# The Penguin Price Guide for Record and Compact Disc Collectors

Nick Hamlyn

PENGUIN BOOKS

PENGUIN BOOKS

Published by the Penguin Group
Penguin Books Ltd, 27 Wrights Lane, London W8 5TZ, England
Penguin Books USA Inc., 375 Hudson Street, New York, New York 10014, USA
Penguin Books Australia Ltd, Ringwood, Victoria, Australia
Penguin Books Canada Ltd, 10 Alcorn Avenue, Toronto, Ontario, Canada M4V 3B2
Penguin Books (NZ) Ltd, 182–190 Wairau Road, Auckland 10, New Zealand

Penguin Books Ltd, Registered Offices: Harmondsworth, Middlesex, England

First published as *The MusicMaster Price Guide for Record Collectors* by Retail Entertainment Data Publishing Ltd 1991
Published in Penguin Books 1997
10 9 8 7 6 5 4 3 2 1

Typeset in Monotype Bembo and Univers by Rowland Phototypesetting Ltd, Bury St Edmunds, Suffolk
Printed in England by Clays Ltd, St Ives plc

# *Contents*

# List of Illustrations

Archie Shepp  *Fire Music*
Sun Ra  *Heliocentric World Vol. 1*
AMM  *AMMMusic*

Keith Tippett  *You Are Here I Am There*
Mike Westbrook  *Love Songs*
Michael Garrick  *Heart Is A Lotus*
Neil Ardley  *Symphony Of Amaranths*
Deep Purple  *Shades Of Purple*
Plastic Penny  *Currency*
Igginbottom  *Igginbottom's Wrench*
Jimi Hendrix  *Band Of Gypsys*

Amon Düül  *Phallus Dei*
Q65  *Afghanistan*
Group 1850  *Agemo's Trip To Mother Earth*
Faust  *Faust*
Culpeper's Orchard  *Second Sight*
Sandrose  *Sandrose*
Audience  *Audience*
Mighty Baby  *Mighty Baby*

End  *Introspection*
Bakerloo  *Bakerloo*
Velvet Opera  *Ride A Hustler's Dream*
Arcadium  *Breathe Awhile*
Fire  *Magic Shoemaker*
Twink  *Think Pink*
T2  *It'll All Work Out In Boomland*
Killing Floor  *Out Of Uranus*

Motherlight  *Bobak, Jons, Malone*
Tea And Symphony  *Asylum For The Musically Insane*
Sandy Coast  *From The Stereo Workshop*
Open Mind  *Open Mind*
Octopus  *Restless Nights*
Fresh Maggots  *Fresh Maggots*
Pete Brown  *Art School Dance Goes On For Ever*
Spring  *Spring*

Jade Warrior  *Released*
Junco Partners  *Junco Partners*
Comus  *First Utterance*
Megaton  *Megaton*
Norman Haines Band  *Den Of Iniquity*
Mellow Candle  *Swaddling Songs*
Dark  *Round The Edges*
Mushroom  *Early One Morning*

Various  *Jug Of Punch*
Ewan MacColl  *Manchester Angel*

Halliard  *It's The Irish In Me*
Copper Family  *Song For Every Season*
Giles Farnaby's Dream Band  *Giles Farnaby's Dream Band*
Nick Drake  *Bryter Layter*
Oddsocks  *Men Of The Moment*
Vikki Clayton  *Lost Lady Found*

Ragged Heroes  *Annual*
Dave Swarbrick & Simon Nicol  *Live At The White Bear*
Queen  'Breakthru'
Madonna  'Who's That Girl'
Def Leppard  *Adrenalize*
Talk Talk  *Laughing Stock*
Christian Marclay  *Record Without A Cover*
Metallica  'Enter Sandman'
Honeycrack  'King Of Misery'

# *Introduction*

Although this book is the first *Penguin Price Guide for Record and Compact Disc Collectors*, it is, of course, the fourth such guide to have been produced by me. The original edition was published near the beginning of 1991 as the very first comprehensive record price guide to be compiled in the UK. Through the nineties, both this and the subsequent Nick Hamlyn price guides have charted the undulating landscape – the rise and rise – of what has become one of the most exciting and widely followed of all collectors' markets.

A couple of years ago, it seemed as though record collecting was beginning to follow the lead set by the shops selling new releases, which have almost entirely swept vinyl off their display racks. The general upward trend in values that had been apparent over the previous decade had largely halted and indeed in some areas prices were beginning to fall. Today, it is still the case that records at the bottom end of the value scale continually teeter and fall off it altogether. Many of the LPs listed at £10 in earlier editions of the *Price Guide* are no longer included in this new edition. A considerably larger number of singles formerly listed at £4 have also now been dropped. At one time, for example, it seemed to make sense that virtually any original single from the fifties or sixties would be worth a minimum of £4 – especially if its status as a chart hit meant that it was likely to appeal to a wide range of collectors. This is not, however, an argument that can any longer be realistically sustained. The fact is that common singles – even ones that are around thirty-five years old, like 'What Do You Want' by Adam Faith or 'I Like It' by Gerry and the Pacemakers – no longer sell for anything like £4, no matter how much a dealer or collector may feel that they should.

Further up the value scale, however, I am happy to report that the prices of a large number of items are once again on the move upwards. Within the key areas of original fifties rock 'n' roll and R&B and the currently fashionable freakbeat genre of the sixties there have been some quite startling price jumps, particularly in the case of very rare singles. Led by a small number of keen collectors who are seemingly prepared to pay almost anything for a record that they do not already own, the auction prices for some singles titles have on occasion far exceeded the previously listed values. As explained below, one must always be very cautious where the results of auctions are concerned, since one or two high bids for a particular record do not necessarily imply that further copies of the same record will attract equal enthusiasm. Nevertheless, this edition of the *Price Guide* does list many greatly increased values, with records showing the greatest movement and likely to continue doing so being indicated by the advisory phrase, 'best auctioned'.

Meanwhile, the albums of certain perennially popular artists – notably the Beatles, the Small Faces, the Who, Jimi Hendrix and some other sixties stars – have also shown marked increases in value. This is a response, no doubt, to the deeper interest in sixties music opened up by successful modern artists like Oasis, Blur, Paul Weller and Kula Shaker, who are only too happy to display their sixties influences openly.

With more specialist genres like jazz, folk, and seventies Euro-rock continuing to attract converts keen to acquire original issues – a development documented within this *Price Guide* both by price rises and by a host of new entries – the market for vinyl can only be described as remarkably buoyant.

At the same time, the introduction of 'Compact Disc' into the guide's title is highly significant. Although a few die-hard vinyl specialists will complain bitterly about the fact, the silver disc has now established a significant place within the collectors' arena. A large number of collectable CD albums and singles have been added to the listings and while their values at the moment cannot compete with those of the most collectable vinyl items, that they are here at all is a demonstration of the way that the market in collectable recorded music is continuing to develop.

The *Penguin Price Guide* presents the record and compact disc collectors' market as it is now. Like its predecessors, it is an essential work of reference for collectors, dealers, and researchers alike.

## HOW ACCURATE ARE THE VALUES LISTED IN THE GUIDE?

The title of this book means what it says: it is a guide to the values of collectable records. Within any collectors' field, an item is essentially worth whatever a collector is prepared to pay for it. When considering items of which several copies are potentially available, however, as is the case with collectors' records, then a few points need to be kept in mind. Let us suppose that Steve Crick, a collector of extraordinary tastes, is desperate to obtain a copy of 'My Old Killarney Hat' by Sister Mary Gertrude. This is not a record that features very often in dealers' lists, so Steve advertises that he is prepared to pay £50 for a copy. Four dealers eventually manage to come across the elusive record: one is delighted to receive £50 from an equally delighted Steve Crick, but the other three find that they are unable to interest anyone at all in the record, at any price. So what is the value of 'My Old Killarney Hat'?

At the other end of the scale, there must be numerous collectors who would like to obtain a copy of the Beatles fan club album, *From Then To You*. This is a record with a listed value of £250 – it is scarce, but copies do turn up, and most dealers will have had at least one passing through their hands. Dave Conroy is a keen Beatles collector and he does not have a copy of *From Then To You*. On the other hand, he does have the actual music in his collection, as he was able to buy an American counterfeit of the record quite cheaply a few years ago. When he sees the real thing in his local collectors' record shop with a price tag of £250, he argues that he has waited nearly thirty years for the record, so he might as well wait a little longer for a copy that is more 'reasonably' priced. In the event, the shop is unable to find a customer for the record. The manager reduces the price to £225, and after a few weeks, with the record still unsold, Dave Conroy offers £200, which is accepted. So again, what is the value of *From Then To You*?

A junk shop, selling all kinds of second-hand goods from shabby premises, and with a box of old records in the corner, would find in all probability that the records would remain unsold if priced according to the values given in this guide. An efficient specialist mail-order company, on the other hand, with a large number of customers in Scandinavia, Germany and Japan, could well be regularly managing to obtain prices in excess of those listed in the guide. The above arguments apply equally well in the case of known rarities being sold at auction. As every rare record dealer is aware, offers made on these occasions can often climb way above the 'book values' of the records in question. There are a number of collectors who, like Steve Crick, are prepared to pay well over the odds to gain the rare records they need. There are also a much larger number of collectors who are of the Dave Conroy persuasion and prepared to temper their enthusiasm. It is important, therefore, to resist the temptation to assume that, simply because one copy of, for example, 'Addicted Man' by the Game has successfully been auctioned for £600, then all subsequent copies of the record will also sell for that figure. To these considerations must be added the fact that the collectors' market is a volatile one. The success of a new group in the charts can send the values of their back catalogue shooting upwards (although a later fall from favour can just as easily send then tumbling back down again); an influential disc jockey can create a collectors' item out of an obscurity simply by deciding to play it (particularly in the case of soul records); or else the reissue of a scarce album can increase the value of the original by making more people aware of its existence. On the other hand, the discovery of a warehouse full of copies of a previously rare record is likely to make the price fall dramatically; or a similar effect can simply result from several people deciding to sell their cherished copies of the same record at the same time. It happens!

To repeat, therefore, this book is a *guide* to the values of collectable records. A large amount of research, however, has gone into making it as accurate as possible, much of it being first-hand – the result of actually selling the records through a successful collectors' record shop to both the home and the international markets over a period of several years. The values are based on actual sales and, within the constraints detailed above, the margin of error is not likely to be large. Comments and corrections are always welcome, however. It should be noted that a price structure is used throughout, along the lines of the discrete price levels used by auctioneers. It starts with the sequence 4, 5, 6, 8, 10, 12, 15, 20 and carries on from there, so that no record is listed as having values such as £7 or £11 or £19. The two values listed for each item refer to two condition categories – 'near mint' (excellent) and the significantly lower 'very good'. To qualify as collectable, a lower price limit was set for near mint items. All the LPs included in the guide are valued at £10 or over; double LPs and CD albums are £12 or over. Seven-inch singles are £4 or over; 7" EPs and CD and cassette singles are £5 and over; 12" singles start at £6.

## HOW IS THE PRICE GUIDE ORGANIZED?

The artists are listed alphabetically, and for each one the collectable records are also listed alphabetically. Where more than one listing appears under the same name, then these are actually the recordings of different artists. It must be remembered that the listings are not complete discographies, but only a catalogue of those items that are valuable enough to be considered collectable. As far as possible, it is the A side that is listed in the case of singles, but if a certain title cannot be found, it is always worth checking to see if the B side has been listed instead. Similarly, where a record has a different artist on each side (a common practice with sixties reggae and ska singles), it will only be listed under one of them. Records featuring several different artists are usually listed under the Various heading. A small number of abbreviations have been used. These are as follows:

**cass**: cassette; **cass-s**: cassingle; **CD-s**: compact disc single; **r-reel**: reel to reel tape.

The extract below shows the different parts of an entry:

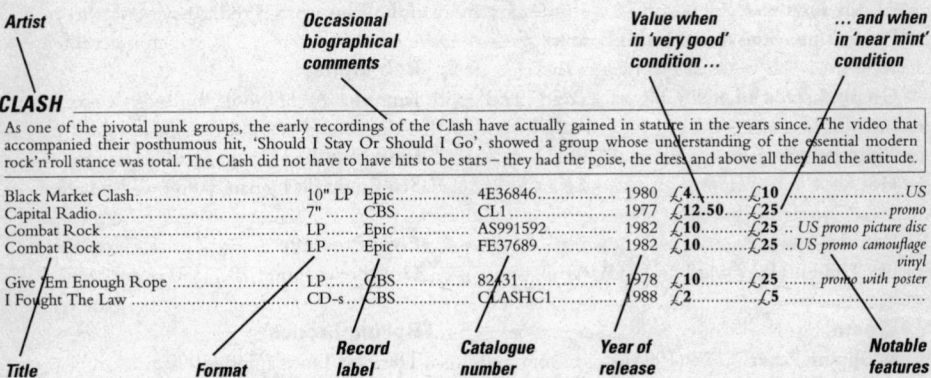

| Artist | | Occasional biographical comments | | | Value when in 'very good' condition ... | | ... and when in 'near mint' condition |

**CLASH**

As one of the pivotal punk groups, the early recordings of the Clash have actually gained in stature in the years since. The video that accompanied their posthumous hit, 'Should I Stay Or Should I Go', showed a group whose understanding of the essential modern rock'n'roll stance was total. The Clash did not have to have hits to be stars – they had the poise, the dress and above all they had the attitude.

| Title | Format | Record label | Catalogue number | Year of release | | | Notable features |
|---|---|---|---|---|---|---|---|
| Black Market Clash | 10" LP | Epic | 4E36846 | 1980 | £4 | £10 | US |
| Capital Radio | 7" | CBS | CL1 | 1977 | £12.50 | £25 | promo |
| Combat Rock | LP | Epic | AS991592 | 1982 | £10 | £25 | US promo picture disc |
| Combat Rock | LP | Epic | FE37689 | 1982 | £10 | £25 | US promo camouflage vinyl |
| Give 'Em Enough Rope | LP | CBS | 82431 | 1978 | £10 | £25 | promo with poster |
| I Fought The Law | CD-s | CBS | CLASHC1 | 1988 | £2 | £5 | |

As a finale to this introduction I would like to offer my grateful thanks to the various dealers and collectors who have helped with information, advice and record sleeves for photographing. An enormous number of people have contacted me after reading the earlier editions of the *Price Guide* and I have talked with a large number of dealers and collectors at different record fairs. I hope that they will have the satisfaction of seeing some of their information included, even if there are far too many names for me to list here! Particular thanks are due, however, to Natalie Round, whose efficient management of Pied Piper Records gives me the time to work on the *Price Guide* database; to the late Michael Gerzon (whose friendship and enthusiasm for the widest range of music imaginable is much missed); to Jon Taylor, and especially to Phil Walker, for helping me to fill the obscurer corners of the discography; to Neil Roddis and Phil Walker again for giving me access to their extensive record collections for photographing; to Steve James for the loan of photographic equipment; and my family – Liz, David and Eileen, Catherine, Fred, and Sarah.

Nick Hamlyn

# Glossary

## ACETATES

Acetates are records made either of hard, brittle plastic or else of metal with a thin vinyl coating. There are two sources of these. Song pluggers in the early sixties would often operate acetate disc-cutters to enable them to easily produce convenient demonstration recordings at a time when cassettes did not exist. Within recording studios, meanwhile, similar quickly produced acetates would be made in order to give the artist or some other interested party some idea of how the finished recording would sound. Where such acetates feature artists whose regular records are collectable, they can also acquire a considerable collectors' interest, especially bearing in mind the fact that, at most, only a handful of copies of any one recording are likely to be in existence. Many commercially released records can be found in acetate form, but values for these tend to be modest, apart from those made by the most collected artists. Examples that have been sold at some of the London rock auctions include the following:

**Beatles:**
All My Loving £260 (1991)
Penny Lane/Strawberry Fields Forever £400 (1990)
Get Back/Don't Let Me Down £225 (1995)

**Marc Bolan:**
Hot Love £120 (1990)

**David Bowie:**
Up The Hill Backwards £35 (1990)

**Cream:**
Wrapping Paper £125 (1994)

**Jimi Hendrix:**
The Wind Cries Mary £50 (1986)

**Buddy Holly:**
Peggy Sue £380 (1987)

**Michael Jackson:**
Bad £220 (1989)

**Madonna:**
True Blue £65 (1989)

**Bob Marley:**
Jamming £90 (1988)

**Pink Floyd:**
See Emily Play £154 (1989)

**Elvis Presley:**
Heartbreak Hotel 78 £380 (1994)

**Rolling Stones:**
The Last Time £330 (1990)

**Sex Pistols:**
Pretty Vacant £200 (1987)

Inevitably, the acetates that are of most interest to collectors are those that contain songs or versions of songs that did not end up as commercial releases. It is in this area that the highest prices have been reached, as the following auction examples make clear:

**Beatles:**
Hey Little Girl/Like Dreamers Do £2500 (1986)
Twelve Bar Original 13.12.65 £1300 (1988)
Yesterday (alternate take) £770 (1989)
Strawberry Fields Forever (alternate take) £560 (1995)

**Bob Dylan:**
Live With The Hawks (2-sided 12″) £1125 (1995)

**Cliff Richard:**
Breathless/Lawdy Miss Clawdy £2800 (1985)
Breathless/Lawdy Miss Clawdy £1000 (1986)

**Rolling Stones:**
Road Runner/Diddley Daddy £1500 (1988)
Soon Forgotten/Close Together/Can't Judge A Book £6000 (1988)
Soon Forgotten/Close Together/Can't Judge A Book £4000 (1989)

It is interesting to see how different acetates of the same recordings can realize quite different prices on different occasions. While some of this discrepancy may be explicable in terms of different playing surface conditions, it also highlights the extent to which the demands of just one or two individual collectors can produce a result that confounds general expectations. A third copy of 'Soon Forgotten' (predating the Rolling Stones' earliest Decca recordings) was subsequently auctioned and failed to reach its reserve price. Perhaps there were, after all, only two collectors prepared to pay substantial four-figure sums for this small chunk of rock music history.

## AUCTIONS

For some time now, rock music auctions have been held once or twice a year by all the major London auction houses. These have tended to concentrate on memorabilia rather than records as such, and they have become the foremost market place for star instruments, stage clothing, star autographs, gold disc awards and the like. A number of scarce acetate recordings have also been sold at auction, but commercial recordings, even when very rare, have played a very limited part on such occasions. At a more private level, however, record auctions are often the most appropriate means of sale for the rarest records. While there is little point in asking for offers on an item whose £20 value is well established and which is relatively often offered for sale, there are a number of more valuable items (notably the rarest rock 'n' roll and R&B singles from the fifties) where the demand by individual collectors can be such as to make them prepared to offer considerably more than the guide value on occasion. Such records are identified in this edition of the *Price Guide* with the cautionary phrase 'best auctioned'.

## AUDIOPHILE PRESSINGS

Hi-fi enthusiasts inevitably maintain that a vinyl record played on a quality system will always sound better than a compact disc. A better sound still is intended to be obtainable from the 'super-stereo', audiophile albums that were issued in the late seventies and eighties. These are mastered at half the usual speed from a tape playing at half the usual speed, which is supposed to create a superior sound quality when played back normally. The records are also pressed on to virgin vinyl, with a high degree of quality control. Despite this, it is actually quite difficult to distinguish most audiophile recordings from their ordinary stereo equivalents on a blindfold test. Curiously, in view of the hype that was originally used to promote the supposedly superior sound quality of compact discs, there also exist a number of audiophile CDs, which are meant to sound even more superior.

## AUTOGRAPHS

Autographs are unfortunately the easiest collecting feature to counterfeit, for which reason autographed records will often attract no more than a slight premium over the normal value of the item, particularly in the case of a modern artist who is still touring and is not of the first stellar magnitude. The situation is different in the case of star or historic names, where the value of an artist's rarest records provides an indication of the likely value of a genuine autograph. The most valuable – by artists like the Beatles and Elvis Presley – are regular features of the London rock auctions, where the authenticity of the autographs will have been verified by experts with experience of what the star signatures actually look like. Other dealers will require some kind of provenance, which may comprise nothing more complicated than a convincing story as to how the autograph was obtained, if the estimated value is not too high. It should be realized, to mention just one area of possible confusion, that signed photographs issued by the Beatles fan club had often never actually been in contact with the pen of a real Beatle, although Ringo Starr apparently quite enjoyed this aspect of fame and would sometimes sign all four names himself! There are, of course, a number of limited-edition releases bearing autographs, and these are listed in the guide where appropriate.

## BBC TRANSCRIPTION DISCS

These records are not listed within the guide, although they are actually highly collectable. In order to sell its programmes to radio stations abroad, the BBC records them on to LPs (CDs in recent times), which can be easily used for broadcast purposes. The records of interest to rock music collectors consist of live recordings from programmes like Radio 1's *In Concert*. Essentially, anyone who is anyone in the eighties and nineties has at least one side of one of these records devoted to their music, while a large number of seventies artists are also represented. Unfortunately, the BBC itself does not approve of the sale of its transcription discs. It will not provide any kind of discography and indeed it actively operates to prevent such records being advertised for sale. Copies do change hands on the collectors' market notwithstanding, although values are kept relatively low by the existence of bootlegs and counterfeits, the average being around £50 to £60. Exceptions to this average are the artists one would expect – *The Beatles At The Beeb* set would be likely to sell for around £500, for example. Any BBC record with a black and white label is definitely a counterfeit, as original labels are green and white (early issues are green and yellow). Also counterfeit are the records that apparently have correct labels, but have hand-scratched matrix numbers on the vinyl.

## BOOTLEGS

A bootleg recording is one that consists of either a live performance or else a set of studio out-takes. Such recordings do not duplicate any official record-company release and, unlike the situation with regard to counterfeits, the issue of whether or not they are genuine does not arise. They are illegal because of the lack of record company involvement, although occasionally the artist is involved and may even get some royalty payment. Lowell George, for example, is known to have mixed two Little Feat live bootlegs himself. Bootlegs are, nevertheless, often keenly sought by collectors for the sake of the otherwise unavailable music they contain. Popular titles are constantly reissued by different manufacturers, but there is some collectors' interest in original labels like Trade Mark of Quality, the Amazing Kornyphone Label and Wizardo Records. Such records, however, have not been listed in this edition of the *Price Guide*.

## CASSETTES

Cassettes are not very well favoured by collectors. Many of the highly priced progressive albums from the early seventies were also issued on cassette, and these are at least as rare as their vinyl equivalents. Despite this, the cassettes do not have a significant collectors' value at all. To illustrate the point, only one such cassette is actually listed in this guide. David Bowie's *The Man Who Sold The World* with the dress cover is listed at £200 for the LP, but a mere £15 for the cassette that was issued at the same time. In the case of modern releases, too, cassette-singles have noticeably failed to maintain an initial interest from collectors, while even the limited privately produced items from early in the careers of subsequently successful groups have much lower values than would vinyl versions if these existed.

## CLASSICAL MUSIC

Although considerations of time and space prevent their inclusion in this edition of the *Price Guide*, collectors and dealers generally should be aware of the high prices being demanded and paid for certain classical records. Realistically, a complete listing of all the collectable classical records would fill a second volume as large as this one. The market as a whole, however, is smaller at present than the rock collectors' market, with many fewer specialist dealers serving the appetites of a small but active body of enthusiasts. The most sought-after are the early stereo recordings made by Decca, the company that pioneered the LP in Britain. Decca were always very concerned to deliver the highest sound quality possible and the stereo records in the SXL2000 and SXL6000 series, together with the boxed sets in the SET200 series, are collected as being among the finest classical recordings ever made. Also in demand are the later Decca issues on the Phase Four label (PFS series) and on all the Argo subsidiary series. The Decca labels, Eclipse (ECS series), Ace Of Diamonds (SDD and GOS series) and World Of (SPA series) reissued the early Decca recordings at a bargain price, but the sound quality is as good as the originals. These records are therefore collected as well, although the values are inevitably rather lower. (Anything in 'electronic stereo', however, is immediately shunned, as such recordings do not have the high sound quality that collectors demand). The Decca company was also responsible for pressing records on certain other labels, which again have become collectable. These are Capitol (CTL series), Lyrita (SRCS series, until as late as 1980), London (American CS, OS, OSA and STS series), and RCA (SB2000, SB6500 and SER4000 series until 1970, together with the 'bargain' Victrola releases bearing a ruby label, VICS1000 series). Mercury *Living Presence* recordings are also renowned for their impressive sound quality, many of them being the result of recordings on to 35 mm magnetic film. The American SR series is very collectable in consequence, as is the British AMS series, whose records were made by EMI, using American masters and machine parts. Other collectable early stereo recordings are to be found on the Angel (SAN and American 35000 series), Columbia (SAX series until 1967; SCX3000 series; TWO series), HMV (ASD series until 1969; CSD series; SLS series of boxed sets), Philips (SABL series) and RCA (LSC 'Living Stereo' series) labels. Some early mono recordings on all these labels are also sought-after by some collectors, although in general the demand for mono records is quite limited, other than for key items that never were issued in stereo.

A few of the most collectable records are listed below. It should be stressed, however, that these represent the merest tip of a considerable iceberg. (It should also be stressed that the small number of dealers working in this area, together with the lack of literature on the subject, results in considerable price variation. The values given here must be viewed as being highly approximate.)

### Ernest Ansermet + Suisse Romande Orchestra:
Tchaikovsky *Sleeping Beauty* Decca stereo SXL2160-2 1959 £400 (3 records)

### Ataulfo Argenta + London Symphony Orchestra:
Concert (Espana!) Decca stereo SXL2020 1958 £400

### Ataulfo Argenta + National Orchestra of Spain:
De Falla *Master Peter's Puppet Show/El Amor Brujo* Decca stereo SXL2260 1961 £400

### Andre Cluytens + Paris Conservatoire Orchestra:
Ravel Concert Columbia stereo SAX2476-9 1963 £400 (4 records)

**Andre Cluytens + Philharmonia Orchestra:**
Concert Columbia stereo SAX2355 1960 £250

**Gioconda de Vito:**
Bach Violin Concerto in E/Mozart Violin Concerto No. 3 HMV stereo ASD429 1961 £1200
   HMV mono ALP1856 1961 £200
Beethoven Violin Sonata No. 9 (Kreutzer) HMV mono ALP1319 1956 £300
Beethoven Violin Sonata No. 7/Brahms Violin Sonata No. 2 HMV mono ALP1521 1958£300
Brahms Violin Sonatas Nos.1 & 3 HMV mono ALP1282 1955 £200

**Øivin Fjeldstad + London Symphony Orchestra:**
Grieg *Peer Gynt* Incidental Music Decca stereo SXL2012 1958 £400

**Wilhelm Furtwangler + Vienna Philharmonic Orchestra:**
Wagner *Die Walküre* HMV mono ALP1257-61 1955 £500 (5 records)

**Vittorio Gui + Glyndebourne Festival Orchestra:**
Mozart Le Nozze di Figaro HMV stereo ASD274-7 1959 £400 (4 records)

**Aram Khachaturian + Vienna Philharmonic Orchestra:**
Khachaturian Spartacus and Gayaneh excerpts Decca stereo SXL6000 1963 £250

**Erich Kleiber + Vienna Philharmonic Orchestra:**
Mozart Le Nozze di Figaro Decca stereo SXL2087-90 1959 £800 (4 records)

**Otto Klemperer + Philharmonia Orchestra:**
Mahler Symphony No. 2 Columbia stereo SAX2473-4 1963 £200 (2 records)

**Leonid Kogan + Constantin Silvestri + Paris Conservatoire Orchestra:**
Beethoven Violin Concerto Columbia stereo SAX2386 1961 £200

**Leonid Kogan + Kyril Kondrashin + Philharmonia Orchestra:**
Brahms Violin Concerto Columbia stereo SAX2307 1960 £200
Lalo *Symphonie Espagnole*/Tchaikovsky Sérénade Mélancolique Columbia stereo SAX2329 1960
   £200

**Josef Krips + Vienna Philharmonic Orchestra:**
Mozart Don Giovanni Decca stereo SXL2117-20 1959 £800 (4 records)

**Rafael Kubelik + Royal Philharmonic Orchestra:**
Beethoven Symphony No. 6 HMV stereo ASD349 1960 £250

**Rafael Kubelik + Vienna Philharmonic Orchestra:**
Mozart Symphonies Nos. 36 & 38 HMV stereo ASD451 1962 £200
Schubert Symphonies Nos. 3 & 4 HMV stereo ASD418 1961 £200

**Peter Maag + London Symphony Orchestra:**
Mendelssohn Midsummer Night's Dream Decca stereo SXL2060 1959 £200

**Johanna Martzy:**
Bach Violin Sonatas Nos. 1-3/Violin Partitas Nos.1-3 Columbia mono 33CX1286-8 1955 £1200
   (3 records)

Schubert *Rondeau Brilliant* in B min/*Fantaisie* in C Columbia mono 33CX1372 1957 £400

**Johanna Martzy + Paul Kletzki + Philharmonia Orchestra:**
Brahms Violin Concerto Columbia mono 33CX1165 1954 £600 (first thick pressing)
Beethoven Romances/Mendelssohn Violin Concerto Columbia mono 33CX1479 1958 £400

**Ginette Neveu:**
Chausson *Poème*/Debussy Violin Sonata No. 3/Ravel *Tzigane* HMV mono ALP1520 1957 £200

**Ginette Neveu + Walter Süsskind + Philharmonia Orchestra:**
Sibelius Violin Concerto/Suk Four Pieces For Violin & Piano HMV mono ALP1479 1957 £200

**Carl Schuricht + Vienna Philharmonic Orchestra:**
Bruckner Symphony No. 8 HMV stereo ASD602–3 1963 £400 (2 records)

**Tullio Serafin + Maria Callas + Orchestra of La Scala:**
Cherubini Medea Columbia stereo SAX2290–2 1959 £300 (3 records)

## COLOURED VINYL

Records made of plastic in colours other than black are considerably older than many collectors appreciate. Though not particularly common, there are 78s made of various different colours. In the rock era, coloured vinyl issues were an occasional occurrence during the fifties and sixties and all of the coloured records with a rock or blues content are now collectable. (A large number of singles and EPs aimed at children were also issued on coloured vinyl – usually red – but these are of no more than novelty value). During the late seventies the use of coloured vinyl became something of an epidemic, to the extent that it ceases to be any guarantee of a record's collectability – a situation that remains true through the eighties, although coloured vinyl had become fairly unusual again by the end of the decade. It remains the case, however, that if an artist's records are collectable anyway, then their coloured vinyl releases are likely to be worth a little more than the equivalent black vinyl issues. With CDs, coloration seems to be restricted so far to the plastic packaging rather than being used for the CDs themselves.

## COMPACT DISCS

Research into the feasibility of the compact disc format began as early as the sixties, but it was not until March 1979 that the first public demonstration took place. In June 1981 a European press conference was held at which some specially produced CDs of opera extracts were on show. These, therefore, are the likely candidates for the first CDs to be made. The first generally available CDs, however, were issued by Sony in Japan in October 1982, following which March 1983 saw the simultaneous release of some 200 different titles in the UK by all the major record companies. The contrast between this and the situation over two decades earlier, when the LP was adopted by different companies at quite different times (some showing a marked reluctance to invest in a medium with what appeared to be an uncertain future), is quite remarkable. CD singles crept on to the market much more surreptitiously than the albums. The first was 'If You're Ready' by Ruby Turner (Jive JIVEX109 1986), although its value has stayed low due to the lack of collectors' interest in Ms Turner. Thus far, the penetration of the collectors' market by compact discs has been limited, but it is growing, as the new inclusion of numerous CDs in this edition of the *Price Guide* demonstrates. Many of the earliest CDs have been deleted for a number of years and are likely soon to begin rising in value above the figures quoted here. This is especially true of CD singles, which have a shorter shelf life to begin with and which are frequently issued in limited edition formats. Candidates for future CD collectability include the limited-edition double-CD sets created by adding a bonus disc of live recordings or out-takes to an album made by a major artist (some of these are already to be found in the listings); the multiple-disc boxed sets designed to provide an overview of the careers of important artists and typically including a number of previously unreleased tracks; and the two-part CD-single releases that aim to boost a single's performance in the charts by persuading fans effectively to buy the single twice (many of these can also be found already in the listings).

## CONDITION

As a description of the condition of a record, the word 'mint' tends to be one of the most misused of all. A record with a light surface mark or two is not mint, even if the marks produce no audible effect. A record whose cover is slightly creased at the corners is not mint – and neither is one where the cover has torn slightly along the top or bottom edge (a condition that is actually suffered by some records bought new from regular record shops). Some collectors would argue that a record ceases to be mint the moment it is played; others would merely insist on a completely blemish-free playing surface and cover. For records with conditions lower than mint, a scale of descriptions operates. The higher values quoted in this guide are for records in excellent, or near mint, condition. Such a record has no scratches or any other mark producing an audible effect that should not be there. The cover is free from tearing and has no more than very slight scuffing or creasing. For a record in worse condition than this, the value will be substantially less than the figure listed. This cannot be stressed too strongly. A record whose music is interrupted by a click that repeats thirty-three or forty-five times every minute is likely to be of interest to a collector only as a stop-gap until he can obtain a better copy. He will certainly not pay a price anywhere approaching the near mint value for such a record. A record whose music is accompanied by what sounds like a frying breakfast is practically worthless. Nor is it possible to use a record's age as an excuse. In many cases, hundreds of thousands of copies of a record may have been sold originally, but a relatively high value is given in the guide precisely because copies in excellent condition are scarce. At the other end of the scale, a record in truly mint condition may sometimes fetch a little more than the listed value. The term 'very good' is used by dealers to indicate a record that, in practice, has several marks on its surface, some of which are audible. The lower values listed in the guide are for very good records. Typically, these are 50% of the near mint values, although the figure is lower than this for the relatively common records at the lower end of the value scale, and higher for the more valuable records, where an appearance on the market in any condition at all is a relatively unusual occurrence. The terms 'good' and 'fair' are seldom used – in most cases they refer to a record from which few collectors would gain much listening pleasure. Exactly the same condition grades are applicable to CDs. It is unfortunate that many CD purchasers have been too ready to take at face value the original company claims with regard to the indestructability of the discs. Scratches do not always cause problems, but they often do make the music on CDs stick or jump.

## COUNTERFEITS

It is a sad fact that some of the rarer records have been counterfeited by unscrupulous individuals wishing to pass off their copies as the real thing. Recognizing a counterfeit can sometimes be a problem. Often the label or the cover simply look 'too new', or the colour or some feature of the design simply does not look quite right. This is no help, however, where one has no idea what the original record should look like. In the case of UK pressings, a good indication is provided by the matrix number, which is to be found on the vinyl in the space occupied by the run-out groove, next to the label. If this is machine printed, then the record is likely to be genuine. If, however, the number is hand scratched, then the record is likely to be a counterfeit. One should also always be suspicious of a record offered for sale far too cheaply, especially if the record is a well-known collectors' item and the dealer is not one with a reputable name. (Although genuine bargains can always be found, of course, amongst the stock of dealers who are simply unaware of its value. It is a matter of judgement.)

High-value collectors' items from the eighties are a particular target for the counterfeiters, as age discrepancies are less likely to arise. 'Mutant Moments' by Soft Cell, 'Damage Done' by the Sisters of Mercy and 'So Young' by the Stone Roses are three rarities of which counterfeits are definitely in circulation, but there are undoubtedly others. In the last few years, a large number of unofficial reissues of scarce albums from the sixties and early seventies have appeared on the market, but the manufacturers of these take care to remove the original record company names from the cover and identification is not a problem.

## DEALERS

The values of the records listed in this guide are the prices that a collector might be expected to pay for a copy of the record concerned in near mint or very good condition. The price that a dealer might pay for the record is another matter altogether. A dealer has to cover the cost of his overheads (which include the rent, rates, and other running expenses of the shop; staff salaries; advertising expenses; and the time and effort spent acquiring the knowledge that he must have) before he can even begin to make a profit. A ten or twenty per cent slice of the record's value is too little to justify the outlay involved. In general, dealers expect to pay around half the anticipated selling price for a record, but this figure may be increased in the case of an item for which there is a waiting customer and decreased for an item whose appeal is rather specialized. It is also likely to be decreased (often considerably) for items at the bottom of the collectors' price scale.

## DEMONSTRATION RECORDS

Demonstration records, or 'demos', are the earliest pressings of a record, used as samples and often made available in advance of the regular commercial copies. Review copies tend to be demos, as do the records sent to radio stations, and collectors' interest centres on those examples where a distinct label design is used. At its most boring, the design simply adds a few printed words to the normal label – something along the lines of 'Demonstration sample. Not for sale'. More excitingly, however, record companies in the sixties, particularly, used demo labels that were striking variations of the issue labels. The EMI group of companies, for example, favoured a white label for their singles, dominated by a big red 'A' on the side that was intended to be the hit. During 1966, this was changed to a green label with a big white 'A'. Pye also favoured a white label, with a black 'A' across the record's centre. The Decca group of companies liked to use a pattern of short radial lines around the edge of the label, and sometimes a colour change: Brunswick from black to red and London from black to orange or yellow, although the Decca label itself retained its blue colour for both issues and demos. Deram kept the same label lay-out, but replaced its brown colour with light blue. The value and collectability of demos varies considerably. Soul collectors prefer demo copies and will pay double the listed price for them (but see the entries for the Action and Tamla Motown labels). This doubling formula works well for other kinds of single too, but only where the artist is generally collectable. A demo copy of 'Bad Blood' by the Paramounts, for example, would be worth around £15, rather than the £8 figure that applies to an issue copy. In the case of one-off or genre singles, however, where the song rather than the singer is important, a demo copy is likely to attract only a modest premium. A copy of 'War Machine' by Leviathan is valued at £20: a demo copy of the record would, perhaps, push the price up to £25. This rule is even more relevant in the case of particularly rare singles, which may originally have sold so poorly that demo copies are actually more common than issue copies. 'She Just Satisfies' by Jimmy Page seldom turns up at all – both demo and issue copies are worth the listed value of £300. To collectors of singles from the fifties, demos are actually inferior to issue copies, so that demonstration copies of rare London singles are worth considerably less than the listed values – probably no more than 50%. Note that fifties demos are often one-sided, a pair of such records being made to demonstrate the A and B sides of the commercial single. (This format is prevalent later in the case of demos of LP releases). In all periods, demo copies of common singles by star artists defy all the usual rules. The values of Beatles demos are listed separately in the guide – hit single demos by the likes of Billy Fury, the Kinks and the Who would fetch around £100 each. Where demos are specifically indicated in the guide, then this is either to draw attention to a value that departs significantly from the guidelines given above or else it is a reference to a record that was withdrawn from issue, with the demonstration copies, therefore, being the only kind in existence. Demonstration albums are less common, but where they do occur, the general guidelines above apply once more. Often the demonstration copies are marked by a label stuck on the sleeve, with the cover and record label being in every other respect identical to those on the issue copies. This procedure is the one commonly followed today in the case of demonstration CDs. Such labels could, of course, be mass-produced by a counterfeiter and stuck on to quantities of regular releases, for which reason demonstration items of this kind attract little or no premium.

## DISCO MIX CLUB

The Disco Mix Club, run by disc jockey Tony Prince, has issued a series of special LPs (now CDs) to accredited DJs who pay to join the club, at the rate of two albums per month from the early eighties. The first of these monthly issues is of no interest to collectors, being merely a compilation of recently issued tracks. The second, however, contains various remixes and megamixes of previously released material, much of it being unavailable in this form anywhere else. Although the individual albums are not listed in the guide, they sell for prices in the range of £10 to £50, depending on the artists involved, on the infrequent occasions when they come on to the open market.

## EXPORT ISSUES

The major British record companies have, from time to time, pressed up special editions of selected domestic records for release overseas. Such records are inevitably scarce in their home country and tend to be sought after by collectors. Usually identifiable by their catalogue numbers, such records are distinguishable from releases made by the actual overseas branches of the record companies concerned, by being marked as 'Manufactured in Great Britain'.

## EXTENDED-PLAY RECORDS

As far as most record collectors are concerned, 'EP' is a technical term. It refers to the 7″ records that were issued during the fifties and sixties with a playing time around twice that of the standard single. In most cases these had four tracks (though some, like *The Spotnicks On The Air*, had six), played at 45 rpm (though some, like *Something Else By The Move*, played at 33 rpm), and had picture sleeves constructed out of thin card, with the front cover edges folded over the back, like the LP sleeves of the time (though many of the early fifties EPs have company covers without pictures). These mini-LPs are widely collected for their own sake, with the result that these listings include many EPs by artists who are otherwise only marginally collectable. During the late seventies, many of the tiny independent labels that emerged in the wake of punk released records containing four or more tracks, often using the 12″ format. Sometimes (though not in this *Price Guide*), these too are described as EPs, but they are not collected as such by EP specialists, and they do not serve the mini-LP function of the earlier records.

## FLEXI-DISCS

Flexi-discs are 7″ singles pressed on to plastic so thin that it is extremely bendy – and extremely easy to damage! Two companies are primarily responsible for making these discs – Lyntone and Sound for Industry – but these are essentially manufacturers and not record companies as such. A variety of sources are responsible for commissioning the flexi-discs in the first place. Record companies use them as promotional devices, typically advertising a forthcoming boxed album set, or else including them as a free extra within the packaging of another record. Magazines, too, use them as a free extra, either on an occasional basis, or with every issue (as in the case of the eighties *Flexipop* magazine). Fan clubs issue them as an exclusive product for their members (the most famous examples of these being the Beatles Christmas flexi-discs). Occasionally, independent record companies will use the flexi-disc format for a cheap, limited-edition run. A few of these different flexi-discs are collectable and are listed in the guide. In many cases, test pressings are made on ordinary hard vinyl and these records are typically worth around three to four times the value of the flexi-disc.

## FOAM-EDGE COVERS

For a few months in 1970-71, one manufacturer of album sleeves decided that it would be a good idea to employ a design in which a cardboard cover like a book cover housed the record in a clear plastic sleeve, along the edge of which was fastened a strip of plastic foam. *Colosseum Live* was one album given such a sleeve; the Pentangle's *Basket Of Light* was another. Sensible purchasers of these records immediately placed a standard paper sleeve inside the plastic one, because although the strip of foam was intended to clean the record as it was pulled out of the sleeve, in practice the foam used was so coarse that it actually damaged the vinyl surface. A similar problem is sometimes found in the case of LPs using polythene-lined inner sleeves. Where the record has not been removed from its sleeve for a period of years, a reaction can take place between the polythene and the vinyl, leaving a thin but visible deposit on the surface of the record. Unlike the foam-edge marking, however, this deposit normally wipes clean and causes minimal effect to the record's sound quality.

## FOLK

Folk music is a collectors' area that tends to get ignored by many people, but there are a large number of valuable albums to be found on the specialist labels. As always, the records issued during the sixties and early seventies are the ones in which there is most interest (a tiny number of folk records dating from the fifties also exist), with anything issued on the Topic label being worth investigating. Other key labels are Acorn, Argo (Decca's home for non-commercial music of various kinds – classical and some jazz as well as folk, and also some spoken word material), Broadside, Cottage, Claddagh (from Ireland), Dolphin (also from Ireland), Folkways (from the US), Free Reed, Leader, Rubber, Saydisc, Tradition, Trailer, Transatlantic (most collectors and dealers do know about that one) and Village Thing. There are also a number of labels responsible for only a handful or fewer releases, which are effectively private pressings. Much of the information on folk releases in this *Price Guide* is derived from two specialist dealers – Peter Loughran and Phil Walker ('Second Spin') – who operate efficient mail order services from Newcastle and Northampton respectively.

## FOREIGN RELEASES

The majority of items listed in the guide are UK issues. A substantial number of releases from other countries, however, have also been included, wherever it is felt that these are of particular interest to the UK collector. Some of these consist of recordings by British artists (by birth or by adoption) that were not actually released in Britain. The rest is a selection of records by artists from other countries that are of particular appeal to collectors in the UK. In particular, a large number of US albums have been included. American LPs have always been imported into Britain in quite large numbers so that they frequently turn up for sale in the collectors' market. Moreover, with so much rock music being American in origin, the first pressing of a large number of releases is actually an American record. In addition, there are key areas of interest (the obscurer regions of West Coast rock, for example), as well as several particularly collectable records, that are exclusively American, yet whose omission in a book seeking to describe the collectors' market would be a nonsense. As a general rule, US albums have been included in this guide either if they have no exact UK equivalent or if the American pressing has a higher value than its British counterpart. (It should be noted that American pressings of many UK original albums are actually less valuable in the UK, especially where the label is a key factor in the collectability of the British record). Recently, there has been an escalation of interest in collectable European albums from the seventies, particularly those originating in Germany. Once again, it would be a nonsense to exclude these records from a comprehensive record Price Guide and it is hoped that every such album has in fact been listed.

## FREAKBEAT

During their brief career, the Beatles presided over a rock music scene that was growing and developing so fast that it was able to move from British beat to psychedelia to progressive rock in the space of just seven years. Of course, rock analysts love categories, and not content with these three to cover the major sixties trends, some have sought to define yet another. 'Freakbeat' attempts to find a genre in the space between British beat and psychedelia – a space that hardly seems big enough to accommodate it. The term is a recent one – no one in the sixties thought it necessary to modify the 'Beat' idea until the sounds heard on such records as the Yardbirds' 'Shapes Of Things' and Jimi Hendrix's 'Purple Haze' made it clear that the description had become inadequate. There is also much disagreement over which records should properly be described as freakbeat, which only goes to highlight the artificial nature of the term.

## FRENCH EPS

France has always been highly resistant to Anglo–American cultural imports and it was not until 1962 that the local record industry paid any attention to the rock music phenomenon. Even then, the French response was typically idiosyncratic. Spurning singles entirely (until 1967), the French record companies decided to concentrate instead on four-track extended-play records. Between 1962 and 1968 a large number of these 7" EPs were issued, featuring both French and some well-known (and not so well-known) British and American artists. The consequence of this was that groups like the Beatles, the Animals and the Rolling Stones had many more EP releases than they did in the UK, and the novelty of both the cover art and the availability of UK album tracks in a unique 7" format has made these records extremely collectable today. Even more sought-after are the EPs by groups like the Creation, the Tony Jackson Group and the Primitives, who had no picture cover releases at all in the UK. The majority of the French EP catalogue is therefore included within this guide – information will be gratefully received from collectors who are in a position to make the listing more nearly complete!

## GATEFOLD SLEEVES

Single-record LP sleeves that open out like a book cover were occasionally used in the fifties and sixties to give a touch of extra class to the records of the biggest stars. Elvis Presley's *Golden Records* and *Elvis Is Back*, Frank Sinatra's *Sinatra-Basie* and *Beatles For Sale* are notable examples. For ten years from the mid sixties, these double sleeves became a common feature and help to make the albums of the period into attractive artefacts in their own right. With the declining influence of progressive rock in the later seventies, however, gatefold sleeves fell out of use and returned to their role of highlighting certain star issues.

## GOLD DISCS

Although there are more copies made of the average gold disc award (or silver or platinum) than many people realize, they are still comparatively uncommon items in the collectors' marketplace. Most often, therefore, they tend to be auctioned rather than offered for a fixed price. In most cases, the values reached are actually quite modest (for items in much shorter supply than the average valuable collectors' record), as the following list of recent auction house sales indicates:

**Bryan Adams:**
Waking Up (platinum) £200

**Beatles:**
Abbey Road (gold) £850
Get Back (gold) £580
Hey Jude (gold) £780

**Bee Gees:**
Too Much Heaven (platinum) £315

**Boomtown Rats:**
A Tonic For The Troops (gold) £130

**Carpenters:**
Please Mr Postman (platinum) £280

**Def Leppard:**
Hysteria (platinum) £200

**Dire Straits:**
Brothers In Arms (platinum) £320

**Frankie Goes To Hollywood:**
Relax (gold) £130

**Guns 'N' Roses:**
Appetite For Destruction (platinum) £350

**House Of Love:**
House Of Love (silver) £100

**Janet Jackson:**
Control (gold) £400

**James:**
Gold Mother (gold) £100

**Elton John:**
The Very Best Of Elton John (platinum)
£350

**Paul McCartney:**
Tripping The Live Fantastic (platinum)
£320

**Metallica:**
Metallica (gold) £350

**Sinead O'Connor:**
The Lion And The Cobra (gold) £140

**Pet Shop Boys:**
Heart (platinum) £90

**Pink Floyd:**
Dark Side Of The Moon (platinum) £280

**Pretenders:**
Pretenders II (silver) £170

**Prince:**
Batdance (gold) £400

**Tears For Fears:**
Seeds Of Love (platinum) £110

Most valuable are those awards presented to the artist themselves, but these are very seldom offered for sale. The products of those companies that offer to make a 'gold disc from your favourite record' are not the same thing at all, of course, and have no value to collectors.

## GOLD LABEL

Just as in the case of the London label, the earliest pressings of singles issued by Columbia, HMV and Parlophone are described as being 'gold label' copies. It is actually the print on the label that is coloured gold, rather than the label itself, but its presence is a good indication of likely value. If the original issue of a single should have a gold label, then this is indicated in the listings if later pressings bearing the same catalogue number exist. In such cases, the later pressing will have a value of only half the value given.

## INTERVIEW RECORDS

As far as copyright law in the UK and US is concerned, the rules that apply to recordings of music do not apply to the spoken word. Accordingly, anyone can issue records containing interviews with the famous, without worrying about the fact that the artists in question have contracts elsewhere. Companies like Baktabak capitalize on this by producing attractive interview picture discs, which can appear to the unwary to be highly desirable collectors' items. In fact, however, few collectors are actually much interested in these items and their values never rise above the cost when new. A small exception to this rule occurs in the case of interview material issued by the artist's record company as a promotional device, although even here interview recordings seldom reach the values of promotional releases containing music.

## JAZZ

For the third edition of the *Price Guide*, a large number of collectable jazz albums by American artists were included for the first time. This did not reflect a new development within the realm of record collecting, but was rather a belated acknowledgement of a collectors' market that had actually been in existence for some time. The emphasis was deliberately placed on UK issues via labels such as Esquire, Vogue and London Jazz, although the highest prices are actually paid for the original American albums that these British labels merely re-packaged. The jazz list has been expanded further still for this fourth edition.

## JAZZ IN BRITAIN

British jazz is a somewhat different animal to its American cousin. From the outset, the restricted market for the music, together with a typically British myopia with regard to the position of jazz's cutting edge, led to a much more intimate relationship between jazz and rock than was ever the case in America. The popularity of traditional jazz was a piece of British idiosyncrasy, for music that was inclined to view jazz as a kind of Music Hall entertainment could have little in common with what had been going on in New York's 52nd Street (the difference between Acker Bilk and Charlie Parker being as great as the difference between Brotherhood of Man and Kurt Cobain's Nirvana). But it was out of trad that the success of Lonnie Donegan was made; out of trad too that Alexis Korner was able to form his launching pad for much of the British R&B and beat boom that followed. During the sixties, musicians like Jack Bruce, Dick Heckstall-Smith, Jon Hiseman and Henry Lowther proved themselves to be equally at home playing both jazz and rock – partly out of necessity, but partly too because they were able to make worthwhile musical statements in both areas. Records by people like Neil Ardley, Mike Westbrook and Ian Carr on the one hand, and Colosseum, Soft Machine and the Battered Ornaments on the other, contain so many overlapping personnel (who feel little need to compromise their playing styles in either area), that it hardly makes sense to differentiate between the two kinds of music. As far as the collectors' market is concerned, it is the overlapping of musical styles and personnel that makes some of the late-sixties/early-seventies British jazz albums so desirable. Most of these are rare and prices remain high – especially since little in this field has ever been reissued.

## LASER-ETCHED RECORDS

In 1980 the first records appeared with laser-etched surfaces. As it happens, neither *True Colours* by Split Enz nor *Paradise Theatre* by Styx is of much more than novelty value these days, despite the attractive designs visible on the playing surface when the records are tilted towards the light. (Neither record was a limited edition, incidentally – all copies have the surface pictures.) The technique has been used very infrequently since 1980, possibly because, although the effect is undoubtedly interesting, it is nevertheless a lot less spectacular than one would imagine.

## LONG PLAY RECORDS

The first LPs were issued in the United States in early 1949 by the Columbia (CBS) record company. In the UK, however, EMI, which was responsible for distributing the Columbia label, prevaricated

– and it was Decca which issued the first LPs in June 1950. The company's initial release sheet comprised fifty-three records, the majority of which were classical, with a sprinkling of light orchestral items, together with gems by such popular artists as Edmundo Ros, the Galloway-Ruault Old Time Dance Orchestra and Troise and His Banjoliers. The claims made on behalf of the new format by advertisers at the time make interesting reading. Superb sound quality, with 'almost silent' playing surfaces, negligible wear during play, unbreakability, and ease of storage are all cited as reasons for purchasing LPs – and all of these will sound very familiar to those who remember the promotion of CDs nearly three and a half decades later.

## MATRIX NUMBERS

The matrix numbers that are to be found on the vinyl surface of a record in between the playing area and the label are sometimes of considerable help in providing information about the record itself. Much of the number will consist of the record's catalogue number, which is itself a piece of vital information in the case of test pressings issued with nothing useful written on the labels themselves. Extra digits, however, provide information about the stampers used to press the records (the 'matrix' being the mould from which the stampers were made). On some occasions, the recorded version of a song has been changed during an extended pressing run, and the corresponding change in the matrix number enables identification of the different versions without the record having to be played (collectable examples of this appear in the listings – see, for example, the Frankie Goes To Hollywood variations where the relevant matrix number differences are given in brackets after the catalogue numbers). In principle, the matrix number can be used to distinguish first and later pressings where the catalogue number is the same, although only classical record collectors seem to be much interested in these fine distinctions. In the case of UK releases, matrix numbers are generally machine stamped. There may also be one or more slogans or messages hand-scratched in the vinyl. A random inspection, for example, reveals the words 'Everything's Jelly' on a Spritualised 12″ test pressing, 'Bilbo' on a copy of the Who's *Live At Leeds* album and both 'Loosely From The Stiff Beach' and 'With Pink Warmth' on a copy of *Psonic Psunspot* by the Dukes of Stratosphear. The ubiquitous 'Townhouse' refers to one of the major studios, while 'A Porky Prime Cut' indicates that the master has been made by the most highly respected cutting engineer, George Peckham.

## MISPRESSED RECORDS

Whenever a record plays music that is not what the label or cover would lead the listener to expect, then this record is said to be a mispress. When pressing plants are producing several different records at the same time, it is an unfortunate but easily understood error if the occasional batch of vinyl is passed under the wrong stamper. Accordingly, records where one side plays what it should, but the other plays something quite different do turn up from time to time. In general, such records are of novelty but little monetary value. The exceptions are those records involving the major collectable artists – a number of Beatles mispressings, for instance, are listed in the guide, as are a few other interesting examples. In the CD age, incidentally, mispressings continue – discs where the musical content bears no relation to what is printed on the disc are in circulation. Errors involving labels on otherwise correctly pressed records are comparatively common. A record may have a side one (or side two) label on both sides; or else the labels for the two sides may be interchanged; or one or both labels may be missing altogether. None of these occurrences creates any increase in value, however, if only because they could be easily reproduced by a counterfeiter. Records where the label is displaced on to the playing surface, preventing play, are virtually worthless, of course.

## NEAR MINT (NM) CONDITION

'Near mint' is used in this guide synonymously with 'excellent', to indicate a record in played, but aurally perfect, condition. Further details are given under the 'Condition' heading.

## ORIGINAL PRESSINGS

The date of publication or the copyright date given on a record usually relates to the original release date, which is not necessarily the date of issue of the particular piece of vinyl in question. Where a record is given a reissue, after having been unavailable for a time, it is usually (though not always, unfortunately) given a new catalogue number. Catalogue numbers are therefore a considerable aid in identifying original pressings, and these are given in the guide wherever possible. Where a record remains in a company's catalogue over an extended period of time, changes in label design can make the first issues distinctive. Some of the most important of these are described under the appropriate record company headings within this guide. Values given in this guide are for original pressings. Later pressings may not be collectable at all, although if the record in question is not easily available in any form, then a later pressing may still command some kind of collectors' value. This, however, will obviously be rather less than for the original.

## PICTURE DISCS

The first picture disc, a 10" 78 rpm recording of 'Cowhand's Last Ride' by Jimmie Rodgers, was issued in America in 1933. At various times after that, further picture discs were issued, but all suffered from the fundamental problem of having poor sound quality, which prevented them from achieving much commercial success. The first rock picture discs (and the earliest to be listed in this guide) date from 1969-70 and comprise two compilation albums alongside LPs by Curved Air and Saturnalia. The sound quality of these was also poor, due to the fact that they are essentially thin, clear flexi-discs glued to a piece of card on which the actual pictures are printed. From the late seventies, picture discs became very much more common and although the sound quality is still inferior compared to the conventional black vinyl equivalents, it is good enough to allow the inherent attractiveness of the discs to become the major consideration. There tends to be a natural bias towards picture discs within the collectors' market, to the extent that for artists who are collected anyway, their picture discs are all sought after. The first shaped picture discs were a series of singles by the Police issued in the US (and widely available on import, albeit at quite high prices). These were cut into the shapes of police badges and were issued within special cardboard folders. For some reason, shaped picture discs did not really catch on in a big way until 1982-3, but they were a common record company gimmick throughout the rest of the eighties. Some of these explicitly recognize their primary function as display items, rather than serious sources of music, by including pieces of cardboard within the packaging that are intended to be folded into stands ('plynths') for the records. Uncut shaped picture discs consist of the twelve-inch record (with seven-inch grooves), from which the shaped disc is cut. They are collected rather in the same way as demonstration copies of regular singles are collected and typically sell for around three times the value of the finished shaped discs.

## PRIVATE PRESSINGS

When a group is unable to gain a recording contract with any established record company and decides to finance the production and distribution of a record itself, then the result is a private pressing. Many singles issued in the post-punk era conform with this description, but the term is most generally used in connection with a fairly large number of more-or-less progressive albums issued during the seventies. Many of these albums have been sold or exchanged for extraordinarily high amounts in the past and although the values of such items have started to fall, prices are still high, as reference to the entries for such groups as the Dark, Ithaca, Toby Jug and Complex will confirm. Arguably, the high values of these records are entirely the result of a skilful exercise in hype on the part of a few specialist dealers, but there have been at least a few transactions now to confirm these as genuine market values. Nevertheless, collectors should be aware that this whole area is something of a minefield, especially if ideas of investment and making a profit are a priority.

## PROMOTIONAL RECORDS

The term 'promo' is often used interchangeably with the term 'demo', even by the record companies themselves. Within this guide, however, the terms have specific, and different, meanings. A demo is a regular commercial release given a special label for the purposes of radio play or review. A promo, on the other hand, is a record (or other item) specially manufactured for advertising or promotional purposes. While being clearly related to a commercial release, the promo will be different in some major way from any version of the release that could be bought in a shop. Such items have long been a feature of the record industry and in the eighties and nineties in particular, a large number have been issued. Sometimes they consist of mixes not available to the general public, to enable radio stations to present something to their listeners that seems exclusive. It is also common for sampler recordings to be issued containing a small number of tracks from a forthcoming album, while the albums themselves may be provided with special packaging as a promotional device. This may range from a simple box containing one of each of the available formats, to the more elaborate affair typified by Talk Talk's *Laughing Stock*, where a picture CD is housed in a wooden box, along with pencils, rubber, ruler and other items of stationery, most stamped with the group's name. The majority of such releases have not been included in this guide, although the intention has been to include collectable items containing music that is not otherwise available, providing that they have values greater than twice any equivalent regular release.

## QUADRAPHONIC RECORDINGS

During the early seventies a number of quadraphonic LPs were issued. When played on a suitable system, incorporating a special decoder, such records enable sounds to be heard from each of four speakers. These are intended to be arranged with two in front of the listener, as in stereo, and a further two behind the listener. The extra two speakers deliver ambient sound in the case of recordings designed to recreate the sound of a live performance; otherwise they can be essential ingredients in a surround-sound experience. Few collectors possess a quadraphonic system – nevertheless, the records are often sought after, since they were designed to be playable on conventional stereo systems and although they do not then provide a quadraphonic effect, they often do contain mixes that sound noticeably different from their stereo equivalents. It should be noted that some US albums – such as many of those on the Impulse label – deliver quadraphonic sound on appropriate systems, even though there is no mention of the fact on either record label or sleeve.

## R.G.M.

The initials 'R.G.M' on a sixties record (whether in a Triumph record catalogue number or a reference to production by R.G.M. Sound) are indicative of the guiding hand of producer Robert George (Joe) Meek. Beginning as an engineer in the fifties, Joe Meek worked on numerous records by the likes of Frankie Vaughan, Shirley Bassey, Petula Clark and Lonnie Donegan, before setting himself up as an independent producer. His concern with creating unusual and distinctive sounds led him continually to push the primitive sound equipment of the time to its limits and it is his reputation as an innovator that is responsible for the considerable interest in his records today. Meek's experiments with speeded-up tape, distortion, close miking, echo and even multi-tracking were certainly some years before his time, but the fact that all this imagination and inventiveness were directed towards the production of what was, for the most part, crassly commercial material, tends to blunt the impact, for modern listeners, of what Meek was achieving. As it happens, Joe Meek did score some considerable commercial successes, including 'Johnny Remember Me' by John Leyton, 'Don't You Think It's Time' by Mike Berry, 'Have I The Right' by the Honeycombs, 'Just Like Eddie' by Heinz and 'Telstar' by the Tornados.

## RADIO TRANSCRIPTION DISCS

The American equivalents of the BBC transcription discs, used to syndicate rock music programmes across a large number of radio stations, are mostly the products of two companies: Westwood One and King Biscuit Flour Hour. Originally issued as two- and three-LP sets, they are now coming out as compact discs. Either way, the values are on a par with the BBC discs, at around £50 to £60 for the average album set or CD (with the same obvious exceptions). These recordings consist of live concerts interspersed with advertisements, ready for broadcast in the US. Other radio show albums contain a mixture of music (some of it previously issued studio material) and interviews. These have lower values than the all-live sets, going down to as little as £10, depending on the amount of unreleased live material they contain.

## REGGAE

Reggae (or ska or rock steady) from the sixties is very collectable and every record released is of value. Listing the records is in some cases quite problematic due to the chaotic nature of the specialist record labels involved. It is common practice for different artists to appear on either side of a single, but it is not always apparent which is intended to be the A side. Artists' names are frequently misspelt or simply change from record to record. Lloyd Charmers, Lloyd Chalmers, Lloyd Tyrell and Lloyd Terrel, for example, are all the same person; so are Roland Alphonso and Rolando Al; so are Jackie, Jackie Edwards, Wilfred, Wilfred Edwards and Wilfred Jackie Edwards! Sometimes the B side of a record changes during the lifetime of a single; sometimes a song is re-attributed to a different artist; and there are numerous examples where the name that appears on the record is simply wrong. It would even appear to be the case that, on occasion, more than one single has been issued with the same catalogue number. The reggae listings in this guide represent the best attempt at making sense of these various difficulties. In practice, sixties reggae collectors are interested in the entire output of the relevant labels and, apart from the special case of records by Bob Marley, which are worth considerably more than their fellows, all the records issued on any particular label have the same value. Singles on the Studio One and Blue Beat labels sell for £12 each. Other key labels are Black Swan, Coxsone, Dice, Doctor Bird, Island, Port-O-Jam, R&B, Rio (from 1963–5), Ska Beat, and Treasure Isle (from 1967–8), all of whose singles sell for £10. The small number of albums on these labels range from expensive to very expensive – typically £50 to £100. Further sixties reggae labels worth looking out for, with singles in the price range £5–£8, are: Aladdin, Amalgamated, Bamboo, Big Shot, Blue Cat, Caltone, Camel, Clan Disc, Columbia Bluebeat (a unique example of a major label taking an interest in the music), Crab, Double D, Duke, Duke Reid, Escort, Gas, Giant, High Note, Jackpot, Jolly, Jump Up, Nu Beat, Pama, Pressure Beat, Punch, Pyramid, Rainbow, Randys, Rio (from 1966), Treasure Isle (1969), Unity and Upsetter. Many of these labels continued into the seventies, but collectors' interest falls off dramatically.

## REMIXES

Ever since Trevor Horn and Frankie Goes To Hollywood hit upon the idea of using multiple remixes as a marketing device, it has been standard practice for modern artists to release several slightly different versions of the same song. A cynic might suggest that the reason for this is primarily to avoid the creative energy necessary in writing more songs and point to the nadir of the practice as being Prince's decision to issue an album-length collection of alternative arrangements of a song that only really consists of a single repeated line in the first place ('The Beautiful Experience'). Collectors, on the other hand, presumably delight in seeking out different mixes, as some of these can reach quite high prices.

## SEVENTY-EIGHTS

To most collectors, 78 rpm recordings are of little interest. They break much too easily for one thing; and hardly anyone has the means to play them these days for another. The age of these records is of no consequence in this respect – indeed it is actually part of the problem, for most 78s contain music from before the rock'n'roll era, which is itself subject to only slight collectors' interest. Even within the rock'n'roll era, the 45 rpm singles are much more collectable than their 78 rpm equivalents, despite what is sometimes suggested by the (non-specialist) media. A small number can be found listed within the pages of this guide, these being either records by particularly collectable artists, like Elvis Presley and Cliff Richard, or else the handful of significant rock'n'roll and R&B songs that were not given a 45 rpm release in the fifties. Apart from these, the general rule is that 78s have a value of about one-quarter of their seven-inch equivalent. It is suggested elsewhere that there is a growing market for 78s from 1959–60, when the format was rapidly dying out. These records are not actually as rare as is sometimes suggested and neither is it true that many were available by special mail order only. It should be realized that many parts of Scotland, for example, were still without mains electricity at this time, so that demand for 78s in these areas was still high.

## SLEEVES

LPs and EPs are supposed to be in sleeves and it should go without saying that a damaged or missing sleeve has a serious effect on the value of a record. As a general rule, the cover should be considered as being responsible for half the value of an item, while the disc is responsible for the other half. An exception to this principle is where a particular sleeve variation is the major factor in a record's rarity – such cases are mentioned explicitly in the listings. Picture sleeves for singles were a comparative rarity prior to the late seventies and were often reserved for promotional issues. In these cases, the effect of the sleeve on the value of a record can be dramatic (see, for example, the Pink Floyd and Tyrannosaurus Rex discographies). Increasingly from about 1978 onwards, it became standard practice for the first several thousand copies of a single to be issued with a picture sleeve. For these, therefore, collectors expect to find such a sleeve and are not very interested in copies without one. Within these listings, singles from 1980 onwards are presumed to come with picture sleeves and no explicit mention is made of the fact. Collectors like to see a company sleeve on singles from the fifties, sixties or seventies, where a picture sleeve is not appropriate, but the absence of a company sleeve has a very minor effect on a single's value. It is possible to obtain very good reproductions of many of the major fifties and sixties company sleeves and many collectors are happy to accept these as an alternative to the real thing. It is worth noting that the construction of LP and EP sleeves made in the UK is a considerable aid in the identification of original issues. During the fifties and sixties, the cardboard edges of the front cover were turned over the outside of the back cover; from the late sixties the edges were glued inside the back cover. In addition, LP covers from the fifties seem to be made of a much thinner, flimsier cardboard than used subsequently.

## STEREO

At the annual Audio Fair held in New York in October 1957, Decca demonstrated the results of its research into the reproduction of stereo sound by records. EMI had, in fact, been recording many of its artists in stereo for over two years previously and was issuing the results on what it called 'stereosonic' tapes. One company in America had issued twin-track stereo discs, which had to be played with two pickups. The first stereo LPs to be issued commercially in the UK were intended to demonstrate the system – Pye CSCL70007, EMI SDD1 and Decca SKL4001 all appearing in mid 1958 and all comprising extracts from various light and classical pieces, together with assorted sound effect recordings. In August, a large number of stereo records, covering various kinds of music, were given a simultaneous release by several different companies, with the first UK stereo LPs appearing a month later (courtesy of EMI and Decca). As a general rule, stereo records from the early years of the medium are worth a little more to collectors than their mono equivalents, due to the rather smaller numbers of them sold at the time. (It should be noted, however, that many jazz collectors prefer the mono versions, as being more faithful to the intentions of the musicians in the studio, so that stereo jazz LPs from the early years are worth a little less than their mono equivalents.) Towards the end of the sixties, when stereo recordings were rapidly becoming the norm, it is the mono versions that are scarcer and in consequence worth a little more to collectors. Mono recordings (other than reissues of earlier material) died out altogether after 1970. There tend to be many differences of detail between mono and stereo versions of the same LP – sometimes different takes are used and on occasion, the artist went back to the studio and re-recorded all the music for stereo. With the advent of multi-track recording, musicians began to take increasing liberties with the technology at their disposal. In order, for example, to record more than four parts on a four track machine, the technique of mixing tracks and bouncing them down to create free tape was invented. The final overdubs would be added at the final mixing stage, so that these would inevitably be different in the case of separately prepared mono and stereo mixes. Well-known examples of different mono and stereo versions resulting from this include the Beatles' 'White Album' (the two recordings of 'Don't Pass Me By' are completely different takes; the mono 'Helter Skelter' lacks Ringo's shouted complaint at the end); Jimi Hendrix's *Axis: Bold As Love* (the stereo 'EXP' is twice as long as the mono); Traffic's *Mr Fantasy* (Steve Winwood plays wildly divergent guitar solos at the ends of Heaven Is In Your Mind); and Pink Floyd's *Saucerful Of Secrets* (the instrumental texture of the two versions of 'Let There Be More Light' is markedly different).

## TEST PRESSINGS

A test pressing is an earlier stage in the production of a record than even the advance demonstration discs. It is made on ordinary vinyl literally to test the fidelity of each component involved, from the master tape itself through to the setting of the cutting equipment. Alternatively, a test pressing may represent a try-out for a proposed record release, the most collectable of these being records that did not, after all, become finished commercial releases. Where these pressings are albums, they may have proof or even finished covers; test pressings generally, however, are distinguished by their plain (usually white) labels. Apart from certain test pressings that are particularly collectable, and are listed as such in the guide, the values for these records are on a par with the values for demonstration records.

## TRI-CENTRES

The earliest singles have triangular centres, which identify original pressings in the case of fifties singles that were reissued with the same catalogue numbers. For most companies, tri-centres were used until the end of 1959, at which time round centres replaced them (the precise situation with regard to London singles is described under the London heading). Capitol, however, were using round centres from as early as 1956.

## TWELVE-INCH SINGLES

The first twelve-inch single was conceived very much as a gimmick. This was a 1976 reissue of the Who's 'Substitute', using exactly the same version as on the original 7″ single. The popularity of late-seventies disco music, however, turned the twelve-inch single into a staple format, since the lengthy playing times possible were ideal for coping with extended dance mixes. The early releases did not often have picture sleeves (RCA used what was essentially a company sleeve for its disco records, with a small picture of the artist at the top). From 1980, however, the majority of twelve-inch singles did have picture sleeves, which form an essential part of the collectors' package.

## VERY GOOD (VG) CONDITION

Very good is a description of a record's condition that is actually less complimentary than it sounds. Further details are given under the Condition heading.

## VINYL

The great majority of dealers will complain that during the last few years, the public demand for vinyl records has plummeted. The collectors' market has actually been less affected than the general second-hand market in records, but it is definitely the case that collectable records sell more reluctantly than they used to. The spiralling upward rise in the values of progressive albums has halted in general and, in some cases, prices have begun to fall. In many other areas too, values in this fourth edition of the guide are lower than those in the second and third editions. In the case of fifties and sixties records, however, demand is still high and in these areas there are a number of trend-bucking price rises. The rarest singles, in particular, are becoming increasingly difficult to find in any condition and several collectors are deciding that they had buy them now while they still can. As a result, the values of these are climbing, most noticeably in the case of the highest price items, where the results of auctions frequently produce very happy surprises for the vendors. Other areas of increasing interest are sixties albums by key artists like the Beatles, the Who and the Small Faces; European progressive albums by artists like Faust, Can and Amon Düül; and a range of jazz albums.

# Labels

### ACTION

Action was a specialist soul label, whose singles issued in 1968 and 1969 (with a distinctive red and black label bearing a shooting-star logo) are all very much in demand. Soul collectors, more than those in other fields, tend to prefer demo copies of singles, arguing that these are the true first pressings. This is particularly true of the Action label, where demos typically have a value of three times that of the standard issues.

### APPLE

The label set up and run by the Beatles is viewed as a legitimate area of interest by Beatles collectors. Quite apart from the records of the Beatles themselves, there are a few considerable rarities on the label, by such names as the Iveys, Delaney and Bonnie, Richard Brautigan and John Tavener. The enormous musical range represented by these and the other names on the label reflects the fact that the Beatles were wealthy enough to issue whatever music took their individual fancies, without commercial success being a particular consideration. The records issued by the Beatles themselves from 1968 onwards were on the Apple label as far as label design was concerned, but the catalogue numbers were actually part of the main Parlophone series.

### ATLANTIC

The Atlantic label's status as one of the most successful independents (until its incorporation within the Kinney organization in 1971) depended on the skill with which its founders, the Ertegun brothers, were able to identify the key developments in jazz and R&B. In the UK, Atlantic releases were originally distributed via the London label, but from 1964 the Atlantic label was issued in its own right. Identification of original pressings is not a problem, since Atlantic obligingly used new catalogue numbers whenever a reissue was made. In particular, the Kinney take-over resulted in the use of a 'K' as prefix to all UK catalogue numbers – so that, *Led Zeppelin IV*, for example, changed from 2401012 to K50008. (There was also a label design change at this time, with the red and plum LP labels becoming green and orange.)

### BLUE HORIZON

Producer Mike Vernon formed the Blue Horizon label as an outlet for his beloved blues music and virtually the entire catalogue is now collectable (the label's one sore thumb, an album by the group Focus, just makes it by the skin of its teeth). The very earliest records to make use of the Blue Horizon name were ten singles and a pair of albums (one by Dr Ross and one a various artists collection) that were sold by mail order in 1965–6. The albums in particular are now extremely rare. In 1967 the signing of Peter Green's new group, Fleetwood Mac, prompted a distribution deal with CBS. The first single releases by Fleetwood Mac and Aynsley Dunbar bore a Blue Horizon logo on an orange CBS label, but by the start of 1968 the familiar light-blue label was in use.

## BLUE NOTE

Blue Note is the most collected jazz label in the UK, with every sixties release being of value (and listed in the guide). The label was founded in 1939 in the US, and the earliest album releases now command high prices. A mint copy of *Genius Of Modern Music Vol.1* by Thelonious Monk (Blue Note BLP5002 1951) sells for £250, for example. Starting in 1961, records released on the label became available in the UK as direct imports. Within this guide, the issue date given often refers to the date of import rather than to the actual release date in the US, which may well have been a few years earlier (this is true for all of the LPs in the BLP15 series). These original US pressings will be worth significantly more than the values listed, which apply to the import copies. Original Blue Note records issued during 1961 to 66 have a blue and white label design with the legend 'Blue Note Records Inc ★ New York USA'; from 1966 to 1970 the legend 'A Division of Liberty Records' appears. The same label design reappeared in 1985, but apart from the fact that the reissues from this time have a generally newer appearance, they also carry the new wording 'The Finest in Jazz Since 1939'.

## CAPITOL

Capitol singles had purple labels in the fifties and black in the sixties. The LPs had turquoise labels in the fifties and black labels with a rainbow border in the sixties. In 1968, the rainbow border was dropped for a short time, before the company switched to a lime green label, with a new deep pink logo.

## CBS

The label that is called Columbia in the US became abbreviated to CBS in the UK (standing for Columbia Broadcasting Systems) to avoid conflict with the UK Columbia label, whose links with its American ancestor became severed during the fifties. The plain orange labels used by CBS on both its singles and LPs in 1962, when the first UK records were released, remained essentially unchanged until 1975, when a new label on which orange shaded into yellow was introduced. As a result, the label design is of limited use in identifying original pressings of records by the likes of Bob Dylan. (The rear fold-over sixties cover design, however, remains a reliable guide in these circumstances). The BPG prefix used for LPs (SBPG for stereo) was dropped at the start of 1968 and reissues from that date onwards have their catalogue numbers amended accordingly.

## CHARISMA

The Charisma label began in 1969 as something of a progressive rock specialist label. Most of the early albums are collectable, although the label lacked the sureness of touch of Island or Vertigo, and a few releases are hardly sought after at all. Until 1972, the label design featured a large scroll logo on a deep pink background and first pressings of early albums by the likes of Audience, Van Der Graaf Generator and Genesis have this label. A new design, featuring a cartoon mad hatter on a pale pink label began with the album *Foxtrot* by Genesis (CAS1058). Albums bearing this label but with lower catalogue numbers are therefore second issues and are worth no more than 50% of the first issue values.

## COLUMBIA

LP labels for the main Columbia SX series were green with gold print until 1963, when they were changed to match the style of EMI's sister label, Parlophone. From 1963 to 1969, this resulted in a black label with silver print and a blue Columbia logo; from 1969 the EMI logo was added to a redesigned black and silver label, with a silver Columbia logo now appearing in a box. Singles also changed from a green to a black label in 1963, with some earlier singles being given later, black label, reissues. Much later reissues using a very similar design to the original green label are easily identifiable by the references to EMI, which are not present on the early labels.

## DANDELION

The Dandelion label was set up and co-financed by disc jockey John Peel in 1969 to enable him to promote the work of artists he felt were worthy of wider exposure, but who may have found some difficulty in gaining record contracts with anyone else! None of the records sold particularly well and the entire catalogue is now collectable. Initially the label was distributed by CBS – the labels for these issues are crimson overlaid with dandelion seed parachutes. In 1971, distribution was taken over by Warner Brothers, whose new label design featured a multi-coloured picture of dandelion flowers on a beige background. None of the CBS records were reissued by Warner Brothers.

## DAWN

Dawn was the specialist progressive label set up by Pye. The label's list of signings somehow lacked the class of rival concerns like Vertigo and Harvest, but the majority of the albums released from 1969 to 1975 are collectable, even if only a handful have managed to reach high values.

## DECCA

Until 1970, Decca used a red label for its mono LPs (LK series) and a blue label for its stereo LPs (SKL series). A few of the mono LPs from the early sixties were still in the catalogue at the end of the decade, but although these later pressings have the same label design as the originals, they no longer use the cover construction in which the edges of the front sheet are folded over the back. From 1970, a blue label is used, but with significantly changed details as compared with the earlier stereo label. The earlier label has a circular 'ffss' logo at the top and a relatively wide 'full frequency stereophonic sound' band immediately adjacent to the centre hole. The later label has a narrow band, with a gap between itself and the hole; there is no circular logo, and the Decca logo is now inside a box. The sleeves for albums released during 1968–70 have a small hole on the back, at the top right corner. The inner sleeves have a red (for mono) or blue (for stereo) coloured band which can be seen through the hole to identify immediately which kind of record it is! Decca singles have a blue label from the early fifties – switching from a tri-centre to a round centre at the end of the decade, and starting to use the boxed Decca logo during 1966.

## DERAM

Decca was the first company to start a specialist progressive label with the release of the first Deram records towards the end of 1966. Of course, in 1966 it was by no means clear what music should actually be included in the definition, with the result that some fairly odd records were given Deram releases (such as those by Whistling Jack Smith and Lionel Bart). Nevertheless, the proportion of musically adventurous releases is high and the label's sixties records are widely collected. Both singles and LPs had a brown and white label – albums bearing a 1970 or 1971 release date with red and white labels are later pressings.

## ECM

ECM is a jazz and contemporary music label run by producer Manfred Eicher, whose direct involvement in the creation of his company's releases is unparalleled in the world of music. From the label's start in 1970, Eicher was determined to enhance the music with as high a recording quality as was possible, combined with superior standards of record pressing. Although there are exceptions – particularly in the early days when avant-garde improvisors like Derek Bailey were recorded – ECM's music is well known for having something of a house style (described in the label's own advertising slogan as 'the most beautiful sound next to silence'). Particularly since the tremendous success (in jazz terms) of Keith Jarrett, and later, that of Pat Metheny and Jan Garbarek, fans of music that somehow manages to be both cutting edge and attractively mellow are content in the knowledge that any record bearing the ECM name is likely to be one that they will like.

## ELEKTRA

From its beginnings as a US folk and roots specialist company, Elektra was held in high regard as a label that could be relied on to issue only artistically worthwhile records. Even when the company began to branch out into the developing rock market, it still seemed to have the knack of finding artists whose role in the development was destined to be a key one – such as the Butterfield Blues Band, the Doors, Love and the Incredible String Band. The earliest Elektra records have gold labels, changing briefly to white in 1966, and then orange to the end of the decade. In 1970, a red label was used, then, following the absorption of the label into the Kinney group in 1971, a mottled green label featuring a butterfly logo was introduced.

## EMBASSY

Embassy was the record label sold by Woolworths during the late fifties and early sixties. Its policy was to issue sound-alike cover versions of the hits of the day, with the result that the label scarcely features in the collectors' market today. A handful of Embassy artists eventually made it on to 'proper' labels – Johnny Worth, Hal Munro, and, most notably, Maureen Evans.

## FACTORY

The label that provided a home for the music of Joy Division and New Order is one of the few modern labels to attract collectors trying to put together a complete run. In practice, however, it is impossible for anyone to collect every Factory catalogue item, due to the label's eccentric habit of giving numbers to assorted items other than music releases. The very first Factory item, in fact, is a concert poster (FAC1). Later catalogue oddities include a badge (FAC21), a computer programme (FAC91), the Hacienda club's first birthday party (FAC83), and, indeed, the Hacienda club itself (FAC51).

## HARVEST

Harvest was set up as EMI's specialist progressive rock label in 1969. Many of the original releases on each of the two number series (SHSP and SHVL) are now collectable, although EMI's high success rate means that there are fewer high value items than are found on many of the other progressive labels. Unfortunately for collectors, Harvest retained its distinctive lime green label throughout the seventies, so that the first pressings of albums selling well enough to stay in the catalogue cannot easily be identified. This is the reason for the omission from the listings of such well-known albums as Pink Floyd's *Umma Gumma* and *Atom Heart Mother* and Deep Purple's *Deep Purple*, *Concerto For Group And Orchestra* and *In Rock*, original copies of all of which might be expected to be sought after.

## HMV

HMV's turquoise-blue labels are a welcome sight on Elvis Presley singles from the fifties, indicating an early release of some value. Sixties HMV labels were black. The LP labels changed from crimson in 1963, acquiring the EMI house-style shown in the Columbia and Parlophone labels of the period. In the case of HMV, this meant a black label with a red His Master's Voice logo. There is no problem with regard to later reissues, since in 1967 HMV became a classical label only.

## INCUS

The Incus label was set up in 1970 by avant-garde improvisors Evan Parker and Derek Bailey as a means of ensuring that rather more of their own difficult music, as well as that of other like-minded musicians, would be recorded than might otherwise be the case. With typically self-deprecating humour, the duo elected to call their parent company Compatible Recording And Publishing Ltd, with the initial capital letters picked out in bold print. The label's releases are, however, definitive statements within their free improvisation genre and are consequently all collected by fans of the style, who know exactly what to expect from an Incus album. The majority of these stayed in the catalogue until the change-over to CDs, but original copies of the earliest issues are particularly sought after, being easily identified by their Edward Road, Bromley, company address, and dark-blue record labels.

## ISLAND

The Island record company was formed in 1962 as an outlet for Caribbean music in the UK – the catalogue number prefix used for singles being WI, standing for West Indies. These singles, with their white and red labels, are all very collectable. During 1967, Island began issuing rock LPs, gaining a significant boost by their successful signing of Stevie Winwood's new group, Traffic. The change in musical emphasis was matched by a change in label design. From 1967 until 1970, Island labels were pink, a fact which easily enables the identification of first pressings. Collectors are not often concerned about the fine differences, but there are actually three different pink label designs. From 1967 until 1969 (beginning with ILP952 by John Martyn), the labels have a distinctive red and black 'eye' logo on the left-hand side. The last album to be issued with this label was ILPS9106 by Dr Strangely Strange, although ILPS9099 (White Noise), ILPS9100 (Clouds), ILPS9104 (Free), and ILPS9105 (Nick Drake) all have the later pink label designs. During 1969 a few issues used a pink label on which an enlarged black-only version of the eye logo appeared at the centre. A few singles, plus copies of *Holidays* and *Unhalfbricking* by Fairport Convention, *Ahead Rings Out* by Blodwyn Pig, and *This Was* by Jethro Tull have been spotted with this label design. The albums are therefore second pressings, although they are actually rarer than the earlier issues. The Clouds and Nick Drake albums mentioned above were first issued with this second pink label design. From 1969 to 1970 the pink labels have a large white 'i' logo below the centre. The last album to be issued with this label was ILPS9135 by Cat Stevens, although one number down, Nick Drake's *Bryter Layter* is not pink, and it is probable that Alan Bown's *Listen* (ILPS9131) is not pink either. From 1970 to 1974, the pink colour was relegated to a circular border for a multi-coloured label bearing a stylized picture of an island in the sun. Many of the earlier alums were reissued with this label, but the values of these later pressings are seldom more than 50% of the original pink label copies. Some albums appear with even later label designs, but unless stated otherwise in the listings, these late issues are of no interest to collectors.

## KEY

Records issued on the Key label during the early seventies were all Christian in content, but many have become collectable as a by-product of the interest in progressive rock and folk music of the period. Most notable in this respect is the album by Out of Darkness, which continues to be one of the more sought-after progressive rarities.

## KINNEY

In 1971, three major US record labels – Elektra, Reprise and Warner Brothers – amalgamated under the Kinney company name. Atlantic joined the fold in early 1972. Records still in the catalogue at that time were immediately given new numbers beginning with a K, a change which is immensely useful to collectors in that it enables the easy identification of original pressings – those without the K numbers. Today the company continues under the name WEA.

## LIBERTY

The bright blue labels on late-sixties Liberty LPs were changed to black during 1970. Collectable albums like the second by the Groundhogs and the first by Hawkwind, which stayed in the catalogue long enough to be issued with both label designs, are only worth the full values listed in this guide if they are the first pressings with the bright blue labels. Second issue, black label copies typically fetch no more than two-thirds of this value. The black label design was short-lived, however, as in 1971 Liberty was absorbed into the United Artists record company.

## LONDON

London was the first label to receive serious attention from collectors due to its policy of issuing in the UK the best of American rock 'n' roll and R&B records. Many collectors try to obtain complete runs of London singles at least up until the mid sixties, when the rise of British beat effectively put an end to the label's importance. Their task in this respect is hindered by the extreme rarity of some of the issues, but they are also safe in the knowledge that a complete collection will contain remarkably few dud recordings. The earliest London singles have gold writing on a black label and these 'gold label' singles are the most highly prized and the most valuable. Where gold label singles have been reissued as later 'silver label' pressings (i.e. they have silver writing on a black label), these are generally worth around only half the value of the first issues. Unfortunately, the London label did not appear to be particularly systematic in its procedures, so that during the early months of 1957 some records were issued on gold labels and some on silver. There are, however, no gold label issues after HLP8420 (which happens to be by Slim Whitman). Within these listings, London singles with gold labels are specifically indicated where it might not be clear whether the first issue is gold or silver. A further design change occurs at the end of the decade, when the original triangular single centres were replaced by a round centre. As before, a round-centre issue of a record that was first issued with a tri-centre is worth only about half the value of the original. The first round centre issue was HLU8903 (Gloria Smith), but the last tri-centre was HLW9050 (Duane Eddy). There is a period of some five months between these two, during which both kinds of centre were being used for new releases. Again, where it would not otherwise be clear in these listings, the existence of a tri-centre is indicated. London EPs have the same label design changes as the singles, but complications with regard to London LPs are restricted to the fact that a few were reissued after 1967 with black labels replacing the original plum-coloured labels.

## MARMALADE

The short-lived and collectable Marmalade label was set up and run by impresario Giorgio Gomelsky, who was the original manager of the Yardbirds amongst other things. The company found some interesting artists to record – Blossom Toes, Julie Driscoll and Brian Auger, and John McLaughlin among them – but the label never really recovered from the failure (or refusal) of Julie Driscoll to become the huge star she could have been.

## MUSHROOM

Three companies have adopted the Mushroom name. A late-seventies US label released albums by the group Heart, and a long-lived Australian Mushroom label is still going. The Mushroom of most interest to collectors, however, is a tiny concern that issued a handful of LPs during 1970–72. The label's varied catalogue of progressive rock, Indian music, and jazz was never available in ordinary record shops, but was advertised in the underground press (notably *Oz* magazine) for sale by mail order. The original asking price of a pound for the albums is now multiplied many times over!

## NEON

Neon was the specialist progressive label set up by RCA at a time when all the majors were doing something similar. RCA was actually a little slow off the mark – the first Neon album was released in 1971 – and although some of the records are rather fine (and have the attractive gatefold sleeves typical of the genre), they sold poorly. All the Neon albums are now collectable – there being just eleven of them in the series.

## NEPENTHA

The short-lived Nepentha label is often described as being a subsidiary of Vertigo, with whom it shared a house-style. In reality, of course, Vertigo is itself a subsidiary of Phonogram, who presumably felt that if one specialist progressive label could prove to be a success, then it was worth trying a second one. In fact, Nepentha never managed to achieve the strong corporate image that Vertigo did (its label design featured a blue quill, whose link with the music's powers of making the listener forget all grief – for such is the label name's arcane meaning – is not a striking one) and it was abandoned after just five album releases. In fact, the label was lucky to last even that long. After minimal sales of the first three Nepentha albums, the cancelled matrix number visible on the fourth, *Earth And Fire*, shows that the record was originally intended for the Mercury label.

## NOVA

Although Deram had originally been conceived as something of a progressive offshoot for Decca records, the flowering of the music in 1969, accompanied by the birth of several specialist labels to feature it, encouraged Decca to try the tactic for a second time. The link with the parent company was made explicit from the outset, and records were issued on labels described either as 'Decca Nova' or 'Deram Nova', although there was only one catalogue number series. Unfortunately, the albums always seemed to convey the impression that Decca's heart was not really in the exercise. Few of the artists were particularly inspiring, and the elaborate gatefold sleeves that were so much a part of the package in the case of rival labels like Vertigo, Harvest and Island were never used. The label was abandoned at the start of 1971.

## OAK

Of the many small private recording studios, catering mainly to young bands without a record contract, that run by R.G. Jones in South London has become the subject of considerable cult interest. Part of this interest derives from the studio's association with the Rolling Stones and the Yardbirds, both of which groups made early recordings there. More, however, is due to the current fascination with any records from the sixties or early seventies that are sufficiently obscure to be suitable candidates for high-priced collectors' items. Oak was the label name given to the small number of records actually pressed up by the R.G. Jones studio. These were paid for by the artists concerned for use as demos – in the same way as modern groups will produce cassettes of their songs in order to obtain a record contract or gigs (or just to sell at those gigs). The small number of collectable Oak records of this kind are listed in the guide. The Bo Street Runners and the Thyrds found some very limited success via the TV rock group contest organized by the *Ready Steady Go* programme, but the majority of the Oak artists were never heard of again. There were also a larger number of Oak label acetates, which occasionally come on to the market at upwards of £25 each (one featuring two unreleased songs by a youthful David Bowie is worth nearer a hundred times this value). Although many of the Oak recordings are decent beat group performances, there is a considerable danger in assuming that everything on the label is worthwhile (and collectable). A recent discovery of a complete Oak album may have whetted a few appetites, but the MOR pop selection that makes up *Wilf Todd And His Music* is not the kind of thing to normally set collectors' pulses racing – a fact which nevertheless proved to be no curb on the hyperbole of one specialist dealer, who managed to describe the record as a 'monster rare Oak label 60s private LP – £400' with a straight face. The R.G. Jones studio is still in operation, incidentally, one of its more recent sucesses being the number one single recorded by Mr Blobby.

## PARLOPHONE

The changes in Parlophone label designs are of particular importance with regard to records by the Beatles. In early 1963, the label used for singles was changed from red to black, so that early pressings of 'Please Please Me' are found with the earlier design and later pressings with the later design. The black label singles, incidentally, all carry the message 'Made In Gt Britain', which is not present on reissue copies from the seventies. Parlophone LPs were also given a label change in 1963. The original labels are black, with all the print being in gold ink. The Parlophone logo is written in gold 3-D effect capitals. The replacement labels were still black, but the print was now silver. Parlophone, now in simple flat capitals, was a bright canary yellow, as was the company's pound-sign logo. Again, the change took place at just the right time for the earliest copies of the Beatles LP *Please Please Me* to have the original label, while most have the newer one. In 1969, the LP labels were changed again, with the yellow Parlophone now being replaced by a silver one in a box.

## PYE

Pye was the third major British record company (after EMI and Decca) and by the early sixties it was issuing singles on a number of related labels – Pye, Pye International, Pye Jazz and Piccadilly (as well as a large number of subsidiary labels licensed from US originals, including Cameo Parkway, Colpix, Red Bird, Chess and Kama Sutra). Only the main Pye and Pye International labels cause much trouble with regard to reissues. Pye labels were purple until 1962; then deep pink until the end of 1967 (with a change of layout at the beginning of 1965, when the Pye moved from the left to the top of the label and gained a wide black band); then sky blue into the seventies. Pye International labels change in tandem: from a greenish-blue, to red and yellow, to red, to sky blue. In both cases, LPs follow through the same label design changes as the corresponding singles. Records by the likes of the Kinks with labels coloured pink shading to mauve, or grey shading to white, or any records mentioning the PRT company, are later pressings from the seventies or eighties and are not collectable.

## RCA

RCA was the company that launched the 45 rpm single in the United States in 1949, as an initial response to its rival, Columbia's, invention of the LP. During the 1950s, the company's records were issued by HMV in the UK (both labels used the distinctive dog and gramophone logo), but in 1957 RCA set up its own UK company. Both singles and LPs used a black label until late 1968, when this was replaced by an orange label.

## RECOMMENDED RECORDS

Some of the most interesting records from the late seventies and early eighties are to be found on the Recommended Records label, co-founded by Henry Cow drummer, Chris Cutler. The company's manifesto included the statement: 'We do not operate R.R. as a business which means we do not have to play the market. We just do what we like.' What they liked was a range of artists who had in common their originality and their defiantly uncommercial bias. The records were often housed in hand-decorated sleeves that were almost works of art in their own right; they were frequently limited editions, and were given catalogue numbers whose logic is hard to identify. They are only just beginning to attract the attention of collectors, but the values are set to rise in the future.

## REGAL ZONOPHONE

The label that was used for Salvation Army records during the fifties was revived by EMI in 1967 as something of a specialist progressive label. The majority of the records released on the label, until its demise in early 1975, are collectable. It is not generally realized that a handful of records were actually issued on Regal Zonophone during 1964–7. Only one of these is listed in the guide (that by the Innocents and the Leroys) – the others continued the label's earlier tradition by featuring the Salvation Army's pop group, the Joystrings.

## REPRISE

Frank Sinatra's Reprise was one of the labels becoming part of the Kinney company in 1971. In addition to its catalogue numbers changing from the RSLP series to the new K series, the label design also changed from yellow and pale green, with a distinctive drawing of a steam-boat, to a plain tawny or orange-yellow.

## STIFF

The Stiff label made an enviable start with its bestselling releases by Elvis Costello, Ian Dury and the Damned and looked set to become one of the most successful of the new breed of record companies to emerge along with punk. The company's unconventional, irreverent approach served as a role model for many later record labels and helped to endear itself to the collectors who tried to amass complete runs of Stiff releases a few years ago. Unfortunately, the label lost much of its prominence when its original stars moved elsewhere and only the Pogues have succeeded in providing much of a boost since. One result is that Stiff is now much less collected than it was and the values of its records have fallen across the board.

## STUDIO 36

The equivalent of Oak records in Northampton was the Studio 36 label, used to issue songs by a tiny number of local beat groups in the sixties made at Northampton Sound Recording. Four records are listed in this *Price Guide* – those by Tony Sands and the Drumbeats, the Quakers, the Blues Five and the Skyliners – and all are extremely scarce, even in the label's home town. There is also an acetate – 'Running Away From Love' by Phoenix – and there are likely to be others as yet unknown to the author.

## SUE

The British Sue label was formed in 1963 as a subsidiary of Island Records, with a policy of leasing US soul records, in contrast to the parent label's West Indian bias. Initially, the label concentrated on records from the American Sue company, but it soon began to cast its net wider. With a label manager, Guy Stevens, who was himself very much a soul fan, the Sue catalogue soon became one of the most impressive of all – and is collected as such by soul enthusiasts today.

## TAMLA MOTOWN

The consistency of Tamla Motown's single release policy during the sixties means that, today, every one of those records is a collectors' item. As with many other specialist soul labels, the most sought-after items are the demonstration copies of the singles. Collectors take the not unreasonable attitude that only these can really be considered to be the first pressings. The consequence for the value of these is that a tripling of the value of the standard issue is a realistic procedure, but only where this takes the value above the following minimum values for demonstration singles: Stateside singles by Motown artists – £50; TMG501-599 – £50; TMG600-635 – £30; TMG636-680 – £20.

## TOPIC

Topic is the oldest specialist folk label, with its first releases appearing on 78 rpm recordings in the mid fifties, and it is by far the most successful. All the fifties and sixties issues are collectable to a greater or lesser extent, and many of the later issues are of interest too. Although the vinyl catalogue has now been deleted in favour of CDs, many of the records remained available for many years. Topic used a plain dark-blue label until the mid seventies, however, and the listed values refer to this label design.

## VERTIGO

The Vertigo label has been of interest to collectors for several years, with many enthusiasts trying to put together a complete run of the original album releases. These are all characterized by a black and white label design intended to induce vertigo when watched spinning round on a turntable. This design is commonly referred to as a 'spiral', although it is actually nothing of the kind – the alternative 'swirl' description is marginally more accurate for a design made up of overlapping circles. Most albums used the 'spiral' design as the entire side one label, with all the track information being included on the side two label, although a few albums have conventional labels on both sides, with the spiral reduced to the status of a logo. The spiral-label albums were nearly all housed in extravagantly designed gatefold sleeves (those by Dr Z and Mike Absalom are more elaborate opening-out creations), which play an essential part in giving these records the special appeal that they have. Vertigo was set up in 1969 as a specialist progressive label for Phonogram (Philips/Fontana) and from the outset, the high proportion of albums by musically interesting artists was a strong indication that the label was destined for long-term success. In fact, it continues today, although inevitably no longer linked to music that might be described as 'progressive'.

## WARNER BROTHERS

The record division of the well-known American film company was begun in 1958, but despite early success with the Everly Brothers and Peter, Paul and Mary, the label did not really start to become a significant force within the industry until its incorporation within the Kinney company in 1971. The green labels in use at the time were not changed until after several months, with the result that some early K series albums can be easily distinguished from the later pressings bearing the 'tree-lined avenue' label.

## ZTT

Both the fortunes and the collectability of the Zang Tumb Tuum label were inextricably linked with the popularity of the company's major asset, Frankie Goes To Hollywood. Whereas at the height of Frankie-mania, it was possible to point to a breed of collector that was interested in the dull music of Andrew Poppy purely because it was to be found on the same label as the star group, this would no longer seem to be the case.

# A

## A – AUSTR

It is appropriate that the first record listed in this guide should be one that typifies exactly what collecting rare records is all about. Produced as a labour of love on an independent label created for the purpose, the record came complete with lavish packaging and sold hardly at all! The music, which is thoughtful and pastoral, is interesting enough to give the record a cult reputation, and the mystique is enhanced for record collectors today by the album being reissued in a very limited facsimile edition, itself being sold at something of a collectors' price.

| | | | | | | | |
|---|---|---|---|---|---|---|---|
| A – Austr | LP | Holyground | HG113 | 1970 | £210 | £350 | |
| A – Austr | LP | Magic Mixture. | MM1 | 1989 | £8 | £20 | |

## A B SKHY

| | | | | | | | |
|---|---|---|---|---|---|---|---|
| Ramblin' On | LP | MGM | SE4676 | 1970 | £4 | £10 | US |
| A B Skhy | LP | MGM | SE4628 | 1969 | £4 | £10 | US |

## A CERTAIN RATIO

| | | | | | | | |
|---|---|---|---|---|---|---|---|
| All Night Party | 7" | Factory | FAC5 | 1979 | £1.50 | £4 | |
| Backs To The Wall | CD-s | A&M | ACRCD517 | 1989 | £2 | £5 | |
| Big E | CD-s | A&M | ACRCD514 | 1989 | £2 | £5 | |
| Four For The Floor EP | CD-s | A&M | ACRCD550 | 1990 | £2 | £5 | |
| Life's A Scream | 7" | Factory | FAC112P | 1984 | £5 | £10 | promo only pack |
| Planet | CD-s | A&M | CDROB2 | 1991 | £2 | £5 | |
| Shack Up | 7" | A&M | ACR590 | 1990 | £2 | £5 | promo only |
| Shack Up | 12" | A&M | ACRY590 | 1990 | £3 | £8 | promo only |
| Twenty Seven Forever | CD-s | A&M | CDROB5 | 1991 | £2 | £5 | |
| Won't Stop Loving You | CD-s | A&M | ACDCD540 | 1990 | £2 | £5 | |

## A HOUSE

| | | | | | | | |
|---|---|---|---|---|---|---|---|
| Kick Me Again Jesus | 12" | Rip | ARIPT1 | 1987 | £2.50 | £6 | |

## A II Z

| | | | | | | | |
|---|---|---|---|---|---|---|---|
| No Fun After Midnight | 12" | Polydor | POSPX243 | 1981 | £3 | £8 | red vinyl |

## AARDVARK

| | | | | | | | |
|---|---|---|---|---|---|---|---|
| Aardvark | LP | Nova | SDN17 | 1970 | £37.50 | £75 | |

## ABACUS

| | | | | | | | |
|---|---|---|---|---|---|---|---|
| Abacus | LP | Polydor | 2371215 | 1971 | £10 | £25 | |
| Everything You Need | LP | Zebra | 2949002 | 1972 | £8 | £20 | German |
| Indian Dancer | 7" | York | YR207 | 1973 | £2 | £5 | |
| Just A Day's Journey Away | LP | Polydor | 2371270 | 1972 | £8 | £20 | German |
| Midway | LP | Zebra | 2949013 | 1974 | £8 | £20 | German |

## ABBA

Scandinavia's most successful pop export continue to enthral a large and loyal following a decade and a half after disbanding. As is well-known, all four members were established artists before joining together in Abba. In addition to the items listed below, therefore, Abba collectors are also interested in the records listed under the Anni-Frid Lyngstad, Agnetha Faltskog, Björn Ulvaeus, Hootenanny Singers, Northern Lights, and Hep Stars headings.

| | | | | | | | |
|---|---|---|---|---|---|---|---|
| Anniversary Boxed Set | 7" | Epic | ABBA26 | 1984 | £50 | £100 | 26 blue vinyl singles |
| Arrival | LP | Nautilus | NR20 | 1981 | £5 | £12 | US audiophile |
| Best Of Abba | LP | Readers Digest. | GABA112 | 1986 | £8 | £20 | 5 LP set |
| Chiquitita (Spanish version) | 7" | Vogue | 45X1188 | 1978 | £2 | £5 | French |
| Dream World | CD-s | Polydor | 8538912 | 1994 | £20 | £40 | promo |
| Estoy Sonando | 7" | Vogue | 101235 | 1979 | £2 | £5 | French |
| I Have A Dream | 7" | Epic | EPC8088 | 1979 | £1.50 | £4 | gatefold picture sleeve |
| I Have A Dream (Shakin' Stevens B side) | 7" | Kelloggs | KELL1 | 1984 | £2.50 | £6 | |
| Ring Ring | LP | Polar | POLS242 | 1973 | £5 | £12 | Swedish |
| Ring Ring | 7" | Epic | EPC1793 | 1973 | £10 | £20 | |
| Ring Ring | 7" | Polar | POS1171 | 1973 | £10 | £10 | Swedish label & language |
| Ring Ring | 7" | Polydor | 2040105 | 1973 | £10 | £20 | sung in German |
| Singles, The First Ten Years | LP | Epic | ABBOX2 | 1983 | £20 | £40 | 2 picture discs, boxed |
| Slipping Through My Fingers | 7" | Discomate | PD105 | 1981 | £15 | £30 | Japanese Coca-Cola picture disc |
| Slipping Through My Fingers | 12" | Discomate | PD1005 | 1981 | £30 | £60 | Japanese, red vinyl |
| So Long | 7" | Epic | EPC2848 | 1974 | £4 | £8 | |
| Super Trouper | LP | Epic | ABBOX1 | 1980 | £20 | £40 | boxed, book, poster |
| Super Trouper | CD | Epic | CDEPC10022 | 1983 | £5 | £12 | |
| Thank You For The Music | 7" | Epic | WA3894 | 1983 | £5 | £10 | shaped picture disc |
| Under Attack | 7" | Epic | EPCA112971 | 1982 | £2.50 | £6 | picture disc |
| Visitors | CD | Epic | CDEPC10032 | 1983 | £5 | £12 | |
| Voulez Vous | LP | Epic | EPC86086 | 1979 | £25 | £50 | picture disc |

| | | | | | | | |
|---|---|---|---|---|---|---|---|
| Waterloo | 7" | Polar | POS1186 | 1974 | £5 | £10 | *Swedish label & language* |
| Waterloo | 7" | Polydor | 2040116 | 1974 | £10 | £20 | *sung in German* |
| Waterloo | 7" | Vogue | 103104 | 1974 | £10 | £20 | *sung in French* |
| Winner Takes It All | 12" | Epic | EPC128835 | 1980 | £15 | £30 | *gatefold picture sleeve* |

## ABBEY TAVERN SINGERS

Collectors of records on a particular label often find themselves buying albums or singles that are not at all to their taste! *We're Off To Dublin In The Green* by the Abbey Tavern Singers is an LP of Irish pub songs that just happens to have been released on a subsidiary of Tamla Motown.

| | | | | | | | |
|---|---|---|---|---|---|---|---|
| We're Off To Dublin In The Green | LP | VIP | VS402 | 1966 | £5 | £12 | *US* |

## ABBOTT, BILL & THE JEWELS

| | | | | | | | |
|---|---|---|---|---|---|---|---|
| Groovy Baby | 7" | Cameo Parkway | P874 | 1963 | £4 | £8 | |

## ABC

| | | | | | | |
|---|---|---|---|---|---|---|
| King Without A Crown | CD-s | Neutron | NTCD113 | 1987 | £2 | £5 |
| When Smokey Sings | CD-s | Neutron | NTCD111 | 1987 | £2 | £5 |

## ABERCROMBIE, JOHN

| | | | | | | | |
|---|---|---|---|---|---|---|---|
| Gateway | LP | ECM | ECM1061ST | 1975 | £5 | £12 | *with Dave Holland & Jack DeJohnette* |
| Sargasso Sea | LP | ECM | ECM1080ST | 1976 | £4 | £10 | *...with Ralph Towner* |
| Timeless | LP | ECM | ECM1047ST | 1974 | £5 | £12 | |

## ABICAIR, SHIRLEY

In the quest to find increasingly rare grooves, some very strange artists become included within the domain of Northern Soul. Hence the unlikely inclusion here of Shirley Abicair, a lady who used to sing rather twee songs on children's television, to the accompaniment of a strummed autoharp.

| | | | | | | |
|---|---|---|---|---|---|---|
| Am I Losing You | 7" | Piccadilly | 7N35364 | 1967 | £2 | £5 |
| Willie Can | 7" | Parlophone | MSP6224 | 1956 | £2 | £5 |

## ABLUTION

| | | | | | | | |
|---|---|---|---|---|---|---|---|
| Ablution | LP | CBS | 80536 | 1974 | £10 | £25 | *Swedish* |

## ABRAHAMS, MICK

| | | | | | | | |
|---|---|---|---|---|---|---|---|
| At Last | LP | Chrysalis | CHR1005 | 1972 | £10 | £25 | *round cover* |
| Learning To Play Guitar With | LP | SRT | SRT73313 | 1975 | £4 | £10 | |
| Mick Abrahams | LP | Chrysalis | ILPS9147 | 1971 | £4 | £10 | |

## ABRAMS, DAVE

| | | | | | | |
|---|---|---|---|---|---|---|
| If I'd Stayed Around | LP | Folksound | FS103 | 1975 | £37.50 | £75 |

## ABRAMS, RICHARD

| | | | | | | |
|---|---|---|---|---|---|---|
| Levels And Degrees Of Light | LP | Delmark | DS413 | 1968 | £5 | £12 |

## ABSALOM, MIKE

| | | | | | | | |
|---|---|---|---|---|---|---|---|
| Hector And Other Peccadillos | LP | Philips | 6308131 | 1972 | £8 | £20 | |
| Mighty Absalom Sings Bathroom Ballads | LP | Sportsdisc | ILP1081 | 196– | £4 | £10 | |
| Mike Absalom | LP | Vertigo | 6360053 | 1971 | £30 | £60 | *spiral label* |
| Save The Last Gherkin For Me | LP | Saydisc | SDL162 | 1969 | £20 | £40 | |

## ABSTRACT TRUTH

| | | | | | | | |
|---|---|---|---|---|---|---|---|
| Abstract Truth | LP | Parlophone | PCSJ12065 | 1970 | £50 | £100 | *South African* |

## ABYSSINIAN BAPTIST CHOIR

| | | | | | | |
|---|---|---|---|---|---|---|
| Abyssinian Baptist Choir | LP | Philips | 847095BY | 1963 | £15 | £30 |

## ABYSSINIANS

| | | | | | | |
|---|---|---|---|---|---|---|
| Arise | LP | Front Line | FL1019 | 1978 | £5 | £12 |
| Forward To Zion | LP | Klik | KLP9023 | 1977 | £5 | £12 |

## AC DONNCA, SEAN

| | | | | | | | |
|---|---|---|---|---|---|---|---|
| An Aill Bain The White Rock | LP | Claddagh | CC9 | 1971 | £5 | £12 | *Irish* |

## ACADEMY

| | | | | | | |
|---|---|---|---|---|---|---|
| Pop Lore According To | LP | Morgan Blue Town | BT5001 | 1969 | £37.50 | £75 |
| Rachel's Dream | 7" | Morgan Blue Town | BTS2 | 1969 | £2.50 | £6 |

## ACCENT

The Accent's one single was produced by Mike Vernon, but it is quite unlike the blues-based material in which Vernon specialized. Instead, crashing guitars and a warbling, distorted guitar solo frame a mysterious unison vocal for a performance that is nowadays described as being psychedelic. The record has a similar feel to the Smoke's greatly superior 'My Friend Jack', which is perhaps the classic of the genre, but it is hardly surprising that the record sunk without trace, given that the Smoke's record was not a UK hit either.

| | | | | | | |
|---|---|---|---|---|---|---|
| Red Sky At Night | 7" | Decca | F12679 | 1967 | £50 | £100 |

## ACCENTS

| | | | | | | |
|---|---|---|---|---|---|---|
| Wiggle Wiggle | 7" | Coral | Q72351 | 1959 | £5 | £10 |

## ACCIDENTS

| Title | Format | Label | Catalogue | Year | | | Notes |
|---|---|---|---|---|---|---|---|
| Blood Spattered With Guitars | 7" | Hook, Line & Sinker | HOOK1 | 1980 | £1.50 | £4 | |
| Kiss Me On The Apocalypse | LP | Hook Line 'n Sinker | | 1980 | £30 | £60 | test pressing |

## ACCOLADE

| Title | Format | Label | Catalogue | Year | | | Notes |
|---|---|---|---|---|---|---|---|
| Accolade | LP | Columbia | SCX6405 | 1970 | £6 | £15 | |
| Accolade 2 | LP | Regal Zonophone | SLRZ1024 | 1971 | £15 | £30 | |
| Natural Day | 7" | Columbia | DB8688 | 1970 | £1.50 | £4 | |

## AC/DC

| Title | Format | Label | Catalogue | Year | | | Notes |
|---|---|---|---|---|---|---|---|
| AC/DC Live | CD | Atlantic | PRCD48182 | 1992 | £20 | £40 | US promo |
| Albert Archives | LP | Albert | APLP037 | 1979 | £5 | £12 | Australian |
| Ballbreakers | CD | East West | SAM1693 | 1995 | £15 | £30 | promo compilation |
| Can I Sit Next To You Girl | 7" | Albert | AP10551 | 1974 | £37.50 | £75 | Australian |
| Danger | 7" | Atlantic | A9532P | 1985 | £5 | £10 | shaped picture disc |
| Danger | 7" | Atlantic | A9532W | 1985 | £1.50 | £4 | poster sleeve |
| Dirty Deeds Done Dirt Cheap | 7" | Atlantic | K10899 | 1977 | £10 | £20 | cartoon schoolboy picture sleeve |
| Flick Of The Switch Interview Album | LP | Atlantic | PR562 | 1983 | £5 | £12 | US promo |
| Girl's Got Rhythm | 7" | Atlantic | K11406E | 1979 | £2 | £5 | envelope sleeve |
| Guns For Hire | 7" | Atlantic | A9774P | 1983 | £5 | £10 | shaped picture disc |
| Heat Seeker | 12" | Atlantic | A9136TP | 1988 | £2.50 | £6 | picture disc |
| Heatseeker | CD-s | Atlantic | A9136CD | 1988 | £2 | £5 | 3" single |
| High Voltage | 7" | Atlantic | K10860 | 1976 | £12.50 | £25 | picture sleeve |
| Highway To Hell | LP | Atlantic | ATL50628 | 1979 | £50 | £100 | German, yellow vinyl |
| Highway To Hell | LP | Atlantic | K50628 | 1979 | £180 | £300 | test pressing with different sleeve |
| If You Want Blood | LP | Atlantic | ATL50532 | 1978 | £100 | £200 | Dutch, red and white vinyl |
| It's A Long Way To The Top | 7" | Atlantic | K10745 | 1976 | £4 | £8 | |
| Jailbreak | 7" | Atlantic | K10805 | 1980 | £2.50 | £6 | |
| Japan Tour '81 | LP | Atlantic | SAM155 | 1981 | £37.50 | £75 | promo picture disc |
| Live From The Atlantic Studios | LP | Atlantic | LAAS001 | 1978 | £37.50 | £75 | US promo |
| Money Talks | CD-s | East West | B8886CD | 1990 | £2 | £5 | |
| Nervous Shakedown | 7" | Atlantic | A9651P | 1984 | £5 | £10 | shaped picture disc |
| Powerage | LP | Atlantic | KSD19180 | 1978 | £20 | £40 | Canadian red vinyl |
| Razor's Edge | CD | Atlantic | ACDC1 | 1990 | £8 | £20 | interview promo |
| Rock 'n' Roll Ain't Noise Pollution | 12" | Atlantic | K11630T | 1980 | £2.50 | £6 | with badge |
| Rock 'n' Roll Damnation | 12" | Atlantic | K11142T | 1978 | £2.50 | £6 | |
| Shake A Leg | 7" | Atlantic | K11600 | 1979 | £15 | £30 | wrong A side |
| Shake Your Foundations | CD-s | Atlantic | A9474CD | 198– | £2 | £5 | |
| Shake Your Foundations | 7" | Atlantic | A9474P | 1986 | £5 | £10 | shaped picture disc |
| That's The Way I Wanna Rock 'n' Roll | CD-s | Atlantic | A9098CD | 1988 | £2 | £5 | |
| That's The Way I Wanna Rock 'n' Roll | 12" | Atlantic | A9098TP | 1988 | £2.50 | £6 | picture disc |
| Thunderstruck | CD-s | Atco | B8907CD | 1990 | £2 | £5 | |
| Touch Too Much | 7" | Atlantic | K11435 | 1980 | £1.50 | £4 | back to front sleeve |
| Who Made Who | CD-s | Atlantic | A9425CD | 198– | £2 | £5 | |
| Who Made Who | 7" | Atlantic | A9425P | 1986 | £5 | £10 | shaped picture disc |
| Who Made Who (Collectors Mix) | 12" | Atlantic | A9425T | 1986 | £2.50 | £6 | with poster |
| Whole Lotta Rosie | 12" | Atlantic | K11207T | 1978 | £2.50 | £6 | |
| You Shook Me All Night Long | 7" | Atlantic | A9377P | 1986 | £4 | £8 | shaped picture disc |

## ACE, BUDDY

| Title | Format | Label | Catalogue | Year | | | Notes |
|---|---|---|---|---|---|---|---|
| Buddy Ace | 7" EP | Vocalion | VEP170164 | 1965 | £20 | £40 | |
| Got To Get Myself Together | 7" | Action | ACT4504 | 1968 | £1.50 | £4 | |

## ACE, CHARLIE

| Title | Format | Label | Catalogue | Year | | | Notes |
|---|---|---|---|---|---|---|---|
| Creeper | 7" | Upsetter | US359 | 1971 | £1.50 | £4 | Upsetters B side |

## ACE, JOHNNY

| Title | Format | Label | Catalogue | Year | | | Notes |
|---|---|---|---|---|---|---|---|
| Johnny Ace | 7" EP | Vogue | VE170150 | 1962 | £30 | £60 | |
| Memorial Album | LP | Duke | DLP71 | 1956 | £50 | £100 | US |
| Memorial Album | LP | Vocalion | VA160177 | 1961 | £30 | £60 | |
| Memorial Album | 10" LP | Duke | DLP70 | 1955 | £150 | £250 | US |
| My Song | 7" | Vogue | V9200 | 1962 | £30 | £60 | demo only |
| Pledging My Love | 7" | Vogue | V9180 | 1961 | £30 | £60 | |

## ACE, RICHARD

| Title | Format | Label | Catalogue | Year | | | Notes |
|---|---|---|---|---|---|---|---|
| Don't Let The Sun Catch You Crying | 7" | Coxsone | CS7031 | 1967 | £5 | £10 | Viceroys B side |
| Hang 'Em High | 7" | Trojan | TR654 | 1969 | £1.50 | £4 | Black & George B side |
| I Need You | 7" | Studio One | SO2022 | 1967 | £6 | £12 | Soul Vendors B side |
| More Reggae | 7" | Studio One | SO2072 | 1969 | £6 | £12 | Gladiators B side |

## ACES

| Title | Format | Label | Catalogue | Year | | | Notes |
|---|---|---|---|---|---|---|---|
| But Say It Isn't So | 7" | Parlophone | R5108 | 1964 | £1.50 | £4 | |
| Wait Till Tomorrow | 7" | Parlophone | R5094 | 1963 | £1.50 | £4 | |

## ACES (2)

| Title | Format | Label | Catalogue | Year | | | Notes |
|---|---|---|---|---|---|---|---|
| One Way Street | 7" | Etc | ETC1 | 1982 | £5 | £10 | |

## ACHE

| Title | Format | Label | Catalogue | Year | | | Notes |
|---|---|---|---|---|---|---|---|
| Bla Som Altid | LP | KHF | ROLP6570 | 1977 | £5 | £12 | Danish |
| De Homine Urbano | LP | Philips | 841906 | 1970 | £5 | £12 | German |
| Green Man | LP | Philips | 6318005 | 1971 | £10 | £25 | German |

| | | | | | | | |
|---|---|---|---|---|---|---|---|
| Pictures From Cyclus 7 | LP | CBS | 81216 | 1974 | £4 | £10 | Dutch |

## ACHES & PAINS
| | | | | | | | |
|---|---|---|---|---|---|---|---|
| Again And Again | 7" | Page One | POF008 | 1966 | £1.50 | £4 | |

## ACHOR
| | | | | | | | |
|---|---|---|---|---|---|---|---|
| End Of My Day | LP | Cedar | CEDAR1 | 1978 | £50 | £100 | |

## ACID GALLERY
| | | | | | | | |
|---|---|---|---|---|---|---|---|
| Dance Around The Maypole | 7" | CBS | 4608 | 1969 | £10 | £20 | |

## ACID SYMPHONY
| | | | | | | | |
|---|---|---|---|---|---|---|---|
| Acid Symphony | LP | private | | 1969 | £75 | £150 | US, three LP set |

## ACINTYA
| | | | | | | | |
|---|---|---|---|---|---|---|---|
| La Cité des dieux oubliés | LP | SRC | 161754 | 1978 | £15 | £30 | French |

## ACKLES, DAVID
| | | | | | | | |
|---|---|---|---|---|---|---|---|
| David Ackles | LP | Elektra | EKL4022/ EKS74022 | 1968 | £6 | £15 | |
| Five and Dime | LP | CBS | 32466 | 1973 | £5 | £12 | US |
| Subway To The Country | LP | Elektra | EKS74060 | 1970 | £6 | £15 | |

## ACKLIN, BARBARA
| | | | | | | | |
|---|---|---|---|---|---|---|---|
| Am I The Same Girl | 7" | MCA | MU1071 | 1969 | £1.50 | £4 | |
| Love Makes A Woman | 7" | MCA | MU1038 | 1968 | £1.50 | £4 | |

## ACQUA FRAGILE
| | | | | | | | |
|---|---|---|---|---|---|---|---|
| Acqua Fragile | LP | Numero Uno | DZSLN55656 | 1973 | £10 | £25 | Italian |
| Mass Media Stars | LP | Dischi | 6150 | 1974 | £6 | £15 | Italian |

## ACRE, SEPH & THE PETS
| | | | | | | | |
|---|---|---|---|---|---|---|---|
| Rock And Roll Cha Cha | 7" | Pye | 7N25001 | 1958 | £1.50 | £4 | |

## ACT
| | | | | | | | |
|---|---|---|---|---|---|---|---|
| Absolutely Immune | 12" | ZTT | TIMM1 | 1987 | £2.50 | £6 | |
| Absolutely Immune | 12" | ZTT | VIMM1 | 1987 | £10 | £20 | |
| Chance | CD-s | ZTT | CDBET1 | 1988 | £50 | £100 | |
| Chance | 7" | ZTT | BET1 | 1988 | £25 | £50 | |
| Chance | 12" | ZTT | BETT1 | 1988 | £37.50 | £75 | |
| I Can't Escape From You | CD-s | ZTT | CDIMM2 | 1987 | £4 | £10 | |
| Laughter, Tears And Rage | CD | ZTT | ZQCD1 | 1988 | £6 | £15 | |
| Snobbery And Decay | CD-s | ZTT | CID28 | 1987 | £10 | £20 | gatefold card sleeve |
| Snobbery And Decay | 12" | ZTT | 12XACT28 | 1987 | £10 | £20 | with poster |
| Snobbery And Decay | 12" | ZTT | 12ZTAS28 | 1987 | £6 | £15 | |
| Snobbery And Decay | 12" | ZTT | CT01 | 1987 | £10 | £20 | promo |

## ACT (2)
| | | | | | | | |
|---|---|---|---|---|---|---|---|
| Cobbled Streets | 7" | Columbia | DB8179 | 1967 | £6 | £12 | |
| Here Come Those Tears | 7" | Columbia | DB8261 | 1967 | £6 | £12 | |
| Just A Little Bit | 7" | Columbia | DB8331 | 1968 | £10 | £20 | |

## ACT (3)
| | | | | | | | |
|---|---|---|---|---|---|---|---|
| Act | 7" EP | Oak | RGJ407 | 1965 | £62.50 | £125 | |

## ACTION
The Action were a mod group with a similar soul/R&B sound to the Who, except that, according to those who saw the group live, the Action were better. Not that this is particularly apparent from the group's records, which are, for the most part, worthy cover versions, but lacking the extra spark of star quality. Sadly, the Action never did get to make an album, although a later incarnation of the group made two, as Mighty Baby.

| | | | | | | | |
|---|---|---|---|---|---|---|---|
| Baby You've Got It | 7" | Parlophone | R5474 | 1966 | £20 | £40 | |
| Harlem Shuffle | 7" | Hansa | 14321AT | 1968 | £20 | £40 | German |
| I'll Keep On Holding On | 7" | Parlophone | R5410 | 1966 | £20 | £40 | |
| Land Of 1000 Dances | 7" | Parlophone | R5354 | 1965 | £20 | £40 | |
| Never Ever | 7" | Parlophone | R5572 | 1967 | £20 | £40 | |
| Shadows And Reflections | 7" EP | Odeon | MOE149 | 1967 | £100 | £200 | French, best auctioned |
| Shadows And Reflections | 7" | Parlophone | R5610 | 1967 | £20 | £40 | |

## ACTIONS
| | | | | | | | |
|---|---|---|---|---|---|---|---|
| Wepp | 7" | Studio One | SO2065 | 1968 | £6 | £12 | Larry & Alvin B side |

## ACTIVE RESTRAINT
| | | | | | | | |
|---|---|---|---|---|---|---|---|
| Terror In My Home | 7" | Sticky | PEELOFF3 | 1983 | £2 | £5 | |

## ACTRESS
| | | | | | | | |
|---|---|---|---|---|---|---|---|
| Good Job With Prospects | 7" | CBS | 4016 | 1969 | £15 | £30 | |

## ACUFF, ROY
| | | | | | | | |
|---|---|---|---|---|---|---|---|
| Favorite Hymns | LP | MGM | E3707 | 1958 | £5 | £12 | US |
| I Like Mountain Music | 7" | Brunswick | 05635 | 1957 | £1.50 | £4 | |
| Old Time Barn Music | 10" LP | Columbia | CL9010 | 195– | £8 | £20 | US |
| Songs Of The Smokey Mountains | LP | Capitol | T617 | 1955 | £5 | £12 | US |
| Songs Of The Smokey Mountains | 10" LP | Columbia | CL9004 | 195– | £8 | £20 | US |

## AD CONSPIRACY
| | | | | | | | |
|---|---|---|---|---|---|---|---|
| Ad Conspiracy | LP | Diamond Age | | 1979 | £6 | £15 | |

## ADAM & THE ANTS

| | | | | | | | |
|---|---|---|---|---|---|---|---|
| Goody Two Shoes | 7" | CBS | A112367 | 1982 | £5 | £10 | *Not credited to 'Adam Ant'* |
| Zerox | 7" | Do-It | DUN8 | 1979 | £1.50 | £4 | *...mispressed B side – plays 'Physical'* |

## ADAM, MIKE & TIM

| | | | | | | | |
|---|---|---|---|---|---|---|---|
| Most Peculiar Man | 7" | Columbia | DB7902 | 1966 | £1.50 | £4 | |

## ADAMO

| | | | | | | | |
|---|---|---|---|---|---|---|---|
| '66 | LP | Electrola | E84070 | 1966 | £5 | £12 | *German* |
| Adamo | LP | HMV | 1044 | 1962 | £8 | £20 | *Dutch* |
| Olympia '67 | LP | HMV | DF321 | 1967 | £15 | £30 | *French* |

## ADAMS, ARTHUR K.

| | | | | | | | |
|---|---|---|---|---|---|---|---|
| She Drives Me Out Of My Mind | 7" | Blue Horizon | 573136 | 1968 | £5 | £10 | |

## ADAMS, BILLY

| | | | | | | | |
|---|---|---|---|---|---|---|---|
| Count Every Star | 7" | Capitol | CL15107 | 1959 | £5 | £10 | |

## ADAMS, BRYAN

| | | | | | | | |
|---|---|---|---|---|---|---|---|
| Bryan Adams | CD | A&M | CDA3100 | 1983 | £5 | £12 | |
| Can't Stop This Thing We Started | CD-s | A&M | AMCD812 | 1991 | £2 | £5 | |
| Cuts Like A Knife | CD | A&M | CDA4919 | 1983 | £5 | £12 | |
| Eighteen Til I Die – The Interview | CD | A&M | BRYANINTCD1 | 1996 | £8 | £20 | *...promo* |
| Everything I Do I Do It For You | CD-s | A&M | AMCD789 | 1991 | £2 | £5 | |
| Hidin' From Love | 7" | A&M | AMS7520 | 1980 | £7.50 | £15 | *... picture sleeve* |
| Into The Fire | CD | A&M | CDA3907 | 1987 | £5 | £12 | |
| It's Only Love (with Tina Turner) | 7" | A&M | AM285 | 1985 | £2 | £5 | *double* |
| Let Me Take You Dancing | 7" | A&M | AMS7460 | 1979 | £4 | £8 | |
| Let Me Take You Dancing | 12" | A&M | AMSP7460 | 1979 | £6 | £15 | |
| One Good Reason | 7" | A&M | AM170 | 1984 | £25 | £50 | |
| Reckless | CD | Mobile Fidelity | UDCD544 | 1991 | £6 | £15 | *.... US audiophile* |
| Somebody | 7" | A&M | AMP236 | 1985 | £1.50 | £4 | *...picture disc* |
| There Will Never Be Another Tonight | CD-s | A&M | AMCD838 | 1991 | £2 | £5 | |
| Waking Up The Neighbourhood | CD | A&M | 3971642 | 1991 | £15 | £30 | *..CD & cass in promo pack* |
| Waking Up The Neighbourhood | CD | A&M | POCM3023/4 | 1991 | £10 | £25 | *....... Japanese with bonus rarities CD* |
| You Want It, You Got It | CD | A&M | CDA3154 | 1983 | £5 | £12 | |

## ADAMS, DANNY & THE CHALLENGERS

| | | | | | | | |
|---|---|---|---|---|---|---|---|
| Bye Bye Baby, Bye Bye | 7" | Philips | BF1346 | 1964 | £1.50 | £4 | |

## ADAMS, FAYE

| | | | | | | | |
|---|---|---|---|---|---|---|---|
| I'll Be True | 7" | London | HLU8339 | 1956 | £250 | £400 | *........ best auctioned* |
| Shake A Hand | LP | Warwick | 2031 | 1961 | £25 | £50 | *US* |

## ADAMS, GLADSTON

| | | | | | | | |
|---|---|---|---|---|---|---|---|
| Dollars And Cents | 7" | Trojan | TR659 | 1969 | £2.50 | £6 | |

## ADAMS, GLEN

| | | | | | | | |
|---|---|---|---|---|---|---|---|
| Cool Cool Rocksteady | 7" | Collins Downbeat | CR006 | 1968 | £4 | £8 | *.... Owen Gray B side* |
| Hold Down Miss Winey | 7" | Island | WI3100 | 1967 | £5 | £10 | *Vincent Gordon B side* |
| My Girl | 7" | Duke | DU58 | 1969 | £1.50 | £4 | *...... Gladiators B side* |
| Rent Too High | 7" | Trojan | TR621 | 1968 | £2.50 | £6 | |
| She | 7" | Island | WI3083 | 1967 | £5 | £10 | *.. Sonny Burke B side* |
| She Is Leaving | 7" | Blue Cat | BS126 | 1968 | £4 | £8 | *...... Uniques B side* |
| She Is So Fine | 7" | Island | WI3120 | 1967 | £4 | £8 | *... Roy Shirley B side* |
| She's So Fine | 7" | Amalgamated | AMG837 | 1969 | £1.50 | £4 | *. Ernest Wilson B side* |
| Silent Lover | 7" | Island | WI3072 | 1967 | £5 | £10 | |

## ADAMS, JOHNNY

| | | | | | | | |
|---|---|---|---|---|---|---|---|
| Come On | 7" | Top Rank | JAR192 | 1959 | £1.50 | £4 | |
| Heart And Soul | LP | SSS | SSS5 | 196– | £5 | £12 | *US* |
| Reconsider Me | 7" | Polydor | 56775 | 1969 | £2.50 | £6 | |

## ADAMS, LLOYD

| | | | | | | | |
|---|---|---|---|---|---|---|---|
| I Wish Your Picture Was You | 7" | Blue Beat | BB366 | 1966 | £6 | £12 | *........Creepers B side* |

## ADAMS, MARIE

| | | | | | | | |
|---|---|---|---|---|---|---|---|
| | 7" | Capitol | CL14963 | 1958 | £7.50 | £15 | |

## ADAMS, MIKE & THE REDJACKETS

| | | | | | | | |
|---|---|---|---|---|---|---|---|
| Surfers Beat | LP | Crown | CST312 | 1963 | £15 | £30 | *US* |

## ADAMS, PAUL & LINDA

| | | | | | | | |
|---|---|---|---|---|---|---|---|
| Far Over The Fell | LP | Sweet Folk | | 1975 | £15 | £30 | |

## ADAMS, PEPPER

| | | | | | | | |
|---|---|---|---|---|---|---|---|
| Cool Sound | LP | Pye | NPL28007 | 1959 | £10 | £25 | |
| Critics' Choice | LP | Vogue | LAE12134 | 1958 | £8 | £20 | |

## ADAMS, RITCHIE

| | | | | | | | |
|---|---|---|---|---|---|---|---|
| Back To School | 7" | London | HLU9200 | 1960 | £6 | £12 | |

## ADAMS, STEVE
Steve Adams .......................................... LP ..... Mind's Ear....... ........................... 1977 £6........ £15 ...............................

## ADAMS, SUZIE & HELEN WATSON
Songbird ............................................... LP ..... Dingles .......... DIN327 ................. 1983 £5.........£12 .....................

## ADAMS, WOODROW
Baby You Just Don't Know...................... 7" ...... Blue Horizon... 451001 ................... 1965 £50.......£100 ...................

## ADDERLEY, CANNONBALL
| | | | | | |
|---|---|---|---|---|---|
| With Sergio Mendes And The Bossa Rio Sextet | LP | Capitol | (S)T2877 | 1968 £5 | £12 |
| Accent On Africa | LP | Capitol | (S)T2987 | 1969 £5 | £12 |
| African Waltz | LP | Riverside | RLP377 | 1961 £6 | £15 |
| At The Lighthouse | LP | Riverside | RLP344 | 1960 £6 | £15 |
| Cannonball | LP | London | LTZC15015 | 1956 £8 | £20 |
| Cannonball Adderley | LP | Emarcy | EJL1261 | 1957 £8 | £20 |
| Cannonball Adderley And The Pollwinners | LP | Riverside | RLP355 | 1961 £6 | £15 |
| Cannonball Adderley Quintet Plus | LP | Riverside | RLP388 | 1961 £6 | £15 |
| Cannonball In Europe | LP | Riverside | RLP499 | 1963 £5 | £12 |
| Cannonball Plays Bossa Nova | LP | Riverside | RM455 | 1963 £5 | £12 |
| Cannonball Takers Charge | LP | Riverside | RLP12303 | 1959 £6 | £15 |
| Cannonball's Sharpshooters | LP | Mercury | MMB12008 | 1959 £5 | £12 |
| Country Preacher | LP | Capitol | EST404 | 1970 £5 | £12 |
| In New York | LP | Riverside | RLP(9)404 | 1962 £6 | £15 |
| In San Francisco | LP | Riverside | RLP12311 | 1962 £6 | £15 |
| Know What I Mean? | LP | Riverside | RLP433 | 1962 £5 | £12 |
| Mercy Mercy Mercy! | LP | Capitol | ST2663 | 1967 £4 | £10 |
| Portrait Of Cannonball | LP | Riverside | RLP12269 | 1958 £6 | £15 |
| San Francisco Revisited | LP | Riverside | RM444 | 1963 £5 | £12 |
| Somethin' Else | LP | Blue Note | BLP/BST81595 | 196– £10 | £25 ..... with Miles Davis |
| Them Dirty Blues | LP | Riverside | RLP12322 | 1960 £6 | £15 |
| Things Are Getting Better | LP | Riverside | RLP12286 | 1958 £6 | £15 |
| Wow! | LP | Fontana | FJL107 | 1965 £5 | £12 |

## ADDERLEY, NAT
| | | | | | |
|---|---|---|---|---|---|
| Nat Adderley | LP | London | LTZC15018 | 1956 £10 | £25 |
| That's Right | LP | Riverside | RLP330 | 1960 £6 | £15 |
| Work Song | LP | Riverside | RLP12318 | 1960 £6 | £15 |

## ADDICTS
Here She Comes ................................... 7" ...... Decca ........... F11902 ................... 1964 £4........ £8

## ADDICTS (2)
Lunch With The Addicts ......................... 7" ...... Dining Out .... TUX1................... 1981 £5.........£10

## ADDRISSI BROTHERS
| | | | | | |
|---|---|---|---|---|---|
| Cherry Stone | 7" | London | HL8922 | 1959 £1.50 | £4 |
| It's Love | 7" | Columbia | DB4370 | 1959 £1.50 | £4 |
| Saving My Kisses | 7" | London | HL8973 | 1959 £1.50 | £4 |

## ADENO, BOBBY
Hands Of Time ...................................... 7" ...... Vocalion ......... VP9279 ................ 1966 £7.50.......£15

## ADLAM, BETH
Seventeen ............................................. 7" ...... Starlite .......... ST45024 .......... 1960 £1.50........£4

## ADLIBS
| | | | | | |
|---|---|---|---|---|---|
| Boy From New York City | 7" | Red Bird | RB10102 | 1966 £7.50 | £15 |
| Giving Up | 7" | Deep Soul | DS9102 | 1970 £2.50 | £6 |

## ADLIBS (2)
Neighbour Neighbour ............................. 7" ...... Fontana.......... TF584 ................... 1965 £12.50....£25 ...........................

## ADMIRALS
Promised Land ....................................... 7" ...... Fontana.......... TF597 .................. 1965 £12.50....£25 ............................

## ADRIAN & THE SUNSETS
| | | | | | |
|---|---|---|---|---|---|
| Breakthrough | LP | Sunset | (SE)63601 | 1963 £15 | £30 ...................US |
| Breakthrough | LP | Sunset | (SE)63601 | 1963 £25 | £50 ....US, multi-coloured vinyl |

## ADULT NET
| | | | | | |
|---|---|---|---|---|---|
| Honey Tangle | CD | Fontana | 8381252 | 1989 £5 | £12 |
| Take Me | CD-s | Fontana | BRXCD1 | 1989 £2 | £5 |
| Waking Up In The Sun | CD-s | Fontana | BRXCD3 | 1989 £2 | £5 |
| Where Were You | CD-s | Fontana | BRXCD2 | 1989 £2 | £5 |

## ADVANCEMENT
Advancement........................................ LP ..... Philips.......... PHS600328 ........... 1969 £15........£30 ...................US

## ADVENTURERS
Can't Stop Twisting................................ LP ..... Columbia ...... CL2147/CS8547..... 1961 £5..........£12 ...................US

## ADVERTS
| | | | | | |
|---|---|---|---|---|---|
| Crossing The Red Sea | LP | Bright | BRL201 | 1978 £5 | £12 .............red vinyl |
| Crossing The Red Sea | LP | Butt | ALSO002 | 1981 £4 | £10 .............red vinyl |

| Title | Format | Label | Cat No | Year | Price 1 | Price 2 | Notes |
|---|---|---|---|---|---|---|---|
| One Chord Wonders | 7" | Stiff | BUY13 | 1977 | £1.50 | £4 | push-out centre |

## ADVOCATES

| Title | Format | Label | Cat No | Year | Price 1 | Price 2 | Notes |
|---|---|---|---|---|---|---|---|
| Advocates | LP | Dovetail | DOVE1 | 1973 | £10 | £25 | |

## AERA

| Title | Format | Label | Cat No | Year | Price 1 | Price 2 | Notes |
|---|---|---|---|---|---|---|---|
| Aera Humanum Est | LP | Erikonig | ERL2001 | 1974 | £4 | £10 | German |
| Hand Und Fuss | LP | Erikonig | ERL2002 | 1976 | £4 | £10 | German |

## AEROSMITH

| Title | Format | Label | Cat No | Year | Price 1 | Price 2 | Notes |
|---|---|---|---|---|---|---|---|
| Angel | CD-s | Geffen | GEF34CD | 1988 | £3 | £8 | 3" single |
| Angel | 12" | Geffen | GEF34TP | 1988 | £2.50 | £6 | picture disc |
| Done With Mirrors | CD | WEA | 9240912 | 1989 | £5 | £12 | |
| Dream On | 7" | CBS | 1898 | 1973 | £2 | £5 | |
| Dude Looks Like A Lady | CD-s | Geffen | GEF72CD | 1990 | £2 | £5 | |
| Dude Looks Like A Lady | 12" | Geffen | GEF29TP | 1987 | £2.50 | £6 | picture disc |
| Get A Grip | CD | Geffen | 24444 | 1994 | £8 | £20 | US promo in calfskin case |
| Get Your Wings | LP | Columbia | KCQ32847 | 1974 | £4 | £10 | US quad |
| Gripping Stuff | CD | Geffen | CDGRIP1 | 1994 | £8 | £20 | promo sampler |
| Janie's Got A Gun | CD-s | Geffen | GEF68CD | 1989 | £3 | £8 | 3" single |
| Janie's Got A Gun | 7" | Geffen | GEF68P | 1989 | £1.50 | £4 | shaped picture disc |
| Livin' On The Edge | CD-s | Geffen | GFSTD35 | 1993 | £4 | £10 | with interview disc |
| Love In An Elevator | CD-s | Geffen | GEF63CD | 1989 | £3 | £8 | 3" single |
| Other Side | CD-s | Geffen | GEF79CD | 1990 | £2 | £5 | |
| Pump | CD | Geffen | 22469DJ | 1989 | £8 | £20 | US promo in leather case |
| Rats In The Cellar | 7" | CBS | AS1 | 1976 | £2.50 | £6 | promo |
| Rock This Way | CD | Columbia | | 1989 | £8 | £20 | US promo compilation |
| Rocks | LP | Columbia | PCQ34165 | 1976 | £4 | £10 | US quad |
| Toys In The Attic | LP | Columbia | JCQ33479 | 1975 | £4 | £10 | US quad |

## AESOP'S FABLES

| Title | Format | Label | Cat No | Year | Price 1 | Price 2 | Notes |
|---|---|---|---|---|---|---|---|
| In Due Time | LP | Cadet Concept | LPS323 | 1969 | £50 | £100 | US |

## AFEX

| Title | Format | Label | Cat No | Year | Price 1 | Price 2 | Notes |
|---|---|---|---|---|---|---|---|
| She Got The Time | 7" | King | KG1058 | 1967 | £20 | £40 | |

## AFFINITY

| Title | Format | Label | Cat No | Year | Price 1 | Price 2 | Notes |
|---|---|---|---|---|---|---|---|
| Affinity | LP | Vertigo | 6360004 | 1970 | £30 | £60 | spiral label |
| Eli's Comin' | 7" | Vertigo | 6059018 | 1970 | £2.50 | £6 | |
| I Wonder If I Care As Much | 7" | Vertigo | 6059007 | 1970 | £2.50 | £6 | |

## AFFLICTED

| Title | Format | Label | Cat No | Year | Price 1 | Price 2 | Notes |
|---|---|---|---|---|---|---|---|
| All Right Boy | 7" | Bonk | AFF2 | 1982 | £2.50 | £6 | |
| I'm Afflicted | 7" | Bonk | AFF1 | 1981 | £2.50 | £6 | |
| untitled | 7" | Bonk | AFF4 | 1982 | £2 | £5 | |

## AFO EXECUTIVES

| Title | Format | Label | Cat No | Year | Price 1 | Price 2 | Notes |
|---|---|---|---|---|---|---|---|
| Compendium | LP | AFO | LP0002 | | £37.50 | £75 | US |

## AFRICAN MUSIC MACHINE

| Title | Format | Label | Cat No | Year | Price 1 | Price 2 | Notes |
|---|---|---|---|---|---|---|---|
| Black Water Gold | 7" | Mojo | 2092046 | 1972 | £1.50 | £4 | |

## AFROTONES

| Title | Format | Label | Cat No | Year | Price 1 | Price 2 | Notes |
|---|---|---|---|---|---|---|---|
| Freedom Sound | 7" | Duke | DU19 | 1969 | £1.50 | £4 | Boys B side |
| Things I Love | 7" | Trojan | TR655 | 1969 | £2 | £5 | Eric Fratter B side |

## AFTER ALL

| Title | Format | Label | Cat No | Year | Price 1 | Price 2 | Notes |
|---|---|---|---|---|---|---|---|
| After All | LP | Athena | | 1970 | £6 | £15 | US |

## AFTER DARK

| Title | Format | Label | Cat No | Year | Price 1 | Price 2 | Notes |
|---|---|---|---|---|---|---|---|
| Evil Woman | 7" | After Dark | AD001 | 1981 | £7.50 | £15 | |

## AFTER TEA

| Title | Format | Label | Cat No | Year | Price 1 | Price 2 | Notes |
|---|---|---|---|---|---|---|---|
| After Tea | LP | Ace Of Clubs | ACL/SCL1251 | 1967 | £6 | £15 | |

## AFTER THE FIRE

| Title | Format | Label | Cat No | Year | Price 1 | Price 2 | Notes |
|---|---|---|---|---|---|---|---|
| 80-F | cass | Epic | EPC84545 | 1980 | £5 | £12 | test pressing |
| 80F | 7" | Epic | XPR104 | 1980 | £2.50 | £6 | promo |
| Love Will Always Make You Cry | 7" | Epic | EPC8394 | 1980 | £2 | £5 | |
| Signs Of Change | LP | Rapid | RR001 | 1978 | £15 | £30 | |

## AFTERGLOW

| Title | Format | Label | Cat No | Year | Price 1 | Price 2 | Notes |
|---|---|---|---|---|---|---|---|
| Afterglow | LP | MTA | MTS5010 | 1967 | £30 | £60 | US |

## AFTERSHAVE

| Title | Format | Label | Cat No | Year | Price 1 | Price 2 | Notes |
|---|---|---|---|---|---|---|---|
| Skin Deep | LP | Splendid | SLP50106 | 1972 | £62.50 | £125 | Swiss, gatefold sleeve |

## AGAPE

| Title | Format | Label | Cat No | Year | Price 1 | Price 2 | Notes |
|---|---|---|---|---|---|---|---|
| Gospel Hard Rock | LP | Mark | 2170 | 1971 | £75 | £150 | US |
| Victims Of Tradition | LP | Renrut | | 1972 | £75 | £150 | US |

## AGE OF REASON

| Title | Format | Label | Cat No | Year | Price 1 | Price 2 | Notes |
|---|---|---|---|---|---|---|---|
| Age Of Reason | LP | Georgetowne | no number | 1969 | £75 | £150 | US |

## AGGREGATION
Mind Odyssey............................................ LP ...... L.H.I. ............ 12008................ 1967 £180 .... £300 ...................... US

## AGINCOURT (ITHACA)
Fly Away .................................................. LP ...... Merlin ........... HF3 ...................... 1970 £250 ..... £400 ........................

## AGITATION FREE
At Last...................................................... LP ...... Barclay .......... XBLY80612 ........... 1976 £10 ........ £25 ....................... French
Malesch ..................................................... LP ...... Vertigo .......... 6360607 ................ 1972 £8 .......... £20 ...................... German
Second Album .......................................... LP ...... Vertigo .......... 6360615 ................ 1973 £8 .......... £20 ...................... German

## AGNES STRANGE
Clever Fool................................................ 7" ...... Birdsnest ........ BN1 ..................... 1975 £5 .......... £10 ........................
Strange Flavour ........................................ LP ...... Birdsnest ........ BRL9000 ............... 1975 £50 ........ £100 ........................

## AGORA
Agora 2 ..................................................... LP ...... Atlantic .......... T50324 ................ 1976 £4 .......... £10 ........................ Italian
Live In Montreux...................................... LP ...... Atlantic .......... T50171 ................ 1975 £5 .......... £12 ........................ Italian

## A-HA
Blood That Moves The Body ................... CD-s .. WEA ............ W7840CD ............. 1988 £2 .......... £5 .........................
Cry Wolf................................................... 12" .... Warner Bros ... W8500TP .............. 1986 £3 .......... £8 ................ picture disc
Crying In The Rain.................................. CD-s .. WEA ............ W9547CD .............. 1990 £2 .......... £5 .........................
Dark Is The Night ................................... CD-s .. WEA ............ W0175CD1/2 ......... 1993 £3 .......... £8 ................. 2 CD set
Early Morning............................................ CD-s .. WEA ............ W0012CD .............. 1991 £2 .......... £5 .........................
East Of The Sun, West Of The Moon....... CD.... Warner Bros ... 263142DJ ............. 1990 £6 .......... £15 ..... US promo picture disc
Hunting High And Low............................ 12" .... Warner Bros ... W8663T .............. 1986 £2.50 ...... £6 .................. with poster
Hunting High And Low............................ 12" .... Warner Bros ... W6663TP ............. 1986 £3 .......... £8 ................ picture disc
I Call Your Name ..................................... CD-s .. WEA ............ W9462CD .............. 1990 £2 .......... £5 .........................
I've Been Losing You ............................... 12" .... Warner Bros ... W8594T .............. 1986 £2.50 ...... £6 .................. with poster
Living Daylights ........................................ 12" .... Warner Bros ... W8305TP .............. 1987 £3 .......... £8 ................ picture disc
Manhattan Skyline ................................... 12" .... Warner Bros ... W8405T .............. 1987 £2.50 ...... £6 .................. with poster
Manhattan Skyline ................................... 12" .... Warner Bros ... W8405TP ............. 1987 £3 .......... £8 ................ picture disc
Move To Memphis ................................... CD-s .. WEA ............ W0070CD .............. 1991 £2 .......... £5 .........................
Stay On These Roads ............................... CD-s .. Warner Bros ... 9256162 .............. 1988 £2.50 ...... £6 ................ picture disc
Stay On These Roads ............................... CD .... Warner Bros ... 9257336 .............. 1988 £6 .......... £15 ..... promo picture disc
Sun Always Shines On TV ....................... 7" ...... Warner Bros ... W8846P .............. 1986 £6 .......... £12 ..... shaped picture disc
Take On Me .............................................. 7" ...... Warner Bros ... W9006 ................ 1985 £2 .......... £5 ................ 2 different
                                                                                                                                    picture sleeves

Take On Me .............................................. 7" ...... Warner Bros ... W9146 ................ 1984 £12.50 .. £25 ........................
Take On Me .............................................. 12" .... Warner Bros ... W9006T ............... 1985 £4 .......... £10 . black & white picture
                                                                                                                                            sleeve
Take On Me .............................................. 12" .... Warner Bros ... W9146T ............... 1984 £20 ........ £40 ........................
Take On Me .............................................. 12" .... Warner Bros ... W9146T ............... 1984 £30 ........ £60 ............... with poster
Touchy ...................................................... CD-s .. Warner Bros ... W7749CD ............. 1988 £2.50 ...... £6 ................. 3" single
Train Of Thought ..................................... 7" ...... Warner Bros ... W8736P ............... 1986 £6 .......... £12 ..... shaped picture disc
You Are The One ...................................... CD-s .. Warner Bros ... W7636CD ............. 1988 £2.50 ...... £6 .........................

## AHAB
Party Girl ........................................................... 7" ...... Chicken Jazz.... JAZZ5 ................... 1982 £2 .......... £5 ........................

## AHORA MAZDA
Ahora Mazda .......................................... LP ...... Catfish ........... 5C05424184 .......... 1970 £50 ........ £100 ...................... Dutch

## AILEACH
Ard Ri ........................................................... LP ..... Leaf ............... 7014 ..................... 1977 £5 .......... £12 ........................ Irish

## AINIGMA
Diluvium........................................................ LP ..... Arc ................. ALPS151715 .......... 1973 £62.50 .. £125 .................. German

## AIRFORCE
Airforce was put together by Ginger Baker as the archetypal supergroup. Graham Bond, Denny Laine, Stevie Winwood, Harold McNair, Rick Grech, and Chris Wood rubbed shoulders within a big band – and achieved very much less than their talents might suggest they should have.

Airforce ..................................................... LP ...... Polydor........... 2662001 ................ 1970 £6 .......... £15 ....................... double
Airforce 2 .................................................. LP ...... Polydor........... 2383029 ................ 1970 £4 .......... £10 ........................

## AIRTO
Fingers ...................................................... LP ...... CTI ............... CTI18 ................ 1973 £4 .......... £10 ........................
Free ........................................................... LP ...... CTI ............... 6020 ................... 1972 £5 .......... £12 ........................ US
In Concert ................................................ LP ...... CTI ............... CTI21 ................ 1974 £4 .......... £10 ........................
Seeds On The Ground............................... LP ...... Polydor .......... 2310040 ............... 1972 £5 .......... £12 ........................
Virgin Land .............................................. LP ...... CTI ............... CTI123 ............... 1974 £4 .......... £10 ........................

## AITKEN, BOBBY
Baby Baby ................................................ 7" ...... Island ............ WI028 ................ 1962 £5 .......... £10 ........................
Don't Leave Me ........................................ 7" ...... Blue Beat ....... BB146 ................ 1963 £6 .......... £12 ........................
Garden Of Eden ....................................... 7" ...... Rio ................ R40 .................... 1964 £5 .......... £10 ........................
I've Told You ........................................... 7" ...... Rio ................ R14 .................... 1963 £5 .......... £10 ........................
It Takes A Friend ..................................... 7" ...... Rio ................ R15 .................... 1963 £5 .......... £10 . Laurel Aitken B side
Jericho....................................................... 7" ...... Black Swan ..... WI441 ................ 1965 £5 .......... £10 . Lester Sterling B side
Kiss Bam Bam ........................................... 7" ...... Island ............ WI3028 ............... 1967 £5 .......... £10 .. Cynthia Richards B
                                                                                                                                            side
Let Them Have A Home .......................... 7" ...... Doctor Bird..... DB1072 ............... 1967 £5 .......... £10 ........................
Little Girl................................................. 7" ...... Rio ................ R50 .................... 1964 £5 .......... £10 ........................

| | | | | | | |
|---|---|---|---|---|---|---|
| Mr. Judge | 7" | Rio | R64 | 1965 | £5 | £10 |
| Never Never | 7" | Blue Beat | BB93 | 1962 | £6 | £12 |
| Rain Came Tumbling Down | 7" | Rio | R52 | 1965 | £5 | £10 _Shenley Lunan B side_ |
| Rolling Stone | 7" | Rio | R34 | 1964 | £5 | £10 _. Lester Sterling B side_ |
| Shame And Scandal | 7" | Blue Beat | BB369 | 1966 | £6 | £12 |
| Sweets For My Sweet | 7" | Doctor Bird | DB1077 | 1967 | £5 | £10 |
| Thunderball | 7" | Ska Beat | JB252 | 1966 | £5 | £10 _..... Originators B side_ |
| What A Fool | 7" | Giant | GN11 | 1967 | £1.50 | £4 |

## AITKEN, LAUREL

| | | | | | | |
|---|---|---|---|---|---|---|
| Adam And Eve | 7" | Rio | R11 | 1963 | £5 | £10 _..Bobby Aitken B side_ |
| Aitken's Boogie | 7" | Kalypso | XX16 | 1960 | £4 | £8 |
| Baby Don't Do It | 7" | Rio | R92 | 1966 | £4 | £8 |
| Bachelor Life | 7" | R&B | JB171 | 1964 | £5 | £10 |
| Bad Minded Woman | 7" | Rio | R13 | 1963 | £5 | £10 |
| Be Mine | 7" | Columbia | DB7280 | 1964 | £4 | £8 |
| Bewildered And Blue | 7" | Rainbow | RAI106 | 1966 | £4 | £8 |
| Boogie In My Bones | 7" | Island | WI198 | 1965 | £5 | £10 |
| Boogie In My Bones | 7" | Starlite | ST45011 | 1960 | £5 | £10 |
| Boogie Rock | 7" | Blue Beat | BB1 | 1960 | £7.50 | £15 |
| Bossa Nova Hop | 7" | Dice | CC13 | 1963 | £5 | £10 |
| Brother David | 7" | Blue Beat | BB84 | 1962 | £6 | £12 |
| Carolina | 7" | Doctor Bird | DB1203 | 1969 | £5 | £10 |
| Clementine | 7" | Blue Beat | BB340 | 1966 | £6 | £12 |
| Daniel Saw The Stone | 7" | Blue Beat | BB194 | 1963 | £6 | £12 |
| Devil Or Angel | 7" | Rio | R17 | 1963 | £5 | £10 |
| Don't Be Cruel | 7" | Nu Beat | NB040 | 1969 | £1.50 | £4 |
| Drinking Whisky | 7" | Starlite | ST45014 | 1960 | £5 | £10 |
| Fire | LP | Doctor Bird | DLM5012 | 1967 | £37.50 | £75 |
| Fire In Your Wire | 7" | Doctor Bird | DB1187 | 1969 | £5 | £10 |
| For Sentimental Reasons | 7" | Fab | FAB45 | 1968 | £4 | £8 |
| Freedom Train | 7" | Rio | R18 | 1963 | £5 | £10 |
| Green Banana | 7" | Ska Beat | JB239 | 1966 | £5 | £10 |
| Haile Haile (The Lion) | 7" | Doctor Bird | DB1202 | 1969 | £5 | £10 _.. Seven Letters B side_ |
| Hailie Selasie | 7" | Nu Beat | NB032 | 1969 | £2 | £5 |
| High Priest Of Reggae | LP | Pama | PSP1012 | 1969 | £20 | £40 |
| How Can I Forget You | 7" | Rio | R91 | 1966 | £4 | £8 |
| I Shall Remove | 7" | Island | WI092 | 1963 | £5 | £10 |
| I'm Still In Love With You Girl | 7" | Columbia | DB106 | 1967 | £4 | £8 |
| In My Soul | 7" | Island | WI099 | 1963 | £5 | £10 |
| Jamaica | 7" | Dice | CC28 | 1964 | £5 | £10 |
| Jamboree | 7" | Ska Beat | JB232 | 1966 | £5 | £10 |
| Jeannie Is Back | 7" | Blue Beat | BB10 | 1960 | £6 | £12 |
| Jesse James | 7" | Nu Beat | NB045 | 1969 | £1.50 | £4 |
| John Saw Them Coming | 7" | Rio | R37 | 1964 | £5 | £10 |
| Judgement Day | 7" | Blue Beat | BB14 | 1960 | £6 | £12 |
| La La La | 7" | Doctor Bird | DB1161 | 1968 | £5 | £10 _..... Detours B side_ |
| Landlords And Tenants | 7" | Nu Beat | NB044 | 1969 | £2 | £5 |
| Last Night | 7" | Rainbow | RAI101 | 1966 | £4 | £8 |
| Lawd Doctor | 7" | Nu Beat | NB033 | 1969 | £2 | £5 |
| Let's Be Lovers | 7" | Rio | R65 | 1965 | £5 | £10 |
| Love Me Baby | 7" | Starlite | ST45034 | 1961 | £5 | £10 |
| Low Down Dirty Girl | 7" | Duke | DK1002 | 1963 | £4 | £8 _.... Duke Reid B side_ |
| Lucille | 7" | Blue Beat | BB109 | 1962 | £6 | £12 |
| Mabel | 7" | Dice | CC1 | 1962 | £5 | £10 |
| Mary | 7" | Rio | R12 | 1963 | £5 | £10 |
| Mary Don't You Weep | 7" | Rio | R53 | 1965 | £5 | £10 |
| Mary Lee | 7" | Melodisc | 1570 | 1960 | £5 | £10 |
| Mary Lou | 7" | Rio | R54 | 1965 | £5 | £10 |
| Mash Potato Boogie | 7" | Blue Beat | BB40 | 1961 | £6 | £12 |
| Mighty Redeemer | 7" | Blue Beat | BB70 | 1961 | £6 | £12 |
| Moon Rock | 7" | Bamboo | BAM16 | 1970 | £1.50 | £4 |
| More Whiskey | 7" | Blue Beat | BB25 | 1960 | £6 | £12 _.. Lloyd Clarke B side_ |
| Mr. Lee | 7" | Doctor Bird | DB1160 | 1968 | £5 | £10 |
| Nebuchnezer | 7" | Kalypso | XX15 | 1960 | £4 | £8 |
| Never You Hurt | 7" | Fab | FAB5 | 1967 | £4 | £8 |
| Nursery Rhyme Boogie | 7" | Blue Beat | BB52 | 1961 | £6 | £12 |
| One More Time | 7" | Rio | R56 | 1965 | £5 | £10 |
| Pick Up Your Bundle And Go | 7" | R&B | JB170 | 1964 | £5 | £10 |
| Propaganda | 7" | Ska Beat | JB236 | 1966 | £5 | £10 |
| Pussy Got Thirteen Life | 7" | Ackee | ACK104 | 1970 | £1.50 | £4 |
| Pussy Price | 7" | Nu Beat | NB046 | 1969 | £2 | £5 |
| Railroad Track | 7" | Blue Beat | BB22 | 1960 | £6 | £12 |
| Reggae Prayer | 7" | Doctor Bird | DB1196 | 1969 | £5 | £10 |
| Remember My Darling | 7" | Black Swan | WI401 | 1964 | £5 | £10 |
| Revival | 7" | Rio | R99 | 1966 | £4 | £8 |
| Rice And Peas | 7" | Doctor Bird | DB1190 | 1969 | £5 | £10 _..... Classics B side_ |
| Rise And Fall | LP | J.J. | | 1969 | £30 | £60 |
| Rise And Fall | 7" | Doctor Bird | DB1197 | 1969 | £5 | £10 |
| Rock Of Ages | 7" | Rio | R35 | 1964 | £5 | £10 |
| Rock Steady | 7" | Columbia | DB102 | 1967 | £4 | £8 |
| Run Powell Run | 7" | Nu Beat | NB035 | 1969 | £2 | £5 _..... Rico B side_ |
| Saint | 7" | Black Swan | WI411 | 1964 | £5 | £10 |
| Save The Last Dance | 7" | Nu Beat | NB039 | 1969 | £1.50 | £4 |
| Scandal In Brixton Market | LP | Pama | ECO8 | 1969 | £20 | £40 |
| Seven Lonely Nights | 7" | Rio | R60 | 1965 | £5 | £10 |
| Shoo Be Doo | 7" | Nu Beat | NB043 | 1969 | £1.50 | £4 |
| Sin Pon You | 7" | Ackee | ACK106 | 1970 | £1.50 | £4 |

| | | | | | | | |
|---|---|---|---|---|---|---|---|
| Sixty Days Sixty Nights | 7" | Blue Beat | BB120 | 1962 | £6 | £12 | |
| Ska With Laurel | LP | Rio | LR1 | 1966 | £50 | £100 | |
| Skinhead Invasion | 7" | Nu Beat | NB048 | 1970 | £4 | £8 | *test pressing* |
| Skinhead Train | 7" | Nu Beat | NB047 | 1969 | £1.50 | £4 | |
| Suffering Still | 7" | Nu Beat | NB025 | 1969 | £2 | £5 | |
| Sweet Precious Love | 7" | Rainbow | RAI111 | 1966 | £4 | £8 | |
| Think Me No Know | 7" | Junior | JR105 | 1969 | £2 | £5 | *Rico B side* |
| This Great Day | 7" | Blue Beat | BB249 | 1964 | £6 | £12 | |
| Tribute To Collie Smith | 7" | Kalypso | XX19 | 1960 | £4 | £8 | |
| We Shall Overcome | 7" | Rio | R97 | 1966 | £4 | £8 | |
| Weary Wanderer | 7" | Blue Beat | BB142 | 1962 | £6 | £12 | *Bandits B side* |
| What A Weeping | 7" | Island | WI095 | 1963 | £5 | £10 | |
| Woppi King | 7" | Nu Beat | NB024 | 1969 | £2 | £5 | |
| You Can't Stop Me From Loving You | 7" | R&B | JB167 | 1964 | £5 | £10 | |
| You Left Me Standing | 7" | Dice | CC31 | 1965 | £5 | £10 | |
| You Left Me Standing | 7" | Rio | R36 | 1964 | £5 | £10 | |
| Zion | 7" | Blue Beat | BB164 | 1963 | £6 | £12 | |

## A-JAES
| | | | | | | | |
|---|---|---|---|---|---|---|---|
| I'm Leaving You | 7" | Oak | RGJ132 | 1964 | £100 | £200 | *best auctioned* |

## AKA & THE CHARLATANS
| | | | | | | | |
|---|---|---|---|---|---|---|---|
| Heroes Are Losers | 12" | Vanity | VANE1 | 1978 | £3 | £8 | |

## AKENS, JEWEL
| | | | | | | | |
|---|---|---|---|---|---|---|---|
| Birds And The Bees | LP | London | HAN8234 | 1965 | £4 | £10 | |
| Birds And The Bees | 7" EP | London | RE10170 | 1965 | £4 | £8 | *French* |
| Birds And The Bees | 7" | London | HLN9954 | 1965 | £1.50 | £4 | |
| Dancing Jenny | 7" | Ember | EMBS219 | 1966 | £2 | £5 | |

## AKIYOSHI, TOSHIKO
| | | | | | | | |
|---|---|---|---|---|---|---|---|
| Newport Jazz Festival 1957 | LP | Columbia | 33CX10101 | 1958 | £6 | £15 | *..Side 2 by Leon Sash* |

## AKRYLYKZ
| | | | | | | | |
|---|---|---|---|---|---|---|---|
| Spyderman | 7" | Red Rhino | RED2 | 1980 | £1.50 | £4 | |

## AKTUALA
| | | | | | | | |
|---|---|---|---|---|---|---|---|
| Tappeto Volante | LP | Bla-Bla | BBXL10009 | 1976 | £10 | £25 | *Italian* |

## AL & THE VIBRATORS
| | | | | | | | |
|---|---|---|---|---|---|---|---|
| Check Up | 7" | High Note | HS005 | 1969 | £1.50 | £4 | |
| Move Up | 7" | Doctor Bird | DB1085 | 1967 | £5 | £10 | |
| Move Up Calypso | 7" | High Note | HS007 | 1969 | £1.50 | £4 | *Patsy Todd B side* |

## AL, ROLANDO & THE SOUL BROTHERS
| | | | | | | | |
|---|---|---|---|---|---|---|---|
| Doctor Ring A Ding | 7" | Doctor Bird | DB1023 | 1966 | £5 | £10 | *Freddie & The Heartaches B side* |
| From Russia With Love | 7" | Doctor Bird | DB1010 | 1966 | £5 | £10 | |
| I Love You | 7" | Doctor Bird | DB1035 | 1966 | £5 | £10 | |
| Phoenix City | 7" | Doctor Bird | DB1020 | 1966 | £5 | £10 | *Deacons B side* |
| Sufferer's Choice | 7" | Doctor Bird | DB1011 | 1966 | £5 | £10 | *Soulettes B side* |
| Sugar And Spice | 7" | Doctor Bird | DB1017 | 1966 | £5 | £10 | |
| VC10 | 7" | Doctor Bird | DB1008 | 1966 | £5 | £10 | *Larry Marshall B side* |

## ALABAMA JUG BAND
| | | | | | | | |
|---|---|---|---|---|---|---|---|
| Alabama Jug Band | 7" EP | Brunswick | OE9161 | 1955 | £4 | £8 | |

## ALABAMA STATE TROUPERS
| | | | | | | | |
|---|---|---|---|---|---|---|---|
| Alabama State Troupers | LP | Elektra | EKS75022 | 1972 | £5 | £12 | *US* |

## ALAIMO, STEVE
| | | | | | | | |
|---|---|---|---|---|---|---|---|
| Every Day I Have To Cry | LP | Checker | LP2986 | 1963 | £10 | £25 | *US* |
| Everyday I Have To Cry | 7" | Pye | 7N25174 | 1963 | £7.50 | £15 | |
| It's A Long Long Way To Happiness | 7" | Pye | 7N25199 | 1963 | £1.50 | £4 | |
| Mashed Potatoes | LP | Checker | LP2983 | 1962 | £8 | £20 | *US* |
| My Friends | 7" | Pye | 7N25161 | 1962 | £1.50 | £4 | |
| Sings And Swings | LP | ABC | (S)551 | 1966 | £5 | £12 | *US* |
| So Much Love | 7" | HMV | POP1531 | 1966 | £2 | £5 | |
| Starring Steve Alaimo | LP | ABC | (S)501 | 1965 | £5 | £12 | *US* |
| Steve Alaimo | LP | Crown | CLP5382 | 1963 | £5 | £12 | *US* |
| Twist With Steve Alaimo | LP | Checker | LP2981 | 1961 | £8 | £20 | *US* |
| Where The Action Is | LP | ABC | (S)531 | 1965 | £5 | £12 | *US* |

## ALAMO
| | | | | | | | |
|---|---|---|---|---|---|---|---|
| Alamo | LP | Atlantic | SD8279 | 1971 | £5 | £12 | *US* |

## ALARCEN, JEAN PIERRE
| | | | | | | | |
|---|---|---|---|---|---|---|---|
| Alarcen | LP | L'Escargot | ESC371 | 1978 | £10 | £25 | *French* |
| Tableau No. 1 | LP | Scoppuzle | ZZ001 | 1980 | £10 | £25 | *French* |

## ALARM
| | | | | | | | |
|---|---|---|---|---|---|---|---|
| 68 Guns | 7" | IRS | PFPC1023 | 1983 | £2 | £5 | *with cassette (CS70504)* |
| Compact Hits | CD-s | A&M | AMCD906 | 1988 | £2 | £5 | |
| Curtain Call | CD | IRS | POPPY1 | 1988 | £10 | £25 | *US promo sampler* |
| Deceiver | 7" | IRS | IRS103 | 1984 | £2 | £5 | *clear vinyl* |
| Deceiver | 7" | IRS | IRS103 | 1984 | £20 | £40 | *mustard vinyl* |
| Deceiver | 7" | IRS | IRSD103 | 1984 | £4 | £8 | *double* |

| Title | Format | Label | Cat. No. | Year | Price | Price | Notes |
|---|---|---|---|---|---|---|---|
| Electric Folklore | CD | IRS | DMIRM5001 | 1988 | £4 | £10 | |
| Eye Of The Hurricane | CD | IRS | DMIRG1023 | 1987 | £5 | £12 | |
| Love Don't Come Easy | CD-s | IRS | EIRSCD134 | 1990 | £2 | £5 | |
| Marching On | 7" | IRS | ILS0032 | 1982 | £6 | £12 | |
| New South Wales | CD-s | IRS | EIRSCD129 | 1989 | £2 | £5 | |
| Presence Of Love | CD-s | IRS | DIRM155 | 1988 | £2 | £5 | |
| Rain In The Summertime | CD-s | IRS | DIRM144 | 1987 | £2 | £5 | promo only |
| Raw | CD-s | IRS | ALARMCD3 | 1991 | £2 | £5 | |
| Sold Me Down The River | CD-s | IRS | EIRSCD123 | 1989 | £2 | £5 | |
| Strength | CD | IRS | DMIRF1004 | 1987 | £5 | £12 | |
| Unsafe Building 1990 | CD-s | IRS | ALARMCD2 | 1990 | £2 | £5 | |
| Unsafe Buildings | 7" | White Cross | 001 | 1981 | £20 | £40 | ..gatefold picture sleeve |

## ALBA
| | | | | | | | |
|---|---|---|---|---|---|---|---|
| Alba | LP | Rubber | RUB021 | 1978 | £8 | £20 | |

## ALBAM, MANNY
| | | | | | | | |
|---|---|---|---|---|---|---|---|
| And The Jazz Greats Of Our Time Vol. 1 | LP | Coral | LVA9064 | 1958 | £5 | £12 | |
| West Side Story | LP | Coral | LVA9097 | 1959 | £5 | £12 | |

## ALBAM, MANNY & ERNIE WILKINS
| | | | | | | | |
|---|---|---|---|---|---|---|---|
| Drum Suite | LP | HMV | CLP1107 | 1957 | £5 | £12 | |

## ALBERT, EDDIE
| | | | | | | | |
|---|---|---|---|---|---|---|---|
| Come Pretty Little Girl | 7" | London | HL8136 | 1955 | £10 | £20 | |
| Jenny Kissed Me (with Sandra Lee) | 7" | London | HLU8241 | 1956 | £6 | £12 | |

## ALBERTO Y LOS TRIOS PARANOIAS
| | | | | | | | |
|---|---|---|---|---|---|---|---|
| Snuff Rock | 12" | Stiff | LAST2 | 1977 | £3 | £8 | promo |

## ALBION BAND
| | | | | | | | |
|---|---|---|---|---|---|---|---|
| Battle Of The Field | LP | Island | HELP25 | 1976 | £5 | £12 | |
| Prospect Before Us | LP | Harvest | SHSP4059 | 1976 | £5 | £12 | |

## ALCAPONE, DENNIS
| | | | | | | | |
|---|---|---|---|---|---|---|---|
| Alpha And Omega | 7" | Upsetter | US377 | 1971 | £1.50 | £4 | ...Junior Byles B side |
| Duppy Serenade | 7" | Banana | BA328 | 1971 | £1.50 | £4 | |
| Fine Style | 7" | Attack | ATT8027 | 1972 | £1.50 | £4 | .....Winston Scotland B side |
| Forever Version | 7" | Banana | BA341 | 1971 | £1.50 | £4 | |
| Great Woggie | 7" | Treasure Isle | TI7069 | 1971 | £1.50 | £4 | |
| Guns Don't Argue | LP | Trojan | TRL187 | 1971 | £4 | £10 | |
| King Of The Track | LP | Magnet | MGT001 | 1973 | £4 | £10 | |
| Let It Roll | 7" | Prince Buster | PB12 | 1971 | £1.50 | £4 | test pressing, Ansell Collins B side |
| Master Key | 7" | Upsetter | US388 | 1972 | £1.50 | £4 | |
| Power Version | 7" | Ackee | ACK146 | 1971 | £1.50 | £4 | Bluesblasters B side |
| Rasta Dub | 7" | Grape | GR3035 | 1972 | £1.50 | £4 | Upsetters B side |
| Shades Of Hudson | 7" | Big Shot | BI565 | 1971 | £1.50 | £4 | |
| Wake Up Jamaica | 7" | Treasure Isle | TI7074 | 1971 | £1.50 | £4 | Tommy McCook B side |
| Well Dread | 7" | Upsetter | US373 | 1971 | £1.50 | £4 | Upsetters B side |
| Wonderman | 7" | Upsetter | US381 | 1972 | £1.50 | £4 | |

## ALDO, STEVE
| | | | | | | | |
|---|---|---|---|---|---|---|---|
| Can I Get A Witness | 7" | Decca | F12041 | 1964 | £10 | £20 | |
| Everybody Has To Cry | 7" | Parlophone | R5432 | 1966 | £10 | £20 | |

## ALDRICH, RONNIE
| | | | | | | | |
|---|---|---|---|---|---|---|---|
| Big Band Beat | 7" | Columbia | DB3945 | 1957 | £2 | £5 | |
| Coach Call Boogie | 7" | Decca | F10248 | 1954 | £2 | £5 | |
| Ko Ko Mo | 7" | Decca | F10494 | 1955 | £4 | £8 | |
| Rhythm 'n Blues | 7" | Decca | F10564 | 1955 | £4 | £8 | |
| Right Now, Right Now | 7" | Columbia | DB3882 | 1957 | £6 | £12 | |
| Rock Candy | 7" | Decca | F10544 | 1955 | £4 | £8 | |
| Wolf On The Prowl | 7" | Decca | F10274 | 1954 | £2 | £5 | |

## ALEANNA
| | | | | | | | |
|---|---|---|---|---|---|---|---|
| Aleanna | LP | Inchecronin | INC7421 | 1978 | £20 | £40 | |

## ALEONG, AKI & THE NOBLES
| | | | | | | | |
|---|---|---|---|---|---|---|---|
| C'mon Baby Let's Dance | LP | Reprise | R(9)6020 | 1962 | £4 | £10 | US |
| Come Surf With Me | LP | Vee Jay | LP/SR1060 | 1963 | £5 | £12 | US |
| Twistin' The Hits | LP | Reprise | R(9)6011 | 1962 | £4 | £10 | US |

## ALEX
| | | | | | | | |
|---|---|---|---|---|---|---|---|
| Alex | LP | Pan | 87305 | 1974 | £10 | £25 | German |
| That's The Deal | LP | Pan | 88831 | 1976 | £6 | £15 | German |

## ALEXANDER, ARTHUR
| | | | | | | | |
|---|---|---|---|---|---|---|---|
| Alexander The Great | 7" EP | London | RED1364 | 1963 | £50 | £100 | |
| Anna | 7" | London | HLD9641 | 1962 | £12.5 | £25 | |
| Black Night | 7" | London | HLD9899 | 1964 | £7.50 | £15 | |
| For You | 7" | London | HLU10023 | 1966 | £7.50 | £15 | |
| Go Home Girl | 7" | London | HLD9667 | 1963 | £10 | £20 | |
| Soldier Of Love | 7" EP | London | RED1401 | 1963 | £50 | £100 | |
| Soldiers Of Love | 7" | London | HLD9566 | 1962 | £12.50 | £25 | |
| You Better Move On | LP | London | HAD2457 | 1962 | £50 | £100 | |

| | | | | | | | |
|---|---|---|---|---|---|---|---|
| You Better Move On | 7" | London | HLD9523 | 1962 | £12.50 | £25 | |

## ALEXANDER'S TIMELESS BLOOZBAND
| | | | | | | | |
|---|---|---|---|---|---|---|---|
| Alexander's Timeless Bloozband | LP | Smack | 1001 | 1967 | £50 | £100 | US |
| For Sale | LP | Uni | 73021 | 1968 | £8 | £20 | US |

## ALEXANDRIA, LOREZ
| | | | | | | | |
|---|---|---|---|---|---|---|---|
| Lorez Sings Pres | 10" LP | Parlophone | PMD1062 | 1958 | £10 | £25 | |

## ALFIE & HARRY
| | | | | | | | |
|---|---|---|---|---|---|---|---|
| Closing Time | 7" | London | HLU8494 | 1957 | £2.50 | £6 | |
| Trouble With Harry | 7" | London | HLU8242 | 1956 | £7.50 | £15 | |

## ALFONSO, CARLTON
| | | | | | | | |
|---|---|---|---|---|---|---|---|
| I Have Changed | 7" | Nu Beat | NB004 | 1968 | £2 | £5 | |

## ALFORD, CLEM
| | | | | | | | |
|---|---|---|---|---|---|---|---|
| Mirror Image | LP | Columbia | SCX6571 | 1974 | £15 | £30 | |
| Music Library Album | LP | KPM | | 1975 | £8 | £20 | |

## ALFRED & MELMOTH
| | | | | | | | |
|---|---|---|---|---|---|---|---|
| I Want Someone | 7" | Island | WI3130 | 1967 | £4 | £8 | |

## ALFRED, SANDRA
| | | | | | | | |
|---|---|---|---|---|---|---|---|
| Rocket And Roll | 7" | Oriole | CB1408 | 1958 | £10 | £20 | |

## ALI, RASHIED
| | | | | | | | |
|---|---|---|---|---|---|---|---|
| Exchange | LP | Survival | SR101 | 1974 | £8 | £20 | US, with Frank Lowe |
| New Directions In Modern Music | LP | Survival | SR104 | 1974 | £8 | £20 | US |
| Rashied Ali Quintet | LP | Survival | SR102 | 1974 | £8 | £20 | US |

## ALICE
| | | | | | | | |
|---|---|---|---|---|---|---|---|
| Alice | LP | Byg | 529016 | 1970 | £8 | £20 | French |
| Arretez le monde | LP | Polydor | 2393043 | 1972 | £5 | £12 | French |

## ALICE THROUGH THE LOOKING GLASS (ITHACA)
| | | | | | | | |
|---|---|---|---|---|---|---|---|
| Alice Through The Looking Glass | LP | SNP | no number | 1969 | £250 | £400 | |

## ALIEN SEX FIEND
| | | | | | | | |
|---|---|---|---|---|---|---|---|
| ASF Box | 12" | Windsong | 02 | 1990 | £10 | £20 | 3 coloured vinyl singles, boxed |
| Dead And Buried | 7" | Anagram | EANA23 | 1984 | £1.50 | £4 | picture disc |
| E.S.T. | 11" | Anagram | 11ANA25 | 1984 | £2.50 | £6 | |
| First Alien Sex Fiend Compact Disc | CD | Anagram | CDGRAM25 | 1987 | £5 | £12 | with poster |
| Haunted House | CD-s | Anagram | CDANA46 | 1989 | £2 | £5 | |
| I Walk The Line | CD-s | Anagram | CDANA53 | 1991 | £2 | £5 | |
| Ignore The Machine | CD-s | Anagram | CDANA11 | 1988 | £2 | £5 | |
| Ignore The Machine | 7" | Anagram | PANA11 | 1985 | £1.50 | £4 | picture disc |
| Now I'm feeling Zombiefied | CD-s | Anagram | CDANA52 | 1990 | £2 | £5 | |

## ALL ABOUT EVE
A comparison between the present edition of the *Price Guide* and the earlier versions will reveal that many bands from the eighties have passed out of fashion, with a corresponding drop in the values of their rarest records. Most dramatic in this respect is perhaps All About Eve, whose list of collector's items is now only a third as long as it used to be.

| | | | | | | | |
|---|---|---|---|---|---|---|---|
| All About Eve | CD | Mercury | 8342602 | 1988 | £5 | £12 | |
| D For Desire | 12" | Eden | EDEN1 | 1985 | £15 | £30 | |
| December | CD-s | Mercury | EVCDX11 | 1989 | £2 | £5 | picture disc |
| Every Angel | CD-s | Mercury | EVNCD7 | 1988 | £2 | £5 | |
| Flowers In Our Hair | 12" | Eden | EVENX4 | 1987 | £3 | £8 | |
| In The Clouds | CD-s | Mercury | EVCDX13 | 1991 | £2 | £5 | picture disc |
| In The Clouds | cass | Mercury | EVCX13 | 1991 | £3 | £8 | 6 tracks |
| In The Clouds | 7" | Mercury | EVENP5 | 1987 | £1.50 | £4 | with poster |
| In The Clouds | 12" | Eden | EDEN2 | 1986 | £5 | £12 | |
| In The Clouds | 12" | Eden | EDEN2 | 1986 | £10 | £20 | with poster |
| Martha's Harbour | CDV | Mercury | 0805222 | 1988 | £3 | £8 | |
| Martha's Harbour | CD-s | Mercury | EVNCD8 | 1988 | £2 | £5 | |
| Martha's Harbour | CD-s | Mercury | EVNCD8 | 1988 | £2.50 | £6 | gatefold sleeve |
| Martha's Harbour | 12" | Mercury | EVNXB2 | 1988 | £2.50 | £6 | boxed with poster, autographed |
| Our Summer | 12" | Eden | EVENX3 | 1987 | £4 | £10 | |
| Road To Your Soul | CD-s | Mercury | EVCDX10 | 1989 | £2 | £5 | gold wallet |
| Scarlet And Other Stories | CD | Mercury | 8389652 | 1989 | £5 | £12 | |
| What Kind Of Fool | CDV | Mercury | 0806182 | 1988 | £10 | £20 | |
| What Kind Of Fool | CD-s | Mercury | EVNCD99 | 1988 | £4 | £10 | with cards |
| Wild Hearted Woman | CD-s | Mercury | EVNCD6 | 1988 | £2 | £5 | |

## ALL DAY
| | | | | | | | |
|---|---|---|---|---|---|---|---|
| York Pop Music Project | LP | private | | 1973 | £180 | £300 | |

## ALL STARS
| | | | | | | | |
|---|---|---|---|---|---|---|---|
| All Stars | LP | Capitol | LCT6110 | 1956 | £6 | £15 | |
| Season At Riverside | LP | Capitol | T761 | 1957 | £5 | £12 | |

## ALLAN, RICHARD
| | | | | | | | |
|---|---|---|---|---|---|---|---|
| As Time Goes By | 7" | Parlophone | R4634 | 1960 | £1.50 | £4 | |

## ALLEN & MILTON
| | | | | | | |
|---|---|---|---|---|---|---|
| It Is I | 7" | Blue Beat | BB348 | 1966 £6 | £12 | |
| Someone Like You | 7" | Blue Beat | BB353 | 1966 £6 | £12 | |

## ALLEN, ANNISTEEN
| | | | | | | |
|---|---|---|---|---|---|---|
| Don't Nobody Move | 7" | Brunswick | 05639 | 1957 £4 | £8 | |
| Fujiyama Mama | 7" | Capitol | CL14264 | 1955 £15 | £30 | |

## ALLEN, CHAD & THE EXPRESSIONS
| | | | | | | |
|---|---|---|---|---|---|---|
| Chad Allen And The Expressions | LP | Scepter | SP533 | 1966 £5 | £12 | US |

## ALLEN, CLAY
| | | | | | | |
|---|---|---|---|---|---|---|
| Crazy Crazy World | 7" | Starlite | ST45106 | 1963 £2 | £5 | |
| I Can't Stop The Blues From Moving | 7" | Starlite | ST45096 | 1963 £2 | £5 | |
| This Time It's Really Goodbye | 7" | Starlite | ST45086 | 1962 £2 | £5 | |

## ALLEN, DAEVID
| | | | | | | |
|---|---|---|---|---|---|---|
| Banana Moon | LP | BYG | 529345 | 1971 £6 | £15 | French |
| Banana Moon | LP | Caroline | C1512 | 1975 £4 | £10 | |
| Good Morning | LP | Virgin | V2054 | 1976 £4 | £10 | |
| It's The Time Of Your Life | 7" | Virgin | VS123 | 1975 £2.50 | £6 | promo |

## ALLEN, DAVE
| | | | | | | |
|---|---|---|---|---|---|---|
| Color Blind | LP | International Artists | IALP11 | 1969 £20 | £40 | US |

## ALLEN, DAVIE & THE ARROWS
| | | | | | | |
|---|---|---|---|---|---|---|
| Apache '65 | LP | Tower | T5002 | 1965 £4 | £10 | US |
| Blues Theme | LP | Tower | (D)T5078 | 1967 £5 | £12 | US |
| Cycledelic Sounds | LP | Tower | DT5094 | 1968 £5 | £12 | US |
| Wild In The Streets | LP | Tower | DT5099 | 1968 £4 | £10 | US |

## ALLEN, DEAN
| | | | | | | |
|---|---|---|---|---|---|---|
| Ooh Ooh Baby Baby | 7" | London | HLM8698 | 1958 £7.50 | £15 | |

## ALLEN, HENRY RED
| | | | | | | |
|---|---|---|---|---|---|---|
| Newport Jazz Festival 1957 | LP | Columbia | 33CX10106 | 1958 £6 | £15 | with Jack Teagarden & Kid Ory |
| Ride, Red, Ride In Hi Fi | LP | RCA | RD27045 | 1958 £8 | £20 | |

## ALLEN, LEE
| | | | | | | |
|---|---|---|---|---|---|---|
| Cat Walk | 7" | Top Rank | JAR265 | 1960 £4 | £8 | |
| Walking With Mr. Lee | LP | Ember | ELP200 | 1958 £50 | £100 | US |
| Walking With Mr. Lee | 7" EP | Top Rank | JKR8020 | 1959 £7.50 | £15 | |
| Walking With Mr. Lee | 7" | HMV | POP452 | 1958 £12.50 | £25 | |

## ALLEN, MAURICE
| | | | | | | |
|---|---|---|---|---|---|---|
| Oooh Baby | 7" | Pye | 7N15128 | 1958 £2 | £5 | |

## ALLEN, RAY & THE UPBEATS
| | | | | | | |
|---|---|---|---|---|---|---|
| Tribute To Six | LP | Blast | BLP6804 | £15 | £30 | US |

## ALLEN, REX
| | | | | | | |
|---|---|---|---|---|---|---|
| Country And Western Aces | 7" EP | Mercury | 10011MCE | 1964 £2 | £5 | |
| Westward Ho The Wagons | 7" EP | Brunswick | OE9317 | 1957 £2 | £5 | |

## ALLEN, RITCHIE
| | | | | | | |
|---|---|---|---|---|---|---|
| Rising Surf | LP | Imperial | LP9229/LP12229 | 1963 £10 | £25 | US |
| Stranger From Durango | LP | Imperial | LP9212/LP12212 | 1963 £10 | £25 | US |
| Surfer's Slide | LP | Imperial | LP9243/LP12243 | 1963 £10 | £25 | US |

## ALLEN, STEVE
| | | | | | | |
|---|---|---|---|---|---|---|
| Ballad Of Davy Crockett | 7" | Vogue Coral | Q72118 | 1956 £1.50 | £4 | |
| Memories Of You | 7" | Vogue Coral | Q72126 | 1956 £1.50 | £4 | |
| Rock And Roll With Tony Allen | LP | Crown | CLP5231 | 1960 £37.50 | £75 | US |
| Time To Swing | 7" EP | Philips | BBE12522 | 1962 £2 | £5 | |

## ALLEN, VERNON
| | | | | | | |
|---|---|---|---|---|---|---|
| Babylon | 7" | R&B | JB169 | 1964 £5 | £10 | |

## ALLEN, WOODY
| | | | | | | |
|---|---|---|---|---|---|---|
| Spot Floyd | 7" | Colpix | PX775 | 1964 £1.50 | £4 | |
| Third Woody Allen Album | LP | Capitol | T2986 | 1968 £5 | £12 | US |
| Wonderful Wacky World | LP | Bell | 6008 | 1968 £4 | £10 | US |
| Woody Allen | LP | Colpix | (S)CP488 | 1964 £5 | £12 | US |
| Woody Allen 2 | LP | Colpix | (S)CP518 | 1965 £5 | £12 | US |

## ALLEY CATS
| | | | | | | |
|---|---|---|---|---|---|---|
| Snap Crackle And Pop | 7" | Vogue | V9155 | 1959 £5 | £10 | |

## ALLISON, GENE
| | | | | | | |
|---|---|---|---|---|---|---|
| Gene Allison | LP | Vee Jay | VJLP1009 | 1959 £30 | £60 | US |
| Hey Hey I Love You | 7" | London | HLU8605 | 1958 £25 | £50 | |

## ALLISON, KEITH
| | | | | | | |
|---|---|---|---|---|---|---|
| In Action | LP | Columbia | CL2641/CS9441 | 1967 £4 | £10 | US |

## ALLISON, LUTHER

| | | | | | | |
|---|---|---|---|---|---|---|
| Luther Allison | LP | Delmark | DS625 | 1971 £4 | £10 | |

## ALLISON, MOSE

Pianist and singer Mose Allison has a distinctively laid-back approach to bluesy jazz (somewhat like a jazz J.J. Cale) that has made him a highly regarded and influential figure. His 'Parchman Farm' was a staple of the sixties R&B scene in Britain, with Georgie Fame in particular borrowing elements of Allison's style wholesale.

| | | | | | | |
|---|---|---|---|---|---|---|
| Autumn Song | LP | Transatlantic | PR7189 | 1967 £6 | £15 | |
| Baby Please Don't Go | 7" | Fontana | H292 | 1961 £2.50 | £6 | |
| Back Country Suite | 7" EP | Esquire | EP221 | 1959 £4 | £8 | |
| Best Of Mose Allison | LP | Atlantic | SD1542 | 1970 £5 | £12 | US |
| Blueberry Hill | 7" EP | Esquire | EP224 | 1960 £4 | £8 | |
| Creek Bank | LP | Esquire | 32094 | 1960 £8 | £20 | |
| Hello There, Universe | LP | Atlantic | SD1550 | 1970 £5 | £12 | US |
| I Don't Worry About A Thing | LP | Atlantic | SD1389 | 1962 £8 | £20 | US |
| I Love The Life I Live | LP | Realm | RM52318 | 1966 £6 | £15 | |
| I Love The Life I Live | 7" | Columbia | DB7330 | 1964 £2.50 | £6 | |
| I've Been Doin' Some Thinkin' | LP | Atlantic | SD1511 | 1969 £6 | £15 | US |
| Local Color | LP | Esquire | 32071 | 1959 £8 | £20 | |
| Mose Alive! | LP | Atlantic | 587/588007 | 1966 £8 | £20 | |
| Mose In Your Ear | LP | Atlantic | SD1627 | 1973 £5 | £12 | US |
| Parchman Farm | 7" EP | Esquire | EP214 | 1959 £4 | £8 | |
| Sings | LP | Stateside | SL10106 | 1964 £8 | £20 | |
| Sings | LP | Transatlantic | PR7279 | 1968 £6 | £15 | |
| Sings The Blues | 7" EP | Columbia | SEG8353 | 1964 £4 | £8 | |
| Swingin' Machine | LP | London | HAK8083 | 1963 £8 | £20 | |
| That Man Mose Again | 7" EP | Esquire | EP231 | 1960 £4 | £8 | |
| V8 Ford | LP | Columbia | SX6058 | 1964 £8 | £20 | |
| Western Man | LP | Atlantic | SD1584 | 1971 £5 | £12 | US |
| Wild Man On The Loose | LP | Atlantic | 587/588031 | 1966 £6 | £15 | |
| Word From Mose | LP | Atlantic | SD1424 | 1966 £6 | £15 | US |

## ALLISONS

| | | | | | | |
|---|---|---|---|---|---|---|
| Allisons | 7" EP | Fontana | TFE17339 | 1961 £5 | £10 | |
| Are You Sure | LP | Fontana | TFL5135/STFL558 | 1961 £8 | £20 | |

## ALLISONS (2)

| | | | | | | |
|---|---|---|---|---|---|---|
| Surfer Street | 7" | Stateside | SS289 | 1964 £1.50 | £4 | |

## ALLMAN, DUANE

| | | | | | | |
|---|---|---|---|---|---|---|
| Anthology | LP | Capricorn | K67502 | 1972 £5 | £12 | double |
| Anthology Vol. 2 | LP | Capricorn | 2659037 | 1974 £5 | £12 | double |

## ALLMAN BROTHERS BAND

| | | | | | | |
|---|---|---|---|---|---|---|
| Allman Brothers Band | LP | Capricorn | 228033 | 1969 £4 | £10 | |
| At Fillmore East | LP | Atlantic | 2659005 | 1971 £5 | £12 | double |
| Beginnings | CD | Polydor | 8275882 | 198– £5 | £12 | |
| Brothers And Sisters | CD | Mobile Fidelity | UDCD617 | 1994 £6 | £15 | US audiophile |
| Brothers And Sisters | CD | Polydor | 8250922 | 1986 £5 | £12 | |
| Eat A Peach | LP | Capricorn | CP40102 | 1972 £6 | £15 | US quad |
| Eat A Peach | LP | Capricorn | K67501 | 1972 £5 | £12 | double |
| Eat A Peach | LP | Mobile Fidelity | MFSL2157 | 1983 £6 | £15 | US audiophile |
| Eat A Peach | CD | Mobile Fidelity | UDCD513 | 1989 £6 | £15 | US audiophile |
| Eat A Peach | CD | Polydor | 8236542 | 1986 £5 | £12 | |
| Idlewild South | LP | Capricorn | 2400032 | 1970 £4 | £10 | |
| Live At Fillmore | CD | Polydor | 8232732 | 1986 £5 | £12 | |

## ALLMAN JOYS

| | | | | | | |
|---|---|---|---|---|---|---|
| Allman Joys | LP | Mercury | 6398005 | 1973 £4 | £10 | |

## ALLSUP, TOMMY

| | | | | | | |
|---|---|---|---|---|---|---|
| Buddy Holly Songbook | LP | Reprise | R(S)6182 | 1965 £10 | £25 | US |

## ALMEIDA, LAURINDO

| | | | | | | |
|---|---|---|---|---|---|---|
| Laurindo Almeida Quartet | LP | Brunswick | LAE12019 | 1956 £10 | £25 | |

## ALMIGHTY

| | | | | | | |
|---|---|---|---|---|---|---|
| Destroyed | 12" | Polydor | PZP60 | 1989 £2.50 | £6 | picture disc |
| Little Lost Sometimes | CD-s | Polydor | PZCD151 | 1991 £2 | £5 | |
| Power | CD-s | Polydor | PZCD66 | 1990 £2 | £5 | |
| Power Trippin'/Live From Donington '92 | CD | Polydor | 5192262 | 1993 £6 | £15 | double |

## ALMOND, JOHNNY

| | | | | | | |
|---|---|---|---|---|---|---|
| Hollywood Blues | LP | Deram | SML1057 | 1970 £6 | £15 | |
| Patent Pending | LP | Deram | DML/SML1043 | 1969 £8 | £20 | |
| Solar Level | 7" | Deram | DM266 | 1969 £1.50 | £4 | |

## ALMOND, MARC

| | | | | | | |
|---|---|---|---|---|---|---|
| Bitter Sweet | CD-s | Parlophone | CDR6194 | 1988 £2 | £5 | |
| Boy Who Came Back | 10" | Some Bizarre | BZS2310 | 1984 £3 | £8 | |
| Days Of Pearly Spencer | CD-s | WEA | YZ638CDX | 1992 £2 | £5 | holographic disc |
| Days Of Pearly Spencer | 12" | Some Bizarre | YZ638T | 1992 £3 | £8 | |
| Desperate Hours | CD-s | Parlophone | CDR6252 | 1990 £2 | £5 | |
| Enchanted | CD | Parlophone | CDPCS7344 | 1990 £5 | £12 | |
| House Is Haunted | 7" | Some Bizarre | GLOW1 | 1985 £2.50 | £6 | promo |

| Title | Format | Label | Catalogue | Year | | | Notes |
|---|---|---|---|---|---|---|---|
| Jacky | CD-s | WEA | YZ610CD | 1991 | £2 | £5 | |
| Kept Boy | 7" | Parlophone | PSR500 | 1988 | £4 | £8 | 1 side etched |
| Love Letter | 10" | Some Bizarre | BONK210 | 1985 | £2.50 | £6 | |
| Lover Spurned | CD-s | Parlophone | CDR6229 | 1990 | £2 | £5 | |
| Mother Fist | 7" | Some Bizarre | GLOW5 | 1987 | £2.50 | £6 | promo |
| My Death | 7" | Gutterhearts | LYN14210 | 1984 | £4 | £8 | flexi |
| Only The Moment | CD-s | Parlophone | CDR6210 | 1989 | £2 | £5 | |
| Something's Gotten Hold Of My Heart | CD-s | Parlophone | CDR6201 | 1989 | £2 | £5 | with Gene Pitney |
| Stars We Are | CD | Parlophone | CDPCS7324 | 1989 | £5 | £12 | |
| Stories Of Johnny | 10" | Some Bizarre | BONK110 | 1985 | £2.50 | £6 | |
| Tears Run Rings | CD-s | Parlophone | CDR6186 | 1988 | £2 | £5 | |
| Tenderness Is A Weakness | 10" | Some Bizarre | BZS2510 | 1984 | £3 | £8 | |
| Waifs And Strays | CD-s | Parlophone | CDR6263 | 1990 | £2 | £5 | |
| Woman's Story | 10" | Some Bizarre | GLOW210 | 1986 | £3 | £8 | |
| You Have | 10" | Some Bizarre | BZS2410 | 1984 | £3 | £8 | |
| Your Aura | 7" | Gutterhearts | | 1986 | £4 | £8 | flexi |

## ALMOND LETTUCE

| Title | Format | Label | Catalogue | Year | | | Notes |
|---|---|---|---|---|---|---|---|
| Magic Circle | 7" | Philips | BF1764 | 1969 | £2.50 | £6 | |

## ALONE AGAIN OR

| Title | Format | Label | Catalogue | Year | | | Notes |
|---|---|---|---|---|---|---|---|
| Drum The Beat | 7" | All One | ALG1 | 1984 | £4 | £8 | |

## ALOVE & PAXTON

| Title | Format | Label | Catalogue | Year | | | Notes |
|---|---|---|---|---|---|---|---|
| Wickeder | 7" | Blue Cat | BS168 | 1969 | £2 | £5 | |

## ALPERT, TRIGGER

| Title | Format | Label | Catalogue | Year | | | Notes |
|---|---|---|---|---|---|---|---|
| Trigger Happy | LP | London | LTZU15096 | 1957 | £10 | £25 | |

## ALPHONSO, CARLTON

| Title | Format | Label | Catalogue | Year | | | Notes |
|---|---|---|---|---|---|---|---|
| Where In This World | 7" | Pama | PM700 | 1967 | £4 | £8 | |

## ALPHONSO, CLYDE

| Title | Format | Label | Catalogue | Year | | | Notes |
|---|---|---|---|---|---|---|---|
| Good Enough | 7" | Studio One | SO2076 | 1969 | £6 | £12 | |

## ALPHONSO, ORVILLE

| Title | Format | Label | Catalogue | Year | | | Notes |
|---|---|---|---|---|---|---|---|
| Belly Lick | 7" | Caribou | CRC1 | 1965 | £1.50 | £4 | |

## ALPHONSO, ROLAND

| Title | Format | Label | Catalogue | Year | | | Notes |
|---|---|---|---|---|---|---|---|
| Blackberry Brandy | 7" | Blue Beat | BB58 | 1961 | £6 | £12 | |
| Cat | 7" | Pyramid | PYR6008 | 1967 | £4 | £8 | Desmond Dekker B side |
| Crime Wave | 7" | R&B | JB164 | 1964 | £5 | £10 | |
| Devoted To You | 7" | Island | WI264 | 1966 | £5 | £10 | Jackie Opel B side |
| El Pussy Cat | 7" | Island | WI217 | 1965 | £5 | £10 | Lord Brynner B side |
| Federal Special | 7" | R&B | JB122 | 1963 | £5 | £10 | |
| Feeling Fine | 7" | Island | WI146 | 1964 | £5 | £10 | Leon & Owen B side |
| Four Corners Of The World | 7" | Blue Beat | BB112 | 1962 | £6 | £12 | Shiners B side |
| Green Door | 7" | Blue Beat | BB63 | 1961 | £6 | £12 | Monty & Roy B side |
| Guantanamera Ska | 7" | Pyramid | PYR6009 | 1967 | £4 | £8 | Spanishtonians B side |
| Jazz Ska | 7" | Rio | R58 | 1965 | £5 | £10 | Hyacinth B side |
| Jericho Chain | 7" | Blue Beat | BB356 | 1966 | £6 | £12 | |
| Jungle Bit | 7" | Pyramid | PYR6007 | 1967 | £4 | £8 | Norman Grant B side |
| Middle East | 7" | Pyramid | PYR6003 | 1967 | £4 | £8 | Desmond Dekker B side |
| Never To Be Mine | 7" | Trojan | TR001 | 1967 | £5 | £10 | Duke Reid B side |
| Nimblefoot | 7" | Ska Beat | JB210 | 1965 | £5 | £10 | Andy And Joey B side |
| Nothing For Nothing | 7" | Pyramid | PYR6011 | 1967 | £4 | £8 | Desmond Dekker B side |
| Nuclear Weapon | 7" | Ska Beat | JB216 | 1965 | £5 | £10 | Stranger Cole B side |
| On The Move | 7" | Pyramid | PYR6006 | 1967 | £4 | £8 | Desmond Dekker B side |
| Peace And Love | 7" | Pyramid | PYR6023 | 1968 | £4 | £8 | |
| Phoenix City | 7" | Trojan | TRM9010 | 1974 | £1.50 | £4 | |
| Reggae In The Grass | 7" | Coxsone | CS7077 | 1968 | £5 | £10 | Roy Richards B side |
| Rinky Dink | 7" | Ska Beat | JB231 | 1966 | £5 | £10 | Scratch & The Dynamites B side |
| Roland Plays The Prince | 7" | Blue Beat | BB286 | 1965 | £6 | £12 | Gaynor & Errol B side |
| Roll On | 7" | Punch | PH39 | 1970 | £1.50 | £4 | |
| Shanty Town Curfew | 7" | Island | WI3055 | 1967 | £5 | £10 | Hopeton Lewis B side |
| Ska Au Go-Go | LP | Coxsone | CSL8003 | 1967 | £50 | £100 | |
| Sock It To Me | 7" | Pyramid | PYR6018 | 1967 | £4 | £8 | Spanishtonians B side |
| Stream Of Life | 7" | Pyramid | PYR6016 | 1967 | £4 | £8 | Austin Faithful B side |
| Thousand Tons Of Megaton | 7" | Gas | GAS112 | 1969 | £1.50 | £4 | |
| Whiter Shade Of Pale | 7" | Pyramid | PYR6022 | 1968 | £4 | £8 | |
| Woman Of The World | 7" | Pyramid | PYR6005 | 1967 | £4 | £8 | Spanishtonians B side |
| Yard Broom | 7" | Ska Beat | JB183 | 1965 | £5 | £10 | Dotty & Bonnie B side |

## ALRUNE ROD

| Title | Format | Label | Catalogue | Year | | | Notes |
|---|---|---|---|---|---|---|---|
| Alrune Rock | LP | Sonet | SLPS1537 | 1971 | £5 | £12 | Danish |
| Alrune Rod | LP | Sonet | SLPS1516 | 1969 | £25 | £50 | Danish |
| Dansk Beat | LP | Sonet | SLPS2413 | 1975 | £5 | £12 | Danish |
| Four | LP | Mandragora | MGLP2 | 1973 | £5 | £12 | Danish |
| Hey Du | LP | Sonet | SLPS1524 | 1970 | £5 | £12 | Danish |
| Spredt For Vinden | LP | Mandragora | MGLP1 | 1973 | £5 | £12 | Danish |
| Tatuba Tapes | LP | Mandragora | MGLP3 | 1975 | £5 | £12 | Danish |

## ALTECS

| Title | Format | Label | Cat# | Year | | | Notes |
|---|---|---|---|---|---|---|---|
| Easy | 7" | London | HLU9387 | 1961 | £1.50 | £4 | |

## ALTERNATIVE TV & HERE AND NOW

| Title | Format | Label | Cat# | Year | | | Notes |
|---|---|---|---|---|---|---|---|
| What You See Is What You Are | LP | Deptford Fun City | DLP02 | 1978 | £4 | £10 | |
| Live At The Rat Club | LP | Crystal | CLP01 | 1979 | £4 | £10 | |

## ALTON & EDDY

| Title | Format | Label | Cat# | Year | | | Notes |
|---|---|---|---|---|---|---|---|
| Muriel | 7" | Blue Beat | BB17 | 1960 | £6 | £12 | |
| My Love Divine | 7" | Island | WI009 | 1962 | £5 | £10 | |

## ALTON & PHYLLIS

| Title | Format | Label | Cat# | Year | | | Notes |
|---|---|---|---|---|---|---|---|
| Love Letters | 7" | Trojan | TR622 | 1968 | £2.50 | £6 | |

## ALTONA

| Title | Format | Label | Cat# | Year | | | Notes |
|---|---|---|---|---|---|---|---|
| Altona | LP | RCA | PPL11049 | 1974 | £5 | £12 | German |
| Chicken Farm | LP | RCA | PPL14129 | 1975 | £6 | £15 | German |

## ALVARO

| Title | Format | Label | Cat# | Year | | | Notes |
|---|---|---|---|---|---|---|---|
| Drinkin My Own Sperm | LP | Squeaky Shoes | SSRDR1 | 1977 | £5 | £12 | |
| Mum's Milk Not Powder | LP | Squeaky Shoes | SSRM2 | 1979 | £4 | £10 | |
| Repetition Kills | LP | Squeaky Shoes | SSR6 | 1982 | £4 | £10 | |
| Working Class | LP | Squeaky Shoes | SSR3 | 1981 | £4 | £10 | |

## ALVYN

| Title | Format | Label | Cat# | Year | | | Notes |
|---|---|---|---|---|---|---|---|
| You've Gotta Have An Image | 7" | Morgan Bluetown | MR18 | 1969 | £1.50 | £4 | |
| Another Time | LP | Vinyl | VS100 | 1976 | £6 | £15 | |

## AMALGAM

| Title | Format | Label | Cat# | Year | | | Notes |
|---|---|---|---|---|---|---|---|
| Close To You | LP | Ogun | OG528 | 1978 | £6 | £15 | |
| Deep | LP | Vinyl | VS108 | 1977 | £6 | £15 | |
| Innovation | LP | Tangent | TGS132 | 1974 | £6 | £15 | |
| Mad | LP | Syntohn | VR20020 | 1976 | £6 | £15 | |
| Over The Rainbow | LP | Arc | ARC01 | 1979 | £6 | £15 | |
| Play Blackwell And Higgins | LP | A Records | A002 | 1973 | £8 | £20 | |
| Prayer For Peace | LP | Transatlantic | TRA196 | 1969 | £15 | £30 | |
| Samanna | LP | Vinyl | VS106 | 1977 | £6 | £15 | |
| Wipe Out | LP | Impetus | IMP47901 | 1979 | £25 | £50 | 4 LP set |

## AMAZIAH

| Title | Format | Label | Cat# | Year | | | Notes |
|---|---|---|---|---|---|---|---|
| Straight Talker | LP | Sunrise | SR001 | 1973 | £75 | £150 | |

## AMAZING BLONDEL

| Title | Format | Label | Cat# | Year | | | Notes |
|---|---|---|---|---|---|---|---|
| Amazing Blondel | LP | Bell | SBLL131 | 1970 | £50 | £100 | |
| Blondel | LP | Island | ILPS9257 | 1973 | £4 | £10 | |
| England | LP | Island | ILPS9205 | 1972 | £4 | £10 | |
| Evensong | LP | Island | ILPS9136 | 1970 | £4 | £10 | |
| Fantasia Lindum | LP | Island | ILPS9156 | 1971 | £4 | £10 | |
| Mulgrave Street | LP | DJM | DJF20442 | 1974 | £4 | £10 | |
| Mulgrave Street | 7" | DJM | DJX503 | 1974 | £2.50 | £6 | promo |

## AMAZING CATSFIELD STEAMERS

| Title | Format | Label | Cat# | Year | | | Notes |
|---|---|---|---|---|---|---|---|
| United Friends | LP | Fat Hen | FH002LP | 1983 | £4 | £10 | |

## AMAZING DANCE BAND

| Title | Format | Label | Cat# | Year | | | Notes |
|---|---|---|---|---|---|---|---|
| Deep Blue Train | 7" | Verve | VS567 | 1968 | £5 | £10 | |

## AMAZING FRIENDLY APPLE

| Title | Format | Label | Cat# | Year | | | Notes |
|---|---|---|---|---|---|---|---|
| Water Woman | 7" | Decca | F12887 | 1969 | £10 | £20 | |

## AMAZING RHYTHM ACES

| Title | Format | Label | Cat# | Year | | | Notes |
|---|---|---|---|---|---|---|---|
| Full House – Aces High | LP | A&M | AMJ2001/2 | 1978 | £20 | £40 | US double |

## AMBER SQUAD

| Title | Format | Label | Cat# | Year | | | Notes |
|---|---|---|---|---|---|---|---|
| Can We Go Dancing? | 7" | Deadgood | DEAD17 | 1980 | £2.50 | £6 | |
| Put My Finger On You | 7" | Sound Of Leicester | ST1 | 1980 | £4 | £8 | |

## AMBOY DUKES

In order to appreciate the Amboy Dukes' tendency to overdo everything, one need look no further than the seminal punk (sixties-style) compilation, *Nuggets*. Here the group turns 'Tobacco Road' into a totally unsuitable vehicle for guitar excess. Lead guitarist Ted Nugent has followed more or less the same approach ever since.

| Title | Format | Label | Cat# | Year | | | Notes |
|---|---|---|---|---|---|---|---|
| All I Need | 7" | Polydor | 56172 | 1967 | £1.50 | £4 | |
| He Came To Me Yesterday | 7" | Polydor | 56281 | 1968 | £1.50 | £4 | |
| High Life In Whitley Wood | 7" | Polydor | 56190 | 1967 | £1.50 | £4 | |
| Judy In Disguise | 7" | Polydor | 56228 | 1968 | £1.50 | £4 | |
| Marriage On The Rocks | LP | Polydor | 244012 | 1970 | £6 | £15 | US |
| Simon Says | 7" | Polydor | 56243 | 1968 | £1.50 | £4 | |
| Turn Back To Me | 7" | Polydor | 56149 | 1966 | £1.50 | £4 | |

## AMBOY DUKES (2)

| Title | Format | Label | Cat# | Year | | | Notes |
|---|---|---|---|---|---|---|---|
| Amboy Dukes | LP | Fontana | (S)TL5468 | 1968 | £20 | £40 | |
| Journey To The Centre Of The Mind | LP | London | HAT/SHT8378 | 1968 | £15 | £30 | |

| | | | | | | |
|---|---|---|---|---|---|---|
| Let's Go Get Stoned | 7" | Fontana | TF971 | 1968 £4 | £8 | |
| Migration | LP | London | HAT/SHT8392 | 1969 £10 | £25 | |

## AMBROSE, SAM
| | | | | | | |
|---|---|---|---|---|---|---|
| Monkey See Monkey Do | 7" | Stateside | SS399 | 1965 £20 | £40 | |
| This Diamond Ring | 7" | Stateside | SS385 | 1965 £15 | £30 | |

## AMBROSE SLADE

Ambrose Slade was the original name of Slade, back in the days when they were being marketed as the first skinhead group (despite the fact that the group's music had nothing in common with the likes of 'Skinhead Moonstomp'). The reissue of the group's LP, on Contour, is as rare as the original – it was withdrawn shortly after release – but the US version of the record, retitled *Ballzy* and given an appropriate cover, is rather more common.

| | | | | | | |
|---|---|---|---|---|---|---|
| Ballzy | LP | Fontana | SRF67598 | 1969 £30 | £60 | US |
| Beginnings | LP | Contour | 6870678 | 1975 £20 | £40 | |
| Beginnings | LP | Fontana | STL5492 | 1969 £100 | £200 | |
| Genesis | 7" | Fontana | TF1015 | 1969 £87.50 | £175 | |

## AMBROSIA
| | | | | | | |
|---|---|---|---|---|---|---|
| Ambrosia | LP | 20th Century | BT434 | 1975 £4 | £10 | |
| Somewhere I've Never Travelled | LP | 20th Century | BT510 | 1976 £4 | £10 | |

## AME SON
| | | | | | | |
|---|---|---|---|---|---|---|
| Ame Son | LP | Byg | 529324 | 1970 £5 | £12 | French |

## AMECHE, LOLA
| | | | | | | |
|---|---|---|---|---|---|---|
| Rock The Joint | 78 | Oriole | CB1143 | 1953 £2 | £5 | |

## AMEN CORNER
| | | | | | | |
|---|---|---|---|---|---|---|
| Farewell Magnificent Seven | LP | Immediate | IMSP028 | 1969 £4 | £10 | |
| National Welsh Coast Live | LP | Immediate | IMSP023 | 1969 £4 | £10 | |
| Round Amen Corner | LP | Deram | DML/SML1021 | 1968 £4 | £10 | |
| So Fine | 7" | Immediate | AS3 | 1969 £7.50 | £15 | promo |

## AMERICAN BLUES

The only UK release of the second American Blues album is a 1987 reissue on the See For Miles label. Although the record is a typically inventive chunk of psychedelia, its real interest, and the reason for the collectibility of the original, lies in the fact that two-thirds of American Blues later became two-thirds of ZZ Top.

| | | | | | | |
|---|---|---|---|---|---|---|
| American Blues Is Here | LP | Karma | KLP1001 | 1968 £75 | £150 | US |
| Do Their Thing | LP | Uni | 73044 | 1969 £20 | £40 | US |

## AMERICAN BLUES EXCHANGE
| | | | | | | |
|---|---|---|---|---|---|---|
| Blueprints | LP | Taylus | TLS1 | 1969 £180 | £300 | US |

## AMERICAN BREED
| | | | | | | |
|---|---|---|---|---|---|---|
| American Breed | LP | Dot | DOLP255 | 1967 £4 | £10 | |
| Bend Me Shape Me | LP | Dot | (S)LPD502 | 1968 £4 | £10 | |
| Bend Me Shape Me | 7" | Stateside | SS2078 | 1968 £1.50 | £4 | |
| Lonely Side Of The City | LP | Dot | (S)LPD526 | 1969 £4 | £10 | |
| Pumpkin Powder,Scarlet & Green | LP | Dot | (S)LPD518 | 1968 £4 | £10 | |
| Step Out Of Your Mind | 7" | CBS | 2888 | 1967 £1.50 | £4 | |

## AMERICAN DREAM
| | | | | | | |
|---|---|---|---|---|---|---|
| American Dream | LP | Ampex | A10101 | 1968 £10 | £25 | US |

## AMERICAN EAGLE
| | | | | | | |
|---|---|---|---|---|---|---|
| American Eagle | LP | Decca | DL75258 | 1970 £4 | £10 | US |

## AMERICAN FOUR

Both Arthur Lee and fellow Love guitarist John Echols were members of the American Four, which stayed together just long enough to make this rare single.

| | | | | | | |
|---|---|---|---|---|---|---|
| Luci Baines | 7" | Selma | 2001 | 1964 £50 | £100 | US |

## AMERICAN GYPSY
| | | | | | | |
|---|---|---|---|---|---|---|
| American Gypsy | LP | BTM | BTM1001GG | 1975 £4 | £10 | |
| Anithesis | LP | RCA | LSP4775 | 1972 £4 | £10 | US |
| Gypsy | LP | CBS | 66270 | 1971 £4 | £10 | |
| In The Garden | LP | Metromedia | 1044 | 1972 £4 | £10 | US |
| Unlock The Dead Gates | LP | RCA | APL10093 | 1973 £4 | £10 | US |

## AMERICAN POETS
| | | | | | | |
|---|---|---|---|---|---|---|
| She Blew A Good Thing | 7" | London | HLC10037 | 1966 £20 | £40 | |

## AMERICAN REVOLUTION
| | | | | | | |
|---|---|---|---|---|---|---|
| American Revolution | LP | Flick | 45002 | 1968 £4 | £10 | US |

## AMERICAN SPRING
| | | | | | | |
|---|---|---|---|---|---|---|
| American Spring | LP | United Artists | UAS29363 | 1972 £6 | £15 | |
| Good Time | 7" | United Artists | UP35376 | 1972 £1.50 | £4 | |
| Mama Said | 7" | United Artists | UP35421 | 1972 £1.50 | £4 | |
| Shyin' Away | 7" | CBS | 1590 | 1973 £1.50 | £4 | |

## AMERICAN TEARS
| | | | | | | |
|---|---|---|---|---|---|---|
| Branded Bad | LP | CBS | 33038 | 1974 £8 | £20 | US |
| Powerhouse | LP | CBS | 34676 | 1977 £8 | £20 | US |

| Teargas | LP | CBS | 33847 | 1975 £8 | £20 | US |

## AMERICAN YOUTH CHOIR
| Together We Can Make It | 7" | Polydor | 2066013 | 1971 £5 | £10 | |

## AMES, NANCY
| Cry Softly | 7" | Columbia | DB8039 | 1966 £15 | £30 | |
| Friends And Lovers Forever | 7" | Columbia | DB7809 | 1966 £2 | £5 | |

## AMES BROTHERS
| Best Of The Ames Brothers | 7" EP | RCA | RCX1047 | 1959 £2.50 | £6 | |
| Boogie Woogie Maxine | 7" | HMV | 7M179 | 1954 £2 | £5 | |
| Exactly Like You | 7" EP | HMV | 7EG8237 | 1957 £2.50 | £6 | |
| Hopelessly | 7" | HMV | 7M253 | 1954 £1.50 | £4 | |
| I'm Gonna Love You | 7" | HMV | POP242 | 1956 £2 | £5 | |
| If You Wanna See Mamie Tonight | 7" | HMV | 7M410 | 1956 £1.50 | £4 | |
| If You Wanna See Mamie Tonight | 7" | HMV | 7MC46 | 1956 £1.50 | £4 | export |
| Man With The Banjo | 7" | HMV | 7M209 | 1954 £1.50 | £4 | |
| Merci Beaucoup | 7" | HMV | 7M322 | 1955 £1.50 | £4 | |
| My Bonnie Lassie | 7" | HMV | 7M331 | 1955 £1.50 | £4 | |
| Naughty Lady Of Shady Lane | 7" | HMV | 7M281 | 1955 £5 | £10 | |
| Rockin' Shoes | 7" | RCA | RCA1015 | 1957 £2 | £5 | |
| Sweet Brown-Eyed Baby | 7" | HMV | 7M310 | 1955 £1.50 | £4 | |
| You You You | 7" | HMV | 7M153 | 1953 £2 | £5 | |

## AMITY
| Amity | LP | Red Rag | | 1976 £15 | £30 | |

## AMM
Apart from being the rarest album on the orange Elektra label, *AMMMusic*, with its distinctive yellow lorry cover, is also a crucial, pioneering landmark within the genre of free improvisation. Instruments like guitar, cello, and saxophone are credited, but so are transistor radios, and in truth it is extremely hard to identify the individual contributions within the maelstrom of sound that the group produces. The album was sponsored by Pink Floyd's management, the kinship with Floyd pieces like *A Saucerful Of Secrets* being clear, but AMM's music proved to be too extreme even in the heady days of the late sixties. Versions of the group have nevertheless continued to perform on occasion ever since.

| AMMMusic | LP | Elektra | EUK(S7)256 | 1966 £50 | £100 | |
| At The Roundhouse | 7" | Incus | EP1 | 1973 £25 | £50 | |
| Crypt – 12th June 1968 | LP | Matchless | MR5 | 1981 £20 | £40 | boxed double |
| Generative Themes | LP | Matchless | MR6 | 1982 £6 | £15 | |
| Inexhaustible Document | LP | Matchless | MR13 | 198– £6 | £15 | |
| It Had Been An Ordinary Enough Day In Pueblo | LP | ECM | 60031 | 1979 £6 | £15 | |
| Live Electronic Music Improvised | LP | Mainstream | MS5002 | 1968 £25 | £50 | US, with MEV |
| To Hear And Back Again | LP | Matchless | MR3 | 1978 £8 | £20 | |

## AMMONS, ALBERT
| Albert Ammons | 7" EP | Vogue | EPV1071 | 1955 £15 | £30 | |
| And His Rhythm Kings | LP | Mercury | MG25012 | 1954 £10 | £25 | |
| Boogie Woogie Stomp | 7" EP | Brunswick | OE9325 | 1957 £5 | £10 | |

## AMMONS, ALBERT, PETE JOHNSON & MEADE LUX LEWIS
| Giants Of Boogie Woogie | LP | Riverside | RLP12106 | 1963 £5 | £12 | |
| Boogie Woogie Trio | LP | Storyville | SLP184 | 1966 £4 | £10 | |
| Shout For Joy | 7" EP | Columbia | SEG7528 | 1954 £7.50 | £15 | |

## AMMONS, GENE
| Ammons Boogie | 7" | Starlite | ST45017 | 1960 £12.50 | £25 | |
| Anna | 7" | Starlite | ST45097 | 1963 £2 | £5 | |
| Bossa Nova By The Boss | 7" EP | Esquire | EP249 | 1962 £2.50 | £6 | |
| Hi Fidelity Jam Session | LP | Esquire | 32047 | 1958 £15 | £30 | |
| Jammin' With Gene | LP | Esquire | 32097 | 1960 £6 | £15 | |
| Soul Summit | LP | Transatlantic | PR7234 | 1968 £5 | £12 | with Sonny Stitt |

## AMON DÜÜL
| Collapsing | LP | Metronome | SMLP012 | 1969 £10 | £25 | German |
| Disaster | LP | BASF | 29290794 | 1971 £10 | £25 | German double |
| Minnelied | LP | Brain | 0040149 | 1975 £8 | £20 | German |
| Paradieswarts | LP | Ohr | OMM56008 | 1969 £15 | £30 | German |
| Psychedelic Underground | LP | Metronome | MLP15332 | 1969 £10 | £25 | German |
| This Is Amon Düül | LP | Brain | 21046 | 1973 £8 | £20 | German double |

## AMON DÜÜL II
Amon Düül II were originally a splinter group away from Amon Düül, following an ideological disagreement, but they rapidly became rather better known than the parent group. Essentially, the group is a German version of Hawkwind, with a similar mystical outlook and fascination with spacey noises. Equally, the music is at root very simply constructed, with single chords being worried half to death for minutes at a time.

| Almost Live | LP | Nova | 623305 | 1977 £5 | £12 | German |
| Carnival In Babylon | LP | United Artists | UAG29327 | 1972 £5 | £12 | |
| Dance Of The Lemmings | LP | United Artists | 60003/4 | 1971 £6 | £15 | double |
| Hi Jack | LP | Atlantic | K50136 | 1974 £5 | £12 | |
| Lemmingmania | LP | United Artists | UAS29723 | 1975 £5 | £12 | |
| Live In London | LP | United Artists | USP102 | 1973 £6 | £15 | |
| Made In Germany | LP | Atlantic | K50182 | 1975 £5 | £12 | |
| Made In Germany | LP | Nova | 628350 | 1975 £8 | £20 | German, double |
| Only Human | LP | Vinyl | LV1004 | 1978 £5 | £12 | |

| | | | | | | | |
|---|---|---|---|---|---|---|---|
| Phallus Dei | LP | Liberty | LBS83279 | 1969 | £15 | £30 | |
| Pyragony | LP | Nova | 622890 | 1976 | £5 | £12 | German |
| Vive La Trance | LP | United Artists | UAS29504 | 1973 | £6 | £15 | |
| Wolf City | LP | United Artists | UAG29406 | 1972 | £5 | £12 | |
| Yeti | LP | Liberty | LSP101/2 | 1970 | £6 | £15 | double |

## AMOS, TORI

Five years before releasing her acclaimed *Little Earthquakes* album, Tori Amos signed a contract with Atlantic, but only made one record with them. *Y Kant Tori Read* presents a startlingly different Tori Amos, casting her in the same mould as Pat Benatar (at least, visually: much of the actual music is close in style to that of her subsequent recordings). The record is extremely scarce, however, and Tori Amos herself disowns it. Even scarcer is the US single 'Baltimore', recorded when Ms Amos was just seventeen. The listed value has to be viewed as highly approximate, since few copies are ever likely to appear on the market.

| | | | | | | | |
|---|---|---|---|---|---|---|---|
| Baltimore | 7" | MEA | 5290 | 1980 | £75 | £150 | . US, credited to Ellen Amos |
| China | CD-s | East West | A7531CD | 1992 | £10 | £20 | |
| Cornflake Girl | CD-s | East West | A7281CDX | 1994 | £6 | £15 | digipak |
| Crucify Live EP | CD-s | East West | A7479CDX | 1992 | £12.50 | £25 | |
| Little Drummer Boy | CD-s | East West | no number | 1992 | £37.50 | £75 | promo |
| Me And A Gun EP (Silent All These Years) | CD-s | East West | YZ618CD | 1991 | £10 | £20 | |
| Me And A Gun EP (Silent All These Years) | 12" | East West | YZ618T | 1991 | £4 | £10 | |
| New Music From Tori Amos | CD | Atlantic | PRCD65352 | 1996 | £6 | £15 | US promo compilation |
| Precious Things | CD-s | Atlantic | PRCD47422 | 1992 | £30 | £60 | US promo picture disc |
| Silent All These Years | CD-s | East West | A7433CDX | 1992 | £12.50 | £25 | fold-out digipak |
| Silent All These Years | CD-s | East West | YZ618CD | 1991 | £5 | £12 | |
| Silent All These Years | 7" | East West | YZ618 | 1991 | £2.50 | £6 | |
| Silent All These Years | 12" | East West | YZ618T | 1991 | £3 | £8 | |
| Tea With The Waitress | CD | Atlantic | PRCD5498 | 1994 | £15 | £30 | ...US interview promo |
| Under The Pink/ More Pink | CD | East West | 7567806072 | 1994 | £10 | £25 | Australian with bonus disc |
| Winter | CD-s | East West | A7504CD | 1992 | £2.50 | £6 | |
| Winter | CD-s | East West | A7504CDX | 1992 | £10 | £20 | |
| Y Kant Tori Read | LP | Atlantic | 81845 | 1988 | £37.50 | £75 | US |
| Y Kant Tori Read | CD | Atlantic | 81845 | 1988 | £50 | £100 | US |

## AMRAM-BARROW QUARTET

| | | | | | | | |
|---|---|---|---|---|---|---|---|
| Jazz Studio Six | LP | Brunswick | LAT8239 | 1958 | £8 | £20 | |

## AMY, CURTIS

| | | | | | | | |
|---|---|---|---|---|---|---|---|
| Katanga | LP | Fontana | 688136ZL | 1966 | £5 | £12 | |

## ANAN

| | | | | | | | |
|---|---|---|---|---|---|---|---|
| Haze Woman | 7" | Pye | 7N17571 | 1968 | £6 | £12 | |
| Madena | 7" | Pye | 7N17642 | 1968 | £5 | £10 | |

## ANCIENT GREASE

| | | | | | | | |
|---|---|---|---|---|---|---|---|
| Women And Children First | LP | Mercury | 6338033 | 1970 | £15 | £30 | |

## ANCIENT MORNING

| | | | | | | | |
|---|---|---|---|---|---|---|---|
| Ancient Morning | LP | Cocaine | | 1979 | £20 | £40 | Swiss |

## AND ALSO THE TREES

| | | | | | | | |
|---|---|---|---|---|---|---|---|
| House Of The Heart | CD-s | Reflex | RE14CD | 1988 | £2 | £5 | |
| Lady D'Arbanville | CD-s | Reflex | RE15CD | 1989 | £2 | £5 | |
| Secret Sea | 7" | Reflex | RE6 | 1984 | £4 | £8 | |
| Secret Sea | 12" | Reflex | 12RE6 | 1984 | £2.50 | £6 | |
| Shantell | 7" | Reflex | FS9 | 1984 | £4 | £8 | |

## ANDERS, CHRISTIAN

| | | | | | | | |
|---|---|---|---|---|---|---|---|
| Beat Gitarren Schule 1 | LP | Joker | SM3037 | 1965 | £15 | £30 | German |

## ANDERSEN, ARILD

| | | | | | | | |
|---|---|---|---|---|---|---|---|
| Clouds In My Head | LP | ECM | ECM1059ST | 1975 | £6 | £15 | |

## ANDERSEN, ERIC

| | | | | | | | |
|---|---|---|---|---|---|---|---|
| 'Bout Changes & Things | LP | Fontana | STFL6068 | 1968 | £5 | £12 | US |
| Avalanche | LP | Warner Bros | WS1748 | 1970 | £5 | £12 | US |
| Best Of Eric Andersen | LP | Vanguard | VSD7/8 | 1973 | £5 | £12 | US, double |
| Blue River | LP | CBS | 65145 | 1973 | £4 | £10 | |
| Country Dream | LP | Vanguard | VSD6540 | 1969 | £5 | £12 | US |
| Eric Andersen | LP | Warner Bros | WS1806 | 1970 | £5 | £12 | US |
| More Hits From Tin Can Alley | LP | Vanguard | VSD79271 | 1968 | £5 | £12 | US |
| Stage | LP | CBS | 65571 | 1974 | £4 | £10 | US |
| Today Is The Highway | LP | Fontana | TFL6061 | 1965 | £5 | £12 | |

## ANDERSON, ALISTAIR

| | | | | | | | |
|---|---|---|---|---|---|---|---|
| Concertina Workshop | LP | Free Reed | FRS501 | 1974 | £4 | £10 | |
| Plays English Concertina | LP | Trailer | LER2074 | 1972 | £4 | £10 | |
| Traditional Tunes | LP | Front Hall | FHR08 | 1976 | £6 | £15 | US |

## ANDERSON, BRUFORD, WAKEMAN & HOWE

| | | | | | | | |
|---|---|---|---|---|---|---|---|
| Anderson, Bruford, Wakeman And Howe | CD | Arista | ARCD90126 | 1989 | £6 | £15 | US promo picture disc |
| Brother Of Mine | CD-s | Arista | 662379 | 1989 | £2 | £5 | picture disc |
| Order Of The Universe | CD-s | Arista | 662693 | 1989 | £2 | £5 | |

## ANDERSON, CASEY

| | | | | | | | |
|---|---|---|---|---|---|---|---|
| Bag I'm In | LP | Atco | (SD)33149 | 1962 | £4 | £10 | US |

| Title | Format | Label | Catalogue | Year | Price | Price | Notes |
|---|---|---|---|---|---|---|---|
| Blues Is A Woman Gone | LP | Atco | (SD)33176 | 1965 | £4 | £10 | US |
| Goin' Places | LP | Elektra | EKL/EKS7192 | 1960 | £4 | £10 | US |
| Live At The Ice House | LP | Atco | (SD)33172 | 1965 | £4 | £10 | US |
| More Pretty Girls Than One | LP | Atco | (SD)33166 | 1964 | £4 | £10 | US |

## ANDERSON, CAT

| Title | Format | Label | Catalogue | Year | Price | Price | Notes |
|---|---|---|---|---|---|---|---|
| Cat On A Hot Tin Horn | LP | Mercury | MMB12006 | 1959 | £6 | £15 | |

## ANDERSON, ERNESTINE

| Title | Format | Label | Catalogue | Year | Price | Price | Notes |
|---|---|---|---|---|---|---|---|
| Azure-Te | 7" EP | Mercury | ZEP10105 | 1961 | £2 | £5 | |
| By Special Request | LP | Pye | NPT19025 | 1958 | £4 | £10 | |
| Ernestine Anderson | LP | Columbia | SX/SCX6145 | 1967 | £4 | £10 | |
| Ernestine Anderson | 7" EP | Mercury | 10007MCE | 1964 | £2.50 | £6 | |
| Fascinating Ernestine | LP | Mercury | MMC14037 | 1960 | £4 | £10 | |
| Jerk And Twine | 7" | Mercury | MF912 | 1965 | £2 | £5 | |
| Just A Swinging | 7" EP | Mercury | ZEP10124 | 1962 | £2 | £5 | |
| Keep An Eye On Love | 7" | Sue | WI309 | 1964 | £6 | £12 | |
| Moanin' | LP | Mercury | MMC14062 | 1961 | £4 | £10 | |
| New Sound Of Ernestine Anderson | LP | Sue | ILP914 | 1964 | £30 | £60 | |
| Runnin' Wild | LP | Mercury | MMC14016 | 1959 | £6 | £15 | |
| Running Wild | 7" EP | Mercury | ZEP10057 | 1960 | £2.50 | £6 | |
| Somebody Told You | 7" | Stateside | SS455 | 1965 | £2 | £5 | |
| Welcome To The Club | 7" EP | Mercury | ZEP10089 | 1960 | £2.50 | £6 | |

## ANDERSON, GLADSTONE

| Title | Format | Label | Catalogue | Year | Price | Price | Notes |
|---|---|---|---|---|---|---|---|
| Judas | 7" | Blue Cat | BS172 | 1969 | £1.50 | £4 | |

## ANDERSON, IAN

| Title | Format | Label | Catalogue | Year | Price | Price | Notes |
|---|---|---|---|---|---|---|---|
| Walking Into Light | CD | Chrysalis | CCD1443 | 1988 | £5 | £12 | |

## ANDERSON, IAN A.

| Title | Format | Label | Catalogue | Year | Price | Price | Notes |
|---|---|---|---|---|---|---|---|
| Almost The Country Blues | 7" EP | Saydisc | EPSD134 | 1969 | £6 | £12 | |
| Book Of Changes | LP | Fontana | STL5542 | 1970 | £8 | £20 | |
| Inverted World | LP | Matchbox | SDM159 | 1968 | £20 | £40 | with Mike Cooper |
| One More Chance | 7" | Village Thing | VTSX1002 | 1971 | £5 | £10 | |
| Royal York Crescent | LP | Village Thing | VTS3 | 1970 | £5 | £12 | |
| Singer Sleeps On As Blaze Rages | LP | Village Thing | VTS18 | 1972 | £4 | £10 | |
| Stereo Death Breakdown | LP | Liberty | LBS83242 | 1969 | £10 | £25 | |
| Vulture Is Not A Bird You Can Trust | LP | Village Thing | VTS9 | 1971 | £4 | £10 | |

## ANDERSON, JON

| Title | Format | Label | Catalogue | Year | Price | Price | Notes |
|---|---|---|---|---|---|---|---|
| Change We Must | CD | EMI | CDC5550882 | 1994 | £10 | £25 | promo CD and video boxed set |
| Evening With Jon Anderson | LP | Atlantic | PR285 | 1976 | £5 | £12 | US promo |
| Hold On To Love | CD-s | Epic | 6515142 | 1988 | £2 | £5 | |
| In The City Of Angels | CD | Epic | 4606932 | 1988 | £5 | £12 | |
| Is It Me | CD-s | Epic | 6529472 | 1988 | £2 | £5 | |

## ANDERSON, JONES, JACKSON

| Title | Format | Label | Catalogue | Year | Price | Price | Notes |
|---|---|---|---|---|---|---|---|
| Anderson, Jones, Jackson | 7" EP | Saydisc | EPSD125 | 1968 | £7.50 | £15 | |

## ANDERSON, LAURIE

| Title | Format | Label | Catalogue | Year | Price | Price | Notes |
|---|---|---|---|---|---|---|---|
| United States Live | LP | Warner Bros | 9251921 | 1984 | £20 | £40 | 5 LP set |

## ANDERSON, LEROY

| Title | Format | Label | Catalogue | Year | Price | Price | Notes |
|---|---|---|---|---|---|---|---|
| Anderson Compositions | 7" EP | Brunswick | OE9021 | 1954 | £2 | £5 | |
| Forgotten Dreams | 7" | Brunswick | 05485 | 1955 | £1.50 | £4 | |
| Pops Concert Pt. 1 | 7" EP | Brunswick | OE9356 | 1958 | £2 | £5 | |
| Pops Concert Pt. 2 | 7" EP | Brunswick | OE9357 | 1958 | £2 | £5 | |

## ANDERSON, MILLER

Miller Anderson was the lead guitarist and singer with the Keef Hartley Band. His solo LP uses the band musicians (but not Hartley himself) to rather less effect than on *Little Big Band*, which was released at the same time.

| Title | Format | Label | Catalogue | Year | Price | Price | Notes |
|---|---|---|---|---|---|---|---|
| Bright City | LP | Deram | SDL3 | 1971 | £15 | £30 | |
| Bright City | 7" | Deram | DM337 | 1971 | £1.50 | £4 | |

## ANDERSON, PINK

| Title | Format | Label | Catalogue | Year | Price | Price | Notes |
|---|---|---|---|---|---|---|---|
| Ballad And Folk Singer | LP | Bluesville | BV1071 | 1963 | £4 | £10 | US |
| Carolina Blues Man | LP | Bluesville | BV1038 | 1961 | £4 | £10 | US |
| Medicine Show Man | LP | Bluesville | BV1051 | 1962 | £4 | £10 | US |

## ANDERSON, REUBEN

| Title | Format | Label | Catalogue | Year | Price | Price | Notes |
|---|---|---|---|---|---|---|---|
| Christmas Time Again | 7" | Doctor Bird | DB1045 | 1966 | £5 | £10 | |

## ANDERSON, SONNY

| Title | Format | Label | Catalogue | Year | Price | Price | Notes |
|---|---|---|---|---|---|---|---|
| Lonely Lonely Train | 7" | London | HLP9036 | 1960 | £15 | £30 | |

## ANDERSON, VICKI

| Title | Format | Label | Catalogue | Year | Price | Price | Notes |
|---|---|---|---|---|---|---|---|
| Super Good | 7" | Polydor | 2001150 | 1971 | £1.50 | £4 | |

## ANDERSON'S ALL STARS

| Title | Format | Label | Catalogue | Year | Price | Price | Notes |
|---|---|---|---|---|---|---|---|
| Intensified Girls | 7" | Blue Cat | BS133 | 1968 | £4 | £8 | |

## ANDREWS, CATHERINE

| Title | Format | Label | Catalogue | Year | Price | Price | Notes |
|---|---|---|---|---|---|---|---|
| Fruits | LP | Cat Tracks | PURRLP2 | 1982 | £87.50 | £175 | |

## ANDREWS, ERNIE

| Title | Format | Label | Cat. No. | Year | | | Notes |
|---|---|---|---|---|---|---|---|
| In The Dark | LP | Vogue | VA160147 | 1959 | £5 | £12 | |
| Round Midnight | 7" | Vogue | V9166 | 1960 | £2 | £5 | |
| Where Were you | 7" | Capitol | CL15407 | 1965 | £5 | £10 | |

## ANDREWS, HARVEY

| Title | Format | Label | Cat. No. | Year | | | Notes |
|---|---|---|---|---|---|---|---|
| Brand New Day | LP | Polydor | 2383595 | 1980 | £4 | £10 | |
| Fantasies From A Corner Seat | LP | Transatlantic | TRA298 | 1975 | £4 | £10 | |
| Friends Of Mine | LP | Fly | HIFLY15 | 1973 | £4 | £10 | |
| Harvey Andrews | 7" EP | Transatlantic | TRAEP133 | 1965 | £7.50 | £15 | |
| Places And Faces | LP | Nova | DN/SND9 | 1969 | £8 | £20 | |
| Soldier | 7" | Cube | BUG20 | 1971 | £1.50 | £4 | |
| Someday | LP | Transatlantic | TRA329 | 1976 | £4 | £10 | |
| Writer Of Songs | LP | Cube | HIFLY10 | 1972 | £4 | £10 | |

## ANDREWS, INEZ & THE ANDREWETTES

| Title | Format | Label | Cat. No. | Year | | | Notes |
|---|---|---|---|---|---|---|---|
| Inez Andrews And The Andrewettes | 7" EP | Vogue | EDVP1283 | 1965 | £15 | £30 | |

## ANDREWS, JOHN & THE LONELY ONES

| Title | Format | Label | Cat. No. | Year | | | Notes |
|---|---|---|---|---|---|---|---|
| Rose Grows In The Ruins | 7" | Parlophone | R5455 | 1966 | £7.50 | £15 | |

## ANDREWS, LEE & THE HEARTS

| Title | Format | Label | Cat. No. | Year | | | Notes |
|---|---|---|---|---|---|---|---|
| Teardrops | 7" | London | HL7031 | 1957 | £37.50 | £75 | export |
| Teardrops | 7" | London | HLM8546 | 1958 | £100 | £200 | best auctioned |
| Try The Impossible | 7" | London | HLU8661 | 1958 | £210 | £300 | best auctioned |

## ANDREWS, PATTY

| Title | Format | Label | Cat. No. | Year | | | Notes |
|---|---|---|---|---|---|---|---|
| Suddenly There's A Valley | 7" | Capitol | CL14374 | 1955 | £2.50 | £6 | |
| Where To My Love? | 7" | Capitol | CL14324 | 1955 | £2.50 | £6 | |

## ANDREWS, WILLIAM & LIAM WALSH

| Title | Format | Label | Cat. No. | Year | | | Notes |
|---|---|---|---|---|---|---|---|
| Classics Of Irish Piping Vol. 2 | LP | Topic | 12T262 | 1976 | £5 | £12 | |

## ANDREWS SISTERS

| Title | Format | Label | Cat. No. | Year | | | Notes |
|---|---|---|---|---|---|---|---|
| Rum And Coca-Cola | 7" | Capitol | CL14705 | 1957 | £1.50 | £4 | |

## ANDROIDS OF MU

| Title | Format | Label | Cat. No. | Year | | | Notes |
|---|---|---|---|---|---|---|---|
| Blood Robots | LP | Fuck Off | FLP001 | 1980 | £4 | £10 | |

## ANDROMEDA

| Title | Format | Label | Cat. No. | Year | | | Notes |
|---|---|---|---|---|---|---|---|
| Andromeda | LP | RCA | SF8031 | 1969 | £62.50 | £125 | |
| Go Your Way | 7" | RCA | RCA1854 | 1969 | £5 | £10 | |

## ANDWELLA

| Title | Format | Label | Cat. No. | Year | | | Notes |
|---|---|---|---|---|---|---|---|
| Are You Ready | 7" | Reflection | RS6 | 1970 | £1.50 | £4 | |
| Peoples People | LP | Reflection | REFL10 | 1971 | £5 | £12 | |
| World's End | LP | Reflection | REF1010 | 1970 | £5 | £12 | |

## ANDWELLA'S DREAM

| Title | Format | Label | Cat. No. | Year | | | Notes |
|---|---|---|---|---|---|---|---|
| Every Little Minute | 7" | Reflection | RS1 | 1970 | £1.50 | £4 | |
| Love And Poetry | LP | CBS | 63673 | 1969 | £150 | £250 | |
| Midday Sun | 7" | CBS | 4301 | 1969 | £10 | £20 | |
| Mr. Sunshine | 7" | CBS | 4634 | 1969 | £5 | £10 | |
| Mrs. Man | 7" | CBS | 4469 | 1969 | £5 | £10 | |

## ANDY, BOB

| Title | Format | Label | Cat. No. | Year | | | Notes |
|---|---|---|---|---|---|---|---|
| Born A Man | 7" | Coxsone | CS7074 | 1968 | £5 | £10 | Marcia Griffiths B side |
| Experience | 7" | Studio One | SO2063 | 1968 | £6 | £12 | |
| Going Home | 7" | Studio One | SO2075 | 1969 | £6 | £12 | Sound Dimension B side |
| Lots Of Love | LP | Sky Note | SKLP15 | 1978 | £5 | £12 | |
| Way I Feel | 7" | Doctor Bird | DB1183 | 1969 | £5 | £10 | Ethiopians B side |

## ANDY, HORACE

| Title | Format | Label | Cat. No. | Year | | | Notes |
|---|---|---|---|---|---|---|---|
| You Are My Angel | LP | Trojan | TBL197 | 1972 | £4 | £10 | |

## ANDY & CLYDE

| Title | Format | Label | Cat. No. | Year | | | Notes |
|---|---|---|---|---|---|---|---|
| I'm So Lonesome | 7" | Rio | R69 | 1965 | £5 | £10 | |
| Never Be A Slave | 7" | Rio | R62 | 1965 | £5 | £10 | |
| We All Have To Part | 7" | Rio | R71 | 1965 | £5 | £10 | |

## ANDY & JOEY

| Title | Format | Label | Cat. No. | Year | | | Notes |
|---|---|---|---|---|---|---|---|
| Have You Ever | 7" | Island | WI056 | 1962 | £5 | £10 | |
| I Want To Know | 7" | Port-O-Jam | PJ4009 | 1964 | £5 | £10 | |
| You'll Never | 7" | R&B | JB162 | 1964 | £5 | £10 | |

## ANGE

| Title | Format | Label | Cat. No. | Year | | | Notes |
|---|---|---|---|---|---|---|---|
| Au delà du délire | LP | Philips | 9101004 | 1974 | £4 | £10 | French |
| Caricatures | LP | Philips | 6325181 | 1972 | £4 | £10 | French |
| Cimetière des arlequins | LP | Philips | 9101022 | 1973 | £4 | £10 | French |
| Emile Jacotey | LP | Philips | 9101012 | 1975 | £4 | £10 | French |
| Par le fils du mandarin | LP | Philips | 9101090 | 1976 | £4 | £10 | French |

## ANGEL

Angel's claim to fame lies not so much in their status as the poor man's Kiss, but rather in being home to Punky Meadows, the guitarist who took exception to being lampooned in Frank Zappa's song, 'Punky's Whips'.

| | | | | | | | |
|---|---|---|---|---|---|---|---|
| Angel | LP | Casablanca | CBC4007 | 1976 | £8 | £20 | |
| Helluva Band | LP | Casablanca | CBC4010 | 1976 | £4 | £10 | |
| Live Without A Net | LP | Casablanca | CALH2703 | 1980 | £6 | £15 | double |
| On Earth As It Is In Heaven | LP | Casablanca | CAL2002 | 1977 | £4 | £10 | |
| Sinful | LP | Casablanca | CAL2046 | 1979 | £5 | £12 | |
| White Hot | LP | Casablanca | CSL2023 | 1978 | £5 | £12 | |

## ANGEL (2)

| | | | | | | |
|---|---|---|---|---|---|---|
| Little Boy Blue | 7" | Cube | BUG51 | 1974 | £2.50 | £6 |

## ANGEL, MARION

| | | | | | | |
|---|---|---|---|---|---|---|
| It's Gonna Be Alright | 7" | Columbia | DB7537 | 1965 | £2 | £5 |

## ANGEL PAVEMENT

| | | | | | | |
|---|---|---|---|---|---|---|
| Baby You've Gotta Stay | 7" | Fontana | TF1059 | 1969 | £1.50 | £4 |
| Tell Me What I've Got To Do | 7" | Fontana | TF1072 | 1970 | £1.50 | £4 |

## ANGELA & THE FANS

This tribute/cash-in song in praise of Illya Kuryakin, the character played by David McCallum in TV's *The Man From U.N.C.L.E.*, was actually performed by Alma Cogan.

| | | | | | | |
|---|---|---|---|---|---|---|
| Love Ya Illya | 7" | Pye | 7N17108 | 1966 | £6 | £12 |

## ANGELIC UPSTARTS

| | | | | | | | |
|---|---|---|---|---|---|---|---|
| Brighton Bomb | 12" | Gas | GM3010 | 1985 | £2.50 | £6 | Thatcher sleeve |
| England | 7" | Regal Zonophone | Z12 | 1980 | £2.50 | £6 | |
| Murder Of Liddle Towers | 7" | Angelic Upstarts | AU1024 | 1978 | £7.50 | £15 | |

## ANGELINA

| | | | | | | |
|---|---|---|---|---|---|---|
| I Just Don't Know How | 7" | Fontana | TF648 | 1965 | £1.50 | £4 |

## ANGELO, BOBBY & THE TUXEDOS

| | | | | | | |
|---|---|---|---|---|---|---|
| Baby Sitting | 7" | HMV | POP892 | 1961 | £7.50 | £15 |
| Don't Stop | 7" | HMV | POP982 | 1961 | £7.50 | £15 |

## ANGELO, MICHAEL

| | | | | | | |
|---|---|---|---|---|---|---|
| Tears | 7" | Columbia | DB4800 | 1962 | £2 | £5 |

## ANGELOU, MAYA

| | | | | | | |
|---|---|---|---|---|---|---|
| Miss Calypso | LP | London | HAU2062 | 1957 | £4 | £10 |

## ANGELS

| | | | | | | | |
|---|---|---|---|---|---|---|---|
| And The Angels Sing | LP | Caprice | (S)LP1001 | 1962 | £15 | £30 | US |
| Everybody Loves A Lover | 7" | Pye | 7N25150 | 1962 | £1.50 | £4 | US |
| Greatest Hits | LP | Ascot | AM13009/ALS6009 | 1964 | £6 | £15 | US |
| Halo To You | LP | Smash | MGS27048/SRS67048 | 1964 | £10 | £25 | US |
| I Adore Him | 7" | Mercury | AMT1215 | 1963 | £1.50 | £4 | |
| My Boyfriend's Back | LP | Smash | MGS27039/SRS67039 | 1963 | £10 | £25 | US |
| My Boyfriend's Back | 7" | Mercury | AMT1211 | 1963 | £1.50 | £4 | |
| Wow Wow Wee | 7" | Philips | BF1312 | 1964 | £1.50 | £4 | |

## ANGELWITCH

| | | | | | | |
|---|---|---|---|---|---|---|
| Angel Witch | 7" | Bronze | BRO108 | 1980 | £2 | £5 |
| Loser | 7" | Bronze | BRO121 | 1981 | £2 | £5 |
| Sweet Danger | 7" | EMI | EMI5064 | 1980 | £2 | £5 |
| Sweet Danger | 12" | EMI | 125064 | 1980 | £4 | £10 |

## ANGLIANS

| | | | | | | |
|---|---|---|---|---|---|---|
| Friend Of Mine | 7" | CBS | 202489 | 1967 | £2 | £5 |

## ANGLOS

The marvelous 'Incense' by the Anglos was issued several times during the sixties and by some means still managed to avoid becoming a hit. The group, however, was purely a studio creation, the intensely soulful singer being Stevie Winwood (who also used the name Steve Anglo for his guest recording with John Mayall, included on the *Raw Blues* compilation album).

| | | | | | | | |
|---|---|---|---|---|---|---|---|
| Incense | 7" | Brit | WI1004 | 1965 | £10 | £20 | |
| Incense | 7" | Fontana | TF561 | 1965 | £15 | £30 | demo only |
| Incense | 7" | Fontana | TF589 | 1965 | £5 | £10 | |
| Incense | 7" | Island | WIP6061 | 1969 | £2 | £5 | |
| Incense | 7" | Sue | WI4033 | 1967 | £10 | £20 | demo only |

## ANIMALS

As with the Beatles and the Rolling Stones, the British and American LPs by the Animals have numerous differences, even where the titles are the same. Five tracks on the first UK album were replaced in the US by the songs from the first two singles, together with a track, 'Blue Feeling', that never did get a British release. The second album, called *Animal Tracks* in the UK, had three of its songs removed and four different ones added for the US version, which was retitled *The Animals On Tour*. An American LP called *Animal Tracks* was also issued, but this was a different record altogether, being a compilation of various singles and LP tracks not already released in the US. The two hits anthologies are inevitably different – the British *Most Of The Animals* (not to be confused with a later Music For Pleasure release with a greatly inferior selection) has fourteen tracks, while the American *Best Of The Animals* has only eleven – and only nine are to be found on both records. *Animalisms* and *Animalization* have four differences in their running orders; the American *Animalism* LP has no British equivalent at all. Of its eleven tracks, nine were not released in the UK, while a tenth, 'Outcast', is a different take to the version found on *Animalisms*.

| Title | Format | Label | Cat. No. | Year | Price | Price | Notes |
|---|---|---|---|---|---|---|---|
| Animal Tracks | LP | Columbia | 33SX1708 | 1965 | £10 | £25 | |
| Animal Tracks | LP | MGM | (S)E4305 | 1965 | £10 | £25 | US |
| Animal Tracks | 7" EP | Columbia | SEG8499 | 1966 | £10 | £20 | |
| Animalism | LP | MGM | (S)E4414 | 1966 | £10 | £25 | US |
| Animalisms | LP | Decca | LK4797 | 1966 | £10 | £25 | |
| Animalization | LP | MGM | (S)E4384 | 1966 | £10 | £25 | US |
| Animals | LP | Columbia | 33SX1669 | 1964 | £8 | £20 | |
| Animals | LP | MGM | (S)E4264 | 1964 | £10 | £25 | US |
| Animals | LP | Regal | SREG104 | 196– | £8 | £20 | export |
| Animals | 7" EP | Columbia | SEG8400 | 1965 | £6 | £12 | |
| Animals Are Back | 7" EP | Columbia | SEG8452 | 1965 | £6 | £12 | |
| Animals Is Here | 7" EP | Columbia | SEG8374 | 1964 | £6 | £12 | |
| Animals No. 2 | 7" EP | Columbia | SEG8439 | 1965 | £6 | £12 | |
| Animals On Tour | LP | MGM | (S)E4281 | 1965 | £10 | £25 | US |
| Baby Let Me Take You Home | 7" | Columbia | DB7247 | 1964 | £1.50 | £4 | |
| Best Of The Animals | LP | MGM | (S)E4324 | 1966 | £6 | £15 | US |
| Best Of The Animals Vol. 2 | LP | MGM | (S)E4454 | 1967 | £6 | £15 | US |
| Boom Boom | 7" EP | Columbia | ESRF1632 | 1964 | £10 | £20 | French |
| Bring It On Home To Me | 7" EP | Columbia | ESRF1671 | 1965 | £10 | £20 | French |
| Bring It On Home To Me | 7" | Columbia | DB7539 | 1965 | £1.50 | £4 | |
| Don't Bring Me Down | 7" EP | Barclay | 071043 | 1966 | £10 | £20 | French |
| Don't Bring Me Down | 7" | Decca | F12407 | 1966 | £1.50 | £4 | |
| Don't Let Me Be Misunderstood | 7" | Columbia | DB7445 | 1965 | £1.50 | £4 | |
| Don't Let Me Be Misunderstood | 7" | Columbia | DB7445 | 1965 | £25 | £50 | demo A side – matrix 1N |
| Help Me Girl | 7" | Decca | F12502 | 1966 | £1.50 | £4 | |
| House Of The Rising Sun | 7" EP | Columbia | ESRF1571 | 1964 | £10 | £20 | French |
| House Of The Rising Sun | 7" | Columbia | DB7301 | 1964 | £1.50 | £4 | |
| I Just Want To Make Love To You | 12" EP | Graphic Sound | ALO10867 | 1963 | £100 | £200 | credited to Alan Price R&B Group |
| I'm Crying | 7" EP | Columbia | ESRF1593 | 1964 | £10 | £20 | French |
| I'm Crying | 7" | Columbia | DB7354 | 1964 | £1.50 | £4 | |
| In The Beginning There Was Early Animals | 7" EP | Decca | DFE8643 | 1965 | £10 | £20 | |
| Inside Looking Out | 7" | Decca | F12332 | 1966 | £1.50 | £4 | |
| It's My Life | 7" EP | Columbia | ESRF1717 | 1965 | £10 | £20 | French |
| It's My Life | 7" | Columbia | DB7741 | 1965 | £1.50 | £4 | |
| Mama Told Me Not To Come | 7" | Decca | F12502 | 1966 | £20 | £40 | |
| Most Of The Animals | LP | Columbia | SX6035 | 1966 | £8 | £20 | |
| Outcast | 7" EP | Barclay | 070970 | 1966 | £10 | £20 | French |
| We've Gotta Get Out Of This Place | CD-s | EMI | CDEM154 | 1990 | £2 | £5 | |
| We've Gotta Get Out Of This Place | 7" | Columbia | DB7639 | 1965 | £1.50 | £4 | |
| We've Gotta Get Out This Place | 7" EP | Columbia | ESRF1692 | 1965 | £10 | £20 | French |

## ANIMALS & OTHERS

| Title | Format | Label | Cat. No. | Year | Price | Price | Notes |
|---|---|---|---|---|---|---|---|
| Get Yourself A College Girl | LP | MGM | (S)E4273 | 1964 | £6 | £15 | US |

## ANIMATED EGG

| Title | Format | Label | Cat. No. | Year | Price | Price | Notes |
|---|---|---|---|---|---|---|---|
| Animated Egg | LP | Alshire | SF5104 | 1967 | £10 | £25 | US |
| Animated Egg | LP | Marble Arch | MAL 890 | 1969 | £10 | £25 | |

## ANKA, PAUL

| Title | Format | Label | Cat. No. | Year | Price | Price | Notes |
|---|---|---|---|---|---|---|---|
| Anka Again | 7" EP | Columbia | SEG7801 | 1958 | £4 | £8 | |
| At The Copa | LP | ABC | (S)353 | 1960 | £6 | £15 | US |
| Can't Get You Out Of My Mind | 7" | RCA | RCA1676 | 1968 | £10 | £20 | |
| Crazy Love | 7" | Columbia | DB4110 | 1958 | £1.50 | £4 | |
| Diana | LP | ABC | (S)420 | 1962 | £8 | £20 | US |
| Diana | 7" EP | Columbia | SEG7747 | 1957 | £5 | £10 | |
| Diana | 7" | Columbia | DB3980 | 1957 | £1.50 | £4 | |
| Excitement On Park Avenue | LP | RCA | RD7700 | 1964 | £4 | £10 | |
| Fly Me To The Moon | 7" EP | RCA | RCX7127 | 1964 | £2.50 | £6 | |
| Four Golden Hits | 7" EP | RCA | RCX7152 | 1964 | £2.50 | £6 | |
| Hello Young Lovers | 7" | Columbia | DB4504 | 1960 | £1.50 | £4 | |
| I Love You Baby | 7" | Columbia | DB4022 | 1957 | £1.50 | £4 | |
| I Miss You So | 7" | Columbia | DB4286 | 1959 | £1.50 | £4 | |
| It's Christmas Everywhere | LP | Columbia | 33SX1287 | 1960 | £6 | £15 | |
| It's Time To Cry | 7" | Columbia | DB4390 | 1960 | £1.50 | £4 | |
| Just Young | 7" | Columbia | DB4199 | 1958 | £1.50 | £4 | |
| Let's Sit This One Out | LP | RCA | RD/SF7533 | 1962 | £4 | £10 | |
| Lonely Boy | 7" | Columbia | DB4324 | 1959 | £1.50 | £4 | |
| Midnight | 7" | Columbia | DB4172 | 1958 | £1.50 | £4 | |
| My Heart Sings | LP | Columbia | 33SX1196 | 1959 | £6 | £15 | |
| My Heart Sings | 7" | Columbia | DB4241 | 1959 | £1.50 | £4 | |
| Our Man Around The World | LP | RCA | RD/SF7547 | 1963 | £4 | £10 | |
| Paul Anka | LP | Columbia | 33SX1092 | 1958 | £6 | £15 | |
| Puppy Love | 7" | Columbia | DB4434 | 1960 | £1.50 | £4 | |
| Put Your Head On My Shoulder | 7" | Columbia | DB4355 | 1959 | £1.50 | £4 | |
| Sing Sing Sing | 7" EP | Columbia | SEG7890 | 1959 | £4 | £8 | |
| Sings His Big 15 | LP | Columbia | 33SX1282 | 1960 | £4 | £10 | |
| Sings His Big 15 Vol. 2 | LP | Columbia | 33SX1395 | 1961 | £4 | £10 | |
| Sings His Big 15 Vol. 3 | LP | Columbia | 33SX1432 | 1962 | £4 | £10 | |
| Sings Songs From Girls Town | 7" EP | Columbia | SEG7985 | 1960 | £4 | £8 | |
| Songs I Wish I'd Written | LP | RCA | RD/SF7613 | 1963 | £4 | £10 | |
| Strictly Instrumental | LP | ABC | (S)371 | 1961 | £8 | £20 | US |
| Strictly Nashville | LP | RCA | LPM/LSP3580 | 1966 | £4 | £10 | US |
| Swings For Young Lovers | LP | Columbia | 33SX1268 | 1960 | £6 | £15 | |
| Sylvia | 7" EP | RCA | RCX7170 | 1964 | £2.50 | £6 | |
| Twenty-One Golden Hits | LP | RCA | RD/SF7573 | 1963 | £4 | £10 | |

| | | | | | | | |
|---|---|---|---|---|---|---|---|
| You Are My Destiny | 7" | Columbia | DB4063 | 1958 | £1.50 | £4 | |
| Young Alive And In Love | LP | RCA | RD27257/SF5129 | 1962 | £4 | £10 | |

## ANKA, PAUL, SAM COOKE & NEIL SEDAKA
| | | | | | | | |
|---|---|---|---|---|---|---|---|
| Three Great Guys | LP | RCA | RD/SF7608 | 1963 | £4 | £10 | |

## ANNETTE
| | | | | | | | |
|---|---|---|---|---|---|---|---|
| Annette | LP | Buena Vista | BV3301 | 1959 | £15 | £30 | US |
| Annette And Hayley Mills | LP | Buena Vista | BV3508 | 196– | £25 | £50 | US |
| Annette At Bikini Beach | LP | Buena Vista | BV/STER.3324 | 1964 | £10 | £25 | US |
| Annette Funicello | LP | Buena Vista | BV4037 | 1962 | £15 | £30 | US |
| Annette On Campus | LP | Buena Vista | BV/STER.3320 | 1964 | £10 | £25 | US |
| Annette Sings Anka | LP | Buena Vista | BV3302 | 1960 | £15 | £30 | US |
| Annette Sings Golden Surfin' Hits | LP | Buena Vista | BV/STER.3327 | 1964 | £10 | £25 | US |
| Annette's Beach Party | LP | HMV | CLP1782 | 1963 | £10 | £25 | |
| Annette's Pajama Party | LP | Buena Vista | BV/STER.3325 | 1964 | £10 | £25 | US |
| Babes In Toyland | LP | Buena Vista | BV(S)4022 | 1961 | £8 | £20 | US |
| Best Of Broadway | LP | Disneyland | DQ1267 | 1965 | £8 | £20 | US |
| Dance Annette | LP | Buena Vista | BV3305 | 1961 | £10 | £25 | US |
| First Name Initial | 7" | Top Rank | JAR233 | 1959 | £2 | £5 | |
| Hawaiiannette | LP | Buena Vista | BV3303 | 1960 | £10 | £25 | US |
| How To Stuff A Wild Bikini | LP | Wand | (S)671 | 1965 | £4 | £10 | |
| Italiannette | LP | Buena Vista | BV3304 | 1960 | £10 | £25 | US |
| Lonely Guitar | 7" | Top Rank | JAR137 | 1959 | £2 | £5 | |
| Merlin Jones | 7" | HMV | POP1322 | 1964 | £1.50 | £4 | |
| Monkey's Uncle | 7" | HMV | POP1447 | 1965 | £5 | £10 | .. with the Beach Boys |
| Muscle Beach Party | LP | Buena Vista | BV/STER.3314 | 1963 | £10 | £25 | US |
| Muscle Beach Party | 7" | HMV | POP1270 | 1964 | £2 | £5 | |
| O Dio Mio | 7" | Top Rank | JAR343 | 1960 | £2 | £5 | |
| Parent Trap | LP | Buena Vista | BV(S)3309 | 1961 | £8 | £20 | US |
| Pineapple Princess | 7" | Pye | 7N25061 | 1960 | £1.50 | £4 | |
| Something Borrowed, Something Blue | LP | Buena Vista | BV3328 | 1964 | £10 | £25 | US |
| Songs From Annette | LP | Mickey Mouse. | MM24 | 196– | £15 | £30 | US |
| State And College Songs | LP | Disneyland | DQ(S)1293 | 1967 | £8 | £20 | US |
| Story Of My Teens | LP | Buena Vista | BV3312 | 1962 | £15 | £30 | US |
| Tall Paul | 7" EP | Gala | 45XP1046 | 196– | £5 | £10 | |
| Teen Street | LP | Buena Vista | BV3313 | 1962 | £10 | £25 | US |
| Thunder Alley | LP | Sidewalk | (S)T5902 | 1967 | £4 | £10 | US |
| Tubby The Tuba | LP | Disneyland | DQ(S)1287 | 1966 | £6 | £15 | US |
| Walt Disney's Wonderful World Of Color | LP | Disneyland | DQ(S)1245 | 1964 | £6 | £15 | US |

## ANNETTE & THE KEYMEN
| | | | | | | | |
|---|---|---|---|---|---|---|---|
| Look Who's Blue | 7" | King | KG1006 | 1964 | £1.50 | £4 | |

## ANNEXUS QUAM
| | | | | | | | |
|---|---|---|---|---|---|---|---|
| Beziehungen | LP | Ohr | OMM56028 | 1972 | £8 | £20 | German |
| Osmose | LP | Ohr | OMM56007 | 1970 | £25 | £50 | German |

## ANNIS
| | | | | | | | |
|---|---|---|---|---|---|---|---|
| Don't Play Your Games | 7" | GTO | 266 | 1979 | £2 | £5 | |

## ANNO DOMINI
| | | | | | | | |
|---|---|---|---|---|---|---|---|
| On The New Day | LP | Deram | SML1085 | 1971 | £50 | £100 | |

## ANONYMOUS
| | | | | | | | |
|---|---|---|---|---|---|---|---|
| Inside The Shadow | LP | A Major Label | AMLS1002 | 1976 | £50 | £100 | US |

## ANOTHER DREAM
| | | | | | | | |
|---|---|---|---|---|---|---|---|
| Forever In Darkness | 7" | Sticky | PEELOFF2 | 198– | £2 | £5 | |

## ANOTHER PRETTY FACE
| | | | | | | | |
|---|---|---|---|---|---|---|---|
| All The Boys Love Carrie | 7" | New Pleasures | Z1 | 1979 | £7.50 | £15 | ...green & white sleeve |
| All The Boys Love Carrie | 7" | New Pleasures | Z1 | 1979 | £4 | £8 | ..... red & white sleeve |
| Heaven Gets Closer Every Day | 7" | Chicken Jazz | JAZZ1 | 1980 | £6 | £12 | |
| I'm Sorry That I Beat You | cass | Chicken Jazz | JAZZ2 | 1981 | £20 | £40 | ... with badge & book |
| Soul To Soul | 7" | Chicken Jazz | JAZZ3 | 1981 | £7.50 | £15 | .gatefold picture sleeve |
| Whatever Happened To The West | 7" | Virgin | VS320 | 1980 | £2.50 | £6 | |

## ANOTHER SUNNY DAY
| | | | | | | | |
|---|---|---|---|---|---|---|---|
| Anorak City | 7" | Sarah | SARAH4 | 1988 | £4 | £8 | flexi |
| I'm In Love With A Girl | 7" | Sarah | SARAH7 | 1988 | £1.50 | £4 | |

## ANSWERS

Lead guitarist with the Answers was Tony Hill, whose talents are heard to best advantage on the more collectable of the group's two singles. Subsequently, Hill was a member of two cult bands, the Misunderstood and High Tide.

| | | | | | | | |
|---|---|---|---|---|---|---|---|
| It's Just A Fear | 7" | Columbia | DB7847 | 1966 | £37.50 | £75 | |
| That's What You're Doing To Me | 7" | Columbia | DB7953 | 1966 | £5 | £10 | |

## ANT, ADAM
| | | | | | | | |
|---|---|---|---|---|---|---|---|
| Apollo 9 | 12" | CBS | TA4719 | 1984 | £4 | £10 | |
| Can't Set Rules About Love | CD-s | MCA | DMCAT1404 | 1990 | £2 | £5 | |
| Desperate But Not Serious | 7" | CBS | A2892 | 1982 | £7.50 | £15 | single sleeve |
| Manners And Physique | CD | MCA | DMCG6068 | 1990 | £5 | £12 | |
| Room At The Top | CD-s | MCA | DMCAT1387 | 1990 | £2 | £5 | |
| Strip | CD | CBS | CD25705 | 1986 | £5 | £12 | |

## ANT TRIP CEREMONY
| | | | | | | | |
|---|---|---|---|---|---|---|---|
| 24 Hours | LP | Resurrection | | 1983 | £10 | £25 | US |
| Twenty-Four Hours | LP | C.R.C. | 2129 | 1967 | £75 | £150 | US |

## ANTEEKS
| | | | | | | |
|---|---|---|---|---|---|---|
| I Don't Want You | 7" | Philips | BF1471 | 1966 | £30 | £60 |

## ANTHEM
| | | | | | | | |
|---|---|---|---|---|---|---|---|
| Anthem | LP | Buddah | BDS5071 | 1970 | £4 | £10 | US |

## ANTHONY, BILLIE
| | | | | | | |
|---|---|---|---|---|---|---|
| Banjo's Back In Town | 7" | Columbia | SCM5191 | 1955 | £2 | £5 |
| Bring Me A Bluebird | 7" | Columbia | SCM5210 | 1955 | £2 | £5 |
| I Dreamed | 7" | Columbia | DB3874 | 1957 | £1.50 | £4 |
| Lay Down Your Arms | 7" | Columbia | DB3818 | 1956 | £2 | £5 |
| No More | 7" | Columbia | SCM5164 | 1955 | £2.50 | £6 |
| Rock A Billy | 7" | Columbia | DB3935 | 1957 | £5 | £10 |
| Something's Gotta Give | 7" | Columbia | SCM5184 | 1955 | £2.50 | £6 |
| Sweet Old Fashioned Girl | 7" | Columbia | SCM5286 | 1956 | £2.50 | £6 |
| Teach Me Tonight | 7" | Columbia | SCM5155 | 1954 | £5 | £10 |
| This Ole House | 7" | Columbia | SCM5143 | 1954 | £7.50 | £15 |
| Tweedle Dee | 7" | Columbia | SCM5174 | 1955 | £4 | £8 |

## ANTHONY, DAVE
| | | | | | | |
|---|---|---|---|---|---|---|
| All Night | 7" | Island | WI3148 | 1968 | £4 | £8 |
| Race With The Wind | 7" | Mercury | MF1031 | 1968 | £4 | £8 |

## ANTHONY, DAVE MOODS
| | | | | | | |
|---|---|---|---|---|---|---|
| New Directions | 7" | Parlophone | R5438 | 1966 | £6 | £12 |

## ANTHONY, RAY
| | | | | | | |
|---|---|---|---|---|---|---|
| Arthur Murray Swing Foxtrots | 10" LP | Capitol | LC6692 | 1955 | £4 | £10 |
| Baby You | 7" | Capitol | CL14275 | 1955 | £2 | £5 |
| Bunny Hop | 7" | Capitol | CL14769 | 1957 | £1.50 | £4 |
| Flip Flop | 7" | Capitol | CL14525 | 1956 | £4 | £8 |
| Girl Can't Help It | 7" EP | Capitol | EAP1823 | 1957 | £7.50 | £15 |
| Heat Wave | 7" | Capitol | CL14243 | 1955 | £4 | £8 |
| Hernando's Hideaway | 7" | Capitol | CL14354 | 1955 | £4 | £8 |
| House Party | 10" LP | Capitol | LC6617 | 1953 | £4 | £10 |
| I Remember Glen Miller | 10" LP | Capitol | LC6653 | 1954 | £4 | £10 |
| Learning The Blues | 7" | Capitol | CL14321 | 1955 | £2.50 | £6 |
| Pete Kelly's Blues | 7" | Capitol | CL14345 | 1955 | £2 | £5 |
| Peter Gunn | 7" EP | Capitol | EAP11181 | 1959 | £2 | £5 |
| Plymouth Rock | 7" | Capitol | CL14703 | 1957 | £1.50 | £4 |
| Ray Anthony's Orchestra | 10" LP | Capitol | LC6570 | 1953 | £4 | £10 |
| Rock And Roll With Ray Anthony | 7" EP | Capitol | EAP1958 | 1957 | £5 | £10 |
| Rock Around The Rockpile | 7" | Capitol | CL14689 | 1957 | £4 | £8 |
| Rockin' Through Dixie | 7" | Capitol | CL14567 | 1956 | £1.50 | £4 |
| Sluefoot | 7" | Capitol | CL14306 | 1955 | £2 | £5 |
| Sweet And Lovely | 10" LP | Capitol | LC6615 | 1953 | £4 | £10 |
| Woman's World | 7" | Capitol | CL14205 | 1954 | £2 | £5 |

## ANTHONY, RAYBURN
| | | | | | | |
|---|---|---|---|---|---|---|
| There's No Tomorrow | 7" | London | HLS9167 | 1960 | £7.50 | £15 |

## ANTHRAX
| | | | | | | | |
|---|---|---|---|---|---|---|---|
| Anti-Social | CD-s | Island | CIDX409 | 1989 | £2 | £5 | |
| Armed And Dangerous | 12" | Megaforce | MRS05P | 1987 | £4 | £10 | picture disc |
| Bring The Noise | CD-s | Island | CID490 | 1991 | £2 | £5 | with Chuck D |
| Got The Time | CD-s | Island | CID476 | 1990 | £2 | £5 | |
| I'm The Man | 7" | Island | ISP338 | 1987 | £1.50 | £4 | shaped picture disc |
| In My World | CD-s | Island | CID470 | 1990 | £2 | £5 | |
| Indians | 7" | Island | ISP325 | 1987 | £1.50 | £4 | picture disc |
| Make Me Laugh | CD-s | Island | CIDP379 | 1988 | £2 | £5 | picture disc |

## ANTI GROUP
| | | | | | | | |
|---|---|---|---|---|---|---|---|
| Big Sex | 7" | Sweatbox | OX011 | 1987 | £2 | £5 | |
| Digitaria | CD | Sweatbox | SACD012 | 1988 | £5 | £12 | |
| Ha | 12" | Sweatbox | SOX009 | 1985 | £2.50 | £6 | with booklet |
| ShT | 12" | Sweatbox | SOX010 | 1986 | £2.50 | £6 | with booklet |

## ANTISOCIAL
| | | | | | | |
|---|---|---|---|---|---|---|
| Traffic Lights | 7" | Dynamite | DRO1 | 1978 | £2 | £5 |

## ANTOINETTE
| | | | | | | |
|---|---|---|---|---|---|---|
| Lullaby Of Love | 7" | Piccadilly | 7N35310 | 1966 | £2 | £5 |
| Why Don't I Run Away From You | 7" | Piccadilly | 7N35293 | 1966 | £1.50 | £4 |

## ANTON, REY
| | | | | | | |
|---|---|---|---|---|---|---|
| Don't Worry Boy | 7" | Parlophone | R5420 | 1966 | £4 | £8 |
| Girl You Don't Know Me | 7" | Parlophone | R5274 | 1965 | £4 | £8 |
| Heard It All Before | 7" | Parlophone | R5172 | 1964 | £4 | £8 |
| Hey Good Looking | 7" | Oriole | CB1771 | 1962 | £2 | £5 |
| Nothing Comes Easy | 7" | Parlophone | R5310 | 1965 | £4 | £8 |
| Peppermint Man | 7" | Oriole | CB1811 | 1963 | £2 | £5 |
| Premeditation | 7" | Parlophone | R5358 | 1965 | £4 | £8 |
| Things Get Better | 7" | Parlophone | R5487 | 1966 | £4 | £8 |

| | | | | | | | |
|---|---|---|---|---|---|---|---|
| Wishbone | 7" | Parlophone | R5245 | 1965 | £4 | £8 | |
| You Can't Judge A Book By The Cover | 7" | Parlophone | R5132 | 1964 | £7.50 | £15 | |

## ANTS
| | | | | | | |
|---|---|---|---|---|---|---|
| Christmas Star | 7" | Parlophone | R5082 | 1963 | £1.50 | £4 |

## ANVIL FLUTES & CAPRICORN VOICES
| | | | | | | |
|---|---|---|---|---|---|---|
| April Showers | 7" | Deram | DM208 | 1968 | £1.50 | £4 |
| Something New Is Coming | LP | Deram | DML/SML1026 | 1968 | £4 | £10 |

## ANY TROUBLE

Any Trouble's first LP was released to a fanfare of critical acclaim. It was as though after bravely withstanding the onslaught of punk for three years or so, the rock weeklies were delighted to find a new group that actually played 'real tunes'. Unfortunately, Any Trouble's material was not really strong enough to take the weight of the praise heaped on it, and although the group carried on for a few years, it was with diminishing success. Clive Gregson, the group's leader, has since established himself in the folk circuit as half a duo with Christine Collister – the pair also finding useful employment as part of the Richard Thompson band.

| | | | | | | |
|---|---|---|---|---|---|---|
| Live At The Venue | LP | Stiff | TRUBZ1 | 1980 | £4 | £10 |
| Nice Girls | 7" | Pennine | PSS165 | 1979 | £5 | £10 |

## AORTA
| | | | | | | | |
|---|---|---|---|---|---|---|---|
| Aorta | LP | Columbia | CS9785 | 1968 | £5 | £12 | US |
| Aorta 2 | LP | Happy Tiger | HT1010 | 1970 | £15 | £30 | US |

## APACHE
| | | | | | | | |
|---|---|---|---|---|---|---|---|
| Maitreya Kali | LP | Akashic | CF2777 | 1971 | £700 | £1000 | US |

## APARTMENT ONE
| | | | | | | | |
|---|---|---|---|---|---|---|---|
| Open House | LP | Pink Elephant | 877013 | 1970 | £10 | £25 | Dutch |

## APEX GROUP

Until the arrival of the chain stores forced its closure, the best-known record shop in Northampton was owned and run by John Lever. As a drummer, Lever was also a member of the Apex Group and Apex Rhythm & Blues All Stars, whose rare singles were recorded privately and sold through the shop. Much of the high value achieved by the All Stars' EP is attributable to a connection with Ian Hunter, the only member of the group to eventually live up to its optimistic name. Unfortunately, Hunter had long departed the group by the time that 'Tall Girl' and its companions were recorded.

| | | | | | | |
|---|---|---|---|---|---|---|
| Caravan | 7" | John Lever | AP100 | 1959 | £12.50 | £25 |

## APEX RHYTHM & BLUES ALL STARS
| | | | | | | | |
|---|---|---|---|---|---|---|---|
| Tall Girl | 7" EP | John Lever | JLEP1 | 1964 | £250 | £400 | best auctioned |

## APHRODITE'S CHILD

To choose a name taken from Greek mythology was rather par for the course in the late sixties – but since the members of Aphrodite's Child did actually come from Greece, they were more entitled than most. Best known for the pop hit, 'Rain And Tears', the group was perhaps an unlikely signing to the progressive Vertigo label. But the group was always something of a compromise between the diverse interests of the singer and the keyboards player – the pop sensibilities of Demis Roussos versus the ambition of Vangelis. Both, of course, became rather better known after the group split up.

| | | | | | | | |
|---|---|---|---|---|---|---|---|
| 666 | LP | Vertigo | 6641581 | 197– | £8 | £20 | double |
| 666 | LP | Vertigo | 6673001 | 1972 | £10 | £25 | spiral label, double |
| End Of The World | LP | Mercury | SMCL20140 | 1969 | £5 | £12 | |
| Rain And Tears | 7" | Mercury | MF1039 | 1968 | £1.50 | £4 | |

## APOLLOS
| | | | | | | |
|---|---|---|---|---|---|---|
| Rocking Horse | 7" | Mercury | AMT1096 | 1960 | £2 | £5 |

## APOSTLES
| | | | | | | | |
|---|---|---|---|---|---|---|---|
| Hour Of Prayer | LP | Sound Recording | 1245 | | £37.50 | £75 | US |

## APOSTOLIC INTERVENTION

Steve Marriott and Ronnie Lane of the Small Faces wrote and produced the single by the Apostolic Intervention. When Marriott formed Humble Pie two years later, he called on the services of the group's drummer, Jerry Shirley.

| | | | | | | |
|---|---|---|---|---|---|---|
| Have You Ever Seen Me | 7" | Immediate | IM043 | 1967 | £62.50 | £125 |

## APPALACHIANS
| | | | | | | |
|---|---|---|---|---|---|---|
| Bony Moronie | 7" | HMV | POP1158 | 1963 | £1.50 | £4 |

## APPALOOSA
| | | | | | | | |
|---|---|---|---|---|---|---|---|
| Appaloosa | LP | Columbia | CS9819 | 1971 | £8 | £20 | US |

## APPELL, DAVE
| | | | | | | | |
|---|---|---|---|---|---|---|---|
| Alone Together | LP | Cameo | C1004 | 1959 | £20 | £40 | US |
| Happy Jose | 7" | Columbia | DB4763 | 1962 | £2 | £5 | |

## APPELL, DAVE & APPLEJACKS
| | | | | | | |
|---|---|---|---|---|---|---|
| Smarter | 7" | Brunswick | 05396 | 1955 | £7.50 | £15 |

## APPLE
| | | | | | | | |
|---|---|---|---|---|---|---|---|
| Apple A Day | LP | Page One | POLS016 | 1968 | £330 | £500 | |
| Dr. Rock | 7" | Page One | POF110 | 1968 | £25 | £50 | |
| Let's Take A Trip Down The Rhine | 7" | Page One | POF101 | 1968 | £25 | £50 | |
| Thank U Very Much | 7" | Smash | 2143 | 1968 | £25 | £50 | US |

## APPLEJACKS

| | | | | | | |
|---|---|---|---|---|---|---|
| Applejacks | LP | Decca | LK4635 | 1964 £37.50 | £75 | |
| Chim Chim Cheree | 7" | Decca | F12050 | 1965 £37.50 | £75 | |
| I Go To Sleep | 7" | Decca | F12216 | 1965 £5 | £10 | |
| I'm Through | 7" | Decca | F12301 | 1965 £1.50 | £4 | |
| It's Not A Game | 7" | Decca | F12106 | 1965 £2.50 | £6 | |
| Like Dreamers Do | 7" | Decca | F11916 | 1964 £1.50 | £4 | |
| Tell Me When | 7" | Decca | F11833 | 1964 £1.50 | £4 | |
| Three Little Words | 7" | Decca | F11981 | 1964 £1.50 | £4 | |
| You've Been Cheatin' | 7" | CBS | 202615 | 1967 £6 | £12 | |

## APPLEJACKS (2)

| | | | | | | |
|---|---|---|---|---|---|---|
| Applejack | 7" | Columbia | DB3894 | 1957 £10 | £20 | |
| Circle Dance | 7" | Top Rank | JAR273 | 1960 £1.50 | £4 | |
| Mexican Hat Rock | 7" | London | HL7063 | 1958 £2 | £5 | export |
| Mexican Hat Rock | 7" | London | HLU8753 | 1958 £4 | £8 | |
| Rock A Conga | 7" | London | HLU8806 | 1959 £4 | £8 | |

## APPLETREE THEATRE

| | | | | | |
|---|---|---|---|---|---|
| Playback | LP | Polydor | 2353051 | 1968 £8 | £20 |

## APPLEWHITE, CHARLIE

| | | | | | |
|---|---|---|---|---|---|
| Blue Star | 7" | Brunswick | 05416 | 1955 £2 | £5 |

## AQUARIAN AGE

This is the first version of a song that Twink – drummer with the Pretty Things and the Pink Fairies and main performer here – later re-recorded for his *Think Pink* album.

| | | | | | |
|---|---|---|---|---|---|
| Ten Thousand Words In A Cardboard Box | 7" | Parlophone | R5700 | 1968 £30 | £60 |

## AQUATONES

| | | | | | |
|---|---|---|---|---|---|
| Aquatones Sing | LP | Fargo | FLP3001 | 1964 £62.50 £125 | US |
| You | 7" | London | HLO8631 | 1958 £12.50 £25 | |

## AQUILA

| | | | | | |
|---|---|---|---|---|---|
| Aquila | LP | RCA | SF8126 | 1970 £15 | £30 |

## AR LOG

| | | | | | | |
|---|---|---|---|---|---|---|
| Ar Log | LP | Dingles | DIN305 | 1979 £4 | £10 | |
| Ar Log II | LP | Dingles | DIN310 | 1983 £4 | £10 | |
| Ar Log II | LP | Sain | 1187M | 1980 £5 | £12 | |
| Ar Log III | LP | Dingles | DIN315 | 1983 £4 | £10 | |
| Ar Log III | LP | Sain | 1218M | 1981 £5 | £12 | |
| Celtic Folk Festival | LP | | CAL30588 | £6 | £15 | |
| Meillionen | LP | Dingles | DID715 | 1983 £4 | £10 | |
| Pedwar | LP | Recordiau Ar Log | RAL001 | 1985 £4 | £10 | |
| Rhwng Hwyl A Thaith | LP | Sain | 1252M | 1982 £5 | £12 | |
| Yma O Hyd | LP | Sain | 1275M | 1983 £5 | £12 | |

## ARANBEE POP SYMPHONY ORCHESTRA

| | | | | | |
|---|---|---|---|---|---|
| Today's Pop Symphony | LP | Immediate | IMLP/IMSP003 | 1966 £62.50 £120 | |

## ARBETE & FRITID

| | | | | | |
|---|---|---|---|---|---|
| Arbete & Fritid | LP | Sonet | SLP2513 | 1970 £10 £25 | Swedish |
| Arbete Och Fritid | LP | MNW | MNW39P | 1973 £6 £15 | Swedish |
| Se Danser Vi Nt | LP | MNW | KRLP3 | 1973 £5 £12 | Swedish double |
| Se Up For Livat | LP | MNW | MNW75P | 1975 £5 £12 | Swedish double |
| Ur Spar | LP | MNW | MNW5F | 1975 £6 £15 | Swedish |

## ARC

| | | | | | |
|---|---|---|---|---|---|
| Arc At This | LP | Decca | SKLR5077 | 1971 £15 | £30 |

## ARCADIA

| | | | | | |
|---|---|---|---|---|---|
| Arcadia | video | PMI | MVP9911382 | 1987 £10 £20 | |
| Election Day | 12" | EMI | 12NSR1 | 1985 £6 £15 | promo, foil picture sleeve |
| Election Day (Cryptic Cut) | 12" | EMI | 12NSRA1 | 1985 £5 £12 | 1 sided promo |
| Election Day (Re-election Day) | 12" | EMI | PSLP393 | 1985 £15 £30 | 1 sided promo |
| Flame | 12" | EMI | 12NSR3 | 1986 £4 £10 | |
| Promise | 12" | EMI | 12NSR2 | 1986 £2.50 £6 | with poster |
| Say The Word | 12" | Atlantic | PR939 | 1986 £37.50 £75 | US promo |

## ARCADIUM

| | | | | | |
|---|---|---|---|---|---|
| Breathe Awhile | LP | Middle Earth | MDLS302 | 1969 £150 £250 | |
| Sing My Song | 7" | Middle Earth | MDS102 | 1969 £10 £20 | |

## ARCHITECTS OF DISASTER

| | | | | | |
|---|---|---|---|---|---|
| Cucumber Sandwich | 7" | Neuter | NEU1 | 1982 £2 £5 | with insert, polythene bag |

## ARCOCHA, JUAN & LESLIE MACKENZIE

| | | | | | |
|---|---|---|---|---|---|
| Book Of Am: Part One | LP | Labo Lab | LTM1016 | 1978 £37.50 £75 | French |

## ARDEN, TONI

| | | | | | |
|---|---|---|---|---|---|
| Little By Little | 7" | Brunswick | 05645 | 1957 £1.50 | £4 |

## ARDLEY, NEIL

The high prices being fetched by British jazz albums from the sixties and early seventies reflects the fact that, with many of the same musicians being involved in both jazz and rock recordings, LPs like those of Neil Ardley are very much part of the progressive rock scene. Certainly, drummer Jon Hiseman viewed his role within Neil Ardley's big band as being no different from that in his own group, Colosseum (most of whose members also played with Neil Ardley). Side two of *Symphony of Amaranths* includes, by way of a contrast, the delightfully eccentric Ivor Cutler reciting Edward Lear's 'The Dong With The Luminous Nose', with Ardley's band performing a suitable accompaniment.

| | | | | | | | |
|---|---|---|---|---|---|---|---|
| Déjeuner sur l'herbe | LP | Verve | SVLP9236 | 1969 | £50 | £100 | |
| Greek Variations | LP | Columbia | SCX6414 | 1970 | £50 | £100 | ....with Ian Carr and Don Rendell |
| Mediterranean Intrigue | LP | KPM | KPM1084 | 1971 | £10 | £25 | . B side by John Leach |
| Symphony Of Amaranths | LP | Regal Zonophone | SLRZ1028 | 1972 | £50 | £100 | |
| Western Reunion London 1965 | LP | Decca | LK/SKL4690 | 1965 | £50 | £100 | |
| Will Power | LP | Argo | ZDA164/5 | 1974 | £75 | £150 | double, with Ian Carr and Mike Gibbs |

## ARDO DOMBEC

| | | | | | | | |
|---|---|---|---|---|---|---|---|
| Ardo Dombec | LP | BASF | 2021095 | 1971 | £5 | £12 | German |

## AREA

| | | | | | | | |
|---|---|---|---|---|---|---|---|
| Arbeit Macht Frei | LP | Cramps | 5205101 | 1973 | £5 | £12 | Italian |
| Areazione | LP | Cramps | 5205104 | 1975 | £4 | £10 | Italian |
| Caution Nacht Frei | LP | Cramps | 5205102 | 1974 | £4 | £10 | Italian |
| Crac | LP | Cramps | 5205103 | 1975 | £4 | £10 | Italian |
| Maledetti | LP | Cramps | 5205105 | 1976 | £5 | £12 | Italian |

## ARENA TWINS

| | | | | | | | |
|---|---|---|---|---|---|---|---|
| Mama, Care Mama | 7" | London | HL7071 | 1959 | £2.50 | £6 | export |

## ARGENT

Argent was formed by the Zombies' keyboard player, Rod Argent, and the group's first LP takes the earlier group's posthumous hit, 'Time Of The Season', as a stylistic jumping-off point. *Argent* emerges, in effect, as the follow up to the Zombies' excellent *Odessey and Oracle*. Subsequent Argent releases were less distinctive, although the group was quite successful in sales terms. Rod Argent's colleagues included Russ Ballard and Bob Henrit, both of whom had been members of the Roulettes.

| | | | | | | | |
|---|---|---|---|---|---|---|---|
| Argent | LP | CBS | 63781 | 1970 | £4 | £10 | |
| In Deep | LP | Epic | Q65475 | 1974 | £4 | £10 | quad |

## ARGONAUTS

| | | | | | | | |
|---|---|---|---|---|---|---|---|
| Apeman | 7" | Lyntone | LYN18249/50 | 1986 | £2.50 | £6 | |

## ARGOSY

| | | | | | | | |
|---|---|---|---|---|---|---|---|
| Mr. Boyd | 7" | DJM | DJS214 | 1969 | £1.50 | £4 | |

## ARISTOCATS

| | | | | | | | |
|---|---|---|---|---|---|---|---|
| Boogie And Blues | LP | Hifi | R610 | | £37.50 | £75 | US |
| Girl With The Laughing Eyes | 7" | Oriole | CB1928 | 1964 | £1.50 | £4 | |

## ARIZONA SWAMP COMPANY

With their hit-making days some way behind them, the Nashville Teens tried an experimental name change: sadly to no great effect.

| | | | | | | | |
|---|---|---|---|---|---|---|---|
| Train Keeps Rollin' | 7" | Parlophone | R5841 | 1970 | £7.50 | £15 | |

## ARKTIS

| | | | | | | | |
|---|---|---|---|---|---|---|---|
| Arktis | LP | Bonnbons | BBR4040 | 1974 | £30 | £60 | German |
| Arktis Tapes | LP | Bonnbons | BBR7502 | 1975 | £20 | £40 | German |

## ARKUS

| | | | | | | | |
|---|---|---|---|---|---|---|---|
| 1914 | LP | Arkus | | 1981 | £6 | £15 | Dutch |

## ARLEN, STEVE

| | | | | | | | |
|---|---|---|---|---|---|---|---|
| That's Love | 7" | Melodisc | 1458 | 1958 | £2.50 | £6 | |

## ARLON, DEKE

| | | | | | | | |
|---|---|---|---|---|---|---|---|
| Can't Make Up My Mind | 7" | Columbia | DB7194 | 1964 | £7.50 | £15 | |
| Hard Times For Young Lovers | 7" | Columbia | DB7841 | 1966 | £1.50 | £4 | |
| I Need You | 7" | HMV | POP1340 | 1964 | £6 | £12 | |
| If I Didn't Have A Dime | 7" | Columbia | DB7487 | 1965 | £1.50 | £4 | |
| Little Piece Of Paper | 7" | Columbia | DB7753 | 1965 | £1.50 | £4 | |

## ARMAGEDDON

| | | | | | | | |
|---|---|---|---|---|---|---|---|
| Armageddon | LP | A&M | AMLH64513 | 1975 | £10 | £25 | |

## ARMAGEDDON (2)

| | | | | | | | |
|---|---|---|---|---|---|---|---|
| Armageddon | LP | Amos | AAS7009 | 1969 | £10 | £25 | US |

## ARMAGEDDON (3)

| | | | | | | | |
|---|---|---|---|---|---|---|---|
| Armageddon | LP | Kuckuck | 2375003 | 1970 | £30 | £60 | German |

## ARMATRADING, JOAN

| | | | | | | | |
|---|---|---|---|---|---|---|---|
| Compact Hits | CD-s | A&M | AMCD903 | 1988 | £2 | £5 | |
| Live At The Bijou, Philadelphia | LP | A&M | SP8414 | 1977 | £8 | £20 | US promo |
| Talk Under Ladders | LP | A&M | SAMP12 | 1981 | £4 | £10 | promo |

## ARMENIAN JAZZ QUARTET
Harem Dance............................................. 7" ...... London ........... HLR8454............... 1957 £1.50 ...... £4 ..................................

## ARMS, RUSSELL
Cinco Robles............................................. 7" ...... London ........... HLB8406............... 1957 £1.50 ...... £4 ..................................

## ARMS & LEGS
Heat Of The Night .................................... 7" ...... MAM ............ MAM147 ................. 1976 £2 ............ £5 ..................................
Is There Any More Wine .......................... 7" ...... MAM ............ MAM156 ................. 1977 £2 ............ £5 ..................................
Janice ........................................................ 7" ...... MAM ............ MAM140 ................. 1976 £2 ............ £5 ..................................

## ARMSTRONG, FRANKIE
And The Music Plays So Grand ................ LP ...... Briar .............. SBR4211 ............... 1980 £4 ............ £10 .............................. US
Lovely On The Water .............................. LP ...... Topic ............. 12TS216 ............... 1972 £4 ............ £10

## ARMSTRONG, FRANKIE, KATHY HENDERSON, SANDRA KERR, ALISON MCMORLAND
My Song Is My Own .................................. LP ...... Plane ............. TPL0001 ............... 1979 £5 ............ £12

## ARMSTRONG, JACK
Celebrated Minstrel .................................. LP ...... Saydisc ........... SDL252 ................. 1974 £5 ............ £12
Northumbrian Pipe Music ........................ 7" EP . Beltona ........... SEP43 .................. 1957 £12.50 ...... £25

## ARMSTRONG, JACK & PATRICIA JENNINGS
Northumbrian Small Pipes ........................ LP ...... Morton ........... MTN3073............... 1969 £4 ............ £10

## ARMSTRONG, LOUIS
Ambassador Satch ..................................... LP ...... Philips............. BBL7091............... 1956 £4 ............ £10
At Pasadena............................................... LP ...... Brunswick ...... LAT8019............... 1952 £5 ............ £12
At Symphony Hall Vol. 1 .......................... LP ...... Brunswick ...... LAT8017............... 1952 £5 ............ £12
At Symphony Hall Vol. 2 .......................... LP ...... Brunswick ...... LAT8018............... 1952 £5 ............ £12
At The Crescendo Vol. 1 ........................... LP ...... Brunswick ...... LAT8084............... 1956 £6 ............ £15
At The Crescendo Vol. 2 ........................... LP ...... Brunswick ...... LAT8085............... 1956 £6 ............ £15
Basin Street Blues ..................................... 10" LP Brunswick ...... LA8691 ................. 1954 £5 ............ £12
Blueberry Hill .......................................... 10" LP Brunswick ...... LA8700 ................. 1955 £5 ............ £12
Classics ..................................................... 10" LP Brunswick ...... LA8528 ................. 1951 £5 ............ £12
I've Got The World On A String.............. LP ...... HMV............ CLP1388/CSD1317 1960 £6 ............ £15
Jazz Classics .............................................. 10" LP Brunswick ...... LA8597 ................. 1953 £5 ............ £12
Jazz Concert ............................................. 10" LP Brunswick ...... LA8534 ................. 1951 £5 ............ £12
Jazzin' With Armstrong............................. 10" LP Columbia ....... 33S1007 ............... 1953 £5 ............ £12
Laughin' Louis .......................................... 10" LP HMV........... DLP1036............... 1954 £5 ............ £12
Louis And The Good Book ....................... LP ...... Brunswick ...... LAT8270............... 1958 £5 ............ £12
Louis Armstrong........................................ 10" LP Columbia ....... 33S1069 ............... 1955 £5 ............ £12
Louis Armstrong And Earl Hines.............. LP ...... Philips............. BBL7046............... 1955 £4 ............ £10
Louis Armstrong And His Hot Five.......... LP ...... Columbia ....... 33SX1029 ............. 1954 £5 ............ £12
Louis Armstrong And His Hot Five.......... 10" LP Fontana .......... TFR6003 ............... 1958 £4 ............ £10
Louis Armstrong Andf His Hot Seven ...... 10" LP Columbia ....... 33S1041 ............... 1954 £5 ............ £12
Louis Armstrong Story Vol. 1 .................. LP ...... Philips............. BBL7134............... 1957 £5 ............ £12
Louis Armstrong Story Vol. 2 .................. LP ...... Philips............. BBL7189............... 1958 £5 ............ £12
Louis Under The Stars .............................. LP ...... HMV........... CLP1247 ............... 1959 £6 ............ £15
Meets Oscar Peterson................................ LP ...... HMV........... CLP1328 ............... 1960 £6 ............ £15
Musical Autobiography ............................. LP ...... Brunswick ...... LAT8211-14......... 1958 £20 .......... £40 .............. 4 LPs, boxed
New Orleans Days...................................... 10" LP Brunswick ...... LA8537 ................. 1952 £5 ............ £12
New York Town Hall Concert 1947 ......... 10" LP HMV........... DLP1015............... 1953 £5 ............ £12
Plays The Blues ......................................... 10" LP London ........... AL3501 ................. 1953 £6 ............ £15
Plays W.C.Handy....................................... LP ...... Philips............. BBL7017............... 1955 £4 ............ £10
Rendezvous At The Sunset Cafe................ 10" LP Columbia ....... 33S1058 ............... 1955 £5 ............ £12
Satch Plays Fats ........................................ LP ...... Philips............. BBL7064............... 1956 £4 ............ £10
Satchmo Plays King Oliver........................ LP ...... Audio Fidelity.. AFLP1930/
                                                                                  AFSD5930.............. 1960 £4 ............ £10
Satchmo Serenades ................................... 10" LP Brunswick ...... LA8679 ................. 1954 £5 ............ £12
Satchmo Session ........................................ 10" LP HMV........... DLP1105............... 1955 £5 ............ £12
Satchmo Sings............................................ LP ...... Brunswick ...... LAT8243............... 1958 £6 ............ £15
Satchmo The Great .................................... LP ...... Philips............. BBL7216............... 1958 £4 ............ £10
We Have All The Time In The World........ 7" ...... United Artists .. JB001 .................... 1969 £7.50 ...... £15 .............. 1 sided promo
We Have All The Time In The World........ 7" ...... United Artists .. UA3172 ................. 1969 £12.50 ...... £25 .............. picture sleeve
We Have All The Time In The World........ 7" ...... United Artists .. UP35059 ................ 1969 £7.50 ...... £15

## ARMY OF LOVERS
Love Me Like A Loaded Gun ................... 7" ...... Ton Son Ton .. SON7 .................... 1988 £1.50 ...... £4
Love Me Like A Loaded Gun ................... 12"...... Ton Son Ton .. SONL7 .................. 1988 £3 ............ £8

## ARNAU, B.J.
Live And Let Die ..................................... 7" ...... RCA ............... RCA2365 .............. 1973 £2 ............ £5

## ARNEZ, CHICO
Yashmak .................................................... 7" ...... Pye ................ 7N15196 ............... 1959 £7.50 ...... £15

## ARNOLD, EDDIE
All-Time Favorites .................................... LP ...... RCA ............... LPM1223 .............. 1955 £6 ............ £15 .............. US
All-Time Favorites .................................... 10" LP RCA ............... LPM3117 .............. 1953 £8 ............ £20 .............. US
All-Time Hits From The Hills .................. 10" LP RCA ............... LPM3031 .............. 1952 £8 ............ £20 .............. US
American Institution .................................. 10" LP RCA ............... LPM3230 .............. 1954 £8 ............ £20 .............. US
Anytime ..................................................... LP ...... RCA ............... LPM1224 .............. 1955 £6 ............ £15 .............. US
Anytime ..................................................... 10" LP RCA ............... LPM3027 .............. 1952 £8 ............ £20 .............. US
Chapel On The Hill ................................. LP ...... RCA ............... LPM1225 .............. 1955 £6 ............ £15 .............. US
Chapel On The Hill ................................. 7" EP . HMV........... 7EG8080............... 1955 £2.50 ...... £6
Chapel On The Hill ................................. 10" LP RCA ............... LPM3219 .............. 1954 £8 ............ £20 .............. US

| | | | | | | | |
|---|---|---|---|---|---|---|---|
| Dozen Hits | LP | RCA | LPM1293 | 1956 £6 | £15 | | US |
| Eddie Arnold | 7" EP | HMV | 7EG8020 | 1954 £2.50 | £6 | | |
| Free Home Demonstrations | 7" | HMV | 7MC16 | 1954 £2.50 | £6 | | export |
| Gonna Find Me A Bluebird | 7" | RCA | RCA1008 | 1957 £1.50 | £4 | | |
| Have Guitar, Will Travel | LP | RCA | LPM/LSP1928 | 1959 £4 | £10 | | US |
| Hep Cat Baby | 7" | HMV | 7MC22 | 1954 £2.50 | £6 | | export |
| In Time | 7" | HMV | 7MC32 | 1955 £2.50 | £6 | | export |
| Little On The Lonely Side | LP | RCA | LPM1377 | 1956 £6 | £15 | | US |
| My Darling, My Darling | LP | RCA | LPM1575 | 1957 £6 | £15 | | US |
| Praise Him, Praise Him | LP | RCA | LPM1733 | 1958 £5 | £12 | | US |
| Prayer | 7" | HMV | 7MC10 | 1954 £2.50 | £6 | | export |
| Richest Man | 7" | HMV | 7M339 | 1955 £1.50 | £4 | | |
| Second Fling | 7" | HMV | 7MC19 | 1954 £2.50 | £6 | | export |
| Tennessee Stud | 7" | RCA | RCA1138 | 1959 £1.50 | £4 | | |
| Thereby Hangs A Tale | LP | RCA | RD27155 | 1959 £4 | £10 | | |
| Wanderin' | LP | RCA | LPM1111 | 1955 £6 | £15 | | US |
| When They Were Young | LP | RCA | LPM1484 | 1957 £6 | £15 | | US |

## ARNOLD, KOKOMO

| | | | | | | | |
|---|---|---|---|---|---|---|---|
| Kokomo Arnold | LP | Saydisc | SDR163 | 1969 £4 | £10 | | |

## ARNOLD, P. P.

Pat Arnold tried hard for solo success with a number of releases on the Immediate label. Despite producing several fondly remembered tracks, however, it was her backing group, the Nice, that achieved the most success. P. P. Arnold returned to session work, although she achieved a brief revival at the end of the eighties. She had originally been a member of Ike and Tina Turner's backing group, the Ikettes.

| | | | | | | | |
|---|---|---|---|---|---|---|---|
| Angel Of The Morning | 7" | Immediate | IM067 | 1968 £1.50 | £4 | | |
| Everything's Gonna Be Alright | 7" | Immediate | IM040 | 1966 £25 | £50 | | |
| First Cut Is The Deepest | 7" EP | Columbia | ESRF1877 | 1967 £7.50 | £15 | | French |
| First Cut Is The Deepest | 7" | Immediate | IM047 | 1967 £1.50 | £4 | | |
| First Cut Is The Deepest | 7" | Immediate | IM079 | 1969 £1.50 | £4 | | |
| First Lady Of Immediate | LP | Immediate | IMLP/IMSP11 | 1967 £10 | £25 | | |
| If You Think You're Groovy | 7" | Immediate | IM061 | 1968 £1.50 | £4 | | |
| Kafunta | LP | Immediate | IMSP17 | 1968 £6 | £15 | | |
| Time Has Come | 7" | Immediate | IM055 | 1967 £1.50 | £4 | | |

## ARNOLD, PAUL

| | | | | | | | |
|---|---|---|---|---|---|---|---|
| Bon Soir Dame | 7" | Pye | 7N17473 | 1968 £1.50 | £4 | | |
| Somewhere In A Rainbow | 7" | Pye | 7N17317 | 1967 £1.50 | £4 | | |

## ARRIVALS

| | | | | | | | |
|---|---|---|---|---|---|---|---|
| Scooby Doo | 7" | Pye | 7N17761 | 1969 £1.50 | £4 | | |

## ARROWS

| | | | | | | | |
|---|---|---|---|---|---|---|---|
| Apache '65 | 7" EP | Capitol | EAP60000 | 1965 £5 | £10 | | French |
| Apache '65 | 7" | Capitol | CL15386 | 1965 £1.50 | £4 | | |

## ARS NOVA

| | | | | | | | |
|---|---|---|---|---|---|---|---|
| Ars Nova | LP | Elektra | EKS74020 | 1968 £4 | £10 | | |
| Sunshine And Shadows | LP | Atlantic | 588196 | 1969 £4 | £10 | | |

## ART

When Chris Blackwell of Island records decided to expand his sphere of operations by entering the rock market place, he demonstrated from the start a remarkable sureness of touch in his decisions regarding which artists to sign. If Island albums seldom reach the high prices regularly achieved by Vertigo and Deram releases, then that is not because their music is uninteresting, but because the company was rather more successful at selling it. The Art LP is a relative obscurity, however, perhaps because the group itself immediately added an extra member and mutated into the rather better-known Spooky Tooth.

| | | | | | | | |
|---|---|---|---|---|---|---|---|
| Supernatural Fairy Tales | LP | Island | ILP967 | 1975 £5 | £12 | | pink rim label |
| Supernatural Fairytales | LP | Island | ILP967 | 1968 £30 | £60 | | pink label |
| What's That Sound | 7" | Island | WIP6019 | 1967 £4 | £8 | | |
| What's That Sound | 7" | Island | WIP6224 | 1975 £1.50 | £4 | | |

## ART ATTACKS

| | | | | | | | |
|---|---|---|---|---|---|---|---|
| I Am A Dalek | 7" | Albatross | TIT1 | 1978 £2.50 | £6 | | |
| Punk Rock Stars | 7" | Fresh | FRESH3 | 1979 £2 | £5 | | |

## ART BEARS

| | | | | | | | |
|---|---|---|---|---|---|---|---|
| Coda To Man And Boy | 7" | Recommended | REH | 1981 £4 | £8 | | 1 side painted |
| Hopes And Fears | LP | Recommended | RE2188 | 1978 £6 | £15 | | 2 different covers |
| Winter Songs | LP | Recommended | RE0618 | 1979 £6 | £15 | | |
| World As It Is Today | LP | Recommended | RE6622 | 1981 £6 | £15 | | |

## ART ENSEMBLE OF CHICAGO

The musicians of the Art Ensemble combined virtuoso avant-garde playing with a highly developed sense of theatricality to emerge as one of the premier jazz groups of the seventies and beyond. Saxophonists Joseph Jarman and Roscoe Mitchell have solo albums listed in the Guide, while trumpeter Lester Bowie has appeared on numerous records over the years, including several of his own and one by his namesake, David Bowie. The trumpeter's wife, Fontella Bass, scored a big hit in the sixties with 'Rescue Me' and appears on a couple of the albums made by the Art Ensemble.

| | | | | | | | |
|---|---|---|---|---|---|---|---|
| Bap Tizum | LP | Atlantic | SD1639 | 1973 £6 | £15 | | US |
| Certain Blacks | LP | America | 30AM6098 | 1970 £8 | £20 | | French |
| Chi Congo | LP | Paula | LPS4001 | 1970 £8 | £20 | | US |
| Fanfare For The Warriors | LP | Atlantic | SD1651 | 1974 £6 | £15 | | US |
| Jackson In Your House | LP | BYG | 529302 | 1969 £8 | £20 | | French |
| Kabalaba | LP | AECO | | 1974 £6 | £15 | | US |
| Les Stances A Sophie | LP | Nessa | N4 | 1970 £8 | £20 | | US |

| | | | | | | | |
|---|---|---|---|---|---|---|---|
| Live At Mundell Hall | LP | Delmark | DS432/3 | 1975 | £8 | £20 | US double |
| Message To Our Folks | LP | BYG | 529328 | 1969 | £8 | £20 | French |
| People In Sorrow | LP | Nessa | N3 | 1969 | £8 | £20 | US |
| Phase One | LP | Prestige | PR10064 | 1971 | £8 | £20 | US |
| Rees And The Smooth Ones | LP | BYG | | 1969 | £8 | £20 | French |
| Spiritual | LP | Polydor | 2383098 | 1974 | £5 | £12 | |
| With Fontella Bass | LP | America | 30AM6117 | 1972 | £8 | £20 | French |

## ART MOVEMENT

| | | | | | | | |
|---|---|---|---|---|---|---|---|
| Game Of Love | 7" | Decca | F12768 | 1968 | £1.50 | £4 | |
| Loving Touch | 7" | Decca | F12836 | 1968 | £1.50 | £4 | |
| Yes Sir No Sir | 7" | Columbia | DB8602 | 1969 | £1.50 | £4 | |

## ART NOUVEAUX

| | | | | | | | |
|---|---|---|---|---|---|---|---|
| Extra Terrestrial Visitations | 7" | Fontana | TF483 | 1964 | £4 | £8 | |

## ART OF LOVIN'

| | | | | | | | |
|---|---|---|---|---|---|---|---|
| Art Of Lovin' | LP | Mainstream | 6613 | 1968 | £15 | £30 | US |

## ART OF NOISE

| | | | | | | | |
|---|---|---|---|---|---|---|---|
| Couldn't Say Goodbye | CD-s | Dover | ROJCD10 | 1991 | £2 | £5 | with Tom Jones |
| Daft | CD | ZTT | ZCIDQ2 | 1987 | £5 | £12 | |
| Into Battle With the Art Of Noise | cass-s | ZTT | CTIS100 | 1983 | £2.50 | £6 | |
| Kiss | CD-s | China | CHICD11 | 1988 | £2 | £5 | with Tom Jones |
| Moments In Love | 7" | ZTT | PZTPS02 | 1985 | £1.50 | £4 | shaped picture disc |
| Paranoimia '89 | CD-s | China | CHICD14 | 1989 | £2 | £5 | |
| Yebo | CD-s | China | CHICD18 | 1989 | £2 | £5 | with Mahotella Queens |

## ART ZOYD

| | | | | | | | |
|---|---|---|---|---|---|---|---|
| Manege | 7" | Recommended | RR14.15 | 1982 | £4 | £8 | 1 side painted |

## ARTERY

| | | | | | | | |
|---|---|---|---|---|---|---|---|
| Mother Moon | 7" | Limited Edition | TAKE1 | 1979 | £4 | £8 | |
| Unbalanced | 7" | Aardvark | STEAL3 | 1980 | £2 | £5 | double |

## ARTHUR

| | | | | | | | |
|---|---|---|---|---|---|---|---|
| Dreams And Images | LP | LHI | 12000 | 1968 | £10 | £25 | US |

## ARTHUR, DAVE & TONI

| | | | | | | | |
|---|---|---|---|---|---|---|---|
| Bushes And Briars | 7" | Trailer | LER1 | 1970 | £1.50 | £4 | |
| Hearken To The Witches' Rune | LP | Trailer | LER2017 | 1970 | £15 | £30 | |
| Lark In The Morning | LP | Topic | 12T190 | 1969 | £10 | £25 | |
| Morning Stands On Tiptoe | LP | Transatlantic | TRA154 | 1967 | £15 | £30 | |
| Sing A Story | LP | Decca | SPA509 | 1977 | £4 | £10 | |

## ARTHURS, ANDY

| | | | | | | | |
|---|---|---|---|---|---|---|---|
| I Can Detect You For A Million Miles | 7" | Radar | ADA7 | 1978 | £4 | £8 | |

## ARTI & MESTIERI

| | | | | | | | |
|---|---|---|---|---|---|---|---|
| Tilt | LP | Cramps | 5501 | 1974 | £5 | £12 | Italian |

## ARTISTICS

| | | | | | | | |
|---|---|---|---|---|---|---|---|
| Girl I Need you | 7" | Coral | Q72492 | 1967 | £7.50 | £15 | |
| I'm Gonna Miss You | 7" | Coral | Q72488 | 1966 | £5 | £10 | |

## ARTWOODS

The Artwoods were typical of the many R&B and beat groups that spent years slogging round the British club circuit without ever really gaining much success. Unlike many, however, two of the group's members did achieve success later – drummer Keef Hartley, who used his stint with John Mayall's Bluesbreakers as a springboard to forming his own band; and organist Jon Lord, the founder member of Deep Purple and Whitesnake. As for poor Art Wood himself, he has been rather eclipsed by his more famous brother, Ron Wood.

| | | | | | | | |
|---|---|---|---|---|---|---|---|
| Art Gallery | LP | Decca | LK4830 | 1966 | £180 | £300 | |
| Art Gallery | LP | Eclipse | ECS2025 | 1974 | £20 | £40 | |
| Artwoods | LP | Spark | SRLM2006 | 1973 | £10 | £25 | |
| Goodbye Sisters | 7" | Decca | F12206 | 1965 | £25 | £50 | |
| I Feel Good | 7" | Decca | F12465 | 1966 | £25 | £50 | |
| I Take What I Want | 7" | Decca | F12384 | 1966 | £25 | £50 | |
| Jazz In Jeans | 7" EP | Decca | DFE8654 | 1966 | £150 | £250 | best auctioned |
| Oh My Love | 7" EP | Decca | 457076 | 1965 | £150 | £250 | French |
| Oh My Love | 7" | Decca | F12091 | 1965 | £25 | £50 | |
| Sweet Mary | 7" | Decca | F12015 | 1964 | £25 | £50 | |
| What Shall I Do | 7" | Parlophone | R5590 | 1967 | £37.50 | £75 | |

## ARZACHEL

The Arzachel LP only received a limited release, but it is a fine and innovative recording. As would be expected from the musicians involved – guitarist Steve Hillage and keyboard wizard Dave Stewart, with Clive Brooks and Hugh Montgomery-Campbell in support. In other words, this is Egg, augmented by guitar. At least one reference book lists an entirely different personnel for the group – these names are taken from the record's sleeve, which includes a set of biographies that are clearly intended as a gentle leg-pull!

| | | | | | | | |
|---|---|---|---|---|---|---|---|
| Arzachel | LP | Evolution | Z1003 | 1969 | £150 | £250 | |
| Arzachel | LP | Roulette | SR42036 | 1969 | £25 | £50 | US |

## ASGARD

| | | | | | | | |
|---|---|---|---|---|---|---|---|
| Children Of A New Born Age | 7" | Threshold | TH10 | 1972 | £1.50 | £4 | |
| In The Realm Of Asgard | LP | Threshold | THS6 | 1972 | £15 | £30 | |

| | | | | | | | | |
|---|---|---|---|---|---|---|---|---|
| In The Realm Of Asgard | 7" | Threshold | TH15 | 1973 | £1.50 | £4 | |

## ASH
| | | | | | | | |
|---|---|---|---|---|---|---|---|
| Petrol | 7" | Infectious | INFECT13S | 1994 | £6 | £12 | |
| Trailer | LP | Infectious | INFECT14LP | 1994 | £5 | £12 | ...with yellow vinyl 7" |
| Uncle Pat | 7" | Infectious | INFECT16S | 1994 | £6 | £12 | |

## ASH, MARVIN
| | | | | | | | |
|---|---|---|---|---|---|---|---|
| New Orleans At Midnight | LP | Brunswick | LAT8191 | 1957 | £5 | £12 | |

## ASH RA TEMPLE
Although synthesizer pioneer Klaus Schulze was involved in the group in the early days, Ash Ra Temple is essentially a vehicle for the playing of German guitarist Manuel Göttsching. Using an E-bow to generate infinite sustain and a fluent playing technique, Göttsching seeks to emulate on guitar what groups like Tangerine Dream and Kraftwerk achieve with synthesizers. Later albums on the Virgin label are quite common and do not qualify for inclusion here, but the early records are becoming increasingly sought after.

| | | | | | | | |
|---|---|---|---|---|---|---|---|
| Ash Ra Temple | LP | Ohr | OMM556013 | 1971 | £15 | £30 | German |
| Discover Music | LP | Ohr | 940101/02X | 1977 | £20 | £40 | French double |
| Inventions For Electric Guitar | LP | Komische | KM58015 | 1975 | £8 | £20 | German |
| Join In | LP | Ohr | OMM556032 | 1973 | £10 | £25 | German |
| Schwingungen | LP | Ohr | OMM556020 | 1972 | £15 | £30 | German |
| Seven Up | LP | Komische | KK58001 | 1973 | £10 | £25 | German, with Timothy Leary |
| Starring Rosi | LP | Komische | KM58007 | 1973 | £10 | £25 | German |

## ASHBY, HAROLD
| | | | | | | | |
|---|---|---|---|---|---|---|---|
| Born To Swing | LP | Columbia | 33SX1257 | 1960 | £4 | £10 | |

## ASHBY, IRVING
| | | | | | | | |
|---|---|---|---|---|---|---|---|
| Big Guitar | 7" | London | HLP8578 | 1958 | £5 | £10 | |

## ASHCROFT, STEVE
| | | | | | | | |
|---|---|---|---|---|---|---|---|
| Keys Of Tomorrow | LP | Wild Dog | DOGLR15 | 1978 | £8 | £20 | |

## ASHES
| | | | | | | | |
|---|---|---|---|---|---|---|---|
| Ashes | LP | Vault | 125 | 1966 | £15 | £30 | US |

## ASHKAN
| | | | | | | | |
|---|---|---|---|---|---|---|---|
| In From The Cold | LP | Nova | (S)RNR1 | 1970 | £25 | £50 | |

## ASHLEY, STEVE
| | | | | | | | |
|---|---|---|---|---|---|---|---|
| Stroll On | LP | Gull | GULP1003 | 1974 | £4 | £10 | |

## ASIA
| | | | | | | | |
|---|---|---|---|---|---|---|---|
| Don't Cry | 7" | Geffen | WA3580 | 1982 | £1.50 | £4 | shaped picture disc |
| Only Time Will Tell | 7" | Geffen | GEFA112228 | 1982 | £1.50 | £4 | picture disc |
| Who Will Stop The Rain | CD-s | Musidisc | 109522 | 1992 | £2 | £5 | |

## ASLAN
| | | | | | | | |
|---|---|---|---|---|---|---|---|
| Paws For Thought | LP | Profile | GMOR006 | 1976 | £37.50 | £75 | |
| Second Helpings | LP | Profile | GMOR144 | 1977 | £37.50 | £75 | |

## ASMUSSEN, SVEND
| | | | | | | | |
|---|---|---|---|---|---|---|---|
| Hot Fiddle | 10" LP | Parlophone | CPMD1 | 1955 | £8 | £20 | |

## ASOKA
| | | | | | | | |
|---|---|---|---|---|---|---|---|
| Asoka | LP | Sonet | SLP2527 | 1973 | £87.50 | £175 | Swedish |

## ASPEY, GARY & VERA
| | | | | | | | |
|---|---|---|---|---|---|---|---|
| From The North | LP | Topic | 12TS255 | 1975 | £4 | £10 | |
| Taste Of Hotpot | LP | Topic | 12TS299 | 1976 | £4 | £10 | |

## ASPEY, VERA
| | | | | | | | |
|---|---|---|---|---|---|---|---|
| Blackbird | LP | Topic | 12TS356 | 1977 | £4 | £10 | |

## ASQUITH, MARY
| | | | | | | | |
|---|---|---|---|---|---|---|---|
| Closing Time | LP | Mother Earth | MUM1204 | 1978 | £30 | £60 | |

## ASSAGAI
| | | | | | | | |
|---|---|---|---|---|---|---|---|
| Assagai | LP | Vertigo | 6360030 | 1971 | £6 | £15 | spiral label |
| Assagai II | LP | Vertigo | 6360058 | 1971 | £25 | £50 | test pressing |
| Zimbabwe | LP | Philips | 6308079 | 1972 | £6 | £15 | |

## ASSOCIATES
| | | | | | | | |
|---|---|---|---|---|---|---|---|
| Affectionate Punch | 7" | Fiction | FICS11 | 1980 | £1.50 | £4 | |
| Boys Keep Swinging | 7" | Double Hip | DHR1 | 1980 | £20 | £40 | |
| Boys Keep Swinging | 7" | MCA | MCA537 | 1980 | £10 | £20 | |
| Country Boy | CD-s | WEA | YZ329CD | 1988 | £20 | £40 | 3" single |
| Country Boy | 12" | WEA | YZ329T | 1988 | £25 | £50 | test pressing |
| Fever | CD-s | Circa | YRCD46 | 1990 | £2 | £5 | |
| Fire To Ice | CD-s | Circa | YRCD49 | 1990 | £2 | £5 | |
| Heart Of Glass | CD-s | WEA | YZ310CD | 1988 | £2 | £5 | |
| Heart Of Glass | 12" | WEA | YZ310TX | 1988 | £4 | £10 | with 3D glasses |
| Just Can't Say Goodbye | CD-s | Circa | YRCD56 | 1991 | £2 | £5 | |
| Peel Sessions | CD-s | Strange Fruit | SFPSCD075 | 1989 | £2 | £5 | |
| Tell Me Easter's On Friday | 7" | Beggars Banquet | BEG86 | 1984 | £7.50 | £15 | test pressing |

| Wild And Lonely | CD-s | Circa | BILLY1 | 1990 £2.50 | £6 | *album sampler* |

## ASSOCIATION

Most of the successful Californian groups that emerged during the late sixties had backgrounds rooted in folk music and naturally tended to favour melodic material and close-harmony singing. The Association were very much a case in point, sustaining a six-year career on the back of four tuneful singles, which if not exactly classics, are at any rate fondly remembered. 'Along Comes Mary', 'Cherish', 'Windy', and 'Never My Love' are to be found scattered through their LP releases alongside similar fare, although, the vagaries of the pop charts being what they are, it was the much less well-known 'Time For Living' that scored in a small way in the UK.

| Along Comes Mary | 7" | London | HLT10054 | 1966 £1.50 | £4 | |
| And Then Along Came Association | LP | London | HAT8305 | 1966 £4 | £10 | |
| Association | LP | Warner Bros | W(S)1800 | 1969 £4 | £10 | |
| Birthday | LP | Warner Bros | W(S)1733 | 1968 £4 | £10 | |
| Cherish | 7" EP | Riviera | 231209 | 1966 £5 | £10 | *French* |
| Cherish | 7" | London | HLT10074 | 1966 £1.50 | £4 | |
| Goodbye Columbus | LP | Warner Bros | W(S)1786 | 1969 £4 | £10 | |
| Greatest Hits | LP | Warner Bros | W(S)1767 | 1969 £4 | £10 | |
| Insight Out | LP | London | HAT/SHT8342 | 1967 £4 | £10 | |
| Live | LP | Warner Bros | 2WS1868 | 1970 £6 | £15 | *US double* |
| Never My Love | 7" | London | HLT10157 | 1967 £1.50 | £4 | |
| No Fair At All | 7" EP | Riviera | 231241 | 1967 £5 | £10 | *French* |
| Pandora's Golden Heebie Jeebies | 7" | London | HLT10098 | 1966 £1.50 | £4 | |
| Renaissance | LP | London | HAT8313 | 1967 £4 | £10 | |
| Stop The Motor | LP | Warner Bros | WS1927 | 1971 £4 | £10 | *US* |
| Windy | 7" EP | Riviera | 231243 | 1967 £5 | £10 | *French* |
| Windy | 7" | London | HLT10140 | 1967 £1.50 | £4 | |

## ASSOCIATION P. C.
| Earwax | LP | Munich | 6802634 | 1969 £15 | £30 | *Dutch* |

## ASTAIRE, FRED
| Funny Face | 7" | HMV | POP337 | 1957 £1.50 | £4 | *Audrey Hepburn B side* |
| Ritz Roll And Rock | 7" | MGM | MGM964 | 1957 £4 | £8 | |

## ASTERIX
| Asterix | LP | Decca | SLK16695P | 1970 £4 | £10 | *German* |

## ASTLEY, EDWIN ORCHESTRA
| Danger Man Theme | 7" | RCA | RCA1492 | 1965 £6 | £12 | |
| Saint | LP | RCA | LPM/LSP3631 | 1966 £15 | £30 | *US* |
| Secret Agent (Danger Man) | LP | RCA | LPM/LSP3630 | 1966 £15 | £30 | *US* |
| Secret Agent Meets The Saint | LP | RCA | LPM/LSP3467 | 1965 £15 | £30 | *US* |

## ASTORS
| Candy | 7" | Atlantic | 584245 | 1969 £1.50 | £4 | |
| Candy | 7" | Atlantic | AT4037 | 1965 £10 | £20 | |

## ASTRAL NAVIGATIONS

The music on the rare *Astral Navigations* album is actually the work of two different bands, who take a side each. Lightyears Away and Thundermother made no other records, although the guitarist with the former band was Bill Nelson. He has recorded prolifically since, as the leader of Bebop Deluxe and as a solo artist.

| Astral Navigations | LP | Holyground | HG114 | 1971 £100 | £200 | |
| Astral Navigations | LP | Magic Mixture | MM2 | 1989 £8 | £20 | |

## ASTRONAUTS
| Banana | 7" | Hala Gala | HG14 | 196– £2.50 | £6 | |
| Before You Leave | 7" | Hala Gala | HG9 | 1966 £2.50 | £5 | |
| Before You Leave | 7" | Island | WI3065 | 1967 £2 | £5 | |
| I'll Be There | 7" | Hala Gala | HG13 | 196– £2.50 | £6 | |
| Oh Why I Still Love You | 7" | Hala Gala | HG12 | 196– £2.50 | £6 | |

## ASTRONAUTS (2)
| Astronauts Go Go Go | LP | RCA | LPM/LSP3307 | 1965 £6 | £15 | *US* |
| Astronauts Orbit Campus | LP | RCA | LPM/LSP2903 | 1964 £6 | £15 | *US* |
| Baja | 7" EP | RCA | 86328 | 1963 £7.50 | £15 | *French* |
| Baju | 7" | RCA | RCA1349 | 1963 £1.50 | £4 | |
| Big Boss Man | 7" EP | RCA | 86367 | 1963 £7.50 | £15 | *French* |
| Competition Coupe | LP | RCA | LPM/LSP2858 | 1964 £6 | £15 | *US* |
| Down The Line | LP | RCA | LPM/LSP3454 | 1965 £6 | £15 | *US* |
| Everything Is A-OK | LP | RCA | LPM/LSP2782 | 1964 £6 | £15 | *US* |
| Favorites For You, Our Fans, From Us | LP | RCA | LPM/LSP3359 | 1965 £6 | £15 | *US* |
| I'm A Rollin' Stone | 7" EP | RCA | 86457 | 1964 £7.50 | £15 | *French* |
| Kuk | 7" EP | RCA | 86334 | 1963 £7.50 | £15 | *French* |
| Rockin' With The Astronauts | LP | RCA | PRM183 | 1964 £6 | £15 | *US* |
| Surf Party | LP | 20th Century | TFM3131/TFS4131 | 1964 £6 | £15 | *US* |
| Surfin' With The Astronauts | LP | RCA | LPM/LSP2760 | 1963 £8 | £20 | *US* |
| Travelin' Men | LP | RCA | LPM/LSP3733 | 1967 £4 | £10 | *US* |
| Wild On The Beach | LP | RCA | LPM/LSP3441 | 1965 £6 | £15 | *US* |
| Wild Wild Winter | LP | Decca | DL(7)4699 | 1966 £4 | £10 | *US* |

## ASTRONAUTS (3)
| All Night Party | 7" | Bugle | BLAST1 | 1979 £4 | £8 | |
| Peter Pan Hits The Suburbs | LP | Bugle | GENIUS001 | 1981 £15 | £30 | |
| We Were Talking | 7" | Bugle | BLAST5 | 1979 £2 | £5 | |

## AT LAST THE 1958 ROCK 'N' ROLL SHOW
I Can't Drive .......................................... 7" .... CBS.............. 3349 ...................... 1968 £6 ......... £12 ...........................

## ATACAMA
Atacama ................................................. LP ..... Charisma ......... CAS1039 ................. 1971 £4 ......... £10 ...........................
Sun Burns Up Above ............................... LP ..... Charisma ......... CAS1060 ................. 1972 £4 ......... £10 ...........................

## ATHENIANS
I've Got Love If You Want It ................... 7" ..... Waverley ......... SLP532 ............... 1964 £20 ....... £40 ...........................
I've Got Love If You Want It ................... 7" ..... Waverley ......... SLP532 ............... 1964 £37.50 .. £75 ........... picture sleeve
Thinking Of Our Love .............................. 7" ..... Waverley ......... SLP533 ............... 1965 £25 ....... £50 ........... picture sleeve
Thinking Of Your Love ............................. 7" ..... Waverley ......... SLP533 ............... 1965 £15 ....... £30 ...........................
You Tell Me ............................................. 7" ..... Edinburgh ....... ESC1 ................. 1964 £25 ....... £50 ...........................
                                                                        Students
                                                                        Charity ...........
You Tell Me ............................................. 7" ..... Edinburgh ....... ESC1 ................. 1964 £37.50 .. £75 ........... picture sleeve
                                                                        Students
                                                                        Charity ...........

## ATHENS, GLENN & THE TROJANS
Glen Athens And The Trojans ................. 7" EP . Spot .............. 7E1018 ............... 1965 £210 ..... £350 ........... best auctioned

## ATILA
Intencion .............................................. LP .... BASF ..................................... 1976 £62.50 .. £125 ................. Spanish
Revlure ................................................. LP .... Odeon ................................... 1978 £62.50 .. £125 ................. Spanish

## ATKIN, PETE
Pete Atkin was the author of some half-dozen LPs, whose stylish and intelligent singer-songwriting was somehow never as popular as it should have been. In the collectors' market too this remains the case, as such classics of the genre as *A King At Nightfall* and *The Road Of Silk* steadfastly refuse to fetch even moderate collectors' prices, despite being long deleted. Not that Atkin himself should worry, having forged a satisfying career as a television producer. The lyricist on the records has done rather well for himself too – his name is Clive James – yes, it is the same one!

Beware Of The Beautiful Stranger ........... LP ..... Fontana ......... 6309011 ............. 1970 £6 ......... £15 ...........................
Beware Of The Beautiful Stranger ........... LP ..... RCA ............... SF8387 ............... 1974 £4 ......... £10 ...........................
Driving Through Mythical America ......... LP ..... Philips .......... 6308070 ............. 1971 £6 ......... £15 ...........................
Driving Through Mythical America ......... LP ..... RCA ............... SF8386 ............... 1974 £4 ......... £10 ...........................
King At Nightfall .................................... LP ..... RCA ............... SF8336 ............... 1973 £4 ......... £10 ...........................
Live Libel ............................................. LP ..... RCA ............... RS1013 ............... 1975 £4 ......... £10 ...........................
Master Of The Revels ............................ LP ..... RCA ............... PL25041 ............. 1977 £4 ......... £10 ...........................
Road Of Silk ......................................... LP ..... RCA ............... LPL15014 ............ 1974 £4 ......... £10 ...........................
Secret Drinker ...................................... LP ..... RCA ............... LPL15062 ............ 1974 £4 ......... £10 ...........................

## ATKINS, BENNY
Lipstick On Your Lips ............................ 7" ..... Mercury ......... AMT1113 ............. 1960 £1.50 ........ £4 ...........................

## ATKINS, CHET
At Home ............................................... LP ..... RCA ............... LPM1544 ............. 1957 £6 ......... £15 ....................... US
Chet Atkins' Gallopin' Guitar ................. 10" LP RCA ............... LPM3079 ............. 1952 £15 ....... £30 ....................... US
Chet Atkins' Workshop .......................... LP ..... RCA ............... RD27214 ............. 1960 £4 ......... £10 ....................... US
Finger Style Guitar ............................... LP ..... RCA ............... LPM1383 ............. 1956 £6 ......... £15 ....................... US
Guitar Genius ....................................... 7" EP . RCA ............... RCX7118 ............. 1963 £2.50 ........ £6 ...........................
Hi Fi In Focus ....................................... LP ..... RCA ............... LPM1577 ............. 1957 £6 ......... £15 ....................... US
In Three Dimensions ............................. LP ..... RCA ............... LPM1197 ............. 1956 £6 ......... £15 ....................... US
Other Chet Atkins ................................. LP ..... RCA ............... RD27194 ............. 1960 £4 ......... £10 ...........................
Picks On The Beatles ............................ LP ..... RCA ............... RD/SF7813 .......... 1966 £4 ......... £10 ...........................
Session With Chet Atkins ....................... LP ..... RCA ............... LPM1090 ............. 1955 £6 ......... £15 ....................... US
String Dustin' ....................................... 10" LP RCA ............... LPM3167 ............. 1953 £10 ....... £25 ....................... US
Stringin' Along ...................................... LP ..... RCA ............... LPM1236 ............. 1956 £6 ......... £15 ....................... US
Stringin' Along ...................................... 10" LP RCA ............... LPM3169 ............. 1953 £10 ....... £25 ....................... US
Teensville ............................................. LP ..... RCA ............... RD27168 ............. 1960 £4 ......... £10 ...........................

## ATLANTIC BRIDGE
Atlantic Bridge ...................................... LP ..... Dawn ............. DNLS3014 ........... 1970 £5 ......... £12 ...........................
I Can't Lie To You ................................. 7" EP . Dawn ............. DNX2507 ............. 1971 £2 ......... £5 ...........................

## ATLANTIC OCEAN
Tranquility Bay ..................................... LP ..... Love ..................................... 1970 £30 ....... £60 ................. Swedish

## ATLANTICS
Bomborra .............................................. LP ..... CBS .............. 233066 ............... 1972 £6 ......... £15 ............. Australian

## ATLANTIS
Atlantis ................................................ LP ..... Vertigo ......... 6360609 ............... 1973 £4 ......... £10 ............. spiral label

## ATLAS
Against All The Odds .............................. LP ..... Atlas ............. WIL001 ............... 1978 £6 ......... £15 ...........................

## ATMOSFEAR
Dancing In Outer Space ......................... 12" .. Elite ............. DAZZ47 ............... 1986 £3 ......... £8 ...........................
Dancing In Outer Space ......................... 12" .. MCA .............. MCA543 .............. 1979 £2.50 ....... £6 ...........................
Entrance ............................................... LP ..... MCA .............. MCF3110 ............. 1981 £4 ......... £10 ...........................

## ATMOSPHERES
Fickle Chicken ...................................... 7" ..... London ........... HLW8977 ............ 1959 £5 ......... £10 ...........................
Telegraph ............................................. 7" ..... London ........... HLW9091 ............ 1960 £4 ......... £8 ...........................

## ATOLL
| | | | | | | | |
|---|---|---|---|---|---|---|---|
| L'araignée mal | LP | Eurodisc | 913002 | 1975 | £4 | £10 | French |
| Musiciens et magiciens | LP | Eurodisc | 87008 | 1974 | £4 | £10 | French |

## ATOMIC ROOSTER
| | | | | | | | |
|---|---|---|---|---|---|---|---|
| Atomic Rooster | LP | B&C | CAS1010 | 1970 | £6 | £15 | |
| Death Walks Behind You | LP | B&C | CAS1026 | 1970 | £6 | £15 | |
| Friday The 13th | 7" | B&C | CB121 | 1970 | £2 | £5 | picture sleeve |
| In Hearing Of | LP | Pegasus | PEG1 | 1971 | £5 | £12 | |
| Made In England | LP | Dawn | DNLS3038 | 1972 | £4 | £10 | |
| Made In England | LP | Dawn | DNLS3038 | 1972 | £15 | £30 | denim cover |
| Nice And Greasy | LP | Dawn | DNLS3049 | 1973 | £10 | £25 | |
| Tell Your Story – Sing Your Song | 7" | Decca | FR13503 | 1974 | £2 | £5 | export |

## ATTACK
The Attack were best known as the performers of the other version of 'Hi Ho Silver Lining', but unfortunately for them, despite receiving fairly extensive radio play, they lost out to Jeff Beck. The guitarist with the Attack was David O'List, who subsequently became a member of the Nice.

| | | | | | | | |
|---|---|---|---|---|---|---|---|
| Created By Clive | 7" | Decca | F12631 | 1967 | £15 | £30 | |
| Hi Ho Silver Lining | 7" | Decca | F12578 | 1967 | £15 | £30 | |
| Neville Thumbcatch | 7" | Decca | F12725 | 1968 | £20 | £40 | |
| Try It | 7" | Decca | F12550 | 1967 | £30 | £60 | |

## ATTACK (2)
| | | | | | | |
|---|---|---|---|---|---|---|
| Please Mr. Phil Spector | 7" | Philips | BF1585 | 1967 | £5 | £10 |

## ATTILA
| | | | | | | | |
|---|---|---|---|---|---|---|---|
| Attila | LP | Epic | E30030 | 1970 | £6 | £15 | US |

## ATTRACTION
| | | | | | | |
|---|---|---|---|---|---|---|
| Party Line | 7" | Columbia | DB8010 | 1966 | £12.50 | £25 |
| Stupid Girl | 7" | Columbia | DB7936 | 1966 | £12.50 | £25 |

## ATTRITION
| | | | | | | | |
|---|---|---|---|---|---|---|---|
| Fear | 7" | Sound For Industry | SFI671 | 1981 | £2 | £5 | flexi |
| Monkey In A Bin | 12" | Uniton | 19841 | 1984 | £4 | £10 | |
| Shrinkwrap | 12" | Third Mind | TMS04 | 1985 | £3 | £8 | |
| Two Traces | 7" | Adventures In Reality | AINR2 | 1982 | £4 | £8 | flexi |
| Voice Of God | 12" | Third Mind | TMS03 | 1984 | £3 | £8 | |

## ATWELL, WINIFRED
| | | | | | | |
|---|---|---|---|---|---|---|
| Boogie With Winifred Atwell | 7" EP | Decca | DFE6099 | 1955 | £2 | £5 |
| Let's Rock 'n' Roll | 7" | Decca | F10852 | 1957 | £2 | £5 |
| Poor People Of Paris | 7" | Decca | F10681 | 1956 | £2 | £5 |
| Spaceship Boogie | 7" | Decca | F10886 | 1957 | £1.50 | £4 |

## AU GO-GO SINGERS
| | | | | | | |
|---|---|---|---|---|---|---|
| San Francisco Bay Blues | 7" | Columbia | DB7493 | 1965 | £2 | £5 |
| They Call Us The Au Go-Go Singers | LP | Columbia | 33SX1696 | 1964 | £25 | £50 |

## AUBREY SMALL
| | | | | | | |
|---|---|---|---|---|---|---|
| Aubrey Small | LP | Polydor | 2383048 | 1971 | £20 | £40 |

## AUDIENCE
As label-mates of Genesis and Van Der Graaf Generator, Audience played very much the same kind of complex structured but essentially melodic material, although with rather less commercial success. The real Audience rarity, however, is the first LP, recorded for Polydor. The scarcity of this record has led some dealers to conclude that the record was withdrawn soon after its release, although the truth is that it was simply deleted after a short time, due to its sales being rather poor.

| | | | | | | | |
|---|---|---|---|---|---|---|---|
| Audience | LP | Polydor | 583065 | 1969 | £30 | £60 | |
| Friends Friends Friends | LP | Charisma | CAS1012 | 1970 | £4 | £10 | |
| House On The Hill | LP | Charisma | CAS1032 | 1971 | £4 | £10 | |
| Indian Summer | 7" | Charisma | CB141 | 1971 | £1.50 | £4 | picture sleeve |
| Lunch | LP | Charisma | CAS1054 | 1972 | £4 | £10 | |

## AUDREY
| | | | | | | | |
|---|---|---|---|---|---|---|---|
| Love Me Tonight | 7" | Downtown | DT414 | 1969 | £1.50 | £4 | Brother Dan Allstars B side |
| Lovers' Concerto | 7" | Downtown | DT418 | 1969 | £1.50 | £4 | Brother Dan Allstars B side |
| Oh I Was Wrong | 7" | Downtown | DT454 | 1969 | £1.50 | £4 | |
| Someday We'll Be Together | 7" | Downtown | DT457 | 1969 | £1.50 | £4 | Music Doctors B side |
| Sweeter Than Sugar | 7" | Downtown | DT452 | 1969 | £1.50 | £4 | |
| You'll Lose A Good Thing | 7" | Downtown | DT436 | 1969 | £1.50 | £4 | Desmond Riley B side |

## AUDSLEY, MICK
| | | | | | | |
|---|---|---|---|---|---|---|
| Dark And Devil Waters | LP | Sonet | SNTF641 | 1973 | £4 | £10 |
| Storyboard | LP | Sonet | SNTF659 | 1974 | £4 | £10 |

## AUGER, BRIAN
Brian Auger's long career as a jazz-rock organist peaked on the recordings made jointly with singer Julie Driscoll. For just a short while, Auger was more than just the skilled craftsman of his recordings before and since, becoming part of a group with real innovative power.

Nothing Julie Driscoll and the Brian Auger Trinity recorded together could quite match the brilliance of 'This Wheel's On Fire', but all the Marmalade recordings contain much worthwhile and memorable music.

| | | | | | | | |
|---|---|---|---|---|---|---|---|
| Befour | LP | RCA | SF8101 | 1970 | £4 | £10 | |
| Definitely What | LP | Marmalade | 607003 | 1968 | £6 | £15 | |
| Don't Send Me No Flowers | LP | Marmalade | 607/608004 | 1968 | £15 | £30 | ...with Jimmy Page & Sonny Boy Williamson |
| Fool Killer | 7" | Columbia | DB7590 | 1965 | £5 | £10 | |
| Green Onions '65 | 7" | Columbia | DB7715 | 1965 | £4 | £8 | |
| I Don't Know Where You Are | 7" | Marmalade | 598006 | 1968 | £1.50 | £4 | |
| Oblivion Express | LP | RCA | SF8170 | 1971 | £4 | £10 | |
| Red Beans And Rice | 7" | Marmalade | 598003 | 1967 | £2 | £5 | |
| Tiger | 7" | Columbia | DB8163 | 1967 | £7.50 | £15 | |
| What You Gonna Do | 7" | Marmalade | 598015 | 1969 | £1.50 | £4 | |

## AULD, GEORGIE

| | | | | | | | |
|---|---|---|---|---|---|---|---|
| Dancing In The Land Of Hi-Fi | LP | Emarcy | EJL1266 | 1958 | £5 | £12 | |
| Georgie Auld | LP | Vogue Coral | LVA9023 | 1956 | £5 | £12 | |
| In The Land Of Hi-Fi | LP | Emarcy | EJL1251 | 1957 | £5 | £12 | with Sarah McLawler |
| Manhattan | 7" | Vogue Coral | Q2002 | 1954 | £1.50 | £4 | |
| With The André Previn Orchestra | LP | Vogue Coral | LVA9012 | 1956 | £5 | £12 | |

## AULD TRIANGLE

| | | | | | | |
|---|---|---|---|---|---|---|
| Auld Triangle | LP | Castle | CASLP008 | | £15 | £30 |

## AULDRIDGE, MIKE

| | | | | | | |
|---|---|---|---|---|---|---|
| Blues And Bluegrass | LP | Sonet | SNTF673 | 1974 | £4 | £10 |

## AUM

| | | | | | | | |
|---|---|---|---|---|---|---|---|
| Bluesvibes | LP | London | HAK/SHK8401 | 1969 | £15 | £30 | |
| Resurrection | LP | Fillmore | 30002 | 1969 | £5 | £12 | US |

## AUNT MARY

| | | | | | | | |
|---|---|---|---|---|---|---|---|
| Aunt Mary | LP | Polydor | 2380002 | 1971 | £37.50 | £75 | German |
| Best Of Vol. 1 | LP | Polydor | 6478009 | 1974 | £25 | £50 | German |
| Best Of Vol. 2 | LP | Polydor | 6478055 | 1975 | £25 | £50 | German |
| Janus | LP | Vertigo | 6317750 | 1973 | £50 | £100 | Norwegian |
| Live Reunion | LP | Philips | 6327059 | 1980 | £15 | £30 | Swedish |
| Loaded | LP | Philips | 6317010 | 1971 | £75 | £150 | Danish |
| Whispering Farewell | LP | Polydor | 2499083 | 1974 | £25 | £50 | German |

## AURA

| | | | | | | |
|---|---|---|---|---|---|---|
| Aura | LP | Mercury | SRM1620 | 1971 | £5 | £12 |

## AUSTIN, CHARLES

| | | | | | | | |
|---|---|---|---|---|---|---|---|
| Home From Home | LP | Ogun | OG522 | 1979 | £5 | £12 | with Roy Babbington & Joe Gallivan |
| Peace On Earth | LP | Compendium | FIDARDO5 | 1977 | £4 | £10 | with Joe Gallivan |

## AUSTIN, CLAIRE

| | | | | | | |
|---|---|---|---|---|---|---|
| Claire Austin Sings The Blues | 10" LP | Good Time Jazz | LDG185 | 1956 | £20 | £40 |
| When Your Lover Has Gone | LP | Contemporary | LAC12139 | 1959 | £8 | £20 |

## AUSTIN, PETER

| | | | | | | |
|---|---|---|---|---|---|---|
| Your Love | 7" | Caltone | TONE125 | 1968 | £2.50 | £6 |

## AUSTIN, REG

| | | | | | | |
|---|---|---|---|---|---|---|
| My Saddest Day | 7" | Pye | 7N15885 | 1965 | £15 | £30 |

## AUSTIN, SIL

| | | | | | | |
|---|---|---|---|---|---|---|
| Band With The Beat | 7" EP | Mercury | MEP9540 | 1958 | £7.50 | £15 |
| Don't You Just Know It | 7" | Mercury | 7MT220 | 1958 | £4 | £8 |
| Go Sil Go | 7" EP | Mercury | MEP9541 | 1958 | £7.50 | £15 |
| Hey Eula | 7" | Mercury | 7MT225 | 1958 | £4 | £8 |
| Slow Walk Rock | LP | Mercury | MPL6534 | 1958 | £10 | £25 |

## AUSTRALIAN JAZZ QUARTET

| | | | | | | |
|---|---|---|---|---|---|---|
| Australian Jazz Quartet | LP | London | LTZN15054 | 1957 | £5 | £12 |
| Australian Jazz Quartet | LP | London | LTZN15065 | 1957 | £5 | £12 |

## AUSTRALIAN JAZZ QUINTET

| | | | | | | |
|---|---|---|---|---|---|---|
| Australian Jazz Quintet Plus One | LP | London | LTZN15089 | 1957 | £5 | £12 |

## AUSTRALIAN PLAYBOYS

| | | | | | | |
|---|---|---|---|---|---|---|
| Black Sheep | 7" | Immediate | IM054 | 1967 | £150 | £250 | best auctioned |

## AUTOSALVAGE

The one LP recorded by Autosalvage is a little like Jefferson Airplane and a little like the Lovin' Spoonful, but with more ambitious arranging than either (including the use of medieval instruments, though not a medieval sound). Unfortunately, the songs are not as strong as they might be, but the record is still very interesting. Frank Zappa is supposed to have had a hand in the group's discovery.

| | | | | | | | |
|---|---|---|---|---|---|---|---|
| Autosalvage | LP | RCA | LSP3940 | 1968 | £15 | £30 | US |

## AUTRY, GENE

| | | | | | | |
|---|---|---|---|---|---|---|
| At The Rodeo | 10" LP | Columbia | JL8001 | 1949 | £10 | £25 | US |

| | | | | | | | |
|---|---|---|---|---|---|---|---|
| Champion Western Adventures | LP | Columbia | CL677 | 1955 £6 | £15 | | US |
| Christmas With Gene Autry | LP | Challenge | CHL600 | 1958 £6 | £15 | | US |
| Gene Autry Sings Peter Cottontail | 10" LP | Columbia | CL2568 | 1955 £10 | £25 | | US |
| Golden Hits | LP | RCA | LPM/LSP2623 | 1962 £5 | £12 | | US |
| Greatest Hits | LP | Columbia | CL1575 | 1961 £6 | £15 | | US |
| Little Johnny Pilgrim | 10" LP | Columbia | MJV83 | 195– £10 | £25 | | US |
| Merry Christmas | 10" LP | Columbia | CL2547 | 1955 £10 | £25 | | US |
| Rusty The Rocking Horse | 10" LP | Columbia | MJV94 | 195– £10 | £25 | | US |
| Stampede | 10" LP | Columbia | JL8009 | 195– £10 | £25 | | US |
| Story Of The Nativity | 10" LP | Columbia | MJV82 | 195– £10 | £25 | | US |
| Western Classic, Vol. 1 | 10" LP | Columbia | HL9001 | 195– £10 | £25 | | US |
| Western Classic, Vol. 2 | 10" LP | Columbia | HL9002 | 195– £10 | £25 | | US |

## AUTUMN
| | | | | | | | |
|---|---|---|---|---|---|---|---|
| My Little Girl | 7" | Pye | 7N45090 | 1970 £1.50 | £4 | | |

## AUTUMN PEOPLE
| | | | | | | | |
|---|---|---|---|---|---|---|---|
| Autumn People | LP | Soundtech | 3020 | 1976 £30 | £60 | | US |

## AVALANCHE
| | | | | | | | |
|---|---|---|---|---|---|---|---|
| Perseverance Kills Our Game | LP | Starlet | | 1979 £330 | £500 | | Dutch |

## AVALANCHES
| | | | | | | | |
|---|---|---|---|---|---|---|---|
| Ski Surfin' | LP | Warner Bros | WS1525 | 1963 £5 | £12 | | US |

## AVALON, FRANKIE
| | | | | | | | |
|---|---|---|---|---|---|---|---|
| And Now About Mr. Avalon | LP | Chancellor | CHL(S)5022 | 1961 £5 | £12 | | US |
| Bobby Sox To Stockings | 7" | HMV | POP636 | 1959 £1.50 | £4 | | |
| Christmas Album | LP | Chancellor | CHL(S)5031 | 1962 £6 | £15 | | US |
| Cleopatra | LP | Chancellor | CHL(S)5032 | 1963 £6 | £15 | | US |
| Darling | 7" | London | HL8636 | 1958 £10 | £20 | | |
| Dede Dinah | 7" | HMV | POP453 | 1958 £4 | £8 | | |
| Don't Throw Away All Those Teardrops | 7" | HMV | POP727 | 1960 £1.50 | £4 | | |
| Fifteen Greatest Hits | LP | United Artists | UAL3382/ UAS6382 | 1964 £4 | £10 | | US |
| Frankie Avalon | LP | Chancellor | CHL5001 | 1958 £8 | £20 | | US |
| Frankie Avalon | 7" EP | HMV | 7EG8471 | 1958 £6 | £12 | | |
| Frankie Avalon No. 2 | 7" EP | HMV | 7EG8482 | 1958 £6 | £12 | | |
| Frankie Avalon No. 3 | 7" EP | HMV | 7EG8507 | 1958 £6 | £12 | | |
| Gingerbread | 7" | HMV | POP517 | 1958 £2 | £5 | | |
| I'll Wait For You | 7" | HMV | POP569 | 1959 £1.50 | £4 | | |
| Italiano | LP | Chancellor | CHL(S)5025 | 1962 £5 | £12 | | US |
| Just Ask Your Heart | 7" | HMV | POP658 | 1959 £1.50 | £4 | | |
| Songs From Muscle Beach Party | LP | United Artists | ULP1078 | 1964 £4 | £10 | | |
| Songs Of The Alamo | 7" EP | HMV | 7EG8632 | 1960 £4 | £8 | | |
| Summer Scene | LP | HMV | CLP1423 | 1960 £6 | £15 | | |
| Swingin' On A Rainbow | LP | HMV | CLP1346 | 1959 £6 | £15 | | |
| Venus | 7" | HMV | POP603 | 1959 £1.50 | £4 | | |
| Whole Lot Of Frankie | LP | Chancellor | CHL5018 | 1961 £6 | £15 | | US |
| Why | 7" | HMV | POP688 | 1960 £1.50 | £4 | | |
| You Are Mine | LP | Chancellor | CHL(S)5027 | 1962 £5 | £12 | | US |
| Young And In Love | LP | HMV | CLP1440/CSD1358 | 1960 £6 | £15 | | |
| Young Frankie Avalon | LP | Chancellor | CHL5002 | 1959 £6 | £15 | | US |

## AVALONS
| | | | | | | | |
|---|---|---|---|---|---|---|---|
| Every Day | 7" | Island | WI263 | 1966 £2 | £5 | | |

## AVANT-GARDE
| | | | | | | | |
|---|---|---|---|---|---|---|---|
| Naturally Stoned | 7" | CBS | 1333160 | 1975 £1.50 | £4 | | |
| Naturally Stoned | 7" | CBS | 3704 | 1968 £1.50 | £4 | | |

## AVENGERS
| | | | | | | | |
|---|---|---|---|---|---|---|---|
| Everyone's Gonna Wonder | 7" | Parlophone | R5661 | 1968 £1.50 | £4 | | |

## AVENGERS (2)
| | | | | | | | |
|---|---|---|---|---|---|---|---|
| American In Me | 12" | White Noise | WNR002 | 1979/ 1981 £5 | £12 | different picture sleeves | |

## AVENGERS (3)

The cult TV programme is represented on vinyl by recordings of its theme tunes. The first series with Patrick McNee and Honor Blackman had a theme by Johnny Dankworth. The second and third series with McNee and Diana Rigg, followed by McNee and Linda Thorson had a theme by Laurie Johnson, and since these series were the ones that achieved the biggest cult following, it is Johnson's music that is most readily associated with the programme. The New Avengers revival in the seventies was rather less popular, but its theme was also by Laurie Johnson. Details of all these records can be found in the *Guide* under the appropriate artist headings.

## AVENGERS VI
| | | | | | | | |
|---|---|---|---|---|---|---|---|
| Real Cool Hits | LP | Mark 56 Records | | 1965 £30 | £60 | | US |

## AVERAGE WHITE BAND
| | | | | | | | |
|---|---|---|---|---|---|---|---|
| Show Your Hand | LP | MCA | MUPS486 | 1973 £4 | £10 | .. white golliwog sleeve | |

## AVON, ALAN & THE TOY SHOP
| | | | | | | | |
|---|---|---|---|---|---|---|---|
| Night To Remember | 7" | Concord | CONC005 | 1974 £25 | £50 | | |

## AVON CITIES JAZZ BAND
| | | | | | | | |
|---|---|---|---|---|---|---|---|
| Avon Cities Jazz Band | 10" LP | Tempo | LAP10 | 1956 £10 | £25 | | |

## AVON CITIES SKIFFLE GROUP

| | | | | | | | |
|---|---|---|---|---|---|---|---|
| Hey Hey Daddy Blues | 7" | Tempo | A146 | 1956 | £1.50 | £4 | |
| How Long Blues | 7" | Tempo | A156 | 1957 | £1.50 | £4 | |
| Lonesome Day Blues | 7" | Tempo | A157 | 1957 | £1.50 | £4 | |
| Ray Bush & The Avon Cities Skiffle Group | 7" EP | Tempo | EXA40 | 1957 | £2 | £5 | |
| Ray Bush & The Avon Cities Skiffle Group No. 2 | 7" EP | Tempo | EXA50 | 1957 | £2 | £5 | |
| This Little Light Of Mine | 7" | Tempo | A149 | 1956 | £1.50 | £4 | |

## AVONS

| | | | | | | | |
|---|---|---|---|---|---|---|---|
| Jerri-Lee | 7" | Columbia | DB4236 | 1959 | £1.50 | £4 | |
| Seven Little Girls Sitting In The Back Seat | 7" | Columbia | DB4363 | 1959 | £1.50 | £4 | |

## AVONS (2)

| | | | | | | | |
|---|---|---|---|---|---|---|---|
| Avons | LP | Hull | HLP1000 | 1960 | £75 | £150 | US |

## AWAY FROM THE SAND

| | | | | | | | |
|---|---|---|---|---|---|---|---|
| Away From The Sand | LP | Beaujangle | DB0003 | 1973 | £62.50 | £125 | |

## AXELROD, DAVID

| | | | | | | | |
|---|---|---|---|---|---|---|---|
| Earth Rot | LP | Capitol | SKAO456 | 1970 | £4 | £10 | US |
| Rock Messiah | LP | RCA | 4636 | 1972 | £4 | £10 | US |
| Songs Of Experience | LP | Capitol | SKAP338 | 1969 | £4 | £10 | US |
| Songs Of Innocence | LP | Capitol | ST2982 | 1968 | £4 | £10 | |

## AXIOM

| | | | | | | | |
|---|---|---|---|---|---|---|---|
| Fools' Gold | LP | Parlophone | PCSO7561 | 1970 | £6 | £15 | Australian |

## AXIS

| | | | | | | | |
|---|---|---|---|---|---|---|---|
| Axis | LP | Riviera | 421088 | 1973 | £6 | £15 | French |
| Axis | LP | Riviera | 95010 | 1971 | £6 | £15 | French |
| Ela Ela | LP | Riviera | 521192 | 1971 | £6 | £15 | French |

## AXTON, HOYT

Apart from being quite well known as a folk and country singer in his own right, Hoyt Axton is also the son of the woman who wrote 'Heartbreak Hotel'. Intending the song as a smooth, sentimental ballad, Mrs Axton was apparently quite upset when she heard what Elvis Presley had done to the song – although she cheered up considerably when the royalties started to arrive!

| | | | | | | | |
|---|---|---|---|---|---|---|---|
| Best Of Hoyt Axton | LP | London | HAF/SHF8276 | 1966 | £5 | £12 | |
| Country Anthem | LP | Capitol | SMAS850 | 1971 | £4 | £10 | US |
| Explodes | LP | Vee Jay | VJS1098 | 1964 | £6 | £15 | US |
| Greenback Dollar | LP | Stateside | SL10082 | 1964 | £4 | £10 | |
| Joy To The World | LP | Capitol | EST788 | 1970 | £4 | £10 | US |
| Less Than A Song | LP | A&M | AMLH64376 | 1973 | £4 | £10 | |
| Saturday's Child | LP | Vee Jay | VJS1127 | 1965 | £6 | £15 | US |
| Sings Betty Smith | LP | Exodus | 301 | 1965 | £5 | £12 | US |
| Thunder And Lightnin' | LP | Stateside | SL10096 | 1964 | £4 | £10 | |

## AYERS, KEVIN

As one of the founders of the 'English eccentric' school of rock music, Kevin Ayers still makes records for the loyal army of fans who have followed his activities since his days as bass player for the Soft Machine. The two earliest albums contain what is arguably his most interesting music, with telling contributions from the supporting musicians, who include Soft Machine on *Joy Of A Toy*, and on *Shooting At The Moon*, saxophonist Lol Coxhill, composer/arranger David Bedford (here playing keyboards), and the youthful Mike Oldfield.

| | | | | | | | |
|---|---|---|---|---|---|---|---|
| As Close As You Think | LP | Illuminated | AMA25 | 1986 | £4 | £10 | |
| Bananamour | LP | Harvest | SHVL807 | 1973 | £4 | £10 | |
| Bananamour | LP | Harvest | SHVL807 | 1973 | £8 | £20 | with booklet |
| Caribbean Moon | 7" | Harvest | HAR5071 | 1973 | £2.50 | £6 | picture sleeve |
| Caribbean Moon | 7" | Harvest | HAR5109 | 1976 | £2.50 | £6 | picture sleeve |
| Joy Of A Toy | LP | Harvest | SHVL763 | 1970 | £6 | £15 | |
| Joy Of A Toy/Shooting At The Moon | LP | Harvest | SHDW407 | 1975 | £5 | £12 | double |
| Puis-Je? | 7" | Harvest | HAR5027 | 1970 | £1.50 | £4 | |
| Shooting At The Moon | LP | Harvest | SHSP4005 | 1971 | £6 | £15 | |
| Singing A Song In The Morning | 7" | Harvest | HAR5011 | 1970 | £2.50 | £6 | |
| Stepping Out | 7" | Illuminated | LEV71 | 1986 | £1.50 | £4 | |
| Whatevershebringswesing | LP | Harvest | SHVL800 | 1973 | £4 | £10 | |

## AYERS, ROY

| | | | | | | | |
|---|---|---|---|---|---|---|---|
| Africa Centre Of The World | LP | Polydor | 2391157 | 1981 | £4 | £10 | |
| Best Of Roy Ayers | LP | Polydor | 2391429 | 1979 | £4 | £10 | |
| Crystal Reflection | LP | Muse | MR5101 | 1977 | £4 | £10 | |
| Daddy Bug And Friend | LP | Atco | SD1692 | 1973 | £6 | £15 | US |
| Everybody Loves The Sunshine | LP | Polydor | PD16070 | 1976 | £4 | £10 | US |
| Evolution | 7" | Polydor | 2066671 | 1976 | £1.50 | £4 | |
| Feelin' Good | LP | Polydor | 2391539 | 1982 | £8 | £20 | |
| Fever | LP | Polydor | 2391396 | 1979 | £4 | £10 | |
| Let's Do It | LP | Polydor | 2490145 | 1978 | £4 | £10 | |
| Lifeline | LP | Polydor | 2391292 | 1977 | £4 | £10 | |
| Mystic Voyage | LP | Polydor | PD6057 | 1975 | £5 | £12 | US |
| Red, Black And Green | LP | Polydor | PD16078 | 1976 | £4 | £10 | US |
| Running Away | 12" | Polydor | POSPX135 | 1980 | £2.50 | £6 | |
| Step Into Our Life | LP | Polydor | 2391380 | 1978 | £4 | £10 | |
| Ubiquity | LP | Polydor | PD6046 | 1974 | £6 | £15 | US |
| Vibrations | LP | Polydor | 2391256 | 1976 | £4 | £10 | |
| Virgo Vibes | LP | Atlantic | SD1488 | 1967 | £8 | £20 | US |
| You Send Me | LP | Polydor | 2391365 | 1978 | £4 | £10 | |

## AYLER, ALBERT

| | | | | | | |
|---|---|---|---|---|---|---|
| At St. Paul De Vence Vol. 1 | LP | Shandar | SR10000 | 1973 £8 £20 | | French |
| At St. Paul De Vence Vol. 2 | LP | Shandar | SR10004 | 1973 £8 £20 | | French |
| Bells | LP | ESP-Disk | 1010 | 1965 £15 £30 | | US |
| Ghosts | LP | Debut | DEB144 | 1956 £25 £50 | | US |
| Ghosts | LP | Fontana | SFJL925 | 1969 £10 £25 | | |
| In Greenwich Village | LP | Impulse | AS9155 | 1967 £10 £25 | | US |
| Last Album | LP | Impulse | AS9208 | 1971 £10 £25 | | US |
| Love Cry | LP | Impulse | AS9165 | 1968 £10 £25 | | US |
| Music Is The Healing Force Of The Universe | LP | Impulse | AS9191 | 1969 £10 £25 | | US |
| My Name Is Albert Ayler | LP | Debut | DEB140 | 1956 £25 £50 | | US |
| My Name Is Albert Ayler | LP | Fantasy | FS6016 | 1965 £10 £25 | | US |
| New Grass | LP | Impulse | AS9175 | 1968 £10 £25 | | US |
| New York Eye And Ear Control | LP | ESP-Disk | 1016 | 1966 £15 £30 | | US |
| Nuits De La Fondation Maeght | LP | Shandar | SHAN83503/4 | 1978 £10 £25 | | French |
| Spirits | LP | Debut | DEB146 | 1956 £25 £50 | | US |
| Spirits Rejoice | LP | ESP-Disk | 1020 | 1966 £15 £30 | | US |
| Spiritual Unity | LP | ESP-Disk | 1002 | 1964 £15 £30 | | US |
| Spiritual Unity | LP | Fontana | SFJL933 | 1969 £10 £25 | | |
| Vibrations | LP | Freedom | | 196– £8 £20 | | |
| Witches And Devils | LP | Freedom | FLP40101 | 1967 £8 £20 | | |

## AYSHEA

| | | | | | | |
|---|---|---|---|---|---|---|
| Ayshea | LP | Polydor | 2384026 | 1970 £4 £10 | | |
| Lift Off With Ayshea | LP | DJM | DJLPS445 | 1974 £4 £10 | | |
| Only Your Love Can Save Me | 7" | Polydor | 56276 | 1968 £4 £8 | | |
| Peep My Love | 7" | Fontana | TF627 | 1965 £1.50 £4 | | |

## AZITIS

| | | | | | | |
|---|---|---|---|---|---|---|
| Help | LP | Elco | SCEC5555 | 1971 £700 £1000 | | US |

## AZTEC CAMERA

| | | | | | | |
|---|---|---|---|---|---|---|
| Crying Scene | CD-s | WEA | YZ492CD | 1990 £2 £5 | | |
| Deep And Wide And Tall | CD-s | WEA | YZ154CD | 1988 £2 £5 | | |
| Good Morning Britain | CD-s | WEA | YZ521CD | 1990 £2 £5 | | with Mick Jones |
| How Men Are | CD-s | WEA | 2480282 | 1988 £2 £5 | | Dutch import |
| Just Like Gold | 7" | Postcard | 81-3 | 1981 £2 £5 | | |
| Just Like Gold | 7" | Postcard | 81-3 | 1981 £5 £10 | | lyric postcard |
| Mattress Of Wire | 7" | Postcard | 81-8 | 1981 £5 £10 | | picture sleeve |
| Oblivious (Langer/Winstanley remix) | 7" | Rainhill | ACFC1 | 1983 £5 £10 | | |
| Pillar To Post | 7" | Rough Trade | RT112P | 1982 £2.50 £6 | | picture disc |
| Retrospect | CD | Sire | | 1993 £8 £20 | | US promo compilation |
| Somewhere In My Heart | CD-s | WEA | YZ181CD | 1988 £2 £5 | | |
| Still On Fire | 7" | WEA | AC2P | 1984 £2 £5 | | shaped picture disc |
| Working In A Goldmine | CD-s | WEA | YZ7199CD | 1988 £2 £5 | | |

## AZTECS

| | | | | | | |
|---|---|---|---|---|---|---|
| Live At The Ad-Lib Club | LP | World Artists | WAM2001 | 1964 £25 £50 | | US |

# B

## B. B. BLUNDER

*Worker's Playtime* is the often overlooked third LP by the Blossom Toes, but sadly it shares few of the inventive qualities of its predecessors. The cover, however, is a delight, being a parody of the Radio Times, with all the song lyrics and credits disguised as programme information.

| | | | | | | | |
|---|---|---|---|---|---|---|---|
| Little Boy | 7" | United Artists | UP35204 | 1971 | £1.50 | £4 | |
| Sticky Living | 7" | United Artists | UP5203 | 1971 | £1.50 | £4 | |
| Workers Playtime | LP | United Artists | UAS29156 | 1971 | £5 | £12 | |

## B-52's

| | | | | | | | |
|---|---|---|---|---|---|---|---|
| B-52's | CD | Island | CID9580 | 1987 | £5 | £12 | |
| Bouncing Off The Satellites | CD | Island | CID9871 | 1987 | £5 | £12 | |
| Channel Z | CD-s | WEA | W2831CD | 1989 | £2 | £5 | |
| Deadbeat Club | CD-s | WEA | W9526CD | 1990 | £2 | £5 | |
| Future Generation | 7" | Island | ISD107 | 1983 | £2.50 | £6 | double |
| Love Shack | CD-s | WEA | W9917CD | 1990 | £2 | £5 | |
| Planet Claire | 7" | Island | WIP6551 | 1980 | £1.50 | £4 | picture disc |
| Roam | CD-s | WEA | W9827CD | 1990 | £2 | £5 | |
| Rock Lobster | 7" | Island | BFTP1/BFTL1/ BFTR1 | 1986 | £5 | £10 | set of 3 rectangular picture discs |
| Wild Planet | LP | Island | ILPS9622 | 1980 | £4 | £10 | with carrying bag, badge |

## B-MOVIE

| | | | | | | | |
|---|---|---|---|---|---|---|---|
| Dead Good Tapes | CD | Wax | WAXCD1 | 1988 | £5 | £12 | |
| Nowhere Girl | 12" | Dead Good | BIGDEAD9 | 1980 | £6 | £15 | |
| Nowhere Girl | 12" | Wax | 12WAX3 | 1988 | £3 | £8 | orange vinyl |
| Nowhere Girl | 12" | Wax | 12WAX3 | 1988 | £2.50 | £6 | pink vinyl |
| Take Three | 7" | Dead Good | DEAD9 | 1980 | £7.50 | £15 | |

## B'S

| | | | | | | | |
|---|---|---|---|---|---|---|---|
| In Your Bonnet | LP | private | | 1974 | £75 | £150 | |

## BABASIN, HARRY

| | | | | | | | |
|---|---|---|---|---|---|---|---|
| For Moderns Only | LP | Emarcy | EJL1265 | 1958 | £8 | £20 | |

## BABE RUTH

| | | | | | | | |
|---|---|---|---|---|---|---|---|
| Amar Caballero | LP | Harvest | SHVL812 | 1973 | £4 | £10 | |
| Babe Ruth | LP | Harvest | SHSP4038 | 1975 | £4 | £10 | |
| First Base | LP | Harvest | SHSP4022 | 1972 | £4 | £10 | |

## BABES IN TOYLAND

| | | | | | | | |
|---|---|---|---|---|---|---|---|
| Live At The Academy | CD | Warner Bros | PROCD5838 | 1992 | £8 | £20 | promo |

## BABY

| | | | | | | | |
|---|---|---|---|---|---|---|---|
| Baby | LP | Lone Star | 6264 | 1974 | £4 | £10 | US |

## BABY BIRD

| | | | | | | | |
|---|---|---|---|---|---|---|---|
| Bad Shave | LP | Baby Bird | LP2 | 1995 | £6 | £15 | |
| Bad Shave | CD | Baby Bird | CD2 | 1995 | £8 | £20 | |
| Fatherhood | LP | Baby Bird | LP3 | 1995 | £6 | £15 | |
| Fatherhood | CD | Baby Bird | CD3 | 1995 | £8 | £20 | |
| Happiest Man Alive | LP | Baby Bird | LP4 | 1995 | £6 | £15 | |
| Happiest Man Alive | CD | Baby Bird | CD4 | 1995 | £8 | £20 | |
| I Was Born A Man | CD | Baby Bird | CD1 | 1995 | £10 | £25 | |
| Snake Caves | 7" | Gorgonzola | REEL01 | 1996 | £7.50 | £15 | blue vinyl |

## BABY HUEY

| | | | | | | | |
|---|---|---|---|---|---|---|---|
| Living Legend | LP | Curtom | CRS8007 | 1970 | £10 | £25 | US |

## BABY RAY & THE FERNS

The single by Baby Ray and the Ferns is one of the early steps in the career of Frank Zappa, who wrote the songs on both sides.

| | | | | | | | |
|---|---|---|---|---|---|---|---|
| How's Your Bird? | 7" | Donna | 1378 | 1963 | £75 | £150 | US |

## BABY SUNSHINE

| | | | | | | | |
|---|---|---|---|---|---|---|---|
| Baby Sunshine | LP | Deroy | DER1301 | 1975 | £30 | £60 | |

## BABYLON

Babylon's lead singer was Carol Grimes, who has managed to maintain a lengthy, if unspectacular career in rock since then.

| | | | | | | | |
|---|---|---|---|---|---|---|---|
| Into The Promised Land | 7" | Polydor | BM56356 | 1969 | £2 | £5 | |

| | | | | | | | | |
|---|---|---|---|---|---|---|---|---|
| Into The Promised Land | 7" | Polydor | BM56356 | 1969 | £4 | £8 | picture sleeve |

## BACH TWO BACH
| | | | | | | | |
|---|---|---|---|---|---|---|---|
| Bach Two Bach | LP | Mushroom | 100MR10 | 1971 | £50 | £100 | |

## BACHARACH, BURT
| | | | | | | | |
|---|---|---|---|---|---|---|---|
| Alfie | 7" | A&M | AMS702 | 1969 | £5 | £10 | |
| Casino Royale | LP | RCA | RD/SF7874 | 1967 | £15 | £30 | |

## BACHDENKEL
| | | | | | | | |
|---|---|---|---|---|---|---|---|
| Lemmings | LP | Initial | IRL001 | 1977 | £8 | £20 | with 7" |
| Stalingrad | LP | Initial | IRL002 | 1977 | £4 | £10 | |

## BACHELOR, JOHNNY
| | | | | | | | |
|---|---|---|---|---|---|---|---|
| Mumbles | 7" | London | HLN9074 | 1960 | £15 | £30 | |

## BACHELORS
| | | | | | | | |
|---|---|---|---|---|---|---|---|
| Ding Ding | 7" | Parlophone | R4547 | 1959 | £4 | £8 | |
| Platter Party | 7" | Parlophone | R4454 | 1958 | £4 | £8 | |

## BACHS
| | | | | | | | |
|---|---|---|---|---|---|---|---|
| Out Of The Bachs | LP | private | | 1968 | £700 | £1000 | US |

## BACK ALLEY CHOIR
| | | | | | | | |
|---|---|---|---|---|---|---|---|
| Back Alley Choir | LP | York | FYK406 | 1972 | £180 | £300 | |
| Nursery Rhyme Song | 7" | York | SYK547 | 1973 | £6 | £12 | |
| Smile Born Of Courtesy | 7" | York | SYK517 | 1972 | £6 | £12 | |

## BACK DOOR
| | | | | | | | |
|---|---|---|---|---|---|---|---|
| Back Door | LP | Blakey | BLP5989 | 1972 | £8 | £20 | |
| Back Door | LP | Warner Bros | K46231 | 1973 | £4 | £10 | |

## BACKBEAT PHILHARMONIC
| | | | | | | | |
|---|---|---|---|---|---|---|---|
| Rock And Roll Symphony | 7" | Top Rank | JAR576 | 1961 | £1.50 | £4 | |

## BACKHOUSE, MIRIAM
| | | | | | | | |
|---|---|---|---|---|---|---|---|
| Gypsy Without A Road | LP | Mother Earth | MUM1203 | 1977 | £100 | £200 | |

## BACKSTREET BAND
| | | | | | | | |
|---|---|---|---|---|---|---|---|
| This Ain't The Road | 7" | Ember | EMBS277 | 1969 | £1.50 | £4 | |
| This Ain't The Road | 7" | Ember | EMBS286 | 1970 | £1.50 | £4 | |

## BACKUS, JIM
| | | | | | | | |
|---|---|---|---|---|---|---|---|
| Delicious | 7" | London | HLJ8674 | 1958 | £1.50 | £4 | |

## BACON, GAR
| | | | | | | | |
|---|---|---|---|---|---|---|---|
| Chains Of Love | 7" | Felsted | AF107 | 1958 | £2.50 | £6 | |
| Marshall Marshall | 7" | Fontana | H196 | 1959 | £10 | £20 | |

## BACON FAT
| | | | | | | | |
|---|---|---|---|---|---|---|---|
| Evil | 7" | Blue Horizon | 573181 | 1971 | £2 | £5 | |
| Grease One For Me | LP | Blue Horizon | 763858 | 1970 | £15 | £30 | |
| Nobody But You | 7" | Blue Horizon | 573171 | 1970 | £2 | £5 | |
| Tough Dude | LP | Blue Horizon | 2431001 | 1971 | £20 | £40 | |

## BAD BOYS
| | | | | | | | |
|---|---|---|---|---|---|---|---|
| Best Of The Bad Boys | LP | Style | STLP8061 | 1966 | £180 | £300 | Italian |
| Owl And The Pussycat | 7" | Piccadilly | 7N35208 | 1964 | £1.50 | £4 | |

## BAD COMPANY
| | | | | | | | |
|---|---|---|---|---|---|---|---|
| Bad Co | LP | Island | ILPS9279 | 1974 | £4 | £10 | |
| Can't Get Enough | CD-s | Atlantic | A7954CD | 1990 | £2 | £5 | |
| Deal With The Preacher | 7" | Island | BCDJ1 | 1976 | £7.50 | £15 | 1 sided promo |
| Straight Shooter | LP | Island | ILPS9304 | 1975 | £4 | £10 | |

## BAD EDGE
| | | | | | | | |
|---|---|---|---|---|---|---|---|
| Bad Edge | LP | private | | 1981 | £8 | £20 | Dutch |

## BAD NEWS REUNION
| | | | | | | | |
|---|---|---|---|---|---|---|---|
| Live Im Logo | LP | Oktave | JFF33781 | 1978 | £8 | £20 | German |

## BADFINGER
| | | | | | | | |
|---|---|---|---|---|---|---|---|
| Apple Of My Eye | 7" | Apple | 49 | 1974 | £4 | £8 | |
| Ass | LP | Apple | SAPCOR27 | 1974 | £8 | £20 | |
| Badfinger | LP | Warner Bros | K56023 | 1974 | £4 | £10 | |
| Come And Get It | 7" | Apple | 20 | 1969 | £2 | £5 | picture sleeve |
| Day After Day | 7" | Apple | 40 | 1972 | £4 | £8 | picture sleeve |
| Magic Christian Music | LP | Apple | SAPCOR12 | 1970 | £15 | £30 | |
| No Dice | LP | Apple | SAPCOR16 | 1970 | £10 | £25 | |
| No Matter What | 7" | Apple | 31 | 1970 | £5 | £10 | picture sleeve |
| Straight Up | LP | Apple | SAPCOR19 | 1972 | £15 | £30 | |
| Wish You Were Here | LP | Warner Bros | K56076 | 1974 | £10 | £25 | |

## BADGE
| | | | | | | | |
|---|---|---|---|---|---|---|---|
| Silver Woman | 7" | Metal Minded | MM2 | 1981 | £7.50 | £15 | |

## BADGER

Badger was the group formed by Tony Kaye after his departure from Yes. *One Live Badger* has a pop-up cover – a badger (naturally) stands up when the gatefold sleeve is opened.

| | | | | | | | |
|---|---|---|---|---|---|---|---|
| One Live Badger | LP | Atlantic | K40473 | 1973 | £6 | £15 | |

## BADGER'S MATE

| | | | | | | | |
|---|---|---|---|---|---|---|---|
| Brighter Than Usual | LP | Cottage | COT521 | 197– | £6 | £15 | |

## BAEZ, JOAN

| | | | | | | | |
|---|---|---|---|---|---|---|---|
| Any Day Now | LP | Vanguard | VSD79306/7 | 1968 | £5 | £12 | double |
| Baptism | LP | Vanguard | SVRL19000 | 1968 | £4 | £10 | |
| Blessed Are | LP | Vanguard | VSD6570/1 | 1971 | £5 | £12 | double |
| Carry It On | LP | Vanguard | VSD519042 | 1972 | £4 | £10 | |
| Come From The Shadows | LP | A&M | AMLH64339 | 1972 | £4 | £10 | |
| David's Album | LP | Vanguard | SVRL19050 | 1969 | £4 | £10 | |
| Don't Think Twice | 7" EP | Fontana | TFE18007 | 1964 | £2 | £5 | |
| Farewell Angelina | LP | Fontana | (S)TFL6058 | 1965 | £4 | £10 | |
| First Ten Years | LP | Vanguard | VSD6560 | 1970 | £5 | £12 | double |
| Hard Rain's Gonna Fall | 7" EP | Fontana | TFE18013 | 1966 | £2 | £5 | |
| In Concert | LP | Fontana | (S)TFL6033 | 1962 | £4 | £10 | |
| In Concert Part 2 | LP | Fontana | (S)TFL6035 | 1962 | £4 | £10 | |
| Joan | LP | Fontana | (S)TFL6082 | 1967 | £4 | £10 | |
| Joan Baez | LP | Fontana | (S)TFL6002 | 1960 | £4 | £10 | |
| Joan Baez 2 | LP | Fontana | (S)TFL6025 | 1961 | £4 | £10 | |
| Joan Baez 5 | LP | Fontana | (S)TFL6043 | 1964 | £4 | £10 | |
| Joan Baez No. 1 | 7" EP | Fontana | TFE18000 | 1964 | £2 | £5 | |
| Joan Baez No. 2 | 7" EP | Fontana | TFE18001 | 1964 | £2 | £5 | |
| Joan Baez Sings Silver Dagger & Other Songs | 7" EP | Fontana | TFE18005 | 1964 | £2 | £5 | |
| Noel | LP | Fontana | (S)TFL6078 | 1966 | £4 | £10 | |
| Once I Had A Sweetheart | 7" EP | Fontana | TFE18006 | 1964 | £2 | £5 | |
| One Day At A Time | LP | Vanguard | VSD23010 | 1970 | £4 | £10 | |
| Portrait | LP | Fontana | (S)TFL6077 | 1966 | £4 | £10 | |
| Pretty Boy Floyd | 7" EP | Fontana | TFE18008 | 1965 | £2 | £5 | |
| With God On Our Side | 7" EP | Fontana | TFE18012 | 1965 | £2 | £5 | |

## BAGDASARIAN, ROSS

| | | | | | | | |
|---|---|---|---|---|---|---|---|
| Crazy, Mixed-Up World | LP | Liberty | LRP3451/LST7451 | 1966 | £8 | £20 | US |

## BAGLEY, DON

| | | | | | | | |
|---|---|---|---|---|---|---|---|
| Jazz On The Rocks | LP | Pye | NPL28008 | 1959 | £8 | £20 | |

## BAILEY, BURR

| | | | | | | | |
|---|---|---|---|---|---|---|---|
| San Francisco Bay | 7" | Decca | F11686 | 1963 | £2.50 | £6 | |
| You Made Me Cry | 7" | Decca | F11846 | 1964 | £6 | £12 | |

## BAILEY, BUSTER

| | | | | | | | |
|---|---|---|---|---|---|---|---|
| All About Memphis | LP | Felsted | FAJ7003 | 1959 | £6 | £15 | |

## BAILEY, CLIVE & RICO

| | | | | | | | |
|---|---|---|---|---|---|---|---|
| Evening Train | 7" | Blue Beat | BB92 | 1962 | £6 | £12 | |

## BAILEY, DEREK

| | | | | | | | |
|---|---|---|---|---|---|---|---|
| Aida | LP | Incus | INCUS40 | 1982 | £5 | £12 | |
| Dart Drug | LP | Incus | INCUS41 | 1983 | £5 | £12 | with Jamie Muir |
| Duo | LP | Incus | INCUS20 | 1976 | £5 | £12 | with Tristan Honsinger |
| Improvisations | LP | ECM | ECM1013ST | 1971 | £8 | £20 | |
| London Concert | LP | Incus | INCUS16 | 197– | £5 | £12 | with Evan Parker |
| Lot 74 Solo Improvisations | LP | Incus | INCUS12 | 1974 | £5 | £12 | |
| Notes | LP | Incus | INCUS48 | 1986 | £5 | £12 | |
| One Music Ensemble | LP | Nondo | 002 | | £6 | £15 | |
| Selections From Live Performances At Verity's Place | LP | Incus | INCUS9 | 1972 | £6 | £15 | |
| Solo Guitar | LP | Incus | INCUS2 | 1971 | £20 | £40 | |

## BAILEY, DEREK & ANTHONY BRAXTON

| | | | | | | | |
|---|---|---|---|---|---|---|---|
| Duo | LP | Emanem | 601 | 1975 | £8 | £20 | double |
| Royal Vol. 1 | LP | Incus | INCUS43 | 1984 | £5 | £12 | |
| Royal Vol. 2 | LP | Incus | INCUS44 | 1984 | £5 | £12 | |

## BAILEY, DEREK & EVAN PARKER

| | | | | | | | |
|---|---|---|---|---|---|---|---|
| Compatibles | LP | Incus | INCUS50 | 1986 | £5 | £12 | |

## BAILEY, MILDRED

| | | | | | | | |
|---|---|---|---|---|---|---|---|
| Mildred Bailey And Her Alley Cats | 7" EP | Parlophone | GEP8600 | 1957 | £4 | £8 | |
| Rockin' Chair Lady | 10" LP | Brunswick | LA8692 | 1954 | £8 | £20 | |

## BAILEY, PEARL

| | | | | | | | |
|---|---|---|---|---|---|---|---|
| That Certain Feeling | 7" EP | London | REU1104 | 1957 | £4 | £8 | |
| That Certain Feeling | 7" | London | HLN8354 | 1956 | £5 | £10 | |

## BAILEY, ROY

| | | | | | | | |
|---|---|---|---|---|---|---|---|
| New Bell Wake | LP | Fuse | AC262 | 1976 | £4 | £10 | |
| Roy Bailey | LP | Trailer | LER3021 | 1971 | £5 | £12 | |

## BAILEY, ROY & LEON ROSSELSON
Love, Loneliness, Laundry ........................ LP ...... Acorn ............. CF271 .................... 1976 £4 .......... £10 .............................

## BAILEY, ROY & VAL & LEON ROSSELSON
Oats And Beans And Kangaroos ................. LP ..... Fontana ........... SFL13061 ............... 1968 £8 .......... £20 .............................

## BAIN, ALY & MIKE WHELLANS
Aly Bain And Mike Whellans ...................... LP ...... Trailer ............. LER2022 ................. 1971 £5 .......... £12 .............................

## BAIN, ALY & TOM ANDERSON
Shetland Folk Fiddling Vol. 1 ..................... LP ...... Topic ............. 12TS281 .......... 1976 £4 .......... £10 ....................
Shetland Folk Fiddling Vol. 2 ..................... LP ...... Topic ............. 12TS379 .......... 1978 £4 .......... £10 ....................

## BAIN, BOB
Rockin', Rollin' ...................................... LP ...... Capitol ........... T965 .................... 1958 £15 ........ £30 .................... US

## BAIRD, ARTHUR SKIFFLE GROUP
Union Train ........................................ 7" ...... Beltona ............. BL2669 ............... 1956 £1.50 ........ £4 ...............................

## BAKER, CHET
At Ann Arbor .......................................... LP ..... Vogue ............. LAE12044 ........ 1957 £10 ........ £25 ....................
Chet Baker And Crew ............................... LP ..... Vogue ............. LAE12076 ........ 1958 £8 .......... £20 ....................
Chet Baker And His Crew .......................... LP ..... Vogue ............. LAE12076/ ....... 1958 £10 ........ £25 ....................
　　　　　　　　　　　　　　　　　　　　　　　　　　　　　　　　　　　SEA5005 ..............
Chet Baker And His Crew .......................... 7" EP . Vogue ............. EPV1186 .......... 1957 £2 ............ £5 ....................
Chet Baker And Strings ............................. 10" LP Philips ........... BBL7022 .......... 1955 £8 .......... £20 ....................
Chet Baker Ensemble ............................... 10" LP Vogue ............. LDE163 ............ 1956 £15 ........ £30 ....................
Chet Baker Ensemble Vol. 1 ...................... 7" EP . Vogue ............. EPV1131 .......... 1956 £2 ............ £5 ....................
Chet Baker Ensemble Vol. 2 ...................... 7" EP . Vogue ............. EPV1132 .......... 1956 £2 ............ £5 ....................
Chet Baker Plays Standards ....................... 7" EP . Felsted ........... ESD3069 .......... 1959 £2 ............ £5 ....................
Chet Baker Quartet .................................. 7" EP . Vogue ............. EPV1007 .......... 1954 £2 ............ £5 ....................
Chet Baker Quartet .................................. 10" LP Vogue ............. LDE045 ............ 1954 £15 ........ £30 ....................
Chet Baker Quartet .................................. 10" LP Vogue ............. LDE116 ............ 1955 £15 ........ £30 ....................
Chet Baker Quartet Vol. 1 ........................ LP ..... Felsted ........... PDL85008 ........ 1956 £10 ........ £25 ....................
Chet Baker Quartet Vol. 2 ........................ LP ..... Felsted ........... PDL85013 ........ 1956 £10 ........ £25 ....................
Chet Baker Sextet ................................... 7" EP . Vogue ............. EPV1121 .......... 1956 £2 ............ £5 ....................
Chet Baker Sextet ................................... 10" LP Vogue ............. LDE159 ............ 1955 £15 ........ £30 ....................
Chet Baker Sings ..................................... LP ..... Vogue ............. LAE12018 ........ 1956 £10 ........ £25 ....................
Chet Baker Sings ..................................... LP ..... Vogue ............. LAE12164 ........ 1959 £8 .......... £20 ....................
Chet Baker Sings ..................................... 10" LP Vogue ............. LDE182 ............ 1956 £15 ........ £30 ....................
Chet Baker Sings And Plays Vol. 1 ............. 7" EP . Vogue ............. EPV1137 .......... 1956 £2 ............ £5 ....................
Chet Baker Sings And Plays Vol. 2 ............. 7" EP . Vogue ............. EPV1138 .......... 1956 £2 ............ £5 ....................
Fabulous Chet Baker Quartet ..................... 7" EP . Vogue ............. EPV1032 .......... 1955 £2 ............ £5 ....................
I Get Chet ............................................. LP ..... Felsted ........... PDL85036 ........ 1957 £10 ........ £25 ....................
Myth ..................................................... 7" EP . Felsted ........... ESD3034 .......... 1957 £2 ............ £5 ....................
Phil's Blues ............................................ LP ..... Vogue ............. LAE12109 ........ 1958 £8 .......... £20 ....................
Playboys ................................................ LP ..... Vogue ............. LAE12183 ........ 1959 £8 .......... £20 ......... with Art Pepper

## BAKER, DESMOND
Rude Boy Gone Jail .................................. 7" ...... Island .............. WI295 ............... 1966 £5 .......... £10 ......... Sharks B side

## BAKER, GEORGE SELECTION
Love In The World ................................... LP ..... Ariola ........... 85132 .................... 1970 £8 .......... £20 .................. German

## BAKER, GINGER
Eleven Sides Of Baker .............................. LP ...... Mountain ........ 5005 ................... 1977 £4 .......... £10 ....................
Fela Ransome Kuti with Ginger Baker ......... LP ...... Regal ............ SLRZ1023 ............. 1972 £4 .......... £10 ....................
　　　　　　　　　　　　　　　　　　　　　　　　　　　　　　　　Zonophone .....
Stratavarious .......................................... LP ...... Polydor .......... 2383133 .............. 1972 £4 .......... £10 ....................

## BAKER, JEANETTE
Crazy With You ....................................... 7" ...... Vogue ............. V9143 ................ 1959 £50 ........ £100 ....................

## BAKER, KENNY
Baker Plays McHugh ................................ 10" LP Pye ................ NJT517 ............. 1959 £5 .......... £12 ....................
Blowin' Up A Storm ................................ 10" LP Columbia ........ 33S1140 ............. 1959 £6 .......... £15 ....................
Kenny Baker Half Dozen .......................... LP ...... Nixa ............... NJL10 ................ 1957 £5 .......... £12 ....................

## BAKER, LAVERN
Best Of Lavern ....................................... 7" EP . Atlantic ........... AET6009 .......... 1965 £20 ........ £40 ....................
Best Of Lavern Baker ............................... LP ..... Atlantic ........... ATL5002 ........... 1964 £25 ........ £50 ....................
Blues Ballads ......................................... LP ..... Atlantic ......... 8030 ................... 1959 £37.50 .. £75 .................... US
Bumble Bee ........................................... 7" ...... London ........... HLK9252 .......... 1960 £7.50 ..... £15 ....................
Game Of Love ........................................ 7" ...... London ........... HLE8442 .......... 1957 £62.50 .. £125 ....................
Get Up Get Up ....................................... 7" ...... London ........... HLE8260 .......... 1956 £75 ........ £150 ....................
Humpty Dumpty Heart ............................. 7" ...... London ........... HLE8524 .......... 1957 £37.50 .. £75 ....................
I Can't Love You Enough .......................... 7" ...... London ........... HLE8396 .......... 1957 £37.50 .. £75 ....................
I Cried A Tear ........................................ 7" ...... London ........... HLE8790 .......... 1959 £15 ........ £30 ....................
I've Waited Too Long ............................... 7" ...... London ........... HLE8871 .......... 1959 £12.50 .. £25 ....................
Jim Dandy ............................................. 7" ...... Columbia ........ DB3879 ............ 1957 £75 ........ £150 ....................
Lavern ................................................... LP ..... Atlantic ......... 8002 ................... 1956 £75 ........ £150 .................... US
Lavern Baker .......................................... LP ..... Atlantic ......... 8007 ................... 1957 £50 ........ £100 .................... US
Learning To Love .................................... 7" ...... London ........... HLE8638 .......... 1958 £30 ........ £60 ....................
Precious Memories ................................... LP ..... Atlantic ......... 8036 ................... 1959 £25 ........ £50 .................... US
Rock And Roll With Lavern Baker ............... LP ..... London ........... HAE2107 .......... 1958 £150 ...... £250 ....................
Saved .................................................... LP ..... London ........... HAE2422 .......... 1961 £37.50 .. £75 ....................
Saved .................................................... 7" ...... London ........... HLK9343 .......... 1961 £7.50 ..... £15 ....................

| See See Rider | LP | Atlantic | 587/588133 | 1968 | £6 | £15 | |
| See See Rider | LP | London | HAK8074 | 1963 | £37.50 | £75 | |
| See See Rider | 7" | London | HLK9649 | 1963 | £10 | £20 | |
| Sings Bessie Smith | LP | London | LTZK15139 | 1958 | £25 | £50 | |
| So High So Low | 7" | London | HLE8945 | 1959 | £10 | £20 | |
| That Lucky Old Sun | 7" | London | HLA8199 | 1955 | £75 | £150 | |
| Tiny Tim | 7" | London | HLE9023 | 1960 | £10 | £20 | |
| Tweedle Dee | 7" | Columbia | SCM5172 | 1955 | £75 | £150 | |
| Voodoo Voodoo | 7" | London | HLK9468 | 1961 | £15 | £30 | |
| Whipper Snapper | 7" | London | HLE8672 | 1958 | £25 | £50 | |
| You're The Boss | 7" | London | HLK9300 | 1961 | £6 | £12 | with Jimmy Ricks |

## BAKER, MICKEY

| But Wild | LP | King | K(S)839 | 1963 | £15 | £30 | US |
| In Blunderland | LP | Major Minor | SMLP67 | 1970 | £4 | £10 | |
| Wildest Guitar | LP | Atlantic | (SD)8035 | 1959 | £30 | £60 | US |

## BAKER, ROBERT

| Pardon Me For Being So Friendly | LP | Crescendo | GNP2027 | 1966 | £8 | £20 | US |

## BAKER, SAM

| I Believe In You | 7" | Monument | MON1009 | 1968 | £2 | £5 | |

## BAKER, TWO TON

| Clink Clank | 7" | London | HL8121 | 1955 | £30 | £60 | |

## BAKERLOO

Bakerloo (originally Bakerloo Blues Line) was one of the many guitarist-led blues groups to surface in the wake of the pioneering work carried out by the various editions of John Mayall's Bluesbreakers. This one featured Dave 'Clem' Clempson, whose name has graced many album sleeves since – most notably during his time as a member of Humble Pie.

| Bakerloo | LP | Harvest | SHVL762 | 1969 | £30 | £60 | |
| Driving Backwards | 7" | Harvest | HAR5004 | 1969 | £12.50 | £25 | |

## BAKERLOO JUNCTION

| Emigrant's Return | LP | Emerald | GES1187 | 1978 | £4 | £10 | |
| Next Stop | LP | Emerald | GES1156 | 1976 | £4 | £10 | |

## BALANCE

| Balance | LP | Incus | INCUS11 | 1973 | £8 | £20 | |
| In For The Count | LP | private | | 1973 | £8 | £20 | |

## BALANCE, BILL

| Bill Balance And The Feminine Look | LP | Mark 56 | NO578 | 1978 | £10 | £25 | US picture disc |

## BALDHEAD GROWLER

| Sausage | 7" | Jump Up | JU531 | 1967 | £1.50 | £4 | |

## BALDO, CHRIS

| Living For Your Love | 7" | Vogue | VRS7029 | 1968 | £5 | £10 | |

## BALDRY, LONG JOHN

John Baldry, known as 'long' because he is indeed something like six foot six tall, has for most of his career sung the blues, for which his distinctive, smokey voice is an ideal instrument. He is featured on Alexis Korner's *R&B At The Marquee* album, and was a member of Cyril Davies's group. When Davies died, Baldry became the leader of the group, which now became called the Hoochie Coochie Men. The earliest recordings in Baldry's name are by this group. With the switch to Pye, Baldry made what was probably a wrong career move when he decided to start singing middle-of-the-road ballad material. Four hits followed, but then nothing, and his attempts to recapture his blues audience in the seventies were not very successful.

| Cuckoo | 7" EP | United Artists | 36108 | 1966 | £7.50 | £15 | French |
| Drifter | 7" | United Artists | UP1136 | 1966 | £7.50 | £15 | |
| How Long Will It Last | 7" | United Artists | UP1107 | 1965 | £10 | £20 | |
| I'm On To You Baby | 7" | United Artists | UP1078 | 1965 | £1.50 | £4 | |
| Let Him Go | 7" | United Artists | UP1204 | 1967 | £2 | £5 | |
| Long John Baldry And The Hoochie Coochie Men | LP | Hallmark | HM560 | 1970 | £6 | £15 | |
| Long John's Blues | LP | United Artists | ULP1081 | 1964 | £20 | £40 | |
| Long John's Blues | 7" EP | United Artists | UEP1013 | 1965 | £7.50 | £15 | |
| Looking At Long John | LP | United Artists | (S)ULP1146 | 1966 | £15 | £30 | |
| Unseen Hands | 7" | United Artists | UP1124 | 1966 | £2 | £5 | |
| Up Above My Head | 7" | United Artists | UP1056 | 1964 | £4 | £8 | |

## BALES, BURT

| Burt Bales | 10" LP | Good Time Jazz | LDG136 | 1955 | £5 | £12 | |
| Jazz From The San Francisco Waterfront | LP | HMV | CLP1218 | 1958 | £6 | £15 | |

## BALFOUR, KEITH

| Dreaming | 7" | Studio One | SO2079 | 1969 | £6 | £12 | |

## BALIN, MARTY

| I Specialize In Love | 7" | Challenge | 9156 | 1962 | £10 | £20 | US |
| Nobody But You | 7" | Challenge | 9146 | 1962 | £10 | £20 | US |

## BALL, KENNY

| Waterloo | 7" | Collector | JDN101 | 1959 | £5 | £10 | |

## BALLARD, FLORENCE
Doesn't Matter How I Say It ..................... 7" ...... Stateside .......... SS2113 .................. 1968 £7.50...... £15 .................................

## BALLARD, FRANK
Rhythm And Blues Party ........................ LP ...... Philips............. 1985 ................. 1962 £150..... £250 ...................... US

## BALLARD, HANK & THE MIDNIGHTERS
| | | | | | | | |
|---|---|---|---|---|---|---|---|
| 1963 Sound Of Hank Ballard.................... | LP ..... | King .......... | 815 ................ | 1963 | £10........ | £25 | ...... US |
| Biggest Hits .................... | LP ..... | King .......... | 867 ................ | 1963 | £10........ | £25 | ...... US |
| Continental Walk.................... | 7" ...... | Parlophone.... | R4771 ............ | 1961 | £2........ | £5 | |
| Finger Popping Time.................... | 7" ...... | Parlophone.... | R4682 ............ | 1960 | £5........ | £10 | |
| Glad Songs, Sad Songs .................... | LP ..... | King .......... | 927 ................ | 1966 | £8........ | £20 | ...... US |
| Hoochi Coochi Coo.................... | 7" ...... | Parlophone.... | R4728 ............ | 1961 | £5........ | £10 | .....Little Willie John B side |
| Jumpin' Hank Ballard .................... | LP ..... | London .......... | HA8101 ............ | 1963 | £15........ | £30 | |
| Let's Go Again .................... | LP ..... | King .......... | 748 ................ | 1961 | £15........ | £30 | ...... US |
| Let's Go Again .................... | 7" ...... | Parlophone.... | R4762 ............ | 1961 | £2........ | £5 | |
| Let's Go Let's Go Let's Go .................... | 7" ...... | Parlophone.... | R4707 ............ | 1960 | £5........ | £10 | |
| Midnighters .................... | LP ..... | Federal.... | 395541 ............ | 1956 | £75........ | £150 | ...... US |
| Midnighters .................... | LP ..... | King .......... | 395541 ............ | 1958 | £30........ | £60 | ...... US |
| Midnighters .................... | 10" LP | Federal.... | 29590 ............ | 1954 | £180.... | £300 | ...... US |
| Midnighters Vol. 2 .................... | LP ..... | Federal.... | 395581 ............ | 1957 | £50........ | £100 | ...... US |
| Midnighters Vol. 2 .................... | LP ..... | King .......... | 395581 ............ | 1958 | £30........ | £60 | ...... US |
| Mr. Rhythm And Blues .................... | LP ..... | King .......... | 700 ................ | 1960 | £210.... | £350 | ...... US |
| One And Only Hank Ballard .................... | LP ..... | King .......... | 674 ................ | 1960 | £15........ | £30 | ...... US |
| Sing Along.................... | LP ..... | King .......... | 759 ................ | 1961 | £15........ | £30 | ...... US |
| Singin' And Swingin'.................... | LP ..... | King .......... | 618 ................ | 1959 | £15........ | £30 | ...... US |
| Spotlight On Hank Ballard .................... | LP ..... | Parlophone.... | PMC1158 ............ | 1961 | £15........ | £30 | |
| Star In Your Eyes .................... | LP ..... | King .......... | 896 ................ | 1964 | £10........ | £25 | ...... US |
| Those Lazy Lazy Days.................... | LP ..... | King .......... | 913 ................ | 1965 | £8........ | £20 | ...... US |
| Twenty-Four Great Songs.................... | LP ..... | King .......... | 981 ................ | 1968 | £6........ | £15 | ...... US |
| Twenty-Four Hit Tunes .................... | LP ..... | King .......... | 950 ................ | 1966 | £8........ | £20 | ...... US |
| Twist .................... | 7" ...... | Parlophone.... | R4558 ............ | 1959 | £12.50........ | £25 | |
| Twist .................... | 7" ...... | Parlophone.... | R4688 ............ | 1960 | £7.50........ | £15 | |
| Twistin' Fools .................... | LP ..... | King .......... | 781 ................ | 1962 | £10........ | £25 | ...... US |
| You Can't Keep A Good Man Down........ | LP ..... | King .......... | KSD1052 ............ | 1969 | £5........ | £12 | ...... US |

## BALLETTO DIBRONZO
Ys.................... LP ...... Polydor ...... 2480127 .................. 1972 £10........ £25 ................ German

## BALLOON FARM
Question Of Temperature........................ 7" ...... London .......... HLP10185 .......... 1968 £20........ £40 .................

## BALLS
Much was expected of the alliance between Denny Laine and the Move's Trevor Burton, but in the end, Balls could only manage one single. This was later reissued under Burton's name.

Fight For My Country ............................ 7" ...... Wizard.......... WIZ101 .......... 1971 £4........ £8 .................

## BALTIK
Baltik .................... LP ...... CBS............. 65581 ................. 1973 £8.......... £20 ................ Swedish

## BALTIMORE & OHIO MARCHING BAND
Lapland .................... LP ...... Stateside ......... SL/SSL10231........ 1968 £10........ £25 .................
Lapland .................... 7" ...... Stateside ......... SS2065 ............. 1967 £30........ £60 .................

## BAMA WINDS
Windy.................... LP ...... Island ............. ILPS9096 .......... 1969 £4........ £10 ................ pink label

## BAMBIS
Baby Blue.................... 7" ...... CBS............. 201778.......... 1965 £5........ £10 .................
Not Wrong.................... 7" ...... Oriole ............. CB1965 .......... 1964 £5........ £10 .................

## BAMBOO SHOOTS
Fox Has Gone To Ground ........................ 7" ...... Columbia .......... DB8370 .......... 1968 £37.50........ £75 .................

## BANANA & THE BUNCH
Mid Mountain Ranch........................ LP ...... Warner Bros .... BS2626 .......... 1973 £6........ £15 ................ US

## BANANARAMA
| | | | | | | | |
|---|---|---|---|---|---|---|---|
| Aie A Mwana.................... | 7" ...... | Demon .... | D1010.......... | 1981 | £2........ | £5 | |
| Aie A Mwana.................... | 7" ...... | Deram .......... | DM446 ............ | 1981 | £1.50........ | £4 | |
| Aie A Mwana.................... | 12" ...... | Deram .......... | DMX446 ............ | 1981 | £2.50........ | £6 | |
| Cruel Summer '89 .................... | CD-s .. | London .......... | NANCD19 ............ | 1989 | £2........ | £5 | |
| Help.................... | CD-s .. | London .......... | LONCD222 ............ | 1989 | £2........ | £5 | ..........with French & Saunders |
| I Can't Help It .................... | CD-s .. | London .......... | NANCD15 ............ | 1988 | £2........ | £5 | |
| I Want You Back .................... | CD-s .. | London .......... | NANCD16 ............ | 1988 | £2........ | £5 | |
| It's Only Your Love .................... | CD-s .. | London .......... | NANCD21 ............ | 1990 | £2........ | £5 | |
| Long Train Running .................... | CD-s .. | London .......... | NANCD24 ............ | 1991 | £2........ | £5 | |
| Love In The First Degree .................... | CD-s .. | London .......... | 0804802 ............ | 1988 | £6........ | £15 | ..........CD video |
| Love, Truth And Honesty .................... | CD-s .. | London .......... | NANCD17 ............ | 1988 | £2........ | £5 | |
| Nathan Jones.................... | CD-s .. | London .......... | NANCD18 ............ | 1988 | £2........ | £5 | |
| Preacher Man .................... | CD-s .. | London .......... | NANCD23 ............ | 1990 | £2........ | £5 | |
| Wow .................... | CD ..... | London .......... | 8280612 ............ | 1987 | £5........ | £12 | |

## BANCHEE

| | | | | | | | | |
|---|---|---|---|---|---|---|---|---|
| Banchee | LP | Atlantic | 8240 | 1969 | £8 | £20 | | US |
| Thinkin' | LP | Polydor | 244066 | 1971 | £20 | £40 | | US |

## BANCO

| | | | | | | | | |
|---|---|---|---|---|---|---|---|---|
| Banco Del Mutuo Soccorso | LP | Orizzonte | ORL8041 | 1972 | £5 | £12 | | Italian |
| Carofano Rosso | LP | Orizzonte | ORL8334 | 1976 | £5 | £12 | | Italian |
| Come In Un Ultima Cena | LP | Manticore | 28004 | 1976 | £8 | £20 | | |
| Darwin | LP | Orizzonte | ORL8094 | 1972 | £10 | £25 | | Italian |
| Lo Sono Nato Libero | LP | Orizzonte | ORL8202 | 1973 | £8 | £20 | | Italian |

## BAND

| | | | | | | | | |
|---|---|---|---|---|---|---|---|---|
| Across The Great Divide | CD | Capitol | | 1994 | £6 | £15 | | US promo sampler |
| Band | LP | Capitol | EST132 | 1969 | £4 | £10 | | |
| Band On CD | CD | Capitol | DPRO79379 | 1990 | £8 | £20 | | US promo sampler |
| Cahoots | LP | Capitol | EAST651 | 1971 | £4 | £10 | | |
| Cahoots | CD | Capitol | CZ138 | 1989 | £5 | £12 | | |
| Islands | CD | Capitol | CZ406 | 1991 | £5 | £12 | | |
| Moondog Matinee | LP | Capitol | ESW11241 | 1973 | £4 | £10 | | |
| Moondog Matinee | CD | Capitol | CZ407 | 1991 | £5 | £12 | | |
| Music From Big Pink | LP | Capitol | (S)T2955 | 1968 | £4 | £10 | | |
| Music From Big Pink | CD | Capitol | CDP7460692 | 1987 | £5 | £12 | | |
| Music From Big Pink | CD | Mobile Fidelity | UDCD527 | 1989 | £6 | £15 | | US audiophile |
| Rock Of Ages | LP | Capitol | ESTSP11 | 1972 | £5 | £12 | | double |
| Rock Of Ages | CD | Capitol | CDP7466172 | 1987 | £5 | £12 | | |
| Stage Fright | LP | Capitol | EASW425 | 1970 | £4 | £10 | | |
| Stage Fright | CD | Capitol | CZ405 | 1991 | £5 | £12 | | |
| Stage Fright | CD | DCC | GZS1061 | 1994 | £6 | £15 | | US audiophile |

## BAND AID

| | | | | | | | | |
|---|---|---|---|---|---|---|---|---|
| Do They Know It's Christmas? | 7" | Mercury | FEEDP1 | 1985 | £2 | £5 | | shaped picture disc |

## BAND OF ANGELS

A Band of Angels wore straw boaters to emphasize their Harrow origins, and it would have been surprising if at least some of them had not achieved success. First up was singer Mike D'Abo, who became the lead singer with Manfred Mann after the departure of Paul Jones. Later, however, the group's guitarist and manager founded EG management, amongst whose signings were King Crimson and Roxy Music.

| | | | | | | | | |
|---|---|---|---|---|---|---|---|---|
| Gonna Make A Woman Of You | 7" | United Artists | UP1066 | 1964 | £6 | £12 | | |
| Invitation | 7" EP | Pye | PNV24162 | 1966 | £15 | £30 | | French |
| Invitation | 7" | Piccadilly | 7N35292 | 1966 | £7.50 | £15 | | |
| Leave It To Me | 7" | Piccadilly | 7N35279 | 1966 | £6 | £12 | | |
| Not True As Yet | 7" | United Artists | UP1049 | 1964 | £6 | £12 | | |
| She'll Never Be You | 7" EP | United Artists | 36050 | 1964 | £15 | £30 | | French |

## BANDOGGS

| | | | | | | | | |
|---|---|---|---|---|---|---|---|---|
| Bandoggs | LP | Transatlantic | LTRA504 | 1978 | £5 | £12 | | |

## BANGLES

| | | | | | | | | |
|---|---|---|---|---|---|---|---|---|
| Be With You | CD-s | CBS | BANGSD6 | 1989 | £2 | £5 | | picture disc |
| Eternal Flame | CD-s | CBS | BANGSC5 | 1989 | £2 | £5 | | |
| Everything | CD | CBS | 4629792 | 1988 | £5 | £12 | | |
| Everything | CD | Columbia | CSK1520 | 1988 | £6 | £15 | US promo picture disc |
| Greatest Hits | CD | CBS | 4666869 | 1990 | £5 | £12 | | picture disc |
| Hazy Shade Of Winter | CD-s | CBS | BANGSC3 | 1988 | £2 | £5 | | |
| I'll Set You Free | CD-s | CBS | BANGSC7 | 1989 | £2 | £5 | | |
| In Your Room | CD-s | CBS | BANGSC4 | 1988 | £2 | £5 | | |
| Walk Like An Egyptian | CD-s | CBS | BANGSC8 | 1990 | £2 | £5 | | |

## BANGOR FLYING CIRCUS

| | | | | | | | |
|---|---|---|---|---|---|---|---|
| Bangor Flying Circus | LP | Stateside | SSL5022 | 1969 | £4 | £10 | |

## BANGS

Debbi and Vicki Peterson and Susanna Hoffs first recorded as the Bangs, before expanding both the size of the group and its name – becoming the Bangles.

| | | | | | | | | |
|---|---|---|---|---|---|---|---|---|
| Getting Out Of Hand | 7" | Downkiddie | 001 | 1981 | £12.50 | £25 | | US |

## BANJO BOYS

| | | | | | | | |
|---|---|---|---|---|---|---|---|
| Hey Mr. Banjo | 7" | Capitol | CL14298 | 1955 | £1.50 | £4 | |

## BANJO KINGS

| | | | | | | | |
|---|---|---|---|---|---|---|---|
| Nostalgia Revisited | LP | Good Time Jazz | LAG12174 | 1959 | £5 | £12 | |

## BANKS, BESSIE

| | | | | | | | |
|---|---|---|---|---|---|---|---|
| Go Now | 7" | Red Bird | BC106 | 1964 | £7.50 | £15 | |
| Go Now | 7" | Soul City | SC105 | 1968 | £2 | £5 | |
| I Can't Make It | 7" | Verve | VS563 | 1967 | £6 | £12 | |

## BANKS, DARRELL

| | | | | | | | | |
|---|---|---|---|---|---|---|---|---|
| Angel Baby | 7" | Atlantic | 584120 | 1967 | £7.50 | £15 | | |
| Here To Stay | LP | Stax | SXATS1011 | 1969 | £6 | £15 | | |
| Just Because Your Love Is Gone | 7" | Stax | STAX124 | 1969 | £6 | £12 | | |
| Open The Door To Your Heart | 7" | London | HL10070 | 1966 | £100 | £200 | | demo only, best auctioned |
| Open The Door To Your Heart | 7" | Stateside | SS536 | 1966 | £5 | £10 | | |

## BANKS, HOMER

| | | | | | | | |
|---|---|---|---|---|---|---|---|
| Hooked By Love | 7" | Liberty | LIB12060 | 1967 | £5 | £10 | |
| Lot Of Love | 7" | Liberty | LIB12028 | 1966 | £6 | £12 | |
| Me Or Your Mama | 7" | Minit | MLF11015 | 1969 | £2 | £5 | |
| Round The Clock Lover Man | 7" | Minit | MLF11004 | 1968 | £2 | £5 | |
| Sixty Minutes Of Your Love | 7" | Liberty | LBF15392 | 1970 | £1.50 | £4 | |
| Sixty Minutes Of Your Love | 7" | Liberty | LIB12047 | 1967 | £5 | £10 | |
| Sixty Minutes Of Your Love | 7" | Minit | MLF11007 | 1968 | £1.50 | £4 | |

## BANKS, LARRY

| | | | | | | | |
|---|---|---|---|---|---|---|---|
| I Don't Wanna Do It | 7" | Stateside | SS579 | 1967 | £2.50 | £6 | |

## BANKS, LLOYD

| | | | | | | | |
|---|---|---|---|---|---|---|---|
| We'll Meet Again | 7" | Reaction | 591008 | 1966 | £2 | £5 | |

## BANKS, PETER

| | | | | | | | |
|---|---|---|---|---|---|---|---|
| Peter Banks | LP | Sovereign | SVNA7256 | 1973 | £8 | £20 | |

## BANNED

| | | | | | | | |
|---|---|---|---|---|---|---|---|
| Little Girl | 7" | Can't Eat | EAT1UP | 1977 | £2.50 | £6 | |

## BANSHEES

Bryan Ferry sung with the Banshees for a time, although he cannot be heard on any of the group's records.

| | | | | | | | |
|---|---|---|---|---|---|---|---|
| Big Buildin' | 7" | Columbia | DB7530 | 1965 | £7.50 | £15 | |
| I Got A Woman | 7" | Columbia | DB7361 | 1964 | £7.50 | £15 | |
| Yes Indeed | 7" | Columbia | DB7752 | 1965 | £7.5 | £15 | |

## BANTAMS

| | | | | | | | |
|---|---|---|---|---|---|---|---|
| Beware The Bantams | LP | Warner Bros | W(S)1625 | 1966 | £6 | £15 | US |
| Over You | 7" EP | Warner Bros | WEP1448 | 1966 | £5 | £10 | French |

## BARA MENYN

| | | | | | | | |
|---|---|---|---|---|---|---|---|
| Bara Menyn | 7" EP | Wren | WRE1065 | 1969 | £7.50 | £15 | |
| Rhagor O'r Bara Menyn | 7" EP | Wren | WRE1072 | 1969 | £7.50 | £15 | |

## BARBARA & BRENDA

| | | | | | | | |
|---|---|---|---|---|---|---|---|
| Never Love A Robin | 7" | Direction | 583799 | 1968 | £2 | £5 | |

## BARBARIANS

| | | | | | | | |
|---|---|---|---|---|---|---|---|
| Are You A Boy Or Are You A Girl | 7" EP | Vogue | INT18027 | 1965 | £50 | £100 | French |
| Are You A Boy Or Are You A Girl | 7" | Stateside | SS449 | 1965 | £7.50 | £15 | |
| Barbarians | LP | Laurie | LLP/SLP2033 | 1966 | £25 | £50 | US |
| Moulty | 7" | Stateside | SS497 | 1966 | £6 | £12 | |

## BARBARIN, PAUL

| | | | | | | | |
|---|---|---|---|---|---|---|---|
| New Orleans Band | 10" LP | Vogue | LDE013 | 1952 | £8 | £20 | |
| New Orleans Jazz | LP | London | LTZK15032 | 1957 | £6 | £15 | |

## BARBARIN, PAUL & PUNCH MILLER

| | | | | | | | |
|---|---|---|---|---|---|---|---|
| Jazz At Preservation Hall Vol. 4 | LP | London | HAK/SHK8164 | 1964 | £4 | £10 | |

## BARBECUE BOB

| | | | | | | | |
|---|---|---|---|---|---|---|---|
| Georgia Blues No. 1 | LP | Kokomo | K1002 | 1967 | £20 | £40 | |

## BARBEE, JOHN HENRY

| | | | | | | | |
|---|---|---|---|---|---|---|---|
| Portraits In Blues Vol. 9 | LP | Storyville | 670171 | 1967 | £4 | £10 | |

## BARBER, CHRIS

| | | | | | | | |
|---|---|---|---|---|---|---|---|
| American Jazz Band | LP | Columbia | 33SX1321/ SCX3376 | 1961 | £4 | £10 | |
| Band Box Vol. 1 | LP | Columbia | 33SX1158 | 1959 | £4 | £10 | |
| Band Box Vol. 2 | LP | Columbia | 33SX1245/ SCX3319 | 1960 | £4 | £10 | |
| Barber's Best | LP | Decca | LK4246 | 1958 | £4 | £10 | |
| Battersea Rain Dance | LP | Marmalade | 608009 | 1969 | £8 | £20 | |
| Battersea Rain Dance | LP | Polydor | 2384020 | 197– | £5 | £12 | |
| Battersea Rain Dance | 7" | Marmalade | 598013 | 1969 | £1.50 | £4 | |
| Best Of Chris Barber | LP | Ace Of Clubs | ACL1037 | 1960 | £4 | £10 | |
| Blues Book | LP | Columbia | 33SX1333/ SCX3384 | 1961 | £4 | £10 | |
| Catcall | 7" | Marmalade | 598005 | 1967 | £15 | £30 | |
| Chris Barber Plays Vol. 1 | 10" LP | Nixa | NJT500 | 1956 | £6 | £15 | |
| Chris Barber Plays Vol. 1 | 10" LP | Polygon | JTL3 | 1955 | £8 | £20 | |
| Chris Barber Plays Vol. 2 | 10" LP | Nixa | NJT502 | 1956 | £6 | £15 | |
| Chris Barber Plays Vol. 3 | 10" LP | Nixa | NJT505 | 1957 | £5 | £12 | |
| Chris Barber Plays Vol. 4 | 10" LP | Nixa | NJT508 | 1957 | £5 | £12 | |
| Chris Barber Skiffle Group | 7" EP | Pye | NJE1025 | 1957 | £5 | £10 | |
| Echoes Of Harlem | LP | Nixa | NJL1 | 1955 | £5 | £12 | |
| Finishing Straight | 7" | Columbia | DB7461 | 1965 | £7.50 | £15 | |
| In Berlin Vol. 1 | LP | Columbia | 33SX1189 | 1959 | £4 | £10 | |
| In Berlin Vol. 2 | LP | Columbia | | 1959 | £4 | £10 | |
| In Concert | LP | Nixa | NJL6 | 1957 | £4 | £10 | |
| In Concert Vol. 2 | LP | Pye | NJL15 | 1958 | £4 | £10 | |
| In Concert Vol. 3 | LP | Pye | NJL17 | 1958 | £4 | £10 | |

| Title | Format | Label | Cat. No. | Year | Price | Price | Notes |
|---|---|---|---|---|---|---|---|
| In Copenhagen | LP | Columbia | 33SX1274/ SCX3342 | 1961 | £4 | £10 | |
| Jazz Sacred And Secular | 10" LP | Columbia | 33S1112 | 1957 | £8 | £20 | |
| New Orleans Joys | 10" LP | Decca | LF1198 | 1954 | £8 | £20 | |
| Plus/Minus One | 7" EP | Polygon | JTE103 | 1956 | £2 | £5 | |

## BARBIERI, GATO

| Title | Format | Label | Cat. No. | Year | Price | Price | Notes |
|---|---|---|---|---|---|---|---|
| Caliente | LP | A&M | AMLH64597 | 1976 | £4 | £10 | |
| Chapter Four: Alive In New York | LP | Impulse | AQD9303 | 1975 | £5 | £12 | US |
| Chapter One: Latin America | LP | Impulse | AS9248 | 1973 | £5 | £12 | US |
| Chapter Three: Viva Emiliano | LP | Impulse | ASD9279 | 1974 | £5 | £12 | US |
| Chapter Two: Hasta Siempre | LP | Impulse | AS9263 | 1974 | £5 | £12 | US |
| El Pampero | LP | Philips | 6369418 | 1973 | £5 | £12 | |
| Fenix | LP | Philips | 6369409 | 1973 | £5 | £12 | |
| In Search Of Mystery | LP | ESP-Disk | 1049 | 1966 | £10 | £25 | US |
| Last Tango In Paris | LP | United Artists | UAGC29440 | 1973 | £5 | £12 | |
| Third World | LP | Philips | 6369403 | 1969 | £6 | £15 | |
| Under Fire | LP | Philips | 6369419 | 1973 | £5 | £12 | |

## BARCLAY, EDDIE

| Title | Format | Label | Cat. No. | Year | Price | Price | Notes |
|---|---|---|---|---|---|---|---|
| Eddie And Quincy | LP | Felsted | PDL85056 | 1959 | £4 | £10 | with Quincy Jones |
| James Dean – Music From His Films | 7" EP | Felsted | ESD3041 | 1957 | £2 | £5 | |

## BARCLAY, RUE & PEGGY DUNCAN

| Title | Format | Label | Cat. No. | Year | Price | Price | Notes |
|---|---|---|---|---|---|---|---|
| Tongue Tied Boy | 7" | London | HL8033 | 1954 | £7.50 | £15 | |

## BARCLAY JAMES HARVEST

| Title | Format | Label | Cat. No. | Year | Price | Price | Notes |
|---|---|---|---|---|---|---|---|
| Another Arable Parable | CD | Harvest | CZ16 | 1987 | £5 | £12 | |
| Barclay James Harvest | LP | Harvest | SHVL770 | 1970 | £4 | £10 | |
| Brother Thrush | 7" | Harvest | HAR5003 | 1969 | £2 | £5 | |
| Cheap The Bullet | CD-s | Polydor | PZCD67 | 1990 | £2 | £5 | |
| Concert For The People | CD | Polydor | 8000262 | 1983 | £5 | £12 | |
| Early Morning | 7" | Parlophone | R5693 | 1968 | £4 | £8 | |
| Gone To Earth | CD | Polydor | 8000922 | 1983 | £5 | £12 | |
| Harvest Years | CD | Nova Lepidoptera | | 1991 | £10 | £25 | double, fan club issue |
| Just A Day Away | 7" | Polydor | POPPX585 | 1983 | £1.50 | £4 | shaped picture disc |
| Live Tapes | CD | Polydor | 8215232 | 198– | £8 | £20 | double |
| Octoberon | CD | Polydor | 8219302 | 1984 | £5 | £12 | |
| Once Again | LP | Harvest | Q4SHVL0788 | 1971 | £6 | £15 | quad |
| Ring Of Changes | CD | Polydor | 8116382 | 1983 | £5 | £12 | |
| Taking Some Time On | 7" | Harvest | HAR5025 | 1970 | £1.50 | £4 | |
| Time Honoured Ghosts | CD | Polydor | 8315432 | 198– | £5 | £12 | |
| Turn Of The Tide | CD | Polydor | 8000132 | 1983 | £5 | £12 | |
| Victims Of Circumstance | CD | Polydor | 8179502 | 198– | £5 | £12 | |
| Victims Of Circumstance | 7" | Polydor | POSPP674 | 1984 | £1.50 | £4 | picture disc |
| Welcome To The Show | CD | Polydor | 8417512 | 1990 | £5 | £12 | |
| XII | CD | Polydor | 8219412 | 198– | £5 | £12 | |

## BARDENS, PETER

| Title | Format | Label | Cat. No. | Year | Price | Price | Notes |
|---|---|---|---|---|---|---|---|
| Answer | LP | Transatlantic | TRA222 | 1970 | £4 | £10 | |
| Peter Bardens | LP | Transatlantic | TRA243 | 1971 | £4 | £10 | |

## BARDOLINI, BAKADI

| Title | Format | Label | Cat. No. | Year | Price | Price | Notes |
|---|---|---|---|---|---|---|---|
| Songs | LP | private | | 1983 | £75 | £150 | Austrian |

## BARDOT, BRIGITTE

| Title | Format | Label | Cat. No. | Year | Price | Price | Notes |
|---|---|---|---|---|---|---|---|
| Brigitte Bardot | LP | Philips | BL7561 | 1963 | £15 | £30 | |
| Harley Davidson | 7" | Pye | 7N25450 | 1968 | £2.50 | £6 | |
| Mr. Sun | 7" | Vogue | VRS7018 | 1966 | £10 | £20 | |
| Mr. Sun | 7" | Vogue | VRS7018 | 1966 | £4 | £8 | picture sleeve |
| Very Private Affair | 7" EP | MGM | MGMEP768 | 1962 | £50 | £100 | |

## BARE, BOBBY

| Title | Format | Label | Cat. No. | Year | Price | Price | Notes |
|---|---|---|---|---|---|---|---|
| Detroit City | 7" EP | RCA | RCX7139 | 1964 | £2 | £5 | |
| Five Hundred Miles Away From Home | LP | RCA | LPM/LSP2835 | 1963 | £4 | £10 | US |
| I'm Hanging Up My Rifle | 7" | Top Rank | JAR310 | 1960 | £2.50 | £6 | |

## BARGE, GENE

| Title | Format | Label | Cat. No. | Year | Price | Price | Notes |
|---|---|---|---|---|---|---|---|
| Dance With Daddy G | LP | Checker | 2994 | 1965 | £8 | £20 | US |

## BARHAM, TINY

| Title | Format | Label | Cat. No. | Year | Price | Price | Notes |
|---|---|---|---|---|---|---|---|
| Tiny Barham | 10" LP | Audubon | | 195– | £8 | £20 | |

## BARK PSYCHOSIS

| Title | Format | Label | Cat. No. | Year | Price | Price | Notes |
|---|---|---|---|---|---|---|---|
| Nothing Feels I Know | CD-s | Cheree | CHEREE010CD | 1990 | £2 | £5 | |

## BARKAN, MARK

| Title | Format | Label | Cat. No. | Year | Price | Price | Notes |
|---|---|---|---|---|---|---|---|
| Pity The Woman | 7" | Stateside | SS2064 | 1967 | £2.50 | £6 | |

## BARKAYS

| Title | Format | Label | Cat. No. | Year | Price | Price | Notes |
|---|---|---|---|---|---|---|---|
| Black Rock | LP | Polydor | 2362003 | 1971 | £5 | £12 | |
| Cold Blooded | LP | Stax | STX1033 | 1976 | £4 | £10 | |
| Do You See What I See? | LP | Polydor | 2325087 | 1972 | £4 | £10 | |
| Give Everybody Some | 7" | Stax | 601025 | 1967 | £1.50 | £4 | |
| Gotta Groove | LP | Stax | STATS1009 | 1969 | £5 | £12 | |
| Hard Day's Night | 7" | Stax | 601036 | 1968 | £1.50 | £4 | |
| Soul Finger | LP | Atco | 228030 | 1969 | £5 | £12 | |

| | | | | | | | |
|---|---|---|---|---|---|---|---|
| Soul Finger | LP | Atlantic | K40184 | 1972 | £4 | £10 | |
| Soul Finger | 7" | Atlantic | 584244 | 1969 | £1.50 | £4 | |
| Soul Finger | 7" | Stax | 601014 | 1967 | £1.50 | £4 | |

## BARKEE, JOHN HENRY
| | | | | | | | |
|---|---|---|---|---|---|---|---|
| Portraits In Blues | LP | Storyville | SLP171 | 1965 | £5 | £12 | |

## BARKER, DAVE
| | | | | | | | |
|---|---|---|---|---|---|---|---|
| Prisoner Of Love | LP | Trojan | TRL127 | 1976 | £6 | £15 | |
| Prisoner Of Love | 7" | Punch | PH20 | 1970 | £1.50 | £4 | Busty & Upsetters B side |
| Shocks Of Mighty | 7" | Punch | PH25 | 1970 | £1.50 | £4 | |
| Shocks Of Mighty | 7" | Upsetter | US331 | 1970 | £1.50 | £4 | |
| Some Sympathy | 7" | Upsetter | US344 | 1970 | £1.50 | £4 | Untouchables B side |
| You Betray Me | 7" | Punch | PH22 | 1970 | £1.50 | £4 | |

## BARNABY BYE
| | | | | | | | |
|---|---|---|---|---|---|---|---|
| Room To Grow | LP | Atlantic | SD7273 | 1973 | £8 | £20 | US |

## BARNES, J. J.
| | | | | | | | |
|---|---|---|---|---|---|---|---|
| Baby Please Come Back Home | 7" | Stax | STAX130 | 1969 | £4 | £8 | |
| Daytripper | 7" | Polydor | 56722 | 1967 | £2.50 | £6 | |
| Rare Stamps | LP | Stax | SXATS1012 | 1969 | £8 | £20 | with Steve Mancha |

## BARNES, LLOYD
| | | | | | | | |
|---|---|---|---|---|---|---|---|
| Time Is Hard | 7" | Blue Beat | BB235 | 1964 | £6 | £12 | Buster's Allstars B side |

## BARNES, MAE
| | | | | | | | |
|---|---|---|---|---|---|---|---|
| Songs By Mae Barnes | 10" LP | Atlantic | ALS404 | 195– | £37.50 | £75 | US |

## BARNES, MYRA
| | | | | | | | |
|---|---|---|---|---|---|---|---|
| Message For The Soul Sisters | 12" | Urban | | 1988 | £2.50 | £6 | |

## BARNET, CHARLIE
| | | | | | | | |
|---|---|---|---|---|---|---|---|
| Cherokee | LP | Top Rank | 35037 | 1960 | £4 | £10 | |
| Classics In Jazz | LP | Capitol | LCT6018 | 1955 | £8 | £20 | |
| Dance Session | 10" LP | Columbia | 33C9024 | 1956 | £8 | £20 | |
| Hop On The Skyliner | LP | Brunswick | LAT8094 | 1956 | £8 | £20 | |

## BARNET, ERIC
| | | | | | | | |
|---|---|---|---|---|---|---|---|
| Horse | 7" | Gas | GAS100 | 1969 | £1.50 | £4 | |
| Quaker City | 7" | Crab | CRAB37 | 1969 | £1.50 | £4 | |
| Te Ta Toe | 7" | Gas | GAS106 | 1969 | £1.50 | £4 | Milton Boothe B side |

## BARNETT, DON
| | | | | | | | |
|---|---|---|---|---|---|---|---|
| Maria | LP | Ovation | OV1725 | 1976 | £8 | £20 | |

## BARNUM, H. B.
| | | | | | | | |
|---|---|---|---|---|---|---|---|
| Big Voice Of Barnum | LP | RCA | RD/SF7500 | 1962 | £4 | £10 | |
| Everybody Loves H.B. | LP | RCA | RD/SF7543 | 1963 | £4 | £10 | |
| Great | 7" EP | RCA | RCX7147 | 1964 | £25 | £50 | |
| Lost Love | 7" | Fontana | H299 | 1961 | £1.50 | £4 | |
| Record | 7" | Capitol | CL15391 | 1965 | £5 | £10 | |

## BAROCK & ROLL ENSEMBLE
Eine Kleine Beatlemusik by the Barock and Roll Ensemble consists of tunes written by the Beatles arranged for a small group of strings as though the music was by Mozart. The joke – perpetrated by musicologist Fritz Spiegl – is a good one, and the record works as music too. The B side is less successful, however; Spiegl knows his Mozart but not his rock music and his arrangements of themes by Wagner as if they were pieces by the Shadows are simply feeble.

| | | | | | | | |
|---|---|---|---|---|---|---|---|
| Eine Kleine Beatlemusik | 7" EP | HMV | 7EG8887 | 1965 | £2 | £5 | |

## BARON, CARL & THE CHEETAHS
| | | | | | | | |
|---|---|---|---|---|---|---|---|
| Beg Borrow Or Steal | 7" | Columbia | DB7162 | 1963 | £4 | £8 | |

## BARON & HIS POUNDING PIANO
| | | | | | | | |
|---|---|---|---|---|---|---|---|
| Is A Bluebird Blue | 7" | Sue | WI398 | 1965 | £7.50 | £15 | with the V.I.P.s |

## BARONS
| | | | | | | | |
|---|---|---|---|---|---|---|---|
| Don't Walk Out | 7" | London | HLP8391 | 1957 | £700 | £1000 | best auctioned |

## BARONS (2)
| | | | | | | | |
|---|---|---|---|---|---|---|---|
| Cossack | 7" | Oriole | CB1608 | 1961 | £2 | £5 | |
| Samurai | 7" | Oriole | CB1620 | 1961 | £4 | £8 | |

## BAROQUES
| | | | | | | | |
|---|---|---|---|---|---|---|---|
| Barbarians With Love | LP | Job | 1002 | 1966 | £6 | £15 | Dutch |
| Baroques | LP | Whamm | PS10001 | 1966 | £15 | £30 | Dutch |
| With Love | LP | Whamm | PS10003 | 1967 | £6 | £15 | Dutch |

## BAROQUES (2)
| | | | | | | | |
|---|---|---|---|---|---|---|---|
| Baroques | LP | Chess | (S)1516 | 1967 | £20 | £40 | US |

## BARRACUDAS
| | | | | | | | |
|---|---|---|---|---|---|---|---|
| Plane View | LP | Justice | 143 | 1968 | £100 | £200 | US |

## BARRACUDAS (2)

| Title | Format | Label | Cat. No. | Year | | | Notes |
|---|---|---|---|---|---|---|---|
| 1965 Again | 7" | Zonophone | Z11 | 1980 | £2.50 | £6 | |
| His Last Summer | 7" | Zonophone | Z8 | 1980 | £2.50 | £6 | |
| I Can't Pretend | 7" | Zonophone | Z17 | 1981 | £2.50 | £6 | |
| I Want My Woody Back | 7" | Cells | CELLOUT1 | 1979 | £4 | £8 | |
| Summer Fun | 7" | Zonophone | Z5 | 1980 | £2.50 | £6 | with sticker sheet |

## BARRETT, RICHARD

| Title | Format | Label | Cat. No. | Year | | |
|---|---|---|---|---|---|---|
| Come Softly To Me | 7" | HMV | POP609 | 1959 | £2 | £5 |

## BARRETT, RITCHIE

| Title | Format | Label | Cat. No. | Year | | |
|---|---|---|---|---|---|---|
| Some Other Guy | 7" | London | HLK9552 | 1962 | £10 | £20 |

## BARRETT, SYD

Syd Barrett was eased out of the Pink Floyd due to his increasingly unreliable behaviour – a guitarist with a tendency to stand still on stage without actually playing anything was something of a liability. Nevertheless, the rest of the Floyd bore him no malice and were happy to turn up to lend support to Barrett's solo recordings (as did Soft Machine too). Whether these records are the work of a brilliant eccentric or merely the last gasp of semi-coherency from an unmitigated loony probably depends on the listener's point of view.

| Title | Format | Label | Cat. No. | Year | | | Notes |
|---|---|---|---|---|---|---|---|
| Barrett | LP | Harvest | SHSP4007 | 1970 | £8 | £20 | |
| Madcap Laughs | LP | Harvest | SHVL765 | 1970 | £8 | £20 | |
| Madcap Laughs/Barrett | LP | Harvest | SHDW404 | 1974 | £6 | £15 | double |
| Octopus | 7" | Harvest | HAR5009 | 1969 | £30 | £60 | |
| Peel Sessions | CD-s | Strange Fruit | SFPSCD043 | 1988 | £2 | £5 | |

## BARRETTO, RAY

| Title | Format | Label | Cat. No. | Year | | |
|---|---|---|---|---|---|---|
| Acid | LP | London | HA/SH8383 | 1969 | £6 | £15 |
| Acid | 7" | London | HL10262 | 1969 | £1.50 | £4 |
| El Watusi | LP | Island | ILP946 | 1967 | £15 | £30 |
| El Watusi | 7" | Columbia | DB7051 | 1963 | £2.50 | £6 |
| El Watusi | 7" | Columbia | DB7684 | 1965 | £2 | £5 |

## BARRIER

| Title | Format | Label | Cat. No. | Year | | |
|---|---|---|---|---|---|---|
| Georgie Brown | 7" | Eyemark | EMS1013 | 1968 | £30 | £60 |
| Spot The Lights | 7" | Philips | BF1731 | 1968 | £7.50 | £15 |
| Tide Is Turning | 7" | Philips | BF1692 | 1968 | £1.50 | £4 |

## BARRON KNIGHTS

| Title | Format | Label | Cat. No. | Year | | | Notes |
|---|---|---|---|---|---|---|---|
| Barron Knights | LP | Columbia | SX6007 | 1966 | £4 | £10 | |
| Call Up The Groups | LP | Columbia | 33SX1048 | 1964 | £5 | £12 | |
| Guying The Top Pops | 7" EP | Columbia | SEG8424 | 1965 | £2 | £5 | |
| Lazy Fat People | 7" EP | Festival | FX1537 | 196– | £4 | £8 | French |
| Scribed | LP | Columbia | SX/SCX6176 | 1967 | £4 | £10 | |
| Those Versatile Barron Knights | 7" EP | Columbia | SEG8526 | 1966 | £2 | £5 | |

## BARROW POETS

The Barrow Poets were a poetry and music group, a little like the Liverpool Scene, but with much less of a rock sound. Where the Liverpool Scene played on the John Peel programme, the Barrow Poets would have turned up on Radio 4. Essentially the records are an extension of the fifties and sixties jazz-and-poetry experiments, in which the words are by far the most important element. Fortunately, they are always well worth hearing.

| Title | Format | Label | Cat. No. | Year | | |
|---|---|---|---|---|---|---|
| At The Printer's Devil | 7" EP | Barrow | BR1 | 1967 | £10 | £20 |
| Barrow Collection | LP | Argo | PLP1072 | 197– | £6 | £15 |
| Entertainment Of Poetry And Music | LP | Argo | R.G360 | 1963 | £10 | £25 |
| Folk Rhymes Tunes And Verses | LP | Fontana | STL5479 | 1968 | £8 | £20 |
| Joker | LP | RCA | SF8110 | 1970 | £6 | £15 |
| Letter In A Bottle | 7" | Fontana | TF939 | 1968 | £1.50 | £4 |
| Magic Egg | LP | Argo | ZSW511 | 1972 | £6 | £15 |
| Outpatients | LP | Argo | ZSW508 | 1972 | £6 | £15 |

## BARRY, DAVE & SARAH BERNER

| Title | Format | Label | Cat. No. | Year | | |
|---|---|---|---|---|---|---|
| Out Of This World With Flying Saucers | 7" | London | HLU8324 | 1956 | £20 | £40 |

## BARRY, JOE

| Title | Format | Label | Cat. No. | Year | | |
|---|---|---|---|---|---|---|
| Fool To Care | 7" EP | Mercury | ZEP10130 | 1962 | £50 | £100 |
| I Started Loving You Again | 7" | Stateside | SS2127 | 1969 | £1.50 | £4 |
| I'm A Fool To Care | 7" | Mercury | AMT1149 | 1961 | £1.50 | £4 |

## BARRY, JOHN

| Title | Format | Label | Cat. No. | Year | | | Notes |
|---|---|---|---|---|---|---|---|
| 007 | 7" | Ember | EMBS243 | 1967 | £1.50 | £4 | |
| 007 | 7" | Ember | EMBS243 | 1967 | £2 | £5 | picture sleeve |
| Americans | LP | Polydor | 2383405 | 1976 | £5 | £12 | |
| Barry Theme Successes | 7" EP | Columbia | SEG8255 | 1963 | £5 | £10 | |
| Beat For Beatniks | 7" | Columbia | DB4446 | 1960 | £1.50 | £4 | |
| Big Beat | 7" EP | Parlophone | GEP8737 | 1958 | £10 | £20 | |
| Big Guitar | 7" | Parlophone | R4418 | 1958 | £7.50 | £15 | |
| Black Stockings | 7" | Columbia | DB4554 | 1960 | £1.50 | £4 | |
| Boom | LP | MCA | MUPS360 | 1969 | £30 | £60 | with Georgie Fame |
| Chase | LP | CBS | (S)BPG62665 | 1966 | £10 | £25 | |
| Concert John Barry | LP | Polydor | 2383156 | 1971 | £4 | £10 | |
| Cutty Sark | 7" | Columbia | DB4806 | 1962 | £1.50 | £4 | |
| Deadfall | LP | Stateside | (S)SL10263 | 1968 | £15 | £30 | |
| Diamonds Are For Ever | LP | United Artists | UAS29216 | 1971 | £4 | £10 | |
| Diamonds Are For Ever | 7" | Polydor | 2058216 | 1972 | £2.50 | £6 | |
| Every Which Way | 7" | Parlophone | R4394 | 1958 | £12.50 | £25 | |
| Farrago | 7" | Parlophone | R4488 | 1958 | £1.50 | £4 | |

| Title | Format | Label | Cat. No. | Year | | | Notes |
|---|---|---|---|---|---|---|---|
| Four In The Morning | LP | Ember | NR56088 | 1965 | £15 | £30 | |
| From Russia With Love | LP | United Artists | (S)ULP1052 | 1963 | £5 | £12 | |
| From Russia With Love | 7" EP | United Artists | UEP1011 | 1965 | £6 | £12 | |
| From Russia With Love | 7" | Ember | EMBS181 | 1963 | £1.50 | £4 | |
| From Russia With Love | 7" | Ember | EMBS181 | 1963 | £4 | £8 | picture sleeve |
| Goldfinger | LP | United Artists | (S)ULP1076 | 1964 | £5 | £12 | |
| Goldfinger | 7" EP | United Artists | UEP1012 | 1965 | £6 | £12 | |
| Goldfinger | 7" | United Artists | UP1068 | 1964 | £1.50 | £4 | |
| Hit And Miss | 7" | Columbia | DB4414 | 1960 | £1.50 | £4 | |
| Human Jungle | 7" | Columbia | DB7003 | 1963 | £1.50 | £4 | |
| Human Jungle | 7" | Columbia | DB7003 | 1963 | £4 | £8 | picture sleeve |
| Ingersoll Trendsetters | 7" | Lyntone | LYN378 | 1963 | £5 | £10 | flexi |
| Ipcress File | LP | CBS | BPG62530 | 1966 | £10 | £25 | |
| James Bond Collection | LP | United Artists | UAD60027/8 | 1973 | £6 | £15 | Double |
| James Bond Is Back | 7" EP | Ember | EMBEP4551 | 1964 | £5 | £10 | |
| James Bond Theme | 7" | CBS | WB730 | 1968 | £2 | £5 | Ray Conniff B side |
| James Bond Theme | 7" | Columbia | DB4898 | 1962 | £1.50 | £4 | |
| John Barry Sound | 7" EP | Columbia | SEG8069 | 1961 | £7.50 | £15 | |
| King Rat | LP | Fontana | (S)TL5302 | 1966 | £10 | £25 | |
| Kinky | 7" | Ember | EMBS178 | 1963 | £1.50 | £4 | |
| Knack | LP | United Artists | ULP1104 | 1965 | £10 | £25 | |
| Last Valley | LP | Probe | SPB1027 | 1971 | £10 | £25 | |
| Lion In Winter | LP | CBS | 70049 | 1969 | £8 | £20 | |
| Lion In Winter | 7" | CBS | 3935 | 1969 | £6 | £12 | |
| Little John | 7" | Parlophone | R4560 | 1959 | £1.50 | £4 | |
| London Theme | 7" | Ember | EMBS183 | 1963 | £1.50 | £4 | |
| Loneliness Of Autumn | 7" EP | Ember | EMBEP4544 | 1964 | £5 | £10 | |
| Long John | 7" | Parlophone | R4530 | 1959 | £1.50 | £4 | |
| Magnificent Seven | 7" | Columbia | DB4598 | 1961 | £1.50 | £4 | |
| Man Alone | 7" | CBS | 201747 | 1965 | £2.50 | £6 | |
| Man In The Middle | LP | Stateside | (S)SL10087 | 1964 | £20 | £40 | |
| Man In The Middle | 7" | Stateside | SS296 | 1964 | £5 | £10 | |
| March Of The Manderins | 7" | Columbia | DB4941 | 1962 | £2 | £5 | |
| Meets Chad And Jeremy | LP | Ember | NR5032 | 1965 | £6 | £15 | |
| Menace | 7" | Columbia | DB4659 | 1961 | £1.50 | £4 | |
| Music Of John Barry | LP | CBS | 22014 | 1976 | £5 | £12 | Double |
| Never Let Go | 7" | Columbia | DB4480 | 1960 | £1.50 | £4 | |
| On Her Majesty's Secret Service | LP | United Artists | UAS29020 | 1969 | £10 | £25 | gatefold sleeve |
| On Her Majesty's Secret Service | 7" | CBS | 4680 | 1969 | £4 | £8 | |
| Pancho | 7" | Parlophone | R4453 | 1958 | £2 | £5 | |
| Play It Again | LP | Polydor | 2383300 | 1974 | £4 | £10 | |
| Plays 007 | LP | Ember | NR5025 | 1964 | £8 | £20 | |
| Quiller Memorandum | LP | CBS | 62869 | 1966 | £8 | £20 | with Matt Monro |
| Ready When You Are JB | LP | CBS | 63952 | 1970 | £4 | £10 | |
| Revisited | LP | Ember | SE8008 | 1971 | £6 | £15 | |
| Seance On A Wet Afternoon | 7" | United Artists | UP1060 | 1964 | £6 | £12 | |
| Seven Faces | 7" | Columbia | DB7414 | 1964 | £6 | £12 | |
| Starfire | 7" | Columbia | DB4699 | 1961 | £1.50 | £4 | |
| Stringbeat | LP | Columbia | 33SX1358/ SCX3401 | 1961 | £15 | £30 | |
| Syndicate | 7" | CBS | 201822 | 1965 | £5 | £10 | |
| Thunderball | LP | United Artists | (S)ULP1110 | 1965 | £5 | £12 | |
| Thunderball | 7" EP | United Artists | UEP1015 | 1966 | £5 | £10 | |
| Twelfth Street Rag | 7" | Parlophone | R4582 | 1959 | £5 | £10 | |
| Walk Don't Run | 7" | Columbia | DB4505 | 1960 | £1.50 | £4 | |
| Watch Your Step | 7" | Columbia | DB4746 | 1961 | £1.50 | £4 | |
| Wednesday's Child | 7" | CBS | 202451 | 1967 | £2.50 | £6 | |
| Whisperers | LP | United Artists | (S)ULP1168 | 1967 | £15 | £30 | |
| Wrong Box | LP | Mainstream | 5/S6088 | 1966 | £75 | £150 | US |
| You Only Live Twice | LP | United Artists | (S)ULP1171 | 1967 | £5 | £12 | |
| You Only Live Twice | 7" | CBS | 2825 | 1967 | £2.50 | £6 | |
| Zip Zip | 7" | Parlophone | R4363 | 1957 | £20 | £40 | |
| Zulu | LP | Ember | NR5012 | 1964 | £8 | £20 | |
| Zulu Stamp | 7" | Ember | EMBS185 | 1963 | £1.50 | £4 | |
| Zulu Stamp | 7" | Ember | EMBS185 | 1963 | £2.50 | £6 | picture sleeve |

## BARRY, LEN

| Title | Format | Label | Cat. No. | Year | | | Notes |
|---|---|---|---|---|---|---|---|
| 1-2-3 | LP | Brunswick | LAT8637 | 1965 | £6 | £15 | |
| 1-2-3 | 7" EP | Brunswick | 10672 | 1965 | £5 | £10 | French |
| 1-2-3 | 7" EP | Decca | 60001 | 1965 | £5 | £10 | French |
| 1-2-3 | 7" | Brunswick | 05942 | 1965 | £1.50 | £4 | |
| Having A Good Time | 7" EP | Cameo Parkway | CPE556 | 1966 | £4 | £8 | with the Dovells |
| Hearts Are Trumps | 7" | Cameo Parkway | P969 | 1965 | £4 | £8 | |
| It's A Crying Shame | 7" EP | Decca | 60005 | 1966 | £4 | £8 | French |
| It's That Time Of The Year | 7" | Brunswick | 05962 | 1966 | £1.50 | £4 | |
| Moving Finger Writes | 7" | RCA | RCA1588 | 1967 | £1.50 | £4 | |
| My Kind Of Soul | LP | RCA | LSP/LSP3823 | 1967 | £4 | £10 | US |
| Sings With The Dovells | LP | Cameo Parkway | C1082 | 1966 | £4 | £10 | |

## BARRY, MARGARET

| Title | Format | Label | Cat. No. | Year | | | Notes |
|---|---|---|---|---|---|---|---|
| Come Back Paddy Reilly | LP | Emerald | GEM1003 | 1968 | £5 | £12 | |

## BARRY, MARGARET & MICHAEL GORMAN

| Title | Format | Label | Cat. No. | Year | | | Notes |
|---|---|---|---|---|---|---|---|
| Blarney Stone | LP | XTRA | XTRA5037 | 1967 | £5 | £12 | |
| Her Mantle So Green | LP | Topic | 12T123 | 1958 | £8 | £20 | |

| | | | | | | |
|---|---|---|---|---|---|---|
| Her Mantle So Green | LP | Topic | 12T123 | 1965 £5 | £12 | .. reissue with different sleeve |
| Ireland's Queen Of The Tinkers Sings | LP | Top Rank | 25020 | 1960 £10 | £25 | |
| Margaret Barry And Michael Gorman | LP | Folkways | FW8729 | 1975 £5 | £12 | US |

## BARRY, SANDRA

'Really Gonna Shake' by Sandra Barry and the Boys represents the first recording by the group that became (without Ms Barry) the Action.

| | | | | | | |
|---|---|---|---|---|---|---|
| End Of The Line | 7" | Pye | 7N15753 | 1965 £2 | £5 | |
| Question | 7" | Pye | 7N15840 | 1965 £2 | £5 | |
| Really Gonna Shake | 7" | Decca | F11851 | 1964 £5 | £10 | with The Boys |
| Stop Thief | 7" | Pye | 7N17102 | 1966 £2 | £5 | |

## BARRY & THE TAMERLANES

| | | | | | | |
|---|---|---|---|---|---|---|
| Butterfly | 7" | Warner Bros | WB124 | 1964 £1.50 | £4 | |
| I Wonder What She's Doing Tonight | 7" | Warner Bros | WB116 | 1963 £7.50 | £15 | |
| I Wonder What She's Doing Tonight | 7" | A&M | W406 | 1963 £20 | £40 | US |
| What She's Doing Tonight | 7" EP | Warner Bros | WEP1429 | 1964 £20 | £40 | French |

## BARRY SISTERS

| | | | | | | |
|---|---|---|---|---|---|---|
| Baby Come A Little Closer | 7" | London | HLA8248 | 1956 £10 | £20 | |
| Intrigue | 7" | London | HLA8304 | 1956 £10 | £20 | |

## BARRY SISTERS (2)

| | | | | | | |
|---|---|---|---|---|---|---|
| Jo Jo | 7" | Decca | F11141 | 1959 £1.50 | £4 | |
| Tall Paul | 7" | Decca | F11118 | 1959 £1.50 | £4 | |

## BART, LIONEL

| | | | | | | |
|---|---|---|---|---|---|---|
| Isn't This Where We Came In | LP | Deram | DML/SML1028 | 1967 £5 | £12 | |

## BARTHOLOMEW, DAVE

| | | | | | | |
|---|---|---|---|---|---|---|
| Fats Domino Presents Dave Bartholomew | LP | Imperial | LP9162/LP12076 | 1961 £10 | £25 | US |
| New Orleans House Party | LP | Imperial | LP9217/LP12217 | 1963 £10 | £25 | US |

## BARTLEY, CHRIS

| | | | | | | |
|---|---|---|---|---|---|---|
| I Found A Goodie | 7" | Bell | BLL1031 | 1968 £2 | £5 | |
| Sweetest Thing This Side Of Heaven | 7" | Cameo Parkway | P101 | 1962 £20 | £40 | |

## BARTOK

| | | | | | | |
|---|---|---|---|---|---|---|
| Insanity | 7" | On | ON1 | 1982 £2 | £5 | |

## BARTON, EILEEN

| | | | | | | |
|---|---|---|---|---|---|---|
| Cry Me A River | 7" | Vogue Coral | Q72122 | 1956 £4 | £8 | |
| Fujiyama Mama | 7" | Vogue Coral | Q72075 | 1955 £7.50 | £15 | |
| Spring It Was | 7" | Vogue Coral | Q72205 | 1956 £1.50 | £4 | |
| Teenage Heart | 7" | Vogue Coral | Q72148 | 1956 £1.50 | £4 | |
| Too Close For Comfort | 7" | Vogue Coral | Q72250 | 1957 £1.50 | £4 | |
| Without Love | 7" | Vogue Coral | Q72270 | 1957 £1.50 | £4 | |
| Year We Fell In Love | 7" | Vogue Coral | Q72060 | 1955 £2 | £5 | |

## BARTY, ALAN

| | | | | | | |
|---|---|---|---|---|---|---|
| Barty's Bow | LP | Kettle | KOP4 | 1980 £4 | £10 | |

## BARTZ, GARY

| | | | | | | |
|---|---|---|---|---|---|---|
| Another Earth | LP | Milestone | MSP901 | 1971 £6 | £15 | |
| I've Known Rivers And Other Bodies | LP | Prestige | 66001 | 1974 £6 | £15 | US |

## BASES

| | | | | | | |
|---|---|---|---|---|---|---|
| Home Sweet Home | 7" | Coxsone | CS7062 | 1968 £5 | £10 | Marcia Griffiths B side |
| I Don't Mind | 7" | Studio One | SO2056 | 1968 £6 | £12 | ...Jackie Mittoo B side |

## BASHO, ROBBIE

| | | | | | | |
|---|---|---|---|---|---|---|
| Basho Sings! | LP | Takoma | C1012 | 1967 £4 | £10 | US |
| Falconer's Arm 1 | LP | Takoma | C1017 | 1967 £4 | £10 | US |
| Falconer's Arm 2 | LP | Takoma | C1018 | 1968 £4 | £10 | US |
| Grail And The Lotus | LP | Takoma | C1007 | 1967 £4 | £10 | US |
| Seal Of The Blue Lotus | LP | Takoma | C1005 | 1965 £4 | £10 | US |
| Song Of The Stallion | LP | Takoma | C1031 | 1972 £4 | £10 | US |
| Venus In Cancer | LP | Blue Thumb | BTS10 | 1969 £4 | £10 | US |
| Zarthus | LP | Vanguard | VSD79339 | 1972 £4 | £10 | US |

## BASIC BLACK & PEARL

| | | | | | | |
|---|---|---|---|---|---|---|
| There'll Come A Time | 7" | Bus Stop | BUS1030 | 1975 £2 | £5 | |

## BASIE, COUNT

| | | | | | | |
|---|---|---|---|---|---|---|
| April In Paris | LP | Columbia | 33CX10088 | 1957 £6 | £15 | |
| At Newport | LP | Columbia | 33CX10110 | 1958 £6 | £15 | |
| Atomic Mr. Basie | LP | Columbia | 33SX1084 | 1958 £6 | £15 | |
| Atomic Mr. Basie | LP | Columbia | 33SX1084/ SCX3265 | 1958 £5 | £12 | |
| Band Of Distinction | LP | HMV | CLP1428 | 1961 £4 | £10 | |
| Basie | LP | Columbia | 33CX10065 | 1957 £6 | £15 | |
| Basie At Birdland | LP | Columbia | 33SX1404 | 1961 £4 | £10 | |
| Basie Plays Hefti | LP | Columbia | 33SX1135 | 1958 £4 | £10 | |
| Basie's Back In Town | LP | Philips | BBL7141 | 1957 £6 | £15 | |
| Basie's Best | 10" LP | Brunswick | LA8589 | 1953 £8 | £20 | |

| | | | | | | |
|---|---|---|---|---|---|---|
| Blues By Basie | LP | Philips | BBL7190 | 1957 | £6 | £15 |
| Breakfast Dance And Barbecue | LP | Columbia | 33SX1209/ SCX3294 | 1959 | £4 | £10 |
| Chairman Of The Board | LP | Columbia | 33SX1224/ SCX3304 | 1960 | £4 | £10 |
| Count | 10" LP | Columbia | 33S1054 | 1955 | £8 | £20 |
| Count Basie | LP | Brunswick | LAT8028 | 1954 | £10 | £25 |
| Count Basie Classics | LP | Fontana | TFL5077 | 1960 | £4 | £10 |
| Count Basie Sextet | 10" LP | Columbia | 33C9010 | 1955 | £8 | £20 |
| Count Basie Story Vol. 1 | LP | Columbia | 33SX1316/ SCX3372 | 1961 | £4 | £10 |
| Count Basie Story Vol. 2 | LP | Columbia | 33SX1317/ SCX3373 | 1961 | £4 | £10 |
| Count Basie Swings And Joe Williams Sings | LP | Columbia | 33CX10026 | 1956 | £6 | £15 |
| Count Basie Swings, Tony Bennett Sings | LP | Columbia | 33SX1174 | 1959 | £4 | £10 |
| Count Basie/Lester Young | 10" LP | Mercury | MG25015 | 1954 | £8 | £20 |
| Dance Along With Basie | LP | Columbia | 33SX1264/ SCX3333 | 1960 | £4 | £10 |
| Dance Session | LP | Columbia | 33CX10007 | 1955 | £6 | £15 |
| Dance Session No. 2 | LP | Columbia | 33CX10044 | 1956 | £6 | £15 |
| Just The Blues | LP | Columbia | 33SX1326/ SCX3380 | 1961 | £4 | £10 |
| Memories Ad-Lib | LP | Columbia | 33SX1175/ SCX3280 | 1959 | £4 | £10 |
| Night At Count Basie's | LP | Vanguard | PPL11005 | 1957 | £6 | £15 |
| Not Now – I'll Tell You When | LP | Columbia | 33SX1293/ SCX3356 | 1961 | £4 | £10 |
| Old Count And The New Count | 10" LP | Philips | BBR8036 | 1955 | £8 | £20 |
| One More Time | LP | Columbia | 33SX1183/ SCX3284 | 1959 | £4 | £10 |
| One O'Clock Jump | LP | Fontana | TFL5046 | 1959 | £4 | £10 |
| String Along With Basie | LP | Columbia | 33SX1151 | 1959 | £4 | £10 |

## BASS, BILLY

| | | | | | | |
|---|---|---|---|---|---|---|
| I'm Coming Too | 7" | Pama | PM761 | 1969 | £4 | £8 |

## BASS, FONTELLA

| | | | | | | | |
|---|---|---|---|---|---|---|---|
| Don't Mess Up A Good Thing | 7" | Chess | CRS8007 | 1965 | £5 | £10 | *with Bobby McClure, 2 different B sides* |
| Fontella Bass & Bobby McClure | 7" EP | Chess | CRE6025 | 1966 | £6 | £12 | |
| Fontella's Hits | 7" EP | Chess | CRE6015 | 1966 | £5 | £10 | |
| I Can't Rest | 7" EP | Chess | CRE6020 | 1966 | £5 | £10 | |
| I Can't Rest | 7" | Chess | CRS8032 | 1966 | £2 | £5 | |
| New Look | LP | Chess | CRL4517 | 1966 | £5 | £12 | |
| Recovery | 7" | Chess | CRS8027 | 1966 | £1.50 | £4 | |
| Rescue Me | 7" | Chess | CRS8023 | 1965 | £1.50 | £4 | |
| Safe And Sound | 7" | Chess | CRS8042 | 1966 | £1.50 | £4 | |

## BASSES

| | | | | | | |
|---|---|---|---|---|---|---|
| River Jordan | 7" | Coxsone | CS7030 | 1967 | £5 | £10 |

## BASSEY, SHIRLEY

| | | | | | | |
|---|---|---|---|---|---|---|
| Banana Boat Song | 7" | Philips | JK1006 | 1957 | £4 | £8 |
| Born To Sing The Blues | 10" LP | Philips | BBR8130 | 1957 | £4 | £10 |
| Diamonds Are Forever | 7" | United Artists | UP35293 | 1972 | £1.50 | £4 |
| Don't Take The Lovers From The World | 7" | United Artists | UP1134 | 1966 | £2 | £5 |
| Goldfinger | 7" | Columbia | DB7360 | 1964 | £1.50 | £4 |
| If I Had A Needle And Thread | 7" | Philips | JK1018 | 1957 | £2.50 | £6 |
| Kiss Me, Honey Honey, Kiss Me | 7" | Philips | PB860 | 1958 | £1.50 | £4 |
| Puh-leeze Mister Brown | 7" | Philips | JK1034 | 1957 | £2.50 | £6 |
| To Give | 7" | United Artists | UP2254 | 1968 | £2.50 | £6 |

## BASSMAN, JOHN GROUP

| | | | | | | | |
|---|---|---|---|---|---|---|---|
| Filthy Sky | LP | ASP | 60600 | 1971 | £30 | £60 | *Dutch* |

## BATAAN, JOE

| | | | | | | |
|---|---|---|---|---|---|---|
| Riot! | LP | London | HA/SH8386 | 1969 | £4 | £10 |

## BATES, COLIN

| | | | | | | |
|---|---|---|---|---|---|---|
| Brew | LP | Fontana | SFJL913 | 1968 | £4 | £10 |

## BATMAN

In 1966 the *Batman* TV series started, complete with its catchy double-note riff theme. A large number of different artists recorded it, entries in this guide being found under the following names: Neal Hefti, Jan and Dean, The Marketts, Nelson Riddle, the Riddlers, the Spacemen, the Spotlights, the Ventures, Link Wray (a latecomer from 1978), and the Who (on their *Ready Steady Who* EP). The stars of the show, Adam West and Burt Ward, made an LP themselves, while Ward followed this up with a single the next year (masterminded by Frank Zappa). A reggae tribute was issued in 1970 by the Sydney All Stars, while the 1989 *Batman* film also turns up in the guide, represented by Prince's LP picture disc.

## BATORS, STIV

| | | | | | | |
|---|---|---|---|---|---|---|
| It's Cold Outside | 7" | London | HLZ10575 | 1979 | £1.50 | £4 |

## BATS

| | | | | | | |
|---|---|---|---|---|---|---|
| Accept It | 7" | Columbia | DB7429 | 1964 | £1.50 | £4 |
| Listen To My Heart | 7" | Decca | F22534 | 1966 | £1.50 | £4 |
| Take Me As I Am | 7" | Decca | F22616 | 1967 | £1.50 | £4 |

| | | | | | | |
|---|---|---|---|---|---|---|
| You Will Won't You | 7" | Decca | F22568 | 1967 £**1.50** | £**4** | |

## BATT, MIKE
| | | | | | | |
|---|---|---|---|---|---|---|
| I See Wonderful Things In You | 7" | Liberty | LBF15122 | 1968 £**1.50** | £**4** | |
| Mr. Poem | 7" | Liberty | LBF15093 | 1968 £**1.50** | £**4** | |
| Your Mother Should Know | 7" | Liberty | LBF15210 | 1969 £**1.50** | £**4** | |

## BATTERED ORNAMENTS
The Battered Ornaments was the group originally brought together by poet Pete Brown. Without him, they still did not have an effective vocalist, but the *Mantle Piece* LP is an interesting and worthwhile addition to the Harvest catalogue.

| | | | | | | |
|---|---|---|---|---|---|---|
| Mantle Piece | LP | Harvest | SHVL758 | 1969 £**30** | £**60** | |

## BATTIN, SKIP
| | | | | | | |
|---|---|---|---|---|---|---|
| Skip | LP | Signpost | SG4255 | 1972 £**4** | £**10** | |

## BATTLEFIELD BAND
| | | | | | | |
|---|---|---|---|---|---|---|
| Scottish Folk | LP | Arfolk | SB349 | 1976 £**5** | £**12** | *French* |

## BAUER, JOE
| | | | | | | |
|---|---|---|---|---|---|---|
| Moonset | LP | Raccoon | N3 | 1971 £**8** | £**20** | *US* |

## BAUHAUS
| | | | | | | |
|---|---|---|---|---|---|---|
| 1979–1983 | CD | Beggars Banquet | BAUCDBOX1 | 1988 £**8** | £**20** | *boxed double* |
| Bela Lugosi's Dead | CD-s | Small Wonder | TEENY2CD | 1988 £**2** | £**5** | |
| Bela Lugosi's Dead | 12" | Small Wonder | TEENY2 | 1979 £**4** | £**10** | *white vinyl* |
| Burning From The Inside | LP | Beggars Banquet | BEGA45P | 1983 £**4** | £**10** | *picture disc* |
| Dark Entries | 7" | 4AD | AD3 | 1980 £**1.50** | £**4** | *blue label* |
| Dark Entries | 7" | 4AD | BEG37 | 1980 £**2.50** | £**6** | |
| Dark Entries | 7" | Axis | AXIS3 | 1980 £**4** | £**8** | |
| Dark Entries | 7" | Beggars Banquet | BEG37 | 1980 £**4** | £**8** | |
| Kick In The Eye | 12" | Beggars Banquet | BEG54T | 1981 £**2.50** | £**6** | |
| Kick In The Eye | 12" | Beggars Banquet | BEG54T | 1981 £**4** | £**10** | *white label, stamped sleeve* |
| Kick In The Eye | 12" | Beggars Banquet | BEG74TA1 | 1983 £**10** | £**20** | *mispress with Poison Pen* |
| Sanity Assassin | 7" | Lyntone | LYN13777/8 | 1983 £**50** | £**100** | |
| She's In Parties | 7" | Beggars Banquet | BEG91P | 1983 £**2** | £**5** | *picture disc* |
| Spirit | 7" | Beggars Banquet | BEG79P | 1982 £**2** | £**5** | *picture disc* |
| Telegram Sam | 12" | 4AD | AD17T | 1980 £**2.50** | £**6** | |
| Terror Couple Kill Colonel (remix) | 7" | 4AD | AD7 | 1980 £**4** | £**8** | |

## BAUMSTAM
| | | | | | | |
|---|---|---|---|---|---|---|
| On Tour | LP | private | BS6232855 | 1976 £**75** | £**150** | *German* |

## BAXTER, ART
| | | | | | | |
|---|---|---|---|---|---|---|
| Don't Knock The Rock | 78 | Philips | PB666 | 1957 £**2.50** | £**6** | |
| Jingle Rock | 78 | Philips | PB652 | 1956 £**2.50** | £**6** | |
| Rock You Sinners | 10" LP | Philips | BBR8107 | 1957 £**30** | £**60** | |

## BAXTER, DAVID
| | | | | | | |
|---|---|---|---|---|---|---|
| Goodbye Dave | LP | Reflection | REFL9 | 1970 £**20** | £**40** | |

## BAXTER, LES
| | | | | | | |
|---|---|---|---|---|---|---|
| Cherry Pink And Apple Blossom White | 7" | Capitol | CL14337 | 1955 £**2** | £**5** | |
| Earth Angel | 7" | Capitol | CL14239 | 1955 £**5** | £**10** | |
| I Ain't Mad At You | 7" | Capitol | CL14249 | 1955 £**2** | £**5** | |
| I Love Paris | 7" | Capitol | CL14166 | 1954 £**2** | £**5** | |
| Midnight On The Cliffs | 7" | Capitol | CL14173 | 1954 £**2** | £**5** | |
| Poor John | 7" | Capitol | CL14533 | 1956 £**1.50** | £**4** | |
| Strike | 7" | Capitol | CL14351 | 1955 £**1.50** | £**4** | |
| Take My Love | 7" | Capitol | CL14358 | 1955 £**1.50** | £**4** | |
| Unchained Melody | 7" | Capitol | CL14257 | 1955 £**4** | £**8** | |
| Wake The Town And Tell The People | 7" | Capitol | CL14344 | 1955 £**2** | £**5** | |
| When You're In Love | 7" | Capitol | CL14217 | 1954 £**2** | £**5** | |

## BAXTER, RONNIE
| | | | | | | |
|---|---|---|---|---|---|---|
| I Finally Found You | 7" | Top Rank | JAR293 | 1960 £**1.50** | £**4** | |

## BAY CITY JAZZ BAND
| | | | | | | |
|---|---|---|---|---|---|---|
| Bay City Jazz Band | LP | Vogue | LAG12093 | 1958 £**5** | £**12** | |

## BAYSIDERS
| | | | | | | |
|---|---|---|---|---|---|---|
| Over The Rainbow | LP | Everest | LPBR/BRST5124 | 1961 £**15** | £**30** | *US* |

## BAYTOWN SINGERS
| | | | | | | |
|---|---|---|---|---|---|---|
| Walkin' Down The Line | 7" | Decca | F12160 | 1965 £**1.50** | £**4** | |

## BBC RADIOPHONIC WORKSHOP
| | | | | | | |
|---|---|---|---|---|---|---|
| Dr. Who | 7" | BBC | RESL11 | 1974 £**1.50** | £**4** | *picture sleeve* |
| Dr. Who | 7" | Decca | F11837 | 1964 £**5** | £**10** | |

# BEACH BOYS

For a group as long-lived and as popular as the Beach Boys, there are surprisingly few hard-core rarities, although all their original issues from the sixties are inevitably collectable. The ultimate Beach Boys rarity has still not been released in full – the LP *Smile* was cancelled by Brian Wilson and would perhaps have included tracks to rival the masterworks 'Good Vibrations', 'Heroes and Villains', and 'Surf's Up', which were all destined for inclusion on the lost album. For collectors who do not actually feel the need to own every note that the group has produced, it should be noted that the World Record Club boxed set *The Capitol Years* is a particularly well-assembled compilation of the group's sixties work, with no major omissions. A bonus LP, moreover, assembles a number of Brian Wilson productions which are otherwise rather difficult to find.

| Title | Format | Label | Cat. No. | Year | | | Notes |
|---|---|---|---|---|---|---|---|
| 20 Golden Greats | LP | EMI | EMTV1 | 1977 | £4 | £10 | blue vinyl |
| 20 Golden Greats Promo | 7" | EMI | PSR402 | 1976 | £4 | £8 | promo |
| 20/20 | LP | Capitol | ET133 | 1969 | £4 | £10 | mono |
| All Summer Long | LP | Capitol | (S)T2110 | 1964 | £6 | £15 | |
| All Summer Long | 7" | Capitol | CL15384 | 1965 | £1.50 | £4 | |
| Ballad Of An Old Car | 7" EP | Capitol | EAP120576 | 1964 | £10 | £20 | French |
| Barbara Ann | 7" EP | Capitol | EAP120762 | 1965 | £7.50 | £15 | French |
| Barbara Ann | 7" | Capitol | CL15432 | 1966 | £1.50 | £4 | |
| Beach Boy Interviews | LP | Caribou | XPR1204 | 1980 | £6 | £15 | promo |
| Beach Boys | CD | Capitol | DPRO79168 | 1990 | £10 | £25 | US promo sampler |
| Beach Boys | CD | Caribou | CD26378 | 1985 | £5 | £12 | |
| Beach Boys Concert | LP | Capitol | (S)T2198 | 1964 | £5 | £12 | |
| Beach Boys Concert | 7" EP | Capitol | EAP42198 | 1964 | £4 | £8 | |
| Beach Boys Party | LP | Capitol | (S)T2398 | 1965 | £4 | £10 | |
| Beach Boys Today | LP | Capitol | (S)T2269 | 1965 | £5 | £12 | |
| Beach Boys' Hits | 7" EP | Capitol | EAP120781 | 1964 | £2.50 | £6 | |
| Bluebirds Over The Mountain | 7" | Capitol | CL15572 | 1968 | £1.50 | £4 | |
| Break Away | 7" | Capitol | CL15598 | 1969 | £1.50 | £4 | |
| California Girls | 7" EP | Capitol | EAP42354 | 1965 | £7.50 | £15 | French |
| California Girls | 7" | Capitol | CL15409 | 1965 | £1.50 | £4 | |
| Capitol Years | LP | World Record Club | SM651-7 | 1981 | £25 | £50 | 7 LPs, boxed |
| Carl And The Passions, So Tough | CD | Epic | 4683492 | 1991 | £5 | £12 | |
| Christmas Album | LP | Capitol | (S)T2164 | 1964 | £8 | £20 | |
| Cottonfields | 7" | Capitol | CL15640 | 1970 | £1.50 | £4 | |
| Dance Dance Dance | 7" EP | Capitol | EAP120648 | 1965 | £7.50 | £15 | French |
| Dance Dance Dance | 7" | Capitol | CL15370 | 1965 | £1.50 | £4 | |
| Darlin' | 7" | Capitol | CL15527 | 1968 | £1.50 | £4 | |
| Deluxe Set | LP | Capitol | DTCL2813 | 1967 | £20 | £40 | US, triple, stereo |
| Deluxe Set | LP | Capitol | TCL2813 | 1967 | £30 | £60 | US, triple, mono |
| Do It Again | CD-s | Capitol | CDEMCT1 | 1991 | £2 | £5 | |
| Do It Again | 7" | Capitol | CL15554 | 1968 | £1.50 | £4 | |
| Don't Go Near The Water | 7" | Stateside | SS2194 | 1971 | £5 | £10 | demo, picture sleeve |
| Driving Cars | 7" EP | Capitol | EAP41998 | 1964 | £10 | £20 | French |
| Four By The Beach Boys | 7" EP | Capitol | EAP15267 | 1964 | £2.50 | £6 | |
| Friends | LP | Capitol | T2895 | 1968 | £4 | £10 | mono |
| Friends | 7" | Capitol | CL15545 | 1968 | £1.50 | £4 | |
| Fun Fun Fun | 7" EP | Capitol | EAP120603 | 1964 | £4 | £8 | |
| Fun Fun Fun | 7" | Capitol | CL15339 | 1964 | £12.50 | £25 | |
| God Only Knows | 7" EP | Capitol | EAP62458 | 1967 | £2.50 | £6 | |
| God Only Knows | 7" | Capitol | CL15459 | 1966 | £1.50 | £4 | |
| Good Vibrations | 7" | Capitol | CL15475 | 1966 | £1.50 | £4 | |
| Help Me Rhonda | 7" | Capitol | CL15392 | 1965 | £1.50 | £4 | |
| Help Me Ronda | 7" EP | Capitol | EAP42269 | 1965 | £7.50 | £15 | French |
| Heroes And Villains | 7" | Capitol | CL15510 | 1967 | £1.50 | £4 | |
| Holland | LP | Reprise | K54008 | 1973 | £4 | £10 | with 7" |
| Holland | LP | Reprise | MS2118 | 1973 | £75 | £150 | US test pressing with 'We Got Love' |
| I Can Hear Music | 7" | Capitol | CL15584 | 1969 | £1.50 | £4 | |
| I Get Around | 7" EP | Capitol | EAP120620 | 1964 | £7.50 | £15 | French, 2 different sleeves |
| I Get Around | 7" | Capitol | CL15350 | 1964 | £1.50 | £4 | |
| L.A. (Light Album) | LP | Caribou | CRB1186081 | 1979 | £4 | £10 | picture disc |
| Little Deuce Coupe | LP | Capitol | (S)T1998 | 1963 | £6 | £15 | |
| Little Girl I Once Knew | 7" | Capitol | CL15425 | 1965 | £1.50 | £4 | |
| Louie Louie | 7" EP | Capitol | EAP120658 | 1965 | £7.50 | £15 | French |
| Pet Sounds | LP | Capitol | (S)T2458 | 1966 | £4 | £10 | |
| Pet Sounds | CD | Capitol | CCM74618 | 1987 | £10 | £25 | US |
| Shut Down Vol. 2 | LP | Capitol | (S)T2027 | 1964 | £6 | £15 | |
| Singles Collection | 7" | Capitol | BBP26 | 1979 | £25 | £50 | 26 singles, boxed |
| Sloop John B | 7" EP | Capitol | EAP120812 | 1966 | £7.50 | £15 | French |
| Sloop John B | 7" | Capitol | CL15441 | 1966 | £1.50 | £4 | |
| Smiley Smile | LP | Capitol | (S)T9001 | 1967 | £4 | £10 | |
| Smiley Smile | LP | Capitol | ST82891 | 1968 | £37.50 | £75 | US, record club issue |
| Stack-O-Tracks | LP | Capitol | DKAO2893 | 1968 | £30 | £60 | US, with booklet |
| Still Cruisin' | CD-s | Capitol | CDCL549 | 1989 | £2 | £5 | |
| Summer Days & Summer Nights | LP | Capitol | (S)T2354 | 1965 | £4 | £10 | |
| Summertime Blues | 7" | Sears | SPS609 | 1970 | £25 | £50 | US |
| Sunflower | LP | Capitol | SKAO93352 | 1970 | £8 | £20 | US, record club issue |
| Sunflower | LP | Stateside | SSLA8251 | 1970 | £4 | £10 | |
| Surf's Up | LP | Asylum | R113793 | 1971 | £25 | £50 | US, record club issue |
| Surfer Girl | LP | Capitol | (S)T1981 | 1963 | £6 | £15 | |
| Surfer Party | 7" EP | Capitol | EAP120561 | 1963 | £10 | £20 | French |
| Surfin' | 7" | Candix | 301 | 1961 | £75 | £150 | US |
| Surfin' | 7" | Candix | 331 | 1961 | £62.50 | £125 | US |
| Surfin' | 7" | X | 301 | 1961 | £100 | £200 | US, best auctioned |
| Surfin' Safari | LP | Capitol | T1808 | 1962 | £8 | £20 | |
| Surfin' Safari | 7" EP | Capitol | EAP51808 | 1962 | £10 | £20 | French |

| | | | | | | |
|---|---|---|---|---|---|---|
| Surfin' Safari | 7" | Capitol | CL15273 | 1962 £6 | £12 | |
| Surfin' USA | LP | Capitol | (S)T1890 | 1963 £6 | £15 | |
| Surfin' USA | 7" EP | Capitol | EAP120504 | 1963 £10 | £20 | French |
| Surfin' USA | 7" EP | Capitol | EAP120540 | 1963 £4 | £8 | |
| Surfin' USA | 7" | Capitol | CL15305 | 1963 £5 | £10 | |
| Surfin' USA/Surfer Girl | CD | Mobile Fidelity | UDCD521 | 1989 £6 | £15 | US audiophile |
| Susie Cincinnatti | 7" | Reprise | K14411 | 1976 £15 | £30 | demo |
| Ten Little Indians | 7" | Capitol | CL15285 | 1963 £20 | £40 | |
| Then I Kissed Her | 7" | Capitol | CL15502 | 1967 £1.50 | £4 | |
| When I Grow Up | 7" | Capitol | CL15361 | 1964 £1.50 | £4 | |
| Wild Honey | LP | Capitol | T2859 | 1968 £4 | £10 | mono |
| Wild Honey | 7" | Capitol | CL15517 | 1967 £30 | £60 | |
| Wild Honey | 7" | Capitol | CL15521 | 1967 £1.50 | £4 | |
| Wouldn't It Be Nice | CD-s | Capitol | CDCL579 | 1990 £2 | £5 | |
| Wouldn't It Be Nice | 7" EP | Capitol | EAP502458 | 1967 £7.50 | £15 | French |
| You Need A Mess of Help | 7" | Reprise | K14173 | 1972 £1.50 | £4 | picture sleeve |
| Out In The Sun | 7" | London | HL9988 | 1965 £2 | £5 | |

## BEACHCOMBERS

An instrumental group whose drummer was Keith Moon, who left to join the High Numbers just as the latter decided to revert to their earlier name of the Who.

| | | | | | | |
|---|---|---|---|---|---|---|
| Mad Goose | 7" | Columbia | DB7124 | 1963 £6 | £12 | |
| Night Train | 7" | Columbia | DB7200 | 1964 £6 | £12 | |

## BEACON STREET UNION

| | | | | | | |
|---|---|---|---|---|---|---|
| Blue Suede Shoes | 7" | MGM | MGM1416 | 1968 £1.50 | £4 | |
| Clown Died In Marvin Gardens | LP | MGM | SE4568 | 1968 £5 | £12 | US |
| Eyes Of The Beacon Street Union | LP | MGM | 8069 | 1968 £5 | £12 | |

## BEAD GAME

| | | | | | | |
|---|---|---|---|---|---|---|
| Welcome | LP | Avco | 33009 | 1970 £15 | £30 | US |

## BEAN, GEORGE

| | | | | | | |
|---|---|---|---|---|---|---|
| Privilege | 7" EP | Vogue | INT18137 | 1967 £4 | £8 | French, B side by Mike Leander Orchestra |
| Sad Story | 7" | Decca | F11922 | 1964 £2.50 | £6 | |
| Secret Love | 7" | Decca | F11762 | 1963 £1.50 | £4 | |
| She Belongs To Me | 7" | Decca | F12228 | 1965 £1.50 | £4 | |
| Will You Be My Lover Tonight | 7" | Decca | F11808 | 1964 £2.50 | £6 | |

## BEAN & LOOPY'S LOT

| | | | | | | |
|---|---|---|---|---|---|---|
| Haywire | 7" | Parlophone | R5458 | 1966 £5 | £10 | |

## BEANS

| | | | | | | |
|---|---|---|---|---|---|---|
| Hey Janey | 7" | Starlite | ST45075 | 1962 £1.50 | £4 | |
| Jumping Beans | 7" | Starlite | ST45071 | 1962 £1.50 | £4 | |

## BEAR

| | | | | | | |
|---|---|---|---|---|---|---|
| Greetings Children Of Paradise | LP | Verve | FTS3059 | 1969 £8 | £20 | |

## BEARCATS

| | | | | | | |
|---|---|---|---|---|---|---|
| Beatlemania | LP | Somerset | P20800 | 1964 £8 | £20 | US |

## BEARD, DEAN & THE CREWCUTS

| | | | | | | |
|---|---|---|---|---|---|---|
| On My Mind Again | 7" | London | HLE8463 | 1957 £100 | £200 | best auctioned |

## BEARZ

| | | | | | | |
|---|---|---|---|---|---|---|
| She's My Girl | 7" | Axis | AXIS2 | 1980 £2.50 | £6 | |

## BEAS

| | | | | | | |
|---|---|---|---|---|---|---|
| Dr. Goodfoot And His Bikini Machine | 7" | Pama | PM744 | 1968 £6 | £12 | |

## BEASLEY, JIMMY

| | | | | | | |
|---|---|---|---|---|---|---|
| Fabulous Jimmy Beasley | LP | Crown | CLP5014 | 1957 £15 | £30 | US |
| Fabulous Jimmy Beasley | LP | Modern | LMP1214 | 1956 £25 | £50 | US |
| Twist With Jimmy Beasley | LP | Crown | CLP5247 | 1961 £8 | £20 | US |

## BEASTIE BOYS

| | | | | | | |
|---|---|---|---|---|---|---|
| Frozen Metal Head EP | CD-s | Capitol | CDCL665 | 1992 £6 | £15 | |
| Frozen Metal Head EP | 12" | Capitol | 12CL665 | 1992 £4 | £10 | white vinyl |
| Girls | 7" | Def Jam | BEASTS3 | 1987 £4 | £8 | shaped picture disc |
| Hey Ladies | CD-s | Capitol | CDCL540 | 1989 £4 | £10 | |
| Licensed To Ill | LP | Def Jam | 4500621 | 1987 £5 | £12 | with poster |
| No Sleep Till Brooklyn | 7" | Def Jam | BEASTP1 | 1987 £4 | £8 | shaped picture disc |
| Pass The Mic | CD-s | Capitol | CDCL653 | 1992 £4 | £10 | |
| Polly Wog Stew | 7" | Rat Cage | MOTR21 | 1982 £4 | £8 | |
| Polly Wog Stew | 12" | Rat Cage | MOTR21T | 1982 £4 | £10 | |
| Sampler | CD | Capitol | GRAND1 | 1994 £8 | £20 | promo compilation |

## BEAT BOYS

| | | | | | | |
|---|---|---|---|---|---|---|
| That's My Plan | 7" | Decca | F11730 | 1963 £6 | £12 | |

## BEAT BROTHERS
Nick Nack Hully Gully.............................. 7" ...... Polydor........... NH52185............... 1963 £10........£20 ...............................

## BEAT CHICS
Skinny Minny ........................................ 7" ...... Decca ............. F12016................... 1964 £2............£5 ...............................

## BEAT MERCHANTS
Pretty Face........................................... 7" ...... Columbia ........ DB7367 ............... 1964 £12.50.... £25
So Fine................................................ 7" ...... Columbia ........ DB7492 ............... 1965 £12.50.... £25

## BEAT MIXERS
Beat ..................................................... LP ...... Baccarola........ 72662.................... 1964 £6............£15 .................. German

## BEAT OF THE EARTH
This Record Is An Artistic Statement ......... LP ...... Radish ............ AS0001 ............... 1968 £75....... £150 ...................... US

## BEAT SIX
Bernadine............................................. 7" ...... Decca ............. F12011................... 1964 £1.50...... £4

## BEATHOVENS
Happy To Be Happy .............................. LP ...... Somerset ........ 650 ...................... 1965 £20........ £40 .................. German

## BEATLES
The Beatles sold so many copies of their singles that it should come as no surprise that few of them have acquired much of a value in the collectors' market. It is a different matter with their LPs, however, especially as so many original copies have been extremely well played over the years! There are also a number of rarer items. The Polydor singles and LP are the first pressings of the material that the Beatles recorded in Germany in 1962 – mainly as a backing group to singer Tony Sheridan, although 'Ain't She Sweet' features a typically gritty John Lennon vocal, and 'Cry For A Shadow' is George Harrison's instrumental tribute to Hank Marvin and company. This material has been reissued on a number of occasions, along with live recordings by the Beatles in Hamburg without Sheridan, but few of these records fetch any kind of collectors' prices, despite the historical importance of the music they present. The Christmas flexi-disc singles were issued each year to members of the fan club and feature specially recorded material not otherwise available, although not very much of this is actually musical. *From Then To You* gathers all these singles together on a highly sought-after LP – inevitably this has been frequently bootlegged, but the copies in recent circulation do not have the Apple label of the original. The US version of the LP has a different cover and title (*The Beatles Christmas Album*) and has also been bootlegged – original copies are on black vinyl, with a clear Apple label and a typically thick cardboard sixties American cover. The limited edition package which combined the *Let It Be* album (whose cover should have a small green apple on the back) with a substantial book has become quite scarce. The catalogue number PXS1 was used in advertising material at the time, but appears nowhere on the package! First pressings of the *Please Please Me* LP have the old Parlophone label design, with gold lettering (the stereo version of this is especially rare) – further details are given in this guide under the Parlophone heading. The infamous American 'butcher cover', hastily withdrawn after the initial release of *Yesterday And Today*, varies considerably in value depending on whether it is mono or stereo and on whether it is 'unpeeled' (i.e. with the replacement cover design pasted on top) or 'peeled' (i.e. with the replacement cover design either successfully removed or never pasted on to begin with). The conversion of an unpeeled copy into a more valuable peeled one is fraught with danger, needless to say, and should be left to a specialist, or not done at all. Reissue copies of the US album *Introducing The Beatles* are common – these have assorted label variants which have a silver VJ logo in large straight brackets. The situation with regard to valuable original pressings is complicated. The values given here are an average for a range of prices attaching to subtle label variations, all of which are extremely rare, especially in the UK. Essentially, however, original pressings have an oval Vee Jay logo, together with a machine-stamped matrix identification ('Audio Matrix', 'MR', or 'ARP'). The much sought-after UK export issues of various of the Beatles' recordings have long been the subject of rumour and misinformation as to what does and does not exist. Claims have been made for the existence of various export albums and singles other than those listed here, but until such time as a collector can confirm ownership of these, one can only remain sceptical. It should be noted, finally, that all original copies of *The Beatles* double album (usually referred to as 'The White Album', after its cover design) were stamped with a unique issue number. Low-numbered copies inevitably come on to the market from time to time and can be expected to fetch considerably higher prices than the norm. Number 000001, autographed by Ringo Starr, was sold at auction in 1985 for $715 and would doubtless sell for rather more today. The values listed below for these records should be taken as points on a sliding scale and are highly approximate – they are all best auctioned.

| | | | | | | | |
|---|---|---|---|---|---|---|---|
| 1962–1970...................................... | 7" ...... | Lyntone ........... | ........................ | 1977 | £4........... | £8 | ............ promo flexi |
| 1962–66......................................... | LP ..... | Apple...... | PCSPR717............. | 1978 | £6........... | £15 | ....... red vinyl, double |
| 1967–70......................................... | LP ..... | Apple...... | PCSPR718............. | 1978 | £6........... | £15 | .....blue vinyl, double |
| 4 garçons dans le vent ..................... | 7" EP . | Odeon.... | SOE3756.............. | 1964 | £10........ | £20 | ...................... French |
| 4 garçons dans le vent ..................... | 7" EP . | Odeon.... | SOE3757.............. | 1964 | £10........ | £20 | ...................... French |
| Abbey Road .................................... | r-reel .. | Apple...... | TAPMC7088........ | 1970 | £50........ | £100 | ...................... mono |
| Abbey Road .................................... | r-reel .. | Apple...... | TDPCS7088......... | 1970 | £15........ | £30 | ...................... stereo |
| Abbey Road .................................... | LP ..... | Apple...... | PCS7088............... | 1969 | £4........... | £10 | ....dark green label |
| Abbey Road .................................... | LP ..... | Apple...... | PCS7088............... | 1978 | £37.50.... | £75 | ................green vinyl |
| Abbey Road .................................... | LP ..... | Apple...... | PHO7088.............. | 1979 | £150..... | £250 | ............... picture disc |
| Abbey Road .................................... | LP ..... | Apple...... | SO383.................. | 1969 | £4........... | £10 | ......................... US |
| Abbey Road .................................... | LP ..... | Capitol.... | SEAX11900......... | 1978 | £8........... | £20 | ..... US picture disc |
| Abbey Road .................................... | LP ..... | EMI........ | 5CP06204243....... | 1979 | £6........... | £15 | ....Dutch picture disc |
| Abbey Road .................................... | LP ..... | Mobile Fidelity | MFSL1023 ............ | 1978 | £15........ | £30 | ...... US audiophile |
| Abbey Road .................................... | LP ..... | Parlophone...... | PPCS7088........... | 1969 | £150..... | £250 | . export, silver & black label |
| Abbey Road .................................... | LP ..... | Parlophone...... | PPCS7088........... | 1969 | £500..... | £750 | export, yellow & black label |
| Abbey Road .................................... | CD ..... | EMI............... | BEACD25/7......... | 1987 | £8........... | £20 | .... HMV box, badge, booklet, 2 posters |
| Abbey Road .................................... | CD ..... | Odeon............ | CP353016 ............ | 1986 | £150..... | £250 | ................Japanese |
| Abbey Road .................................... | CD ..... | Parlophone...... | CDP7464462......... | 1987 | £20........ | £40 | ...mispressing – plays Edith Piaf |
| All My Loving ................................ | 7" EP . | Odeon.... | SOE3751.............. | 1964 | £10........ | £20 | ...................... French |
| All My Loving ................................ | 7" EP . | Parlophone...... | GEP8891............. | 1964 | £5........... | £10 | |
| All You Need Is Love ...................... | CD-s .. | Parlophone...... | CD3R5620........... | 1989 | £2........... | £5 | ..................... 3" single |
| All You Need Is Love ...................... | 7" ...... | Parlophone...... | R5620 ................... | 1967 | £1.50...... | £4 | |
| All You Need Is Love ...................... | 7" ...... | Parlophone...... | R5620 ................... | 1967 | £150..... | £250 | ...................... demo |
| All You Need Is Love ...................... | 7" ...... | Parlophone...... | R5620 ................... | 1967 | £5........... | £10 | ...no reference to TV transmission |
| All You Need Is Love ...................... | 7" ...... | Parlophone...... | RP5620 ................. | 1987 | £5........... | £10 | ................picture disc |

57

| Title | Format | Label | Catalog | Year | Price | Price | Notes |
|---|---|---|---|---|---|---|---|
| Amazing Beatles | LP | Clarion | 601 | 1966 | £20 | £40 | US, mono |
| Amazing Beatles | LP | Clarion | SD601 | 1966 | £30 | £60 | US, stereo |
| Another Beatles Christmas Record | 7" | Lyntone | LYN757 | 1964 | £15 | £30 | picture sleeve, flexi |
| Another Beatles Christmas Record | 7" | Lyntone | LYN757 | 1964 | £25 | £50 | picture sleeve, flexi, newsletter |
| Anthology 2 | CD | Apple | ANTH2 | 1996 | £30 | £60 | 10 track promo sampler, booklet |
| Anthology 2 | CD | Apple | no number | 1996 | £37.50 | £75 | US promo CD-ROM press kit |
| Anthology 3 | CD | Apple | ANTH3 | 1996 | £50 | £100 | 5 track promo sampler, press kit |
| Baby It's You | CD-s | Capitol | DPRO79553 | 1995 | £25 | £50 | US promo, Valentine's card sleeve |
| Ballad Of John And Yoko | CD-s | Parlophone | CD3R5786 | 1989 | £2 | £5 | 3" single |
| Ballad Of John And Yoko | 7" | Apple | R5786 | 1969 | £1.50 | £4 | |
| Ballad Of John And Yoko | 7" | Apple | R5786 | 1969 | £150 | £250 | demo, best auctioned |
| Ballad Of John And Yoko | 7" | Apple | RP5786 | 1989 | £5 | £10 | picture disc |
| Beatles | LP | Deutscher Bucherclub | H052 | 1965 | £30 | £60 | German, club pressing |
| Beatles | LP | Deutscher Bucherclub | J033 | 1964 | £37.50 | £75 | German, club pressing |
| Beatles (White Album) | r-reel | Apple | DTAPMC/DTDPCS7067/8 | 1969 | £15 | £30 | |
| Beatles (White Album) | LP | Apple | PCS7067/8 | 1968 | £20 | £40 | stereo |
| Beatles (White Album) | LP | Apple | PCS7067/8 | 1978 | £37.50 | £75 | white vinyl |
| Beatles (White Album) | LP | Apple | PMC/PCS7067/8 | 1968 | £3500 | £5000 | cover number 000001-00010 |
| Beatles (White Album) | LP | Apple | PMC/PCS7067/8 | 1968 | £1400 | £2000 | cover number 000011-00020 |
| Beatles (White Album) | LP | Apple | PMC/PCS7067/8 | 1968 | £700 | £1000 | cover number 000021-00100 |
| Beatles (White Album) | LP | Apple | PMC/PCS7067/8 | 1968 | £500 | £750 | cover number 000101-01000 |
| Beatles (White Album) | LP | Apple | PMC/PCS7067/8 | 1968 | £330 | £500 | cover number 001001-10000 |
| Beatles (White Album) | LP | Apple | PMC7067/8 | 1968 | £75 | £150 | mono |
| Beatles (White Album) | LP | Apple | SWBO101 | 1968 | £10 | £25 | US, double |
| Beatles (White Album) | LP | Mobile Fidelity | MFSL2072 | 1982 | £20 | £40 | US audiophile |
| Beatles (White Album) | LP | Parlophone | PCSJ7067/8 | 1969 | £250 | £400 | double export |
| Beatles (White Album) | LP | Parlophone | PPCS7067/8 | 1968 | £400 | £600 | export, yellow & black label |
| Beatles (White Album) | LP | Parlophone | PPCS7067/8 | 1969 | £250 | £400 | double export, silver & black label |
| Beatles (White Album) | CD | EMI | BEACD25/4 | 1987 | £20 | £40 | HMV box, badge, booklet |
| Beatles 1962 | 7" | Baktabak | TABOKS1001 | 1988 | £25 | £50 | 15 singles, boxed |
| Beatles '65 | LP | Capitol | ST2228 | 1964 | £8 | £20 | US, stereo |
| Beatles '65 | LP | Capitol | T2228 | 1964 | £10 | £25 | US, mono |
| Beatles '65 | LP | Odeon | SMO83917 | 1965 | £50 | £100 | German, white & gold label |
| Beatles VI | LP | Capitol | ST2358 | 1965 | £8 | £20 | US, stereo |
| Beatles VI | LP | Capitol | ST82358 | 1965 | £25 | £50 | US, Record Club issue |
| Beatles VI | LP | Capitol | T2358 | 1965 | £10 | £25 | US, mono |
| Beatles VI | LP | Parlophone | CPCS104 | 1966 | £250 | £400 | export |
| Beatles VI | LP | Parlophone | CPCS104 | 1969 | £100 | £200 | export, black & silver label |
| Beatles & Frank Ifield On Stage | LP | Vee Jay | LP1085 | 1964 | £700 | £1000 | US, Beatles on cover |
| Beatles & Frank Ifield On Stage | LP | Vee Jay | LP1085 | 1964 | £25 | £50 | US, old man on cover, mono |
| Beatles & Frank Ifield On Stage | LP | Vee Jay | LPS1085 | 1964 | £75 | £150 | US, old man on cover, stereo |
| Beatles At The Beeb | LP | BBC | CN3970 | 1982 | £330 | £500 | transcription disc |
| Beatles At The Beeb | CD | Apple | | | £2000 | £3000 | promo only 140 CD set |
| Beatles At The Hollywood Bowl | 7" | Parlophone | EMTV4 | 1977 | £25 | £50 | promo boxed set |
| Beatles Beat | LP | Odeon | O83692 | 1964 | £37.50 | £75 | German, green label |
| Beatles Box | LP | World Record Club | SM701-8 | 1980 | £25 | £50 | 8 LPs, boxed |
| Beatles' Christmas Album | LP | Apple | SBC100 | 1970 | £100 | £200 | US |
| Beatles' Christmas Record | 7" | Lyntone | LYN492 | 1963 | £37.50 | £75 | picture sleeve, flexi |
| Beatles Collection | LP | Mobile Fidelity | | 1982 | £180 | £300 | US audiophile, 14 LPs, boxed |
| Beatles Collection | LP | Parlophone | BC13 | 1978 | £50 | £100 | 13 LPs (1 double), boxed |
| Beatles Collection | 7" | Lyntone | LYN9657 | 1978 | £1.50 | £4 | flexi |
| Beatles Collection | 7" | Lyntone | LYNSF165 | 1978 | £4 | £8 | promo flexi, poster |
| Beatles Collection | 7" | World Record Club | | 1977 | £20 | £40 | 24 singles, boxed |
| Beatles Collection | 7" | World Record Club | | 1978 | £20 | £40 | 25 singles, boxed |
| Beatles Conquer America | 7" | Baktabak | BAKPAK1004 | 1989 | £4 | £8 | 4 single pack |
| Beatles EP Collection | 7" EP | Parlophone | BEP14 | 1981 | £30 | £60 | 14 EPs |
| Beatles Fifth Christmas Record | 7" | Lyntone | LYN1360 | 1967 | £15 | £30 | picture sleeve, flexi |
| Beatles Fifth Christmas Record | 7" | Lyntone | LYN1360 | 1967 | £25 | £50 | picture sleeve, flexi, newsletter |
| Beatles For Sale | r-reel | Parlophone | TAPMC1240/TDPCS3062 | 1965 | £10 | £25 | |
| Beatles For Sale | LP | Mobile Fidelity | MFSL1104 | 1984 | £8 | £20 | US audiophile |

| Title | Format | Label | Cat. No. | Year | Price | Price | Notes |
|---|---|---|---|---|---|---|---|
| Beatles For Sale | LP | Parlophone | PCS3062 | 1964 | £30 | £60 | stereo |
| Beatles For Sale | LP | Parlophone | PCS3062 | 1969 | £4 | £10 | reissue, exposed edges on inside of cover, 'Made in Gt Britain' on label |
| Beatles For Sale | LP | Parlophone | PMC1240 | 1964 | £15 | £30 | mono |
| Beatles For Sale | 7" EP | Parlophone | GEP8931 | 1965 | £5 | £10 | |
| Beatles For Sale No. 2 | 7" EP | Parlophone | GEP8938 | 1965 | £7.50 | £15 | |
| Beatles Fourth Christmas Record | 7" | Lyntone | LYN1145 | 1966 | £15 | £30 | picture sleeve, flexi |
| Beatles Fourth Christmas Record | 7" | Lyntone | LYN1145 | 1966 | £25 | £50 | picture sleeve, flexi, newsletter |
| Beatles Greatest Hits | LP | Parlophone | EMTVS34 | 1982 | £50 | £100 | double, test pressing |
| Beatles Hits | 7" EP | Parlophone | GEP8880 | 1963 | £5 | £10 | |
| Beatles Million Sellers | 7" EP | Parlophone | GEP8946 | 1965 | £7.50 | £15 | |
| Beatles Mono Collection | LP | Parlophone | BMC10 | 1982 | £62.50 | £125 | 10 LPs, boxed |
| Beatles No. 1 | 7" EP | Parlophone | GEP8883 | 1963 | £5 | £10 | |
| Beatles' Rock 'n' Roll Medley | 7" | EMI | PSR401 | 1976 | £25 | £50 | 1 sided promo |
| Beatles Second Album | LP | Capitol | ST2080 | 1964 | £8 | £20 | US, stereo |
| Beatles Second Album | LP | Capitol | ST82080 | 1964 | £25 | £50 | US, Record Club issue |
| Beatles Second Album | LP | Capitol | T2080 | 1964 | £10 | £25 | US, mono |
| Beatles' Second Album | LP | Parlophone | CPCS103 | 1966 | £250 | £400 | export |
| Beatles Second Album | LP | Parlophone | CPCS103 | 1969 | £100 | £200 | export, silver & black label |
| Beatles Seventh Christmas Record | 7" | Lyntone | LYN1970/1 | 1969 | £15 | £30 | picture sleeve, flexi |
| Beatles Seventh Christmas Record | 7" | Lyntone | LYN1970/1 | 1969 | £25 | £50 | picture sleeve, flexi, newsletter |
| Beatles Singles Collection | 7" | EMI | BSC1 | 1982 | £20 | £40 | 26 singles, boxed |
| Beatles Singles Collection | 7" | EMI | BSCP1 | 1982 | £25 | £50 | 27 singles, boxed, export |
| Beatles Singles Collection | 7" | Lyntone | LYNSF1291 | 1977 | £5 | £10 | promo flexi, poster |
| Beatles Singles Collection | 7" | Parlophone | BSCP1 | 1982 | £37.50 | £75 | box set with mispressed picture disc – 'Love Me Do' both sides |
| Beatles Singles Collection | 7" | Parlophone/Apple | BS24 | 1976 | £25 | £50 | 24 singles, boxed |
| Beatles Sixth Christmas Record | 7" | Lyntone | LYN1743/4 | 1968 | £15 | £30 | picture sleeve, flexi |
| Beatles Sixth Christmas Record | 7" | Lyntone | LYN1743/4 | 1968 | £25 | £50 | picture sleeve, flexi, sales insert |
| Beatles Story | LP | Capitol | STBO2222 | 1964 | £8 | £20 | US, stereo |
| Beatles Story | LP | Capitol | TBO2222 | 1964 | £10 | £25 | US, mono |
| Beatles Tapes (David Wigg Interviews) | LP | Polydor | 2683068 | 1976 | £5 | £12 | double |
| Beatles Third Christmas Record | 7" | Lyntone | LYN948 | 1965 | £15 | £30 | picture sleeve, flexi |
| Beatles Third Christmas Record | 7" | Lyntone | LYN948 | 1965 | £25 | £50 | picture sleeve, flexi, newsletter |
| Beatles Vs. The Four Seasons | LP | Vee Jay | DX30 | 1964 | £875 | £1250 | US double |
| Beatles With Tony Sheridan | LP | MGM | E4215 | 1964 | £25 | £50 | US, mono |
| Beatles With Tony Sheridan | LP | MGM | SE4215 | 1964 | £50 | £100 | US, stereo |
| Can't Buy Me Love | CD-s | Parlophone | CD3R5114 | 1989 | £2 | £5 | 3" single |
| Can't Buy Me Love | 7" EP | Odeon | SOE3750 | 1964 | £10 | £20 | French |
| Can't Buy Me Love | 7" | Parlophone | R5114 | 1964 | £1.50 | £4 | |
| Can't Buy Me Love | 7" | Parlophone | R5114 | 1964 | £210 | £350 | demo |
| Can't Buy Me Love | 7" | Parlophone | RP5114 | 1984 | £5 | £10 | picture disc |
| Chansons du film Help | 7" EP | Odeon | SOE3771 | 1965 | £10 | £20 | French |
| Collection Of Beatles Oldies | r-reel | Parlophone | TAPMC/TDPCS7016 | 1967 | £10 | £25 | |
| Collection Of Beatles Oldies | LP | Parlophone | PCS7016 | 1967 | £25 | £50 | stereo |
| Collection Of Beatles Oldies | LP | Parlophone | PCS7016 | 1969 | £4 | £10 | reissue, exposed edges on back cover, 'Made in Gt Britain' on label |
| Collection Of Beatles Oldies | LP | Parlophone | PMC7016 | 1967 | £12 | £25 | mono |
| Day Tripper | 78 | Parlophone | R5389 | 196– | £150 | £250 | Indian, best auctioned |
| Day Tripper | 7" | Parlophone | R5389 | 1965 | £1.50 | £4 | |
| Day Tripper | 7" | Parlophone | R5389 | 1965 | £210 | £350 | demo |
| Day Tripper | 7" | Parlophone | RP5389 | 1985 | £5 | £10 | picture disc |
| Devil In Her Heart | 7" EP | Odeon | SOE3777 | 1965 | £15 | £30 | French |
| Dizzy Miss Lizzy | 78 | Parlophone | DPE183 | 196– | £150 | £250 | Indian, best auctioned |
| Do You Want To Know A Secret | 7" | Odeon | 22710 | 1964 | £5 | £10 | German import |
| Early Beatles | LP | Capitol | ST2309 | 1965 | £8 | £20 | US, stereo |
| Early Beatles | LP | Capitol | T2309 | 1965 | £10 | £25 | US, mono |
| Eight Days A Week | 7" EP | Odeon | SOE3764 | 1965 | £10 | £20 | French |
| From Me To You | CD-s | Parlophone | CD3R5015 | 1988 | £2 | £5 | 3" single |
| From Me To You | 7" EP | Odeon | SOE3739 | 1963 | £10 | £20 | French |
| From Me To You | 7" EP | Odeon | SOE3739 | 1963 | £330 | £500 | French, Beatles in French costume on sleeve |
| From Me To You | 7" | Parlophone | R5015 | 1963 | £1.50 | £4 | |
| From Me To You | 7" | Parlophone | R5015 | 1963 | £210 | £350 | demo |
| From Me To You | 7" | Parlophone | RP5015 | 1983 | £7.50 | £15 | picture disc |
| From Then To You | LP | Apple | LYN2153/4 | 1970 | £150 | £250 | green Apple label |
| Get Back | CD-s | Parlophone | CD3R5777 | 1989 | £2 | £5 | 3" single |
| Get Back | 7" | Apple | R5777 | 1969 | £1.50 | £4 | |
| Get Back | 7" | Apple | R5777 | 1978 | £7.50 | £15 | mispress – B side plays 'I've Had Enough' by Wings |
| Get Back | 7" | Apple | R5779 | 1969 | £150 | £250 | demo |
| Get Back | 7" | Apple | RP5777 | 1989 | £5 | £10 | picture disc |
| Girl | 78 | Parlophone | DPE188 | 196– | £150 | £250 | Indian, best auctioned |

| Title | Format | Label | Catalogue | Year | | | Notes |
|---|---|---|---|---|---|---|---|
| Hard Day's Night | r-reel | Parlophone | TAPMC1230/ TDPCS3058 | 1964 | £10 | £25 | |
| Hard Day's Night | LP | Mobile Fidelity | MFSL1103 | 1984 | £8 | £20 | US audiophile |
| Hard Day's Night | LP | Parlophone | PCS3058 | 1964 | £30 | £60 | stereo |
| Hard Day's Night | LP | Parlophone | PCS3058 | 1969 | £4 | £10 | reissue, exposed edges on back cover, 'Made in Gt Britain' on label |
| Hard Day's Night | LP | Parlophone | PMC1230 | 1964 | £15 | £30 | mono |
| Hard Day's Night | LP | United Artists | SP2359 | 1964 | £150 | £250 | US promo with script |
| Hard Day's Night | LP | United Artists | UAL3366 | 1964 | £15 | £30 | US, mono |
| Hard Day's Night | LP | United Artists | UAS6366 | 1964 | £10 | £25 | US, stereo |
| Hard Day's Night | CD-s | Parlophone | CD3R5160 | 1989 | £2 | £5 | 3" single |
| Hard Day's Night | CD | Liberty | CDP7460792 | 1987 | £20 | £40 | mispressed on to James Bond CD |
| Hard Day's Night | 7" EP | Parlophone | GEP8920 | 1964 | £5 | £10 | |
| Hard Day's Night | 7" | Parlophone | R5160 | 1964 | £1.50 | £4 | |
| Hard Day's Night | 7" | Parlophone | R5160 | 1964 | £210 | £350 | demo |
| Hard Day's Night | 7" | Parlophone | RP5160 | 1984 | £5 | £10 | picture disc |
| Hard Day's Night No. 2 | 7" EP | Parlophone | GEP8924 | 1964 | £10 | £20 | |
| Hello Goodbye | CD-s | Parlophone | CD3R5655 | 1989 | £2 | £5 | 3" single |
| Hello Goodbye | 7" | Parlophone | R5655 | 1967 | £1.50 | £4 | |
| Hello Goodbye | 7" | Parlophone | R5655 | 1967 | £150 | £250 | demo |
| Hello Goodbye | 7" | Parlophone | RP5655 | 1987 | £5 | £10 | picture disc |
| Help! | r-reel | Parlophone | TAPMC1255/ TDPCS3071 | 1965 | £10 | £25 | |
| Help! | LP | Capitol | MAS2386 | 1965 | £10 | £25 | US, mono |
| Help! | LP | Capitol | SMAS2386 | 1965 | £8 | £20 | US, stereo |
| Help! | LP | Capitol | SMAS82386 | 1965 | £25 | £50 | US, Record Club issue |
| Help! | LP | Mobile Fidelity | MFSL1105 | 1984 | £8 | £20 | US audiophile |
| Help! | LP | Odeon | SMO84008 | 1965 | £37.50 | £75 | German, white and gold label |
| Help! | LP | Odeon | SMO984008 | 1965 | £100 | £200 | German, club pressing |
| Help! | LP | Parlophone | PCS3071 | 1965 | £30 | £60 | stereo |
| Help! | LP | Parlophone | PCS3071 | 1969 | £4 | £10 | reissue, exposed edges on back cover, 'Made in Gt Britain' on label |
| Help! | LP | Parlophone | PMC1255 | 1965 | £15 | £30 | mono |
| Help! | CD-s | Parlophone | CD3R5305 | 1989 | £2 | £5 | 3" single |
| Help! | 78 | Parlophone | R5305 | 196– | £150 | £250 | Indian, best auctioned |
| Help! | 7" EP | Odeon | SOE3769 | 1965 | £10 | £20 | French |
| Help! | 7" | Parlophone | R5305 | 1965 | £1.50 | £4 | |
| Help! | 7" | Parlophone | R5305 | 1965 | £210 | £350 | demo |
| Help! | 7" | Parlophone | RP5305 | 1985 | £5 | £10 | picture disc |
| Help!/Rubber Soul/Revolver | CD | EMI | BEACD25/2 | 1987 | £37.50 | £75 | HMV red box, magazine |
| Here, There And Everywhere | 78 | Parlophone | DPE189 | 196– | £150 | £250 | Indian, best auctioned |
| Hey Jude | LP | Apple | CPCS106 | 197– | £8 | £20 | export |
| Hey Jude | LP | Apple | CPCS106 | 1970 | £25 | £50 | dark green Apple label |
| Hey Jude | LP | Parlophone | CPCS106 | 1970 | £100 | £200 | export, silver & black label |
| Hey Jude | LP | Parlophone | PCSJ149 | 1970 | £8 | £20 | export |
| Hey Jude | CD-s | Parlophone | CD3R5722 | 1989 | £2 | £5 | 3" single |
| Hey Jude | 78 | Parlophone | DPE190 | 196– | £150 | £250 | Indian, best auctioned |
| Hey Jude | 7" | Apple | R5722 | 1968 | £1.50 | £4 | |
| Hey Jude | 7" | Apple | RP5722 | 1988 | £5 | £10 | picture disc |
| Hey Jude | 7" | Parlophone | DP570 | 1968 | £20 | £40 | export |
| Hey Jude | 7" | Parlophone | R5722 | 1968 | £150 | £250 | demo |
| Hey Jude | 12" | Apple | 12RP5722 | 1988 | £3 | £8 | picture disc |
| Hey Jude/The Beatles Again | LP | Apple | SO/SW385 | 1970 | £6 | £15 | US, labels read 'The Beatles Again' |
| History Of Rock Vol. 26 | LP | Orbis | HRL026 | 1984 | £6 | £15 | double |
| Honey Don't | 7" EP | Odeon | SOE3779 | 1965 | £15 | £30 | French |
| I Feel Fine | CD-s | Parlophone | CD3R5200 | 1989 | £2 | £5 | 3" single |
| I Feel Fine | 78 | Parlophone | R5200 | 196– | £150 | £250 | Indian, best auctioned |
| I Feel Fine | 7" EP | Odeon | SOE3760 | 1964 | £10 | £20 | French |
| I Feel Fine | 7" | Parlophone | R5200 | 1964 | £1.50 | £4 | |
| I Feel Fine | 7" | Parlophone | R5200 | 1964 | £210 | £350 | demo |
| I Feel Fine | 7" | Parlophone | RP5200 | 1984 | £5 | £10 | picture disc |
| I Saw Her Standing There | 78 | Parlophone | DPE159 | 196– | £150 | £250 | Indian, best auctioned |
| I Should Have Known Better | 78 | Parlophone | DPE168 | 196– | £150 | £250 | Indian, best auctioned |
| I Wanna Be Your Man | 7" | Odeon | 22681 | 1964 | £5 | £10 | German import |
| I Want To Hold Your Hand | CD-s | Parlophone | CD3R5084 | 1989 | £2 | £5 | 3" single |
| I Want To Hold Your Hand | 7" EP | Odeon | SOE3745 | 1963 | £10 | £20 | French |
| I Want To Hold Your Hand | 7" | Odeon | 22623 | 1964 | £5 | £10 | German import |
| I Want To Hold Your Hand | 7" | Parlophone | R5084 | 1963 | £1.50 | £4 | |
| I Want To Hold Your Hand | 7" | Parlophone | R5084 | 1963 | £210 | £350 | demo |
| I Want To Hold Your Hand | 7" | Parlophone | RP5084 | 1983 | £5 | £10 | picture disc |
| I'm A Loser | 78 | Parlophone | DPE178 | 196– | £150 | £250 | Indian, best auctioned |
| I'm A Loser | 7" | HMV | MQ20007 | 1964 | £5 | £10 | Italian import |
| I'm Looking Through You | 78 | Parlophone | DPE193 | 196– | £150 | £250 | Indian, best auctioned |
| If I Fell | 78 | Parlophone | DPE167 | 196– | £150 | £250 | Indian, best auctioned |
| If I Fell | 7" | Parlophone | DP562 | 1964 | £20 | £40 | export |
| Impression | LP | Parlophone | 6086 | 1965 | £400 | £600 | German, club pressing |
| Impression | LP | Parlophone | 6279 | 1965 | £250 | £400 | German, club pressing |
| In The Beginning | LP | Polydor | 244504 | 1970 | £6 | £15 | US, red label |
| Introducing The Beatles | LP | Vee Jay | LP1062 | 1963 | £180 | £300 | US, with 'Love Me Do', blank back cover, mono |

| Title | Format | Label | Cat. No. | Year | Price | Price | Notes |
|---|---|---|---|---|---|---|---|
| Introducing The Beatles | LP | Vee Jay | LP1062 | 1963 | £50 | £100 | ...US, with 'Love Me Do', songs listed on back |
| Introducing The Beatles | LP | Vee Jay | LP1062 | 1964 | £25 | £50 | ...... US, with 'Please Please Me', mono |
| Introducing The Beatles | LP | Vee Jay | LPS1062 | 1963 | £400 | £600 | ...US, with 'Love Me Do', blank back cover, stereo |
| Introducing The Beatles | LP | Vee Jay | LPS1062 | 1964 | £180 | £300 | ...... US, with 'Please Please Me', stereo |
| Kansas City | 7" EP | Odeon | SOE3776 | 1965 | £15 | £30 | ......................French |
| Komm Gib Mir Deine Hand | 7" | Odeon | 22671 | 1964 | £25 | £50 | ...... German import, picture sleeve |
| Lady Madonna | CD-s | Parlophone | CD3R5675 | 1989 | £2 | £5 | ..........................3" single |
| Lady Madonna | 7" | Parlophone | R5675 | 1968 | £1.50 | £4 | |
| Lady Madonna | 7" | Parlophone | R5675 | 1968 | £150 | £250 | ......................demo |
| Lady Madonna | 7" | Parlophone | RP5675 | 1988 | £5 | £10 | ..............picture disc |
| Les Beatles | LP | Odeon | OSX222 | 1963 | £37.50 | £75 | ........................ French |
| Let It Be | r-reel | Apple | TAPMC7096 | 1970 | £25 | £50 | ............................mono |
| Let It Be | r-reel | Apple | TDPCS7096 | 1970 | £15 | £30 | ..............................stereo |
| Let It Be | LP | Apple | AR34001 | 1970 | £4 | £10 | ...US, 'a subsidiary of Capitol' |
| Let It Be | LP | Apple | PCS7096 | 1970 | £4 | £10 | . orange Apple on back cover |
| Let It Be | LP | Apple | PCS7096 | 1978 | £30 | £60 | ......... white vinyl |
| Let It Be | LP | Apple | PPCS7096 | 1970 | £8 | £20 | ...................export |
| Let It Be | LP | Apple | PXS1/PCS7096 | 1970 | £100 | £200 | ....... boxed with book |
| Let It Be | LP | Mobile Fidelity | MFSL1109 | 1984 | £8 | £20 | ........US audiophile |
| Let It Be | LP | Parlophone | PPCS7096 | 1970 | £100 | £200 | . export, silver & black label |
| Let It Be | LP | Parlophone | PPCS7096 | 1970 | £250 | £400 | export, yellow & black label |
| Let It Be | CD-s | Parlophone | CD3R5833 | 1989 | £2 | £5 | ..........................3" single |
| Let It Be | CD | EMI | BEACD25/8 | 1987 | £8 | £20 | ...... HMV boxed set, poster, booklet, badge |
| Let It Be | CD | Parlophone | CDP7464472 | 1988 | £62.50 | £125 | ......promo, green disc, boxed |
| Let It Be | 7" | Apple | PR5833 | 1970 | £37.50 | £75 | ............................export |
| Let It Be | 7" | Apple | R5833 | 1970 | £1.50 | £4 | |
| Let It Be | 7" | Apple | R5833 | 1970 | £150 | £250 | ....................demo |
| Let It Be | 7" | Apple | R5833 | 1970 | £2 | £5 | ........ picture sleeve |
| Let It Be | 7" | Apple | RP5833 | 1990 | £5 | £10 | ...............picture disc |
| Let It Be | 7" | Parlophone | PR5833 | 1970 | £25 | £50 | ..................export |
| Live At The BBC | CD | Apple | 724383179626 | 1994 | £10 | £25 | double, mis-titled track 17, disc 2 |
| Live At The BBC | CD | Apple | CDPCSPDJ7261 | 1994 | £37.50 | £75 | ........promo sampler in fold-out package |
| Long Tall Sally | 78 | Parlophone | DPE164 | 196– | £150 | £250 | Indian, best auctioned |
| Long Tall Sally | 7" EP | Odeon | SOE3755 | 1964 | £7.50 | £15 | ........................ French |
| Long Tall Sally | 7" EP | Parlophone | GEP8913 | 1964 | £5 | £10 | |
| Long Tall Sally | 7" | Odeon | 22745 | 1964 | £6 | £12 | ......German import |
| Love Me Do | CD-s | Parlophone | CD3R4949 | 1988 | £2 | £5 | .......................3" single |
| Love Me Do | 7" | Parlophone | R4949 | 1962 | £700 | £1000 | ........................demo |
| Love Me Do | 7" | Parlophone | R4949 | 1962 | £12.50 | £25 | .................red label |
| Love Me Do | 7" | Parlophone | R4949 | 1963 | £25 | £50 | .black label, 2 versions |
| Love Me Do | 7" | Parlophone | R4949 | 1982 | £7.50 | £15 | Ardmore & Beechwood credit |
| Love Me Do | 7" | Parlophone | RP4949 | 1982 | £7.50 | £15 | Ardmore & Beechwood credit, picture disc |
| Love Me Do | 7" | Parlophone | RP4949 | 1982 | £10 | £20 | .picture disc mispress – 2 A sides |
| Love Me Do | 12" | Parlophone | 12R4949 | 1982 | £2.50 | £6 | |
| Magical Mystery Tour | LP | Capitol | MAL2835 | 1967 | £30 | £60 | .................US, mono |
| Magical Mystery Tour | LP | Capitol | SMAL2835 | 1967 | £6 | £15 | ..................US, stereo |
| Magical Mystery Tour | LP | Mobile Fidelity | MFSL1047 | 1981 | £10 | £25 | ...........US audiophile |
| Magical Mystery Tour | LP | Parlophone | PCTC255 | 1978 | £25 | £50 | .............. yellow vinyl |
| Magical Mystery Tour | CD | EMI | BEACD25/6 | 1987 | £10 | £25 | .... HMV box, badge, booklet, poster |
| Magical Mystery Tour | 7" EP | Odeon | MEOHS39501/2 | 1967 | £10 | £20 | .......French double |
| Magical Mystery Tour | 7" EP | Parlophone | MMT1 | 1967 | £10 | £20 | ... double, mono, blue lyric sheet |
| Magical Mystery Tour | 7" EP | Parlophone | MMT1 | 1967 | £15 | £30 | . mispress, Beach Boys 'Darlin'' on B side of 'Walrus' |
| Magical Mystery Tour | 7" EP | Parlophone | SMMT1 | 1967 | £7.50 | £15 | .... double, stereo, blue lyric sheet |
| Magical Mystery Tour | 7" EP | Parlophone | SMMT1 | 197– | £5 | £10 | ........ yellow lyric sheet |
| Meet The Beatles | LP | Capitol | ST2047 | 1964 | £10 | £25 | US, brown title, stereo |
| Meet The Beatles | LP | Capitol | ST2047 | 1964 | £8 | £20 | .US, green title, stereo |
| Meet The Beatles | LP | Capitol | ST82047 | 1964 | £25 | £50 | US, Record Club issue |
| Meet The Beatles | LP | Capitol | T2047 | 1964 | £15 | £30 | US, brown title, mono |
| Meet The Beatles | LP | Capitol | T2047 | 1964 | £10 | £25 | .US, green title, mono |
| Michelle | 78 | Parlophone | DPE186 | 196– | £150 | £250 | Indian, best auctioned |
| Michelle | 78 | Parlophone | DPE187 | 196– | £150 | £250 | Indian, best auctioned |
| Michelle | 7" EP | Odeon | MEO102 | 1965 | £7.50 | £15 | ......................French |
| Michelle | 7" | Parlophone | DP564 | 1966 | £30 | £60 | ..................export |
| Michelle | 7" | Odeon |  | 1965 | £10 | £30 | ......................French |
| Misery | 7" EP | Odeon | SOE3778 | 1964 | £15 | £30 | ......................French |
| Money | 7" | Odeon | 22638 | 1964 | £5 | £10 | .........German import |

| Title | Format | Label | Cat. No. | Year | | | Notes |
|---|---|---|---|---|---|---|---|
| No Reply | 7" | Odeon | 22893 | 1964 | £5 | £10 | German import |
| No. 1 | LP | Odeon | OSX225 | 1963 | £62.50 | £125 | French |
| Nowhere Man | 7" EP | Parlophone | GEP8952 | 1966 | £12.50 | £25 | |
| Ob-La-Di, Ob-La-Da | 78 | Parlophone | DPE192 | 196– | £150 | £250 | Indian, best auctioned |
| Only The Beatles | cass | EMI | SMMC151 | 1986 | £6 | £15 | Heineken promotion |
| Original Master Records | LP | Mobile Fidelity | 0575 | 1984 | £210 | £350 | US 13 LP box set, audiophile |
| Paperback Writer | CD-s | Parlophone | CD3R5452 | 1989 | £2 | £5 | 3" single |
| Paperback Writer | 7" EP | Odeon | MEO119 | 1966 | £7.50 | £15 | French |
| Paperback Writer | 7" | Parlophone | R5452 | 1966 | £1.50 | £4 | |
| Paperback Writer | 7" | Parlophone | R5452 | 1966 | £210 | £350 | demo |
| Paperback Writer | 7" | Parlophone | RP5452 | 1986 | £5 | £10 | picture disc |
| Paperback Writer | 7" | Parlophone | RP5452 | 1986 | £12.50 | £25 | picture disc mispress – A side plays Queen track |
| Past Masters Vol. 1 | CD | EMI | BEACD25/9 | 1987 | £8 | £20 | HMV box, booklet, badge |
| Past Masters Vol. 2 | CD | EMI | BEACD25/10 | 1987 | £8 | £20 | HMV box, booklet, badge |
| Penny Lane | CD-s | Parlophone | CD3R5570 | 1989 | £2 | £5 | 3" single |
| Penny Lane | 7" | Parlophone | R5570 | 1967 | £1.50 | £4 | |
| Penny Lane | 7" | Parlophone | R5570 | 1967 | £180 | £300 | demo |
| Penny Lane | 7" | Parlophone | R5570 | 1967 | £7.50 | £15 | picture sleeve |
| Penny Lane | 7" | Parlophone | RP5570 | 1987 | £5 | £10 | picture disc |
| Please Please Me | r-reel | Parlophone | TAPMC1202/ TDPCS3042 | 1963 | £10 | £25 | |
| Please Please Me | LP | Mobile Fidelity | MFSL1101 | 1984 | £8 | £20 | US audiophile |
| Please Please Me | LP | Odeon | ZTOX5550 | 1963 | £87.50 | £175 | German export |
| Please Please Me | LP | Parlophone | PCS3042 | 1963 | £1050 | £1500 | gold label stereo |
| Please Please Me | LP | Parlophone | PCS3042 | 1963 | £62.50 | £125 | stereo |
| Please Please Me | LP | Parlophone | PCS3042 | 1969 | £4 | £10 | reissue, exposed edges on back cover, 'Made in Gt Britain' on label |
| Please Please Me | LP | Parlophone | PMC1202 | 1963 | £15 | £30 | mono |
| Please Please Me | LP | Parlophone | PMC1202 | 1963 | £100 | £200 | mono, gold label |
| Please Please Me | CD-s | Parlophone | CD3R4983 | 1988 | £2 | £5 | 3" single |
| Please Please Me | CD | Parlophone | CDP7463452 | 1987 | £25 | £50 | mispressing – plays A Hard Day's Night |
| Please Please Me | CD | Parlophone | CDP7463452 | 1987 | £25 | £50 | mispressing – plays Beatles For Sale |
| Please Please Me | 78 | Parlophone | | 196– | £150 | £250 | Indian, best auctioned |
| Please Please Me | 7" | Parlophone | R4983 | 1963 | £1.50 | £4 | black label |
| Please Please Me | 7" | Parlophone | R4983 | 1963 | £400 | £600 | demo |
| Please Please Me | 7" | Parlophone | R4983 | 1963 | £15 | £30 | red label |
| Please Please Me | 7" | Parlophone | RP4983 | 1982 | £7.50 | £15 | picture disc mispress, plays 'From Me To You' |
| Please Please Me | 7" | Parlophone | RP4983 | 1983 | £5 | £10 | picture disc |
| Please Please Me/With /Hard Day's Night/ For Sale | CD | EMI | BEACD25 | 1987 | £100 | £200 | HMV black box, book, leaflet |
| Rarities | LP | Capitol | SN12009 | 1978 | £20 | £40 | US green label |
| Reel Music | LP | Capitol | SV12199 | 1982 | £8 | £20 | US gold vinyl |
| Reel Music | LP | Capitol | SV12199 | 1982 | £15 | £30 | US gold vinyl, numbered |
| Revolver | r-reel | Parlophone | TAPMC/ TDPCS7009 | 1966 | £10 | £25 | |
| Revolver | LP | Capitol | ST2576 | 1966 | £8 | £20 | US, stereo |
| Revolver | LP | Capitol | ST82576 | 1966 | £25 | £50 | US, record club issue |
| Revolver | LP | Capitol | T2576 | 1966 | £10 | £25 | US, mono |
| Revolver | LP | Mobile Fidelity | MFSL1107 | 1984 | £8 | £20 | US audiophile |
| Revolver | LP | Odeon | SMO74161 | 1966 | £37.50 | £75 | German, white and gold label |
| Revolver | LP | Parlophone | PCS7009 | 1966 | £30 | £60 | stereo |
| Revolver | LP | Parlophone | PCS7009 | 1969 | £4 | £10 | reissue, exposed edges on back cover, 'Made in Gt Britain' on label |
| Revolver | LP | Parlophone | PMC7009 | 1966 | £15 | £30 | mono |
| Revolver | CD | Decca | 4177182 | 1987 | £20 | £40 | mispressed on to Haydn CD |
| Rock And Roll Music | 78 | Parlophone | DPE179 | 196– | £150 | £250 | Indian, best auctioned |
| Roll Over Beethoven | 7" EP | Odeon | SOE3746 | 1963 | £10 | £20 | French |
| Rubber Soul | r-reel | Parlophone | TAPMC1267/ TDPCS3075 | 1966 | £10 | £25 | |
| Rubber Soul | LP | Capitol | ST2442 | 1965 | £8 | £20 | US, stereo |
| Rubber Soul | LP | Capitol | ST82442 | 1965 | £25 | £50 | US, Record Club issue |
| Rubber Soul | LP | Capitol | T2442 | 1965 | £10 | £25 | US, mono |
| Rubber Soul | LP | Mobile Fidelity | MFSL1106 | 1984 | £8 | £20 | US audiophile |
| Rubber Soul | LP | Odeon | SMO984066 | 1965 | £75 | £150 | German, club pressing |
| Rubber Soul | LP | Parlophone | PCS3075 | 1966 | £30 | £60 | stereo |
| Rubber Soul | LP | Parlophone | PCS3075 | 1969 | £4 | £10 | reissue, exposed edges on back cover, 'Made in Gt Britain' on label |
| Rubber Soul | LP | Parlophone | PMC1267 | 1966 | £15 | £30 | mono |
| Rubber Soul | CD | Parlophone | CDP7464402 | 1987 | £20 | £40 | mispressing – plays Wilson-Phillips |
| Searchin' | 7" | AFE | AFS1 | 1982 | £4 | £8 | |
| Second Album | LP | Odeon | ZTOX5558 | 1964 | £50 | £100 | German, export |
| Sgt. Pepper's Lonely Hearts Club Band | r-reel | Parlophone | TAPMC7027 | 1967 | £10 | £25 | mono |

| Title | Format | Label | Catalogue | Year | | | Notes |
|---|---|---|---|---|---|---|---|
| Sgt. Pepper's Lonely Hearts Club Band | r-reel | Parlophone | TDPCS7027 | 1967 | £15 | £30 | stereo |
| Sgt. Pepper's Lonely Hearts Club Band | LP | Capitol | MAS2653 | 1967 | £25 | £50 | US, mono |
| Sgt. Pepper's Lonely Hearts Club Band | LP | Capitol | SEAV11840 | 1978 | £10 | £25 | Canadian, marbled vinyl |
| Sgt. Pepper's Lonely Hearts Club Band | LP | Capitol | SEAX11840 | 1978 | £10 | £25 | US picture disc |
| Sgt. Pepper's Lonely Hearts Club Band | LP | Capitol | SMAS2653 | 1967 | £10 | £25 | US, stereo |
| Sgt. Pepper's Lonely Hearts Club Band | LP | Mobile Fidelity | MFSL1100 | 1982 | £8 | £20 | US audiophile |
| Sgt. Pepper's Lonely Hearts Club Band | LP | Mobile Fidelity | UHQR1100 | 1982 | £100 | £200 | US audiophile, quarter-inch thick vinyl |
| Sgt. Pepper's Lonely Hearts Club Band | LP | Parlophone | PCS7027 | 1967 | £15 | £30 | stereo |
| Sgt. Pepper's Lonely Hearts Club Band | LP | Parlophone | PCS7027 | 1969 | £4 | £10 | reissue, exposed edges on inside of cover, 'Made in Gt Britain' on label |
| Sgt. Pepper's Lonely Hearts Club Band | LP | Parlophone | PHO7027 | 1979 | £10 | £25 | picture disc |
| Sgt. Pepper's Lonely Hearts Club Band | LP | Parlophone | PMC7027 | 1967 | £25 | £50 | mono |
| Sgt. Pepper's Lonely Hearts Club Band | LP | Parlophone | PMC7027 | 1982 | £5 | £12 | from BMC10, but with stereo B side |
| Sgt. Pepper's Lonely Hearts Club Band | CD | EMI | BEACD25/3 | 1987 | £10 | £25 | HMV box, badge, booklet, cutouts |
| Sgt. Pepper's Lonely Hearts Club Band | CD | Parlophone | CDP7464422 | 1987 | £20 | £40 | mispressing – plays classical album |
| Sgt. Pepper's Lonely Hearts Club Band | CD | Parlophone | CDP7464422 | 1987 | £20 | £40 | mispressing – plays Now 18 |
| Sgt. Pepper's Lonely Hearts Club Band | CD | Parlophone | CDP7464422 | 1987 | £25 | £50 | mispressing – plays Revolver |
| Sgt. Pepper's Lonely Hearts Club Band | CD | Virgin | CDV2421 | 1987 | £20 | £40 | mispressed on to In Tua Nua CD |
| She Loves You | CD-s | Parlophone | CD3R5055 | 1988 | £2 | £5 | 3" single |
| She Loves You | 7" EP | Odeon | SOE3741 | 1963 | £10 | £20 | French, 2 slightly different sleeves |
| She Loves You | 7" | Parlophone | R5055 | 1963 | £1.50 | £4 | |
| She Loves You | 7" | Parlophone | R5055 | 1963 | £210 | £350 | demo |
| She Loves You | 7" | Parlophone | RP5055 | 1983 | £7.50 | £15 | picture disc |
| Singles Collection | CD-s | Parlophone/Apple | CDBSC1 | 1989 | £25 | £50 | boxed set of 22 3" singles |
| Something | CD-s | Parlophone | CD3R5814 | 1989 | £2 | £5 | 3" single |
| Something | 7" | Apple | R5814 | 1969 | £1.50 | £4 | |
| Something | 7" | Apple | R5814 | 1969 | £150 | £250 | demo |
| Something | 7" | Apple | RP5814 | 1989 | £5 | £10 | picture disc |
| Something New | LP | Capitol | ST2108 | 1964 | £8 | £20 | US, stereo |
| Something New | LP | Capitol | ST82108 | 1964 | £25 | £50 | US, Record Club issue |
| Something New | LP | Capitol | T2108 | 1964 | £10 | £25 | US, mono |
| Something New | LP | Parlophone | CPCS101 | 1965 | £250 | £400 | export |
| Something New | LP | Parlophone | CPCS101 | 1969 | £100 | £200 | export, silver & black label |
| Songs, Pictures And Stories | LP | Vee Jay | LP1092 | 1964 | £37.50 | £75 | US, fold-open cover |
| Strawberry Fields Forever | 7" EP | Odeon | MEO134 | 1967 | £7.50 | £15 | French |
| Tell Me What You See | 7" EP | Odeon | SOE3775 | 1965 | £10 | £20 | French |
| Tell Me Why | 78 | Parlophone | DPE172 | 196– | £150 | £250 | Indian, best auctioned |
| Their Greatest Hits | cass | St. Michael | 13615701 | 1984 | £8 | £20 | boxed with book |
| Ticket To Ride | CD-s | Parlophone | CD3R5265 | 1989 | £2 | £5 | 3" single |
| Ticket To Ride | 7" EP | Odeon | SOE3766 | 1965 | £10 | £20 | French |
| Ticket To Ride | 7" | Parlophone | R5265 | 1965 | £1.50 | £4 | |
| Ticket To Ride | 7" | Parlophone | R5265 | 1965 | £210 | £350 | demo |
| Ticket To Ride | 7" | Parlophone | RP5265 | 1985 | £5 | £10 | picture disc |
| Ticket To Ride | 7" | Parlophone | RP5265 | 1985 | £7.50 | £15 | picture disc mispress, B side plays Power Station track |
| Twist And Shout | 7" EP | Parlophone | GEP8882 | 1963 | £5 | £10 | |
| Twist And Shout | 7" | Lingasong | NB1 | 1977 | £4 | £8 | |
| Twist And Shout | 7" | Odeon | 22581 | 1964 | £5 | £10 | German import |
| Volume 1 | 7" EP | Odeon | MOE21001 | 1965 | £30 | £60 | French |
| Volume 2 | 7" EP | Odeon | MOE21002 | 1965 | £30 | £60 | French |
| Volume 3 | 7" EP | Odeon | MOE21003 | 1965 | £50 | £100 | French |
| Volume 4 | 7" EP | Odeon | MOE21004 | 1965 | £30 | £60 | French |
| We Can Work It Out | CD-s | Parlophone | CD3R5389 | 1989 | £2 | £5 | 3" single |
| We Can Work It Out | 7" EP | Odeon | MEO107 | 1965 | £7.50 | £15 | French |
| With The Beatles | r-reel | Parlophone | TAPMC1206/TDPCS3045 | 1964 | | £25 | |
| With The Beatles | LP | Mobile Fidelity | MFSL1102 | 1984 | £20 | £40 | US audiophile |
| With The Beatles | LP | Parlophone | PCS3045 | 1963 | £30 | £60 | stereo |
| With The Beatles | LP | Parlophone | PCS3045 | 1969 | £4 | £10 | reissue, exposed edges on back cover, 'Made in Gt Britain' on label |
| With The Beatles | LP | Parlophone | PMC1206 | 1963 | £15 | £30 | mono |
| Words Of Love | 78 | Parlophone | DPE180 | 196– | £150 | £250 | Indian, best auctioned |
| World Records Presents The Music Of The Beatles | 7" | Lyntone | LYN8982 | 1980 | £4 | £8 | promo flexi |
| Yellow Submarine | r-reel | Apple | TAPMC/TDPCS7070 | 1969 | £15 | £30 | |
| Yellow Submarine | LP | Apple | PCS7070 | 1969 | £6 | £15 | stereo |
| Yellow Submarine | LP | Apple | PMC7070 | 1969 | £62.50 | £125 | mono |
| Yellow Submarine | LP | Apple | SW153 | 1968 | £5 | £12 | US |
| Yellow Submarine | LP | Mobile Fidelity | MFSL1108 | 1984 | £8 | £20 | US audiophile |
| Yellow Submarine | LP | Odeon | PPCS7070 | 1969 | £330 | £500 | export |
| Yellow Submarine | LP | Parlophone | PPCS7070 | 1969 | £100 | £200 | export, silver & black label |

| Title | Format | Label | Cat. No. | Year | | | Notes |
|---|---|---|---|---|---|---|---|
| Yellow Submarine | LP | Parlophone | PPCS7070 | 1969 | £500 | £750 | export, yellow & black label |
| Yellow Submarine | CD-s | Parlophone | CD3R5493 | 1989 | £2 | £5 | 3" single |
| Yellow Submarine | CD | EMI | BEACD25/5 | 1987 | £25 | £50 | HMV box, badge, cutout, leaflet |
| Yellow Submarine | CD | Parlophone | CDP7464452 | 1987 | £25 | £50 | mispressing – plays Sgt. Pepper |
| Yellow Submarine | 7" EP | Odeon | MEO126 | 1966 | £7.50 | £15 | French |
| Yellow Submarine | 7" | Parlophone | R5493 | 1966 | £1.50 | £4 | |
| Yellow Submarine | 7" | Parlophone | R5493 | 1966 | £180 | £300 | demo |
| Yellow Submarine | 7" | Parlophone | RP5493 | 1986 | £5 | £10 | picture disc |
| Yesterday | 78 | Parlophone | DPE184 | 196– | £150 | £250 | Indian, best auctioned |
| Yesterday | 7" EP | Odeon | MEO105 | 1965 | £7.50 | £15 | French |
| Yesterday | 7" EP | Odeon | SOE3772 | 1965 | £10 | £20 | French |
| Yesterday | 7" EP | Parlophone | GEP8948 | 1966 | £12.50 | £25 | |
| Yesterday | 7" | Parlophone | DP563 | 1965 | £30 | £60 | export |
| Yesterday And Today | LP | Capitol | ST2553 | 1966 | £2100 | £3000 | US, peeled butcher sleeve, stereo |
| Yesterday And Today | LP | Capitol | ST2553 | 1966 | £8 | £20 | US, stereo |
| Yesterday And Today | LP | Capitol | ST2553 | 1966 | £400 | £600 | US, unpeeled butcher sleeve, stereo |
| Yesterday And Today | LP | Capitol | ST2553 | 198– | £100 | £200 | Japanese butcher sleeve reissue |
| Yesterday And Today | LP | Capitol | ST82553 | 1966 | £25 | £50 | US, Record Club issue |
| Yesterday And Today | LP | Capitol | T2553 | 1966 | £700 | £1000 | US peeled butcher sleeve |
| Yesterday And Today | LP | Capitol | T2553 | 1966 | £100 | £200 | US unpeeled butcher sleeve |
| Yesterday And Today | LP | Capitol | T2553 | 1966 | £10 | £25 | US, mono |
| You Like Me Too Much | 78 | Parlophone | DPE185 | 196– | £150 | £250 | Indian, best auctioned |
| You've Got To Hide Your Love Away | 7" EP | Odeon | SOE3772 | 1965 | £15 | £30 | French |

## BEATLES & OTHERS

| Title | Format | Label | Cat. No. | Year | | | Notes |
|---|---|---|---|---|---|---|---|
| Our First Four | 7" | Apple | | 1968 | £500 | £750 | promo, pack with 4 x 7" |

## BEATLES WITH TONY SHERIDAN

| Title | Format | Label | Cat. No. | Year | | | Notes |
|---|---|---|---|---|---|---|---|
| Ain't She Sweet | LP | Atco | 33169 | 1964 | £30 | £60 | US, mono |
| Ain't She Sweet | LP | Atco | SD33169 | 1964 | £37.50 | £75 | US, stereo |
| Ain't She Sweet | 7" EP | Polydor | 21965 | 1964 | £20 | £40 | French |
| Ain't She Sweet | 7" | Polydor | NH52317 | 1964 | £20 | £40 | orange label |
| Ain't She Sweet | 7" | Polydor | NH52317 | 1964 | £50 | £100 | picture sleeve |
| Ain't She Sweet | 7" | Polydor | NH52317 | 1967 | £6 | £12 | red label |
| Beatles' First | LP | Polydor | 236201 | 1964 | £25 | £50 | rough red label |
| Beatles' First | LP | Polydor | 236201 | 1967 | £15 | £30 | smooth red label |
| Beatles' First | LP | Polydor | POLD666 | 197– | £15 | £30 | |
| Beatles' First | CD | Polydor | 8237012 | 1984 | £5 | £12 | |
| Beatles' First | CD | Polydor | 8237012 | 1984 | £25 | £50 | withdrawn sleeve with wrong line-up |
| Cry For A Shadow | 7" | Polydor | NH52275 | 1964 | £20 | £40 | orange label |
| Cry For A Shadow | 7" | Polydor | NH52275 | 1964 | £50 | £100 | picture sleeve |
| Cry For A Shadow | 7" | Polydor | NH52275 | 1967 | £4 | £8 | red label |
| Meet The Beat | 10" LP | Polydor | J74557 | 1965 | £150 | £250 | German |
| Mister Twist | 7" EP | Polydor | 21914 | 1962 | £25 | £50 | French |
| My Bonnie | 7" | Polydor | NH66833 | 1962 | £25 | £50 | orange label |
| My Bonnie | 7" | Polydor | NH66833 | 1967 | £4 | £8 | red label |
| Sweet Georgia Brown | 7" | Polydor | NH52906 | 1964 | £37.50 | £75 | orange label |
| Sweet Georgia Brown | 7" | Polydor | NH52906 | 1967 | £12.50 | £25 | red label |
| Tony Sheridan With The Beatles | 7" EP | Polydor | EPH21610 | 1963 | £25 | £50 | |
| When The Saints | 7" EP | Polydor | 21914 | 1963 | £20 | £40 | French, 2 different sleeves |

## BEATMEN

| Title | Format | Label | Cat. No. | Year | | | Notes |
|---|---|---|---|---|---|---|---|
| You Can't Sit Down | 7" | Pye | 7N15659 | 1964 | £2 | £5 | |

## BEATSTALKERS

| Title | Format | Label | Cat. No. | Year | | | Notes |
|---|---|---|---|---|---|---|---|
| Everybody's Talkin' About My Baby | 7" | Decca | F12259 | 1965 | £10 | £20 | |
| Everything Is You | 7" | CBS | 3557 | 1968 | £10 | £20 | |
| Left Right Left | 7" | Decca | F12352 | 1966 | £10 | £20 | |
| Love Like Yours | 7" | Decca | F12460 | 1966 | £10 | £20 | |
| My One Chance | 7" | CBS | 2732 | 1967 | £12.50 | £25 | |
| Silver Tree Top School For Boys | 7" | CBS | 3105 | 1967 | £20 | £40 | |
| When I'm Five | 7" | CBS | 3936 | 1969 | £10 | £20 | |
| You'd Better Get A Better Hold On | 7" EP | Decca | 457112 | 1966 | £100 | £200 | French |

## BEATTY, E. C.

| Title | Format | Label | Cat. No. | Year | | | Notes |
|---|---|---|---|---|---|---|---|
| Ski King | 7" | Felsted | AF127 | 1959 | £4 | £8 | |

## BEAU

C. J. T. Midgley (Beau) was a singer-songwriter whose songs would have benefited from more fully worked-out arrangements than they actually got. No doubt John Peel's Dandelion label could not afford the expense of a cast of session musicians. Nevertheless, '1917 Revolution' with its taut strummed twelve-string guitar echoing across the sound-stage is quite wonderful.

| Title | Format | Label | Cat. No. | Year | | | Notes |
|---|---|---|---|---|---|---|---|
| 1917 Revolution | 7" | Dandelion | K4403 | 1970 | £1.50 | £4 | |
| Beau | LP | Dandelion | 63751 | 1969 | £8 | £20 | |
| Creation | LP | Dandelion | DAN8006 | 1971 | £8 | £20 | |

## BEAU BRUMMELS

The natural response of America to the initial furore surrounding the Beatles was for the record-buying public to embrace a number of home-grown talents, whose sound and style owed everything to their Liverpudlian rivals. The Beau Brummels were probably the most successful of these, although they inevitably meant little in Britain. As a result, one of the classic albums of the late sixties has been largely ignored – for *Triangle* is an immaculate collection of imaginatively arranged songs to rival Love's *Forever Changes*.

| | | | | | | |
|---|---|---|---|---|---|---|
| Beau Brummels | LP | Pye | NPL28062 | 1965 | £10 ... £25 | |
| Beau Brummels 66 | LP | Warner Bros | W(S)1644 | 1966 | £10 ... £25 | US |
| Beau Brummels Vol. 2 | LP | Autumn | (S)LP104 | 1966 | £8 ... £20 | US |
| Best Of The Beau Brummels | LP | Vault | LPS114 | 1967 | £15 ... £30 | US |
| Bradley's Barn | LP | Warner Bros | WS1760 | 1968 | £8 ... £20 | US |
| Don't Talk To Strangers | 7" | Pye | 7N25333 | 1965 | £1.50 ... £4 | |
| Good Time Music | 7" | Pye | 7N25342 | 1966 | £1.50 ... £4 | |
| Here We Are Again | 7" EP | Warner Bros | WB112 | 1966 | £12.50 ... £25 | French |
| Just A Little | 7" EP | Vogue | INT18010 | 1965 | £12.50 ... £25 | French |
| Just A Little | 7" | Pye | 7N25306 | 1965 | £1.50 ... £4 | |
| Laugh Laugh | 7" EP | Vogue | INT18002 | 1965 | £12.50 ... £25 | French |
| Laugh Laugh | 7" | Pye | 7N25293 | 1965 | £1.50 ... £4 | |
| Triangle | LP | Warner Bros | W(S)1692 | 1967 | £8 ... £20 | US |
| Vol. 44 | LP | Vault | LPS121 | 1967 | £10 ... £25 | US |
| You Tell Me Why | 7" | Pye | 7N25318 | 1965 | £1.50 ... £4 | |

## BEAUMARKS

| | | | | | |
|---|---|---|---|---|---|
| Clap Your Hands | 7" | Top Rank | JAR377 | 1960 | £5 ... £10 |

## BEAUMONT, JIMMY

| | | | | | |
|---|---|---|---|---|---|
| You Got Too Much Going For You | 7" | London | HLZ10059 | 1966 | £15 ... £30 |

## BEAUREGARDE

| | | | | | |
|---|---|---|---|---|---|
| Beauregarde | LP | F-Empire | 1001 | 1969 | £30 ... £60 | US |

## BEAUTIFUL SOUTH

| | | | | | | |
|---|---|---|---|---|---|---|
| Carry On Continues | CD | Go! Discs | TNTBS1 | 1996 | £8 ... £20 | promo compilation |
| Cary On Up The Charts | CD | Go! Discs | 8285692 | 1994 | £6 ... £15 | double |
| I'll Sail This Ship Alone | CD-s | Go! Discs | GODCD38 | 1989 | £2 ... £5 | |
| My Book | CD-s | Go! Discs | GODCD48 | 1990 | £2 ... £5 | |

## BEAVER, PAUL

| | | | | | |
|---|---|---|---|---|---|
| Perchance To Dream | LP | Rapture | 11111 | | £5 ... £12 | US |

## BEAVER-KRAUSE

Paul Beaver and Bernie Krause were the other pair of synthesizer pioneers, but, unlike the records by Tonto's Expanding Headband, theirs mix the electronics with conventional instruments. Particularly recommended is the music to be found on side two of *Gandharva*, where saxophonist Gerry Mulligan meets the duo in church to glorious effect. *The Guide To Electronic Music* is by way of being an aural handbook, recorded for an avant-garde classical label.

| | | | | | | |
|---|---|---|---|---|---|---|
| All Good Men | LP | Warner Bros | K46184 | 1972 | £4 ... £10 | |
| Gandharva | LP | Warner Bros | K46130 | 1971 | £4 ... £10 | |
| In A Wild Sanctuary | LP | Warner Bros | WS1850 | 1970 | £4 ... £10 | US |
| Nonesuch Guide To Electronic Music | LP | Nonesuch | HC73018 | 1968 | £6 ... £15 | 2 LP boxed set |
| Ragnarok Electronic Funk | LP | Limelight | 86069 | 1969 | £5 ... £12 | US |

## BEAZERS (CHRIS FARLOWE)

| | | | | | |
|---|---|---|---|---|---|
| Blue Beat | 7" | Decca | F11827 | 1964 | £6 ... £12 |

## BEBOP DELUXE

| | | | | | |
|---|---|---|---|---|---|
| Between Two Worlds | 7" | Harvest | HAR5091 | 1975 | £15 ... £30 |
| Teenage Archangel | 7" | Smile | LAFS001 | 1973 | £7.50 ... £15 |

## BEBOP PRESERVATION SOCIETY

| | | | | | |
|---|---|---|---|---|---|
| Bebop Preservation Society | LP | Dawn | DNLS3027 | 1971 | £5 ... £12 |

## BECHET, SIDNEY

| | | | | | | |
|---|---|---|---|---|---|---|
| At Storyville | 10" LP | Vogue | LDE132 | 1955 | £20 ... £40 | |
| At Storyville | 10" LP | Vogue | LDE149 | 1955 | £20 ... £40 | |
| Blue Note Jazz Men | 10" LP | Vogue | LDE025 | 1953 | £25 ... £50 | |
| Blue Note Jazzmen | 10" LP | Vogue | LDE127 | 1955 | £20 ... £40 | |
| Blue Note Jazzmen Vol. 2 | 10" LP | Vogue | LDE086 | 1954 | £20 ... £40 | |
| Fabulous | LP | Blue Note | BLP/BST81207 | 196– | £8 ... £20 | |
| Festival de Jazz 1958 | LP | Vogue | LAE12168 | 1959 | £6 ... £15 | |
| Giant Of Jazz Vol. 1 | LP | Blue Note | BLP/BST81203 | 196– | £8 ... £20 | |
| Giant Of Jazz Vol. 2 | LP | Blue Note | BLP/BST81204 | 196– | £8 ... £20 | |
| Golden Disc Concert | LP | Vogue | LAE12010 | 1956 | £10 ... £25 | |
| Golden Disc Concert | LP | Vogue | LAE12011 | 1956 | £10 ... £25 | |
| Hot Six | 10" LP | Vogue | LDE138 | 1955 | £20 ... £40 | |
| Jazz Classics Vol. 1 | LP | Blue Note | BLP/BST81201 | 196– | £8 ... £20 | |
| Jazz Classics Vol. 2 | LP | Blue Note | BLP/BST81202 | 196– | £8 ... £20 | |
| Jazz Concert Vol. 1 | 10" LP | Vogue | LDE018 | 1953 | £20 ... £40 | |
| Jazz Concert Vol. 2 | 10" LP | Vogue | LDE019 | 1953 | £20 ... £40 | |
| Jazz Concert Vol. 3 | 10" LP | Vogue | LDE027 | 1953 | £20 ... £40 | |
| Last Show | LP | Pye | NPL28006 | 1959 | £6 ... £15 | |
| New Orleans In Paris | 10" LP | Vogue | LDE069 | 1954 | £20 ... £40 | |
| Shake It And Break It | 10" LP | HMV | DLP1042 | 1954 | £20 ... £40 | |
| Sidney Bechet | 10" LP | Columbia | 33S1042 | 1954 | £20 ... £40 | |
| Sidney Bechet | 10" LP | Vogue | LDE001 | 1952 | £20 ... £40 | |
| Vogue Jazzmen | 10" LP | Vogue | LDE119 | 1955 | £20 ... £40 | |

| | | | | | | | |
|---|---|---|---|---|---|---|---|
| With Sammy Price's Bluesicians | LP | Vogue | LAE12037 | 1957 £10 | £25 | |
| With The Claude Luter Orchestra | LP | Vogue | LAE12003 | 1955 £10 | £25 | |
| With The Claude Luter Orchestra | LP | Vogue | LAE12024 | 1956 £10 | £25 | |

## BECK, BOGERT & APPICE

| | | | | | | |
|---|---|---|---|---|---|---|
| Beck, Bogert & Appice | LP | CBS | Q65455 | 1975 £4 | £10 | quad |
| Live In Japan | LP | CBS/Sony | ECPJ11/12 | 1973 £6 | £15 | Japanese double |

## BECK, ELDER CHARLES

| | | | | | |
|---|---|---|---|---|---|
| RCA Victor Race Series Vol. 5 | 7" EP . RCA | RCX7176 | 1965 £2 | £5 |

## BECK, GORDON

| | | | | | | |
|---|---|---|---|---|---|---|
| All In The Morning | cass | Jaguar | JS1 | 1974 £5 | £12 | |
| Beck-Matthewson-Humair Trio | LP | Dire | FO341 | 1972 £15 | £30 | |
| Experiments With Pops | LP | Major Minor | MMLP/SMLP21 | 1969 £15 | £30 | |
| Gyroscope | LP | Morgan | MJ1 | 1968 £20 | £40 | |
| One, Two, Three Go! | cass | Jaguar | JS2 | 1974 £5 | £12 | credited to Gyroscope |
| Plays Dr. Doolittle | LP | Major Minor | SML88 | 1968 £15 | £30 | |
| Plays Half A Jazz Sixpence | LP | Major Minor | MMLP/SMLP22 | 1968 £15 | £30 | |
| Seven Ages Of Man | LP | Rediffusion | ZS115 | 1972 £10 | £25 | |

## BECK, JEFF

When the *Observer* surveyed a number of well-known rock guitarists to discover who the 'guitarists' guitarist' was, the consensus of opinion was Jeff Beck. Notoriously difficult to work with, Beck's career has been notable for the instability of his group line-ups and also for his apparent difficulty in deciding on the best music style to display his talents. He has, nevertheless, managed to create the occasional masterpiece along the way, of which the most obvious examples are the electric jazz album *Blow By Blow* (too common to be valuable, unfortunately) and the blues-rock *Truth*. This record, which included Rod Stewart and Ron Wood as members of a fine band, was a direct influence on Led Zeppelin, not least with regard to Jimmy Page's guitar playing, in which the Jeff Beck approach is very apparent.

| | | | | | | |
|---|---|---|---|---|---|---|
| Beck-ola | LP | Columbia | SCX6351 | 1969 £4 | £10 | |
| Beckology | CD | Epic | 4692622 | 1992 £20 | £40 | Boxed 3 CD set |
| Beckology – The Sampler | CD | Epic | ESK4275 | 1992 £8 | £20 | US promo sampler |
| Blow By Blow | LP | Epic | PEQ33409 | 1975 £5 | £12 | US quad |
| Day In The House | CD-s | Epic | BECK1CD | 1989 £2 | £5 | |
| Fire Meets The Fury | CD | Epic | ESK1901 | 1989 £8 | £20 | US promo sampler, with Stevie Ray Vaughan |
| Guitar Shop | CD-s | Epic | CDBECK1 | 1989 £2 | £5 | |
| Hi Ho Silver Lining | 7" | Columbia | DB8151 | 1967 £1.50 | £4 | |
| Hi Ho Silver Lining | 7" | RAK | RRP3 | 1982 £1.50 | £4 | picture disc |
| Jeff Beck Group | LP | Epic | EQ31331 | 1974 £5 | £12 | US quad |
| Live | LP | Epic | PEQ34433 | 1977 £5 | £12 | US quad |
| Love Is Blue | 7" | Columbia | DB8359 | 1968 £1.50 | £4 | |
| Mustang Sally | CD-s | Silvertone | ORECD30 | 1991 £2 | £5 | with Buddy Guy |
| Plinth | 7" | Columbia | DB8590 | 1968 £20 | £40 | demo only |
| Rough And Ready | LP | Epic | Q64619 | 1974 £5 | £12 | quad |
| Tallyman | 7" | Columbia | DB8227 | 1967 £2.50 | £6 | |
| There And Back | CD | Epic | CD83288 | 1984 £5 | £12 | |
| Truth | LP | Columbia | SCX6293 | 1968 £6 | £15 | |
| Truth | 7" | Columbia | PSR317 | 1968 £7.50 | £15 | promo |
| Wired | LP | Epic | PEQ33849 | 1976 £5 | £12 | US quad |
| Wired | CD | Epic | CD86012 | 1988 £5 | £12 | |
| Wired | CD | Mobile Fidelity | MFCD531 | 1988 £6 | £15 | US audiophile |

## BECKETT, HAROLD

Harold Beckett is a jazz trumpeter whose playing seems to be included somewhere on most British rock LPs made in the early seventies! His own records, which feature the usual familiar jazz faces of the period, are actually remarkably free from rock influence, which is the reason for their relatively low collectors' values today.

| | | | | | | |
|---|---|---|---|---|---|---|
| Flare Up | LP | Philips | 6308026 | 1971 £8 | £20 | |
| Got It Made | LP | Ogun | OG020 | 1977 £5 | £12 | |
| Joy Unlimited | LP | Cadillac | SGC1004 | 1975 £6 | £15 | |
| Memories Of Bacares | LP | Ogun | OG800 | 1976 £5 | £12 | |
| Theme For Fega | LP | RCA | SF8264 | 1973 £8 | £20 | |
| Warm Smiles | LP | RCA | SF8225 | 1972 £8 | £20 | |

## BECKFORD, KEITH

| | | | | | |
|---|---|---|---|---|---|
| Suzy Wong | 7" | Big Shot | BI521 | 1969 £1.50 | £4 |

## BECKFORD, LYN

| | | | | | | |
|---|---|---|---|---|---|---|
| Kiss Me Quick | 7" | Jackpot | JP707 | 1969 £1.50 | £4 | Mr. Miller B side |
| Combination | 7" | Island | WI3144 | 1968 £4 | £8 | |

## BECKFORD, THEO

| | | | | | | |
|---|---|---|---|---|---|---|
| Bollerman | 7" | Island | WI106 | 1963 £5 | £10 | |
| Bringing In The Sheep | 7" | Blue Beat | BB132 | 1962 £6 | £12 | |
| Brother Ram Goat | 7" | Crab | CRAB25 | 1969 £1.50 | £4 | Starlights B side |
| Dig The Dig | 7" | Blue Beat | BB303 | 1965 £6 | £12 | |
| Don't Worry To Cry | 7" | Blue Beat | BB257 | 1964 £6 | £12 | |
| Easy Snappin' | 7" | Nu Beat | NB009 | 1968 £2 | £5 | Eric Morris B side |
| Easy Snapping | 7" | Blue Beat | BB15 | 1960 £6 | £12 | |
| Georgie And The Old Shoes | 7" | Blue Beat | BB50 | 1961 £6 | £12 | |
| I Don't Want You | 7" | Island | WI026 | 1962 £5 | £10 | |
| If Life Was A Thing | 7" | Island | WI246 | 1965 £5 | £10 | Lloyd Clarke B side |
| Jack And Jill Shuffle | 7" | Blue Beat | BB33 | 1961 £6 | £12 | |
| On Your Knees | 7" | Blue Beat | BB287 | 1965 £6 | £12 | |
| She's Gone | 7" | Blue Beat | BB250 | 1964 £6 | £12 | |

| Take Your Time | | 7" | Black Swan | WI452 | 1965 £5 | £10 | ..Stranger Cole B side |
|---|---|---|---|---|---|---|---|
| Trench Town People | | 7" | Island | WI238 | 1965 £5 | £10 | ...Pioneers B side |
| Walking Down King Street | | 7" | Blue Beat | BB87 | 1962 £6 | £12 | ....Sir Dee's Group B side |
| What A Woe | | 7" | Island | WI248 | 1965 £5 | £10 | |
| You Are The One | | 7" | Island | WI243 | 1965 £5 | £10 | |

## BEDFORD, DAVID

David Bedford is an avant-garde composer whose sympathy for rock music has led to his gaining much employment as an arranger. In particular, he has worked extensively with Mike Oldfield, producing an orchestral version of *Tubular Bells* and writing a guitar concerto for him (the superb *Star's End*, which should be required listening for Jon Lord, Keith Emerson and other rock-classical fusionists whose ideas of how classical music is constructed are still rooted in the nineteenth century). *Nurses Song With Elephants* is less accessible than later Bedford works, but is still crammed with original ideas.

| Music For Albion Moonlight | | LP | Argo | ZRG638 | 1970 £8 | £20 | ...other side Elizabeth Lutyens |
|---|---|---|---|---|---|---|---|
| Nurses Song With Elephants | | LP | Dandelion | 2310165 | 1972 £8 | £20 | |

## BEDLAM

| Bedlam | | LP | Chrysalis | CHR1048 | 1973 £5 | £12 | |
|---|---|---|---|---|---|---|---|

## BEDROCKS

| Ob La Di Ob La Da | | 7" | Columbia | DB8516 | 1968 £1.50 | £4 | |
|---|---|---|---|---|---|---|---|

## BEE, EDWIN

| I've Been Loving You | | 7" | Decca | F12781 | 1968 £1.50 | £4 | |
|---|---|---|---|---|---|---|---|

## BEE, MOLLY

| Since I Met You Baby | | 7" | London | HLD8400 | 1957 £4 | £8 | |
|---|---|---|---|---|---|---|---|

## BEE GEES

Despite a long and very successful hit-making career, the Bee Gees have proved to be of limited interest to collectors. There are one or two high-priced items, but the albums issued prior to the leap into the premier division occasioned by the *Saturday Night Fever* soundtrack struggle to be included in the list below (many are not) despite being quite hard to find. The first UK album is actually something of a period classic, standing shoulder-to-shoulder with other post-Sgt Pepper albums like the Hollies' *Butterfly* or the Rainbow Ffolly's *Sallies Forth*.

| Bee Gees First | | LP | Polydor | 582/583012 | 1967 £4 | £10 | |
|---|---|---|---|---|---|---|---|
| Boogie Child | | 7" | RSO | 2090224 | 1977 £4 | £8 | promo only |
| Cucumber Castle | | LP | Polydor | 2383010 | 1970 £4 | £10 | |
| Horizontal | | LP | Polydor | 582/583020 | 1968 £4 | £10 | |
| How Deep Is Your Love | | CD-s | Polydor | PZCD110 | 1990 £2 | £5 | |
| Idea | | LP | Polydor | 582/583036 | 1968 £4 | £10 | |
| Inception And Nostalgia | | LP | Karussell | 2674002 | 1973 £37.50 | £75 | German double |
| New York Mining Disaster 1941 | | 7" EP | Polydor | 27806 | 1967 £7.50 | £15 | French |
| Odessa | | LP | Polydor | 583049/050 | 1969 £6 | £15 | felt sleeve |
| Odessa | | CD | Polydor | 8254512 | 1985 £5 | £12 | |
| Odessa | | 7" | Polydor | 56304 | 1969 £10 | £20 | |
| One | | CD-s | WEA | W2916CD | 1989 £2 | £5 | |
| Ordinary Lives | | CD-s | WEA | W7523CD | 1989 £2 | £5 | |
| Rare Precious & Beautiful Vol. 1 | | LP | Polydor | 236221 | 1968 £4 | £10 | |
| Rare Precious & Beautiful Vol. 2 | | LP | Polydor | 236513 | 1968 £4 | £10 | |
| Rare Precious & Beautiful Vol. 3 | | LP | Polydor | 236556 | 1969 £4 | £10 | |
| Secret Love | | CD-s | WEA | W0014CD | 1991 £2 | £5 | |
| Short Cuts | | LP | RSO | BGPLP1 | 1979 £4 | £10 | promo |
| Sing & Play 14 Barry Gibb Songs | | LP | Calendar | R66241 | 1968 £20 | £40 | Australian reissue |
| Sing & Play 14 Barry Gibb Songs | | LP | Leedon | LL31801 | 1965 £50 | £100 | Australian |
| Spicks And Specks | | LP | Spin | EL32031 | 1966 £25 | £50 | Australian |
| Spicks And Specks | | 7" | Polydor | 56727 | 1967 £1.50 | £4 | |
| Spirits Having Flown | | LP | Nautilus | NR17 | 1981 £4 | £10 | US audiophile |
| To Love Somebody | | 7" EP | Polydor | 27811 | 1967 £7.50 | £15 | French |
| Trafalgar | | LP | Polydor | 2383052 | 1971 £4 | £10 | |
| Two Years On | | LP | Polydor | 2310069 | 1970 £4 | £10 | |

## BEEFEATERS

| Please Let Me Love You | | 7" | Elektra | 2101007 | 1970 £5 | £10 | |
|---|---|---|---|---|---|---|---|
| Please Let Me Love You | | 7" | Pye | 7N25277 | 1964 £25 | £50 | |

## BEEFEATERS (2)

| Beefeaters | | LP | Sonet | SLPS1242 | 1967 £10 | £25 | Danish |
|---|---|---|---|---|---|---|---|
| Meet You There | | LP | Sonet | SLPS1509 | 1967 £5 | £12 | Danish |
| Meet You There | | LP | Sonet | SPLP1509 | 1969 £5 | £12 | |
| Soul In | | LP | Karussell | 635078 | 1968 £15 | £30 | German |

## BEER, MARK

| Dust On The Road | | LP | My China | TAO001 | 1981 £8 | £20 | |
|---|---|---|---|---|---|---|---|

## BEES

| Jesse James Rides Again | | 7" | Blue Beat | BB386 | 1967 £6 | £12 | |
|---|---|---|---|---|---|---|---|
| Jesse James Rides Again | | 7" | Columbia | DB101 | 1967 £2 | £5 | |
| Prisoner From Alcatraz | | 7" | Columbia | DB111 | 1968 £2 | £5 | |

## BEES MAKE HONEY

| Music Every Night | | LP | EMI | EMC3013 | 1972 £6 | £15 | |
|---|---|---|---|---|---|---|---|

## BEETHOVEN SOUL

| Beethoven Soul | | LP | Dot | DLP25821 | 1967 £6 | £15 | US |
|---|---|---|---|---|---|---|---|

## BEGGARS FARM

| Title | Format | Label | Cat# | Year | | | Notes |
|---|---|---|---|---|---|---|---|
| Depth Of A Dream | LP | White Rabbit | WR1001 | 1984 | £15 | £30 | |

## BEGGAR'S HILL

| Title | Format | Label | Cat# | Year | | | Notes |
|---|---|---|---|---|---|---|---|
| Beggar's Hill | LP | Moonshine | MS60 | 1976 | £100 | £200 | |

## BEGGARS MANTLE

| Title | Format | Label | Cat# | Year | | | Notes |
|---|---|---|---|---|---|---|---|
| Beggars Mantle | LP | Milestone | CM5001R | 1984 | £10 | £25 | |

## BEGGARS OPERA

| Title | Format | Label | Cat# | Year | | | Notes |
|---|---|---|---|---|---|---|---|
| Act One | LP | Vertigo | 6360018 | 1970 | £8 | £20 | spiral label |
| Get Your Dog Off Me | LP | Vertigo | 6360090 | 1973 | £4 | £10 | |
| Pathfinder | LP | Vertigo | 6360073 | 1972 | £6 | £15 | spiral label |
| Sagittary | LP | Jupiter | 88907 | 1974 | £6 | £15 | German |
| Sarabande | 7" | Vertigo | 6059026 | 1970 | £2 | £5 | |
| Waters Of Change | LP | Vertigo | 6360054 | 1971 | £8 | £20 | spiral label |

## BEGINNING OF THE END

| Title | Format | Label | Cat# | Year | | | Notes |
|---|---|---|---|---|---|---|---|
| Funky Nassau | LP | Atlantic | K40304 | 1971 | £5 | £12 | |
| Funky Nassau | 7" | Atlantic | 2091097 | 1971 | £1.50 | £4 | |

## BEHAN, BRENDAN

| Title | Format | Label | Cat# | Year | | | Notes |
|---|---|---|---|---|---|---|---|
| Hostage | LP | Argo | RG239 | 1960 | £8 | £20 | |

## BEHAN, DOMINIC

| Title | Format | Label | Cat# | Year | | | Notes |
|---|---|---|---|---|---|---|---|
| Arkle | 7" | Piccadilly | 7N35238 | 1965 | £1.50 | £4 | |
| Bells Of Hell | 7" | Decca | F11147 | 1959 | £1.50 | £4 | |
| Cosmopolitan Man | LP | Folklore | FLEUT4 | 1962 | £20 | £40 | |
| Down By The Liffeyside | LP | Topic | 12T35 | 1960 | £15 | £30 | |
| Easter Week And After | LP | Topic | 12T44 | 1961 | £15 | £30 | |
| Finnegan's Wake | 7" EP | Collector | JEI4 | 1960 | £7.50 | £15 | |
| Ireland Sings | LP | Pye | NPL18134 | 1965 | £10 | £25 | |
| Irish Rover | LP | Folklore | FLEUT2 | 1961 | £20 | £40 | |
| Liverpool Lou | 7" | Piccadilly | 7N35172 | 1964 | £1.50 | £4 | |
| Lots Of Fun At Finnegan's Wake | 7" EP | Collector | JEI1 | 1959 | £7.50 | £15 | |
| McCafferty | 7" EP | Collector | JEI2 | 1959 | £7.50 | £15 | |
| Patriot Game | 7" | Topic | STOP115 | 1964 | £1.50 | £4 | |
| Rifles Of The IRA | 7" | Major Minor | MM575 | 1968 | £1.50 | £4 | |
| Songs Of The Streets | 7" EP | Collector | JEI3 | 1959 | £7.50 | £15 | |

## BEIDERBECKE, BIX

| Title | Format | Label | Cat# | Year | | | Notes |
|---|---|---|---|---|---|---|---|
| Bix Beiderbecke | 7" EP | Columbia | SEG7577 | 1956 | £2 | £5 | |
| Bix Beiderbecke And His Orchestra | 7" EP | Columbia | SEG7523 | 1955 | £2 | £5 | |
| Bix Beiderbecke And The Wolverines | 10" LP | London | AL3532 | 1954 | £10 | £25 | |
| Great Bix | 10" LP | Columbia | 33S1035 | 1954 | £6 | £15 | |

## BEIRACH, RICHARD

| Title | Format | Label | Cat# | Year | | | Notes |
|---|---|---|---|---|---|---|---|
| Eon | LP | ECM | ECM1054ST | 1975 | £6 | £15 | |

## BEL CANTOS

| Title | Format | Label | Cat# | Year | | | Notes |
|---|---|---|---|---|---|---|---|
| Feel Alright | 7" | R&B | MRB5003 | 1965 | £2.50 | £6 | |

## BELAFONTE, HARRY

| Title | Format | Label | Cat# | Year | | | Notes |
|---|---|---|---|---|---|---|---|
| Banana Boat Song | 7" | HMV | POP308 | 1957 | £2 | £5 | |
| Calypso | 7" EP | HMV | 7EG8211 | 1957 | £2 | £5 | |
| Close Your Eyes | 7" EP | Capitol | EAP1619 | 1956 | £2 | £5 | |
| Close Your Eyes | 7" | Capitol | CL14312 | 1955 | £1.50 | £4 | |
| Hold 'Em Joe | 7" | HMV | 7M202 | 1954 | £1.50 | £4 | |
| I'm Just A Country Boy | 7" | HMV | 7M224 | 1954 | £1.50 | £4 | |
| Mathilda Mathilda | 7" EP | HMV | 7EG8259 | 1957 | £2 | £5 | |
| Scarlet Ribbons | 7" | HMV | POP360 | 1957 | £1.50 | £4 | |
| Versatile Mr. Belafonte | 10" LP | HMV | DLP1147 | 1957 | £4 | £10 | |

## BELFAST GYPSIES

| Title | Format | Label | Cat# | Year | | | Notes |
|---|---|---|---|---|---|---|---|
| Belfast Gypsies | LP | Grand Prix | GP9923 | 1967 | £25 | £50 | Swedish |
| Gloria's Dream | 7" EP | Vogue | INT18079 | 1966 | £30 | £60 | French |
| Gloria's Dream | 7" | Island | WI3007 | 1966 | £7.50 | £15 | |

## BELIN, ED TEX

| Title | Format | Label | Cat# | Year | | | Notes |
|---|---|---|---|---|---|---|---|
| Ed Tex Belin | 7" EP | Starlite | GRK509 | 1966 | £2 | £5 | |
| Ed Tex Belin | 7" EP | Starlite | STEP39 | 1963 | £4 | £8 | |

## BELL, ALEXANDER

| Title | Format | Label | Cat# | Year | | | Notes |
|---|---|---|---|---|---|---|---|
| Alexander Bell Believes | 7" | CBS | 2977 | 1967 | £2 | £5 | |

## BELL, ARCHIE & THE DRELLS

| Title | Format | Label | Cat# | Year | | | Notes |
|---|---|---|---|---|---|---|---|
| I Can't Stop Dancing | 7" | Atlantic | 584217 | 1968 | £1.50 | £4 | |
| Tighten Up | LP | Atlantic | | 1968 | £6 | £15 | |
| Tighten Up | 7" | Atlantic | 2091156 | 1971 | £1.50 | £4 | |
| Tighten Up | 7" | Atlantic | 584185 | 1968 | £1.50 | £4 | |

## BELL, BELINDA

| Title | Format | Label | Cat# | Year | | | Notes |
|---|---|---|---|---|---|---|---|
| Stone Valley | LP | Columbia | SCXA9255 | 1973 | £10 | £25 | |

## BELL, BENNY & THE BLOCKBUSTERS

| Title | Format | Label | Cat# | Year | | | Notes |
|---|---|---|---|---|---|---|---|
| Sack Dress | 7" | Parlophone | R4372 | 1957 | £1.50 | £4 | |

## BELL, CAREY
Carey Bell.................................................. LP ..... Delmark ........ DS622 ..................... 1971 £5 ........ £12 ...............................

## BELL, FREDDY & THE BELL BOYS
| | | | | | | |
|---|---|---|---|---|---|---|
| Bells Are Swinging ..................................... | LP ..... | 20th Century ... | (S)4146 ............ | 1964 | £5 ........ £12 | ................ US |
| Big Bad Wolf ............................................ | 78...... | Mercury ......... | MT149 ............ | 1957 | £2.50 ..... £6 | |
| Giddy-Up-A-Ding-Dong............................... | 78...... | Mercury ......... | MT122 ............ | 1956 | £2.50 ..... £6 | |
| Hucklebuck .............................................. | 78...... | Mercury ......... | MT141 ............ | 1957 | £2.50 ..... £6 | |
| Rock And Roll – All Flavors ...................... | LP ..... | Mercury ......... | MG20289 ...... | 1958 | £25 ........ £50 | ................ US |
| Rock With The Bell Boys ......................... | 7" EP . | Mercury ......... | MEP9508 ...... | 1956 | £12.50 ..... £25 | |
| Rock With The Bell Boys Vol. 2............... | 7" EP . | Mercury ......... | MEP9512 ...... | 1957 | £20 ........ £40 | |
| Rockin' Is My Business ............................. | 78...... | Mercury ......... | MT159 ............ | 1957 | £2.50 ..... £6 | |
| Teach You To Rock ................................. | 78...... | Mercury ......... | MT146 ............ | 1957 | £2.50 ..... £6 | |

## BELL, FREDERICK
Rocksteady Cool............................................ 7" ...... Nu Beat ........ NB004 ..................... 1968 £2 ........ £5

## BELL, GRAHAM
Graham Bell................................................ LP ..... Charisma........ CAS1061 ............ 1972 £4 ........ £10
How Can You Say I Don't Love You ....... 7" ..... Polydor........... 56067 ..................... 1966 £2 ........ £5

## BELL, MADELINE
| | | | | | |
|---|---|---|---|---|---|
| Because You Didn't Care ........................ | 7" ...... | HMV ............. | POP1215 ....... | 1963 | £1.50 ........ £4 |
| Bells A-Poppin' ....................................... | LP ..... | Philips ........... | (S)BL7818 ..... | 1967 | £5 ........ £12 |
| Daytime .................................................. | 7" ...... | Columbia ....... | DB7512 ......... | 1965 | £1.50 ........ £4 |
| Doin' Things ........................................... | LP ..... | Philips ........... | SBL7865 ........ | 1969 | £4 ........ £10 |
| Don't Come Running To Me .................... | 7" ...... | Philips ........... | BF1501 .......... | 1966 | £2 ........ £5 |
| I'm Gonna Make You Love Me................. | 7" ...... | Philips ........... | BF1656 .......... | 1968 | £1.50 ........ £4 |
| One Step At A Time ................................ | 7" ...... | Philips ........... | BF1526 .......... | 1966 | £1.50 ........ £4 |
| Picture Me Gone ..................................... | 7" ...... | Philips ........... | BF1611 .......... | 1967 | £4 ........ £8 |
| Thinkin' .................................................. | 7" ...... | Philips ........... | BF1688 .......... | 1968 | £1.50 ........ £4 |
| What The World Needs Now .................... | 7" ...... | Philips ........... | BF1448 .......... | 1965 | £4 ........ £8 |
| You Don't Love Me No More .................. | 7" ...... | Columbia ....... | DB7257 ......... | 1964 | £1.50 ........ £4 |

## BELL, PADDIE
I Know Where I'm Going........................ LP ..... Waverley......... (S)ZLP2104 ........ 1968 £6 ........ £15

## BELL, WILLIAM
| | | | | | |
|---|---|---|---|---|---|
| Bound To Happen ................................... | LP ..... | Stax .............. | SXATS1016 ..... | 1970 | £4 ........ £10 |
| Eloise ..................................................... | 7" ..... | Stax .............. | 601019 ........... | 1967 | £1.50 ........ £4 |
| Every Day Will Be Like A Holiday ........... | 7" ..... | Atlantic .......... | 584259 ........... | 1969 | £1.50 ........ £4 |
| Happy ..................................................... | 7" ..... | Stax .............. | STAX128 ........ | 1969 | £2 ........ £5 |
| I Forgot How To Be Your Lover ............. | 7" ..... | Stax .............. | STAX110 ........ | 1969 | £1.50 ........ £4 |
| My Whole World Is Falling Down............. | 7" ..... | Stax .............. | STAX121 ........ | 1969 | £1.50 ........ £4 |
| Never Like This Before............................. | 7" ..... | Atlantic .......... | 584076 ........... | 1967 | £1.50 ........ £4 |
| Tribute To A King .................................. | LP ..... | Atco .............. | 228003 ........... | 1969 | £4 ........ £10 |
| Tribute To A King .................................. | 7" ..... | Stax .............. | 601038 ........... | 1968 | £1.50 ........ £4 |

## BELL BROTHERS
Tell Him No ............................................. 7" ...... Action............ ACT4510 ............ 1968 £1.50 ........ £4

## BELL SOUNDS
Marching Guitars....................................... 7" ...... HMV ............. POP685 ............... 1959 £1.50 ........ £4

## BELLAMY, GEORGE
Where I'm Bound ..................................... 7" ...... Parlophone...... R5282 ................. 1965 £2 ........ £5

## BELLAMY, PETER
| | | | | | | |
|---|---|---|---|---|---|---|
| Barrack Room Ballads................................ | LP ..... | Free Reed ...... | FRR014 .......... | 1977 | £5 ........ £12 | |
| Both Sides Then....................................... | LP ..... | Topic.............. | 12TS400 ......... | 1979 | £4 ........ £10 | |
| Fair England's Shore ................................ | LP ..... | XTRA............. | XTRA1075 ....... | 1969 | £10 ........ £25 | |
| Fox Jumps Over The Parson's Gate........... | LP ..... | Topic.............. | 12T200 ........... | 1970 | £10 ........ £25 | |
| Keep On Kipling ...................................... | LP ..... | Fellside........... | FE032 ............ | 1982 | £5 ........ £12 | |
| Mainly Norfolk ........................................ | LP ..... | XTRA............. | XTRA1060 ....... | 1968 | £8 ........ £20 | |
| Merlin's Isle Of Gramarye ........................ | LP ..... | Argo .............. | ZFB81 ............ | 1972 | £10 ........ £25 | |
| Oak, Ash And Thorn ............................... | LP ..... | Argo .............. | ZFB11 ............ | 1970 | £8 ........ £20 | |
| Peter Bellamy........................................... | LP ..... | Green Linnet ... | SIF1001 .......... | 1975 | £5 ........ £12 | US |
| Rudyard Kipling Made Exceedingly Good Songs .................................................. | LP ..... | Dambuster....... | DAM019 .......... | 1989 | £4 ........ £10 | |
| Second Wind ........................................... | LP ..... | EFDSS ........... | ES002 ............ | 1985 | £4 ........ £10 | |
| Tell It Like It Was ................................. | LP ..... | Trailer............. | LER2089 ......... | 1975 | £5 ........ £12 | |
| Transports................................................ | LP ..... | Free Reed ...... | FRR021/2 ....... | 1977 | £8 ........ £20 | Double |
| Won't You Go My Way............................ | LP ..... | Argo .............. | ZFB37 ............ | 1970 | £8 ........ £20 | with Louis Killen |

## BELLETTO, AL
Half And Half ........................................... LP ..... Capitol ........... T751 ................... 1957 £6 ........ £15

## BELLINE, DENNY & THE RICH KIDS
Denny Belline And The Rich Kids ........... LP ..... RCA .............. LPM/LSP3655........ 1966 £15 ........ £30 ............... US

## BELLSON, LOUIS
| | | | | | | |
|---|---|---|---|---|---|---|
| At The Flamingo ...................................... | LP ..... | Columbia ........ | 33CX10142........ | 1959 | £6 ........ £15 | |
| Brilliant Bellson Sound............................. | LP ..... | HMV ............. | CLP1343.......... | 1960 | £6 ........ £15 | |
| Louis Bellson ........................................... | LP ..... | Columbia ........ | 33CX10083........ | 1957 | £6 ........ £15 | |
| Louis Bellson ........................................... | 10" LP | Columbia ........ | 33C9017........... | 1956 | £20 ........ £40 | |

## BELLUS, TONY
| | | | | | | | |
|---|---|---|---|---|---|---|---|
| Robbing The Cradle | LP | NRC | LPA8 | 1960 £25 | £50 | | US |
| Robbing The Cradle | 7" | London | HL8933 | 1959 £10 | £20 | | |

## BELMONTS
| | | | | | | | |
|---|---|---|---|---|---|---|---|
| Carnival Of Hits | LP | Sabina | SALP5001 | 1962 £37.50 | £75 | | US |
| Cigars, Acappella, Candy | LP | Buddah | BDS5123 | 1972 £5 | £12 | | US |
| Come On Little Angel | 7" | Stateside | SS128 | 1962 £2 | £5 | | |
| Summer Love | LP | Dot | DLP25949 | 1969 £5 | £12 | | US |
| Tell Me Why | 7" | Pye | 7N25094 | 1961 £5 | £10 | | |

## BELOVED
| | | | | | | | |
|---|---|---|---|---|---|---|---|
| Forever Dancing | 12" | Flim Flam | HARP7T | 1987 £2.50 | £6 | | |
| Hello | CD-s | WEA | YZ426CD | 1990 £2.50 | £6 | | |
| Hundred Words | 12" | Flim Flam | HARP2T | 1986 £2.50 | £6 | | |
| It's Alright Now | CD-s | East West | YZ541CD | 1990 £3 | £8 | | |
| Loving Feeling | CD-s | WEA | YZ311CD | 1989 £10 | £20 | | 3" single |
| Sun Rising | CD-s | WEA | YZ414CD | 1989 £4 | £10 | | 3" single |
| Time After Time | CD-s | East West | YZ482CD | 1990 £2 | £5 | | |
| Time After Time | 7" | WEA | YZ482X | 1990 £1.50 | £4 | | picture disc |
| Where It Is | CD | Orange | HARPCD2 | 1990 £10 | £25 | | |
| Your Love Takes Me Higher | CD-s | WEA | YZ357CD | 1989 £10 | £20 | | 3" single |
| Your Love Takes Me Higher | CD-s | WEA | YZ463CD | 1990 £2 | £5 | | |

## BELTONES
| | | | | | | | |
|---|---|---|---|---|---|---|---|
| Home Without You | 7" | Duke | DU17 | 1969 £1.50 | £4 | | |
| Mary Mary | 7" | High Note | HS017 | 1969 £1.50 | £4 | | |
| No More Heartaches | 7" | Blue Cat | BS142 | 1968 £2.50 | £6 | | |
| No More Heartaches | 7" | Trojan | TR628 | 1968 £2 | £5 | | |

## BELVIN, JESSE
| | | | | | | | |
|---|---|---|---|---|---|---|---|
| Best Of Jesse Belvin | LP | Camden | CAS960 | 1966 £6 | £15 | | US |
| But Not Forgotten | LP | United | 7220 | 1968 £5 | £12 | | US |
| Casual | LP | Crown | CLP5145 | 1960 £6 | £15 | | US |
| Funny | 7" | RCA | RCA1119 | 1959 £4 | £8 | | |
| Just Jesse Belvin | LP | RCA | LPM/LSP2089 | 1959 £15 | £30 | | US |
| Mr. Easy | LP | RCA | LPM/LSP2105 | 1960 £10 | £25 | | US |
| Unforgettable | LP | Crown | CLP5187 | 1960 £6 | £15 | | US |

## BEN
| | | | | | | | |
|---|---|---|---|---|---|---|---|
| Ben | LP | Vertigo | 6360052 | 1971 £75 | £150 | | spiral label |

## BENATAR, PAT
| | | | | | | | |
|---|---|---|---|---|---|---|---|
| Don't Walk Away | CD-s | Chrysalis | PATCD6 | 1988 £2 | £5 | | |
| Get Nervous | CD | Chrysalis | ACCD1396 | 1982 £5 | £12 | | |
| If You Think You Know How To Love Me | 7" | Chrysalis | CHS2373 | 1979 £1.50 | £4 | | |
| In The Heat Of The Night | LP | Mobile Fidelity | MFSL1057 | 1981 £5 | £12 | | US audiophile |
| In The Heat Of The Night | CD | Chrysalis | ACCD1236 | 1985 £5 | £12 | | |
| Live From Earth | CD | Chrysalis | ACCD1451 | 1983 £5 | £12 | | |
| One Love | CD-s | Chrysalis | PATCD7 | 1988 £2 | £5 | | |
| Precious Time | CD | Chrysalis | ACCD1346 | 1986 £5 | £12 | | |
| Seven The Hard Way | CD | Chrysalis | ACCD1507 | 1986 £5 | £12 | | |
| Shadows Of The Night | 7" | Chrysalis | CHSP2662 | 1983 £2 | £5 | | shaped picture disc |
| Treat Me Right | 7" | Chrysalis | CHS2511 | 1981 £2 | £5 | | clear vinyl |
| Tropico | CD | Chrysalis | ACCD1471 | 1984 £3 | £12 | | |
| True Love | CD-s | Chrysalis | PATCD8 | 1991 £2 | £5 | | |
| Wide Awake In Dreamland | CD | Chrysalis | ACCD1628 | 1988 £5 | £12 | | |

## BENBOW, STEVE
| | | | | | | | |
|---|---|---|---|---|---|---|---|
| Captain Kidd | 7" EP | Collector | JEB2 | 1960 £2 | £5 | | |
| Of Situations And Predicaments | LP | Decca | LK4881 | 1967 £5 | £12 | | |
| Whaling In Greenland | 7" EP | Collector | JEB1 | 1959 £2 | £5 | | |

## BENNETT, BOBBY
| | | | | | | | |
|---|---|---|---|---|---|---|---|
| Big New York | 7" | London | HLZ10274 | 1969 £2 | £5 | | |

## BENNETT, BOBBY (2)
| | | | | | | | |
|---|---|---|---|---|---|---|---|
| All My Life Is You | 7" | Columbia | DB8435 | 1968 £1.50 | £4 | | |
| Just Say Goodbye | 7" | CBS | 202511 | 1967 £1.50 | £4 | | |
| You're Ready Now | 7" | Columbia | DB8532 | 1969 £7.50 | £15 | | |

## BENNETT, BOYD & HIS ROCKETS
| | | | | | | | |
|---|---|---|---|---|---|---|---|
| Banjo Rock And Roll | 7" | Parlophone | MSP6203 | 1956 £75 | £150 | | |
| Blue Suede Shoes | 7" | Parlophone | MSP6233 | 1956 £62.50 | £125 | | |
| Boogie At Midnight | 7" | Parlophone | MSP6161 | 1955 £100 | £200 | | best auctioned |
| Boyd Bennett | LP | King | 594 | 1957 £400 | £600 | | US |
| Hi That Jive Jack | 7" | Parlophone | R4214 | 1956 £50 | £100 | | with Big Moe |
| Move | 7" | Parlophone | R4423 | 1958 £37.50 | £75 | | |
| Rocking Up A Storm | 7" | Parlophone | R4252 | 1957 £50 | £100 | | with Big Moe |
| Seventeen | 7" | Parlophone | MSP6180 | 1955 £75 | £150 | | |
| Tight Tights | 7" | Mercury | AMT1031 | 1959 £25 | £50 | | |

## BENNETT, BRIAN

Brian Bennett replaced original drummer with the Shadows, Tony Meehan, in 1962, and has played with the group ever since. He has also done a considerable amount of production and session work, of which the collectable records issued under his own name and listed below are but a small fraction.

| | | | | | | | |
|---|---|---|---|---|---|---|---|
| Canvas | 7" | Columbia | DB8294 | 1967 | £4 | £8 | |
| Change Of Direction | LP | Columbia | SX/SCX6144 | 1968 | £10 | £25 | |
| Chase Side Shoot Up | 7" | Fontana | 6007040 | 1974 | £2 | £5 | |
| Illustrated London Noise | LP | Studio Two | TWO268 | 1969 | £25 | £50 | |

## BENNETT, CLIFF

| | | | | | | | |
|---|---|---|---|---|---|---|---|
| Branches Out | LP | Parlophone | PMC/PCS7054 | 1968 | £10 | £25 | |
| I'll Take Good Care Of You | 7" EP | Odeon | MEO149 | 1967 | £12.50 | £25 | French |
| One More Heartache | 7" | Parlophone | R5728 | 1968 | £1.50 | £4 | |

## BENNETT, CLIFF & REBEL ROUSERS

| | | | | | | | |
|---|---|---|---|---|---|---|---|
| Cliff Bennett & The Rebel Rousers | LP | Parlophone | PMC1242 | 1964 | £15 | £30 | |
| Cliff Bennett & The Rebel Rousers | 7" EP | Parlophone | GEP8923 | 1964 | £10 | £20 | |
| Everybody Loves A Lover | 7" | Parlophone | R5046 | 1963 | £5 | £10 | |
| Got My Mojo Working | 7" | Parlophone | R5119 | 1964 | £1.50 | £4 | |
| Got To Get You into My Life | 7" | Parlophone | R5489 | 1966 | £1.50 | £4 | |
| Got To Get You Into Our Lives | LP | Parlophone | PMC/PCS7017 | 1967 | £15 | £30 | |
| I'll Take Good Care Of You | 7" | Parlophone | R5565 | 1967 | £1.50 | £4 | |
| One Way Love | 7" | Parlophone | R5173 | 1964 | £1.50 | £4 | |
| Poor Joe | 7" | Parlophone | R4895 | 1962 | £5 | £10 | |
| Three Rooms With Running Water | 7" | Parlophone | R5259 | 1965 | £1.50 | £4 | |
| Try It Baby | 7" EP | Parlophone | GEP8936 | 1965 | £10 | £20 | |
| We're Gonna Make It | 7" EP | Parlophone | GEP8955 | 1966 | £20 | £50 | |
| When I Get Paid | 7" | Parlophone | R4836 | 1961 | £5 | £10 | |
| You Got What I Like | 7" | Parlophone | R4793 | 1961 | £5 | £10 | |
| You Really Got A Hold On Me | 7" | Parlophone | R5080 | 1963 | £1.50 | £4 | |
| Cliff Bennett | LP | Regal | REG1039 | 1966 | £5 | £12 | export |

## BENNETT, DICKIE

| | | | | | | | |
|---|---|---|---|---|---|---|---|
| Dungaree Doll | 7" | Decca | F10697 | 1956 | £1.50 | £4 | |

## BENNETT, DUSTER

Using his nickname to avoid an obvious confusion, Tony Bennett was a one-man band who played the blues, and played it rather well. Although a few supporting musicians are used in places on his records, what one hears is essentially Duster Bennett's voice and harmonica, his guitar, and his bass drum. If the format sounds limited, then Bennett proves that it need not be. He was an unlikely addition to John Mayall's band in the early seventies, but this facet of his career was never recorded.

| | | | | | | | |
|---|---|---|---|---|---|---|---|
| 12 dBs | LP | Blue Horizon | 763868 | 1970 | £10 | £25 | |
| Act Nice And Gentle | 7" | Blue Horizon | 573179 | 1970 | £2 | £5 | |
| Bright Lights | LP | Blue Horizon | 763221 | 1969 | £20 | £40 | |
| Bright Lights, Big City | 7" | Blue Horizon | 573154 | 1969 | £2.50 | £6 | |
| Comin' Home | 7" | RAK | RAK177 | 1974 | £4 | £8 | |
| Fingertips | LP | Mushroom | L35436 | 1974 | £8 | £20 | Australian |
| I Chose To Sing The Blues | 7" | Blue Horizon | 573173 | 1970 | £2 | £5 | |
| I'm Gonna Wind Up Endin' Up | 7" | Blue Horizon | 573164 | 1969 | £5 | £10 | |
| It's A Man Down There | 7" | Blue Horizon | 573141 | 1967 | £2.50 | £6 | |
| Raining In My Heart | 7" | Blue Horizon | 573148 | 1967 | £4 | £8 | |
| Smiling Like I'm Happy | LP | Blue Horizon | 763208 | 1968 | £15 | £30 | |

## BENNETT, JO JO

| | | | | | | | |
|---|---|---|---|---|---|---|---|
| Groovy Jo Jo | LP | Trojan | TBL133 | 1970 | £6 | £15 | |
| Leaving Rome | 7" | Trojan | TR7774 | 1970 | £1.50 | £4 | |
| Lecture | 7" | Doctor Bird | DB1097 | 1967 | £5 | £10 | |
| Rocksteady | 7" | Doctor Bird | DB1117 | 1967 | £5 | £10 | |

## BENNETT, JOE & THE SPARKLETONES

| | | | | | | | |
|---|---|---|---|---|---|---|---|
| Black Slacks | 7" | HMV | POP399 | 1957 | £37.50 | £75 | |
| Rocket | 7" | HMV | POP445 | 1958 | £50 | £100 | |

## BENNETT, RAY

| | | | | | | | |
|---|---|---|---|---|---|---|---|
| Introducing Ray Bennett | 7" EP | Decca | DFE8516 | 1962 | £4 | £8 | |

## BENNETT, TONY

| | | | | | | | |
|---|---|---|---|---|---|---|---|
| Stranger In Paradise | 7" EP | Philips | BBE12009 | 1955 | £2 | £5 | |
| Whatever Lola Wants | 7" | Philips | JK1008 | 1957 | £2 | £5 | |

## BENNETT, VAL

| | | | | | | | |
|---|---|---|---|---|---|---|---|
| All In The Game | 7" | Trojan | TR625 | 1968 | £2.50 | £6 | George Penny B side |
| Any More | 7" | Fab | FAB131 | 1970 | £1.50 | £4 | |
| Baby Baby | 7" | Trojan | TR640 | 1968 | £2.50 | £6 | |
| Jumping With Mr. Lee | 7" | Island | WI3113 | 1967 | £5 | £10 | Roy Shirley B side |
| Midnight Spin | 7" | Camel | CA24 | 1969 | £1.50 | £4 | Soul Cats B side |
| My Girl | 7" | Trojan | TR649 | 1969 | £1.50 | £4 | Clancy Eccles B side |
| Reggae City | 7" | Crab | CRAB6 | 1969 | £1.50 | £4 | Cannon King B side |
| Russians Are Coming | 7" | Island | WI3146 | 1968 | £5 | £10 | Lester Stirling B side |
| Soul Survivor | 7" | Island | WI3116 | 1967 | £5 | £10 | Lloyd Clarke B side |
| South Parkway Rock | 7" | Trojan | TR626 | 1968 | £2.50 | £6 | Derrick Morgan B side |
| Spanish Harlem | 7" | Trojan | TR611 | 1968 | £2.50 | £6 | Roy Shirley B side |

## BENNINGS, JOHN & HIS RHYTHM & BLUES BAND

| | | | | | | | |
|---|---|---|---|---|---|---|---|
| Timber | 78 | Esquire | 10376 | 1954 | £7.50 | £15 | |

## BENNY & TINA

| | | | | | | | |
|---|---|---|---|---|---|---|---|
| This Love Is Real | 7" | Mercury | MF1133 | 1969 | £1.50 | £4 | |

## BENSON, BARRY
| Title | | | | | | | |
|---|---|---|---|---|---|---|---|
| Cousin Jane | 7" | Parlophone | R5578 | 1967 | £1.50 | £4 | |
| Stay A Little While | 7" | Parlophone | R5446 | 1966 | £5 | £10 | |
| Sunshine Child | 7" | Parlophone | R5484 | 1966 | £1.50 | £4 | |

## BENSON, MARIE
| Mambo Italiano | 7" | Decca | F10452 | 1955 | £1.50 | £4 | |

## BENSUSAN, PIERRE
| Solilai | LP | Rounder | 3068 | 1982 | £10 | £25 | US |

## BENT WIND
| Sussex | LP | Trend | | 1972 | £700 | £1000 | Canadian |

## BENTINE, MICHAEL
| It's A Square World | LP | Parlophone | PMC1179/ PCS3031 | 1962 | £5 | £12 | |

## BENTLEY, BRIAN & THE BACHELORS
| Caramba | 7" | Salvo | SLO1813 | 1962 | £2 | £5 | |

## BENTLEY, JAY & THE JET SET
| Watusi '64 | 7" | Vocalion | VN9230 | 1964 | £2 | £5 | |
| Watusi 64 | 7" EP | Vogue | 18006 | 1964 | £10 | £20 | French |

## BENTON, BROOK
| Boll Weevil Song | LP | Mercury | MMC14090/ CMS18060 | 1961 | £4 | £10 | |
| Brook Benton & Jesse Belvin | LP | Crown | CST350 | 1963 | £6 | £15 | US |
| Caressing Voice Of Brook Benton | 7" EP | Mercury | ZEP10023 | 1959 | £2 | £5 | |
| Endlessly | LP | Mercury | MMC14022 | 1959 | £4 | £10 | |
| I Love You In So Many Ways | LP | Mercury | MMC14042 | 1960 | £4 | £10 | |
| It's Just A Matter Of Time | LP | Mercury | MMC14015 | 1958 | £4 | £10 | |
| Make A Date With Brook Benton | 7" EP | Mercury | ZEP10046 | 1959 | £2 | £5 | |
| So Warm | 7" EP | Mercury | SEZ19024 | 1962 | £2 | £5 | stereo |
| Songs I Love To Sing | LP | Mercury | MMC14060/ CMS18041 | 1960 | £4 | £10 | |
| There Goes That Song Again | LP | Mercury | MMC14108/ CMS18068 | 1961 | £4 | £10 | |
| When I Fall In Love | 7" EP | Mercury | SEZ19009 | 1961 | £2 | £5 | stereo |
| When You're In Love | 7" EP | Mercury | SEZ19019 | 1961 | £2 | £5 | stereo |

## BENTON, BROOK & DINAH WASHINGTON
| Baby | 7" | Mercury | AMT1083 | 1960 | £1.50 | £4 | |
| Rockin' Good Way | 7" EP | Mercury | SEZ19022 | 1961 | £6 | £12 | stereo |
| Rockin' Good Way | 7" EP | Mercury | ZEP10120 | 1961 | £4 | £8 | |
| Rockin' Good Way | 7" | Mercury | AMT1099 | 1960 | £4 | £8 | |

## BENTON, OSCAR BLUES BAND
| Benton '71 | LP | Decca | 641900 | 1971 | £4 | £10 | Dutch |
| Blues Is Gonna Wreck My Life | LP | Decca | XBY846521 | 1969 | £5 | £12 | Dutch |
| Feel So Good | LP | Decca | XBY846510 | 1969 | £4 | £10 | Dutch |

## BENTON, WALTER
| Out Of This World | LP | Jazzland | JLP28 | 1960 | £8 | £20 | with Freddie Hubbard |

## BERBERIAN, JOHN
| Impressions East | LP | Mainstream | S6123 | 1969 | £30 | £60 | US |
| Middle Eastern Rock | LP | Verve | FTS3073 | 1969 | £15 | £30 | US |

## BERGER, GABY
| Die Grossen Erfolge | LP | Ariola | 80886AT | 1970 | £6 | £15 | German |

## BERGIN, MARY
| Feadoga Stain | LP | Gael-Linn | CEF071 | 1979 | £4 | £10 | |

## BERIGAN, BUNNY
| Bunny Berigan | LP | Philips | BBL7086 | 1956 | £8 | £20 | |
| Plays Again | 10" LP | HMV | DLP1018 | 1953 | £8 | £20 | |

## BERKERS, JERRY
| Unterwegs | LP | Pilz | 20291316 | 1972 | £8 | £20 | German |

## BERLE, MILTON
| In The Middle Of The House | 7" | Vogue Coral | Q72197 | 1956 | £2.50 | £6 | |

## BERMUDAS
| Donnie | 7" | London | HLN9894 | 1964 | £2.50 | £6 | |

## BERNARD, KENNY
| Ain't No Sole Left In These Old Shoes | 7" | Pye | 7N17233 | 1967 | £7.50 | £15 | |
| I Do | 7" | Pye | 7N17284 | 1967 | £1.50 | £4 | |
| Nothing Can Change That Love | 7" | Pye | 7N17131 | 1966 | £6 | £12 | |
| Somebody | 7" | CBS | 2936 | 1967 | £15 | £30 | |
| Tracker | 7" | Pye | 7N15920 | 1965 | £2.50 | £6 | |
| Victim Of Perfume And Lace | 7" | CBS | 3860 | 1968 | £15 | £30 | |

## BERNARD, ROD

| | | | | | | | |
|---|---|---|---|---|---|---|---|
| One More Chance | 7" | Mercury | AMT1070 | 1959 | £2 | £5 | |
| Rod Bernard | LP | Jin | LP4007 | 1966 | £20 | £40 | US |
| This Should Go On Forever | 7" | London | HLM8849 | 1959 | £10 | £20 | |

## BERNHARDT, CLYDE

| | | | | | | | |
|---|---|---|---|---|---|---|---|
| Sittin' On Top Of The World | LP | Wam | 780061 | 1975 | £10 | £25 | German |

## BERNIE & THE BUZZ BAND

| | | | | | | | |
|---|---|---|---|---|---|---|---|
| House That Jack Built | 7" | Decca | F22829 | 1968 | £1.50 | £4 | B side by Pete Kelly's Soulution |
| When Something's Wrong With My Baby | 7" | Deram | DM181 | 1968 | £1.50 | £4 | |

## BERNSTEIN, ELMER

| | | | | | | | |
|---|---|---|---|---|---|---|---|
| Rat Race | 7" | MGM | MGM1238 | 1963 | £2.50 | £6 | |
| Staccato | 7" EP | Capitol | EAP11287 | 1960 | £2 | £5 | |

## BERNSTEIN, LEONARD

| | | | | | | | |
|---|---|---|---|---|---|---|---|
| What Is Jazz? | LP | Philips | BBL7149 | 1957 | £6 | £15 | |

## BERRY, CHU

| | | | | | | | |
|---|---|---|---|---|---|---|---|
| Stompy Stevedores | LP | Philips | BBL7054 | 1955 | £10 | £25 | |

## BERRY, CHUCK

Although Elvis Presley defined the rock'n'roll image, it was Chuck Berry who invented the actual music – a fact recognized both by the enormous number of cover versions of his best-known songs and by the inclusion of 'Johnny B. Goode' as one of the cultural artefacts included in the Voyagers I and II spacecraft.

| | | | | | | | |
|---|---|---|---|---|---|---|---|
| After School Session | LP | Chess | LP1426 | 1958 | £25 | £50 | US |
| Back To Memphis | 7" | Mercury | MF994 | 1967 | £1.50 | £4 | |
| Beautiful Delilah | 7" | London | HL8677 | 1958 | £20 | £40 | |
| Berry Is On Top | LP | Chess | LP1435 | 1959 | £20 | £40 | US |
| Best Of Chuck Berry | 7" EP | Pye | NEP44018 | 1964 | £4 | £8 | |
| Blue Mood | 7" EP | Pye | NEP44033 | 1964 | £4 | £8 | |
| Bye Bye Johnny | 7" | London | HLM9159 | 1960 | £5 | £10 | |
| Carol | 7" | London | HL8712 | 1958 | £15 | £30 | |
| Chuck Berry | LP | Pye | NPL28024 | 1963 | £5 | £12 | |
| Chuck Berry | 7" EP | Pye | NEP44011 | 1963 | £4 | £8 | |
| Chuck Berry Hits | 7" EP | Pye | NEP44028 | 1964 | £4 | £8 | |
| Chuck In London | LP | Chess | CRL4005 | 1965 | £4 | £10 | |
| Club Nitty Gritty | 7" | Mercury | MF958 | 1966 | £1.50 | £4 | |
| Come On | 7" EP | Chess | CRE6005 | 1965 | £7.50 | £15 | |
| Concerto In B.Goode | LP | Mercury | 20162SMCL | 1969 | £4 | £10 | |
| Dear Dad | 7" | Chess | CRS8012 | 1965 | £1.50 | £4 | |
| Fresh Berrys | LP | Chess | CRL4506 | 1965 | £4 | £10 | |
| Go Go Go | 7" | Pye | 7N25209 | 1963 | £1.50 | £4 | |
| Golden Decade | LP | Chess | 6641018 | 1972 | £5 | £12 | double |
| I Got A Booking | 7" EP | Chess | CRE6012 | 1966 | £7.50 | £15 | |
| I'm Talking About You | 7" | Pye | 7N25100 | 1961 | £4 | £8 | |
| In Memphis | LP | Mercury | (S)MCL20110 | 1967 | £4 | £10 | |
| It Wasn't Me | 7" | Chess | CRS8022 | 1965 | £1.50 | £4 | |
| Johnny B Goode | 7" | London | HLM8629 | 1958 | £7.50 | £15 | |
| Johnny B.Goode | 7" | Chess | CRS8075 | 1968 | £1.50 | £4 | |
| Latest And The Greatest | LP | Pye | NPL28031 | 1964 | £5 | £12 | |
| Let It Rock | 7" | London | HLM9069 | 1960 | £5 | £10 | |
| Little Marie | 7" | Pye | 7N25271 | 1964 | £1.50 | £4 | |
| Little Queenie | 7" | London | HLM8853 | 1959 | £7.50 | £15 | |
| Live At Fillmore Auditorium | LP | Mercury | 20112MCL | 1967 | £4 | £10 | with the Steve Miller Band |
| Lonely School Days | 7" | Chess | CRS8006 | 1965 | £1.50 | £4 | |
| Memphis Tennessee | 7" | London | HLM8921 | 1959 | £12.50 | £25 | |
| Memphis Tennessee | 7" | Pye | 7N25218 | 1963 | £1.50 | £4 | |
| More Chuck Berry | LP | Pye | NPL28028 | 1963 | £4 | £10 | |
| Nadine | 7" | Pye | 7N25236 | 1964 | £1.50 | £4 | |
| New Juke Box Hits | LP | Pye | NPL28019 | 1962 | £8 | £20 | |
| No Money Down | 7" | London | HLU8275 | 1956 | £330 | £500 | gold label, best auctioned |
| No Particular Place To Go | 7" | Chess | CRS8089 | 1969 | £1.50 | £4 | |
| No Particular Place To Go | 7" | Pye | 7N25242 | 1964 | £1.50 | £4 | |
| On Stage | LP | Pye | NPL28027 | 1963 | £4 | £10 | |
| One Dozen Berrys | LP | London | HAM2132 | 1958 | £30 | £60 | |
| Promised Land | 7" EP | Chess | CRE6002 | 1965 | £7.50 | £15 | |
| Promised Land | 7" | Pye | 7N25285 | 1965 | £1.50 | £4 | |
| Ramona Say Yes | 7" | Chess | CRS8037 | 1966 | £1.50 | £4 | |
| Reeling And Rocking | 7" EP | London | REM1188 | 1960 | £50 | £100 | tri-centre |
| Rhythm And Blues With Chuck Berry | 7" EP | London | REU1053 | 1956 | £75 | £150 | gold label |
| Rock & Roll Music | 7" | London | HLM8531 | 1957 | £20 | £40 | |
| Rockin' At The Hops | LP | Chess | LP1448 | 1960 | £20 | £40 | US |
| Roll Over Beethoven | 7" | London | HLU8428 | 1957 | £37.50 | £75 | |
| Roll Over Beethoven | 7" | Mercury | MF1102 | 1969 | £1.50 | £4 | |
| Run Rudolph Run | 7" | Pye | 7N25228 | 1963 | £1.50 | £4 | |
| Saint Louis To Frisco | 7" | Mercury | MF1057 | 1968 | £1.50 | £4 | |
| Schooldays | 7" | Columbia | DB3951 | 1957 | £50 | £100 | |
| Sweet Little Rock and Roller | 7" | London | HLM8767 | 1958 | £7.50 | £15 | |
| Sweet Little Sixteen | 7" | London | HLM8585 | 1958 | £10 | £20 | |
| This Is Chuck Berry | 7" EP | Pye | NEP44013 | 1963 | £4 | £8 | |

| | | | | | | | |
|---|---|---|---|---|---|---|---|
| You Came A Long Way From Saint Louis.. | 7" EP | Chess | CRE6016 | 1966 | £7.50 | £15 | |
| You Can't Catch Me | 7" | London | HLN8375 | 1957 | £75 | £150 | *gold label* |
| You Never Can Tell | LP | Pye | NPL28039 | 1964 | £5 | £12 | |
| You Never Can Tell | 7" | Pye | 7N25257 | 1964 | £1.50 | £4 | |

## BERRY, CHUCK & BO DIDDLEY

| | | | | | | | |
|---|---|---|---|---|---|---|---|
| Chuck And Bo Vol. 1 | 7" EP | Pye | NEP44009 | 1963 | £4 | £8 | |
| Chuck And Bo Vol. 2 | 7" EP | Pye | NEP44012 | 1963 | £4 | £8 | |
| Chuck And Bo Vol. 3 | 7" EP | Pye | NEP44017 | 1964 | £4 | £8 | |
| Two Great Guitars | LP | Pye | NPL28047 | 1964 | £6 | £15 | |

## BERRY, DAVE

| | | | | | | | |
|---|---|---|---|---|---|---|---|
| Baby It's You | 7" | Decca | F11876 | 1964 | £1.50 | £4 | |
| Can I Get It From You | 7" EP | Decca | DFE8625 | 1965 | £6 | £12 | |
| Dave Berry | LP | Decca | LK4653 | 1964 | £15 | £30 | |
| Dave Berry | 7" EP | Decca | DFE8601 | 1964 | £7.50 | £15 | |
| Dave Berry '68 | LP | Decca | LK/SKL4932 | 1968 | £8 | £20 | |
| Dozen Berrys | LP | Ace Of Clubs | ACL/SCL1218 | 1966 | £5 | £12 | |
| Little Things | 7" EP | Decca | 457071 | 1965 | £7.50 | £15 | *French* |
| Mama | 7" EP | Decca | 457124 | 1966 | £7.50 | £15 | *French* |
| Memphis Tennessee | 7" | Decca | F11734 | 1963 | £1.50 | £4 | |
| My Baby Left Me | 7" | Decca | F11803 | 1963 | £1.50 | £4 | |
| Special Sound Of Dave Berry | LP | Decca | LK4823 | 1966 | £8 | £20 | |

## BERRY, EMMETT

| | | | | | | | |
|---|---|---|---|---|---|---|---|
| Beauty And The Blues | LP | Columbia | 33SX1246 | 1960 | £5 | £12 | *side 2 by Buddy Tate* |
| Emmett Berry Orchestra | 10" LP | Columbia | 33S1107 | 1957 | £4 | £10 | |

## BERRY, HEIDI

| | | | | | | | |
|---|---|---|---|---|---|---|---|
| Below The Waves | CD-s | Creation | CRE047CD | 1989 | £2 | £5 | |

## BERRY, MIKE

| | | | | | | | |
|---|---|---|---|---|---|---|---|
| Don't You Think It's Time | 7" | HMV | POP1105 | 1962 | £1.50 | £4 | |
| Every Little Kiss | 7" | HMV | POP1042 | 1962 | £6 | £12 | |
| It Really Doesn't Matter | 7" | HMV | POP1194 | 1963 | £2 | £5 | |
| It's Just A Matter Of Time | 7" | HMV | POP979 | 1962 | £2 | £5 | |
| It's Time For Mike Berry | 7" EP | HMV | 7EG8793 | 1963 | £10 | £20 | |
| Lovesick | 7" | HMV | POP1284 | 1964 | £2 | £5 | |
| My Little Baby | 7" | HMV | POP1142 | 1963 | £2 | £5 | |
| Raining In My Heart | 7" | Polydor | 56182 | 1967 | £1.50 | £4 | |
| Talk | 7" | HMV | POP1314 | 1964 | £2 | £5 | |
| This Little Girl | 7" | HMV | POP1257 | 1964 | £2 | £5 | |
| Tribute To Buddy Holly | 7" EP | HMV | 7EG8808 | 1963 | £12.50 | £25 | |
| Tribute To Buddy Holly | 7" | HMV | POP912 | 1961 | £2 | £5 | |
| Will You Love Me Tomorrow | 7" | Decca | F11314 | 1961 | £6 | £12 | |

## BERRY, RICHARD

| | | | | | | | |
|---|---|---|---|---|---|---|---|
| Live At The Century Club | LP | Pam | 1001 | | £15 | £30 | *US* |
| Rhythm And Blues Vol. 3 | 7" EP | Ember | EMBEP4527 | 1964 | £62.50 | £125 | |
| Richard Berry And The Dreamers | LP | Crown | CLP5371 | 1963 | £6 | £15 | *US* |
| Wild Berry | LP | Pam | 1002 | | £15 | £30 | *US* |

## BERRYMAN, PETE

| | | | | | | | |
|---|---|---|---|---|---|---|---|
| Pete Berryman And Guitar | LP | Autogram | FLLP509 | 1978 | £5 | £12 | *German* |

## BERT, EDDIE

| | | | | | | | |
|---|---|---|---|---|---|---|---|
| Encore | LP | London | LTZC15060 | 1957 | £8 | £20 | |
| Musician Of The Year | LP | London | LTZC15040 | 1957 | £8 | £20 | |

## BESSON, CLAUDE

| | | | | | | | |
|---|---|---|---|---|---|---|---|
| Instrumental | LP | Pendes | 13NP609 | 197– | £10 | £25 | *French* |
| Instrumental Vol. 2 | LP | Pendes | 13NP637 | 197– | £10 | £25 | *French* |
| N'Oubliez pas l'amour | LP | Pendes | 13NP605 | 197– | £10 | £25 | *French* |

## BEST, JON

| | | | | | | | |
|---|---|---|---|---|---|---|---|
| Young Boy Blues | 7" | Decca | F12077 | 1965 | £2.50 | £6 | |

## BEST, PETE

Pete Best was the original drummer with the Beatles, who is still understandably bitter at the way he was sacked to make way for Ringo Starr just as the group was about to make its first record for Parlophone. The American LP was given a deliberately misleading title – these are not Beatles recordings.

| | | | | | | | |
|---|---|---|---|---|---|---|---|
| Anyway | 7" | Beatles | 800 | 1964 | £25 | £50 | *US* |
| Best Of The Beatles | LP | Savage | BM71 | 1965 | £37.50 | £75 | *US* |
| Boys | 7" | Cameo | 391 | 1966 | £12.50 | £25 | *US* |
| Casting My Spell | 7" | Mr. Maestro | 712 | 1965 | £12.50 | £25 | *US* |
| I Can't Do Without You Now | 7" | Mr. Maestro | 711 | 1964 | £25 | £50 | *US* |
| I'm Gonna Knock On Your Door | 7" | Decca | F11929 | 1964 | £15 | £30 | *US* |
| If You Can't Get Her | 7" | Happening | 117/8 | 1964 | £25 | £50 | *US* |
| If You Can't Get Her | 7" | Happening | 405 | 1964 | £25 | £50 | *US* |

## BETHEA, H. & THE AGENTS

| | | | | | | | |
|---|---|---|---|---|---|---|---|
| Got To Find A Sweet Name | LP | Reprise | MS3239 | 1972 | £8 | £20 | *US* |

## BETHNAL

| | | | | | | | |
|---|---|---|---|---|---|---|---|
| Fiddler | 7" | Bethnal | VIOL1 | 1977 | £1.50 | £4 | |

## BETTERDAYS
| | | | | | | | |
|---|---|---|---|---|---|---|---|
| Don't Want That | 7" | Polydor | 56024 | 1965 | £75 | £150 | |
| Down On The Waterfront | 7" EP | NTB | 1002 | 1992 | £2 | £5 | |
| Howl Of The Streets | 7" EP | NTB | 001 | 1991 | £2 | £5 | |

## BETTERS, HAROLD
| | | | | | | | |
|---|---|---|---|---|---|---|---|
| Do Anything You Wanna | 7" | Sue | WI378 | 1965 | £5 | £10 | |

## BETWEEN
| | | | | | | | |
|---|---|---|---|---|---|---|---|
| And The Waters Opened | LP | Vertigo | 6360612 | 1973 | £6 | £15 | German |
| Contemplation | LP | Wergo | WER1012 | 1976 | £6 | £15 | German |
| Dharana | LP | Vertigo | 6360619 | 1974 | £6 | £15 | German |
| Einstieg | LP | Wergo | WER1001 | 1971 | £8 | £20 | German |
| Hesse Between Music | LP | EMI | 1C06229546 | 1974 | £6 | £15 | German |

## BEVERLEY

Beverley became Beverley Martyn when she married John Martyn. The pair recorded two fine albums together.

| | | | | | | | |
|---|---|---|---|---|---|---|---|
| Happy New Year | 7" | Deram | DM101 | 1966 | £4 | £8 | |
| Museum | 7" | Deram | DM137 | 1967 | £2 | £5 | |

## BEVERLEY SISTERS
| | | | | | | | |
|---|---|---|---|---|---|---|---|
| Beverley Sisters | 7" EP | Decca | DFE6307 | 1956 | £2 | £5 | |
| Beverley Sisters No. 2 | 7" EP | Decca | DFE6401 | 1957 | £2 | £5 | |
| Beverley Sisters No. 3 | 7" EP | Decca | DFE6402 | 1957 | £2 | £5 | |
| Beverley Sisters No. 4 | 7" EP | Decca | DFE6512 | 1958 | £2 | £5 | |
| Bevs For Christmas | 7" EP | Decca | DFE6611 | 1959 | £2 | £5 | |
| Born To Be With You | 7" | Decca | F10770 | 1956 | £1.50 | £4 | |
| Bye Bye Love | 7" | Decca | F10909 | 1957 | £1.50 | £4 | |
| Date With The Bevs | 10" LP | Philips | BBR8052 | 1955 | £6 | £15 | |
| Enchanting Beverley Sisters | LP | Columbia | 33SX1285 | 1960 | £4 | £10 | |
| Long Black Nylons | 7" | Decca | F10971 | 1958 | £2 | £5 | |
| Those Beverley Sisters | LP | Ace Of Clubs | ACL1048 | 1960 | £4 | £10 | |
| Three's Company | 7" EP | Columbia | SEG7602 | 1956 | £2 | £5 | |
| Willie Can | 7" | Decca | F10705 | 1956 | £2 | £5 | |

## BEVERLEY'S ALL STARS
| | | | | | | | |
|---|---|---|---|---|---|---|---|
| Double Shot | 7" | Trojan | TR683 | 1969 | £1.50 | £4 | |
| Go Home | 7" | Black Swan | WI449 | 1965 | £5 | £10 | |

## BEVIS FROND

Nick Salomon knows about record collecting from two different sides. Starting as a dealer, he was able to put his love and knowledge of psychedelic music to good use. As an artist, demonstrating that love by playing the same style himself, he has seen his limited-edition record releases acquiring a cult reputation and hence an increase in value. Woronzow is Salomon's own label, which he uses to issue recordings by several like-minded groups as well as his own efforts, which appear under the name of the Bevis Frond.

| | | | | | | | |
|---|---|---|---|---|---|---|---|
| Bevis Through The Looking Glass | LP | Woronzow | WOO51/2 | 1987 | £25 | £50 | double, booklet |
| Inner Marshland | LP | Woronzow | WOO4 | 1987 | £4 | £10 | |
| Miasma | LP | Woronzow | WOO3 | 1987 | £4 | £10 | |
| Triptych | LP | Woronzow | WOO8 | 1988 | £4 | £10 | |

## BEWES, RODNEY
| | | | | | | | |
|---|---|---|---|---|---|---|---|
| Dear Mother Love Albert | 7" | Revolution | REVP1001 | 1970 | £1.50 | £4 | |
| Remember When | 7" | Revolution | REV1003 | 1969 | £1.50 | £4 | |

## BIANCHI, MAURICIO
| | | | | | | | |
|---|---|---|---|---|---|---|---|
| Sympathy For A Genocide | LP | Sterile | SR2 | 1981 | £25 | £50 | |

## BIANCO, GENE
| | | | | | | | |
|---|---|---|---|---|---|---|---|
| Alarm Clock Boogie | 7" | Vogue | V9167 | 1960 | £5 | £10 | |

## BIBBY
| | | | | | | | |
|---|---|---|---|---|---|---|---|
| Rub It Down | 7" | Blue Beat | BB289 | 1965 | £6 | £12 | |

## BIBLE
| | | | | | | | |
|---|---|---|---|---|---|---|---|
| Bible | CD | Ensign | CCD1727 | 1989 | £5 | £12 | |
| Crystal Palace | CD-s | Chrysalis | BIBCD2 | 1988 | £2 | £5 | |
| Eureka | CD | Chrysalis | CCD1646 | 1988 | £5 | £12 | |
| Graceland (New Version) | CD-s | Chrysalis | BIBCD4 | 1989 | £2 | £5 | |
| Honey Be Good | CD-s | Chrysalis | BIBCD3 | 1988 | £2 | £5 | |
| Honey Be Good | CD-s | Ensign | BIBCD5 | 1989 | £2 | £5 | |

## BIFF BANG POW!

Creation is that true rarity – a record label with a player-manager. For Alan McGee, when not keeping an eye on the likes of Teenage Fanclub and Ride, plays guitar and sings for his own group, Biff Bang Pow!

| | | | | | | | |
|---|---|---|---|---|---|---|---|
| Fifty Years Of Fun | 7" | Creation | CRE003 | 1984 | £2 | £5 | |
| Sleep | 7" | Caff | CAFF13 | 1991 | £6 | £12 | Times B side |
| There Must Be A Better Life | 7" | Creation | CRE007 | 1984 | £5 | £10 | |

## BIG AUDIO DYNAMITE
| | | | | | | | |
|---|---|---|---|---|---|---|---|
| Ally Pally Paradiso | LP | CBS | BIG11 | 1990 | £4 | £10 | promo |
| Ally Pally Paradiso | LP | CBS | BIG11 | 1990 | £4 | £10 | promo |
| Ally Pally Paradiso | CD | Columbia | CSK4271 | 1991 | £8 | £20 | US promo |
| Contact | CD-s | CBS | CDBAAD6 | 1989 | £2 | £5 | |
| Just Play Music | CD-s | CBS | CDBAAD4 | 1988 | £2 | £5 | |

| Title | Format | Label | Catalogue | Year | | | Notes |
|---|---|---|---|---|---|---|---|
| Kool Aid | CD | CBS | 4674662 | 1990 | £5 | £12 | |
| Looking For A Song | CD | Epic | ZSK6587 | 1994 | £10 | £25 | US double promo |
| Medicine Show | 12" | CBS | DTA7181 | 1985 | £2.50 | £6 | double |
| Megatop Phoenix | CD | CBS | 4657902 | 1989 | £5 | £12 | |
| Other 99 | CD-s | CBS | CDBAAD5 | 1988 | £2 | £5 | |
| Rush | CD-s | CBS | 6576402 | 1991 | £2 | £5 | |

## BIG BEATS

| Title | Format | Label | Catalogue | Year | | | Notes |
|---|---|---|---|---|---|---|---|
| Live | LP | Liberty | LRP/LST7407 | 1965 | £5 | £12 | US |

## BIG BEN ACCORDION BAND

| Title | Format | Label | Catalogue | Year | | | Notes |
|---|---|---|---|---|---|---|---|
| Rock 'n' Roll Medley No. 1 | 7" | Columbia | DB3835 | 1956 | £2 | £5 | |
| Rock 'n' Roll Medley No. 2 | 7" | Columbia | DB3856 | 1957 | £2 | £5 | |

## BIG BERTHA

This group was formed by the original Move bass player, Ace Kefford, as the Ace Kefford Stand, becoming Big Bertha when Kefford himself left. The drummer for a short while was Cozy Powell. The single would appear to have been withdrawn – or else never given a full release in the first place, as it bears the same catalogue number as a single by Yes.

| Title | Format | Label | Catalogue | Year | | | Notes |
|---|---|---|---|---|---|---|---|
| Munich City | 7" | United Artists | UA35142 | 1969 | £6 | £12 | German, picture sleeve |
| World's An Apple | 7" | Atlantic | 584298 | 1969 | £6 | £12 | |

## BIG BLACK

| Title | Format | Label | Catalogue | Year | | | Notes |
|---|---|---|---|---|---|---|---|
| Headache | 12" | Blast First | BFFP14T | 1987 | £20 | £40 | red vinyl, with booklet, poster, 7" |
| Pigpile | LP | Touch & Go | TG81 | 1992 | £6 | £15 | with video & T shirt, boxed |
| Sound Of Impact | LP | | NOT2(BUT1) | 1986 | £25 | £50 | nos 1-1000 |
| Sound Of Impact | LP | | NOT2(BUT1) | 1987 | £15 | £30 | nos 1001-1500 |

## BIG BOB

| Title | Format | Label | Catalogue | Year | | | Notes |
|---|---|---|---|---|---|---|---|
| Your Line Was Busy | 7" | Top Rank | JAR185 | 1959 | £7.50 | £15 | |

## BIG BOPPER

| Title | Format | Label | Catalogue | Year | | | Notes |
|---|---|---|---|---|---|---|---|
| Big Bopper | 7" EP | Mercury | ZEP10004 | 1959 | £50 | £100 | |
| Big Bopper's Wedding | 7" | Mercury | AMT1017 | 1958 | £5 | £10 | |
| Chantilly Lace | LP | Contour | 6870531 | 1974 | £4 | £10 | |
| Chantilly Lace | LP | Mercury | MMC14008 | 1958 | £75 | £150 | |
| Chantilly Lace | 7" | Mercury | AMT1002 | 1958 | £5 | £10 | |
| It's The Truth Ruth | 7" | Mercury | AMT1046 | 1959 | £6 | £12 | |
| Pink Petticoats | 7" EP | Mercury | ZEP10027 | 1959 | £87.50 | £175 | |

## BIG BORIS

| Title | Format | Label | Catalogue | Year | | | Notes |
|---|---|---|---|---|---|---|---|
| Big Country | 7" | RCA | RCA2187 | 1972 | £1.50 | £4 | |

## BIG BOY PETE

| Title | Format | Label | Catalogue | Year | | | Notes |
|---|---|---|---|---|---|---|---|
| Cold Turkey | 7" | Camp | 602005 | 1968 | £25 | £50 | |

## BIG BROTHER

| Title | Format | Label | Catalogue | Year | | | Notes |
|---|---|---|---|---|---|---|---|
| Confusion | LP | All American | 5570 | 1970 | £37.50 | £75 | US |

## BIG BROTHER & THE HOLDING CO.

Big Brother and the Holding Co. had Janis Joplin as their lead singer, but were far from being just her backing group. The first LP, recorded before Cream toured America with their amplifiers turned up to maximum, sounds weak. The partly live *Cheap Thrills*, however, is an exciting and vital recording. Janis Joplin without the Holding Co. failed to achieve this power, but equally, the Holding Co. without Janis Joplin (as on the 1971 recordings) lacked distinction.

| Title | Format | Label | Catalogue | Year | | | Notes |
|---|---|---|---|---|---|---|---|
| Be A Brother | LP | CBS | 64118 | 1971 | £4 | £10 | |
| Big Brother & The Holding Co. | LP | Fontana | (S)TL5457 | 1967 | £8 | £20 | |
| Big Brother & The Holding Co. | LP | London | HAT/SHT8377 | 1968 | £5 | £12 | |
| Bye Bye Baby | 7" | Fontana | TF881 | 1967 | £2.50 | £6 | |
| Cheap Thrills | LP | CBS | 63392 | 1968 | £4 | £10 | |
| Cheap Thrills | LP | Columbia | KCL2900 | 1968 | £15 | £30 | US mono |
| Down On Me | 7" | London | HLT10226 | 1969 | £2 | £5 | |
| How Hard It Is | LP | CBS | 30738 | 1971 | £5 | £12 | US |
| Light Is Faster Than Sound | 7" EP | Vogue | INT18147 | 1967 | £12.50 | £25 | French |
| Piece Of My Heart | 7" | CBS | 3683 | 1968 | £1.50 | £4 | |
| Piece Of My Heart | 7" | CBS | 3683 | 1968 | £5 | £10 | picture sleeve |

## BIG CARROT

The single credited to Big Carrot is actually the work of T Rex, being designed as a showcase for Marc Bolan's increasing desire to be taken seriously as a lead guitarist.

| Title | Format | Label | Catalogue | Year | | | Notes |
|---|---|---|---|---|---|---|---|
| Blackjack | 7" | EMI | EMI2047 | 1973 | £7.50 | £15 | |

## BIG CHARLIE

| Title | Format | Label | Catalogue | Year | | | Notes |
|---|---|---|---|---|---|---|---|
| Red Sea | 7" | Blue Beat | BB241 | 1964 | £6 | £12 | |

## BIG COUNTRY

| Title | Format | Label | Catalogue | Year | | | Notes |
|---|---|---|---|---|---|---|---|
| Beautiful People | CD-s | Vertigo | BICD2 | 1991 | £2 | £5 | |
| Broken Heart | CD-s | Mercury | BIGCD6 | 1988 | £2 | £5 | |
| Chance | 12" | Mercury | COUP4 | 1983 | £4 | £10 | picture disc |
| Crossing | LP | Mercury | MERS27 | 1983 | £4 | £10 | white sleeve |
| Fields Of Fire | 7" | Mercury | COUP2 | 1983 | £4 | £8 | shaped picture disc |
| Fields Of Fire | 12" | Mercury | COUNX2 | 1983 | £4 | £10 | clear vinyl |
| Harvest Home | 12" | Mercury | COUNX1 | 1982 | £4 | £10 | clear vinyl |
| In A Big Country | 12" | Mercury | COUNT313 | 1983 | £3 | £8 | red sleeve |

| | | | | | | | |
|---|---|---|---|---|---|---|---|
| King Of Emotion | CD-s | Mercury | BIGCD5 | 1988 £2 | £5 | |
| Look Away | 7" | Mercury | BIGCP1 | 1986 £2.50 | £6 | .... shaped picture disc |
| One Great Thing | CD-s | Mercury | BIGCD3 | 1986 £2 | £5 | |
| Peace In Our Time | CD-s | Mercury | BIGCD7 | 1989 £2 | £5 | |
| Republican Party Reptile | CD-s | Mercury | BICD1 | 1991 £2 | £5 | |
| Save Me | CD-s | Mercury | BIGCD8 | 1990 £2 | £5 | |
| Twelve Inch Singles | 12" | Mercury | | £30 | £60 | box set |
| Where The Rose Is Sown | 7" | Mercury | MERD185 | 1984 £4 | £8 | double |

## BIG DADDY
| | | | | | | | |
|---|---|---|---|---|---|---|---|
| Big Daddy's Blues | LP | Gee | (S)G704 | 1960 £8 | £20 | US |
| Twist Party | LP | Regent | 6106 | 1962 £6 | £15 | US |

## BIG DAVE & HIS ORCHESTRA
| | | | | | | | |
|---|---|---|---|---|---|---|---|
| Cat From Coos Bay | 7" | Capitol | CL14195 | 1954 £4 | £8 | |
| Rock And Roll Party | 7" | Capitol | CL14245 | 1955 £7.50 | £15 | |
| Rock, Roll, Ball And Wail | 78 | Capitol | CL14156 | 1954 £3 | £8 | |

## BIG FLAME
| | | | | | | | |
|---|---|---|---|---|---|---|---|
| Rigour | 7" | Ron Johnson | ZRON3 | 1985 £2 | £5 | |
| Sink | 7" | Plaque | 001 | 1984 £5 | £10 | |
| Tough | 7" | Ron Johnson | ZRON4 | 1985 £1.50 | £4 | |
| Why Pop Stars Can't Dance | 7" | Ron Johnson | ZRON7 | 1986 £1.50 | £4 | |

## BIG FOOT
| | | | | | | | |
|---|---|---|---|---|---|---|---|
| Big Foot | LP | Winro | 1004 | 1968 £8 | £20 | US |

## BIG GROUP
| | | | | | | | |
|---|---|---|---|---|---|---|---|
| Big Hammer | LP | Peer International Library | PIL9009 | 1971 £50 | £100 | |

## BIG IN JAPAN
Various people passing through the ranks of Big In Japan went on to be fairly big in lots of places – most notably Budgie (Siouxsie and the Banshees), David Balfe (Teardrop Explodes, then founder of the Food label), Holly Johnson (Frankie Goes To Hollywood), Bill Drummond (KLF and manager of Zoo label), and Ian Broudie (production work and the Lightning Seeds).

| | | | | | | | |
|---|---|---|---|---|---|---|---|
| Big In Japan | 7" | Erics | ERICS001 | 1977 £2.50 | £6 | |
| From Y To Z And Never Again | 7" | Zoo | CAGE001 | 1978 £4 | £8 | |

## BIG LOST RAINBOW
| | | | | | | | |
|---|---|---|---|---|---|---|---|
| Big Lost Rainbow | LP | private | | 1973 £700 | £1000 | US |

## BIG MAYBELLE
| | | | | | | | |
|---|---|---|---|---|---|---|---|
| All Of Me | 7" | London | HLC8447 | 1957 £12.50 | £25 | |
| Baby Won't You Please Come Home | 7" | London | HLC8854 | 1959 £6 | £12 | |
| Blues, Candy And Big Maybelle | LP | Savoy | MG14011 | 1958 £15 | £30 | US |
| Careless Love | 7" | London | HL9941 | 1965 £2.50 | £6 | |
| Gospel Soul | LP | Brunswick | BL754142 | 1968 £5 | £12 | US |
| Got A Brand New Bag | LP | Rajac | (S)S122 | 1967 £4 | £10 | US |
| Mama He Treats Your Daughter Mean | 7" | CBS | 2926 | 1967 £1.50 | £4 | |
| Pure Soul Of Big Maybelle | LP | CBS | 62999 | 1967 £8 | £20 | |
| Quittin' Time | 7" | Direction | 583312 | 1968 £5 | £10 | |
| Sings | LP | Savoy | MG14005 | 1958 £15 | £30 | US |
| Soul Of Big Maybelle | LP | Scepter | (S)S522 | 1964 £6 | £15 | US |
| Turn The World Around | 7" | CBS | 2735 | 1967 £6 | £12 | |
| What More Can A Woman Do | LP | Brunswick | BL(7)54107 | 1962 £8 | £20 | US |

## BIG MOOSE
| | | | | | | | |
|---|---|---|---|---|---|---|---|
| Puppy Howl Blues | 7" | Python | PKM1 | 1968 £6 | £12 | |

## BIG SLEEP
| | | | | | | | |
|---|---|---|---|---|---|---|---|
| Bluebell Wood | LP | Pegasus | PEG4 | 1971 £20 | £40 | |

## BIG STAR
Big Star, the group led by Alex Chilton following the disbanding of the Box Tops, has acquired a formidable cult reputation wholly unjustified by the actual music to be found on the records. The songs are rather ordinary and Big Star's lack of success is not at all surprising.

| | | | | | | | |
|---|---|---|---|---|---|---|---|
| Big Star | LP | Ardent | ADS1501 | 1971 £8 | £20 | US |
| Radio City | LP | Ardent | ADS2803 | 1971 £8 | £20 | US |
| Radio City/Big Star | LP | Stax | SXSP302 | 1978 £8 | £20 | double |
| Third Album | LP | Aura | AUL703 | 1978 £4 | £10 | |

## BIG THREE
By all accounts, the Big Three were, on stage, the most impressive Liverpool group of them all. Their records, however, never did them justice – even with the live At The Cavern EP, it is clearly a case of 'you had to be there'. Bass player Johnny Gustafson has been ubiquitous ever since, however, playing, among others, with Quatermass, Hard Stuff, Gillan and Roxy Music.

| | | | | | | | |
|---|---|---|---|---|---|---|---|
| At The Cavern | 7" EP | Decca | DFE8552 | 1963 £6 | £12 | |
| By The Way | 7" | Decca | F11689 | 1963 £1.50 | £4 | |
| I'm With You | 7" | Decca | F11752 | 1963 £2.50 | £6 | |
| If You Ever Change Your Mind | 7" | Decca | F11927 | 1964 £2.50 | £6 | |
| Resurrection | LP | Polydor | 2383199 | 1973 £8 | £20 | |
| Some Other Guy | 7" | Decca | F11614 | 1963 £2.50 | £6 | |
| What'd I Say | 7" EP | Decca | 457029 | 1964 £12.50 | £25 | French |

## BIG THREE (CASS ELLIOTT, JIM HENDRICKS, TIM ROSE)

| | | | | | | | |
|---|---|---|---|---|---|---|---|
| Big Three | LP | FM | (FS)307 | 1963 | £6 | £15 | US |
| Big Three Featuring Cass Elliott | LP | Roulette | RCP1003 | 1967 | £4 | £10 | |
| Live At The Recording Studio | LP | FM | (FS)311 | 1964 | £6 | £15 | US |

## BIG YOUTH

Of the many toasting DJs to emerge in the wake of U Roy's first successes, Big Youth was the most idiosyncratic and the most spectacular. His 'Ace 90 Skank' set the pattern – a roaring motor bike engine is overlaid by thickly accented Jamaican voices; then a lanky bass guitar begins its deep descent as Big Youth unleashes a stream of words that manage to sound lazy even while tumbling over each other.

| | | | | | | | |
|---|---|---|---|---|---|---|---|
| A So We Say | 7" | Summit | SUM8542 | 1973 | £1.50 | £4 | Winston Scotland B side |
| Ace 90 Skank | 7" | Downtown | DT492 | 1972 | £1.50 | £4 | |
| Can You Keep A Secret | 7" | Pyramid | PYR7015 | 1974 | £1.50 | £4 | with Keith Hudson |
| Cane And Abel | 7" | Prince Buster | PB50 | 1973 | £1.50 | £4 | |
| Chi Chi Run | LP | Fab | MS8 | 1972 | £8 | £20 | |
| Chi Chi Run | 7" | Blue Beat | BB424 | 1972 | £6 | £12 | John Holt B side |
| Chi Chi Run | 7" | Prince Buster | PB46 | 1972 | £1.50 | £4 | |
| Concrete Jungle | 7" | Grape | GR3061 | 1973 | £1.50 | £4 | |
| Cool Breeze | 7" | Green Door | GD4051 | 1973 | £1.50 | £4 | Crystalites B side |
| Dock Of The Bay | 7" | Downtown | DT497 | 1972 | £1.50 | £4 | Crystalites B side |
| Dreadlocks Dread | LP | Front Line | FL1014 | 1978 | £5 | £12 | |
| Dreadlocks Dread | LP | Klik | KLP9001 | 1976 | £6 | £15 | |
| Foreman v. Frazier | 7" | Grape | GR3040 | 1973 | £1.50 | £4 | |
| Hit The Road Jack | LP | Trojan | TRLS137 | 1976 | £6 | £15 | |
| Isaiah First Prophet Of Old | LP | Front Line | FL1011 | 1978 | £5 | £12 | |
| JA To UK | 7" | Grape | GR3044 | 1973 | £1.50 | £4 | |
| Leggo Beast | 7" | Prince Buster | PB48 | 1973 | £1.50 | £4 | |
| Medicine Doctor | 7" | Gayfeet | CS206 | 1969 | £1.50 | £4 | |
| Natty Cultural Dread | LP | Trojan | TRLS123 | 1976 | £6 | £15 | |
| Opportunity Rock | 7" | Grape | GR3051 | 1973 | £1.50 | £4 | |
| Reggae Phenomenon | LP | Big Youth | BYD1 | 1977 | £5 | £12 | |
| Screaming Target | LP | Trojan | TRLS61 | 1973 | £6 | £15 | |

## BIGLIETTO PER L'INFERNO

| | | | | | | | |
|---|---|---|---|---|---|---|---|
| Biglietto Per L'Inferno | LP | Trident | TRI1005 | 1973 | £75 | £150 | Italian |

## BIKINIS

| | | | | | | |
|---|---|---|---|---|---|---|
| Bikini | 7" | Columbia | DB4149 | 1958 | £2.50 | £6 |

## BILLIE & EDDIE

| | | | | | | |
|---|---|---|---|---|---|---|
| King Is Coming Back | 7" | Top Rank | JAR249 | 1959 | £2.50 | £6 |

## BILLIE & LILLIE

| | | | | | | |
|---|---|---|---|---|---|---|
| Bells Bells Bells | 7" | Top Rank | JAR157 | 1959 | £1.50 | £4 |
| Creeping Crawling Crying | 7" | London | HLU8630 | 1958 | £10 | £20 |
| Hanging On To You | 7" | London | HLU8689 | 1958 | £5 | £10 |
| La Dee Dah | 7" | London | HLU8564 | 1958 | £10 | £20 |
| Lucky Ladybug | 7" | London | HLU8795 | 1959 | £5 | £10 |

## BILLIE & THE ESSENTIALS

| | | | | | | |
|---|---|---|---|---|---|---|
| Maybe You'll be There | 7" | London | HLW9657 | 1963 | £15 | £30 |

## BILLMUSS, TREVOR

| | | | | | | |
|---|---|---|---|---|---|---|
| Family Apology | LP | Charisma | CAS1017 | 1970 | £4 | £10 |

## BINTANGS

| | | | | | | | |
|---|---|---|---|---|---|---|---|
| Blues On The Ceiling | LP | Decca | XBY846514 | 1969 | £5 | £12 | Dutch |
| Down South Blues | LP | Decca | PD12032 | 1973 | £5 | £12 | German |
| Genuine Bull | LP | RCA | YHPL10982 | 1975 | £4 | £10 | Dutch |
| Ridin' With The Bintangs | LP | Decca | 6454420 | 1970 | £6 | £15 | Dutch |
| Travelling In The USA | LP | Decca | 6440677 | 1970 | £6 | £15 | Dutch |

## BIOTA

The albums issued by the musicians and artists involved in both Biota and Mnemonists are conceived as general art packages, in which the cover art, the elaborate art print inserts, and the music itself are of equal importance. The concept becomes a little subverted in the compact disc age, so that although the majority of the albums listed are available on CD, along with some more recent releases, the original vinyl issues are definitely the ones to get. The music itself is instrumental and consists of dense, fascinating soundscapes produced by a large number of different instrumental sounds, without, however, including anything that might be described as a synthesizer.

| | | | | | | | |
|---|---|---|---|---|---|---|---|
| Bellowing Room | LP | Recommended | RRC27 | 1987 | £5 | £12 | |
| Biota | LP | Dys | BIOTA | 1982 | £6 | £15 | US |
| Rackabones | LP | Dys | DYS12/13 | 1985 | £8 | £20 | US double |
| Tinct | LP | Recommended | RRC31 | 1988 | £5 | £12 | |

## BIRD, IVOR

| | | | | | | |
|---|---|---|---|---|---|---|
| Over The Wall We Go | 7" | RSO | 2090270 | 1978 | £1.50 | £4 |

## BIRD, RONNIE

| | | | | | | | |
|---|---|---|---|---|---|---|---|
| Adieu à un ami | 7" EP | Decca | 460844 | 196– | £12.50 | £25 | French |
| Chante | 7" EP | Philips | 437220 | 196– | £7.50 | £15 | French |
| Elle m'attend | LP | Decca | 154134 | 196– | £25 | £50 | French |
| Elle m'attend | 7" EP | Decca | 460918 | 196– | £7.50 | £15 | French |
| L'Amour nous rend fou | 7" EP | Decca | 460889 | 196– | £7.50 | £15 | French |
| La Surprise | 7" EP | Philips | 437353 | 196– | £7.50 | £15 | French |
| Le Pivert | 7" EP | Philips | 437403 | 196– | £7.50 | £15 | French |

| | | | | | | | |
|---|---|---|---|---|---|---|---|
| N'Ecoute pas ton coeur | 7" EP | Philips | 437239 | 196– £7.50 | £15 | | *French* |
| Où va-t-elle? | 7" EP | Decca | 460946 | 196– £7.50 | £15 | | *French* |
| Tu en dis trop | 7" EP | Philips | 437327 | 196– £7.50 | £15 | | *French* |

## BIRD, TONY

| | | | | | | |
|---|---|---|---|---|---|---|
| Bird Of Paradise | LP | CBS | 82498 | 1978 £4 | £10 | |
| Tony Bird | LP | CBS | 81183 | 1976 £4 | £10 | |

## BIRDLEGS & PAULINE

| | | | | | | |
|---|---|---|---|---|---|---|
| Spring | 7" | Sue | WI4014 | 1966 £5 | £10 | |

## BIRDS

The Birds started playing together at art college in Middlesex, the three singles featuring their typical British R&B. They had shortened their name from the Thunderbirds, a move that brought the group into legal conflict with the more successful Byrds. This gave them a modicum of publicity, but it was not translated into sales. A fourth single was credited to Bird's Birds, but the group split up soon afterwards. Bass player Kim Gardner achieved chart success a few years later as a member of Ashton, Gardner and Dyke, while the Birds' guitarist did even better when he joined successively the Jeff Beck Group, the Faces and the Rolling Stones – his name being Ron Wood.

| | | | | | | |
|---|---|---|---|---|---|---|
| Leavin' Here | 7" | Decca | F12140 | 1965 £20 | £40 | |
| No Good Without You Baby | 7" EP | Decca | 457114 | 1966 £100 | £200 | *French, best auctioned* |
| No Good Without You Baby | 7" | Decca | F12257 | 1965 £20 | £40 | |
| You're On My Mind | 7" | Decca | F12031 | 1964 £37.50 | £75 | |

## BIRD'S BIRDS

| | | | | | | |
|---|---|---|---|---|---|---|
| Say Those Magic Words | 7" | Reaction | 591005 | 1966 £250 | £400 | *best auctioned* |

## BIRDS OF A FEATHER

| | | | | | | |
|---|---|---|---|---|---|---|
| All God's Children | 7" | Page One | POF179 | 1970 £1.50 | £4 | |
| Birds Of A Feather | LP | Page One | POLS027 | 1970 £25 | £50 | |
| Blacksmith Blues | 7" | Page One | POF156 | 1969 £1.50 | £4 | |

## BIRKIN, JANE & SERGE GAINSBOURG

| | | | | | | |
|---|---|---|---|---|---|---|
| Jane Birkin And Serge Gainsbourg | LP | Fontana | STL5493 | 1969 £8 | £20 | |
| Je t'aime moi non plus | 7" | Antic | K11511 | 1974 £5 | £10 | *picture sleeve* |
| Je t'aime moi non plus | 7" | Fontana | TF1042 | 1969 £1.50 | £4 | |
| Je t'aime moi non plus | 7" | Major Minor | MM645 | 1969 £1.50 | £4 | |

## BIRMINGHAM

| | | | | | | |
|---|---|---|---|---|---|---|
| Birmingham | LP | Grosvenor | GRS1011 | 1971 £62.50 | £125 | |

## BIRTH CONTROL

| | | | | | | |
|---|---|---|---|---|---|---|
| Backdoor Possibilities | LP | Brain | 60019 | 1976 £5 | £12 | *German* |
| Believe In The Pill | LP | Ohr | OMM556025 | 1972 £6 | £15 | *German* |
| Birth Control | LP | Charisma | CAS1036 | 1971 £6 | £15 | |
| Birth Control | LP | Metronome | MLP15366 | 1970 £15 | £30 | *German* |
| Hoodoo Man | LP | CBS | 65316 | 1972 £6 | £15 | *German* |
| Live | LP | CBS | 88088 | 1974 £8 | £20 | *German double* |
| Operation | LP | Ohr | OMM556015 | 1971 £8 | £20 | *German double* |
| Plastic People | LP | CBS | 80921 | 1975 £5 | £12 | *German* |
| Re-birth | LP | CBS | 65963 | 1974 £6 | £15 | *German* |

## BIRTHDAY PARTY

| | | | | | | |
|---|---|---|---|---|---|---|
| Friend Catcher | 7" | 4AD | AD12 | 1980 £2 | £5 | |
| Mr. Clarinet | 7" | 4AD | AD114 | 1981 £2 | £5 | |
| Peel Sessions | CD-s | Strange Fruit | SFPSCD020 | 1988 £2 | £5 | |
| Release The Bats | 7" | 4AD | AD111 | 1981 £1.50 | £4 | |

## BISCAYNES

The recordings by the Biscaynes are the first by the group that found success when they changed their name to the Walker Brothers.

| | | | | | | |
|---|---|---|---|---|---|---|
| Church Key | 7" | Northridge | 1001 | 1963 £10 | £20 | *US* |
| Midnight In Montevideo | 7" | Co-En | 01 | 196– £10 | £20 | *US* |

## BISHOP, DICKIE & HIS SIDEKICKS

| | | | | | | |
|---|---|---|---|---|---|---|
| Cumberland Gap | 7" | Decca | F10869 | 1957 £4 | £8 | |
| Jumping Judy | 7" | Decca | F11028 | 1958 £2 | £5 | |
| No Other Baby | 7" | Decca | F10981 | 1958 £2 | £5 | |
| Prisoners Song | 7" | Decca | F10959 | 1957 £4 | £8 | |

## BISHOP, ELVIN

| | | | | | | |
|---|---|---|---|---|---|---|
| Elvin Bishop | LP | Fillmore | 30001 | 1969 £5 | £12 | *US* |

## BISHOP, JOHN

| | | | | | | |
|---|---|---|---|---|---|---|
| Plays His Guitar (Doesn't He?) | LP | Tangerine | 6495002 | 1971 £4 | £10 | |

## BISHOP, TOMMY RICOCHETS

| | | | | | | |
|---|---|---|---|---|---|---|
| I Should Have Known | 7" | Decca | F12238 | 1965 £1.50 | £4 | |

## BIT 'A SWEET

| | | | | | | |
|---|---|---|---|---|---|---|
| Hypnotic 1 | LP | ABC | ABCS640 | 1968 £10 | £25 | *US* |

## BITCHES SIN

| | | | | | | |
|---|---|---|---|---|---|---|
| Predator | LP | Heavy Metal | HMRLP4 | 1982 £4 | £10 | |

## BIVOUAC

| | | | | | | |
|---|---|---|---|---|---|---|
| Tuber | CD | Elemental | ELM11CD | 1993 £5 | £12 | *...with 6 bonus tracks* |

# BJORK

| | | | | | | | |
|---|---|---|---|---|---|---|---|
| Björk | LP | Falkinn | FA006 | 1977 | £75 | £150 | ... Icelandic, credited to Björk Gudmundsdottir |
| Enjoy (The Beats Mix) | 12" | One Little Indian | 193TP12DM | 1996 | £12.50 | £25 | |
| Possibly Maybe | 12" | One Little Indian | | 1996 | £12.50 | £25 | |
| Post | CD | One Little Indian | TPLP51CDX | 1995 | £5 | £12 | .. fold-out cover, poster |

# BLACK

| | | | | | | | |
|---|---|---|---|---|---|---|---|
| Human Features | 7" | Rox | ROX17 | 1981 | £10 | £20 | |
| More Than The Sun | 7" | Wonderful World Of | WW3 | 1982 | £2 | £5 | |

# BLACK, BILL COMBO

| | | | | | | | |
|---|---|---|---|---|---|---|---|
| Bill Black's Combo | 7" EP | London | REU1277 | 1960 | £5 | £10 | |
| Blue Tango | 7" | London | HLU9267 | 1961 | £1.50 | £4 | |
| Don't Be Cruel | 7" | London | HLU9212 | 1960 | £1.50 | £4 | |
| Goes Big Band | LP | Hi | HLP32020 | 1964 | £4 | £10 | US |
| Greatest Hits | LP | London | HAU8113 | 1963 | £4 | £10 | |
| Hearts Of Stone | 7" | London | HLU9306 | 1961 | £1.50 | £4 | |
| Josephine | 7" | London | HLU9156 | 1960 | £1.50 | £4 | |
| Let's Twist | LP | London | HAU2427/ SAHU6222 | 1962 | £5 | £12 | |
| Little Queenie | 7" | London | HLU9925 | 1964 | £6 | £12 | |
| More Solid And Raunchy | LP | Hi | HLP32023 | 1965 | £4 | £10 | US |
| Movin' | LP | London | HAU2433 | 1962 | £5 | £12 | |
| Moving | 7" | London | HLU9436 | 1961 | £2 | £5 | |
| Mr. Beat | LP | Hi | HLP32027 | 1965 | £4 | £10 | US |
| My Girl Josephine | 7" | London | HLU9479 | 1961 | £1.50 | £4 | |
| Ole Buttermilk Sky | 7" | London | HLU9383 | 1961 | £1.50 | £4 | |
| Plays Chuck Berry | LP | London | HAU8187 | 1964 | £6 | £15 | |
| Plays The Blues | LP | Hi | HLP32015 | 1964 | £6 | £15 | US |
| Record Hop | LP | Hi | HLP32006 | 1961 | £8 | £20 | US |
| Saxy Jazz | LP | Hi | HLP32002 | 1960 | £8 | £20 | US |
| Smokie | LP | Hi | HLP12001 | 1960 | £8 | £20 | US |
| Smokie | 7" | Felsted | AF129 | 1959 | £2 | £5 | |
| Solid & Raunchy | LP | London | HAU2310 | 1962 | £8 | £20 | |
| Tequila | 7" | London | HLU9903 | 1964 | £1.50 | £4 | |
| That Wonderful Feeling | LP | Hi | HLP32004 | 1962 | £5 | £12 | US |
| Untouchable Sound | 7" EP | London | REU1369 | 1963 | £5 | £10 | |
| Untouchable Sound Of Bill Black | LP | London | HAU8080 | 1963 | £4 | £10 | |
| White Silver Sands | 7" | London | HLU9090 | 1960 | £1.50 | £4 | |

# BLACK, CILLA

Nothing detracts from an artist's collectability as much as their becoming a popular entertainer and interest in Cilla Black's recordings has plummeted since her emergence as a television personality. She was, however, an integral part of the Merseybeat phenomenon and her first LP, in particular, stands up well.

| | | | | | | | |
|---|---|---|---|---|---|---|---|
| Alfie | 7" EP | Odeon | MEO114 | 1966 | £4 | £8 | French |
| Anyone Who Had A Heart | 7" EP | Odeon | SOE3747 | 1963 | £2.50 | £6 | French |
| Anyone Who Had A Heart | 7" EP | Parlophone | GEP8901 | 1964 | £2 | £5 | |
| Cilla | LP | Parlophone | PCS3063 | 1965 | £5 | £12 | stereo |
| Cilla | LP | Parlophone | PMC1243 | 1965 | £4 | £10 | mono |
| Cilla | LP | World Record Club | STP1036 | 1966 | £4 | £10 | |
| Cilla Sings A Rainbow | LP | Parlophone | PCS7004 | 1966 | £4 | £10 | stereo |
| Cilla's Hits | 7" EP | Parlophone | GEP8954 | 1966 | £2.50 | £6 | |
| It's For You | 7" EP | Parlophone | GEP8916 | 1964 | £2.50 | £6 | |
| Love Of The Loved | 7" | Parlophone | R5065 | 1963 | £1.50 | £4 | |
| Sheroo! | LP | Parlophone | PMC/PCS7041 | 1968 | £4 | £10 | |
| Time For Cilla | 7" EP | Parlophone | GEP8967 | 1967 | £6 | £12 | |
| You're My World | 7" EP | Odeon | SOE3758 | 1964 | £4 | £8 | French |
| You've Lost That Lovin' Feelin' | 7" EP | Odeon | SOE3765 | 1965 | £4 | £8 | French |

# BLACK, FRANK

| | | | | | | | |
|---|---|---|---|---|---|---|---|
| Conversation | CD | Elektra | PRCD88292 | 1993 | £8 | £20 | US promo |
| Teenager Of The Year | CD | Elektra | PRCD9000 | 1994 | £8 | £20 | US promo |

# BLACK ABBOTTS

| | | | | | | | |
|---|---|---|---|---|---|---|---|
| Love Is Alive | 7" | Evolution | E3004 | 1971 | £2.50 | £6 | |

# BLACK ACE

| | | | | | | | |
|---|---|---|---|---|---|---|---|
| Black Ace | LP | Heritage | HLP1006 | 1962 | £10 | £25 | |
| Black Ace | 7" EP | XX | MIN701 | 1961 | £2 | £5 | |

# BLACK AXE

| | | | | | | | |
|---|---|---|---|---|---|---|---|
| Red Lights | 7" | Metal | MELT1 | 1980 | £2 | £5 | picture sleeve |

# BLACK CAT BONES

| | | | | | | | |
|---|---|---|---|---|---|---|---|
| Barbed Wire Sandwich | LP | Nova | SDN15 | 1970 | £30 | £60 | |

# BLACK COUNTRY THREE

| | | | | | | | |
|---|---|---|---|---|---|---|---|
| Black Country Three | LP | Transatlantic | TRA140 | 1966 | £15 | £30 | |

## BLACK CROWES

| | | | | | | | |
|---|---|---|---|---|---|---|---|
| Grits 'n' Gravy | CD | Reprise | PROCD7102 | 1994 | £8 | £20 | US promo compilation |
| Hard To Handle | CD-s | Def American | DEFAC6 | 1990 | £2.50 | £6 | |
| Hard To Handle | 7" | Def American | DEFAP10 | 1991 | £1.50 | £4 | .... shaped picture disc |
| Hard To Handle | 12" | Def American | DEFAP612 | 1990 | £2.50 | £6 | .... shaped picture disc |
| Jealous Again | CD-s | Def American | DEFAC4 | 1990 | £3 | £8 | |
| Jealous Again | CD-s | Def American | DEFAC8 | 1991 | £2 | £5 | |
| Jealous Again | 12" | Def American | DEFAP412 | 1990 | £3 | £8 | .............picture disc |
| Twice As Hard | CD-s | Def American | DEFAC7 | 1991 | £2 | £5 | |
| Twice As Hard | 12" | Def American | DEFA712 | 1991 | £2.50 | £6 | |
| Twice As Hard | 12" | Def American | DEFAP712 | 1991 | £2.50 | £6 | .............picture disc |

## BLACK DYKE MILLS BAND

| | | | | | | | |
|---|---|---|---|---|---|---|---|
| Thingumybob | 7" | Apple | 4 | 1968 | £12.50 | £25 | |

## BLACK DYNAMITES

| | | | | | | | |
|---|---|---|---|---|---|---|---|
| Brush Those Tears | 7" | Top Rank | JAR319 | 1960 | £6 | £12 | |

## BLACK FLAG

| | | | | | | | |
|---|---|---|---|---|---|---|---|
| Annihilate This Week | CD-s | SST | SST081CD | 1988 | £2 | £5 | |
| I Can See You | CD-s | SST | SST226CD | 1990 | £2 | £5 | |

## BLACK KNIGHTS

| | | | | | | | |
|---|---|---|---|---|---|---|---|
| I Got A Woman | 7" | Columbia | DB7443 | 1965 | £5 | £10 | |

## BLACK MERDA

| | | | | | | | |
|---|---|---|---|---|---|---|---|
| Black Merda | LP | Chess | 569517 | 1970 | £15 | £30 | US |
| Long Burn The Fire | LP | Janus | JLS3042 | 1971 | £8 | £20 | US |

## BLACK OAK ARKANSAS

| | | | | | | | |
|---|---|---|---|---|---|---|---|
| Black Oak Arkansas | LP | Atlantic | 2400180 | 1971 | £4 | £10 | |

## BLACK PEARL

| | | | | | | | |
|---|---|---|---|---|---|---|---|
| Live | LP | Prophesy | PRS1001 | 1970 | £4 | £10 | US |

## BLACK SABBATH

Black Sabbath were hated by the critics in the early days, so that the latter were disconcerted to see the group's first LP release climb high in the album charts. The achievement was based on the group's sheer hard work in building up a large and loyal following through live performance. Essentially, the group also invented the heavy metal genre, or at any rate solidified the style into the riff-based music that it has remained ever since.

| | | | | | | | |
|---|---|---|---|---|---|---|---|
| Black Sabbath | LP | Vertigo | VO6 | 1970 | £5 | £12 | .............spiral label |
| Black Sabbath | CD | Nems | NELCD6002 | 1986 | £5 | £12 | |
| Black Sabbath 4 | LP | Vertigo | 6360071 | 1972 | £5 | £12 | .... spiral label, booklet |
| Black Sabbath Vol. 4 | CD | Nems | NELCD6005 | 1988 | £5 | £12 | |
| Children Of The Grave | 7" | Phonogram | DJ005 | 1974 | £100 | £200 | promo, Status Quo B side |
| Cross Purposes Live | CD | EMI | | 1994 | £15 | £30 | . promo CD and video boxed set |
| Evil Woman | 7" | Fontana | TF1067 | 1970 | £20 | £40 | |
| Evil Woman | 7" | Vertigo | V2 | 1970 | £2.50 | £6 | |
| Feels Good To Me | CD-s | IRS | EIRSCD148 | 1990 | £2 | £5 | |
| Greatest Hits | CD | Nems | NELCD6009 | 1985 | £5 | £12 | |
| Heaven And Hell | CD | Vertigo | 8301712 | 1987 | £5 | £12 | |
| Live At Last | CD | Nems | NELCD6001 | 1989 | £5 | £12 | |
| Master Of Insanity | CD-s | IRS | EIRSDJ180 | 1992 | £3 | £8 | ...... promo only |
| Master Of Reality | LP | Vertigo | 6360050 | 1971 | £15 | £30 | ......spiral label, poster |
| Master Of Reality | CD | Nems | NELCD6004 | 1985 | £5 | £12 | |
| Paranoid | LP | Nems | NEP6003 | 1977 | £4 | £10 | .............picture disc |
| Paranoid | LP | Vertigo | 6360011 | 1970 | £4 | £10 | .............spiral label |
| Paranoid | LP | Warner Bros | K3104 | 1970 | £5 | £12 | ...............US quad |
| Paranoid | CD | Nems | NELCD6003 | 1986 | £5 | £12 | |
| Paranoid | 7" | NEMS | NEP1 | 1982 | £1.50 | £4 | .............picture disc |
| Sabbath Bloody Sabbath | CD | Nems | NELCD6017 | 1985 | £5 | £12 | |
| Sabotage | CD | Nems | NELCD6018 | 1986 | £5 | £12 | |
| Technical Ecstasy | CD | Vertigo | 8382242 | 1989 | £5 | £12 | |
| Tomorrow's Dream | 7" | Vertigo | 6059061 | 1972 | £2 | £5 | |
| Turn Up The Night | 7" | Vertigo | SABP6 | 1982 | £1.50 | £4 | .............picture disc |
| We Sold Our Soul For Rock 'n' Roll | CD | Raw Power | RAWCD017 | 1986 | £5 | £12 | |

## BLACK SHEEP

| | | | | | | | |
|---|---|---|---|---|---|---|---|
| Black Sheep | LP | Capitol | 11369 | 1975 | £6 | £15 | US |

## BLACK SPIRIT

| | | | | | | | |
|---|---|---|---|---|---|---|---|
| Black Spirit | LP | Brutkasten | 850006 | 1978 | £30 | £60 | German |

## BLACK UHURU

| | | | | | | | |
|---|---|---|---|---|---|---|---|
| Love Crisis | LP | Third World | TWS925 | 1978 | £5 | £12 | |

## BLACK VELVET

| | | | | | | | |
|---|---|---|---|---|---|---|---|
| Can You Feel It | LP | Seven Sun | SUNLP1 | 1973 | £20 | £40 | |
| People Of The World | LP | Pye | NSPL18392 | 1972 | £15 | £30 | |
| This Is Black Velvet | LP | Beacon | BEAS16 | 1971 | £10 | £25 | |

## BLACK WIDOW

| | | | | | | | |
|---|---|---|---|---|---|---|---|
| Black Widow | LP | CBS | 64133 | 1970 | £8 | £20 | |

| | | | | | | |
|---|---|---|---|---|---|---|
| Come To The Sabbat | 7" | CBS | 5031 | 1970 £10 | £20 | |
| Sacrifice | LP | CBS | 63948 | 1970 £8 | £20 | |
| Three | LP | CBS | 64562 | 1971 £8 | £20 | |
| Wish You Would | 7" | CBS | 7596 | 1971 £1.50 | £4 | |

## BLACKBIRDS
| | | | | | | |
|---|---|---|---|---|---|---|
| No Destination | LP | Saga | FID2113 | 1968 £10 | £25 | |
| No Destination | 7" | Saga | OPP3 | 1968 £7.50 | £15 | |
| Touch Of Music | LP | Opp | 534 | 1971 £10 | £25 | German |

## BLACKBURDS
| | | | | | | |
|---|---|---|---|---|---|---|
| Play The Bugaloo | 7" EP | Philips | 437323 | 196– £4 | £8 | French |

## BLACKBURN, TONY
| | | | | | | |
|---|---|---|---|---|---|---|
| Don't Get Off That Train | 7" | Fontana | TF562 | 1965 £1.50 | £4 | |
| Meets Matt Monro | LP | Fontana | SFL13161 | 1966 £4 | £10 | |
| Tony Blackburn Sings | LP | MGM | C(S)8062 | 1968 £4 | £10 | |

## BLACKBYRDS
| | | | | | | |
|---|---|---|---|---|---|---|
| Action | LP | Fantasy | FT534 | 1977 £4 | £10 | |
| Blackbyrds | LP | Fantasy | FT9444 | 1975 £5 | £12 | |
| City Life | LP | Fantasy | FTA3003 | 1976 £5 | £12 | |
| Flying Start | LP | Fantasy | FT522 | 1974 £5 | £12 | |
| Night Grooves | LP | Fantasy | FT555 | 1979 £4 | £10 | |

## BLACKFEATHER
| | | | | | | |
|---|---|---|---|---|---|---|
| At The Mountains Of Madness | LP | Festival | 34159 | 1970 £25 | £50 | Australian |
| Boppin' The Blues | LP | Infinity | 34731 | 1972 £25 | £50 | Australian |
| Live | LP | Festival | 25095 | 1972 £25 | £50 | Australian |

## BLACKFOOT, J. D.
| | | | | | | |
|---|---|---|---|---|---|---|
| Song Of Crazy Horse | LP | Fantasy | 9468 | 1974 £6 | £15 | US |
| Southbound And Gone | LP | Fantasy | 9487 | 1975 £4 | £10 | US |
| Ultimate Prophecy | LP | Mercury | 6338031 | 1970 £20 | £40 | |

## BLACKFOOT SUE
| | | | | | | |
|---|---|---|---|---|---|---|
| Gun Running | LP | DJM | DJLPS455 | 1975 £15 | £30 | |
| Nothing To Hide | LP | Jam | JAL104 | 1973 £4 | £10 | |

## BLACKJACK
The lead singer of this otherwise obscure American AOR group was Michael Bolton.

| | | | | | | |
|---|---|---|---|---|---|---|
| Blackjack | LP | Polydor | 2391411 | 1979 £4 | £10 | |
| Worlds Apart | LP | Polydor | PD16279 | 1980 £6 | £15 | US |

## BLACKJACKS
| | | | | | | |
|---|---|---|---|---|---|---|
| Woo Hoo | 7" EP | Pye | PNV24117 | 1964 £6 | £12 | French |
| Woo Hoo | 7" | Pye | 7N15586 | 1963 £3 | £8 | |

## BLACKMAN, HONOR
| | | | | | | |
|---|---|---|---|---|---|---|
| Before Today | 7" | CBS | 3896 | 1968 £5 | £10 | |
| Everything I've Got | LP | Decca | LK4642 | 1964 £8 | £20 | |
| Kinky Boots | CD-s | London | KINCD1 | 1990 £2 | £5 | . with Patrick MacNee |
| Kinky Boots | 7" | Decca | F11843 | 1964 £6 | £12 | . with Patrick MacNee |

## BLACKMORE, RITCHIE
| | | | | | | |
|---|---|---|---|---|---|---|
| Getaway | 7" | Oriole | CB314 | 1965 £210 | £350 | best auctioned |

## BLACKTHORN
| | | | | | | |
|---|---|---|---|---|---|---|
| Blackthorn | LP | WHM | 1921 | 1977 £37.50 | £75 | |
| Blackthorn II | LP | WHM | 1923 | 1978 £37.50 | £75 | |

## BLACKTHORN (2)
| | | | | | | |
|---|---|---|---|---|---|---|
| Blackthorn | LP | Homespun | HRL118 | 1976 £4 | £10 | Irish |

## BLACKWATER PARK
| | | | | | | |
|---|---|---|---|---|---|---|
| Dirt Box | LP | BASF | 20212386 | 1971 £30 | £60 | German |

## BLACKWELL, CHARLES
| | | | | | | |
|---|---|---|---|---|---|---|
| Freight Train | 7" | Columbia | DB4919 | 1962 £1.50 | £4 | |
| Supercar | 7" | Columbia | DB4839 | 1962 £5 | £10 | |
| Taboo | 7" | HMV | POP977 | 1962 £10 | £20 | |

## BLACKWELL, OTIS
| | | | | | | |
|---|---|---|---|---|---|---|
| Make Ready For Love | 7" | London | HLE8616 | 1958 £12.50 | £25 | |
| Singin' The Blues | LP | Davis | 109 | 1956 £50 | £100 | US |

## BLACKWELL, RORY & THE BLACKJACKS
| | | | | | | |
|---|---|---|---|---|---|---|
| Bye Bye love | 7" | Parlophone | R4326 | 1957 £5 | £10 | |

## BLACKWELL, SCRAPPER
| | | | | | | |
|---|---|---|---|---|---|---|
| Blues Before Sunrise | LP | 77 | LA124 | 1961 £6 | £15 | |
| Longtime Blues | 7" EP | Collector | JEN7 | 1962 £2 | £5 | |
| Mr. Scrapper's Blues | LP | XTRA | XTRA5011 | 1966 £4 | £10 | |

## BLACKWELLS
| | | | | | | |
|---|---|---|---|---|---|---|
| Why Don't You Love Me | 7" | Columbia | DB7442 | 1965 £7.50 | £15 | |

## BLACKWELLS (2)
| | | | | | | | |
|---|---|---|---|---|---|---|---|
| Love Or Money | 7" | London | HLW9334 | 1961 | £2 | £5 | |
| Unchained Melody | 7" | London | HLW9135 | 1960 | £1.50 | £4 | |

## BLAH BLAH BLAH
| | | | | | | | |
|---|---|---|---|---|---|---|---|
| Blah Blah Blah | LP | Some Bizarre | | 1981 | £15 | £30 | *test pressing* |

## BLAINE, HAL
| | | | | | | | |
|---|---|---|---|---|---|---|---|
| Deuces, T's, Roadsters And Drums | LP | RCA | RD7624 | 1964 | £10 | £25 | |
| Gear Stripper | 7" | RCA | RCA1379 | 1963 | £4 | £8 | |

## BLAIR
| | | | | | | |
|---|---|---|---|---|---|---|
| Night Life | 12" | Miracle | M4 | 1979 | £2.50 | £6 |

## BLAIR, SALLIE
| | | | | | | |
|---|---|---|---|---|---|---|
| Squeeze Me | LP | Parlophone | PMC1083 | 1959 | £6 | £15 |

## BLAKE, ERIC
| | | | | | | |
|---|---|---|---|---|---|---|
| Sin City | 7" | Carrere | CAR141 | 1980 | £2 | £5 |

## BLAKE, KEITH
| | | | | | | | |
|---|---|---|---|---|---|---|---|
| Musically | 7" | Blue Cat | BS102 | 1968 | £4 | £8 | |
| Woo Oh Oh | 7" | Amalgamated | AMG809 | 1968 | £4 | £8 | *Overtakers B side* |

## BLAKE, RALPH
| | | | | | | |
|---|---|---|---|---|---|---|
| High Blood Pressure | 7" | Coxsone | CS7063 | 1968 | £5 | £10 |

## BLAKE, SONNY
| | | | | | | |
|---|---|---|---|---|---|---|
| Harmonica Blues | 7" EP | Rooster | R706 | 1980 | £2 | £5 |

## BLAKE, TIM
Going under the name of Hi-T Moonweed when a member of Gong, Tim Blake contributed greatly to that group's science-fiction ambience with his arsenal of synthesizer sounds. For his solo recordings, the synthesizer takes over completely, with Blake covering similar territory to that explored by Tangerine Dream.

| | | | | | | | |
|---|---|---|---|---|---|---|---|
| Blake's New Jerusalem | LP | Barclay | CLAY7005 | 1978 | £6 | £15 | |
| Crystal Machine | LP | Egg | 900545 | 1977 | £6 | £15 | *French* |

## BLAKEY, ART
| | | | | | | | |
|---|---|---|---|---|---|---|---|
| African Beat | LP | Blue Note | BLP/BST84097 | 196– | £8 | £20 | |
| Are You Real | 7" EP | Fontana | TFE17364 | 1961 | £2 | £5 | |
| Art Blakey Jazz Messengers | LP | HMV | CLP1532/CSD1423 | 1962 | £6 | £15 | |
| Art Blakey's Big Band | LP | Parlophone | PMC1099 | 1959 | £10 | £25 | |
| At The Cafe Bohemia Vol. 1 | LP | Blue Note | BLP/BST81507 | 196– | £10 | £25 | |
| At The Cafe Bohemia Vol. 2 | LP | Blue Note | BLP/BST81508 | 196– | £10 | £25 | |
| At The Jazz Corner Of The World Vol. 1 | LP | Blue Note | BLP/BST84015 | 196– | £10 | £25 | |
| At The Jazz Corner Of The World Vol. 2 | LP | Blue Note | BLP/BST84016 | 196– | £10 | £25 | |
| Big Beat | LP | Blue Note | BLP/BST84029 | 196– | £10 | £25 | |
| Blue Monk | LP | Atlantic | 590009 | 1967 | £5 | £12 | *with Thelonious Monk* |
| Blues March | 7" EP | Fontana | TFE17257 | 1960 | £2 | £5 | |
| Buhaina's Delight | LP | Blue Note | BLP/BST84104 | 1963 | £8 | £20 | |
| Buttercorn Lady | LP | Mercury | (S)LML4021 | 1966 | £5 | £12 | |
| Caravan | LP | Riverside | RLP438 | 1964 | £6 | £15 | |
| Cu-Bop | LP | London | LTZJ15110 | 1958 | £8 | £20 | |
| Drum Suite | LP | Philips | BBL7196 | 1958 | £6 | £15 | |
| Free For All | LP | Blue Note | BLP/BST84170 | 1966 | £8 | £20 | |
| Freedom Rider | LP | Blue Note | BLP/BST84156 | 1964 | £8 | £20 | |
| Hard Bop | LP | Philips | BBL7212 | 1958 | £8 | £20 | |
| Hard Bop | LP | Philips | BBL7220 | 1958 | £8 | £20 | |
| Hard Drive | LP | Parlophone | PMC1084 | 1959 | £8 | £20 | |
| Hold On, I'm Comin' | LP | Mercury | (S)LML4023 | 1967 | £5 | £12 | |
| Holiday For Skins Vol. 1 | LP | Blue Note | BLP/BST84004 | 196– | £10 | £25 | |
| Holiday For Skins Vol. 2 | LP | Blue Note | BLP/BST84005 | 196– | £10 | £25 | |
| I Remember Clifford | 7" EP | Fontana | TFE17337 | 1961 | £2 | £5 | |
| Indestructable | LP | Blue Note | BLP/BST84193 | 1965 | £8 | £20 | |
| Jazz Message | LP | HMV | CLP1760 | 1964 | £6 | £15 | |
| Jazz Messengers | LP | Philips | BBL7121 | 1957 | £8 | £20 | |
| Jazz Messengers With Thelonious Monk | LP | London | LTZK15157/ SAHK6017 | 1959 | £8 | £20 | |
| Kyoto | LP | Storyville | 673013 | 1969 | £4 | £10 | |
| Les Liaisons dangereuses | LP | Fontana | TFL5184 | 1962 | £6 | £15 | |
| Like Someone In Love | LP | Blue Note | BLP/BST84245 | 1967 | £6 | £15 | |
| Meet You At The Jazz Corner Of The World Vol. 1 | LP | Blue Note | BLP/BST84054 | 196– | £8 | £20 | |
| Meet You At The Jazz Corner Of The World Vol. 2 | LP | Blue Note | BLP/BST84055 | 196– | £8 | £20 | |
| Message From Kenya | 7" | Blue Note | 451626 | 1964 | £1.50 | £4 | |
| Moanin' | LP | Blue Note | BLP/BST84003 | 1963 | £10 | £25 | |
| Moanin' | 7" | Blue Note | 451735 | 1962 | £1.50 | £4 | |
| Mosaic | LP | Blue Note | BLP/BST84090 | 1962 | £8 | £20 | |
| Night At Birdland Vol. 1 | LP | Blue Note | BLP/BST81521 | 1964 | £10 | £25 | |
| Night At Birdland Vol. 2 | LP | Blue Note | BLP/BST81522 | 1964 | £10 | £25 | |
| Night In Tunisia | LP | Blue Note | BLP/BST84049 | 1962 | £10 | £25 | |
| Night In Tunisia | 7" | Blue Note | 451796 | 1961 | £1.50 | £4 | |
| Olympia Concert | LP | Fontana | TFL5116 | 1961 | £6 | £15 | |
| Orgy In Rhythm Vol. 1 | LP | Blue Note | BLP/BST81554 | 1962 | £10 | £25 | |

| Title | Format | Label | Catalogue | Year | | | Notes |
|---|---|---|---|---|---|---|---|
| Orgy In Rhythm Vol. 2 | LP | Blue Note | BLP/BST81555 | 1965 | £10 | £25 | |
| Ritual | LP | Vogue | LAE12096 | 1958 | £10 | £25 | |
| Roots And Herbs | LP | Blue Note | BST84347 | 1969 | £5 | £12 | |
| 'S Make It | LP | Mercury | (S)LML4000 | 1965 | £5 | £12 | |
| Soul Finger | LP | Mercury | (S)LML4012 | 1966 | £5 | £12 | |
| Three Blind Mice | LP | United Artists | (S)ULP1017 | 1963 | £8 | £20 | |
| Ugetsu | LP | Riverside | RLP464 | 1964 | £6 | £15 | |
| Witch Doctor | LP | Blue Note | BLP/BST84258 | 1967 | £6 | £15 | |

## BLANC, MEL

| Title | Format | Label | Catalogue | Year | | | Notes |
|---|---|---|---|---|---|---|---|
| Bugs Bunny | 7" EP | Capitol | EAP56 | 1958 | £2 | £5 | |
| I Taut I Taw A Puddy Tat | 7" | Capitol | CL14950 | 1958 | £2 | £5 | |
| Tweety Pie | 7" EP | Capitol | EAP57 | 1958 | £2 | £5 | |
| Tweety Pie | 7" EP | Capitol | EAP59 | 1958 | £2 | £5 | |
| Woody Woodpecker | 7" EP | Capitol | EAP58 | 1958 | £2 | £5 | |
| Woody Woodpecker's Family Album No. 1 | 7" EP | Brunswick | OE9397 | 1959 | £2 | £5 | |
| Woody Woodpecker's Family Album No. 2 | 7" EP | Brunswick | OE9398 | 1959 | £2 | £5 | |
| Woody Woodpecker's Family Album No. 3 | 7" EP | Brunswick | OE9399 | 1959 | £2 | £5 | |

## BLANCA, BURT

| Title | Format | Label | Catalogue | Year | | | Notes |
|---|---|---|---|---|---|---|---|
| Texas Rider | 7" | Zodiac | ZR004 | 1960 | £4 | £8 | |

## BLANCMANGE

| Title | Format | Label | Catalogue | Year | | | Notes |
|---|---|---|---|---|---|---|---|
| Irene And Mavis | 7" | Blahh | no number | 1979 | £4 | £8 | |

## BLAND, BILLY

| Title | Format | Label | Catalogue | Year | | | Notes |
|---|---|---|---|---|---|---|---|
| Let The Little Girl Dance | 7" | London | HL9096 | 1960 | £4 | £8 | |

## BLAND, BOBBY

| Title | Format | Label | Catalogue | Year | | | Notes |
|---|---|---|---|---|---|---|---|
| Ain't Doing Too Bad | 7" EP | Vocalion | VEP170157 | 1964 | £15 | £30 | |
| Ain't Nothin' You Can Do | LP | Vocalion | VAP8027 | 1964 | £15 | £30 | |
| Best Of Bobby Bland | LP | Duke | DLP(S)84 | 1967 | £5 | £12 | US |
| Best Of Bobby Bland Vol. 2 | LP | Duke | DLP(S)86 | 1968 | £5 | £12 | US |
| Blue Moon | 7" | Vogue | V9192 | 1962 | £5 | £10 | |
| Call On Me | LP | Vocalion | VAP8034 | 1965 | £15 | £30 | |
| Chains Of Love | 7" | Action | ACT4553 | 1969 | £2.50 | £6 | |
| Cry Cry Cry | 7" | Vogue | V9178 | 1961 | £6 | £12 | |
| Don't Cry No More | 7" | Vogue | V9188 | 1961 | £5 | £10 | |
| Good Time Charlie | 7" | Vocalion | VP9273 | 1966 | £4 | £8 | |
| Gotta Get To Know You | 7" | Action | ACT4538 | 1969 | £5 | £10 | |
| Here's The Man | LP | Vocalion | VAP8041 | 1962 | £15 | £30 | |
| His California Album | LP | ABC | ABCL5044 | 1973 | £4 | £10 | |
| His California Album | LP | Probe | SPB1088 | 1973 | £4 | £10 | |
| Honey Child | 7" | Vocalion | VP9222 | 1964 | £4 | £8 | |
| I Wouldn't Treat A Dog | 7" | ABC | ABC4030 | 1975 | £2 | £5 | |
| I'm Too Far Gone | 7" | Vocalion | VP9262 | 1966 | £4 | £8 | |
| If Loving You Is Wrong | LP | Duke | X90 | 1970 | £5 | £12 | US |
| Lead Me On | 7" | Vogue | V9182 | 1961 | £6 | £12 | |
| Piece Of Gold | LP | Action | ACLP4006 | 1969 | £8 | £20 | |
| Rockin' In The Same Old Boat | 7" | Action | ACT4524 | 1969 | £2.50 | £6 | |
| Share Your Love With Me | 7" | Action | ACT4548 | 1969 | £2.50 | £6 | |
| Share Your Love With Me | 7" | Vocalion | VP9229 | 1964 | £4 | £8 | |
| Soul Of The Man | LP | Duke | DLP(S)79 | 1966 | £10 | £25 | US |
| Spotlighting The Man | LP | Duke | DLPS89 | 1969 | £20 | £20 | US |
| These Hands | 7" | Vocalion | VP9251 | 1965 | £4 | £8 | |
| Touch Of The Blues | LP | Island | ILP974 | 1968 | £10 | £25 | pink label |
| Touch Of The Blues | 7" | Sue | WI4044 | 1968 | £7.50 | £15 | |
| Two Steps From The Blues | LP | Vogue | VAP160183 | 1961 | £15 | £30 | |
| Yield Not To Temptation | 7" EP | Vocalion | VEP170153 | 1963 | £15 | £30 | |
| Yield Not To Temptation | 7" | Vocalion | VP9232 | 1965 | £4 | £8 | |
| You're The One That I Need | 7" | Vogue | V9190 | 1962 | £5 | £10 | |

## BLANE, MARCIE

| Title | Format | Label | Catalogue | Year | | | Notes |
|---|---|---|---|---|---|---|---|
| Bobby's Girl | 7" | London | HLU9599 | 1962 | £5 | £10 | |
| How Can I Tell Him | 7" | London | HLU9673 | 1963 | £1.50 | £4 | |
| Little Miss Fool | 7" | London | HLU9744 | 1963 | £1.50 | £4 | |
| Marcie Blane | 7" EP | London | REU1413 | 1964 | £15 | £30 | |
| You Gave My Number To Billy | 7" | London | HLU9787 | 1963 | £2 | £5 | |

## BLANKE, TOTO

| Title | Format | Label | Catalogue | Year | | | Notes |
|---|---|---|---|---|---|---|---|
| Spider's Dance | LP | Vertigo | 6360623 | 1975 | £6 | £15 | German |

## BLANKS

| Title | Format | Label | Catalogue | Year | | | Notes |
|---|---|---|---|---|---|---|---|
| Northern Ripper | 7" | Void | SRTS79CUS560 | 1979 | £4 | £8 | |

## BLAST FURNACE

| Title | Format | Label | Catalogue | Year | | | Notes |
|---|---|---|---|---|---|---|---|
| Blast Furnace | LP | Polydor | 2380013 | 1971 | £37.50 | £75 | Danish |

## BLASTERS

| Title | Format | Label | Catalogue | Year | | | Notes |
|---|---|---|---|---|---|---|---|
| American Music | LP | Rollin' Rock | 021 | 1980 | £10 | £25 | US |

## BLAZERS

| Title | Format | Label | Catalogue | Year | | | Notes |
|---|---|---|---|---|---|---|---|
| Rock And Roll | 10" LP | Fontana | TFR6010 | 1958 | £20 | £40 | |

## BLAZING SONS
Chant Down The National Front ............. 7" ...... Cool Ghoul..... COOL002............ 1983 £2.50........£6 ...............................

## BLEAK HOUSE
Chase The Wind .................................... 7" ...... Buzzard.......... BUZZ2................ 1982 £12.50....£25 ...............................

## BLEECHERS
Come Into My Parlour ........................... 7" ...... Upsetter.......... US314................. 1969 £1.50........£4 .......Melotones B side
Ease Up ............................................. 7" ...... Trojan............ TR679................. 1969 £1.50........£4 ...............................
Send Me The Pillow.............................. 7" ...... Columbia ........ DB118 ................ 1970 £1.50........£4 ...............................

## BLEGVAD, PETER
Alcohol .............................................. 7" ...... Recommended RR5.75 ................ 1981 £4............£8 .......... 1 side engraved

## BLENDELLS
Dance With Me .................................... 7" ...... Reprise .......... R20340................ 1964 £2.50........£6 ...............................
Lalalalalala ......................................... 7" ...... Reprise .......... R20291................ 1964 £2...........£5 ...............................

## BLESSED END
Movin' On .......................................... LP...... Tns................. J248................... 1971 £75...........£150 ......................... US

## BLESSING, MICHAEL
Before becoming a Monkee, Mike Nesmith recorded as Michael Blessing.

New Recruit ........................................ 7" ...... Colpix ............ 787 ....................... 1965 £12.50....£25 .. US, probably promo
only
Until It's Time For You To Go ................ 7" ...... Colpix ............ 792 ....................... 1965 £12.50....£25 .. US, probably promo
only

## BLEY, CARLA
Carla Bley's *Escalator Over The Hill* is a jazz opera, covering a range of musical styles, and bringing together some unlikely combinations of musicians. Linda Ronstadt and John McLaughlin, Don Cherry and Jack Bruce, Paul Jones and Gato Barbieri all have key roles in a work that continues to grow in stature. Carla Bley has never quite achieved this greatness again, and few other composers have either.

Escalator Over The Hill ......................... LP...... JCOA ............ EOTH3 ............. 1972 £8...........£20 .............triple, boxed

## BLEY, PAUL
Pianist Paul Bley is a major, though often unheralded, figure within jazz. Playing with Ornette Coleman in the fifties (documented rather belatedly on the *Fabulous Paul Bley Quintet* album), Bley went on to become a very early synthesizer pioneer, touring with the huge, distinctly user-unfriendly machines that were the early seventies state of the art.

Ballads .............................................. LP...... ECM ............ ECM1010ST .......... 1971 £8...........£20 .............................
Barrage .............................................. LP...... ESP-Disk ........ 1008 .................. 1965 £8...........£20 ..................... US
Fabulous Paul Bley Quintet ................... LP...... America ........ 30AM6120 ............ 1972 £6...........£15 .............................
Mr. Joy ............................................. LP...... Mercury ........ SMWL21050 .......... 1969 £10..........£25 .............................
Open, To Love .................................... LP...... ECM ............ ECM1023ST ........ 1973 £5...........£12 .............................
Pastorius/Metheny/Ditmas/Bley.............. LP...... Improvising 373846 .................. 1976 £5...........£12 ..................... US
Artists ...........
Paul Bley .......................................... 10" LP Vogue............ LDE171 ............. 1956 £25..........£50 .............................
Paul Bley Synthesizer Show ................... LP...... Milestone ........ MSP9033 .......... 1971 £15..........£30 ..................... US
Paul Bley With Gary Peacock.................. LP...... ECM ............ ECM1003ST ........ 1970 £5...........£12 .............................
Scorpio.............................................. LP...... Milestone ....... MSP9046 .......... 1973 £6...........£15 ..................... US
Touching............................................ LP...... Fontana.......... SFJL929 ........... 1969 £10..........£25 .............................

## BLEY, PAUL & ANNETTE PEACOCK
Dual Unity ......................................... LP...... Freedom ........ 2383105 .......... 1972 £15..........£30 .............................
Improvisie .......................................... LP...... America ........ 30AM6121 ............ 1973 £15..........£30 ..................... French
Revenge............................................. LP...... Polydor .......... 2425043 ........... 1971 £20..........£40 .............................

## BLEYER, ARCHIE
Amber............................................... 7" ...... London .......... HL8035............ 1954 £10..........£20 .............................
Bridge Of Happiness............................ 7" ...... London .......... HLA8263 ........... 1956 £5...........£10 .............................
Hernando's Hideaway ........................... 7" ...... London .......... HLA8176 .......... 1955 £6...........£12 .............................
Naughty Lady Of Shady Lane ................. 7" ...... London .......... HL8111............ 1954 £7.50........£15 .............................
Nothin' To Do .................................... 7" ...... London .......... HLA8243 ........... 1956 £5...........£10 .............................

## BLIND BLAKE
Blind Blake ........................................ 10" LP Collector........ JFL2001 ............ 1960 £8...........£20 .............................
Blind Blake 1927-30 ............................ LP...... Whoopee ........ 101 .................. 196– £4...........£10 .............................
Blues In Chicago ................................. LP...... Riverside ........ RLP8804 .......... 1967 £6...........£15 .............................
Hey Hey Daddy Blues .......................... 78....... Tempo ........... R23 ................. 1950 £2...........£5 .............................
Legendary Blind Blake .......................... 10" LP Ristic............. LP18 ................ 1958 £15..........£30 .............................

## BLIND BLAKE & CHARLIE JACKSON
Blind Blake And Charlie Jackson............. LP...... Heritage .......... HLP1011 ........... 1960 £10..........£25 .............................

## BLIND BLAKE & RAMBLING THOMAS
Male Blues Vol. 3................................. 7" EP . Collector........ JEL4 ................ 1959 £2.50........£6 .............................

## BLIND FAITH
Blind Faith.......................................... LP...... Polydor .......... 583059 ............ 1969 £4............£10 .............gatefold sleeve
Blind Faith.......................................... CD...... Mobile Fidelity UDCD507 ........... 1988 £6...........£15 .... US audiophile
instrumental (Change Of Address).............. 7" ...... Island .......... no number ......... 1969 £75........£150 ..................... promo

## BLIND RAVAGE
Blind Ravage ....................................... LP...... Crescent Street CS1874 ................ 1972 £10..........£25 ................ Canadian

## BLINKERS
Original Sin ....................................................... 7" ...... Pye ................ 7N17752 ............... 1969 £15 ........ £30 ...........................

## BLISS
Bliss .................................................................. LP ...... Canyon ........... 7707 ..................... 1969 £30 ........ £60 ........................ US

## BLITZ
All Out Attack ................................................ 7" ...... No Future ....... OI1 .................... 1982 £1.50 ...... £4 ...........................

## BLITZ BOYS
Eddy's New Shoes ............................................ 12" ..... Told You So ... TYS001 ............... 1981 £3 ........... £8 ...........................

## BLITZKRIEG BOP
Let's Go .......................................................... 7" ...... Mortonsound ... MTN3172/3 ....... 1977 £5 ........... £10 ...........................

## BLIZZARDS
I'm Your Guy .................................................. LP ...... Fontana ........... 885424 ................. 1966 £50 .......... £100 .............. German

## BLODWYN PIG
The natural successor to the bluesy, jazzy music to be found on Jethro Tull's first LP, *This Was*, is Blodwyn Pig's *Ahead Rings Out*, rather than the later recordings of Ian Anderson and his cohorts. The common factor, of course, is guitarist Mick Abrahams, whose distinctive playing-style dominates both records. For Blodwyn Pig, he found an ideal foil in Jack Lancaster, whose fluent work on saxophones and flute is far more noteworthy than Ian Anderson's flautistry.

Ahead Rings Out ............................................. LP ...... Island ............. ILPS9101 ............. 1969 £8 ........... £20 .............. pink label
Dear Jill ......................................................... 7" ...... Island ............. WIP6059 .............. 1969 £2 ........... £5
Getting To This .............................................. LP ...... Chrysalis ......... ILPS9122 ............. 1970 £5 ........... £12
Same Old Story ............................................... 7" ...... Island ............. WIP6078 .............. 1969 £2 ........... £5
Walk On The Water ........................................ 7" ...... Island ............. WIP6069 .............. 1969 £2 ........... £5

## BLOND
Blond ............................................................... LP ...... Fontana ........... SRF67607 ............. 1969 £5 ........... £12 ........................ US
Lilac Years ...................................................... LP ...... Fontana ........... STL5515 .............. 1969 £50 .......... £100
Wake Up And Call ......................................... 7" ...... Fontana ........... TF1040 ............... 1969 £2.50 ...... £6

## BLONDE ON BLONDE
All Day All Night ........................................... 7" ...... Pye ................ 7N17637 .............. 1968 £12.50 .... £25
Blonde On Blonde .......................................... LP ...... Ember ............. NR50 ................... 1972 £10 .......... £25
Castles In The Sky .......................................... 7" ...... Ember ............. EMBS279 ............. 1970 £1.50 ...... £4
Contrasts ........................................................ LP ...... Pye ................ NSPL18288 .......... 1969 £15 .......... £30
Rebirth ........................................................... LP ...... Ember ............. NR5049 ............... 1970 £10 .......... £25
Reflections On A Life ...................................... LP ...... Ember ............. NR5058 ............... 1971 £10 .......... £25

## BLONDIE
Auto-American Interview ................................ 7" ...... Fan Club ......... FLX146 ............... 1980 £2 ........... £5 ....................... flexi
Blondie ........................................................... LP ...... Private Stock ... PVLP1017 ............ 1977 £4 ........... £10
Call Me ........................................................... CD-s .. Chrysalis ......... CHSCD3342 ......... 1989 £2 ........... £5
Denis 88 ......................................................... CD-s .. Chrysalis ......... CHSCD3328 ......... 1988 £2 ........... £5
Encounters With Blondie ................................. LP ...... Chrysalis ......... CDMR1 ................ ........ £25 .......... £50 .................. double
Hunter ............................................................ LP ...... Chrysalis ......... PCDL1384 ............ 1982 £4 ........... £10 .............. picture disc
In The Flesh ................................................... 7" ...... Private Stock ... PVT105 ............... 1977 £6 ........... £12 ........ no picture sleeve
Once More Into The Bleach ............................ CD ..... Chrysalis ......... CDJB2 ................. 1988 £5 ........... £12
Parallel Lines .................................................. LP ...... Chrysalis ......... PCDL1192 ............ 1978 £4 ........... £10 ........ US picture disc
Parallel Lines .................................................. LP ...... Mobile Fidelity  MFSL1050 ............ 1981 £5 ........... £12 ........ US audiophile
Parallel Lines .................................................. CD ..... Chrysalis ......... CCD1192 ............. 1983 £5 ........... £12
Parallel Lines .................................................. CD ..... Chrysalis ......... CCD1192 ............. 1994 £5 ........... £12 ..... Chrysalis 25 pack
Rip Her To Shreds .......................................... 7" ...... Chrysalis ......... CHS2180 ............. 1977 £2 ........... £5
X Offender ..................................................... 7" ...... Private Stock ... PVT90 ................. 1977 £50 .......... £100

## BLOOD
Se Parare Nex ................................................. LP ...... Conquest ......... QUEST3 ............... 1985 £6 ........... £15

## BLOOD, SWEAT & TEARS
Blood, Sweat & Tears ..................................... LP ...... Columbia ......... CQ30994 .............. 1973 £4 ........... £10 ............... US quad
Child Is Father To The Man ........................... LP ...... Columbia ......... HC49619 .............. 1981 £4 ........... £10 ......... US audiophile
Greatest Hits .................................................. LP ...... Columbia ......... CQ31170 .............. 1973 £4 ........... £10 ............... US quad
I Can't Quit Her ............................................ 7" ...... CBS ................ 3563 ..................... 1968 £1.50 ...... £4
Child Is Father To The Man ........................... LP ...... CBS ................ 63296 ................... 1968 £4 ........... £10

## BLOODROCK
Bloodrock ....................................................... LP ...... Capitol ............ ST435 .................. 1969 £5 ........... £12 ........................ US
Bloodrock 'n' Roll ......................................... LP ...... Capitol ............ SM11417 .............. 1975 £4 ........... £10 ........................ US
Bloodrock Three ............................................. LP ...... Capitol ............ EST765 ................ 1971 £4 ........... £10 ........................ US
Bloodrock Two ............................................... LP ...... Capitol ............ ST491 .................. 1970 £4 ........... £10 ........................ US
Live ................................................................ LP ...... Capitol ............ SVBB11038 .......... 1972 £4 ........... £10 ........................ US
Passage ........................................................... LP ...... Capitol ............ EST11109 ............ 1973 £4 ........... £10 ........................ US
USA ............................................................... LP ...... Capitol ............ SM645 ................. 1971 £4 ........... £10 ........................ US
Whirlwind Tongues ........................................ LP ...... Capitol ............ EST11259 ............ 1973 £4 ........... £10 ........................ US

## BLOODY MARY
Bloody Mary .................................................. LP ...... Family ............. 2707 ..................... 1972 £15 .......... £30 ........................ US

## BLOOM, ROGER HAMMER
Out Of The Blue ............................................ 7" ...... CBS ................ 202654 ................. 1967 £2.50 ...... £6

## BLOOMFIELD, MIKE

| | | | | | | | | |
|---|---|---|---|---|---|---|---|---|
| Analine | LP | Sonet | SNTF749 | 1977 | £4 | £10 | |
| If You Love Those Blues | LP | Sonet | SNTF726 | 1977 | £4 | £10 | |
| It's Not Killing Me | LP | CBS | 63652 | 1969 | £4 | £10 | |
| Live At Bill Graham's Fillmore West | LP | CBS | 63816 | 1969 | £4 | £10 | |
| Try It Before You Buy It | LP | Columbia | PC33173 | 1973 | £4 | £10 | US |

## BLOOMFIELD, MIKE & AL KOOPER

| | | | | | | | | |
|---|---|---|---|---|---|---|---|---|
| Live Adventures | LP | CBS | 66216 | 1969 | £8 | £20 | double |
| Weight | 7" | CBS | 4094 | 1969 | £2 | £5 | |

## BLOOMFIELD, MIKE, DR. JOHN, JOHN HAMMOND

| | | | | | | | |
|---|---|---|---|---|---|---|---|
| Triumvirate | LP | CBS | 65659 | 1973 | £4 | £10 | |

## BLOSSOM TOES

Blossom Toes was one of the most interesting groups to emerge out of the psychedelic period, but failed to find the success it deserved. The first album contains inspired pop, imaginatively arranged in the *Sgt Pepper* manner. The second is very different in sound, presenting guitar-based rock with a hard edge, but with all the creative imagination still intact. The group members all managed to sustain subsequent careers, especially guitarists Jim Cregan and Brian Godding – the former playing for Family and Rod Stewart amongst others, while the latter has placed his increasingly finely honed technique and imagination at the disposal of such diverse employers as Keith Tippett, Mike Westbrook and Kevin Coyne, before recording an impressive solo album in 1988. What is in effect a third Blossom Toes LP was issued under the name of B. B. Blunder in 1971.

| | | | | | | | | |
|---|---|---|---|---|---|---|---|---|
| I'll Be Your Baby Tonight | 7" | Marmalade | 598009 | 1968 | £6 | £12 | |
| If Only For A Moment | LP | Marmalade | 608010 | 1969 | £30 | £60 | |
| New Day | 7" | Marmalade | 598022 | 1969 | £25 | £50 | test pressing only |
| Peace Loving Man | 7" | Marmalade | 598014 | 1969 | £4 | £8 | |
| Postcard | 7" | Marmalade | 598012 | 1969 | £4 | £8 | |
| We Are Ever So Clean | LP | Marmalade | 607/608001 | 1967 | £25 | £50 | |
| What On Earth | 7" | Marmalade | 598002 | 1967 | £4 | £8 | |
| What On Earth | 7" | Marmalade | 598002 | 1967 | £15 | £30 | picture sleeve |

## BLOSSOMS

Led by Darlene Love, the Blossoms provided backing vocals for a vast number of other artists, including Elvis Presley. The high value of 'Things Are Changing', however, derives from the fact that it is a rare collaboration between Phil Spector, who produced, and Brian Wilson, who played piano.

| | | | | | | | | |
|---|---|---|---|---|---|---|---|---|
| Baby Daddy-o | 7" | Capitol | CL14947 | 1958 | £10 | £20 | |
| Blossoms | LP | MGM | LN1007 | 1972 | £6 | £15 | US |
| Little Louie | 7" | Capitol | CL14856 | 1958 | £10 | £20 | |
| Move On | 7" | Capitol | CL14833 | 1958 | £10 | £20 | |
| Things Are Changing | 7" | EOEOC | | 1965 | £100 | £200 | US |

## BLOSSOMS (2)

| | | | | | | | |
|---|---|---|---|---|---|---|---|
| Stand By | 7" | Pama | PM814 | 1971 | £5 | £10 | |

## BLOSSOMS (3)

| | | | | | | | |
|---|---|---|---|---|---|---|---|
| Twiddy Dee | 7" | MGM | MGM1435 | 1968 | £1.50 | £4 | |

## BLOUNT, MICHAEL

| | | | | | | | |
|---|---|---|---|---|---|---|---|
| Fantasies | LP | York | FYK414 | 1973 | £5 | £12 | |
| Patchwork | LP | CBS | 64230 | 1970 | £6 | £15 | |
| Souvenirs | LP | York | FYK401 | 1972 | £5 | £12 | |

## BLOW MONKEYS

| | | | | | | | | |
|---|---|---|---|---|---|---|---|---|
| Celebrate The Day | CD-s | RCA | MONKC6 | 1989 | £2 | £5 | |
| Celebrate The Day After You | 10" | RCA | MONKX6 | 1987 | £6 | £15 | |
| Choice | CD-s | RCA | PD42886 | 1989 | £2 | £5 | |
| Forbidden Fruit | 12" | RCA | PT40334 | 1985 | £2.50 | £6 | double |
| It Pays To Be Twelve | 12" | RCA | PT42232R | 1988 | £3 | £8 | |
| It Pays To Belong | CD-s | RCA | PD42232 | 1988 | £2 | £5 | in tin box |
| Limping For A Generation | CD | RCA | ND71495 | 1987 | £5 | £12 | |
| Live Today Love Tomorrow | 7" | Parasol | PAR1 | 1980 | £4 | £8 | |
| Out With Her | CD-s | RCA | MONKC5 | 1987 | £2 | £5 | |
| Passionara | CD-s | RCA | PD43864 | 1990 | £2 | £5 | |
| She Was Only A Grocer's Daughter | CD | RCA | PD71245 | 1987 | £5 | £12 | |
| Slaves No More | CD-s | RCA | PD43202 | 1989 | £2 | £5 | with Sylvia Tella |
| Springtime For The World | CD-s | RCA | PD43624 | 1990 | £2 | £5 | |
| This Is Your Life | CD-s | RCA | PD42150 | 1988 | £2 | £5 | |
| This Is Your Life | CD-s | RCA | PD42696 | 1989 | £2 | £5 | |

## BLUE, BABBITY

| | | | | | | | |
|---|---|---|---|---|---|---|---|
| Don't Hurt Me | 7" | Decca | F12149 | 1965 | £1.50 | £4 | |
| Don't Make Me | 7" | Decca | F12053 | 1965 | £1.50 | £4 | |

## BLUE, DAVID

| | | | | | | | | |
|---|---|---|---|---|---|---|---|---|
| 23 Days In September | LP | Reprise | RS6293 | 1968 | £5 | £12 | US |
| David Blue | LP | Elektra | EKS74003 | 1966 | £5 | £12 | US |
| Me | LP | Reprise | RS6375 | 1970 | £5 | £12 | US |

## BLUE, PAMELA

| | | | | | | | |
|---|---|---|---|---|---|---|---|
| My Friend Bobby | 7" | Decca | F11761 | 1963 | £20 | £40 | |

## BLUE, TIMOTHY

| | | | | | | | |
|---|---|---|---|---|---|---|---|
| Room At The Top Of The Stairs | 7" | Spark | SRL1014 | 1968 | £5 | £10 | |

## BLUE & FERRIS
You Stole My Money .............................. 7" ...... Blue Cat ........ BS147 ................... 1968 £2.50 ....... £6 ...............................

## BLUE ACES
All I Want ............................................. 7" ...... Columbia ....... DB7755 ................. 1965 £10 ......... £20 ...............................
I Beat You To It ................................... 7" ...... Pye ................ 7N15713 .............. 1964 £1.50 ...... £4
Land Of Love ...................................... 7" ...... Pye ................ 7N15672 .............. 1964 £1.50 ...... £4
Talk About My Baby ........................... 7" ...... Columbia ....... DB7954 ................. 1966 £25 ......... £50
You Don't Care ................................... 7" ...... Pye ................ 7N15821 .............. 1965 £1.50 ...... £4

## BLUE ANGEL
Blue Angel made an album and two singles, but the group's lead singer only found success once she had decided to go solo. Her name: Cyndi Lauper.

Blue Angel ........................................... LP ..... Polydor .......... 2391486 ............... 1980 £6 ......... £15
I Had A Love ....................................... 7" ..... Polydor ......... POSP241 ............. 1981 £6 ......... £12
I'm Gonna Be Strong ......................... 7" ..... Polydor ......... POSP212 ............. 1980 £6 ......... £12
I'm Gonna Be Strong ......................... 7" ..... Polydor ......... POSP212 ............. 1984 £2.50 ....... £6 .. reissue, picture sleeve

## BLUE BARONS
Twist To The Great Blues Hits ................. LP ..... Philips............ PHM2/PHS600017. 1962 £10 ......... £25 ................................. US

## BLUE BEATS
Beatle Beat .......................................... LP ..... A.A. .............. 133 ................... 1964 £15 ......... £30 ................................. US

## BLUE BLOOD
Blue Blood .......................................... LP ..... Sonet ............. SNTF615 ............. 1970 £4 ......... £10

## BLUE CATS
Beat Beat Beat...................................... LP ..... Starlet ............ 3261 .................... 1965 £6 ......... £15 ................................. German

## BLUE CHEER
Blue Cheer .......................................... LP ..... Philips ............ 6336001 ............... 1969 £6 ......... £15
Feathers From Your Tree ..................... 7" ...... Philips ............ BF1711 ............... 1968 £1.50 ...... £4
Just A Little Bit ................................... 7" ...... Philips ............ BF1684 ............... 1968 £1.50 ...... £4
New Improved ..................................... LP ..... Philips ............ SBL7896 ............. 1969 £6 ......... £15
Oh Pleasant Hope ............................... LP ..... Philips ............ PHS600350 ......... 1971 £15 ......... £30 ................................. US
Original Human Being......................... LP ..... Philips ............ 6336004 ............... 1970 £8 ......... £20
Outside Inside ..................................... LP ..... Philips ............ SBL7860 ............. 1968 £15 ......... £30
Pilot..................................................... 7" ...... Philips ............ 6051010 ............... 1971 £1.50 ...... £4
Summertime Blues .............................. 7" ...... Philips ............ BF1646 ............... 1968 £2 ......... £5
Vincebus Eruptum................................ LP ..... Philips ............ (S)BL7839 ........... 1967 £6 ......... £15
West Coast Child Of Sunshine ................ 7" ...... Philips ............ BF1778 ............... 1969 £1.50 ...... £4

## BLUE CHIPS
I'm On The Right Side ........................ 7" ...... Pye ................ 7N15970 .............. 1965 £7.50 ...... £15
Some Kind Of Lovin' .......................... 7" ...... Pye ................ 7N17111 .............. 1966 £7.50 ...... £15
Tell Her ............................................... 7" ...... Pye ................ 7N17155 .............. 1966 £7.50 ...... £15

## BLUE DIAMONDS
Always ................................................. 10" LP Decca ............. 60413 ................. 1962 £15 ......... £30 .................Dutch
I'm Forever Blowing Bubbles ................. 7" EP . Decca ............. DFE6675............... 1960 £2 ......... £5
Ramona ............................................... LP ..... Fontana ........... ST701595 ............. 1969 £5 ......... £12 .................German
Weltschlager ....................................... LP ..... Fontana ........... 680517 ................ 1963 £20 ......... £40 .................German

## BLUE EFFECT
Kingdom Of Life.................................. LP ..... Supraphon ....... 1131023 ................ 1971 £10 ......... £25 ....... Czechoslovakian

## BLUE EPITAPH
Ode ...................................................... LP ...... Holyground..... HG117 ................ 1974 £180 ..... £300

## BLUE FLAMES
J. A. Blues........................................... 7" ...... R&B ............... JB114 ................. 1963 £10 ......... £20
Stop Right Here................................... 7" ...... R&B ............... JB126 ................. 1963 £10 ......... £20

## BLUE GOOSE
Blue Goose.......................................... LP ..... Anchor ............ ANCL2005 ........... 1975 £5 ......... £12
Loretta ................................................. 7" ...... Anchor ............ ANC1015 ............. 1975 £1.50 ...... £4

## BLUE JEANS
Hey Mrs. Housewife............................ 7" ...... Columbia ....... DB8555 ............... 1969 £5 ......... £10

## BLUE MEN
I Hear A New World ........................... LP ..... Triumph .......... TRXST9000 ......... 1960 £400 ..... £600 .. demo, best auctioned
I Hear A New World ........................... 7" EP . Triumph ......... RGXST5000 ......... 1960 £250 ..... £400 ............ best auctioned

## BLUE MOUNTAIN EAGLE
Blue Mountain Eagle ........................... LP ..... Atco .............. SD33324 ............. 1970 £4 ......... £10 ................................. US

## BLUE NILE
Downtown Lights ................................ CD-s .. Linn................ LKSCD3 ............. 1989 £2 ......... £5 ... promo in round box
Hats ..................................................... CD.... Linn................ LKHCD2 ............ 1990 £6 ......... £15 ... promo in round box
Headlights On The Parade .................. CD-s .. Linn................ LKSCD4 ............. 1990 £2 ......... £5
I Love This Life .................................. 7" ...... RSO................ RSO84 ................ 1981 £5 ......... £10
Saturday Night..................................... CD-s .. Linn................ LKSCD5 ............. 1991 £2 ......... £5

## BLUE NOTES
| | | | | | | | |
|---|---|---|---|---|---|---|---|
| For Johnny | LP | Ogun | OG532 | 1987 | £5 | £12 | |
| For Mongezi | LP | Ogun | OGD001/002 | | £8 | £20 | double |
| In Concert Vol. 1 | LP | Ogun | OG220 | 1978 | £6 | £15 | |

## BLUE OYSTER CULT
| | | | | | | | |
|---|---|---|---|---|---|---|---|
| Agents Of Fortune | CD | CBS | CD32221 | 1989 | £5 | £12 | |
| Astronomy | CD-s | CBS | 6529852 | 1988 | £2 | £5 | |
| Career Of Evil | CD | CBS | 4659292 | 1990 | £5 | £12 | |
| Club Ninja | CD | CBS | CD26775 | 1987 | £5 | £12 | |
| Don't Fear The Reaper/Tattoo Vampire | 7" | CBS | 4483 | 1976 | £2.50 | £6 | demo |
| Imaginos | CD | CBS | 4600362 | 1988 | £5 | £12 | |
| Live Bootleg | 10" LP | Columbia | AS40 | 1973 | £6 | £15 | US promo |
| Secret Treaties | LP | CBS | PCQ32858 | 1974 | £4 | £10 | US quad |
| Tyranny and Mutation | LP | CBS | PCQ32017 | 1973 | £4 | £10 | US quad |

## BLUE PHANTOM
| | | | | | | | |
|---|---|---|---|---|---|---|---|
| Distortions | LP | Kaleidoscope | KAL101 | 1972 | £30 | £60 | |

## BLUE RONDOS
| | | | | | | | |
|---|---|---|---|---|---|---|---|
| Don't Want Your Lovin' | 7" | Pye | 7N15833 | 1965 | £10 | £20 | |
| Little Baby | 7" | Pye | 7N15734 | 1964 | £25 | £50 | |

## BLUE STARS
| | | | | | | | |
|---|---|---|---|---|---|---|---|
| I Can Take It | 7" | Decca | F12303 | 1965 | £50 | £100 | |

## BLUE SUN
| | | | | | | | |
|---|---|---|---|---|---|---|---|
| Blue Sun | LP | Parlophone | 1019 | 1971 | £8 | £20 | Danish |
| Peace Be Unto You | LP | Spectator | SL1013 | 1970 | £8 | £20 | Danish |

## BLUE THINGS
| | | | | | | | |
|---|---|---|---|---|---|---|---|
| Blue Things | LP | RCA | LPM/LSP3603 | 1966 | £37.50 | £75 | US |

## BLUE VELVET BAND
| | | | | | | | |
|---|---|---|---|---|---|---|---|
| Sweet Moments | LP | Warner Bros | WS1802 | 1969 | £8 | £20 | US |

## BLUE ZONE
| | | | | | | | |
|---|---|---|---|---|---|---|---|
| Thinking About His Baby | CD-s | Rockin' Horse | RHCD115 | 1987 | £2.50 | £6 | 3" single |

## BLUEBEARD
| | | | | | | | |
|---|---|---|---|---|---|---|---|
| Bluebeard | LP | Ember | LT7004 | 1971 | £250 | £400 | test pressing |

## BLUEBEATS
| | | | | | | | |
|---|---|---|---|---|---|---|---|
| Fabulous Bluebeats Vol. 1 | 7" EP | Ember | EMBEP4525 | 1962 | £15 | £30 | |
| Fabulous Bluebeats Vol. 2 | 7" EP | Ember | EMBEP4526 | 1962 | £15 | £30 | |

## BLUEBELLS
| | | | | | | | |
|---|---|---|---|---|---|---|---|
| Young At Heart | 7" | London | LON49 | 1984 | £1.50 | £4 | shaped picture disc |

## BLUEBERRIES
| | | | | | | | |
|---|---|---|---|---|---|---|---|
| It's Gonna Work Out Fine | 7" | Mercury | MF894 | 1965 | £10 | £20 | |

## BLUES ADDICTS
| | | | | | | | |
|---|---|---|---|---|---|---|---|
| Blues Addicts | LP | Spectator | 1015 | 1970 | £75 | £150 | Danish |

## BLUES BAND
| | | | | | | | |
|---|---|---|---|---|---|---|---|
| Official Bootleg Album | LP | Arista | BBBP101 | 1980 | £4 | £10 | autographed |

## BLUES BLENDERS
| | | | | | | | |
|---|---|---|---|---|---|---|---|
| Girl Next Door | 7" | Rio | R93 | 1966 | £2.50 | £6 | |

## BLUES BROTHERS
| | | | | | | | |
|---|---|---|---|---|---|---|---|
| Everybody Needs Somebody To Love | CD-s | Atlantic | A7951CD | 1990 | £2 | £5 | |
| Soul Man | CD-s | Atlantic | A7897CD | 1990 | £2 | £5 | |

## BLUES BUSTERS
| | | | | | | | |
|---|---|---|---|---|---|---|---|
| Behold! | LP | Island | ILP923 | 1965 | £50 | £100 | |
| Blues Busters | LP | Doctor Bird | DLM5008 | 1966 | £37.50 | £75 | |
| Donna | 7" | Blue Beat | BB55 | 1961 | £6 | £12 | |
| How Sweet It Is | 7" | Island | WI214 | 1965 | £5 | £10 | |
| I've Been Trying | 7" | Doctor Bird | DB1030 | 1966 | £5 | £10 | |
| Little Vilma | 7" | Limbo | XL101 | 1960 | £5 | £10 | |
| Oh Baby | 7" | Island | WI023 | 1962 | £5 | £10 | |
| Philip And Lloyd | LP | Dynamic | DYLP3007 | 1976 | £4 | £10 | |
| Spiritual | 7" | Starlite | ST45031 | 1961 | £5 | £10 | |
| Tell Me Why | 7" | Blue Beat | BB102 | 1962 | £6 | £12 | |
| There's Always A Sunshine | 7" | Doctor Bird | DB1078 | 1967 | £5 | £10 | |
| There's Always Sunshine | 7" | Blue Beat | BB73 | 1962 | £6 | £12 | |
| Wings Of A Dove | 7" | Island | WI222 | 1965 | £5 | £10 | Byron Lee B side |
| Your Love | 7" | Starlite | ST45072 | 1962 | £4 | £8 | |

## BLUES BY FIVE
| | | | | | | | |
|---|---|---|---|---|---|---|---|
| Boom Boom | 7" | Decca | F12029 | 1964 | £15 | £30 | |

## BLUES CLIMAX
| | | | | | | | |
|---|---|---|---|---|---|---|---|
| Blues Climax | LP | Horn | JC888 | 1972 | £6 | £15 | US |

## BLUES COUNCIL
| | | | | | | |
|---|---|---|---|---|---|---|
| Baby Don't Look Down | 7" | Parlophone | R5264 | 1965 £20 | £40 | |

## BLUES DIMENSION
| | | | | | | |
|---|---|---|---|---|---|---|
| Blues Dimension | LP | Decca | ND254 | 1969 £4 | £10 | German |

## BLUES FIVE
| | | | | | | |
|---|---|---|---|---|---|---|
| Running Away From Love | 7" | Studio 36 | | 1965 £30 | £60 | |

## BLUES IMAGE
| | | | | | | |
|---|---|---|---|---|---|---|
| Blues Image | LP | Atco | SD33300 | 1969 £4 | £10 | US |
| Open | LP | Atco | 33317 | 1970 £4 | £10 | US |
| Red, White, & Blues Image | LP | Atlantic | 2400120 | 1971 £4 | £10 | |

## BLUES MAGOOS
| | | | | | | |
|---|---|---|---|---|---|---|
| Basic Blues Magoos | LP | Mercury | MG2/SR61167 | 1968 £15 | £30 | US |
| Blues Magoos | LP | Fontana | (S)TL5402 | 1966 £20 | £40 | |
| Electric Comic Book | LP | Mercury | MG2/SR61104 | 1967 £25 | £50 | US, with comic |
| Gulf Coast Bound | LP | ABC | ABCS710 | 1970 £8 | £20 | US |
| Never Going Back To Georgia | LP | ABC | S697 | 1969 £8 | £20 | US |
| One By One | 7" | Fontana | TF848 | 1967 £5 | £10 | |
| Psychedelic Lollipop | LP | Mercury | MG2/SR61096 | 1966 £20 | £40 | US |
| We Ain't Got Nothin' Yet | 7" EP | Mercury | 126221 | 1967 £25 | £50 | French |
| We Ain't Got Nothin' Yet | 7" | Mercury | MF954 | 1966 £10 | £20 | |

## BLUES MESSAGE
| | | | | | | |
|---|---|---|---|---|---|---|
| Golden Cups Album | LP | Capitol | CPC8005 | 1969 £10 | £25 | Japanese |

## BLUES PROJECT
| | | | | | | |
|---|---|---|---|---|---|---|
| Blues Project | LP | Capitol | EST11017 | 1972 £4 | £10 | US |
| Flanders, Kalb, Katz | LP | Verve | FTS3069 | 1969 £5 | £12 | US |
| I Can't Keep From Crying | 7" | Verve | VS1505 | 1967 £5 | £10 | |
| Lazarus | LP | Capitol | ST872 | 1971 £5 | £12 | US |
| Live At The Cafe Au Go-Go | LP | Verve | FT(S)3000 | 1966 £10 | £25 | US |
| Live At Town Hall | LP | Verve | FT(S)3025 | 1967 £10 | £25 | US |
| No Time Like The Right Time | 7" EP | Verve | 519905 | 1967 £25 | £50 | French |
| Planned Obsolescence | LP | Verve | FTS3046 | 1968 £8 | £20 | US |
| Projections | LP | Verve | (S)VLP6009 | 1967 £8 | £20 | |
| Reunion In Central Park | LP | MCA | 8003 | 1973 £5 | £12 | US |

## BLUES SECTION
| | | | | | | |
|---|---|---|---|---|---|---|
| Once More On The Road | LP | Love | 2 | 1967 £8 | £20 | Finnish |

## BLUESBREAKERS
| | | | | | | |
|---|---|---|---|---|---|---|
| Curly | 7" | Decca | F12588 | 1967 £2 | £5 | |

## BLUESOLOGY

Bluesology worked as the backing group for Long John Baldry when the singer was still performing rhythm and blues. The group's pianist was Reg Dwight – or rather Elton John, as he subsequently chose to be known.

| | | | | | | |
|---|---|---|---|---|---|---|
| Come Back Baby | 7" | Fontana | TF594 | 1965 £150 | £250 | best auctioned |
| Mr. Frantic | 7" | Fontana | TF668 | 1966 £150 | £250 | best auctioned |
| Since I Found You Baby | 7" | Polydor | 56195 | 1967 £150 | £250 | with Stu Brown, best auctioned |

## BLUETONES
| | | | | | | |
|---|---|---|---|---|---|---|
| Are You Blue Or Are You Blind? | CD-s | Superior Quality Recordings | BLUE001CD | 1995 £4 | £10 | |
| Are You Blue Or Are You Blind? | 7" | Superior Quality Recordings | BLUE001X | 1995 £6 | £12 | |
| Are You Blue Or Are You Blind? | 12" | Superior Quality Recordings | BLUE001T | 1995 £4 | £10 | |
| Bluetonic | CD-s | Superior Quality Recordings | BLUE002CD | 1995 £2 | £5 | |
| Bluetonic | 7" | Superior Quality Recordings | BLUE002X | 1995 £1.50 | £4 | |
| Bluetonic | 12" | Superior Quality Recordings | BLUE002T | 1995 £2.50 | £6 | |
| Expecting To Fly | LP | Superior Quality Recordings | BLUELPX004 | 1996 £6 | £15 | with plastic sleeve |
| Slight Return | 7" | Superior Quality Recordings | TONE001 | 1995 £30 | £60 | red vinyl, export |
| Slight Return | 7" | Superior Quality Recordings | TONE001 | 1995 £20 | £40 | blue vinyl |

## BLUEWATER FOLK
| | | | | | | |
|---|---|---|---|---|---|---|
| Bluewater Folk | LP | Folk Heritage | | 197– £15 | £30 | |

## BLUR

The media-provoked competition between Blur and Oasis in 1995 did Blur few favours, since their more thoughtful, less bombastic material was always likely to be overshadowed in such a contest. In fact, however, Blur's development from the laddish guitar pop of their first singles to the carefully constructed arrangements of their more recent music has been remarkable. It is likely that Damon Albarn and his colleagues will be a musical force to be reckoned with for a considerable time to come.

| Title | Format | Label | Cat. No. | Year | | | Notes |
|---|---|---|---|---|---|---|---|
| Bang | CD-s | Food | CDFOOD31 | 1991 | £10 | £20 | |
| Basically Blur | CD | SBK | | 1992 | £15 | £30 | US promo |
| Bet Bet Bet | CD-s | EMI | SPCD1736 | 1995 | £30 | £60 | 4 track French promo |
| Blue To Go | CD | SBK | DPRO5455 | 1993 | £6 | £15 | US promo |
| Chemical World | CD-s | Food | CDFOOD45 | 1993 | £10 | £20 | 2 versions |
| Focusing In With Blur | CD | SBK | DPRO5424 | 1993 | £6 | £15 | US promo |
| For Tomorrow | CD-s | Food | CDFOOD40 | 1993 | £10 | £20 | 2 versions |
| Girls And Boys | CD-s | Food | CDFOOD(S)47 | 1994 | £3 | £8 | 2 versions |
| High Cool | 12" | Food | 12BLUR4 | 1991 | £4 | £10 | promo |
| Parklife | CD-s | Food | CDFOODS53 | 1994 | £2 | £5 | 2 versions |
| Parklife | CD | Food | PCD0476 | 1994 | £25 | £50 | Japanese electronic pack with 5 extra tracks |
| Popscene | CD-s | Food | CDFOOD37 | 1992 | £12.50 | £25 | |
| She's So High | CD-s | Food | CDFOOD26 | 1990 | £12.50 | £25 | |
| Special Collectors' Edition | CD | Food | TOCP8395 | 1994 | £15 | £30 | Japanese compilation from 1st 3 albums |
| Sunday Sunday | CD-s | Food | CDFOOD46 | 1993 | £10 | £20 | 2 versions |
| There's No Other Way | CD-s | Food | CDFOOD29 | 1991 | £10 | £20 | |
| There's No Other Way (remix) | 12" | Food | 12FOODX29 | 1991 | £10 | £20 | |
| To The End | CD-s | Food | CDFOOD50 | 1994 | £3 | £8 | |
| To The End | CD-s | Food | CDFOODS50 | 1994 | £2 | £5 | |
| Wassailing Song | 7" | Food | BLUR6 | 1992 | £7.50 | £15 | 1 sided promo |

## BLYTHE, JIMMY

| Title | Format | Label | Cat. No. | Year | | |
|---|---|---|---|---|---|---|
| South Side Blues Piano | 10" LP | London | AL3527 | 1954 | £8 | £20 |
| South Side Chicago Jazz | 10" LP | London | AL3529 | 1954 | £8 | £20 |

## BO & PEEP

| Title | Format | Label | Cat. No. | Year | | |
|---|---|---|---|---|---|---|
| Young Love | 7" | Decca | F11968 | 1964 | £7.50 | £15 |

## BO STREET RUNNERS

When the cult TV show *Ready Steady Go* organized a beat group talent contest in 1964, the Bo Street Runners were the winners. (The various-artists' LP *Ready Steady Win* documents the affair). As is usually the case with talent contests, however, the win yielded nothing in terms of subsequent success for the Bo Street Runners. The group was led by organist Tim Hinkley, while both Mick Fleetwood and Mike Patto were members for a time.

| Title | Format | Label | Cat. No. | Year | | | Notes |
|---|---|---|---|---|---|---|---|
| Baby Never Say Goodbye | 7" | Columbia | DB7640 | 1965 | £15 | £30 | |
| Bo Street Runner | 7" | Decca | F11986 | 1964 | £20 | £40 | |
| Bo Street Runners | 7" EP | Oak | RGJ131 | 1964 | £500 | £750 | best auctioned |
| Drive My Car | 7" | Columbia | DB7901 | 1966 | £15 | £30 | |
| Tell Me What You're Gonna Do | 7" | Columbia | DB7488 | 1965 | £25 | £50 | |

## BOA

| Title | Format | Label | Cat. No. | Year | | | Notes |
|---|---|---|---|---|---|---|---|
| Wrong Road | LP | Snakefield | SN001 | 1969 | £150 | £250 | US |

## BOARDMAN, HARRY

| Title | Format | Label | Cat. No. | Year | | |
|---|---|---|---|---|---|---|
| Lancashire Mon | LP | Topic | 12TS236 | 1974 | £4 | £10 |

## BOARDMAN, HARRY & DAVE HILLERY

| Title | Format | Label | Cat. No. | Year | | |
|---|---|---|---|---|---|---|
| Trans Pennine | LP | Topic | 12TS215 | 1971 | £8 | £20 |

## BOB

| Title | Format | Label | Cat. No. | Year | | | Notes |
|---|---|---|---|---|---|---|---|
| Esmerelda Brooklyn | 7" | House Of Teeth | HOT003 | 1989 | £2.50 | £6 | |
| Prune | 7" | House Of Teeth | | 1988 | £2 | £5 | flexi |

## BOB & BOBBY

The single by Bob and Bobby is one of the small number of outside productions undertaken by Beach Boy Brian Wilson in the sixties.

| Title | Format | Label | Cat. No. | Year | | | Notes |
|---|---|---|---|---|---|---|---|
| Twelve-O-Four | 7" | Tower | 154 | 1965 | £12.50 | £25 | US |

## BOB & EARL

| Title | Format | Label | Cat. No. | Year | | |
|---|---|---|---|---|---|---|
| Baby I'm Satisfied | 7" | Sue | WI393 | 1965 | £6 | £12 |
| Don't Ever Leave Me | 7" | Sue | WI4030 | 1967 | £6 | £12 |
| Harlem Shuffle | LP | Sue | ILP951 | 1967 | £15 | £30 |
| Harlem Shuffle | 7" | Island | WIP6053 | 1969 | £1.50 | £4 |
| Harlem Shuffle | 7" | Sue | WI374 | 1965 | £5 | £10 |

## BOB & JERRY

| Title | Format | Label | Cat. No. | Year | | |
|---|---|---|---|---|---|---|
| Ghost Satellite | 7" | Pye | 7N25003 | 1958 | £2 | £5 |
| We're The Guys | 7" | Philips | PB1205 | 1961 | £1.50 | £4 |

## BOB & MARCIA

| Title | Format | Label | Cat. No. | Year | | |
|---|---|---|---|---|---|---|
| Pied Piper | LP | Trojan | TRLS26 | 1971 | £4 | £10 |
| Really Together | 7" | Bamboo | BAM40 | 1970 | £2 | £5 |
| Young Gifted And Black | 7" | Harry J | HJ6605 | 1970 | £1.50 | £4 |
| Young, Gifted And Black | LP | Trojan | TBL122 | 1970 | £5 | £12 |

## BOB & SHERI

The ultra-rare single by Bob and Sheri is a Brian Wilson production.

| | | | | | | | |
|---|---|---|---|---|---|---|---|
| Surfer Moon | 7" | Safari | 101 | 1962 | £500 | £750 | ... US, blue label, best auctioned |

## BOB & TYRONE

| | | | | | | | |
|---|---|---|---|---|---|---|---|
| I Don't Care | 7" | Coxsone | CS7086 | 1969 | £5 | £10 | |

## BOBBETTES

| | | | | | | | |
|---|---|---|---|---|---|---|---|
| Come A Come A Come A | 7" | London | HLE8597 | 1958 | £15 | £30 | |
| Have Mercy Baby | 7" | London | HLU9248 | 1960 | £7.50 | £15 | |
| I Shot Mr. Lee | 7" | London | HLK9173 | 1960 | £10 | £20 | |
| I Shot Mr. Lee | 7" | Pye | 7N25060 | 1960 | £7.50 | £15 | |
| Mr. Lee | 7" | London | HLE8477 | 1957 | £15 | £30 | |
| That's A Bad Thing To Know | 7" | Action | ACT4603 | 1972 | £2.50 | £6 | |

## BOBBSEY TWINS

| | | | | | | | |
|---|---|---|---|---|---|---|---|
| Change Of Heart | 7" | London | HLA8474 | 1957 | £6 | £12 | |

## BOBBY & LAURIE

| | | | | | | | |
|---|---|---|---|---|---|---|---|
| Hitch Hiker | 7" | Parlophone | R5480 | 1966 | £1.50 | £4 | |

## BOBCATS

| | | | | | | | |
|---|---|---|---|---|---|---|---|
| Can't See For Looking | 7" | Pye | 7N17242 | 1967 | £4 | £8 | |

## BOCKY & THE VISIONS

| | | | | | | | |
|---|---|---|---|---|---|---|---|
| I Go Crazy | 7" | Atlantic | AT4049 | 1965 | £5 | £10 | |

## BODINES

| | | | | | | | |
|---|---|---|---|---|---|---|---|
| God Bless | 7" | Creation | CRE016 | 1985 | £2 | £5 | |

## BODKIN

| | | | | | | | |
|---|---|---|---|---|---|---|---|
| Bodkin | LP | West | CSA104 | 1972 | £250 | £400 | |

## BODY

| | | | | | | | |
|---|---|---|---|---|---|---|---|
| Body Album | LP | Recession | REC01 | 1981 | £20 | £40 | |

## BOFFALONGO

| | | | | | | | |
|---|---|---|---|---|---|---|---|
| Beyond Your Head | LP | United Artists | UAG29130 | 1970 | £4 | £10 | |
| Boffalongo | LP | United Artists | 6726 | 1969 | £5 | £12 | US |

## BOGARDE, DIRK

| | | | | | | | |
|---|---|---|---|---|---|---|---|
| Darling | 7" | Fontana | TF615 | 1965 | £1.50 | £4 | |
| Lyrics For Lovers | LP | Decca | LK4373 | 1960 | £6 | £15 | |

## BOGIES

| | | | | | | | |
|---|---|---|---|---|---|---|---|
| 'Bye 'Bye | LP | private | no number | 1964 | £100 | £200 | |
| On Campus | LP | private | no number | 1964 | £100 | £200 | |

## BOHEMIAN VENDETTA

| | | | | | | | |
|---|---|---|---|---|---|---|---|
| Bohemian Vendetta | LP | Mainstream | (S)6106 | 1968 | £37.50 | £75 | US |

## BOINES, HOUSTON

| | | | | | | | |
|---|---|---|---|---|---|---|---|
| Superintendant Blues | 7" | Blue Horizon | 451006 | 1966 | £50 | £100 | |

## BOKAJ RETSIEM

| | | | | | | | |
|---|---|---|---|---|---|---|---|
| Psychedelic Underground | LP | Fass | 1532WY | 1969 | £6 | £15 | German |

## BOLAN, MARC

For an artist with an essentially rather limited talent, Marc Bolan has managed to attract an extraordinarily devoted following. Part of this is no doubt the direct consequence of Bolan's premature death. In any event, there are a number of quite valuable recordings to be found scattered through Bolan's catalogue. These include the original issue of his *Zinc Alloy* LP, which has an individually numbered poster sleeve, and the early solo singles (whose lack of chart success is not hard to understand once they are heard; they are somewhat less than inspiring). Records made with John's Children and Tyrannosaurus Rex are listed under those headings.

| | | | | | | | |
|---|---|---|---|---|---|---|---|
| Beginning Of Doves | LP | Track | 2410201 | 1974 | £6 | £15 | |
| Hippy Gumbo | 7" | Parlophone | R5539 | 1966 | £330 | £500 | best auctioned |
| Jasper C. Debussy | 7" | Track | 2094013 | 1974 | £6 | £12 | picture sleeve |
| Road I'm On | 7" | Archive Jive | TOBY1 | 1990 | £4 | £8 | as Toby Tyler |
| Third Degree | 7" | Decca | F12413 | 1966 | £330 | £500 | best auctioned |
| Wizard | 7" | Decca | F12288 | 1965 | £180 | £300 | best auctioned |
| You Scare Me To Death | LP | Cherry Red | PERED20 | 1981 | £4 | £10 | picture disc |
| You Scare Me To Death | CD-s | Cherry Red | CDCHERRY29 | 1989 | £2 | £5 | |
| You Scare Me To Death | 7" | Cherry Red | CHERRY29 | 1981 | £1.50 | £4 | with flexi (LYN10086) |
| You Scare Me To Death | 7" | Cherry Red | CHERRYP29 | 1981 | £1.50 | £4 | picture disc |

## BOLAN, MARC & T REX

| | | | | | | | |
|---|---|---|---|---|---|---|---|
| Celebrate Summer | 7" | EMI | MARC18 | 1977 | £1.50 | £4 | picture sleeve |
| Chariot Choogle | 7" | EMI | SPSR346 | 1972 | £50 | £100 | promo |
| Children Of Rarn | 10" | Marc | ABOLAN2 | 1982 | £6 | £15 | with book |
| Electric Warrior | LP | Fly | HIFLY6 | 1971 | £4 | £10 | with inner & poster |
| Essential Collection | CD | Relativity | | 1991 | £8 | £20 | US promo sampler |

| Title | Format | Label | Cat. No. | Year | | | Notes |
|---|---|---|---|---|---|---|---|
| Get It On | 7" | Fly | BUG10 | 1971 | £4 | £8 | picture sleeve, silver fly on label, handwritten credits |
| Great Hits | LP | EMI | BLN5003 | 1972 | £4 | £10 | with poster |
| Hard On Love | LP | Track | 2406101 | 1972 | £100 | £200 | test pressing |
| History Of T Rex | LP | Marc On Wax | WARRIOR1-4 | 1986 | £8 | £20 | 4 picture discs, boxed |
| Jeepster | 7" | Fly | GRUB1 | 1971 | £50 | £100 | promo |
| Jeepster | 7" | Fly | GRUB1 | 1971 | £62.50 | £125 | promo, pink sleeve |
| Life's A Gas | 12" | Cube | ANTS001 | 1979 | £3 | £8 | |
| Metal Guru | CD-s | Total | CDMARC502 | 1991 | £2 | £5 | |
| Ride A White Swan | 7" | Fly | BUG1 | 1970 | £5 | £10 | picture sleeve, purple label |
| Ride A White Swan | 7" | Octopus | OCTO1 | 1970 | £500 | £750 | test pressing, best auctioned |
| Sing Me A Song | 12" | Rarn | MBFS001P | 1981 | £4 | £10 | picture disc, black rim |
| Singles Collection Vol. 1 | CD | Marc On Wax | MARCD510 | 1987 | £8 | £20 | double |
| Solid Gold Easy Action | CD-s | Old Gold | OG6134 | 1989 | £2 | £5 | |
| T Rex EP | CD-s | Special Edition | CD313 | 1988 | £2 | £5 | |
| T Rex In Concert | LP | Marc | ABOLAN1 | 1981 | £6 | £15 | promo, no applause |
| Tanx | LP | EMI | BLN5002 | 1972 | £4 | £10 | with inner & poster |
| Twentieth Century Boy | CD-s | Total | CDMARC501 | 1991 | £2 | £5 | |
| Words And Music Of Marc Bolan | LP | Cube | HIFLY1 | 1978 | £6 | £15 | double, with 7" (BINT1) |
| Zinc Alloy & Hidden Riders Of Tomorrow | LP | EMI | BLNA7751 | 1974 | £62.50 | £125 | fold-out numbered sleeve |
| Zinc Alloy & Hidden Riders Of Tomorrow | LP | EMI | BLNA7751 | 1974 | £4 | £10 | with inner |
| Zip Gun | LP | EMI | BLN7752 | 1975 | £5 | £12 | diamond cut sleeve, inner |

## BOLD

| Title | Format | Label | Cat. No. | Year | | | Notes |
|---|---|---|---|---|---|---|---|
| Bold | LP | ABC | ABCS705 | 1969 | £6 | £15 | US |

## BOLDER DAMN

| Title | Format | Label | Cat. No. | Year | | | Notes |
|---|---|---|---|---|---|---|---|
| Mourning | LP | private | | 1971 | £700 | £1000 | US |

## BOLIVAR, SIMON

| Title | Format | Label | Cat. No. | Year | | | Notes |
|---|---|---|---|---|---|---|---|
| Merengue Holiday | 7" | London | HLG8245 | 1956 | £6 | £12 | |

## BOLOTIN, MICHAEL

Bolotin is, of course, Michael Bolton, performing in much the same style as was successful for him several years later.

| Title | Format | Label | Cat. No. | Year | | | Notes |
|---|---|---|---|---|---|---|---|
| Every Day Of My Life | LP | RCA | APL11550 | 1976 | £5 | £12 | US |
| Michael Bolotin | LP | RCA | SF8451 | 1975 | £5 | £12 | |

## BOLTON, POLLY

| Title | Format | Label | Cat. No. | Year | | | Notes |
|---|---|---|---|---|---|---|---|
| No Going Back | LP | Making Waves | SPIN134 | 1989 | £15 | £30 | |

## BOMBAY DUCKS

| Title | Format | Label | Cat. No. | Year | | | Notes |
|---|---|---|---|---|---|---|---|
| Dance Music | LP | United Dairies | UP05 | 198– | £6 | £15 | |
| Sympathy For The Devil | 7" | Complete Control | CON1 | 1980 | £2 | £5 | |

## BON BONS

| Title | Format | Label | Cat. No. | Year | | | Notes |
|---|---|---|---|---|---|---|---|
| Circle | 7" | London | HLU8262 | 1956 | £7.50 | £15 | |
| That's The Way Love Goes | 7" | London | HL8139 | 1955 | £10 | £20 | |

## BON JOVI

The music of Bon Jovi defines modern American stadium rock. Histrionic lead vocals, with stirring chorus support, declaim anthems that are custom-written for arenas holding thousands of fans, while the lead guitar delivers the sustain-drenched tone, with all the whammy bar dives and tricky tapped figures that are expected of the style. *Slippery When Wet* was the biggest-selling rock album of 1987, the group's continued success since inspiring considerable collectors' interest in its growing back catalogue.

| Title | Format | Label | Cat. No. | Year | | | Notes |
|---|---|---|---|---|---|---|---|
| Bad Medicine | CD-s | Vertigo | JOVCD3 | 1988 | £2 | £5 | |
| Blaze Of Glory | CD-s | Vertigo | JBJCD1 | 1990 | £2 | £5 | |
| Born To Be My Baby | CD-s | Vertigo | JOVCD4 | 1988 | £2 | £5 | |
| Born To Be My Baby | 12" | Vertigo | JOVR412 | 1988 | £5 | £12 | picture disc |
| Essential Bon Jovi | CD | Mercury | JOVI1989 | 1989 | £10 | £25 | promo |
| Hardest Part Is The Night | 7" | Vertigo | VER22 | 1985 | £2.50 | £6 | |
| Hardest Part Is The Night | 7" | Vertigo | VERDP22 | 1985 | £7.50 | £15 | double |
| Hardest Part Is The Night | 12" | Vertigo | VERX22 | 1985 | £5 | £12 | |
| Hardest Part Is The Night | 12" | Vertigo | VERXR22 | 1985 | £10 | £20 | red vinyl |
| I'll Be There For You | CD-s | Vertigo | JOVCD5 | 1989 | £2 | £5 | |
| In And Out Of Love | 7" | Vertigo | VER19 | 1985 | £4 | £8 | |
| In And Out Of Love | 7" | Vertigo | VERP19 | 1985 | £15 | £30 | picture disc |
| In And Out Of Love | 12" | Vertigo | VERX19 | 1985 | £6 | £15 | |
| Interview | CD | Mercury | CDP1371 | 1995 | £8 | £20 | US promo |
| Keep The Faith | CD | Mercury | PHCR16003 | 1993 | £10 | £25 | Japanese, with bonus live disc |
| Lay Your Hands On Me | CD-s | Vertigo | JOVCD6 | 1989 | £2 | £5 | |
| Lay Your Hands On Me | 7" | Vertigo | JOV6 | 1989 | £6 | £15 | triple pack, red, white, blue vinyls |
| Living In Sin | CD-s | Vertigo | JOVCD7 | 1989 | £2 | £5 | boxed |
| Living On A Prayer | 7" | Vertigo | VERP28 | 1986 | £7.50 | £15 | picture disc |
| Living On A Prayer | 7" | Vertigo | VERPA28 | 1986 | £1.50 | £4 | with patch |
| Living On A Prayer | 12" | Vertigo | VERXG28 | 1986 | £3 | £8 | double |
| Living On A Prayer | 12" | Vertigo | VERXR28 | 1986 | £5 | £12 | green vinyl |

| | | | | | | | |
|---|---|---|---|---|---|---|---|
| Miracle | CD-s | Vertigo | JBJCD2 | 1990 | £6 | £15 | *picture disc* |
| Never Say Goodbye | CD-s | Polygram | 0802262 | 1987 | £15 | £30 | *CD video* |
| Runaway | 7" | Vertigo | VER14 | 1984 | £7.50 | £15 | |
| Runaway | 12" | Vertigo | VERX14 | 1984 | £15 | £30 | |
| She Don't Know Me | 7" | Vertigo | VER11 | 1984 | £7.50 | £15 | |
| She Don't Know Me | 12" | Vertigo | VERX11 | 1984 | £15 | £30 | |
| Slippery When Wet | LP | Vertigo | VERHP38 | 1988 | £4 | £10 | *picture disc, poster* |
| Someday I'll Be Saturday Night | CD-s | Vertigo | | 1994 | £3 | £8 | *in red tin* |
| These Days | CD | Mercury | | 1995 | £15 | £30 | *interview promo* |
| These Days | CD | Mercury | 5326442 | 1996 | £6 | £15 | *double* |
| Volkswagen Presents These Days | CD-s | Mercury | JOVVW1 | 1996 | £15 | £30 | *promo* |
| Wanted Dead Or Alive | CD-s | Vertigo | JOVCD1 | 1987 | £2.50 | £6 | |
| Wanted Dead Or Alive | 12" | Vertigo | JOVR112 | 1987 | £6 | £15 | *silver vinyl* |
| Wanted Dead Or Alive | CD-s | Mercury | 0800522 | 1987 | £15 | £30 | *CD video* |
| You Give Love A Bad Name | 12" | Vertigo | VERX26 | 1986 | £2.50 | £6 | *with poster* |
| You Give Love A Bad Name | 12" | Vertigo | VERXR26 | 1986 | £6 | £15 | *blue vinyl* |
| You Give Love A Bad Name | 10" | Vertigo | VERP26 | 1986 | £4 | £10 | *shaped picture disc* |

## BONANO, SHARKEY

| | | | | | | | |
|---|---|---|---|---|---|---|---|
| At The Round Table | LP | Columbia | 33SX1255/ SCX3327 | 1960 | £4 | £10 | |

## BOND, BOBBY

| | | | | | | | |
|---|---|---|---|---|---|---|---|
| Sweet Love | 7" | Pye | 7N25081 | 1961 | £2 | £5 | |

## BOND, BRIGITTE

| | | | | | | | |
|---|---|---|---|---|---|---|---|
| Blue Beat Baby | 7" | Blue Beat | BB212 | 1964 | £6 | £12 | |

## BOND, EDDIE

| | | | | | | | |
|---|---|---|---|---|---|---|---|
| Greatest Country Gospel Hits | LP | Philips | 1980 | 1961 | £25 | £50 | *US* |

## BOND, GRAHAM

Although he was undoubtedly a major influence within the development of sixties rock, Bond's tragedy was to see his ideas developed more successfully by others. Few of his records really do justice to his undoubted talents, partly because despite being a good alto sax jazz player (as his work on both the Don Rendell Quintet LP of 1962 and on the early Organization tracks included on *Solid Bond* prove), he constantly compromised his art in a desperate search for commercial success. Unfortunately, he never did find it, and yet all his sixties sidemen managed to – Ginger Baker and Jack Bruce with Cream; Jon Hiseman and Dick Heckstall-Smith with Colosseum; and John McLaughlin with Mahavishnu Orchestra. Bond himself stumbled through increasingly marginal musical projects, in which personal and drug problems did not help, until he fell under a train in 1974.

| | | | | | | | |
|---|---|---|---|---|---|---|---|
| Bond In America | LP | Mercury | 6499200/1 | 1971 | £10 | £25 | *double* |
| Holy Magick | LP | Vertigo | 6360021 | 1971 | £8 | £20 | *spiral label* |
| Lease On Love | 7" | Columbia | DB7647 | 1965 | £15 | £30 | |
| Long Tall Shorty | 7" | Decca | F11909 | 1964 | £20 | £40 | |
| Love Is The Law | LP | Pulsar | AR10604 | 1968 | £8 | £20 | *US* |
| Mighty Graham Bond | LP | Pulsar | AR10606 | 1968 | £8 | £20 | *US* |
| Solid Bond | LP | Warner Bros | WS3001 | 1970 | £10 | £25 | *double* |
| Sound Of '65 | LP | Columbia | 33SX1711 | 1965 | £37.50 | £75 | |
| St. James Infirmary | 7" | Columbia | DB7838 | 1966 | £15 | £30 | |
| Tammy | 7" | Columbia | DB7471 | 1965 | £15 | £30 | |
| Tell Me | 7" | Columbia | DB7528 | 1965 | £15 | £30 | |
| There's A Bond Between Us | LP | Columbia | 33SX1750 | 1966 | £30 | £60 | |
| This Is Graham Bond | LP | Philips | 6382010 | 1972 | £4 | £10 | |
| Walking In The Park | 7" | Warner Bros | WB8004 | 1970 | £5 | £10 | |
| We Put Our Magick On You | LP | Vertigo | 6360042 | 1971 | £8 | £20 | *spiral label* |
| You've Gotta Have Love Babe | 7" | Page One | POF014 | 1967 | £15 | £30 | |

## BOND, GRAHAM & PETE BROWN

| | | | | | | | |
|---|---|---|---|---|---|---|---|
| Lost Tribe | 7" | Greenwich | GSS104 | 1972 | £15 | £30 | |
| Two Heads Are Better Than One | LP | Chapter One | CHSR813 | 1972 | £30 | £60 | |

## BOND, ISABELLA

| | | | | | | | |
|---|---|---|---|---|---|---|---|
| Surfin' 66 | LP | Decca | SLK16410 | 1966 | £10 | £25 | *German* |

## BOND, JAMES

Records associated with the James Bond films are widely collected and are listed in the *Price Guide* under the names of the relevant artists. Much of the soundtrack music has been written and recorded by John Barry. Other relevant entries are as follows: Monty Norman (*Dr No*); Matt Monro (*From Russia With Love*); Shirley Bassey (*Goldfinger* and *Diamonds Are Forever*); Tom Jones (*Thunderball*); Burt Bacharach (*Casino Royale*); Dusty Springfield ('The Look Of Love', from *Casino Royale*, is the B side of 'Give Me Time'); Nancy Sinatra (*You Only Live Twice*); Louis Armstrong ('We Have All The Time In The World' from *On Her Majesty's Secret Service*); Lulu (*The Man With The Golden Gun*); Michel Legrand (*Never Say Never Again*); and A-Ha (*The Living Daylights*). A large number of other artists have also issued cover versions of the various Bond theme songs and other songs associated with, or inspired by James Bond.

## BOND, JACKI

| | | | | | | | |
|---|---|---|---|---|---|---|---|
| He Say | 7" | Strike | JH320 | 1966 | £7.50 | £15 | |
| Tell Him To Go Away | 7" | Strike | JH302 | 1966 | £1.50 | £4 | |

## BOND, JOHNNY

| | | | | | | | |
|---|---|---|---|---|---|---|---|
| Hot Rod Jalopy | 7" | London | HLU9189 | 1960 | £4 | £8 | |
| Hot Rod Lincoln | 7" | London | HL7100 | 1960 | £5 | £10 | *export* |
| Live It Up | LP | London | HAB8098 | 1963 | £4 | £10 | |
| Songs That Made Him Famous | LP | London | HAB8228 | 1965 | £6 | £15 | |
| Ten Little Bottles | 7" | London | HLB9957 | 1965 | £1.50 | £4 | |
| That Wild, Wicked But Wonderful West | LP | Stateside | SL10008 | 1962 | £4 | £10 | |

## BOND, JOYCE

| | | | | | | | |
|---|---|---|---|---|---|---|---|
| Back To School | 7" | Pama | PM718 | 1968 | £1.50 | £4 | |

| | | | | | | |
|---|---|---|---|---|---|---|
| Do The Teasy | 7" | Island | WIP6010 | 1967 £1.50 | £4 | |
| It's Alright | 7" | Airborn | NBP0011 | 1967 £4 | £8 | |
| Mr. Pitiful | 7" | Pama | PM770 | 1969 £1.50 | £4 | |
| Ob La Di Ob La Da | 7" | Island | WIP6051 | 1968 £1.50 | £4 | |
| Soul And Ska | LP | Island | ILP968 | 1968 £30 | £60 | *pink label* |
| Tell Me What It's All About | 7" | Island | WI3019 | 1966 £2 | £5 | |
| This Train | 7" | Island | WIP6018 | 1967 £1.50 | £4 | |

## BOND, MARGARET
| | | | | | |
|---|---|---|---|---|---|
| Your Love Is My Love | 7" | Parlophone | R4283 | 1957 £1.50 | £4 |

## BOND, OLIVER
| | | | | | |
|---|---|---|---|---|---|
| Let Me Love You | 7" | Parlophone | R5476 | 1966 £2.50 | £6 |

## BOND, PETER
| | | | | | |
|---|---|---|---|---|---|
| Awkward Age | LP | Totem | STO813 | 1983 £6 | £15 |
| It's Alright For Some | LP | Trailer | LER2108 | 1977 £6 | £15 |

## BOND, RONNIE
| | | | | | |
|---|---|---|---|---|---|
| Anything For You | 7" | Page One | POF123 | 1969 £7.50 | £15 |

## BONDS, GARY (U.S.)
| | | | | | |
|---|---|---|---|---|---|
| Dance Till Quarter To Three | LP | Legrand | LLP3001 | 1961 £25 | £50 | US |
| Dance Till Quarter To Three | LP | Top Rank | 35114 | 1961 £15 | £30 | |
| Dear Lady Twist | 7" | Top Rank | JAR602 | 1962 £1.50 | £4 | |
| Do The Limbo With Me | 7" | Stateside | SS179 | 1963 £1.50 | £4 | |
| Ella Is Yella | 7" | Stateside | SS308 | 1964 £1.50 | £4 | |
| Greatest Hits | LP | Stateside | SL10037 | 1962 £6 | £15 | |
| New Orleans | 7" | Top Rank | JAR527 | 1961 £1.50 | £4 | |
| Not Me | 7" | Top Rank | JAR566 | 1961 £1.50 | £4 | |
| Quarter To Three | 7" | Top Rank | JAR575 | 1961 £1.50 | £4 | |
| School Is In | 7" | Top Rank | JAR595 | 1961 £1.50 | £4 | |
| School Is Out | 7" | Top Rank | JAR581 | 1961 £1.50 | £4 | |
| Send Her To Me | 7" | Stateside | SS2025 | 1967 £4 | £8 | |
| Seven Day Weekend | 7" | Stateside | SS111 | 1962 £1.50 | £4 | |
| Twist Twist Senora | 7" | Top Rank | JAR615 | 1962 £1.50 | £4 | |
| Twist Up Calypso | LP | Stateside | SL10001 | 1962 £6 | £15 | |

## BONE, OLIVER
| | | | | | |
|---|---|---|---|---|---|
| Knock On Wood | 7" | Parlophone | R5527 | 1966 £2 | £5 |

## BONFIRE, MARS
| | | | | | |
|---|---|---|---|---|---|
| Faster Than The Speed Of Life | LP | Columbia | CS9834 | 1969 £5 | £12 | US |
| Mars Bonfire | LP | UNI | 73027 | 1968 £4 | £10 | US |

## BONNER, JUKE BOY
| | | | | | |
|---|---|---|---|---|---|
| One Man Trio | LP | Flyright | LP3501 | 1968 £8 | £20 |
| Runnin' Shoes | 7" | Blue Horizon | 573163 | 1969 £6 | £12 |
| Things Ain't Right | LP | Liberty | LBS83319 | 1969 £5 | £12 |

## BONNET, GRAHAM
| | | | | | |
|---|---|---|---|---|---|
| Graham Bonnet | LP | Ring O' | 2320103 | 1977 £4 | £10 |

## BONNEVILLES
| | | | | | |
|---|---|---|---|---|---|
| Meet The Bonnevilles | LP | Drum Boy | DLM/LS1001 | 1963 £8 | £20 | US |

## BONNEY, GRAHAM
| | | | | | |
|---|---|---|---|---|---|
| Get Ready | 7" | Columbia | DB8531 | 1969 £1.50 | £4 |
| No One Knows | 7" | Columbia | DB8005 | 1966 £1.50 | £4 |
| Sign On The Dotted Line | 7" | Columbia | DB8648 | 1970 £1.50 | £4 |
| Super Girl | 7" | Columbia | DB7843 | 1966 £1.50 | £4 |
| Supergirl | LP | Columbia | SX6052 | 1966 £5 | £12 |

## BONNIE
| | | | | | |
|---|---|---|---|---|---|
| Did You Get The Message | 7" | Ska Beat | JB270 | 1967 £5 | £10 |
| Lovin' You | 7" | Jolly | JY014 | 1968 £2 | £5 |

## BONNIE & THE TREASURES
| | | | | | |
|---|---|---|---|---|---|
| Home Of The Brave | 7" | London | HLU9998 | 1965 £7.50 | £15 |

## BONNIWELL, T.S.
| | | | | | |
|---|---|---|---|---|---|
| Close | LP | Capitol | ST277 | 1969 £15 | £30 | US |

## BONUS, JACK
| | | | | | |
|---|---|---|---|---|---|
| Jack Bonus | LP | Grunt | FTR1005 | 1972 £6 | £15 | US |

## BONZO DOG (DOO-DAH) BAND & OTHERS
| | | | | | |
|---|---|---|---|---|---|
| Alberts,The Bonzo Dog Band,& The Temperance Seven | LP | Starline | SRS5151 | 1973 £4 | £10 | |
| Alley Oop | 7" | Parlophone | R5499 | 1966 £7.50 | £15 | |
| Best Of The Bonzos | LP | Liberty | LBS83332 | 1970 £4 | £10 | |
| Doughnut In Granny's Greenhouse | LP | Liberty | LBL/LBS83158 | 1968 £8 | £20 | *with booklet* |
| Equestrian Statue | 7" | Liberty | LBF15040 | 1967 £1.50 | £4 | |
| Gorilla | LP | Liberty | LBL/LBS83056 | 1967 £8 | £20 | *with booklet* |
| History Of The Bonzos | LP | United Artists | UAD60071/2 | 1974 £6 | £15 | *double* |
| I Want To Be With You | 7" | Liberty | LBF15273 | 1969 £1.50 | £4 | |
| Keynsham | LP | Liberty | LBS83290 | 1969 £5 | £12 | |
| Let's Make Up & Be Friendly | LP | United Artists | UAS29288 | 1972 £5 | £12 | |

| Title | Format | Label | Catalogue | Year | | | Notes |
|---|---|---|---|---|---|---|---|
| Mr. Apollo | 7" | Liberty | LBF15201 | 1969 | £1.50 | £4 | |
| My Brother Makes The Noises For The Talkies | 7" | Parlophone | R5430 | 1966 | £7.50 | £15 | |
| Tadpoles | LP | Liberty | LBS83257 | 1969 | £4 | £10 | |
| Urban Spaceman | 7" | Liberty | LBF15144 | 1968 | £1.50 | £4 | 2 versions of B-side |
| You Done My Brain In | 7" | Liberty | LBF15314 | 1970 | £1.50 | £4 | |

## BOO RADLEYS

| Title | Format | Label | Catalogue | Year | | | Notes |
|---|---|---|---|---|---|---|---|
| Boo Up! | CD-s | Rough Trade | R2753 | 1991 | £2 | £5 | |
| Every Heaven | CD-s | Rough Trade | R20112713 | 1991 | £3 | £8 | |
| Ichabod And I | LP | Action | TAKE4 | 1990 | £6 | £15 | |
| Kaleidoscope | CD-s | Rough Trade | RTT241CD | 1990 | £3 | £8 | |
| Kaleidoscope | 12" | Rough Trade | RTT241 | 1990 | £2.50 | £6 | |

## BOOGIE KINGS

| Title | Format | Label | Catalogue | Year | | | Notes |
|---|---|---|---|---|---|---|---|
| Blue Eyed Soul | LP | Montel-Michelle | 109 | 1967 | £4 | £10 | US |
| Boogie Kings | LP | Montel-Michelle | 104 | 1966 | £4 | £10 | US |

## BOOGIE WOOGIE COMPANY

| Title | Format | Label | Catalogue | Year | | | Notes |
|---|---|---|---|---|---|---|---|
| Live For Dancing | LP | Electrola | 1C06291783 | 1971 | £20 | £40 | German |

## BOOK OF A.M.

| Title | Format | Label | Catalogue | Year | | | Notes |
|---|---|---|---|---|---|---|---|
| Dawn And Morning | LP | LMT | 1016 | 1978 | £6 | £15 | French |

## BOOKER, BERYL

| Title | Format | Label | Catalogue | Year | | | Notes |
|---|---|---|---|---|---|---|---|
| Beryl Booker Trio | 10" LP | London | HBA1054 | 1956 | £20 | £40 | |

## BOOKER, JAMES

| Title | Format | Label | Catalogue | Year | | | Notes |
|---|---|---|---|---|---|---|---|
| Cool Turkey | 7" | Vogue | V9177 | 1961 | £5 | £10 | |
| Gonzo | 7" EP | Vocalion | VEP170154 | 1963 | £20 | £40 | |

## BOOKER T & THE MG'S

| Title | Format | Label | Catalogue | Year | | | Notes |
|---|---|---|---|---|---|---|---|
| And Now | LP | Stax | 589002 | 1966 | £5 | £12 | |
| Back To Back (with Markeys) | LP | Stax | (STS)720 | 1967 | £4 | £10 | US |
| Best Of Booker T And The MG's | LP | Atlantic | 228015 | 1968 | £4 | £10 | |
| Booker T Set | LP | Stax | SXATS1015 | 1970 | £4 | £10 | |
| Bootleg | 7" | Atlantic | AT4033 | 1965 | £2 | £5 | |
| Chinese Checkers | 7" | London | HLK9784 | 1963 | £2 | £5 | |
| Chinese Checkers | 7" | Stax | 601026 | 1967 | £1.50 | £4 | |
| Doin' Our Thing | LP | Atlantic | 2464011 | 1968 | £5 | £12 | |
| Get Ready | LP | Atco | 228004 | 1969 | £4 | £10 | |
| Green Onions | LP | Atlantic | 587/588033 | 1966 | £4 | £10 | |
| Green Onions | LP | London | HAK8182 | 1964 | £8 | £20 | |
| Green Onions | 7" | Atlantic | 584088 | 1967 | £1.50 | £4 | |
| Green Onions | 7" | London | HLK9595 | 1962 | £2 | £5 | |
| Hip Hug-Her | LP | Stax | (STS)717 | 1967 | £4 | £10 | US |
| Hip Hugger | 7" | Stax | 601009 | 1967 | £1.50 | £4 | |
| In The Christmas Spirit | LP | Stax | (STS)713 | 1966 | £4 | £10 | US |
| Jelly Bread | 7" | London | HLK9670 | 1963 | £2 | £5 | |
| Jingle Bells | 7" | Atlantic | 584060 | 1966 | £1.50 | £4 | |
| McLemore Avenue | LP | Stax | SXATS1031 | 1970 | £4 | £10 | |
| My Sweet Potato | 7" | Atlantic | 584044 | 1966 | £1.50 | £4 | |
| R&B With Booker T Vol. 1 | 7" EP | London | REK1367 | 1963 | £6 | £12 | |
| R&B With Booker T Vol. 2 | 7" EP | Atlantic | AET6002 | 1964 | £6 | £12 | |
| Red Beans And Rice | 7" | Atlantic | AT4063 | 1966 | £2 | £5 | |
| Slim Jenkins' Place | 7" | Stax | 601018 | 1967 | £1.50 | £4 | |
| Soul Christmas | LP | Stax | 589013 | 1967 | £4 | £4 | |
| Soul Clap '69 | 7" | Stax | STAX127 | 1969 | £1.50 | £4 | |
| Soul Dressing | LP | Atlantic | 587047 | 1967 | £4 | £10 | |
| Soul Dressing | LP | Atlantic | ATL5027 | 1965 | £5 | £12 | |
| Soul Limbo | LP | Stax | (S)XATS1001 | 1968 | £5 | £12 | |
| Soul Limbo | 7" | Stax | STAX102 | 1968 | £1.50 | £4 | |
| Time Is Tight | 7" | Stax | STAX119 | 1969 | £1.50 | £4 | |
| Uptight | LP | Stax | (S)XATS1005 | 1968 | £5 | £12 | |

## BOOMERANGS

| Title | Format | Label | Catalogue | Year | | | Notes |
|---|---|---|---|---|---|---|---|
| Another Tear Falls | 7" | Fontana | TF555 | 1965 | £5 | £10 | |
| Rockin' Robin | 7" | Fontana | TF507 | 1964 | £7.50 | £15 | |

## BOOMERANGS (2)

| Title | Format | Label | Catalogue | Year | | | Notes |
|---|---|---|---|---|---|---|---|
| Beat Live | LP | Baccarola | S72660 | 1966 | £6 | £15 | German |
| Dream World | 7" | Pye | 7N17049 | 1966 | £2 | £5 | |

## BOOMTOWN RATS

| Title | Format | Label | Catalogue | Year | | | Notes |
|---|---|---|---|---|---|---|---|
| Rat Pack | 7" | Ensign | | 1978 | £4 | £8 | 6 singles in plastic wallet |

## BOONE, PAT

| Title | Format | Label | Catalogue | Year | | | Notes |
|---|---|---|---|---|---|---|---|
| Ain't That A Shame | 7" | London | HLD8172 | 1955 | £10 | £20 | |
| All Hands On Deck | 7" EP | London | RED1294 | 1961 | £2 | £5 | |
| Always You And Me | 7" EP | London | RED1384 | 1963 | £2 | £5 | |
| April Love | LP | London | HAD2078 | 1958 | £4 | £10 | |
| April Love | LP | London | HAD2078 | 1958 | £4 | £10 | |
| April Love | 7" | London | HLD8512 | 1957 | £1.50 | £4 | |

| Title | Format | Label | Catalogue | Year | | | Notes |
|---|---|---|---|---|---|---|---|
| Beach Girl | 7" | Dot | DS16658 | 1964 | £1.50 | £4 | |
| Boss Beat | LP | Dot | (D)DLP3594 | 1965 | £4 | £10 | |
| Don't Forbid Me | 7" | London | HLD8370 | 1957 | £4 | £8 | |
| Down Lovers Lane | 7" EP | London | RED1359 | 1963 | £2 | £5 | |
| Easy | 7" EP | London | RED1255 | 1960 | £2 | £5 | |
| For A Penny | 7" | London | SLD4002 | 1959 | £7.50 | £15 | export, stereo |
| Four By Pat | 7" EP | London | RED1109 | 1957 | £2 | £5 | |
| Friendly Persuasion | 7" | London | HLD8346 | 1956 | £4 | £8 | |
| Gee Whittakers | 7" | London | HLD8233 | 1956 | £5 | £10 | |
| Golden Hits | LP | London | HAD/SHD8031 | 1962 | £4 | £10 | |
| Good Rockin' Tonight | 7" | London | HLD8824 | 1959 | £1.50 | £4 | |
| Hey Baby | 7" EP | Dot | DEP20008 | 1966 | £2 | £5 | |
| Howdy | LP | London | HAD2030 | 1957 | £4 | £10 | |
| Howdy Part 1 | 7" EP | London | RED1081 | 1957 | £2 | £5 | |
| Howdy Part 2 | 7" EP | London | RED1082 | 1957 | £2 | £5 | |
| Howdy Part 3 | 7" EP | London | RED1119 | 1958 | £2 | £5 | |
| I Almost Lost My Mind | 7" | London | HLD8303 | 1956 | £4 | £8 | |
| I Love You Truly | LP | London | HAD/SHD8053 | 1963 | £4 | £10 | |
| I'll Be Home | 7" | London | HLD8253 | 1956 | £5 | £10 | |
| I'll See You In My Dreams | LP | London | HAD2452/ SAHD6240 | 1962 | £4 | £10 | |
| Johnny Will | 7" | London | HLD9461 | 1961 | £1.50 | £4 | |
| Just A Closer Walk With Thee | 7" EP | London | RED1095 | 1957 | £2 | £5 | |
| Latest And Greatest | 7" EP | London | RED1281 | 1961 | £2 | £5 | |
| Latest And Greatest No. 2 | 7" EP | London | RED1335 | 1962 | £2 | £5 | |
| Long Tall Sally | 7" | London | HLD8291 | 1956 | £5 | £10 | |
| Love Letters In The Sand | 7" | London | HLD8445 | 1957 | £1.50 | £4 | |
| Make The World Go Away | 7" EP | Dot | DEP20012 | 1966 | £2 | £5 | |
| Merry Christmas | 7" EP | London | RED1128 | 1958 | £2 | £5 | |
| Mexican Joe | 7" | London | HLD7121 | 1963 | £2.50 | £6 | export |
| Moody River | LP | London | HAD2382/ SAHD6182 | 1961 | £4 | £10 | |
| Moody River | 7" EP | London | RED1302 | 1961 | £2 | £5 | |
| Moonglow | LP | London | HAD2265/ SAHD6085 | 1960 | £4 | £10 | |
| Moonglow Pt. 1 | 7" EP | London | RED1267 | 1961 | £2 | £5 | |
| Moonglow Pt. 2 | 7" EP | London | RED1268 | 1961 | £2 | £5 | |
| No Arms Could Ever Hold You | 7" | London | HLD8197 | 1955 | £10 | £20 | |
| On Mike | 7" EP | London | RED1069 | 1957 | £2 | £5 | |
| Pat! | LP | London | HAD2049 | 1957 | £4 | £10 | |
| Pat Boone Sings The Hits | 7" EP | London | RED1063 | 1956 | £2 | £5 | |
| Pat Boone Sings The Hits No. 2 | 7" EP | London | RED1086 | 1957 | £2 | £5 | |
| Pat Boone Sings The Hits No. 3 | 7" EP | London | RED1112 | 1958 | £2 | £5 | |
| Pat Boone's Hits | 7" EP | Dot | DEP20001 | 1965 | £2 | £5 | |
| Pat Boone's Hits Vol. 2 | 7" EP | Dot | DEP20005 | 1965 | £2 | £5 | |
| Pat Part 1 | 7" EP | London | RED1132 | 1958 | £2.50 | £6 | |
| Pat Part 2 | 7" EP | London | RED1133 | 1958 | £2 | £5 | |
| Pat Sings | LP | London | HAD2161/ SAHD6013 | 1959 | £4 | £10 | |
| Pat Sings Movie Themes | 7" EP | London | RED1391 | 1963 | £2 | £5 | |
| Pat's Big Hits | LP | London | HAD2024 | 1957 | £5 | £12 | |
| Pat's Big Hits | 7" EP | London | RED1118 | 1958 | £2 | £5 | |
| Pat's Big Hits Vol. 2 | LP | London | HAD2098 | 1958 | £5 | £12 | |
| Remember You're Mine | 7" | London | HLD8479 | 1957 | £1.50 | £4 | |
| Rich In Love | 7" | London | HLD8316 | 1956 | £4 | £8 | |
| Send Me The Pillow You Dream On | 7" | London | HL7118 | 1963 | £2 | £5 | export |
| Side By Side | LP | London | HAD2210/ SAHD6057 | 1960 | £4 | £10 | with Shirley Boone |
| Side By Side | 7" EP | London | RED1220 | 1959 | £2 | £5 | with Shirley Boone |
| Sings Guess Who? | LP | London | HAD/SHD8109 | 1963 | £8 | £20 | |
| Sings Irving Berlin | LP | London | HAD2082/ SAHD6038 | 1958 | £4 | £10 | |
| Sings Irving Berlin Pt. 1 | 7" EP | London | RED1164 | 1958 | £2 | £5 | |
| Sings Irving Berlin Pt. 2 | 7" EP | London | RED1165 | 1958 | £2 | £5 | |
| Sings Irving Berlin Pt. 3 | 7" EP | London | RED1166 | 1958 | £2 | £5 | |
| Songs From Friendly Persuasion | 7" EP | London | RED1068 | 1957 | £2 | £5 | |
| Songs From Mardi Gras | 7" EP | London | RED1194 | 1959 | £2 | £4 | |
| Speedy Gonzales | 7" | London | HLD9573 | 1962 | £1.50 | £4 | |
| Stardust | LP | London | HAD2127/ SAHD6001 | 1958 | £4 | £10 | |
| Stardust Part 1 | 7" EP | London | RED1177 | 1959 | £2 | £5 | |
| Stardust Part 2 | 7" EP | London | RED1178 | 1959 | £2 | £5 | |
| Stardust Part 3 | 7" EP | London | RED1179 | 1959 | £2 | £5 | |
| State Fair | LP | London | HAD2453/ SAHD6241 | 1962 | £4 | £10 | |
| Sweet Little Sixteen | 7" EP | Dot | DEP20013 | 1966 | £2 | £5 | |
| Tenderly | LP | London | HAD2204/ SAHD6053 | 1960 | £4 | £10 | |
| This And That | LP | London | HAD2305 | 1961 | £4 | £10 | |
| Touch Of Your Lips | LP | London | HAD/SHD8153 | 1964 | £4 | £10 | |
| White Christmas | 7" | London | HLD8520 | 1957 | £1.50 | £4 | |
| Why Baby Why | 7" | London | HLD8404 | 1957 | £4 | £8 | |
| Wonderful Time Up There | 7" | London | HLD8574 | 1958 | £1.50 | £4 | |
| Yes Indeed | LP | London | HAD2144/ SAHD6010 | 1959 | £4 | £10 | |
| Yes Indeed Part 1 | 7" EP | London | RED1190 | 1959 | £2 | £5 | |
| Yes Indeed Part 2 | 7" EP | London | RED1191 | 1959 | £2 | £5 | |
| Yes Indeed Part 3 | 7" EP | London | RED1192 | 1959 | £2 | £5 | |

## BOOT

| Title | Format | Label | Cat. No. | Year | | | Notes |
|---|---|---|---|---|---|---|---|
| Boot | LP | Agape | 2601 | 1972 | £8 | £20 | US |

## BOOTH, BARRY

| Title | Format | Label | Cat. No. | Year | | | Notes |
|---|---|---|---|---|---|---|---|
| Diversions! | LP | Pye | NPL18216 | 1968 | £4 | £10 | |

## BOOTHE, KEN

| Title | Format | Label | Cat. No. | Year | | | Notes |
|---|---|---|---|---|---|---|---|
| Be Yourself | 7" | Bamboo | BAM8 | 1969 | £1.50 | £4 | Sound Dimension B side |
| Everybody Knows | 7" | Coxsone | CS7041 | 1968 | £5 | £10 | Gaylads B side |
| Feel Good | 7" | Studio One | SO2000 | 1967 | £6 | £12 | |
| Girl I Left Behind | 7" | Studio One | SO2041 | 1968 | £6 | £12 | Termites B side |
| Home Home Home | 7" | Coxsone | CS7020 | 1967 | £5 | £10 | Soul Brothers B side |
| I Remember Someone | 7" | Fab | FAB63 | 1968 | £4 | £8 | |
| Lady With The Starlight | 7" | High Note | HS003 | 1969 | £2.50 | £6 | Leslie Butler & Count Ossie B side |
| Lonely Teardrops | 7" | Coxsone | CS7006 | 1967 | £5 | £10 | |
| Mr. Rock Steady | LP | Studio One | SOL9001 | 1967 | £50 | £100 | |
| One I Love | 7" | Caltone | TONE107 | 1967 | £4 | £8 | |
| Original Six | 7" | Banana | BA352 | 1971 | £1.50 | £4 | |
| Pleading | 7" | Bamboo | BAM4 | 1969 | £1.50 | £4 | Sound Dimension B side |
| Puppet On A String | 7" | Studio One | SO2012 | 1967 | £6 | £12 | Roland Alphonso B side |
| Say You | 7" | Doctor Bird | DB1110 | 1967 | £5 | £10 | Lyn Taitt B side |
| Sherry | 7" | Coxsone | CS7094 | 1969 | £5 | £10 | |
| Tomorrow | 7" | Studio One | SO2053 | 1968 | £6 | £12 | |
| Train Is Coming | 7" | Island | WI3020 | 1966 | £5 | £10 | |
| When I Fall In Love | 7" | Studio One | SO2039 | 1968 | £6 | £12 | Heptones B side |
| Why Baby Why | 7" | Trojan | TR7716 | 1970 | £1.50 | £4 | |
| You Keep Me Hanging On | 7" | Coxsone | CS7043 | 1968 | £5 | £10 | Charmers B side |
| You're No Good | 7" | Ska Beat | JB248 | 1966 | £5 | £10 | Soulettes B side |
| You're On My Mind | 7" | Studio One | SO2073 | 1969 | £6 | £12 | Richard Ace B side |

## BOOTHE, MILTON

| Title | Format | Label | Cat. No. | Year | | | Notes |
|---|---|---|---|---|---|---|---|
| Lonely And Blue | 7" | Gas | GAS106 | 1969 | £2 | £5 | |

## BOOTLES

| Title | Format | Label | Cat. No. | Year | | | Notes |
|---|---|---|---|---|---|---|---|
| I'll Let You Hold My Hand | 7" | Vocalion | VN9216 | 1964 | £4 | £8 | |

## BOOTS

| Title | Format | Label | Cat. No. | Year | | | Notes |
|---|---|---|---|---|---|---|---|
| Animal In Me | 7" | CBS | 3550 | 1968 | £4 | £8 | |
| Beat With The Boots | LP | Telefunken | SLE14457 | 1965 | £37.50 | £75 | German |
| Here Are The Boots | LP | Telefunken | SLE14399 | 1966 | £25 | £50 | German |
| Keep Your Lovelight Burning | 7" | CBS | 3833 | 1968 | £5 | £10 | |

## BOOTS, DAVE

| Title | Format | Label | Cat. No. | Year | | | Notes |
|---|---|---|---|---|---|---|---|
| Green Satin And Gold | LP | Solent | SM013 | 196– | £50 | £100 | |

## BOOTSY'S RUBBER BAND

| Title | Format | Label | Cat. No. | Year | | | Notes |
|---|---|---|---|---|---|---|---|
| Ahh The Name Is Bootsy, Baby | LP | Warner Bros | K56302 | 1977 | £4 | £10 | |
| Bootsy? Player Of The Year | LP | Warner Bros | K56424 | 1978 | £4 | £10 | |
| One Giveth, The Count Taketh Away | LP | Warner Bros | K56998 | 1981 | £4 | £10 | |
| Stretchin' Out | LP | Warner Bros | K56200 | 1976 | £4 | £10 | |
| This Boot Is Made For Fonk-n | LP | Warner Bros | K56615 | 1979 | £4 | £10 | |
| Ultra Wave | LP | Warner Bros | BSK3433 | 1980 | £4 | £10 | US |

## BOOZE HOISTER BAND

| Title | Format | Label | Cat. No. | Year | | | Notes |
|---|---|---|---|---|---|---|---|
| Tavern Tales | LP | Peace Pie | | 1980 | £20 | £40 | Dutch |

## BOOZE HOISTER FOLK GROUP

| Title | Format | Label | Cat. No. | Year | | | Notes |
|---|---|---|---|---|---|---|---|
| More You Booze, The Double You See | LP | Crossroad | | 1978 | £100 | £200 | Dutch |

## BOOZERS

| Title | Format | Label | Cat. No. | Year | | | Notes |
|---|---|---|---|---|---|---|---|
| No No No | 7" EP | DiscAZ | | 1967 | £4 | £8 | French |

## BOP & THE BELTONES

| Title | Format | Label | Cat. No. | Year | | | Notes |
|---|---|---|---|---|---|---|---|
| Smile Like An Angel | 7" | Coxsone | CS7007 | 1967 | £5 | £10 | Soul Agents B side |

## BORBETOMAGUS

Borbetomagus are a band of extreme noise terrorists with a side-line in vaguely unsettling album covers, typically involving worms. Depending on one's point of view, the music is either extremely exhilarating or else nothing but a racket, but it has proved to be remarkably influential. The group's two saxophonists, Jim Sauter and Donald Dietrich, can also be found on an album (*Barefoot In The Head*) with Sonic Youth's Thurston Moore, who has no difficulty slotting his abrasive guitar into the general mêlée.

| Title | Format | Label | Cat. No. | Year | | | Notes |
|---|---|---|---|---|---|---|---|
| Barbed Wire Maggots | LP | Agaric | AG1983 | 1983 | £8 | £20 | US |
| Borbeto Jam | LP | Cadence | 1026 | 198– | £8 | £20 | US |
| Borbetomagus | LP | Agaric | AG1980 | 1980 | £10 | £25 | US |
| Borbetomagus | LP | Agaric | AG1982 | 1982 | £10 | £25 | US |
| Fish That Sparkling Bubble | LP | Agaric | AG1987 | 1987 | £8 | £20 | US |
| Industrial Strength | LP | Leo | 113 | 1984 | £8 | £20 | |
| New York Performances | LP | Agaric | AG1986 | 1986 | £8 | £20 | US |
| Seven Reasons For Tears | LP | Purge | 027 | 1986 | £8 | £20 | US |
| Work On What Has Been Spoiled | LP | Agaric | AG1981 | 1981 | £10 | £25 | US |
| Zurich | LP | Agaric | AG1984 | 1984 | £10 | £25 | US double |

## BORDERSONG

| | | | | | | | |
|---|---|---|---|---|---|---|---|
| Morning | LP | Real Good | 1001 | 1975 | £8 | £20 | US |

## BOSTIC, EARL

| | | | | | | | |
|---|---|---|---|---|---|---|---|
| Alto Magic | 7" EP | Parlophone | GEP8754 | 1958 | £2.50 | £6 | |
| Alto Magic In Hi-Fi | LP | King | 597 | 1958 | £8 | £20 | US |
| Alto Sax And Mambo Strings | 7" EP | Parlophone | GEP8565 | 1956 | £2 | £5 | |
| Alto-Tude | LP | King | 515 | 195– | £8 | £20 | US |
| Best Of Bostic | LP | King | 500 | 195– | £8 | £20 | US |
| Beyond The Blue Horizon | 7" | Parlophone | R4232 | 1956 | £1.50 | £4 | |
| Big Bostic Beat | 7" EP | Parlophone | GEP8701 | 1958 | £2 | £5 | |
| Blue Skies | 7" | Parlophone | MSP6119 | 1954 | £2.50 | £6 | |
| Bo Do Rock | 7" | Parlophone | R4208 | 1956 | £2 | £5 | |
| Bostic In Harlem | 7" EP | Parlophone | GEP8637 | 1957 | £2 | £5 | |
| Bostic Meets Doggett | 10" LP | Parlophone | PMD1054 | 1958 | £8 | £20 | |
| Bostic Rocks | LP | King | 571 | 1958 | £8 | £20 | US |
| Bostic Rocks | 10" LP | Parlophone | PMD1068 | 1958 | £8 | £20 | |
| Bostic Showcase Of Swinging Dance Hits | LP | King | 583 | 1958 | £8 | £20 | US |
| Bostic Workshop | LP | King | 613 | 1959 | £8 | £20 | US |
| Bubbin's Rock | 7" | Parlophone | R4278 | 1957 | £2 | £5 | |
| C'mon Dance With Earl Bostic | LP | King | 558 | 1958 | £8 | £20 | US |
| Dance Time | LP | King | 525 | 195– | £8 | £20 | US |
| Deep Purple | 7" | Parlophone | MSP6089 | 1954 | £4 | £8 | |
| Don't You Do It | 7" | Parlophone | MSP6105 | 1954 | £2.50 | £6 | |
| Earl Bostic | 7" EP | Parlophone | GEP8520 | 1955 | £2.50 | £6 | |
| Earl Bostic | 7" EP | Vogue | EPV1010 | 1955 | £5 | £10 | |
| Earl Bostic | 10" LP | Parlophone | PMD1016 | 1954 | £8 | £20 | |
| Earl Bostic And His Alto Sax No. 2 | 10" LP | Parlophone | PMD1040 | 1956 | £8 | £20 | |
| Earl Bostic And His Orchestra | 10" LP | Vogue | LDE100 | 1954 | £8 | £20 | |
| Earl's Imagination | 7" EP | Parlophone | GEP8548 | 1956 | £2 | £5 | |
| Flamingo | 7" EP | Parlophone | GEP8506 | 1954 | £2.50 | £6 | |
| Flamingo | 7" | Vogue | V2145 | 1956 | £4 | £8 | |
| For You | LP | King | 503 | 195– | £8 | £20 | US |
| Harlem Nocturne | 7" | Parlophone | R4263 | 1957 | £1.50 | £4 | |
| Honeymoon Night | 7" | Island | WI271 | 1966 | £2.50 | £6 | |
| Invitation To Dance | LP | King | 547 | 1957 | £8 | £20 | US |
| Jungle Drums | 7" | Parlophone | MSP6110 | 1954 | £2.50 | £6 | |
| Let's Dance With Earl Bostic | LP | King | 529 | 195– | £8 | £20 | US |
| Linger Awhile | 7" EP | Parlophone | GEP8513 | 1955 | £2.50 | £6 | |
| Mambostic | 7" | Parlophone | MSP6131 | 1954 | £4 | £8 | |
| Melody Of love | 7" | Parlophone | MSP6162 | 1955 | £2.50 | £6 | |
| Moonglow | 7" | Vogue | V2148 | 1956 | £4 | £8 | |
| Music A La Bostic No. 1 | 7" EP | Parlophone | GEP8571 | 1956 | £2 | £5 | |
| Music A La Bostic No. 2 | 7" EP | Parlophone | GEP8574 | 1956 | £2.50 | £6 | |
| Music A La Bostic No. 3 | 7" EP | Parlophone | GEP8603 | 1957 | £2.50 | £6 | |
| Off Shore | 7" | Parlophone | MSP6075 | 1954 | £4 | £8 | |
| Over The Waves Rock | 7" | Parlophone | R4460 | 1958 | £2 | £5 | |
| Plays The Sweet Side Of The Fantastic 50's | LP | King | 602 | 1959 | £8 | £20 | US |
| Rocking With Bostic | 7" EP | Parlophone | GEP8741 | 1958 | £2.50 | £6 | |
| Showcase Of Swinging Dance Hits | 10" LP | Parlophone | PMD1071 | 1959 | £5 | £12 | |
| Sweet Tunes Of The Fantastic Fifties | 10" LP | Parlophone | PMD1074 | 1959 | £5 | £12 | |
| Temptation | 7" | Parlophone | R4370 | 1957 | £1.50 | £4 | |
| Too Fine For Crying | 7" | Parlophone | R4305 | 1957 | £1.50 | £4 | |
| Tuxedo Junction | 7" | Ember | JBS708 | 1962 | £1.50 | £4 | |
| Velvet Sunset | 7" EP | Vogue | EPV1111 | 1956 | £2.50 | £6 | |
| Wrap It Up | 7" EP | Parlophone | GEP8539 | 1955 | £2.50 | £6 | |

## BOSTON

| | | | | | | | |
|---|---|---|---|---|---|---|---|
| Boston | LP | Epic | E99-34188 | 1978 | £4 | £10 | US picture disc |
| Can'tcha Say | CD-s | MCA | DMCA1150 | 1987 | £2 | £5 | |

## BOSTON CRABS

In an effort to make themselves stand out from the mass of mid-sixties British beat groups, the Boston Crabs favoured an intriguing assortment of stage costumes – the lead guitarist dressed as a country bumpkin, the drummer wore an asbestos fire-fighting suit, and the lead singer posed as a blind man in a wheelchair! Uniform red shirts and blue jeans for the second half proved the last to be indeed a pose. Not that any of this did the group much good, for even substantial airplay on pirate radio for their cover of the Lovin' Spoonful's 'You Didn't Have To Be So Nice' failed to give the Boston Crabs the success they sought.

| | | | | | | |
|---|---|---|---|---|---|---|
| As Long As I Have You | 7" | Columbia | DB7679 | 1965 | £4 | £8 |
| Down In Mexico | 7" | Columbia | DB7586 | 1965 | £4 | £8 |
| You Didn't Have To Be So Nice | 7" | Columbia | DB7830 | 1966 | £2.50 | £6 |

## BOSTON DEXTERS

| | | | | | | |
|---|---|---|---|---|---|---|
| I've Got Something To Tell You | 7" | Columbia | DB7498 | 1965 | £10 | £20 |
| I've Got Troubles Of My Own | 7" | Contemporary | CR103 | 1964 | £20 | £40 |
| La Bamba | 7" | Contemporary | CR101 | 1964 | £20 | £40 |
| Try Hard | 7" | Columbia | DB7641 | 1965 | £10 | £20 |
| You've Been Talking About Me | 7" | Contemporary | CR102 | 1964 | £20 | £40 |

## BOSWELL, CONNIE

| | | | | | | |
|---|---|---|---|---|---|---|
| If I Give My Heart To You | 7" | Brunswick | 05319 | 1954 | £1.50 | £4 |

## BOSWELL, EVE

| | | | | | | |
|---|---|---|---|---|---|---|
| Bobby | 7" | Parlophone | R4401 | 1958 | £1.50 | £4 |
| Chantez Chantez | 7" | Parlophone | R4299 | 1957 | £2.50 | £6 |
| Cookie | 7" | Parlophone | MSP6220 | 1956 | £5 | £10 |

| | | | | | | | |
|---|---|---|---|---|---|---|---|
| Enchanting Eve | 7" EP | Parlophone | GEP8601 | 1957 | £5 | £10 | |
| Following The Sun Around | LP | Parlophone | PMC1105 | 1959 | £8 | £20 | |
| Gypsy In My Soul | 7" | Parlophone | R4341 | 1957 | £2 | £5 | |
| Keeping Cool With Lemonade | 7" | Parlophone | MSP6245 | 1956 | £2.50 | £6 | |
| Left Right Out Of Your Heart | 7" | Parlophone | R4455 | 1958 | £1.50 | £4 | |
| Love Me Again | 7" | Parlophone | R4414 | 1958 | £1.50 | £4 | |
| Pam-Poo-Dey | 7" | Parlophone | MSP6158 | 1955 | £5 | £10 | |
| Saries Marais | 7" | Parlophone | MSP6250 | 1956 | £2.50 | £6 | |
| Sentimental Eve | LP | Parlophone | PMC1038 | 1957 | £8 | £20 | |
| Showcase | 7" EP | Parlophone | GEP8690 | 1958 | £5 | £10 | |
| Showcase No. 2 | 7" EP | Parlophone | GEP8717 | 1958 | £5 | £10 | |
| Sugar And Spice | 10" LP | Parlophone | PMD1039 | 1957 | £10 | £25 | |
| Sugar Bush | 7" | Parlophone | MSP6006 | 1953 | £6 | £12 | |
| Swedish Polka | 7" | Parlophone | R4362 | 1957 | £1.50 | £4 | |
| Tika Tika Tok | 7" | Parlophone | MSP6160 | 1955 | £5 | £10 | |
| Tra La La | 7" | Parlophone | R4275 | 1957 | £4 | £8 | |
| True Love | 7" | Parlophone | R4230 | 1956 | £2.50 | £6 | |
| With All My Heart | 7" | Parlophone | R4328 | 1957 | £2 | £5 | |
| Young And Foolish | 7" | Parlophone | MSP6208 | 1956 | £5 | £10 | |

## BOTHY BAND

| | | | | | | | |
|---|---|---|---|---|---|---|---|
| Afterhours | LP | Polydor | 2383530 | 1979 | £4 | £10 | |
| Bothy Band | LP | Polydor | 2383379 | 1975 | £4 | £10 | |
| Old Hag You Have Killed Me | LP | Polydor | 2383417 | 1976 | £4 | £10 | |
| Out Of The Wind And Into The Sun | LP | Polydor | 2383456 | 1977 | £4 | £10 | |

## BOTTCHER, GERD

| | | | | | | | |
|---|---|---|---|---|---|---|---|
| Die Grossen Efolge | LP | Decca | 357 | 1966 | £20 | £40 | German |
| Gerd Bottcher | LP | Decca | BLK16217P | 1963 | £15 | £30 | German |

## BOUDEWIJN DE GROOT

| | | | | | | | |
|---|---|---|---|---|---|---|---|
| Nacht En Outiz | LP | Decca | | 1969 | £30 | £60 | Dutch |

## BOURBON STREET ALL STAR DIXIELANDERS

| | | | | | | | |
|---|---|---|---|---|---|---|---|
| Bourbon Street All Star Dixielanders | LP | HMV | CLP1121 | 1957 | £4 | £10 | |

## BOW STREET RUNNERS

| | | | | | | | |
|---|---|---|---|---|---|---|---|
| Bow Street Runners | LP | B.T.Puppy | BTPS1026 | 1969 | £700 | £1000 | US |

## BOW WOW WOW

| | | | | | | | |
|---|---|---|---|---|---|---|---|
| Mile High Club | 7" | Tour D'Eiffel | TE001 | 1981 | £2 | £5 | |

## BOWEN, JIMMY

| | | | | | | | |
|---|---|---|---|---|---|---|---|
| Crossover | 7" | Columbia | DB4027 | 1957 | £7.50 | £15 | |
| I'm Sticking With You | 7" | Columbia | DB3915 | 1957 | £15 | £30 | |
| Jimmy Bowen | LP | Roulette | R.25004 | 1957 | £25 | £50 | US |
| Meet Jimmy Bowen | 7" EP | Columbia | SEG7757 | 1958 | £25 | £50 | |
| Meet Jimmy Bowen No. 2 | 7" EP | Columbia | SEG7793 | 1958 | £25 | £50 | |
| Spanish Cricket | 7" | Reprise | RS23043 | 1965 | £15 | £30 | |
| Sunday Morning With The Comics | LP | Reprise | R(S)6210 | 1966 | £6 | £15 | US |
| Two Step | 7" | Columbia | DB4184 | 1958 | £5 | £10 | |
| Warm Up To Me Baby | 7" | Columbia | DB3984 | 1957 | £12.50 | £25 | |

## BOWERS, BEN

| | | | | | | | |
|---|---|---|---|---|---|---|---|
| Big Ben Blues | 7" EP | Pye | NJE1001 | 1956 | £2 | £5 | |
| Country Boy | 7" | Parlophone | R4317 | 1957 | £1.50 | £4 | |
| Kentuckian Song | 7" | Columbia | SCM5192 | 1955 | £2.50 | £6 | |
| Kings Of Calypso Vol. 4 | 7" EP | Pye | NEP24069 | 1958 | £2 | £5 | |

## BOWIE, DAVID

David Bowie achieved popularity a fairly long time after starting to make records, so that there are a considerable number of rare and expensive records from the early years of his career for the Bowie completist to obtain. Perhaps the most famous of these is the original cover of the LP *The Man Who Sold The World*, which portrays Bowie casually attired in a dress. 'It's a man's dress,' he explained at the time. The uncensored cover of *Diamond Dogs*, on which Bowie is painted as a creature half man and half dog, has the dog's genitalia intact – these were airbrushed out on all but the first issues. More recently, Bowie's RCA albums were issued on compact disc and then speedily withdrawn due to a royalty dispute. These became, in consequence, among the first CDs to acquire collectors' values.

| | | | | | | | |
|---|---|---|---|---|---|---|---|
| 1980 All Clear | LP | RCA | DJL13545 | 1980 | £8 | £20 | US promo |
| Absolute Beginners | CD-s | Virgin | CDT20 | 1988 | £2 | £5 | 3" single |
| Absolute Beginners | 7" | Virgin | VSS838 | 1986 | £1.50 | £4 | square picture disc |
| Aladdin Sane | LP | RCA | BOPIC1 | 1984 | £6 | £15 | picture disc |
| Aladdin Sane | CD | RCA | PD83890 | 1985 | £15 | £30 | |
| All Saints | CD | private | | 1993 | £180 | £300 | |
| Black Tie, White Noise | CD | Savage | | 1993 | £25 | £50 | US promo with interview |
| Black Tie, White Noise | CD | Savage | | 1994 | £20 | £40 | Japanese with 4 extra tracks |
| Can't Help Thinking About Me | 7" | Pye | 7N17020 | 1966 | £75 | £150 | |
| ChangesOneBowie | LP | RCA | RS1055 | 1976 | £8 | £20 | with sax version of 'John' |
| ChangesOneBowie | CD | RCA | PD81732 | 1985 | £15 | £30 | |
| ChangesTwoBowie | LP & cass | RCA | DF1 | 1983 | £6 | £15 | LP & cassette in holder |
| ChangesTwoBowie | CD | RCA | PD84202 | 1985 | £15 | £30 | |
| China Girl | CD-s | Virgin | VVCS8 | 1990 | £2 | £5 | |
| David Bowie | LP | Deram | DML1007 | 1967 | £100 | £200 | mono |
| David Bowie | LP | Deram | SML1007 | 1967 | £150 | £250 | stereo |

| Title | Format | Label | Catalogue | Year | | | Notes |
|---|---|---|---|---|---|---|---|
| David Bowie | LP | Philips | SBL7912 | 1969 | £75 | £150 | |
| David Bowie | CD | Deram | 8000872 | 1984 | £30 | £60 | white title |
| David Bowie Now | LP | RCA | DJL12697 | 1977 | £10 | £25 | US promo |
| David Bowie Radio Special Vol. 1 | LP | RCA | DJL13829 | 1980 | £10 | £25 | US promo |
| David Live | CD | RCA | PD80771 | 1985 | £15 | £30 | |
| Diamond Dogs | LP | RCA | APL10576 | 1974 | £150 | £250 | uncensored cover |
| Diamond Dogs | LP | RCA | BOPIC5 | 1984 | £6 | £15 | picture disc |
| Diamond Dogs | CD | RCA | PD83859 | 1985 | £15 | £30 | |
| DJ | 7" | RCA | BOW3 | 1979 | £7.50 | £15 | picture sleeve, green vinyl |
| Do Anything You Say | 7" | Pye | 7N17079 | 1966 | £210 | £350 | best auctioned |
| Do Anything You Say | 7" | Pye | 7NX8002 | 1972 | £5 | £10 | picture sleeve |
| Evening With David Bowie | LP | RCA | DJL13016 | 1978 | £10 | £25 | US promo |
| Fame 90 | CD-s | EMI | CDFAME90 | 1990 | £2 | £5 | |
| Fame And Fashion | LP | RCA | PD84919 | 1985 | £30 | £60 | |
| Fashions | 7" | RCA | BOW100 | 1982 | £20 | £40 | set of 10 picture discs in folder |
| Golden Years | CD | RCA | PD84792 | 1985 | £8 | £20 | |
| Heart's Filthy Lesson | CD-s | fan club | | 1995 | £4 | £10 | shaped disc |
| Helden | 7" | RCA | PB9168 | 1978 | £2 | £5 | sung in German |
| Heroes | CD | RCA | PD83857 | 1985 | £8 | £20 | |
| Heros | 7" | RCA | PB9167 | 1978 | £2 | £5 | sung in French |
| Holy Holy | 7" | Mercury | 6052049 | 1971 | £75 | £150 | |
| Hunky Dory | LP | RCA | BOPIC2 | 1984 | £6 | £15 | picture disc |
| Hunky Dory | CD | RCA | PD84623 | 1985 | £15 | £30 | |
| I Dig Everything | 7" | Pye | 7N17157 | 1966 | £210 | £350 | best auctioned |
| I Pity The Fool | 7" | Parlophone | R5250 | 1965 | £210 | £350 | credited to the Manish Boys, best auctioned |
| I Pity The Fool | CD-s | See For Miles... | SEACD1 | 1985 | £2 | £5 | credited to the Manish Boys |
| Laughing Gnome | 7" | Deram | DM123 | 1967 | £37.50 | £75 | matrix no. upside down on label |
| Let's Dance | LP | Mobile Fidelity | MFSL1083 | 1982 | £5 | £12 | US audiophile |
| Let's Dance | LP | RCA | UK83 | 1983 | £100 | £200 | numbered promo |
| Let's Dance | CD | EMI | CDP7460022 | 1984 | £5 | £12 | |
| Let's Talk | LP | EMI | SPRO9960/1 | 1983 | £10 | £25 | US promo |
| Life On Mars | 7" | RCA | RCA2316 | 1973 | £2.50 | £6 | picture sleeve |
| Lifetimes | LP | RCA | LIFETIMES1 | 1983 | £10 | £25 | promo |
| Liza Jane | 7" | Vocalion | V9221 | 1964 | £400 | £600 | credited to Davie Jones & The King Bees, best auctioned |
| Lodger | CD | RCA | PD84234 | 1985 | £8 | £20 | |
| Love You Till Tuesday | 7" | Deram | DM135 | 1967 | £75 | £150 | |
| Loving The Alien | 7" | EMI | EAP195 | 1984 | £1.50 | £4 | shaped picture disc |
| Low | CD | RCA | PD83856 | 1985 | £10 | £25 | |
| Man Of Words, Man Of Music | LP | Mercury | SR61246 | 1969 | £50 | £100 | US |
| Man Who Sold The World | LP | Mercury | 61325 | 1971 | £10 | £25 | US, cartoon cover, stamped matrix no. |
| Man Who Sold The World | LP | Mercury | 6338041 | 1970 | £180 | £300 | German, round sleeve |
| Man Who Sold The World | LP | Mercury | 6338041 | 1971 | £100 | £200 | dress cover |
| Man Who Sold The World | LP | RCA | LSP4816 | 1971 | £4 | £10 | with inner and poster |
| Man Who Sold The World | CD | RCA | PD84654 | 1985 | £15 | £30 | |
| Man Who Sold The World | cass | Mercury | 6338041 | 1971 | £6 | £15 | dress cover |
| Memory Of A Free Festival | 7" | Mercury | 6052026 | 1970 | £75 | £150 | |
| Narrates Peter And The Wolf | LP | RCA | ARLI2743 | 1978 | £4 | £10 | US green vinyl |
| Narrates Peter And The Wolf | CD | RCA | PD82743 | 1985 | £8 | £20 | |
| Never Let Me Down | CD | EMI | CDAMLS3117 | 1987 | £5 | £12 | |
| Pin-Ups | LP | RCA | BOPIC4 | 1984 | £6 | £15 | picture disc |
| Pin-Ups | CD | RCA | PD84653 | 1985 | £15 | £30 | |
| Portrait Of A Star | LP | RCA | PL37700 | 1982 | £10 | £25 | French 3 LP boxed set |
| Prettiest Star | 7" | Mercury | MF1135 | 1970 | £75 | £150 | |
| Ragazza Sola, Ragazza Solo | 7" | Philips | BW704208 | 1969 | £50 | £100 | sung in Italian |
| Ragazza Sola, Ragazza Solo | 7" | Philips | BW704208 | 1969 | £75 | £150 | sung in Italian, picture sleeve, black label |
| Ragazza Sola, Ragazza Solo | 7" | Philips | BW704208 | 1969 | £62.50 | £125 | sung in Italian, picture sleeve, blue label |
| Rare Bowie | LP | RCA | PL45406 | 1982 | £8 | £20 | hand stamped edition |
| Rubber Band | 7" | Deram | DM107 | 1966 | £75 | £150 | |
| Scary Monsters | LP | RCA | BOWLP2 | 1980 | £100 | £200 | purple vinyl |
| Scary Monsters | CD | RCA | PD83647 | 1985 | £15 | £30 | |
| Scary Monsters Interview | LP | RCA | DJL13840 | 1980 | £10 | £25 | US promo |
| Selections From The Singles Collection | CD | EMI | BOWIE1 | 1993 | £8 | £20 | promo sampler |
| Sound And Vision | CD | Ryko | | 1989 | £100 | £200 | US triple CDV box set, wooden box, signed certificate |
| Space Oddity | CD | RCA | PD84813 | 1985 | £15 | £30 | |
| Space Oddity | 7" | Philips | BF1801 | 1969 | £2 | £5 | |
| Space Oddity | 7" | Philips | BF1801 | 1969 | £2.50 | £6 | stereo |
| Space Oddity | 7" | RCA | RCA2593 | 1975 | £2 | £5 | picture sleeve |
| Stage | LP | RCA | PL02913 | 1978 | £8 | £20 | double, green or blue vinyl |
| Stage | LP | RCA | PL02913 | 1978 | £6 | £15 | double, yellow vinyl |
| Stage | CD | RCA | PD89002 | 1985 | £15 | £30 | |
| Starman | 7" | RCA | RCA2199 | 1972 | £15 | £30 | picture sleeve |
| Station To Station | LP | RCA | APLI1327 | 1976 | £100 | £200 | US multicoloured vinyl |
| Station To Station | CD | RCA | PD81327 | 1985 | £15 | £30 | |
| Suffragette City | 7" | RCA | RCA2726 | 1976 | £4 | £8 | picture sleeve |
| Tonight | CD | EMI | CDP7460472 | 1984 | £5 | £12 | |

## BOYLES BROTHERS
Introducing The Boyles Brothers ............... LP ...... International      6801 ..................... 1968 £62.50.. £125 ........................ US
                                                                     Artists .............

## BOYS
The Boys, who released 'It Ain't Fair' in 1964, became the Action shortly afterwards.

It Ain't Fair............................................. 7" ......· Pye ................. 7N15726 ............. 1964 £15......... £30 ............................

## BOYS (2)
Kamikaze................................................. 7" ...... Safari ............. SAFE21................. 1979 £1.50....... £4 .............with booklet

## BOYS (3)
Polaris .................................................... 7" ...... Parlophone...... R5027 ................... 1963 £6............ £12 ...............................

## BOYS (4)
Happy Days ............................................ 7" ...... private............. .............................. 1988 £5............ £10 ...............................

## BOYS BLUE
Take A Heart........................................... 7" ...... HMV............... POP1427 ............. 1965 £20............ £40 ...............................

## BOYS OF THE LOUGH
Boys Of The Lough................................. LP ...... Trailer............. LER2086 ............. 1973 £4............ £10 ...............................
Good Friends Good Music ....................... LP ...... Transatlantic ... TRA354 ............. 1977 £4............ £10 ...............................
Piper's Broken Finger ............................. LP ...... Transatlantic ... TRA333 ............. 1976 £4............ £10 ...............................
Recorded Live ........................................ LP ...... Transatlantic ... TRA296 ............. 1975 £4............ £10 ...............................
Second Album ........................................ LP ...... Trailer............. LER2090 ............. 1974 £4............ £10 ...............................

## BOYZONE
Working My Way Back To You .............. CD-s .. Polydor........... 8532462 ................. 1994 £6............ £15 ........................Irish

## BOZ
Baby Song.............................................. 7" ...... Columbia ...... DB7972 ............... 1966 £1.50....... £4 ...............................
I Shall Be Released ................................ 7" ...... Columbia ...... DB8406 ............... 1968 £1.50....... £4 ...............................
Isn't That So ......................................... 7" ...... Columbia ...... DB7832 ............... 1966 £1.50....... £4 ...............................
Light My Fire ........................................ 7" ...... Columbia ...... DB8468 ............... 1968 £1.50....... £4 ...............................
Meeting Time ........................................ 7" ...... Columbia ...... DB7889 ............... 1966 £1.50....... £4 ...............................
Pinnochio .............................................. 7" ...... Columbia ...... DB7941 ............... 1966 £1.50....... £4 ...............................

## BRACE, JANET
Teach Me Tonight .................................. 7" ...... Brunswick ...... 05272................... 1955 £1.50....... £4 ...............................

## BRACEY, ISHMAN
RCA Victor Race Series Vol. 1 ............... 7" EP . RCA .............. RCX7167 ............. 1964 £2............ £5 ...............................

## BRACKEN
Prince Of The Northlands........................ LP ...... Look............... LKLP6438 ............. 1979 £37.50.... £75 ...............................

## BRADFORD, BOBBY
Love's Dream.......................................... LP ...... Emanem........... 302 ..................... 1974 £6............ £15 ...............................

## BRADFORD, PROFESSOR ALEX
Angel On Vacation.................................. LP ...... Stateside ......... SL10083................. 1964 £4............ £10 ...............................
One Step ................................................ LP ...... Stateside ......... SL10047................. 1963 £4............ £10 ...............................
Too Close To Heaven ............................. 7" EP . London .......... REU1357............... 1963 £2............ £5 ...............................

## BRADLEY, JAN
Mama Didn't Lie ................................... 7" ...... Pye ................. 7N25182 ............... 1963 £5............ £10 ...............................

## BRADLEY, OWEN
Big Guitar.............................................. 7" ...... Brunswick ...... 05736................... 1958 £2.50....... £6 ...............................

## BRADSHAW, SONNY
Festival Jump Up.................................... 7" ...... Duke .............. DK1003 ............... 1963 £2............ £5 ...............................

## BRADSHAW, TINY
Breaking Up The House .......................... 78...... Vogue.............. V2146.................. 1952 £2............ £5 ...............................
Great Composer...................................... LP ...... King ............... 653 ..................... 1959 £10............ £25 ........................ US
Off And On............................................ 10" LP King ............... 29574.................. 195– £50............ £100 ........................ US
Overflow................................................ 7" ...... Parlophone...... MSP6145 ............. 1955 £4............ £8 ...............................
Pompton Turnpike .................................. 7" EP . Parlophone...... GEP8552.............. 1956 £6............ £12 ...............................
Selections............................................... LP ...... King ............... 395501................. 195– £20............ £40 ........................ US
Spider Web............................................. 7" ...... Parlophone...... MSP6118 ............. 1954 £5............ £10 ...............................
Train Kept A Rolling ............................. 7" EP . Parlophone...... GEP8507.............. 1954 £10............ £20 ...............................
Twenty-Four Great Songs ....................... LP ...... King ............... 953 ..................... 1966 £5............ £12 ........................ US

## BRADSHAW, TINY & WYNONIE HARRIS
Kings Of Rhythm And Blues.................... LP ...... Polydor........... 623273 ................. 1970 £4............ £10 ...............................

## BRADY, BOB & THE CONCHORDS
Everybody Goin' To A Love-In ............... 7" ...... Bell................. BLL1025 ............. 1968 £2............ £5 ...............................

## BRADY, PAUL
Welcome Here Kind Stranger................... LP ...... Mulligan ......... LUN024 ............. 1974 £5............ £12 ........................Irish

## BRAFF, RUBY

| | | | | | | |
|---|---|---|---|---|---|---|
| Hustlin' And Bustlin' | LP | Vogue | LAE12051 | 1957 | £10 | £25 |
| Inventions In Jazz Part 2 | 10" LP | Vanguard | PPT12022 | 1958 | £10 | £25 ..... *with Ellis Larkins* |
| Newport Jazz Festival 1957 | LP | Columbia | 33CX10104 | 1958 | £6 | £15 ...... *side 2 by Bobby Henderson* |
| Ruby Braff All Stars | LP | Philips | BBL7130 | 1957 | £5 | £12 |
| Ruby Braff And The Dixie Victors | LP | HMV | CLP1091 | 1956 | £6 | £15 |
| Ruby Braff Orchestra | 10" LP | London | LZN14022 | 1956 | £10 | £25 |
| Ruby Braff Sextet | 10" LP | London | LZN14028 | 1956 | £10 | £25 |
| Ruby Braff Special | LP | Vanguard | PPL11003 | 1956 | £6 | £15 |

## BRAGG, BILLY

| | | | | | | |
|---|---|---|---|---|---|---|
| Peel Sessions | CD-s | Strange Fruit | SFPSCD027 | 1988 | £2 | £5 |
| Sexuality | CD-s | Go! Discs | GODCD56 | 1991 | £2 | £5 |
| You Woke Up My Neighbourhood | CD-s | Go! Discs | GODCD60 | 1991 | £2 | £5 |

## BRAGGS, AL TNT

| | | | | | | |
|---|---|---|---|---|---|---|
| Al TNT Braggs | 7" EP | Vocalion | VEP170163 | 1965 | £10 | £20 |
| Earthquake | 7" | Action | ACT4506 | 1968 | £2 | £5 |
| Earthquake | 7" | Vocalion | VP9278 | 1966 | £2.50 | £6 |
| I'm A Good Man | 7" | Action | ACT4526 | 1969 | £1.50 | £4 |

## BRAHAM, ERNEL

| | | | | | | |
|---|---|---|---|---|---|---|
| Musical Fight | 7" | Rio | R79 | 1966 | £2.50 | £6 |

## BRAIN

The Brain's 'Nightmares In Red' is not so much psychedelic as lunatic. It is in fact an early recorded effort by the brothers Giles – prior to them joining forces with guitarist Robert Fripp and beginning the rehearsals that led to the debut of King Crimson.

| | | | | | | |
|---|---|---|---|---|---|---|
| Nightmares In Red | 7" | Parlophone | R5595 | 1967 | £37.50 | £75 |

## BRAINBOX

| | | | | | | |
|---|---|---|---|---|---|---|
| Best Of Brainbox | LP | EMI | 05424327 | 1972 | £6 | £15 ..... *German* |
| Brainbox | LP | Parlophone | PCS7094 | 1970 | £15 | £30 |
| Down Man | 7" | Parlophone | R5775 | 1969 | £2 | £5 |
| Parts | LP | Harvest | 05624551 | 1972 | £6 | £15 ..... *German* |
| To You | 7" | Parlophone | R5842 | 1970 | £1.50 | £4 |

## BRAINCHILD

| | | | | | | |
|---|---|---|---|---|---|---|
| Healing Of The Lunatic Owl | LP | A&M | AMLS979 | 1970 | £20 | £40 |

## BRAINIAC FIVE

| | | | | | | |
|---|---|---|---|---|---|---|
| Mushy Doubt | 7" | Roach | RREP5001 | 1978 | £2.50 | £6 |
| Working | 7" | Roach | RR5002 | 1980 | £2 | £5 |

## BRAINSTORM

| | | | | | | |
|---|---|---|---|---|---|---|
| Second Smile | LP | Spiegelei | 28596 | 1974 | £4 | £10 ..... *German* |
| Smile A While | LP | Spiegelei | 28505 | 1972 | £4 | £10 ..... *German* |

## BRAINTICKET

| | | | | | | |
|---|---|---|---|---|---|---|
| Celestial Ocean | LP | RCA | SF8398 | 1974 | £6 | £15 |
| Cotton Wood Hill | LP | Bellaphon | BLPS19019 | 1971 | £8 | £20 ..... *German double* |
| Psychonaut | LP | Bellaphon | BLPS19104 | 1972 | £6 | £15 ..... *German* |

## BRAITH, GEORGE

| | | | | | | |
|---|---|---|---|---|---|---|
| Extension | LP | Blue Note | BLP/BST84171 | 1964 | £15 | £30 |
| Soul Dream | LP | Blue Note | BLP/BST84161 | 1964 | £15 | £30 |
| Two Souls In One | LP | Blue Note | BLP/BST84148 | 1963 | £15 | £30 |

## BRAM STOKER

| | | | | | | |
|---|---|---|---|---|---|---|
| Hard Rock Spectacular | LP | Windmill | WMD117 | 1972 | £20 | £40 |

## BRAMLETT, DELANEY

| | | | | | | |
|---|---|---|---|---|---|---|
| Heartbreak Hotel | 7" | Vocalion | VN9227 | 1964 | £4 | £8 |
| Liverpool Lou | 7" | Vocalion | VN9237 | 1965 | £7.50 | £15 |

## BRAN

| | | | | | | |
|---|---|---|---|---|---|---|
| Ail Ddechra | LP | Sain | 1038M | 1974 | £10 | £25 |
| Hedfan | LP | Sain | 1070M | 1976 | £10 | £25 |

## BRAND

| | | | | | | |
|---|---|---|---|---|---|---|
| I'm A Lover Not A Fighter | 7" | Piccadilly | 7N35216 | 1965 | £37.50 | £75 ..... *2 different B sides* |

## BRAND, DOLLAR

| | | | | | | |
|---|---|---|---|---|---|---|
| Anatomy Of A South African Village | LP | Fontana | 688314ZL | 1964 | £4 | £10 |

## BRANDON, JOHNNY

| | | | | | | |
|---|---|---|---|---|---|---|
| Hits | 7" EP | Pye | NEP24003 | 1955 | £5 | £10 |
| Shim Sham Shuffle | 7" | Parlophone | R4207 | 1956 | £2 | £5 |

## BRANDON, VERN

| | | | | | | |
|---|---|---|---|---|---|---|
| Gotta Know The Reason | 7" | Decca | F11472 | 1962 | £5 | £10 |

## BRANDY BOYS

| | | | | | | |
|---|---|---|---|---|---|---|
| Gale Winds | 7" | Columbia | DB7507 | 1965 | £2.50 | £6 |

## BRANDYWINE BRIDGE
| | | | | | | | | |
|---|---|---|---|---|---|---|---|---|
| English Meadow | LP | Cottage | COT321 | 1978 | £8 | £20 | | |
| Grey Lady | LP | Cottage | COT311 | 1977 | £8 | £20 | | |

## BRANTLEY, JOHNNY
| | | | | | | | |
|---|---|---|---|---|---|---|---|
| Place | 7" | London | HLU8606 | 1958 | £5 | £10 | |

## BRASS MONKEY
| | | | | | | | |
|---|---|---|---|---|---|---|---|
| Brass Monkey | LP | Topic | 12TS431 | 1983 | £4 | £10 | |

## BRASS TACKS
| | | | | | | | |
|---|---|---|---|---|---|---|---|
| I'll Keep Holding On | 7" | Transatlantic | BIG110 | 1968 | £1.50 | £4 | |

## BRASSEUR, ANDRE
| | | | | | | | |
|---|---|---|---|---|---|---|---|
| Early Bird | 7" | Pye | 7N25332 | 1965 | £2 | £5 | |

## BRAUN, CHRIS
| | | | | | | | | |
|---|---|---|---|---|---|---|---|---|
| Both Sides | LP | BASF | 20213994 | 1972 | £4 | £10 | | German |
| Foreign Lady | LP | Pan | 87586 | 1973 | £4 | £10 | | German |

## BRAUTIGAN, RICHARD
Richard Brautigan is an American writer whose whimsically poetic prose style struck something of a chord in the late sixties and early seventies. *Trout Fishing In America* is perhaps his best-known book, but his reading of extracts from it failed to achieve the success on Apple that was intended.

| | | | | | | | | |
|---|---|---|---|---|---|---|---|---|
| Listening To Richard Brautigan | LP | Apple | ZAPPLE03 | 1969 | £150 | £250 | | test pressing |
| Listening To Richard Brautigan | LP | Straight | ST424 | 1969 | £6 | £15 | | US |

## BRAVE NEW WORLD
| | | | | | | | | |
|---|---|---|---|---|---|---|---|---|
| Impressions On Reading Aldous Huxley | LP | Vertigo | 6360606 | 1972 | £25 | £50 | | German |

## BRAVO, CEDRIC
| | | | | | | | |
|---|---|---|---|---|---|---|---|
| Merry Christmas | 7" | Ska Beat | JB229 | 1965 | £5 | £10 | |

## BRAXTON, ANTHONY
Anthony Braxton's forbiddingly intellectual approach to jazz improvisation and composition is shot through with a pleasing eccentricity. Many of his pieces have titles that are like molecular diagrams or mathematical formulae – some even comprise little pictures of people and buildings and suchlike. Then there is his plan to write music for orchestras situated on different planets . . . The collectable albums listed here are just the earliest in a huge and still growing catalogue.

| | | | | | | | | |
|---|---|---|---|---|---|---|---|---|
| Anthony Braxton | LP | BYG | 529315 | 1970 | £6 | £15 | | French |
| Donna Lee | LP | America | 30AM6122 | 1972 | £5 | £12 | | |
| For Alto | LP | Delmark | DS420/1 | 1971 | £8 | £20 | | double |
| This Time | LP | BYG | 529347 | 1971 | £6 | £15 | | French |
| Three Compositions Of New Jazz | LP | Delmark | DS415 | 1968 | £6 | £15 | | |

## BRAZIER, PRISCILLA
| | | | | | | | |
|---|---|---|---|---|---|---|---|
| Priscilla Brazier | LP | Dovetail | DOVE9 | 1974 | £8 | £20 | |
| Something Beautiful | LP | Key | KL038 | 1976 | £8 | £20 | |

## BREAD, LOVE & DREAMS
| | | | | | | | |
|---|---|---|---|---|---|---|---|
| Amarylis | LP | Decca | SKL5081 | 1971 | £150 | £250 | |
| Bread, Love & Dreams | LP | Decca | SKL5008 | 1969 | £20 | £40 | |
| Strange Tale Of Captain Shannon | LP | Decca | LK/SKL5048 | 1970 | £20 | £40 | |
| Switch Out The Sun | 7" | Decca | F12958 | 1969 | £1.50 | £4 | |

## BREAD & BEER BAND
The high value of the Bread and Beer Band's single derives from the fact that the band's pianist was one Reg Dwight (who was shortly to adopt the stage name Elton John). There is an LP by the band, but it is believed that only one copy of this exists. It came up for sale at one of the London rock auctions at the end of the eighties and fetched £1700.

| | | | | | | | |
|---|---|---|---|---|---|---|---|
| Dick Barton Theme | 7" | Decca | F12891 | 1969 | £50 | £100 | |
| Dick Barton Theme | 7" | Decca | F13354 | 1973 | £20 | £40 | |

## BREAKAWAYS
| | | | | | | | | |
|---|---|---|---|---|---|---|---|---|
| Danny Boy | 7" | Pye | 7N15973 | 1965 | £1.50 | £4 | | |
| He Doesn't Love Me | 7" | Pye | 7N15618 | 1964 | £1.50 | £4 | | |
| He's A Rebel | 7" | Pye | 7N15471 | 1962 | £1.50 | £4 | | |
| Here She Comes | 7" | Pye | 7N15585 | 1963 | £1.50 | £4 | | |
| That Boy Of Mine | 7" EP | Pye | PNV24119 | 1964 | £10 | £20 | | French |

## BREAKDOWN
| | | | | | | | |
|---|---|---|---|---|---|---|---|
| Meet Me On The Highway | LP | private | | 1977 | £20 | £40 | |

## BREAKTHRU
| | | | | | | | |
|---|---|---|---|---|---|---|---|
| Ice Cream Tree | 7" | Mercury | MF1066 | 1968 | £2.50 | £6 | |

## BREATHLESS
| | | | | | | | | |
|---|---|---|---|---|---|---|---|---|
| Nobody Leaves This Song Alive | LP | EMI | SW17041 | 1980 | £25 | £50 | | US |

## BRECKER, RANDY
| | | | | | | | | |
|---|---|---|---|---|---|---|---|---|
| Score | LP | Solid State | 18051 | 1968 | £6 | £15 | | US |

## BREEDLOVE, JIMMY
| | | | | | | | |
|---|---|---|---|---|---|---|---|
| Over Somebody Else's Shoulder | 7" | London | HLE8490 | 1957 | £37.50 | £75 | |
| You're Following Me | 7" | Pye | 7N25121 | 1962 | £2 | £5 | |

## BREEZIN
Breezin........................................ LP ...... Plahadima........ .................. 1983 £6........... £15 ....................Dutch

## BREGMAN, BUDDY
Buddy Bregman And His Orchestra .......... LP ...... HMV.............. CLP1154................ 1958 £6........... £15

## BREL, JACQUES
A L'Olympia ..................................... LP ...... Fontana........... SFJL967 ................ 1968 £6........... £15

## BREMERS, BEVERLY
Get Smart Girl .................................. 7" ...... Wand.............. WN18 ................ 1972 £2.50........ £6

## BRENDA & THE TABULATIONS
Baby You're So Right For Me................... 7" ...... Direction ....... 583678................ 1968 £2.50........ £6
Dry Your Eyes.................................. LP ...... Action............ ACLP6003 ............ 1969 £6........... £15
Dry Your Eyes.................................. 7" ...... London........... HL10127............. 1967 £4........... £8
That's In The Past .............................. 7" ...... Action............ ACT4541 ............. 1969 £7.50........ £15
When You're Gone.............................. 7" ...... London........... HL10174............. 1967 £5........... £10

## BRENNAN, ROSE
Band Of Gold ................................... 7" ...... HMV.............. 7M383 ................ 1956 £4........... £8
Courtin' In The Kitchen ....................... 7" ...... HMV.............. 7M392 ................ 1956 £1.50........ £4
Sincerely........................................ 7" ...... HMV.............. 7M299 ................ 1955 £4........... £8
Ten Little Kisses ............................... 7" ...... HMV.............. 7M328 ................ 1955 £2.50........ £6
Tra La La ....................................... 7" ...... HMV.............. POP302 ................ 1957 £2........... £5
You Are My Love ............................... 7" ...... HMV.............. 7M360 ................ 1956 £2.50........ £6

## BRENNAN, WALTER
Dutchman's Gold ............................... 7" ...... London........... HLD9148 ............. 1960 £1.50........ £4

## BRENT, FRANKIE
Rockin' Shoes................................... 78...... Pye .................. N15102 ................ 1957 £1.50........ £4

## BRENT, TONY
Amore........................................... 7" ...... Columbia ....... DB3884 ................ 1957 £2........... £5
Big Hits......................................... LP ...... Columbia ....... 33SX5001 ............ 195– £8........... £20
Butterfly........................................ 7" ...... Columbia ....... DB3918 ................ 1957 £2.50........ £6
Cindy, Oh Cindy ............................... 7" ...... Columbia ....... DB3844 ................ 1956 £2.50........ £6
Dark Moon...................................... 7" ...... Columbia ....... DB3950 ................ 1957 £2........... £5
Deep Within Me ................................ 7" ...... Columbia ....... DB3987 ................ 1957 £1.50........ £4
Ding Dong Boogie .............................. 7" ...... Columbia ....... SCM5029 ............. 1953 £7.50........ £15
Have You Heard ................................ 7" ...... Columbia ....... SCM5042 ............. 1953 £7.50........ £15
I Understand Just How You Feel .............. 7" ...... Columbia ....... SCM5135 ............. 1954 £5........... £10
It's A Woman's World .......................... 7" ...... Columbia ....... SCM5160 ............. 1955 £5........... £10
Love By The Jukebox Light .................... 7" ...... Columbia ....... DB4043 ................ 1957 £1.50........ £4
Mirror Mirror .................................. 7" ...... Columbia ....... SCM5188 ............. 1955 £4........... £8
My Little Angel................................. 7" ...... Columbia ....... SCM5272 ............. 1956 £2.50........ £6
Nicolette ........................................ 7" ...... Columbia ....... SCM5146 ............. 1954 £4........... £8
Off Stage ....................................... 7" EP . Columbia ....... SEG8019 ............. 1960 £5........... £10
Off Stage ....................................... 10" LP Columbia ....... 33S1125 ............. 1958 £10........... £25
Off Stage No. 2................................. 7" EP . Columbia ....... SEG8040 ............. 1960 £5........... £10
Open Up Your Heart ........................... 7" ...... Columbia ....... SCM5170 ............. 1955 £6........... £12
Sooner Or Later ................................ 7" ...... Columbia ....... SCM5245 ............. 1956 £2.50........ £6
Time For Tony .................................. 7" EP . Columbia ....... SEG7869 ............. 1957 £5........... £10
Tony Calls The Tune ........................... 7" EP . Columbia ....... SEG7824 ............. 1958 £5........... £10
Tony Takes Five ................................ LP ...... Columbia ....... 33SX1200/ ........... 1960 £6........... £15
................................................................................ SCX3288
Which Way The Wind Blows ................. 7" ...... Columbia ....... SCM5057............. 1953 £6........... £12
With Your Love ................................. 7" ...... Columbia ....... SCM5200............. 1955 £2.50........ £6

## BRENTWOOD ROAD ALL STARS
Love At First Sight.............................. 7" ...... Bamboo ......... BAM23................ 1970 £1.50........ £4
Soul Shake ...................................... 7" ...... Bamboo ......... BAM25................ 1970 £1.50........ £4

## BRESSLAW, BERNARD
I Only Arsked .................................. 7" EP . HMV............ 7EG8439 ............. 1957 £2........... £5

## BRETT, PAUL
Jubilation Foundry.............................. LP ...... Dawn............. DNLS3021 ............ 1971 £4........... £10
Paul Brett ....................................... LP ...... Bradleys ........ BRAD1001 ............ 1973 £4........... £10
Paul Brett Sage ................................. LP ...... Pye ............... NSPL18347 .......... 1970 £5........... £12
Phoenix Future ................................. LP ...... Phoenix Future PF001 ................ 1975 £5........... £12
Schizophrenia .................................. LP ...... Dawn............. DNLS3032 ............ 1972 £5........... £12
Very Strange Brew .............................. LP ...... ABC.............. 672 ................ 1969 £6........... £15 ...................... US

## BRETT, STEVE & THE MAVERICKS
Chains On My Heart ........................... 7" ...... Columbia ....... DB7794................ 1965 £50........... £100
Sad Lonely And Blue ........................... 7" ...... Columbia ....... DB7581................ 1965 £50........... £100
Wishing......................................... 7" ...... Columbia ....... DB7470................ 1965 £50........... £100

## BREVETT, LLOYD
Wayward Ska.................................... 7" ...... Ska Beat........ JB213................ 1965 £5........... £10 ...... Winston Samuels
............................................................................................................................................................ B side

## BREWER, TERESA
Aloha From Teresa ............................. LP ...... Coral ...... LVA9152 ............. 1962 £5........... £12
And The Dixieland Band ...................... LP ...... Coral ...... LVA9107 ............. 1959 £5........... £12

| | | | | | | |
|---|---|---|---|---|---|---|
| And The Dixieland Band Pt. 1 | 7" EP | Coral | FEP2047 | 1960 | £2.50 .... £6 | |
| And The Dixieland Band Pt. 2 | 7" EP | Coral | FEP2048 | 1960 | £2.50 .... £6 | |
| At Christmas Time | LP | Coral | LVA9091 | 1958 | £6 ...... £15 | |
| Au Revoir | 7" | Vogue Coral | Q2029 | 1954 | £5 ...... £10 | |
| Banjo's Back In Town | 7" | Vogue Coral | Q72098 | 1955 | £2.50 .... £6 | |
| Bouquet Of Hits | LP | Coral | CRL56072 | 1954 | £6 ...... £15 | US |
| Bye Bye Baby Goodbye | 7" | Coral | Q72375 | 1959 | £1.50 .... £4 | |
| Crazy With Love | 7" | Vogue Coral | Q72213 | 1956 | £2 ...... £5 | |
| Don't Mess Around With Tess | LP | Coral | LVA9204 | 1962 | £5 ...... £12 | |
| Empty Arms | 7" | Vogue Coral | Q72251 | 1957 | £1.50 .... £4 | |
| For Teenagers In Love | LP | Coral | LVA9075 | 1957 | £6 ...... £15 | |
| Good Man Is Hard To Find | 7" | Vogue Coral | Q72130 | 1956 | £2.50 .... £6 | |
| Heavenly Lover | 7" | Coral | Q72364 | 1959 | £1.50 .... £4 | |
| How Do You Know It's Love | 7" EP | Coral | FEP2061 | 1960 | £2.50 .... £6 | |
| How Important Can It Be? | 7" | Vogue Coral | Q72065 | 1955 | £4 ...... £8 | |
| Hula Hoop Song | 7" | Coral | Q72340 | 1958 | £1.50 .... £4 | |
| Hula Hoop Time | 7" EP | Coral | FEP2013 | 1959 | £4 ...... £8 | |
| I'm Drowning My Sorrows | 7" | Vogue Coral | Q72239 | 1957 | £1.50 .... £4 | |
| Jilted | 78 | Vogue Coral | Q2001 | 1954 | £1.50 .... £4 | |
| Jingle Bell Rock | 7" | Coral | Q72349 | 1958 | £1.50 .... £4 | |
| Keep Your Cotton Pickin' Paddies | 7" | Vogue Coral | Q72199 | 1956 | £1.50 .... £4 | |
| Let Me Go Lover | 7" | Vogue Coral | Q72043 | 1955 | £6 ...... £12 | |
| Lula Rock-a-Hula | 7" | Vogue Coral | Q72278 | 1957 | £2.50 .... £6 | |
| Music! Music! Music! | LP | Coral | LVA9020 | 1956 | £6 ...... £15 | |
| Mutual Admiration Society | 7" | Coral | Q72301 | 1958 | £1.50 .... £4 | |
| My Golden Favourites | LP | Coral | LVA9131 | 1960 | £4 ...... £10 | |
| Naughty Naughty Naughty | LP | Coral | LVA9138 | 1960 | £5 ...... £12 | |
| Nora Malone | 7" | Vogue Coral | Q72224 | 1957 | £2 ...... £5 | |
| Pickle Up A Doodle | 7" | Coral | Q72336 | 1958 | £1.50 .... £4 | |
| Pledging My Love | 7" | Vogue Coral | Q72077 | 1955 | £5 ...... £10 | |
| Remembering | 7" | Vogue Coral | Q72139 | 1956 | £4 ...... £8 | |
| Ridin' High | LP | Coral | LVA9129 | 1960 | £5 ...... £12 | |
| Rock Love | 7" | Vogue Coral | Q72066 | 1955 | £6 ...... £12 | |
| Saturday Dance | 7" | Coral | Q72320 | 1958 | £1.50 .... £4 | |
| Showcase | 10" LP | London | HAPB1006 | 1951 | £10 ...... £25 | |
| Skinny Minnie | 7" | Vogue Coral | Q2011 | 1954 | £6 ...... £12 | |
| Songs Everybody Knows | LP | Coral | LVA9145 | 1961 | £5 ...... £12 | |
| Sweet Old-Fashioned Girl | 7" | Vogue Coral | Q72172 | 1956 | £4 ...... £8 | |
| Tear Fell | 7" | Vogue Coral | Q72146 | 1956 | £5 ...... £10 | |
| Till I Waltz Again With You | LP | Coral | CRL56093 | 1954 | £6 ...... £15 | US |
| Time For Teresa Brewer | LP | Coral | LVA9095 | 1959 | £5 ...... £12 | |
| When Your Lover Has Gone | LP | Coral | LVA9100/SVL3003 | 1959 | £5 ...... £12 | |
| When Your Lover Has Gone Pt. 1 | 7" EP | Coral | FEP2036 | 1959 | £2.50 .... £6 | |
| When Your Lover Has Gone Pt. 2 | 7" EP | Coral | FEP2037 | 1959 | £2.50 .... £6 | |
| When Your Lover Has Gone Pt. 3 | 7" EP | Coral | FEP2038 | 1959 | £2.50 .... £6 | |
| You Send Me | 7" | Vogue Coral | Q72292 | 1957 | £2 ...... £5 | |
| You're Telling Our Secret | 7" | Vogue Coral | Q72083 | 1955 | £4 ...... £8 | |

## BREWER & FARNER

| | | | | | | |
|---|---|---|---|---|---|---|
| Monumental Funk | LP | Quadico | QLP7401 | 1974 | £5 ...... £12 | US |

## BREWERS DROOP

| | | | | | | |
|---|---|---|---|---|---|---|
| Opening Time | LP | RCA | SF8301 | 1972 | £4 ...... £10 | |

## BRIDES OF FUNKENSTEIN

| | | | | | | |
|---|---|---|---|---|---|---|
| Funk Or Walk | LP | Atlantic | K50545 | 1978 | £6 ...... £15 | |

## BRIDGES

| | | | | | | |
|---|---|---|---|---|---|---|
| Fakkeltog | LP | Vakenatt | VN01 | 1979 | £50 ... £100 | Norwegian |

## BRIERLEY, MARC

| | | | | | | |
|---|---|---|---|---|---|---|
| Autograph Of Time | 7" | CBS | 3857 | 1968 | £1.50 .... £4 | |
| Hello | LP | CBS | 63835 | 1969 | £10 ...... £25 | |
| Welcome To The Citadel | LP | CBS | 63478 | 1967 | £6 ...... £15 | |

## BRIGADE

| | | | | | | |
|---|---|---|---|---|---|---|
| Last Laugh | LP | Band N Vocal | 1066 | 1970 | £700 ... £1000 | US |

## BRIGG

| | | | | | | |
|---|---|---|---|---|---|---|
| Brigg | LP | private | | 1972 | £180 ..... £300 | US |

## BRIGGS, ANNE

Richard Thompson's song, 'Beeswing', the tale of a woman possessed of an incurable restlessness, is supposed to be inspired by the life of Anne Briggs. Her handful of recordings (which include 'Bird In The Bush', a collaboration with A. L. Lloyd, listed in this guide under his name) are widely regarded as folk masterpieces. Her treatments of traditional material are definitive, while her own songs – some of which were covered by Bert Jansch – are highly memorable. Her version of the traditional tune 'Blackwater Side' inspired Bert Jansch to record the piece also, from where it found its way into the repertoire of Led Zeppelin (as 'Black Mountain Side'). Anne Briggs's lack of interest in establishing any kind of career as a singer, however, is highlighted by the fact that her own daughter apparently only discovered her mother's recordings when a compilation CD was issued in 1990.

| | | | | | | |
|---|---|---|---|---|---|---|
| Anne Briggs | LP | Topic | 12TS207 | 1971 | £50 ...... £100 | |
| Hazards Of Love | 7" EP | Topic | TOP94 | 1963 | £30 ...... £60 | |
| Time Has Come | LP | CBS | 64612 | 1971 | £50 ...... £100 | |

## BRIGGS, BILLY

| | | | | | | |
|---|---|---|---|---|---|---|
| Chew Tobacco Rag | 78 | Columbia | DB2938 | 1951 | £2.50 ...... £6 | |

## BRIGHT, RONNELL
Bright Flight ............................................. LP...... Vanguard ........ PPL11016............... 1958 £5.........£12 ...............................

## BRIGMAN, GEORGE
Jungle Rot................................................ LP...... Solid............... SR001 .................. 1975 £37.50....£75 ....................... US
Second Album ....................................... cass ..... ................................ 1977 £10.........£25 ....................... US

## BRILLIANT, ASHLEIGH
In The Haight-Ashbury ........................... LP...... Dorash ............ 1001 ...................... 1967 £15.........£30 ....................... US

## BRILLIANT CORNERS
Big Hip ................................................... 7"...... SS20 ............. SS22 ................... 1984 £2............£5 ...............................
My Baby's In Black ................................. 12".... SS20 ............. SS23T ................. 1984 £3............£8 ...............................
She's Got Fever....................................... 7"...... SS20 ............. SS21 ................... 1984 £7.50......£15 ...............................

## BRIMSTONE
Paper Winged Dreams ............................ LP...... Brimstone ....... ............................ 196– £50........£100 ....................... US

## BRIMSTONE, DEREK
Derek Brimstone .................................... LP...... Fontana............ STL5478 ................. 1969 £5.........£12 ...............................

## BRINDLEY BRAE
Village Music .......................................... LP...... Harmony ........ DB0002 ................ 197– £10.........£25 ...............................

## BRINSLEY SCHWARZ
Forever damned as the group whose manager virtually invented the concept of hype (when he chartered a plane-load of journalists to watch his clients perform at the bottom of the Fillmore bill), Brinsley Schwarz never quite managed to find the acclaim that their frequently fine material deserved. Bassist Nick Lowe, however, went on to do quite well for himself, while other members of the group, including guitarist Schwarz himself, found employment as members of Graham Parker's Rumour.

Brinsley Schwarz ................................... LP ..... United Artists .. UAS29111............... 1970 £5.........£12 ...............................
Country Girl........................................... 7".... Liberty ............ LBY15419.............. 1970 £1.50.......£4 ...............................
Despite It All ......................................... LP ..... Liberty ............ LBG83427.............. 1970 £5.........£12 ...............................
Nervous On The Road............................ LP ..... United Artists .. UAS29374.............. 1972 £4.........£10 ...............................
New Favourites ...................................... LP ..... United Artists .. UAS29641.............. 1974 £4.........£10 ...............................
Please Don't Ever Change ...................... LP ..... United Artists .. UAS29489.............. 1973 £5.........£12 ...............................
Shining Brightly ..................................... 7".... United Artists .. UP35118............... 1970 £1.50.......£4 ...............................
Silver Pistol .......................................... LP .... United Artists .. UAS29217.............. 1972 £5.........£12 ..............with poster

## BRITISH WALKERS
I Found You........................................... 7"...... Pye ................ 7N25298.............. 1965 £7.50......£15 ...............................

## BRITT
Leave My Baby Alone.............................. 7"...... Piccadilly........ 7N35273.............. 1966 £2.............£5 ...............................

## BRITT, ELTON
Wandering Cowboy ................................ LP ..... ABC-           (S)293 ................... 1959 £4.........£10 ....................... US
                                                    Paramount.......
Yodel Songs........................................... LP ..... RCA .............. LPM1288 .............. 1956 £6.........£15 ....................... US
Yodel Songs........................................... 10" LP RCA .............. LPM3222 .............. 1954 £10.........£25 ....................... US

## BRITT, TINA
Real Thing.............................................. 7"...... London ........... HLC9974............... 1965 £7.50......£15 ...............................

## BRITTEN, BUDDY & THE REGENTS
Don't Spread It Around ......................... 7" ..... Decca ........... F11435............. 1962 £1.50......£4 ...............................
Hey There............................................. 7" ..... Oriole ............ CB1839 .............. 1963 £1.50......£4 ...............................
I Guess I'm In The Way.......................... 7" ..... Oriole ............ CB1911 .............. 1964 £1.50......£4 ...............................
If You've Gotta Make A Fool Of .............. 7" ..... Oriole ............ CB1827 .............. 1963 £1.50......£4 ...............................
   Somebody........................................
Money ................................................... 7" ..... Oriole ............ CB1889 .............. 1963 £1.50......£4 ...............................
My Pride And Joy................................... 7" ..... Piccadilly........ 7N35075.............. 1962 £1.50......£4 ...............................
My Resistance Is Low............................. 7" ..... Oriole ............ CB1859 .............. 1963 £1.50......£4 ...............................
Right Now.............................................. 7" ..... Piccadilly........ 7N35257.............. 1965 £1.50......£4 ...............................
She's About A Mover .............................. 7" ..... Piccadilly........ 7N35241.............. 1965 £2............£5 ...............................

## BRITTON, CHRIS
As I Am.................................................. LP ..... Page One ........ POLS022 .............. 1969 £37.50....£75 ...............................

## BROADBENT, TIM
Female Drummer ................................... LP...... Longman......... LM4004 .............. 1976 £15.........£30 ...............................

## BROADSIDE
To Drive The Dark Away......................... LP...... Guildhall ......... 12........................ 1975 £5.........£12 ...............................

## BROCK, B. & THE SULTANS
Do The Beetle ........................................ LP...... Crown ............. CST399 ................ 1964 £8.........£20 ....................... US

## BROCK, DAVE
Social Alliance....................................... 7" ...... Flicknife.......... FLS024P .............. 1983 £1.50.......£4 ...............picture disc

## BROCKETT, JAIME
Remember The Wind And The Rain ........ LP ...... Capitol............ ST678 .................. 1968 £4.........£10 ....................... US

## BROCKSTEDT, NORAH
Big Boy.................................................. 7" ...... Top Rank ....... JAR353................ 1960 £2.50.......£6 ...............................

## BROGUES

Greg Elmore and Gary Duncan played as members of the Brogues before helping to form the Quicksilver Messenger Service.

| | | | | | | |
|---|---|---|---|---|---|---|
| But Now I'm Fine | 7" | Challenge | | 1965 £12.50 | £25 | US |
| But Now I'm Fine | 7" | Twilight | 408 | 1965 £20 | £40 | US |
| I Ain't No Miracle Worker | 7" | Challenge | 59316 | 1965 £7.50 | £15 | US |

## BROMLEY, JOHN

| | | | | | |
|---|---|---|---|---|---|
| Sing | LP | Polydor | 583048 | 1969 £6 | £15 |

## BRONCO

Jess Roden, former singer with Alan Bown, hit on the idea of a group that could rock hard on acoustic guitars. Live, Bronco played sitting down, which was certainly a novelty, and their records, particularly *Country Home*, still have a remarkable freshness. Guitarist Robbie Blunt is also an impressive electric player, as he later proved as a member of the Robert Plant band.

| | | | | | | |
|---|---|---|---|---|---|---|
| Ace Of Sunlight | LP | Island | ILPS9161 | 1971 £4 | £10 | |
| Country Home | LP | Island | ILPS9124 | 1970 £5 | £12 | pink label |

## BRONX CHEER

| | | | | | |
|---|---|---|---|---|---|
| Greatest Hits | LP | Dawn | DNLS3034 | 1972 £4 | £10 |

## BROOK, PATTI

'I Love You, I Need You' has the rare songwriting credit, 'Cliff Richard'. The song is not especially distinguished, and Cliff Richard's own opinion of it can be gauged by the fact that he did not record it himself.

| | | | | | |
|---|---|---|---|---|---|
| I Love You, I Need You | 7" | Pye | 7N15422 | 1962 £10 | £20 |

## BROOK, TONY & THE BREAKERS

| | | | | | | |
|---|---|---|---|---|---|---|
| Love Dances On | 7" | Columbia | DB7444 | 1965 £2 | £5 | |
| Meanie Genie | 7" | Columbia | DB7279 | 1964 £30 | £60 | |
| Meanie Genie | 7" | Columbia | DB7279 | 1964 £50 | £100 | picture sleeve |

## BROOK BROTHERS

| | | | | | | |
|---|---|---|---|---|---|---|
| Ain't Gonna Wash For A Week | 7" | Pye | 7N15369 | 1961 £1.50 | £4 | |
| Brook Brothers | LP | Pye | NPL18067 | 1961 £15 | £30 | |
| Brook Brothers | 7" EP | Pye | NEP24155 | 1962 £5 | £10 | |
| Hit Parade | 7" EP | Pye | NEP24140 | 1961 £5 | £10 | |
| Hit Parade Vol. 2 | 7" EP | Pye | NEP24148 | 1961 £5 | £10 | |
| Warpaint | 7" | Pye | 7N15333 | 1961 £1.50 | £4 | |

## BROOKLYN

| | | | | | |
|---|---|---|---|---|---|
| Hollywood | 7" | Rondelet | ROUND6 | 1981 £1.50 | £4 |
| I Wanna Be A Detective | 7" | Rondelet | ROUND3 | 1980 £1.50 | £4 |

## BROOKMEYER, BOB

| | | | | | | |
|---|---|---|---|---|---|---|
| Blues Hot And Cold | LP | HMV | CLP1438/CSD1356 | 1961 £6 | £15 | |
| Bob Brookmeyer Quartet | 10" LP | Vogue | LDE131 | 1955 £20 | £40 | |
| Bob Brookmeyer Quartet | 10" LP | Vogue | LDE164 | 1956 £20 | £40 | |
| Portrait Of The Artist | LP | London | LTZK15208/SAHK6125 | 1961 £6 | £15 | |
| Street Swingers | LP | Vogue | LAE12147 | 1959 £8 | £20 | |
| Tonight's Jazz Today | LP | Vogue | LAE12047 | 1957 £10 | £25 | with Zoot Sims |
| Traditionalism Revisited | LP | Vogue | LAE12108 | 1958 £8 | £20 | |
| Whooeeee | LP | Vogue | LAE12053 | 1957 £10 | £25 | with Zoot Sims |
| Dual Roll | 10" LP | Esquire | 20084 | 1957 £10 | £25 | |

## BROOKS, BABA

| | | | | | | |
|---|---|---|---|---|---|---|
| Baby Elephant Walk | 7" | Black Swan | WI466 | 1965 £5 | £10 | Don Drummond B side |
| Bank To Bank | 7" | Island | WI096 | 1963 £5 | £10 | |
| Catch A Fire | 7" | Island | WI150 | 1964 £5 | £10 | Eric Morris B side |
| Clock | 7" | Doctor Bird | DB1042 | 1966 £5 | £10 | Lyn Taitt B side |
| Cork Foot | 7" | Black Swan | WI438 | 1964 £5 | £10 | Hersang Combo B side |
| Duck Soup | 7" | Island | WI235 | 1965 £5 | £10 | Zodiacs B side |
| Eighth Games | 7" | Doctor Bird | DB1043 | 1966 £5 | £10 | Joe White B side |
| Ethiopia | 7" | Black Swan | WI451 | 1965 £5 | £10 | Archibald Trott B side |
| Faberge | 7" | Doctor Bird | DB1081 | 1967 £5 | £10 | Monty Morris B side |
| First Session | 7" | Doctor Bird | DB1001 | 1966 £5 | £10 | Joe White B side |
| Girls Town Ska | 7" | Ska Beat | JB218 | 1965 £5 | £10 | Derrick Morgan B side |
| Guns Fever | 7" | Island | WI229 | 1965 £5 | £10 | Dotty & Bonnie B side |
| Independence Ska | 7" | Island | WI233 | 1965 £5 | £10 | Strangher & Claudette B side |
| Jelly Beans | 7" | Black Swan | WI412 | 1964 £5 | £10 | Eric Morris B side |
| King Size | 7" | Doctor Bird | DB1009 | 1966 £5 | £10 | Saints B side |
| Mattie Rag | 7" | Ska Beat | JB217 | 1965 £5 | £10 | Lord Tanamo B side |
| Musical Workshop | 7" | Black Swan | WI442 | 1965 £5 | £10 | Duke White B side |
| One Eyed Giant | 7" | Ska Beat | JB220 | 1965 £5 | £10 | Dynamites B side |
| One Eyed Giant | 7" | Ska Beat | JB268 | 1967 £5 | £10 | Dynamites B side |
| Open The Door | 7" | Doctor Bird | DB1067 | 1966 £5 | £10 | Monty Morris B side |
| Our Man Flint | 7" | High Note | HS030 | 1969 £1.50 | £4 | Hippy Boys B side |
| Party Time | 7" | Doctor Bird | DB1064 | 1966 £5 | £10 | Aston & Yen B side |
| Roll Call | 7" | Doctor Bird | DB1062 | 1966 £5 | £10 | |
| Scratch | 7" | Doctor Bird | DB1065 | 1966 £5 | £10 | Valentines B side |
| Shock Resistance | 7" | Island | WI078 | 1963 £5 | £10 | |

| | | | | | | | |
|---|---|---|---|---|---|---|---|
| Skank J. Sheck | 7" | Rio | R61 | 1965 | £5 | £10 | ...Shenley & Hiacinth B side |
| Spider | 7" | Black Swan | WI434 | 1964 | £5 | £10 | |
| Teenage Ska | 7" | Island | WI241 | 1965 | £5 | £10 | ..... Alton Ellis B side |
| Three Blind Mice | 7" | Island | WI127 | 1963 | £5 | £10 | .Billy & Bobby B side |
| Virginia Ska | 7" | Island | WI247 | 1965 | £5 | £10 | ...............Riots B side |
| Water Melon Man | 7" | R&B | JB125 | 1963 | £5 | £10 | .. Stranger Cole B side |

## BROOKS, CHUCK
| | | | | | | |
|---|---|---|---|---|---|---|
| Black Sheep | 7" | Soul City | SC116 | 1969 | £2 | £5 |

## BROOKS, DALE
| | | | | | | |
|---|---|---|---|---|---|---|
| I Wanna Be Your Girl | 7" | Stateside | SS553 | 1966 | £1.50 | £4 |

## BROOKS, DONNIE
| | | | | | | |
|---|---|---|---|---|---|---|
| Happiest | LP | London | HAN2391 | 1961 | £8 | £20 |
| Oh You Beautiful Doll | 7" | London | HLN9572 | 1962 | £1.50 | £4 |

## BROOKS, ELKIE
| | | | | | | | |
|---|---|---|---|---|---|---|---|
| All Of My Life | 7" | HMV | POP1480 | 1965 | £2.50 | £6 | |
| Baby Let Me Love You | 7" | HMV | POP1512 | 1966 | £2.50 | £6 | |
| Elkie Brooks | LP | A&M | ELKIE1 | 1978 | £6 | £15 | ..... promo compilation |
| He's Gotta Love Me | 7" | HMV | POP1431 | 1965 | £4 | £8 | |
| Nothing Left To Do But Cry | 7" | Decca | F11983 | 1964 | £2.50 | £6 | |
| Something's Got A Hold On Me | 7" | Decca | F11928 | 1964 | £2.50 | £6 | |
| Way You Do The Things You do | 7" | Decca | F12061 | 1965 | £4 | £8 | |

## BROOKS, HADDA
| | | | | | | | |
|---|---|---|---|---|---|---|---|
| Boogie | LP | Crown | CLP5058 | 1958 | £8 | £20 | US |
| Femme Fatale | LP | Crown | CLP5010 | 1957 | £8 | £20 | US |
| Femme Fatale | LP | Modern | LMP1210 | 1956 | £30 | £60 | US |
| Sings And Swings | LP | Crown | CLP5374 | 1963 | £5 | £12 | US |

## BROOKS, NORMAN
| | | | | | | |
|---|---|---|---|---|---|---|
| Baby Mine | 7" EP | London | REP1021 | 1955 | £12.50 | £25 |
| Back In Circulation | 7" | London | HL8115 | 1955 | £7.50 | £15 |
| Hello Sunshine | 7" | London | L1166 | 1954 | £10 | £20 |
| I Can't Give You Anything But Love | 7" | London | HL8041 | 1954 | £7.50 | £15 |
| I'd Like To Be In Your Shoes Baby | 7" | London | HL8015 | 1954 | £7.50 | £15 |
| My Three D Sweetie | 7" | London | HL8051 | 1954 | £7.50 | £15 |
| Skyblue Shirt & A Rainbow Tie | 7" | London | L1228 | 1954 | £10 | £20 |
| Vol. 1 | 7" EP | London | REP1004 | 1954 | £12.50 | £25 |
| You Shouldn't Have Kissed Me | 7" | London | L1202 | 1954 | £10 | £20 |

## BROOKS, ROSA LEE
The collaboration between Love's Arthur Lee and Jimi Hendrix, which produced, in the song 'The Everlasting First', a particularly noteworthy addition to the careers of both musicians, was not the first time they worked together. 'My Diary' was written by Arthur Lee and features Jimi Hendrix's guitar. Like all of Hendrix's early work, it is not exactly essential, but the single has not been reissued and seldom appears in the market place.

| | | | | | | | |
|---|---|---|---|---|---|---|---|
| My Diary | 7" | Revis | 1013 | 1964 | £180 | £300 | .... US, best auctioned |

## BROOKS, TERRY & STRANGE
| | | | | | | | |
|---|---|---|---|---|---|---|---|
| High Flyer | LP | Star People | | 198– | £8 | £20 | US |
| Raw Power | LP | Outer Galaxie | OG1001 | 1976 | £37.50 | £75 | US |
| Translucent World | LP | Outer Galaxie | TW1000 | 1973 | £37.50 | £75 | US |

## BROOKS, TINA
| | | | | | | |
|---|---|---|---|---|---|---|
| True Blue | LP | Blue Note | BLP/BST84041 | 196– | £62.50 | £125 |

## BROONZY, BIG BILL
| | | | | | | | |
|---|---|---|---|---|---|---|---|
| Back Water Blues | 78 | Vogue | V2068 | 1951 | £2.50 | £6 | |
| Big Bill Blues | LP | Vogue | LAE12009 | 1956 | £8 | £20 | |
| Big Bill Blues | 78 | Vogue | V2075 | 1951 | £2.50 | £6 | |
| Big Bill Broonzy | LP | Philips | BBL7113 | 1957 | £15 | £30 | |
| Big Bill Broonzy | 7" EP | Columbia | SEG7674 | 1957 | £4 | £8 | |
| Big Bill Broonzy & Washboard Sam | LP | Chess | LP1468 | 1962 | £8 | £20 | US |
| Big Bill Broonzy No. 2 | 7" EP | Columbia | SEG7790 | 1958 | £4 | £8 | |
| Big Bill Broonzy Sings | 10" LP | Period | 1114 | 195– | £8 | £20 | US |
| Big Bill Broonzy, Sonny Terry & Brownie McGhee | LP | Folkways | FA3817 | 1959 | £5 | £12 | US |
| Big Bill's Blues | LP | Columbia | WL111 | 1958 | £8 | £20 | US |
| Bill Bailey Won't You Please Come Home | 7" EP | Tempo | EXA61 | 1957 | £2 | £5 | |
| Black, Brown And White | 78 | Vogue | V2077 | 1951 | £2.50 | £6 | |
| Blues | LP | Vogue | LAE12063 | 1958 | £8 | £20 | |
| Blues Anthology Vol. 3 | 7" EP | Storyville | SEP383 | 1962 | £2 | £5 | |
| Blues By Broonzy | LP | EmArcy | MG26137 | 1957 | £8 | £20 | US |
| Country Blues | LP | Folkways | FA2326 | 195– | £5 | £12 | US |
| Do You Remember Big Bill Broonzy | 7" EP | Emarcy | YEP9508 | 1959 | £2 | £5 | |
| Evening With Big Bill Broonzy | LP | Storyville | SLP114 | 1964 | £4 | £10 | |
| Evening With Big Bill Broonzy | LP | Tempo | TAP23 | 1959 | £15 | £30 | |
| Five Foot Seven | 78 | Melodisc | 1203 | 1952 | £2.50 | £6 | |
| Folk Blues | LP | EmArcy | MG26034 | 1957 | £8 | £20 | US |
| Guitar Shuffle | 7" EP | Vogue | EPV1107 | 1956 | £4 | £8 | |
| Guitar Shuffle | 7" | Vogue | V2351 | 1958 | £2.50 | £6 | |
| Hey Bud Blues | 7" EP | Vogue | EPV1024 | 1955 | £2.50 | £6 | |
| His Songs And Story | LP | Folkways | FA3586 | 195– | £5 | £12 | US |

| Title | Format | Label | Catalogue | Year | | | Notes |
|---|---|---|---|---|---|---|---|
| Hollering Blues | 7" EP | Mercury | ZEP10093 | 1960 | £2 | £5 | |
| House Rent Stomp | 78 | Vogue | V2076 | 1951 | £2.50 | £6 | |
| In Concert | LP | Verve | VLP5006/SVLP506 | 1966 | £4 | £10 | with Pete Seeger |
| In Concert | LP | XTRA | XTRA1006 | 1964 | £5 | £12 | with Pete Seeger |
| In Paris | LP | Vogue | LO60530 | 1956 | £8 | £20 | US |
| In The Evenin' | 78 | Vogue | V2073 | 1951 | £2.50 | £6 | |
| John Henry | 78 | Vogue | V2074 | 1951 | £2.50 | £6 | |
| Keep Your Hands Off | 78 | Melodisc | 1191 | 1951 | £2.50 | £6 | |
| Keep Your Hands Off | 7" EP | Melodisc | EPM765 | 1956 | £2 | £5 | |
| Last Session Part 1 | LP | HMV | CLP1544 | 1961 | £4 | £10 | |
| Last Session Part 2 | LP | HMV | CLP1551 | 1961 | £4 | £10 | |
| Last Session Part 3 | LP | HMV | CLP1562 | 1961 | £4 | £10 | |
| Make My Getaway | 78 | Vogue | V2078 | 1952 | £2.50 | £6 | |
| Memorial | LP | Mercury | MG2/SR60822 | 1963 | £4 | £10 | US |
| Midnight Special | 7" | Storyville | A45053 | 1961 | £2 | £5 | |
| Mississippi Blues Vol. 1 | 7" EP | Pye | NJE1005 | 1956 | £2 | £5 | |
| Mississippi Blues Vol. 2 | 7" EP | Pye | NJE1015 | 1956 | £2 | £5 | |
| Portraits In Blues | LP | Storyville | SLP154 | 1964 | £4 | £10 | |
| Portraits In Blues Vol. 2 | LP | Storyville | 670154 | 1967 | £4 | £10 | |
| Remembering Broonzy | LP | Mercury | 20044MCL | 1966 | £4 | £10 | |
| Sings The Blues | 7" EP | Vogue | EPV1074 | 1956 | £4 | £8 | |
| South Bound Train | 78 | Pye | NJ2016 | 1957 | £2 | £5 | |
| Southern Saga | 7" EP | Pye | NJE1047 | 1957 | £2 | £5 | |
| Tribute To Big Bill | LP | Nixa | NJL16 | 1958 | £8 | £20 | |
| Trouble In Mind | LP | Fontana | 688206ZL | 1965 | £6 | £15 | |
| Walking Down A Lonesome Road | 7" EP | Mercury | 10003MCE | 1964 | £2 | £5 | |
| Walking Down A Lonesome Road | 7" EP | Mercury | ZEP10065 | 1960 | £2 | £5 | |
| When Do I Get To Be Called A Man | 78 | Pye | NJ2012 | 1957 | £2 | £5 | |

### BROONZY, BIG BILL & JOSH WHITE

| Title | Format | Label | Catalogue | Year | | | |
|---|---|---|---|---|---|---|---|
| Blues | 7" EP | Pieces Of 8 | PEP605 | 1961 | £2 | £5 | |

### BROONZY, BIG BILL & SONNY BOY WILLIAMSON

| Title | Format | Label | Catalogue | Year | | | |
|---|---|---|---|---|---|---|---|
| Big Bill And Sonny Boy | LP | RCA | RD7685 | 1965 | £6 | £15 | |

### BROSELMASCHINE

| Title | Format | Label | Catalogue | Year | | | |
|---|---|---|---|---|---|---|---|
| Broselmaschine | LP | Pilz | 20211002 | 1971 | £10 | £25 | German |

### BROTH

| Title | Format | Label | Catalogue | Year | | | |
|---|---|---|---|---|---|---|---|
| Broth | LP | Mercury | 6338032 | 1970 | £6 | £15 | |

### BROTHER DAN ALL STARS

| Title | Format | Label | Catalogue | Year | | | |
|---|---|---|---|---|---|---|---|
| Another Saturday Night | 7" | Trojan | TR608 | 1968 | £2.50 | £6 | |
| Donkey Returns | 7" | Trojan | TR601 | 1968 | £2.50 | £6 | |
| Eastern Organ | 7" | Trojan | TR602 | 1968 | £2.50 | £6 | |
| Follow That Donkey | LP | Trojan | TRL1 | 1969 | £6 | £15 | |
| Hold Pon Them | 7" | Trojan | TR603 | 1968 | £2.50 | £6 | |
| Let's Catch The Beat | LP | Trojan | TBL101 | 1968 | £8 | £20 | |
| Read Up | 7" | Trojan | TR607 | 1968 | £2.50 | £6 | |

### BROTHER FOX AND THE TAR BABY

| Title | Format | Label | Catalogue | Year | | | |
|---|---|---|---|---|---|---|---|
| Brother Fox And The Tar Baby | LP | Capitol | ST544 | 1969 | £5 | £12 | US |

### BROTHERHOOD

| Title | Format | Label | Catalogue | Year | | | |
|---|---|---|---|---|---|---|---|
| Brotherhood | LP | RCA | LSP4092 | 1968 | £5 | £12 | US |
| Brotherhood Brotherhood | LP | RCA | LSP4228 | 1969 | £5 | £12 | US |
| Paper Man | 7" | Philips | BF1766 | 1969 | £2 | £5 | |

### BROTHERHOOD OF MAN

| Title | Format | Label | Catalogue | Year | | | |
|---|---|---|---|---|---|---|---|
| Good Things Happening | LP | Dawn | DNLS3063 | 1970 | £4 | £10 | |
| United We Stand | LP | Deram | SML1066 | 1970 | £5 | £12 | |
| Brotherhood | LP | RCA | LSP4092 | 1968 | £5 | £12 | US |

### BROTHERS

| Title | Format | Label | Catalogue | Year | | | |
|---|---|---|---|---|---|---|---|
| Disco Soul | LP | People | PLEO25 | 1975 | £8 | £20 | |

### BROTHERS AND SISTERS

| Title | Format | Label | Catalogue | Year | | | |
|---|---|---|---|---|---|---|---|
| Are Watching You | LP | private | | 1968 | £25 | £50 | |

### BROTHERS FOUR

| Title | Format | Label | Catalogue | Year | | | |
|---|---|---|---|---|---|---|---|
| Sing Bob Dylan | 7" EP | CBS | EP6063 | 1965 | £2 | £5 | |
| Song Book | LP | CBS | BPG62012 | 1961 | £4 | £10 | |

### BROTHERS GRIMM

| Title | Format | Label | Catalogue | Year | | | |
|---|---|---|---|---|---|---|---|
| Looky Looky | 7" | Ember | EMBS222 | 1966 | £25 | £50 | |

### BROTHERS TWO

| Title | Format | Label | Catalogue | Year | | | |
|---|---|---|---|---|---|---|---|
| Here I Am In Love Again | 7" | Action | ACT4513 | 1968 | £2 | £5 | |

### BROTHERS WILLIAM

| Title | Format | Label | Catalogue | Year | | | |
|---|---|---|---|---|---|---|---|
| Honey Love | 7" | Parlophone | R5293 | 1965 | £1.50 | £4 | |

### BROUGHTON, EDGAR BAND

The Edgar Broughton Band were a staple feature of the open-air festivals and free concerts of 1969–70. They were supremely good at giving an audience a good time, but on record their musical limitations become rather glaringly obvious. The crowd-pleasing chant, 'Out Demons Out', with which they always ended their stage act, sounds rather weak on cold vinyl, while the fusion of Captain Beefheart with the Shadows on 'Apache Drop Out' sounds silly. Nevertheless, the track 'Love In The Rain', on the first LP, provides for an exhilarating three minutes or so, and would do Motorhead proud.

| | | | | | | | | |
|---|---|---|---|---|---|---|---|---|
| Apache Drop Out | 7" | Harvest | HAR5032 | 1970 | £1.50 | £4 | |
| Bandages | LP | Nems | NEL6006 | 1975 | £4 | £10 | |
| Edgar Broughton Band | LP | Harvest | SHVL791 | 1971 | £5 | £12 | |
| Evil | 7" | Harvest | HAR5001 | 1969 | £1.50 | £4 | |
| Inside Out | LP | Harvest | SHTC252 | 1972 | £6 | £15 | |
| Legendary | LP | Babylon | DB80073 | 1984 | £5 | £12 | German double |
| Live Hits Harder | LP | BB | BB201009 | 1979 | £4 | £10 | |
| Oora | LP | Harvest | SHVL810 | 1973 | £5 | £12 | |
| Out Demons Out | 7" | Harvest | HAR5015 | 1970 | £1.50 | £4 | |
| Sing Brother Sing | LP | Harvest | SHVL772 | 1970 | £6 | £15 | |
| Super Chip | LP | Sheet | SHEET2 | 1982 | £4 | £10 | |
| Wasa Wasa | LP | Harvest | SHVL757 | 1969 | £6 | £15 | |

## BROWN, AL & HIS TUNE TOPPERS

| | | | | | | | | |
|---|---|---|---|---|---|---|---|---|
| Madison Dance Party | LP | Amy | A(S)1 | 1960 | £8 | £20 | US |

## BROWN, ARTHUR

Arthur Brown's stage act, which began with his being lowered on to the stage with his head-dress on fire, was legendary during 1967–8. His album, *The Crazy World Of Arthur Brown* (which was actually the name of his group) easily matches the visual bombast, emerging as one of the classic recordings of the period. The music is guitar-free, which is often a recipe for dullness, but Vincent Crane's organ playing is so full of imagination, and Arthur Brown's singing so powerful, that guitars are not missed. The non-album 'Devil's Grip' is in the same league, although the jokey B side, 'Give Him A Flower', is a bit of a throw-away. Brown's contribution to the soundtrack records of the Roger Vadim film *The Game Is Over/La Curée* is uncredited, but consists of two songs in a style close to that of the Crazy World.

| | | | | | | | | |
|---|---|---|---|---|---|---|---|---|
| Complete Tapes Of Atoya | LP | Plexus | KMH709223 | 1984 | £4 | £10 | Dutch |
| Crazy World Of Arthur Brown | LP | Track | 612/613005 | 1968 | £6 | £15 | |
| Devil's Grip | 7" | Track | 604008 | 1967 | £1.50 | £4 | |
| Faster Than The Speed Of Sound | LP | WEA | 58088 | 1980 | £4 | £10 | Dutch |
| Fire | 7" | Track | 604022 | 1968 | £1.50 | £4 | |
| Game Is Over (La Curee) | LP | Atco | 33205 | 1966 | £30 | £60 | US |
| La Curee | 7" EP | Barclay | 71026 | 1966 | £37.50 | £75 | French |
| Nightmare | 7" | Track | 604026 | 1968 | £1.50 | £4 | |
| Requiem | LP | Remote | REM101 | 1982 | £4 | £10 | |
| You Don't Know | 7" | Reading Rag Record | LYN771 | 1965 | £30 | £60 | flexi, with The Diamonds |

## BROWN, BEN

| | | | | | | | | |
|---|---|---|---|---|---|---|---|---|
| Ask The Lonely | 7" | Polydor | 56198 | 1967 | £7.50 | £15 | |

## BROWN, BOBBY

| | | | | | | | | |
|---|---|---|---|---|---|---|---|---|
| Enlightening Beam Of Axonda | LP | Destiny | 4002 | 1972 | £50 | £100 | US |
| Live | LP | Destiny | 4001 | 1972 | £30 | £60 | US |

## BROWN, BOOTS

| | | | | | | | | |
|---|---|---|---|---|---|---|---|---|
| Rock That Beat | LP | RCA | LG1000 | 1958 | £8 | £20 | US |

## BROWN, BUSTER

| | | | | | | | | |
|---|---|---|---|---|---|---|---|---|
| B. & Buster Brown | 7" EP | XX | MIN713 | 196– | £2.50 | £6 | with B. Brown |
| Fannie Mae | 7" | Melodisc | 1559 | 1960 | £20 | £40 | |
| Fannie Mae | 7" | Sue | WI368 | 1965 | £6 | £12 | |
| My Blue Heaven | 7" | Island | WI3031 | 1967 | £7.50 | £15 | |
| New King Of The Blues | LP | Fire | FLP102 | 1960 | £37.50 | £75 | US |
| Sugar Babe | 7" | Blue Horizon | 573147 | 1969 | £4 | £8 | |

## BROWN, BUSTY

| | | | | | | | | |
|---|---|---|---|---|---|---|---|---|
| Broken Heart | 7" | Punch | PH10 | 1969 | £1.50 | £4 | |
| Here Comes The Night | 7" | Doctor Bird | DB1158 | 1968 | £5 | £10 | |
| To Love Somebody | 7" | Upsetter | US308 | 1969 | £1.50 | £4 | Bleechers B side |
| What A Price | 7" | Upsetter | US304 | 1969 | £1.50 | £4 | |

## BROWN, CHARLES

| | | | | | | | | |
|---|---|---|---|---|---|---|---|---|
| Ballads My Way | LP | Mainstream | 6035 | 1965 | £4 | £10 | US |
| Christmas Question | 7" | Parlophone | R4848 | 1961 | £10 | £20 | |
| Confidential | 7" | Vogue | V9065 | 1957 | £150 | £250 | best auctioned |
| Driftin' Blues | LP | Score | SLP4011 | 1957 | £37.50 | £75 | US |
| Great Charles Brown | LP | King | 878 | 1963 | £10 | £25 | US |
| Legend | LP | Bluesway | 6039 | 1970 | £5 | £12 | US |
| Million Sellers | LP | Imperial | A9178 | 1961 | £20 | £40 | US |
| Mood Music | LP | Aladdin | 809 | 1956 | £62.50 | £125 | US |
| Mood Music | 10" LP | Aladdin | 702 | 1954 | £87.50 | £175 | US |
| Mood Music | 10" LP | Aladdin | 702 | 1954 | £180 | £300 | US, red vinyl |
| Sings Christmas Songs | LP | King | 775 | 1961 | £15 | £30 | US |
| Soothe Me | 7" | Vogue | V9061 | 1956 | £150 | £250 | best auctioned |

## BROWN, CLARENCE 'GATEMOUTH'

| | | | | | | | | |
|---|---|---|---|---|---|---|---|---|
| Vol 1: 1948–1953 | LP | Python | PLP26 | 1972 | £8 | £20 | |
| Vol 2: 1956–1965 | LP | Python | PLP27 | 1972 | £8 | £20 | |
| Clarence Gatemouth Brown | 7" EP | Vocalion | VE170161 | 1965 | £20 | £40 | |

## BROWN, CLIFFORD

| | | | | | | | | |
|---|---|---|---|---|---|---|---|---|
| At Basin Street | LP | Emarcy | EJL1253 | 1957 | £15 | £30 | with Max Roach |
| Clifford Brown – Gigi Gryce Orchestra | 7" EP | Vogue | EPV1027 | 1955 | £2 | £5 | |
| Clifford Brown And Art Farmer Vol. 1 | 7" EP | Esquire | EP3 | 1954 | £2 | £5 | |
| Clifford Brown And Art Farmer Vol. 2 | 7" EP | Esquire | EP4 | 1954 | £2 | £5 | |

| | | | | | | | |
|---|---|---|---|---|---|---|---|
| Clifford Brown And Max Roach | 7" EP | Emarcy | ERE1572 | 1958 | £2 | £5 | |
| Clifford Brown And Tadd Dameron | 7" EP | Esquire | EP71 | 1955 | £2 | £5 | |
| Clifford Brown Ensemble | 7" EP | Vogue | EPV1119 | 1956 | £2 | £5 | |
| Clifford Brown Ensemble | 10" LP | Vogue | LDE158 | 1955 | £20 | £40 | |
| Clifford Brown Quartet | 10" LP | Vogue | LDE042 | 1954 | £10 | £25 | |
| Clifford Brown Sextet | 10" LP | Vogue | LDE121 | 1955 | £10 | £25 | |
| Conception | 7" EP | Vogue | EPV1041 | 1955 | £2 | £5 | |
| Memorial Album | LP | Blue Note | BLP/BST81526 | 1963 | £10 | £25 | |
| Remember Clifford | LP | Mercury | 20022MCL | 1964 | £6 | £15 | |
| Study In Brown | LP | Emarcy | EJL1278 | 1958 | £8 | £20 | |
| Study In Brown Vol. 1 | 7" EP | Emarcy | ERE1565 | 1958 | £2 | £5 | |
| Study In Brown Vol. 2 | 7" EP | Emarcy | ERE1566 | 1958 | £2 | £5 | |
| Sweet Clifford | 7" EP | Emarcy | ERE1501 | 1956 | £2 | £5 | |

## BROWN, DAVID

| | | | | | | | |
|---|---|---|---|---|---|---|---|
| All My Life | 7" | Island | WI3112 | 1967 | £5 | £10 | *Ron Wilson B side* |

## BROWN, DENNIS

| | | | | | | | |
|---|---|---|---|---|---|---|---|
| Black Magic Woman | 7" | Explosion | EX2068 | 1972 | £1.50 | £4 | |
| Just Dennis | LP | Trojan | TRLS107 | 1975 | £4 | £10 | |
| Little Green Apples | 7" | Ocean | OC001 | 1971 | £1.50 | £4 | *Sound Dimension B side* |
| Love Grows | 7" | Bamboo | BAM56 | 1970 | £1.50 | £4 | *Sound Dimension B side* |
| Money In My Pocket | 7" | Pressure Beat | PB5513 | 1972 | £1.50 | £4 | *Joe Gibbs B side* |
| Never Fall In Love | 7" | Banana | BA336 | 1971 | £1.50 | £4 | |
| No Man Is An Island | 7" | Banana | BA309 | 1970 | £1.50 | £4 | *Soul Sisters B side* |
| Super Reggae And Soul Hits | LP | Trojan | TRLS57 | 1973 | £5 | £12 | |
| Visions | LP | Lightning | LIP7 | 1978 | £4 | £10 | |
| West Bound Train | LP | Third World | TWS934 | 1977 | £4 | £10 | |
| Words Of Wisdom | LP | Laser | LASL1 | 1979 | £4 | £10 | |

## BROWN, DUSTY

| | | | | | | | |
|---|---|---|---|---|---|---|---|
| Please Don't Go | 7" | Starlite | ST45058 | 1961 | £10 | £20 | |

## BROWN, FAY

| | | | | | | | |
|---|---|---|---|---|---|---|---|
| Unchained Melody | 7" | Columbia | SCM5185 | 1955 | £5 | £10 | |

## BROWN, FRANK

| | | | | | | | |
|---|---|---|---|---|---|---|---|
| Some Come Some Go | 7" | Island | WI3103 | 1967 | £5 | £10 | |

## BROWN, GERRY

| | | | | | | | |
|---|---|---|---|---|---|---|---|
| It's Trad Time | LP | Fontana | TFL5165 | 1961 | £6 | £15 | |

## BROWN, GLEN, JOE WHITE & TREVOR

| | | | | | | | |
|---|---|---|---|---|---|---|---|
| Way Of Life | 7" | Blue Cat | BS131 | 1968 | £2.50 | £6 | *Carl Bryan & Lyn Taitt B side* |

## BROWN, GLENMORE & HOPETON LEWIS

| | | | | | | | |
|---|---|---|---|---|---|---|---|
| Girl You're Cold | 7" | Fab | FAB42 | 1968 | £2.50 | £6 | |

## BROWN, HENRY

| | | | | | | | |
|---|---|---|---|---|---|---|---|
| Blues | LP | 77 | LA125 | 1961 | £6 | £15 | |

## BROWN, IRVING

| | | | | | | | |
|---|---|---|---|---|---|---|---|
| I'm Still Around | 7" | Bamboo | BAM58 | 1970 | £1.50 | £4 | |
| Now I'm Alone | 7" | Bamboo Now | BN1003 | 1971 | £1.50 | £4 | |
| Today | 7" | Bamboo | BAM36 | 1970 | £1.50 | £4 | |

## BROWN, JAMES

James Brown is the most sampled artist of all for the simple reason that, as the inventor of funk, he has also made the records that are the best examples of it. From 'Think' to 'Papa's Got A Brand New Bag' to 'Cold Sweat' to 'Give It Up Or Turn It A-Loose' and beyond, Brown's skill at winding up the rhythmic tension has always been totally unsurpassed. Of course, within the mêlée of brittle drum beats, scratchy guitar patterns, and moon-booted bass riffs, Brown apparently does nothing more than oversee. He does, of course, have an emotion-wrenching soul voice, as early ballads like 'Prisoner Of Love' and 'It's A Man's Man's World' confirm, but he more often chooses to employ a series of ecstatic calls and rhythmic vocal adjuncts than to deliver anything resembling a melody. In reality, however, the music is as much in his control as that of an orchestra stands or falls according to the talents of its conductor. For proof of this, the lower level of inspiration apparent in the work of Brown's musicians playing without the man himself easily suffices (Maceo and the King's Men, the JBs, and even Bootsy Collins's groups cannot compare to the man they call the Godfather for the rhythmic impact, the sheer funk of the music).

| | | | | | | | |
|---|---|---|---|---|---|---|---|
| Ain't It Funky | LP | Polydor | 2343010 | 1970 | £10 | £25 | |
| Ain't It Funky Now | 7" | Polydor | 56793 | 1970 | £1.50 | £4 | |
| Ain't That A Groove | 7" | Pye | 7N25367 | 1966 | £2 | £5 | |
| Always Amazing James Brown | LP | King | LP743 | 1961 | £15 | £30 | *US* |
| At The Apollo | LP | London | HA8184 | 1964 | £15 | £30 | |
| At The Apollo | LP | Polydor | 582703 | 1967 | £6 | £15 | |
| At The Apollo Vol. 2 | LP | Polydor | 583729/730 | 1969 | £10 | £25 | *double* |
| Best Of James Brown | LP | Polydor | 583765 | 1969 | £5 | £12 | |
| Black Caesar | LP | Polydor | 2490117 | 1974 | £15 | £30 | |
| Bodyheat | LP | Polydor | 2391258 | 1977 | £4 | £10 | |
| Bodyheat | 7" | Polydor | 2066763 | 1977 | £1.50 | £4 | |
| Bring It Up | 7" EP | Pye | NEP44088 | 1967 | £5 | £10 | |
| Bring It Up | 7" | Pye | 7N25411 | 1967 | £2 | £5 | |
| Christmas Album | LP | Pye | NPL28097 | 1966 | £10 | £25 | |
| Cold Sweat | 7" | Pye | 7N25430 | 1967 | £2.50 | £6 | |
| Don't Be A Drop-Out | 7" | Pye | 7N25394 | 1966 | £2.50 | £6 | |

| Title | Format | Label | Catalogue | Year | | | Notes |
|---|---|---|---|---|---|---|---|
| Everybody's Doin' The Hustle | LP | Polydor | 2391197 | 1975 | £5 | £12 | |
| Exciting James Brown | LP | King | LP780 | 1962 | £15 | £30 | US |
| Eyesight | 7" | Polydor | 2066915 | 1978 | £1.50 | £4 | |
| Funky President | 7" | Polydor | 2066520 | 1975 | £1.50 | £4 | |
| Get Involved | 7" | Polydor | 2001190 | 1971 | £1.50 | £4 | |
| Get It Together | 7" | Pye | 7N25441 | 1967 | £2 | £5 | |
| Get On The Good Foot | LP | Polydor | 2659018 | 1973 | £15 | £30 | double |
| Get On The Good Foot | 7" | Polydor | 2066231 | 1972 | £1.50 | £4 | |
| Get Up Offa That Thing | LP | Polydor | 2391228 | 1976 | £4 | £10 | |
| Get Up Offa That Thing | 7" | Polydor | 2066687 | 1976 | £1.50 | £4 | |
| Gettin' Down To It | LP | Polydor | 583742 | 1970 | £10 | £25 | |
| Greatest Hits | LP | Polydor | 623017 | 1968 | £5 | £12 | |
| Grits And Soul | LP | Philips | BL7664 | 1965 | £10 | £25 | |
| Handful Of Soul | LP | Philips | (S)BL7761 | 1967 | £8 | £20 | |
| Have Mercy Baby | 7" | London | HL9945 | 1965 | £5 | £10 | |
| Hell | LP | Polydor | 2659036 | 1974 | £20 | £40 | double |
| Hey America | 7" | Mojo | 2093006 | 1971 | £1.50 | £4 | |
| Honky Tonk | 7" | Polydor | 2066216 | 1972 | £1.50 | £4 | |
| Honky Tonk | 7" | Polydor | 2066834 | 1977 | £1.50 | £4 | |
| Hot | LP | Polydor | 2391214 | 1976 | £5 | £12 | |
| Hot | 7" | Polydor | 2066642 | 1976 | £1.50 | £4 | |
| Hot Pants | LP | Polydor | 2425086 | 1971 | £6 | £15 | |
| Hot Pants | 7" | Polydor | 2001213 | 1971 | £1.50 | £4 | |
| How Long Darling | 7" EP | Pye | NEP44076 | 1967 | £5 | £10 | |
| I Can't Stand Myself | LP | Polydor | 184136 | 1968 | £10 | £25 | |
| I Can't Stand Myself | 7" | Polydor | 56787 | 1970 | £2 | £5 | |
| I Do Just What I Want | 7" EP | Ember | EMBEP4549 | 1964 | £6 | £12 | |
| I Got A Bag Of My Own | 7" | Polydor | 2066285 | 1973 | £1.50 | £4 | |
| I Got A Feeling | 7" | Polydor | 56743 | 1968 | £2.50 | £6 | |
| I Got Ants In My Pants | 7" | Polydor | 2066296 | 1973 | £1.50 | £4 | |
| I Got You | 7" EP | Pye | NEP44059 | 1966 | £5 | £10 | |
| I Got You | 7" | Pye | 7N25350 | 1966 | £4 | £8 | |
| I Got You (I Feel Good) | LP | Pye | NPL28074 | 1966 | £10 | £25 | |
| I'll Go Crazy | 7" EP | Pye | NEP44068 | 1966 | £5 | £10 | |
| I'm A Greedy Man | 7" | Polydor | 2066153 | 1971 | £1.50 | £4 | |
| In The Jungle Groove | LP | Urban | URBLP11 | 1988 | £6 | £15 | double |
| It's A Man's Man's Man's World | LP | Pye | NPL28079 | 1966 | £8 | £20 | |
| It's A Man's Man's Man's World | 7" | Pye | 7N25371 | 1966 | £4 | £8 | |
| It's A Mother | LP | Polydor | 583768 | 1969 | £10 | £25 | |
| It's A New Day | LP | Polydor | 2310029 | 1971 | £10 | £25 | |
| It's A New Day | 7" | Polydor | 2001018 | 1970 | £1.50 | £4 | |
| It's Hell | 7" | Polydor | 2066513 | 1974 | £1.50 | £4 | |
| Jump Around | LP | King | LP/KS771 | 1962 | £15 | £30 | US |
| Kansas City | 7" | Pye | 7N25418 | 1967 | £2.50 | £6 | |
| King Heroin | 7" | Polydor | 2066185 | 1972 | £1.50 | £4 | |
| King Of Soul | LP | Polydor | 184159 | 1969 | £8 | £20 | |
| Let A Man Come In | 7" | Polydor | 56783 | 1969 | £2 | £5 | |
| Let Yourself Go | 7" | Pye | 7N25423 | 1967 | £2.50 | £6 | |
| Licking Stick | 7" | Polydor | 56744 | 1968 | £2 | £5 | |
| Live At The Apollo | LP | Polydor | 2482184 | 1975 | £4 | £10 | |
| Live At The Apollo 1962 | CD | Mobile Fidelity | UDCD583 | 1993 | £6 | £15 | US audiophile |
| Live At The Apollo Vol. 2 | LP | Polydor | 2612005 | 1970 | £6 | £15 | double |
| Live At The Garden | LP | Pye | NPL28104 | 1967 | £10 | £25 | |
| Make It Funky | 7" | Polydor | 2001223 | 1971 | £1.50 | £4 | |
| Mighty Instrumentals | LP | Pye | NPL28093 | 1967 | £8 | £20 | |
| Money Won't Change You | 7" | Pye | 7N25379 | 1966 | £2.50 | £6 | |
| Mother Popcorn | 7" | Polydor | 56776 | 1969 | £1.50 | £4 | |
| Mr. Dynamite | LP | Polydor | 623032 | 1968 | £8 | £20 | |
| Mr. Excitement | LP | Pye | NPL28100 | 1967 | £8 | £20 | |
| Mr. Soul | LP | Polydor | 184100 | 1968 | £8 | £20 | |
| Mutha Nature | LP | Polydor | 2391300 | 1977 | £5 | £12 | |
| My Thing | 7" | Polydor | 2066485 | 1974 | £1.50 | £4 | |
| Nature | 7" | Polydor | 2066984 | 1978 | £1.50 | £4 | |
| New Breed | 7" | Philips | BF1481 | 1966 | £2.50 | £6 | |
| Night Train | 7" | Parlophone | R4922 | 1962 | £10 | £20 | |
| Night Train | 7" | Sue | WI360 | 1964 | £10 | £20 | |
| Out Of Sight | LP | Mercury | SMCL20133 | 1969 | £8 | £20 | |
| Out Of Sight | 7" | Philips | BF1368 | 1964 | £5 | £10 | |
| Papa's Got A Brand New Bag | LP | London | HA8262 | 1966 | £10 | £25 | |
| Papa's Got A Brand New Bag | LP | Polydor | 2334009 | 1970 | £6 | £15 | |
| Papa's Got A Brand New Bag | LP | Pye | NPL28099 | 1967 | £8 | £20 | |
| Papa's Got A Brand New Bag | 7" | London | HL9990 | 1965 | £4 | £8 | |
| Papa's Got A Brand New Bag | 7" | Polydor | 2141008 | 1973 | £1.50 | £4 | |
| Payback | LP | Polydor | 2659030 | 1974 | £20 | £40 | double |
| Plays James Brown Today & Yesterday | LP | Philips | BL7697 | 1966 | £8 | £20 | |
| Plays New Breed | LP | Philips | BL7718 | 1966 | £8 | £20 | |
| Plays The Real Thing | LP | Philips | (S)BL7823 | 1967 | £8 | £20 | |
| Please Please Please | LP | King | 395610 | 1959 | £30 | £60 | US |
| Please Please Please | LP | London | HA8231 | 1965 | £10 | £25 | |
| Popcorn | LP | Polydor | 184319 | 1970 | £15 | £30 | |
| Prisoner Of Love | LP | King | LP/KS851 | 1963 | £15 | £30 | US |
| Prisoner Of Love | 7" EP | London | RE1410 | 1964 | £12.50 | £25 | |
| Prisoner Of Love | 7" EP | Pye | NEP44072 | 1967 | £5 | £10 | |
| Prisoner Of Love | 7" | London | HL9730 | 1963 | £7.50 | £15 | |
| Pure Dynamite | LP | London | HA8177 | 1964 | £10 | £25 | |
| Raw Soul | LP | Pye | NPL28103 | 1967 | £8 | £20 | |
| Reality | LP | Polydor | 2391164 | 1975 | £6 | £15 | |
| Revolution Of The Mind | LP | Polydor | 2659011 | 1972 | £15 | £30 | double |

| Title | Format | Label | Catalogue | Year | | | Notes |
|---|---|---|---|---|---|---|---|
| Say It Loud I'm Black & I'm Proud | LP | Polydor | 583741 | 1969 | £10 | £25 | |
| Say It Loud, I'm Black And I'm Proud | 7" | Polydor | 56752 | 1968 | £2.50 | £6 | |
| Sex Machine | LP | Polydor | 2625004 | 1971 | £10 | £25 | double |
| Sex Machine | 7" | Polydor | 2001071 | 1970 | £1.50 | £4 | |
| Sex Machine Today | LP | Polydor | 2391175 | 1975 | £5 | £12 | |
| Shout And Shimmy | 7" | Parlophone | R4952 | 1962 | £7.50 | £15 | |
| Showtime | LP | Philips | BL7630 | 1964 | £10 | £25 | |
| Slaughter's Big Rip-Off | LP | Polydor | 2391084 | 1973 | £10 | £25 | |
| Soul Brother No. 1 | LP | Polydor | 2343036 | 1971 | £5 | £12 | |
| Soul Classics | LP | Polydor | 2391057 | 1973 | £5 | £12 | |
| Soul Classics Vol. 2 | LP | Polydor | 2391116 | 1974 | £5 | £12 | |
| Soul Classics Vol. 3 | LP | Polydor | 2391166 | 1975 | £5 | £12 | |
| Soul Fire | LP | Polydor | 184148 | 1969 | £8 | £20 | |
| Soul On Top | LP | Polydor | 2310022 | 1971 | £10 | £25 | |
| Soul Power | 7" | Polydor | 2001163 | 1971 | £1.50 | £4 | |
| Stone To The Bone | 7" | Polydor | 2066411 | 1974 | £1.50 | £4 | |
| Super Bad | LP | Polydor | 2310089 | 1971 | £8 | £20 | |
| Super Bad | 7" | Polydor | 2001097 | 1970 | £1.50 | £4 | |
| Tell Me What You're Gonna Do | LP | Ember | EMB3357 | 1964 | £10 | £25 | |
| Tell Me What You're Gonna Do | 7" | Ember | EMBS216 | 1965 | £5 | £10 | |
| That's Life | 7" | Polydor | 56540 | 1970 | £1.50 | £4 | |
| There It Is | LP | Polydor | 2391033 | 1972 | £15 | £30 | |
| There It Is | 7" | Polydor | 2066210 | 1972 | £1.50 | £4 | |
| There Was A Time | 7" | Polydor | 56740 | 1968 | £2.50 | £6 | |
| These Foolish Things | 7" | London | HL9775 | 1963 | £6 | £12 | |
| Think | LP | King | LP683 | 1960 | £25 | £50 | US |
| Think | 7" | Parlophone | R4667 | 1960 | £10 | £20 | |
| Think | 7" | Polydor | 2066329 | 1973 | £1.50 | £4 | |
| This Is James Brown | LP | Philips | 6336201 | 1972 | £4 | £10 | |
| This Is James Brown | LP | Polydor | 643317 | 1969 | £6 | £15 | |
| This Old Heart | 7" | Fontana | H273 | 1960 | £10 | £20 | |
| Tours The USA | LP | London | HA8240 | 1965 | £10 | £25 | |
| Try Me | LP | King | 395635 | 1959 | £30 | £60 | US |
| Try Me | 7" | Philips | BF1458 | 1965 | £2.50 | £6 | |
| Turn It Loose | LP | Polydor | 580701 | 1970 | £10 | £25 | |
| Unbeatable Sixteen Hits | LP | London | HA8203 | 1965 | £10 | £25 | |
| What My Baby Needs Now | 7" | Polydor | 2066283 | 1972 | £1.50 | £4 | |
| Woman | 7" | Polydor | 2066370 | 1973 | £1.50 | £4 | |
| World | 7" | Polydor | 56780 | 1969 | £1.50 | £4 | |

## BROWN, JIM EDWARD

| Title | Format | Label | Catalogue | Year | | |
|---|---|---|---|---|---|---|
| Introducing | 7" EP | RCA | RCX7179 | 1965 | £2 | £5 |

## BROWN, JIM EDWARD & MAXINE

| Title | Format | Label | Catalogue | Year | | |
|---|---|---|---|---|---|---|
| Country Songs | 7" EP | London | REP1024 | 1955 | £5 | £10 |
| Country Songs Vol. 3 | 7" EP | London | REU1044 | 1955 | £5 | £10 |
| Here Today And Gone Tomorrow | 7" EP | London | HLU8200 | 1955 | £7.50 | £15 |
| Itsy Witsy Bitsy Me | 7" | London | HL8123 | 1955 | £10 | £20 |
| Your Love Is Wild As The West Wind | 7" | London | HLU8166 | 1955 | £10 | £20 |

## BROWN, JOE

As the guitarist on Billy Fury's highly regarded *Sound Of Fury* album, Joe Brown had considerable credibility, yet his own records are wildly variable in quality. The problem was that Brown seemed to be determined to prove his versatility, but when this included the performance of old music-hall songs and an instrumental version of 'All Things Bright And Beautiful', then the effort did not seem to be particularly worthwhile. At his best, however, such as on the succession of hit singles begun with 'A Picture Of You', Brown created an effective form of robust pop-country that could, perhaps, have become a significant influence if only he had developed it further.

| Title | Format | Label | Catalogue | Year | | | Notes |
|---|---|---|---|---|---|---|---|
| All Things Bright And Beautiful | 7" EP | Piccadilly | NEP34026 | 1962 | £2 | £5 | |
| Darktown Strutters Ball | 7" | Decca | F11207 | 1960 | £2.50 | £6 | |
| Here Comes Joe Brown | LP | Golden Guinea | GGL0231 | 1963 | £4 | £10 | |
| Hit Parade | 7" EP | Piccadilly | NEP34025 | 1962 | £2 | £5 | |
| It Only Took A Minute | 7" | Piccadilly | 7N35082 | 1962 | £1.50 | £4 | |
| Jellied Eels | 7" | Decca | F11246 | 1960 | £2 | £5 | |
| Live | LP | Piccadilly | NPL38006 | 1963 | £4 | £10 | |
| Mrs O's Theme | 7" EP | Pye | PNV24195 | 1967 | £5 | £10 | French |
| People Gotta Talk | 7" | Decca | F11185 | 1959 | £2.50 | £6 | |
| Picture Of Joe Brown | LP | Ace Of Clubs | ACL1127 | 1962 | £4 | £10 | |
| Picture Of Joe Brown | 7" EP | Decca | DFE8500 | 1962 | £2.50 | £6 | |
| Picture Of You | LP | Golden Guinea | GGL0146 | 1962 | £4 | £10 | |
| Picture Of You | 7" | Piccadilly | 7N35047 | 1962 | £1.50 | £4 | |
| Satisfied Mind | 7" | Pye | 7N17184 | 1966 | £1.50 | £4 | |
| Shine | 7" | Pye | 7N15322 | 1960 | £1.50 | £4 | |
| That's What Love Will Do | 7" | Piccadilly | 7N35106 | 1963 | £1.50 | £4 | |

## BROWN, JOE & MARK WYNTER

| Title | Format | Label | Catalogue | Year | | |
|---|---|---|---|---|---|---|
| Big Hits | 7" EP | Golden Guinea | WO1 | 1963 | £2 | £5 |
| Just For Fun | 7" EP | Pye | NEP24167 | 1963 | £2 | £5 |

## BROWN, K.

| Title | Format | Label | Catalogue | Year | | |
|---|---|---|---|---|---|---|
| Pocket Money | 7" | Blue Beat | BB66 | 1961 | £6 | £12 |

## BROWN, KENT & THE RAINBOWS

| Title | Format | Label | Catalogue | Year | | |
|---|---|---|---|---|---|---|
| Come Ya Come Ya | 7" | Fab | FAB53 | 1968 | £2 | £5 |

## BROWN, LAWRENCE

| Title | Format | Label | Catalogue | Year | | |
|---|---|---|---|---|---|---|
| Slide Trombone | LP | Columbia | 33CX10046 | 1956 | £6 | £15 |

## BROWN, LES

| | | | | | | | |
|---|---|---|---|---|---|---|---|
| Forty Cups Of Coffee | 7" | Vogue Coral | Q72242 | 1957 | £2 | £5 | |
| Frenesi | 7" | Capitol | CL14331 | 1955 | £1.50 | £4 | |
| He Needs Me | 7" | Capitol | CL14350 | 1955 | £1.50 | £4 | |
| Les Brown Band | 10" LP | Vogue Coral | LVC10017 | 1955 | £5 | £12 | |
| Les Brown Band | 10" LP | Vogue Coral | LVC10033 | 1956 | £5 | £12 | |
| Les Brown Orchestra | 10" LP | Vogue Coral | LVC10002 | 1955 | £5 | £12 | |

## BROWN, MARION

| | | | | | | | |
|---|---|---|---|---|---|---|---|
| Afternoon Of A Georgia Faun | LP | ECM | ECM1004ST | 1970 | £5 | £12 | |
| Geechee Recollections | LP | Impulse | AS9252 | 1973 | £6 | £15 | US |
| Marion Brown Quartet | LP | Fontana | SFJL930 | 1967 | £6 | £15 | |
| Porto Novo | LP | Polydor | 583724 | 1969 | £8 | £20 | |

## BROWN, MARK

| | | | | | | | |
|---|---|---|---|---|---|---|---|
| Brown Low Special | 7" | Island | WI3097 | 1967 | £5 | £10 | ...Dawn Penn B side |

## BROWN, MAXINE

| | | | | | | | |
|---|---|---|---|---|---|---|---|
| All In My Mind | 7" | London | HLU9286 | 1961 | £5 | £10 | |
| Fabulous Sound Of Maxine Brown | LP | Wand | WD656 | 1963 | £5 | £12 | US |
| Greatest Hits | LP | Wand | WD(S)684 | 1967 | £5 | £12 | US |
| I've Got A Lot Of Love Left In Me | 7" | Pye | 7N25410 | 1967 | £2 | £5 | |
| It's Gonna Be Alright | 7" | Pye | 7N25299 | 1965 | £2 | £5 | |
| Oh No Not My Baby | 7" | Pye | 7N25272 | 1964 | £4 | £8 | |
| One Step At A Time | 7" | Pye | 7N25311 | 1965 | £4 | £8 | |
| Promise Me Anything | 7" | HMV | POP1102 | 1962 | £15 | £30 | |
| Since I Found You | 7" | Pye | 7N25434 | 1967 | £2.50 | £6 | |
| Spotlight On Maxine Brown | LP | Wand | WD(S)663 | 1965 | £5 | £12 | US |
| Yesterday's Kisses | 7" | Stateside | SS188 | 1963 | £5 | £10 | |

## BROWN, NAPPY

| | | | | | | | |
|---|---|---|---|---|---|---|---|
| Don't Be Angry | 7" | London | HL8145 | 1955 | £210 | £350 | ...best auctioned |
| It Don't Hurt No More | 7" | London | HLC8760 | 1958 | £20 | £40 | |
| Little By Little | 7" | London | HLC8384 | 1957 | £100 | £200 | ...best auctioned |
| Nappy Brown Sings | LP | Savoy | MG14002 | 1958 | £37.50 | £75 | US |
| Pitter Patter | 7" | London | HLC8182 | 1955 | £150 | £250 | ...best auctioned |
| Right Time | LP | Savoy | MG14025 | 1960 | £25 | £50 | US |

## BROWN, NOEL

| | | | | | | | |
|---|---|---|---|---|---|---|---|
| Man's Temptation | 7" | Island | WI3149 | 1968 | £4 | £8 | |

## BROWN, PETE

Pete Brown was one of the first poets to attempt to make a living by giving readings of his work, but achieved his greatest success as lyricist for Cream and for Jack Bruce solo. His own rock groups – Battered Ornaments and Piblokto – were interesting and featured strong contributions from musicians with their feet in both the jazz and rock camps, such as Chris Spedding, Jim Mullen and George Khan. They were ultimately handicapped, however, by their vocalist's (Brown himself) inability to sing.

| | | | | | | | |
|---|---|---|---|---|---|---|---|
| Art School Dance Goes On Forever | LP | Harvest | SHVL768 | 1970 | £25 | £50 | |
| Can't Get Off The Planet | 7" | Harvest | HAR5023 | 1970 | £2 | £5 | |
| Flying Hero Sandwich | 7" | Harvest | HAR5028 | 1970 | £2 | £5 | |
| Living Life Backwards | 7" | Harvest | HAR5008 | 1970 | £2 | £5 | |
| Meal You Can Shake Hands With In The Dark | LP | Harvest | SHVL752 | 1969 | £25 | £50 | |
| My Last Band | LP | Harvest | SHSM2017 | 1977 | £6 | £15 | |
| Not Forgotten Association | LP | Deram | SML1103 | 1973 | £30 | £60 | |
| Thousands On A Raft | LP | Harvest | SHVL782 | 1970 | £25 | £50 | |
| Week Looked Good On Paper | 7" | Parlophone | R5767 | 1969 | £5 | £10 | |
| Week Looked Good On Paper | 7" | Parlophone | R5767 | 1969 | £15 | £30 | ... demo, picture sleeve |

## BROWN, PETE & IAN LYNN

| | | | | | | | |
|---|---|---|---|---|---|---|---|
| Party In The Rain | LP | Discs International | INTLP1 | 1982 | £20 | £40 | |

## BROWN, PETE (2)

| | | | | | | | |
|---|---|---|---|---|---|---|---|
| Pete Brown Sextet | 10" LP | London | LZN14002 | 1955 | £15 | £30 | |

## BROWN, RAY

| | | | | | | | |
|---|---|---|---|---|---|---|---|
| Bass Hit | 10" LP | Columbia | 33C9037 | 1957 | £8 | £20 | |

## BROWN, RICKY & THE HI-LITES

| | | | | | | | |
|---|---|---|---|---|---|---|---|
| Liverpool Beat! | LP | CBS | 62262 | 1965 | £50 | £100 | ...German |

## BROWN, ROY

| | | | | | | | |
|---|---|---|---|---|---|---|---|
| Blues Are All Brown | LP | Bluesway | BLS6019 | 1968 | £5 | £12 | US |
| Hard Luck Blues | LP | King | KS1130 | 1971 | £5 | £12 | US |
| Hard Times | LP | Bluesway | BLS6056 | 1973 | £5 | £12 | US |
| Live At Monterey | LP | Epic | BG30473 | 1971 | £5 | £12 | US |
| Party Doll | 7" | London | HLP8399 | 1957 | £150 | £250 | ...best auctioned |
| Saturday Night | 7" | London | HLP8448 | 1957 | £210 | £350 | ...best auctioned |
| Sings 24 Hits | LP | King | (KS)956 | 1966 | £8 | £20 | US |

## BROWN, ROY & WYNONIE HARRIS

| | | | | | | | |
|---|---|---|---|---|---|---|---|
| Battle Of The Blues Vol. 1 | LP | King | 607 | 1958 | £75 | £150 | US |
| Battle Of The Blues Vol. 2 | LP | King | 627 | 1959 | £75 | £150 | US |

## BROWN, ROY, WYNONIE HARRIS & EDDIE VINSON
Battle Of The Blues Vol. 4 ....................... LP ...... King .............. 668 ....................... 1960 £180 ..... £300 ........................ US

## BROWN, RUTH
| | | | | | | | | |
Along Comes Ruth ....................... LP ..... Philips .......... 652012BL ........... 1962 £10 ......... £25
As Long As I'm Moving.................. 7" ..... London .......... HLE8210 ........... 1955 £87.50 .. £175
Best Of Ruth Brown ....................... LP ..... Atlantic .......... ATL5007 ........... 1964 £25 ......... £50
Don't Deceive Me............................ 7" ..... London .......... HLE9093 ........... 1960 £7.50 ..... £15
Gospel Time ....................... LP ..... Philips .......... 652020BL ........... 1963 £10 ......... £25
Gospel Time ....................... 7" EP . Philips .......... BE12537 ........... 1963 £12.50 .... £25
I Don't Know ....................... 7" ..... London .......... HLE8946 ........... 1959 £10 ......... £20
I Want To Do More .................. 7" ..... London .......... HLE8310 ........... 1956 £37.50 ... £75
Jack Of Diamonds ....................... 7" ..... London .......... HLE8887 ........... 1959 £15 ......... £30
Just Too Much ....................... 7" ..... London .......... HLE8645 ........... 1958 £20 ......... £40
Late Date.............................. LP ..... Atlantic .......... (S)1308 ........... 1959 £30 ......... £60 ........................ US
Late Date.............................. LP ..... London .......... LTZK15187 ........... 1960 £15 ......... £30
Lucky Lips.......................... 7" ..... Columbia .......... DB3913 ........... 1957 £62.50 .. £125
Mambo Baby ....................... 7" ..... London .......... HL8153 ........... 1955 £87.50 .. £175
Miss Rhythm ....................... LP ..... Atlantic .......... 8026 .......... ----- ........... 1959 £30 ......... £60 ........................ US
Mom Oh Mom ....................... 7" ..... London .......... HLE8401 ........... 1957 £37.50 ... £75
New Love ....................... 7" ..... London .......... HLE8552 ........... 1958 £20 ......... £40
One More Time ....................... 7" ..... London .......... HLE8483 ........... 1957 £20 ......... £40
Queen Of R&B....................... 7" EP . London .......... REE1038 ........... 1955 £50 ......... £100
Rockin' With Ruth........................ LP ..... London .......... HAE2106 ........... 1958 £50 ......... £100
Ruth Brown ....................... LP ..... Atlantic .......... 8004 ........... 1957 £37.50 ... £75 ........................ US
Ruth Brown '65 ....................... LP ..... Mainstream ..... 1/S6044 ........... 1965 £5 ......... £12 ........................ US
Ruth Brown Sings ..................... 10" LP Atlantic .......... 115 ........... 1956 £400 ......... £600 ........................ US
Sure Nuff ....................... 7" ..... London .......... HLK9304 ........... 1961 £7.50 ..... £15
This Little Girl's Gone Rocking............ 7" ..... London .......... HL7061 ........... 1958 £10 ......... £20 ........................ export
This Little Girl's Gone Rocking............ 7" ..... London .......... HLE8757 ........... 1958 £20 ......... £40
Yes Sir That's My Baby .................. 7" ...... Brunswick ...... 05904 ........... 1964 £5 ......... £10

## BROWN, RUTH & JOE TURNER
King And Queen Of R&B ....................... 7" EP . London .......... REE1047 ........... 1956 £75 ......... £150

## BROWN, SANDY
Doctor McJazz ............................... LP ..... Columbia ........ 33SX1306/ ........... 1961 £5 ......... £12 ...with Al Fairweather
                                                                         SCX3367 ...............
McJazz .......................... LP ..... Nixa .......... NJL9............... 1957 £6 ......... £15
Playing Compositions By Al Fairweather .... LP ..... Tempo .......... TAP3............... 1956 £15 ......... £30
Traditional Jazz Vol. 2 ............................ 10" LP Esquire............ 20022............... 1953 £8 ......... £20

## BROWN, TINY
No More Blues ................................. 78....... Capitol.......... CL13306 ........... 1950 £6 ......... £12

## BROWN BROTHERS
Let The Good Times Roll.................. 7" ...... Vogue .......... V9131 ................... 1959 £50 ......... £100

## BROWNE, DUNCAN
Duncan Browne ............................... LP ..... Rak .......... SRKA6754 ........... 1973 £4 ......... £10
Give Me Take You ............................ LP ..... Immediate ...... IMSP018 ........... 1968 £10 ......... £25
On The Bombsite ............................ 7" ..... Immediate ...... IM070............... 1968 £2 ......... £5

## BROWNE, FRIDAY
Ask Any Woman............................... 7" ...... Fontana .......... TF851............... 1967 £1.50 ......... £4
Getting Nowhere .......................... 7" ...... Parlophone ..... R5396 ............... 1966 £1.50 ......... £4
Thirty Second Love Affair .................. 7" ...... Fontana .......... TF736................... 1966 £1.50 ......... £4

## BROWNE, JACKSON
Jackson Browne ............................... LP ..... Asylum .......... SD5051 ........... 1972 £5 ......... £12 ........canvas cover, US
Late For The Sky ............................ LP ..... Asylum .......... K243007 ........... 1974 £4 ......... £10 ........................ quad
Pretender................................ LP ..... Mobile Fidelity MFSL1055 ............. 1981 £4 ......... £10 ......... US audiophile

## BROWNE, SANDRA
Johnny Boy ............................... 7" ...... Columbia ........ DB4998 ........... 1963 £1.50 ......... £4
Knock On Any Door .......................... 7" ...... Columbia ........ DB7465 ........... 1965 £2 ......... £5
You'd Think He Didn't Know Me ........... 7" ...... Columbia ........ DB7109 ........... 1963 £1.50 ......... £4

## BROWNE, TEDDY
Pretty Little Baby ...................... 7" ...... Starlite ............ ST45033 ........... 1961 £2 ......... £5

## BROWNE, THOMAS F.
Wednesday's Child .......................... LP ..... Vertigo .......... 6343700 ................. 1972 £20 ......... £40 ........spiral label

## BROWNHILL STAMP DUTY
Maxwell's Silver Hammer ...................... 7" ...... Columbia ........ DB8625 ........... 1969 £1.50 ......... £4

## BROWNS
In The Country ....................... 7" EP . RCA .......... RCX187 ............. 1960 £2.50 ......... £6
Sweet Sounds By The Browns.................. LP ..... RCA .......... RD27153/SF5052... 1959 £5 ......... £12

## BROWNSVILLE STATION
Brownsville Station.................. LP ..... Palladium ........ P1004 ................. 1970 £4 ......... £10 ........................ US

## BROX, VICTOR & ANNETTE
Rollin' Back ....................... LP ..... Sonet .......... SNTF663 ........... 1974 £5 ......... £12
Wake Me And Shake Me ....................... 7" ...... Fontana.......... TF536................. 1965 £1.50 ......... £4

## BRUBECK, DAVE

| | | | | | | | |
|---|---|---|---|---|---|---|---|
| At Storyville | LP | Philips | BBL7018 | 1955 | £6 | £15 | |
| Bernstein Plays Brubeck Plays Bernstein | LP | Fontana | TFL5114/STFL542 | 1960 | £4 | £10 | |
| Best Of Brubeck | LP | Fontana | TFL5136 | 1961 | £4 | £10 | |
| Brubeck And Rushing | LP | Fontana | TFL5126/STFL550 | 1961 | £4 | £10 | |
| Dave Brubeck | LP | Philips | BBL7116 | 1957 | £5 | £12 | |
| Dave Brubeck And Jay And Kai At Newport | LP | Philips | BBL7147 | 1957 | £6 | £15 | ...with J. J. Johnson & Kai Winding |
| Dave Brubeck Quartet | LP | Philips | BBL7041 | 1955 | £6 | £15 | |
| Dave Brubeck Quartet | LP | Philips | BBL7060 | 1956 | £6 | £15 | |
| Dave Brubeck Quartet | LP | Vogue | LAE12105 | 1959 | £4 | £10 | |
| Dave Brubeck Quartet | 10" LP | Vogue | LDE095 | 1954 | £10 | £25 | |
| Dave Brubeck Quartet Featuring Paul Desmond | LP | Vogue | LAE12114 | 1959 | £6 | £15 | |
| Dave Brubeck Quartet Vol. 2 | 10" LP | Vogue | LDE104 | 1954 | £10 | £25 | |
| Dave Brubeck Quartet Vol. 3 | 10" LP | Vogue | LDE114 | 1955 | £10 | £25 | |
| Dave Brubeck Trio | 10" LP | Vogue | LDE090 | 1954 | £10 | £25 | |
| Dave Digs Disney | LP | Fontana | TFL5017 | 1957 | £5 | £12 | |
| Fabulous Trio And Octet | LP | Vogue | LAE12008 | 1956 | £8 | £20 | |
| Gone With The Wind | LP | Fontana | TFL5071 | 1960 | £4 | £10 | |
| Gone With The Wind | LP | Fontana | TFL5071/STFL501 | 1959 | £5 | £12 | |
| In Europe | LP | Fontana | TFL5034 | 1959 | £4 | £10 | |
| Jazz At Oberlin | LP | Vogue | LAE12048 | 1957 | £8 | £20 | |
| Jazz At The Black Hawk | LP | Vogue | LAE12094 | 1958 | £5 | £12 | |
| Jazz At The College Of The Pacific | LP | Vogue | LAE12110 | 1960 | £5 | £12 | |
| Jazz Goes To College | LP | Philips | BBL7447 | 1960 | £4 | £10 | |
| Jazz Goes To Junior College | LP | Fontana | TFL5002 | 1958 | £5 | £12 | |
| Jazz Impressions Of Eurasia | LP | Fontana | TFL5051 | 1959 | £4 | £10 | |
| Jazz Impressions Of The USA | LP | Philips | BBL7171 | 1957 | £5 | £12 | |
| Newport 1958 | LP | Fontana | TFL5059 | 1959 | £4 | £10 | |
| Riddle | LP | Fontana | TFL5101/STFL532 | 1960 | £4 | £10 | |
| Southern Scene | LP | Fontana | TFL5099/STFL530 | 1960 | £4 | £10 | |
| Time Further Out | LP | CBS | BPG62078 | 1962 | £4 | £10 | |
| Time In | LP | CBS | 62757 | 1966 | £4 | £10 | |
| Time Out | LP | Fontana | TFL5085/STFL523 | 1960 | £5 | £10 | |
| Tonight Only! | LP | Fontana | STFL566 | 1961 | £4 | £10 | . with Carmen McRae |

## BRUCE, JACK

As a member of the Graham Bond Organization, John Mayall's Bluesbreakers (briefly) and Cream, Jack Bruce was perhaps the first rock bass player to attract notice for the excellence of his musicianship. At the same time, he was playing jazz with the likes of Mike Taylor, Mike Gibbs and John McLaughlin, as well as developing a fruitful songwriting partnership with poet Pete Brown. The solo albums from 1969 and 1971 (as well as the impressive *Out Of The Storm* from 1974) combine all these talents in magnificent manner and make it all the more a matter of regret that Bruce's career since then has consisted largely of a catalogue of lost opportunities.

| | | | | | | | |
|---|---|---|---|---|---|---|---|
| Consul At Sunset | 7" | Polydor | 2058153 | 1971 | £1.50 | £4 | |
| Harmony Row | LP | Polydor | 2310107 | 1971 | £4 | £10 | |
| I'm Gettin' Tired | 7" | Polydor | 56036 | 1965 | £30 | £60 | |
| Songs For A Tailor | LP | Polydor | 583058 | 1969 | £5 | £12 | |
| Songs For A Tailor | CD | Polydor | 8352422 | 1988 | £5 | £12 | |
| Things We Like | LP | Polydor | 2343033 | 1970 | £4 | £10 | |

## BRUCE, LENNY

| | | | | | | | |
|---|---|---|---|---|---|---|---|
| Berkeley Concert | LP | Transatlantic | TRA195 | 1969 | £10 | £25 | double |
| Best Of Lenny Bruce | LP | Fantasy | 7012 | 1962 | £8 | £20 | US |
| Carnegie Hall February 4,1961 | LP | United Artists | UAS9800 | 1971 | £8 | £20 | US triple |
| Essential Lenny Bruce | LP | Douglas | SD788 | 1968 | £6 | £15 | US |
| I Am Not A Nut, Elect Me | LP | Fantasy | 7007 | 1959 | £8 | £20 | US |
| Interviews Of Our Times | LP | Fantasy | 7001 | 1958 | £8 | £20 | US |
| Law, Language And Lenny Bruce | LP | Spector | SP9101 | 1974 | £5 | £12 | US |
| Lenny Bruce | LP | United Artists | UAL3580 | 1967 | £6 | £15 | US |
| Lenny Bruce Is Out Again | LP | Philles | PHLP4010 | 1966 | £30 | £60 | US |
| Lenny Bruce, American | LP | Fantasy | 7011 | 1962 | £8 | £20 | US |
| Live At The Curran Theatre | LP | Fantasy | 34201 | 1972 | £5 | £12 | US |
| Midnight Concert | LP | United Artists | UAS6794 | 196– | £5 | £12 | US |
| Recordings Submitted As Evidence | 10" LP | private | | 1962 | £37.50 | £75 | US |
| Sick Humor Of Lenny Bruce | LP | Fantasy | 7003 | 1958 | £8 | £20 | US |
| Thank You, Masked Man | LP | Fantasy | F7017 | 1972 | £5 | £12 | US |
| To Is A Preposition, Come Is A Verb | LP | Douglas | 2KZ30872 | 1970 | £6 | £15 | US |
| What I Was Arrested For | LP | Douglas | 2KZ30872 | 1971 | £5 | £12 | US |

## BRUCE, TOMMY

| | | | | | | | |
|---|---|---|---|---|---|---|---|
| Boom Boom | 7" | Polydor | BM56006 | 1965 | £2.50 | £6 | |
| Broken Doll | 7" | Columbia | DB4498 | 1960 | £1.50 | £4 | |
| Knockout | 7" EP | Columbia | SEG8077 | 1961 | £25 | £50 | |

## BRUFORD, BILL

| | | | | | | | |
|---|---|---|---|---|---|---|---|
| Bruford Tapes | LP | Canadian Imps. | BRUBOOT28 | 1980 | £4 | £10 | |
| Dig | CD | Editions EG | EEGCD60 | 1989 | £5 | £12 | |
| Feels Good To Me | LP | Polydor | 2302075 | 1978 | £4 | £10 | |
| Gradually Going Tornado | LP | Editions EG | EGLP104 | 1980 | £4 | £10 | |
| One Of A Kind | LP | Polydor | POLD5020 | 1979 | £4 | £10 | |

## BRUISERS

| | | | | | | | |
|---|---|---|---|---|---|---|---|
| Blue Girl | 7" | Parlophone | R5042 | 1963 | £1.50 | £4 | |
| Your Turn To Cry | 7" | Parlophone | R5092 | 1963 | £1.50 | £4 | |

## BRUMBEATS
Cry Little Girl, Cry...................................... 7" ...... Decca ............. F11834................... 1964 £5.......... £10 .................

## BRUMMELL, BEAU
Better Man Than I ................................. 7" ...... Columbia .... DB7675 ................. 1965 £1.50......... £4
I Know Know Know.............................. 7" ...... Columbia .... DB7447 ................. 1965 £1.50......... £4
Next Kiss.............................................. 7" ...... Columbia .... DB7538 ................. 1965 £1.50......... £4
Take Me Like I Am................................ 7" ...... Columbia .... DB7878 ................. 1966 £1.50......... £4 .................

## BRUNNING HALL SUNFLOWER BLUES BAND
Saga was a bargain-priced label, specializing in cheaply produced cash-ins of the prevailing trends. The Brunning Hall Band was Saga's blues band, and by having their records released on the label, the group was fighting a losing battle from the outset with regard to being taken as serious rivals for the likes of Fleetwood Mac or Savoy Brown. In fact, Bob Brunning had been the original bass player with Fleetwood Mac (and plays on one track on the group's debut LP), while Bob Hall played piano on all Savoy Brown's early records, albeit without ever being counted as a member of the group.

Bullen Street Blues ............................. LP ...... Boulevard........ 4032 ............... 1971 £4 .......... £10 ..................
Bullen Street Blues ............................. LP ...... Saga................ FID2118............ 1968 £5 .......... £12 ..................
I Wish You Would................................ LP ...... Saga................ SAGA8150 .......... 1970 £20 ...... £40 ..................
Sunflower Blues Band ......................... LP ...... Gemini ............ GM2010 ........... 1969 £25 ...... £50 ..................
Trackside Blues .................................. LP ...... Saga................ EROS8132............ 1969 £10 ...... £25 ..................

## BRUT
Brut ..................................................... LP ...... Philips............ 6305045 ................ 1970 £5 .......... £12 ................. German

## BRUTE FORCE
Extemporaneous................................... LP ...... B.T.Puppy ...... BTPS1015 ............. 1971 £700 ... £1000 ...................... US
King Of Fuh ......................................... 7" ...... Apple ............. 8 ........................... 1969 £250 .... £400 ......... best auctioned

## BRYAN, CANNONBALL
Man About The Town ......................... 7" ...... Amalgamated... AMG829................. 1968 £2.50..... £6 ........ Hugh Malcolm
                                                                                                                                B side
Red Ash............................................... 7" ...... Trojan............. TR673 ................ 1969 £1.50..... £4 ..... Silvertones B side

## BRYAN, CARL
Run For Your Life ............................... 7" ...... Camel............. CA22 ................. 1969 £1.50..... £4 ... Two Sparks B side

## BRYAN, FITZVAUGHN ORCHESTRA
Evening News....................................... 7" ...... Melodisc ......... 1560 ................. 1960 £2 ............ £5

## BRYAN, WES
Honey Baby.......................................... 7" ...... London ........... HLU8978.......... 1959 £12.50... £25
Lonesome Lover.................................... 7" ...... London ........... HLU8607.......... 1958 £7.50..... £15 .................

## BRYAN & THE BRUNELLES
Jacqueline ........................................... 7" ...... HMV.............. POP1394 .......... 1965 £15......... £20 .................

## BRYANT, ANITA
In My Little Corner Of The World.......... LP ...... London ............. HAL2381 .......... 1961 £10......... £25
Kisses Sweeter Than Wine ................... 7" EP . CBS................ AGG20005 .......... 1962 £2.50....... £6
My Little Corner Of The World.............. 7" ...... London ............. HLL9171............ 1960 £1.50........ £4
My Mind's Playing Tricks On Me Again .... 7" ...... CBS................ 202026............ 1966 £12.50..... £25

## BRYANT, LAURA K.
Bobby .................................................. 7" ...... London ........... HLU8551 .......... 1958 £6.......... £12

## BRYANT, MARIE
Calypso's Too Hot To Handle.................. 7" EP . Kalypso ......... XXEP7 ............. 1963 £4............. £8
Don't Touch Me Nylons ....................... LP ...... Melodisc ......... MLP132.......... 196— £6............ £15
Don't Touch My Nylon ........................ 7" ...... Kalypso ......... XX28 ............... 1961 £1.50........ £4
Water Melon ......................................... 7" ...... Kalypso ......... XX27 ................. 1961 £1.50........ £4

## BRYANT, RAY
Alone With The Blues............................ LP ...... Esquire............ 32106.............. 1960 £15......... £30
Ray Bryant Trio.................................... LP ...... Esquire............ 32066.............. 1958 £20......... £40

## BRYANT, RUSTY
All Night Long...................................... LP ...... Dot ............. DLP3006........... 1956 £8.......... £20 ................... US
Rock 'n' Roll With Rusty Bryant............. 10" LP London ........... HBD1066 ......... 1956 £15......... £30

## BRYANT, SANDRA
Out To Get You ................................... 7" ...... Major Minor ... MM553................. 1968 £1.50....... £4

## BRYARS, GAVIN
Sinking Of The Titanic/Jesus Blood............ LP ...... Obscure .......... OBS1 ............ 1975 £5 .......... £12

## BRYCE, CALUM
Love Maker .......................................... 7" ...... Condor ............ PS1001 ............. 1968 £15......... £30

## BRYDEN, BERYL
Casey Jones......................................... 7" ...... Decca ............. F10823.............. 1956 £2 ............ £5

## BRYE, BETSY
Sleep Walk ........................................... 7" ...... Columbia ........ DB4350 ........... 1959 £1.50........ £4 .................

## BUBBLE PUPPY
Gathering Of Promises.............................. LP ...... International ....... IALP10 ................. 1969 £20........£40 ........................US
........................................................................ Artists ............

## BUBBLEMEN
Bubblemen Rap!........................................ CD-s .. Beggars ........... BULB1CD............ 1988 £2........£5
........................................................................ Banquet ..........

## BUBBLES
Bopping In The Barnyard.......................... 7" ...... Duke .............. DK1001 ................. 1963 £2.50........£6

## BUCCHI, J.-L.
Sunflower.................................................. LP ...... De L'Autre ...... 0047 ..................... 1978 £6........£15 ........................French

## BUCHANAN, ROY
In The Beginning....................................... LP ...... Polydor........... PD6035................ 1975 £4........£10 ........................US
Live Stock ............................................... LP ...... Polydor........... 2391192............... 1975 £4........£10
Loading Zone .......................................... LP ...... Polydor........... 2391295............... 1977 £4........£10
Rescue Me ............................................... LP ...... Polydor........... 2391152............... 1975 £4........£10
Roy Buchanan .......................................... LP ...... Polydor........... 2391042............... 1972 £5........£12
Roy Buchanan .......................................... LP ...... Polydor........... 2482275............... 1976 £4........£10
Second Album .......................................... LP ...... Polydor........... 2391062............... 1973 £5........£12
Street Called Straight ................................ LP ...... Polydor........... 2391233............... 1976 £4........£10
That's What I'm Here For.......................... LP ...... Polydor........... 2391114............... 1974 £4........£10
You're Not Alone ..................................... LP ...... Atlantic ........... SD19170............... 1978 £4........£10 ........................US

## BUCHANAN BROTHERS
Medicine Man............................................ LP ...... Event.............. ES101 ................ 1969 £8........£20 ........................US

## BUCKINGHAM-NICKS
Lindsey Buckingham and Stevie Nicks achieved little success with their LP, yet its sound is almost exactly that of the LPs *Fleetwood Mac* and *Rumours*, with which the Buckingham-Nicks team managed so spectacularly to restore Fleetwood Mac's fortunes. The earlier LP was reissued in 1981, when it might have been expected to do very well, and yet once again the record sank without a trace.

Buckingham-Nicks.................................... LP ...... Polydor ..... 2391093............... 1973 £15........£30
Buckingham-Nicks.................................... LP ...... Polydor ..... 2482378............... 1981 £8........£20
Don't Let Me Down Again ....................... 7" ...... Polydor ..... 2066398............... 1974 £2........£5

## BUCKINGHAMS
Back In Love Again .................................. 7" ...... CBS............. 3559 ................ 1968 £1.50........£4
Don't You Care ........................................ 7" ...... CBS............. 2640 ................ 1968 £2.50........£6
Greatest Hits ............................................ LP ...... Columbia ..... CS9812............ 1969 £5........£12 ........................US
Hey Baby ................................................. 7" ...... CBS............. 2995 ................ 1967 £1.50........£4
I Call Your Name ..................................... 7" ...... Stateside ...... SS529.............. 1966 £1.50........£4
In One Ear And Gone Tomorrow ............ LP ...... Columbia ..... CS9703............ 1968 £5........£12 ........................US
Kind Of A Drag ....................................... LP ...... USA ............ 107 ................ 1967 £6........£15 ........................US
Kind Of A Drag ....................................... LP ...... USA ............ 107 ................ 1967 £8........£20 ..... US, with 'I'm A
........................................................................................................................................................................ Man'
Kind Of A Drag ....................................... 7" EP . Columbia ...... ESRF1841............ 1967 ££10........£20 ........................French
Kind Of A Drag ....................................... 7" ...... Stateside ...... SS588............... 1967 £1.50........£4
Making Up And Breaking Up ................... 7" ...... Stateside ...... SS2011............. 1967 £1.50........£4
Mercy Mercy Mercy................................ 7" ...... CBS............. 2859 ................ 1967 £1.50........£4
Portraits.................................................. LP ...... Columbia ...... CL2798/CS9598.. 1968 £4........£10 ........................US
Susan....................................................... 7" ...... CBS............. 3195 ................ 1967 £1.50........£4
Time And Charges .................................... LP ...... Columbia ...... CL2669/CS9469.. 1967 £4........£10 ........................US

## BUCKINGHAMS (2)
I'll Never Hurt You No More..................... 7" ...... Pye ................ 7N15848............ 1965 £1.50........£4
To Be Or Not To Be ................................ 7" ...... Pye ................ 7N15921............ 1965 £1.50........£4

## BUCKLE, BOB
Come Listen To Bob Buckle ..................... LP ...... Ash................ ALP1075............ 1973 £4........£10

## BUCKLEY, JEFF
Although he disliked the comparison, Jeff Buckley inherited his father's astonishing voice and was able to flex its powers on a set of self-composed songs that, for melodic invention allied to emotional strength, make most others sound a little inadequate. *Grace* is one of the towering albums of the nineties, while the live tours that Buckley undertook in its support showed him to have the same kind of charisma and vitality as the young Bruce Springsteen. The promotional *Album Sampler* emphasizes Columbia's faith in their signing by actually consisting of the entire *Grace* album. Jeff Buckley will be greatly missed.

Album Sampler ........................................ CD..... Columbia........ SAMPCD2281 ........ 1994 £8........£20 ..................promo

## BUCKLEY, SEAN & THE BREADCRUMBS
It Hurts Me When I Cry............................ 7" ...... Stateside .......... SS421.................. 1965 £20........£40 ....................

## BUCKLEY, TIM
It would have been easy for Tim Buckley to stay as the conventional singer-songwriter of *Goodbye And Hello* and his first LP. Instead, he chose to let the incredible range and power of his tenor voice lead him into unexplored territory. *Lorca* and *Starsailor*, with members of the Mothers of Invention amongst its cast of backing musicians, are brave, inspirational recordings, in which Buckley's voice really does function as an instrument – its player an improvising virtuoso of the highest order.

Aren't You The Girl ................................. 7" ...... Elektra ......... EKSN45008 ........... 1967 £1.50........£4
Blue Afternoon ........................................ LP ...... Straight ........... STS1060 ............. 1969 £15........£30
Goodbye And Hello ................................. LP ...... Elektra .......... EKL/EKS318 ......... 1967 £6........£15
Greetings From L.A................................. LP ...... Warner Bros.... K46176 ................. 1972 £4........£10
Happy Sad .............................................. LP ...... Elektra ........... EKS74045 ............. 1968 £8........£20

| Title | Format | Label | Catalogue | Year | | | Notes |
|---|---|---|---|---|---|---|---|
| Happy Time | 7" | Straight | 4799 | 1970 | £1.50 | £4 | |
| Look At The Fool | LP | Discreet | K59204 | 1974 | £4 | £10 | |
| Lorca | LP | Elektra | 2410005 | 1970 | £10 | £25 | |
| Morning Glory | 7" | Elektra | EKSN45018 | 1967 | £1.50 | £4 | |
| Once I Was | 7" | Elektra | EKSN45023 | 1968 | £1.50 | £4 | |
| Peel Sessions | CD-s | Strange Fruit | SFPSCD082 | 1991 | £2 | £5 | |
| Pleasant Street | 7" | Elektra | EKSN45041 | 1968 | £1.50 | £4 | |
| Sefronia | LP | Discreet | K49201 | 1973 | £4 | £10 | |
| Starsailor | LP | Straight | STS1064 | 1970 | £10 | £25 | |
| Tim Buckley | LP | Elektra | EKL/EKS4004 | 1966 | £15 | £30 | |
| Wings | 7" | Elektra | EKSN45031 | 1968 | £1.50 | £4 | |

## BUCKNER, MILT

| Title | Format | Label | Catalogue | Year | | | Notes |
|---|---|---|---|---|---|---|---|
| Rockin' Hammond | 10" LP | Capitol | T722 | 1956 | £5 | £12 | |
| Rocking With Milt | 7" EP | Capitol | EAP1000 | 1956 | £2 | £5 | |

## BUCKNER, TEDDY

| Title | Format | Label | Catalogue | Year | | | Notes |
|---|---|---|---|---|---|---|---|
| Dixieland Jubilee | 10" LP | Vogue | LDE175 | 1956 | £4 | £10 | |
| Salute To Louis Armstrong | LP | Vogue | LAE12129 | 1958 | £4 | £10 | |
| Teddy Buckner | LP | Vogue | LAE12026 | 1957 | £4 | £10 | |

## BUCKY & THE STRINGS

| Title | Format | Label | Catalogue | Year | | | Notes |
|---|---|---|---|---|---|---|---|
| Lolitas On The Loose | 7" | Salvo | SLO1807 | 1962 | £1.50 | £4 | |

## BUDD, HAROLD

| Title | Format | Label | Catalogue | Year | | | Notes |
|---|---|---|---|---|---|---|---|
| Pavilion Of Dreams | LP | Obscure | OBS10 | 1978 | £4 | £10 | |

## BUDD, ROY

| Title | Format | Label | Catalogue | Year | | | Notes |
|---|---|---|---|---|---|---|---|
| Birth Of The Budd | 7" | Pye | 7N15807 | 1965 | £1.50 | £4 | |

## BUDDIES

| Title | Format | Label | Catalogue | Year | | | Notes |
|---|---|---|---|---|---|---|---|
| Buddies And The Compacts | LP | Wing | MGW12293/ SRW16293 | 1965 | £6 | £15 | US |
| Go Go | LP | Wing | MGW12306/ SRW16306 | 1965 | £6 | £15 | US |

## BUDGIE

| Title | Format | Label | Catalogue | Year | | | Notes |
|---|---|---|---|---|---|---|---|
| Budgie | LP | MCA | MCF2506 | 1974 | £4 | £10 | |
| Budgie | LP | MCA | MKPS2018 | 1971 | £8 | £20 | |
| Crash Course In Brain Surgery | 7" | MCA | MK5072 | 1971 | £2.50 | £6 | |
| Crime Against The World | 12" | Active | BUDGIE2 | 1980 | £2.50 | £6 | |
| If Swallowed Do Not Induce Vomiting | 12" | Active | BUDGIE1 | 1980 | £2.50 | £6 | |
| Never Turn Your Back On A Friend | LP | MCA | MDKS8010 | 1973 | £4 | £10 | |
| Squawk | LP | MCA | MKPS2023 | 1972 | £5 | £12 | |

## BUENA VISTAS

| Title | Format | Label | Catalogue | Year | | | Notes |
|---|---|---|---|---|---|---|---|
| Hot Shot | 7" | Stateside | SS525 | 1966 | £5 | £10 | |

## BUFFALO

| Title | Format | Label | Catalogue | Year | | | Notes |
|---|---|---|---|---|---|---|---|
| Average Rock 'n' Roller | LP | Vertigo | 6357104 | 1977 | £20 | £40 | Australian |
| Dead Forever | LP | Vertigo | 6357007 | 1971 | £30 | £60 | Australian |
| Mother's Choice | LP | Vertigo | 6357103 | 1976 | £25 | £50 | Australian |
| Volcanic Rock | LP | Vertigo | 6357101 | 1973 | £30 | £60 | Australian |

## BUFFALO (2)

| Title | Format | Label | Catalogue | Year | | | Notes |
|---|---|---|---|---|---|---|---|
| Battle Torn Heroes | 7" | Heavy Metal | HEAVY3 | 1981 | £2 | £5 | |
| Mean Machine | 7" | Heavy Metal | HEAVY15 | 1982 | £2.50 | £6 | |

## BUFFALO NICKEL JUGBAND

| Title | Format | Label | Catalogue | Year | | | Notes |
|---|---|---|---|---|---|---|---|
| Buffalo Nickel Jugband | LP | Happy Tiger | 1018 | 1971 | £5 | £12 | US |

## BUFFALO SPRINGFIELD

The uneasy alliance that existed between Buffalo Springfield's three major talents – Neil Young, Steve Stills and Richie Furay – meant that the group was never destined to last very long. The competition, however, inspired the three into producing some particularly inventive material, which turns *Buffalo Springfield Again* into one of the key albums of the late sixties. By comparison, the eponymous first album is strictly formative, while *Last Time Around*, released when the group had already split, suffers from being compiled from the material that the three songwriters did not particularly want to keep for their next projects.

| Title | Format | Label | Catalogue | Year | | | Notes |
|---|---|---|---|---|---|---|---|
| Beginning | LP | Atlantic | K30028 | 1973 | £4 | £10 | |
| Best Of/Retrospective | LP | Atlantic | K40071 | 1972 | £4 | £10 | |
| Bluebird | 7" | Atlantic | K10237 | 1972 | £1.50 | £4 | picture sleeve |
| Buffalo Springfield | LP | Atlantic | 587/588070 | 1967 | £8 | £20 | |
| Buffalo Springfield | LP | Atlantic | 587/588070 | 1967 | £20 | £40 | with 'Baby Don't Scold Me' |
| Buffalo Springfield | LP | Atlantic | K70001 | 1973 | £6 | £15 | double |
| Buffalo Springfield Again | LP | Atlantic | 587/588091 | 1968 | £6 | £15 | |
| Buffalo Springfield Again | LP | Atlantic | K40014 | 1971 | £4 | £10 | |
| Expecting To Fly | LP | Atlantic | 2462012 | 1970 | £4 | £10 | |
| Expecting To Fly | 7" | Atlantic | 584165 | 1968 | £1.50 | £4 | |
| For What It's Worth | 7" EP | Atco | 123 | 1967 | £37.50 | £75 | French |
| For What It's Worth | 7" | Atlantic | 584077 | 1967 | £1.50 | £4 | |
| Last Time Around | LP | Atco | 228024 | 1969 | £6 | £15 | |
| Last Time Around | LP | Atlantic | K40077 | 1971 | £5 | £12 | |
| Pretty Girl Why | 7" | Atco | 226006 | 1969 | £1.50 | £4 | |
| Retrospective | LP | Atco | 228012 | 1969 | £5 | £12 | |
| Rock 'n' Roll Woman | 7" | Atlantic | 584145 | 1967 | £1.50 | £4 | |
| Uno Mundo | 7" | Atlantic | 584189 | 1968 | £1.50 | £4 | |

## BUFFOONS
| | | | | | | | |
|---|---|---|---|---|---|---|---|
| Girls Beat | LP | Hor Zu | SHZE234 | 1967 £10 | £25 | | German |
| My World Fell Down | 7" | Columbia | DB8317 | 1967 £1.50 | £4 | | |

## BUGGS
| | | | | | | | |
|---|---|---|---|---|---|---|---|
| Beetle Beat | LP | Coronet | 212 | 1964 £6 | £15 | | US |

## BULL
| | | | | | | | |
|---|---|---|---|---|---|---|---|
| This Is Bull | LP | Paramount | PAS5028 | 1970 £8 | £20 | | US |

## BULL, SANDY
| | | | | | | | |
|---|---|---|---|---|---|---|---|
| E Pluribus Unum | LP | Vanguard | SVRL19040 | 1969 £4 | £10 | | |
| Fantasias | LP | Vanguard | VSD79119 | 1963 £5 | £12 | | US |
| Inventions | LP | Vanguard | VSD79191 | 1965 £5 | £12 | | US |

## BULLDOG BREED
| | | | | | | | |
|---|---|---|---|---|---|---|---|
| Made In England | LP | Nova | (S)DN5 | 1970 £15 | £30 | | |
| Portcullis Gate | 7" | Deram | DM270 | 1969 £10 | £20 | | |

## BULLDOGS
| | | | | | | | |
|---|---|---|---|---|---|---|---|
| John, Paul, George, and Ringo | 7" | Mercury | MF808 | 1964 £2.50 | £6 | | |

## BULLET
| | | | | | | | |
|---|---|---|---|---|---|---|---|
| Hobo | 7" | Purple | PUR101 | 1971 £1.50 | £4 | | |

## BULLET (2)
| | | | | | | | |
|---|---|---|---|---|---|---|---|
| Hanged Man | LP | Contour | 2870437 | 1975 £10 | £25 | | |

## BULLY WEE BAND
| | | | | | | | |
|---|---|---|---|---|---|---|---|
| Bully Wee | LP | Folksound | FS102AB | 1975 £10 | £25 | | |
| Enchanted Lady | LP | Red Rag | RRR007 | 1976 £6 | £15 | | |
| Madmen Of Gotham | LP | Red Rag | | 1981 £6 | £15 | | |
| Silvermines | LP | Red Rag | RRR017 | 1978 £6 | £15 | | |

## BUMBLE, B. & THE STINGERS
| | | | | | | | |
|---|---|---|---|---|---|---|---|
| Bumble Boogie | 7" | Top Rank | JAR561 | 1961 £1.50 | £4 | | |
| Nut Rocker | 7" EP | Pathe | EMF316 | 1962 £10 | £20 | | French |
| Piano Stylings Of B. Bumble | 7" EP | Stateside | SE1001 | 1962 £7.50 | £15 | | |

## BUMP
| | | | | | | | |
|---|---|---|---|---|---|---|---|
| Bump | LP | Pioneer | PRSD2150 | 1970 £250 | £400 | | US |

## BUNCH
The Bunch was not a real group as such, but rather members and friends of Fairport Convention on holiday. *Rock On* contains their versions of a number of rock'n'roll classics – and it has to be admitted that once the novelty of hearing these particular musicians tackling this kind of material has worn off, the results are not especially impressive.

| | | | | | | | |
|---|---|---|---|---|---|---|---|
| Rock On | LP | Island | ILPS9189 | 1972 £10 | £25 | | with flexi |

## BUNCH (2)
| | | | | | | | |
|---|---|---|---|---|---|---|---|
| Birthday | 7" | CBS | 3692 | 1968 £4 | £8 | | |
| Birthday | 7" | CBS | 3709 | 1968 £2.50 | £6 | | |
| Spare A Shilling | 7" | CBS | 3060 | 1967 £20 | £40 | | |
| You Can't Do This | 7" | CBS | 2740 | 1967 £2.50 | £6 | | |
| You Never Came Home | 7" | CBS | 202506 | 1967 £15 | £30 | | |

## BUNCH OF FIVES
| | | | | | | | |
|---|---|---|---|---|---|---|---|
| Go Home Baby | 7" | Parlophone | R5494 | 1966 £10 | £20 | | |

## BUNN, ROGER
| | | | | | | | |
|---|---|---|---|---|---|---|---|
| Piece Of Mind | LP | Major Minor | SMLP70 | 1971 £6 | £15 | | |

## BUNNY & RUDDY
| | | | | | | | |
|---|---|---|---|---|---|---|---|
| On The Town | 7" | Nu Beat | NB011 | 1968 £2.50 | £6 | . Monty Morris B side | |
| True Romance | 7" | Nu Beat | NB007 | 1968 £2.50 | £6 | Bobby Kalphat B side | |

## BUNTING, BOB
| | | | | | | | |
|---|---|---|---|---|---|---|---|
| You've Got To Go Down This Way | LP | Transatlantic | TRA166 | 1968 £8 | £20 | | |

## BUNYAN, VASHTI
| | | | | | | | |
|---|---|---|---|---|---|---|---|
| Just Another Diamond Day | LP | Philips | 6308019 | 1971 £250 | £400 | | |

## BURCHETTE, WILBURN
| | | | | | | | |
|---|---|---|---|---|---|---|---|
| Guitar Grimoire | LP | Burchette | 001 | 1973 £50 | £100 | | US |
| Mind Storm | LP | Burchette | 007 | 1977 £50 | £100 | | US |
| Music Of The Godhead | LP | Burchette | 003 | 1975 £50 | £100 | | US |
| Occult Concert | LP | Ames | 7014 | 1971 £50 | £100 | | US |
| Opens The Seven Gates | LP | Ebos | 0001 | 1972 £50 | £100 | | US |
| Psychic Meditation Music | LP | Burchette | 002 | 1974 £50 | £100 | | US |
| Transcendental Music For Meditation | LP | Burchette | 004 | 1976 £50 | £100 | | US |

## BURDON, ERIC
| | | | | | | | |
|---|---|---|---|---|---|---|---|
| Guilty | LP | United Artists | UAG29251 | 1971 £5 | £12 | | with Jimmy Witherspoon |

## BURDON, ERIC & THE ANIMALS

| Title | Format | Label | Cat. No. | Year | | | Notes |
|---|---|---|---|---|---|---|---|
| Eric Is Here | LP | MGM | (S)E4433 | 1967 | £8 | £20 | US |
| Everyone Of Us | LP | MGM | (S)E4553 | 1968 | £6 | £15 | US |
| Good Times | 7" | MGM | MGM1344 | 1967 | £1.50 | £4 | |
| Hey Gyp | 7" EP | Barclay | 071121 | 1967 | £10 | £20 | French |
| Love Is | LP | MGM | 2354006/7 | 1971 | £8 | £20 | double |
| Love Is | LP | MGM | CS8105 | 1968 | £5 | £12 | |
| Love Is | LP | MGM | SE4591/2 | 1968 | £10 | £25 | US double |
| Monterey | 7" | MGM | MGM1412 | 1968 | £1.50 | £4 | |
| Ring Of Fire | 7" | MGM | MGM1461 | 1969 | £1.50 | £4 | |
| River Deep Mountain High | 7" | MGM | MGM1481 | 1969 | £1.50 | £4 | |
| San Franciscan Nights | 7" | MGM | MGM1359 | 1967 | £1.50 | £4 | |
| See See Rider | 7" EP | Barclay | 071081 | 1966 | £10 | £20 | French |
| Sky Pilot | 7" | MGM | MGM1373 | 1968 | £1.50 | £4 | |
| Twain Shall Meet | LP | MGM | CS8074 | 1968 | £6 | £15 | |
| When I Was Young | 7" | MGM | MGM1340 | 1967 | £1.50 | £4 | |
| Winds Of Change | LP | MGM | 2354001 | 1971 | £4 | £10 | |
| Winds Of Change | LP | MGM | C(S)8052 | 1967 | £6 | £15 | |
| Winds Of Change | CD | Polydor | 8257122 | 1985 | £5 | £12 | |

## BURDON, ERIC & WAR

| Title | Format | Label | Cat. No. | Year | | | Notes |
|---|---|---|---|---|---|---|---|
| Blackman's Burdon | LP | Liberty | LDS8400 | 1970 | £6 | £15 | double |
| Eric Burdon Declares War | LP | Polydor | 2310041 | 1970 | £4 | £10 | |

## BURGESS, DAVE

| Title | Format | Label | Cat. No. | Year | | |
|---|---|---|---|---|---|---|
| I Love Paris | 7" | London | HLB8175 | 1955 | £10 | £20 |
| I'm Available | 7" | Oriole | CB1413 | 1957 | £30 | £60 |

## BURGESS, JOHN

| Title | Format | Label | Cat. No. | Year | | |
|---|---|---|---|---|---|---|
| King Of Highland Pipers | LP | Topic | 12T199 | 1969 | £5 | £12 |

## BURGESS, SONNY

| Title | Format | Label | Cat. No. | Year | | |
|---|---|---|---|---|---|---|
| Sadie's Back In Town | 7" | London | HLS9064 | 1960 | £75 | £150 |

## BURKE, JOE, ANDY MCGANN & FELIX DOLAN

| Title | Format | Label | Cat. No. | Year | | |
|---|---|---|---|---|---|---|
| Tribute To Michael Coleman | LP | Shaskeen | 05360 | 1970 | £6 | £15 |

## BURKE, KEVIN & JACKIE DALY

| Title | Format | Label | Cat. No. | Year | | | Notes |
|---|---|---|---|---|---|---|---|
| Eavesdropper | LP | Mulligan | LUN039 | 1981 | £5 | £12 | Irish |

## BURKE, KEVIN & MICHAEL O DOMHNAILL

| Title | Format | Label | Cat. No. | Year | | | Notes |
|---|---|---|---|---|---|---|---|
| Promenade | LP | Mulligan | LUN028 | 1979 | £5 | £12 | Irish |

## BURKE, SOLOMON

| Title | Format | Label | Cat. No. | Year | | | Notes |
|---|---|---|---|---|---|---|---|
| Baby Come On Home | 7" | Atlantic | AT4073 | 1966 | £1.50 | £4 | |
| Best Of Solomon Burke | LP | Atlantic | 587/588016 | 1966 | £5 | £12 | |
| Can't Nobody Love You | 7" | London | HLK9763 | 1963 | £2.50 | £6 | |
| Cry To Me | 7" | London | HLK9512 | 1962 | £4 | £8 | |
| Down In The Valley | 7" | London | HLK9560 | 1962 | £2.50 | £6 | |
| Everybody Needs Somebody To Love | 7" | Atlantic | AT4004 | 1964 | £2 | £5 | |
| Greatest | LP | London | HAK8018 | 1963 | £8 | £20 | |
| He'll Have To Go | 7" | London | HLK9849 | 1964 | £2.50 | £6 | |
| I Feel A Sin Comin' On | 7" | Atlantic | 584005 | 1966 | £1.50 | £4 | |
| I Wish I Knew | LP | Atlantic | 587/588117 | 1968 | £5 | £12 | |
| I Wish I Knew | 7" | Atlantic | 584191 | 1968 | £1.50 | £4 | |
| If You Need Me | LP | Atlantic | (SD)8085 | 1963 | £10 | £25 | US |
| If You Need Me | 7" | London | HLK9715 | 1963 | £2.50 | £6 | |
| Just Out Of Reach | 7" | London | HLK9454 | 1961 | £6 | £12 | |
| Keep A Light In The Window | 7" | Atlantic | 584100 | 1967 | £1.50 | £4 | |
| Keep Lookin' | 7" | Atlantic | 584026 | 1966 | £1.50 | £4 | |
| King Of Rock 'n' Soul | LP | Atlantic | 590004 | 1966 | £5 | £12 | |
| King Solomon | LP | Atlantic | 587105 | 1968 | £5 | £12 | |
| Maggie's Farm | 7" | Atlantic | AT4030 | 1965 | £2 | £5 | |
| More Rocking Soul | 7" | Atlantic | AT4014 | 1964 | £2 | £5 | |
| Only Love | 7" | Atlantic | AT4061 | 1965 | £2 | £5 | |
| Peepin' | 7" | Atlantic | AT4022 | 1965 | £1.50 | £4 | |
| Proud Mary | LP | Bell | MBLL/SBLL118 | 1969 | £5 | £12 | |
| Proud Mary | 7" | Bell | BLL1062 | 1969 | £1.50 | £4 | |
| Rock 'n' Soul | LP | Atlantic | ATL5009 | 1964 | £8 | £20 | |
| Rock 'n' Soul | 7" EP | Atlantic | AET6008 | 1965 | £5 | £10 | |
| Save It | 7" | Atlantic | 584204 | 1968 | £1.50 | £4 | |
| Solomon Burke | LP | Apollo | ALP498 | 1962 | £20 | £40 | US |
| Someone Is Watching | 7" | Atlantic | AT4044 | 1965 | £1.50 | £4 | |
| Someone To Love | 7" | London | HLK9887 | 1964 | £2.50 | £6 | |
| Take Me | 7" | Atlantic | 584122 | 1967 | £1.50 | £4 | |
| Tonight My Heart She Is Crying | 7" EP | London | REK1379 | 1963 | £10 | £20 | |
| Uptight Good Woman | 7" | Bell | BLL1047 | 1968 | £1.50 | £4 | |

## BURKE, SONNY

| Title | Format | Label | Cat. No. | Year | | | Notes |
|---|---|---|---|---|---|---|---|
| Blue Island | 7" | Blue Beat | BB363 | 1966 | £6 | £12 | |
| Choo Choo Train | 7" | Island | WI3082 | 1967 | £5 | £10 | Ken Parker B side |
| Dance With Me | 7" | Black Swan | WI470 | 1965 | £5 | £10 | |
| Glad | 7" | Black Swan | WI469 | 1965 | £5 | £10 | |
| Grandpa | 7" | Island | WI221 | 1965 | £5 | £10 | |
| Have Faith | 7" | Ska Beat | JB272 | 1967 | £5 | £10 | |
| Life Without Fun | 7" | Island | WI134 | 1963 | £5 | £10 | |
| Rudy Girl | 7" | Island | WI3040 | 1967 | £5 | £10 | Bob Andy B side |

| | | | | | | | |
|---|---|---|---|---|---|---|---|
| Sounds Of Sonny Burke | LP | Island | ILP972 | 1968 | £25 | £50 | *pink label* |
| Wicked People | 7" | Black Swan | WI471 | 1965 | £5 | £10 | |
| You Rule My Heart | 7" | Island | WI3022 | 1966 | £5 | £10 | *Gaylads B side* |

## BURKE, VINNIE

| | | | | | | | |
|---|---|---|---|---|---|---|---|
| String Jazz Quartet | LP | HMV | CLP1163 | 1958 | £6 | £15 | |
| Vinnie Burke All Stars | LP | HMV | CLP1217 | 1958 | £6 | £15 | |

## BURLAND, DAVE

| | | | | | | | |
|---|---|---|---|---|---|---|---|
| Dalesman's Litany | LP | Trailer | LER2029 | 1971 | £5 | £12 | |
| Dave Burland | LP | Trailer | LER2082 | 1972 | £5 | £12 | |
| Double Take | LP | Rubber | RUB012/036 | 1980 | £8 | £20 | *double* |
| Rollin' | LP | Moonraker | MOO6 | 1985 | £4 | £10 | |
| Songs And Buttered Haycocks | LP | Rubber | RUB012 | 1975 | £5 | £12 | |
| You Can't Fool The Fat Man | LP | Rubber | RUB036 | 1979 | £5 | £12 | |

## BURLAND, DAVE, TONY CAPSTICK & DICK GAUGHAN

| | | | | | | | |
|---|---|---|---|---|---|---|---|
| Songs Of Ewan MacColl | LP | Rubber | RUB027 | 1978 | £4 | £10 | |

## BURMOE BROTHERS

| | | | | | | | |
|---|---|---|---|---|---|---|---|
| Skin | 12" | Some Bizarre | WBY121 | 1985 | £2.50 | £6 | |

## BURNEL, J. J.

| | | | | | | | |
|---|---|---|---|---|---|---|---|
| Girl From The Snow Country | 7" | United Artists | BP361 | 1980 | £100 | £200 | |

## BURNEL, JEAN-JACQUES

| | | | | | | | |
|---|---|---|---|---|---|---|---|
| Euroman Cometh | LP | Mau Mau | PMAU601 | 1988 | £4 | £10 | *picture disc* |

## BURNETTE, DORSEY

| | | | | | | | |
|---|---|---|---|---|---|---|---|
| Dorsey Burnette | LP | London | HAD8050 | 1963 | £20 | £40 | |
| Dorsey Burnette Sings | 7" EP | London | RED1402 | 1963 | £12.50 | £25 | |
| Greatest Hits | LP | Era | ES800 | 1969 | £6 | £15 | *US* |
| Greatest Love | 7" | Liberty | LIB15190 | 1969 | £2 | £5 | |
| Hey Little One | 7" | London | HLN9160 | 1960 | £4 | £8 | |
| It's No Sin | 7" | London | HLN9365 | 1961 | £2.50 | £6 | |
| Jimmy Brown | 7" | Tamla Motown | TMG534 | 1965 | £20 | £40 | |
| Tall Oak Tree | LP | Era | EL(S)102 | 1960 | £37.50 | £75 | *US* |
| Tall Oak Tree | 7" | London | HLN9047 | 1960 | £4 | £8 | |

## BURNETTE, JAN

| | | | | | | | |
|---|---|---|---|---|---|---|---|
| Boy I Used To Know | 7" | Oriole | CB1807 | 1963 | £1.50 | £4 | |
| I Could Have Loved You So Well | 7" | Oriole | CB1716 | 1962 | £1.50 | £4 | |
| Let Me Make You Smile Again | 7" | Oriole | CB1905 | 1964 | £1.50 | £4 | |
| Too Young | 7" | Oriole | CB1920 | 1964 | £1.50 | £4 | |

## BURNETTE, JOHNNY

Johnny Burnette's original rock'n'roll trio played rockabilly to rival that of Elvis Presley. Like Presley, however, Burnette rapidly descended into trite pop music – there is simply no comparison between 'You're Sixteen' and 'Train Kept A-Rollin''. Not for nothing has the latter song inspired furious cover versions by the Yardbirds and Motorhead.

| | | | | | | | |
|---|---|---|---|---|---|---|---|
| All Week Long | 7" | Capitol | CL15322 | 1963 | £2.50 | £6 | |
| Big Big World | 7" EP | London | REG1309 | 1961 | £15 | £30 | |
| Clown Shoes | 7" | Liberty | LIB55416 | 1962 | £1.50 | £4 | |
| Damn The Defiant | 7" | Liberty | LIB55489 | 1962 | £1.50 | £4 | |
| Dreamin' | LP | London | HAG2306 | 1961 | £25 | £50 | |
| Dreamin' | LP | Sunset | SLS50007 | 1969 | £4 | £10 | |
| Dreamin' | 7" EP | London | REG1263 | 1960 | £15 | £30 | |
| Dreamin' | 7" | Liberty | LIB10235 | 1966 | £1.50 | £4 | |
| Dreamin' | 7" | London | HLG9172 | 1960 | £1.50 | £4 | |
| Eager Beaver Baby | 7" | Vogue Coral | Q72283 | 1957 | £87.50 | £175 | |
| Fool | 7" | London | HLG9473 | 1961 | £2 | £5 | |
| Four By Johnny Burnette | 7" EP | Capitol | EAP120645 | 1964 | £25 | £50 | |
| Girls | 7" | London | HLG9388 | 1961 | £1.50 | £4 | |
| God, Country And My Baby | 7" | London | HLG9453 | 1961 | £1.50 | £4 | |
| Hit After Hit | 7" EP | Liberty | LEP2091 | 1963 | £7.50 | £15 | |
| Hits And Other Favourites | LP | Liberty | LBY1006 | 1961 | £10 | £25 | |
| I Wanna Thank Your Folks | 7" | Pye | 7N25158 | 1962 | £1.50 | £4 | |
| I'm The One Who Loves You | 7" | Pye | 7N25187 | 1963 | £1.50 | £4 | |
| Johnny Burnette | 7" EP | London | REG1327 | 1961 | £15 | £30 | |
| Johnny Burnette Sings | LP | London | HAG2375 | 1961 | £25 | £50 | |
| Johnny Burnette Sings | LP | London | SAHG6175 | 1961 | £30 | £60 | *stereo* |
| Johnny Burnette Story | LP | Liberty | LBY1231 | 1964 | £20 | £40 | |
| Johnny Burnette/You're 16 | LP | London | HAG2349 | 1961 | £25 | £50 | |
| Little Boy Sad | 7" EP | London | REG1291 | 1961 | £15 | £30 | |
| Little Boy Sad | 7" | London | HLG9315 | 1961 | £1.50 | £4 | |
| Lonesome Train | LP | Vogue Coral | Q72227 | 1957 | £100 | £200 | *best auctioned* |
| Rock 'n' Roll Trio | LP | Ace Of Hearts | AH120 | 1966 | £6 | £15 | |
| Rock 'n' Roll Trio | LP | Coral | CRL57080 | 1956 | £400 | £600 | *US* |
| Rock 'n' Roll Trio | 10" LP | Coral | LVC10041 | 1956 | £400 | £600 | |
| Roses Are Red | LP | Liberty | LRP3083/LST7255 | 1962 | £10 | £25 | *US* |
| Setting The Woods On Fire | 7" | London | HLG9458 | 1961 | £1.50 | £4 | |
| Tear It Up | LP | Coral | CP15 | 1969 | £4 | £10 | |
| Tear It Up | 7" | Vogue Coral | Q72177 | 1956 | £180 | £300 | *best auctioned* |
| Walking Talking Doll | 7" | Capitol | CL15347 | 1964 | £4 | £8 | |
| You're Sixteen | 7" | London | HLG9254 | 1960 | £1.50 | £4 | |
| You're Undecided | 7" | Von | 1006 | 1954 | £330 | £500 | *US, best auctioned* |

## BURNETTE, JOHNNY & DORSEY
| | | | | | | | |
|---|---|---|---|---|---|---|---|
| Hey Sue | 7" | Reprise | R20153 | 1963 | £10 | £20 | |

## BURNETTE, SMILEY
| | | | | | | | |
|---|---|---|---|---|---|---|---|
| Chugging On Down Sixty-Six | 7" | London | HL8085 | 1954 | £20 | £40 | |
| Lazy Locomotive | 7" | London | HL8071 | 1954 | £20 | £40 | |
| Rudolph The Red-Nosed Reindeer | 78 | Capitol | CL13388 | 1950 | £2 | £5 | |

## BURNIN' RED IVANHOE
| | | | | | | | |
|---|---|---|---|---|---|---|---|
| 6 Elefantskovcikadeviser | LP | Sonet | SLSP1528 | 1971 | £10 | £25 | Danish |
| Burnin' Red Ivanhoe | LP | Warner Bros | K44062 | 1970 | £6 | £15 | |
| Dansk Beat | LP | Sonet | SLPS2140 | 1974 | £8 | £20 | Danish |
| M144 | LP | Sonet | SLPS1512/3 | 1969 | £10 | £25 | Danish double |
| Miley Smile/Stage Recall | LP | Sonet | SLSP1540 | 1972 | £6 | £15 | Danish |
| Right On | LP | Sonet | SLSP1549 | 1974 | £10 | £25 | Danish |
| W.W.W. | LP | Dandelion | 2310145 | 1971 | £6 | £15 | |

## BURNING PLAGUE
| | | | | | | | |
|---|---|---|---|---|---|---|---|
| Burning Plague | LP | CBS | 65664 | 1973 | £8 | £20 | Dutch |

## BURNING SPEAR
| | | | | | | | |
|---|---|---|---|---|---|---|---|
| Dry And Heavy | LP | Island | ILPS9431 | 1977 | £5 | £12 | |
| Garvey's Ghost | LP | Island | ILPS9382 | 1976 | £6 | £15 | |
| Hail HIM | LP | Radic | RDC2003 | 1980 | £4 | £10 | |
| Harder Than The Rest | LP | Island | ILPS9567 | 1979 | £4 | £10 | |
| Live | LP | Island | ILPS9513 | 1977 | £5 | £12 | |
| Man In The Hills | LP | Island | ILPS9412 | 1976 | £5 | £12 | |
| Marcus Garvey | LP | Island | ILPS9377 | 1975 | £5 | £12 | |
| Social Living | LP | Island | ILPS9556 | 1980 | £4 | £10 | |

## BURNS, EDDIE 'GUITAR'
| | | | | | | | |
|---|---|---|---|---|---|---|---|
| Bottle Up And Go | LP | Action | ACMP100 | 1972 | £8 | £20 | |

## BURNS, JACKIE & THE BELLS
| | | | | | | | |
|---|---|---|---|---|---|---|---|
| He's My Guy | 7" | MGM | MGM1226 | 1963 | £25 | £50 | |

## BURNS, RALPH
| | | | | | | | |
|---|---|---|---|---|---|---|---|
| Jazz Studio Five | LP | Brunswick | LAT8121 | 1956 | £10 | £25 | |
| Ralph Burns Group | LP | Columbia | 33CX10017 | 1955 | £10 | £25 | |
| Very Warm For Jazz | LP | Brunswick | LAT8289 | 1959 | £6 | £15 | |

## BURNS, RAY
| | | | | | | | |
|---|---|---|---|---|---|---|---|
| Condemned For Life | 7" | Columbia | DB3811 | 1956 | £2 | £5 | |
| Ray Burns | 7" EP | Columbia | SEG7594 | 1955 | £2.50 | £6 | |

## BURNT SUITE
| | | | | | | | |
|---|---|---|---|---|---|---|---|
| Burnt Suite | LP | B.J.W. | CSS9 | 1968 | £50 | £100 | US |

## BURRAGE, HAROLD
| | | | | | | | |
|---|---|---|---|---|---|---|---|
| I'll Take One | 7" | Sue | WI353 | 1965 | £5 | £10 | |

## BURRELL, KENNY
| | | | | | | | |
|---|---|---|---|---|---|---|---|
| All Day Long | LP | Esquire | 32107 | 1960 | £10 | £25 | |
| All Night Long | LP | Esquire | 32140 | 1961 | £6 | £15 | |
| Asphalt Canyon Suite | LP | Verve | SVLP9250 | 1970 | £4 | £10 | |
| Blue Bash | LP | Verve | VLP9058 | 1964 | £5 | £12 | with Jimmy Smith |
| Blue Nights Vol. 1 | LP | Blue Note | BLP/BST81596 | 196- | £10 | £25 | |
| Blue Nights Vol. 2 | LP | Blue Note | BLP/BST81597 | 196- | £10 | £25 | |
| Blues, The Common Ground | LP | Verve | (S)VLP9217 | 1968 | £5 | £12 | |
| Bluesy Burrell | LP | XTRA | XTRA5048 | 1968 | £5 | £12 | |
| Crash | LP | Stateside | SL10163 | 1966 | £6 | £15 | with Jack McDuff |
| Guitar Forms | LP | Verve | VLP9099 | 1965 | £5 | £12 | |
| Introducing | LP | Blue Note | BLP/BST81523 | 196- | £10 | £25 | |
| Kenny Burrell Vol. 2 | LP | Blue Note | BLP/BST81543 | 196- | £10 | £25 | |
| Midnight Blue | LP | Blue Note | BLP/BST84123 | 1964 | £8 | £20 | |
| On View At The Five Spot Cafe | LP | Blue Note | BLP/BST84021 | 1961 | £10 | £25 | |

## BURROUGHS, WILLIAM
| | | | | | | | |
|---|---|---|---|---|---|---|---|
| Call Me Burroughs | LP | ESP-Disk | 1050 | 1968 | £10 | £25 | US |
| Nothing Here Now But The Recordings | LP | Industrial | IR0016 | 1980 | £6 | £15 | |

## BURTON, GARY

The track 'General Mojo Cuts Up' on the album *Lofty Fake Anagram* has the dubious distinction of featuring the first burst of guitar feedback on a jazz record. Courtesy of Larry Coryell, the sound is actually a fairly modest one, more reminiscent of what the Beatles had pioneered some years earlier on 'I Feel Fine' than the extravagances of the contemporary Jimi Hendrix. Burton himself is a vibraphone player of astonishing virtuosity – he is capable of playing with three mallets in each hand. His own skill, together with his knack for finding inspirational colleagues to work with – bass player Steve Swallow, composer/arranger Michael Gibbs, and guitarist Pat Metheny among them – has assured Burton's status as a premier-league jazz musician.

| | | | | | | | |
|---|---|---|---|---|---|---|---|
| Alone At Last | LP | Atlantic | K40305 | 1972 | £4 | £10 | |
| Country Roads And Other Places | LP | RCA | SF8042 | 1969 | £4 | £10 | |
| Crystal Silence | LP | ECM | ECM1024ST | 1972 | £5 | £12 | with Chick Corea |
| Dreams So Real | LP | ECM | ECM1072ST | 1975 | £6 | £15 | |
| Duster | LP | RCA | LPM/LSP3835 | 1967 | £6 | £15 | US |
| Gary Burton And Keith Jarrett | LP | Atlantic | K40208 | 1971 | £5 | £12 | US |
| Genuine Tong Funeral | LP | RCA | SF8015 | 1969 | £6 | £15 | with Carla Bley |

| | | | | | | | |
|---|---|---|---|---|---|---|---|
| Good Vibes | LP | Atlantic | K40110 | 1971 | £5 | £12 | US |
| Groovy Sound Of Music | LP | RCA | LPM/LSP3360 | 1965 | £6 | £15 | US |
| Hotel Hello | LP | ECM | ECM1055ST | 1975 | £6 | £15 | ... with Steve Swallow |
| Hotel Hello/Matchbook | LP | ECM | ECM1055/6ST | 1975 | £15 | £30 | ... special double sleeve |
| In Concert | LP | RCA | LPM/LSP3985 | 1968 | £6 | £15 | US |
| Lofty Fake Anagram | LP | RCA | RD/SF7923 | 1968 | £4 | £10 | |
| Matchbook | LP | ECM | ECM1056ST | 1975 | £5 | £12 | ... with Ralph Towner |
| New Quartet | LP | ECM | ECM1030ST | 1973 | £6 | £15 | |
| New Vibe Man In Town | LP | RCA | LPM/LSP2420 | 1961 | £8 | £20 | US |
| Paris Encounter | LP | Atlantic | K40378 | 1972 | £4 | £10 | ... with Stephane Grappelli |
| Passengers | LP | ECM | ECM1092ST | 1976 | £4 | £10 | |
| Ring | LP | ECM | ECM1051ST | 1974 | £6 | £15 | |
| Seven Songs For Quartet And Chamber Orchestra | LP | ECM | ECM1040ST | 1974 | £8 | £20 | ... with Michael Gibbs |
| Something's Coming | LP | RCA | LPM/LSP2880 | 1964 | £6 | £15 | US |
| Tennessee Firebird | LP | RCA | LPM/LSP3719 | 1966 | £6 | £15 | US |
| Throb | LP | Atlantic | 588203 | 1969 | £6 | £15 | |
| Time Machine | LP | RCA | LPM/LSP3642 | 1966 | £6 | £15 | US |
| Who Is Gary Burton? | LP | RCA | LPM/LSP2665 | 1963 | £8 | £20 | US |

## BURTON, JAMES

James Burton's legendary reputation as an ace guitarist is entirely justified by his playing on record. Largely content to work for others – most notably Rick Nelson and Elvis Presley – his two solo LPs are quite scarce (and undervalued).

| | | | | | | | |
|---|---|---|---|---|---|---|---|
| Corn Pickin' And Slick Slidin' | LP | Capitol | ST2822 | 1968 | £20 | £40 | US |
| Guitar Sounds Of James Burton | LP | A&M | AMLS64293 | 1971 | £20 | £40 | |

## BURTON, LORI

| | | | | | | | |
|---|---|---|---|---|---|---|---|
| Breakout | LP | Mercury | SR61136 | 1967 | £10 | £25 | US |

## BURTON, TOMMY

| | | | | | | | |
|---|---|---|---|---|---|---|---|
| I'm Walking | 7" | Blue Beat | BB237 | 1964 | £6 | £12 | |

## BUSCH, LOU

| | | | | | | | |
|---|---|---|---|---|---|---|---|
| Wild Ones | 7" | Capitol | CL14730 | 1957 | £1.50 | £4 | |
| Zambesi | 7" | Capitol | CL14504 | 1956 | £2.50 | £6 | |

## BUSH

| | | | | | | | |
|---|---|---|---|---|---|---|---|
| Bush | LP | Dunhill | DS50086 | 1970 | £8 | £20 | US |

## BUSH, KATE

When Kate Bush first appeared on TV's *Top Of The Pops* wailing to Heathcliff in that extraordinary high voice, it seemed impossible that she could ever turn out to be more than a one-hit-wonder novelty act. Instead, of course, it turned out that she was possessed of a rare talent – as a singer, as a dancer, as a performance artist, and above all as a composer and musician. Each of her album releases has been more impressive than the one before it and she is without doubt one of the most important rock artists of the eighties and nineties. Many of her records have become collectable, with picture-sleeve copies of all her early singles rising steadily in value.

| | | | | | | | |
|---|---|---|---|---|---|---|---|
| Amiga | LP | EMI | 856072 | 1984 | £15 | £30 | German |
| Best Works 1978–1993 | CD | EMI | SPCD1402/3 | 1994 | £330 | £500 | Japanese double promo compilation |
| Big Sky | 7" | EMI | KB4P | 1986 | £4 | £8 | picture disc |
| Breathing | 7" | EMI | EMI5058 | 1980 | £20 | £40 | bat picture sleeve |
| Dreaming | 7" | EMI | EMI5296 | 1982 | £1.50 | £4 | picture sleeve |
| Hammer Horror | 7" | EMI | EMI2887 | 1978 | £1.50 | £4 | picture sleeve |
| Hounds Of Love | LP | EMI | ST17171 | 1985 | £15 | £30 | US, coloured vinyl |
| Hounds Of Love | CD | EMI | CDP7461642 | 1986 | £5 | £12 | cover reference to 12" mix of 'Running Up That Hill' |
| Hounds Of Love | CD | EMI | CDP7461642 | 1987 | £25 | £50 | US mispressing – plays Beatles A Hard Day's Night |
| Interview With Kate Bush | LP | EMI | SPRO282 | 1985 | £100 | £200 | Canadian promo |
| Kate Bush | LP | EMI | MLP19004 | 1984 | £30 | £60 | Canadian 6 track LP, brown or clear vinyl |
| Kate Bush | LP | EMI | MLP19004 | 1984 | £15 | £30 | Canadian 6 track LP, green, yellow, blue, or white vinyl |
| Kick Inside | LP | EMI | 5C06206603 | 1978 | £25 | £50 | coloured vinyl, Dutch |
| Kick Inside | LP | EMI | EMCP3223 | 1978 | £50 | £100 | picture disc, same picture both sides |
| Kick Inside | LP | EMI | EMCP3223 | 1979 | £20 | £40 | picture disc |
| Kick Inside | LP | EMI/ Harvest | EMC3223/ SW11761 | 1978 | £6 | £15 | different US sleeve on UK record |
| Love And Anger | CD-s | EMI | CDEM134 | 1990 | £2 | £5 | |
| Man With The Child In His Eyes | 7" | EMI | EMI2806 | 1978 | £4 | £8 | picture sleeve |
| Ne t'en fui pas | 7" | EMI | PM102 | 1983 | £5 | £10 | sung in French |
| Never For Ever | LP | EMI | SFI562 | 1980 | £7.50 | £15 | promo, flexi |
| Night Of The Swallow | 7" | EMI | 1EMI9001 | 1983 | £25 | £50 | Irish |
| On Stage | 7" | EMI | PSR442/443 | 1979 | £20 | £40 | promo, double |
| Red Shoes | CD | EMI | CDEMD1047 | 1993 | £87.50 | £175 | promo shoe box with CD, video, slide, pen, biog |
| Rocket Man | CD-s | Mercury | TRICD2 | 1991 | £2 | £5 | |
| Self Portrait | LP | EMI | SSA3020 | 1979 | £100 | £200 | US promo |
| Sensual World | CD-s | EMI | EMCD102 | 1989 | £2 | £5 | |

| Title | Format | Label | Cat. No. | Year | | | Notes |
|---|---|---|---|---|---|---|---|
| Sensual World | CD | EMI | CDEMD1010 | 1989 | £62.50 | £125 | ... promo box set, with cassette, biog, lyric book |
| Single File | 7" | EMI | KBS1 | 1984 | £50 | £100 | ... boxed with booklet |
| There Goes A Tenner | 7" | EMI | EMI5350 | 1982 | £1.50 | £4 | picture sleeve |
| This Woman's Work | LP | EMI | KBBX1 | 1990 | £37.50 | £75 | box set |
| This Woman's Work | CD-s | EMI | CDEM119 | 1989 | £2 | £5 | |
| This Woman's Work | CD | EMI | CDKBBX1 | 1990 | £50 | £100 | box set |
| This Woman's Work | 7" | EMI | EMPD119 | 1989 | £1.50 | £4 | picture disc |
| Wow | 7" | EMI | EMI2911 | 1979 | £1.50 | £4 | picture sleeve |
| Wuthering Heights | 7" | EMI | EMI2719 | 1978 | £10 | £20 | picture sleeve |

## BUSHKIN, JOE

| Title | Format | Label | Cat. No. | Year | | | Notes |
|---|---|---|---|---|---|---|---|
| Joe Bushkin Orchestra | LP | Capitol | LCT6126 | 1957 | £4 | £10 | |
| Piano After Midnight | LP | Fontana | TFL5014 | 1958 | £4 | £10 | |

## BUSKER

| Title | Format | Label | Cat. No. | Year | | | Notes |
|---|---|---|---|---|---|---|---|
| Mowrey Junior And Watson | LP | Riverdale | | 1976 | £37.50 | £75 | |
| Buskers | LP | Hawk | HALPX142 | 1975 | £5 | £12 | |

## BUSKERS

| Title | Format | Label | Cat. No. | Year | | | Notes |
|---|---|---|---|---|---|---|---|
| Life Of A Man | LP | Rubber | RUB007 | 1973 | £5 | £12 | |

## BUSTERS

| Title | Format | Label | Cat. No. | Year | | | Notes |
|---|---|---|---|---|---|---|---|
| Bust Out | 7" | Stateside | SS231 | 1963 | £1.50 | £4 | |

## BUTALA, TONY

| Title | Format | Label | Cat. No. | Year | | | Notes |
|---|---|---|---|---|---|---|---|
| Long Black Stockings | 7" | Salvo | SLO1801 | 1962 | £4 | £8 | |

## BUTCHER, EDDIE

| Title | Format | Label | Cat. No. | Year | | | Notes |
|---|---|---|---|---|---|---|---|
| I Once Was A Daysman | LP | Free Reed | FRR003 | 1976 | £5 | £12 | |
| Shamrock, Rose And Thistle | LP | Leader | LED2070 | 1976 | £4 | £10 | |

## BUTERA, SAM & THE WITNESSES

| Title | Format | Label | Cat. No. | Year | | | Notes |
|---|---|---|---|---|---|---|---|
| Big Horn | LP | Capitol | T1098 | 1959 | £6 | £15 | |
| Bim Bam | 7" | Capitol | CL14913 | 1958 | £37.50 | £75 | |
| Good Gracious Baby | 7" | HMV | POP476 | 1958 | £10 | £20 | |
| Handle With Care | 7" | Capitol | CL14988 | 1959 | £5 | £10 | |
| Rat Race | LP | London | HAD2288 | 1960 | £5 | £12 | |
| Sax Serenade | 7" EP | HMV | 7EG8087 | 1955 | £10 | £20 | |

## BUTLER, BILLY

| Title | Format | Label | Cat. No. | Year | | | Notes |
|---|---|---|---|---|---|---|---|
| Right Track | LP | Soul City | | 196– | £8 | £20 | |
| Right Track | 7" | Soul City | SC113 | 1969 | £4 | £8 | |

## BUTLER, JERRY

| Title | Format | Label | Cat. No. | Year | | | Notes |
|---|---|---|---|---|---|---|---|
| Are You Happy | 7" | Mercury | MF1078 | 1969 | £1.50 | £4 | |
| Aware Of Love | LP | Vee Jay | LP/SR1038 | 1961 | £8 | £20 | US |
| Best Of Jerry Butler | LP | Vee Jay | LP/SR1048 | 1962 | £6 | £15 | US |
| Brand New Me | 7" | Mercury | MF1132 | 1969 | £1.50 | £4 | |
| Folk Songs | LP | Stateside | SL10050 | 1963 | £6 | £15 | |
| For Your Precious Love | LP | Vee Jay | LP/VJS1075 | 1963 | £6 | £15 | US |
| For Your Precious Love | 7" | London | HL8697 | 1958 | £37.50 | £75 | |
| Give Me Your Love | 7" | Stateside | SS252 | 1964 | £2.50 | £6 | |
| Giving Up On Love | LP | Vee Jay | LP/VJS1076 | 1963 | £6 | £15 | US |
| Good Times | 7" | Fontana | TF553 | 1965 | £2.50 | £6 | |
| He Will Break Your Heart | LP | Stateside | SL10032 | 1963 | £8 | £20 | |
| He Will Break Your Heart | 7" | Top Rank | JAR531 | 1961 | £12.50 | £25 | |
| Hey Mr. Western Union Man | 7" | Mercury | MF1058 | 1968 | £2 | £5 | |
| Hey Mr. Western Union Man | 7" | Mercury | MF1058 | 1968 | £1.50 | £4 | |
| I Can't Stand To See You Cry | 7" | Fontana | TF588 | 1965 | £2.50 | £6 | |
| I Dig You Baby | 7" | Mercury | MF964 | 1967 | £2 | £5 | |
| I Found A Love | 7" | Top Rank | JAR389 | 1960 | £7.50 | £15 | |
| I Stand Accused | 7" | Sue | WI4003 | 1966 | £7.50 | £15 | |
| I've Been Trying | 7" | Stateside | SS300 | 1964 | £2.50 | £6 | |
| Ice Man Cometh | LP | Mercury | 20154SML | 1969 | £4 | £10 | |
| Jerry Butler Esquire | LP | Abner | R2001 | 1959 | £37.50 | £75 | US |
| Jerry Butler Esquire | LP | Vee Jay | LP1027 | 1961 | £10 | £25 | US |
| Just For You | 7" | Sue | WI4009 | 1966 | £4 | £8 | |
| Love | 7" | Mercury | MF932 | 1965 | £1.50 | £4 | |
| Love Me | LP | Fontana | (S)TL5264 | 1968 | £4 | £10 | |
| Make It Easy On Yourself | 7" | President | PT299 | 1970 | £1.50 | £4 | |
| Make It Easy On Yourself | 7" | Stateside | SS121 | 1962 | £4 | £8 | |
| Moody Woman | 7" | Mercury | MF1122 | 1969 | £1.50 | £4 | |
| Moon River | LP | Vee Jay | LP/SR1046 | 1962 | £8 | £20 | US |
| Moon River | 7" | Columbia | DB4743 | 1961 | £4 | £8 | |
| More Of The Best Of Jerry Butler | LP | Vee Jay | (VJS)1119 | 1965 | £4 | £10 | US |
| Mr. Dream Merchant | 7" | Mercury | MF1005 | 1967 | £1.50 | £4 | |
| Never Give You up | 7" | Mercury | MF1035 | 1968 | £1.50 | £4 | |
| Only The Strong Survive | 7" | Mercury | MF1094 | 1969 | £1.50 | £4 | |
| When Trouble Calls | 7" | Top Rank | JAR562 | 1961 | £6 | £12 | |
| You Can Run | 7" | Stateside | SS158 | 1963 | £2.50 | £6 | |
| You Go Right Through Me | 7" | Stateside | SS170 | 1963 | £2.50 | £6 | |
| You Won't Be Sorry | 7" | Stateside | SS195 | 1963 | £2.50 | £6 | |

## BUTLER, LESLIE

| Title | Format | Label | Cat. No. | Year | | | Notes |
|---|---|---|---|---|---|---|---|
| Ramona | 7" | Doctor Bird | DB1083 | 1967 | £5 | £10 | |
| Revival | 7" | High Note | HS009 | 1969 | £2.50 | £6 | |
| Soul Drums | 7" | High Note | HS001 | 1969 | £2.50 | £6 | Gaylads B side |

| | | | | | |
|---|---|---|---|---|---|
| Top Cat | 7" | High Note | HS008 | 1969 £2.50 | £6 |
| You Don't Have To Say You Love Me | 7" | Island | WI3069 | 1967 £5 | £10 |

## BUTTERCUPS

| | | | | | |
|---|---|---|---|---|---|
| Come Put My Life In Order | 7" | Pama | PM760 | 1969 £2 | £5 |
| If I Love You | 7" | Pama | PM742 | 1968 £4 | £8 |

## BUTTERFIELD, BILLY

| | | | | | |
|---|---|---|---|---|---|
| Ballads For Sweethearts | 10" LP | Nixa | WLPY6729 | 1955 £5 | £12 |
| Billy Butterfield Orchestra | 10" LP | London | HBF1043 | 1956 £5 | £12 |
| Classics In Jazz | 10" LP | Capitol | LC6684 | 1955 £6 | £15 |
| Magnificent Matador | 7" | London | HLF8181 | 1955 £5 | £10 |
| That Butterfield Bounce | 10" LP | Nixa | WLPY6720 | 1955 £5 | £12 |

## BUTTERFIELD, PAUL BLUES BAND

Paul Butterfield occupied a very similar position within American rock music to that of John Mayall in Britain. Both were virtuoso harmonica players; both chose to surround themselves with a continually evolving team of inspirational musicians; and both adopted an imaginative approach to the blues, in which improvised solos were a key element. Butterfield's masterpiece came early – *East West* is an essential sixties album, if only for the freshness of the guitar-playing by Michael Bloomfield and Elvin Bishop on the two long instrumental tracks.

| | | | | | |
|---|---|---|---|---|---|
| All These Blues | 7" | Elektra | EKSN45007 | 1967 £1.50 | £4 |
| Come On In | 7" | London | HLZ10100 | 1966 £2.50 | £6 |
| East West | LP | Elektra | EKL/EKS315 | 1966 £8 | £20 |
| East West | LP | Elektra | K42006 | 1971 £4 | £10 |
| Get Yourself Together | 7" | Elektra | EKSN45047 | 1968 £1.50 | £4 |
| Golden Butter | LP | Elektra | K62011 | 1972 £5 | £12 ......... double |
| I Got My Mojo Working | 7" EP | Vogue | INT18063 | 1965 £12.50 | £25 ......... French |
| In My Own Dream | LP | Elektra | EKL/EKS74025 | 1968 £5 | £12 |
| In My Own Dream | LP | Elektra | K42042 | 1971 £4 | £10 |
| Keep On Moving | LP | Elektra | EKS74053 | 1969 £5 | £12 |
| Keep On Moving | LP | Elektra | K42033 | 1971 £4 | £10 |
| Live | LP | Elektra | EKS2001 | 1970 £5 | £12 ......... double |
| Live | LP | Elektra | K62001 | 1971 £5 | £12 ......... double |
| Offer You Can't Refuse | LP | Red Lightnin' | R008 | 1972 £4 | £10 |
| Paul Butterfield Blues Band | LP | Elektra | EKL/EKS7294 | 1965 £8 | £20 |
| Paul Butterfield Blues Band | LP | Elektra | K42004 | 1971 £4 | £10 |
| Resurrection Of Pigboy Crabshaw | LP | Elektra | EKL/EKS74015 | 1967 £5 | £12 |
| Resurrection Of Pigboy Crabshaw | LP | Elektra | K42017 | 1971 £4 | £10 |
| Run Out Of Time | 7" | Elektra | EKSN45020 | 1967 £1.50 | £4 |
| Where Did My Baby Go | 7" | Elektra | EKSN45069 | 1968 £1.50 | £4 |

## BUTTERFLYS

| | | | | | |
|---|---|---|---|---|---|
| Goodnight Baby | 7" | Red Bird | RB10009 | 1964 £5 | £10 |

## BUTTHOLE SURFERS

| | | | | | |
|---|---|---|---|---|---|
| Double Live | LP | LBV | | 198– £6 | £15 ......... double |
| Hurdy Gurdy Man | CD-s | Rough Trade | RTT240CD | 1990 £2 | £5 |
| Widowmaker | CD-s | Blast First | BFFP41CD | 1989 £2 | £5 |

## BUXTON, SHEILA

| | | | | | |
|---|---|---|---|---|---|
| Charm | 7" | Columbia | DB4051 | 1957 £1.50 | £4 |
| Perfect Love | 7" | Columbia | DB3887 | 1957 £1.50 | £4 |
| Thank You For The Waltz | 7" | Columbia | SCM5193 | 1955 £1.50 | £4 |

## BUZZ

| | | | | | |
|---|---|---|---|---|---|
| You're Holding Me Down | 7" | Columbia | DB7887 | 1966 £62.50 | £125 |

## BUZZ & BUCKY

| | | | | | |
|---|---|---|---|---|---|
| Tiger A-Go-Go | 7" | Stateside | SS428 | 1965 £5 | £10 |

## BUZZCOCKS

The Buzzcocks' *Spiral Scratch* EP was the first self-produced record to emerge out of punk and was an early collectors' item. A reissue brought the record's value down to its current level, although the two issues are easily distinguished by the original making no specific reference to Howard Devoto on the front cover.

| | | | | | |
|---|---|---|---|---|---|
| Another Music In A Different Kitchen | LP | United Artists | UAG30159 | 1978 £8 | £20 with printed carrier bag |
| Fab Four | CD-s | EMI | CDEM104 | 1989 £2 | £5 |
| Moving Away From The Pulsebeat | 12" | United Artists | UALP15 | 1978 £6 | £15 ......... 1 sided promo |
| Spiral Scratch | 7" EP | Document | DPRO1 | 1991 £2 | £5 ......... promo |
| Spiral Scratch | 7" EP | New Hormones | ORG1 | 1977 £5 | £10 no Devoto reference on sleeve |

## BYAS, DON

| | | | | | |
|---|---|---|---|---|---|
| Don Byas | 10" LP | Esquire | 20005 | 1953 £20 | £40 |
| Don Byas | 10" LP | Felsted | EDL87004 | 1954 £20 | £40 |

## BYLES, JUNIOR

| | | | | | |
|---|---|---|---|---|---|
| Beat Down Babylon | LP | Trojan | TRL52 | 1972 £4 | £10 |
| Beat Down Babylon | 7" | Bullet | BU499 | 1971 £1.50 | £4 ......... Upsetters B side |
| Festival Da Da | 7" | Upsetter | US387 | 1971 £1.50 | £4 ......... Upsetters B side |
| Fever | 7" | Pama | PM857 | 1972 £1.50 | £4 ......... Groovers B side |

## BYRD, BOBBY

| | | | | | |
|---|---|---|---|---|---|
| Back From The Dead | 7" | Seville | SEV1003 | 1975 £1.50 | £4 |
| I Know You Got Soul | 7" | Mojo | 2027003 | 1971 £2 | £5 |
| I Know You Got Soul | 12" | Urban | URBX8 | 1987 £2.50 | £6 |

| I Need Help | 7" | Polydor | 2001118 | 1971 £1.50 | £4 | |
| I Need Help – Live | LP | Mojo | 2918002 | 1972 £25 | £50 | |

## BYRD, CHARLIE
| Blues Sonata | LP | Riverside | OLP(9)3009 | 1963 £4 | £10 | |
| Guitar Artistry | LP | Riverside | OLP(9)3007 | 1963 £4 | £10 | |

## BYRD, DONALD
| And Then Some | LP | Eros | ERL50067 | 1962 £4 | £10 | |
| At The Half Note Cafe | LP | Blue Note | BLP/BST84060 | 1961 £10 | £25 | |
| At The Half Note Cafe Vol. 2 | LP | Blue Note | BLP/BST84061 | 1961 £15 | £30 | |
| Black Byrd | LP | Blue Note | BNLA047F | 1973 £5 | £12 | US |
| Black Jack | LP | Blue Note | BLP/BST84259 | 1967 £6 | £15 | |
| Boom Boom | 7" | Verve | VS532 | 1966 £1.50 | £4 | |
| Byrd In Flight | LP | Blue Note | BLP/BST84048 | 196– £10 | £25 | |
| Cat Walk | LP | Blue Note | BLP/BST84075 | 1961 £8 | £20 | |
| Child's Play | LP | Polydor | 423/623224 | 1967 £4 | £10 | |
| Donald Byrd And Gigi Gryce | 7" EP | Philips | BBE12274 | 1959 £2 | £5 | |
| Donald Byrd Group | LP | Esquire | 32013 | 1956 £15 | £30 | |
| Donald Byrd Group | LP | London | LTZC15039 | 1957 £15 | £30 | |
| Donald Byrd Sextet | LP | Esquire | 32019 | 1956 £15 | £30 | |
| Donald Byrd's Jazz Group | 7" EP | Esquire | EP139 | 1957 £2 | £5 | |
| Donald Byrd's Jazz Group | 7" EP | Esquire | EP149 | 1957 £2 | £5 | |
| Electric Byrd | LP | Blue Note | BST84349 | 1970 £6 | £15 | |
| Ethiopian Nights | LP | Blue Note | BST84380 | 1970 £6 | £15 | |
| Fancy Free | LP | Blue Note | BST84319 | 1969 £6 | £15 | |
| Free Form | LP | Blue Note | BLP/BST84118 | 1962 £8 | £20 | |
| Fuego | LP | Blue Note | BLP/BST84026 | 1961 £10 | £25 | |
| Fuego | 7" | Blue Note | 451764 | 1962 £1.50 | £4 | |
| I'm Trying To Get Home | LP | Blue Note | BLP/BST84188 | 1965 £8 | £20 | |
| Jazz Lab | LP | Philips | BBL7210 | 1958 £10 | £25 | with Gigi Gryce |
| Modern Jazz Perspective | LP | Philips | BBL7244 | 1958 £8 | £20 | with Gigi Gryce |
| Mustang | LP | Blue Note | BLP/BST84238 | 1966 £8 | £20 | |
| New Perspective | LP | Blue Note | BLP/BST84124 | 1963 £10 | £25 | |
| Places And Spaces | LP | United Artists | UAG20001 | 197– £8 | £20 | |
| Royal Flush | LP | Blue Note | BLP/BST84101 | 1962 £8 | £20 | |
| Slow Drag | LP | Blue Note | BST84292 | 1968 £6 | £15 | |
| Street Lady | LP | Blue Note | BNLA140F | 1974 £5 | £12 | US |
| Three Trumpets | LP | Esquire | 32093 | 1960 £6 | £15 | with Art Farmer & Idrees Sulieman |
| Up With Donald Byrd | LP | Verve | VLP9104 | 1965 £6 | £15 | |

## BYRD, JOE & THE FIELD HIPPIES

*American Metaphysical Circus* is, in effect, the follow-up to the innovative LP made by the United States Of America. With only Joe Byrd remaining from the original line-up, however, a change of name was clearly appropriate.

| American Metaphysical Circus | LP | CBS | 7317 | 1969 £15 | £30 | US |

## BYRD, RUSSELL
| Hitch Hike | 7" | Sue | WI305 | 1964 £7.50 | £15 | |

## BYRDS
| All I Really Want To Do | 7" | CBS | 201796 | 1965 £1.50 | £4 | |
| Back Pages | CD | Columbia | CSK2239 | 1990 £8 | £20 | US promo sampler |
| Bad Night At The Whisky | 7" | CBS | 4055 | 1969 £1.50 | £4 | |
| Ballad Of Easy Rider | LP | CBS | 63795 | 1970 £4 | £10 | |
| Byrdmaniax | LP | CBS | 64389 | 1971 £4 | £10 | |
| Byrds | LP | Asylum | SYLA8754 | 1973 £4 | £10 | |
| Dr. Byrds & Mr. Hyde | LP | CBS | 63545 | 1969 £4 | £10 | mono |
| Early Flight | LP | Together | ST1014 | 1969 £8 | £20 | US |
| Eight Miles High | 7" EP | CBS | EP6077 | 1966 £7.50 | £15 | |
| Eight Miles High | 7" | CBS | 202067 | 1966 £1.50 | £4 | |
| Farther Along | LP | CBS | 64676 | 1972 £4 | £10 | |
| Fifth Dimension | LP | CBS | (S)BPG62783 | 1966 £5 | £12 | |
| Fifth Dimension | 7" | CBS | 202259 | 1966 £1.50 | £4 | |
| Four Dimensions | CD-s | CBS | 6565445 | 1990 £2 | £5 | picture disc |
| Goin' Back | 7" | CBS | 3093 | 1967 £1.50 | £4 | |
| I Am A Pilgrim | 7" | CBS | 3752 | 1968 £1.50 | £4 | |
| It Won't Be Wrong | 7" EP | CBS | 5668 | 1966 £10 | £20 | French |
| Lady Friend | 7" | CBS | 2924 | 1967 £4 | £8 | |
| Lay Lady Lay | 7" | CBS | 4284 | 1969 £1.50 | £4 | |
| Mr. Spaceman | 7" | CBS | 202295 | 1966 £1.50 | £4 | |
| Mr. Tambourine Man | LP | CBS | (S)BPG62571 | 1965 £5 | £12 | |
| Mr. Tambourine Man | 7" EP | CBS | 6100 | 1965 £10 | £20 | French, 2 different track listings |
| Mr. Tambourine Man | 7" | CBS | 201765 | 1965 £1.50 | £4 | |
| My Back Pages | 7" | CBS | 2648 | 1967 £1.50 | £4 | |
| Notorious Byrd Brothers | LP | CBS | (S)BPG63169 | 1968 £5 | £12 | |
| Preflyte | LP | Bumble | GEXP8001 | 196– £10 | £25 | US |
| Preflyte | LP | CBS | KC32183 | 1972 £8 | £20 | US |
| Preflyte | LP | Together | ST1001 | 1969 £10 | £25 | US |
| Set You Free This Time | 7" | CBS | 202037 | 1966 £2 | £5 | |
| So You Want To Be A Rock 'n' Roll Star | 7" | CBS | 202559 | 1967 £1.50 | £4 | |
| Sweetheart Of The Rodeo | LP | CBS | 63353 | 1968 £4 | £10 | |
| Things Will Be Better | 7" | Asylum | AYM516 | 1973 £5 | £10 | demo, picture sleeve |
| Times They Are A Changing | 7" EP | CBS | EP6069 | 1966 £5 | £10 | |
| Turn Turn Turn | LP | CBS | (S)BPG62652 | 1966 £5 | £12 | |

| | | | | | | | | |
|---|---|---|---|---|---|---|---|---|
| Turn Turn Turn | 7" EP | CBS | 6521 | 1965 | £10 | £20 | | French |
| Turn! Turn! Turn! | 7" | CBS | 202008 | 1965 | £1.50 | £4 | | |
| Untitled | LP | CBS | 66253 | 1970 | £5 | £12 | | double |
| Wasn't Born To Follow | 7" | CBS | 4572 | 1969 | £1.50 | £4 | | |
| You Ain't Goin' Nowhere | 7" | CBS | 3411 | 1968 | £1.50 | £4 | | |
| Younger Than Yesterday | LP | CBS | (S)BPG62988 | 1967 | £5 | £12 | | |

## BYRNE, BRIAN

| | | | | | | | | |
|---|---|---|---|---|---|---|---|---|
| Brian Byrne | LP | Hawk | HALP105 | 1976 | £5 | £12 | | Irish |

## BYRNE, DAVID

| | | | | | | | | |
|---|---|---|---|---|---|---|---|---|
| Rei Momo | CD | Sire | | 1989 | £8 | £20 | | US promo with artwork on case |
| Words And Music | CD | Sire | PROCD3820 | 1989 | £8 | £20 | | US interview promo |

## BYRNE, JERRY

| | | | | | | | |
|---|---|---|---|---|---|---|---|
| Lights Out | 7" | Speciality | SON5011 | 1976 | £1.50 | £4 | |

## BYRNE, PACKIE

| | | | | | | | |
|---|---|---|---|---|---|---|---|
| Packie Byrne | LP | EFDSS | LP1009 | 1969 | £5 | £12 | |
| Songs Of A Donegal Man | LP | Topic | 12TS257 | 1975 | £5 | £12 | |

## BYRNE, PACKIE & BONNIE SHALJEAN

| | | | | | | | |
|---|---|---|---|---|---|---|---|
| Half Door | LP | Dingles | DIN302 | 1977 | £4 | £10 | |
| Roundtower | LP | Dingles | DIN311 | 1981 | £4 | £10 | |

## BYRNES, EDDIE

| | | | | | | | | |
|---|---|---|---|---|---|---|---|---|
| Kookie | LP | Warner Bros | W(S)1309 | 1959 | £6 | £15 | | US |
| Kookie | 7" EP | Warner Bros | WEP6010 | 1960 | £4 | £8 | | |
| Kookie Vol. 2 | 7" EP | Warner Bros | WEP6108 | 1963 | £4 | £8 | | |
| Kookie, Kookie, Lend Me Your Comb | 7" | Warner Bros | WB5 | 1960 | £1.50 | £4 | | |

## BYRNES, MARTIN

| | | | | | | | |
|---|---|---|---|---|---|---|---|
| Martin Byrnes | LP | Leader | LEA2004 | 1969 | £8 | £20 | |

## BYRON, PAUL

| | | | | | | | |
|---|---|---|---|---|---|---|---|
| Pale Moon | 7" | Decca | F11210 | 1960 | £2 | £5 | |

## BYSTANDERS

There were a number of sixties groups who eventually achieved some measure of success in the seventies by effecting a dramatic change of style. Status Quo are the obvious example, yet the Bystanders are another good one. In their case, the change from their original harmony vocal approach was so great that they found it necessary to change their name too – to Man.

| | | | | | | | |
|---|---|---|---|---|---|---|---|
| 98.6 | 7" | Piccadilly | 7N35363 | 1967 | £2.50 | £6 | |
| My Love Come Home | 7" | Piccadilly | 7N35351 | 1966 | £6 | £12 | |
| Pattern People | 7" | Piccadilly | 7N35399 | 1967 | £4 | £8 | |
| Royal Blue Summer Sunshine Day | 7" | Piccadilly | 7N35382 | 1967 | £6 | £12 | |
| That's The End | 7" | Pylot | 501 | 1965 | £37.50 | £75 | |
| This World Is My World | 7" | Pye | 7N17540 | 1968 | £5 | £10 | |
| When Jezamine Goes | 7" | Pye | 7N17476 | 1968 | £10 | £20 | |
| You're Gonna Hurt Yourself | 7" | Piccadilly | 7N35330 | 1966 | £5 | £10 | |

## BYZANTIUM

| | | | | | | | |
|---|---|---|---|---|---|---|---|
| Byzantium | LP | A&M | AMLS68104 | 1972 | £6 | £15 | |
| Live and Studio | LP | private | | 1972 | £50 | £100 | |
| Seasons Changing | LP | A&M | AMLH68163 | 1972 | £15 | £30 | |
| What A Coincidence | 7" | A&M | AMS7064 | 1973 | £1.50 | £4 | |

# C

## C, FANTASTIC JOHNNY
| | | | | | | | |
|---|---|---|---|---|---|---|---|
| Boogaloo Down Broadway | LP | Action | ACLP6001 | 1969 | £6 | £15 | |
| Boogaloo Down Broadway | 7" | London | HL10169 | 1967 | £2 | £5 | |
| Hitch It To The Horse | 7" | London | HL10212 | 1968 | £2 | £5 | |
| New Love | 7" | Action | ACT4543 | 1969 | £2 | £5 | |

## C, ROY
| | | | | | | | |
|---|---|---|---|---|---|---|---|
| Shotgun Wedding | 7" | Island | WI273 | 1966 | £2.50 | £6 | 2 different B sides |
| That Shotgun Wedding Man | LP | Ember | NR5055 | 1966 | £4 | £10 | |
| Twistin' Pneumonia | 7" | Ember | EMBS230 | 1967 | £1.50 | £4 | |

## C. A. QUINTET
| | | | | | | | |
|---|---|---|---|---|---|---|---|
| Live | LP | private | | 1985 | £10 | £25 | US |
| Trip Thru' Hell | LP | Candy Floss | 7764 | 1968 | £875 | £1250 | US |
| Trip Thru' Hell | LP | Psycho | PSYCHO12 | 1983 | £6 | £15 | |

## C JAM BLUES
| | | | | | | |
|---|---|---|---|---|---|---|
| Candy | 7" | Columbia | DB8064 | 1966 | £4 | £8 |

## C. M. J.
| | | | | | | |
|---|---|---|---|---|---|---|
| I Can't Do It All BY Myself | 7" | Impression | IMP102 | 1968 | £7.50 | £15 |
| Live At The Bankhouse | LP | Impression | IMPL1001 | 1969 | £100 | £200 |

## C.O.B. (CLIVE'S OWN BAND)

Singer and banjo player Clive Palmer seemed to be a man who was scared of success. As a founder member of the Incredible String Band, he played on their first album, yet left just as they began to gain a following. He then formed the Famous Jug Band, recorded a promising LP, but again left when it began to seem as though the band might actually live up to its name. Finally, he formed C.O.B., and was no doubt highly gratified when neither of the group's albums sold more than a handful of copies.

| | | | | | | |
|---|---|---|---|---|---|---|
| Blue Morning | 7" | Polydor | 2058260 | 1972 | £7.50 | £15 |
| Moyshe McStiff | LP | Polydor | 2383161 | 1972 | £100 | £200 |
| Spirit Of Love | LP | CBS | 69010 | 1971 | £25 | £50 |

## C. O. D.'S
| | | | | | | |
|---|---|---|---|---|---|---|
| Michael | 7" | Stateside | SS489 | 1966 | £5 | £10 |

## CABARET VOLTAIRE
| | | | | | | | |
|---|---|---|---|---|---|---|---|
| Code | CD | Parlophone | CDPCS7312 | 1987 | £5 | £12 | |
| Easy Life | CD-s | Parlophone | CDR6261 | 1990 | £2 | £5 | |
| Eddie's Out | 12" | Rough Trade | RT096T | 1981 | £2.50 | £6 | ...with pink vinyl 7" (RT095) |
| Groovy Laidback And Nasty | CD | Parlophone | CDPCS7338 | 1990 | £5 | £12 | |
| Here To Go | CD-s | Parlophone | CDR6166 | 1987 | £6 | £15 | |
| Hypnotised | CD-s | Parlophone | CDR6227 | 1989 | £2 | £5 | |
| Keep On | CD-s | Parlophone | CDR6250 | 1990 | £2 | £5 | |
| Limited Edition | cass | private | | 1976 | £20 | £40 | |
| What Is Real | CD-s | Crepuscule | TWI9482 | 1991 | £2 | £5 | |

## CABLES
| | | | | | | |
|---|---|---|---|---|---|---|
| Be A Man | 7" | Studio One | SO2060 | 1968 | £6 | £12 |
| Got To Find Someone | 7" | Studio One | SO2085 | 1969 | £6 | £12 |
| How Can I Trust You? | 7" | Bamboo | BAM19 | 1970 | £1.50 | £4 |
| Love Is A Pleasure | 7" | Studio One | SO2071 | 1968 | £6 | £12 |
| So Long | 7" | Bamboo | BAM12 | 1969 | £1.50 | £4 |
| What Kind Of World | 7" | Coxsone | CS7072 | 1968 | £5 | £10 |

## CACCIAPAGEIA, ROBERTO
| | | | | | | | |
|---|---|---|---|---|---|---|---|
| Sonanze | LP | Cosmic Music | PDU6025 | 1975 | £15 | £30 | Italian |

## CACTUS
| | | | | | | |
|---|---|---|---|---|---|---|
| Cactus | LP | Atlantic | 2400020 | 1970 | £4 | £10 |

## CADDICK, BILL
| | | | | | | |
|---|---|---|---|---|---|---|
| Duck On His Head | LP | Highway | SHY7012 | 1980 | £4 | £10 |
| Rough Music | LP | Park | SHP102 | 1976 | £4 | £10 |
| Sunny Memories | LP | Trailer | LER2097 | 1977 | £4 | £10 |

## CADDY, ALAN
| | | | | | | |
|---|---|---|---|---|---|---|
| Workout | 7" | HMV | POP1286 | 1964 | £10 | £20 |

## CADETS
| | | | | | | | |
|---|---|---|---|---|---|---|---|
| Cadets | LP | Crown | CLP5370/CST370 | 1963 | £10 | £25 | US |

| | | | | | | | |
|---|---|---|---|---|---|---|---|
| Rockin' 'n' Reelin' | LP | Crown | CLP5015 | 1957 | £37.50 | £75 | US |
| Stranded In The Jungle | 7" | London | HLU8313 | 1956 | £210 | £350 | gold label, best auctioned |

## CADILLACS

| | | | | | | | |
|---|---|---|---|---|---|---|---|
| Cadillacs Meet The Orioles | LP | Jubilee | JGM1117 | 1961 | £30 | £60 | US |
| Crazy Cadillacs | LP | Jubilee | JGM1089 | 1959 | £50 | £100 | US |
| Fabulous Cadillacs | LP | Jubilee | JGM1045 | 1957 | £75 | £150 | US |
| Peek A Boo | 7" | London | HLJ8786 | 1959 | £12.50 | £25 | |
| Twisting With The Cadillacs | LP | Jubilee | JGM5009 | 1962 | £25 | £50 | US |

## CAEDMON

| | | | | | | | |
|---|---|---|---|---|---|---|---|
| Caedmon | LP | private | | 1978 | £180 | £300 | with 7" |

## CAESAR & CLEO

| | | | | | | |
|---|---|---|---|---|---|---|
| Letter | 7" | Vocalion | VP9247 | 1965 | £1.50 | £4 |
| Love Is Strange | 7" | Reprise | R20419 | 1965 | £1.50 | £4 |

## CAESARS

| | | | | | | |
|---|---|---|---|---|---|---|
| Five In The Morning | 7" | Decca | F12462 | 1966 | £2 | £5 |
| On The Outside Looking In | 7" | Decca | F12251 | 1965 | £2.50 | £6 |

## CAFE SOCIETY

Café Society included Tom Robinson in its line-up, but the collectability of the group's records has more to do with the fact that they were among the few releases on the label founded by the Kinks' Ray Davies.

| | | | | | | |
|---|---|---|---|---|---|---|
| Café Society | LP | Konk | KONK102 | 1975 | £4 | £10 |

## CAGE, BUTCH & MABEL LEE WILLIAMS

| | | | | | | |
|---|---|---|---|---|---|---|
| Country Blues | LP | Storyville | SLP129 | 1964 | £4 | £10 |

## CAGE, JOHN

| | | | | | | | |
|---|---|---|---|---|---|---|---|
| Cartridge Music | LP | Deutsche Grammophon | 137009 | 1969 | £6 | £15 | |
| Concerto For Piano & Orchestra | LP | EMI | C165289547 | | £6 | £15 | |
| Concerto For Prepared Piano & Orchestra | LP | Nonesuch | H71202 | 1968 | £6 | £15 | other side Lukas Foss |
| Fontana Mix | LP | Turnabout | TV34046 | 196– | £6 | £15 | |
| HPSCHD | LP | Nonesuch | H71224 | 1970 | £6 | £15 | other side Ben Johnston |
| Sonatas & Interludes For Prepared Piano | LP | Decca | HEAD9 | 1976 | £6 | £15 | |
| Variations | LP | Everest | 3132 | | £6 | £15 | |
| Variations II | LP | Columbia | MS7051 | | £6 | £15 | US |

## CAGLE, AUBREY

| | | | | | | | |
|---|---|---|---|---|---|---|---|
| Come Along Little Girl | 7" | Starlite | ST45082 | 1962 | £100 | £200 | best auctioned |

## CAHILL, PATRICIA

| | | | | | | |
|---|---|---|---|---|---|---|
| Summer's Daughter | LP | Nova | SDN22 | 1970 | £6 | £15 |

## CAIN

| | | | | | | |
|---|---|---|---|---|---|---|
| Her Emotion | 7" | Page One | POF054 | 1968 | £2 | £5 |

## CAIN, JACKIE & ROY KRAL

| | | | | | | |
|---|---|---|---|---|---|---|
| Bits And Pieces | LP | HMV | CLP1187 | 1958 | £6 | £15 |
| Free And Easy | LP | HMV | CLP1232 | 1959 | £6 | £15 |
| Glory Of Love | LP | HMV | CLP1219 | 1958 | £6 | £15 |
| Jackie And Roy | LP | Vogue | VA160111 | 1958 | £4 | £10 |

## CAIN, JEFFREY

| | | | | | | | |
|---|---|---|---|---|---|---|---|
| For You | LP | Warner Bros | WS1880 | 1970 | £8 | £20 | US |
| Whispering Thunder | LP | Raccoon | 12 | 1972 | £6 | £15 | US |

## CAIOLA, AL

| | | | | | | |
|---|---|---|---|---|---|---|
| Bonanza | 7" | London | HLT9325 | 1961 | £4 | £8 |
| Deep In A Dream | LP | London | HAC2017 | 1956 | £4 | £10 |
| Flamenco Love | 7" | London | HLC8285 | 1956 | £7.50 | £15 |
| Hit TV Themes | 7" EP | United Artists | UEP1018 | 1966 | £2.50 | £6 |
| Serenade In Blue | LP | London | HAC2022 | 1957 | £4 | £10 |

## CAKE

| | | | | | | |
|---|---|---|---|---|---|---|
| Cake | LP | MCA | MUPS303 | 1968 | £4 | £10 |
| Slice Of Cake | LP | MCA | MUPS390 | 1969 | £4 | £10 |

## CALDWELL, LOUISE HARRISON

| | | | | | | | |
|---|---|---|---|---|---|---|---|
| All About The Beatles | LP | Recar | 2012 | 1964 | £37.50 | £75 | US |

## CALE, J. J.

| | | | | | | | |
|---|---|---|---|---|---|---|---|
| J. J. Cale | LP | Shelter | ISADJ1 | 1976 | £4 | £10 | promo |
| Outside Looking In | 7" | Liberty | LBY55881 | 1966 | £2 | £5 | |

## CALE, JOHN

| | | | | | | | |
|---|---|---|---|---|---|---|---|
| Hear Fear | LP | Island | IXP2 | 1976 | £4 | £10 | US promo |
| Jack The Ripper | 7" | Illegal | IL006 | 1977 | £4 | £8 | demo |
| Vintage Violence | LP | CBS | 64256 | 1970 | £4 | £10 | |

## CALE, JOHN & TERRY RILEY

| | | | | | | |
|---|---|---|---|---|---|---|
| Church Of Anthrax | LP | CBS | 64259 | 1971 | £5 | £12 |

## CALEB
Woman Of Distinction .......................... 7" ...... Philips............ BF1588 ................ 1967 £75....... £150 .......................

## CALEDONIANS
Funny Way Of Laughing ........................ 7" ...... Fab .............. FAB103................ 1969 £1.50........ £4

## CALIFORNIA IN CROWD
Questions And Answers ........................... 7" ...... Fontana ........... TF779 ................ 1966 £12.50.... £25

## CALIFORNIANS
Congratulations................................ 7" ...... Decca ......... F12758 ................ 1968 £1.50..... £4
Cooks Of Cake And Kindness ................... 7" ...... Fontana ....... TF991 ........... 1969 £12.50.... £25
Follow Me.................................... 7" ...... Decca ......... F12678 .......... 1967 £2 .......... £5
Golden Apples ................................ 7" ...... CBS............ 202263 .......... 1967 £7.50..... £15
Golden Apples ................................ 7" ...... CBS............ 2663 .......... 1969 £1.50..... £4
Out In The Sun ............................... 7" ...... Decca ......... F12802 .......... 1968 £1.50..... £4
Sad Old Song................................. 7" ...... Fontana ....... TF1052 .......... 1969 £1.50..... £4
Sunday Will Never Be The Same............... 7" ...... Decca ......... F12712 .......... 1967 £1.50..... £4

## CALL GIRLS
Primal World ................................ 7" ...... 53rd and 3rd.... AGAR001 .......... 1988 £2.50..... £6

## CALLAN & JOHN
House Of Delight................................ 7" ...... CBS............ 4447 ......... 1969 £2.50..... £6

## CALLENDER, BOBBY
Rainbow ..................................... LP ..... MGM............ SE4557 ......... 1968 £30..... £60 ....................... US
Way ........................................ LP ..... MGM............ ................. 1971 £15..... £30 ................ US double

## CALLICOTT, MISSISSIPPI JOE
Deal Gone Down ............................. LP ..... Revival ........ RVS1002 ......... 1972 £5..... £12
Presenting The Country Blues.................. LP ..... Blue Horizon... 763227 ......... 1968 £15..... £30

## CALLIES
On Your Side ................................. LP ..... Rubber .......... RUB001 ......... 1971 £8..... £20

## CALLINAN FLYNN
Freedom's Lament............................. LP ..... Mushroom ...... 150MR18 .......... 1972 £100.... £200
Freedom's Lament............................. CD .... Blast From The BFTP002CD .......... 1991 £6..... £15
                                                      Past
We Are The People............................ 7" ..... Mushroom ..... 50MR17 .......... 1972 £25..... £50

## CALLIOPE
Steamed..................................... LP ..... Buddah .......... 203016 ......... 1968 £4..... £10

## CALLOWAY, CAB
Cab Calloway ............................... 7" EP . Fontana ....... TFE17216 ......... 1960 £7.50.... £15
Cab Calloway ............................... 7" EP . Gala............ 45XP1016 ......... 1958 £2..... £5
Cabulous Calloway ........................... 7" EP . Vintage Jazz.... VEP22 .......... 196– £2..... £5
Cabulous Calloway Vol. 2 ..................... 7" EP . Vintage Jazz.... VEP35 .......... 196– £2..... £5
Minnie The Moocher ......................... 78...... Brunswick ....... 05022.......... 1952 £1.50.... £4

## CALVERT, EDDIE
Ave Maria.................................... 7" ...... Columbia ....... SCM5004 .......... 1953 £1.50.... £4
Cherry Pink And Apple Blossom White ..... 7" ...... Columbia ....... SCM5168 .......... 1955 £2.50.... £6
Man With The Golden Arm................... 7" ...... Columbia ....... SCM5237 .......... 1956 £1.50.... £4
My Son, My Son............................ 7" ...... Columbia ....... SCM5129 .......... 1954 £1.50.... £4
My Yiddishe Momma ......................... 7" ...... Columbia ....... SCM5003 .......... 1953 £1.50.... £4

## CALVERT, ROBERT
At The Queen Elizabeth Hall ................. LP ..... Clear........... BLACK1 .......... 1989 £8........ £20 . with badge & T shirt
Captain Lockheed & The Starfighters......... LP ..... United Artists .. UAG29507............ 1974 £8........ £20 ... inner sleeve, booklet
Captain Lockheed And The Starfighters..... LP ..... United Artists .. UAG29507............ 1974 £10........ £25 ............. with booklet
Ejection.................................... 7" ...... United Artists .. UP35543 .......... 1973 £2.50....... £6 ............. different mix
Ejection.................................... 7" ...... United Artists .. UP35543 .......... 1973 £6........ £12 .picture sleeve, credited
                                                                                                                    to Captain Lockheed
Hype....................................... LP ..... A Side........... IFO311 .......... 1980 £4........ £10
Lucky Leif & The Longships................. LP ..... United Artists .. UAG29852.......... 1975 £8........ £20

## CALVIN, TABBY & THE ROUNDERS
False Alarm ................................. 7" ...... Capitol........... CL14640 .......... 1956 £1.50....... £4

## CALYX
Just A Dream ................................ LP ..... ALG ............ ................. 1976 £37.50.... £75 ................. Dutch

## CAMARATA
Velvet Gentleman............................ LP ..... Deram ......... SML1101 .......... 1973 £25..... £50

## CAMEL
Camel...................................... LP ..... MCA............ MUPS473 ......... 1973 £4..... £10
Mirage..................................... LP ..... Deram ......... SML1107 ......... 1974 £4..... £10
Moon Madness............................... CD .... Decca ......... 8108792 ......... 1983 £5..... £12
Never Let Go............................... 7" ..... MCA............ MU1177 ......... 1973 £1.50.... £4
Nude....................................... CD .... Decca ......... 8108802 ......... 1987 £5..... £12
Single Factor ............................... CD .... Decca ......... 8000812 ......... 1983 £5..... £12
Snow Goose ................................ CD .... Deram ......... 8000802 ......... 1988 £5..... £12
Stationary Traveller ......................... CD .... Decca ......... 8200202 ......... 1983 £5..... £12

## CAMEO
| | | | | | | | |
|---|---|---|---|---|---|---|---|
| Cardiac Arrest | LP | Casablanca | CAL2015 | 1977 | £4 | £10 | |

## CAMEOS
| | | | | | | | |
|---|---|---|---|---|---|---|---|
| My Baby's Coming Home | 7" | Columbia | DB7201 | 1964 | £10 | £20 | |
| Powercut | 7" | Columbia | DB7092 | 1963 | £12.50 | £25 | |

## CAMEOS (2)
| | | | | | | | |
|---|---|---|---|---|---|---|---|
| On The Good Ship Lollipop | 7" | Toast | TT508 | 1968 | £1.50 | £4 | |
| Pretty Shade Of Blue | 7" | Toast | TT503 | 1967 | £1.50 | £4 | |

## CAMERON, DION
| | | | | | | | |
|---|---|---|---|---|---|---|---|
| Get Ready | 7" | Rio | R111 | 1966 | £4 | £8 | |
| Miserable Friday | 7" | Doctor Bird | DB1101 | 1967 | £5 | £10 | |

## CAMERON, ISLA
| | | | | | | | |
|---|---|---|---|---|---|---|---|
| Lost Love | 7" EP | Transatlantic | TRAEP109 | 1964 | £2.50 | £6 | |

## CAMERON, ISLA, GUY CARAWAN, PEGGY SEEGER
| | | | | | | | |
|---|---|---|---|---|---|---|---|
| Origins Of Skiffle | 7" EP | Pye | NJE1043 | 1957 | £4 | £8 | |

## CAMERON, JOHN
| | | | | | | | |
|---|---|---|---|---|---|---|---|
| Cover Lover | LP | Columbia | SCX6116 | 1967 | £8 | £20 | |
| Off Centre | LP | Deram | DML/SML1044 | 1969 | £20 | £40 | |
| Troublemaker | 7" | Deram | DM256 | 1969 | £1.50 | £4 | |
| Walk Small | 7" | Columbia | DB8120 | 1967 | £1.50 | £4 | |

## CAMERON, RAY
| | | | | | | | |
|---|---|---|---|---|---|---|---|
| Doin' My Time | 7" | Island | WIP6003 | 1967 | £1.50 | £4 | |

## CAMERON, TED & THE DEEJAYS
| | | | | | | | |
|---|---|---|---|---|---|---|---|
| Early In The Morning | 7" | Pye | 7N15292 | 1960 | £4 | £8 | |

## CAMPBELL, AL & THE THRILLERS
| | | | | | | | |
|---|---|---|---|---|---|---|---|
| Heart For Sale | 7" | Blue Cat | BS118 | 1968 | £4 | £8 | Zoot Sims B side |

## CAMPBELL, ALEX
| | | | | | | | |
|---|---|---|---|---|---|---|---|
| Alex Campbell | LP | XTRA | XTRA1041 | 1966 | £4 | £10 | |
| Alex Campbell And Friends | LP | Saga | EROS8021 | 1967 | £8 | £20 | with Sandy Denny |
| At His Best | LP | Boulevard | 4073 | 1972 | £4 | £10 | |
| Been On The Road So Long | 7" | Transatlantic | TRASP4 | 1965 | £1.50 | £4 | |
| Best Loved Songs Of Bonnie Scotland | LP | Society | SOC936 | 1963 | £4 | £10 | |
| Big Daddy Of Folk Music | LP | Antagon | LP3206 | 1976 | £5 | £12 | German |
| Folk Session | LP | Society | SOC960 | 1963 | £4 | £10 | |
| In Copenhagen | LP | Polydor | 623035 | 1965 | £8 | £20 | |
| No Regrets | LP | Look | LKLP6043 | 1976 | £6 | £15 | |
| Out West | 7" | Arc | ARC36 | 196– | £1.50 | £4 | |
| This Is Alex Campbell 1 | LP | Ad Rhythm-Tepee | ARPS1 | 1971 | £15 | £30 | |
| This Is Alex Campbell 2 | LP | Ad Rhythm-Tepee | ARPS2 | 1971 | £15 | £30 | |
| Victoria Dines Alone | 7" | Saga | OPP2 | 1968 | £1.50 | £4 | |
| With The Greatest Respect | LP | Sundown | SDLP2048 | 1987 | £5 | £12 | double |

## CAMPBELL, ALEX, ALAN ROBERTS, DOUGIE MACLEAN
| | | | | | | | |
|---|---|---|---|---|---|---|---|
| Alex Campbell, Alan Roberts, Dougie Maclean | LP | Burlington | BURL002 | 1979 | £5 | £12 | |

## CAMPBELL, ALEX, COLIN WILKIE & SHIRLEY HART
| | | | | | | | |
|---|---|---|---|---|---|---|---|
| Sing Folk | LP | Presto | PRE648 | 1965 | £5 | £12 | |

## CAMPBELL, CHOKER
| | | | | | | | |
|---|---|---|---|---|---|---|---|
| Hits Of The Sixties | LP | Tamla Motown | TML11011 | 1965 | £50 | £100 | |
| Mickey's Monkey | 7" | Tamla Motown | TMG517 | 1965 | £30 | £60 | |

## CAMPBELL, CORNELL
| | | | | | | | |
|---|---|---|---|---|---|---|---|
| Cornell Campbell | LP | Trojan | TBL199 | 1972 | £5 | £12 | |
| Each Lonely Night | 7" | Island | WI083 | 1963 | £5 | £10 | |
| Gloria | 7" | Rio | R38 | 1964 | £5 | £10 | |
| Jericho Road | 7" | Port-O-Jam | PJ4008 | 1964 | £5 | £10 | |
| Rosahelle | 7" | Island | WI039 | 1962 | £5 | £10 | |

## CAMPBELL, DAVID
| | | | | | | | |
|---|---|---|---|---|---|---|---|
| Young Blood | LP | Transatlantic | TRA141 | 1967 | £10 | £25 | |

## CAMPBELL, DICK
| | | | | | | | |
|---|---|---|---|---|---|---|---|
| Sings Where It's At | LP | Mercury | MG2/SR61060 | 1965 | £4 | £10 | US |

## CAMPBELL, DOREEN
| | | | | | | | |
|---|---|---|---|---|---|---|---|
| Rude Girls | 7" | Rainbow | RAI117 | 1967 | £2.50 | £6 | |

## CAMPBELL, ETHNA
| | | | | | | | |
|---|---|---|---|---|---|---|---|
| What's Easy For Two | 7" | Mercury | MF804 | 1964 | £2.50 | £6 | |

## CAMPBELL, GLEN

Glen Campbell is dismissed as unredeemably middle-of-the-road by rock music collectors, yet his versions of songs by Jimmy Webb are always worth hearing and include at least one genuine classic in 'Wichita Lineman'. In 1965 he turned down the chance to become a full-time Beach Boy, but did record Brian Wilson's 'Guess I'm Dumb' with the writer in the producer's chair.

| | | | | | | | |
|---|---|---|---|---|---|---|---|
| Guess I'm Dumb | 7" | Capitol | 5441 | 1965 | £15 | £30 | US |
| Turn Around, Look At Me | 7" | Top Rank | JAR596 | 1961 | £2 | £5 | |

## CAMPBELL, IAN

The Ian Campbell Folk Group recorded prolifically during the sixties to considerable acclaim, but lost momentum thereafter – finally disbanding in 1978. Star fiddler Dave Swarbrick was a member of the group on the majority of the recordings listed below, while bass player Dave Pegg was a member during the late sixties. Swarbrick and Pegg went on to play together in Fairport Convention. Ian Campbell's sons have gained considerable success with their group UB40, although it is said that the father does not really approve of the commercial direction they have taken.

| | | | | | | | |
|---|---|---|---|---|---|---|---|
| Across The Hills | LP | Transatlantic | TRA118 | 1964 | £8 | £20 | |
| Adam's Rib | LP | | | 1976 | £20 | £40 | |
| Break My Mind | 7" | Major Minor | MM639 | 1969 | £1.50 | £4 | |
| Ceilidh At The Crown | 7" EP | Topic | TOP76 | 1962 | £10 | £20 | |
| Circle Game | LP | Transatlantic | TRA163 | 1968 | £6 | £15 | |
| Coaldust Ballads | LP | Transatlantic | TRA123 | 1965 | £10 | £25 | |
| Cock Doth Craw | LP | XTRA | XTRA1061 | 1968 | £6 | £15 | |
| Come Kiss Me | 7" | Transatlantic | TRASP6 | 1966 | £1.50 | £4 | |
| Contemporary Campbells | LP | Transatlantic | TRA137 | 1965 | £8 | £20 | |
| Guantanamera | 7" | Transatlantic | TRASP7 | 1966 | £1.50 | £4 | |
| Ian Campbell Folk Group | LP | MFP | MFP1349 | 1969 | £4 | £10 | |
| Ian Campbell Folk Group | 7" EP | Decca | DFE8592 | 1964 | £2.50 | £6 | |
| Kelly From Killane | 7" | Transatlantic | TRASP2 | 1965 | £1.50 | £4 | |
| Lover Let Me In | 7" | Transatlantic | BIG103 | 1968 | £1.50 | £4 | |
| Marilyn Monroe | 7" | Decca | F11802 | 1964 | £1.50 | £4 | |
| New Impressions | LP | Transatlantic | TRA151 | 1967 | £6 | £15 | |
| One Eyed Reilly | 7" | Transatlantic | TRASP10 | 1966 | £1.50 | £4 | |
| Presenting The Ian Campbell Folk Group | LP | Contour | 2870314 | 197– | £4 | £10 | |
| Sampler | LP | Transatlantic | TRASAM4 | 1969 | £5 | £12 | |
| Sampler | 7" EP | Transatlantic | TRAEP128 | 1965 | £2 | £5 | |
| Sampler 2 | LP | Transatlantic | TRASAM12 | 1969 | £5 | £12 | |
| Something To Sing About | LP | Pye | PKL5506 | 1972 | £8 | £20 | |
| Sun Is Burning | LP | Argo | ZFB13 | 1971 | £8 | £20 | |
| Sun Is Burning | 7" | Topic | STOP102 | 1964 | £4 | £8 | picture sleeve |
| Tam O'Shanter | LP | XTRA | XTRA1074 | 1968 | £6 | £15 | |
| This Is The Ian Campbell Folk Group | LP | Transatlantic | TRA110 | 1963 | £8 | £20 | |
| Times They Are A–Changin' | 7" | Transatlantic | TRASP5 | 1965 | £1.50 | £4 | |

## CAMPBELL, JIMMY

| | | | | | | | |
|---|---|---|---|---|---|---|---|
| Album | LP | Philips | 6308100 | 1972 | £4 | £10 | |
| Half Baked | LP | Vertigo | 6360010 | 1970 | £4 | £10 | with Merseybeats |
| Songs Of Anastasia | LP | Fontana | STL5508 | 1969 | £4 | £10 | |

## CAMPBELL, JO ANN

| | | | | | | | |
|---|---|---|---|---|---|---|---|
| All The Hits | LP | Cameo | (S)C1026 | 1962 | £8 | £20 | US |
| I Changed My Mind Jack | 7" | HMV | POP1003 | 1962 | £1.50 | £4 | |
| I'm Nobody's Baby | LP | End | LP306 | 1959 | £15 | £30 | US |
| Kookie Little Paradise | 7" | HMV | POP776 | 1960 | £1.50 | £4 | |
| Mister Fixit Man | 7" | Cameo Parkway | C237 | 1962 | £1.50 | £4 | |
| Mother Please | 7" | Cameo Parkway | C249 | 1963 | £1.50 | £4 | |
| Motorcycle Michael | 7" | HMV | POP873 | 1961 | £1.50 | £4 | |
| Starring | LP | Coronet | CX(S)199 | 1964 | £10 | £25 | US |
| Twistin' And Listenin' | LP | ABC | (S)393 | 1962 | £10 | £25 | US |
| Wait A Minute | 7" | London | HLU8536 | 1958 | £10 | £20 | |

## CAMPBELL, NOLA

| | | | | | | | |
|---|---|---|---|---|---|---|---|
| Pictures Of You | 7" | Gas | GAS107 | 1969 | £1.50 | £4 | |

## CAMPBELL, ROY

| | | | | | | | |
|---|---|---|---|---|---|---|---|
| Another Saturday Night | 7" | Giant | GN41 | 1968 | £1.50 | £4 | |
| Engine Number Nine | 7" | Jolly | JY003 | 1968 | £1.50 | £4 | |

## CAMPBELL FAMILY

| | | | | | | | |
|---|---|---|---|---|---|---|---|
| Singing Campbells | LP | Topic | 12T120 | 1965 | £10 | £25 | |

## CAMPBELL-LYONS, PATRICK

| | | | | | | | |
|---|---|---|---|---|---|---|---|
| Electric Plough | LP | Public | PUBL1 | 1981 | £4 | £10 | |
| Everybody Should Fly A Kite | 7" | Sovereign | SOV115 | 1973 | £4 | £8 | |
| Me And My Friend | LP | Sovereign | SVNA7258 | 1973 | £50 | £100 | |
| Out On The Road | 7" | Sovereign | SOV119 | 1973 | £4 | £8 | |

## CAN

| | | | | | | | |
|---|---|---|---|---|---|---|---|
| Cannibalism | LP | United Artists | UDM105/6 | 1978 | £5 | £12 | double |
| Ege Bamyasi | LP | United Artists | UAS29414 | 1972 | £6 | £15 | |
| Flow Motion | LP | Virgin | V2071 | 1976 | £4 | £10 | |
| Flow Motion | CD | Virgin | CDV2071 | 1988 | £5 | £12 | |
| Future Days | LP | United Artists | UAS29505 | 1973 | £5 | £12 | |
| Landed | LP | Virgin | V2041 | 1975 | £5 | £12 | |
| Limited Edition | LP | United Artists | USP103 | 1974 | £5 | £12 | |
| Monster Movie | LP | Music Factory | SRS001 | 1969 | £37.50 | £75 | German |
| Monster Movie | LP | United Artists | UAS29094 | 1969 | £8 | £20 | |
| Only You | cass | Pure Freude | PF23 | 1982 | £15 | £30 | tin container |

| | | | | | | | |
|---|---|---|---|---|---|---|---|
| Opener | LP | Sunset | SLS50400 | 1976 | £4 | £10 | |
| Saw Delight | LP | Virgin | V2079 | 1977 | £4 | £10 | |
| Saw Delight | CD | Virgin | CDV2079 | 1988 | £5 | £12 | |
| Soon Over Babaluma | LP | United Artists | UAG29673 | 1974 | £5 | £12 | |
| Soundtracks | LP | United Artists | UAS29283 | 1970 | £8 | £20 | |
| Tago Mago | LP | United Artists | UAD60009/10 | 1971 | £10 | £25 | double |
| Unlimited Edition | LP | Caroline | CAD3001 | 1976 | £6 | £15 | double |

## CANAAN
| | | | | | | | |
|---|---|---|---|---|---|---|---|
| Canaan | LP | Dovetail | DOVE3 | 1973 | £25 | £50 | |
| Out Of The Wilderness | LP | Myrrh | | 197– | £15 | £30 | |

## CANADIAN BEATLES
| | | | | | | | |
|---|---|---|---|---|---|---|---|
| Three Faces North | LP | Tide | 2005 | 1964 | £20 | £40 | US |

## CANADIAN SQUIRES

Levon and the Hawks – later to become the Band – recorded as the Canadian Squires for one single.

| | | | | | | | |
|---|---|---|---|---|---|---|---|
| Uh Uh Uh | 7" | Ware | 6002 | 1965 | £10 | £20 | US |

## CANARIES
| | | | | | | | |
|---|---|---|---|---|---|---|---|
| Flying High | LP | B.T.Puppy | BTPS1007 | 1970 | £4 | £10 | US |

## CANDIDO
| | | | | | | | |
|---|---|---|---|---|---|---|---|
| Beautiful | LP | Blue Note | BST84357 | 1970 | £5 | £12 | |
| Candido In Indigo | LP | HMV | CLP1265 | 1959 | £6 | £15 | |
| Candido The Volcanic | 10" LP | HMV | DLP1182 | 1958 | £6 | £15 | |

## CANDLE FACTORY
| | | | | | | | |
|---|---|---|---|---|---|---|---|
| Nightshift | LP | Cavs | | 197– | £25 | £50 | |

## CANDOLI, CONTE
| | | | | | | | |
|---|---|---|---|---|---|---|---|
| Sincerely, Conte | 10" LP | London | LZN14010 | 1956 | £8 | £20 | |
| Toots Sweet | LP | London | LTZN15036 | 1957 | £6 | £15 | |

## CANDOLI, PETE
| | | | | | | | |
|---|---|---|---|---|---|---|---|
| St. Louis Blues Boogie | 7" | Capitol | CL14615 | 1956 | £2 | £5 | |

## CANDY & THE KISSES
| | | | | | | | |
|---|---|---|---|---|---|---|---|
| Do The 81 | 7" | Cameo Parkway | C336 | 1965 | £20 | £40 | |
| Mr. Creator | 7" | Kent | TOWN104 | 1985 | £5 | £10 | Chuck Jackson B side |

## CANDY CHOIR
| | | | | | | | |
|---|---|---|---|---|---|---|---|
| Shake Hands And Come Out Crying | 7" | Parlophone | R5472 | 1966 | £4 | £8 | |

## CANDY DATES
| | | | | | | | |
|---|---|---|---|---|---|---|---|
| Day Just Like That | 7" | Pye | 7N15944 | 1965 | £1.50 | £4 | |
| Some Other Time | 7" | Pye | 7N17000 | 1965 | £1.50 | £4 | |

## CANDYMEN
| | | | | | | | |
|---|---|---|---|---|---|---|---|
| De Manchester A Paris | 7" EP | Barclay | 70806 | 1965 | £5 | £10 | French |
| Georgia Pines | 7" | HMV | POP1612 | 1967 | £1.50 | £4 | |

## CANE
| | | | | | | | |
|---|---|---|---|---|---|---|---|
| 3 X 3 | 7" | Lightning | GIL531 | 1978 | £2 | £5 | |

## CANNED HEAT

At their best (*Boogie With Canned Heat*), Canned Heat were one of the most interesting white blues groups. Bob Hite and Henry Vestine had a collection of blues records of legendary proportions, so they were not short of good examples to follow. They did have a liking, however, for what they called 'boogie', by which they meant a string of extremely long and extremely tedious instrumental solos played over an elemental riff. Both extremes can be found on the double *Living The Blues*. There is a boogie of record-breaking length, but also some short experimental tracks that take interesting liberties with the blues format. The record made with John Lee Hooker, listed under that name, also shows Canned Heat's abilities well. They let Hooker run the show, but by virtue of their telling support, they push him into making one of his very best records.

| | | | | | | | |
|---|---|---|---|---|---|---|---|
| Boogie With Canned Heat | LP | Liberty | LBL/LBS83103 | 1968 | £5 | £12 | |
| Canned Heat | LP | Liberty | LBL/LBS83059 | 1967 | £6 | £15 | |
| Canned Heat '70: Live In Europe | LP | Liberty | LBS83333 | 1970 | £5 | £12 | |
| Cookbook | LP | Liberty | LBS83303 | 1970 | £4 | £10 | |
| Future Blues | LP | Liberty | LBS83364 | 1970 | £5 | £12 | |
| Going Up The Country | 7" | Liberty | LBF15169 | 1968 | £1.50 | £4 | |
| Hallelujah | LP | Liberty | LBS83239 | 1969 | £5 | £12 | |
| Let's Work Together | CD-s | Liberty | CDEM100 | 1989 | £2 | £5 | |
| Let's Work Together | 7" | Liberty | LBF15302 | 1969 | £1.50 | £4 | |
| Live At Topanga Canyon | LP | Wand | WDS693 | 1970 | £5 | £12 | US |
| Living The Blues | LP | Liberty | LDS84001 | 1969 | £8 | £20 | double |
| Living The Blues | LP | United Artists | UAS29258/9 | 1972 | £6 | £15 | double |
| On The Road Again | 7" | Liberty | LBS15090 | 1968 | £1.50 | £4 | |
| Spoonful | 7" | Pye | 7N25513 | 1970 | £1.50 | £4 | |
| Vintage Heat | LP | Pye | NSPL28129 | 1970 | £5 | £12 | |

## CANNED HEAT & CLARENCE GATEMOUTH BROWN
| | | | | | | | |
|---|---|---|---|---|---|---|---|
| Gate's On Heat | LP | Barclay | 80603 | 1973 | £6 | £15 | French |

## CANNED HEAT & MEMPHIS SLIM
| | | | | | | | |
|---|---|---|---|---|---|---|---|
| Memphis Heat | LP | Barclay | 80607 | 1975 | £6 | £15 | French |

## CANNIBAL & THE HEADHUNTERS
| | | | | | | | |
|---|---|---|---|---|---|---|---|
| Land Of 1000 Dances | LP | CBS | 62942 | 1967 | £6 | £15 | |
| Land Of 1000 Dances | 7" | Stateside | SS403 | 1965 | £5 | £10 | |

## CANNIBALS
| | | | | | | | |
|---|---|---|---|---|---|---|---|
| Good Guys | 7" | Big Cock | FUK1 | 1978 | £2 | £5 | |

## CANNON, ACE
| | | | | | | | |
|---|---|---|---|---|---|---|---|
| Blues Stay Away From Me | 7" | London | HLU9546 | 1962 | £1.50 | £4 | |
| Cottonfields | 7" | London | HLU9745 | 1963 | £1.50 | £4 | |
| Searching | 7" | London | HLU9866 | 1964 | £1.50 | £4 | |
| Tuff | LP | Hi | HLP32007 | 1961 | £4 | £10 | US |
| Tuff | 7" | London | HLU9498 | 1962 | £1.50 | £4 | |

## CANNON, FREDDIE
| | | | | | | | |
|---|---|---|---|---|---|---|---|
| Action | LP | Warner Bros | W(S)1612 | 1965 | £6 | £15 | US |
| Bang On | LP | Stateside | SL10013 | 1963 | £10 | £25 | |
| Blast Off | 7" EP | Stateside | SE1002 | 1962 | £7.50 | £15 | |
| Buzz Buzz A Diddle It | 7" | Top Rank | JAR568 | 1961 | £5 | £10 | |
| California Here I Come | 7" | Top Rank | JAR309 | 1960 | £1.50 | £4 | |
| Chattanooga Shoeshine Boy | 7" | Top Rank | JAR334 | 1960 | £1.50 | £4 | |
| Dedication Song | 7" | Warner Bros | WB5693 | 1966 | £1.50 | £4 | |
| Explosive Freddie Cannon | LP | Top Rank | 25018 | 1960 | £8 | £20 | |
| Explosive Freddie Cannon | 7" EP | Top Rank | JKP2058 | 1960 | £10 | £20 | |
| Four Direct Hits | 7" EP | Top Rank | JKP2066 | 1960 | £7.50 | £15 | |
| Freddie Cannon | LP | Warner Bros | WM/WS8153 | 1964 | £8 | £20 | |
| Freddie Cannon Favourites | LP | Top Rank | 35113 | 1961 | £10 | £25 | |
| Greatest Hits | LP | Warner Bros | W(S)1628 | 1966 | £6 | £15 | US |
| Happy Shades Of Blue | LP | Top Rank | 35106 | 1961 | £10 | £25 | |
| Humdinger | 7" | Top Rank | JAR518 | 1960 | £1.50 | £4 | |
| Okefenokee | 7" | Top Rank | JAR207 | 1959 | £2 | £5 | |
| On Target | 7" EP | Top Rank | JKP3010 | 1961 | £7.50 | £15 | |
| Palisades Park | 7" | Stateside | SS101 | 1962 | £1.50 | £4 | |
| Patty Baby | 7" | Stateside | SS201 | 1963 | £1.50 | £4 | |
| Steps Out | LP | Stateside | SL10062 | 1964 | £15 | £30 | |
| Tallahassee Lassie | 7" | Top Rank | JAR135 | 1959 | £1.50 | £4 | |
| Teen Queen Of The Week | 7" | Top Rank | JAR609 | 1962 | £1.50 | £4 | |
| Transistor Sister | 7" | Top Rank | JAR579 | 1961 | £1.50 | £4 | |
| Urge | 7" | Top Rank | JAR369 | 1960 | £1.50 | £4 | |
| Way Down Yonder In New Orleans | 7" | Top Rank | JAR247 | 1959 | £1.50 | £4 | |

## CANNON, GUS
| | | | | | | | |
|---|---|---|---|---|---|---|---|
| Cannon's Jug Stompers/Clifford's Louisville Jug Band | LP | Tax | LP2 | 1966 | £6 | £15 | |
| Walk Right In | LP | Stax | 702 | 1962 | £8 | £20 | US |

## CANNON, JUDY
| | | | | | | | |
|---|---|---|---|---|---|---|---|
| Very First Day I Met You | 7" | Pye | 7N15900 | 1965 | £5 | £10 | |

## CANNON, SEAN
| | | | | | | | |
|---|---|---|---|---|---|---|---|
| Erin The Green | LP | Ogham | BLB5004 | 1979 | £4 | £10 | Irish |
| Roving Journey Man | LP | Cottage | COT411 | 1977 | £4 | £10 | |

## CANNON BROTHERS
| | | | | | | | |
|---|---|---|---|---|---|---|---|
| Turn Your Eyes To Me | 7" | Brit | WI1003 | 1965 | £4 | £8 | |

## CANNONBALL & JOHNNY MELODY
| | | | | | | | |
|---|---|---|---|---|---|---|---|
| Cool Hand Luke | 7" | Big Shot | BI518 | 1969 | £1.50 | £4 | |

## CANNONBALLS
| | | | | | | | |
|---|---|---|---|---|---|---|---|
| Calliope Boogie | 7" | Coral | Q72431 | 1961 | £4 | £8 | |
| New Orleans Beat | 7" | Coral | Q72428 | 1961 | £4 | £8 | |

## CANNONS
| | | | | | | | |
|---|---|---|---|---|---|---|---|
| Bush Fire | 7" | Columbia | DB4724 | 1961 | £4 | £8 | |
| I Didn't Know The Gun Was Loaded | 7" | Decca | F11269 | 1960 | £4 | £8 | |

## CANNY FETTLE
| | | | | | | | |
|---|---|---|---|---|---|---|---|
| Varry Canny | LP | Tradition | TSR023 | 1975 | £5 | £12 | |

## CANTELON, WILLARD
| | | | | | | | |
|---|---|---|---|---|---|---|---|
| LSD Battle For The Mind | LP | Supreme | M/S113 | 1966 | £4 | £10 | US |

## CANTOR, EDDIE
| | | | | | | | |
|---|---|---|---|---|---|---|---|
| Ma He's Making Eyes At Me | 7" EP | Capitol | EAP120113 | 1961 | £2 | £5 | |

## CAPE KENNEDY CONSTRUCTION CO.
| | | | | | | | |
|---|---|---|---|---|---|---|---|
| First Step On The Moon | 7" | President | PT265 | 1969 | £5 | £10 | |

## CAPITOLS
| | | | | | | | |
|---|---|---|---|---|---|---|---|
| Cool Jerk | 7" | Atlantic | 584004 | 1966 | £2 | £5 | |
| Cool Jerk | 7" | Atlantic | 584251 | 1969 | £1.50 | £4 | |
| Dance The Cool Jerk | LP | Atlantic | 587/588019 | 1966 | £6 | £15 | |
| I Got To Handle It | 7" | Atlantic | 584043 | 1966 | £1.50 | £4 | |
| We Got A Thing | LP | Atco | (SD33)201 | 1966 | £5 | £12 | US |

## CAPITOLS (2)
Honey And Wine.................................... 7" ...... Pye ................ 7N17025 ................ 1966 £2 ............ £5 ................

## CAPP, ANDY
Law............................................................. 7" ...... Duke ............ DU69 .................... 1970 £1.50 .......... £4 .....................

## CAPRIS
There's A Moon Out Tonight .................. 7" ...... Columbia ....... DB4605 ................. 1961 £30 ....... £60 .........................

## CAPSTICK, TONY
Punch And Judy Man .............................. LP ..... Rubber .......... RUB008 ................ 1974 £4 .......... £10 .......................

## CAPTAIN BEEFHEART
Don Van Vliet followed his own wayward path through rock music, before deciding that he would much rather make a living as a full-time artist (and has apparently become far wealthier through his painting than he ever did through his music). Evolving from an idiosyncratic approach to the blues, the music made by the Magic Band on the ground-breaking albums *Strictly Personal* and *Trout Mask Replica* has strong parallels within a rock context to the harmelodic jazz approach developed by Ornette Coleman. The rhythms and harmonies sound fractured and chaotic at first, but they have their own logic and are very far from being dismissable as the weird ramblings of an eccentric. Indeed, Van Vliet's influence has become increasingly noticeable in the work of various adventurous post-punk groups. As it happens, *Trout Mask Replica*, produced by Van Vliet's schoolfriend Frank Zappa, sold well enough to enter the lower reaches of the album charts, and later pressings are fairly common.

| | | | | | | | |
|---|---|---|---|---|---|---|---|
| Bluejeans And Moonbeams | LP | Virgin | V2123 | 1974 | £4 | £10 | |
| Clear Spot | LP | Reprise | K54007 | 1972 | £4 | £10 | |
| Diddy Wah Diddy | 7" EP | A&M | AME600 | 1971 | £100 | £200 | |
| Lick My Decals Off | LP | Reprise | K44244 | 1973 | £5 | £12 | |
| Lick My Decals Off | LP | Straight | STS1063 | 1970 | £10 | £25 | |
| Mirror Man | LP | Buddah | 2365022 | 1971 | £5 | £12 | |
| Moonchild | 7" | A&M | AMS726 | 1968 | £7.50 | £15 | |
| Safe As Milk | LP | Buddah | 623171 | 1969 | £4 | £10 | |
| Safe As Milk | LP | Pye | NPL28110 | 1968 | £8 | £20 | |
| Sixpack | 7" | Virgin | SIXPACK1 | 1979 | £5 | £10 | picture disc |
| Spotlight Kid | LP | Reprise | K44162 | 1972 | £4 | £10 | |
| Spotlight Kid/Clear Spot | CD | Reprise | 26249 | 1990 | £6 | £15 | US promo picture disc |
| Stand Up To Be Discontinued | CD | Cantz | 398013203X | 1993 | £25 | £50 | German, with hard-cover book |
| Sure 'Nuff 'N Yes I Do | 7" | Buddah | BDS466 | 1978 | £1.50 | £4 | |
| Strictly Personal | LP | Liberty | LBL/LBS83172 | 1968 | £10 | £25 | |
| Too Much Time | 7" | Reprise | K14233 | 1973 | £1.50 | £4 | |
| Trout Mask Replica | LP | Reprise | K64026 | 1975 | £5 | £12 | double |
| Trout Mask Replica | LP | Straight | STS1053 | 1969 | £10 | £25 | double |
| Unconditionally Guaranteed | LP | Virgin | V2015 | 1974 | £4 | £10 | |
| Upon The My-Oh-My | 7" | Virgin | VS110 | 1974 | £1.50 | £4 | |
| Yellow Brick Road | 7" | Pye | 7N25443 | 1968 | £5 | £10 | |

## CAPTAIN BEYOND
| | | | | | | | |
|---|---|---|---|---|---|---|---|
| Captain Beyond | LP | Capricorn | K47503 | 1972 | £4 | £10 | 3-D cover |

## CAPTAIN NOAH & HIS FLOATING ZOO
| | | | | | | |
|---|---|---|---|---|---|---|
| Captain Noah & His Floating Zoo | LP | Argo | ZDA149 | 1972 | £4 | £10 |

## CARAVAN
The unrecorded Canterbury group, Wilde Flowers, evolved into both Soft Machine and Caravan. Not surprisingly, therefore, these two groups have many similarities in their sound, although Caravan always had rather more of a pop sensibility. Unusual time signatures and improvised solos abound in Caravan's music, but always wedded to easily attractive melodies. Like Soft Machine too, Caravan's long career was distinguished by numerous personnel changes, which served to dilute the group's impact. The most effective recordings are the first three albums, made by the original line-up. The Verve LP has become quite scarce, although it is an essential sixties document. Like many albums of the period, the mono and stereo mixes are noticeably different.

| | | | | | | | |
|---|---|---|---|---|---|---|---|
| Caravan | LP | MGM | 2353058 | 1972 | £8 | £20 | |
| Caravan | LP | Verve | SVLP6011 | 1968 | £30 | £60 | |
| Caravan | LP | Verve | VLP6011 | 1968 | £37.50 | £75 | Mono |
| For Girls Who Grow Plump In The Night | LP | Deram | SDL12 | 1973 | £4 | £10 | |
| If I Could Do It All Over Again | 7" | Decca | F13063 | 1970 | £1.50 | £4 | |
| If I Could Do It All Over Again | LP | Decca | SKL5052 | 1970 | £6 | £15 | |
| In The Land Of Grey And Pink | LP | Deram | SDLR1 | 1971 | £5 | £12 | |
| Love To Love You | 7" | Decca | F23125 | 1971 | £1.50 | £4 | |
| Place Of My Own | 7" | Verve | VS1518 | 1968 | £5 | £10 | |
| Waterloo Lily | LP | Deram | SDL8 | 1972 | £4 | £10 | |

## CARAVELLES
| | | | | | | |
|---|---|---|---|---|---|---|
| Caravelles | LP | Decca | LK4565 | 1963 | £10 | £25 |
| Hey Mama You've Been On My Mind | 7" | Polydor | BM56137 | 1966 | £2.50 | £6 |
| Other Side Of Love | 7" | Pye | 7N17654 | 1968 | £1.50 | £4 |
| You Are Here | 7" | Fontana | TF466 | 1964 | £1.50 | £4 |
| You Don't Have to Be A Baby To Cry | 7" | Decca | F11697 | 1963 | £1.50 | £4 |

## CARAWAN, GUY
| | | | | | | | |
|---|---|---|---|---|---|---|---|
| Guy Carawan Sings | LP | Folkways | 3548 | 1959 | £4 | £10 | US |
| Old Man Atom | 7" | Pye | 7N15132 | 1958 | £1.50 | £4 | |
| Songs From The South | 7" EP | Collector | JEA4 | 1961 | £2 | £5 | |

## CARDBOARD ORCHESTRA
| | | | | | | |
|---|---|---|---|---|---|---|
| Nothing But A Sad Sad Show | 7" | CBS | 4633 | 1969 | £1.50 | £4 |
| Zebady Zak | 7" | CBS | 4176 | 1969 | £1.50 | £4 |

## CARDEILHAC
Cardeilhac ............................................. LP ...... Olabel............ 703721 ................ 1972 £**50** ....... £**100** ...................... *Swiss*

## CARDEW, CORNELIUS
Thalmann Variations ............................ LP ...... Matchless ...... MR10 ...................... 1986 £**5** .......... £**12**

## CARDIAC ARREST
Bus For A Bus On A Bus ..................... 7" ...... Torch .......... TOR002 ................ 1979 £**4** .......... £**8**
Running In The Street ......................... 7" ...... Another ....... AN1 ...................... 1981 £**2** .......... £**5**
..................................................................... Record ...........

## CARDIACS
Seaside Treats ........................................ 12" ..... Alphabet ...... ALPH002 ............ 1986 £**2.50** ..... £**6**
Toy World ............................................. cass .... Cardiacs ........ .............................. 1981 £**4** .......... £**10**

## CARDIGANS
Poor Boy .............................................. 7" ...... Mercury ......... AMT1007 ............ 1958 £**1.50** ..... £**4**

## CAREFREES
We Love You All .................................. LP ..... London ........ LL3/PS379 .............. 1964 £**15** ....... £**30** ...................... *US*
We Love You Beatles ........................... 7" ...... Oriole ............ CB1916 ................. 1964 £**2.50** ..... £**6**

## CAREY, DAVE
Broken Wings ....................................... 7" ...... Columbia ........ SCM5030 ............. 1953 £**1.50** ..... £**4**

## CAREY, MARIAH
Can't Let Go ......................................... CD-s .. CBS ............. 6576622 ............... 1991 £**6** .......... £**15**
Emotions .............................................. CD-s .. CBS ............. 6574032 ............... 1991 £**5** .......... £**12**
I'll Be There .......................................... CD-s .. CBS ............. 6581372 ............... 1992 £**3** .......... £**8**
I'll Be There .......................................... CD-s .. CBS ............. 6581379 ............... 1992 £**10** ....... £**20** ........ *picture disc, live tracks*
Love And Dreams – The Best Collection ... CD ..... Sony ............. XACS90032 .......... 1996 £**75** ..... £**150** .......... *Japanese promo*
  1990–1995
Love Takes Time .................................. CD-s .. CBS ............. 6563642 ............... 1990 £**6** .......... £**15**
Love Takes Time .................................. CD-s .. CBS ............. 6563645 ............... 1990 £**10** ....... £**20** .................. *picture disc*
Make It Happen .................................... CD-s .. CBS ............. 6579412 ............... 1992 £**5** .......... £**12**
Someday ............................................... CD-s .. CBS ............. 6565832 ............... 1991 £**6** .......... £**15**
Someday ............................................... CD-s .. CBS ............. 6565835 ............... 1991 £**12.50** ... £**25** .................. *picture disc*
There's Got To Be A Way .................... CD-s .. CBS ............. 6569312 ............... 1991 £**6** .......... £**15**
There's Got To Be A Way .................... CD-s .. CBS ............. 6569315 ............... 1991 £**10** ....... £**20** .................. *picture disc*
Vision Of Love ..................................... CD-s .. CBS ............. 6559322 ............... 1990 £**6** .......... £**15**

## CARGO
Cargo .................................................... LP ..... Harvest ........... 5C05224582 ........... 1971 £**100** ..... £**200** ...................... *Dutch*

## CARIBBEANS
Let Me Walk By .................................... 7" ...... Doctor Bird .... DB1181 ............... 1969 £**5** .......... £**10** ...... *Amblings B side*
Please Please ........................................ 7" ...... Crab ............. CRAB14 .............. 1969 £**1.50** ..... £**4** ........ *Matadors B side*

## CARIBBEATS
Bells Of Saint Mary's Ska .................... 7" ...... Ska Beat ........ JB246 .................. 1966 £**5** .......... £**10** .. *Winston Richards B*
..................................................................................................................................................................................... *side*
Highway 300 ......................................... 7" ...... Double D ....... DD101 ................ 1967 £**4** .......... £**8**
I'll Try ................................................... 7" ...... Double D ........ DD103 ................ 1967 £**4** .......... £**8**

## CARIBS
Taboo .................................................... 7" ...... Starlite ......... ST45012 .............. 1960 £**1.50** ..... £**4**

## CARL & THE COMMANDERS
Farmer John .......................................... 7" ...... Columbia ........ DB4719 ............... 1961 £**2.50** ..... £**6**

## CARLISLE, BELINDA
Belinda .................................................. CD .... MCA ........... DMIRL1505 ....... 1990 £**5** .......... £**12**
Circle In The Sand ............................... CD-s .. Virgin .......... VSCD1074 ........... 1987 £**10** ....... £**20**
Circle In The Sand ............................... 12" .... Virgin .......... VSTY1074 ............ 1988 £**4** .......... £**10** .................. *picture disc*
Half The World ..................................... CD-s .. Virgin .......... VSCDG1388 ........ 1992 £**2** .......... £**5** ...................... *digipak*
Heaven Is A Place On Earth ................. CD-s .. Virgin .......... VSCD1036 ........... 1987 £**10** ....... £**20**
Heaven On Earth ................................... CD .... Virgin .......... CDVP2496 .......... 1988 £**5** .......... £**12** .................. *picture disc*
I Get Weak ........................................... CD-s .. Virgin .......... VSCD1046 ........... 1988 £**6** .......... £**15** .................. *picture disc*
La Luna ................................................. CD-s .. Virgin .......... VSCD1230 ........... 1989 £**2** .......... £**5** ..................... *3" single*
La Luna ................................................. CD-s .. Virgin .......... VSCD1230DJ ....... 1989 £**20** ....... £**40** ..... *promo picture disc*
Leave A Light On .................................. CD-s .. Virgin .......... VSCD1210 ........... 1989 £**2.50** ..... £**6**
Leave A Light On .................................. 7" ...... Virgin .......... VSP1210 ............. 1989 £**1.50** ..... £**4** ...... *poster picture sleeve*
Little Black Book .................................. CD-s .. Virgin .......... VSCDG1428 ........ 1992 £**2.50** ..... £**6** ...................... *digipak*
Live Your Life Be Free ......................... CD-s .. Virgin .......... VSCDG1370 ........ 1991 £**2** .......... £**5** ...................... *digipak*
Love Never Dies .................................... CD-s .. Virgin .......... VSCD1150 ........... 1988 £**3** .......... £**8**
Mad About You ..................................... CD-s .. IRS ............. DIRM118 ............. 1988 £**20** ....... £**40** ..................... *3" single*
Real ....................................................... CD .... Virgin .......... CDVDJ2725 ......... 1993 £**8** .......... £**20** .. *promo in rubber case*
Runaway Horses ................................... CD-s .. Virgin .......... VSCD1244 ........... 1990 £**2.50** ..... £**6**
Runaway Horses ................................... CD .... Virgin .......... CDV2599 ............ 1989 £**5** .......... £**12**
Summer Rain ........................................ CD-s .. Virgin .......... VSCDT1323 ........ 1990 £**3** .......... £**8** ........................ *boxed*
Summer Rain ........................................ CD-s .. Virgin .......... VSCDX1323 ........ 1990 £**2.50** ..... £**6** ...................... *digipak*
Vision Of You ....................................... CD-s .. Virgin .......... VSCDT1264 ........ 1990 £**2.50** ..... £**6**
We Want The Same Thing (Summer Mix) . CD-s .. Virgin .......... VSCDP1291 ......... 1990 £**2** .......... £**5**
Woman And A Man .............................. CD .... Chrysalis ....... .............................. 1996 £**30** ....... £**60** ... *promo box set, with*
..................................................................................................................................................................................... *video*
World Without You ............................... CD-s .. Virgin .......... VSCD1114 ........... 1988 £**4** .......... £**10**
World Without You ............................... 7" ...... Virgin .......... VSX1114 ............. 1988 £**4** .......... £**8** ........................ *boxed*

World Without You................................ 12".... Virgin ............. VST1114............... 1988 £3............£8 ............. poster sleeve

## CARLISLE, BILLY
Down Boy ......................................... 7"...... Mercury.......... AMT1063 ............. 1959 £7.50....£15 ......................

## CARLISLE BROTHERS
Fresh From The Country ......................... 7" EP . Parlophone...... GEP8799 .............. 1959 £4.............£8 .....................

## CARLSEN, DAVE
Pale Horse ........................................ LP..... Spark ............. SRLP110 .............. 1973 £5............£12 .....................

## CARLTON, EDDIE
It Will Be Done ................................... 7"...... Cream............. 5001 ................ 1976 £2............£5 ......................

## CARLTON, LITTLE CARL
46 Drums 1 Guitar ............................... 7"...... Action............. ACT4514 ............. 1968 £1.50........£4
Competition Ain't Nothing...................... 7"...... Action............. ACT4501 ............. 1968 £7.50....£15
Look At Mary Wonder............................ 7"...... Action............. ACT4537 ............. 1969 £2............£5

## CARLTON & HIS SHOES
Love Me Forever.................................. LP..... Studio One..... PSOL003 .............. 197– £4............£10
Love Me Forever.................................. 7"...... Coxsone ......... CS7065 .............. 1968 £5............£10
This Feeling...................................... 7"..... Studio One..... SO2062 .............. 1968 £6............£12

## CARMEN
Dancing On A Cold Wind...................... LP..... Regal
                                                      Zonophone ..... SLRZ1040 ............. 1975 £8............£20
Fandangos In Space............................. LP..... Regal
                                                      Zonophone ..... SRZA8518............. 1973 £6............£15

## CARMICHAEL, HOAGY
Hoagy Carmichael............................... 7" EP . Vogue............. VE170113 ............. 1958 £2............£5
Stardust .......................................... 7" EP . HMV............. 7EG8037............. 1954 £2............£5
Stardust Road .................................... 7" EP . Brunswick....... OE9023 .............. 1954 £2............£5

## CARNABY
Jump And Dance ................................. 7"...... Piccadilly......... 7N35272 .............. 1965 £15............£30

## CARNABY STREET POP
Carnaby Street Pop.............................. LP..... Carnaby .......... CNLS6003 ............. 1969 £25............£50

## CARNATIONS
Mighty Man ...................................... 7"...... Blue Beat ....... BB285................. 1965 £6............£12 ......................

## CARNE, JUDY
Sock It To Me .................................... 7"...... Reprise .......... RS20680 ............. 1968 £1.50........£4

## CARNEGY HALL
Bells Of San Francisco........................... 7"...... Polydor........... 56224.............. 1968 £5............£10

## CARNES, KIM
Rest On Me ....................................... LP..... Amos ............. 7016 ............... 1970 £4............£10 ......................... US

## CAROL, BOBBI
Will You Love Me Tomorrow .................... 7"...... Fontana........... 267260TF............. 1963 £1.50........£4

## CAROL & THE MEMORIES
Tears On My Pillow .............................. 7"...... CBS............... 202086.............. 1966 £2............£5

## CAROLINA SLIM
Carolina Blues And Boogie ..................... LP..... Flyright .......... LP4702 .............. 1972 £5............£12

## CARPENTER, IKE
Lights Out ........................................ LP..... Aladdin .......... LP811 .............. 1956 £50........£100 ......................... US
Lights Out ........................................ LP..... Score ............. SLP4010............. 1957 £30........£60 ......................... US

## CARPENTER, KAREN
I'll Be Yours ..................................... 7"...... Magic Lamp .... 704 ................ 196– £150....£250 .... US, best auctioned

## CARPENTER, THELMA
Back Street ...................................... 7"...... Coral ............. Q72442............. 1961 £1.50........£4
Yes I'm Lonesome Tonight ...................... 7"...... Coral ............. Q72422............. 1961 £1.50........£4

## CARPENTERS
Carpenters ....................................... LP..... A&M ............. QU53502 ............. 1971 £4............£10 ......................... US quad
Close To You..................................... LP..... A&M ............. QU54271 ............. 1970 £4............£10 ......................... US quad
Close To You..................................... CD–s .. A&M ............. AMCD558 ............. 1990 £2............£5
Compact Hits.................................... CD–s .. A&M ............. AMCD901 ............. 1988 £2............£5
Horizon.......................................... LP..... A&M ............. QU54530 ............. 1975 £4............£10 ......................... US quad
Now And Then ................................. LP..... A&M ............. QU53519 ............. 1973 £4............£10 ......................... US quad
Singles 1969–1973 .............................. LP..... A&M ............. QU53601 ............. 1973 £4............£10 ......................... US quad
Song For You .................................... LP..... A&M ............. QU53511 ............. 1972 £4............£10 ......................... US quad
Song For You .................................... CD.... Mobile Fidelity UDCD525 ............. 1990 £6............£15 ......................... US audiophile

## CARPET BAGGERS
Flea Teacher ..................................... 7"...... Spin.............. SP2006............. 1967 £2............£5 ......................

## CARR, CATHY
Ivory Tower ........................................... 7" ...... London ........... HLH8274 .............. 1956 £12.50 .... £25 ..............................................

## CARR, GEORGIA
| | | | | | | | |
|---|---|---|---|---|---|---|---|
| Rocks In My Bed | LP | Vee Jay | LP/VJS1105 | 1964 | £4 | £10 | US |
| Shy | LP | Roulette | (S)R25077 | 196– | £4 | £10 | US |
| Songs By A Moody Miss | LP | Tops | 1617 | 1958 | £6 | £15 | US |

## CARR, HELEN
Why Do I Love You? ............................... LP ...... London ........... HAN2065 .............. 1957 £4 ........... £10

## CARR, JAMES
| | | | | | | | |
|---|---|---|---|---|---|---|---|
| Baby You've Got My Mind Messed Up | 7" | Stateside | SS507 | 1966 | £10 | £20 | |
| Dark End Of The Street | 7" | Stateside | SS2001 | 1967 | £2.50 | £6 | |
| Freedom Train | 7" | B&C | CB101 | 1969 | £1.50 | £4 | |
| I'm A Fool For You | 7" | Stateside | SS2052 | 1967 | £1.50 | £4 | |
| Let It Happen | 7" | Stateside | SS2038 | 1967 | £2.50 | £6 | |
| Love Attack | 7" | Stateside | SS535 | 1966 | £4 | £8 | |
| Man Needs A Woman | LP | Bell | MBLL/SBLL113 | 1968 | £6 | £15 | |
| Pouring Water On A Drowning Man | 7" | Stateside | SS545 | 1966 | £2.50 | £6 | |
| You Got My Mind Messed Up | LP | Stateside | SL10205 | 1967 | £20 | £40 | |

## CARR, JOE 'FINGERS'
| | | | | | | | |
|---|---|---|---|---|---|---|---|
| Barky-Roll Stomp | 7" | Capitol | CL14359 | 1955 | £2 | £5 | |
| Give Me A Band And My Baby | 7" | Capitol | CL14372 | 1955 | £1.50 | £4 | |
| Let Me Be Your Honey, Honey | 7" | Capitol | CL14535 | 1956 | £1.50 | £4 | |
| Memories Of You | 7" | Capitol | CL14520 | 1956 | £1.50 | £4 | |
| Piccadilly Rag | 7" | Capitol | CL14169 | 1954 | £2.50 | £6 | |
| Portuguese Washerwoman | 7" | Capitol | CL14587 | 1956 | £1.50 | £4 | |

## CARR, JOHNNY
| | | | | | | | |
|---|---|---|---|---|---|---|---|
| Do You Love That Girl | 7" | Fontana | TF600 | 1965 | £2 | £5 | |
| Respectable | 7" | Decca | F11854 | 1964 | £2.50 | £6 | |
| Then So Do I | 7" | Fontana | TF681 | 1966 | £1.50 | £4 | |
| Things Get Better | 7" | Fontana | TF823 | 1967 | £5 | £10 | |

## CARR, LEROY
| | | | | | | | |
|---|---|---|---|---|---|---|---|
| Blues Before Sunrise | LP | CBS | BPG62206 | 1963 | £8 | £20 | |
| RCA Victor Race Series Vol. 2 | 7" EP | RCA | RCX7168 | 1964 | £4 | £8 | |
| Treasures Of North American Negro Music | 7" EP | Fontana | TFE17051 | 1958 | £5 | £10 | |

## CARR, LINDA
Everytime ............................................. 7" ...... Stateside ........ SS2058 .................... 1967 £2.50 ....... £6

## CARR, MIKE
| | | | | | | | |
|---|---|---|---|---|---|---|---|
| Hammond Under Pressure | LP | Columbia | S(C)X6248 | 1968 | £6 | £15 | ...with Tony Crombie |
| Mike Carr | LP | Ad-Rhythm | ARPS1020 | 1973 | £6 | £15 | |
| Mike Carr And His Trio | LP | Spotlite | SPJ517 | 1980 | £5 | £12 | |

## CARR, ROMEY
These Things Will Keep Me Loving You ... 7" ...... Columbia ....... DB8710 .............. 1970 £5 ........... £10

## CARR, VALERIE
When The Boys Talk About The Girls ....... 7" ...... Columbia ....... DB4131 .................. 1958 £1.50 ....... £4

## CARR, WYNONA
I Gotta Stand Tall ................................... 7" ...... Reprise .......... R20033 ................... 1961 £5 ........... £10

## CARROLL, ANDREA
It Hurts To Be Sixteen ............................ 7" ...... London ........... HLX9772 ......... 1963 £1.50 ....... £4

## CARROLL, BARBARA
North By Northwest ................................ 7" ...... London ........... HLR8981 .......... 1959 £1.50 ....... £4

## CARROLL, BERNADETTE
Party Girl .............................................. 7" ...... Stateside ........ SS311 ................... 1964 £1.50 ....... £4

## CARROLL, BOB
| | | | | | | | |
|---|---|---|---|---|---|---|---|
| Hi Ho Silver | 7" | London | HLT8724 | 1958 | £2 | £5 | |
| I Can't Get You Out Of My Life | 7" | London | HLT8888 | 1959 | £1.50 | £4 | |
| I Love You So Much It Hurts | 7" | MGM | SP1132 | 1955 | £1.50 | £4 | |
| Red Confetti, Pink Balloons, & Tambourines | 7" | London | HLU8299 | 1956 | £7.50 | £15 | |

## CARROLL, DIAHANN
| | | | | | | | |
|---|---|---|---|---|---|---|---|
| Big Country | 7" | London | HLT8788 | 1959 | £1.50 | £4 | |
| Sings Harold Arlen | LP | RCA | LPM1467 | 1956 | £8 | £20 | US |

## CARROLL, JOHNNY & THE HOT ROCKS
| | | | | | | | |
|---|---|---|---|---|---|---|---|
| Hot Rock | 7" | Brunswick | 05603 | 1956 | £180 | £300 | best auctioned |
| Wild Wild Women | 7" | Brunswick | 05580 | 1956 | £180 | £300 | best auctioned |

## CARROLL, PAT
To The Sun ............................................ 7" ...... Pye ................ 7N25592 .............. 1972 £5 ........... £10

## CARROLL, RONNIE
From Ten Till One .................................. 10" LP Philips ........... BBR8105 .............. 1956 £6 ........... £15 .....with Bill McGuffie

| Lucky Thirteen | LP | Philips | BBL7236 | 1958 £5 £12 | |
|---|---|---|---|---|---|
| Mr. And Mrs. Is The Name | LP | Philips | (S)BL7591 | 1964 £4 £10 | .with Millicent Martin |
| Sometimes I'm Happy, Sometimes I'm Blue | LP | Philips | BL7563 | 1963 £4 £10 | |
| Walk Hand In Hand | 7" EP | Philips | BBE12074 | 1956 £2.50 £6 | |

## CARROLLS

| Carrolls | 10" LP | Electrocord | EDD1150 | 1966 £50 £100 | Romanian |
|---|---|---|---|---|---|
| Come On | 7" | CBS | 3710 | 1968 £1.50 £4 | |
| Surrender Your Love | 7" | Polydor | BM56081 | 1966 £2 £5 | |

## CARRUTHERS, BEN & THE DEEP

The 'Jack O'Diamonds' single is of special interest to Bob Dylan collectors, as the song consists of a setting of part of the poetry written by Bob Dylan as sleeve notes for his *Another Side* album. An effective version of the song was also recorded by Fairport Convention on their debut LP.

| Jack O'Diamonds | 7" | Parlophone | R5295 | 1965 £12.50 £25 | |
|---|---|---|---|---|---|

## CARS

| Candy O | LP | Nautilus | NR49 | 1981 £4 £10 | US audiophile |
|---|---|---|---|---|---|
| Cars | LP | Nautilus | NR14 | 1981 £4 £10 | US audiophile |
| Double Life | 7" | Elektra | K12385P | 1979 £1.50 £4 | picture disc |
| Just What I Needed | 7" | Elektra | K12301 | 1978 £2.50 £6 | |

## CARSON, CHAD

| Don't Pick On Me | 7" | HMV | POP1156 | 1963 £12.50 £25 | |
|---|---|---|---|---|---|

## CARSON, KEN

| Daniel Boone | 7" | London | HLF8237 | 1956 £12.50 £25 | |
|---|---|---|---|---|---|
| Hawkeye | 7" | London | HLF8213 | 1955 £12.50 £25 | |

## CARSON, KIT

| Band Of Gold | 7" | Capitol | CL14524 | 1956 £2 £5 | |
|---|---|---|---|---|---|

## CARTER, ANITA

| Blue Doll | 7" | London | HLA8693 | 1958 £5 £10 | |
|---|---|---|---|---|---|
| Moon Girl | 7" | London | HLW9102 | 1960 £2.50 £6 | |

## CARTER, BENNY

| Aspects | LP | London | LTZT15169 | 1959 £6 £15 | |
|---|---|---|---|---|---|
| Benny Carter Orchestra | 10" LP | Columbia | 33C9002 | 1955 £20 £40 | |
| Jazz Giant | LP | Contemporary | LAC12188 | 1959 £6 £15 | |
| Swingin' The Twenties | LP | Contemporary | LAC12225 | 1959 £6 £15 | |

## CARTER, BETTY

| Good Life | 7" | London | HLK9748 | 1963 £1.50 £4 | |
|---|---|---|---|---|---|

## CARTER, CALVIN

| Twist Along | LP | Vee Jay | LP/SR1041 | 1962 £6 £15 | US |
|---|---|---|---|---|---|

## CARTER, CAROLYN

| I'm Thru | 7" | London | HL9959 | 1965 £7.50 £15 | |
|---|---|---|---|---|---|

## CARTER, CLARENCE

| Dynamic | LP | Atlantic | 588172 | 1968 £5 £12 | |
|---|---|---|---|---|---|
| Looking For A Fox | 7" | Atlantic | 584176 | 1968 £2 £5 | |
| Patches | 7" | Atlantic | 2091030 | 1970 £1.50 £4 | |
| Slip Away | 7" | Atlantic | 584187 | 1968 £1.50 £4 | |
| Testifyin' | LP | Atlantic | 588191 | 1969 £5 £12 | |
| This Is Clarence Carter | LP | Atlantic | 588152 | 1968 £5 £12 | |
| Thread The Needle | 7" | Atlantic | 584154 | 1968 £1.50 £4 | |
| Too Weak To Fight | 7" | Atlantic | 584223 | 1968 £1.50 £4 | |

## CARTER, HERBIE

| Happy Time | 7" | Duke | DU4 | 1968 £2.50 £6 | |
|---|---|---|---|---|---|

## CARTER, JEAN

| No Good Jim | 7" | Stateside | SS2114 | 1968 £1.50 £4 | |
|---|---|---|---|---|---|

## CARTER, JOHN & RUSS ALQUIST

| Laughing Man | 7" | Spark | SRL1017 | 1968 £5 £10 | |
|---|---|---|---|---|---|

## CARTER, MARTIN

| Ups And Downs | LP | Tradition | TSR012 | 1972 £20 £40 | |
|---|---|---|---|---|---|

## CARTER, MEL

| Easy Listening | LP | Imperial | 12319 | 1966 £4 £10 | US |
|---|---|---|---|---|---|
| Hold Me, Thrill Me, Kiss Me | LP | Imperial | 12289 | 1965 £4 £10 | US |
| My Heart Sings | LP | Imperial | 12300 | 1965 £4 £10 | US |
| When A Boy Falls In Love | LP | Derby | LPM702 | 1963 £25 £50 | US |
| When A Boy Falls In Love | 7" | Pye | 7N25212 | 1963 £1.50 £4 | |

## CARTER, SONNY

| There Is No Greater Love | 7" | Parlophone | MSP6167 | 1955 £2 £5 | with Earl Bostic |
|---|---|---|---|---|---|

## CARTER, SYDNEY

| Lord Of The Dance | 7" EP | Elektra | EPK801 | 1966 £4 £8 | |
|---|---|---|---|---|---|

## CARTER FAMILY

| Title | Format | Label | Cat# | Year | | | Notes |
|---|---|---|---|---|---|---|---|
| Mean As Hell | 7" EP | CBS | EP6073 | 1966 | £2 | £5 | |
| Mountain Music Vol. 2 | 7" EP | Brunswick | OE9168 | 1955 | £2 | £5 | |
| Original And Great Carter Family Vol. 1 | 7" EP | RCA | RCX7100 | 1962 | £2 | £5 | |
| Original And Great Carter Family Vol. 2 | 7" EP | RCA | RCX7101 | 1962 | £2 | £5 | |
| Original And Great Carter Family Vol. 3 | 7" EP | RCA | RCX7102 | 1962 | £2 | £5 | |
| Original And Great Carter Family Vol. 4 | 7" EP | RCA | RCX7109 | 1963 | £2 | £5 | |
| Original And Great Carter Family Vol. 5 | 7" EP | RCA | RCX7110 | 1963 | £2 | £5 | |
| Original And Great Carter Family Vol. 6 | 7" EP | RCA | RCX7111 | 1963 | £2 | £5 | |

## CARTER LEWIS & THE SOUTHERNERS

| Title | Format | Label | Cat# | Year | | | Notes |
|---|---|---|---|---|---|---|---|
| Poor Joe | 7" | Piccadilly | 7N35085 | 1962 | £7.50 | £15 | |
| Skinnie Minnie | 7" | Oriole | CB1919 | 1964 | £6 | £12 | |
| So Much in Love | 7" | Piccadilly | 7N35004 | 1961 | £7.50 | £15 | |
| Sweet And Tender Romance | 7" | Oriole | CB1835 | 1963 | £5 | £10 | |
| Tell Me | 7" | Ember | EMBS165 | 1962 | £12.50 | £25 | |
| Two Timing Baby | 7" | Ember | EMBS145 | 1961 | £12.50 | £25 | |
| Your Mama's Out Of Town | 7" | Oriole | CB1868 | 1963 | £7.50 | £15 | |

## CARTER THE UNSTOPPABLE SEX MACHINE

| Title | Format | Label | Cat# | Year | | | Notes |
|---|---|---|---|---|---|---|---|
| 1992 The Love Album | CD | Chrysalis | CD25CR24 | 1994 | £5 | £12 | Chrysalis 25 pack |
| After The Watershed | CD-s | Chrysalis | USMCD2 | 1991 | £3 | £8 | |
| Anytime Anyplace Anywhere | CD-s | Chrysalis | CDUSM7 | 1993 | £4 | £10 | |
| Bloodsports For All | CD-s | Rough Trade | R20112683 | 1991 | £4 | £10 | |
| Christmas Shoppers Paradise | 7" | Rough Trade | GIFT1 | 1990 | £7.50 | £15 | |
| Handbuilt For Perverts | LP | Big Cat | ABB103X | 1990 | £4 | £10 | export |
| Handbuilt For Perverts | CD | Big Cat | ABB103XCD | 1990 | £5 | £12 | export |
| Rubbish | CD-s | Big Cat | ABB102CD | 1990 | £2 | £5 | |
| Sheriff Fat Man | CD-s | Chrysalis | USMCD1 | 1991 | £2 | £5 | |
| Worry Bomb | CD | Chrysalis | 724383211722 | 1995 | £6 | £15 | double |

## CARTHY, MARTIN

| Title | Format | Label | Cat# | Year | | | Notes |
|---|---|---|---|---|---|---|---|
| Bonny Lass Of Anglesey | 7" | Topic | STOP7002 | 196– | £1.50 | £4 | |
| Brigg Fair | LP | Fontana | 6857010 | 1967 | £6 | £15 | same LP as Byker Hill |
| But Two Came By | LP | Fontana | STL5477 | 1968 | £10 | £25 | with Dave Swarbrick |
| Byker Hill | LP | Fontana | (S)TL5434 | 1967 | £10 | £25 | with Dave Swarbrick |
| Landfall | LP | Philips | 6308049 | 1971 | £6 | £15 | |
| Martin Carthy | LP | Fontana | (S)TL5269 | 1965 | £10 | £25 | |
| Prince Heathen | LP | Fontana | STL5529 | 1969 | £6 | £15 | |
| Second Album | LP | Fontana | (S)TL5362 | 1966 | £10 | £25 | |
| Selections | LP | Pegasus | PEG6 | 1971 | £6 | £15 | with Dave Swarbrick |
| Shearwater | LP | Mooncrest | CREST25 | 1974 | £4 | £10 | |
| Shearwater | LP | Pegasus | PEG12 | 1972 | £6 | £15 | |
| Sweet Wivelsfield | LP | Deram | SML1111 | 1974 | £6 | £15 | |
| This Is Martin Carthy | LP | Philips | 6282022 | 1972 | £4 | £10 | |

## CARTHY, MARTIN & DAVE SWARBRICK

| Title | Format | Label | Cat# | Year | | |
|---|---|---|---|---|---|---|
| No Songs | 7" EP | Fontana | | 196– | £6 | £12 |

## CARTOONE

| Title | Format | Label | Cat# | Year | | |
|---|---|---|---|---|---|---|
| Cartoone | LP | Atlantic | 588174 | 1969 | £8 | £20 |
| Penny for The Sun | 7" | Atlantic | 584240 | 1969 | £1.50 | £4 |

## CARTWRIGHT, DAVE

| Title | Format | Label | Cat# | Year | | |
|---|---|---|---|---|---|---|
| In The Middle Of The Road | LP | Harmony | DB0001 | 1970 | £20 | £40 |

## CARTY, PADDY & MICK O'CONNOR

| Title | Format | Label | Cat# | Year | | | Notes |
|---|---|---|---|---|---|---|---|
| Traditional Music of Ireland | LP | Morning Star | 1 | 1974 | £5 | £12 | US |

## CASCADES

| Title | Format | Label | Cat# | Year | | | Notes |
|---|---|---|---|---|---|---|---|
| I Bet You Won't Stay | 7" | Liberty | LIB55822 | 1965 | £1.50 | £4 | |
| Maybe The Rain Will Fall | LP | Uni | 73069 | 1969 | £4 | £10 | US |
| Rhythm Of The Rain | LP | Warner Bros | WM8127 | 1963 | £8 | £20 | |
| Rhythm Of The Rain | 7" EP | Warner Bros | WEP1419 | 1963 | £10 | £20 | French |
| Rhythm Of The Rain | 7" EP | Warner Bros | WEP6106 | 1963 | £7.50 | £15 | |
| Rhythm Of The Rain | 7" | Warner Bros | WB88 | 1963 | £1.50 | £4 | |
| Vol. 2 | 7" EP | Warner Bros | WEP1421 | 1963 | £10 | £20 | French |
| What Goes On | LP | Cascade | 681001 | 1968 | £10 | £25 | US |

## CASEY, AL & THE K.C.ETTES

| Title | Format | Label | Cat# | Year | | |
|---|---|---|---|---|---|---|
| Surfing Hootenanny | 7" | Pye | 7N25215 | 1963 | £2 | £5 |

## CASEY, HOWIE & THE SENIORS

| Title | Format | Label | Cat# | Year | | |
|---|---|---|---|---|---|---|
| Bony Moronie | 7" | Fontana | TF403 | 1963 | £4 | £8 |
| Double Twist | 7" | Fontana | H364 | 1962 | £5 | £10 |
| I Ain't Mad At You | 7" | Fontana | H381 | 1962 | £4 | £8 |
| Let's Twist | LP | Wing | WL1022 | 1965 | £6 | £15 |
| Twist At The Top | LP | Fontana | TFL5180 | 1962 | £15 | £30 |

## CASH, ALVIN

| Title | Format | Label | Cat# | Year | | |
|---|---|---|---|---|---|---|
| Philly Freeze | LP | President | PTL1000 | 1966 | £5 | £12 |
| Philly Freeze | 7" | Stateside | SS543 | 1966 | £5 | £10 |
| Twine Time | 7" | Stateside | SS386 | 1965 | £10 | £20 |

## CASH, JOHNNY

| Title | Format | Label | Cat# | Year | | | Notes |
|---|---|---|---|---|---|---|---|
| All Aboard the Blue Train | LP | Sun | 1270 | 1963 | £6 | £15 | US |
| All Over Again | 7" | Philips | PB874 | 1958 | £2 | £5 | |

| | | | | | | | |
|---|---|---|---|---|---|---|---|
| Ballad Of A Teenage Queen | 7" | London | HL7032 | 1958 | £4 | £8 | *export* |
| Ballad Of A Teenage Queen | 7" | London | HLS8586 | 1958 | £5 | £10 | |
| Bitter Tears | LP | CBS | (S)BPG62463 | 1964 | £4 | £10 | |
| Blood, Sweat And Tears | LP | CBS | BPG62119 | 1963 | £4 | £10 | |
| Christmas Spirit | LP | CBS | (S)BPG62284 | 1963 | £4 | £10 | |
| Country Boy | 7" EP | London | RES1212 | 1959 | £10 | £20 | *tri-centre* |
| Don't Take Your Guns To Town | 7" | Philips | PB897 | 1959 | £2 | £5 | |
| Down The Street To 301 | 7" | London | HLS9182 | 1960 | £2 | £5 | |
| Fabulous Johnny Cash | LP | CBS | (S)BPG62042 | 1961 | £4 | £10 | |
| Fabulous Johnny Cash | LP | Philips | BBL7298/SBBL554 | 1959 | £5 | £12 | |
| Folsom Prison Blues | 7" EP | CBS | EP6601 | 1969 | £4 | £8 | |
| Forty Shades Of Green | 7" EP | CBS | AGG20050 | 1964 | £5 | £10 | |
| Forty Shades Of Green | 7" | Philips | PB1148 | 1961 | £1.50 | £4 | |
| Frankie's Man, Johnny | 7" | Philips | PB928 | 1959 | £2 | £5 | |
| Going To Memphis | 7" | Philips | PB1075 | 1960 | £1.50 | £4 | |
| Guess Things Happen That Way | 7" | London | HLS8656 | 1958 | £4 | £8 | |
| Holy Land | LP | CBS | 63428 | 1968 | £4 | £10 | |
| Holy Land | LP | Columbia | CS9726 | 1969 | £5 | £12 | *US, 3D cover* |
| Home Of The Blues | 7" | London | HL7023 | 1957 | £5 | £10 | *export* |
| Home Of The Blues | 7" | London | HLS8514 | 1957 | £6 | £12 | |
| Hymns By Johnny Cash | LP | Philips | BBL7373 | 1960 | £4 | £10 | |
| I Got Stripes | 7" | Philips | PB953 | 1959 | £2 | £5 | |
| I Walk The Line | LP | CBS | (S)BPG62371 | 1964 | £4 | £10 | |
| I Walk The Line | 7" | London | HL8358 | 1957 | £30 | £60 | *gold label* |
| It Ain't Me Babe | 7" EP | CBS | EP6061 | 1965 | £4 | £8 | |
| It's Just About Time | 7" | London | HLS8789 | 1959 | £2.50 | £6 | |
| Johnny Cash | 7" EP | London | RES1120 | 1958 | £12.50 | £25 | *tri-centre* |
| Johnny Cash No. 2 | 7" EP | London | RES1230 | 1959 | £10 | £20 | *tri-centre* |
| Johnny Cash Sings Hank Williams | LP | Sun | 1245 | 1960 | £8 | £20 | *US* |
| Johnny Cash Sings Hank Williams | 7" EP | London | RES1193 | 1959 | £10 | £20 | *tri-centre* |
| Johnny Cash With His Hot And Blue Guitar | LP | Sun | 1220 | 1956 | £20 | £40 | *US* |
| Johnny Cash's Greatest | LP | Sun | 1240 | 1959 | £15 | £30 | *US* |
| Katy Too | 7" | London | HLS8928 | 1959 | £2.50 | £6 | |
| Little Drummer Boy | 7" | Philips | PB979 | 1959 | £1.50 | £4 | |
| Live At San Quentin | LP | CBS | Q63629 | 1973 | £4 | £10 | *quad* |
| Lonesome Me | LP | London | HAS8253 | 1966 | £5 | £12 | |
| Lure Of The Grand Canyon | LP | Columbia | CL1622/CS8422 | 1961 | £6 | £15 | *US* |
| Luther Played The Boogie | 7" | London | HLS8847 | 1959 | £5 | £10 | |
| Mean As Hell | 7" EP | CBS | EP6073 | 1966 | £4 | £8 | |
| Next In Line | 7" | London | HL7020 | 1957 | £5 | £10 | *export* |
| Next In Line | 7" | London | HLS8461 | 1957 | £10 | £20 | |
| Now Here's Johnny Cash | LP | Sun | 1255 | 1961 | £8 | £20 | *US* |
| Now There Was A Song | LP | Philips | BBL7358/SBBL580 | 1960 | £4 | £10 | |
| Oh Lonesome Me | 7" | London | HLS9314 | 1961 | £1.50 | £4 | |
| Original Sun Sound Of Johnny Cash | LP | London | HAS8220 | 1965 | £5 | £12 | |
| Ride This Train | LP | Philips | BBL7417 | 1960 | £4 | £10 | |
| Ring Of Fire | LP | CBS | (S)BPG62171 | 1963 | £4 | £10 | |
| Rock Island Line | LP | London | HAS2179 | 1959 | £6 | £15 | |
| Seasons Of My Heart | 7" | Philips | PB1017 | 1960 | £1.50 | £4 | |
| Songs Of Our Soil | LP | Philips | BBL7353 | 1959 | £4 | £10 | |
| Songs Of Our Soil | 7" EP | Philips | BBE12395 | 1960 | £5 | £10 | |
| Songs That Made Him Famous | LP | London | HAS2157 | 1959 | £8 | £20 | |
| Songs That Made Him Famous | LP | Sun | 1235 | 1958 | £15 | £30 | *US* |
| Sound Of Johnny Cash | LP | CBS | (S)BPG62073 | 1962 | £4 | £10 | |
| Straight A's In Love | 7" | London | HLS9070 | 1960 | £2.50 | £6 | |
| Strictly Cash | 7" EP | Philips | BBE12494 | 1961 | £5 | £10 | |
| Train Of Love | 7" | London | HLS8427 | 1957 | £15 | £30 | |
| Troubadour | 7" EP | Philips | BBE12377 | 1960 | £5 | £10 | |
| Ways Of A Woman In Love | 7" | London | HL70533 | 1958 | £2.50 | £6 | *export* |
| Ways Of A Woman In Love | 7" | London | HLS8709 | 1958 | £2.50 | £6 | |
| You Tell Me | 7" | London | HLS8979 | 1959 | £2 | £5 | |

## CASINOS

| | | | | | | | |
|---|---|---|---|---|---|---|---|
| That's The Way | 7" | Ember | EMBS241 | 1967 | £10 | £20 | |
| Then You Can Tell Me Goodbye | LP | President | PTL1007 | 1967 | £4 | £10 | |
| Then You Can Tell Me Goodbye | 7" | President | PT123 | 1968 | £2.50 | £6 | |

## CASSIBER

| | | | | | | | |
|---|---|---|---|---|---|---|---|
| Beauty And The Beast | LP | Recommended | RE0110 | 1984 | £5 | £12 | |
| Perfect Worlds | LP | Recommended | RE0000 | 1986 | £4 | £10 | |
| Time Running Out | 7" | Recommended | RE21 | 1984 | £4 | £8 | *blue vinyl, 1 side painted* |

## CASSIDY, TED

| | | | | | | | |
|---|---|---|---|---|---|---|---|
| Lurch | 7" | Capitol | CL15423 | 1965 | £6 | £12 | |

## CAST

| | | | | | | | |
|---|---|---|---|---|---|---|---|
| All Change | CD | Polydor | CASTCD1 | 1995 | £8 | £20 | *promo sampler in tin* |
| Finetime | CD-s | Polydor | 5795072 | 1995 | £3 | £8 | |
| Finetime | 7" | Polydor | 5795067 | 1995 | £5 | £10 | *green vinyl, with stencil* |
| Sandstorm | CD-s | Polydor | | 1995 | £4 | £10 | *in tin* |

## CAST OF THOUSANDS

| | | | | | | | |
|---|---|---|---|---|---|---|---|
| My Jeannie Wears A Mini | 7" | Stateside | SS546 | 1966 | £4 | £8 | |

## CASTANARC
Journey To The East................................ LP...... Peninsula......... PENCIL010 ........... 1986 £10.........£25 ...............................

## CASTAWAYS
Liar Liar.................................................... 7"...... London.......... HL10003 ........... 1965 £5..........£10 ...............................

## CASTELL, JOEY
I'm Left, You're Right, She's Gone............ 7"...... Decca ............. F10966 .......... 1957 £20.........£40 ...............................

## CASTELLS
Sacred ....................................................... 7"...... London .......... HLN9392............ 1961 £7.50.....£15 ...............................
So This Is Love ........................................ LP..... Era ................. EL/ES109 ............. 1962 £20.........£40 .................................. US
So This Is Love ........................................ 7"...... London .......... HLN9551............ 1962 £7.50.....£15 ...............................

## CASTLE, LEE & THE BARONS
Love She Can Count On ......................... 7"...... Parlophone...... R5151 ............... 1964 £4.............£8 ...............................

## CASTLE FARM
Mascot .................................................... 7"...... private.............. ....................... 1972 £10.........£20 ...............................

## CASTLE JAZZ BAND
Famous Castle Jazz Band In Hi Fi ............. LP..... Good Time   LAG12176............. 1959 £5..........£12 ...............................
                                                              Jazz.................
Five Pennies............................................. LP..... Good Time   LAG12207.............. 1960 £5..........£12 ...............................
                                                              Jazz.................

## CASTLE ROCK
Nottingham Castle Festival Fringe............... LP...... private...... ....................... 1974 £100.....£200 ...............................

## CASTLE SISTERS
Stop Your Lying ...................................... 7"...... Ska Beat ........ JB257 ................. 1966 £5..........£10 ...............................

## CASTOR, JIMMY
Hey Leroy ............................................... LP..... Smash ............ MGS2/SRW67091 . 1967 £4.........£10 ............................ US
Hey Leroy ............................................... 7"...... Philips.............. BF1543 ............... 1967 £1.50........£4 ...............................
Magic Saxophone ................................... 7"...... Philips............. BF1590 ................. 1967 £7.50.....£15 ...............................

## CASUALS
Hour World............................................. LP..... Decca ............. SKL5001 ............ 1969 £5..........£12 ...............................
If You Walk Out....................................... 7"...... Fontana......... TF635 ................. 1965 £1.50........£4 ...............................
Toy........................................................... 7"...... Decca ............. F22852 ............... 1968 £2.............£5 ......... picture sleeve

## CAT
Run Run Run............................................ 7"...... Reaction ......... ....................... 196– £62.50.. £125 ...............................

## CAT IRON
Cat Iron .................................................. LP..... XTRA........... XTRA1087............ 1969 £15.........£30 ...............................

## CAT MOTHER & THE ALL NIGHT NEWSBOYS
The first LP by Cat Mother and the All Night Newsboys was produced by Jimi Hendrix, a fact which once gave the record a higher
collectors' value than it now has. The problem is that the group sounds extremely ordinary. Hendrix does not play on the record and the
production wizardry that he brought to his own records is nowhere in evidence.

Street Giveth........................................... LP...... Polydor........... 184300................. 1969 £4.............£10 ...............................

## CATALINAS
Fun Fun Fun............................................ LP...... Ric................. M1006 ................. 1964 £20.........£40 ........................ US

## CATAPILLA
Catapilla ................................................. LP..... Vertigo ........... 6360029................ 1971 £20.........£40 ............. spiral label
Changes .................................................. LP..... Vertigo ........... 6360074 ............... 1972 £100.....£200 ............. spiral label

## CATCH
Borderline .............................................. 7"...... Logo............. GO103................. 1977 £20.........£40 ...............................

## CATHARSIS
32 Mars .................................................. LP..... Galloway........ GB600507 ......... 1973 £4.........£10 ............. French
Catharsis.................................................. LP..... Explosive ........ 558004............... 1971 £6..........£15 ............. French
Catharsis.................................................. LP..... Saravah ........... SH10035 ............ 1971 £5..........£12 ............. French
Et s'aimer et mourir ............................... LP..... Festival .......... 678 ................... 1978 £4.........£10 ............. French
Illuminations........................................... LP..... Festival .......... 655 ................... 1974 £4.........£10 ............. French
Le Bolero ............................................... LP..... Festival .......... 676 ................... 1976 £4.........£10 ............. French
Les Chevrons ......................................... LP..... Festival .......... 651 ................... 1972 £5..........£12 ............. French
Mars........................................................ LP..... Festival .......... 652 ................... 1973 £4.........£10 ............. French

## CATHODE, RAY
Time Beat............................................... 7"...... Parlophone...... R4901 ................ 1962 £1.50........£4 ...............................

## CATHY JEAN & THE ROOMATES
At The Hop!............................................ LP...... Valmor............ 789 ................... 1961 £37.50.... £75 ........................ US

## CATS EYES
Come Away Melinda................................ 7"...... MCA............. MK5043 ............. 1970 £1.50........£4 ...............................
I Thank You Marianne ........................... 7"...... Deram ........... DM209 ............... 1968 £1.50........£4 ...............................
Loser ...................................................... 7"...... MCA............. MK5028 ............. 1970 £1.50........£4 ...............................
Smile Girl For Me ................................... 7"...... Deram ........... DM190 ............... 1968 £1.50........£4 ...............................

| | | | | | | | | | |
|---|---|---|---|---|---|---|---|---|---|
| Where Is She Now | 7" | Deram | DM251 | 1969 | £5 | £10 | |
| Wizard | 7" | MCA | MK5056 | 1970 | £2.50 | £6 | |

## CATS PYJAMAS
| | | | | | | | |
|---|---|---|---|---|---|---|---|
| Camera Man | 7" | Direction | 583482 | 1968 | £5 | £10 | |
| Virginia Waters | 7" | Direction | 583235 | 1968 | £5 | £10 | |

## CATTINI, CLEM
| | | | | | | | |
|---|---|---|---|---|---|---|---|
| No Time To Think | 7" | Decca | F12135 | 1965 | £6 | £12 | |

## CATTOUSE, NADIA
| | | | | | | | |
|---|---|---|---|---|---|---|---|
| Beautiful Barbados | 7" | Reality | RE503 | 1966 | £1.50 | £4 | |
| Earth Mother | LP | RCA | SF8070 | 1969 | £6 | £50 | |
| Nadia Cattouse | LP | Reality | RY1001 | 1966 | £30 | £60 | |

## CAVALLI, PIERRE
| | | | | | | | |
|---|---|---|---|---|---|---|---|
| Strictly Guitar | 7" EP | HMV | 7EG8817 | 1963 | £2 | £5 | |

## CAVE, EDDIE & THE FIX
| | | | | | | | |
|---|---|---|---|---|---|---|---|
| Fresh Out Of Tears | 7" | Pye | 7N17161 | 1966 | £10 | £20 | |

## CAVE, NICK
| | | | | | | | |
|---|---|---|---|---|---|---|---|
| Murder Ballads – The Interview | CD | Mute | CAVESPEAK1CD | 1996 | £6 | £15 | promo |
| Ship Song | CD-s | Mute | CDMUTE108 | 1990 | £2 | £5 | |
| Weeping Song | CD-s | Mute | CDMUTE118 | 1990 | £2 | £5 | 4 track single |

## CAVELL, ANDY
| | | | | | | | |
|---|---|---|---|---|---|---|---|
| Always On Saturday | 7" | HMV | POP1080 | 1962 | £7.50 | £15 | |
| Andy | 7" | Pye | 7N15539 | 1963 | £7.50 | £15 | |
| Hey There Cruel Heart | 7" | HMV | POP1024 | 1962 | £7.50 | £15 | |
| Tell The Truth | 7" | Pye | 7N15610 | 1964 | £7.50 | £15 | |

## CAVELLO, JIMMY & THE HOUSE ROCKERS
| | | | | | | | |
|---|---|---|---|---|---|---|---|
| Footstomping | 7" | Vogue Coral | Q72240 | 1957 | £75 | £150 | |
| Rock Rock Rock | 7" | Vogue Coral | Q72226 | 1957 | £75 | £150 | |

## CAZAZZA, MONTE
| | | | | | | | |
|---|---|---|---|---|---|---|---|
| Something For Nobody | 7" | Industrial | IR0010 | 1980 | £2 | £5 | |
| To Mom On Mother's Day | 7" | Industrial | IR0005 | 1979 | £4 | £8 | |

## CCS
| | | | | | | | |
|---|---|---|---|---|---|---|---|
| CCS | LP | RAK | SRKA6751 | 1970 | £4 | £10 | |

## CECCARELLI, ANDRE
| | | | | | | | |
|---|---|---|---|---|---|---|---|
| André Ceccarelli | LP | Carla | CAR500002 | 1977 | £10 | £25 | French |

## CEDARS
| | | | | | | | |
|---|---|---|---|---|---|---|---|
| For Your Information | 7" | Decca | F22720 | 1968 | £10 | £20 | |
| I Like The Way | 7" | Decca | F22772 | 1968 | £10 | £20 | |

## CELEBRATED RATLIFFE STOUT BAND

The Celebrated Ratliffe Stout Band was formed by eccentric folk singer-songwriter Tom Hall and includes the playing of Gerald Claridge, Mark Griffiths and other stalwarts of the Northampton music scene. The earliest recording, *Songs And Tales*, is a duo Hall/Jay Woodhall venture, the mis-spelling of the album's title being a feature of the album and not a mistake in this guide!

| | | | | | | | |
|---|---|---|---|---|---|---|---|
| Behind The Mask | LP | Plant Life | PLR020 | 1981 | £10 | £25 | |
| Dan Half Dan And The Spaceman | LP | private | | 1976 | £62.50 | £125 | |
| Songs And Tales From Greenwood Egde | LP | private | DT21 | 1976 | £75 | £150 | |
| Vanlag | LP | Plant Life | PLR030 | 1981 | £10 | £25 | |

## CELESTIN, OSCAR 'PAPA'
| | | | | | | | |
|---|---|---|---|---|---|---|---|
| New Orleans Band | 10" LP | Melodisc | MLP506 | 1956 | £6 | £15 | |

## CELIA & THE MUTATIONS
| | | | | | | | |
|---|---|---|---|---|---|---|---|
| You Better Believe Me | 7" | United Artists | UP36318 | 1977 | £2 | £5 | |

## CELTIC FOLKWEAVE
| | | | | | | | |
|---|---|---|---|---|---|---|---|
| Celtic Folkweave | LP | Polydor | | 1974 | £15 | £30 | |

## CENOTAPH CORNER
| | | | | | | | |
|---|---|---|---|---|---|---|---|
| Every Day But Wednesday | LP | Cottage | COT031 | 1979 | £8 | £20 | |
| Ups And Downs | LP | Cottage | COT501 | 1976 | £8 | £20 | |

## CENTAURUS
| | | | | | | | |
|---|---|---|---|---|---|---|---|
| Centaurus | LP | Azra | 61549 | 1978 | £20 | £40 | US picture disc |

## CENTIPEDE

Centipede was so named because of its huge line-up: fifty-five people play on the record, not including Robert Fripp, who played guitar with the band on stage, but who remains in the producer's chair here. Centipede was the inspiration of jazz pianist Keith Tippett, as a piece of mad indulgence that would be unlikely to make anyone's fortune. *Septober Energy* is a single piece of music spread over four sides of vinyl, but it falls naturally into sections, which enable different combinations of musicians to be highlighted.

| | | | | | | | |
|---|---|---|---|---|---|---|---|
| Septober Energy | LP | Neon | NE9 | 1971 | £25 | £50 | double |
| Septober Energy | LP | RCA | DPS2054 | 1974 | £15 | £30 | different cover |

## CENTURIANS
| | | | | | | | |
|---|---|---|---|---|---|---|---|
| Surfers' Pajama Party | LP | Del Fi | DFST128 | 1964 | £10 | £25 | US |

## CENTURY 21

| Title | Format | Label | Cat. No. | Year | | | |
|---|---|---|---|---|---|---|---|
| Alias Mister Hackenbacker | 7" EP | Century 21 | MA123 | 1967 | £10 | £20 | |
| Atlantic Inferno | 7" EP | Century 21 | MA125 | 1967 | £10 | £20 | |
| Brink Of Disaster | 7" EP | Century 21 | MA124 | 1967 | £10 | £20 | |
| Captain Scarlet & The Mysterons | 7" EP | Century 21 | MA132 | 1967 | £7.50 | £15 | |
| Captain Scarlet Is Indestructable | 7" EP | Century 21 | MA133 | 1967 | £7.50 | £15 | |
| Captain Scarlet Of Spectrum | 7" EP | Century 21 | MA134 | 1967 | £7.50 | £15 | |
| Captain Scarlet Vs Captain Black | 7" EP | Century 21 | MA135 | 1967 | £7.50 | £15 | |
| Chain Chain | 7" EP | Century 21 | MA122 | 1967 | £10 | £20 | |
| Daleks | 7" EP | Century 21 | MA106 | 1966 | £15 | £30 | |
| Day Of Disaster | 7" EP | Century 21 | MA121 | 1967 | £10 | £20 | |
| Desperate Intruder | 7" EP | Century 21 | MA119 | 1966 | £7.50 | £15 | |
| Fab | 7" EP | Century 21 | MA107 | 1966 | £6 | £12 | |
| Favourite Television Themes | LP | Century 21 | LA6 | 1966 | £10 | £25 | |
| Great Themes From Thunderbirds | 7" EP | Century 21 | MA116 | 1966 | £6 | £12 | |
| Imposters | 7" EP | Century 21 | MA120 | 1966 | £7.50 | £15 | |
| Into Action With Troy Tempest | 7" EP | Century 21 | MA101 | 1965 | £5 | £10 | |
| Introducing Captain Scarlet | 7" EP | Century 21 | MA131 | 1967 | £7.50 | £15 | |
| Introducing Thunderbirds | 7" EP | Century 21 | MA103 | 1965 | £5 | £10 | |
| Jeff Tracy Introduces International Rescue | LP | Century 21 | LA3 | 1966 | £15 | £30 | |
| Journey To The Moon | LP | Century 21 | LA100 | 1965 | £20 | £40 | |
| Journey To The Moon | 7" EP | Century 21 | MA100 | 1965 | £5 | £10 | |
| Lady Penelope & Other TV Themes | 7" EP | Century 21 | MA111 | 1966 | £6 | £12 | |
| Lady Penelope Investigates | LP | Century 21 | LA4 | 1966 | £15 | £30 | |
| Lady Penelope Presents | LP | Century 21 | LA2 | 1966 | £15 | £30 | |
| Marina Speaks | 7" EP | Century 21 | MA104 | 1965 | £5 | £10 | |
| One Move And You're Dead | 7" EP | Century 21 | MA128 | 1967 | £10 | £20 | |
| Perils Of Penelope | 7" EP | Century 21 | MA114 | 1966 | £6 | £12 | |
| Ricochet | 7" EP | Century 21 | MA126 | 1967 | £10 | £20 | |
| Space Age Nursery Rhymes | 7" | Century 21 | MA117 | 1966 | £7.50 | £15 | |
| Stately Home Robberies | 7" EP | Century 21 | MA110 | 1966 | £6 | £12 | |
| Thirty Minutes After Noon | 7" EP | Century 21 | MA129 | 1967 | £10 | £20 | |
| Thunderbird Four | 7" EP | Century 21 | MA113 | 1966 | £6 | £12 | |
| Thunderbird One | 7" EP | Century 21 | MA108 | 1966 | £6 | £12 | |
| Thunderbird Three | 7" EP | Century 21 | MA112 | 1966 | £6 | £12 | |
| Thunderbird Two | 7" EP | Century 21 | MA109 | 1966 | £6 | £12 | |
| Thunderbirds And Captain Scarlet | LP | Hallmark | HMA227 | 1973 | £6 | £15 | |
| Tingha And Tucker And The Wombaville Band | 7" EP | Century 21 | MA127 | 1967 | £10 | £20 | |
| Tingha And Tucker Club Song Book | LP | Century 21 | LA5 | 1966 | £8 | £20 | |
| Tingha And Tucker In Nursery Rhyme Time | 7" EP | Century 21 | MA130 | 1967 | £7.50 | £15 | |
| Top Gigio In London | 7" EP | Century 21 | MA115 | 1966 | £6 | £12 | |
| Trip To Marineville | 7" EP | Century 21 | MA102 | 1965 | £5 | £10 | |
| TV Favourites Vol. 1 | LP | Marble Arch | MAL770 | 1968 | £8 | £20 | |
| TV Favourites Vol. 2 | LP | Marble Arch | MAL771 | 1968 | £8 | £20 | |
| TV Themes | 7" EP | Century 21 | MA136 | 1967 | £7.50 | £15 | |
| TV21 Themes | 7" EP | Century 21 | MA105 | 1965 | £5 | £10 | |
| Vault Of Death | 7" EP | Century 21 | MA118 | 1966 | £10 | £20 | |
| World Of Tomorrow | LP | Century 21 | LA1 | 1965 | £10 | £25 | |

## CESANA

| Title | Format | Label | Cat. No. | Year | | | |
|---|---|---|---|---|---|---|---|
| Tender Emotions | LP | Modern | M100 | 1964 | £4 | £10 | US |

## CEYLEIB PEOPLE

| Title | Format | Label | Cat. No. | Year | | | |
|---|---|---|---|---|---|---|---|
| Tanyet | LP | Vault | LP117 | 1968 | £37.50 | £75 | US |

## CHAFFIN, ERNIE

| Title | Format | Label | Cat. No. | Year | | | |
|---|---|---|---|---|---|---|---|
| Lonesome For My Baby | 7" | London | HLS8409 | 1957 | £67.50 | £125 | |

## CHAIRMEN OF THE BOARD

| Title | Format | Label | Cat. No. | Year | | | |
|---|---|---|---|---|---|---|---|
| Chairmen Of The Board | LP | Invictus | SVT1002 | 1970 | £5 | £12 | |
| Give Me Just A Little More Time | 7" | Invictus | INV501 | 1970 | £1.50 | £4 | |
| In Session | LP | Invictus | SVT1003 | 1971 | £5 | £12 | |

## CHAKACHAS

| Title | Format | Label | Cat. No. | Year | | | |
|---|---|---|---|---|---|---|---|
| Jungle Fever | LP | Polydor | 2489050 | 1972 | £4 | £10 | |

## CHAKIRIS, GEORGE

| Title | Format | Label | Cat. No. | Year | | | |
|---|---|---|---|---|---|---|---|
| Cool | 7" | Saga | SAG452905 | 1959 | £2 | £5 | |
| I'm Always Chasing Rainbows | 7" | Triumph | RGM1010 | 1960 | £12.50 | £25 | |

## CHALIBAUCHE

| Title | Format | Label | Cat. No. | Year | | | |
|---|---|---|---|---|---|---|---|
| Les noces du papillon | LP | CEZ | 1017 | 1976 | £6 | £15 | French |

## CHALKER, BRYAN

| Title | Format | Label | Cat. No. | Year | | | |
|---|---|---|---|---|---|---|---|
| Bryan Chalker | LP | Chapter One | CMS1017 | 1973 | £4 | £10 | |
| Daddy Sing Me A Song | LP | Chapter One | CMS1020 | 1974 | £4 | £10 | |
| Hanging Of Samuel Hall | LP | Avenue | AVE071 | 1971 | £75 | £150 | |
| New Frontier | LP | Chapter One | CMS1010 | 1972 | £10 | £25 | |

## CHALLENGERS

| Title | Format | Label | Cat. No. | Year | | | |
|---|---|---|---|---|---|---|---|
| At The Teenage Fair | LP | GNP-Crescendo | (S)2010 | 1965 | £6 | £15 | US |
| Billy Strange And The Challengers | LP | GNP-Crescendo | (S)2030 | 1966 | £6 | £15 | US |
| Bulldog | 7" | Stateside | SS177 | 1963 | £1.50 | £4 | |

| Title | Format | Label | Catalog | Year | Price | Price | Notes |
|---|---|---|---|---|---|---|---|
| California Kicks | LP | GNP-Crescendo | (S)2025 | 1966 | £6 | £15 | US |
| Challengers Au Go-Go | LP | Vault | LP/VS110 | 1966 | £8 | £20 | US |
| Greatest Hits | LP | Vault | LP/VS111 | 1967 | £6 | £15 | US |
| K-39 | LP | Vault | LP107 | 1964 | £10 | £25 | US |
| Light My Fire | LP | GNP-Crescendo | S2045 | 1968 | £4 | £10 | US |
| Man From UNCLE | LP | GNP-Crescendo | (S)2018 | 1965 | £8 | £20 | US |
| Man From UNCLE | 7" | Vocalion | VN9253 | 1965 | £4 | £8 | |
| On The Move | LP | Vault | LP/VS102 | 1963 | £8 | £20 | US |
| Sidewalk Surfing | LP | Triumph | (TR)100 | 1965 | £8 | £20 | US |
| Surf 's Up | LP | Vault | LP/VS109 | 1965 | £8 | £20 | US |
| Surfbeat | LP | Stateside | SL10030 | 1963 | £8 | £20 | |
| Surfing | LP | Vault | LP/VS101 | 1963 | £8 | £20 | US |
| Twenty-Five Great Instrumental Hits | LP | GNP-Crescendo | (S)609 | 1967 | £5 | £12 | US |
| Vanilla Funk | LP | GNP-Crescendo | S2056 | 1970 | £4 | £10 | US |
| Walk With Me | 7" | Vocalion | VN9270 | 1966 | £1.50 | £4 | |
| Wipe Out | LP | Vocalion | VAN/SAVN8069 | 1967 | £8 | £20 | |
| Wipe Out | 7" EP | Vogue | INT18094 | 1966 | £10 | £20 | French |

## CHALLENGERS (2)

| Title | Format | Label | Catalog | Year | Price | Price | Notes |
|---|---|---|---|---|---|---|---|
| Cry Of The Wild Goose | 7" | Parlophone | R4773 | 1961 | £2 | £5 | |

## CHALMERS, LLOYD

| Title | Format | Label | Catalog | Year | Price | Price | Notes |
|---|---|---|---|---|---|---|---|
| Cooyah | 7" | Duke | DU15 | 1969 | £1.50 | £4 | Uniques B side |
| Death A Come | 7" | Explosion | EX2001 | 1969 | £1.50 | £4 | |
| Duckey Luckey | 7" | Songbird | SB1007 | 1969 | £1.50 | £4 | |
| Five To Five | 7" | Duke | DU25 | 1969 | £1.50 | £4 | |
| Follow This Sound | 7" | Duke | DU16 | 1969 | £1.50 | £4 | |
| For The Good Times | 7" | Duke | DU162 | 1973 | £1.50 | £4 | |
| I'm Gonna Love You Just A Little | 7" | Trojan | MJ6662 | 1974 | £1.50 | £4 | |
| Reggae Charm | LP | Trojan | TTL30 | 1970 | £5 | £12 | |
| Reggae Is Tight | LP | Trojan | TTL25 | 1970 | £5 | £12 | |
| Safari | 7" | Duke | DU36 | 1969 | £1.50 | £4 | |
| Time Is Getting Hard | 7" | Coxsone | CS7023 | 1967 | £5 | £10 | Tony Gregory B side |
| Why Baby | 7" | Gas | GAS114 | 1969 | £2 | £5 | |

## CHALOFF, SERGE

| Title | Format | Label | Catalog | Year | Price | Price | Notes |
|---|---|---|---|---|---|---|---|
| Blue Serge | LP | Capitol | T742 | 1956 | £8 | £20 | |
| Fable Of Mabel | LP | Vogue | LAE12052 | 1957 | £20 | £40 | |
| Lestorian Mode | LP | Realm | RM113 | 1963 | £5 | £12 | ...with tracks by Stan Getz & Brew Moore |

## CHAMAELEON CHURCH

Film star Chevy Chase was the drummer with this obscure pop band, while the two guitarists became part of the line-up of the second, less interesting version of cult band Ultimate Spinach.

| Title | Format | Label | Catalog | Year | Price | Price | Notes |
|---|---|---|---|---|---|---|---|
| Chamaeleon Church | LP | MGM | SE4574 | 1968 | £10 | £25 | US |

## CHAMBER POP ENSEMBLE

| Title | Format | Label | Catalog | Year | Price | Price | Notes |
|---|---|---|---|---|---|---|---|
| Chamber Pop Ensemble | LP | Decca | SKL4933 | 1968 | £5 | £12 | |
| Walk Away Renee | 7" | Decca | F12789 | 1968 | £1.50 | £4 | |

## CHAMBERLAIN, RICHARD

| Title | Format | Label | Catalog | Year | Price | Price | Notes |
|---|---|---|---|---|---|---|---|
| Richard Chamberlain Hits | 7" EP | MGM | MGMEP776 | 1963 | £2 | £5 | |
| Richard Chamberlain Sings | LP | MGM | C923 | 1963 | £4 | £10 | |

## CHAMBERS, JACK & RALPH HODGE

| Title | Format | Label | Catalog | Year | Price | Price | Notes |
|---|---|---|---|---|---|---|---|
| Country & Western Express Vol. 2 | 7" EP | Top Rank | JKP2056 | 1960 | £2 | £5 | |

## CHAMBERS, PAUL

| Title | Format | Label | Catalog | Year | Price | Price | Notes |
|---|---|---|---|---|---|---|---|
| Bass On Top | LP | Blue Note | BLP/BST81569 | 196- | £10 | £25 | |
| Whims Of Chambers | LP | Blue Note | BLP/BST81534 | 196- | £10 | £25 | |

## CHAMBERS BROTHERS

| Title | Format | Label | Catalog | Year | Price | Price | Notes |
|---|---|---|---|---|---|---|---|
| Call Me | 7" | Vocalion | VP9276 | 1966 | £1.50 | £4 | |
| Feelin' The Blues | LP | Liberty | LBS83276 | 1970 | £4 | £10 | |
| Greatest Hits | LP | Vault | 135 | 1970 | £4 | £10 | US |
| Love Me Like The Rain | 7" | Vocalion | VP9267 | 1966 | £1.50 | £4 | |
| Love, Peace And Happiness | LP | CBS | 66228 | 1970 | £5 | £12 | double |
| New Generation | LP | CBS | 64156 | 1971 | £4 | £10 | |
| New Time – A New Day | LP | Direction | 863451 | 1969 | £4 | £10 | |
| Now | LP | Vault | 115 | 1967 | £6 | £15 | US |
| Oh My God | LP | Columbia | KC31158 | 1972 | £4 | £10 | US |
| People Get Ready | LP | Vocalion | VAL/SAVL8058 | 1966 | £8 | £20 | |
| Shout | LP | Vault | 120 | 1968 | £5 | £12 | US |
| Time Has Come Today | LP | Direction | 863407 | 1968 | £4 | £10 | |

## CHAMBLEE, EDDIE

| Title | Format | Label | Catalog | Year | Price | Price | Notes |
|---|---|---|---|---|---|---|---|
| Blues For Eddie | 78 | Esquire | 10330 | 1953 | £3 | £8 | |
| Chamblee Music | LP | Emarcy | EJL1281 | 1958 | £6 | £15 | |
| Cradle Rock | 78 | Esquire | 10340 | 1953 | £3 | £8 | |

## CHAMELEONS
| | | | | | | | |
|---|---|---|---|---|---|---|---|
| As High As You Can Go | 7" | Statik | STAT30 | 1983 | £2.50 | £6 | |
| As High As You Can Go | 12" | Statik | STAT3012 | 1983 | £4 | £10 | |
| In Shreds | 7" | Epic | EPCA2210 | 1982 | £7.50 | £15 | |
| In Shreds | 7" | Statik | TAK29 | 1985 | £4 | £8 | double |
| In Shreds | 12" | Statik | TAK2912 | 1985 | £5 | £12 | |
| Person Isn't Safe Anywhere These Days | 7" | Statik | TAK6 | 1983 | £2.50 | £6 | |
| Person Isn't Safe Anywhere These Days | 12" | Statik | TAK612 | 1983 | £4 | £10 | |
| Script Of The Bridge | LP | Statik | STATP17 | 1985 | £6 | £15 | picture disc |
| Singing Rule Britannia | 12" | Statik | TAK3512 | 1985 | £2.50 | £6 | |
| Tears | 7" | Geffen | GEF4/SAM287 | 1986 | £4 | £8 | double |
| Tony Fletcher Walked On Water | CD-s | Glass Pyramid | EMCD1 | 1990 | £12.50 | £25 | |
| Tony Fletcher Walked On Water | 12" | Glass Pyramid | EMC1 | 1990 | £10 | £20 | |

## CHAMPIONS
| | | | | | | |
|---|---|---|---|---|---|---|
| Circlorama | 7" | Oriole | CB1854 | 1963 | £1.50 | £4 |

## CHAMPS
| | | | | | | | |
|---|---|---|---|---|---|---|---|
| All American Music | LP | Challenge | CHL/CHS614 | 1962 | £8 | £20 | US |
| Another Four By The Champs | 7" EP | London | REH1209 | 1959 | £10 | £20 | |
| Beatnick | 7" | London | HLH8811 | 1959 | £2 | £5 | |
| Cantina | 7" | London | HLH9430 | 1961 | £1.50 | £4 | |
| Caramba | 7" | London | HLH8864 | 1959 | £2 | £5 | |
| Chariot Rock | 7" | London | HL8715 | 1958 | £2.50 | £6 | |
| El Rancho Rock | 7" | London | HL8655 | 1958 | £4 | £8 | |
| Everybody's Rockin' | LP | London | HAH2184 | 1959 | £10 | £25 | |
| Experiment In Terror | 7" | London | HLH9539 | 1962 | £1.50 | £4 | |
| Four By The Champs | 7" EP | London | RE1176 | 1959 | £10 | £20 | |
| Go Champs Go | LP | London | HAH2152 | 1958 | £10 | £25 | |
| Great Dance Hits | LP | London | HAH2451 | 1962 | £6 | £15 | |
| Knockouts | 7" EP | London | REH1250 | 1961 | £10 | £20 | |
| Latin Limbo | 7" | London | HLH9604 | 1962 | £1.50 | £4 | |
| Limbo Rock | 7" | London | HLH9506 | 1962 | £1.50 | £4 | |
| Still More By The Champs | 7" EP | London | REH1223 | 1959 | £10 | £20 | |
| Tequila | 7" | London | HLU8580 | 1958 | £2.50 | £6 | |
| Too Much Tequila | 7" | London | HL9052 | 1960 | £1.50 | £4 | |

## CHAMPS (2)
| | | | | | | |
|---|---|---|---|---|---|---|
| Walk Between Your Enemies | 7" | Blue Beat | BB267 | 1964 | £6 | £12 |

## CHANCE, ROB & CHANCES R
| | | | | | | |
|---|---|---|---|---|---|---|
| At The End Of The Day | 7" | CBS | 3130 | 1967 | £1.50 | £4 |

## CHANCES ARE
| | | | | | | |
|---|---|---|---|---|---|---|
| Fragile Child | 7" | Columbia | DB8144 | 1967 | £7.50 | £15 |

## CHANCES R
| | | | | | | |
|---|---|---|---|---|---|---|
| Do It Yourself | 7" | CBS | 2940 | 1967 | £1.50 | £4 |
| Talking Out The Back Of My Head | 7" | CBS | 202614 | 1967 | £1.50 | £4 |

## CHANDELLE, DANY
| | | | | | | |
|---|---|---|---|---|---|---|
| Lying Awake | 7" | Columbia | DB7540 | 1965 | £4 | £8 |

## CHANDLER, BARBARA
| | | | | | | |
|---|---|---|---|---|---|---|
| Do You Really Love Me Too | 7" | London | HLR9823 | 1963 | £1.50 | £4 |
| Lonely New Year | 7" | London | HLR9861 | 1964 | £1.50 | £4 |

## CHANDLER, GENE
| | | | | | | | |
|---|---|---|---|---|---|---|---|
| Bless Our Love | 7" | Stateside | SS364 | 1964 | £1.50 | £4 | |
| Duke Of Earl | LP | Fontana | TL5247 | 1962 | £15 | £30 | |
| Duke Of Earl | 7" | Columbia | DB4793 | 1962 | £7.50 | £15 | |
| Duke Of Soul | LP | Checker | LP(S)3003 | 1967 | £4 | £10 | US |
| Fool For You | 7" | Stateside | SS500 | 1966 | £2 | £5 | |
| Girl Don't Care | 7" | Coral | Q72490 | 1967 | £4 | £8 | |
| Good Times | 7" | Stateside | SS458 | 1965 | £2.50 | £6 | |
| Greatest Hits | LP | Constellation | LP1421 | 1964 | £6 | £15 | US |
| I Can't Save It | 7" | Action | ACT4551 | 1969 | £6 | £12 | |
| Just Be True | LP | Constellation | LP1423 | 1964 | £6 | £15 | US |
| Live On Stage | LP | Action | ACLP6010 | 1969 | £6 | £15 | |
| Nothing Can Stop Me | 7" | Soul City | SC102 | 1968 | £2.50 | £6 | |
| Nothing Can Stop Me | 7" | Stateside | SS425 | 1965 | £10 | £20 | |
| Song Called Soul | 7" | Stateside | SS331 | 1964 | £2 | £5 | |
| Such A Pretty Thing | 7" | Chess | CRS8047 | 1966 | £7.50 | £15 | |
| There Was A Time | LP | MCA | MUPS367 | 1968 | £4 | £10 | |
| What Now | 7" | Stateside | SS388 | 1965 | £2.50 | £6 | |
| You Can't Hurt Me No More | 7" | Stateside | SS401 | 1965 | £2 | £5 | |
| You Threw A Lucky Punch | 7" | Stateside | SS185 | 1963 | £1.50 | £4 | |
| You're A Lady | 7" | Mercury | 6052098 | 1971 | £1.50 | £4 | |

## CHANDLER, JEFF
| | | | | | | |
|---|---|---|---|---|---|---|
| Everything Happens To Me | 7" | Brunswick | 05380 | 1955 | £2 | £5 |
| Half Of My Heart | 7" | London | HLU8484 | 1957 | £2 | £5 |
| I Should Care | 7" | Brunswick | 05264 | 1954 | £2 | £5 |
| My Prayer | 7" | Brunswick | 05417 | 1955 | £1.50 | £4 |
| Sings To You | LP | London | HAU2100 | 1958 | £4 | £10 |

## CHANDLER, KAREN
My Own True Love ............................. 7" ...... Salvo ............... SLO1803 ................... 1962 £1.50 ........ £4 ................

## CHANDLER, KENNY
Beyond Love .................................... 7" ...... Stateside .......... SS2110 ..................... 1968 £15 ......... £30 ................

## CHANNEL, BRUCE
| Blue And Lonesome ........................... | 7" | London | HLU9776 | 1963 £1.50 | £4 | |
| Going Back To Louisiana ..................... | 7" | London | HLU9841 | 1964 £1.50 | £4 | |
| Hey Baby ..................................... | 7" | Mercury | AMT1171 | 1962 £1.50 | £4 | |
| Hey Baby! .................................... | LP | Mercury | MMC14104 | 1962 £6 | £15 | |
| Keep On ...................................... | LP | Bell | MBLL/SBLL111 | 1969 £5 | £12 | |

## CHANTAYS
| Beyond ....................................... | 7" | King | KG1018 | 1965 £4 | £8 | |
| Pipeline ..................................... | LP | Downey | DLP1002 | 1963 £37.50 | £75 | US |
| Pipeline ..................................... | LP | London | HAD/SHD8087 | 1963 £10 | £25 | |
| Pipeline ..................................... | 7" EP | London | RED1397 | 1963 £15 | £30 | |
| Pipeline ..................................... | 7" | Dot | DS26757 | 1967 £1.50 | £4 | |
| Pipeline ..................................... | 7" | London | HLD9696 | 1963 £1.50 | £4 | |
| Two Sides Of The Chantays ................... | LP | Dot | DLP3771/25771 | 1966 £10 | £25 | US |

## CHANTELLES
| Blue Moon .................................... | 7" | CBS | 2777 | 1967 £2 | £5 | |
| Gonna Get Burned ............................. | 7" | Parlophone | R5350 | 1965 £2 | £5 | |
| I Think Of You ............................... | 7" | Parlophone | R5431 | 1966 £1.50 | £4 | |
| I Want That Boy .............................. | 7" | Parlophone | R5271 | 1965 £2.50 | £6 | |
| There's Something About You .................. | 7" | Polydor | 56119 | 1966 £2.50 | £6 | |

## CHANTELS
| Eternally .................................... | 7" | Capitol | CL15297 | 1963 £2 | £5 | |
| Look In My Eyes .............................. | 7" | London | HLL9428 | 1961 £6 | £12 | |
| Maybe ........................................ | 7" | London | HLU8561 | 1958 £180 | £300 | best auctioned |
| On Tour ...................................... | LP | Carlton | (ST)LP144 | 1961 £30 | £60 | US |
| Still ........................................ | 7" | London | HLL9480 | 1962 £5 | £10 | |
| Summertime ................................... | 7" | London | HLL9532 | 1962 £5 | £10 | |
| There's Our Song Again ....................... | LP | End | LP312 | 1962 £10 | £25 | US |
| We're The Chantels ........................... | LP | End | LP301 | 1958 £180 | £300 | US, group photo cover |
| We're The Chantels ........................... | LP | End | LP301 | 1959 £67.50 | £125 | US, jukebox cover |

## CHANTER
Suburban Ethnia ............................... LP ...... private ................................. 1977 £8 .......... £20 ................

## CHANTERS
| Every Night I Sit And Cry ................... | 7" | CBS | 202454 | 1966 £1.50 | £4 | |
| My Love Is For You ........................... | 7" | CBS | 3668 | 1968 £1.50 | £4 | |
| What's Wrong With You ........................ | 7" | CBS | 3400 | 1968 £1.50 | £4 | |
| You Can't Fool Me ............................ | 7" | CBS | 202616 | 1967 £2.50 | £6 | |

## CHANTS
| Ain't Nobody Home ............................ | 7" | Page One | POF016 | 1967 £1.50 | £4 | |
| Come Back & Get This Loving Boy .............. | 7" | Fontana | TF716 | 1966 £2 | £5 | |
| I Could Write A Book ......................... | 7" | Pye | 7N15591 | 1964 £1.50 | £4 | |
| I Don't Care ................................. | 7" | Pye | 7N15557 | 1963 £1.50 | £4 | |
| I Get The Sweetest Feeling ................... | 7" | RCA | RCA1823 | 1969 £2.50 | £6 | |
| I've Been Trying ............................. | 7" | Chipping Norton | CHIP2 | 1976 £7.50 | £15 | |
| Lover's Story ................................ | 7" | Decca | F12650 | 1967 £1.50 | £4 | |
| Man Without A Face ........................... | 7" | RCA | RCA1754 | 1968 £10 | £20 | |
| She's Mine ................................... | 7" | Pye | 7N15643 | 1964 £1.50 | £4 | |
| Sweet Was The Wine ........................... | 7" | Pye | 7N15691 | 1964 £1.50 | £4 | |

## CHANTS (2)
Close Friends ................................. 7" ...... Capitol ............ CL14876 ................ 1958 £2 ............ £5 ................

## CHAPIN BROTHERS
Chapin Music .................................. LP ..... Rockland ........ 66 ...................... 1967 £20 ......... £40 ................ US

## CHAPLAIN, PAUL & THE EMERALDS
Shortning Bread ............................... 7" ...... London ............ HLU9205 ............... 1960 £10 ......... £20 ................

## CHAPMAN, GENE
Oklahoma Blues ................................ 7" ...... Starlite ............. ST45102 ............... 1963 £50 ........ £100 ................

## CHAPMAN, MICHAEL
| Almost Alone ................................. | LP | Black Crow | CRO202 | 1981 £4 | £10 | |
| Deal Gone Down ............................... | LP | Deram | SML1114 | 1974 £4 | £10 | |
| Fully Qualified Survivor ..................... | LP | Harvest | SHVL764 | 1969 £5 | £12 | |
| Guitars ...................................... | LP | Standard | ESL146 | 197– £25 | £50 | |
| Lady On The Rocks ............................ | LP | Intercord | 126309 | 1980 £4 | £10 | German |
| Life On The Ceiling .......................... | LP | Criminal | STEAL5 | 1978 £4 | £10 | |
| Lived Here ................................... | LP | Cube | GNAT1 | 1977 £4 | £10 | |
| Looking For Eleven ........................... | LP | Criminal | STEAL9 | 1980 £4 | £10 | |
| Man Who Hated Mornings ....................... | LP | Decca | SKLR5290 | 1977 £4 | £10 | |
| Millstone Grit ............................... | LP | Deram | SML1105 | 1973 £5 | £12 | |
| Playing Guitar The Easy Way .................. | LP | Criminal | STEAL2 | 1978 £4 | £10 | |
| Pleasures Of The Street ...................... | LP | Nova | 622321 | 1975 £4 | £10 | German |

| | | | | | | | |
|---|---|---|---|---|---|---|---|
| Rainmaker | LP | Harvest | SHVL755 | 1969 | £5 | £12 | |
| Savage Amusement | LP | Decca | SKLR5242 | 1976 | £5 | £12 | |
| Window | LP | Harvest | SHVL786 | 1971 | £5 | £12 | |
| Wrecked Again | LP | Harvest | SHVL798 | 1971 | £5 | £12 | |

## CHAPMAN, TRACY

| | | | | | | | |
|---|---|---|---|---|---|---|---|
| Baby Can I Hold You | CD-s | Elektra | EKR82CD | 1988 | £2 | £5 | |
| Fast Car | CD-s | Elektra | EKR73CD | 1988 | £2 | £5 | 3" single |
| Talkin' 'Bout A Revolution | CD-s | Elektra | EKR78CD | 1988 | £2 | £5 | |

## CHAPS

| | | | | | | | |
|---|---|---|---|---|---|---|---|
| Popping Medley | 7" | Parlophone | R4979 | 1962 | £5 | £10 | |

## CHAPTER FIVE

| | | | | | | | |
|---|---|---|---|---|---|---|---|
| Anything That You Do | 7" | CBS | 202395 | 1966 | £250 | £400 | best auctioned |
| One In A Million | 7" | CBS | 2696 | 1967 | £75 | £150 | |

## CHAPTER FOUR

| | | | | | | | |
|---|---|---|---|---|---|---|---|
| In My Life | 7" | United Artists | UP1143 | 1966 | £75 | £150 | |

## CHAPTER TWO

| | | | | | | | |
|---|---|---|---|---|---|---|---|
| Page One | LP | Philips | 655023 | 1966 | £20 | £40 | Dutch |

## CHAPTERHOUSE

| | | | | | | | |
|---|---|---|---|---|---|---|---|
| Free Fall | CD-s | Dedicated | STONE001CD | 1990 | £3 | £8 | |
| Free Fall | 12" | Dedicated | STONE001T | 1990 | £2.50 | £6 | |
| Mesmerise | CD-s | Dedicated | HOUSE001CD | 1991 | £2 | £5 | |
| Pearl | CD-s | Dedicated | STONE003CD | 1991 | £2 | £5 | |
| Sunburst EP | CD-s | Dedicated | STONE002CD | 1990 | £2 | £5 | |

## CHAPTERS

| | | | | | | | |
|---|---|---|---|---|---|---|---|
| Can't Stop Thinking About Her | 7" | Pye | 7N15815 | 1965 | £12.50 | £25 | |

## CHARIG, MARC

| | | | | | | | |
|---|---|---|---|---|---|---|---|
| Pipedream | LP | Ogun | OG710 | 1977 | £5 | £12 | with Keith Tippett & Ann Winter |

## CHARIOT

| | | | | | | | |
|---|---|---|---|---|---|---|---|
| Chariot | LP | National General | NG2003 | 1968 | £30 | £60 | US |

## CHARLATANS

The original Charlatans were one of the great, pioneering San Franciso groups, but only the Kapp single comes anywhere near to capturing them at their peak. By the time the Charlatans got to make an album, several of the founder members had departed and the moment had passed.

| | | | | | | | |
|---|---|---|---|---|---|---|---|
| 32:20 | 7" | Kapp | 779 | 1966 | £10 | £20 | US |
| Alabama Bound | LP | Eva | 12017 | 1983 | £5 | £12 | French |
| Charlatans | LP | Groucho Marx | | 1979 | £8 | £20 | Italian |
| Charlatans | LP | Philips | SBL7903 | 1969 | £30 | £60 | |

## CHARLATANS (2)

| | | | | | | | |
|---|---|---|---|---|---|---|---|
| Indian Rope | 12" | Dead Dead Good | GOOD ONE | 1990 | £3 | £8 | |
| Isolation (Live At Chicago Metro) | LP | Live Live Good | CB2 | 1991 | £5 | £12 | fan club issue |
| Me In Time | CD-s | Situation 2 | SIT84CD | 1991 | £2 | £5 | |
| Melting Pot | CD | Beggars Banquet | CHAR14 | 1995 | £8 | £20 | promo sampler |
| Only One I Know | CD-s | Situation 2 | SIT70CD | 1990 | £2 | £5 | |
| Over Rising | CD-s | Situation 2 | SIT76CD | 1991 | £2 | £5 | |
| Some Friendly | CD | Situation 2 | SITU30CD | 1990 | £5 | £12 | |
| Subterranean (Live) | CD-s | Beggars Banquet | CHAR7 | 1993 | £3 | £8 | with fan club magazine |
| Then | CD-s | Situation 2 | SIT74CD | 1990 | £2 | £5 | |

## CHARLEE

| | | | | | | | |
|---|---|---|---|---|---|---|---|
| Charlee | LP | Mind Dust | MDM1001 | 1976 | £6 | £15 | Canadian |
| Charlee | LP | RCA | LSP4809 | 1972 | £20 | £40 | Canadian |

## CHARLES, BOBBY

'See You Later Alligator' by Bobby Charles has the distinction of being the most valuable single issued commercially in the UK. One of the few copies to appear on the market has sold for £2000 and one London dealer maintains that this copy is the only surviving one, having changed hands on a number of occasions, with the price climbing steadily each time. Another dealer, however, insists with equal certainty that he has personally handled six different copies!

| | | | | | | | |
|---|---|---|---|---|---|---|---|
| Bobby Charles | LP | Bearsville | K45516 | 1972 | £4 | £10 | |
| See You Later Alligator | 7" | London | HLU8247 | 1956 | £1050 | £1500 | best auctioned |

## CHARLES, DON

| | | | | | | | |
|---|---|---|---|---|---|---|---|
| Angel Of Love | 7" | Decca | F11602 | 1963 | £5 | £10 | |
| Don Charles | 7" EP | Decca | DFE8530 | 1963 | £30 | £60 | |
| Drifter | 7" | Parlophone | R5688 | 1968 | £7.50 | £15 | |
| Have I Told You Lately | LP | Parlophone | PMC/PCS7021 | 1967 | £8 | £20 | |
| Heart's Ice Cold | 7" | Decca | F11645 | 1963 | £7.50 | £15 | |
| Hermit Of Misty Mountain | 7" | Decca | F11464 | 1962 | £4 | £8 | |
| It's My Way Of Loving You | 7" | Decca | F11528 | 1962 | £4 | £8 | |

| Title | Format | Label | Catalogue | Year | | | |
|---|---|---|---|---|---|---|---|
| She's Mine | 7" | HMV | POP1332 | 1964 | £4 | £8 | |
| Walk With Me My Angel | 7" | Decca | F11424 | 1962 | £4 | £8 | |

## CHARLES, JIMMY

| Title | Format | Label | Catalogue | Year | | | |
|---|---|---|---|---|---|---|---|
| Million To One | 7" | London | HLU9206 | 1960 | £1.50 | £4 | |

## CHARLES, RAY

Ray Charles is the man who invented soul music, brought it into the entertainment mainstream, and, some would say, sold out. Charles himself sees it differently – he has never deliberately sought to be a champion for black culture, but has simply played what he enjoys. Having been exposed to a wide range of styles during childhood – across blues, jazz and country – he does in fact enjoy an equally wide range and has been happy to perform it all. It is fair to say, however, that the influence and reputation that he enjoys amongst rock musicians and collectors is based on the earlier, blacker material. Even so, the music played by Ray Charles in the fifties has nothing to do with rock'n'roll and has little in common with the work of most other R&B artists – the main reason, no doubt, for the values of his records remaining relatively low. The songs and instrumental pieces on Charles's recordings for Atlantic (issued on London in the UK) swing rather than rock, have a line-up modelled on that of Count Basie, and include many straightforward hard bop pieces, with Charles playing fluent solos on the alto saxophone.

| Title | Format | Label | Catalogue | Year | | | |
|---|---|---|---|---|---|---|---|
| Baby Don't You Cry | 7" | HMV | POP1272 | 1964 | £1.50 | £4 | |
| Baby It's Cold Outside | 7" EP | HMV | 7EG8807 | 1963 | £2 | £5 | |
| Ballad Style Of Ray Charles | 7" EP | HMV | 7EG8783 | 1963 | £2 | £5 | |
| Busted | 7" EP | HMV | 7EG8841 | 1964 | £2 | £5 | |
| Busted | 7" | HMV | POP1221 | 1963 | £1.50 | £4 | |
| C&W Meets R&B | LP | HMV | CLP1914/CSD1630 | 1965 | £4 | £10 | |
| Cincinnati Kid | LP | MGM | (S)E4313 | 1965 | £4 | £10 | US |
| Cincinnati Kid | 7" | HMV | POP1484 | 1965 | £1.50 | £4 | |
| Come Rain Or Come Shine | 7" | London | HLK9251 | 1960 | £1.50 | £4 | |
| Cry | 7" | HMV | POP1392 | 1965 | £1.50 | £4 | |
| Cryin' Time | 7" | HMV | POP1502 | 1966 | £1.50 | £4 | |
| Crying Time | LP | HMV | CLP/CSD3533 | 1966 | £4 | £10 | |
| Dedicated To You | LP | HMV | CLP1449/CSD1362 | 1961 | £4 | £10 | |
| Don't Set Me Free | 7" | HMV | POP1133 | 1963 | £1.50 | £4 | |
| Early In The Mornin' | 7" | London | HLK9364 | 1961 | £1.50 | £4 | |
| Genius After Hours | LP | London | HAK8035 | 1963 | £5 | £12 | |
| Genius Hits The Road | LP | HMV | CLP1387/CSD1320 | 1960 | £4 | £10 | |
| Genius Of Ray Charles | LP | London | LTZK15190 | 1960 | £8 | £20 | |
| Genius Sings The Blues | LP | London | LTZK15238 | 1960 | £6 | £15 | |
| Genius + Soul = Jazz | LP | HMV | CLP1475/CSD1384 | 1961 | £4 | £10 | |
| Georgia On My Mind | 7" | HMV | POP792 | 1960 | £1.50 | £4 | |
| Great Ray Charles | LP | London | LTZK15134 | 1958 | £10 | £25 | |
| Great Ray Charles | 7" EP | London | EZK19043 | 1959 | £4 | £8 | |
| Greatest Hits | LP | HMV | CLP1626/CSD1482 | 1962 | £4 | £10 | |
| Have A Smile With Me | LP | HMV | CLP1795/CSD1566 | 1964 | £4 | £10 | |
| Hide Nor Hair | 7" | HMV | POP1017 | 1962 | £1.50 | £4 | |
| Hit the Road Jack | 7" EP | HMV | 7EG8729 | 1962 | £2 | £5 | |
| Hit The Road Jack | 7" | HMV | POP935 | 1961 | £1.50 | £4 | |
| I Can't Stop Loving You | 7" EP | HMV | 7EG8781 | 1962 | £2 | £5 | |
| I Can't Stop Loving You | 7" | HMV | POP1034 | 1962 | £1.50 | £4 | |
| I Chose To Sing The Blues | 7" | HMV | POP1551 | 1966 | £1.50 | £4 | |
| I Gotta Woman | 7" | HMV | POP1437 | 1965 | £1.50 | £4 | |
| I Wonder Who | 7" | London | HLK9435 | 1961 | £1.50 | £4 | |
| I'm Movin' On | 7" | London | HLE9009 | 1959 | £2 | £5 | |
| In Person | LP | London | HAK2284 | 1960 | £6 | £15 | |
| In The Heat Of The Night | LP | United Artists | 5160 | 1967 | £4 | £10 | US |
| Ingredients In A Recipe For Soul | LP | HMV | CLP1678 | 1963 | £4 | £10 | |
| Let The Good Times Roll | 7" | London | HLE9058 | 1960 | £2 | £5 | |
| Let's Go Get Stoned | 7" | HMV | POP1537 | 1966 | £1.50 | £4 | |
| Light Out Of Darkness | 7" | HMV | POP1414 | 1965 | £1.50 | £4 | |
| Listen | LP | HMV | CLP/CSD3630 | 1967 | £4 | £10 | |
| Live In Concert | LP | HMV | CLP1872/CSD1606 | 1965 | £4 | £10 | |
| Love's Gonna Live Here | 7" | HMV | POP1457 | 1965 | £1.50 | £4 | |
| Makin' Whoopee | 7" | HMV | POP1383 | 1965 | £1.50 | £4 | |
| Man And His Soul | LP | ABC | (S)590 | 1967 | £4 | £10 | US |
| Memories Of A Middle-Aged Man | LP | Atlantic | SD263 | 1968 | £4 | £10 | US |
| Modern Sounds In C&W | LP | HMV | CLP1580/CSD1451 | 1961 | £5 | £12 | |
| Modern Sounds In C&W 2 | LP | HMV | CLP1613/CSD1477 | 1962 | £4 | £10 | |
| My Baby Don't Dig Me | 7" | HMV | POP1315 | 1964 | £1.50 | £4 | |
| No One | 7" | HMV | POP1202 | 1963 | £1.50 | £4 | |
| No One To Cry To | 7" | HMV | POP1333 | 1964 | £1.50 | £4 | |
| One Mint Julep | 7" | HMV | POP862 | 1961 | £1.50 | £4 | |
| Original Ray Charles | LP | London | HAB8022 | 1962 | £6 | £15 | |
| Original Ray Charles Vol. 1 | 7" EP | London | REB1407 | 1963 | £4 | £8 | |
| Original Ray Charles Vol. 2 | 7" EP | London | REB1408 | 1963 | £4 | £8 | |
| Original Ray Charles Vol. 3 | 7" EP | London | REB1409 | 1963 | £4 | £8 | |
| Please Say You're Fooling | 7" | HMV | POP1566 | 1966 | £7.50 | £15 | |
| Ray Charles & Betty Carter | LP | HMV | CLP1520/CSD1414 | 1961 | £4 | £10 | |
| Ray Charles At Newport | LP | London | LTZK15149/SAHK6008 | 1959 | £6 | £15 | |
| Ray Charles At Newport | 7" EP | London | REK1317 | 1961 | £2.50 | £6 | |
| Ray Charles Live | 7" EP | HMV | 7EG8932 | 1966 | £2 | £5 | |
| Ray Charles Sextet | LP | London | LTZK15178 | 1960 | £6 | £15 | |
| Ray Charles Sings | 7" EP | HMV | 7EG8861 | 1964 | £2 | £5 | |
| Ray Charles Story Vol. 1 | LP | London | HAK8023 | 1962 | £4 | £10 | |
| Ray Charles Story Vol. 2 | LP | London | HAK8024 | 1962 | £4 | £10 | |
| Ray Charles Story Vol. 3 | LP | Atlantic | (SD)8083 | 1963 | £4 | £10 | US |
| Ray Charles Story Vol. 4 | LP | Atlantic | (SD)8094 | 1964 | £4 | £10 | US |
| Ray Charles/Rock And Roll | LP | Atlantic | 8006 | 1957 | £10 | £25 | US |
| Ray's Moods | LP | HMV | CLP/CSD3574 | 1966 | £4 | £10 | |

| Title | Format | Label | Catalog | Year | Price1 | Price2 | Notes |
|---|---|---|---|---|---|---|---|
| Rockhouse | 7" | London | HLE8768 | 1958 | £7.50 | £15 | |
| Ruby | 7" | HMV | POP825 | 1961 | £1.50 | £4 | |
| Sings Songs Of Buck Owens | 7" EP | HMV | 7EG8951 | 1966 | £2 | £5 | |
| Smack Dab In The Middle | 7" | HMV | POP1350 | 1964 | £1.50 | £4 | |
| Soul Brothers | LP | London | LTZK15146/SAHK6030 | 1959 | £6 | £15 | |
| Soul Brothers | 7" EP | London | EZK19048 | 1959 | £4 | £8 | |
| Soul Meeting | LP | London | HAK/SHK8045 | 1963 | £5 | £12 | ...with Milt Jackson |
| Sticks And Stones | 7" | HMV | POP774 | 1960 | £1.50 | £4 | |
| Sweet & Sour Tears | LP | HMV | CLP1728/CSD1537 | 1963 | £4 | £10 | |
| Swinging Style Of Ray Charles | 7" EP | HMV | 7EG8801 | 1963 | £2 | £5 | |
| Take These Chains From My Heart | 7" EP | HMV | 7EG8812 | 1963 | £2 | £5 | |
| Take These Chains From My Heart | 7" | HMV | POP1161 | 1963 | £1.50 | £4 | |
| Tell The Truth | 7" | London | HLK9181 | 1960 | £2 | £5 | |
| That Lucky Old Sun | 7" | HMV | POP1251 | 1964 | £1.50 | £4 | |
| Them That Got | 7" | HMV | POP838 | 1961 | £1.50 | £4 | |
| Together Again | LP | ABC | (S)520 | 1966 | £4 | £10 | US |
| Together Again | 7" | HMV | POP1519 | 1966 | £1.50 | £4 | |
| Unchain My Heart | 7" | HMV | POP969 | 1962 | £1.50 | £4 | |
| What I Say | 7" | Atlantic | 584093 | 1967 | £1.50 | £4 | |
| What I Say | 7" | London | HLE8917 | 1959 | £5 | £10 | |
| What'd I Say | LP | London | HAK2226 | 1959 | £6 | £15 | |
| What'd I Say | 7" EP | London | REK1306 | 1961 | £2.50 | £6 | |
| Yes Indeed | LP | London | HAE2168 | 1958 | £6 | £15 | |
| You Don't Know Me | 7" | HMV | POP1064 | 1962 | £1.50 | £4 | |
| Young Ray Charles | 7" EP | Realm | REP4001 | 1964 | £2.50 | £6 | |
| Your Cheating Heart | 7" | HMV | POP1099 | 1962 | £1.50 | £4 | |

## CHARLES, SONNY

| Title | Format | Label | Catalog | Year | Price1 | Price2 |
|---|---|---|---|---|---|---|
| Black Pearl | 7" | A&M | AMS752 | 1969 | £1.50 | £4 |
| Mastered The Art Of Love | 7" | Ember | EMBS240 | 1967 | £5 | £10 |

## CHARLES, TEDDY

| Title | Format | Label | Catalog | Year | Price1 | Price2 | Notes |
|---|---|---|---|---|---|---|---|
| New Directions | 10" LP | Esquire | 20034 | 1954 | £20 | £40 | |
| New Directions Quartet | 10" LP | Esquire | 20043 | 1955 | £20 | £40 | |
| Teddy Charles Quartet | 10" LP | Atlantic | ATLLP3 | 1955 | £25 | £50 | |
| Teddy Charles Tentet | LP | London | LTZK15034 | 1957 | £6 | £15 | |
| Three For Duke | LP | London | LTZJ15119 | 1958 | £6 | £15 | ...with Hal Overton & Oscar Pettiford |

## CHARLIE PARKAS

| Title | Format | Label | Catalog | Year | Price1 | Price2 |
|---|---|---|---|---|---|---|
| Ballad Of Robin Hood | 7" | Paranoid Plastics | PPS1 | 1980 | £2 | £5 |

## CHARMERS

| Title | Format | Label | Catalog | Year | Price1 | Price2 | Notes |
|---|---|---|---|---|---|---|---|
| Oh Yes | 7" | Vogue | V9095 | 1958 | £150 | £250 | best auctioned |

## CHARMERS (2)

| Title | Format | Label | Catalog | Year | Price1 | Price2 | Notes |
|---|---|---|---|---|---|---|---|
| Angel Love | 7" | R&B | JB118 | 1963 | £5 | £10 | |
| Back To Back | 7" | Melodisc | CAL9 | 1963 | £4 | £8 | |
| Dig Them Prince | 7" | Blue Beat | BB251 | 1964 | £6 | £12 | |
| Done Me Wrong | 7" | Blue Beat | BB157 | 1963 | £6 | £12 | |
| Glamour Girl | 7" | Blue Beat | BB256 | 1964 | £6 | £12 | ...Prince Buster B side |
| I Am Through | 7" | R&B | JB151 | 1964 | £5 | £10 | |
| I'm Back | 7" | Blue Beat | BB204 | 1964 | £6 | £12 | |
| In My Soul | 7" | R&B | JB156 | 1964 | £5 | £10 | |
| Keep On Going | 7" | Treasure Isle | TI7036 | 1968 | £5 | £10 | |
| Lonely Boy | 7" | Blue Beat | BB42 | 1961 | £6 | £12 | |
| Now You Want To Cry | 7" | Blue Beat | BB114 | 1962 | £6 | £12 | |
| Oh My Baby | 7" | Blue Beat | BB315 | 1965 | £6 | £12 | Spanishtonians B side |
| Oh Why Baby | 7" | R&B | JB121 | 1963 | £5 | £10 | ...Roland Alphonso B side |
| Skinhead Train | 7" | Explosion | EX2045 | 1970 | £1.50 | £4 | |
| Stone Cold Man | 7" | Melodisc | CAL8 | 1963 | £4 | £8 | |
| Waiting For You | 7" | Blue Beat | BB238 | 1964 | £6 | £12 | |
| You Don't Know | 7" | Rio | R78 | 1966 | £4 | £8 | |

## CHARMETTES

| Title | Format | Label | Catalog | Year | Price1 | Price2 |
|---|---|---|---|---|---|---|
| Please Don't Kiss Me Again | 7" | London | HLR9820 | 1963 | £2.50 | £6 |

## CHARMS

| Title | Format | Label | Catalog | Year | Price1 | Price2 |
|---|---|---|---|---|---|---|
| Carry, Go, Bring, Come | 7" | Island | WI154 | 1964 | £5 | £10 |
| Everybody Say Yeah | 7" | Rio | R98 | 1966 | £4 | £8 |

## CHARMS (2)

The rare single, 'Hearts Of Stone', is listed in the guide under the name used on other singles by the group – Otis Williams and the Charms.

## CHARMS, TEDDY

| Title | Format | Label | Catalog | Year | Price1 | Price2 |
|---|---|---|---|---|---|---|
| I Want It Girl | 7" | Blue Cat | BS141 | 1968 | £4 | £8 |

## CHARTBUSTERS

| Title | Format | Label | Catalog | Year | Price1 | Price2 |
|---|---|---|---|---|---|---|
| She's The One | 7" | London | HLU9906 | 1964 | £1.50 | £4 |
| Why | 7" | London | HLU9934 | 1964 | £1.50 | £4 |

## CHASE

| Title | Format | Label | Catalog | Year | Price1 | Price2 | Notes |
|---|---|---|---|---|---|---|---|
| Chase | LP | Epic | EQ30472 | 1971 | £5 | £12 | US quad |

## CHASE, LINCOLN

| | | | | | | | |
|---|---|---|---|---|---|---|---|
| Explosive | LP | Liberty | LRP3076 | 1958 | £6 | £15 | US |
| Johnny Klingeringding | 7" | London | HLU8495 | 1957 | £2 | £5 | |

## CHASERS

| | | | | | | | |
|---|---|---|---|---|---|---|---|
| Hey Little Girl | 7" | Decca | F12302 | 1965 | £25 | £50 | |
| Hey Little Girl | 7" | Decca | F12302 | 1965 | £30 | £60 | picture sleeve |
| Inspiration | 7" | Parlophone | R5451 | 1966 | £37.50 | £75 | |
| Ways Of A Man | 7" | Philips | BF1546 | 1967 | £7.50 | £15 | |

## CHAUSETTES

| | | | | | | | |
|---|---|---|---|---|---|---|---|
| Noire's Party | LP | Barclay | 80197 | 1963 | £8 | £20 | French |

## CHEAP TRICK

| | | | | | | | |
|---|---|---|---|---|---|---|---|
| At The Budokan | CD | Epic | CD86083 | 1986 | £5 | £12 | |
| Don't Be Cruel | CD-s | Epic | 6528962 | 1988 | £2 | £5 | |
| Flame | CD-s | Epic | 6514662 | 1988 | £2 | £5 | |
| So Good To See You | 7" | Epic | EPC6199 | 1978 | £2.50 | £6 | |

## CHEATIN' HEARTS

| | | | | | | | |
|---|---|---|---|---|---|---|---|
| Bad Kind | 7" | Columbia | DB8048 | 1966 | £1.50 | £4 | |

## CHECKER, CHUBBY

| | | | | | | | |
|---|---|---|---|---|---|---|---|
| All The Hits | LP | Cameo Parkway | P7014 | 1963 | £5 | £12 | |
| Beach Party | LP | Parkway | (S)P7030 | 1963 | £5 | £12 | US |
| Biggest Hits | LP | Parkway | (S)P7022 | 1962 | £5 | £12 | US |
| Chubby Checker | LP | Cameo Parkway | P7036 | 1963 | £5 | £12 | |
| Chubby Checker | LP | Parkway | 5001 | 1960 | £15 | £30 | US |
| Class | 7" | Top Rank | JAR154 | 1959 | £10 | £20 | |
| Dancing Party | 7" EP | Cameo Parkway | CPE550 | 1963 | £4 | £8 | |
| Dancing Party | 7" | Columbia | DB4876 | 1962 | £1.50 | £4 | |
| Discotheque | LP | Parkway | (S)P7045 | 1965 | £5 | £12 | US |
| Discotheque | 7" | Cameo Parkway | P949 | 1965 | £7.50 | £15 | |
| Don't Knock The Twist | LP | Parkway | P7011 | 1962 | £5 | £12 | US |
| Eighteen Golden Hits | LP | Parkway | (S)P7048 | 1966 | £5 | £12 | US |
| Everything's Wrong | 7" | Cameo Parkway | P959 | 1965 | £6 | £12 | |
| Fly | 7" | Columbia | DB4728 | 1961 | £1.50 | £4 | |
| Folk Album | LP | Parkway | (S)P7040 | 1963 | £5 | £12 | US |
| For Twisters Only | LP | Columbia | 33SX1341 | 1961 | £6 | £15 | |
| Good Good Loving | 7" | Columbia | DB4652 | 1961 | £1.50 | £4 | |
| Hey You Little Boogaloo | 7" | Cameo Parkway | P989 | 1965 | £4 | £8 | |
| Hucklebuck | 7" | Columbia | DB4541 | 1960 | £2 | £5 | |
| In Person | LP | Parkway | (S)P7026 | 1963 | £5 | £12 | US |
| It's Pony Time | LP | Columbia | 33SX1365 | 1961 | £6 | £15 | |
| King Of The Twist | 7" EP | Columbia | SEG8155 | 1962 | £4 | £8 | |
| Let's Limbo Some More | LP | Parkway | (S)P7027 | 1963 | £5 | £12 | US |
| Let's Twist Again | LP | Columbia | 33SX1411 | 1961 | £5 | £12 | |
| Let's Twist Again | 7" | Cameo Parkway | P824 | 1961 | £1.50 | £4 | |
| Let's Twist Again | 7" | Columbia | DB4691 | 1961 | £1.50 | £4 | |
| Limbo Party | LP | Cameo Parkway | P7020 | 1963 | £5 | £12 | |
| Limbo Rock | 7" | Cameo Parkway | P849 | 1962 | £1.50 | £4 | |
| Loddy Lo | 7" | Cameo Parkway | P890 | 1964 | £1.50 | £4 | |
| Lovely Lovely | 7" | Cameo Parkway | P936 | 1965 | £2 | £5 | |
| Pony Time | 7" | Columbia | DB4591 | 1961 | £1.50 | £4 | |
| Slow Twisting | 7" | Columbia | DB4808 | 1962 | £1.50 | £4 | |
| Twist | 7" | Columbia | DB4503 | 1960 | £1.50 | £4 | |
| Twist Along With Chubby Checker | LP | Columbia | 33SX1445 | 1962 | £5 | £12 | |
| Twist With Chubby Checker | LP | Columbia | 33SX1315 | 1961 | £6 | £15 | |
| Twistin' Around The World | LP | Golden Guinea | GGL0236 | 1962 | £4 | £10 | |
| Twistin' Around The World | LP | Parkway | P7008 | 1962 | £5 | £12 | US |
| Two Hearts Make One Love | 7" | Cameo Parkway | P965 | 1965 | £37.50 | £75 | |
| Your Twist Party | LP | Parkway | P7007 | 1961 | £5 | £12 | US |

## CHECKER, CHUBBY & BOBBY RYDELL

| | | | | | | | |
|---|---|---|---|---|---|---|---|
| Bobby Rydell/Chubby Checker | LP | Cameo | C1013 | 1961 | £5 | £12 | US |
| Chubby Checker & Bobby Rydell In London | 7" EP | Cameo Parkway | CPE554 | 1964 | £6 | £12 | |
| Chubby Checker And Bobby Rydell | LP | Columbia | 33SX1424 | 1962 | £5 | £12 | |
| Jingle Bell Rock | 7" | Cameo Parkway | C205 | 1962 | £1.50 | £4 | |
| Teach Me To Twist | 7" | Columbia | DB4802 | 1962 | £1.50 | £4 | |

## CHECKER, CHUBBY & DEE DEE SHARP

| | | | | | | | |
|---|---|---|---|---|---|---|---|
| Down To Earth | LP | Cameo Parkway | C1029 | 1963 | £5 | £12 | |

## CHECKMATES

| Title | Format | Label | Cat. No. | Year | | | Notes |
|---|---|---|---|---|---|---|---|
| Around | 7" | Decca | F12114 | 1965 | £2.50 | £6 | |
| Checkmates | LP | Pye | NPL18061 | 1961 | £6 | £15 | |
| Every Day Is Just The Same | 7" | Parlophone | R5495 | 1966 | £4 | £8 | |
| Rocking Minstrel | 7" | Piccadilly | 7N35010 | 1961 | £2 | £5 | |
| Sticks And Stones | 7" | Decca | F11844 | 1964 | £1.50 | £4 | |
| Stop That Music | 7" | Parlophone | R5337 | 1965 | £4 | £8 | |
| You Got The Gamma Goochie | 7" | Parlophone | R5402 | 1966 | £5 | £10 | |
| You've Gotta Have A Gimmick Today | 7" | Decca | F11603 | 1963 | £4 | £8 | |

## CHECKMATES (2)

| Title | Format | Label | Cat. No. | Year | | | Notes |
|---|---|---|---|---|---|---|---|
| Invisible Ska | 7" | Ska Beat | JB225 | 1965 | £5 | £10 | Winston Richards B side |

## CHECKMATES LTD.

| Title | Format | Label | Cat. No. | Year | | | Notes |
|---|---|---|---|---|---|---|---|
| Do The Walk | 7" | Ember | EMBS235 | 1967 | £1.50 | £4 | |
| I Keep Forgettin' | 7" | A&M | AMS780 | 1970 | £1.50 | £4 | |
| Live At Caesar's Palace | LP | Capitol | ST2840 | 1967 | £6 | £15 | US |
| Love Is All I Have To Give | 7" | A&M | AMS747 | 1969 | £1.50 | £4 | |
| Love Is All We Have To Give | LP | A&M | AMLS943 | 1969 | £6 | £15 | |

## CHECKPOINT CHARLY

| Title | Format | Label | Cat. No. | Year | | | Notes |
|---|---|---|---|---|---|---|---|
| Frühling Der Krüppel | LP | Schneeball | 2015 | 1978 | £8 | £20 | German |
| Gruss Gott Mit Hellem Klang | LP | CPM | LPS003 | 1970 | £10 | £25 | German |

## CHEERS

| Title | Format | Label | Cat. No. | Year | | | Notes |
|---|---|---|---|---|---|---|---|
| Bazoom I Need Your Loving | 7" | Capitol | CL14189 | 1954 | £15 | £30 | |
| Black Denim Trousers | 7" | Capitol | CL14377 | 1955 | £12.50 | £25 | |
| Blueberries | 7" | Capitol | CL14280 | 1955 | £10 | £20 | |
| Cheers | 7" EP | Capitol | EAP1584 | 1956 | £20 | £40 | |
| Chicken | 7" | Capitol | CL14561 | 1956 | £7.50 | £15 | |
| I Must Be Dreaming | 7" | Capitol | CL14337 | 1955 | £10 | £20 | |
| Que Pasa Muchacha | 7" | Capitol | CL14601 | 1956 | £5 | £10 | Bert Convy B side |
| Whadya Want | 7" | Capitol | CL14248 | 1955 | £10 | £20 | |

## CHEETAHS

| Title | Format | Label | Cat. No. | Year | | | Notes |
|---|---|---|---|---|---|---|---|
| Goodbye Baby | 7" | Philips | BF1412 | 1965 | £1.50 | £4 | |
| Mecca | 7" | Philips | BF1362 | 1964 | £1.50 | £4 | |
| Russian Boat Song | 7" | Philips | BF1499 | 1966 | £1.50 | £4 | |
| Soldier Boy | 7" | Philips | BF1383 | 1965 | £1.50 | £4 | |
| Whole Lotta Love | 7" | Philips | BF1453 | 1965 | £1.50 | £4 | |

## CHELSEA

| Title | Format | Label | Cat. No. | Year | | | Notes |
|---|---|---|---|---|---|---|---|
| Alternative Hits | LP | Step Forward | SFLP5 | 1981 | £4 | £10 | |
| Chelsea | LP | Step Forward | SFLP2 | 1979 | £4 | £10 | |

## CHELSEA LADS

| Title | Format | Label | Cat. No. | Year | | | Notes |
|---|---|---|---|---|---|---|---|
| English Teas | 7" | CBS | 202047 | 1966 | £1.50 | £4 | |

## CHENE NOIR

| Title | Format | Label | Cat. No. | Year | | | Notes |
|---|---|---|---|---|---|---|---|
| Orphée 2000 | LP | Disque Chêne Noir | CN002 | 1977 | £8 | £20 | French |

## CHENIER, CLIFTON

| Title | Format | Label | Cat. No. | Year | | | Notes |
|---|---|---|---|---|---|---|---|
| Black Girl | 7" | Action | ACT4550 | 1969 | £1.50 | £4 | |
| Very Best | LP | Harvest | SHSP4002 | 1970 | £6 | £15 | |

## CHER

| Title | Format | Label | Cat. No. | Year | | | Notes |
|---|---|---|---|---|---|---|---|
| 3614 Jackson Highway | LP | Atlantic | 226026 | 1969 | £4 | £10 | |
| After All | CD-s | Geffen | GEF52CD | 1989 | £2 | £5 | with Peter Cetera |
| Alfie | 7" EP | Polydor | 27788 | 1966 | £2.50 | £6 | French |
| All I Really Want To Do | LP | Liberty | LBY3058 | 1965 | £4 | £10 | |
| All I Really Want To Do | 7" EP | Polydor | 27771 | 1965 | £2.50 | £6 | French |
| Baby I'm Yours | CD-s | Geffen | GEF84CD | 1990 | £2 | £5 | |
| Backstage | LP | Liberty | LBL/LBS83156 | 1968 | £4 | £10 | |
| Bang Bang | 7" EP | Polydor | 27782 | 1966 | £4 | £8 | French, 2 different sleeves |
| Cher | LP | Liberty | (S)LBY3081 | 1967 | £4 | £10 | |
| Cher | LP | MCA | MUPS438 | 1971 | £4 | £10 | |
| Golden Greats | LP | Liberty | LBL/LBS83105 | 1968 | £4 | £10 | |
| Heart Of Stone | CD-s | Geffen | GEF75CD | 1990 | £2 | £5 | |
| Hits Of Cher | 7" EP | Liberty | LEP4047 | 1966 | £2 | £5 | |
| If I Could Turn Back Time | CD-s | Geffen | GEF59CD | 1989 | £2 | £5 | |
| Just Like Jesse James | CD-s | Geffen | GEF69CD | 1990 | £2 | £5 | |
| Love And Understanding | CD-s | Geffen | GFSXD5 | 1991 | £2 | £5 | heart-shaped pack |
| Love Hurts | CD | Geffen | 243692DJ | 1991 | £8 | £20 | US promo picture disc in wooden box |
| Mama | 7" EP | Polydor | 27797 | 1966 | £2 | £5 | French |
| Skin Deep | CD-s | Geffen | GEF44CD | 1988 | £2 | £5 | |
| Sonny Side Of Cher | LP | Liberty | (S)LBY3072 | 1966 | £4 | £10 | |
| Take Me Home | LP | Casablanca | NBPIX7133 | 1979 | £5 | £12 | picture disc |
| Turning Back Time | CD | Geffen | CHERCD1 | 1992 | £8 | £20 | promo sampler |
| We All Sleep Alone | CD-s | Geffen | GEF35CD | 1988 | £2 | £5 | |
| With Love | LP | Liberty | LBL/LBS83051 | 1967 | £4 | £10 | |
| You Wouldn't Know Love | CD-s | Geffen | GEF77CD | 1990 | £2 | £5 | |

## CHEROKEES

| | | | | | | | |
|---|---|---|---|---|---|---|---|
| Dig A Little Deeper | 7" | Columbia | DB7704 | 1965 | £1.50 | £4 | |
| Land Of A Thousand Dances | 7" | Columbia | DB7822 | 1966 | £2 | £5 | |
| Seven Daffodils | 7" | Columbia | DB7341 | 1964 | £1.50 | £4 | |
| Wondrous Place | 7" | Columbia | DB7473 | 1965 | £1.50 | £4 | |
| You've Done It Again Little Girl | 7" | Decca | F11915 | 1964 | £1.50 | £4 | |

## CHEROKEES (2)

| | | | | | | | |
|---|---|---|---|---|---|---|---|
| Cherokee | 7" | Pye | 7N25066 | 1961 | £1.50 | £4 | |

## CHERRY, DON

The Don Cherry who recorded pop songs during the fifties has no connection at all with the jazz trumpeter who participated in pioneering recordings by Ornette Coleman and John Coltrane, before embarking on his own solo career. Much of this has taken trumpeter Cherry out of a strictly jazz context, embracing instead a range of influences taken directly from African and Oriental musics. Cherry's role as one of the first Western musicians to be seriously interested in World Music has clearly been well understood by his step-daughter Neneh.

| | | | | | | | |
|---|---|---|---|---|---|---|---|
| Complete Communion | LP | Blue Note | BLP/BST84226 | 1966 | £8 | £20 | |
| Don Cherry | LP | Horizon | SP717 | 1976 | £5 | £12 | US |
| Eternal Now | LP | Sonet | SNTF653 | 1973 | £6 | £15 | |
| Eternal Rhythm | LP | BASF | 20680 | 1968 | £8 | £20 | German |
| Mu First Part | LP | BYG | 529301 | 1970 | £8 | £20 | French |
| Mu Second Part | LP | BYG | 529331 | 1970 | £8 | £20 | French |
| Symphony For Improvisors | LP | Blue Note | BLP/BST84247 | 1966 | £8 | £20 | |
| Where Is Brooklyn? | LP | Blue Note | BST84311 | 1969 | £8 | £20 | |

## CHERRY, DON (2)

| | | | | | | | |
|---|---|---|---|---|---|---|---|
| Last Dance | 7" | Philips | JK1013 | 1957 | £1.50 | £4 | |
| Wanted Someone To Love | 7" | Brunswick | 05538 | 1956 | £1.50 | £4 | |

## CHERRY, NENEH

| | | | | | | | |
|---|---|---|---|---|---|---|---|
| Buffalo Stance | CD-s | Circa | YRCD21 | 1989 | £2 | £5 | 3" single |
| I've Got You Under My Skin | CD-s | Circa | YRCD53 | 1990 | £2 | £5 | |
| Inna City Mamma | CD-s | Circa | YRCD42 | 1989 | £2 | £5 | |
| Kisses On The Wind | CD-s | Circa | YRCD33 | 1989 | £2 | £5 | 3" single |
| Manchild | CD-s | Circa | YRCD30 | 1989 | £2 | £5 | 3" single |

## CHERRY PEOPLE

| | | | | | | | |
|---|---|---|---|---|---|---|---|
| And Suddenly | 7" | MGM | MGM1438 | 1968 | £10 | £20 | |
| Cherry People | LP | Heritage | HTS35000 | 1968 | £5 | £12 | US |
| Gotta Get Back | 7" | MGM | MGM1472 | 1969 | £1.50 | £4 | |
| Light Of Love | 7" | MGM | MGM1489 | 1969 | £1.50 | £4 | |

## CHERRY SMASH

| | | | | | | | |
|---|---|---|---|---|---|---|---|
| Fade Away Maureen | 7" | Decca | F12884 | 1969 | £4 | £8 | |
| Goodtime Sunshine | 7" | Decca | F12838 | 1968 | £2.50 | £6 | |
| Sing Songs Of Love | 7" | Track | 604017 | 1967 | £2 | £5 | |

## CHESTER, GARY

| | | | | | | | |
|---|---|---|---|---|---|---|---|
| Yeah Yeah Yeah | LP | DCP | D(S)6803 | 1964 | £4 | £10 | US |

## CHESTER, PETE

| | | | | | | | |
|---|---|---|---|---|---|---|---|
| Forest Fire | 7" | Pye | 7N25074 | 1961 | £5 | £10 | |
| Ten Swinging Bottles | 7" | Pye | 7N15305 | 1960 | £5 | £10 | |

## CHESTER, VIC

| | | | | | | | |
|---|---|---|---|---|---|---|---|
| Rock A Billy | 7" | Decca | F10882 | 1957 | £6 | £12 | |

## CHESTERFIELDS

| | | | | | | | |
|---|---|---|---|---|---|---|---|
| A Guitar In Your Bath | 7" | Subway | SUBWAY3 | 1986 | £1.50 | £4 | |

## CHEVIOT RANTERS

| | | | | | | | |
|---|---|---|---|---|---|---|---|
| Cheviot Barn Dance | LP | Topic | 12TS245 | 1974 | £5 | £12 | |
| Cheviot Hills | LP | Topic | 12TS222 | 1973 | £5 | £12 | |
| Sound Of The Cheviots | LP | Topic | 12T214 | 1972 | £5 | £12 | |

## CHEVLONS

| | | | | | | | |
|---|---|---|---|---|---|---|---|
| Too Long Alone | 7" | Pye | 7N17145 | 1966 | £1.50 | £4 | |

## CHEVRONS

| | | | | | | | |
|---|---|---|---|---|---|---|---|
| Lullaby | 7" | Top Rank | JAR308 | 1960 | £1.50 | £4 | |
| Sing Along Rock And Roll | LP | Time | T10008 | 1961 | £8 | £20 | US |

## CHEVY

| | | | | | | | |
|---|---|---|---|---|---|---|---|
| Taker | 7" | Avatar | AAA107 | 1980 | £2.50 | £6 | |

## CHEYNES

A well-respected but ultimately unsuccessful R&B group, the Cheynes included Peter Bardens and Mick Fleetwood, whose next project was the Peter Bs, and Phil Sawyer, who later turned up as a member of the second Spencer Davis Group.

| | | | | | | | |
|---|---|---|---|---|---|---|---|
| Down And Out | 7" | Columbia | DB7464 | 1965 | £15 | £30 | |
| Going To The River | 7" | Columbia | DB7368 | 1964 | £15 | £30 | |
| Respectable | 7" | Columbia | DB7153 | 1963 | £15 | £30 | |

## CHI-LITES

| | | | | | | | |
|---|---|---|---|---|---|---|---|
| Give It Away | LP | MCA | MUPS397 | 1968 | £4 | £10 | |
| Pretty Girl | 7" | Beacon | BEA119 | 1968 | £2.50 | £6 | |

# CHICAGO

Chicago have fallen into almost as much disfavour as Blood, Sweat and Tears, but many of their records are actually rather fine. The presence of brass instruments, however, does not make the group's music jazz-rock. The primary function of the brass is to give the music power, in the manner of the Atlantic recordings by Otis Redding and Wilson Pickett. Meanwhile, the most dominant solo voice is that of Terry Kath's guitar, which is fluent and exciting, though without, perhaps, being particularly individual.

| | | | | | | | |
|---|---|---|---|---|---|---|---|
| Chicago At Carnegie Hall | LP | Columbia | CQ30865 | 1974 | £10 | £25 | US quad, 4 LPs |
| Chicago II | LP | Columbia | GQ33258 | 1975 | £5 | £12 | US quad, double |
| Chicago III | LP | Columbia | C2Q30110 | 1974 | £5 | £12 | US quad, double |
| Chicago Transit Authority | LP | Columbia | GQ33255 | 1975 | £5 | £12 | US quad, double |
| Chicago Transit Authority | LP | Mobile Fidelity | MFSL2218 | 1983 | £5 | £12 | US audiophile, double |
| I'm A Man | 7" | CBS | 4503 | 1969 | £2.50 | £6 | |
| Live In Japan 1972 | LP | CBS/Sony | SCPS31 | 1975 | £5 | £12 | Japanese |

# CHICAGO LINE

| | | | | | | | |
|---|---|---|---|---|---|---|---|
| Shimmy Shimmy Ko Ko Bop | 7" | Philips | BF1488 | 1966 | £50 | £100 | |

# CHICKEN BONES

| | | | | | | | |
|---|---|---|---|---|---|---|---|
| Hard Rock In Concert | LP | Procom | 027606 | 1973 | £150 | £250 | German |

# CHICKEN SHACK

As the second most successful group signed to Blue Horizon (behind Fleetwood Mac), Chicken Shack relied heavily on the blues guitar of Stan Webb. He was not, however, as talented as he thought he was, as his embarrassing attempts to prove his versatility via live versions of Davey Graham's tricky instrumental, 'Angie', showed only too clearly. The real talent in the group was singer and pianist Christine Perfect (later Christine McVie), but she defected to Fleetwood Mac after the first two LPs.

| | | | | | | | |
|---|---|---|---|---|---|---|---|
| 100 Ton Chicken | LP | Blue Horizon | 763218 | 1969 | £10 | £25 | |
| 40 Blue Fingers Freshly Packed And Ready To Serve | LP | Blue Horizon | 763203 | 1968 | £15 | £30 | |
| Accept | LP | Blue Horizon | 763861 | 1970 | £10 | £25 | |
| Goodbye (Live) | LP | Nova | 621579 | 1974 | £5 | £12 | |
| Imagination Lady | LP | Deram | SDL5 | 1971 | £8 | £20 | |
| It's OK With Me Baby | 7" | Blue Horizon | 573135 | 1967 | £2 | £5 | |
| Maudie | 7" | Blue Horizon | 573168 | 1970 | £1.50 | £4 | |
| O.K. Ken? | 7" | Blue Horizon | 763209 | 1968 | £10 | £25 | |
| Sad Clown | 7" | Blue Horizon | 573176 | 1970 | £1.50 | £4 | |
| Tears In The Wind | 7" | Blue Horizon | 573160 | 1969 | £1.50 | £4 | |
| Unlucky Boy | LP | Deram | SML1100 | 1973 | £4 | £10 | |
| When The Train Comes Back | 7" | Blue Horizon | 573146 | 1968 | £1.50 | £4 | |
| Worried About My Woman | 7" | Blue Horizon | 573143 | 1968 | £2 | £5 | |

# CHICKEN SHED

| | | | | | | | |
|---|---|---|---|---|---|---|---|
| Alice | LP | Colby | AJ370 | 1977 | £25 | £50 | |
| Rock | LP | Colby | AJ371 | 1978 | £6 | £15 | |

# CHIEFS

| | | | | | | | |
|---|---|---|---|---|---|---|---|
| Apache | 7" | London | HLU8624 | 1958 | £10 | £20 | |
| Enchiladas | 7" | London | HLU8720 | 1958 | £6 | £12 | |

# CHIEFTAINS

| | | | | | | | |
|---|---|---|---|---|---|---|---|
| Chieftains | LP | Claddagh | CC2 | 1965 | £6 | £15 | |
| Chieftains Vol. 2 | LP | Claddagh | CC7 | 1969 | £5 | £12 | |
| Chieftains Vol. 3 | LP | Claddagh | CC10 | 1971 | £5 | £12 | |
| Chieftains Vol. 4 | LP | Claddagh | CC14 | 1973 | £5 | £12 | |

# CHIFFONS

| | | | | | | | |
|---|---|---|---|---|---|---|---|
| Chiffons | LP | Stateside | SL10040 | 1963 | £15 | £30 | |
| He's So Fine | LP | Laurie | LLP2018 | 1963 | £15 | £30 | US |
| He's So Fine | 7" | Stateside | SS172 | 1963 | £1.50 | £4 | |
| I Have A Boyfriend | 7" | Stateside | SS254 | 1964 | £1.50 | £4 | |
| Love So Fine | 7" | Stateside | SS230 | 1963 | £1.50 | £4 | |
| My Boyfriend's Back | 7" | Stateside | SS578 | 1967 | £4 | £8 | |
| My Secret Love | LP | B.T.Puppy | S1011 | 1970 | £6 | £15 | US |
| Nobody Knows What's Goin' On | 7" | Stateside | SS437 | 1965 | £5 | £10 | |
| One Fine Day | LP | Laurie | LLP2020 | 1963 | £15 | £30 | US |
| One Fine Day | 7" | Stateside | SS202 | 1963 | £1.50 | £4 | |
| Out Of This World | 7" | Stateside | SS533 | 1966 | £2 | £5 | |
| Sailor Boy | 7" | Stateside | SS332 | 1964 | £1.50 | £4 | |
| Stop, Look, & Listen | 7" | Stateside | SS559 | 1966 | £2 | £5 | |
| Sweet Talkin' Guy | LP | Stateside | (S)SL10190 | 1966 | £15 | £30 | |
| Sweet Talkin' Guy | 7" | Stateside | SS512 | 1966 | £1.50 | £4 | |
| They're So Fine | 7" EP | Stateside | SE1012 | 1964 | £15 | £30 | |

# CHILD

| | | | | | | | |
|---|---|---|---|---|---|---|---|
| Child | LP | Jubilee | JGS5673 | 1969 | £15 | £30 | US |

# CHILDE, SONNY

| | | | | | | | |
|---|---|---|---|---|---|---|---|
| Giving Up On Love | 7" | Decca | F12218 | 1965 | £2.50 | £6 | |
| Heartbreak | 7" | Polydor | 56141 | 1966 | £5 | £10 | |
| To Be Continued | LP | Polydor | 582003 | 1966 | £4 | £10 | |
| Two Lovers | 7" | Polydor | 56108 | 1966 | £7.50 | £15 | |

# CHILDREN

Bass player with the Children was Cassell Webb, who has subsequently enjoyed a moderately successful solo career.

| | | | | | | | |
|---|---|---|---|---|---|---|---|
| Rebirth | LP | Atco | SD33271 | 1968 | £25 | £50 | US |

| | | | | | | | |
|---|---|---|---|---|---|---|---|
| Rebirth | LP | Cinema | CLP1 | 1967 | £50 | £100 | US |

## CHILDREN OF ONE
| | | | | | | | |
|---|---|---|---|---|---|---|---|
| Children Of One | LP | Real | 101 | 1968 | £50 | £100 | US |

## CHILDREN OF THE NIGHT
| | | | | | | | |
|---|---|---|---|---|---|---|---|
| Dinner With Dracula | LP | Pip | PIP6822 | 1977 | £8 | £20 | US |

## CHILLI WILLI & THE RED HOT PEPPERS
| | | | | | | |
|---|---|---|---|---|---|---|
| Bongos Over Balham | LP | Mooncrest | CREST21 | 1974 | £4 | £10 |
| Kings Of The Robot Rhythm | LP | Revelation | REV002 | 1972 | £5 | £12 |

## CHILLIWACK
| | | | | | | | |
|---|---|---|---|---|---|---|---|
| All Over You | LP | A&M | 4375 | 1972 | £4 | £10 | US |
| Chilliwack | LP | London | SHU8418 | 1971 | £4 | £10 | |

## CHILLUM
| | | | | | | |
|---|---|---|---|---|---|---|
| Chillum | LP | Mushroom | 100MR11 | 1971 | £10 | £25 |

## CHIMERA
| | | | | | | | |
|---|---|---|---|---|---|---|---|
| Obstakel | LP | Spoof | | 1981 | £30 | £60 | Dutch |

## CHIMES
| | | | | | | |
|---|---|---|---|---|---|---|
| Once In A While | 7" | London | HLU9283 | 1961 | £7.50 | £15 |

## CHIMES FEATURING DENISE
| | | | | | | |
|---|---|---|---|---|---|---|
| I'll Be Waiting, I'll Be There | 7" | Decca | F11885 | 1964 | £1.50 | £4 |
| Say It Again | 7" | Decca | F11783 | 1963 | £1.50 | £4 |

## CHINA DOLLS
| | | | | | | |
|---|---|---|---|---|---|---|
| One Hit Wonder | 7" | Speed | FIRED001 | 1982 | £5 | £10 |

## CHINATOWN
| | | | | | | |
|---|---|---|---|---|---|---|
| Short And Sweet | 7" | Airship | AP138 | 1981 | £10 | £20 |

## CHIPMUNKS
| | | | | | | | |
|---|---|---|---|---|---|---|---|
| All My Loving | 7" | Liberty | LIB10170 | 1964 | £1.50 | £4 | |
| Chipmunk Song | 7" | London | HLU8762 | 1958 | £1.50 | £4 | |
| Sing The Beatles Hits | 7" EP | Liberty | LEP2188 | 1964 | £4 | £8 | French |

## CHIRCO
| | | | | | | | |
|---|---|---|---|---|---|---|---|
| Visitation | LP | Crested Butte | 701598 | 1972 | £20 | £40 | US |

## CHISHOLM, GEORGE
| | | | | | | |
|---|---|---|---|---|---|---|
| George Chisholm Sextet | LP | Decca | LK4147 | 1956 | £5 | £12 |
| Honky Tonk | 7" | Beltona | BL2671 | 1956 | £1.50 | £4 |

## CHITINOUS ENSEMBLE
| | | | | | | |
|---|---|---|---|---|---|---|
| Chitinous Ensemble | LP | Deram | SML1093 | 1971 | £30 | £60 |

## CHOCOLATE FROG
| | | | | | | |
|---|---|---|---|---|---|---|
| Butchers And Bakers | 7" | Atlantic | 584207 | 1968 | £6 | £12 |

## CHOCOLATE MILK
| | | | | | | |
|---|---|---|---|---|---|---|
| Actions Speak Louder Than Words | 7" | RCA | RCA2592 | 1975 | £1.50 | £4 |
| Comin' | LP | RCA | PL11830 | 1977 | £8 | £20 |

## CHOCOLATE WATCH BAND
| | | | | | | | |
|---|---|---|---|---|---|---|---|
| Inner Mystique | LP | Tower | ST5106 | 1968 | £100 | £200 | US |
| No Way Out | LP | Tower | (S)T5096 | 1967 | £100 | £200 | US |
| One Step Beyond | LP | Tower | ST5153 | 1969 | £37.50 | £75 | US |

## CHOCOLATE WATCH BAND (2)
| | | | | | | |
|---|---|---|---|---|---|---|
| Requiem | 7" | Decca | F12704 | 1967 | £7.50 | £15 |
| Sound Of The Summer | 7" | Decca | F12649 | 1967 | £7.50 | £15 |

## CHOIR
| | | | | | | |
|---|---|---|---|---|---|---|
| It's Cold Outside | 7" | Major Minor | MM537 | 1968 | £12.50 | £25 |
| When You Were With Me | 7" | Major Minor | MM557 | 1968 | £10 | £20 |

## CHOPYN
| | | | | | | |
|---|---|---|---|---|---|---|
| Grand Slam | LP | Jet | LP08 | 1975 | £6 | £15 |

## CHORDETTES
| | | | | | | | |
|---|---|---|---|---|---|---|---|
| Baby Of Mine | 7" | London | HLA8566 | 1958 | £5 | £10 | |
| Born To Be With You | 7" | London | HA7011 | 1956 | £6 | £12 | export |
| Born To Be With You | 7" | London | HLA8302 | 1956 | £12.50 | £25 | |
| Chordettes | LP | London | HAA2088 | 1958 | £20 | £40 | |
| Chordettes | 7" EP | London | REA1228 | 1960 | £15 | £30 | |
| Chordettes Sing | LP | London | HAA2441 | 1962 | £10 | £25 | |
| Close Harmony | LP | Cadence | CLP3002 | 1957 | £20 | £40 | US |
| Duddlesack Polka | 7" | London | HLA8217 | 1956 | £10 | £20 | |
| Girl's Work Is Never Done | 7" | London | HLA8926 | 1959 | £2.50 | £6 | |
| Harmony Encores | 10" LP | Columbia | CL6218 | 1953 | £20 | £40 | US |
| Harmony Time | 10" LP | Columbia | CL6111 | 1950 | £20 | £40 | US |
| Harmony Time Vol. 2 | 10" LP | Columbia | CL6170 | 1951 | £20 | £40 | US |
| Hummingbird | 7" | London | HLA8169 | 1955 | £12.50 | £25 | |
| Just Between You And Me | 7" | London | HLA8473 | 1957 | £5 | £10 | |

| | | | | | | |
|---|---|---|---|---|---|---|
| Lay Down Your Arms | 7" | London | HLA8323 | 1956 | £10 | £20 | |
| Like A Baby | 7" | London | HLA8497 | 1957 | £5 | £10 | |
| Listen | LP | Columbia | CL956 | 1954 | £20 | £40 | *US* |
| Lollipop | 7" | London | HLA8584 | 1958 | £4 | £8 | |
| Love Is A Two Way Street | 7" | London | HLA8654 | 1958 | £4 | £8 | |
| Mister Sandman | 7" | Columbia | SCM5158 | 1954 | £62.50 | £125 | |
| Never On Sunday | LP | Cadence | CLP3062/25062 | 1962 | £8 | £20 | *US* |
| Never On Sunday | 7" | London | HLA9400 | 1961 | £1.50 | £4 | |
| No Other Arms No Other Lips | 7" | London | HLA8809 | 1959 | £2 | £5 | |
| Our Melody | 7" | London | HLA8264 | 1956 | £12.50 | £25 | |
| Your Requests | 10" LP | Columbia | CL6285 | 1953 | £20 | £40 | *US* |

## CHORDS
| | | | | | | |
|---|---|---|---|---|---|---|
| Sh'boom | 7" | Columbia | SCM5133 | 1954 | £700 | £1000 | *best auctioned* |

## CHORDS FIVE
| | | | | | | |
|---|---|---|---|---|---|---|
| I'm Only Dreaming | 7" | Island | WI3044 | 1967 | £15 | £30 | |
| Same Old Fat Man | 7" | Polydor | 56261 | 1968 | £20 | £40 | |
| Some People | 7" | Jayboy | BOY6 | 1968 | £10 | £20 | |

## CHOSEN FEW
The Chosen Few eventually evolved into Skip Bifferty. The guitarist, however, who was the composer of all the songs on the two singles, went his own way, eventually forming a successful folk-rock group. They were Lindisfarne – he, of course, was Alan Hull.

| | | | | | | |
|---|---|---|---|---|---|---|
| I Won't Be Around You Anymore | 7" | Pye | 7N15905 | 1965 | £4 | £8 | |
| So Much To Look Forward To | 7" | Pye | 7N15942 | 1965 | £4 | £8 | |

## CHOSEN FEW (2)
| | | | | | | |
|---|---|---|---|---|---|---|
| I Can Make Your Dreams Come True | 7" | Polydor | 2058721 | 1976 | £2.50 | £6 | |
| You Mean Everything To Me | 7" | Polydor | 2058975 | 1978 | £2.50 | £6 | |

## CHRIS, PETER & THE OUTCASTS
| | | | | | | |
|---|---|---|---|---|---|---|
| Over The Hill | 7" | Columbia | DB7923 | 1966 | £7.50 | £15 | |

## CHRIS & COSEY
| | | | | | | |
|---|---|---|---|---|---|---|
| Sweet Surprise | cass | Electronic Soundmaker | | 198– | £6 | £15 | *with magazine* |

## CHRIS & STUDENTS
| | | | | | | |
|---|---|---|---|---|---|---|
| Lass Of Richmond Hill | 7" | Parlophone | R4806 | 1961 | £5 | £10 | |

## CHRISTIAN, BOBBY
| | | | | | | |
|---|---|---|---|---|---|---|
| Crickets On Parade | 7" | Oriole | CB1384 | 1957 | £7.50 | £15 | |

## CHRISTIAN, CHARLIE
| | | | | | | |
|---|---|---|---|---|---|---|
| Profoundly Blue | 7" | Blue Note | 451634 | 1964 | £1.50 | £4 | *Ike Quebec B side* |
| With The Benny Goodman Sextet And Orchestra | LP | Philips | BBL7172 | 1957 | £5 | £12 | |

## CHRISTIAN, HANS
This was, for a short time, the stage name of the future lead singer of Yes, Jon Anderson.

| | | | | | | |
|---|---|---|---|---|---|---|
| Mississippi Hobo | 7" | Parlophone | R5698 | 1968 | £20 | £40 | |
| Never My Love | 7" | Parlophone | R5676 | 1968 | £20 | £40 | |

## CHRISTIAN, LIZ
| | | | | | | |
|---|---|---|---|---|---|---|
| Suddenly You Find Love | 7" | CBS | 202520 | 1967 | £15 | £30 | |

## CHRISTIAN, NEIL
Lead guitarist for a time with Neil Christian's group, the Crusaders, was the young Jimmy Page (or Elmer Twitch, as he liked to be known at the time), although he does not play on many of the singles.

| | | | | | | |
|---|---|---|---|---|---|---|
| All Things Bright And Beautiful | 7" | Pye | 7N17372 | 1967 | £2 | £5 | |
| Big Beat Drum | 7" | Columbia | DB4938 | 1962 | £6 | £12 | |
| Get A Load Of This | 7" | Columbia | DB7075 | 1963 | £2 | £5 | |
| Honey Hush | 7" | Columbia | DB7289 | 1964 | £2.50 | £6 | |
| Little Bit Of Something Else | 7" EP | Columbia | SEG8492 | 1966 | £15 | £30 | |
| Oops | 7" | Strike | JH313 | 1966 | £1.50 | £4 | |
| That's Nice | 7" EP | Riviera | 231161 | 1966 | £15 | £30 | *French* |
| That's Nice | 7" | Strike | JH301 | 1966 | £1.50 | £4 | |
| Two At A Time | 7" | Strike | JH319 | 1966 | £1.50 | £4 | |

## CHRISTIAN DEATH
| | | | | | | |
|---|---|---|---|---|---|---|
| Official Anthology Of Live Bootlegs | LP | Jungle | NOS006 | 1986 | £8 | £20 | *black & yellow cover* |
| Only Theatre Of Pain | LP | No Future | FL2 | 1983 | £8 | £20 | |
| Zero Sex | CD-s | Jungle | JUNG050CD | 1989 | £2 | £5 | |

## CHRISTIE, JOHN
| | | | | | | |
|---|---|---|---|---|---|---|
| Fourth Of July | 7" | Polydor | 2058496 | 1974 | £2.50 | £6 | |
| Fourth Of July | 7" | Polydor | 2058496 | 1974 | £6 | £12 | *picture sleeve* |

## CHRISTIE, KEITH
| | | | | | | |
|---|---|---|---|---|---|---|
| Homage To The Duke | 10" LP | Esquire | 20047 | 1955 | £6 | £15 | |

## CHRISTIE, LOU
| | | | | | | |
|---|---|---|---|---|---|---|
| All That Glitters Isn't Gold | 7" | King | KG1036 | 1966 | £1.50 | £4 | |
| Lightnin' Strikes | LP | MGM | C(S)8008 | 1966 | £4 | £10 | |

| | | | | | | | | |
|---|---|---|---|---|---|---|---|---|
| Lou Christie | LP | Roulette | (S)R25208 | 1963 | £5 | £12 | US |
| Lou Christie Strikes Back | LP | Co & Ce | LP1231 | 1966 | £5 | £12 | US |
| Strikes Again | LP | Colpix | PXL551 | 1966 | £4 | £10 | |

## CHRISTMAS
| | | | | | | | |
|---|---|---|---|---|---|---|---|
| Lies To Live By | LP | Daffodil | 10047 | 1974 | £25 | £50 | US |

## CHRISTMAS, JOHNNY & THE SUNSPOTS
| | | | | | | |
|---|---|---|---|---|---|---|
| I'm Gonna Sing Sing Sing | 7" EP | Starlite | STEP5 | 1958 | £2 | £5 |

## CHRISTMAS, KEITH
| | | | | | | |
|---|---|---|---|---|---|---|
| Fable Of The Wings | LP | B&C | CAS1015 | 1971 | £4 | £10 |
| Pigmy | LP | B&C | CAS1041 | 1971 | £4 | £10 |
| Stimulus | LP | RCA | SF8059 | 1969 | £15 | £30 |

## CHRISTOPHER
| | | | | | | | |
|---|---|---|---|---|---|---|---|
| Whatcha Gonna Do | LP | Chris-tee | PRP12411 | 1970 | £1050 | £1500 | US |
| Whatcha Gonna Do | LP | Rockadelic | | 1991 | £5 | £12 | US |

## CHRISTOPHER (2)
| | | | | | | | |
|---|---|---|---|---|---|---|---|
| Christopher | LP | Metromedia | 1024 | 1970 | £75 | £150 | US |

## CHRISTY, JUNE
| | | | | | | | |
|---|---|---|---|---|---|---|---|
| Duet | LP | Capitol | T656 | 1955 | £6 | £15 | US |
| Gone For The Day | LP | Capitol | T902 | 1957 | £6 | £15 | |
| June Fair And Warmer | LP | Capitol | T833 | 1957 | £6 | £15 | US |
| June's Got Rhythm | LP | Capitol | T1076 | 1959 | £4 | £10 | |
| Misty Miss Christy | LP | Capitol | T725 | 1956 | £6 | £15 | US |
| Pete Kelly's Blues | 7" | Capitol | CL14355 | 1955 | £1.50 | £4 | |
| Something Cool | LP | Capitol | T516 | 1955 | £6 | £15 | US |
| Something Cool | 7" EP | Capitol | EAP1516 | 1955 | £2 | £5 | |
| Something Cool | 10" LP | Capitol | LC6682 | 1954 | £8 | £20 | |
| This Is June Christy | LP | Capitol | T1006 | 1959 | £6 | £15 | |

## CHROME
| | | | | | | | |
|---|---|---|---|---|---|---|---|
| Alien Soundtracks | LP | Siren | DE2100 | 1978 | £6 | £15 | US |
| Firebomb | 7" | Don't Fall Off The Mountain | Z17 | 1982 | £2 | £5 | |
| Inworlds | 12" | Don't Fall Off The Mountain | Y3 | 1981 | £3 | £8 | |
| New Age | 7" | Beggars Banquet | BEG36 | 1980 | £1.50 | £4 | |
| No Humans Allowed | LP | Siren | 7140 | 1981 | £6 | £15 | US |
| Read Only Memory | 12" | Siren | RS12007 | 1980 | £3 | £8 | with poster |
| Visitation | LP | Siren | DE1000 | 1977 | £6 | £15 | US |

## CHRYSTAL BAND
| | | | | | | |
|---|---|---|---|---|---|---|
| Chrystal Band | LP | Carole | | | £25 | £50 |

## CHUBBY & THE HONEYSUCKERS
| | | | | | | |
|---|---|---|---|---|---|---|
| Emergency Ward | 7" | Rio | R75 | 1966 | £2.50 | £6 |

## CHUCK & BETTY
| | | | | | | |
|---|---|---|---|---|---|---|
| Sissy Britches | 7" | Brunswick | 05815 | 1959 | £10 | £20 |

## CHUCK & DOBBY
| | | | | | | |
|---|---|---|---|---|---|---|
| Cool School | 7" | Blue Beat | BB23 | 1960 | £6 | £12 |
| Do Du Wap | 7" | Blue Beat | BB39 | 1961 | £6 | £12 |
| Lovey Dovey | 7" | Starlite | ST45044 | 1961 | £5 | £10 |
| Oh Fanny | 7" | Blue Beat | BB59 | 1961 | £6 | £12 |
| Sweeter Than Honey | 7" | Starlite | ST45043 | 1961 | £5 | £10 |
| Till The End Of Time | 7" | Blue Beat | BB19 | 1960 | £6 | £12 |

## CHUCK & GARY
| | | | | | | |
|---|---|---|---|---|---|---|
| Teenie Weenie Jeannie | 7" | HMV | POP466 | 1958 | £10 | £20 |

## CHUCKS
| | | | | | | |
|---|---|---|---|---|---|---|
| Chucks | 7" EP | Decca | DFE8562 | 1964 | £7.50 | £15 |

## CHURCH
| | | | | | | | |
|---|---|---|---|---|---|---|---|
| Almost With You | 7" | Carrere | CAR247 | 1982 | £2.50 | £6 | |
| Different Man | 7" | Carrere | CHURCHR5A | 1983 | £5 | £10 | no picture sleeve |
| It's No Reason | 12" | Carrere | CART336 | 1984 | £2.50 | £6 | |
| Metropolis | CD-s | Arista | 663086 | 1990 | £2 | £5 | |
| She Never Said | 7" | Parlophone | A367 | 1981 | £20 | £40 | Australian |
| Sing Songs | 12" | Carrere | CHURCH5 | 1983 | £5 | £12 | |
| Starfish | LP | Arista | 208895 | 1988 | £5 | £12 | with bonus 12" |
| Too Fast For You | 7" | Parlophone | A536/525 | 1981 | £20 | £40 | Australian double |
| Under The Milky Way | CD-s | Arista | 659778 | 1988 | £2 | £5 | |
| Unguarded Moment | 7" | Carrere | CAR212 | 1982 | £2.50 | £6 | |
| Unguarded Moment | 7" | Carrere | CAR257 | 1982 | £1.50 | £4 | |
| Unguarded Moment | 10" | Carrere | CAREP257 | 1982 | £4 | £10 | |

## CHURCH, EUGENE
| | | | | | | | |
|---|---|---|---|---|---|---|---|
| Miami | 7" | London | HL8940 | 1959 | £15 | £30 | |

## CHURCHILL, SAVANNAH
| | | | | | | |
|---|---|---|---|---|---|---|
| I Want To Be Loved | 7" | London | HLW9273 | 1961 | £1.50 | £4 |

## CHURLS
Churls .................................... LP ...... A&M ............. SP4169 ................. 1969 £5 .......... £12 ........................ US

## CHWYS
Gwr Bonheddig Hael ................................ 7" ...... Afon .............. RAS001 .............. 1975 £2.50 ....... £6

## CICERO
Dave Cicero's handful of single releases bear the Pet Shop Boys' Spaghetti Recordings imprint. Apart from the first, the singles are also produced by the duo, the connection being the reason for collectors seeking them out.

Heaven Must Have Sent You Back To Me . CD-s .. Polydor .......... CIOCD1 .............. 1991 £3 .......... £8
Heaven Must Have Sent You Back To Me . CD-s .. Polydor .......... CIOCD5 .............. 1992 £2 .......... £5
Live For Today ..................................... CD-s .. Polydor .......... CIOCD7 .............. 1992 £2.50 ....... £6
Love Is Everywhere .............................. CD-s .. Polydor .......... CIOCD3 .............. 1992 £2 .......... £5
That Loving Feeling ............................. CD-s .. Polydor .......... CIOCD4 .............. 1992 £2.50 ....... £6

## CIGARETTES
Can't Sleep At Night .............................. 7" ...... Dead Good ...... DEAD10 .............. 1980 £2.50 ....... £6
They're Back Again, Here They Come ...... 7" ...... Company ........ CIGCO008 ........... 1979 £5 .......... £10

## CIMARONS
Bad Day At Black Rock ........................... 7" ...... Reggae .......... REG3003 .............. 1970 £1.50 ....... £4
In Time ............................................... LP ...... Trojan............. TRLS87 ................. 1974 £4 .......... £10

## CINDERELLAS
Baby Baby I Still Love You ...................... 7" ...... Colpix .......... PX11126 .............. 1964 £20 .......... £40
Mr. Dee-Jay .......................................... 7" ...... Brunswick ...... 05794 .................. 1959 £7.50 ...... £15
Trouble With Boys ................................. 7" ...... Philips .......... PB1012 ................ 1960 £4 .......... £8

## CINDY
Let Me Serve You .................................. LP ...... York ................................................ £30 ....... £60

## CINDY & LINDY
Saturday Night In Tiajuana ..................... 7" ...... Coral ............ Q72368 ............... 1959 £1.50 ....... £4

## CINEMA FACE
Cinema Face ......................................... LP ........................ RS2 ........................ £8 ....... £20 .............. Canadian

## CINNAMOND, ROBERT
You Rambling Boys Of Pleasure ............... LP ...... Topic.............. 12T269 ................ 1976 £4 .......... £10

## CIRCLE
Paris Concert ....................................... LP ...... ECM ............ ECM1018/9ST ....... 1972 £6 .......... £15 .................... double

## CIRCLES
Take Your Time ..................................... 7" ...... Island ............ WI279 ................ 1966 £15 .......... £30

## CIRCLES (2)
Circles ................................................ 7" ...... Graduate ........ GRAD17 .............. 1985 £1.50 ....... £4

## CIRCULATION
Circulation .......................................... LP ...... Deroy ............................... 1969 £330 ..... £500

## CIRCUS
Circus played a serviceable rock style with jazz overtones and were chiefly notable for launching the career of Mel Collins, whose saxophone and flute have been used to spice literally dozens of records since.

Circus ................................................. LP ...... Transatlantic .... TRA207 ................ 1969 £15 ......... £30
Do You Dream ...................................... 7" ...... Parlophone ...... R5672 ................ 1968 £12.50 .... £25
Sink Or Swim ....................................... 7" ...... Parlophone ...... R5633 ................ 1967 £2.50 ....... £6

## CIRCUS 2000
Circus 2000 ......................................... LP ...... Rift .......... RFLLP14049 ......... 1969 £75 ....... £150 .................... Italian
Escape From A Box ................................ LP ...... Rift .............................. 1970 £50 ....... £100

## CIRCUS MAXIMUS
Circus Maximus .................................... LP ...... Vanguard ........ VSD79260 ............ 1967 £8 .......... £20 ........................ US
Neverland Revisited ............................... LP ...... Vanguard ........ VSD79274 ............ 1968 £6 .......... £15 ........................ US

## CIRKEL
First Goodbye ...................................... LP ...... Goodbye ........................... 1983 £8 .......... £20 .................. Dutch

## CIRKUS
Future Shock ....................................... LP ...... Shock ............ SHOCK1 .............. 1977 £75 ....... £150
Melissa ............................................... 7" ...... Guardian ........ GRCA4 .............. 1970 £20 ........ £40
One .................................................... LP ...... RCB ............ RCB1 ................ 1973 £50 ....... £100

## CITATIONS
Moon Race .......................................... 7" ...... Columbia ........ DB7068 .............. 1963 £2.50 ....... £6

## CITY
Carole King's first LP was issued under the name of a group, City, but the sound is the same as on its successors. Following her success with *Tapestry*, the City album was counterfeited – copies with black and white covers are the unofficial ones.

Now That Everything's Been Said ............. LP ...... Ode ............... Z1244012 .............. 1969 £6 .......... £15 .............. colour cover

## CITY OF WESTMINSTER STRING BAND
| | | | | | | |
|---|---|---|---|---|---|---|
| Touch Of Velvet A Sting Of Brass | 7" | Pye | 7N17620 | 1968 | £2 | £5 |

## CITY PREACHERS
| | | | | | | |
|---|---|---|---|---|---|---|
| Back To The City | LP | Hor Zu | SHZM265 | 1972 | £6 | £15 | German |
| City Preachers | LP | Decca | SLK16435 | 1966 | £6 | £15 | German |
| Cool Water | LP | Decca | SLK16482P | 1966 | £6 | £15 | German |
| Folk Songs | LP | Decca | SLK16382 | 1966 | £6 | £15 | German |
| Warum | LP | Philips | 843798PY | 1966 | £8 | £20 | German |

## CITY RAMBLERS SKIFFLE GROUP
| | | | | | | |
|---|---|---|---|---|---|---|
| Delia's Gone | 7" EP | Tempo | EXA77 | 1958 | £2.50 | £6 |
| Delia's Gone | 7" | Tempo | A165 | 1957 | £1.50 | £4 |
| Ella Speed | 7" | Tempo | A158 | 1957 | £1.50 | £4 |
| Good Morning Blues | 7" EP | Tempo | EXA71 | 1957 | £2.50 | £6 |
| I Shall Not Be Moved | 7" EP | Storyville | SEP345 | 195– | £4 | £8 |
| I Want A Girl | 7" EP | Storyville | SEP327 | 195– | £4 | £8 |
| I Want A Girl | 7" EP | Tempo | EXA59 | 1957 | £2.50 | £6 |
| Mama Don't Allow | 7" | Tempo | A161 | 1957 | £1.50 | £4 |

## CITY WAITES
| | | | | | | |
|---|---|---|---|---|---|---|
| City Waites | LP | Decca | SKL5264 | 1976 | £37.50 | £75 |
| Fox | 7" | EMI | EMI2149 | 1974 | £1.50 | £4 |
| Gorgeous Gallery Of Gallant Inventions | LP | EMI | EMC3017 | 1974 | £30 | £60 |

## CLAGUE

The two singles credited to Clague were the work of the same band that played on John Peel's radio show as Coyne-Clague and then made two LPs as Siren.

| | | | | | | |
|---|---|---|---|---|---|---|
| Bottle Up And Go | 7" | Dandelion | K4493 | 1970 | £1.50 | £4 |
| Stride | 7" | Dandelion | K4494 | 1970 | £1.50 | £4 |

## CLANCY, WILLIE
| | | | | | | |
|---|---|---|---|---|---|---|
| Minstrel From Clare | LP | Topic | 12T175 | 1967 | £6 | £15 |

## CLANCY, WILLY & MICHAEL GORMAN
| | | | | | | |
|---|---|---|---|---|---|---|
| Irish Jigs, Reels And Hornpipes | 10" LP | Folkways | FW6819 | 1956 | £15 | £30 | US |

## CLANCY BROTHERS & TOMMY MAKEM
| | | | | | | |
|---|---|---|---|---|---|---|
| At Home With The Clancy Brothers | LP | Emerald | GEM/S1006 | 1968 | £4 | £10 |
| Boys Won't Leave The Girls Alone | LP | CBS | (S)BPG62164 | 1963 | £4 | £10 |
| First Hurrah! | LP | CBS | (S)BPG62283 | 1964 | £4 | £10 |
| Freedom's Sons | LP | CBS | 62775 | 1967 | £4 | £10 |
| Hearty And Hellish | LP | CBS | BPG62020 | 1962 | £4 | £10 |
| In Concert | LP | CBS | (S)BPG63070 | 1967 | £4 | £10 |
| In Ireland! | LP | CBS | (S)BPG62479 | 1965 | £4 | £10 |
| In Person At Carnegie Hall | LP | CBS | (S)BPG62192 | 1963 | £4 | £10 |
| Isn't It Grand Boys | LP | CBS | 62674 | 1966 | £4 | £10 |

## CLANNAD
| | | | | | | |
|---|---|---|---|---|---|---|
| Clannad | LP | Philips | 6392013 | 1973 | £6 | £15 | Irish |
| Clannad 2 | LP | Gael-Linn | CEF041 | 1974 | £6 | £15 | Irish |
| Dulaman | LP | Gael Linn | CEF058 | 1976 | £4 | £10 | Irish |
| Hourglass | CD-s | RCA | PD43076 | 1989 | £2 | £5 | |
| In A Lifetime | CD-s | RCA | PD42874 | 1989 | £2 | £5 | with Bono |
| In Concert | LP | Ogham | BLB5001 | 1978 | £4 | £10 | Irish |

## CLANTON, JIMMY
| | | | | | | |
|---|---|---|---|---|---|---|
| Another Sleepless Night | 7" | Top Rank | JAR382 | 1960 | £1.50 | £4 | |
| Best Of Jimmy Clanton | LP | Philips | PHM2/PHS600154 | 1964 | £8 | £20 | US |
| Come Back | 7" | Top Rank | JAR509 | 1960 | £1.50 | £4 | |
| Go Jimmy Go | 7" | Top Rank | JAR269 | 1960 | £1.50 | £4 | |
| Jimmy's Blue | LP | Ace | 1008 | 1960 | £10 | £25 | US |
| Jimmy's Blue | LP | Ace | 1008 | 1960 | £20 | £40 | US, blue vinyl |
| Jimmy's Happy | LP | Ace | 1007 | 1960 | £10 | £25 | US |
| Jimmy's Happy | LP | Ace | 1007 | 1960 | £20 | £40 | US, red vinyl |
| Just A Dream | LP | Ace | 1001 | 1959 | £15 | £30 | US |
| Just A Dream | 7" EP | London | RES1224 | 1959 | £15 | £30 | |
| Just A Dream | 7" | London | HLS8699 | 1958 | £5 | £10 | |
| Letter To An Angel | 7" | London | HL7066 | 1958 | £4 | £8 | export |
| Letter To An Angel | 7" | London | HLS8779 | 1959 | £10 | £20 | |
| My Best To You | LP | Ace | 1011 | 1961 | £15 | £30 | US |
| My Own True Love | 7" | Top Rank | JAR189 | 1959 | £1.50 | £4 | |
| Teenage Millionaire | LP | Ace | 1014 | 1961 | £15 | £30 | US |
| Venus In Blue Jeans | LP | Ace | 1026 | 1962 | £15 | £30 | US |
| What Am I Gonna Do | 7" | Top Rank | JAR544 | 1961 | £1.50 | £4 | |

## CLAP
| | | | | | | |
|---|---|---|---|---|---|---|
| Have You Reached Yet? | LP | Nova Sol | 1001 | | £50 | £100 | US |

## CLAPTON, ERIC

Anyone attempting to collect a complete set of the records with which Eric Clapton has been involved is facing an extremely difficult task. For Clapton probably holds the prize for the highest number of guest appearances, including some on records that have become extremely rare. The compilation album *Clapton* was withdrawn and supposedly only four copies were left undestroyed. In fact many more than this have appeared on the market and the value of the record remains stubbornly low.

| | | | | | | | |
|---|---|---|---|---|---|---|---|
| 461 Ocean Boulevard | LP | RSO | QD4801 | 1974 | £6 | £15 | US quad |
| 461 Ocean Boulevard | CD | Mobile Fidelity | UDCD594 | 1993 | £6 | £15 | US audiophile |
| After Midnight | CD-s | Polydor | PZCD8 | 1988 | £2 | £5 | |
| After Midnight | 12" | Polydor | PZ8 | 1988 | £2.50 | £6 | |
| Bad Love | CD-s | Duck | W2644CD | 1990 | £2 | £5 | |
| Bad Love | 12" | Duck | W2644T | 1990 | £2.50 | £6 | |
| Behind The Mask | 12" | Duck | W8461T | 1987 | £2.50 | £6 | |
| Clapton | LP | RSO | 2479702 | 1978 | £10 | £25 | |
| Cream Of Eric Clapton | CD | Polydor | 8335192 | 1987 | £30 | £60 | promo box set with album & cassette |
| Edge Of Darkness | CD-s | BBC | CDRSL178 | 1989 | £10 | £20 | 3" single |
| Edge Of Darkness | 7" | BBC | RESL178 | 1985 | £2.50 | £6 | |
| Edge Of Darkness | 12" | BBC | 12RSL178 | 1985 | £3 | £8 | |
| Forever Man | 12" | Duck | W9069T | 1985 | £2.50 | £6 | |
| Holy Mother | 12" | Duck | W8141T | 1987 | £2.50 | £6 | |
| I've Got A Rock And Roll Heart | 12" | Duck | W9780T | 1983 | £2.50 | £6 | |
| It's In The Way That You Use It | 12" | Duck | W8397T | 1987 | £2.50 | £6 | |
| Journeyman | 7" | Duck | ECBOX2 | 1989 | £30 | £60 | promo 6 single boxed set |
| Just One Night | LP | Nautilus | NR32 | 1981 | £6 | £15 | US audiophile double |
| Just One Night | CD | Mobile Fidelity | UDCD2608 | 1994 | £10 | £25 | US audiophile double |
| Layla | CD-s | Polydor | PZCD163 | 1991 | £2 | £5 | |
| Layla And Other Assorted Love Songs | CD | Mobile Fidelity | UDCD585 | 1993 | £8 | £20 | US audiophile, original mix |
| No Alibis | CD-s | WEA | W9981CD | 1990 | £2 | £5 | |
| No Alibis | 12" | Duck | W9981T | 1990 | £2.50 | £6 | |
| Pretending | 12" | Duck | W9770T | 1990 | £2.50 | £6 | |
| Shape You're In | 12" | Duck | W9701T | 1983 | £2.50 | £6 | |
| Slow Down Linda | 12" | Duck | W9651T | 1983 | £2.50 | £6 | |
| Slowhand | LP | Mobile Fidelity | MFSL1030 | 1979 | £5 | £12 | US audiophile |
| Slowhand | CD | Mobile Fidelity | UDCD553 | 1991 | £6 | £15 | US audiophile |
| Tearing Us Apart | 12" | WEA | W8299T | 1987 | £2.50 | £6 | with Tina Turner |
| Tearing Us Apart | 12" | WEA | W8299TP | 1987 | £3 | £8 | with Tina Turner, picture disc |
| Tears In Heaven | CD-s | Reprise | W0081CD | 1992 | £2 | £5 | |
| Tears In Heaven | 12" | Reprise | W0081T | 1992 | £2.50 | £6 | |
| There's One In Every Crowd | LP | RSO | QD4806 | 1974 | £5 | £12 | US quad |
| Twenty-Four Nights | 7" | Duck | ECB3/ECL1/7 | 1991 | £20 | £40 | promo 7 single boxed set |
| Wonderful Tonight | 12" | Polydor | POSPX881 | 1987 | £2.50 | £6 | |
| Wonderful Tonight (live) | 12" | RSO | JONX001 | 1979 | £3 | £8 | promo |

## CLARE, ALAN

| | | | | | | | |
|---|---|---|---|---|---|---|---|
| Jazz Around The Clock | LP | Decca | LK4260 | 1959 | £6 | £15 | |

## CLARENDONIANS

| | | | | | | | |
|---|---|---|---|---|---|---|---|
| Baby Baby | 7" | Caltone | TONE114 | 1968 | £4 | £8 | |
| Baby Don't Do It | 7" | Trojan | TR7719 | 1970 | £1.50 | £4 | |
| Come Along | 7" | Duke | DU97 | 1970 | £1.50 | £4 | |
| Goodbye Forever | 7" | Island | WI3041 | 1967 | £5 | £10 | |
| He Who Laughs Last | 7" | Studio One | SO2007 | 1967 | £6 | £12 | Gaylads B side |
| I Can't Go On | 7" | Studio One | SO2004 | 1967 | £6 | £12 | |
| I'll Never Change | 7" | Island | WI3005 | 1966 | £5 | £10 | |
| Jerk | 7" | Ska Beat | JB261 | 1966 | £5 | £10 | |
| Little Girl | 7" | Island | WI180 | 1965 | £5 | £10 | |
| Ma Bien | 7" | Ska Beat | JB219 | 1965 | £5 | £10 | |
| Musical Train | 7" | Rio | R115 | 1967 | £4 | £8 | |
| Rudie Bam Bam | 7" | Rio | R112 | 1966 | £4 | £8 | |
| Sweetheart Of Beauty | 7" | Island | WI3032 | 1967 | £5 | £10 | |
| Try Me One More Time | 7" | Island | WI284 | 1966 | £5 | £10 | |

## CLARK, CHRIS

| | | | | | | | |
|---|---|---|---|---|---|---|---|
| C C Rides Again | LP | Weed | WS801 | 1967 | £20 | £40 | US |
| From Head To Toe | 7" | Tamla Motown | TMG624 | 1967 | £10 | £20 | |
| I Want To Go Back There Again | 7" | Tamla Motown | TMG638 | 1968 | £7.50 | £15 | |
| Love's Gone Bad | 7" | Tamla Motown | TMG591 | 1967 | £15 | £30 | |
| Soul Sounds | LP | Tamla Motown | (S)TML11069 | 1968 | £20 | £40 | |

## CLARK, CLAUDINE

| | | | | | | | |
|---|---|---|---|---|---|---|---|
| Party Lights | LP | Chancellor | CHL5029 | 1962 | £15 | £30 | US |
| Party Lights | 7" | Pye | 7N25157 | 1962 | £1.50 | £4 | |
| Strength To Be Strong | 7" | Sue | WI4039 | 1967 | £5 | £10 | |
| Walk Me Home From The Party | 7" | Pye | 7N25186 | 1963 | £1.50 | £4 | |

## CLARK, DAVE FIVE

Anyone watching the repeat showings of the influential *Ready Steady Go* TV programme would be forgiven for presuming that the biggest stars of the sixties were the Dave Clark Five. In truth, the group was very successful, particularly in America, but the reason for their dominance of the *RSG* videos lies in Clark's astute purchase of the rights to the show back when few people would have predicted a nostalgia boom for all things sixties. At the time, Clark had apparently epitomized the rock music cliché of the thick drummer, with singer Mike Smith appearing to be the group's real leader. However, Dave Clark was actually highly adept at managing the fortunes of his own group. Unlike many of the sixties stars, who fell victim to highly disadvantageous royalty deals, Clark was clever enough to retain the rights to his own material and merely leased it to his record company.

| | | | | | | | |
|---|---|---|---|---|---|---|---|
| 5 By 5 – Go! | LP | Epic | LN24/BN26236 | 1967 | £8 | £20 | US |
| 5 By 5 – Go! (14 Titles By Dave Clark) | LP | Columbia | SCX6309 | 1968 | £5 | £15 | |
| All Time Greats | 7" | Columbia | DB8963 | 1972 | £1.50 | £4 | picture sleeve |
| American Tour | LP | Epic | LN24/BN26117 | 1964 | £8 | £20 | US |

## DAVE CLARK FIVE (continued)

| Title | Format | Label | Cat No | Year | | | Notes |
|---|---|---|---|---|---|---|---|
| Bits And Pieces | 7" EP | Columbia | ESRF1525 | 1964 | £10 | £20 | French |
| Bits And Pieces | 7" | Columbia | DB7210 | 1964 | £1.50 | £4 | |
| Catch Us If You Can | LP | Columbia | SX1756 | 1965 | £8 | £20 | |
| Catch Us If You Can | 7" EP | Columbia | ESRF1699 | 1965 | £10 | £20 | French |
| Chaquita | 7" | Ember | EMBS156 | 1962 | £12.50 | £25 | |
| Coast To Coast | LP | Epic | LN24/BN26128 | 1965 | £8 | £20 | US |
| Dave Clark 5 & Washington DCs | LP | Ember | FA2003 | 1965 | £10 | £25 | |
| Dave Clark And Friends | LP | Columbia | SCX6494 | 1972 | £5 | £12 | |
| Dave Clark Five | LP | Epic | EG30434 | 1971 | £8 | £20 | US double |
| Dave Clark Five | 7" EP | Columbia | SEG8289 | 1964 | £4 | £8 | |
| Do You Love Me | 7" | Columbia | DB7112 | 1963 | £1.50 | £4 | |
| Everybody Knows | LP | Columbia | SX6207 | 1968 | £6 | £15 | |
| Everybody Knows | 7" | Columbia | DB7453 | 1965 | £1.50 | £4 | |
| Everybody Knows | 7" | Polydor | 2058953 | 1977 | £4 | £8 | picture sleeve |
| First Love | 7" | Piccadilly | 7N35088 | 1962 | £12.50 | £25 | |
| Get It On Now | 7" | Columbia | DB8591 | 1969 | £37.50 | £75 | test pressing |
| Glad All Over | LP | Epic | LN24/BN26093 | 1964 | £8 | £20 | US |
| Glad All Over | 7" EP | Columbia | ESRF1489 | 1964 | £10 | £20 | French |
| Glad All Over | 7" | Columbia | DB7154 | 1963 | £1.50 | £4 | |
| Good Old Rock 'n' Roll | 7" | Columbia | DB8638 | 1969 | £1.50 | £4 | picture sleeve |
| Greatest Hits | LP | Columbia | SX6105 | 1966 | £5 | £12 | |
| Having A Wild Weekend | LP | Epic | LN24/BN26162 | 1965 | £8 | £20 | US |
| Hits Of The Dave Clark Five | 7" EP | Columbia | SEG8381 | 1965 | £5 | £10 | |
| I Knew It All The Time | 7" | Piccadilly | 7N35500 | 1962 | £12.50 | £25 | |
| I Like It Like That | LP | Epic | LN24/BN26178 | 1966 | £8 | £20 | US |
| If Somebody Loves You | LP | Columbia | SCX6437 | 1971 | £5 | £12 | |
| In Session | LP | Regal | REG2017 | 1965 | £10 | £25 | export |
| Julia | 7" | Columbia | DB8681 | 1970 | £1.50 | £4 | |
| More Greatest Hits | LP | Epic | LN24/BN26221 | 1966 | £6 | £15 | US |
| Mulberry Bush | 7" | Columbia | DB7011 | 1963 | £7.50 | £15 | |
| Over And Over | 7" EP | Columbia | ESRF1727 | 1965 | £10 | £20 | French |
| Please Tell Me Why | 7" EP | Columbia | ESRF1795 | 1966 | £10 | £20 | French |
| Reelin' And Rockin' | 7" EP | Columbia | ESRF1647 | 1964 | £10 | £20 | French |
| Return | LP | Epic | LN24/BN26104 | 1964 | £8 | £20 | US |
| Satisfied With You | LP | Epic | LN24/BN26212 | 1966 | £8 | £20 | US |
| Session With The Dave Clark Five | LP | Columbia | 33SX1598 | 1964 | £8 | £20 | |
| Thinking Of You Baby | 7" EP | Columbia | ESRF1581 | 1964 | £10 | £20 | French |
| Try Too Hard | LP | Epic | LN24/BN26198 | 1966 | £8 | £20 | US |
| Weekend In London | LP | Epic | LN24/BN26139 | 1965 | £8 | £20 | US |
| Wild Weekend | 7" EP | Columbia | SEG8447 | 1965 | £5 | £10 | |
| You Got What It Takes | LP | Epic | LN24/BN26312 | 1967 | £8 | £20 | US |
| You Got What It Takes | 7" EP | Columbia | ESRF1871 | 1967 | £10 | £20 | French |
| You Knew It All The Time | 7" EP | Palette | 22009 | 1963 | £10 | £20 | French, B side by the Ravens |

## CLARK, DEE

| Title | Format | Label | Cat No | Year | | | Notes |
|---|---|---|---|---|---|---|---|
| At My Front Door | 7" | Top Rank | JAR373 | 1960 | £6 | £12 | |
| Best Of Dee Clark | LP | Vee Jay | LP/SR1047 | 1964 | £6 | £15 | US |
| Dee Clark | LP | Abner | LP/SR2000 | 1959 | £10 | £25 | US |
| Dee Clark | LP | Vee Jay | LP1028 | 1961 | £8 | £20 | US |
| Don't Walk Away From Me | 7" | Columbia | DB4768 | 1962 | £2 | £5 | |
| Heartbreak | 7" | Stateside | SS355 | 1964 | £1.50 | £4 | |
| Hey Little Girl | 7" | Top Rank | JAR196 | 1959 | £5 | £10 | |
| Hold On, It's Dee Clark | LP | Vee Jay | LP/SR1037 | 1961 | £8 | £20 | US |
| How About That | LP | Top Rank | BUY044 | 1960 | £8 | £20 | |
| How About That | 7" | Top Rank | JAR284 | 1960 | £2.50 | £6 | |
| I'm A Soldier Boy | 7" | Stateside | SS180 | 1963 | £5 | £10 | |
| Just Keep It Up | 7" | London | HL8915 | 1959 | £6 | £12 | |
| Raindrops | 7" | Top Rank | JAR570 | 1961 | £1.50 | £4 | |
| T.C.B. | 7" | Stateside | SS400 | 1965 | £5 | £10 | |
| When I Call On You | 7" | London | HL8802 | 1959 | £5 | £10 | |
| You're Looking Good | LP | Vee Jay | LP1019 | 1960 | £8 | £20 | US |
| You're Looking Good | 7" | Top Rank | JAR501 | 1960 | £1.50 | £4 | |
| Your Friends | 7" | Top Rank | JAR551 | 1961 | £1.50 | £4 | |

## CLARK, GENE

| Title | Format | Label | Cat No | Year | | | Notes |
|---|---|---|---|---|---|---|---|
| Early L.A. Sessions | LP | CBS | 31123 | 1972 | £6 | £15 | US |
| Echoes | 7" | CBS | 202523 | 1967 | £2 | £5 | |
| Gene Clark And The Gosdin Brothers | LP | CBS | 62934 | 1967 | £6 | £15 | |
| Road Master | LP | Ariola | 87584 | 1973 | £6 | £15 | Dutch |

## CLARK, MICHAEL

| Title | Format | Label | Cat No | Year | | | Notes |
|---|---|---|---|---|---|---|---|
| None Of These Girls | 7" | Liberty | LIB5893 | 1966 | £2 | £5 | |

## CLARK, PETULA

| Title | Format | Label | Cat No | Year | | | Notes |
|---|---|---|---|---|---|---|---|
| A Date With Pet | 10" LP | Pye | NPT19014 | 1956 | £37.50 | £75 | |
| Alone | 7" | Pye | 7N15112 | 1957 | £1.50 | £4 | |
| Baby Lover | 7" | Pye | 7N15126 | 1958 | £1.50 | £4 | |
| Beautiful Sounds | LP | Pet Projects | PP2 | 1976 | £8 | £20 | |
| C'est ma chanson | LP | Pye-Vogue | VRL3030 | 1967 | £4 | £10 | |
| C'est ma chanson | 7" EP | Pye-Vogue | VRE5025 | 1967 | £2 | £5 | |
| Call Me | 7" EP | Pye | NEP24237 | 1966 | £2 | £5 | |
| Chante en italien | 7" EP | Vogue | VRE5007 | 1965 | £4 | £8 | |
| Children's Choice | 7" EP | Pye | NEP24006 | 1956 | £10 | £20 | |
| Christmas Carol | 7" EP | Pye | NEP24094 | 1958 | £5 | £10 | |
| Christmas Carol | 7" EP | Pye | NSEP85001 | 1958 | £7.50 | £15 | stereo |
| Cinderella Jones | 7" | Pye | 7N15281 | 1960 | £1.50 | £4 | |

| Title | Format | Label | Cat. No. | Year | | | Notes |
|---|---|---|---|---|---|---|---|
| Colour My World | LP | Pye | N(S)PL18171 | 1967 | £4 | £10 | with 'England Swings' & 'Reach Out' |
| Devotion | 7" | Pye | 7N15152 | 1958 | £1.50 | £4 | |
| Dis moi au revoir | 7" EP | Vogue | VRE5028 | 1968 | £2 | £5 | |
| Don't Give Up | LP | Pye | NPL18114 | 1965 | £4 | £10 | |
| Downtown | LP | Pye | NPL18114 | 1965 | £4 | £10 | |
| Downtown | 7" EP | Pye | NEP24206 | 1965 | £2 | £5 | |
| Downtown '88 | CD-s | PRT | PYD19 | 1988 | £2 | £5 | |
| En francais | 7" EP | Pye | NEP24182 | 1963 | £2.50 | £6 | |
| Encore | 7" EP | Pye | NEP24121 | 1959 | £2 | £5 | |
| Encore en francais | 7" EP | Pye | NEP24189 | 1964 | £2 | £5 | |
| Ever Been In Love | 7" | Pye | 7N15182 | 1959 | £1.50 | £4 | |
| Fibbin' | 7" | Pye | 7N15168 | 1958 | £1.50 | £4 | |
| Finian's Rainbow | LP | Warner Bros | WF(S)2550 | 1968 | £6 | £15 | |
| Goodbye Mr. Chips | LP | MGM | CS8113 | 1969 | £6 | £15 | |
| Hello Dolly In French | 7" EP | Pye | NEP24194 | 1964 | £2 | £5 | |
| Hello Mr. Brown | 7" | Pye-Vogue | VRE5023 | 1966 | £2.50 | £6 | |
| Hello Paris Vol. 1 | LP | Pye-Vogue | VRL3016 | 1966 | £5 | £12 | |
| Hello Paris Vol. 2 | LP | Pye-Vogue | VRL3019 | 1966 | £4 | £10 | |
| Here, There And Everywhere | 7" EP | Pye | NEP24286 | 1968 | £2 | £5 | |
| Hit Parade | 7" EP | Pye | NEP24016 | 1956 | £6 | £12 | |
| Hit Parade 4 | 7" EP | Pye | NEP24137 | 1961 | £4 | £8 | |
| Hit Parade 5 | 7" EP | Pye | NEP24150 | 1961 | £2 | £5 | |
| Hit Parade No. 2 | 7" EP | Pye | NEP24056 | 1957 | £2 | £5 | |
| Hit Parade No. 3 | 7" EP | Pye | NEP24080 | 1958 | £2 | £5 | |
| Hits | 7" EP | Pye | NEP24163 | 1962 | £2 | £5 | |
| I Am Your Song | 7" | Polydor | 2058560 | 1975 | £2.50 | £6 | |
| I Couldn't Live Without Your Love | LP | Pye | N(S)PL18148 | 1966 | £4 | £10 | |
| I Couldn't Live Without Your Love | 7" EP | Pye | NEP24266 | 1966 | £2 | £5 | |
| I Couldn't Live Without Your Love ('89 Mix) | CD-s | Legacy | LGYCD100 | 1989 | £2.50 | £6 | |
| I Love A Violin | 7" | Pye | 7N15244 | 1960 | £1.50 | £4 | |
| I'm The Woman You Need | LP | Polydor | 2383324 | 1975 | £5 | £12 | |
| In Other Words | LP | Pye | NPL18070 | 1962 | £6 | £15 | |
| Jumble Sale | 7" | Pye | 7N15456 | 1962 | £1.50 | £4 | |
| Just Say Goodbye | 7" EP | Pye | NEP24259 | 1966 | £2 | £5 | |
| L'Agent secret | 7" EP | Pye-Vogue | VRE5019 | 1966 | £2.50 | £6 | |
| L'Amour viendra | 7" EP | Vogue | VRE5026 | 1968 | £2 | £5 | |
| Lead Me On | 7" | Polydor | 2058413 | 1973 | £5 | £10 | |
| Les Disques d'or de la chanson | 7" EP | Vogue | VRE5004 | 1965 | £2 | £5 | |
| Les James Dean | LP | Pye-Vogue | VRL3001 | 1964 | £4 | £10 | |
| Let's Sing A Love Song | 7" | Polydor | 2058519 | 1974 | £2 | £5 | |
| Live In London | LP | Polydor | 2383303 | 1974 | £4 | £10 | |
| Many Faces | 7" EP | Pye | NEP24280 | 1967 | £2 | £5 | |
| My Love | LP | Pye | NPL18141 | 1966 | £4 | £10 | |
| My Love | 7" EP | Pye | NEP24246 | 1966 | £2 | £5 | |
| New Petula Clark Album | LP | Pye | N(S)PL18118 | 1965 | £4 | £10 | |
| Noel | LP | Pet Projects | PP1 | 1975 | £8 | £20 | |
| Pet Ooh La La | 7" EP | Pye | NEP24157 | 1962 | £2 | £5 | |
| Petula | LP | Pye | NPL18089 | 1962 | £4 | £10 | |
| Petula '65 | LP | Pye-Vogue | VRL3010 | 1965 | £6 | £15 | |
| Petula '66 | LP | Pye-Vogue | VRL3022 | 1966 | £4 | £10 | |
| Petula '71 | LP | Pye | NSPL18370 | 1971 | £4 | £10 | |
| Petula Clark In Hollywood | LP | Pye | NPL18039 | 1959 | £15 | £30 | |
| Petula Clark Sings | 10" LP | Pye | NPT19002 | 1956 | £37.50 | £75 | |
| Road | 7" | Pye | 7N15478 | 1962 | £1.50 | £4 | |
| Sign Of The Times | 7" | Pye | 7N17071 | 1966 | £1.50 | £4 | |
| Sings In French | 7" EP | Pye | NEP24089 | 1958 | £4 | £8 | |
| Sings The International Hits | LP | Pye | NPL18123 | 1965 | £4 | £10 | |
| This Is My Song | 7" EP | Pye | NEP24279 | 1967 | £2 | £5 | |
| Today | LP | Pye | PKL5502 | 1971 | £4 | £10 | |
| Valentino | 7" | Pye | 7N15517 | 1963 | £4 | £8 | |
| Watch Your Heart | 7" | Pye | 7N15191 | 1959 | £1.50 | £4 | |
| Where Do I Go From Here? | 7" | Pye | 7N15208 | 1959 | £1.50 | £4 | |
| Whistlin' For The Moon | 7" | Pye | 7N15437 | 1962 | £1.50 | £4 | |
| With All My Heart | 7" | Pye | 7N15096 | 1957 | £5 | £10 | |
| You Are My Lucky Star | LP | Pye | NPL18007 | 1957 | £15 | £30 | |
| You Are My Lucky Star Part 1 | 7" EP | Pye | NEP24060 | 1957 | £5 | £10 | |
| You Are My Lucky Star Part 2 | 7" EP | Pye | NEP24061 | 1957 | £5 | £10 | |
| You Are My Lucky Star Part 3 | 7" EP | Pye | NEP24062 | 1957 | £5 | £10 | |
| You're the One | 7" EP | Pye | NEP24233 | 1965 | £2 | £5 | |

## CLARK, ROY

| Title | Format | Label | Cat. No. | Year | | | Notes |
|---|---|---|---|---|---|---|---|
| Lightning Fingers | LP | Capitol | (S)T1780 | 1962 | £4 | £10 | |
| Please Mr. Mayor | 7" | HMV | POP581 | 1959 | £15 | £30 | |
| Texas Twist | 7" | Capitol | CL15288 | 1963 | £2 | £5 | |
| Tips Of My Fingers | 7" | Capitol | CL15317 | 1963 | £1.50 | £4 | |

## CLARK, SANFORD

| Title | Format | Label | Cat. No. | Year | | | Notes |
|---|---|---|---|---|---|---|---|
| Fool | 7" | London | HL7014 | 1956 | £12.50 | £25 | export |
| Fool | 7" | London | HLD8320 | 1956 | £37.50 | £75 | |
| Lowdown Blues | 7" EP | London | REW1256 | 1960 | £12.50 | £25 | |
| Pledging My Love | 7" | London | HLW9095 | 1960 | £4 | £8 | |
| Presenting Sanford Clark | 7" EP | London | RED1105 | 1957 | £20 | £40 | |
| Run Boy Run | 7" | London | HLW8959 | 1959 | £7.50 | £15 | |
| Shades | 7" | Ember | EMBS250 | 1968 | £1.50 | £4 | |
| Son Of A Gun | 7" | London | HLW9026 | 1960 | £4 | £8 | |

## CLARK, SONNY

| | | | | | | | |
|---|---|---|---|---|---|---|---|
| Cool Struttin' | LP | Blue Note | BLP/BST81588 | 196– | £10 | £25 | |
| Leapin' And Lopin' | LP | Blue Note | BLP/BST84091 | 1961 | £15 | £30 | |

## CLARK, TREVOR

| | | | | | | | |
|---|---|---|---|---|---|---|---|
| Sufferer | 7" | Studio One | SO2082 | 1969 | £6 | £12 | ...Jackie Mittoo B side |

## CLARK-HUTCHINSON

The Clark-Hutchinson LP, *A=MH2*, was probably the best selling record on Decca's progressive offshoot, Nova, although as most of the records on the label sank without trace, this is not saying very much. The duo turned themselves into a group by extensive multi-tracking, concentrating on Mick Hutchinson's guitar playing to provide a focus of interest. In truth, he was not that remarkable a player and although Clark-Hutchinson got to make two more LPs, they have not been heard from since.

| | | | | | | | |
|---|---|---|---|---|---|---|---|
| A=MH2 | LP | Nova | (S)DNR2 | 1970 | £6 | £15 | |
| Gestalt | LP | Deram | SML1090 | 1971 | £6 | £15 | |
| Retribution | LP | Deram | SML1076 | 1970 | £6 | £15 | |

## CLARK SISTERS

| | | | | | | | |
|---|---|---|---|---|---|---|---|
| Beauty Shop Beat | LP | Coral | CRL(7)57290 | 1960 | £5 | £12 | US |
| Chicago | 7" | London | HLD8791 | 1959 | £2.50 | £6 | |
| Sing Sing Sing | LP | London | HAD2128 | 1958 | £5 | £12 | |
| Sing Sing Sing | 7" EP | London | RED1198 | 1959 | £5 | £10 | |
| Swing Again | LP | London | HAD2177/ SAHD6025 | 1959 | £6 | £15 | |

## CLARKE, ALICE

| | | | | | | | |
|---|---|---|---|---|---|---|---|
| You Got A Deal | 7" | Action | ACT4520 | 1969 | £2 | £5 | |

## CLARKE, ALLAN

| | | | | | | | |
|---|---|---|---|---|---|---|---|
| My Real Name Is 'Arold | LP | RCA | SF8283 | 1972 | £4 | £10 | |

## CLARKE, JOHN COOPER

| | | | | | | | |
|---|---|---|---|---|---|---|---|
| Suspended Sentence | 7" | Rabid | TOSH103 | 1977 | £1.50 | £4 | ...orange picture sleeve |

## CLARKE, JOHNNY

| | | | | | | | |
|---|---|---|---|---|---|---|---|
| Authorised Versions | LP | Virgin | V2076 | 1977 | £5 | £12 | |
| Enter Into His Gates | LP | Attack | ATLP1015 | 1975 | £6 | £15 | |
| Put It On | LP | Vulcan | VULP001 | 1975 | £6 | £15 | |
| Rockers Time Now | LP | Virgin | V2058 | 1976 | £5 | £12 | |

## CLARKE, KENNY

| | | | | | | | |
|---|---|---|---|---|---|---|---|
| Jacksonville | LP | Realm | RM124 | 1963 | £5 | £12 | |
| Jazz International | LP | Vogue | LAE12029 | 1957 | £10 | £25 | |
| Jazz Is Universal | LP | London | HAK8085 | 1963 | £6 | £15 | |
| Kenny Clarke | LP | London | LTZC15038 | 1957 | £10 | £25 | |
| Kenny Clarke | LP | London | LTZC15047 | 1957 | £10 | £25 | |
| Kenny Clarke Quartet | 7" EP | Columbia | SEG7830 | 1957 | £2 | £5 | |
| Kenny Clarke Sextet | LP | London | LTZC15004 | 1956 | £10 | £25 | |
| Klook's Clique | LP | Realm | RM156 | 1963 | £5 | £12 | |
| Plenty For Kenny | LP | London | LTZC15008 | 1956 | £10 | £25 | ... with Ernie Wilkins |
| What's New | LP | Realm | RM115 | 1963 | £5 | £12 | |

## CLARKE, KENNY & FRANCY BOLAND

| | | | | | | | |
|---|---|---|---|---|---|---|---|
| All Blues | LP | BASF | BMP29747 | 1973 | £5 | £12 | |
| All Smiles | LP | Polydor | 583727 | 1969 | £6 | £15 | |
| At Her Majesty's Pleasure | LP | Black Lion | 2460131 | 1971 | £5 | £12 | |
| Faces | LP | Polydor | | 1968 | £6 | £15 | |
| Fellini 712 | LP | Polydor | | 1968 | £6 | £15 | |
| Golden Eight | LP | Blue Note | BLP/BST84092 | 1961 | £15 | £30 | |
| Latin Kaleidoscope | LP | Polydor | 583726 | 1969 | £5 | £12 | |
| Live At Ronnie Scotts Vol. 1 | LP | Polydor | | 1969 | £6 | £15 | |
| Live At Ronnie Scotts Vol. 2 | LP | Polydor | | 1969 | £6 | £15 | |
| More | LP | Polydor | | 1968 | £6 | £15 | |
| More Smiles | LP | BASF | BMP29746 | 1972 | £5 | £12 | |
| Off Limits | LP | Polydor | 2310147 | 1972 | £5 | £12 | |

## CLARKE, LLOYD

| | | | | | | | |
|---|---|---|---|---|---|---|---|
| Fellow Jamaican | 7" | Rio | R24 | 1964 | £5 | £10 | ...Patrick & George B side |
| Fools Day | 7" | Blue Beat | BB104 | 1962 | £6 | £12 | |
| Good Morning | 7" | Blue Beat | BB99 | 1962 | £6 | £12 | |
| Japanese Girl | 7" | Island | WI045 | 1962 | £5 | £10 | |
| Love Is Strange | 7" | Blue Beat | BB371 | 1967 | £6 | £12 | .. Sonny Burke B side |
| Love Me | 7" | Rio | R16 | 1963 | £5 | £10 | |
| Love You The Most | 7" | Island | WI007 | 1962 | £5 | £10 | Lloyd Robinson B side |
| Stop Your Talking | 7" | Rio | R23 | 1964 | £5 | £10 | |
| Young Love | 7" | Blue Cat | BS136 | 1968 | £4 | £8 | .. Untouchables B side |

## CLARKE, STANLEY

| | | | | | | | |
|---|---|---|---|---|---|---|---|
| Stanley Clarke | LP | Atlantic | K5010 | 1975 | £4 | £10 | |

## CLARKE, TONY

| | | | | | | | |
|---|---|---|---|---|---|---|---|
| Ain't Love Good Ain't Love Proud | 7" | Pye | 7N25251 | 1964 | £4 | £8 | |
| Entertainer | 7" | Chess | CRS8011 | 1965 | £5 | £10 | |
| Entertainer | 7" | Chess | CRS8091 | 1969 | £2.50 | £6 | |

## CLASH

As one of the pivotal punk groups, the early recordings of the Clash have actually gained in stature in the years since. The video that accompanied their posthumous hit, 'Should I Stay Or Should I Go', showed a group whose understanding of the essential modern rock'n'roll stance was total. The Clash did not have to have hits to be stars – they had the poise, the dress and above all they had attitude.

| | | | | | | | |
|---|---|---|---|---|---|---|---|
| Black Market Clash | 10" LP | Epic | 4E36846 | 1980 | £4 | £10 | US |
| Capital Radio | 7" | CBS | CL1 | 1977 | £12.50 | £25 | promo |
| Combat Rock | LP | Epic | AS991592 | 1982 | £10 | £25 | US promo picture disc |
| Combat Rock | LP | Epic | FE37689 | 1982 | £10 | £25 | US promo camoflague vinyl |
| Give 'Em Enough Rope | LP | CBS | 82431 | 1978 | £10 | £25 | promo with poster |
| I Fought The Law | CD-s | CBS | CLASHC1 | 1988 | £2 | £5 | |
| If Music Could Talk | LP | Epic | AS952 | 1981 | £8 | £20 | US promo |
| London Calling | CD-s | CBS | 6569465 | 1991 | £2 | £5 | in round tin |
| London Calling | CD-s | CBS | CLASHC2 | 1988 | £2 | £5 | |
| London Calling | 12" | CBS | 128087 | 1979 | £2.50 | £6 | |
| Remote Control | 12" | CBS | 125293 | 1978 | £6 | £15 | promo |
| Return To Brixton | CD-s | CBS | 6560722 | 1990 | £2 | £5 | |
| Rock The Casbah | CD-s | CBS | 6568142 | 1991 | £2 | £5 | |
| Rock The Casbah | CD-s | CBS | 6568145 | 1991 | £2 | £5 | |
| Sandinista Now! | LP | Epic | AS913 | 1980 | £8 | £20 | US single LP promo |
| Should I Stay Or Should I Go | CD-s | CBS | 6566672 | 1991 | £2 | £5 | |
| Should I Stay Or Should I Go | CD-s | CBS | 6566675 | 1991 | £2 | £5 | |
| Should I Stay Or Should I Go | 7" | CBS | A112646 | 1982 | £1.50 | £4 | picture disc |
| Take A Gamble | 12" | CBS | | 1980 | £2.50 | £6 | promo |
| Train In Vain | CD-s | CBS | 6574302 | 1991 | £2 | £5 | |
| World According To The Clash | LP | Epic | AS1574 | 1982 | £20 | £40 | US promo |

## CLASSICS

| | | | | | | | |
|---|---|---|---|---|---|---|---|
| Life Is But A Dream | 7" | Mercury | AMT1152 | 1961 | £20 | £40 | |
| Pollyanna | 7" | Capitol | CL15470 | 1966 | £2 | £5 | |
| Till Then | 7" | Stateside | SS215 | 1963 | £2 | £5 | |

## CLASSICS IV

| | | | | | | | |
|---|---|---|---|---|---|---|---|
| Golden Greats | LP | Imperial | 16000 | 1969 | £4 | £10 | US |
| Mamas And Papas Soul Train | LP | Imperial | 12407 | 1968 | £4 | £10 | US |
| Spooky | LP | Imperial | 12371 | 1968 | £4 | £10 | US |
| Spooky | 7" | Liberty | LBF15051 | 1968 | £1.50 | £4 | |

## CLASSMATES

| | | | | | | | |
|---|---|---|---|---|---|---|---|
| Go Away | 7" | Decca | F12047 | 1964 | £2.50 | £6 | |

## CLAUDETTE & THE CORPORATION

| | | | | | | | |
|---|---|---|---|---|---|---|---|
| Skinheads A Bash Them | 7" | Grape | GR3020 | 1970 | £2 | £5 | |

## CLAY, CASSIUS

If the idea of Cassius Clay (or Mohammed Ali as he became better known) wailing 'Stand By Me' seems hard to take, then the single's B side may be more to the point – 'I Am The Greatest', it is called.

| | | | | | | | |
|---|---|---|---|---|---|---|---|
| I Am The Greatest! | LP | Columbia | CL2093/CS8893 | 1963 | £10 | £25 | US |
| Stand By Me | 7" | CBS | 202190 | 1966 | £2.50 | £6 | |
| Stand By Me | 7" | CBS | AAG190 | 1964 | £5 | £10 | |

## CLAY, JUDY

| | | | | | | | |
|---|---|---|---|---|---|---|---|
| You Can't Run Away From Your Heart | 7" | Stax | 601022 | 1967 | £1.50 | £4 | |

## CLAY, JUDY & WILLIAM BELL

| | | | | | | | |
|---|---|---|---|---|---|---|---|
| Private Number | 7" | Stax | STAX101 | 1968 | £1.50 | £4 | |

## CLAY, OTIS

| | | | | | | | |
|---|---|---|---|---|---|---|---|
| Baby Jane | 7" | Atlantic | 584282 | 1969 | £1.50 | £4 | |
| Lasting Love | 7" | President | PT176 | 1968 | £1.50 | £4 | |

## CLAYRE, ALASDAIR

| | | | | | | | |
|---|---|---|---|---|---|---|---|
| Adam And The Beasts | LP | Acorn | CF252 | 1976 | £10 | £25 | |
| Alasdair Clayre | LP | Elektra | EUK255 | 1967 | £15 | £30 | |

## CLAYTON, BUCK

| | | | | | | | |
|---|---|---|---|---|---|---|---|
| All The Cats Join In | LP | Philips | BBL7129 | 1957 | £5 | £12 | |
| Buck | LP | Vogue | LAE12032 | 1957 | £5 | £12 | |
| Buck Clayton | LP | Philips | BBL7068 | 1956 | £5 | £15 | |
| Buck Clayton | 10" LP | Vogue | LDE140 | 1955 | £8 | £20 | |
| Buck Clayton Special | LP | Philips | BBL7217 | 1958 | £5 | £12 | |
| Buck Meets Ruby | 10" LP | Vanguard | PPT12006 | 1956 | £8 | £20 | with Ruby Braff |
| Buckin' The Blues | LP | Vanguard | PPL11010 | 1958 | £5 | £12 | |
| Jam Session | LP | Philips | BBL7032 | 1955 | £6 | £15 | |
| Jam Session | LP | Philips | BBL7040 | 1955 | £6 | £15 | |
| Jam Session | LP | Philips | BBL7446 | 1961 | £4 | £10 | |
| Jumpin' At The Woodside | LP | Philips | BBL7087 | 1956 | £5 | £12 | |
| Newport Jazz Festival All Stars | LP | London | LTZK15202/SAHK6116 | 1961 | £4 | £10 | |
| Songs For Swingers | LP | Philips | BBL7317 | 1959 | £4 | £10 | |

## CLAYTON, PAUL

| | | | | | | | |
|---|---|---|---|---|---|---|---|
| Paul Clayton | 7" EP | London | REU1276 | 1960 | £7.50 | £15 | |
| Wings Of A Dove | 7" | London | HLU9285 | 1961 | £2 | £5 | |

## CLAYTON, PAUL (2)
Dulcimer Songs And Solos ...................... LP ...... Folkways ......... FG3571 ................. 1962 £6 ......... £15 ...................... US

## CLAYTON, VIKKI
Lost Lady Found ................................. LP ...... Dambuster ....... DAM021 .............. 1988 £50 ....... £100 ......................

## CLAYTON SQUARES
Come And Get It .................................... 7" ...... Decca ............. F12250 .................. 1965 £6 ......... £12
There She Is ......................................... 7" ...... Decca ............. F12456 .................. 1966 £15 ......... £30

## CLEANERS FROM VENUS
Anyone who has read Giles Smith's entertaining book, *Lost In Music*, knows all about the Cleaners From Venus, the group in which Smith played. Despite good reviews, the album did not sell well in 1987 and has consequently become rather scarce. It is, however, well worth seeking out.

Going To England ................... LP ...... Ammunition .... CLEANLP1 ............ 1987 £4 ......... £10 ......................

## CLEANLINESS & GODLINESS SKIFFLE BAND
Greatest Hits ...................................... LP ...... Vanguard ...... SVRL19043 ............ 1968 £4 ......... £10 ......................

## CLEAR BLUE SKY
Clear Blue Sky ..................................... LP ...... Vertigo .......... 6360013 ............. 1971 £30 ......... £60 ............ spiral label

## CLEAR LIGHT
Black Roses ......................................... 7" ...... Elektra ......... EKSN45019 .......... 1967 £2.50 ..... £6
Clear Light .......................................... LP ..... Elektra ......... EKL/EKS74011 ...... 1967 £8 ......... £20
Night Sounds Loud ................................ 7" ...... Elektra ......... EKSN45027 .......... 1968 £1.50 ..... £4

## CLEARLIGHT
Clearlight Symphony ......................... LP ...... Virgin ............ V2029 .................. 1975 £5 ......... £12
Forever Blowing Bubbles ................... LP ...... Virgin ............ V2039 .................. 1975 £5 ......... £12
Les Contes du singe fou .................... LP ...... Isadora ......... 9009 ................... 1976 £5 ......... £12 ............ French
Visions ............................................... LP ...... Polydor ........... 2393185 ............... 1978 £5 ......... £12 ............ French

## CLEARWAYS
I'll Be Here ......................................... 7" ...... Columbia ....... DB7333 ................ 1964 £1.50 ....... £4 ......................

## CLEESE, JOHN & OTHERS
I'm Sorry, I'll Read That Again ................ LP ...... Parlophone ...... PMC7024 ........... 1967 £4 ......... £10 ......................

## CLEFS
Dream Train Special ............................ 7" ...... Salvo ............. SLO1810 ............... 1962 £5 ......... £10 ......................

## CLEFTONES
For Sentimental Reasons ...................... LP ...... Gee ............. (S)GLP707 ............. 1962 £50 ..... £100 ...................... US
Heart And Soul ................................... LP ...... Gee ............. (S)GLP705 ............. 1961 £50 ..... £100 ...................... US
Heart And Soul ................................... 7" ...... Columbia ....... DB4678 .............. 1961 £37.50 ... £75
I Love You For Sentimental Reasons ...... 7" ...... Columbia ....... DB4720 .............. 1961 £25 ..... £50
Little Girl Of Mine .............................. 7" ...... Columbia ....... DB3801 .............. 1956 £150 .... £250 ............ best auctioned
Lover Come Back To Me ...................... 7" ...... Columbia ....... DB4988 .............. 1963 £25 ..... £50

## CLEMENT, JACK
Ten Years .......................................... 7" ...... London ........... HLS8691 ............... 1958 £15 ......... £30 ......................

## CLEMENTS, SOUL JOE
Never Never ...................................... 7" ...... Plexium ......... PXM10 ................. 1968 £50 ....... £100 ......................

## CLEMENTS, VASSAR
Bluegrass Session ............................... LP ...... Sonet ............. SNTF748 .............. 1977 £4 ......... £10 ......................

## CLEVELAND, JIMMY
Jimmy Cleveland ................................ LP ..... Mercury ......... MMB12012 .......... 1959 £8 ......... £20
Map Of Jimmy Cleveland .................... LP ..... Mercury ......... MMC14023 ........... 1959 £5 ......... £12
Trombones ........................................ LP ..... London ........... LTZC15088 ........... 1958 £8 ......... £20 ... with Henry Coker, Bill Hughes, Benny Powell

## CLIFF, JIMMY
Another Cycle ..................................... LP ...... Island .............. ILPS9159 .......... 1971 £4 ......... £10
Give And Take ..................................... 7" ...... Island .............. WIP6004 ........... 1967 £1.50 ....... £4
Hard Road To Travel ............................. LP ...... Island .............. ILP962 .............. 1968 £20 ......... £40 ............ pink label
Harder They Come ............................... LP ...... Island .............. ILPS9202 .......... 1972 £4 ......... £10 ..... with other artists
Harder They Come ............................... 7" ...... Island .............. WIP6139 ........... 1972 £1.50 ....... £4
Huricane Hatty ................................... 7" ...... Island .............. WI1012 ............. 1962 £5 ......... £10
I Got A Feeling .................................... 7" ...... Island .............. WIP6011 ........... 1967 £1.50 ....... £4
I'm Sorry ............................................ 7" ...... Blue Beat ......... BB78 ................. 1962 £6 ......... £12 ....... Red Price B side
Jimmy Cliff ......................................... LP ...... Trojan ............ TRLS16 .............. 1969 £6 ......... £15
King Of Kings ...................................... 7" ...... Island .............. WI070 ............... 1963 £5 ......... £10 .......... Sir Percy B side
Man .................................................. 7" ...... Black Swan ...... WI403 ............... 1964 £5 ......... £10
Miss Jamaica ...................................... 7" ...... Island .............. WI016 ............... 1962 £5 ......... £10
Miss Universe ..................................... 7" ...... Island .............. WI112 ............... 1963 £5 ......... £10
My Lucky Day ..................................... 7" ...... Island .............. WI062 ............... 1962 £5 ......... £10
One Eyed Jacks ................................... 7" ...... Stateside ......... SS342 ............... 1964 £2.50 ....... £6
Pride And Passion ............................... 7" ...... Fontana ........... TF641 ............... 1966 £2.50 ....... £6
Since Lately ........................................ 7" ...... Island .............. WI025 ............... 1962 £5 ......... £10
Struggling Man .................................... LP ...... Island .............. ILPS9235 ............ 1974 £4 ......... £10

| | | | | | | |
|---|---|---|---|---|---|---|
| That's The Way Life Goes | 7" | Island | WIP6024 | 1967 £1.50 | £4 | |
| Trapped | 7" | Island | WIP6132 | 1972 £1.50 | £4 | |
| Unlimited | LP | EMI | EMA757 | 1973 £4 | £10 | |
| Vietnam | 7" | Trojan | TR7722 | 1970 £1.50 | £4 | |
| Waterfall | 7" | Island | WIP6039 | 1968 £2.50 | £6 | |
| Wild World | 7" | Island | WIP6087 | 1970 £1.50 | £4 | |
| Wonderful World | LP | A&M | SP4251 | 1970 £4 | £10 | US |
| Wonderful World Beautiful People | 7" | Trojan | TR690 | 1969 £1.50 | £4 | |

## CLIFFORD, BILLY
| | | | | | |
|---|---|---|---|---|---|
| Irish Traditional Flute Solos | LP | Topic | 12TS312 | 1977 £4 | £10 |

## CLIFFORD, BUZZ
| | | | | | |
|---|---|---|---|---|---|
| Baby Sittin' Boogie | 7" | Fontana | H297 | 1961 £2 | £5 |
| Baby Sittin' With Buzz | LP | Fontana | TFL5147/STFL567 | 1961 £25 | £50 |
| Nobody Loves Me Like You | 7" | Columbia | DB4903 | 1962 £1.50 | £4 |
| Three Little Fishes | 7" | Fontana | H312 | 1961 £1.50 | £4 |

## CLIFFORD, MIKE
| | | | | | |
|---|---|---|---|---|---|
| For The Love Of Mike | LP | United Artists | UAL/UAS6409 | 1965 £4 | £10 | US |

## CLIFTERS
| | | | | | |
|---|---|---|---|---|---|
| Amapola | 7" | Philips | PB1242 | 1962 £1.50 | £4 |

## CLIFTON, BILL
| | | | | | |
|---|---|---|---|---|---|
| Beatle Crazy | 7" | Decca | F11793 | 1963 £1.50 | £4 |
| Bill Clifton | 7" EP | Mercury | MEP9546 | 1958 £2 | £5 |
| Blue River Hoedown | 7" EP | Melodisc | EPM7102 | 195– £2.50 | £6 | with Jim Eanes |
| You Don't Think About Me | 7" | Melodisc | 1554 | 1960 £1.50 | £4 |

## CLIFTON, BILL & GEORGE JONES
| | | | | | |
|---|---|---|---|---|---|
| Country & Western Trailblazers No. 2 | 7" EP | Mercury | ZEP10052 | 1960 £2.50 | £6 |

## CLIMAX BLUES BAND
| | | | | | |
|---|---|---|---|---|---|
| Climax Chicago Blues Band | LP | Parlophone | PMC/PCS7069 | 1969 £8 | £20 |
| Like Uncle Charlie | 7" | Parlophone | R5809 | 1969 £1.50 | £4 |
| Lot Of Bottle | LP | Harvest | SHSP4009 | 1970 £4 | £10 |
| Plays On | LP | Parlophone | PCS7084 | 1969 £6 | £15 |
| Rich Man | LP | Harvest | SHSP4024 | 1972 £4 | £10 |
| Tightly Knit | LP | Harvest | SHSP4015 | 1971 £4 | £10 |

## CLINE, PATSY
| | | | | | |
|---|---|---|---|---|---|
| Crazy | 7" | Brunswick | 05861 | 1961 £2.50 | £6 |
| Cry Not For Me | 7" EP | Ember | EMBEP4552 | 1964 £2 | £5 |
| Heartaches | 7" | Brunswick | 05878 | 1962 £1.50 | £4 |
| I Fall To Pieces | 7" | Brunswick | 05855 | 1961 £2.50 | £6 |
| Leaving On Your Mind | 7" | Brunswick | 05883 | 1963 £1.50 | £4 |
| Patsy Cline | LP | Decca | DL8611 | 1957 £10 | £25 | US |
| Patsy Cline Showcase | LP | Brunswick | LAT8344 | 1959 £6 | £15 |
| Patsy Cline Story | LP | Decca | D(S)XB(7)176 | 1963 £6 | £15 | US, with booklet |
| Portrait Of Patsy Cline | LP | Brunswick | LAT/STA8589 | 1964 £6 | £15 |
| Sentimentally Yours | LP | Brunswick | LAT/STA8510 | 1962 £6 | £15 |
| She's Got You | 7" | Brunswick | 05866 | 1962 £1.50 | £4 |
| So Wrong | 7" | Brunswick | 05874 | 1962 £1.50 | £4 |
| Sweet Dreams | 7" EP | Brunswick | OE9490 | 1962 £2.50 | £6 |
| Sweet Dreams | 7" | Brunswick | 05888 | 1963 £1.50 | £4 |
| That's How A Heartache Begins | LP | Decca | DL(7)4586 | 1964 £5 | £12 | US |
| Tribute To Patsy Cline | LP | Brunswick | LAT8549 | 1963 £5 | £12 |
| Walkin' After Midnight | 7" | Brunswick | 05660 | 1957 £5 | £10 |
| When I Get Through With You | 7" | Brunswick | 05869 | 1962 £1.50 | £4 |

## CLIQUE
| | | | | | |
|---|---|---|---|---|---|
| Clique | 7" EP | private | | 196– £330 | £500 | promo, best auctioned |
| She Ain't No Good | 7" | Pye | 7N15786 | 1965 £30 | £60 |
| We Didn't Kiss | 7" | Pye | 7N15853 | 1965 £75 | £150 |

## CLIQUE (2)
| | | | | | |
|---|---|---|---|---|---|
| Sugar On Sunday | 7" | London | HLU10286 | 1969 £5 | £10 |

## CLIVE & GLORIA
| | | | | | |
|---|---|---|---|---|---|
| Change Of Plan | 7" | R&B | JB113 | 1963 £5 | £10 |
| Do The Ska | 7" | King | KG1004 | 1964 £5 | £10 |
| Have I Told You Lately That I Love You? | 7" | Ska Beat | JB173 | 1964 £5 | £10 |

## CLIVE & NAOMI
| | | | | | |
|---|---|---|---|---|---|
| Open The Door | 7" | Ska Beat | JB181 | 1965 £5 | £10 |

## CLIVE ALL STARS
| | | | | | |
|---|---|---|---|---|---|
| Donkey Trot | 7" | Big Shot | BI501 | 1968 £4 | £8 | Tennors B side |

## CLOCK DVA
| | | | | | |
|---|---|---|---|---|---|
| Four Hours | 7" | Fetish | FET008 | 1981 £2 | £5 |
| White Souls In Black Suits | cass | Indutrial | IRC31 | 1981 £4 | £10 |

## CLOCKWORK ORANGES
| | | | | | |
|---|---|---|---|---|---|
| Ready Steady | 7" | Ember | EMBS227 | 1966 £4 | £8 |

## CLOONEY, ROSEMARY

| | | | | | | |
|---|---|---|---|---|---|---|
| At The London Palladium | 10" LP | Philips | BBR8073 | 1956 | £6 | £15 |
| Blues In The Night | 7" | Columbia | SCM5049 | 1953 | £2.50 | £6 |
| Children's Favourites | LP | Philips | BBL7191 | 1957 | £4 | £10 |
| Date With The King | 10" LP | Columbia | CL2572 | 195– | £8 | £20 | US |
| Half As Much | 7" | Columbia | SCM5019 | 1953 | £5 | £10 |
| Hey Baby | LP | Philips | BBL7090 | 1956 | £4 | £10 |
| I Still Feel The Same About You | 7" | Columbia | SCM5093 | 1954 | £1.50 | £4 |
| I'm The One Who Loves You | 7" | Columbia | SCM5040 | 1953 | £1.50 | £4 |
| If I Had A Penny | 7" | Columbia | SCM5027 | 1953 | £2 | £5 |
| Mangos | 7" | Philips | JK1010 | 1957 | £4 | £8 |
| On The First Warm Day | 7" | Columbia | SCM5028 | 1953 | £2.50 | £6 |
| Ring Around Rosie | LP | Philips | BBL7156 | 1957 | £4 | £10 | ..... with The Hi-Lo's |
| Rosemary Clooney | 7" EP | Philips | BBE12004 | 1955 | £4 | £8 |
| Rosemary Clooney | 7" EP | Philips | BBE12051 | 1956 | £2.50 | £6 |
| Rosemary Clooney | 10" LP | Philips | BBR8047 | 1955 | £6 | £15 |
| Rosemary Clooney & Benny Goodman | 7" EP | Philips | BBE12038 | 1956 | £2 | £5 |
| Rosemary Clooney & Harry James | 7" EP | Columbia | SEG7552 | 1954 | £2.50 | £6 |
| Showcase Of Hits | LP | Philips | BBL7301 | 1958 | £4 | £10 |
| Sings For You | 7" EP | MGM | MGMEP721 | 1960 | £2 | £5 |
| Swing Around Rosie | LP | Coral | LVA9112 | 1959 | £4 | £10 |
| Swing Around Rosie Vol. 1 | 7" EP | Coral | FEP2045 | 1960 | £2 | £5 |
| Swing Around Rosie Vol. 2 | 7" EP | Coral | FEP2046 | 1960 | £2 | £5 |
| Swings Softly No. 1 | 7" EP | MGM | ES3514 | 1961 | £2 | £5 | .....stereo |
| Swings Softly No. 1 | 7" EP | MGM | MGMEP758 | 1961 | £2 | £5 |
| Tenderly | 10" LP | Columbia | CL2525 | 195– | £8 | £20 | US |
| Too Old To Cut The Mustard | 7" | Columbia | SCM5010 | 1953 | £4 | £8 |
| White Christmas | 10" LP | Philips | BBR8022 | 1954 | £8 | £20 |

## CLOUD

| | | | | | | |
|---|---|---|---|---|---|---|
| Watered Garden | LP | Dovetail | | | £20 | £40 |

## CLOUD, CLAUDE

| | | | | | | |
|---|---|---|---|---|---|---|
| Beat | 7" | MGM | MGM946 | 1957 | £2 | £5 |
| Let's Get Catstatic No. 1 | 7" EP | MGM | MGMEP517 | 1955 | £10 | £20 |
| Rock 'n' Roll Music For Dancing | 10" LP | MGM | D142 | 1956 | £15 | £30 |

## CLOUDS

As 1-2-3, the organ trio that became Clouds pioneered a brand of underground music that was unfortunately not properly represented by the records that the group made. To quote organist Billy Ritchie, 'The records are a very poor record of a good live group. On a good night, we could kill anybody, and often did, especially in the States.' It seems that Clouds suffered from the sadly familiar record company behaviour whereby they were signed on the basis of an exciting live sound and then forced to change style for their records.

| | | | | | | |
|---|---|---|---|---|---|---|
| Make No Bones About It | 7" | Island | WIP6055 | 1969 | £1.50 | £4 |
| Scrapbook | LP | Island | ILPS9100 | 1969 | £6 | £15 | .....pink label |
| Scrapbook | 7" | Island | WIP6067 | 1969 | £1.50 | £4 |
| Up Above Our Heads | LP | Deram | DES18044 | 1969 | £10 | £25 | US |
| Watercolour Days | LP | island | ILPS9151 | 1971 | £6 | £15 |

## CLOUGH, TOM, NED PEARSON, BILLY BALLANTINE

| | | | | | | |
|---|---|---|---|---|---|---|
| Holey Ha'penny | LP | Topic | 12T283 | 1978 | £4 | £10 |

## CLOVEN HOOF

| | | | | | | |
|---|---|---|---|---|---|---|
| Opening Ritual | 7" | Cloven Hoof | TOA1402 | 1982 | £4 | £8 |

## CLOVER

| | | | | | | |
|---|---|---|---|---|---|---|
| Clover | LP | Liberty | LBS83340 | 1970 | £4 | £10 |
| Forty-Niner | LP | Liberty | LBS83487 | 1971 | £4 | £10 |
| Wade In The Water | 7" | Liberty | LBF15341 | 1970 | £1.50 | £4 |

## CLOVERLEAFS

| | | | | | | |
|---|---|---|---|---|---|---|
| Step Right Up And say Howdy | 7" | MGM | MGM933 | 1956 | £1.50 | £4 |

## CLOVERS

| | | | | | | |
|---|---|---|---|---|---|---|
| Clovers | LP | Atlantic | LP1248 | 1956 | £150 | £250 | US |
| Clovers | LP | Atlantic | LP8009 | 1957 | £87.50 | £175 | US |
| Dance Party | LP | Atlantic | LP8034 | 1959 | £62.50 | £125 | US |
| Easy Loving | 7" | London | HLT9154 | 1960 | £10 | £20 |
| From The Bottom Of My Heart | 7" | London | HLE8334 | 1956 | £180 | £300 | .....best auctioned |
| Honey Dripper | 7" | HMV | POP883 | 1961 | £5 | £10 |
| In Clover | LP | Poplar | 1001 | 1958 | £62.50 | £125 | US |
| In Clover | LP | United Artists | UAL3033/ UAS6033 | 1959 | £62.50 | £125 | US |
| In The Good Old Summertime | 7" | HMV | POP542 | 1958 | £7.50 | £15 |
| Love Bug | LP | Atlantic | 587162 | 1969 | £10 | £25 |
| Love Love Love | 7" | London | HLE8314 | 1956 | £180 | £300 | .....best auctioned |
| Love Potion No. 9 | LP | United Artists | UAL3/UAS6099 | 1960 | £50 | £100 | US |
| Love Potion No. 9 | 7" | London | HLT8949 | 1959 | £20 | £40 |
| Nip Sip | 7" | London | HLE8229 | 1956 | £330 | £500 | .....gold label, best auctioned |
| One Mint Julep | 7" | London | HLT9122 | 1960 | £12.50 | £25 |
| Original Love Potion No. 9 | LP | Grand Prix | K428 | 1964 | £8 | £20 | US |
| Wishing For Your Love | 7" | London | HL7048 | 1958 | £62.50 | £125 | .....export |
| Your Cash Ain't Nothin' But Trash | 7" | Atlantic | 584160 | 1968 | £2.50 | £6 |

170

## CLUE J & HIS BLUES BUSTERS
| | | | | | | |
|---|---|---|---|---|---|---|
| Little Willie | 7" | Blue Beat | BB60 | 1961 | £6 | £12 |
| Lovers' Jive | 7" | Blue Beat | BB37 | 1961 | £6 | £12 |

## CLUSTER
| | | | | | | | |
|---|---|---|---|---|---|---|---|
| After The Heat | LP | Sky | SKY021 | 1979 | £5 | £12 | German |
| Cluster | LP | Philips | 6305074 | 1971 | £8 | £20 | German |
| Cluster 2 | LP | Brain | 1006 | 1972 | £8 | £20 | German |
| Cluster And Eno | LP | Sky | SKY010 | 1977 | £5 | £12 | German |
| Curiosum | LP | Sky | SKY063 | 1981 | £4 | £10 | German |
| Grosses Wasser | LP | Sky | SKY027 | 1979 | £5 | £12 | German |
| Klopfzeichen | LP | Schwann | STUDIO511 | 1970 | £15 | £30 | German |
| Sowieso | LP | Sky | SKY005 | 1976 | £5 | £12 | German |
| Stimmungen | LP | Sky | SKY093 | 1984 | £4 | £10 | German |
| Zuckerzeit | LP | Brain | 0001065 | 1974 | £6 | £15 | German |
| Zwei Osterie | LP | Schwann | STUDIO512 | 1970 | £15 | £30 | German |

## CLUTHA
| | | | | | | |
|---|---|---|---|---|---|---|
| Bonnie Mill Dams | LP | Topic | 12TS330 | 1977 | £4 | £10 |
| Scotia! | LP | Argo | ZFB18 | 1971 | £6 | £15 |

## CLYDE VALLEY STOMPERS
| | | | | | | |
|---|---|---|---|---|---|---|
| Clyde Valley Stompers | 10" LP | Beltona | ABL524 | 1958 | £4 | £10 |

## CLYNE, JEFF & OTHERS
| | | | | | | |
|---|---|---|---|---|---|---|
| Springboard | LP | Polydor | 545007 | 1966 | £20 | £40 |

## CMU
| | | | | | | |
|---|---|---|---|---|---|---|
| Heart Of The Sun | 7" | Transatlantic | BIG508 | 1972 | £2 | £5 |
| Open Spaces | LP | Transatlantic | TRA237 | 1971 | £30 | £60 |
| Space Cabaret | LP | Transatlantic | TRA259 | 1972 | £20 | £40 |

## COACHMEN
| | | | | | | |
|---|---|---|---|---|---|---|
| Here Come The Coachmen | LP | Vogue | VA16062 | 1960 | £4 | £10 |
| Here Come The Coachmen | 7" EP | Vogue | VE170149 | 1962 | £2.50 | £6 |
| Those Brown Eyes | 7" | Vogue | V9154 | 1959 | £2 | £5 |

## COAST ROAD DRIVE
| | | | | | | |
|---|---|---|---|---|---|---|
| Delicious And Refreshing | LP | Deram | SML1113 | 1974 | £15 | £30 |

## COASTERS
| | | | | | | | |
|---|---|---|---|---|---|---|---|
| Ain't That Just Like Me | 7" | London | HLK9493 | 1962 | £1.50 | £4 | |
| All Time Great Hits | LP | Atlantic | 590015 | 1967 | £6 | £15 | |
| Along Came Jones | 7" | London | HLE8882 | 1959 | £4 | £8 | |
| Besame Mucho | 7" | London | HLK9111 | 1960 | £2 | £5 | |
| Charlie Brown | 7" | London | HL7073 | 1959 | £1.50 | £4 | |
| Charlie Brown | 7" | London | HLE8819 | 1959 | £2 | £5 | |
| Coasters | LP | Atco | 33101 | 1958 | £50 | £100 | US |
| Coasters | 7" EP | London | REE1203 | 1959 | £20 | £40 | |
| Coastin' Along | LP | Atlantic | 587134 | 1968 | £6 | £15 | |
| Coastin' Along | LP | London | HAK8033 | 1963 | £20 | £40 | |
| Cool Jerk | 7" | Stateside | SS2201 | 1972 | £2.50 | £6 | |
| Girls Girls Girls | 7" | London | HLK9413 | 1961 | £1.50 | £4 | |
| Greatest Hits | LP | Atco | 33111 | 1959 | £25 | £50 | US |
| Greatest Hits | LP | London | HAE2237 | 1960 | £20 | £40 | |
| Little Egypt | 7" | London | HLK9349 | 1961 | £1.50 | £4 | |
| One By One | LP | Atco | (SD)33129 | 1960 | £8 | £20 | US |
| Poison Ivy | 7" | London | HLE8938 | 1959 | £2 | £5 | |
| Searchin' | 7" | Atlantic | 584087 | 1967 | £1.50 | £4 | |
| Searchin' | 7" | London | HL7021 | 1957 | £5 | £10 | export |
| Searchin' | 7" | London | HLE8450 | 1957 | £12.50 | £25 | |
| Shadow Knows | 7" | London | HLE8729 | 1958 | £7.50 | £15 | |
| She Can | 7" | Direction | 583701 | 1968 | £1.50 | £4 | |
| She's A Yum Yum | 7" | Atlantic | 584033 | 1966 | £1.50 | £4 | |
| Shopping For Clothes | 7" | London | HLK9208 | 1960 | £2 | £5 | |
| Soul Pad | 7" | CBS | 2749 | 1967 | £1.50 | £4 | |
| Stewball | 7" | London | HLK9151 | 1960 | £2 | £5 | |
| T'ain't Nothing To Me | 7" | London | HLK9863 | 1964 | £1.50 | £4 | |
| Thumbin' A Ride | 7" | London | HLK9293 | 1961 | £1.50 | £4 | |
| What About Us | 7" | London | HLE9020 | 1960 | £2 | £5 | |
| Yakety Yak | 7" | London | HLE8665 | 1958 | £5 | £10 | |

## COBB, ARNETT
| | | | | | | | |
|---|---|---|---|---|---|---|---|
| Blow Arnett, Blow | LP | Esquire | 32114 | 1961 | £8 | £20 | with Eddie 'Lockjaw' Davis |

## COBBLERS LAST
| | | | | | | |
|---|---|---|---|---|---|---|
| Boot In The Door | LP | Banshee | BAN1012 | 1979 | £75 | £150 |

## COBBS
| | | | | | | |
|---|---|---|---|---|---|---|
| Hot Buttered Corn | 7" | Amalgamated | AMG845 | 1969 | £2 | £5 |
| Space Doctor | 7" | Amalgamated | AMG849 | 1969 | £2 | £5 |

## COBHAM, BILLY
| | | | | | | | |
|---|---|---|---|---|---|---|---|
| Crosswinds | LP | Atlantic | K50037 | 1974 | £4 | £10 | |
| Spectrum | LP | Atlantic | K40406 | 1973 | £4 | £10 | |
| Stratus | LP | In-Akustic | INAK813 | 1981 | £6 | £15 | German, direct to disc |

| Total Eclipse | LP | Atlantic | K50098 | 1974 £4 | £10 | |

## COCHISE
| Cochise | LP | United Artists | UAS29117 | 1970 £4 | £10 | |

## COCHRAN, DIB & THE EARWIGS
This mysterious pseudonym actually hides the identity of Tyrannosaurus Rex, having fun with Rick Wakeman and Tony Visconti. It has often been thought that David Bowie appears on the record too, but this would seem not to be the case.

| Oh Baby | 7" | Bell | BLL1121 | 1970 £62.50 | £125 | |

## COCHRAN, EDDIE
| C'mon Again | 7" EP | Liberty | LEP2165 | 1964 £15 | £30 | |
| C'mon Everybody | 7" EP | Liberty | LEP2111 | 1963 £7.50 | £15 | |
| C'mon Everybody | 7" EP | London | REU1214 | 1959 £30 | £60 | tri-centre |
| C'mon Everybody | 7" | Liberty | LBF15366 | 1970 £2.50 | £6 | |
| C'mon Everybody | 7" | Liberty | LIB10233 | 1966 £7.50 | £15 | |
| C'mon Everybody | 7" | London | HLU8792 | 1959 £10 | £20 | |
| Cherished Memories | LP | Liberty | LBL/LBS83072 | 1967 £4 | £10 | |
| Cherished Memories | LP | Liberty | LBY1109 | 1962 £6 | £15 | |
| Cherished Memories Of Eddie Cochran | 7" EP | Liberty | LEP2123 | 1963 £12.50 | £25 | |
| Cherished Memories Of Eddie Cochran | 7" EP | London | REG1301 | 1961 £30 | £60 | |
| Cherished Memories Vol. 1 | 7" EP | Liberty | LEP2090 | 1963 £12.50 | £25 | |
| Drive In Show | 7" | Liberty | LIB10108 | 1963 £7.50 | £15 | |
| Eddie's Hits | 7" EP | Liberty | LEP2124 | 1963 £10 | £20 | |
| Eddie's Hits | 7" EP | London | REG1262 | 1960 £30 | £60 | |
| Hallelujah I Love Her So | 7" | London | HLW9022 | 1960 £4 | £8 | |
| Hallelujah I Love Her So | 7" | London | HLW9022 | 1960 £20 | £40 | tricentre |
| Jeannie Jeannie Jeannie | 7" | London | HLG9460 | 1961 £7.50 | £15 | |
| Legendary Masters | LP | United Artists | UAD60017/8 | 1972 £5 | £12 | double |
| Memorial Album | LP | Liberty | LBL/LBS83009 | 1967 £4 | £10 | |
| Memorial Album | LP | Liberty | LBY1127 | 1963 £6 | £15 | |
| Memorial Album | LP | London | HAG2267 | 1960 £20 | £40 | |
| My Way | LP | Liberty | LBL83104 | 1968 £4 | £10 | |
| My Way | LP | Liberty | LBY1205 | 1964 £15 | £30 | |
| My Way | 7" | Liberty | LIB10088 | 1963 £4 | £8 | |
| Never To Be Forgotten | LP | Liberty | LRP3220 | 1962 £15 | £30 | US |
| Never To Be Forgotten | 7" EP | Liberty | LEP2052 | 1962 £10 | £20 | |
| Pretty Girl | 7" | London | HLG9464 | 1961 £10 | £20 | |
| Singing To My Baby | LP | Liberty | LBL/LBS83152 | 1968 £4 | £10 | |
| Singing To My Baby | LP | Liberty | LBY1158 | 1963 £8 | £20 | |
| Singing To My Baby | LP | Liberty | LRP3061 | 1958 £62.50 | £125 | US |
| Singing To My Baby | LP | London | HAU2093 | 1958 £50 | £100 | |
| Sitting In The Balcony | 7" | London | HLU8433 | 1957 £100 | £200 | |
| Skinny Jim | 7" | Crest | 1026 | 1956 £87.50 | £175 | US |
| Skinny Jim | 7" | Crest | 1026 | 1956 £330 | £500 | US, red vinyl, best auctioned |
| Skinny Jim | 7" | Liberty | LIB10151 | 1964 £12.50 | £25 | |
| Somethin' Else | 7" EP | Liberty | LEP2122 | 1963 £10 | £20 | |
| Somethin' Else | 7" EP | London | REU1239 | 1960 £30 | £60 | |
| Somethin' Else | 7" | Liberty | LBF15109 | 1968 £2.50 | £6 | |
| Somethin' Else | 7" | London | HLU8944 | 1959 £20 | £40 | tri-centre |
| Stockings And Shoes | 7" EP | Liberty | LEP2180 | 1964 £10 | £20 | |
| Stockings And Shoes | 7" | London | HLG9467 | 1961 £10 | £20 | |
| Summertime Blues | 7" | Liberty | LBF15071 | 1968 £2.50 | £6 | |
| Summertime Blues | 7" | London | HLU8702 | 1958 £10 | £20 | |
| Sweetie Pie | 7" | London | HLG9196 | 1960 £5 | £10 | |
| Teenage Heaven | 7" | London | HL7082 | 1959 £30 | £60 | export |
| Teenage Heaven | 7" | London | HLU8880 | 1959 £10 | £20 | |
| Think Of Me | 7" | Liberty | LIB10049 | 1962 £5 | £10 | |
| Three Stars | 7" | Liberty | LIB10249 | 1966 £15 | £30 | |
| Three Steps To Heaven | 7" | Liberty | LIB10276 | 1967 £12.50 | £25 | |
| Three Steps To Heaven | 7" | London | HLG9115 | 1960 £4 | £8 | |
| Twentieth Anniversary Album | LP | United Artists | ECSP20 | 1980 £15 | £30 | 4 LPs, boxed |
| Twenty Flight Rock | 7" | London | HLU8386 | 1957 £50 | £100 | tri-centre |
| Weekend | 7" | London | HLG9362 | 1961 £4 | £8 | |

## COCHRAN, JACKIE LEE
| Mama Don't You Think I Know | 7" | Brunswick | 05669 | 1957 £500 | £750 | best auctioned |

## COCHRAN, WAYNE
| Wayne Cochran | LP | Chess | LP(S)1519 | 1967 £5 | £12 | US |

## COCHRAN BROTHERS
Though sharing a surname, Hank and Eddie Cochran were not actually related at all.

| Guilty Conscience | 7" | Ekko | 1005 | 1955 £75 | £150 | US |
| Mr. Fiddle | 7" | Ekko | 1003 | 1955 £75 | £150 | US |
| Tired And Sleepy | 7" | Ekko | 3001 | 1956 £87.50 | £175 | US |

## COCK SPARRER
| Cock Sparrer | LP | Decca | TXS3103 | 1978 £20 | £40 | Spanish |
| England Belongs To Me | 7" | Carrere | CAR255 | 1982 £10 | £20 | |
| Running Riot | 7" | Decca | FR13710 | 1977 £2.50 | £6 | |
| Running Riot | 7" | Decca | FR13710 | 1977 £12.50 | £25 | picture sleeve |
| We Love You | 7" | Decca | FR13732 | 1977 £2 | £5 | |
| We Love You | 12" | Decca | FR13732 | 1977 £3 | £8 | |

## COCKBURN, BRUCE

Bruce Cockburn is a Canadian singer-songwriter who, since first issuing LPs on his own True North label at the start of the seventies, seems to have grown in stature with each passing year. His most impressive recordings are the most recent ones, the earliest records being interesting mainly for the glimpses they afford of a great artist in the making. This, of course, is the exact reverse of the usual state of affairs where rock performers are concerned.

| | | | | | | | |
|---|---|---|---|---|---|---|---|
| Bruce Cockburn | LP | True North | TN1 | 1970 | £6 | £15 | Canadian |
| Circles In The Stream | LP | Island | ILTA9475 | 1977 | £6 | £15 | US double |
| Further Adventures | LP | True North | TN33 | 1976 | £6 | £15 | Canadian |
| Hand Dancing | LP | True North | TN13 | 1974 | £6 | £15 | Canadian |
| High Winds White Sky | LP | True North | TN3 | 1971 | £6 | £15 | Canadian |
| In The Falling Dark | LP | True North | TN26 | 1976 | £6 | £15 | Canadian |
| Joy Will Find A Way | LP | True North | TN23 | 1975 | £6 | £15 | Canadian |
| Night Vision | LP | True North | TN11 | 1973 | £6 | £15 | Canadian |
| Salt, Sun And Time | LP | True North | TN16 | 1974 | £6 | £15 | Canadian |
| Sunwheel Dance | LP | Epic | 65187 | 1972 | £6 | £15 | |

## COCKER, JOE

| | | | | | | | |
|---|---|---|---|---|---|---|---|
| Best Of Joe Cocker Live | CD | EMI | | 1994 | £10 | £25 | CD & video boxed set |
| Don't You Love Me Anymore | CD-s | Capitol | CDCL493 | 1988 | £2 | £5 | |
| I'll Cry Instead | 7" | Decca | F11974 | 1964 | £12.50 | £25 | |
| Joe Cocker | LP | Regal Zonophone | SLRZ1011 | 1969 | £4 | £10 | |
| Joe Cocker | 7" EP | Oak | | 196– | £100 | £200 | best auctioned |
| Luxury You Can Afford | LP | Asylum | DP400 | 1978 | £5 | £12 | US promo picture disc |
| Marjorine | 7" | Regal Zonophone | RZ3006 | 1968 | £1.50 | £4 | |
| Rag Goes Mad At The Mojo | 7" | Action | ACT002 | 1967 | £20 | £40 | with other artists |
| Sheffield Steel | CD | Mobile Fidelity | | 1995 | £6 | £15 | US audiophile |
| Unchain My Heart | CD-s | Capitol | CDCL465 | 1987 | £2 | £5 | |
| When The Night Comes | CD-s | Capitol | CDCL535 | 1989 | £2 | £5 | |
| With A Little Help From My Friends | LP | Regal Zonophone | SLRZ1006 | 1969 | £5 | £12 | |
| With A Little Help From My Friends | 7" | MagniFly | ECHO103 | 1972 | £1.50 | £4 | picture sleeve |
| With A Little Help From My Friends | 7" | Regal Zonophone | RZ3013 | 1968 | £1.50 | £4 | |

## COCKNEY REBEL

| | | | | | | | |
|---|---|---|---|---|---|---|---|
| Best Years Of Our Lives | 7" | EMI | EMI2673 | 1977 | £2.50 | £6 | picture sleeve |
| Human Menagerie | LP | EMI | EMA759 | 1973 | £8 | £20 | with booklet |
| Psychomodo | 7" | EMI | EMI2191 | 1974 | £25 | £50 | demo |

## COCKNEYS

| | | | | | | | |
|---|---|---|---|---|---|---|---|
| After Tomorrow | 7" | Philips | BF1303 | 1964 | £2 | £5 | |
| After Tomorrow | 7" | Philips | BF1338 | 1964 | £2 | £5 | |
| I Know You're Gonna Be Mine | 7" | Philips | BF1360 | 1964 | £2 | £5 | |

## COCKTAIL CABINET

| | | | | | | | |
|---|---|---|---|---|---|---|---|
| Puppet On A String | 7" | Page One | POF23046 | 1967 | £5 | £10 | |

## COCTEAU TWINS

| | | | | | | | |
|---|---|---|---|---|---|---|---|
| Cocteau Twins | CD | Capitol | DPRO79065 | 1991 | £10 | £25 | US promo sampler |
| Echoes In A Shallow Bay | CD-s | 4AD | BAD511CD | 1985 | £2 | £5 | |
| EP Box Set | CD-s | 4AD | CTBOX1 | 1991 | £10 | £20 | |
| Ice Blink Luck | CD-s | 4AD | BADCD0011 | 1990 | £2 | £5 | |
| Peppermint Pig | 7" | 4AD | AD303 | 1983 | £6 | £12 | |
| Sugar Hiccup | 7" | 4AD | AD314 | 1984 | £5 | £10 | 1 sided promo |
| Tiny Dynamite | CD-s | 4AD | BAD510CD | 1988 | £2 | £5 | |

## CODA

| | | | | | | | |
|---|---|---|---|---|---|---|---|
| Sounds Of Passion | LP | Boni | 2860481 | 1986 | £6 | £15 | Dutch |

## CODE III

| | | | | | | | |
|---|---|---|---|---|---|---|---|
| Planet Of Man | LP | Delta-Akustik | 251251 | 1974 | £25 | £50 | German |

## COE, DAVID ALAN

| | | | | | | | |
|---|---|---|---|---|---|---|---|
| Penitentiary Blues | LP | SSS | 9 | 1968 | £4 | £10 | US |
| Requiem For A Harlequin | LP | SSS | 31 | 1969 | £4 | £10 | US |

## COE, JAMIE

| | | | | | | | |
|---|---|---|---|---|---|---|---|
| Fool | 7" | London | HLX9713 | 1963 | £4 | £8 | |
| How Low Is Low | 7" | HMV | POP991 | 1961 | £4 | £8 | |
| Schoolday Blues | 7" | Parlophone | R4621 | 1960 | £12.50 | £25 | |
| Summertime Symphony | 7" | Parlophone | R4600 | 1959 | £37.50 | £75 | |

## COE, PETE & CHRIS

| | | | | | | | |
|---|---|---|---|---|---|---|---|
| Game Of All Fours | LP | Highway | SHY7007 | 1979 | £4 | £10 | |
| Open The Door And Let Us In | LP | Leader | LER2077 | 1972 | £5 | £12 | |
| Out Of Season Out Of Rhyme | LP | Trailer | LER2098 | 1976 | £5 | £12 | |

## COE, TONY

| | | | | | | | |
|---|---|---|---|---|---|---|---|
| Existence | LP | Leelambert | LAM100 | 1978 | £6 | £15 | |
| Le Chat se retourne | LP | Nato | 257 | 1984 | £5 | £12 | |
| Nutty On Willisau | LP | Hat Art | 2004 | 1983 | £5 | £12 | |
| Pop Makes Progress | LP | Chapter One | CHS804 | 1970 | £15 | £30 | with Robert Farnon |
| Swingin' Till The Girls Come Home | LP | Philips | B10784L | 1962 | £15 | £30 | |

| Title | Format | Label | Catalogue | Year | Price | Price | Notes |
|---|---|---|---|---|---|---|---|
| Tony Coe And The Brian Lemon Trio | LP | 77 | SEU1241 | 1971 | £10 | £25 | |
| Tony's Basement | LP | Columbia | S(C)X6170 | 1967 | £15 | £30 | |
| Tournée du chat | LP | Nato | 19 | 1982 | £5 | £12 | |
| Zeitgeists | LP | EMI | EMC3207 | 1977 | £6 | £15 | |

## COE, TONY & DEREK BAILEY

| Title | Format | Label | Catalogue | Year | Price | Price | Notes |
|---|---|---|---|---|---|---|---|
| Time | LP | Incus | INCUS34 | 1979 | £5 | £12 | |

## COEUR MAGIQUE

| Title | Format | Label | Catalogue | Year | Price | Price | Notes |
|---|---|---|---|---|---|---|---|
| Wankan Tanka | LP | Byg | 529018 | 1971 | £6 | £15 | French |

## COGAN, ALMA

| Title | Format | Label | Catalogue | Year | Price | Price | Notes |
|---|---|---|---|---|---|---|---|
| Alma | LP | Columbia | SX6130 | 1967 | £15 | £30 | |
| Alma Sings With You In Mind | LP | Columbia | 33SX1345 | 1961 | £20 | £40 | |
| Alma Sings With You In Mind | LP | Columbia | SCX3391 | 1961 | £30 | £60 | stereo |
| Bell Bottom Blues | 7" | HMV | 7M188 | 1954 | £10 | £20 | |
| Birds And The Bees | 7" | HMV | 7M415 | 1956 | £7.50 | £15 | |
| Chantez Chantez | 7" | HMV | POP336 | 1957 | £4 | £8 | |
| Chee Chee Oo Chee | 7" | HMV | 7M293 | 1955 | £7.50 | £15 | |
| Do Do Do Do Do Do Do It Again | 7" | HMV | 7M226 | 1954 | £5 | £10 | with Frankie Vaughan |
| Eight Days A Week | 7" | Columbia | DB7786 | 1965 | £1.50 | £4 | |
| Fabulous | 7" | HMV | POP367 | 1957 | £5 | £10 | |
| Fly Away Lovers | 7" | HMV | POP500 | 1958 | £1.50 | £4 | |
| Girl With The Laugh In Her Voice | LP | MFP | MFP1377 | 1970 | £4 | £10 | |
| Girl With The Laugh In Her Voice | 7" EP | HMV | 7EG8122 | 1955 | £5 | £10 | |
| Girl With The Laugh In Her Voice No. 2 | 7" EP | HMV | 7EG8151 | 1955 | £5 | £10 | |
| Girl With The Laugh In Her Voice No. 3 | 7" EP | HMV | 7EG8169 | 1956 | £5 | £10 | |
| Got 'n Idea | 7" | HMV | 7M316 | 1955 | £7.50 | £15 | |
| Hits From My Fair Lady | 7" EP | HMV | 7EG8352 | 1957 | £2 | £5 | ...with Ronnie Hilton |
| How About Love | LP | Columbia | 33SX1465 | 1962 | £20 | £40 | |
| How About Love | LP | Columbia | SCX3459 | 1962 | £30 | £60 | stereo |
| I Can't Tell A Waltz From A Tango | 7" | HMV | 7M271 | 1954 | £7.50 | £15 | |
| I Love To Sing | LP | HMV | CLP1152 | 1958 | £20 | £40 | |
| I Went To Your Wedding | 7" | HMV | 7M106 | 1953 | £10 | £20 | |
| In The Middle Of The House | 7" | HMV | POP261 | 1956 | £10 | £20 | |
| It's All Been Done Before | 7" | HMV | 7M390 | 1956 | £10 | £20 | ...with Ronnie Hilton |
| It's You | 7" | Columbia | DB7390 | 1964 | £1.50 | £4 | |
| Last Night On The Back Porch | 7" | HMV | POP573 | 1959 | £2 | £5 | |
| Little Shoemaker | 7" | HMV | 7M219 | 1954 | £10 | £20 | |
| Little Things Mean A Lot | 7" | HMV | 7M228 | 1954 | £7.50 | £15 | |
| Love And Marriage | 7" | HMV | 7M367 | 1956 | £7.50 | £15 | |
| Make Love To Me | 7" | HMV | 7M196 | 1954 | £7.50 | £15 | |
| Mama Teach Me To Dance | 7" | HMV | POP239 | 1956 | £7.50 | £15 | |
| More Than Ever Now | 7" | HMV | 7M301 | 1955 | £7.50 | £15 | |
| Must Be Santa | 7" | HMV | POP815 | 1960 | £1.50 | £4 | |
| Never Do A Tango With An Eskimo | 7" | HMV | 7M337 | 1955 | £7.50 | £15 | |
| Now That I've Found You | 7" | Columbia | DB8088 | 1966 | £1.50 | £4 | |
| O Dio Mio | 7" | HMV | POP728 | 1960 | £1.50 | £4 | |
| Oliver | LP | HMV | CLP1459 | 1961 | £15 | £30 | mono |
| Oliver | LP | HMV | CSD1370 | 1961 | £20 | £40 | stereo |
| Over And Over Again | 7" | HMV | 7M166 | 1953 | £7.50 | £15 | with Les Howard |
| Paper Kisses | 7" | HMV | 7M286 | 1955 | £7.50 | £15 | |
| Party Time | 7" | HMV | POP415 | 1957 | £2.50 | £6 | |
| Pink Shoelaces | 7" | HMV | POP608 | 1959 | £2 | £5 | |
| Ricochet | 7" | HMV | 7M173 | 1954 | £10 | £20 | |
| She Loves To Sing | 7" EP | HMV | 7EG8437 | 1957 | £5 | £10 | |
| Snakes And Snails | 7" | Columbia | DB7652 | 1965 | £1.50 | £4 | |
| Stairway Of Love | 7" | HMV | POP482 | 1958 | £4 | £8 | |
| Story Of My Life | 7" | HMV | POP433 | 1958 | £4 | £8 | |
| Sugartime | 7" | HMV | POP450 | 1958 | £5 | £10 | |
| Tennessee Waltz | 7" | Columbia | DB7233 | 1964 | £1.50 | £4 | |
| That's Happiness | 7" | HMV | POP392 | 1957 | £2.50 | £6 | |
| There's Never Been A Night | 7" | HMV | POP531 | 1958 | £2 | £5 | |
| This Ole House | 7" | HMV | 7M269 | 1954 | £10 | £20 | |
| To Be Loved By You | 7" | HMV | 7M107 | 1953 | £10 | £20 | |
| Train Of Love | 7" | HMV | POP760 | 1960 | £1.50 | £4 | |
| We Got Love | 7" | HMV | POP670 | 1959 | £1.50 | £4 | |
| What Am I Gonna Do, Ma? | 7" | HMV | 7M239 | 1954 | £12.50 | £25 | |
| Whatever Lola Wants | 7" | HMV | POP317 | 1957 | £5 | £10 | |
| You Me And Us | 7" | HMV | POP284 | 1957 | £5 | £10 | |

## COHEN, ALAN

| Title | Format | Label | Catalogue | Year | Price | Price | Notes |
|---|---|---|---|---|---|---|---|
| Duke Ellington's Black, Brown & Beige | LP | Argo | ZDA159 | 1973 | £5 | £12 | |

## COHEN, LEONARD

| Title | Format | Label | Catalogue | Year | Price | Price | Notes |
|---|---|---|---|---|---|---|---|
| Ain't No Cure For Love | CD-s | CBS | 6515992 | 1988 | £2 | £5 | |
| Bird On The Wire | 7" | CBS | 4245 | 1969 | £1.50 | £4 | |
| First We Take Manhattan | CD-s | CBS | 6513522 | 1988 | £2 | £5 | |
| Live From The Complex, Los Angeles | CD | Columbia | CSK5249 | 1993 | £8 | £20 | US promo |
| Live Songs | CD | CBS | CD65224 | 1988 | £5 | £12 | |
| McCabe & Mrs. Miller | 7" EP | CBS | 7684 | 1972 | £2 | £5 | |
| Songs From A Room | LP | CBS | 63587 | 1968 | £4 | £10 | |
| Songs Of Leonard Cohen | LP | CBS | 63241 | 1968 | £4 | £10 | |
| Songs Of Leonard Cohen | LP | Columbia | CL2733 | 1968 | £50 | £100 | US, mono |
| Songs Of Love And Hate | LP | CBS | 69004 | 1970 | £4 | £10 | with booklet |
| Suzanne | 7" | CBS | 3337 | 1968 | £1.50 | £4 | |

## COHEN, LEONARD & OTHERS
Canadian Poets 1 .......................................... LP ..... CBC ........... ..................... 1966 £20 .... £40 .............. Canadian
Six Montreal Poets ................................. LP ..... Folkways ..... FL9805 ................ 1957 £20 .... £40 ..................... US

## COHN, AL
Al Cohn Orchestra .............................. 10" LP HMV ............ DLP1107 .......... 1955 £20 .... £40 ..........................

## COIL
Anal Staircase ...................................... 12" ..... Force & Form.. ROTA121 ........... 1986 £2.50 ..... £6 ..........................
Anal Staircase ...................................... 12" ..... Force & Form.. ROTA121 ........... 1986 £4 ......... £10 .............. clear vinyl
Gold Is The Metal ............................... LP ..... Threshold LOCI1 ................. 1988 £100 .... £200 boxed with 7", poster,
House ............ booklet, linen folder
Gold Is The Metal ............................... LP ..... Threshold LOCI1 ................. 1988 £6 ......... £15 ....... red or clear vinyl
House ............
Gold Is The Metal ............................... LP ..... Threshold LOCI1 ................. 1988 £8 ......... £20 red or clear vinyl, with
House ............ bonus 7"
Gold Is The Metal ............................... CD .... Threshold LOCICD1 ........... 1987 £5 ......... £12
House ............
Hellraiser ............................................. 10" .... Solar Lodge .... COIL001 ............ 198– £2.50 ...... £6 ..... clear or pink vinyl
How To Destroy Angels ..................... CD-s .. Laylah ............ LAY005CD ......... 1988 £2 ........... £5
Panic .................................................... 12" ..... Force & Form.. FFK512 ............ 1985 £2.50 ...... £6
Panic .................................................... 12" ..... Force & Form.. FFK512 ............ 1985 £4 ........... £10 ............... red vinyl
Wrong Eye ........................................... 7" ...... Shock ............. SX002 ............... 1989 £10 ......... £20 ... individually lettered
Wrong Eye ........................................... 7" ...... Shock ............. SX002 ............... 1989 £4 ........... £8 individually numbered

## COIL (2)
Motor Industry ..................................... 7" ...... Northampton HAV1 ................... 1979 £2 ........... £5
Wood Hill .......

## COINCIDENCE
Coincidence ......................................... LP ..... Tromblas ......... 1133 ................... 1976 £6 ........... £15 ..................... French

## COKER, ALVADEAN
We're Gonna Bop .................................. 7" ...... London ........... HLU8191 ........... 1955 £100 ..... £200 ........... best auctioned

## COKER, SANDY
Meadowlark Melody ............................. 7" ...... London ........... HL8109 ............. 1954 £10 ......... £20

## COLBECK, RIC
Sun Is Coming Up ................................ LP ..... Fontana ........... 63883001 .......... 1970 £8 ........... £20

## COLD BLOOD
First Blood ........................................... LP ..... Atlantic ........... 588218 .............. 1970 £4 ........... £10
First Taste Of Sin ................................ LP ..... Reprise ........... 2074 ................. 1972 £4 ........... £10 ..................... US
Lydia .................................................... LP ..... Warner Bros .. K56047 ............. 1974 £4 ........... £10
Sisyphus ............................................... LP ..... Atlantic ........... 2400102 ............ 1971 £4 ........... £10

## COLD CUTS
Cold Cuts ............................................. LP ..... Pink Elephant .. 8777099 ............ 1973 £6 ........... £15 ..................... Dutch

## COLD STEEL
Cold Steel ............................................ LP ..... Ariola ............. 87736 ............... 1974 £4 ........... £10 ..................... Dutch

## COLD SUN
Dark Shadows ...................................... LP ..... private ............. ........................ 1969 £1400 . £2000 ........... US acetate
Dark Shadows ...................................... LP ..... Rockadelic ...... ........................ 1991 £15 ......... £30 ..................... US

## COLDER, BEN
Make The World Go Away .................... 7" EP . MGM ............ MGMEP791 ...... 1964 £2.50 ...... £6

## COLDMAN, RICHARD & JOHN RUSSELL
Homecooking and Richard Coldman ........ LP ..... Incus ............... INCUS31 ............ 1979 £5 ........... £12

## COLDWATER ARMY
Peace .................................................... LP ..... Agape ............. 2600 ................. 1972 £8 ........... £20 ......................... US

## COLE, B. J.
New Hovering Dog ............................... LP ..... United Artists .. UAS29418 .......... 1972 £4 ........... £10

## COLE, CINDY
Just Being Your Baby ........................... 7" ...... Columbia ........ DB7973 ............. 1966 £2.50 ...... £6

## COLE, CLAY
Twist Around The Clock ....................... 7" ...... London ........... HLP9499 ............ 1962 £1.50 ...... £4

## COLE, COZY
Cozy Cole All Stars ............................. 7" EP . MGM ............ MGMEP622 ...... 1957 £2.50 ...... £6
Father Cooperates ................................ 7" ...... Mercury .......... AMT1015 .......... 1958 £1.50 ...... £4
Topsy .................................................... 7" ...... London ........... HL7065 ............. 1958 £1.50 ...... £4 ..................... export
Topsy .................................................... 7" ...... London ........... HL8750 ............. 1958 £2 ........... £5
Turvy ................................................... 7" ...... London ........... HL8843 ............. 1959 £1.50 ...... £4

## COLE, JERRY
Hot Rod Dance Party ............................ LP ..... Capitol ............ (S)T2061 ........... 1964 £5 ........... £12 ..................... US
Outer Limits ........................................ LP ..... Capitol ............ (S)T2044 ........... 1963 £5 ........... £12 ..................... US
Surf Age ............................................... LP ..... Capitol ............ (S)T2112 ........... 1964 £8 ........... £20 .US, with bonus Dick
Dale 7"

## COLE, LLOYD & THE COMMOTIONS

| Title | Format | Label | Cat No | Year | | | |
|---|---|---|---|---|---|---|---|
| Are You Ready To Be Heartbroken? | 7" | Welcome To Las Vegas | LC1 | 1984 | £20 | £40 | |

## COLE, NAT 'KING'

| Title | Format | Label | Cat No | Year | | | |
|---|---|---|---|---|---|---|---|
| After Midnight | LP | Capitol | LCT6133 | 1957 | £4 | £10 | |
| After Midnight Part 1 | 7" EP | Capitol | EAP1782 | 1957 | £2 | £5 | |
| After Midnight Part 2 | 7" EP | Capitol | EAP2782 | 1957 | £2 | £5 | |
| After Midnight Part 3 | 7" EP | Capitol | EAP3782 | 1957 | £2 | £5 | |
| After Midnight Part 4 | 7" EP | Capitol | EAP4782 | 1958 | £2 | £5 | |
| Annabelle | 7" | Capitol | CL14317 | 1955 | £2.50 | £6 | |
| Around The World | 7" EP | Capitol | EAP1813 | 1957 | £2 | £5 | |
| At The Piano | 10" LP | Capitol | H156 | 1952 | £8 | £20 | US |
| Ballads Of The Day | LP | Capitol | T680 | 1956 | £5 | £12 | US |
| Ballads Of The Day | 10" LP | Capitol | LC6818 | 1956 | £4 | £10 | |
| Blossom Fell | 7" | Capitol | CL14235 | 1955 | £4 | £8 | |
| Capitol Presents Nat King Cole | 10" LP | Capitol | LC6569 | 1953 | £6 | £15 | |
| Capitol Presents Nat King Cole & His Trio Vol. 1 | 10" LP | Capitol | LC6587 | 1953 | £4 | £10 | |
| Capitol Presents Nat King Cole & His Trio Vol. 2 | 10" LP | Capitol | LC6594 | 1953 | £4 | £10 | |
| Capitol Presents Nat King Cole At The Piano | 10" LP | Capitol | LC6593 | 1953 | £4 | £10 | |
| Christmas Song | 7" EP | Capitol | EAP1036 | 1956 | £2 | £5 | |
| Cole Español | LP | Capitol | LCT6166 | 1958 | £4 | £10 | |
| Cole Español Part 1 | 7" EP | Capitol | EAP11031 | 1959 | £2 | £5 | |
| Cole Español Part 2 | 7" EP | Capitol | EAP21031 | 1959 | £2 | £5 | |
| Dreams Can Tell A Lie | 7" | Capitol | CL14513 | 1956 | £2 | £5 | |
| Every Time I Feel The Spirit | LP | Capitol | LCT6187 | 1959 | £4 | £10 | |
| I Am In Love | 7" | Capitol | CL14172 | 1954 | £2.50 | £6 | |
| If I Give My Heart To You | 7" | Capitol | CL14203 | 1954 | £2.50 | £6 | |
| If I May | 7" | Capitol | CL14295 | 1955 | £2.50 | £6 | |
| In The Beginning | LP | Brunswick | LAT8123 | 1956 | £6 | £15 | |
| Instrumental Classics | LP | Capitol | T592 | 1955 | £5 | £12 | US |
| Just One Of Those Things | LP | Capitol | (S)LCT6149 | 1958 | £4 | £10 | |
| King Cole Trio | 10" LP | Capitol | H8 | 1950 | £8 | £20 | US |
| King Cole Trio | 10" LP | Score | SLP4019 | 1950 | £30 | £60 | US |
| King Cole Trio Vol. 2 | 10" LP | Capitol | H29 | 1950 | £8 | £20 | US |
| King Cole Trio Vol. 3 | 10" LP | Capitol | H59 | 1950 | £8 | £20 | US |
| King Cole Trio Vol. 4 | 10" LP | Capitol | H139 | 1951 | £8 | £20 | US |
| Long Long Ago | 7" | Capitol | CL14215 | 1955 | £4 | £8 | |
| Looking Back | 7" EP | Capitol | EAP1960 | 1958 | £2 | £5 | |
| Love Is A Many Splendored Thing | 7" EP | Capitol | EAP1010 | 1956 | £2 | £5 | |
| Love Is A Many Splendored Thing | 7" | Capitol | CL14364 | 1955 | £2.50 | £6 | |
| Love Is Here To Stay | 7" EP | Capitol | EAP120151 | 1961 | £2 | £5 | |
| Love Is The Thing | LP | Capitol | (S)LCT6129 | 1957 | £4 | £10 | |
| Love Is The Thing Part 1 | 7" EP | Capitol | EAP1824 | 1957 | £2 | £5 | |
| Love Is The Thing Part 2 | 7" EP | Capitol | EAP2824 | 1957 | £2 | £5 | |
| Love Is The Thing Part 3 | 7" EP | Capitol | EAP3824 | 1957 | £2 | £5 | |
| Love Me As Though There Were No Tomorrow | 7" | Capitol | CL14621 | 1956 | £2 | £5 | |
| Midnight Flyer | 7" EP | Capitol | EAP11317 | 1960 | £2 | £5 | |
| Moods In Song | 7" EP | Capitol | EAP1633 | 1956 | £2 | £5 | |
| My One Sin | 7" | Capitol | CL14327 | 1955 | £4 | £8 | |
| Nat King Cole And George Shearing Part 1 | 7" EP | Capitol | EAP41675 | 1961 | £2 | £5 | |
| Nat King Cole And George Shearing Part 2 | 7" EP | Capitol | EAP51675 | 1963 | £2 | £5 | |
| Nat King Cole Trio | 10" LP | Capitol | H177 | 1952 | £8 | £20 | US |
| Nat King Cole Trio | 10" LP | Capitol | H220 | 1952 | £8 | £20 | US |
| Night Lights | 7" EP | Capitol | EAP1801 | 1957 | £2 | £5 | |
| Night Of The Quarter Moon | 7" EP | Capitol | EAP11211 | 1959 | £2 | £5 | |
| Non Domenticar | 7" EP | Capitol | EAP11138 | 1959 | £2 | £5 | |
| Penthouse Serenade | LP | Capitol | T332 | 1953 | £5 | £12 | US |
| Penthouse Serenade | 10" LP | Capitol | H332 | 1953 | £8 | £20 | US |
| Piano Style Of Nat King Cole | LP | Capitol | W689 | 1956 | £5 | £12 | US |
| Piano Style Of Nat King Cole | 10" LP | Capitol | LC6830 | 1956 | £4 | £10 | |
| Ramblin' Rose | 7" EP | Capitol | EAP51793 | 1963 | £2 | £5 | |
| Sand And The Sea | 7" | Capitol | CL14251 | 1955 | £2.50 | £6 | |
| Sings For Two In Love | LP | Capitol | T420 | 1954 | £5 | £12 | US |
| Sings For Two In Love | 10" LP | Capitol | LC6627 | 1953 | £4 | £10 | |
| Smile | 7" | Capitol | CL14149 | 1954 | £4 | £8 | |
| Someone You Love | 7" | Capitol | CL14378 | 1955 | £2.50 | £6 | |
| St. Louis Blues | LP | Capitol | (S)LCT6156 | 1958 | £4 | £10 | |
| St. Louis Blues Part 1 | 7" EP | Capitol | EAP1993 | 1958 | £2 | £5 | |
| St. Louis Blues Part 2 | 7" EP | Capitol | EAP2993 | 1958 | £2 | £5 | |
| St. Louis Blues Part 3 | 7" EP | Capitol | EAP3993 | 1958 | £2 | £5 | |
| Strip For Action | 7" EP | Capitol | EAP1040 | 1956 | £2 | £5 | |
| Teach Me Tonight | 7" | Capitol | CL14207 | 1954 | £4 | £8 | |
| Tenderly | 7" EP | Capitol | EAP120108 | 1961 | £2 | £5 | |
| Tenth Anniversary Album | LP | Capitol | LCT6003 | 1954 | £6 | £15 | |
| Tenth Anniversary Album Part 1 | 7" EP | Capitol | EAP1514 | 1955 | £2 | £5 | |
| Tenth Anniversary Album Part 2 | 7" EP | Capitol | EAP2514 | 1955 | £2 | £5 | |
| Tenth Anniversary Album Part 3 | 7" EP | Capitol | EAP3514 | 1955 | £2 | £5 | |
| Tenth Anniversary Album Part 4 | 7" EP | Capitol | EAP4514 | 1955 | £2 | £5 | |
| This Is Nat King Cole | LP | Capitol | LCT6142 | 1957 | £4 | £10 | |
| To Whom It May Concern | LP | Capitol | (S)LCT6182 | 1959 | £4 | £10 | |
| To Whom It May Concern Part 1 | 7" EP | Capitol | EAP11190 | 1959 | £2 | £5 | |
| To Whom It May Concern Part 2 | 7" EP | Capitol | EAP21190 | 1959 | £2 | £5 | |

| | | | | | | | |
|---|---|---|---|---|---|---|---|
| To Whom It May Concern Part 3 | 7" EP | Capitol | EAP31190 | 1959 | £2 | £5 | |
| Too Young To Go Steady | 7" | Capitol | CL14573 | 1956 | £1.50 | £4 | |
| Unbelievable | 7" | Capitol | CL14155 | 1954 | £2.50 | £6 | |
| Unforgettable | LP | Capitol | T357 | 1953 | £5 | £12 | US |
| Unforgettable | 7" EP | Capitol | EAP120053 | 1961 | £2 | £5 | |
| Unforgettable | 10" LP | Capitol | H357 | 1953 | £8 | £20 | US |
| Very Thought Of You | LP | Capitol | (S)LCT6173 | 1959 | £4 | £10 | |
| Very Thought Of You Part 1 | 7" EP | Capitol | EAP11084 | 1959 | £2 | £5 | |
| Very Thought Of You Part 2 | 7" EP | Capitol | EAP21084 | 1959 | £2 | £5 | |
| Vocal Classics | LP | Capitol | T591 | 1955 | £5 | £12 | US |
| Welcome To The Club | LP | Capitol | (S)LCT6176 | 1959 | £4 | £10 | |
| Welcome To The Club | 7" EP | Capitol | EAP11120 | 1959 | £2 | £5 | |
| When I Fall In Love | 7" | Capitol | CL14709 | 1957 | £1.50 | £4 | |
| When Rock And Roll Came To Trinidad | 7" | Capitol | CL14733 | 1957 | £1.50 | £4 | |

## COLE, NATALIE

| | | | | | | | |
|---|---|---|---|---|---|---|---|
| Party Lights | 7" | Capitol | CL15929 | 1977 | £1.50 | £4 | demo only |

## COLE, STRANGER

| | | | | | | | |
|---|---|---|---|---|---|---|---|
| All Your Friends | 7" | R&B | JB120 | 1963 | £5 | £10 | with Ken |
| Cherry May | 7" | Island | WI162 | 1964 | £5 | £10 | Don Drummond B side |
| Cow In A Pasture | 7" | Island | WI169 | 1965 | £5 | £10 | Gloris & Dreamletts B side |
| Darling Please | 7" | Songbird | SB1008 | 1969 | £1.50 | £4 | |
| Down The Train Line | 7" | Doctor Bird | DB1087 | 1967 | £5 | £10 | with Patsy Todd |
| Drop The Rachet | 7" | Doctor Bird | DB1040 | 1966 | £5 | £10 | |
| Give Me One More Chance | 7" | Rio | R81 | 1966 | £4 | £8 | with Patsy Cole |
| Give Me The Right | 7" | Doctor Bird | DB1050 | 1966 | £5 | £10 | with Patsy Todd |
| Glad You're Living | 7" | Duke | DU27 | 1969 | £1.50 | £4 | |
| Hey Little Girl | 7" | Black Swan | WI462 | 1965 | £5 | £10 | with Patsy Todd, Cornell Campbell B side |
| I Want To Go Home | 7" | Black Swan | WI465 | 1965 | £5 | £10 | |
| Jeboza Macod | 7" | Island | WI3154 | 1968 | £5 | £10 | |
| Just Like A River | 7" | Amalgamated | AMG801 | 1968 | £4 | £8 | Leaders B side |
| Last Love | 7" | Island | WI114 | 1963 | £5 | £10 | Stranger & Ken B side |
| Leana Leana | 7" | Escort | ES819 | 1969 | £1.50 | £4 | |
| Little Boy Blue | 7" | Black Swan | WI435 | 1964 | £5 | £10 | Eric Morris B side |
| Morning Star | 7" | R&B | JB129 | 1963 | £5 | £10 | |
| Night After Night | 7" | Black Swan | WI461 | 1965 | £5 | £10 | |
| Oh Oh I Need You | 7" | Island | WI141 | 1964 | £5 | £10 | Don Drummond B side |
| Out Of Many | 7" | R&B | JB133 | 1963 | £5 | £10 | |
| Over And Over Again | 7" | Island | WI3128 | 1967 | £5 | £10 | |
| Pretty Cottage | 7" | Escort | ES810 | 1969 | £1.50 | £4 | |
| Pussy Cat | 7" | Ska Beat | JB192 | 1965 | £5 | £10 | Maytals B side |
| Remember | 7" | Escort | ES826 | 1969 | £1.50 | £4 | |
| Rolling On | 7" | Island | WI126 | 1963 | £5 | £10 | |
| Run Joe | 7" | Island | WI177 | 1965 | £5 | £10 | |
| Seeing Is Knowing | 7" | Amalgamated | AMG806 | 1968 | £4 | £8 | Roy Shirley B side |
| Senor Senorita | 7" | Island | WI113 | 1963 | £5 | £10 | with Patsy Todd, Don Drummond B side |
| Stranger At The Door | 7" | Island | WI110 | 1963 | £5 | £10 | |
| Summer Day | 7" | Black Swan | WI415 | 1964 | £5 | £10 | |
| Tell It To Me | 7" | Doctor Bird | DB1084 | 1967 | £5 | £10 | with Patsy Todd |
| Things Come To Those Who Wait | 7" | Island | WI160 | 1964 | £5 | £10 | with Patsy Todd |
| Till My Dying Days | 7" | Island | WI133 | 1963 | £5 | £10 | Stranger & Patsy B side |
| Tom Dick And Harry | 7" | Island | WI144 | 1964 | £5 | £10 | with Patsy Todd |
| Uno-Dos-Tres | 7" | Black Swan | WI413 | 1964 | £5 | £10 | |
| We Shall Overcome | 7" | Doctor Bird | DB1025 | 1966 | £5 | £10 | |
| What Moma No Want She Get | 7" | Amalgamated | AMG838 | 1969 | £2.50 | £6 | |
| When I Get My Freedom | 7" | Unity | UN514 | 1969 | £1.50 | £4 | |
| When The Party Is Over | 7" | Blue Beat | BB345 | 1966 | £6 | £12 | Charmers B side |
| Yea Yea Baby | 7" | Island | WI152 | 1964 | £5 | £10 | with Patsy Todd, Baba Brooks B side |
| You Took My Love | 7" | Doctor Bird | DB1066 | 1966 | £5 | £10 | |

## COLEMAN, BOBBY

| | | | | | | | |
|---|---|---|---|---|---|---|---|
| You Don't Have To Tell Me | 7" | Pye | 7N25365 | 1966 | £25 | £50 | |

## COLEMAN, FITZROY

| | | | | | | | |
|---|---|---|---|---|---|---|---|
| Lucille | 7" | Starlite | ST45064 | 1961 | £1.50 | £4 | |

## COLEMAN, LONNIE & JESSE ROBERTSON

| | | | | | | | |
|---|---|---|---|---|---|---|---|
| Dolores Diana | 7" | London | HLU8335 | 1956 | £12.50 | £25 | |

## COLEMAN, MICHAEL

| | | | | | | | |
|---|---|---|---|---|---|---|---|
| Irish Jigs And Reels | LP | Ace Of Hearts | AH56 | 1963 | £10 | £25 | |
| Legacy Of Michael Coleman | LP | Shanachie | 33002 | 1976 | £4 | £10 | US |

## COLEMAN, ORNETTE

| | | | | | | | |
|---|---|---|---|---|---|---|---|
| Art Of The Improvisors | LP | Atlantic | 2400109 | 1971 | £6 | £15 | |
| At The Golden Circle, Stockholm, Vol. 1 | LP | Blue Note | BLP/BST84224 | 1966 | £8 | £20 | |
| At The Golden Circle, Stockholm, Vol. 2 | LP | Blue Note | BLP/BST84225 | 1966 | £8 | £20 | |
| Change Of The Century | LP | London | LTZK15199/ SAHK6099 | 1961 | £10 | £25 | |

| Title | Format | Label | Catalogue | Year | | | Notes |
|---|---|---|---|---|---|---|---|
| Chappaqua Suite | LP | CBS | 66203 | 1967 | £15 | £30 | double |
| Crisis | LP | Impulse | AS9187 | 1972 | £6 | £15 | US |
| Dancing In Your Head | LP | Horizon | SP722 | 1977 | £6 | £15 | US |
| Empty Foxhole | LP | Blue Note | BLP/BST84246 | 1967 | £8 | £20 | |
| Evening With Ornette Coleman | LP | Polydor | 623246/7 | 1968 | £15 | £30 | boxed double |
| Free Jazz | LP | Atlantic | (SD)1364 | 1961 | £10 | £25 | US |
| Love Call | LP | Blue Note | BST84356 | 1970 | £6 | £25 | |
| Music Of Ornette Coleman | LP | RCA | RD/SF7944 | 1970 | £6 | £15 | |
| New York Is Now | LP | Blue Note | BST84287 | 1968 | £10 | £25 | |
| Ornette | LP | London | LTZK15241/ SAHK6235 | 1962 | £10 | £25 | |
| Ornette At Twelve | LP | Impulse | M/SIPL518 | 1969 | £6 | £15 | |
| Ornette On Tenor | LP | Atlantic | (SD)1394 | 1962 | £10 | £25 | US |
| Ornette On Tenor | LP | Atlantic | 588121 | 1968 | £6 | £15 | |
| Science Fiction | LP | CBS | 64774 | 1972 | £6 | £15 | |
| Shape Of Jazz To Come | LP | Atlantic | (SD)1317 | 1959 | £10 | £25 | US |
| Shape Of Jazz To Come | LP | Atlantic | 587/588022 | 1966 | £6 | £15 | |
| Skies Of America | LP | CBS | 64147 | 1972 | £8 | £20 | |
| Something Else | LP | Contemporary | LAC12170 | 1959 | £10 | £25 | |
| This Is Our Music | LP | London | LTZK15228/ SAHK6181 | 1961 | £10 | £25 | |
| Tomorrow Is The Question | LP | Contemporary | LAC12228 | 1960 | £10 | £25 | |
| Town Hall 1962 | LP | Fontana | SFJL923 | 1969 | £6 | £15 | |
| Twins | LP | Atlantic | K40278 | 1972 | £6 | £15 | |

## COLEMAN TRADITIONAL SOCIETY

| Title | Format | Label | Catalogue | Year | | | Notes |
|---|---|---|---|---|---|---|---|
| Music From The Coleman Country | LP | Leader | LEA2044 | 1972 | £4 | £10 | |

## COLES, JOHNNY

| Title | Format | Label | Catalogue | Year | | | Notes |
|---|---|---|---|---|---|---|---|
| Little Johnny C | LP | Blue Note | BLP/BST84144 | 1963 | £20 | £40 | |

## COLLAGE

| Title | Format | Label | Catalogue | Year | | | Notes |
|---|---|---|---|---|---|---|---|
| Misty | LP | Studio Two | TWO410 | 1973 | £4 | £10 | |

## COLLECTORS

| Title | Format | Label | Catalogue | Year | | | Notes |
|---|---|---|---|---|---|---|---|
| Collectors | LP | Warner Bros | WS1746 | 1968 | £8 | £20 | US |
| Grass And Wild Strawberries | LP | Warner Bros | WS1774 | 1968 | £6 | £15 | |

## COLLEGE BOYS

| Title | Format | Label | Catalogue | Year | | | Notes |
|---|---|---|---|---|---|---|---|
| Someone Will Be There | 7" | Blue Beat | BB202 | 1963 | £6 | £12 | |

## COLLEN, SHARON

| Title | Format | Label | Catalogue | Year | | | Notes |
|---|---|---|---|---|---|---|---|
| Travelling People | LP | HMV | CLP3592 | 1966 | £4 | £10 | |

## COLLETTE, BUDDY

| Title | Format | Label | Catalogue | Year | | | Notes |
|---|---|---|---|---|---|---|---|
| Man Of Many Parts | LP | Contemporary | LAC12090 | 1958 | £6 | £15 | |
| Nice Day With Buddy Collette | LP | Contemporary | LAC12092 | 1958 | £6 | £15 | |
| Porgy And Bess | LP | Top Rank | 25003 | 1960 | £5 | £12 | |
| Swinging Shepherds | LP | Mercury | MMB12001 | 1959 | £5 | £12 | |

## COLLIER, GRAHAM

| Title | Format | Label | Catalogue | Year | | | Notes |
|---|---|---|---|---|---|---|---|
| Darius | LP | Mosaic | GCM741 | 1974 | £5 | £12 | |
| Day Of The Dead | LP | Mosaic | GCMD783/4 | 1978 | £8 | £20 | double |
| Deep Dark Blue Centre | LP | Deram | DML/SML1005 | 1967 | £15 | £30 | |
| Down Another Road | LP | Fontana | SFJL922 | 1969 | £15 | £30 | |
| Jazz Illustrations | LP | Cambridge University | 521205646 | 1975 | £8 | £20 | |
| Jazz Lecture Concert | LP | Cambridge University | 051205638 | 1975 | £8 | £20 | |
| Jazz Rhythm Section | LP | Cambridge University | 05212056033 | 1976 | £8 | £20 | |
| Midnight Blue | LP | Mosaic | GCM751 | 1975 | £5 | £12 | |
| Mosaics | LP | Philips | 6308051 | 1971 | £15 | £30 | |
| New Conditions | LP | Mosaic | GCM761 | 1976 | £5 | £12 | |
| Portraits | LP | Saydisc | SDL244 | 1972 | £15 | £30 | |
| Songs For My Father | LP | Polydor | 6309006 | 1970 | £15 | £30 | |
| Symphony Of Scorpions | LP | Mosaic | GCM773 | 1977 | £5 | £12 | |

## COLLIER, MITTY

| Title | Format | Label | Catalogue | Year | | | Notes |
|---|---|---|---|---|---|---|---|
| I Had A Talk With My Man | 7" | Pye | 7N25275 | 1964 | £10 | £20 | |

## COLLINS, AL JAZZBO

| Title | Format | Label | Catalogue | Year | | | Notes |
|---|---|---|---|---|---|---|---|
| East Coast Jazz Scene | LP | Vogue Coral | LVA9030 | 1956 | £15 | £30 | |

## COLLINS, ALBERT

Albert Collins was one of the great blues guitarists, with an easily recognizable sound of his own derived from an oddly tuned Telecaster played without a plectrum. After some success with his earliest recordings, Collins hardly recorded at all during the seventies, but found himself becoming a considerable blues star towards the end of his life, thanks in no small part to the enthusiastic support of Robert Cray and Gary Moore, who featured him on their records, and jazz composer John Zorn, who wrote an extended showcase for his guitar playing (included on the album *Spillane*).

| Title | Format | Label | Catalogue | Year | | | Notes |
|---|---|---|---|---|---|---|---|
| Compleat Albert Collins | LP | Imperial | 12445 | 1969 | £8 | £20 | US |
| Cool Sound Of Albert Collins | LP | TCF Hall | 8002 | 1965 | £8 | £20 | US |
| Love Can Be Found Anywhere | LP | Liberty | LBS83238 | 1969 | £6 | £15 | |
| There's Gotta Be A Change | LP | Tumbleweed | TW3501 | 1971 | £6 | £15 | |
| Trash Talkin' | LP | Imperial | 12438 | 1969 | £8 | £20 | US |
| Truckin' | LP | Blue Thumb | 8758 | 197– | £6 | £15 | US |

## COLLINS, ANSELL

| | | | | | | | |
|---|---|---|---|---|---|---|---|
| Cock Robin | 7" | J-Dan | JDN4401 | 1970 | £1.50 | £4 | |
| My Last Waltz | 7" | Amalgamated | AMG851 | 1969 | £2.50 | £6 | *Immortals B side* |
| Night Of Love | 7" | Trojan | TR699 | 1969 | £1.50 | £4 | |

## COLLINS, DAVE & ANSELL

| | | | | | | | |
|---|---|---|---|---|---|---|---|
| Double Barrel | LP | Trojan | TBL162 | 1971 | £4 | £10 | |
| Double Barrel | 7" | Technique | TE901 | 1971 | £1.50 | £4 | |
| Monkey Spanner | 7" | Technique | TE914 | 1971 | £1.50 | £4 | |

## COLLINS, DONNIE SHOW BAND

| | | | | | | | |
|---|---|---|---|---|---|---|---|
| Get Down With It | 7" | Pye | 7N17628 | 1968 | £2 | £5 | |

## COLLINS, DOROTHY

| | | | | | | | |
|---|---|---|---|---|---|---|---|
| At Home With Dorothy And Raymond | LP | Coral | LVA9058 | 1957 | £4 | £10 | |
| Baby Can Rock | 7" | Vogue Coral | Q72232 | 1957 | £4 | £8 | |
| Cool It Baby | 7" | Vogue Coral | Q72198 | 1956 | £7.50 | £15 | |
| Dorothy Collins Sings | 7" EP | London | REP1025 | 1955 | £5 | £10 | |
| Four Walls | 7" | Vogue Coral | Q72262 | 1957 | £1.50 | £4 | |
| Moments To Remember | 7" | Vogue Coral | Q72116 | 1956 | £2.50 | £6 | |
| Mr. Wonderful | 7" | Vogue Coral | Q72252 | 1957 | £1.50 | £4 | |
| My Boy Flat Top | 7" | Vogue Coral | Q72111 | 1955 | £7.50 | £15 | |
| Rock And Roll Train | 7" | Vogue Coral | Q72193 | 1956 | £7.50 | £15 | |
| Seven Days | 7" | Vogue Coral | Q72137 | 1956 | £4 | £8 | |
| Soft Sands | 7" | Vogue Coral | Q72287 | 1957 | £1.50 | £4 | |
| Treasure Of Love | 7" | Vogue Coral | Q72173 | 1956 | £5 | £10 | |
| Twelve Gifts Of Christmas | 7" | Vogue Coral | Q72208 | 1956 | £1.50 | £4 | |

## COLLINS, EDWYN

| | | | | | | | |
|---|---|---|---|---|---|---|---|
| Don't Shilly Shally | 12" | Creation | CRE047T | 1987 | £15 | £30 | *test pressing* |
| Fifty Shades Of Blue | CD-s | Demon | D1065CD | 1989 | £2 | £5 | |
| My Beloved Girl | 7" | Elevation | ACID6B | 1987 | £2 | £5 | *boxed with 3 cards* |

## COLLINS, GLENDA

| | | | | | | | |
|---|---|---|---|---|---|---|---|
| Age For Love | 7" | Decca | F11321 | 1961 | £1.50 | £4 | |
| Baby It Hurts | 7" | HMV | POP1283 | 1964 | £5 | £10 | |
| Head Over Heels In Love | 7" | Decca | F11417 | 1961 | £1.50 | £4 | |
| I Lost My Heart In The Fairground | 7" | HMV | POP1163 | 1963 | £15 | £30 | |
| If You've Got To Pick A Baby | 7" | HMV | POP1233 | 1963 | £5 | £10 | |
| It's Hard To Believe It | 7" | Pye | 7N17150 | 1966 | £5 | £10 | |
| Johnny Loves Me | 7" | HMV | POP1439 | 1965 | £7.50 | £15 | |
| Lollipop | 7" | HMV | POP1323 | 1964 | £5 | £10 | |
| Something I've Got To Tell You | 7" | Pye | 7N17044 | 1966 | £5 | £10 | |
| Take A Chance | 7" | Decca | F11280 | 1960 | £1.50 | £4 | |
| Thou Shalt Not Steal | 7" | HMV | POP1475 | 1965 | £4 | £8 | |

## COLLINS, JOHNNY

| | | | | | | | |
|---|---|---|---|---|---|---|---|
| Johnny's Private Army | LP | Tradition | TSR020 | 1975 | £4 | £10 | |
| Traveller's Rest | LP | Tradition | TSR014 | 1973 | £4 | £10 | |

## COLLINS, JUDY

| | | | | | | | |
|---|---|---|---|---|---|---|---|
| Concert | LP | Elektra | EKL/EKS7280 | 1964 | £4 | £10 | |
| Fifth Album | LP | Elektra | EKL/EKS7300 | 1965 | £4 | £10 | |
| Golden Apples Of The Sun | LP | Elektra | EKL/EKS7222 | 1962 | £4 | £10 | |
| I'll Keep It With Mine | 7" | London | HLZ10029 | 1966 | £1.50 | £4 | |
| In My Life | LP | Elektra | EKL/EKS7320 | 1967 | £4 | £10 | |
| Maid Of Constant Sorrow | LP | Elektra | EKL/EKS7209 | 1962 | £4 | £10 | |
| Third Album | LP | Elektra | EKL/EKS7243 | 1964 | £4 | £10 | |
| Who Knows Where The Time Goes | LP | Elektra | EKL/EKS74033 | 1969 | £4 | £10 | |
| Wild Flowers | LP | Elektra | EKL/EKS74012 | 1968 | £4 | £10 | |

## COLLINS, LYN

| | | | | | | | |
|---|---|---|---|---|---|---|---|
| Check Me Out If You Don't Know Me By Now | LP | People | PE6605 | 1975 | £15 | £30 | *US* |
| Female Preacher | LP | Urban | URBLP7 | 1988 | £4 | £10 | |
| Rock Me Again And Again | 7" | Polydor | 2066490 | 1974 | £2.50 | £6 | |
| Think | LP | Polydor | 2918006 | 1972 | £15 | £30 | |
| Think | 7" | Mojo | 2093029 | 1974 | £2 | £5 | |

## COLLINS, PETER

| | | | | | | | |
|---|---|---|---|---|---|---|---|
| First Album | LP | Nova | SDN21 | 1970 | £4 | £10 | |

## COLLINS, PHIL

| | | | | | | | |
|---|---|---|---|---|---|---|---|
| Another Day In Paradise | CD-s | Virgin | VSC1234 | 1989 | £2 | £5 | |
| Do You Remember (live) | CD-s | Virgin | VSCD1305 | 1990 | £2 | £5 | |
| Do You Remember (live) | CD-s | Virgin | VSCDX1305 | 1990 | £2.50 | £6 | *picture disc* |
| Groovy Kind Of Love | CD-s | Virgin | VSCD1117 | 1988 | £2 | £5 | |
| Hang In Long Enough | CD-s | Virgin | VSCDX1300 | 1990 | £2.50 | £6 | *picture disc* |
| I Wish It Would Rain Down | CD-s | Virgin | VSCD1240 | 1990 | £2 | £5 | |
| In The Air Tonight | CD-s | Virgin | VSCD1200 | 1988 | £2 | £5 | |
| In The Air Tonight | 7" | Virgin | VSK102 | 1981 | £2 | £5 | *with booklet* |
| One More Night | 7" | Virgin | VSS755 | 1985 | £2 | £5 | *shaped picture disc* |
| Profiled! | CD | Atlantic | PR30922 | 1989 | £8 | £20 | *US interview promo* |
| Separate Lives | 7" | Virgin | VSSD818 | 1985 | £2.50 | £6 | *2 picture discs* |
| Serious Hits | CD | Virgin | PCVCD1 | 1990 | £30 | £60 | *promo box set with video, tour programme* |

| Title | Format | Label | Cat. No. | Year | | | Notes |
|---|---|---|---|---|---|---|---|
| Something Happened On The Way To Heaven | CD-s | Virgin | VSCDT1251 | 1990 | £2 | £5 | |
| Story Interview Disc | CD | Atlantic | PR53702 | 1993 | £8 | £20 | ...US interview promo |
| Story So Far | CD | Virgin | PC001 | 1993 | £15 | £30 | ..... promo compilation |
| Sussudio | 7" | Virgin | VSY73612 | 1985 | £2 | £5 | ...... shaped picture disc |
| That's Just The Way It Is | CD-s | Virgin | VSCD1277 | 1990 | £2 | £5 | |
| Thru' These Walls | 7" | Virgin | VSY524 | 1982 | £1.50 | £4 | .................picture disc |
| Twelve Inchers | CD-s | Virgin | CDEP4 | 1988 | £2 | £5 | |
| Two Hearts | CD-s | Virgin | VSCD1142 | 1988 | £2 | £5 | ...............3" single |
| You Can't Hurry Love | 7" | Virgin | VSY531 | 1982 | £2 | £5 | .................picture disc |

## COLLINS, ROGER

| | | | | | | | |
|---|---|---|---|---|---|---|---|
| She's Looking Good | 7" | Vocalion | VP9285 | 1967 | £2.50 | £6 | |

## COLLINS, SHIRLEY

| | | | | | | | |
|---|---|---|---|---|---|---|---|
| Adieu To Old England | LP | Topic | 12T238 | 1974 | £10 | £25 | |
| Amaranth | LP | Harvest | SHSM2008 | 1976 | £8 | £20 | |
| Anthems In Eden | LP | Harvest | SHVL754 | 1969 | £25 | £50 | .... with Dolly Collins |
| English Songs Vol. 2 | 7" EP | Collector | JEB9 | 1964 | £20 | £40 | |
| False True Lovers | LP | Folkways | FG3564 | 1959 | £75 | £150 | ...... US |
| Favourite Garland | LP | Deram | SML1117 | 1975 | £6 | £15 | |
| Foggy Dew | 7" EP | Collector | JEB3 | 1960 | £20 | £40 | |
| For As Many As Will | LP | Topic | 12T380 | 1978 | £4 | £10 | ... with Dolly Collins |
| Heroes In Love | 7" EP | Topic | TOP95 | 1963 | £20 | £40 | |
| Love, Death And The Lady | LP | Harvest | SHVL771 | 1970 | £25 | £50 | ... with Dolly Collins |
| No Roses | LP | Mooncrest | CREST11 | 1974 | £4 | £10 | ... with Albion Band |
| No Roses | LP | Pegasus | PEG7 | 1971 | £10 | £25 | ..... with Albion Band |
| Power Of The True Love Knot | LP | Hannibal | HNBL1327 | 198– | £4 | £10 | |
| Power Of The True Love Knot | LP | Polydor | 583025 | 1968 | £30 | £60 | |
| Sweet England | LP | Argo | RG150 | 1960 | £50 | £100 | |
| Sweet Primroses | LP | Topic | 12TS170 | 1967 | £20 | £40 | |
| Unquiet Grave | 7" EP | Collector | JEB5 | 1961 | £20 | £40 | |

## COLLINS, TOMMY

| | | | | | | | |
|---|---|---|---|---|---|---|---|
| Dynamic Tommy Collins | LP | Columbia | CL2510/CS9310 | 1966 | £8 | £20 | US |
| Let Down | 7" | Capitol | CL14894 | 1958 | £1.50 | £4 | |
| Let's Live A Little | LP | Tower | (D)T5021 | 1966 | £4 | £10 | US |
| Light Of The Lord | LP | Capitol | T1125 | 1959 | £10 | £25 | US |
| Little June | 7" | Capitol | CL15076 | 1959 | £2 | £5 | |
| On Tour | LP | Columbia | CL2778/CS9578 | 1968 | £8 | £20 | US |
| Shindig | LP | Tower | (D)T5107 | 1968 | £4 | £10 | US |
| Songs I Love To Sing | LP | Capitol | (S)T1436 | 1961 | £8 | £20 | US |
| Think It Over Boys | 7" | Capitol | CL14838 | 1958 | £1.50 | £4 | |
| This Is Tommy Collins | LP | Capitol | T1196 | 1959 | £8 | £20 | |
| Words And Music Country Style | LP | Capitol | T776 | 1957 | £8 | £20 | |
| Wreck Of The Old '97 | 7" | Capitol | CL15118 | 1960 | £1.50 | £4 | |

## COLONNA, JERRY

| | | | | | | | |
|---|---|---|---|---|---|---|---|
| Chicago Style | 7" | London | HL8143 | 1955 | £6 | £12 | |
| Ebb Tide | 7" | Brunswick | 05243 | 1954 | £4 | £8 | |
| It Might As Well Be Spring | 7" | Brunswick | 05342 | 1954 | £2.50 | £6 | |
| Let Me Go Lover | 7" | Parlophone | MSP6165 | 1955 | £1.50 | £4 | |
| Let's All Sing | LP | London | HAU2190 | 1959 | £5 | £12 | |
| Shifting Whispering Sands | 7" | HMV | 7M369 | 1956 | £1.50 | £4 | |

## COLORADOS

| | | | | | | | |
|---|---|---|---|---|---|---|---|
| Lips Are Redder On You | 7" | Oriole | CB1972 | 1964 | £2 | £5 | |

## COLOSSEUM

| | | | | | | | |
|---|---|---|---|---|---|---|---|
| Collectors' Colosseum | LP | Bronze | ILPS9173 | 1971 | £4 | £10 | |
| Daughter Of Time | LP | Vertigo | 6360017 | 1970 | £4 | £10 | .................spiral label |
| Live | LP | Bronze | ICD1 | 1971 | £5 | £12 | ................. double |
| Those About To Die Salute You | LP | Fontana | STL5510 | 1969 | £5 | £12 | |
| Those Who Are About To Die | 7" | Fontana | TF1029 | 1969 | £1.50 | £4 | |
| Valentyne Suite | LP | Vertigo | VO1 | 1969 | £5 | £12 | ...............spiral label |

## COLOURBOX

| | | | | | | | |
|---|---|---|---|---|---|---|---|
| Breakdown | 7" | 4AD | AD215 | 1982 | £2.50 | £6 | |
| Breakdown | 12" | 4AD | BAD215 | 1982 | £4 | £10 | |

## COLOURS OF LOVE

Although collectors' interest in the singles made by Colours of Love is slight, one of the singers was Elaine Page.

| | | | | | | | |
|---|---|---|---|---|---|---|---|
| I'm A Train | 7" | Page One | POF060 | 1968 | £1.50 | £4 | |
| Just Another Fly | 7" | Page One | POF086 | 1968 | £1.50 | £4 | |
| Mother Of Convention | 7" | Page One | POF124 | 1969 | £1.50 | £4 | |

## COLT, CHRISTOPHER

| | | | | | | | |
|---|---|---|---|---|---|---|---|
| Virgin Sunrise | 7" | Decca | F12726 | 1968 | £5 | £10 | |

## COLTON, TONY

| | | | | | | | |
|---|---|---|---|---|---|---|---|
| I Stand Accused | 7" | Pye | 7N15886 | 1965 | £30 | £60 | |
| I've Laid Some Down In My Time | 7" | Pye | 7N17117 | 1966 | £7.50 | £15 | |
| In The World Of Marnie Dreaming | 7" | Columbia | DB8385 | 1968 | £2.50 | £6 | |
| Lose My Mind | 7" | Decca | F11879 | 1964 | £2.50 | £6 | |
| You're Wrong There Baby | 7" | Pye | 7N17046 | 1966 | £7.50 | £15 | |

## COLTRANE, ALICE

John Coltrane's wife played piano on her husband's last recordings, and expanded her range to include organ and harp on the music she made after his death. Her albums tend to have a mystical slant which makes them fit well into the ethos of much seventies progressive music, although the sound is closer to the emotional out-pouring of John Coltrane than to a superficially similar hippy group like Gong. Nevertheless, Alice Coltrane did later make an album with Carlos Santana, though it is not listed here.

| Title | Format | Label | Cat. No. | Year | | | Notes |
|---|---|---|---|---|---|---|---|
| Eternity | LP | Warner Bros | BS2916 | 1976 | £5 | £12 | US |
| Journey In Satchidananda | LP | Impulse | AS9203 | 1971 | £8 | £20 | US |
| Lord Of Lords | LP | Impulse | AS9224 | 1973 | £6 | £15 | US |
| Monastic Trio | LP | Impulse | AS9156 | 1968 | £8 | £20 | US |
| Ptah The El Daoud | LP | Impulse | AS9196 | 1970 | £8 | £20 | US |
| Reflection On Creation And Space | LP | Impulse | AS92322 | 1973 | £10 | £25 | US |
| Universal Consciousness | LP | Impulse | AS9210 | 1971 | £8 | £20 | US |

## COLTRANE, JOHN

In the sixties, John Coltrane's passionate brand of modal improvisation often appealed to rock fans who did not otherwise like jazz. And when rock groups started to introduce long improvised solos, it was invariably the Coltrane style that they adopted. (This was made explicit by Mike Bloomfield and Al Kooper in their Coltrane tribute track 'His Holy Modal Majesty'.) There is one oddity in the Coltrane discography – some copies of *Kulu Se Mama* actually play the album *Om*, which was not otherwise given a UK release. There are likely to be some owners of *Kulu Se Mama* who are unaware that the music they know by that title is actually something totally different!

| Title | Format | Label | Cat. No. | Year | | | Notes |
|---|---|---|---|---|---|---|---|
| Africa/Brass | LP | HMV | CLP1548/CSD1431 | 1962 | £8 | £20 | |
| Afro Blue | LP | Probe | SPB1025 | 1971 | £6 | £15 | |
| Alternate Takes | LP | Atlantic | SD1668 | 1975 | £5 | £12 | US |
| Ascension | LP | HMV | CLP/CSD3543 | 1966 | £8 | £20 | |
| Atlantic Years | LP | Atlantic | K60052 | 1974 | £6 | £15 | double |
| Avant-Garde | LP | Atlantic | 587/588004 | 1966 | £8 | £20 | with Don Cherry |
| Bags And Trane | LP | London | LTZK15232/ SAHK6192 | 1962 | £10 | £25 | with Milt Jackson |
| Bahia | LP | Stateside | SL10162 | 1966 | £6 | £15 | |
| Ballads | LP | HMV | CLP1647/CSD1496 | 1963 | £8 | £20 | |
| Bass Blues | 7" EP | Esquire | EP239 | 1961 | £2 | £5 | |
| Black Pearls | LP | Prestige | PR24037 | 1974 | £5 | £12 | double |
| Black Pearls | LP | Stateside | SL10124 | 1965 | £6 | £15 | |
| Blue Train | LP | Blue Note | BLP/BST81577 | 1961 | £15 | £30 | |
| Cattin' | LP | Esquire | 32101 | 1960 | £8 | £20 | |
| Coltrane | LP | HMV | CLP1629/CSD1483 | 1963 | £8 | £20 | |
| Coltrane Jazz | LP | Atlantic | ATL/SAL1354 | 1967 | £6 | £15 | |
| Coltrane Jazz | LP | London | LTZK15219/ SAHK6162 | 1961 | £10 | £25 | |
| Coltrane Plays The Blues | LP | London | HAK/SHK8017 | 1963 | £10 | £25 | |
| Coltrane Time | LP | United Artists | (S)ULP1018 | 1963 | £8 | £20 | |
| Coltrane's Sound | LP | Atlantic | 587/588039 | 1966 | £6 | £15 | |
| Concert In Japan | LP | Impulse | AS9246 | 1973 | £15 | £30 | US triple |
| Cosmic Music | LP | Impulse | M/SIPL515 | 1969 | £8 | £20 | ... with Alice Coltrane |
| Crescent | LP | HMV | CLP1799/CSD1567 | 1965 | £8 | £20 | |
| Dakar | LP | Transatlantic | PR7280 | 1968 | £6 | £15 | |
| Duke Ellington And John Coltrane | LP | HMV | CLP1657/CSD1502 | 1963 | £8 | £20 | |
| Expression | LP | Impulse | M/SIPL502 | 1968 | £8 | £20 | |
| First Trane | LP | Esquire | 32079 | 1958 | £10 | £25 | |
| Giant Steps | LP | Atlantic | 588168 | 1969 | £4 | £10 | |
| Giant Steps | LP | Atlantic | ATL1311 | 1967 | £6 | £15 | |
| Giant Steps | LP | London | LTZK15197 | 1960 | £10 | £25 | |
| Impressions | LP | HMV | CLP1695/CSD1509 | 1964 | £8 | £20 | |
| Infinity | LP | Impulse | AS9225 | 1973 | £6 | £15 | US |
| Interstellar Space | LP | Impulse | ASD9277 | 1974 | £6 | £15 | US |
| John Coltrane | LP | Prestige | PR24003 | 1973 | £5 | £12 | double |
| John Coltrane Quartet Plays | LP | HMV | CLP1897/CSD1619 | 1965 | £8 | £20 | |
| John Coltrane With Johnny Hartman | LP | HMV | CLP1700 | 1964 | £8 | £20 | |
| Kulu Se Mama | LP | HMV | CLP/CSD3617 | 1967 | £8 | £20 | |
| Kulu Se Mama | LP | HMV | CLP/CSD3617 | 1967 | £10 | £25 | mispress – plays Coltrane's Om LP |
| Last Trane | LP | Transatlantic | PR7378 | 1968 | £6 | £15 | |
| Live At Birdland | LP | HMV | CLP1741/CSD1544 | 1964 | £8 | £20 | |
| Live At The Village Vanguard | LP | HMV | CLP1590/CSD1456 | 1962 | £8 | £20 | |
| Live At The Village Vanguard Again | LP | HMV | CLP/CSD3599 | 1967 | £8 | £20 | |
| Live In Seattle | LP | Impulse | AS92022 | 1971 | £10 | £25 | US double |
| Love Supreme | LP | HMV | CLP1869/CSD1605 | 1965 | £8 | £20 | |
| Lush Life | LP | Esquire | 32129 | 1961 | £10 | £25 | |
| Meditation | LP | HMV | CLP/CSD3575 | 1966 | £8 | £20 | |
| Moment's Notice | 7" | Blue Note | 451718 | 1964 | £2 | £5 | |
| More Lasting Than Bronze | LP | Prestige | PR24014 | 1973 | £5 | £12 | double |
| My Favorite Things | LP | Atlantic | 588146 | 1969 | £4 | £10 | |
| My Favorite Things | LP | Atlantic | ATL/SAL5022 | 1965 | £6 | £15 | |
| New Thing At Newport | LP | HMV | CLP/CSD3551 | 1966 | £8 | £20 | with Archie Shepp |
| Olé Coltrane | LP | London | LTZK15239/ SAHK6223 | 1962 | £10 | £25 | |
| On West 42nd Street | LP | Realm | RM157 | 1964 | £6 | £15 | |
| Other Village Vanguard Tapes | LP | Impulse | AS9325 | 1977 | £5 | £12 | US |
| Selflessness | LP | Impulse | SIPL522 | 1969 | £8 | £20 | |
| Soul Of Trane | 7" EP | Esquire | EP229 | 1960 | £2 | £5 | |
| Soultrane | LP | Esquire | 32089 | 1959 | £10 | £25 | |
| Soultrane | LP | Transatlantic | PR7531 | 1968 | £5 | £12 | |
| Standard Coltrane | LP | Esquire | 32179 | 1963 | £8 | £20 | |
| Sun Ship | LP | Impulse | AS9211 | 1973 | £6 | £15 | US |
| Tanganyika Strut | LP | Realm | RM52226 | 1965 | £6 | £15 | |

| Title | Format | Label | Catalogue | Year | | | Notes |
|---|---|---|---|---|---|---|---|
| Tenor Conclave | LP | Esquire | 32059 | 1958 | £8 | £20 | |
| Trane Ride | LP | Realm | RM181 | 1964 | £6 | £15 | |
| Traneing In | LP | Esquire | 32091 | 1959 | £10 | £25 | |
| Transition | LP | Impulse | AS9195 | 1970 | £8 | £20 | US |
| While My Lady Sleeps | 7" EP | Fontana | 469203TE | 1964 | £2 | £5 | |

## COLTS

| Title | Format | Label | Catalogue | Year | | | |
|---|---|---|---|---|---|---|---|
| San Miguel | 7" | Pye | 7N15955 | 1965 | £1.50 | £4 | |

## COLUMBUS

| Title | Format | Label | Catalogue | Year | | | |
|---|---|---|---|---|---|---|---|
| Everybody Loves The US Marshall | 7" | Deram | DM294 | 1970 | £1.50 | £4 | |

## COLWELL BROTHERS

| Title | Format | Label | Catalogue | Year | | | |
|---|---|---|---|---|---|---|---|
| Africa's Got The Answer | 7" EP | Philips | NBE11117 | 1959 | £2 | £5 | |
| Colwell Brothers | 7" EP | Philips | NBE11047 | 195– | £2 | £5 | |
| Colwell Brothers | 7" EP | Philips | NBE11048 | 195– | £2 | £5 | |
| There'll Be A New World | 7" EP | Philips | NBE11118 | 1959 | £2 | £5 | |

## COLWELL-WINFIELD BLUES BAND

| Title | Format | Label | Catalogue | Year | | | |
|---|---|---|---|---|---|---|---|
| Live Bust | LP | Zazoo | 1. | 1971 | £5 | £12 | US |

## COLYER, KEN

| Title | Format | Label | Catalogue | Year | | | |
|---|---|---|---|---|---|---|---|
| And Back To New Orleans Vol. 1 | 7" EP | Decca | DFE6268 | 1955 | £2 | £5 | |
| And Back To New Orleans Vol. 2 | 7" EP | Decca | DFE6299 | 1956 | £2 | £5 | |
| And His Omega Brass | 7" EP | Decca | DFE6435 | 1957 | £2 | £5 | |
| Back To The Delta | 10" LP | Decca | LF1196 | 1954 | £8 | £20 | |
| Club Session | LP | Decca | LK4178 | 1957 | £5 | £12 | |
| Dippermouth Blues | 7" | Decca | FJ10755 | 1956 | £1.50 | £4 | |
| Early Hours | 7" | Decca | F10504 | 1955 | £1.50 | £4 | |
| If I Ever Cease To Love | 7" | Decca | F10519 | 1955 | £1.50 | £4 | |
| In Hamburg | 10" LP | Decca | LF1319 | 1959 | £6 | £15 | |
| In New Orleans | 7" EP | Tempo | EXA53 | 1957 | £2.50 | £6 | |
| In New Orleans | 7" EP | Vogue | EPV1102 | 1956 | £2 | £5 | |
| In New Orleans | 10" LP | Vogue | LDE161 | 1955 | £8 | £20 | |
| In New Orleans Pt. 2 | 7" EP | Vogue | EPV1202 | 1958 | £2 | £5 | |
| Isle Of Capri | 7" | Tempo | A120 | 1956 | £1.50 | £4 | |
| Ken Colyer | 7" EP | Melodisc | EPM7105 | 195– | £2 | £5 | |
| Ken Colyer Jazzmen | 7" EP | Storyville | SEP301 | 1960 | £2 | £5 | |
| Ken Colyer Jazzmen | 7" EP | Tempo | EXA26 | 1956 | £2.50 | £6 | |
| Ken Colyer Jazzmen | 7" EP | Tempo | EXA31 | 1956 | £2.50 | £6 | |
| Ken Colyer Jazzmen & Crane River Jazz Band | 7" EP | Melodisc | EPM759 | 1956 | £2 | £5 | |
| Ken Colyer's Jazzmen | 7" EP | Storyville | SEP305 | 196– | £2 | £5 | |
| Ken Colyer's Jazzmen | 7" EP | Storyville | SEP309 | 196– | £2 | £5 | |
| Ken Colyer's Jazzmen | 10" LP | Tempo | LAP11 | 1956 | £15 | £30 | |
| Marching To New Orleans | 10" LP | Decca | LF1301 | 1958 | £6 | £15 | |
| Maryland My Maryland | 7" | Tempo | A136 | 1956 | £1.50 | £4 | |
| New Orleans To London | 10" LP | Decca | LF1152 | 1954 | £8 | £20 | |
| Plays Standards | LP | Decca | LK4294 | 1959 | £5 | £12 | |
| Red Wing | 7" | Decca | F10565 | 1955 | £1.50 | £4 | |
| Rum And Coca Cola | 7" EP | Esquire | EP233 | 1960 | £2 | £5 | |
| Sheik Of Araby | 7" | Tempo | A117 | 1956 | £1.50 | £4 | |
| Stomping | 7" EP | Esquire | EP243 | 1961 | £2 | £5 | |
| They All Played Ragtime | 7" EP | Decca | DFE6466 | 1958 | £2 | £5 | |
| This Is Jazz | LP | Columbia | 33SX1220 | 1960 | £4 | £10 | |
| This Is Jazz | 7" EP | Columbia | SEG8038 | 1960 | £2 | £5 | |
| This Is Jazz Vol. 1 No. 2 | 7" EP | Columbia | SEG8104 | 1961 | £2 | £5 | |
| This Is Jazz Vol. 2 | LP | Columbia | 33SX1297/ SCX3360 | 1961 | £4 | £10 | |
| This Is Jazz Vol. 2 | 7" EP | Columbia | SEG8145 | 1962 | £2 | £5 | |
| Too Busy | 7" EP | Columbia | SEG8180 | 1962 | £2 | £5 | |
| Trad Jazz Scene In Europe Vol. 2 | 7" EP | Storyville | SEP392 | 1961 | £2 | £5 | |
| Wabash Blues | 7" | Tempo | A126 | 1956 | £1.50 | £4 | |
| Walking The Blues | 7" EP | Decca | DFE6645 | 1960 | £2 | £5 | |
| Walking The Blues | 7" EP | Decca | STO143 | 1960 | £2 | £5 | |
| Wildcat Blues | 7" EP | Storyville | SEP412 | 1961 | £2 | £5 | |

## COLYER, KEN SKIFFLE GROUP

| Title | Format | Label | Catalogue | Year | | | |
|---|---|---|---|---|---|---|---|
| Downbound Train | 7" | Decca | FJ10751 | 1956 | £2 | £5 | |
| Ella Speed | 7" | Decca | FJ10972 | 1958 | £1.50 | £4 | |
| Green Corn | 7" EP | KC | KCS11EP | 195– | £2 | £5 | |
| Grey Goose | 7" | Decca | FJ10889 | 1957 | £1.50 | £4 | |
| House Rent Stomp | 7" | Decca | FJ10926 | 1957 | £1.50 | £4 | |
| Ken Colyer Skiffle Group In Hamburg | 7" EP | Decca | DFE6563 | 1959 | £4 | £8 | |
| Ken Colyer's Skiffle Group | 7" EP | Decca | DFE6286 | 1956 | £2.50 | £6 | |
| Ken Colyer's Skiffle Group No. 2 | 7" EP | Decca | DFE6444 | 1957 | £2.50 | £6 | |
| Ole Riley | 7" | Decca | FJ10772 | 1956 | £2 | £5 | |
| Streamline Train | 7" | Decca | F10711 | 1956 | £2 | £5 | |
| Take This Hammer | 7" | Decca | F10631 | 1955 | £2 | £5 | |

## COMBAT 84

| Title | Format | Label | Catalogue | Year | | | |
|---|---|---|---|---|---|---|---|
| Orders Of The Day | 7" | Victory | VIC1 | 1983 | £4 | £8 | |
| Rapist | 7" | Victory | VIC2 | 1983 | £2 | £5 | |

## COME

| Title | Format | Label | Catalogue | Year | | | |
|---|---|---|---|---|---|---|---|
| Come Sunday | 7" | Come Org | WDC88001 | 1979 | £12.50 | £25 | |
| I'm Jack | LP | Come Org | WDC880012 | 1981 | £20 | £40 | orange vinyl |
| Rampton | LP | Come Org | WDC88002 | 1979 | £25 | £50 | |

## COMFORTABLE CHAIR
Comfortable Chair ........................................ LP ...... Ode ............... 21244005 ............... 1969 £8 .......... £20 ........................... US

## COMICS, ARTHUR
Isgodaman? ................................................... 7" ..... XS ..................................... 1977 £5 ........... £10 ...........................

## COMMANDERS
Cat From Coos Bay ...................................... 7" ...... Brunswick ...... 05433 ............ 1955 £1.50 ..... £4 ...........................
Meet The Commanders ............................. 7" EP . Brunswick ...... OE9037 .............. 1955 £2 .......... £5 ...........................
Monster ........................................................ 7" ...... Brunswick ...... 05467 .............. 1955 £1.50 ..... £4 ...........................

## COMMODORES
Riding On A Train ....................................... 7" ...... London ........... HLD8209 ............... 1955 £250 ..... £400 ........... best auctioned
Speedo .......................................................... 7" ...... London ........... HLD8251 ............... 1956 £250 ..... £400 ........... best auctioned

## COMMON BOND
Faces ............................................................. LP ...... Word ............... WST9569 ............... 1975 £15 .......... £30 ...........................

## COMMON PEOPLE
Of The People, By The People, For The ....... LP ...... Capitol ........... ST266 ............... 1969 £37.50 .... £75 ........................... US
  People ........................................................

## COMMON ROUND
Four Pence A Day ....................................... LP ...... Galliard .......... GAL4015 ............... 197– £5 ........... £12 ...........................

## COMMUNARDS
Don't Leave Me This Way ........................ CD-s .. Polygram ...... 0804782 ............... 1988 £3 ........... £8 ........... CD video
For A Friend ................................................ CD-s .. London ........... LONCD166 ............... 1988 £2 ........... £5 ...........................
Never Can Say Goodbye ............................ CD-s .. London ........... LONCD158 ............... 1988 £2 ........... £5 ...........................
There's More To Love ............................... CD-s .. London ........... LONCD173 ............... 1988 £2 ........... £5 ...........................
You Are My World ..................................... CD-s .. London ........... LONFC123 ............... 1988 £2 ........... £5 ...........................

## COMO, PERRY
All At Once You Love Her ....................... 7" ...... HMV ............ POP394 ............... 1957 £1.50 ..... £4 ...........................
Bushel And A Peck ..................................... 7" ...... HMV ............ 7M138 ............... 1953 £5 ........... £10 ...........................
Como Sings ................................................. 7" EP . HMV ............ 7EG8192 ............... 1956 £2 ........... £5 ...........................
Don't Let The Stars Get In Your Eyes ..... 7" ...... HMV ............ 7M118 ............... 1953 £6 ........... £12 ...........................
Door Of Dreams .......................................... 7" ...... HMV ............ 7M305 ............... 1955 £2.50 ..... £6 ...........................
Frosty The Snowman .................................. 7" ...... HMV ............ 7M278 ............... 1954 £2.50 ..... £6 ...........................
Glendora ...................................................... 7" ...... HMV ............ 7MC49 ............... 1956 £5 ........... £10 ...........................
Hello Young Lovers .................................... 7" ...... HMV ............ 7M155 ............... 1953 £2.50 ..... £6 ...........................
Hot Diggity ................................................. 7" ...... HMV ............ 7M404 ............... 1956 £4 ........... £8 ...........................
Idle Gossip .................................................. 7" ...... HMV ............ 7M200 ............... 1954 £4 ........... £8 ...........................
If You Were Only Mine ............................ 7" ...... HMV ............ 7M241 ............... 1954 £4 ........... £8 ...........................
Juke Box Baby ............................................ 7" ...... HMV ............ 7MC39 ............... 1956 £12.50 ... £25 ........... export
Ko Ko Mo .................................................... 7" ...... HMV ............ 7M296 ............... 1955 £4 ........... £8 ...........................
Moonlight Love ........................................... 7" ...... HMV ............ POP271 ............... 1956 £2 ........... £5 ...........................
More ............................................................. 7" ...... HMV ............ POP240 ............... 1956 £4 ........... £8 ...........................
Papa Loves Mambo ..................................... 7" ...... HMV ............ 7M263 ............... 1954 £5 ........... £10 ...........................
Perry Como ................................................. 7" EP . HMV ............ 7EG8013 ............... 1954 £2 ........... £5 ...........................
Perry Como Sings ...................................... 10" LP HMV ............ DLP1026 ............... 1954 £4 ........... £10 ...........................
Rose Tattoo ................................................. 7" ...... HMV ............ 7M366 ............... 1956 £2.50 ..... £6 ...........................
Round And Round ...................................... 7" ...... HMV ............ POP328 ............... 1957 £2 ........... £5 ...........................
Ruby And The Pearl ................................... 7" ...... HMV ............ 7M102 ............... 1953 £2.50 ..... £6 ...........................
Say You're Mine Again .............................. 7" ...... HMV ............ 7M149 ............... 1953 £4 ........... £8 ...........................
Silk Stockings ............................................ 7" ...... HMV ............ POP369 ............... 1957 £1.50 ..... £4 ...........................
So Smooth ................................................... 7" EP . HMV ............ 7EG8171 ............... 1956 £2 ........... £5 ...........................
Some Enchanted Evening .......................... 7" ...... HMV ............ 7M110 ............... 1953 £4 ........... £8 ...........................
Somebody Up There Likes Me ................ 7" ...... HMV ............ 7MC51 ............... 1957 £4 ........... £8 ........... export
Somebody Up There Likes Me ................ 7" ...... HMV ............ POP304 ............... 1957 £2 ........... £5 ...........................
Tina Marie ................................................... 7" ...... HMV ............ 7M326 ............... 1955 £4 ........... £8 ...........................
Wanted ......................................................... 7" ...... HMV ............ 7M215 ............... 1954 £4 ........... £8 ...........................
Why Did You Leave Me? ........................... 7" ...... HMV ............ 7M163 ............... 1953 £2.50 ..... £6 ...........................
Wild Horses ................................................. 7" ...... HMV ............ 7M124 ............... 1953 £4 ........... £8 ...........................
With A Song In My Heart ......................... 7" EP . HMV ............ 7EG8244 ............... 1957 £2 ........... £5 ...........................
You Alone .................................................... 7" ...... HMV ............ 7M175 ............... 1954 £4 ........... £8 ...........................

## COMPANY
Company 1 .................................................... LP ...... Incus ........... INCUS21 ............... 1977 £5 ........... £12 ...........................
Company 2 .................................................... LP ..... Incus ........... INCUS23 ............... 1977 £5 ........... £12 ...........................
Company 3 .................................................... LP ..... Incus ........... INCUS25 ............... 1977 £5 ........... £12 ...........................
Company 4 .................................................... LP ..... Incus ........... INCUS26 ............... 1977 £5 ........... £12 ...........................
Company 5 .................................................... LP ..... Incus ........... INCUS28 ............... 1978 £5 ........... £12 ...........................
Company 6 .................................................... LP ..... Incus ........... INCUS29 ............... 1978 £5 ........... £12 ...........................
Company 7 .................................................... LP ..... Incus ........... INCUS30 ............... 1978 £5 ........... £12 ...........................
Epiphany ...................................................... LP ..... Incus ........... INCUS46/7 ............... 1985 £8 ........... £20 ........... double
Fables ........................................................... LP ..... Incus ........... INCUS36 ............... 1980 £5 ........... £12 ...........................
Fictions ........................................................ LP ..... Incus ........... INCUS38 ............... 1981 £5 ........... £12 ...........................
Trios ............................................................. LP ..... Incus ........... INCUS51 ............... 1986 £5 ........... £12 ...........................

## COMPETITORS
Hits Of The Street And Strip ................... LP ...... Dot ............... DLP3542/25542 ..... 1963 £10 .......... £25 ........................... US

## COMPLEX
Complex ....................................................... LP ...... Halpix ........... CLPM001 ............... 1970 £400 ..... £600 ...........................
Way We Feel ............................................... LP ...... Deroy ............ ............... 1971 £330 ..... £500 ...........................

## COMPROMISE
You Will Think Of Me ............................ 7" ...... CBS............... 202050.................. 1966 £1.50.... £4 ...............

## COMSAT ANGELS
Red Planet............................................ 7" ...... Junta ............. JUNTA1 ............... 1979 £2................ £5 ................ *red vinyl*

## COMSTOCK, BOBBY
I'm A Man............................................. 7" ...... United Artists .. UP1086................. 1965 £5............ £10 ..........
Jambalaya............................................. 7" ...... London ........... HLE9080 ........... 1960 £5............ £10 ..........
Let's Stomp.......................................... 7" ...... Stateside ......... SS163.................. 1963 £2.50........ £6 ..........
Out Of Sight......................................... LP ...... Ascot ............. ALM13/ALS16026.. 1966 £5............ £12 ........... *US*
Susie Baby ........................................... 7" ...... Stateside ......... SS221.................. 1963 £1.50........ £4 ..........
Tennessee Waltz................................... 7" ...... Top Rank ........ JAR223................. 1959 £1.50........ £4 ..........

## COMUS
Comus were like a folky version of Family, with the group's singer adopting the same gargling tones as Roger Chapman. The largely acoustic instrumentation, however, gives the vocals a considerable dramatic emphasis, especially when underscored by a female singer. *First Utterance* is not exactly a classic, but it is certainly interesting.

Diana ................................................... 7" ...... Dawn.............. DNX2506 ........... 1971 £5........... £10 ........... *picture sleeve*
First Utterance ..................................... LP ...... Dawn.............. DNLS3019 ............ 1971 £30.......... £60 ..........
To Keep From Crying ........................... LP ...... Virgin ............. V2018 .................. 1974 £4........... £10 ..........

## CONCEPT
Invasion................................................ LP ..... R.C. ............... 772 ...................... 1977 £15.......... £30 ...........*Canadian*

## CONCHORDS
You Can't Take It Away.......................... 7" ...... Polydor ........... BM56059 ............. 1965 £2............ £5 ..........

## CONCORDS
I Need Your Loving............................... 7" ...... Blue Cat........... BS170 .................. 1969 £2............ £5 ..........

## CONDELLO, MIKE
Phase One ............................................ LP ...... Scepter............ SPS542.................. 1968 £10........... £25 ...................... *US*

## CONDON, EDDIE
Dixieland.............................................. LP ...... Philips............. BBL7109 .............. 1957 £6............ £15 ..........
Dixieland Dance Party ......................... LP ...... London ........... LTZD15158/ ........ 1959 £5............ £12 ..........
                                                     SAHD6014...........
Eddie Condon All Stars......................... LP ...... Philips............. BBL7031 .............. 1955 £6............ £15 ..........
Eddie Condon Is Uptown Now.............. LP ...... MGM ............. C768................... 1958 £4............ £10 ..........
Eddie Condon Orchestra...................... 10" LP London ........... LZC14024............. 1956 £6............ £15 ..........
Eddie Condon Quartet......................... LP ...... Philips............. BBL7061 .............. 1956 £6............ £15 ..........
Gershwin Jazz...................................... 10" LP Brunswick ...... LA8518 ................. 1951 £8............ £20 ..........
Jazz Band Ball Vol. 1 ........................... 10" LP Brunswick ...... LA8549 ................. 1952 £8............ £20 ..........
Jazz Concert ........................................ 10" LP Brunswick ...... LA8577 ................. 1953 £8............ £20 ..........
Ringside At Condon's Vol. 1.................. 10" LP London ........... LZC14004.............. 1955 £6............ £15 ..........
Roaring Twenties.................................. LP ...... Philips............. BBL7227 .............. 1958 £6............ £15 ..........
That Toddlin' Town .............................. LP ...... Warner Bros ... WM4009/WS8009 . 1960 £5............ £12 ..........
Treasury Of Jazz ................................... LP ...... Philips............. BBL7131 .............. 1957 £6............ £15 ..........
We Called It Music .............................. 10" LP Brunswick ...... LA8542 ................. 1952 £8............ £20 ..........

## CONDOR, HOWIE G.
Big Noise From Winnetka ..................... 7" ...... Fontana........... TF613................... 1965 £2............ £5 ..........

## CONEY ISLAND KIDS
Baby Baby You ..................................... 7" ...... London ........... HLJ8207 ............... 1955 £6............ £12 ..........

## CONLEY, ARTHUR
Aunt Dora's Love Soul Shack ................ 7" ...... Atlantic ........... 584224.................. 1968 £1.50........ £4 ..........
Funky Street ......................................... 7" ...... Atlantic ........... 584175.................. 1968 £1.50........ £4 ..........
More Sweet Soul.................................. LP ...... Atco ............... 228019.................. 1969 £5............ £12 ..........
People Sure Act Funny ......................... 7" ...... Atlantic ........... 584197.................. 1968 £1.50........ £4 ..........
Shake Rattle And Roll........................... 7" ...... Atlantic ........... 584121.................. 1967 £1.50........ £4 ..........
Shake, Rattle And Roll.......................... LP ...... Atlantic ........... 587084.................. 1967 £4............ £10 ..........
Soul Directions .................................... LP ...... Atlantic ........... 587128.................. 1968 £4............ £10 ..........
Sweet Soul Music ................................ LP ...... Atlantic ........... 587069.................. 1967 £6............ £15 ..........
Sweet Soul Music ................................ 7" ...... Atlantic ........... 584083.................. 1967 £1.50........ £4 ..........
Whole Lotta Woman ............................ 7" ...... Atlantic ........... 584143.................. 1967 £1.50........ £4 ..........

## CONNELL, BRIAN & THE ROUND SOUND
Considerable confusion exists as to whether Brian Connell is the same person as Brian Connolly, the lead singer of the Sweet. Some authorities state that Connell is Connolly, while others are equally certain that he is not. Brian Connolly himself was no help in the matter, unfortunately, having made contrary statements to his Dutch fan club when they tried to determine the facts once and for all!

I Know.................................................. 7" ...... Philips............. BF1718 ................. 1968 £2............ £5 ..........
Just My Kind Of Loving ........................ 7" ...... Mercury.......... MF956 ................. 1966 £2............ £5 ..........
Same Thing Happened To Me .............. 7" ...... Mercury.......... MF991 ................. 1966 £2............ £5 ..........
What Good Am I ................................... 7" ...... Philips............. BF1661 ................. 1968 £2............ £5 ..........

## CONNIFF, RAY & HIS ROCKING RHYTHM BOYS
Piggy Bank Boogie................................ 7" ...... Vogue Coral.... QW5001 ............... 1955 £4............ £8 ..........

## CONNOLLY, BRIAN
Hypnotised ........................................... 7" ...... Carrere ........... CAR231 ................ 1981 £2.50........ £6 ..........

## CONNOR, CHRIS

| | | | | | | | |
|---|---|---|---|---|---|---|---|
| Ballad Of The Sad Cafe | LP | London | LTZK15183 | 1960 £4 | £10 | |
| Bethlehem Girls | LP | Bethlehem | BCP6006 | 1956 £6 | £15 | US |
| Chris | LP | Bethlehem | BCP56 | 1956 £6 | £15 | US |
| Chris | 10" LP | London | HBN1074 | 1956 £6 | £15 | |
| Chris Connor | LP | Atlantic | 1228 | 1957 £6 | £15 | US |
| Chris Connor | LP | London | LZN14007 | 1956 £6 | £15 | |
| Chris Craft | LP | London | LTZK15151 | 1959 £6 | £15 | |
| Chris In Person | LP | London | LTZK15195/ SAHK6088 | 1960 £4 | £10 | |
| George Gershwin Almanac Of Songs | LP | Atlantic | 2601 | 1957 £8 | £20 | US |
| Hallelujah I Love Him So | 7" | London | HLE8869 | 1959 £1.50 | £4 | |
| He Loves Me, He Loves Me Not | LP | London | HAK2066 | 1957 £6 | £15 | |
| I Miss You So | LP | Atlantic | 8014 | 1956 £6 | £15 | US |
| I Only Want Some | 7" | London | HLK9124 | 1960 £1.50 | £4 | |
| Jazz Date | LP | London | LTZK15142 | 1959 £6 | £15 | |
| London's Girl Friends No. 2 | 7" EP | London | REN1093 | 1957 £2.50 | £6 | |
| Lullaby Of Birdland | 7" EP | London | EZN19010 | 1956 £2.50 | £6 | |
| Lullabys For Lovers | LP | Bethlehem | BCP6005 | 1956 £6 | £15 | US |
| Lullabys For Lovers | 10" LP | Bethlehem | 1002 | 1954 £8 | £20 | US |
| Lullabys Of Birdland | LP | Parlophone | PMC1082 | 1959 £6 | £15 | |
| Lullabys Of Birdland | 10" LP | Bethlehem | 1001 | 1954 £8 | £20 | US |
| Meets J And Kai | 7" EP | Parlophone | GEP8767 | 1958 £2 | £5 | |
| Presenting | LP | London | HAK2020/ SHK6032 | 1957/ 1959 £6 | £15 | |
| This Is Chris | LP | Bethlehem | BCP20 | 1955 £6 | £15 | US |
| This Is Chris | 7" EP | Parlophone | GEP8778 | 1958 £2 | £5 | |
| Witchcraft | LP | London | LTZK15185 | 1960 £4 | £10 | |

## CONNORS, BILL

| | | | | | | |
|---|---|---|---|---|---|---|
| Theme To The Guardian | LP | ECM | ECM1057ST | 1975 £5 | £12 | |

## CONNY

| | | | | | | |
|---|---|---|---|---|---|---|
| Gino | 7" | Columbia | DB4845 | 1962 £4 | £8 | |

## CONQUERORS

| | | | | | | |
|---|---|---|---|---|---|---|
| If You Can't Beat Them Join Them | 7" | High Note | HS016 | 1969 £1.50 | £4 | |
| Jumpy Jumpy Girl | 7" | Amalgamated | AMG832 | 1968 £2.50 | £6 | |
| Lonely Street | 7" | Treasure Isle | TI7035 | 1968 £5 | £10 | |
| Mr. D.J. | 7" | High Note | HS025 | 1969 £1.50 | £4 | |
| What A Agony | 7" | Doctor Bird | DB1046 | 1966 £5 | £10 | Baba Brooks B side |
| Won't You Come Home Now | 7" | Doctor Bird | DB1119 | 1967 £5 | £10 | |

## CONRAD, JESS

| | | | | | | |
|---|---|---|---|---|---|---|
| Hey Little Girl | 7" | Decca | F11412 | 1961 £2 | £5 | picture sleeve |
| Human Jungle | 7" EP | Decca | DFE8524 | 1963 £2 | £5 | |
| Hurt Me | 7" | Pye | 7N15849 | 1965 £4 | £8 | |
| Jess Conrad | 7" EP | Decca | DFE6666 | 1960 £2.50 | £6 | |
| Jess For You | LP | Decca | LK4390 | 1961 £8 | £20 | |
| Twist My Wrist | 7" EP | Decca | DFE6702 | 1962 £2 | £5 | |

## CONRAD, TONY & FAUST

Tony Conrad was a member of La Monte Young's Theatre Of Eternal Music in 1962, playing violin and bowed guitar alongside John Cale. Later, he played in a group called the Primitives, with both Cale and Lou Reed. Despite these Velvet Underground connections, however, the increasing interest in Conrad's album derives mainly from the fact that it is a collaborative work with the German avant-garde group, Faust.

| | | | | | |
|---|---|---|---|---|---|
| Outside The Dream Syndicate | LP | Caroline | C1501 | 1972 £8 | £20 |

## CONROY

The value of the once-legendary *London Underground* LP has been steadily falling since collectors have realized that this is not actually the work of a forgotten progressive group. The 'Conroy Recorded Music Library' is not a group at all, in fact, but a series of records produced by anonymous session musicians for use in film and TV work.

| | | | | | |
|---|---|---|---|---|---|
| Background Action | LP | Berry Music Co. | | 197– £25 | £50 |
| Far West/Far East | LP | Berry Music Co. | BMLP155 | 1976 £4 | £10 |
| Indian Suite | LP | Berry Music Co. | | 197– £4 | £10 |
| London's Underground | LP | Berry Music Co. | BMLP092 | 1972 £25 | £50 |
| London's Underground No. 2 | LP | Berry Music Co. | BMLP115 | 1975 £15 | £30 |
| Psychosis Suite | LP | Berry Music Co. | | 197– £4 | £10 |
| Way In Way Out | LP | Berry Music Co. | | 197– £4 | £10 |

## CONSORTIUM

| | | | | | |
|---|---|---|---|---|---|
| All The Love In The World | 7" | Pye | 7N17635 | 1968 £1.50 | £4 |

## CONSUMATES

| | | | | | |
|---|---|---|---|---|---|
| What Is It | 7" | Coxsone | CS7054 | 1968 £5 | £10 |

## CONTINENTALS
Going Crazy .................................... 7" ...... Island ............. WI010 ................... 1962 £5.......... £10 .......................................

## CONTINUUM
Autumn Grass ................................. LP ..... RCA ............. SF8196.................. 1971 £4......... £10 .................................
Continuum..................................... LP ..... RCA ............. SF8157.................. 1970 £4......... £10 .................................

## CONTOURS
Can You Do It.................................. 7" ...... Stateside ........ SS299................... 1964 £12.50.... £25 .................................
Can You Jerk Like Me...................... 7" ...... Stateside ........ SS381................... 1965 £10......... £20 .................................
Contours ......................................... 7" EP . Tamla Motown TME2002.......... 1965 £20......... £40 .................................
Determination.................................. 7" ...... Tamla Motown TMG564............ 1966 £12.50.... £25 .................................
Do You Love Me .............................. LP ..... Oriole ............. PS40043............. 1963 £37.50.... £75 .................................
Do You Love Me .............................. 7" ...... Oriole ............. CBA1763............ 1962 £10......... £20 .................................
Don't Let Her Be Your Baby ............ 7" ...... Oriole ............. CBA1831............ 1963 £25......... £50 .................................
First I Look At The Purse................. 7" ...... Tamla Motown TMG531............ 1965 £12.50.... £25 .................................
It's So Hard Being A Loser ............... 7" ...... Tamla Motown TMG605............ 1967 £10......... £20 .................................
Shake Sherry.................................... 7" ...... Oriole ............. CBA1799............ 1963 £15......... £30 .................................

## CONTRABAND
Contraband..................................... LP ..... Transatlantic ... TRA278............. 1974 £4......... £10 .................................

## CONTRASTS
What A Day ..................................... 7" ...... Monument ...... MON1018........... 1968 £1.50....... £4 .................................

## CONTROLLED BLEEDING
Headcrack ....................................... LP ..... Sterile ............. SR11................. 1986 £8......... £20 .................................

## CONVAIRS
Mignight Mary................................. 7" ...... HMV.............. POP1549 ............. 1966 £2......... £5 .................................

## CONVY, BERT & THE THUNDERBIRDS
Come On Back................................. 7" ...... London ........... HLB8190 ............. 1955 £62.50.. £125 .................................

## COODER, RY
Borderlive....................................... LP ..... Warner Bros .... ......................... 1981 £6......... £15 .................. US promo
Chicken Skin Music .......................... 7" ...... Reprise ............ PRO644 ............. 1977 £1.50....... £4 .........................promo
Jazz ................................................ LP ..... Mobile Fidelity MFSL1085 ......... 1982 £4......... £10 ..... US audiophile
Ry Cooder ...................................... LP ..... Reprise .......... RSLP6402.......... 1971 £4......... £10 .................................
Ry Cooder Radio Show .................... LP ..... Reprise ........... PRO558 ............. 1976 £6......... £15 ................. US promo

## COOK, LITTLE JOE
Don't You Have Feelings................... 7" ...... Sonet ............. SON2002............. 1973 £2.50....... £6 .................................

## COOK, LITTLE JOE (CHRIS FARLOWE)
Stormy Monday Blues........................ 7" ...... Sue ................. WI385 ............... 1965 £12.50.... £25 .................................

## COOK, PETER
Ballad Of Spotty Muldoon ............... 7" ...... Decca ............. F12182............... 1965 £1.50....... £4 .................................
Beyond The Fringe .......................... LP ..... Parlophone ...... PMC1145 ............ 1961 £4......... £10 ..... with other artists
Bridge On The River Wye ................ LP ..... Parlophone ...... PMC1190/.......... 1962 £4......... £10 ..... with other artists
                                                          PCS3036
Peter Cook Presents The Establishment ...... LP ..... Parlophone ...... PMC1198 ............ 1963 £4......... £10 ...... with other artists
Presents Misty Mr. Wisty .................. LP ..... Decca ............. LK4722 .............. 1965 £4......... £10 .................................
Private Eye's Blue Record................. LP ..... Transatlantic ... TRA131 ............. 1965 £4......... £10 ................with others
Sitting On The Bench ........................ 7" ...... Parlophone ...... R4969 ............... 1962 £1.50....... £4 ................with others

## COOK, PETER (2)
Georgia ........................................... 7" ...... Pye ................. 7N15847............. 1965 £4......... £8 .................................

## COOK, PETER & DUDLEY MOORE
The duo's comedy records include a drug-culture spoof, 'L. S. Bumble Bee', that was given a perfect punch-line by being included on several Beatles bootleg albums in the seventies under the guise of a supposed *Sgt Pepper* out-take.

Bedazzled ........................................ LP ..... Decca ............. LK/SKL4923.......... 1968 £10......... £25 .................................
By Appointment............................... 7" EP . Decca ............. DFE8644.............. 1965 £2......... £5 .................................
Goodbye-ee..................................... 7" ...... Decca ............. F12158................ 1965 £1.50....... £4 .................................
L. S. Bumble Bee ............................ 7" ...... Decca ............. F12551................ 1967 £4......... £8 .................................
Not Only But Also ........................... LP ..... Decca ............. LK4703 .............. 1965 £4......... £10 .................................
Once Moore With Cook .................... LP ..... Decca ............. LK4785 .............. 1966 £4......... £10 .................................
Peter Cook & Dudley Moore ............ 7" EP . Parlophone ...... GEP8940.............. 1965 £2......... £5 .................................

## COOK, ROGER
Meanwhile Back At The World............ LP ..... Regal ............. SRZA8508............ 1972 £5......... £12 .................................
                                        Zonophone .....
Minstrel In Flight ............................ LP ..... Regal ............. SLRZ1035 .......... 1973 £6......... £15 .................................
                                        Zonophone .....
Study .............................................. LP ..... Columbia........ SCX6388 ............ 1970 £4......... £10 .................................

## COOKE, SAM
Ain't That Good News ...................... LP ..... RCA ............. RD/SF7635 .......... 1964 £8......... £20 .................................
Another Saturday Night .................... 7" ...... RCA ............. RCA1341 ........... 1963 £1.50....... £4 .................................
Another Saturday Night .................... 7" ...... RCA ............. RCA1701 ............ 1968 £4......... £8 ....Duane Eddy B side
At The Copa..................................... LP ..... RCA ............. RD/SF7674 .......... 1965 £8......... £20 .................................
Best Of Sam Cooke .......................... LP ..... RCA ............. LPM/LSP2625........ 1962 £8......... £20 ........................... US
Best Of Sam Cooke Vol. 2 ................ LP ..... RCA ............. LPM/LSP3373........ 1965 £8......... £20 ........................... US

| | | | | | | | |
|---|---|---|---|---|---|---|---|
| Bring It On Home To Me | 7" | RCA | RCA1296 | 1962 | £1.50 | £4 | |
| Chain Gang | 7" | RCA | RCA1202 | 1960 | £1.50 | £4 | |
| Cooke's Tour | LP | RCA | RD27190/SF5076 | 1961 | £15 | £30 | |
| Cousin Of Mine | 7" | RCA | RCA1420 | 1964 | £1.50 | £4 | |
| Cupid | 7" | RCA | RCA1242 | 1961 | £1.50 | £4 | |
| Encore | LP | HMV | CLP1273 | 1959 | £25 | £50 | |
| Feel It | 7" | RCA | RCA1260 | 1961 | £1.50 | £4 | |
| Frankie And Johnny | 7" | RCA | RCA1361 | 1963 | £1.50 | £4 | |
| Good News | 7" | RCA | RCA1386 | 1964 | £1.50 | £4 | |
| Good Times | 7" | RCA | RCA1405 | 1964 | £1.50 | £4 | |
| Heart And Soul | 7" EP | RCA | RCX7117 | 1963 | £7.50 | £15 | |
| Hit Kit | LP | Keen | 86101 | 1959 | £25 | £50 | US |
| Hits Of The Fifties | LP | RCA | RD27215/SF5098 | 1961 | £15 | £30 | |
| I Need You Now | 7" | London | HLU9046 | 1960 | £5 | £10 | |
| I Thank God | LP | Keen | 86103 | 1960 | £15 | £30 | US |
| It's Got The Whole World Shakin' | 7" | RCA | RCA1452 | 1965 | £1.50 | £4 | |
| Little Red Rooster | 7" | RCA | RCA1367 | 1963 | £1.50 | £4 | |
| Little Things You Do | 7" | HMV | POP610 | 1959 | £5 | £10 | |
| Love Me | 7" | RCA | RCA1221 | 1961 | £1.50 | £4 | |
| Love You Most Of All | 7" | HMV | POP568 | 1958 | £5 | £10 | |
| Man Who Invented Soul | LP | RCA | LSP3991 | 1968 | £6 | £15 | US |
| Mr. Soul | LP | RCA | RD/SF7539 | 1963 | £10 | £25 | |
| My Kind Of Blues | LP | RCA | RD27245/SF5120 | 1962 | £10 | £25 | |
| Night Beat | LP | RCA | RD/SF7583 | 1963 | £15 | £30 | |
| Nothing Can Change This Love | 7" | RCA | RCA1310 | 1962 | £1.50 | £4 | |
| One Hour Ahead | 7" | HMV | POP675 | 1959 | £4 | £8 | |
| Only Sixteen | 7" | HMV | POP642 | 1959 | £5 | £10 | |
| Sam Cooke | LP | HMV | CLP1261 | 1958 | £30 | £60 | |
| Send Me Some Loving | 7" | RCA | RCA1327 | 1963 | £1.50 | £4 | |
| Shake | LP | RCA | RD7730 | 1965 | £8 | £20 | |
| Shake | 7" | RCA | RCA1436 | 1965 | £1.50 | £4 | |
| Sugar Dumpling | 7" | RCA | RCA1476 | 1965 | £1.50 | £4 | |
| Swing Low | LP | RCA | RD27222 | 1960 | £15 | £30 | |
| Swing Sweetly | 7" EP | RCA | RCX7128 | 1964 | £7.50 | £15 | |
| Teenage Sonata | 7" | RCA | RCA1184 | 1960 | £1.50 | £4 | |
| That's All I Need To Know | 7" | London | HLU8615 | 1958 | £10 | £20 | |
| That's Heaven To Me | 7" | Immediate | | 1966 | £12.50 | £25 | demo only |
| That's It I Quit, I'm Moving On | 7" | RCA | RCA1230 | 1961 | £1.50 | £4 | |
| Tribute To The Lady | LP | Keen | 2004 | 1959 | £25 | £50 | US |
| Try A Little Love | LP | RCA | RD/SF7764 | 1965 | £6 | £15 | |
| Twistin' The Night Away | LP | RCA | RD27263/SF5133 | 1962 | £8 | £20 | |
| Twistin' The Night Away | 7" | RCA | RCA1277 | 1962 | £1.50 | £4 | |
| Unforgettable Sam Cooke | LP | RCA | LPM/LSP3517 | 1966 | £8 | £20 | US |
| Wonderful World | 7" | HMV | POP754 | 1960 | £2 | £5 | |
| Wonderful World Of Sam Cooke | LP | Immediate | IMLP002 | 1966 | £8 | £20 | |
| You Send Me | 7" | London | HLU8506 | 1957 | £15 | £30 | |

## COOKIES

| | | | | | | | |
|---|---|---|---|---|---|---|---|
| Chains | 7" | London | HLU9634 | 1962 | £2.50 | £6 | |
| Don't Say Nothing Bad About My Baby | 7" | London | HLU9704 | 1963 | £2.50 | £6 | |
| Girls Grow Up Faster Than Boys | 7" | Colpix | PX11020 | 1964 | £1.50 | £4 | |
| Willpower | 7" | Colpix | PX11012 | 1963 | £1.50 | £4 | |

## COOL BREEZE

| | | | | | | | |
|---|---|---|---|---|---|---|---|
| People Ask What Love Is | 7" | Pathway | PAT103 | 197– | £5 | £10 | |

## COOL CATS

| | | | | | | | |
|---|---|---|---|---|---|---|---|
| Hold Your Love | 7" | Jolly | JY009 | 1968 | £4 | £8 | Helmsley Morris B side |
| What Kind Of Man | 7" | Jolly | JY007 | 1968 | £4 | £8 | |

## COOL MEN

| | | | | | | | |
|---|---|---|---|---|---|---|---|
| Cool For Cats No. 1 | 7" EP | Parlophone | GEP8739 | 1958 | £4 | £8 | |
| Cool For Cats No. 2 | 7" EP | Parlophone | GEP8752 | 1958 | £4 | £8 | |

## COOL SPOON

| | | | | | | | |
|---|---|---|---|---|---|---|---|
| Yakety Yak | 7" | Coxsone | CS7032 | 1967 | £5 | £10 | |

## COOL STICKY

| | | | | | | | |
|---|---|---|---|---|---|---|---|
| Train To Soulville | 7" | Amalgamated | AMG825 | 1968 | £4 | £8 | Eric Morris B side |

## COOLEY, EDDIE & THE DIMPLES

| | | | | | | | |
|---|---|---|---|---|---|---|---|
| Got A Little Woman | 7" | Columbia | DB3873 | 1957 | £50 | £100 | |

## COOMBES, CHRIS

| | | | | | | | |
|---|---|---|---|---|---|---|---|
| Where It's At | 7" EP | Holyground | HG110 | 1965 | £12.50 | £25 | |

## COOPER, ALICE

| | | | | | | | |
|---|---|---|---|---|---|---|---|
| Alice Cooper Reads Stoopid News | CD | Epic | | 1991 | £8 | £20 | US promo |
| Be My Lover | 7" | Warner Bros | K16154 | 1972 | £1.50 | £4 | |
| Bed Of Nails | CD-s | Epic | ALICEC3 | 1989 | £2 | £5 | |
| Billion Dollar Babies | LP | Warner Bros | BS42685 | 1973 | £4 | £10 | US quad |
| Clones | 7" | Warner Bros | K17598 | 1980 | £1.50 | £4 | |
| Easy Action | LP | Straight | STS1061 | 1969 | £10 | £25 | |
| Eighteen | 7" | Straight | S7209 | 1971 | £30 | £60 | |
| Elected | 7" | Warner Bros | K16214 | 1972 | £2.50 | £6 | picture sleeve |
| Greatest Hits | LP | Warner Bros | W42803 | 1974 | £4 | £10 | US quad |
| Hey Stoopid | CD-s | Epic | 6569839 | 1991 | £2 | £5 | |

| Title | Format | Label | Catalogue | Year | £ | £ | Notes |
|---|---|---|---|---|---|---|---|
| House Of Fire | CD-s | Epic | ALICEC4 | 1989 | £2 | £5 | |
| House Of Fire | 7" | Epic | ALICEP4 | 1989 | £1.50 | £4 | ... shaped picture disc |
| I Love America | 12" | Warner Bros | ALICE1T | 1983 | £2.50 | £6 | |
| Killer | LP | Warner Bros | K56005 | 1971 | £4 | £10 | calendar cover |
| Last Temptation | CD | Epic | | 1994 | £10 | £25 | ..Japanese, with bonus live CD |
| Last Temptation | CD | Epic | EPC4765942 | 1994 | £5 | £12 | ... with comic |
| Love It To Death | LP | Straight | STS1065 | 1971 | £10 | £25 | |
| Love It To Death | LP | Warner Bros | K46177 | 1971 | £4 | £10 | |
| Love's Like A Loaded Gun | CD-s | Epic | 6574389 | 1991 | £4 | £10 | gun-shaped sleeve |
| Muscle Of Love | LP | Warner Bros | BS42748 | 1974 | £4 | £10 | US quad |
| Poison | CD-s | Epic | 6551652 | 1989 | £4 | £10 | bottle sleeve |
| Pretties For You | LP | Straight | STS1051 | 1969 | £10 | £25 | |
| School's Out | LP | Warner Bros | K56007 | 1972 | £4 | £10 | with panties |
| School's Out | 7" | Warner Bros | K16188 | 1972 | £2 | £5 | picture sleeve |
| Schooldays | LP | Warner Bros | K66021 | 1973 | £5 | £12 | double |
| Trash | CD | Epic | | 1989 | £25 | £50 | US promo trash can with tape, video, biog |
| Under My Wheels | 7" | Warner Bros | K16127 | 1971 | £1.50 | £4 | |
| Welcome To My Nightmare | LP | Mobile Fidelity | MFSL1063 | 1980 | £4 | £10 | US audiophile |
| Welcome To My Nightmare | 12" | Anchor | ANE12001 | 1977 | £2.50 | £6 | |
| Who Do You Think We Are? | 12" | Warner Bros | K17940T | 1982 | £3 | £8 | |

## COOPER, BOB

| Title | Format | Label | Catalogue | Year | £ | £ | Notes |
|---|---|---|---|---|---|---|---|
| Bob Cooper Sextet | 10" LP | Capitol | KPL102 | 1955 | £8 | £20 | |
| Coop | LP | Contemporary | LAC12157 | 1959 | £6 | £15 | |

## COOPER, GARNELL & KINFOLK

| Title | Format | Label | Catalogue | Year | £ | £ | Notes |
|---|---|---|---|---|---|---|---|
| Green Monkey | 7" | London | HL9757 | 1963 | £1.50 | £4 | |

## COOPER, JIM

| Title | Format | Label | Catalogue | Year | £ | £ | Notes |
|---|---|---|---|---|---|---|---|
| Jim Cooper Band | LP | Jim Cooper Band | JCB1 | 1979 | £8 | £20 | |

## COOPER, JIMMY

| Title | Format | Label | Catalogue | Year | £ | £ | Notes |
|---|---|---|---|---|---|---|---|
| Dulcimer Player | LP | Forest Tracks | FTS3009 | 1976 | £4 | £10 | |

## COOPER, LES & THE SOUL ROCKERS

| Title | Format | Label | Catalogue | Year | £ | £ | Notes |
|---|---|---|---|---|---|---|---|
| Wiggle Wobble | 7" | Stateside | SS142 | 1962 | £2 | £5 | |

## COOPER, LINDSAY

| Title | Format | Label | Catalogue | Year | £ | £ | Notes |
|---|---|---|---|---|---|---|---|
| Pictures From The Great Exhibition | 7" | Recommended | RE1851 | 1983 | £4 | £8 | 1 side painted |

## COOPER, MARTY

| Title | Format | Label | Catalogue | Year | £ | £ | Notes |
|---|---|---|---|---|---|---|---|
| If You Were A Singer | LP | EMI | 1C06445413 | 1979 | £6 | £15 | German |

## COOPER, MIKE

| Title | Format | Label | Catalogue | Year | £ | £ | Notes |
|---|---|---|---|---|---|---|---|
| Do I Know You | LP | Dawn | DNLS3005 | 1970 | £5 | £12 | |
| Life & Death In Paradise | LP | Fresh Air | 6370500 | 1974 | £4 | £10 | |
| Machine Gun Company | LP | Dawn | DNLS3031 | 1972 | £5 | £12 | |
| Oh Really | LP | Pye | NSPL18281 | 1969 | £8 | £20 | |
| Places I Know | LP | Dawn | DNLS3026 | 1971 | £5 | £12 | |
| Trout Steel | LP | Dawn | DNLS3011 | 1970 | £5 | £12 | |
| Up The Country Blues | 7" EP | Saydisc | SD137 | 196- | £7.50 | £15 | |
| Watching You Fall | 7" | Dawn | DNX2511 | 1971 | £1.50 | £4 | |
| Your Lovely Ways | 7" | Dawn | DNX2501 | 1970 | £1.50 | £4 | |

## COOPER, TOMMY

| Title | Format | Label | Catalogue | Year | £ | £ | Notes |
|---|---|---|---|---|---|---|---|
| Don't Jump Off The Roof Dad | 7" | Palette | PG9019 | 1961 | £2.50 | £6 | |

## COPAS, COWBOY

| Title | Format | Label | Catalogue | Year | £ | £ | Notes |
|---|---|---|---|---|---|---|---|
| Alabam | 7" | Melodisc | 1566 | 1960 | £2 | £5 | |
| Best Of American Country Music Vol. 3 | 7" EP | Ember | EMBEP4547 | 1964 | £2 | £5 | |
| Country Entertainer No. 1 | LP | London | HAB8088 | 1963 | £4 | £10 | |
| Country Hits | 7" EP | Stateside | SE1003 | 1963 | £2 | £5 | |
| Country Music | 7" EP | Top Rank | JKP3014 | 1962 | £2 | £5 | |
| Cowboy Copas | LP | Melodisc | MLP12119 | 1961 | £4 | £10 | |
| Favourite Cowboy Songs | 7" EP | Parlophone | GEP8527 | 1955 | £2.50 | £6 | |
| Heartbreak Ago | 7" | Parlophone | MSP6109 | 1954 | £6 | £12 | |
| Return To Sender | 7" | Parlophone | MSP6164 | 1955 | £6 | £12 | |
| Star Of The Grand Ole Opry | LP | London | HAB8180 | 1964 | £4 | £10 | |
| Tennessee Senorita | 7" | Parlophone | MSP6079 | 1954 | £6 | £12 | |
| Unforgettable Vol. 1 | 7" EP | London | REB1418 | 1964 | £2 | £5 | |
| Unforgettable Vol. 2 | 7" EP | London | REB1419 | 1964 | £2 | £5 | |
| Unforgettable Vol. 3 | 7" EP | London | REB1420 | 1964 | £2 | £5 | |
| Western Style | 7" EP | Parlophone | GEP8575 | 1956 | £2.50 | £6 | |

## COPE, JULIAN

| Title | Format | Label | Catalogue | Year | £ | £ | Notes |
|---|---|---|---|---|---|---|---|
| Beautiful Love | CD-s | Island | CID483 | 1991 | £2 | £5 | |
| Charlotte Anne | CD-s | Island | CIDP380 | 1988 | £2 | £5 | picture disc |
| China Doll | CD-s | Island | CID406 | 1989 | £2 | £5 | |
| Droolian | LP | Mofo | MOFOCOLP90 | 1990 | £4 | £10 | |
| Droolian | CD | Mofo | MOFOCOCD90 | 1990 | £6 | £15 | |
| East Easy Rider | CD-s | Island | CID492 | 1991 | £2 | £5 | |
| Eve's Volcano | CD-s | Island | CID318 | 1987 | £2 | £5 | |
| Five O'Clock World | CD-s | Island | CIDP399 | 1988 | £2 | £5 | picture disc |
| Head | CD-s | Island | CID497 | 1991 | £2 | £5 | |
| Safesurfer | 7" | Island | JC1 | 1991 | £5 | £10 | |

| | | | | | | | | |
|---|---|---|---|---|---|---|---|---|
| Saint Julian | LP | Island | ILPS9861 | 1987 | £6 | £15 | .. with bonus interview LP |
| Skellington | LP | Copeco | JULP89 | 1989 | £4 | £10 | |
| Skellington | CD | Copeco | JUCD89 | 1989 | £6 | £15 | |
| Sunspots | 7" | Mercury | MER1822 | 1985 | £2 | £5 | double |

## COPE, SUZY
| | | | | | | | |
|---|---|---|---|---|---|---|---|
| You Can't Say I Never Told You | 7" | CBS | 201792 | 1965 | £1.50 | £4 | |

## COPELAND, ALAN
| | | | | | | | |
|---|---|---|---|---|---|---|---|
| Feeling Happy | 7" | Vogue Coral | Q72237 | 1957 | £2.50 | £6 | |
| Flip Flop | 7" | Pye | 7N25007 | 1959 | £1.50 | £4 | |
| How Will I Know? | 7" | Vogue Coral | Q72277 | 1957 | £1.50 | £4 | |

## COPELAND, JOHNNY
| | | | | | | | |
|---|---|---|---|---|---|---|---|
| Sufferin' City | 7" | Atlantic | K10242 | 1972 | £2.50 | £6 | |

## COPELAND, KEN
| | | | | | | | |
|---|---|---|---|---|---|---|---|
| Pledge Of Love | 7" | London | HLP8423 | 1957 | £150 | £250 | Mints B side, best auctioned |

## COPELAND, MARTHA
| | | | | | | | |
|---|---|---|---|---|---|---|---|
| RCA Victor Race Series Vol. 8 | 7" EP | RCA | RCX7183 | 1966 | £2 | £5 | |

## COPPER, BOB
| | | | | | | | |
|---|---|---|---|---|---|---|---|
| Sweet Rose In June | LP | Topic | 12TS328 | 1977 | £4 | £10 | |

## COPPER FAMILY
| | | | | | | | |
|---|---|---|---|---|---|---|---|
| Song For Every Season | LP | Leader | LEAB404 | 1971 | £50 | £100 | 4 LP box set |

## COPPERFIELD
| | | | | | | | |
|---|---|---|---|---|---|---|---|
| Any Old Time | 7" | Instant | IN004 | 1969 | £2.50 | £6 | |
| I'll Hold Out My Hand | 7" | Parlophone | R5818 | 1969 | £1.50 | £4 | |

## COPS & ROBBERS
| | | | | | | | |
|---|---|---|---|---|---|---|---|
| I Could Have Danced All Night | 7" EP | Pye | PNV24148 | 1965 | £25 | £50 | French |
| I Could Have Danced All Night | 7" | Pye | 7N15870 | 1965 | £6 | £12 | |
| It's All Over Now Baby Blue | 7" | Pye | 7N15928 | 1965 | £5 | £10 | |
| St. James Infirmary | 7" | Decca | F12019 | 1964 | £12.50 | £25 | |

## CORBAN
| | | | | | | | |
|---|---|---|---|---|---|---|---|
| Break In The Clouds | LP | Acorn | | 1978 | £8 | £20 | |

## CORBETT, HARRY H. & WILFRED BRAMBELL
| | | | | | | | |
|---|---|---|---|---|---|---|---|
| Gems From The Steptoe Scrap Heap | LP | Pye | NPL18153 | 1966 | £4 | £10 | |
| Love And Harold Steptoe | LP | Pye | NPL18135 | 1965 | £4 | £10 | |
| Steptoe And Son | LP | Pye | NPL18081 | 1962 | £4 | £10 | |

## CORBITT, JERRY
| | | | | | | | |
|---|---|---|---|---|---|---|---|
| Jerry Corbitt | LP | Capitol | ST771 | 1971 | £8 | £20 | US |

## CORDELL, PHIL
| | | | | | | | |
|---|---|---|---|---|---|---|---|
| Chevy Van | 7" | Mowest | MW3026 | 1975 | £2 | £5 | demo |

## CORDES
| | | | | | | | |
|---|---|---|---|---|---|---|---|
| Give Her Time | 7" | Cavern Sound | IMSTL1 | 1965 | £10 | £20 | |

## CORDET, LOUISE
| | | | | | | | |
|---|---|---|---|---|---|---|---|
| Don't Let The Sun Catch You Crying | 7" | Decca | F11824 | 1964 | £1.50 | £4 | |
| Don't Make Me Over | 7" | Decca | F11875 | 1964 | £1.50 | £4 | |
| I'm Just A Baby | 7" | Decca | F11476 | 1962 | £1.50 | £4 | |
| Sweet Beat Of Louise Cordet | 7" EP | Decca | DFE8515 | 1962 | £7.50 | £15 | |
| Sweet Enough | 7" | Decca | F11524 | 1962 | £1.50 | £4 | |
| Which Way The Wind Blows | 7" | Decca | F11673 | 1963 | £1.50 | £4 | |

## CORDUROYS
| | | | | | | | |
|---|---|---|---|---|---|---|---|
| Tick Tock | 7" | Planet | PLF122 | 1966 | £10 | £20 | |

## COREA, CHICK
| | | | | | | | |
|---|---|---|---|---|---|---|---|
| ARC | LP | ECM | ECM1009ST | 1971 | £5 | £12 | |
| Hymn Of The Seventh Galaxy | LP | Polydor | 2310283 | 1973 | £6 | £15 | credited to Return To Forever |
| Inner Space | LP | Atlantic | K60081 | 1974 | £6 | £15 | double |
| Is | LP | Solid State | SS18055 | 1969 | £8 | £20 | US |
| Light As A Feather | LP | Polydor | 2310247 | 1972 | £6 | £15 | credited to Return To Forever |
| Now He Sings Now He Sobs | LP | Solid State | SS18039 | 1968 | £8 | £20 | US |
| Piano Improvisations Vol. 1 | LP | ECM | ECM1014ST | 1971 | £5 | £12 | |
| Piano Improvisations Vol. 2 | LP | ECM | ECM1020ST | 1972 | £5 | £12 | |
| Return To Forever | LP | ECM | ECM1022ST | 1972 | £5 | £12 | |
| Song Of Singing | LP | Blue Note | BST84353 | 1971 | £6 | £15 | US |
| Tones For Joan's Bones | LP | Vortex | 2004 | 1966 | £20 | £40 | US |
| Where Have I Known You Before | LP | Polydor | 2310354 | 1974 | £5 | £12 | credited to Return To Forever |

## CORKSCREW
| | | | | | | | |
|---|---|---|---|---|---|---|---|
| For Openers | LP | Highway | SHY7005 | 1979 | £10 | £25 | |

## CORNELL, DON

| | | | | | | | |
|---|---|---|---|---|---|---|---|
| But Love Me | 7" | Vogue Coral | Q72164 | 1956 | £2 | £5 | |
| Don Cornell | 7" EP | HMV | 7EG8105 | 1955 | £2 | £5 | |
| For You | 10" LP | Vogue Coral | LVC10004 | 1955 | £8 | £20 | |
| Heaven Only Knows | 7" | Vogue Coral | Q72203 | 1956 | £1.50 | £4 | |
| Hold My Hand | 7" | Vogue Coral | Q2013 | 1954 | £10 | £20 | |
| I've Got Bells On My Heart | 7" | Coral | Q72313 | 1958 | £1.50 | £4 | |
| Let's Be Friends | 7" | Vogue Coral | Q72234 | 1957 | £1.50 | £4 | |
| Let's Get Lost | LP | Coral | LVA9037 | 1956 | £6 | £15 | |
| Love Is A Many Splendoured Thing | 7" | Vogue Coral | Q72104 | 1955 | £4 | £8 | |
| Mailman Bring Me No More Blues | 7" | Coral | Q72308 | 1958 | £4 | £8 | |
| Mama Guitar | 7" | Vogue Coral | Q72276 | 1957 | £5 | £10 | |
| No Man Is An Island | 7" | Vogue Coral | Q72058 | 1955 | £2 | £5 | |
| Rock Island Line | 7" | Vogue Coral | Q72152 | 1956 | £4 | £8 | |
| S'posin' | 7" | Vogue Coral | Q2037 | 1954 | £2.50 | £6 | |
| See-saw | 7" | Vogue Coral | Q72218 | 1956 | £2.50 | £6 | |
| Sempre Amore | 7" | Pye | 7N25041 | 1959 | £1.50 | £4 | |
| Sittin' In The Balcony | 7" | Vogue Coral | Q72257 | 1957 | £4 | £8 | |
| Size Twelve | 7" | Vogue Coral | Q72071 | 1955 | £2 | £5 | |
| Stranger In Paradise | 7" | Vogue Coral | Q72073 | 1955 | £4 | £8 | |
| Teenage Meeting | 7" | Vogue Coral | Q72144 | 1956 | £6 | £12 | |
| There Once Was A Beautiful | 7" | Vogue Coral | Q72132 | 1956 | £2 | £5 | |
| There's Only You | 7" | Vogue Coral | Q72291 | 1957 | £1.50 | £4 | |
| This Earth Is Mine | 7" | London | HLD8937 | 1959 | £1.50 | £4 | |
| Unchained Melody | 7" | Vogue Coral | Q72080 | 1955 | £2.50 | £6 | |
| When You Are In Love | 7" | Vogue Coral | Q72070 | 1955 | £2 | £5 | |

## CORNELL, JERRY

| | | | | | | |
|---|---|---|---|---|---|---|
| Please Don't Talk About Me | 7" | London | HL8157 | 1955 | £10 | £20 |

## CORNELLS

| | | | | | | | |
|---|---|---|---|---|---|---|---|
| Beach Bound | LP | Garex | 100 | 1963 | £75 | £150 | US |

## CORNS, ARNOLD

The records issued by Arnold Corns are actually songwriting demos recorded by David Bowie (and re-recorded later for inclusion on his *Ziggy Stardust* album).

| | | | | | | |
|---|---|---|---|---|---|---|
| Hang On To Yourself | 7" | B&C | CB189 | 1971 | £10 | £20 |
| Hang On To Yourself | 7" | Mooncrest | MOON25 | 1974 | £2.50 | £6 |
| Moonage Daydream | 7" | B&C | CB149 | 1971 | £20 | £40 |

## CORNUCOPIA

| | | | | | | | |
|---|---|---|---|---|---|---|---|
| Full Horn | LP | Brain | 1030 | 1973 | £5 | £12 | German |

## CORNWELL, HUGH

| | | | | | | | |
|---|---|---|---|---|---|---|---|
| Another Kind Of Love | CD-s | Virgin | VSCD94512 | 1988 | £2 | £5 | 3" single |
| Dreaming Again | CD-s | Virgin | VSCD1093 | 1988 | £2 | £5 | |

## CORONADOES

| | | | | | | |
|---|---|---|---|---|---|---|
| Love Me With All Your Heart | 7" | London | HL9895 | 1964 | £1.50 | £4 |

## CORONETS

| | | | | | | |
|---|---|---|---|---|---|---|
| Do Do Do It Again | 7" | Columbia | SCM5117 | 1954 | £2.50 | £6 |
| Lizzie Borden | 7" | Columbia | SCM5235 | 1956 | £2.50 | £6 |
| Magic Touch | 7" | Columbia | SCM5261 | 1956 | £4 | £8 |
| Perfect Combination | 7" EP | Columbia | SEG7621 | 1956 | £2 | £5 |
| Rhythm And Blues | 7" EP | Columbia | SEG7603 | 1956 | £2.50 | £6 |
| Someone To Love | 7" | Columbia | DB3827 | 1956 | £1.50 | £4 |

## CORPORATION

| | | | | | | | |
|---|---|---|---|---|---|---|---|
| Corporation | LP | Capitol | ST175 | 1969 | £15 | £30 | |
| Get On Our Swing | LP | Age Of Aquarius | 4150 | 1969 | £10 | £25 | US |
| Hassels In My Mind | LP | Age Of Aquarius | 4250 | 1969 | £10 | £25 | US |

## CORPUS

| | | | | | | | |
|---|---|---|---|---|---|---|---|
| Creation A Child | LP | Acorn | 1001 | 1970 | £50 | £100 | US |

## CORRIB FOLK

| | | | | | | | |
|---|---|---|---|---|---|---|---|
| Corrib Folk | LP | Homespun | HRL107 | 1975 | £4 | £10 | Irish |

## CORRIE FOLK TRIO

| | | | | | | | |
|---|---|---|---|---|---|---|---|
| Cam Ye By Atholl | LP | Philips | 6382083 | 1973 | £4 | £10 | reissue of Those Wild Corries! |
| Corrie Folk Trio And Paddie Bell | LP | Waverley | ZLP2042/ SZLP2043 | 1964 | £6 | £15 | |
| Promise Of The Day | LP | Waverley | (S)ZLP2050 | 1965 | £6 | £15 | |
| Those Wild Corries! | LP | Fontana | STL5337 | 1966 | £6 | £15 | |

## CORRIE FOLK TRIO AND PADDY BELL

| | | | | | | |
|---|---|---|---|---|---|---|
| In Retrospect | LP | Talisman | STAL5005 | 1970 | £6 | £15 |

## CORRIES

| | | | | | | |
|---|---|---|---|---|---|---|
| Bonnet, Belt And Sword | LP | Fontana | STL5401 | 1967 | £6 | £15 |
| Bonnet, Belt And Sword | LP | Philips | 8220841 | | £4 | £10 |

| | | | | | | | |
|---|---|---|---|---|---|---|---|
| In Concert | LP | Fontana | STL5484 | 1969 | £5 | £12 | |
| Kishmul's Galley | LP | Fontana | STL5465 | 1968 | £6 | £15 | |
| Little Of What You Fancy | LP | Columbia | SCX6546 | 1973 | £4 | £10 | |
| Live At The Royal Lyceum Theatre Edinburgh | LP | Columbia | SCX6468 | 1971 | £6 | £15 | |
| Live At The Royal Lyceum Theatre Edinburgh | LP | EMI | NTS109 | 197– | £4 | £10 | |
| Scottish Love Songs | LP | Fontana | | 1970 | £5 | £12 | |
| Sound The Pibroch | LP | Columbia | SCX6511 | 1972 | £4 | £10 | |
| Spotlight On The Corries | LP | Philips | 6625035 | 1977 | £6 | £15 | double |
| Strings And Things | LP | Columbia | SCX6442 | 1970 | £4 | £10 | |
| These Are The Corries Vol. 2 | LP | Philips | 6382059 | 1969 | £4 | £10 | |

## CORSAIRS

| | | | | | | |
|---|---|---|---|---|---|---|
| I'll Take You Home | 7" | Pye | 7N25142 | 1962 | £1.50 | £4 |

## CORSAIRS (2)

| | | | | | | |
|---|---|---|---|---|---|---|
| I'm Gonna Shut You Down | 7" | CBS | 202624 | 1967 | £2 | £5 |

## CORT, BOB

| | | | | | | |
|---|---|---|---|---|---|---|
| Ain't It A Shame | LP | Decca | LK4222 | 1958 | £6 | £15 |
| Ark | 7" | Decca | F10989 | 1958 | £1.50 | £4 |
| Don't You Rock Me Daddy-O | 7" | Decca | FJ10831 | 1957 | £4 | £8 |
| El Paso | 7" | Decca | F11197 | 1960 | £1.50 | £4 |
| Eskimo Nell | LP | Decca | LK4301 | 1959 | £6 | £15 |
| Kissin' Time | 7" | Decca | F11160 | 1959 | £1.50 | £4 |
| Mule Skinner Blues | 7" | Decca | F11256 | 1960 | £1.50 | £4 |
| On Top Of Old Smokey | 7" | Decca | F11109 | 1959 | £1.50 | £4 |
| Schoolday | 7" | Decca | F10905 | 1957 | £4 | £8 |
| Six Five Special | 7" | Decca | F10892 | 1957 | £4 | £8 |
| Skiffle Party | 7" | Decca | F10951 | 1957 | £1.50 | £4 |
| Waterloo | 7" | Decca | F11145 | 1959 | £1.50 | £4 |

## CORTEZ, DAVE BABY

| | | | | | | | |
|---|---|---|---|---|---|---|---|
| And His Happy Organ | LP | RCA | LPM/LSP2099 | 1959 | £8 | £20 | US |
| Countdown | 7" | Roulette | RK7001 | 1966 | £1.50 | £4 | |
| Dave Baby Cortez | LP | Clock | C331 | 1960 | £8 | £20 | US |
| Dave Baby Cortez | 7" EP | London | REU1233 | 1960 | £12.50 | £25 | |
| Deep In The Heart Of Texas | 7" | London | HLU9126 | 1960 | £4 | £8 | |
| Golden Hits | LP | London | HAU8142 | 1964 | £8 | £20 | |
| Happy Organ | 7" | London | HLU8852 | 1959 | £4 | £8 | |
| In Orbit | LP | Roulette | (S)R25328 | 1966 | £4 | £10 | US |
| Organ Shindig | LP | Roulette | (S)R25298 | 1965 | £6 | £15 | US |
| Piano Shuffle | 7" | Columbia | DB4404 | 1960 | £2 | £5 | |
| Rinky Dink | LP | Chess | LP1473 | 1962 | £8 | £20 | US |
| Rinky Dink | 7" | Pye | 7N25159 | 1962 | £4 | £8 | |
| Tweety Pie | LP | Roulette | (S)R25315 | 1966 | £4 | £10 | US |
| Whistling Organ | 7" | London | HLU8919 | 1959 | £4 | £8 | |

## CORTINAS

| | | | | | | |
|---|---|---|---|---|---|---|
| Phoebe's Flower Shop | 7" | Polydor | 56255 | 1968 | £1.50 | £4 |

## CORYELL, LARRY

Larry Coryell caused much comment as the first guitarist in a jazz group to employ feedback, but the offending track, Gary Burton's 'General Mojo Cuts Up', is actually a very mild-mannered affair. Ever since, Coryell has languished in the shade of John McLaughlin, who is the real innovator where the use of a highly amplified guitar in jazz is concerned. There is a reasonable sampler of his work – the double *Essential Larry Coryell* on Vanguard. Otherwise, he has made a great many records, of which the scarcer, earlier ones listed here are just the start.

| | | | | | | | |
|---|---|---|---|---|---|---|---|
| Coryell | LP | Vanguard | SVRL19059 | 1969 | £4 | £10 | |
| Introducing The Eleventh House | LP | Vanguard | VSD79342 | 1974 | £4 | £10 | quad |
| Lady Coryell | LP | Vanguard | SVRL19051 | 1969 | £4 | £10 | |
| Live At The Village Gate | LP | Vanguard | VSD6573 | 1971 | £4 | £10 | quad |
| Offering | LP | Vanguard | VSD79319 | 1972 | £4 | £10 | quad |
| Spaces | LP | Philips | 6359005 | 1970 | £4 | £10 | with John McLaughlin |

## COSBY, BILL

| | | | | | | | |
|---|---|---|---|---|---|---|---|
| Little Ole Man | 7" | Warner Bros | WB7072 | 1967 | £4 | £8 | picture sleeve |

## COSMIC DEALER

| | | | | | | | |
|---|---|---|---|---|---|---|---|
| Crystallization | LP | Negram | NQ20015 | 1971 | £62.50 | £125 | Dutch |

## COSMIC EYE

Cosmic Eye represented an attempt on the part of some of the second division of British jazz musicians – basically John Mayer's Indo-jazz group – to break directly into the progressive rock market.

| | | | | | | |
|---|---|---|---|---|---|---|
| Dream Sequence | LP | Regal Zonophone | SLRZ1030 | 1972 | £62.50 | £125 |

## COSMIC JOKERS

| | | | | | | | |
|---|---|---|---|---|---|---|---|
| Cosmic Jokers | LP | Metronome | KM58008 | 1974 | £8 | £20 | German |
| Planet Sit In | LP | Metronome | KM58013 | 1974 | £6 | £15 | German |

## COSMIC SOUNDS

*The Zodiac* was the first electronic rock record and featured spoken verses, one for each Zodiacal sign, behind which Paul Beaver put his new synthesizer through its paces.

| | | | | | | | |
|---|---|---|---|---|---|---|---|
| Zodiac | LP | Elektra | EKL/EKS74009 | 1967 | £6 | £15 | |

## COSMO, FRANK

| | | | | | | | |
|---|---|---|---|---|---|---|---|
| Alone | 7" | Black Swan | WI446 | 1965 | £5 | £10 | |
| Better Get Right | 7" | Island | WI135 | 1964 | £5 | £10 | |
| Gypsy Woman | 7" | Blue Beat | BB175 | 1963 | £6 | £12 | |
| I Love You | 7" | R&B | JB119 | 1963 | £5 | £10 | Don Drummond B side |
| Merry Christmas | 7" | Island | WI100 | 1963 | £5 | £10 | |
| Revenge | 7" | Island | WI058 | 1963 | £5 | £10 | |

## COSTA, DON

| | | | | | | | |
|---|---|---|---|---|---|---|---|
| I Walk The Line | 7" | London | HLT8992 | 1959 | £1.50 | £4 | |
| Love Is A Many Splendoured Thing | 7" | London | HLF8186 | 1955 | £6 | £12 | |

## COSTA, EDDIE

| | | | | | | | |
|---|---|---|---|---|---|---|---|
| Eddie Costa Quintet | 10" LP | Top Rank | 25017 | 1960 | £6 | £15 | |
| Newport Jazz Festival 1957 | LP | Columbia | 33CX10108 | 1958 | £6 | £15 | with Mat Matthews & Don Elliott |

## COSTANZO, JACK

| | | | | | | | |
|---|---|---|---|---|---|---|---|
| Mr. Bongo | LP | Vogue | VA160150 | 1959 | £8 | £20 | |

## COSTELLO, CECILIA

| | | | | | | | |
|---|---|---|---|---|---|---|---|
| Recordings From The Sound Archives Of The BBC | LP | Leader | LEE4054 | 1975 | £5 | £12 | |

## COSTELLO, DAY

Despite its early date, the Beatles cover credited to 'Day Costello' was long thought to have been attributable to the young Declan McManus. It is not, but the guess was not so very wide of the mark, as the name actually hides the identity of Elvis Costello's father, the former singer with the Joe Loss Orchestra, Ross McManus.

| | | | | | | | |
|---|---|---|---|---|---|---|---|
| Long And Winding Road | 7" | Spark | SRL1042 | 1970 | £2 | £5 | |

## COSTELLO, ELVIS

Two of Elvis Costello's limited-edition releases are vital additions to any collection of his work. *A Conversation With Elvis Costello* spreads the contents of his *Imperial Bedroom* LP over two records, adding a substantial amount of interview material in which Costello explains the genesis of each of the songs, prior to each one being heard. (The promo version of *Almost Blue* gives the same treatment to that album, but the interview segments are much shorter and much less interesting.) *Live At The El Mocambo*, meanwhile, contains a brilliant live reworking of some of the songs from Costello's first two LPs. Most copies that appear on the market are actually counterfeits, although this has little effect on their value. (As usual, the counterfeits are readily identified by their hand-written matrix numbers.) The original pressing of the *Armed Forces* LP, complete with its opening-out cover and its EP record and postcard inserts, is nothing like as rare as some people seem to imagine. The record was included in earlier editions of the price guide, but has now become a victim of the general fall in vinyl prices at the bottom end of the market.

| | | | | | | | |
|---|---|---|---|---|---|---|---|
| Alison | 7" | Stiff | BUY14 | 1977 | £12.50 | £25 | white vinyl A side |
| Armed Forces | LP | CBS | JC35709 | 1979 | £4 | £10 | Canadian, yellow vinyl |
| Armed Forces | CD | Demon | IMPFIENDCD21 | 1986 | £5 | £12 | with 'Peace, Love & Understanding' |
| Baby Plays Around | CD-s | WEA | W2949CD | 1989 | £2 | £5 | |
| Big Sister | 7" | F-Beat | | 1982 | £2 | £5 | 1 sided promo |
| Blood And Chocolate | cass | Demon | XFIENDCASS80 | 1986 | £5 | £12 | 'chocolate bar' package |
| Conversation With Elvis Costello | LP | F-Beat | ECCHAT2 | 1982 | £25 | £50 | double promo |
| Costello Hour | CD | Warner Bros | PROCD3426 | 1989 | £8 | £20 | US promo |
| Don't Let Me Be Misunderstood (Live) | 12" | Columbia | CAS2310 | 1986 | £6 | £15 | US promo |
| Excerpts from Almost Blue | 7" | F-Beat | EC1 | 1981 | £12.50 | £25 | promo |
| Excerpts from Trust | 12" | F-Beat | EL2 | 1981 | £15 | £30 | promo |
| Get Happy | LP | F-Beat | XXPROMO1 | 1980 | £20 | £40 | double 12" promo |
| Good Year For The Roses | 7" | F-Beat | XX17 | 1981 | £7.50 | £15 | picture sleeve |
| Highlights From Blood And Chocolate | 7" | Imp | CHOC1 | 1986 | £2.50 | £6 | red vinyl promo |
| I Can't Stand Up For Falling Down | 7" | 2-Tone | CHSTT7 | 1980 | £6 | £12 | |
| I Can't Stand Up For Falling Down | 7" | 2-Tone | CHSTT7 | 1980 | £4 | £8 | matrix No. XX1 |
| I Wanna Be Loved (Radio Version) | 7" | F-Beat | XX35DJ | 1984 | £2 | £5 | promo |
| I Wanna Be Loved (Radio Version) | 12" | F-Beat | XX35Z | 1984 | £4 | £10 | promo |
| Imperial Bedroom | LP | Columbia | HC48157 | 1982 | £5 | £12 | US audiophile |
| Imperial Bedroom/Almost Blue | CD | Demon | ECPROMO2 | 1994 | £6 | £15 | promo sampler |
| Introduces The Tracks From Almost Blue | LP | F-Beat | ECCHAT1 | 1981 | £25 | £50 | |
| Live At Hollywood High | 12" | Columbia | AS529 | 1979 | £6 | £15 | US promo |
| Live At The El Mocambo | LP | Columbia | CDN10 | 1978 | £25 | £50 | Canadian promo |
| Mighty Like A Rose | CD | Warner Bros | | 1991 | £6 | £15 | US promo picture disc |
| My Aim Is True/This Year's Model | LP | Columbia | no number | 1978 | £75 | £150 | US promo picture disc |
| New Amsterdam | 7" | F-Beat | XX5P | 1980 | £2.50 | £6 | picture disc, black rim |
| New Amsterdam | 7" | F-Beat | XX5P | 1980 | £1.50 | £4 | picture disc, white rim |
| Other Side Of Summer | CD-s | WEA | W0025CD | 1991 | £2 | £5 | |
| Punch The Clock | 7" | F-Beat | | 1983 | £12.50 | £25 | 2 x 7" in plastic wallet, promo |
| Radio Radio | 12" | Columbia | AS443 | 1978 | £5 | £12 | US promo, orange vinyl, with other artists |
| Radio Radio | 12" | Radar | ADA24 | 1978 | £5 | £12 | promo |
| Spike | CD | Warner Bros | PROCD3426 | 1989 | £6 | £15 | US promo in tartan cover |
| Stiff Singles Four Pack | 7" | Stiff | GRAB3 | 1980 | £6 | £12 | |
| Taking Liberties | LP | Columbia | JC36939 | 1980 | £4 | £10 | US |
| Taking Liberties | 12" | Columbia | AS847 | 1980 | £6 | £15 | US promo, Costello label |
| Talking In The Dark | 7" | Radar | RG1 | 1978 | £2.50 | £6 | |

| | | | | | | | |
|---|---|---|---|---|---|---|---|
| Ten Bloody Marys And Ten How's Your Fathers | cass ..... | F-Beat | XXC6 | 1980 £4 | £10 | ...gold cassette & case |
| Tom Snyder Interview | 12" ..... | Columbia | AS958 | 1980 £6 | £15 | US promo |
| Two And A Half Years In Thirty-One Minutes | CD .... | Demon | | 1993 £8 | £20 | promo sampler |
| Veronica | CD-s .. | WEA | W7558CD | 1989 £2 | £5 | |
| Words And Music | CD .... | Warner Bros .... | PROCD6955 | 1994 £8 | £20 | US promo |

## COTSWOLD FOLK
| | | | | | | |
|---|---|---|---|---|---|---|
| Collection | LP ..... | Deroy | | 1977 £25 | £50 | |

## COTTON, BILLY
| | | | | | | |
|---|---|---|---|---|---|---|
| Friends And Neighbours | 7" ..... | Decca | F10299 | 1954 £1.50 | £4 | |
| This Ole House | 7" ..... | Decca | F10377 | 1954 £1.50 | £4 | |

## COTTON, JAMES BLUES BAND
| | | | | | | |
|---|---|---|---|---|---|---|
| Cotton In Your Ears | LP ..... | Verve | FTS3060 | 1969 £4 | £10 | US |
| Cut You Loose | LP ..... | Vanguard | SVRL19035 | 1968 £4 | £10 | |
| James Cotton Blues Band | LP ..... | Verve | FT(S)3023 | 1967 £4 | £10 | US |
| Pure Cotton | LP ..... | Verve | FTS3038 | 1968 £4 | £10 | US |
| Taking Care Of Business | LP ..... | Capitol | SM814 | 1970 £4 | £10 | US |

## COTTON, JIMMY
| | | | | | | |
|---|---|---|---|---|---|---|
| Chris Barber Presents Jimmy Cotton | 7" EP . | Columbia | SEG8141 | 1962 £2 | £5 | |
| Chris Barber Presents Jimmy Cotton No. 2. | 7" EP . | Columbia | SEG8189 | 1962 £2 | £5 | |

## COTTON, MIKE JAZZMEN
| | | | | | | |
|---|---|---|---|---|---|---|
| Ain't Misbehavin' | 7" ..... | Columbia | DB4779 | 1962 £1.50 | £4 | |
| Cobbler's Song | 7" ..... | Columbia | DB4821 | 1962 £1.50 | £4 | |
| Cotton Picking | 7" EP . | Columbia | SEG8144 | 1962 £10 | £20 | |
| Senora | 7" ..... | Columbia | DB4697 | 1961 £1.50 | £4 | |
| Swing That Hammer | 7" ..... | Columbia | DB7029 | 1963 £2 | £5 | |
| Wild And The Willing | 7" EP . | Columbia | SEG8190 | 1962 £10 | £20 | |
| Zulu Warrior | 7" ..... | Columbia | DB4910 | 1962 £1.50 | £4 | |

## COTTON, MIKE SOUND
| | | | | | | |
|---|---|---|---|---|---|---|
| Harlem Shuffle | 7" ..... | Polydor | 56096 | 1966 £7.50 | £15 | |
| I Don't Wanna Know | 7" ..... | Columbia | DB7267 | 1964 £10 | £20 | |
| Make Up Your Mind | 7" EP . | Festival | 452433 | 1965 £25 | £50 | French |
| Make Up Your Mind | 7" ..... | Columbia | DB7623 | 1965 £7.50 | £15 | |
| Midnight Flyer | 7" ..... | Columbia | DB7134 | 1963 £2 | £5 | |
| Mike Cotton Sound | LP ..... | Columbia | 33SX1647 | 1964 £180 | £300 | |
| Round And Round | 7" ..... | Columbia | DB7382 | 1964 £15 | £30 | |

## COUGAR (MELLENCAMP), JOHN
| | | | | | | |
|---|---|---|---|---|---|---|
| Biography | LP ..... | Riva | RVLP9 | 1979 £6 | £15 | |

## COUGARS
| | | | | | | |
|---|---|---|---|---|---|---|
| Caviare And Chips | 7" ..... | Parlophone | R5115 | 1964 £2.50 | £6 | |
| Red Square | 7" ..... | Parlophone | R5038 | 1963 £1.50 | £4 | |
| Saturday Night At The Duckpond | 7" ..... | Parlophone | R4989 | 1963 £1.50 | £4 | |
| Saturday Night With The Cougars | 7" EP . | Parlophone | GEP8886 | 1963 £15 | £30 | |

## COUGHLAN, CATHAL
| | | | | | | |
|---|---|---|---|---|---|---|
| I'm Long Me Measaim | 7" ..... | Caff | CAFF1 | 198– £2.50 | £6 | flexi, East Village B side |

## COULDRY, DENIS & SMILE
| | | | | | | |
|---|---|---|---|---|---|---|
| James In The Basement | 7" ..... | Decca | F12734 | 1968 £1.50 | £4 | |
| Penny For The Wind | 7" ..... | Decca | F12786 | 1968 £1.50 | £4 | |

## COUNCE, CURTIS
| | | | | | | |
|---|---|---|---|---|---|---|
| Carl's Blues | LP ..... | Contemporary . | LAC12263 | 1961 £8 | £20 | |
| Curtis Counce Group | LP ..... | Contemporary . | LAC12073 | 1958 £8 | £20 | |
| You Get More Bounce With Curtis Counce | LP ..... | Contemporary . | LAC12133 | 1959 £8 | £20 | |

## COUNT DOWN & THE ZEROS
| | | | | | | |
|---|---|---|---|---|---|---|
| Hello My Angel | 7" ..... | Ember | EMBS189 | 1964 £10 | £20 | |

## COUNT FIVE
| | | | | | | |
|---|---|---|---|---|---|---|
| Psychotic Reaction | LP ..... | Double Shot .... | DSM1001/DSS5001 | 1966 £15 | £30 | US |
| Psychotic Reaction | 7" EP . | DiscAZ | 1058 | 1966 £25 | £50 | French |
| Psychotic Reaction | 7" ..... | Pye | 7N25393 | 1966 £5 | £10 | |

## COUNT OSSIE
Count Ossie and the Mystic Revelation of Rastafari are members of an isolated rural Rastafarian community in Jamaica. Their music is rather different from that of other reggae groups – the several percussionists that form the central strand give it a pronounced African flavour; the horns and acoustic double bass add a jazz flavour; the poets and chanters turn the whole thing into pure Count Ossie.

| | | | | | | |
|---|---|---|---|---|---|---|
| Grounation | LP ..... | Ashanti | NTI301 | 1973 £10 | £25 | triple, with the Mystic Revelation Of Rastafari |
| Nyiah Bongo | 7" ..... | Doctor Bird .... | DB1086 | 1967 £5 | £10 | |
| Pure Soul | 7" ..... | Doctor Bird .... | DB1113 | 1967 £5 | £10 | Patsy Todd B side |
| Tales Of Mozambique | LP ..... | Dynamic | DNYLS1001 | 1975 £6 | £15 | with the Mystic Revelation Of Rastafari |

| Turn Me On | 7" | Doctor Bird | DB1018 | 1966 £5 | £10 | |

## COUNT VICTORS
| Peeping And Hiding | 7" | Coral | Q72456 | 1962 £1.50 | £4 | |
| Road Runner | 7" | Coral | Q72462 | 1963 £2 | £5 | |

## COUNTRY BOY
| I'm A Lonely Boy | 7" | Blue Beat | BB236 | 1964 £6 | £12 | |

## COUNTRY GENTLEMEN
| Greensleeves | 7" | Decca | F11766 | 1963 £10 | £20 | |

## COUNTRY HAMS
| Walking In The Park With Eloise | 7" | EMI | EMI2220 | 1974 £12.50 | £25 | red & brown label |
| Walking In The Park With Eloise | 7" | EMI | EMI2220 | 1982 £2 | £5 | straw label |

## COUNTRY JOE & THE FISH

The album that most clearly epitomizes the spirit of the 1967 'summer of love' is *I Feel Like I'm Fixin' To Die* by Country Joe and the Fish. The combination of electric guitar wizardry, political protest, and general psychedelia lends credence to the legend that the whole thing was recorded while the band was tripping on acid, but it also happens to be one of the finest albums of the period. Country Joe McDonald himself had a background in folk and country – and returned to this as a solo artist after the Fish disbanded in 1970. His early career is documented by the self-produced Rag Baby series of EPs and also by a recently discovered solo album from 1965 – listed under his own name.

| Best Of Country Foe And The Fish | LP | Vanguard | SVRL19058 | 1969 £4 | £10 | |
| C. J. Fish | LP | Vanguard | 6369002 | 1970 £4 | £10 | |
| Country Joe And The Fish | 7" EP | Rag Baby | RAG1002 | 1965 £25 | £50 | US |
| Electric Music For The Mind & Body | LP | Fontana | (S)TFL6081 | 1967 £8 | £20 | |
| Electric Music For The Mind & Body | LP | Vanguard | SVRL19026 | 1967 £5 | £12 | |
| Electric Music For The Mind And Body | LP | Vanguard | VSD79244 | 1972 £4 | £10 | |
| Here I Go Again | 7" | Vanguard | VA3 | 1969 £2 | £5 | |
| Here We Are Again | LP | Vanguard | SVRL19048 | 1969 £5 | £12 | |
| I Feel Like I'm Fixin' To Die | LP | Vanguard | VSD79266 | 1971 £4 | £10 | |
| I Feel Like I'm Fixin' To Die | 7" | Vanguard | 6076250 | 1970 £2 | £5 | |
| I Feel Like I'm Fixing To Die | LP | Fontana | (S)TFL6087 | 1967 £8 | £20 | |
| I Feel Like I'm Fixing To Die | LP | Vanguard | SVRL19029 | 1967 £5 | £12 | |
| Life And Times Of Country Joe And The Fish | LP | Vanguard | VSD27/28 | 1973 £6 | £15 | double |
| Life And Times Of Country Joe And The Fish | LP | Vanguard | VSQ40004/5 | 1973 £10 | £25 | quad, double |
| Not So Sweet Martha Lorraine | 7" | Fontana | TF882 | 1967 £2.50 | £6 | |
| Rag Baby Talking Issue | 7" EP | Rag Baby | RAG1001 | 1965 £25 | £50 | US |
| Resist | 7" EP | Rag Baby | RAG1003 | 1971 £15 | £30 | US |
| Together | LP | Vanguard | SVRL19006 | 1968 £5 | £12 | |

## COUNTRY LANE
| Substratum | LP | Splendid | SLP50108 | 1973 £100 | £200 | Swiss |

## COURIERS
| Take Away | 7" | Ember | EMBS218 | 1966 £30 | £60 | |
| Take Away | 7" | Ember | EMBS218 | 1966 £37.50 | £75 | picture sleeve |

## COURTNEY, PETER
| Docteur David's Private Papers | 7" EP | Fontana | 469210 | 1967 £4 | £8 | French |

## COUSIN EMMY & HER KINFOLK
| Kentucky Mountain Ballads Vol. 1 | 7" EP | Brunswick | OE9258 | 1956 £2.50 | £6 | |
| Kentucky Mountain Ballads Vol. 2 | 7" EP | Brunswick | OE9259 | 1956 £2.50 | £6 | |

## COUSINS
| Greatest Hits | LP | Palette | PPB225 | 1966 £6 | £15 | Belgian |
| Live | LP | Palette | MGPB9449 | 1964 £6 | £15 | Dutch |

## COUSINS, DAVE
| Old School Songs | LP | Slurp | 1 | 1980 £8 | £20 | |
| Two Weeks Last Summer | LP | A&M | AMLS68118 | 1972 £10 | £25 | |

## COVAY, DON
| Different Strokes | LP | Janus | 3038 | 1970 £4 | £10 | US |
| Forty Days – Forty Nights | 7" | Atlantic | 584114 | 1967 £1.50 | £4 | |
| House Of Blue Light | LP | Atlantic | K50225 | 1969 £4 | £10 | |
| Mercy | LP | Atlantic | ATL5025 | 1965 £20 | £40 | |
| Mercy Mercy | 7" | Atlantic | 584094 | 1967 £1.50 | £4 | |
| Mercy Mercy | 7" | Atlantic | AT4006 | 1964 £1.50 | £4 | |
| Pony Time | 7" | Pye | 7N25075 | 1961 £2 | £5 | |
| Popeye Waddle | 7" | Cameo Parkway | C239 | 1962 £7.50 | £15 | |
| See Saw | 7" | Atlantic | 584059 | 1966 £1.50 | £4 | |
| See Saw | 7" | Atlantic | AT4056 | 1965 £1.50 | £4 | |
| See-Saw | LP | Atlantic | 587062 | 1967 £5 | £12 | |
| Shake Wid The Shake | 7" | Philips | PB1140 | 1961 £2.50 | £6 | |
| Shing-A-Ling '67 | 7" | Atlantic | 584082 | 1967 £1.50 | £4 | |
| Sookie Sookie | 7" | Atlantic | AT4078 | 1966 £1.50 | £4 | |
| Take This Hurt Off Me | 7" | Atlantic | AT4016 | 1965 £1.50 | £4 | |
| You Put Something On Me | 7" | Atlantic | 584025 | 1966 £1.50 | £4 | |

## COVERDALE, DAVID
Last Note Of Freedom ............................ CD-s .. Epic .............. 6562922 ................... 1990 £2 .......... £5

## COVEY, JULIAN & THE MACHINE
Little Bit Hurt .................................................. 7" ...... Island ............. WIP6009 ............. 1967 £6 .......... £12

## COVINGTON, JULIE
Beautiful Changes.................................... LP ..... Columbia ..... SCX6466 ........... 1971 £50 ...... £100
Magic Wasn't There .................................. 7" ...... Columbia ..... DB8649 ............ 1970 £2.50 ..... £6
Tonight Your Love Is Over ...................... 7" ...... Columbia ..... DB8705 ............ 1970 £2.50 ..... £6

## COVINGTON, JULIE & PETE ATKIN
While The Music Lasts........................... LP ..... MJB............ BEVLP1009 .......... 1967 £50 ...... £100

## COWELL, STANLEY
Illusion Suite ............................................ LP ..... ECM ............ ECM1026ST ....... 1973 £6 .......... £15

## COWSILLS
Captain Sad And His Ship Of Fools............ LP ..... MGM ........... CS8095 .................. 1968 £4 .......... £10
Cowsills........................................................ LP ..... MGM ........... C(S)8059 ............... 1967 £4 .......... £10
Cowsills And The Lincoln Park Zoo ........ LP ..... Fontana ....... SFL13055 ............ 1968 £4 .......... £10
In Concert.................................................... LP ..... MGM ........... SE4619 ................. 1969 £4 .......... £10 ............. US
On My Side................................................. LP ..... London ........ SHU8421 ............. 1971 £4 .......... £10
Rain, The Park And Other Things........... 7" ...... MGM ........... MGM1353 .......... 1967 £1.50 ..... £4
Two By Two................................................. LP ..... MGM ........... SE4639 ................. 1970 £4 .......... £10 ............. US
We Can Fly ................................................ LP ..... MGM ........... CS8077 .................. 1968 £4 .......... £10

## COX, BILLY
Immediately after the death of his employer, Jimi Hendrix, bassist Billy Cox recorded what amounts to a tribute LP before effectively vanishing from the music scene. For *Nitro Function*, he recruited a rather fine lady guitarist, who manages to convey the spirit of Jimi Hendrix rather better than most, although she too subsequently disappeared. The record cover, incidentally, is a creation by the same man who was responsible for the series of distinctive Yes sleeves – Roger Dean.

Nitro Function.......................................... LP ..... Pye ............. NSPL28158 .......... 1971 £10 ....... £25

## COX, HARRY
Sings English Love Songs ......................... LP ..... DTS ............ LFX4 ................... 1965 £8 .......... £20

## COX, IDA
Blues For Rampart Street ........................ LP ..... Riverside ....... RLP374 ................ 1961 £6 .......... £15
Female Blues Vol. 1.................................. 7" EP . Collector........ JEL12 .................. 1960 £4 .......... £8 ........ *with Ma Rainey*
Ida Cox..................................................... 7" EP . Fontana ........ TFE17136 ........... 1959 £2.50 ..... £6
Ida Cox Vol. 1 ......................................... LP ..... Fountain ....... FB301 ................. 1974 £4 .......... £10
Ida Cox Vol. 2 ......................................... LP ..... Fountain ....... FB304 ................. 1975 £4 .......... £10
Sings The Blues ...................................... 10" LP London ......... AL3517 ................ 1954 £8 .......... £20

## COX, IDA & ETHEL WATERS
Ida Cox And Ethel Waters ..................... LP ..... Poydras ....... 104 ...................... 195– £10 ....... £25

## COX, KENNY
Introducing............................................... LP ..... Blue Note ....... BST84302 ............ 1968 £5 .......... £12
Multidirection......................................... LP ..... Blue Note ....... BST84339 ............ 1969 £5 .......... £12

## COX, MICHAEL
Along Came Caroline ............................. 7" ...... HMV ............ POP789 ................ 1960 £5 .......... £10
Angela Jones ........................................... 7" ...... Ember........... EMBS103 .......... 1960 £12.50 ... £25
Angela Jones ........................................... 7" ...... Triumph ........ RGM1011........... 1960 £2.50 ..... £6
Boy Meets Girl......................................... 7" ...... Decca ........... F11166.................. 1959 £2.50 ..... £6
Don't You Break My Heart...................... 7" ...... HMV ............ POP1137 .............. 1963 £5 .......... £10
Gee What A Party ..................................... 7" ...... HMV ............ POP1220 .............. 1963 £5 .......... £10
Gypsy ......................................................... 7" ...... HMV ............ POP1417 ............. 1965 £5 .......... £10
I Hate Getting Up In The Morning .......... 7" ...... Parlophone...... R5436 .................. 1966 £1.50 ..... £4
Rave On ..................................................... 7" ...... HMV ............ POP1293 ............. 1964 £6 .......... £12
Stand Up ................................................... 7" ...... HMV ............ POP1065 ............. 1962 £5 .......... £10
Sweet Little Sixteen ............................... 7" ...... HMV ............ POP905 ................ 1961 £2.50 ..... £6
Teenage Love ........................................... 7" ...... HMV ............ POP830 ................ 1961 £2.50 ..... £6
Too Hot To Handle ................................. 7" ...... Decca ........... F11182.................. 1959 £2.50 ..... £6
Young Only Once ..................................... 7" ...... HMV ............ POP972 ................ 1962 £5 .......... £10

## COX, WALLY
I Can't Help It ......................................... 7" ...... Vogue ............ V9175 ................. 1961 £5 .......... £10

## COXHILL, LOL
Lol Coxhill is as great an eccentric as he is a saxophone player – and his work on that instrument is very fine indeed! The Dandelion double album *Ear Of Beholder* is the ideal introduction to both the man and the musician. It contains free group improvisation; recordings of Coxhill busking on the streets of London (he is supposed to be the inspiration behind Joni Mitchell's 'For Free', although he was apparently mildly insulted by this); Victorian music-hall songs interpreted by the Coxhill-Bedford duo; and a group of school children singing 'I Am The Walrus'. The later *Murder In The Air* consists of a radio play with all the parts accompanied by what amount to saxophone sub-titles!

10:02.......................................................... LP ..... Nato ............. 439 ...................... 1986 £5 .......... £12
Cafe De La Place ..................................... LP ..... Nato ............. ......................... 1988 £5 .......... £12
Chantenay '80 .......................................... LP ..... Nato ............. 10 ....................... 1980 £5 .......... £12
Couscous ................................................... LP ..... Nato ............. 157 ...................... 1983 £5 .......... £12
Coxhill Miller .......................................... LP ..... Caroline ........ C1503 .................. 1973 £4 .......... £10 ....... *with Stephen Miller*
Digwell Duets ........................................... LP ..... Random Radar RR005 ................. 1979 £5 .......... £12
Diverse........................................................ LP ..... Ogun ............ OG510.................. 1976 £5 .......... £12

| Title | Format | Label | Cat. No. | Year | Price | Price | Notes |
|---|---|---|---|---|---|---|---|
| Dunois Solos | LP | Nato | 95 | 1981 | £5 | £12 | |
| Ear Of Beholder | LP | Dandelion | 69001 | 1971 | £20 | £40 | double |
| Fleas In The Custard | LP | Caroline | C1515 | 1975 | £4 | £10 | |
| French Gigs | LP | AAA | A02 | 1982 | £5 | £12 | |
| Frogdance | LP | Impetus | 1085 | 1984 | £5 | £12 | |
| Inimitable | LP | Chabada | OH9 | 1986 | £5 | £12 | French |
| Instant Replay | LP | Nato | 25/32 | 1982 | £5 | £12 | |
| Johnny Rondo Duo Plus Mike Cooper | LP | FMP | SAJ29 | 1982 | £5 | £12 | German, with David Holland |
| Joy Of Paranoia | LP | Ogun | OG525 | 1978 | £5 | £12 | |
| Lid | LP | Ictus | 0011 | 1978 | £6 | £15 | |
| Lol Coxhill & Welfare State | LP | Caroline | C1514 | 1975 | £4 | £10 | |
| Moot | LP | Ictus | 0008 | 1978 | £6 | £15 | |
| Murder In The Air | 12" | Chiltern Sound | CS100 | 1978 | £4 | £10 | |
| Slow Music | LP | Pipe | 1 | 1980 | £5 | £12 | with Morgan Fisher |
| Story So Far Oh Really? | LP | Caroline | C1507 | 1974 | £4 | £10 | with Stephen Miller |
| Toverbal Sweet | LP | Mushroom | 150MR23 | 1972 | £37.50 | £75 | |

## COXHILL, LOL & DAVID BEDFORD

| Title | Format | Label | Cat. No. | Year | Price | Price |
|---|---|---|---|---|---|---|
| Pretty Little Girl | 7" | Polydor | 2001253 | 1971 | £1.50 | £4 |

## COXSONE, LLOYD

| Title | Format | Label | Cat. No. | Year | Price | Price |
|---|---|---|---|---|---|---|
| Cruising | 7" | Pyramid | PYR7003 | 1973 | £1.50 | £4 |

## COYNE, KEVIN

| Title | Format | Label | Cat. No. | Year | Price | Price | Notes |
|---|---|---|---|---|---|---|---|
| Blame It On The Night | LP | Virgin | V2012 | 1974 | £4 | £10 | |
| Case History | LP | Dandelion | 2310228 | 1972 | £20 | £40 | |
| Cheat Me | 7" | Polydor | 2001357 | 1972 | £1.50 | £4 | |
| Heartburn | LP | Virgin | V2047 | 1976 | £4 | £10 | |
| In Living Black And White | LP | Virgin | VD2505 | 1976 | £5 | £12 | double |
| Marjory Razorblade | LP | Virgin | VD2501 | 1973 | £5 | £12 | double |
| Matching Head And Feet | LP | Virgin | V2033 | 1975 | £4 | £10 | |

## CRACKED MIRROR

| Title | Format | Label | Cat. No. | Year | Price | Price |
|---|---|---|---|---|---|---|
| Cracked Mirror | LP | private | CMLP001 | 1983 | £25 | £50 |

## CRACKERS

The single credited to the Crackers was actually made by the Merseys.

| Title | Format | Label | Cat. No. | Year | Price | Price |
|---|---|---|---|---|---|---|
| Honey Do | 7" | Fontana | TF995 | 1969 | £1.50 | £4 |

## CRACKNELL, SARAH

| Title | Format | Label | Cat. No. | Year | Price | Price |
|---|---|---|---|---|---|---|
| Love Is All You Need | 7" | Three Bears | TED001 | 1987 | £2.50 | £6 |

## CRADDOCK, BILLY 'CRASH'

| Title | Format | Label | Cat. No. | Year | Price | Price | Notes |
|---|---|---|---|---|---|---|---|
| Boom Boom Baby | 7" | Philips | PB966 | 1959 | £5 | £10 | |
| Goodtime Billy | 7" | Philips | PB1092 | 1961 | £4 | £8 | |
| I'm Tore Up | LP | King | 912 | 1964 | £10 | £25 | US |
| Since She Turned Seventeen | 7" | Philips | PB1006 | 1960 | £5 | £10 | |
| Truly True | 7" | Mercury | AMT1146 | 1961 | £2.50 | £6 | |

## CRAIG

| Title | Format | Label | Cat. No. | Year | Price | Price |
|---|---|---|---|---|---|---|
| I Must Be Mad | 7" | Fontana | TF715 | 1966 | £87.50 | £175 |
| Little Bit Of Soap | 7" | Fontana | TF665 | 1966 | £30 | £60 |

## CRAIG (2)

| Title | Format | Label | Cat. No. | Year | Price | Price |
|---|---|---|---|---|---|---|
| Ain't That A Shame | 7" | King | KG1022 | 1965 | £4 | £8 |

## CRAMER, FLOYD

| Title | Format | Label | Cat. No. | Year | Price | Price |
|---|---|---|---|---|---|---|
| Fancy Pants | 7" | London | HL8012 | 1954 | £12.50 | £25 |
| Flip Flop And Bop | 7" | RCA | RCA1050 | 1958 | £7.50 | £15 |
| Jolly Cholly | 7" | London | HL8062 | 1954 | £12.50 | £25 |
| Last Date | 7" | RCA | RCA1211 | 1960 | £1.50 | £4 |
| On The Rebound | LP | RCA | RD27221/SF5103 | 1961 | £4 | £10 |
| Piano Hayride | 7" EP | London | REP1023 | 1955 | £12.50 | £25 |
| Rag A Tag | 7" | London | HLU8195 | 1955 | £10 | £20 |
| That Handsome Piano | 7" EP | RCA | RCX7120 | 1963 | £4 | £8 |

## CRAMPS

| Title | Format | Label | Cat. No. | Year | Price | Price | Notes |
|---|---|---|---|---|---|---|---|
| All Women Are Bad | CD-s | Enigma | ENVCD19 | 1990 | £2 | £5 | |
| Bikini Girls With Machine Guns | CD-s | Enigma | ENVCD17 | 1990 | £2 | £5 | |
| Creature From The Black Leather Lagoon | CD-s | Enigma | ENVCD22 | 1990 | £2 | £5 | |
| Crusher | 12" | IRS | PFSX1008 | 1981 | £4 | £10 | |
| Drug Train | 7" | Illegal | ILS021 | 1980 | £4 | £8 | |
| Eyeball In My Martini | CD-s | Big Beat | CDNST135 | 1991 | £2 | £5 | |
| Fever | 7" | Illegal | ILS017 | 1980 | £2.50 | £6 | band picture sleeve |
| Flamejob | CD | Creation | CRECD170 | 1994 | £8 | £20 | US promo with extra tracks |
| Garbageman/Mystery Plane | 7" | Illegal | ILS017 | 1980 | £6 | £12 | demo |
| Goo Goo Muck | 7" | IRS | PFS1003 | 1981 | £2.50 | £6 | yellow vinyl |
| Gravest Hits | 12" | Illegal | ILS12013 | 1979 | £2.50 | £6 | |
| Gravest Hits | 12" | Illegal | ILS12013 | 1979 | £4 | £10 | blue vinyl |
| Off The Bone | LP | Illegal | ILP012 | 1983 | £4 | £10 | picture disc |
| Smell Of Female | LP | Big Beat | BEDP6 | 1984 | £4 | £10 | picture disc |
| Songs The Lord Taught Us | LP | Illegal | ILP005 | 1980 | £25 | £50 | test pressing with 'Drug Train' |

## CRANBERRIES

Seldom has the Irish accent found so mellifluous a setting as in the singing of Dolores O'Riordan with the music of the Cranberries. Whether her songwriting abilities will prove sufficient to sustain the group through a long career remains to be proved, but the Cranberries have already earned their place within the rock encyclopaedias of the next century – if only for the powerful 'Zombie', whose reverberations continue to be felt. In addition to the collectables listed below, there is also supposed to be a demo three-track tape, including the song 'Nothing Left At All', issued in 1991 when the group still used the original punning version of their name, the Cranberry Saw Us. Further information on this item will be gratefully received.

| | | | | | | | |
|---|---|---|---|---|---|---|---|
| Dreams | CD–s | Island | CID548 | 1992 | £2 | £5 | |
| No Need To Argue | CD–s | Island | 4373 | 1994 | £12.50 | £25 | French live promo |
| To The Faithful Departed Interview | CD | Island | CDINTCRAN | 1996 | £10 | £25 | promo |
| Uncertain | CD–s | Xeric | XER014CD | 1991 | £20 | £40 | |
| Uncertain | 7" | Xeric | XER014 | 1991 | £10 | £20 | |
| Uncertain | 12" | Xeric | XER014T | 1991 | £15 | £30 | |
| Zombie | CD–s | Island | CID600/CIDX600 | 1994 | £4 | £10 | boxed double |

## CRANE, DON & THE NEW DOWNLINERS SECT

| | | | | | | |
|---|---|---|---|---|---|---|
| I Can't Get Away From You | 7" | Pye | 7N17261 | 1967 | £37.50 | £75 |

## CRANE, TONY

| | | | | | | |
|---|---|---|---|---|---|---|
| Anonymous Mr. Brown | 7" | Pye | 7N17337 | 1967 | £1.50 | £4 |
| Even The Bravest | 7" | CBS | 202022 | 1965 | £1.50 | £4 |
| Ideal Love | 7" | Polydor | BM56008 | 1965 | £1.50 | £4 |
| If I Ever Get To Saginaw Again | 7" | Pye | 7N17645 | 1968 | £1.50 | £4 |
| Scratchin' Ma Head | 7" | Pye | 7N17517 | 1968 | £1.50 | £4 |

## CRANE, VINCENT & CHRIS FARLOWE

| | | | | | | |
|---|---|---|---|---|---|---|
| Can't Find A Reason | 7" | Dawn | DNS1034 | 1972 | £1.50 | £4 |

## CRANE RIVER JAZZ BAND

| | | | | | | |
|---|---|---|---|---|---|---|
| Crane River Jazz Band | 7" EP | Parlophone | GEP8652 | 1957 | £2 | £5 |

## CRANES

| | | | | | | |
|---|---|---|---|---|---|---|
| Fuse | cass | Biteback | | 1987 | £10 | £20 |

## CRANNOG

| | | | | | | |
|---|---|---|---|---|---|---|
| Crannog | LP | private | CR1 | 1980 | £25 | £50 |

## CRASHERS

| | | | | | | |
|---|---|---|---|---|---|---|
| Off Track | 7" | Amalgamated | AMG834 | 1969 | £1.50 | £4 |

## CRASS

| | | | | | | |
|---|---|---|---|---|---|---|
| Feeding Of The Five Thousand | 12" | Small Wonder | WEENY2 | 1978 | £2.50 | £6 |

## CRAVINKEL

| | | | | | | |
|---|---|---|---|---|---|---|
| Cravinkel | LP | Philips | 6305055 | 1970 | £6 | £15 | German |
| Garden Of Loneliness | LP | Philips | 6305124 | 1971 | £5 | £12 | German |

## CRAWFORD BROTHERS

| | | | | | | |
|---|---|---|---|---|---|---|
| I Ain't Guilty | 7" | Vogue | V9140 | 1959 | £50 | £100 |
| Midnight Mover Groover | 7" | Vogue | V9077 | 1957 | £50 | £100 |

## CRAWFORD, CAROLYN

| | | | | | | |
|---|---|---|---|---|---|---|
| When Someone's Good To You | 7" | Stateside | SS384 | 1965 | £50 | £100 |

## CRAWFORD, GLORIA

| | | | | | | |
|---|---|---|---|---|---|---|
| Sad Movies | 7" | Doctor Bird | DB1057 | 1966 | £5 | £10 | Lester Sterling B side |

## CRAWFORD, JIMMY

| | | | | | | |
|---|---|---|---|---|---|---|
| Long Stringy Baby | 7" | Columbia | DB4525 | 1960 | £7.50 | £15 |

## CRAWFORD, JOHNNY

| | | | | | | |
|---|---|---|---|---|---|---|
| Captivating Johnny Crawford | LP | Del-Fi | LP1220 | 1962 | £8 | £20 | US |
| Greatest Hits | LP | Del-Fi | LP/ST1229 | 1963 | £6 | £15 | US |
| Greatest Hits Vol. 2 | LP | Del-Fi | LP/ST1248 | 1964 | £6 | £15 | US |
| His Greatest Hits | LP | London | HA8197 | 1964 | £6 | £15 | |
| Johnny Crawford | 7" EP | London | RE1343 | 1962 | £6 | £12 | |
| Rumors | LP | London | HA8060 | 1963 | £6 | £15 | |
| When I Fall In Love | 7" EP | London | RE1416 | 1964 | £6 | £12 | |
| Young Man's Fancy | LP | Del-Fi | LP/ST1223 | 1963 | £6 | £15 | US |

## CRAYTON, PEE WEE

| | | | | | | |
|---|---|---|---|---|---|---|
| Pee Wee Crayton | LP | Crown | CLP5175 | 1959 | £10 | £25 | US |

## CRAZY CASEY

| | | | | | | |
|---|---|---|---|---|---|---|
| Beast And I | LP | Polydor | 236148 | 1967 | £8 | £20 | Dutch |

## CRAZY ELEPHANT

| | | | | | | |
|---|---|---|---|---|---|---|
| Crazy Elephant | LP | Major Minor | SMLP62 | 1969 | £4 | £10 | |

## CRAZY ROCKERS

| | | | | | | |
|---|---|---|---|---|---|---|
| Best Of Crazy Rockers | LP | Negram | NYN218 | 1973 | £15 | £30 | Dutch |
| Out Of Sight | LP | CNR | 657580 | 1981 | £6 | £15 | Dutch |
| Successen Van Crazy Rockers | LP | Delta | HJD102 | 1964 | £30 | £60 | Dutch |

# CREAM

Cream are not highly regarded by those who feel that improvisation has no place in rock music, but on a good night the interplay between the three virtuoso musicians, each trying to outplay the others, was thrilling. Inevitably this approach does not always work, but when it does, the risks are entirely justified. 'Crossroads' is an electric blues masterpiece, while the long modal improvisation on 'Spoonful' (also included on *Wheels Of Fire*) is as inspirational as the lengthy drum solo on 'Toad' is tedious. The other side of Cream was their ability to create intelligent pop music with an attractive blues edge – *Disraeli Gears* was quite rightly hailed as one of the most impressive recordings of 1967 – in a year when the competition was extremely stiff.

| Title | Format | Label | Cat. No. | Year | Price1 | Price2 | Notes |
|---|---|---|---|---|---|---|---|
| Anyone For Tennis | 7" | Polydor | 56258 | 1968 | £1.50 | £4 | |
| Badge | 7" | Polydor | 56315 | 1969 | £1.50 | £4 | |
| Cream | LP | RSO | 2658142 | 198– | £20 | £40 | German 6 LP boxed set |
| Disraeli Gears | LP | Reaction | 593003 | 1967 | £6 | £15 | mono |
| Disraeli Gears | LP | Reaction | 594003 | 1967 | £5 | £12 | stereo |
| Disraeli Gears | CD | Mobile Fidelity | UDCD562 | 1992 | £8 | £20 | US audiophile, mono & stereo mixes |
| Fresh Cream | LP | Reaction | 593001 | 1966 | £6 | £15 | mono |
| Fresh Cream | LP | Reaction | 594001 | 1966 | £5 | £12 | stereo |
| Fresh Cream | CD | DCC | GZS1022 | 1992 | £6 | £15 | US audiophile |
| Goodbye | LP | Polydor | 583053 | 1969 | £4 | £10 | |
| Goodbye | CD | Polydor | 8236602 | 1984 | £5 | £12 | |
| I Feel Free | 7" EP | Polydor | 27798 | 1966 | £15 | £30 | French |
| I Feel Free | 7" | Reaction | 591011 | 1966 | £1.50 | £4 | |
| Live Cream Vols 1 & 2 | CD | Mobile Fidelity | UDCD2625 | 1995 | £10 | £25 | US double audiophile |
| On Top | LP | Polydor | 2855002 | 1969 | £5 | £12 | |
| Strange Brew | 7" EP | Polydor | 27810 | 1967 | £15 | £30 | French |
| Strange Brew | 7" | Reaction | 591015 | 1967 | £1.50 | £4 | |
| Sunshine Of Your Love | 7" | Polydor | 56286 | 1968 | £1.50 | £4 | |
| Wheels Of Fire | LP | Mobile Fidelity | MFSL2066 | 1982 | £8 | £20 | US audiophile |
| Wheels Of Fire | LP | Polydor | 582031/2 | 1968 | £8 | £20 | double, mono |
| Wheels Of Fire | LP | Polydor | 583031/2 | 1968 | £6 | £15 | double, stereo |
| Wheels Of Fire | CD | DCC | GZS21020 | 1992 | £10 | £25 | US double audiophile |
| Wheels Of Fire In The Studio | LP | Polydor | 582033 | 1968 | £5 | £12 | mono |
| Wheels Of Fire In The Studio | LP | Polydor | 583033 | 1968 | £4 | £10 | stereo |
| Wheels Of Fire Live At Fillmore | LP | Polydor | 582040 | 1968 | £5 | £12 | mono |
| Wheels Of Fire Live At Fillmore | LP | Polydor | 583040 | 1968 | £4 | £10 | stereo |
| White Room | 7" | Polydor | 56300 | 1968 | £1.50 | £4 | |
| Wrapping Paper | 7" EP | Polydor | 27791 | 1966 | £15 | £30 | French |
| Wrapping Paper | 7" | Reaction | 591007 | 1966 | £1.50 | £4 | |

# CREAMERS

| Title | Format | Label | Cat. No. | Year | Price1 | Price2 | Notes |
|---|---|---|---|---|---|---|---|
| Sunday Head | 7" | Fierce | FRIGHT045 | 1989 | £2.50 | £6 | |

# CREARY SISTERS

| Title | Format | Label | Cat. No. | Year | Price1 | Price2 | Notes |
|---|---|---|---|---|---|---|---|
| Oh What A Glory | 7" | High Note | HS020 | 1969 | £1.50 | £4 | |

# CREATION

The Creation have acquired the status of one of the great groups of the sixties, with guitarist Eddie Phillips being a pioneer in the use of feedback and violin bow techniques. The group failed to find much success, however, and in all honesty they are not well served by their records, which are much less impressive than those of their rivals, the Who.

| Title | Format | Label | Cat. No. | Year | Price1 | Price2 | Notes |
|---|---|---|---|---|---|---|---|
| 1966–67 | LP | Charisma | CS8 | 1973 | £10 | £25 | |
| Best Of The Creation | LP | Pop Schallplaten | ZS10168 | 1968 | £25 | £50 | German |
| How Does It Feel To Feel | 7" | Polydor | 56230 | 1968 | £7.50 | £15 | |
| If I Stay Too Long | 7" | Polydor | 56177 | 1967 | £7.50 | £15 | |
| Making Time | 7" EP | Vogue | INT18098 | 1966 | £180 | £300 | French, best auctioned |
| Making Time | 7" | Charisma | CB213 | 1973 | £1.50 | £4 | |
| Making Time | 7" | Planet | PLF116 | 1966 | £15 | £30 | |
| Midway Down | 7" | Polydor | 56246 | 1968 | £7.50 | £15 | |
| Painter Man | 7" | Planet | PLF119 | 1966 | £15 | £30 | |
| Through My Eyes | 7" | Polydor | 56207 | 1967 | £10 | £20 | |
| Tom Tom | 7" EP | Vogue | INT18144 | 1967 | £180 | £300 | French, best auctioned |
| We Are The Paintermen | LP | Hitton | HTSLP340037 | 1967 | £50 | £100 | German |
| We Are The Paintermen | LP | Sonet | SLPS1251 | 1967 | £50 | £100 | Danish |

# CREATION (2)

| Title | Format | Label | Cat. No. | Year | Price1 | Price2 | Notes |
|---|---|---|---|---|---|---|---|
| I Got The Fever | 7" | Stateside | SS2205 | 1972 | £1.50 | £4 | |

# CREATION OF SUNLIGHT

| Title | Format | Label | Cat. No. | Year | Price1 | Price2 | Notes |
|---|---|---|---|---|---|---|---|
| Creation Of Sunlight | LP | Windi | 1001 | 1968 | £180 | £300 | US |

# CREATIONS

| Title | Format | Label | Cat. No. | Year | Price1 | Price2 | Notes |
|---|---|---|---|---|---|---|---|
| Get On Up | 7" | Amalgamated | AMG818 | 1968 | £4 | £8 | |
| Meet Me At Eight | 7" | Rio | R133 | 1967 | £4 | £8 | |

# CREATIVE ROCK

| Title | Format | Label | Cat. No. | Year | Price1 | Price2 | Notes |
|---|---|---|---|---|---|---|---|
| Gorilla | LP | Brain | 1017 | 1973 | £4 | £10 | German |
| Lady Pig | LP | Brain | 1061 | 1974 | £5 | £12 | German |

# CREATURES

| Title | Format | Label | Cat. No. | Year | Price1 | Price2 | Notes |
|---|---|---|---|---|---|---|---|
| Fury Eyes | CD-s | Polydor | SHECD18 | 1990 | £2 | £5 | |
| Standing There | CD-s | Polydor | SHECD17 | 1989 | £2 | £5 | |
| Wild Things | 7" | Polydor | POSPD354 | 1981 | £2 | £5 | double, single picture sleeve |

| | | | | | | | |
|---|---|---|---|---|---|---|---|
| Wild Things | 7" | Polydor | POSPG354 | 1981 | £2 | £5 | *double, gatefold picture sleeve* |

## CREATURES (2)

| | | | | | | | |
|---|---|---|---|---|---|---|---|
| Looking At Tomorrow | 7" | CBS | 2666 | 1967 | £1.50 | £4 | |
| String Along | 7" | CBS | 202350 | 1966 | £1.50 | £4 | |
| Turn Out The Light | 7" | CBS | 202048 | 1966 | £1.50 | £4 | |

## CREEDENCE CLEARWATER REVIVAL

| | | | | | | | |
|---|---|---|---|---|---|---|---|
| Bayou Country | LP | Liberty | LBS83261 | 1969 | £4 | £10 | |
| Cosmo's Factory | LP | Liberty | LBS83388 | 1970 | £4 | £10 | |
| Cosmo's Factory | LP | Mobile Fidelity | MFSL1037 | 1979 | £5 | £12 | *US audiophile* |
| Cosmo's Factory | CD | DCC | GZS1031 | 1992 | £6 | £15 | *US audiophile* |
| Creedence Clearwater Revival | LP | Liberty | LBS83259 | 1969 | £4 | £10 | |
| Green River | LP | Liberty | LBS83273 | 1969 | £4 | £10 | |
| Green River | CD | DCC | GZS1064 | 1994 | £6 | £15 | *US audiophile* |
| Long As I Can See The Light | 7" | Liberty | LBF15384 | 1970 | £2 | £5 | *picture sleeve* |
| Pendulum | LP | Liberty | LBS83400 | 1971 | £4 | £10 | |
| Porterville | 7" | Scorpio | 412 | 1967 | £12.50 | £25 | *US* |
| Proud Mary/I Put A Spell On You | 7" | Liberty | LBF15223 | 1969 | £7.50 | £15 | |
| Up Around The Bend | 7" | Liberty | LBF15354 | 1970 | £2 | £5 | *picture sleeve* |
| Willie & The Poor Boys | LP | Liberty | LBS83338 | 1970 | £4 | £10 | |
| Willy And The Poor Boys | CD | DCC | GZS1070 | 1994 | £6 | £15 | *US audiophile* |

## CREME SODA

| | | | | | | | |
|---|---|---|---|---|---|---|---|
| Tricky Zingers | LP | Trinity | CST11 | 1975 | £180 | £300 | *US* |

## CRESCENDOES

| | | | | | | | |
|---|---|---|---|---|---|---|---|
| Crescendoes | LP | Metronome | MLP15200 | 1966 | £25 | £50 | *German* |

## CRESCENDOS

| | | | | | | | |
|---|---|---|---|---|---|---|---|
| Oh Julie | LP | Guest Star | G1453 | 196– | £15 | £30 | *US* |
| Oh Julie | 7" | London | HLU8563 | 1958 | £15 | £30 | |

## CRESCENDOS (2)

| | | | | | | | |
|---|---|---|---|---|---|---|---|
| Presenting | LP | Gallotone | GALP1458 | 1966 | £50 | £100 | *South African* |

## CRESCENTS

| | | | | | | | |
|---|---|---|---|---|---|---|---|
| Baby Baby Baby | 7" | Columbia | DB4093 | 1958 | £20 | £40 | |

## CRESCENTS (2)

| | | | | | | | |
|---|---|---|---|---|---|---|---|
| Pink Dominoes | 7" | London | HLN9851 | 1964 | £2 | £5 | |

## CRESSIDA

| | | | | | | | |
|---|---|---|---|---|---|---|---|
| Asylum | LP | Vertigo | 6360025 | 1971 | £37.50 | £75 | *spiral label* |
| Cressida | LP | Vertigo | VO7 | 1970 | £25 | £50 | *spiral label* |

## CRESTAS

| | | | | | | | |
|---|---|---|---|---|---|---|---|
| I Want To Be Loved | 7" | Fontana | TF551 | 1965 | £6 | £12 | |

## CRESTERS

| | | | | | | | |
|---|---|---|---|---|---|---|---|
| I Just Don't Understand | 7" | HMV | POP1249 | 1964 | £1.50 | £4 | |
| Put Your Arms Around Me | 7" | HMV | POP1296 | 1964 | £1.50 | £4 | |

## CRESTS

| | | | | | | | |
|---|---|---|---|---|---|---|---|
| Angels Listened In | 7" | London | HL8954 | 1959 | £12.50 | £25 | |
| Best Of The Crests | LP | Coed | LPC/LPS904 | 1961 | £50 | £100 | *US* |
| Crests Sing All The Biggies | LP | Coed | LPC901 | 1960 | £62.50 | £125 | *US* |
| Flower Of Love | 7" | Top Rank | JAR150 | 1959 | £2.50 | £6 | |
| Gee | 7" | Top Rank | JAR372 | 1960 | £6 | £12 | |
| Guilty | 7" | London | HLU9671 | 1963 | £2.50 | £6 | |
| Isn't It Amazing | 7" | HMV | POP808 | 1960 | £2.50 | £6 | |
| Little Miracles | 7" | HMV | POP976 | 1962 | £2.50 | £6 | |
| Model Girl | 7" | HMV | POP848 | 1961 | £2.50 | £6 | |
| Paper Crown | 7" | Top Rank | JAR302 | 1960 | £6 | £12 | |
| Six Nights A Week | 7" | Top Rank | JAR168 | 1959 | £5 | £10 | |
| Sixteen Candles | 7" | London | HL8794 | 1959 | £15 | £30 | |
| Trouble in Paradise | 7" | HMV | POP768 | 1960 | £6 | £12 | |

## CREW

| | | | | | | | |
|---|---|---|---|---|---|---|---|
| Cecilia | 7" | Decca | F13000 | 1970 | £1.50 | £4 | |
| Marty | 7" | Plexium | PXM12 | 1969 | £1.50 | £4 | |

## CREWCUTS

| | | | | | | | |
|---|---|---|---|---|---|---|---|
| Angels In The Sky | 7" | Mercury | 7MT2 | 1956 | £6 | £12 | *export* |
| Crewcut Capers | LP | Mercury | MG20143 | 1954 | £20 | £40 | *US* |
| Crewcuts | LP | Wing | MGW12177 | 1959 | £10 | £25 | *US* |
| Crewcuts | 7" EP | Mercury | MEP9002 | 1956 | £15 | £30 | *US* |
| Crewcuts Go Longhair | LP | Mercury | MG20067 | 1954 | £20 | £40 | *US* |
| Crewcuts On The Campus | LP | Mercury | MG20140 | 1954 | £20 | £40 | *US* |
| Crewcuts Sing | LP | RCA | LPM/LSP2037 | 1959 | £10 | £25 | *US* |
| Crewcuts Sing Folk | LP | Camay | CA1/CA3002 | 196– | £8 | £20 | *US* |
| Hey Stella | 7" | RCA | RCA1075 | 1958 | £10 | £20 | |
| High School Favorites | LP | Wing | MGW12180 | 1959 | £10 | £25 | *US* |
| Music A La Carte | LP | Mercury | MG20199 | 1955 | £20 | £40 | *US* |
| On Parade | 10" LP | Mercury | MPT7501 | 1956 | £20 | £40 | |
| Rock And Roll Bash | LP | Mercury | MG21044 | 1955 | £25 | £50 | *US* |
| Surprise Package | LP | RCA | LPM/LSP1933 | 1958 | £10 | £25 | *US* |

| | | | | | | | |
|---|---|---|---|---|---|---|---|
| Susie-Q | 78 | Mercury | MT161 | 1957 £2.50 | £6 | |
| You Must Have Been A Beautiful Baby | LP | RCA | LPM/LSP2067 | 1960 £8 | £20 | US |

## CREWE, BOB

| | | | | | | |
|---|---|---|---|---|---|---|
| Maggie Maggie May | 7" | Stateside | SS356 | 1964 £1.50 | £4 | |

## CRIBBINS, BERNARD

| | | | | | | |
|---|---|---|---|---|---|---|
| Combination Of Cribbins | LP | Parlophone | PMC1186 | 1962 £4 | £10 |
| Hole In The Ground | 7" EP | Parlophone | GEP8859 | 1962 £2 | £5 |
| Hole In The Ground | 7" | Parlophone | R4869 | 1962 £1.50 | £4 |
| Right Said Fred | 7" | Parlophone | R4923 | 1962 £1.50 | £4 |

## CRICKETS

| | | | | | | |
|---|---|---|---|---|---|---|
| April Avenue | 7" | Liberty | LIB55603 | 1966 £1.50 | £4 |
| Baby My Heart | 7" | Coral | Q72395 | 1960 £1.50 | £4 |
| Collection | LP | Liberty | LBY1258 | 1965 £6 | £15 |
| Come On | 7" EP | Liberty | LEP2173 | 1964 £5 | £10 |
| Crickets | 7" EP | Coral | FEP2053 | 1960 £10 | £20 |
| Crickets Don't Ever Change | 7" EP | Coral | FEP2064 | 1961 £6 | £12 |
| Don't Ever Change | 7" | Liberty | LIB55441 | 1962 £1.50 | £4 |
| Don't Try To Change Me | 7" | Liberty | LIB10092 | 1963 £1.50 | £4 |
| He's Old Enough To Know Better | 7" | London | HLG9486 | 1961 £2 | £5 |
| I Fought The Law | 7" | Coral | Q72440 | 1961 £2 | £5 |
| I Think I've Got The Blues | 7" | Liberty | LIB10174 | 1964 £1.50 | £4 |
| In Style With | LP | Coral | LVA9142 | 1959 £10 | £25 |
| La Bamba | 7" | Liberty | LIB55696 | 1964 £1.50 | £4 |
| Little Hollywood Girl | 7" | Liberty | LIB55495 | 1962 £2 | £5 |
| Love's Made A Fool Of You | 7" | Coral | Q72365 | 1959 £2 | £5 |
| Now Hear This | 7" | Liberty | LIB10196 | 1965 £1.50 | £4 |
| Peggy Sue Got Married | 7" | Coral | Q72417 | 1961 £2 | £5 |
| Something Old Something New | LP | Liberty | (S)LBY1120 | 1962 £6 | £15 |
| Straight No Strings | 7" EP | Liberty | LEP2094 | 1963 £6 | £12 |
| Straight No Strings | 7" EP | Liberty | SLEP2094 | 1963 £10 | £20 | stereo |
| When You Ask About Love | 7" | Coral | Q72382 | 1959 £2 | £5 |

## CRIMSON BRIDGE

| | | | | | | |
|---|---|---|---|---|---|---|
| Crimson Bridge | LP | Myrrh | MST6503 | 1972 £6 | £15 |

## CRISIS

| | | | | | | |
|---|---|---|---|---|---|---|
| Alienation | 7" | Ardkor | CRI004 | 1981 £2.50 | £6 |
| Holocaust | 12" | Crisis | NOTH1/CRI002 | 1982 £3 | £8 |
| Hymns Of Faith | 12" | Ardkor | CRI003 | 1980 £3 | £8 |
| No Town Hall (Southwark) | 7" | Peckham Action Group | NOTH1 | 1982 £2.50 | £6 |
| UK '79 | 7" | Ardkor | CRI002 | 1979 £2 | £5 |

## CRISIS (2)

| | | | | | | |
|---|---|---|---|---|---|---|
| Another Fine Mess | LP | private | | 197– £25 | £50 |

## CRISPY AMBULANCE

| | | | | | | |
|---|---|---|---|---|---|---|
| Four Minutes From The Frontline | 7" | Aural Assault | AAR001 | 1976 £2.50 | £6 |

## CRISS, GARY

| | | | | | | |
|---|---|---|---|---|---|---|
| Our Favourite Melodies | 7" | Stateside | SS104 | 1962 £1.50 | £4 |

## CRISS, SONNY

| | | | | | | |
|---|---|---|---|---|---|---|
| Sonny Criss Plays Cole Porter | LP | London | LTZP15094 | 1957 £25 | £50 |

## CRISTINA

| | | | | | | |
|---|---|---|---|---|---|---|
| Is That All There Is | 12" | Ze | WIP6560T | 1980 £2.50 | £6 |

## CRISTO, BOBBY & THE REBELS

| | | | | | | |
|---|---|---|---|---|---|---|
| Other Side Of The Track | 7" | Decca | F11913 | 1964 £7.50 | £15 |

## CRISTY, MARY

| | | | | | | |
|---|---|---|---|---|---|---|
| Thank You For Rushing Into My Life | 7" | Polydor | 2056513 | 1976 £2.50 | £6 |

## CRITICS GROUP

| | | | | | | |
|---|---|---|---|---|---|---|
| Merry Progress To London | LP | Argo | (Z)DA46 | 1966 £10 | £25 |
| Sweet Thames Flow Softly | LP | Argo | (Z)DA47 | 1966 £10 | £25 |

## CRITTERS

| | | | | | | |
|---|---|---|---|---|---|---|
| Heart Of Love, Head Of Stone | 7" EP | Kapp | KEV13028 | 1966 £7.50 | £15 | French |
| Mr. Dieingly Sad | 7" EP | Kapp | KEV13031 | 1966 £7.50 | £15 | French |
| Mr. Dieingly Sad | 7" | London | HLR10071 | 1966 £1.50 | £4 |
| Younger Girl | LP | London | HAR8302 | 1966 £5 | £12 |
| Younger Girl | 7" | London | HLR10047 | 1966 £1.50 | £4 |

## CROCE, JIM

| | | | | | | |
|---|---|---|---|---|---|---|
| Croce (with Ingrid Croce) | LP | Capitol | ST315 | 1969 £10 | £25 | US |
| You Don't Mess Around With Jim | LP | Vertigo | 6360700 | 1971 £4 | £10 | spiral label |

## CROCHETED DOUGHNUT RING

| | | | | | | |
|---|---|---|---|---|---|---|
| Havana Anna | 7" | Deram | DM169 | 1967 £10 | £20 |
| Maxine's Parlour | 7" | Deram | DM180 | 1968 £5 | £10 |
| Two Little Ladies | 7" | Polydor | 56204 | 1967 £10 | £20 |

## CROFTERS
Crofters ............................................ LP ...... Beltona ........... SBE103 ................... 1969 £15 ......... £30 ....................................

## CROMAGNON
Cromagnon ......................................... LP ...... ESP-Disk ........ 2001 ...................... 1969 £15 ......... £30 ....................... US

## CROMBIE, TONY
| | | | | | | |
|---|---|---|---|---|---|---|
| Atmosphere | LP | Columbia | 33SX1119 | 1958 | £15 | £30 |
| Atmosphere | 7" EP | Columbia | SEG7918/ESG7753 | 1959 | £2 | £5 |
| Brighton Rock | 7" | Columbia | DB3921 | 1957 | £7.50 | £15 |
| Drums! Drums! Drums! | LP | Top Rank | BUY027 | 1960 | £5 | £12 |
| Dumplin's | 7" | Columbia | DB4076 | 1958 | £2 | £5 |
| Flying Hickory | 7" | Decca | F10592 | 1955 | £2.50 | £6 |
| Flying Home | 7" | Decca | F10547 | 1955 | £2 | £5 |
| Four Favourite Film Themes | 7" EP | Decca | DFE6670 | 1960 | £2 | £5 |
| Gigglin' Gurgleburp | 7" | Columbia | DB4189 | 1958 | £1.50 | £4 |
| Gutbucket | 7" | Ember | JBS706 | 1962 | £1.50 | £4 |
| I Want You To Be My Baby | 7" | Decca | F10637 | 1955 | £2.50 | £6 |
| Jazz Inc | LP | Tempo | TAP30 | 1960 | £10 | £25 |
| Let's You And I Rock | 7" EP | Columbia | SEG7686 | 1957 | £15 | £30 |
| Let's You And I Rock | 7" | Columbia | DB3859 | 1956 | £7.50 | £15 |
| Lonesome Train | 7" | Columbia | DB3881 | 1957 | £7.50 | £15 |
| Man From Interpol | LP | Top Rank | 35043 | 1959 | £6 | £15 |
| Presenting Tony Crombie No. 1 | 7" EP | Decca | DFE6247 | 1956 | £4 | £8 |
| Presenting Tony Crombie No. 2 | 7" EP | Decca | DFE6281 | 1956 | £4 | £8 |
| Rock Rock Rock | 7" EP | Columbia | SEG7676 | 1957 | £15 | £30 |
| Rock Rock Rock | 7" | Columbia | DB3880 | 1957 | £7.50 | £15 |
| Rockin' With The Rockets | 10" LP | Columbia | 33S1108 | 1957 | £50 | £100 |
| Stop It | 7" | Decca | F10424 | 1954 | £2 | £5 |
| Sweet And Rhythmic | 7" EP | Columbia | SEG7769 | 1958 | £2 | £5 |
| Sweet Beat | 7" | Columbia | DB4000 | 1957 | £2.50 | £6 |
| Sweet, Wild And Blue | LP | Decca | SKL4114 | 1961 | £6 | £15 |
| Swinging Dance Beat No. 1 | 7" EP | Columbia | SEG7882/ESG7768 | 1959 | £2 | £5 |
| Swinging Dance Beat No. 2 | 7" EP | Columbia | SEG7896 | 1959 | £2 | £5 |
| Teach You To Rock | 7" | Columbia | DB3822 | 1956 | £10 | £20 |
| Twelve Favourite Film Themes | LP | Decca | LK4385/SKL4127 | 1961 | £4 | £10 |
| Ungaua | 7" | Columbia | DB4145 | 1958 | £1.50 | £4 |

## CROME CYRCUS
Love Cycle ........................................ LP ...... Command ....... 925 ...................... 1968 £10 ........ £25 ....................... US

## CROMPTON, BILL
Hoot An' A Holler ............................ 7" ...... Fontana ........... H152 .................... 1958 £1.50 ....... £4

## CROMWELL

This pleasant but unexceptional album is undoubtedly rare, but its value has been considerably boosted by claims that the music is like that of the Rolling Stones on *Exile On Main Street*. In fact, the resemblance is limited to the fact that both groups play guitars and drums and sing. If a comparison is really required for Cromwell, then a name like Edison Lighthouse would be far more appropriate.

At The Gallop ................................... LP ...... private ............ WELL005 ............. 1975 £75 ....... £150

## CROMWELL, LINK
Crazy Like A Fox .............................. 7" ...... London ........... HLB10040 ............. 1966 £2.50 ....... £6

## CRONSHAW, ANDREW
A Is For Andrew Z Is For Zither .......... LP ...... Transatlantic .... XTRA1139 ........... 1974 £6 ......... £15

## CROOKED OAK
Foot O'Wor Stairs ............................. LP ...... Eron .............. 019 .................. 1979 £15 ......... £30
From Little Acorns Grow .................... LP ...... Folkland ........... FL0102 ............... 1976 £87.50 .. £175

## CROOKS
All The Time In The World .................. 7" ...... Blue Print ....... BLU2006 ............. 1980 £2 ......... £5

## CROPPER, STEVE
With A Little Help From My Friends ...... LP ...... Stax .............. SXATS1008 .......... 1971 £4 ......... £10

## CROPPER, STEVE, ALBERT KING & POP STAPLES
Jammed Together ............................. LP ...... Stax .............. SXATS1020 .......... 1971 £4 ......... £10

## CROSBY, BING
| | | | | | | | |
|---|---|---|---|---|---|---|---|
| Bing And Connie | 10" LP | Brunswick | LA8558 | 1953 | £4 | £10 | ...with Connie Boswell |
| Bing Crosby And The Dixieland Bands | 10" LP | Brunswick | LA8579 | 1953 | £4 | £10 | |
| Bing Sings The Hits | 10" LP | Brunswick | LA8674 | 1954 | £4 | £10 | |
| Blue Of The Night | 10" LP | Brunswick | LA8595 | 1953 | £4 | £10 | |
| Blue Skies | 10" LP | Brunswick | LA8602 | 1953 | £4 | £10 | ...... with Fred Astaire |
| Changing Partners | 7" | Brunswick | 05244 | 1954 | £1.50 | £4 | |
| Collectors' Classics Vol. 1 | 10" LP | Brunswick | LA8687 | 1954 | £4 | £10 | |
| Collectors' Classics Vol. 2 | 10" LP | Brunswick | LA8723 | 1955 | £4 | £10 | |
| Collectors' Classics Vol. 3 | 10" LP | Brunswick | LA8726 | 1955 | £4 | £10 | |
| Collectors' Classics Vol. 4 | 10" LP | Brunswick | LA8727 | 1955 | £4 | £10 | |
| Count Your Blessings Instead Of Sheep | 7" | Brunswick | 05339 | 1954 | £1.50 | £4 | |
| Country Girl | 10" LP | Brunswick | LA8714 | 1955 | £4 | £10 | |
| Country Style | 10" LP | Brunswick | LA8724 | 1955 | £4 | £10 | |
| Crosby Classics | 10" LP | Columbia | 33S1036 | 1954 | £4 | £10 | |
| Don't Bingle | 10" LP | Fontana | TFR.6000 | 1958 | £4 | £10 | |

| | | | | | | |
|---|---|---|---|---|---|---|
| Down Memory Lane | 10" LP | Brunswick | LA8620 | 1953 £4 | £10 | |
| Down Memory Lane Vol. 2 | 10" LP | Brunswick | LA8624 | 1953 £4 | £10 | |
| Early Thirties Vol. 1 | 10" LP | Brunswick | LA8740 | 1956 £4 | £10 | |
| Early Thirties Vol. 2 | 10" LP | Brunswick | LA8741 | 1956 £4 | £10 | |
| El Bingo | 10" LP | Brunswick | LA8529 | 1951 £4 | £10 | |
| Favourite Hawaiian Songs | 10" LP | Brunswick | LA8730 | 1956 £4 | £10 | |
| George Gershwin Songs | 10" LP | Brunswick | LA8666 | 1954 £4 | £10 | |
| Holiday Inn | 10" LP | Brunswick | LA8592 | 1953 £4 | £10 | *...with Fred Astaire* |
| Merry Christmas | 10" LP | Brunswick | LA8686 | 1954 £4 | £10 | |
| Old Lang Syne | 10" LP | Brunswick | LA8585 | 1953 £4 | £10 | |
| Quiet Man | 10" LP | Brunswick | LA8584 | 1953 £4 | £10 | |
| Secret Love | 7" | Brunswick | 05269 | 1954 £2 | £5 | |
| Silent Night | 7" | Brunswick | 03929 | 1954 £1.50 | £4 | |
| Sings Cole Porter Songs | 10" LP | Brunswick | LA8513 | 1951 £4 | £10 | |
| Sings Jerome Kern Songs | 10" LP | Brunswick | LA8505 | 1951 £4 | £10 | |
| Sings Victor Herbert Songs | 10" LP | Brunswick | LA8600 | 1953 £4 | £10 | |
| Some Fine Old Chestnuts | 10" LP | Brunswick | LA8673 | 1954 £4 | £10 | |
| Song Hits From Broadway Shows | 10" LP | Brunswick | LA8675 | 1954 £4 | £10 | |
| Song Hits Of Paris | 10" LP | Brunswick | LA8645 | 1954 £4 | £10 | |
| Stardust | 10" LP | Brunswick | LA8514 | 1951 £4 | £10 | |
| Stephen Foster Songs | 10" LP | Brunswick | LA8571 | 1953 £4 | £10 | |
| Stranger In Paradise | 7" | Brunswick | 05410 | 1955 £1.50 | £4 | |
| True Love (with Grace Kelly) | 7" | Capitol | CL14645 | 1956 £1.50 | £4 | |
| Way Back Home | 10" LP | Brunswick | LA8656 | 1954 £4 | £10 | |
| When Irish Eyes Are Smiling | 10" LP | Brunswick | LA8606 | 1953 £4 | £10 | |
| White Christmas | 7" | Brunswick | 03384 | 1954 £1.50 | £4 | |
| Young At Heart | 7" | Brunswick | 05277 | 1954 £1.50 | £4 | |
| Yours Is My Heart Alone | 10" LP | Brunswick | LA8684 | 1954 £4 | £10 | |

## CROSBY, BOB

| | | | | | | |
|---|---|---|---|---|---|---|
| Bob Crosby And His Bobcats | 10" LP | Capitol | LC6553 | 1952 £6 | £15 | |
| Bob Crosby's Bobcats | LP | Brunswick | LAT8050 | 1955 £5 | £12 | |
| Dark At The Top Of The Stairs | 7" | London | HLD9228 | 1960 £1.50 | £4 | |
| Great Hits | LP | London | HAD2293/ SAHD6105 | 1960 £4 | £10 | |
| In Hi-Fi | LP | Coral | LVA9083 | 1958 £4 | £10 | |
| Petite Fleur | 7" | London | HLD8828 | 1959 £1.50 | £4 | |

## CROSBY, DAVID

| | | | | | | |
|---|---|---|---|---|---|---|
| If I Could Only Remember My Name | LP | Atlantic | 2401005 | 1971 £4 | £10 | |

## CROSBY, GARY

| | | | | | | |
|---|---|---|---|---|---|---|
| Ayuh Ayuh | 7" | Brunswick | 05446 | 1955 £2 | £5 | |
| Gary Crosby | LP | Vogue | VA160118 | 1957 £4 | £10 | |
| Give Me A Band And My Baby | 7" | Brunswick | 05496 | 1955 £2 | £5 | |
| Happy Bachelor | 7" | HMV | POP648 | 1959 £1.50 | £4 | |
| Judy Judy | 7" | HMV | POP550 | 1958 £2 | £10 | |
| Ko Ko Mo | 7" | Brunswick | 05400 | 1955 £4 | £8 | *with Louis Armstrong* |
| Mambo In The Moonlight | 7" | Brunswick | 05340 | 1954 £2 | £5 | |
| Palsy Walsy | 7" | Brunswick | 05365 | 1955 £2 | £5 | |
| Ready, Willing And Able | 7" | Brunswick | 05378 | 1955 £4 | £8 | |
| Yaller Yaller Gold | 7" | Brunswick | 05546 | 1956 £1.50 | £4 | |

## CROSBY, STILLS & NASH

| | | | | | | |
|---|---|---|---|---|---|---|
| Crosby, Stills And Nash | CD | Atlantic | PR4283 | 1991 £8 | £20 | *...US promo sampler* |
| Crosby, Stills, & Nash | LP | Atlantic | 588189 | 1969 £4 | £10 | *...............lyric sheet* |

## CROSBY, STILLS, NASH & YOUNG

| | | | | | | |
|---|---|---|---|---|---|---|
| American Dream | CD | Atlantic | PR24972 | 1988 £6 | £15 | *US promo picture disc, hard cloth cover* |
| Celebration Record | LP | Atlantic | PR165 | 1971 £10 | £25 | *...............US promo* |
| Déjà Vu | LP | Atlantic | 2401001 | 1970 £4 | £10 | |
| Déjà Vu | LP | Mobile Fidelity | MFSL1088 | 1982 £5 | £12 | *.........US audiophile* |
| Déjà Vu | LP | Atlantic | SD19118 | 197– £6 | £15 | *... Dutch, brown vinyl* |
| Four Way Street | LP | Atlantic | 2657004 | 1972 £5 | £12 | *.................double* |
| In Synch | CD | Atlantic | PR2575 | 1988 £6 | £15 | *...US interview promo* |
| Rap With Crosby, Stills, Nash And Young | LP | Atlantic | 18102 | 1973 £6 | £15 | *...............US promo* |

## CROSS

| | | | | | | |
|---|---|---|---|---|---|---|
| Cowboys And Indians | CD-s | Virgin | CDEP10 | 1987 £15 | £30 | *.................promo* |
| Cowboys And Indians | 7" | Virgin | VS1007 | 1987 £1.50 | £4 | |
| Cowboys And Indians | 12" | Virgin | VST1007 | 1987 £2.50 | £6 | |
| Heaven For Everyone | 7" | Virgin | VS1062 | 1988 £1.50 | £4 | |
| Heaven For Everyone | 12" | Virgin | VST1062 | 1988 £2.50 | £6 | |
| Life Changes | CD-s | Electrola | 5602045472 | 1991 £30 | £60 | *.................Dutch* |
| Mad, Bad And Dangerous To Know | CD | Parlophone | CDPCS7342 | 1990 £6 | £15 | |
| Power To Love | CD-s | Parlophone | CDR6251 | 1990 £15 | £30 | |
| Shove It | CD-s | Virgin | CDEP20 | 1988 £15 | £30 | |
| Shove It | CD | Virgin | CDV2477 | 1988 £6 | £15 | |
| Shove It | 7" | Virgin | VS1026 | 1988 £1.50 | £4 | |
| Shove It | 12" | Virgin | VST1026 | 1988 £5 | £12 | |

## CROSS, JIMMIE

| | | | | | | |
|---|---|---|---|---|---|---|
| Super Duper Man | 7" | Red Bird | RB10042 | 1966 £4 | £8 | |

## CROSS, KEITH & PETER ROSS

| | | | | | | |
|---|---|---|---|---|---|---|
| Bored Civilians | LP | Decca | SKL5129 | 1972 £25 | £50 | |
| Can You Believe It? | 7" | Decca | F13224 | 1971 £1.50 | £4 | |

| Peace In The End | 7" | Decca | F13316 | 1972 £1.50 | £4 | |

## CROSSBEATS
| Crazy Mixed Up Generation | LP | Pilgrim | KLP12 | 1967 £8 | £20 | |

## CROW, SHERYL

Having apparently had to fend off the unwelcome advances of Michael Jackson's bodyguard while on tour as one of the star's backing singers, and having been told, in effect, that failure to give in to the advances would seriously affect the success of her music career (as described in the song 'What I Can Do For You'), it must have been particularly gratifying for Sheryl Crow when her debut album and its attendant singles managed to catapult her into the ranks of stardom in her own right. The album's success has produced two interesting variations. A limited-edition double-disc package, issued some time after the original release of the studio album, adds a set of six live recordings made by the BBC at a London concert. A limited US version, meanwhile, houses the disc in an envelope glued inside the front cover of a ring-bound book, printed to look like Sheryl Crow's own scrapbook, with photographs, song lyrics, and even a printed coffee-cup stain on the front.

| Tuesday Night Music Club | CD | A&M | 3145401262 | 1993 £6 | £15 | US, scrapbook packaging |
| Tuesday Night Music Club | CD | A&M | 5401262/5403682 | 1991 £6 | £15 | double |

## CROWBAR
| Hippie Punks | 7" | Skinhead | SKIN1 | 1984 £4 | £8 | |

## CROWDED HOUSE
| Better Be Home Soon | CD-s | Capitol | CDCL498 | 1988 £10 | £20 | |
| Chocolate Cake | CD-s | EMI | CDCL618 | 1991 £2 | £5 | |
| Conversation With Neil Finn | CD-s | EMI | FINNTERVIEW1 | 1993 £8 | £20 | promo |
| Fall At Your Feet | CD-s | Capitol | CDCL626 | 1991 £5 | £12 | double |
| Final Interview ? | CD-s | EMI | FINNTERVIEW2 | 1996 £8 | £20 | promo |
| Four Seasons In One Day | CD-s | Capitol | CDCLS655 | 1992 £5 | £12 | double |
| Full House | CD | Capitol | CDCHDJ1 | 1994 £10 | £25 | promo compilation |
| It's Only Natural | CD-s | Capitol | CDCL655 | 1992 £5 | £12 | 2 single set |
| Live At The Town And Country Club | CD | Capitol | CH1 | 1992 £20 | £40 | double promo |
| Locked Out | CD | Capitol | DPRO79297 | 1993 £20 | £40 | US promo with bonus CD album |
| Recurring Dream | CD | Capitol | 724385224829 | 1996 £6 | £15 | double |
| Sister Madly | CD-s | Capitol | CDCL509 | 1988 £6 | £15 | |
| Weather With You | CD-s | Capitol | CDCLS643 | 1992 £5 | £12 | double |
| Woodface | CD | Capitol | CDP7935592 | 1991 £5 | £12 | foldout pack |
| Woodface – The Singles Collection | CD-s | Capitol | | 1991 £37.50 | £75 | 8 CD single boxed set |
| World Where You Live | CD-s | Capitol | CDCL416 | 1986 £10 | £20 | |
| World Where You Live | 12" | Capitol | 12CL416 | 1986 £2.50 | £6 | |

## CROWDY CRAWN
| No Song To Sing | LP | Sentinel | SENS1021 | 1974 £37.50 | £75 | |

## CROWS
| Gee | 7" | Columbia | SCM5119 | 1954 £700 | £1000 | best auctioned |

## CRUCIFIXION
| Green Eyes | 12" | Neat | NEAT3712 | 1984 £2.50 | £6 | |

## CRUDUP, ARTHUR
| Crudup's Mood | LP | Delmark | DS621 | 1971 £4 | £10 | |
| Father Of Rock 'n' Roll | LP | RCA | RD8224 | 1971 £4 | £10 | |
| Look On Yonder's Wall | LP | Delmark | DS614 | 1970 £4 | £10 | |
| Mean Ole Frisco | LP | Blue Horizon | 763855 | 1969 £20 | £40 | |
| My Baby Left Me | 7" | RCA | RCA1401 | 1964 £6 | £12 | |
| Rhythm And Blues Vol. 4 | 7" EP | RCA | RCX7161 | 1964 £5 | £10 | |

## CRUISERS
| It Ain't Me Babe | 7" | Decca | F12098 | 1965 £4 | £8 | |

## CRUM, SIMON
| Enormity In Motion | 7" | Capitol | CL15183 | 1961 £4 | £8 | |
| Morgan Poisoned The Waterhole | 7" | Capitol | CL15077 | 1959 £4 | £8 | |
| Stand Up Sit Down | 7" | Capitol | CL14965 | 1958 £10 | £20 | |

## CRUSADERS
| Crusaders | LP | Blue Thumb | ILPS9218 | 1972 £5 | £12 | double |
| Hollywood | LP | Mowest | MWS7004 | 1973 £6 | £15 | |
| Old Socks, New Shoes | LP | Rare Earth | SRE3001 | 1971 £4 | £10 | |

## CRYAN SHAMES
| Scratch In The Sky | LP | CBS | CL/CS9586 | 1967 £10 | £25 | US |
| Sugar And Spice | LP | CBS | CL2589/CS9389 | 1966 £10 | £25 | US |
| Sugar And Spice | 7" | CBS | 202344 | 1966 £7.50 | £15 | |
| Synthesis | LP | CBS | CS9719 | 1968 £10 | £25 | US |

## CRYCH, TALCEN
| Angharad | 7" | Afon | RAS002 | 1975 £2 | £5 | |

## CRYER, BARRY
| Nothin' Shakin' | 7" | Fontana | H151 | 1958 £1.50 | £4 | |

## CRYIN' SHAMES
| Nobody Waved Goodbye | 7" | Decca | F12425 | 1966 £6 | £12 | |
| Please Stay | 7" | Decca | F12340 | 1966 £5 | £10 | |

## CRYSTALITES

| | | | | | | | |
|---|---|---|---|---|---|---|---|
| Biafra | 7" | Big Shot | BI510 | 1969 | £1.50 | £4 | |
| Ilya Kuryakin | 7" | Island | WI3134 | 1968 | £4 | £8 | |
| James Ray | 7" | Island | WI3153 | 1968 | £4 | £8 | Derrick Harriott B side |
| Splashdown | 7" | Nu Beat | NB036 | 1969 | £1.50 | £4 | |
| Try A Little Merriness | 7" | Island | WI3151 | 1968 | £2.50 | £6 | |

## CRYSTALS

| | | | | | | | |
|---|---|---|---|---|---|---|---|
| All Grown Up | 7" | London | HLU9909 | 1964 | £4 | £8 | |
| Da Doo Ron Ron | 7" EP | London | REU1381 | 1963 | £20 | £40 | |
| Da Doo Ron Ron | 7" | London | HLU9732 | 1963 | £1.50 | £4 | |
| Do The Screw | 7" | Philles | 111 | 1963 | £700 | £1000 | . US, promo only, best auctioned |
| Greatest Hits | LP | Philles | PHLP4003 | 1963 | £50 | £100 | US |
| He Sure Is The Boy I Love | 7" | London | HLU9661 | 1963 | £5 | £10 | |
| He's A Rebel | LP | London | HAU8120 | 1963 | £37.50 | £75 | |
| He's A Rebel | 7" | London | HLU9611 | 1962 | £4 | £8 | |
| I Wonder | 7" | London | HLU9852 | 1964 | £4 | £8 | |
| Little Boy | 7" | London | HLU9837 | 1964 | £15 | £30 | |
| My Place | 7" | United Artists | UP1110 | 1965 | £10 | £20 | |
| Then He Kissed Me | 7" | London | HLU9773 | 1963 | £1.50 | £4 | |
| There's No Other | 7" | Parlophone | R4867 | 1962 | £37.50 | £75 | |
| Twist Uptown | LP | Philles | PHLP4000 | 1962 | £50 | £100 | US |

## CUBY & THE BLIZZARDS

| | | | | | | | |
|---|---|---|---|---|---|---|---|
| Afscheids-Koncert | LP | Philips | 6343229 | 1974 | £5 | £12 | Dutch |
| Appleknockers Flophouse | LP | Philips | SBL7918 | 1969 | £6 | £15 | |
| Appleknockers Flophouse | 7" | Philips | BF1827 | 1969 | £2 | £5 | |
| Best Of 66–68 | LP | Philips | 6677023 | 1974 | £5 | £12 | Dutch double |
| Desolation | LP | Philips | SBL7874 | 1968 | £6 | £15 | |
| Distant Smile | 7" | Philips | BF1638 | 1968 | £2 | £5 | |
| Groeten Uit Grollo | LP | Philips | 855040XPY | 1967 | £6 | £15 | Dutch |
| King Of The World | LP | Philips | 6314002 | 1970 | £6 | £15 | Dutch |
| Live | LP | Philips | 6440091 | 1968 | £6 | £15 | Dutch |
| On The Road | LP | Philips | K1014 | 1968 | £5 | £12 | Dutch |
| Praise The Blues | LP | Philips | 6440308 | 1968 | £6 | £15 | Dutch |
| Simple Man | LP | Philips | 6413014 | 1971 | £4 | £10 | Dutch |
| Sometimes | LP | Philips | 6413026 | 1972 | £4 | £10 | Dutch |
| Soul | LP | Philips | 044054 | 1968 | £6 | £15 | Dutch |
| Too Blind To See | LP | Philips | 6413002 | 1969 | £6 | £15 | Dutch |
| Trippin' Thru A Midnight Blues | LP | Philips | 6343228 | 1967 | £6 | £15 | Dutch |
| Windows Of My Eyes | 7" | Philips | BF1719 | 1968 | £1.50 | £4 | |
| With Regards From Grollo | LP | Philips | 6343227 | 1967 | £6 | £15 | Dutch |

## CUD

| | | | | | | | |
|---|---|---|---|---|---|---|---|
| Haywire | 12" | Imaginary | MIRAGE18T | 1990 | £3 | £8 | signed |
| Hey Wire | CD-s | Imaginary | MIRAGE018CD | 1990 | £2 | £5 | |
| Magic | CD-s | Imaginary | MIRACD027 | 1991 | £2 | £5 | |
| Oh No Won't Do | CD-s | A&M | AMCD829 | 1991 | £2 | £5 | |
| Robinson Crusoe | CD-s | Imaginary | MIRACD021 | 1990 | £2 | £5 | |
| Slack Time | 12" | Dug | DUGNI001T | 1988 | £4 | £10 | |
| Under My Hat | 12" | Ediesta | CALC049 | 1988 | £4 | £10 | |
| You're The Boss | 12" | Reception | REC007 | 1987 | £5 | £12 | |

## CUDDLY DUDLEY

| | | | | | | | |
|---|---|---|---|---|---|---|---|
| Blarney Blues | 7" | Oriole | ICB9 | 1964 | £2 | £5 | |
| Later | 7" | HMV | POP586 | 1959 | £2 | £5 | |
| Too Pooped To Pop | 7" | HMV | POP725 | 1960 | £2 | £5 | |
| Way Of Life | 7" | Oriole | ICB10 | 1964 | £2 | £5 | |

## CUES

| | | | | | | | |
|---|---|---|---|---|---|---|---|
| Burn That Candle | 7" | Capitol | CL14501 | 1956 | £62.50 | £125 | |
| Crackerjack | 7" | Capitol | CL14651 | 1956 | £62.50 | £125 | |
| Prince Or Pauper | 7" | Capitol | CL14682 | 1957 | £50 | £100 | |

## CULPEPER'S ORCHARD

| | | | | | | | |
|---|---|---|---|---|---|---|---|
| 1971–73 | LP | Polydor | 2444032 | 1975 | £6 | £15 | Danish |
| All Dressed Up And Nowhere To Go | LP | Sonet | SLP1558 | 1977 | £8 | £20 | Danish |
| Culpeper's Orchard | LP | Polydor | 2380006 | 1971 | £50 | £100 | German |
| Going For A Song | LP | Polydor | 2308020 | 1972 | £15 | £30 | German |
| Second Sight | LP | Polydor | 2480123 | 1972 | £30 | £60 | |

## CULT

| | | | | | | | |
|---|---|---|---|---|---|---|---|
| Ceremony | CD-s | Beggars Banquet | CULT14 | 1991 | £2.50 | £6 | promo only |
| Cult | CD | Beggars Banquet | | 1994 | £8 | £20 | Australian with bonus 'Live At The Marquee' CD |
| Dreamtime | LP | Beggars Banquet | BEGA57 | 1984 | £5 | £12 | with live LP |
| Dreamtime | LP | Beggars Banquet | BEGA57P | 1984 | £4 | £10 | picture disc |
| Dreamtime | CD | Beggars Banquet | BEGA57CD | 1984 | £5 | £12 | |
| Edie (Ciao Baby) | CD-s | Beggars Banquet | BEG230CD | 1989 | £2 | £5 | |

| Title | Format | Label | Catalogue | Year | Price | Price | Notes |
|---|---|---|---|---|---|---|---|
| Edie (Ciao Baby) | CD-s | Beggars Banquet | BEG230CP | 1989 | £2.50 | £6 | picture disc |
| Electric | LP | Beggars Banquet | BEGA80 | 1987 | £4 | £10 | gold vinyl |
| Electric | LP | Beggars Banquet | CULTLP12 | 1987 | £5 | £12 | interview & music promo |
| Fire Woman | CD-s | Beggars Banquet | BEG228CD | 1989 | £2 | £5 | black plastic wallet |
| Li'l Devil | CD-s | Beggars Banquet | BEG188CD | 1987 | £3 | £8 | |
| Singles Collection | CD-s | Beggars Banquet | CBOX1 | 1991 | £15 | £30 | 10 picture disc singles, boxed |
| Soldier Blue | CD-s | Beggars Banquet | BEG205CD | 1987 | £2 | £5 | |
| Sonic Temple | LP | Beggars Banquet | BEGA98 | 1989 | £4 | £10 | red vinyl |
| Sonic Temple | CD | Beggars Banquet | BEGA98CH | 1989 | £6 | £15 | hologram pack |
| Sun King | CD-s | Beggars Banquet | BEG235CD | 1989 | £2 | £5 | |
| Sweet Soul Sister | CD-s | Beggars Banquet | BEG241CR | 1990 | £2 | £5 | |
| Wild Hearted Son | CD-s | Beggars Banquet | BEG255CD | 1991 | £2 | £5 | |
| Wildflower | CD-s | Beggars Banquet | BEG195CD | 1987 | £2 | £5 | |

## CULT HERO
| Title | Format | Label | Catalogue | Year | Price | Price | Notes |
|---|---|---|---|---|---|---|---|
| I'm A Cult Hero | 7" | Fiction | FICS006 | 1979 | £20 | £40 | |

## CULTURE
| Title | Format | Label | Catalogue | Year | Price | Price | Notes |
|---|---|---|---|---|---|---|---|
| Baldhead Bridge | LP | Laser | LASL7 | 1980 | £4 | £10 | |
| Cumbolo | LP | Front Line | FL1040 | 1979 | £4 | £10 | |
| Harder Than The Rest | LP | Front Line | FL1016 | 1978 | £5 | £12 | |
| International Herb | LP | Front Line | FL1047 | 1979 | £4 | £10 | |
| Two Sevens Clash | LP | Lightning | LIP1 | 1977 | £5 | £12 | |

## CULTURE CLUB
| Title | Format | Label | Catalogue | Year | Price | Price | Notes |
|---|---|---|---|---|---|---|---|
| God Thank You Woman | 7" | Virgin | VSY861 | 1986 | £2.50 | £6 | picture disc |
| Waking Up With The House On Fire | CD | Virgin | CDV2330 | 1984 | £6 | £15 | |
| War Song | 7" | Virgin | VSY694 | 1984 | £20 | £40 | picture disc |

## CULVER STREET PLAYGROUND
| Title | Format | Label | Catalogue | Year | Price | Price | Notes |
|---|---|---|---|---|---|---|---|
| Alley Pond Park | 7" | President | PT145 | 1968 | £2 | £5 | |

## CUMBERLAND THREE
| Title | Format | Label | Catalogue | Year | Price | Price | Notes |
|---|---|---|---|---|---|---|---|
| Civil War Almanac – Rebels | LP | Columbia | 33SX1325 | 1961 | £4 | £10 | |
| Civil War Almanac – Yankees | LP | Columbia | 33SX1318 | 1961 | £4 | £10 | |
| Folk Scene USA | LP | Columbia | 33SX1302/ SCX3364 | 1961 | £4 | £10 | |

## CUMBERLAND THREE (2)
| Title | Format | Label | Catalogue | Year | Price | Price | Notes |
|---|---|---|---|---|---|---|---|
| Cumberland Three | LP | Parlophone | PMC1223 | 1964 | £4 | £10 | |

## CUPIDS
| Title | Format | Label | Catalogue | Year | Price | Price | Notes |
|---|---|---|---|---|---|---|---|
| Lillie Mae | 7" | Vogue | V9102 | 1958 | £180 | £300 | best auctioned |

## CUPID'S INSPIRATION
| Title | Format | Label | Catalogue | Year | Price | Price | Notes |
|---|---|---|---|---|---|---|---|
| Yesterday Has Gone | LP | Nems | 63553 | 1968 | £4 | £10 | |

## CUPOL
| Title | Format | Label | Catalogue | Year | Price | Price | Notes |
|---|---|---|---|---|---|---|---|
| Like This For Ages | 12" | 4AD | BAD9 | 1980 | £2.50 | £6 | |

## CUPPA T
| Title | Format | Label | Catalogue | Year | Price | Price | Notes |
|---|---|---|---|---|---|---|---|
| Miss Pinkerton | 7" | Deram | DM144 | 1967 | £4 | £8 | |
| Streatham Hippodrome | 7" | Deram | DM185 | 1968 | £4 | £8 | |

## CUPS
| Title | Format | Label | Catalogue | Year | Price | Price | Notes |
|---|---|---|---|---|---|---|---|
| Good As Gold | 7" | Polydor | 56777 | 1968 | £2.50 | £6 | |

## CURE
| Title | Format | Label | Catalogue | Year | Price | Price | Notes |
|---|---|---|---|---|---|---|---|
| Boys Don't Cry | CD-s | Fiction | 8150112 | 1986 | £5 | £12 | non-picture disc |
| Boys Don't Cry | 7" | Fiction | FICS002 | 1979 | £5 | £10 | |
| Catch | CD-s | Fiction | 0801862 | 1987 | £15 | £30 | CD video |
| Catch | 7" | Fiction | FICS26 | 1987 | £1.50 | £4 | |
| Catch | 7" | Fiction | FICSC26 | 1987 | £4 | £8 | clear vinyl |
| Caterpillar | 7" | Fiction | FICSP20 | 1984 | £10 | £20 | picture disc |
| Charlotte Sometimes | 7" | Fiction | FICS14 | 1981 | £2 | £5 | |
| Charlotte Sometimes | 12" | Fiction | FICSX14 | 1981 | £5 | £12 | |
| Close To Me | CD-s | Fiction | 0801802 | 1989 | £15 | £30 | CD video |
| Close To Me | CD-s | Fiction | FICCD36 | 1990 | £2 | £5 | picture disc single |
| Close To Me | CD-s | Fiction | FICCD36 | 1990 | £2.50 | £6 | poster pack |
| Close To Me | 7" | Fiction | FICSG23 | 1985 | £1.50 | £4 | poster picture sleeve |
| Close To Me | 7" | Fiction | FICSP23 | 1985 | £2.50 | £6 | poster sleeve, sticker |
| Close To Me | 10" | Fiction | FICST23 | 1985 | £4 | £10 | |
| Disintegration | LP | Fiction | FIXHP14 | 1990 | £4 | £10 | picture disc |
| Disintegration | CD | Fiction | 8393532 | 1989 | £15 | £30 | promo pack |
| Entreat | CD | Fiction | FIXCD17 | 1990 | £6 | £15 | promo |

| | | | | | | | |
|---|---|---|---|---|---|---|---|
| Faith | CD | Fiction | 8276872 | 1985 | £5 | £12 | non-picture disc |
| Forest | 7" | Fiction | FICS10 | 1980 | £2 | £5 | 'radio' sleeve, silver label |
| Forest | 7" | Fiction | FICS10 | 1980 | £4 | £8 | picture sleeve, blue label |
| Forest | 12" | Fiction | FICSX10 | 1980 | £10 | £20 | |
| Friday I'm In Love | CD-s | Fiction | 8630012 | 1992 | £3 | £8 | |
| Grinding Halt | 12" | Fiction | CUR1 | 1979 | £20 | £40 | promo |
| Hanging Garden | 7" | Fiction | FICG15 | 1982 | £6 | £12 | double |
| Hanging Garden | 7" | Fiction | FICS15 | 1982 | £2.50 | £6 | |
| Hot! Hot! Hot! | CD-s | Fiction | FIXCD28 | 1988 | £3 | £8 | |
| Hot! Hot! Hot! | 7" | Fiction | FICS28 | 1988 | £2.50 | £6 | promo |
| In Between Days | CD-s | Polygram | 0801822 | 1988 | £15 | £30 | CD video |
| Interview | CD | Fiction | CUREPROCD3 | 1990 | £15 | £30 | promo |
| Japanese Whispers | CD | Fiction | 8174702 | 1987 | £5 | £12 | non-picture disc |
| Jumping Someone Else's Train | 7" | Fiction | FICS005 | 1979 | £6 | £12 | |
| Just Like Heaven | CD-s | Fiction | FIXCD27 | 1987 | £5 | £12 | |
| Just Like Heaven | 7" | Fiction | FICSP27 | 1987 | £4 | £8 | picture disc |
| Just Like Heaven | 7" | Fiction | FICSW27 | 1987 | £2 | £5 | white vinyl |
| Killing An Arab | 7" | Fiction | FICS001 | 1979 | £5 | £10 | |
| Killing An Arab | 7" | Small Wonder | SMALL11 | 1978 | £6 | £12 | |
| Killing An Arab (Peel Sessions) | 7" | Strange Fruit | 671002 | 1991 | £1.50 | £4 | shaped picture disc |
| Kiss Me Kiss Me Kiss Me | LP | Fiction | FIXH13 | 1987 | £6 | £15 | with orange vinyl disc in cellophane |
| Kiss Me Kiss Me Kiss Me | CD | Elektra | | 1987 | £75 | £150 | US promo box set, with LP and cassette |
| Kiss Me Kiss Me Kiss Me Interview | LP | Fiction | KSME2 | 1987 | £4 | £10 | promo |
| Lament | 7" | Lyntone | LYN12011 | 1982 | £2.50 | £6 | Flexipop green flexi |
| Lament | 7" | Lyntone | LYN12011 | 1982 | £4 | £8 | Flexipop red flexi |
| Let's Go To Bed | 12" | Fiction | FICSX17 | 1982 | £2.50 | £6 | |
| Limited Edition CD Box | CD | Fiction | 5136000 | 1992 | £75 | £150 | 15 CD boxed set |
| Love Cats | 7" | Fiction | FICSP19 | 1983 | £12.50 | £25 | picture disc |
| Love Song | CD-s | Fiction | FICCD30 | 1989 | £3 | £8 | |
| Lovesong | 12" | Fiction | FICSX30 | 1989 | £20 | £40 | picture disc test pressing |
| Lullaby | CD-s | Fiction | 0813982 | 1989 | £15 | £30 | CD video |
| Lullaby | 7" | Fiction | FICSP29 | 1989 | £2.50 | £6 | clear vinyl |
| Lullaby | 12" | Fiction | FICVX29 | 1989 | £3 | £8 | pink vinyl |
| Lullaby (Remix) | CD-s | Fiction | FICCD29 | 1989 | £2 | £5 | 3" single |
| Never Enough | CD-s | Fiction | FICCD35 | 1990 | £3 | £8 | |
| One Hundred Years | 12" | Fiction | CURE1 | 1982 | £15 | £30 | promo |
| Peel Sessions | CD-s | Strange Fruit | SFPSCD050 | 1988 | £2 | £5 | |
| Pictures Of You | CD-s | Fiction | FICDA34 | 1990 | £2.50 | £6 | |
| Pictures Of You | CD-s | Fiction | FICDB34 | 1990 | £3 | £8 | |
| Pictures Of You | 7" | Fiction | FICPB34 | 1990 | £2 | £5 | purple vinyl |
| Pictures Of You | 12" | Fiction | FIXPB34 | 1990 | £3 | £8 | purple vinyl |
| Pornography | CD | Fiction | 8276882 | 1986 | £5 | £12 | non-picture disc |
| Primary | 7" | Fiction | FICS12 | 1981 | £2.50 | £6 | |
| Primary | 12" | Fiction | FICSX12 | 1981 | £6 | £15 | |
| Retrospective | CD | Elektra | PRCD95522 | 1996 | £8 | £20 | US promo compilation |
| Seventeen Seconds | CD | Fiction | 8253542 | 1985 | £5 | £12 | non-picture disc |
| Stranger Than Fiction | CD | Fiction | SCIFCD301 | 1989 | £37.50 | £75 | promo sampler |
| Three Imaginary Boys | LP | Fiction | FIX1 | 1979 | £4 | £10 | with postcard |
| Walk | 7" | Fiction | FICS18 | 1983 | £4 | £8 | poster sleeve |
| Walk | 7" | Fiction | FICSP18 | 1983 | £12.50 | £25 | picture disc |
| Walk | 12" | Fiction | FICSX18 | 1983 | £2.50 | £6 | |
| Why Can't I Be You | 7" | Fiction | FICSG25 | 1987 | £2.50 | £6 | double |
| Why Can't I Be You? | CD-s | Fiction | 0801842 | 1990 | £15 | £30 | CD video |
| Wish | CD | Fiction | PK1 | 1992 | £20 | £40 | promo box set, with cassette and video |
| Wish Interview | CD | Fiction | CID1 | 1992 | £8 | £20 | promo |

## CURE, MARTIN & THE PEEPS

| | | | | | | | |
|---|---|---|---|---|---|---|---|
| It's All Over Now | 7" | Philips | BF1605 | 1967 | £7.50 | £15 | |

## CURFEW

| | | | | | | | |
|---|---|---|---|---|---|---|---|
| Let There Be Dark And There Was Dark | LP | United Artists | UAS6746 | 1970 | £6 | £15 | US |

## CURIOSITY SHOPPE

| | | | | | | | |
|---|---|---|---|---|---|---|---|
| Baby I Need You | 7" | Deram | DM220 | 1968 | £7.50 | £15 | |

## CURIOUS, JOHNNY & THE STRANGERS

| | | | | | | | |
|---|---|---|---|---|---|---|---|
| In Tune | 7" | Illegal | IL009 | 1978 | £1.50 | £4 | |
| Someone Else's Home | 7" | Bugle | BLAST2 | 1979 | £4 | £8 | |

## CURLY CURVE

| | | | | | | | |
|---|---|---|---|---|---|---|---|
| Curly Curve | LP | Brain | 1040 | 1974 | £10 | £25 | German |

## CURRANT KRAZE

| | | | | | | | |
|---|---|---|---|---|---|---|---|
| Lady Pearl | 7" | Deram | DM292 | 1970 | £2 | £5 | |

## CURRENT 93

| | | | | | | | |
|---|---|---|---|---|---|---|---|
| Christ And The Pale Queen | LP | Maldoror | MAL666 | 1988 | £25 | £50 | |
| Crowleymass | 12" | Maldoror | MAL108 | 1987 | £2.50 | £6 | |
| Faith's Favourites | 7" | Yangki | 002 | 1988 | £2.50 | £6 | |
| Live At Bar Maldoror | LP | Durtro | DURTRO001 | 1989 | £10 | £25 | |
| She Is Dead And All Fall Down | 7" | Shock | SX003 | 1990 | £4 | £8 | |
| She Is Dead And All Fall Down | 7" | Shock | SX003 | 1990 | £7.50 | £15 | individually lettered |
| This Ain't The Summer Of Love | 7" | Cerne | 004 | 1990 | £2.50 | £6 | Sol Invictus B side |

## CURRY, CLIFFORD
I Can't Get A Hold Of Myself ..................... 7" ...... Pama ............. PM797 ................... 1969 £2 ............ £5 ...................
She Shot A Hole In My Soul ..................... 7" ...... Action ............. ACT4549 ............. 1969 £1.50 ........ £4 ...................
You Turn Out The Light ........................ 7" ...... Pama ............. PM793 ................... 1969 £1.50 ........ £4 ...................

## CURSON, TED
Tears For Dolphy ............................ LP ..... Fontana ............ 688310ZL ............. 1964 £4 ............ £10 ...................

## CURTIS, CHRIS
Aggravation ............................... 7" ...... Pye ............. 7N17132 ............... 1966 £12.50 .... £25 ...................

## CURTIS, JOHNNY
Our Love's Disintegrating ....................... 7" ...... Parlophone .... R5529 ................... 1966 £7.50 .... £15 ...................

## CURTIS, KING
Arthur Murray's Music For Dancing – The    LP ...... RCA ............. RD27252 ............. 1962 £6 ............ £15 ...................
   Twist.
Azure ................................... LP ...... Everest ............ DBR1121 ............. 1961 £8 ............ £20 ............. US
Best Of King Curtis ........................... LP ...... Atlantic ............ 228002 ............... 1968 £5 ............ £12 ...................
Doin' The Dixie Twist ......................... LP ...... Tru-Sound ..... (S)TS15009 ............. 1962 £6 ............ £15 ............. US
Good To Me ............................... 7" ...... Atlantic ............ 584109 ............... 1967 £1.50 ........ £4 ...................
Have Tenor Sax Will Blow ..................... 7" EP . London ......... REK1307 ............. 1961 £6 ............ £12 ...................
Have Tenor Sax, Will Blow ..................... LP ...... London ......... HAK2247 ............. 1960 £8 ............ £20 ...................
Hits Made Famous By Sam Cooke ............ LP ...... Capitol ......... (S)T2341 ............. 1965 £6 ............ £15 ............. US
Instant Groove ............................. LP ...... Atlantic ............ 228027 ............... 1968 £5 ............ £12 ...................
It's Party Time ............................. LP ...... Tru-Sound ..... (S)TS15008 ............. 1962 £6 ............ £15 ............. US
Kingsize Soul ............................. LP ...... Atlantic ............ 587043 ............... 1967 £4 ............ £10 ...................
La Jeanne ................................ 7" ...... Atlantic ............ 584287 ............... 1969 £1.50 ........ £4 ...................
Live At Small's Paradise ...................... LP ...... Atco ............ (SD)33198 ............. 1966 £6 ............ £15 ............. US
Memphis Soul Stew .......................... 7" ...... Atlantic ............ 584134 ............... 1967 £1.50 ........ £4 ...................
New Scene ............................... LP ...... Esquire ......... 32161 ............... 1962 £6 ............ £15 ...................
Plays Great Memphis Hits ..................... LP ...... Atlantic ............ 587067 ............... 1967 £4 ............ £10 ...................
Soul Serenade ............................. LP ...... Capitol ......... (S)T2095 ............. 1964 £6 ............ £15 ............. US
Soul Serenade ............................. LP ...... Ember ......... SPE/LP6600 ............. 1968 £4 ............ £10 ...................
Soul Serenade ............................. 7" ...... Capitol ......... CL15346 ............. 1964 £2.50 ........ £6 ...................
Soul Twist ............................... 7" ...... London ......... HLU9547 ............. 1962 £4 ............ £8 ...................
Sweet Soul ............................... LP ...... Atlantic ............ 587115 ............... 1968 £5 ............ £12 ...................
That Lovin' Feeling .......................... LP ...... Atco ............ (SD)33189 ............. 1966 £6 ............ £15 ............. US
Wiggle Wobble ............................. 7" ...... Speciality ......... SPE1000 ............. 1967 £2 ............ £5 ...................

## CURTIS, KING, OLIVER NELSON, JIMMY FORREST
Soul Battle ............................... LP ..... Esquire ............ 32189 ............... 1963 £6 ............ £15 ...................

## CURTIS, LEE & THE ALL STARS
Ecstasy .................................. 7" ...... Philips ......... BF1385 ............... 1964 £5 ............ £10 ...................
It's Lee .................................. LP ...... Star-Club ......... 158017STY ............. 1965 £30 ............ £60 ............. German
Let's Stomp ............................... 7" ...... Decca ............. F11690 ............... 1963 £5 ............ £10 ...................
Little Girl ................................ 7" ...... Decca ............. F11622 ............... 1963 £4 ............ £8 ...................
Star-Club Show 3 ........................... LP ...... Star-Club ......... 158002STY ............. 1965 £30 ............ £60 ............. German
What About Me ............................. 7" ...... Decca ............. F11830 ............... 1964 £4 ............ £8 ...................

## CURTIS, MAC
You Ain't Treating Me Right ..................... 7" ...... Parlophone .... R4279 ................... 1957 £700 ... £1000 ........... best auctioned

## CURTIS, SONNY
Beatle Hits Flamenco Guitar Style ............ LP ...... Imperial ......... LP9276/LP12276 .... 1964 £6 ............ £15 ............. US
Beatle I Want To Be .......................... 7" ...... Colpix ......... PX11024 ............. 1964 £4 ............ £8 ...................
Bo Diddley Bach ............................ 7" ...... Liberty ......... LIB55710 ............. 1964 £4 ............ £8 ...................
Red Headed Stranger ......................... 7" ...... Coral ............. Q72400 ............... 1960 £7.50 .... £15 ...................

## CURTISS, DAVE & THE TREMORS
Summertime Blues ........................... 7" ...... Philips ......... BF1330 ............... 1964 £1.50 ........ £4 ...................
What Kind of Girl Are You ..................... 7" ...... Philips ......... BF1285 ............... 1963 £1.50 ........ £4 ...................
You Don't Love Me .......................... 7" ...... Philips ......... BF1257 ............... 1963 £1.50 ........ £4 ...................

## CURVE
Blindfold ................................ CD-s .. Anxious .......... ANXCD27 ............. 1991 £2 ............ £5 ...................
Clipped .................................. CD-s .. Anxious .......... ANXCD35 ............. 1991 £2 ............ £5 ...................
Coast Is Clear ............................. CD-s .. Anxious .......... ANXCD30 ............. 1991 £2 ............ £5 ...................
Ten Little Girls ............................. 7" ...... Anxious .......... ANXP27 ............. 1991 £1.50 ........ £4 ............. picture disc

## CURVED AIR
Curved Air (named after the Terry Riley piece) were more successful than most at integrating elements of classical music within a rock format and both Francis Monkman and Darryl Way have worked extensively with the same approach ever since the group's first release. The first LP, *Air Conditioning*, was issued as a limited-edition picture disc – probably the first rock record to be released in this form. Its value has been kept low, however, by the fact that a small number of playings causes a drastic deterioration in sound quality.

Air Conditioning .......................... LP ...... Warner Bros .... WSX3012 ............. 1970 £6 ............ £15 ............. picture disc
Air Cut .................................. LP ...... Warner Bros .... K46224 ............... 1973 £4 ............ £10 ...................
Phantasmagoria ............................ LP ...... Warner Bros .... K46158 ............... 1972 £4 ............ £10 ...................
Second Album ............................. LP ...... Warner Bros .... K46092 ............... 1971 £4 ............ £10 ...................

## CUT AND DRY BAND
Cut And Dry Dolly .......................... LP ...... Topic ............ 12TS278 ............. 1976 £4 ............ £10 ...................
Cut And Dry No. 2 .......................... LP ...... Topic ............ 12TS413 ............. 1980 £4 ............ £10 ...................

## CUTLER, CHRIS & FRED FRITH
Limoges .................................................. 7" ...... Recommended REDUO ............... 1983 £4 ........... £8 .............. clear vinyl
Live In Prague And Washington ............... LP ..... Recommended RE1729 ................. 1983 £5 ........... £12 ...............

## CUTLER, CHRIS & LINDSAY COOPER
News From Babel ................................ LP ..... Recommended RE6116 .............. 1984 £5 ........... £12

## CUTLER, CHRIS & OTHERS
News From Babel: Contraries ................. 7" ...... Recommended RE£ .................... 1984 £4 ............ £8 ........... 1 side painted

## CUTLER, IVOR
Get Away From The Wall ........................ 7" EP . Decca ............ DFE6677 ............... 1961 £10 ....... £20
Great Grey Grasshopper ...................... 7" ...... Parlophone ...... R5624 ............... 1967 £1.50 ...... £4
Ludo ....................................................... LP ..... Parlophone ...... PCS7040 .............. 1967 £15 ...... £30
Of Y'hup ............................................... 7" EP . Fontana ........... TFE17144 .......... 1959 £10 ...... £20
Who Tore Your Trousers ....................... LP ..... Decca ............ LK4405 ................. 1961 £15 ...... £30

## CUTTERS
I've Had It ............................................ 7" ...... Decca ............ F11110 ............... 1959 £1.50 ...... £4

## CUTTY, GORDON
Grand Old Fashioned Dance .................. LP ..... Free Reed ....... FRR006 ............. 1976 £5 .......... £12

## CWT
Hundredweight ...................................... LP ..... Kuckuck ........ 2375022 ............... 1973 £30 ........ £60 ............... German

## CYAN THREE
Since I Lost My Baby ............................ 7" ...... Decca ............ F12371 ............ 1966 £5 .......... £10

## CYBERMEN
Cybermen .............................................. 7" ...... Rockaway ...... AERE101 ............... 1978 £2 ........... £5

## CYCLONES
Nobody .................................................. 7" ...... Oriole ............ CB1898 ............... 1964 £6 .......... £12

## CYKLE
Cykle .................................................... LP ..... Label .............. 9261 ............... 1969 £330 ..... £500 ............... US

## CYMANDE
Cymande ................................................ LP ..... Alaska ........... ALKA100 ............ 1973 £6 ......... £15
Promised Height ................................... LP ..... Contempo ....... CLP508 ............. 1974 £6 ......... £15

## CYMBAL, JOHNNY
Cymbal Smashes ................................... 7" EP . London ........... RER1406 ......... 1963 £10 ....... £20
Dum Dum De Dum ................................ 7" ...... London ........... HLR9762 ........ 1963 £2 .......... £5
Go VW Go ............................................ 7" ...... United Artists .. UP1093 ........... 1965 £5 .......... £10
It'll Be Me ............................................ 7" ...... MGM .......... MGM1106 ......... 1960 £4 .......... £8
Mister Bass Man ................................... LP ..... Kapp ........... KL1324/KS3324 .... 1963 £15 ....... £30 ............... US
Mister Bass Man ................................... 7" EP . London ....... RER1375 ............ 1963 £10 ....... £20
Mister Bass Man ................................... 7" ...... London ........... HLR9682 ....... 1963 £1.50 ...... £4
Robinson Crusoe On Mars ..................... 7" ...... London ........... HLR9911 ........ 1964 £4 ......... £8
Teenage Heaven .................................... 7" ...... London ........... HLR9731 ......... 1963 £4 .......... £8

## CYMBALINE
Down By The Seaside ............................ 7" ...... Philips ........... BF1681 .............. 1968 £1.50 ...... £4
I Don't Want It ..................................... 7" ...... Mercury ......... MF961 ............. 1967 £1.50 ...... £4
Matrimonial Fears ................................. 7" ...... Philips ........... BF1624 ............. 1967 £10 ........ £20
Peanuts And Chewy Macs ...................... 7" ...... Mercury ......... MF975 ............ 1967 £1.50 ...... £4
Please Little Girl .................................. 7" ...... Pye ............... 7N15916 ........... 1965 £7.50 ...... £15
Top Girl ............................................... 7" ...... Mercury ......... MF918 .............. 1965 £1.50 ...... £4
Turn Around ......................................... 7" ...... Philips ........... BF1749 ............. 1969 £1.50 ...... £4

## CYMERONS
Everyday ............................................... 7" ...... Polydor ........... 56098 ............ 1966 £1.50 ...... £4
I'll Be There ......................................... 7" ...... Decca ............. F11976 ............ 1964 £1.50 ...... £4

## CYNARA
Cynara .................................................. LP ..... Capitol ........... ST547 ............. 1968 £20 ........ £40 ............... US

## CYRKLE
Neon ..................................................... LP ..... CBS ............... 62977 ............... 1967 £6 ......... £15
Red Rubber Ball .................................... LP ..... CBS ............... CL2544/CS9344 .... 1966 £10 ....... £25 ............... US
Red Rubber Ball .................................... 7" ...... CBS ............... 202064 ............ 1966 £1.50 ...... £4

## CZAR
Oh Lord I'm Getting Heavy .................... 7" ...... Philips ........... 6006071 ............ 1970 £10 ........ £20
Tread Softly On My Dreams ................... LP ..... Fontana ........... 6309009 ............... 1970 £75 ....... £150

## CZUKAY, HOLGER & ROLF DAMMERS
Canaxis 5 .............................................. LP ..... Music Factory .. SRS002 ............... 1969 £75 ....... £150

# D

**D, KIM**
Real Thing ................................. 7" ...... Pye ................. 7N15953 ................ 1965 £2 ........... £5 .............................

**D, TONY & THE SHAKEDOWNS**
Is It True ................................... 7" ...... Piccadilly ......... 7N35168 ............... 1964 £1.50 ...... £4

**D JUNIOR, DON**
Dirty Dozen .............................. 7" ...... Caltone ........... TONE124 ........... 1968 £4 ............ £8 ...... *Phil Pratt B side*

**D'ABO, MICHAEL**
Gulliver's Travels ....................... 7" ...... Immediate ...... IM075 ................ 1969 £2.50 ...... £6

**D'ABO, MIKE**
D'Abo ....................................... LP ...... Uni ............... UNLS114 ........... 1970 £5 ........... £12
Down At Rachel's Place ............................ LP ...... A&M ............. AMLH68097 ......... 1972 £4 ........... £10

**DADA**
Dada was an ambitious big band that unfortunately found the costs of maintaining a large line-up too great to continue when their LP failed to set the country alight. A slimmed-down version of the group continued as Vinegar Joe. The singer in both cases was Elkie Brooks and, at the end, Dada's second singer was Robert Palmer, although he makes no more than a passing appearance on the album.

Dada ........................................ LP ...... Atco .............. 2400030 ................. 1970 £5 ........... £12

**DADDY LONGLEGS**
Daddy Longlegs ......................... LP ...... Warner Bros .... WS3004 .............. 1970 £4 ........... £10
Oakdown Farm ........................... LP ...... Vertigo ......... 6360038 .............. 1971 £6 ........... £15 ........ *spiral label*
Shifting Sands ........................... LP ...... Polydor ......... 2371323 .............. 1972 £4 ........... £10
Three Musicians ......................... LP ...... Polydor ......... 2371261 .............. 1972 £4 ........... £10

**DADDY-O'S**
Got A Match? ............................ 7" ...... Oriole ............ CB1454 ............. 1958 £1.50 ...... £4

**DADDY'S ACT**
Eight Days A Week ..................... 7" ...... Columbia ........ DB8242 ............. 1967 £2.50 ...... £6

**DAFOS, CALVIN**
Brown Sugar ............................. 7" ...... Blue Beat ....... BB347 ............... 1966 £6 ........... £12
Lash Them ................................ 7" ...... Doctor Bird ..... DB1174 ............. 1969 £5 ........... £10

**DAGABAND**
Second Time Around ................... 7" ...... MHM ............ AM094 ............... 1983 £1.50 ...... £4

**DAGGERMEN**
Introducing The Daggermen .......... 7" ...... Empire ........... UPW258J ........... 1986 £2 ........... £5

**DAILY, PETE**
Dixie By Daily ........................... 10" LP Capitol ........ LC6603 .............. 1953 £5 ........... £12
Dixieland Band .......................... 10" LP Capitol ........ LC6525 .............. 1951 £5 ........... £12
Pete Daily And Phil Napoleon ........ 10" LP Brunswick ...... LA8515 ............... 1951 £6 ........... £15

**DAINTEES**
Roll On Summertime .................... 7" ...... Kitchenware .... SK3 ...................... 1984 £2 ........... £5

**DAISY PLANET**
Daisy Planet .............................. 7" EP . Oak ............... no number ........... 196– £20 ....... £40 ........ *no picture sleeve*

**DAKOTAS**
Cruel Sea .................................. 7" ...... Parlophone ...... R5044 ............... 1963 £1.50 ...... £4
I Can't Break The News To Myself ......... 7" ...... Philips ............ BF1645 .............. 1968 £15 ........ £30
I'm An 'Ardworkin' Barrow Boy .............. 7" ...... Page One ........ POF018 ............. 1967 £6 ........... £12
Magic Carpet ............................. 7" ...... Parlophone ...... R5064 ............... 1963 £1.50 ...... £4
Meet The Dakotas ....................... 7" EP . Parlophone ...... GEP8888 ............ 1963 £12.50 .... £25
Oyeh ....................................... 7" ...... Parlophone ...... R5203 ............... 1964 £4 ........... £8

**DAKOTA'S ALL STARS**
Call Me Master .......................... 7" ...... Blue Beat ....... BB358 ............... 1966 £6 ........... £12

**DALE, ALAN**
Cherry Pink And Apple Blossom White ..... 7" ...... Vogue Coral .... Q72072 ............. 1955 £2.50 ...... £6
Don't Knock The Rock .................. 7" ...... Vogue Coral .... Q72225 ............. 1957 £4 ........... £8
Lonesome Road .......................... 7" ...... Vogue Coral .... Q72231 ............. 1957 £4 ........... £8
Robin Hood ............................... 7" ...... Vogue Coral .... Q72121 ............. 1956 £7.50 ...... £15

| | | | | | | | |
|---|---|---|---|---|---|---|---|
| Rockin' The Cha–Cha | 7" | Vogue Coral | Q72105 | 1955 | £2 | £5 | |
| Sweet And Gentle | 7" | Vogue Coral | Q72089 | 1955 | £1.50 | £4 | |
| Test Of Time | 7" | Vogue Coral | Q72194 | 1956 | £1.50 | £4 | |

## DALE, DICK & THE DELTONES

| | | | | | | | |
|---|---|---|---|---|---|---|---|
| Checkered Flag | LP | Capitol | (S)T2002 | 1963 | £20 | £40 | US |
| King Of The Surf Guitar | LP | Capitol | (S)T1930 | 1963 | £20 | £40 | US |
| Mr. Eliminator | LP | Capitol | (S)T2053 | 1964 | £20 | £40 | US |
| Peppermint Man | 7" | Capitol | CL15296 | 1963 | £4 | £8 | |
| Rock Out | LP | Capitol | (S)T2293 | 1965 | £20 | £40 | US |
| Scavenger | 7" | Capitol | CL15320 | 1963 | £4 | £8 | |
| Summer Surf | LP | Capitol | (S)T2111 | 1964 | £15 | £30 | US |
| Surfer's Choice | LP | Capitol | T1886 | 1963 | £15 | £30 | US |
| Surfer's Choice | LP | Deltone | LPM1001 | 1962 | £25 | £50 | US |

## DALE, JIM

| | | | | | | | |
|---|---|---|---|---|---|---|---|
| Be My Girl | 7" | Parlophone | R4343 | 1957 | £1.50 | £4 | |
| Jim | 10" LP | Parlophone | PMD1055 | 1958 | £20 | £40 | |
| Jim Dale | 7" EP | Parlophone | GEP8656 | 1957 | £6 | £12 | |
| Just Born | 7" | Parlophone | R4376 | 1957 | £1.50 | £4 | |
| Piccadilly Line | 7" | Parlophone | R4329 | 1957 | £2 | £5 | |
| Somewhere There's A Someone | 7" | Academy | AD001 | 196– | £1.50 | £4 | |
| Sugartime | 7" | Parlophone | R4402 | 1958 | £1.50 | £4 | |
| Top Ten Special | 7" | Parlophone | R4356 | 1957 | £2 | £5 | with the Vipers & King Brothers |

## DALE & GRACE

| | | | | | | | |
|---|---|---|---|---|---|---|---|
| Dale And Grace No. 1 | 7" EP | London | RE1428 | 1964 | £6 | £12 | |
| Dale And Grace No. 2 | 7" EP | London | RE1429 | 1964 | £6 | £12 | |
| Dale And Grace No. 3 | 7" EP | London | RE1430 | 1964 | £6 | £12 | |
| I'm Leaving It Up To You | LP | Montel | LP100 | 1964 | £20 | £40 | US |
| I'm Leaving It Up To You | 7" | London | HL10249 | 1969 | £1.50 | £4 | |
| I'm Leaving It Up To You | 7" | London | HL9807 | 1963 | £2.50 | £6 | |
| Stop And Think It Over | 7" | London | HL9857 | 1964 | £2 | £5 | |

## DALE SISTERS

| | | | | | | | |
|---|---|---|---|---|---|---|---|
| Kiss | 7" | HMV | POP781 | 1960 | £2 | £5 | |
| My Sunday Baby | 7" | Ember | EMBS140 | 1961 | £1.50 | £4 | |
| Secrets | 7" | Ember | EMBS151 | 1962 | £1.50 | £4 | |

## DALEY, BASIL

| | | | | | | | |
|---|---|---|---|---|---|---|---|
| Born To Love | 7" | Studio One | SO2054 | 1968 | £6 | £12 | |

## DALEY, JIMMY & THE DING-A-LINGS

| | | | | | | | |
|---|---|---|---|---|---|---|---|
| Rock, Pretty Baby | LP | Brunswick | LAT8162 | 1957 | £37.50 | £75 | |
| Rock, Pretty Baby | 7" | Brunswick | 05648 | 1957 | £37.50 | £75 | |

## DALI, SALVADOR

| | | | | | | | |
|---|---|---|---|---|---|---|---|
| Dali In Venice | LP | Decca | SET230 | 1962 | £6 | £15 | |

## DALLON, MIKI

| | | | | | | | |
|---|---|---|---|---|---|---|---|
| Cheat And Lie | 7" | Strike | JH306 | 1966 | £2 | £5 | |
| Do You Call That Love? | 7" | RCA | RCA1438 | 1965 | £7.50 | £15 | |
| I Care About You | 7" | RCA | RCA1478 | 1965 | £10 | £20 | |
| What Will Your Mama Say | 7" | Strike | JH318 | 1966 | £1.50 | £4 | |

## DALMOUR, DAVID & MARIANNE

| | | | | | | | |
|---|---|---|---|---|---|---|---|
| Introducing | LP | Columbia | 33SX1715 | 1965 | £20 | £40 | |

## DALTONS

| | | | | | | | |
|---|---|---|---|---|---|---|---|
| Never Kiss You Again | 7" | Fab | FAB30 | 1967 | £4 | £8 | .. Righteous Flames B side |

## DALTREY, ROGER

| | | | | | | | |
|---|---|---|---|---|---|---|---|
| Say It Ain't So/Satin And Lace | 7" | Polydor | 2058948 | 1976 | £5 | £10 | |
| Under A Raging Moon | 7" | 10 | TEN(G)81 | 1986 | £2 | £5 | double |
| Under A Raging Moon | 10" | 10 | TEN(G)8112 | 1986 | £2.50 | £6 | double |

## DALY, JACKIE

| | | | | | | | |
|---|---|---|---|---|---|---|---|
| Music From Sliabh Luachra Vol. 6 | LP | Topic | 12TS358 | 1977 | £4 | £10 | |

## DAMERON, TADD

| | | | | | | | |
|---|---|---|---|---|---|---|---|
| Fontainebleau | LP | Esquire | 32034 | 1957 | £10 | £25 | |
| Tadd Dameron Band | 10" LP | Esquire | 20044 | 1955 | £20 | £40 | |
| Tadd's Delight | 7" EP | Capitol | EAP120388 | 1962 | £2 | £5 | |

## DAMIAN

| | | | | | | | |
|---|---|---|---|---|---|---|---|
| Time Warp | 7" | Jive | JIVE160 | 1987 | £1.50 | £4 | |
| Time Warp | 7" | Jive | JIVE182 | 1988 | £1.50 | £4 | |
| Time Warp | 12" | Jive | JIVET160 | 1987 | £2.50 | £6 | |
| Time Warp | 12" | Sedition | EDITL3311 | 1986 | £2.50 | £6 | |

## DAMNED

The thing about the Damned is that, for all their anti-progressive rock establishment stance and their iconic status as the first punk group to issue a record, they were actually pretty good musicians. Punk classics like 'I Just Can't Be Happy Today' and 'Smash It Up' work on wider terms too, because they are interesting songs, well played. Even that first punk record, 'New Rose', has an authority – a grandeur even – that is lacking in most of the records made by the style's camp followers. These days, of course, punk – and especially the Damned

– has taken its own place within the rock establishment. This is emphasized by the sight of Captain Sensible making star appearances at a number of VIP record fairs during 1997 – playing wah-wah lead-guitar solos of a distinctly virtuoso nature.

| | | | | | | | |
|---|---|---|---|---|---|---|---|
| Alone Again Or | CD-s | MCA | DGRIM7 | 1987 | £2 | £5 | 7" sleeve |
| Black Album | LP | Chiswick | CWK3015 | 1980 | £5 | £12 | double |
| Damned Damned Damned | LP | Stiff | SEEZ1 | 1977 | £10 | £25 | Eddie & Hot Rods photo |
| Damned Damned Damned | LP | Stiff | SEEZ1 | 1977 | £20 | £40 | Eddie & Hot Rods photo, with red sticker |
| Damned Damned Damned | CD | Demon | FIENDCD91 | 1990 | £8 | £20 | picture disc |
| Damned Damned Damned/Music For Pleasure | LP | Stiff | MAIL2 | 1986 | £5 | £12 | double, yellow vinyl |
| Don't Cry Wolf | 7" | Stiff | BUY24 | 1977 | £2 | £5 | pink vinyl |
| Four Pack | 7" | Stiff | GRAB2 | 1981 | £10 | £20 | BUY6,10,18,24 in plastic wallet |
| Fun Factory | CD-s | Deltic | DELT7C | 1991 | £2 | £5 | |
| Generals | 7" | Bronze | BRO159 | 1982 | £4 | £8 | |
| Grimly Fiendish | 7" | MCA | GRIM1 | 1985 | £2 | £5 | gatefold picture sleeve, autographed |
| Grimly Fiendish | 7" | MCA | GRIMP1 | 1985 | £1.50 | £4 | picture disc |
| Grimly Fiendish | 12" | MCA | GRIMT1 | 1985 | £2.50 | £6 | autographed |
| Grimly Fiendish | 12" | MCA | GRIMX1 | 1985 | £2.50 | £6 | white vinyl |
| I Just Can't Be Happy Today | 7" | Chiswick | CHIS120 | 1979 | £2 | £5 | |
| Live In Newcastle | LP | Damned | DAMU2 | 1983 | £10 | £25 | |
| Live In Newcastle | LP | Damned | PDAMU2 | 1983 | £6 | £15 | picture disc |
| Lively Arts | 7" | Big Beat | NS80 | 1982 | £2 | £5 | green vinyl |
| Lively Arts | 10" | Big Beat | NST80 | 1982 | £2.50 | £6 | |
| Love Song | 7" | Dodgy Demo | SGS105 | 1978 | £10 | £20 | |
| Lovely Money | 7" | Bronze | BROP149 | 1982 | £2 | £5 | picture disc |
| Neat Neat Neat | 7" | Stiff | BUY10 | 1977 | £2 | £5 | 'Damned' in fancy text on label |
| New Rose | 7" | Stiff | BUY6 | 1976 | £2 | £5 | press-out centre |
| Peel Sessions | CD-s | Strange Fruit | SFPSCD002 | 1988 | £2 | £5 | |
| Problem Child | 7" | Stiff | BUY18 | 1977 | £1.50 | £4 | press-out centre |
| Shadow Of Love | 7" | MCA | GRIM2 | 1985 | £2.50 | £6 | gatefold picture sleeve 7 (GRIMY2) |
| Stretcher Case Baby | 7" | Stiff | DAMNED1 | 1977 | £12.50 | £25 | |
| Thanks For The Night | 7" | Plus One | DAMNED1P | 1986 | £12.50 | £25 | shaped picture disc, plinth |
| Wait For The Blackout | 7" | Big Beat | NS77 | 1982 | £1.50 | £4 | red/black Damned labels |
| Wait For The Blackout | 7" | Big Beat | NSP77 | 1982 | £2 | £5 | picture disc |
| White Rabbit | 7" | Chiswick | CHIS130 | 1980 | £20 | £40 | 2 x 1 sided test pressings only |

## DAMON
| | | | | | | | |
|---|---|---|---|---|---|---|---|
| Song Of A Gypsy | LP | ANKH | | 1970 | £1050 | £1500 | US |
| Song Of A Gypsy | LP | private | | 1993 | £5 | £12 | US |

## DAMON, RUSS
| | | | | | | |
|---|---|---|---|---|---|---|
| Hip Huggers | 7" | Stateside | SS258 | 1964 | £1.50 | £4 |

## DAMONE, VIC
| | | | | | | |
|---|---|---|---|---|---|---|
| All-Time Song Hits | 10" LP | Mercury | MPT7514 | 1957 | £6 | £15 |
| Closer Than A Kiss | LP | Philips | BBL7259 | 1958 | £4 | £10 |
| That Towering Feeling | LP | Philips | BBL7144 | 1957 | £4 | £10 |
| Walking My Baby Back Home | 7" EP | Mercury | EP13121 | 1954 | £2.50 | £6 |

## DANCE CHAPTER
| | | | | | | | |
|---|---|---|---|---|---|---|---|
| Anonymity | 7" | 4AD | AD18 | 1980 | £2 | £5 | insert |

## DANCING DID
| | | | | | | |
|---|---|---|---|---|---|---|
| Dancing Did | 7" | Fruit And Veg | F&V1 | 1979 | £2 | £5 |

## DANDO SHAFT
| | | | | | | | |
|---|---|---|---|---|---|---|---|
| Dando Shaft | LP | Neon | NE5 | 1971 | £30 | £60 | |
| Evening With | LP | Youngblood | SSYB6 | 1970 | £20 | £40 | |
| Kingdom | LP | Rubber | RUB034 | 1978 | £30 | £60 | |
| Lantaloon | LP | RCA | SF8256 | 1972 | £30 | £60 | with poster |
| Sun Clog Dance | 7" | RCA | RCA2246 | 1972 | £2 | £5 | |

## DANDY
| | | | | | | | |
|---|---|---|---|---|---|---|---|
| Baby Don't Go | 7" | Dice | CC21 | 1963 | £5 | £10 | |
| Be Natural Be Proud | 7" | Downtown | DT434 | 1969 | £1.50 | £4 | |
| Charlie Brown | 7" | Giant | GN20 | 1968 | £2 | £5 | |
| Come On Home | 7" | Downtown | DT437 | 1969 | £1.50 | £4 | |
| Dandy Livingstone | LP | Trojan | TRL45 | 1972 | £4 | £10 | |
| Everybody Loves A Winner | 7" | Downtown | DT442 | 1969 | £1.50 | £4 | |
| Fight | 7" | Ska Beat | JB247 | 1966 | £5 | £10 | |
| Games People Play | 7" | Downtown | DT421 | 1969 | £1.50 | £4 | |
| Hey Boy Hey Girl | 7" | Blue Beat | BB319 | 1965 | £6 | £12 | |
| I Found Love | 7" | Blue Beat | BB336 | 1966 | £6 | £12 | |
| I Need You | LP | Trojan | TRL17 | 1969 | £5 | £12 | with Audrey |
| I'm Back with A Bang Bang | 7" | Giant | GN36 | 1968 | £2 | £5 | |
| I'm In The Mood | 7" | Giant | GN19 | 1968 | £2 | £5 | |
| I'm Looking For Love | 7" | Blue Beat | BB308 | 1965 | £6 | £12 | |
| I'm Your Puppet | 7" | Downtown | DT416 | 1969 | £1.50 | £4 | |

| | | | | | | |
|---|---|---|---|---|---|---|
| In The Mood | 7" | Caltone | TONE103 | 1967 £4 | £8 | .. *Honeyboy Martin B side* |
| Let's Go Rocksteady | 7" | Giant | GN7 | 1967 £2 | £5 | |
| Little More Ska | 7" | Dice | CC29 | 1964 £5 | £10 | |
| Morning Side Of The Mountain | LP | Trojan | TBL118 | 1970 £5 | £12 | *with Audrey* |
| Move Your Mule | 7" | Downtown | DT401 | 1969 £1.50 | £4 | |
| My Babe | 7" | Blue Beat | BB327 | 1965 £6 | £12 | |
| My Time Now | 7" | Giant | GN3 | 1967 £2 | £5 | |
| Now I Have You | 7" | Dice | CC24 | 1964 £5 | £10 | |
| One Scotch, One Bourbon, One Beer | 7" | Ska Beat | JB269 | 1967 £5 | £10 | |
| People Get Ready | 7" | Downtown | DT429 | 1969 £1.50 | £4 | |
| Play It Cool | 7" | Columbia | DB112 | 1969 £2.50 | £6 | |
| Propogandist | 7" | Giant | GN23 | 1968 £2 | £5 | |
| Puppet On A String | 7" | Giant | GN5 | 1967 £2 | £5 | |
| Reggae In Your Jeggae | 7" | Downtown | DT410 | 1969 £1.50 | £4 | |
| Returns | LP | Trojan | TRL2 | 1969 £6 | £15 | |
| Rocksteady With Dandy | LP | Giant | GNL1000 | 1967 £20 | £40 | |
| Rudy A Message To You | 7" | Ska Beat | JB273 | 1967 £5 | £10 | |
| Sentence | 7" | Trojan | TR629 | 1968 £2.50 | £6 | *Lee Perry B side* |
| Shake Me Wake Me | 7" | Downtown | DT402 | 1969 £1.50 | £4 | |
| Somewhere My Love | 7" | Giant | GN10 | 1967 £2 | £5 | |
| Sweet Ride | 7" | Giant | GN27 | 1968 £2 | £5 | |
| Tears On My Pillow | 7" | Giant | GN30 | 1968 £2 | £5 | |
| Tell Me Darling | 7" | Downtown | DT404 | 1969 £1.50 | £4 | |
| There Is A Mountain | 7" | Giant | GN15 | 1967 £2 | £5 | |
| Toast | 7" | Trojan | TR618 | 1968 £2.50 | £6 | |
| Trier | 7" | Downtown | DT411 | 1969 £1.50 | £4 | |
| Vipers | 7" | Carnival | CV7020 | 1965 £4 | £8 | |
| Won't You Come Home | 7" | Downtown | DT453 | 1969 £1.50 | £4 | |
| You're No Hustler | 7" | Ska Beat | JB279 | 1967 £5 | £10 | |
| Your Musical Doctor | LP | Trojan | TTL26 | 1970 £5 | £12 | |

## DANE, CHRIS

| | | | | | |
|---|---|---|---|---|---|
| Cynthia's In Love | 7" | London | HLA8165 | 1955 £6 | £12 |

## DANE, SHELLEY

| | | | | | |
|---|---|---|---|---|---|
| Hannah Lee | 7" | Pye | 7N25064 | 1960 £1.50 | £4 |

## DANGER

| | | | | | |
|---|---|---|---|---|---|
| Danger | LP | Cow | | 1973 £50 | £100 *Dutch* |

## DANGER, CAL

| | | | | | |
|---|---|---|---|---|---|
| Teenage Girlie Blues | 7" | Fontana | 267225TF | 1962 £15 | £30 |

## DANGERFIELD, A. P.

| | | | | | |
|---|---|---|---|---|---|
| Conversations | 7" | Fontana | TF935 | 1968 £5 | £10 |

## DANGERFIELD, KEITH

The Keith Dangerfield single owes its high value to the once-held belief that the Dangerfield name was a pseudonym for the Yardbirds' vocalist, Keith Relf. This was very much a case of wishful thinking, however. Relf did attempt a solo career while still with the Yardbirds, but his singles have the obvious credit – Keith Relf.

| | | | | | |
|---|---|---|---|---|---|
| No Life Child | 7" | Plexium | P1237 | 1968 £50 | £100 |

## DANGERFIELD, TONY

| | | | | | |
|---|---|---|---|---|---|
| She's Too Way Out | 7" | Pye | 7N15695 | 1964 £15 | £30 |

## DANI

| | | | | | |
|---|---|---|---|---|---|
| That Old Familiar Feeling | 7" | Pye | 7N25667 | 1974 £4 | £8 |

## DANIELS, BILLY

| | | | | | |
|---|---|---|---|---|---|
| At The Crescendo | LP | Vogue | LAE12021 | 1956 £4 | £10 |
| Best Of Billy Daniels | 7" EP | HMV | 7EG8485 | 1958 £2 | £5 |
| Songs At Midnight | 10" LP | Mercury | MG25163 | 1954 £8 | £20 |
| Songs At Midnight | 10" LP | Mercury | MPT7505 | 1956 £6 | £15 |
| That Old Black Magic | 7" EP | Mercury | MEP9001 | 1956 £2.50 | £6 |
| That Old Black Magic | 7" EP | Mercury | ZEP10066 | 1960 £2 | £5 |
| That Old Black Magic | 7" | Vogue | V9172 | 1960 £2.50 | £6 |
| Torch Hour | 10" LP | Mercury | MG10003 | 1953 £8 | £20 |
| Torch Hour | 10" LP | Mercury | MG25163 | 1954 £6 | £15 |
| Torch Hour | 10" LP | Mercury | MPT7006 | 1956 £4 | £10 |
| You Go To My Head | 10" LP | HMV | DLP1174 | 1958 £4 | £10 |

## DANIELS, JULIUS

| | | | | | |
|---|---|---|---|---|---|
| RCA Victor Race Series Vol. 4 | 7" EP | RCA | RCX7175 | 1965 £5 | £10 |

## DANIELS, ROLY 'YO YO'

| | | | | | |
|---|---|---|---|---|---|
| Yo Yo Boy | 7" | Decca | F11501 | 1962 £1.50 | £4 |
| Yo Yo Boy | 7" | Stardisc | SD101 | 196– £4 | £8 |

## DANIELS, SAM

| | | | | | |
|---|---|---|---|---|---|
| Tell Me Baby | 7" | Sway | SW003 | 1963 £2 | £5 |

## DANISH SHARKS

| | | | | | |
|---|---|---|---|---|---|
| Ready Steady Go | LP | Ariola | TD209 | 196– £6 | £15 *German* |

## DANKWORTH, JOHNNY

| | | | | | | |
|---|---|---|---|---|---|---|
| African Waltz | 7" EP . | Columbia | SEG8137 | 1961 £2 | £5 | |
| Avengers | 7" | Columbia | DB4695 | 1961 £2.50 | £6 | |
| Avengers | 7" | Fontana | TF422 | 1963 £2.50 | £6 | |
| Criminal | 7" EP . | Columbia | SEG8037/ESG7825. | 1960 £2 | £5 | |
| Dankworth Workshop No. 1 | 7" EP . | Parlophone | GEP8653 | 1958 £2 | £5 | |
| Dankworth Workshop No. 2 | 7" EP . | Parlophone | GEP8697 | 1958 £2 | £5 | |
| Experiments With Mice | 7" | Parlophone | MSP6255 | 1956 £1.50 | £4 | |
| Five Steps To Dankworth | LP | Parlophone | PMC1043 | 1957 £8 | £20 | |
| Jazz Routes | LP | Columbia | 33SX1280/ SCX3347 | 1961 £6 | £15 | |
| London To Newport | LP | Top Rank | 25019 | 1960 £6 | £15 | |
| London To Newport | LP | Top Rank | 30019 | 1960 £5 | £12 | |
| Million Dollar Collection | LP | Fontana | TL5445 | 1968 £5 | £12 | |
| Modesty Blaise Theme | 7" | Fontana | TF700 | 1966 £1.50 | £4 | |
| Movies And Me | LP | Sepia | RSR1005 | 1974 £4 | £10 | |
| Vintage Years | LP | Parlophone | PMC1076 | 1959 £8 | £20 | |
| What The Dickens | LP | Fontana | TL/STL5203 | 1964 £5 | £12 | |
| Zodiac Variations | LP | Fontana | TL5229 | 1965 £5 | £12 | |

## DANLEERS

| | | | | | | |
|---|---|---|---|---|---|---|
| One Summer Night | 7" | Mercury | AMT1003 | 1958 £50 | £100 | |

## DANNY & THE JUNIORS

| | | | | | | |
|---|---|---|---|---|---|---|
| At The Hop | 7" | HMV | POP436 | 1958 £7.50 | £15 | |
| Back To The Hop | 7" | Top Rank | JAR587 | 1961 £2.50 | £6 | |
| Dottie | 7" | HMV | POP504 | 1958 £7.50 | £15 | |
| Oo-La-La-Limbo | 7" | London | HL9666 | 1963 £1.50 | £4 | |
| Pony Express | 7" | Top Rank | JAR552 | 1961 £2.50 | £6 | |
| Rock And Roll Is Here To Stay | 7" | HMV | POP467 | 1958 £12.50 | £25 | |
| Twisting All Night Long | 7" | Top Rank | JAR604 | 1962 £2 | £5 | |
| Twisting USA | 7" | Top Rank | JAR510 | 1960 £2.50 | £6 | |

## DANSE SOCIETY

| | | | | | | |
|---|---|---|---|---|---|---|
| 2000 Light Years From Home | 12" | Arista | SOCV127 | 1984 £3 | £8 | blue marble vinyl |
| Clock | 7" | North | SOC381 | 1981 £4 | £8 | |
| There Is No Shame In Death | 12" | Pax | PAX2 | 1981 £2.50 | £6 | |
| There Is No Shame In Death | 12" | Pax | PAX2 | 1981 £15 | £30 | blue vinyl |
| Woman's Own | 7" | Pax | PAX5 | 1982 £2.50 | £6 | |
| Woman's Own | 12" | Pax | PAX5 | 1982 £3 | £8 | |

## DANTALIAN'S CHARIOT

With the arrival of psychedelia, Zoot Money was able to indulge his penchant for on-stage flamboyance and, with the aid of his latest re-named version of the Big Roll Band, recorded one of the classic singles of the genre. The drummer, Colin Allen, subsequently played with John Mayall and Stone the Crows; bassist Pat Donaldson joined Fotheringay and has been a busy session musician ever since; while guitarist Andy Summers eventually found mega-stardom as a member of the Police.

| | | | | | | |
|---|---|---|---|---|---|---|
| Madman Running Through The Fields | 7" | Columbia | DB8260 | 1967 £25 | £50 | |

## DANTE, TROY & THE INFERNOS

| | | | | | | |
|---|---|---|---|---|---|---|
| This Little Girl | 7" | Fontana | TF477 | 1964 £2 | £5 | |

## DANTE & THE EVERGREENS

| | | | | | | |
|---|---|---|---|---|---|---|
| Alley Oop | 7" | Top Rank | JAR402 | 1960 £6 | £12 | |
| Dante & The Evergreens | LP | Madison | MA1002 | 1961 £75 | £150 | US |

## D'ARBY, TERENCE TRENT

| | | | | | | |
|---|---|---|---|---|---|---|
| Introducing The Hardline | CD | CBS | 4509119 | 1987 £5 | £12 | picture disc |
| Sign Your Name | CD-s | CBS | TRENTC4 | 1988 £2 | £5 | picture disc |

## DARIN, BOBBY

| | | | | | | |
|---|---|---|---|---|---|---|
| 25th Day Of December | 7" EP | London | REK1321 | 1961 £10 | £20 | |
| At The Copa | LP | London | HAK2291 | 1960 £6 | £15 | |
| At The Copa | LP | London | SAHK6103 | 1960 £10 | £25 | stereo |
| Be Mad Little Girl | 7" | Capitol | CL15328 | 1963 £1.50 | £4 | |
| Beachcomber | 7" | London | HLK9197 | 1960 £1.50 | £4 | |
| Best Of Bobby Darin | LP | Capitol | T2571 | 1966 £4 | £10 | |
| Bobby Darin | LP | London | HAE2140 | 1958 £20 | £40 | |
| Bobby Darin | LP | Motown | M753L | 1972 £4 | £10 | US |
| Bobby Darin | 7" EP | London | REE1173 | 1959 £15 | £30 | |
| Bobby Darin No. 2 | 7" EP | London | REE1225 | 1959 £12.50 | £25 | |
| Born Robert Walden Cassotto | LP | Bell | MBLL/SBLL112 | 1969 £4 | £10 | |
| Commitment | LP | Bell | SBLL128 | 1970 £4 | £10 | |
| Dream Lover | 7" | London | HLE8867 | 1959 £1.50 | £4 | |
| Early in The Morning | 7" | London | HLE8679 | 1958 £20 | £40 | |
| Earthy | LP | Capitol | T1826 | 1963 £6 | £15 | |
| Eighteen Yellow Roses | LP | Capitol | ST1942 | 1963 £6 | £15 | stereo |
| Eighteen Yellow Roses | LP | Capitol | T1942 | 1963 £6 | £15 | |
| For Teenagers Only | LP | London | HAK2311 | 1960 £8 | £20 | |
| For Teenagers Only | 7" EP | London | REK1286 | 1961 £10 | £20 | |
| From Hello Dolly To Goodbye Charlie | LP | Capitol | T2194 | 1964 £4 | £10 | |
| Golden Folk Hits | LP | Capitol | ST2007 | 1964 £8 | £20 | stereo |
| Golden Folk Hits | LP | Capitol | T2007 | 1964 £6 | £15 | |
| Hear Them Bells | 7" | Brunswick | 05831 | 1960 £2.50 | £6 | |
| I Wanna Be Around | LP | Capitol | T2322 | 1965 £5 | £12 | |
| If I Were A Carpenter | LP | Atlantic | 587/588051 | 1966 £4 | £10 | |

| | | | | | | | |
|---|---|---|---|---|---|---|---|
| In A Broadway Bag | LP | Atlantic | 587/588020 | 1966 £5 | £12 | |
| Inside Out | LP | Atlantic | 587076 | 1967 £5 | £12 | |
| It's You Or No One | LP | London | HAK8102 | 1963 £6 | £15 | |
| It's You Or No One | LP | London | SHK8102 | 1963 £8 | £20 | stereo |
| Keep A Walking | 7" | London | HLK9663 | 1963 £1.50 | £4 | |
| Lost Love | 7" | London | HL7060 | 1958 £5 | £10 | export |
| Love Swings | LP | London | HAK2394 | 1961 £6 | £15 | mono |
| Love Swings | LP | London | SAHK6194 | 1961 £8 | £20 | stereo |
| Love Swings | 7" EP | London | REK1334 | 1961 £5 | £10 | |
| Mack The Knife | 7" | London | HLE8939 | 1959 £1.50 | £4 | |
| Mighty Mighty Man | 7" | London | HLE8793 | 1959 £12.50 | £25 | |
| Milord | 7" EP | Atlantic | AET6013 | 1965 £4 | £8 | |
| Milord | 7" | Atlantic | AT4002 | 1964 £1.50 | £4 | |
| Oh Look At Me Now | LP | Capitol | T1791 | 1962 £6 | £15 | |
| Plain Jane | 7" | London | HL7078 | 1959 £5 | £10 | export |
| Plain Jane | 7" | London | HLE8815 | 1959 £10 | £20 | |
| Queen Of The Hop | 7" | London | HLE8737 | 1958 £10 | £20 | |
| Rock Island Line | 7" | Brunswick | 05561 | 1956 £30 | £60 | |
| Shadow Of Your Smile | LP | Atlantic | 587/588014 | 1966 £5 | £12 | |
| Sings Dr. Doolittle | LP | Atlantic | 587089 | 1968 £4 | £10 | |
| Sings Ray Charles | LP | London | HAK2456 | 1962 £6 | £15 | |
| Sings Ray Charles | LP | London | SAHK6243 | 1962 £8 | £20 | stereo |
| Something Special | LP | Atlantic | 587073 | 1967 £8 | £20 | |
| Splish Splash | 7" | London | HLE8666 | 1958 £10 | £20 | |
| Story | LP | Atlantic | 587065 | 1967 £5 | £12 | |
| Story | LP | London | HAK2372 | 1961 £8 | £20 | |
| That's All | LP | London | HAE2172 | 1959 £8 | £20 | |
| That's All | 7" EP | London | REK1243 | 1960 £7.50 | £15 | |
| Theme From Come September | 7" | London | HLK9407 | 1961 £1.50 | £4 | |
| Things | 7" EP | London | REK1342 | 1962 £5 | £10 | |
| Things | 7" | London | HLK9575 | 1962 £1.50 | £4 | |
| Things And Other Things | LP | London | HAK8030 | 1962 £6 | £15 | |
| This Is Bobby Darin | LP | London | HAK2235 | 1959 £6 | £15 | |
| This Is Bobby Darin | LP | London | SAHK6067 | 1960 £10 | £25 | stereo |
| Twist With Bobby Darin | 7" EP | London | REK1338 | 1962 £5 | £10 | |
| Two Of A Kind | LP | London | HAK2363 | 1961 £6 | £15 | ... with Johnny Mercer |
| Two Of A Kind | LP | London | SAHK6164 | 1961 £8 | £20 | .. with Johnny Mercer, stereo |
| Two Of A Kind | 7" EP | London | REK1310 | 1961 £5 | £10 | ... with Johnny Mercer |
| Up A Lazy River | 7" EP | London | REK1290 | 1961 £5 | £10 | |
| We Didn't Ask To Be Brought Here | 7" | Atlantic | AT4046 | 1965 £1.50 | £4 | |
| Winners | LP | Atlantic | ATL5014 | 1965 £5 | £12 | |

## DARIUS

| | | | | | | | |
|---|---|---|---|---|---|---|---|
| Darius | LP | Chartmaker | 1102 | 1968 £50 | £100 | US |

## DARK

The high value attaching to privately pressed progressive albums by groups like the Dark, Forever Amber and Complex depends in part on the mystique woven around them by collectors and dealers alike. The records are certainly rare and when so few people have actually heard them, it is difficult to gainsay claims that they are masterpieces. Now these records are being reissued, but in tiny limited editions and at prices that are often themselves well into the realm of serious collecting. Thus the mystique continues. Original copies of the Dark album exist in four different forms. The first ten or twelve copies came in a colour gatefold sleeve; the next edition of around thirty copies had a black and white gatefold sleeve; and a final run of about thirty-five copies had a black and white single sleeve. Meanwhile, just one eight-track cartridge was made for a friend who wanted it to play in his car! The record's status as the most valuable of the private pressings is supported by the fact that it is actually a very decent set of progressive hard rock performances – certainly at least as good as many records of the period that were issued by major record companies. Encouraged by the publicity surrounding their rare private pressing, the Dark reformed in 1994 and recorded *Anonymous Days*, a long-delayed follow-up that does the legend no harm at all.

| | | | | | | |
|---|---|---|---|---|---|---|
| Round The Edges | LP | Darkside | 001 | 1991 £10 | £25 | |
| Round The Edges | LP | S.I.S. | SR0102S | 1972 £875 | £1250 | |

## DARK (2)

| | | | | | | |
|---|---|---|---|---|---|---|
| Living End | LP | Fallout | FALLLP005 | 1982 £4 | £10 | |

## DARK STAR

| | | | | | | |
|---|---|---|---|---|---|---|
| Lady Of Mars | 12" | Avatar | AAA105 | 1981 £3 | £8 | |

## DARKSIDE

| | | | | | | |
|---|---|---|---|---|---|---|
| Waiting For The Angels | CD-s | Situation 2 | SIT72CD | 1990 £2 | £5 | |

## DARLING BUDS

| | | | | | | |
|---|---|---|---|---|---|---|
| Burst | CD-s | Epic | BLONDC1 | 1988 £2 | £5 | |
| Hit The Ground | CD-s | Epic | BLONDC2 | 1988 £2 | £5 | |
| If I Said | 7" | Darling Buds | DAR1 | 1987 £5 | £10 | |
| Let's Go Round There | CD-s | Epic | BLONDC3 | 1989 £2 | £5 | |
| You've Gotta Choose | CD-s | Epic | BLONDC4 | 1989 £2 | £5 | |

## DARNELL, BILL

| | | | | | | |
|---|---|---|---|---|---|---|
| Guilty Lips | 7" | London | HLU8267 | 1956 £10 | £20 | |
| Last Frontier | 7" | London | HLU8234 | 1956 £10 | £20 | |
| My Little Mother | 7" | London | HLU8204 | 1955 £10 | £20 | |
| Tell Me More | 7" | London | HLU8292 | 1956 £10 | £20 | |

## DARRELL, GUY

| | | | | | | |
|---|---|---|---|---|---|---|
| Evil Woman | 7" | Piccadilly | 7N35406 | 1967 £7.50 | £15 | |
| Go Home Girl | 7" | Oriole | CB1932 | 1964 £1.50 | £4 | |
| Guy Darrell | LP | CBS | 53364 | 196– £4 | £10 | |

| | | | | | | |
|---|---|---|---|---|---|---|
| I've Been Hurt | 7" | CBS | 202082 | 1966 £4 | £8 | |
| Sorry | 7" | Oriole | CB1964 | 1964 £1.50 | £4 | |

## DARREN, JAMES
| | | | | | | |
|---|---|---|---|---|---|---|
| Album No. 1 | LP | Colpix | CP406 | 1960 £5 | £12 | US |
| All | LP | Warner Bros | WS1688 | 1967 £5 | £12 | US |
| Angel Face | 7" | Pye | 7N25034 | 1959 £1.50 | £4 | |
| Gidget | 7" | Pye | 7N25019 | 1959 £1.50 | £4 | |
| James Darren Hit Parade | 7" EP | Pye | NEP44008 | 1962 £5 | £10 | |
| Love Among The Young | LP | Pye | NPL28021 | 1963 £5 | £12 | |
| P.S. I Love You | 7" EP | Pye | NEP44004 | 1959 £4 | £8 | |
| Sings For All Sizes | LP | Colpix | CP424 | 1962 £5 | £12 | US |
| Sings The Movies | LP | Colpix | CP418 | 1961 £5 | £12 | US |

## DARTELLS
| | | | | | | |
|---|---|---|---|---|---|---|
| Dartell Stomp | 7" | London | HLD9719 | 1963 £4 | £8 | |
| Hot Pastrami | LP | Dot | DLP3522/25522 | 1963 £6 | £15 | US |

## DARTS
| | | | | | | |
|---|---|---|---|---|---|---|
| Hollywood Drag | LP | Del-Fi | DF(ST)1244 | 1963 £5 | £12 | US |

## DARVELL, BARRY
| | | | | | | |
|---|---|---|---|---|---|---|
| How Will It End | 7" | London | HL9191 | 1960 £15 | £30 | |

## DARWIN'S THEORY
| | | | | | | |
|---|---|---|---|---|---|---|
| Daytime | 7" | Major Minor | MM503 | 1967 £10 | £20 | |

## DAS FENSTER
| | | | | | | |
|---|---|---|---|---|---|---|
| Doch Wir | LP | BASF | | 1970 £25 | £50 | German |

## DASGUPTA, NATAI
| | | | | | | |
|---|---|---|---|---|---|---|
| Songs Of India | LP | Mushroom | 100MR22 | 1972 £8 | £20 | |

## DATE WITH SOUL
This single is a reissue of one originally credited to Hale and the Hushabyes.

| | | | | | | |
|---|---|---|---|---|---|---|
| Yes Sir That's My Baby | 7" | Stateside | SS2062 | 1967 £10 | £20 | |

## DAUGHTERS OF THE ALBION
| | | | | | | |
|---|---|---|---|---|---|---|
| Daughters Of The Albion | LP | Fontana | STL5486 | 1968 £6 | £15 | |

## DAUNER, WOLFGANG
| | | | | | | |
|---|---|---|---|---|---|---|
| Et Cetera | LP | Intercord | 26001 | 1971 £5 | £12 | German |
| Et Cetera Live | LP | MPS | 2921754 | 1973 £5 | £12 | German double |
| Khirsh | LP | MPS | 2121432 | 1972 £5 | £12 | German |
| Output | LP | ECM | ECM1006ST | 1971 £8 | £20 | |
| Rischkas Soul | LP | Brain | 1016 | 1972 £5 | £12 | German |

## DAVANI, DAVE
| | | | | | | |
|---|---|---|---|---|---|---|
| Don't Fool Around | 7" | Columbia | DB7125 | 1963 £2 | £5 | |
| Four Faced | LP | Parlophone | | 1962 £10 | £25 | |
| Fused | LP | Parlophone | PMC1258 | 1965 £8 | £20 | |
| Midnight Special | 7" | Decca | F11896 | 1964 £2.50 | £6 | |
| One Track Mind | 7" | Parlophone | R5525 | 1966 £5 | £10 | |
| Top Of The Pops | 7" | Parlophone | R5329 | 1965 £4 | £8 | |
| Tossin' And Turnin' | 7" | Parlophone | R5490 | 1966 £4 | £8 | |

## DAVE & THE DIAMONDS
| | | | | | | |
|---|---|---|---|---|---|---|
| I Walk The Lonely Night | 7" | Columbia | DB7692 | 1965 £2 | £5 | |

## DAVE DEE, DOZY, BEAKY, MICK & TICH
| | | | | | | |
|---|---|---|---|---|---|---|
| All I Want | 7" | Fontana | TF586 | 1965 £4 | £8 | |
| Bend It | 7" EP | Fontana | 465324 | 1966 £4 | £8 | French |
| Dave Dee,Dozy,Beaky,Mick & Tich | LP | Fontana | (S)TL5350 | 1966 £4 | £10 | |
| DDDBMT | LP | Fontana | SFL13002 | 1968 £4 | £10 | |
| Golden Hits | LP | Fontana | (S)TL5441 | 1967 £4 | £10 | |
| Hideaway | 7" EP | Fontana | 465312 | 1966 £4 | £8 | French |
| If Music Be The Food Of Love | LP | Fontana | (S)TL5388 | 1966 £4 | £10 | |
| If No One Sang | LP | Fontana | (S)TL5471 | 1968 £4 | £10 | |
| Legend Of | LP | Fontana | SFL13063 | 1969 £4 | £10 | |
| Loos Of England | 7" EP | Fontana | TE17488 | 1967 £2.50 | £6 | |
| No Time | 7" | Fontana | TF531 | 1965 £5 | £10 | |
| Save Me | 7" EP | Fontana | 465349 | 1966 £4 | £8 | French |
| Together | LP | Fontana | SFL13173 | 1969 £4 | £10 | |
| Touch Me Touch Me | 7" EP | Fontana | 465372 | 1966 £4 | £8 | French |
| You Make It Move | 7" | Fontana | TF630 | 1965 £1.50 | £4 | |

## DAVENPORT, BOB
| | | | | | | |
|---|---|---|---|---|---|---|
| And The Marsden Rattlers | LP | Trailer | LER3008 | 1971 £10 | £25 | |
| Bob Davenport And The Rakes | LP | Columbia | SX1786 | 1965 £10 | £25 | |
| Bob Davenport And The Rakes | LP | Topic | 12TS350 | 1977 £4 | £10 | |
| Down The Long Road | LP | Topic | 12TS274 | 1975 £5 | £12 | |
| Geordie Songs | 7" EP | Collector | JEB4 | 1959 £5 | £10 | |
| Postcards Home | LP | Topic | 12TS318 | 1977 £4 | £10 | |

## DAVEY & MORRIS
| | | | | | | |
|---|---|---|---|---|---|---|
| Davey & Morris | LP | York | FYK417 | 1973 £10 | £25 | |

## DAVEY & THE BADMEN
Wanted .................................................. LP ...... KRW ............. WA63054.................... £15.........£30 ...................... US

## DAVID
Another Day, Another Lifetime ................ LP ..... Vance Music    VS124................... 1967 £37.50....£75 ...................... US
                                                                Co. ................

## DAVID (2)
Please Mr. Postman ............................... 7" ...... Philips............. BF1776 ................. 1969 £10.........£20

## DAVID & JONATHAN
David & Jonathan ...................................... LP ..... Columbia ........ SX/SCX6031 ........ 1967 £5.........£12
Lovers Of The World Unite ................. 7" EP . Columbia ........ ESRF1807.......... 1966 £5.........£10 ......................French
Ten Storeys High ............................... 7" ...... Columbia ........ DB8035 ............. 1966 £1.50.......£4

## DAVID & ROZAA
Spark That Lights The Flame.................... 7" ...... Philips............ 6006094 ............. 1971 £4.........£8
Time Of Our Life ................................ 7" ...... Philips............ 6006040 ............. 1970 £4.........£8

## DAVIDSON, DIANE
Sympathy ............................................. 7" ...... Janus............... no number ............ 1972 £4.........£8 demo, 2 tracks by other
                                                                                                                                    artists

## DAVIDSON, FRANKIE & THE HI MARKS
You're Driving Me Crazy ........................ 7" ...... Starlite ............ ST45037 ............. 1961 £5.........£10

## DAVIDSON, TOMMY
Half Past Kissing Time ......................... 7" ...... London ........... HLU8219 ............. 1956 £12.50....£25

## DAVIE, HUTCH & HIS HONKY TONKERS
At The Woodchoppers' Ball ...................... 7" ...... London ........... HLE8667 ............. 1958 £2.50.......£6

## DAVIES, BOB
Rock And Roll Show ............................ 7" ...... London ........... HLU9767 ............. 1963 £7.50....£15

## DAVIES, CYRIL
Country Line Special................................ 7" ...... Pye...... 7N17663 ............. 1969 £2.50.......£6
Country Line Special................................ 7" ...... Pye...... 7N25194 ............. 1963 £6.........£12
Legendary Cyril Davies ............................. LP ..... Folklore ...... FLEUT9 ............. 1970 £25.......£50
Legendary Cyril Davies ......................... 10" LP 77...... LP2 ............. 1957 £150.....£250
Preaching The Blues ............................ 7" ...... Pye...... 7N25221 ............. 1963 £6.........£12
Sound Of Davies .................................. 7" EP . Pye...... NEP44025 ............. 1964 £20.......£40

## DAVIES, DAVE
Dave Davies Hits...................................... 7" EP . Pye...... NEP24289.......... 1968 £180.....£300 .........best auctioned
Death Of A Clown.................................... 7" EP . Pye...... PNV24196 ......... 1967 £15.........£30 . French, B side by the
                                                                                                                                    Kinks
Death Of A Clown .............................. 7" ...... Pye...... 7N17356 ............. 1967 £1.50.......£4
Hold My Hand .................................... 7" ...... Pye...... 7N17678 ............. 1969 £2.50.......£6
Lincoln County .................................... 7" ...... Pye...... 7N17514 ............. 1968 £2.50.......£6
Susannah's Still Alive ........................ 7" ...... Pye...... 7N17429 ............. 1967 £1.50.......£4

## DAVIES, MIAR
I Hear You Knocking................................ 7" ...... Decca ............ F11894.............. 1964 £1.50.......£4

## DAVIS, BARRINGTON
Tracks Of Mind ................................. LP ..... Montague........ MONS2................ 1972 £100.....£200

## DAVIS, BETTE & DEBBIE BURTON
Whatever Happened To Baby Jane ............ 7" ...... London ........... HLU9711.............. 1963 £1.50.......£4

## DAVIS, BETTY
Betty Davis............................................. LP ..... Just Sunshine ... JSS5 ................... 1973 £6.........£15 ...................... US
Nasty Gal................................................ LP ..... Island ............. ILPS9329 ........... 1975 £5.........£12
They Say I'm Different ......................... LP ..... Polydor........... 2933402 ............. 1974 £5.........£12

## DAVIS, BILLIE
Angel Of The Morning............................. 7" ...... Decca ............ F12696.............. 1967 £1.50.......£4
Billie Davis............................................. LP ..... Decca ............ SKL5029 ............ 1970 £8.........£20
Heart And Soul....................................... 7" ...... Piccadilly ....... 7N35308 ............. 1966 £1.50.......£4
Can Remember ...................................... 7" ...... Decca ............ F12923.............. 1969 £2.........£5
Just Walk In My Shoes............................ 7" ...... Piccadilly ....... 7N35350 ............. 1966 £4.........£8
Say Nothing........................................... 7" ...... Columbia ........ DB7195 ............. 1964 £1.50.......£4
School Is Over ....................................... 7" ...... Columbia ........ DB7246 ............. 1964 £1.50.......£4
Tell Him ............................................... 7" ...... Decca ............ F11572............... 1963 £1.50.......£4
Wasn't It You ....................................... 7" ...... Decca ............ F12620.............. 1967 £1.50.......£4
Whatcha Gonna Do................................. 7" ...... Columbia ........ DB7346 ............. 1964 £1.50.......£4
You And I .............................................. 7" ...... Columbia ........ DB7115 ............. 1963 £1.50.......£4

## DAVIS, BOBBY
Hype You Into Selling Your Head............. 7" ...... Starlite ............ ST45056 ............. 1961 £10.........£20

## DAVIS, BONNIE
Pepperhot Baby....................................... 7" ...... Brunswick ....... 05507................. 1955 £10.........£20

## DAVIS, CLIFFORD
Before the Beginning................................ 7" ...... Reprise ............ RS27003 ............. 1969 £1.50.......£4

## DAVIS, DANNY
Rome Wasn't Built In A Day .................... 7" ...... Pye ................ 7N15427 ................ 1962 £1.50.....£4 ................

## DAVIS, DANNY ORCHESTRA
Main Theme From The Saint .................... 7" ...... MGM ............ MGM1277 ............ 1965 £1.50........£4 ................

## DAVIS, EDDIE 'LOCKJAW'
| | | | | | | |
|---|---|---|---|---|---|---|
| Count Basie Presents The Eddie Davis Trio | LP ..... | Columbia ....... | 33SX1117 | 1959 | £6 | £15 |
| Eddie 'Lockjaw' Davis Cookbook ........... | LP ..... | Esquire ........ | 32104 | 1960 | £6 | £15 |
| Eddie Lockjaw Davis ........................... | 7" EP . | Esquire ........ | EP217 | 1959 | £2 | £5 |
| Eddie Lockjaw Davis Quartet ............... | 7" EP . | Esquire ........ | EP237 | 1961 | £2 | £5 |
| Eddie Lockjaw Davis Trio ................... | 7" EP . | Parlophone .... | GEP8587 | 1956 | £2 | £5 |
| Eddie Lockjaw Davis Trio ................... | 7" EP . | Parlophone .... | GEP8685 | 1958 | £2 | £5 |
| First Set (Live At Minton's) ............... | LP ..... | Stateside ....... | SL10102 | 1964 | £6 | £15 |
| Jaws In Orbit .................................... | LP ..... | Esquire ........ | 32128 | 1961 | £6 | £15 |
| Lockjaw ........................................... | 7" EP . | Parlophone .... | GEP8678 | 1957 | £2 | £5 |
| Very Saxy ........................................ | LP ..... | Esquire ........ | 32117 | 1960 | £6 | £15 |

## DAVIS, JACKIE
Land Of Make Believe ............................. 7" ...... Pye ............... .................... 196– £5...........£10 ................

## DAVIS, JIMMY
Maxwell Street Jimmy Davis .................... LP ...... Bounty........... BY6009.................... 1966 £5.........£12 ................

## DAVIS, KIM
Don't Take Your Lovin' Away ................. 7" ...... Decca ....... F12387 .............. 1966 £5.........£10 ................
Tell It Like It Is ................................. 7" ...... CBS.............. 202568.................... 1967 £2...........£5 ................

## DAVIS, LARRY & FENTON ROBINSON
Larry Davis And Fenton Robinson............. LP ...... Python........... PLP24.................. 1972 £8...........£20 ................

## DAVIS, MELVIN
Save It.............................................. 7" ...... Action............. ACT4531.............. 1969 £5..........£10 ................

## DAVIS, MILES

The changing styles of jazz presented by Miles Davis during his four-and-a-half-decade career give his many fans a uniquely varied listening experience if they follow it all through. During the forties, Davis was a member of Charlie Parker's crucially important quintet, helping to invent the modern jazz music called bebop. Through the fifties, leading his own groups, Miles Davis began by developing the cool jazz style (*Birth Of The Cool*). The formation of his first permanent line-up – a quintet with saxophonist John Coltrane – sparked a lucrative recording deal with CBS. The four albums still owed to Prestige were dashed off in just two sessions, yet such was the level of inspiration in the quintet, that these four – *Cookin'*, *Relaxin'*, *Workin'* and *Steamin'* – emerged as the definitive hard bop recordings. The big band albums made with Gil Evans (notably *Miles Ahead*, *Porgy And Bess* and *Sketches Of Spain*) set new standards in harmonic and textural invention, while the sextet recording with John Coltrane and Cannonball Adderley (*Kind Of Blue*) pioneered a new, modal approach to improvisation. The live recordings of the early sixties (particularly *My Funny Valentine* and *Four And More*) stretched the concept of improvising around jazz standards as far as it could go. Then the formation of the second great Miles Davis quintet, with Wayne Shorter and Herbie Hancock, spurred a succession of magisterial albums (*Miles Smiles*, *ESP*, and their successors) that define a free jazz alternative to the jagged music of Ornette Coleman and Cecil Taylor – free, yet still clearly melodic. From the late sixties until a serious car crash put a temporary halt to his career in 1975, Miles Davis maintained a remarkable creative run in which he not only invented the fusion genre, but also began to explore most of the possibilities inherent in it. He released an unusually large number of records during this period, and every one is different. Of the rarities listed here, the quadrophonic mix of *Bitches Brew* is significantly different from the stereo, with extra percussion and a frequent doubling-up of melodic phrases to create an echo effect. The Japanese double albums are all live recordings – *Black Beauty*, with Chick Corea, Jack DeJohnette and Steve Grossman, is close to the jazz avant-garde in places; *Dark Magus* is a densely rhythmic work-out from a 1974 Carnegie Hall concert; while *Pangaea* is a companion set to the UK release *Agharta* – the second set from the same evening's performance. It is magnificent, powerful music, though not for the faint-hearted. The Session Disc LP, a poorly recorded set from 1971, would qualify as a bootleg if it was a rock album – in the jazz world, however, such live recordings have always been accepted as part of the natural scheme of things.

| | | | | | | | |
|---|---|---|---|---|---|---|---|
| Back To Back .............................. | LP ...... | Fontana........... | FJL135 | 1966 | £4 | £10 | ..side 2 by Art Blakey |
| Bags' Groove ............................... | LP ...... | Esquire........... | 32090 | 1959 | £10 | £25 | |
| Birth Of The Cool ........................ | LP ...... | Capitol............ | T1974 | 1966 | £5 | £12 | |
| Birth Of The Cool ........................ | LP ...... | Capitol............ | T762 | 1957 | £20 | £40 | |
| Bitches Brew ............................... | LP ...... | CBS................. | 66236 | 1970 | £5 | £12 | double |
| Bitches Brew ............................... | LP ...... | CBS................. | QBL30998/9 | 1971 | £10 | £25 | quad double |
| Black Beauty ............................... | LP ...... | CBS-Sony ....... | SOPJ39/40 | 1973 | £10 | £25 | Japanese double |
| Blue Changes ............................... | 7" EP . | Esquire............ | EP242 | 1961 | £2 | £5 | |
| Blue Haze ................................... | LP ...... | Esquire............ | 32088 | 1960 | £15 | £30 | |
| Blue Miles .................................. | 7" EP . | Esquire............ | EP232 | 1960 | £2 | £5 | |
| Blue Moods ................................ | LP ...... | Vocalion .......... | LAEF584 | 1964 | £8 | £20 | |
| Changes ...................................... | LP ...... | Esquire............ | 32028 | 1957 | £10 | £25 | |
| Classics In Jazz ........................... | 10" LP | Capitol............ | LC6683 | 1954 | £15 | £30 | |
| Collectors' Item ........................... | LP ...... | Esquire............ | 32030 | 1957 | £20 | £40 | |
| Cookin'....................................... | LP ...... | Esquire............ | 32048 | 1958 | £10 | £25 | |
| Dark Magus ................................ | LP ...... | CBS-Sony ....... | 40AP741/2 | 1977 | £10 | £25 | Japanese double |
| Davis Cup ................................... | 7" EP . | Philips............. | BBE12418 | 1961 | £2 | £5 | |
| Dig............................................. | 10" LP | Esquire............ | 20017 | 1953 | £15 | £30 | |
| E.S.P.......................................... | LP ...... | CBS................. | (S)BPG62577 | 1966 | £5 | £12 | |
| Early Miles ................................. | LP ...... | Esquire............ | 32118 | 1961 | £10 | £25 | |
| Essential Miles Davis .................... | LP ...... | CBS................. | 66310 | 1973 | £20 | £40 | 3 LP boxed set, bonus single |
| Ezz-thetic.................................. | LP ...... | XTRA............... | XTRA5004 | 1966 | £5 | £12 | ..with Lee Konitz, B side by Teddy Charles |
| Filles De Kilimanjaro ................... | LP ...... | CBS................. | 63551 | 1969 | £4 | £10 | |
| Four And More ............................ | LP ...... | CBS................. | (S)BPG62655 | 1966 | £5 | £12 | |
| Friday Night At The Blackhawk ..... | LP ...... | CBS................. | (S)BPG62306 | 1964 | £5 | £12 | |
| Friday Night At The Blackhawk ..... | LP ...... | Fontana........... | TFL5163/STFL580 | 1961 | £8 | £20 | |
| HiFi Modern Jazz Jam Session ..... | 10" LP | Esquire............ | 20052 | 1955 | £15 | £30 | |

| Title | Format | Label | Catalogue | Year | | | Notes |
|---|---|---|---|---|---|---|---|
| Hooray For Miles Davis | LP | Session Disc | 123 | 1972 | £6 | £15 | |
| In A Silent Way | LP | CBS | 63630 | 1970 | £4 | £10 | |
| Isle Of Wight | LP | CBS | 4504721 | 1987 | £6 | £15 | French |
| Jazz Track | LP | Fontana | TFL5081 | 1960 | £10 | £25 | |
| Kind Of Blue | LP | CBS | (S)BPG62066 | 1966 | £4 | £10 | |
| Kind Of Blue | LP | Fontana | TFL5072/STFL513 | 1960 | £8 | £20 | |
| Live/Evil | LP | CBS | QBL30954 | 1973 | £6 | £15 | quad double |
| Miles Ahead | LP | CBS | (S)BPG62496 | 1966 | £4 | £10 | |
| Miles Ahead | LP | Fontana | TFL5007 | 1957 | £10 | £25 | |
| Miles And Monk At Newport | LP | CBS | (S)BPG62389 | 1964 | £6 | £15 | with Thelonious Monk |
| Miles Davis | LP | Esquire | 32021 | 1957 | £20 | £40 | |
| Miles Davis | 7" EP | Esquire | EP152 | 1957 | £2 | £5 | |
| Miles Davis | 7" EP | Fontana | TFE17119 | 1959 | £2 | £5 | |
| Miles Davis | 7" EP | Philips | BBE12266 | 1959 | £2 | £5 | |
| Miles Davis | 7" EP | Philips | BBE12351 | 1960 | £2 | £5 | |
| Miles Davis | 7" EP | Vogue | EPV1191 | 1958 | £2 | £5 | |
| Miles Davis All Stars | 10" LP | Esquire | 20021 | 1953 | £15 | £30 | |
| Miles Davis All Stars | 10" LP | Vogue | LDE028 | 1953 | £25 | £50 | |
| Miles Davis All Stars Sextet | 10" LP | Esquire | 20062 | 1956 | £15 | £30 | |
| Miles Davis And His Orchestra | 10" LP | Vogue | LDE064 | 1954 | £15 | £30 | |
| Miles Davis And John Coltrane Play Richard Rogers | LP | Pacific Jazz | 688204ZL | 1965 | £6 | £15 | |
| Miles Davis And John Coltrane Play Richard Rogers | LP | Stateside | SL10111 | 1965 | £6 | £15 | |
| Miles Davis And John Coltrane Play Richard Rogers | LP | Transatlantic | PR7322 | 1968 | £5 | £12 | |
| Miles Davis And The Modern Jazz Giants | LP | Esquire | 32100 | 1960 | £10 | £25 | |
| Miles Davis At Carnegie Hall | LP | CBS | (S)BPG62081 | 1962 | £6 | £15 | |
| Miles Davis In Europe | LP | CBS | (S)BPG62390 | 1964 | £6 | £15 | |
| Miles Davis New Quartet | 7" EP | Esquire | EP212 | 1959 | £2 | £5 | |
| Miles Davis No. 2 | 7" EP | Fontana | TFE17223 | 1960 | £2 | £5 | |
| Miles Davis No. 3 | 7" EP | Fontana | TFE17225 | 1960 | £2 | £5 | |
| Miles Davis Orchestra | 7" EP | Capitol | EAP1459 | 1954 | £2 | £5 | |
| Miles Davis Orchestra | 7" EP | Capitol | EAP2459 | 1954 | £2 | £5 | |
| Miles Davis Plays For Lovers | LP | Stateside | SL10168 | 1966 | £6 | £15 | |
| Miles Davis Quartet | 7" EP | Esquire | EP12 | 195– | £2 | £5 | |
| Miles Davis Quartet | 7" EP | Esquire | EP132 | 1957 | £2 | £5 | |
| Miles Davis Quartet | 7" EP | Esquire | EP172 | 1958 | £2 | £5 | |
| Miles Davis Quartet | 7" EP | Fontana | TFE17359 | 1961 | £2 | £5 | |
| Miles Davis Quintet | 10" LP | Esquire | 20041 | 1955 | £15 | £30 | |
| Miles Davis Quintet | 10" LP | Esquire | 20072 | 1956 | £15 | £30 | |
| Miles Davis Sextet | 7" EP | Vogue | EPV1075 | 1956 | £2 | £5 | |
| Miles Davis Vol. 1 | LP | Blue Note | BLP/BST81501 | 1961 | £10 | £25 | |
| Miles Davis Vol. 2 | LP | Blue Note | BLP/BST81502 | 1964 | £10 | £25 | |
| Miles In The Sky | LP | CBS | 63352 | 1969 | £4 | £10 | |
| Miles Smiles | LP | CBS | (S)BPG62933 | 1967 | £5 | £12 | |
| Miles Theme | 7" EP | Esquire | EP222 | 1959 | £2 | £5 | |
| Milestones | LP | CBS | 62308 | 1967 | £4 | £10 | |
| Milestones | LP | Fontana | TFL5035 | 1958 | £8 | £20 | |
| Modern Jazz Giants | LP | Transatlantic | PR7150 | 1967 | £5 | £12 | |
| More Miles | 7" EP | Fontana | TFE17195 | 1959 | £2 | £5 | |
| Most Of Miles | LP | Fontana | TFL5089 | 1960 | £6 | £15 | |
| Musings Of Miles | LP | Esquire | 32012 | 1956 | £15 | £30 | |
| My Funny Valentine | LP | CBS | (S)BPG62510 | 1965 | £5 | £12 | |
| Nature Boy | 10" LP | Vogue | LDE191 | 1957 | £20 | £40 | |
| Nefertiti | LP | CBS | 63248 | 1968 | £4 | £10 | |
| Odyssey! | LP | XTRA | XTRA5050 | 1968 | £5 | £12 | |
| Pangaea | LP | CBS-Sony | 36AP1789/90 | 1975 | £10 | £25 | Japanese double |
| Porgy And Bess | LP | CBS | (S)BPG62108 | 1966 | £4 | £10 | |
| Porgy And Bess | LP | Fontana | TFL5056 | 1959 | £8 | £20 | |
| Porgy And Bess | 7" EP | Fontana | TFE17247 | 1960 | £2 | £5 | |
| Quiet Nights | LP | CBS | (S)BPG62213 | 1964 | £6 | £15 | |
| Relaxin' | LP | Esquire | 32068 | 1958 | £10 | £25 | |
| Round About Midnight | LP | Philips | BBL7140 | 1957 | £8 | £20 | |
| Saturday Night At The Blackhawk | LP | CBS | (S)BPG62307 | 1964 | £5 | £12 | |
| Saturday Night At The Blackhawk | LP | Fontana | TFL5164/STFL581 | 1961 | £8 | £20 | |
| Second HiFi Modern Jazz Jam Session | 10" LP | Esquire | 20056 | 1955 | £15 | £30 | |
| Seven Steps To Heaven | LP | CBS | (S)BPG62170 | 1964 | £6 | £15 | |
| Sketches Of Spain | LP | CBS | (S)BPG62327 | 1964 | £4 | £10 | |
| Sketches Of Spain | LP | Fontana | TFL5100/STFL531 | 1961 | £10 | £25 | |
| Someday My Prince Will Come | LP | CBS | (S)BPG62104 | 1966 | £4 | £10 | |
| Someday My Prince Will Come | LP | Fontana | TFL5172/STFL587 | 1962 | £8 | £20 | |
| Sorcerer | LP | CBS | 63097 | 1968 | £4 | £10 | |
| Steamin' With The Miles Davis Quintet | LP | Esquire | 32138 | 1961 | £10 | £25 | |
| Straight No Chaser | 7" EP | Fontana | TFE17197 | 1959 | £2 | £5 | |
| Walkin' | LP | Esquire | 32098 | 1960 | £10 | £25 | |
| Workin' With The Miles Davis Quintet | LP | Esquire | 32108 | 1960 | £10 | £25 | |

## DAVIS, REV. GARY

| Title | Format | Label | Catalogue | Year | | | Notes |
|---|---|---|---|---|---|---|---|
| Bring Your Money Honey | LP | Fontana | SFJL914 | 1969 | £4 | £10 | |
| Harlem Street Singer | LP | Fontana | 688303ZL | 1964 | £4 | £10 | |
| Little More Faith | LP | XTRA | XTRA5042 | 1968 | £6 | £15 | |
| Lo I Be With You Always | LP | Kicking Mule | SNKD1 | 1974 | £5 | £12 | double |
| Lord I Wish I Could See | LP | Biograph | BLP12034 | 1971 | £4 | £10 | US |
| Pure Religion And Bad Company | LP | 77 | LA1214 | 1963 | £6 | £15 | |
| Say No To The Devil | LP | XTRA | XTRA5014 | 1966 | £6 | £15 | |

## DAVIS, SAMMY JR.

| Title | Format | Label | Cat. No. | Year | | | Notes |
|---|---|---|---|---|---|---|---|
| All Of You | 7" | Brunswick | 05629 | 1956 | £1.50 | £4 | |
| Azure | 7" | Capitol | CL14562 | 1956 | £1.50 | £4 | |
| Because Of You | 7" | Brunswick | 05326 | 1954 | £1.50 | £4 | |
| Birth Of The Blues | 7" | Brunswick | 05383 | 1955 | £1.50 | £4 | |
| Hey There | 7" | Brunswick | 05469 | 1955 | £4 | £8 | |
| In A Persian Market | 7" | Brunswick | 05518 | 1956 | £1.50 | £4 | |
| Love Me Or Leave Me | 7" | Brunswick | 05428 | 1955 | £4 | £8 | |
| Not For Me | 7" | Reprise | R20289 | 1964 | £2 | £5 | |
| Six Bridges To Cross | 7" | Brunswick | 05389 | 1955 | £1.50 | £4 | |
| That Old Black Magic | 7" | Brunswick | 05450 | 1955 | £4 | £8 | |

## DAVIS, SKEETER

| Title | Format | Label | Cat. No. | Year | | | Notes |
|---|---|---|---|---|---|---|---|
| Cloudy, With Occasional Tears | LP | RCA | RD/SF7604 | 1963 | £4 | £10 | |
| End Of The World | LP | RCA | RD/SF7563 | 1963 | £4 | £10 | |
| End Of The World | 7" | RCA | RCA1328 | 1963 | £1.50 | £4 | |
| Here's The Answer | LP | RCA | LPM2327 | 1961 | £5 | £12 | US |
| I Can't Stay Mad At You | 7" | RCA | RCA1363 | 1963 | £1.50 | £4 | |
| I'll Sing You A Song And Harmonize Too | LP | RCA | LPM2197 | 1960 | £5 | £12 | US |
| I'm Falling Too | 7" | RCA | RCA1201 | 1960 | £1.50 | £4 | |
| Let Me Get Close To You | LP | RCA | RD7676 | 1964 | £4 | £10 | |
| My Last Date With You | 7" | RCA | RCA1222 | 1961 | £1.50 | £4 | |
| Silver Threads And Golden Needles | 7" EP | RCA | RCX7153 | 1964 | £2.50 | £6 | |

## DAVIS, SKEETER & BOBBY BARE

| Title | Format | Label | Cat. No. | Year | | |
|---|---|---|---|---|---|---|
| Tunes For Two | LP | RCA | RD7711 | 1965 | £4 | £10 |

## DAVIS, SKEETER & PORTER WAGONER

| Title | Format | Label | Cat. No. | Year | | | Notes |
|---|---|---|---|---|---|---|---|
| Duets | LP | RCA | LPM/LSP2529 | 1962 | £5 | £12 | US |

## DAVIS, SPENCER GROUP

Spencer Davis had no dominant role within the group that bore his name, which is probably why his solo career in the seventies and eighties has been such a low-key affair. Originally, the Spencer Davis Group focused on its dynamic young singer, Stevie Winwood, who was also a talented guitarist and keyboard player. Winwood shines throughout the group's sturdy R&B material and in particular on the impressive series of singles, which includes some real classics. Remarkably, when Winwood left to form Traffic, Spencer Davis was able to find a replacement, Eddie Hardin, whose singing and keyboard playing was almost as fine. 'Time Seller' and 'Mr Second Class' are a worthy continuation of the singles series, being soulful performances tinged with psychedelia. They are included on the album *With Their New Face On*, which is itself a very under-rated recording.

| Title | Format | Label | Cat. No. | Year | | | Notes |
|---|---|---|---|---|---|---|---|
| After Tea | 7" | United Artists | UP2213 | 1968 | £1.50 | £4 | |
| Autumn 66 | LP | Fontana | STL5359 | 1966 | £10 | £25 | |
| Best Of The Spencer Davis Group | LP | Island | ILP970/ILPS9070 | 1968 | £8 | £20 | pink label |
| Dimples | 7" | Fontana | TF471 | 1964 | £2 | £5 | |
| Every Little Bit Hurts | 7" EP | Fontana | TE17450 | 1965 | £7.50 | £15 | |
| Every Little Bit Hurts | 7" | Fontana | TF530 | 1965 | £2 | £5 | |
| Gimme Some Lovin' | LP | United Artists | UAL3578/ UAS6578 | 1967 | £6 | £15 | US |
| Gimme Some Lovin' | 7" | Fontana | TF762 | 1966 | £1.50 | £4 | |
| Gimme Some Loving | 7" EP | Fontana | 465337 | 1966 | £10 | £20 | French |
| Hits Of The Spencer Davis Group | cass-s | Philips | MCF5003 | 1968 | £3 | £8 | |
| I Can't Stand It | 7" | Fontana | TF499 | 1964 | £2 | £5 | |
| I'm A Man | LP | United Artists | UAL3589/ UAS6589 | 1967 | £6 | £15 | US |
| I'm A Man | 7" EP | Fontana | 465360 | 1966 | £10 | £20 | French |
| I'm A Man | 7" | Fontana | TF785 | 1967 | £1.50 | £4 | |
| Keep On Running | CD-s | Island | CID487 | 1991 | £2 | £5 | |
| Keep On Running | 7" EP | Fontana | 465297 | 1965 | £10 | £20 | French |
| Keep On Running | 7" | Fontana | TF632 | 1965 | £1.50 | £4 | |
| Letters From Edith | LP | CBS | 63842 | 1969 | £30 | £60 | test pressing |
| Mr. Second Class | 7" | United Artists | UP1203 | 1967 | £1.50 | £4 | |
| Second Album | LP | Fontana | TL5295 | 1966 | £10 | £25 | |
| Sitting And Thinking | 7" EP | Fontana | TE17463 | 1966 | £7.50 | £15 | |
| Somebody Help Me | 7" EP | Fontana | 465305 | 1966 | £10 | £20 | French |
| Somebody Help Me | 7" | Fontana | TF679 | 1966 | £1.50 | £4 | |
| Strong Love | 7" | Fontana | TF571 | 1965 | £1.50 | £4 | |
| Their First Album | LP | Fontana | TL5242 | 1965 | £10 | £25 | |
| Their First Album | LP | Wing | WL1165 | 1968 | £4 | £10 | |
| Time Seller | 7" | Fontana | TF854 | 1967 | £1.50 | £4 | |
| When I Come Home | 7" EP | Fontana | 465318 | 1966 | £10 | £20 | French |
| When I Come Home | 7" | Fontana | TF739 | 1966 | £1.50 | £4 | |
| With Their New Face On | LP | United Artists | SULP1192 | 1968 | £6 | £15 | |
| You Put The Hurt On Me | 7" EP | Fontana | TE17444 | 1965 | £7.50 | £15 | |

## DAVIS, SPENCER GROUP & TRAFFIC

| Title | Format | Label | Cat. No. | Year | | |
|---|---|---|---|---|---|---|
| Here We Go Round The Mulberry Bush | LP | United Artists | SULP1186 | 1968 | £6 | £15 |

## DAVIS, STEVE

| Title | Format | Label | Cat. No. | Year | | |
|---|---|---|---|---|---|---|
| Takes Time To Know Her | 7" | Fontana | TF922 | 1968 | £12.50 | £25 |

## DAVIS, TYRONE

| Title | Format | Label | Cat. No. | Year | | |
|---|---|---|---|---|---|---|
| Can I Change My Mind | 7" | Atlantic | 584253 | 1969 | £1.50 | £4 |
| Is It Something You've Got | 7" | Atlantic | 584265 | 1969 | £1.50 | £4 |
| Turn Back The Hands Of Time | LP | Atlantic | 2465021 | 1970 | £4 | £10 |
| Turn Back The Hands Of Time | 7" | Atlantic | 2091003 | 1970 | £1.50 | £4 |
| What If A Man | 7" | Stateside | SS2092 | 1968 | £2.50 | £6 |

## DAVIS, WALTER
RCA Victor Race Series Vol. 3 ................. 7" EP . RCA .............. RCX7169 .............. 1964 £4 ........ £8 ......................................

## DAVIS, WARREN MONDAY BAND
Love Is A Hurting Thing ........................ 7" ...... Columbia ........ DB8270 ............... 1967 £2 ............ £5 ......................................
Wait For Me ............................................. 7" ...... Columbia ........ DB8190 .............. 1967 £5 ............ £10 ......................................

## DAVIS, WILD BILL
Wild Bill Davis ........................................ 10" LP Philips ............. BBR8079 .............. 1956 £8 ........... £20 ......................................

## DAVIS SISTERS
Rock-a-bye Boogie ................................... 78 ...... HMV ............. B10582 ............... 1953 £5 ........... £10 ......................................

## DAVISON, BRIAN
Every Which Way ..................................... LP ...... Charisma ......... CAS1021 ............... 1970 £4 ........... £10 ......................................

## DAVISON, WILD BILL
Greatest Of The Greats ........................... LP ...... Vogue ............ LAE12217 ............... 1960 £4 ........... £10 ......................................
Wild BIll Davison .................................... LP ...... London ........... LTZU15068 ........... 1957 £5 ........... £12 ......................................
Wild Bill Davison Band ......................... 10" LP Melodisc ....... MLP501 ............... 1955 £8 ........... £20 ......................................
With Strings Attached ............................. LP ...... Philips ............ BBL7104 .............. 1957 £5 ........... £12 ......................................

## DAWE, TIM
Penrod ..................................................... LP ...... Straight ........... ST1058 .............. 1969 £6 ........... £15 ......................... US

## DAWKINS, CARL
All Of A Sudden .................................... 7" ...... Rio ............ R136 ............... 1967 £4 ........... £8 ......................................
Baby I Love You ..................................... 7" ...... Rio ............ R137 ............... 1967 £4 ........... £8 ......................................
Hot And Sticky ....................................... 7" ...... Rio ............ R138 ............... 1967 £4 ........... £8 ......... Rulers B side
I Love The Way You Are ........................ 7" ...... Blue Cat ....... BS114 ............... 1968 £4 ........... £8  Dermott Lynch B side
I'll Make It Up ....................................... 7" ...... Duke ........... DU3 ............... 1968 £2.50 ....... £6 ...J. J. Allstars B side
Rodney's History .................................... 7" ...... Nu Beat ......... NB030 ............... 1969 £1.50 ....... £4 ......Dynamites B side

## DAWKINS, HORELL
Butterfly ................................................. 7" ...... Ska Beat ........ JB240 ............... 1966 £5 ........... £10 ......................................

## DAWKINS, JIMMY
Fast Fingers ............................................ LP ...... Delmark ......... DS623 ............... 1971 £5 ........... £12 ......................................

## DAWKINS, RUSS & THE WAILERS
Picture On The Wall ............................... 7" ...... Upsetter ......... US368 ............... 1971 £5 ........... £10 ...... Upsetters B side

## DAWN, JULIE
Wild Horses ............................................. 7" ...... Columbia ........ SCM5035 ............... 1953 £1.50 ....... £4 ......................................

## DAWNWIND
Looking Back On The Future ................... LP ...... Amron .......... ARD5003 .............. 1976 £50 ........... £100 ......................................

## DAWSON, JULIET
Boo ......................................................... LP ...... Sovereign ............................ 1972 £20 ........... £40 ......................................

## DAWSON, LES SYNDICATE
Last Chicken In The Shop ........................ 7" ...... Melodisc ......... 1586 .............. 1964 £2 ........... £5 ......................................

## DAWSON, LESLEY
Just Say Goodbye ................................... 7" ...... Mercury .......... MF946 .............. 1967 £1.50 ....... £4 ......................................
Run For Shelter ...................................... 7" ...... Mercury .......... MF965 ............... 1967 £4 ........... £8 ......................................

## DAX, DANIELLE
Pop-Eyes .................................................. LP ...... Initial ............. IRC009 .............. 1983 £10 ........... £25 ......................................
Tomorrow Never Knows .......................... CD-s . Sire .............. W9529CD ............. 1990 £2 ........... £5 ......................................

## DAY, BING
I Can't Help It ........................................ 7" ...... Mercury .......... AMT1047 .............. 1959 £20 ........... £40 ......................................

## DAY, BOBBY
Bluebird Buzzard And Oriole .................. 7" ...... London ........... HL8800 ............. 1959 £12.50 .. £25 ......................................
Little Bitty Pretty One .......................... 7" ...... HMV ............. POP425 .............. 1957 £50 ........... £100 ......................................
Love Is A One Time Affair ..................... 7" ...... London ........... HL8964 ............. 1959 £6 ........... £12 ......................................
My Blue Heaven ...................................... 7" ...... London ........... HLY9044 .............. 1960 £6 ........... £12 ......................................
Over And Over ....................................... 7" ...... Top Rank ...... JAR538 ............... 1961 £4 ........... £8 ......................................
Rockin' Robin ......................................... 7" ...... London ........... HL8726 .............. 1958 £10 ........... £20 ......................................
Rockin' Robin ......................................... 7" ...... Sue .............. WI388 ............... 1965 £6 ........... £12 ......................................
Rockin' With Robin ................................ LP ...... Class .............. LP5002 ............. 1959 £50 ........... £100 ......................... US

## DAY, DORIS
Annie Get Your Gun ............................... LP ...... CBS ............. (S)BPG62129 ...... 1963 £4 ........... £10 ......................................
April In Paris .......................................... 7" ...... Columbia ........ SCM5038 ............. 1953 £2.50 ....... £6 ......................................
Boys And Girls Together ......................... 10" LP Columbia ....... CL2530 ............. 195– £6 ........... £15 ......................... US
Bright And Shiny .................................... LP ...... Philips ............ BBL7471/SBBL619. 1961 £6 ........... £15 ......................................
Bushel And A Peck .................................. 7" ...... Columbia ........ SCM5044 ............. 1953 £5 ........... £10 ......................................
By The Light Of The Silvery Moon ........ 10" LP Columbia ....... CL6248 .............. 1953 £10 ........... £25 ......................... US
Calamity Jane (with Howard Keel) .......... 10" LP Philips ......... BBR8104 ............. 1956 £6 ........... £15 ......................................
Canadian Capers .................................... 7" EP . Columbia ........ SEG7507 .............. 1954 £2 ........... £5 ......................................
Cherries .................................................. 7" ...... Columbia ........ SCM5059 .............. 1953 £2 ........... £5 ......................................
Christmas Album ..................................... LP ...... CBS ............. (S)BPG62712 ...... 1966 £4 ........... £10 ......................................
Cuttin' Capers ........................................ LP ...... Philips ............ BBL7296/SBBL540. 1959 £4 ........... £10 ......................................

| Title | Format | Label | Catalogue | Year | | | Notes |
|---|---|---|---|---|---|---|---|
| Day By Day | LP | Philips | BBL7142 | 1957 | £10 | £25 | |
| Day By Night | LP | Philips | BBL7211 | 1958 | £10 | £25 | |
| Day By Night | LP | Philips | SBBL548 | 1959 | £6 | £15 | stereo, 1 different track |
| Day Dreams | LP | Philips | BBL7120 | 1957 | £6 | £15 | |
| Day Dreams | 7" EP | Philips | BBE12151 | 1957 | £2 | £5 | |
| Day In Hollywood | LP | Philips | BBL7175 | 1957 | £6 | £15 | |
| Doris | 7" EP | Philips | BBE12167 | 1958 | £2 | £5 | |
| Doris And Frank | LP | Philips | BBL7137 | 1957 | £5 | £12 | with Frank Sinatra |
| Doris Day | 7" EP | Philips | BBE12007 | 1955 | £4 | £8 | |
| Doris Day No. 2 | 7" EP | Philips | BBE12089 | 1956 | £2 | £5 | |
| Dream A Little Dream Of Me | 7" EP | Philips | BBE12213 | 1958 | £2 | £5 | |
| Duet | LP | CBS | (S)BPG62010 | 1962 | £4 | £10 | with André Previn |
| Duet | 7" EP | CBS | AGG20018 | 1962 | £2 | £5 | with André Previn |
| Duet No. 2 | 7" EP | CBS | AGG20029 | 1963 | £2 | £5 | with André Previn |
| Favourites | 10" LP | Philips | BBR8094 | 1956 | £6 | £15 | |
| Hooray For Hollywood | LP | Philips | SBBL519 | 1959 | £5 | £12 | stereo |
| Hooray For Hollywood Vol. 1 | LP | Philips | BBL7247 | 1958 | £6 | £15 | |
| Hooray For Hollywood Vol. 2 | LP | Philips | BBL7248 | 1958 | £6 | £15 | |
| Hot Canaries | 10" LP | Columbia | CL2534 | 195– | £6 | £15 | US, with Peggy Lee |
| I Have Dreamed | LP | Philips | BBL7496/SBBL643 | 1961 | £6 | £15 | |
| I Have Dreamed | 7" EP | CBS | AGG20009 | 1962 | £2 | £5 | |
| I'll Never Stop Loving You | 7" EP | Philips | BBE12011 | 1955 | £4 | £8 | |
| I'll See You In My Dreams | 10" LP | Columbia | CL6198 | 1951 | £10 | £25 | US |
| In The Still Of The Night | LP | Philips | SBBL537 | 1960 | £6 | £15 | |
| Jumbo | LP | CBS | (S)BPG62118 | 1962 | £4 | £10 | |
| Just One Of Those Things | 7" | Columbia | SCM5171 | 1955 | £2.50 | £6 | |
| Latin For Lovers | LP | CBS | (S)BPG62502 | 1965 | £4 | £10 | |
| Let's Fly Away | 7" EP | Philips | BBE12298 | 1959 | £2 | £5 | |
| Let's Fly Away | 7" EP | Philips | SBBE9006 | 1960 | £4 | £8 | stereo |
| Lights, Cameras, Action | 10" LP | Columbia | CL2518 | 195– | £6 | £15 | US |
| Load Of Hay | 7" | Columbia | SCM5087 | 1954 | £2.50 | £6 | |
| Love Him | LP | CBS | (S)BPG62226 | 1964 | £10 | £25 | |
| Love Me Or Leave Me | LP | Philips | BBL7047 | 1955 | £10 | £25 | |
| Love Me Or Leave Me/Young At Heart | LP | CBS | 63528 | 1969 | £10 | £25 | |
| Lullaby Of Broadway | 10" LP | Columbia | CL6168 | 1951 | £10 | £25 | US |
| Lullaby Of Broadway (Doris Day Hits) | 10" LP | Columbia | 33S1038 | 1954 | £8 | £20 | |
| Ma Says, Pa Says | 7" | Columbia | SCM5033 | 1953 | £4 | £8 | |
| Mister Tap-Toe | 7" | Columbia | SCM5062 | 1953 | £2 | £5 | |
| Move Over Darling | 7" EP | CBS | AGG20048 | 1964 | £2 | £5 | |
| Nobody's Sweetheart | 7" | Columbia | SEG7531 | 1954 | £2 | £5 | |
| On Moonlight Bay | 10" LP | Columbia | CL6186 | 1951 | £10 | £25 | US |
| Party's Over | 7" | Philips | JK1031 | 1957 | £2 | £5 | juke-box issue |
| Pillow Talk | 7" EP | Philips | BBE12339 | 1959 | £2 | £5 | |
| Pyjama Game | LP | Philips | BBL7197 | 1957 | £4 | £10 | |
| Second Star To The Right | 7" | Columbia | SCM5045 | 1953 | £2 | £5 | |
| Sentimental Journey | LP | CBS | (S)BPG62562 | 1966 | £4 | £10 | |
| Show Time | LP | Philips | BBL7392/SBBL577 | 1960 | £4 | £10 | |
| Show Time No. 1 | 7" EP | Philips | SBBE9034 | 1961 | £2 | £5 | stereo |
| Showcase Of Hits | LP | Philips | BBL7297 | 1959 | £4 | £10 | |
| Sings Her Great Movie Hits | LP | CBS | BPG62785 | 1966 | £4 | £10 | |
| Sometimes I'm Happy | 7" EP | Columbia | SEG7546 | 1954 | £2 | £5 | |
| Song Is You | 7" EP | Philips | BBE12187 | 1958 | £2 | £5 | |
| Tea For Two | 10" LP | Columbia | CL6149 | 1950 | £10 | £25 | US |
| That's The Way He Does It | 7" | Columbia | SCM5075 | 1953 | £2.50 | £6 | |
| That's What Makes Paris Paree | 7" | Columbia | SCM5039 | 1953 | £2 | £5 | |
| Twelve O'Clock Tonight | 7" | Philips | JK1020 | 1957 | £2 | £5 | juke-box issue |
| Vocal Gems From The Film Young Man Of Music | 7" EP | Columbia | SEG7572 | 1955 | £2 | £5 | |
| Voice Of Your Choice | 10" LP | Philips | BBR8026 | 1954 | £6 | £15 | |
| We Kiss In A Shadow | 7" EP | Columbia | SEG7515 | 1954 | £2 | £5 | |
| We Kiss In A Shadow | 7" | Columbia | SCM5067 | 1953 | £2 | £5 | |
| What Every Girl Should Know | LP | Philips | BBL7377/SBBL563 | 1960 | £4 | £10 | |
| With A Smile And A Song | LP | CBS | (S)BPG62461 | 1965 | £8 | £20 | |
| You Can't Have Everything | 7" EP | Philips | BBE12388 | 1960 | £2 | £5 | |
| You Can't Have Everything | 7" EP | Philips | SBBE9021 | 1960 | £4 | £8 | stereo |
| You'll Never Walk Alone | LP | CBS | (S)BPG62101 | 1963 | £10 | £25 | |
| You're My Thrill | 10" LP | Columbia | CL6071 | 1949 | £8 | £20 | US |
| Young At Heart | 10" LP | Philips | BBR8040 | 1955 | £6 | £15 | with Frank Sinatra |
| Young Man With A Horn | LP | Columbia | CL582 | 1954 | £6 | £15 | US |
| Young Man With A Horn | 10" LP | Columbia | CL6106 | 1950 | £10 | £25 | US |

## DAY, JACKIE

| Title | Format | Label | Catalogue | Year | | | |
|---|---|---|---|---|---|---|---|
| Before It's Too Late | 7" | Sue | WI4040 | 1967 | £25 | £50 | |

## DAY, JILL

| Title | Format | Label | Catalogue | Year | | | |
|---|---|---|---|---|---|---|---|
| I Hear You Knocking | 7" | HMV | 7M362 | 1956 | £4 | £8 | |
| Mangos | 7" | HMV | POP320 | 1957 | £1.50 | £4 | |
| Promises | 7" | Parlophone | MSP6177 | 1955 | £2 | £5 | |
| Sincerely | 7" | Parlophone | MSP6169 | 1955 | £2.50 | £6 | |
| Tear Fell | 7" | HMV | 7M391 | 1956 | £2 | £5 | |

## DAY, MURIEL

| Title | Format | Label | Catalogue | Year | | | |
|---|---|---|---|---|---|---|---|
| Nine Times Out Of Ten | 7" | Page One | POF151 | 1969 | £7.50 | £15 | |
| Wages Of Love | 7" | CBS | 4115 | 1969 | £2 | £5 | |

## DAY, TANYA

| Title | Format | Label | Catalogue | Year | | | |
|---|---|---|---|---|---|---|---|
| His Lips Get In The Way | 7" | Polydor | NH52331 | 1964 | £1.50 | £4 | |

## DAY, TERRY
That's All I Want........................ 7" ...... CBS.............. AAG104................ 1962 £2............£5 ....................

## DAY BLINDNESS
Day Blindness ........................ LP ...... Studio 10 ........ DBX101 ............... 1969 £30......£60 ...................... US

## DAY OF THE PHOENIX
Neighbour's Son ...................... LP ..... Chapter One ... CNSR812.................... 1972 £20........£40 ...................
Wide Open N–Way ................................ LP ...... Greenwich ...... GSLPR1002 ........... 1970 £15........£30 ...................

## DAYLIGHT
Daylight ............................ LP ..... RCA ............... SF8194................ 1971 £15........£30 ..............
Lady Of St. Clare ................ 7" ...... RCA ............... RCA2106 .............. 1971 £1.50........£4 .............

## DAYLIGHTERS
Oh Mom Teach Me How...................... 7" ...... Sue ........... WI343 ................. 1964 £4............£8 ..............

## DAYS
Bacchus Is Back................... LP ...... Sonet ......... SLPS1701.............. 1975 £25.........£50 .................. Danish

## DE BURGH, CHRIS
Compact Hits.......................... CD–s .. A&M.............. AMCD915 ........... 1988 £2............£5 ...............
Tender Hands ...................... CD–s .. A&M.............. CDEE486 .......... 1988 £2............£5 .......... 3" single

## DE BYL, FRANZ
Franz De Byl.......................... LP ..... Metronome .... MLP15383 ......... 1970 £6............£15 .............. German
Und ............................ LP ..... Thorofon ........ ATH114 .......... 1972 £8.........£20 ................... German

## DE CASTRO SISTERS
Boom Boom Boomerang ...................... 7" ...... London ......... HL8137.............. 1955 £12.50....£25 .............
Christmas Is Coming ............................ 7" ...... London ......... HLU8212............. 1955 £10........£20 ..............
Give Me Time ................................ 7" ...... London ......... HLU8228............ 1956 £10........£20 ..............
I'm Bewildered .................................. 7" ...... London ......... HL8158.............. 1955 £12.50....£25 .............
If I Ever Fall In Love ...................... 7" ...... London ......... HLU8189............ 1955 £10........£20 ..............
No One To Blame But You ............... 7" ...... London ......... HLU8296............ 1956 £10........£20 ..............
Red Sails In The Sunset ................... 7" ...... Capitol ......... CL15199 .............. 1961 £1.50.......£4 ..............
Teach Me Tonight ........................ 7" ...... London ......... HL8104.............. 1954 £12.50....£25 .............
Teach Me Tonight Cha–Cha ............ 7" ...... HMV............. POP583 .............. 1959 £2............£5 ...............
Who Are They To Say ...................... 7" ...... HMV............. POP527 .............. 1958 £2............£5 ...............

## DE DANAAN
Banks Of The Nile ........................ LP ..... Decca ......... SKL5318 .............. 1980 £4............£10 ..............
De Danann ............................ LP ..... Decca ............. SKL5287 .......... 1977 £6............£15 ..............
De Danann ............................ LP ..... Polydor ........... 2904005 ........... 1975 £5............£12 .................. Irish

## DE FRANCO, BUDDY
Buddy DeFranco ....................... 10" LP Columbia ... 33C9022 .............. 1956 £10........£25 ..............
Buddy DeFranco Wailers ..................... LP ..... Columbia ...... 33CX10091 ......... 1957 £8.........£20 ..............
King Of The Clarinet ...................... 10" LP MGM............. D112 ................ 1953 £15........£30 ..............
Plays Benny Goodman ...................... LP ..... HMV............. CLP1215 .......... 1958 £6............£15 ..............
Takes You To The Stars ...................... 10" LP Vogue............ LDE077 .............. 1954 £15........£30 ..............
With Oscar Peterson ...................... LP ..... Columbia ...... 33CX10003 ......... 1955 £10........£25 ..............

## DE GALLIER, ZION
Dream Dream Dream ...................... 7" ...... Parlophone .... R5710 .............. 1968 £2.50........£6 ..............
Winter Will Be Cold ........................ 7" ...... Parlophone..... R5686 .............. 1968 £2.50........£6 ..............

## DE LORY, AL
Yesterday............................ 7" ...... London ........... HLU9999................ 1965 £5............£10 ..............

## DE LUGG, MILTON ORCHESTRA
Addams Family Theme ...................... 7" ...... Columbia ....... DB7474 .............. 1965 £2............£5 ..............
Munsters Theme ...................... 7" ...... Columbia ....... DB7762 ................ 1966 £2.50........£6 ..............

## DE MARCO SISTERS
Bouillabasse ...................... 7" ...... MGM........... SP1043 .............. 1953 £2............£5 ..............
Dreamboat............................ 7" ...... Brunswick ..... 05425.............. 1955 £4............£8 ..............
Hot Barcarolle.......................... 7" ...... Brunswick ..... 05474.............. 1955 £2.50........£6 ..............
Love Me.......................... 7" ...... Brunswick ..... 05349.............. 1954 £2.50........£6 ..............
Romance Me.......................... 7" ...... Brunswick ..... 05526.............. 1956 £2............£5 ..............

## DE PARIS, SIDNEY
DeParis Dixie ............................ LP ...... Blue Note ...... B6501 .............. 1969 £4............£10 ..............

## DE PARIS, WILBUR
At Symphony Hall........................ LP ...... London ......... LTZK15086/ ...... 1957 £6............£15 ..............
                                                                    SAHK6016...........
New Orleans Jazz ........................ LP ..... London ......... LTZK15024 ......... 1957 £6............£15 ..............
Plays Cole Porter ........................ LP ..... London ......... LTZK15156 ........ 1959 £5............£12 ..............
Something Old, New, Gay Blue ........ LP ..... London ......... LTZK15175/ ...... 1960 £5............£12 ..............
                                                                    SAHK6060...........
That's A Plenty ......................... LP ..... London ......... LTZK15192/ ...... 1960 £5............£12 ..............
                                                                    SAHK6079.............
Wild Jazz Age ......................... LP ..... London ......... LTZK15201/ ...... 1961 £4............£10 ..............
                                                                    SAHK6115.............

## DE ROSA, FRANK
Big Guitar................................ 7" ...... London .......... HLD8576................. 1958 £7.50......£15 ............................

## DE VIVRE, JOY
Our Wedding ........................... 7" ...... Crass............... ENVY1..................... 1981 £7.50 ....£15 ............white flexi

## DE VORZON, BARRY
Barbara Jean ........................... 7" ...... RCA.............. RCA1066............. 1958 £25.......£50 . B side by Jimmy Bell
Betty Betty ............................. 7" ...... Philips........... PB993................. 1960 £2.50......£6 ............................

## DEACON, BOBBY
Fool Was I................................ 7" ...... Pye ............... 7N15270............. 1960 £2...........£5 ............................

## DEACON, GEORGE & MARION ROSS
Sweet William's Ghost ................ LP ...... XTRA............ XTRA1130............. 1973 £50.......£100 ............................

## DEACON BLUE
| | | | | | | |
|---|---|---|---|---|---|---|
| Chocolate Girl | CD-s .. | CBS. | CDDEAC6 | 1988 | £5 | £12 |
| Chocolate Girl | 7" EP . | CBS. | DEACEP6 | 1988 | £2.50 | £6 |
| Closing Time | CD-s .. | CBS. | 6575022 | 1991 | £2 | £5 |
| Cover From The Sky | CD-s .. | CBS. | 6576732 | 1991 | £2 | £5 |
| Dignity | CD-s .. | CBS. | CDDEAC4 | 1988 | £4 | £10 |
| Dignity | 7" EP . | CBS. | DEACEP4 | 1988 | £2 | £5 |
| Dignity | 7" ...... | CBS. | DEAC1 | 1987 | £1.50 | £4 | with cassette XPC4011 |
| Dignity | 10" ...... | CBS. | DEACQ4 | 1988 | £3 | £8 |
| Fergus Sings The Blues | CD-s .. | CBS. | CDDEAC9 | 1989 | £2 | £5 |
| Four Bacharach And David Songs | CD-s .. | CBS. | CDDEAC12 | 1990 | £2 | £5 |
| Love And Regret | CD-s .. | CBS. | DEACC10 | 1989 | £2 | £5 |
| Queen Of The New Year | CD-s .. | CBS. | CDDEAC11 | 1990 | £3 | £8 |
| Raintown | CD ...... | CBS. | 4505499 | 1990 | £5 | £12 | picture disc |
| Raintown | cass ...... | CBS. | 4505498 | 1988 | £6 | £15 | with Riches cassette |
| Raintown/Riches | LP ...... | CBS. | 4505491/XPR1361. | 1988 | £10 | £25 | double |
| Raintown/Riches | CD ...... | CBS. | 4505490/XPCD277 | 1988 | £15 | £30 | double |
| Real Gone Kid | CD-s .. | CBS. | CDDEAC7 | 1988 | £5 | £12 |
| Real Gone Kid | 7" EP . | CBS. | DEACEP7 | 1988 | £2 | £5 |
| Real Gone Kid | 12" ...... | CBS. | DEACQT7 | 1988 | £2.50 | £6 | with poster |
| Riches | LP ...... | CBS. | XPR1361 | 1988 | £6 | £15 |
| Twist And Shout | CD-s .. | CBS. | 6573022 | 1991 | £2 | £5 |
| Wages Day | CD-s .. | CBS. | CDDEAC8 | 1989 | £2 | £5 | wallet sleeve |
| Wages Day | 7" ...... | CBS. | DEACQ8 | 1989 | £1.50 | £4 |
| When Will You Make My Telephone Ring | CD-s .. | CBS. | CDDEAC5 | 1988 | £6 | £15 |
| When Will You Make My Telephone Ring | CD-s .. | CBS. | CPDEAC5 | 1988 | £5 | £12 | picture disc |
| When Will You Make My Telephone Ring | 7" ...... | CBS. | DEACB5 | 1988 | £1.50 | £4 | boxed set |
| Your Swaying Arms | CD-s .. | CBS. | 6568932 | 1991 | £2 | £5 |

## DEAD BOYS
| | | | | | | |
|---|---|---|---|---|---|---|
| Sonic Reducer | 12" ...... | Sire | 6078609 | 1977 | £3 | £8 |
| Tell Me | 7" ...... | Sire | SRE1029 | 1978 | £1.50 | £4 |
| We Have Come For Your Children | LP ...... | Sire | SRK6054 | 1978 | £4 | £10 |
| Young Loud And Snotty | LP ...... | Sire | 9103329 | 1977 | £4 | £10 |

## DEAD KENNEDYS
| | | | | | | |
|---|---|---|---|---|---|---|
| Give Me Convenience Or Give Me Death . | CD ...... | Alternative Tentacles | VIRUS57CD | 1987 | £5 | £12 |
| Holiday In Cambodia | CD-s .. | Cherry Red | CDCHERRY13 | 1988 | £2 | £5 |

## DEAD OR ALIVE
| | | | | | | |
|---|---|---|---|---|---|---|
| Baby Don't Say Goodbye | CD-s .. | Epic | BURNSC6 | 1989 | £2 | £5 |
| Come Home With Me Baby | CD-s .. | Epic | BURNSC5 | 1989 | £4 | £10 |
| I'd Do Anything | 7" ...... | Epic | A4069 | 1984 | £1.50 | £4 |
| I'd Do Anything | 10" ...... | Epic | QA4069 | 1984 | £3 | £8 |
| I'm Falling | 7" ...... | Inevitable | INEV005 | 1980 | £4 | £8 |
| Lover Come Back To Me | 7" ...... | Epic | A6086 | 1985 | £12.50 | £25 |
| Lover Come Back To Me | 7" ...... | Epic | WA6086 | 1985 | £2 | £5 | shaped picture disc |
| Lover Come Back To Me | 12" ...... | Epic | QTA6086 | 1985 | £3 | £8 | poster sleeve |
| Mad, Bad And Dangerous To Know | CD ...... | Epic | 4502572 | 1987 | £5 | £12 |
| Mighty Mix | 12" ...... | Epic | XPR1257 | 1984 | £10 | £25 | promo |
| Misty Circles | 7" ...... | Epic | A3399 | 1983 | £2 | £5 |
| Misty Circles | 12" ...... | Epic | TA3399 | 1983 | £4 | £10 |
| My Heart Goes Bang | 7" ...... | Epic | DA6571 | 1985 | £1.50 | £4 | double |
| Nowhere To Nowhere | 12" ...... | Black Eyes | BE1 | 1982 | £4 | £10 |
| Nude | CD ...... | Epic | 4650792 | 1989 | £5 | £12 |
| Number Eleven | 7" ...... | Inevitable | INEV008 | 1981 | £2 | £5 |
| Something In My House (Clean & Dirty Mix) | 12" ...... | Epic | XPR1328 | 1987 | £30 | £60 | promo |
| Stranger | 7" ...... | Black Eyes | BE2 | 1982 | £2.50 | £6 |
| That's The Way | 7" ...... | Epic | WA4271 | 1984 | £1.50 | £4 | picture disc |
| Turn Around And Count To Ten | CD-s . | Epic | BURNSC4 | 1988 | £10 | £20 | picture disc |
| Turn Around And Count To Ten | 12" ...... | Epic | BURNSQ4 | 1988 | £15 | £30 |
| What I Want | 7" ...... | Epic | A3676 | 1983 | £5 | £10 | black picture sleeve |
| What I Want | 7" ...... | Epic | A3676 | 1983 | £10 | £20 | floppy hat picture sleeve |
| What I Want | 12" ...... | Epic | TA3676 | 1983 | £2.50 | £6 |

| | | | | | | | |
|---|---|---|---|---|---|---|---|
| What I Want | 12" | Epic | TA3676 | 1983 | £4 | £10 | ...with poster |
| What I Want (Dance Mix) | 12" | Epic | TA4510 | 1984 | £2.50 | £6 | ...with poster |
| What I Want (Remix) | 7" | Epic | A4510 | 1984 | £2.50 | £6 | poster sleeve |
| You Spin Me Round | 7" | Epic | DA4861 | 1984 | £1.50 | £4 | double |
| Youthquake | CD | Epic | EPC26420 | 1985 | £15 | £30 | 2 extra 12" mixes |

## DEAD SEA FRUIT

| | | | | | | | |
|---|---|---|---|---|---|---|---|
| Dead Sea Fruit | LP | Camp | 603001 | 1967 | £20 | £40 | |
| Kensington High Street | 7" | Camp | 602001 | 1967 | £4 | £8 | |
| Loulou Put Another Record On | 7" EP | DiscAZ | 1126 | 1967 | £10 | £20 | French, 2 different sleeves |
| Love At The Hippiedrome | 7" | Camp | 602004 | 1968 | £4 | £8 | |

## DEADLY ONES

| | | | | | | | |
|---|---|---|---|---|---|---|---|
| It's Monster Surfing Time | LP | Vee Jay | LP/VS1090 | 1964 | £6 | £15 | US |

## DEAL, BILL & THE RHONDELLS

| | | | | | | |
|---|---|---|---|---|---|---|
| I've Been Hurt | 7" | MGM | MGM1479 | 1969 | £2 | £5 |

## DEAN, ALAN

| | | | | | | |
|---|---|---|---|---|---|---|
| Rock 'n' Roll Tarantella | 7" | Columbia | DB3932 | 1957 | £4 | £8 |

## DEAN, ALAN & THE PROBLEMS

| | | | | | | |
|---|---|---|---|---|---|---|
| Thunder And Rain | 7" | Pye | 7N15749 | 1965 | £15 | £30 |
| Time It Takes | 7" | Decca | F11947 | 1964 | £4 | £8 |

## DEAN, ELTON

Elton Dean (from whom Reg Dwight pinched half of his stage name) was the saxophonist with Soft Machine during the early seventies. Since leaving the group he has followed a busy jazz career, including the recording of several albums in his own name.

| | | | | | | |
|---|---|---|---|---|---|---|
| Bologna Tapes | LP | Ogun | OG530 | 1985 | £4 | £10 |
| Boundaries | LP | Japo | 60033 | 1980 | £4 | £10 |
| Cheque Is In The Mail | LP | Ogun | OG610 | 1977 | £5 | £12 |
| Elton Dean | LP | CBS | 64539 | 1971 | £8 | £20 |
| Happy Daze | LP | Ogun | OG910 | 1977 | £5 | £12 |
| Mercy Dash | LP | Culture Press | CP2001 | 1985 | £4 | £10 |
| Oh! For The Edge | LP | Ogun | OG900 | 1976 | £5 | £12 |
| They All Be On This Old Road | LP | Ogun | OG410 | 1977 | £5 | £12 |
| Welcome Live In Brazil 1986 | LP | Impetus | IMP18126 | 1987 | £4 | £10 |

## DEAN, JIMMY

| | | | | | | | |
|---|---|---|---|---|---|---|---|
| Best Of Jimmy Dean | 7" EP | CBS | EP6075 | 1966 | £2.50 | £6 | |
| Big Bad John | LP | Philips | BBL7537 | 1961 | £8 | £20 | |
| Big Bad John | 7" | Philips | PB1187 | 1961 | £1.50 | £4 | |
| Hour Of Prayer | LP | Columbia | CL1025 | 1957 | £4 | £10 | US |
| Jimmy Dean | 7" EP | Philips | BBE12501 | 1961 | £4 | £8 | |
| Little Black Book | 7" | CBS | AAG122 | 1962 | £1.50 | £4 | |
| Smoke Smoke That Cigarette | 7" | Philips | PB1223 | 1962 | £1.50 | £4 | |
| Weekend Blues | 7" | Philips | PB940 | 1959 | £1.50 | £4 | |

## DEAN, JOHNNY & THE APACHES

| | | | | | | | |
|---|---|---|---|---|---|---|---|
| Johnny Dean And The Apaches | LP | Rave | RMG1194 | 1964 | £50 | £100 | South African |

## DEAN, LITTLE BILLY

| | | | | | | |
|---|---|---|---|---|---|---|
| That's Always Like You | 7" | Strike | JH325 | 1967 | £7.50 | £15 |

## DEAN, NORA

| | | | | | | |
|---|---|---|---|---|---|---|
| Same Thing You Gave To Daddy | 7" | Upsetter | US322 | 1969 | £1.50 | £4 |

Upsetter Pilgrims B side

## DEAN, PAUL

Although these singles sank without trace, Paul Beuselinck went on to achieve considerable success as an actor and a singer, after changing his stage surname from Dean to Nicholas.

| | | | | | | | |
|---|---|---|---|---|---|---|---|
| She Can Build A Mountain | 7" | Reaction | 591002 | 1966 | £2 | £5 | with the Soul Savages |
| You Don't Own Me | 7" | Decca | F12136 | 1965 | £4 | £8 | ...with the Thoughts |

## DEAN, ROGER

Roger Dean is a painter, whose science-fantasy landscapes were commissioned on several occasions through the seventies for use on LP sleeves. The most well-known of these are the series he produced for Yes, but Dean's sleeves are also to be found on records by the likes of Osibisa, Greenslade, Badger, Keith Tippett, Billy Cox, Paladin, The Gun, Ramases, and, more recently, Asia. All of these are collected by fans of Dean. As it happens, he can also be heard on record – he is the guitarist with John Mayall's Bluesbreakers on the group's first album, *John Mayall Plays John Mayall*.

## DEAN & JEAN

| | | | | | | |
|---|---|---|---|---|---|---|
| Hey Jean Hey Dean | 7" | Stateside | SS283 | 1964 | £2 | £5 |
| I Love The Summertime | 7" | Stateside | SS249 | 1964 | £2.50 | £6 |
| I Wanna Be Loved | 7" | Stateside | SS313 | 1964 | £2.50 | £6 |

## DEANE, JASON

| | | | | | | |
|---|---|---|---|---|---|---|
| Down In The Street | 7" | King | KG1060 | 1967 | £15 | £30 |
| Make Believe | 7" | King | KG1049 | 1966 | £7.50 | £15 |

## DEAR MR. TIME

| | | | | | | |
|---|---|---|---|---|---|---|
| Grandfather | LP | Square | SQA101 | 1970 | £37.50 | £75 |

## DEARIE, BLOSSOM

| | | | | | |
|---|---|---|---|---|---|
| Blossom Dearie | LP | Fontana | STL5454 | 1968 £4 | £10 |
| Hey John | 7" | Fontana | TF986 | 1968 £1.50 | £4 |
| I'm Hip | 7" | Fontana | TF719 | 1966 £1.50 | £4 |
| Plays For Dancing | 10" LP | Felsted | SDL86034 | 1956 £6 | £15 |
| Sweet Georgie Fame | 7" | Fontana | TF788 | 1967 £1.50 | £4 |

## DEARLY BELOVED

| | | | | | |
|---|---|---|---|---|---|
| Peep Peep Pop Pop | 7" | CBS | 202398 | 1966 £2.50 | £6 |

## DEATH IN JUNE

| | | | | | | |
|---|---|---|---|---|---|---|
| And Murder Love | 7" | New European | BADVC73 | 1985 £4 | £8 | |
| And Murder Love | 12" | New European | BADVC73T | 1985 £4 | £10 | |
| Born Again | 12" | Cenaz | CENAZ09 | 1988 £3 | £8 | picture disc |
| Born Again | 12" | New European | BADVC69 | 1985 £4 | £10 | |
| Burial | LP | New European | UBADVC4 | 199– £6 | £15 | brown vinyl |
| Burial | LP | New European | UBADVC4 | 199– £10 | £25 | white vinyl |
| Heaven Street | 7" | New European | SA29634 | 1984 £10 | £20 | |
| Heaven Street | 12" | New European | SA29634 | 1984 £10 | £20 | blue & white sleeve |
| Heaven Street | 12" | New European | SA29634 | 1984 £15 | £30 | brown & gold sleeve |
| Holy Water | 7" | New European | SA30634 | 1982 £7.50 | £15 | |
| Nada | LP | New European | BADVC13 | 1985 £8 | £20 | blue sleeve |
| Nada | LP | New European | BADVC13 | 1985 £4 | £10 | brown sleeve |
| She Said Destroy | 7" | New European | BADVC6 | 1984 £5 | £10 | |
| She Said Destroy | 12" | New European | BADVC6T | 1984 £6 | £15 | |
| To Drown A Rose | 10" | New European | BADVC10 | 1987 £3 | £8 | |
| Wall Of Sacrifice | LP | New European | BADVC88 | 1988 £15 | £30 | green & yellow sleeve |
| Wall Of Sacrifice | LP | New European | BADVC88 | 1988 £20 | £40 | red sleeve |
| World That Summer | LP | New European | BADVC9 | 199– £5 | £12 | double |

## DEBONAIRES

| | | | | | |
|---|---|---|---|---|---|
| I'm In Love Again | 7" | Track | 604035 | 1970 £5 | £10 |

## DEB-TONES

| | | | | | |
|---|---|---|---|---|---|
| Knock, Knock, Who's There? | 7" | RCA | RCA1137 | 1959 £5 | £10 |

## DEBRIS

| | | | | | | |
|---|---|---|---|---|---|---|
| Debris | LP | Static Disposal | PIG0000 | 1976 £37.50 | £75 | US |

## DEBS

| | | | | | |
|---|---|---|---|---|---|
| Sloopy's Gonna Hang On | 7" | Mercury | MF888 | 1965 £1.50 | £4 |

## DECEMBER'S CHILDREN

| | | | | | | |
|---|---|---|---|---|---|---|
| December's Children | LP | Mainstream | 6128 | 1968 £30 | £60 | US |

## DECKER, DIANA

| | | | | | |
|---|---|---|---|---|---|
| Abracadabra | 7" | Columbia | SCM5145 | 1954 £2.50 | £6 |
| Apples, Peaches And Cherries | 7" | Columbia | SCM5173 | 1955 £1.50 | £4 |
| Happy Wanderer | 7" | Columbia | SCM5096 | 1954 £1.50 | £4 |
| Kitty In The Basket | 7" | Columbia | SCM5123 | 1954 £4 | £8 |
| Mama Mia | 7" | Columbia | SCM5130 | 1954 £2 | £5 |
| Man With The Banjo | 7" | Columbia | SCM5120 | 1954 £2 | £5 |
| Oh My Papa | 7" | Columbia | SCM5083 | 1954 £2.50 | £6 |
| Open The Window Of Your Heart | 7" | Columbia | SCM5166 | 1955 £1.50 | £4 |
| Rock-a-Boogie Baby | 7" | Columbia | SCM5246 | 1956 £6 | £12 |

## DEDE LIND

| | | | | | | |
|---|---|---|---|---|---|---|
| Io Non So Da | LP | Mercury | 6323093 | 1972 £75 | £150 | Italian |

## DEDICATED MEN'S JUG BAND

| | | | | | |
|---|---|---|---|---|---|
| Boodle Am Shake | 7" | Piccadilly | 7N35245 | 1965 £1.50 | £4 |
| Don't Come Knocking | 7" | Piccadilly | 7N35283 | 1966 £1.50 | £4 |

## DEE, JEANNIE

| | | | | | |
|---|---|---|---|---|---|
| Don't Come Home My Little Darling | 7" | Beacon | BEA142 | 1969 £2 | £5 |

## DEE, JOEY & THE STARLIGHTERS

| | | | | | | |
|---|---|---|---|---|---|---|
| All The World Is Twistin' | LP | Columbia | 33SX1502 | 1962 £5 | £12 | |
| Back To The Peppermint Lounge Twistin' | LP | Roulette | (S)R25173 | 1962 £5 | £12 | US |
| Dance Dance Dance | 7" | Columbia | DB7102 | 1963 £1.50 | £4 | |
| Dance, Dance, Dance | LP | Roulette | (S)R25221 | 1963 £4 | £10 | US |
| Doin' The Twist | LP | Columbia | 33SX1406 | 1961 £5 | £12 | |
| Hey Let's Twist | LP | Columbia | 33SX1421 | 1962 £5 | £12 | |
| Joey Dee | LP | Roulette | (S)R25197 | 1963 £4 | £10 | US |
| Peppermint Twist | 7" | Columbia | DB4758 | 1962 £1.50 | £4 | |
| Two Tickets To Paris | LP | Roulette | (S)R25182 | 1962 £4 | £10 | US |

## DEE, JOHNNY

| | | | | | |
|---|---|---|---|---|---|
| Sitting In The Balcony | 7" | Oriole | CB1367 | 1957 £37.50 | £75 |

## DEE, KIKI

| | | | | | | |
|---|---|---|---|---|---|---|
| Baby I Don't Care | 7" | Fontana | TF490 | 1964 £1.50 | £4 | |
| Early Night | 7" | Fontana | TF394 | 1963 £1.50 | £4 | |
| En francais | 7" EP | Fontana | 465323 | 1966 £7.50 | £15 | French |
| Great Expectations | LP | Tamla Motown | STML11158 | 1970 £10 | £25 | |
| I Was Only Kidding | 7" | Fontana | TF414 | 1963 £1.50 | £4 | |
| I'm Kiki Dee | LP | Fontana | (S)TL5455 | 1968 £6 | £15 | |

| Title | Format | Label | Cat. No. | Year | | | Notes |
|---|---|---|---|---|---|---|---|
| Kiki Dee | 7" EP | Fontana | TE17443 | 1965 | £7.50 | £15 | |
| Kiki Dee In Clover | 7" EP | Fontana | TE17470 | 1966 | £7.50 | £15 | |
| Now The Flowers Cry | 7" | Fontana | TF983 | 1968 | £15 | £30 | |
| Our Day Will Come Between Monday & Sunday | 7" | Tamla Motown | TMG739 | 1970 | £1.50 | £4 | |
| Running Out Of Fools | 7" | Fontana | TF596 | 1965 | £1.50 | £4 | |
| That's Right Walk On By | 7" | Fontana | TF443 | 1964 | £1.50 | £4 | |
| Why Don't I Run Away From You | 7" | Fontana | TF669 | 1966 | £1.50 | £4 | |

## DEE, LENNY

| Title | Format | Label | Cat. No. | Year | | | Notes |
|---|---|---|---|---|---|---|---|
| Plantation Boogie | 7" | Brunswick | 05440 | 1955 | £1.50 | £4 | |

## DEE, RICKY & THE EMBERS

| Title | Format | Label | Cat. No. | Year | | | Notes |
|---|---|---|---|---|---|---|---|
| Workout | 7" | Stateside | SS136 | 1962 | £2 | £5 | |

## DEE, SANDRA

| Title | Format | Label | Cat. No. | Year | | | Notes |
|---|---|---|---|---|---|---|---|
| Tammy Tell Me | 7" | Brunswick | 05858 | 1961 | £1.50 | £4 | |

## DEE, TOMMY & THE TEEN TONES

| Title | Format | Label | Cat. No. | Year | | | Notes |
|---|---|---|---|---|---|---|---|
| Three Stars | 7" | Melodisc | 1516 | 1959 | £25 | £50 | |

## DEE DEE

| Title | Format | Label | Cat. No. | Year | | | Notes |
|---|---|---|---|---|---|---|---|
| Love Is Always | 7" | Palette | PB25579 | 1968 | £7.50 | £15 | |

## DEE SET

| Title | Format | Label | Cat. No. | Year | | | Notes |
|---|---|---|---|---|---|---|---|
| I Know A Place | 7" | Blue Cat | BS146 | 1968 | £2.50 | £6 | |

## DEEJAYS

| Title | Format | Label | Cat. No. | Year | | | Notes |
|---|---|---|---|---|---|---|---|
| Black-Eyed Woman | 7" | Polydor | 56501 | 1965 | £37.50 | £75 | |
| Blackeyed Woman | 7" EP | Polydor | 27773 | 1965 | £50 | £100 | French |
| Deejays | LP | Polydor | LPHM46254 | 1966 | £50 | £100 | Swedish |
| Dimples | 7" | Polydor | 56034 | 1965 | £20 | £40 | |
| Haze | LP | Hep House | HLP02 | 1967 | £30 | £60 | Swedish |

## DEELEY, ANTHONY

| Title | Format | Label | Cat. No. | Year | | | Notes |
|---|---|---|---|---|---|---|---|
| Anytime Man | 7" | Pama | PM728 | 1968 | £1.50 | £4 | |

## DEENE, CAROL

| Title | Format | Label | Cat. No. | Year | | | Notes |
|---|---|---|---|---|---|---|---|
| I Can't Forget Someone Like You | 7" | HMV | POP1405 | 1965 | £1.50 | £4 | |
| Love Affair | LP | World Records | ST1031 | 1970 | £6 | £15 | |
| Love Not Have I | 7" | Columbia | DB8107 | 1967 | £1.50 | £4 | |
| Norman | 7" | HMV | POP973 | 1962 | £1.50 | £4 | |
| Sad Movies | 7" | HMV | POP922 | 1961 | £1.50 | £4 | |
| Who's Been Sleeping In My Bed | 7" | HMV | POP1275 | 1964 | £1.50 | £4 | |

## DEEP

| Title | Format | Label | Cat. No. | Year | | | Notes |
|---|---|---|---|---|---|---|---|
| Psychedelic Moods | LP | Parkway | 7051 | 1966 | £150 | £250 | US |

## DEEP FEELING

| Title | Format | Label | Cat. No. | Year | | | Notes |
|---|---|---|---|---|---|---|---|
| Deep Feeling | LP | DJM | DJLPS419 | 1971 | £10 | £25 | |
| Do You Love Me | 7" | Page One | POF23165 | 1970 | £1.50 | £4 | |
| Skyline Pigeon | 7" | Page One | POF23177 | 1970 | £1.50 | £4 | |

## DEEP FREEZE MICE

| Title | Format | Label | Cat. No. | Year | | | Notes |
|---|---|---|---|---|---|---|---|
| Gates Of Lunch | LP | Mole Embalming | MOLE3 | 1981 | £4 | £10 | |
| Hang On Constance Let Me Hear The News | 7" | Cordelia | ERICAT004 | 198– | £2 | £5 | |
| I Love You Little Bo Bo With Your Delicate Golden Lions | LP | Cordelia | ERICAT001 | 198– | £5 | £12 | double |
| My Geraniums Are Bulletproof | LP | Mole Embalming | MOLE1 | 1979 | £10 | £25 | |
| My Geraniums Are Bulletproof | LP | Mole Embalming | MOLE1 | 1979 | £25 | £50 | .. various inserts, DIY sleeve |
| Rain Is When The Earth Is Television | 7" | Cordelia | ERICAT013 | 198– | £1.50 | £4 | |
| Saw A Ranch Burning Last Night | LP | Mole Embalming | MOLE4 | 1983 | £4 | £10 | |
| Teenage Head In My Refrigerator | LP | Mole Embalming | MOLE2 | 1981 | £10 | £25 | |
| These Floors Are Smooth | 7" | Cordelia | ERICAT002 | 198– | £2.50 | £6 | |

## DEEP PURPLE

Deep Purple are one of the definitive founding fathers of heavy metal, if only for having created the bane of guitar-shop proprietors, 'Smoke On The Water'. The earliest Deep Purple recordings, however, follow much more of a progressive rock policy, with keyboard player Jon Lord trying very hard, if seldom very successfully, to integrate rock with classical music. The group underwent numerous personnel changes during its long life, with only Lord and drummer Ian Paice giving continuity to the different line-ups. What is viewed as the classic version of Deep Purple, with Ian Gillan and Ritchie Blackmore, came together when Gillan joined the band just in time to contribute to Lord's failed experiment, *Concerto For Group And Orchestra*, following which the group turned towards Blackmore's preferred direction, delivering the heavy metal master-work, *Deep Purple In Rock*.

| Title | Format | Label | Cat. No. | Year | | | Notes |
|---|---|---|---|---|---|---|---|
| Bad Attitude | CD-s | Polygram | 0800882 | 1988 | £20 | £40 | CD video |
| Book Of Taliesyn | CD | Harvest | CDP7924082 | 1989 | £5 | £12 | |
| Concerto For Group And Orchestra | 7" | Harvest | PSR325 | 1970 | £5 | £10 | promo |
| Deep Purple In Rock | CD | Harvest | CDP7462392 | 1988 | £5 | £12 | |
| Deep Purple Mark 2 Singles | LP | Purple | TPS3514 | 1979 | £4 | £10 | purple vinyl |
| Deepest Purple | CD | Harvest | CDP7460322 | 1984 | £5 | £12 | |
| Emmaretta | 7" | Parlophone | R5763 | 1969 | £15 | £30 | |

| Title | Format | Label | Catalogue | Year | Price | Price | Notes |
|---|---|---|---|---|---|---|---|
| Fireball | LP | EMI | EJ2603440 | 1984 | £4 | £10 | *..... picture disc, poster* |
| Hallelujah | 7" | Harvest | HAR5006 | 1969 | £1.50 | £4 | |
| Hallelujah | 7" | Harvest | HAR5006 | 1969 | £7.50 | £15 | *.. promo, picture sleeve* |
| Hush | CD-s | Polydor | PZCD4 | 1988 | £2 | £5 | |
| Hush | 7" | Parlophone | R5708 | 1968 | £15 | £30 | |
| Hush | 7" | Parlophone | R5708 | 1968 | £30 | £60 | *... demo, picture sleeve* |
| In Rock | LP | EMI | EJ2603430 | 1984 | £4 | £10 | *..... picture disc, poster* |
| Kentucky Woman | 7" | Parlophone | R5745 | 1968 | £10 | £20 | |
| King Of Dreams | CD-s | RCA | PD49248 | 1990 | £2 | £5 | |
| Love Conquers All | CD-s | RCA | PD49226 | 1991 | £2 | £5 | |
| Machine Head | LP | EMI | EJ2603450 | 1984 | £4 | £10 | *..... picture disc, poster* |
| Machine Head | LP | Harvest | Q4SHVL7504 | 1974 | £15 | £30 | *.................quad* |
| Machine Head | CD | EMI | CZ83 | 1987 | £5 | £12 | |
| Shades Of Deep Purple | LP | Parlophone | PCS7055 | 1968 | £20 | £40 | *.................stereo* |
| Shades Of Deep Purple | LP | Parlophone | PMC/PCS7055 | 1968 | £6 | £15 | *... black & white label* |
| Shades Of Deep Purple | LP | Parlophone | PMC7055 | 1968 | £37.50 | £75 | *.................mono* |
| Shades Of Deep Purple | CD | Parlophone | CZ170 | 1989 | £5 | £12 | |
| Singles A's And B's | LP | Harvest | SHSM2026 | 1978 | £4 | £10 | *....... purple vinyl* |
| Stormbringer | LP | Warner Bros | PR42832 | 1975 | £8 | £20 | *.............US quad* |
| Woman From Tokyo | 7" | Purple | PUR112 | 1973 | £10 | £20 | |

## DEEP RIVER BOYS

| Title | Format | Label | Catalogue | Year | Price | Price | Notes |
|---|---|---|---|---|---|---|---|
| Deep River Boys | LP | Vik | LXA1019 | 1956 | £25 | £50 | *.................US* |
| Deep River Boys | 7" EP | HMV | 7EG8133 | 1955 | £2 | £5 | |
| Ezikiel Saw The Wheel | 7" EP | Nixa | 45EP131 | 1955 | £2 | £5 | |
| Go On Board Little Children | 7" EP | Nixa | 45EP113 | 1955 | £2 | £5 | |
| Itchy Twitchy Feeling | 7" | HMV | POP537 | 1958 | £2.50 | £6 | |
| Midnight Magic | LP | Que | FLS104 | 1957 | £20 | £40 | *.................US* |
| Negro Spirituals | 7" EP | HMV | 7EG8445 | 1957 | £2 | £5 | |
| Nola | 7" | Top Rank | JAR172 | 1959 | £1.50 | £4 | |
| Not Too Old To Rock And Roll | 7" | HMV | POP449 | 1958 | £4 | £8 | |
| Presenting The Deep River Boys | LP | Camden | CAL303 | 1956 | £20 | £40 | *.................US* |
| Presenting The Deep River Boys | LP | Capitol | T6050 | 195– | £6 | £15 | *.................US* |
| Rock A Beating Boogie | 7" | HMV | 7M361 | 1956 | £7.50 | £15 | |
| Romance A La Mode | 7" EP | HMV | 7EG8321 | 1957 | £2 | £5 | |
| Settle Down | 7" | HMV | POP1081 | 1962 | £2 | £5 | |
| Shake Rattle And Roll | 7" | HMV | 7M280 | 1954 | £7.50 | £15 | |
| Spirituals | 10" LP | Nixa | XLPY135 | 1954 | £5 | £12 | |
| Spirituals | 10" LP | Pye | XLTY138 | 1954 | £4 | £10 | |
| Spirituals | 10" LP | Waldorf | 120 | 1956 | £25 | £50 | *.................US* |
| Spirituals And Jubilees | 10" LP | Waldorf | 108 | 1956 | £25 | £50 | *.................US* |
| Sweet Mama Tree Top Tall | 7" | HMV | 7M174 | 1954 | £6 | £12 | |
| Swing Low Sweet Chariot | 7" EP | Nixa | 45EP114 | 1955 | £2 | £5 | |
| That's Right | 7" | HMV | POP263 | 1956 | £7.50 | £15 | |
| Timbers Gotta Roll | 7" | Top Rank | JAR174 | 1959 | £1.50 | £4 | |
| Walk Together Children | 7" EP | Nixa | 45EP130 | 1955 | £2 | £5 | |
| Whole Lotta Shaking Going On | 7" | HMV | POP395 | 1957 | £7.50 | £15 | |

## DEEP SET

| Title | Format | Label | Catalogue | Year | Price | Price | Notes |
|---|---|---|---|---|---|---|---|
| I Started A Joke | 7" | Major Minor | MM607 | 1969 | £1.50 | £4 | |
| That's The Way Life Goes | 7" | Pye | 7N17594 | 1968 | £1.50 | £4 | |

## DEEP SIX

| Title | Format | Label | Catalogue | Year | Price | Price | Notes |
|---|---|---|---|---|---|---|---|
| Deep Six | LP | Liberty | LRP3475/LST7475 | 1966 | £5 | £12 | *.................US* |

## DEERFIELD

| Title | Format | Label | Catalogue | Year | Price | Price | Notes |
|---|---|---|---|---|---|---|---|
| Nil Desperandum | LP | Flat Rock | | 1971 | £50 | £100 | *.................US* |

## DEES, SAM

| Title | Format | Label | Catalogue | Year | Price | Price | Notes |
|---|---|---|---|---|---|---|---|
| Handle With Care | 7" | Atlantic | K10676 | 1975 | £2.50 | £6 | |
| Show Must Go On | LP | Atlantic | K50142 | 1975 | £6 | £15 | |
| Storybook Children | 7" | Atlantic | K10719 | 1976 | £2 | £5 | *....with Bettye Swann* |

## DEF LEPPARD

It would be nice to think that the rise to megastardom of Def Leppard had at least something to do with the public's appreciation of the way the group stood by their drummer, Rick Allen, when he lost an arm in an accident. In any event, as with other rock stars of the eighties, Def Leppard have released a multitude of picture discs and special packages geared directly at the collector. There is also a genuine rarity (i.e. one not expressly created by the record company) in the first single, 'Getcha Rocks Off', which was a private pressing running to three separate issues.

| Title | Format | Label | Catalogue | Year | Price | Price | Notes |
|---|---|---|---|---|---|---|---|
| Action | CD-s | Phonogram | LEPCD13 | 1994 | £4 | £10 | *.... boxed with booklet* |
| Adrenalize Collectors Box | CD | Bludgeon Riffola | ACB1/2 | 1994 | £75 | £150 | *. 2 CD wooden boxed set with booklets, certificate, plectrum* |
| Adrenalize Collectors Box | CD | Bludgeon Riffola | ACB1/2 | 1994 | £100 | £200 | *. 2 CD wooden boxed set, Honorary Edition* |
| Adrenalize Interview With Joe Elliott | CD | Mercury | SACD508 | 1992 | £6 | £15 | *.................US promo* |
| Adrenalize Mega Edition | CD | Mercury | PHCR16001 | 1993 | £10 | £25 | *...Japanese with bonus live disc* |
| Animal | CD-s | Phonogram | LEPCD1 | 1987 | £6 | £15 | |
| Animal | CD-s | Polygram | 0806262 | 1989 | £30 | £60 | *.................CD video* |
| Animal | 12" | Vertigo | LEPC1 | 1987 | £5 | £12 | *.................red vinyl* |
| Armageddon It | CD-s | Phonogram | LEPCD4 | 1988 | £12.50 | £25 | |
| Armageddon It | 12" | Phonogram | LEPXB4 | 1988 | £4 | £10 | *boxed, poster, badge, 5 cards* |
| Bringin' On The Heartbreak | 7" | Vertigo | LEPP3 | 1982 | £10 | £20 | |
| Bringin' On The Heartbreak | 12" | Vertigo | LEPP312 | 1982 | £5 | £12 | |

| Title | Format | Label | Catalogue | Year | Price | Price | Notes |
|---|---|---|---|---|---|---|---|
| First Strike | LP | Flash | 843007 | 1984 | £37.50 | £75 | Belgian |
| Four Albums | CD | Phonogram | 8366062 | 1989 | £20 | £40 | 4 CD boxed set |
| Getcha Rocks Off | 7" | Bludgeon Riffola | MSB001 | 1979 | £5 | £10 | yellow label, no picture sleeve |
| Getcha Rocks Off | 7" | Bludgeon Riffola | SRTS78CUS232 | 1979 | £100 | £200 | picture sleeve, lyric insert, red label |
| Getcha Rocks Off | 7" | Bludgeon Riffola | SRTS78CUS232 | 1979 | £50 | £100 | picture sleeve, red label |
| Getcha Rocks Off | 7" | Phonogram | 6059240 | 1979 | £7.50 | £15 | mispress with 2 B sides |
| Getcha Rocks Off | 7" | Vertigo | 6059240 | 1979 | £2 | £5 | no picture sleeve |
| Greatest Hits – Vault 1980-1995 | CD | Mercury | 5286572 | 1995 | £6 | £15 | double |
| Hello America | 7" | Vertigo | LEPP1 | 1980 | £2.50 | £6 | |
| Hysteria | LP | Phonogram | HYSPD1 | 1987 | £5 | £12 | picture disc |
| Hysteria | CD-s | Phonogram | LEPCD3 | 1988 | £5 | £12 | |
| Hysteria | CD | Mobile Fidelity | UDCD580 | 1993 | £6 | £15 | US audiophile |
| Hysteria | 12" | Phonogram | LEPX313 | 1987 | £3 | £8 | envelope sleeve, poster |
| Interview With Joe Elliott and Rick Savage | CD | Mercury | DLINT3 | 1996 | £8 | £20 | promo |
| Let It Go | 7" | Vertigo | LEPP2 | 1981 | £2.50 | £6 | |
| Let It Go | 7" | Vertigo | LEPP2 | 1981 | £5 | £10 | with patch |
| Let's Get Rocked | CD-s | Phonogram | DEFCD7 | 1992 | £20 | £40 | boxed set of 4 picture discs |
| Let's Get Rocked | 12" | Phonogram | DEFXP7 | 1992 | £2.50 | £6 | picture disc |
| Love Bites | CD-s | Phonogram | LEPCD5 | 1988 | £6 | £15 | |
| Love Bites | 12" | Phonogram | LEPXB5 | 1988 | £4 | £10 | boxed, 4 cards |
| Photograph | 7" | Vertigo | VER5 | 1983 | £2.50 | £6 | |
| Photograph | 7" | Vertigo | VER9 | 1984 | £2 | £5 | wallet picture sleeve |
| Photograph | 7" | Vertigo | VERG9 | 1984 | £15 | £30 | gatefold wallet picture sleeve |
| Photograph | 7" | Vertigo | VERP5 | 1983 | £10 | £20 | 3-D sleeve |
| Photograph | 7" | Vertigo | VERQ5 | 1983 | £7.50 | £15 | 3-D sleeve |
| Photograph | 12" | Vertigo | VERX5 | 1983 | £5 | £12 | |
| Photograph | 12" | Vertigo | VERX9 | 1984 | £5 | £12 | same sleeve as VERX5 |
| Pour Some Sugar On Me | 7" | Phonogram | LEPS2 | 1987 | £4 | £8 | shaped picture disc |
| Pyromania | CD | Mobile Fidelity | UDCD520 | 1989 | £6 | £15 | US audiophile |
| Release Me (Stumpus Maximus) | 12" | Phonogram | LEPDK6 | 1989 | £3 | £8 | promo |
| Rock Of Ages | CD | Polygram | 0800342 | 1989 | £8 | £20 | CD video |
| Rock Of Ages | 7" | Vertigo | VERP6 | 1983 | £4 | £8 | shaped picture disc |
| Rock Of Ages | 7" | Vertigo | VERQ6 | 1983 | £12.50 | £25 | cube sleeve |
| Rock Of Ages | 12" | Vertigo | VERX6 | 1983 | £4 | £10 | |
| Rocket | CD-s | Phonogram | LEPCD6 | 1989 | £10 | £20 | |
| Rocket | CD | Polygram | 0809902 | 1989 | £6 | £15 | CD video |
| Rocket | 12" | Phonogram | LEPXP6 | 1989 | £5 | £12 | numbered picture disc |
| Rocket | 12" | Phonogram | LEPXP6 | 1989 | £2.50 | £6 | picture disc |
| Slang | CD | Mercury | 5324932 | 1996 | £6 | £15 | double |
| Tonight | CD-s | Phonogram | LEPCD10 | 1993 | £12.50 | £25 | double single, etched case |
| Too Late For Love | 7" | Vertigo | VER8 | 1983 | £2.50 | £6 | |
| Too Late For Love | 7" | Vertigo | VER8 | 1983 | £20 | £40 | soccer strip picture sleeve |
| Too Late For Love | 12" | Vertigo | VERX8 | 1983 | £4 | £10 | |
| Two Steps Behind | CD-s | Phonogram | LEPTN12 | 1993 | £2 | £5 | metal tin |
| Wasted | 7" | Vertigo | 6059247 | 1979 | £2.50 | £6 | picture sleeve |

## DEFENDERS

| Title | Format | Label | Catalogue | Year | Price | Price | Notes |
|---|---|---|---|---|---|---|---|
| Drag Beat | LP | Del-Fi | DFLP1242 | 1964 | £15 | £30 | US |

## DEFENDERS (2)

| Title | Format | Label | Catalogue | Year | Price | Price | Notes |
|---|---|---|---|---|---|---|---|
| Set Them Free | 7" | Doctor Bird | DB1104 | 1967 | £5 | £10 | |

## DEFINITION OF SOUND

| Title | Format | Label | Catalogue | Year | Price | Price | Notes |
|---|---|---|---|---|---|---|---|
| Now Is Tomorrow | CD-s | Circa | YRCD54 | 1990 | £2 | £5 | |
| Wear Your Love Like Heaven | CD-s | Circa | YRCD61 | 1991 | £2 | £5 | |

## DEINING

| Title | Format | Label | Catalogue | Year | Price | Price | Notes |
|---|---|---|---|---|---|---|---|
| Deining | LP | Crossroad | | 1982 | £25 | £50 | Dutch |

## DEIRDRE

| Title | Format | Label | Catalogue | Year | Price | Price | Notes |
|---|---|---|---|---|---|---|---|
| Deidre | LP | Philips | | 1977 | £50 | £100 | Dutch |
| Deidre | LP | Polydor | | 1972 | £75 | £150 | Irish |

## DEJOHNETTE, JACK

| Title | Format | Label | Catalogue | Year | Price | Price | Notes |
|---|---|---|---|---|---|---|---|
| Untitled | LP | ECM | ECM1074ST | 1976 | £6 | £15 | |

## DEKKER, DESMOND

| Title | Format | Label | Catalogue | Year | Price | Price | Notes |
|---|---|---|---|---|---|---|---|
| 007 | 7" | Pyramid | PYR6004 | 1967 | £1.50 | £4 | Roland Alphonso B side |
| 007 Shanty Town | LP | Doctor Bird | DLM5007 | 1967 | £30 | £60 | |
| Beautiful And Dangerous | 7" | Pyramid | PYR6031 | 1968 | £4 | £8 | |
| Bongo Gal | 7" | Pyramid | PYR6035 | 1968 | £4 | £8 | |
| Christmas Day | 7" | Pyramid | PYR6059 | 1969 | £2 | £5 | |
| Double Dekker | LP | Trojan | TRLD401 | 1973 | £5 | £12 | double |
| Dracula | 7" | Black Swan | WI455 | 1965 | £5 | £10 | Don Drummond B side |
| Get Up Edna | 7" | Island | WI181 | 1965 | £5 | £10 | |
| Hey Grandma | 7" | Pyramid | PYR6047 | 1968 | £4 | £8 | |
| Honour Your Mother And Father | 7" | Island | WI054 | 1963 | £5 | £10 | |
| Israelites | LP | Doctor Bird | DLM5013 | 1969 | £20 | £40 | |

228

| | | | | | | | |
|---|---|---|---|---|---|---|---|
| Israelites | 7" | Pyramid | PYR6058 | 1969 | £1.50 | £4 | *Beverley's Allstars B side* |
| It Mek | 7" | Pyramid | PYR6054 | 1968 | £4 | £8 | |
| It Mek | 7" | Pyramid | PYR6068 | 1969 | £1.50 | £4 | |
| It Pays | 7" | Pyramid | PYR6026 | 1968 | £4 | £8 | |
| Jeserene | 7" | Island | WI158 | 1964 | £5 | £10 | |
| Mother Pepper | 7" | Pyramid | PYR6044 | 1968 | £4 | £8 | |
| Mother's Young Gal | 7" | Pyramid | PYR6012 | 1967 | £4 | £8 | *Soul Brothers B side* |
| Music Like Dirt | 7" | Pyramid | PYR6051 | 1968 | £4 | £8 | |
| Parents | 7" | Island | WI111 | 1963 | £5 | £10 | |
| Pickney Girl | 7" | Pyramid | PYR6078 | 1970 | £1.50 | £4 | |
| Sabotage | 7" | Pyramid | PYR6020 | 1967 | £4 | £8 | |
| This Is Desmond Dekker | LP | Trojan | TTL4 | 1969 | £5 | £12 | |
| This Woman | 7" | Island | WI202 | 1965 | £5 | £10 | *Lee Perry B side* |
| To Sir With Love | 7" | Pyramid | PYR6037 | 1968 | £4 | £8 | |
| Unity | 7" | Pyramid | PYR6017 | 1967 | £4 | £8 | |
| You Can Get It If You Really Want | LP | Trojan | TBL146 | 1970 | £5 | £12 | |
| You Can Get It If You Really Want | 7" | Trojan | TR7777 | 1970 | £1.50 | £4 | |

## DEL AMITRI

| | | | | | | | |
|---|---|---|---|---|---|---|---|
| Kiss This Thing Goodbye | CD-s | A&M | AMCD551 | 1990 | £2 | £5 | |
| Move Away Jimmy Blue | CD-s | A&M | AMCD555 | 1990 | £2 | £5 | |
| Sense Sickness | 7" | No Strings | NOSP1 | 1983 | £5 | £10 | |
| Spit In The Rain | CD-s | A&M | AMCD589 | 1990 | £2 | £5 | |
| Stone Cold Sober | CD-s | A&M | CDEE527 | 1989 | £2 | £5 | |
| Twisted | CD | A&M | 5403962 | 1995 | £6 | £15 | *double* |

## DEL FUEGO, TERESA

| | | | | | | | |
|---|---|---|---|---|---|---|---|
| Don't Hang Up | 7" | Satril | HH155 | 1981 | £2 | £5 | |

## DEL SATINS

| | | | | | | | |
|---|---|---|---|---|---|---|---|
| Out To Lunch | LP | B.T.Puppy | BTPS1019 | 1972 | £8 | £20 | *US* |

## DEL VIKINGS

| | | | | | | | |
|---|---|---|---|---|---|---|---|
| Angel Up In Heaven | 7" | HMV | POP1145 | 1963 | £2.50 | £6 | *US* |
| Come Go With Me | LP | Dot | DLP3695 | 1966 | £37.50 | £75 | *gold label* |
| Come Go With Me | 7" | London | HLD8405 | 1957 | £50 | £100 | |
| Come Go With The Del Vikings | LP | Luniverse | LP1000 | 1957 | £150 | £250 | *US* |
| Confession Of Love | 7" | HMV | POP1072 | 1962 | £2.50 | £6 | |
| Cool Shake | 78 | Mercury | MT169 | 1957 | £5 | £10 | |
| Del Vikings And The Sonnets | LP | Crown | CLP5368 | 1963 | £8 | £20 | *US* |
| Flat Tyre | 7" | Mercury | AMT1027 | 1959 | £15 | £30 | |
| Swinging, Singing Record Session | LP | Mercury | MG20353 | 1958 | £75 | £150 | *US* |
| They Sing They Swing | LP | Mercury | MG20314 | 1957 | £75 | £150 | *US* |
| Voodoo Man | 7" | Mercury | 7MT199 | 1958 | £20 | £40 | |
| Whispering Bells | 7" | London | HLD8464 | 1957 | £12.50 | £25 | |

## DELACARDOS

| | | | | | | | |
|---|---|---|---|---|---|---|---|
| Mister Dillon | 7" | HMV | POP890 | 1961 | £7.50 | £15 | |

## DELANEY & BONNIE

The sense of well-being and fun that spills over from Delaney and Bonnie's records attracted some famous names to their cause – George Harrison, Dave Mason and Eric Clapton were all perfectly content to play as sidemen within the band for a while. The LP *Accept No Substitute* was to have appeared on the Apple label, but was eventually released on Elektra. Apple test pressings exist, but no cover has ever been found. Meanwhile, Eric Clapton's thrilling contributions to the Delaney and Bonnie sound can be sampled on the LP *On Tour*.

| | | | | | | | |
|---|---|---|---|---|---|---|---|
| Accept No Substitute (The Original Delaney & Bonnie) | LP | Apple | SAPCOR7 | 1969 | £400 | £600 | *test pressing, no sleeve* |
| Accept No Substitute (The Original Delaney & Bonnie) | LP | Elektra | EKS74039 | 1969 | £4 | £10 | |
| On Tour | LP | Atlantic | 2400013 | 1970 | £4 | £10 | |

## DELFONICS

| | | | | | | | |
|---|---|---|---|---|---|---|---|
| La La Means I Love You | LP | Bell | SBLL106 | 1968 | £4 | £10 | |
| Sound Of Sexy Soul | LP | Bell | SBLL121 | 1969 | £4 | £10 | |

## DELICATES

| | | | | | | | |
|---|---|---|---|---|---|---|---|
| Ronnie Is My Lover | 7" | London | HLT8953 | 1959 | £37.50 | £75 | |
| Too Young To Date | 7" | London | HLT9176 | 1960 | £15 | £30 | |

## DELIRIUM

| | | | | | | | |
|---|---|---|---|---|---|---|---|
| Three | LP | Fonit | LPX29 | 1974 | £50 | £100 | *Italian* |

## D'ELL, DENNIS

| | | | | | | | |
|---|---|---|---|---|---|---|---|
| It Breaks My Heart In Two | 7" | CBS | 202605 | 1967 | £75 | £150 | |
| It Breaks My Heart In Two | 7" | CBS | 202605 | 1967 | £30 | £60 | *demo* |

## DELLO, PETE

| | | | | | | | |
|---|---|---|---|---|---|---|---|
| Into Your Ears | LP | Nepentha | 6437001 | 1971 | £20 | £40 | |

## DELLS

| | | | | | | | |
|---|---|---|---|---|---|---|---|
| Bossa Nova Bird | 7" | Pye | 7N25178 | 1963 | £2.50 | £6 | |
| Greatest Hits | LP | Chess | CRLS4554 | 1968 | £4 | £10 | |
| It's All Up To You | 7" | Chess | 6145008 | 1972 | £1.50 | £4 | |
| It's Not Unusual | LP | Vee Jay | LP(S)1141 | 1965 | £6 | £15 | *US* |
| Like It Is | LP | Cadet | 837 | 1969 | £4 | £10 | *US* |
| Love Is Blue – I Can Sing A Rainbow | LP | Chess | CRLS4555 | 1969 | £4 | £10 | |

| | | | | | | | |
|---|---|---|---|---|---|---|---|
| Musical Menu | LP | Cadet | 822 | 1968 £4 | £10 | | US |
| Oh What A Nite | LP | Vee Jay | VJLP1010 | 1959 £50 | £100 | | US |
| Do I Love You | 7" | Chess | CRS8066 | 1967 £1.50 | £4 | | |
| Stay In My Corner | 7" | Chess | CRS8079 | 1968 £1.50 | £4 | | |
| There Is | LP | Cadet | 804 | 1968 £4 | £10 | | US |
| Wear It On Our Face | 7" | Chess | CRS8071 | 1968 £2 | £5 | | |

## DELMORE BROTHERS

| | | | | | | | |
|---|---|---|---|---|---|---|---|
| Country And Western | 7" EP | Parlophone | GEP8728 | 1958 £6 | £12 | | |
| In Memory | LP | King | 910 | 1964 £5 | £12 | | US |
| In Memory Vol. 2 | LP | King | 920 | 1964 £5 | £12 | | US |
| Songs By The Delmore Brothers | LP | King | 589 | 1958 £15 | £30 | | US |
| Thirtieth Anniversary Album | LP | King | 785 | 1962 £10 | £25 | | US |
| Twenty-Four Great Country Songs | LP | King | (S)983 | 1966 £5 | £12 | | US |

## DELTA BLUES BAND

| | | | | | | | |
|---|---|---|---|---|---|---|---|
| Delta Blues Band | LP | Parlophone | 6E06237038 | 1969 £75 | £150 | | Danish |
| No Overdubs | LP | KB | KBLP4 | 1979 £8 | £20 | | Danish |
| Rave On | LP | Medley | 6031 | 1979 £8 | £20 | | Danish |

## DELTA CATS

| | | | | | | | |
|---|---|---|---|---|---|---|---|
| I Can't Re-Live | 7" | Bamboo | BAM3 | 1969 £1.50 | £4 | | |
| Unworthy Baby | 7" | Blue Cat | BS128 | 1968 £4 | £8 | | Thrillers B side |

## DELTA KINGS

| | | | | | | |
|---|---|---|---|---|---|---|
| At Sundown | 7" EP | London | RER1318 | 1961 £2 | £5 | |
| Down The River | LP | London | LTZR15180 | 1960 £4 | £10 | |

## DELTA RHYTHM BOYS

| | | | | | | |
|---|---|---|---|---|---|---|
| Mood Indigo | 7" | Brunswick | 05353 | 1954 £1.50 | £4 | |
| Sixteen Tons | 7" EP | Felsted | ESD3064 | 1958 £2 | £5 | |

## DELTA SKIFFLE GROUP

| | | | | | | |
|---|---|---|---|---|---|---|
| Delta Skiffle Group | 7" EP | Esquire | EP162 | 1958 £5 | £10 | |

## DELTAS

| | | | | | | | |
|---|---|---|---|---|---|---|---|
| Georgia | 7" | Blue Beat | BB265 | 1964 £6 | £12 | | |
| Visitor | 7" | Blue Beat | BB275 | 1965 £6 | £12 | | Skatalites B side |

## DELTONES

| | | | | | | |
|---|---|---|---|---|---|---|
| Rocking Blues | 7" | Top Rank | JAR171 | 1959 £20 | £40 | |

## DELUSION

| | | | | | | |
|---|---|---|---|---|---|---|
| Pessimists Paradise | 7" | Wizzo | WIZZO2 | 198– £2 | £5 | |

## DEMENSIONS

| | | | | | | |
|---|---|---|---|---|---|---|
| Count Your Blessings Instead Of Sheep | 7" | Coral | Q72437 | 1961 £1.50 | £4 | |
| Over The Rainbow | 7" | Top Rank | JAR505 | 1960 £10 | £20 | |

## DEMIAN

| | | | | | | | |
|---|---|---|---|---|---|---|---|
| Demian | LP | ABC | ABC5718 | 1971 £20 | £40 | | US |

## DEMIAN (BUBBLE PUPPY)

| | | | | | | | |
|---|---|---|---|---|---|---|---|
| Demian | LP | ABC | S718 | 1971 £6 | £15 | | US |

## DEMON FUZZ

| | | | | | | |
|---|---|---|---|---|---|---|
| Afreaka | LP | Dawn | DNLS3013 | 1971 £5 | £12 | |

## DEMON PACT

| | | | | | | | |
|---|---|---|---|---|---|---|---|
| Eaten Alive | 7" | Slime | PACT1 | 1981 £5 | £10 | | |
| Escape | 7" | Slime | PACT2 | 1981 £7.50 | £15 | | test pressing only |

## DEMON PREACHER

| | | | | | | |
|---|---|---|---|---|---|---|
| Little Miss Perfect | 7" | Small Wonder | SMALL10 | 1978 £2.50 | £6 | |
| Royal Northern | 7" | Illegal | SRTS78110 | 1978 £4 | £8 | |

## DEMON THOR

| | | | | | | |
|---|---|---|---|---|---|---|
| Anno 1972 | LP | United Artists | UAS29393 | 1972 £10 | £25 | |
| Written In The Sky | LP | United Artists | UAS29496 | 1974 £10 | £25 | |

## DEMONS

| | | | | | | |
|---|---|---|---|---|---|---|
| Action By Example | 7" | Crypt Music | DEM1 | 1980 £2 | £5 | |
| Bless You | 7" | Big Shot | BI523 | 1969 £1.50 | £4 | |

## DEMPSEY, TOMMY & JOHN SWIFT

| | | | | | | |
|---|---|---|---|---|---|---|
| Green Grow The Laurel | LP | Trailer | LER2096 | 1976 £4 | £10 | |

## DENE, TERRY

| | | | | | | | |
|---|---|---|---|---|---|---|---|
| Bimbombey | 7" | Decca | F11100 | 1959 £2 | £5 | | |
| Come And Get It | 7" | Decca | F10938 | 1957 £4 | £8 | | |
| Come In And Be Loved | 7" | Decca | F10977 | 1958 £4 | £8 | | |
| Feminine Look | 7" | Aral | PS107 | 1963 £2.50 | £6 | | picture sleeve |
| Geraldine | 7" | Oriole | CB1562 | 1960 £4 | £8 | | |
| Golden Disc | 7" EP | Decca | DFE6427 | 1957 £10 | £20 | | |
| I've Come Of Age | 7" | Decca | F11136 | 1959 £2 | £5 | | |
| Like A Baby | 7" | Oriole | CB1594 | 1961 £4 | £8 | | |
| Lucky Lucky Bobby | 7" | Decca | F10964 | 1957 £5 | £10 | | |
| Pretty Little Pearly | 7" | Decca | F11076 | 1958 £2.50 | £6 | | |

| | | | | | | | | |
|---|---|---|---|---|---|---|---|---|
| Seven Steps To Love | 7" | Decca | F11037 | 1958 | £2.50 | £6 | |
| Stairway Of Love | 7" | Decca | F11016 | 1958 | £2 | £5 | |
| Start Moving | 7" | Decca | F10914 | 1957 | £6 | £12 | |
| Terry Dene No. 1 | 7" EP | World Records | DFE6459 | 1958 | £10 | £20 | |
| Terry Dene No. 2 | 7" EP | Decca | DFE6507 | 1958 | £10 | £20 | |
| Terry Dene Now | 7" EP | Herald | ELR107 | 1966 | £2.50 | £6 | |
| Thank You Pretty Baby | 7" | Decca | F11154 | 1959 | £2.50 | £6 | |
| White Sports Coat | 7" | Decca | F10895 | 1957 | £10 | £20 | |

## DENE BOYS

| | | | | | | | |
|---|---|---|---|---|---|---|---|
| Bye Bye Love | 7" | HMV | POP374 | 1957 | £2.50 | £6 | |

## DENE FOUR

| | | | | | | | |
|---|---|---|---|---|---|---|---|
| Hush-a-Bye | 7" | HMV | POP666 | 1959 | £2 | £5 | |

## DENIMS

| | | | | | | | |
|---|---|---|---|---|---|---|---|
| I'm Your Man | 7" | CBS | 201807 | 1965 | £10 | £20 | |

## DENISON, ROGER

| | | | | | | | |
|---|---|---|---|---|---|---|---|
| I'm On An Island | 7" | Parlophone | R5545 | 1966 | £2.50 | £6 | |
| She Wanders Through My Mind | 7" | Parlophone | R5566 | 1967 | £1.50 | £4 | |

## DENNIS, CATHY

| | | | | | | | |
|---|---|---|---|---|---|---|---|
| Irresistible | 12" | Polydor | CATHX7 | 1992 | £6 | £15 | |
| Just Another Dream | 12" | Polydor | CATHR1 | 1989 | £2.50 | £6 | |

## DENNIS, DENZIL

| | | | | | | | |
|---|---|---|---|---|---|---|---|
| Donkey Train | 7" | Trojan | TR614 | 1968 | £2.50 | £6 | |
| Hush Don't You Cry | 7" | Trojan | TR615 | 1968 | £2.50 | £6 | |
| Oh Carol | 7" | Jolly | JY011 | 1968 | £2 | £5 | |
| Seven Nights In Rome | 7" | Blue Beat | BB181 | 1963 | £6 | £12 | |

## DENNIS, JACKIE

| | | | | | | | |
|---|---|---|---|---|---|---|---|
| Gingerbread | 7" | Decca | F11090 | 1958 | £1.50 | £4 | |
| Jackie Dennis No. 1 | 7" EP | Decca | DFE6513 | 1958 | £5 | £10 | |
| La Dee Dah | 7" | Decca | F10992 | 1958 | £2 | £5 | |
| Miss Valerie | 7" | Decca | F11011 | 1958 | £2 | £5 | |
| More Than Ever | 7" | Decca | F11060 | 1958 | £1.50 | £4 | |
| Purple People Eater | 7" | Decca | F11033 | 1958 | £2.50 | £6 | |

## DENNISONS

| | | | | | | | |
|---|---|---|---|---|---|---|---|
| Be My Girl | 7" | Decca | F11691 | 1963 | £2.50 | £6 | |
| Nobody Like My Babe | 7" | Decca | F11990 | 1964 | £2.50 | £6 | |
| Walking The Dog | 7" | Decca | F11880 | 1964 | £2.50 | £6 | |

## DENNY, MARTIN

| | | | | | | | |
|---|---|---|---|---|---|---|---|
| Afrodesia | LP | London | SAHU6048 | 1959 | £5 | £12 | stereo |
| Enchanted Sea | LP | London | SAHG6098 | 1960 | £4 | £10 | |
| Exotic Percussion | LP | London | SAHG6187 | 1961 | £4 | £10 | |
| Exotic Sounds | 7" EP | London | REU1241 | 1960 | £2.50 | £6 | |
| Exotica | 10" LP | London | HBU1079 | 1957 | £6 | £15 | |
| Exotica Vol. 2 | LP | London | SAHG6076 | 1960 | £4 | £10 | |
| Exotica Vol. 3 | LP | London | SAHW6089 | 1960 | £4 | £10 | |
| Forbidden Island | LP | London | SAHU6004 | 1958 | £5 | £12 | |
| Quiet Village | LP | London | SAHU6055 | 1960 | £4 | £10 | |
| Quiet Village | 7" | London | SLW4004 | 1959 | £7.50 | £15 | stereo |
| Romantica | LP | London | SAHG6215 | 1962 | £4 | £10 | |
| Silver Screen | LP | London | SAHG6122 | 1961 | £4 | £10 | |

## DENNY, SANDY

Sandy Denny was something of a limited singer: hopeless on up-tempo rock material, she nevertheless sounded gorgeous on a slow ballad – as her recording of 'The Sea' with Fotheringay proves at a stroke. The small number of early, pre-Fairport Convention tracks are spread somewhat thinly over various LPs. The album with Johnny Silvo, for example, is not a collaboration, but merely includes songs recorded by each separately. The Strawbs LP, however, is a true joint effort.

| | | | | | | | |
|---|---|---|---|---|---|---|---|
| Candle In The Wind | 7" | Island | WIP6391 | 1977 | £25 | £50 | demo only |
| Like An Old Fashioned Waltz | LP | Island | ILPS9258 | 1973 | £6 | £15 | |
| Make Me A Pallet On Your Floor | 7" | Mooncrest | MOON54 | 1976 | £1.50 | £4 | |
| Northstar Grass Man & The Ravens | LP | Island | ILPS9165 | 1971 | £6 | £15 | |
| Pass Of Arms EP | 7" | Island | WIP6141 | 1972 | £37.50 | £75 | picture sleeve |
| Rendezvous | LP | Island | ILPS9433 | 1977 | £4 | £10 | with insert |
| Sandy | LP | Island | ILPS9207 | 1972 | £6 | £15 | |
| Sandy And Johnny | LP | Saga | EROS8041 | 1967 | £15 | £30 | with Johnny Silvo |
| Sandy Denny | LP | Mooncrest | CREST28 | 1978 | £10 | £25 | 1 extra track |
| Sandy Denny | LP | Saga | EROS8153 | 1970 | £15 | £30 | |
| Whispering Grass | 7" | Island | WIP6176 | 1973 | £2 | £5 | picture sleeve |
| Who Knows Where The Time Goes | LP | Island | SDSP100 | 1985 | £10 | £25 | 4 LP box set |

## DENNY, SANDY & STRAWBS

| | | | | | | | |
|---|---|---|---|---|---|---|---|
| All Our Own Work | LP | Pickwick | SHM813 | 1973 | £5 | £12 | |

## DENVER, KARL

| | | | | | | | |
|---|---|---|---|---|---|---|---|
| At The Yew Tree | LP | Decca | LK4540 | 1963 | £5 | £12 | |
| By A Sleepy Lagoon | 7" EP | Decca | DFE8501 | 1962 | £2.50 | £6 | |
| Karl Denver | LP | Ace Of Clubs | ACL1131 | 1962 | £4 | £10 | |
| Karl Denver Hits | 7" EP | Decca | DFE8504 | 1962 | £2.50 | £6 | |
| Wimoweh | LP | Decca | ACL1098 | 1961 | £6 | £15 | |

| | | | | | | | |
|---|---|---|---|---|---|---|---|
| Wimoweh | 7" | Decca | F11420 | 1962 | £1.50 | £4 | |

## DENVER, NIGEL

| | | | | | | | |
|---|---|---|---|---|---|---|---|
| Borderline | LP | Decca | LK5014 | 1969 | £4 | £10 | |
| Folk, Old And New | LP | Decca | SKL4943 | 1968 | £5 | £12 | |
| Rebellion | LP | Decca | SKL4844 | 1967 | £5 | £12 | |
| Scottish Nationalist Songs | LP | Major Minor | MMLP1 | 1967 | £5 | £12 | |
| There Was A Lad | LP | Major Minor | MMLP38 | 1968 | £5 | £12 | |

## DENVERS

| | | | | | | | |
|---|---|---|---|---|---|---|---|
| Do You Love Me | 7" EP | Polydor | 27114 | 1964 | £5 | £10 | French |
| Liverpool Party | LP | Polydor | 46144 | 1964 | £25 | £50 | French |

## DENZIL & PAT

| | | | | | | | |
|---|---|---|---|---|---|---|---|
| Dream | 7" | Downtown | DT403 | 1969 | £1.50 | £4 | |

## DEPECHE MODE

| | | | | | | | |
|---|---|---|---|---|---|---|---|
| Behind The Wheel | CD-s | Mute | CDBONG15 | 1988 | £2 | £5 | |
| Behind The Wheel (Beatmasters Mix) | 12" | Mute | L12BONG15 | 1988 | £2.50 | £6 | |
| Behind The Wheel (Shep Pettibone Mix) | 12" | Mute | DBONG15 | 1987 | £2.50 | £6 | promo |
| Blasphemous Rumours | CD-s | Mute | INT826839 | 1987 | £2 | £5 | German import |
| Broken Frame | CD | Mute | CDSTUMM9 | 1988 | £5 | £12 | |
| Construction Time Again | CD | Mute | CDSTUMM13 | 1988 | £5 | £12 | |
| Depeche Mode | CD-s | Mute | DMBX1 | 1991 | £10 | £20 | 6 CD singles, boxed |
| Depeche Mode | CD-s | Mute | DMBX2 | 1991 | £10 | £20 | 6 CD singles, boxed |
| Depeche Mode | CD-s | Mute | DMBX3 | 1991 | £10 | £20 | 6 CD singles, boxed |
| Enjoy The Silence | CD-s | Mute | CDBONG18 | 1990 | £2 | £5 | |
| Enjoy The Silence | CD-s | Mute | LCDBONG18 | 1990 | £4 | £10 | |
| Enjoy The Silence | 12" | Mute | P12BONG18 | 1990 | £2.50 | £6 | promo |
| Enjoy The Silence (The Quad) | CD-s | Mute | XLCDBONG18 | 1990 | £6 | £15 | 3" single |
| Everything Counts (Absolute Mix) | 10" | Mute | 10BONG16 | 1989 | £2.50 | £6 | |
| Everything Counts (edit) | 7" | Mute | 7BONG16R | 1989 | £2 | £5 | promo |
| Everything Counts (live) | CD-s | Mute | CDBONG16 | 1989 | £2 | £5 | |
| Everything Counts (Simenon & Saunders Mix) | CD-s | Mute | LCDBONG16 | 1989 | £10 | £20 | 3" single |
| Everything Counts (Simenon & Saunders Mix) | 12" | Mute | P12BONG16 | 1989 | £2.50 | £6 | promo |
| Leave In Silence | CD-s | Intercord | INT826807 | 1988 | £2 | £5 | |
| Love In Itself | CD-s | Intercord | INT826836 | 1987 | £2 | £5 | German import |
| Master And Servant | 12" | Mute | L12BONG6 | 1984 | £2.50 | £6 | |
| Music For The Masses | LP | Mute | STUMM47 | 1987 | £4 | £10 | clear or blue vinyl |
| Music For The Masses | LP | Mute | STUMM47 | 1987 | £4 | £10 | HMV ltd edn with promo 12" (HMV1) |
| Music For The Masses | CD | Mute | CDSTUMM47 | 1987 | £8 | £20 | test pressing with 10 tracks |
| Never Let Me Down Again | CD-s | Mute | CDBONG14 | 1987 | £2.50 | £6 | |
| Never Let Me Down Again | 12" | Mute | P12BONG14 | 1987 | £2.50 | £6 | promo |
| People Are People (On U Sound Mix) | 12" | Mute | L12BONG5 | 1984 | £2.50 | £6 | |
| Personal Jesus | CD-s | Mute | CDBONG17 | 1989 | £2 | £5 | 3" single |
| Personal Jesus | CD-s | Mute | LCDBONG17 | 1989 | £5 | £12 | |
| Personal Jesus | 12" | Mute | P12BONG17 | 1989 | £2.50 | £6 | promo |
| Policy Of Truth | CD-s | Mute | CDBONG19 | 1990 | £2 | £5 | |
| Policy Of Truth (Capitol Mix) | 12" | Mute | P12BONG19 | 1990 | £2.50 | £6 | promo |
| Policy Of Truth (Trancentral Mix) | CD-s | Mute | LCDBONG19 | 1990 | £2.50 | £6 | |
| Sometimes I Wish I Was Dead | 7" | Lyntone | LYN10209 | 1981 | £2.50 | £6 | Flexipop flexi |
| Speak And Spell | CD | Mute | CDSTUMM5 | 1988 | £5 | £12 | 5 extra tracks |
| Strangelove | CD-s | Mute | CDBONG13 | 1987 | £2 | £5 | |
| Strangelove (Blind Mix) | 12" | Mute | L12BONG13 | 1987 | £2.50 | £6 | |
| Strangelove (Fresh Ground Mix) | 12" | Mute | DANCEBONG13 | 1987 | £10 | £25 | promo |
| Strangelove (Hijack MIx) | 12" | Mute | PP12BONG16 | 1989 | £3 | £8 | promo |
| Strangelove (Maxi-Mix) | 12" | Mute | S12BONG13 | 1987 | £2.50 | £6 | promo |
| Stripped | 12" | Mute | 12BONG10 | 1986 | £2.50 | £6 | promo |
| Violator | CD | Mute | CDSTUMM64 | 1989 | £50 | £100 | promo box set, with LP and cassette |
| Violator | 12" | Mute | PSTUMM64 | 1990 | £3 | £8 | promo sampler |
| World In My Eyes | CD-s | Mute | CDBONG20 | 1990 | £2 | £5 | |
| World In My Eyes (Dub In My Eyes) | CD-s | Mute | LCDBONG20 | 1990 | £10 | £20 | |
| World In My Eyes (Mayhem Mode) | 12" | Mute | P12BONG20 | 1990 | £2.50 | £6 | promo |

## DEPUTIES

| | | | | | | | |
|---|---|---|---|---|---|---|---|
| Given Half A Chance | 7" | Strike | JH305 | 1966 | £5 | £10 | |

## DEREK, JON

| | | | | | | | |
|---|---|---|---|---|---|---|---|
| Songs I Have Written | LP | Westwood | WR5098 | 1976 | £8 | £20 | |

## DEREK & THE DOMINOES

| | | | | | | | |
|---|---|---|---|---|---|---|---|
| Tell The Truth | 7" | Polydor | 2058057 | 1970 | £7.50 | £15 | |

## DEREK & THE FRESHMEN

| | | | | | | | |
|---|---|---|---|---|---|---|---|
| Gone Away | 7" | Oriole | CB305 | 1965 | £2 | £5 | |

## DESANTO, SUGAR PIE

| | | | | | | | |
|---|---|---|---|---|---|---|---|
| I Don't Wanna Fuss | 7" | Pye | 7N25267 | 1964 | £4 | £8 | |
| Soulful Dress | 7" | Chess | CRS8093 | 1969 | £2 | £5 | |
| Soulful Dress | 7" | Pye | 7N25249 | 1964 | £5 | £10 | |
| Sugar Pie | LP | Checker | LP2979 | 1961 | £10 | £25 | US |
| There's Gonna Be Trouble | 7" | Chess | CRS8034 | 1966 | £2.50 | £6 | |

## DESCENDANTS
| | | | | | | |
|---|---|---|---|---|---|---|
| Garden Of Eden | 7" | CBS | 202545 | 1967 £20 | £40 | |

## DESHANNON, JACKIE
| | | | | | | |
|---|---|---|---|---|---|---|
| Are You Ready For This? | LP | Liberty | (S)BLY3085 | 1966 £4 | £10 | |
| Breakin' It Up On The Beatles Tour | LP | Liberty | LRP3390/LST7390. | 1964 £8 | £20 | US |
| C'Mon Let's Live A Little | LP | Liberty | LRP3430/LST7430. | 1966 £4 | £10 | US |
| Come On Down | 7" | Liberty | LIB66224 | 1966 £5 | £10 | |
| Don't Turn Your Back On Me | LP | Liberty | LBY1245 | 1965 £5 | £12 | |
| Don't Turn Your Back On Me | 7" | Liberty | LIB10175 | 1964 £1.50 | £4 | |
| Great Performances | LP | Liberty | LBS83117 | 1968 £4 | £10 | |
| In The Wind | LP | Imperial | LP9296/12296 | 1965 £4 | £10 | US |
| Jackie | 7" EP | Liberty | LEP2233 | 1965 £6 | £12 | |
| Jackie DeShannon | LP | Liberty | LRP3320/LST7320. | 1963 £6 | £15 | US |
| Needles And Pins | 7" | Liberty | LIB55563 | 1963 £1.50 | £4 | |
| This Is Jackie DeShannon | LP | Liberty | LBY1182 | 1965 £4 | £10 | |
| When You Walk In The Room | 7" | Liberty | LIB55645 | 1964 £1.50 | £4 | |
| You Won't Forget Me | LP | Imperial | LP9294/12294 | 1965 £4 | £10 | US |

## DESIGN
| | | | | | | |
|---|---|---|---|---|---|---|
| Day Of The Fox | LP | Regal Zonophone | SLRZ1037 | 1973 £6 | £15 | |
| Design | LP | Epic | 64322 | 1970 £8 | £20 | |
| Tomorrow Is So Far Away | LP | Epic | 64653 | 1971 £8 | £20 | |

## DESMOND, ANDY
| | | | | | | |
|---|---|---|---|---|---|---|
| Living On A Shoe String | LP | Konk | KONK103 | 1975 £4 | £10 | |

## DESMOND, JOHNNY
| | | | | | | |
|---|---|---|---|---|---|---|
| Bushel And A Peck | 7" | MGM | SP1042 | 1953 £1.50 | £4 | B side by Art Lund |
| Eighteenth Century Music Box | 7" | Vogue Coral | Q72235 | 1957 £1.50 | £4 | |
| Sixteen Tons | 7" | Vogue Coral | Q72115 | 1956 £1.50 | £4 | |
| White Sports Coat | 7" | Vogue Coral | Q72261 | 1957 £1.50 | £4 | |
| Yellow Rose Of Texas | 7" | Vogue Coral | Q72099 | 1955 £1.50 | £4 | |

## DESMOND, LORRAE
| | | | | | | |
|---|---|---|---|---|---|---|
| Ding Dong Rock-a-Billy | 7" | Parlophone | R4361 | 1957 £5 | £10 | |
| Heartbroken | 7" | Decca | F10533 | 1955 £2 | £5 | |
| Hold My Hand | 7" | Decca | F10375 | 1954 £2.50 | £6 | |
| House With Love In It | 7" | Parlophone | R4239 | 1956 £1.50 | £4 | |
| I Can't Tell A Waltz From A Tango | 7" | Decca | F10404 | 1954 £2.50 | £6 | |
| Kansas City Special | 7" | Parlophone | R4320 | 1957 £2 | £5 | |
| No One But You | 7" | Decca | F10398 | 1954 £2.50 | £6 | |
| Secret Of Happiness | 7" | Parlophone | R4430 | 1958 £1.50 | £4 | |
| Soda Pop Hop | 7" | Parlophone | R4463 | 1958 £1.50 | £4 | |
| Tall Paul | 7" | Parlophone | R4534 | 1959 £1.50 | £4 | |
| Two Ships | 7" | Parlophone | R4400 | 1958 £1.50 | £4 | |
| Wake The Town And Tell The People | 7" | Decca | F10612 | 1955 £2.50 | £6 | |
| Where Will The Dimple Be? | 7" | Decca | F10510 | 1955 £2.50 | £6 | |
| Why Oh Why? | 7" | Decca | F10461 | 1955 £2.50 | £6 | |
| You Won't Be Around | 7" | Parlophone | R4287 | 1957 £1.50 | £4 | |

## DESMOND, PAUL
| | | | | | | |
|---|---|---|---|---|---|---|
| Paul Desmond And Friends | LP | Warner Bros | WM4020/WS8020 . | 1961 £6 | £15 | |
| Two Of A Mind | LP | RCA | RD7525 | 1962 £6 | £15 | ...with Gerry Mulligan |

## DESTROYERS
| | | | | | | |
|---|---|---|---|---|---|---|
| Niney Special | 7" | Amalgamated | AMG856 | 1969 £1.50 | £4 | |

## DETERGENTS
| | | | | | | |
|---|---|---|---|---|---|---|
| I Don't Know | 7" | Columbia | DB7591 | 1965 £1.50 | £4 | |
| Leader Of The Laundromat | 7" | Columbia | DB7513 | 1965 £2.50 | £6 | |
| Many Faces Of The Detergents | LP | Roulette | (S)R25308 | 1965 £6 | £15 | US |

## DETOURS
| | | | | | | |
|---|---|---|---|---|---|---|
| Run To Me Baby | 7" | CBS | 3213 | 1968 £7.50 | £15 | |
| Whole Lotta Lovin' | 7" | CBS | 3401 | 1968 £12.50 | £25 | |

## DETROIT
| | | | | | | |
|---|---|---|---|---|---|---|
| Detroit | LP | Paramount | SPFL277 | 1971 £4 | £10 | |

## DETROIT SPINNERS
| | | | | | | |
|---|---|---|---|---|---|---|
| Detroit Spinners | LP | Tamla Motown | (S)TML11060 | 1968 £10 | £25 | |
| For All We Know | 7" | Tamla Motown | TMG627 | 1967 £4 | £8 | |
| I'll Always Love You | 7" | Tamla Motown | TMG523 | 1965 £15 | £30 | |
| Sweet Thing | 7" | Tamla Motown | TMG514 | 1965 £15 | £30 | |

## DEUCHAR, JIMMY
| | | | | | | |
|---|---|---|---|---|---|---|
| Jimmy Deuchar Ensemble | 10" LP | Tempo | LAP2 | 1955 £20 | £40 | |
| Jimmy Deuchar Quartet | 10" LP | Esquire | 20059 | 1956 £8 | £20 | |
| Pal Jimmy | LP | Tempo | TAP20 | 1958 £20 | £40 | |
| Showcase | 10" LP | Vogue | LDE023 | 1953 £15 | £30 | |

## DEUTER
| | | | | | | |
|---|---|---|---|---|---|---|
| Aum | LP | Kuckuck | 2375017 | 1972 £6 | £15 | German |
| Celebration | LP | Kuckuck | 2375040 | 1976 £5 | £12 | German |
| Deuter | LP | Kuckuck | 2375009 | 1971 £6 | £15 | German |

## DEUTSCHER, DRAFI
Drafi ............... LP ...... Decca ............. SLK16380 ............. 1966 £15 ......... £30 ................. *German*

## DEVIANTS
The Deviants, masterminded (if the word is appropriate to such a chaotic organization) by Mick Farren, were more about social revolution than about music. Pieces like 'Let's Loot The Supermarket' describe the group's stance, although they were too disorganized and too full of drugs and alcohol to have ever achieved even this much of a blow against society. Amazingly, many of the original group members managed to continue with some kind of career in rock music – Farren with new versions of the Deviants (and he also became a successful writer) and Duncan Sanderson, Russ Hunter, and Paul Rudolph with the Pink Fairies.

Deviants ..................... LP ...... Transatlantic .... TRA204 ................. 1969 £15 ......... £30 ..........................
Deviants ..................... LP ...... Transatlantic .... TRA204 ................. 1969 £20 ......... £40 ............. *with booklet*
Disposable ................. LP ...... Stable ............. SLP7001 .............. 1968 £25 ......... £50 ..........................
Ptooff ....................... LP ...... Decca ............. LKR/SKLR4993 .... 1969 £15 ......... £30 ..........................
Ptooff ....................... LP ...... Underground Impressarios ..... IMP1 ................. 1967 £30 ......... £60 ............. *poster sleeve*
Ptooff! ...................... LP ...... Psycho ........... PSYCHO16 ........... 1983 £5 ......... £12 ..........................
You've Got To Hold On ......................... 7" ...... Stable ............. STA5601 ................ 1968 £10 ......... £20 ..........................

## DEVILED HAM
I Had Too Much To Dream Last Night ..... LP ...... Super K .......... 6003 ................ 1968 £5 ......... £12 ................. *US*

## DEVIL'S ANVIL
Hardrock From The Middle East ............... LP ...... Columbia ........ CL2664/CS9464 ..... 1968 £10 ......... £25 ....................... *US*

## DEVON
Making Love ................................ 7" ...... Nu Beat .......... NB021 ................. 1968 £2 ......... £5 ..........................
What A Sin Thing ....................... 7" ...... Blue Cat .......... BS158 ..................... 1969 £2 ......... £5 ..........................

## DEVOTED
I Love George Best ....................... 7" ...... Page One ....... POF076 ................. 1968 £2 ......... £5 ......... *picture sleeve*

## DEVOTIONS
For Sentimental Reasons ......................... 7" ...... Columbia ........ DB7256 ................. 1964 £6 ......... £12 ..........................

## DEW DROPS
Somebody Is Knocking ......................... 7" ...... Blue Beat ....... BB381 .................. 1967 £6 ......... £12 ..........................

## DEWHURST, BRIAN
Hunter And The Hunted ......................... LP ...... Folk Heritage .. FHR075 ................. 1975 £8 ......... £20 ..........................

## DEXTER, DANNY
Sweet Mama ......................... 7" ...... London ........... HLU9690 ............... 1963 £2.50 ......... £6 ..........................

## DEXTER, RAY & THE LAYABOUTS
Coalman's Lament ......................... 7" ...... Decca ............. F11538 ............. 1962 £5 ......... £10 ..........................

## DEXY'S MIDNIGHT RUNNERS
It seems incredible that a group with the inspiration and brilliance that Dexy's Midnight Runners had at the beginning of the eighties could so rapidly and so completely fall from favour in the aftermath of a number one hit. The group is now represented by just two collectors' items, the rarity of the listed LP being considerably greater than might be suggested by its low value. On the eve of the group's second album being released, Kevin Rowland had still not come up with his Celtic Soul identity, although the actual music was in place. Accordingly, test pressings of the album that was actually issued as *Too Rye Aye* have a different title and completely different artwork.

Come On Eileen ............................. CD-s .. Mercury .......... MERCD347 ........... 1991 £2 ......... £5 ..........................
Hey Where Are You Going With That Suitcase ............................. LP ...... Mercury .......... MERS5 ................. 1982 £8 ......... £20 ...... *promo of 2nd LP*

## DEY, TRACY
Go Away ......................... 7" ...... Stateside .......... SS287 ..................... 1964 £5 ......... £10 ..........................

## DHARMA BLUES
The music of the Dharma Blues is a reasonably faithful copy of the country blues – piano and harmonica to the fore – but suffers badly from the perennial problem of white blues records: the vocals are totally unconvincing. The sleeve notes go on at length about how exciting the music is and how relevant it is to the present age, but in truth these versions of some well-known traditional songs are a bit boring. That anyone should be willing to pay a substantial collectors' price for the record, when for a fraction of the price they could buy a good compilation of music by the likes of Memphis Slim or Sonny Terry and Brownie McGhee, is one of the mysteries of record collecting.

Dharma Blues ............................. LP ...... Major Minor ... SMCP5017 ............. 1969 £30 ......... £60 ..........................

## DIALOGUE
Dialogue ............................. LP ...... Cold Studio ..... DM68425 ............... 1968 £100 ..... £200 ..........................

## DIAMOND, BRIAN & THE CUTTERS
Big Bad Wolf ............................. 7" ...... Pye ............ 7N15779 ............. 1965 £2 ......... £5 ..........................
Bone Idol ............................. 7" ...... Pye ............ 7N15952 ............. 1965 £2 ......... £5 ..........................
Jealousy Will Get You Nowhere ............... 7" ...... Decca .......... F11724 ............. 1963 £2 ......... £5 ..........................
Shake Shout And Go ............................. 7" ...... Fontana ........... TF452 ............. 1964 £2 ......... £5 ..........................

## DIAMOND, JERRY
Sunburned Lips ............................. 7" ...... London ........... HLE8496 ............. 1957 £7.50 ......... £15 ..........................

## DIAMOND, LEE
I'll Step Down ............................. 7" ...... Fontana ........... H310 ............. 1961 £1.50 ......... £4 ..........................
Stop Your Crying ............................. 7" ...... Fontana ........... H345 .................... 1961 £1.50 ......... £4 ..........................

## DIAMOND, NEIL

| | | | | | | | |
|---|---|---|---|---|---|---|---|
| Best Years Of Our Lives | CD | CBS | XPCD113 | 1989 | £8 | £20 | promo compilation |
| Clown Town | 7" | Columbia | 42809 | 1963 | £62.50 | £125 | US |
| Heartlight | 12" | Columbia | AS991586 | 1982 | £4 | £10 | US 1 sided promo picture disc |
| Hot August Night | LP | Mobile Fidelity | MFSL2024 | 1978 | £4 | £10 | US audiophile |
| Hot August Night | CD | Mobile Fidelity | UDCD589 | 1993 | £6 | £15 | US audiophile |
| In My Lifetime Sampler | CD | Columbia | CSK8877 | 1996 | £8 | £20 | promo |
| Jazz Singer | LP | Mobile Fidelity | MFSL2071 | 1982 | £4 | £10 | US audiophile |
| Jonathan Livingstone Seagull | LP | Columbia | HC42550 | 1981 | £4 | £10 | US audiophile |
| Neil Diamond Songbook | CD | CBS | XPCD708 | 1996 | £8 | £20 | promo |
| Open Ended Interview | LP | Uni | LP1913 | 1968 | £6 | £15 | US promo |
| Solitary Man | 7" | London | HLZ10049 | 1966 | £1.50 | £4 | |
| This Time And All The Hits | CD | Columbia | | 1989 | £8 | £20 | US promo compilation |
| You Don't Bring Me Flowers | LP | Columbia | HC45625 | 1980 | £4 | £10 | US audiophile |

## DIAMOND BOYS

| | | | | | | | |
|---|---|---|---|---|---|---|---|
| Hey Little Girl | 7" | RCA | RCA1351 | 1963 | £1.50 | £4 | |

## DIAMOND HEAD

| | | | | | | | |
|---|---|---|---|---|---|---|---|
| Diamond Lights | 12" | Windsong | DHM005 | 1981 | £3 | £8 | |
| Kingmaker | 7" | MCA | DHMP104 | 1983 | £1.50 | £4 | picture disc |
| Lightning To The Nations | LP | Happy Face | MMDHLP105 | 1981 | £10 | £25 | plain white sleeve |
| Living On Borrowed Time | LP | MCA | DH1001 | 1981 | £5 | £12 | with poster |
| Out Of Phase | 12" | MCA | DHMT104 | 1983 | £2.50 | £6 | |
| Shoot Out the Lights | 7" | Happy Face | MMDH120 | 1980 | £2.50 | £6 | |
| Sweet And Innocent | 7" | Media | SCREEN1 | 1980 | £2 | £5 | |
| Waited Too Long | 7" | DHM | DHM004 | 1981 | £1.50 | £4 | |

## DIAMONDS

| | | | | | | | |
|---|---|---|---|---|---|---|---|
| Black Denim Trousers & Motorcycle Boots | 7" | Vogue Coral | Q72109 | 1955 | £15 | £30 | |
| Collection Of Golden Hits | LP | Mercury | MG20213 | 1956 | £30 | £60 | US |
| Diamonds | LP | Mercury | MG20309 | 1958 | £25 | £50 | US |
| Diamonds | LP | Wing | MGW12114 | 1958 | £10 | £25 | US |
| Diamonds | 10" LP | Mercury | MPT7526 | 1957 | £37.50 | £75 | |
| Diamonds Are Trumps | 7" EP | Mercury | ZEP10026 | 1959 | £10 | £20 | |
| Diamonds Meet Pete Rugulo | LP | Mercury | MG20368/SR60076 | 1958 | £10 | £25 | US |
| Diamonds Meet Pete Rugulo | 7" EP | Mercury | ZEP10020 | 1959 | £6 | £12 | |
| Diamonds Vol. 1 | 7" EP | Mercury | MEP9523 | 1957 | £7.50 | £15 | |
| Diamonds Vol. 2 | 7" EP | Mercury | MEP9527 | 1958 | £7.50 | £15 | |
| Diamonds Vol. 3 | 7" EP | Mercury | MEP9530 | 1958 | £7.50 | £15 | |
| Dig The Diamonds | 7" EP | Mercury | ZEP10003 | 1959 | £10 | £20 | |
| Don't Say Goodbye | 78 | Mercury | MT167 | 1957 | £2 | £5 | |
| Eternal Lovers | 7" | Mercury | AMT1004 | 1958 | £4 | £8 | |
| High Sign | 7" | Mercury | 7MT207 | 1958 | £7.50 | £15 | |
| Kathy O | 7" | Mercury | 7MT233 | 1958 | £2.50 | £6 | |
| Love Love Love | 78 | Mercury | MT121 | 1956 | £2.50 | £6 | |
| Oh How I Wish | 78 | Mercury | MT179 | 1957 | £2.50 | £6 | |
| One Summer Night | 7" | Mercury | AMT1156 | 1961 | £4 | £8 | |
| Pete Rugolo Leads The Diamonds | 7" EP | Mercury | SEZ19012 | 1961 | £10 | £20 | stereo |
| Pete Rugolo Leads The Diamonds | 7" EP | Mercury | ZEP10097 | 1961 | £7.50 | £15 | |
| Pop Hits By The Diamonds | LP | Wing | MGW12178 | 1959 | £8 | £20 | US |
| Presenting The Diamonds | 7" EP | Mercury | MEP9515 | 1957 | £7.50 | £15 | |
| She Say Oom Dooby Oom | 7" | Mercury | AMT1024 | 1959 | £4 | £8 | |
| Silhouettes | 7" | Mercury | 7MT187 | 1958 | £7.50 | £15 | |
| Songs From The Old West | LP | Mercury | MMC14039 | 1960 | £6 | £15 | |
| Star Studded Diamonds | 7" EP | Mercury | ZEP10053 | 1960 | £7.50 | £15 | |
| Straight Skirts | 7" | Mercury | 7MT208 | 1958 | £10 | £20 | |
| Stroll | 7" | Mercury | 7MT195 | 1958 | £6 | £12 | |
| Surprise Package | 7" EP | Mercury | ZEP10088 | 1960 | £10 | £20 | with Ben Hewitt |
| Tell The Truth | 7" | Mercury | AMT1086 | 1960 | £5 | £10 | |

## DIAMONDS (2)

| | | | | | | | |
|---|---|---|---|---|---|---|---|
| Lost City | 7" | Philips | BF1264 | 1963 | £1.50 | £4 | |

## DIANE & THE JAVELINS

| | | | | | | | |
|---|---|---|---|---|---|---|---|
| Heart And Soul | 7" | Columbia | DB7819 | 1966 | £10 | £20 | |

## DI'ANNO, PAUL

| | | | | | | | |
|---|---|---|---|---|---|---|---|
| Di'Anno | LP | FM | WKFMPD1 | 1984 | £4 | £10 | picture disc |

## DIATONES

| | | | | | | | |
|---|---|---|---|---|---|---|---|
| Ruby Has Gone | 7" | Starlite | ST45057 | 1961 | £2.50 | £6 | |

## DIBANGO, MANU

| | | | | | | | |
|---|---|---|---|---|---|---|---|
| Soul Makossa | LP | Atlantic | SD7267 | 1972 | £4 | £10 | US |

## DICE THE BOSS

| | | | | | | | |
|---|---|---|---|---|---|---|---|
| Brixton Cat | LP | Trojan | TBL106 | 1969 | £6 | £15 | |
| Brixton Cat | 7" | Joe | DU50 | 1969 | £2.50 | £6 | |
| But Officer | 7" | Joe | DU52 | 1969 | £2.50 | £6 | |
| Gun The Man Down | 7" | Duke | DU51 | 1969 | £1.50 | £4 | |
| Your Boss DJ | 7" | Joe | DU57 | 1969 | £2.50 | £6 | |

## DICK & DEE DEE

| | | | | | | | |
|---|---|---|---|---|---|---|---|
| All My Trials | 7" | Warner Bros | WB126 | 1964 | £1.50 | £4 | |
| Be My Baby | 7" | Warner Bros | WB156 | 1965 | £1.50 | £4 | |

| | | | | | | | |
|---|---|---|---|---|---|---|---|
| Goodbye To Love | 7" | London | HLG9483 | 1962 | £2 | £5 | |
| Mountain's High | 7" | London | HLG9408 | 1961 | £2.50 | £6 | |
| Remember When | 7" | Warner Bros | WB138 | 1964 | £1.50 | £4 | |
| Songs We've Sung On Shindig | LP | Warner Bros | W(S)1623 | 1965 | £5 | £12 | US |
| Tell Me | LP | Liberty | LRP3236/LST7236. | 1962 | £6 | £15 | US |
| Thou Shalt Not Steal | LP | Warner Bros | W(S)1586 | 1965 | £5 | £12 | US |
| Turn Around | LP | Warner Bros | WM/WS8150 | 1963 | £6 | £15 | |
| Young And In Love | LP | Warner Bros | WM/WS8132 | 1963 | £6 | £15 | |

## DICKENS

| | | | | | | | |
|---|---|---|---|---|---|---|---|
| Standing Out | LP | Hawkmoon | ROCK101P | 1985 | £8 | £20 | |

## DICKENS, CHARLES

| | | | | | | | |
|---|---|---|---|---|---|---|---|
| So Much In Love | 7" | Immediate | IM025 | 1966 | £2.50 | £6 | |

## DICKENSON, VIC

| | | | | | | | |
|---|---|---|---|---|---|---|---|
| Mainstream | LP | London | LTZK15182/ SAHK6066 | 1960 | £6 | £15 | with Joe Thomas |
| Vic Dickenson Septet | 10" LP | Vanguard | PPT12000 | 1955 | £8 | £20 | |
| Vic Dickenson Septet | 10" LP | Vanguard | PPT12005 | 1956 | £8 | £20 | |
| Vic Dickenson Septet | 10" LP | Vanguard | PPT12015 | 1957 | £8 | £20 | |
| Vol. 4 | 10" LP | Vanguard | PPT12019 | 1958 | £8 | £20 | |

## DICKIES

| | | | | | | | |
|---|---|---|---|---|---|---|---|
| Dawn Of The Dickies | LP | A&M | AMLH68510 | 1979 | £4 | £10 | ... blue or yellow vinyl |
| Incredible Shrinking Dickies | LP | A&M | AMLH64742 | 1979 | £4 | £10 | blue, yellow, or orange vinyl |
| Paranoid | 10" | A&M | 12008 | 1978 | £2.50 | £6 | .... promo, white vinyl |

## DICKINSON, BRUCE

| | | | | | | | |
|---|---|---|---|---|---|---|---|
| All The Young Dudes | CD-s | EMI | CDEM142 | 1990 | £2 | £5 | |
| Born In '58 | CD-s | EMI | CDEM185 | 1991 | £2 | £5 | |
| Dive Dive Dive | CD-s | EMI | CDEM151 | 1990 | £2 | £5 | |
| Tattooed Millionaire | CD-s | EMI | CDEM138 | 1990 | £2 | £5 | |

## DICKSON, BARBARA

At the start of her career, Barbara Dickson was a folk singer, this being the style to be found on her collectable Trailer and Decca albums. Her commercial breakthrough came when she was asked to perform the music for the hit stage show about the Beatles – *John, Paul, George, Ringo and Bert*. Her subsequent recordings have found their way into far too many people's homes to have any kind of rarity value.

| | | | | | | | |
|---|---|---|---|---|---|---|---|
| Do Right Woman | LP | Decca | SKL5058 | 1970 | £25 | £50 | |
| Fate O' Charlie | LP | Trailer | LER3002 | 1969 | £15 | £30 | . with Archie Fisher & John MacKinnon |
| From The Beggar's Mantle | LP | Celtic | CM029 | | £4 | £10 | |
| From The Beggar's Mantle | LP | Decca | SKL5116 | 1972 | £25 | £50 | |
| Golden Bird | LP | Oliver And Boyd | | 1969 | £50 | £100 | |
| John, Paul, George, Ringo & Bert | LP | RSO | 2394167 | 1975 | £4 | £10 | |
| Through The Recent Years | LP | Decca | SKL5041 | 1970 | £15 | £30 | .....with Archie Fisher |

## DIDDLEY, BO

Although he has recorded numerous songs that do not use it, Bo Diddley's name will forever be associated with a particular rhythm – the one used on his eponymous first single and translated by band-leader Johnny Otis as 'shave and a haircut, two bits'. It is extremely unlikely that Bo Diddley thought of the rhythm himself, indeed there is evidence that it goes right back to Africa, but it has become his anyway, the 'Bo Diddley beat' being borrowed at intervals ever since by artists as varied as the Rolling Stones, Bruce Springsteen and the Smiths. Bo Diddley is also famous for his unusual guitars – one was covered in fake fur, one was rectangular in shape – but he is not a lead player and his playing has not been an influence on anyone else. Apart, that is, from that rhythm.

| | | | | | | | |
|---|---|---|---|---|---|---|---|
| 16 All Time Hits | LP | Pye | NPL28049 | 1964 | £6 | £15 | |
| 500 Per Cent More Man | 7" | Chess | CRS8026 | 1966 | £1.50 | £4 | |
| Another Sugar Daddy | 7" | Chess | CRS8078 | 1968 | £1.50 | £4 | |
| Beach Party | LP | Checker | LP(S)2988 | 1963 | £15 | £30 | US |
| Beach Party | LP | Pye | NPL28032 | 1963 | £5 | £12 | |
| Black Gladiator | LP | Checker | LP(S)3013 | 1969 | £5 | £12 | US |
| Bo Diddley | LP | Checker | LP2984 | 1962 | £8 | £20 | US |
| Bo Diddley | LP | Chess | LP1431 | 1957 | £25 | £50 | US |
| Bo Diddley | LP | Pye | NPL28026 | 1963 | £6 | £15 | |
| Bo Diddley | 7" | Pye | 7N25210 | 1963 | £2.50 | £6 | |
| Bo Diddley 1969 | 7" | Chess | CRS8088 | 1969 | £1.50 | £4 | |
| Bo Diddley And Company | LP | Checker | LP2985 | 1963 | £20 | £40 | US |
| Bo Diddley Is A Gunslinger | LP | Checker | LP2977 | 1961 | £20 | £40 | US |
| Bo Diddley Is A Gunslinger | LP | Pye | NJL33 | 1963 | £10 | £25 | |
| Bo Diddley Is A Lover | LP | Checker | LP2980 | 1961 | £15 | £30 | US |
| Bo Diddley Is A Lover | 7" | Pye | 7N25227 | 1963 | £2 | £5 | |
| Bo Diddley Is A Twister | LP | Checker | LP2982 | 1962 | £8 | £20 | US |
| Bo Diddley Rides Again | LP | Pye | NPL28029 | 1963 | £6 | £15 | |
| Bo's A Lumberjack | 7" EP | Pye | NEP44031 | 1964 | £6 | £12 | |
| Boss Man | LP | Checker | LP(S)3007 | 1967 | £15 | £30 | US |
| Diddling | 7" EP | Pye | NEP44036 | 1964 | £4 | £8 | |
| Five Hundred Per Cent More Man | LP | Checker | LP(S)2996 | 1964 | £6 | £15 | US |
| Go Bo Diddley | LP | London | HAM2230 | 1959 | £50 | £100 | |
| Great Grandfather | 7" | London | HLM8913 | 1959 | £15 | £30 | |
| Have Guitar, Will Travel | LP | Checker | LP2974 | 1959 | £15 | £30 | US |
| Hey Bo Diddley | LP | Pye | NPL28025 | 1963 | £6 | £15 | |
| Hey Bo Diddley | 7" EP | Pye | NEP44014 | 1963 | £4 | £8 | |
| Hey Good Looking | LP | Chess | CRL4002 | 1964 | £5 | £12 | |
| Hey Good Looking | 7" | Chess | CRS8000 | 1965 | £1.50 | £4 | |

236

| Title | Format | Label | Catalog | Year | | | Notes |
|---|---|---|---|---|---|---|---|
| I'm A Man | LP | MF | 2002 | 1977 | £25 | £50 | US |
| I'm A Man | 7" EP | Chess | CRE6008 | 1965 | £4 | £8 | |
| In The Spotlight | LP | Checker | LP2976 | 1960 | £8 | £20 | US |
| In The Spotlight | LP | Pye | NPL28034 | 1964 | £6 | £15 | |
| Let Me Pass | LP | Chess | CRL4507 | 1965 | £5 | £12 | |
| Let The Kids Dance | 7" | Chess | CRS8021 | 1965 | £1.50 | £4 | |
| Mama Keep Your Big Mouth Shut | 7" | Pye | 7N25258 | 1964 | £2 | £5 | |
| Memphis | 7" | Pye | 7N25235 | 1964 | £2 | £5 | |
| Mona | 7" | Pye | 7N25243 | 1964 | £2.50 | £6 | |
| Ooh Baby | 7" | Chess | CRS8053 | 1967 | £1.50 | £4 | |
| Originator | LP | Chess | CRL4526 | 1967 | £5 | £12 | |
| Rhythm And Blues With Bo Diddley | 7" EP | London | REU1054 | 1956 | £75 | £150 | |
| Road Runner | LP | Checker | LP2982 | 1962 | £15 | £30 | US |
| Road Runner | 7" | London | HLM9112 | 1960 | £15 | £30 | |
| Road Runner | 7" | Pye | 7N25217 | 1963 | £2.50 | £6 | |
| Rooster Stew | 7" EP | Chess | CRE6023 | 1966 | £4 | £8 | |
| Say Man | 7" | London | HLM8975 | 1959 | £15 | £30 | |
| Say Man Back Again | 7" | London | HLM9035 | 1960 | £15 | £30 | |
| Somebody Beat Me | 7" | Chess | CRS8014 | 1965 | £1.50 | £4 | |
| Story Of Bo Diddley | 7" EP | Pye | NEP44019 | 1964 | £4 | £8 | |
| Surfin' With Bo Diddley | LP | Checker | LP(S)2987 | 1963 | £8 | £20 | US |
| We're Gonna Get Married | 7" | Chess | CRS8036 | 1966 | £1.50 | £4 | |
| Where It All Began | LP | Chess | CH50016 | 1972 | £8 | £20 | US |
| Who Do You Love | 7" | Pye | 7N25193 | 1963 | £2.50 | £6 | |
| Wrecking My Love Life | 7" | Chess | CRS8057 | 1967 | £1.50 | £4 | |
| You Can't Judge A Book By Its Cover | 7" | Pye | 7N25165 | 1962 | £4 | £8 | |
| You Can't Judge A Book By The Cover | 7" | Pye | 7N25216 | 1963 | £2 | £5 | |

## DIDI & HIS ABC BOYS

| Title | Format | Label | Catalog | Year | | | Notes |
|---|---|---|---|---|---|---|---|
| Beat Aus Berlin | LP | Telefunken | BLE14340P | 1966 | £87.50 | £175 | German |
| Beat Beat Beat | LP | Gong | 74999 | 1967 | £15 | £30 | German |

## DIED PRETTY

| Title | Format | Label | Catalog | Year | | |
|---|---|---|---|---|---|---|
| Whitlam Square | CD-s | Beggars Banquet | BEG238CD | 1990 | £2 | £5 |

## DIES IRAE

| Title | Format | Label | Catalog | Year | | | Notes |
|---|---|---|---|---|---|---|---|
| First | LP | Pilz | 20201147 | 1971 | £6 | £15 | German |

## DIETRICH, MARLENE

| Title | Format | Label | Catalog | Year | | |
|---|---|---|---|---|---|---|
| At The Café De Paris | 10" LP | Philips | BBR8006 | 1954 | £4 | £10 |
| Marlene Dietrich | 7" EP | HMV | 7EG8257 | 1957 | £2 | £5 |
| Marlene Dietrich | 7" EP | London | RED1146 | 1958 | £2 | £5 |
| Marlene Returns To Germany | 7" EP | HMV | 7EG8844 | 1964 | £2 | £5 |
| Near You | 7" | London | HLD8492 | 1957 | £1.50 | £4 |
| Souvenir Album | 10" LP | Brunswick | LA8591 | 1953 | £4 | £10 |

## DIF JUZ

| Title | Format | Label | Catalog | Year | | |
|---|---|---|---|---|---|---|
| Huremics | 12" | 4AD | BAD109 | 1981 | £4 | £10 |
| Vibrating Air | 12" | 4AD | BAD116 | 1981 | £3 | £8 |

## DIGA RHYTHM BAND

| Title | Format | Label | Catalog | Year | | |
|---|---|---|---|---|---|---|
| Diga | LP | Round | UAS29975 | 1976 | £5 | £12 |

## DILLARD, DOUG

| Title | Format | Label | Catalog | Year | | | Notes |
|---|---|---|---|---|---|---|---|
| Banjo Album | LP | Together | STT1003 | 1970 | £15 | £30 | US |

## DILLARD, MOSES & JOSHUA

| Title | Format | Label | Catalog | Year | | |
|---|---|---|---|---|---|---|
| My Elusive Dreams | 7" | Stateside | SS2059 | 1967 | £2.50 | £6 |

## DILLARD & CLARK

| Title | Format | Label | Catalog | Year | | | Notes |
|---|---|---|---|---|---|---|---|
| Fantastic Expedition Of Dillard And Clark | LP | A&M | AMLS939 | 1969 | £4 | £10 | |
| Kansas City Southern | LP | Ariola | 86436 | 1975 | £4 | £10 | Dutch |
| Through The Morning | LP | A&M | AMLS966 | 1969 | £4 | £10 | |

## DILLARDS

| Title | Format | Label | Catalog | Year | | | Notes |
|---|---|---|---|---|---|---|---|
| Back Porch Blue Grass | LP | Elektra | EKL/EKS7232 | 1963 | £6 | £15 | US |
| Copperfields | LP | Elektra | EKS74054 | 1970 | £4 | £10 | |
| Live Almost | LP | Elektra | EKL/EKS7265 | 1964 | £6 | £15 | US |
| Pickin' And Fiddlin' | LP | Elektra | EKL/EKS7285 | 1965 | £6 | £15 | US |
| Wheatsheaf Suite | LP | Elektra | EKS74035 | 1968 | £4 | £10 | |

## DILLINGER

| Title | Format | Label | Catalog | Year | | |
|---|---|---|---|---|---|---|
| Answer Me Question | LP | Third World | TWS928 | 1978 | £4 | £10 |
| Bionic Dread | LP | Island | ILPS9455 | 1976 | £5 | £12 |
| CB200 | LP | Island | ILPS9385 | 1976 | £5 | £12 |
| Talking Blues | LP | Magnum | DEAD1001 | 1977 | £4 | £10 |
| Top Ranking | LP | Third World | TWS919 | 1977 | £4 | £10 |
| Trinity Versus Clash | LP | Burning Sounds | BSLP1003 | 1978 | £4 | £10 |

## DILLON, PHYLLIS

| Title | Format | Label | Catalog | Year | | | Notes |
|---|---|---|---|---|---|---|---|
| Don't Stay Away | 7" | Doctor Bird | DB1061 | 1966 | £5 | £10 | Tommy McCook B side |
| Get On The Right Track | 7" | Trojan | TR671 | 1969 | £2.50 | £6 | Tommy McCook B side |
| I Wear This Ring | 7" | Treasure Isle | TI7041 | 1968 | £5 | £10 | |
| It's Rocking Time | 7" | Treasure Isle | TI7015 | 1967 | £5 | £10 | |

| | | | | | | | |
|---|---|---|---|---|---|---|---|
| Lipstick On Your Collar | 7" | Trojan | TR686 | 1969 £2 | £5 | *Tommy McCook*<br>*B side* |
| Love Is All I Had | 7" | Trojan | TR651 | 1969 £2.50 | £6 | |
| Midnight Confession | 7" | Treasure Isle | TI7070 | 1971 £1.50 | £4 | *Tommy McCook*<br>*B side* |
| One Life To Live | LP | Trojan | TRL41 | 1972 £8 | £20 | |
| One Life To Live One Love To Give | 7" | Treasure Isle | TI7058 | 1970 £1.50 | £4 | *Tommy McCook*<br>*B side* |
| Things Of The Past | 7" | Treasure Isle | TI7003 | 1967 £5 | £10 | |
| This Is A Lovely Way | 7" | Trojan | TR006 | 1967 £4 | £8 | |
| This Is Me | 7" | Duke Reid | DR2508 | 1970 £1.50 | £4 | |

## DIMENSIONS
| | | | | | | | |
|---|---|---|---|---|---|---|---|
| Tears On My Pillow | 7" | Parlophone | R5294 | 1965 £4 | £8 | |

## DIMENSIONS (2)
| | | | | | | | |
|---|---|---|---|---|---|---|---|
| From All Dimensions | LP | private | 1666 | 1966 £500 | £750 | *US* |

## DIMPLES
| | | | | | | | |
|---|---|---|---|---|---|---|---|
| Love Of A Lifetime | 7" | Decca | F12537 | 1966 £7.50 | £15 | |

## DINGER
| | | | | | | | |
|---|---|---|---|---|---|---|---|
| Air Of Mystery | 7" | Face Value | FVRA221 | 1985 £12.50 | £25 | |
| Air Of Mystery | 7" | SRT | SRT394 | 1985 £12.50 | £25 | |

## DINGLE BROTHERS
| | | | | | | | |
|---|---|---|---|---|---|---|---|
| Tank De Lard | 7" | Doctor Bird | DB1026 | 1966 £5 | £10 | |

## DINGLE SPIKE
| | | | | | | | |
|---|---|---|---|---|---|---|---|
| Dingle Spike | LP | SRTX | 78CUS185 | 1978 £5 | £12 | |

## DINNING, MARK
Mark Dinning is responsible for what is undoubtedly the worst record ever released. Forget all the other candidates for the accolade – 'Teen Angel' is the one! The song has one of those lyrics that deal with death – on this occasion, the singer's girlfriend has apparently rushed back into a burning building in order to save a ring that the singer had bought her. The symbol of the romance was more important than the romance itself! Meanwhile, the singer laments: 'I'll never kiss your lips again, they buried you today'. The epitome of bad taste – and all delivered in a thin, quavery voice so as to pile the pathos on really thick. Needless to say, the record was an American number one!

| | | | | | | | |
|---|---|---|---|---|---|---|---|
| Teen Angel | LP | MGM | (S)E3828 | 1960 £15 | £30 | *US* |
| Teen Angel | 7" | MGM | MGM1053 | 1960 £2 | £5 | |
| Wanderin' | LP | MGM | (S)E3855 | 1960 £8 | £20 | *US* |

## DINNING SISTERS
| | | | | | | | |
|---|---|---|---|---|---|---|---|
| Drifting And Dreaming | 7" | London | HLF8179 | 1955 £12.50 | £25 | |
| Hold Me Tight | 7" | London | HLF8218 | 1956 £12.50 | £25 | |

## DINO, DESI & BILLY
| | | | | | | | |
|---|---|---|---|---|---|---|---|
| I'm A Fool | 7" EP | Reprise | RVEP60072 | 1965 £2 | £5 | *French* |

## DINO, KENNY
| | | | | | | | |
|---|---|---|---|---|---|---|---|
| Your Ma Said You Cried In Your Sleep<br>Last Night | 7" | HMV | POP960 | 1961 £1.50 | £4 | |

## DINO & DEL
| | | | | | | | |
|---|---|---|---|---|---|---|---|
| Hey Little Girl Hey Little Boy | 7" | Carnival | CV7026 | 1965 £1.50 | £4 | |

## DINOSAUR
| | | | | | | | |
|---|---|---|---|---|---|---|---|
| Kiss Me Again | 7" | Sire | SRE1034 | 1979 £2 | £5 | |
| Kiss Me Again | 12" | Sire | SRE1034 | 1979 £3 | £8 | |

## DINOSAUR JR.
| | | | | | | | |
|---|---|---|---|---|---|---|---|
| Dinosaur Jr. | CD-s | SST | SST152CD | 1988 £2 | £5 | |
| Just Like Heaven | CD-s | Blast First | BFFP47CD | 1989 £2 | £5 | |
| Just Like Heaven | CD-s | SST | SST244CD | 1990 £2 | £5 | |
| Wagon | CD-s | Blanco Y<br>Negro | NEG48CD | 1991 £2 | £5 | |
| Without A Sound | CD | Warner Bros | | 1994 £10 | £25 | *Australian double tour*<br>*CD* |

## DIO
| | | | | | | | |
|---|---|---|---|---|---|---|---|
| Hey Angel | CD-s | Vertigo | DIOCD9 | 1990 £2 | £5 | |
| Last In Line | CD | Vertigo | 8223662 | 1984 £5 | £12 | |
| Sacred Heart | CD | Vertigo | 8348482 | 1985 £5 | £12 | |

## DION
| | | | | | | | |
|---|---|---|---|---|---|---|---|
| Alone With Dion | LP | Laurie | LLP2004 | 1960 £10 | £25 | *US* |
| Be Careful Of The Stones That You<br>Throw | 7" | CBS | AAG161 | 1963 £1.50 | £4 | |
| Berimbau | 7" | HMV | POP1565 | 1966 £1.50 | £4 | |
| By Special Request | LP | Laurie | LLP2016 | 1963 £10 | £25 | *US* |
| Come Go With Me | 7" | Stateside | SS209 | 1963 £2 | £5 | |
| Dion | LP | London | HAP/SHP8390 | 1969 £4 | £10 | |
| Dion Sings The Fifteen Million Sellers | LP | Laurie | LLP2019 | 1963 £8 | £20 | *US* |
| Dion Sings To Sandy & All Other Girls | LP | Laurie | LLP2017 | 1963 £8 | £20 | *US* |
| Dion's Hits | 7" EP | Stateside | SE1006 | 1963 £15 | £30 | |
| Don't Pity Me | 7" | London | HL8799 | 1959 £12.50 | £25 | |
| Donna La Prima Donna | 7" | CBS | 121053 | 1963 £2.50 | £6 | *sung in Italian* |

| Title | Format | Label | Catalog | Year | | | Notes |
|---|---|---|---|---|---|---|---|
| Donna The Prima Donna | LP | CBS | (S)BPG62203 | 1964 | £6 | £15 | |
| Donna The Prima Donna | 7" | CBS | AAG169 | 1963 | £1.50 | £4 | |
| Drip Drop | 7" | CBS | AAG177 | 1963 | £2 | £5 | |
| Greatest Hits | LP | Laurie | LLP2013 | 1962 | £8 | £20 | US |
| Having Fun | 7" | Top Rank | JAR545 | 1961 | £2 | £5 | |
| I Can't Go On | 7" | London | HL8718 | 1958 | £15 | £30 | |
| I Wonder Why | 7" | London | HLH8646 | 1958 | £25 | £50 | |
| I'm Your Hoochie Coochie Man | 7" | CBS | AAG188 | 1964 | £2 | £5 | |
| In The Still Of The Night | 7" | Top Rank | JAR503 | 1960 | £2.50 | £6 | |
| Johnny B.Goode | 7" | CBS | AAG224 | 1964 | £2 | £5 | |
| Little Diane | 7" | Stateside | SS115 | 1962 | £1.50 | £4 | |
| Lonely Teenager | 7" | Top Rank | JAR521 | 1960 | £2 | £5 | |
| Love Came To Me | LP | Laurie | LLP2015 | 1963 | £8 | £20 | US |
| Love Came To Me | 7" | Stateside | SS139 | 1962 | £1.50 | £4 | |
| Lover's Prayer | 7" | Pye | 7N25038 | 1959 | £7.50 | £15 | |
| Lovers Who Wander | LP | Stateside | SL10034 | 1962 | £10 | £25 | |
| Lovers Who Wander | 7" | HMV | POP1020 | 1962 | £2 | £5 | |
| More Greatest Hits | LP | Laurie | LLP2022 | 1963 | £6 | £15 | US |
| Movin' Man | 7" | HMV | POP1586 | 1967 | £1.50 | £4 | |
| Presenting Dion And The Belmonts | LP | Laurie | LLP2002 | 1959 | £37.50 | £75 | US |
| Presenting Dion And The Belmonts | LP | London | HAU2194 | 1959 | £75 | £150 | |
| Ruby Baby | LP | CBS | (B)PG62137 | 1963 | £6 | £15 | |
| Ruby Baby | 7" | CBS | AAG133 | 1963 | £1.50 | £4 | |
| Runaround Sue | LP | HMV | CLP1539 | 1961 | £20 | £40 | |
| Runaround Sue | LP | Laurie | LLP2009 | 1961 | £25 | £50 | US, blue vinyl |
| Runaround Sue | 7" | Top Rank | JAR586 | 1961 | £1.50 | £4 | |
| Sandy | 7" | Stateside | SS161 | 1963 | £1.50 | £4 | |
| Spoonful | 7" | CBS | 201780 | 1965 | £1.50 | £4 | |
| Sweet Sweet Baby | 7" | CBS | 201728 | 1965 | £2 | £5 | |
| Swing Along With Dion | 7" EP | HMV | 7EG8745 | 1962 | £15 | £30 | |
| Teenager In Love | 7" | London | HLU8874 | 1959 | £10 | £20 | |
| This Little Girl | 7" | CBS | AAG145 | 1963 | £1.50 | £4 | |
| Together Again | LP | HMV | CLP/CSD3618 | 1967 | £8 | £20 | |
| Toppermost Vol. 1 | LP | Top Rank | 25027 | 1960 | £20 | £40 | |
| Wanderer | 7" | HMV | POP971 | 1962 | £1.50 | £4 | |
| When You Wish Upon A Star | 7" | Top Rank | JAR368 | 1960 | £2.50 | £6 | |
| Where Or When | 7" | London | HLU9030 | 1960 | £4 | £8 | |
| Wish Upon A Star | LP | Laurie | LLP2006 | 1960 | £10 | £25 | US |

## DION, CELINE

| Title | Format | Label | Catalog | Year | | | |
|---|---|---|---|---|---|---|---|
| Last To Know | CD-s | Epic | 6573332 | 1991 | £2 | £5 | |
| Where Does My Heart Beat Now? | CD-s | Epic | 6563262 | 1991 | £2 | £5 | |

## DIONYSOS

| Title | Format | Label | Catalog | Year | | | Notes |
|---|---|---|---|---|---|---|---|
| Le Grand jeu | LP | Jupiter | 8032 | 1970 | £6 | £15 | Canadian |

## DIPLOMATS

| Title | Format | Label | Catalog | Year | | | |
|---|---|---|---|---|---|---|---|
| I Can Give You Love | 7" | Direction | 583899 | 1968 | £1.50 | £4 | |

## DIRE STRAITS

| Title | Format | Label | Catalog | Year | | | Notes |
|---|---|---|---|---|---|---|---|
| Brothers In Arms | 7" | Vertigo | DSPIC11 | 1985 | £5 | £10 | shaped picture disc |
| Brothers In Arms Special Edition | CD | Vertigo | 8842852 | 1985 | £15 | £30 | promo |
| Calling Elvis | CD-s | Vertigo | DSCD16 | 1991 | £2 | £5 | |
| Dire Straits Live | LP | Warner Bros | WBMS109 | 1980 | £10 | £25 | US promo |
| Heavy Fuel | CD-s | Vertigo | DSHAM17 | 1991 | £2 | £5 | |
| Money For Nothing | 7" | Vertigo | DSPIC10 | 1985 | £5 | £10 | shaped picture disc |
| On Every Street | CD | Vertigo | 5101602 | 1991 | £25 | £50 | promo box set with cassette |
| Sultans Of Swing | CD-s | Vertigo | DSCD15 | 1988 | £5 | £12 | card sleeve |
| Telegraph Road | 12" | Vertigo | | 1982 | £4 | £10 | promo |

## DIRECT HITS

| Title | Format | Label | Catalog | Year | | | |
|---|---|---|---|---|---|---|---|
| Blow Up | LP | Whaam | BIG7 | 1984 | £10 | £25 | |
| Christopher Cooper | 7" | Direct | POP001 | 1985 | £1.50 | £4 | |
| Modesty Blaise | 7" | Whaam | WHAAM7 | 1982 | £2.50 | £6 | |

## DIRECTIONS

| Title | Format | Label | Catalog | Year | | | |
|---|---|---|---|---|---|---|---|
| Three Bands Tonite | 7" | Tortch | TOR004 | 1979 | £15 | £30 | |

## DIRTY BLUES BAND

| Title | Format | Label | Catalog | Year | | | |
|---|---|---|---|---|---|---|---|
| Dirty Blues Band | LP | Stateside | (S)SL10234 | 1968 | £5 | £12 | |
| Stone Dirt | LP | Stateside | (S)SL10268 | 1969 | £4 | £10 | |

## DIRTY FILTHY MUD

| Title | Format | Label | Catalog | Year | | | Notes |
|---|---|---|---|---|---|---|---|
| Dirty Filthy Mud | 7" EP | Worex | 2340 | 1967 | £180 | £300 | US |

## DISCO 2000

| Title | Format | Label | Catalog | Year | | | Notes |
|---|---|---|---|---|---|---|---|
| I Gotta CD | 7" | KLF | D2001 | 1987 | £5 | £10 | white label |
| I Gotta CD | 12" | KLF | D2000 | 1987 | £4 | £10 | |
| One Love Nation | 12" | KLF | D2002 | 1988 | £2.50 | £6 | |
| Uptight | 12" | KLF | D2003T | 1989 | £2.50 | £6 | |

## DISCO ZOMBIES

| Title | Format | Label | Catalog | Year | | | |
|---|---|---|---|---|---|---|---|
| Drums Over London | 7" | South Circular | SGS106 | 1979 | £4 | £8 | |
| Here Come The Buts | 7" | Dining Out | TUX2 | 1981 | £2 | £5 | |
| Invisible EP | 7" | Wizzo | WIZZO1 | 1979 | £2.50 | £6 | |

## DISGUISE IN LOVE
Ross Was My Best Friend .......................... 7" ...... Purple Snow.... FLAKE1 ................. 1982 £2 .......... £5 ............ *purple vinyl*

## DISSING, POVL
| | | | | | | | |
|---|---|---|---|---|---|---|---|
| Dansk Beat | LP | Sonet | SLPS2412 | 1975 | £6 | £15 | *Danish* |
| Mor Danmark | LP | Hookfarm | HKLP3 | 1973 | £6 | £15 | *Danish* |
| Svantes Visir | LP | Metronome | BP7739 | 1973 | £8 | £20 | *Danish* |

## DIVINE COMEDY
| | | | | | | | |
|---|---|---|---|---|---|---|---|
| Indulgence No. 1 | 7" | Setanta | DC1 | 1993 | £2.50 | £6 | *picture disc* |
| Walk Like A Man | 7" | Proto | ENAP125 | 1985 | £1.50 | £4 | *shaped picture disc* |

## DIXIE BELLES
| | | | | | | | |
|---|---|---|---|---|---|---|---|
| Dixie Belles | 7" EP | London | REU1434 | 1964 | £2.50 | £6 | |
| Down At Papa Joe's | LP | London | HAU/SHU8152 | 1964 | £4 | £10 | |
| Down At Poppa Joe's | 7" | London | HLU9797 | 1963 | £1.50 | £4 | |

## DIXIE CUPS
| | | | | | | | |
|---|---|---|---|---|---|---|---|
| Chapel Of Love | LP | Red Bird | RB(S)20100 | 1965 | £10 | £25 | US |
| Chapel Of Love | 7" | Pye | 7N25245 | 1964 | £2 | £5 | |
| Gee The Moon Is Shining Bright | 7" | Red Bird | RB10032 | 1965 | £5 | £10 | |
| Iko Iko | LP | Red Bird | RB(S)20103 | 1965 | £8 | £20 | US |
| Iko Iko | 7" | Red Bird | RB10024 | 1965 | £1.50 | £4 | |
| Little Bell | 7" | Red Bird | RB10017 | 1964 | £2 | £5 | |
| Love Ain't So Bad | 7" | HMV | POP1557 | 1966 | £1.50 | £4 | |
| People Say | 7" | Red Bird | RB10006 | 1964 | £2 | £5 | |
| Riding High | LP | HMV | CLP1916 | 1966 | £6 | £15 | |
| Two Way Poc-A-Way | 7" | HMV | POP1453 | 1965 | £1.50 | £4 | |
| What Kind Of Fool | 7" | HMV | POP1524 | 1966 | £2 | £5 | |
| | 7" | Red Bird | RB10012 | 1964 | £1.50 | £4 | |

## DIXIE DRIFTER
Soul Heaven .......................................... 7" ...... Columbia ........ DB7710 ................. 1965 £4 .......... £8

## DIXIE FOUR
Dixie Four .......................................... 7" EP . Rarities ........... RA3 ................. 196– £7.50 .......... £15

## DIXIE HUMMINGBIRDS
| | | | | | | | |
|---|---|---|---|---|---|---|---|
| Dixie Hummingbirds | 7" EP | Vocalion | EPVP1277 | 1964 | £4 | £8 | |
| Final Edition | 7" EP | Vocalion | EPVP1281 | 1964 | £4 | £8 | |
| Have A Talk With Jesus | 7" | Vogue | V2422 | 1964 | £2 | £5 | |

## DIXIELAND ALL STARS
Dixiecats .......................................... LP ...... Columbia ........ 33SX1080 ................. 1958 £5 .......... £12

## DIXIELAND JUG BLOWERS
| | | | | | | | |
|---|---|---|---|---|---|---|---|
| Boodle-am-Shake | 7" | HMV | 7M223 | 1954 | £2 | £5 | |
| Hen Party Blues | 7" | HMV | 7M233 | 1954 | £2 | £5 | |

## DIXIELANDERS
Cyclone .......................................... 7" ...... Vocalion ........ V9209 ................. 1963 £1.50 .......... £4

## DIXON, BILLY & THE TOPICS
This was one of a number of names tried out by the group that eventually settled on the Four Seasons.

| | | | | | | | |
|---|---|---|---|---|---|---|---|
| I Am All Alone | 7" | Topix | 6002 | 1960 | £30 | £60 | US |
| Lost Lullabye | 7" | Topix | 6008 | 1960 | £30 | £60 | US |

## DIXON, ERROL
| | | | | | | | |
|---|---|---|---|---|---|---|---|
| Back To The Chicken Shack | 7" | Decca | F12826 | 1968 | £4 | £8 | |
| Bad Bad Woman | 7" | Blue Beat | BB86 | 1962 | £6 | £12 | |
| Blues In The Pot | LP | Decca | LK/SKL4962 | 1968 | £25 | £50 | ...*with Chicken Shack* |
| Errol Sings Fats | 7" EP | Decca | DFE8626 | 1965 | £10 | £20 | |
| Gloria | 7" | Blue Beat | BB337 | 1966 | £6 | £12 | |
| Hoop | 7" | Direct | DS5002 | 1967 | £2.50 | £6 | |
| I Love You | 7" | Island | WI069 | 1963 | £5 | £10 | |
| I Need Someone To Love Me | 7" | Rainbow | RAI104 | 1966 | £2.50 | £6 | |
| I Want | 7" | Fab | FAB1 | 1966 | £2 | £5 | |
| Mama Shut Your Door | 7" | Blue Beat | BB46 | 1961 | £6 | £12 | |
| Mean And Evil Woman | 7" | Carnival | CV7004 | 1963 | £4 | £8 | |
| Midnight Party | 7" | Ska Beat | JB271 | 1967 | £5 | £10 | |
| Midnight Train | 7" | Blue Beat | BB27 | 1960 | £6 | £12 | |
| Morning Train | 7" | Island | WI017 | 1962 | £5 | £10 | |
| Oo Wee Baby | 7" | Carnival | CV7001 | 1963 | £4 | £8 | |
| Rocks In My Pillow | 7" | Oriole | CB1914 | 1964 | £7.50 | £15 | |
| Six Questions | 7" | Decca | F12613 | 1967 | £4 | £8 | |
| That's How You Got Killed | LP | Transatlantic | TRA225 | 1970 | £8 | £20 | |
| True Love Never Runs Smooth | 7" | Decca | F12717 | 1967 | £4 | £8 | |
| Why Hurt Yourself | 7" | Doctor Bird | DB1197 | 1969 | £5 | £10 | |
| You're No Good | 7" | Blue Beat | BB344 | 1966 | £6 | £12 | |

## DIXON, JEFF
| | | | | | | | |
|---|---|---|---|---|---|---|---|
| Rock | 7" | Coxsone | CS7015 | 1967 | £5 | £10 | |
| Tickle Me | 7" | Studio One | SO2051 | 1968 | £6 | £12 | |

## DIXON, WILLIE

| | | | | | | |
|---|---|---|---|---|---|---|
| Catalyst | LP | Ovation | OVQD1433 | 1973 £4 | £10 | US quad |
| I Am The Blues | LP | Columbia | CS9987 | 1970 £5 | £12 | US |
| Walking The Blues | 7" | London | HLU8297 | 1956 £700 | £1000 | best auctioned |
| Walking The Blues | 7" | Pye | 7N25270 | 1964 £6 | £12 | |

## DIXON, WILLIE & MEMPHIS SLIM

| | | | | | | |
|---|---|---|---|---|---|---|
| Blues Every Which Way | LP | Verve | V(6)3007 | 1961 £6 | £15 | US |
| In Paris | LP | Battle | BV(S)6122 | 1963 £6 | £15 | US |
| Willie's Blues | LP | Bluesville | BV1003 | 1960 £8 | £20 | US |

## DIXXY SISTERS

| | | | | | |
|---|---|---|---|---|---|
| Game Of Broken Hearts | 7" | Columbia | SCM5105 | 1954 £1.50 | £4 |

## DIZZY, JOHNNY

| | | | | | | |
|---|---|---|---|---|---|---|
| Sudden Destruction | 7" | Ska Beat | JB204 | 1965 £5 | £10 | Soulettes B side |

## DMOCHOWSKI, JED

| | | | | | |
|---|---|---|---|---|---|
| Sha La La | 7" | Whaam! | WHAAM9 | 1983 £2.50 | £6 |

## DNV

| | | | | | | |
|---|---|---|---|---|---|---|
| Mafia | 7" | New Pleasures | Z2 | 1979 £12.50 | £25 | fold-out picture sleeve |

## D.O.A.

| | | | | | |
|---|---|---|---|---|---|
| Disco Sucks | 7" | Quintessence | QEP002 | 1979 £10 | £20 |
| Disco Sucks | 7" | Sudden Death | 3097 | 1978 £12.50 | £25 |
| Hardcore '81 | LP | Friends | FR010 | 1981 £30 | £60 |
| Positively D.O.A. | 7" | Alternative Tentacles | VIRUS7 | 1981 £2 | £5 |
| Something Better Change | LP | Friends | FR003 | 1980 £20 | £40 |
| Triumph Of The Ignoroids | 12" | Friends | | 198– £20 | £40 |
| War On 45 | 12" | Alternative Tentacles | VIRUS24 | 1984 £2.50 | £6 |

## DOBKINS, CARL

| | | | | | |
|---|---|---|---|---|---|
| Exclusively Yours | 7" | Brunswick | 05832 | 1960 £1.50 | £4 |
| If You Don't Want My Lovin' | 7" | Brunswick | 05811 | 1959 £6 | £12 |
| Lucky Devil | 7" | Brunswick | 05817 | 1960 £2 | £5 |
| My Heart Is An Open Book | LP | Brunswick | LAT8329 | 1959 £8 | £20 |
| My Heart Is An Open Book | 7" | Brunswick | 05804 | 1959 £2 | £5 |

## DOBSON, ANITA

| | | | | | |
|---|---|---|---|---|---|
| In One Of My Weaker Moments | 7" | MCA | MCA1260 | 1988 £1.50 | £4 |
| In One Of My Weaker Moments | 12" | MCA | MCAT1260 | 1988 £4 | £10 |
| To Know Him Is To Love Him | 7" | Odeon | ODO111 | 1988 £2 | £5 |

## DOBSON, DOBBY

| | | | | | | |
|---|---|---|---|---|---|---|
| Cry A Little Cry | 7" | King | KG1008 | 1965 £2 | £5 | |
| Loving Pauper | 7" | Trojan | TR011 | 1967 £5 | £10 | Tommy McCook B side |
| Seems To Me I'm Losing You | 7" | Coxsone | CS7058 | 1968 £5 | £10 | Gaylads B side |
| Strange | LP | Pama | SECO33 | 1969 £8 | £20 | |
| Strange | 7" | Blue Cat | BS171 | 1969 £2 | £5 | |
| Tell Me | 7" | Blue Beat | BB246 | 1964 £6 | £12 | |
| That Wonderful Sound | LP | Trojan | TBL145 | 1970 £6 | £15 | |
| Walking In The Footsteps | 7" | Studio One | SO2068 | 1968 £6 | £12 | Soul Vendors B side |

## DOCKER, ROY

| | | | | | |
|---|---|---|---|---|---|
| I'm An Outcast | 7" | Pama | PM756 | 1968 £1.50 | £4 |
| When | 7" | Pama | PM750 | 1968 £1.50 | £4 |

## DOCTOR ALIMANTADO

| | | | | | |
|---|---|---|---|---|---|
| Best Dressed Chicken In Town | LP | Greensleeves | GREL1 | 1978 £4 | £10 |
| King's Bread | LP | Ital Sounds | ISDA5000 | 1979 £4 | £10 |

## DOCTOR & THE MEDICS

| | | | | | |
|---|---|---|---|---|---|
| Druids Are Here | 7" | Whaam! | WHAAM6 | 1982 £4 | £8 |

## DOCTOR CLAYTON

| | | | | | |
|---|---|---|---|---|---|
| RCA Victor Race Series Vol. 6 | 7" EP | RCA | RCX7177 | 1965 £5 | £10 |

## DOCTOR FATHER

| | | | | | |
|---|---|---|---|---|---|
| Umbopo | 7" | Pye | 7N17977 | 1970 £1.50 | £4 |

## DOCTOR FEELGOOD

| | | | | | | |
|---|---|---|---|---|---|---|
| Something To Take Up Time | LP | Number One | | 1969 £10 | £25 | US |

## DODD, DICK

| | | | | | | |
|---|---|---|---|---|---|---|
| First Evolution Of Dick Dodd | LP | Tower | ST5142 | 1968 £10 | £25 | US |

## DODD, PAT

| | | | | | |
|---|---|---|---|---|---|
| Stag Party | 7" | Pye | 7N25030 | 1959 £1.50 | £4 |

## DODD ALL STARS

| | | | | | |
|---|---|---|---|---|---|
| Hip Shuffle | 7" | Coxsone | CS7076 | 1968 £5 | £10 |
| Mother Aitken | 7" | Coxsone | CS7096 | 1969 £5 | £10 |

## DODDS, JOHNNY

| | | | | | | |
|---|---|---|---|---|---|---|
| Johnny Dodds And Kid Ory | LP | Philips | BBL7136 | 1957 £6 | £15 | |
| Johnny Dodds Vol. 1 | 10" LP | London | AL3505 | 1953 £8 | £20 | |
| Johnny Dodds Vol. 1 | 10" LP | Vogue Coral | LRA10025 | 1955 £8 | £20 | |
| Johnny Dodds Vol. 2 | 10" LP | London | AL3513 | 1954 £8 | £20 | |
| Johnny Dodds Vol. 3 | 10" LP | London | AL3555 | 1956 £8 | £20 | |
| Johnny Dodds Vol. 4 | 10" LP | London | AL3560 | 1957 £8 | £20 | |
| Johnny Dodds Washboard Band | 10" LP | HMV | DLP1073 | 1955 £8 | £20 | |

## DODDS, NELLA

| | | | | | | |
|---|---|---|---|---|---|---|
| Come See About Me | 7" | Pye | 7N25281 | 1965 £5 | £10 | |
| Finders Keepers Losers Weepers | 7" | Pye | 7N25291 | 1965 £5 | £10 | |

## DODGERS

| | | | | | | |
|---|---|---|---|---|---|---|
| Let's Make A Whole Lot Of Love | 7" | Downbeat | CHA2 | 1960 £5 | £10 | |

## DODGY

| | | | | | | |
|---|---|---|---|---|---|---|
| Summer Fayre | 12" | Bostin | BTN001T | 1991 £3 | £8 | |

## DODOS

| | | | | | | |
|---|---|---|---|---|---|---|
| I Made Up My Mind | 7" | Polydor | 56153 | 1967 £2 | £5 | |

## DOE, ERNIE K

| | | | | | | |
|---|---|---|---|---|---|---|
| Certain Girl | 7" | London | HLP9487 | 1962 £4 | £8 | |
| Dancing Man | 7" | Action | ACT4502 | 1968 £2 | £5 | |
| Gotta Pack My Bags | 7" | Action | ACT4512 | 1968 £1.50 | £4 | |
| Mother In Law | LP | Minit | LP0002 | 1961 £20 | £40 | US |
| Mother In Law | 7" | London | HLU9330 | 1961 £4 | £8 | |
| My Mother In Law | 7" | Vocalion | VP9233 | 1965 £2 | £5 | |
| Te Ta Te Ta Ta | 7" | London | HLU9390 | 1961 £2.50 | £6 | |

## DOG THAT BIT PEOPLE

| | | | | | | |
|---|---|---|---|---|---|---|
| Dog That Bit People | LP | Parlophone | PCS7125 | 1971 £180 | £300 | |
| Lovely Lady | 7" | Parlophone | R5880 | 1971 £7.50 | £15 | |

## DOGFEET

| | | | | | | |
|---|---|---|---|---|---|---|
| Dogfeet | LP | Reflection | REFL8 | 1970 £180 | £300 | |
| Sad Story | 7" | Reflection | RS7 | 1970 £12.50 | £25 | |

## DOGGEREL BANK

The two little-known LPs by Doggerel Bank continue the experiments in mixing poetry, wit, and music carried out by the Barrow Poets, with many of the same personnel.

| | | | | | | |
|---|---|---|---|---|---|---|
| Mister Skillicorn Dances | LP | Charisma | CAS1102 | 1975 £4 | £10 | |
| Silver Faces | LP | Charisma | CAS1079 | 1973 £4 | £10 | |

## DOGGETT, BILL

| | | | | | | |
|---|---|---|---|---|---|---|
| 3046 People Danced Till 4 a.m. | LP | Warner Bros | WM4042 | 1961 £4 | £10 | |
| As You Desire Me | LP | King | 523 | 1955 £15 | £30 | US |
| Back Again With More | LP | King | 723 | 1960 £6 | £15 | US |
| Back With More Bill Doggett | LP | Parlophone | PMC1165 | 1962 £4 | £10 | |
| Band With The Beat | LP | Warner Bros | WS8056 | 1962 £4 | £10 | stereo |
| Best Of Bill Doggett | LP | King | 908 | 1964 £4 | £10 | US |
| Big City Dance Party | LP | King | 641 | 1959 £8 | £20 | US |
| Bill Doggett | 7" EP | Parlophone | GEP8711 | 1958 £4 | £8 | |
| Candle Glow | LP | King | 563 | 1958 £8 | £20 | US |
| Christmas | LP | King | 600 | 1959 £8 | £20 | US |
| Dame Dreaming | LP | King | 532 | 1956 £15 | £30 | US |
| Dame Dreaming | 10" LP | Parlophone | PMD1067 | 1958 £8 | £20 | |
| Dance Awhile | LP | King | 585 | 1958 £8 | £20 | US |
| Dance Awhile | 10" LP | Parlophone | PMD1073 | 1959 £8 | £20 | |
| Doggett Beat | LP | King | 557 | 1958 £15 | £30 | US |
| Doggett's Big City Dance Party | LP | Parlophone | PMC1118 | 1960 £5 | £12 | |
| Everybody Dance The Honky Tonk | LP | King | 531 | 1956 £15 | £30 | US |
| Flute Cocktail | 7" EP | Parlophone | GEP8694 | 1958 £2 | £5 | |
| For Reminiscent Lovers | LP | King | 706 | 1960 £8 | £20 | US |
| High And Wide | LP | King | 633 | 1959 £8 | £20 | US |
| Hold It | LP | King | 609 | 1959 £8 | £20 | US |
| Honky Tonk | 7" EP | Parlophone | GEP8644 | 1957 £4 | £8 | |
| Honky Tonk | 7" | Parlophone | R4231 | 1956 £10 | £20 | gold label |
| Hot Doggett | LP | King | 514 | 1954 £15 | £30 | US |
| Hot Ginger | 7" | Parlophone | R4379 | 1957 £5 | £10 | |
| Jolly Christmas | 7" EP | Parlophone | GEP8771 | 1958 £2.50 | £6 | |
| Leaps And Bounds | 7" | Parlophone | R4413 | 1958 £2.50 | £6 | |
| Many Moods | LP | King | 778 | 1961 £6 | £15 | US |
| Moondust | LP | King | 502 | 1954 £15 | £30 | US |
| On Tour | LP | Parlophone | PMC1124 | 1960 £6 | £15 | |
| Plays Duke Ellington | 7" EP | Parlophone | GEP8674 | 1957 £2.50 | £6 | |
| Prelude To The Blues | LP | Columbia | 1942 | 1962 £5 | £12 | US |
| Rainbow Riot | 7" EP | Parlophone | GEP8727 | 1958 £2.50 | £6 | |
| Ram Bunk Shush | 7" | Parlophone | R4306 | 1957 £5 | £10 | |
| Salute To Ellington | LP | King | 533 | 1956 £15 | £30 | US |
| Slow Walk | 7" | Parlophone | R4265 | 1957 £5 | £10 | |
| Smoke | 7" | Parlophone | R4629 | 1960 £2 | £5 | |
| Swingin' Easy | LP | King | 582 | 1958 £8 | £20 | US |
| Swings | LP | Warner Bros | 1452 | 1963 £4 | £10 | US |

| Wow | LP | HMV | CLP1884 | 1965 £4 | £10 | |
| You Can't Sit Down | 7" | Warner Bros | WB46 | 1961 £1.50 | £4 | |

## DOGS D'AMOUR

| (Un)authorised Bootleg | LP | China | WOL7 | 1988 £10 | £25 | |
| Back On The Juice | CD-s | China | CHICD30 | 1990 £2 | £5 | |
| Empty World | CD-s | China | CHICD27 | 1990 £2 | £5 | |
| How Come It Never Rains | CD-s | China | CHICD13 | 1989 £2 | £5 | |
| How Come It Never Rains | 7" | Supertrack | DOGS1 | 1987 £4 | £8 | |
| How Do You Fall In Love | 7" | Kumibeat | JOM3 | 1984 £20 | £40 | Finnish |
| Satellite Kid | CD-s | China | CHICD17 | 1989 £2 | £5 | |
| State We're In | LP | Kumibeat | | 1984 £25 | £50 | Finnish |
| Trail Of Tears | CD-s | China | CHICD20 | 1989 £2 | £5 | |

## DOGWATCH

| Penfriend | LP | Bridgehouse | BHLP002 | 1979 £25 | £50 | |

## DOLBY, THOMAS

| Urges | 7" | Armageddon | AS7 | 1981 £2.50 | £6 | |
| Urges | 7" | Statik | TAK4 | 1982 £1.50 | £4 | |

## DOLDINGER, KLAUS

| Blues Happening | LP | World Pacific | 20167 | 1968 £6 | £15 | German |
| Doldinger's Motherhood | LP | Liberty | LBS83426 | 1970 £6 | £15 | German |
| In Südamerika | LP | Philips | 843728 | 1965 £6 | £15 | German |
| Made In Germany | LP | Philips | 48024 | 1963 £6 | £15 | German |

## DOLENZ, JONES, BOYCE & HART

| Dolenz, Jones, Boyce & Hart | LP | Capitol | ST11513 | 1976 £5 | £12 | US |

## DOLENZ, MICKEY

| Don't Do It | 7" | London | HLH10117 | 1967 £2.50 | £6 | B side by Finders Keepers |
| Huff Puff | 7" | London | HLH10152 | 1967 £2 | £5 | Obvious B side |

## DOLL, ANDY

| On Stage | LP | Starlite | STLP11 | 1963 £6 | £15 | |
| Wild Desire | 7" | Starlite | ST45068 | 1962 £2.50 | £6 | |

## DOLLIES

| You Touch Me Baby | 7" | CBS | 201788 | 1965 £1.50 | £4 | |

## DOLPHIN

| Molecules | LP | Gale | LP02 | 1980 £6 | £15 | |

## DOLPHY, ERIC

| At The Five Spot | LP | Transatlantic | PR7294 | 1967 £6 | £15 | |
| Eric Dolphy And Booker Little Memorial Album | LP | Stateside | SL10160 | 1966 £6 | £15 | |
| Out To Lunch | LP | Blue Note | BLP/BST84163 | 1964 £10 | £25 | |
| Outward Bound | LP | Transatlantic | PR7311 | 1969 £6 | £15 | |
| Screamin' The Blues | LP | Esquire | | 1962 £8 | £20 | with Oliver Nelson |
| Screamin' The Blues | LP | XTRA | XTRA5039 | 1968 £5 | £12 | with Oliver Nelson |

## DOM

| Edge Of Time | LP | Melocord | STLPD001 | 1971 £50 | £100 | German |

## DOME

| 3R4 | 12" | 4AD | CAD16 | 1980 £2.50 | £6 | |
| Dome | LP | Dome | DOME1 | 1980 £4 | £10 | |
| Dome 2 | LP | Dome | DOME2 | 1980 £4 | £10 | |
| Dome 3 | LP | Dome | DOME3 | 1981 £4 | £10 | |

## DOMINO, FATS

With a hit-making career that began as early as 1949 (with music that differs hardly at all from the rock'n'roll that exploded into the American charts some half a dozen years later), Fats Domino had achieved more million-selling gold discs than any other artist apart from Elvis Presley by the time that the arrival of the Beatles effectively consigned him to the nostalgia circuit. The fact of his records being issued in the UK on the London label would have made him a collectable artist in any case, but the matter is clinched by the status of songs like 'Blue Monday', 'Ain't That A Shame', and above all, 'Blueberry Hill', as classic recordings of the fifties.

| Ain't That A Shame | 7" | London | HLU8173 | 1955 £25 | £50 | gold label |
| Ain't That Just Like A Woman | 7" | London | HLP9301 | 1961 £2.50 | £6 | |
| Be My Guest | 7" EP | London | REP1261 | 1960 £7.50 | £15 | |
| Be My Guest | 7" | London | HLP9005 | 1959 £2.50 | £6 | |
| Be My Guest | 7" | London | HLP9005 | 1959 £12.50 | £25 | tri-centre |
| Big Beat | 7" | London | HL7054 | 1958 £4 | £8 | export |
| Big Beat | 7" | London | HLP8575 | 1958 £6 | £12 | |
| Blue Monday | 7" | London | HLP8377 | 1957 £20 | £40 | gold label |
| Blueberry Hill | 7" | London | HLU8330 | 1956 £25 | £50 | gold label |
| Blues For Love Vol. 1 | 7" EP | London | REP1022 | 1955 £25 | £50 | gold label |
| Blues For Love Vol. 2 | 7" EP | London | REU1062 | 1956 £25 | £50 | gold label |
| Blues For Love Vol. 3 | 7" EP | London | REP1117 | 1958 £10 | £20 | |
| Blues For Love Vol. 4 | 7" EP | London | REP1121 | 1958 £10 | £20 | |
| Bo Weevil | 7" | London | HLU8256 | 1956 £37.50 | £75 | gold label |
| Carry On Rocking | LP | London | HAU2041 | 1956 £15 | £30 | |
| Carry On Rocking part 1 | 7" EP | London | REP1115 | 1958 £10 | £20 | |
| Carry On Rocking part 2 | 7" EP | London | REP1116 | 1958 £10 | £20 | |

| Title | Format | Label | Catalogue | Year | | | Notes |
|---|---|---|---|---|---|---|---|
| Country Boy | 7" | London | HLP9073 | 1960 | £2.50 | £6 | |
| Domino '65 | LP | Mercury | (S)MCL20070 | 1965 | £4 | £10 | |
| Don't Leave Me This Way | 78 | London | HL8096 | 1954 | £10 | £20 | |
| Everybody's Got Something To Hide | 7" | Reprise | RS20810 | 1969 | £1.50 | £4 | |
| Fabulous Mr. D | LP | London | HAP2135 | 1958 | £10 | £25 | |
| Fantastic Fats | LP | Stateside | (S)SL10240 | 1968 | £4 | £10 | |
| Fats | LP | Reprise | RS6439 | 1971 | £180 | £300 | US |
| Fats | 7" EP | London | REU1073 | 1957 | £37.50 | £75 | gold label |
| Fats Domino | LP | Imperial | LP9009 | 1956 | £30 | £60 | US |
| Fats Domino Swings | LP | Imperial | LP9062 | 1959 | £10 | £25 | US |
| Fats On Fire | LP | HMV | CLP1740/CSD1543 | 1963 | £6 | £15 | |
| Getaway With Fats | LP | HMV | CLP1821/CSD1580 | 1966 | £6 | £15 | |
| Here Comes Fats | LP | HMV | CLP1690/CSD1520 | 1963 | £6 | £15 | |
| Here Comes Fats Vol. 1 | 7" EP | London | REP1079 | 1957 | £10 | £20 | |
| Here Comes Fats Vol. 2 | 7" EP | London | REP1080 | 1957 | £10 | £20 | |
| Here Comes Fats Vol. 3 | 7" EP | London | REP1138 | 1958 | £10 | £20 | |
| Here He Comes Again | LP | Imperial | LP9248 | 1963 | £6 | £15 | US |
| Here Stands Fats Domino | LP | Imperial | LP9038 | 1957 | £30 | £60 | US |
| Here Stands Fats Domino | LP | London | HAU2052 | 1957 | £15 | £30 | |
| Honest Mamas Love Their Papas | 7" | Reprise | R20696 | 1968 | £2.50 | £6 | |
| Honey Chile | 7" | London | HLU8356 | 1957 | £20 | £40 | gold label |
| I Don't Want To Set The World On Fire | 7" | HMV | POP1281 | 1964 | £1.50 | £4 | |
| I Know | 7" | London | HL8133 | 1955 | £50 | £100 | gold label |
| I Left My Heart In San Francisco | 7" | Mercury | MF869 | 1965 | £2.50 | £6 | |
| I Miss You So | LP | London | HAP2364 | 1961 | £15 | £30 | |
| I Want To Walk You Home | 7" | London | HLP8942 | 1959 | £5 | £10 | |
| I'm Livin' Right | 7" | HMV | POP1582 | 1967 | £1.50 | £4 | |
| I'm Ready | 7" | Liberty | LIB15274 | 1969 | £2.50 | £6 | |
| I'm Walking | 7" | London | HLP8407 | 1957 | £7.50 | £15 | |
| It Keeps Raining | 7" | Liberty | LIB12055 | 1967 | £1.50 | £4 | |
| It Keeps Raining | 7" | London | HLP9374 | 1961 | £7.50 | £15 | |
| Jambalaya | 7" | London | HLP9520 | 1962 | £2 | £5 | |
| Just A Lonely Man | 7" | HMV | POP1265 | 1963 | £1.50 | £4 | |
| Just Domino | LP | London | HAP8039 | 1963 | £15 | £30 | |
| Kansas City | 7" | HMV | POP1370 | 1964 | £1.50 | £4 | |
| Lady Madonna | 7" | Reprise | RS20763 | 1968 | £1.50 | £4 | |
| Let The Four Winds Blow | LP | London | HAP2420 | 1961 | £15 | £30 | |
| Let The Four Winds Blow | 7" | London | HLP9415 | 1961 | £2.50 | £6 | |
| Let's Dance With Domino | LP | Imperial | LP9239 | 1963 | £8 | £20 | US |
| Let's Play Fats Domino | LP | London | HAP2223 | 1959 | £10 | £25 | |
| Little Mary | 7" | London | HLP8663 | 1958 | £7.50 | £15 | |
| Lot Of Domino's | LP | London | HAP2312 | 1960 | £10 | £25 | |
| Love Me | 7" | London | HL8124 | 1955 | £62.50 | £125 | gold label |
| Margie | 7" | London | HLP8865 | 1959 | £6 | £12 | |
| Mary Oh Mary | 7" | HMV | POP1324 | 1964 | £1.50 | £4 | |
| Million Record Hits | LP | Imperial | LP9103/12103 | 1960 | £10 | £25 | US |
| Million Sellers Vol. 1 | LP | Liberty | LBY3033 | 1965 | £4 | £10 | |
| Million Sellers Vol. 2 | LP | Liberty | LBY3046 | 1965 | £4 | £10 | |
| Million Sellers Vol. 3 | LP | Liberty | LBL83101 | 1968 | £4 | £10 | |
| My Blue Heaven | 7" EP | Liberty | LEP4026 | 1965 | £4 | £8 | |
| My Blue Heaven | 7" | London | HLU8280 | 1956 | £30 | £60 | gold label |
| My Girl Josephine | 7" | London | HLP9244 | 1960 | £2 | £5 | |
| My Real Name | 7" | London | HLP9557 | 1962 | £4 | £8 | |
| Nothing New | 7" | London | HLP9590 | 1962 | £4 | £8 | |
| Red Sails In The Sunset | 7" EP | HMV | 7EG8862 | 1964 | £4 | £8 | |
| Red Sails In The Sunset | 7" | HMV | POP1219 | 1963 | £1.50 | £4 | |
| Rock And Rollin' | LP | Imperial | LP9004 | 1956 | £25 | £50 | US |
| Rock And Rollin' | LP | London | HAU2028 | 1956 | £15 | £30 | |
| Rocking Mister D Vol. 1 | 7" EP | London | REP1206 | 1959 | £10 | £20 | |
| Rocking Mister D Vol. 2 | 7" EP | London | REP1207 | 1959 | £10 | £20 | |
| Rocking Mister D Vol. 3 | 7" EP | London | REP1265 | 1960 | £7.50 | £15 | |
| Rolling | 7" EP | Liberty | LEP4045 | 1966 | £4 | £8 | |
| Shurah | 7" | London | HLP9327 | 1961 | £4 | £8 | |
| Sick And Tired | 7" | London | HL7040 | 1958 | £4 | £8 | export |
| Sick And Tired | 7" | London | HLP8628 | 1958 | £6 | £12 | |
| Something You Got Baby | 7" | HMV | POP1303 | 1964 | £2 | £5 | |
| Stop The Clock | 7" | London | HLP9616 | 1962 | £4 | £8 | |
| Tell Me That You Love Me | 7" | London | HLP9133 | 1960 | £5 | £10 | |
| There Goes My Heart Again | 7" | HMV | POP1164 | 1963 | £2.50 | £6 | |
| This Is Fats | LP | Imperial | LP9040 | 1957 | £25 | £50 | US |
| This Is Fats | LP | London | HAP2087 | 1958 | £15 | £30 | |
| This Is Fats Domino | LP | Imperial | LP9028 | 1957 | £25 | £50 | US |
| This Is Fats Domino | LP | London | HAP2073 | 1956 | £15 | £30 | |
| Three Nights A Week | 7" | London | HLP9198 | 1960 | £2.50 | £6 | |
| Twistin' The Stomp | LP | London | HAP2447 | 1962 | £15 | £30 | |
| Valley Of Tears | 7" | London | HLP8449 | 1957 | £7.50 | £15 | |
| Wait And See | 7" | London | HL7028 | 1957 | £4 | £8 | export |
| Wait And See | 7" | London | HLP8519 | 1957 | £7.50 | £15 | |
| Walking To New Orleans | LP | London | HAP8084 | 1963 | £15 | £30 | |
| Walking To New Orleans | 7" | London | HLP9163 | 1960 | £2.50 | £6 | |
| What A Party | LP | London | HAP2426 | 1961 | £15 | £30 | |
| What A Party | 7" EP | London | REP1340 | 1962 | £6 | £12 | |
| What A Party | 7" | London | HLP9456 | 1961 | £2.50 | £6 | |
| What's That You Got | 7" | Mercury | MF1104 | 1969 | £2 | £5 | |
| What's That You Got | 7" | Mercury | MF873 | 1965 | £2 | £5 | |
| When I See You | 7" | London | HLP8471 | 1957 | £10 | £20 | |
| When I'm Walking | 7" | HMV | POP1197 | 1963 | £2 | £5 | |
| When My Dreamboat Comes Along | 7" | London | HLU8309 | 1956 | £25 | £50 | gold label |

| | | | | | | | |
|---|---|---|---|---|---|---|---|
| When The Saints Go Marching In | 7" | London | HLP8822 | 1959 | £6 | £12 | |
| Whole Lotta Loving | 7" | London | HLP8759 | 1958 | £7.50 | £15 | |
| Why Don't You Do Right | 7" | HMV | POP1421 | 1965 | £1.50 | £4 | |
| You Always Hurt The One You Love | 7" | London | HLP9738 | 1963 | £2.50 | £6 | |
| You Done Me Wrong | 78 | London | HL8063 | 1954 | £12.50 | £25 | |
| You Said You Loved Me | 78 | London | HL8007 | 1954 | £12.50 | £25 | |
| Young School Girl | 7" | London | HLP8727 | 1958 | £7.50 | £15 | |

## DOMINOES & SWALLOWS
| | | | | | | | |
|---|---|---|---|---|---|---|---|
| Rhythm And Blues | 7" EP | Vogue | EPV1113 | 1956 | £62.50 | £125 | |

## DOMINOES (2)
| | | | | | | | |
|---|---|---|---|---|---|---|---|
| Tribute | 7" | Melody | MRC002 | 1968 | £2.50 | £6 | |

## DON, DICK & JIMMY
| | | | | | | | |
|---|---|---|---|---|---|---|---|
| Angela Mia | 7" | Columbia | SCM5110 | 1954 | £5 | £10 | |
| Don, Dick & Jimmy | 7" EP | London | REU1043 | 1955 | £7.50 | £15 | |
| Make Yourself Comfortable | 7" | London | HL8144 | 1955 | £6 | £12 | |
| Spring Fever | LP | Modern | LMP1205 | 1956 | £10 | £25 | US |
| That's The Way I Feel | 7" | HMV | POP280 | 1956 | £2 | £5 | |
| You Can't Have Your Cake & Eat It Too | 7" | London | HL8117 | 1955 | £6 | £12 | |

## DON & DEWEY
| | | | | | | | |
|---|---|---|---|---|---|---|---|
| Get Your Hat | 7" | London | HL9897 | 1964 | £2.50 | £6 | |
| Soul Motion | 7" | Cameo Parkway | CP750 | 1966 | £5 | £10 | |
| Soul Motion | 7" | Sue | WI4032 | 1967 | £4 | £8 | |

## DON & JUAN
| | | | | | | | |
|---|---|---|---|---|---|---|---|
| What's Your Name | 7" | London | HLX9529 | 1962 | £7.50 | £15 | |

## DON & THE GOODTIMES
| | | | | | | | |
|---|---|---|---|---|---|---|---|
| Greatest Hits | LP | Burdette | 300 | 1966 | £8 | £20 | US |
| So Good | LP | Epic | BN26311 | 1967 | £6 | £15 | US |
| Where The Action Is | LP | Wand | WDS679 | 1966 | £8 | £20 | US |

## DON BRADSHAW LEATHER
| | | | | | | | |
|---|---|---|---|---|---|---|---|
| Distance Between Us | LP | Distance | no number | 1972 | £20 | £40 | double |

## DONAHUE, JERRY
| | | | | | | | |
|---|---|---|---|---|---|---|---|
| Theme From Catlow | 7" | Philips | 6006219 | 1972 | £2 | £5 | |

## DONAHUE, SAM
| | | | | | | | |
|---|---|---|---|---|---|---|---|
| Sam Donahue Orchestra | 10" LP | Capitol | LCT6019 | 1955 | £6 | £15 | |
| Saxaboogie | 7" | Capitol | CL14349 | 1955 | £4 | £8 | |

## DONALD, MIKE
| | | | | | | | |
|---|---|---|---|---|---|---|---|
| North By North East | LP | Galliard | GAL4020 | 1972 | £6 | £15 | |
| Yorkshire Songs Of The Broad Acres | LP | Folk Heritage | FHR021 | 1971 | £4 | £10 | |

## DONALDSON, BOBBY
| | | | | | | | |
|---|---|---|---|---|---|---|---|
| Dixieland – New York! | LP | London | SAHC6007 | 1959 | £5 | £12 | |

## DONALDSON, ERIC
| | | | | | | | |
|---|---|---|---|---|---|---|---|
| Cherry Oh Baby | 7" | Dynamic | DYN420 | 1971 | £1.50 | £4 | Lloyd Charmers B side |
| Eric Donaldson | LP | Trojan | TRL42 | 1972 | £6 | £15 | |

## DONALDSON, JULIA & MICHAEL
| | | | | | | | |
|---|---|---|---|---|---|---|---|
| First Fourteen | LP | Longmans | | 1979 | £15 | £30 | |

## DONALDSON, LOU
| | | | | | | | |
|---|---|---|---|---|---|---|---|
| Alligator Boogaloo | LP | Blue Note | BLP/BST84263 | 1967 | £8 | £20 | |
| Blues Walk | LP | Blue Note | BLP/BST81593 | 196– | £10 | £25 | |
| Cosmos | LP | Blue Note | BST84370 | 1970 | £5 | £12 | |
| Everything I Play Is Funky | LP | Blue Note | BST84337 | 1969 | £6 | £15 | |
| Good Gracious | LP | Blue Note | BLP/BST84125 | 1963 | £15 | £30 | |
| Gravy Train | LP | Blue Note | BLP/BST84079 | 196– | £10 | £25 | |
| Here 'Tis | LP | Blue Note | BLP/BST84066 | 196– | £10 | £25 | |
| Hot Dog | LP | Blue Note | BST84318 | 1969 | £6 | £15 | |
| Light Foot | LP | Blue Note | BLP/BST84053 | 196– | £15 | £30 | |
| Midnight Creeper | LP | Blue Note | BST84280 | 1968 | £6 | £15 | |
| Mr. Shing-A-Ling | LP | Blue Note | BLP/BST84271 | 1967 | £8 | £20 | |
| Natural Soul | LP | Blue Note | BLP/BST84108 | 1962 | £10 | £25 | |
| Pretty Things | LP | Blue Note | BST84359 | 1970 | £5 | £12 | |
| Say It Loud | LP | Blue Note | BST84299 | 1968 | £6 | £15 | |
| Sunny Side Up | LP | Blue Note | BLP/BST84036 | 196– | £15 | £30 | |
| Sweet Slumber | LP | Blue Note | BLP/BST84254 | 1967 | £8 | £20 | |
| Time Is Right | LP | Blue Note | BLP/BST84025 | 196– | £15 | £30 | |

## DONAYS
| | | | | | | | |
|---|---|---|---|---|---|---|---|
| Devil In His Heart | 7" | Oriole | CB1770 | 1962 | £50 | £100 | |

## DONEGAN, DOROTHY
| | | | | | | | |
|---|---|---|---|---|---|---|---|
| Dorothy Donegan Trio | 7" EP | MGM | MGMEP532 | 1956 | £2 | £5 | |

## DONEGAN, LONNIE
To anyone who grew up with the rock music of the sixties, Lonnie Donegan was essentially a novelty figure – the man who recorded weak musical jokes like 'My Old Man's A Dustman' and 'Does Chewing Gum Lose Its Flavour On The Bedpost Overnight?'. In fact,

Donegan actually deserves as much respect as Elvis Presley as a vital rock pioneer. Musicians like Brian May and Rory Gallagher have spoken in glowing terms of the man who introduced the sound of the blues to British listeners, single-handedly inventing the skiffle genre in the process, and thereby inspiring them to pick up a guitar. As the banjo player with Chris Barber's traditional jazz band in the early fifties, Donegan would also entertain audiences during set breaks by trading his banjo for an acoustic guitar and bashing his way through enthusiastic renditions of Leadbelly songs. Someone decided that one of these, an extraordinary and rather thrilling version of 'Rock Island Line' included on Barber's LP, *New Orleans Joys*, would make a good single. It became the first of an incredible run of twenty-six British chart hits that ended only with the arrival of the Beatles.

| | | | | | | | |
|---|---|---|---|---|---|---|---|
| Backstairs Session | 7" EP | Polygon | JTE107 | 1956 | £7.50 | £15 | |
| Backstairs Session | 7" EP | Pye | NJE1014 | 1956 | £2.50 | £6 | |
| Digging My Potatoes | 7" | Decca | FJ10695 | 1956 | £4 | £8 | |
| Folk Album | LP | Pye | NPL18126 | 1965 | £6 | £15 | |
| Grand Coulee Dam | 7" | Pye | 7N15129 | 1958 | £1.50 | £4 | |
| Jack O'Diamonds | 7" | Pye | 7N15116 | 1957 | £1.50 | £4 | |
| Kevin Barry | 7" | Pye | 7N15219 | 1959 | £4 | £8 | |
| Lonesome Traveller | 7" | Pye | 7N15158 | 1958 | £1.50 | £4 | |
| Lonnie | 10" LP | Pye | NPT19027 | 1957 | £6 | £15 | |
| Lonnie Donegan Hit Parade | 7" EP | Pye | NEP24031 | 1957 | £2 | £5 | |
| Lonnie Donegan Hit Parade Vol. 2 | 7" EP | Pye | NEP24040 | 1957 | £2 | £5 | |
| Lonnie Donegan Hit Parade Vol. 3 | 7" EP | Pye | NEP24067 | 1958 | £2 | £5 | |
| Lonnie Donegan Hit Parade Vol. 4 | 7" EP | Pye | NEP24081 | 1958 | £2 | £5 | |
| Lonnie Donegan Hit Parade Vol. 5 | 7" EP | Pye | NEP24104 | 1959 | £2 | £5 | |
| Lonnie Donegan Hit Parade Vol. 6 | 7" EP | Pye | NEP24114 | 1959 | £2 | £5 | |
| Lonnie Donegan Hit Parade Vol. 7 | 7" EP | Pye | NEP24134 | 1961 | £2 | £5 | |
| Lonnie Donegan Hit Parade Vol. 8 | 7" EP | Pye | NEP24149 | 1961 | £2 | £5 | |
| Lonnie Donegan On Stage | 7" EP | Pye | NEP24075 | 1958 | £2 | £5 | |
| Lonnie Donegan Skiffle Group | 7" EP | Decca | DFE6345 | 1956 | £4 | £8 | tri-centre |
| Lonnie's Skiffle Party | 7" | Pye | 7N15165 | 1958 | £1.50 | £4 | |
| Midnight Special | 7" | Pye | 7NJ2006 | 1958 | £2 | £5 | |
| More Tops With Lonnie | LP | Pye | NPL18063 | 1961 | £4 | £10 | |
| Passing Stranger | 78 | Oriole | CB1329 | 1956 | £4 | £8 | B side by Tommy Reilly |
| Pick A Bale Of Cotton | 7" | Pye | 7N15455 | 1962 | £1.50 | £4 | |
| Pick A Bale Of Cotton | 7" | Pye | 7N15455 | 1962 | £4 | £8 | picture sleeve |
| Relax With Lonnie | 7" EP | Pye | NEP24107 | 1959 | £2 | £5 | |
| Rides Again | LP | Pye | NPL18043 | 1959 | £4 | £10 | |
| Rock Island Line | 7" | Decca | FJ10647 | 1955 | £5 | £10 | |
| Sally Don't You Grieve | 7" | Pye | 7N15148 | 1958 | £1.50 | £4 | |
| Showcase | 10" LP | Pye | NPT19012 | 1956 | £6 | £15 | |
| Sing Hallelujah | LP | Pye | NPL18073 | 1962 | £4 | £10 | |
| Skiffle Session | 7" EP | Pye | NJE1017 | 1956 | £2 | £5 | |
| Take My Hand | 7" | Columbia | DB3850 | 1956 | £5 | £10 | |
| Tops With Lonnie | LP | Pye | NPL18034 | 1958 | £4 | £10 | |
| Yankee Doodle Donegan | 7" EP | Pye | NEP24127 | 1960 | £2 | £5 | |

## DONLEY, JIMMY

| | | | | | | | |
|---|---|---|---|---|---|---|---|
| Shape You Left Me In | 7" | Brunswick | 05807 | 1959 | £37.50 | £75 | |
| South Of The Border | 7" | Brunswick | 05715 | 1957 | £4 | £8 | |

## DONNER, RAL

| | | | | | | | |
|---|---|---|---|---|---|---|---|
| Bells Of Love | 7" | Stateside | SS109 | 1962 | £4 | £8 | |
| I Don't Need You | 7" | Parlophone | R4889 | 1962 | £2.50 | £6 | |
| I Got Burned | 7" | Reprise | R20141 | 1963 | £6 | £12 | |
| Please Don't Go | 7" | Parlophone | R4859 | 1961 | £2 | £5 | |
| Takin' Care Of Business | LP | Gone | LP5012 | 1961 | £37.50 | £75 | US |
| You Don't Know What You Got | 7" | Parlophone | R4820 | 1961 | £1.50 | £4 | |

## DONNIE & THE DREAMERS

| | | | | | | | |
|---|---|---|---|---|---|---|---|
| Count Every Star | 7" | Top Rank | JAR571 | 1961 | £2.50 | £6 | |

## DONOVAN

Donovan is often viewed as a bit of a joke these days, seeming to epitomize all the more pretentious, self-conscious aspects of hippy culture. His achievement in moving onwards from being a pale shadow of Bob Dylan into creating music of genuine invention and charm is considerable, however. The UK album, *Sunshine Superman*, which combines the best tracks of two albums issued in America, is like a folk version of *Sgt Pepper*, while the double *Gift From A Flower To A Garden*, despite being inevitably too long, is almost as good. This latter album, which was issued as a boxed set, is becoming increasingly scarce, especially with its numerous poetic inserts intact.

| | | | | | | | |
|---|---|---|---|---|---|---|---|
| 7-Tease | LP | Epic | SEPC69104 | 1974 | £4 | £10 | |
| Barabajagal | LP | Epic | BN26481 | 1968 | £4 | £10 | US |
| Brother Sun, Sister Moon | LP | HMV | 3C06493393 | 1970 | £10 | £25 | German |
| Catch The Wind | 7" EP | Pye | NEP24287 | 1968 | £2.50 | £6 | |
| Catch The Wind | 7" EP | Pye | PNV24138 | 1965 | £4 | £8 | French |
| Catch The Wind | 7" | Pye | 7N15801 | 1965 | £1.50 | £4 | |
| Colours | 7" EP | Pye | NEP24229 | 1965 | £4 | £8 | |
| Colours | 7" EP | Pye | PNV24153 | 1965 | £5 | £10 | French |
| Cosmic Wheels | LP | Epic | SEPC65450 | 1973 | £4 | £10 | |
| Donovan | LP | World Records | ST951 | 1965 | £4 | £10 | |
| Donovan Vol. 1 | 7" EP | Pye | NEP24239 | 1966 | £2.50 | £6 | |
| Epistle To Dippy | 7" EP | Epic | 9064 | 1967 | £6 | £12 | French |
| Essence To Essence | LP | Epic | SEPC69050 | 1973 | £4 | £10 | |
| Fairytale | LP | Pye | NPL18128 | 1965 | £4 | £10 | |
| For Little Ones | LP | Epic | LN24/BN26350 | 1967 | £4 | £10 | US |
| Gift From A Flower To A Garden | LP | Pye | NPL20000 | 1968 | £25 | £50 | 2 LPs, boxed, mono |
| Gift From A Flower To A Garden | LP | Pye | NSPL20000 | 1968 | £15 | £30 | double, boxed |
| Greatest Hits | LP | Pye | N(S)PL18283 | 1969 | £4 | £10 | |
| HMS Donovan | LP | Dawn | DNLD4001 | 1971 | £30 | £60 | double |
| Hurdy Gurdy Donovan | 7" EP | Pye | NEP24299 | 1968 | £4 | £8 | |

| | | | | | | | | |
|---|---|---|---|---|---|---|---|---|
| Hurdy Gurdy Man | LP | Epic | BN26420 | 1968 | £4 | £10 | | US |
| Hurdy Gurdy Man | 7" | Pye | 7N17537 | 1968 | £1.50 | £4 | | |
| In Concert | LP | Pye | N(S)PL18237 | 1968 | £4 | £10 | | |
| Jennifer Juniper | 7" | Epic | | 1967 | £4 | £8 | | sung in Italian |
| Jennifer Juniper | 7" | Pye | 7N17457 | 1968 | £1.50 | £4 | | |
| Live In Japan, Spring Tour 1973 | LP | Epic | ECPM25 | 1973 | £8 | £20 | | Japanese |
| Mellow Yellow | LP | Epic | LN24/BN26239 | 1967 | £6 | £15 | | US |
| Mellow Yellow | 7" | Pye | 7N17267 | 1967 | £1.50 | £4 | | |
| Open Road | LP | Dawn | DNLS3009 | 1970 | £6 | £15 | | |
| Remember The Alamo | 7" | Pye | 7N17088 | 1966 | £4 | £8 | | |
| Slow Down World | LP | Epic | SEPC86011 | 1976 | £4 | £10 | | |
| Summer Day Reflection Song | 7" EP | Pye | PNV24170 | 1966 | £6 | £12 | | French |
| Sunshine Superman | LP | Epic | LN24/BN26217 | 1966 | £6 | £15 | | US, different tracks |
| Sunshine Superman | LP | Pye | NPL18181 | 1967 | £6 | £15 | | |
| Sunshine Superman | CD-s | EMI | CDEM98 | 1989 | £2 | £5 | | |
| Sunshine Superman | 7" | Pye | 7N17241 | 1966 | £1.50 | £4 | | |
| There Is A Mountain | 7" | Pye | 7N17403 | 1967 | £1.50 | £4 | | |
| To Susan On The West Coast Waiting | 7" | Pye | 7N17660 | 1968 | £6 | £12 | | |
| Trip | CD | EMI | CDEM1385 | 1991 | £5 | £12 | | |
| Turquoise | 7" EP | Pye | PNV24158 | 1965 | £5 | £10 | | French |
| Universal Soldier | 7" EP | Pye | NEP24219 | 1965 | £2.50 | £6 | | |
| Universal Soldier | 7" EP | Pye | PNV24149 | 1965 | £4 | £8 | | French |
| Wear Your Love Like Heaven | LP | Epic | LN24/BN26349 | 1967 | £4 | £10 | | US |
| What's Bin Did And What's Bin Hid | LP | Pye | NPL18117 | 1965 | £5 | £12 | | |

## DONOVAN & JEFF BECK GROUP

| | | | | | | | | |
|---|---|---|---|---|---|---|---|---|
| Goo Goo Barabajagal | 7" | Pye | 7N17778 | 1969 | £1.50 | £4 | | |
| Goo Goo Barabajagal | 7" | Pye | 7N17778 | 1969 | £2 | £5 | | 'Bed With Me' B side |

## DONOVAN, JASON

| | | | | | | | | |
|---|---|---|---|---|---|---|---|---|
| Angel | CD-s | Polydor | PZCD295 | 1994 | £4 | £10 | | |

## DONTELLS

| | | | | | | | | |
|---|---|---|---|---|---|---|---|---|
| In Your Heart | 7" | Fontana | TF566 | 1965 | £12.50 | £25 | | |

## DOO, DICKIE & THE DONTS

| | | | | | | | | |
|---|---|---|---|---|---|---|---|---|
| Click Clack | 7" | London | HLU8589 | 1958 | £12.50 | £25 | | |
| Leave Me Alone | 7" | London | HLU8754 | 1958 | £12.50 | £25 | | |
| Madison | LP | United Artists | UAL3094/ UAS6094 | 1960 | £8 | £20 | | US |
| Teen Scene | LP | United Artists | UAL3097/ UAS6097 | 1960 | £8 | £20 | | US |
| Wabash Cannonball | 7" | Top Rank | JAR318 | 1960 | £1.50 | £4 | | |

## DOOLEY SISTERS

| | | | | | | | | |
|---|---|---|---|---|---|---|---|---|
| Ko Ko Mo | 7" | London | HL8128 | 1955 | £10 | £20 | | |

## DOONAN, JOHN

| | | | | | | | | |
|---|---|---|---|---|---|---|---|---|
| At The Feis | LP | Topic | 12TS368 | 1978 | £10 | £25 | | |
| Flute For The Feis | LP | Leader | LEA2043 | 1972 | £5 | £12 | | |

## DOORFIELD

| | | | | | | | | |
|---|---|---|---|---|---|---|---|---|
| Nil Desperandum | LP | Flatrock | | 1971 | £15 | £30 | | US |

## DOORS

For the most part, the success of the Doors represented a triumph of image over content. Certainly to British ears, the simple blues-based material in which the group specialized sounded distinctly ordinary in comparison with either the other West Coast bands or the more searching local groups. The Doors had two effective hit singles – 'Light My Fire' and 'Riders On The Storm', together with a first album that was interesting in parts, but the rest was largely built on the repetition of a few tried formulae. Live, however, the group had an aggressive macho image, with lead singer Jim Morrison wearing an all-leather outfit and gaining a reputation for exposing himself on stage. His stance at the microphone has become widely copied by charismatic singers in groups like the Stone Roses and Oasis, so that, in combination with the fact that fans have never become disillusioned by seeing Morrison grow old and tired, the Doors are made to seem like a more important sixties group than they were at the time.

| | | | | | | | | |
|---|---|---|---|---|---|---|---|---|
| 13 | LP | Elektra | K42062 | 1971 | £4 | £10 | | |
| Absolutely Live | LP | Elektra | 2665002 | 1970 | £6 | £15 | | double |
| Absolutely Live | CD | Elektra | K262005 | 1987 | £8 | £20 | | double |
| Alabama Song | 7" | Elektra | EKSN45012 | 1967 | £1.50 | £4 | | |
| American Prayer | LP | Elektra | K52111 | 1978 | £4 | £10 | | with booklet |
| Best Of The Doors | LP | Elektra | K242143 | 1974 | £5 | £12 | | quad |
| Break On Through | CD-s | Elektra | EKR121CD | 1991 | £2 | £5 | | |
| Break On Through | 7" EP | Vogue | INT18129 | 1967 | £100 | £200 | | French |
| Break On Through | 7" | Elektra | EKSN45009 | 1967 | £2.50 | £6 | | |
| Doors | LP | Elektra | EKL4007 | 1967 | £15 | £30 | | mono |
| Doors | LP | Elektra | EKS74007 | 1967 | £8 | £20 | | stereo |
| Doors | LP | Elektra | EKS74007 | 1970 | £4 | £10 | | red label |
| Doors | LP | Mobile Fidelity | MFSL1051 | 1980 | £5 | £12 | | US audiophile |
| Doors | CD | DCC | GZS1023 | 1992 | £6 | £15 | | US audiophile |
| Doors | CD | Elektra | K242012 | 1985 | £5 | £12 | | |
| Hello I Love You | 7" | Elektra | EKSN45037 | 1968 | £1.50 | £4 | | |
| L.A. Woman | CD | DCC | GZS1034 | 1993 | £6 | £15 | | US audiophile |
| L.A. Woman | CD | Elektra | C8816 | 1988 | £5 | £12 | | HMV boxed set |
| L.A. Woman | CD | Elektra | K242090 | 1985 | £5 | £12 | | |
| L.A. Woman | LP | Elektra | K42090 | 1971 | £6 | £15 | | clear window sleeve |
| Light My Fire | CD-s | Elektra | EKR1235CD | 1991 | £2 | £5 | | |
| Light My Fire | 7" EP | Vogue | INT18145 | 1967 | £50 | £100 | | French |
| Light My Fire | 7" | Elektra | EKSN45014 | 1967 | £2 | £5 | | |

| | | | | | | | |
|---|---|---|---|---|---|---|---|
| Live At The Hollywood Bowl | LP | Elektra | EKT40F | 1987 | £8 | £20 | ..promo with interview LP |
| Love Her Madly | 7" | Elektra | EK45726 | 1971 | £1.50 | £4 | |
| Love Me Two Times | 7" | Elektra | EKSN45022 | 1967 | £1.50 | £4 | |
| Love Me Two Times | 7" | Elektra | K12215 | 1979 | £1.50 | £4 | double |
| Morrison Hotel | LP | Elektra | EKS75007 | 1970 | £5 | £12 | |
| Morrison Hotel | CD | Elektra | K242080 | 1985 | £5 | £12 | |
| People Are Strange | 7" | Elektra | EKSN45017 | 1967 | £2 | £5 | |
| Riders On The Storm | CD-s | Elektra | EKR131CD | 1991 | £2 | £5 | |
| Roadhouse Blues | 7" | Elektra | 2101008 | 1970 | £1.50 | £4 | |
| Soft Parade | LP | Elektra | EKS75005 | 1969 | £6 | £15 | |
| Strange Days | LP | Elektra | EKL4014 | 1968 | £15 | £30 | mono |
| Strange Days | LP | Elektra | EKS74014 | 1968 | £8 | £20 | stereo |
| Strange Days | CD | DCC | GZS1026 | 1992 | £6 | £15 | US audiophile |
| Strange Days | CD | Elektra | K242016 | 1985 | £5 | £12 | |
| Tell All The People | 7" | Elektra | EKSN45065 | 1969 | £1.50 | £4 | |
| Touch Me | 7" | Elektra | EKSN45050 | 1969 | £1.50 | £4 | |
| Unknown Soldier | 7" | Elektra | EKSN45030 | 1968 | £1.50 | £4 | |
| Waiting For The Sun | LP | Elektra | EKL4024 | 1968 | £8 | £20 | mono |
| Waiting For The Sun | LP | Elektra | EKS74024 | 1968 | £6 | £15 | stereo |
| Waiting For The Sun | CD | Elektra | K242041 | 1985 | £5 | £12 | |
| Wishful Sinful | 7" | Elektra | EKSN45059 | 1969 | £1.50 | £4 | |
| You Make Me Real | 7" | Elektra | 2101004 | 1970 | £1.50 | £4 | |

## DORAN, FELIX

| | | | | | | |
|---|---|---|---|---|---|---|
| Last Of The Travelling Pipers | LP | Topic | 12TS288 | 1976 | £4 | £10 |

## DOREEN

| | | | | | | |
|---|---|---|---|---|---|---|
| Rude Girls | 7" | Rainbow | RAI114 | 1967 | £2.50 | £6 |

## DOREEN & JACKIE

| | | | | | | |
|---|---|---|---|---|---|---|
| Welcome Home | 7" | Ska Beat | JB208 | 1965 | £5 | £10 |

## DORHAM, KENNY

| | | | | | | |
|---|---|---|---|---|---|---|
| Jazz Contrasts | LP | London | LTZU15133 | 1958 | £8 | £20 |
| Kenny Dorham Anmd The Jazz Prophets | 10" LP | HMV | DLP1184 | 1958 | £8 | £20 |
| Trompeta Toccata | LP | Blue Note | BLP/BST84181 | 1964 | £10 | £25 |
| Unas Mas | LP | Blue Note | BLP/BST84127 | 1963 | £8 | £20 |
| Whistle Stop | LP | Blue Note | BLP/BST84063 | 1961 | £10 | £25 |

## DORIAN GRAY

| | | | | | | | |
|---|---|---|---|---|---|---|---|
| Idaho Transfer | LP | New Blood | PA476 | 1976 | £50 | £100 | German |

## DORMAN, HAROLD

| | | | | | | |
|---|---|---|---|---|---|---|
| Mountain Of Love | 7" | Top Rank | JAR357 | 1960 | £4 | £8 |
| There They Go | 7" | London | HLS9386 | 1961 | £6 | £12 |

## DOROTHY

| | | | | | | |
|---|---|---|---|---|---|---|
| I Confess | 7" | Industrial | IR0014 | 1980 | £2.50 | £6 |

## DORPER, RALPH

| | | | | | | |
|---|---|---|---|---|---|---|
| Eraserhead | 12" | Operation Twilight | OPT18 | 1983 | £2.50 | £6 |

## DORS, DIANA

| | | | | | | |
|---|---|---|---|---|---|---|
| Swingin' Dors | LP | Pye | NPL18044 | 1960 | £10 | £25 |

## DORSETS

| | | | | | | |
|---|---|---|---|---|---|---|
| Pork Chops | 7" | Sue | WI391 | 1965 | £4 | £8 |

## DORSEY, GERRY

| | | | | | | |
|---|---|---|---|---|---|---|
| Baby Turn Around | 7" | Hickory | 451337 | 1965 | £2.50 | £6 |

## DORSEY, JACK ORCHESTRA

| | | | | | | |
|---|---|---|---|---|---|---|
| Dance Of The Daleks | 7" | Polydor | 56020 | 1965 | £2.50 | £6 |

## DORSEY, JIMMY

| | | | | | | |
|---|---|---|---|---|---|---|
| Dixie By Dorsey | 10" LP | Columbia | 33S1026 | 1954 | £6 | £15 |
| Jay Dee's Boogie Woogie | 7" | HMV | POP383 | 1957 | £4 | £8 |
| So Rare | 7" | HMV | POP324 | 1957 | £1.50 | £4 |

## DORSEY, LEE

| | | | | | | | |
|---|---|---|---|---|---|---|---|
| Best Of Lee Dorsey | LP | Sue | ILP924 | 1965 | £15 | £30 | |
| Confusion | 7" | Stateside | SS506 | 1966 | £1.50 | £4 | |
| Do Re Mi | 7" | Top Rank | JAR606 | 1962 | £2.50 | £6 | |
| Get Out Of My Life Woman | 7" | Stateside | SS485 | 1966 | £1.50 | £4 | |
| Holy Cow | 7" | Stateside | SS552 | 1966 | £1.50 | £4 | |
| Lee Dorsey | LP | Stateside | (S)SL10177 | 1966 | £6 | £15 | |
| Messed Around | 7" | Sue | WI399 | 1966 | £4 | £8 | |
| New Lee Dorsey | LP | Stateside | (S)SL10192 | 1966 | £6 | £15 | |
| Rain Rain Go Away | 7" | Stateside | SS593 | 1967 | £1.50 | £4 | |
| Ride Your Pony | 7" EP | Stateside | SE1038 | 1966 | £5 | £10 | |
| Ride Your Pony | 7" | Stateside | SS441 | 1965 | £1.50 | £4 | |
| Work Work Work | 7" | Stateside | SS465 | 1965 | £1.50 | £4 | |
| Working In A Coalmine | 7" | Stateside | SS528 | 1966 | £1.50 | £4 | |
| Ya Ya | LP | Fury | 1002 | 1962 | £10 | £25 | US |
| Ya Ya | 7" | Sue | WI367 | 1965 | £4 | £8 | |
| You're Breaking Me Up | 7" EP | Stateside | SE1043 | 1966 | £5 | £10 | |

## DORSEY, TOMMY

| | | | | | | |
|---|---|---|---|---|---|---|
| And His Orchestra Vol. 1 | 7" EP | Brunswick | OE9012 | 1954 | £2 | £5 |
| Best Of Tommy Dorsey | 7" EP | Ember | EMBEP4513 | 1961 | £2 | £5 |
| Dixieland Jazz Vol. 1 | 10" LP | Brunswick | LA8524 | 1951 | £6 | £15 |
| Ecstasy | 10" LP | Brunswick | LA8669 | 1954 | £4 | £10 |
| Tenderly | 10" LP | Brunswick | LA8640 | 1954 | £4 | £10 |
| Tommy Dorsey | 10" LP | Brunswick | LA8610 | 1953 | £4 | £10 |
| Tommy Dorsey And His Orchestra | 7" EP | HMV | 7EG8004 | 1954 | £2 | £5 ...with Frank Sinatra |
| Tommy Dorsey And His Orchestra | 7" EP | HMV | 7EG8011 | 1954 | £2 | £5 |
| Tommy Dorsey No. 1 | 7" EP | RCA | RCX1002 | 1958 | £2 | £5 |
| Tommy Dorsey No. 3 | 7" EP | RCA | RCX1023 | 1959 | £2 | £5 |

## DOT, JOHNNY & THE DASHERS

| | | | | | | |
|---|---|---|---|---|---|---|
| I Love An Angel | 7" | Salvo | SLO1805 | 1962 | £1.50 | £4 |

## DOTTIE & BONNIE

| | | | | | | |
|---|---|---|---|---|---|---|
| Bunch Of Roses | 7" | Island | WI161 | 1964 | £5 | £10 ...Don Drummond B side |
| Dearest | 7" | Island | WI148 | 1964 | £5 | £10 |
| I'll Know | 7" | Ska Beat | JB274 | 1967 | £5 | £10 |
| I'm So Glad | 7" | Rio | R43 | 1964 | £5 | £10 ...Douglas Brothers B side |
| Sun Rises | 7" | Island | WI149 | 1964 | £5 | £10 ...Don Drummond B side |
| Your Kisses | 7" | Island | WI143 | 1964 | £5 | £10 |

## DOUBLE FEATURE

| | | | | | | |
|---|---|---|---|---|---|---|
| Baby Get Your Head Screwed On | 7" | Deram | DM115 | 1967 | £7.50 | £15 |
| Handbags And Gladrags | 7" | Deram | DM165 | 1967 | £2.50 | £6 |
| Tide Turned | LP | Marathon | | 1987 | £8 | £20 ...Dutch |

## DOUBLES

| | | | | | | |
|---|---|---|---|---|---|---|
| Hey Girl | 7" | HMV | POP613 | 1959 | £30 | £60 |

## DOUGHNUT RING

| | | | | | | |
|---|---|---|---|---|---|---|
| Dance Around Julie | 7" | Deram | DM215 | 1968 | £6 | £12 |

## DOUGLAS, CARL

| | | | | | | |
|---|---|---|---|---|---|---|
| Crazy Feeling | 7" | Go | AJ11401 | 1966 | £2.50 | £6 ...Peter Perry B side |
| Let The Birds Sing | 7" | Go | AJ11408 | 1967 | £2.50 | £6 |
| Nobody Cries | 7" | United Artists | UP1206 | 1967 | £20 | £40 |
| Sell My Soul To The Devil | 7" | United Artists | UP2227 | 1968 | £2 | £5 |

## DOUGLAS, CRAIG

| | | | | | | |
|---|---|---|---|---|---|---|
| Are You Really Mine | 7" | Decca | F11075 | 1958 | £2.50 | £6 |
| Bandwagon Ball | LP | Top Rank | 35103 | 1961 | £6 | £15 |
| Come Softly To Me | 7" | Top Rank | JAR110 | 1959 | £1.50 | £4 |
| Craig | 7" EP | Decca | DFE6633 | 1960 | £5 | £10 |
| Craig Douglas | LP | Top Rank | BUY049 | 1960 | £8 | £20 |
| Craig Sings For Roxy | 7" EP | Top Rank | JKR8033 | 1959 | £5 | £10 |
| Craig's Movie Songs | 7" EP | Columbia | SEG8219 | 1963 | £6 | £12 |
| Cuddle Up With Craig | 7" EP | Decca | DFE8509 | 1962 | £5 | £10 |
| Hundred Pounds Of Clay | 7" | Top Rank | JAR555 | 1961 | £1.50 | £4 |
| Hundred Pounds Of Clay (censored version) | 7" | Top Rank | JAR556 | 1961 | £2 | £5 |
| Hundred Pounds Of Clay (censored version) | 7" | Top Rank | JAR556 | 1961 | £4 | £8 ...picture sleeve |
| Only Sixteen | 7" | Top Rank | JAR159 | 1959 | £1.50 | £4 |
| Our Favourite Melodies | LP | Columbia | 33SX1468 | 1962 | £25 | £50 |
| Our Favourite Melodies | 7" | Columbia | DB4854 | 1962 | £1.50 | £4 |
| Sitting In A Tree House | 7" | Decca | F11055 | 1958 | £2 | £5 |
| Teenager In Love | 7" | Top Rank | JAR133 | 1959 | £1.50 | £4 |

## DOUGLAS, MARK

| | | | | | | |
|---|---|---|---|---|---|---|
| It Matters Not | 7" | Ember | EMBS166 | 1962 | £10 | £20 |

## DOUGLAS, NORMA

| | | | | | | |
|---|---|---|---|---|---|---|
| Be It Resolved | 7" | London | HLZ8475 | 1957 | £2 | £5 |

## DOUGLAS BROTHERS

| | | | | | | |
|---|---|---|---|---|---|---|
| Down And Out | 7" | Rio | R63 | 1965 | £5 | £10 Ronald Wilson B side |
| Valley Of Tears | 7" | Rio | R57 | 1965 | £5 | £10 ...Charmers B side |

## DOVELLS

| | | | | | | |
|---|---|---|---|---|---|---|
| All The Hits Of The Teen Groups | LP | Parkway | P7010 | 1962 | £8 | £20 ...US |
| Betty In Bermudas | 7" | Cameo Parkway | P882 | 1963 | £1.50 | £4 |
| Biggest Hits | LP | Wyncote | (SW)9114 | 1965 | £4 | £10 ...US |
| Bristol Stomp | LP | Parkway | P7006 | 1961 | £10 | £25 ...US |
| Bristol Stomp | 7" | Columbia | DB4718 | 1961 | £2 | £5 |
| Bristol Twistin' Annie | 7" | Columbia | DB4877 | 1962 | £1.50 | £4 |
| Discotheque | LP | Wyncote | (S)W9052 | 1965 | £4 | £10 ...US |
| Doin' The New Continental | 7" | Columbia | DB4810 | 1962 | £1.50 | £4 |
| Don't Knock The Twist | LP | Parkway | P7011 | 1962 | £8 | £20 ...US |
| Dragster On The Prowl | 7" | Cameo Parkway | P901 | 1963 | £2 | £5 |

| | | | | | | | |
|---|---|---|---|---|---|---|---|
| For Your Hully Gully Party | LP | Parkway | P7021 | 1963 | £8 | £20 | US |
| Hully Gully Baby | 7" | Cameo Parkway | P845 | 1962 | £1.50 | £4 | |
| You Can't Run Away From Yourself | 7" | Cameo Parkway | P861 | 1963 | £1.50 | £4 | |
| You Can't Sit Down | 7" | Cameo Parkway | P867 | 1963 | £1.50 | £4 | |

## DOW, NICK
| | | | | | | | |
|---|---|---|---|---|---|---|---|
| Burd Margaret | LP | Dingle | DIN306 | 1978 | £4 | £10 | |

## DOWELL, JOE
| | | | | | | | |
|---|---|---|---|---|---|---|---|
| Wooden Heart | LP | Smash | SRS67000 | 1961 | £8 | £20 | US |

## DOWLANDS
| | | | | | | | |
|---|---|---|---|---|---|---|---|
| All My Loving | 7" | Oriole | CB1897 | 1964 | £5 | £10 | |
| Breakups | 7" | Oriole | CB1815 | 1963 | £12.50 | £25 | |
| Don't Ever Change | 7" | Oriole | CB1781 | 1962 | £37.50 | £75 | |
| Don't Make Me Over | 7" | Columbia | DB7547 | 1965 | £5 | £10 | |
| I Walk The Line | 7" | Oriole | CB1926 | 1964 | £10 | £20 | |
| Julie | 7" | Oriole | CB1748 | 1962 | £12.50 | £25 | |
| Lucky Johnny | 7" | Oriole | CB1892 | 1963 | £100 | £200 | best auctioned |
| Wishing And Hoping | 7" | Oriole | CB1947 | 1964 | £20 | £40 | |

## DOWNBEATS
| | | | | | | | |
|---|---|---|---|---|---|---|---|
| Thinking Of You | 7" | Starlite | ST45051 | 1961 | £5 | £10 | |

## DOWNBEATS (2)
| | | | | | | | |
|---|---|---|---|---|---|---|---|
| Chantent en francais | 7" EP | Philips | 434932 | 196– | £2.50 | £6 | French |
| Dans la rue | 7" EP | Philips | 434990 | 196– | £2.50 | £6 | French |

## DOWNES, BOB

Bob Downes was an averagely talented flautist who attempted to haul himself into the first division by surrounding himself with the best British jazz musicians of the time and adopting a suitably 'progressive' image. So far, so good, but he also frequently insisted on opening his mouth to sing. Bob Downes has a terrible voice!

| | | | | | | | |
|---|---|---|---|---|---|---|---|
| Deep Down Heavy | LP | MFP | MFP1412 | 1970 | £4 | £10 | |
| Diversions | LP | Ophenian | BDOM001 | 1973 | £8 | £20 | |
| Electric City | LP | Vertigo | 6360005 | 1970 | £10 | £25 | spiral label |
| Episodes At 4am | LP | Ophenian | BDOM002 | 1974 | £8 | £20 | |
| Hell's Angels | LP | Ophenian | BDOM003 | 1975 | £8 | £20 | |
| Open Music – Dream Journey | LP | Philips | SBL7922 | 1970 | £30 | £60 | |
| Solo | LP | Openian | BDOM004 | 1976 | £8 | £20 | |

## DOWNES, JULIA
| | | | | | | | |
|---|---|---|---|---|---|---|---|
| Let Sleeping Dogs Lie | LP | Naive | NAVI2 | 1982 | £20 | £40 | |

## DOWNING, AL
| | | | | | | | |
|---|---|---|---|---|---|---|---|
| Yes I'm Loving You | 7" | Sue | WI341 | 1964 | £6 | £12 | |

## DOWNLINERS SECT
| | | | | | | | |
|---|---|---|---|---|---|---|---|
| All Night Worker | 7" | Columbia | DB7817 | 1966 | £6 | £12 | |
| Baby What's Wrong | 7" | Columbia | DB7300 | 1964 | £6 | £12 | |
| Bad Storm Coming | 7" | Columbia | DB7712 | 1965 | £6 | £12 | |
| Cost Of Living | 7" | Columbia | DB8008 | 1966 | £7.50 | £15 | |
| Country Sect | LP | Columbia | 33SX1745 | 1965 | £20 | £40 | |
| Downliners Sect | LP | HMV | SGLP534 | 1964 | £50 | £100 | Swedish |
| Find Out What's Happening | 7" | Columbia | DB7415 | 1964 | £6 | £12 | |
| Glendora | 7" | Columbia | DB7939 | 1966 | £10 | £20 | |
| I Got Mine | 7" | Columbia | DB7597 | 1965 | £6 | £12 | |
| Little Egypt | 7" | Columbia | DB7347 | 1964 | £6 | £12 | |
| Nite In Great Newport Street | 7" EP | Contrast | RBCSP001 | 1964 | £62.50 | £125 | |
| Rock Sect's In | LP | Columbia | SX/SCX6028 | 1966 | £25 | £50 | |
| Sect | LP | Columbia | 33SX1658 | 1964 | £25 | £50 | |
| Sect Sing Sick Songs | 7" EP | Columbia | SEG8438 | 1965 | £25 | £50 | |
| Wreck Of The Old '97 | 7" | Columbia | DB7509 | 1965 | £6 | £12 | |

## DOWNTOWN ALL STARS
| | | | | | | | |
|---|---|---|---|---|---|---|---|
| Downtown Jump | 7" | Downtown | DT426 | 1969 | £1.50 | £4 | |

## DOYLE, DANNY
| | | | | | | | |
|---|---|---|---|---|---|---|---|
| Highwaymen | LP | Granvaile | GRLP001 | 1981 | £4 | £10 | Irish |

## DR. CALCULUS
| | | | | | | | |
|---|---|---|---|---|---|---|---|
| Designer Beatnik | CD | Ten | DIXCD45 | 1986 | £5 | £12 | |

## DR. FEELGOOD & THE INTERNS
| | | | | | | | |
|---|---|---|---|---|---|---|---|
| Blang Dong | 7" | Columbia | DB7228 | 1964 | £2.50 | £6 | |
| Doctor Feelgood | LP | OKeh | M12/S14101 | 1962 | £10 | £25 | US |
| Don't Tell Me No Dirty | 7" | CBS | 202099 | 1966 | £4 | £8 | |
| Dr. Feelgood | 7" | Columbia | DB4838 | 1962 | £2.50 | £6 | |
| Dr. Feelgood & The Interns | 7" EP | Columbia | SEG8310 | 1964 | £20 | £40 | |
| Sugar Bee | 7" | Capitol | CL15569 | 1968 | £5 | £10 | |

## DR. HOOK
| | | | | | | | |
|---|---|---|---|---|---|---|---|
| Cover Of Radio Times | 7" | CBS | 1037 | 1973 | £4 | £8 | 1 sided promo |

## DR. JOHN

Mac Rebennack achieved early notoriety as the only white musician to break into the tough New Orleans R&B session world. With the advent of flower power, he reinvented himself as the voodoo magician, Dr. John, and recorded the weirdly mystical 'Gris Gris' album. Three other LPs followed in similar style, before Rebennack reverted to R&B, while still retaining the Dr. John pseudonym. He continues to be a prolific maker of records, both his own and other people's, for which he is an in-demand session pianist.

| | | | | | | | |
|---|---|---|---|---|---|---|---|
| Babylon | LP | Atlantic | 228018 | 1969 | £8 | £20 | |
| Gris Gris | LP | Atlantic | 587147 | 1968 | £8 | £20 | |
| Gris Gris | LP | Atlantic | K40168 | 1972 | £5 | £12 | |
| Gumbo | LP | Atlantic | K40384 | 1972 | £6 | £15 | |
| In The Right Place | LP | Atlantic | K50017 | 1973 | £4 | £10 | |
| Remedies | LP | Atlantic | 2400015 | 1970 | £8 | £20 | |
| Sun, Moon, & Herbs | LP | Atlantic | 2400161 | 1971 | £8 | £20 | |
| Sun, Moon, & Herbs | LP | Atlantic | K40250 | 1971 | £5 | £12 | |

## DR. K'S BLUES BAND

| | | | | | | | |
|---|---|---|---|---|---|---|---|
| Dr. K's Blues Band | LP | Spark | UK101 | 1968 | £10 | £25 | |

## DR. MARIGOLD'S PRESCRIPTION

| | | | | | | | |
|---|---|---|---|---|---|---|---|
| Pictures Of Life | LP | Marble Arch | MALS1222 | 1969 | £5 | £12 | |

## DR. STRANGELY STRANGE

Dr. Strangely Strange attempted to play the same kind of eccentrically pitched folk music as the Incredible String Band, but found that the market was only big enough for one. *Kip Of The Serenes* is one of the rarest rock releases on the Island label, although one track is well known to the many people who bought the *Nice Enough To Eat* sampler LP.

| | | | | | | | |
|---|---|---|---|---|---|---|---|
| Heavy Petting | LP | Vertigo | 6360009 | 1970 | £30 | £60 | *spiral label* |
| Kip Of The Serenes | LP | Island | ILPS9106 | 1969 | £37.50 | £75 | *pink label* |

## DR. TECHNICAL & THE MACHINES

| | | | | | | | |
|---|---|---|---|---|---|---|---|
| Zones | 7" | Hawkfan | HWFB1 | 1983 | £2.50 | £6 | *1 sided* |

## DR. WEST'S MEDICINE SHOW & JUNK BAND

| | | | | | | | |
|---|---|---|---|---|---|---|---|
| Bullets La Verne | 7" | Page One | POF23061 | 1968 | £7.50 | £15 | |
| Eggplant That Ate Chicago | LP | Page One | POLS17 | 1968 | £10 | £25 | |

## DR. Z

The rarest album on the Vertigo 'spiral' label is the work of a typical keyboard trio from the period and is housed in an elaborate opening out sleeve. Legend suggests that only eighty copies of the record were sold, and it is certainly scarce enough today for this to be true.

| | | | | | | | |
|---|---|---|---|---|---|---|---|
| Lady Ladybird | 7" | Fontana | 6007023 | 1970 | £10 | £20 | |
| Three Parts To My Soul | LP | Vertigo | 6360048 | 1971 | £150 | £250 | *spiral label* |

## DRAG SET

| | | | | | | | |
|---|---|---|---|---|---|---|---|
| Day And Night | 7" | Go | AJ11405 | 1966 | £62.50 | £125 | |

## DRAGON

| | | | | | | | |
|---|---|---|---|---|---|---|---|
| Dragon | LP | Acorn | CF268 | 1976 | £20 | £40 | |
| Scented Gardens For The Blind | LP | Vertigo | 6360903 | 1974 | £30 | £60 | *French* |
| Universal Radio | LP | Vertigo | 6360902 | 1971 | £25 | £50 | *New Zealand* |

## DRAGONFLY

| | | | | | | | |
|---|---|---|---|---|---|---|---|
| Almost Abandoned | LP | Retreat | 6002 | 1974 | £4 | £10 | |

## DRAGONFLY (2)

| | | | | | | | |
|---|---|---|---|---|---|---|---|
| Dragonfly | LP | Megaphone | 1202 | 1970 | £100 | £200 | *US* |
| Dragonfly | LP | Megaphone | MS1202 | 1968 | £15 | £30 | *US* |

## DRAGONWYCK

| | | | | | | | |
|---|---|---|---|---|---|---|---|
| Dragonwyck | LP | private | | 1970 | £700 | £1000 | *US* |
| Dragonwyck | LP | private | | 1972 | £1400 | £2000 | *US acetate* |

## DRAKE, CHARLIE

| | | | | | | | |
|---|---|---|---|---|---|---|---|
| Hello My Darlings | 7" EP | Parlophone | GEP8720 | 1958 | £2 | £5 | |
| Hits From The Man In The Moon | 7" EP | Parlophone | GEP8903 | 1964 | £2 | £5 | |
| Naughty | 7" EP | Parlophone | GEP8812 | 1960 | £2 | £5 | |
| Sea Cruise | 7" | Parlophone | R4552 | 1959 | £1.50 | £4 | |
| Splish Splash | 7" | Parlophone | R4461 | 1958 | £1.50 | £4 | |
| You Never Know | 7" | Charisma | CB270 | 1975 | £2 | £5 | *with Peter Gabriel* |

## DRAKE, NICK

Nick Drake's shyly melodic music has had a considerable cult following for some time. The three original albums that he recorded before his death of a drug overdose have long remained collectable, despite the ready availability of reissue copies on vinyl and CD. When producer Joe Boyd sold his Witchseason company, which included the rights to Drake's records, to Island, he made it a condition of sale that Nick Drake's music should never become unavailable. Listening to the late-night beauty of the *Five Leaves Left* arrangements, to the sparkling playing by the likes of Richard Thompson, John Cale, and Chris McGregor on *Bryter Layter*, to the stark introspection of *Pink Moon*, and to the musical and lyrical poetry throughout, it is easy to understand Boyd's enthusiasm.

| | | | | | | | |
|---|---|---|---|---|---|---|---|
| Bryter Layter | LP | Island | ILPS9134 | 1970 | £10 | £25 | |
| Five Leaves Left | LP | Island | ILPS9105 | 1969 | £10 | £25 | *pink label* |
| Fruit Tree | LP | Island | NDSP100 | 1979 | £25 | £50 | *triple, boxed* |
| Island LP Sampler | LP | Island | RSS7 | 1979 | £10 | £25 | *promo* |
| Pink Moon | LP | Island | ILPS9184 | 1972 | £10 | £25 | |

## DRAMA

| | | | | | | | |
|---|---|---|---|---|---|---|---|
| Drama | LP | Philips | 6413021 | 1971 | £62.50 | £125 | *Dutch* |

## DRAMATICS
Whatcha See Is Whatcha Get...................... LP ..... Stax ............... 2362025 ................. 1972 £4.......... £10 .......................

## DRANSFIELD, BARRY
Barry Dransfield ................................. LP ..... Polydor.......... 2383160 ............... 1972 £150..... £250 ........................
Bowin' And Scrapin' ........................... LP ..... Topic.............. 12TS386 ............... 1978 £10......... £25 ........................

## DRANSFIELD, ROBIN
Tidewave.......................................... LP ..... Topic.............. 12TS414 ............... 1980 £4........... £10 ........................

## DRANSFIELD, ROBIN & BARRY
Fiddler's Dream ................................. LP ..... Transatlantic .... TRA322 ............... 1976 £10......... £25 . credited to Dransfield
Lord Of All I Behold .......................... LP ..... Trailer............ LER2026 ............... 1971 £20......... £40 ........................
Popular To Contrary Belief ................... LP ..... Free Reed ...... FRR018 ............... 1977 £5........... £12 ........................
Rout Of The Blues ............................. LP ..... Trailer............ LER2011 ............... 1970 £20......... £40 ........................

## DRAPER, RUSTY
Chicken Picking Hawk ......................... 7" ...... Mercury.......... 7MT229........... 1958 £2.50........ £6 ........................
Folsom Prison Blues............................ 7" ...... London ........... HLU9989......... 1965 £2............. £5 ........................
Gambling Gal..................................... 7" ...... Mercury.......... 7MT211........... 1958 £2.50........ £6 ........................
Hits That Sold A Million....................... LP ..... Mercury.......... MMC14040....... 1960 £5........... £12 ........................
Mule Skinner Blues ............................. 7" EP . Mercury.......... ZEP10095........ 1960 £2.50........ £6 ........................
Mule Skinner Blues ............................. 7" ...... Mercury.......... AMT1101......... 1960 £2............. £5 ........................
Presenting Rusty Draper ...................... 7" EP . Mercury.......... MEP9506......... 1956 £6........... £12 ........................
Rock And Roll Ruby ........................... 78 ...... Mercury.......... MT113............ 1956 £2.50........ £6 ........................
Rusty Draper .................................... 7" EP . Mercury.......... ZEP10016........ 1959 £2.50........ £6 ........................
Rusty Draper No. 1 ............................ 7" EP . London ........... REU1431.......... 1964 £5........... £10 ........................
Rusty Draper No. 2 ............................ 7" EP . London ........... REU1432.......... 1964 £5........... £10 ........................
Rusty In Gambling Mood ...................... 7" EP . Mercury.......... ZEP10059........ 1960 £2.50........ £6 ........................
Shopping Around ............................... 7" ...... Mercury.......... AMT1019......... 1959 £5........... £10 ........................
Sun Will Always Shine ........................ 7" ...... Mercury.......... AMT1033......... 1959 £1.50........ £4 ........................
That's Why I Love You Like I Do ............ 7" ...... London ........... HLU9786.......... 1963 £2.50........ £6 ........................

## DREAM
Guitarist with Dream was Terje Rypdal, later to make many highly acclaimed albums for the ECM label.

Dream............................................. LP ..... Karussell......... 2915068 ........... 1976 £25.......... £50 ................. German
Get Dreamy ...................................... LP ..... Polydor.......... SLPHM184099....... 1967 £50..... £100 ................. German

## DREAM POLICE
The Dream Police achieved little success in their own right, but managed to provide members for two much more successful groups – the Sensational Alex Harvey Band and the Average White Band.

I've Got No Choice ............................. 7" ...... Decca ............ F13105............ 1970 £1.50........ £4 ........................
Living Is Easy.................................... 7" ...... Decca ............ F12998............ 1970 £4............. £8 ........................
Our Song .......................................... 7" ...... Decca ............ F13078............ 1970 £1.50........ £4 ........................

## DREAMERS
Maybe Song....................................... 7" ...... Columbia ........ DB8340 ........... 1968 £1.50........ £4 ........................

## DREAMERS (2)
Dear Love......................................... 7" ...... Downtown...... DT408 ............ 1969 £1.50........ £4 ........................
Sweet Chariot .................................... 7" ...... Downtown...... DT407 ............ 1969 £1.50........ £4 ........................

## DREAMIES
Auralgraphic Entertainment...................... LP ..... Stone Theatre.. DM68481............... 1968 £75........ £150 ........................ US

## DREAMLETS
Really Now ........................................ 7" ...... Ska Beat .......... JB182..................... 1965 £5........... £10 ....... Skatalites B side

## DREAMLOVERS
Bird .............................................. LP ..... Columbia ........ CL2020/CS8820..... 1963 £8........... £20 ........................ US
When We Get Married........................... 7" ...... Columbia ........ DB4711 ........... 1961 £25.......... £50 ........................

## DREAMS
Best Of Dreams.................................. LP ..... Dolphin .......... DOLB7002 ........ 1969 £6........... £15 ........................ Irish

## DREAMS DIE FIRST?
Dare To Dream.................................. LP ..... Serial ............ ....................... 1986 £6........... £15 ........................ Dutch

## DREAMTIMERS
Dancin' Lady ..................................... 7" ...... London .......... HLU9368.............. 1961 £2.50........ £6 ........................

## DREAMWEAVERS
It's Almost, Tomorrow ......................... 7" ...... Brunswick ...... 05515.................. 1956 £12.50...... £25 ........................
Little Love Can Go A Long Long Way....... 7" ...... Brunswick ...... 05568.................. 1956 £10......... £20 ........................
You're Mine....................................... 7" ...... Brunswick ...... 05607.................. 1956 £5........... £10 ........................

## DREGS
Dregs .............................................. 7" ...... Disturbing ...... DRO1 ................. 1979 £2............. £5 ........................

## DREVAR, JOHN EXPRESSION
Closer She Gets.................................. 7" ...... MGM ............. MGM1367 ............ 1967 £20......... £40 ........................

## DREW, PATTI
Workin' On A Groovy Thing ................... 7" ...... Capitol............ CL15557 ............... 1968 £1.50........ £4 ........................

# DRIFTERS

| Title | Format | Label | Cat. No. | Year | | | Notes |
|---|---|---|---|---|---|---|---|
| At The Club | 7" | Atlantic | AT4019 | 1965 | £1.50 | £4 | |
| Baby What I Mean | 7" | Atlantic | 584065 | 1967 | £1.50 | £4 | |
| Clyde McPhatter & The Drifters | LP | Atlantic | 8003 | 1956 | £62.50 | £125 | US |
| Come On Over To My Place | 7" | Atlantic | AT4023 | 1965 | £1.50 | £4 | |
| Dance With Me | 7" | London | HLE8988 | 1959 | £5 | £10 | |
| Drifters | LP | Clarion | (SD)608 | 1964 | £6 | £15 | US |
| Drifters | 7" EP | London | REK1355 | 1963 | £10 | £20 | |
| Drifting | 7" EP | London | REK1385 | 1963 | £10 | £20 | |
| Drifting Vol. 2 | 7" EP | London | AET6003 | 1964 | £6 | £12 | |
| Follow Me | 7" | Atlantic | AT4034 | 1965 | £4 | £8 | |
| Good Gravy | LP | Atlantic | 587144 | 1968 | £6 | £15 | |
| Good Life | LP | Atlantic | ATL5023 | 1965 | £4 | £10 | |
| Greatest Hits | LP | London | HAK2318 | 1960 | £10 | £25 | |
| I Count The Tears | 7" | London | HLK9287 | 1961 | £1.50 | £4 | |
| I'll Take You Home | 7" | London | HLK9785 | 1963 | £1.50 | £4 | |
| I'll Take You Where The Music's Playing | LP | Atlantic | 587061 | 1967 | £4 | £10 | |
| I'll Take You Where The Music's Playing | LP | Atlantic | ATL/STL5039 | 1966 | £5 | £12 | |
| I'll Take You Where The Music's Playing | 7" | Atlantic | 584152 | 1968 | £1.50 | £4 | |
| I'll Take You Where The Music's Playing | 7" | Atlantic | AT4040 | 1965 | £1.50 | £4 | |
| I've Got Sand In My Shoes | 7" | Atlantic | AT4008 | 1964 | £1.50 | £4 | |
| In The Land Of Make Believe | 7" | London | HLK9848 | 1964 | £1.50 | £4 | |
| Lonely Winds | 7" | London | HLK9145 | 1960 | £5 | £10 | |
| Memories Are Made Of This | 7" | Atlantic | AT4084 | 1966 | £1.50 | £4 | |
| Moonlight Bay | 7" | London | HLE8686 | 1958 | £37.50 | £75 | |
| On Broadway | 7" | London | HLK9699 | 1963 | £1.50 | £4 | |
| One Way Love | 7" | London | HLK9886 | 1964 | £1.50 | £4 | |
| Our Biggest Hits | LP | Atlantic | 587038 | 1966 | £4 | £10 | |
| Our Biggest Hits | LP | Atlantic | ATL5015 | 1965 | £5 | £12 | |
| Please Stay | 7" | London | HLK9382 | 1961 | £1.50 | £4 | |
| Rat Race | 7" | London | HLK9750 | 1963 | £1.50 | £4 | |
| Rockin' And Driftin' | LP | Atlantic | 587123 | 1968 | £4 | £10 | |
| Rockin' And Driftin' | LP | Atlantic | 8022 | 1958 | £62.50 | £125 | US |
| Room Full Of Tears | 7" | London | HLK9500 | 1962 | £1.50 | £4 | |
| Saturday Night At The Movies | 7" | Atlantic | AT4012 | 1964 | £1.50 | £4 | |
| Save The Last Dance For Me | LP | Atlantic | 587063 | 1967 | £4 | £10 | |
| Save The Last Dance For Me | LP | London | HAK2450 | 1962 | £8 | £20 | |
| Save The Last Dance For Me | 7" EP | London | REK1282 | 1961 | £10 | £20 | |
| Save The Last Dance For Me | 7" | London | HLK9201 | 1960 | £1.50 | £4 | |
| Soldier Of Fortune | 7" | London | HLE8344 | 1956 | £210 | £350 | best auctioned |
| Some Kind Of Wonderful | 7" | London | HLK9326 | 1961 | £2 | £5 | |
| Souvenirs | LP | Atlantic | 590010 | 1966 | £4 | £10 | |
| Stranger On The Shore | 7" | London | HLK9554 | 1962 | £1.50 | £4 | |
| Sweets For My Sweet | 7" | London | HLK9427 | 1961 | £1.50 | £4 | |
| There Goes My Baby | 7" | London | HLE8892 | 1959 | £10 | £20 | |
| This Magic Moment | 7" | London | HLE9081 | 1960 | £5 | £10 | |
| Tonight | 7" EP | London | AET6012 | 1965 | £6 | £12 | |
| Under The Boardwalk | LP | Atlantic | (SD)8099 | 1964 | £10 | £25 | US |
| Under The Boardwalk | 7" | Atlantic | AT4001 | 1964 | £1.50 | £4 | |
| Up On The Roof | LP | Atlantic | (SD)8073 | 1963 | £10 | £25 | US |
| Up On The Roof | LP | Atlantic | 587/588160 | 1969 | £4 | £10 | |
| Up On The Roof | 7" | London | HLK9626 | 1962 | £1.50 | £4 | |
| We Gotta Sing | 7" | Atlantic | AT4062 | 1966 | £1.50 | £4 | |
| When My Little Girl Is Smiling | 7" | London | HLK9522 | 1962 | £1.50 | £4 | |

# DRIFTERS (UK)

Cliff Richard's backing group was originally called the Drifters, and they released two singles under that name in their own right, before changing name to the Shadows, in order to avoid confusion with the more famous American Drifters. In America, a change was made for them for the single 'Jet Black' (the B side of the UK 'Drifting' single), as this was credited to the Four Jets.

| Title | Format | Label | Cat. No. | Year | | | |
|---|---|---|---|---|---|---|---|
| Drifting | 7" | Columbia | DB4325 | 1959 | £15 | £30 | |
| Feeling Fine | 7" | Columbia | DB4263 | 1959 | £25 | £50 | |

# DRIFTING SLIM

| Title | Format | Label | Cat. No. | Year | | | |
|---|---|---|---|---|---|---|---|
| Good Morning Baby | 7" | Blue Horizon | 451005 | 1966 | £50 | £100 | |

# DRIFTWOOD

| Title | Format | Label | Cat. No. | Year | | | |
|---|---|---|---|---|---|---|---|
| Driftwood | LP | Decca | SKL5069 | 1970 | £6 | £15 | |

# DRIFTWOOD, JIMMY

| Title | Format | Label | Cat. No. | Year | | | |
|---|---|---|---|---|---|---|---|
| Country Guitar Vol. 13 | 7" EP | RCA | RCX191 | 1960 | £2 | £5 | |
| Tall Tales In Song Vol. 1 | 7" EP | RCA | RCX193 | 1960 | £2 | £5 | |
| Tall Tales In Song Vol. 2 | 7" EP | RCA | RCX195 | 1960 | £2 | £5 | |
| Tall Tales In Song Vol. 3 | 7" EP | RCA | RCX198 | 1960 | £2 | £5 | |

# DRISCOLL, JULIE

As far as the general public is concerned, Julie Driscoll is something of a one-hit wonder, having topped the charts with a superb version of Bob Dylan's 'This Wheel's On Fire' and then having apparently dropped from sight. In fact, she married jazz pianist Keith Tippett, and as Julie Tippett has appeared on a number of jazz records by her husband and by others. 'This Wheel's On Fire' was the most visible product of a profitable association with the Brian Auger Trinity, documented by the various Marmalade recordings credited to one or both of them, and going back, through her membership of Steampacket, to the single 'Don't Do It No More'.

| Title | Format | Label | Cat. No. | Year | | | |
|---|---|---|---|---|---|---|---|
| 1969 | LP | Polydor | 2383077 | 1971 | £5 | £12 | |
| 1969 | LP | Polydor | 2480074 | 1971 | £6 | £15 | |
| Don't Do It No More | 7" | Parlophone | R5296 | 1965 | £5 | £10 | |
| I Didn't Want To Have To Do It | 7" | Parlophone | R5444 | 1966 | £2 | £5 | |

| | | | | | | | | |
|---|---|---|---|---|---|---|---|---|
| I Know You Love Me Not | 7" | Parlophone | R5588 | 1967 | £2 | £5 | |
| Take Me By The Hand | 7" | Columbia | DB7118 | 1963 | £4 | £8 | |

## DRISCOLL, JULIE & BRIAN AUGER

| | | | | | | | | |
|---|---|---|---|---|---|---|---|---|
| Julie Driscoll And Brian Auger | LP | MFP | MFP1265 | 1968 | £4 | £10 | |
| Open | LP | Marmalade | 607/608002 | 1967 | £8 | £20 | |
| Road To Cairo | 7" | Marmalade | 598011 | 1969 | £1.50 | £4 | |
| Save Me | 7" | Marmalade | 598004 | 1967 | £1.50 | £4 | |
| Streetnoise | LP | Marmalade | 608005/6 | 1968 | £10 | £25 | double |
| Streetnoise Part 1 | LP | Marmalade | 608014 | 1969 | £4 | £10 | |
| Streetnoise Part 2 | LP | Marmalade | 608015 | 1969 | £4 | £10 | |
| Take Me To The Water | 7" | Marmalade | 598018 | 1969 | £1.50 | £4 | |
| This Wheel's On Fire | 7" | Marmalade | 598006 | 1968 | £1.50 | £4 | |

## DRIVE

| | | | | | | | |
|---|---|---|---|---|---|---|---|
| No Girls | 7" | First Strike | FST007 | 1990 | £4 | £8 | |

## DRNWYN

| | | | | | | | |
|---|---|---|---|---|---|---|---|
| Gypsies In The Mist | LP | Wilderland | 31778 | 1978 | £30 | £60 | US |

## D-ROK

| | | | | | | | |
|---|---|---|---|---|---|---|---|
| Get Out Of My Way | CD-s | Warhammer | DROK08724 | 1991 | £3 | £8 | |
| Get Out Of My Way | 12" | Warhammer | DROK08722 | 1991 | £2.50 | £6 | |

## DRONES

| | | | | | | | |
|---|---|---|---|---|---|---|---|
| Be My Baby | 12" | Valer | VRSP1 | 1977 | £10 | £20 | test pressing |
| Bone Idol | 7" | Valer | VRS1 | 1977 | £2 | £5 | |
| Can't See | 7" | Fabulous | JC4 | 1980 | £1.50 | £4 | |
| Further Temptations | LP | Valer | VRLP1 | 1977 | £6 | £15 | |
| Temptations Of A White Collar Worker | 7" | Ohms | GOODMIX1 | 1977 | £1.50 | £4 | picture sleeve, plastic bag |

## DROSSELBART

| | | | | | | | |
|---|---|---|---|---|---|---|---|
| Drosselbart | LP | Polydor | 2371126 | 1970 | £10 | £25 | German |

## DRUGSTORE

| | | | | | | | |
|---|---|---|---|---|---|---|---|
| Drugstore | CD | Honey | 8286170 | 1995 | £5 | £12 | with CD single (8500662) |
| Injection | CD-s | Honey | HONCD8 | 1995 | £2 | £5 | |
| Injection | 7" | Honey | HON8 | 1995 | £2 | £5 | clear vinyl |
| Xmas At The Drugstore | 7" | Honey | DXMAS95 | 1995 | £4 | £8 | 1 sided freebie |

## DRUID

| | | | | | | | |
|---|---|---|---|---|---|---|---|
| Fluid Druid | LP | EMI | EMC3128 | 1976 | £4 | £10 | |
| Towards The Sun | LP | EMI | EMC3081 | 1975 | £4 | £10 | |

## DRUID CHASE

| | | | | | | | |
|---|---|---|---|---|---|---|---|
| Take Me In Your Garden | 7" | CBS | 3053 | 1967 | £5 | £10 | |

## DRUIDS

| | | | | | | | |
|---|---|---|---|---|---|---|---|
| It's Just A Little Bit Too Late | 7" | Parlophone | R5134 | 1964 | £2.50 | £6 | |
| Long Tall Texan | 7" | Parlophone | R5097 | 1964 | £1.50 | £4 | |

## DRUIDS (2)

| | | | | | | | |
|---|---|---|---|---|---|---|---|
| Burnt Offering | LP | Argo | ZFB22 | 1970 | £50 | £100 | |
| Pastime With Good Company | LP | Argo | ZFB39 | 1972 | £37.50 | £75 | |

## DRUIDS OF STONEHENGE

| | | | | | | | |
|---|---|---|---|---|---|---|---|
| Creation | LP | Uni | (7)3004 | 1968 | £30 | £60 | US |

## DRUMBAGO

| | | | | | | | |
|---|---|---|---|---|---|---|---|
| Dulcimania | 7" | Trojan | TR638 | 1968 | £2 | £5 | Clancy Eccles B side |
| I Am Drunk | 7" | Island | WI085 | 1963 | £5 | £10 | |
| I'm Not Worthy | 7" | Blue Beat | BB51 | 1961 | £6 | £12 | Magic Notes B side |
| Reggae Jeggae | 7" | Blue Cat | BS145 | 1968 | £2.50 | £6 | Tyrone Taylor B side |

## DRUMMOND, DON

| | | | | | | | |
|---|---|---|---|---|---|---|---|
| Allepon | 7" | Ska Beat | JB187 | 1965 | £5 | £10 | Justin Hinds B side |
| Best Of Don Drummond | LP | Studio One | SOL9008 | 1968 | £50 | £100 | |
| Cool Smoke | 7" | Island | WI231 | 1965 | £5 | £10 | Techniques B side |
| Coolie Boy | 7" | Island | WI204 | 1965 | £5 | £10 | Lord Antics B side |
| Doctor Dekker | 7" | Ska Beat | JB189 | 1965 | £5 | £10 | Owen & Leon B side |
| Don De Lion | 7" | Ska Beat | JB191 | 1965 | £5 | £10 | Movers B side |
| Far East | 7" | Blue Beat | BB179 | 1963 | £6 | £12 | |
| Heavenless | 7" | Studio One | SO2078 | 1969 | £6 | £12 | Glen Brown B side |
| Looking Through The Window | 7" | Island | WI294 | 1966 | £5 | £10 | Soul Brothers B side |
| Man In The Street | 7" | Island | WI208 | 1965 | £5 | £10 | Rita & Bunny B side |
| Memorial Album | LP | Trojan | TTL23 | 1969 | £10 | £25 | |
| Memory Of Don | 7" | Trojan | TR678 | 1969 | £2.50 | £6 | John Holt B side |
| Musical Storeroom | 7" | Island | WI153 | 1964 | £5 | £10 | Stranger Cole B side |
| Scandal | 7" | Island | WI094 | 1963 | £5 | £10 | W.Sparks B side |
| Schooling The Duke | 7" | Island | WI021 | 1962 | £5 | £10 | |
| Scrap Iron | 7" | Black Swan | WI406 | 1963 | £5 | £10 | |
| Shock | 7" | R&B | JB105 | 1963 | £5 | £10 | Tonettes B side |
| Ska Town | 7" | Blue Beat | BB298 | 1965 | £6 | £12 | Eric Morris B side |
| Stampede | 7" | Island | WI192 | 1965 | £5 | £10 | Justin Hinds B side |
| Treasure Island | 7" | Island | WI195 | 1965 | £5 | £10 | Riots B side |
| University Goes Ska | 7" | Island | WI242 | 1965 | £5 | £10 | Derrick Morgan B side |

## DRUSKY, ROY
| | | | | | | | |
|---|---|---|---|---|---|---|---|
| Just About That Time | 7" | Brunswick | 05785 | 1959 | £1.50 | £4 | |

## DRY ICE
| | | | | | | | |
|---|---|---|---|---|---|---|---|
| Running To The Convent | 7" | B&C | CB115 | 1970 | £5 | £10 | |

## DRY RIB
| | | | | | | | |
|---|---|---|---|---|---|---|---|
| Dry Season | 7" | Clockwork | COR001 | 1979 | £7.50 | £15 | |

## DSCHINN
| | | | | | | | |
|---|---|---|---|---|---|---|---|
| Dschinn | LP | Bacillus | BLPS19120 | 1972 | £8 | £20 | German |

## D'SILVA, AMANCIO
| | | | | | | | |
|---|---|---|---|---|---|---|---|
| Integration | LP | Columbia | SX/SCX6322 | 1969 | £25 | £50 | |
| Reflections | LP | Columbia | SCX6465 | 1970 | £25 | £50 | |

## DUALS
| | | | | | | | |
|---|---|---|---|---|---|---|---|
| Stick Shift | LP | Sue | LP2002 | 1961 | £25 | £50 | US |
| Stick Shift | 7" | London | HL9450 | 1961 | £6 | £12 | |

## DUBLINERS
| | | | | | | | |
|---|---|---|---|---|---|---|---|
| At Home With The Dubliners | LP | Columbia | SCX6380 | 1969 | £6 | £15 | |
| At It Again | LP | Major Minor | SMLP34 | 1968 | £4 | £10 | |
| Drop Of The Dubliners | LP | Major Minor | (S)MCP5024 | 1969 | £4 | £10 | |
| Drop Of The Hard Stuff | LP | Major Minor | MMLP3 | 1967 | £5 | £12 | |
| Dubliners | LP | Major Minor | GOL200 | 1968 | £4 | £10 | |
| Dubliners Now | LP | Polydor | 2383329 | 1975 | £4 | £10 | |
| Dubliners With Luke Kelly | LP | Transatlantic | TRA116 | 1964 | £6 | £15 | |
| Fifteen Years On | LP | Polydor | 2683070 | 1977 | £5 | £12 | double |
| Finnegan Wakes | LP | Hallmark | CHM695 | 1966 | £4 | £10 | |
| Finnegan Wakes | LP | Transatlantic | TRA139 | 1966 | £6 | £15 | |
| In Concert | LP | Transatlantic | TRA124 | 1965 | £6 | £15 | |
| Live At The Albert Hall London | LP | Major Minor | SMLP44 | 1969 | £4 | £10 | |
| More Of The Hard Stuff | LP | Major Minor | MMLP/SMLP5 | 1967 | £5 | £12 | |
| Plain And Simple | LP | Polydor | 2383235 | 1973 | £4 | £10 | |
| Revolution | LP | Columbia | SCX6423 | 1970 | £6 | £15 | |

## DUBS
| | | | | | | | |
|---|---|---|---|---|---|---|---|
| Could This Be Magic | 7" | London | HLU8526 | 1957 | £62.50 | £125 | |
| Dubs Meet The Shells | LP | Josie | JM/JSS4001 | 195– | £25 | £50 | US |
| Gonna Make A Change | 7" | London | HL8684 | 1958 | £100 | £200 | best auctioned |

## DUCKS DELUXE
Ducks Deluxe was one of the better 'pub rock' bands to emerge during the seventies. The group included Martin Belmont, Sean Tyla and Andy McMaster, all of whom found a little success in subsequent years (Belmont with Graham Parker's Rumour, Tyler as a solo artist, McMaster with the Motors).

| | | | | | | | |
|---|---|---|---|---|---|---|---|
| Ducks Deluxe | LP | RCA | PL5008 | 1974 | £4 | £10 | |
| Taxi To The Terminal Zone | LP | RCA | SF8402 | 1974 | £4 | £10 | |

## DUDLEY
| | | | | | | | |
|---|---|---|---|---|---|---|---|
| El Pizza | 7" | Vogue | V9171 | 1960 | £4 | £8 | |

## DUFFAS, SHENLEY
| | | | | | | | |
|---|---|---|---|---|---|---|---|
| Big Mouth | 7" | R&B | JB146 | 1964 | £5 | £10 | Frankie Anderson B side |
| Christopher Columbus | 7" | R&B | JB152 | 1964 | £5 | £10 | Carl Bryan B side |
| Digging A Ditch | 7" | Black Swan | WI440 | 1964 | £5 | £10 | |
| Easy Squeal | 7" | Island | WI125 | 1963 | £5 | £10 | |
| Fret Man Fret | 7" | Island | WI063 | 1963 | £5 | £10 | |
| Gather Them In | 7" | Black Swan | WI443 | 1964 | £5 | £10 | |
| Give To Get | 7" | Island | WI036 | 1962 | £5 | £10 | |
| I Will Be Glad | 7" | Rio | R41 | 1964 | £5 | £10 | |
| Know The Lord | 7" | Island | WI115 | 1963 | £5 | £10 | Tommy McCook B side |
| La La La La | 7" | Island | WI182 | 1965 | £5 | £10 | Upcoming Willows B side |
| Mother-In-Law | 7" | R&B | JB154 | 1964 | £5 | £10 | Don Drummond B side |
| No More Wedding Bells | 7" | R&B | JB134 | 1963 | £5 | £10 | |
| Rukembine | 7" | Island | WI186 | 1965 | £5 | £10 | |
| What A Disaster | 7" | Island | WI093 | 1963 | £5 | £10 | |
| You Are Mine | 7" | Island | WI184 | 1965 | £5 | £10 | Upcoming Willows B side |

## DUFFY
| | | | | | | | |
|---|---|---|---|---|---|---|---|
| Joker | 7" | Chapter One | CH184 | 1973 | £4 | £8 | |
| Just In Case You're Interested | LP | Ariola | 85846 | 1975 | £6 | £15 | German |
| Scruffy Duffy | LP | Chapter One | CHSR814 | 1970 | £37.50 | £75 | |

## DUFFY'S NUCLEUS
| | | | | | | | |
|---|---|---|---|---|---|---|---|
| Hound Dog | 7" EP | Decca | 457142 | 1967 | £20 | £40 | French |
| Hound Dog | 7" | Decca | F22547 | 1967 | £4 | £8 | |

## DUKE, DENVER & JEFFREY NULL BLUEGRASS BOYS
| | | | | | | | |
|---|---|---|---|---|---|---|---|
| Denver Duke & Jeffrey Null Bluegrass Boys | 7" EP | Starlite | STEP33 | 1963 | £4 | £8 | |

## DUKE, DORIS
I'm A Loser ........................................... LP ..... Mojo ............. 2916001 ................. 1971 £4......... £10 ............................................
Woman ................................................... LP ..... Contempo........ CLP519................. 1975 £4......... £10 ............................................

## DUKE, GEORGE
Aura Will Prevail.................................... LP ..... BASF............ BAP5064................. 1974 £4......... £10 ......................... German
Feel.......................................................... LP ..... MPS ............. 23124....................... 1974 £4......... £10 ......................... German
I Love The Blues, She Heard My Cry ....... LP ..... BASF............ BAP5071................. 1975 £4......... £10 ......................... German
Live In Los Angeles ............................... LP ..... Sunset .......... SLS50232............... 1971 £4......... £10 ............................... US

## DUKE ALL STARS
Letter To Mummy And Daddy................. 7" ...... Blue Cat....... BS111 ..................... 1968 £4......... £8 ................................................

## DUKE & DUCHESS
Get Ready For Love............................... 7" ...... London.......... HLU8206................. 1955 £6......... £12 ............................................

## DUKES, AGGIE
John John ............................................... 7" ...... Vogue............ V9090..................... 1957 £62.50.. £125 .........................................

## DUKES OF STRATOSFEAR
As is well known, the Dukes are actually XTC, using the alias to produce one and a half albums' worth of material that would be hailed as
true masterpieces of sixties psychedelia, if only they had actually been recorded in the sixties!

Psonic Psunspot....................................... LP ..... Virgin ........... VP2440................... 1987 £4......... £10 ... multi-coloured vinyl
You're A Good Man Albert Brown............ 7" ...... Virgin ........... VSY982................... 1987 £1.50........ £4 ... multi-coloured vinyl

## DULCIMER
And I Turned As I Had Turned As A Boy .. LP ..... Nepentha ........ 6437003 ................. 1971 £25......... £50 .........................................
Land Fit For Heroes............................... LP ..... Happy Face ..... MMLP1021.......... 1980 £5......... £12 .........................................

## DUMB ANGELS
Love And Mercy ..................................... 7" ...... Fierce ............ FRIGHT033 .......... 1988 £2.50........ £6 ...................................

## DUMBELLS (ROXY MUSIC)
Giddy Up .................................................. 7" ...... Editions EG..... EGO3 ...................... 1976 £2.50........ £6 ...................................
Giddy Up .................................................. 7" ...... Polydor ........... POSP209 ............... 1981 £2......... £5 .........................................

## DUMMER, JOHN
Blue........................................................... LP ..... Vertigo .......... 6360055 .................. 1972 £30......... £60 ................ spiral label
Cabal ........................................................ LP ..... Mercury.......... SMCL20136.......... 1969 £25......... £50 .........................................
Famous Music Band ............................... LP ..... Fontana .......... 6309008 ................. 1970 £25......... £50 .........................................
John Dummer's Blues Band.................... LP ..... Mercury.......... SMCL20167.......... 1969 £37.50..... £75 .........................................
Medicine Weasel ..................................... 7" ...... Philips ............ 6006176 .................. 1971 £1.50........ £4 ...................................
Nine By Nine ........................................... 7" ...... Philips ............ 6006111 .................. 1970 £2......... £5 .........................................
Oobleedooblee Jubilee ........................... LP ..... Vertigo .......... 6360083 .................. 1973 £15......... £30 ................ spiral label
Oobleedooblee Jubilee ........................... 7" ...... Vertigo .......... 6059074 .................. 1972 £1.50........ £4 ...................................
This Is John Dummer ............................. LP ..... Philips ............ 6382039 .................. 1972 £15......... £30 .........................................
Travelling Man ........................................ 7" ...... Mercury.......... MF1040 ................. 1968 £2......... £5 .........................................
Try Me One More Time .......................... LP ..... Philips ............ 6382040 .................. 1973 £15......... £30 .........................................
Try Me One More Time .......................... 7" ...... Mercury.......... MF1119 ................. 1969 £2......... £5 .........................................

## DUMMIES
Desperate for some more chart success, Slade tried the stratagem of issuing singles under the name of the Dummies. They hoped that radio
programmers who responded with disinterest to the name of Slade would hear the music of the Dummies with unprejudiced ears. They
may have done just that, but unfortunately they still did not appear to like what they heard.

Maybe Tonite .......................................... 7" ...... Cheapskate ...... CHEAP14............... 1981 £4......... £8 .........................................

## DUMPY'S RUSTY NUTS
Boxhill Or Bust....................................... 7" ...... Cool King....... CNK008 ................. 1982 £2......... £5 ............... with patch
Just For Kicks.......................................... 7" ...... Cool King....... CNK006 ................. 1981 £2.50........ £6 ...................................

## DUNBAR, AYNSLEY
Frank Zappa once described Aynsley Dunbar as the only drummer capable of playing the complicated rhythms some of his pieces contained.
A graduate of the John Mayall blues school, Dunbar tried for a couple of years to make his own group a success, before accepting that he
could do very well playing drums for other people (Zappa, Jefferson Starship and Journey). The Aynsley Dunbar Retaliation was a fairly
routine blues group, but Blue Whale was a more ambitious affair, being a big band with an open, improvisational approach.

Aynsley Dunbar Retaliation.................... LP ..... Liberty ........... LBL/LBS83154....... 1968 £8......... £20 ...................................
Blue Whale............................................... LP ..... Warner Bros..... K46062 ................. 1971 £5......... £12 ...................................
Blue Whale............................................... LP ..... Warner Bros..... WS3010 ................. 1971 £6......... £15 ...................................
Doctor Dunbar's Prescription .................. LP ..... Liberty ........... LBL/LBS83177....... 1968 £10......... £25 ...................................
Remains To Be Heard............................. LP ..... Liberty ........... LBS83316............... 1970 £8......... £20 ...................................
To Mum From Aynsley & The Boys......... LP ..... Liberty ........... LBS83223............... 1969 £8......... £20 ...................................
Warning.................................................... 7" ...... Blue Horizon.... 453109 ................... 1967 £5......... £10 ...................................
Warning.................................................... 7" ...... Blue Horizon.... 453109 ................... 1967 £15......... £30 ........... picture sleeve
Watch 'n' Chain...................................... 7" ...... Liberty ........... LBF15132 .............. 1968 £1.50........ £4 ...................................

## DUNBAR, SCOTT
From Lake Mary ...................................... LP ..... Ahura Mazda ... AMSSDS1 .............. 1971 £8......... £20 ...................................

## DUNCAN, JOHNNY
All Of The Monkeys Ain't In The Zoo ...... 7" ...... Columbia ........ DB4167 ................. 1958 £1.50........ £4 ...................................
Ballad Of Jed Clampett .......................... 7" ...... Columbia ........ DB7164 ................. 1963 £1.50........ £4 ...................................
Beyond The Sunset ................................. LP ..... Columbia ........ 33SX1328 ............. 1961 £5......... £12 ...................................
Blue Blue Heartaches.............................. 7" ...... Columbia ........ DB3996 ................. 1957 £2......... £5 .........................................

| | | | | | | |
|---|---|---|---|---|---|---|
| Footprints In The Snow | 7" EP | Columbia | SEG7753 | 1958 £5 | £10 | |
| Footprints In The Snow | 7" | Columbia | DB4029 | 1957 £1.50 | £4 | |
| Goodnight Irene | 7" | Columbia | DB4074 | 1958 £4 | £8 | |
| Itching For My Baby | 7" | Columbia | DB4118 | 1958 £2 | £5 | |
| Johnny Duncan & His Blue Grass Boys | 7" EP | Columbia | SEG7708 | 1957 £5 | £10 | |
| Johnny Duncan & His Blue Grass Boys No. 2. | 7" EP | Columbia | SEG7733 | 1957 £5 | £10 | |
| Kansas City | 7" | Columbia | DB4311 | 1959 £1.50 | £4 | |
| Kawliga | 7" | Columbia | DB3925 | 1957 £2.50 | £6 | |
| Last Train To San Fernando | 7" | Columbia | DB3959 | 1957 £4 | £8 | |
| Legend Of Gunga Din | 7" | Pye | 7N15380 | 1961 £1.50 | £4 | |
| Long Time Gone | 7" | Pye | 7N15420 | 1962 £1.50 | £4 | |
| My Lucky Love | 7" | Columbia | DB4179 | 1958 £1.50 | £4 | |
| Rosalie | 7" | Columbia | DB4282 | 1959 £1.50 | £4 | |
| Salute To Hank Williams | LP | Encore | ENC190 | 1959 £6 | £15 | |
| Salutes Hank Williams | 10" LP | Columbia | 33S1129 | 1958 £10 | £25 | |
| Tennessee Sing Song | 7" EP | Columbia | SEG7850 | 1958 £4 | £8 | |
| Tennessee Song Bag | 10" LP | Columbia | 33S1122 | 1957 £10 | £25 | |
| Tobacco Road | 7" | Pye | 7N15358 | 1961 £1.50 | £4 | |

## DUNCAN, LESLEY

Despite making several fine records in the late sixties and early seventies, Ms Duncan's most collectable recording, a charity remake of her 'Sing Children Sing', is sought after primarily because Kate Bush is one of the singers participating in the ensemble – despite the fact that her voice cannot actually be distinguished!

| | | | | | | |
|---|---|---|---|---|---|---|
| Hey Boy | 7" | Mercury | MF939 | 1965 £1.50 | £4 | |
| I Want A Steady Guy | 7" | Parlophone | R5034 | 1963 £1.50 | £4 | |
| Just For The Boy | 7" | Mercury | MF847 | 1965 £1.50 | £4 | |
| Lullaby | 7" | RCA | RCA1746 | 1968 £1.50 | £4 | |
| Road To Nowhere | 7" | RCA | RCA1783 | 1969 £1.50 | £4 | |
| Run To Love | 7" | Mercury | MF876 | 1965 £1.50 | £4 | |
| Sing Children Sing | LP | CBS | 64202 | 1971 £4 | £10 | |
| Sing Children Sing | 7" | CBS | 8061 | 1979 £7.50 | £15 | picture sleeve |
| Tell Him | 7" | Parlophone | R5106 | 1964 £1.50 | £4 | |
| When My Baby Cries | 7" | Mercury | MF830 | 1964 £1.50 | £4 | |

## DUNCAN, TOMMY

| | | | | | | |
|---|---|---|---|---|---|---|
| Dance Dance Dance | 7" | Sue | WI4002 | 1966 £5 | £10 | |

## DUNGEON FOLK

| | | | | | | |
|---|---|---|---|---|---|---|
| Country Meets Folk | LP | Crown Folk | REC365 | £10 | £25 | |

## DUNKLEY, ERROL

| | | | | | | |
|---|---|---|---|---|---|---|
| Having A Party | 7" | Jackpot | JP702 | 1969 £2.50 | £6 | |
| I Am Not Your Man | 7" | Amalgamated | AMG805 | 1968 £4 | £8 | |
| I Am Not Your Man | 7" | Island | WI3150 | 1968 £5 | £10 | |
| I Spy | 7" | Amalgamated | AMG820 | 1968 £4 | £8 | |
| Love Me Forever | 7" | Rio | R109 | 1966 £4 | £8 | Vietnam Allstars B side |
| Please Stop Your Lying | 7" | Amalgamated | AMG800 | 1968 £4 | £8 | |
| Scorcher | 7" | Amalgamated | AMG807 | 1968 £4 | £8 | |
| You're Gonna Need Me | 7" | Rio | R131 | 1967 £4 | £8 | |

## DUNKLEY, ERROLL

| | | | | | | |
|---|---|---|---|---|---|---|
| I'll Take You In My Arms | 7" | Fab | FAB117 | 1969 £1.50 | £4 | King Cannon B side |

## DUNN, BLIND WILLIE

| | | | | | | |
|---|---|---|---|---|---|---|
| Jet Black Blues | 7" | Columbia | SCM5100 | 1954 £4 | £8 | |

## DUNN, GEORGE

| | | | | | | |
|---|---|---|---|---|---|---|
| George Dunn | LP | Leader | LEE4042 | 1973 £10 | £25 | |

## DUNNE, PECKER

| | | | | | | |
|---|---|---|---|---|---|---|
| Introducing The Pecker | LP | Emerald | GES1152 | 1976 £4 | £10 | |

## DUPREE, CHAMPION JACK

| | | | | | | |
|---|---|---|---|---|---|---|
| Ba' La Fouche | 7" | Blue Horizon | 573152 | 1969 £4 | £8 | |
| Barrelhouse Woman | 7" | Decca | F12611 | 1967 £4 | £8 | |
| Blues Anthology Vol. 1 | 7" EP | Storyville | SEP381 | 1961 £5 | £10 | |
| Blues From The Gutter | LP | London | LTZK15171 | 1959 £15 | £30 | |
| Cabbage Greens | LP | XTRA | XTRA1028 | 1965 £4 | £10 | |
| Champion Jack Dupree | LP | Storyville | 670194 | 1967 £4 | £10 | |
| Champion Jack Dupree | LP | Storyville | SLP107 | 1964 £4 | £10 | |
| Champion Jack Dupree | 7" EP | XX | MIN716 | 196– £2 | £5 | |
| Champion Jack Dupree And His Blues Band | LP | Decca | SKL4871 | 1967 £20 | £40 | |
| Champion Of The Blues | LP | Atlantic | (SD)8056 | 1961 £8 | £20 | US |
| Fisherman's Blues | 78 | Jazz Parade | B16 | 1951 £3 | £8 | |
| From New Orleans To Chicago | LP | Decca | LK/SKL4747 | 1966 £20 | £40 | |
| I Haven't Done No One No Harm | 7" | Blue Horizon | 573140 | 1968 £4 | £8 | |
| I Want To Be A Hippy | 7" | Blue Horizon | 573158 | 1968 £4 | £8 | |
| Jack Dupree | 7" EP | Ember | EMBEP4564 | 1965 £5 | £10 | |
| London Special | 7" EP | Decca | DFE8586 | 1964 £10 | £20 | |
| Natural And Soulful Blues | LP | London | LTZK15217/ SAHK6151 | 1961 £15 | £30 | |
| Portraits In Blues | LP | Storyville | SLP161 | 1964 £4 | £10 | |
| Rhythm And Blues Vol. 1 | 7" EP | RCA | RCX7137 | 1964 £4 | £8 | |

| Scooby Dooby Doo | LP | Blue Horizon | 763214 | 1969 | £25 | £50 | |
| Sings The Blues | LP | King | 735 | 1961 | £15 | £30 | US |
| Trouble Trouble | LP | Storyville | SLP145 | 1964 | £4 | £10 | |
| Two Shades Of Blue | LP | Ember | CJS800 | 1962 | £4 | £10 | ..with Jimmy Rushing |
| When You Feel The Feeling You Was Feeling | LP | Blue Horizon | 763206 | 1968 | £25 | £50 | |
| Whiskey Head Woman | 7" | Storyville | A45051 | 1962 | £5 | £10 | |
| Women Blues | LP | Folkways | FS3825 | 1961 | £8 | £20 | US |

## DUPREE, CHAMPION JACK & TONY MCPHEE

| Get Your Head Happy | 7" | Blue Horizon | 451007 | 1966 | £50 | £100 | |

## DUPREE, SIMON & THE BIG SOUND

| Broken Hearted Pirates | 7" | Parlophone | R5757 | 1969 | £1.50 | £4 | |
| Day Time, Night Time | 7" | Parlophone | R5594 | 1967 | £1.50 | £4 | |
| Eagle Flies Tonight | 7" | Parlophone | R5816 | 1969 | £1.50 | £4 | |
| For Whom The Bell Tolls | 7" | Parlophone | R5670 | 1968 | £1.50 | £4 | |
| I See The Light | 7" | Parlophone | R5542 | 1966 | £2 | £5 | |
| Kites | 7" | Parlophone | R5646 | 1967 | £1.50 | £4 | |
| Part Of My Past | 7" | Parlophone | R5697 | 1968 | £1.50 | £4 | |
| Reservations | 7" | Parlophone | R5574 | 1967 | £1.50 | £4 | |
| Thinking About My Life | 7" EP | Odeon | FO135 | 1968 | £10 | £20 | French |
| Thinking About My Life | 7" | Parlophone | R5727 | 1968 | £1.50 | £4 | |
| Without Reservations | LP | Parlophone | PCS7029 | 1969 | £4 | £10 | black & white label |
| Without Reservations | LP | Parlophone | PMC/PCS7029 | 1967 | £8 | £20 | |

## DUPREES

| Gone With the Wind | 7" | London | HLU9709 | 1963 | £2 | £5 | |
| Have You Heard | LP | Coed | LPC906 | 1963 | £15 | £30 | US |
| Have You Heard | 7" EP | London | RE10157 | 1964 | £10 | £20 | French |
| Have You Heard | 7" | London | HLU9813 | 1963 | £2 | £5 | |
| I'd Rather Be Here In Your Arms | 7" | London | HLU9678 | 1963 | £2 | £5 | |
| It's No Sin | 7" | London | HLU9843 | 1964 | £2 | £5 | |
| My Own True Love | 7" | Stateside | SS143 | 1962 | £2 | £5 | |
| Why Don't You Believe Me | 7" | London | HLU9774 | 1963 | £2 | £5 | |
| You Belong To Me | LP | Coed | LPC905 | 1962 | £15 | £30 | US |
| You Belong To Me | 7" | HMV | POP1073 | 1962 | £5 | £10 | |

## DURAN DURAN

| All She Wants Is | CD-s | EMI | CDDD11 | 1988 | £6 | £15 | 3" single |
| Big Thing | CD | Parlophone | CDDDB33 | 1988 | £25 | £50 | promo box set with cassette, badge, booklet |
| Big Thing | 7" | EMI | | 1988 | £4 | £8 | promo |
| Burning The Ground | CD-s | EMI | CDDD13 | 1989 | £20 | £40 | |
| Careless Memories | 12" | EMI | 12EMI5168 | 1981 | £2.50 | £6 | |
| Come Undone | CD-s | EMI | CDDD17 | 1993 | £3 | £8 | double pack |
| Decade | CD | Capitol | DPRO79607 | 1993 | £8 | £20 | US promo with 4 versions of 'Ordinary World' |
| Do You Believe In Shame? | CD-s | Parlophone | CDDD12 | 1989 | £6 | £15 | 3" single |
| Do You Believe In Shame? | 7" | Parlophone | DDA/B/C12 | 1989 | £4 | £8 | triple |
| I Don't Want Your Love | CD-s | EMI | CDYOUR1 | 1988 | £5 | £12 | |
| Liberty | CD | Parlophone | CDPCSD112 | 1990 | £25 | £50 | promo box set with cassette, biog, photo |
| Master Mixes | LP | EMI | | 1987 | £8 | £20 | double |
| My Own Way (3 versions) | 12" | EMI | | 1982 | £3 | £8 | promo |
| Notorious (Latin Rascals mix) | 12" | EMI | 12DDN45 | 1986 | £3 | £8 | |
| Ordinary World | CD-s | EMI | CDDDPD16 | 1993 | £2 | £5 | picture disc |
| Ordinary World | CD-s | Parlophone | CDDDS16 | 1992 | £5 | £12 | |
| Perfect Day | CD-s | EMI | | 1995 | £12.50 | £25 | 'choc ice' promo |
| Presidential Suite | CD-s | Parlophone | CDTOUR1 | 1987 | £2 | £5 | |
| Reflex | 7" | EMI | DURANP2 | 1984 | £1.50 | £4 | poster sleeve |
| Serious | CD-s | EMI | CDDD15 | 1990 | £4 | £10 | |
| Sing Blue Silver | video | PMI | MVP9910632 | 1984 | £10 | £20 | |
| Skin Trade | 7" | Parlophone | TRADE1 | 1987 | £4 | £8 | bum picture sleeve |
| Sound Of Thunder | 12" | EMI | PSLP344 | 1981 | £10 | £20 | promo sampler |
| Tour Sampler | CD | Capitol | DPRO79786 | 1993 | £8 | £20 | US promo |
| Violence Of Summer | CD-s | Parlophone | CDD14 | 1990 | £2 | £5 | |

## DURANTE, JIMMY

| In Person | 10" LP | MGM | MGMD102 | 1952 | £4 | £10 | |
| It's Bigger Than Both Of Us | 7" | Brunswick | 05445 | 1955 | £1.50 | £4 | |
| Jimmy Durante | 7" EP | MGM | MGMEP508 | 1954 | £2 | £5 | |
| Jimmy Durante Sings | 10" LP | Brunswick | LA8582 | 1953 | £4 | £10 | |
| Pupalina | 7" | Brunswick | 05395 | 1955 | £1.50 | £4 | |
| Schnozzles | 7" EP | MGM | MGMEP597 | 1957 | £2 | £5 | |
| Swingin' With Rhythm And Blues | 7" | Brunswick | 05495 | 1955 | £1.50 | £4 | |

## DURHAM, JUDITH

| Again And Again | 7" | Columbia | DB8290 | 1967 | £1.50 | £4 | |
| For Christmas With Love | LP | Columbia | SCX6374 | 1969 | £4 | £10 | |

## DURHAM, TERRY

| Crystal Telephone | LP | Deram | DML/SML1042 | 1969 | £5 | £12 | |

## DURUTTI COLUMN

| Enigma | 7" | Sordide Sentimentale | SS45005 | 1981 | £7.50 | £15 | French |

| | | | | | | | |
|---|---|---|---|---|---|---|---|
| For Patti | 7" | Factory Benelux | FBN100 | 1982 | £10 | £20 | |
| Live At The Venue London | LP | VU | VINI1 | 1983 | £4 | £10 | |
| Return Of The Durutti Column | LP | Factory | FACT14 | 1980 | £6 | £15 | *sandpaper sleeve, with flexi (FACT14C)* |

## DURY, IAN
| | | | | | | | |
|---|---|---|---|---|---|---|---|
| Sex & Drugs & Rock 'n' Roll | 7" | Stiff | FREEBIE1 | 1978 | £1.50 | £4 | *flexi* |

## DUST
| | | | | | | | |
|---|---|---|---|---|---|---|---|
| Dust | LP | Kama Sutra | 2319014 | 1971 | £6 | £15 | |

## DUSTY, SLIM
| | | | | | | | |
|---|---|---|---|---|---|---|---|
| Pub With No Beer | 7" | Columbia | DB4212 | 1958 | £1.50 | £4 | |
| Slim Dusty And His Country Rockers | 7" EP | Columbia | SEG8009 | 1960 | £4 | £8 | |

## DUTCH SWING COLLEGE
| | | | | | | | |
|---|---|---|---|---|---|---|---|
| Dutch Swing College | LP | Philips | BBL7099 | 1956 | £4 | £10 | |
| Dutch Swing College | 10" LP | Philips | BBR8021 | 1954 | £6 | £15 | |
| Gems Of Jazz Vol. 1 | 10" LP | Philips | BBR8018 | 1954 | £6 | £15 | |

## DUTY CYCLE
| | | | | | | | |
|---|---|---|---|---|---|---|---|
| Nero | LP | Mirasound | MS5030 | 1976 | £37.50 | £75 | *Dutch* |

## DUVAL, JOSE
| | | | | | | | |
|---|---|---|---|---|---|---|---|
| Message Of Love | 7" | London | HLR8458 | 1957 | £2 | £5 | |

## DUVEEN, BOEING & THE BEAUTIFUL SOUP
The psychedelic single by Boeing Duveen, which sets two Lewis Carroll poems to music, is actually the work of Dr Sam Hutt. Hutt, who specialized in helping people overcome drug addictions (notably at many of the rock festivals, starting at the Isle of Wight in 1969), was one of the many lesser names with a significant role in the sixties and early-seventies counter-culture. During the eighties and nineties, while continuing to work as a doctor, Hutt has also worked extensively as a country singer – music that he is inclined to tackle for its comic potential – using the name Hank Wangford.

| | | | | | | | |
|---|---|---|---|---|---|---|---|
| Jabberwock | 7" | Parlophone | R5696 | 1968 | £25 | £50 | |
| Jabberwock | 7" | Parlophone | R5696 | 1968 | £50 | £100 | *picture sleeve* |

## DWYER, FINBARR
| | | | | | | | |
|---|---|---|---|---|---|---|---|
| Irish Traditional Accordionist | LP | Outlet | OLP1004 | 1970 | £4 | £10 | *Irish* |

## DYKE & THE BLAZERS
| | | | | | | | |
|---|---|---|---|---|---|---|---|
| Funky Broadway | LP | Original Sound | LP(S)8876 | 1967 | £10 | £25 | *US* |
| Funky Broadway | 7" | Pye | 7N25413 | 1967 | £5 | £10 | |
| Greatest Hits | LP | Original Sound | LPS8877 | 1969 | £8 | £20 | *US* |

## DYLAN, BOB
Bob Dylan has recorded so prolifically over the years that collecting him consists to a large extent of trying to obtain some of the large number of bootleg LPs that have been issued. Apart from documenting some crucially important live performances (such as the famous Albert Hall concert with the Band, albums of which probably have total sales to rival those of Dylan's CBS recordings), these also allow Dylan's many studio out-takes to be heard. Many of these are arguably better than the tracks that were released. A few out-takes are also officially available on scarce promotional releases and on the very first American issue of *Freewheelin'*, which included four songs that are not on any of the subsequent releases of the record. These are 'Rocks And Gravel' (called 'Solid Gravel' on some pressings), 'Let Me Die In My Footsteps', 'Gamblin' Willie's Dead Man's Hand', and 'Talkin' John Birch Society Blues'. It should be stressed that only copies playing these tracks, which are not actually listed on the sleeve, are worth the large sums of money quoted below.

| | | | | | | | |
|---|---|---|---|---|---|---|---|
| All I Really Want To Do | 7" EP | CBS | 5923 | 1964 | £20 | £40 | *French* |
| Another Side Of Bob Dylan | LP | CBS | (S)BPG62429 | 1964 | £6 | £15 | |
| Blonde On Blonde | LP | CBS | 66012 | 1966 | £15 | £30 | *double, mono* |
| Blonde On Blonde | LP | CBS | 66012 | 1966 | £8 | £20 | *double, stereo* |
| Blood On The Tracks | LP | Columbia | PC33235 | 1974 | £1750 | £2500 | *test pressing with different versions of 5 tracks* |
| Blowin' In The Wind | 7" EP | CBS | 5688 | 1964 | £20 | £40 | *French* |
| Blowin' In The Wind | 7" | Columbia | 42856 | 1963 | £75 | £150 | *US* |
| Blowing In The Wind | 7" EP | Fontana | TFE18010 | 1965 | £20 | £40 | *with other artists* |
| Bob Dylan | LP | CBS | (S)BPG62022 | 1962 | £6 | £15 | |
| Bob Dylan | LP | Columbia | CL1779 | 1962 | £37.50 | £75 | *US mono, 6 eye logos on label* |
| Bob Dylan | LP | Columbia | CS8579 | 1962 | £50 | £100 | *US stereo, 6 eye logos on label* |
| Bob Dylan | 7" EP | CBS | EP6051 | 1965 | £7.50 | £15 | |
| Bob Dylan And The Grateful Dead | CD | Columbia | CSK1435 | 1989 | £6 | £15 | *US promo picture disc* |
| Bob Dylan In Concerto | 12" | Gong | 5A/6B | 1976 | £25 | £50 | *Italian* |
| Bringing It All Back Home | LP | CBS | (S)BPG62515 | 1965 | £6 | £15 | |
| Can You Please Crawl Out Your Window | 7" EP | CBS | 6265 | 1965 | £20 | £40 | *French* |
| Can You Please Crawl Out Your Window | 7" | CBS | 201900 | 1965 | £1.50 | £4 | |
| Desire | LP | CBS | Q86003 | 1976 | £6 | £15 | *quad* |
| Everything Is Broken | CD-s | CBS | 6553582 | 1989 | £3 | £8 | |
| Forever Young | CD | CBS | XPCD116 | 1990 | £8 | £20 | *13 track promo sampler* |
| Forever Young | CD | Columbia | CSK1157 | 1988 | £10 | £25 | *US 18 track promo sampler* |
| Four Songs From Renaldo And Clara | 12" | Columbia | AS422 | 1978 | £20 | £40 | *US promo* |
| Freewheelin' | LP | CBS | (S)BPG62193 | 1963 | £6 | £15 | |
| Freewheelin' | LP | Columbia | CL1986 | 1963 | £3500 | £5000 | *US mono, 4 different tracks* |

| Title | Format | Label | Cat. No. | Year | Price | Price | Notes |
|---|---|---|---|---|---|---|---|
| Freewheelin' | LP | Columbia | CS8786 | 1963 | £10000 | £12000 | US stereo, 4 different tracks |
| George Jackson | 7" | CBS | 7688 | 1971 | £2 | £5 | |
| Highway 61 Revisited | LP | CBS | BPG62572 | 1965 | £6 | £15 | mono |
| Highway 61 Revisited | LP | CBS | SBPG62572 | 1965 | £5 | £12 | stereo |
| Highway 61 Revisited | LP | Columbia | CS9189 | 1965 | £50 | £100 | US, alternate take of 'From A Buick 6' |
| Highway 61 Revisited | CD | DCC | GZS1021 | 1992 | £6 | £15 | US audiophile |
| Hurricane | 7" | CBS | 3878 | 1976 | £2 | £5 | picture sleeve |
| I Want You | 7" EP | CBS | 5769 | 1966 | £15 | £30 | French |
| I Want You | 7" | CBS | 202258 | 1966 | £1.50 | £4 | |
| It's Unbelievable | CD-s | CBS | 6563042 | 1990 | £3 | £8 | |
| John Wesley Harding | LP | CBS | 63252 | 1968 | £5 | £12 | mono |
| Just Like Tom Thumb's Blues | 7" EP | CBS | 6270 | 1966 | £20 | £40 | French |
| Leopard-Skin Pill-Box Hat | 7" EP | CBS | 6345 | 1967 | £20 | £40 | French |
| Leopardskin Pillbox Hat | 7" | CBS | 2700 | 1967 | £1.50 | £4 | |
| Leopardskin Pillbox Hat | 7" | CBS | 2700 | 1967 | £12.50 | £25 | picture sleeve |
| Like A Rolling Stone | 7" EP | CBS | 6107 | 1965 | £20 | £40 | French |
| Like A Rolling Stone | 7" | CBS | 201811 | 1965 | £1.50 | £4 | |
| Maggie's Farm | 7" | CBS | 201781 | 1965 | £1.50 | £4 | |
| Mixed Up Confusion | 7" | CBS | 2476 | 196– | £12.50 | £25 | Dutch, picture sleeve |
| Mixed Up Confusion | 7" | Columbia | 442656 | 1963 | £100 | £200 | US, best auctioned |
| Mr. Tambourine Man | 7" EP | CBS | EP6078 | 1966 | £7.50 | £15 | |
| Nashville Skyline | LP | CBS | 63601 | 1969 | £4 | £10 | mono |
| Nashville Skyline | LP | CBS | CQ32872 | 1974 | £8 | £20 | US quad |
| Nashville Skyline | LP | Columbia | HC49825 | 1981 | £8 | £20 | US audiophile |
| Nine Song Publisher's Sampler | LP | Warner Bros | XTD221567 | 1963 | £400 | £600 | US promo |
| One Of Us Must Know | 7" | CBS | 202053 | 1966 | £1.50 | £4 | |
| One Too Many Mornings | 7" EP | CBS | EP6070 | 1966 | £7.50 | £15 | |
| Planet Waves | LP | Ashes And Sands | 7E501 | 1973 | £30 | £60 | US own label |
| Planet Waves | LP | Asylum | EQ1003 | 1974 | £10 | £25 | US quad |
| Political World | CD-s | CBS | 6556435 | 1990 | £3 | £8 | |
| Positively Fourth Street | 7" EP | CBS | 6210 | 1965 | £20 | £40 | French |
| Positively Fourth Street | 7" | CBS | 201824 | 1965 | £1.50 | £4 | |
| Positively Fourth Street | 7" | Columbia | 43389 | 1965 | £50 | £100 | US mispress, plays alternate 'Crawl Out Your Window' |
| Rainy Day Women | 7" | CBS | 202307 | 1966 | £1.50 | £4 | |
| Rainy Day Women No. 12 & 35 | 7" EP | CBS | 5660 | 1966 | £20 | £40 | French |
| Rita May | 7" | CBS | 4859 | 1977 | £2 | £5 | picture sleeve |
| Subterranean Homesick Blues | 7" EP | CBS | 6096 | 1965 | £20 | £40 | French |
| Subterranean Homesick Blues | 7" | CBS | 201753 | 1965 | £1.50 | £4 | |
| Thirtieth Anniversary Concert | CD | Columbia | XPCD308 | 1993 | £8 | £20 | US promo sampler |
| Times They Are A-Changin' | LP | CBS | (S)BPG62251 | 1964 | £6 | £15 | |
| Times They Are A-Changin' | LP | Mobile Fidelity | MFSL1114 | 1984 | £5 | £12 | US audiophile |
| Times They Are A-Changin' | 7" | CBS | 201751 | 1965 | £1.50 | £4 | |
| Vs. A. J. Weberman | LP | Folkways | FB5322 | 1971 | £50 | £100 | US |
| Watching The River Flow | 7" | CBS | 7329 | 1971 | £2 | £5 | |
| Wigwam | 7" | CBS | 5122 | 1970 | £1.50 | £4 | |
| With God On Our Side | 7" EP | CBS | 6266 | 1965 | £20 | £40 | French |
| With God On Our Side | 7" EP | Fontana | TFE18009 | 1965 | £20 | £40 | with other artists |
| World Of Folk Music | LP | Warner Bros | XGPB508 | 1964 | £100 | £200 | US promo, with other artists |
| Ye Playboys And Playgirls | 7" EP | Fontana | TFE18011 | 1965 | £20 | £40 | with other artists |

## DYMON, FRANKIE

| Title | Format | Label | Cat. No. | Year | Price | Price | Notes |
|---|---|---|---|---|---|---|---|
| Let It Out | LP | BASF | 20212416 | 1971 | £6 | £15 | German |

## DYNAMICS

| Title | Format | Label | Cat. No. | Year | Price | Price | Notes |
|---|---|---|---|---|---|---|---|
| Ice Cream Song | 7" | Atlantic | 584270 | 1969 | £2 | £5 | |
| Misery | 7" | London | HLX9809 | 1963 | £6 | £12 | |
| So In Love With Me | 7" | King | KG1007 | 1964 | £4 | £8 | |

## DYNAMICS (2)

| Title | Format | Label | Cat. No. | Year | Price | Price | Notes |
|---|---|---|---|---|---|---|---|
| Dynamics With Jimmy Hannah | LP | Bolo | BLP8001 | 1962 | £8 | £20 | US |

## DYNAMICS (3)

| Title | Format | Label | Cat. No. | Year | Price | Price | Notes |
|---|---|---|---|---|---|---|---|
| My Friends | 7" | Blue Cat | BS104 | 1968 | £4 | £8 | Neville Irons B side |

## DYNAMITES

| Title | Format | Label | Cat. No. | Year | Price | Price | Notes |
|---|---|---|---|---|---|---|---|
| Fire Corner | LP | Trojan | TTL21 | 1969 | £6 | £15 | |
| John Public | 7" | Duke | DU30 | 1969 | £1.50 | £4 | |
| Mr. Midnight | 7" | Clandisc | CLA200 | 1969 | £1.50 | £4 | King Stitt B side |
| Rahtid | 7" | Trojan | TR647 | 1969 | £1.50 | £4 | Clancy Eccles B side |

## DYNAMITES (2)

| Title | Format | Label | Cat. No. | Year | Price | Price | Notes |
|---|---|---|---|---|---|---|---|
| Someone Like Me | 7" EP | Columbia | ESRF1729 | 1965 | £5 | £10 | French |

## DYNATONES

| Title | Format | Label | Cat. No. | Year | Price | Price | Notes |
|---|---|---|---|---|---|---|---|
| Fife Piper | 7" | Pye | 7N25389 | 1966 | £15 | £30 | |
| Steel Guitar Rag | 7" | Top Rank | JAR149 | 1959 | £2 | £5 | |

## DYSON, ALAN

| Title | Format | Label | Cat. No. | Year | Price | Price | Notes |
|---|---|---|---|---|---|---|---|
| Still Small Voice Of Alan Dyson | LP | Pye | NPL18212 | 1968 | £8 | £20 | |

## DYSON, RONNIE
We Can Make It Last Forever.................... 7" ....... CBS................ 2430 ...................... 1974 £2............ £5 ............................

## DZYAN
Dzyan ................................................... LP ...... Aronda............ 10006................... 1972 £5........... £12 ................ German
Electric Silence......................................... LP ...... Bacillus ........... 19202................... 1975 £4........... £10 ................ German
Time Machine ......................................... LP ...... Bacillus ........... BLPS19161............. 1973 £6........... £15 ................ German

# E

## E. F. BAND

| | | | | | | | |
|---|---|---|---|---|---|---|---|
| Night Angel | 7" | Aerco | EF1 | 1980 | £2.50 | £6 | |
| Self Made Suicide | 7" | Redball | RR026 | 1980 | £2.50 | £6 | |

## EAGER, VINCE

| | | | | | | | |
|---|---|---|---|---|---|---|---|
| Five Days Five Days | 7" | Parlophone | R4482 | 1958 | £6 | £12 | |
| Lonely Blue Boy | 7" | Top Rank | JAR307 | 1960 | £2 | £5 | |
| Making Love | 7" | Top Rank | JAR191 | 1959 | £1.50 | £4 | |
| No Other Arms, No Other Lips | 7" | Parlophone | R4550 | 1959 | £4 | £8 | |
| Tread Softly Stranger | 7" | Decca | F11023 | 1958 | £15 | £30 | 2 x 1 sided demos only |
| Vince Eager & The Vagabonds No. 1 | 7" EP | Decca | DFE6504 | 1958 | £20 | £40 | |
| When's Your Birthday Baby | 7" | Parlophone | R4531 | 1959 | £4 | £8 | |
| Why | 7" | Top Rank | JAR275 | 1960 | £1.50 | £4 | |

## EAGLE

| | | | | | | | |
|---|---|---|---|---|---|---|---|
| Come Under Mrs. Nancy's Tent | LP | Pye | NSPL28138 | 1969 | £6 | £15 | |
| Kickin' It Back To You | 7" | Pye | 7N25530 | 1970 | £1.50 | £4 | |

## EAGLES

| | | | | | | | |
|---|---|---|---|---|---|---|---|
| 1994 Tour Collection Airplay Sampler | CD | Elektra | PRCD89832 | 1994 | £6 | £15 | US promo |
| Common Thread – The Songs Of The Eagles | CD | Giant | CTDX93 | 1993 | £10 | £25 | Canadian promo double – one disc covers, one disc originals |
| Hotel California | LP | Mobile Fidelity | MFSL1126 | 1981 | £4 | £10 | US audiophile |
| Hotel California | CD | Asylum | C8815 | 1988 | £6 | £15 | HMV boxed set |
| Hotel California | CD | DCC | GZS1024 | 1992 | £6 | £15 | US audiophile |
| On The Border | LP | Asylum | EQ1004 | 1975 | £4 | £10 | US quad |
| One Of These Nights | LP | Asylum | EQ1039 | 1975 | £4 | £10 | US quad |

## EAGLES (2)

| | | | | | | | |
|---|---|---|---|---|---|---|---|
| Andorra | 7" | Pye | 7N15613 | 1964 | £1.50 | £4 | |
| Bristol Express | 7" | Pye | 7N15451 | 1962 | £1.50 | £4 | |
| Come On Baby | 7" | Pye | 7N15550 | 1963 | £1.50 | £4 | |
| Desperadoes | 7" | Pye | 7N15503 | 1962 | £1.50 | £4 | |
| Eagles Nest | 7" | Pye | 7N15571 | 1963 | £1.50 | £4 | |
| Exodus | 7" | Pye | 7N15473 | 1962 | £1.50 | £4 | |
| New Sound TV Themes | 7" EP | Pye | NEP24166 | 1962 | £5 | £10 | |
| Smash Hits | LP | Pye | NPL18084 | 1963 | £10 | £25 | |
| Wishing And Hoping | 7" | Pye | 7N15650 | 1964 | £2.50 | £6 | |

## EAGLIN, SNOOKS

| | | | | | | | |
|---|---|---|---|---|---|---|---|
| Blues Anthology Vol. 6 | 7" EP | Storyville | SEP386 | 1963 | £2.50 | £6 | |
| Country Boy | 7" | Storyville | A45056 | 196- | £4 | £8 | |
| Message From New Orleans | LP | Heritage | HLP1002 | 1961 | £8 | £20 | |
| New Orleans Street Singer | LP | Folkways | FA2476 | 1961 | £8 | £20 | |
| New Orleans Street Singer | LP | Storyville | SLP119 | 1964 | £4 | £10 | |
| Portraits In Blues Vol. 1 | LP | Storyville | SLP146 | 1964 | £4 | £10 | |
| Vol. 2 – Blues From New Orleans | LP | Storyville | SLP140 | 1964 | £4 | £10 | |

## EANES, JIM

| | | | | | | | |
|---|---|---|---|---|---|---|---|
| Christmas Doll | 7" | Melodisc | 1530 | 1959 | £1.50 | £4 | |

## EARDLEY, JOHN

| | | | | | | | |
|---|---|---|---|---|---|---|---|
| Down East | LP | Esquire | 32040 | 1958 | £15 | £30 | |

## EARLS

| | | | | | | | |
|---|---|---|---|---|---|---|---|
| Never | 7" | London | HL9702 | 1963 | £10 | £20 | |
| Remember Me Baby | LP | Old Town | LP104 | 1963 | £30 | £60 | US |
| Remember Then | 7" | Stateside | SS153 | 1963 | £7.50 | £15 | |

## EARTH

| | | | | | | | |
|---|---|---|---|---|---|---|---|
| Resurrection City | 7" | CBS | 4671 | 1969 | £10 | £20 | |
| Stranger Of Fortune | 7" | Decca | F22908 | 1969 | £2.50 | £6 | |

## EARTH & FIRE

| | | | | | | | |
|---|---|---|---|---|---|---|---|
| Atlantis | LP | Polydor | 2925013 | 1973 | £5 | £12 | Dutch |
| Best Of Earth And Fire | LP | Polydor | 2491004 | 1975 | £4 | £10 | Dutch |
| Earth And Fire | LP | Nepentha | 6437004 | 1971 | £75 | £150 | |
| Earth And Fire | LP | Polydor | 2441011 | 1971 | £37.50 | £75 | Dutch |
| Invitation | 7" | Nepentha | 6129001 | 1971 | £10 | £20 | |
| Song Of Marching Children | LP | Polydor | 2925003 | 1971 | £6 | £15 | Dutch |

| | | | | | | | |
|---|---|---|---|---|---|---|---|
| To The World A Future | LP | Polydor | 2925033 | 1975 | £4 | £10 | *Dutch* |

## EARTH BOYS
| | | | | | | |
|---|---|---|---|---|---|---|
| Space Girl | 7" | Capitol | CL14979 | 1959 | £2 | £5 |

## EARTH OPERA
| | | | | | | |
|---|---|---|---|---|---|---|
| Earth Opera | LP | Elektra | EKS74016 | 1968 | £5 | £12 |
| Great American Eagle Tragedy | LP | Elektra | EKS74038 | 1969 | £4 | £10 |

## EARTH, WIND & FIRE
| | | | | | | | |
|---|---|---|---|---|---|---|---|
| Head To The Sky | LP | Columbia | CQ32194 | 1974 | £4 | £10 | *US quad* |
| Last Days And Time | LP | CBS | 65208 | 1973 | £4 | £10 | |
| Open Our Eyes | LP | Columbia | CQ32712 | 1974 | £4 | £10 | *US quad* |

## EARTHBOUND (PRODIGY)
| | | | | | | | |
|---|---|---|---|---|---|---|---|
| One Love | 12" | XL | EB1 | 1993 | £10 | £20 | *white label* |
| One Love (remix) | 12" | XL | EB2 | 1993 | £10 | £20 | *white label* |

## EARTHLINGS
| | | | | | | |
|---|---|---|---|---|---|---|
| Landing Of The Daleks | 7" | Parlophone | R5242 | 1965 | £10 | £20 |

## EARTHQUAKE
| | | | | | | |
|---|---|---|---|---|---|---|
| Live | LP | United Artists | UAS29853 | 1975 | £6 | £15 |

## EARTHQUAKERS
| | | | | | | |
|---|---|---|---|---|---|---|
| Whistling In The Sunshine | 7" | Stateside | SS2050 | 1967 | £1.50 | £4 |

## EARTHQUAKES
| | | | | | | |
|---|---|---|---|---|---|---|
| Brother Moses | 7" | Duke | DU55 | 1969 | £1.50 | £4 |
| Earth Quake | 7" | Duke | DU56 | 1969 | £1.50 | £4 |
| I Can't Stop Loving You | 7" | Duke | DU54 | 1969 | £1.50 | £4 |

## EAST 17
| | | | | | | |
|---|---|---|---|---|---|---|
| Gold | CD-s | London | LONCD331 | 1992 | £2 | £5 |
| House Of Love | CD-s | London | LONCD325 | 1992 | £2 | £5 |

## EAST OF EDEN

East Of Eden were virtually two separate groups, with only violinist Dave Arbus being a member of both. The Harvest recordings, made after the group gained a chart hit with the atypical 'Jig A Jig', are routine seventies rock. The Deram LPs, on the other hand, contain fiercely experimental music in which Don Drummond rubs shoulders with Charles Mingus, and saxophones, flutes and violins jostle with each other for supremacy.

| | | | | | | |
|---|---|---|---|---|---|---|
| East Of Eden | LP | Harvest | SHVL792 | 1971 | £6 | £15 |
| King Of Siam | 7" | Atlantic | 584198 | 1968 | £4 | £8 |
| Mercator Projected | LP | Deram | DML/SML1038 | 1969 | £6 | £15 |
| New Leaf | LP | Harvest | SHVL796 | 1971 | £4 | £10 |
| Northern Hemisphere | 7" | Deram | DM242 | 1969 | £4 | £8 |
| Ramadhan | 7" | Deram | DM338 | 1971 | £1.50 | £4 |
| Snafu | LP | Deram | SML1050 | 1970 | £6 | £15 |

## EAST VILLAGE OTHER
| | | | | | | | |
|---|---|---|---|---|---|---|---|
| Electric Newspaper | LP | ESP-Disk | 1034 | 1966 | £25 | £50 | *US* |

## EASTERHOUSE
| | | | | | | | |
|---|---|---|---|---|---|---|---|
| In Our Own Hands | 12" | Easterhouse | EIREX1 | 1985 | £2.50 | £6 | *hand stencilled picture sleeve* |

## EASTWOOD, CLINT
| | | | | | | | |
|---|---|---|---|---|---|---|---|
| Cowboy Favorites | LP | Cameo | C(S)1056 | 1963 | £8 | £20 | *US* |

## EASYBEATS

The Easybeats were responsible for one of the classic beat singles, 'Friday On My Mind'. Originally from Australia, the group gained considerable success there, but were unable to find a satisfactory follow-up to their big hit single in the UK. Guitarists Harry Vanda and George Young (brother of AC/DC's Angus and Malcolm) managed to maintain successful careers as songwriters and producers, however, and recorded further albums in the eighties as members of the group Flash and the Pan.

| | | | | | | | |
|---|---|---|---|---|---|---|---|
| Best Of The Easybeats | LP | Parlophone | PMEO9958 | 1967 | £25 | £50 | *Australian* |
| Come And See Her | 7" | United Artists | UP1144 | 1966 | £2 | £5 | |
| Falling Off The Edge Of The World | LP | United Artists | UAS6667 | 1968 | £10 | £25 | *US* |
| Friday On My Mind | LP | United Artists | UAL3/UAS6588 | 1967 | £15 | £30 | *US* |
| Friday On My Mind | 7" EP | United Artists | 36106 | 1966 | £15 | £30 | *French* |
| Friday On My Mind | 7" | United Artists | UP1157 | 1966 | £1.50 | £4 | |
| Friends | LP | Polydor | 2482010 | 1970 | £15 | £30 | |
| Friends | 7" | Polydor | 2001028 | 1970 | £1.50 | £4 | |
| Good Friday | LP | United Artists | (S)ULP1167 | 1967 | £30 | £60 | |
| Good Times | 7" | United Artists | UP2243 | 1969 | £1.50 | £4 | |
| Heaven & Hell | 7" EP | United Artists | 36117 | 1967 | £15 | £30 | *French* |
| Heaven And Hell | 7" | United Artists | UP1183 | 1967 | £1.50 | £4 | |
| Hello How Are You | 7" | United Artists | UP2209 | 1968 | £1.50 | £4 | |
| I Love Marie | 7" | Polydor | 56357 | 1969 | £1.50 | £4 | |
| Land Of Make Believe | 7" | United Artists | UP2219 | 1968 | £1.50 | £4 | |
| Music Goes Round My Head | 7" | United Artists | UP1201 | 1967 | £1.50 | £4 | |
| St. Louis | 7" | Polydor | 56335 | 1969 | £1.50 | £4 | |
| Vigil | LP | United Artists | (S)ULP1193 | 1968 | £15 | £30 | |
| Volume Three | LP | Parlophone | PMCO7537 | 1966 | £25 | £50 | *Australian* |
| Who'll Be The One | 7" EP | United Artists | 36112 | 1966 | £15 | £30 | *French* |
| Who'll Be The One | 7" | United Artists | UP1175 | 1966 | £1.50 | £4 | |

## EAT

| | | | | | | | |
|---|---|---|---|---|---|---|---|
| Autogift | CD-s | Fiction | WANCD100 | 1989 | £2 | £5 | |
| Plastic Bag | CD-s | Fiction | CIFCD1 | 1989 | £2 | £5 | |
| Psycho Couch | CD-s | Non Fiction | YESCD3 | 1990 | £2 | £5 | |
| Sell Me A God | CD-s | Fiction | 8389442 | 1989 | £2 | £5 | |
| Summer In The City | CD-s | Fiction | CIFCD2 | 1989 | £2 | £5 | |

## EATER

| | | | | | | | |
|---|---|---|---|---|---|---|---|
| Album | LP | The Label | TLRLP001 | 1978 | £6 | £15 | |
| Lock It Up | 12" | The Label | TLR004 | 1977 | £2.50 | £6 | |

## EBONIES

| | | | | | | | |
|---|---|---|---|---|---|---|---|
| Never Gonna Break Your Heart Again | 7" | Philips | BF1648 | 1968 | £1.50 | £4 | |

## ECCENTRICS

| | | | | | | | |
|---|---|---|---|---|---|---|---|
| What You Got | 7" | Pye | 7N15850 | 1965 | £10 | £20 | |

## ECCLES, CLANCY

| | | | | | | | |
|---|---|---|---|---|---|---|---|
| Auntie Lulu | 7" | Duke | DU9 | 1969 | £1.50 | £4 | Slickers B side |
| Beat Dance | 7" | Clandisc | CLA206 | 1969 | £1.50 | £4 | King Stitt B side |
| C.N.Express | 7" | Pama | PM722 | 1968 | £2.50 | £6 | |
| Constantinople | 7" | Trojan | TR648 | 1969 | £1.50 | £4 | |
| Fattie Fattie | 7" | Trojan | TR658 | 1969 | £1.50 | £4 | Silverstars B side |
| Feel The Rhythm | 7" | Doctor Bird | DB1156 | 1968 | £5 | £10 | |
| Festival '68 | 7" | Nu Beat | NB006 | 1968 | £2.50 | £6 | |
| Fight | 7" | Pama | PM712 | 1968 | £2.50 | £6 | |
| Freedom | LP | Trojan | TTL22 | 1969 | £6 | £15 | |
| Freedom | 7" | Blue Beat | BB67 | 1961 | £6 | £12 | |
| Glory Hallelujah | 7" | Island | WI098 | 1963 | £5 | £10 | |
| Judgement | 7" | Island | WI044 | 1963 | £5 | £10 | |
| Miss Ida | 7" | Ska Beat | JB198 | 1965 | £5 | £10 | King Rocky B side |
| Mother's Advice | 7" | Pama | PM703 | 1967 | £2.50 | £6 | |
| Open Up | 7" | Clandisc | CLA209 | 1969 | £1.50 | £4 | Higgs & Wilson B side |
| River Jordan | 7" | Blue Beat | BB34 | 1961 | £6 | £12 | |
| Sammy No Dead | 7" | Ska Beat | JB194 | 1965 | £5 | £10 | |
| Shu Be Do | 7" | Duke | DU31 | 1969 | £1.50 | £4 | |
| Sweet Africa | 7" | Trojan | TR639 | 1968 | £2.50 | £6 | |
| What Will Your Mama Say | 7" | Pama | PM701 | 1967 | £2.50 | £6 | |
| World Needs Loving | 7" | Clandisc | CLA201 | 1969 | £1.50 | £4 | |

## ECHO & THE BUNNYMEN

| | | | | | | | |
|---|---|---|---|---|---|---|---|
| Bring On The Dancing Horses | 7" | Korova | KOW43 | 1988 | £2 | £5 | shaped picture disc |
| Crocodiles | 7" | Korova | ECHO1 | 1981 | £2 | £5 | promo |
| Cutter | 12" | Korova | KOW26T | 1983 | £2.50 | £6 | with cassette and poster |
| Echo And The Bunnymen | CD | WEA | 2421372 | 1987 | £20 | £40 | promo canvas hold-all, with cassette and video |
| Peel Sessions | CD-s | Strange Fruit | SFPSCD060 | 1989 | £2 | £5 | |
| Pictures On My Wall | CD-s | Document | DC003 | 1991 | £2 | £5 | |
| Pictures On My Wall | 7" | Zoo | CAGE004 | 1979 | £2.50 | £6 | |
| Puppet | 7" | Korova | KOW11 | 1980 | £2.50 | £6 | |
| Rescue | 12" | Korova | KOW1T | 1980 | £2.50 | £6 | |

## ECHOES

| | | | | | | | |
|---|---|---|---|---|---|---|---|
| Baby Blue | 7" | Top Rank | JAR553 | 1961 | £2.50 | £6 | |
| Born To Be With You | 7" | Top Rank | JAR399 | 1960 | £2.50 | £6 | |

## ECHOES (2)

| | | | | | | | |
|---|---|---|---|---|---|---|---|
| Searchin' For You Baby | 7" | Philips | BF1683 | 1968 | £2.50 | £6 | |

## ECHOES (3)

| | | | | | | | |
|---|---|---|---|---|---|---|---|
| Are You Mine | 7" | Blue Beat | BB89 | 1962 | £6 | £12 | |

## ECKSTINE, BILLY

| | | | | | | | |
|---|---|---|---|---|---|---|---|
| At Basin Street East | LP | Mercury | MMC14100/ CMS18066 | 1962 | £4 | £10 | |
| Basie-Eckstine Incorporated | 7" EP | Columbia | SEG8043/ESG7827 | 1960 | £2 | £5 | |
| Best Of Mister B No. 1 | 7" EP | Mercury | ZEP10005 | 1959 | £2 | £5 | |
| Best Of Mister B No. 2 | 7" EP | Emarcy | YEP9509 | 1959 | £2 | £5 | |
| Billy Eckstine | 7" EP | MGM | MGMEP511 | 1954 | £2 | £5 | |
| Billy Eckstine's Imagination | LP | Mercury | MMB12002 | 1959 | £4 | £10 | |
| Billy's Best | LP | Mercury | MMC14043 | 1960 | £4 | £10 | |
| Cashmere Voice | 7" EP | MGM | MGMEP523 | 1955 | £2 | £5 | |
| Count Basie And Billy Eckstine | LP | Columbia | 33SX1202/ SCX3290 | 1960 | £4 | £10 | with Count Basie |
| Date With Rhythm | 7" EP | Parlophone | GEP8672 | 1957 | £2 | £5 | |
| Enchantment No. 1 | 7" EP | MGM | MGMEP545 | 1956 | £2 | £5 | |
| Four Great Standards | 7" EP | MGM | MGMEP598 | 1957 | £2 | £5 | |
| Gentle On My Mind | LP | Tamla Motown | (S)TML11101 | 1969 | £8 | £20 | |
| Golden Saxophones | LP | London | HAD2241/ SAHD6070 | 1960 | £4 | £10 | |
| Had You Been Around | 7" | Tamla Motown | TMG533 | 1965 | £15 | £30 | |
| Kiss Of Fire | 7" | MGM | SP1011 | 1953 | £2 | £5 | |
| Love Me Or Leave Me | 7" | MGM | SP1136 | 1955 | £1.50 | £4 | |
| My Way | LP | Tamla Motown | (S)TML11046 | 1967 | £15 | £30 | |
| No Cover, No Minimum | LP | Columbia | 33SX1327/ SCX3381 | 1961 | £4 | £10 | |

| | | | | | | | | |
|---|---|---|---|---|---|---|---|---|
| No One But You | 7" | MGM | SP1101 | 1954 | £1.50 | £4 | |
| Once More With Feeling | LP | Columbia | 33SX1249/ SCX3322 | 1960 | £4 | £10 | |
| Prime Of My Life | LP | Tamla Motown | TML11025 | 1966 | £20 | £40 | |
| Tenderly | 10" LP | MGM | MGMD126 | 1954 | £4 | £10 | |
| That Old Feeling | 10" LP | MGM | MGMD138 | 1956 | £4 | £10 | |
| Weaver Of Dreams | 10" LP | MGM | MGMD151 | 1958 | £4 | £10 | |

## ECKSTINE, BILLY & SARAH VAUGHAN

| | | | | | | | | |
|---|---|---|---|---|---|---|---|---|
| Best Of Berlin | 7" EP | Mercury | SEZ19016 | 1961 | £2 | £5 | stereo |
| Best Of Irving Berlin | LP | Mercury | MPL6530 | 1958 | £4 | £10 | |
| Billy Eckstine And Sarah Vaughan | 7" EP | MGM | MGMEP690 | 1959 | £2 | £5 | |
| More Of Irving Berlin | 7" EP | Mercury | SEZ19023 | 1962 | £2 | £5 | stereo |
| Passing Strangers | 7" EP | Mercury | 10025MCE | 1965 | £2 | £5 | |
| Passing Strangers | 7" | Mercury | AMT1071 | 1959 | £1.50 | £4 | |

## ECLECTION

Eclection had a very similar sound to the early Fairport Convention and two of its members – Trevor Lucas and Gerry Conway – played with the more famous group in later years. When singer Kerilee Male left in October 1968, the group took the unusual step of re-recording their current single with Male's replacement, Dorris Henderson. Despite this, however, neither version sold particularly well.

| | | | | | | | | |
|---|---|---|---|---|---|---|---|---|
| Another Time Another Place | 7" | Elektra | EKSN45040 | 1968 | £1.50 | £4 | |
| Eclection | LP | Elektra | EKL4023 | 1968 | £25 | £50 | mono |
| Eclection | LP | Elektra | EKS74023 | 1968 | £20 | £40 | |
| Nevertheless | 7" | Elektra | EKSN45033 | 1968 | £1.50 | £4 | |
| Please | 7" | Elektra | EKSN45042 | 1968 | £1.50 | £4 | |
| Please | 7" | Elektra | EKSN45046 | 1968 | £1.50 | £4 | |

## EDDIE, JASON

Even a Joe Meek production (on 'Singing The Blues') could not give Al Wycherley the kind of success enjoyed by his elder brother, Ron – who used the stage name Billy Fury.

| | | | | | | | | |
|---|---|---|---|---|---|---|---|---|
| Heart And Soul | 7" | Tangerine | DP0010 | 1969 | £4 | £8 | |
| Singing The Blues | 7" | Parlophone | R5473 | 1966 | £50 | £100 | |
| Whatcha Gonna Do Baby | 7" | Parlophone | R5388 | 1965 | £37.50 | £75 | |

## EDDIE AND THE HOT RODS

| | | | | | | | | |
|---|---|---|---|---|---|---|---|---|
| Writing On The Wall | 7" | Island | WIP6270 | 1976 | £5 | £10 | picture sleeve |

## EDDIE'S CROWD

| | | | | | | | | |
|---|---|---|---|---|---|---|---|---|
| Baby Don't Look Down | 7" | CBS | 202078 | 1966 | £10 | £20 | |

## EDDY, DUANE

| | | | | | | | | |
|---|---|---|---|---|---|---|---|---|
| 1,000,000 Dollars Of Twang | LP | London | HAW2325 | 1961 | £4 | £10 | |
| 1,000,000 Dollars Of Twang Vol. 2 | LP | London | HAW2435 | 1964 | £5 | £12 | |
| Avenger | 7" | London | HLW9477 | 1961 | £1.50 | £4 | |
| Because They're Young | 7" EP | London | REW1252 | 1960 | £3 | £8 | |
| Because They're Young | 7" | London | HL7096 | 1960 | £1.50 | £4 | export |
| Biggest Twang Of All | LP | Reprise | R(S)LP6218 | 1967 | £4 | £10 | |
| Bonnie Come Back | 7" | London | HL7090 | 1960 | £7.50 | £15 | export |
| Break My Mind | 7" | CBS | 3962 | 1969 | £4 | £8 | |
| Cannonball | 7" | London | HL8764 | 1958 | £2 | £5 | tri-centre |
| Caravan | 7" | Parlophone | R4826 | 1961 | £1.50 | £4 | |
| Cottonmouth | 7" EP | Colpix | PXE304 | 1965 | £10 | £20 | |
| Country Twang | 7" EP | RCA | RCX7115 | 1963 | £5 | £10 | |
| Dance With The Guitar Man | LP | RCA | RD7545 | 1963 | £4 | £10 | |
| Dance With The Guitar Man | LP | RCA | SF7545 | 1963 | £6 | £15 | stereo |
| Daydream | 7" | Reprise | RS20504 | 1966 | £2.50 | £6 | |
| Duane A Go Go | LP | Colpix | PXL490 | 1965 | £4 | £10 | |
| Duane Does Dylan | LP | Colpix | PXL494 | 1965 | £6 | £15 | |
| Duane Does Dylan | LP | Golden Guinea | GGL10337 | 1968 | £4 | £10 | |
| Duane Does Dylan | LP | Golden Guinea | GGSL10337 | 1968 | £6 | £15 | stereo |
| Especially For You | LP | London | HAW2191 | 1959 | £4 | £10 | |
| Especially For You | LP | London | SAHW6045 | 1959 | £6 | £15 | stereo |
| Forty Miles Of Bad Road | 7" | London | HL7080 | 1959 | £1.50 | £4 | export |
| Girls Girls Girls | LP | London | HAW2373 | 1961 | £4 | £10 | |
| Girls Girls Girls | LP | London | SAHW6173 | 1961 | £6 | £15 | stereo |
| Guitar Star | 7" | RCA | RCA1425 | 1964 | £1.50 | £4 | |
| Guitared And Feathered | 7" | RCA | RCA1369 | 1963 | £1.50 | £4 | |
| Have Twangy Guitar Will Travel | LP | London | HAW2160 | 1958 | £8 | £20 | |
| House Of The Rising Sun | 7" | Colpix | PX788 | 1964 | £1.50 | £4 | |
| Lonely Guitar | LP | RCA | RD/SF7621 | 1964 | £6 | £15 | |
| Lonely One | 7" EP | London | REW1216 | 1959 | £3 | £8 | |
| Lonely One | 7" | London | HL7072 | 1959 | £1.50 | £4 | export |
| Lonely One | 7" | London | HLW8821 | 1959 | £2 | £5 | tri-centre |
| Love Confusion | 7" | Target | 101 | 1975 | £2 | £5 | |
| Mister Twang | 7" EP | RCA | RCX7129 | 1963 | £6 | £12 | |
| Monsoon | 7" | Reprise | RS20557 | 1967 | £2.50 | £6 | |
| Movie Themes | 7" EP | London | REW1303 | 1961 | £3 | £8 | |
| Niki Hoeky | 7" | Reprise | RS20690 | 1968 | £2.50 | £6 | |
| Pepe | 7" EP | London | REW1287 | 1961 | £3 | £8 | |
| Peter Gunn | 7" | London | SLW4001 | 1959 | £20 | £40 | stereo |
| Ramrod | 7" | Ford | 500 | 1957 | £75 | £150 | US |
| Ramrod | 7" | London | HL7057 | 1958 | £1.50 | £4 | export |
| Ramrod | 7" | London | HL8723 | 1958 | £2 | £5 | tri-centre |
| Rebel Rouser | 7" EP | London | RE1175 | 1958 | £3 | £8 | |
| Rebel Rouser | 7" | London | HL8669 | 1958 | £2.50 | £6 | tri-centre |

| Title | Format | Label | Catalogue | Year | Price 1 | Price 2 | Notes |
|---|---|---|---|---|---|---|---|
| Roarin' Twangies | LP | Reprise | R(S)LP6240 | 1967 | £8 | £20 | |
| Son Of Rebel Rouser | 7" | RCA | RCA1389 | 1964 | £1.50 | £4 | |
| Songs Of Our Heritage | LP | London | HAW2285 | 1960 | £4 | £10 | |
| Songs Of Our Heritage | LP | London | SAHW6119 | 1960 | £6 | £15 | stereo |
| Trash | 7" | Colpix | PX779 | 1964 | £1.50 | £4 | |
| Twangin' Golden Hits | LP | RCA | RD7689 | 1964 | £4 | £10 | |
| Twangin' Golden Hits | LP | RCA | SF7689 | 1965 | £6 | £15 | stereo |
| Twangin' Up A Small Storm | 7" EP | RCA | RCX7146 | 1964 | £7.50 | £15 | |
| Twangin' Up A Storm | LP | RCA | RD7568 | 1963 | £4 | £10 | |
| Twangin' Up A Storm | LP | RCA | SF7568 | 1963 | £6 | £15 | stereo |
| Twangs A Country Song | LP | RCA | RD7560 | 1963 | £4 | £10 | |
| Twangs A Country Song | LP | RCA | SF7560 | 1963 | £6 | £15 | stereo |
| Twang's The Thang | LP | London | HAW2236 | 1960 | £4 | £10 | |
| Twang's The Thang | LP | London | SAHW6068 | 1960 | £6 | £15 | stereo |
| Twangsville | LP | RCA | RD7754 | 1965 | £6 | £15 | |
| Twangsville | LP | RCA | SF7754 | 1965 | £8 | £20 | stereo |
| Twangy | 7" EP | London | REW1257 | 1960 | £3 | £8 | |
| Twangy Guitar Silky Strings | LP | RCA | RD7510 | 1962 | £4 | £10 | |
| Twangy Guitar Silky Strings | LP | RCA | SF7510 | 1962 | £6 | £15 | stereo |
| Twangy No. 2 | 7" EP | London | REW1341 | 1961 | £3 | £8 | |
| Twistin' And Twangin' | LP | RCA | RD27264 | 1962 | £4 | £10 | |
| Twistin' And Twangin' | LP | RCA | SF5134 | 1962 | £6 | £15 | stereo |
| Water Skiing | LP | RCA | RD7656 | 1964 | £6 | £15 | |
| Water Skiing | LP | RCA | SF7656 | 1964 | £8 | £20 | stereo |
| Yep | 7" EP | London | REW1217 | 1959 | £3 | £8 | |
| Yep! | 7" | London | HL7076 | 1959 | £7.50 | £15 | export |

## EDDY, PEARL

| Title | Format | Label | Catalogue | Year | Price 1 | Price 2 | Notes |
|---|---|---|---|---|---|---|---|
| That's What A Heart Is For | 7" | HMV | 7M262 | 1954 | £1.50 | £4 | |

## EDEN

| Title | Format | Label | Catalogue | Year | Price 1 | Price 2 | Notes |
|---|---|---|---|---|---|---|---|
| Eden | LP | Total | 22009 | 1975 | £6 | £15 | Canadian |

## EDEN, TONI

| Title | Format | Label | Catalogue | Year | Price 1 | Price 2 | Notes |
|---|---|---|---|---|---|---|---|
| Grown Up Dreams | 7" | Columbia | DB4458 | 1960 | £1.50 | £4 | |
| Teen Street | 7" | Columbia | DB4409 | 1960 | £2 | £5 | |

## EDEN ROSE

| Title | Format | Label | Catalogue | Year | Price 1 | Price 2 | Notes |
|---|---|---|---|---|---|---|---|
| On The Way To Eden | LP | Katema | KA33507 | 1970 | £100 | £200 | French |

## EDEN'S CHILDREN

| Title | Format | Label | Catalogue | Year | Price 1 | Price 2 | Notes |
|---|---|---|---|---|---|---|---|
| Eden's Children | LP | Stateside | (S)SL10235 | 1968 | £15 | £30 | |
| Sure Looks Real | LP | ABC | S652 | 1969 | £8 | £20 | US |

## EDGE

| Title | Format | Label | Catalogue | Year | Price 1 | Price 2 | Notes |
|---|---|---|---|---|---|---|---|
| Edge | LP | Nose | NRS48003 | 1970 | £15 | £30 | US |

## EDISON, HARRY

| Title | Format | Label | Catalogue | Year | Price 1 | Price 2 | Notes |
|---|---|---|---|---|---|---|---|
| Gee Baby Ain't I Good To You | LP | HMV | CLP1350 | 1960 | £8 | £20 | |
| Harry Edison Quartet | 10" LP | Vogue | LDE118 | 1955 | £20 | £40 | |
| Sweets | LP | Columbia | 33CX10087 | 1957 | £8 | £20 | |
| Swinger | LP | HMV | CLP1277 | 1959 | £8 | £20 | |
| Swings Buck Clayton | LP | HMV | CLP1321 | 1960 | £8 | £20 | |

## EDMUNDS, DAVE

| Title | Format | Label | Catalogue | Year | Price 1 | Price 2 | Notes |
|---|---|---|---|---|---|---|---|
| College Radio Network Presents Dave Edmunds | LP | Swansong | PR320 | 1978 | £6 | £15 | US promo |
| Information | 12" | Columbia | AS991725 | 1983 | £10 | £20 | US promo picture disc |
| Rockpile | LP | Regal Zonophone | SLRZ1026 | 1971 | £10 | £25 | |
| Rockpile Collection | LP | Regal Zonophone | SRZA8503 | 1971 | £25 | £50 | |

## EDSELS

| Title | Format | Label | Catalogue | Year | Price 1 | Price 2 | Notes |
|---|---|---|---|---|---|---|---|
| Rama Lama Ding Dong | 7" | Pye | 7N25086 | 1961 | £25 | £50 | |

## EDWARD BEAR

| Title | Format | Label | Catalogue | Year | Price 1 | Price 2 | Notes |
|---|---|---|---|---|---|---|---|
| Bearings | LP | Capitol | ST426 | 1969 | £4 | £10 | |

## EDWARD H. DAFIS

| Title | Format | Label | Catalogue | Year | Price 1 | Price 2 | Notes |
|---|---|---|---|---|---|---|---|
| Ffordd Newydd Eingl-Americanaidd Gret O Fyw | LP | Sain | 1034M | 1975 | £10 | £25 | |
| Hen Ffordd Gymreig O Fyw | LP | Sain | 1016M | 1974 | £15 | £30 | |
| Plant Y Fflam | LP | Sain | 1196M | 1980 | £5 | £12 | |
| Sneb Yn Becso Dam | LP | Sain | 1053M | 1976 | £5 | £12 | |
| Yn Erbyn Y Ffactore | LP | Sain | 1144M | 1979 | £5 | £12 | |

## EDWARDS, BOBBY

| Title | Format | Label | Catalogue | Year | Price 1 | Price 2 | Notes |
|---|---|---|---|---|---|---|---|
| You're The Reason | 7" | Top Rank | JAR584 | 1961 | £2 | £5 | |

## EDWARDS, BRENT

| Title | Format | Label | Catalogue | Year | Price 1 | Price 2 | Notes |
|---|---|---|---|---|---|---|---|
| Pride | 7" | Pye | 7N25197 | 1963 | £1.50 | £4 | |

## EDWARDS, CHUCK

| Title | Format | Label | Catalogue | Year | Price 1 | Price 2 | Notes |
|---|---|---|---|---|---|---|---|
| Downtown Soulville | 7" | Soul City | SC104 | 1968 | £2.50 | £6 | |

## EDWARDS, GARY

| Title | Format | Label | Catalogue | Year | Price 1 | Price 2 | Notes |
|---|---|---|---|---|---|---|---|
| Africa | 7" | Oriole | CB1733 | 1962 | £1.50 | £4 | |

266

| Title | Format | Label | Cat. No. | Year | | | Notes |
|---|---|---|---|---|---|---|---|
| Hopscotch | 7" | Oriole | CB1759 | 1962 | £1.50 | £4 | |
| Twist Or Bust | 7" | Oriole | CB1700 | 1962 | £1.50 | £4 | |

## EDWARDS, JACKIE & JIMMY CLIFF

| Title | Format | Label | Cat. No. | Year | | | Notes |
|---|---|---|---|---|---|---|---|
| Set Me Free | 7" | Island | WIP6036 | 1968 | £1.50 | £4 | |

## EDWARDS, JACKIE & MILLIE

| Title | Format | Label | Cat. No. | Year | | | Notes |
|---|---|---|---|---|---|---|---|
| Best Of Jackie & Millie | LP | Island | ILP963 | 1968 | £30 | £60 | pink label |
| Jackie And Millie | LP | Trojan | TBL155 | 1970 | £6 | £15 | |
| Pledging My Love | LP | Island | ILP941 | 1966 | £30 | £60 | |
| All My Days | 7" | Island | WI008 | 1962 | £5 | £10 | |
| Best Of Jackie Edwards | LP | Island | ILP936 | 1966 | £25 | £50 | |
| By Demand | LP | Island | ILP940 | 1966 | £25 | £50 | |
| By Demand | LP | Trojan | TTL46 | 1970 | £6 | £15 | |
| Come Back Girl | 7" | Island | WIP6008 | 1967 | £1.50 | £4 | |
| Come On Home | LP | Island | ILP931 | 1966 | £25 | £50 | |
| Come On Home | LP | Trojan | TTL45 | 1970 | £6 | £15 | |
| He'll Have To Go | 7" | Aladdin | WI601 | 1965 | £2 | £5 | |
| Heaven Just Knows | 7" | Starlite | ST45046 | 1961 | £5 | £10 | |
| Hush | 7" EP | Island | IEP708 | 1966 | £10 | £20 | |
| Hush | 7" | Aladdin | WI605 | 1965 | £2 | £5 | |
| I Feel So Bad | 7" | Island | WI3006 | 1966 | £20 | £40 | |
| Julie On My Mind | 7" | Island | WIP6026 | 1968 | £1.50 | £4 | |
| Let It Be Me | LP | Direction | 863977 | 1969 | £4 | £10 | |
| Lonely Game | 7" | Decca | F11547 | 1962 | £1.50 | £4 | |
| L-O-V-E | 7" | Island | WI274 | 1966 | £5 | £10 | |
| More Than Words Can Say | 7" | Starlite | ST45062 | 1961 | £5 | £10 | |
| Most Of Wilfred Jackie Edwards | LP | Island | ILP906 | 1964 | £25 | £50 | |
| Most Of Wilfred Jackie Edwards | LP | Trojan | TTL40 | 1970 | £6 | £15 | |
| One More Week | 7" | Island | WI019 | 1962 | £5 | £10 | |
| Only A Fool Breaks His Own Heart | 7" | Island | WI3030 | 1967 | £5 | £10 | |
| Premature Golden Sands | LP | Island | ILP960/ILPS9060 | 1967 | £20 | £40 | pink label |
| Premature Golden Sands | LP | Trojan | TTL57 | 1970 | £6 | £15 | |
| Put Your Tears Away | LP | Island | IWPS4 | 1969 | £10 | £25 | |
| Royal Telephone | 7" | Island | WI3018 | 1966 | £5 | £10 | |
| Sacred Songs Vol. 1 | 7" EP | Island | IEP701 | 1966 | £5 | £10 | no picture sleeve |
| Sacred Songs Vol. 2 | 7" EP | Island | IEP702 | 1966 | £5 | £10 | no picture sleeve |
| Same One | 7" | Aladdin | WI611 | 1965 | £2 | £5 | |
| Sea Cruise | 7" | Fontana | TF465 | 1964 | £5 | £10 | |
| Sometimes | 7" | Island | WI270 | 1966 | £5 | £10 | |
| Stagger Lee | 7" | Sue | WI329 | 1964 | £5 | £10 | |
| Stand Up For Jesus | LP | Island | ILP912 | 1964 | £20 | £40 | |
| Things You Do | 7" | Black Swan | WI416 | 1964 | £5 | £10 | |
| Think Twice | 7" | Island | WI287 | 1966 | £5 | £10 | |
| White Christmas | 7" | Island | WI255 | 1965 | £5 | £10 | |
| Why Make Believe | 7" | Black Swan | WI404 | 1963 | £5 | £10 | |
| You're My Girl | 7" | Island | WI3157 | 1968 | £5 | £10 | |
| You're My Girl | 7" | Island | WIP6042 | 1968 | £1.50 | £4 | |

## EDWARDS, JIMMY

| Title | Format | Label | Cat. No. | Year | | | Notes |
|---|---|---|---|---|---|---|---|
| Love Bug Crawl | 7" | Mercury | 7MT193 | 1958 | £180 | £300 | best auctioned |

## EDWARDS, NOKIE

| Title | Format | Label | Cat. No. | Year | | | Notes |
|---|---|---|---|---|---|---|---|
| Again | LP | Cream | ISP80546 | 1972 | £8 | £20 | Japanese |
| King Of Guitars | LP | Stateside | 80859 | 1973 | £8 | £20 | Japanese |
| Nokie | LP | Cream | CR9006 | 1971 | £4 | £10 | US |
| Nokie Edwards | LP | Stateside | 97019 | 1974 | £8 | £20 | Japanese |

## EDWARDS, PAUL

| Title | Format | Label | Cat. No. | Year | | | Notes |
|---|---|---|---|---|---|---|---|
| Longstone Farm | LP | Cottage | COT301 | 1976 | £10 | £25 | |

## EDWARDS, RUPIE

| Title | Format | Label | Cat. No. | Year | | | Notes |
|---|---|---|---|---|---|---|---|
| Guilty Convict | 7" | Blue Beat | BB90 | 1962 | £6 | £12 | |
| I Can't Forget | 7" | Doctor Bird | DB1163 | 1968 | £5 | £10 | |
| Long Lost Love | 7" | Crab | CRAB35 | 1969 | £1.50 | £4 | |

## EDWARDS, SAMUEL

| Title | Format | Label | Cat. No. | Year | | | Notes |
|---|---|---|---|---|---|---|---|
| Israel | 7" | Blue Cat | BS159 | 1969 | £1.50 | £4 | |

## EDWARDS, TOMMY

| Title | Format | Label | Cat. No. | Year | | | Notes |
|---|---|---|---|---|---|---|---|
| Baby Let Me Take You Dreaming | 7" | MGM | SP1168 | 1956 | £1.50 | £4 | |
| Fool Such As I | 7" | MGM | SP1030 | 1953 | £2 | £5 | |
| For Young Lovers | LP | MGM | C791 | 1959 | £8 | £20 | |
| I've Been There | 7" EP | MGM | MGMEP707 | 1959 | £6 | £12 | |
| It's All In The Game | LP | MGM | C734 | 1959 | £10 | £25 | |
| Tommy Edwards | LP | Lion | 70120 | 195– | £10 | £25 | US |
| Tommy Edwards Sings | LP | Regent | MG6096 | 195– | £10 | £25 | US |
| Ways Of Love | 7" EP | MGM | MGMEP712 | 1960 | £6 | £12 | |
| You Started Me Dreaming | LP | MGM | C824 | 1960 | £6 | £15 | |

## EDWARDS, VINCE

| Title | Format | Label | Cat. No. | Year | | | Notes |
|---|---|---|---|---|---|---|---|
| County Durham Dream | 7" | United Artists | UP2230 | 1968 | £1.50 | £4 | |
| I Can't Turn Back Time | 7" | United Artists | UP1179 | 1967 | £2 | £5 | |

## EDWARDS, VINCE (2)

| Title | Format | Label | Cat. No. | Year | | | Notes |
|---|---|---|---|---|---|---|---|
| No Not Much | 7" | Colpix | PX771 | 1964 | £1.50 | £4 | |

## EDWARDS, WILFRED & THE CARIBS

| | | | | | | |
|---|---|---|---|---|---|---|
| Little Bitty Girl | 7" | Starlite | ST45076 | 1962 £5 | £10 | |
| Tell Me Darling | 7" | Starlite | ST45026 | 1960 £5 | £10 | |
| We're Gonna Love | 7" | Starlite | ST45016 | 1960 £5 | £10 | |

## EDWARD'S GROUP

| | | | | | | |
|---|---|---|---|---|---|---|
| Dear Hearts | 7" | Island | WI040 | 1963 £5 | £10 | .... Osbourne Graham B side |
| He Gave You To Me | 7" | Island | WI082 | 1963 £5 | £10 | |
| Hey Girl | 7" | Island | WI087 | 1963 £5 | £10 | |
| Russian Roulette | 7" | Island | WI047 | 1963 £5 | £10 | |

## EDWARDS HAND

| | | | | | | |
|---|---|---|---|---|---|---|
| Edwards Hand | LP | GRT | 10005 | 1969 £5 | £12 | US |
| Rainshine | LP | Regal Zonophone | SRZA8513 | 1973 £25 | £50 | |
| Stranded | LP | RCA | SF8154 | 1971 £4 | £10 | |

## EDWICK RUMBOLD

| | | | | | | |
|---|---|---|---|---|---|---|
| Shades Of Grey | 7" | Parlophone | R5622 | 1967 £25 | £50 | |
| Specially When | 7" | CBS | 202393 | 1966 £25 | £50 | |

## EELA CRAIG

| | | | | | | |
|---|---|---|---|---|---|---|
| Eela Craig | LP | Pro Disc | 208711 | 1971 £37.50 | £75 | Austrian |
| Hats Of Glass | LP | Vertigo | 6360638 | 1977 £10 | £25 | German |
| Missa Universalis | LP | Vertigo | 6360639 | 1978 £10 | £25 | German |
| One Nighter | LP | Vertigo | 6360635 | 1976 £10 | £25 | German |

## EFENDI'S GARDEN

| | | | | | | |
|---|---|---|---|---|---|---|
| Efendi's Garden | LP | Babylon | 80004 | 1979 £10 | £25 | German |

## EGANS, WILLIE

| | | | | | | |
|---|---|---|---|---|---|---|
| Willie Egans | 7" EP | XX | MIN714 | 196– £4 | £8 | |

## EGG

The records made by Egg contain the most impressive music of any made by those groups whose dominant voice is that of the keyboards. Organist Dave Stewart has been making records ever since, with Hatfield and the North and other related groups (he's even been in the charts a few times, but not as a member of the Eurythmics!), but he has arguably never bettered the youthful enthusiasm of his work with Egg. The group's music is difficult in places, but only in the same way that Soft Machine's music is. It utilizes awkward time signatures and convoluted melody lines, but never forgets its essential function of communicating with an audience.

| | | | | | | |
|---|---|---|---|---|---|---|
| Civil Surface | LP | Caroline | C1510 | 1974 £4 | £10 | |
| Egg | LP | Nova | SDN14 | 1970 £6 | £15 | |
| Polite Force | LP | Deram | SML1074 | 1970 £6 | £15 | |
| Seven Is A Jolly Good Time | 7" | Deram | DM269 | 1969 £2.50 | £6 | |

## EGGY

| | | | | | | |
|---|---|---|---|---|---|---|
| You're Still Mine | 7" | Spark | SRL1024 | 1970 £5 | £10 | |

## EIGHT-EYED SPY

| | | | | | | |
|---|---|---|---|---|---|---|
| Diddy Wah Diddy | 7" | Fetish | FE19 | 1982 £2 | £5 | |
| Eight-Eyed Spy | LP | Fetish | FR2003 | 1981 £4 | £10 | |

## EIGHT-O-EIGHT STATE

| | | | | | | |
|---|---|---|---|---|---|---|
| Let Yourself Go | 12" | Creed | STATE003 | 1988 £2.50 | £6 | |
| Newbuild | LP | Creed | STATE002 | 1988 £5 | £12 | |

## EIGHT-OH-EIGHT STATE

| | | | | | | |
|---|---|---|---|---|---|---|
| Cubik Olympic | CD-s | ZTT | ZANG5CD | 1990 £2 | £5 | |
| In Yer Face | CD-s | ZTT | ZANG14CD | 1991 £2 | £5 | |
| Lift | CD-s | ZTT | ZANG20CD | 1991 £2 | £5 | |
| Ooops | CD-s | ZTT | ZANG19CD | 1991 £2 | £5 | with Björk |

## EIGHTH WONDER

| | | | | | | |
|---|---|---|---|---|---|---|
| Baby Baby | CD-s | CBS | BABECD1 | 1988 £2 | £5 | |
| Baby Baby | 12" | CBS | BABEQT1 | 1988 £5 | £12 | |
| Cross My Heart | CD-s | CBS | 6515522 | 1988 £2 | £5 | |
| Fearless | CD | CBS | 4606282 | 1988 £5 | £12 | |
| I'm Not Scared | CD-s | CBS | SCAREC1 | 1988 £6 | £15 | |
| I'm Not Scared | 7" | CBS | SCAREQ1 | 1988 £1.50 | £4 | poster sleeve |
| I'm Not Scared | 10" | CBS | SCAREY1 | 1988 £4 | £10 | |
| Stay With Me | 12" | CBS | QTX6594 | 1985 £6 | £15 | poster picture sleeve |

## EIGHTIES LADIES

| | | | | | | |
|---|---|---|---|---|---|---|
| Turned On To You | 12" | Music Of Life | MOLIF6 | 1986 £4 | £10 | |

## EIH, DAMIN, A.L.K. AND BROTHER CLARK

| | | | | | | |
|---|---|---|---|---|---|---|
| Never Mind | LP | Demelot | NS7310 | 1973 £50 | £100 | US |

## EILIFF

| | | | | | | |
|---|---|---|---|---|---|---|
| Eiliff | LP | Philips | 6305103 | 1971 £25 | £50 | German |
| Girlrls | LP | Philips | 6305145 | 1972 £8 | £20 | German |

## EIRE APPARENT

| | | | | | | |
|---|---|---|---|---|---|---|
| Follow Me | 7" | Track | 604019 | 1967 £2.50 | £6 | |
| Rock 'n' Roll Band | 7" | Buddah | 201039 | 1969 £2 | £5 | |

| | | | | | | | |
|---|---|---|---|---|---|---|---|
| Sunrise | LP | Buddah | 203021 | 1969 | £15 | £30 | |

## EKSEPTION

| | | | | | | | |
|---|---|---|---|---|---|---|---|
| 3 | LP | Philips | 6423005 | 1971 | £5 | £12 | *Dutch* |
| 4 | LP | Philips | 6423019 | 1972 | £5 | £12 | *Dutch* |
| 5 | LP | Philips | 6423042 | 1972 | £5 | £12 | *Dutch* |
| Beggar Julia's Time Trip | LP | Philips | 6314001 | 1969 | £5 | £12 | |
| Ekseption | LP | Philips | 6314005 | 1970 | £5 | £12 | |
| Trinity | LP | Philips | 6423056 | 1973 | £4 | £10 | *Dutch* |

## EL SHALOM

| | | | | | | | |
|---|---|---|---|---|---|---|---|
| Frost | LP | Attacca | 27625 | 1976 | £15 | £30 | *German* |

## ELASTIC BAND

| | | | | | | | |
|---|---|---|---|---|---|---|---|
| Do Unto Others | 7" | Decca | F12815 | 1968 | £7.50 | £15 | |
| Expansions On Life | LP | Nova | DN/SND6 | 1969 | £15 | £30 | |
| Think Of You Baby | 7" | Decca | F12763 | 1968 | £7.50 | £15 | |

## ELASTICA

| | | | | | | | |
|---|---|---|---|---|---|---|---|
| Connection | 7" | Deceptive | BLUFF010 | 1994 | £4 | £8 | |
| Line Up | 7" | Deceptive | BLUFF004 | 1994 | £5 | £10 | |
| Stutter | 7" | Deceptive | BLUFF003 | 1993 | £10 | £20 | |

## ELASTICK BAND

| | | | | | | | |
|---|---|---|---|---|---|---|---|
| Spazz | 7" | Stateside | SS2056 | 1967 | £15 | £30 | *demo* |

## ELBERT, DONNIE

| | | | | | | | |
|---|---|---|---|---|---|---|---|
| Get Ready | 7" | CBS | 2807 | 1967 | £1.50 | £4 | |
| In Between The Heartaches | 7" | Polydor | 56234 | 1968 | £1.50 | £4 | |
| Let's Do The Stroll | 7" | Parlophone | R4403 | 1958 | £15 | £30 | |
| Little Piece Of Leather | 7" | Sue | WI377 | 1965 | £6 | £12 | |
| Sensational Donnie Elbert Sings | LP | King | 629 | 1959 | £37.50 | £75 | *US* |
| This Old Heart Of Mine | 7" | Polydor | 56265 | 1968 | £1.50 | £4 | |
| You Can Push It Or Pull It | 7" | Sue | WI396 | 1965 | £6 | £12 | |

## ELCORT

| | | | | | | | |
|---|---|---|---|---|---|---|---|
| Tammy | 7" | Parlophone | R5447 | 1966 | £2.50 | £6 | |

## ELDERBERRY JAK

| | | | | | | | |
|---|---|---|---|---|---|---|---|
| Elderberry Jak | LP | Forest | AW14019 | 1968 | £37.50 | £75 | *US* |
| Long Overdue | LP | Electric Fox | LP555 | 1975 | £15 | £30 | *US* |

## ELDORADOS

| | | | | | | | |
|---|---|---|---|---|---|---|---|
| Crazy Little Mama | LP | Vee Jay | VJLP1001 | 1959 | £87.50 | £175 | *US* |

## ELDORADOS (2)

| | | | | | | | |
|---|---|---|---|---|---|---|---|
| Eldorados | 7" EP | Decca | DFE8543 | 1963 | £12.50 | £25 | |

## ELDRIDGE, ROY

| | | | | | | | |
|---|---|---|---|---|---|---|---|
| Roy And Diz No. 2 | LP | Columbia | 33CX10084 | 1957 | £15 | £30 | *with Dizzy Gillespie* |
| Roy Eldridge | 10" LP | Columbia | 33C9031 | 1957 | £15 | £30 | |
| Roy Eldridge And Dizzy Gillespie | LP | Columbia | 33CX10025 | 1956 | £20 | £40 | |
| Roy Eldridge Quintet | 10" LP | Columbia | 33C9005 | 1955 | £20 | £40 | |

## ELECAMPANE

| | | | | | | | |
|---|---|---|---|---|---|---|---|
| Further Adventures Of Mr. Punch | LP | Dame Jane | ODJ2 | 1978 | £10 | £25 | |
| When God's On The Water | LP | Dame Jane | ODJ1 | 1975 | £30 | £60 | |

## ELECTRAS

| | | | | | | | |
|---|---|---|---|---|---|---|---|
| Electras | LP | private | | 196– | £180 | £300 | *US* |

## ELECTRIC BANANA

The library records credited to Electric Banana, and intended for use as background film and TV music, are actually the work of the Pretty Things.

| | | | | | | | |
|---|---|---|---|---|---|---|---|
| Electric Banana | LP | De Wolfe | DWSLP3040 | 1967 | £8 | £20 | |
| Even More Electric Banana | LP | De Wolfe | DWSLP3282 | 1969 | £4 | £10 | |
| Hot Licks | LP | De Wolfe | DWSLP3284 | 1973 | £4 | £10 | |
| More Electric Banana | LP | De Wolfe | DWSLP3069 | 1968 | £8 | £20 | |
| Return Of The Electric Banana | LP | De Wolfe | DWSLP3381 | 1979 | £5 | £12 | |

## ELECTRIC BLUES

| | | | | | | | |
|---|---|---|---|---|---|---|---|
| Still Going Strong | LP | private | | 1979 | £50 | £100 | *Dutch* |

## ELECTRIC CRAYONS

| | | | | | | | |
|---|---|---|---|---|---|---|---|
| Hip Shake Junkie | 7" | Emergency | MIV3 | 1989 | £4 | £8 | |

## ELECTRIC FLAG

At its best, Mike Bloomfield's big band sounds marvellous – the driving 'Killing Floor' or the long, crafted 'Another Country' (both on *A Long Time Comin'*) – but the Electric Flag's music was extremely uneven. Calling itself An American Music Band, the Electric Flag really wanted to play everything. It would probably have been better, however, if it had not tried to cast its net so wide. As it is, the band seems to lack focus. *Electric Flag* was recorded after many of the original members, including Bloomfield, had left. *The Trip* is a film soundtrack and contains a large number of very short tracks – frustrating.

| | | | | | | | |
|---|---|---|---|---|---|---|---|
| Electric Flag | LP | CBS | 63462 | 1969 | £4 | £10 | |
| Groovin' Is Easy | 7" | CBS | 3584 | 1968 | £1.50 | £4 | |
| Long Time Comin' | LP | CBS | 63294 | 1968 | £5 | £12 | |

| Title | Format | Label | Cat. No. | Year | | | Notes |
|---|---|---|---|---|---|---|---|
| Sunny | 7" | CBS | 4066 | 1969 | £1.50 | £4 | |
| Trip | LP | Sidewalk | (S)T5908 | 1967 | £8 | £20 | US |

## ELECTRIC JOHNNY

| | | | | | | | |
|---|---|---|---|---|---|---|---|
| Black Eyes Rock | 7" | London | HLU9384 | 1961 | £7.50 | £15 | |

## ELECTRIC JUNKYARD

| | | | | | | | |
|---|---|---|---|---|---|---|---|
| Electric Junkyard | LP | RCA | LSP4158 | 1969 | £6 | £15 | US |

## ELECTRIC LIGHT ORCHESTRA

| | | | | | | | |
|---|---|---|---|---|---|---|---|
| All Over The World | 10" | Jet | JET10195 | 1980 | £2.50 | £6 | blue vinyl |
| Can't Get It Out Of My Head | 7" | Jet | ELO1JB | 1977 | £2 | £5 | juke box issue |
| Discovery | LP | Jet | HZ45769 | 1981 | £5 | £12 | US audiophile |
| Eldorado | LP | Jet | | 1981 | £5 | £12 | US audiophile |
| Eldorado | LP | Jet | JETLP203 | 1978 | £4 | £10 | yellow vinyl |
| Electric Light Orchestra | LP | Harvest | Q4SHVL797 | 1974 | £4 | £10 | quad |
| Face The Music | LP | Jet | JETLP201 | 1978 | £5 | £12 | green vinyl |
| Four Little Diamonds | 12" | Jet | TA3869 | 1983 | £2.50 | £6 | |
| Getting To The Point | 12" | Epic | QTA7317 | 1986 | £2.50 | £6 | |
| Greatest Hits | LP | Jet | HZ46310 | 1981 | £5 | £12 | US audiophile |
| Livin' Thing | 7" | United Artists | UP36184 | 1976 | £2 | £5 | blue vinyl |
| New World Record | LP | Jet | JETLP200 | 1978 | £4 | £10 | red vinyl |
| Night The Light Went Out In Long Beach. | LP | Warner Bros | WBK56058 | 1974 | £4 | £10 | German |
| Ole Elo | LP | Jet/United Artists | SP123 | 1976 | £6 | £15 | US promo, gold vinyl |
| On The Third Day | LP | Jet | LP202 | 1978 | £4 | £10 | clear vinyl |
| Out Of The Blue | LP | Jet | JETDP400 | 1978 | £5 | £12 | blue vinyl double |
| Roll Over Beethoven | 12" | Harvest | PSLP213 | 1977 | £2.50 | £6 | promo |
| Roll Over Beethoven/Manhattan Rumble. | 7" | Harvest | HAR5063 | 1973 | £2 | £5 | |
| Secret Messages | LP | Jet | HZ48490 | 1983 | £5 | £12 | US audiophile |
| Secret Messages | 7" | Jet | PA3720 | 1983 | £1.50 | £4 | picture disc |
| Strange Magic | 7" | Jet | ELO2JB | 1977 | £2 | £5 | juke box issue |
| Sweet Talking Woman | 12" | Jet | SJET12121 | 1978 | £2.50 | £6 | mauve vinyl |
| Ticket To The Moon | 12" | Jet | JET127018 | 1981 | £2.50 | £6 | picture disc |
| Time | LP | Jet | HZ47371 | 1981 | £5 | £12 | US audiophile |
| Wild West Hero | 12" | Jet | SJET12109 | 1978 | £2.50 | £6 | yellow vinyl, Jet label |
| Xanadu | 10" | MCA | 2315 | 1980 | £75 | £150 | US promo picture disc |

## ELECTRIC PRUNES

The Electric Prunes were two groups, both in style and in personnel, for sometime during the recording of *Mass In F Minor* there was a complete change in membership. The 1966–7 releases contain many prime examples of psychedelia, most notably the quartet of singles. *Mass In F Minor*, on the other hand, is exactly what it says it is – a rock mass. The album is an interesting and reasonably successful experiment, but it is very short on playing time.

| | | | | | | | |
|---|---|---|---|---|---|---|---|
| Everybody Knows | 7" | Reprise | RS20652 | 1968 | £5 | £10 | |
| Get Me To The World On Time | 7" | Reprise | RS20564 | 1967 | £2.50 | £6 | |
| Great Banana Hoax | 7" | Reprise | RS20607 | 1967 | £2.50 | £6 | |
| I Had Too Much To Dream | LP | Reprise | R(S)6248 | 1967 | £15 | £30 | US |
| I Had Too Much To Dream | 7" EP | Reprise | RVEP60098 | 1966 | £25 | £50 | French |
| I Had Too Much To Dream | 7" | Reprise | RS20532 | 1966 | £2.50 | £6 | |
| Just Good Old Rock 'n' Roll | LP | Reprise | RS6342 | 1969 | £8 | £20 | US |
| Long Day's Flight | CD | Edsel | EDCD179 | 1989 | £5 | £12 | |
| Long Day's Flight | 7" EP | Reprise | RVEP60110 | 1967 | £25 | £50 | French |
| Long Day's Flight | 7" | Reprise | RS23212 | 1967 | £4 | £8 | |
| Mass In F Minor | LP | Reprise | R(S)LP6275 | 1968 | £6 | £15 | |
| Release Of An Oath | LP | Reprise | R(S)LP6316 | 1968 | £6 | £15 | |
| Underground | LP | Reprise | R(S)6262 | 1967 | £25 | £50 | US |

## ELECTRIC SANDWICH

| | | | | | | | |
|---|---|---|---|---|---|---|---|
| Electric Sandwich | LP | Brain | 1018 | 1972 | £10 | £25 | German |

## ELECTRIC TOILET

| | | | | | | | |
|---|---|---|---|---|---|---|---|
| In The Hands Of Karma | LP | Nasco | 9004 | 1970 | £50 | £100 | US |
| In The Hands Of Karma | LP | Psycho | PSYCHO8 | 1983 | £6 | £15 | |

## ELECTRONIC

| | | | | | | | |
|---|---|---|---|---|---|---|---|
| Feel Every Beat | CD-s | Factory | FAC328C | 1991 | £2 | £5 | |
| Get The Message | CD-s | Factory | FAC287C | 1991 | £2 | £5 | |
| Getting Away With It | CD-s | Factory | FACD257 | 1989 | £2 | £5 | |

## ELEGANTS

| | | | | | | | |
|---|---|---|---|---|---|---|---|
| Little Star | 7" | HMV | POP520 | 1958 | £10 | £20 | |
| Please Believe Me | 7" | HMV | POP551 | 1958 | £12.50 | £25 | |

## ELEPHANT BAND

| | | | | | | | |
|---|---|---|---|---|---|---|---|
| Stone Penguin | 7" | Mojo | 2092036 | 1972 | £2 | £5 | |

## ELEPHANT'S MEMORY

| | | | | | | | |
|---|---|---|---|---|---|---|---|
| Elephant's Memory | LP | Apple | SAPCOR22 | 1972 | £6 | £15 | |
| Power Boogie | 7" | Apple | 45 | 1972 | £2 | £5 | |

## ELEVEN FIFTY-NINE

| | | | | | | | |
|---|---|---|---|---|---|---|---|
| This Is Our Sacrifice Of Praise | LP | Dovetail | DOVE4 | 1974 | £50 | £100 | |

## ELF

| | | | | | | | |
|---|---|---|---|---|---|---|---|
| Carolina Country Ball | LP | Purple | TPSA3506 | 1974 | £8 | £20 | |
| Elf | LP | Epic | KE31789 | 1972 | £8 | £20 | US |

| | | | | | | | | |
|---|---|---|---|---|---|---|---|---|
| Trying To Burn The Sun | LP | MGM | M3G4994 | 1975 | £5 | £12 | | US |

## ELFENBIEN

| | | | | | | | | |
|---|---|---|---|---|---|---|---|---|
| Made In Rock | LP | MDM | 011246 | 1977 | £6 | £15 | | German |

## ELGINS

| | | | | | | | |
|---|---|---|---|---|---|---|---|
| Darling Baby | LP | Tamla Motown | (S)TML11081 | 1968 | £15 | £30 | |
| Heaven Must Have Sent You | 7" | Tamla Motown | TMG583 | 1966 | £10 | £20 | |
| It's Been A Long Time | 7" | Tamla Motown | TMG615 | 1967 | £6 | £12 | |
| Put Yourself In My Place | 7" | Tamla Motown | TMG551 | 1966 | £15 | £30 | |
| Put Yourself In My Place | 7" | Tamla Motown | TMG642 | 1968 | £4 | £8 | |

## ELIAS & HIS ZIG ZAG JIVE FLUTES

| | | | | | | | |
|---|---|---|---|---|---|---|---|
| Tom Hark | 7" | Columbia | DB4109 | 1958 | £1.50 | £4 | |

## ELIAS HULK

| | | | | | | | |
|---|---|---|---|---|---|---|---|
| Unchained | LP | Youngblood | SSYB8 | 1970 | £75 | £150 | |

## ELIZABETH

| | | | | | | | |
|---|---|---|---|---|---|---|---|
| Elizabeth | LP | Vanguard | SVRL19010 | 1968 | £30 | £60 | |

## ELLEDGE, JIMMY

| | | | | | | | |
|---|---|---|---|---|---|---|---|
| Funny How Time Slips Away | 7" EP | RCA | RCX7132 | 1964 | £5 | £10 | |
| Pink Dally Rue | 7" | Hickory | 451363 | 1965 | £1.50 | £4 | |
| Swanee River Rocket | 7" | RCA | RCA1274 | 1962 | £2.50 | £6 | |

## ELLIE POP

| | | | | | | | | |
|---|---|---|---|---|---|---|---|---|
| Ellie Pop | LP | Mainstream | S6115 | 1968 | £30 | £60 | | US |

## ELLINGTON, DUKE

| | | | | | | | | |
|---|---|---|---|---|---|---|---|---|
| Anatomy Of A Murder | LP | Philips | BBL7338 | 1959 | £6 | £15 | | |
| Anatomy Of A Murder | LP | Philips | SBBL514 | 1960 | £6 | £15 | | |
| At His Very Best | LP | RCA | RD27133 | 1959 | £6 | £15 | | |
| At Newport | LP | Philips | BBL7133 | 1957 | £6 | £15 | | |
| At The Bal Masque | LP | Philips | BBL7315/SBBL543 | 1960 | £5 | £12 | | |
| Back To Back | LP | HMV | CLP1316 | 1959 | £6 | £15 | with Johnny Hodges | |
| Black, Brown And Beige | LP | Philips | BBL7251/SBBL506 | 1958 | £4 | £10 | | |
| Blues In Orbit | LP | Philips | BBL7381/SBBL567 | 1960 | £5 | £12 | | |
| Blues Serenade | 10" LP | HMV | DLP1172 | 1958 | £6 | £15 | | |
| Caravan | 7" EP | RCA | RCX1022 | 1959 | £2 | £5 | | |
| Cosmic Scene | LP | Philips | BBL7287 | 1959 | £8 | £20 | | |
| Dance To The Duke | 7" EP | Capitol | EAP1004 | 1957 | £2 | £5 | | |
| Dance To The Duke | 7" EP | Capitol | EAP1637 | 1956 | £2 | £5 | | |
| Dance To The Duke No. 2 | 7" EP | Capitol | EAP2637 | 1956 | £2 | £5 | | |
| Dance To The Duke No. 3 | 7" EP | Capitol | EAP3637 | 1956 | £2 | £5 | | |
| Drum Is A Woman | LP | Philips | BBL7179 | 1957 | £6 | £15 | | |
| Duke – 1926 | 10" LP | London | AL3551 | 1956 | £8 | £20 | | |
| Duke Ellington | 7" EP | RCA | RCX1006 | 1958 | £2 | £5 | | |
| Duke Ellington | 10" LP | Philips | BBR8060 | 1955 | £10 | £25 | | |
| Duke Ellington – Betty Roche | 7" EP | Philips | BBE12002 | 1955 | £2 | £5 | | |
| Duke Ellington – Billy Strayhorn | 7" EP | Vogue | EPV1051 | 1955 | £2 | £5 | | |
| Duke Ellington And Al Hibbler | 7" EP | HMV | 7EG8158 | 1955 | £2 | £5 | | |
| Duke Ellington And His Orchestra | 7" EP | HMV | 7EG8033 | 1954 | £2 | £5 | | |
| Duke Ellington And His Orchestra Vol. 1 | 10" LP | Vogue Coral | LRA10027 | 1955 | £8 | £20 | | |
| Duke Ellington And His Orchestra Vol. 2 | 10" LP | Vogue Coral | LRA10028 | 1955 | £8 | £20 | | |
| Duke Ellington And Jimmy Blanton | 7" EP | HMV | 7EG8189 | 1956 | £2 | £5 | | |
| Duke Ellington And The Coronets | 7" EP | Vogue | EPV1060 | 1955 | £2 | £5 | | |
| Duke Ellington And The Coronets | 10" LP | Vogue | LDE035 | 1953 | £8 | £20 | | |
| Duke Ellington Orchestra | 10" LP | Philips | BBR8086 | 1956 | £10 | £25 | | |
| Duke Ellington Presents | LP | London | LTZN15078 | 1957 | £6 | £15 | | |
| Duke Ellington Presents | LP | Parlophone | PMC1136 | 1961 | £5 | £12 | | |
| Duke Ellington Presents Ivie Anderson | 7" EP | HMV | 7EG8209 | 1957 | £2 | £5 | | |
| Duke In London | 7" EP | Decca | DFE6376 | 1957 | £2 | £5 | | |
| Duke Plays Ellington | 7" EP | Capitol | EAP1477 | 1954 | £2 | £5 | | |
| Duke Plays Ellington | 10" LP | Capitol | LC6670 | 1954 | £8 | £20 | | |
| Duke Plays Ellington Part 2 | 7" EP | Capitol | EAP2477 | 1954 | £2 | £5 | | |
| Ellington '55 | LP | Capitol | LCT6008 | 1955 | £6 | £15 | | |
| Ellington '55 Part 1 | 7" EP | Capitol | EAP1521 | 1955 | £2 | £5 | | |
| Ellington '55 Part 2 | 7" EP | Capitol | EAP2521 | 1955 | £2 | £5 | | |
| Ellington '55 Part 3 | 7" EP | Capitol | EAP3521 | 1955 | £2 | £5 | | |
| Ellington Highlights, 1940 | 10" LP | HMV | DLP1034 | 1954 | £8 | £20 | | |
| Ellington Jazz Party | LP | Philips | BBL7324/SBBL516 | 1959 | £4 | £10 | | |
| Ellington Showcase | LP | Capitol | T679 | 1956 | £6 | £15 | | |
| Ellington Sidemen | LP | Philips | BBL7163 | 1957 | £6 | £15 | | |
| Ellington Uptown | LP | Philips | BBL7003 | 1954 | £6 | £15 | | |
| Ellington Uptown | LP | Philips | BBL7443 | 1961 | £5 | £12 | | |
| Ellington's Greatest | 10" LP | HMV | DLP1007 | 1953 | £8 | £20 | | |
| Festival Session | LP | Philips | BBL7355/SBBL556 | 1960 | £5 | £12 | | |
| Great Ellington Soloists | 10" LP | HMV | DLP1025 | 1954 | £8 | £20 | | |
| Harlem Twist | 7" EP | Fontana | TFE17117 | 1959 | £2 | £5 | | |
| Historically Speaking | LP | Parlophone | PMC1116 | 1960 | £4 | £10 | | |
| Historically Speaking – The Duke | LP | London | LTZN15029 | 1957 | £6 | £15 | | |
| In A Mellotone | LP | RCA | RD27134 | 1959 | £6 | £15 | | |
| Jazz Cocktail | 10" LP | Columbia | 33S1044 | 1954 | £8 | £20 | | |
| Masterpieces By Ellington | LP | Columbia | 33SX1022 | 1954 | £10 | £25 | | |
| Mood Ellington | 10" LP | Philips | BBR8044 | 1955 | £8 | £20 | | |
| Newport 1958 | LP | Philips | BBL7279 | 1959 | £4 | £10 | | |

| Newport Jazz Festival | LP | Philips | BBL7152 | 1957 | £6 | £15 | ........ side 2 by Buck Clayton |
|---|---|---|---|---|---|---|---|
| Nutcracker Suite | LP | Philips | BBL7418/SBBL594 | 1961 | £6 | £15 | |
| Perfume Suite/Black Brown And Beige | 10" LP | HMV | DLP1070 | 1955 | £8 | £20 | |
| Piano In THe Background | LP | Philips | BBL7460 | 1961 | £5 | £12 | |
| Premiered By Ellington | 10" LP | Capitol | LC6616 | 1953 | £8 | £20 | |
| Saturday Night Function | 10" LP | HMV | DLP1094 | 1955 | £8 | £20 | |
| Side By Side | LP | HMV | CLP1374 | 1961 | £6 | £15 | .. with Johnny Hodges |
| Solitude | LP | Philips | BBL7229 | 1958 | £6 | £15 | |
| Such Sweet Thunder | LP | Philips | BBL7203 | 1958 | £6 | £15 | |
| Such Sweet Thunder | LP | Realm | RM52421 | 1967 | £5 | £12 | |
| Ultra Deluxe | 7" EP | Capitol | EAP120114 | 1961 | £2 | £5 | |

## ELLINGTON, MARC

| Marc Ellington | LP | Philips | SBL7883 | 1969 | £10 | £25 | |
|---|---|---|---|---|---|---|---|
| Marc Time | LP | Xtra | XTRA1154 | 1972 | £5 | £12 | |
| Question Of Roads | LP | Philips | 6308120 | 1972 | £6 | £15 | |
| Rains/Reins Of Change | LP | B&C | CAS193 | 1971 | £6 | £15 | |
| Restoration | LP | Philips | 6308143 | 1972 | £6 | £15 | |

## ELLINGTON, RAY

| ABC Boogie | 7" | Columbia | SCM5147 | 1954 | £4 | £8 | |
|---|---|---|---|---|---|---|---|
| All's Going Well | 7" | Columbia | SCM5088 | 1954 | £1.50 | £4 | |
| Charlie Brown | 7" | Pye | 7N15189 | 1959 | £1.50 | £4 | |
| Cloudburst | 7" | Columbia | SCM5199 | 1955 | £1.50 | £4 | |
| Giddy-Up A Ding Dong | 7" | Columbia | DB3838 | 1956 | £4 | £8 | |
| Keep That Coffee Hot | 7" | Columbia | SCM5274 | 1956 | £1.50 | £4 | |
| Ko Ko Mo | 7" | Columbia | SCM5177 | 1955 | £4 | £8 | |
| Little Red Monkey | 7" | Columbia | SCM5050 | 1953 | £1.50 | £4 | |
| Long Black Nylons | 7" | Columbia | DB4057 | 1958 | £2.50 | £6 | |
| Madison | 7" | Ember | EMBS102 | 1960 | £1.50 | £4 | |
| Owl Song | 7" | Columbia | SCM5104 | 1954 | £1.50 | £4 | |
| Play It Boy Play | 7" | Columbia | SCM5187 | 1955 | £1.50 | £4 | |
| Stranded In The Jungle | 7" | Columbia | DB3821 | 1956 | £4 | £8 | |
| That Rock 'n' Rollin' Man | 7" | Columbia | DB3905 | 1957 | £4 | £8 | |
| Who's Got The Money? | 7" | Columbia | SCM5250 | 1956 | £1.50 | £4 | |

## ELLIOT, DEREK & DOROTHY

| Derek And Dorothy Elliot | LP | Trailer | LER2023 | 1972 | £4 | £10 | |
|---|---|---|---|---|---|---|---|
| Yorkshire Relish | LP | Tradition | TSR025 | 1976 | £4 | £10 | |

## ELLIOT, JACK

| Jack Elliot Of Birtley | LP | Leader | LER4001 | 1969 | £4 | £10 | |
|---|---|---|---|---|---|---|---|

## ELLIOTS OF BIRTLEY

| Elliots Of Birtley | LP | Folkways | FG3565 | 1961 | £10 | £25 | US |
|---|---|---|---|---|---|---|---|
| Musical Portrait Of A Durham Mining Family | LP | XTRA | XTRA1091 | 1969 | £5 | £12 | |

## ELLIOTT, BERN

| Guess Who | 7" | Decca | F12051 | 1965 | £1.50 | £4 | |
|---|---|---|---|---|---|---|---|
| Voodoo Woman | 7" | Decca | F12171 | 1965 | £1.50 | £4 | |

## ELLIOTT, BERN & THE CLAN

| Good Times | 7" | Decca | F11970 | 1964 | £1.50 | £4 | |
|---|---|---|---|---|---|---|---|

## ELLIOTT, BERN & THE FENMEN

| Bern Elliott & The Fenmen Play | 7" EP | Decca | DFE8561 | 1964 | £7.50 | £15 | |
|---|---|---|---|---|---|---|---|
| Money | 7" | Decca | F11770 | 1963 | £1.50 | £4 | |
| New Orleans | 7" | Decca | F11852 | 1964 | £1.50 | £4 | |

## ELLIOTT, BILL & ELASTIC OZ BAND

| God Save Us | 7" | Apple | 36 | 1971 | £2.50 | £6 | |
|---|---|---|---|---|---|---|---|
| God Save Us | 7" | Apple | 36 | 1971 | £7.50 | £15 | ........... picture sleeve |

## ELLIOTT, DON

| Don Elliott | 10" LP | London | LZN14037 | 1957 | £4 | £10 | |
|---|---|---|---|---|---|---|---|
| Don Elliott And His Choir | LP | Brunswick | LAT8263 | 1958 | £4 | £10 | |
| Musical Offering | LP | HMV | CLP1186 | 1958 | £4 | £10 | |
| Six Valves | 10" LP | London | LZU14034 | 1956 | £15 | £30 | ... with Rusty Dedrick |

## ELLIOTT, JACK

| Jack Elliott | LP | Leader | LEA4001 | 1969 | £6 | £15 | |
|---|---|---|---|---|---|---|---|

## ELLIOTT, MARI

| Silly Billy | 7" | GTO | GT58 | 1976 | £5 | £10 | |
|---|---|---|---|---|---|---|---|

## ELLIOTT, PETER

| Devotion | 7" | Parlophone | R4457 | 1958 | £1.50 | £4 | |
|---|---|---|---|---|---|---|---|
| To The Aisle | 7" | Parlophone | R4355 | 1957 | £1.50 | £4 | |

## ELLIOTT, RAMBLING JACK

| Blues And Country | 7" EP | Collector | JEA6 | 1964 | £2.50 | £6 | |
|---|---|---|---|---|---|---|---|
| Bull Durham Sacks And Railroad Tracks | LP | Reprise | RSLP6387 | 1970 | £4 | £10 | |
| Country Style | LP | Stateside | SL10143 | 1965 | £4 | £10 | |
| In London | LP | Columbia | 33SX1166 | 1959 | £10 | £25 | |
| In London | LP | Encore | ENC194 | 196– | £6 | £15 | |
| Jack Elliott | LP | Fontana | TFL6044 | 1965 | £4 | £10 | |

| Title | Format | Label | Cat No | Year | Price1 | Price2 | Notes |
|---|---|---|---|---|---|---|---|
| Jack Takes The Floor | 10" LP | Topic | 10T15 | 1958 | £10 | £25 | |
| Kids Stuff | 7" EP | Columbia | SEG8046 | 1960 | £2 | £5 | |
| More Pretty Girls | 7" | Fontana | TF575 | 1965 | £1.50 | £4 | |
| Muleskinner | LP | Topic | 12T106 | 1964 | £6 | £15 | |
| Rambling Boys | 10" LP | Topic | 10T14 | 1958 | £10 | £25 | ...with Derroll Adams |
| Rambling Jack Elliott | LP | Vanguard | | 1964 | £4 | £10 | US |
| Rambling Jack Elliott | 7" EP | Collector | JEA5 | 1963 | £2.50 | £6 | |
| Roll On Buddy | LP | Topic | 12T105 | 1964 | £6 | £15 | ...with Derroll Adams |
| Rusty Jigs And Sandy Sam | 7" | Columbia | DB7593 | 1965 | £1.50 | £4 | |
| Sings | LP | Columbia | 33SX1291 | 1961 | £6 | £15 | |
| Sings The Songs Of Woody Guthrie | LP | Stateside | SL10167 | 1966 | £4 | £10 | |
| Talking Woody Guthrie | LP | Topic | 12T93 | 1963 | £6 | £15 | |
| Woody Guthrie's Blues | 8' LP | Topic | T5 | 195– | £10 | £25 | |

## ELLIOTT, RON

| Title | Format | Label | Cat No | Year | Price1 | Price2 | Notes |
|---|---|---|---|---|---|---|---|
| Candlestick Maker | LP | Warner Bros | WS1833 | 1969 | £6 | £15 | US |

## ELLIOTT, SHAWN

| Title | Format | Label | Cat No | Year | Price1 | Price2 | Notes |
|---|---|---|---|---|---|---|---|
| My Girl | 7" | Columbia | DB7418 | 1964 | £1.50 | £4 | |

## ELLIOTT'S SUNSHINE

| Title | Format | Label | Cat No | Year | Price1 | Price2 | Notes |
|---|---|---|---|---|---|---|---|
| It Is Too Late | 7" | Philips | BF1649 | 1968 | £1.50 | £4 | |

## ELLIS, ALTON

| Title | Format | Label | Cat No | Year | Price1 | Price2 | Notes |
|---|---|---|---|---|---|---|---|
| Ain't That Loving You | 7" | Treasure Isle | TI7016 | 1967 | £5 | £10 | Tommy McCook B side |
| Ain't That Loving You | 7" | Trojan | TR004 | 1967 | £5 | £10 | Tommy McCook B side |
| Better Example | 7" | Bamboo | BAM2 | 1969 | £1.50 | £4 | Duke Morgan B side |
| Blessings Of Love | 7" | Doctor Bird | DB1044 | 1966 | £5 | £10 | |
| Breaking Up | 7" | Trojan | TR642 | 1968 | £4 | £8 | |
| Bye Bye Love | 7" | Nu Beat | NB013 | 1968 | £2.50 | £6 | Monty Morris B side |
| Change Of Plans | 7" | Studio One | SO2084 | 1969 | £6 | £12 | Cables B side |
| Cry Tough | 7" | Island | WI3046 | 1967 | £5 | £10 | Tommy McCook B side |
| Dance Crasher | 7" | Island | WI239 | 1965 | £5 | £10 | Baba Brooks B side |
| Diana | 7" | Duke | DU14 | 1969 | £1.50 | £4 | |
| Diana | 7" | Gas | GAS105 | 1969 | £1.50 | £4 | |
| Don't Gamble With Love | 7" | Island | WI230 | 1965 | £5 | £10 | |
| Duke Of Earl | 7" | Treasure Isle | TI7010 | 1967 | £5 | £10 | |
| Easy Squeeze | 7" | Studio One | SO2003 | 1967 | £6 | £12 | Mr. Foundation B side |
| Fool | 7" | Coxsone | CS7071 | 1968 | £5 | £10 | Soul Vendors B side |
| Girl I've Got A Date | 7" | Doctor Bird | DB1059 | 1966 | £5 | £10 | Lyn Taitt & Tommy McCook B side |
| Greatest Hits | LP | Count Shelly | SSLO02 | 1973 | £8 | £20 | |
| I Am Just A Guy | 7" | Studio One | SO2028 | 1967 | £6 | £12 | Soul Vendors B side |
| I Am Still In Love | 7" | Studio One | SO2020 | 1967 | £6 | £12 | Roy Richards B side |
| I Can't Stand It | 7" | Nu Beat | NB010 | 1968 | £2.50 | £6 | |
| I Can't Stand It | 7" | Trojan | TR630 | 1968 | £4 | £8 | |
| La–La Means I Love You | 7" | Nu Beat | NB014 | 1968 | £2.50 | £6 | |
| Laba Laba Reggae | 7" | Trojan | TR634 | 1968 | £4 | £8 | |
| Live And Learn | 7" | Studio One | SO2037 | 1968 | £6 | £12 | Heptones B side |
| Message | 7" | Pama | PM707 | 1968 | £2.50 | £6 | |
| Mr. Soul Of Jamaica | LP | Treasure Isle | 013 | 196– | £50 | £100 | |
| My Time Is The Right Time | 7" | Pama | PM717 | 1968 | £2.50 | £6 | Johnny Moore B side |
| Oowee Baby | 7" | Treasure Isle | TI7030 | 1968 | £5 | £10 | |
| Preacher | 7" | Doctor Bird | DB1049 | 1966 | £5 | £10 | Lyn Taitt B side |
| Rock Steady | 7" | Treasure Isle | TI7004 | 1967 | £5 | £10 | Tommy McCook B side |
| Shake It | 7" | Doctor Bird | DB1055 | 1966 | £5 | £10 | Silvertones B side |
| Sings Rock And Soul | LP | Coxsone | CSL8008 | 1967 | £50 | £100 | |
| Sunday Coming | LP | Bamboo | BDLPS214 | 1971 | £10 | £25 | |
| What Does It Take | 7" | Duke Reid | DR2501 | 1970 | £1.50 | £4 | Tommy McCook B side |
| Willow Tree | 7" | Treasure Isle | TI7044 | 1968 | £5 | £10 | |
| Wise Birds Follow Spring | 7" | Trojan | TR009 | 1967 | £5 | £10 | Tommy McCook B side |
| You Made Me So Very Happy | 7" | Duke Reid | DR2512 | 1970 | £1.50 | £4 | Tommy McCook B side |

## ELLIS, BOBBY

| Title | Format | Label | Cat No | Year | Price1 | Price2 | Notes |
|---|---|---|---|---|---|---|---|
| Dollar A Head | 7" | Island | WI3136 | 1968 | £5 | £10 | Rudy Mills B side |
| Emperor | 7" | Island | WI3089 | 1967 | £5 | £10 | Derrick Harriott B side |
| Feeling Peckish | 7" | Island | WI3091 | 1967 | £5 | £10 | Keith & Tex B side |
| Now We Know | 7" | Island | WI3092 | 1967 | £5 | £10 | Rudy Mills B side |
| Shuntin' | 7" | Island | WI3135 | 1968 | £5 | £10 | Derrick Harriott B side |

## ELLIS, DON

Don Ellis's updating of the big band sound won many fans from the progressive rock genre, who could readily appreciate Ellis's musical games with unusual time signatures as well the electronics he introduced via his specially built four-valve amplified trumpet. *Autumn* was produced by Al Kooper, who must have realized that his own big band experiments with Blood, Sweat and Tears were made to sound a little ordinary by comparison. Drummer Ralph Humphrey went from Don Ellis to the only other band that could possibly provide him with the same rhythmic challenge – that of Frank Zappa.

| Title | Format | Label | Cat No | Year | Price1 | Price2 | Notes |
|---|---|---|---|---|---|---|---|
| At Fillmore | LP | CBS | 66261 | 1969 | £8 | £20 | double |
| Autumn | LP | CBS | 63503 | 1968 | £6 | £15 | |
| Don Ellis Orchestra Live | LP | Liberty | LBL/LBS83060 | 1968 | £8 | £20 | |

| | | | | | | | |
|---|---|---|---|---|---|---|---|
| Electric Bath | LP | CBS | 63230 | 1968 £6 | £15 | |
| Goes Underground | LP | CBS | 63680 | 1969 £5 | £12 | |
| Haiku | LP | BASF | MC25341 | 1974 £6 | £15 | German |
| Live At Monterey | LP | Fontana | (S)TL5426 | 1967 £8 | £20 | |
| Shock Treatment | LP | CBS | 63356 | 1968 £6 | £15 | |
| Soaring | LP | BASF | 21251233 | 1973 £6 | £15 | German |
| Tears Of Joy | LP | Columbia | CG30927 | 1971 £6 | £15 | US |

## ELLIS, HERB

| | | | | | | |
|---|---|---|---|---|---|---|
| Herb Ellis | LP | Columbia | 33CX10066 | 1957 £6 | £15 | |
| Meets Jimmy Giuffre | LP | HMV | CLP1337 | 1960 £5 | £12 | |
| Nothing But The Blues | LP | Columbia | 33CX10139 | 1959 £6 | £15 | |

## ELLIS, HORTENSE

| | | | | | | |
|---|---|---|---|---|---|---|
| Groovy Kind Of Love | 7" | Coxsone | CS7033 | 1968 £5 | £10 | Three Tops B side |
| I'll Come Softly | 7" | R&B | JB101 | 1963 £5 | £10 | |
| I've Been A Fool | 7" | Blue Beat | BB295 | 1965 £6 | £12 | |
| Midnight Train | 7" | Blue Beat | BB119 | 1962 £6 | £12 | Duke Reid B side |

## ELLIS, JIMMY

| | | | | | | |
|---|---|---|---|---|---|---|
| Ellis Sings Elvis By Request | LP | Boblo | 78829 | £8 | £20 | US |

## ELLIS, LARRY

| | | | | | | |
|---|---|---|---|---|---|---|
| Nothing You Can Do | 7" | Felsted | AF110 | 1958 £2.50 | £6 | |

## ELLIS, MATTHEW

| | | | | | | |
|---|---|---|---|---|---|---|
| Am I | LP | Regal Zonophone | SRZA8505 | 1971 £8 | £20 | |
| Matthew Ellis | LP | Regal Zonophone | SRZA8501 | 1971 £4 | £10 | |

## ELLIS, SHIRLEY

| | | | | | | |
|---|---|---|---|---|---|---|
| Clapping Song | 7" | London | HLR9961 | 1965 £1.50 | £4 | |
| Ever See A Diver Kiss His Wife | 7" | London | HLR10021 | 1966 £1.50 | £4 | |
| In Action | LP | Congress | CGL/CGS3002 | 1964 £6 | £15 | US |
| Name Game | LP | Congress | CGL/CGS3003 | 1965 £6 | £15 | US |
| Name Game | 7" | London | HLR9946 | 1965 £1.50 | £4 | |
| Nitty Gritty | 7" | London | HLR9824 | 1963 £1.50 | £4 | |
| Puzzle Song | 7" | London | HLR9973 | 1965 £1.50 | £4 | |
| Soul Time | LP | CBS | (S)BPG63044 | 1967 £6 | £15 | |
| Soul Time | 7" | CBS | 202606 | 1967 £4 | £8 | |
| Sugar Let's Shing A Ling | 7" | CBS | 2817 | 1967 £2.50 | £6 | |
| Sugar, Let's Shing A Ling | LP | Columbia | CL2679/CS9479 | 1967 £6 | £15 | US |

## ELLIS, STEVE & THE STARFIRES

| | | | | | | |
|---|---|---|---|---|---|---|
| Steve Ellis Songbook | LP | IGL | 105 | 1967 £700 | £1000 | US |

## ELLIS, WAYGOOD

| | | | | | | |
|---|---|---|---|---|---|---|
| I Like What I'm Trying To Do | 7" | Polydor | 56729 | 1967 £4 | £8 | |

## ELLISON, ANDY

| | | | | | | |
|---|---|---|---|---|---|---|
| Been A Long Time | 7" | Track | 604018 | 1967 £12.50 | £25 | John's Children B side |
| Fool From Upper Eden | 7" | CBS | 3357 | 1968 £15 | £30 | |
| You Can't Do That | 7" | SNB | 553308 | 1968 £20 | £40 | |

## ELLISON, LORRAINE

| | | | | | | |
|---|---|---|---|---|---|---|
| Call Me Any Time You Need Some Lovin' | 7" | Mercury | 6052073 | 1971 £2 | £5 | |
| Stay With Me | LP | Warner Bros | WB1821 | 1970 £4 | £10 | |
| Stay With Me | 7" | Warner Bros | WB5850 | 1966 £2 | £5 | |
| Try A Little Bit Harder | 7" | Warner Bros | WB2094 | 1968 £1.50 | £4 | |

## ELLUFFANT

The most sought-after of the privately pressed albums issued in the Netherlands contains improvised music, recorded live on behalf of the drug-help organization Release. The keyboard/percussion duo played on equipment they had built themselves, which helped to give them a very individual sound.

| | | | | | | |
|---|---|---|---|---|---|---|
| Release Concert | LP | Disko Thiel | | 1972 £500 | £1000 | Dutch |

## ELMER GANTRY'S VELVET OPERA

Lead singer Dave Terry was reported in the press at the time as being the only man in the country legally allowed to smoke marijuana – having been prescribed it as a calming aid for an occasionally violent personality. The group's song 'Mary Jane' is by way of being a tribute to this state of affairs, but their finest three minutes is undoubtedly the driving 'Flames', which by rights should have been an enormous chart hit. The group's second album was recorded as just Velvet Opera, with Terry replaced by Paul Brett. Subsequently, the rhythm section of John Ford and Richard Hudson joined the Strawbs and later formed a successful band of their own, Hudson-Ford.

| | | | | | | |
|---|---|---|---|---|---|---|
| Elmer Gantry's Velvet Opera | LP | Direction | 863300 | 1968 £20 | £40 | |
| Flames | 7" | Direction | 583083 | 1967 £2 | £5 | |
| Mary Jane | 7" | Direction | 583481 | 1968 £1.50 | £4 | |
| Volcano | 7" | Direction | 583924 | 1969 £1.50 | £4 | |

## ELOY

| | | | | | | |
|---|---|---|---|---|---|---|
| Eloy | LP | Philips | 6305089 | 1971 £50 | £100 | bin cover |
| Inside | LP | Electrola | 1C06429479 | 1973 £4 | £10 | German |
| Planets | LP | Heavy Metal | HMIPD1 | 1982 £4 | £10 | picture disc |

## ELROY, JEFF & THE BLUE BOYS

| | | | | | | |
|---|---|---|---|---|---|---|
| Honey Machine | 7" | Philips | BF1533 | 1966 £6 | £12 | |

## ELVES
Amber Velvet.................................. 7" ..... MCA............. MU1114 ............... 1970 £1.50.....£4 ........................................

## EMANON
Raging Pain.................................. 7" ..... Clubland ......... SJP777 ................ 1977 £2.........£5

## EMBERS
Chelsea Boots ............................. 7" ..... Decca............. F11625 .............. 1963 £2.........£5

## EMBERS (2)
Rock And Roll Eleven ........................ LP..... JCP Recording  2006 ..................... ......£37.50....£75 ......................US

## EMBRYO
| | | | | | | | |
|---|---|---|---|---|---|---|---|
| Apo Calypso............................. | LP..... | April................ | 0010 | ......... | 1977 | £5.........£12 | German |
| Bad Heads And Bad Cats................... | LP..... | April................ | 005 | ......... | 1976 | £5.........£12 | German |
| Embryo's Rache............................ | LP..... | United Artists .. | UAS29239........ | | 1971 | £10.......£25 | German |
| Father, Son And Holy Ghosts .............. | LP..... | United Artists .. | UAS29344........ | | 1972 | £8.........£20 | German |
| Live .................................... | LP..... | April................ | 003 | ......... | 1976 | £5.........£12 | German |
| Opal..................................... | LP..... | Ohr ................ | OMM56003 ...... | | 1970 | £15.......£30 | German |
| Rocksession.............................. | LP..... | Brain ............. | 1036 | ......... | 1973 | £6.........£15 | German |
| Rocksession.............................. | LP..... | Brain ............. | 201109 ......... | | 1975 | £5.........£12 | German |
| Steig Aus ............................... | LP..... | Brain ............. | 1023 | ......... | 1973 | £6.........£15 | German |
| Surfin'.................................. | LP..... | BASF............ | 223853 ......... | | 1975 | £5.........£12 | German |
| We Keep On .............................. | LP..... | BASF............ | 20218653 ....... | | 1974 | £6.........£15 | German |

## EMERALD WEB
Dragon Wings And Wizard Tales............ LP ..... Stargate ...... AR4230 ............. 1979 £8.........£20 ..........................US

## EMERALDS
King Lonely The Blue ......................... 7" ..... Decca ............. F12304 ............. 1965 £10.......£20

## EMERGENCY
| | | | | | | | |
|---|---|---|---|---|---|---|---|
| Emergency................................ | LP..... | CBS............... | 64381 | .......... | 1971 | £5.........£12 | German |
| Entrance................................. | LP..... | CBS............... | 64928 | .......... | 1972 | £4.........£10 | German |
| Get To The Country ...................... | LP..... | Brain ............. | 1037 | .......... | 1973 | £4.........£10 | German |
| Gold Rock ............................... | LP..... | Brain ............. | 201104 ......... | | 1973 | £4.........£10 | German |
| No Compromise .......................... | LP..... | Brain ............. | 1052 | .......... | 1974 | £4.........£10 | German |

## EMERSON, KEITH
Christmas Album.............................. CD..... Priority ........... KEITHCD1 ........... 1988 £5.........£12

## EMERSON, LAKE & PALMER
| | | | | | | | |
|---|---|---|---|---|---|---|---|
| Emerson, Lake & Palmer.................... | LP ..... | Island ............. | ILPS9132 ....... | | 1970 | £4.........£10 | pink label |
| Fanfare For The Common Man................ | 12".... | Atlantic ........... | K10946T......... | | 1977 | £4.........£10 | |
| Pictures At An Exhibition ................ | LP..... | Mobile Fidelity | MFSL1031 ....... | | 1979 | £5.........£12 | US audiophile |
| Tarkus................................... | CD..... | Mobile Fidelity | UDCD598 ........ | | 1994 | £6.........£15 | US audiophile |
| Trilogy.................................. | CD..... | Mobile Fidelity | UDCD621 ........ | | 1995 | £6.........£15 | US audiophile |
| Works Volume One ....................... | LP..... | Atlantic ........... | | | 1976 | £4.........£10 | promo |

## EMILY
Old Stone Bridge ........................... 7" ..... Big Fun.......... 001 ..................... 1987 £1.50.....£4 ................flexi
Old Stone Bridge ........................... 7" ..... Sha La La ...... 007 ..................... 1987 £1.50.....£4 .....flexi, B side by
                                                                                                              Remember Fun

## EMJAYS
All My Love All My Life...................... 7" ..... Top Rank ....... JAR145............... 1959 £2.50.....£6 ....................................

## EMLYN, ENDAF
Hiraeth................................... LP..... Wren ............. WRL537........... 1972 £20.......£40 ....................................
Salem .................................... LP..... Sain ............... 1012M............ 1974 £8.........£20
Syrffio (Mewn Cariad) .................... LP..... Sain ............... 1051M............ 1976 £6.........£15

## EMMET SPICELAND
Emmet Spiceland........................... LP..... Page One ...... POLS011 .......... 1968 £25.......£50
Emmet Spiceland Album.................... LP..... Hawk ........... HALP166 .......... 1977 £20.......£40 ........................Irish
Lowlands ................................. 7" ..... Page One ...... POF089 ........... 1968 £1.50.....£4
So Long Marianne ........................ 7" ..... Page One ...... POF143 ........... 1969 £1.50.....£4

## EMOTIONS
Come Dance Baby ......................... 7" ..... London ......... HLR9640........... 1962 £4.........£8
Love ..................................... 7" ..... London ......... HLR9701........... 1963 £4.........£8
Somebody New ........................... 7" ..... Deep Soul ..... DS9104............ 1970 £2.50.....£6
Story Untold.............................. 7" ..... Stateside ........ SS237............. 1963 £2.50.....£6

## EMOTIONS (2)
Careless Hands ........................... 7" ..... Caltone........... TONE120.......... 1968 £4.........£8
Rainbow................................. 7" ..... Caltone........... TONE100.......... 1967 £4.........£8
Rudeboy Confession .................... 7" ..... Ska Beat ........ JB263............. 1966 £5.........£10
Rumbay .................................. 7" ..... High Note ...... HS026............. 1969 £1.50.....£4
Soulful Music ............................ 7" ..... Caltone........... TONE118.......... 1968 £4.........£8
Storm.................................... 7" ..... High Note ...... HS018............. 1969 £1.50.....£4

## EMPERORS
Karate ................................... 7" ..... Pama ............. PM786............. 1969 £1.50.....£4
Karate ................................... 7" ..... Stateside ........ SS565............. 1966 £2.50.....£6

## EMTIDI

| | | | | | | | |
|---|---|---|---|---|---|---|---|
| Emtidi | LP | Thorofon | ATH109 | 1970 | £30 | £60 | German |
| Saat | LP | Pilz | 20290778 | 1972 | £20 | £40 | German |

## ENCHANTED FOREST

| | | | | | | | |
|---|---|---|---|---|---|---|---|
| You're Never Gonna Get My Lovin' | 7" | Stateside | SS2080 | 1968 | £1.50 | £4 | |

## ENCHANTERS

| | | | | | | | |
|---|---|---|---|---|---|---|---|
| We Got Love | 7" | Warner Bros | WB2054 | 1967 | £2 | £5 | |

## END

The End were managed and produced by Bill Wyman, but his patronage brought them little success. A change of name to Tucky Buzzard brought more recordings in the seventies, but only a small increase in sales.

| | | | | | | | |
|---|---|---|---|---|---|---|---|
| I Can't Get Any Joy | 7" | Philips | BF1444 | 1965 | £4 | £8 | |
| Introspection | LP | Decca | LK/SKL5015 | 1969 | £37.50 | £75 | |
| Shades Of Orange | 7" | Decca | F12750 | 1968 | £7.50 | £15 | |

## ENDLE ST. CLOUD

| | | | | | | | |
|---|---|---|---|---|---|---|---|
| Thank You All Very Much | LP | International Artists | IALP12 | 1970 | £20 | £40 | US |

## ENDSLEY, MELVIN

| | | | | | | | |
|---|---|---|---|---|---|---|---|
| I Got A Feeling | 7" | RCA | RCA1051 | 1958 | £7.50 | £15 | |
| I Like Your Kind Of Love | 7" | RCA | RCA1004 | 1957 | £10 | £20 | |

## ENERGY

| | | | | | | | |
|---|---|---|---|---|---|---|---|
| Energy | LP | Harvest | 34893 | 1974 | £10 | £25 | Spanish |

## ENEVOLDSEN, BOB

| | | | | | | | |
|---|---|---|---|---|---|---|---|
| Bob Enevoldsen Quintet | 10" LP | London | LZU14035 | 1956 | £20 | £40 | |

## ENFORCERS

| | | | | | | | |
|---|---|---|---|---|---|---|---|
| Musical Fever | 7" | Blue Cat | BS120 | 1968 | £4 | £8 | Ed Nangle B side |

## ENGEL, SCOTT

| | | | | | | | |
|---|---|---|---|---|---|---|---|
| Charlie Bop | 7" | Vogue | V9150 | 1959 | £75 | £150 | |
| Living End | 7" | Vogue | V9145 | 1959 | £75 | £150 | |
| Paper Doll | 7" | Vogue | V9125 | 1958 | £75 | £150 | |
| Scott Engel | 7" EP | Liberty | LEP2261 | 1966 | £10 | £20 | |

## ENGEL, SCOTT & JOHN STEWART

| | | | | | | | |
|---|---|---|---|---|---|---|---|
| I Only Came To Dance With You | LP | Tower | ST5026 | 1965 | £10 | £25 | US |
| I Only Came To Dance With You | 7" | Capitol | CL15440 | 1966 | £2.50 | £6 | |

## ENGLAND

| | | | | | | | |
|---|---|---|---|---|---|---|---|
| England | LP | Deroy | DER1356 | 1976 | £150 | £250 | |
| Garden Shed | LP | Arista | ARTY153 | 1977 | £15 | £30 | |

## ENGLAND SISTERS

| | | | | | | | |
|---|---|---|---|---|---|---|---|
| Heartbeat | 7" | HMV | POP710 | 1960 | £7.50 | £15 | |

## ENGLAND'S GLORY

| | | | | | | | |
|---|---|---|---|---|---|---|---|
| England's Glory | LP | Venus | VEN105 | 1973 | £180 | £300 | pink label |

## ENGLEBERG, FRED

| | | | | | | | |
|---|---|---|---|---|---|---|---|
| Songs Of Fred Engleberg | LP | Elektra | EKL247 | 1964 | £5 | £12 | US |

## ENID

Masterminded by keyboard player Robert John Godfrey, the Enid have produced a succession of elaborately arranged progressive rock albums, in defiance of the prevailing fashions, for over twenty years. Noted for his refusal to compromise, Godfrey has devoted everything to his art, issuing albums himself and selling them by mail order when unable to find a regular record company. Though uncredited, the Enid were also the backing group on the earliest recordings by Kim Wilde.

| | | | | | | | |
|---|---|---|---|---|---|---|---|
| Dambusters March | 7" | Pye | 7P106 | 1979 | £2.50 | £6 | |
| Fand | LP | Enid | ENID9 | 1985 | £4 | £10 | |
| Fool | 7" | Pye | 7P187 | 1980 | £2 | £5 | |
| Golden Earrings | 7" | EMI | EMI5109 | 1980 | £2 | £5 | |
| Golden Earrings | 7" | EMI | INTS540 | 1977 | £2.50 | £6 | |
| Heigh Ho | 7" | Bronze | BRO134 | 1981 | £1.50 | £4 | |
| In The Region Of The Summer Stars | LP | Buk | BULP2014 | 1977 | £4 | £10 | Decca distribution |
| Jubilee | 7" | EMI | INT534 | 1977 | £1.50 | £4 | |
| Live At Hammersmith Vol. 1 | LP | Enid | ENID1 | 1984 | £4 | £10 | |
| Live At Hammersmith Vol. 2 | LP | Enid | ENID2 | 1984 | £4 | £10 | |
| Liverpool Album | LP | The Stand | LE1 | 198– | £4 | £10 | |
| Lovers | 7" | Buk | BUK3002 | 1976 | £4 | £8 | |
| Salome | LP | Enid | ENID10 | 1986 | £4 | £10 | |
| Salome | CD-s | Wonderful Music Co. | ENID2999 | 1990 | £2 | £5 | |
| Six Pieces | LP | Enid | ENID4 | 1984 | £4 | £10 | |
| Six Pieces | LP | Pye | NH116 | 1979 | £4 | £10 | |
| Spell | LP | Enid | ENID8 | 1984 | £4 | £10 | |
| The Stand | LP | The Stand | THESTAND1 | 1983 | £10 | £25 | 2 x 45rpm discs |
| The Stand 2 | LP | The Stand | STAND2 | 1985 | £10 | £25 | |
| Then There Were None | 7" | Rak | RAK349 | 1982 | £1.50 | £4 | |
| Touch Me | LP | Enid | ENID5 | 1984 | £4 | £10 | |

When You Wish Upon A Star................. 7" ...... Bronze ............ BRO127 ................ 1981 £1.50........£4 ..........................

## ENNIS, RAY & THE BLUE JEANS
What Have They Done To Hazel ............. 7" ...... Columbia ........ DB8431 ................ 1968 £7.50........£15

## ENNIS, SEAMUS
Bonnie Bunch Of Roses ........................ LP ..... Tradition........ TLP1013 ................ 1959 £10........£25
Feidlim Tonn Ri's Castle ...................... LP ..... Claddagh........ CC19.................... 1977 £5.........£12 ...................Irish
Forty Years Of Irish Piping.................. LP ..... Free Reed ...... FR001/2 ........ 1976 £10........£25 .................double
Fox Chase ......................................... LP ..... Tara............... 1009 .................... 1977 £5.........£12 ...................Irish
Irish Pipe And Tin Whistle Songs ........ LP ..... Olympic....... ALTLAS6129 ....... 1976 £5.........£12 ....................US
Masters Of Irish Music ........................ LP ..... Leader............ LEA2003 ............... 1969 £6.........£15
Pure Drop ........................................ LP ..... Tara............... 1002 .................... 1973 £5.........£12 ...................Irish
Wandering Minstrel.............................. LP ..... Topic ........... 12TS250 ............... 1974 £5.........£12

## ENO, BRIAN
When his task was to make some sense of the controls of a distinctly non-user-friendly synthesizer as a member of Roxy Music, Brian Eno always used to describe himself as a non-musician. If this was in any way an accurate description, then the lack of preconceptions has clearly been an advantage for Eno, for his solo career has been distinguished by some very interesting ideas. The novelty of his approach is typified by his experiments with creative muzak – what he calls 'ambient' music – where the listener is not intended to listen at all closely. Eno's career has thrown up one ultra-rarity: an early, alternative version of his *Music For Films* LP, which was limited to around a hundred copies.

Another Green World.......................... CD-s .. Virgin ............ CDT41 ................ 1989 £2...........£5 ................3" single
Before And After Science .................... LP ..... Polydor.......... 2302071 ............... 1977 £4...........£10 ........with 4 prints
Discreet Music .................................. LP ..... Obscure ........ OBS3 .................... 1975 £4...........£10
Here Come The Warm Jets ................. CD ..... Editions EG.... EGCD11 ............... 1986 £5...........£12
Music For Films ................................ LP ..... Editions EG.... EGM1................... 1976 £100..... £200 . *different tracks to '78 issue*
My Life In The Bush Of Ghosts............ CD ..... Editions EG.... EGCD48 ............... 1987 £5...........£12 ... *with David Byrne*
My Squelchy Life ............................... CD ..... Opal .............. ...................... 1990 £15........£30 ............ *demo only*
One Word ......................................... CD-s .. Land .............. LANDH04 ........... 1990 £2...........£5 .......... *with John Cale*
Taking Tiger Mountain By Strategy ......... CD ..... Editions EG.... EGCD17 ............... 1986 £5...........£12
Thursday Afternoon............................. CD ..... Editions EG.... EGCD64 ............... 1987 £5...........£12

## ENOS & SHEILA
La La Bamba ...................................... 7" ...... Blue Cat........ BS135 .................... 1968 £4...........£8
Tonight You're Mine ........................... 7" ...... Blue Cat........ BS138 .................... 1968 £4...........£8

## ENOUGH'S ENOUGH
Please Remember.:............................... 7" ...... Tattoo............ TT101 ................ 1968 £20........£40

## ENTICERS
Calling For Your Love......................... 7" ...... Atlantic .......... 2091136 ............... 1971 £2...........£5

## ENTWISTLE, JOHN
Backtrack 14 (The Ox) ........................ LP ..... Track ............. 2407014 ............... 1971 £5...........£12
Rigor Mortis Sets In ........................... LP ..... Track ............. 2406106 ............... 1973 £4...........£10
Too Late The Hero ............................. 7" ...... WEA ............. K79249P .............. 1981 £2...........£5 ... *autographed picture disc*

## ENYA
Caribbean Blue .................................. CD-s .. WEA ............. YZ604CD............ 1991 £2...........£5
Celts ............................................... CD ..... BBC ............. BBCCD605......... 1987 £5...........£12
Evening Falls .................................... CD-s .. WEA ............. YZ356CD............ 1988 £2...........£5
How Can I Keep From Singing ............. CD-s .. WEA ............. YZ635CD............ 1991 £2...........£5
I Want Tomorrow................................ CD-s .. BBC ............. CDRSL201 ........... 1987 £12.50....£25
Orinoco Flow .................................... CD-s .. WEA ............. YZ312CD............ 1988 £2...........£5
Storms In Africa ................................ CD-s .. WEA ............. YZ368CD............ 1989 £2...........£5 ................3" single
Storms In Africa ................................ CD-s .. WEA ............. YZ368CDX........... 1989 £6...........£15 ...........picture disc

## EPICS
Henry Long ....................................... 7" ...... CBS ............. 3564 .................... 1968 £1.50........£4
How Wrong Can You Be ..................... 7" ...... Pye ................ 7N17053 ............... 1966 £1.50........£4
There's No Pleasing You ..................... 7" ...... Pye ................ 7N15829 ............... 1965 £1.50........£4

## EPIDAURUS
Earthly Paradise ................................ LP ..... private............ E1004 ................ 1977 £50........£100 ................German

## EPIDERMIS
Genius Of Original Force..................... LP ..... Kerston ........... FK65063 ............ 1977 £10........£25 ................German

## EPILEPTICS
1970s Have Been Made In Hong Kong ...... 7" ...... Stortbeat ........ BEAT8 ................ 1979 £1.50........£4

## EPISODE SIX
Episode Six's pleasant but undistinguished harmony music would be very much less collectable were it not for the fact that the group's vocalist was Ian Gillan (and the bass player was Roger Glover), although the likes of 'Here There And Everywhere' are light years away from the dynamism of Deep Purple's 'Sweet Child In Time' and 'Speed King'.

Episode Six............................. 7" EP . ...................... ........................ 196– £100..... £200 ........ *Portuguese, best auctioned*
Here There And Everywhere .................. 7" EP. Pye ..... PNV24175 ........... 1966 £100..... £200 ................French
Here, There, And Everywhere.............. 7" ...... Pye ................ 7N17147 ............... 1966 £5.........£10
I Can See Through You ....................... LP ..... Pye ................ 260404 ................ 1969 £8...........£20 ....................US
I Can See Through You ....................... 7" ...... Pye ................ 7N17376 ............... 1967 £5...........£10
I Hear Trumpets Blow......................... 7" ...... Pye ................ 7N17110 ............... 1966 £5...........£10
I Will Warm Your Heart...................... 7" ...... Pye ................ 7N17194 ............... 1966 £10........£20 .....*with Sheila Carter*

| Title | Format | Label | Cat. No. | Year | Price 1 | Price 2 | Notes |
|---|---|---|---|---|---|---|---|
| Little One | 7" | MGM | MGM1409 | 1968 | £10 | £20 | |
| Love, Hate, Revenge | 7" | Pye | 7N17244 | 1967 | £7.50 | £15 | |
| Lucky Sunday | 7" | Chapter One | CH103 | 1968 | £5 | £10 | |
| Morning Dew | 7" | Pye | 7N17330 | 1967 | £5 | £10 | |
| Mozart Versus The Rest | 7" | Chapter One | CH104 | 1969 | £5 | £10 | |
| Put Yourself In My Place | 7" | Pye | 7N17018 | 1966 | £5 | £10 | |

## EPITAPH

| Title | Format | Label | Cat. No. | Year | Price 1 | Price 2 | Notes |
|---|---|---|---|---|---|---|---|
| Epitaph | LP | Polydor | 2371225 | 1971 | £6 | £15 | German |
| Outside The Law | LP | Membran | 221311 | 1974 | £5 | £12 | German |
| Stop, Look And Listen | LP | Polydor | 2371274 | 1972 | £5 | £12 | German |

## EPPERSON, MINNIE

| Title | Format | Label | Cat. No. | Year | Price 1 | Price 2 | Notes |
|---|---|---|---|---|---|---|---|
| Grab Your Clothes | 7" | Action | ACT4503 | 1968 | £2.50 | £6 | |

## EPPS, PRESTON

| Title | Format | Label | Cat. No. | Year | Price 1 | Price 2 | Notes |
|---|---|---|---|---|---|---|---|
| Bongo Bongo Bongo | LP | Original Sound | (S)8851 | 1960 | £6 | £15 | US |
| Bongo Bongo Bongo | 7" | Top Rank | JAR413 | 1960 | £1.50 | £4 | |
| Bongo Boogie | 7" | Top Rank | JAR345 | 1960 | £1.50 | £4 | |
| Bongo Rock | 7" | Top Rank | JAR140 | 1959 | £4 | £8 | |
| Surfin' Bongos | LP | Original Sound | (S)8872 | 1963 | £5 | £12 | US |

## EPSILON

| Title | Format | Label | Cat. No. | Year | Price 1 | Price 2 | Notes |
|---|---|---|---|---|---|---|---|
| Epsilon | LP | Bacillus | BLPS19070 | 1971 | £4 | £10 | German |
| Move On | LP | Bacillus | BLPS19078 | 1972 | £5 | £12 | German |
| Off | LP | Philips | 6305216 | 1974 | £4 | £10 | German |

## EQUALS

| Title | Format | Label | Cat. No. | Year | Price 1 | Price 2 | Notes |
|---|---|---|---|---|---|---|---|
| Baby Come Back | 7" EP | President | PTE1 | 1968 | £2 | £5 | |
| Equals | 7" EP | President | PTE2 | 1969 | £2 | £5 | |
| I Can See But You Don't Know | 7" | President | PT303 | 1970 | £4 | £8 | |
| Unequalled | LP | President | PTL1006 | 1967 | £4 | £10 | |

## EQUINOX

| Title | Format | Label | Cat. No. | Year | Price 1 | Price 2 | Notes |
|---|---|---|---|---|---|---|---|
| Hard Rock | LP | Boulevard | 4118 | 1973 | £6 | £15 | |

## EQUIPE 84

| Title | Format | Label | Cat. No. | Year | Price 1 | Price 2 | Notes |
|---|---|---|---|---|---|---|---|
| Auschwitz | 7" | Major Minor | MM517 | 1967 | £5 | £10 | |
| Dr. Jekyll And Mr. Hyde | LP | Ariston | ARLP12107 | 1973 | £8 | £20 | Italian |

## ERASURE

| Title | Format | Label | Cat. No. | Year | Price 1 | Price 2 | Notes |
|---|---|---|---|---|---|---|---|
| Abbaesque (Club Mixes) | 12" | Mute | ERAS4 | 1992 | £6 | £15 | promo |
| Am I Right | CD-s | Mute | CDMUTE134 | 1991 | £2 | £5 | |
| Blue Savannah | CD-s | Mute | LCDMUTE109 | 1990 | £2 | £5 | |
| Blue Savannah (Der Deutsche Mixes) | 12" | Mute | XL12MUTE109 | 1990 | £3 | £8 | |
| Blue Savannah (Deutsch Mix Part 1) | 12" | Mute | P12MUTE109 | 1990 | £2.50 | £6 | promo |
| Chains Of Love | CD-s | Mute | CDMUTE83 | 1988 | £2 | £5 | |
| Chains Of Love (Marx Brothers & Foghorn Mixes) | 12" | Mute | D12MUTE83 | 1988 | £2.50 | £6 | promo |
| Chorus | CD-s | Mute | CDMUTE125 | 1991 | £2 | £5 | |
| Chorus | CD | Mute | STUMM95 | 1991 | £5 | £12 | box set with prints |
| Chorus Software Installation Guide User Manual | CD | Sire | | 1991 | £37.50 | £75 | US promo 'hardback book' holding CD and cassette |
| Circus (Live In Hamburg) | LP | Mute | LIVE1 | 1987 | £4 | £10 | promo |
| Circus (Two Ring Edition) | 12" | Mute | LSTUMM35 | 1987 | £6 | £15 | double promo sampler |
| Crackers International | CD-s | Mute | CDMUTE93 | 1988 | £2 | £5 | |
| Crackers International Part II: Stop (Remix) | CD-s | Mute | LCDMUTE93 | 1988 | £4 | £10 | with card & gift label, 6x3" sleeve |
| Drama | CD-s | Mute | CDMUTE89 | 1989 | £2 | £5 | |
| Drama (Act 2) | 12" | Mute | P12MUTE89 | 1989 | £2.50 | £6 | promo |
| Eras 5 | CD | Mute | ERAS5CD | | £20 | £40 | promo compilation |
| Heavenly Action | 12" | Mute | D12MUTE42 | 1985 | £20 | £40 | double |
| Heavenly Action (Yellow Brick Mix) | 12" | Mute | L12MUTE42 | 1985 | £30 | £60 | |
| Interview | CD | Mute | ERASSAY1 | 1994 | £25 | £50 | promo |
| It Doesn't Have To Be This Way | CD-s | Mute | CDMUTE56 | 1987 | £4 | £10 | |
| Little Respect | CD-s | Mute | LCDMUTE85 | 1988 | £2.50 | £6 | |
| Little Respect (Big Train Mix) | 12" | Mute | L12MUTE85 | 1988 | £2.50 | £6 | |
| Love To Hate You | CD-s | Mute | CDMUTE131 | 1991 | £2 | £5 | |
| Oh L'Amour | CD-s | Intercord | INT826840 | 1988 | £2 | £5 | |
| Oh L'Amour | 7" | Mute | MUTE45 | 1986 | £2.50 | £6 | Thomas The Tank Engine picture sleeve |
| Oh L'Amour | 12" | Mute | 12MUTE45 | 1986 | £10 | £20 | blue vinyl promo |
| Oh L'Amour (Funky Sisters Mix) | 12" | Mute | L12MUTE45 | 1986 | £6 | £15 | |
| Oh L'Amour (remix) | 12" | Mute | 12MUTE45 | 1986 | £6 | £15 | Thomas The Tank Engine picture sleeve |
| Push Me Shove Me (Moonbeam Mix) | 12" | Mute | ERAS1 | 1990 | £10 | £20 | promo |
| Ship Of Fools | CD-s | Mute | CDMUTE74 | 1988 | £2 | £5 | 3" single |
| Ship Of Fools (Orbital Mix) | 12" | Mute | ERAS2 | 1990 | £10 | £20 | promo |
| Ship Of Fools (Stephen Hague Remix) | 12" | Mute | D12MUTE74 | 1988 | £2.50 | £6 | promo |
| Sometimes | CD-s | Intercord | INT826854 | 1988 | £2 | £5 | |
| Sometimes (Danny Rampling Mix) | 12" | Mute | ERAS3 | 1990 | £10 | £20 | promo |
| Sometimes (Shiver Mix) | 12" | Mute | L12MUTE51 | 1986 | £2.50 | £6 | |
| Star | CD-s | Mute | CDMUTE111 | 1990 | £2 | £5 | |
| Star (Mark Saunders Mix) | 12" | Mute | P12MUTE111 | 1990 | £2.50 | £6 | promo |
| Stop | 7" | Mute | DJMUTE93 | 1988 | £2.50 | £6 | promo |
| Stop | 12" | Mute | P12MUTE93 | 1988 | £2.50 | £6 | promo |

| | | | | | | | |
|---|---|---|---|---|---|---|---|
| Supernature (Daniel Miller & Phil Legg Mix) | 12" | Mute | XL12MUTE99 | 1990 | £4 | £10 | ...with outer envelope |
| Who Needs Love Like That (Mexican Mix) | 12" | Mute | L12MUTE40 | 1985 | £10 | £25 | |
| Wild | CD | Mute | STUMM75 | 1989 | £37.50 | £75 | ... promo box set, with LP, cassette, inserts |
| You Surround Me | CD-s | Mute | LCDMUTE99 | 1989 | £2.50 | £6 | |
| You Surround Me (Remix) | 12" | Mute | P12MUTE99 | 1989 | £2.50 | £6 | promo |
| You Surround Me (Syrinx Mix) | 12" | Mute | S12MUTE99 | 1989 | £2.50 | £6 | promo |

## ERGO SUM

| | | | | | | | |
|---|---|---|---|---|---|---|---|
| Mexico | LP | Theleme | 6332500 | 1972 | £37.50 | £75 | French |

## ERICA

| | | | | | | | |
|---|---|---|---|---|---|---|---|
| You Used To Think | LP | ESP-Disk | 1099 | 1968 | £15 | £30 | US |

## ERICKSON, ROKY

| | | | | | | | |
|---|---|---|---|---|---|---|---|
| Beauty And The Beast | LP | One Big Guitar | OBG9003 | 1987 | £8 | £20 | test pressing only |

## ERICSON, ROLF

| | | | | | | | |
|---|---|---|---|---|---|---|---|
| Transatlantic Wail | LP | Nixa | NJL5 | 1957 | £6 | £15 | |

## EROC

| | | | | | | | |
|---|---|---|---|---|---|---|---|
| Eroc | LP | Brain | 1069 | 1975 | £4 | £10 | German |
| Zwei | LP | Brain | 0060007 | 1976 | £4 | £10 | German |

## ERROL & HIS GROUP

| | | | | | | | |
|---|---|---|---|---|---|---|---|
| Gypsy | 7" | Blue Beat | BB284 | 1965 | £6 | £12 | |

## ERVIN, BOOKER

| | | | | | | | |
|---|---|---|---|---|---|---|---|
| In Between | LP | Blue Note | BST84283 | 1969 | £10 | £25 | |

## ERWIN, BLUEGRASS

| | | | | | | | |
|---|---|---|---|---|---|---|---|
| I Won't Cry Alone | 7" | Top Rank | JAR252 | 1959 | £1.50 | £4 | |

## ERWIN, PEE WEE

| | | | | | | | |
|---|---|---|---|---|---|---|---|
| Oh Play That Thing! | LP | London | LTZT15153/ SAH6011 | 1959 | £4 | £10 | |

## ESCORTS

| | | | | | | | |
|---|---|---|---|---|---|---|---|
| C'mon Home Baby | 7" | Fontana | TF570 | 1965 | £4 | £8 | |
| Dizzie Miss Lizzie | 7" | Fontana | TF453 | 1964 | £4 | £8 | |
| From Head To Toe | 7" | Columbia | DB8061 | 1966 | £6 | £12 | |
| I Can Tell | 7" | Lyntone | LYN509 | 1964 | £5 | £10 | flexi, Lance Harvey B side |
| I Don't Want To Go On Without You | 7" | Fontana | TF516 | 1964 | £2.50 | £6 | |
| Let It Be Me | 7" | Fontana | TF651 | 1966 | £4 | £8 | |
| One To Cry | 7" | Fontana | TF474 | 1964 | £4 | £8 | |

## ESPERANTO ROCK ORCHESTRA

| | | | | | | | |
|---|---|---|---|---|---|---|---|
| Danse Macabre | LP | A&M | AMLH63624 | 1974 | £4 | £10 | |
| Esperanto Rock Orchestra | LP | A&M | AMLH68175 | 1973 | £4 | £10 | |
| Last Tango | LP | A&M | AMLH68294 | 1975 | £4 | £10 | |

## ESPRIT DE CORPS

| | | | | | | | |
|---|---|---|---|---|---|---|---|
| If (Would It Turn Out Wrong) | 7" | Jam | JAM24 | 1972 | £5 | £10 | |
| Lonely | 7" | Jam | JAM32 | 1973 | £2.50 | £6 | |

## ESQUEIXADA SNIFF

| | | | | | | | |
|---|---|---|---|---|---|---|---|
| En Concert | LP | Edigsa | UM2055 | 1979 | £4 | £10 | Spanish |
| Ocells | LP | Edigsa | CM456 | 1979 | £4 | £10 | Spanish |

## ESQUERITA

| | | | | | | | |
|---|---|---|---|---|---|---|---|
| Esquerita | LP | Capitol | T1186 | 1959 | £150 | £250 | US |
| Rocking The Joint | 7" | Capitol | CL14938 | 1958 | £30 | £60 | |
| Wildcat Shakeout | LP | Ember | SPE6603 | 196– | £6 | £15 | |

## ESQUIRES

| | | | | | | | |
|---|---|---|---|---|---|---|---|
| And Get Away | 7" | Stateside | SS2077 | 1968 | £1.50 | £4 | |
| Get On Up | 7" | Stateside | SS2048 | 1967 | £2.50 | £6 | |

## ESSEX

| | | | | | | | |
|---|---|---|---|---|---|---|---|
| Easier Said Than Done | LP | Columbia | 33SX1593 | 1963 | £6 | £15 | |
| Easier Said Than Done | 7" | Columbia | DB7077 | 1963 | £2.50 | £6 | |
| She's Got Everything | 7" | Columbia | DB7178 | 1963 | £1.50 | £4 | |
| Walkin' Miracle | LP | Columbia | 33SX1613 | 1964 | £5 | £12 | |
| Walkin' Miracle | 7" | Columbia | DB7122 | 1963 | £2.50 | £6 | |
| Young And Lively | LP | Roulette | (S)R25246 | 1964 | £5 | £12 | US |

## ESSEX, DAVID

| | | | | | | | |
|---|---|---|---|---|---|---|---|
| And The Tears Came Tumbling Down | 7" | Fontana | TF559 | 1965 | £10 | £20 | |
| Can't Nobody Love You | 7" | Fontana | TF620 | 1965 | £10 | £20 | |
| Day The Earth Stood Still | 7" | Decca | F12967 | 1969 | £6 | £12 | |
| Just For Tonight | 7" | Pye | 7N17621 | 1968 | £2.50 | £6 | |
| Love Story | 7" | Uni | UN502 | 1968 | £4 | £8 | |
| That Takes Me Back | 7" | Decca | F12935 | 1969 | £6 | £12 | |
| Thigh High | 7" | Fontana | TF733 | 1966 | £7.50 | £15 | |
| This Little Girl Of Mine | 7" | Fontana | TF680 | 1966 | £10 | £20 | |

## ESTABLISHMENT

| | | | | | | | |
|---|---|---|---|---|---|---|---|
| Bad Catholics | LP | Phaeton | SPIN992 | 1981 | £8 | £20 | |
| Unfree Child | LP | EMI | SPLEAF7018 | 1977 | £25 | £50 | |

## ESTEFAN, GLORIA

| | | | | | | | |
|---|---|---|---|---|---|---|---|
| 1-2-3 | 7" | Epic | 6529580 | 1988 | £1.50 | £4 | poster sleeve |
| Anything For You | CD-s | Epic | 6516732 | 1988 | £2 | £5 | |
| Anything For You | 12" | Epic | 6516739 | 1988 | £2.50 | £6 | |
| Betcha Say That | 7" | Epic | 6511257 | 1987 | £1.50 | £4 | |
| Can't Stay Away From You | CD-s | Epic | 6514442 | 1988 | £2.50 | £6 | 3" single |
| Can't Stay Away From You | CD-s | Epic | 6514442 | 1988 | £2 | £5 | 3" single |
| Can't Stay Away From You | 7" | Epic | 6514440 | 1988 | £1.50 | £4 | poster sleeve |
| Can't Stay Away From You | 7" | Epic | 6531957 | 1989 | £1.50 | £4 | shaped picture disc |
| Can't Stay Away From You | 12" | Epic | 6514449 | 1988 | £2.50 | £6 | |
| Don't Wanna Lose You | CD-s | Epic | 6550543 | 1989 | £2 | £5 | 3" single |
| Get On Your Feet | CD-s | Epic | 6554502 | 1989 | £2 | £5 | |
| Gloria Estefan & Miami Sound Machine | CD | Epic | ESK1336 | 1988 | £8 | £12 | US promo sampler |
| Hold Me, Thrill Me, Ask Me | CD | Epic | | 1994 | £6 | £15 | US interview promo |
| Into The Light | CD | Epic | | 1991 | £10 | £25 | Australian, with bonus Love Songs CD |
| Into The Light | CD | Epic | ESK3028 | 1991 | £6 | £15 | US promo with bonus track |
| Let It Loose | CD | Epic | 4509102 | 1987 | £6 | £15 | |
| One Two Three | CD-s | Epic | 6529582 | 1988 | £2 | £5 | |
| Oye Mi Canto | CD-s | Epic | 6552875 | 1989 | £3 | £8 | picture disc |
| Rhythm Is Gonna Get You | CD-s | Epic | 6545142 | 1988 | £2 | £5 | |
| Rhythm Is Gonna Get You | 7" | Epic | 6545140 | 1988 | £1.50 | £4 | calendar picture sleeve |
| Rhythm Is Gonna Get You | 7" | Epic | 6545147 | 1988 | £2 | £5 | with badge |
| Rhythm Is Gonna Get You | 7" | Epic | 6545149 | 1988 | £2 | £5 | poster picture sleeve |

## ESTES, SLEEPY JOHN

| | | | | | | | |
|---|---|---|---|---|---|---|---|
| 1929–1940 | LP | Folkways | RF8 | 1967 | £4 | £10 | |
| Broke And Hungry | LP | Delmark | DL608 | 1964 | £6 | £15 | |
| Brownsville Blues | LP | Delmark | DL613 | 1965 | £6 | £15 | |
| Electric Sleep | LP | Delmark | DL619 | 1966 | £4 | £10 | |
| In Europe | LP | Delmark | DL611 | 1965 | £4 | £10 | |
| Legend | LP | Delmark | DL603 | 1961 | £6 | £15 | |
| Legend Of Sleepy John Estes | LP | Esquire | 32195 | 1963 | £10 | £25 | |
| Portraits In Blues Vol. 10 | LP | Storyville | SLP172 | 1965 | £4 | £10 | |
| Sleepy John's Got The Blues | 7" EP | Delmark | DJB3 | 1966 | £2.50 | £6 | |
| Tennessee Jug Busters | LP | 77 | LA1227 | 1964 | £6 | £15 | |

## ESTICK, JACKIE

| | | | | | | | |
|---|---|---|---|---|---|---|---|
| Boss Girl | 7" | Blue Beat | BB64 | 1961 | £6 | £12 | Count Ossie B side |
| Since You've Been Gone | 7" | Island | WI042 | 1963 | £5 | £10 | |
| Ska | 7" | Ska Beat | JB256 | 1966 | £5 | £10 | |

## ETCETERAS

| | | | | | | | |
|---|---|---|---|---|---|---|---|
| Little Lady | 7" | Oriole | CB1973 | 1964 | £5 | £10 | |
| Where Is My Love | 7" | Oriole | CB1950 | 1964 | £5 | £10 | |

## ETERNALS

| | | | | | | | |
|---|---|---|---|---|---|---|---|
| Rocking In The Jungle | 7" | London | HL8995 | 1959 | £30 | £60 | tri-centre |

## ETERNALS (2)

| | | | | | | | |
|---|---|---|---|---|---|---|---|
| Queen Of The Minstrels | 7" | Coxsone | CS7091 | 1969 | £5 | £10 | |

## ETERNITY'S CHILDREN

| | | | | | | | |
|---|---|---|---|---|---|---|---|
| Eternity's Children | LP | Tower | ST5123 | 1968 | £5 | £12 | US |
| Timeless | LP | Tower | ST5144 | 1968 | £5 | £12 | US |

## ETHEL THE FROG

| | | | | | | | |
|---|---|---|---|---|---|---|---|
| Ethel The Frog | LP | EMI | EMC3329 | 1980 | £6 | £15 | |

## ETHERIDGE, MELISSA

| | | | | | | | |
|---|---|---|---|---|---|---|---|
| Angels | CD-s | Island | CID440 | 1989 | £2 | £5 | |
| Bring Me Some Water | CD-s | Island | CID393 | 1989 | £2 | £5 | |
| Don't You Need | CD-s | Island | CID376 | 1988 | £2 | £5 | |
| No Souvenirs | CD-s | Island | CID431 | 1989 | £2 | £5 | |
| Similar Features | CD-s | Island | CID356 | 1988 | £2 | £5 | |

## ETHIOPIANS

| | | | | | | | |
|---|---|---|---|---|---|---|---|
| Buss Your Mouth | 7" | Nu Beat | NB038 | 1969 | £1.50 | £4 | Reggae Boys B side |
| Come On Now | 7" | Doctor Bird | DB1141 | 1968 | £5 | £10 | |
| Do It Sweet | 7" | Doctor Bird | DB1092 | 1967 | £5 | £10 | |
| Engine 54 | 7" | Doctor Bird | DB1147 | 1968 | £5 | £10 | |
| Everyday Talking | 7" | Doctor Bird | DB1199 | 1969 | £5 | £10 | |
| Everything Crash | 7" | Doctor Bird | DB1169 | 1968 | £5 | £10 | |
| Fire A Muss Muss Tail | 7" | Crab | CRAB2 | 1968 | £2.50 | £6 | |
| For You | 7" | Island | WI3036 | 1967 | £5 | £10 | Soul Brothers B side |
| Go Rock Steady | LP | Doctor Bird | DLM5011 | 1968 | £50 | £100 | |
| Hong Kong Flu | 7" | Doctor Bird | DB1185 | 1969 | £5 | £10 | |
| I Am Free | 7" | Island | WI3015 | 1966 | £5 | £10 | Soul Brothers B side |
| I'm A King | 7" | Crab | CRAB7 | 1969 | £2.50 | £6 | |
| I'm Gonna Take Over Now | 7" | Rio | R114 | 1967 | £4 | £8 | Jackie Mittoo B side |
| Leave Me Business Alone | 7" | Studio One | SO2035 | 1967 | £6 | £12 | Soul Vendors B side |
| Let's Get Together | 7" | Coxsone | CS7022 | 1967 | £5 | £10 | Hamlins B side |

| | | | | | | | |
|---|---|---|---|---|---|---|---|
| Live Good | 7" | Ska Beat | JB260 | 1966 | £5 | £10 | Soul Brothers B side |
| Monkey Money | 7" | Fab | FAB180 | 1971 | £1.50 | £4 | |
| Mother's Tender Care | 7" | Duke Reid | DR2507 | 1970 | £1.50 | £4 | Tommy McCook B side |
| Mr. Tom | 7" | Randys | RAN512 | 1969 | £1.50 | £4 | |
| My Testimony | 7" | Nu Beat | NB031 | 1969 | £1.50 | £4 | J. J. Allstars B side |
| Not Me | 7" | Doctor Bird | DB1172 | 1969 | £5 | £10 | |
| Owe Me No Pay Me | 7" | Rio | R110 | 1966 | £4 | £8 | |
| Pirate | 7" | Treasure Isle | TI7067 | 1971 | £1.50 | £4 | Tommy McCook B side |
| Reggae Hit The Town | 7" | Crab | CRAB4 | 1968 | £2.50 | £6 | |
| Reggae Power | LP | Trojan | TTL10 | 1969 | £8 | £20 | |
| Stay In My Lonely Arms | 7" | Rio | R126 | 1967 | £4 | £8 | |
| Train To Glory | 7" | Doctor Bird | DB1148 | 1968 | £5 | £10 | |
| Train To Skaville | 7" | Rio | R130 | 1967 | £4 | £8 | |
| True Man | 7" | Randys | RAN510 | 1969 | £1.50 | £4 | Randy's Allstars B side |
| Walkie Talkie | 7" | Bamboo | BAM26 | 1970 | £1.50 | £4 | Sound Dimension B side |
| Well Red | 7" | Trojan | TR697 | 1969 | £1.50 | £4 | J. J. Allstars B side |
| What A Fire | 7" | Doctor Bird | DB1186 | 1969 | £5 | £10 | |
| What To Do | 7" | Rio | R123 | 1967 | £4 | £8 | Jackie Mittoo B side |
| Whip | 7" | Doctor Bird | DB1096 | 1967 | £5 | £10 | |
| Woman Capture Man | LP | Trojan | TBL112 | 1970 | £8 | £20 | |
| Woman Capture Man | 7" | Trojan | TR666 | 1969 | £1.50 | £4 | |
| World Goes Ska | 7" | Doctor Bird | DB1103 | 1967 | £5 | £10 | |
| You'll Want To Come Back | 7" | Bamboo | BAM38 | 1970 | £1.50 | £4 | Jackie Mittoo B side |

## ETNA
| | | | | | | | |
|---|---|---|---|---|---|---|---|
| Etna | LP | Catoca | CTL1002 | 1975 | £10 | £25 | Italian |

## ETRON FOU LELOUBLAN
| | | | | | | | |
|---|---|---|---|---|---|---|---|
| Batelages | LP | Gratte-Ciel | CIEL2001 | 1976 | £4 | £10 | French |
| En direct | LP | Celluloid | CEL6572 | 1979 | £4 | £10 | |
| Les trois fou's perdegagnent | LP | L'Orchestra | OLPS55002 | 1979 | £4 | £10 | Italian |

## ETTA & HARVEY
| | | | | | | | |
|---|---|---|---|---|---|---|---|
| If I Can't Have You | 7" | London | HLM9180 | 1960 | £7.50 | £15 | |

## EUBANKS, JACK
| | | | | | | | |
|---|---|---|---|---|---|---|---|
| Searchin' | 7" | London | HLU9501 | 1962 | £1.50 | £4 | |
| What'd I Say | 7" | London | HLU9312 | 1961 | £1.50 | £4 | |

## EULENSPYGEL
| | | | | | | | |
|---|---|---|---|---|---|---|---|
| 2 | LP | Spiegelei | 287607 | 1971 | £8 | £20 | German |
| Ausschuss | LP | Spiegelei | 287807 | 1972 | £10 | £25 | German |

## EUPHONIOUS WAIL
| | | | | | | | |
|---|---|---|---|---|---|---|---|
| Euphonious Wail | LP | Kapp | KS3668 | 1973 | £8 | £20 | US |

## EUPHORIA
| | | | | | | | |
|---|---|---|---|---|---|---|---|
| Euphoria | LP | Heritage | HTS35005 | 1969 | £10 | £25 | US |

## EUPHORIA (2)
| | | | | | | | |
|---|---|---|---|---|---|---|---|
| Gift From Euphoria | LP | Capitol | SKAO363 | 1969 | £37.50 | £75 | US |
| Lost In Trance | LP | Rainbow | 1003 | 1973 | £50 | £100 | US |

## EUREKA BRASS BAND
| | | | | | | | |
|---|---|---|---|---|---|---|---|
| Jazz At Preservation Hall Vol. 1 | LP | London | HAK/SHK8162 | 1964 | £5 | £12 | |
| New Orleans Parade | LP | Melodisc | MLP12101 | 1955 | £5 | £12 | |

## EURYTHMICS
| | | | | | | | |
|---|---|---|---|---|---|---|---|
| Angel | CD-s | RCA | DACD21 | 1990 | £2 | £5 | |
| Angel (Remix) | 12" | RCA | DAT25 | 1990 | £2.50 | £6 | |
| Beethoven | CD-s | RCA | DA11CD | 1987 | £2 | £5 | |
| Beethoven | 7" | RCA | DA11P | 1987 | £2.50 | £6 | poster sleeve |
| Belinda | 7" | RCA | RCA115 | 1981 | £7.50 | £15 | |
| Don't Ask Me Why | CD-s | RCA | DACD19 | 1989 | £2 | £5 | |
| Don't Ask Me Why | CD-s | RCA | DACD20 | 1989 | £2 | £5 | black box, poster |
| I Need A Man (live) | CD-s | RCA | DA15CD | 1988 | £2 | £5 | metal tin |
| I'm Never Gonna Cry Again | 7" | RCA | RCA68 | 1981 | £2 | £5 | |
| I'm Never Gonna Cry Again | 12" | RCA | RCAT68 | 1981 | £10 | £20 | |
| It's Alright | 7" | RCA | PB40375 | 1985 | £1.50 | £4 | double |
| It's Alright | 12" | RCA | PB40376 | 1985 | £2.50 | £6 | double |
| Julia | 7" | Virgin | VSY734 | 1985 | £1.50 | £4 | picture disc |
| Julia | 12" | Virgin | VS73412 | 1985 | £2.50 | £6 | picture disc |
| King And Queen Of America | CD-s | RCA | DACD23 | 1990 | £2 | £5 | in wooden box |
| Love Is A Stranger | 7" | RCA | DAP1 | 1982 | £1.50 | £4 | picture disc |
| Miracle Of Love | 7" | RCA | DA9P | 1986 | £1.50 | £4 | picture disc |
| Revival | CD-s | RCA | DACD17 | 1989 | £2 | £5 | |
| Right By Your Side | 7" | RCA | DA4 | 1983 | £10 | £20 | with 4 track cassette |
| Right By Your Side | 7" | RCA | DAP4 | 1983 | £1.50 | £4 | picture disc |
| Rough And Tough | CD | RCA | CP353016 | 1987 | £25 | £50 | US live promo |
| Sexcrime (1984) | CD-s | Virgin | CDT22 | 1988 | £2 | £5 | 3" single |
| Sexcrime (1984) | CD-s | Virgin | VVCS2 | 1988 | £2 | £5 | |
| Sweet Dreams | LP | RCA | RCALP6063 | 1983 | £4 | £10 | picture disc |
| Sweet Dreams | 7" | RCA | DAP2 | 1983 | £2 | £5 | picture disc |
| Sweet Dreams Are Made Of This | CD-s | RCA | PD42651 | 1989 | £2 | £5 | |

| | | | | | | | |
|---|---|---|---|---|---|---|---|
| This Is The House | 7" | RCA | RCA199 | 1982 | £4 | £8 | |
| This Is The House | 12" | RCA | RCAT199 | 1982 | £10 | £25 | |
| Walk | 7" | RCA | RCA230 | 1982 | £4 | £8 | |
| Walk | 12" | RCA | RCAT230 | 1982 | £15 | £30 | |
| We Two Are One | CD | RCA | PD74251 | 1989 | £20 | £40 | ... promo box set, with video and interview cassette |
| We Two Are One Two | CD | BMG | 780349 | 1991 | £10 | £25 | laser disc |
| Who's That Girl | 7" | RCA | DAP3 | 1983 | £1.50 | £4 | picture disc |
| You Have Placed A Chill In My Heart | CD-s | RCA | DA16CD | 1988 | £2.50 | £6 | black metal tin |

## EVANS, BILL

| | | | | | | |
|---|---|---|---|---|---|---|
| Alone | LP | Verve | SVLP9251 | 1970 | £4 | £10 |
| At The Montreux Jazz Festival | LP | Verve | (S)VLP9243 | 1969 | £5 | £12 |
| Conversations With Myself | LP | Verve | VLP9054 | 1963 | £6 | £15 |
| Dig It | LP | Fontana | FJL104 | 1964 | £4 | £10 |
| Everybody Digs Bill Evans | LP | Riverside | RLP12291 | 1958 | £6 | £15 |
| Explorations | LP | Riverside | RLP351 | 1961 | £6 | £15 |
| Further Conversations With Myself | LP | Verve | (S)VLP9198 | 1968 | £5 | £12 |
| Portrait In Jazz | LP | Riverside | RLP12315 | 1959 | £6 | £15 |
| Waltz For Debby | LP | Riverside | RLP(9)399 | 1961 | £6 | £15 |

## EVANS, CHRISTINE

| | | | | | | |
|---|---|---|---|---|---|---|
| Somewhere There's Love | 7" | Philips | BF1496 | 1966 | £4 | £8 |

## EVANS, DAVE

| | | | | | | |
|---|---|---|---|---|---|---|
| Elephantasia | LP | Village Thing | VTS14 | 1972 | £4 | £10 |
| Words In Between | LP | Village Thing | VTS6 | 1971 | £4 | £10 |

## EVANS, GIL

Although technically an arranger, Gil Evans produced jazz that was so individual that it effectively amounted to recomposition. At his best when creating music around a star soloist (*New Bottle Old Wine* featured Cannonball Adderley; *Miles Ahead, Porgy And Bess* and *Sketches Of Spain* featured Miles Davis and are listed under his name), Evans was ready to record an album with Jimi Hendrix, when the guitarist's untimely end aborted the project. Evans went on to record many of Hendrix's tunes anyway, but although these work very well as modern jazz pieces, they offer no more than a tantalizing glimpse of what might have been.

| | | | | | | | |
|---|---|---|---|---|---|---|---|
| Gil Evans And Ten | LP | Esquire | 32070 | 1959 | £8 | £20 | |
| Great Jazz Standards | LP | Fontana | 688000ZL | 1965 | £5 | £12 | |
| Great Jazz Standards | LP | Vogue | LAE12234 | 1960 | £8 | £20 | |
| Great Jazz Standards | 7" EP | Vogue | EPV1266 | 1960 | £2 | £5 | |
| New Bottle, Old Wine | LP | Vogue | LAE12173 | 1959 | £8 | £20 | |
| Out Of The Cool | LP | HMV | CLP1456 | 1961 | £6 | £15 | |
| Plays The Music Of Jimi Hendrix | LP | RCA | LSA3197 | 1974 | £5 | £12 | US |
| Roots (New Bottle, Old Wine) | LP | Fontana | 688003ZL | 1965 | £5 | £12 | |
| Svengali | LP | Atlantic | AD1643 | 1974 | £5 | £12 | US |

## EVANS, LARRY

| | | | | | | | |
|---|---|---|---|---|---|---|---|
| Crazy About My Baby | 7" | London | HLU8269 | 1956 | £100 | £200 | best auctioned |

## EVANS, MAUREEN

| | | | | | | |
|---|---|---|---|---|---|---|
| All The Angels Sang | 7" | CBS | 201773 | 1965 | £1.50 | £4 |
| Like I Do | LP | Oriole | PS40046 | 1963 | £15 | £30 |
| Melancholy Me | 7" EP | Oriole | EP7076 | 1963 | £7.50 | £15 |
| Never Let Him Go | 7" | CBS | 201752 | 1965 | £1.50 | £4 |
| Somewhere There's Love | 7" | CBS | 202621 | 1967 | £2 | £5 |

## EVANS, MAUREEN & DAVID KOSSOFF

| | | | | | | |
|---|---|---|---|---|---|---|
| Oliver | 7" EP | Oriole | EP7039 | 1961 | £2 | £5 |

## EVANS, PAUL

| | | | | | | | |
|---|---|---|---|---|---|---|---|
| 21 Years In A Tennessee Jail | LP | Kapp | KL1346/KS3346 | 1964 | £6 | £15 | US |
| Another Town, Another Jail | LP | Kapp | KL1475/KS3475 | 1966 | £5 | £12 | US |
| Brigade Of Broken Hearts | 7" | London | HLL9183 | 1960 | £2 | £5 | |
| Folk Songs Of Many Lands | LP | Carlton | (STLP)130 | 1961 | £6 | £15 | US |
| Happy Go Lucky Me | 7" | London | HLL9129 | 1960 | £2 | £5 | |
| Hear Paul Evans In Your Home Tonight | LP | Carlton | (STLP)129 | 1961 | £6 | £15 | US |
| Hushabye Little Guitar | 7" | London | HLL9239 | 1960 | £2 | £5 | |
| Midnight Special | 7" | London | HLL9045 | 1960 | £4 | £8 | |
| Paul Evans | 7" EP | London | RER1349 | 1962 | £12.50 | £25 | |
| Seven Little Girls Sitting In The Back Seat | 7" | London | HLL8968 | 1959 | £2 | £5 | |
| Sings The Fabulous Teens | LP | London | HAL2248 | 1960 | £20 | £40 | |

## EVANS, RUSSELL & THE NITEHAWKS

| | | | | | | |
|---|---|---|---|---|---|---|
| Send Me Some Cornbread | 7" | Atlantic | 584010 | 1966 | £2 | £5 |

## EVEN DOZEN JUG BAND

The Even Dozen Jug Band, while in itself having little to distinguish it from the many other folk groups playing in America during the early sixties, was nevertheless a remarkably effective training school for some later well-known musicians. Playing in the group were John Sebastian (soon to form the Lovin' Spoonful), Maria D'Amato (famous later under her married name, Maria Muldaur), Steve Katz (guitarist with the Blues Project and Blood, Sweat and Tears), guitarist Stefan Grossman, and Joshua Rifkin (later responsible for bringing the works of Scott Joplin to public notice).

| | | | | | | | |
|---|---|---|---|---|---|---|---|
| Even Dozen Jug Band | LP | Bounty | BY6023 | 1966 | £6 | £15 | |
| Even Dozen Jug Band | LP | Elektra | EKS7246 | 1964 | £8 | £20 | US |
| Jug Band Songs Of The Southern Mountains | LP | Legacy | LEG119 | 1965 | £6 | £15 | US |

## EVERETT, BETTY

| | | | | | | | |
|---|---|---|---|---|---|---|---|
| Getting Mighty Crowded | 7" | Fontana | TF520 | 1964 | £1.50 | £4 | |
| I Can't Hear You | 7" | Stateside | SS321 | 1964 | £2 | £5 | |
| I've Got A Claim On You | 7" | Sue | WI352 | 1965 | £5 | £10 | |
| It's In His Kiss | LP | Fontana | TL5136 | 1965 | £10 | £25 | |
| It's In His Kiss | 7" | Stateside | SS280 | 1964 | £1.50 | £4 | |
| Very Best Of Betty Everett | LP | Vee Jay | VJLP/VJS1122 | 1965 | £4 | £10 | US |
| You're No Good | 7" | Stateside | SS259 | 1964 | £2.50 | £6 | |
| Your Loving Arms | 7" | King | KG1002 | 1964 | £1.50 | £4 | |

## EVERETT, BETTY & JERRY BUTLER

| | | | | | | | |
|---|---|---|---|---|---|---|---|
| Delicious Together | LP | Fontana | TL5237 | 1965 | £4 | £10 | |
| Let It Be Me | 7" | Stateside | SS339 | 1964 | £1.50 | £4 | |
| Smile | 7" | Fontana | TF528 | 1965 | £1.50 | £4 | |

## EVERETT, VINCE

| | | | | | | | |
|---|---|---|---|---|---|---|---|
| Every Now And Then | 7" | Fontana | TF915 | 1968 | £5 | £10 | |

## EVERGREEN BLUES

| | | | | | | | |
|---|---|---|---|---|---|---|---|
| Laura | 7" | Mercury | MF1025 | 1968 | £1.50 | £4 | |
| Midnight Confessions | 7" | Mercury | MF1012 | 1967 | £1.50 | £4 | |
| Seven Do Eleven | LP | Mercury | SMCL20122 | 1968 | £4 | £10 | |

## EVERGREEN BLUESHOES

| | | | | | | | |
|---|---|---|---|---|---|---|---|
| Ballad Of Evergreen Blueshoes | LP | London | HAU/SHU8399 | 1969 | £4 | £10 | |

## EVERLY, DON

| | | | | | | | |
|---|---|---|---|---|---|---|---|
| Don Everly | LP | A&M | AMLH2007 | 1971 | £6 | £15 | |
| Sunset Towers | LP | Ode | 77023 | 1974 | £4 | £10 | US |

## EVERLY, PHIL

| | | | | | | | |
|---|---|---|---|---|---|---|---|
| Ich Bin Dein | 7" | Elektra | ELK12381 | 1977 | £2 | £5 | sung in German |
| Mystic Line | LP | Pye | NSPL18473 | 1975 | £4 | £10 | |
| Nothing's Too Good For My Baby | LP | Pye | NSPL18448 | 1974 | £4 | £10 | |
| Star Spangled Springer | LP | RCA | SF8370 | 1973 | £6 | £15 | |

## EVERLY BROTHERS

| | | | | | | | |
|---|---|---|---|---|---|---|---|
| Ain't That Lovin' You Baby | 7" | Warner Bros | WB129 | 1964 | £1.50 | £4 | |
| All I Have To Do Is Dream | 7" | London | HLA8618 | 1958 | £4 | £8 | tri-centre |
| Beat 'n' Soul | LP | Warner Bros | W(S)1605 | 1965 | £6 | £15 | |
| Bird Dog | 7" | London | HLA8685 | 1958 | £4 | £8 | tri-centre |
| Both Sides Of An Evening | LP | Warner Bros | WS8052 | 1961 | £10 | £25 | stereo |
| Both Sides Of An Evening | LP | Warner Bros | WM4052 | 1961 | £8 | £20 | |
| Both Sides Of An Evening Vol. 1 | 7" EP | Warner Bros | WEP6115 | 1963 | £10 | £20 | |
| Both Sides Of An Evening Vol. 1 | 7" EP | Warner Bros | WSE6115 | 1963 | £20 | £40 | stereo |
| Both Sides Of An Evening Vol. 2 | 7" EP | Warner Bros | WEP6117 | 1964 | £10 | £20 | |
| Both Sides Of An Evening Vol. 2 | 7" EP | Warner Bros | WSE6117 | 1964 | £20 | £40 | stereo |
| Both Sides Of An Evening Vol. 3 | 7" EP | Warner Bros | WEP6138 | 1965 | £10 | £20 | |
| Bowling Green | 7" | Warner Bros | WB7020 | 1967 | £1.50 | £4 | |
| Bye Bye Love | 7" | London | HLA8440 | 1957 | £7.50 | £15 | |
| Cathy's Clown | 7" | Warner Bros | WB1 | 1960 | £1.50 | £4 | |
| Christmas With The Everly Brothers | LP | Warner Bros | WS8116 | 1962 | £10 | £25 | stereo |
| Christmas With The Everly Brothers | LP | Warner Bros | WM8116 | 1962 | £8 | £20 | |
| Crying In The Rain | 7" | Warner Bros | WB56 | 1962 | £1.50 | £4 | |
| Date With The Everly Brothers | LP | Warner Bros | WS8028 | 1960 | £10 | £25 | stereo |
| Date With The Everly Brothers | LP | Warner Bros | WM4028 | 1960 | £8 | £20 | |
| Date With The Everly Brothers Vol. 1 | 7" EP | Warner Bros | WEP6107 | 1963 | £10 | £20 | |
| Date With The Everly Brothers Vol. 1 | 7" EP | Warner Bros | WSE6107 | 1963 | £20 | £40 | stereo |
| Date With The Everly Brothers Vol. 2 | 7" EP | Warner Bros | WEP6109 | 1963 | £10 | £20 | |
| Date With The Everly Brothers Vol. 2 | 7" EP | Warner Bros | WSE6109 | 1963 | £20 | £40 | stereo |
| Especially For You | 7" EP | Warner Bros | WEP6034 | 1961 | £7.50 | £15 | |
| Especially For You | 7" EP | Warner Bros | WSEP2034 | 1961 | £15 | £30 | stereo |
| Everly Brothers | LP | Cadence | CLP3003 | 1958 | £20 | £40 | US |
| Everly Brothers | LP | London | HAA2081 | 1958 | £20 | £40 | |
| Everly Brothers | 7" EP | London | REA1113 | 1958 | £7.50 | £15 | |
| Everly Brothers' Best | LP | Cadence | CLP3025 | 1959 | £20 | £40 | US |
| Everly Brothers No. 2 | 7" EP | London | REA1148 | 1958 | £7.50 | £15 | |
| Everly Brothers No. 3 | 7" EP | London | REA1149 | 1958 | £7.50 | £15 | |
| Everly Brothers No. 4 | 7" EP | London | REA1174 | 1959 | £10 | £20 | |
| Everly Brothers No. 5 | 7" EP | London | REA1229 | 1960 | £10 | £20 | |
| Everly Brothers No. 6 | 7" EP | London | REA1311 | 1961 | £10 | £20 | |
| Everly Brothers Show | LP | Warner Bros | WS1858 | 1970 | £5 | £12 | |
| Everly Brothers Sing | LP | Warner Bros | W(S)1708 | 1967 | £6 | £15 | |
| Everly Brothers Single Set | 7" | Lightning | SET1 | 1980 | £10 | £20 | 15 x 7", boxed book |
| Fabulous Style Of The Everly Brothers | LP | Cadence | CLP3040/25040 | 1960 | £15 | £30 | US |
| Fabulous Style Of The Everly Brothers | LP | London | HAA2266 | 1960 | £10 | £25 | |
| Ferris Wheel | 7" | Warner Bros | WB135 | 1964 | £1.50 | £4 | |
| Fifteen Everly Hits Fifteen | LP | Cadence | CLP3062/25062 | 1963 | £10 | £25 | US |
| Folk Songs Of The Everly Brothers | LP | Cadence | CLP3059/25059 | 1962 | £15 | £30 | US |
| Foreverly Yours | 7" EP | Warner Bros | WEP6049 | 1962 | £7.50 | £15 | |
| Foreverly Yours | 7" EP | Warner Bros | WSEP2049 | 1962 | £20 | £40 | stereo |
| Girl Sang The Blues | 7" | Warner Bros | WB109 | 1963 | £1.50 | £4 | |
| Golden Hits | LP | Warner Bros | WM/WS8108 | 1962 | £4 | £10 | |
| Gone Gone Gone | LP | Warner Bros | WS8169 | 1965 | £8 | £20 | stereo |
| Gone Gone Gone | LP | Warner Bros | WM8169 | 1965 | £6 | £15 | |
| Gone Gone Gone | 7" | Warner Bros | WB146 | 1964 | £1.50 | £4 | |
| Hit Sound Of The Everly Brothers | LP | Warner Bros | WS1676 | 1967 | £8 | £20 | stereo |

283

| | | | | | | | |
|---|---|---|---|---|---|---|---|
| Hit Sound Of The Everly Brothers | LP | Warner Bros | W1676 | 1967 | £5 | £12 | |
| How Can I Meet Her | 7" | Warner Bros | WB67 | 1962 | £1.50 | £4 | |
| I'll Never Get Over You | 7" | Warner Bros | WB5639 | 1965 | £1.50 | £4 | |
| I've Been Wrong Before | 7" | Warner Bros | WB5754 | 1966 | £1.50 | £4 | |
| In Our Image | LP | Warner Bros | W1620 | 1965 | £6 | £15 | mono |
| In Our Image | LP | Warner Bros | WS1620 | 1965 | £8 | £20 | stereo |
| Instant Party | LP | Warner Bros | WS8061 | 1962 | £8 | £20 | stereo |
| Instant Party | LP | Warner Bros | WM4061 | 1962 | £6 | £15 | |
| Instant Party | 7" EP | Warner Bros | WEP6111 | 1963 | £10 | £12 | |
| Instant Party | 7" EP | Warner Bros | WSE6111 | 1963 | £20 | £40 | stereo |
| Instant Party Vol. 2 | 7" EP | Warner Bros | WEP6113 | 1963 | £10 | £20 | |
| Instant Party Vol. 2 | 7" EP | Warner Bros | WSE6113 | 1963 | £20 | £40 | stereo |
| It's Been Nice | 7" | Warner Bros | WB99 | 1963 | £1.50 | £4 | |
| It's Everly Time | LP | Warner Bros | WS8012 | 1960 | £10 | £25 | stereo |
| It's Everly Time | LP | Warner Bros | WM4012 | 1960 | £8 | £20 | |
| It's Everly Time | 7" EP | Warner Bros | WEP6056 | 1962 | £7.50 | £15 | |
| It's Everly Time | 7" EP | Warner Bros | WSEP2056 | 1962 | £20 | £40 | stereo |
| It's My Time | 7" | Warner Bros | WB7192 | 1968 | £1.50 | £4 | |
| Leave My Girl Alone | 7" EP | Warner Bros | WEP622 | 1967 | £10 | £20 | |
| Let It Be Me | 7" | London | HLA9039 | 1960 | £1.50 | £4 | |
| Lightning Express | 7" | London | | 1962 | £30 | £60 | test pressing |
| Like Strangers | 7" | London | HLA9250 | 1960 | £2 | £5 | |
| Love Is Strange | 7" EP | Warner Bros | WEP610 | 1966 | £10 | £20 | |
| Love Is Strange | 7" | Warner Bros | WB5649 | 1965 | £1.50 | £4 | |
| Love Of The Common People | 7" | Warner Bros | WB7088 | 1967 | £1.50 | £4 | |
| Mary Jane | 7" | Warner Bros | WB7062 | 1967 | £1.50 | £4 | |
| Milk Train | 7" | Warner Bros | WB7226 | 1968 | £1.50 | £4 | |
| Muskrat | 7" | Warner Bros | WB50 | 1961 | £1.50 | £4 | |
| No One Can Make My Sunshine Smile | 7" | Warner Bros | WB79 | 1962 | £1.50 | £4 | |
| Oh Boy | 7" | Warner Bros | WB6074 | 1967 | £1.50 | £4 | |
| Pass The Chicken And Listen | LP | RCA | SF8332 | 1973 | £4 | £10 | |
| People Get Ready | 7" EP | Warner Bros | WEP612 | 1966 | £7.50 | £15 | |
| Poor Jenny | 7" | London | HLA8863 | 1959 | £4 | £8 | tri-centre |
| Power Of Love | 7" | Warner Bros | WB5743 | 1966 | £1.50 | £4 | |
| Price Of Love | 7" EP | Warner Bros | WEP604 | 1965 | £6 | £12 | |
| Price Of Love | 7" | Warner Bros | WB161 | 1965 | £1.50 | £4 | |
| Price Of Love | 7" | Warner Bros | WB5628 | 1965 | £1.50 | £4 | |
| Problems | 7" | London | HLA8781 | 1958 | £4 | £8 | tri-centre |
| Ridin' High | 7" | RCA | RCA2232 | 1972 | £1.50 | £4 | |
| Rock 'n' Soul | 7" EP | Warner Bros | WEP608 | 1965 | £6 | £12 | |
| Rock 'n' Soul Vol. 2 | 7" EP | Warner Bros | WEP609 | 1965 | £6 | £12 | |
| Rock 'n' Soul | LP | Warner Bros | W(S)1578 | 1965 | £6 | £15 | |
| Rock 'n' Soul | LP | Warner Bros | WM/WS8171 | 1965 | £6 | £15 | |
| Roots | LP | Warner Bros | W(S)1752 | 1968 | £6 | £15 | |
| See See Rider | 7" EP | Warner Bros | WEP618 | 1966 | £10 | £20 | |
| Sing Great Country Hits | LP | Warner Bros | WM/WS8138 | 1963 | £6 | £15 | |
| Sing Great Country Hits Vol. 1 | 7" EP | Warner Bros | WEP6128 | 1964 | £10 | £20 | |
| Sing Great Country Hits Vol. 2 | 7" EP | Warner Bros | WEP6131 | 1964 | £10 | £20 | |
| Sing Great Country Hits Vol. 3 | 7" EP | Warner Bros | WEP6132 | 1964 | £10 | £20 | |
| So It Will Always Be | 7" | Warner Bros | WB94 | 1963 | £1.50 | £4 | |
| So Sad | 7" | Warner Bros | WB19 | 1960 | £1.50 | £4 | |
| Somebody Help Me | 7" EP | Warner Bros | WEP623 | 1967 | £7.50 | £15 | |
| Songs Our Daddy Taught Us | LP | London | HAA2150 | 1958 | £20 | £40 | |
| Songs Our Daddy Taught Us Part 1 | 7" EP | London | REA1195 | 1959 | £12.50 | £25 | |
| Songs Our Daddy Taught Us Part 2 | 7" EP | London | REA1196 | 1959 | £12.50 | £25 | |
| Songs Our Daddy Taught Us Part 3 | 7" EP | London | REA1197 | 1959 | £12.50 | £25 | |
| Sun Keeps Shining | 7" | Columbia | 21496 | 1956 | £150 | £250 | US, best auctioned |
| Temptation | 7" | Warner Bros | WB42 | 1961 | £1.50 | £4 | |
| That'll Be The Day | 7" | Warner Bros | WB158 | 1965 | £1.50 | £4 | |
| This Little Girl Of Mine | 7" | London | HLA8554 | 1958 | £7.50 | £15 | |
| Till I Kissed You | 7" | London | HLA8934 | 1959 | £4 | £8 | tri-centre |
| Two Yanks In England | LP | Warner Bros | WS1646 | 1965 | £8 | £20 | stereo |
| Two Yanks In England | LP | Warner Bros | W1646 | 1965 | £6 | £15 | with the Hollies |
| Wake Up Little Susie | 7" EP | Warner Bros | K16407 | 1974 | £2 | £5 | |
| Wake Up Little Suzie | 7" | London | HLA8498 | 1957 | £4 | £8 | |
| Walk Right Back | 7" | Warner Bros | WB33 | 1961 | £1.50 | £4 | |
| When Will I Be Loved | 7" | London | HLA9157 | 1960 | £2 | £5 | |
| You're My Girl | 7" | Warner Bros | WB154 | 1965 | £1.50 | £4 | |
| You're The One I Love | 7" | Warner Bros | WB143 | 1964 | £2.50 | £6 | |
| Yves | 7" | Warner Bros | WB7425 | 1970 | £1.50 | £4 | |

## EVERPRESENT FULLNESS

| | | | | | | | |
|---|---|---|---|---|---|---|---|
| Everpresent Fullness | LP | White Whale | 7132 | 1970 | £8 | £20 | US |

## EVERY MOTHER'S SON

| | | | | | | | |
|---|---|---|---|---|---|---|---|
| Come And Take A Ride In My Boat | 7" | MGM | MGM1341 | 1967 | £2.50 | £6 | |
| Every Mother's Son | LP | MGM | C(S)8044 | 1967 | £4 | £10 | US |
| Pony With The Golden Mane | 7" | MGM | MGM1372 | 1967 | £2 | £5 | |
| Put Your Mind At Ease | 7" | MGM | MGM1350 | 1967 | £2 | £5 | |

## EVERYONE

| | | | | | | | |
|---|---|---|---|---|---|---|---|
| Everyone | LP | B&C | CAS1028 | 1971 | £4 | £10 | |

## EVERYONE INVOLVED

| | | | | | | | |
|---|---|---|---|---|---|---|---|
| Circus Keeps On Turning | 7" | Arcturus | ARC3 | 1972 | £10 | £20 | |
| Either Or | LP | Arcturus | ARC4 | 1972 | £210 | £350 | |

## EVERYTHING BUT THE GIRL

| | | | | | | | |
|---|---|---|---|---|---|---|---|
| Driving | CD-s | Blanco Y Negro | NEG40CD | 1989 | £2 | £5 | |
| I Always Was Your Girl | CD-s | Blanco Y Negro | NEG33CD | 1988 | £2 | £5 | |
| I Don't Want To Talk About It | CD-s | Blanco Y Negro | NEG34CD | 1988 | £2 | £5 | *3" single* |
| Night And Day | CD-s | Cherry Red | CDCHERRY37 | 1989 | £2 | £5 | |

## EWAN & DENVER

| | | | | | | | |
|---|---|---|---|---|---|---|---|
| I Want You So Bad | 7" | Giant | GN17 | 1967 | £2 | £5 | |

## EWAN & GERRY

| | | | | | | | |
|---|---|---|---|---|---|---|---|
| Oh Babe | 7" | Blue Beat | BB385 | 1967 | £6 | £12 | |
| Right Track | 7" | Giant | GN4 | 1967 | £2.50 | £6 | |
| Rock Steady Train | 7" | Giant | GN9 | 1967 | £2.50 | £6 | |
| Tennessee Waltz | 7" | Giant | GN14 | 1967 | £2.50 | £6 | |

## EWELL, DON

| | | | | | | | |
|---|---|---|---|---|---|---|---|
| Piano Solos Of King Oliver Tunes | LP | Tempo | TAP7 | 1957 | £10 | £25 | |

## EXCALIBUR

| | | | | | | | |
|---|---|---|---|---|---|---|---|
| First Album | LP | Reprise | REP44163 | 1972 | £50 | £100 | *German* |

## EXCALIBUR (2)

| | | | | | | | |
|---|---|---|---|---|---|---|---|
| Sceptre | LP | Yarmouth | 01 | 1970 | £180 | £300 | |

## EXCELSIOR SPRING

| | | | | | | | |
|---|---|---|---|---|---|---|---|
| Happy Miranda | 7" | Instant | IN002 | 1968 | £4 | £8 | |

## EXCEPTIONS

Dave Pegg, the bass player with Fairport Convention and Jethro Tull, was a member of the Exceptions, while his colleague Roger Hill has also played for Fairport.

| | | | | | | | |
|---|---|---|---|---|---|---|---|
| Eagle Flies On Sunday | 7" | CBS | 202632 | 1967 | £5 | £10 | |
| Exceptional Exceptions | LP | President | PTLS1026 | 1969 | £6 | £15 | |
| Gaberdine Saturday Night | 7" | CBS | 2830 | 1967 | £6 | £12 | |
| Pendulum | 7" | President | PT271 | 1969 | £2.50 | £6 | |

## EXCEPTIONS (2)

| | | | | | | | |
|---|---|---|---|---|---|---|---|
| What More Do You Want | 7" | Decca | F12100 | 1965 | £2.50 | £6 | |

## EXCHECKERS

Drummer with this third-division Merseybeat group was Aynsley Dunbar, whose subsequent career included stints with John Mayall, Frank Zappa, Journey and Jefferson Starship.

| | | | | | | | |
|---|---|---|---|---|---|---|---|
| All The World Is Mine | 7" | Decca | F11871 | 1964 | £2 | £5 | |

## EXCITERS

| | | | | | | | |
|---|---|---|---|---|---|---|---|
| Do Wah Diddy | 7" | United Artists | UP2274 | 1969 | £1.50 | £4 | |
| Doo Wah Diddy Diddy | 7" EP | United Artists | UEP1005 | 1965 | £15 | £30 | |
| Doo Wah Diddy Diddy | 7" | United Artists | UP1041 | 1964 | £4 | £8 | |
| Exciters | LP | Roulette | (S)R25326 | 1966 | £8 | £20 | *US* |
| Exciters | LP | United Artists | ULP1032 | 1964 | £25 | £50 | |
| He's Got The Power | 7" | United Artists | UP1017 | 1963 | £1.50 | £4 | |
| I Want You To Be My Boy | 7" | Columbia | DB7479 | 1965 | £1.50 | £4 | |
| It's So Exciting | 7" | United Artists | UP1026 | 1963 | £1.50 | £4 | |
| Just Not Ready | 7" | Columbia | DB7544 | 1965 | £2 | £5 | |
| Little Bit Of Soap | 7" | London | HLZ10018 | 1966 | £2 | £5 | |
| Run Mascara | 7" | Columbia | DB7606 | 1965 | £2.50 | £6 | |
| Tell Him | LP | United Artists | UAL3264/ UAS6264 | 1963 | £15 | £30 | *US* |
| Tell Him | 7" | United Artists | UP1011 | 1963 | £2 | £5 | |
| Weddings Make Me Cry | 7" | London | HLZ10038 | 1966 | £4 | £8 | |

## EXCURSION

| | | | | | | | |
|---|---|---|---|---|---|---|---|
| Night Train | LP | Gemini | GMX5029 | 1970 | £8 | £20 | |

## EXECUTIVES

| | | | | | | | |
|---|---|---|---|---|---|---|---|
| Gaza Strip | 7" | CBS | 3067 | 1967 | £1.50 | £4 | |
| I Ain't Got Nobody | 7" | CBS | 4013 | 1969 | £1.50 | £4 | |
| It's Been So Long | 7" | Columbia | DB7573 | 1965 | £1.50 | £4 | |
| Lock Your Door | 7" | Columbia | DB7919 | 1966 | £1.50 | £4 | |
| March Of The Mods | 7" | Columbia | DB7323 | 1964 | £1.50 | £4 | |
| Return Of The Mods | 7" | Columbia | DB7770 | 1965 | £2 | £5 | |
| Smokey Atmosphere | 7" | CBS | 202652 | 1967 | £1.50 | £4 | |
| Strictly For The Beat | 7" | Columbia | DB7393 | 1964 | £1.50 | £4 | |
| Tracy Took A Trip | 7" | CBS | 3431 | 1968 | £2.50 | £6 | |
| Tracy Took A Trip | 7" | CBS | 3431 | 1968 | £10 | £20 | *... demo, picture sleeve* |

## EXILE

| | | | | | | | |
|---|---|---|---|---|---|---|---|
| Don't Tax Me | 7" | Boring | BO1 | 1977 | £2.50 | £6 | |

## EXILES

| | | | | | | | |
|---|---|---|---|---|---|---|---|
| Freedom, Come All Ye | LP | Topic | 12T143 | 1966 | £10 | £25 | |

## EXIT
Exit ........................................................ LP ...... Better Daze ..... XPL1008 ................ 1969 £8 ......... £20 ........................ US

## EXITS
Yodelling ................................................ 7" ...... Way Out ........ WOO1 ................ 1978 £10 ......... £20

## EXITS (2)
Fashion Plague ........................................ 7" ...... Lightning ........ GIL519 ................ 1978 £2 ........... £5

## EXMAGMA
Exmagma ................................................ LP ...... Neusi ............ B204 ................ 1973 £8 ......... £20 ................. German
Goldball ................................................ LP ...... Disjuncta ......... 0009 ................ 1973 £6 ......... £15 ................. French

## EXPEDITION
Live ........................................................ LP ...... Cegep ............. 1653 ................ 1972 £6 ......... £15 ................. Canadian

## EXPERIMENTS WITH ICE
Experiments With Ice ............................... LP ...... United Dairies . EX001 ................ 1981 £6 ......... £15

## EXPLOSIVE
Cities Make The Country Colder .............. 7" ...... President ......... PT244 .................... 1969 £2 ............. £5
Who Planted Thorns In Alice's Garden ...... 7" ...... President ......... PT262 .................... 1969 £2 ............. £5

## EXPORT
Export ...................................................... LP ...... His Master's .... VICE1 ................ 1980 £4 ......... £10
.................................................................................... Vice ................
Wheeler Dealer ........................................ 7" ...... His Master's .... VICE2 ................ 1981 £1.50 ......... £4
.................................................................................... Vice ................

## EXTREEM
On The Beach ........................................ 7" ...... Strike ............. JH326 ................ 1966 £1.50 ......... £4

## EXTREME
Holehearted ............................................ CD-s .. A&M ............ AMCD839 .......... 1991 £2 ............. £5
More Than Words .................................... CD-s .. A&M ............ AMCD792 .......... 1991 £2.50 ......... £6
Song For Love ........................................ CD-s .. A&M ............ AMCD698 .......... 1992 £2 ............. £5

## EXUMA
Exuma ...................................................... LP ...... Mercury .......... 6338018 ............. 1970 £4 ......... £10
Exuma II ................................................ LP ...... Mercury .......... SR61314 ............. 1971 £4 ......... £10 ................. US
Snake ...................................................... LP ...... Kama Sutra ...... KSBS2052 ............. 1972 £4 ......... £10 ................. US

## EYE FULL TOWER
How About Me ........................................ 7" ...... Polydor ........... 56734 ................ 1967 £1.50 ......... £4

## EYELESS IN GAZA
Kodak Ghosts Run Amok ........................ 7" ...... Ambivalent ...... ASR002 ................ 1980 £5 ......... £10
.................................................................................... Scale ................

## EYES
Mod band the Eyes owed everything to the Who – even going so far as to record a Who sound-alike under the title 'My Degeneration'. Their handful of singles, and the EP which comprises the tracks from the first two singles, are now extremely collectable as prime examples of the freakbeat genre. The group also recorded an album, but this was a quickly and cheaply recorded exploitation affair, issued under the thin disguise of a pseudonym – *Tribute To The Rolling Stones* by the Pupils.

Arrival Of The Eyes .................................. 7" EP . Mercury .......... MCE10035 ............. 1966 £250 ..... £400
Good Day Sunshine .................................. 7" ...... Mercury .......... MF934 .................... 1966 £37.50 .... £75
Man With Money ...................................... 7" ...... Mercury .......... MF910 .................... 1966 £75 ......... £150
My Immediate Pleasure .............................. 7" ...... Mercury .......... MF897 .................... 1966 £50 ......... £100
When The Night Falls ............................... 7" ...... Mercury .......... MF881 .................... 1965 £50 ......... £100

## EYES OF BLUE
Crossroads Of Time .................................. LP ...... Mercury .......... SMCL20134 ........ 1968 £15 ......... £30
In Fields Of Ardath .................................. LP ...... Mercury .......... SMCL20164 ........ 1969 £15 ......... £30
Largo ...................................................... 7" ...... Mercury .......... MF1049 ............. 1968 £2 ............. £5
Supermarket Full Of Cans ........................ 7" ...... Deram ............ DM114 ............. 1967 £7.50 ......... £15
Up And Down ........................................ 7" ...... Deram ............ DM106 ............. 1966 £7.50 ......... £15

## EZELL, WILL
Chicago Piano .......................................... LP ...... Gannet ............ 12002 .................... 1973 £4 ......... £10
Gin Mill Jazz .......................................... 10" LP London .......... AL3539 ................ 1955 £8 ......... £20

# F

## FABARES, SHELLEY
| | | | | | | | |
|---|---|---|---|---|---|---|---|
| Johnny Angel | 7" | Pye | 7N25132 | 1962 | £2 | £5 | |
| Johnny Loves Me | 7" | Pye | 7N25151 | 1962 | £1.50 | £4 | |
| My Prayer | 7" | Fontana | TF592 | 1965 | £1.50 | £4 | |
| Shelley | LP | Colpix | CLP/CST426 | 1962 | £8 | £20 | US |
| Things We Did Last Summer | LP | Colpix | CLP/CST431 | 1962 | £8 | £20 | US |

## FABIAN
| | | | | | | | |
|---|---|---|---|---|---|---|---|
| Fabulous Fabian | LP | HMV | CLP1345 | 1960 | £15 | £30 | |
| Good Old Summertime | LP | Chancellor | CHL(S)5012 | 1960 | £10 | £25 | US |
| Got The Feeling | 7" | HMV | POP659 | 1959 | £4 | £8 | |
| Grapevine | 7" | HMV | POP869 | 1961 | £1.50 | £4 | |
| High Time | LP | RCA | LPM/LSP2314 | 1960 | £8 | £20 | US |
| Hold That Tiger | LP | HMV | CLP1301 | 1959 | £20 | £40 | |
| Hound Dog Man | 7" | HMV | POP695 | 1960 | £4 | £8 | |
| I'm A Man | 7" | HMV | POP587 | 1959 | £10 | £20 | |
| I'm Gonna Sit Right Down And Write Myself A Letter | 7" | HMV | POP778 | 1960 | £1.50 | £4 | |
| Kissin' And Twistin' | 7" | HMV | POP810 | 1960 | £1.50 | £4 | |
| Rockin' Hot | LP | Chancellor | CHL5019 | 1961 | £15 | £30 | US |
| Sixteen Fabulous Hits | LP | Chancellor | CHL5024 | 1962 | £10 | £25 | US |
| String Along | 7" | HMV | POP724 | 1960 | £1.50 | £4 | |
| Tiger | 7" | HMV | POP643 | 1959 | £5 | £10 | |
| Tomorrow | 7" | HMV | POP800 | 1960 | £1.50 | £4 | |
| Turn Me Loose | 7" | HMV | POP612 | 1959 | £7.50 | £15 | |
| You Know You Belong To Somebody Else | 7" | HMV | POP829 | 1961 | £1.50 | £4 | |
| You're Only Young Once | 7" | HMV | POP934 | 1961 | £1.50 | £4 | |
| Young And Wonderful | LP | HMV | CLP1433 | 1961 | £10 | £25 | |
| Young And Wonderful | LP | HMV | CSD1352 | 1961 | £15 | £30 | stereo |

## FABIAN & FRANKIE AVALON
| | | | | | | | |
|---|---|---|---|---|---|---|---|
| Hit Makers | LP | Chancellor | CHL5009 | 1960 | £10 | £25 | US |

## FABULOUS DIALS
| | | | | | | | |
|---|---|---|---|---|---|---|---|
| Bossa Nova Stomp | 7" | Pye | 7N25200 | 1963 | £5 | £10 | |

## FACE TO FACE
| | | | | | | | |
|---|---|---|---|---|---|---|---|
| Turning To You | LP | Acorn | AC001 | 1978 | £37.50 | £75 | |

## FACES
| | | | | | | | |
|---|---|---|---|---|---|---|---|
| Borstal Boys | 7" | Warner Bros | K16281 | 1973 | £5 | £10 | |
| First Step | LP | Warner Bros | K46053 | 1970 | £4 | £10 | |
| First Step | LP | Warner Bros | WS3000 | 1970 | £4 | £10 | |
| Long Player | LP | Warner Bros | K46064 | 1971 | £4 | £10 | |
| Long Player | LP | Warner Bros | W3011 | 1971 | £4 | £10 | |
| Nod Is As Good As A Wink | LP | Warner Bros | K56006 | 1971 | £4 | £10 | |
| Nod Is As Good As A Wink | LP | Warner Bros | K56006 | 1971 | £5 | £12 | with poster |
| Ooh La La | LP | Warner Bros | K56011 | 1973 | £4 | £10 | |

## FACTORY
| | | | | | | | |
|---|---|---|---|---|---|---|---|
| Path Through the Forest | 7" | MGM | MGM1444 | 1968 | £100 | £200 | best auctioned |
| Try A Little Sunshine | 7" | CBS | 4540 | 1969 | £100 | £200 | best auctioned |

## FACTORY (2)
| | | | | | | | |
|---|---|---|---|---|---|---|---|
| Time Machine | 7" | Oak | RGJ718 | 1970 | £50 | £100 | |

## FACTOTUMS
| | | | | | | | |
|---|---|---|---|---|---|---|---|
| Cloudy | 7" | Pye | 7N17402 | 1967 | £1.50 | £4 | |
| Here Today | 7" | Piccadilly | 7N35333 | 1966 | £1.50 | £4 | |
| I Can't Give You Anything | 7" | Piccadilly | 7N35355 | 1966 | £1.50 | £4 | |
| In My Lonely Room | 7" | Immediate | IM009 | 1965 | £4 | £8 | |
| Mr. And Mrs. Regards | 7" | CBS | 4140 | 1969 | £1.50 | £4 | |
| You're So Good To Be | 7" | Immediate | IM022 | 1965 | £4 | £8 | |

## FADING COLOURS
| | | | | | | | |
|---|---|---|---|---|---|---|---|
| Just Like Romeo And Juliet | 7" | Ember | EMBS229 | 1966 | £1.50 | £4 | |

## FAGEN, DONALD
| | | | | | | | |
|---|---|---|---|---|---|---|---|
| Kamakiriad | CD | Reprise | 245230DJ | 1993 | £10 | £25 | US gold promo, autographed |
| Words And Music | CD | Reprise | PROCD6161 | 1993 | £8 | £20 | US promo |

## FAHEY, BRIAN ORCHESTRA

'At The Sign Of The Swinging Cymbal' is the theme tune of radio's *Pick Of The Pops*, although it inevitably sounds incomplete without Alan Freeman's perfectly timed interjections.

| | | | | | | | |
|---|---|---|---|---|---|---|---|
| At The Sign Of The Swinging Cymbal | 7" | Parlophone | R4686 | 1960 £2 | £5 | | |
| At The Sign Of The Swinging Cymbal | 7" | Parlophone | R4909 | 1962 £1.50 | £4 | | |
| Twang | 7" | United Artists | UP1115 | 1965 £1.50 | £4 | | |

## FAHEY, JOHN

| | | | | | | | |
|---|---|---|---|---|---|---|---|
| Blind Joe Death | LP | Takoma | C1002 | 1967 £6 | £15 | | US |
| Dance Of Death | LP | Takoma | 1004 | 1967 £6 | £15 | | US |
| Days Have Gone By | LP | Takoma | 1014 | 1967 £6 | £15 | | US |
| Death Chants, Breakdowns & Military Waltzes | LP | Sonet | SNTF608 | 1969 £4 | £10 | | |
| Death Chants, Breakdowns And Military Waltzes | LP | Takoma | C1003 | 1967 £6 | £15 | | US |
| Essential John Fahey | LP | Vanguard | VSD55/56 | 1974 £5 | £12 | | double |
| Great San Bernadino Birthday Party (Guitar Vol. 4) | LP | Takoma | 1008 | 1967 £6 | £15 | | US |
| New Possibility | LP | Takoma | 1020 | 1968 £6 | £15 | | US |
| Requia | LP | Vanguard | SVRL19055 | 1968 £5 | £12 | | |
| Transfiguration Of Blind Joe Death | LP | Sonet | SNTF607 | 1969 £5 | £12 | | |
| Transfiguration Of Blind Joe Death | LP | Transatlantic | TRA173 | 1967 £5 | £12 | | |
| Transfiguration Of Blind Joe Death | LP | Transatlantic | TRA173 | 1967 £8 | £20 | with booklet | |
| Voice Of The Turtle | LP | Takoma | 1019 | 1968 £6 | £15 | | US |
| Yellow Princess | LP | Vanguard | SVRL19033 | 1968 £5 | £12 | | |

## FAINE JADE

| | | | | | | | |
|---|---|---|---|---|---|---|---|
| Introspection: A Faine Jade Recital | LP | R.S.V.P. | 8002 | 1968 £250 | £400 | | US |

## FAIR, JAD

| | | | | | | | |
|---|---|---|---|---|---|---|---|
| Zombies Of Mora–Tau | 7" | Armageddon | AEP003 | 1980 £5 | £10 | | |

## FAIR, YVONNE

| | | | | | | | |
|---|---|---|---|---|---|---|---|
| Bitch Is Black | LP | Tamla Motown | STML12008 | 1975 £4 | £10 | | |

## FAIR SET

| | | | | | | |
|---|---|---|---|---|---|---|
| Honey And Wine | 7" | Decca | F12168 | 1965 £2 | £5 | |

## FAIRBURN, WERLY

| | | | | | | |
|---|---|---|---|---|---|---|
| All The Time | 7" | London | HLC8349 | 1956 £500 | £750 | best auctioned |

## FAIRE, JOHNNY

| | | | | | | |
|---|---|---|---|---|---|---|
| Bertha Lou | 7" | London | HLU8569 | 1958 £150 | £250 | best auctioned |

## FAIRFIELD PARLOUR

*From Home To Home* is the third LP by the English Kaleidoscope. The change of name to Fairfield Parlour brought no more than a marginal improvement to the group's fortunes, however, and the record today is almost as scarce as the first two.

| | | | | | | |
|---|---|---|---|---|---|---|
| Bordeaux Rose | 7" | Prism | PR11 | 1976 £2 | £5 | |
| Bordeaux Rose | 7" | Vertigo | 6059003 | 1970 £1.50 | £4 | |
| From Home To Home | LP | Vertigo | 6360001 | 1970 £30 | £60 | spiral label |
| Just Another Day | 7" | Vertigo | 6059008 | 1970 £5 | £10 | |

## FAIRGROUND ATTRACTION

| | | | | | | |
|---|---|---|---|---|---|---|
| Clare | CD-s | RCA | PD42608 | 1989 £2 | £5 | |
| Find My Love | CD-s | RCA | PD42080 | 1988 £2 | £5 | |
| Perfect | CD-s | RCA | PD41846 | 1988 £2 | £5 | |
| Perfect | CD-s | RCA | PD42649 | 1988 £2 | £5 | |
| Smile In A Whisper | CD-s | RCA | PD42250 | 1988 £2 | £5 | |
| Walking After Midnight | CD-s | RCA | PD43654 | 1990 £2 | £5 | |

## FAIRIES

| | | | | | | |
|---|---|---|---|---|---|---|
| Don't Mind | 7" | HMV | POP1445 | 1965 £25 | £50 | |
| Don't Think Twice It's Alright | 7" | Decca | F11943 | 1964 £25 | £50 | |
| Get Yourself Home | 7" | HMV | POP1404 | 1965 £50 | £100 | |

## FAIRPORT CONVENTION

On their first LP Fairport Convention sound like an English Jefferson Airplane. The folk music influence begins to be felt on *What We Did On Our Holidays* and takes over altogether on *Liege and Lief*. Thus over the course of four LPs, recorded in a period of not much more than a year, it is possible to hear the genesis of a new kind of rock music. The personnel changes in the group became rather complicated after this, but the various editions of Fairport Convention – and indeed the many groups derived from it – were able to explore the possibilities of the folk-rock fusion in many fruitful ways. The success of Fairport Convention's annual 'reunion' at Copredy testifies to the tremendous loyalty of their considerable number of both fans and past members! Virtually all of the group's records are now collectable to a greater or lesser extent. It should be noted that, unlike many late sixties albums, the mono version of the Polydor LP does not appear to contain any different mixes to the stereo version, but it does somehow manage to deliver a crisper, more dynamic sound, which justifies its higher value.

| | | | | | | |
|---|---|---|---|---|---|---|
| Airing Cupboard Tapes | cass | Woodworm | | 1981 £6 | £15 | |
| Angel Delight | LP | Island | ILPS9162 | 1971 £5 | £12 | |
| AT2 | LP | Woodworm | WR1 | 1984 £5 | £12 | |
| Babbacombe Lee | LP | Island | ILPS9176 | 1971 £5 | £12 | |
| Bonny Bunch Of Roses | LP | Vertigo | 9102015 | 1977 £5 | £12 | |
| Expletive Delighted | LP | Woodworm | WR009 | 1986 £5 | £12 | |
| Fairport Convention | LP | Polydor | 582035 | 1968 £20 | £40 | mono |
| Fairport Convention | LP | Polydor | 583035 | 1968 £15 | £30 | |

| | | | | | | | | |
|---|---|---|---|---|---|---|---|---|
| Farewell Farewell | LP | Simons | GAMA1 | 1979 | £5 | £12 | |
| Full House | LP | Island | ILPS9130 | 1970 | £6 | £15 | pink label |
| Full House | LP | Island | ILPS9130 | 1970 | £150 | £250 | test pressing with 'Poor Will & The Jolly Hangman' |
| Gladys Leap | CD | Woodworm | WRCD007 | 1985 | £5 | £12 | |
| Gottle O'Geer | LP | Island | ILPS9389 | 1976 | £6 | £15 | |
| History Of Fairport Convention | LP | Island | ICD4 | 1972 | £6 | £15 | |
| History Of Fairport Convention | LP | Island | ICD4 | 1972 | £6 | £15 | double |
| If I Had A Ribbon Bow | 7" | Track | 604020 | 1968 | £5 | £10 | |
| If (Stomp) | 7" | Polydor | 2058014 | 1970 | £4 | £8 | |
| In Real Time | LP | Island | ILPS9883 | 1987 | £5 | £12 | |
| John Lee | 7" | Island | WIP6128 | 1971 | £2 | £5 | picture sleeve |
| Liege And Lief | LP | Island | ILPS9115 | 1969 | £6 | £15 | pink label |
| Liege And Lief | CD | Island | CID9115 | 1986 | £5 | £12 | |
| Live A Movable Feast | LP | Island | ILPS9285 | 1974 | £5 | £12 | |
| Live At Broughton Castle | LP | Stony Plain | SP51052 | 1985 | £5 | £12 | |
| Live At L.A. Troubadour | LP | Island | HELP28 | 1976 | £10 | £25 | |
| Meet On The Ledge | 7" | Island | WIP6047 | 1968 | £2.50 | £6 | |
| Moat On The Ledge | LP | Woodworm | WR001 | 1982 | £5 | £12 | |
| Nine | LP | Island | ILPS9246 | 1973 | £5 | £12 | |
| Red And Gold | CD | New Routes | RUECD002 | 1989 | £5 | £12 | |
| Rising For The Moon | LP | Island | ILPS9313 | 1975 | £5 | £12 | |
| Rosie | LP | Island | ILPS9208 | 1973 | £5 | £12 | |
| Rubber Band | 7" | Simons | PMW1 | 1979 | £1.50 | £4 | |
| Tippler's Tales | LP | Vertigo | 9102022 | 1978 | £5 | £12 | |
| Tour Sampler | LP | Island | ISS2 | 1975 | £50 | £100 | |
| Unhalfbricking | LP | Island | ILPS9102 | 1969 | £6 | £15 | pink label |
| What We Did On Our Holidays | LP | Island | ILPS9092 | 1968 | £6 | £15 | pink label |

## FAIRWAYS

| | | | | | | | |
|---|---|---|---|---|---|---|---|
| Yoko Ono | 7" | Mercury | MF1116 | 1969 | £2 | £5 | |

## FAIRWEATHER

Named after lead singer Andy Fairweather-Low, Fairweather were essentially a slimmed down version of Amen Corner. Seeing the way that rock music was going, the group attempted to put their pop past behind it by signing to RCA's new progressive label, Neon. They blew it, however, by gaining a hit single!

| | | | | | | | |
|---|---|---|---|---|---|---|---|
| Beginning From An End | LP | Neon | NE1 | 1971 | £4 | £10 | |

## FAIRWEATHER, AL

| | | | | | | | |
|---|---|---|---|---|---|---|---|
| Al And Sandy | LP | Columbia | 33SX1159 | 1959 | £6 | £15 | with Sandy Brown |
| Al's Pals | LP | Columbia | 33SX1221 | 1960 | £6 | £15 | |
| Fairweather Friends | 10" LP | Nixa | NJT511 | 1958 | £5 | £12 | |

## FAIRY TALE

| | | | | | | | |
|---|---|---|---|---|---|---|---|
| Once Upon A Time | LP | Blossom | 17001 | 1969 | £8 | £20 | Dutch |

## FAIRY'S MOKE

| | | | | | | | |
|---|---|---|---|---|---|---|---|
| Fairy's Moke | LP | Deroy | DER1175 | 1975 | £50 | £100 | |

## FAIRYTALE

| | | | | | | | |
|---|---|---|---|---|---|---|---|
| Guess I Was Dreaming | 7" | Decca | F12644 | 1967 | £20 | £40 | |
| Lovely People | 7" | Decca | F12665 | 1967 | £20 | £40 | |

## FAITH, ADAM

Adam Faith has remained a public figure ever since his first forays into the charts – though not in general as a singer, but rather as an actor and a financial commentator. His first recordings took the soft pop-and-strings sound of Buddy Holly's 'It Doesn't Matter Any More' as their starting point – the weakness of using as the basis for an entire style what Holly undoubtedly viewed as a limited novelty reached by the rather low collectors' values reached by Faith's records today. It was to his credit, however, that with the arrival of British beat, Faith's response was to find a beat backing group, the Roulettes, for himself. On records like 'The First Time', the results were quite successful, although collectors are more interested in the records made by the Roulettes without their employer.

| | | | | | | | |
|---|---|---|---|---|---|---|---|
| Adam | LP | Parlophone | PCS3010 | 1960 | £6 | £15 | stereo |
| Adam | LP | Parlophone | PMC1128 | 1960 | £4 | £10 | mono |
| Adam | LP | Regal | (S)REG1033 | 1960 | £4 | £10 | export |
| Adam | 7" EP | Parlophone | GEP8824 | 1960 | £2.50 | £6 | |
| Adam | 7" EP | Parlophone | SGE2014 | 1960 | £5 | £10 | stereo |
| Adam Faith | LP | Amy | 8005 | 1965 | £8 | £20 | US |
| Adam Faith | LP | Parlophone | PCS3025 | 1961 | £6 | £15 | stereo |
| Adam Faith | LP | Parlophone | PMC1162 | 1961 | £4 | £10 | mono |
| Adam No. 2 | 7" EP | Parlophone | GEP8826 | 1960 | £2.50 | £6 | |
| Adam No. 2 | 7" EP | Parlophone | SGE2015 | 1960 | £5 | £10 | stereo |
| Adam No. 3 | 7" EP | Parlophone | GEP8831 | 1960 | £2.50 | £6 | |
| Adam No. 3 | 7" EP | Parlophone | SGE2018 | 1960 | £5 | £10 | stereo |
| Adam's Hit Parade | 7" EP | Parlophone | GEP8811 | 1960 | £2.50 | £6 | |
| Adam's Hit Parade Vol. 2 | 7" EP | Parlophone | GEP8841 | 1961 | £2.50 | £6 | |
| Adam's Hit Parade Vol. 3 | 7" EP | Parlophone | GEP8862 | 1962 | £4 | £8 | |
| Adam's Latest Hits | 7" EP | Parlophone | GEP8877 | 1963 | £4 | £8 | |
| All These Things | 7" EP | Parlophone | GEP8852 | 1961 | £2.50 | £6 | |
| Beat Girl | 7" EP | Columbia | SEG8138 | 1962 | £12.50 | £25 | with John Barry |
| Beat Girl | LP | Columbia | 33SX1225 | 1960 | £10 | £25 | with John Barry |
| Cheryl's Going Home | 7" | Parlophone | R5516 | 1966 | £1.50 | £4 | |
| Daddy What'll Happen To Me | 7" | Parlophone | R5635 | 1967 | £1.50 | £4 | |
| England's Top Singer | LP | MGM | (S)E3591 | 1961 | £8 | £20 | US |
| Faith Alive | LP | Parlophone | PMC1249 | 1965 | £15 | £30 | |
| For You | LP | Parlophone | PMC1213 | 1963 | £4 | £10 | |

*289*

| Title | Format | Label | Catalogue | Year | | | Notes |
|---|---|---|---|---|---|---|---|
| For You – Adam | 7" EP | Parlophone | GEP8904 | 1964 | £4 | £8 | |
| From Adam With Love | LP | Parlophone | PCS3038 | 1962 | £6 | £15 | stereo |
| From Adam With Love | LP | Parlophone | PMC1192 | 1962 | £4 | £10 | mono |
| Heartsick Feeling | 7" | HMV | POP438 | 1958 | £30 | £60 | |
| Hey Little Lovin' Girl | 7" | Parlophone | R5673 | 1968 | £1.50 | £4 | |
| High School Confidential | 7" | HMV | POP557 | 1958 | £20 | £40 | |
| Message To Martha – From Adam | 7" EP | Parlophone | GEP8929 | 1965 | £4 | £8 | |
| On The Move | LP | Parlophone | PMC1228 | 1964 | £8 | £20 | |
| Poor Me | 78 | Parlophone | R4623 | 1960 | £7.50 | £15 | |
| Runk Bunk | 78 | Top Rank | JAR126 | 1959 | £10 | £20 | |
| Runk Bunk | 7" | Top Rank | JAR126 | 1959 | £7.50 | £15 | |
| Songs And Things | 7" EP | Parlophone | GEP8939 | 1965 | £5 | £10 | |
| Sure Know A Lot About Love | 7" EP | Parlophone | GEP8854 | 1961 | £2.50 | £6 | |
| Time Has Come | 7" EP | Parlophone | GEP8851 | 1961 | £2.50 | £6 | |
| To Hell With Love | 7" | Parlophone | R5649 | 1967 | £1.50 | £4 | |
| Top Of The Pops | 7" EP | Parlophone | GEP8893 | 1964 | £5 | £10 | |
| What Do You Want? | 78 | Parlophone | R4591 | 1959 | £7.50 | £15 | |
| What More Can Anyone Do | 7" | Parlophone | R5556 | 1967 | £1.50 | £4 | |

## FAITH, GEORGE

| Title | Format | Label | Catalogue | Year | | | Notes |
|---|---|---|---|---|---|---|---|
| To Be A Lover | LP | Island | ILPS9504 | 1977 | £4 | £10 | |

## FAITH, HORACE

| Title | Format | Label | Catalogue | Year | | | Notes |
|---|---|---|---|---|---|---|---|
| Black Pearl | 7" | Trojan | TR7790 | 1970 | £1.50 | £4 | |
| Daddy's Home | 7" | Downtown | DT446 | 1969 | £1.50 | £4 | |
| Spinning Wheel | 7" | B&C | CB104 | 1969 | £1.50 | £4 | |

## FAITH NO MORE

| Title | Format | Label | Catalogue | Year | | | Notes |
|---|---|---|---|---|---|---|---|
| Anne's Song | 7" | Slash | LASHP18 | 1988 | £4 | £8 | picture disc |
| Anne's Song | 12" | Slash | LASHX18 | 1988 | £3 | £8 | |
| Epic | CD-s | Slash | LASCD21 | 1990 | £6 | £15 | |
| Epic | CD-s | Slash | LASCD26 | 1990 | £2 | £5 | |
| Epic | 7" | Slash | LASPD21 | 1990 | £2.50 | £6 | shaped picture disc |
| From Out Of Nowhere | CD-s | Slash | LASCD24 | 1990 | £2 | £5 | |
| King For A Day | CD | Slash | | 199– | £6 | £15 | Australian with bonus 6 track CD of B sides and alternate versions |
| Real Thing | LP | Slash | 8282171 | 1989 | £4 | £10 | picture disc |
| We Care A Lot | 12" | Slash | LASHX17 | 1988 | £3 | £8 | |

## FAITHFUL, AUSTIN

| Title | Format | Label | Catalogue | Year | | | Notes |
|---|---|---|---|---|---|---|---|
| Ain't That Peculiar | 7" | Pyramid | PYR6042 | 1968 | £4 | £8 | |
| Eternal Love | 7" | Pyramid | PYR6028 | 1968 | £4 | £8 | Roland Alphonso B side |
| Uncle Joe | 7" | Blue Cat | BS140 | 1968 | £2.50 | £6 | |

## FAITHFUL BREATH

| Title | Format | Label | Catalogue | Year | | | Notes |
|---|---|---|---|---|---|---|---|
| Fading Beauty | LP | Fb | AA6963233 | 1973 | £15 | £30 | German |

## FAITHFULL, MARIANNE

| Title | Format | Label | Catalogue | Year | | | Notes |
|---|---|---|---|---|---|---|---|
| A Bientôt nous deux | 7" EP | Decca | 457094 | 1965 | £10 | £20 | French |
| As Tears Go By | 7" | Decca | F11923 | 1964 | £1.50 | £4 | |
| Blowing In The Wind | 7" | Decca | F12007 | 1964 | £2 | £5 | |
| Come And Stay With Me | 7" EP | Decca | 457068 | 1965 | £7.50 | £15 | French |
| Come And Stay With Me | 7" | Decca | F12075 | 1965 | £1.50 | £4 | |
| Come My Way | LP | Decca | LK4688 | 1965 | £10 | £25 | |
| Conversation With Marianne Faithfull | CD | Island | MFCCD1 | 1987 | £8 | £20 | promo |
| Coquillages | 7" EP | Decca | 457119 | 1966 | £10 | £20 | French |
| Counting | 7" EP | Decca | 457125 | 1966 | £7.50 | £15 | French |
| Counting | 7" | Decca | F12443 | 1966 | £1.50 | £4 | |
| Faithful Forever | LP | London | LL3/PS482 | 1966 | £8 | £20 | US |
| Go Away From My World | LP | London | LL3/PS452 | 1965 | £8 | £20 | US |
| Greensleeves | 7" EP | Decca | 457049 | 1964 | £12.50 | £25 | French |
| Hier ou demain | 7" EP | Decca | 457139 | 1967 | £10 | £20 | French |
| Is This What I Get For Loving You | 7" | Decca | F12524 | 1966 | £1.50 | £4 | |
| Love In A Mist | LP | Decca | LK/SKL4854 | 1967 | £15 | £30 | |
| Marianne Faithfull | LP | Decca | LK4689 | 1965 | £10 | £25 | |
| Marianne Faithfull | 7" EP | Decca | DFE8624 | 1965 | £6 | £12 | |
| North Country Maid | LP | Decca | LK4778 | 1966 | £15 | £30 | |
| Sister Morphine | 7" | Decca | F12889 | 1969 | £10 | £20 | |
| Summer Nights | 7" EP | Decca | 457085 | 1965 | £7.50 | £15 | French |
| Summer Nights | 7" | Decca | F12193 | 1965 | £1.50 | £4 | |
| This Little Bird | 7" | Decca | F12162 | 1965 | £1.50 | £4 | |
| Tomorrow's Calling | 7" | Decca | F12408 | 1966 | £1.50 | £4 | |
| Yesterday | 7" EP | Decca | 457097 | 1965 | £7.50 | £15 | French |
| Yesterday | 7" | Decca | F12268 | 1965 | £1.50 | £4 | |

## FALCONS

| Title | Format | Label | Catalogue | Year | | | Notes |
|---|---|---|---|---|---|---|---|
| Billy The Kid | 7" | London | HLU10146 | 1967 | £2 | £5 | |

## FALCONS (2)

| Title | Format | Label | Catalogue | Year | | | Notes |
|---|---|---|---|---|---|---|---|
| Stampede | 7" | Philips | BF1297 | 1964 | £2 | £5 | |

## FALCONS (3)

| Title | Format | Label | Catalogue | Year | | | Notes |
|---|---|---|---|---|---|---|---|
| Fever | LP | Ariola | 85067 | 1970 | £6 | £15 | German |
| I Found A Love | 7" | London | HLK9565 | 1962 | £12.50 | £25 | |
| You're So Fine | 7" | London | HLT8876 | 1959 | £25 | £50 | |

# FALL

| | | | | | | | |
|---|---|---|---|---|---|---|---|
| Bingo Masters Breakout | 7" | Step Forward | SF7 | 1978 | £2 | £5 | |
| Fall In A Hole | LP | Flying Nun | MARK1/2 | 1983 | £15 | £30 | *New Zealand, with 12"* |
| Fiery Jack | 7" | Step Forward | SF13 | 1980 | £2 | £5 | *2 picture sleeves* |
| Grotesque | LP | Rough Trade | ROUGH18 | 1980 | £4 | £10 | |
| It's The New Thing | 7" | Step Forward | SF9 | 1978 | £1.50 | £4 | |
| Kicker Conspiracy | 7" | Rough Trade | RT143 | 1983 | £2.50 | £6 | *double picture sleeve* |
| Marquis Cha Cha | 7" | Kamera | ERA014 | 1982 | £7.50 | £15 | |
| Popcorn Double Feature | CD-s | Cog Sinister | SINCD5 | 1990 | £2 | £5 | |
| Rowche Rumble | 7" | Step Forward | SF11 | 1979 | £1.50 | £4 | |
| Selections From The Infotainment Scan | CD | Matador | PRCD5094 | 1993 | £8 | £20 | *with new live track* |
| Slates | 10" | Rough Trade | RT071 | 1981 | £2.50 | £6 | |
| Telephone Thing | CD-s | Cog Sinister | SINCD4 | 1990 | £2 | £5 | |
| Totale's Turns | LP | Rough Trade | ROUGH10 | 1980 | £4 | £10 | |
| White Lightning | CD-s | Cog Sinister | SINCD6 | 1990 | £2 | £5 | |

# FALLEN ANGELS

| | | | | | | | |
|---|---|---|---|---|---|---|---|
| Fallen Angels | LP | London | HAZ/SHZ8359 | 1968 | £15 | £30 | |
| It's A Long Way Down | LP | Roulette | SR42011 | 1968 | £50 | £100 | *US* |

# FALLIN, JOHNNY

| | | | | | | | |
|---|---|---|---|---|---|---|---|
| Party Kiss | 7" | Capitol | CL15043 | 1959 | £5 | £10 | |
| Wild Streak | 7" | Capitol | CL15091 | 1959 | £7.50 | £15 | |

# FALLING LEAVES

| | | | | | | | |
|---|---|---|---|---|---|---|---|
| Beggar's Parade | 7" | Decca | F12420 | 1966 | £5 | £10 | |
| She Loves To Be Loved | 7" | Parlophone | R5233 | 1965 | £12.50 | £25 | |

# FALLOUT

| | | | | | | | |
|---|---|---|---|---|---|---|---|
| Butchery | LP | I | FLP2 | 1984 | £8 | £20 | |

# FALTSKOG, AGNETHA

The blonde singer from Abba was an established solo artist in Sweden before becoming a member of the successful group, and has reverted to her solo career since Abba disbanded.

| | | | | | | | |
|---|---|---|---|---|---|---|---|
| Agnetha | LP | Cupol | CLP64 | 1968 | £10 | £25 | *Swedish* |
| Agnetha | LP | Cupol | CLPL1002 | 197– | £5 | £12 | *Swedish* |
| Agnetha | LP | Embassy | EMB31094 | 1974 | £20 | £40 | |
| Agnetha Faltskog | LP | Cupol | | 1972 | £5 | £12 | *Swedish* |
| Agnetha Vol. 2 | LP | Cupol | CLP80 | 1969 | £8 | £20 | *Swedish* |
| Agnetha Vol. 2 | LP | Cupol | CLPL1003 | 197– | £5 | £12 | *Swedish* |
| Basta | LP | Cupol | CLPL1023 | 1973 | £15 | £30 | *Swedish* |
| Can't Shake Loose | 7" | Epic | EPCA3812 | 1983 | £1.50 | £4 | *poster picture sleeve* |
| Elva Kvinnor I Ett Hus | LP | Cupol | CLPS351 | 1975 | £5 | £12 | *Swedish* |
| Eyes Of A Woman | CD | Epic | CD26446 | 1987 | £5 | £12 | |
| I Stand Alone | CD | WEA | 2422312 | 1988 | £5 | £12 | |
| Nar En Vacker Tanke Blir En Sang | LP | Cupol | CLPN348 | 1971 | £15 | £30 | *Swedish* |
| Som Jag Ar | LP | Cupol | CLPL1016 | 197– | £5 | £12 | *Swedish* |
| Som Jag Ar | LP | Cupol | CLPN345 | 1970 | £10 | £25 | *Swedish* |
| Tio Ar Med | LP | Cupol | CLPS352 | 1979 | £5 | £12 | *Swedish* |
| Wrap Your Arms Around Me | CD | Epic | CD25505 | 1983 | £5 | £12 | |

# FAME, GEORGIE

Georgie Fame's lengthy and still-flourishing career (his earliest recordings are as a member of Billy Fury's backing group) has produced few real collectors' items. Of his series of distinctive, jazz-inflected albums, only the first is in the same price league as his contemporaries – the others sold well when new, but are clearly considered by modern collectors to be too polished and too far removed from how British R&B should sound. Two scarce early singles were credited to the Blue Flames, with no mention of Georgie Fame's name. They are listed in this guide under the Blue Flames.

| | | | | | | | |
|---|---|---|---|---|---|---|---|
| Bend A Little | 7" | Columbia | DB7328 | 1964 | £1.50 | £4 | |
| Do Re Mi | 7" | Columbia | DB7255 | 1964 | £1.50 | £4 | |
| Do The Dog | 7" EP | Columbia | ESRF1516 | 1964 | £7.50 | £15 | *French* |
| Fame At Last | LP | Columbia | 33SX1638 | 1964 | £6 | £15 | |
| Fame At Last | 7" EP | Columbia | SEG8393 | 1964 | £2.50 | £6 | |
| Fats For Fame | 7" EP | Columbia | SEG8406 | 1965 | £4 | £8 | |
| Get Away | LP | Imperial | LP9331/12331 | 1966 | £5 | £12 | *US* |
| Get Away | 7" EP | Columbia | ESRF1796 | 1966 | £5 | £10 | *French* |
| Get Away | 7" EP | Columbia | SEG8518 | 1966 | £2.50 | £6 | |
| Get Away | 7" | 208 Luxembourg | | 1964 | £2 | £5 | *1 sided promo* |
| Hall Of Fame | LP | Columbia | SX6120 | 1967 | £4 | £10 | |
| In The Meantime | 7" EP | Columbia | ESRF1645 | 1964 | £7.50 | £15 | *French* |
| In The Meantime | 7" | Columbia | DB7494 | 1965 | £1.50 | £4 | |
| Knock On Wood | 7" EP | CBS | EP6363 | 1967 | £2 | £5 | |
| Like We Used To Be | 7" EP | Columbia | ESRF1706 | 1965 | £5 | £10 | *French* |
| Like We Used To Be | 7" | Columbia | DB7633 | 1965 | £1.50 | £4 | |
| Move It On Over | 7" EP | Columbia | SEG8454 | 1965 | £4 | £8 | |
| R&B At The Flamingo | LP | Columbia | SX1599 | 1964 | £15 | £30 | |
| R&B At The Flamingo | 7" EP | Columbia | SEG8382 | 1964 | £5 | £10 | |
| Rhythm And Blue Beat | 7" EP | Columbia | SEG8334 | 1964 | £6 | £12 | |
| Seventh Son | LP | CBS | 63786 | 1969 | £4 | £10 | |
| Shop Around | 7" | Columbia | DB7193 | 1964 | £2 | £5 | |
| Shorty | LP | Epic | BN26563 | 1968 | £15 | £30 | *German* |
| Sitting In The Park | 7" EP | Columbia | ESRF1848 | 1967 | £5 | £10 | *French* |
| Sitting In The Park | 7" | Columbia | DB8096 | 1966 | £1.50 | £4 | |

| Something | 7" EP | Columbia | ESRF1751 | 1966 | £5 | £10 | French |
|---|---|---|---|---|---|---|---|
| Something | 7" | Columbia | DB7727 | 1965 | £1.50 | £4 | |
| Sound Venture | LP | Columbia | SX6076 | 1966 | £5 | £12 | |
| Sunny | 7" | Columbia | DB8015 | 1966 | £1.50 | £4 | |
| Sweet Things | LP | Columbia | SX6043 | 1966 | £5 | £12 | |
| Two Faces Of Fame | LP | CBS | 63018 | 1967 | £4 | £10 | |
| Yeh Yeh | LP | Imperial | LP9282/12282 | 1965 | £5 | £12 | US |
| Yeh Yeh | 7" EP | Columbia | ESRF1618 | 1964 | £6 | £12 | French |

## FAMILY

Family's first single, 'Scene Thru The Eye Of A Lens', is something of a psychedelic classic, and has not been reissued. All the members of Traffic were also involved in the making of the record, with Stevie Winwood playing the vital mellotron part. *Music In A Doll's House* continued the Traffic connection, being to some extent taken over by Dave Mason, who produced the record and played on it. It is a wonderful LP, however, and proof that the real sixties gems have already been discovered, and do not cost a fortune. Subsequent Family records are increasingly ordinary, although each undoubtedly has its moments, and they are all highlighted by the extraordinary Roger Chapman voice.

| Family Entertainment | LP | Reprise | RLP6340 | 1969 | £10 | £25 | with poster, mono |
|---|---|---|---|---|---|---|---|
| Family Entertainment | LP | Reprise | RSLP6340 | 1969 | £6 | £15 | with poster, stereo |
| Larf And Sing | 7" | Reprise | SAM1 | 1971 | £4 | £8 | promo |
| Me My Friend | 7" | Reprise | RS23270 | 1968 | £1.50 | £4 | |
| Music In A Doll's House | LP | Reprise | RLP6312 | 1968 | £8 | £20 | with poster, mono |
| Music In A Doll's House | LP | Reprise | RSLP6312 | 1968 | £6 | £15 | with poster, stereo |
| No Mule's Fool | 7" | Reprise | RS27001 | 1969 | £2 | £5 | picture sleeve |
| Scene Thru The Eye Of A Lens | 7" | Liberty | LBF15031 | 1967 | £37.50 | £75 | |
| Second Generation Woman | 7" | Reprise | RS23315 | 1968 | £1.50 | £4 | |
| Song For Me | LP | Reprise | RSLP9001 | 1970 | £4 | £10 | |
| Today | 7" | Reprise | RS27005 | 1970 | £2 | £5 | picture sleeve |

## FAMILY DOGG

| Family Dogg | 7" | MGM | MGM1360 | 1967 | £1.50 | £4 | |
|---|---|---|---|---|---|---|---|

## FAMILY OF APOSTOLIC

| Family Of Apostolic | LP | Vanguard | SDVL1 | 1969 | £8 | £20 | double |
|---|---|---|---|---|---|---|---|

## FAMOUS JUG BAND

| Chameleon | LP | Liberty | LBS83355 | 1970 | £6 | £15 | |
|---|---|---|---|---|---|---|---|
| Only Friend I Own | 7" | Liberty | LBF15224 | 1969 | £1.50 | £4 | |
| Sunshine Possibilities | LP | Liberty | LBS83263 | 1969 | £10 | £25 | |

## FAMOUS WARD SINGERS

| Famous Ward Singers Vol. 1 | 7" EP | London | EZC19024 | 1958 | £4 | £8 | |
|---|---|---|---|---|---|---|---|
| Famous Ward Singers Vol. 2 | 7" EP | London | EZC19033 | 1958 | £4 | £8 | |
| Famous Ward Singers Vol. 3 | 7" EP | London | EZC19034 | 1958 | £5 | £10 | |
| I Knew It Was The Lord | 78 | London | HL8065 | 1954 | £10 | £20 | |

## FAN CLUB

| Avenue | 7" | M&S | SJP791 | 1978 | £4 | £8 | |
|---|---|---|---|---|---|---|---|

## FANATICS

| Suburban Love Songs | 12" | Chapter 22 | 12CHAP38 | 1989 | £4 | £10 | |
|---|---|---|---|---|---|---|---|

## FANKHAUSER, MERRELL

| Merrell Fankhauser | LP | Maui | 101 | 1976 | £8 | £20 | US |
|---|---|---|---|---|---|---|---|
| Merrell Fankhauser & His HMS Bounty | LP | Shamley | SS701 | 1968 | £8 | £20 | US |

## FANTASTIC BAGGYS

| Summer Means Fun | 7" | United Artists | UP36142 | 1976 | £2 | £5 | Jan And Dean B side |
|---|---|---|---|---|---|---|---|
| Tell 'Em I'm Surfin' | LP | Imperial | LP9270/12270 | 1964 | £25 | £50 | US |

## FANTASTIC DEE-JAYS

| Fantastic Dee-Jays | LP | Stone | | 1966 | £250 | £400 | US |
|---|---|---|---|---|---|---|---|

## FANTASTIC FOUR

| Fantastic Four | LP | Tamla Motown | (S)TML11105 | 1969 | £8 | £20 | |
|---|---|---|---|---|---|---|---|
| I Love You Madly | 7" | Tamla Motown | TMG678 | 1968 | £5 | £10 | |

## FANTASTICS

| Baby Make Your Own Sweet Music | 7" | MGM | MGM1434 | 1968 | £1.50 | £4 | |
|---|---|---|---|---|---|---|---|

## FANTASY

| Paint A Picture | LP | Polydor | 2383246 | 1973 | £100 | £200 | |
|---|---|---|---|---|---|---|---|
| Politely Insane | 7" | Polydor | 2058405 | 1973 | £10 | £20 | |

## FANTONI, BARRY

| Little Man In A Little Box | 7" | Fontana | TF707 | 1966 | £5 | £10 | |
|---|---|---|---|---|---|---|---|

## FAPARDOKLY

| Fapardokly | LP | Psycho | PSYCHO5 | 1983 | £15 | £30 | |
|---|---|---|---|---|---|---|---|
| Fapardokly | LP | V.I.P. | 250 | 1966 | £700 | £1000 | US |

## FAR CRY

| Far Cry | LP | Vanguard | SVRL19041 | 1969 | £15 | £30 | |
|---|---|---|---|---|---|---|---|

## FAR EAST FAMILY BAND

| Cave Down To Earth | LP | Muland | CD7139M | 1975 | £10 | £25 | Japanese |
|---|---|---|---|---|---|---|---|
| Far Out | LP | Denon | 5047 | 1975 | £10 | £25 | Japanese |

| | | | | | | | |
|---|---|---|---|---|---|---|---|
| Nipponjin | LP | Vertigo | 6370850 | 1975 | £10 | £25 | |
| Parallel World | LP | Muland | LQ7002M | 1976 | £10 | £25 | Japanese |
| Tenkeyin | LP | All Ears | 114797 | 1977 | £8 | £20 | US |
| Torn Hatano | LP | Muland | 7024 | 1977 | £10 | £25 | Japanese |

## FAR OUT

| | | | | | | | |
|---|---|---|---|---|---|---|---|
| Far Out | LP | Denon | | 1972 | £100 | £200 | Japanese |

## FARAWAY FOLK

| | | | | | | | |
|---|---|---|---|---|---|---|---|
| Introducing The Faraway Folk | 7" EP | RA | EP7001 | 197– | £7.50 | £15 | |
| Live At Bolton | LP | RA | LP6006ST | 1970 | £30 | £60 | |
| On The Radio | LP | RA | LP6019 | 1974 | £15 | £30 | |
| Only Authorised Employees To Break Bottles | LP | RA | LP6022 | 1974 | £10 | £25 | |
| Seasonal Man | LP | Ra | RALP6029 | 1975 | £75 | £150 | |
| Shadow Of A Pie | 7" | Tabitha | TAB3 | 197– | £2 | £5 | |
| Time And Tide | LP | RA | LP6012ST | 1972 | £37.50 | £75 | |

## FARDON, DON

| | | | | | | | |
|---|---|---|---|---|---|---|---|
| Indian Reservation | 7" | Pye | 7N25437 | 1967 | £1.50 | £4 | |
| Indian Reservation | 7" | Pye | 7N25475 | 1968 | £1.50 | £4 | |
| Lament Of The Cherokee Indian Reservation | LP | GNP | 2044 | 1968 | £4 | £10 | US |
| Letter | 7" EP | Vogue | EPL8583 | 1967 | £7.50 | £15 | French |

## FARINA, RICHARD & MIMI

Richard and Mimi Farina were a folk duo typical of the many folk acts that were a dominant strain within the American music of the early sixties. Most managed to come up with a significant song or two – the Farinas' included 'Pack Up All Your Sorrows' and 'Hard Lovin' Loser', which were recorded by Judy Collins. Richard Farina was killed in a motor-cycle accident in 1966, but his wife Mimi, who is Joan Baez's sister, has managed to follow a reasonably successful career since as a musician and actress.

| | | | | | | | |
|---|---|---|---|---|---|---|---|
| Best Of Richard And Mimi Farina | LP | Vanguard | VSD21/22 | 1973 | £5 | £12 | double |
| Celebrations For A Grey Day | LP | Fontana | (S)TFL6060 | 1965 | £4 | £10 | |
| Memories | LP | Vanguard | VSD79263 | 1968 | £4 | £10 | US |
| Refelections In A Crystal Wind | LP | Fontana | (S)TFL6075 | 1965 | £4 | £10 | |
| Richard & Mimi Farina | LP | Vanguard | VSD79174 | 1965 | £4 | £10 | US |
| Richard Farina | LP | Vanguard | VSD79281 | 1968 | £4 | £10 | US |

## FARINAS

The Farinas were a blues and soul group from Leicester, but as soon as they began to write their own material, they changed their name – to Family.

| | | | | | | | |
|---|---|---|---|---|---|---|---|
| I Like It Like That | 7" | Fontana | TF493 | 1964 | £30 | £60 | |

## FARLOW, TAL

| | | | | | | | |
|---|---|---|---|---|---|---|---|
| Interpretations | LP | Columbia | 33CX10029 | 1956 | £15 | £30 | |
| Swinging Guitar | LP | Columbia | 33CX10132 | 1959 | £6 | £15 | |
| Tal Farlow | 10" LP | Columbia | 33C9041 | 1957 | £10 | £25 | |
| Tal Farlow | 10" LP | Columbia | 33C9052 | 1957 | £6 | £15 | |

## FARLOWE, CHRIS

| | | | | | | | |
|---|---|---|---|---|---|---|---|
| 14 Things To Think About | LP | Immediate | IMLP005 | 1966 | £10 | £25 | |
| Air Travel | 7" | Decca | F11536 | 1962 | £7.50 | £15 | |
| Art Of Chris Farlowe | LP | Immediate | IMLP006 | 1966 | £10 | £25 | |
| Buzz With The Fuzz | 7" | Columbia | DB7614 | 1965 | £62.50 | £125 | |
| Chris Farlowe | LP | Regal | REG2025 | 1968 | £4 | £10 | export |
| Chris Farlowe | 7" EP | Decca | DFE8665 | 1965 | £15 | £30 | |
| Chris Farlowe And The Thunderbirds | LP | Columbia | SX/SCX6034 | 1966 | £15 | £30 | |
| Dawn | 7" | Immediate | IM074 | 1969 | £1.50 | £4 | |
| Fool | 7" | Immediate | IM016 | 1965 | £2 | £5 | |
| From Here To Mama Rosa | LP | Polydor | 2425029 | 1970 | £4 | £10 | |
| Girl Trouble | 7" | Columbia | DB7237 | 1964 | £4 | £8 | |
| Handbags And Gladrags | 7" | Immediate | IM065 | 1967 | £1.50 | £4 | |
| Hits | 7" EP | Immediate | IMEP004 | 1966 | £7.50 | £15 | |
| Hound Dog | 7" | Columbia | DB7379 | 1964 | £4 | £8 | |
| I Remember | 7" | Columbia | DB7120 | 1963 | £4 | £8 | |
| In The Midnight Hour | 7" EP | Immediate | IMEP001 | 1965 | £7.50 | £15 | |
| Just A Dream | 7" | Columbia | DB7311 | 1964 | £4 | £8 | |
| Just A Dream | 7" | Columbia | DB7983 | 1966 | £2.50 | £6 | |
| Last Goodbye | LP | Immediate | IMLP021 | 1969 | £15 | £30 | |
| Moanin' | 7" | Immediate | IM056 | 1967 | £1.50 | £4 | |
| My Way Of Giving | 7" | Immediate | IM041 | 1967 | £2 | £5 | |
| Out Of Time | 7" EP | Columbia | ESRF1806 | 1966 | £10 | £20 | French |
| Out Of Time | 7" | Immediate | IM035 | 1966 | £1.50 | £4 | |
| Paint It Black | 7" | Immediate | IM071 | 1968 | £1.50 | £4 | |
| Paperman Fly In The Sky | 7" | Immediate | IM066 | 1968 | £2 | £5 | |
| Ride On Baby | 7" EP | Columbia | ESRF1837 | 1966 | £10 | £20 | French |
| Ride On Baby | 7" | Immediate | IM038 | 1966 | £1.50 | £4 | |
| Stormy Monday | LP | MFP | MFP1186 | 1967 | £4 | £10 | |
| Stormy Monday | 7" EP | Island | IEP709 | 1966 | £20 | £40 | |
| Think | 7" | Immediate | IM023 | 1966 | £1.50 | £4 | |
| Yesterday's Paper | 7" EP | Columbia | ESRF1875 | 1967 | £10 | £20 | French |
| Yesterday's Papers | 7" | Immediate | IM049 | 1967 | £1.50 | £4 | |

## FARM

| | | | | | | | |
|---|---|---|---|---|---|---|---|
| Hearts And Minds | 12" | Skysaw | END1 | 1984 | £2.50 | £6 | |

## FARM BAND
Farm Band .............................................. LP ..... Mescalero ........ S334 ..................... 1972 £15 .......... £30 .............. *US double*

## FARMER, ART
| | | | | | | | |
|---|---|---|---|---|---|---|---|
| Art Farmer ............................................... | 7" EP . | Vogue ............. | EPV1045 ............... | 1955 | £2 .......... | £5 | |
| Art Farmer Quintet ................................ | 10" LP | Esquire ............ | 20087 ................... | 1957 | £20 ....... | £40 | |
| Art Farmerr Quintet .............................. | 10" LP | Esquire ............ | 20057 ................... | 1956 | £25 ....... | £50 | |
| Aztec Suite ............................................ | LP ..... | London .......... | LTZT15198 ......... | 1960 | £8 ......... | £20 | |
| Brass Shout ............................................ | LP ..... | London .......... | LTZT15184 ......... | 1960 | £8 ......... | £20 | |
| Charts .................................................... | LP ..... | Esquire ............ | 32042 ................... | 1958 | £8 ......... | £20 | |
| Early Art ................................................ | LP ..... | Esquire ............ | 32120 ................... | 1961 | £8 ......... | £20 | |
| Interaction ............................................. | LP ..... | London ...... | HAK/SHK8135 ...... | 1964 | £6 ......... | £15 | |
| Modern Art ............................................ | LP ..... | London ........ | LTZT15167/ SAHT6028 ........... | 1959 | £8 ......... | £20 | |
| Music For That Wild Party ..................... | LP ..... | Esquire ............ | 32037 ................... | 1958 | £10 ....... | £25 | |
| Plays The Great Jazz Hits ...................... | LP ..... | CBS ................ | (S)BPG63113 ...... | 1968 | £5 ......... | £12 | |
| Portrait .................................................. | LP ..... | Contemporary . | LAC12197 ............. | 1959 | £8 ......... | £20 | |
| Work Of Art ........................................... | 10" LP | Esquire ............ | 20033 ................... | 1954 | £20 ....... | £40 | |

## FARMER, JULES
Love Me Now .......................................... 7" ...... London ............ HLP8967 .............. 1959 £1.50 ..... £4

## FARMER, MYLENE
| | | | | | | | |
|---|---|---|---|---|---|---|---|
| Ainsi sois-je ........................................... | CD .... | Polydor .......... | 8355642 ................. | 1990 | £8 ......... | £20 | |
| Ainsi sois-je ........................................... | CD-s .. | Polydor .......... | 0803602 ................. | 1989 | £15 ....... | £30 | *CD video* |

## FARMLIFE
Big Country .............................................. 7" ...... Whaam! ......... WHAAM13 .......... 1983 £15 ........ £30 ............. *test pressing*

## FARNER, MARK & DON BREWER
Monumental Funk ..................................... LP ..... Quadico .......... Q7401 ................... 1974 £8 .......... £20 ..... *US picture disc*

## FARO, WAYNE SCHMALTZ BAND
There's Still Time ..................................... 7" ...... Deram ............ DM222 ................. 1969 £2 .......... £5

## FARON'S FLAMINGOES
See If She Cares ....................................... 7" ...... Oriole .......... CB1834 ............... 1963 £4 .......... £8
Shake Sherry ............................................ 7" ...... Oriole .......... CB1867 ............... 1963 £5 .......... £10

## FARR, GARY
| | | | | | | | |
|---|---|---|---|---|---|---|---|
| Addressed To The Censors Of Love ........... | LP ..... | Atco ............. | SD7034 ............. | 1973 | £5 ......... | £12 | *US* |
| Everyday ................................................ | 7" ...... | Marmalade ....... | 598007 .......... | 1968 | £1.50 ..... | £4 | *with Kevin Westlake* |
| Hey Daddy .............................................. | 7" ...... | Marmalade ....... | 598017 .......... | 1969 | £2 .......... | £5 | |
| Strange Fruit .......................................... | LP ..... | CBS .............. | 64138 ........... | 1971 | £10 ....... | £25 | |
| Take Something With You ....................... | LP ..... | Marmalade ....... | 608013 ........... | 1969 | £15 ....... | £30 | |

## FARR, GARY & THE T-BONES
Dem Bones Dem Bones Dem T-Bones ... 7" EP . Columbia ....... SEG8414 .......... 1965 £50 ...... £100
Give All She's Got .................................... 7" ...... Columbia ....... DB7608 ............... 1965 £10 ....... £20

## FARRELL, DO & DENA
Young Magic ............................................ 7" ...... HMV .............. POP427 ............... 1957 £2 .......... £5

## FARRELL, JOE
Joe Farrell Quartet ................................... LP ...... Philips ............ 6308046 ............... 1970 £4 .......... £10

## FARREN, MICK
Carnivorous Circus (Mona) ....................... LP ..... Transatlantic .... TRA212 ............... 1970 £20 ....... £40
Vampires Stole My Lunch Money .............. LP ..... Logo ............... LOGO2010 ............ 1978 £4 .......... £10

## FARRIERS
Farriers ................................................... LP ..... Broadside ........ BRO112 ............... 1969 £6 .......... £15

## FARRIERS & KEMPION
Brummagem Ballads .............................. LP ..... Broadside ........ BRO119 ............... 1976 £5 .......... £12

## FASCINATIONS
Girls Are Out To Get You .......................... 7" ...... Mojo ............ 2092004 ............... 1971 £1.50 ..... £4
Girls Are Out To Get You .......................... 7" ...... Stateside ........ SS594 ................... 1967 £15 ....... £30
Girls Are Out To Get You .......................... 7" ...... Sue ............... WI4049 ................. 1968 £7.50 ..... £15

## FASCINATORS
Chapel Bells ............................................ 7" ...... Capitol ........... CL14942 ............... 1958 £75 ...... £150
Oh Rose Marie ......................................... 7" ...... Capitol ........... CL15062 ............... 1959 £15 ....... £30

## FASHIONS
I.O.U. ..................................................... 7" ...... Evolution ........ E2444 ................... 1969 £1.50 ..... £4
I.O.U. ..................................................... 7" ...... Stateside ......... SS2115 ................. 1968 £2 .......... £5

## FAST BREEDER & THE RADIO ACTORS
Nuclear Waste ......................................... 7" ...... Virgin ............ NONUKE235 ....... 1978 £2.50 ..... £6
Nuclear Waste ......................................... 7" ...... Virgin ............ NONUKE235 ....... 1978 £7.50 ..... £15 ........... *picture sleeve*

## FAST SET
Junction One ........................................... 7" ...... Axis ............... AXIS1 .................. 1980 £5 .......... £10

## FAT

| | | | | | | | |
|---|---|---|---|---|---|---|---|
| Fat | LP | RCA | LPS4368 | 1970 | £6 | £15 | |

## FAT LADY SINGS

| | | | | | | | |
|---|---|---|---|---|---|---|---|
| Be Still | 7" | Harbour Sound | HSS1 | 1988 | £2 | £5 | |
| Fear And Favour | 7" | Good Vibrations | FLS1 | 1986 | £4 | £8 | |

## FAT MATTRESS

Even while still a member of the Jimi Hendrix Experience, bassist Noel Redding began playing with his own group in order to switch back to the guitar he had always really preferred. Fat Mattress inevitably attracted attention simply because of Redding's presence, but the sad fact was that the most interesting aspect of the group was the cover of the first LP, which opens out into a two-foot-square sheet of card.

| | | | | | | | |
|---|---|---|---|---|---|---|---|
| Fat Mattress | LP | Polydor | 583056 | 1969 | £5 | £12 | |
| Fat Mattress 2 | LP | Polydor | 2383025 | 1970 | £4 | £10 | |
| Highway | 7" | Polydor | 2058053 | 1970 | £2 | £5 | |
| Magic Forest | 7" | Polydor | 56367 | 1969 | £2 | £5 | |
| Naturally | 7" | Polydor | 56352 | 1969 | £1.50 | £4 | |

## FATHERS ANGELS

| | | | | | | | |
|---|---|---|---|---|---|---|---|
| Bok To Bach | 7" | MGM | MGM1459 | 1968 | £37.50 | £75 | |

## FATS & THE CHESSMEN

| | | | | | | | |
|---|---|---|---|---|---|---|---|
| Big Ben Twist | 7" | Pye | 7N25122 | 1962 | £1.50 | £4 | |

## FAUN

| | | | | | | | |
|---|---|---|---|---|---|---|---|
| Faun | LP | Gregar | GG70000 | 1969 | £20 | £40 | US |

## FAUST

The first record issued by the German group, Faust, was a clear vinyl disc, housed in a clear plastic sleeve printed with the X-ray photograph of a hand, and with a clear plastic insert containing red printed sleeve notes, mostly in German, and having no obvious connection with the music. With expectations raised for the record's contents to be somewhat on the weird side, the music does not disappoint. Constructed as a collage, the music places an emphasis on interesting sounds rather than obvious melodies or rhythms, shifting rapidly through a succession of different short segments. Almost before the listener has time to work out what is going on at any one time, Faust have shifted on to something else. A similar approach has been followed by artists like Henry Cow and John Zorn, both of whom have actually been rather better at it, but then they were not playing in 1971. Faust are becoming increasingly collectable, with even the once ubiquitous *Faust Tapes* (originally sold for the price of a single) now qualifying for inclusion in this guide.

| | | | | | | | |
|---|---|---|---|---|---|---|---|
| Extracts From Faust Party 3 | 7" | Recommended | RR1.5 | 1980 | £4 | £8 | |
| Faust | LP | Polydor | 2310142 | 1971 | £8 | £20 | |
| Faust | LP | Polydor | 2310142 | 1971 | £15 | £30 | clear vinyl |
| Faust | LP | Recommended | RRONE | 1979 | £6 | £15 | clear vinyl |
| Faust 4 | LP | Virgin | V2004 | 1973 | £8 | £20 | |
| Faust Party 3 Extracts #2 | 7" | Recommended | RR6.5 | 1981 | £4 | £8 | |
| Faust Tapes | LP | Recommended | RRSIX | 1980 | £5 | £12 | in plastic bag |
| Faust Tapes | LP | Virgin | VC501 | 1973 | £4 | £10 | |
| Last LP | LP | Recommended | ReR36 | 1988 | £10 | £25 | |
| Last LP | LP | Recommended | ReR36 | 1988 | £20 | £40 | with print |
| Munic & Elsewhere | LP | Recommended | RR25 | 1986 | £10 | £25 | white vinyl |
| So Far | LP | Polydor | 2310196 | 1972 | £25 | £50 | with 10 prints |
| So Far | LP | Recommended | RR2 | 1979 | £8 | £20 | with 10 prints |

## FAVOURITE SONS

| | | | | | | | |
|---|---|---|---|---|---|---|---|
| That Driving Beat | 7" | Mercury | MF911 | 1965 | £25 | £50 | |

## FAWKES, WALLY

| | | | | | | | |
|---|---|---|---|---|---|---|---|
| Fawkes On Holiday | 10" LP | Decca | LF1312 | 1958 | £6 | £15 | |

## FAWKES, WALLY & BRUCE TURNER

| | | | | | | | |
|---|---|---|---|---|---|---|---|
| Fawkes-Turner Sextet | 10" LP | Decca | LF1214 | 1956 | £10 | £25 | |

## FAY, BILL

| | | | | | | | |
|---|---|---|---|---|---|---|---|
| Bill Fay | LP | Nova | SDN12 | 1970 | £10 | £25 | |
| Some Good Advice | 7" | Deram | DM143 | 1967 | £15 | £30 | |
| Time Of Last Persecution | LP | Deram | SML1079 | 1971 | £25 | £50 | |

## FAYE, FRANCIS

| | | | | | | | |
|---|---|---|---|---|---|---|---|
| Frenesi | 7" | HMV | POP898 | 1961 | £1.50 | £4 | |
| I Wish I Could Shimmy Like My Sister Kate | 7" | Vogue | V9186 | 1961 | £2.50 | £6 | |

## FEAR OF FALLING

| | | | | | | | |
|---|---|---|---|---|---|---|---|
| Like A Lion | 7" | Excellent | XL7 | 1983 | £7.50 | £15 | |

## FEARNS BRASS FOUNDRY

| | | | | | | | |
|---|---|---|---|---|---|---|---|
| Don't Change It | 7" | Decca | F12721 | 1968 | £2.50 | £6 | |
| Love, Sink And Drown | 7" | Decca | F12835 | 1968 | £2 | £5 | |

## FEATHER, LEONARD

| | | | | | | | |
|---|---|---|---|---|---|---|---|
| Hi Fi Suite | LP | MGM | C762 | 1957 | £4 | £10 | with Dick Hyman |
| One World Jazz | LP | Philips | BBL7361 | 1960 | £4 | £10 | |
| Winter Sequence | 10" LP | MGM | D135 | 1955 | £20 | £40 | |

## FEATHERS, CHARLIE & MAC CURTIS

| | | | | | | | |
|---|---|---|---|---|---|---|---|
| Rockabilly Kings | LP | Polydor | 2310293 | 1974 | £4 | £10 | |

## FEDERAL DUCK
Federal Duck ............................................. LP ...... Musicor .......... MS3162 ................. 1968 £8 .......... £20 ...................... US

## FEDERALS
Boot Hill ................................................. 7" ...... Parlophone ...... R5013 ................. 1963 £2 .......... £5
Brazil .................................................... 7" ...... Parlophone ...... R4988 ................. 1963 £2 .......... £5
Bucket Full Of Love .................................. 7" ...... Parlophone ...... R5320 ................. 1965 £2.50 .......... £6
Climb ................................................... 7" ...... Parlophone ...... R5100 ................. 1964 £2 .......... £5
Marlena ................................................. 7" ...... Parlophone ...... R5139 ................. 1964 £2 .......... £5
Twilight Time .......................................... 7" ...... Parlophone ...... R5193 ................. 1964 £2 .......... £5

## FEDERALS (2)
Federals ................................................ LP ...... Electrocord ..... EDE0202 ......... 1966 £25 .......... £50 ................. Romanian
I've Passed This Way Before .................... 7" ...... Island .............. WI3126 ............. 1967 £5 .......... £10
In This World .......................................... 7" ...... Camel .............. CA40 ............... 1970 £1.50 .......... £4
Shocking Love .......................................... 7" ...... Island .............. WI3152 ............. 1968 £5 .......... £10
Wailing Festival ........................................ 7" ...... High Note ...... HS024 ............... 1969 £1.50 .......... £4

## FELDER'S ORIOLES
Backstreet ................................................ 7" ...... Piccadilly ...... 7N35332 .......... 1966 £5 .......... £10
Down Home Girl ...................................... 7" ...... Piccadilly ...... 7N35247 .......... 1965 £5 .......... £10
I Know You Don't Love Me No More ...... 7" ...... Piccadilly ...... 7N35311 .......... 1966 £5 .......... £10
Sweet Tasting Wine ................................... 7" ...... Piccadilly ...... 7N35269 .......... 1965 £5 .......... £10

## FELDMAN, MARTY
I Feel A Song Going Off ........................... LP ...... Decca ............. LK/SKL4983 ...... 1969 £4 .......... £10
Marty .................................................... LP ...... Pye ............... NPL18258 ......... 1968 £4 .......... £10

## FELDMAN, MARTY, JOHN CLEESE & OTHERS
At Last The 1948 Show ............................. LP ...... Pye ............... NPL18198 ......... 1967 £4 .......... £10

## FELDMAN, VICTOR
Arrival Of Victor Feldman ........................ LP ...... Contemporary . LAC12172 ........ 1959 £8 .......... £20
In London Vol. 1 ...................................... LP ...... Tempo ........... TAP8 ............... 1957 £20 .......... £40
In London Vol. 2 ...................................... LP ...... Tempo ........... TAP12 ............. 1957 £20 .......... £40
Multi-Recording Session ............................ 10" LP Esquire ......... 20046 ............... 1955 £20 .......... £40
Transatlantic Alliance ............................... LP ...... Tempo ........... TAP19 ............. 1958 £20 .......... £40
Vibes To The Power Of Three .................... LP ...... Top Rank ...... 30007 ............... 1960 £8 .......... £20 ...with Terry Gibbs & Larry Bunker
Victor Feldman Modern Jazz Quartet ......... 10" LP Tempo ........... LAP6 ............... 1956 £20 .......... £40
Victor Feldman's Sextet ............................ 10" LP Tempo ........... LAP5 ............... 1955 £20 .......... £40
With Kenny Graham ................................. 10" LP Esquire ......... 20064 ............... 1956 £10 .......... £25

## FELICE, DEE TRIO
In The Heat ............................................. LP ...... Bethlehem ...... B1000 ............... 1969 £8 .......... £20 ...................... US

## FELIUS ANDROMEDA
Meditations ............................................. 7" ...... Decca .............. F12694 ............. 1967 £15 .......... £30

## FELIX, JULIE
Changes ................................................. LP ...... Fontana ........... (S)TL5368 ........ 1966 £4 .......... £10
Flowers .................................................. LP ...... Fontana ........... (S)TL5437 ........ 1967 £4 .......... £10
Julie Felix ............................................... LP ...... Decca ............. LK4626 ............. 1964 £4 .......... £10
Julie Felix In Concert ............................... LP ...... World Record Club .............. ST842 ............... 1968 £4 .......... £10
Second Album .......................................... LP ...... Decca ............. LK4724 ............. 1965 £4 .......... £10
Sings Dylan & Guthrie .............................. LP ...... Decca ............. LK4683 ............. 1965 £4 .......... £10
Third Album ............................................ LP ...... Decca ............. LK4820 ............. 1966 £4 .......... £10
This World Goes Round And Round ......... LP ...... Fontana ........... (S)TL5473 ........ 1968 £4 .......... £10

## FELIX, LENNIE
Cat Meets Mice ........................................ LP ...... Columbia ......... 33SX1298 ......... 1961 £4 .......... £10
Cat On A Hot Tin Piano ........................... 10" LP Columbia ......... 33S1144 ............ 1959 £4 .......... £10
Let's Put Out The Cat ............................... LP ...... Top Rank ......... 35034 ............... 1960 £4 .......... £10
That Cat Felix ......................................... 10" LP Nixa ............. NJT514 ............. 1958 £6 .......... £15

## FELIX & HIS GUITAR
Chili Beans ............................................. 7" ...... London ........... HLU8875 .......... 1959 £2 .......... £5

## FELT
Index .................................................... 7" ...... Shanghai ........ CUS321 ............ 1979 £15 .......... £30
My Face Is On Fire ................................... 7" ...... Cherry Red ..... CHERRY45 ...... 1982 £2 .......... £5
Primitive Painters .................................... CD-s .. Cherry Red ..... CDCHERRY89 .... 1988 £2 .......... £5
Something Sends Me To Sleep .................. 7" ...... Cherry Red ..... CHERRY26 ......... 1981 £2.50 .......... £6

## FELT (2)
Felt ....................................................... LP ...... Nasco ............. 9006 ................. 1971 £75 ....... £150 ...................... US

## FENCE
The lone single release by the Fence is collected by fans of the Levellers, due to the fact that the latter's drummer Charlie Heather and bass player Jeremy Cunningham made their recording debut here.

Frozen Water .......................................... 7" ...... Hag ............... HAG1 ............... 1987 £10 .......... £20

## FENDA, JAYMES & THE VULCANS
Mistletoe Love ......................................... 7" ...... Parlophone ...... R5210 ................. 1964 £2 .......... £5

### FENDER, JAN & BUSTER
Sweet Pea ............................................. 7" ...... Fab ................ FAB164 ................. 1971 £1.50 ........ £4 ....................................

### FENDERMEN
Don't You Just Know It .......................... 7" ...... Top Rank ....... JAR513 ................ 1960 £2.50 ....... £6 ....................................
Mule Skinner Blues .............................. LP ..... Soma ............. MG1240 ............... 1960 £250 .... £400 ........................... US
Mule Skinner Blues .............................. 7" ...... Top Rank ....... JAR395 ................ 1960 £2 .......... £5 ....................................

### FENMEN
Be My Girl ........................................... 7" ...... Decca ............ F11955 ................. 1964 £4 .......... £8 .....................................
California Dreamin' ............................... 7" ...... CBS ............... 202075 ................. 1966 £1.50 ........ £4 ....................................
I've Got Everything You Need ................. 7" ...... Decca ............ F12269 ................. 1965 £1.50 ........ £4 ....................................
Rejected ............................................... 7" ...... CBS ............... 202236 ................. 1966 £7.50 ........ £15 ..................................

### FENTON, SHANE & THE FENTONES
Bernard Jewry has had two separate singing careers. Best known as Alvin Stardust in the seventies, he was also Shane Fenton in the early sixties, achieving a few minor successes in a style which owed everything to Cliff Richard and Billy Fury.

Don't Do That ...................................... 7" ...... Parlophone ..... R5047 .................. 1963 £1.50 ........ £4 ....................................
Eastern Seaboard ................................. 7" ...... Fury ................ FY305 .................. 1972 £2.50 ....... £6 ....................................
Fool's Paradise ..................................... 7" ...... Parlophone ..... R5020 .................. 1963 £1.50 ........ £4 ....................................
Good Rocking Tonight ......................... LP ..... Contour .......... 2870409 ............... 1974 £4 .......... £10 ..................................
Hey Lulu ............................................. 7" ...... Parlophone ..... R5131 .................. 1964 £1.50 ........ £4 ....................................
I Ain't Got Nobody .............................. 7" ...... Parlophone ..... R4982 .................. 1963 £1.50 ........ £4 ....................................
I'm A Moody Guy ................................ 7" ...... Parlophone ..... R4827 .................. 1961 £1.50 ........ £4 ....................................
It's All Over Now ................................ 7" ...... Parlophone ..... R4883 .................. 1962 £2 .......... £5 ....................................
It's Gonna Take Magic .......................... 7" ...... Parlophone ..... R4921 .................. 1962 £1.50 ........ £4 ....................................
Too Young For Sad Memories ................ 7" ...... Parlophone ..... R4951 .................. 1962 £1.50 ........ £4 ....................................
Walk Away ........................................... 7" ...... Parlophone ..... R4866 .................. 1962 £2 .......... £5 ....................................

### FENTONES
Breeze And I ........................................ 7" ...... Parlophone ..... R4937 .................. 1962 £1.50 ........ £4 ....................................
Mexican ............................................... 7" ...... Parlophone ..... R4899 .................. 1962 £2 .......... £5 ....................................

### FENWAYS
Walk ................................................... 7" ...... Liberty ............ LIB66082 ............... 1965 £2.50 ....... £6 ....................................

### FENWICK, RAY
Keep America Beautiful .......................... LP ..... Decca ............ SKL5090 ............... 1971 £10 ........ £25 ..................................

### FENWYCK
Many Sides Of Jerry Raye Featuring ....... LP ..... De Ville .......... LP101 ................... 1967 £180 .... £300 ........... US, red vinyl
   Fenwyck ...........................................

### FERGUSON, H-BOMB
Feel Like I Do ...................................... 78 ...... Esquire ........... 10372 ................... 1954 £7.50 ........ £15 ..................................

### FERGUSON, HELENA
Where Is The Party ............................... 7" ...... London ........... HLZ10164 ............. 1967 £7.50 ........ £15 ..................................

### FERGUSON, JOHNNY
Angela Jones ........................................ 7" ...... MGM ............. MGM1059 ............. 1960 £1.50 ........ £4 ....................................

### FERGUSON, MAYNARD
Around The Horn .................................. LP ..... Emarcy .......... EJL1275 ................ 1958 £6 .......... £15 ..................................
Boy With Lots Of Brass ........................ LP ..... Mercury ......... MMC14050 .......... 1960 £5 .......... £12 ..................................
Boy With Lots Of Brass ........................ LP ..... Mercury ......... MMC14050/ ......... 1960 £5 .......... £12 ..................................
                                                                                           CMS18034 ............
Dimensions ........................................... LP ..... Emarcy .......... EJL1287 ................ 1958 £8 .......... £20 ..................................
Jam Session .......................................... LP ..... Emarcy .......... EJL1270 ................ 1958 £6 .......... £15 ..................................
Jazz For Dancing .................................. LP ..... Columbia ....... 33SX1270/ ............. 1960 £5 .......... £12 ..................................
                                                                                           SCX3338 ..............
Message From Birdland ......................... LP ..... Columbia ....... 33SX1210/ ............. 1960 £5 .......... £12 ..................................
                                                                                           SCX3245 ..............
Message From Newport .......................... LP ..... Columbia ....... 33SX1146 .............. 1959 £6 .......... £15 ..................................
Newport Suite ...................................... LP ..... Columbia ....... 33SX1301/ ............. 1961 £5 .......... £12 ..................................
                                                                                           SCX3363 ..............
Newport Suite ...................................... LP ..... Columbia ....... 33SX1301/ ............. 1961 £5 .......... £12 ..................................
                                                                                           SCX3368 ..............
Swingin' My Way Through College .......... LP ..... Columbia ....... 33SX1173 .............. 1959 £5 .......... £12 ..................................

### FERKO STRING BAND
Alabama Jubilee .................................... 7" ...... London ........... HL8140 ................. 1955 £6 .......... £12 ..................................
Happy Days Are Here Again .................. 7" ...... London ........... HL7052 ................. 1958 £1.50 ........ £4 ...................... export
Happy Days Are Here Again .................. 7" ...... London ........... HLF8215 ............... 1955 £5 .......... £10 ..................................
Ma She's Making Eyes At Me ................. 7" ...... London ........... HLF8183 ............... 1955 £5 .......... £10 ..................................
Philadelphia Mummers Parade Vol. 1 ........ 7" EP . London ........... REF1041 ............... 1956 £2.50 ....... £6 ....................................
Philadelphia Mummers Parade Vol. 2 ........ 7" EP . London ........... REF1052 ............... 1956 £2.50 ....... £6 ....................................

### FERLINGHETTI, LAWRENCE
Impeachment Of President Eisenhower ...... LP ..... Fantasy .......... 7004 ..................... 1958 £15 ........ £30 ........... US, red vinyl
Poetry Readings In The Cellar ................ LP ..... Fantasy .......... 7002 ..................... 1957 £15 ......... £30 ........... US, red vinyl

### FERNANDO, PHIL
Make Ready For Love ............................ 7" ...... Pye ................. 7N15142 ............... 1958 £1.50 ........ £4 ....................................

## FERNBACH, ANDY
If You Miss Your Connection .................. LP ..... Liberty ............ LBS83233 ............... 1969 £30 ......... £60 ............................

## FERRER, JOE DEVILS BOYS
Rocking Crickets ..................................... 7" ..... Oriole ............. CB1629 ................. 1961 £2 ......... £5

## FERRER, NINO
Metronomie ............................................ LP ..... Riviera ............ XCED421082U ...... 1972 £6 .......... £15 .................... French

## FERRIS, EUGENE
There Was A Smile In Your Eyes ............. 7" ...... Planet ............ PLF112 ................ 1966 £4 ......... £8

## FERRIS WHEEL
Can't Break The Habit ............................ LP ..... Pye .............. NPL18203 ............. 1967 £6 ......... £15
Can't Stop Now ...................................... 7" ..... Polydor ......... 56366 ................ 1969 £1.50 ...... £4
Ferris Wheel .......................................... LP ..... Polydor ......... 583086 ............... 1970 £4 ......... £10
Let It Be Me .......................................... 7" ..... Pye .............. 7N17538 ............. 1968 £1.50 ...... £4
Na Na Song ........................................... 7" ..... Pye .............. 7N17631 ............. 1968 £1.50 ...... £4
Number One Guy ................................... 7" ..... Pye .............. 7N17387 ............. 1967 £6 ......... £12

## FERRY, BRYAN
Bete Noire ............................................. CD ..... Virgin ........... CDVP2474 .......... 1988 £5 ......... £12 ................... picture disc
Bride Stripped Bare ................................ LP ..... Polydor ......... POLD5003 ........... 1978 £50 ....... £100 ....... test pressing with
                                                                                                                                                      2 different tracks
Bride Stripped Bare ................................ LP ..... Polydor ......... POLD5003 ........... 1978 £100 ..... £200 ....... test pressing with
                                                                                                                                                      2 different tracks, proof
                                                                                                                                                      sleeve
Bryan Ferry Box Set ............................... CD ..... Editions EG .... EGBC5 ............... 1989 £10 ......... £25 ................ 3 disc set
Don't Stop The Dance ............................ 12" .... Editions EG .... FERPX2 ............. 1985 £2.50 ...... £6 ................ picture disc
He'll Have To Go .................................... CD-s .. Editions EG .... EGOCD48 .......... 1989 £2 .......... £5 ................ 3" single
Hold On I'm Coming .............................. 12" .... Polydor ......... PPSP10 ............. 1978 £4 .......... £10 ................... promo
Interview .............................................. CD ..... Virgin ........... DPRO12699 ....... 1994 £6 .......... £15 ... US promo
Kiss And Tell ......................................... CD-s .. Virgin ........... CDEP19 ............ 1988 £2 .......... £5
Let's Stick Together ............................... CD-s .. Virgin ........... CDT10 .............. 1988 £2 .......... £5 ................ 3" single
Let's Stick Together (remix) .................... CD-s .. Editions EG .... EGOCD44 .......... 1988 £2 .......... £5
Limbo (Latin Mix) .................................. CD-s .. Virgin ........... VSCD1066 ......... 1988 £2 .......... £5
Price Of Love ......................................... CD-s .. Editions EG .... EGOCD46 .......... 1989 £2 .......... £5
Right Stuff ............................................ CD-s .. Virgin ........... CDEP8 ............... 1988 £2 .......... £5
These Foolish Things .............................. CD ..... Polydor ......... 8230212 ............. 1984 £5 ......... £12

## FERRY, CATHERINE
One Two Three ...................................... 7" ..... Barclay ........... BAR42 ................ 1976 £4 ......... £8

## FEVER TREE
Fever Tree were one of the many San Francisco groups who got to make a few records, but never managed to consolidate them into a long-term career. The group was responsible for a terrific single, 'San Francisco Girls', which was something of a Haight-Ashbury response to the Beach Boys, with gritty vocals and a keening guitar reclaiming the California girls as their own. In general, however, Fever Tree did not feature the guitar playing enough, preferring a pseudo-classical approach which squandered the group's real strengths without replacing them with anything that was not done better by others.

Another Time Another Place .................... LP ..... MCA ............. MUPS374 ............. 1968 £8 ......... £20
Creation ............................................... LP ..... Uni .............. 73067 ................. 1969 £8 ......... £20 ..................... US
Fever Tree ............................................ LP ..... UNI .............. UNL102 .............. 1968 £10 ......... £25 ................. mono
Fever Tree ............................................ LP ..... Uni .............. UNLS102 ............ 1968 £8 ......... £20
For Sale ............................................... LP ..... Ampex .......... A10113 ............... 1970 £6 ......... £15 ..................... US
San Francisco Girls ................................ 7" ..... MCA ............. MU1043 ............. 1968 £2.50 ...... £6

## FEZA, MONGEZI
Music For Xaba ...................................... LP ..... Sonet ............. SNTF642 ............. 1975 £5 ......... £12

## FI-DELS
Try A Little Harder ................................. 7" ..... Jay Boy .......... BOY69 .......... 1973 £1.50 ...... £4

## FICHTE, HUBERT
Beat And Prosa Im Star Club Hamburg ...... LP ...... Philips ............ 843933 ............ 1964 £37.50 ... £75 . German, with Ian &
                                                                                                                                                      The Zodiacs

## FICKLE PICKLE
American Pie ......................................... 7" ..... B&C ............. CB177 ............... 1972 £1.50 ...... £4
California Calling .................................... 7" ..... B&C ............. CB178 ............... 1972 £1.50 ...... £4
Millionaire ............................................ 7" ..... Fontana ......... TF1069 .............. 1970 £2 .......... £5
Sinful Skinful ........................................ LP ..... Negram .......... EQ20049 ........... 1970 £20 ......... £40 .................... Dutch

## FIDDLER'S DRAM
Fiddler's Dram ...................................... LP ..... Dingles .......... DID711 ............. 1980 £4 ......... £10
To See The Play ..................................... LP ..... Dingles .......... DIN304 ............. 1978 £5 ......... £12

## FIELD, KEITH
Day That War Broke Out ......................... 7" ..... Polydor .......... 56278 ............. 1968 £2.50 ...... £6

## FIELD MICE
I Can See Myself ..................................... 7" ..... Caff .............. CAFF2 ............... 1990 £7.50 ...... £15

## FIELDING, ALAN
How Many Nights, How Many Days ......... 7" ..... Decca ........... F11404 ............. 1962 £1.50 ...... £4
Too Late To Worry, Too Blue To Cry ...... 7" ..... Decca ........... F11518 .............. 1962 £1.50 ...... £4

## FIELDING, JERRY ORCHESTRA

| | | | | | | | |
|---|---|---|---|---|---|---|---|
| Dance Date Vol. 1 | 7" EP | London | REP1026 | 1955 | £2.50 | £6 | |
| Faintly Reminiscent | 7" | London | HL7001 | 1955 | £1.50 | £4 | export |
| Gypsy In My Soul | 7" | Brunswick | 05399 | 1955 | £1.50 | £4 | |
| I'm In Love | 7" | London | HL7004 | 1955 | £1.50 | £4 | |
| Peanut Vendor | 7" | London | HL7002 | 1955 | £1.50 | £4 | |
| Tea For Two | 7" | London | HL7003 | 1955 | £1.50 | £4 | |
| When I Grow Too Old To Dream | 7" | London | HL8017 | 1954 | £6 | £12 | |

## FIELDS

| | | | | | | | |
|---|---|---|---|---|---|---|---|
| Fields | LP | CBS | 69009 | 1971 | £10 | £25 | with poster |

## FIELDS (2)

| | | | | | | | |
|---|---|---|---|---|---|---|---|
| Fields | LP | Uni | UNLS104 | 1969 | £4 | £10 | |

## FIELDS, ERNIE

| | | | | | | | |
|---|---|---|---|---|---|---|---|
| Chattanooga Choo Choo | 7" | London | HL9100 | 1960 | £2 | £5 | |
| In The Mood | LP | London | HA2263 | 1960 | £6 | £15 | |
| In The Mood | 7" | London | HL8985 | 1959 | £1.50 | £4 | |
| Raunchy | 7" | London | HL9227 | 1960 | £1.50 | £4 | |
| Saxy | 7" EP | London | RE1260 | 1960 | £10 | £20 | |

## FIELDS, KANSAS & MILTON SEALEY

| | | | | | | | |
|---|---|---|---|---|---|---|---|
| Kansas Fields & Milton Sealey | 7" EP | Ducretet | DEP95017 | 1956 | £2 | £5 | |

## FIELDS OF THE NEPHILIM

| | | | | | | | |
|---|---|---|---|---|---|---|---|
| Blue Water | 7" | Situation 2 | SIT48 | 1987 | £4 | £8 | |
| Blue Water | 12" | Situation 2 | SIT48T | 1987 | £4 | £10 | with poster |
| Burning The Fields | 12" | Tower | N1 | 1984 | £20 | £40 | red sleeve |
| Burning The Fields | 12" | Tower | N1 | 1985 | £3 | £8 | coloured vinyl |
| Burning The Fields | 12" | Tower | N1 | 1985 | £6 | £15 | green sleeve, label with band photos |
| Chord Of Souls | 12" | Situation 2 | | 1988 | £5 | £12 | promo |
| For Her Light | CD-s | Beggars Banquet | BEG244CD | 1990 | £2 | £5 | |
| Preacher Man | 7" | Situation 2 | SIT46 | 1987 | £7.50 | £15 | |
| Psychonaut Lib III | CD-s | Situation 2 | SIT057CD | 1989 | £2 | £5 | |
| Summerland (Dreamed) | CD-s | Beggars Banquet | BEG250CD | 1990 | £2 | £5 | |

## FIESTA MOBILE

| | | | | | | | |
|---|---|---|---|---|---|---|---|
| Diario | LP | RCA | DPSL10605 | 1973 | £25 | £50 | Italian |

## FIESTAS

| | | | | | | | |
|---|---|---|---|---|---|---|---|
| So Fine | 7" | London | HL8870 | 1959 | £7.50 | £15 | |

## FIFTEENTH

| | | | | | | | |
|---|---|---|---|---|---|---|---|
| Andelain | 12" | Tanz | TANZ3 | 1986 | £2.50 | £6 | |

## FIFTH AVENUE

| | | | | | | | |
|---|---|---|---|---|---|---|---|
| Bells Of Rhymney | 7" | Immediate | IM002 | 1965 | £7.50 | £15 | |

## FIFTH COLUMN

Gerry Rafferty and Joe Egan later formed Stealer's Wheel.

| | | | | | | | |
|---|---|---|---|---|---|---|---|
| Benjamin Day | 7" | Columbia | DB8068 | 1966 | £5 | £10 | |

## FIFTH DIMENSION

| | | | | | | | |
|---|---|---|---|---|---|---|---|
| Go Where You Wanna Go | 7" | Liberty | LIB12051 | 1967 | £5 | £10 | |
| I'll Be Loving You For Ever | 7" | Liberty | LBF15356 | 1970 | £2.50 | £6 | |

## FIFTH ESTATE

| | | | | | | | |
|---|---|---|---|---|---|---|---|
| Ding Dong The Witch Is Dead | LP | Jubilee | JGM/JGS8005 | 1967 | £6 | £15 | US |

## FIFTY FANTASTICS

| | | | | | | | |
|---|---|---|---|---|---|---|---|
| God's Got Religion | 7" | Dining Out | TUX5 | 1980 | £2 | £5 | |
| God's Got Religion | 7" | South Circular | SGS108 | 1979 | £2.50 | £6 | B side by Steppes |

## FIFTY FOOT HOSE

Along with the group the United States of America, the Fifty Foot Hose were early pioneers in the use of electronics within a general rock group sound. The results are undoubtedly dated to modern ears, and the album *Cauldron* is apparently a mere blueprint compared to the sonic experiments that the group performed live. *Cauldron* is nevertheless a vital sixties artefact with far more to offer than some of the more celebrated rarities from the period.

| | | | | | | | |
|---|---|---|---|---|---|---|---|
| Cauldron | LP | Limelight | 86062 | 1969 | £30 | £60 | US |

## FIFTY YEAR VOID (SAINT ETIENNE)

| | | | | | | | |
|---|---|---|---|---|---|---|---|
| Blade's Love Machine | 12" | Blade | BLADE1 | 1992 | £10 | £20 | promo only |

## FILBY, PAULINE

| | | | | | | | |
|---|---|---|---|---|---|---|---|
| Show Me A Rainbow | LP | Herald | LLR567 | 1969 | £180 | £300 | |

## FILET OF SOUL

| | | | | | | | |
|---|---|---|---|---|---|---|---|
| Freedom | LP | Monoquid Squid | ST4857 | 1968 | £30 | £60 | US |

## FINCHLEY BOYS
Everlasting Tribute .................................. LP ...... Golden Throat. 20019.................... 1972 £50........£100 ..................... US

## FINDERS KEEPERS
Bass player Glen Hughes was later a member of Deep Purple.

Light ......................................... 7" ...... CBS.............. 202249.................... 1966 £2.50........£6 .....................
Light/Power Of Love .......................... 7" ...... CBS.............. 202249.................... 1966 £20........£40 .............. demo only
On The Beach .................................. 7" ...... Fontana........... TF892.................... 1967 £7.50........£15 .....................
Sadie The Cleaning Lady....................... 7" ...... Fontana........... TF938.................... 1968 £2.50........£6 .....................

## FINE WINE
Fine Wine ...................................... LP ...... Polydor........... 2310438 ................. 1976 £5..........£12 ................. German

## FINE YOUNG CANNIBALS
Don't Look Back.............................. CD-s .. London ........ LONCD220 .......... 1989 £2.........£5 .....................
Ever Fallen In Love ......................... CD-s .. London ........ LONCD121 .......... 1987 £2.........£5 .....................
Good Thing................................... CD-s .. London ........ LONCD218 .......... 1989 £2.........£5 .....................
I'm Not Satisfied ........................... CD-s .. London ........ LONCD252 .......... 1990 £2.........£5 .....................
I'm Not The Man I Used To Be.............. CD-s .. London ........ LONCD244 .......... 1989 £2.........£5 .....................
She Drives Me Crazy ........................ CD-s .. London ........ 8863612 .......... 1989 £2.........£5 .....................
She Drives Me Crazy ........................ CD-s .. London ........ LONCD199 .......... 1988 £2.........£5 .....................
Suspicious Minds ........................... CD-s .. Polygram....... 0804882 .......... 1988 £3.........£8 .............CD video

## FINGERS
All Kinds Of People.............................. 7" ...... Columbia ........ DB8112 ................. 1967 £5........£10 .....................

## FINN, LEE & THE RHYTHM MEN
High Class Feeling............................... 7" ...... Starlite ........... ST45103 ............... 1963 £75........£150 .....................

## FINN, MICKEY & THE BLUE MEN
Pills ........................................... 7" ...... Oriole ........... CB1927 ............... 1964 £15........£30 .....................
Reeling And Rocking........................... 7" ...... Oriole ........... CB1940 ............... 1964 £15........£30 .....................
Tom Hark ...................................... 7" ...... Blue Beat ........ BB203................. 1964 £12.50........£25 .....................

## FINN, SIMON
Pass The Distance................................ LP ...... Mushroom ...... 100MR2 ............... 1970 £30........£60 .....................

## FINN, TIM
How'm I Gonna Sleep ........................... CD-s .. Capitol........... CDCL542 ............... 1989 £2.........£5 .....................
Live At The Borderline ......................... CD ..... Capitol........... FINN1 ............... 1993 £10.........£25 ..................,promo

## FINN MACCULL
Sink Ye – Swim Ye ............................... LP ...... private............. REL460 ................. 1978 £100.....£200 .....................

## FINNEGAN, LARRY
Dear One ...................................... 7" ...... HMV........... POP1022 ............... 1962 £2.50........£6 .....................
It's Walking Talking Time ...................... 7" ...... London ........ HLU9613............... 1962 £2.........£5 .....................
Larry Finnegan ................................ LP ...... MFP ........... 50136................ 1966 £10.........£25 ................. Swedish
Other Ringo ................................... 7" ...... Ember ........... EMBS207............... 1965 £2.........£5 .....................

## FINNEGAN, MIKE
Just One Minute More............................ 7" ...... CBS ........... 6656 ................. 1978 £2.........£5 .....................

## FIRE
Father's Name Is Dad............................ 7" ...... Decca ........... F12753.................... 1968 £50........£100 .....................
Magic Shoemaker................................ LP ...... Pye ........... NSPL18343.......... 1970 £100........£200 .....................
Round The Gum Tree ........................... 7" ...... Decca ........... F12856.................. 1968 £10........£20 .....................

## FIRE (2)
Could You Understand Me ...................... LP ...... Killroy ........... ............... 1973 £150.....£250 .................Dutch

## FIRE ESCAPE
Love Special Delivery ............................ 7" EP . Vogue............. INT18117 ............. 1966 £12.50....£25 .............French
Psychotic Reaction.............................. LP ...... GNP ........... 2034 ................... 1966 £10.....£25 ..................... US
                                                           Crescendo .......

## FIREBALLS
Bottle Of Wine ................................ LP ...... Stateside ........ (S)SL10237 ........... 1968 £6.........£15 .....................
Bulldog ....................................... 7" ...... Top Rank ........ JAR276................ 1960 £1.50........£4 .....................
Fireballs...................................... LP ...... Top Rank ........ RM324................ 1960 £15.........£30 ..................... US
Foot Patter ................................... 7" ...... Top Rank ........ JAR354................ 1960 £1.50........£4 .....................
Here Are The Fireballs......................... LP ...... Warwick ........ W2042................. 1961 £10.........£25 ..................... US
Quite A Party ................................. 7" ...... Pye ........... 7N25092 ............... 1961 £1.50........£4 .....................
Torquay ...................................... 7" ...... Top Rank ........ JAR218................ 1959 £1.50........£4 .....................
Vaquero ...................................... LP ...... Top Rank ........ 25105.................. 1961 £10.........£25 .....................
Vaquero ...................................... 7" ...... Top Rank ........ JAR507................ 1960 £1.50........£4 .....................

## FIREBIRDS
Light My Fire .................................. LP ...... Crown ........... CST589 ............... 1968 £25........£50 ..................... US

## FIRECLOWN
Fireclown ..................................... 10" ..... Fireclown ........... ................ 1983 £30........£40 .....................

## FIREFLIES
I Can't Say Goodbye ............................ 7" ...... London ........... HLU9057............... 1960 £4........£8 .....................

| | | | | | | | |
|---|---|---|---|---|---|---|---|
| You Were Mine | LP | Taurus | (S)1002 | 1961 | £25 | £50 | US |
| You Were Mine | 7" | Top Rank | JAR198 | 1959 | £4 | £8 | |

## FIREHOUSE FIVE PLUS TWO

| | | | | | | | |
|---|---|---|---|---|---|---|---|
| Crashes A Party | LP | Good Time Jazz | LAG12236/ SGA5012 | 1960 | £4 | £10 | |
| Firehouse Five Plus Two | LP | Good Time Jazz | LAG12079 | 1958 | £4 | £10 | |
| Firehouse Five Plus Two | 10" LP | Vogue | LDE183 | 1956 | £4 | £10 | |
| Firehouse Five Plus Two Vol. 2 | LP | Good Time Jazz | LAG12089 | 1958 | £4 | £10 | |
| Firehouse Five Story Vol. 3 | LP | Good Time Jazz | LAG12099 | 1958 | £4 | £10 | |
| For Lovers | LP | Good Time Jazz | LAG12074 | 1958 | £4 | £10 | |
| Goes South | LP | Good Time Jazz | LAG12087 | 1958 | £4 | £10 | |
| Goes South Vol. 1 | 10" LP | Good Time Jazz | LDG036 | 1954 | £5 | £12 | |
| Goes South Vol. 2 | 10" LP | Good Time Jazz | LDG079 | 1954 | £5 | £12 | |
| Goes South Vol. 3 | 10" LP | Good Time Jazz | LDG094 | 1954 | £5 | £12 | |
| Goes South Vol. 4 | 10" LP | Good Time Jazz | LDG169 | 1955 | £5 | £12 | |
| Goes To Sea | LP | Good Time Jazz | LAG12150/ SGA5003 | 1958 | £4 | £10 | |

## FIREMAN

One of the more surprising album releases of 1993 was one whose origin would be guessed by few casual listeners. For the ambient work credited to the Fireman is actually the work of none other than Paul McCartney, working in collaboration with Youth, the producer who has, of course, worked with the Orb. The LP version of *Strawberries* . . . was issued on clear vinyl only for a very limited period. By the time that most McCartney collectors had realized the involvement of their hero, the record had already been deleted.

| | | | | | | | |
|---|---|---|---|---|---|---|---|
| Strawberries Oceans Ships Forest | LP | EMI | PCSD145 | 1993 | £6 | £15 | *clear vinyl double, red sleeve* |
| Strawberries Oceans Ships Forest | LP | Parlophone | PMCD1452 | 1993 | £20 | £40 | *clear vinyl double, white sleeve* |
| Strawberries Oceans Ships Forest | CD | EMI | CDPCSD145 | 1993 | £6 | £15 | |

## FIRESIGN THEATRE

| | | | | | | | |
|---|---|---|---|---|---|---|---|
| Dear Friends | LP | CBS | 31099 | 1972 | £5 | £12 | US, double |
| Don't Crush That Dwarf | LP | CBS | 30102 | 1970 | £5 | £12 | US |
| Everything You Know Is Wrong | LP | CBS | 33141 | 1974 | £4 | £10 | US |
| How Can You Be In Two Places At Once | LP | CBS | 65130 | 1968 | £6 | £15 | |
| I Think We're All Bozos On This Bus | LP | CBS | 30737 | 1971 | £5 | £12 | US |
| In The Next World | LP | CBS | 31383 | 1972 | £4 | £10 | US |
| Not Insane | LP | Columbia | 31585 | 1972 | £5 | £12 | US |
| Not Insane Or Anything You Want | LP | CBS | 31585 | 1972 | £4 | £10 | US |
| Tale Of The Giant Rat | LP | CBS | 32370 | 1974 | £4 | £10 | US |
| TV Or Not TV | LP | CBS | 32199 | 1973 | £4 | £10 | US |
| Waiting For The Electrician Or Someone Like Him | LP | CBS | 65129 | 1968 | £6 | £15 | |

## FIRING SQUAD

| | | | | | | |
|---|---|---|---|---|---|---|
| Little Bit More | 7" | Parlophone | R5152 | 1964 | £6 | £12 |

## FIRKIN THE FOX

| | | | | | | |
|---|---|---|---|---|---|---|
| Behind Bars | LP | Woodworm | WR005 | 1984 | £25 | £50 |

## FIRM

| | | | | | | |
|---|---|---|---|---|---|---|
| Firm | CD | Atlantic | 7812392 | 1985 | £5 | £12 |
| Firm Mean Business | CD | Atlantic | 7816282 | 1986 | £5 | £12 |

## FIRST AID

| | | | | | | |
|---|---|---|---|---|---|---|
| Nostradamus | LP | Decca | TXS117 | 1977 | £6 | £15 |

## FIRST CHOICE

| | | | | | | | |
|---|---|---|---|---|---|---|---|
| This Is The House Where Love Died | 7" | Pye | 7N25613 | 1973 | £50 | £100 | demo only |

## FIRST GEAR

| | | | | | | |
|---|---|---|---|---|---|---|
| In Crowd | 7" | Pye | 7N15763 | 1965 | £7.50 | £15 |
| Leave My Kitten Alone | 7" | Pye | 7N15703 | 1964 | £50 | £100 |

## FIRST MODERN PIANO QUARTET

| | | | | | | |
|---|---|---|---|---|---|---|
| Gallery Of Gershwin | LP | Coral | LVA9110/SVL3002 | 1959 | £5 | £12 |

## FIRST MYSTERIOUS APPEARANCE

| | | | | | | | |
|---|---|---|---|---|---|---|---|
| First Mysterious Appearance | LP | Impossible | | 1983 | £10 | £25 | Dutch |

## FIRST STEPS

| | | | | | | |
|---|---|---|---|---|---|---|
| Anywhere Else But Here | 7" | English Rose | ER3 | 1981 | £2 | £5 |
| Beat Is Back | 7" | English Rose | ER1 | 1980 | £1.50 | £4 |

## FISCHER, WILD MAN

| | | | | | | | |
|---|---|---|---|---|---|---|---|
| Evening With Wild Man Fischer | LP | Reprise | RSLP6332 | 1970 | £15 | £30 | |
| Wildmania | LP | Rhino | RNLP001 | 1977 | £4 | £10 | US |

## FISCHER & EPSTEIN
| | | | | | | | | |
|---|---|---|---|---|---|---|---|---|
| It's A Beatle World | LP | Swan | 514 | 1964 | £6 | £15 | | US |

## FISH
| | | | | | | | | |
|---|---|---|---|---|---|---|---|---|
| Big Wedge | CD-s | EMI | CDEM125 | 1990 | £2 | £5 | | |
| Company | CD-s | EMI | | 1990 | £4 | £10 | | German |
| Funny Farm Interview | CD | Dick Brothers | DDICK15CD | 1995 | £8 | £20 | | promo |
| Gentleman's Excuse Me | CD-s | EMI | CDEM135 | 1990 | £2 | £5 | | |
| Internal Exile | CD-s | EMI | FISCD1 | 1991 | £2 | £5 | | |
| State Of Mind | CD-s | EMI | CDEM109 | 1989 | £2 | £5 | | |

## FISHER, ARCHIE
| | | | | | | | | |
|---|---|---|---|---|---|---|---|---|
| Archie Fisher | LP | XTRA | XTRA1070 | 1968 | £10 | £25 | | |
| Man With A Rhyme | LP | Folk Legacy | FSS61 | 1976 | £10 | £25 | | US |
| Orfeo | LP | Decca | SKL5057 | 1970 | £10 | £25 | | |

## FISHER, CHIP
| | | | | | | | |
|---|---|---|---|---|---|---|---|
| At The Sugar Bowl | 7" EP | RCA | RCX143 | 1959 | £10 | £20 | |

## FISHER, CILLA & ARTIE TREZISE
| | | | | | | | |
|---|---|---|---|---|---|---|---|
| Balcanquhal | LP | Trailer | LER2100 | 1976 | £10 | £25 | |
| For Foul Day And Fair | LP | Kettle | KAC1 | 1979 | £4 | £10 | |

## FISHER, EDDIE
| | | | | | | | |
|---|---|---|---|---|---|---|---|
| Bundle Of Joy | 7" EP | HMV | 7EG8207 | 1957 | £2 | £5 | |
| Cindy Oh Cindy | 7" | HMV | POP273 | 1956 | £6 | £12 | |
| Count Your Blessings Instead Of Sheep | 7" | HMV | 7M266 | 1954 | £2.50 | £6 | |
| Downhearted | 7" | HMV | 7M126 | 1953 | £4 | £8 | |
| Dungaree Doll | 7" | HMV | 7M374 | 1956 | £5 | £10 | |
| Even Now | 7" | HMV | 7M125 | 1953 | £5 | £10 | |
| Everything I Have Is Yours | 7" | HMV | 7M115 | 1953 | £5 | £10 | |
| Girl, A Girl | 7" | HMV | 7M212 | 1954 | £4 | £8 | |
| Green Years | 7" | HMV | 7M257 | 1954 | £2.50 | £6 | |
| How Deep Is The Ocean | 7" | HMV | 7M185 | 1954 | £4 | £8 | |
| How Do You Speak To An Angel? | 7" | HMV | 7M242 | 1954 | £2.50 | £6 | |
| I Need You Now | 7" | HMV | 7M251 | 1954 | £2.50 | £6 | |
| I'm Walking Behind You | 7" | HMV | 7M133 | 1953 | £4 | £8 | |
| I'm Yours | 7" | HMV | 7M101 | 1953 | £6 | £12 | |
| Just Another Polka | 7" | HMV | 7M146 | 1953 | £5 | £10 | |
| Just To Be With You | 7" | HMV | 7M201 | 1954 | £4 | £8 | |
| Kari Waits For Me | 7" | RCA | RCA1061 | 1958 | £1.50 | £4 | |
| Magic Fingers | 7" | HMV | 7M353 | 1956 | £2.50 | £6 | |
| Many Times | 7" | HMV | 7M168 | 1953 | £4 | £8 | |
| My Friend | 7" | HMV | 7M235 | 1954 | £4 | £8 | |
| My Serenade Is You | 10" LP | HMV | DLP1074 | 1955 | £8 | £20 | |
| Night And Day | 7" EP | HMV | 7EG8026 | 1954 | £2.50 | £6 | |
| No Other One | 7" | HMV | 7M402 | 1956 | £2.50 | £6 | |
| Oh My Papa | 7" | HMV | 7M172 | 1953 | £4 | £8 | |
| Outside Of Heaven | 7" | HMV | 7M117 | 1953 | £5 | £10 | |
| Sayonara | 7" | RCA | RCA1030 | 1958 | £1.50 | £4 | |
| Sings Academy Award Winning Songs | LP | HMV | CLP1095 | 1956 | £4 | £10 | |
| Some Day Soon | 7" | HMV | POP296 | 1957 | £1.50 | £4 | |
| Sweet Heartaches | 7" | HMV | 7M421 | 1956 | £2.50 | £6 | |
| Time For Romance | 10" LP | HMV | DLP1040 | 1954 | £8 | £20 | |
| Tonight My Heart She Is Crying | 7" | HMV | POP342 | 1957 | £2 | £5 | |
| Trust In Me | 7" | HMV | 7M116 | 1953 | £6 | £12 | |
| Wedding Bells | 7" | HMV | 7M294 | 1955 | £2.50 | £6 | |
| Wish You Were Here | 7" | HMV | 7M159 | 1953 | £4 | £8 | |

## FISHER, RAY
| | | | | | | | |
|---|---|---|---|---|---|---|---|
| Bonny Birdy | LP | Trailer | LER2038 | 1972 | £10 | £25 | |

## FISHER, RAY & ARCHIE
| | | | | | | | |
|---|---|---|---|---|---|---|---|
| Far Over The Forth | 7" EP | Topic | TOP67 | 1961 | £15 | £30 | |

## FISHER, TONI
| | | | | | | | |
|---|---|---|---|---|---|---|---|
| Big Hurt | 7" | Top Rank | JAR261 | 1960 | £1.50 | £4 | |

## FISHER FAMILY
| | | | | | | | |
|---|---|---|---|---|---|---|---|
| Fisher Family | LP | Topic | 12T137 | 1965 | £10 | £25 | |

## FISHERS
| | | | | | | | |
|---|---|---|---|---|---|---|---|
| Hide In The Rock | LP | Sharing | SC008 | 1978 | £8 | £20 | |

## FISK JUBILEE SINGERS
| | | | | | | | |
|---|---|---|---|---|---|---|---|
| Fisk Jubilee Singers | LP | Topic | 12T39 | 1959 | £6 | £15 | |

## FIST
| | | | | | | | |
|---|---|---|---|---|---|---|---|
| Forever Amber | 7" | MCA | MCA640 | 1980 | £1.50 | £4 | |
| Name, Rank And Serial Number | 7" | MCA | MCA615 | 1980 | £2.50 | £6 | |

## FITCH, JOHN & ASSOCIATES
| | | | | | | | |
|---|---|---|---|---|---|---|---|
| Stoned Out Of It | 7" | Beacon | BEA118 | 1971 | £2 | £5 | |

## FITZ & COOZERS
| | | | | | | | |
|---|---|---|---|---|---|---|---|
| Cover Me | 7" | Nu Beat | NB003 | 1968 | £2.50 | £6 | |

## FITZGERALD, ELLA

| Title | Format | Label | Catalogue | Year | | | Notes |
|---|---|---|---|---|---|---|---|
| At Newport | LP | Columbia | 33CX10100 | 1958 | £6 | £15 | side 2 by Billie Holiday |
| At The Opera House | LP | Columbia | 33CX10126 | 1958 | £8 | £20 | ... with Oscar Peterson |
| Cole Porter Songbook Vol. 1 | LP | HMV | CLP1083 | 1956 | £8 | £20 | |
| Cole Porter Songbook Vol. 2 | LP | HMV | CLP1084 | 1956 | £8 | £20 | |
| Duke Ellington Songbook Vol. 1 | LP | HMV | CLP1213/4 | 1958 | £15 | £30 | double |
| Duke Ellington Songbook Vol. 2 | LP | HMV | CLP1227/8 | 1958 | £15 | £30 | double |
| Ella And Her Fellas | LP | Brunswick | LAT8223 | 1957 | £6 | £15 | |
| Ella And Louis | LP | HMV | CLP1098 | 1956 | £6 | £15 | with Louis Armstrong |
| Ella And Louis Again No. 1 | LP | HMV | CLP1146 | 1957 | £6 | £15 | with Louis Armstrong |
| Ella And Louis Again No. 2 | LP | HMV | CLP1147 | 1957 | £6 | £15 | with Louis Armstrong |
| Ella At Juan–Les Pins | LP | Verve | VLP9083 | 1965 | £4 | £10 | |
| Ella Sings Gershwin | 10" LP | Brunswick | LA8648 | 1954 | £15 | £30 | |
| Ella Swings Brightly With Nelson | LP | Verve | (S)VLP9001 | 1962 | £5 | £12 | |
| Ella Swings Lightly | LP | HMV | CLP1267 | 1959 | £8 | £20 | |
| Ella Wishes You A Swinging Christmas | LP | HMV | CLP1397 | 1960 | £8 | £20 | |
| First Lady Of Song | LP | Brunswick | LAT8264 | 1958 | £6 | £15 | |
| Get Ready | 7" | Reprise | R20850 | 1969 | £1.50 | £4 | |
| Hello Love | LP | HMV | CLP1383/CSD1315 | 1960 | £8 | £20 | |
| Irving Berlin Songbook Vol. 1 | LP | HMV | CLP1183 | 1958 | £8 | £20 | |
| Irving Berlin Songbook Vol. 2 | LP | HMV | CLP1184 | 1958 | £8 | £20 | |
| Let No Man Write My Epitaph | LP | HMV | CLP1396 | 1960 | £8 | £20 | |
| Like Someone In Love | LP | HMV | CLP1166 | 1958 | £8 | £20 | |
| Lover, Come Back To Me | 7" | Brunswick | 05468 | 1955 | £1.50 | £4 | |
| Lullabies Of Birdland | LP | Brunswick | LAT8115 | 1956 | £8 | £20 | |
| Lullaby Of Birdland | 7" | Brunswick | 05392 | 1955 | £1.50 | £4 | |
| Mack The Knife | LP | HMV | CLP1391 | 1960 | £8 | £20 | |
| Moanin' Low | 7" | Brunswick | 05427 | 1955 | £1.50 | £4 | |
| My One And Only Love | 7" | Brunswick | 05514 | 1956 | £1.50 | £4 | |
| Pete Kelly's Blues | 7" | Brunswick | 05473 | 1955 | £1.50 | £4 | |
| Porgy And Bess Vol. 1 | LP | HMV | CLP1245 | 1959 | £6 | £15 | with Louis Armstrong |
| Porgy And Bess Vol. 2 | LP | HMV | CLP1246 | 1959 | £6 | £15 | with Louis Armstrong |
| Rhythm Is My Business | LP | Verve | VLP9020 | 1963 | £5 | £12 | |
| Rodgers And Hart Songbook Vol. 1 | LP | HMV | CLP1116 | 1957 | £8 | £20 | |
| Rodgers And Hart Songbook Vol. 2 | LP | HMV | CLP1117 | 1957 | £8 | £20 | |
| Sings Gershwin Vol. 1 | LP | HMV | CLP1338/CSD1292 | 1959 | £8 | £20 | |
| Sings Gershwin Vol. 2 | LP | HMV | CLP1339/CSD1293 | 1959 | £8 | £20 | |
| Sings Gershwin Vol. 3 | LP | HMV | CLP1347/CSD1299 | 1960 | £8 | £20 | |
| Sings Gershwin Vol. 4 | LP | HMV | CLP1348/CSD1300 | 1960 | £8 | £20 | |
| Sings Gershwin Vol. 5 | LP | HMV | CLP1353/CSD1304 | 1960 | £8 | £20 | |
| Soldier Boy | 7" | Brunswick | 05477 | 1955 | £1.50 | £4 | |
| Songs In A Mellow Mood | LP | Brunswick | LAT8056 | 1955 | £8 | £20 | |
| Souvenir Album | 10" LP | Brunswick | LA8581 | 1953 | £15 | £30 | |
| Souvenir Album | 10" LP | Brunswick | LA8665 | 1954 | £8 | £20 | |
| Sweet And Hot | LP | Brunswick | LAT8091 | 1956 | £8 | £20 | |
| Sweet Songs For Swingers | LP | HMV | CLP1322/CSD1287 | 1960 | £8 | £20 | |
| Who's Afraid | 7" | Brunswick | 05324 | 1954 | £1.50 | £4 | |
| You'll Never Know | 7" | Brunswick | 05584 | 1956 | £1.50 | £4 | |

## FITZGERALD, G. F.

| Title | Format | Label | Catalogue | Year | | | |
|---|---|---|---|---|---|---|---|
| Mouseproof | LP | Uni | UNLS115 | 1970 | £20 | £40 | |

## FIVE & A PENNY

| Title | Format | Label | Catalogue | Year | | | |
|---|---|---|---|---|---|---|---|
| You Don't Know Where Your Interest Lies | 7" | Polydor | 56282 | 1968 | £7.50 | £15 | |

## FIVE A.M. EVENT

| Title | Format | Label | Catalogue | Year | | | |
|---|---|---|---|---|---|---|---|
| Hungry | 7" | Pye | 7N17154 | 1966 | £62.50 | £125 | |

## FIVE AMERICANS

| Title | Format | Label | Catalogue | Year | | | Notes |
|---|---|---|---|---|---|---|---|
| Evol, Not Love | 7" | Pye | 7N25373 | 1966 | £7.50 | £15 | |
| I See The Light | LP | Hanna Barbera | LP8503/ST9503 | 1966 | £15 | £30 | US |
| I See The Light | 7" EP | Vogue | INT18087 | 1966 | £7.50 | £15 | French |
| I See The Light | 7" | Pye | 7N25354 | 1966 | £4 | £8 | |
| Now And Then | LP | Abnak | ABST2071 | 1968 | £5 | £12 | US |
| Progressions | LP | Abnak | AB(ST)2069 | 1967 | £5 | £12 | US |
| Sound Of Love | 7" EP | Stateside | FSE1007 | 1967 | £7.50 | £15 | French |
| Western Union | LP | Abnak | AB(ST)2067 | 1967 | £6 | £15 | US |
| Western Union | 7" EP | Stateside | FSE102 | 1967 | £6 | £12 | French |

## FIVE BLIND BOYS

| Title | Format | Label | Catalogue | Year | | | |
|---|---|---|---|---|---|---|---|
| Five Blind Boys | 7" EP | Vocalion | EPVP1282 | 1964 | £4 | £8 | |

## FIVE BLOBS

| Title | Format | Label | Catalogue | Year | | | |
|---|---|---|---|---|---|---|---|
| Blob | 7" | Philips | PB881 | 1958 | £1.50 | £4 | |

## FIVE BY FIVE

| Title | Format | Label | Catalogue | Year | | | Notes |
|---|---|---|---|---|---|---|---|
| Fire | 7" | Pye | 7N25477 | 1968 | £7.50 | £15 | |
| Next Exit | LP | Paula | LPS2202 | 1968 | £6 | £15 | US |

## FIVE CHESTERNUTS

The Five Chesternuts were together for less than four months, but managed to make one (now rare) single during that time. Hank Marvin and Bruce Welch, who subsequently formed the Shadows, were both members.

| Title | Format | Label | Catalogue | Year | | | |
|---|---|---|---|---|---|---|---|
| Jean Dorothy | 7" | Columbia | DB4165 | 1958 | £50 | £100 | |

## FIVE COUNTS
| | | | | | | | |
|---|---|---|---|---|---|---|---|
| Watermelon Walk | 7" | Oriole | CBA1769 | 1962 | £1.50 | £4 | |

## FIVE DALLAS BOYS
| | | | | | | |
|---|---|---|---|---|---|---|
| Big Man | 7" | Columbia | DB4154 | 1958 | £1.50 | £4 |
| Fatty Patty | 7" | Columbia | DB4231 | 1958 | £2 | £5 |
| Five Dallas Boys | 7" EP | Columbia | SEG8035 | 1960 | £2 | £5 |

## FIVE DAY RAIN
| | | | | | | |
|---|---|---|---|---|---|---|
| Five Day Rain | LP | private | | 1970 | £500 | £750 |

## FIVE DAY WEEK STRAW PEOPLE
| | | | | | | |
|---|---|---|---|---|---|---|
| Five Day Week Straw People | LP | Saga | FID2123 | 1968 | £30 | £60 |

## FIVE DU-TONES
| | | | | | | |
|---|---|---|---|---|---|---|
| Shake A Tail Feather | 7" | President | PT134 | 1968 | £1.50 | £4 |
| Shake A Tail Feather | 7" | Stateside | SS206 | 1963 | £4 | £8 |

## FIVE EMPREES
| | | | | | | | |
|---|---|---|---|---|---|---|---|
| Five Emprees | LP | Freeport | FR3001/FRS4001 | 1965 | £15 | £30 | US |
| Little Miss Sad | LP | Freeport | FR3002/FRS4002 | 1966 | £6 | £15 | US |

## FIVE FLEETS
| | | | | | | |
|---|---|---|---|---|---|---|
| Oh What A Feeling | 7" | Felsted | AF103 | 1958 | £62.50 | £125 |

## FIVE HAND REEL
| | | | | | | |
|---|---|---|---|---|---|---|
| Five Hand Reel | LP | Rubber | RUB019 | 1976 | £4 | £10 |

## FIVE KEYS
| | | | | | | | |
|---|---|---|---|---|---|---|---|
| Best Of The Five Keys | LP | Aladdin | 806 | 1956 | £250 | £400 | US |
| Blues Don't Care | 7" | Capitol | CL14756 | 1957 | £30 | £60 | |
| Cos You're My Love | 7" | Capitol | CL14545 | 1956 | £87.50 | £175 | |
| Doggone It | 7" | Capitol | CL14325 | 1955 | £250 | £400 | best auctioned |
| Fantastic Five Keys | LP | Capitol | T1769 | 1962 | £50 | £100 | US |
| Five Keys | LP | King | 688 | 1960 | £75 | £150 | US |
| Five Keys On Stage | LP | Capitol | T828 | 1957 | £75 | £150 | US |
| Five Keys On The Town | LP | Score | LP4003 | 1957 | £180 | £300 | US |
| Four Walls | 7" | Capitol | CL14736 | 1957 | £25 | £50 | |
| From Me To You | 7" | Capitol | CL14829 | 1958 | £30 | £60 | |
| Ling Ting Tong | 78 | Capitol | CL14184 | 1954 | £25 | £50 | |
| Really O Truly Oh | 7" | Capitol | CL14967 | 1958 | £30 | £60 | |
| Rhythm And Blues Hits Past And Present | LP | King | 692 | 1960 | £75 | £150 | US |
| She's The Most | 7" | Capitol | CL14582 | 1956 | £87.50 | £175 | |
| That's Right | 7" | Capitol | CL14639 | 1956 | £37.50 | £75 | |
| Verdict | 7" | Capitol | CL14313 | 1955 | £330 | £500 | best auctioned |
| Wisdom Of A Fool | 7" | Capitol | CL14686 | 1957 | £37.50 | £75 | |

## FIVE LIVERPOOLS
| | | | | | | | |
|---|---|---|---|---|---|---|---|
| Tokio International | LP | CBS | 62460 | 1965 | £150 | £250 | German |

## FIVE MAN ELECTRICAL BAND
| | | | | | | | |
|---|---|---|---|---|---|---|---|
| Five Man Electrical Band | LP | Capitol | ST165 | 1969 | £5 | £12 | US |

## FIVE OF DIAMONDS
| | | | | | | | |
|---|---|---|---|---|---|---|---|
| Five Of Diamonds | 7" EP | Oak | RGJ150FD | 1965 | £150 | £250 | best auctioned |

## FIVE ROYALES
Within Greil Marcus's collection or rock essays, *Stranded*, Ed Ward writes an account of the recording career of the Five Royales. It is a moving story, a piece of great rock writing that makes the reader want to seek out immediately the group's records – and as Ward admits at the end, it is completely made up. The music that inspired Ward, however, is likely to inspire any fan of the period. The Five Royales perform superior doo-wop with the added distinction of fiery blues guitar, courtesy of Lowman Pauling, who also managed to write two classic songs – 'Think', covered by James Brown, and 'Dedicated To The One I Love', made into a big hit by the Mamas and the Papas.

| | | | | | | | |
|---|---|---|---|---|---|---|---|
| Dedicated To The One I Love | 7" | Ember | EMBS124 | 1960 | £30 | £60 | |
| Dedicated To You | LP | King | 580 | 1957 | £75 | £150 | US |
| Five Royales | LP | King | 678 | 1960 | £50 | £100 | US |
| Five Royales Sing For You | LP | King | 616 | 1959 | £62.50 | £125 | US |
| Rockin' Five Royales | LP | Apollo | LP488 | 1956 | £180 | £300 | US |
| Twenty-Four All Time Hits | LP | King | 955 | 1966 | £8 | £20 | US |

## FIVE SATINS
| | | | | | | | |
|---|---|---|---|---|---|---|---|
| Encore | LP | Ember | ELP401 | 1960 | £15 | £30 | US |
| Five Satins Sing | LP | Ember | ELP100 | 1957 | £75 | £150 | US |
| Five Satins Sing | LP | Ember | ELP100 | 1957 | £330 | £500 | US, blue vinyl |
| Five Satins Sing | LP | Mount Vernon | 108 | 196– | £8 | £20 | US |
| Shadows | 7" | Top Rank | JAR239 | 1959 | £6 | £12 | |
| To The Aisle | 7" | London | HL8501 | 1957 | £180 | £300 | best auctioned |
| Wonderful Girl | 7" | Top Rank | JAR199 | 1959 | £7.50 | £15 | |
| Your Memory | 7" | MGM | MGM1087 | 1960 | £12.50 | £25 | |

## FIVE SMITH BROTHERS
| | | | | | | |
|---|---|---|---|---|---|---|
| ABC Boogie | 7" | Decca | F10403 | 1954 | £5 | £10 |
| I'm In Favour Of Friendship | 7" | Decca | F10527 | 1955 | £2.50 | £6 |
| You're As Sweet Today | 7" | Decca | F10507 | 1955 | £1.50 | £4 |

## FIVE STAIRSTEPS & CUBIE
| | | | | | | |
|---|---|---|---|---|---|---|
| Million To One | 7" | Pye | 7N25448 | 1968 | £2 | £5 |
| We Must Be In Love | 7" | Buddah | 201070 | 1969 | £2 | £5 |

## FIVE STEPS BEYOND
| | | | | | | |
|---|---|---|---|---|---|---|
| Not So Young Today | 7" | CBS | 202490 | 1967 | £1.50 | £4 |

## FIVE THIRTY
| | | | | | | |
|---|---|---|---|---|---|---|
| Abstain | CD-s | East West | YZ530CD | 1990 | £2 | £5 |
| Air Conditioned Nightmare | CD-s | East West | YZ543CD | 1990 | £2 | £5 |
| Catcher In The Rye | 12" | Other | 12OTH2 | 1985 | £6 | £15 |
| Supernova | CD-s | East West | YZ594CD | 1991 | £2 | £5 |
| You EP | CD-s | East West | YZ624CD | 1991 | £2 | £5 |

## FIVE'S COMPANY
| | | | | | | |
|---|---|---|---|---|---|---|
| Ballad Of Fred The Pixie | LP | Saga | FID2151 | 1969 | £4 | £10 |
| Session Man | 7" | Pye | 7N17199 | 1966 | £4 | £8 |
| Some Girls | 7" | Pye | 7N17162 | 1966 | £1.50 | £4 |
| Sunday For Seven Days | 7" | Pye | 7N17118 | 1966 | £2 | £5 |

## FIZZBOMBS
| | | | | | | |
|---|---|---|---|---|---|---|
| Sign On The Line | 7" | Narodnik | NRK003 | 1987 | £2 | £5 |

## FLACK, ROBERTA
| | | | | | | |
|---|---|---|---|---|---|---|
| First Take | LP | Atlantic | 588204 | 1969 | £4 | £10 |

## FLACK, ROBERTA & DONNY HATHAWAY
| | | | | | | |
|---|---|---|---|---|---|---|
| Roberta Flack And Donny Hathaway | LP | Atlantic | K40380 | 1972 | £4 | £10 |

## FLAIRS
| | | | | | | | |
|---|---|---|---|---|---|---|---|
| Flairs | LP | Crown | CLP5356 | 1963 | £15 | £30 | US |
| Swing Pretty Mama | 7" | Oriole | CB1392 | 1957 | £210 | £350 | best auctioned |

## FLAKY PASTRY
| | | | | | | |
|---|---|---|---|---|---|---|
| Ingredients | LP | Flaky Pastry | FALP001 | 1976 | £6 | £15 |

## FLAME
| | | | | | | |
|---|---|---|---|---|---|---|
| Flame | LP | Stateside | SSL10312 | 1971 | £5 | £12 |
| See The Light | 7" | Stateside | SS2183 | 1970 | £1.50 | £4 |

## FLAMES
| | | | | | | | |
|---|---|---|---|---|---|---|---|
| Broadway Jungle | 7" | Island | WI139 | 1964 | £5 | £10 | |
| He's The Greatest | 7" | Island | WI130 | 1964 | £5 | £10 | |
| Helena Darling | 7" | Blue Beat | BB205 | 1964 | £6 | £12 | |
| It Takes Time | 7" | Blue Beat | BB300 | 1965 | £6 | £12 | Liges B side |
| Little Flea | 7" | Island | WI136 | 1964 | £5 | £10 | |
| When I Get Home | 7" | Island | WI138 | 1964 | £5 | £10 | |
| You've Lost Your Date | 7" | Nu Beat | NB028 | 1969 | £2.50 | £6 | |

## FLAMIN' GROOVIES
| | | | | | | | |
|---|---|---|---|---|---|---|---|
| Feel A Whole Lot Better | 7" | Sire | 6078619 | 1978 | £1.50 | £4 | picture sleeve |
| Flamin' Groovies | LP | Kama Sutra | 2683003 | 1971 | £5 | £12 | double |
| Flamingo | LP | Kama Sutra | KSBS2021 | 1971 | £4 | £10 | US |
| Married Woman | 7" | United Artists | UP35464 | 1972 | £2 | £5 | |
| Slow Death | 7" | United Artists | REM406 | 1976 | £2 | £5 | |
| Slow Death | 7" | United Artists | UP35392 | 1972 | £1.50 | £4 | |
| Sneekers | 10" LP | Snazz | R2371 | 1969 | £8 | £20 | US |
| Supersnazz | LP | Epic | BN26487 | 1969 | £6 | £15 | US |
| Teenage Head | LP | Kama Sutra | KSBS2031 | 1971 | £4 | £10 | US |
| Teenage Head | 7" | Kama Sutra | 2013031 | 1971 | £1.50 | £4 | |

## FLAMING LIPS
| | | | | | | | |
|---|---|---|---|---|---|---|---|
| This Here Giraffe | CD-s | Warner Bros | W0335CDX | 1996 | £2 | £5 | shaped pic disc |

## FLAMING YOUTH
Flaming Youth's *Ark II* was a *Melody Maker* album of the month, but its remarkable lack of commercial success probably goes to show that the music press is very much less influential than it would like to believe. The group's drummer, however, has done very well subsequently – he is Phil Collins, albeit almost unrecognizable from the picture on the LP cover.

| | | | | | | | |
|---|---|---|---|---|---|---|---|
| Ark 2 | LP | Fontana | STL5533 | 1969 | £8 | £20 | |
| From Now On | 7" | Fontana | 6001003 | 1970 | £5 | £10 | |
| Guide Me Orion | 7" | Fontana | TF1057 | 1969 | £7.50 | £15 | picture sleeve |
| Man, Woman And Child | 7" | Fontana | 6001002 | 1970 | £5 | £10 | |

## FLAMINGO, JOHNNY
| | | | | | | |
|---|---|---|---|---|---|---|
| My Teenage Girl | 7" | Vogue | V9089 | 1957 | £37.50 | £75 |
| So Long | 7" | Vogue | V9100 | 1958 | £30 | £60 |

## FLAMINGOS
John Peel once presented a radio programme in which he outlined the history of the falsetto male vocal within black pop music. His choice of 'I Only Have Eyes For You' by the Flamingos as an early milestone in this history was confirmed as a wise one by the memorable inclusion of the song at a key point in the film, *American Graffiti*. It is a doo-wop performance of remarkable power and beauty – a fact that was further acknowledged by Art Garfunkel's hit cover of the song, using an identical arrangement. The Flamingos were actually unusually long-lived for a doo-wop group, and their biggest hit is just one high point within an extensive catalogue.

| | | | | | | |
|---|---|---|---|---|---|---|
| At Night | 7" | Top Rank | JAR519 | 1960 | £7.50 | £15 |

| Title | Format | Label | Catalogue | Year | | | Notes |
|---|---|---|---|---|---|---|---|
| Boogaloo Party | 7" | Philips | BF1483 | 1966 | £4 | £8 | |
| Favorites | LP | End | LP(S)307 | 1960 | £20 | £40 | US |
| Flamingos | LP | Checker | LP1433/LPS3005 | 1959 | £62.50 | £125 | US |
| Flamingos | LP | Constellation | CS3 | 1964 | £20 | £20 | US |
| Flamingos Meet The Moonglows | LP | Vee Jay | LP1052 | 1962 | £15 | £30 | US |
| I Only Have Eyes For You | 7" | Top Rank | JAR263 | 1960 | £30 | £60 | |
| Just For A Kick | 7" | London | HLN8373 | 1957 | £210 | £350 | best auctioned |
| Ladder Of Love | 7" | Brunswick | 05696 | 1957 | £210 | £350 | best auctioned |
| Love Walked In | 7" | Top Rank | JAR213 | 1959 | £7.50 | £15 | |
| Nobody Loves Me Like You | 7" | Top Rank | JAR367 | 1960 | £7.50 | £15 | |
| Requestfully Yours | LP | End | LP(S)308 | 1960 | £20 | £40 | US |
| Serenade | LP | End | LP(S)304 | 1959 | £25 | £50 | US |
| Sound Of The Flamingos | LP | End | LP(S)316 | 1962 | £20 | £40 | US |
| Their Hits – Then And Now | LP | Philips | 2/PHS600206 | 1966 | £6 | £15 | US |

## FLAMMA – SHERMAN
| Title | Format | Label | Catalogue | Year | | | Notes |
|---|---|---|---|---|---|---|---|
| Move Me | 7" | SNB | 554142 | 1969 | £7.50 | £15 | |

## FLANAGAN, TOMMY
| Title | Format | Label | Catalogue | Year | | | Notes |
|---|---|---|---|---|---|---|---|
| Jazz It's Magic! | LP | Pye | NPL28009 | 1960 | £8 | £20 | |

## FLANAGAN BROTHERS
| Title | Format | Label | Catalogue | Year | | | Notes |
|---|---|---|---|---|---|---|---|
| Salton City | 7" | Coral | Q72342 | 1958 | £4 | £8 | |

## FLANAGAN BROTHERS (2)
| Title | Format | Label | Catalogue | Year | | | Notes |
|---|---|---|---|---|---|---|---|
| Irish Delight | LP | Topic | 12T365 | 1979 | £4 | £10 | |

## FLANDERS, MICHAEL & DONALD SWANN
| Title | Format | Label | Catalogue | Year | | | Notes |
|---|---|---|---|---|---|---|---|
| At The Drop Of A Hat | LP | Parlophone | PMC1033/ PCS3001 | 1957 | £4 | £10 | |
| At The Drop Of Another Hat | LP | Parlophone | PMC1216 | 1964 | £4 | £10 | |
| Bestiary Of Flanders And Swann | LP | Parlophone | PMC1164 | 1961 | £4 | £10 | |

## FLANDERS, TOMMY
| Title | Format | Label | Catalogue | Year | | | Notes |
|---|---|---|---|---|---|---|---|
| Moonstone | LP | Verve | SVLP6020 | 1969 | £5 | £12 | |

## FLARES
| Title | Format | Label | Catalogue | Year | | | Notes |
|---|---|---|---|---|---|---|---|
| Foot Stompin' Hits | LP | London | HAU8034 | 1963 | £10 | £25 | |
| Foot Stomping | 7" | London | HLU9441 | 1961 | £6 | £12 | |

## FLASH
| Title | Format | Label | Catalogue | Year | | | Notes |
|---|---|---|---|---|---|---|---|
| Flash | LP | Sovereign | SVNA7251 | 1972 | £5 | £12 | |
| Flash In The Can | LP | Sovereign | SVNA7255 | 1972 | £5 | £12 | |
| Out Of Our Hands | LP | Sovereign | SVNA7260 | 1973 | £5 | £12 | |

## FLASH & THE BOARD OF DIRECTORS
| Title | Format | Label | Catalogue | Year | | | Notes |
|---|---|---|---|---|---|---|---|
| Busy Signal | 7" | Bell | BLL1007 | 1968 | £1.50 | £4 | |

## FLASKET BRINNER
| Title | Format | Label | Catalogue | Year | | | Notes |
|---|---|---|---|---|---|---|---|
| Flasket Brinner | LP | Silence | SRS4606 | 1971 | £15 | £30 | Swedish |

## FLAT EARTH SOCIETY
| Title | Format | Label | Catalogue | Year | | | Notes |
|---|---|---|---|---|---|---|---|
| Waleeco | LP | Fleetwood | 3027 | 1968 | £50 | £100 | US |
| Waleeco | LP | Psycho | PSYCHO17 | 1983 | £6 | £15 | |

## FLATT & SCRUGGS
| Title | Format | Label | Catalogue | Year | | | Notes |
|---|---|---|---|---|---|---|---|
| Ballad Of Jed Clampett | 7" | CBS | 201793 | 1965 | £1.50 | £4 | |
| Country & Western Aces | 7" EP | Mercury | 10010MCE | 1964 | £2 | £5 | |
| Country & Western Trailblazers No. 4 | 7" EP | Mercury | ZEP10106 | 1961 | £2 | £5 | |
| Folk Songs Of Our Land | LP | CBS | BPG62095 | 1963 | £4 | £10 | |

## FLAVOUR
| Title | Format | Label | Catalogue | Year | | | Notes |
|---|---|---|---|---|---|---|---|
| Sally Had A Party | 7" | Direction | 583597 | 1968 | £2 | £5 | |

## FLAX
| Title | Format | Label | Catalogue | Year | | | Notes |
|---|---|---|---|---|---|---|---|
| One | LP | Vertigo | | 1976 | £75 | £150 | |

## FLEE REKKERS
| Title | Format | Label | Catalogue | Year | | | Notes |
|---|---|---|---|---|---|---|---|
| Blue Tango | 7" | Pye | 7N15326 | 1960 | £2 | £5 | |
| Fabulous Flee Rekkers | 7" EP | Pye | NEP24141 | 1961 | £15 | £30 | |
| Fireball | 7" | Piccadilly | 7N35109 | 1963 | £2.50 | £6 | |
| Green Jeans | 7" | Top Rank | JAR431 | 1960 | £12.50 | £25 | |
| Green Jeans | 7" | Triumph | RGM1008 | 1960 | £7.50 | £15 | |
| Lone Rider | 7" | Piccadilly | 7N35006 | 1961 | £4 | £8 | |
| Stage To Cimmaron | 7" | Piccadilly | 7N35048 | 1962 | £4 | £8 | |
| Sunburst | 7" | Piccadilly | 7N35081 | 1962 | £2.50 | £6 | |
| Sunday Date | 7" | Pye | 7N15288 | 1960 | £2 | £5 | |

## FLEETWOOD MAC

Most of the collectable Fleetwood Mac records come from the first part of the group's career, when its sound was very different to the commercial pop style that later became its forte. The Blue Horizon recordings – and especially the eponymous first LP – are probably the most authentic blues recordings to have been made by white, English musicians. Remarkably, that first LP climbed to number four in the album charts, although mint copies of the record have become surprisingly scarce these days.

| Title | Format | Label | Catalogue | Year | | | Notes |
|---|---|---|---|---|---|---|---|
| As Long As You Follow | CD-s | Warner Bros | W7644CD | 1988 | £2 | £5 | 3" single |
| Behind The Mask | CD | Warner Bros | 9267602DJ | 1990 | £8 | £20 | US promo picture disc |
| Big Love | 12" | Warner Bros | W8398TP | 1987 | £2.50 | £6 | picture disc |

| Title | Format | Label | Catalog | Year | | | Notes |
|---|---|---|---|---|---|---|---|
| Black Magic Woman | 7" | Blue Horizon | 573138 | 1968 | £1.50 | £4 | |
| Blues Jam At Chess | LP | Blue Horizon | 766227 | 1969 | £20 | £40 | double, with other artists |
| Everywhere | CD-s | Warner Bros | W8143CD | 1988 | £2 | £5 | 3" single |
| Fleetwood Mac | LP | Blue Horizon | 763200 | 1968 | £10 | £25 | |
| Fleetwood Mac | LP | Mobile Fidelity | MFSL1012 | 1978 | £5 | £12 | US audiophile |
| Fleetwood Mac | LP | Reprise | K54043 | 1975 | £4 | £10 | white vinyl |
| Green Manalishi | 7" | Reprise | RS27007 | 1970 | £2.50 | £6 | picture sleeve |
| Hold Me | CD-s | Warner Bros | W7528CD | 1989 | £2 | £5 | 3" single |
| I Believe My Time Ain't Long | 7" | Blue Horizon | 573051 | 1967 | £2 | £5 | |
| I Believe My Time Ain't Long | 7" | Blue Horizon | 573051 | 1967 | £10 | £20 | picture sleeve |
| In The Back Of My Mind | CD-s | Warner Bros | W9739CDX | 1990 | £2 | £5 | foldout sleeve |
| Isn't It Midnight | CD-s | Warner Bros | W7860CD | 1988 | £2 | £5 | 3" single |
| Kiln House | LP | Reprise | RSLP9004 | 1970 | £4 | £10 | |
| Little Lies | 12" | Warner Bros | W8291TP | 1987 | £2.50 | £6 | picture disc |
| Man Of The World | 7" | Immediate | IM080 | 1969 | £1.50 | £4 | |
| Mirage | LP | Mobile Fidelity | MFSL1119 | 1984 | £4 | £10 | US audiophile |
| Mr. Wonderful | LP | Blue Horizon | 763205 | 1968 | £10 | £25 | |
| Mr. Wonderful | CD | Essential | ESSCD010 | 1989 | £5 | £12 | |
| Need Your Love So Bad | 7" | Blue Horizon | 573139 | 1968 | £1.50 | £4 | |
| Need Your Love So Bad | 7" | Blue Horizon | 573157 | 1969 | £1.50 | £4 | |
| Oh Diane | 7" | Warner Bros | FLEET1P | 1982 | £1.50 | £4 | picture disc |
| Oh Well | 7" | Reprise | RS27000 | 1969 | £1.50 | £4 | |
| Original Fleetwood Mac | LP | Blue Horizon | 763875 | 1971 | £4 | £10 | |
| Pious Bird Of Good Omen | LP | Blue Horizon | 763215 | 1969 | £6 | £15 | |
| Rumours | LP | Nautilus | NR 8 | 1981 | £5 | £12 | US audiophile |
| Rumours | CD | Reprise | | 1988 | £6 | £15 | HMV box set |
| Save Me | CD-s | Warner Bros | W9866CDX | 1990 | £2 | £5 | foldout sleeve |
| Selections From 25 Years – The Chain | CD | Warner Bros | PROCD5905 | 1992 | £8 | £20 | |
| Seven Wonders | 12" | Warner Bros | W8317TP | 1987 | £2.50 | £6 | picture disc |
| Sky's The Limit | CD-s | WEA | W9740CD | 1990 | £2 | £5 | |
| Then Play On | LP | Reprise | RSLP9000 | 1969 | £4 | £10 | |
| Tusk | LP | Warner Bros | PROA866 | 1979 | £4 | £10 | US promo sampler |

## FLEETWOODS

| Title | Format | Label | Catalog | Year | | | Notes |
|---|---|---|---|---|---|---|---|
| Almost There | 7" | Liberty | LIB10191 | 1965 | £1.50 | £4 | US |
| Before And After | LP | Dolton | BLP2/BST8030 | 1965 | £6 | £15 | US |
| Best Of The Oldies | LP | Dolton | BLP2/BST8011 | 1962 | £8 | £20 | US |
| Come Softly To Me | 7" | London | HLU8841 | 1959 | £4 | £8 | |
| Come Softly To Me | 7" | London | SLU4003 | 1959 | £12.50 | £25 | stereo |
| Deep In A Dream | LP | London | HAG2419 | 1961 | £8 | £20 | |
| Fleetwoods | LP | Dolton | BLP2/BST8002 | 1960 | £10 | £25 | US |
| Fleetwoods Sing For Lovers By Night | LP | Dolton | BLP2/BST8020 | 1963 | £8 | £20 | US |
| Folk Rock | LP | Dolton | BLP2/BST8039 | 1965 | £6 | £15 | US |
| Goodnight My Love | LP | Dolton | BLP2/BST8025 | 1963 | £8 | £20 | US |
| Goodnight My Love | 7" | Liberty | LIB75 | 1964 | £1.50 | £4 | |
| Graduation's Here | 7" | London | HLU8895 | 1959 | £4 | £8 | |
| Greatest Hits | LP | Dolton | BLP2/BST8018 | 1962 | £8 | £20 | US |
| He's The Great Imposter | 7" | London | HLG9426 | 1961 | £2.50 | £6 | |
| Mr. Blue | LP | Top Rank | BUY028 | 1960 | £8 | £20 | |
| Mr. Blue | 7" | Top Rank | JAR202 | 1959 | £2.50 | £6 | |
| Outside My Window | 7" | Top Rank | JAR294 | 1960 | £1.50 | £4 | |
| Outside My Window | 7" | Top Rank | JAR294 | 1960 | £4 | £8 | picture sleeve |
| Ruby Red Baby Blue | 7" | Liberty | LIB93 | 1964 | £1.50 | £4 | |
| Runaround | 7" | Top Rank | JAR383 | 1960 | £2 | £5 | |
| Softly | LP | London | HAG2388 | 1961 | £15 | £30 | |
| Softly | LP | London | SAHG6188 | 1961 | £20 | £40 | stereo |
| They Tell Me It's Summer | 7" | Liberty | LIB62 | 1964 | £1.50 | £4 | |
| Tragedy | 7" | London | HLG9341 | 1961 | £2.50 | £6 | |

## FLEMING, HELEN

| Title | Format | Label | Catalog | Year | | | Notes |
|---|---|---|---|---|---|---|---|
| Eve's Ten Commandments | 7" | Blue Beat | BB341 | 1966 | £6 | £12 | |

## FLEMONS, WADE

| Title | Format | Label | Catalog | Year | | | Notes |
|---|---|---|---|---|---|---|---|
| Easy Loving | 7" | Top Rank | JAR371 | 1960 | £1.50 | £4 | |
| Slow Motion | 7" | Top Rank | JAR206 | 1959 | £1.50 | £4 | |
| Wade Flemons | LP | Vee Jay | LP1011 | 1959 | £15 | £30 | US |
| What's Happening | 7" | Top Rank | JAR327 | 1960 | £1.50 | £4 | |

## FLESH FOR LULU

| Title | Format | Label | Catalog | Year | | | Notes |
|---|---|---|---|---|---|---|---|
| Subterraneans | 7" | Polydor | FFLD1 | 1984 | £2 | £5 | double |

## FLETCHER, DARROW

| Title | Format | Label | Catalog | Year | | | Notes |
|---|---|---|---|---|---|---|---|
| Pain Gets A Little Deeper | 7" | London | HLU10024 | 1966 | £20 | £40 | |

## FLETCHER, DON

| Title | Format | Label | Catalog | Year | | | Notes |
|---|---|---|---|---|---|---|---|
| Two Wrongs Don't Make A Right | 7" | Vocalion | VP9271 | 1966 | £4 | £8 | |

## FLEUR DE LYS

A legendary psychedelic group, the Fleur De Lys recorded both under their own name and as backing group to singer Sharon Tandy. They produced a number of striking singles, but with little commercial impact. Bryn Haworth, however, began a solo career during the seventies, while Pete Sears ended up as a member of Jefferson Starship.

| Title | Format | Label | Catalog | Year | | | Notes |
|---|---|---|---|---|---|---|---|
| Circles | 7" | Immediate | IM032 | 1966 | £50 | £100 | |
| Dong With A Luminous Nose | 7" | Polydor | 56251 | 1968 | £20 | £40 | |
| I Can See A Light | 7" | Polydor | 56200 | 1967 | £20 | £40 | |
| Moondreams | 7" | Immediate | IM020 | 1965 | £50 | £100 | |

| | | | | | | | | |
|---|---|---|---|---|---|---|---|---|
| Mud In Your Eye | 7" | Polydor | 56124 | 1966 | £150 | £250 | best auctioned |
| Stop Crossing The Bridge | 7" | Atlantic | 584193 | 1968 | £20 | £40 | |
| You're Just A Liar | 7" | Atlantic | 584243 | 1969 | £20 | £40 | |

## FLICK, VIC SOUND
| | | | | | | | |
|---|---|---|---|---|---|---|---|
| Hang On | 7" | Chapter One | CH136 | 1970 | £2 | £5 | |

## FLIED EGG
| | | | | | | | |
|---|---|---|---|---|---|---|---|
| Dr. Siegel's Fried Egg Shooting Machine | LP | Philips | | 1971 | £50 | £100 | Japanese |
| Goodbye | LP | Philips | 55504 | 1972 | £75 | £150 | Japanese |

## FLIES
| | | | | | | | |
|---|---|---|---|---|---|---|---|
| House Of Love | 7" | Decca | F12594 | 1967 | £15 | £30 | |
| I'm Not Your Stepping Stone | 7" | Decca | F12533 | 1966 | £20 | £40 | |
| Magic Train | 7" | RCA | RCA1757 | 1968 | £10 | £20 | |

## FLINGELS
| | | | | | | | |
|---|---|---|---|---|---|---|---|
| Ireland Awake | LP | Saga | EROS8095 | 1969 | £6 | £15 | |

## FLINT, SHELBY
| | | | | | | | |
|---|---|---|---|---|---|---|---|
| Angel On My Shoulder | 7" | Warner Bros | WB30 | 1961 | £1.50 | £4 | |

## FLINTLOCK
| | | | | | | | |
|---|---|---|---|---|---|---|---|
| Hot From The Lock | LP | Pinnacle | PLP8309 | 1976 | £5 | £12 | |
| On The Way | LP | Pinnacle | PLP8307 | 1975 | £5 | £12 | |
| Tears 'n' Cheers | LP | Pinnacle | PLP8310 | 1977 | £5 | £12 | |

## FLINTSTONES
| | | | | | | | |
|---|---|---|---|---|---|---|---|
| Workout | 7" | HMV | POP1266 | 1964 | £4 | £8 | |

## FLIP & THE DATELINERS
| | | | | | | | |
|---|---|---|---|---|---|---|---|
| My Johnny Doesn't Come Around Anymore | 7" | HMV | POP1359 | 1964 | £12.50 | £25 | |

## FLIPS
| | | | | | | | |
|---|---|---|---|---|---|---|---|
| Rockin' Twist | 7" | London | HLU9490 | 1962 | £2 | £5 | |

## FLIRTATIONS
| | | | | | | | |
|---|---|---|---|---|---|---|---|
| Sounds Like The Flirtations | LP | Deram | DML/SML1046 | 1969 | £4 | £10 | |

## FLOATING BRIDGE
| | | | | | | | |
|---|---|---|---|---|---|---|---|
| Floating Bridge | LP | Liberty | LBS83271 | 1969 | £6 | £15 | |

## FLOCK
The Flock were one of the crop of rock big bands to emerge at the end of the sixties. They were made distinctive by the presence of a violin as a lead instrument; its wielder, Jerry Goodman, later found a context in which he could shine even brighter, as a member of John McLaughlin's Mahavishnu Orchestra.

| | | | | | | | |
|---|---|---|---|---|---|---|---|
| Flock | LP | CBS | 63733 | 1969 | £5 | £12 | |

## FLOH DE COLOGNE
| | | | | | | | |
|---|---|---|---|---|---|---|---|
| Fliessbandbabys Beat Show | LP | Ohr | OMM556000 | 1970 | £8 | £20 | German |
| Geler Symphonie | LP | Ohr | OMM556033 | 1973 | £6 | £15 | German |
| Lucky Streik | LP | Ohr | OMM556029 | 1973 | £8 | £20 | German double |
| Munien | LP | Plane | 99201 | 1974 | £5 | £12 | German |
| Profitgier | LP | Ohr | OMM556010 | 1971 | £10 | £25 | German, red vinyl |
| Rotkäppchen | LP | Plane | 20905 | 1977 | £5 | £12 | German |
| Tilt | LP | Plane | 99202 | 1975 | £5 | £12 | German |
| Vietnam | LP | Plane | 33101 | 1968 | £10 | £25 | German |

## FLOOD, DICK
| | | | | | | | |
|---|---|---|---|---|---|---|---|
| Three Bells | 7" | Felsted | AF125 | 1959 | £1.50 | £4 | |

## FLOOR
| | | | | | | | |
|---|---|---|---|---|---|---|---|
| First Floor | LP | Philips | XPY855701 | 1967 | £20 | £40 | Dutch |

## FLORIAN GEYER
| | | | | | | | |
|---|---|---|---|---|---|---|---|
| Beggars' Pride | LP | private | 6621284 | 1976 | £87.50 | £175 | German |

## FLOWER TRAVELLING BAND
| | | | | | | | |
|---|---|---|---|---|---|---|---|
| Anywhere | LP | Philips | 8507 | 1970 | £75 | £150 | Japanese |
| Made In Japan | LP | Atlantic | S8187 | 1972 | £50 | £100 | Japanese |
| Make Up | LP | Atlantic | 5073/4 | 1973 | £75 | £150 | Japanese double |
| Satori | LP | Atlantic | S8056 | 1971 | £50 | £100 | Japanese |

## FLOWERPOT MEN
| | | | | | | | |
|---|---|---|---|---|---|---|---|
| Man Without A Woman | 7" | Deram | DM183 | 1968 | £1.50 | £4 | |
| Walk In The Sky | 7" | Deram | DM160 | 1967 | £1.50 | £4 | |

## FLOWERS
| | | | | | | | |
|---|---|---|---|---|---|---|---|
| Challenge | LP | CBS | 10063 | 1969 | £50 | £100 | Japanese |

## FLOWERS, LLOYD
| | | | | | | | |
|---|---|---|---|---|---|---|---|
| Lovers Town | 7" | Blue Beat | BB88 | 1962 | £6 | £12 | |

## FLOWERS AND FROLICS
| | | | | | | | |
|---|---|---|---|---|---|---|---|
| Bees On Horseback | LP | Free Reed | FRR016 | 1977 | £5 | £12 | |

## FLOYD, EDDIE

| | | | | | | | |
|---|---|---|---|---|---|---|---|
| Big Bird | 7" | Stax | 601035 | 1968 | £1.50 | £4 | |
| Bye Bye Baby | 7" | Speciality | SPE1001 | 1967 | £4 | £8 | |
| California Girl | LP | Stax | SXATS1036 | 1970 | £4 | £10 | |
| I've Never Found A Girl | LP | Stax | SXATS1003 | 1968 | £4 | £10 | |
| Knock On Wood | LP | Atco | 228014 | 1967 | £5 | £12 | |
| Knock On Wood | LP | Stax | 589006 | 1967 | £5 | £12 | |
| Knock On Wood | 7" | Atlantic | 584041 | 1966 | £1.50 | £4 | |
| On A Saturday Night | 7" | Stax | 601024 | 1967 | £1.50 | £4 | |
| Raise Your Hand | 7" | Stax | 601001 | 1967 | £1.50 | £4 | |
| Set My Soul On Fire | 7" | London | HL10129 | 1967 | £1.50 | £4 | |
| Things Get Better | 7" | Stax | 601016 | 1967 | £1.50 | £4 | |

## FLUTE & VOICE

| | | | | | | | |
|---|---|---|---|---|---|---|---|
| Imaginations Of Light | LP | Pilz | 20210882 | 1971 | £20 | £40 | German |

## FLUX

| | | | | | | | |
|---|---|---|---|---|---|---|---|
| Grand Result | LP | Rosegarden | | 1982 | £25 | £50 | Dutch |

## FLYING BURRITO BROTHERS

| | | | | | | | |
|---|---|---|---|---|---|---|---|
| Burrito Deluxe | LP | A&M | AMLS983 | 1970 | £4 | £10 | |
| Flying Burrito Brothers | LP | A&M | AMLS64295 | 1971 | £4 | £10 | |
| Gilded Palace Of Sin | LP | A&M | AMLS931 | 1969 | £5 | £12 | |
| Last Of The Red Hot Burritos | LP | A&M | AMLS64343 | 1971 | £4 | £10 | |
| Live In Amsterdam | LP | Bumble | GEXD301 | 1973 | £5 | £12 | double |
| Train Song | 7" | A&M | AMS756 | 1969 | £1.50 | £4 | |
| Tried So Hard | 7" | A&M | AMS816 | 1970 | £1.50 | £4 | |

## FLYING CIRCUS

| | | | | | | | |
|---|---|---|---|---|---|---|---|
| Prepared In Peace | LP | Harvest | SHSP4010 | 1970 | £4 | £10 | |

## FLYING MACHINE

| | | | | | | | |
|---|---|---|---|---|---|---|---|
| Down To Earth | LP | Pye | NSPL18328 | 1970 | £4 | £10 | |
| Hanging On The Edge Of Sadness | 7" | Pye | 7N17914 | 1970 | £1.50 | £4 | |
| Send My Baby Home Again | 7" | Pye | 7N17811 | 1969 | £2 | £5 | |
| Smile A Little Smile For Me | 7" | Pye | 7N17722 | 1969 | £2 | £5 | 2 different B sides |

## FLYING SAUCER ATTACK

| | | | | | | | |
|---|---|---|---|---|---|---|---|
| Soaring High | 7" | Heartbeat | FSA6 | 1993 | £15 | £30 | 3 different sleeves |

## FLYNN, STEVE

| | | | | | | | |
|---|---|---|---|---|---|---|---|
| Mr. Rainbow | 7" | Parlophone | R5625 | 1967 | £6 | £12 | |
| Your Life And My Life | 7" | Parlophone | R5689 | 1968 | £1.50 | £4 | |

## FLYS

| | | | | | | | |
|---|---|---|---|---|---|---|---|
| Bunch Of Five | 7" | Zama | ZA10 | 1977 | £2 | £5 | |

## FLYTE

| | | | | | | | |
|---|---|---|---|---|---|---|---|
| Dawn Dancer | LP | Don Quixote | | 1979 | £10 | £25 | Dutch |

## FOCAL POINT

| | | | | | | | |
|---|---|---|---|---|---|---|---|
| Love You Forever | 7" | Deram | DM186 | 1968 | £10 | £20 | |

## FOCUS

| | | | | | | | |
|---|---|---|---|---|---|---|---|
| Hocus Pocus | 7" | Blue Horizon | 2096004 | 1971 | £1.50 | £4 | |
| Moving Waves | LP | Blue Horizon | 2931002 | 1971 | £4 | £10 | with poster |
| Tommy | 7" | Blue Horizon | 2096008 | 1972 | £2.50 | £6 | |

## FOCUS & P. J. PROBY

| | | | | | | | |
|---|---|---|---|---|---|---|---|
| Focus Con Proby | LP | EMI | 5C06425713 | 1977 | £5 | £12 | European |

## FOCUS THREE

| | | | | | | | |
|---|---|---|---|---|---|---|---|
| Ten Thousand Years Behind My Mind | 7" | Columbia | DB8279 | 1967 | £12.50 | £25 | |

## FOETUS

The aggressively avant-garde rock songs made by Jim Thirlwell (or Clint Ruin, as he sometimes likes to be known) are credited to a bewildering variety of names, of which the common denominator is the 'Foetus' ingredient. For the sake of imposing some kind of order on the chaos that Thirlwell loves, records originally issued under such diverse descriptions as Foetus Corruptus, Foetus Over Frisco, Foetus Under Glass, Philip ans His Foetus Vibrations, and You've Got Foetus On Your Breath are all listed here. Other records have been released using still further variations of the Foetus idea.

| | | | | | | | |
|---|---|---|---|---|---|---|---|
| Ache | LP | Self Immolation | WOMBOYBL2 | 1982 | £30 | £60 | |
| Butterfly Potion | CD-s | Big Cat | ABBCD16 | 1990 | £2 | £5 | as Foetus Inc. |
| Custom Built For Capitalism | 12" | Self Immolation | WOMBWSUSC125 | 1982 | £10 | £25 | |
| Deaf | LP | Self Immolation | WOMBOYBL1 | 1981 | £30 | £60 | |
| OKFM | 7" | Self Immolation | WOMBS201 | 1981 | £12.50 | £25 | |
| Rife | LP | Rifle | RIFLE1 | 198– | £8 | £20 | double |
| Tell Me, What Is The Bane Of Your Life | 7" | Self Immolation | WOMBKX07 | 1982 | £10 | £20 | |
| Wash It All Off | 7" | Self Immolation | WOMBALL007 | 1981 | £10 | £20 | |

## FOGCUTTERS
Cry Cry Cry .................................................. 7" ...... Liberty ........... LIB55793 ............... 1964 £2 ........ £5 ..................................................

## FOGERTY, TOM & THE BLUE VELVETS
Come On, Baby ............................................ 7" ...... Orchestra ........ 617 ...................... 1961 £20 ...... £40 ...................................... US
Have You Ever Been Lonely? ................... 7" ...... Orchestra ....... 1010 ..................... 1961 £20 ...... £40 ...................................... US
Yes You Did .............................................. 7" ...... Orchestra ........ ......................... 1962 £20 ...... £40 ...................................... US

## FOGGY
How Come The Sun ................................. 7" ...... York ............. SYK534 ................... 1972 £1.50 ...... £4 ........................................
Kitty Starr ................................................. 7" ...... York ............. SYK542 ................... 1972 £1.50 ...... £4 ........................................
Patchwork Album .................................... LP ...... Canon ........... CNN5957 ............... 1976 £10 ........ £25 ........................................
Simple Gifts ............................................. LP ...... York ............. FYK411 .................. 1972 £20 ........ £40 ........................................

## FOGGY DEW-O
Born To Take The Highway .................. LP ...... Decca ........... LK/SKL5035 ......... 1969 £6 .......... £15 ........................................
Foggy Dew-O ........................................... LP ...... Decca ........... LK/SKL4940 ......... 1968 £8 .......... £20 ........................................
Reflections ............................................... 7" ...... Decca ........... F12776 .................. 1968 £1.50 ...... £4 ........................................

## FOKAL POINT
Fokal Point .............................................. LP ...... Midas ........... ......................... 197- £100 ...... £200 ........................................

## FOLEY, RED
Beyond The Sunset ................................. LP ...... Decca ........... DL8296 .................. 1958 £6 .......... £15 ...................................... US
Company's Comin' .................................. LP ...... Decca ........... DL(7)4140 ............. 1961 £5 .......... £12 ...................................... US
Country Double Date ............................. 7" EP . Brunswick ...... OE9148 ................. 1955 £4 .......... £8 ..... with Ernest Tubb
Dear Hearts And Gentle People ........... LP ...... Decca ........... DL(7)4290 ............. 1962 £5 .......... £12 ...................................... US
Golden Favorites .................................... LP ...... Decca ........... DL4107 .................. 1961 £5 .......... £12 ...................................... US
He Walks With Thee ............................... LP ...... Decca ........... DL8767 .................. 1958 £6 .......... £15 ...................................... US
Hearts Of Stone ...................................... 7" ...... Brunswick ...... 05363 .................... 1955 £5 .......... £10 ........................................
Let's All Sing To Him ............................ LP ...... Decca ........... DL(7)8903 ............. 1959 £5 .......... £12 ...................................... US
Let's All Sing With Red Foley ............. LP ...... Decca ........... DL(7)8847 ............. 1959 £6 .......... £15 ...................................... US
Lift Up Your Voice ................................ 10" LP Decca ........... DL5338 .................. 1954 £15 ........ £30 ...................................... US
My Keepsake Album ............................... LP ...... Decca ........... DL8806 .................. 1958 £6 .......... £15 ...................................... US
Night Watch ............................................ 7" ...... Brunswick ...... 05508 .................... 1955 £2 .......... £5 ........................................
Red And Ernie ......................................... LP ...... Brunswick ...... LAT8206 ................ 1957 £6 .......... £15 ..... with Ernest Tubb
Sing Along ................................................ LP ...... Brunswick ...... LAT8343/STA3034 1960 £4 .......... £10 ........................................
Skinnie Minnie Fishtail ......................... 7" ...... Brunswick ...... 05321 .................... 1954 £2 .......... £5 ........................................
Songs Of Devotion .................................. LP ...... Decca ........... DL(7)4198 ............. 1961 £5 .......... £12 ...................................... US
Souvenir Album ...................................... LP ...... Decca ........... DL8294 .................. 1958 £8 .......... £20 ...................................... US
Souvenir Album ...................................... 10" LP Decca ........... DL5303 .................. 1951 £15 ........ £30 ...................................... US

## FOLK BLUES INC.
Don't Hide .............................................. 7" ...... Eyemark ........ EMS1006 ............... 1966 £2 .......... £5 ........................................
F.B.I. ....................................................... LP ...... Good Earth ..... GDS802 ................. 1977 £20 ........ £40 ........................................

## FOLK STOW
Folk Stow ................................................ LP ...... Stoof ............. MU7456 ................. 1978 £25 ........ £50 ........................................

## FOLKCORN
Goedenavond Spielman ............................ LP ...... Spoof ............. ......................... 1978 £15 ........ £30 ........................................

## FOLKES, CALVIN
Hello Everybody ..................................... 7" ...... Port-O-Jam ..... PJ4118 .................. 1964 £5 .......... £10 ........ Irving Six B side
My Bonnie ............................................... 7" ...... Port-O-Jam ..... PJ4117 .................. 1964 £5 .......... £10 ........................................
Someone .................................................. 7" ...... Rio ............. R5 ........................ 1963 £5 .......... £10 ........................................
You'll Never Know ................................. 7" ...... Rio ............. R8 ........................ 1963 £5 .......... £10 ........................................

## FOLKLANDERS
Two Little Fishes ................................... 7" EP . Urban ............. PB001 ................... 196- £2 .......... £5 ........................................

## FOLKLORDS
Release The Sunshine ............................. LP ...... Allied ............. 11 ........................ 1969 £30 ........ £60 ............... Canadian

## FOLKLORE
Room For Company ................................ LP ...... Tank ............. BSS210 .................. 1977 £30 ........ £60 ........................................

## FOLKS BROTHERS
Carolina .................................................. 7" ...... Blue Beat ........ BB30 .................... 1961 £6 .......... £12 ..... Eric Morris B side

## FOLKWAYS
No Other Name ...................................... LP ...... Folk Heritage .. ......................... 1972 £4 .......... £10 ........................................

## FOLLY'S FOOL
Folly's Fool ............................................ LP ...... Century ........ ......................... 1975 £37.50 ...... £75 ...................................... US

## FOLQUE
Folque .................................................... LP ...... Phonogram ...... ......................... 1974 £75 ........ £150 ............... Norwegian

## FONTAINE, EDDIE
Cool It Baby ........................................... 7" ...... Brunswick ...... 05624 .................... 1956 £37.50 ...... £75 ........................................
Nothing Shaking ..................................... 7" ...... London ........... HLM8711 ............. 1958 £12.50 ...... £25 ........................................
Rock Love ............................................... 7" ...... HMV ............. 7M304 ................... 1955 £100 ...... £200 ........................................

## FONTANA, ARLENE
I'm In Love ............................................ 7" ...... Pye ............. 7N25010 ............... 1959 £1.50 ...... £4 ........................................

## FONTANA, WAYNE

| | | | | | | | |
|---|---|---|---|---|---|---|---|
| Charlie Cass/Linda | 7" | Fontana | TF1054 | 1969 | £2.50 | £6 | |
| Come On Home | 7" EP | Fontana | 465307 | 1966 | £10 | £20 | French |
| Give Me Just A Little More Time | 7" | Philips | 6006035 | 1970 | £15 | £30 | |
| Wayne One | LP | Fontana | (S)TL5351 | 1966 | £4 | £10 | |

## FONTANA, WAYNE & THE MINDBENDERS

| | | | | | | | |
|---|---|---|---|---|---|---|---|
| Eric,Rick,Wayne,& Bob | LP | Fontana | TL5257 | 1966 | £25 | £50 | |
| For You For You | 7" | Fontana | TF418 | 1963 | £1.50 | £4 | |
| Game Of Love | 7" EP | Fontana | 465272 | 1965 | £10 | £20 | French |
| Game Of Love | 7" EP | Fontana | TE17449 | 1965 | £5 | £10 | |
| Hello Josephine | 7" | Fontana | TF404 | 1963 | £1.50 | £4 | |
| Just A Little Bit Too Late | 7" | Fontana | TF579 | 1965 | £1.50 | £4 | |
| Little Darling | 7" | Fontana | TF436 | 1964 | £1.50 | £4 | |
| Road Runner | 7" EP | Fontana | TE17421 | 1964 | £12.50 | £25 | |
| She Needs Love | 7" EP | Fontana | 465295 | 1965 | £10 | £20 | French |
| She Needs Love | 7" | Fontana | TF611 | 1965 | £1.50 | £4 | |
| Stop Look And Listen | 7" | Fontana | TF451 | 1964 | £1.50 | £4 | |
| Um Um Um Um Um | 7" EP | Fontana | TE17435 | 1964 | £5 | £10 | |
| Walking On Air | 7" EP | Fontana | TE17453 | 1965 | £15 | £30 | |
| Wayne Fontana & The Mindbenders | LP | Fontana | SFL13106 | 1969 | £4 | £10 | |
| Wayne Fontana & The Mindbenders | LP | Fontana | TL5230 | 1965 | £10 | £25 | |
| Wayne Fontana & The Mindbenders | LP | Wing | WL1166 | 1967 | £6 | £15 | |

## FONTANE SISTERS

| | | | | | | | |
|---|---|---|---|---|---|---|---|
| Adorable | 7" | London | HLD8225 | 1956 | £12.50 | £25 | |
| Banana Boat Song | 7" | London | HLD8378 | 1957 | £7.50 | £15 | |
| Billy Boy | 7" | London | HLD8861 | 1959 | £4 | £8 | |
| Chanson D'Amour | 7" | London | HLD8621 | 1958 | £4 | £8 | |
| Eddie My Love | 7" | London | HL7009 | 1956 | £2.50 | £6 | export |
| Eddie My Love | 7" | London | HLD8265 | 1956 | £20 | £40 | |
| Fontane Sisters | LP | Dot | DLP3004 | 1956 | £20 | £40 | US |
| Fontane Sisters No. 1 | 7" EP | London | RED1029 | 1955 | £25 | £50 | |
| Fontane Sisters No. 2 | 7" EP | London | RED1037 | 1955 | £20 | £40 | |
| Fontanes Sing | LP | London | HAD2053 | 1957 | £37.50 | £75 | |
| Fool Around | 7" | London | HLD8488 | 1957 | £6 | £12 | |
| Happy Days And Lonely Nights | 7" | London | HL8099 | 1954 | £15 | £30 | |
| Hearts Of Stone | 7" | London | HL8113 | 1955 | £37.50 | £75 | |
| I'm In Love Again | 7" | London | HLD8289 | 1956 | £10 | £20 | |
| Listen To Your Heart | 7" | London | HLD9037 | 1960 | £2 | £5 | |
| Please Don't Leave Me | 7" | London | HLD8415 | 1957 | £7.50 | £15 | |
| Rock Love | 7" | London | HL8126 | 1955 | £37.50 | £75 | |
| Rolling Stone | 7" | London | HLD8211 | 1955 | £25 | £50 | |
| Seventeen | 7" | London | HLD8177 | 1955 | £30 | £60 | |
| Silver Bells | 7" | London | HLD8343 | 1956 | £7.50 | £15 | |
| Theme From A Summer Place | 7" | London | HLD9078 | 1960 | £1.50 | £4 | |
| Tips Of My Fingers | LP | Dot | DLP3531/25531 | 1963 | £6 | £15 | US |
| Voices | 7" | London | HLD8318 | 1956 | £10 | £20 | with Pat Boone |

## FOOD

| | | | | | | | |
|---|---|---|---|---|---|---|---|
| Forever Is A Dream | LP | Capitol | ST304 | 1969 | £15 | £30 | US |

## FOOD BRAIN

| | | | | | | | |
|---|---|---|---|---|---|---|---|
| Social Gathering | LP | Polydor | 2310072 | 1970 | £37.50 | £75 | German |

## FOOL

Simon and Marijke of the Fool were a design team (the Beatles' shop mural; Eric Clapton's guitar; the Incredible String Band's second LP cover), rather than musicians, but they nevertheless recorded two interesting and eclectic LPs (the second was credited to 'Simon and Marijke'), the first being produced by the Hollies' Graham Nash.

| | | | | | | | |
|---|---|---|---|---|---|---|---|
| Fool | LP | Mercury | SMCL20138 | 1969 | £20 | £40 | |

## FOOLS DANCE

| | | | | | | | |
|---|---|---|---|---|---|---|---|
| Fools Dance | LP | Top Hat | TH22 | 1986 | £4 | £10 | |
| Fools Dance | LP | Top Hole Turn | TURN19 | 1985 | £6 | £15 | |
| They'll Never Know | 7" | Lambs To The Slaughter | LTS22 | 1987 | £2.50 | £6 | |
| They'll Never Know | 12" | Lambs To The Slaughter | LTS22T | 1987 | £4 | £10 | |

## FOOT IN COLD WATER

| | | | | | | | |
|---|---|---|---|---|---|---|---|
| Foot In Cold Water | LP | Elektra | K52011 | 1974 | £6 | £15 | |
| Second Foot | LP | Daffodil | 16028 | 1973 | £8 | £20 | Canadian |

## FOOTE, CHUCK

| | | | | | | | |
|---|---|---|---|---|---|---|---|
| You're Running Out Of Kisses | 7" | London | HLU9495 | 1962 | £1.50 | £4 | |

## FORBES

| | | | | | | | |
|---|---|---|---|---|---|---|---|
| Beatles | 7" | Power Exchange | PX253 | 1977 | £1.50 | £4 | |

## FORBES, BILL

| | | | | | | | |
|---|---|---|---|---|---|---|---|
| Once More | 7" | Columbia | DB4269 | 1959 | £2 | £5 | |
| You're Sixteen | 7" | Columbia | DB4566 | 1961 | £1.50 | £4 | |

## FORCE, ROBERT & ALBERT D'OSSCHE
| | | | | | | |
|---|---|---|---|---|---|---|
| Cross Over | LP | Sonet | SNKF168 | 1980 | £4 | £10 |

## FORCE FIVE
| | | | | | | |
|---|---|---|---|---|---|---|
| Baby Don't Care | 7" | United Artists | UP1102 | 1965 | £10 | £20 |
| Don't Know Which Way To Turn | 7" | United Artists | UP1141 | 1966 | £7.50 | £15 |
| Don't Make My Baby Blue | 7" | United Artists | UP1051 | 1964 | £4 | £8 |
| I Want You Babe | 7" | United Artists | UP1118 | 1965 | £7.50 | £15 |
| Yeah I'm Waiting | 7" | United Artists | UP1089 | 1965 | £5 | £10 |

## FORCE WEST
| | | | | | | |
|---|---|---|---|---|---|---|
| All The Children Sleep | 7" | Columbia | DB8174 | 1967 | £2.50 | £6 |
| Gotta Find Another Baby | 7" | Columbia | DB7908 | 1966 | £2.50 | £6 |
| I Can't Give What I Haven't Got | 7" | Decca | F12223 | 1965 | £2 | £5 |
| I'll Be Moving On | 7" | CBS | 3798 | 1968 | £1.50 | £4 |
| I'll Walk In The Rain | 7" | CBS | 3632 | 1968 | £1.50 | £4 |
| Sherry | 7" | CBS | 4385 | 1969 | £2 | £5 |
| When the Sun Comes Out | 7" | Columbia | DB7963 | 1966 | £2 | £5 |

## FORD, CLINTON
| | | | | | | |
|---|---|---|---|---|---|---|
| Dandy | 7" EP | Piccadilly | NEP34057 | 1966 | £2 | £5 |
| Old Shep | 7" | Oriole | CB1500 | 1959 | £1.50 | £4 |

## FORD, DEAN & THE GAYLORDS
| | | | | | | |
|---|---|---|---|---|---|---|
| Mr. Heartbreak's Here Instead | 7" | Columbia | DB7402 | 1964 | £5 | £10 |
| Name Game | 7" | Columbia | DB7610 | 1965 | £5 | £10 |
| Twenty Miles | 7" | Columbia | DB7264 | 1964 | £5 | £10 |

## FORD, DEE DEE
| | | | | | | |
|---|---|---|---|---|---|---|
| Good Morning Blues | 7" | London | HLU9245 | 1960 | £12.50 | £25 |

## FORD, EMILE
| | | | | | | |
|---|---|---|---|---|---|---|
| Emile | LP | Piccadilly | NPL38001 | 1961 | £6 | £15 |
| Emile | 7" EP | Pye | NEP24119 | 1959 | £2 | £5 |
| Emile Ford Hit Parade | 7" EP | Pye | NEP24124 | 1960 | £2.50 | £6 |
| Emile Ford Hit Parade Vol. 2 | 7" EP | Pye | NEP24133 | 1960 | £2.50 | £6 |
| New Tracks With Emile | LP | Pye | NPL18049 | 1959 | £5 | £12 |

## FORD, FRANKIE
| | | | | | | | |
|---|---|---|---|---|---|---|---|
| Alimony | 7" | Top Rank | JAR186 | 1959 | £4 | £8 | |
| Cheating Woman | 7" | Top Rank | JAR282 | 1960 | £7.50 | £15 | Huey Piano Smith B side |
| Let's Take A Sea Cruise | LP | Ace | LP1005 | 1959 | £62.50 | £125 | US |
| Sea Cruise | 7" | London | HL8850 | 1959 | £20 | £40 | |
| Sea Cruise | 7" | Sue | WI366 | 1965 | £4 | £8 | |
| Time After Time | 7" | Top Rank | JAR299 | 1960 | £2 | £5 | |
| What's Going On | 7" | Sue | WI369 | 1965 | £7.50 | £15 | |
| You Talk Too Much | 7" | London | HLP9222 | 1960 | £7.50 | £15 | |

## FORD, JON
| | | | | | | | |
|---|---|---|---|---|---|---|---|
| Two's Company, Three's A Crowd | 7" | Philips | BF1690 | 1968 | £1.50 | £4 | |
| You Got Me Where You Want Me | 7" | Philips | 6006030 | 1970 | £20 | £40 | |

## FORD, NEAL & THE FANATICS
| | | | | | | | |
|---|---|---|---|---|---|---|---|
| Neal Ford And The Fanatics | LP | Hickory | LPS141 | 1967 | £15 | £30 | US |

## FORD, PERRY
| | | | | | | |
|---|---|---|---|---|---|---|
| Prince Of Fools | 7" | Decca | F11497 | 1962 | £1.50 | £4 |

## FORD, ROCKY
| | | | | | | | |
|---|---|---|---|---|---|---|---|
| New Singing Star | LP | Audio Lab | AL1561 | 1960 | £10 | £25 | US |

## FORD, TENNESSEE ERNIE
| | | | | | | | |
|---|---|---|---|---|---|---|---|
| Anticipation Blues | 7" EP | Capitol | EAP120067 | 1961 | £6 | £12 | |
| Ballad Of Davy Crockett | 7" | Capitol | CL14506 | 1956 | £4 | £8 | |
| Blackeyed Susie | 7" | Capitol | CL15010 | 1959 | £1.50 | £4 | |
| Capitol Presents | 10" LP | Capitol | LC6573 | 1952 | £15 | £30 | |
| Catfish Boogie | 7" | Capitol | CL14006 | 1953 | £10 | £20 | |
| Gather Round | 7" EP | Capitol | EAP11227 | 1960 | £4 | £8 | |
| Give Me Your Word | 7" | Capitol | CL14005 | 1953 | £5 | £10 | |
| His Hands | 7" | Capitol | CL14261 | 1955 | £2.50 | £6 | |
| In The Middle Of An Island | 7" | Capitol | CL14759 | 1957 | £1.50 | £4 | |
| Little Red Rocking Hood | 7" | Capitol | CL15210 | 1961 | £2.50 | £6 | |
| Ol' Rockin' Ern | LP | Capitol | T888 | 1958 | £10 | £25 | |
| Sixteen Tons | LP | Capitol | T1380 | 1960 | £8 | £20 | |
| Sixteen Tons | 7" EP | Capitol | EAP1014 | 1956 | £4 | £8 | |
| Sixteen Tons | 7" | Capitol | CL14500 | 1956 | £4 | £8 | |
| Star Carol | 7" EP | Capitol | SEP11071 | 1961 | £2 | £5 | stereo |
| Sunday Barbecue | 7" | Capitol | CL14896 | 1958 | £1.50 | £4 | |
| Tennessee Ernie Ford | 7" EP | Capitol | EAP1639 | 1956 | £2.50 | £6 | |
| That's All | 7" | Capitol | CL14557 | 1956 | £2 | £5 | |
| There Is Beauty In Everything | 7" | Capitol | CL14273 | 1955 | £2.50 | £6 | |
| This Lusty Land | 10" LP | Capitol | LC6825 | 1956 | £6 | £15 | |
| This Must Be The Place | 7" | Capitol | CL14133 | 1954 | £4 | £8 | with Betty Hutton |
| Who Will Shoe Your Pretty Little Foot | 7" | Capitol | CL14616 | 1956 | £1.50 | £4 | |

## FORD THEATRE
Trilogy For The Masses............................ LP ..... ABC .............. ABCS658 .............. 1968 £15........ £30 ........................ US

## FOREHAND, EDDIE BUSTER
Young Boy Blues ................................. 7" ...... Action............ ACT4519 .............. 1969 £2........ £5

## FOREIGNER
Double Vision.................................... LP ..... Mobile Fidelity MFSL1052 ............ 1982 £5........ £12 ........ US audiophile
I Don't Want To Live Without You ......... CD-s .. Atlantic .......... A9101CD ............. 1988 £2........ £5
Inside Information ............................. CD .... Atlantic .......... 7818082 .............. 1987 £20........ £40 ... promo box set, with
                                                                                                                 cassette, single, press
                                                                                                                 kit
Profiled! ........................................ CD .... Atlantic .......... PRCD4007 .......:... 1991 £8........ £20 .............. US promo

## FORELAND
Foreland ........................................ LP ..... private............ GL1 .................... 1975 £50........ £100 ....................

## FORERUNNERS
Bony Moronie ................................. 7" ...... Solar ............ SRP100 .................. 1964 £1.50........ £4

## FOREST
Forest ........................................... LP ..... Harvest .......... SHVL760 .............. 1969 £30........ £60
Forest ........................................... LP ..... Zap.............. ZAP2 ................ 1987 £4........ £10
Full Circle ...................................... LP ..... Harvest .......... SHVL784 .............. 1970 £37.50.. £75
Full Circle ...................................... LP ..... Zap.............. ZAP3 ................ 1988 £4........ £10
Searching For Shadows ....................... 7" ...... Harvest .......... HAR5007 .............. 1969 £5........ £10

## FORESTERS
Broken Hearted Clown......................... 7" ...... Polydor .......... 56038................ 1965 £1.50........ £4
Early Morning Hours........................... 7" ...... Polydor .......... 56104................ 1966 £1.50........ £4
How Can I Tell Her............................. 7" ...... Polydor .......... 56057................ 1965 £1.50........ £4
Sometimes When You're Lonely ............. 7" ...... Columbia ........ DB8040 ................ 1966 £1.50........ £4

## FOREVER AMBER
Love Cycle ..................................... LP ..... Advance .......... no number ............ 1969 £875... £1250

## FOREVER MORE
Words On Black Plastic ....................... LP ..... RCA .............. 3015 ................ 1971 £4........ £10
Yours Forever More ........................... LP ..... RCA .............. SF8016 ................ 1969 £4........ £10

## FORK IN THE ROAD
Can't Turn Around ............................ 7" ...... Ember............ EMBS131 .............. 1961 £62.50.. £125

## FORMAT
Maxwell's Silver Hammer ..................... 7" ...... CBS.............. 4600 ................ 1969 £1.50........ £4

## FORMATIONS
At The Top Of The Stairs...................... 7" ...... MGM ............ MGM1399 .............. 1968 £25........ £50

## FORMERLY FAT HARRY
Formerly Fat Harry ............................ LP ..... Harvest .......... SHSP4016 .............. 1971 £5........ £12

## FORMULA ONE
I Just Can't Go To Sleep ...................... 7" ...... Warner Bros .... WB155 .............. 1965 £5........ £10

## FORRAY, ANDY
Dream With Me................................. 7" ...... Decca ............ F12733.................. 1968 £10........ £20
Proud One ..................................... 7" ...... Parlophone ...... R5729 .................. 1968 £1.50........ £4
Sarah Jane ...................................... 7" ...... Parlophone ...... R5715 .................. 1968 £1.50........ £4

## FORT MUDGE MEMORIAL DUMP
Fort Mudge Memorial Dump .................. LP ..... Mercury.......... 61256.................. 1970 £15........ £30 ........................ US

## FORTES MENTUM
Gotta Go ........................................ 7" ...... Parlophone...... R5768 .............. 1969 £2........ £5
I Can't Go On .................................. 7" ...... Parlophone...... R5726 .............. 1968 £2........ £5
Saga Of A Wrinkled Man...................... 7" ...... Parlophone...... R5684 ................ 1968 £7.50........ £15

## FORTUNA
From The Edinburgh Festival Fringe 1976 .. LP ..... Sweet Folk SFA058 ................ 1976 £4........ £10
                                                     And Country ...

## FORTUNE, JOHNNY
Soul Surfer...................................... LP ..... Park Avenue.... 401 .................... 1963 £10........ £25 ........................ US

## FORTUNE, LANCE
Be Mine ........................................ 7" ...... Pye .............. 7N15240 .............. 1960 £1.50........ £4
This Love I Have For You ..................... 7" ...... Pye .............. 7N15260 .............. 1960 £1.50........ £4

## FORTUNE, SONNY
Awakening ...................................... LP ..... Horizon .......... SP704 .................. 1975 £5........ £12 ........................ US

## FORTUNES
Caroline ........................................ 7" ...... Decca ............ F11809.................. 1964 £6........ £12
Fortunes ........................................ LP ..... Decca ............ LK4736 ................ 1965 £10........ £25
Freedom ........................................ LP ..... Capitol............ ST647 .................. 1971 £5........ £12 ........................ US

| Title | Format | Label | Catalogue | Year | | | Notes |
|---|---|---|---|---|---|---|---|
| Here Comes That Rainy Day Feeling Again | LP | Capitol | ST809 | 1971 | £5 | £12 | US |
| Here It Comes Again | 7" | Decca | F12243 | 1965 | £1.50 | £4 | |
| I Like The Look Of You | 7" | Decca | F11912 | 1964 | £1.50 | £4 | |
| Idol | 7" EP | United Artists | 36119 | 1967 | £10 | £20 | French |
| Is It Really Worth Your While | 7" | Decca | F12485 | 1966 | £1.50 | £4 | |
| Look Homeward Angel | 7" | Decca | F11985 | 1964 | £1.50 | £4 | |
| Our Love Has Gone | 7" | Decca | F12612 | 1967 | £1.50 | £4 | |
| Our Love Has Gone | 7" | Decca | F12874 | 1969 | £1.50 | £4 | |
| Silent Street | 7" | Decca | F12429 | 1966 | £1.50 | £4 | |
| Summertime Summertime | 7" | Decca | F11718 | 1963 | £4 | £8 | |
| Summertime Summertime | 7" | Decca | F11718 | 1963 | £7.50 | £15 | picture sleeve |
| That Same Old Feeling | LP | World Pacific | WPS21904 | 1970 | £5 | £12 | US |
| This Golden Ring | 7" EP | Decca | 457105 | 1966 | £10 | £20 | French |
| This Golden Ring | 7" | Decca | F12321 | 1966 | £1.50 | £4 | |
| You've Got Your Troubles | 7" EP | Decca | 457089 | 1965 | £10 | £20 | French |

## FORTY-FIVES

| Title | Format | Label | Catalogue | Year | | | Notes |
|---|---|---|---|---|---|---|---|
| Couldn't Believe A Word | 7" | Chopper | CHEAP5 | 1979 | £1.50 | £4 | |

## FORTY-NINTH PARALLEL

| Title | Format | Label | Catalogue | Year | | | Notes |
|---|---|---|---|---|---|---|---|
| Forty-Ninth Parallel | LP | Maverick | MAS7001 | 1969 | £62.50 | £125 | US |

## FORWOOD, SHIRLEY

| Title | Format | Label | Catalogue | Year | | | Notes |
|---|---|---|---|---|---|---|---|
| Two Hearts | 7" | London | HLD8402 | 1957 | £4 | £8 | |

## FOSTER, FRANK

| Title | Format | Label | Catalogue | Year | | | Notes |
|---|---|---|---|---|---|---|---|
| Frank Foster Quartet | 10" LP | Vogue | LDE112 | 1955 | £50 | £100 | |
| Frank Foster With Elmo Hope | LP | Esquire | 32033 | 1957 | £20 | £40 | |
| Manhattan Fever | LP | Blue Note | BST84278 | 1968 | £10 | £25 | |

## FOSTER, JOHN

| Title | Format | Label | Catalogue | Year | | | Notes |
|---|---|---|---|---|---|---|---|
| John Foster Sings | LP | Island | ILP939 | 1966 | £10 | £25 | |

## FOSTER, LES

| Title | Format | Label | Catalogue | Year | | | Notes |
|---|---|---|---|---|---|---|---|
| Do It Nice | 7" | Big Shot | BI529 | 1969 | £1.50 | £4 | |
| Muriel | 7" | Jolly | JY022 | 1968 | £2 | £5 | |

## FOSTERCHILD

| Title | Format | Label | Catalogue | Year | | | Notes |
|---|---|---|---|---|---|---|---|
| Fosterchild | LP | Columbia | PES90382 | 1977 | £15 | £30 | Canadian |
| Troubled Child | LP | Columbia | PCC80003 | 1978 | £15 | £30 | Canadian |

## FOTHERINGAY

The group formed by Sandy Denny after leaving Fairport Convention for the first time operated in very much the same folk-rock area, but included some of Denny's most winning material on its only album. Sadly the group came apart during sessions for a second album, leaving the members to join the Fairport team pool.

| Title | Format | Label | Catalogue | Year | | | Notes |
|---|---|---|---|---|---|---|---|
| Fotheringay | LP | Island | ILPS9125 | 1970 | £8 | £20 | pink label |
| Peace In The End | 7" | Island | WIP6085 | 1970 | £1.50 | £4 | |

## FOUNDATIONS

| Title | Format | Label | Catalogue | Year | | | Notes |
|---|---|---|---|---|---|---|---|
| Baby Now That I've Found You | 7" EP | Pye | PNV24199 | 1967 | £4 | £8 | French |
| Digging The Foundations | LP | Pye | NPL18290 | 1969 | £4 | £10 | |
| From The Foundations | LP | Pye | NPL18206 | 1967 | £4 | £10 | |
| It's All Right | 7" EP | Pye | NEP24297 | 1968 | £2 | £5 | |
| Rocking The Foundations | LP | Pye | NPL18227 | 1968 | £4 | £10 | |

## FOUNTAIN, PETE

| Title | Format | Label | Catalogue | Year | | | Notes |
|---|---|---|---|---|---|---|---|
| Salutes The Great Clarinettists | LP | Coral | LVA9132 | 1960 | £4 | £10 | |

## FOUR

| Title | Format | Label | Catalogue | Year | | | Notes |
|---|---|---|---|---|---|---|---|
| It's Alright | 7" | Decca | F11999 | 1964 | £1.50 | £4 | |

## FOUR ACES

| Title | Format | Label | Catalogue | Year | | | Notes |
|---|---|---|---|---|---|---|---|
| Bahama Mama | 7" | Brunswick | 05663 | 1957 | £1.50 | £4 | |
| Beyond The Blue Horizon | LP | Decca | DL(7)8944 | 1959 | £5 | £12 | US |
| Four Aces | 7" EP | Brunswick | OE9458 | 1959 | £2 | £5 | |
| Four Aces | 10" LP | Decca | DL5429 | 195– | £8 | £20 | US |
| Friendly Persuasion | 7" | Brunswick | 05623 | 1956 | £1.50 | £4 | |
| Gal With The Yaller Shoes | 7" | Brunswick | 05566 | 1956 | £1.50 | £4 | |
| Gang That Sang | 7" | Brunswick | 05256 | 1954 | £1.50 | £4 | |
| Golden Hits | LP | Decca | DL(7)4013 | 1960 | £5 | £12 | US |
| Hanging Up A Horseshoe | 7" | Brunswick | 05758 | 1958 | £1.50 | £4 | |
| Heart | 7" | Brunswick | 05651 | 1957 | £1.50 | £4 | |
| Heart And Soul | LP | Decca | DL8228 | 1956 | £6 | £15 | US |
| Hits From Broadway | LP | Decca | DL(7)8855 | 1959 | £5 | £12 | US |
| Hits From Hollywood | LP | Decca | DL8693 | 1958 | £6 | £15 | US |
| I'm Yours | 7" | Decca | A73010 | 195– | £2.50 | £6 | export |
| If You Can Dream | 7" | Brunswick | 05573 | 1956 | £1.50 | £4 | |
| It Shall Come To Pass | 7" | Brunswick | 05322 | 1954 | £1.50 | £4 | |
| It's A Woman's World | 7" | Brunswick | 05348 | 1954 | £2 | £5 | |
| Just Squeeze Me | 10" LP | Brunswick | LA8614 | 1953 | £6 | £15 | |
| Love Is A Many Splendoured Thing | 7" | Brunswick | 05480 | 1955 | £4 | £8 | |
| Melody Of Love | 7" | Brunswick | 05379 | 1955 | £2 | £5 | |
| Mood For Love | LP | Decca | DL8122 | 1956 | £6 | £15 | US |
| Mood For Love Vol. 1 | 7" EP | Brunswick | OE9157 | 1955 | £2 | £5 | |
| Mood For Love Vol. 2 | 7" EP | Brunswick | OE9192 | 1955 | £2 | £5 | |

| Title | Format | Label | Cat. No. | Year | Price 1 | Price 2 | Notes |
|---|---|---|---|---|---|---|---|
| Mr. Sandman | 7" | Brunswick | 05355 | 1954 | £4 | £8 | |
| Presenting | 7" EP | Brunswick | OE9090 | 1955 | £2.50 | £6 | |
| Rock and Roll Rhapsody | 7" | Brunswick | 05743 | 1958 | £1.50 | £4 | |
| Sentimental Souvenirs | LP | Decca | DL8191 | 1956 | £6 | £15 | US |
| She Sees All The Hollywood Hits | LP | Decca | DL8312 | 1957 | £6 | £15 | US |
| Shuffling Along | LP | Decca | DL8567 | 1958 | £6 | £15 | US |
| Sing Film Titles | 7" EP | Brunswick | OE9324 | 1957 | £2 | £5 | |
| Slewfoot | 7" | Brunswick | 05429 | 1955 | £1.50 | £4 | |
| Stranger In Paradise | 7" | Brunswick | 05418 | 1955 | £4 | £8 | |
| Swingin' Aces | LP | Decca | DL(7)8766 | 1958 | £5 | £12 | US |
| There Goes My Heart | 7" | Brunswick | 05401 | 1955 | £1.50 | £4 | |
| Three Coins In The Fountain | 7" | Brunswick | 05308 | 1954 | £5 | £10 | |
| To Love Again | 7" | Brunswick | 05562 | 1956 | £1.50 | £4 | |
| Woman In Love | 7" | Brunswick | 05589 | 1956 | £2 | £5 | |
| World Outside | 7" | Brunswick | 05767 | 1958 | £1.50 | £4 | |
| Written On The Wind | LP | Decca | DL8424 | 1957 | £6 | £15 | US |

## FOUR ACES (2)

| Title | Format | Label | Cat. No. | Year | Price 1 | Price 2 | Notes |
|---|---|---|---|---|---|---|---|
| River Bank Coberley Again | 7" | Island | WI178 | 1965 | £5 | £10 | |
| Sweet Chariot | 7" | Island | WI179 | 1965 | £5 | £10 | |

## FOUR COINS

| Title | Format | Label | Cat. No. | Year | Price 1 | Price 2 | Notes |
|---|---|---|---|---|---|---|---|
| World Outside | 7" | Fontana | H168 | 1958 | £1.50 | £4 | |

## FOUR ESQUIRES

| Title | Format | Label | Cat. No. | Year | Price 1 | Price 2 | Notes |
|---|---|---|---|---|---|---|---|
| Act Your Age | 7" | Pye | 7N25027 | 1959 | £1.50 | £4 | |
| Adorable | 7" | London | HLA8224 | 1956 | £10 | £20 | |
| Always And Forever | 7" | London | HLO8579 | 1958 | £2 | £5 | |
| Hideaway | 7" | London | HL8746 | 1958 | £1.50 | £4 | |
| Look Homeward Angel | 7" | London | HL8376 | 1957 | £15 | £30 | demo |
| Love Me Forever | 7" | London | HLO8533 | 1958 | £4 | £8 | |
| Sphinx Won't Tell | 7" | London | HL8152 | 1955 | £12.50 | £25 | |
| Wouldn't It Be Wonderful | 7" | Pye | 7N25049 | 1960 | £1.50 | £4 | |

## FOUR FOLK

| Title | Format | Label | Cat. No. | Year | Price 1 | Price 2 | Notes |
|---|---|---|---|---|---|---|---|
| Hard Cases | LP | Reality | RY1003 | 1966 | £25 | £50 | |

## FOUR FRESHMEN

| Title | Format | Label | Cat. No. | Year | Price 1 | Price 2 | Notes |
|---|---|---|---|---|---|---|---|
| Four Freshmen And Five Guitars | 7" EP | Capitol | SEP11255 | 1961 | £2 | £5 | stereo |
| Four Freshmen And Five Guitars Pt. 2 | 7" EP | Capitol | SEP21255 | 1961 | £2 | £5 | stereo |
| Four Freshmen And Five Guitars Pt. 3 | 7" EP | Capitol | SEP31255 | 1961 | £2 | £5 | stereo |
| Four Freshmen And Five Saxes | LP | Capitol | T844 | 1957 | £4 | £10 | |
| Four Freshmen And Five Trombones | LP | Capitol | LC6812 | 1956 | £4 | £10 | |
| Four Freshmen And Five Trumpets | LP | Capitol | T763 | 1957 | £4 | £10 | |
| Freshmen Favorites | LP | Capitol | T743 | 1956 | £4 | £10 | US |
| Voices In Latin | LP | Capitol | T992 | 1958 | £4 | £10 | US |
| Voices In Modern | LP | Capitol | T522 | 1955 | £4 | £10 | US |
| Voices In Modern | 10" LP | Capitol | LC6685 | 1954 | £4 | £10 | |

## FOUR GIBSON GIRLS

| Title | Format | Label | Cat. No. | Year | Price 1 | Price 2 | Notes |
|---|---|---|---|---|---|---|---|
| June, July And August | 7" | Oriole | CB1447 | 1958 | £2 | £5 | |
| Safety Sue | 7" | Oriole | CB1453 | 1958 | £1.50 | £4 | |

## FOUR GUYS

| Title | Format | Label | Cat. No. | Year | Price 1 | Price 2 | Notes |
|---|---|---|---|---|---|---|---|
| Mine | 7" | Vogue Coral | Q72054 | 1955 | £2.50 | £6 | |

## FOUR JACKS

| Title | Format | Label | Cat. No. | Year | Price 1 | Price 2 | Notes |
|---|---|---|---|---|---|---|---|
| Hey Baby | 7" EP | Decca | DFE6460 | 1958 | £6 | £12 | |
| Hey Baby | 7" | Decca | F10984 | 1958 | £1.50 | £4 | |

## FOUR JONES BOYS

| Title | Format | Label | Cat. No. | Year | Price 1 | Price 2 | Notes |
|---|---|---|---|---|---|---|---|
| Certain Smile | 7" | Columbia | DB4170 | 1958 | £1.50 | £4 | |
| Day The Rains Came | 7" | Columbia | DB4217 | 1958 | £1.50 | £4 | |
| Rock-a-Hula Baby | 7" | Columbia | DB4046 | 1957 | £1.50 | £4 | |
| Tutti Frutti | 7" | Decca | F10717 | 1956 | £2.50 | £6 | |

## FOUR JUST MEN

| Title | Format | Label | Cat. No. | Year | Price 1 | Price 2 | Notes |
|---|---|---|---|---|---|---|---|
| That's My Baby | 7" | Parlophone | R5186 | 1964 | £20 | £40 | |

## FOUR KENTS

| Title | Format | Label | Cat. No. | Year | Price 1 | Price 2 | Notes |
|---|---|---|---|---|---|---|---|
| Moving Finger Writes | 7" | RCA | RCA1705 | 1968 | £1.50 | £4 | |

## FOUR KINSMEN

| Title | Format | Label | Cat. No. | Year | Price 1 | Price 2 | Notes |
|---|---|---|---|---|---|---|---|
| It Looks Like The Daybreak | 7" | Decca | F22671 | 1967 | £1.50 | £4 | |

## FOUR KNIGHTS

| Title | Format | Label | Cat. No. | Year | Price 1 | Price 2 | Notes |
|---|---|---|---|---|---|---|---|
| Foolish Tears | 7" | Coral | Q72355 | 1959 | £1.50 | £4 | |
| Foolishly Yours | 7" | Capitol | CL14290 | 1955 | £2 | £5 | |
| Four Knights | LP | Coral | CRL52221 | 195– | £8 | £20 | US |
| Four Knights | 7" EP | Capitol | EAP1506 | 1955 | £12.50 | £25 | |
| Honey Bunch | 7" | Capitol | CL14244 | 1955 | £10 | £20 | |
| In The Chapel In The Moonlight | 7" | Capitol | CL14154 | 1954 | £4 | £8 | |
| Million Dollar Baby | LP | Coral | CRL(7)57309 | 1960 | £6 | £15 | US |
| Saw Your Eyes | 7" | Capitol | CL14204 | 1954 | £2.50 | £6 | |
| Spotlight Songs | LP | Capitol | T345 | 1953 | £15 | £30 | US |
| Spotlight Songs | 10" LP | Capitol | H345 | 1953 | £37.50 | £75 | US |
| Spotlight Songs | 10" LP | Capitol | LC6604 | 1953 | £10 | £25 | |
| Till Then | 7" | Capitol | CL14076 | 1954 | £5 | £10 | |

You ...................................................... 7" ...... Capitol............ CL14516 ................ 1956 £1.50........£4 ................................

## FOUR LADS
Four Hits ................................................ 7" EP . London ............ RER1289 ............. 1961 £4..........£8 ................................
Four Lads ............................................... LP ...... Philips............. BBL7256 ............. 1958 £4..........£10 ................................
Golly........................................................ 7" ...... Philips............. JK1021 ................ 1957 £2..........£5 ................................
Moments To Remember ....................... 7" EP . Philips............. BBE12044 ........... 1956 £2.50........£6 ................................
Standing On The Corner ........................ 7" ...... Philips............. PB1000 ............... 1960 £1.50........£4 ................................

## FOUR LEAVED CLOVER
Why ........................................................ 7" ...... Oak ................ RGJ207.......... 1965 £150 ..... £250 ........... best auctioned

## FOUR LOVERS
The earliest recordings made by the group that later became the Four Seasons were these.

Joyride .................................................... LP ..... RCA ............... LPM1317 .............. 1956 £250..... £400 .... US, best auctioned
My Life For Your Love........................... 7" ..... Epic ............... 9255 ................... 1957 £250..... £400 .... US, best auctioned
Shake A Hand ........................................ 7" ..... RCA ............... 476812............... 1957 £12.50.....£25 ................................ US

## FOUR MATADORS
Man's Gotta Stand Tall ......................... 7" ...... Columbia ........ DB7806 ............... 1966 £15.........£30

## FOUR PALMS
Jeannie, Joanie, Shirley & Tony ................ 7" ...... Vogue ............ V9116.................. 1958 £150 ..... £250 ........... best auctioned

## FOUR PENNIES
Do You Want Me To.............................. 7" ..... Philips ....... BF1296 ......... 1964 £1.50........£4 ...........
Four Pennies........................................... 7" EP . Philips............. BE12561 ............. 1964 £4..........£8 ...........
Juliet ...................................................... LP ..... Wing ............. WL1146 ............. 1967 £6..........£15 ...........
Keep The Freeway Open ......................... 7" ..... Philips............. BF1491 .............. 1966 £1.50........£4 ...........
Mixed Bag .............................................. LP ..... Philips............. BL7734 ............... 1966 £30..........£60 ...........
No Sad Songs For Me............................ 7" ..... Philips............. BF1519 .............. 1966 £1.50........£4 ...........
Smooth Side Of The Four Pennies......... 7" EP . Philips............. BE12571 ............. 1964 £2.50........£6 ...........
Spin With The Four Pennies.................... 7" EP . Philips............. BE12562 ............. 1964 £5..........£10 ...........
Swinging Side Of The Four Pennies......... 7" EP . Philips............. BE12570 ............. 1964 £5..........£10 ...........
Two Sides Of The Four Pennies ............... LP ..... Philips............. BL7642 ............... 1964 £8..........£20 ...........

## FOUR PENNIES (2)
My Block ................................................ 7" ...... Stateside ......... SS198................ 1963 £5..........£10 ...........
When The Boys Are Happy ..................... 7" ...... Stateside ......... SS244................ 1963 £5..........£10 ...........

## FOUR PERFECTIONS
I'm Not Strong Enough.......................... 7" ...... Cream........... CRM5006............. 1976 £1.50........£4 ...........

## FOUR PLUS ONE
The group that issued its first single under the name Four Plus One, issued its second as the In Crowd, and eventually, after a few changes in personnel, got round to making an LP – as Tomorrow.

Time Is On My Side............................... 7" ...... Parlophone...... R5221 .................. 1965 £20..........£40

## FOUR PREPS
Big Man .................................................. 7" EP . Capitol............ EAP11064 ........... 1959 £2..........£5 ...........
Campus Encores...................................... 7" EP . Capitol............ EAP11647 ........... 1961 £2..........£5 ...........
Dreamy Eyes .......................................... 7" EP . Capitol............ EAP1862............. 1957 £2..........£5 ...........
Four Preps .............................................. LP ..... Capitol............ T994.................. 1958 £4..........£10 ................................ US
Lazy Summer Nights ............................. 7" EP . Capitol............ EAP11139 ........... 1959 £2..........£5 ...........
Things We Did Last Summer ................. LP ..... Capitol............ T1090................ 1958 £4..........£10 ...........
Twenty Six Miles ................................... 7" EP . Capitol............ EAP11015 ........... 1958 £2..........£5 ...........
Twenty Six Miles ................................... 7" ...... Capitol............ CL14815 ............. 1957 £1.50........£4 ...........

## FOUR SAXOPHONES
Four Saxophones In Twelve Tones ........... 10" LP Vogue............. LDE170 ............... 1956 £5..........£12

## FOUR SEASONS
Ain't That A Shame................................ LP ..... Stateside ......... SL10042 ............. 1963 £6..........£15 ...........
Ain't That A Shame................................ 7" ..... Stateside ......... SS194................ 1963 £1.50........£4 ...........
All The Song Hits .................................. LP ..... Philips............. 2/600150 ........... 1964 £4..........£10 ................................ US
Alone ...................................................... 7" ..... Stateside ......... SS315................ 1964 £2..........£5 ...........
Big Girls Don't Cry................................ LP ..... Vee Jay .......... LP/SR1056 ........ 1963 £6..........£15 ................................ US
Big Girls Don't Cry................................ 7" ..... Stateside ......... SS145................ 1963 £1.50........£4 ...........
Born To Wander...................................... LP ..... Philips............. BL7611 ............... 1964 £5..........£12 ...........
Bye Bye Baby ......................................... 7" ..... Philips............. BF1395 .............. 1965 £1.50........£4 ...........
C'mon Marianne ..................................... 7" ..... Philips............. BF1584 .............. 1967 £1.50........£4 ...........
Candy Girl.............................................. 7" ..... Stateside ......... SS216................ 1963 £2..........£5 ...........
Christmas Album.................................... LP ..... Philips............. (S)BL7753 ........... 1966 £4..........£10 ...........
Dawn ...................................................... LP ..... Philips............. BL7621 ............... 1964 £4..........£10 ...........
Dawn ...................................................... 7" ..... Philips............. BF1317 .............. 1964 £1.50........£4 ...........
Don't Think Twice ................................ 7" EP . Philips............. 452049............... 1965 £7.50........£15 ................................ French
Electric Stories ....................................... 7" ..... Philips............. BF1743 .............. 1969 £2..........£5 ...........
Entertain You ......................................... LP ..... Philips............. BL7663 ............... 1965 £4..........£10 ...........
Four Seasons Sing .................................. 7" EP . Stateside ......... SE1011 ............... 1964 £5..........£10 ...........
Gold Vault Of Hits................................ LP ..... Philips............. (S)BL7719 .......... 1966 £4..........£10 ...........
Golden Hits............................................ LP ..... Vee Jay .......... LP/SR1065 ........ 1963 £5..........£12 ................................ US
Greetings ................................................ LP ..... Stateside ......... SL10051 ............. 1963 £6..........£15 ...........
Hits Of The Four Seasons ..................... cass-s . Philips............. MCP1000 ............ 1968 £2.50........£6 ...........
I've Got You Under My Skin ................. 7" EP . Philips............. 452060............... 1966 £7.50........£15 ................................ French
I've Got You Under My Skin ................. 7" ...... Philips............. BF1511 .............. 1966 £1.50........£4 ...........

| | | | | | | | |
|---|---|---|---|---|---|---|---|
| Let's Hang On | 7" | Philips | BF1439 | 1965 | £1.50 | £4 | |
| Looking Back | LP | Philips | (S)BL7752 | 1966 | £4 | £10 | |
| More Golden Hits | LP | Vee Jay | LP/SR1088 | 1964 | £5 | £12 | US |
| More Great Hits Of 1964 | LP | Vee Jay | LP/SR1136 | 1965 | £5 | £12 | US |
| Opus 17 | 7" | Philips | BF1493 | 1966 | £1.50 | £4 | |
| Peanuts | 7" | Stateside | SS262 | 1964 | £2 | £5 | |
| Rag Doll | LP | Philips | BL7643 | 1964 | £4 | £10 | |
| Rag Doll | 7" EP | Philips | 452030 | 1964 | £7.50 | £15 | French |
| Rag Doll | 7" | Philips | BF1347 | 1964 | £1.50 | £4 | |
| Rag Doll | 7" | Philips | BF1763 | 1969 | £1.50 | £4 | picture sleeve |
| Recorded Live On Stage | LP | Vee Jay | LP/SR1154 | 1965 | £5 | £12 | US |
| Ronnie | 7" | Philips | BF1334 | 1964 | £1.50 | £4 | |
| Santa Claus Is Coming To Town | 7" | Stateside | SS241 | 1963 | £2 | £5 | |
| Seasoned Hits | LP | Fontana | SFJL952 | 1968 | £4 | £10 | |
| Second Vault Of Golden Hits | LP | Philips | (S)BL7751 | 1967 | £4 | £10 | |
| Sherry | LP | Stateside | SL10033 | 1963 | £6 | £15 | |
| Sherry | 7" EP | Pathe | EMF332 | 1962 | £7.50 | £15 | French |
| Sherry | 7" | Stateside | SS122 | 1962 | £1.50 | £4 | |
| Since I Don't Have You | 7" | Stateside | SS343 | 1964 | £2 | £5 | |
| Sing Big Hits | LP | Philips | (S)BL7687 | 1965 | £4 | £10 | |
| Stay | LP | Vee Jay | LP/SR1082 | 1964 | £5 | £12 | US |
| Walk Like a Man | 7" | Stateside | SS169 | 1963 | £1.50 | £4 | |
| Watch The Flowers Grow | 7" | Philips | BF1621 | 1967 | £1.50 | £4 | |
| We Love Girls | LP | Vee Jay | LP/SR1121 | 1965 | £5 | £12 | US |
| Whatever You Say | 7" | Warner Bros | K16107 | 1971 | £5 | £10 | |
| Working My Way Back To You | LP | Philips | BL7699 | 1965 | £4 | £10 | |
| Working My Way Back To You | 7" | Philips | BF1474 | 1966 | £1.50 | £4 | |

## FOUR SKINS

| | | | | | | | |
|---|---|---|---|---|---|---|---|
| One Law For Them | 7" | Clockwork Fun | CF101 | 1981 | £1.50 | £4 | |

## FOUR SPICES

| | | | | | | |
|---|---|---|---|---|---|---|
| Fire Engine Boogie | 7" | MGM | MGM944 | 1957 | £10 | £20 |

## FOUR SQUARES

| | | | | | | |
|---|---|---|---|---|---|---|
| Four Squares | 7" EP | Hollick & Taylor | HT1009 | 1964 | £20 | £40 |

## FOUR TONES

| | | | | | | |
|---|---|---|---|---|---|---|
| Voom Ba Voom | 7" | Decca | F11074 | 1958 | £1.50 | £4 |

## FOUR TOPHATTERS

| | | | | | | | |
|---|---|---|---|---|---|---|---|
| Go Baby Go | 7" | London | HLA8163 | 1955 | £100 | £200 | best auctioned |
| Wild Rosie | 7" | London | HLA8198 | 1955 | £100 | £200 | best auctioned |

## FOUR TOPS

| | | | | | | | |
|---|---|---|---|---|---|---|---|
| 7 Rooms Of Gloom | 7" | Tamla Motown | TMG612 | 1967 | £2 | £5 | |
| Ask The Lonely | 7" | Tamla Motown | TMG507 | 1965 | £12.50 | £25 | |
| Baby I Need Your Loving | CD-s | Motown | ZD41947 | 1989 | £2 | £5 | |
| Baby I Need Your Loving | 7" | Stateside | SS336 | 1964 | £10 | £20 | |
| Do What You Gotta Do | 7" | Tamla Motown | TMG710 | 1969 | £1.50 | £4 | |
| Four Tops | LP | Tamla Motown | TML11010 | 1965 | £15 | £30 | |
| Four Tops | 7" EP | Tamla Motown | TME2012 | 1966 | £5 | £10 | |
| Four Tops Hits | 7" EP | Tamla Motown | TME2018 | 1967 | £4 | £8 | |
| I Can't Help Myself | 7" | Tamla Motown | TMG515 | 1965 | £2.50 | £6 | |
| I'm In A Different World | 7" | Tamla Motown | TMG675 | 1968 | £1.50 | £4 | |
| It's The Same Old Song | 7" | Tamla Motown | TMG528 | 1965 | £4 | £8 | |
| Jazz Impressions | LP | Workshop | 217 | 1962 | £180 | £300 | US |
| Live | LP | Tamla Motown | (S)TML11041 | 1967 | £4 | £10 | |
| Loving You Is Sweeter Than Ever | 7" | Tamla Motown | TMG568 | 1966 | £2 | £5 | |
| On Broadway | LP | Motown | (MS)657 | 1967 | £5 | £12 | US |
| On Top | LP | Tamla Motown | (S)TML11037 | 1966 | £5 | £12 | |
| Reach Out | LP | Tamla Motown | (S)TML11056 | 1967 | £4 | £10 | |
| Reach Out & I'll Be There | 7" | Tamla Motown | TMG579 | 1966 | £1.50 | £4 | |
| Second Album | LP | Tamla Motown | TML11021 | 1966 | £10 | £25 | |
| Shake Me Wake Me | 7" | Tamla Motown | TMG553 | 1966 | £5 | £10 | |
| Something About You | 7" | Tamla Motown | TMG542 | 1965 | £4 | £8 | |
| Standing In The Shadows Of Love | 7" | Tamla Motown | TMG589 | 1967 | £1.50 | £4 | |
| Without The One You Love | 7" | Stateside | SS371 | 1965 | £12.50 | £25 | |
| You Keep Running Away | 7" | Tamla Motown | TMG623 | 1967 | £1.50 | £4 | |

## FOUR TUNES

| | | | | | | | |
|---|---|---|---|---|---|---|---|
| 12 X 4 | LP | Jubilee | LP1039 | 195– | £30 | £60 | US |
| I Gambled With Love | 78 | London | L1231 | 1954 | £10 | £20 | |
| I Sold My Heart To The Junkman | 7" | London | HL8151 | 1955 | £37.50 | £75 | |
| Tired Of Waiting | 7" | London | HLJ8164 | 1955 | £15 | £30 | |

## FOUR WINDS

| | | | | | | |
|---|---|---|---|---|---|---|
| Short Shorts | 7" | London | HLU8556 | 1958 | £10 | £20 |

## FOURMOST

| | | | | | | |
|---|---|---|---|---|---|---|
| Apples, Peaches, Pumpkin Pie | 7" | CBS | 3814 | 1968 | £4 | £8 |
| Auntie Maggie's Remedy | 7" | Parlophone | R5528 | 1966 | £2.50 | £6 |
| Baby I Need Your Lovin' | 7" | Parlophone | R5194 | 1964 | £1.50 | £4 |
| Easy Squeezy | 7" | CBS | 4461 | 1969 | £4 | £8 |
| Everything In The Garden | 7" | Parlophone | R5304 | 1965 | £1.50 | £4 |
| First And Fourmost | LP | Parlophone | PMC1259 | 1965 | £30 | £60 |

| | | | | | | | | |
|---|---|---|---|---|---|---|---|---|
| Fourmost Sound | 7" EP | Parlophone | GEP8892 | 1964 | £15 | £30 | |
| Girls Girls Girls | 7" | Parlophone | R5379 | 1965 | £1.50 | £4 | |
| Hello Little Girl | 7" EP | Odeon | SOE3748 | 1963 | £25 | £50 | French |
| Here There And Everywhere | 7" | Parlophone | R5491 | 1966 | £2 | £5 | |
| How Can I Tell Her | 7" EP | Parlophone | GEP8917 | 1964 | £15 | £30 | |
| How Can I Tell Her | 7" | Parlophone | R5157 | 1964 | £1.50 | £4 | |
| Rosetta | 7" | CBS | 4041 | 1969 | £5 | £10 | |

## FOURMYULA

| | | | | | | | |
|---|---|---|---|---|---|---|---|
| Honey Chile | 7" | Columbia | DB8549 | 1969 | £1.50 | £4 | |

## FOURTEEN

| | | | | | | | |
|---|---|---|---|---|---|---|---|
| Easy To Fool | 7" | Olga | S051 | 1968 | £2 | £5 | |
| Through My Door | 7" | Olga | OLE002 | 1968 | £2 | £5 | |
| Umbrella | 7" | Olga | OLE006 | 1968 | £2 | £5 | |

## FOURTEEN ICED BEARS

| | | | | | | | |
|---|---|---|---|---|---|---|---|
| Balloon Song | 7" | Penetration | | 1987 | £2 | £5 | flexi |
| Come Get Me | 7" | Sarah | SARAH5 | 1988 | £4 | £8 | |
| Falling Backwards | 7" | Thunderball Surfacer | 002 | 198– | £2 | £5 | ...B side by Crocodile Ride |
| Inside | 12" | Frank | COPPOLA1 | 1986 | £3 | £8 | |
| Like A Dolphin | 12" | Frank | CAPRA202 | 1987 | £2.50 | £6 | |
| Mother Sleep | 7" | Thunderball | 7TBL2 | 1989 | £10 | £20 | test pressing |

## FOURTH CEKCION

| | | | | | | | |
|---|---|---|---|---|---|---|---|
| Fourth Ceksion | LP | Solar | 110 | 1970 | £25 | £50 | US |

## FOURTH WAY

| | | | | | | | |
|---|---|---|---|---|---|---|---|
| Fourth Way | LP | Capitol | ST317 | 1970 | £4 | £10 | US |
| Sun And Moon Have Come Together | LP | Harvest | SKAO423 | 1970 | £4 | £10 | US |
| Werewolf | LP | Harvest | ST666 | 1971 | £4 | £10 | US |

## FOURUM

| | | | | | | | |
|---|---|---|---|---|---|---|---|
| Fourum | LP | Sirius | | 197– | £25 | £50 | |
| Gunnerside Gill Remembered | LP | Guardian | GRF54 | 1980 | £8 | £20 | |

## FOWLEY, KIM

| | | | | | | | |
|---|---|---|---|---|---|---|---|
| Born To Be Wild | LP | Imperial | LP12413 | 1968 | £6 | £15 | US |
| Day The Earth Stood Still | LP | Silence | MNWLP7P | 1970 | £37.50 | £75 | Swedish |
| Good Clean Fun | LP | Imperial | LP12443 | 1969 | £6 | £15 | US |
| I'm Bad | LP | Capitol | ST11075 | 1972 | £8 | £20 | US |
| International Heroes | LP | Capitol | ST11159 | 1973 | £5 | £12 | US |
| Lights | 7" | Parlophone | R5521 | 1966 | £5 | £10 | |
| Lights The Blind Can See | 7" | CBS | 202338 | 1966 | £2.50 | £6 | |
| Lijud Fran Waholm | LP | Silence | MNW14P | 1970 | £8 | £20 | Swedish |
| Love Is Alive And Well | LP | Tower | (S)T5080 | 1967 | £15 | £30 | US |
| Outrageous | LP | Imperial | LP12423 | 1969 | £8 | £20 | US |
| They're Coming To Take Me Away | 7" | CBS | 202243 | 1966 | £2 | £5 | |
| Trip | 7" EP | Vogue | INT18086 | 1966 | £30 | £60 | French |
| Trip | 7" | Island | WI278 | 1966 | £2.50 | £6 | |
| Underground All Stars | LP | Dot | 25964 | 1969 | £10 | £25 | US |

## FOX

| | | | | | | | |
|---|---|---|---|---|---|---|---|
| Mr. Carpenter | 7" | CBS | 3381 | 1968 | £10 | £20 | |

## FOX (2)

| | | | | | | | |
|---|---|---|---|---|---|---|---|
| For Fox Sake | LP | Fontana | 6309007 | 1970 | £30 | £60 | |
| Second Hand Love | 7" | Fontana | 6007016 | 1970 | £7.50 | £15 | |

## FOX, DON

| | | | | | | | |
|---|---|---|---|---|---|---|---|
| Be My Girl | 7" | Decca | F10927 | 1957 | £1.50 | £4 | |
| Party Time | 7" | Decca | F10955 | 1957 | £1.50 | £4 | |
| Pretend You Don't See Her | 7" | Decca | F10983 | 1958 | £1.50 | £4 | |
| She Was Only Seventeen | 7" | Decca | F11057 | 1958 | £1.50 | £4 | |
| T'Ain't What You Do | 7" | Triumph | RGM1022 | 1960 | £4 | £8 | |

## FOXX, INEZ

| | | | | | | | |
|---|---|---|---|---|---|---|---|
| You Hurt Me For The Last Time | 7" | Stax | 2025151 | 1973 | £2 | £5 | |

## FOXX, INEZ & CHARLIE

| | | | | | | | |
|---|---|---|---|---|---|---|---|
| Baby Give It To Me | 7" | Direction | 584042 | 1969 | £1.50 | £4 | |
| Come By Here | LP | Direction | 863085 | 1968 | £4 | £10 | |
| Come On In | 7" | Direction | 583816 | 1968 | £1.50 | £4 | |
| Count The Days | 7" | Direction | 583192 | 1967 | £1.50 | £4 | |
| Greatest Hits | LP | Direction | 863281 | 1968 | £4 | £10 | |
| Here We Go Round | 7" | Sue | WI307 | 1964 | £5 | £10 | |
| Hi Diddle Diddle | 7" | Sue | WI314 | 1964 | £5 | £10 | |
| Hummingbird | 7" | London | HLC10009 | 1965 | £1.50 | £4 | |
| Hurt By Love | 7" | Sue | WI323 | 1964 | £5 | £10 | |
| I Ain't Going For That | 7" | Direction | 582712 | 1967 | £1.50 | £4 | |
| Inez & Charles Foxx | LP | London | SHA8241 | 1965 | £6 | £15 | |
| Jaybirds | 7" | Sue | WI304 | 1964 | £6 | £12 | |
| La De Da I Love You | 7" | United Artists | UP35013 | 1970 | £1.50 | £4 | |
| La De Dah I Love You | 7" | Sue | WI356 | 1964 | £5 | £10 | |
| Mockingbird | LP | Sue | ILP911 | 1964 | £15 | £30 | |
| Mockingbird | 7" | Sue | WI301 | 1963 | £5 | £10 | |
| Mockingbird | 7" | United Artists | UP2269 | 1969 | £1.50 | £4 | |

| My Momma Told Me | | 7" | London | HLC9971 | 1965 | £2 | £5 | |
|---|---|---|---|---|---|---|---|---|
| No Stranger To Love | | 7" | Stateside | SS556 | 1966 | £2 | £5 | |
| Tightrope | | 7" | Pye | 7N25561 | 1971 | £1.50 | £4 | |
| Tightrope | | 7" | Stateside | SS586 | 1967 | £5 | £10 | |

## FOXX, JOHN
| No-one Driving | | 7" | Virgin | VS338 | 1980 | £5 | £10 | double |
|---|---|---|---|---|---|---|---|---|

## FOYER DES ARTS
| Su Seltsame Sekretarin | | 10" LP | Aronda | 002 | 1980 | £10 | £25 | German |
|---|---|---|---|---|---|---|---|---|

## FRABJOY & THE RUNCIBLE SPOON

The tracks credited to Graham Gouldman and Kevin Godley on the Marmalade label sampler LP were actually by Frabjoy and the Runcible Spoon. The group also included Lol Creme in its line-up and can be viewed, therefore, as a first dry-run for Ten cc. An album was apparently recorded, but was lost when the Marmalade label folded.

| I'm Beside Myself | | 7" | Marmalade | 598019 | 1969 | £5 | £10 | |
|---|---|---|---|---|---|---|---|---|

## FRACTION
| Moon Blood | | LP | Angelus | 571 | 1971 | £700 | £1000 | |
|---|---|---|---|---|---|---|---|---|

## FRAGILE
| Fragile | | LP | private | | 1976 | £150 | £250 | Dutch |
|---|---|---|---|---|---|---|---|---|

## FRAME
| Doctor Doctor | | 7" | RCA | RCA1571 | 1967 | £20 | £40 | |
|---|---|---|---|---|---|---|---|---|
| My Feet Don't Fit His Shoes | | 7" | RCA | RCA1556 | 1966 | £2.50 | £6 | |

## FRAME (2)
| Frame Of Mind | | LP | Bellaphon | BLPS19107 | 1972 | £10 | £25 | German |
|---|---|---|---|---|---|---|---|---|

## FRAMPTON, PETER
| Frampton Comes Alive (edited) | | LP | A&M | PR3703 | 1978 | £4 | £10 | US picture disc |
|---|---|---|---|---|---|---|---|---|

## FRANC, PETER
| En Route | | LP | Dawn | DNLS3051 | 1973 | £4 | £10 | |
|---|---|---|---|---|---|---|---|---|
| Profile | | LP | Dawn | DNLS3043 | 1972 | £4 | £10 | |

## FRANCIS, BOBBY
| Chain Gang | | 7" | Doctor Bird | DB1153 | 1968 | £5 | £10 | |
|---|---|---|---|---|---|---|---|---|
| Judy Drowned | | 7" | Ska Beat | JB193 | 1965 | £5 | £10 | |

## FRANCIS, CONNIE
| All Time International Hits | | LP | MGM | C1012 | 1965 | £4 | £10 | |
|---|---|---|---|---|---|---|---|---|
| All Time International Hits | | LP | MGM | CS6083 | 1965 | £6 | £15 | stereo |
| Another Page | | 7" | MGM | MGM1334 | 1967 | £1.50 | £4 | |
| At The Copa | | LP | MGM | C861 | 1961 | £4 | £10 | |
| At The Copa | | LP | MGM | CS6035 | 1961 | £6 | £15 | stereo |
| Award-Winning Motion Picture Hits | | LP | MGM | C940 | 1963 | £4 | £10 | |
| Award-Winning Motion Picture Hits | | LP | MGM | CS6070 | 1963 | £6 | £15 | stereo |
| Be Anything | | 7" | MGM | MGM1236 | 1963 | £1.50 | £4 | |
| Best Of Connie Francis | | LP | MGM | C8041 | 1967 | £4 | £10 | |
| Best Of Connie Francis | | LP | Readers Digest | GBCFA106 | 1981 | £10 | £25 | 4 LP set |
| Blue Winter | | 7" | MGM | MGM1224 | 1963 | £1.50 | £4 | |
| Christmas With Connie | | LP | MGM | C797 | 1959 | £10 | £25 | |
| Connie And Clyde | | LP | MGM | C(S)8086 | 1968 | £6 | £15 | |
| Connie Francis | | 7" EP | MGM | MGMEP686 | 1958 | £7.50 | £15 | |
| Connie Francis | | 7" EP | MGM | MGMEP792 | 1965 | £7.50 | £15 | |
| Connie Francis Favourites | | 7" EP | MGM | MGMEP759 | 1961 | £7.50 | £15 | |
| Connie Sings For Mama | | 7" EP | MGM | MGMEP789 | 1964 | £7.50 | £15 | |
| Connie's American Hits | | 7" EP | MGM | MGMEP769 | 1963 | £7.50 | £15 | |
| Connie's Greatest Hits | | LP | MGM | C831 | 1960 | £4 | £10 | |
| Country And Western Golden Hits | | LP | MGM | C812 | 1960 | £10 | £25 | |
| Country Music Connie Style | | LP | MGM | C916 | 1962 | £6 | £15 | |
| Country Music Connie Style | | LP | MGM | CS6062 | 1962 | £8 | £20 | stereo |
| Do The Twist | | LP | MGM | C879 | 1961 | £10 | £25 | |
| Don't Break The Heart That Loves You | | 7" | MGM | MGM1157 | 1962 | £1.50 | £4 | |
| Don't Ever Leave Me | | 7" | MGM | MGM1253 | 1964 | £1.50 | £4 | |
| Drowning My Sorrows | | 7" | MGM | MGM1207 | 1963 | £1.50 | £4 | |
| Exciting Connie Francis | | LP | MGM | C786 | 1959 | £6 | £15 | |
| Faded Orchid | | 7" | MGM | MGM962 | 1957 | £10 | £20 | |
| First Lady Of Record | | 7" EP | MGM | MGMEP742 | 1960 | £6 | £12 | |
| Folk Song Favourites | | LP | MGM | C883 | 1962 | £4 | £10 | |
| Folk Song Favourites | | LP | MGM | CS6054 | 1962 | £6 | £15 | stereo |
| Follow The Boys | | LP | MGM | C931 | 1963 | £4 | £10 | |
| Follow The Boys | | LP | MGM | CS6068 | 1963 | £6 | £15 | stereo |
| Follow The Boys | | 7" | MGM | MGM1193 | 1962 | £1.50 | £4 | |
| For Mama | | LP | MGM | C1006/CS6082 | 1965 | £6 | £15 | |
| Forget Domani | | 7" | MGM | MGM1265 | 1965 | £1.50 | £4 | |
| From Italy With Love | | 7" EP | MGM | MGMEP783 | 1963 | £7.50 | £15 | |
| Fun Songs For Children | | LP | MGM | C819 | 1960 | £25 | £50 | |
| Girl In Love | | 7" EP | MGM | MGMEP658 | 1956 | £7.50 | £15 | |
| Great American Waltzes | | LP | MGM | C958 | 1964 | £4 | £10 | |
| Great American Waltzes | | LP | MGM | CS6075 | 1964 | £6 | £15 | stereo |
| Great Country Hits Vol. 2 | | LP | MGM | ACB00167 | 1975 | £4 | £10 | |
| Hawaii Connie | | LP | MGM | C(S)8110 | 1969 | £10 | £25 | |
| Heartaches | | 7" EP | MGM | MGMEP677 | 1958 | £6 | £12 | |

| Title | Format | Label | Catalogue | Year | | | Notes |
|---|---|---|---|---|---|---|---|
| Hey Ring A Ding | 7" EP | MGM | MGMEP773 | 1963 | £7.50 | £15 | |
| I Never Had A Sweetheart | 7" | MGM | MGM945 | 1957 | £12.50 | £25 | |
| I Was Such A Fool | 7" | MGM | MGM1171 | 1962 | £1.50 | £4 | |
| I'll Get By | 7" | MGM | MGM993 | 1958 | £1.50 | £4 | |
| I'm Gonna Be Warm This Winter | 7" | MGM | MGM1185 | 1962 | £1.50 | £4 | |
| If I Didn't Care | 7" EP | MGM | MGMEP697 | 1959 | £7.50 | £15 | |
| If My Pillow Could Talk | 7" | MGM | MGM1202 | 1963 | £1.50 | £4 | |
| Irish Favourites | LP | MGM | C898 | 1962 | £8 | £20 | |
| Irish Favourites | LP | MGM | CS6056 | 1962 | £10 | £25 | stereo |
| Italian Favourites | LP | MGM | C821/CS6002 | 1960 | £6 | £15 | |
| Italian Favourites | 7" EP | MGM | MGMEP760 | 1961 | £7.50 | £15 | |
| Jealous Heart | LP | MGM | C(S)8009 | 1966 | £6 | £15 | |
| Jealous Heart | 7" | MGM | MGM1293 | 1966 | £1.50 | £4 | |
| Jewish Favourites | LP | MGM | C845 | 1961 | £4 | £10 | |
| Jewish Favourites | LP | MGM | CS6021 | 1961 | £6 | £15 | stereo |
| Live At Sahara In Las Vegas | LP | MGM | C(S)8036 | 1967 | £6 | £15 | |
| Looking For Love | LP | MGM | C983/CS6079 | 1965 | £6 | £15 | |
| Love Is Me, Love Is You | 7" | MGM | MGM1305 | 1966 | £1.50 | £4 | |
| Love Italian Style | LP | MGM | C(S)8050 | 1968 | £4 | £10 | |
| Majesty Of Love | 7" | MGM | MGM969 | 1957 | £10 | £20 | with Marvin Rainwater |
| Mala Femmena | 7" EP | MGM | MGMEP780 | 1963 | £7.50 | £15 | |
| Mama | 7" | MGM | MGM1070 | 1960 | £15 | £30 | |
| More Italian Favourites | LP | MGM | C854 | 1961 | £4 | £10 | |
| More Italian Favourites | LP | MGM | CS6029 | 1961 | £6 | £15 | stereo |
| More Italian Hits | LP | MGM | C930 | 1963 | £4 | £10 | |
| More Italian Hits | LP | MGM | CS6067 | 1963 | £6 | £15 | stereo |
| Movie Greats Of The Sixties | LP | MGM | C(S)8027 | 1966 | £6 | £15 | |
| Mr. Love | 7" | MGM | MGM1493 | 1969 | £1.50 | £4 | |
| Mr. Twister | 7" | MGM | MGM1151 | 1962 | £1.50 | £4 | |
| My Child | 7" | MGM | MGM1271 | 1965 | £1.50 | £4 | |
| My First Real Love | 7" | MGM | SP1169 | 1956 | £37.50 | £75 | |
| My Heart Cries For You | LP | MGM | C(S)8054 | 1968 | £4 | £10 | |
| My Heart Cries For You | 7" | MGM | MGM1347 | 1967 | £1.50 | £4 | |
| My Sailor Boy | 7" | MGM | MGM932 | 1956 | £30 | £60 | |
| My Thanks To You | LP | MGM | C782 | 1959 | £8 | £20 | |
| My Thanks To You | LP | World Record Club | TP618 | 1966 | £4 | £10 | |
| My World Is Slipping Away | 7" | MGM | MGM1381 | 1968 | £1.50 | £4 | |
| Never On Sunday | LP | MGM | C875 | 1961 | £4 | £10 | |
| Never On Sunday | LP | MGM | CS6047 | 1961 | £6 | £15 | stereo |
| New Kind Of Connie | LP | MGM | C998/CS6080 | 1965 | £4 | £10 | |
| Phoenix Love Theme | 7" | MGM | MGM1295 | 1966 | £1.50 | £4 | |
| Plenty Good Lovin' | 7" | MGM | MGM1036 | 1959 | £1.50 | £4 | |
| Rock And Roll Million Sellers | LP | MGM | C804 | 1960 | £10 | £25 | |
| Rock And Roll Million Sellers | 7" EP | MGM | MGMEP717 | 1960 | £7.50 | £15 | |
| Rock And Roll Million Sellers No. 2 | 7" EP | MGM | MGMEP720 | 1960 | £7.50 | £15 | |
| Rock And Roll Million Sellers No. 3 | 7" EP | MGM | MGMEP731 | 1960 | £7.50 | £15 | |
| Roundabout | 7" | MGM | MGM1282 | 1965 | £1.50 | £4 | |
| Sings Great Country Favourites | LP | MGM | C1003/CS6081 | 1965 | £6 | £15 | with Hank Williams Jr |
| Sixteen Of Connie's Greatest Hits | LP | MGM | C970 | 1964 | £4 | £10 | |
| Somebody Else Is Takin' My Place | 7" | MGM | MGM1446 | 1968 | £1.50 | £4 | |
| Somewhere My Love | 7" | MGM | MGM1320 | 1966 | £1.50 | £4 | |
| Songs Of Les Reed | LP | MGM | CS8117 | 1969 | £6 | £15 | |
| Songs To A Swinging Band | LP | MGM | C870 | 1961 | £4 | £10 | |
| Songs To A Swinging Band | LP | MGM | CS6044 | 1961 | £6 | £15 | stereo |
| Spanish And Latin American Favourites | LP | MGM | C836 | 1960 | £4 | £10 | |
| Spanish And Latin American Favourites | LP | MGM | CS6012 | 1960 | £6 | £15 | stereo |
| Spanish Nights And You | 7" | MGM | MGM1327 | 1966 | £1.50 | £4 | |
| Summer Of His Years | 7" | MGM | MGM1220 | 1963 | £1.50 | £4 | |
| Time Alone Will Tell | 7" | MGM | MGM1336 | 1967 | £1.50 | £4 | |
| Toward The End Of The Day | 7" | MGM | MGM1012 | 1959 | £1.50 | £4 | |
| Vacation | 7" | MGM | MGM1165 | 1962 | £1.50 | £4 | |
| Valentino | 7" | MGM | MGM1060 | 1960 | £1.50 | £4 | |
| Wedding Cake | 7" | MGM | MGM1471 | 1969 | £1.50 | £4 | |
| What Kind Of Fool Am I | 7" EP | MGM | MGMEP775 | 1963 | £7.50 | £15 | |
| Whatever Happened To Rosemary | 7" | MGM | MGM1212 | 1963 | £1.50 | £4 | |
| When The Boys Meet The Girls | LP | MGM | C(S)8006 | 1966 | £4 | £10 | |
| Where The Boys Are | 7" EP | MGM | MGMEP756 | 1961 | £7.50 | £15 | |
| Who's Happy Now? | LP | United Artists | ULP30182 | 1978 | £50 | £100 | withdrawn sleeve |
| Who's Sorry Now | 10" LP | MGM | MGMD153 | 1958 | £25 | £50 | |
| Why Say Goodbye | 7" | MGM | MGM1407 | 1968 | £1.50 | £4 | |
| You Always Hurt The One You Love | 7" | MGM | MGM998 | 1958 | £1.50 | £4 | |
| You're My Everything | 7" EP | MGM | MGMEP711 | 1960 | £7.50 | £15 | |

## FRANCIS, JOE 'KING'

| Title | Format | Label | Catalogue | Year | | | |
|---|---|---|---|---|---|---|---|
| Have Me Baby | 7" | Rio | R90 | 1966 | £2.50 | £6 | |
| I Don't Want You No More | 7" | Ska Beat | JB184 | 1965 | £5 | £10 | |
| I Got A Ska | 7" | Ska Beat | JB262 | 1966 | £5 | £10 | |
| Pull It Out | 7" | Rainbow | RAI114 | 1967 | £2.50 | £6 | |
| Wicked Woman | 7" | Blue Beat | BB323 | 1965 | £6 | £12 | |

## FRANCIS, LITTLE WILLIE

| Title | Format | Label | Catalogue | Year | | | |
|---|---|---|---|---|---|---|---|
| I'm Ashamed | 7" | Blue Beat | BB151 | 1963 | £6 | £12 | |

## FRANCIS, NAT

| Title | Format | Label | Catalogue | Year | | | |
|---|---|---|---|---|---|---|---|
| Just To Keep You | 7" | Blue Beat | BB361 | 1966 | £6 | £12 | |

| Title | Format | Label | Cat. No. | Year | Price | Price | Notes |
|---|---|---|---|---|---|---|---|
| Mama Kiss Him Goodnight | 7" | Blue Beat | BB346 | 1966 | £6 | £12 | |
| Three Nights Of Love | 7" | Blue Beat | BB376 | 1967 | £6 | £12 | |

## FRANCIS, RITCHIE

| Title | Format | Label | Cat. No. | Year | Price | Price | Notes |
|---|---|---|---|---|---|---|---|
| Songbird | LP | Pegasus | PEG11 | 1971 | £5 | £12 | |

## FRANCIS, WILBERT

| Title | Format | Label | Cat. No. | Year | Price | Price | Notes |
|---|---|---|---|---|---|---|---|
| Memories Of You | 7" | Ska Beat | JB267 | 1966 | £5 | £10 | |

## FRANCIS, WINSTON

| Title | Format | Label | Cat. No. | Year | Price | Price | Notes |
|---|---|---|---|---|---|---|---|
| California Dreaming | LP | Bamboo | BDLPS216 | 1971 | £10 | £25 | |
| Games People Play | 7" | Studio One | SO2086 | 1969 | £6 | £12 | Albert Griffiths B side |
| If Your Heart Be Lonely | 7" | Coxsone | CS7087 | 1969 | £5 | £10 | |
| Mr. Fix It | LP | Bamboo | BDLP207 | 1970 | £15 | £30 | |
| Reggae And Cry | 7" | Coxsone | CS7089 | 1969 | £5 | £10 | Freedom Singers B side |
| Same Old Song | 7" | Bamboo | BAM10 | 1969 | £1.50 | £4 | Sound Dimension B side |
| Too Experienced | 7" | Punch | PH5 | 1969 | £1.50 | £4 | ...Jackie Mittoo B side |
| Turn Back The Hands Of Time | 7" | Bamboo | BAM46 | 1970 | £1.50 | £4 | |

## FRANCIS & THE SWINGERS

| Title | Format | Label | Cat. No. | Year | Price | Price | Notes |
|---|---|---|---|---|---|---|---|
| Warn The People | 7" | Blue Beat | BB379 | 1967 | £6 | £12 | |

## FRANCISCO

| Title | Format | Label | Cat. No. | Year | Price | Price | Notes |
|---|---|---|---|---|---|---|---|
| Cosmic Beam Experience | LP | Cosmic Beam | 001 | 1976 | £30 | £60 | US |

## FRANK, JACKSON C.

The album made by the otherwise obscure Mr Frank is collectable as a rare outside production by Paul Simon. One track also features the young Al Stewart.

| Title | Format | Label | Cat. No. | Year | Price | Price | Notes |
|---|---|---|---|---|---|---|---|
| Again | LP | B&C | BCLP4 | 1978 | £37.50 | £75 | |
| Blues Run The Game | 7" | Columbia | DB7795 | 1965 | £5 | £10 | |
| Jackson C.Frank | LP | Columbia | 33SX1788 | 1965 | £75 | £150 | |

## FRANKIE & JOHNNY

'Frankie' was singer Maggie Bell, who was later the vocalist with Stone the Crows.

| Title | Format | Label | Cat. No. | Year | Price | Price | Notes |
|---|---|---|---|---|---|---|---|
| Climb Every Mountain | 7" | Parlophone | R5518 | 1966 | £2.50 | £6 | |
| I'll Hold You | 7" | Decca | F22376 | 1966 | £37.50 | £75 | |

## FRANKIE & THE CLASSICALS

| Title | Format | Label | Cat. No. | Year | Price | Price | Notes |
|---|---|---|---|---|---|---|---|
| I Only Have Eyes For You | 7" | Philips | BF1586 | 1967 | £37.50 | £75 | |

## FRANKIE GOES TO HOLLYWOOD

As record companies became aware of the collectors' market during the eighties, they realized that it was possible to create instant collectors' items by issuing various limited-edition versions of each potential hit record. Arguably the most thorough exploration of the possibilities of this tactic was carried out by ZTT records and Frankie Goes To Hollywood. Each single by the group comes in a bewildering variety of alternative mixes, and different shaped picture discs, with a correspondingly wide range of values. In fact, due to Trevor Horn's skill as a producer, the different mixes make sense on musical grounds, but this is very much a happy accident.

| Title | Format | Label | Cat. No. | Year | Price | Price | Notes |
|---|---|---|---|---|---|---|---|
| Pleasurefix/Starfix | 12" | ZTT | FGTH1 | 1985 | £4 | £10 | pink label promo |
| Power Of Love | 12" | ZTT | 12XZTAS5 | 1984 | £2.50 | £6 | gatefold sleeve, 5 photos |
| Rage Hard | CD-s | ZTT | ZCID22 | 1986 | £5 | £12 | |
| Relax | cass-s | ZTT | CTIS102 | 1984 | £2.50 | £6 | |
| Relax | 7" | ZTT | PZTAS1 | 1983 | £2 | £5 | picture disc |
| Relax (live version) | cass | Ocean | no number | 1985 | £6 | £15 | with FGTH computer game |
| Relax (Original Mix) | 12" | ZTT | 12ZTAS1 (1A1U) | 1983 | £10 | £20 | 33rpm |
| Relax (Original Mix) | 12" | ZTT | 12ZTAS1 (1A5) | 1984 | £5 | £12 | |
| Relax (remixes) | 12" | ZTT | SAM1231 | 1993 | £20 | £40 | double promo |
| Relax (Sex Mix) | 12" | ZTT | 12PZTAS1 | 1983 | £2.50 | £6 | picture disc |
| Relax (Sex Mix) | 12" | ZTT | 12ZTAS1 (1A2U) | 1983 | £6 | £15 | |
| Relax (The Last Seven Inches) | 7" | ZTT | ZTAS1DJ | 1983 | £2 | £5 | promo |
| Relax (The Last Seven Inches) | 7" | ZTT | ZTAS1DJ | 1983 | £2.50 | £6 | promo, mispressed B side – plays 'Ferry(Go)' |
| Relax (US Mix)/Two Tribes (Carnage) | 12" | ZTT | XZTAS3DJ | 1984 | £4 | £10 | promo, grey ZTT sleeve |
| Relax (Warp Mix) | 7" | ZTT | ZTAS1 | 1983 | £4 | £8 | white label promo |
| Two Tribes | 7" | ZTT | PZTAS3 | 1984 | £2 | £5 | picture disc |
| Two Tribes | 12" | ZTT | SAM1301 | 1993 | £20 | £40 | double promo |
| Two Tribes (Carnage)/War (Hidden) | 12" | ZTT | WARTZ3 | 1984 | £2.50 | £6 | picture disc |
| Two Tribes (Hibakusha) | 12" | ZTT | XZIP1 | 1984 | £6 | £15 | ZTT sleeve |
| Warriors | CD-s | ZTT | ZCID25 | 1986 | £4 | £10 | |
| Warriors (Attack Mix) | 12" | ZTT | 12ZTAK25 | 1986 | £3 | £8 | white label promo |
| Watching The Wildlife (Die Letzen Mix) | 12" | ZTT | ZTE26 | 1987 | £2.50 | £6 | |
| Welcome To The Pleasure Dome | LP | ZTT | NEAT1 | 1984 | £6 | £15 | double picture disc |
| Welcome To The Pleasure Dome | CD | ZTT | CID101 | 1984 | £10 | £25 | with San Jose, not Happy Hi |
| Welcome To The Pleasure Dome | CD | ZTT | CID101 | 1985 | £5 | £12 | |
| Welcome To The Pleasure Dome | 7" | ZTT | PZTAS7 | 1985 | £2 | £5 | shaped picture disc |
| Welcome To The Pleasure Dome | 7" | ZTT | ZTAS7 (7A7U) | 1985 | £4 | £8 | blue label |
| Welcome To The Pleasure Dome (Tribal/ Urban Mix) | 12" | ZTT | 12ZTAJ7 | 1985 | £6 | £15 | promo |
| Welcome To The Pleasuredome (remixes) | 12" | ZTT | SAM1275 | 1993 | £20 | £40 | double promo |

## FRANKLIN, ALAN EXPLOSION
Blues Climax ......................................... LP ...... Horne ............ ...................... 1970 £50 ...... £100 ...................... US

## FRANKLIN, ARETHA
Few of Aretha Franklin's earliest recordings are particularly valuable, despite the fact that they seldom appear on the market. There is a staggering lack of direction on the CBS recordings, as for six years neither Miss Franklin herself nor the record company seemed to have any idea as to the most effective setting for that extraordinary voice. Signing with Atlantic at the end of 1966, Aretha Franklin immediately struck gold with the powerful Southern soul sound of 'I Never Loved A Man', a sound that seemed to have been waiting for Aretha Franklin as much as she had been waiting for the sound.

| | | | | | | | |
|---|---|---|---|---|---|---|---|
| Amazing Grace | LP | Atlantic | K60023 | 1972 | £6 | £15 | double |
| Aretha | LP | Fontana | TFL5173 | 1961 | £6 | £15 | |
| Aretha Arrives | LP | Atlantic | 587/588085 | 1967 | £6 | £15 | |
| Aretha Franklin Now/Lady Soul | CD | Mobile Fidelity | UDCD623 | 1995 | £6 | £15 | US audiophile |
| Aretha Gold | LP | Atlantic | 588192 | 1969 | £4 | £10 | |
| Aretha Now | LP | Atlantic | 587/588114 | 1968 | £4 | £10 | |
| Baby I Love You | 7" | Atlantic | 584127 | 1967 | £1.50 | £4 | |
| Best Of Aretha Franklin | LP | Atlantic | QD8295 | 1971 | £4 | £10 | US quad |
| Can't You See Me | 7" | CBS | 201732 | 1965 | £1.50 | £4 | |
| Don't Play That Song | LP | Atlantic | 2400021 | 1970 | £4 | £10 | |
| Electrifying Aretha Franklin | LP | Columbia | CL1761/CS8561 | 1962 | £5 | £12 | US |
| Freeway Of Love | 7" | Arista | ARIST22624 | 1986 | £2 | £5 | pink vinyl |
| I Never Loved A Man | LP | Atlantic | 587/588066 | 1967 | £6 | £15 | |
| I Never Loved A Man | CD | Mobile Fidelity | UDCD574 | 1992 | £6 | £15 | US audiophile |
| I Never Loved A Man | 7" | Atlantic | 584084 | 1967 | £1.50 | £4 | |
| I Say A Little Prayer | LP | Atlantic | 2464007 | 1970 | £4 | £10 | |
| I Say A Little Prayer | 7" | Atlantic | 584206 | 1968 | £1.50 | £4 | |
| Lady Soul | LP | Atlantic | 587/588099 | 1968 | £4 | £10 | |
| Laughing On The Outside | LP | Columbia | CL2079/CS8879 | 1963 | £5 | £12 | US |
| Lee Cross | LP | CBS | 63160 | 1967 | £4 | £10 | |
| Lee Cross | 7" | CBS | 3059 | 1967 | £1.50 | £4 | |
| Live At Paris Olympia | LP | Atlantic | 587/588149 | 1968 | £6 | £15 | |
| Live At The Fillmore West | LP | Atlantic | 2400136 | 1971 | £4 | £10 | |
| Live At The Fillmore West | LP | Atlantic | QD7205 | 1971 | £5 | £12 | US quad |
| Love Is The Only Thing | 7" | Fontana | H271 | 1961 | £4 | £8 | |
| Natural Woman | 7" | Atlantic | 584141 | 1967 | £1.50 | £4 | |
| Operation Heartbreak | 7" | Fontana | H343 | 1961 | £2 | £5 | |
| Queen Of Soul | CD | Atlantic | PRO290126 | 1992 | £6 | £15 | US promo sampler |
| Respect | 7" | Atlantic | 584115 | 1967 | £1.50 | £4 | |
| Runnin' Out Of Fools | LP | Columbia | CL2281/CS9081 | 1964 | £5 | £12 | US |
| Satisfaction/Chain Of Fools | 7" | Atlantic | 584157 | 1967 | £1.50 | £4 | |
| Satisfaction/Night Life | 7" | Atlantic | 584157 | 1967 | £2.50 | £6 | |
| Since You've Been Gone | 7" | Atlantic | 584172 | 1968 | £1.50 | £4 | |
| Songs Of Faith | LP | Chess | CRL(S)54550 | 1967 | £4 | £10 | |
| Soul '69 | LP | Atlantic | 588163 | 1969 | £4 | £10 | |
| Soul Sister | LP | CBS | (S)BPG62744 | 1966 | £4 | £10 | |
| Take A Look | LP | CBS | 63269 | 1967 | £4 | £10 | |
| Take It Like You Give It | LP | CBS | (S)BPG62969 | 1967 | £4 | £10 | |
| Tender Swinging Aretha Franklin | LP | Columbia | CL1876/CS8676 | 1962 | £5 | £12 | US |
| Think | 7" | Atlantic | 584186 | 1968 | £1.50 | £4 | |
| This Girl's In Love With You | LP | Atlantic | 2400004 | 1969 | £4 | £10 | |
| Today I Sing The Blues | 7" EP | Fontana | TE467217 | 1962 | £4 | £8 | |
| Unforgettable | LP | Columbia | CL2163/CS8963 | 1964 | £5 | £12 | US |
| Yeah/In Person | LP | CBS | (S)BPG62556 | 1965 | £4 | £10 | |
| Young, Gifted And Black | LP | Atlantic | 2400188 | 1971 | £4 | £10 | |

## FRANKLIN, ERMA

| | | | | | | | |
|---|---|---|---|---|---|---|---|
| Gotta Find Me A Lover | 7" | MCA | MU1073 | 1969 | £1.50 | £4 | |
| Her Name Is Erma | LP | Epic | LN3824/BN619 | 1962 | £6 | £15 | US |
| Open Up Your Soul | 7" | London | HLZ10201 | 1968 | £2 | £5 | |
| Piece Of My Heart | 7" | London | HLZ10170 | 1967 | £2.50 | £6 | |
| Right To Cry | 7" | London | HLZ10220 | 1968 | £2 | £5 | |
| Soul Sister | LP | MCA | MUPS394 | 1970 | £6 | £15 | |
| Time After Time | 7" | Soul City | SC118 | 1969 | £1.50 | £4 | |

## FRANKS, JOHNNY

| | | | | | | | |
|---|---|---|---|---|---|---|---|
| Good Old Country Music | 7" | Melodisc | 1459 | 1958 | £1.50 | £4 | |
| Tweedle Dee | 78 | Melodisc | P230 | 1955 | £3 | £8 | |

## FRANKSON, BONNIE

| | | | | | | | |
|---|---|---|---|---|---|---|---|
| Dearest | 7" | Columbia | DB114 | 1969 | £2 | £5 | |
| Dearest | 7" | Jolly | JY021 | 1968 | £2 | £5 | |

## FRANTIC

| | | | | | | | |
|---|---|---|---|---|---|---|---|
| Conception | LP | Lizard | 20103 | 1971 | £8 | £20 | US |

## FRANTIC ELEVATORS
Mick Hucknall was the leader of the Frantic Elevators, who began as a punk group, but who had anticipated the smooth soul sound of Hucknall's Simply Red by the end of their career. The song 'Holding Back The Years' was, in fact, recorded by both groups.

| | | | | | | | |
|---|---|---|---|---|---|---|---|
| Holding Back The Years | 7" | No Waiting | WAIT1 | 1982 | £10 | £20 | |
| Hunchback Of Notre Dame | 7" | TJM | TJM6 | 1980 | £50 | £100 | demo |
| Searching For The Only One | 7" | Crackin' Up | CRACK1 | 1980 | £5 | £10 | |
| Voice In The Dark | 7" | TJM | TJM5 | 1979 | £5 | £10 | |
| You Know What You Told Me | 7" | Erics | 006 | 1980 | £5 | £10 | |

## FRANZ K

| | | | | | | | |
|---|---|---|---|---|---|---|---|
| Rock In Deutsch | LP | Zebra | 2949014 | 1973 | £5 | £12 | German |
| Sensemann | LP | Ruhr | 007 | 1972 | £25 | £50 | German |
| Sensermann | LP | Philips | 6305127 | 1972 | £20 | £40 | German |

## FRASER, JOHN

| | | | | | | | |
|---|---|---|---|---|---|---|---|
| Presenting | 7" EP | Pye | NEP24068 | 1958 | £2 | £5 | |

## FRASER, NORMA

| | | | | | | | |
|---|---|---|---|---|---|---|---|
| Everybody Loves A Lover | 7" | Ska Beat | JB223 | 1965 | £5 | £10 | |
| First Cut Is The Deepest | 7" | Coxsone | CS7017 | 1967 | £5 | £10 | Bumps Oakley B side |
| Heartaches | 7" | Coxsone | CS7049 | 1968 | £5 | £10 | Righteous Flames B side |
| Heartaches | 7" | Doctor Bird | DB1032 | 1966 | £5 | £10 | Tommy McCook B side |
| Respect | 7" | Coxsone | CS7060 | 1968 | £5 | £10 | |
| Telling Me Lies | 7" | Studio One | SO2025 | 1967 | £6 | £12 | Viceroys B side |

## FRATERNITY OF MAN

The group's 'Don't Bogart Me' was included in the soundtrack of the film *Easy Rider*, although their records are otherwise little known. Guitarist Elliot Ingber had previously played with Frank Zappa's Mothers of Invention, while drummer Richard Hayward subsequently joined Little Feat.

| | | | | | | | |
|---|---|---|---|---|---|---|---|
| Don't Bogart Me | 7" | Stateside | SS2166 | 1970 | £1.50 | £4 | |
| Fraternity Of Man | LP | ABC | S647 | 1968 | £6 | £15 | US |
| Get It On | LP | Dot | DLP25955 | 1969 | £8 | £20 | US |

## FRAYS

Singer Mike Patto was a member of this collectable group.

| | | | | | | | |
|---|---|---|---|---|---|---|---|
| For Your Precious Love | 7" | Decca | F12229 | 1965 | £12.50 | £25 | |
| Walk On | 7" | Decca | F12153 | 1965 | £75 | £150 | |

## FRAZIER CHORUS

| | | | | | | | |
|---|---|---|---|---|---|---|---|
| Sloppy Heart | 7" | 4AD | AD708 | 1987 | £2 | £5 | promo |

## FREAK SCENE

| | | | | | | | |
|---|---|---|---|---|---|---|---|
| Psychedelic Psoul | LP | Columbia | CL2556/CS9356 | 1967 | £37.50 | £75 | US |

## FREAKS OF NATURE

The rare Island single credited to the Freaks of Nature actually features members of Them (after Van Morrison had left the group), backed by the Soft Machine, at a time when Daevid Allen contributions on guitar made the band into a four-piece. Production was by the maverick Kim Fowley.

| | | | | | | | |
|---|---|---|---|---|---|---|---|
| People Let's Freak Out | 7" | Island | WI3017 | 1966 | £20 | £40 | |

## FREBERG, STAN

| | | | | | | | |
|---|---|---|---|---|---|---|---|
| Any Requests | 7" EP | Capitol | EAP1496 | 1955 | £2 | £5 | |
| Banana Boat Song | 7" | Capitol | CL14712 | 1957 | £2 | £5 | |
| Best Of Stan Freberg | LP | Capitol | T2020 | 1964 | £4 | £10 | |
| Best Of The Stan Freberg Show | LP | Capitol | WBO1035 | 1958 | £5 | £12 | US |
| Child's Garden Of Freberg | LP | Capitol | T777 | 1957 | £6 | £15 | US |
| Comedy Caravan | LP | Capitol | T732 | 1956 | £6 | £15 | US |
| Face The Funnies | LP | Capitol | T1694 | 1962 | £5 | £12 | US |
| Freberg Again | 7" EP | Capitol | EAP120115 | 1961 | £2 | £5 | |
| Great Pretender | 7" EP | Capitol | EAP120050 | 1961 | £2.50 | £6 | |
| Great Pretender | 7" | Capitol | CL14571 | 1956 | £4 | £8 | |
| Green Christmas | 7" | Capitol | CL14966 | 1958 | £2 | £5 | |
| Heartbreak Hotel | 7" | Capitol | CL14608 | 1956 | £5 | £10 | |
| Lone Psychiatrist | 7" | Capitol | CL14316 | 1955 | £4 | £8 | |
| Madison Avenue Werewolf | LP | Capitol | T1816 | 1962 | £5 | £12 | US |
| Mickey Mouse's Birthday Party | LP | Capitol | J3264 | 1963 | £5 | £12 | US |
| Old Payola Roll Blues | 7" | Capitol | CL15122 | 1960 | £4 | £8 | |
| Omaha | 7" EP | Capitol | EAP11101 | 1959 | £2 | £5 | |
| Real Saint George | 7" EP | Capitol | EAP1628 | 1956 | £2.50 | £6 | |
| Sh'boom | 7" | Capitol | CL14187 | 1954 | £6 | £12 | |
| Stan Freberg | LP | Capitol | LCT6170/1 | 1959 | £8 | £20 | double |
| Stan Freberg With The Original Cast | LP | Capitol | T1242 | 1959 | £5 | £12 | US |
| Underground Show Number One | LP | Capitol | (S)T2551 | 1966 | £4 | £10 | US |
| United States Of America | LP | Capitol | (S)W1573 | 1961 | £5 | £12 | US |
| Yellow Rose Of Texas | 7" | Capitol | CL14509 | 1956 | £4 | £8 | |

## FRED, JOHN & HIS PLAYBOY BAND

| | | | | | | | |
|---|---|---|---|---|---|---|---|
| 34:40 Of John Fred | LP | Paula | LP(S)2193 | 1967 | £5 | £12 | US |
| Agnes English | LP | Pye | NPL28111 | 1967 | £4 | £10 | |
| John Fred & His Playboys | LP | Paula | LP(S)2191 | 1966 | £5 | £12 | US |
| Judy In Disguise | LP | Paula | LPS2197 | 1968 | £5 | £12 | US |
| Permanently Stated | LP | Paula | LPS2201 | 1968 | £4 | £10 | US |
| Shirley | 7" | CBS | 3475 | 1968 | £2 | £5 | |

## FREDDIE & THE DREAMERS

| | | | | | | | |
|---|---|---|---|---|---|---|---|
| Do The Freddie | LP | Mercury | MG2/SR61026 | 1965 | £4 | £10 | US |
| Frantic Freddie | LP | Mercury | MG2/SR61053 | 1965 | £4 | £10 | US |
| Freddie And The Dreamers | LP | Columbia | 33SX1577 | 1963 | £4 | £10 | |
| Freddie And The Dreamers | LP | Mercury | MG2/SR61017 | 1965 | £4 | £10 | US |
| Freddie And The Dreamers | 7" EP | Columbia | SEG8323 | 1964 | £2.50 | £6 | |

| | | | | | | | |
|---|---|---|---|---|---|---|---|
| Freddie And The Dreamers | 7" EP | Columbia | SEG8457 | 1965 | £5 | £10 | |
| Freddie Sings Just For You | 7" EP | Columbia | SEG8349 | 1964 | £2.50 | £6 | |
| Fun Lovin' Freddie | LP | Mercury | MG2/SR61061 | 1966 | £4 | £10 | US |
| Gabardine Mac | 7" | Columbia | DB8517 | 1968 | £1.50 | £4 | |
| Get Around Downtown Girl | 7" | Columbia | DB8606 | 1969 | £1.50 | £4 | |
| I'm Tellin' You Now | 7" EP | Columbia | ESRF1654 | 1964 | £6 | £12 | French |
| I'm Telling You Now | LP | Tower | (D)T5003 | 1965 | £4 | £10 | US |
| If You Gotta Make A Fool Of Somebody | 7" EP | Columbia | SEG8275 | 1963 | £2.50 | £6 | |
| If You Gotta Make A Fool Of Somebody | 7" | Columbia | DB7032 | 1963 | £1.50 | £4 | |
| In Disneyland | LP | Columbia | SX/SCX6069 | 1966 | £4 | £10 | |
| Just For You | 7" EP | Columbia | SEG8337 | 1964 | £2.50 | £6 | 2 tracks by Peter & Gordon |
| King Freddie & Dreaming Knights | LP | Columbia | SX6177 | 1967 | £4 | £10 | |
| Little Big Time | 7" | Columbia | DB8496 | 1968 | £1.50 | £4 | |
| Ready Freddie Go | 7" EP | Columbia | SEG8403 | 1965 | £5 | £10 | |
| Seaside Swingers | LP | Mercury | MG2/SR61031 | 1965 | £4 | £10 | US |
| Sing Along Party | LP | Columbia | SX1785 | 1965 | £4 | £10 | |
| Some Other Guy | 7" EP | Columbia | ESRF1486 | 1963 | £6 | £12 | French |
| Songs From What A Crazy World | 7" EP | Columbia | SEG8287 | 1963 | £4 | £8 | |
| You Were Mad For Me | LP | Columbia | 33SX1663 | 1964 | £4 | £10 | |
| You Were Made For Me | 7" EP | Columbia | SEG8302 | 1964 | £2.50 | £6 | |

## FREDDY & FITZY
| | | | | | | | |
|---|---|---|---|---|---|---|---|
| Do Good | 7" | Doctor Bird | DB1033 | 1966 | £5 | £10 | |

## FREDERICKS, BILL
| | | | | | | | |
|---|---|---|---|---|---|---|---|
| Almost | 7" | Polydor | 2059035 | 1978 | £2.50 | £6 | |

## FREDERICKS, DOLORES
| | | | | | | | |
|---|---|---|---|---|---|---|---|
| Cha Cha Joe | 7" | Brunswick | 05540 | 1956 | £7.50 | £15 | |

## FREDERICKS, DOTTY
| | | | | | | | |
|---|---|---|---|---|---|---|---|
| Just Wait | 7" | Top Rank | JAR106 | 1959 | £2 | £5 | |

## FREDERICKS, MARC
| | | | | | | | |
|---|---|---|---|---|---|---|---|
| Mystic Midnight | 7" | London | HLD8281 | 1956 | £4 | £8 | |

## FREDERICKS, TOMMY
| | | | | | | | |
|---|---|---|---|---|---|---|---|
| Prince Of Players | 7" | London | HLU8555 | 1958 | £20 | £40 | |

## FREDRIC
| | | | | | | | |
|---|---|---|---|---|---|---|---|
| Phases And Faces | LP | Forte | 80461 | 1968 | £330 | £500 | US |

## FREE

With an average age of around eighteen, the members of the newly formed Free had amazingly still managed to acquire some professional experience – most notably in the case of Andy Fraser, who had played bass (albeit briefly) with John Mayall. They could have been enormous (and the classic 'All Right Now' – included in extended form on *Fire And Water* – was indeed a considerable hit), but dissipated their momentum in a welter of petty disputes, leading to members leaving and returning in a quite bewildering manner. The most collectable record remaining from all this is *Kossoff, Kirke, Tetsu And Rabbit*, which is prevented from being a Free LP only by the absence of singer Paul Rodgers.

| | | | | | | | |
|---|---|---|---|---|---|---|---|
| All Right Now | CD-s | Island | CID486 | 1991 | £2 | £5 | |
| All Right Now | 7" | Island | WIP6082 | 1970 | £1.50 | £4 | |
| Broad Daylight | 7" | Island | WIP6054 | 1969 | £10 | £20 | |
| Fire And Water | LP | Island | ILPS9120 | 1970 | £6 | £15 | pink label |
| Fire And Water | CD | Island | CID9120 | 1986 | £5 | £12 | |
| Free | LP | Island | ILPS9104 | 1969 | £8 | £20 | pink label |
| Free At Last | CD | Island | CID9192 | 1988 | £5 | £12 | |
| Free Live | CD | Island | CID9160 | 1988 | £5 | £12 | |
| Free Story | LP | Island | ISLD4 | 1973 | £6 | £15 | double |
| Heartbreaker | CD | Island | CID9217 | 1988 | £5 | £12 | |
| Highway | LP | Island | ILPS9138 | 1970 | £4 | £10 | |
| Highway | CD | Island | CID9138 | 1988 | £5 | £12 | |
| I'll Be Creepin' | CD | Island | CID9104 | 1988 | £5 | £12 | |
| I'll Be Creeping | 7" | Island | WIP6062 | 1969 | £10 | £20 | |
| I'll Be Creeping | 7" | Island | WIP6062 | 1969 | £20 | £40 | picture sleeve |
| Live | LP | Island | ILPS9160 | 1971 | £4 | £10 | |
| My Brother Jake | CD-s | Island | CID495 | 1991 | £2 | £5 | |
| Stealer | 7" | Island | WIP6093 | 1970 | £1.50 | £4 | |
| Tons Of Sobs | LP | Island | ILPS9089 | 1969 | £8 | £20 | pink label |
| Tons Of Sobs | CD | Island | CID9089 | 1988 | £5 | £12 | |
| Travellin' In Style | 7" | Island | WIP6160 | 1973 | £1.50 | £4 | |

## FREE (2)
| | | | | | | | |
|---|---|---|---|---|---|---|---|
| Keep In Touch | 7" | Philips | BF1754 | 1969 | £10 | £20 | |

## FREE AGENTS
| | | | | | | | |
|---|---|---|---|---|---|---|---|
| Free Agents | LP | Groovy | STP1 | 1980 | £6 | £15 | |

## FREE FERRY
| | | | | | | | |
|---|---|---|---|---|---|---|---|
| Mary What Have You Become | 7" | CBS | 4456 | 1969 | £2 | £5 | |

## FREE SOULS
| | | | | | | | |
|---|---|---|---|---|---|---|---|
| I Want To Be Free | 7" | Blue Beat | BB264 | 1964 | £6 | £12 | |

## FREE SPIRITS
| | | | | | | | |
|---|---|---|---|---|---|---|---|
| Out Of Sight And Sound | LP | ABC | (S)593 | 1967 | £4 | £10 | US |

## FREEBORNE
| | | | | | | |
|---|---|---|---|---|---|---|
| Peak Impression | LP | Monitor | MPS607 | 1967 £37.50 | £75 | US |

## FREED, ALAN
| | | | | | | |
|---|---|---|---|---|---|---|
| Presents The King's Henchmen | LP | Coral | CRL57216 | 195– £25 | £50 | US |
| Right Now Right Now | 7" | Vogue Coral | Q72219 | 1957 £25 | £50 | |
| Rock 'n' Roll Boogie | 7" | Vogue Coral | Q72230 | 1957 £25 | £50 | |
| Rock Around The Block | LP | Coral | CRL57213 | 195– £25 | £50 | US |
| Rock 'n' Roll Dance Party | LP | Vogue Coral | LVA9033 | 1957 £20 | £40 | |
| Rock 'n' Roll Dance Party Vol. 2 | LP | Vogue Coral | LVA9066 | 1957 £25 | £50 | |
| Rock 'n' Roll Show | LP | Brunswick | BL54043 | 1958 £25 | £50 | US |
| TV Record Hop | LP | Coral | CRL57177 | 195– £25 | £50 | US |

## FREEDOM
| | | | | | | |
|---|---|---|---|---|---|---|
| At Last | LP | Metronome | MLP15371 | 1970 £10 | £25 | |
| Escape While You Can | 7" | Plexium | PXM3 | 1968 £2 | £5 | |
| Freedom | LP | Probe | SPBA6252 | 1970 £8 | £20 | |
| Is More Than A Word | LP | Vertigo | 6360072 | 1972 £30 | £60 | spiral label |
| Through The Years | LP | Vertigo | 6360049 | 1971 £20 | £40 | spiral label |
| Where Will You Be Tonight | 7" | Mercury | MF1033 | 1968 £2.50 | £6 | |

## FREEDOM CRY
| | | | | | | |
|---|---|---|---|---|---|---|
| In Disneyland | LP | Columbia | SCX6069 | 1966 £15 | £30 | |

## FREEDOM SINGERS
| | | | | | | |
|---|---|---|---|---|---|---|
| I Want Money | 7" | Coxsone | CS7016 | 1967 £5 | £10 | Slim Smith B side |
| Work Crazy | 7" | Studio One | SO2011 | 1967 £6 | £12 | |

## FREEDOM SOUNDS
| | | | | | | |
|---|---|---|---|---|---|---|
| People Get Ready | LP | Atlantic | SD1492 | 1968 £6 | £15 | |

## FREEDOM'S CHILDREN
| | | | | | | |
|---|---|---|---|---|---|---|
| Astra | LP | Parlophone | PCSJ12066 | 1970 £100 | £200 | South African |

## FREEMAN, ART
| | | | | | | |
|---|---|---|---|---|---|---|
| Slipping Around | 7" | Atlantic | 584053 | 1966 £20 | £40 | |

## FREEMAN, BOBBY
| | | | | | | |
|---|---|---|---|---|---|---|
| Betty Lou Got A New Pair Of Shoes | 7" | London | HLJ8721 | 1958 £12.50 | £25 | |
| C'mon And Swim | LP | Autumn | LP102 | 1964 £8 | £20 | US |
| C'mon And Swim | 7" | Pye | 7N25260 | 1964 £4 | £8 | |
| Do You Wanna Dance | LP | Jubilee | (SD)JLP1086 | 1959 £15 | £30 | US |
| Do You Wanna Dance | 7" | London | HLJ8644 | 1958 £10 | £20 | |
| Duck | 7" | Pye | 7N25347 | 1966 £2.50 | £6 | 2 B sides |
| Ebb Tide | 7" | London | HLJ9031 | 1960 £2 | £5 | |
| Get In The Swim | LP | Josie | JM/JGS4007 | 1965 £8 | £20 | US |
| Lovable Style Of Bobby Freeman | LP | King | 930 | 1965 £10 | £25 | US |
| Mary Ann Thomas | 7" | London | HLJ8898 | 1959 £7.50 | £15 | |
| Need Your Love | 7" | London | HLJ8782 | 1959 £10 | £20 | |
| Shimmy Shimmy | 7" | Parlophone | R4684 | 1960 £2 | £5 | |
| Swim | 7" | Pye | 7N25280 | 1964 £5 | £10 | |
| Twist With Bobby Freeman | LP | Jubilee | JGM5010 | 1962 £10 | £25 | US |

## FREEMAN, BUD
| | | | | | | |
|---|---|---|---|---|---|---|
| Bud Freeman | LP | London | LTZN15030 | 1957 £6 | £15 | |
| Chicago Style | 7" EP | Fontana | TFE17082 | 1958 £2 | £5 | |
| Classics In Jazz | 10" LP | Capitol | LC6706 | 1955 £8 | £20 | |
| Comes Jazz | 10" LP | Columbia | 33S1016 | 1954 £10 | £25 | |
| Jazz For Sale | 7" EP | Top Rank | JKR8021 | 1959 £2 | £5 | |
| Jazz Scene | 7" EP | Parlophone | GEP8783 | 1959 £2 | £5 | |
| Midnight At Eddie Condon's | LP | Emarcy | EJL1257 | 1957 £6 | £15 | |
| Wolverine Jazz | 10" LP | Brunswick | LA8526 | 1951 £8 | £20 | |

## FREEMAN, CAROL
| | | | | | | |
|---|---|---|---|---|---|---|
| Rolling Sea | 7" | CBS | 202579 | 1967 £2.50 | £6 | |

## FREEMAN, ERNIE
| | | | | | | |
|---|---|---|---|---|---|---|
| Big River | 7" | London | HLP9041 | 1960 £1.50 | £4 | |
| Dumplin's | 7" | London | HL7029 | 1957 £1.50 | £4 | export |
| Dumplings | 7" | London | HLP8558 | 1958 £2.50 | £6 | |
| Ernie Freeman & His Rhythm Guitar | 7" EP | London | REU1059 | 1956 £12.50 | £25 | |
| Ernie Freeman Vol. 2 | 7" EP | London | REP1210 | 1959 £7.50 | £15 | |
| Indian Love Call | 7" | London | HLP8660 | 1958 £1.50 | £4 | |
| Raunchy | 7" | London | HLP8523 | 1957 £4 | £8 | |
| Raunchy '65 | 7" | London | HLA9944 | 1965 £2 | £5 | |

## FREEMAN, MARGARET
| | | | | | | |
|---|---|---|---|---|---|---|
| Mister Ting-a-ling | 7" | Starlite | ST45040 | 1961 £2 | £5 | |

## FREEMAN, RUSS & CHET BAKER
| | | | | | | |
|---|---|---|---|---|---|---|
| Freeman/Baker Quartet | LP | Vogue | LAE12119 | 1959 £8 | £20 | |

## FREEMAN, STAN
| | | | | | | |
|---|---|---|---|---|---|---|
| Piano Moods | 10" LP | Columbia | 33S1056 | 1955 £5 | £12 | |

## FREEWHEELERS
| | | | | | | |
|---|---|---|---|---|---|---|
| Why Do You Treat Me Like A Fool | 7" | HMV | POP1406 | 1965 £1.50 | £4 | |

## FRENCH, DON
Goldilocks ................................ 7" ..... London ........... HLW8884 .............. 1959 £37.50... £75
Little Blonde Girl ....................... 7" ..... London ........... HLW8989 .............. 1959 £30 ........ £60

## FRENCH, RAY
Since I Lost My Baby ................... 7" ..... Pye ................ 7N17215 .............. 1966 £2 ........... £5

## FRENCH IMPRESSIONISTS
Santa Baby ............................. 7" ..... Operation ...... OPT20 ................ 1982 £1.50 ...... £4
                                                Twilight ..........

## FRENCH REVOLUTION
Nine Till Five ........................... 7" ..... Decca ............ F22898 ............... 1969 £20 ........ £40

## FRENZY
This Is The Last Time ................... 7" ..... Frenzy ............ FRENZY1 ............. 1981 £2 ........... £5

## FRESH
Fresh Out Of Borstal .................. LP ..... RCA .............. SF8122 ............... 1970 £4 .......... £10
Fresh Today ........................... LP ..... RCA .............. LSA3027 ............. 1971 £4 .......... £10

## FRESH AIR
Running Wild ........................... 7" ..... Pye ................ 7N17736 .............. 1969 £30 ........ £60

## FRESH MAGGOTS
Car Song .............................. 7" ..... RCA .............. RCA2150 ............ 1971 £5 .......... £10
Fresh Maggots ......................... LP ..... RCA .............. SF8205 .............. 1971 £62.50 . £125

## FRESH WINDOWS
Fashion Conscious ..................... 7" ..... Fontana ......... TF839 ............... 1967 £37.50... £75

## FRESHIES
Baiser ................................ 7" ..... Razz .............. RAZZXEP1 .......... 1978 £5 .......... £10 ... Chris Sievey B side
I'm In Love With The Girl ............... 7" ..... Razz .............. RAZZ12 .............. 1980 £2.50 ....... £6 ............... promo
Men From Banana Island ............... 7" ..... Razz .............. RAZZ3 ............... 1979 £1.50 ....... £4
Straight In At No. 2 .................... 7" ..... Razz .............. RAZZEP2 ............ 1979 £2.50 ....... £6

## FRESHMEN
Go Granny Go .......................... 7" ..... Pye ................ 7N17592 ............. 1968 £1.50 ...... £4
Just To See You Smile .................. 7" ..... Pye ................ 7N17689 ............. 1969 £1.50 ...... £4
Movin' On ............................. LP ..... Pye ................ N(S)PL18263 ......... 1968 £20 ........ £40
Papa Oom Mow Mow ................... 7" ..... Pye ................ 7N17432 ............. 1967 £1.50 ...... £4
Peace On Earth ........................ LP ..... CBS ............... 64099 ............... 1970 £15 ........ £30
She Sang Hymns Out Of Tune .......... 7" ..... Pye ................ 7N17757 ............. 1969 £1.50 ...... £4

## FRIAR TUCK
And His Psychedelic Guitar ............. LP ..... Mercury ......... MG21111/SR61111 1968 £6 ........... £15 ............... US

## FRIDAY, CAROL
Everybody I Know ...................... 7" ..... Parlophone ...... R5369 ............... 1965 £7.50 ...... £15

## FRIEDHOF
Friedhof .............................. LP ..... Sound-Star- .... 0103 ................ 1971 £62.50.. £125 ............... German
                                                Ton ...............

## FRIEDMAN, PERRY
Vive La Canadienne ..................... 7" EP . Topic ............ TOP56 .............. 1961 £2 ........... £5

## FRIENDS
Friends To Friends ..................... LP ..... TVO .............. ..................... 1980 £10 ....... £25 ............... Dutch
Piccolo Man ........................... 7" ..... Deram ............ DM198 ............. 1968 £7.50 ...... £15

## FRIENDS BY FEATHER
Friends By Feather ..................... LP ..... Columbia ........ CS30137 ............. 1969 £6 ........... £15 ............... US

## FRIENDS O'MINE
Friends O'Mine ......................... LP ..... Westwood ........ ..................... 1972 £150 ..... £250

## FRIJID PINK
All Pink Inside ......................... LP ..... Fantasy .......... 9464 ................ 1975 £6 ........... £15 ............... US
Defrosted ............................. LP ..... Deram ............ SML1077 ............ 1970 £6 ........... £15
Earth Omen ........................... LP ..... Lionel ............ 1004 ................ 1973 £6 ........... £15 ............... US
Frijid Pink ............................ LP ..... Deram ............ SML1062 ............ 1970 £6 ........... £15
House Of The Rising Sun ................ 7" ..... Deram ............ DM288 ............. 1970 £1.50 ...... £4

## FRISCO, JACKIE
Sugar Baby ............................ 7" ..... Decca ............ F11566 ............... 1963 £1.50 ...... £4

## FRITCHIE, VONNIE
Sugar Booger Avenue ................... 7" ..... London ........... HLU8178 ............. 1955 £12.50 .... £25

## FRITH, FRED
Gravity ............................... LP ..... Ralph ............ FF8057L ............. 1980 £4 .......... £10 ............... US
Guitar Solos .......................... LP ..... Caroline ......... C1508 ............... 1974 £4 .......... £10
Guitar Solos 2 ........................ LP ..... Caroline ......... C1518 ............... 1976 £4 .......... £10 with G. F. Fitzgerald,
                                                                                              Hans Reichel, Derek
                                                                                              Bailey

| | | | | | | | | |
|---|---|---|---|---|---|---|---|---|
| Live In Japan | LP | Recommended | RRJ003/004 | 1982 | £15 | £30 | *Japanese double, mailing envelope cover, 2 posters, 2 booklets* |
| Speechless | LP | Ralph | FF8106 | 1981 | £4 | £10 | *US* |

### FRIZZELL, LEFTY

| | | | | | | | |
|---|---|---|---|---|---|---|---|
| Greatest Hits | LP | Columbia | CL2488/CS9288 | 1966 | £5 | £12 | *US* |
| Listen To Lefty | 10" LP | Columbia | HL9021 | 1952 | £15 | £30 | *US* |
| One And Only | LP | Columbia | CL1342 | 1959 | £10 | £25 | *US* |
| Puttin' On | LP | Columbia | CL2772/CS9572 | 1967 | £5 | £12 | *US* |
| Sad Side Of Love | LP | Columbia | CL2386/CS9186 | 1965 | £5 | £12 | *US* |
| Saginaw, Michigan | LP | Columbia | CL2169/CS8969 | 1964 | £5 | £12 | *US* |
| Songs Of Jimmie Rodgers | 10" LP | Columbia | HL9019 | 1951 | £15 | £30 | *US* |

### FRIZZLE, REV. DWIGHT

| | | | | | | | |
|---|---|---|---|---|---|---|---|
| Beyond The Black Crack | LP | | | | £20 | £40 | *US* |

### FROBOESS, CORNELIA

| | | | | | | | |
|---|---|---|---|---|---|---|---|
| German Teenagers | LP | HMV | 1671 | 1962 | £20 | £40 | *with Rex Gildo* |

### FROEBA, FRANK

| | | | | | | | |
|---|---|---|---|---|---|---|---|
| Back Room Piano | 10" LP | Brunswick | LA8547 | 1952 | £5 | £12 | |
| Moonlight Playing Time | 10" LP | Brunswick | LA8611 | 1953 | £5 | £12 | |
| Parlor Piano | 10" LP | Brunswick | LA8555 | 1953 | £5 | £12 | |

### FROG, WYNDER K.

| | | | | | | | |
|---|---|---|---|---|---|---|---|
| Green Door | 7" EP | Fontana | 460221 | 1967 | £10 | £20 | *French* |
| Green Door | 7" | Island | WIP6006 | 1967 | £2.50 | £6 | |
| I Am A Man | 7" | Island | WIP6014 | 1967 | £2 | £5 | |
| Into The Fire | LP | United Artists | 6740 | 1970 | £5 | £12 | *US* |
| Jumping Jack Flash | 7" | Island | WIP6044 | 1968 | £2 | £5 | |
| Out Of The Frying Pan | LP | Island | ILP982/ILPS9082 | 1968 | £8 | £20 | *pink label* |
| Sunshine Super Frog | LP | Island | ILP944/ILPS9044 | 1967 | £10 | £25 | |
| Sunshine Superman | 7" | Island | WI3011 | 1966 | £1.50 | £4 | |
| Turn On Your Lovelight | 7" | Island | WI280 | 1966 | £2 | £5 | |

### FROGGATT, RAYMOND

| | | | | | | | |
|---|---|---|---|---|---|---|---|
| Bleach | LP | Bell | BELLS207 | 1972 | £6 | £15 | |
| Voice And Writing Of Raymond Froggatt | LP | Polydor | 583044 | 1969 | £6 | £15 | |

### FROGGIE BEAVER

| | | | | | | | |
|---|---|---|---|---|---|---|---|
| From The Pond | LP | Froggie Beaver | 7301 | 1973 | £37.50 | £75 | *US* |

### FROGMEN

| | | | | | | | |
|---|---|---|---|---|---|---|---|
| Underwater | 7" | Oriole | CB1617 | 1961 | £6 | £12 | |

### FROGMORTON

| | | | | | | | |
|---|---|---|---|---|---|---|---|
| At Last | LP | Philips | 6308261 | 1976 | £6 | £15 | |

### FROHMADER, PETER

| | | | | | | | |
|---|---|---|---|---|---|---|---|
| Nekropolis 2 | LP | Hasch Platten | KIF002 | 1982 | £30 | £60 | *German* |

### FROLK HEAVEN

The obscure progressive album by the extraordinarily named Frolk Heaven derives much of its value from the fact that Stewart Copeland, who was later with Curved Air and the Police, is the drummer.

| | | | | | | | |
|---|---|---|---|---|---|---|---|
| At The Apex Of High | LP | LRS | RT6032 | 197– | £180 | £300 | *US* |

### FROMAN, JANE

| | | | | | | | |
|---|---|---|---|---|---|---|---|
| Finger Of Suspicion Points At You | 7" | Capitol | CL14209 | 1954 | £4 | £8 | |
| I Wonder | 7" | Capitol | CL14254 | 1955 | £4 | £8 | |
| Jane Froman | 7" EP | Capitol | EAP1600 | 1956 | £2 | £5 | |
| Song From Desiree | 7" | Capitol | CL14208 | 1954 | £2 | £5 | |
| Songs At Sunset Pt. 1 | 7" EP | Capitol | EAP1889 | 1957 | £2 | £5 | |
| Songs At Sunset Pt. 2 | 7" EP | Capitol | EAP2889 | 1957 | £2 | £5 | |
| Songs At Sunset Pt. 3 | 7" EP | Capitol | EAP3889 | 1957 | £2 | £5 | |
| Summertime In Venice | 7" | Capitol | CL14340 | 1956 | £1.50 | £4 | |

### FRONT LINE

| | | | | | | | |
|---|---|---|---|---|---|---|---|
| Got Love | 7" | Atlantic | AT4057 | 1965 | £12.50 | £25 | |

### FRONTIERE, DOM

| | | | | | | | |
|---|---|---|---|---|---|---|---|
| Jet Rink Ballad | 7" | London | HLU8385 | 1957 | £10 | £20 | |

### FROST

| | | | | | | | |
|---|---|---|---|---|---|---|---|
| Frost Music | LP | Vanguard | VSD6520 | 1969 | £5 | £12 | *US* |
| Rock and Roll Music | LP | Vanguard | SVRL19056 | 1969 | £5 | £12 | |
| Through The Eyes Of Love | LP | Vanguard | VSD6556 | 1970 | £5 | £12 | *US* |

### FROST, DAVID

| | | | | | | | |
|---|---|---|---|---|---|---|---|
| Deck Of Cards | 7" | Parlophone | R5441 | 1966 | £1.50 | £4 | |
| Frost Report On Britain | LP | Parlophone | PMC7005 | 1966 | £4 | £10 | |
| Frost Report On Everything | LP | Pye | NPL18199 | 1967 | £4 | £10 | |

## FROST, DAVID & OTHERS
That Was The Week That Was ................ LP ..... Parlophone ...... PMC1197/          1963 £4 .......... £10 ...............................
                                                     PCS3040 ...............

## FROST, FRANK & THE NIGHTHAWKS
Hey Boss Man! ....................................... LP ..... Philips ............. 1975 ..................... 1961 £250 ..... £400 ........................... US

## FROST, MAX & THE TROOPERS
Shape Of Things To Come ..................... LP ..... Tower ........... ST5147 .................... 1968 £15 .......... £30 ........................... US
Shape Of Things To Come ..................... 7" ...... Capitol .......... CL15565 ................ 1968 £5 .......... £10

## FROST LANE
Frost Lane ............................................. LP ..... Cutty Wren ..... no number ........... 1971 £30 ......... £60

## FRUIT MACHINE
Follow Me .............................................. 7" ...... Spark ............. SRL1003 ................ 1969 £10 .......... £20
I'm Alone Today ..................................... 7" ...... Spark ............. SRL1027 ................ 1970 £30 ......... £60

## FRUMIOUS BANDERSNATCH
Limited Edition ...................................... 7" EP . Muggles                            196– £180 ..... £300 ........................... US
                                                  Gramophone
                                                  Works ..............

## FRUMMOX
Here To There ....................................... LP ..... Probe ............ SPB1007 ............... 1969 £5 .......... £12

## FRUMPY
All Will Be Changed ............................... LP ..... Philips ........... 6305067 ................ 1971 £6 .......... £15
By The Way ........................................... LP ..... Vertigo ......... 6360604 ................ 1972 £5 .......... £12 ........................... German
Frumpy 2 .............................................. LP ..... Philips ........... 6305098 ................ 1972 £8 .......... £20 ..... blue & black vinyl
In And Out Of Studios ........................... LP ..... Fontana ......... 643401 .................. 1972 £4 .......... £10 ........................... German
Live ...................................................... LP ..... Philips ........... 6623022 ................ 1972 £5 .......... £12 ........... German double

## FRUSCELLA, TONY
Tony Fruscella ...................................... LP ..... London .......... LTZK15044 .......... 1957 £10 ......... £25

## FRUUPP
Future Legends ..................................... LP ..... Dawn ............ DNLS3053 ............. 1973 £10 .......... £25
Modern Masquerades .............................. LP ..... Dawn ............ DNLS3070 ............. 1975 £10 .......... £25
Prince Of Heaven ................................... 7" ...... Dawn ............ DNS1087 .............. 1974 £1.50 .......... £4
Prince Of Heaven's Eyes ........................ LP ..... Dawn ............ DNLH2 ................. 1974 £10 .......... £25 ........... with booklet
Seven Secrets ....................................... LP ..... Dawn ............ DNLS3058 ............. 1974 £10 .......... £25

## FUCHS, PAUL & LIMPE (ANIMA SOUND)
Anima .................................................... LP ..... Pilz ............... 20290972 ............... 1972 £8 .......... £20 ........................... German
Anima Sound (Echolette) ........................ LP ..... Melocord ....... STLPNB0027 ......... 1971 £20 .......... £40 ........................... German
Sturmischer Himmel ............................... LP ..... Ohr .............. OMM56011 ........... 1974 £8 .......... £20 ........................... German

## FUCHSIA
Fuchsia ................................................. LP ..... Pegasus ......... PEG8 ................... 1971 £20 .......... £40

## FUGI
Red Moon .............................................. 7" ...... Blue Horizon... 2096005 ................ 1971 £2.50 .......... £6

## FUGITIVES
Fugitive ................................................ 7" ...... Vogue ............ V9176 ................... 1961 £6 .......... £12

## FUGITIVES (2)
Musical Pressure .................................... 7" ...... Doctor Bird ..... DB1082 ................ 1967 £5 .......... £10
Real Gone Loser ..................................... 7" ...... Doctor Bird ..... DB1116 ................ 1967 £5 .......... £10

## FUGITIVES (3)
The Fugitives who made the extremely rare album, *Fugitives At Dave's Hideout*, evolved into the important psychedelic band, SRC.

Friday At The Cafe A GoGo (Long Hot      LP ..... Westchester .... 1005 ..................... 1965 £150 ..... £250 . US, with other artists
   Summer) .............................................
Fugitives At Dave's Hideout .................... LP ..... Hideout .......... 1001 ..................... 1965 £700 ... £1000 ........................... US

## FUGITIVES (4)
On The Run ............................................ LP ..... Justice ........... 141 .......................... £75 ..... £150 ........................... US

## FUGS
Ballads Of Contemporary Protest ............. LP ..... Broadside ....... 304 ...................... 1966 £15 .......... £30 ........................... US
Belle Of Avenue A ................................. LP ..... Reprise .......... RS6359 ................ 1969 £4 .......... £10 ........................... US
Crystal Liaison ....................................... 7" ...... Transatlantic .... BIG115 ................ 1968 £1.50 ...... £4
First Album ............................................ LP ..... Fontana .......... (S)TL5513 ............ 1965 £8 .......... £20
Fugs 4 Rounders Score ........................... LP ..... ESP-Disk ........ 2018 ..................... 1967 £6 .......... £15 ........................... US
Fugs II .................................................. LP ..... Fontana .......... (S)TL5524 ............ 1966 £8 .......... £20
Golden Filth .......................................... LP ..... Reprise .......... RS6396 ................ 1970 £4 .......... £10 ........................... US
It Crawled Into My Hand Honest ............. LP ..... Transatlantic ... TRA181 ................ 1968 £5 .......... £12
Tenderness Junction ............................... LP ..... Transatlantic ... TRA180 ............... 1968 £5 .......... £12
Virgin Fugs ............................................ LP ..... Fontana .......... (S)TL5501 ............ 1967 £6 .......... £15

## FULHAM FURIES
These Boots Are Made For Walking .......... 7" ...... GM ............... GMS9050 ............. 1978 £4 .......... £8

## FULL MOON

| Title | Format | Label | Cat. No. | Year | | | |
|---|---|---|---|---|---|---|---|
| Moon Fools | LP | Amor Sound | FM001 | 1977 | £37.50 | £75 | Dutch |
| Nothing Ventured, Nothing Gained | LP | Amor Sound | | 197– | £37.50 | £75 | Dutch |
| What's Going On | LP | Amor Sound | | 197– | £25 | £50 | Dutch |

## FULLER, BLIND BOY

| Title | Format | Label | Cat. No. | Year | | | |
|---|---|---|---|---|---|---|---|
| 1935–40 | LP | Philips | BBL7510 | 1957 | £15 | £30 | |
| On Down Vol. 1 | LP | Saydisc | SDR143 | 1968 | £4 | £10 | |
| On Down Vol. 2 | LP | Saydisc | SDR168 | 1969 | £4 | £10 | |

## FULLER, BOBBY

| Title | Format | Label | Cat. No. | Year | | | |
|---|---|---|---|---|---|---|---|
| I Fought The Law | LP | Mustang | M(S)901 | 1966 | £15 | £30 | US |
| I Fought The Law | 7" | London | HLU10030 | 1966 | £6 | £12 | |
| KRLA King Of The Wheels | LP | Mustang | M(S)900 | 1966 | £20 | £40 | US |
| Love's Made A Fool Of You | 7" EP | London | RE10179 | 1966 | £30 | £60 | French |
| Love's Made A Fool Of You | 7" | London | HLU10041 | 1966 | £2.50 | £6 | |
| Memorial Album | LP | President | PTL1003 | 1967 | £4 | £10 | |

## FULLER, GIL

| Title | Format | Label | Cat. No. | Year | | | |
|---|---|---|---|---|---|---|---|
| Man From Monterey | LP | Fontana | 688147ZL | 1966 | £5 | £12 | with Dizzy Gillespie |

## FULLER, JERRY

| Title | Format | Label | Cat. No. | Year | | | |
|---|---|---|---|---|---|---|---|
| Guilty Of Loving You | 7" | London | HLN9439 | 1961 | £1.50 | £4 | |
| Mother Goose At The Bandstand | 7" | Salvo | SLO1802 | 1962 | £2 | £5 | |
| Teenage Love | LP | Lin | LP100 | 1960 | £6 | £15 | US |
| Tennessee Waltz | 7" | London | HLH8982 | 1959 | £2 | £5 | |

## FULLER, JESSE

| Title | Format | Label | Cat. No. | Year | | | |
|---|---|---|---|---|---|---|---|
| Favourites | LP | Stateside | SL10154 | 1965 | £4 | £10 | |
| Frisco Bound | LP | Cavalier | 6009 | 195– | £15 | £30 | US |
| Frisco Bound | 10" LP | Cavalier | 5006 | 195– | £20 | £40 | US |
| Going Back To My Old Used To Be | 7" | Fontana | TF821 | 1967 | £4 | £8 | |
| Jesse Fuller | LP | Good Time Jazz | LAG12159 | 1958 | £5 | £12 | |
| Lone Cat | LP | Good Time Jazz | LAG12279 | 1960 | £5 | £12 | |
| Move On Down The Line | LP | Topic | 12T134 | 1965 | £8 | £20 | |
| Runnin' Wild | 7" | Good Time Jazz | GV2427 | 1967 | £1.50 | £4 | |
| San Francisco Bay Blues | LP | Good Time Jazz | LAG574 | 1963 | £5 | £12 | |
| San Francisco Bay Blues | LP | Stateside | SL10166 | 1966 | £4 | £10 | |
| San Francisco Bay Blues | LP | Vocalion | VRLP574 | 196– | £4 | £10 | |
| San Francisco Bay Blues | 7" | Good Time Jazz | GV2426 | 1965 | £1.50 | £4 | |
| Session | LP | Fontana | TL5313 | 1966 | £4 | £10 | |
| Working On The Railroad | 10" LP | Topic | 10T59 | 1960 | £8 | £20 | |

## FULLER, RANDY

| Title | Format | Label | Cat. No. | Year | | | |
|---|---|---|---|---|---|---|---|
| It's Love Come What May | 7" | President | PTL111 | 1967 | £2 | £5 | |

## FULSON, LOWELL

| Title | Format | Label | Cat. No. | Year | | | |
|---|---|---|---|---|---|---|---|
| Black Nights | 7" | Polydor | 56515 | 1970 | £4 | £8 | |
| Hung Down Head | LP | Chess | 408 | 196– | £8 | £20 | US |
| I Love My Baby | 78 | London | L1199 | 1953 | £7.50 | £15 | |
| Lowell Fulson | LP | Kent | KLP5016 | 1965 | £8 | £20 | US |
| Lowell Fulson Now | LP | Kent | KST531 | 1969 | £5 | £12 | US |
| San Francisco Blues | LP | Fontana | SFJL920 | 1969 | £6 | £15 | |
| Stop And Think | 7" | Outasite | 45502 | 1966 | £12.50 | £25 | with Leon Blue |
| Talking Woman | 7" | Sue | WI4023 | 1966 | £10 | £20 | |
| Too Many Drivers | 7" | Sue | WI375 | 1965 | £5 | £10 | |
| Tramp | LP | Kent | KLP/KST520 | 1967 | £8 | £20 | US |
| Tramp | 7" | Fontana | TF795 | 1967 | £7.50 | £15 | |

## FUMBLE

| Title | Format | Label | Cat. No. | Year | | | |
|---|---|---|---|---|---|---|---|
| Fumble | LP | Sovereign | SVNA7254 | 1972 | £5 | £12 | |
| Poetry In Lotion | LP | RCA | SF8403 | 1974 | £4 | £10 | |

## FUN FOUR

| Title | Format | Label | Cat. No. | Year | | | |
|---|---|---|---|---|---|---|---|
| Singing In The Showers | 7" | NMC | NMC010 | 1980 | £1.50 | £4 | |

## FUNGUS

| Title | Format | Label | Cat. No. | Year | | | |
|---|---|---|---|---|---|---|---|
| Fungus | LP | Negram | NR102 | 1974 | £15 | £30 | Dutch |
| Lief Ende Leid | LP | Negram | NR115 | 1975 | £15 | £30 | Dutch |
| Van De Kiel Naar Vlaring | LP | Negram | NK211 | 1976 | £15 | £30 | Dutch |

## FUNHOUSE

| Title | Format | Label | Cat. No. | Year | | | |
|---|---|---|---|---|---|---|---|
| Out Of Control | 7" | Ensign | ENY22 | 1982 | £6 | £12 | |
| Out Of Control | 12" | Ensign | ENY22 | 1982 | £6 | £15 | |

## FUNKADELIC

The records made by Funkadelic represent one of the main branches of George Clinton's P-Funk organization – other records being listed under the Parliament name.

| Title | Format | Label | Cat. No. | Year | | | |
|---|---|---|---|---|---|---|---|
| America Eats Its Young | LP | Westbound | 2WB2020 | 1972 | £15 | £30 | US |
| Can You Get To That | 7" | Janus | 6146001 | 1974 | £1.50 | £4 | |

| | | | | | | | |
|---|---|---|---|---|---|---|---|
| Cosmic Slop | LP | Westbound | WB2022 | 1973 £8 | £20 | | US |
| Electric Spanking Of War Babies | LP | Warner Bros | K56874 | 1981 £5 | £12 | | |
| Free Your Mind & Your Ass Will Follow | LP | Pye | NSPL28144 | 1971 £15 | £30 | | |
| Funkadelic | LP | Pye | NSPL28137 | 1970 £15 | £30 | | |
| Greatest Hits | LP | Westbound | 1004 | 1975 £6 | £15 | | US |
| Hardcore Jollies | LP | Warner Bros | K56299 | 1978 £6 | £15 | | |
| I Got A Thing, You Got A Thing | 7" | Pye | 7N25519 | 1970 £2.50 | £6 | | |
| Let's Take It To The Stage | LP | 20th Century | W215 | 1975 £6 | £15 | | |
| Maggot Brain | LP | Westbound | 6310201 | 1971 £10 | £25 | | |
| One Nation Under A Groove | LP | Warner Bros | K56359 | 1978 £5 | £12 | | with 12" |
| Standing On The Verge Of Getting It On | LP | Westbound | 1001 | 1974 £10 | £25 | | US |
| Tales Of Kidd Funkadelic | LP | Westbound | 227 | 1976 £8 | £20 | | US |
| Uncle Jam Wants You | LP | Warner Bros | K56712 | 1979 £6 | £15 | | |
| You And Your Folks, Me And Mine | 7" | Pye | 7N25548 | 1971 £2.50 | £6 | | |

## FUREKAABEN

| | | | | | | | |
|---|---|---|---|---|---|---|---|
| Prinsesse Vaerelset | LP | Spectator | 1017 | 1970 £30 | £60 | | Danish |

## FUREY, FINBAR

| | | | | | | | |
|---|---|---|---|---|---|---|---|
| Prince Of Pipers | LP | Polydor | 2908023 | 1974 £6 | £15 | | Irish |
| Traditional Irish Pipe Music | LP | XTRA | XTRA1077 | 1969 £10 | £25 | | |

## FUREY, FINBAR & BOB STEWART

| | | | | | | |
|---|---|---|---|---|---|---|
| Tomorrow We Part | LP | Broadside | BRO133 | 1979 £4 | £10 | |

## FUREY, FINBAR & EDDIE

| | | | | | | | |
|---|---|---|---|---|---|---|---|
| Dawning Of The Day | LP | Dawn | DNLS3037 | 1972 £10 | £25 | | |
| Dream In My Hand | LP | Interchord | 264291U | 1974 £5 | £12 | | German |
| Finbar And Eddie Furey | LP | Transatlantic | TRA168 | 1968 £8 | £20 | | |
| Four Green Fields | LP | Plane | S12F200 | 1972 £5 | £12 | | German |
| Lonesome Boatman | LP | Transatlantic | TRA191 | 1969 £6 | £15 | | |
| Town Is Not Their Own | LP | Harp | HPE613 | 1969 £5 | £12 | | Irish |

## FUREY, TED

| | | | | | | | |
|---|---|---|---|---|---|---|---|
| Traditional Fiddle | LP | Outlet | OLP1020 | 1973 £10 | £25 | | Irish |

## FURNITURE

| | | | | | | |
|---|---|---|---|---|---|---|
| Shaking Story | 7" | Guy From Paraguay | PARA1 | 1980 £2.50 | £6 | |

## FURTADO, TOMMY

| | | | | | | |
|---|---|---|---|---|---|---|
| Sun Tan Sam | 7" | London | HLA8418 | 1957 £4 | £8 | |

## FURY, BILLY

Billy Fury is held in high regard as one of the most convincing British rock'n'rollers and yet the proportion of rock to ballads in his output is far too small for the reputation to be sustained by deep enquiry. *The Sound Of Fury* is certainly a competent slice of rockabilly, and Fury wrote much of the material himself, but to release an album in this style in 1960 was to indulge in a piece of historical re-creation rather than to be part of the development of something new. Cliff Richard's exploration of the Buddy Holly style was much more to the point, and it is significant that he survived the onslaught of the Beatles, whereas Billy Fury did not.

| | | | | | | | |
|---|---|---|---|---|---|---|---|
| All The Way To The USA | 7" | Parlophone | R5819 | 1969 £7.50 | £15 | | |
| Am I Blue | 7" EP | Decca | DFE8558 | 1963 £15 | £30 | | |
| Angel Face | 78 | Decca | F11158 | 1959 £20 | £40 | | |
| Angel Face | 7" | Decca | F11158 | 1959 £12.50 | £25 | | tri-centre |
| Because Of Love | 7" | Decca | F11508 | 1962 £1.50 | £4 | | |
| Best Of Billy Fury | LP | Ace Of Clubs | ACL1229 | 1967 £8 | £20 | | |
| Beyond The Shadow Of A Doubt | 7" | Parlophone | R5658 | 1967 £5 | £10 | | |
| Billy | LP | Decca | LK4533 | 1963 £15 | £30 | | |
| Billy Fury | LP | Ace Of Clubs | ACL1047 | 1960 £10 | £25 | | |
| Billy Fury | 7" EP | Decca | DFE6694 | 1961 £20 | £40 | | |
| Billy Fury And The Gamblers | 7" EP | Decca | DFE8641 | 1965 £30 | £60 | | |
| Billy Fury And The Tornadoes | 7" EP | Decca | DFE8525 | 1963 £12.50 | £25 | | |
| Billy Fury Hits | 7" EP | Decca | DFE8505 | 1962 £7.50 | £15 | | |
| Billy Fury No. 2 | 7" EP | Decca | DFE6699 | 1962 £20 | £40 | | |
| Colette | 7" | Decca | F11200 | 1960 £10 | £20 | | tri-centre |
| Do You Really Love Me Too | 7" | Decca | F11792 | 1963 £1.50 | £4 | | |
| Don't Let A Little Pride | 7" | Decca | F12409 | 1966 £1.50 | £4 | | |
| Don't Worry | 7" | Decca | F11334 | 1961 £2 | £5 | | |
| Give Me Your Word | 7" | Decca | F12459 | 1966 £1.50 | £4 | | |
| Halfway To Paradise | LP | Ace Of Clubs | ACL1083 | 1961 £10 | £25 | | |
| Halfway To Paradise | 7" | Decca | F11349 | 1961 £1.50 | £4 | | |
| Halfway To Paradise | 7" | NEMS | NES018 | 1976 £1.50 | £4 | | |
| Hippy Hippy Shake | 7" | Decca | F40719 | 1964 £10 | £20 | | export |
| Hippy Hippy Shake | 7" | Decca | F40719 | 1964 £20 | £40 | | export, picture sleeve |
| Hurtin' Is Lovin' | 7" | Parlophone | R5560 | 1967 £5 | £10 | | |
| I Call For My Rose | 7" | Parlophone | R5788 | 1969 £5 | £10 | | |
| I Will | 7" | Decca | F11888 | 1964 £1.50 | £4 | | |
| I'd Never Find Another You | 7" | Decca | F11409 | 1961 £1.50 | £4 | | |
| I'll Be Your Sweetheart | 7" | Warner Bros | K16402 | 1974 £1.50 | £4 | | |
| I'll Never Quite Get Over You | 7" | Decca | F12325 | 1966 £1.50 | £4 | | |
| I'm Lost Without You | 7" | Decca | F12048 | 1965 £1.50 | £4 | | |
| I've Got A Horse | LP | Decca | LK4677 | 1965 £20 | £40 | | |
| In Summer | 7" | Decca | F11701 | 1963 £1.50 | £4 | | |
| In Thoughts Of You | 7" | Decca | F12178 | 1965 £1.50 | £4 | | |
| Interview With Stuart Colman | 10" LP | Polydor | | 1982 £6 | £15 | | promo |
| It's Only Make Believe | 7" | Decca | F11939 | 1964 £1.50 | £4 | | |
| Jealousy | 7" | Decca | F11384 | 1961 £1.50 | £4 | | |

| Title | Format | Label | Cat. No. | Year | | | Notes |
|---|---|---|---|---|---|---|---|
| Lady | 7" | Parlophone | R5747 | 1968 | £5 | £10 | |
| Last Night Was Made For Love | 7" | Decca | F11458 | 1962 | £1.50 | £4 | |
| Letter Full Of Tears | 7" | Decca | F11437 | 1962 | £1.50 | £4 | |
| Like I've Never Been Gone | 7" | Decca | F11582 | 1963 | £1.50 | £4 | |
| Long Live Rock | 7" EP | Ronco | MREP001 | 1973 | £5 | £10 | with other artists, no picture sleeve |
| Loving You | 7" | Parlophone | R5605 | 1967 | £5 | £10 | |
| Margo | 78 | Decca | F11128 | 1959 | £10 | £20 | |
| Margo | 7" | Decca | F11128 | 1959 | £7.50 | £15 | tri-centre |
| Maybe Tomorrow | 78 | Decca | F11102 | 1959 | £10 | £20 | |
| Maybe Tomorrow | 7" EP | Decca | DFE6597 | 1959 | £30 | £60 | tri-centre |
| Maybe Tomorrow | 7" | Decca | F11102 | 1959 | £7.50 | £15 | tri-centre |
| My Christmas Prayer | 78 | Decca | F11189 | 1959 | £30 | £60 | |
| My Christmas Prayer | 7" EP | Decca | DFE8686 | 1983 | £2 | £5 | |
| My Christmas Prayer | 7" | Decca | F11189 | 1959 | £25 | £50 | tri-centre |
| Once Upon A Dream | 7" | Decca | F11485 | 1962 | £1.50 | £4 | |
| Paradise Alley | 7" | Parlophone | R5874 | 1970 | £10 | £20 | |
| Phone Box | 7" | Parlophone | R5723 | 1968 | £6 | £12 | |
| Play It Cool | 7" EP | Decca | DFE6708 | 1962 | £7.50 | £15 | |
| Run To My Lovin' Arms | 7" | Decca | F12230 | 1965 | £1.50 | £4 | |
| Silly Boy Blue | 7" | Parlophone | R5681 | 1968 | £10 | £20 | |
| Somebody Else's Girl | 7" | Decca | F11744 | 1963 | £1.50 | £4 | |
| Sound Of Fury | CD | Decca | 8206272 | 1988 | £5 | £12 | |
| Sound Of Fury | 10" LP | Decca | LF1329 | 1960 | £20 | £40 | |
| Suzanne In The Mirror | 7" | Parlophone | R5634 | 1967 | £5 | £10 | |
| That's Love | 7" | Decca | F11237 | 1960 | £2.50 | £6 | |
| Thousand Stars | 7" | Decca | F11311 | 1960 | £2.50 | £6 | |
| We Want Billy | LP | Decca | LK4548 | 1963 | £15 | £30 | with the Tornados |
| We Want Billy | LP | Decca | SKL4548 | 1963 | £20 | £40 | with the Tornados, stereo |
| When Will You Say I Love You | 7" | Decca | F11655 | 1963 | £1.50 | £4 | |
| Why Are You Leaving | 7" | Parlophone | R5845 | 1970 | £7.50 | £15 | |
| Will The Real Man Stand Up | 7" | Fury | FY301 | 1972 | £5 | £10 | |
| Wondrous Place | 7" | Decca | F11267 | 1960 | £2.50 | £6 | |

## FURYS

| Title | Format | Label | Cat. No. | Year | | | Notes |
|---|---|---|---|---|---|---|---|
| Never More | 7" EP | Columbia | ESDF1488 | 1963 | £5 | £10 | French |

## FUSE

This hard rock band included guitarist Rick Nielsen (who did not, however, have the lead guitar role) and bassist Tom Peterson, who subsequently enjoyed considerable success as members of Cheap Trick.

| Title | Format | Label | Cat. No. | Year | | | Notes |
|---|---|---|---|---|---|---|---|
| Fuse | LP | Epic | 26502 | 1968 | £15 | £30 | US |

## FUSION

The private pressing issued by the group Fusion is much rarer than its modest value would suggest. The guitarist was Nik Kershaw, and his later solo single, 'Human Racing', appears here in a very similar version.

| Title | Format | Label | Cat. No. | Year | | | Notes |
|---|---|---|---|---|---|---|---|
| Till I Hear from You | LP | Telephone | TEL101 | 1980 | £6 | £15 | blue vinyl |

## FUSION ORCHESTRA

| Title | Format | Label | Cat. No. | Year | | | Notes |
|---|---|---|---|---|---|---|---|
| Skeleton In Armour | LP | EMI | EMA758 | 1973 | £25 | £50 | |
| When My Mama's Not At Home | 7" | EMI | EMI2056 | 1973 | £1.50 | £4 | |

## FUT

Desperate to believe in the existence of rare Beatles out-takes, collectors seized on 'Have You Heard The Word' as being one such. Unless, of course, it was really the Bee Gees – or, again, perhaps it was actually the Bee Gees and the Beatles singing together? Actually, it was the Fut (whoever they were), just as the label said.

| Title | Format | Label | Cat. No. | Year | | | Notes |
|---|---|---|---|---|---|---|---|
| Have You Heard The Word | 7" | Beacon | BEA160 | 1971 | £7.50 | £15 | |

## FUTURE SOUND OF LONDON

| Title | Format | Label | Cat. No. | Year | | | Notes |
|---|---|---|---|---|---|---|---|
| ISDN | CD | Virgin | CDV2755 | 1994 | £8 | £20 | black card cover |

## FUTURES

| Title | Format | Label | Cat. No. | Year | | | Notes |
|---|---|---|---|---|---|---|---|
| You Better Be Certain | 7" | Buddah | BDS430 | 1975 | £2.50 | £6 | |

## FUZZY DUCK

| Title | Format | Label | Cat. No. | Year | | | Notes |
|---|---|---|---|---|---|---|---|
| Big Brass Band | 7" | Mam | MAM51 | 1971 | £5 | £10 | |
| Double Time Woman | 7" | Mam | MAM37 | 1971 | £5 | £10 | |
| Fuzzy Duck | LP | MAM | MAM1005 | 1971 | £75 | £150 | |
| Fuzzy Duck | LP | Reflection | MM05 | 1990 | £6 | £15 | with 7" |

## FYNN MCCOOL

| Title | Format | Label | Cat. No. | Year | | | Notes |
|---|---|---|---|---|---|---|---|
| Fynn McCool | LP | RCA | SF8112 | 1970 | £20 | £40 | |
| US Thumbstyle | 7" | RCA | RCA1956 | 1970 | £1.50 | £4 | |

# G

## G, TOMMY & THE CHARMS
| | | | | | | |
|---|---|---|---|---|---|---|
| I Know What I Want | 7" | London | HLB10107 | 1967 | £2.50 | £6 |

## G, WINSTON
| | | | | | | |
|---|---|---|---|---|---|---|
| Cloud Nine | 7" | Decca | F12444 | 1966 | £2.50 | £6 |
| Mother Ferguson's Love Dust | 7" | Decca | F12559 | 1967 | £4 | £8 |
| Riding With The Milkman | 7" | Decca | F12623 | 1967 | £4 | £8 |

## G, WINSTON & THE WICKED
| | | | | | | |
|---|---|---|---|---|---|---|
| Like A Baby | 7" | Parlophone | R5266 | 1965 | £4 | £8 |
| Until You Were Gone | 7" | Parlophone | R5330 | 1966 | £2 | £5 |

## GABBIDON, BASIL
| | | | | | | | |
|---|---|---|---|---|---|---|---|
| Ena Mena | 7" | Blue Beat | BB155 | 1963 | £6 | £12 | |
| I Bet You Don't Know | 7" | Island | WI076 | 1963 | £5 | £10 | |
| I Found My Baby | 7" | Island | WI033 | 1962 | £5 | £10 | |
| I Was Wrong | 7" | Blue Beat | BB69 | 1961 | £6 | £12 | |
| I'll Find Love | 7" | Blue Beat | BB161 | 1963 | £6 | £12 | ...Mellow Larks B side |
| Independence Blues | 7" | Blue Beat | BB124 | 1962 | £6 | £12 | |
| Iverene | 7" | Blue Beat | BB111 | 1962 | £6 | £12 | |
| No More Wedding | 7" | Blue Beat | BB38 | 1961 | £6 | £12 | |
| Our Melody | 7" | Blue Beat | BB129 | 1962 | £6 | £12 | |
| St. Louis Woman | 7" | Island | WI089 | 1963 | £5 | £10 | |
| Tic Toc | 7" | Blue Beat | BB288 | 1965 | £6 | £12 | |

## GABERLUNZIE
| | | | | | | |
|---|---|---|---|---|---|---|
| Freedom's Sword | LP | Revival | RVS1010 | 1974 | £6 | £15 |

## GABRIEL, PETER
| | | | | | | | |
|---|---|---|---|---|---|---|---|
| Before Us – A Brief History | CD | Geffen | PROCD4412 | 1992 | £8 | £20 | .....US promo sampler |
| Big Time | CDV | Virgin | VVD241 | 1988 | £6 | £15 | |
| Big Time | CD-s | Virgin | GAIL312 | 1987 | £3 | £8 | |
| Biko (live) | CD-s | Virgin | CDPGS612 | 1987 | £2 | £5 | |
| D.I.Y. | 7" | Charisma | CB311 | 1978 | £2 | £5 | |
| D.I.Y. (remix) | 7" | Charisma | CB319 | 1978 | £12.50 | £25 | |
| Deutsches Album | LP | Charisma | 6302221 | 1982 | £4 | £10 | 4th LP in German |
| Ein Deutsches Album | LP | Charisma | 6302035 | 1980 | £4 | £10 | 3rd LP in German |
| Games Without Frontiers (live) | 12" | Virgin | GAB122 | 1983 | £2.50 | £6 | double |
| Live – Secret World Tour | CD | Virgin | | 1994 | £20 | £40 | .. Japanese double CD |
| Modern Love | 7" | Charisma | CB302 | 1977 | £15 | £30 | picture label |
| Peter Gabriel 1 | CD | Charisma | 8000912 | 1983 | £5 | £12 | |
| Peter Gabriel 4 | LP | Charisma | | 1982 | £5 | £12 | audiophile |
| Peter Gabriel Plays Live | LP | Charisma | PGDL1 | 1983 | £25 | £50 | .. double, test pressing, original mixes |
| Schock Den Affen | 7" | Charisma | 60000876 | 1982 | £4 | £8 | German |
| Shaking The Tree | CD-s | Virgin | VSCD1167 | 1989 | £2 | £5 | with Youssou N'Dour |
| Shaking The Tree – Sixteen Golden Greats. | CD | Virgin | PGTVD6 | 1990 | £5 | £12 | . with album version of 'Games Without Frontiers' |
| Shock The Monkey | 7" | Charisma | SHOCK122 | 1982 | £2 | £5 | ...........picture disc |
| Shock The Monkey/instrumental | 7" | Charisma | SHOCK1 | 1982 | £2.50 | £6 | |
| Sledgehammer | CD-s | Virgin | CDT4 | 1988 | £2 | £5 | 3" single |
| Solsbury Hill | CD-s | Virgin | CDT33 | 1988 | £3 | £8 | 3" single |
| Solsbury Hill | CD-s | Virgin | VSCDT1322 | 1990 | £2 | £5 | |
| Solsbury Hill | 7" | Charisma | CB301 | 1977 | £2.50 | £6 | picture sleeve |
| Solsbury Hill | 7" | Sound For Industry | SFI381 | 1978 | £1.50 | £4 | flexi |
| Spiel Ohne Grenzen | 7" | Charisma | 6000448 | 1980 | £4 | £8 | German |
| Us | CD | Real World | PGCD7 | 1992 | £20 | £40 | ... promo box set, with prints, press sheet, photo |

## GABRIEL & THE ANGELS
| | | | | | | |
|---|---|---|---|---|---|---|
| Don't Wanna Twist No More | 7" | Stateside | SS150 | 1963 | £1.50 | £4 |

## GABRIELLI BRASS
| | | | | | | |
|---|---|---|---|---|---|---|
| Canterbury Tales Theme | 7" | Polydor | 56252 | 1968 | £1.50 | £4 |
| Ride Your Pony | 7" | Polydor | 56047 | 1965 | £1.50 | £4 |

## GADGETS
The Gadgets performed improvised industrial music which was released on three limited-edition albums. One of the trio was Matt Johnson, subsequently the central pillar of The The.

| | | | | | | |
|---|---|---|---|---|---|---|
| Gadgetree ................................................. | LP ...... | Final Solution .. | FSLP001 ................ | 1979 | £6 ........ £15 | .... *blue or brown cover design/insert* |
| Love, Curiosity, Freckles, & Doubt ........... | LP ...... | Final Solution . | FSLP002 ................ | 1980 | £6 ........ £15 | ............................ |

## GADSON, MEL

| | | | | | | |
|---|---|---|---|---|---|---|
| Comin' Down With Love ......................... | 7" ...... | London .......... | HLX9105 ............. | 1960 | £1.50 .... £4 | ............................ |

## GAGALACTYCA

| | | | | | | |
|---|---|---|---|---|---|---|
| Gagalactyca ........................................... | LP ...... | Holyground ..... | HG1135 ............... | 1990 | £6 ........ £15 | |

## GAGS

| | | | | | | |
|---|---|---|---|---|---|---|
| Death In Buzzard's Gulch ....................... | LP ...... | Look ............ | LKLP6312 ............ | 1979 | £50 .... £100 | |

## GAILLARD, SLIM

| | | | | | | |
|---|---|---|---|---|---|---|
| Central Avenue Boogie ........................... | 78 ...... | Vogue ............ | V2044 ............... | 1951 | £1.50 .... £4 | |
| Jam Man ................................................. | 78 ...... | Parlophone ..... | R3291 ............... | 1950 | £5 ........ £10 | |
| Musical Aggregations ............................. | 7" EP . | Columbia ..... | SEB10046 ........... | 1957 | £7.50 .... £15 | |
| Slim Gaillard No. 1 ................................. | 7" EP . | Parlophone ..... | GEP8595 ............. | 1957 | £6 ........ £12 | |
| Slim Gaillard Rides Again ..................... | 7" EP . | London .......... | RED1251 ............ | 1960 | £7.50 .... £15 | |
| Voot Boogie ........................................... | 78 ...... | Vogue ............ | V2029 ............... | 1951 | £1.50 .... £4 | |

## GAINORS

| | | | | | | |
|---|---|---|---|---|---|---|
| Secret ..................................................... | 7" ...... | London .......... | HLU8734 ............. | 1958 | £50 .... £100 | |

## GALACTIC FEDERATION

| | | | | | | |
|---|---|---|---|---|---|---|
| March Of The Sky People ........................ | 7" ...... | Polydor .......... | 56093 ............... | 1966 | £6 ........ £12 | |

## GALACTIC SUPERMARKET

| | | | | | | |
|---|---|---|---|---|---|---|
| Galactic Supermarket ............................. | LP ...... | Komische ..... | KM58010 ............ | 1974 | £8 ........ £20 | ................ German |

## GALACTUS

| | | | | | | |
|---|---|---|---|---|---|---|
| Cosmic Force Field ................................. | LP ...... | Airship .......... | | 1971 | £10 ........ £25 | ................ US |

## GALADRIEL

| | | | | | | |
|---|---|---|---|---|---|---|
| Galadriel ............................................... | LP ...... | Polydor .......... | 2480059 ............. | 1970 | £87.50 .. £175 | ................ German |

## GALAHADS

| | | | | | | |
|---|---|---|---|---|---|---|
| Galahads ............................................... | LP ...... | Liberty .......... | LRP3371/LST7371. | 1964 | £5 ........ £12 | ................ US |

## GALAXIE 500

| | | | | | | |
|---|---|---|---|---|---|---|
| Blue Thunder ......................................... | 7" ...... | Rough Trade ... | G5SFI ............... | 1990 | £2 ........ £5 | ................ *promo* |
| Rain ....................................................... | 7" ...... | Caff .............. | CAFF9 .............. | 1988 | £7.50 .... £15 | |

## GALAXY

| | | | | | | |
|---|---|---|---|---|---|---|
| Day Without The Sun ............................. | LP ...... | Sky Queen ...... | SQR1677 ............ | 1976 | £150 .... £250 | ................ US |

## GALAXY-LIN

| | | | | | | |
|---|---|---|---|---|---|---|
| G ........................................................... | LP ...... | Polydor .......... | 2925037 ............. | 1975 | £5 ........ £12 | ................ Dutch |
| Galaxy-Lin ............................................. | LP ...... | Polydor .......... | 2480259 ............. | 1974 | £5 ........ £12 | ................ German |

## GALBRAITH, BARRY

| | | | | | | |
|---|---|---|---|---|---|---|
| Guitar And The Wind ............................. | LP ...... | Brunswick ..... | LAT8273 ............. | 1959 | £6 ........ £15 | ............................ |

## GALE, EDDIE

| | | | | | | |
|---|---|---|---|---|---|---|
| Black Rhythm Happening ........................ | LP ...... | Blue Note ...... | BST84320 ............ | 1969 | £6 ........ £15 | |
| Ghetto Music .......................................... | LP ...... | Blue Note ...... | BST84294 ............ | 1968 | £6 ........ £15 | |

## GALE, SUNNY

| | | | | | | |
|---|---|---|---|---|---|---|
| C'Est La Vie ........................................... | 7" ...... | HMV .............. | 7M344 ............... | 1955 | £2 ........ £5 | |
| Certain Smile .......................................... | 7" ...... | Brunswick ..... | 05753 ............... | 1958 | £1.50 .... £4 | |
| Come Go With Me ................................... | 7" ...... | Brunswick ..... | 05661 ............... | 1957 | £1.50 .... £4 | |
| Goodnight, Well It's Time To Go ............ | 7" ...... | HMV .............. | 7M243 ............... | 1954 | £2.50 .... £6 | |
| Send My Baby Back To Me ..................... | 7" ...... | HMV .............. | 7M147 ............... | 1953 | £2.50 .... £6 | |
| Sunny And Blue ...................................... | LP ...... | RCA .............. | LPM1277 ............ | 1956 | £6 ........ £15 | ................ US |
| Two Hearts .............................................. | 7" ...... | Brunswick ..... | 05659 ............... | 1957 | £1.50 .... £4 | |

## GALL, FRANCE

| | | | | | | |
|---|---|---|---|---|---|---|
| 1968 ....................................................... | LP ...... | Philips .......... | 844706 ............... | 1968 | £15 ........ £30 | ................ Canadian |
| Et des baisers ......................................... | 7" EP . | Philips .......... | 437095 ............... | 1964 | £15 ........ £30 | ................ French |
| Poupée de lire ......................................... | LP ...... | Barclay .......... | 77728L ................ | 1965 | £10 ........ £25 | ................ French |

## GALLAGHER, RORY

Rory Gallagher's brand of tough blues-rock continues to have a significant following despite the fairly low profile that the man himself adopted at the end of his career. His earliest recordings with Taste scrape into the collectors' price bracket, but his seventies albums sold too well to be rare. They remain steady sellers, however, at around the £8 price level.

| | | | | | | |
|---|---|---|---|---|---|---|
| In The Beginning .................................... | LP ...... | Emerald .......... | GES1110 ............. | 1974 | £5 ........ £12 | ............................ |

## GALLAGHER & LYLE

| | | | | | | |
|---|---|---|---|---|---|---|
| Trees ....................................................... | 7" ...... | Polydor .......... | 56170 ............... | 1967 | £2 ........ £5 | ............................ |

## GALLAHADS

| | | | | | | |
|---|---|---|---|---|---|---|
| Ooh-Ah .................................................. | 7" ...... | Capitol .......... | CL14282 ............. | 1955 | £1.50 .... £4 | ............................ |

## GALLANTS

| | | | | | | |
|---|---|---|---|---|---|---|
| Man From UNCLE Theme ....................... | 7" ...... | Capitol .......... | CL15408 ............. | 1965 | £2.50 .... £6 | ............................ |

## GALLERY
Barley................................................................. LP...... ................. ..................... 197– £87.50.. £175 .................................

## GALLEY
Smiling Morn ................................................... LP...... ................. ..................... 197– £50....... £100 .................................

## GALLIARD
I Wrapped Her In Ribbons ...................... 7"...... Deram ............ DM306 ............... 1970 £1.50...... £4
New Dawn .............................................. LP...... Deram ............ SML1075 ............ 1970 £30........ £60
Strange Pleasures .................................. LP...... Nova ............. SDN4 ................. 1969 £8 .......... £20

## GALLION, BOB
Froggy Went A Courtin'............................. 7"...... MGM ............ MGM1057 ........... 1960 £2........... £5
You Take The Table ................................ 7"...... MGM ............ MGM1028 ........... 1959 £1.50...... £4

## GALLION, BOB & RAMSEY KEARNEY
Two Country Greats ................................ 7" EP . Hickory .......... LPE1508 ............ 1965 £2........... £5

## GALT, JAMES
Comes The Dawn ................................... 7"...... Pye .............. 7N15936 ............. 1965 £2........... £5
With My Baby ........................................ 7"...... Pye .............. 7N17021 ............. 1965 £10........ £20

## GAMBLERS
Cry Me A River........................................ 7"...... Parlophone...... R5557 ................ 1967 £6.......... £12
Dr. Goldfoot........................................... 7"...... Decca ............ F12399 .............. 1966 £5.......... £10
Nobody But Me........................................ 7"...... Decca ............ F11872............... 1964 £4............ £8
Now I'm All Alone .................................. 7"...... Decca ............ F12060............... 1965 £2.50...... £6
You've Really Got A Hold On Me............ 7"...... Decca ............ F11780............... 1963 £2.50...... £6

## GAMBRELL, FREDDIE
Freddie Gambrell..................................... LP...... Vogue ............ LAE12205 ........... 1960 £5.......... £12

## GAME
The inclusion of the Game's 'Addicted Man' on the programme caused a section of television's *Juke Box Jury* to be edited out, second thoughts deciding that it was not appropriate to publicize a song about drug taking. Parlophone was persuaded to withdraw the single, which is now understandably rare. All four of the group's Who–influenced singles, however, have become very collectable. Lead singer Tony Bird, who was only fifteen at the time of the 'Addicted Man' debacle, recorded as a solo artist for CBS in the late seventies – the resulting albums are listed under his name.

Addicted Man ......................................... 7"...... Parlophone...... R5553 ................ 1967 £250..... £400 ........... *best auctioned*
But I Do.................................................. 7"...... Pye .............. 7N15889 ............. 1965 £25........ £50
Gonna Get Me Someone .......................... 7"...... Decca ............ F12469 .............. 1966 £30........ £60
It's Shocking What They Call Me ............ 7"...... Parlophone...... R5569 ................ 1967 £75........ £150

## GAMMA
Alpha ..................................................... LP...... GA ................. ..................... 1973 £25........ £50 ................. *Dutch*
Darts ..................................................... LP...... GA ................. ..................... 1974 £10........ £25 ................. *Dutch*

## GAMMA GOOCHEE
Gamma Goochee ..................................... 7" EP . Colpix ............ 8007 .................. 1966 £4............ £8 ...... *French, B side by Nooney Rickett*

## GAMMER & HIS FAMILIARS
Rocket Ticket........................................... LP...... Gammer........... EJ9851 .............. 1981 £4............ £10
Will The New Baby ................................ 12".... Gammer........... GAMMER5 .......... 1984 £2.50...... £6
Won't Look Out...................................... LP...... Gammer........... EJ9699 .............. 1981 £4............ £10

## GANDALF
Gandalf................................................... LP...... Capitol............ ST121 ................ 1969 £37.50.... £75 ..................... US

## GANDALF THE GREY
Grey Wizard Am I..................................... LP...... Grey Wizard .. 7........................ 1972 £250.. £400 ..................... US
                                                               Records ..........

## GANDERTON, RON WARREN
Guitar Star ............................................. LP...... Celestial Sound LPRWG1............. 1973 £6.......... £15
Precious As England .............................. LP...... Celestial Sound LPRWG3............. 1981 £6.......... £15
Sound Ceremony ................................... LP...... Celestial Sound LPRWG2............. 1974 £6.......... £15

## GANIM'S ASIA MINORS
Daddy Lolo............................................. 7"...... London ........... HLE8637 ............ 1958 £1.50...... £4

## GANT, CECIL
Cecil Gant .............................................. LP...... King ............... 671 .................... 1960 £20........ £40 ..................... US
Incomparable Cecil Gant........................ LP...... Sound ............ 601 .................... 1957 £20........ £40 ..................... US
Rock Little Baby .................................... LP...... Flyright ........... LP4710 .............. 1974 £4............ £10

## GANT, DON
Early In The Morning................................ 7"...... Hickory .......... 451297 .............. 1965 £2.50...... £6

## GANTS
Gants Again ........................................... LP...... Liberty ............ LRP3473/LSP7473 . 1966 £6.......... £15 ..................... US
Gants Galore .......................................... LP...... Liberty ............ LRP3455/LSP7455. 1966 £6.......... £15 ..................... US
Greener Days ......................................... 7"...... Liberty ............ LIB55940 ........... 1967 £1.50...... £4
Road Runner .......................................... LP...... Liberty ............ LRP3432/LST7432. 1965 £8.......... £20 ..................... US
Road Runner .......................................... 7"...... Liberty ............ LIB55829 ........... 1965 £5.......... £10

## GARBAGE

When premier-league producer Butch Vig (Nirvana, the Smashing Pumpkins, Sonic Youth) decided to form his own group, it should have come as a surprise to no one that he managed to find some considerable extra mileage in the grunge formula. Some specially packaged items have helped to boost the group's collectability, but the strength of the music would have been enough in any case. Vocalist Shirley Manson was previously a member of Scottish group Goodbye Mr MacKenzie, though not the lead singer.

| | | | | | | | |
|---|---|---|---|---|---|---|---|
| Garbage | 7" | Mushroom | LX31450 | 1995 | £10 | £20 | ....album on boxed set of 6 singles |
| Only Happy When It Rains | 7" | Mushroom | SX1199 | 1995 | £2.50 | £6 | |
| Subhuman | CD-s | Mushroom | D1138 | 1995 | £5 | £12 | |
| Subhuman | 7" | Mushroom | S1138 | 1995 | £5 | £10 | |
| Subhuman | 7" | Mushroom | SX1138 | 1995 | £7.50 | £15 | ........rubber sleeve |
| Vow | 7" | Discordant | CORD001 | 1995 | £7.50 | £15 | |
| Vow | 7" | Discordant | CORD001 | 1995 | £25 | £50 | ........metal case |

## GARBAREK, JAN

| | | | | | | | |
|---|---|---|---|---|---|---|---|
| Afric Pepperbird | LP | ECM | ECM1007ST | 1971 | £8 | £20 | |
| Dansere | LP | ECM | ECM1075ST | 1976 | £4 | £10 | .... with Bobo Stenson |
| Dis | LP | ECM | ECM1093T | 1977 | £4 | £10 | |
| Esoteric Circle | LP | Freedom | 147300 | 1976 | £10 | £25 | ...German, with Terje Rypdal |
| Red Lanta | LP | ECM | ECM1038ST | 1974 | £5 | £12 | ........ with Art Lande |
| Sart | LP | ECM | ECM1015ST | 1972 | £5 | £12 | |
| Til Vigris | LP | NJF | LP1 | 1967 | £25 | £50 | ........Norwegian |
| Triptykon | LP | ECM | ECM1029ST | 1973 | £8 | £20 | |
| Walking Muza | LP | Polydor | XLP0342 | 1966 | £25 | £50 | ........Norwegian |
| Witchi-Tai-To | LP | ECM | ECM1041ST | 1974 | £5 | £12 | .... with Bobo Stenson |

## GARBUTT, VIN

| | | | | | | | |
|---|---|---|---|---|---|---|---|
| Valley Of Tees | LP | Trailer | LER2078 | 1972 | £5 | £12 | |
| Young Tin Whistle Pest | LP | Trailer | LER2081 | 1975 | £4 | £10 | |

## GARDEN ODYSSEY ENTERPRISE

| | | | | | | | |
|---|---|---|---|---|---|---|---|
| Sad And Lonely | 7" | Deram | DM267 | 1969 | £2.50 | £6 | |

## GARDINER, PAUL

The collectability of Paul Gardiner's promotional issue of 'Stormtrooper In Drag' derives from the identity of the lead singer on the track, who is Gardiner's friend, Gary Numan.

| | | | | | | | |
|---|---|---|---|---|---|---|---|
| Stormtrooper In Drag | 12" | Beggars Banquet | BEG61T | 1981 | £75 | £150 | ........promo |

## GARDNER, BORIS

| | | | | | | | |
|---|---|---|---|---|---|---|---|
| Elizabethan Reggae | 7" | Doctor Bird | DB1205 | 1969 | £2.50 | £6 | |
| Hooked On A Feeling | 7" | Treasure Isle | TI7056 | 1969 | £2.50 | £6 | |
| Lucky Is The Boy | 7" | High Note | HS010 | 1968 | £4 | £8 | |
| Never My Love | 7" | Duke | DU21 | 1969 | £1.50 | £4 | |
| Reggae Happening | LP | Trojan | TBL121 | 1970 | £4 | £10 | |

## GARDNER, DAVE

| | | | | | | | |
|---|---|---|---|---|---|---|---|
| All By Myself | 7" | Brunswick | 05740 | 1958 | £10 | £20 | |

## GARDNER, DON & DEE DEE FORD

| | | | | | | | |
|---|---|---|---|---|---|---|---|
| Don't You Worry | 7" | Soul City | SC101 | 1968 | £2 | £5 | |
| Don't You Worry | 7" | Stateside | SS130 | 1962 | £2.50 | £6 | |
| I Need Your Loving | 7" | Stateside | SS114 | 1962 | £2 | £5 | |
| In Sweden | LP | Sue | LP1044 | 1965 | £10 | £25 | US |
| Need Your Lovin' | LP | Fire | LP105 | 1962 | £25 | £50 | US |

## GARFIELD

| | | | | | | | |
|---|---|---|---|---|---|---|---|
| Out There Tonight | LP | Capricorn | CPO193 | 1977 | £5 | £12 | US |
| Strange Streets | LP | Mercury | SRM11082 | 1976 | £5 | £12 | US |

## GARFIELD, JOHNNY

| | | | | | | | |
|---|---|---|---|---|---|---|---|
| Stranger In Paradise | 7" | Pye | 7N15758 | 1965 | £5 | £10 | |

## GARLAND, JUDY

| | | | | | | | |
|---|---|---|---|---|---|---|---|
| Alone | LP | Capitol | LCT6136 | 1957 | £4 | £10 | |
| At The Grove | LP | Capitol | ST1118 | 1959 | £4 | £10 | ........stereo |
| Born In A Trunk | 7" EP | Philips | BBE12012 | 1955 | £2 | £5 | |
| Born To Sing | 10" LP | MGM | MGMD1334 | 1955 | £4 | £10 | |
| Couple Of Swells | 7" | MGM | SP1001 | 1953 | £1.50 | £4 | ...... with Fred Astaire |
| Garland For Judy | 7" EP | Capitol | EAP120051 | 1961 | £2 | £5 | |
| Judy | LP | Capitol | LCT6121 | 1957 | £4 | £10 | |
| Judy At Carnegie Hall Pt. 1 | 7" EP | Capitol | EAP71569 | 1961 | £2 | £5 | |
| Judy At Carnegie Hall Pt. 2 | 7" EP | Capitol | EAP81569 | 1961 | £2 | £5 | |
| Judy At The Palace | 10" LP | Brunswick | LA8725 | 1955 | £6 | £15 | |
| Judy In Love | LP | Capitol | ST1036 | 1959 | £4 | £10 | ........stereo |
| Judy In Love Pt. 1 | 7" EP | Capitol | EAP11036 | 1959 | £2 | £5 | |
| Judy In Love Pt. 2 | 7" EP | Capitol | EAP21036 | 1959 | £2 | £5 | |
| Judy In Love Pt. 3 | 7" EP | Capitol | EAP31036 | 1959 | £2 | £5 | |
| Letter | LP | Capitol | ST1188 | 1959 | £4 | £10 | ........stereo |
| Look For The Silver Lining | 7" | MGM | SP1157 | 1956 | £1.50 | £4 | |
| Miss Show Business | LP | Capitol | LCT6103 | 1956 | £4 | £10 | |
| Star Is Born | LP | Philips | BBL7007 | 1955 | £4 | £10 | |

## GARLAND, RED

| | | | | | | | |
|---|---|---|---|---|---|---|---|
| All Morning Long | LP | Esquire | 32099 | 1960 | £8 | £20 | *with John Coltrane &* |
| | | | | | | | *Donald Byrd* |
| At The Prelude | LP | Esquire | 32126 | 1961 | £5 | £12 | |
| Manteca | LP | Esquire | 32096 | 1960 | £6 | £15 | *.... with Ray Barreto* |
| Red In Bluesville | LP | Esquire | 32116 | 1961 | £6 | £15 | |

## GARNER, ERROLL

| | | | | | | | |
|---|---|---|---|---|---|---|---|
| Afternoon Of An Elf | LP | Mercury | MPL6539 | 1958 | £6 | £15 | |
| At The Piano | LP | Mercury | MPL6507 | 1957 | £6 | £15 | |
| At The Piano | LP | Philips | BBL7078 | 1956 | £6 | £15 | |
| Concert By The Sea | LP | Philips | BBL7106 | 1957 | £5 | £12 | |
| Errol | LP | Mercury | MMB12010 | 1959 | £5 | £12 | |
| Errol Garner Trio | LP | Vogue | LAE12209 | 1960 | £5 | £12 | |
| Errol Garner Trio Vol. 1 | 10" LP | Vogue | LDE034 | 1953 | £8 | £20 | |
| Erroll Garner | LP | London | LTZC15126 | 1958 | £5 | £12 | |
| Erroll Garner | 10" LP | Felsted | L87002 | 195– | £8 | £20 | |
| Garner Touch | LP | Philips | BBL7193 | 1957 | £5 | £12 | |
| Giant Jazz Gallery | LP | Philips | BBL7448 | 1961 | £4 | £10 | |
| Gone Garner Gonest | LP | Philips | BBL7034 | 1955 | £5 | £12 | |
| Gone With Garner | 10" LP | Oriole | MG26042 | 1955 | £8 | £20 | |
| Mambo Moves Garner | LP | Mercury | MPL6501 | 1956 | £8 | £20 | |
| Margie | 10" LP | Felsted | EDL87002 | 195– | £8 | £20 | |
| Most Happy Piano | LP | Philips | BBL7282 | 1958 | £5 | £12 | |
| Music Maestro Please | LP | Philips | BBL7426 | 1961 | £4 | £10 | |
| Other Voices | LP | Philips | BBL7204 | 1958 | £5 | £12 | |
| Paris Impressions Vol. 1 | LP | Philips | BBL7313 | 1959 | £4 | £10 | |
| Paris Impressions Vol. 2 | LP | Philips | BBL7314 | 1959 | £4 | £10 | |
| Passport To Fame | 10" LP | Felsted | EDL87015 | 1955 | £8 | £20 | |
| Penthouse Serenade | LP | London | LTZC15125 | 1958 | £5 | £12 | |
| Piano Gems | 10" LP | Columbia | 33S1059 | 1955 | £8 | £20 | |
| Piano Moods | 10" LP | Columbia | 33S1050 | 1955 | £8 | £20 | |
| Piano Wizardry | 7" EP | London | REU1066 | 1956 | £2 | £5 | |
| Plays For Dancing | 10" LP | Philips | BBR8002 | 1954 | £8 | £20 | |
| Soliloquy | LP | Philips | BBL7226 | 1958 | £5 | £12 | |
| Solo Flight | 10" LP | Philips | BBR8045 | 1955 | £8 | £20 | |
| Undecided | 7" EP | CBS | REP4006 | 196– | £2 | £5 | |

## GARNETT, COL

| | | | | | | | |
|---|---|---|---|---|---|---|---|
| With A Girl Like You | 7" | Page One | POF002 | 1966 | £2 | £5 | |

## GARNETT, GALE

| | | | | | | | |
|---|---|---|---|---|---|---|---|
| I'll Cry Alone | 7" | RCA | RCA1451 | 1965 | £1.50 | £4 | |

## GARON, JESSE & DESPERADOS

| | | | | | | | |
|---|---|---|---|---|---|---|---|
| Splashing Along | 7" | Narodnik | NRK001 | 1986 | £1.50 | £4 | |

## GARR, ARTIE

This was the name first used by Art Garfunkel.

| | | | | | | | |
|---|---|---|---|---|---|---|---|
| Dream Alone | 7" | Warwick | 515 | 1959 | £12.50 | £25 | US |
| Private World | 7" | Octavia | 8002 | 1960 | £10 | £20 | US |

## GARRETT, VERNON

| | | | | | | | |
|---|---|---|---|---|---|---|---|
| If I Could Turn Back The Hands Of Time | 7" | Stateside | SS2006 | 1967 | £5 | £10 | |
| Shine It On | 7" | Action | ACT4508 | 1968 | £1.50 | £4 | |
| Shine It On | 7" | Stateside | SS2026 | 1967 | £2.50 | £6 | |

## GARRICK, DAVID

| | | | | | | | |
|---|---|---|---|---|---|---|---|
| A Boy Called David | LP | Piccadilly | NPL38024 | 1967 | £4 | £10 | |
| David | 7" EP | Piccadilly | NEP34056 | 1966 | £15 | £30 | |
| Dear Mrs. Applebee | 7" EP | Pye | PNV24182 | 1966 | £5 | £10 | French |
| Don't Go Out Into The Rain Sugar | LP | Piccadilly | N(S)PL38035 | 1968 | £4 | £10 | |
| I've Found A Love | 7" EP | Pye | PNV24187 | 1967 | £5 | £10 | French |
| Lady Jane | 7" | Piccadilly | 7N35317 | 1966 | £1.50 | £4 | |

## GARRICK, MICHAEL

Garrick is a British jazz pianist who recorded prolifically for the Don Rendell-Ian Carr group and under his own name, but despite the considerable efforts of Argo records on his behalf – including frequent full-page adverts in relevant publications like *Jazz Journal* – his record sales were rather poor. His rare albums are actually well worth seeking out, as they are consistently inventive and thought-provoking. His albums integrating poetry with jazz broke new ground, while later extravaganzas like *Mr Smith's Apocalypse* transcend the jazz category altogether, emerging as more like particularly fine pieces of early-seventies progressive music.

| | | | | | | | |
|---|---|---|---|---|---|---|---|
| Anthem | LP | Argo | EAF/ZFA92 | 1965 | £30 | £60 | |
| Before Night/Day | LP | Argo | EAF115 | 1966 | £30 | £60 | |
| Black Marigolds | LP | Argo | (Z)DA88 | 1968 | £30 | £60 | |
| Case Of Jazz | LP | Airborne | | 1963 | £37.50 | £75 | |
| Cold Mountain | LP | Argo | ZDA153 | 1972 | £30 | £60 | |
| Epiphany | 7" | Argo | AFW105 | 1971 | £2 | £5 | |
| Heart Is A Lotus | LP | Argo | ZDA135 | 1970 | £25 | £50 | *with Norma Winstone* |
| Home Stretch Blues | LP | Argo | ZDA154 | 1972 | £30 | £60 | |
| Illumination | LP | Impulse | AS49 | 1973 | £10 | £25 | |
| Jazz Praises At St. Pauls | LP | Airborne | NBP0021 | 1968 | £30 | £60 | |
| Kronos | LP | Hep | 2013 | 1982 | £10 | £25 | |
| Michael Garrick Quartet | 7" EP | Argo | EAF92 | 1965 | £7.50 | £15 | |
| Moonscape | LP | Airborne | | 1964 | £37.50 | £75 | |

| | | | | | | |
|---|---|---|---|---|---|---|
| Mr. Smith's Apocalypse | LP | Argo | ZAGF1 | 1971 £30 | £60 | |
| October Woman | LP | Argo | (Z)DA33 | 1964 £30 | £60 | |
| Poetry And Jazz In Concert | LP | Argo | (Z)DA26/27 | 1964 £50 | £100 | ...double, with Adrian Mitchell |
| Poetry And Jazz In Concert 250 | LP | Argo | ZPR264/5 | 1969 £37.50 | £75 | double |
| Promises | LP | Argo | (Z)DA36 | 1965 £30 | £60 | |
| Troppo | LP | Argo | ZDA163 | 1974 £20 | £40 | |
| You've Changed | LP | Hep | 2011 | 1978 £10 | £25 | |

## GARRIE, NICK
| | | | | | | |
|---|---|---|---|---|---|---|
| Nightmare Of J.B.Stanislas | LP | A-Z | STECLP107 | 1970 £6 | £15 | French |

## GARRITY, FREDDIE
| | | | | | | |
|---|---|---|---|---|---|---|
| Little Red Donkey | 7" | Columbia | DB8348 | 1968 £1.50 | £4 | |
| Oliver In The Overworld | LP | Starline | SRS5019 | 1970 £4 | £10 | |

## GARSIDE, ROBIN & PAUL GOUGH
| | | | | | | |
|---|---|---|---|---|---|---|
| Sea Songs | LP | Northern Sound | NSR01 | 1977 £10 | £25 | |

## GARVIN, REX
| | | | | | | |
|---|---|---|---|---|---|---|
| I Gotta Go Now | 7" | Atlantic | 584097 | 1967 £2 | £5 | |
| Sock It To Them JB | 7" | Atlantic | 584028 | 1966 £2 | £5 | |

## GARY & STU
| | | | | | | |
|---|---|---|---|---|---|---|
| Harlan Fare | LP | Carnaby | 6302012 | 1971 £20 | £40 | |

## GARY & THE ARIELS
| | | | | | | |
|---|---|---|---|---|---|---|
| Say You Love Me | 7" | Fontana | TF476 | 1964 £1.50 | £4 | |

## GARYBALDI
| | | | | | | |
|---|---|---|---|---|---|---|
| Astrolabia | LP | Fonit | LPO09075 | 1973 £62.50 | £125 | Italian |
| Nuda | LP | CGD | FGL5113 | 1972 £37.50 | £75 | Italian |

## GAS WORKS
| | | | | | | |
|---|---|---|---|---|---|---|
| Gas Works | LP | Regal Zonophone | SLRZ1036 | 1973 £6 | £15 | |

## GASH
| | | | | | | |
|---|---|---|---|---|---|---|
| Young Man's Gash | LP | Brain | 1014 | 1972 £10 | £25 | German |

## GASKIN
| | | | | | | |
|---|---|---|---|---|---|---|
| End Of The World | LP | Rondelet | ABOUT4 | 1981 £6 | £15 | |
| I'm No Fool | 7" | Rondelet | ROUND7 | 1981 £2.50 | £6 | |
| Mony Mony | 7" | Rondelet | ROUND21 | 1982 £2.50 | £6 | |

## GASLIGHT CHOIR
| | | | | | | |
|---|---|---|---|---|---|---|
| Gaslight Choir | LP | private | | 1970 £100 | £200 | double |

## GASOLIN
| | | | | | | |
|---|---|---|---|---|---|---|
| Gasolin | LP | CBS | 80470 | 1974 £37.50 | £75 | German |

## GASS
| | | | | | | |
|---|---|---|---|---|---|---|
| Juju | LP | Polydor | 2383022 | 1970 £8 | £20 | |
| New Breed | 7" | Parlophone | R5456 | 1966 £7.50 | £15 | |
| One Of These Days | 7" | Parlophone | R5344 | 1965 £2.50 | £6 | |

## GASS COMPANY
| | | | | | | |
|---|---|---|---|---|---|---|
| Everybody Needs Love | 7" | President | PT170 | 1968 £5 | £10 | |

## GATES, DAVID
| | | | | | | |
|---|---|---|---|---|---|---|
| Happiest Man Alive | 7" | Top Rank | JAR504 | 1960 £4 | £8 | |

## GATES OF EDEN
| | | | | | | |
|---|---|---|---|---|---|---|
| In Your Love | 7" | Pye | 7N17252 | 1967 £2.50 | £6 | |
| Mini Shirts | 7" EP | Pye | PNV24181 | 1966 £10 | £20 | French |
| One To Seven | 7" | Pye | 7N17278 | 1967 £5 | £10 | |
| Too Much On My Mind | 7" | Pye | 7N17195 | 1966 £4 | £8 | |

## GATOR CREEK
| | | | | | | |
|---|---|---|---|---|---|---|
| Gator Creek | LP | Mercury | 6338035 | 1970 £4 | £10 | |

## GATORS
| | | | | | | |
|---|---|---|---|---|---|---|
| In Concert | LP | Bulletin | | 1967 £6 | £15 | US |

## GAUCHOS
| | | | | | | |
|---|---|---|---|---|---|---|
| Gauchos Featuring Jim Doval | LP | ABC | (S)506 | 1965 £6 | £15 | US |

## GAUGERS
| | | | | | | |
|---|---|---|---|---|---|---|
| Beware Of The Aberdonian | LP | Topic | 12TS284 | 1976 £6 | £15 | |

## GAUGHAN, DICK
| | | | | | | |
|---|---|---|---|---|---|---|
| Coppers And Brass | LP | Topic | 12TS315 | 1977 £4 | £10 | |
| Gaughan | LP | Topic | 12TS384 | 1978 £4 | £10 | |
| Handful Of Earth | CD | Topic | TSCD419 | 1989 £5 | £12 | |
| Kist O'Gold | LP | Trailer | LER2103 | 1977 £4 | £10 | |
| No More Forever | LP | Trailer | LER2072 | 1972 £5 | £12 | |

## GAUGHAN, DICK & ANDY IRVINE

| | | | | | | | |
|---|---|---|---|---|---|---|---|
| Parallel Lines | LP | Folk Freak | FF4007 | 1982 | £4 | £10 | German |

## GAVIN, FRANKIE & ALEC FINN

| | | | | | | | |
|---|---|---|---|---|---|---|---|
| Frankie Gavin And Alec Finn | LP | Shanachie | 29008 | 1977 | £4 | £10 | US |

## GAVIN, JIMMY

| | | | | | | |
|---|---|---|---|---|---|---|
| I Sit In My Window | 7" | London | HLU8478 | 1957 | £25 | £50 |

## GAYDEN, MAC

| | | | | | | |
|---|---|---|---|---|---|---|
| McGavock Gayden | LP | EMI | EMA760 | 1973 | £8 | £20 |

## GAYE, MARVIN

| | | | | | | | |
|---|---|---|---|---|---|---|---|
| Abraham, Martin And John | 7" | Tamla Motown | TMG734 | 1970 | £1.50 | £4 | |
| Ain't That Peculiar | 7" | Tamla Motown | TMG539 | 1965 | £4 | £8 | |
| Can I Get A Witness | 7" | Stateside | SS243 | 1963 | £12.50 | £25 | |
| Chained | 7" | Tamla Motown | TMG676 | 1968 | £2.50 | £6 | |
| Greatest Hits | LP | Tamla Motown | (S)TML11065 | 1968 | £4 | £10 | |
| Hello Broadway | LP | Tamla Motown | TML11015 | 1965 | £25 | £50 | |
| How Sweet It Is | LP | Tamla Motown | TML11004 | 1965 | £15 | £30 | |
| How Sweet It Is | 7" | Stateside | SS360 | 1964 | £10 | £20 | |
| I Heard It Through The Grapevine | 7" | Tamla Motown | TMG686 | 1969 | £1.50 | £4 | |
| I'll Be Doggone | 7" | Tamla Motown | TMG510 | 1965 | £12.50 | £25 | |
| In The Groove | LP | Tamla Motown | (S)TML11091 | 1969 | £8 | £20 | |
| Let's Get It On | 7" | Tamla Motown | TMG868 | 1973 | £6 | £12 | demo, picture sleeve |
| Little Darling | 7" | Tamla Motown | TMG574 | 1966 | £5 | £10 | |
| Marvin Gaye | LP | Stateside | SL10100 | 1964 | £30 | £60 | |
| Marvin Gaye | 7" EP | Tamla Motown | TME2016 | 1966 | £10 | £20 | |
| Marvin Gaye & His Girls | LP | Tamla Motown | (S)TML11123 | 1969 | £4 | £10 | |
| Moods Of Marvin Gaye | LP | Tamla Motown | (S)TML11033 | 1966 | £15 | £30 | |
| MPG | LP | Tamla Motown | (S)TML11119 | 1969 | £6 | £15 | |
| On Stage Recorded Live | LP | Tamla | 242 | 1963 | £25 | £50 | US |
| One More Heartache | 7" | Tamla Motown | TMG552 | 1966 | £5 | £10 | |
| Originals From Marvin Gaye | 7" EP | Tamla Motown | TME2019 | 1967 | £10 | £20 | |
| Pretty Little Baby | 7" | Tamla Motown | TMG524 | 1965 | £7.50 | £15 | |
| Pride And Joy | 7" | Oriole | CBA1846 | 1963 | £25 | £50 | |
| Soulful Moods Of Marvin Gaye | LP | Tamla | 221 | 1961 | £50 | £100 | US |
| Stubborn Kind Of Fellow | 7" | Oriole | CBA1803 | 1963 | £25 | £50 | |
| Take This Heart Of Mine | 7" | Tamla Motown | TMG563 | 1966 | £5 | £10 | |
| That Stubborn Kind Of Fella | 7" | Tamla | 239 | 1963 | £37.50 | £75 | US |
| That's The Way Love Is | LP | Tamla Motown | (S)TML11136 | 1970 | £6 | £15 | |
| That's The Way Love Is | 7" | Tamla Motown | TMG718 | 1969 | £1.50 | £4 | |
| Too Busy Thinking About My Baby | 7" | Tamla Motown | TMG705 | 1969 | £1.50 | £4 | |
| Tribute To The Great Nat King Cole | LP | Tamla Motown | STML11022 | 1966 | £30 | £60 | stereo |
| Tribute To The Great Nat King Cole | LP | Tamla Motown | TML11022 | 1966 | £25 | £50 | mono |
| Try It Baby | 7" | Stateside | SS326 | 1964 | £10 | £20 | |
| What's Going On | LP | Tamla Motown | STML11190 | 1971 | £4 | £10 | |
| What's Going On | CD | Motown | C8818 | 1988 | £6 | £15 | HMV box set |
| When I'm Alone I Cry | LP | Tamla | 251 | 1964 | £20 | £40 | US |
| You | 7" | Tamla Motown | TMG640 | 1968 | £2.50 | £6 | |
| You're A Wonderful One | 7" | Stateside | SS284 | 1964 | £10 | £20 | |
| Your Unchanged Love | 7" | Tamla Motown | TMG618 | 1967 | £2.50 | £6 | |

## GAYE, MARVIN & KIM WESTON

| | | | | | | |
|---|---|---|---|---|---|---|
| It Takes Two | 7" | Tamla Motown | TMG590 | 1967 | £2 | £5 |
| Take Two | LP | Tamla Motown | (S)TML11049 | 1967 | £6 | £15 |
| What Good Am I Without You | 7" | Stateside | SS363 | 1964 | £10 | £20 |

## GAYE, MARVIN & MARY WELLS

| | | | | | | |
|---|---|---|---|---|---|---|
| Once Upon A Time | 7" | Stateside | SS316 | 1964 | £7.50 | £15 |
| Together | LP | Stateside | SL10097 | 1964 | £30 | £60 |

## GAYE, MARVIN & TAMMI TERRELL

| | | | | | | |
|---|---|---|---|---|---|---|
| Ain't No Mountain High Enough | 7" | Tamla Motown | TMG611 | 1967 | £2 | £5 |
| Ain't Nothing Like The Real Thing | 7" | Tamla Motown | TMG655 | 1968 | £1.50 | £4 |
| Easy | LP | Tamla Motown | (S)TML11132 | 1970 | £4 | £10 |
| Good Lovin' Ain't Easy To Come By | 7" | Tamla Motown | TMG697 | 1969 | £1.50 | £4 |
| Greatest Hits | LP | Tamla Motown | (S)TML11153 | 1970 | £4 | £10 |
| If I Could Build My Whole World Around You | 7" | Tamla Motown | TMG635 | 1967 | £1.50 | £4 |
| Onion Song | 7" | Tamla Motown | TMG715 | 1969 | £1.50 | £4 |
| United | LP | Tamla Motown | (S)TML11062 | 1968 | £6 | £15 |
| You Ain't Livin' Till You're Lovin' | 7" | Tamla Motown | TMG681 | 1969 | £1.50 | £4 |
| You're All I Need To Get By | LP | Tamla Motown | (S)TML11084 | 1968 | £5 | £12 |
| You're All I Need To Get By | 7" | Tamla Motown | TMG668 | 1968 | £1.50 | £4 |
| Your Precious Love | 7" | Tamla Motown | TMG625 | 1967 | £2 | £5 |

## GAYLADS

| | | | | | | | |
|---|---|---|---|---|---|---|---|
| Go Away | 7" | Blue Cat | BS110 | 1968 | £4 | £8 | Soul Vendors B side |
| Goodbye Daddy | 7" | Island | WI281 | 1966 | £5 | £10 | |
| I'm Free | 7" | Studio One | SO2038 | 1968 | £6 | £12 | Soul Vendors B side |
| It's Hard To Confess | 7" | Doctor Bird | DB1124 | 1968 | £5 | £10 | |
| Lady With The Red Dress On | 7" | Doctor Bird | DB1014 | 1966 | £5 | £10 | |
| Looking For A Girl | 7" | Fab | FAB62 | 1968 | £4 | £8 | |
| Love Me With All Your Heart | 7" | Studio One | SO2017 | 1967 | £6 | £12 | |
| No Good Girl | 7" | Island | WI3025 | 1967 | £5 | £10 | |
| Put On Your Style | 7" | Rio | R125 | 1967 | £4 | £8 | Soul Brothers B side |

| | | | | | | |
|---|---|---|---|---|---|---|
| Rock Steady | LP | Coxsone | CSL8005 | 1967 | £50 | £100 | |
| Same Things | 7" | Upsetter | US323 | 1969 | £1.50 | £4 |
| She Want It | 7" | Doctor Bird | DB1145 | 1968 | £5 | £10 |
| Stop Making Love | 7" | Island | WI3002 | 1966 | £5 | £10 |
| Sunshine Golden 18 | LP | Coxsone | CSL8006 | 1967 | £30 | £60 |
| Tears From My Eyes | 7" | Studio One | SO2002 | 1967 | £6 | £12 |
| There'll Come A Day | 7" | R&B | JB159 | 1964 | £5 | £10 | *Billy Cooke B side* |
| Whap Whap | 7" | R&B | JB165 | 1964 | £5 | £10 |
| You Had Your Chance | 7" | Trojan | TR688 | 1969 | £1.50 | £4 |
| You Should Never Do That | 7" | Doctor Bird | DB1031 | 1966 | £5 | £10 | *Winston Stewart* |
| | | | | | | | *B side* |
| You'll Never Leave Him | 7" | Island | WI291 | 1966 | £5 | £10 |

### GAYLETTS

| | | | | | | |
|---|---|---|---|---|---|---|
| I Like Your World | 7" | Island | WI3141 | 1968 | £5 | £10 |
| If You Can't Be Good | 7" | Big Shot | BI502 | 1968 | £2 | £5 |
| Silent River Runs Deep | 7" | Island | WI3129 | 1968 | £5 | £10 |
| Son Of A Preacher Man | 7" | Big Shot | BI516 | 1969 | £1.50 | £4 |
| Son Of A Preacher Man | 7" | London | HLJ10302 | 1970 | £1.50 | £4 |

### GAYLORDS

| | | | | | | |
|---|---|---|---|---|---|---|
| He's A Good Face | 7" | Columbia | DB7805 | 1966 | £5 | £10 |

### GAYLORDS (2)

| | | | | | | |
|---|---|---|---|---|---|---|
| Chipmunk Ska | 7" | Island | WI269 | 1966 | £5 | £10 |

### GAYNAIR, WILTON

| | | | | | | |
|---|---|---|---|---|---|---|
| Blue Bogey | LP | Tempo | TAP25 | 1960 | £20 | £40 |

### GAYNOR, ROSEMARY

| | | | | | | |
|---|---|---|---|---|---|---|
| Ain't That A Shame | 7" | Columbia | SCM5196 | 1955 | £1.50 | £4 |

### GAYTEN, PAUL

| | | | | | | |
|---|---|---|---|---|---|---|
| Hunch | 7" | London | HLM8998 | 1959 | £37.50 | £75 |

### G-CLEFS

| | | | | | | |
|---|---|---|---|---|---|---|
| Girl Has To Know | 7" | London | HLU9530 | 1962 | £4 | £8 |
| I Understand | 7" | London | HLU9433 | 1961 | £1.50 | £4 |
| Ka Ding Dong | 7" | Columbia | DB3851 | 1956 | £180 | £300 | *best auctioned* |
| Make Up Your Mind | 7" | London | HLU9563 | 1962 | £4 | £8 |
| Ronnie | 7" | Oriole | CB1456 | 1958 | £2 | £5 |

### GEDDES AXE

| | | | | | | |
|---|---|---|---|---|---|---|
| Return Of The Gods | 7" | ACS | ACS1 | 1981 | £4 | £8 |
| Sharpen Your Wits | 7" | Steel City | AXE1 | 1982 | £2 | £5 |

### GEE, MATTHEW

| | | | | | | |
|---|---|---|---|---|---|---|
| Jazz By Gee | LP | London | LTZU15075 | 1957 | £10 | £25 |

### GEESIN, RON

| | | | | | | |
|---|---|---|---|---|---|---|
| As He Stands | LP | Ron | RON28 | 1973 | £5 | £12 |
| Atmospheres | LP | KPM | KPM1201 | 1977 | £5 | £12 |
| Electrosound | LP | KPM | KPM1102 | 1972 | £5 | £12 |
| Electrosound (Volume 2) | LP | KPM | KPM1154 | 1975 | £5 | £12 |
| Mr. Mayor Stamp Your Foot | 7" EP | private | RRG319/320 | 1965 | £20 | £40 |
| Patruns | LP | Ron | RON31 | 1975 | £5 | £12 |
| Raise Of The Eyebrows | LP | Transatlantic | TRA161 | 1967 | £8 | £20 |
| Right Through | LP | Ron | RON323 | 1977 | £5 | £12 |

### GEESIN, RON & ROGER WATERS

| | | | | | | |
|---|---|---|---|---|---|---|
| Body | LP | Harvest | SHSP4008 | 1970 | £4 | £10 |

### GEISLER, LADI

| | | | | | | |
|---|---|---|---|---|---|---|
| Alte Kameraden Beaten Zum Tanz | LP | Ariola | 72643 | 1965 | £20 | £40 | *German* |
| Gitarrenmethode | LP | Polydor | 004525 | 1965 | £8 | £20 | *German, with booklet* |
| Guitar A La Carte | LP | Polydor | 249292 | 1967 | £5 | £12 | *German* |
| Happy Guitar | LP | Ariola | 72157IU | 1964 | £6 | £15 | *German* |
| Mister Guitar | LP | Polydor | 237117 | 1962 | £15 | £30 | *German, stereo* |
| Mister Guitar | LP | Polydor | 46617 | 1962 | £6 | £15 | *German, mono* |

### GELLER, HERB

| | | | | | | |
|---|---|---|---|---|---|---|
| Fire In The West | LP | Stateside | (S)SL10249 | 1963 | £4 | £10 |
| Herb Geller | LP | Emarcy | EJL1268 | 1958 | £8 | £20 |

### GEMINI

| | | | | | | |
|---|---|---|---|---|---|---|
| Space Walk | 7" | Columbia | DB7638 | 1965 | £7.50 | £15 |

### GENE

| | | | | | | |
|---|---|---|---|---|---|---|
| Be My Light, Be My Guide | CD-s | Costermonger | COST2CD | 1994 | £5 | £12 |
| Be My Light, Be My Guide | 7" | Costermonger | COST2 | 1994 | £7.50 | £15 |
| For The Dead | CD-s | Costermonger | COST1CD | 1994 | £20 | £40 |
| For The Dead | 7" | Costermonger | COST1 | 1994 | £25 | £50 |
| Sleep Well Tonight | CD-s | Costermonger | COST3CD | 1994 | £3 | £8 |
| Sleep Well Tonight | 7" | Costermonger | COST3 | 1994 | £4 | £8 |

### GENE & DEBBE

| | | | | | | |
|---|---|---|---|---|---|---|
| Go With Me | 7" | London | HLE10165 | 1967 | £1.50 | £4 |
| Lovin' Season | 7" | London | HLE10203 | 1968 | £1.50 | £4 |

339

| | | | | | | | |
|---|---|---|---|---|---|---|---|
| Playboy | 7" | London | HLE10179 | 1968 | £2 | £5 | |

## GENE & EUNICE

| | | | | | | | |
|---|---|---|---|---|---|---|---|
| Bom Bom Lulu | 7" | Vogue | V9136 | 1959 | £12.50 | £25 | |
| Doodle Doodle Do | 7" | Vogue | V9083 | 1957 | £37.50 | £75 | |
| I Gotta Go Home | 7" | Vogue | V9062 | 1956 | £50 | £100 | |
| I Mean Love | 7" | Vogue | V9106 | 1958 | £37.50 | £75 | |
| Let's Get Together | 7" | Vogue | V9071 | 1957 | £37.50 | £75 | |
| Poco Loco | 7" | London | HL8956 | 1959 | £12.50 | £25 | |
| This Is My Story | 7" | Vogue | V9066 | 1957 | £50 | £100 | |
| Vow | 7" | Vogue | V9126 | 1958 | £15 | £30 | |

## GENE LOVES JEZEBEL

| | | | | | | | |
|---|---|---|---|---|---|---|---|
| Bruises | 12" | Situation 2 | SIT24T | 1983 | £2.50 | £6 | |
| Cow | 12" | Situation 2 | SIT36T | 1985 | £2.50 | £6 | with poster |
| Gorgeous | CD-s | Beggars Banquet | BEG202CD | 1987 | £2 | £5 | |
| Screaming | 12" | Situation 2 | SIT20T | 1982 | £2.50 | £6 | |
| Shaving My Neck | 12" | Situation 2 | SIT18T | 1982 | £10 | £20 | |
| Sweetest Thing | 7" | Beggars Banquet | BEG156 | 1986 | £2 | £5 | with cassette (161F) |

## GENERAL HUMBERT

| | | | | | | | |
|---|---|---|---|---|---|---|---|
| General Humbert | LP | Dolphin | DOLM5015 | 1976 | £8 | £20 | Irish |
| General Humbert II | LP | Gael Linn | CEF095 | 1982 | £4 | £10 | Irish |

## GENERATION X

| | | | | | | | |
|---|---|---|---|---|---|---|---|
| Wild Youth | 7" | Chrysalis | CHS2189 | 1977 | £6 | £12 | mispressed B-side, plays 'No No No' |

## GENESIS

Genesis's first LP was produced by Jonathan King – an unlikely choice for a determinedly progressive group, except that King and Genesis were all ex-pupils of Charterhouse. The record has been reissued several times – the first being as early as 1973 – but the original *From Genesis To Revelation* is quite scarce. Even more so are the early singles, of which 'Happy The Man', 'I Know What I Like' and 'The Carpet Crawlers' all have non-album B sides. The albums *Trespass* and *Nursery Cryme* remained in the catalogue for years, of course, but their inclusion here refers to the original pressings with their deep pink Charisma labels.

| | | | | | | | |
|---|---|---|---|---|---|---|---|
| 3 X 3 | 7" EP | Charisma | GEN1 | 1982 | £2 | £5 | picture disc |
| Carpet Crawlers | 7" | Charisma | CB251 | 1975 | £7.50 | £15 | |
| Counting Out Time | 7" | Charisma | CB238 | 1974 | £4 | £8 | |
| Firth Of Fifth | 7" | Genesis Information | GI01 | 1983 | £2 | £5 | flexi |
| Foxtrot/Selling England By The Pound | LP | Charisma | CGS103 | 1975 | £37.50 | £75 | boxed, poster |
| From Genesis To Revelation | LP | Decca | LK4990 | 1969 | £75 | £150 | mono |
| From Genesis To Revelation | LP | Decca | SKL4990 | 1969 | £15 | £30 | stereo |
| Happy The Man | 7" | Charisma | CB181 | 1972 | £25 | £50 | |
| Happy The Man | 7" | Charisma | CB181 | 1972 | £100 | £200 | picture sleeve |
| Hold On My Heart | CD-s | Virgin | GENDG8 | 1992 | £2 | £5 | with 4 cards |
| I Know What I Like | 7" | Charisma | CB224 | 1974 | £2 | £5 | |
| Illegal Alien | 7" | Charisma | ALS1 | 1984 | £2 | £5 | shaped picture disc |
| In The Beginning | LP | Decca | SKL4990 | 1974 | £6 | £15 | |
| Invisible Touch | CD | Virgin | GENPCD2 | 1986 | £5 | £12 | picture disc |
| Invisible Touch (Live) | CD-s | Virgin | GENDX10 | 1992 | £2 | £5 | boxed |
| Knife | 7" | Charisma | CB152 | 1971 | £25 | £50 | |
| Knife | 7" | Charisma | CB152 | 1971 | £100 | £200 | picture sleeve |
| Land Of Confusion | CD-s | Virgin | SNEG312 | 1986 | £2 | £5 | |
| Looking For Someone | 7" | Charisma | GS1 | 1970 | £150 | £250 | |
| Mama | CD-s | Virgin | CDT5 | 1988 | £2 | £5 | 3" single |
| Man On The Corner | 7" | Charisma | CB393 | 1982 | £2.50 | £6 | picture sleeve |
| Nursery Cryme | LP | Charisma | CAS1052 | 1971 | £6 | £15 | dark pink label |
| Nursery Cryme | LP | Charisma | CAS1052 | 1972 | £15 | £30 | with tour label |
| Paperlate | 7" | Charisma | JBGEN1 | 1982 | £1.50 | £4 | juke box issue |
| Silent Sun | 7" | Decca | F12735 | 1968 | £50 | £100 | |
| Spot The Pigeon EP | CD-s | Virgin | CDT40 | 1988 | £2 | £5 | 3" single |
| That's All | 7" | Charisma/ Virgin | TATA1 | 1983 | £2 | £5 | picture disc |
| Tonight Tonight Tonight | CD-s | Virgin | CDEP1 | 1987 | £15 | £30 | with Invisible Touch |
| Tonight Tonight Tonight | CD-s | Virgin | DRAW412 | 1987 | £2 | £5 | |
| Trespass | LP | Charisma | CAS1020 | 1970 | £6 | £15 | dark pink label |
| Trespass/Nursery Cryme | LP | Charisma | CGS102 | 1975 | £37.50 | £75 | boxed, poster |
| Trick Of The Tail | LP | Mobile Fidelity | MFSL1062 | 1981 | £8 | £20 | US audiophile |
| Trick Of The Tail | 7" | Charisma | CB277 | 1976 | £1.50 | £4 | juke box issue, purple label |
| Twilight Alehouse | 7" | Charisma | no number | 1975 | £7.50 | £15 | flexi |
| We Can't Dance | CD | Virgin | DJGCD1 | 1991 | £20 | £40 | promo box set, with cassette and prints |
| We Can't Dance | CD | Virgin | DJGCD1 | 1991 | £6 | £15 | promo with card cover |
| When The Sour Turns To Sweet | LP | Metal Masters | MACHMP4 | 1986 | £4 | £10 | |
| Where The Sour Turns To Sweet | 7" | Decca | F12949 | 1969 | £50 | £100 | picture disc |
| Winter's Tale | 7" | Decca | F12775 | 1968 | £50 | £100 | |

## GENESIS (2)

| | | | | | | | |
|---|---|---|---|---|---|---|---|
| In The Beginning | LP | Mercury | SR61175 | 1968 | £8 | £20 | US |

## GENGHIS KHAN

| | | | | | | | |
|---|---|---|---|---|---|---|---|
| Love You | 7" | Wabbit | WAB61/63 | 1983 | £2.50 | £6 | double |

## GENTILES
Goodbye Baby ........................................ 7" ...... Pye ................ 7N17530 ............... 1968 £2 ............ £5 ....................................

## GENTLE, JOHNNY
Gentle Touch ........................................ 7" EP . Philips ............. BBE12345 ............. 1959 £12.50 .... £25 ...............................

## GENTLE, TIM & THE GENTLEMEN
Without You ......................................... 7" ...... Oriole ............ CB1988 ................. 1965 £4 ............ £8 ....................................

## GENTLE GIANT
Gentle Giant's intricately constructed and faultlessly performed music seems to epitomize what the Vertigo label was all about. The album *Octopus*, in particular, stands as something of a landmark within the progressive rock genre. One can hear the band, on successive albums, learning how to create music that requires a high degree of skill for its execution and an even higher degree of inventiveness for its original creation. At the same time, the music is perfectly accessible, if a little hard to dance to! Gentle Giant's ancestor, by the way, was Simon Dupree and the Big Sound, both groups revolving around the Shulman brothers, although they have little in common musically.

Acquiring The Taste ............................. LP ...... Vertigo .......... 6360041 ........... 1971 £6 ............ £15 ............... *spiral label*
Gentle Giant ......................................... LP ...... Vertigo .......... 6360020 ........... 1970 £6 ............ £15 ............... *spiral label*
In A Glass House .................................. LP ...... WWA ......... WWA002 ............ 1973 £8 ............ £20 ..........................
Octopus ................................................ LP ...... Vertigo .......... 6360080 ........... 1972 £6 ............ £15 ............... *spiral label*
Power And The Glory ........................... LP ...... WWA ......... WWA010 ............ 1974 £5 ............ £12 ..........................
Three Friends ....................................... LP ...... Vertigo .......... 6360070 ........... 1972 £6 ............ £15 ............... *spiral label*

## GENTLE INFLUENCE
Always Be A Part Of My Living ............... 7" ...... Pye ............. 7N17743 ......... 1969 £2 ............ £5 ..........................
Never Trust In Tomorrow ..................... 7" ...... Pye ............. 7N17666 ......... 1969 £2 ............ £5 ..........................

## GENTLE PEOPLE
It's Too Late ........................................ 7" ...... Columbia ....... DB8276 ............. 1967 £2 ............ £5 ..........................

## GENTLE REIGN
Gentle Reign ......................................... LP ...... Vanguard ....... ..................... 1968 £5 ............ £12 ................... *US*

## GENTRY, BOBBIE
Ode To Billy Joe ................................... 7" ...... Capitol .......... CL15511 ............. 1967 £1.50 ....... £4 ..........................

## GENTRYS
Brown Paper Sack ................................. 7" ...... MGM ............ MGM1296 ......... 1966 £5 ............ £10 ..........................
Everyday I Have To Cry ......................... 7" ...... MGM ............ MGM1312 ......... 1966 £1.50 ..... £4 ..........................
Gentrys ................................................ LP ...... MGM ............ GAS127 ............. 1966 £8 ............ £20 ................... *US*
Gentrys ................................................ LP ...... Sun .............. 117 ................... 1970 £5 ............ £12 ................... *US*
Keep On Dancing .................................. LP ...... MGM ............ (S)E4336 ........... 1965 £8 ............ £20 ................... *US*
Keep On Dancing .................................. 7" EP . MGM ............ 63628 ............... 1965 £7.50 ..... £15 ............... *French*
Keep On Dancing .................................. 7" ...... MGM ............ MGM1284 ......... 1965 £1.50 ..... £4 ..........................
Time .................................................... LP ...... MGM ............ (S)E4346 ........... 1966 £8 ............ £20 ................... *US*

## GENTS
Faker ................................................... 7" ...... Posh ............. POSH001 ............ 1981 £1.50 ....... £4 ..........................

## GEORDIE
Don't Be Fooled By The Name ............... LP ...... EMI ............. EMA764 ............. 1974 £4 ............ £10 ..........................
Save The World .................................... LP ...... EMI ............. EMC3134 ............ 1976 £6 ............ £15 ..........................

## GEORGE, BARBARA
I Know .................................................. 7" ...... London ......... HL9513 ............. 1962 £4 ............ £8 ..........................
I Know You Don't Love Me Anymore ...... LP ...... A.F.O. ........... 5001 ................... 1962 £30 ........... £60 ................... *US*
Send For Me ......................................... 7" ...... Sue ............... WI316 ............... 1964 £6 ............ £12 ..........................

## GEORGE, LLOYD
Sing Real Loud ..................................... 7" ...... London ......... HLP9562 ........... 1962 £10 ........... £20 ..........................

## GEORGE, RENE
Messengers Of Autumn .......................... LP ...... RCS ............. ..................... 1981 £20 ........... £40 ................... *Dutch*

## GEORGE & BEN
Boa Constrictions Natural Vine ............... LP ...... Vanguard ....... ..................... 1968 £5 ............ £12 ..........................

## GEORGE & CAROLE
At Pythingdean ..................................... LP ...... Decca ............ LK4999 ............. 1969 £8 ............ £20 ..........................

## GEORGETTES
Down By The River ............................... 7" ...... Pye ............. 7N25058 ............. 1960 £2 ............ £5 ..........................
Love Like A Fool .................................. 7" ...... London ......... HL8548 ............. 1958 £12.50 .... £25 ..........................

## GEORGIA TOM
Georgia Tom And Friends ...................... LP ...... Riverside ....... RLP8803 ............ 1967 £6 ............ £15 ..........................

## GEORGIE & THE MONARCHS
The rare single by Georgie and the Monarchs features the recording debut of Van Morrison, who played saxophone for the band.

Boo-Zooh ............................................. 7" ...... CBS ............. 1307 ................... 1963 £15 ........... £30 *picture sleeve, German or Dutch*

## GERMAN BLUE FLAMES
German Blue Flames .............................. LP ...... Ariola ............ 72256IT .............. 1965 £50 ........ £100 ................... *German*

## GERMAN OAK
| | | | | | | | |
|---|---|---|---|---|---|---|---|
| German Oak | LP | Bunker | BU172 | 1972 | £20 | £40 | German |

## GERMS
| | | | | | | | |
|---|---|---|---|---|---|---|---|
| Forming | 7" | What | WHAT01 | 1977 | £5 | £10 | |

## GERONIMO BLACK
| | | | | | | | |
|---|---|---|---|---|---|---|---|
| Geronimo Black | LP | MCA | MCF2683 | 1974 | £4 | £10 | |

## GERRARD, DENNY
| | | | | | | | |
|---|---|---|---|---|---|---|---|
| Sinister Morning | LP | Nova | SDN10 | 1970 | £15 | £30 | with 'High Tide' |

## GERRY & THE HOLOGRAMS

Here is a record to file next to the Stiff album *The Wit And Wisdom Of Ronald Reagan*, an LP that is completely silent. It is impossible to tell what, if anything, is recorded on the single by Gerry and the Holograms. For the record is painted and glued into its sleeve, rendering it completely unplayable. As concepts go, this one has a kind of anarchic brilliance about it!

| | | | | | | | |
|---|---|---|---|---|---|---|---|
| Emperor's New Music | 7" | Absurd | A5 | 1979 | £2.50 | £6 | unplayable record |

## GERRY & THE PACEMAKERS
| | | | | | | | |
|---|---|---|---|---|---|---|---|
| Don't Let The Sun Catch You Crying | LP | Laurie | LLP/SLP2024 | 1964 | £8 | £20 | US |
| Don't Let The Sun Catch You Crying | 7" EP | Columbia | ESRF1549 | 1964 | £7.50 | £15 | French |
| Don't Let The Sun Catch You Crying | 7" EP | Columbia | SEG8346 | 1964 | £5 | £10 | |
| Ferry Cross The Mersey | LP | Columbia | 33SX1693/ SCX3544 | 1965 | £8 | £20 | |
| Ferry Cross The Mersey | 7" EP | Columbia | ESRF1637 | 1964 | £7.50 | £15 | French |
| Gerry In California | 7" EP | Columbia | SEG8388 | 1965 | £7.50 | £15 | |
| Girl On A Swing | LP | Laurie | LLP/SLP2037 | 1965 | £8 | £20 | US |
| Girl On The Swing | 7" | Columbia | DB8044 | 1966 | £1.50 | £4 | |
| Greatest Hits | LP | Laurie | LLP/SLP2031 | 1965 | £6 | £15 | US |
| Hits From Ferry Cross The Mersey | 7" EP | Columbia | SEG8397 | 1965 | £7.50 | £15 | |
| How Do You Do It | 7" EP | Columbia | ESDF1490 | 1963 | £7.50 | £15 | French |
| How Do You Do It | 7" EP | Columbia | SEG8257 | 1963 | £5 | £10 | |
| How Do You Like It | LP | Columbia | 33SX1546 | 1963 | £6 | £15 | mono |
| How Do You Like It | LP | Columbia | SCX3492 | 1963 | £10 | £25 | stereo |
| I'll Be There | LP | Laurie | LLP/SLP2030 | 1964 | £8 | £20 | US |
| I'm The One | 7" EP | Columbia | SEG8311 | 1964 | £5 | £10 | |
| It's Gonna Be Alright | 7" EP | Columbia | SEG8367 | 1964 | £6 | £12 | |
| Rip It Up | 7" EP | Columbia | SEG8426 | 1965 | £10 | £20 | |
| Second Album | LP | Laurie | LLP/SLP2027 | 1964 | £8 | £20 | US |
| You'll Never Walk Alone | LP | Regal | SREG1070 | 1967 | £8 | £20 | export |
| You'll Never Walk Alone | 7" EP | Columbia | ESRF1446 | 1963 | £7.50 | £15 | French |
| You'll Never Walk Alone | 7" EP | Columbia | SEG8295 | 1963 | £5 | £10 | |

## GERVASE
| | | | | | | | |
|---|---|---|---|---|---|---|---|
| Pepper Grinder | 7" | Decca | F12822 | 1968 | £2.50 | £6 | |

## GESTURES
| | | | | | | | |
|---|---|---|---|---|---|---|---|
| Run Run Run | 7" | Stateside | SS379 | 1965 | £5 | £10 | |

## GETZ, STAN
| | | | | | | | |
|---|---|---|---|---|---|---|---|
| At Storyville | 10" LP | Vogue | LDE089 | 1954 | £20 | £40 | |
| At Storyville Vol. 1 | LP | Vogue | LAE12158 | 1959 | £8 | £20 | |
| At Storyville Vol. 2 | LP | Vogue | LAE12199 | 1959 | £8 | £20 | |
| At The Opera House | LP | Columbia | 33CX10127 | 1958 | £8 | £20 | with J. J. Johnson |
| At The Shrine No. 1 | LP | Columbia | 33CX10000 | 1955 | £15 | £30 | |
| At The Shrine No. 2 | LP | Columbia | 33CX10001 | 1955 | £15 | £30 | |
| Big Band Bossa Nova | LP | Verve | VLP9024 | 1963 | £4 | £10 | with Gary McFarland |
| Captain Marvel | LP | Verve | 2304225 | 1975 | £5 | £12 | with Chick Corea |
| Didn't We | LP | Verve | SVLP9081 | 1970 | £5 | £12 | |
| Dynasty | LP | Verve | V688022 | 1972 | £8 | £20 | double |
| Focus | LP | HMV | CLP1577 | 1962 | £5 | £12 | |
| Getz Au Go Go | LP | Verve | VLP9081 | 1964 | £5 | £12 | |
| Girl From Ipanema | 7" | Verve | VS520 | 1964 | £1.50 | £4 | with Astrud & Joao Gilberto |
| Greatest Hits | LP | Stateside | SL10161 | 1966 | £4 | £10 | |
| Imported From Europe | LP | HMV | CLP1351 | 1960 | £6 | £15 | |
| Interpretations | LP | Columbia | 33CX10057 | 1956 | £20 | £40 | |
| Jazz Samba | LP | Verve | (S)VLP9013 | 1962 | £4 | £10 | with Charlie Byrd |
| Jazz Samba Encore | LP | Verve | (S)VLP9038 | 1963 | £4 | £10 | with Luiz Bonfa |
| Soft Swing | LP | HMV | CLP1320 | 1960 | £6 | £15 | |
| Stan Getz | LP | Columbia | 33CX10082 | 1957 | £8 | £20 | |
| Stan Getz Plays | 10" LP | Esquire | 20007 | 1953 | £20 | £40 | |
| Stan Getz Quartet | LP | Esquire | 32011 | 1956 | £15 | £30 | |
| Stan Getz Quartet | 10" LP | Vogue | LDE147 | 1955 | £15 | £30 | |
| Stan Meets Chet | LP | HMV | CLP1292 | 1959 | £10 | £25 | with Chet Baker |
| Steamer | LP | HMV | CLP1276 | 1959 | £8 | £20 | |
| What The World Needs Now | LP | Verve | (S)VLP9232 | 1969 | £5 | £12 | |

## GHOST
| | | | | | | | |
|---|---|---|---|---|---|---|---|
| I've Got To Get To Know You | 7" | Gemini | GMS014 | 1970 | £5 | £10 | |
| When You're Dead | 7" | Gemini | GMS007 | 1969 | £7.50 | £15 | |
| When You're Dead – One Second | LP | Gemini | GME1004 | 1970 | £75 | £150 | |

## GHOST DANCE
| | | | | | | | |
|---|---|---|---|---|---|---|---|
| Celebrate | CD-s | Chrysalis | CHSCD3402 | 1989 | £2 | £5 | |

| | | | | | | |
|---|---|---|---|---|---|---|
| Grip Of Love | 7" | Karbon | KAR604 | 1986 £2 | £5 | |
| Grip Of Love | 12" | Karbon | KAR604T | 1986 £2.50 | £6 | |
| Heart Full Of Soul | 7" | Karbon | KAR606 | 1986 £2.50 | £6 | promo |
| River Of No Return | 12" | Karbon | KAR602T | 1986 £2.50 | £6 | |
| Stop The World | CD-s | Chrysalis | CCD1706 | 1989 £2 | £5 | |
| When I Call | 7" | Karbon | KAR608 | 1987 £2.50 | £6 | promo |

## GHOULS
| | | | | | | |
|---|---|---|---|---|---|---|
| Dracula's Deuce | LP | Capitol | (S)T2215 | 1965 £5 | £12 | US |

## GIANT CRAB
| | | | | | | |
|---|---|---|---|---|---|---|
| Cool It Helios | LP | Uni | 73057 | 1969 £5 | £12 | US |
| Giant Crab Comes Forth | LP | Uni | 73037 | 1968 £5 | £12 | US |

## GIANT SUNFLOWER
| | | | | | | |
|---|---|---|---|---|---|---|
| Big Apple | 7" | CBS | 2805 | 1967 £2 | £5 | |
| Mark Twain | 7" | CBS | 3033 | 1967 £1.50 | £4 | |

## GIANTS
| | | | | | | |
|---|---|---|---|---|---|---|
| Live | LP | Polydor | 237626 | 1964 £10 | £25 | German |

## GIANTS (2)
| | | | | | | |
|---|---|---|---|---|---|---|
| Giants | LP | International | ZO201V | 1976 £25 | £50 | French |

## GIBB, MAURICE
| | | | | | | |
|---|---|---|---|---|---|---|
| Sing A Rude Song | LP | Polydor | 2383018 | 1970 £8 | £20 | |

## GIBB, ROBIN
| | | | | | | |
|---|---|---|---|---|---|---|
| Robin's Reign | LP | Polydor | 583085 | 1970 £4 | £10 | |
| Saved By The Bell/Alexandria Good Time | 7" | Polydor | BM56337 | 1969 £5 | £10 | |

## GIBBONS, STEVE
| | | | | | | |
|---|---|---|---|---|---|---|
| Short Stories | LP | Wizard | SWZA5501 | 1971 £25 | £50 | |

## GIBBS, GEORGIA
| | | | | | | |
|---|---|---|---|---|---|---|
| Arrivederci Roma | 7" | Mercury | 7MT210 | 1958 £2 | £5 | |
| Balling The Jack | 7" | Vogue Coral | Q72088 | 1955 £5 | £10 | |
| Great Balls Of Fire | 7" | RCA | RCA1029 | 1958 £5 | £10 | |
| Happiness Street | 7" EP | Mercury | MEP9505 | 1956 £2 | £5 | |
| Her Nibbs Miss Gibbs | 10" LP | Mercury | MPT7511 | 1957 £10 | £25 | |
| Hucklebuck | 7" | Columbia | DB4259 | 1959 £2 | £5 | |
| Hula Hoop Song | 7" | Columbia | DB4201 | 1958 £1.50 | £4 | |
| I'll Be Seeing You | 7" EP | Mercury | EP13265 | 1955 £2 | £5 | |
| I'll Know | 7" | Vogue Coral | Q72182 | 1956 £2.50 | £6 | |
| Silent Lips | 7" EP | Mercury | MEP9516 | 1957 £4 | £8 | |
| Sings The Oldies | 10" LP | Mercury | MPT7500 | 1956 £10 | £25 | |
| Stroll That Stole My Heart | 7" | London | HLP9098 | 1960 £1.50 | £4 | |
| Sugar Candy | 7" | RCA | RCA1011 | 1957 £1.50 | £4 | |
| Swinging With Her Nibbs | LP | Mercury | MPL6508 | 1957 £6 | £15 | |

## GIBBS, JOE
| | | | | | | |
|---|---|---|---|---|---|---|
| African Dub Chapter One | LP | Lightning | LIP10 | 1978 £6 | £15 | |
| African Dub Chapter Three | LP | Lightning | LIP12 | 1979 £6 | £15 | |
| African Dub Chapter Two | LP | Lightning | LIP11 | 1979 £6 | £15 | |
| Majestic Dub | LP | Laser | LASL3 | 1979 £5 | £12 | |

## GIBBS, MICHAEL

Michael Gibbs is a jazz composer and arranger of major importance. Unfortunately, he is not at all prolific and of what he has recorded, much is hard to find. The vital early albums are listed below – other Gibbs creations can be found scattered through various records by Gary Burton, while his arranging skills have been employed by such diverse artists as John McLaughlin and Joni Mitchell.

| | | | | | | |
|---|---|---|---|---|---|---|
| Just Ahead | LP | Polydor | 2683011 | 1972 £15 | £30 | double |
| Michael Gibbs | LP | Deram | SML1063 | 1970 £25 | £50 | |
| Tanglewood '63 | LP | Deram | SML1087 | 1971 £15 | £30 | |

## GIBBS, SIR
| | | | | | | |
|---|---|---|---|---|---|---|
| People Grudgeful | 7" | Amalgamated | AMG822 | 1968 £4 | £8 | |

## GIBBS, TERRY
| | | | | | | |
|---|---|---|---|---|---|---|
| Launching A New Sound In Music | LP | Mercury | MMC14018 | 1959 £5 | £12 | |
| Swing Is Here | LP | HMV | CLP1394/CSD1324 | 1960 £5 | £12 | |
| Swingin' With Terry Gibbs | LP | Emarcy | EJL1263 | 1957 £6 | £15 | |
| Terry Gibbs | LP | Emarcy | EJL1269 | 1958 £6 | £15 | |
| Terry Gibbs | LP | Emarcy | EJT752 | 1957 £6 | £15 | |
| Terry Gibbs | LP | Vogue Coral | LVA9013 | 1956 £6 | £15 | |
| Terry Gibbs | 10" LP | Vogue Coral | LRA10035 | 1955 £15 | £30 | |

## GIBSON, BOB
| | | | | | | |
|---|---|---|---|---|---|---|
| Where I'm Bound | LP | Bounty | BY6006 | 1966 £10 | £25 | |

## GIBSON, DEBBIE
| | | | | | | |
|---|---|---|---|---|---|---|
| Anything Is Possible | CD-s | East West | A7735CD | 1991 £2 | £5 | |
| Electric Youth | LP | WEA | WX231Y | 1988 £6 | £15 | yellow vinyl, poster |
| Electric Youth | CD-s | WEA | A8919CDP | 1989 £2 | £5 | picture disc |
| Foolish Beat | CD-s | WEA | A9059CD | 1988 £2.50 | £6 | |
| Foolish Beat | 12" | WEA | A9059TP | 1988 £2.50 | £6 | picture disc |
| Lost In Your Eyes | CD-s | Atlantic | A8970CD | 1989 £2 | £5 | |

| | | | | | | | |
|---|---|---|---|---|---|---|---|
| Lost In Your Eyes | 12" | WEA | A8970TP | 1989 | £2.50 | £6 | *picture disc* |
| Only In My Dreams | 7" | WEA | A9322P | 1988 | £1.50 | £4 | *picture disc* |
| Only In My Dreams | 7" | WEA | A9322W | 1988 | £1.50 | £4 | *... poster picture sleeve* |
| Only In My Dreams | 12" | Atlantic | A9322TP | 1987 | £6 | £15 | *picture disc* |
| Only In My Dreams | 12" | WEA | A9322T | 1987 | £15 | £30 | |
| Out Of The Blue | CD-s | Atlantic | A9091CD | 1988 | £3 | £8 | |
| Out Of The Blue | 12" | Atlantic | A9091T | 1988 | £4 | £10 | *with poster* |
| Shake Your Love | 12" | WEA | A9187T | 1987 | £2.50 | £6 | *with poster* |
| Shake Your Love | 12" | WEA | A9187TP | 1987 | £3 | £8 | *picture disc* |
| Staying Together | CD-s | WEA | A9020CD | 1988 | £3 | £8 | |
| We Could Be Together | CD-s | Atlantic | 7567887 | 1989 | £2 | £5 | |
| We Could Be Together | CD-s | Atlantic | A8896CD | 1989 | £2 | £5 | |
| We Could Be Together | 7" | WEA | A8896P | 1989 | £1.50 | £4 | *picture disc* |

## GIBSON, DON

| | | | | | | | |
|---|---|---|---|---|---|---|---|
| Big Hearted Me | 7" | RCA | RCA1158 | 1959 | £1.50 | £6 | |
| Blue And Lonesome | 7" EP | RCA | RCX1050 | 1960 | £2.50 | £6 | |
| Blue Blue Day | 7" | RCA | RCA1073 | 1958 | £1.50 | £4 | |
| Don't Tell Me Your Trouble | 7" | RCA | RCA1150 | 1959 | £1.50 | £4 | |
| Give Myself A Party | 7" | RCA | RCA1098 | 1958 | £1.50 | £4 | |
| God Walks These Hills | LP | RCA | RD7641 | 1964 | £4 | £10 | |
| I Wrote A Song | LP | RCA | RD/SF7576 | 1963 | £4 | £10 | |
| Look Who's Blue | LP | RCA | LPM/LSP2184 | 1960 | £6 | £15 | US |
| Look Who's Blue | 7" EP | RCA | RCX213 | 1962 | £2.50 | £6 | |
| May You Never Be Alone | 7" EP | RCA | RCX7122 | 1963 | £2.50 | £6 | |
| No One Stands Alone | LP | RCA | LPM/LSP1918 | 1959 | £6 | £15 | US |
| Oh Lonesome Me | LP | RCA | LPM1743 | 1958 | £8 | £20 | US |
| Oh Lonesome Me | 7" | RCA | RCA1056 | 1958 | £1.50 | £4 | |
| Sea Of Heartbreak | 7" | RCA | RCA1243 | 1961 | £1.50 | £4 | |
| Some Favourites Of Mine | LP | RCA | RD/SF7506 | 1962 | £4 | £10 | |
| Songs By Don Gibson | LP | Lion | 70069 | 1958 | £15 | £30 | US |
| Sweet Dreams | LP | RCA | LPM/LSP2269 | 1960 | £6 | £15 | US |
| Sweet Dreams | 7" | MGM | SP1177 | 1956 | £37.50 | £75 | |
| That Gibson Boy | LP | RCA | RD27158 | 1960 | £4 | £10 | |
| That Gibson Boy | 7" EP | RCA | RCX214 | 1962 | £2.50 | £6 | |

## GIBSON, HENRY

| | | | | | | | |
|---|---|---|---|---|---|---|---|
| Grass Menagerie | LP | Epic | 15120 | 1969 | £5 | £12 | US |

## GIBSON, JODY & THE MULESKINNERS

| | | | | | | | |
|---|---|---|---|---|---|---|---|
| Kissin' Time | 7" | Parlophone | R4579 | 1959 | £1.50 | £4 | |
| So You Think You've Got Troubles | 7" | Parlophone | R4645 | 1960 | £1.50 | £4 | |

## GIBSON, STEVE & THE RED CAPS

| | | | | | | | |
|---|---|---|---|---|---|---|---|
| Silhouettes | 7" | HMV | POP417 | 1957 | £37.50 | £75 | |
| Steve Gibson & The Red Caps | 10" LP | Mercury | MG25116 | 195– | £75 | £150 | US |

## GIBSON, WAYNE

| | | | | | | | |
|---|---|---|---|---|---|---|---|
| Come On Let's Go | 7" | Decca | F11800 | 1964 | £2.50 | £6 | |
| Ding Dong The Witch Is Dead | 7" | Parlophone | R5357 | 1965 | £7.50 | £15 | |
| For No One | 7" | Columbia | DB7998 | 1966 | £1.50 | £4 | |
| Kelly | 7" | Pye | 7N15680 | 1964 | £1.50 | £4 | |
| Linda Lu | 7" | Decca | F11713 | 1963 | £2.50 | £6 | |
| One Little Smile | 7" | Columbia | DB7683 | 1965 | £10 | £20 | |
| Portland Town | 7" | Pye | 7N15798 | 1965 | £1.50 | £4 | |
| Under My Thumb | 7" | Columbia | DB7911 | 1966 | £5 | £10 | |

## GIDIAN

| | | | | | | | |
|---|---|---|---|---|---|---|---|
| Feeling | 7" | Columbia | DB8041 | 1966 | £1.50 | £4 | |
| Fight For Your Love | 7" | Columbia | DB7916 | 1966 | £1.50 | £4 | |
| Try Me Out | 7" | Columbia | DB7826 | 1966 | £5 | £10 | |

## GIFT

| | | | | | | | |
|---|---|---|---|---|---|---|---|
| Blue Apple | LP | Nova | SDL8002 | 1974 | £30 | £60 | German |
| Gift | LP | Telefunken | SLE14680 | 1972 | £8 | £20 | German |

## GIFTED CHILDREN

| | | | | | | | |
|---|---|---|---|---|---|---|---|
| Painting By Numbers | 7" | Whaam! | WHAAM001 | 1981 | £10 | £20 | |

## GIGGETTY

| | | | | | | | |
|---|---|---|---|---|---|---|---|
| Dawn To Dusk In The Black Country | LP | private | | 1975 | £37.50 | £75 | |

## GIGUERE, RUSS

| | | | | | | | |
|---|---|---|---|---|---|---|---|
| Hexagram II | LP | Warner Bros | WS1910 | 1971 | £5 | £12 | US |

## GIGYMEN

| | | | | | | | |
|---|---|---|---|---|---|---|---|
| Gigymen | LP | Spaceward | 3S3/EDENLP76 | 1975 | £6 | £15 | |

## GILA

| | | | | | | | |
|---|---|---|---|---|---|---|---|
| Bury My Heart At Wounded Knee | LP | Warner Bros | 46234 | 1973 | £10 | £25 | German |
| Gila | LP | BASF | 20211096 | 1971 | £50 | £100 | German |

## GILBERT

| | | | | | | | |
|---|---|---|---|---|---|---|---|
| Disappear | 7" | CBS | 3089 | 1967 | £4 | £8 | |
| Mister Moody's Garden | 7" | Major Minor | MM613 | 1969 | £4 | £8 | |
| What Can I Do | 7" | CBS | 3399 | 1968 | £4 | £8 | |

## GILBERT, GEORGE
Medway Flows Softly ............................. LP ..... private ............. 1974 £20 ........ £40

## GILBERT & LEWIS
Ends With The Sea .............................. 7" .... 4AD ............. AD106 ............. 1981 £1.50 .... £4

## GILBERTO, ASTRUD
Astrud Gilberto Album ........................... LP ..... Verve ........... SVLP9087 ...... 1969 £4 ........ £10
Beach Samba ..................................... LP ..... Verve ........... SVLP9187 ...... 1968 £4 ........ £10
I Haven't Got Anything Better To Do ....... LP ..... Verve ........... SVLP9242 ...... 1969 £4 ........ £10
Shadow Of Your Smile ........................ LP ..... Verve ........... SVLP9107 ...... 1970 £4 ........ £10
Windy ........................................... LP ..... Verve ........... SVLP9233 ...... 1969 £4 ........ £10

## GILDED CAGE
Long Long Road ................................. 7" ...... Tepee ............ TPR1003 ............. 1969 £1.50 .... £4

## GILES, GILES & FRIPP
Although this is the group that evolved into King Crimson, little of the music on *Cheerful Insanity* sounds much like that produced by any King Crimson line-up. Instead, much of it is of the novelty-song variety, with flat English vocals conveying lyrics that aim to be whimsical, but which mostly sound embarrassing. The record is certainly distinctive, however, and in places Robert Fripp does reveal himself to be a highly talented guitarist, even if conveying no hint that he would ever become a major influence within seventies rock and beyond.

Cheerful Insanity Of Giles, Giles And Fripp LP ..... Deram ............ DML/SML1022 ...... 1968 £25 ........ £50
Cheerful Insanity Of Giles, Giles And Fripp LP ..... Deram ............ SPA423 ............. 1970 £15 ........ £30
One In A Million ................................ 7" ...... Deram ............ DM188 ............. 1968 £37.50 .... £75
Thursday Morning .............................. 7" ...... Deram ............ DM210 ............. 1968 £37.50 .... £75

## GILES FARNABY'S DREAM BAND
Giles Farnaby was an English composer of madrigals and dance tunes who lived from about 1563 until 1640. Clearly, therefore, his Dream Band was not one that he had any hand in assembling personally. With much 'traditional' material actually dating from Farnaby's era, the folk-rock interpretations of his music on this album fall in naturally alongside recordings by Ashley Hutchings and the Albion Band. Some well-known British jazz musicians make up the rhythm section, playing behind an amalgamation of medieval music specialists St George's Canzona and folk group Trevor Crozier's Broken Consort, with singing group the Druids making an occasional appearance.

Giles Farnaby's Dream Band .................... LP ..... Argo ............. ZDA158 ............. 1973 £50 ........ £100

## GILFELLON, TOM
In The Middle Of The Tune ................... LP ..... Topic ............ 12TS282 ............. 1976 £6 ........ £15
Loving Mad Tom ............................... LP ..... Trailer ............ LER2079 ............. 1972 £5 ........ £12

## GILGAMESH
Gilgamesh ....................................... LP ..... Caroline ........... CA2007 ............. 1975 £4 ........ £10

## GILKYSON, TERRY & THE EASYRIDERS
Golden Minutes Of Folk Music ................ 10" LP Brunswick ....... LA8618 ............. 1953 £6 ........ £15
Lonesome Rider ................................ 7" EP . Fontana ........... TFE17327 ............. 1960 £2 ........ £5
Marianne ....................................... 7" ...... Philips ............ JK1007 ............. 1958 £4 ........ £8
Remember The Alamo .......................... LP ..... London ........... HAR2323 ............. 1961 £4 ........ £10
Rolling .......................................... LP ..... London ........... HAR2301/
SAHR6111 ............
Rolling .......................................... 7" EP . London ........... RER1333 ............. 1961 £2.50 ........ £6
Strolling Blues ................................. 7" EP . Fontana ........... TFE17326 ............. 1960 £2 ........ £5

## GILL, COLIN & DESMOND
History Of Lore ................................. LP ..... Profile ............ GMOR142 ............. 1977 £25 ........ £50

## GILLAN, IAN
Child In Time ................................... LP ..... Polydor ........... ACBR261 ............. 1976 £4 ........ £10
Living For The City ........................... 7" ...... Virgin ............ VSY519 ............. 1982 £2 ........ £5 ......... *picture disc*
Mad Elaine ..................................... 7" ...... Island ............ WIP6423 ............. 1978 £1.50 .... £4
No Good Luck .................................. CD-s . East West ........ YZ513CD ............. 1990 £2 ........ £5
What I Did On My Vacation .................. CD .... 10 ............... DXDCD39 ............. 1986 £5 ........ £12

## GILLES ZEITSCHIFF
Gilles Zeitschiff ................................ LP ..... Kosmische ....... KM58012 ............. 1974 £6 ........ £15 ........... *German*

## GILLESPIE, DANA
Andy Warhol .................................... 7" ...... RCA ............. RCA2446 ............. 1974 £2 ........ £5
Box Of Surprises ............................... LP ..... Decca ............ SKL5012 ............. 1969 £20 ........ £40
Donna Donna .................................... 7" ...... Pye ............... 7N15872 ............. 1965 £2 ........ £5
Pay You Back With Interest .................. 7" ...... Pye ............... 7N17280 ............. 1967 £1.50 .... £4
Thank You Boy ................................. 7" ...... Pye ............... 7N15962 ............. 1965 £1.50 .... £4

## GILLESPIE, DARLENE
Darlene Of The Teens .......................... LP ..... Disneyland ...... WDL3010 ....... £10 ........ £25 ........... *US*

## GILLESPIE, DIZZY
Always .......................................... 7" EP . Verve ............ VRE5022 ............. 1966 £2 ........ £5
Be Bop .......................................... 7" EP . Philips ............ BE12552 ............. 1964 £2 ........ £5
Birks Works ..................................... 7" EP . Columbia ......... SEB10096 ............. 1957 £2 ........ £5
Champ .......................................... 7" EP . Vogue ............ EPV1094 ............. 1956 £2 ........ £5
Diz 'n' Bird In Concert ........................ LP ..... Vogue ............ LAE12252 ............. 1961 £4 ........ £10 ...*with Charlie Parker*
Diz And Don .................................... 7" EP . MGM ............ MGMEP579 ............. 1957 £2 ........ £5  *2 tracks by Don Byas*
Dizzy Atmosphere .............................. LP ..... London ........... LTZU15121 ............. 1958 £8 ........ £20
Dizzy Gillespie ................................. LP ..... RCA ............. RD7827 ............. 1965 £4 ........ £10
Dizzy Gillespie ................................. 7" EP . Vogue ............ EPV1022 ............. 1955 £2 ........ £5

| | | | | | | | |
|---|---|---|---|---|---|---|---|
| Dizzy Gillespie | 7" EP | Vogue | EPV1078 | 1956 | £2 | £5 | |
| Dizzy Gillespie | 10" LP | Columbia | 33C9030 | 1957 | £20 | £40 | |
| Dizzy Gillespie And His Orchestra | LP | Columbia | 33CX10002 | 1955 | £15 | £30 | |
| Dizzy Gillespie And His Orchestra | 7" EP | Vogue | EPV1157 | 1956 | £2 | £5 | |
| Dizzy Gillespie And His Orchestra | 7" EP | Vogue | EPV1158 | 1956 | £2 | £5 | |
| Dizzy Gillespie And His Orchestra | 10" LP | HMV | DLP1047 | 1954 | £20 | £40 | |
| Dizzy Gillespie And His Orchestra | 10" LP | Vogue | LDE076 | 1954 | £20 | £40 | |
| Dizzy Gillespie And His Orchestra | 10" LP | Vogue | LDE135 | 1955 | £20 | £40 | |
| Dizzy Gillespie And Stuff Smith | LP | HMV | CLP1291 | 1959 | £8 | £20 | |
| Dizzy Gillespie Plays | 10" LP | Vogue | LDE017 | 1953 | £20 | £40 | |
| Dizzy Gillespie Plays – Johnny Richards Conducts | 10" LP | Vogue | LDE033 | 1953 | £20 | £40 | |
| Dizzy Gillespie With Strings | 7" EP | Vogue | EPV1049 | 1955 | £2 | £5 | |
| Dizzy Gillespie-Stan Getz Sextet | 10" LP | Columbia | 33C9027 | 1956 | £37.50 | £75 | |
| Dizzy Gillespie/Stan Getz Sextet | 7" EP | HMV | 7EG8596 | 1960 | £2 | £5 | |
| Dizzy Gillespie/Stan Getz Sextet | 10" LP | Columbia | 33C9009 | 1955 | £20 | £40 | |
| Dizzy In Greece | LP | Columbia | 33CX10144 | 1959 | £8 | £20 | |
| Dizzy With Strings | 7" EP | Esquire | EP193 | 1958 | £2 | £5 | |
| Duets | LP | Columbia | 33CX10121 | 1958 | £15 | £30 | with Sonny Rollins & Sonny Stitt |
| Film Themes | 7" EP | Philips | BE12583 | 1965 | £2 | £5 | |
| For Musicians Only | LP | Columbia | 33CX10095 | 1958 | £8 | £20 | .. with Stan Getz and Sonny Stitt |
| Gillespiana | LP | HMV | CLP1484/CSD1392 | 1962 | £8 | £20 | |
| Greatest | LP | RCA | RD27242 | 1961 | £4 | £10 | |
| Greatest Trumpet Of Them All | LP | HMV | CLP1381 | 1960 | £8 | £20 | |
| Have Trumpet, Will Excite | LP | HMV | CLP1318 | 1959 | £8 | £20 | |
| Mellow Sounds | 7" EP | HMV | 7EG8577 | 1960 | £2 | £5 | |
| More Mellow Sounds | 7" EP | HMV | 7EG8646 | 1961 | £2 | £5 | |
| New Sound In Jazz | 7" EP | Philips | 430793BE | 1963 | £2 | £5 | |
| Newport Jazz Festival 1957 | LP | Columbia | 33CX10111 | 1958 | £6 | £15 | Side 2 by Count Basie |
| One More Time | 7" EP | Columbia | SEB10087 | 1957 | £2 | £5 | ... with Charlie Parker |
| Operatic Strings | LP | Fontana | TL5343 | 1967 | £4 | £10 | |
| Operatic Strings | 10" LP | Esquire | 20003 | 1953 | £20 | £40 | |
| Operatic Strings – Jealousy | 10" LP | Felsted | EDL87006 | 1954 | £20 | £40 | |
| Paris Concert | 10" LP | Vogue | LDE039 | 1954 | £20 | £40 | |
| Pile Driver | 7" EP | Columbia | SEB10075 | 1957 | £2 | £5 | |
| Portrait Of Duke Ellington | LP | HMV | CLP1431 | 1961 | £8 | £20 | |
| Two By Two | 7" EP | MGM | MGMEP681 | 1958 | £2 | £5 | 2 tracks by Kai Winding |

## GILLEY, MICKEY

| | | | | | | | |
|---|---|---|---|---|---|---|---|
| Lonely Wine | LP | Astro | 101 | 1964 | £100 | £200 | US |

## GILLUM, JAZZ

| | | | | | | | |
|---|---|---|---|---|---|---|---|
| 1938-47 | LP | RCA | RD7816 | 1968 | £5 | £12 | |
| Jazz Gillum | LP | Folkways | FS3826 | 1961 | £8 | £20 | |

## GILMER, JIMMY

| | | | | | | | |
|---|---|---|---|---|---|---|---|
| Ain't Gonna Tell Nobody | 7" | London | HLD9872 | 1964 | £1.50 | £4 | |
| Buddy's Buddy | LP | Dot | DLP3577 | 1964 | £8 | £20 | |
| Campusology | LP | Dot | DLP3709/25709 | 1966 | £8 | £20 | US |
| Daisy Petal Picking | 7" | London | HLD9827 | 1964 | £1.50 | £4 | |
| Firewater | LP | Dot | DLP25856 | 1968 | £4 | £10 | US |
| Folkbeat | LP | Dot | DLP3668/25668 | 1965 | £8 | £20 | US |
| I'm Gonna Go Walkin' | 7" | London | HLD9632 | 1962 | £1.50 | £4 | |
| Look At Me | 7" | London | HLD9898 | 1964 | £1.50 | £4 | |
| Lucky 'Leven | LP | Dot | DLP3643/25643 | 1965 | £8 | £20 | US |
| She Belongs To Me | 7" | Stateside | SS472 | 1965 | £1.50 | £4 | |
| Sugar Shack | LP | London | HAD/SHD8150 | 1964 | £10 | £25 | |
| Sugar Shack | 7" EP | London | RE10154 | 1964 | £10 | £20 | French, B side by the Surfaris |
| Sugar Shack | 7" | London | HLD9789 | 1963 | £1.50 | £4 | |
| Thunder 'n' Lightnin' | 7" | Stateside | SS418 | 1965 | £1.50 | £4 | |
| Torquay | LP | Dot | DLP3512/25512 | 1963 | £8 | £20 | US |

## GILMOUR, DAVE

| | | | | | | | |
|---|---|---|---|---|---|---|---|
| Blue Light | 12" | Harvest | 12HAR5226 | 1984 | £2.50 | £6 | |
| Love On The Air | 7" | Harvest | HARP5229 | 1984 | £1.50 | £4 | ... shaped picture disc |

## GILREATH, JAMES

| | | | | | | | |
|---|---|---|---|---|---|---|---|
| Little Band Of Gold | 7" | Pye | 7N25190 | 1963 | £1.50 | £4 | |
| Lollipops, Lace And Lipstick | 7" | Pye | 7N25213 | 1963 | £1.50 | £4 | |

## GILTRAP, GORDON

| | | | | | | | |
|---|---|---|---|---|---|---|---|
| Giltrap | LP | Philips | 6308175 | 1973 | £8 | £20 | |
| Gordon Giltrap | LP | Transatlantic | TRA175 | 1968 | £10 | £25 | |
| Portrait | LP | Transatlantic | TRA202 | 1969 | £8 | £20 | |
| Testament Of Time | LP | MCA | MKPS2020 | 1971 | £8 | £20 | |

## GIN BOTTLE SEVEN

| | | | | | | | |
|---|---|---|---|---|---|---|---|
| Gin Bottle Jazz | LP | London | LTZU15115 | 1958 | £6 | £15 | |

## GINGER & THE SNAPS

This is an alternative name used by the Honeys and, like those records, these are keenly sought by Beach Boys completists.

| | | | | | | | |
|---|---|---|---|---|---|---|---|
| Love Me The Way That I Love You | 7" | Tore | 1008 | 1961 | £15 | £30 | US |

| | | | | | | | |
|---|---|---|---|---|---|---|---|
| Seven Days In September | 7" | LP | MGM | 13413 | 1965 £30 | £60 | US |

## GINGER JUG BAND
| | | | | | | |
|---|---|---|---|---|---|---|
| Ginger Jug Band | LP | private | GJB001 | 197– £25 | £50 | |

## GINHOUSE
| | | | | | | |
|---|---|---|---|---|---|---|
| Ginhouse | LP | B&C | CAS1031 | 1971 £20 | £40 | |

## GINNY & GALLIONS
| | | | | | | |
|---|---|---|---|---|---|---|
| Two Sides | LP | Downey | DS1003 | 1964 £6 | £15 | US |

## GINO & GINA
| | | | | | | |
|---|---|---|---|---|---|---|
| Pretty Baby | 7" | Mercury | 7MT230 | 1958 £12.50 | £25 | |

## GINSBERG, ALLEN
| | | | | | | |
|---|---|---|---|---|---|---|
| Allen Ginsberg Reads Kaddish | LP | Atlantic | 4001 | 1966 £8 | £20 | US |
| At The ICA | LP | Saga | | 1967 £8 | £20 | |
| Ginsberg Thing | LP | Douglas | 801 | 1968 £8 | £20 | US |
| Howl And Other Poems | LP | Fantasy | 7006 | 1959 £20 | £40 | US, red vinyl |
| Songs Of Innocence And Experience | LP | Forecast | FVS3083 | 1969 £8 | £20 | US |

## GIORDANO, LOU
This very rare single was co-produced by Buddy Holly and Phil Everly, who can also be heard on both sides of the record.

| | | | | | | |
|---|---|---|---|---|---|---|
| Stay Close To Me | 7" | Brunswick | 955115 | 1959 £330 | £500 | US, best auctioned |

## GIORGIO
| | | | | | | |
|---|---|---|---|---|---|---|
| Baby I Need You | 7" | Electratone | EP1003 | 1968 £5 | £10 | |
| Bla Bla Diddley | 7" | Page One | POF028 | 1967 £1.50 | £4 | |
| Bla Bla Diddly | 7" EP | DiscAZ | 1093 | 1967 £6 | £15 | French |
| Full Stop | 7" | Page One | POF003 | 1966 £1.50 | £4 | |
| Girl Without A Heart | 7" | Polydor | 56101 | 1966 £1.50 | £4 | |

## GIRARD, GEORGE
| | | | | | | |
|---|---|---|---|---|---|---|
| Stompin' At The Famous Door | LP | HMV | CLP1123 | 1957 £6 | £15 | |

## GIRL SATCHMO
| | | | | | | |
|---|---|---|---|---|---|---|
| Blue Beat Chariot | 7" | Blue Beat | BB227 | 1964 £6 | £12 | |
| Don't Be Sad | 7" | Blue Beat | BB156 | 1963 £6 | £12 | |
| Mash Potato | 7" | Blue Beat | BB45 | 1961 £6 | £12 | |
| Take You For A Ride | 7" | Fab | FAB111 | 1969 £1.50 | £4 | |
| Twist Around The Town | 7" | Blue Beat | BB79 | 1962 £6 | £12 | |

## GIRL WONDER
| | | | | | | |
|---|---|---|---|---|---|---|
| Mommy Out Of The Light | 7" | Doctor Bird | DB1015 | 1966 £5 | £10 | |

## GIRLFRIENDS
| | | | | | | |
|---|---|---|---|---|---|---|
| Jimmy Boy | 7" | Colpix | PX712 | 1963 £4 | £8 | |

## GIRLIE
| | | | | | | |
|---|---|---|---|---|---|---|
| African Meeting | 7" | Duke | DU42 | 1969 £1.50 | £4 | |
| Boss Cocky | 7" | Treasure Isle | TI7053 | 1969 £2 | £5 | Love Shocks B side |
| Madame Straggae | 7" | Bullet | BU400 | 1969 £1.50 | £4 | Laurel Aitken B side |

## GIRLS TOGETHER OUTRAGEOUSLY
| | | | | | | |
|---|---|---|---|---|---|---|
| Permanent Damage | LP | Straight | STS1059 | 1969 £20 | £40 | |

## GITTE
| | | | | | | |
|---|---|---|---|---|---|---|
| Favoriter | LP | HMV | KELP117 | 1968 £5 | £12 | Danish |
| Gitte | LP | Capitol | ST10424 | 1965 £5 | £12 | German |
| Gitte Haenning | LP | HMV | KELP102 | 1964 £6 | £15 | Danish |
| Greatest Hits | LP | Odeon | BOKS20 | 1965 £37.50 | £75 | Danish |
| Red Mantle | LP | RCA | LSP4815 | 1972 £20 | £40 | US |

## GIUFFRE, JIMMY
| | | | | | | |
|---|---|---|---|---|---|---|
| Easy Way | LP | HMV | CLP1344 | 1960 £6 | £15 | |
| Jimmy Giuffre | 10" LP | Capitol | LC6699 | 1955 £15 | £30 | |
| Jimmy Giuffre Clarinet | LP | London | LTZK15059 | 1957 £6 | £15 | |
| Jimmy Giuffre Three | LP | London | LTZK15130 | 1958 £6 | £15 | |
| Music Man | LP | London | LTZK15216 | 1961 £6 | £15 | |
| Train And The River | LP | Atlantic | 590011 | 1968 £6 | £15 | |
| Trav'lin' Light | LP | London | LTZK15137 | 1958 £6 | £15 | |

## GIZMO
| | | | | | | |
|---|---|---|---|---|---|---|
| Just Like Master Bates | LP | Ace | ACE001 | 1979 £15 | £30 | white vinyl |
| Just Like Master Bates/Victims | LP | Gizmo | | 198– £25 | £50 | autographed double |
| Psychedelic Rock And Roll | 7" | MCM | 4 | 197– £2.50 | £6 | |
| Victims | LP | Sleep 'n' Eat | | 1979 £15 | £30 | |

## GLACIERS
| | | | | | | |
|---|---|---|---|---|---|---|
| From Sea To Sky | LP | Mercury | MG2/SR60895 | 1964 £6 | £15 | US |

## GLACKIN, PADDY & PADDY KEENAN
| | | | | | | |
|---|---|---|---|---|---|---|
| Doublin | LP | Tara | 2007 | 1979 £4 | £10 | Irish |

## GLACKIN, PADDY, MICK GAVIN, MICHAEL O'BRIEN
| | | | | | | |
|---|---|---|---|---|---|---|
| Flags Of Dublin | LP | Topic | 12TS383 | 1978 £4 | £10 | |

## GLADIATORS
| | | | | | | | |
|---|---|---|---|---|---|---|---|
| Bleak House | 7" | HMV | POP1134 | 1963 | £5 | £10 | |

## GLADIATORS (2)
| | | | | | | | |
|---|---|---|---|---|---|---|---|
| Girl Don't Make Me Wait | 7" | Direction | 583854 | 1968 | £1.50 | £4 | |
| Gladiators | LP | Virgin | V2161 | 1980 | £4 | £10 | |
| Naturality | LP | Front Line | FL1035 | 1978 | £5 | £12 | |
| Proverbial Reggae | LP | Front Line | FL1002 | 1978 | £5 | £12 | |
| Sweet So Till | LP | Front Line | FL1048 | 1979 | £5 | £12 | |
| Train Is Coming | 7" | Doctor Bird | DB1114 | 1967 | £5 | £10 | |
| Trenchtown Mix Up | LP | Virgin | V2062 | 1976 | £5 | £12 | |
| Waiting On The Shores Of Nowhere | 7" | Direction | 584308 | 1969 | £1.50 | £4 | |

## GLADIOLAS
| | | | | | | | |
|---|---|---|---|---|---|---|---|
| Little Darling | 7" | London | HLO8435 | 1957 | £150 | £200 | |

## GLANS OVER SJO OCH STRAND
| | | | | | | | |
|---|---|---|---|---|---|---|---|
| First | LP | Silence | MNW13P | 1970 | £15 | £30 | Swedish |
| Second | LP | Silence | MNW22P | 1971 | £20 | £40 | Swedish |

## GLASEL, JOHNNY
| | | | | | | | |
|---|---|---|---|---|---|---|---|
| Jazz Session | 10" LP | HMV | DLP1198 | 1958 | £8 | £20 | |

## GLASER, TOMPALL
| | | | | | | | |
|---|---|---|---|---|---|---|---|
| Land – Folk Songs | LP | Decca | DL(7)4041 | 1960 | £6 | £15 | US |

## GLASS, PHILIP
Philip Glass is one of the pioneering minimalist composers, whose knack of finding easily attractive riffs for development has made his career prosper to the point where he has become probably the best known modern composer. Some of his work overlaps with rock – he produced the album by Polyrock (listed under their name) and set lyrics by the likes of Paul Simon and David Byrne, using the warm tones of Linda Ronstadt to deliver them, on his album *Songs From Liquid Days*. His success must be particularly gratifying given that his earliest works were considered so *outré* by the classical establishment, that Glass was forced to issue them on his own Chatham Square label.

| | | | | | | | |
|---|---|---|---|---|---|---|---|
| Music In Fifths/Music In Similar Motion | LP | Chatham Square | LP1003 | 1973 | £8 | £20 | US |
| Music In Twelve Parts | CD | Charisma | CACD2010 | 1986 | £5 | £12 | |
| Music With Changing Parts | LP | Chatham Square | LP1001/2 | 197– | £15 | £30 | US double |
| Two Pages | LP | Folkways | FTS33902 | 197– | £4 | £10 | US |

## GLASS FAMILY
| | | | | | | | |
|---|---|---|---|---|---|---|---|
| Electric Band | LP | Warner Bros | WS1776 | 1968 | £8 | £20 | US |

## GLASS MENAGERIE
| | | | | | | | |
|---|---|---|---|---|---|---|---|
| Do My Thing Myself | 7" | Polydor | 56341 | 1969 | £1.50 | £4 | |
| Frederick Jordan | 7" | Pye | 7N17615 | 1968 | £10 | £20 | |
| Have You Forgotten Who You Are | 7" | Polydor | 56318 | 1969 | £1.50 | £4 | |
| She's A Rainbow | 7" | Pye | 7N17518 | 1968 | £2 | £5 | |
| You Didn't Have To Be So Nice | 7" | Pye | 7N17568 | 1968 | £1.50 | £4 | |

## GLASS OPENING
| | | | | | | | |
|---|---|---|---|---|---|---|---|
| Silver Bells And Cockle Shells | 7" | Plexium | P1236 | 1968 | £75 | £150 | |

## GLASS PRISM
| | | | | | | | |
|---|---|---|---|---|---|---|---|
| On Joy And Sorrow | LP | RCA | LSP4270 | 1970 | £5 | £12 | US |
| Poe Through The Glass Prism | LP | RCA | LSP4201 | 1969 | £5 | £12 | US |

## GLEASON, JACKIE
| | | | | | | | |
|---|---|---|---|---|---|---|---|
| Rain | 7" | Capitol | CL14289 | 1955 | £1.50 | £4 | |
| What Is A Boy? | 7" | Brunswick | 04775 | 1960 | £1.50 | £4 | |

## GLEEMEN
| | | | | | | | |
|---|---|---|---|---|---|---|---|
| Gleemen | LP | CGD | FGS5073 | 1970 | £50 | £100 | Italian |

## GLEN & LLOYD
| | | | | | | | |
|---|---|---|---|---|---|---|---|
| Feel Good Now | 7" | Doctor Bird | DB1099 | 1967 | £5 | £10 | |
| Live And Let Others Live | 7" | Ska Beat | JB250 | 1966 | £5 | £10 | |

## GLENCOE
| | | | | | | | |
|---|---|---|---|---|---|---|---|
| Glencoe | LP | Epic | EPC65207 | 1972 | £4 | £10 | |
| Spirit Of Glencoe | LP | Epic | EPC65717 | 1973 | £4 | £10 | |

## GLENN, LLOYD
| | | | | | | | |
|---|---|---|---|---|---|---|---|
| Chica Boo | LP | Aladdin | 808 | 1956 | £15 | £30 | US |
| Chica Boo | LP | Aladdin | 808 | 1956 | £50 | £100 | US, red vinyl |

## GLENN, TYREE
| | | | | | | | |
|---|---|---|---|---|---|---|---|
| At The Embers | LP | Esquire | 32061 | 1958 | £5 | £12 | |

## GLITTER, GARY
Records by the man who was christened Paul Gadd can also be found listed in the guide under the names Paul Raven, Paul Monday and Rubber Bucket.

| | | | | | | | |
|---|---|---|---|---|---|---|---|
| Boys Will Be Boys | CD | Arista | 8225712 | 1984 | £5 | £12 | |
| When I'm On I'm On | 7" | Eagle | ERS009 | 1981 | £2 | £5 | |

## GLITTERHOUSE
Barbarella................................. 7" ...... Stateside .......... SS2129 .................. 1968 £1.50.......£4 ..... 2 different B sides

## GLOBAL VILLAGE TRUCKING CO.
Global Village Trucking Co....................... LP ..... Caroline ....... C1516 ................... 1976 £4.........£10 ................................

## GLOOMYS
Daybreak .................................. LP ..... Columbia ...... SMC74360............ 1967 £6.........£15 .................. German
Daybreak .................................. 7" ...... Columbia ....... DB8391 ............... 1968 £2.............£5 ................................
II ............................................ LP ..... Columbia ...... 1C05228406 ........... 1969 £5.........£12 .................. German

## GLORIES
I Love You But Give Me My Freedom ...... 7" ...... Direction ....... 583084 ............... 1967 £2.............£5 ................................
I Stand Accused...................................... 7" ...... CBS............... 2736 ................... 1967 £5.........£10 ................................

## GLORY
Meat Music Sampler ......................... LP ..... Texas ........... TRR69................. 1969 £30.........£60 ........................... US
........................................................................ Revolution......

## GLOVE
Like An Animal............................. 7" .... Wonderland .... SHE3 .................. 1983 £2.50........£6 ................................
Like An Animal............................. 12".... Wonderland .... SHEX3 ................. 1983 £4.........£10 ................................
Punish Me With Kisses .......................... 7" ...... Wonderland .... SHE5 .................. 1983 £4.........£8 ................................

## GLOVER, ROGER
Butterfly Ball................................. LP ..... Purple ......... TPSA7514............ 1974 £6.........£15 ................................

## GMT
One By One ..................................... 12".... Mausoleum ..... BONE1283102 ....... 1991 £2.50........£6 ................................

## GNIDROLOG
Gnidrolog played an idiosyncratic form of progressive rock, characterized by abrupt tempo and key changes that gave their music an interestingly fractured feel. The group's extraordinary name was actually an imperfect anagram of the surname of the Goldring brothers who were the front men.

In Spite Of Harry's Toenail ....................... LP ..... RCA ............. SF8261 ................. 1971 £10.........£25 ................................
Lady Lake ............................................. LP ..... RCA ............. SF8322 ................. 1972 £37.50.....£75 ................................

## GNOMES OF ZURICH
Hang On Baby................................ 7" ...... CBS............... 202556................. 1967 £4.............£8 ................................
High Hopes.................................... 7" ...... CBS............... 2694 ................... 1967 £4.............£8 ................................
Please Mr. Sun ............................... 7" ...... Planet .......... PLF121 ............... 1966 £10.........£20 ................................
Second Fiddle ............................... 7" ...... RCA ............. RCA1606 ............. 1967 £5.........£10 ................................

## GO-BETWEENS
I Need Two Heads............................ 7" ...... Postcard ....... 80-4................. 1980 £2.50........£6 cream or brown sleeves
Peel Sessions ................................. CD-s .. Strange Fruit.... SFPSCD074 ......... 1989 £2.............£5 ................................
Streets Of Your Town ..................... CD-s .. Beggars ........ BEG218CD........... 1988 £2.............£5 ................................
........................................................................ Banquet ..........
Was There Anything I Could Do.............. CD-s .. Beggars ........ BEG219CD........... 1988 £2.............£5 ................................
........................................................................ Banquet ..........

## GO-GO'S
Automatic....................................... 7" ...... Initial ............ IRS101 ............... 1981 £1.50.......£4 ...................picture disc
Our Lips Are Sealed............................ 7" ...... IRS .............. PFP1007 ............. 1981 £2.50........£6 ................. pink vinyl
Return To The Valley Of The Go-Go's..... CD .... IRS .............. ....................... 199– £15.........£30 ...US with bonus CD
We Got The Beat................................. 7" ...... Stiff .............. BUY78 ................ 1980 £2.............£5 ................................

## GO-GO'S (2)
I'm Gonna Spend My Christmas With A ... 7" ...... Oriole ............ CB1982 ................ 1964 £7.50......£15 ................................
  Dalek...................
I'm Gonna Spend My Christmas With A ... 7" ...... Oriole ............ CB1982 ................ 1964 £12.50.....£25 ......... picture sleeve
  Dalek...................
Swim ............................................. LP ..... RCA ............. LPM/LSP2930........ 1964 £8.........£20 ............................... US

## GOBBLEDEGOOKS
Where Have You Been........................ 7" ...... Decca ............ F12023................. 1964 £2.............£5 ................................

## GOBLIN
Suspiria........................................ LP ..... EMI............... EMC3222 ........... 1977 £8.........£20 ................................

## GOD'S GIFT
These Days ................................... 7" ...... Newmarket ..... ....................... 1979 £2.50........£6 ................................

## GODDARD, GEOFF
Girl Bride .................................... 7" ...... HMV............. POP938 ............. 1961 £7.50......£15 ................................
My Little Girl's Come Home .................. 7" ...... HMV............. POP1068 ............ 1962 £10.........£20 ................................
Saturday Dance .............................. 7" ...... HMV............. POP1160 ............ 1963 £10.........£20 ................................
Sky Man ....................................... 7" ...... HMV............. POP1213 ............. 1963 £37.50.....£75 ................................

## GODDING, BRIAN
For those of us who waited years for guitarist Brian Godding's solo LP (after admiring his playing in Blossom Toes and the Mike Westbrook band), it is rather distressing to find the record becoming unavailable only months after its release. Reckless Records is not the first collectors' shop to try its hand at running its own record label and neither is it the first to find that the problems of distribution and achieving actual sales can be enormous.

Slaughter On Shaftesbury Avenue ............. LP ..... Reckless .......... RECK16 ................ 1989 £4 ........ £10 ...............

## GODFATHERS
Cause I Said So .................................... CD-s .. Epic ................ CDGFT2 ............... 1988 £2 .......... £5 ..............
I'm Lost And Then I'm Found ................ CD-s .. Epic ................ GFTC5 ................ 1990 £2 .......... £5 ..............
Lonely Man .......................................... 12" .... Corporate ......... GFTR010 ........... 1985 £2.50 ....... £6 ..............
                           Image .............
Love Is Dead ........................................ CD-s .. Epic ................ CDGFT3 ............... 1988 £2 .......... £5 ..............
Night Tracks ........................................ CD-s .. Strange Fruit .... SFNTCD019 ....... 1989 £2 .......... £5 ..............
She Gives Me Love ............................. CD-s .. Epic ................ CDGFT4 ............... 1989 £2 .......... £5 ..............

## GODFREY, HUGH
A Dey Pon Dem .................................. 7" ...... Coxsone ........... CS7001 ............... 1967 £5 ........... £10 ... Soul Brothers B side
Go Tell Him ........................................ 7" ...... Studio One ....... SO2015 ............... 1967 £6 ........... £12 ..............

## GODFREY, ROBERT JOHN
To all intents and purposes, Robert John Godfrey is the Enid. His solo album is effectively the first Enid album, therefore, and the hardest to find of the fully released series as it was not reissued on vinyl.

Fall Of Hyperion .................................. LP ..... Charisma ......... CAS1084 ............... 1974 £10 ........ £25 ..............

## GODFREY & STEWART
Joined By The Heart ............................ LP ..... The Stand ....... HEARTLP ........... 198– £6 .......... £15 ..............
Seed And The Sower ........................... LP ..... Enid ............... ENID11 ............... 1986 £4 .......... £10 ..............

## GODLEY & CREME
Consequences ...................................... LP ..... Mercury .......... CONS017 ........... 1977 £8 .......... £20 ............. triple, boxed
Consequences – Edited Highlights ........... LP ..... Mercury .......... LKP001 ............... 1977 £5 .......... £12 ............. promo

## GODS
Ken Hensley, the leader of Uriah Heep, began his career as a member of the Gods. The original line-up also included guitarist Mick Taylor, who can be heard playing on the Polydor single.

Baby's Rich .......................................... 7" ...... Columbia ......... DB8486 ............... 1968 £2.50 ....... £6 ..............
Come On Down To My Boat Baby .......... 7" ...... Polydor ........... 56168 ............... 1967 £50 ......... £100 ..............
Genesis ............................................... LP ..... Columbia ......... SX/SCX6286 ...... 1968 £37.50 ..... £75 ..............
Hey Bulldog ........................................ 7" ...... Columbia ......... DB8544 ............... 1969 £4 .......... £8 ..............
Maria ................................................. 7" ...... Columbia ......... DB8572 ............... 1969 £2.50 ....... £6 ..............
To Samuel A Son ................................ LP ..... Columbia ......... SCX6372 ............ 1970 £37.50 ..... £75 ..............

## GODZ
Contact High ....................................... LP ..... Fontana .......... STL5500 ............. 1967 £6 .......... £15 ..............
Godz 2 ............................................... LP ..... Fontana .......... STL5512 ............. 1969 £6 .......... £15 ..............
Godzundheit ........................................ LP ..... ESP-Disk ........ 2017 ............... 1970 £6 .......... £15 ............. US
Third Testament .................................. LP ..... ESP-Disk ........ 1077 ............... 1969 £6 .......... £15 ............. US

## GOGMAGOG
I Will Be There .................................... 12" .... Food For ......... YUMT109 ........... 1985 £4 .......... £10 ..............
                           Thought ..........

## GOINS, HERBIE & NIGHT-TIMERS
Incredible Miss Brown .......................... 7" EP . Odeon ............ MEO133 ............... 1966 £15 ......... £30 ............. French
Incredible Miss Brown .......................... 7" ...... Parlophone ....... R5533 ............... 1966 £6 .......... £12 ..............
Number One In Your Heart .................... LP ..... Parlophone ....... PMC7026 ........... 1967 £37.50 ..... £75 ..............
Number One in Your Heart .................... 7" ...... Parlophone ....... R5478 ............... 1966 £25 ......... £50 ..............

## GOLDBERG, BARRY
Another Day ........................................ 7" ...... Pye ................. 7N25465 ............ 1968 £1.50 ....... £4 ..............
Blowing My Mind ................................ LP ..... Epic ................ LN24/BN26199 ... 1966 £6 .......... £15 ............. US
Reunion .............................................. LP ..... Pye ................. NSPL28116 ......... 1968 £5 .......... £12 ..............
Two Jews Blues .................................. LP ..... Buddah .......... 203020 ............... 1969 £4 .......... £10 ..............

## GOLDEN APPLES OF THE SUN
Monkey Time ...................................... 7" ...... Decca ............. F12194 ............... 1965 £15 ......... £30 ............. demo
Monkey Time ...................................... 7" ...... Immediate ....... IM010 ............... 1965 £10 ......... £20 ..............

## GOLDEN CRUSADERS
Hey Good Looking .............................. 7" ...... Columbia ......... DB7357 ............... 1964 £4 .......... £8 ..............
I Don't Care ........................................ 7" ...... Columbia ......... DB7485 ............... 1965 £4 .......... £8 ..............
I'm In Love With You .......................... 7" ...... Columbia ......... DB7232 ............... 1964 £4 .......... £8 ..............

## GOLDEN DAWN
Power Plant ........................................ LP ..... International ..... IA4 ............... 1967 £37.50 ..... £75 ............. US
                           Artists ............

## GOLDEN DAWN (2)
My Secret World .................................. 7" ...... Sarah .............. 009 ............... 1988 £1.50 ....... £4 ............. with poster

## GOLDEN EARRING
Golden Earring are best known in the UK for their powerful hit single, 'Radar Love', but in their native Holland they are a star group with a long and successful career. The list of collectables below is just a small part of a huge discography extending over thirty years.

Another Forty-Five Miles ...................... 7" ...... Major Minor ... MM679 ............... 1970 £1.50 ....... £4 ..............
Back Home ........................................ 7" ...... Polydor ........... 2001073 ............. 1970 £1.50 ....... £4 ..............
Eight Miles High ................................ LP ..... Major Minor ... SMLP65 ............. 1969 £8 .......... £20 ..............
Eight Miles High ................................ LP ..... Polydor ........... 656019 ............... 1969 £6 .......... £15 ..............
It's Alright But It Could Be Better ........... 7" ...... Major Minor ... MM633 ............... 1969 £1.50 ....... £4 ..............

| | | | | | | |
|---|---|---|---|---|---|---|
| Just A Little Bit Of Peace | 7" | Major Minor | MM601 | 1969 £1.50 | £4 | |
| Just Earring | LP | Polydor | 736007 | 1964 £10 | £25 | Dutch |
| Miracle Mirror | LP | Polydor | 1236283 | 1968 £8 | £20 | Dutch |
| On The Double | LP | Polydor | 2653001 | 1969 £15 | £30 | Dutch double |
| Seven Tears | LP | Polydor | 2310135 | 1971 £5 | £12 | |
| That Day | 7" | Polydor | 56514 | 1970 £4 | £8 | |
| Together | LP | Polydor | 2310210 | 1972 £4 | £10 | |
| Winter Harvest | LP | Polydor | 736068 | 1967 £10 | £25 | Dutch |

## GOLDEN GATE QUARTET

| | | | | | |
|---|---|---|---|---|---|
| Get On Board | LP | Columbia | 33SX1370 | 1961 £4 | £10 |
| Shout For Joy! | LP | Columbia | 33SX1172 | 1959 £4 | £10 |
| Sings Great Spirituals | 7" EP | Columbia | SEG7700 | 1957 £2 | £5 |
| That Golden Chariot | 10" LP | Fontana | TFR6009 | 1958 £4 | £10 |

## GOLDEN GATE STRINGS

| | | | | | |
|---|---|---|---|---|---|
| Mr. Tambourine Man | 7" | Columbia | DB7634 | 1965 £1.50 | £4 |

## GOLDENROD

| | | | | | | |
|---|---|---|---|---|---|---|
| Goldenrod | LP | Chartmaker | CSG1101 | 1967 £75 | £150 | US |

## GOLDIE

| | | | | | |
|---|---|---|---|---|---|
| Going Back | 7" | Immediate | IM026 | 1966 £7.50 | £15 |
| I Do | 7" | Fontana | TF693 | 1966 £2.50 | £6 |

## GOLDIE & THE GINGERBREADS

| | | | | | | |
|---|---|---|---|---|---|---|
| Can't You Hear My Heartbeat | 7" EP | Decca | 457072 | 1965 £12.50 | £25 | French |
| Can't You Hear My Heartbeat | 7" | Decca | F12070 | 1965 £2 | £5 | |
| Sailor Boy | 7" | Decca | F12199 | 1965 £1.50 | £4 | |
| That's Why I Love You | 7" | Decca | F12126 | 1965 £1.50 | £4 | |

## GOLDING, JOHN

| | | | | | |
|---|---|---|---|---|---|
| Discarded Verse | LP | Cottage | 101S | 1974 £4 | £10 |

## GOLDSBORO, BOBBY

| | | | | | | |
|---|---|---|---|---|---|---|
| Autumn Of My Life | 7" | United Artists | UP2223 | 1968 £1.50 | £4 | |
| Bobby Goldsboro Album | LP | United Artists | UAL3/UAS6358 | 1964 £6 | £15 | US |
| Honey | LP | United Artists | (S)ULP1195 | 1968 £4 | £10 | |
| I Can't Stop Loving You | LP | United Artists | UAL3/UAS6381 | 1964 £6 | £15 | US |
| It's Too Late | LP | United Artists | (S)ULP1135 | 1966 £4 | £10 | |
| It's Too Late | 7" | United Artists | UP1128 | 1966 £2 | £5 | |
| Little Things | LP | United Artists | UAL3/UAS6425 | 1965 £6 | £15 | US |
| Little Things | 7" EP | United Artists | UEP1006 | 1965 £6 | £12 | |
| Little Things | 7" | United Artists | UP1079 | 1965 £2 | £5 | |
| Runaround | 7" | Stateside | SS193 | 1963 £2.50 | £6 | |
| Solid Goldsboro | LP | United Artists | (S)ULP1163 | 1967 £4 | £10 | |
| Take Your Love | 7" | United Artists | UP1146 | 1966 £2.50 | £6 | |
| Talented Bobby Goldsboro | 7" EP | United Artists | UEP1016 | 1966 £6 | £12 | |
| Too Many People | 7" | United Artists | UP1177 | 1967 £10 | £20 | |

## GOLDSMITH

| | | | | | |
|---|---|---|---|---|---|
| Life Is Killing Me | 7" | Bedlam | BLM001 | 1983 £5 | £10 |

## GOLDTONES

| | | | | | | |
|---|---|---|---|---|---|---|
| Goldtones Featuring Randy Seol | LP | LaBrea | L8011 | 1966 £6 | £15 | US |

## GOLEM

| | | | | | | |
|---|---|---|---|---|---|---|
| Golem | LP | Delta | 251281 | 1974 £10 | £25 | German |

## GOLIATH

| | | | | | |
|---|---|---|---|---|---|
| Goliath | LP | CBS | 64229 | 1970 £20 | £40 |
| Port And Lemon Lady | 7" | CBS | 5312 | 1971 £1.50 | £4 |

## GOLLIWOGS

The Golliwogs were the same group that later found considerable success as Creedence Clearwater Revival.

| | | | | | | |
|---|---|---|---|---|---|---|
| Brown-Eyed Girl | 7" | Vocalion | VF9266 | 1966 £10 | £20 | |
| Don't Tell Me No Lies | 7" | Fantasy | 590 | 1964 £10 | £20 | US |
| Fight Fire | 7" | Vocalion | VF9283 | 1967 £10 | £20 | |
| Walking On The Water | 7" | Scorpio | 408 | 1966 £10 | £20 | US |
| You Came Walking | 7" | Fantasy | 597 | 1965 £10 | £20 | US |
| You Got Nothin' On Me | 7" | Fantasy | 599 | 1965 £10 | £20 | US |

## GOLOWIN, SERGIUS

| | | | | | | |
|---|---|---|---|---|---|---|
| Lord Krishna Von Goloka | LP | Kosmische | KM58002 | 1973 £8 | £20 | German |

## GOLSON, BENNY

| | | | | | | |
|---|---|---|---|---|---|---|
| Benny Golson And The Philadelphians | LP | London | LTZK15176/ SAHT6061 | 1960 £8 | £20 | |
| Groovin' With Golson | LP | Esquire | 32105 | 1960 £8 | £20 | |
| Stockholm Sojourn | LP | Stateside | SL10150 | 1965 £4 | £10 | with Art Farmer |

## GOMORRHA

| | | | | | | |
|---|---|---|---|---|---|---|
| Gomorrha | LP | Cornet | 15038 | 1970 £10 | £25 | German |
| I Turned To See Whose Voice It Was | LP | Brain | 1003 | 1971 £8 | £20 | German |
| Trauma | LP | BASF | 20204138 | 1972 £6 | £15 | German |

## GONDOLIERS
God's Green Acres.................................................. 7" ...... Starlite ............ ST45001 ................ 1958 £1.50........ £4 ...............................

## GONELLA, NAT
Salute To Satchmo .................................. 10" LP Columbia........ 33S1146 ................ 1959 £5........ £12

## GONG
Gong's eccentric blend of hippy humour and electric jazz is very early seventies, yet is becoming of increasing interest to modern listeners, who appreciate the influence that the band has had on groups like Ozric Tentacles and Porcupine Tree. All the collectable early albums are masterminded by Daevid Allen (an original member of Soft Machine), although the group's creative peak was arguably reached on later albums like *You* and *Shamal*. Allen had departed by the time of the latter album, although in more recent times he has reclaimed the Gong name as his own.

Angel's Egg.................................... LP ..... Virgin ............ V2007 .................... 1973 £15........ £30 ................ with book
Camembert Electrique ..................... LP ..... Byg............ 529353 ................ 1971 £8........ £20 .... French, with insert
Continental Circus ........................... LP ..... Philips............ 6332033 ................ 1971 £8........ £20 ......................... French
Flying Teapot.................................... LP ..... Virgin ............ V2002 ................ 1973 £4........ £10 ..black and white label
Magick Brother................................ LP ..... Byg............ 529029 ................ 1970 £15........ £30 ........................ French
Magick Brother................................ LP ..... Byg............ 529305 ................ 1970 £10........ £25 ........................ French

## GONKS
That's All Right Mama ......................... 7" ...... Decca ............ F11984................ 1964 £4........ £8

## GONSALVES, PAUL
Boom Jackie Boom................................ LP ..... Vocalion ..... LAE587................ 1964 £30........ £60
Hummingbird .................................... LP ..... Deram ............ SML1064 ................ 1970 £8........ £20

## GONZALEZ
Gonzalez .......................................... LP ..... EMI............ EMC3046 ................ 1974 £10........ £25

## GONZALEZ, BELLE
Belle ........................................... LP ..... Columbia........ SCX6484 ................ 1971 £30........ £60

## GOOD, JACK FAT NOISE
Fat Noise...................................... 7" ...... Decca ............ F11233................ 1960 £2........ £5

## GOOD EARTH
It's Hard Rock & All That ....................... LP ..... Saga ............ FID2112................ 1968 £5........ £12

## GOOD SHIP LOLLIPOP
Maxwell's Silver Hammer ...................... 7" ...... Ember............ EMBS276............... 1970 £1.50........ £4

## GOOD TIME LOSERS
Trafalgar Square ................................ 7" ...... Fontana............ TF791 ................ 1967 £1.50........ £4

## GOODBYE MR. MACKENZIE
Death Of A Salesman............................. 7" ...... Scruples............ YTS1 ................ 1984 £10........ £20
Face To Face ..................................... 12" .... Claude ............ MAC1 ................ 1986 £3........ £8
Rattler........................................... 7" ...... Precious ......... JEWEL2................ 1986 £2........ £5
Rattler........................................... 12" .... Precious ......... JEWEL2T ................ 1986 £3........ £8
Blacker Than Black ............................ CD-s .. Parlophone ..... CDR6257 ............ 1990 £2........ £5
Goodbye Mr. Mackenzie ...................... CD-s .. Capitol............ CDCL501 ................ 1988 £2........ £5
Goodwill City .................................. CD-s .. Capitol............ CDCL538 ................ 1989 £2........ £5
Love Child ...................................... CD-s .. Parlophone ..... CDR6247 ............ 1990 £2........ £5
Open Your Arms .............................. CD-s .. Capitol............ CDCL513 ................ 1988 £2........ £5
Rattler........................................... CD-s .. Capitol............ CDCL522 ................ 1989 £2........ £5

## GOODEES
Condition Red.................................... 7" ...... Stax ............ STAX113 ................ 1969 £4........ £8

## GOODHAND-TAIT, PHILIP
I'm Gonna Put Some Hurt On You ........... 7" ...... Parlophone ..... R5448 ................ 1966 £2.50........ £6
Love Has Got A Hold On Me ................... 7" ...... Decca ............ F12868................ 1969 £1.50........ £4
No Problem...................................... 7" ...... Parlophone ..... R5498 ................ 1966 £2........ £5
You Can't Take Love ........................... 7" ...... Parlophone ..... R5547 ................ 1966 £2.50........ £6

## GOODISON, JOHNNY
Little Understanding ............................ 7" ...... Deram ............ DM319 ................ 1970 £1.50........ £4

## GOODMAN, BENNY
1937–1938 Jazz Concert No. 2 Vol. 1 ........ LP ..... Philips............ BBL7009 ................ 1955 £8........ £20
1937–1938 Jazz Concert No. 2 Vol. 2 ........ LP ..... Philips............ BBL7010 ................ 1955 £8........ £20
After Hours..................................... 10" LP Capitol............ LC6565 ................ 1952 £8........ £20
Benny Goodman Band.......................... 10" LP Capitol............ LC6831 ................ 1956 £6........ £15
Benny Goodman Orchestra .................. LP ..... Capitol............ LCT6012 ................ 1955 £8........ £20
Benny Goodman Orchestra .................. 10" LP HMV............ DLP1112 ................ 1956 £8........ £20
Benny Goodman Orchestra .................. 10" LP HMV............ DLP1116 ................ 1956 £6........ £15
Benny Goodman Orchestra And Quartet.... LP ..... Capitol............ LCT6104 ................ 1956 £6........ £15
Benny Goodman Quartet....................... 10" LP HMV............ DLPC6 ................ 1955 £8........ £20
Benny Goodman Sextet........................ LP ..... Philips............ BBL7021 ................ 1955 £5........ £12
Benny Goodman Sextet........................ 10" LP Fontana............ TFR6006 ................ 1958 £6........ £15
Benny Goodman Small Groups............... 10" LP Capitol............ LC6810 ................ 1956 £6........ £15
Benny Goodman Story Vol. 1................. LP ..... Brunswick ..... LAT8102 ................ 1956 £6........ £15
Benny Goodman Story Vol. 2................. LP ..... Brunswick ..... LAT8103 ................ 1956 £6........ £15
Benny Goodman Trio.......................... 10" LP Fontana............ TFR6022 ................ 1959 £5........ £12
Benny Goodman Trio.......................... 10" LP HMV............ DLPC11 ................ 1956 £6........ £15

| | | | | | | |
|---|---|---|---|---|---|---|
| Benny In Brussels | LP | Philips | BBL7299 | 1959 | £4 | £10 |
| Benny In Brussels | LP | Philips | BBL7300 | 1959 | £4 | £10 |
| Benny Rides Again | LP | Columbia | 33SX1038 | 1955 | £6 | £15 |
| Carnegie Hall Jazz Concert Vol. 1 | LP | Philips | BBL7000 | 1954 | £8 | £20 |
| Carnegie Hall Jazz Concert Vol. 2 | LP | Philips | BBL7001 | 1954 | £8 | £20 |
| Classics In Jazz | 10" LP | Capitol | LC6680 | 1954 | £8 | £20 |
| Dizzy Fingers | 10" LP | Capitol | LC6601 | 1953 | £8 | £20 |
| Easy Does It | 10" LP | Capitol | LC6557 | 1952 | £8 | £20 |
| Goodman Touch | 10" LP | Capitol | LC6620 | 1953 | £8 | £20 |
| Happy Session | LP | Philips | BBL7318 | 1959 | £4 | £10 |
| Let's Hear The Melody | 10" LP | Philips | BBR8064 | 1955 | £6 | £15 |
| Makes History | LP | Philips | BBL7073 | 1956 | £6 | £15 |
| Plays For Fletcher Henderson Fund | LP | Columbia | 33SX1020 | 1954 | £8 | £20 |
| Presents Eddie Sauter Arrangements | LP | Philips | BBL7043 | 1955 | £6 | £15 |
| Session For Sextet | 10" LP | Columbia | 33S1048 | 1954 | £8 | £20 |
| Session For Sextet No. 2 | LP | Columbia | 33SX1035 | 1955 | £6 | £15 |
| Session For Six | 10" LP | Capitol | LC6526 | 1951 | £8 | £20 |

## GOODMAN, DAVE

| | | | | | | | |
|---|---|---|---|---|---|---|---|
| Justifiable Homicide | 7" | The Label | TLR008 | 1978 | £15 | £30 | *Steve Jones & Paul Jones named on sleeve* |

## GOODWIN, RON

| | | | | | | |
|---|---|---|---|---|---|---|
| Limelight | 7" | Parlophone | MSP6035 | 1953 | £1.50 | £4 |

## GOOFERS

| | | | | | | |
|---|---|---|---|---|---|---|
| Dipsy Doodle | 7" | Vogue Coral | Q72289 | 1957 | £7.50 | £15 |
| Flip Flop And Fly | 7" | Vogue Coral | Q72074 | 1955 | £20 | £40 |
| Goofie Dry Bones | 7" | Vogue Coral | Q72094 | 1955 | £7.50 | £15 |
| Hearts Of Stone | 7" | Vogue Coral | Q72051 | 1955 | £20 | £40 |
| Push Push Push Cart | 7" | Vogue Coral | Q72267 | 1957 | £7.50 | £15 |
| Sick Sick Sick | 7" | Vogue Coral | Q72124 | 1956 | £7.50 | £15 |
| Tennessee Rock And Roll | 7" | Vogue Coral | Q72171 | 1956 | £12.50 | £25 |

## GOONS

| | | | | | | |
|---|---|---|---|---|---|---|
| Best Of The Goon Shows | LP | Parlophone | PMC1108 | 1959 | £4 | £10 |
| Best Of The Goon Shows No. 2 | LP | Parlophone | PMC1129 | 1960 | £4 | £10 |
| Eeh Ah Oh Oooh | 7" | Decca | F10885 | 1957 | £1.50 | £4 |
| Goons | 7" EP | Decca | DFE6396 | 1956 | £2 | £5 |
| I'm Walking Backwards For Christmas | 7" | Decca | F10756 | 1956 | £2 | £5 |
| My September Love | 7" | Parlophone | R4251 | 1956 | £2 | £5 |
| Russian Love Song | 7" | Decca | F10945 | 1957 | £1.50 | £4 |
| Unchained Melodies | 10" LP | Decca | LF1332 | 1964 | £6 | £15 |
| Ying Tong Song | 7" | Decca | F10780 | 1956 | £2 | £5 |

## GOPAL, SAM

Sam Gopal is a percussionist whose work can be found on several albums by the likes of Daevid Allen, G. F. Fitzgerald, and Isaac Guillory. The demand for his solo album, however, derives primarily from the fact that it is Lemmy, of future Motorhead fame, who plays guitar on the album.

| | | | | | | | |
|---|---|---|---|---|---|---|---|
| Escalator | LP | Stable | SLE8001 | 1969 | £30 | £60 | |
| Escalator | 7" | Stable | SLE8001 | 1969 | £10 | £20 | *promo sampler* |
| Horse | 7" | Stable | STA5602 | 1969 | £12.50 | £25 | |

## GORDON, DEXTER

| | | | | | | |
|---|---|---|---|---|---|---|
| Daddy Plays The Horn | LP | London | LTZN15098 | 1957 | £20 | £40 |
| Dexter Calling | LP | Blue Note | BLP/BST84083 | 1961 | £10 | £25 |
| Doin' Alright | LP | Blue Note | BLP/BST84077 | 1961 | £15 | £30 |
| Gettin' Around | LP | Blue Note | BLP/BST84204 | 1965 | £10 | £25 |
| Go! | LP | Blue Note | BLP/BST84112 | 1962 | £10 | £25 |
| One Flight Up | LP | Blue Note | BLP/BST84176 | 1964 | £10 | £25 |
| Our Man In Paris | LP | Blue Note | BLP/BST84146 | 1963 | £10 | £25 |
| Swingin' Affair | LP | Blue Note | BLP/BST84133 | 1963 | £10 | £25 |

## GORDON, JOE FOLK FOUR

| | | | | | | |
|---|---|---|---|---|---|---|
| Gay Gordons | LP | HMV | CLP1379/CSD1314 | 1960 | £4 | £10 |
| Johnnie Lad | 7" EP | HMV | 7EG8454 | 1960 | £2 | £5 |

## GORDON, PHIL

| | | | | | | |
|---|---|---|---|---|---|---|
| Down The Road Apiece | 7" | Brunswick | 05545 | 1956 | £2 | £5 |

## GORDON, RABBI JOSEPH

| | | | | | | | |
|---|---|---|---|---|---|---|---|
| Competition | 7" | Bam Caruso | NRIC030 | 1985 | £4 | £8 | *no picture sleeve* |

## GORDON, RONNIE

| | | | | | | |
|---|---|---|---|---|---|---|
| Coming Home | 7" | R&B | JB127 | 1963 | £5 | £10 |

## GORDON, ROSCOE

| | | | | | | |
|---|---|---|---|---|---|---|
| Just A Little Bit | 7" | Stateside | SS204 | 1963 | £7.50 | £15 |
| Just A Little Bit | 7" | Top Rank | JAR332 | 1960 | £7.50 | £15 |
| Keep On Doggin' | 7" | Vocalion | VP9245 | 1965 | £7.50 | £15 |
| No More Doggin' | 7" | Island | WI272 | 1966 | £7.50 | £15 |
| Surely I Love You | 7" | Island | WI256 | 1965 | £5 | £10 |

## GORDON, VINCENT

| | | | | | | | |
|---|---|---|---|---|---|---|---|
| Everybody Bawlin' | 7" | Duke | DU37 | 1969 | £1.50 | £4 | *Silvertones B side* |
| Soul Trombone | 7" | Coxsone | CS7085 | 1969 | £5 | £10 | *Larry & Alvin B side* |

## GORE, LESLEY

| | | | | | | | |
|---|---|---|---|---|---|---|---|
| All About Love | LP | Mercury | 20076MCL | 1965 | £5 | £12 | |
| Boys Boys Boys | LP | Mercury | 20020MCL | 1964 | £5 | £12 | |
| California Nights | LP | Mercury | MG2/SR61120 | 1967 | £4 | £10 | US |
| Girl Talk | LP | Mercury | 20033MCL | 1964 | £5 | £12 | |
| Girl Talk | LP | Wing | WL1183 | 1967 | £4 | £10 | |
| Golden Hits | LP | Mercury | MG2/SR61024 | 1965 | £4 | £10 | US |
| Golden Hits Vol. 2 | LP | Mercury | SR61185 | 1968 | £4 | £10 | US |
| I Won't Love You Any More | 7" | Mercury | MF889 | 1965 | £1.50 | £4 | |
| I'll Cry If I Want To | LP | Mercury | MMC14127 | 1963 | £6 | £15 | |
| I'm Fallin' Down | 7" | Mercury | MF984 | 1966 | £2 | £5 | |
| It's My Party | 7" | Mercury | AMT1205 | 1963 | £1.50 | £4 | |
| Lesley Gore | 7" EP | Mercury | 10017MCE | 1964 | £5 | £10 | |
| Maybe I Know | 7" | Mercury | MF829 | 1964 | £1.50 | £4 | |
| My Town, My Guy And Me | LP | Mercury | 20071MCL | 1965 | £5 | £12 | |
| My Town, My Guy, And Me | 7" | Mercury | MF872 | 1965 | £2.50 | £6 | |
| Sings Of Mixed-Up Hearts | LP | Mercury | 20001MCL | 1963 | £5 | £12 | |
| You Don't Own Me | 7" | Mercury | MF803 | 1964 | £1.50 | £4 | |

## GORME, EYDIE

| | | | | | | | |
|---|---|---|---|---|---|---|---|
| Climb Up The Wall | 7" | Vogue Coral | Q2014 | 1954 | £2 | £5 | |
| Everybody Go Home | 7" | CBS | AAG170 | 1963 | £1.50 | £4 | |
| Eydie Gorme | LP | HMV | CLP1156 | 1958 | £4 | £10 | |
| Eydie Gorme's Delight | LP | Coral | LVA9086 | 1958 | £4 | £10 | |
| Eydie In Love | LP | HMV | CLP1250 | 1959 | £4 | £10 | |
| Eydie Swings The Blues | LP | HMV | CLP1170 | 1958 | £4 | £10 | |
| Give A Fool A Chance | 7" | Vogue Coral | Q72092 | 1955 | £1.50 | £4 | |
| Gorme Sings Showstoppers | LP | HMV | CLP1257 | 1959 | £4 | £10 | |
| I'll Remember April | 7" EP | HMV | GES5795 | 1959 | £2 | £5 | stereo |
| Kiss In Your Eyes | 7" | HMV | POP400 | 1957 | £1.50 | £4 | |
| Love Is A Season | LP | HMV | CLP1290 | 1959 | £4 | £10 | |
| Love Is A Season | 7" EP | HMV | GES5789 | 1959 | £2 | £5 | stereo |
| Love Me Forever | 7" | HMV | POP432 | 1958 | £2 | £5 | |
| Make Yourself Comfortable | 7" | Vogue Coral | Q72044 | 1955 | £1.50 | £4 | |
| Sincerely Yours | 7" | London | HL8227 | 1956 | £4 | £8 | |
| Soldier Boy | 7" | Vogue Coral | Q72103 | 1955 | £1.50 | £4 | |
| Sure | 7" | Vogue Coral | Q2027 | 1954 | £1.50 | £4 | |
| Take A Deep Breath | 7" | Vogue Coral | Q72085 | 1955 | £1.50 | £4 | |
| Vamps The Roaring Twenties | LP | HMV | CLP1201 | 1958 | £4 | £10 | |
| Yes My Darling Daughter | 7" | CBS | AAG105 | 1962 | £1.50 | £4 | |

## GORME, EYDIE & STEVE LAWRENCE

| | | | | | | | |
|---|---|---|---|---|---|---|---|
| Cozy | LP | HMV | CLP1463 | 1962 | £4 | £10 | |
| Golden Hits | LP | HMV | CLP1404/CSD1329 | 1961 | £4 | £10 | |
| Steve And Eydie | 7" EP | CBS | AGG20035 | 1963 | £2 | £5 | |
| Steve Lawrence And Eydie Gorme | 7" EP | Coral | FEP2017 | 1959 | £2 | £5 | |
| We Got Us | LP | HMV | CLP1372/CSD1310 | 1960 | £4 | £10 | |

## GORSHIN, FRANK

| | | | | | | | |
|---|---|---|---|---|---|---|---|
| Riddler | 7" | Pye | 7N25402 | 1966 | £2 | £5 | |
| Riddler | 7" | Pye | 7N25402 | 1966 | £5 | £10 | picture sleeve |

## GOSPEL CLASSICS

| | | | | | | | |
|---|---|---|---|---|---|---|---|
| More Love That's What We Need | 7" | Chess | CRS8080 | 1968 | £10 | £20 | |

## GOSPEL GARDEN

| | | | | | | | |
|---|---|---|---|---|---|---|---|
| Finders Keepers | 7" | Camp | 602006 | 1968 | £2 | £5 | |

## GOSPEL OAK

| | | | | | | | |
|---|---|---|---|---|---|---|---|
| Gospel Oak | LP | Uni | UNLS113 | 1970 | £10 | £25 | |

## GOSPELFOLK

| | | | | | | | |
|---|---|---|---|---|---|---|---|
| Prodigal | LP | private | | 1969 | £100 | £200 | |

## GOTHIC HORIZON

| | | | | | | | |
|---|---|---|---|---|---|---|---|
| Girl With Guitar | 7" | Argo | AFW108 | 1972 | £4 | £8 | |
| If You Can Smile | 7" | Argo | AFW107 | 1973 | £2.50 | £6 | |
| Jason Lodge Poetry Book | LP | Argo | ZFB26 | 1970 | £50 | £100 | |
| Jason Lodge Poetry Book | 7" | Argo | AFW102 | 1970 | £4 | £8 | |
| Marjorie | 7" | Argo | AFW104 | 1971 | £4 | £8 | |
| Tomorrow Is Another Day | LP | Argo | ZDA150 | 1972 | £37.50 | £75 | |

## GOULDER, DAVE

| | | | | | | | |
|---|---|---|---|---|---|---|---|
| Requiem For Steam | LP | Big Ben | BB004 | 1973 | £4 | £10 | |

## GOULDER, DAVE & LIZ DYER

| | | | | | | | |
|---|---|---|---|---|---|---|---|
| January Man | LP | Argo | ZFB10 | 1970 | £6 | £15 | |
| Raven And The Crow | LP | Argo | ZFB30 | 1971 | £6 | £15 | |

## GOULDMAN, GRAHAM

| | | | | | | | |
|---|---|---|---|---|---|---|---|
| Graham Gouldman Thing | LP | RCA | LPM/LSP3954 | 1968 | £10 | £25 | US |
| Stop Stop Stop | 7" | Decca | F12334 | 1966 | £10 | £20 | |
| Upstairs Downstairs | 7" | RCA | RCA1667 | 1968 | £5 | £10 | |
| Windmills Of Your Mind | 7" | Spark | SRL1026 | 1969 | £2.50 | £6 | |

## GOVE

| | | | | | | | |
|---|---|---|---|---|---|---|---|
| Dead Letter Blues | 7" | London | HLE10295 | 1969 | £2 | £5 | |

## GOWEN, ALAN
| | | | | | | | |
|---|---|---|---|---|---|---|---|
| Before A Word Is Said | LP | Europa | JF2007 | 1981 | £4 | £10 | French |
| Two Rainbows Daily | LP | Red | ROUGE1 | 1980 | £4 | £10 | |

## GRAAS, JOHN
| | | | | | | | |
|---|---|---|---|---|---|---|---|
| Jazz Studio 2 | LP | Brunswick | LAT8046 | 1954 | £8 | £20 | with Herb Geller |
| Jazz Studio 3 | LP | Brunswick | LAT8069 | 1955 | £8 | £20 | ..with Gerry Mulligan |

## GRABHAM, MICK
| | | | | | | | |
|---|---|---|---|---|---|---|---|
| Mick The Lad | LP | United Artists | UAS29341 | 1972 | £4 | £10 | |

## GRACIE, CHARLIE
| | | | | | | | |
|---|---|---|---|---|---|---|---|
| Angel Of Love | 7" | Coral | Q72373 | 1959 | £5 | £10 | |
| Butterfly | 7" | Parlophone | R4290 | 1957 | £15 | £30 | gold label |
| Cool Baby | 7" | London | HLU8521 | 1957 | £10 | £20 | |
| Crazy Girl | 7" | London | HLU8596 | 1958 | £12.50 | £25 | |
| Doodlebug | 7" | Coral | Q72362 | 1959 | £5 | £10 | |
| Fabulous | 7" | London | HLU10563 | 1978 | £4 | £8 | tri-centre! |
| Fabulous | 7" | Parlophone | R4313 | 1957 | £15 | £30 | gold label |
| Fabulous Charlie Gracie | 7" EP | Parlophone | GEP8630 | 1957 | £15 | £30 | |
| He'll Never Love You Like I Do | 7" | Stateside | SS402 | 1965 | £15 | £30 | |
| Night And Day USA | 7" | London | HLU9603 | 1962 | £5 | £10 | |
| Oh Well-a | 7" | Coral | Q72381 | 1959 | £5 | £10 | |
| Race | 7" | Columbia | DB4477 | 1960 | £5 | £10 | |
| Wandering Eyes | 7" | London | HL8467 | 1957 | £10 | £20 | |

## GRACIOUS
| | | | | | | | |
|---|---|---|---|---|---|---|---|
| Beautiful | 7" | Polydor | 56333 | 1968 | £7.50 | £15 | |
| Gracious | LP | Vertigo | 6360002 | 1970 | £25 | £50 | spiral label |
| Once On A Windy Day | 7" | Vertigo | 6059009 | 1970 | £2 | £5 | |
| This Is Gracious | LP | Philips | 6382004 | 1972 | £30 | £60 | |

## GRADUATE
Rock musicians whose respected careers start from shaky beginnings have difficulty forgetting the fact when they are unwise enough to commit them to vinyl. Two of the grinning mod revivalists on the cover of the Graduate LP are Roland Orzabel and Curt Smith, later of Tears For Fears. The extraordinary perfectionism applied to the recording of the *Seeds Of Love* album shows how these two like to be taken seriously. With Graduate's forgettable music in their past, however, it is hard.

| | | | | | | | |
|---|---|---|---|---|---|---|---|
| Ambition | 7" | Precision | PAR111 | 1980 | £2 | £5 | |
| Ever Met A Day | 7" | Precision | PAR104 | 1980 | £2 | £5 | |
| Made One | 7" | Blue Hat | 5BHR | 198– | £4 | £8 | |

## GRAHAM, BOBBY
Interest in the two singles released by drummer Bobby Graham is due primarily to the fact that they were co-recordings with guitarist Jimmy Page.

| | | | | | | | |
|---|---|---|---|---|---|---|---|
| Skin Deep | 7" | Fontana | TF521 | 1965 | £5 | £10 | |
| Teensville | 7" | Fontana | TF667 | 1966 | £5 | £10 | |

## GRAHAM, CHICK & THE COASTERS
| | | | | | | | |
|---|---|---|---|---|---|---|---|
| Dance Baby Dance | 7" | Decca | F11932 | 1964 | £1.50 | £4 | |
| Education | 7" | Decca | F11859 | 1964 | £1.50 | £4 | |

## GRAHAM, DAVEY
The number of recordings made by innovative folk-blues guitarist Davey Graham has been limited by his belief that acts of creativity are inevitably balanced by acts of destruction elsewhere in the world. His playing was nevertheless a major influence on the likes of Bert Jansch and John Renbourn, with his difficult instrumental 'Angie' being a required test piece for acoustic guitarists in the sixties (his own version can be found on the *3/4 AD* EP).

| | | | | | | | |
|---|---|---|---|---|---|---|---|
| 3/4 AD | 7" EP | Topic | TOP70 | 1962 | £25 | £50 | with Alexis Korner |
| All That Moody | LP | Eron | 007 | 1976 | £62.50 | £125 | |
| Both Sides Now | 7" | Decca | F12841 | 1968 | £1.50 | £4 | |
| Complete Guitarist | LP | Kicking Mule | SNKF138 | 1978 | £4 | £10 | |
| Dance For Two People | LP | Kicking Mule | SNKF158 | 1979 | £4 | £10 | |
| Folk Blues & Beyond | LP | Decca | LK4649 | 1964 | £20 | £40 | |
| Folk Roots New Routes | LP | Decca | LK4652 | 1964 | £50 | £100 | with Shirley Collins |
| Folk Roots New Routes | LP | Righteous | GDC001 | 1980 | £6 | £15 | with Shirley Collins |
| From A London Hootenanny | 7" EP | Decca | DFE8538 | 1963 | £7.50 | £15 | 2 tracks by The Thamesiders |
| Godington Boundary | LP | President | PTLS1039 | 1970 | £8 | £20 | |
| Guitar Player | LP | Golden Guinea | GGL0224 | 1962 | £10 | £25 | |
| Hat | LP | Decca | SKL5011 | 1969 | £25 | £50 | |
| Holly Kaleidoscope | LP | Decca | SKL5056 | 1970 | £25 | £50 | |
| Large As Life & Twice As Natural | LP | Decca | SKL4969 | 1968 | £20 | £40 | |
| Midnight Man | LP | Decca | LK4780 | 1966 | £25 | £50 | |

## GRAHAM, ERNIE
| | | | | | | | |
|---|---|---|---|---|---|---|---|
| Ernie Graham | LP | Liberty | LBS83485 | 1971 | £10 | £25 | |

## GRAHAM, KENNY
| | | | | | | | |
|---|---|---|---|---|---|---|---|
| Afro-Cubists | 10" LP | Esquire | 20012 | 1953 | £8 | £20 | |
| Afro-Cubists | 10" LP | Esquire | 20023 | 1953 | £8 | £20 | |
| Kenny Graham And His Satellites | LP | MGM | C764 | 1958 | £6 | £15 | |
| Kenny Graham's Afro Cubists | LP | Nixa | NJL12 | 1957 | £6 | £15 | |

## GRAHAM, LEN
Wind And Water ........................................ LP ...... Topic ............. 12TS334 ................ 1977 £4 .......... £10 ...................

## GRAHAM, LOU
Wee Willie Brown ....................................... 7" ...... Coral ............. Q72322 ............... 1958 £100 ..... £200 ...................

## GRAIL
Grail ...................................................... LP ...... Metronome ..... 15393 ....................... 1971 £50 ..... £100 .................. German

## GRAINER, RON ORCHESTRA
Man In A Suitcase ..................................... 7" ...... Pye ................. 7N17383 .............. 1967 £2 ........... £5
Prisoner .................................................. 7" ...... RCA ............... RCA1635 ............. 1967 £15 ......... £30
Prisoner Arrival ....................................... 7" . EP . Six Of One ... 6OF1 ................. 1979 £5 ........... £10
That Was The Week That Was ................. 7" . Decca ............. F11597 ............... 1963 £1.50 ........ £4
Theme Music From Inspector Maigret ....... 7" . EP . Warner Bros .... WEP6012 ........... 1960 £2.50 ........ £6

## GRAMMER, BILLY
Billy Grammer Hits ................................. 7" . EP . Felsted ......... GEP1005 ............. 1959 £15 ......... £30
Gotta Travel On ...................................... 7" ...... London ............. HLU8752 ............. 1958 £2.50 ........ £6
Kissing Tree ............................................ 7" ...... Felsted ............. AF121 ................. 1959 £2.50 ........ £6
Rainbow Round My Shoulder ................... 7" ...... Brunswick ......... 05851 ................. 1961 £2 ........... £5
Travellin' On .......................................... LP ...... Monument ..... MLP/SLP14000 ...... 1961 £8 ........... £20 ...................... US
Willy, Quit Your Playing .......................... 7" ...... Felsted ............. AF128 ................. 1959 £2.50 ........ £6

## GRANAHAN, GERRY
It Hurts .................................................. 7" ...... Top Rank ...... JAR262 ................ 1960 £4 ........... £8 ...Richie Robin B side
No Chemise Please ................................... 7" ...... London ............. HL8668 ................ 1958 £7.50 ........ £15

## GRAND FUNK RAILROAD
Closer To Home ...................................... LP ...... Capitol ............. EST471 ................ 1970 £4 ........... £10
E Pluribus Funk ...................................... LP ...... Capitol ............. EAS853 ............... 1972 £4 ........... £10
Grand Funk ............................................ LP ...... Capitol ............. EST406 ............... 1970 £4 ........... £10
Live ....................................................... LP ...... Capitol ............. EST633 ............... 1971 £5 ........... £12 ........................ double
Mark,Don,& Mel 1969-71 ........................ LP ...... Capitol ............. ESTSP10 ............. 1972 £5 ........... £12 ........................ double
On Time ................................................ LP ...... Capitol ............. EST307 ............... 1969 £4 ........... £10
Survival ................................................. LP ...... Capitol ............. ESW764 .............. 1971 £4 ........... £10
We're An American Band ......................... LP ...... Capitol ............. SMAS11207 ........... 1973 £4 ........... £10 ..... US, yellow vinyl

## GRANDISONS
All Right ................................................ 7" ...... RCA ............. RCA1339 ............. 1963 £1.50 ........ £4

## GRANDMA'S ROCKERS
Homemade Apple Pie ............................... LP ...... Fredlo ............. 6727 .................. 1967 £150 ..... £250 ...................... US

## GRANFALLOON
Laser Pace ............................................. LP ...... Takoma ......... 9021 .................. 1973 £20 ......... £40 ...................... US

## GRANGER, GERRI
Just Tell Him Jane Said Hello ................... 7" ...... London ......... HLX9759 ............. 1963 £1.50 ........ £4

## GRANICUS
Granicus ................................................ LP ...... RCA ............. AFL10321 ............ 1973 £10 ......... £25 ...................... US

## GRANNIE
Grannie ................................................. LP ...... SRT ............. SRT71138 ............ 1971 £330 ..... £500 ...................

## GRANNY'S INTENTIONS
Hilda The Builder .................................... 7" ...... Deram ............. DM214 ................ 1968 £1.50 ........ £4
Honest Injun .......................................... LP ...... Deram ............. SML1060 .............. 1970 £15 ......... £30
Julie Don't Love Me Anymore ................... 7" ...... Deram ............. DM184 ................ 1968 £1.50 ........ £4
Story Of David ........................................ 7" ...... Deram ............. DM158 ................ 1967 £2 ........... £5
Take Me Back ......................................... 7" ...... Deram ............. DM293 ................ 1970 £1.50 ........ £4

## GRANT, EARL
Earl Grant .............................................. 7" . EP . Brunswick ..... OE9460 ............... 1960 £2.50 ........ £6
End ....................................................... LP ...... Brunswick ..... LAT8297 .............. 1959 £4 ........... £10
End ....................................................... 7" ...... Brunswick ..... 05762 ................. 1958 £1.50 ........ £4
House Of Bamboo .................................... 7" ...... Brunswick ..... 05824 ................. 1960 £5 ........... £10
Nothin' But The Blues .............................. LP ...... Brunswick ..... LAT8332 .............. 1960 £4 ........... £10
Stand By Me ........................................... 7" ...... Brunswick ..... 05945 ................. 1965 £1.50 ........ £4
Swinging Gently ...................................... 7" . EP . Brunswick ..... OE9493 ............... 1963 £2 ........... £5

## GRANT, ERKEY & THE EARWIGS
I'm A Hog For You ................................... 7" ...... Pye ................. 7N15521 .............. 1963 £7.50 ........ £15

## GRANT, GOGI
Both Ends Of The Candle .......................... LP ...... RCA ............. RD27054 .............. 1958 £4 ........... £10
Gigi ....................................................... LP ...... RCA ............. RD27097 .............. 1959 £4 ........... £10 ..... with Tony Martin
Goin' Home ............................................ 7" ...... London ............. HLG9185 ............. 1960 £1.50 ........ £4
Golden Ladder ........................................ 7" ...... London ............. HLB8550 ............. 1958 £2.50 ........ £6
If You Want To Get To Heaven – Shout! .. LP ...... London ............. HAG2242/ .......... 1960 £4 ........... £10
   SAHG6072 ............
Kiss Me, Honey Honey, Kiss Me ............... 7" ...... RCA ............. RCA1105 ............. 1959 £1.50 ........ £4
Suddenly There's A Valley ....................... 7" ...... London ............. HLB8192 ............. 1955 £6 ........... £12
Suddenly There's Gogi Grant ................... LP ...... London ............. HAB2032 ............. 1957 £6 ........... £15
Wayward Wind ....................................... 7" ...... London ............. HLB8282 ............. 1956 £5 ........... £10
We Believe In Love .................................. 7" ...... London ............. HLB8257 ............. 1956 £5 ........... £10

| | | | | | | | |
|---|---|---|---|---|---|---|---|
| You're In Love | 7" | London | HLB8364 | 1957 | £4 | £8 | |

## GRANT, JULIE
| | | | | | | | |
|---|---|---|---|---|---|---|---|
| Baby Baby | 7" | Pye | 7N15756 | 1965 | £1.50 | £4 | |
| Count On Me | 7" | Pye | 7N15508 | 1963 | £1.50 | £4 | |
| This Is Julie Grant | 7" EP | Pye | NEP24171 | 1962 | £4 | £8 | |

## GRANT, LEE & THE CAPITOLS
| | | | | | | | |
|---|---|---|---|---|---|---|---|
| Breaking Point | 7" | Parlophone | R5531 | 1966 | £6 | £12 | |

## GRANT, NORMAN ORCHESTRA
| | | | | | | | |
|---|---|---|---|---|---|---|---|
| Jive Medley | 7" | Starlite | ST45060 | 1961 | £1.50 | £4 | |

## GRANT, TOP
| | | | | | | | |
|---|---|---|---|---|---|---|---|
| Money Money Money | 7" | Island | WI074 | 1963 | £2 | £5 | |
| Riverbank Cobberley | 7" | Island | WI072 | 1963 | £2 | £5 | |
| Searching | 7" | Island | WI034 | 1962 | £2 | £5 | |
| Suzie | 7" | Island | WI052 | 1962 | £2 | £5 | |
| War In Africa | 7" | Island | WI077 | 1963 | £2 | £5 | |

## GRANZ, NORMAN
Norman Granz was a major force within fifties jazz without playing a note himself. His Clef label (issued in the UK on the Columbia 33CX100 series) was an important showcase for a large number of artists. All the records on the label are now sought after by jazz collectors. Alongside this, Granz organized a series of concerts in which he encouraged various well-known musicians from different areas of jazz to play together. The recorded evidence of these concerts is listed in this Guide under the heading Jazz at the Philharmonic.

## GRANTCHESTER MEADOW
| | | | | | | | |
|---|---|---|---|---|---|---|---|
| Candlelight | 7" | Amber | ABR004 | 1971 | £10 | £20 | |

## GRAPE
| | | | | | | | |
|---|---|---|---|---|---|---|---|
| Baby In A Plastic Bag | 7" | Pencil Toast | PENT001 | 1992 | £10 | £20 | |

## GRAPEFRUIT
| | | | | | | | |
|---|---|---|---|---|---|---|---|
| Around Grapefruit | LP | Stateside | (S)SL5008 | 1969 | £6 | £15 | |
| C'mon Marianne | 7" | RCA | RCA1716 | 1968 | £1.50 | £4 | |
| Dear Delilah | 7" | RCA | RCA1656 | 1968 | £1.50 | £4 | |
| Deep Water | LP | RCA | SF8030 | 1969 | £6 | £15 | |
| Deep Water | 7" | RCA | RCA1855 | 1969 | £1.50 | £4 | |
| Elevator | 7" | RCA | RCA1677 | 1968 | £1.50 | £4 | |
| Lady Godiva | 7" | RCA | RCA1907 | 1969 | £1.50 | £4 | |
| Round Going Round | 7" | Stateside | SS8011 | 1969 | £1.50 | £4 | |
| Someday Soon | 7" | Stateside | SS8005 | 1968 | £1.50 | £4 | |

## GRAPPELLY, STEPHANE
| | | | | | | | |
|---|---|---|---|---|---|---|---|
| Stephane Grappelly | 10" LP | Felsted | SDL86048 | 1956 | £8 | £20 | |
| Stephane Grappelly And His Quintet | LP | Felsted | PDL85027 | 1957 | £8 | £20 | |

## GRASS ROOTS
| | | | | | | | |
|---|---|---|---|---|---|---|---|
| Golden Grass | LP | Dunhill | (S)SL5005 | 1969 | £4 | £10 | |
| Leaving It Behind | LP | Stateside | SSL5012 | 1969 | £4 | £10 | |
| Let's Live For Today | LP | Dunhill | D(S)50020 | 1967 | £4 | £10 | US |
| Let's Live For Today | 7" | Pye | 7N25422 | 1967 | £2.50 | £6 | |
| Midnight Confessions | 7" | RCA | RCA1737 | 1968 | £1.50 | £4 | |
| Things I Should Have Said | 7" | Pye | 7N25431 | 1967 | £1.50 | £4 | |
| Where Were You When I Needed You | LP | Dunhill | D(S)50011 | 1966 | £4 | £10 | US |
| Where Were You When I Needed You | 7" EP | RCA | 86906 | 1966 | £7.50 | £15 | French |

## GRATEFUL DEAD
It used to be maintained that the Grateful Dead found it difficult to transfer the sparkle and uplift of their best live performances on to vinyl. This is actually hardly surprising, since supremely amongst the groups evolving out of the late-sixties period of rock experimentation, the Grateful Dead took risks. (The past tense has to be sadly appropriate since, with the death of guitarist Jerry Garcia, the rest of the band will not be the Grateful Dead even if they decide to perform together.) During their long live shows, the Dead would use much of their studio material as skeletons around which to fashion long improvisations. Insofar as they got better at it as they went along, the best Grateful Dead showcase is probably the late live album, *Without A Net*, but the group's style changed very little over the years and *Anthem Of The Sun*, which is mostly live, is almost as good (albeit strangely underrated when first released). Especially recommended too, as a very fine example of the Dead aiming high in the studio, is the scarce single 'Born Cross-Eyed'. This is different to the version on *Anthem Of The Sun* and has a non-album B side, a studio recording of 'Dark Star'. Both songs can also be found on the anthology, *What A Long Strange Trip It's Been*. Records of interest to Grateful Dead collectors can also be found listed under the names of Mickey Hart, Ned Lagin and Ken Kesey.

| | | | | | | | |
|---|---|---|---|---|---|---|---|
| American Beauty | LP | Mobile Fidelity | MFSL1014 | 1978 | £6 | £15 | US audiophile |
| American Beauty | LP | Warner Bros | WS1893 | 1971 | £4 | £10 | |
| Ante Up | CD | Arista | ASCD9921 | 1989 | £8 | £20 | ...US interview promo |
| Anthem Of The Sun | LP | Warner Bros | WS1749 | 1968 | £6 | £15 | |
| Aoxomoxoa | LP | Warner Bros | WS1790 | 1969 | £6 | £15 | |
| Aoxomoxoa | CD | WEA | 9271782 | 1989 | £5 | £12 | |
| Blues For Allah | CD | Grateful Dead | GDPD4001 | 1990 | £6 | £15 | ...picture disc |
| Born Cross-Eyed | 7" | Warner Bros | WB7186 | 1967 | £10 | £20 | |
| Built To Last | CD | Arista | ADP8575 | 1989 | £8 | £20 | US promo picture disc, playing cards |
| Dark Star | 7" | Warner Bros | SAM79 | 1977 | £2 | £5 | |
| Dead Zone | CD | Arista | | 1986 | £50 | £100 | 6 discs, booklet, poster |
| Europe '72 | LP | Warner Bros | K66019 | 1972 | £6 | £15 | triple |
| From The Mars Hotel | LP | Mobile Fidelity | MFSL1172 | 1980 | £6 | £15 | US audiophile |
| Grateful Dead | LP | Warner Bros | W1689 | 1967 | £15 | £30 | mono |
| Grateful Dead | LP | Warner Bros | WS1689 | 1967 | £8 | £20 | |

| Title | Format | Label | Cat No | Year | | | Notes |
|---|---|---|---|---|---|---|---|
| Grateful Dead | CD | Atlantic | K259302 | 1988 | £5 | £12 | |
| Grateful Dead Live | LP | Warner Bros | K66009 | 1971 | £6 | £15 | double |
| Greetings From The Mars Hotel | CD | Grateful Dead | GDPD4007 | 1990 | £6 | £15 | picture disc |
| Greetings From The Mars Hotel | CD | Mobile Fidelity | MFCD830 | 1985 | £6 | £15 | US audiophile |
| Historic Dead | LP | Polydor | 2310171 | 1972 | £8 | £20 | |
| Historic Dead | LP | Sunflower | SNF5004 | 1971 | £15 | £30 | US |
| History Of The Grateful Dead (Bear's Choice) | LP | Warner Bros | K46246 | 1973 | £4 | £10 | |
| Let Me Sing Your Blues Away | 7" | Warner Bros | K19301 | 1973 | £1.50 | £4 | |
| Live Dead | LP | Warner Bros | K66002 | 1971 | £5 | £12 | green label, double |
| Live Dead | LP | Warner Bros | WS1830 | 1970 | £8 | £20 | double |
| One More Saturday Night | 7" | Warner Bros | K16167 | 1972 | £1.50 | £4 | |
| Steal Your Face | LP | United Artists | UAD60131/2 | 1976 | £8 | £20 | double bonus LP |
| Steal Your Face | CD | Grateful Dead | GDPD4006 | 1990 | £6 | £15 | picture disc |
| Stealin' | 7" | Scorpio | 201 | 1966 | £150 | £250 | US |
| Terrapin Station | LP | Direct Disk | SD16619 | 1979 | £15 | £30 | US audiophile |
| U.S. Blues | 7" | United Artists | UP36030 | 1974 | £1.50 | £4 | |
| Uncle John's Band | 7" | Warner Bros | WB7410 | 1970 | £2 | £5 | |
| Vintage Dead | LP | Polydor | 2310172 | 1972 | £8 | £20 | |
| Vintage Dead | LP | Sunflower | SNF5001 | 1970 | £15 | £30 | US |
| Wake Of The Flood | CD | Grateful Dead | GDPD4002 | 1990 | £6 | £15 | picture disc |
| Workingman's Dead | LP | Warner Bros | WS1869 | 1970 | £4 | £10 | |

## GRAVENITES, NICK

| Title | Format | Label | Cat No | Year | | | Notes |
|---|---|---|---|---|---|---|---|
| My Labours | LP | CBS | 63818 | 1969 | £5 | £12 | |
| Steelyard Blues | LP | Liberty | 352662 | 1973 | £4 | £10 | US |

## GRAVES, CONLEY

| Title | Format | Label | Cat No | Year | | | Notes |
|---|---|---|---|---|---|---|---|
| Genius At Work | LP | Brunswick | LAT8116 | 1956 | £5 | £12 | |

## GRAVESTONE

| Title | Format | Label | Cat No | Year | | | Notes |
|---|---|---|---|---|---|---|---|
| Doomsday | LP | AVC | 793102 | 1979 | £15 | £30 | German |
| War | LP | AVC | 80020 | 1972 | £15 | £30 | German |

## GRAVY TRAIN

| Title | Format | Label | Cat No | Year | | | Notes |
|---|---|---|---|---|---|---|---|
| Ballad Of A Peaceful Man | LP | Vertigo | 6360051 | 1971 | £75 | £150 | spiral label |
| Climb Aboard The Gravy Train | 7" | Dawn | DNS1115 | 1975 | £1.50 | £4 | |
| Gravy Train | LP | Vertigo | 6360023 | 1970 | £15 | £30 | spiral label |
| Second Birth | LP | Dawn | DNLS3046 | 1973 | £15 | £30 | |
| Staircase To The Day | LP | Dawn | DNLH1 | 1974 | £15 | £30 | |
| Starbright Starlight | 7" | Dawn | DNS1058 | 1974 | £1.50 | £4 | |
| Strength Of A Dream | 7" | Dawn | DNS1036 | 1973 | £1.50 | £4 | |

## GRAY, BARRY

| Title | Format | Label | Cat No | Year | | | Notes |
|---|---|---|---|---|---|---|---|
| Adventures Of Twizzle | 7" EP | HMV | 7EG8339 | 1957 | £5 | £10 | |
| Captain Scarlet | 7" | Pye | 7N17391 | 1967 | £2 | £5 | |
| Fireball XL5 | 7" | Melodisc | 1591 | 1964 | £2.50 | £6 | |
| Fireball XL5 | 7" | Melodisc | 1591 | 1964 | £10 | £20 | picture sleeve |
| Joe 90 | 7" | Pye | 7N17625 | 1969 | £4 | £8 | |
| Robot Man | 7" | Philips | 326587BF | 1963 | £10 | £20 | picture sleeve, with Mary Jane |
| Robot Man | 7" | Philips | 326587BF | 1963 | £2.50 | £6 | with Mary Jane |
| Supercar Club | 7" | National | LYN250 | 1962 | £6 | £12 | |
| Supercar: Flight Of Fancy | LP | Golden Guinea | GGL0106 | 1961 | £15 | £30 | stereo |
| Thunderbirds Are Go! | LP | United Artists | SULP1159 | 1967 | £37.50 | £75 | stereo |
| Thunderbirds Are Go! | LP | United Artists | ULP1159 | 1966 | £30 | £60 | mono |
| Thunderbirds Theme | 7" | Pye | 7N17016 | 1965 | £4 | £8 | |
| Thunderbirds Theme | 7" | Pye | 7N17016 | 1965 | £10 | £20 | picture sleeve |
| Twizzle: Stories And Songs | 7" EP | HMV | 7EG8417 | 1957 | £5 | £10 | |

## GRAY, CLAUDE

| Title | Format | Label | Cat No | Year | | | Notes |
|---|---|---|---|---|---|---|---|
| Country And Western Aces | 7" EP | Mercury | 10012MCE | 1964 | £4 | £8 | |

## GRAY, DOBIE

| Title | Format | Label | Cat No | Year | | | Notes |
|---|---|---|---|---|---|---|---|
| Dobie Gray Sings For In Crowders | LP | Charger | CHRM/CHRS2002 | 1965 | £6 | £15 | US |
| In Crowd | 7" | London | HL9953 | 1965 | £2 | £5 | |
| See You At The Go-Go | 7" | Pye | 7N25307 | 1965 | £6 | £12 | |

## GRAY, DOLORES

| Title | Format | Label | Cat No | Year | | | Notes |
|---|---|---|---|---|---|---|---|
| After You Get What You Want | 7" | Brunswick | 05382 | 1955 | £1.50 | £4 | |
| Rock Love | 7" | Brunswick | 05407 | 1955 | £5 | £10 | |
| There'll Be Some Changes Made | 7" | Capitol | CL14732 | 1957 | £1.50 | £4 | |

## GRAY, GLENN

| Title | Format | Label | Cat No | Year | | | Notes |
|---|---|---|---|---|---|---|---|
| Glenn Gray And The Casa Loma Orchestra | LP | Capitol | LCT6128 | 1957 | £4 | £10 | |

## GRAY, HERBIE

| Title | Format | Label | Cat No | Year | | | Notes |
|---|---|---|---|---|---|---|---|
| We're Staying Here | 7" | Giant | GN38 | 1968 | £2 | £5 | |

## GRAY, JERRY

| Title | Format | Label | Cat No | Year | | | Notes |
|---|---|---|---|---|---|---|---|
| Jerry Gray And His Orchestra | LP | Brunswick | LAT8164 | 1957 | £5 | £12 | |

## GRAY, JOHNNIE

| Title | Format | Label | Cat No | Year | | | Notes |
|---|---|---|---|---|---|---|---|
| Apache | 7" | Fontana | H134 | 1958 | £4 | £8 | |
| Tequila | 7" | Fontana | H123 | 1958 | £4 | £8 | |

# GRAY, OWEN

| Title | Format | Label | Cat# | Year | | | Notes |
|---|---|---|---|---|---|---|---|
| Am Satisfy | 7" | Collins Downbeat | CR007 | 1968 | £4 | £8 | Sir Collins B side |
| Ay Ay Ay | 7" | Fab | FAB96 | 1969 | £1.50 | £4 | |
| Best Twist | 7" | Blue Beat | BB113 | 1962 | £6 | £12 | |
| Big Mabel | 7" | Blue Beat | BB147 | 1963 | £6 | £12 | |
| Call Me My Pet | 7" | Blue Beat | BB188 | 1963 | £6 | £12 | |
| Collins Greetings | 7" | Collins Downbeat | CR003 | 1967 | £4 | £8 | |
| Come On Baby | 7" | Chek | TD101 | 1962 | £4 | £8 | |
| Cupid | LP | Melodisc | MLP12153 | 196– | £6 | £15 | |
| Cutest Little Woman | 7" | Blue Beat | BB8 | 1960 | £6 | £12 | |
| Days I'm Living | 7" | Blue Beat | BB365 | 1966 | £6 | £12 | |
| Do You Want To Jump | 7" | Blue Beat | BB108 | 1962 | £6 | £12 | |
| Dolly Baby | 7" | Island | WI020 | 1962 | £5 | £10 | |
| Don't Take Your Love Away | 7" | Camel | CA34 | 1969 | £1.50 | £4 | |
| Draw Me Nearer | 7" | Blue Beat | BB217 | 1964 | £6 | £12 | |
| Every Beat Of My Heart | 7" | Camel | CA37 | 1969 | £1.50 | £4 | |
| Experienced | 7" | Trojan | TR670 | 1969 | £1.50 | £4 | |
| Get Drunk | 7" | Blue Beat | BB43 | 1961 | £6 | £12 | |
| Girl What You Doing To Me | 7" | Camel | CA25 | 1969 | £1.50 | £4 | |
| Give It To Me | 7" | Coxsone | CS7053 | 1968 | £5 | £10 | |
| Give Me A Little Sign | 7" | Coxsone | CS7047 | 1968 | £5 | £10 | |
| Groovin'. | 7" | Downtown | DT423 | 1969 | £1.50 | £4 | Herbie Gray B side |
| Help Me | 7" | Island | WIP6000 | 1967 | £5 | £10 | |
| I Can't Stop Loving You | 7" | Blue Cat | BS156 | 1969 | £2.50 | £6 | |
| I Can't Stop Loving You | 7" | Trojan | TR650 | 1969 | £1.50 | £4 | |
| I Feel Good | 7" | Starlite | ST45078 | 1962 | £4 | £8 | |
| I'm Gonna Take You Back | 7" | Collins Downbeat | CR010 | 1968 | £4 | £8 | Glen Adams B side |
| I'm So Lonely | 7" | Collins Downbeat | CR004 | 1967 | £4 | £8 | Sir Collins B side |
| I'm Still Waiting | 7" | Island | WI048 | 1962 | £5 | £10 | |
| In My Dreams | 7" | Starlite | ST45088 | 1962 | £4 | £8 | |
| It's Gonna Work Out Fine | 7" | Aladdin | WI603 | 1965 | £2.50 | £6 | |
| Jenny Lee | 7" | Starlite | ST45019 | 1960 | £5 | £10 | |
| Linda Lu | 7" | Island | WI607 | 1965 | £2.50 | £6 | |
| Lovey Dovey | 7" | Downtown | DT428 | 1969 | £1.50 | £4 | Herbie Gray B side |
| Lovey Dovey | 7" | Trojan | TR632 | 1968 | £1.50 | £4 | |
| Mash It | 7" | Starlite | ST45032 | 1961 | £4 | £8 | |
| Midnight Track | 7" | Island | WI030 | 1962 | £5 | £10 | |
| No Good Woman | 7" | Blue Beat | BB103 | 1962 | £6 | £12 | |
| On The Beach | 7" | Dice | CC3 | 1962 | £5 | £10 | |
| Paradise | 7" | Island | WI267 | 1966 | £5 | £10 | |
| Please Let Me Go | 7" | Starlite | ST45015 | 1960 | £5 | £10 | |
| Pretty Girl | 7" | Blue Beat | BB127 | 1962 | £6 | £12 | |
| Reggae Dance | 7" | Duke | DU12 | 1969 | £1.50 | £4 | |
| Reggae With Soul | LP | Trojan | TTL24 | 1969 | £4 | £10 | |
| Rocking In My Feet | 7" | Blue Beat | BB75 | 1962 | £6 | £12 | |
| Seven Lonely Days | 7" | Duke | DU33 | 1969 | £1.50 | £4 | with Laurel Aitken |
| She's Gone To Napoli | 7" | Blue Beat | BB149 | 1963 | £6 | £12 | |
| Shook Shimmy And Shake | 7" | Island | WI252 | 1965 | £5 | £10 | |
| Sings | LP | Starlite | STLP5 | 1961 | £50 | £100 | |
| Snow Falling | 7" | Blue Beat | BB201 | 1963 | £6 | £12 | |
| Sugar Dumpling | 7" | Pama | PM810 | 1970 | £1.50 | £4 | |
| Swing Low | 7" | Fab | FAB126 | 1969 | £1.50 | £4 | |
| These Foolish Things | 7" | Blue Cat | BS123 | 1968 | £2.50 | £6 | |
| They Got To Move | 7" | Blue Beat | BB136 | 1962 | £6 | £12 | |
| Three Coins In The Fountain | 7" | Fab | FAB90 | 1969 | £1.50 | £4 | |
| Tree In The Meadow | 7" | Blue Beat | BB139 | 1962 | £6 | £12 | |
| Twist Baby | 7" | Island | WI002 | 1962 | £5 | £10 | |
| Understand My Love | 7" | Fab | FAB120 | 1969 | £1.50 | £4 | |
| You Don't Know Like I Know | 7" | Island | WI258 | 1965 | £5 | £10 | |

# GRAY, WARDELL

| Title | Format | Label | Cat# | Year | | | Notes |
|---|---|---|---|---|---|---|---|
| Chase And Steeplechase | 10" LP | Brunswick | LA8646 | 1954 | £30 | £60 | with Dexter Gordon |
| Memorial Album Vol. 1 | LP | Stateside | SL10144 | 1965 | £4 | £10 | |
| Memorial Album Vol. 2 | LP | Stateside | SL10145 | 1965 | £4 | £10 | |
| Memorial Vol. 1 | LP | Esquire | 32016 | 1956 | £15 | £30 | |
| Memorial Vol. 2 | LP | Esquire | 32023 | 1957 | £15 | £30 | |

# GRAY BROTHERS

| Title | Format | Label | Cat# | Year | | |
|---|---|---|---|---|---|---|
| Always | 7" | Blue Cat | BS124 | 1968 | £2.50 | £6 |

# GRAYZELL, RUDY

| Title | Format | Label | Cat# | Year | | |
|---|---|---|---|---|---|---|
| Looking At The Moon | 7" | London | HL8094 | 1954 | £30 | £60 |

# GRAZINA

| Title | Format | Label | Cat# | Year | | |
|---|---|---|---|---|---|---|
| Be My Baby | 7" | HMV | POP1212 | 1963 | £2.50 | £6 |
| Don't Be Shy | 7" | HMV | POP1149 | 1963 | £2.50 | £6 |
| Lover Please Believe Me | 7" | HMV | POP1094 | 1962 | £2.50 | £6 |

# GREASE BAND

| Title | Format | Label | Cat# | Year | | |
|---|---|---|---|---|---|---|
| Grease Band | LP | Harvest | SHVL790 | 1971 | £4 | £10 |

# GREAT, JOHNNY B

| Title | Format | Label | Cat# | Year | | |
|---|---|---|---|---|---|---|
| School Is In | 7" | Decca | F11740 | 1963 | £1.50 | £4 |

You'll Never Leave Me............................ 7" .... Decca ............ F11804.................. 1964 £1.50........£4

## GREAT AWAKENING

The instrumental version of 'Amazing Grace' credited to the Great Awakening starts with a single electric guitar, then rapidly adds further guitars until a whole choir of them are wailing away at the traditional theme. Then the guitars are stripped away until the solo guitar is left to finish the piece. It is extraordinarily effective – and the 'Cohen' arranging credit has led many observers, including disc jockey John Peel when playing the record at the time of its first release and the present author, to assume that this must be David Cohen from Country Joe and the Fish. Further research by *Q* magazine, however, revealed that this is actually an altogether less celebrated David Cohen, who worked as a session musician in the late sixties.

Amazing Grace......................................... 7" ...... London ........... HLU10284............. 1969 £1.50.....£4 ...............................

## GREAT DJELI
Great Djeli........................................... LP ...... Gawsounds ........................ 1981 £25.........£50 ...............Dutch
Productions ......

## GREAT LEAP FORWARD
Controlling The Edges Of Tone ............... 7" ...... Ron Johnson ... ZRON20............. 1987 £1.50......£4

## GREAT SATURDAY NIGHT SWINDLE
Great Saturday Night Swindle.................... LP ...... CBS............................. 1977 £15.........£30 ......................Irish

## GREAT SOCIETY

The Great Society was one of the first and best known locally of the San Francisco bands, but its career was halted when singer Grace Slick was invited to join the rival Jefferson Airplane. During its short life, the band only recorded the one single, but a good live recording produced enough material for the two posthumous albums listed. These reveal the group to be a tight, efficient unit that would undoubtedly have sounded very impressive indeed had a studio album ever been recorded. Particularly interesting are the early versions of two songs that Jefferson Airplane made their own – 'White Rabbit' and 'Somebody To Love'.

Conspicuous Only In Its Absence.............. LP ...... CBS............... 63476.................. 1968 £6.........£15
How It Was...................................... LP ...... CBS............... CS9702.................. 1968 £8.........£20 ...............US
Someone To Love.................................. 7" ...... North Beach.... 1001 ..................... 1966 £25.........£50 ...............US

## GREATEST SHOW ON EARTH
Going's Easy ................................... LP ...... Harvest ....... SHVL783 ............. 1970 £10.........£25
Greatest Show On Earth ...................... LP ...... Harvest ....... SHSM2004............. 1975 £6.........£15 ............, double
Horizons .......................................... LP ...... Harvest ....... SHVL769 ............. 1970 £10.........£25

## GRECO, BUDDY
At Mister Kelly's ............................... LP ...... Vogue Coral.... LVA9021 ......... 1956 £4.........£10
I've Grown Accustomed To Her Face ........ 7" ...... London ........... HLR8613............. 1958 £1.50.........£4
My Buddy ........................................ LP ...... Fontana ....... TFL5098 ............. 1960 £4.........£10
Songs For Swinging Losers ................. LP ...... Fontana ....... TFL5125/STFL552. 1961 £4.........£10
With All My Heart............................... 7" ...... London ........... HLR8452............. 1957 £5.........£10

## GRECO, JULIETTE
Juliette Greco Sings ......................... 10" LP Philips ............ BBR8023.................. 1954 £5.........£12

## GREEK FOUNTAIN RIVER FRONT BAND
Takes Requests ................................. LP ...... Montel........... LLP110 ................. 1965 £25.........£50 ...............US

## GREEN, AL
Back Up Train................................... LP ...... Action............ ACLP6008 ............. 1969 £6.........£15
Back Up Train................................... 7" ...... Bell............... BLL1188 ............. 1971 £1.50......£4
Back Up Train................................... 7" ...... Stateside ....... SS2079............. 1968 £4.........£8
Don't Hurt Me No More......................... 7" ...... Action............ ACT4540 ............. 1969 £1.50......£4
Full Of Fire (extended) ....................... 7" ...... London ........... HLU10511 ............. 1975 £2.............£5 ............. promo only

## GREEN, GRANT
Alive............................................... LP ...... Blue Note ...... BST84360 ............. 1970 £5.........£12
Am I Blue.......................................... LP ...... Blue Note ...... BLP/BST84139 ...... 1965 £15.........£30
Carryin' On ...................................... LP ...... Blue Note ...... BST84327 ............. 1969 £6.........£15
Feelin' The Spirit .............................. LP ...... Blue Note ...... BLP/BST84132 ...... 1963 £15.........£30
Goin' West ........................................ LP ...... Blue Note ...... BST84310 ............. 1969 £6.........£15
Grant's First Stand ............................ LP ...... Blue Note ...... BLP/BST84064 ...... 1961 £20.........£40
Grantstand........................................ LP ...... Blue Note ...... BLP/BST84086 ...... 196– £15.........£30
Green Is Beautiful.............................. LP ...... Blue Note ...... BST84342 ............. 1970 £5.........£12
Green Street...................................... LP ...... Blue Note ...... BLP/BST84071 ...... 1962 £15.........£30
I Want To Hold Your Hand ................... LP ...... Blue Note ...... BLP/BST84202 ...... 1966 £15.........£30
Idle Moments..................................... LP ...... Blue Note ...... BLP/BST84154 ...... 1964 £15.........£30
Latin Bit .......................................... LP ...... Blue Note ...... BLP/BST84111 ...... 1963 £15.........£30
Shades Of Green ............................... LP ...... Blue Note ...... BST84413 ............. 1970 £5.........£12
Street Of Dreams ............................... LP ...... Blue Note ...... BLP/BST84253 ...... 1968 £8.........£20
Sunday Mornin' .................................. LP ...... Blue Note ...... BLP/BST84099 ...... 1962 £20.........£40
Talkin' About! ................................... LP ...... Blue Note ...... BLP/BST84183 ...... 1964 £20.........£40
Visions ............................................ LP ...... Blue Note ...... BST84373 ............. 1970 £5.........£12

## GREEN, IAN
Last Pink Rose .................................. 7" ...... Polydor ........ 56194.................. 1967 £1.50......£4
Revelation........................................ LP ...... CBS............... 63840.................. 1970 £4.........£10

## GREEN, KATHE
If I Thought You'd Ever Change Your ....... 7" ...... Deram ............ DM279 .................. 1969 £1.50......£4
Mind ..............................................
Run The Length Of Your Wildness........... LP ...... Deram ............ SML1039 ............. 1969 £15.........£30

## GREEN, PETER

Like B. B. King before him, Peter Green discovered the knack of playing a single note on the guitar with real soul. Performances like 'The Supernatural', with John Mayall, or 'I Loved Another Woman' and 'Love That Burns' with Fleetwood Mac are testimony and tribute to an outstanding blues guitar voice. *The End Of The Game* is a different kind of guitar playing. In place of soul and beauty, there is anger and anguish, burning out of every twisted note of these largely improvised instrumentals. It is no wonder that Green's next act was to quit the music business, give away all his money, and embark on a life of withdrawn paranoia from which he has never really recovered, despite the occasional foray back into the recording studio.

| | | | | | | |
|---|---|---|---|---|---|---|
| Beast Of Burden | 7" | Reprise | K14141 | 1972 £1.50 | £4 | |
| Blue Guitar | LP | Creole | CRX5 | 1981 £4 | £10 | blue vinyl |
| End Of The Game | LP | Reprise | RSLP9006 | 1970 £4 | £10 | |
| Heavy Heart | 7" | Reprise | K14092 | 1971 £1.50 | £4 | |
| Heavy Heart | 7" | Reprise | RS27012 | 1971 £1.50 | £4 | |
| In The Skies | LP | PVK | PVLS101 | 1979 £4 | £10 | green vinyl |

## GREEN, URBIE

| | | | | | | |
|---|---|---|---|---|---|---|
| All About Urbie Green | LP | HMV | CLP1158 | 1958 £6 | £15 | |
| Urbie Green Orchestra | LP | London | LTZN15002 | 1956 £8 | £20 | |

## GREEN ANGELS

| | | | | | | |
|---|---|---|---|---|---|---|
| Let It Happen | 7" | Parlophone | R5390 | 1965 £1.50 | £4 | |

## GREEN BULLFROG

| | | | | | | |
|---|---|---|---|---|---|---|
| Green Bullfrog | LP | MCA | MKPS2021 | 1972 £8 | £20 | |

## GREEN GINGER TREE

| | | | | | | |
|---|---|---|---|---|---|---|
| From The Land Of Green Ginger | 7" EP | Decca | DFE8623 | 1965 £37.50 | £75 | |

## GREEN ON RED

| | | | | | | |
|---|---|---|---|---|---|---|
| Two Bibles | LP | private | | 1981 £8 | £20 | US |

## GREEN RIVER BOYS

| | | | | | | |
|---|---|---|---|---|---|---|
| Big Bluegrass Special | LP | Capitol | (S)T1810 | 1962 £10 | £25 | US |

## GREENBAUM, NORMAN

| | | | | | | |
|---|---|---|---|---|---|---|
| Spirit In The Sky | LP | Reprise | RS6365 | 1969 £5 | £12 | US |

## GREENBEATS

| | | | | | | |
|---|---|---|---|---|---|---|
| Pretty Woman | 7" | Spin | SP2007 | 1967 £1.50 | £4 | |

## GREENE, BERNIE & HIS STEREO MAD-MEN

| | | | | | | |
|---|---|---|---|---|---|---|
| Musically Mad | LP | RCA | LPM/LSP1929 | 1958 £8 | £20 | US |

## GREENE, CLAUDE 'FATS'

| | | | | | | |
|---|---|---|---|---|---|---|
| Fats Shake 'Em Up | 7" | Island | WI290 | 1966 £2 | £5 | |

## GREENE, DODO

| | | | | | | |
|---|---|---|---|---|---|---|
| My Hour Of Need | LP | Blue Note | BLP/BST9001 | 1962 £20 | £40 | |

## GREENGAGE

| | | | | | | |
|---|---|---|---|---|---|---|
| Greengage | LP | Look | LKLP6414 | 1979 £6 | £15 | |

## GREENSLADE

| | | | | | | |
|---|---|---|---|---|---|---|
| Bedside Manners Are Extra | LP | Warner Bros | K46259 | 1973 £4 | £10 | |
| Greenslade | LP | Warner Bros | K46207 | 1973 £4 | £10 | |
| Spyglass Guest | LP | Warner Bros | K56055 | 1974 £4 | £10 | |
| Time And Tide | LP | Warner Bros | K56126 | 1975 £4 | £10 | |

## GREENSLADE, ARTHUR

| | | | | | | |
|---|---|---|---|---|---|---|
| Rockin' Susannah | 7" | Decca | F11363 | 1961 £1.50 | £4 | |

## GREENSLADE, DAVE

*The Pentateuch* is not so much a double LP that includes a book, as a book that just happens to have a couple of records tucked into pockets in its cover. The illustrations, packed with a wealth of often disturbing detail, are the essence of *The Pentateuch* – Dave Greenslade's rather simple keyboard music just cannot match their impact. Now if only Patrick Woodruffe, or some other talented illustrator, would get together with Vangelis, or, better still, Tomita . . .

| | | | | | | |
|---|---|---|---|---|---|---|
| Pentateuch | LP | EMI | EMC3321/2 | 1979 £10 | £25 | double with book |

## GREENWICH, ELLIE

| | | | | | | |
|---|---|---|---|---|---|---|
| Composes, Produces And Sings | LP | United Artists | UAS6648 | 1968 £5 | £12 | US |
| I Want You To Be My Baby | 7" | United Artists | UP1180 | 1967 £1.50 | £4 | |
| Sunshine After The Rain | 7" | United Artists | UP2214 | 1968 £1.50 | £4 | |

## GREENWOOD, NICK

Although Vincent Crane was perfectly capable of supplying a bass line with his organ pedals, Arthur Brown's management insisted on adding a bass player to the Crazy World. This was Nick Greenwood – later a member of Khan. Kingdom records issued his solo LP in 1972, which is now extremely scarce.

| | | | | | | |
|---|---|---|---|---|---|---|
| Cold Cuts | LP | Kingdom | KVLP9002 | 1972 £180 | £300 | |

## GREENWOOD, STOCKER & FRIENDS

| | | | | | | |
|---|---|---|---|---|---|---|
| Billy And Nine | LP | Changes | | 1979 £25 | £50 | |

## GREGG, BOBBY & FRIENDS

| | | | | | | |
|---|---|---|---|---|---|---|
| Jam | 7" | Columbia | DB4825 | 1962 £2 | £5 | |

## GREGORY, IAN

| | | | | | | | |
|---|---|---|---|---|---|---|---|
| Can't You Hear The Beat | 7" | Pye | 7N15397 | 1961 | £7.50 | £15 | |
| How Many Times | 7" | Columbia | DB7085 | 1963 | £2.50 | £6 | |
| Mr. Lovebug | 7" | Pye | 7N15435 | 1962 | £7.50 | £15 | |
| Time Will Tell | 7" | Pye | 7N15295 | 1960 | £7.50 | £15 | |

## GREGORY, JOHNNY ORCHESTRA

| | | | | | | | |
|---|---|---|---|---|---|---|---|
| Bonanza | 7" | Fontana | H286 | 1960 | £2 | £5 | |
| Bonanza | 7" EP | Fontana | TFE17331 | 1960 | £4 | £8 | |
| Maverick | 7" EP | Fontana | TFE17325 | 1960 | £4 | £8 | |
| Route Sixty-Six | 7" EP | Fontana | TFE17382 | 1962 | £2 | £5 | |
| Route 66 | 7" | Fontana | H341 | 1961 | £2 | £5 | |
| TV Thrillers | 7" EP | Fontana | TFE17389 | 1962 | £4 | £8 | |
| Wagon Train | 7" | Fontana | H288 | 1961 | £2 | £5 | |

## GREGORY, TONY

| | | | | | | | |
|---|---|---|---|---|---|---|---|
| Baby Come On Home | 7" | Doctor Bird | DB1007 | 1966 | £5 | £10 | |
| Get Out Of My Life | 7" | Island | WI3029 | 1967 | £5 | £10 | Soul Brothers B side |
| Give Me One More Chance | 7" | Doctor Bird | DB1016 | 1966 | £5 | £10 | |
| Only A Fool | 7" | Coxsone | CS7013 | 1967 | £5 | £10 | |
| Sings | LP | Coxsone | CSL8011 | 1967 | £25 | £50 | |

## GREMLINS

| | | | | | | | |
|---|---|---|---|---|---|---|---|
| Coming Generation | 7" | Mercury | MF981 | 1966 | £4 | £8 | |
| You Gotta Believe It | 7" | Mercury | MF1004 | 1967 | £4 | £8 | |

## GREY, RONNIE & THE JETS

| | | | | | | | |
|---|---|---|---|---|---|---|---|
| Run Manny Run | 7" | Capitol | CL14329 | 1955 | £10 | £20 | |

## GREYHOUND

| | | | | | | | |
|---|---|---|---|---|---|---|---|
| Black And White | LP | Trojan | TRLS27 | 1971 | £4 | £10 | |

## GRIER, ROOSEVELT

| | | | | | | | |
|---|---|---|---|---|---|---|---|
| C'mon Cupid | 7" | Pama | PM784 | 1969 | £1.50 | £4 | |
| People Make The World | 7" | Action | ACT4515 | 1968 | £1.50 | £4 | |
| Who's Got The Ball Y'All | 7" | Pama | PM774 | 1969 | £1.50 | £4 | |

## GRIFFIN

| | | | | | | | |
|---|---|---|---|---|---|---|---|
| I Am The Noise In Your Head | 7" | Bell | BLL1075 | 1969 | £10 | £20 | |
| In The Darkness | 7" | MGM | 2006088 | 1972 | £2 | £5 | |

## GRIFFIN, JAMES

| | | | | | | | |
|---|---|---|---|---|---|---|---|
| Summer Holiday | LP | Reprise | R(9)6091 | 1963 | £5 | £12 | US |

## GRIFFIN, JOHNNY

| | | | | | | | |
|---|---|---|---|---|---|---|---|
| Big Soul-Band | LP | Riverside | RLP12331 | 1960 | £6 | £15 | |
| Change Of Pace | LP | Riverside | RLP368 | 1961 | £6 | £15 | |
| Lookin' At Monk | LP | Jazzland | JLP39 | 1961 | £8 | £20 | with Eddie 'Lockjaw' Davis |
| Man I Love | LP | Polydor | 583734 | 1969 | £8 | £20 | |
| Tough Tenors | LP | Jazzland | JLP31 | 1960 | £8 | £20 | with Eddie 'Lockjaw' Davis |

## GRIFFITH, ANDY

| | | | | | | | |
|---|---|---|---|---|---|---|---|
| Andy Griffith | 7" EP | Capitol | EAP1630 | 1956 | £2 | £5 | |
| Ko Ko Mo | 7" | Capitol | CL14263 | 1955 | £2.50 | £6 | |
| Mama Guitar | 7" | Capitol | CL14766 | 1957 | £2 | £5 | |
| Midnight Special | 7" | Capitol | CL14936 | 1958 | £1.50 | £4 | |
| No Time For Sergeants | 7" | Capitol | CL14619 | 1956 | £1.50 | £4 | |

## GRIFFITH, NANCI

| | | | | | | | |
|---|---|---|---|---|---|---|---|
| From A Distance | CD-s | MCA | DMCA1282 | 1988 | £2 | £5 | |
| It's A Hard Life | CD-s | MCA | DMCAT1358 | 1989 | £2 | £5 | |
| Portrait Of An Artist | CD | MCA | CD451693 | 1989 | £8 | £20 | US promo sampler |
| Present Echoes | CD | Elektra | | 1993 | £8 | £20 | US promo, 6 Other Voices tracks with 6 original versions |

## GRIFFITHS, MARCIA

| | | | | | | | |
|---|---|---|---|---|---|---|---|
| Don't Let Me Down | 7" | Escort | ES808 | 1969 | £1.50 | £4 | Reggaeites B side |
| Feel Like Jumping | 7" | Coxsone | CS7055 | 1968 | £5 | £10 | Horace Taylor B side |
| Funny | 7" | Island | WI285 | 1966 | £5 | £10 | King Sparrow B side |
| Hound Dog | 7" | Studio One | SO2008 | 1967 | £6 | £12 | Hugh Godfrey B side |
| Mojo Girl | 7" | Coxsone | CS7035 | 1968 | £5 | £10 | Hamlins B side |
| Mr. Everything | 7" | Rio | R121 | 1966 | £4 | £8 | Soul Brothers B side |
| Naturally | LP | Sky Note | SKYLP9 | 1978 | £4 | £10 | |
| Put A Little Love In Your Heart | 7" | Trojan | TR693 | 1969 | £1.50 | £4 | J Boys B side |
| Talk | 7" | High Note | HS029 | 1969 | £2.50 | £6 | |
| Tell Me Now | 7" | Gas | GAS111 | 1969 | £2.50 | £6 | Stan Hope B side |
| Truly | 7" | Studio One | SO2059 | 1968 | £6 | £12 | Simms & Robinson B side |
| Words | 7" | Studio One | SO2047 | 1968 | £6 | £12 | Sharks B side |
| You Keep Me On The Move | 7" | Studio One | SO2069 | 1968 | £6 | £12 | Mr. Foundation B side |

## GRIFFITHS, MARI

| | | | | | | | |
|---|---|---|---|---|---|---|---|
| Mari Griffiths | LP | Rediffusion | Z5131 | 1973 | £15 | £30 | |

## GRIGNARD, FERRE
| | | | | | | | |
|---|---|---|---|---|---|---|---|
| Hash Bamboo Shuffle | 7" EP | Philips | 434337 | 196– £2.50 | £6 | French |
| La Si Do 25 | 7" EP | Barclay | 71199 | 1968 £4 | £8 | French |
| Ring Ring I've Got To Sing | 7" EP | Philips | 434330 | 196– £2.50 | £6 | French |

## GRIMES, CAROL
| | | | | | | | |
|---|---|---|---|---|---|---|---|
| Fools Meeting | LP | B&C | CAS1023 | 1970 £15 | £30 | with Delivery |
| Warm Blood | LP | Caroline | CA2001 | 1974 £4 | £10 | |

## GRIMES, TINY
| | | | | | | |
|---|---|---|---|---|---|---|
| Callin' The Blues | LP | Esquire | 32092 | 1960 £6 | £15 | |

## GRIMMS
| | | | | | | |
|---|---|---|---|---|---|---|
| Grimms | LP | Island | HELP11 | 1973 £4 | £10 | |
| Rocking Duck | LP | Island | ILPS9248 | 1973 £4 | £10 | |

## GRIN
| | | | | | | |
|---|---|---|---|---|---|---|
| Grin | LP | Epic | 64272 | 1971 £4 | £10 | |
| One Plus One | LP | Epic | 64652 | 1972 £4 | £10 | |

## GRIN (2)
| | | | | | | |
|---|---|---|---|---|---|---|
| View From The Valley | LP | Hasznee | | 1985 £10 | £25 | Dutch |

## GRINGO
| | | | | | | |
|---|---|---|---|---|---|---|
| Gringo | LP | MCA | MKPS2017 | 1971 £4 | £10 | |

## GRINNE, JOE
| | | | | | | |
|---|---|---|---|---|---|---|
| Mr. Editor | 7" | Coxsone | CS7098 | 1969 £5 | £10 | |

## GRISBY DYKE
| | | | | | | |
|---|---|---|---|---|---|---|
| Adventures Of Miss Rosemary La Page | 7" | Deram | DM232 | 1969 £1.50 | £4 | |

## GROBSCHNITT
| | | | | | | | |
|---|---|---|---|---|---|---|---|
| Ballermann | LP | Brain | 21050 | 1974 £8 | £20 | German double |
| Grobschnitt | LP | Brain | 1008 | 1972 £10 | £25 | German |
| Jumbo (English Lyrics) | LP | Brain | 0001076 | 1975 £6 | £15 | German |
| Jumbo (German Lyrics) | LP | Brain | 0001081 | 1975 £6 | £15 | German |

## GRODECK WHIPPERJENNY
| | | | | | | |
|---|---|---|---|---|---|---|
| Grodeck Whipperjenny | LP | People | 3000 | 1970 £37.50 | £75 | US |

## GROOM, DEWEY
| | | | | | | |
|---|---|---|---|---|---|---|
| Butane Blues | 7" | Starlite | ST45085 | 1962 £4 | £8 | |
| Heartaches For Sale | 7" | Starlite | ST45105 | 1963 £2 | £5 | |
| Walking Papers | 7" | Starlite | ST45095 | 1963 £2.50 | £6 | |

## GROOP
| | | | | | | |
|---|---|---|---|---|---|---|
| Lovin' Tree | 7" | CBS | 3351 | 1968 £1.50 | £4 | |

## GROOV-U
| | | | | | | |
|---|---|---|---|---|---|---|
| On Campus | LP | Gateway | GLP3010 | £6 | £15 | US |

## GROOVE
| | | | | | | |
|---|---|---|---|---|---|---|
| Wind | 7" | Parlophone | R5783 | 1969 £2 | £5 | |

## GROOVE FARM
| | | | | | | | |
|---|---|---|---|---|---|---|---|
| Baby Blue Marine | 7" | Lyntone | LYN18632 | 1988 £4 | £8 | flexi, B side by Sea Urchins, no picture sleeve |
| Baby Blue Marine | 7" | Lyntone | LYN18632 | 1988 £5 | £10 | flexi, B side by Sea Urchins, picture sleeve |
| Driving In Your New Car | 7" | Subway Organisation | SUBWAY22N | 1988 £6 | £12 | promo |
| Only The Most Ignorant | 7" | Raving Pop Blast | RPBGF2 | 1989 £2 | £5 | |
| Sore Heads And Happy Hearts | 7" | Raving Pop Blast | RPBGF1 | 1987 £2.50 | £6 | |

## GROOVERS
| | | | | | | | |
|---|---|---|---|---|---|---|---|
| You've Got To Cry | 7" | Island | WI3080 | 1967 £5 | £10 | Alva Lewis B side |

## GROOVEY, WINSTON
| | | | | | | | |
|---|---|---|---|---|---|---|---|
| Free The People | LP | Pama | PMP2011 | 1969 £4 | £10 | |
| Funky Chicken | 7" | Jackpot | JP708 | 1969 £1.50 | £4 | Cimarrons B side |
| Funny | 7" | Jackpot | JP709 | 1969 £1.50 | £4 | Cimarrons B side |
| Island In The Sun | 7" | Nu Beat | NB041 | 1969 £1.50 | £4 | |
| Josephine | 7" | Nu Beat | NB042 | 1969 £1.50 | £4 | |
| You Can't Turn Your Back On Me | 7" | Attack | ATT8019 | 1969 £1.50 | £4 | Pama Dice B side |

## GROSSETT, G. G.
| | | | | | | | |
|---|---|---|---|---|---|---|---|
| Greater Sounds | 7" | Crab | CRAB33 | 1969 £1.50 | £4 | |
| Run Girl Run | 7" | Crab | CRAB10 | 1969 £1.50 | £4 | Dennis Walks B side |

## GROSSMAN, STEFAN
| | | | | | | | |
|---|---|---|---|---|---|---|---|
| Gramercy Park Sheik | LP | Fontana | STLS485 | 1969 £6 | £15 | |
| Ragtime Cowboy Jew | LP | Transatlantic | TRA223 | 1970 £6 | £15 | double |

## GROSSMAN, STEVE
Some Shapes To Come............................ LP ...... P.M. Records .. PMR002................ 1975 £5........... £12 ......................... US

## GROSVENOR, LUTHER
Under Open Skies.................................... LP ...... Island .............. ILPS9168 ............... 1971 £4........... £10 ........................

## GROUNDHOGS
Tony McPhee is a guitarist with a particularly good understanding of the blues, as his numerous session appearances on records by people like John Lee Hooker and Champion Jack Dupree testify. He was also one of the first musicians involved in the British blues boom of the late sixties to realize that it would not be possible to keep recycling the same twelve-bar repertoire indefinitely without the public losing interest. *Blues Obituary* announced the end of an era with music that while obviously inspired by a love of the blues, nevertheless ranged very much more widely. Subsequently, McPhee became a little too convinced that he could play like Jimi Hendrix, but each Groundhogs LP still has its moments, with *Split* being something of a minor classic.

| | | | | | | | |
|---|---|---|---|---|---|---|---|
| BDD ................................................ | 7" ...... | Liberty ........... | LBF15263 .............. | 1969 | £2.50....... | £6 | ........................... |
| Best Of 1969–72 ............................. | LP ...... | United Artists .. | 600063/4 ........... | 1974 | £4........... | £10 | ......................... double |
| Blues Obituary ................................ | LP ...... | Liberty ........... | LBS83253............. | 1969 | £15......... | £30 | ........................... |
| Eccentric Man................................. | 7" ...... | Liberty ........... | LBF15346 ............ | 1970 | £2.50....... | £6 | ........................... |
| Hoggin' The Stage .......................... | LP ...... | Psycho ........... | PSYCHO24 ......... | 1984 | £8........... | £20 | ....... double with EP |
| Hogwash ........................................ | LP ...... | United Artists .. | UAG29419......... | 1972 | £4........... | £10 | ........................... |
| I'll Never Fall In Love Again .......... | 7" ...... | Planet ............ | PLF104 ................ | 1966 | £20......... | £40 | . credited to John Lee's |
| | | | | | | | Groundhogs |
| Live At Leeds ................................. | LP ...... | Liberty ........... | | 1971 | £100 ...... | £200 | ......................... promo |
| Scratching The Surface .................... | LP ...... | Liberty ........... | LBL/LBS83199....... | 1968 | £20......... | £40 | ........................... |
| Solid ............................................. | LP ...... | WWA ............ | WWA004............ | 1974 | £4........... | £10 | ........................... |
| Split .............................................. | LP ...... | Liberty ........... | LBS83401............. | 1971 | £4........... | £10 | ........................... |
| Thank Christ For The Bomb ............ | LP ...... | Liberty ........... | LBS83295............. | 1970 | £4........... | £10 | ........................... |
| Who Will Save The World .............. | LP ...... | United Artists .. | UAG29237........... | 1972 | £4........... | £10 | ........................... |
| You Don't Love Me........................ | 7" ...... | Liberty ........... | LBF15174 ............ | 1968 | £2.50....... | £6 | ........................... |

## GROUP 1850
| | | | | | | | |
|---|---|---|---|---|---|---|---|
| Agemo's Trip To Mother Earth ................ | LP ...... | Philips ........... | SBL7884 ............. | 1968 | £37.50... | £75 | ........................... |
| Live ............................................... | LP ...... | Orange .......... | OP1.................... | 1975 | £5........... | £12 | ......................... Dutch |
| Live 2............................................ | LP ...... | Rubber .......... | RR1852............... | 1974 | £10......... | £25 | ......................... Dutch |
| Live On Tour .................................. | LP ...... | Rubber .......... | ME5 .................... | 1973 | £10......... | £25 | ......................... Dutch |
| Paradise Now .................................. | LP ...... | Discofoon ...... | VD7063 ............... | 1969 | £25......... | £50 | ......................... Dutch |
| Polyandri ....................................... | LP ...... | Rubber .......... | RR1851............... | 1974 | £10......... | £25 | ......................... Dutch |

## GROUP 5
En direct de Liverpool ........................ LP ...... Barclay .......... 80230 ................ 1964 £50....... £100 ....................... French

## GROUP IMAGE
Mouth In The Clouds.......................... LP ...... Stable ............ SLE8005 ............. 1969 £8........... £20 .........................

## GROUP ONE
| | | | | | | | |
|---|---|---|---|---|---|---|---|
| Chanson D'Amour ........................... | 7" ...... | HMV.............. | POP492 ............... | 1958 | £1.50....... | £4 | ........................... |
| She's Neat ...................................... | 7" ...... | HMV.............. | POP463 ............... | 1958 | £4........... | £8 | ........................... |

## GROUP SIX
Rock A Boogie .................................. 7" ...... Oriole............ CB1488 .............. 1959 £6........... £12 .........................

## GROUP X
| | | | | | | | |
|---|---|---|---|---|---|---|---|
| Roti Calliope .................................. | 7" ...... | Fontana.......... | TF417.................. | 1963 | £2........... | £5 | ........................... |
| There Are 8 Million Cossack Melodies....... | 7" ...... | Fontana.......... | 267274TF............ | 1963 | £2........... | £5 | ........................... |
| There Are 8 Million Cossack Melodies....... | 7" ...... | Fontana.......... | 267274TF............ | 1963 | £5........... | £10 | ................. picture sleeve |

## GROVE, BOBBY
It Was For You ................................. LP ...... King .............. 831 ................. 1963 £5........... £12 ......................... US

## GROWING CONCERN
Growing Concern .............................. LP ...... Mainstream ..... S6108.................... 1968 £30......... £60 ......................... US

## GRUMBLE
The single credited to Grumble was actually made by Ten cc.

Da Doo Ron Ron .............................. 7" ...... RCA .............. RCA2384 ............. 1973 £1.50....... £4 .........................

## GRUNBLATT, GEORGES
K-Priss .......................................... LP ...... Polydor .......... 2473911 ............. 1980 £6........... £15 ......................... French

## GRUNSKY, JACK
Toronto .......................................... LP ...... Kuckuck ......... 2375002 ............. 1970 £4........... £10 ......................... German

## GRUNT FUTTOCK
Rock 'n' Roll Christian ....................... 7" ...... Regal ............. RZ3042 .............. 1972 £7.50...... £15 .........................
Zonophone .....

## GRUPO SINTESIS
Aqui Estamos .................................... LP ...... Egrem ............ LD3951 ................. 1981 £15......... £30 ......................... Cuban

## GRYCE, GIGI
| | | | | | | | |
|---|---|---|---|---|---|---|---|
| Gigi Gryce Octet.............................. | 10" LP | Vogue............ | LDE113 .............. | 1955 | £20......... | £40 | ........................... |
| Gigi Gryce Orchestra........................ | 10" LP | Vogue............ | LDE070 .............. | 1954 | £20......... | £40 | ........................... |
| Jazz Time Paris Vol. 2....................... | 10" LP | Vogue............ | LDE048 .............. | 1954 | £20......... | £40 | .. with Clifford Brown |

## GRYPHON

The growing influence of folk music during the early seventies led a few groups to try the integration of medieval instruments into a folk-rock setting. The most successful of these was Gryphon, whose *Midnight Mushrumps* in particular is something of a landmark. Later albums found the group retreating to a more ordinary rock sound, but Richard Harvey subsequently made much use of his love for medieval music in his solo career.

| | | | | | | | |
|---|---|---|---|---|---|---|---|
| Gryphon | LP | Transatlantic | TRA262 | 1973 | £4 | £10 | |
| Midnight Mushrumps | LP | Transatlantic | TRA282 | 1974 | £4 | £10 | |
| Raindance | LP | Transatlantic | TRA302 | 1975 | £4 | £10 | |
| Red Queen To Gryphon Three | LP | Transatlantic | TRA287 | 1974 | £4 | £10 | |

## GRYPHON (2)
| | | | | | | | |
|---|---|---|---|---|---|---|---|
| Gryphon | LP | NR | 12497 | 197– | £30 | £60 | US |

## G.T.O.'S
| | | | | | | | |
|---|---|---|---|---|---|---|---|
| She Rides With Me | 7" | Polydor | 56721 | 1967 | £2 | £5 | |

## GUARNIERI, JOHNNY
| | | | | | | | |
|---|---|---|---|---|---|---|---|
| Songs Of Will Hudson And Eddie De Lange | LP | Vogue Coral | LVA9049 | 1957 | £6 | £15 | |

## GUDIBRALLAN
| | | | | | | | |
|---|---|---|---|---|---|---|---|
| Gudibrallan | LP | Silence | SRS4612 | 1971 | £15 | £30 | Swedish |

## GUESS WHO
| | | | | | | | |
|---|---|---|---|---|---|---|---|
| Hey Ho What You Do To Me | 7" EP | Vogue | INT18038 | 1965 | £7.50 | £15 | French |
| His Girl | 7" | King | KG1044 | 1966 | £5 | £10 | |
| Miss Felicity Grey | 7" | Fontana | TF861 | 1967 | £2 | £5 | |
| Shakin' All Over | 7" | Pye | 7N25305 | 1965 | £4 | £8 | |
| This Time Long Ago | 7" | Fontana | TF831 | 1967 | £2.50 | £6 | |

## GUEST, EARL
| | | | | | | | |
|---|---|---|---|---|---|---|---|
| Foxy | 7" | Columbia | DB7212 | 1964 | £2 | £5 | |
| Winkle Picker Stomp | 7" | Columbia | DB4707 | 1962 | £1.50 | £4 | |

## GUEST, REG SYNDICATE
| | | | | | | | |
|---|---|---|---|---|---|---|---|
| Reg Guest Trio | 7" EP | NFS | 68CFH1002 | 1968 | £25 | £50 | |
| Underworld | LP | Mercury | 20089MCL | 1966 | £6 | £15 | |
| Underworld | 7" | Mercury | MF927 | 1965 | £25 | £50 | |

## GUGGENHEIM
| | | | | | | | |
|---|---|---|---|---|---|---|---|
| Guggenheim | LP | Indigo | GOLP7001 | 197– | £37.50 | £75 | |

## GUILLOTEENS
| | | | | | | | |
|---|---|---|---|---|---|---|---|
| I Don't Believe | 7" | Pye | 7N25324 | 1965 | £12.50 | £25 | |

## GUITAR, BONNIE
| | | | | | | | |
|---|---|---|---|---|---|---|---|
| Dark Moon | LP | Dot | DLP3335/25335 | 1962 | £4 | £10 | US |
| Moonlight And Shadows | LP | London | HAD2122 | 1958 | £5 | £12 | |
| Very Precious Love | 7" | London | HLD8591 | 1958 | £2 | £5 | |
| Whispering Hope | LP | Dot | DLP3151/ DLP25151 | 1959 | £5 | £12 | US |

## GUITAR CRUSHER WITH JIMMY SPRUILL
| | | | | | | | |
|---|---|---|---|---|---|---|---|
| Since My Baby Hit The Numbers | 7" | Blue Horizon | 573149 | 1969 | £7.50 | £15 | |

## GUITAR JUNIOR
| | | | | | | | |
|---|---|---|---|---|---|---|---|
| Pick Me Up On Your Way Down | LP | Goldband | 1085 | 1960 | £5 | £12 | US |

## GUITAR NUBBIT
| | | | | | | | |
|---|---|---|---|---|---|---|---|
| Georgia Chain Gang | 7" | Bootleg | 501 | 1964 | £10 | £20 | |

## GUITAR RED
| | | | | | | | |
|---|---|---|---|---|---|---|---|
| Just You And I | 7" | Pye | 7N25219 | 1963 | £2.50 | £6 | |

## GUITAR SHORTY
| | | | | | | | |
|---|---|---|---|---|---|---|---|
| Carolina Slide Guitar | LP | Flyright | LP500 | 1972 | £4 | £10 | |

## GUITAR SLIM
| | | | | | | | |
|---|---|---|---|---|---|---|---|
| Things That I Used To Do | LP | Speciality | 2120 | 1964 | £6 | £15 | US |

## GULDA, FRIEDRICH
| | | | | | | | |
|---|---|---|---|---|---|---|---|
| At Birdland | LP | Decca | LK4188 | 1958 | £8 | £20 | |
| Man Of Letters | LP | Decca | LK4189 | 1958 | £8 | £20 | |

## GULLIN, LARS
| | | | | | | | |
|---|---|---|---|---|---|---|---|
| Holiday For Piano | 10" LP | Esquire | 20015 | 1953 | £25 | £50 | |
| Lars Gullin Compositions | 10" LP | Esquire | 20019 | 1953 | £25 | £50 | |
| New Sounds From Europe Vol. 3 | 10" LP | Vogue | LDE052 | 1954 | £25 | £50 | |

## GULLIVER
| | | | | | | | |
|---|---|---|---|---|---|---|---|
| Gulliver | LP | Elektra | 2410006 | 1970 | £4 | £10 | |

## GULLIVER'S TRAVELS
| | | | | | | | |
|---|---|---|---|---|---|---|---|
| Gulliver's Travels | LP | Instant | INLP003 | 1968 | £20 | £40 | |

## GUN

The Gun were a guitar trio fronted by Adrian Gurvitz, who has popped up periodically ever since. 'Race With The Devil' was the Gun's calling card, a classic piece of hard rock, powered by one of those simple guitar riffs that seems to have been waiting around for ever for someone to just come along and play it. Not much of the rest of the Gun's material is in the same class, unfortunately.

| Title | Format | Label | Cat. | Year | Low | High | Notes |
|---|---|---|---|---|---|---|---|
| Drives You Mad | 7" | CBS | 4052 | 1969 | £1.50 | £4 | |
| Gun | LP | CBS | 63552 | 1968 | £6 | £15 | |
| Gunsight | LP | CBS | 63683 | 1969 | £10 | £25 | |
| Hobo/Long Hair Wild Man | 7" | CBS | 4443 | 1969 | £2 | £5 | |
| Race With The Devil | 7" | CBS | 3764 | 1968 | £1.50 | £4 | 2 different B sides |
| Running Wild | 7" | CBS | 4952 | 1970 | £1.50 | £4 | |

## GUN (2)

| Title | Format | Label | Cat. | Year | Low | High |
|---|---|---|---|---|---|---|
| Better Days | CD-s | A&M | CDEE505 | 1989 | £2 | £5 |
| Higher Ground | CD-s | A&M | AMCD869 | 1991 | £2 | £5 |
| Inside Out | CD-s | A&M | CDEE531 | 1989 | £2 | £5 |
| Money (Everybody Loves Her) | CD-s | A&M | CDEE520 | 1989 | £2 | £5 |
| Shame On You | CD-s | A&M | AMCD573 | 1990 | £2 | £5 |
| Taking On The World | CD-s | A&M | CDEE541 | 1990 | £2 | £5 |

## GUNN, JON

| Title | Format | Label | Cat. | Year | Low | High |
|---|---|---|---|---|---|---|
| I've Just Made My Mind Up | 7" | Deram | DM133 | 1967 | £2 | £5 |

## GUNNER, JIM

| Title | Format | Label | Cat. | Year | Low | High |
|---|---|---|---|---|---|---|
| Desperado | 7" | Fontana | H313 | 1961 | £2.50 | £6 |
| Hoolee Jump | 7" | Decca | F11276 | 1960 | £2.50 | £6 |

## GUNS 'N' ROSES

With a raunchy image and music to match, Guns 'n' Roses have slipped effortlessly into the niche left vacant by the semi-retired Rolling Stones. The fact that the group is too young to have a particularly extensive back catalogue is no problem for collectors. The record company is only too willing to provide instant collectors' items in the form of limited-edition releases of one sort or another. (The US promotional doormat – definitely an item for the collector who must have everything – was selling for £60 when first produced!)

| Title | Format | Label | Cat. | Year | Low | High | Notes |
|---|---|---|---|---|---|---|---|
| Civil War | 12" | WEA | SAM694 | 1991 | £6 | £15 | promo |
| Don't Cry | CD-s | Geffen | GFSTD9 | 1991 | £3 | £8 | |
| Guns 'n' Radio | CD | Geffen | PROCD4340 | 1991 | £10 | £25 | US promo |
| It's So Easy | 7" | Geffen | GEF22 | 1987 | £4 | £8 | |
| It's So Easy | 12" | Geffen | GEF22T | 1987 | £4 | £10 | |
| It's So Easy | 12" | Geffen | GEF22TP | 1987 | £15 | £30 | picture disc |
| Live ?!*@ Like A Suicide | LP | Uzi Suicide | USR001 | 1986 | £50 | £100 | US |
| Live And Let Die | CD-s | Geffen | GFSTD17 | 1991 | £2.50 | £6 | |
| Night Train | CD-s | Geffen | GEF60CD | 1989 | £2.50 | £6 | |
| Nightrain | 7" | Geffen | GEF60P | 1989 | £2.50 | £6 | shaped picture disc |
| November Rain | CD-s | Geffen | GFSTD18 | 1992 | £3 | £8 | picture disc |
| On Tour Now! | CD | Geffen | PROCD4441 | 1993 | £8 | £20 | US promo |
| Paradise City | CD-s | Geffen | GEF50CD | 1989 | £3 | £8 | 3" single |
| Paradise City | 7" | Geffen | GEF50P | 1989 | £4 | £8 | shaped picture disc, clear background |
| Paradise City | 7" | Geffen | GEF50P | 1989 | £5 | £10 | shaped picture disc, white background |
| Paradise City | 7" | Geffen | GEF50X | 1989 | £4 | £8 | holster pack |
| Patience | CD-s | Geffen | GEF56CD | 1989 | £3 | £8 | 3" single |
| Sample Your Illusion | CD | Geffen | | 1991 | £8 | £20 | promo sampler |
| Since I Don't Have You | CD-s | Geffen | GFSXD70 | 1993 | £4 | £10 | in tin |
| Spaghetti Incident | CD | Geffen | | 1993 | £10 | £25 | US promo in spaghetti tin |
| Sweet Child O' Mine | CD-s | Geffen | GEF55CD | 1989 | £3 | £8 | 3" single |
| Sweet Child Of Mine | 7" | Geffen | GEF55P | 1989 | £4 | £8 | shaped picture disc |
| Sweet Child Of Mine | 12" | Geffen | GEF43TV | 1988 | £4 | £10 | metallic sleeve |
| Sweet Child Of Mine | 10" | Geffen | GEF43TE | 1988 | £10 | £20 | revolving sleeve |
| Use Your Illusion World Tour I | CD | Geffen | GEI39521 | 1993 | £10 | £25 | laser disc |
| Use Your Illusion World Tour II | CD | Geffen | GEI39522 | 1993 | £10 | £25 | laser disc |
| Welcome To The Jungle | CD-s | Geffen | GEF47CD | 1988 | £5 | £12 | 3" single |
| Welcome To The Jungle | 7" | Geffen | GEF30 | 1987 | £2.50 | £6 | |
| Welcome To The Jungle | 12" | Geffen | GEF30T | 1987 | £10 | £25 | |
| Welcome To The Jungle | 12" | Geffen | GEF30TP | 1987 | £15 | £30 | picture disc |
| Welcome To The Jungle | 12" | Geffen | GEF30TW | 1987 | £6 | £15 | poster sleeve |
| Welcome To The Jungle | 12" | Geffen | GEF47T | 1988 | £4 | £10 | with patch |
| Welcome To The Jungle | 12" | Geffen | GEF47P | 1988 | £4 | £10 | picture disc |
| Welcome To The Jungle | 12" | Geffen | GEF47TW | 1988 | £2.50 | £6 | poster sleeve |
| You Could Be Mine | CD-s | Geffen | GFSTD6 | 1991 | £4 | £10 | card sleeve |

## GUNTER, ARTHUR

| Title | Format | Label | Cat. | Year | Low | High | Notes |
|---|---|---|---|---|---|---|---|
| Black And Blues | LP | Excello | 8017 | 1970 | £37.50 | £75 | US |
| Blues After Hours | LP | Blue Horizon | 2431012 | 1971 | £20 | £40 | |

## GUNTHER, HARDROCK

| Title | Format | Label | Cat. | Year | Low | High |
|---|---|---|---|---|---|---|
| Mountain Music | 7" EP | Brunswick | OE9167 | 1955 | £5 | £10 |

## GURU GURU

| Title | Format | Label | Cat. | Year | Low | High | Notes |
|---|---|---|---|---|---|---|---|
| Dance Of The Flames | LP | Atlantic | K50044 | 1974 | £5 | £12 | |
| Der Elektrolurch | LP | Brain | 21057 | 1974 | £6 | £15 | German double |
| Don't Call Us We'll Call You | LP | Atlantic | K50022 | 1973 | £6 | £15 | |
| Guru Guru | LP | Brain | 1025 | 1973 | £6 | £15 | German |
| Hinten | LP | Ohr | 556017 | 1971 | £10 | £25 | German |
| Kan Guru | LP | Brain | 1007 | 1972 | £6 | £15 | German |

| | | | | | | | |
|---|---|---|---|---|---|---|---|
| This Is Guru Guru | LP | Brain | 200145 | 1973 £5 | £12 | | *German* |
| UFO | LP | Ohr | 556005 | 1970 £15 | £30 | | *German* |

## GURUS
| | | | | | | |
|---|---|---|---|---|---|---|
| Blue Snow Night | 7" | United Artists | UP1160 | 1966 £5 | £10 | |

## GUSTAFSON, JOHNNY
| | | | | | | |
|---|---|---|---|---|---|---|
| Just To Be With You | 7" | Polydor | 56022 | 1965 £2 | £5 | |
| Take Me For A Little While | 7" | Polydor | 56043 | 1965 £4 | £8 | |

## GUTHRIE, ARLO
| | | | | | | |
|---|---|---|---|---|---|---|
| Alice's Restaurant | LP | Reprise | RLP6267 | 1967 £4 | £10 | |
| Alice's Restaurant Soundtrack | LP | United Artists | UAS29061 | 1969 £4 | £10 | |
| Arlo | LP | Reprise | RSLP6299 | 1968 £4 | £10 | |
| Motorcycle Song | 7" | Reprise | RS20644 | 1967 £2 | £5 | |
| Valley Of Pray | 7" | Reprise | RS20951 | 1970 £1.50 | £4 | *demo* |

## GUTHRIE, WOODY
| | | | | | | |
|---|---|---|---|---|---|---|
| Bound For Glory | LP | Topic | 12T21 | 1958 £10 | £25 | |
| Dust Bowl Ballads | LP | RCA | RD7642 | 1964 £8 | £20 | |
| Greatest Songs | LP | Vanguard | VSD35/36 | 1972 £5 | £12 | *US double* |
| Guthrie's Story | LP | Topic | 12T31 | 1958 £10 | £25 | |
| Hard It Ain't Hard | 7" EP | Melodisc | EPM784 | 1958 £4 | £8 | |
| Hey Lolly Lolly | 7" EP | Melodisc | EPM791 | 1959 £4 | £8 | |
| More Songs By Guthrie | LP | Melodisc | MLP12106 | 1955 £10 | £25 | |
| Poor Boy | LP | XTRA | XTRA1065 | 1968 £4 | £10 | |
| Songs To Grow On Vol. 1 | LP | XTRA | XTRA1067 | 1968 £4 | £10 | |
| Woody Guthrie | LP | XTRA | XTRA1012 | 1965 £4 | £10 | |
| Worried Man Blues | 7" EP | Melodisc | EPM785 | 1958 £2 | £5 | |

## GUY, BARRY
| | | | | | | |
|---|---|---|---|---|---|---|
| Ode | LP | Incus | INCUS6/7 | 197– £10 | £25 | *double* |
| Statement V–XI | LP | Incus | INCUS22 | 1977 £5 | £12 | |

## GUY, BOB
'Dear Jeepers' is an early Frank Zappa composition.

| | | | | | | |
|---|---|---|---|---|---|---|
| Dear Jeepers | 7" | Donna | 1380 | 1963 £75 | £150 | *US* |

## GUY, BUDDY
| | | | | | | |
|---|---|---|---|---|---|---|
| Blues Today | LP | Vanguard | SVRL19004 | 1968 £4 | £10 | |
| Buddy And The Juniors | LP | Harvest | SHSP4006 | 1970 £6 | £15 | |
| Buddy Guy & Junior Wells Play The Blues | LP | Atlantic | K40240 | 1972 £4 | £10 | |
| Coming At You | LP | Vanguard | SVRL19001 | 1968 £4 | £10 | |
| Crazy Music | 7" EP | Chess | CRE6004 | 1965 £5 | £10 | |
| First Time I Met The Blues | LP | Python | KM2 | 1969 £8 | £20 | |
| Hold That Plane | LP | Vanguard | VSD79323 | 1972 £4 | £10 | |
| Hot And Cool | LP | Vanguard | SVRL79290 | 1969 £4 | £10 | |
| I Was Walking Through The Woods | LP | Chess | LP409 | 196– £8 | £20 | *US* |
| Left My Blues In San Francisco | LP | Chess | CRL(S)4546 | 1969 £5 | £12 | |
| Let Me Love You Baby | 7" | Chess | CRS8004 | 1965 £2.50 | £6 | |
| Man And His Blues | LP | Vanguard | SVRL19002 | 1968 £6 | £15 | |
| Mary Had A Little Lamb | 7" | Fontana | TF951 | 1968 £2.50 | £6 | |
| This Is Buddy Guy | LP | Vanguard | SVRL19008 | 1969 £6 | £15 | |

## GUYS
| | | | | | | |
|---|---|---|---|---|---|---|
| You Go Your Way | 7" | Tepee | TPRSP1001 | 1969 £2 | £5 | |

## GYGAFO
| | | | | | | |
|---|---|---|---|---|---|---|
| Legend Of The Kingfisher | LP | Holyground | HG1155 | 1989 £25 | £50 | *. 1973 LP with 1989 cover* |

## GYPSIES
| | | | | | | |
|---|---|---|---|---|---|---|
| Jerk It | 7" | CBS | 2785 | 1967 £7.50 | £15 | |

## GYPSY
| | | | | | | |
|---|---|---|---|---|---|---|
| Brenda And The Rattlesnake | LP | United Artists | UAS29420 | 1972 £4 | £10 | |
| Gypsy | LP | United Artists | UAS29155 | 1971 £4 | £10 | |

# H

## H. P. LOVECRAFT

H. P. Lovecraft was a writer of gothic fiction and not responsible for the music of the group that borrowed his name. In fact, the two albums made by the original line-up are highly inventive collections of songs, which graft some of the psychedelic pop trappings of UK groups like the Blossom Toes or Family on to the West Coast group sound of the late sixties, complete with a vocal sound that owes much to the power harmonies of Jefferson Airplane. The albums are much less celebrated than those of people like Country Joe and the Fish and Quicksilver Messenger Service, but are well worth investigation. A third album was made by a revised version of the group, and is listed in this guide under the name Lovecraft, but sadly this is a very disappointing affair.

| | | | | | |
|---|---|---|---|---|---|
| H. P. Lovecraft | LP | Philips | (S)BL7830 | 1967 £20 | £40 |
| H. P. Lovecraft 2 | LP | Philips | SBL7872 | 1968 £10 | £25 |
| This Is H. P. Lovecraft – Sailing On The White Ship | LP | Philips | 6336210 | 1970 £6 | £15 |
| This Is H. P. Lovecraft Vol. 2 – Spin Spin Spin | LP | Philips | 6336213 | 1970 £6 | £15 |
| Wayfarin' Stranger | 7" | Philips | BF1620 | 1967 £1.50 | £4 |
| White Ship | 7" | Philips | BF1639 | 1968 £1.50 | £4 |

## HAACK, BRUCE

| | | | | | |
|---|---|---|---|---|---|
| Electric Luzifer | LP | Columbia | 9991 | 1970 £8 | £20 ............ US |

## HABIBIYYA

| | | | | | |
|---|---|---|---|---|---|
| If Man But Knew | LP | Island | HELP7 | 1972 £5 | £12 |

## HABITS

The drummer with the Nice, Brian Davidson, was previously a member of the Habits.

| | | | | | |
|---|---|---|---|---|---|
| Elbow Baby | 7" | Decca | F12348 | 1966 £6 | £12 |

## HACKENSACK

| | | | | | |
|---|---|---|---|---|---|
| Here Comes The Judge | LP | Zel | UZ003 | 197– £37.50 | £75 |
| Moving On | 7" | Island | WIP6149 | 1972 £4 | £8 |
| Up The Hardway | LP | Polydor | 2383263 | 1974 £30 | £60 |

## HACKETT, BOBBY

| | | | | | |
|---|---|---|---|---|---|
| At The Embers | LP | Capitol | T1077 | 1959 £4 | £10 |
| Bobby Hackett Jazz Band | 10" LP | Capitol | LC6824 | 1956 £5 | £12 |
| Gotham Jazz Scene | LP | Capitol | T857 | 1958 £4 | £10 |
| Jazz Session | 10" LP | Columbia | 33S1053 | 1955 £6 | £15 |
| Rendezvous | LP | Capitol | T719 | 1956 £4 | £10 |
| Trumpet Solos | 10" LP | Brunswick | LA8587 | 1953 £6 | £15 |

## HACKETT, STEVE

| | | | | | |
|---|---|---|---|---|---|
| Cell 151 | 12" | Charisma | CELL12/13 | 1983 £4 | £10 ............ double |
| Clocks – The Angel Of Mons | 12" | Charisma | CB34112 | 1979 £2.50 | £6 |
| Till We Have Faces | CD | Lambourghini | CDLMG4000 | 1985 £5 | £12 |

## HADDOCK

| | | | | | |
|---|---|---|---|---|---|
| Dockside | LP | Seagull | | 1981 £10 | £25 ............ Dutch |
| Still Alive | LP | Seagull | | 1986 £10 | £25 ............ Dutch |

## HADEN, CHARLIE

| | | | | | |
|---|---|---|---|---|---|
| Closeness Duets | LP | Horizon | SP710 | 1976 £5 | £12 ............ US |
| Liberation Music Orchestra | LP | Probe | SPB1037 | 1969 £8 | £20 |

## HADLEY, TONY

| | | | | | |
|---|---|---|---|---|---|
| For Your Blue Eyes Only | CD-s | EMI | CDEM234 | 1992 £2 | £5 |
| Game Of Love | CD-s | EMI | CDEM254 | 1992 £2 | £5 |
| Lost In Your Love | CD-s | EMI | CDEM222 | 1992 £2 | £5 |
| State Of Play | CD | EMI | CDEMC3619 | 1992 £15 | £30 |

## HAFLER TRIO

| | | | | | |
|---|---|---|---|---|---|
| Bang! – An Open Letter | LP | Doublevision | DVR4 | 1984 £4 | £10 |
| Three Ways Of Saying Two | LP | Charrm | 3 | 1986 £4 | £10 |

## HAGAR, SAMMY

| | | | | | |
|---|---|---|---|---|---|
| Sammy Hagar | LP | Capitol | EST11599 | 1977 £4 | £10 ............ red vinyl |
| Sammy Hagar Returns | CD | Geffen | | 1988 £8 | £20 ............ US promo |

## HAGER, JOAN

| | | | | | |
|---|---|---|---|---|---|
| Happy Is A Girl Named Me | 7" | Brunswick | 05650 | 1957 £2.50 | £6 |

## HAGGIS
Live ............................................................. LP ...... Univers ...................................... 1977 £100 ..... £200 ........................ Dutch

## HAHN, JERRY BROTHERHOOD
Jerry Hahn Brotherhood ......................... LP ...... Columbia ........ CS1044 ................ 1970 £4 ........... £10 ........................ US

## HAHN, JOYCE
Gonna Find Me A Bluebird ..................... 7" ...... London .......... HLA8453 .............. 1957 £1.50 ..... £4

## HAIG, AL
Al Haig Trio ............................................ 10" LP Vogue ............ LDE092 ................ 1954 £20 ........ £40
Jazz Will O' The Wisp ............................ LP ..... XTRA ............ XTRA1125 ............ 1971 £4 ........... £10

## HAIKARA
Iso Iintu ................................................. LP ..... Satril ............ SATLP1016 ............ 1975 £37.50 .... £75 ................... Finnish

## HAINES, NORMAN
Daffodil ................................................. 7" ...... Parlophone ...... R5871 ................ 1970 £10 .......... £20
Den Of Iniquity ..................................... LP ...... Parlophone ...... PCS7130 ............ 1971 £250 ..... £400
Den Of Iniquity ..................................... 7" ...... Parlophone ...... SPSR338 ............ 1971 £12.50 .... £25 .............. promo only
Give To You Girl ................................... 7" ...... Parlophone ...... R5960 ................ 1972 £10 .......... £20

## HAIR
Hair Piece ............................................. LP ...... Columbia ......... SCX6452 ............ 1970 £50 ........ £100

## HAIR (2)
Rave Up ................................................ LP ...... Pye .............. NSPL18314 .......... 1969 £25 ........ £50

## HAIRBAND
Band On The Wagon ............................ LP ...... Bell .............. SBLL69 ............... 1969 £15 ........ £30
Big Louis .............................................. 7" ...... Bell .............. BLL1076 ............. 1969 £2.50 ..... £6

## HAIRCUT 100
Blue Hat For A Blue Day ....................... LP ...... Arista ............. HCC101 ............. 1982 £4 ........... £10 ...... test pressing only

## HAIRY CHAPTER
Can't Get Through ............................... LP ...... Bacillus .......... 6494002 ............. 1971 £8 ........... £20 ................. German
Can't Get Through ............................... LP ...... Bacillus .......... BLPS19074 .......... 1971 £6 ........... £15 ................. German
Eyes ..................................................... LP ...... Opp .............. 521 .................... 1970 £8 ........... £20 ................. German

## HAIRY ONES
Get Off My Cloud ................................ 7" EP . Barclay ........... 70898 ................. 1965 £5 ........... £10 ................... French

## HAL HOPPERS
Baby I've Had It .................................... 7" ...... London .......... HL8129 .............. 1955 £10 .......... £20
Do Nothing Blues ................................. 7" ...... London .......... HL8107 .............. 1954 £12.50 .... £25

## HALE & THE HUSHABYES
The group name disguises the combined forces of Jackie DeShannon, Sonny and Cher, the Blossoms, and Brian Wilson.

Yes Sir, That's My Baby ......................... 7" ...... Apogee ........... 104 ..................... 1964 £50 ...... £100 ............. US
Yes Sir, That's My Baby ......................... 7" ...... Reprise ........... 0299 .................... 1964 £20 ........ £40 ............. US

## HALEY, BILL
Bill Haley & His Comets ....................... 7" EP . Brunswick ...... OE9459 .............. 1959 £15 ........ £30 ............. tri-centre
Bill Haley And His Comets .................... 7" EP . Warner Bros .... WEP6001 ............ 1960 £5 ........... £10
Bill Haley And The Comets ................... LP ...... Valiant ........... VS103 ................. 1970 £4 ........... £10
Bill Haley And The Comets ................... LP ...... Warner Bros .... W(S)1738 ............ 1960 £8 ........... £20 ............. US
Bill Haley And The Comets ................... LP ...... XTRA ............ XTRA1027 ............ 1965 £6 ........... £15
Bill Haley Vol. 1 ................................... 7" EP . Warner Bros .... WEP6133 ............ 1964 £7.50 ..... £15
Bill Haley Vol. 2 ................................... 7" EP . Warner Bros .... WEP6136 ............ 1964 £7.50 ..... £15
Bill Haley's Chicks ............................... LP ...... Ace Of Hearts .. AH66 ................. 1964 £4 ........... £10
Bill Haley's Chicks ............................... LP ...... Brunswick ...... LAT8295 ............. 1959 £15 ........ £30
Bill Haley's Chicks ............................... LP ...... Brunswick ...... STA3011 ............. 1959 £20 ........ £40 ................. stereo
Bill Haley's Chicks ............................... LP ...... Decca ........... DL(7)8821 ............ 1959 £20 ........ £40 ............. US
Bill Haley's Juke Box ............................ LP ...... Warner Bros .... W1391 ............... 1960 £10 .......... £25
Bill Haley's Juke Box ............................ 7" EP . Warner Bros .... WEP6025 ............ 1961 £5 ........... £10
Bill Haley's Juke Box ............................ 7" EP . Warner Bros .... WSEP2025 .......... 1961 £10 .......... £20 ................. stereo
Billy Goat ............................................. 7" ...... Brunswick ...... 05688 ................ 1957 £5 ........... £10
Birth Of The Boogie ............................ 7" ...... Brunswick ...... 05910 ................ 1964 £4 ........... £8
Caldonia .............................................. 7" ...... Brunswick ...... 05805 ................ 1959 £6 ........... £12
Candy Kisses ....................................... 7" ...... Warner Bros .... WB6 ................. 1960 £2 ........... £5
Crazy Man Crazy .................................. 78 ....... London .......... L1190 ................ 1953 £10 .......... £20
Crazy Man, Crazy ................................. 7" ...... Pye .............. 7N25455 ............. 1968 £5 ........... £10
Dim Dim The Lights ............................. 7" EP . Brunswick ...... OE9129 .............. 1955 £10 .......... £20 ............... gold label
Dim Dim The Lights ............................. 7" ...... Brunswick ...... 05373 ................ 1955 £20 ........ £40 ............... gold label
Dipsy Doodle ...................................... 7" ...... Brunswick ...... 05719 ................ 1957 £7.50 ..... £15
Don't Knock The Rock ......................... 7" ...... Brunswick ...... 05640 ................ 1957 £7.50 ..... £15
Farewell So Long Goodbye .................. 7" ...... London .......... HLF8161 ............. 1955 £50 ...... £100 ............. gold label
Forty Cups Of Coffee ........................... 7" ...... Brunswick ...... 05658 ................ 1957 £7.50 ..... £15
Goofing Around ................................... 7" ...... Brunswick ...... 05641 ................ 1957 £7.50 ..... £15
Green Door .......................................... 7" ...... Brunswick ...... 05917 ................ 1964 £4 ........... £8
Greentree Boogie ................................ 7" ...... London .......... HL8142 .............. 1955 £50 ...... £100 ............. gold label
He Digs Rock And Roll ......................... LP ...... Decca ........... DL8315 .............. 1956 £37.50 .... £75 ............. US
I Got A Woman ................................... 7" ...... Brunswick ...... 05788 ................ 1959 £5 ........... £10
I'm Gonna Dry Every Little Tear ............ 78 ....... Melodisc ........ 1376 ................... 1956 £7.50 ..... £15

| | | | | | | | | |
|---|---|---|---|---|---|---|---|---|
| Lean Jean | 7" | Brunswick | 05752 | 1958 | £5 | £10 | |
| Live It Up | 10" LP | London | HAPB1042 | 1955 | £50 | £100 | gold label |
| Live It Up Pt. 1 | 7" EP | London | REF1049 | 1956 | £12.50 | £25 | |
| Live It Up Pt. 2 | 7" EP | London | REF1050 | 1956 | £12.50 | £25 | |
| Live It Up Pt. 3 | 7" EP | London | REF1058 | 1956 | £12.50 | £25 | |
| Mambo Rock | 7" | Brunswick | 05405 | 1955 | £20 | £40 | gold label |
| Mary Mary Lou | 7" | Brunswick | 05735 | 1958 | £5 | £10 | |
| Ooh Looka There Ain't She Pretty | 7" | Brunswick | 05810 | 1959 | £4 | £8 | |
| Pat-A-Cake | 78 | London | L1216 | 1953 | £10 | £20 | |
| Razzle Dazzle | 7" | Brunswick | 05453 | 1955 | £15 | £30 | gold label |
| Rip It Up | 7" | Brunswick | 05615 | 1956 | £7.50 | £15 | |
| Rock 'n' Roll | 7" EP | Brunswick | OE9214 | 1956 | £7.50 | £15 | |
| Rock 'n' Roll | 7" EP | London | REF1031 | 1955 | £20 | £40 | |
| Rock 'n' Roll Stage Show | LP | Brunswick | LAT8139 | 1956 | £10 | £25 | |
| Rock 'n' Roll Stage Show | LP | Decca | DL8345 | 1956 | £37.50 | £75 | US |
| Rock 'n' Roll Stage Show Pt. 1 | 7" EP | Brunswick | OE9278 | 1956 | £7.50 | £15 | |
| Rock 'n' Roll Stage Show Pt. 2 | 7" EP | Brunswick | OE9279 | 1956 | £7.50 | £15 | |
| Rock 'n' Roll Stage Show Pt. 3 | 7" EP | Brunswick | OE9280 | 1956 | £7.50 | £15 | |
| Rock Around The Clock | LP | Ace Of Hearts | AH13 | 1961 | £5 | £12 | |
| Rock Around The Clock | LP | Brunswick | LAT8117 | 1956 | £10 | £25 | |
| Rock Around The Clock | LP | Decca | DL8225 | 1955 | £50 | £100 | US |
| Rock Around The Clock | 7" EP | Brunswick | OE9250 | 1956 | £7.50 | £15 | 2 covers |
| Rock Around The Clock | 7" | Brunswick | 05317 | 1954 | £25 | £50 | gold label |
| Rock Around The Clock | 7" | Decca | AD1010 | 1968 | £2 | £5 | export |
| Rock Around The Clock | 7" | Warner Bros | WB133 | 1964 | £2.50 | £6 | |
| Rock The Joint | LP | Golden Guinea | GGL0282 | 1963 | £4 | £10 | |
| Rock The Joint | LP | London | HAF2037 | 1957 | £25 | £50 | |
| Rock The Joint | 7" | London | HLF8371 | 1957 | £50 | £100 | gold label |
| Rock With Bill Haley & The Comets | LP | Essex | LP202 | 1956 | £50 | £100 | US |
| Rock With Bill Haley & The Comets | LP | Somerset | P4600 | 1956 | £10 | £25 | US |
| Rock With Bill Haley And The Comets | LP | Trans World | 202 | 1956 | £20 | £40 | US |
| Rock-A-Beatin' Boogie | 7" | Brunswick | 05509 | 1955 | £15 | £30 | gold label |
| Rockin' Around The World | LP | Decca | DL8692 | 1957 | £20 | £40 | US |
| Rockin' Around The World | 7" EP | Brunswick | OE9446 | 1959 | £15 | £30 | |
| Rockin' Chair On The Moon | 7" | London | HLF8194 | 1955 | £62.50 | £125 | gold label |
| Rockin' The Joint | LP | Brunswick | LAT8268 | 1957 | £15 | £30 | |
| Rockin' The Joint | LP | Decca | DL8775 | 1958 | £20 | £40 | US |
| Rockin' The Oldies | LP | Ace Of Hearts | AH35 | 1962 | £4 | £10 | |
| Rockin' The Oldies | LP | Brunswick | LAT8219 | 1957 | £15 | £30 | |
| Rockin' The Oldies | LP | Decca | DL8569 | 1957 | £20 | £40 | US |
| Rockin' The Oldies Pt. 1 | 7" EP | Brunswick | OE9349 | 1958 | £10 | £20 | |
| Rockin' The Oldies Pt. 2 | 7" EP | Brunswick | OE9350 | 1958 | £10 | £20 | |
| Rockin' The Oldies Pt. 3 | 7" EP | Brunswick | OE9351 | 1958 | £10 | £20 | |
| Rockin' Through The Rye | 7" | Brunswick | 05582 | 1956 | £7.50 | £15 | |
| Rudy's Rock | 7" | Brunswick | 05616 | 1956 | £7.50 | £15 | |
| Saints Rock 'n' Roll | 7" | Brunswick | 05565 | 1956 | £7.50 | £15 | |
| See You Later Alligator | 7" | Brunswick | 05530 | 1956 | £15 | £30 | gold label |
| Shake, Rattle And Roll | 7" | Brunswick | 05338 | 1954 | £20 | £40 | gold label |
| Shake, Rattle And Roll | 10" LP | Decca | DL5560 | 1954 | £210 | £350 | US |
| Skinnie Minnie | 7" | Brunswick | 05742 | 1958 | £6 | £12 | |
| Skokiaan | 7" | Brunswick | 05818 | 1960 | £3 | £6 | |
| Spanish Twist | 7" | London | HLU9471 | 1961 | £4 | £8 | |
| Strictly Instrumental | LP | Brunswick | LAT8326 | 1960 | £15 | £30 | |
| Strictly Instrumental | LP | Decca | DL(7)8964 | 1959 | £20 | £40 | US |
| Tenor Man | 7" | Stateside | SS196 | 1963 | £1.50 | £4 | |
| They Sold A Million No. 15 | 7" EP | Brunswick | OE9431 | 1959 | £5 | £10 | 2 tracks by the Four Aces |
| Twisting Knights At The Round Table | LP | Columbia | 33SX1460 | 1962 | £8 | £20 | |
| Whoa Mabel | 7" | Brunswick | 05766 | 1958 | £6 | £12 | |

## HALF NELSON

Half Nelson was the name originally used by Sparks. The one LP made under this name was reissued as *Sparks* a year later.

| | | | | | | | | |
|---|---|---|---|---|---|---|---|---|
| Half Nelson | LP | Bearsville | BV2048 | 1972 | £6 | £15 | US |

## HALF TRIBE

| | | | | | | | | |
|---|---|---|---|---|---|---|---|---|
| Only Starting | LP | private | | 1965 | £330 | £500 | US |

## HALL, CONNIE & JAMES O'GWYNN

| | | | | | | | | |
|---|---|---|---|---|---|---|---|---|
| Country And Western Trailblazers No. 3 | 7" EP | Mercury | ZEP10080 | 1960 | £2 | £5 | |

## HALL, DARYL & JOHN OATES

| | | | | | | | | |
|---|---|---|---|---|---|---|---|---|
| Voices | CD | Mobile Fidelity | UDCD830 | 1990 | £6 | £15 | US audiophile |

## HALL, DEREK & MIKE COOPER

| | | | | | | | | |
|---|---|---|---|---|---|---|---|---|
| Out Of The Shades | 7" EP | Kennet | KRS766 | 196– | £2.50 | £6 | |

## HALL, DICKSON

| | | | | | | | | |
|---|---|---|---|---|---|---|---|---|
| Fabulous Country Hits No. 1 | 7" EP | London | RER1158 | 1958 | £2.50 | £6 | |
| Fabulous Country Hits No. 2 | 7" EP | London | RER1159 | 1958 | £2.50 | £6 | |
| Fabulous Country Hits No. 3 | 7" EP | London | RER1160 | 1958 | £2.50 | £6 | |
| Fabulous Country Hits Way Out West | LP | Kapp | KL1067 | 1957 | £4 | £10 | US |
| Outlaws Of The Old West | LP | MGM | E3263 | 1956 | £5 | £12 | US |
| Outlaws Of The Old West | 7" EP | MGM | MGMEP626 | 1957 | £4 | £8 | |
| Outlaws Of The Old West | 10" LP | MGM | E329 | 1954 | £6 | £15 | US |
| Twenty-Five All-Time Country & Western Hits | LP | Epic | LN3427 | 1958 | £4 | £10 | US |

## HALL, EDMOND
Celestial Express ........................................... LP ...... Blue Note ....... B6505 ................... 1969 £5 .......... £12 ........................................
Petite Fleur ...................................................... LP ...... London .......... LTZT15166 ...... 1959 £4 .......... £10 ........................................
Rumpus On Rampart Street ...................... LP ...... Top Rank ...... 35050 ................... 1960 £4 .......... £10 ........................................

## HALL, EDMUND
Edmund Hall All Stars .......................... 10" LP London .......... LZC14005 ............ 1955 £6 .......... £15

## HALL, GERRI
Who Can I Run To ................................. 7" ...... Sue .............. WI4026 ............... 1966 £25 ........ £50 ...................... demo

## HALL, JIM
Jazz Guitar .................................................. LP ...... Vogue .......... LAE12072 .......... 1958 £8 .......... £20

## HALL, JIMMY GRAY
Be That Way .................................................. 7" ...... Epic .......... EPC2312 ........... 1974 £4 .......... £8

## HALL, JUANITA
Sings The Blues ........................................... LP ...... Storyville ...... SLP113 ............. 1964 £6 .......... £15
Storyville Blues Anthology Vol. 2 .......... 7" EP . Storyville ...... SEP382 ............. 1962 £2 .......... £5

## HALL, LARRY
Ladder Of Love ............................................ 7" ...... Salvo .......... SLO1811 ............. 1962 £1.50 ...... £4

## HALL, RENE
Twitchy ....................................................... 7" ...... London .......... HLU8581 ............. 1958 £15 ........ £30

## HALL, ROBIN
Last Leaves Of Traditional Ballads ............ 10" LP Collector ........ JFS4002 ............ 1961 £5 .......... £12

## HALL, ROBIN & JIMMIE MACGREGOR
Football Crazy .............................................. 7" ...... Decca ............ F11266 .............. 1960 £1.50 ...... £4 .......... picture sleeve
Scottish Choice ........................................... LP ...... Ace Of Clubs .. ACL1065 .............. 1961 £4 .......... £10

## HALL, RONNIE
I'll Stand Aside ........................................... 7" ...... Fontana .......... TF569 ............... 1965 £4 .......... £8

## HALL, ROY
Blue Suede Shoes ......................................... 7" ...... Brunswick ...... 05555 .............. 1956 £150 .... £250 .......... best auctioned
See You Later Alligator .............................. 7" ...... Brunswick ...... 05531 .............. 1956 £250 .... £400 .......... best auctioned
Three Alley Cats .......................................... 7" ...... Brunswick ...... 05627 .............. 1956 £150 .... £250 .......... best auctioned

## HALL, TERRY
Lenny The Lion ........................................... 7" EP . Decca .......... DFE/STO8554 ...... 1963 £2 .......... £5

## HALL, TERRY (2)
Missing ......................................................... CD-s .. Chrysalis ......... CHSCD3381 ....... 1989 £2 .......... £5

## HALL, TONY
Fieldvole Music ........................................... LP ...... Free Reed ....... FRR012 ............ 1977 £8 .......... £20

## HALLADAY, CHANCE
John Henry ................................................... 7" ...... Vogue .......... V9203 ............... 1962 £1.50 ...... £4

## HALLBERG, BENGT
New Sounds From Sweden ...................... 10" LP Esquire .......... 20014 .................... 1953 £25 ........ £50

## HALLELUJAH
Hallelujah Babe ........................................... LP ...... Metronome ...... LMLP15805 .......... 1971 £10 ........ £25 ................ German

## HALLELUJAH SKIFFLE GROUP
I Saw The Light ........................................... 7" ...... Oriole .......... CB1429 .............. 1958 £1.50 ...... £4

## HALLIARD
The Halliard were a folk trio led by Nic Jones, whose later solo work consists of particularly fine traditional interpretations. Tragically, Jones's career was cut short by a serious car accident, which left him unable to play the guitar.

Halliard And Jon Raven ............................ LP ...... Broadside ....... BRO106 ............... 1968 £37.50 .... £75
It's The Irish In Me ................................... LP ...... Saga .......... SOC1058 .............. 1967 £25 .... £50

## HALLYDAY, JOHNNY
America's Rockin' Hits ................................ LP ...... Philips .......... BBL7556 ............ 1961 £37.50 .... £75
Chante ......................................................... LP ...... Philips .......... 77746L ............. 1965 £15 .... £30 ................ French
Hey Little Girl ........................................... 7" ...... Philips .......... 373012BF .......... 1963 £2 .......... £5
Johnny Hallyday ........................................ 7" EP . Vogue .......... VRE5013 ............ 1966 £37.50 .... £75
L'Idole des jeunes ....................................... LP ...... Mode .......... MDINT9095 ...... 1964 £5 .......... £12 ................ French
La Génération perdue ................................ LP ...... Philips .......... 70381L ............. 1967 £6 .......... £15 ........ French, mono
La Génération perdue ................................ LP ...... Philips .......... 840586 ............. 1967 £8 .......... £20 ........ French, stereo
Le Disque d'or ........................................... LP ...... Vogue .......... 16009 ............... 1973 £15 .... £30 ................ French
Olympia '64 ................................................ LP ...... Philips .......... B77987L ............ 1964 £8 .......... £20 ................ French
Pour moi tu es la seule ................................ 7" ...... Philips .......... BF1449 ............. 1965 £2.50 .... £6
Rocking ....................................................... 7" EP . Philips .......... 432813BE .......... 1962 £37.50 .... £75
Shake The Hand Of A Fool ...................... 7" ...... Philips .......... PB1238 ............. 1962 £2 .......... £5
Twistin' The Rock ....................................... LP ...... Vogue .......... MDINT9059 .......... 1962 £8 .......... £20 ................ French

## HALOS

| | | | | | | | |
|---|---|---|---|---|---|---|---|
| Halos | LP | Warwick | W2046 | 1962 | £30 | £60 | US |
| Nag | 7" | London | HLU9424 | 1961 | £7.50 | £15 | |

## HAMBLEN, STUART

| | | | | | | | |
|---|---|---|---|---|---|---|---|
| Go On By | 7" | HMV | 7MC30 | 1955 | £2.50 | £6 | export |
| Hell Train | 7" | HMV | 7M394 | 1956 | £2 | £5 | |
| This Ole House | 7" | HMV | 7MC20 | 1954 | £5 | £10 | export |

## HAMBRO, LENNY

| | | | | | | |
|---|---|---|---|---|---|---|
| Lenny Hambro And Eddie Bert | 10" LP | London | LZC14025 | 1956 | £8 | £20 |
| Message From Hambro | LP | Philips | BBL7161 | 1957 | £6 | £15 |

## HAMEL, PETER MICHAEL

| | | | | | | | |
|---|---|---|---|---|---|---|---|
| Buddhist Meditation East West | LP | Harmonia Mundi | 29222926 | 1975 | £5 | £12 | German double |
| Hamel | LP | Vertigo | 67641055 | 1972 | £8 | £20 | German double |
| Voice Of Silence | LP | Vertigo | 6360613 | 1973 | £5 | £12 | German |

## HAMFATS, HARLEM

| | | | | | | |
|---|---|---|---|---|---|---|
| Harlem Hamfats | LP | Ace Of Hearts | AH27 | 1962 | £4 | £10 |

## HAMILL, CLAIRE

| | | | | | | |
|---|---|---|---|---|---|---|
| Abracadabra | LP | Konk | KONK104 | 1975 | £4 | £10 |
| October | LP | Island | ILPS9225 | 1973 | £4 | £10 |
| One House Left Standing | LP | Island | ILPS9182 | 1971 | £4 | £10 |
| Stage Door Johnnies | LP | Konk | KONK101 | 1974 | £4 | £10 |

## HAMILTON, CHICO

| | | | | | | |
|---|---|---|---|---|---|---|
| Chico Hamilton Quintet | LP | Vogue | LAE12039 | 1957 | £8 | £20 |
| Chico Hamilton Quintet | LP | Vogue | LAE12045 | 1957 | £8 | £20 |
| Chico Hamilton Trio | LP | Vogue | LAE12077 | 1958 | £8 | £20 |
| Chico Hamnilton Quintet | LP | Vogue | LAE12085 | 1958 | £6 | £15 |
| Ellington Suite | LP | Vogue | LAE12210 | 1960 | £6 | £15 |
| Introducing Freddie Gambrell | LP | Vogue | LAE12160 | 1959 | £6 | £15 |
| Original | LP | Vogue | LAE12239 | 1961 | £5 | £12 |

## HAMILTON, GAVIN

| | | | | | | |
|---|---|---|---|---|---|---|
| It Won't Be The Same | 7" | King | KG1067 | 1967 | £7.50 | £15 |

## HAMILTON, GUY

| | | | | | | |
|---|---|---|---|---|---|---|
| Lifetime Of Loneliness | 7" | HMV | POP1418 | 1965 | £2 | £5 |

## HAMILTON, M.

| | | | | | | |
|---|---|---|---|---|---|---|
| Something Gotta Ring | 7" | Ska Beat | JB265 | 1967 | £5 | £10 |

## HAMILTON, ROY

| | | | | | | |
|---|---|---|---|---|---|---|
| Come Out Swinging | 7" EP | Fontana | TFE17170 | 1959 | £4 | £8 |
| Crazy Feeling | 7" | Fontana | H143 | 1958 | £4 | £8 |
| Dark End Of The Street | 7" | Deep Soul | DS9106 | 1970 | £4 | £8 |
| Don't Let Go | 7" | Fontana | H113 | 1958 | £6 | £12 |
| I Need Your Loving | 7" | Fontana | H193 | 1959 | £2.50 | £6 |
| Mood Moves | 7" EP | Fontana | TFE17163 | 1959 | £2.50 | £6 |
| Pledging My Love | 7" | Fontana | H180 | 1959 | £4 | £8 |
| Theme From The VIPs | 7" | MGM | MGM1210 | 1963 | £1.50 | £4 |
| There She Is | 7" | MGM | MGM1251 | 1964 | £37.50 | £75 |
| Thousand Years Ago | 7" | MGM | MGM1268 | 1965 | £2 | £5 |
| Warm Soul | LP | MGM | C960 | 1964 | £6 | £15 |
| Why Fight The Feeling | 7" EP | Fontana | TFE17160 | 1959 | £4 | £8 |
| You Can Have Her | 7" | Fontana | H298 | 1961 | £4 | £8 |
| You're Gonna Need Magic | 7" | Fontana | H320 | 1961 | £2.50 | £6 |

## HAMILTON, RUSS

| | | | | | | | |
|---|---|---|---|---|---|---|---|
| It's A Sin To Tell A Lie | 7" | Oriole | CB1531 | 1960 | £1.50 | £4 | |
| My Unbreakable Heart | 7" | Oriole | CB1506 | 1959 | £1.50 | £4 | |
| Rainbow | LP | Kapp | KL1076 | 1957 | £15 | £30 | US |
| Russ Hamilton | 7" EP | Oriole | EP7005 | 1958 | £5 | £10 | |
| Smile Smile Smile | 7" | Oriole | CB1508 | 1959 | £1.50 | £4 | |
| Things No Money Can Buy | 7" | Oriole | CB1527 | 1960 | £1.50 | £4 | |
| We Will Make Love | LP | Oriole | MG20031 | 1958 | £15 | £30 | |
| We Will Make Love | 7" | Oriole | CB1359 | 1957 | £1.50 | £4 | |
| Wedding Ring | 7" | Oriole | CB1388 | 1957 | £1.50 | £4 | |

## HAMILTON, SARA

| | | | | | | |
|---|---|---|---|---|---|---|
| Someone Ought To Care | LP | Polydor | 2310261 | 1973 | £8 | £20 |

## HAMILTON IV, GEORGE

| | | | | | | | |
|---|---|---|---|---|---|---|---|
| Before This Day Ends | 7" | HMV | POP813 | 1960 | £1.50 | £4 | |
| I Know Where I'm Going | 7" | HMV | POP505 | 1958 | £1.50 | £4 | |
| On Campus | LP | HMV | CLP1202 | 1958 | £5 | £12 | |
| Rose And A Candy Bar | 7" | London | HL8361 | 1957 | £50 | £100 | gold label |
| Sing Me A Sad Song | LP | HMV | CLP1263 | 1959 | £5 | £12 | |
| Why Don't They Understand | 7" | HMV | POP429 | 1957 | £2.50 | £6 | |
| Your Cheatin' Heart | 7" | HMV | POP534 | 1958 | £1.50 | £4 | |

## HAMILTON & THE MOVEMENT

| | | | | | | |
|---|---|---|---|---|---|---|
| I'm Not the Marrying Kind | 7" | CBS | 202573 | 1967 | £7.50 | £15 |

Really Saying Something .......................... 7" ...... Polydor .......... BM56026 ................ 1965 £10 ......... £20 ..........................................

## HAMLINS
Everyone Got To Be There ...................... 7" ...... Studio One ... SO2036 ............... 1967 £6 ......... £12 ...... *Minstrels B side*
Sentimental Reasons ............................. 7" ...... Coxsone ....... CS7048 .............. 1968 £5 ......... £10 .. *Soul Vendors B side*
Sugar And Spice ..................................... 7" ...... Blue Cat ....... BS115 ................ 1968 £4 ......... £8 .. *Soul Vendors B side*

## HAMMER, JACK
Brave New World ................................... LP ...... Polydor .......... 582001 .............. 1966 £15 ......... £30 ..........................................
Crazy Twist ............................................ 7" ...... Oriole ........... CB1728 .............. 1962 £1.50 ......... £4 ..........................................
Kissing Twist ......................................... 7" ...... Oriole ........... CB1645 .............. 1961 £1.50 ......... £4 ..........................................
Number 2539 ........................................ 7" ...... Oriole ........... CB1753 .............. 1962 £1.50 ......... £4 ..........................................
Thanks ................................................... 7" ...... Polydor .......... 56091 ................ 1966 £1.50 ......... £4 ..........................................
What Greater Love ............................... 7" ...... United Artists .. UP35029 ........... 1969 £7.50 ......... £15 ..........................................
Young Only Once .................................. 7" ...... Oriole ........... CB1634 .............. 1961 £1.50 ......... £4 ..........................................

## HAMMER, JAN
First Seven Days .................................... LP ...... Atlantic .......... K50184 .............. 1975 £4 ......... £10 ..........................................
Like Children ........................................ LP ...... Atlantic .......... K50092 .............. 1974 £4 ......... £10 ..........................................

## HAMMERSMITH
Hammersmith ........................................ LP ...... Mercury ........ SRM11040 ......... 1975 £5 ......... £12 ...................................... US
It's For You ........................................... LP ...... Mercury ........ SRM11102 ......... 1976 £4 ......... £10 ...................................... US

## HAMMERSMITH GORILLAS
You Really Got Me ............................... 7" ...... Penny Farthing PEN849 .............. 1974 £2.50 ......... £6

## HAMMILL, PETER
Chameleon In The Shadow Of The Night . LP ...... Charisma ........ CAS1067 ............ 1973 £4 ......... £10 ..........................................
Fool's Mate ........................................... LP ...... Charisma ........ CAS1037 ............ 1971 £6 ......... £15 ..........................................
Future Now ........................................... LP ...... Charisma ........ CAS1137 ............ 1978 £4 ......... £10 ..........................................
In Camera ............................................. LP ...... Charisma ........ CAS1089 ............ 1974 £4 ......... £10 ..........................................
Nadir's Last Chance .............................. LP ...... Charisma ........ CAS1099 ............ 1975 £4 ......... £10 ..........................................
Over ...................................................... LP ...... Charisma ........ CAS1125 ............ 1977 £4 ......... £10 ..........................................
PH7 ....................................................... LP ...... Charisma ........ CAS1146 ............ 1979 £4 ......... £10 ..........................................
Polaroid ................................................. 7" ...... Charisma ........ CB339 ............... 1979 £2.50 ......... £6 *credited to Rikki Nadir*
Silent Corner And The Empty Stage ........ LP ...... Charisma ........ CAS1083 ............ 1974 £4 ......... £10 ..........................................
Vision ................................................... LP ...... GIR ............... 92111016 ........... 1978 £4 ......... £10 ......... *US compilation*

## HAMMOND, JOHN
Best Of (Southern Fried) ...................... LP ...... Vanguard ....... VSD11/12 .......... 1974 £5 ......... £12 ................................ *double*
Big City Blues ....................................... LP ...... Fontana ......... TFL6046 ............ 1964 £8 ......... £20 ..........................................
Brown Eyed Handsome Man ................ 7" ...... Atlantic .......... 584190 .............. 1968 £2 ......... £5 ..........................................
Country Blues ....................................... LP ...... Vanguard ....... VRS/VSD79198 ... 1965 £8 ......... £20 ...................................... US
I Can Tell ............................................. LP ...... Atlantic .......... SD8152 .............. 1968 £8 ......... £20 ...................................... US
I Live The Life I Love ......................... 7" ...... Fontana ......... TF560 ............... 1965 £4 ......... £8 ..........................................
I'm Satisfied ......................................... LP ...... CBS ............... 65051 ................ 1972 £6 ......... £15 ..........................................
John Hammond ..................................... LP ...... Vanguard ....... VRS9132 ........... 1963 £8 ......... £20 ...................................... US
Little Big Man ...................................... LP ...... CBS ............... 30545 ................ 1971 £6 ......... £15 ...................................... US
Mirrors .................................................. LP ...... Vanguard ....... VRS/VSD79245 ... 1968 £8 ......... £20 ...................................... US
So Many Roads ..................................... LP ...... Fontana ......... TFL6059 ............ 1965 £8 ......... £20 ..........................................
Sooner Or Later ................................... LP ...... Atlantic .......... SD8206 .............. 1968 £8 ......... £20 ...................................... US
Source Point ......................................... LP ...... CBS ............... 64365 ................ 1971 £6 ......... £15 ..........................................
Southern Fried ...................................... LP ...... Atlantic .......... SD8251 .............. 1970 £6 ......... £15 ...................................... US
When I Need ......................................... LP ...... CBS ............... 30549 ................ 1971 £6 ......... £15 ...................................... US

## HAMNER, CURLEY
Twistin' And Turnin' ............................. 7" ...... Felsted ........... SD80061 ............ 1959 £1.50 ......... £4

## HAMPSHIRE, SUSAN
When Love Is True ............................... 7" ...... Decca ............. F12185 .............. 1965 £1.50 ......... £4

## HAMPTON, LIONEL
All American Award Concert ................ LP ...... Brunswick ....... LAT8086 ............ 1956 £6 ......... £15
Apollo Hall Concert 1954 ...................... LP ...... Philips ........... BBL7015 ............ 1955 £6 ......... £15
At The Pasadena Auditorium ................ LP ...... Vogue ........... LAE12014 .......... 1956 £6 ......... £15
At The Pasadena Auditorium ................ 7" EP. Vogue ........... EPV1161 ........... 1957 £2 ......... £5
Hamp 1956 ............................................ LP ...... Oriole ........... MG20012 .......... 1956 £6 ......... £15
Hamp's Big Band .................................. LP ...... Audio Fidelity.. AFLP1913/ ......... 1960 £5 ......... £12
........................................................................................ AFSD5913 ...........
Hamp's Boogie Woogie ......................... 7" EP. Columbia ....... SEB10108 .......... 1959 £2 ......... £5
Hamp's Boogie Woogie ......................... 7" ...... Vogue ........... V2406 ............... 1957 £6 ......... £12
Hamp's Boogie Woogie ......................... 10" LP Brunswick ....... LA8527 .............. 1951 £10 ......... £25
Hampton And The Old World ............... LP ...... Philips ........... BBL7119 ............ 1957 £6 ......... £15
High And The Mighty ........................... LP ...... Columbia ....... 33CX10146 ........ 1959 £6 ......... £15
Hot Mallets ........................................... LP ...... HMV .............. CLP1023 ............ 1955 £6 ......... £15
In Paris Vol. 1 ...................................... 10" LP Felsted ........... EDL87007 .......... 1954 £10 ......... £25
In Paris Vol. 2 ...................................... 10" LP Felsted ........... EDL87008 .......... 1954 £10 ......... £25
Jazz Flamenco ...................................... LP ...... RCA ............... RD27006 ........... 1957 £6 ......... £15
Jazz Time Paris Vol. 1 .......................... 10" LP Vogue ........... LDE043 ............. 1954 £10 ......... £25
Jivin' The Vibes .................................... LP ...... Camden .......... CDN129 ............ 1959 £4 ......... £10
Lionel Hampton .................................... LP ...... Felsted ........... PDL85006 .......... 1956 £8 ......... £20
Lionel Hampton And His All Stars ........ LP ...... Columbia ....... 33CX10086 ........ 1957 £8 ......... £20
Lionel Hampton And His Orchestra ........ 7" EP. MGM ............. MGMEP552 ....... 1956 £2 ......... £5
Lionel Hampton And Stan Getz ............ LP ...... Columbia ....... 33CX10041 ........ 1956 £15 ......... £30
Lionel Hampton Group .......................... LP ...... Vogue ........... LAE12034 .......... 1957 £6 ......... £15
Lionel Hampton Orchestra .................... 7" EP. Oriole ........... EP7046 .............. 1962 £2 ......... £5
Lionel Hampton Plays Love Songs .......... LP ...... HMV .............. CLP1136 ............ 1957 £6 ......... £15

| | | | | | | | |
|---|---|---|---|---|---|---|---|
| Lionel Hampton Quartet | LP | Columbia | 33CX10006 | 1955 £10 | £25 | |
| Lionel Hampton Quartet | 10" LP | Columbia | 33C9011 | 1955 £10 | £25 | |
| Lionel Hampton Vol. 3 | 10" LP | Vogue | LDE063 | 1954 £10 | £25 | |
| Lionel Hampton–Art Tatum–Buddy Rich Trio | LP | Columbia | 33CX10045 | 1956 £8 | £20 | |
| Many Splendored Vibes | LP | Columbia | 33SX1500 | 1962 £4 | £10 | |
| Moonglow | 10" LP | Brunswick | LA8551 | 1952 £10 | £25 | |
| New French Sound Vol. 1 | LP | Felsted | PDL85002 | 1955 £6 | £15 | |
| New Sounds From Europe Vol. 2 | 10" LP | Vogue | LDE051 | 1954 £10 | £25 | |
| One And Only Lionel Hampton | LP | Fontana | Z4053 | 1961 £4 | £10 | |
| Open House | LP | Camden | CDN138 | 1960 £4 | £10 | |
| Perdido | 7" | Vogue | V2405 | 1957 £5 | £10 | |

## HAMPTON, SLIDE

| | | | | | |
|---|---|---|---|---|---|
| Jazz With A Twist | LP | London | HAK/SHK8008 | 1962 £5 | £12 |

## HANCOCK, HERBIE

Jazz pianist Herbie Hancock has tried his hand at a particularly wide range of styles over the years, from straightforward modern jazz to hiphop. The trilogy of early-seventies recordings, *Mwandishi*, *Crossings* and *Sextant* finds him entering the composed electric jazz world defined by Weather Report. Typically, they are amongst the most impressive jazz recordings of the period, and arguably they are Hancock's personal best. *Crossings* is especially fine. *Treasure Chest* is an anthology of music taken from these electric jazz recordings and from Hancock's sixties work. It also includes a short track whose music is taken from *Crossings*, but in a remixed form not otherwise available.

| | | | | | | |
|---|---|---|---|---|---|---|
| Blind Man, Blind Man | 7" | Blue Note | 451887 | 1963 £1.50 | £4 | |
| Crossings | LP | Warner Bros | K46164 | 1972 £5 | £12 | |
| Death Wish | LP | CBS | 80546 | 1974 £5 | £12 | |
| Direct Step | LP | CBS Sony | 30AP1032 | 1979 £6 | £15 | Japanese |
| Empyrean Isles | LP | Blue Note | BLP/BST84175 | 1965 £10 | £25 | |
| Fat Albert Rotunda | LP | Warner Bros | K46039 | 1974 £6 | £15 | |
| Fat Albert Rotunda | LP | Warner Bros | WS1834 | 1971 £8 | £20 | |
| Fat Mama | 7" | Warner Bros | WB7358 | 1970 £1.50 | £4 | |
| Head Hunters | LP | CBS | 65928 | 1973 £4 | £10 | |
| Inventions And Dimensions | LP | Blue Note | BLP/BST84147 | 1964 £10 | £25 | |
| Live In Japan | LP | CBS Sony | 98/99 | 1975 £10 | £25 | Japanese double |
| Live Under The Sky | LP | CBS Sony | 1037875 | 1976 £6 | £15 | Japanese |
| Maiden Voyage | LP | Blue Note | BLP/BST84195 | 1966 £10 | £25 | |
| Mwandishi | LP | Warner Bros | K46077 | 1971 £5 | £12 | |
| My Point Of View | LP | Blue Note | BLP/BST84126 | 1964 £10 | £25 | |
| Prisoner | LP | Blue Note | BST84321 | 1969 £6 | £15 | |
| Sextant | LP | CBS | 65582 | 1972 £5 | £12 | |
| Speak Like A Child | LP | Blue Note | BST84279 | 1968 £6 | £15 | |
| Takin' Off | LP | Blue Note | BLP/BST84109 | 1964 £15 | £30 | |
| Thrust | LP | CBS | 80193 | 1974 £4 | £10 | |
| Treasure Chest | LP | Warner Bros | 2WS2807 | 1974 £6 | £15 | US double |

## HANCOCK, TONY

| | | | | | | |
|---|---|---|---|---|---|---|
| Blood Donor | 7" EP | Pye | NEP24175 | 1963 £2 | £5 | |
| Blood Donor & Radio Ham | LP | Pye | NPL18068 | 1961 £4 | £10 | |
| Hancock's Half Hour | 7" EP | Pye | NEP24170 | 1963 £2 | £5 | |
| It's Hancock | LP | Decca | LK4740 | 1965 £4 | £10 | |
| Little Pieces Of Hancock | 7" EP | Pye | NEP24146 | 1961 £2 | £5 | |
| Little Pieces Of Hancock Vol. 2 | 7" EP | Pye | NEP24161 | 1962 £2 | £5 | |
| Pieces Of Hancock | LP | Pye | NPL18054 | 1960 £4 | £10 | |
| This Is Hancock | LP | Pye | NPL18045 | 1960 £4 | £10 | |

## HAND, OWEN

| | | | | | |
|---|---|---|---|---|---|
| Something New | LP | Transatlantic | TRA127 | 1966 £25 | £50 |

## HANDLE, JOHNNY

| | | | | | |
|---|---|---|---|---|---|
| Collier Lad | LP | Topic | 12TS270 | 1975 £4 | £10 |

## HANDSOME BEASTS

| | | | | | | |
|---|---|---|---|---|---|---|
| All Riot Now | 7" | Heavy Metal | HEAVY1 | 1981 £1.50 | £4 | |
| Breaker | 7" | Heavy Metal | HEAVY2 | 1981 £1.50 | £4 | |
| Sweeties | 7" | Heavy Metal | HEAVY11 | 1982 £1.50 | £4 | |

## HANDY, WAYNE

| | | | | | | |
|---|---|---|---|---|---|---|
| Say Yeah | 7" | London | HL8547 | 1958 £180 | £300 | best auctioned |

## HANFORD, PAUL

| | | | | | |
|---|---|---|---|---|---|
| Minute You're Gone | 7" | Oriole | CB1866 | 1963 £1.50 | £4 |

## HANGMEN

| | | | | | | |
|---|---|---|---|---|---|---|
| Bitter Sweet | LP | Monument | SLP18077 | 1966 £6 | £15 | US |

## HANK & THE MELLOWMEN

| | | | | | | |
|---|---|---|---|---|---|---|
| Santa Anno | 7" | Lyntone | LYN153/4 | 196– £1.50 | £4 | flexi |
| So In Love With You | 7" | Lyntone | LYN201 | 196– £1.50 | £4 | flexi |

## HANLY, MICHAEL

| | | | | | | |
|---|---|---|---|---|---|---|
| As I Went Over Blackwater | LP | Mulligan | LUN040 | 1980 £4 | £10 | Irish |
| Kiss In The Morning Early | LP | Mulligan | LUN005 | 1976 £4 | £10 | Irish |

## HANLY, MICHAEL & MICHAEL O'DONNEL

| | | | | | | |
|---|---|---|---|---|---|---|
| Celtic Folkweave | LP | Polydor | 2908013 | 1974 £20 | £40 | Irish |

## HANNA, BOBBY
| | | | | | | |
|---|---|---|---|---|---|---|
| Blame It On Me | 7" | Decca | F12695 | 1967 £2 | £5 | |
| Written On The Wind | 7" | Decca | F12783 | 1968 £2 | £5 | |

## HANNA, GEORGE & SARAH ANNE O'NEILL
| | | | | | | |
|---|---|---|---|---|---|---|
| On The Shores Of Lough Neagh | LP | Topic | 12TS372 | 1978 £5 | £12 | |

## HANNA, JOSH
| | | | | | | |
|---|---|---|---|---|---|---|
| Shut Your Mouth | 7" | Decca | F12532 | 1966 £4 | £8 | |

## HANNA, KEN
| | | | | | | |
|---|---|---|---|---|---|---|
| Ken Hanna Orchestra | 10" LP | London | HAPB1031 | 1954 £4 | £10 | |

## HANNA BARBERA
| | | | | | | |
|---|---|---|---|---|---|---|
| Flintstones – Goldilocks & The Bearosauruses | 7" EP | Hanna Barbera | HBE3 | 1966 £2 | £5 | |
| Flintstones – Hansel And Gretel | 7" EP | Hanna Barbera | HBE1 | 1966 £2 | £5 | |
| Flintstones – Mary Poppins | 7" EP | Hanna Barbera | HBE6 | 1966 £2 | £5 | |
| Flintstones – Three Little Pigs | 7" EP | Hanna Barbera | HBE9 | 1966 £2 | £5 | |
| Snagglepuss Tales – Wizard Of Oz | 7" EP | Hanna Barbera | HBE4 | 1966 £2 | £5 | |
| Top Cat – Robin Hood | 7" EP | Hanna Barbera | HBE7 | 1966 £2 | £5 | |
| Uncle Remus – Brer Rabbit & The Tar Baby | 7" EP | Hanna Barbera | HBE2 | 1966 £2 | £5 | |
| Yogi Bear & Boo Boo – Jack & The Beanstalk | 7" EP | Hanna Barbera | HBE5 | 1966 £2 | £5 | |
| Yogi Bear & Boo Boo – Little Red Riding Hood | 7" EP | Hanna Barbera | HBE8 | 1966 £2 | £5 | |

## HANNIBAL

Hannibal's only album is definitely a neglected gem from the progressive era. Occasionally let down a little by the lyrics, the music is nevertheless sparkling and inventive, these qualities being enhanced by fluent jazz-rock playing from all concerned. The keyboard player turned up on a few Roy Wood records, but remarkably none of the members of Hannibal was able to sustain a career in music.

| | | | | | | |
|---|---|---|---|---|---|---|
| Hannibal | LP | B&C | CAS1022 | 1970 £10 | £25 | |
| Winds Of Change | 7" | B&C | HB1 | 1974 £1.50 | £4 | |

## HANNIBAL, LANCE
| | | | | | | |
|---|---|---|---|---|---|---|
| Read The News | 7" | Blue Cat | BS148 | 1968 £1.50 | £4 | Rico B side |

## HANOI ROCKS
| | | | | | | |
|---|---|---|---|---|---|---|
| Best Of Hanoi Rocks | CD | Lick | LICCD8 | 1988 £5 | £12 | |
| Don't You Ever Leave Me | 12" | CBS | TA4885 | 1984 £3 | £8 | |
| Don't You Ever Leave Me | 12" | CBS | WA4885 | 1984 £4 | £10 | picture disc |
| Malibu Beach | 7" | Lick | LIXPD1 | 1983 £4 | £10 | picture disc |
| Underwater World | 12" | CBS | TA4732 | 1984 £2.50 | £6 | |
| Underwater World | 12" | CBS | WA4732 | 1984 £4 | £10 | picture disc |
| Up Around The Bend | 7" | CBS | DA4513 | 1984 £5 | £10 | double |
| Up Around The Bend | 12" | CBS | TA4513 | 1984 £2.50 | £6 | with transfer |

## HANSSON & KARLSSON
| | | | | | | |
|---|---|---|---|---|---|---|
| Man At The Moon | LP | Polydor | 46265 | 1968 £5 | £12 | Swedish |
| Monument | LP | Polydor | 46260 | 1969 £5 | £12 | |
| Rex | LP | Polydor | 46264 | 1968 £6 | £15 | Swedish |
| Swedish Underground | LP | Polydor | 184196 | 1967 £6 | £15 | |

## HANUMAN
| | | | | | | |
|---|---|---|---|---|---|---|
| Hanuman | LP | Kuckuck | 2375012 | 1972 £6 | £15 | German |

## HA'PENNYS
| | | | | | | |
|---|---|---|---|---|---|---|
| Love Is Not The Same | LP | Fersch | 1110 | 1968 £75 | £150 | US |

## HAPPENINGS
| | | | | | | |
|---|---|---|---|---|---|---|
| Go Away Little Girl | 7" EP | Vogue | INT18100 | 1966 £2.50 | £6 | French |
| Go Away Little Girl | 7" | Fontana | TF766 | 1966 £1.50 | £4 | |
| Golden Hits | LP | B.T.Puppy | BTLPS1004 | 1968 £5 | £12 | US |
| Greatest Hits | LP | Jubilee | JGS8030 | 1969 £5 | £12 | US |
| Happenings | LP | B.T.Puppy | (S)1001 | 1966 £5 | £12 | US |
| I Got Rhythm | 7" EP | B.T.Puppy | 701 | 1967 £2.50 | £6 | French |
| Piece Of Mind | LP | Jubilee | JGS8028 | 1969 £5 | £12 | US |
| Psycle | LP | B.T.Puppy | (S)1003 | 1967 £5 | £12 | US |
| See You In September | LP | Fontana | TL5383 | 1967 £5 | £12 | |
| See You In September | 7" EP | Vogue | INT18090 | 1966 £2.50 | £6 | French, B side by Jimmy Mays & Soul Breed |
| See You In September | 7" | Fontana | TF735 | 1966 £1.50 | £4 | |

## HAPPENINGS & TOKENS
| | | | | | | |
|---|---|---|---|---|---|---|
| Back To Back | LP | B.T.Puppy | (S)1002 | 1967 £5 | £12 | US |

## HAPPY DRAGON BAND
| | | | | | | |
|---|---|---|---|---|---|---|
| Happy Dragon Band | LP | Fiddlers Music Company | | 1978 £30 | £60 | US |

## HAPPY FAMILY
| | | | | | | |
|---|---|---|---|---|---|---|
| Puritans | 7" | 4AD | AD204 | 1982 £2 | £5 | |

## HAPPY MAGAZINE
| | | | | | | | |
|---|---|---|---|---|---|---|---|
| Satisfied Street | 7" | Polydor | 56233 | 1968 | £2 | £5 | |
| Who Belongs To You | 7" | Polydor | 56307 | 1968 | £1.50 | £4 | |

## HAPPY MONDAYS
| | | | | | | | |
|---|---|---|---|---|---|---|---|
| Bummed | CD | Factory | FACD220 | 1988 | £5 | £12 | |
| Judge Fudge | CD-s | Factory | FACD332 | 1991 | £2 | £5 | |
| Kinky Afro | CD-s | Factory | FACD302 | 1990 | £2 | £5 | |
| Live | CD | Factory | FACT322C | 1991 | £5 | £12 | |
| Loose Fit | CD-s | Factory | FACD312 | 1991 | £2 | £5 | |
| Madchester, Rave On | CD-s | Factory | FACD242 | 1989 | £2 | £5 | |
| Peel Sessions | CD-s | Strange Fruit | SFPSCD077 | 1990 | £2 | £5 | |
| Peel Sessions 2 | CD-s | Strange Fruit | SFPSCD084 | 1991 | £2 | £5 | |
| Pills 'n' Thrills And Bellyaches | CD | Factory | FACD320 | 1990 | £5 | £12 | |
| Squirrel And G Man | CD | Factory | FACD170 | 1990 | £5 | £12 | |
| Squirrel And G Man | LP | Factory | FACT170 | 1987 | £4 | £10 | ... plastic sleeve, with 'Desmond' |
| Step On | CD-s | Factory | FACD272 | 1990 | £2 | £5 | |
| Step On (Melon Mix) | 12" | Factory | FAC272 | 1990 | £4 | £10 | 1 sided promo |
| Sunshine And Love EP | CD-s | Factory | FACD372 | 1992 | £2 | £5 | |
| Wrote For Luck | CD-s | Factory | FACD232 | 1989 | £2 | £5 | |
| Yes Please | CD-s | Factory | FACD420D | 1992 | £2 | £5 | |

## HAPSHASH & THE COLOURED COAT
| | | | | | | | |
|---|---|---|---|---|---|---|---|
| Colinda | 7" | Liberty | LBF15188 | 1969 | £5 | £10 | |
| Human Host And Heavy Metal Kids | LP | Liberty | MLL/MLS40001E | 1967 | £15 | £30 | red vinyl |
| Human Host And The Heavy Metal Kids | LP | Liberty | MLS40001E | 1967 | £8 | £20 | |
| Western Flyer | LP | Liberty | LBL/LBS83212 | 1969 | £6 | £15 | |

## HARBOUR LITES
| | | | | | | | |
|---|---|---|---|---|---|---|---|
| I Would Give All | 7" | HMV | POP1465 | 1965 | £1.50 | £4 | |
| Run For Your Life | 7" | Fontana | TF682 | 1966 | £2 | £5 | |

## HARD CORPS
| | | | | | | | |
|---|---|---|---|---|---|---|---|
| Dirty | 7" | Survival | SUR026 | 1984 | £2.50 | £6 | |
| Dirty | 12" | Hard Corps | 1 | 1984 | £15 | £30 | |
| Dirty | 12" | Survival | SUR12026 | 1984 | £3 | £8 | |
| Je Suis Passee | 12" | Immaculate | 12IMMAC2 | 1985 | £4 | £10 | |
| Je Suis Passee | 12" | Polydor | HARDA1 | 1985 | £10 | £20 | ... plastic sleeve, poster |
| To Breathe | 7" | Polydor | HARD2 | 1985 | £12.50 | £25 | |
| To Breathe | 12" | Polydor | HARDX2 | 1985 | £15 | £30 | |

## HARD MEAT
| | | | | | | | |
|---|---|---|---|---|---|---|---|
| Hard Meat | LP | Warner Bros | WS1852 | 1970 | £5 | £12 | |
| Rain | 7" | Island | WIP6066 | 1969 | £2.50 | £6 | |
| Through A Window | LP | Warner Bros | WS1879 | 1970 | £8 | £20 | |

## HARD ROAD
| | | | | | | | |
|---|---|---|---|---|---|---|---|
| No Problem | LP | Goodstuff | LP1002 | 1979 | £8 | £20 | |

## HARD STUFF
| | | | | | | | |
|---|---|---|---|---|---|---|---|
| Bolex Dementia | LP | Purple | TPSA7507 | 1973 | £6 | £15 | |
| Bullet Proof | LP | Purple | TPSA7505 | 1972 | £6 | £15 | |

## HARD TIMES
| | | | | | | | |
|---|---|---|---|---|---|---|---|
| Blew Mind | LP | World Pacific | WPS21867 | 1968 | £6 | £15 | US |

## HARD TRAVELLIN'
| | | | | | | | |
|---|---|---|---|---|---|---|---|
| Hard Travellin' | LP | Flams Ltd | PR1065 | 1971 | £50 | £100 | |

## HARD WATER
| | | | | | | | |
|---|---|---|---|---|---|---|---|
| Hard Water | LP | Capitol | ST2954 | 1968 | £8 | £20 | US |

## HARDCAKE SPECIAL
| | | | | | | | |
|---|---|---|---|---|---|---|---|
| Hardcake Special | LP | Brain | 1060 | 1974 | £4 | £10 | German |

## HARDEN, WILBUR
| | | | | | | | |
|---|---|---|---|---|---|---|---|
| Mainstream 1958 | LP | London | LTZC15159 | 1959 | £8 | £20 | with John Coltrane |

## HARDIN, EDDIE
| | | | | | | | |
|---|---|---|---|---|---|---|---|
| Home Is Where You Find It | LP | Decca | TXS106 | 1972 | £4 | £10 | |

## HARDIN, TIM

Tim Hardin's fragile voice made his own interpretations of his best material the most moving versions of all – and he wrote some classic songs; 'Hang On To A Dream', 'If I Were A Carpenter' and 'Reason To Believe' among them. Particularly moving is his 'Suite For Susan Moore and Damian', which is a kind of stream-of-consciousness tribute to his wife and child. It was a real tragedy when this precious talent succumbed to heroin addiction in 1980.

| | | | | | | | |
|---|---|---|---|---|---|---|---|
| Bird On A Wire | LP | CBS | 64335 | 1970 | £4 | £10 | |
| Don't Make Promises | 7" | Verve | VS1516 | 1968 | £1.50 | £4 | |
| Hang On To a Dream | 7" | Verve | VS1504 | 1966 | £1.50 | £4 | |
| Lady Came From Baltimore | 7" | Verve | VS1511 | 1967 | £1.50 | £4 | |
| Live In Concert | LP | Verve | (S)VLP6010 | 1968 | £6 | £15 | |
| Suite For Susan Moore & Damian | LP | CBS | 63571 | 1970 | £10 | £25 | |
| This Is Tim Hardin | LP | Atco | 587/588082 | 1967 | £8 | £20 | |
| Tim Hardin 1 | LP | Verve | (S)VLP5018 | 1966 | £6 | £15 | |

| | | | | | | | | |
|---|---|---|---|---|---|---|---|---|
| Tim Hardin 1/Tim Hardin 2 | LP | Verve | 2683048 | 1974 | £6 | £15 | double |
| Tim Hardin 2 | LP | Verve | (S)VLP6002 | 1967 | £6 | £15 | |
| Tim Hardin 4 | LP | Verve | (S)VLP6016 | 1969 | £6 | £15 | |

## HARDIN & YORK

| | | | | | | | |
|---|---|---|---|---|---|---|---|
| For The World | LP | Decca | SKL5095 | 1971 | £4 | £10 | |
| Tomorrow Today | LP | Bell | SBLL125 | 1969 | £4 | £10 | |
| World's Smallest Big Band | LP | Bell | SBLL136 | 1970 | £4 | £10 | |

## HARDING, RICHARD

| | | | | | | | |
|---|---|---|---|---|---|---|---|
| Jezebel | 7" | HMV | POP887 | 1961 | £1.50 | £4 | |

## HARDMAN, ROSEMARY

| | | | | | | | |
|---|---|---|---|---|---|---|---|
| Eagle Over Blue Mountain | LP | Plant Life | PLR014 | 1978 | £5 | £12 | |
| Firebird | LP | Trailer | LER2075 | 1972 | £6 | £15 | |
| Jerseyburger | LP | Alida Star Cottage | ASC7754 | 1975 | £75 | £150 | |
| Queen Of Hearts | LP | Folk Heritage | FHR002M | 1969 | £37.50 | £75 | |
| Second Season Came | LP | Trailer | LER3018 | 1971 | £6 | £15 | with Bob Axford |
| Stopped In My Tracks | LP | Plant Life | PLR023 | 1980 | £5 | £12 | |
| Weakness Of Eve | LP | Plant Life | PLR053 | 1983 | £5 | £12 | |

## HARDY, DAVE

| | | | | | | | |
|---|---|---|---|---|---|---|---|
| Leaving The Dales | LP | Red Rag | RRR008 | 1976 | £15 | £30 | |

## HARDY, FRANÇOISE

As one of France's top sixties pop-music stars, Françoise Hardy also gained a considerable following in Britain. The EPs *C'est fab* and *C'est Françoise* in particular sold well enough to enter the lower reaches of the charts – a rare feat for records sung in a language other than English. After some years of retirement from the music business, Françoise Hardy was persuaded to add vocals to a version of Blur's 'To The End', the success of which encouraged her to record a whole new album – the excellent *Le Danger*.

| | | | | | | | |
|---|---|---|---|---|---|---|---|
| All Because Of You | 7" | United Artists | UP35070 | 1969 | £1.50 | £4 | |
| All Over The World | 7" | Pye | 7N15802 | 1965 | £1.50 | £4 | |
| Autumn Rendezvous | 7" EP | Vogue | VRE5018 | 1967 | £2 | £5 | |
| Autumn Rendezvous | 7" | Vogue | VRS7014 | 1966 | £1.50 | £4 | |
| C'est fab | 7" EP | Pye | NEP24188 | 1964 | £2.50 | £6 | |
| C'est Françoise | 7" EP | Pye | NEP24193 | 1964 | £2.50 | £6 | |
| Catch A Falling Star | 7" | Pye | 7N15612 | 1964 | £1.50 | £4 | |
| Chante en allemand | 7" EP | Vogue | VRE5012 | 1966 | £2 | £5 | |
| Comment te dire adieu | 7" | United Artists | UP35011 | 1969 | £1.50 | £4 | |
| Dis lui non | 7" EP | Vogue | VRE5003 | 1965 | £2 | £5 | |
| Et même | 7" | Pye | 7N15740 | 1964 | £1.50 | £4 | |
| Françoise | LP | Vogue | VRL3028 | 1967 | £4 | £10 | |
| Françoise | 7" EP | Vogue | VRE5000 | 1965 | £2 | £5 | |
| Françoise Hardy | LP | Pye | NPL18094 | 1964 | £4 | £10 | |
| Françoise Hardy | LP | Vogue | VRL3000 | 1965 | £4 | £10 | |
| Françoise Hardy | LP | Vogue | VRL3021 | 1966 | £4 | £10 | |
| Françoise Hardy | 7" EP | Vogue | VRE5001 | 1965 | £2 | £5 | |
| Françoise Hardy Sings In English | LP | Vogue | VRL3025 | 1966 | £4 | £10 | |
| Françoise Sings In English | 7" EP | Pye | NEP24192 | 1964 | £2.50 | £6 | |
| In Vogue | LP | Pye | NPL18099 | 1964 | £4 | £10 | |
| Just Call And I'll Be There | 7" | Vogue | VRS7001 | 1966 | £1.50 | £4 | |
| L'Amitié | 7" EP | Vogue | VRE5015 | 1966 | £2 | £5 | |
| La Maison où j'ai grandi | 7" | Vogue | VRS7011 | 1966 | £1.50 | £4 | |
| Le Meilleur de Françoise Hardy | LP | Vogue | VRL3023 | 1966 | £4 | £10 | |
| Le Temps des souvenirs | 7" EP | Vogue | VRE5008 | 1965 | £2 | £5 | |
| Mon Amie la rose | 7" EP | Vogue | VRE5017 | 1967 | £2 | £5 | |
| Now You Want To Be Loved | 7" | United Artists | UP1208 | 1968 | £1.50 | £4 | |
| On se quitte toujours | 7" | Vogue | VRS7026 | 1967 | £1.50 | £4 | |
| Pourtant tu m'aimes | 7" | Pye | 7N15696 | 1964 | £1.50 | £4 | |
| Si c'est ça | 7" | Vogue | VRS7020 | 1966 | £1.50 | £4 | |
| So Many Friends | 7" | Vogue | VRS7004 | 1966 | £1.50 | £4 | |
| Soon Is Slipping Away | 7" | United Artists | UP35105 | 1970 | £1.50 | £4 | |
| This Little Heart | 7" | Vogue | VRS7010 | 1966 | £1.50 | £4 | |
| Tous les garçons et les filles | 7" | Pye | 7N15653 | 1964 | £1.50 | £4 | |
| Voilà | 7" | Vogue | VRS7025 | 1966 | £1.50 | £4 | |
| Voilà! | LP | Vogue | VRL3031 | 1967 | £4 | £10 | |
| Will You Love Me Tomorrow | 7" | United Artists | UP2253 | 1968 | £1.50 | £4 | |

## HARE, COLIN

Colin Hare was the second guitarist with the Honeybus, whose best material was written by the first, Pete Dello. Sadly, Hare's solo album rather shows why this was.

| | | | | | | | |
|---|---|---|---|---|---|---|---|
| Didn't I Tell You | 7" | Warner Bros | K16203 | 1972 | £1.50 | £4 | |
| March Hare | LP | Penny Farthing | PELS516 | 1971 | £15 | £30 | |

## HARGRAVE, RON

| | | | | | | | |
|---|---|---|---|---|---|---|---|
| Latch On | 7" | MGM | MGM956 | 1957 | £875 | £1250 | best auctioned |

## HARLEY, STEVE

| | | | | | | | |
|---|---|---|---|---|---|---|---|
| Big Big Deal | 7" | EMI | EMI2233 | 1974 | £5 | £10 | |
| Lighthouse | CD-s | Food For Thought | no number | 1993 | £2.50 | £6 | promo only |

## HARLOWE, RAY & GYP FOX

| | | | | | | | |
|---|---|---|---|---|---|---|---|
| First Rays | LP | Water Wheel | WR711 | 1978 | £20 | £40 | US |

## HARMONIA

| Title | Format | Label | Cat. | Year | | | Notes |
|---|---|---|---|---|---|---|---|
| De Luxe | LP | Brain | 1073 | 1975 | £6 | £15 | German |
| Harmonia | LP | Brain | 1044 | 1974 | £6 | £15 | German |

## HARMONICA FATS

| Title | Format | Label | Cat. | Year | | | Notes |
|---|---|---|---|---|---|---|---|
| Tore Up | 7" | Action | ACT4507 | 1968 | £5 | £10 | |
| Tore Up | 7" | Stateside | SS184 | 1963 | £6 | £12 | |

## HARMONICA FRANK

In the pages of *Mystery Train*, the acclaimed sociological study of American themes as revealed in the work of various rock musicians, Greil Marcus chooses the almost forgotten figure of white bluesman Frank Floyd to illustrate his thesis. As it happens, the single that Harmonica Frank recorded for Sun is one of the rarest releases on a particularly collectable label – anyone in possession of a copy can virtually name their own price.

| Title | Format | Label | Cat. | Year | | | Notes |
|---|---|---|---|---|---|---|---|
| Rockin' Chair Daddy | 7" | Sun | 205 | 1954 | £1050 | £1500 | US, best auctioned |

## HARMONISERS

| Title | Format | Label | Cat. | Year | | | Notes |
|---|---|---|---|---|---|---|---|
| Mother Hen | 7" | Duke | DU32 | 1969 | £1.50 | £4 | Winston Sinclair B side |

## HARMONY

| Title | Format | Label | Cat. | Year | | | Notes |
|---|---|---|---|---|---|---|---|
| Harmony | LP | Breakthrough | | 1972 | £20 | £40 | |

## HARMONY FLAMES

| Title | Format | Label | Cat. | Year | | |
|---|---|---|---|---|---|---|
| USA Hit Parade No. 1 | 7" EP | Fontana | TFE17152 | 1959 | £2 | £5 |

## HARNER, BILLY

| Title | Format | Label | Cat. | Year | | | Notes |
|---|---|---|---|---|---|---|---|
| What About The Music | 7" | Kama Sutra | 2013029 | 1971 | £1.50 | £4 | |
| What About The Music | 7" | Kama Sutra | 2013029 | 1971 | £150 | £250 | with instrumental version |

## HARPER, BUD

| Title | Format | Label | Cat. | Year | | |
|---|---|---|---|---|---|---|
| Mr. Soul | 7" | Vocalion | VP9252 | 1965 | £7.50 | £15 |

## HARPER, DON

| Title | Format | Label | Cat. | Year | | |
|---|---|---|---|---|---|---|
| Dr. Who Theme | 7" | Columbia | DB9023 | 1973 | £5 | £10 |
| Homo Electronicus | LP | Columbia | SCX6559 | 1974 | £8 | £20 |

## HARPER, HERBIE

| Title | Format | Label | Cat. | Year | | |
|---|---|---|---|---|---|---|
| Herbie Harper Octet | 10" LP | London | LZN14031 | 1956 | £10 | £25 |

## HARPER, JOE 'HARMONICA'

| Title | Format | Label | Cat. | Year | | |
|---|---|---|---|---|---|---|
| Lazy Train | 7" | MGM | MGM983 | 1958 | £1.50 | £4 |

## HARPER, MIKE

| Title | Format | Label | Cat. | Year | | |
|---|---|---|---|---|---|---|
| You've Got Too Much Going For You | 7" | Concord | CON026 | 197– | £5 | £10 |

## HARPER, ROY

| Title | Format | Label | Cat. | Year | | | Notes |
|---|---|---|---|---|---|---|---|
| Born In Captivity | LP | Hardup | PUB5002 | 1984 | £8 | £20 | |
| Bullinamingvase | LP | Harvest | SHSP4060 | 1977 | £5 | £12 | with 'Watford Gap' |
| Bullinamingvase | LP | Harvest | SHSP4060 | 1977 | £8 | £20 | with 7" (PSR407) |
| Come Out Fighting Ghengis Smith | LP | CBS | (S)BPG63184 | 1967 | £8 | £20 | |
| Commercial Break | LP | Harvest | SHSP4077 | 1977 | £100 | £200 | test pressing |
| Descendants Of Smith | CD | EMI | CDEMC3524 | 1988 | £5 | £12 | |
| Flashes From The Archives Of Oblivion | LP | Harvest | SHDW405 | 1974 | £8 | £20 | double |
| Flat Baroque And Beserk | LP | Harvest | SHVL776 | 1970 | £4 | £10 | |
| Flat, Baroque And Beserk | CD | Hard Up | HUCD003 | 1993 | £5 | £12 | boxed, with 40 page booklet & poster, signed |
| Folkjokeopus | LP | Liberty | LBS83231 | 1969 | £6 | £15 | |
| Introducing Roy Harper | LP | Chrysalis | PRO620 | 1977 | £15 | £30 | US promo |
| Life Goes By | 7" | CBS | 3371 | 1968 | £5 | £10 | |
| Lifemask | LP | Harvest | SHVL808 | 1973 | £4 | £10 | |
| Midspring Dithering | 7" | CBS | 203001 | 1967 | £7.50 | £15 | |
| Mrs. Space | 7" | Harvest | PSR408 | 1977 | £1.50 | £4 | promo |
| Playing Games | 7" | Harvest | HAR5203 | 1980 | £1.50 | £4 | |
| Return Of The Sophisticated Beggar | LP | Birth | RAB3 | 1972 | £6 | £15 | |
| Return Of The Sophisticated Beggar | LP | Youngblood | SYB7 | 1970 | £8 | £20 | |
| Sail Away | 7" | Harvest | HAR5140 | 1977 | £1.50 | £4 | |
| Sophisticated Beggar | LP | Strike | JHL105 | 1967 | £30 | £60 | |
| Stormcock | LP | Harvest | SHVL789 | 1971 | £4 | £10 | |
| Take Me In Your Eyes | 7" | Strike | JH304 | 1966 | £12.50 | £25 | picture sleeve |
| Valentine | LP | Harvest | SHSP4027 | 1974 | £5 | £12 | lyric booklet |
| Work Of Heart | LP | Awareness | AWL1002 | 1988 | £4 | £10 | with 2 singles |

## HARPERS BIZARRE

| Title | Format | Label | Cat. | Year | | | Notes |
|---|---|---|---|---|---|---|---|
| 59th Street Bridge Song | 7" EP | Warner Bros | WEP1454 | 1967 | £10 | £20 | French |
| 59th Street Bridge Song | 7" | Warner Bros | WB5890 | 1967 | £1.50 | £4 | |
| Anything Goes | LP | Warner Bros | WS1716 | 1967 | £5 | £12 | US |
| Anything Goes | 7" | Warner Bros | WB7063 | 1967 | £1.50 | £4 | |
| Anything Goes | 7" | Warner Bros | WB7388 | 1970 | £1.50 | £4 | |
| Battle Of New Orleans | 7" | Warner Bros | WB7223 | 1968 | £1.50 | £4 | |
| Best Of Harpers Bizarre | LP | Warner Bros | K56044 | 1974 | £4 | £10 | |
| Come To The Sunshine | 7" | Warner Bros | WB7528 | 1967 | £1.50 | £4 | |
| Cotton Candy Sandman | 7" | Warner Bros | WB7172 | 1968 | £1.50 | £4 | |
| Feelin' Groovy | LP | Warner Bros | WS1693 | 1967 | £5 | £12 | US |

| | | | | | | | |
|---|---|---|---|---|---|---|---|
| Harpers Bizarre 4 | LP | Warner Bros | WS1784 | 1969 £5 | £12 | | US |
| I Love You Alice B.Toklas | 7" | Warner Bros | WB7238 | 1969 £1.50 | £4 | | |
| Secret Life Of Harpers Bizarre | LP | Warner Bros | W(S)1739 | 1968 £5 | £12 | | |

## HARPO, SLIM

| | | | | | | | |
|---|---|---|---|---|---|---|---|
| Baby Scratch My Back | LP | Excello | LP8005 | 1966 £10 | £25 | | US |
| Baby Scratch My Back | 7" | Stateside | SS491 | 1966 £4 | £8 | | |
| Best Of Slim Harpo | LP | Excello | LP8010 | 1969 £5 | £12 | | US |
| Folsom Prison Blues | 7" | Blue Horizon | 573175 | 1970 £5 | £10 | | |
| He Knew The Blues | LP | Blue Horizon | 763854 | 1970 £20 | £40 | | |
| I'm A King Bee | 7" | Stateside | SS557 | 1966 £6 | £12 | | |
| I'm Gonna Keep What I've Got | 7" | President | PT164 | 1968 £1.50 | £4 | | |
| I'm Your Breadmaker Baby | 7" | Stateside | SS581 | 1967 £5 | £10 | | |
| Long Drink Of The Blues | LP | Stateside | SL10135 | 1965 £10 | £25 | | ...with Lightnin' Slim |
| Raining In My Heart | LP | Excello | LP8003 | 1961 £20 | £40 | | US |
| Raining In My Heart | 7" | Pye | 7N25098 | 1961 £2.50 | £6 | | |
| Raining In My Heart | 7" | Pye | 7N25220 | 1963 £4 | £8 | | |
| Shake Your Hips | 7" | Stateside | SS527 | 1966 £7.50 | £15 | | |
| Slim Harpo Knew The Blues | LP | Excello | LP8013 | 1970 £5 | £12 | | US |
| Something Inside Me | 7" | Liberty | LBF15176 | 1968 £4 | £8 | | .Papa Lightfoot B side |
| Tip On In | 7" | President | PT187 | 1968 £1.50 | £4 | | |
| Trigger Finger | LP | Blue Horizon | 2431013 | 1971 £20 | £40 | | |

## HARRIOTT, DERRICK

| | | | | | | | |
|---|---|---|---|---|---|---|---|
| Another Lonely Night | 7" | Big Shot | BI511 | 1969 £1.50 | £4 | | |
| Be True | 7" | Blue Beat | BB178 | 1963 £6 | £12 | | |
| Best Of Derrick Harriott | LP | Island | ILP928 | 1965 £30 | £60 | | |
| Best Of Derrick Harriott | LP | Trojan | TTL43 | 1970 £6 | £15 | | |
| Best Of Derrick Harriott Vol. 2 | LP | Island | ILP983 | 1968 £30 | £60 | | pink label |
| Born To Love You | 7" | Island | WI3147 | 1968 £5 | £10 | | Ike & Crystalites B side |
| Derrick | 7" | Ska Beat | JB199 | 1965 £5 | £10 | | |
| Happy Times | 7" | Island | WI3064 | 1967 £5 | £10 | | |
| Have Faith In Me | 7" | Blue Beat | BB131 | 1962 £6 | £12 | | |
| I'm Only Human | 7" | Island | WI170 | 1965 £5 | £10 | | |
| John Tom | 7" | Doctor Bird | DB1002 | 1966 £5 | £10 | | Audrey Williams B side |
| Loser | 7" | Island | WI3063 | 1967 £5 | £10 | | |
| Message From A Black Man | 7" | Song Bird | SB1028 | 1970 £1.50 | £4 | | |
| My Three Loves | 7" | Island | WI237 | 1965 £5 | £10 | | |
| Psychedelic Train | LP | Trojan | TBL141 | 1970 £6 | £15 | | |
| Reggae Hits | LP | Trojan | TBL116 | 1970 £6 | £15 | | |
| Riding For A Fall | 7" | Songbird | SB1013 | 1969 £1.50 | £4 | | |
| Rock Steady Party | LP | Island | ILP955 | 1967 £50 | £100 | | pink label |
| Rocksteady Party | LP | Trojan | TTL54 | 1970 £15 | £30 | | |
| Sings Jamaica Reggae | LP | Pama | SECO13 | 1969 £20 | £40 | | |
| Sitting On Top | 7" | Songbird | SB1014 | 1969 £1.50 | £4 | | |
| Standing In | 7" | Big Shot | BI505 | 1968 £2.50 | £6 | | |
| Together | 7" | Island | WI245 | 1965 £5 | £10 | | |
| Undertaker | LP | Trojan | TBL114 | 1970 £6 | £15 | | |
| Walk The Streets | 7" | Island | WI3077 | 1967 £5 | £10 | | Bobby Ellis B side |
| What Can I Do | 7" | Island | WI157 | 1964 £5 | £10 | | |

## HARRIOTT, JOE

Jamaican saxophonist Joe Harriott was perhaps the first jazz player working in Britain to break free from the prevailing trad/mainstream orthodoxy. His *Free Form* album pioneered an approach to free improvisation – had Harriott been an American he would undoubtedly have received as much acclaim as fellow adventurers John Coltrane and Ornette Coleman. Later, he linked up with violinist John Mayer for a series of equally ground-breaking experiments in fusing jazz with Indian music (*Indo-Jazz Suite* is listed here – other albums appear under Mayer's name). Most sought-after of all, however, is the last album made by Harriott before his death of cancer in 1973, *Hum-Dono*, containing uplifting music made in collaboration with guitarist Amancio D'Silva.

| | | | | | | | |
|---|---|---|---|---|---|---|---|
| Abstract | LP | Columbia | 33SX1477 | 1963 £25 | £50 | | |
| Blue Harriott | 7" EP | Columbia | SEG7939 | 1959 £7.50 | £15 | | |
| Cool Jazz With Joe | 7" EP | Melodisc | EPM7117 | 195– £7.50 | £15 | | |
| Free Form | LP | Jazzland | JLP49 | 1961 £25 | £50 | | |
| Guy Called Joe | 7" EP | Columbia | SEG8070 | 1961 £7.50 | £15 | | |
| High Spirits | LP | Columbia | 33SX1692 | 1964 £25 | £50 | | |
| Hum-Dono | LP | Columbia | SCX6354 | 1969 £50 | £100 | | |
| Indo-Jazz Suite | LP | Columbia | SX/SCX6025 | 1966 £25 | £50 | | with John Mayer |
| Joe Harriott | 7" EP | Polygon | JTE106 | 195– £7.50 | £15 | | |
| Joe Harriott Quartet | 7" EP | Columbia | SEG7665 | 1957 £7.50 | £15 | | |
| Memorial | LP | One Up | OU2011 | 1973 £20 | £40 | | |
| Movement | LP | Columbia | 33SX1627 | 1963 £25 | £50 | | |
| No Strings | 7" EP | Pye | NJE1003 | 195– £7.50 | £15 | | |
| Personal Portrait | LP | Columbia | SX/SCX6249 | 1968 £20 | £40 | | |
| Southern Horizons | LP | Jazzland | JLP37 | 1961 £25 | £50 | | |
| Swings High | LP | Melodisc | SLP12150 | 1967 £25 | £50 | | |
| Tony Kinsey Trio And Joe Harriott | 7" EP | Esquire | EP36 | 195– £7.50 | £15 | | |
| Tony Kinsey Trio And Joe Harriott | 7" EP | Esquire | EP52 | 195– £7.50 | £15 | | |
| Tony Kinsey Trio And Joe Harriott | 7" EP | Esquire | EP82 | 195– £7.50 | £15 | | |

## HARRIS, ANITA

| | | | | | | | |
|---|---|---|---|---|---|---|---|
| Something Must Be Done | 7" | Pye | 7N17069 | 1966 £1.50 | £4 | | |
| Willingly | 7" | Decca | F12082 | 1965 £1.50 | £4 | | |

## HARRIS, BARRY

| | | | | | | | |
|---|---|---|---|---|---|---|---|
| Preminado | LP | Riverside | RLP354 | 1961 £6 | £15 | | |

## HARRIS, BETTY
| | | | | | | | |
|---|---|---|---|---|---|---|---|
| Cry To Me | 7" | London | HL9796 | 1963 | £2.50 | £6 | |
| Nearer To You | 7" | Stateside | SS2045 | 1967 | £5 | £10 | |
| Ride Your Pony | 7" | Action | ACT4535 | 1969 | £2.50 | £6 | |
| Soul Perfection | LP | Action | ACLP6007 | 1969 | £6 | £15 | |
| What A Sad Feeling | 7" | Stateside | SS475 | 1965 | £4 | £8 | |

## HARRIS, BILL
| | | | | | | | |
|---|---|---|---|---|---|---|---|
| Bill Harris | LP | Emarcy | EJL1267 | 1958 | £5 | £12 | |

## HARRIS, BRENDA JO
| | | | | | | | |
|---|---|---|---|---|---|---|---|
| I Can Remember | 7" | Roulette | RO503 | 1968 | £1.50 | £4 | |

## HARRIS, DON 'SUGARCANE'
| | | | | | | | |
|---|---|---|---|---|---|---|---|
| Cupful Of Dreams | LP | BASF | MPS68030 | 1973 | £4 | £10 | |
| Don 'Sugarcane' Harris | LP | Epic | 26286 | 1970 | £4 | £10 | US |
| Fiddler On The Rock | LP | BASF | MPS68028 | 1970 | £4 | £10 | |
| Got The Blues | LP | BASF | MPS68029 | 1972 | £4 | £10 | |
| Keep On Driving | LP | BASF | MPS68027 | 1970 | £4 | £10 | |
| Sugarcane | LP | Epic | 30027 | 1971 | £4 | £10 | |

## HARRIS, EDDIE
| | | | | | | | |
|---|---|---|---|---|---|---|---|
| Breakfast At Tiffany's | LP | Stateside | SL10009 | 1962 | £5 | £12 | |
| Electrifying Eddie Harris | LP | Atlantic | 781985 | 1968 | £5 | £12 | |
| Goes To The Movies | LP | Stateside | SL10049 | 1963 | £5 | £12 | |
| In Sound | LP | Atlantic | SD1448 | 1966 | £5 | £12 | US |
| Mean Greens | LP | Atlantic | SD1453 | 1966 | £5 | £12 | US |
| Mighty Like A Rose | LP | Stateside | SL10018 | 1963 | £5 | £12 | |
| Plug Me In | LP | Atlantic | SD1506 | 1969 | £5 | £12 | US |
| Silver Cycles | LP | Atlantic | 588177 | 1969 | £4 | £10 | |
| Tender Storm | LP | Atlantic | SD1478 | 1967 | £5 | £12 | US |

## HARRIS, EMMYLOU
| | | | | | | | |
|---|---|---|---|---|---|---|---|
| Gliding Bird | LP | Jubilee | JGS8031 | 1969 | £25 | £50 | US, colour cover |
| Quarter Moon In A Ten Cent Town | LP | Mobile Fidelity | MFSL1015 | 1978 | £4 | £10 | US audiophile |

## HARRIS, JET
| | | | | | | | |
|---|---|---|---|---|---|---|---|
| Anniversary Album | LP | Q | LPMM1038 | 197– | £6 | £15 | |
| Besame Mucho | 7" | Decca | F11466 | 1962 | £1.50 | £4 | |
| Big Bad Bass | 7" | Decca | F11841 | 1964 | £1.50 | £4 | |
| Inside Jet Harris | LP | Ellie Jay | EJSP8622 | 1978 | £6 | £15 | |
| Jet Harris | 7" EP | Decca | DFE8502 | 1962 | £6 | £12 | |
| Main Title Theme | 7" | Decca | F11488 | 1962 | £1.50 | £4 | |
| My Lady | 7" | Fontana | TF849 | 1967 | £4 | £8 | |
| Theme For A Fallen Idol | 7" | SRT | SRTS75355 | 1975 | £1.50 | £4 | |

## HARRIS, JET & TONY MEEHAN
| | | | | | | | |
|---|---|---|---|---|---|---|---|
| Applejack | 7" | Decca | F11710 | 1963 | £1.50 | £4 | |
| Diamonds | 7" EP | Decca | DFE7099 | 1963 | £25 | £50 | export |
| Jet And Tony | 7" EP | Decca | DFE8528 | 1963 | £6 | £12 | |

## HARRIS, JOHNNY
| | | | | | | | |
|---|---|---|---|---|---|---|---|
| Movements | LP | Warner Bros | K46054 | 1972 | £8 | £20 | |

## HARRIS, JUNE
| | | | | | | | |
|---|---|---|---|---|---|---|---|
| Over And Over Again | 7" | CBS | 201774 | 1965 | £2.50 | £6 | |

## HARRIS, PAT
| | | | | | | | |
|---|---|---|---|---|---|---|---|
| Hippy Hippy Shake | 7" | Pye | 7N15567 | 1963 | £2.50 | £6 | |

## HARRIS, PEPPERMINT
| | | | | | | | |
|---|---|---|---|---|---|---|---|
| Peppermint Harris | LP | Time | 5 | 1962 | £5 | £12 | US |

## HARRIS, PHIL
| | | | | | | | |
|---|---|---|---|---|---|---|---|
| I Guess I'll Have To Change My Plan | 7" | HMV | 7M231 | 1954 | £1.50 | £4 | |
| I Wouldn't Touch You With A Ten Foot Pole | 7" | HMV | 7M289 | 1955 | £1.50 | £4 | |
| Take Your Girlie To The Movies | 7" | HMV | 7M199 | 1954 | £1.50 | £4 | |

## HARRIS, RICHARD
| | | | | | | | |
|---|---|---|---|---|---|---|---|
| Tramp Shining | LP | RCA | RD/SF7947 | 1968 | £4 | £10 | |
| Tramp Shining | LP | Stateside | SSL5019 | 1969 | £4 | £10 | |
| Yard Went On Forever | LP | Stateside | SSL5001 | 1968 | £4 | £10 | |

## HARRIS, ROLF
| | | | | | | | |
|---|---|---|---|---|---|---|---|
| Favourites | 7" EP | Columbia | SEG8531 | 1967 | £2 | £5 | |
| Jake The Peg | 7" EP | Columbia | SEG8516 | 1966 | £2 | £5 | |
| Sun Arise | 7" | Columbia | DB4888 | 1962 | £1.50 | £4 | |
| Tie Me Kangaroo Down Sport | 7" | Columbia | DB4483 | 1960 | £1.50 | £4 | |

## HARRIS, RONNIE
| | | | | | | | |
|---|---|---|---|---|---|---|---|
| Cabaret | 7" | Columbia | SCM5206 | 1955 | £1.50 | £4 | |
| Cry Upon My Shoulder | 7" | Columbia | DB3814 | 1956 | £1.50 | £4 | |
| Don't Go To Strangers | 7" | Columbia | SCM5159 | 1955 | £1.50 | £4 | |
| Hello Mrs. Jones | 7" | Columbia | SCM5178 | 1955 | £1.50 | £4 | |
| Hold My Hand | 7" | Columbia | SCM5138 | 1954 | £1.50 | £4 | |
| I Love Paris | 7" | Columbia | SCM5139 | 1954 | £1.50 | £4 | |

| | | | | | | |
|---|---|---|---|---|---|---|
| I've Changed My Mind A Thousand Times | 7" | Columbia | SCM5242 | 1956 £**1.50** | £**4** | |
| On The Way To Your Heart | 7" | Columbia | SCM5189 | 1955 £**1.50** | £**4** | |
| Stranger In Paradise | 7" | Columbia | SCM5176 | 1955 £**2** | £**5** | |
| That's Right | 7" | Columbia | DB3836 | 1956 £**2** | £**5** | |
| What Is The Reason? | 7" | Columbia | SCM5266 | 1956 £**1.50** | £**4** | |

## HARRIS, ROY
| | | | | | | |
|---|---|---|---|---|---|---|
| Bitter And The Sweet | LP | Topic | 12TS217 | 1972 £**4** | £**10** | |
| Champions Of Folly | LP | Topic | 12TS256 | 1975 £**4** | £**10** | |

## HARRIS, SHAKEY JAKE
| | | | | | | |
|---|---|---|---|---|---|---|
| Devil's Harmonica | LP | Polydor | 2391015 | 1972 £**6** | £**15** | |
| Further On Up The Road | LP | Liberty | 83217 | 1969 £**6** | £**15** | |

## HARRIS, SUE
| | | | | | | |
|---|---|---|---|---|---|---|
| Hammers And Tongues | LP | Free Reed | FRR020 | 1978 £**5** | £**12** | |

## HARRIS, THURSTON
| | | | | | | |
|---|---|---|---|---|---|---|
| Be Baba Leba | 7" | Vogue | V9108 | 1958 £**87.50** | £**175** | |
| Do What You Did | 7" | Vogue | V9098 | 1958 £**87.50** | £**175** | |
| Hey Little Girl | 7" | Vogue | V9146 | 1959 £**30** | £**60** | |
| In The Bottom Of My Heart | 7" | Vogue | V9144 | 1959 £**20** | £**40** | |
| Little Bitty Pretty One | 7" | Sue | WI4016 | 1966 £**5** | £**10** | |
| Little Bitty Pretty One | 7" | Vogue | V9092 | 1957 £**30** | £**60** | |
| Purple Stew | 7" | Vogue | V9139 | 1959 £**25** | £**50** | |
| Runk Bunk | 7" | Vogue | V9149 | 1959 £**50** | £**100** | |
| Slip Slop | 7" | Vogue | V9151 | 1959 £**30** | £**60** | |
| Smokey Joes | 7" | Vogue | V9122 | 1958 £**30** | £**60** | |
| Tears From My Heart | 7" | Vogue | V9127 | 1958 £**20** | £**40** | |

## HARRIS, WEE WILLIE
| | | | | | | |
|---|---|---|---|---|---|---|
| Listen To The River Roll Along | 7" | Polydor | 56140 | 1966 £**2.50** | £**6** | |
| Love Bug Crawl | 7" | Decca | F10980 | 1958 £**12.50** | £**25** | |
| No Chemise Please | 7" | Decca | F11044 | 1958 £**10** | £**20** | |
| Rocking At The Two I's | 7" | Decca | F10970 | 1957 £**12.50** | £**25** | |
| Rocking With Wee Willie | 7" EP | Decca | DFE6465 | 1958 £**37.50** | £**75** | |
| Someone's In The Kitchen With Diana | 7" | Parlophone | R5504 | 1966 £**2.50** | £**6** | |
| Wild One | 7" | Decca | F11217 | 1960 £**4** | £**8** | |
| You Must Be Joking | 7" | HMV | POP1198 | 1963 £**2.50** | £**6** | |

## HARRIS, WYNONIE
| | | | | | | |
|---|---|---|---|---|---|---|
| Adam Come And Get Your Rib | 78 | Vogue | V2166 | 1953 £**5** | £**10** | |
| Battle Of The Blues | 7" EP | Bluebeat | BBEP301 | 1961 £**30** | £**60** | |
| Bloodshot Eyes | 78 | Vogue | V2127 | 1952 £**5** | £**10** | |
| Bloodshot Eyes | 7" | Vogue | V2127 | 1956 £**37.50** | £**75** | tri-centre |
| Do It Again Please | 78 | Vogue | V2133 | 1952 £**5** | £**10** | |
| Drinkin' Wine Spo Dee O Dee | 78 | Vogue | V2006 | 1951 £**5** | £**10** | |
| Good Morning Judge | 78 | Vogue | V2128 | 1952 £**5** | £**10** | |
| Good Rockin' Blues | LP | King | KS1086 | 1970 £**5** | £**12** | US |
| Lovin' Machine | 78 | Vogue | V2111 | 1952 £**5** | £**10** | |
| Put It Back | 78 | Vogue | V2134 | 1952 £**5** | £**10** | |
| Teardrops From My Eyes | 78 | Vogue | V2144 | 1952 £**5** | £**10** | |
| Wynonie Mister Blues Harris | 7" EP | Vogue | EPV1103 | 1956 £**75** | £**150** | |

## HARRIS, WYNONIE, AMOS MILBURN & PRINCE WATERFORD
| | | | | | | |
|---|---|---|---|---|---|---|
| Party After Hours | 10" LP | Aladdin | 703 | 1956 £**87.50** | £**175** | US |
| Party After Hours | 10" LP | Aladdin | 703 | 1956 £**180** | £**300** | US, red vinyl |

## HARRIS SISTERS
| | | | | | | |
|---|---|---|---|---|---|---|
| Kissing Bug | 7" | Capitol | CL14232 | 1955 £**4** | £**8** | |

## HARRISON, DANNY
| | | | | | | |
|---|---|---|---|---|---|---|
| I'm A Rolling Stone | 7" | Coral | Q72479 | 1965 £**2.50** | £**6** | |
| Introducing Danny Harrison | 7" EP | Starlite | STEP23 | 1962 £**2.50** | £**6** | |

## HARRISON, EARL
| | | | | | | |
|---|---|---|---|---|---|---|
| Humphrey Stomp | 7" | London | HL10121 | 1967 £**12.50** | £**25** | |

## HARRISON, GEORGE

*Songs By George Harrison* consists of three out-takes from *Somewhere In England* together with a live version of 'For You Blue'. It is available as either a CD or a vinyl single, but in either case only as a bonus within a deluxe, partly hand-made, edition of a book of George Harrison's lyrics. £250 was the new selling price of the last sets to be available in 1992 and they were produced as a limited edition of 2,500 copies. (A few promotional copies extra to the main edition were also made available.) The value of the set may well not rise any further, since it is likely that all collectors interested in the set will already have acquired one during the lengthy period of time it took for the edition to sell out.

| | | | | | | |
|---|---|---|---|---|---|---|
| All Things Must Pass | LP | Apple | STCH639 | 1971 £**6** | £**15** | 3 LP box, poster |
| Bangla Desh | 7" | Apple | R5912 | 1971 £**25** | £**50** | picture sleeve |
| Best Of Dark Horse | CD | Dark Horse | 257262DJ | 1987 £**8** | £**20** | US promo picture disc |
| Cloud Nine | CD | Dark Horse | 256432 | 1987 £**8** | £**20** | US promo picture disc |
| Dark Horse | 7" | Apple | R6001 | 1975 £**2.50** | £**6** | picture sleeve |
| Dark Horse Radio Special | LP | Dark Horse | SP22002 | 1974 £**100** | £**200** | US promo |
| Electronic Sound | LP | Apple | ZAPPLE2 | 1969 £**25** | £**50** | |
| Faster | 7" | Dark Horse | K17423 | 1979 £**2.50** | £**6** | |
| Faster | 7" | Dark Horse | K17423P | 1979 £**7.50** | £**15** | picture disc |
| Gone Troppo | LP | Dark Horse | 9237341 | 1982 £**6** | £**15** | US audiophile promo |
| Got My Mind Set On You | 7" | Dark Horse | W8178 | 1987 £**5** | £**10** | green label |

| | | | | | | | |
|---|---|---|---|---|---|---|---|
| Got My Mind Set On You | 7" | Dark Horse | W8178 | 1987 | £1.50 | £4 | red label |
| Got My Mind Set On You | 7" | Dark Horse | W8178B | 1987 | £2 | £5 | boxed set |
| Got My Mind Set On You | 12" | Dark Horse | W8178T | 1987 | £5 | £12 | with poster |
| Got My Mind Set On You | 12" | Dark Horse | W8178TP | 1987 | £4 | £10 | picture disc |
| Is This Love | CD-s | Dark Horse | W7913CD | 1988 | £2 | £5 | 3" single |
| My Sweet Lord | 7" | Apple | R5884 | 1971 | £7.50 | £15 | picture sleeve, colour head shot of George |
| Somewhere In England | LP | Dark Horse | DHK3472 | 1980 | £15 | £30 | US original issue with 4 different tracks |
| Songs By George Harrison | CD | Genesis Publications | SGHCD777 | 1988 | £150 | £250 | issued with ltd edn book |
| Songs By George Harrison | 7" | Genesis Publications | SGH777 | 1988 | £150 | £250 | issued with ltd edn book |
| Songs By George Harrison Vol. 2 | CD | Genesis Publications | SGHCD778 | 1992 | £150 | £250 | issued with ltd edn book |
| Thirty-Three And A Third Dialogue Album | LP | Dark Horse | PRO649 | 1976 | £15 | £30 | US promo |
| This Guitar | 7" | Apple | R6012 | 1976 | £4 | £8 | |
| When We Was Fab | 12" | Dark Horse | W8131TP | 1988 | £3 | £6 | picture disc |
| Wonderwall | LP | Apple | APCOR1 | 1968 | £30 | £60 | mono |
| Wonderwall | LP | Apple | SAPCOR1 | 1968 | £10 | £25 | stereo |
| You | 7" | Apple | R6007 | 1975 | £2.50 | £6 | picture sleeve |

## HARRISON, GEORGE & OTHERS

| | | | | | | | |
|---|---|---|---|---|---|---|---|
| Concert For Bangla Desh | LP | Apple | STCX3385 | 1972 | £6 | £15 | 3 LPs, booklet, boxed |

## HARRISON, GEORGE & VICKI BROWN

| | | | | | | | |
|---|---|---|---|---|---|---|---|
| Shanghai Surprise | 7" | Ganga Publishing | SHANGHAI1 | 1986 | £180 | £300 | promo only |

## HARRISON, MIKE

| | | | | | | |
|---|---|---|---|---|---|---|
| Mike Harrison | LP | Island | ILPS9170 | 1971 | £4 | £10 |
| Smokestack Lightning | LP | Island | ILPS9209 | 1972 | £4 | £10 |

## HARRISON, NOEL

| | | | | | | |
|---|---|---|---|---|---|---|
| At The Blue Angel | LP | Philips | BBL7399 | 1960 | £4 | £10 |
| Great Electric Experiment Is Over | LP | Reprise | RSLP6321 | 1969 | £5 | £12 |
| It's All Over Now Baby Blue | 7" | Decca | F12345 | 1966 | £1.50 | £4 |
| Love Minus Zero/No Limit | 7" | Decca | F12918 | 1969 | £1.50 | £4 |
| Noel Harrison | 7" EP | Decca | DFE8616 | 1965 | £2 | £5 |
| Noel Harrison | 7" EP | HMV | 7EG8383 | 1957 | £2 | £5 |
| To Ramona | 7" EP | Decca | DFE8639 | 1965 | £2 | £5 |
| Trees | 7" | Decca | F12201 | 1965 | £1.50 | £4 |
| Windmills Of Your Mind | 7" | Reprise | RS20758 | 1969 | £1.50 | £4 |
| Young Girl Of Sixteen | 7" | Decca | F12314 | 1966 | £1.50 | £4 |

## HARRISON, WILBERT

| | | | | | | | |
|---|---|---|---|---|---|---|---|
| Battle Of The Giants | LP | Joy | JOYS191 | 1971 | £4 | £10 | with Baby Washington |
| I'm Broke | 7" | Island | WI031 | 1962 | £5 | £10 | |
| Kansas City | LP | Sphere Sound | (S)SR7000 | 1964 | £10 | £25 | US |
| Kansas City | 7" | Top Rank | JAR132 | 1959 | £4 | £8 | |
| Let's Stick Together | 7" | Sue | WI363 | 1965 | £5 | £10 | |
| Let's Work Together | LP | London | HA/SH8415 | 1969 | £6 | £15 | |
| Let's Work Together | 7" | London | HL10307 | 1970 | £2 | £5 | |

## HARRISON, YVONNE

| | | | | | | |
|---|---|---|---|---|---|---|
| Chase | 7" | Caltone | TONE102 | 1967 | £4 | £8 |

## HARRY, DEBBIE

| | | | | | | | |
|---|---|---|---|---|---|---|---|
| Def Dumb And Blonde | CD | Reprise | 259382 | 1989 | £8 | £20 | US promo, 3D insert |
| I Want That Man | CD-s | Chrysalis | CHSCD3369 | 1989 | £2 | £5 | |

## HARSH REALITY

Guitarist and bass player Mark Griffiths made his first solo album in 1996, having long been associated with both Ian Matthews and Cliff Richard. His recording debut is here, as a member of obscure underground band, Harsh Reality.

| | | | | | | |
|---|---|---|---|---|---|---|
| Heaven And Hell | LP | Philips | SBL7891 | 1969 | £37.50 | £75 |
| Heaven And Hell | 7" | Philips | BF1769 | 1969 | £2.50 | £6 |
| Tobacco Ash Sunday | 7" | Philips | BF1710 | 1968 | £2 | £5 |

## HART, BOB, PERCY WEBB, ERNEST AUSTIN

| | | | | | | |
|---|---|---|---|---|---|---|
| Flash Company | LP | Topic | 12TS243 | 1974 | £4 | £10 |

## HART, CAJUN

| | | | | | | |
|---|---|---|---|---|---|---|
| Got To Find A Way | 7" | Warner Bros | WB7258 | 1969 | £50 | £100 |

## HART, DERRY & THE HARTBEATS

| | | | | | | |
|---|---|---|---|---|---|---|
| Come On Baby | 7" | Decca | F11138 | 1959 | £5 | £10 |

## HART, MICKEY

| | | | | | | |
|---|---|---|---|---|---|---|
| Rolling Thunder | LP | Warner Bros | K46182 | 1972 | £5 | £12 |

## HART, MIKE

| | | | | | | |
|---|---|---|---|---|---|---|
| Basher, Chalky, Pongo, & Me | LP | Polydor | 2310211 | 1972 | £6 | £15 |
| Mike Hart Bleeds | LP | Dandelion | 63756 | 1970 | £6 | £15 |
| Yawney Morning Song | 7" | Dandelion | 4781 | 1970 | £1.50 | £4 |

## HART, TIM
Tim Hart................................................ LP..... Chrysalis ......... CHR1218 .............. 1979 £5.......... £12 ..............................

## HART, TIM & MADDY PRIOR
Folk Songs Of Olde England 1 ................ LP..... Tepee ............ ARPS3 ............... 1968 £10........ £25 ..............................
Folk Songs Of Olde England 2 ................ LP..... Tepee ............ ARPS4 ............... 1969 £10........ £25 ..............................
Summer Solstice.................................... LP..... B&C ............... CAS1035............ 1971 £5.......... £12 ..............................

## HARTE, FRANK
Daybreak And A Candle-End.................... LP..... Spin ............... 995 .................... 1987 £4.......... £10 ......................Irish
Through Dublin City .............................. LP..... Topic .............. 12T218 ............... 1973 £4.......... £10 ..............................

## HARTFORD, JOHN
Earthwords And Music .......................... LP..... RCA ............... LSP3796............. 1967 £4.......... £10 ...........................US
Gentle On My Mind ............................... LP..... RCA ............... LSP4068............. 1968 £4.......... £10 ...........................US
Housing Project .................................... LP..... RCA ............... LSP3998............. 1968 £4.......... £10 ...........................US
Iron Mountain Depot ............................ LP..... RCA ............... LSP4337............. 1970 £4.......... £10 ...........................US
John Hartford....................................... LP..... RCA ............... LSP4156............. 1969 £4.......... £10 ...........................US
Looks At Life ........................................ LP..... RCA ............... LSP3687............. 1967 £4.......... £10 ...........................US
Love Album .......................................... LP..... RCA ............... LSP3884............. 1968 £4.......... £10 ...........................US

## HARTH, ALFRED
Just Music............................................ LP..... ECM .............. ECM1002ST ......... 1970 £8.......... £20 ..............................

## HARTLEY, KEEF
The Keef Hartley Band was one of the many groups to emerge from the John Mayall school of blues, and one of the best. They favoured a tough, riff-based approach to blues-rock, and by gradually adding brass instruments the group became a key element within the growth of jazz-rock. The first two albums are the best – after that Miller Anderson, who was both the lead singer and the lead guitarist, became a little too fond of writing sensitive, reflective material, which did not really suit the band. *Little Big Band*, however, which presents the group's most exciting music re-arranged for a much bigger unit, is a splendid return to form.

Battle Of North West Six........................ LP..... Deram ............ DML1054 ............. 1969 £6.......... £15 ......................mono
Battle Of North West Six........................ LP..... Deram ............ SML1054 ............. 1969 £5.......... £12 ..............................
Best Of The Keef Hartley Band ............... LP..... Deram ............ DPA3011/2........ 1974 £5.......... £12 ...................double
Dance To The Music............................... 7"...... Deram ............ DM380 ............... 1973 £1.50........ £4 ..............................
Halfbreed............................................. LP..... Deram ............ SML1037 ............. 1969 £6.......... £15 ..............................
Lancashire Hustler ................................ LP..... Deram ............ SDL13 ............... 1973 £4.......... £10 ..............................
Leave It Till The Morning ...................... 7"...... Deram ............ DM250 ............... 1969 £1.50........ £4 ..............................
Little Big Band ...................................... LP..... Deram ............ SDL4 ................. 1971 £6.......... £15 ..............................
Overdog............................................... LP..... Deram ............ SDL2 ................. 1971 £5.......... £12 ..............................
Roundabout .......................................... 7"...... Deram ............ DM316 ............... 1970 £1.50........ £4 ..............................
Seventy Second Brave ............................ LP..... Deram ............ SDL9 ................. 1972 £4.......... £10 ..............................
Time Is Near ........................................ LP..... Deram ............ DML1037 ............. 1969 £8.......... £20 ......................mono
Time Is Near ........................................ LP..... Deram ............ SML1071 ............. 1970 £5.......... £12 ..............................
Waiting Around ..................................... 7"...... Deram ............ DM273 ............... 1969 £1.50........ £4 ..............................

## HARUMI
Harumi ................................................ LP..... Verve ............. FT30302 ............. 1968 £10........ £25 ...............US double

## HARVEST OF DREAMS
Harvest Of Dreams................................ LP..... private............ ........................ 1982 £50........ £100 ..........................US

## HARVEY & THE MOONGLOWS
Ten Commandments Of Love .................. 7"...... London ............ HLM8730 ............. 1958 £100..... £200 ..........best auctioned

## HARVEY, ALEX
Agent OO Soul ...................................... 7"...... Fontana............ TF610 ................ 1965 £15........ £30 ..............................
Ain't That Just Too Bad.......................... 7"...... Polydor............ 56017................ 1965 £30........ £60 ..............................
Alex Harvey And His Soul Band ............... LP..... Polydor............ LPHM46424 ......... 1964 £50........ £100 ..............................
Blues................................................... LP..... Polydor............ LPHM46441 ......... 1964 £50........ £100 ..............................
Framed ................................................ LP..... Vertigo ........... 6360081 ............. 1972 £20........ £40 ...............spiral label
Got My Mojo Working ............................ 7"...... Polydor............ NH52907............ 1964 £25........ £50 ..............................
I Just Wanna Make Love To You ............. 7"...... Polydor............ NH52264............ 1964 £15........ £30 ..............................
Maybe Someday .................................... 7"...... Decca ............. F12660............... 1967 £15........ £30 ..............................
Midnight Moses .................................... 7"...... Fontana............ TF1063 .............. 1969 £15........ £30 ..............................
Next .................................................... 7"...... Vertigo ........... 6360103 ............. 1974 £4.......... £10 ..............................
Presents The Loch Ness Monster ............ LP..... K-Tel .............. NE984 ................ 1977 £15........ £30 ..............................
Roman Wall Blues ................................. LP..... Fontana............ (S)TL5534 ........... 1969 £75........ £150 ..............................
Sunday Song ......................................... 7"...... Decca ............. F12640............... 1967 £15........ £30 ..............................
Work Song ........................................... 7"...... Fontana............ TF764 ................ 1966 £15........ £30 ..............................

## HARVEY, JANCIS
Distance Of Doors.................................. LP..... Pilgrim King.... KLP5 .................. 1973 £15........ £30 ..............................
Portrait Of Jancis Harvey....................... LP..... Westwood......... ........................ 1976 £10........ £25 ..............................
Time Was Now ...................................... LP..... Westwood......... WR5054 .............. 1975 £20........ £40 ..............................

## HARVEY, P. J.
Dress................................................... CD-s .. Too Pure ....... PURECD5 ............ 1992 £4.......... £10 ..............................
Dry ..................................................... LP..... Too Pure ....... PURED10 ............ 1992 £10........ £25 ...........with demos LP
Dry ..................................................... CD.... Too Pure ....... PURECDD10 ......... 1992 £15........ £30 ...........with demos CD
Interview ............................................. CD.... Island............. PJICD1 ............... 1995 £8.......... £20 ......................promo
Sheela Na Gig ....................................... CD-s .. Too Pure ....... PURECD8 ............ 1992 £10........ £20 ..............................
Sheela-Na-Gig ...................................... 7"...... Too Pure ....... PURES8 ............. 1992 £4.......... £8 ..............................

## HARVEY, PETER
Rainin' In My Heart............................... 7"...... Columbia ........ DB4873 .............. 1962 £1.50........ £4 ..............................

## HARVEY, PHIL

The name of Phil Harvey (also appearing as Harvey and Doc) covers the identity of Phil Spector.

| | | | | | | | |
|---|---|---|---|---|---|---|---|
| Bumbershoot | 7" | Imperial | 5583 | 1959 | £25 | £50 | US |

## HARVEY, RICHARD

Richard Harvey was the dominant influence within Gryphon and his interest in, knowledge of and skill with medieval instruments has kept him busy as a session musician and soundtrack composer ever since. *A New Way Of Seeing* was produced specially for a new equipment launch by the computer company ICL and has never been issued commercially, although the considerable number of copies that have found their way on to the collectors' market since attention was drawn to the record in the first edition of this *Price Guide* have had the effect of depressing the record's value.

| | | | | | | |
|---|---|---|---|---|---|---|
| Brass At La Sauve-Majeure | LP | ASV | ALH926 | 1983 | £6 | £15 |
| Divisions On A Ground | LP | Transatlantic | TRA292 | 1975 | £25 | £50 |
| New Way Of Seeing | LP | ICL | ICL001 | 1979 | £10 | £25 |

## HARVEY BOYS

| | | | | | | |
|---|---|---|---|---|---|---|
| Nothing Is Too Good For You | 7" | London | HLA8397 | 1957 | £7.50 | £15 |

## HARVEY'S FOLK

| | | | | | | |
|---|---|---|---|---|---|---|
| Songs Of Sister | LP | Galliard | | | £20 | £40 |

## HARWOOD, CHRIS

| | | | | | | |
|---|---|---|---|---|---|---|
| Nice To Meet Miss Christine | LP | Birth | RAB1 | 1970 | £25 | £50 |

## HASKELL, GORDON

| | | | | | | |
|---|---|---|---|---|---|---|
| It Is And It Isn't | LP | Atlantic | K40311 | 1972 | £6 | £15 |
| Sail In My Boat | LP | CBS | 63741 | 1969 | £62.50 | £125 |

## HASKELL, JACK

| | | | | | | |
|---|---|---|---|---|---|---|
| Around The World | 7" | London | HL8426 | 1957 | £5 | £10 |

## HASLAM, MICHAEL

| | | | | | | |
|---|---|---|---|---|---|---|
| There Goes The Forgotten Man | 7" | Parlophone | R5267 | 1965 | £2 | £5 |

## HASSLES

The first recordings by Billy Joel (apart from a little unspecified session work) were with the Hassles, whose only claim to fame this is.

| | | | | | | | |
|---|---|---|---|---|---|---|---|
| Hassles | LP | United Artists | UAS6631 | 1968 | £6 | £15 | US |
| Hassles | CD | EMI | | 1992 | £8 | £20 | US |
| Hour Of The Wolf | LP | United Artists | UAS6699 | 1969 | £6 | £15 | US |
| You Got Me Humming | 7" | United Artists | UP1199 | 1967 | £4 | £8 | |

## HAT & TIE

| | | | | | | |
|---|---|---|---|---|---|---|
| Bread To Spend | 7" | President | PT122 | 1967 | £10 | £20 |
| Chance For Romance | 7" | President | PT105 | 1966 | £2.50 | £6 |

## HATCH, TONY ORCHESTRA

| | | | | | | | |
|---|---|---|---|---|---|---|---|
| Crossroads | 7" | Pye | 7N15754 | 1965 | £2 | £5 | picture sleeve |

## HATE

| | | | | | | |
|---|---|---|---|---|---|---|
| Hate Kills | LP | Famous | SFMA5752 | 1970 | £20 | £40 |

## HATFIELD & THE NORTH

| | | | | | | |
|---|---|---|---|---|---|---|
| Afters | LP | Virgin | VR5 | 1980 | £8 | £20 |
| Hatfield & The North | LP | Virgin | V2008 | 1974 | £4 | £10 |
| Rotters Club | LP | Virgin | V2030 | 1975 | £4 | £10 |

## HATHAWAY, DONNY

| | | | | | | |
|---|---|---|---|---|---|---|
| Donny Hathaway | LP | Atlantic | K40241 | 1970 | £5 | £12 |
| Everything Is Everything | LP | Atlantic | K40063 | 1970 | £5 | £12 |
| Extension Of A Man | LP | Atlantic | K40487 | 1973 | £4 | £10 |
| Ghetto | 7" | Atco | 226010 | 1970 | £1.50 | £4 |
| Live | LP | Atlantic | K40369 | 1972 | £4 | £10 |

## HAVEN, ALAN

| | | | | | | |
|---|---|---|---|---|---|---|
| Images | 7" | Fontana | TF542 | 1965 | £1.50 | £4 |

## HAVENS, RICHIE

| | | | | | | | |
|---|---|---|---|---|---|---|---|
| 1983 | LP | Verve | 2610001 | 1969 | £6 | £15 | double |
| Alarm Clock | LP | Polydor | 2310080 | 1971 | £4 | £10 | |
| Electric Havens | LP | Transatlantic | TRA187 | 1966 | £5 | £12 | |
| Great Blind Degree | LP | Polydor | 2480049 | 1972 | £4 | £10 | |
| Lady Madonna | 7" | Verve | VS1519 | 1969 | £1.50 | £4 | |
| Live On Stage | LP | Polydor | 2659015 | 1972 | £5 | £12 | double |
| Mixed Bag | LP | Verve | (S)VLP6008 | 1967 | £5 | £12 | |
| Mixed Bag 2 | LP | Polydor | 2310356 | 1974 | £4 | £10 | |
| Portfolio | LP | Polydor | 2480166 | 1973 | £4 | £10 | |
| Richie Havens' Record | LP | Transatlantic | TRA199 | 1965 | £5 | £12 | |
| Something Else Again | LP | Verve | (S)VLP6005 | 1968 | £5 | £12 | |
| State Of Mind | LP | Verve | 2304050 | 1971 | £4 | £10 | |
| Stonehenge | LP | Verve | (S)VLP6021 | 1968 | £5 | £12 | |
| Three Day Eternity | 7" | Verve | VS1512 | 1968 | £1.50 | £4 | |

## HAWES, HAMPTON
| | | | | | | | |
|---|---|---|---|---|---|---|---|
| All Night Session Vol. 1 | LP | Contemporary | LAC12161 | 1959 | £6 | £15 | |
| All Night Session Vol. 2 | LP | Contemporary | LAC12162 | 1959 | £6 | £15 | |
| All Night Session Vol. 3 | LP | Contemporary | LAC12163 | 1959 | £6 | £15 | |
| Everybody Likes Hampton Hawes | LP | Contemporary | LAC12091 | 1958 | £6 | £15 | |
| Hampton Hawes Quartet | 10" LP | Esquire | 20079 | 1956 | £10 | £25 | |
| Here And Now | LP | Contemporary | LAC602 | 1966 | £4 | £10 | |
| This Is Hampton Hawes | LP | Contemporary | LAC12081 | 1958 | £8 | £20 | |
| Trio Vol. 1 | LP | Vogue | LAE12059 | 1957 | £8 | £20 | |
| Vol. 1 – The Trio | LP | Contemporary | LAC12056 | 1957 | £8 | £20 | |

## HAWKE, TOMMY
| | | | | | | | |
|---|---|---|---|---|---|---|---|
| Good Gravy | 7" | Top Rank | JAR348 | 1960 | £2 | £5 | |

## HAWKES, CHIP
| | | | | | | | |
|---|---|---|---|---|---|---|---|
| Nashville Album | LP | RCA | PL25044 | 1977 | £15 | £30 | |

## HAWKINS, BUDDY BOY & WILLIAM MOORE
| | | | | | | | |
|---|---|---|---|---|---|---|---|
| Buddy Boy Hawkins/William Moore | 7" EP | Heritage | RE102 | 195– | £5 | £10 | |

## HAWKINS, COLEMAN
| | | | | | | | |
|---|---|---|---|---|---|---|---|
| Alive At The Village Gate | LP | Verve | VLP9044 | 1963 | £5 | £12 | |
| Back In Bean's Bag | LP | CBS | BPG62157 | 1964 | £4 | £10 | |
| Bean And The Boys | 7" EP | Esquire | EP192 | 1958 | £2 | £5 | |
| Blue Saxophones | LP | Columbia | 33CX10143 | 1959 | £8 | £20 | with Ben Webster |
| Capitol Presents Coleman Hawkins & Sonny Greer | 10" LP | Capitol | LC6650 | 1954 | £20 | £40 | |
| Cattin' | LP | Fontana | SJL131 | 1966 | £4 | £10 | |
| Classics In Jazz | 10" LP | Capitol | LC6580 | 1953 | £20 | £40 | |
| Coleman Hawkins | LP | Moodsville | MV7 | 1961 | £6 | £15 | |
| Coleman Hawkins | 7" EP | Vogue | EPV1021 | 1955 | £2 | £5 | |
| Coleman Hawkins All Stars | LP | Swingsville | SV2005 | 1962 | £6 | £15 | |
| Coleman Hawkins Group | LP | London | LTZC15048 | 1957 | £8 | £20 | |
| Coleman Hawkins Group | 7" EP | Mercury | EP16029 | 195– | £2 | £5 | |
| Coleman Hawkins Sextet | 7" EP | Esquire | EP235 | 1961 | £2 | £5 | |
| Desafinado | LP | HMV | CLP1630/CSD1484 | 1963 | £5 | £12 | |
| Genius Of Coleman Hawkins | LP | HMV | CLP1293 | 1959 | £8 | £20 | |
| Gilded Hawk | LP | Capitol | T819 | 1957 | £8 | £20 | |
| Hawk Eyes | LP | Esquire | 32102 | 1960 | £8 | £20 | |
| Hawk Flies High | LP | London | LTZU15117 | 1958 | £8 | £20 | |
| Hawk Returns | 7" EP | London | EZC19020 | 1958 | £2 | £5 | |
| Hawk Talks | LP | Brunswick | LAT8242 | 1958 | £10 | £25 | |
| Hawk Talks | 7" EP | Brunswick | OE9166 | 1955 | £2 | £5 | |
| High And Mighty Hawk | LP | Felsted | FAJ7005/SJA2005 | 1958 | £15 | £30 | |
| Lucky Duck | 7" | Brunswick | 05459 | 1955 | £2.50 | £6 | |
| Meditations | LP | Fontana | TL5273 | 1965 | £4 | £10 | |
| Newport Jazz Festival 1957 | LP | Columbia | 33CX10103 | 1958 | £6 | £15 | with Roy Eldridge |
| Soul | LP | Esquire | 32095 | 1960 | £8 | £20 | |
| Stasch | LP | Swingsville | SVLP2013 | 1962 | £6 | £15 | |
| Swing! | LP | Fontana | FJL102 | 1964 | £4 | £10 | |
| Ten Coleman Hawkins Specials | 10" LP | HMV | DLP1055 | 1954 | £20 | £40 | |
| Today And Now | LP | HMV | CLP1689 | 1964 | £5 | £12 | |
| With The Red Garland Trio | LP | Swingsville | SV2001 | 1962 | £6 | £15 | |

## HAWKINS, DALE
| | | | | | | | |
|---|---|---|---|---|---|---|---|
| Hot Dog | 7" | London | HLM9060 | 1960 | £12.50 | £25 | |
| La Do Da Da | 7" | London | HLM8728 | 1958 | £15 | £30 | |
| LA, Memphis & Tyler, Texas | LP | Bell | SBLL127 | 1970 | £5 | £12 | |
| Let's All Twist | LP | Roulette | (S)R25175 | 1962 | £20 | £40 | US |
| Liza Jane | 7" | London | HLM9016 | 1959 | £12.50 | £25 | |
| Susie Q | 7" | Janus | no number | 1971 | £10 | £20 | promo, plus 3 tracks by other artists |
| Susie Q | 7" | London | HL8482 | 1957 | £100 | £200 | best auctioned |
| Suzie-Q | LP | Chess | 1429 | 1958 | £150 | £250 | US |
| Yea Yea Classcutter | 7" | London | HLM8842 | 1959 | £15 | £30 | |

## HAWKINS, HAWKSHAW
| | | | | | | | |
|---|---|---|---|---|---|---|---|
| All New Hawkshaw Hawkins | LP | London | HA8181 | 1964 | £5 | £12 | |
| Country And Western | 7" EP | Parlophone | GEP8742 | 1958 | £6 | £12 | |
| Grand Ole Opry Favorites | LP | King | 592 | 1958 | £8 | £20 | US |
| Hawkshaw Hawkins | LP | King | 587 | 1958 | £8 | £20 | US |
| Hawkshaw Hawkins | LP | King | 599 | 1959 | £8 | £20 | US |
| Hawkshaw Hawkins – Country And Western | 7" EP | Vogue | VE170117 | 1958 | £10 | £20 | |
| Lonesome 7-7203 | 7" | London | HL9737 | 1963 | £2 | £5 | |
| Taken From Our Vaults Vol. 1 | LP | King | (S)858 | 1963 | £4 | £10 | US |
| Taken From Our Vaults Vol. 2 | LP | King | (S)870 | 1963 | £4 | £10 | US |
| Taken From Our Vaults Vol. 3 | LP | King | (S)873 | 1963 | £4 | £10 | US |

## HAWKINS, RONNIE
| | | | | | | | |
|---|---|---|---|---|---|---|---|
| Arkansas Rockpile | LP | Roulette | RCP1003 | 1970 | £4 | £10 | |
| Best Of Ronnie Hawkins & His Band | LP | Roulette | SR42045 | 1970 | £5 | £12 | US |
| Clara | 7" | Columbia | DB4442 | 1960 | £7.50 | £15 | |
| Folk Ballads | LP | Columbia | 33SX1295 | 1960 | £15 | £30 | mono |
| Folk Ballads | LP | Columbia | SCX3358 | 1960 | £20 | £40 | stereo |
| Forty Days | 7" | Columbia | DB4319 | 1959 | £20 | £40 | |
| Hawk | LP | Cotillion | SD9039 | 1971 | £4 | £10 | US |

| | | | | | | | |
|---|---|---|---|---|---|---|---|
| Hey, Bo Diddley | 7" | Quality | 6128 | 1959 | £50 | £100 | Canadian |
| Mary Lou | 7" | Columbia | DB4345 | 1959 | £10 | £20 | |
| Mojo Man | LP | Roulette | R25390 | 1964 | £8 | £20 | US |
| Mr. Dynamo | LP | Columbia | 33SX1238 | 1960 | £25 | £50 | mono |
| Mr. Dynamo | LP | Columbia | SCX3315 | 1960 | £37.50 | £75 | stereo |
| Mr. Dynamo | LP | Roulette | SR25102 | 1960 | £75 | £150 | US, red vinyl |
| Rock 'n' Roll Resurrection | LP | Monument | MNT65122 | 1972 | £4 | £10 | |
| Rocking With Ronnie | 7" EP | Columbia | ESG7792 | 1960 | £37.50 | £75 | stereo |
| Rocking With Ronnie | 7" EP | Columbia | SEG7983 | 1960 | £25 | £50 | |
| Rocking With Ronnie No. 2 | 7" EP | Columbia | ESG7795 | 1960 | £37.50 | £75 | stereo |
| Rocking With Ronnie No. 2 | 7" EP | Columbia | SEG7988 | 1960 | £25 | £50 | |
| Ronnie Hawkins | LP | Atlantic | 2400009 | 1970 | £5 | £12 | |
| Ronnie Hawkins | LP | Roulette | (S)R25078 | 1959 | £30 | £60 | US |
| Ronnie Hawkins | LP | Roulette | SR25078 | 1959 | £75 | £150 | US, red vinyl |
| Ronnie Hawkins | LP | Yorkville | YVS33002 | 1968 | £5 | £12 | US |
| Rrrracket Time | LP | WLW | WLW101 | 1965 | £8 | £20 | Canadian |
| Songs Of Hank Williams | LP | Roulette | (S)R25137 | 1960 | £10 | £25 | US |
| Southern Love | 7" | Columbia | DB4412 | 1960 | £5 | £10 | |
| Who Do You Love | 7" | Columbia | DB7036 | 1963 | £6 | £12 | |

## HAWKINS, SCREAMING JAY

| | | | | | | | |
|---|---|---|---|---|---|---|---|
| At Home | LP | Epic | LN3448 | 1956 | £330 | £500 | US |
| I Hear Voices | 7" | Sue | WI379 | 1965 | £6 | £12 | |
| I Put A Spell On You | LP | Direction | 863481 | 1969 | £8 | £20 | |
| I Put A Spell On You | LP | Epic | LN3457 | 1957 | £75 | £150 | US |
| I Put A Spell On You | 78 | Fontana | H107 | 1958 | £30 | £60 | |
| I Put A Spell On You | 7" | Direction | 584097 | 1969 | £4 | £8 | |
| Night And Day | LP | Planet | PLL1001 | 1966 | £25 | £50 | |
| Night At Forbidden City | LP | Sounds Of Hawaii | 5015 | 196– | £10 | £25 | US |
| Screaming Jay Hawkins | LP | Philips | PHS600336 | 1970 | £5 | £12 | US |
| Whammy | 7" | Columbia | DB7460 | 1965 | £5 | £10 | |
| What That Is | LP | Mercury | SMCL20178 | 1969 | £4 | £10 | |

## HAWKS

| | | | | | | | |
|---|---|---|---|---|---|---|---|
| Grissle | 7" | Stateside | SS2147 | 1968 | £2 | £5 | ... B side by the Sheep |

## HAWKS (2)

| | | | | | | | |
|---|---|---|---|---|---|---|---|
| Words Of Hope | 7" | Five Believers | FB001 | 198– | £2.50 | £6 | |

## HAWKSHAW, ALAN

| | | | | | | | |
|---|---|---|---|---|---|---|---|
| Big Beat | LP | KPM | KPM1044 | 1969 | £20 | £40 | |
| Music For A Young Generation | LP | KPM | KPM1086 | 1971 | £10 | £25 | |
| Soul Organ | LP | KPM | KPM1027 | 1967 | £10 | £25 | |

## HAWKSWORTH, JOHNNY ORCHESTRA

| | | | | | | | |
|---|---|---|---|---|---|---|---|
| Lunar Walk | 7" | Pye | 7N15969 | 1965 | £2 | £5 | |

## HAWKWIND

By overlaying simple riff music with electronic noise Hawkwind succeeded in creating the perfect backdrop for Michael Moorcock's science fiction and sword-and-sorcery novels. The link was cemented by Moorcock himself contributing to many of the group's records; by Hawkwind returning the favour in supplying the music for Moorcock's own *New World's Fair* LP; and by Moorcock inspiring the creation of a science fiction novel in which the members of Hawkwind were the main characters. Here is the origin of the close interrelation between fantasy and heavy metal music. The perfect artefact to summarize all this is the Hawkwind LP *Warrior On The Edge Of Time*, whose cover, showing a mounted hero waiting on the edge of a precipice, opens out into a cardboard shield.

| | | | | | | | |
|---|---|---|---|---|---|---|---|
| Approved History Of Hawkwind | LP | Samurai | SAMR046 | 1986 | £15 | £30 | set of 3 picture discs |
| Choose Your Masques | LP | RCA | RCALP6055 | 1982 | £4 | £10 | |
| Chronicle Of The Black Sword | CD | Flicknife | SHARP033CD | 1985 | £5 | £12 | with 3 extra tracks |
| Church Of Hawkwind | LP | RCA | RCALP9004 | 1982 | £6 | £15 | with booklet |
| Doremi Fasolatido | LP | United Artists | UAG29364 | 1972 | £5 | £12 | with poster |
| Hall Of The Mountain Grill | LP | United Artists | UAG29672 | 1974 | £4 | £10 | |
| Hawkfan 12 | LP | Hawkfan | HWFB2 | 1986 | £15 | £30 | with poster, insert, bag |
| Hawkwind | LP | Liberty | LBS83348 | 1970 | £6 | £15 | black label |
| Hawkwind | LP | Liberty | LBS83348 | 1970 | £8 | £20 | blue label |
| Hawkwind | LP | Liberty | SLSP1972921 | 1984 | £4 | £10 | picture disc |
| Hurry On Hawkwind | 7" EP | United Artists | USEP1 | 1973 | £25 | £50 | |
| Hurry On Sundown | 7" | Liberty | LBF15382 | 1970 | £37.50 | £75 | |
| In Search Of Space | LP | United Artists | UAG29202 | 1971 | £5 | £12 | with booklet |
| Kings Of Speed | 7" | United Artists | UP35808 | 1975 | £12.50 | £25 | picture sleeve |
| Levitation | LP | Bronze | BRON530 | 1980 | £4 | £10 | blue vinyl |
| Official Picture Log Book | LP | Flicknife | HWBOX01 | 1987 | £20 | £40 | 3 picture discs, interview LP, boxed |
| Orgasmatron | CD | Cargo | CD22 | 1992 | £5 | £12 | |
| PXR5 | LP | Charisma | CDS4016 | 1979 | £4 | £10 | with poster |
| Roadhawks | LP | United Artists | UAK29919 | 1976 | £4 | £10 | with poster |
| Silver Machine | 7" | RCA | RCAP267 | 1982 | £2.50 | £6 | picture disc |
| Silver Machine | 7" | Samurai | HW001 | 1986 | £2 | £5 | shaped picture disc |
| Silver Machine | 7" | United Artists | UP35381 | 1972 | £2.50 | £6 | silver & blue picture sleeve |
| Silver Machine | 7" | United Artists | UPP35381 | 1982 | £5 | £10 | mispress – B side plays Beatles 'Ask Me Why' |
| Silver Machine | 7" | United Artists | UPP35381 | 1983 | £2 | £5 | picture disc |
| Sonic Attack | LP | RCA | RCALP6004 | 1981 | £4 | £10 | with insert |
| Sonic Attack | 7" | United Artists | WD3637 | 1973 | £50 | £100 | 1 sided promo, cloth sleeve |

| Title | Format | Label | Cat. No. | Year | | | Notes |
|---|---|---|---|---|---|---|---|
| Space Ritual | LP | United Artists | UAD60037/8 | 1973 | £6 | £15 | double |
| Urban Guerilla | 7" | United Artists | UP35566 | 1973 | £2.50 | £6 | |
| Warrior On The Edge Of Time | LP | United Artists | UAG29766 | 1975 | £6 | £15 | shield cover |
| Who's Gonna Win The War | 7" | Bronze | BRO109 | 1980 | £2.50 | £6 | cream label |

## HAX CEL
| | | | | | | | |
|---|---|---|---|---|---|---|---|
| Zwai Life | LP | Dizzy | DS726 | 1972 | £6 | £15 | German |

## HAY, BARRY
| | | | | | | | |
|---|---|---|---|---|---|---|---|
| Only Parrots, Frogs And Angels | LP | Polydor | 2925006 | 1972 | £15 | £30 | Dutch |

## HAYDOCK'S ROCKHOUSE
| | | | | | | | |
|---|---|---|---|---|---|---|---|
| Cupid | 7" | Columbia | DB8050 | 1966 | £10 | £20 | |
| Lovin' You | 7" | Columbia | DB8135 | 1967 | £10 | £20 | |

## HAYES, BILL
| | | | | | | | |
|---|---|---|---|---|---|---|---|
| Ballad Of Davy Crockett | 7" | London | HLA8220 | 1956 | £10 | £20 | |
| Berry Tree | 7" | London | HL8149 | 1955 | £10 | £20 | |
| Das Ist Musik | 7" | London | HLA8300 | 1956 | £5 | £10 | |
| Donkey Song | 7" | MGM | SP1036 | 1953 | £7.50 | £15 | |
| Great Pioneers Of The West | 7" EP | London | REA1051 | 1956 | £10 | £20 | |
| Kwela Kwela | 7" | London | HLA8239 | 1956 | £7.50 | £15 | |
| Legend Of Wyatt Earp | 7" | London | HLA8325 | 1956 | £5 | £10 | |
| Sings The Best Of Disney | 7" EP | HMV | 7EG8355 | 1957 | £2 | £5 | |
| Wimoweh | 7" | London | HLR8833 | 1959 | £2 | £5 | |
| Wringle Wrangle | 7" | London | HL8430 | 1957 | £4 | £8 | |

## HAYES, ISAAC
| | | | | | | | |
|---|---|---|---|---|---|---|---|
| Black Moses | LP | Stax | 2628004 | 1972 | £5 | £12 | double |
| Blue Hayes | LP | Stax | 2465016 | 1971 | £5 | £12 | |
| Chocolate Chip | LP | ABC | ABCL5129 | 1975 | £4 | £10 | |
| Groove-A-Thon | LP | ABC | ABCL5155 | 1975 | £4 | £10 | |
| Hot Buttered Soul | LP | Stax | 2325011 | 1971 | £5 | £12 | |
| Hot Buttered Soul | LP | Stax | SXATS1028 | 1969 | £6 | £15 | |
| I Stand Accused | 7" | Stax | STAX154 | 1970 | £1.50 | £4 | |
| Isaac Hayes Movement | LP | Stax | 2325014 | 1971 | £5 | £12 | |
| Isaac Hayes Movement | LP | Stax | SXATS1032 | 1970 | £6 | £15 | |
| Joy | LP | Stax | 2325111 | 1974 | £4 | £10 | |
| Live At The Sahara Tahoe | LP | Stax | 2659026 | 1973 | £5 | £12 | double |
| Presenting Isaac Hayes | LP | Stax | | 1967 | £6 | £15 | |
| Shaft | LP | Stax | 2659007 | 1971 | £5 | £12 | double |
| To Be Continued | LP | Stax | 2325016 | 1971 | £5 | £12 | |
| Tough Guys | LP | Stax | STXH5001 | 1974 | £4 | £10 | |
| Truck Turner | LP | Stax | STXD4001/2 | 1974 | £5 | £12 | double |
| Use Me | LP | Stax | STX1043 | 1975 | £4 | £10 | |
| Walk On By | 7" | Stax | STAX133 | 1969 | £1.50 | £4 | |

## HAYES, LINDA & THE PLATTERS
| | | | | | | | |
|---|---|---|---|---|---|---|---|
| Please Have Mercy | 7" | Parlophone | MSP6174 | 1955 | £100 | £200 | |

## HAYES, TUBBY
| | | | | | | | |
|---|---|---|---|---|---|---|---|
| 100% Proof | LP | Fontana | (S)TL5410 | 1966 | £37.50 | £75 | |
| 100% Proof | LP | Philips | 6382041 | 1973 | £15 | £30 | |
| Change Of Setting | LP | World Record Club | T631 | 196– | £6 | £15 | ...with Paul Gonsalves |
| Down In The Village | LP | Fontana | 680998TL/886163TY | 1963 | £75 | £150 | |
| Eighth Wonder | 7" EP | Tempo | EXA82 | 1958 | £10 | £20 | |
| Equation In Rhythm | LP | Fontana | TFL5190/STFL598 | 1962 | £20 | £40 | ...with Jack Costanzo |
| Evening With Mr. Percussion | LP | Ember | EMB3337 | 1961 | £15 | £30 | ...with Tony Kinsey |
| Jazz Tête-à-Tête | LP | 77 | ELEU1221 | 1966 | £37.50 | £75 | |
| Just Friends | LP | Columbia | SX6003 | 196– | £8 | £20 | ...with Paul Gonsalves |
| Late Spot At Scott's | LP | Fontana | TL5200 | 1964 | £37.50 | £75 | |
| Mexican Green | LP | Fontana | SFJL911 | 1969 | £37.50 | £75 | |
| Modern Jazz Scene | 7" EP | Tempo | EXA36 | 1956 | £10 | £20 | |
| Ode To Ernie | 7" | Tempo | A148 | 1957 | £2 | £5 | |
| Palladium Jazz Date | LP | Fontana | (S)TFL570 | 196– | £6 | £15 | ...with Cleo Laine |
| Return Visit | LP | Fontana | (S)TL5195 | 1964 | £37.50 | £75 | |
| Sally | 7" | Fontana | H397 | 1962 | £1.50 | £4 | |
| Tubbs | LP | Fontana | TFL5142/STFL562 | 1961 | £37.50 | £75 | |
| Tubbs In New York | LP | Fontana | TFL5183/STFL595 | 1961 | £37.50 | £75 | |
| Tubbs In New York | LP | Wing | WL1162 | 1967 | £8 | £20 | |
| Tubby Hayes And His Orchestra | 7" EP | Tempo | EXA14 | 1955 | £10 | £20 | |
| Tubby Hayes And His Orchestra | 7" EP | Tempo | EXA17 | 1955 | £10 | £20 | |
| Tubby Hayes Orchestra | LP | Fontana | 6309002 | 1970 | £30 | £60 | |
| Tubby Hayes Quartet | LP | Fontana | TFL5151 | 1961 | £37.50 | £75 | |
| Tubby Hayes Quartet | 7" EP | Tempo | EXA27 | 1956 | £10 | £20 | |
| Tubby Hayes Quartet | 7" EP | Tempo | EXA28 | 1956 | £10 | £20 | |
| Tubby Hayes Quintet | LP | Tempo | TAP6 | 1956 | £50 | £100 | |
| Tubby Hayes Quintet | 7" EP | Tempo | EXA55 | 1957 | £10 | £20 | |
| Tubby Tours | LP | Fontana | (S)TL5221 | 1966 | £37.50 | £75 | |
| Tubby's Groove | LP | Tempo | TAP29 | 1961 | £50 | £100 | |

## HAYMARKET SQUARE
| | | | | | | | |
|---|---|---|---|---|---|---|---|
| Magic Lantern | LP | Chaparral | CRM201 | 1968 | £700 | £1000 | US |

## HAYNES, ROY
| | | | | | | | |
|---|---|---|---|---|---|---|---|
| Roy Haynes Band | 10" LP | Vogue | LDE130 | 1955 | £20 | £40 | |

387

| | | | | | | | |
|---|---|---|---|---|---|---|---|
| We Three | LP | Esquire | 32103 | 1960 | £15 | £30 | with Phineas Newborn & Paul Chambers |

## HAYSTACK

| | | | | | | |
|---|---|---|---|---|---|---|
| Letter To Josephine | 7" | United Artists | UP35024 | 1969 | £1.50 | £4 |
| Tahiti Farewell | 7" | United Artists | UP35035 | 1969 | £1.50 | £4 |

## HAYSTACKS BALBOA

| | | | | | | |
|---|---|---|---|---|---|---|
| Haystacks Balboa | LP | Polydor | 2489002 | 1970 | £50 | £100 |

## HAYWARD, JUSTIN

| | | | | | | |
|---|---|---|---|---|---|---|
| I Can't Face The World Without You | 7" | Parlophone | R5496 | 1966 | £37.50 | £75 |
| London Is Behind Me | 7" | Pye | 7N17014 | 1965 | £30 | £60 |
| Moving Mountains | CD | Towerbell | TOWCD15 | 1985 | £10 | £25 |
| Songwriter | CD | Deram | 8204922 | 1987 | £5 | £12 |

## HAYWARD, RICK

| | | | | | | |
|---|---|---|---|---|---|---|
| Rick Hayward | LP | Blue Horizon | 2431006 | 1971 | £20 | £40 |

## HAYWARD, SUSAN

| | | | | | | |
|---|---|---|---|---|---|---|
| I'll Cry Tomorrow | 7" EP | MGM | MGMEP555 | 1956 | £2 | £5 |

## HAYWOOD, JOE

| | | | | | | |
|---|---|---|---|---|---|---|
| Warm And Tender Love | 7" | Island | WI218 | 1965 | £2 | £5 |

## HAYWOOD, LEON

| | | | | | | |
|---|---|---|---|---|---|---|
| Ain't No Use | 7" | Vocalion | VP9280 | 1966 | £2 | £5 |
| Ever Since You Were Sweet Sixteen | 7" | Vocalion | VP9288 | 1967 | £5 | £10 |
| Soul Cargo | LP | Vocalion | VAL8064 | 1967 | £6 | £15 |

## HAZE

| | | | | | | | |
|---|---|---|---|---|---|---|---|
| Hazecolor Dia | LP | Bacillus | 6494007 | 1971 | £4 | £10 | German |

## HAZEL & THE JOLLY BOYS

| | | | | | | |
|---|---|---|---|---|---|---|
| Stop Them | 7" | Doctor Bird | DB1063 | 1966 | £5 | £10 |

## HAZELWOOD, LEE

| | | | | | | | |
|---|---|---|---|---|---|---|---|
| Friday's Child | LP | Reprise | RS6163 | 1964 | £8 | £20 | US |
| Words Mean Nothing | 7" | London | HLW9223 | 1960 | £4 | £8 | |
| Love And Other Crimes | LP | Reprise | RSLP6297 | 1968 | £6 | £15 | |
| My Baby Cried All Night Long | 7" | MGM | MGM1348 | 1967 | £2 | £5 | |
| Ode To Billie Joe | 7" | Reprise | RS20613 | 1967 | £1.50 | £4 | |
| Poet, Fool Or Bum | LP | Stateside | SSL10315 | 1974 | £6 | £15 | |
| Rainbow Woman | 7" | Reprise | RS20667 | 1968 | £1.50 | £4 | |
| Sand | 7" | MGM | MGM1310 | 1966 | £1.50 | £4 | |
| Trouble Is A Lonesome Town | LP | London | HAN/SHN8398 | 1970 | £6 | £15 | |

## HEAD

| | | | | | | |
|---|---|---|---|---|---|---|
| G.T.F. | LP | SRT | 72254 | 1973 | £10 | £25 |

## HEAD, MURRAY

| | | | | | | | |
|---|---|---|---|---|---|---|---|
| Nigel Lived | LP | CBS | 65503 | 1973 | £4 | £10 | |
| She Was Perfection | 7" | Immediate | IM053 | 1967 | £7.50 | £15 | |
| Superstar | 7" | MCA | MK5019 | 1969 | £1.50 | £4 | picture sleeve |

## HEAD, ROY

| | | | | | | | |
|---|---|---|---|---|---|---|---|
| Apple Of My Eye | 7" | Vocalion | VP9254 | 1966 | £1.50 | £4 | |
| Just A Little Bit | 7" | Pye | 7N25340 | 1965 | £2.50 | £6 | |
| Just A Little Bit Of Roy Head | 7" EP | Pye | NEP44053 | 1966 | £5 | £10 | |
| Most Wanted Woman In Town | 7" | London | HLD10487 | 1975 | £2 | £5 | |
| Roy Head And The Traits | LP | TNT | 101 | 1965 | £25 | £50 | US |
| To Make A Big Man Cry | 7" | London | HLZ10097 | 1966 | £1.50 | £4 | |
| Treat Her Right | 7" | Vocalion | VP9248 | 1965 | £1.50 | £4 | |
| Treat Me Right | LP | Scepter | (S)S532 | 1965 | £5 | £12 | US |

## HEAD MACHINE

| | | | | | | |
|---|---|---|---|---|---|---|
| Orgasm | LP | Major Minor | SMLP79 | 1970 | £62.50 | £125 |

## HEAD SHOP

| | | | | | | | |
|---|---|---|---|---|---|---|---|
| Head Shop | LP | Epic | BN26476 | 1969 | £10 | £25 | US |

## HEADBAND

| | | | | | | | |
|---|---|---|---|---|---|---|---|
| Song For Tooley | LP | Polydor | 2907008 | 1971 | £37.50 | £75 | Australian |

## HEADHUNTERS

| | | | | | | |
|---|---|---|---|---|---|---|
| Straight From The Gate | LP | Arista | SPART1046 | 1977 | £6 | £15 |
| Survival Of The Fittest | LP | Arista | ARTY116 | 1975 | £10 | £25 |

## HEADS, HANDS & FEET

| | | | | | | |
|---|---|---|---|---|---|---|
| Heads, Hands & Feet | LP | Island | ILPS9149 | 1971 | £6 | £15 |
| On The Tracks | LP | Island | ILPS9185 | 1972 | £5 | £12 |

## HEADSTONE

| | | | | | | | |
|---|---|---|---|---|---|---|---|
| Still Looking | LP | Starr | SLP1056 | 1971 | £100 | £200 | US |

## HEALY, PAT

| | | | | | | |
|---|---|---|---|---|---|---|
| Just Before Dawn | LP | Vogue | VA160131 | 1959 | £6 | £15 |

## HEANEY, JOE

| | | | | | | | |
|---|---|---|---|---|---|---|---|
| As I Roved Out | 7" EP | Collector | JEI7 | 1961 | £2 | £5 | |
| Irish Traditional Songs In Gaelic And English | LP | Topic | 12T91 | 1963 | £5 | £12 | |
| Morrissey And The Russian Sailor | 7" EP | Collector | JEI5 | 1960 | £2 | £5 | |
| O Mo Dhuchas | LP | Gael-Linn | CEF051 | 1976 | £4 | £10 | Irish |

## HEART

| | | | | | | | |
|---|---|---|---|---|---|---|---|
| All I Wanna Do Is Make Love To You | CD-s | Capitol | CDCL569 | 1990 | £2 | £5 | |
| Brigade | CD | Capitol | DPRO79967 | 1990 | £6 | £15 | US promo picture disc |
| Dreamboat Annie | LP | Mushroom | MRS5005 | 1976 | £8 | £20 | US picture disc |
| Dreamboat Annie | LP | Nautilus | NR 3 | 1979 | £5 | £12 | US audiophile |
| Dreamboat Annie | CD | Capitol | CDEST2042 | 1987 | £5 | £12 | |
| Heart Box Set | LP | Capitol | HGIFT1 | 1990 | £8 | £20 | 3 LPs, boxed, booklet |
| Heart Box Set | CD | Capitol | CDHGIFT1 | 1990 | £10 | £25 | 3 CDs boxed |
| I Didn't Want To Need You | CD-s | Capitol | CDCL580 | 1990 | £2 | £5 | |
| Little Queen | LP | Portrait | HR 44799 | 1981 | £5 | £12 | US audiophile |
| Magazine | LP | Arista | SPART1024 | 1977 | £6 | £15 | 1st version, without 1978 recordings |
| Magazine | LP | Mushroom | MRS1SP | 1978 | £5 | £12 | US picture disc |
| Magazine | CD | Capitol | CDEST2041 | 1987 | £5 | £12 | |
| Never | CD-s | Capitol | CDCL482 | 1988 | £2 | £5 | |
| Nothin' At All | CD-s | Capitol | CDCL507 | 1988 | £2 | £5 | |
| Nothin' At All | 7" | Capitol | CL406 | 1986 | £1.50 | £4 | ... heart shaped picture disc |
| Radio Star Audio Cue Card | CD | Capitol | | 1987 | £6 | £15 | ...US interview promo |
| Secret | CD-s | Capitol | CDCL603 | 1991 | £2 | £5 | |
| Stranded | CD-s | Capitol | CDCL595 | 1990 | £2 | £5 | |
| There's The Girl | CD-s | Capitol | CDCL473 | 1987 | £2 | £5 | |
| These Dreams | CD-s | Capitol | CDCL477 | 1988 | £2 | £5 | |
| What About Love? | CD-s | Capitol | CDCL487 | 1988 | £2 | £5 | |
| With Love From Heart | LP | Capitol | LOVE2 | 1988 | £6 | £15 | 2 LPs, boxed, inserts |
| With Love From Heart | CD | Capitol | CDLOVE2 | 1988 | £8 | £20 | 2 CDs boxed |
| You're The Voice | CD-s | Capitol | CDCL624 | 1991 | £2 | £5 | |

## HEARTBEATS

| | | | | | | | |
|---|---|---|---|---|---|---|---|
| Thousand Miles Away | LP | Roulette | (S)R25107 | 1960 | £25 | £50 | US |

## HEARTBREAKERS

| | | | | | | | |
|---|---|---|---|---|---|---|---|
| It's Not Enough | 7" | Track | 2094142 | 1977 | £25 | £50 | picture sleeve |
| One Track Mind | 7" | Track | 2094137 | 1977 | £1.50 | £4 | |

## HEARTBREAKERS (2)

Frank Zappa plays guitar on 'Every Time I See You'.

| | | | | | | | |
|---|---|---|---|---|---|---|---|
| Every Time I See You | 7" | Donna | 1381 | 1964 | £75 | £150 | US |

## HEARTS

| | | | | | | | |
|---|---|---|---|---|---|---|---|
| Dear Abby | 7" | Stateside | SS268 | 1964 | £1.50 | £4 | |

## HEARTS (2)

| | | | | | | | |
|---|---|---|---|---|---|---|---|
| Young Woman | 7" | Parlophone | R5147 | 1964 | £10 | £20 | |

## HEARTS & FLOWERS

| | | | | | | | |
|---|---|---|---|---|---|---|---|
| Now Is The Time | LP | Capitol | (S)T2762 | 1967 | £20 | £40 | US |
| Of Horses, Kids, & Forgotten Women | LP | Capitol | ST2868 | 1968 | £20 | £40 | US |
| Rock 'n' Roll Gypsies | 7" | Capitol | CL15492 | 1967 | £2 | £5 | |
| She Sang Hymns Out Of Tune | 7" | Capitol | CL15549 | 1968 | £1.50 | £4 | |

## HEARTS OF SOUL

| | | | | | | | |
|---|---|---|---|---|---|---|---|
| Waterman | 7" | Columbia | DB8670 | 1970 | £4 | £8 | |

## HEATH, JIMMY

| | | | | | | | |
|---|---|---|---|---|---|---|---|
| Really Big | LP | Riverside | RLP333 | 1960 | £6 | £15 | |
| Triple Threat | LP | Riverside | RLP400 | 1962 | £6 | £15 | |

## HEATH, TED

| | | | | | | | |
|---|---|---|---|---|---|---|---|
| Al Jolson Classics No. 1 | 7" EP | Decca | DFE6510 | 1958 | £2 | £5 | |
| At Carnegie Hall | LP | Decca | LK4165 | 1957 | £4 | £10 | |
| At The London Palladium | LP | Decca | LK4062 | 1953 | £4 | £10 | |
| At The London Palladium Vol. 3 | LP | Decca | LK4097 | 1955 | £4 | £10 | |
| At The London Palladium Vol. 4 | LP | Decca | LK4134 | 1956 | £4 | £10 | |
| Australian Suite | 7" EP | Decca | DFE6300 | 1956 | £4 | £8 | |
| Beaulieu Festival Suite | 7" EP | Decca | DFE6625 | 1960 | £2 | £5 | |
| Beaulieu Festival Suite | 7" EP | Decca | STO135 | 1960 | £4 | £8 | stereo |
| Bell Bell Boogie | 7" | Decca | F10540 | 1955 | £1.50 | £4 | |
| Creep | 7" | Decca | F10222 | 1954 | £1.50 | £4 | |
| Dig Deep | 7" | Decca | F10425 | 1955 | £1.50 | £4 | |
| Faithful Hussar | 7" | Decca | F10746 | 1956 | £1.50 | £4 | |
| Fats Waller Album | LP | Decca | LK4074 | 1954 | £4 | £10 | |
| Fats Waller Album | 7" EP | Decca | DFE6159 | 1955 | £4 | £8 | |
| Fats Waller Album No. 2 | 7" EP | Decca | DFE6160 | 1955 | £2 | £5 | |
| First American Tour | LP | Decca | LK4167 | 1957 | £4 | £10 | |
| Four Classics | 7" EP | Decca | DFE6323 | 1956 | £2 | £5 | |
| Four Hits From The All Time Top Twelve | 7" EP | Decca | DFE6579 | 1959 | £2 | £5 | |
| Four Hits From The All Time Top Twelve | 7" EP | Decca | STO122 | 1959 | £2.50 | £6 | stereo |

| Title | Format | Label | Cat No | Year | Price | Price | Notes |
|---|---|---|---|---|---|---|---|
| Gershwin For Moderns | LP | Decca | LK4098 | 1955 | £4 | £10 | |
| Gershwin For Moderns No. 1 | 7" EP | Decca | DFE6290 | 1956 | £2 | £5 | |
| Gershwin For Moderns No. 2 | 7" EP | Decca | DFE6354 | 1956 | £2 | £5 | |
| Great Film Hits | 7" EP | Decca | STO155 | 1961 | £2 | £5 | stereo |
| Haitian Ritual | 7" | Decca | F10477 | 1955 | £1.50 | £4 | |
| Hits I Missed | LP | Decca | LK4275 | 1958 | £4 | £10 | |
| Hits I Missed | LP | Decca | SKL4003 | 1958 | £4 | £10 | stereo |
| Hits I Missed | 7" EP | Decca | STO103 | 1958 | £2 | £5 | stereo |
| Hits I Missed No. 1 | 7" EP | Decca | DFE6509 | 1958 | £2 | £5 | |
| Hundredth London Palladium Sunday Concert | LP | Decca | LK4075 | 1954 | £4 | £10 | |
| Hundredth London Palladium Sunday Concert Vol. 1 | 7" EP | Decca | DFE6189 | 1955 | £2 | £5 | |
| Hundredth London Palladium Sunday Concert Vol. 2 | 7" EP | Decca | DFE6190 | 1955 | £2 | £5 | |
| Hundredth London Palladium Sunday Concert Vol. 3 | 7" EP | Decca | DFE6191 | 1955 | £2 | £5 | |
| Kern For Moderns | LP | Decca | LK4121 | 1956 | £4 | £10 | |
| Kern For Moderns No. 1 | 7" EP | Decca | DFE6304 | 1956 | £2 | £5 | |
| Kern For Moderns No. 2 | 7" EP | Decca | DFE6305 | 1956 | £2 | £5 | |
| Kern For Moderns No. 3 | 7" EP | Decca | DFE6306 | 1956 | £2 | £5 | |
| Listen To My Music | 10" LP | Decca | LF1060 | 1952 | £4 | £10 | |
| London Palladium Highlights | 7" EP | Decca | DFE6120 | 1955 | £2 | £5 | |
| London Palladium Highlights No. 2 | 7" EP | Decca | DFE6317 | 1956 | £2 | £5 | |
| London Palladium Highlights No. 3 | 7" EP | Decca | DFE6346 | 1956 | £2 | £5 | |
| London Palladium Highlights No. 4 | 7" EP | Decca | DFE6373 | 1956 | £2 | £5 | |
| Lush Slide | 7" | Decca | F10273 | 1954 | £1.50 | £4 | |
| Moments At Montreux | 7" EP | Decca | STO8532 | 1963 | £2 | £5 | stereo |
| My Very Good Friends The Bandleaders | 7" EP | Decca | DFE6642 | 1960 | £2 | £5 | |
| Old English No. 1 | 7" EP | Decca | DFE6511 | 1958 | £2 | £5 | |
| Olde Englyshe | LP | Decca | LK4280 | 1958 | £4 | £10 | |
| Our Kind Of Jazz | 7" EP | Decca | DFE6500 | 1958 | £2 | £5 | |
| Peg O' My Heart | 7" | Decca | F10447 | 1955 | £1.50 | £4 | |
| Recalls The Fabulous Dorseys No. 1 | 7" EP | Decca | DFE6451 | 1957 | £2 | £5 | |
| Rodgers For Moderns | LP | Decca | LK4148 | 1956 | £4 | £10 | |
| Selection | 10" LP | Decca | LF1064 | 1952 | £4 | £10 | |
| Seven Eleven | 7" | Decca | F10200 | 1954 | £1.50 | £4 | |
| Skin Deep | 7" | Decca | F10246 | 1954 | £1.50 | £4 | |
| Spotlight On Sidemen | LP | Decca | LK4204 | 1957 | £4 | £10 | |
| Strike Up The Band | LP | Decca | LK4064 | 1953 | £4 | £10 | |
| Swing Session | LP | Decca | SKL4030 | 1959 | £4 | £10 | stereo |
| Swing Session | 7" EP | Decca | STO109 | 1959 | £4 | £8 | stereo |
| Swings In Hi Stereo | 7" EP | Decca | STO113 | 1959 | £2 | £5 | stereo |
| Swings In Hi-Stereo | LP | Decca | SKL4023 | 1958 | £4 | £10 | |
| Ted Heath And His Music | 7" EP | Decca | DFE6025 | 1955 | £4 | £8 | |
| Ted Heath And His Music No. 2 | 7" EP | Decca | DFE6027 | 1955 | £4 | £8 | |
| Ted Heath And His Music No. 3 | 7" EP | Decca | DFE6403 | 1957 | £2 | £5 | |
| Ted Heath And His Music No. 4 | 7" EP | Decca | DFE6432 | 1957 | £2 | £5 | |
| Ted Heath And His Music No. 5 | 7" EP | Decca | DFE6487 | 1958 | £2 | £5 | |
| Tempo For Dancers | 10" LP | Decca | LF1037 | 1951 | £6 | £15 | |
| Viva Verrell | 7" | Decca | F10272 | 1954 | £1.50 | £4 | |

## HEATHCOTE, GEORGE & SHARON PEOPLE

| Title | Format | Label | Cat No | Year | Price | Price | Notes |
|---|---|---|---|---|---|---|---|
| Freely Freely | LP | Genesis | GENESIS1 | 1975 | £50 | £100 | |

## HEATHER BLACK

| Title | Format | Label | Cat No | Year | Price | Price | Notes |
|---|---|---|---|---|---|---|---|
| Heather Black | LP | American Playboy | 1001 | 196– | £25 | £50 | US |

## HEAVEN

| Title | Format | Label | Cat No | Year | Price | Price | Notes |
|---|---|---|---|---|---|---|---|
| Brass Rock | LP | CBS | 66293 | 1971 | £6 | £15 | double |

## HEAVEN 17

| Title | Format | Label | Cat No | Year | Price | Price | Notes |
|---|---|---|---|---|---|---|---|
| Height Of The Fighting | 7" | Virgin | VS483 | 1982 | £5 | £10 | |
| Temptation | CD-s | Virgin | CDT19 | 1988 | £2 | £5 | 3" single |
| We Don't Need This Fascist Groove Thang | CD-s | Virgin | CDT21 | 1988 | £2 | £5 | 3" single |

## HEAVY BALLOON

| Title | Format | Label | Cat No | Year | Price | Price | Notes |
|---|---|---|---|---|---|---|---|
| 32000 Pound | LP | Elephant | EVS104 | 1968 | £30 | £60 | US |

## HEAVY JELLY

A joke review of an imaginary band called 'Heavy Jelly' in one of the rock weeklies led to the formation of two separate bands, adopting the name in an attempt to make the joke real. The first of these became familiar to many people through a track included on the Island sampler album *Nice Enough To Eat*. Also released as a single, 'I Keep Singing The Same Old Song' was actually the work of the group Skip Bifferty, who never seriously intended to use the new name for subsequent work. As it happens, the single is rather good. A second Heavy Jelly, in which John Mayall's departing bass player Steve Thompson joined singer Jackie Lomax and members of Aynsley Dunbar's Retaliation, did actually gig for a short while, and issued the single 'Chewn In' on the Head label together with an album that failed to be given a full release.

| Title | Format | Label | Cat No | Year | Price | Price | Notes |
|---|---|---|---|---|---|---|---|
| I Keep Singing The Same Old Song | 7" | Island | WIP6049 | 1968 | £2.50 | £6 | |

## HEAVY JELLY (2)

| Title | Format | Label | Cat No | Year | Price | Price | Notes |
|---|---|---|---|---|---|---|---|
| Chewn In | 7" | Head | HDS4001 | 1969 | £4 | £8 | |
| Take Me Down To The Water | LP | Head | | 1969 | £50 | £100 | demo |

## HEBB, BOBBY

| Title | Format | Label | Cat No | Year | Price | Price | Notes |
|---|---|---|---|---|---|---|---|
| I Love Everything About You | 7" | Philips | BF1570 | 1967 | £1.50 | £4 | |

| | | | | | | | |
|---|---|---|---|---|---|---|---|
| Love Me | 7" | Philips | BF1541 | 1967 | £2 | £5 | |
| Satisfied Mind | 7" | Philips | BF1522 | 1966 | £1.50 | £4 | |
| Sunny | LP | Philips | 2/PHS600212 | 1966 | £5 | £12 | US |
| Sunny | 7" EP | Philips | 452056 | 1966 | £5 | £10 | French |
| You Want To Change Me | 7" | Philips | BF1702 | 1968 | £7.50 | £15 | |

## HEBBERT, MICHAEL

| | | | | | | | |
|---|---|---|---|---|---|---|---|
| Rampin Cat | LP | Free Reed | FRR009 | 1977 | £4 | £10 | |

## HECKSTALL-SMITH, DICK

Colosseum broke apart during the extensive rehearsals of the difficult 'Pirate's Dream', but the piece was rescued for Dick Heckstall-Smith's solo LP. This is close enough to the sound of Colosseum to make it the legitimate follow-up to *Colosseum Live* and is something of an odd record for a saxophonist to have made, as Heckstall-Smith's own contributions do not exactly dominate the centre stage. The record is, however, a fine addition to the small body of adventurous songwriting otherwise largely occupied by the works of Jack Bruce. Meanwhile the very scarce Heckstall-Smith EP provides a kind of glimpse of an alternative world; the start of the career of a straight-ahead jazz saxophonist, that actually proceeded on rather different lines. (Although, in the nineties, Heckstall-Smith has unexpectedly decided to reclaim his jazz career – his *Woza Nasu* album in particular is rather fine.)

| | | | | | | | |
|---|---|---|---|---|---|---|---|
| Jazz Gumbo Vol. 2 | LP | Nixa | NJT510 | 1958 | £15 | £30 | side 2 by Wally Fawkes & Bruce Turner |
| Story Ended | LP | Bronze | ILPS9196 | 1972 | £6 | £15 | |
| Very Special Old Jazz | 7" EP | Pye | NJE1037 | 1957 | £12.50 | £25 | |

## HEDAYAT, DASHIELL (DAEVID ALLEN)

| | | | | | | | |
|---|---|---|---|---|---|---|---|
| Melmoth La Devanture | LP | Arion | 30T079 | 1969 | £15 | £30 | French |
| Obsolete | LP | Shandar | SR83512 | 1971 | £8 | £20 | French |

## HEDGEHOG PIE

| | | | | | | | |
|---|---|---|---|---|---|---|---|
| Green Lady | LP | Rubber | RUB014 | 1975 | £10 | £25 | |
| Hedgehog Pie | LP | Rubber | RUB009 | 1975 | £6 | £15 | |
| His Round | LP | Rubber | RUB002 | 1972 | £6 | £15 | |
| Just Act Normal | LP | Rubber | RUB024 | 1978 | £8 | £20 | |
| Lambton Worm | 7" EP | Rubber | TUB12 | 1976 | £10 | £20 | |

## HEDGEHOPPERS ANONYMOUS

| | | | | | | | |
|---|---|---|---|---|---|---|---|
| It's Good News Week | 7" | Decca | F12241 | 1965 | £1.50 | £4 | |

## HEDLUND, SVEN

| | | | | | | | |
|---|---|---|---|---|---|---|---|
| Sings Elvis | LP | Olga | 005 | 1973 | £6 | £15 | Swedish |

## HEFTI, NEAL

| | | | | | | | |
|---|---|---|---|---|---|---|---|
| Batman | LP | RCA | LPM/LSP3573 | 1966 | £10 | £25 | US |
| Batman Theme | 7" | RCA | RCA1521 | 1966 | £4 | £8 | |

## HEIGHT, DONALD

| | | | | | | | |
|---|---|---|---|---|---|---|---|
| 365 Days | 7" | London | HLZ10116 | 1967 | £7.50 | £15 | |
| Rags To Riches | 7" | Avco | 6105005 | 1971 | £2.50 | £6 | |
| Talk Of The Grapevine | 7" | London | HLZ10062 | 1966 | £12.50 | £25 | |

## HEINZ

Heinz Burt's good looks and spiky dyed blond hair ensured his promotion from bass player with the Tornados, but after a good start with the top five single, 'Just Like Eddie', his career fizzled out. Although Heinz mimed the Eddie Cochran guitar style on television, it was actually the future Deep Purple star, Ritchie Blackmore, who played the lead breaks on the record.

| | | | | | | | |
|---|---|---|---|---|---|---|---|
| Country Boy | 7" | Decca | F11768 | 1963 | £1.50 | £4 | |
| Diggin' My Potatoes | 7" | Columbia | DB7482 | 1965 | £6 | £12 | |
| Don't Think Twice It's Alright | 7" | Columbia | DB7559 | 1965 | £5 | £10 | |
| Dreams Do Come True | 7" | Decca | F11652 | 1963 | £5 | £10 | |
| End Of The World | 7" | Columbia | DB7656 | 1965 | £6 | £12 | |
| Heart Full Of Sorrow | 7" | Columbia | DB7779 | 1965 | £6 | £12 | |
| Heinz | 7" EP | Decca | DFE8545 | 1963 | £15 | £30 | |
| Just Like Eddie | 7" | Decca | F11693 | 1963 | £1.50 | £4 | |
| Live It Up | 7" EP | Decca | DFE8559 | 1963 | £12.50 | £25 | |
| Movin' In | 7" | Columbia | DB7942 | 1966 | £7.50 | £15 | |
| Please Little Girl | 7" | Decca | F11920 | 1964 | £4 | £8 | |
| Questions I Can't Answer | 7" | Columbia | DB7374 | 1964 | £5 | £10 | |
| Tribute To Eddie | LP | Decca | LK4599 | 1964 | £25 | £50 | |
| You Were There | 7" | Decca | F11831 | 1964 | £2.50 | £6 | |

## HELDEN

| | | | | | | | |
|---|---|---|---|---|---|---|---|
| Holding On | 7" | Zica | ZICA01 | 1983 | £2 | £5 | |
| Holding On | 12" | Zica | 12ZICA01 | 1983 | £4 | £10 | |

## HELDON

| | | | | | | | |
|---|---|---|---|---|---|---|---|
| Agneta Nilsson (IV) | LP | Urus | 000011 | 1976 | £5 | £12 | French |
| Allez Teja | LP | Disjuncta | 000002 | 1975 | £5 | £12 | French |
| Guérilla électronique | LP | Disjuncta | 000001 | 1974 | £5 | £12 | French |
| Interface | LP | Cobra | 37013 | 1976 | £5 | £12 | French |
| It's Always Rock And Roll | LP | Disjuncta | 000006/7 | 1975 | £6 | £15 | French double |
| Stand By | LP | Egg | 900578 | 1979 | £4 | £10 | French |
| Un Rêve sans conséquence spéciale | LP | Cobra | 37002 | 1976 | £5 | £12 | French |

## HELL, RICHARD

It was the American Richard Hell who invented the punk style. The ripped clothing comes from him, as does the nihilist attitude – Richard Hell's theme song is 'Blank Generation'. He was originally the bass player for Television, which is presumably why that group tend to be classed as punk/new wave, despite a fascination with long guitar solos.

| | | | | | | | |
|---|---|---|---|---|---|---|---|
| Blank Generation | LP | Sire | SR6037 | 1977 | £5 | £12 | *...... with inner sleeve* |
| Blank Generation | 7" | Ork | 81976 | 1976 | £5 | £10 | *US* |
| Blank Generation | 7" | Sire | 6078608 | 1977 | £2.50 | £6 | |
| I Could Live With You In Another World | 7" | Stiff | BUY7 | 1976 | £2 | £5 | |

## HELL PREACHERS INC.

| | | | | | | |
|---|---|---|---|---|---|---|
| Supreme Psychedelic Underground | LP | Marble Arch | MALS1169 | 1969 | £10 | £25 |

## HELLING, DAVE

| | | | | | | |
|---|---|---|---|---|---|---|
| Christine | 7" | Planet | PLF101 | 1966 | £5 | £10 |
| It Ain't Me Babe | 7" | Stateside | SS409 | 1965 | £1.50 | £4 |

## HELLIONS

Three singles, but all of them unsuccessful, for a group that included two future members of Traffic (Dave Mason and Jim Capaldi) and one future member of Spooky Tooth and Mott the Hoople (Luther Grosvenor/Ariel Bender).

| | | | | | | |
|---|---|---|---|---|---|---|
| Daydreaming Of You | 7" | Piccadilly | 7N35213 | 1965 | £6 | £12 |
| Little Lovin' | 7" | Piccadilly | 7N35265 | 1965 | £6 | £12 |
| Tomorrow Never Comes | 7" | Piccadilly | 7N35232 | 1965 | £6 | £12 |

## HELLO

| | | | | | | |
|---|---|---|---|---|---|---|
| Another School Day | 7" | Bell | BLL1333 | 1973 | £5 | £10 |
| You Move Me | 7" | Bell | BLL1238 | 1972 | £5 | £10 |

## HELMS, BOBBY

| | | | | | | | |
|---|---|---|---|---|---|---|---|
| Best Of Bobby Helms | LP | Columbia | CL2060/CS8860 | 1963 | £6 | £15 | *US* |
| Bobby Helms | 7" EP | Brunswick | OE9461 | 1960 | £12.50 | £25 | |
| Fraulein | 7" | Brunswick | 05711 | 1957 | £1.50 | £4 | |
| Jacqueline | 7" | Brunswick | 05748 | 1958 | £2 | £5 | |
| Jingle Bell Rock | 7" | Brunswick | 05765 | 1958 | £4 | £8 | |
| Love My Lady | 7" | Brunswick | 05741 | 1958 | £1.50 | £4 | |
| My Special Agent | 7" | Brunswick | 05721 | 1957 | £2.50 | £6 | |
| New River Train | 7" | Brunswick | 05786 | 1959 | £1.50 | £4 | |
| No Other Baby | 7" | Brunswick | 05730 | 1958 | £2 | £5 | |
| Schoolboy Crush | 7" | Brunswick | 05754 | 1958 | £2.50 | £6 | |
| To My Special Angel | LP | Brunswick | LAT8250 | 1957 | £20 | £40 | |

## HELP

| | | | | | | | |
|---|---|---|---|---|---|---|---|
| Help | LP | Decca | DL75257 | 1971 | £15 | £30 | *US* |
| Second Coming | LP | Decca | DL75304 | 1971 | £15 | £30 | *US* |

## HELP YOURSELF

| | | | | | | | |
|---|---|---|---|---|---|---|---|
| Beware Of The Shadow | LP | United Artists | UAS29413 | 1972 | £4 | £10 | |
| Help Yourself | LP | Liberty | LIBS83484 | 1971 | £15 | £30 | |
| Return Of Ken Whaley/Happy Days | LP | United Artists | UDG4001 | 1973 | £10 | £25 | *double* |
| Running Down Deep | 7" | Liberty | LBF15459 | 1971 | £1.50 | £4 | |
| Strange Affair | LP | United Artists | UAS29287 | 1972 | £4 | £10 | |

## HEMLOCK

| | | | | | | |
|---|---|---|---|---|---|---|
| Hemlock | LP | Deram | SML1102 | 1973 | £15 | £30 |
| Mr. Horizontal | 7" | Deram | DM379 | 1973 | £1.50 | £4 |

## HEMMINGS, DAVID

| | | | | | | | |
|---|---|---|---|---|---|---|---|
| Happens | LP | MGM | 4490 | 1968 | £8 | £20 | *..US, with The Byrds* |

## HENDERSON, BERTHA & ROSA HENDERSON

| | | | | | | |
|---|---|---|---|---|---|---|
| Female Blues Vol. 2 | 7" EP | Collector | JEL14 | 1961 | £4 | £8 |

## HENDERSON, BILL

| | | | | | | |
|---|---|---|---|---|---|---|
| Sweet Pumpkin | 7" | Top Rank | JAR412 | 1960 | £4 | £8 |

## HENDERSON, BOBBY

| | | | | | | |
|---|---|---|---|---|---|---|
| Handful Of Keys | LP | Vanguard | PPL11007 | 1957 | £6 | £15 |

## HENDERSON, BRIAN

| | | | | | | |
|---|---|---|---|---|---|---|
| Folk's In A Hurry | 7" | Columbia | DB8006 | 1966 | £1.50 | £4 |

## HENDERSON, DORRIS

Dorris Henderson was the second female lead singer to be employed by folk-rock pioneers, the Eclection. She had earlier made two very scarce folk LPs on which she is backed by John Renbourn and Danny Thompson.

| | | | | | | |
|---|---|---|---|---|---|---|
| Hangman | 7" | Columbia | DB7567 | 1965 | £4 | £8 |
| Message To Pretty | 7" | Fontana | TF811 | 1967 | £4 | £8 |
| There You Go | LP | Columbia | SX6001 | 1965 | £75 | £150 |
| Watch The Stars | LP | Fontana | (S)TL5385 | 1967 | £75 | £150 |

## HENDERSON, FLETCHER

| | | | | | | | |
|---|---|---|---|---|---|---|---|
| At Connie's Inn | 10" LP | HMV | DLP1066 | 1955 | £10 | £25 | |
| Big Band Story Vol. 1 | 7" EP | Collector | JE115 | 1959 | £2 | £5 | |
| Birth Of Big Band Jazz | 10" LP | London | AL3547 | 1955 | £10 | £25 | |
| Fletcher Henderson | 10" LP | Audubon | AAF-AAK | 195– | £50 | £100 | *6 LP set* |
| Fletcher Henderson Jazz Group | 7" EP | Collector | JE111 | 1959 | £2 | £5 | |

## HENDERSON, JOE

| | | | | | | | |
|---|---|---|---|---|---|---|---|
| In 'n' Out | LP | Blue Note | BLP/BST84166 | 1964 | £8 | £20 | |
| Inner Urge | LP | Blue Note | BLP/BST84189 | 1965 | £8 | £20 | |
| Joe Henderson | 7" EP | London | REU1376 | 1963 | £2.50 | £6 | |

| | | | | | | | |
|---|---|---|---|---|---|---|---|
| Kicker | LP | Milestone | MSP9008 | 1971 | £5 | £12 | |
| Mode For Joe | LP | Blue Note | BLP/BST84227 | 1966 | £8 | £20 | |
| Our Thing | LP | Blue Note | BLP/BST84152 | 1963 | £10 | £25 | |
| Page One | LP | Blue Note | BLP/BST84140 | 1963 | £8 | £20 | |
| Power To The People | LP | CBS | 64068 | 1970 | £5 | £12 | |

## HENDRICKS, BOBBY

| | | | | | | | |
|---|---|---|---|---|---|---|---|
| I'm Coming Home | 7" | Mercury | AMT1163 | 1961 | £1.50 | £4 | |
| Itchy Twitchy Feeling | 7" | London | HL8714 | 1958 | £30 | £60 | |
| Itchy Twitchy Feeling | 7" | Sue | WI315 | 1964 | £4 | £8 | |
| Little John Green | 7" | Top Rank | JAR193 | 1959 | £2 | £5 | |

## HENDRICKS, JON

| | | | | | | | |
|---|---|---|---|---|---|---|---|
| Good Git-Together | LP | Vogue | LAE12231 | 1960 | £4 | £10 | |

## HENDRIK, TONY FIVE

| | | | | | | | |
|---|---|---|---|---|---|---|---|
| Nightflight | LP | Columbia | SMC74255 | 1966 | £6 | £15 | German |

## HENDRIX, JIMI

Collecting Jimi Hendrix begins with a copy of *Electric Ladyland*, which is as good a demonstration of the power and potential of rock music as one is likely to find anywhere. There are any number of examples of Hendrix's genius as a guitarist to be found amongst the double album's tracks, while for those who still believe that Hendrix was all about noise and bombast, there is '1983 . . . A Merman I Should Turn To Be', an extended composition in which the resources of the recording studio are tested to the limit, yet to a largely gentle and subtle effect. With regard to actual collectors' items, there is the original 'puppet' cover for *Band Of Gypsies*; the first pressing of *Axis: Bold As Love* with its rare red vinyl; the scarce red vinyl edition of *The Cry Of Love*; and the even scarcer record club compilation *Electric Hendrix*. None, however, can give the excitement and emotional impact of an hour and a half spent in *Electric Ladyland*.

| | | | | | | | |
|---|---|---|---|---|---|---|---|
| 6 Singles Pack | 7" | Polydor | 2608001 | 1980 | £7.50 | £15 | 6 x 7" |
| All Along The Watchtower | CD-s | Polydor | PZCD100 | 1990 | £3 | £8 | |
| All Along The Watchtower | 7" | Track | 604025 | 1968 | £1.50 | £4 | |
| All I Want | 7" EP | Visadisc | 348 | 1967 | £7.50 | £15 | French |
| And A Happy New Year | 7" | Reprise | PRO595 | 196– | £25 | £50 | US promo |
| Angel | 7" | Track | 2094007 | 1971 | £1.50 | £4 | |
| Are You Experienced | LP | Track | 612001 | 1967 | £15 | £30 | mono |
| Are You Experienced | LP | Track | 613001 | 1967 | £20 | £40 | stereo |
| Are You Experienced? | CD | Polydor | C88CD111 | 1988 | £5 | £12 | HMV boxed set |
| Axis: Bold As Love | LP | Reprise | R6281 | 1968 | £75 | £150 | US mono |
| Axis: Bold As Love | LP | Track | 612003 | 1967 | £20 | £40 | mono |
| Axis: Bold As Love | LP | Track | 612003 | 1967 | £37.50 | £75 | with lyric sheet |
| Axis: Bold As Love | LP | Track | 613003 | 1967 | £15 | £30 | stereo |
| Band Of Gypsys | LP | Track | 2406002 | 1970 | £6 | £15 | kaftan gatefold |
| Band Of Gypsys | LP | Track | 2406002 | 1970 | £20 | £40 | puppet cover |
| Between The Lines | CD | Reprise | PROCD4541 | 1990 | £10 | £25 | US promo sampler |
| Burning Of The Midnight Lamp | 7" | Track | 604007 | 1967 | £1.50 | £4 | |
| Calling Long Distance | CD | Univibes | UV001 | 1992 | £10 | £25 | Irish |
| Cornerstones | CD | Polydor | 8472312 | 1990 | £30 | £60 | promo box set with video |
| Crash Landing | LP | Polydor | 2310398 | 1975 | £4 | £10 | |
| Crosstown Traffic | 7" | Track | 604029 | 1969 | £2 | £5 | |
| Cry Of Love | LP | Track | 2408101 | 1971 | £6 | £15 | |
| Cry Of Love | LP | Track | 2408101 | 1971 | £500 | £750 | red vinyl |
| Electric Hendrix | LP | Track | 2856002 | 1968 | £330 | £500 | |
| Electric Ladyland | LP | Track | 613008/9 | 1968 | £150 | £250 | mono double |
| Electric Ladyland Part 1 | LP | Track | 613010 | 1968 | £8 | £20 | |
| Electric Ladyland Part 2 | LP | Track | 613017 | 1968 | £8 | £20 | |
| Exp Over Sweden | CD | Univibes | UV002 | 1994 | £10 | £25 | Irish |
| Fire | 7" | Track | 604033 | 1969 | £2 | £5 | |
| Gloria | 7" | Polydor | JIMI1 | 1978 | £2 | £5 | 1 sided |
| Gypsy Eyes | 7" | Track | 2094010 | 1971 | £4 | £8 | picture sleeve |
| Hear My Train A-Comin' | 7" EP | Reprise | K14286 | 1973 | £1.50 | £4 | |
| Hey Joe | 7" EP | Barclay | 071111 | 1967 | £20 | £40 | French |
| Hey Joe | 7" | Polydor | 56139 | 1966 | £2 | £5 | |
| In The West | CD | Polydor | 8313122 | 1989 | £5 | £12 | |
| Isle Of Wight | LP | Polydor | 2302016 | 1971 | £4 | £10 | |
| Jimi Hendrix | LP | Polydor | 2625038 | 1980 | £37.50 | £75 | German, 12 LP boxed set |
| Jimi Hendrix | LP | St. Michael | 2891139 | 1978 | £25 | £50 | |
| Jimi In Denmark | CD | Univibes | UV003 | 1995 | £10 | £25 | Irish |
| Jimi Plays Berkeley | CD-s | BMG | 791168 | 1992 | £2 | £5 | |
| Johnny B Goode | 7" | Polydor | 2001277 | 1972 | £1.50 | £4 | |
| Nine To The Universe | LP | Polydor | 2344155 | 1980 | £5 | £12 | |
| Peel Sessions | CD-s | Strange Fruit | SFPSCD065 | 1988 | £2 | £5 | |
| Purple Haze | CD-s | Polydor | PZCD33 | 1989 | £2 | £5 | |
| Purple Haze | 7" | Track | 604001 | 1967 | £1.50 | £4 | |
| Purple Haze | 7" | Track | 604001 | 1967 | £2.50 | £6 | white Track label |
| Radio One | CD | Ryko | | 1989 | £20 | £40 | US promo picture disc, alternate Drivin' South |
| Smash Hits | LP | Reprise | MS2025 | 1969 | £20 | £40 | US, with poster |
| Smash Hits | LP | Track | 612/613004 | 1968 | £8 | £20 | |
| Stages 1967–1970 | CD | Reprise | PROCD5194 | 1991 | £10 | £25 | US promo sampler |
| Ultimate Experience | CD | Polydor | 5172352 | 1992 | £5 | £12 | picture disc |
| Voodoo Chile | 7" | Track | 2095001 | 1970 | £2 | £5 | picture sleeve |
| War Heroes | LP | Polydor | 2302020 | 1972 | £4 | £10 | |
| Wind Cries Mary | 7" EP | Barclay | 071157 | 1967 | £20 | £40 | French |
| Wind Cries Mary | 7" | Track | 604004 | 1967 | £1.50 | £4 | |

## HENDRIX, JIMI & CURTIS KNIGHT

| | | | | | |
|---|---|---|---|---|---|
| Ballad Of Jimi | 7" | London | HL10321 | 1970 £1.50 £4 | |
| Get That Feeling | LP | London | HAU/SHU8349 | 1968 £5 £12 | |
| How Would You Feel | 7" | Track | 604009 | 1967 £2 £5 | |
| Hush Now | 7" | London | HL10160 | 1967 £2 £5 | |
| No Such Animal | 7" | RCA | RCA2033 | 1970 £4 £8 | picture sleeve |
| Strange Things | LP | London | HAU/SHU8369 | 1968 £5 £12 | |

## HENDRIX, MARGIE

| | | | | | |
|---|---|---|---|---|---|
| I Call You Lover | 7" | Mercury | MF976 | 1966 £1.50 £4 | |
| Restless | 7" | Mercury | MF1001 | 1967 £4 £8 | |

## HENKE, MEL

| | | | | | |
|---|---|---|---|---|---|
| Mel Henke | LP | Contemporary | LAC12112 | 1958 £8 £20 | |

## HENLEY, LARRY

| | | | | | |
|---|---|---|---|---|---|
| My Reasons For Living | 7" | Hickory | 451272 | 1964 £5 £10 | |

## HENNESSYS

| | | | | | |
|---|---|---|---|---|---|
| Road And The Miles | LP | Cambrian | | 1969 £30 £60 | |

## HENNIG, SONNY

| | | | | | |
|---|---|---|---|---|---|
| Tranengas | LP | Kuckuck | 2375008 | 1971 £15 £30 | German |

## HENRI, ADRIAN

| | | | | | |
|---|---|---|---|---|---|
| Adrian Henri | LP | Charivari | | 196– £15 £30 | |
| Adrian Henri And Hugo Williams | LP | Argo | PLP1194 | 196– £15 £30 | |

## HENRY, BOB

| | | | | | |
|---|---|---|---|---|---|
| I Need Someone | 7" | Philips | BF1450 | 1965 £2.50 £6 | |

## HENRY, CLARENCE 'FROGMAN'

| | | | | | |
|---|---|---|---|---|---|
| Ain't Got No Home | 7" | London | HLN8389 | 1957 £75 £150 | |
| Ain't Got No Home | 7" | London | HLU10025 | 1966 £1.50 £4 | |
| Alive And Well And Living In New Orleans | LP | Roulette | SR42039 | 1969 £4 £10 | US |
| But I Do | 7" | Pye | 7N25078 | 1961 £1.50 £4 | |
| Clarence Henry Hit Parade | 7" EP | Pye | NEP44007 | 1961 £15 £30 | |
| Dream Myself A Sweetheart | 7" | Pye | 7N25141 | 1962 £1.50 £4 | |
| Jealous Kind | 7" | Pye | 7N25169 | 1962 £1.50 £4 | |
| Little Green Frog | 7" | London | HLU9936 | 1964 £1.50 £4 | |
| Little Too Much | 7" | Pye | 7N25123 | 1962 £1.50 £4 | |
| Lonely Street | 7" | Pye | 7N25108 | 1961 £1.50 £4 | |
| Standing In The Need Of Love | 7" | Pye | 7N25115 | 1961 £1.50 £4 | |
| You Always Hurt The One You Love | LP | Pye | NPL28017 | 1961 £15 £30 | |
| You Always Hurt The One You Love | 7" | Pye | 7N25089 | 1961 £1.50 £4 | |

## HENRY, PIERRE

| | | | | | |
|---|---|---|---|---|---|
| Messe de Liverpool | LP | Philips | 6510001 | 1970 £4 £10 | French |
| Messe pour le temps présent | LP | Philips | 836893 | 1965 £5 £12 | French |

## HENRY, ROBERT

| | | | | | |
|---|---|---|---|---|---|
| Walk Away Like A Winner | 7" | Philips | BF1476 | 1966 £12.50 £25 | |

## HENRY III

| | | | | | |
|---|---|---|---|---|---|
| I'll Reach The End | 7" | Island | WI3081 | 1967 £5 £10 | Don Tony Lee B side |
| So Much Love | 7" | RCA | RCA1568 | 1967 £2.50 £6 | |
| Thank You Girl | 7" | Island | WI3078 | 1967 £5 £10 | |

## HENRY COW

Of all the groups that followed in the wake of Soft Machine, Henry Cow presented the most avant-garde approach. The music on *Legend* and its companions was marketed as rock for want of an alternative category, but in truth the distance between it and *Johnny B. Goode* is about as far as one can get. In essence, the group achieved the difficult feat of creating an extensively improvised music that sounds very little like jazz, partly through the use of unusual timbres – bassoon as a leading voice, for instance – and partly through the use of spiky melody lines and lop-sided rhythms. (Drummer Chris Cutler refers to the album as *Leg End*, incidentally, which is why the cover design features a sock!) Henry Cow's musicians, who include Cutler, guitarist Fred Frith and reed player Lindsay Cooper, have been extraordinarily prolific ever since – to the extent that an entire rock music genre has developed around them – much of it being released through the label that Cutler co-founded, Recommended Records.

| | | | | | |
|---|---|---|---|---|---|
| Concerts | LP | Caroline | CAD3002 | 1976 £5 £12 | double |
| In Praise Of Learning | LP | Virgin | V2027 | 1975 £4 £10 | with Slapp Happy |
| Legend | LP | Virgin | V2005 | 1973 £4 £10 | |
| Unrest | LP | Virgin | V2011 | 1974 £4 £10 | |
| Western Culture | LP | Broadcast | BC1 | 1978 £4 £10 | |

## HENRY TREE

| | | | | | |
|---|---|---|---|---|---|
| Electric Holy Man | LP | Mainstream | S6129 | 1970 £30 £60 | US |

## HENSKE, JUDY

| | | | | | |
|---|---|---|---|---|---|
| Death Defying | LP | Reprise | RS6203 | 1965 £6 £15 | |
| High Flying Bird | LP | Elektra | EKL/EKS7241 | 1964 £6 £15 | US |
| Judy Henske | LP | Elektra | EKL/EKS7231 | 1963 £6 £15 | US |
| Little Bit Of Sunshine | LP | Mercury | MG2/SR61010 | 1965 £6 £15 | US |

## HENSKE, JUDY & JERRY YESTER

| | | | | | |
|---|---|---|---|---|---|
| Farewell Aldebaran | LP | Straight | STS1052 | 1969 £10 £25 | |

| | | | | | | | |
|---|---|---|---|---|---|---|---|
| Road To Nowhere | 7" | Reprise | RS20485 | 1966 | £1.50 | £4 | |
| Rosebud | LP | Reprise | RS6426 | 1971 | £6 | £15 | *US* |

## HENSLEY, ROBERT HENRY

| | | | | | | |
|---|---|---|---|---|---|---|
| You're Gonna See Me Cry | 7" | Polydor | 56295 | 1968 | £2 | £5 |

## HENSON, NICKY

| | | | | | | |
|---|---|---|---|---|---|---|
| Till I See You Cry | 7" | Parlophone | R4976 | 1963 | £1.50 | £4 |

## HEP STARS

This Swedish group had future Abba star Benny Andersson as keyboard player and songwriter.

| | | | | | | | |
|---|---|---|---|---|---|---|---|
| Hep Stars | LP | Olga | LP004 | 1966 | £10 | £25 | *Swedish* |
| It's Been A Long Long Time | LP | Cupol | CLPNS342 | 1968 | £6 | £15 | *Swedish* |
| Jul Med | LP | Olga | LP006 | 1966 | £6 | £15 | *Swedish* |
| Let It Be Me | 7" | Olga | OLE13 | 1968 | £20 | £40 | |
| Malaika | 7" | Olga | OLE14 | 1968 | £5 | £10 | |
| Malaika | 7" | Olga | OLE14 | 1968 | £10 | £20 | *picture sleeve* |
| Pa Svenska | LP | Olga | LP011 | 196– | £8 | £20 | *Swedish* |
| Songs We Sang | LP | Olga | LP007 | 196– | £8 | £20 | *Swedish* |
| Sunny Girl | 7" | Decca | F22446 | 1966 | £10 | £20 | |
| Wedding | 7" | Olga | OLE001 | 1967 | £5 | £10 | |

## HEPTONES

| | | | | | | | |
|---|---|---|---|---|---|---|---|
| Better Days | LP | Third World | TDWD1 | 1978 | £4 | £10 | |
| Change Is Gonna Come | 7" | Studio One | SO2005 | 1967 | £6 | £12 | |
| Cool Rasta | LP | Trojan | TRLS128 | 1976 | £5 | £12 | |
| Cry Baby Cry | 7" | Studio One | SO2049 | 1968 | £6 | £12 | |
| Dock Of The Bay | 7" | Studio One | SO2052 | 1968 | £6 | £12 | *King Rocky B side* |
| Equal Rights | 7" | Coxsone | CS7068 | 1968 | £5 | £10 | |
| Fat Girl | 7" | Studio One | SO2014 | 1967 | £6 | £12 | *Delroy Wilson B side* |
| Good Life | LP | Greensleeves | GREL6 | 1979 | £4 | £10 | |
| Gunmen Coming To Town | 7" | Rio | R104 | 1966 | £4 | £8 | *Tommy McCook B side* |
| Heptones | LP | Studio One | SOL9002 | 1967 | £50 | £100 | |
| Heptones And Friends | LP | Trojan | TBL183 | 1972 | £6 | £15 | |
| Heptones And Friends Vol. 2 | LP | Attack | ATLP1001 | 1975 | £6 | £15 | |
| Hurry Up | 7" | Upsetter | US339 | 1970 | £1.50 | £4 | |
| I Shall Be Released | 7" | Bamboo | BAM11 | 1969 | £1.50 | £4 | |
| I Shall Be Released | 7" | Studio One | SO2083 | 1969 | £6 | £12 | |
| If I Knew | 7" | Studio One | SO2021 | 1967 | £6 | £12 | |
| Love Won't Come Easy | 7" | Coxsone | CS7052 | 1968 | £5 | £10 | |
| Nightfood | LP | Island | ILPS9381 | 1976 | £5 | £12 | |
| On Top | LP | Studio One | SOL9010 | 1968 | £50 | £100 | |
| Only Sixteen | 7" | Studio One | SO2033 | 1967 | £6 | £12 | |
| Party Time | LP | Island | ILPS9456 | 1977 | £5 | £12 | |
| Party Time | 7" | Studio One | SO2055 | 1968 | £6 | £12 | |
| Schoolgirls | 7" | Caltone | TONE105 | 1967 | £4 | £8 | |
| Soul Power | 7" | Coxsone | CS7082 | 1968 | £5 | £10 | |
| We've Got Love | 7" | Ska Beat | JB266 | 1967 | £5 | £10 | |
| Why Did You Leave | 7" | Studio One | SO2026 | 1967 | £6 | £12 | *Gaylads B side* |
| Why Must I | 7" | Studio One | SO2027 | 1967 | £6 | £12 | *Slim Smith B side* |

## HERB & KAY

| | | | | | | |
|---|---|---|---|---|---|---|
| This Ole House | 7" | Parlophone | MSP6127 | 1954 | £5 | £10 |

## HERBAL MIXTURE

Blues guitarist Tony McPhee led this psychedelic pop band, which also included fellow member of the Groundhogs, bass player Pete Cruickshank.

| | | | | | | |
|---|---|---|---|---|---|---|
| Love That's Died | 7" | Columbia | DB8021 | 1966 | £37.50 | £75 |
| Machines | 7" | Columbia | DB8083 | 1966 | £37.50 | £75 |

## HERBIE & THE ROYALISTS

| | | | | | | |
|---|---|---|---|---|---|---|
| Soul Of The Matter | LP | Saga | FID2121 | 1968 | £6 | £15 |

## HERBIE'S PEOPLE

| | | | | | | |
|---|---|---|---|---|---|---|
| One Little Smile | 7" | CBS | 202058 | 1966 | £2 | £5 |
| Residential Area | 7" | CBS | 202584 | 1967 | £2 | £5 |
| Sweet And Tender Romance | 7" | CBS | 202005 | 1965 | £7.50 | £15 |

## HERD

| | | | | | | | |
|---|---|---|---|---|---|---|---|
| From The Underworld | 7" | Fontana | TF856 | 1967 | £1.50 | £4 | |
| Game | 7" | Fontana | TF1011 | 1969 | £1.50 | £4 | |
| Goodbye Baby Goodbye | 7" | Parlophone | R5284 | 1965 | £5 | £10 | |
| I Can Fly | 7" | Fontana | TF819 | 1967 | £1.50 | £4 | |
| I Don't Want Our Loving To Die | 7" | Fontana | TF925 | 1968 | £1.50 | £4 | |
| Lookin' Thru You | LP | Fontana | SRF67579 | 1968 | £8 | £20 | *US* |
| Nostalgia | LP | Bumble | GEMP5001 | 1972 | £5 | £12 | |
| Paradise Lost | LP | Fontana | (S)TL5458 | 1968 | £10 | £25 | |
| Paradise Lost | 7" | Fontana | TF887 | 1967 | £1.50 | £4 | |
| She Was Really Saying Something | 7" | Parlophone | R5353 | 1965 | £7.50 | £15 | |
| So Much In Love | 7" | Parlophone | R5413 | 1966 | £10 | £20 | |
| Sunshine Cottage | 7" | Fontana | TF975 | 1968 | £1.50 | £4 | |

## HERDSMEN

| | | | | | | |
|---|---|---|---|---|---|---|
| Blow In Paris | 10" LP | Vogue | LDE058 | 1954 | £5 | £12 |

| | | | | | | | |
|---|---|---|---|---|---|---|---|
| Blow In Paris Vol. 2 | 10" LP | Vogue | LDE091 | 1954 | £5 | £12 | |

## HERETICS
| | | | | | | | |
|---|---|---|---|---|---|---|---|
| Evening With The Heretics | LP | Heritage | 101 | 1975 | £8 | £20 | |

## HERITAGE
| | | | | | | | |
|---|---|---|---|---|---|---|---|
| Remorse Code | LP | Rondelet | | 1982 | £4 | £10 | |
| Strange Place To Be | 7" | Rondelet | ROUND8 | 1981 | £2.50 | £6 | |

## HERMAN, BONGO
| | | | | | | | |
|---|---|---|---|---|---|---|---|
| True Grit | 7" | Song Bird | SB1018 | 1970 | £1.50 | £4 | |

## HERMAN, WOODY
| | | | | | | | |
|---|---|---|---|---|---|---|---|
| At Carnegie Hall Vol. 1 | 10" LP | MGM | D108 | 1952 | £8 | £20 | |
| At Carnegie Hall Vol. 2 | 10" LP | MGM | D110 | 1953 | £8 | £20 | |
| At The Monterey Jazz Festival | LP | London | LTZK15200/ SAHK6100 | 1960 | £5 | £12 | |
| Blues Groove | LP | Capitol | T784 | 1957 | £6 | £15 | |
| Classics In Jazz | LP | Capitol | T20809 | 1965 | £4 | £10 | |
| Classics In Jazz | 10" LP | Capitol | LC6560 | 1952 | £8 | £20 | |
| Fancy Woman | 7" | London | HL8031 | 1954 | £7.50 | £15 | |
| Fourth Herd | LP | Jazzland | JLP17 | 1960 | £5 | £12 | |
| Girl Upstairs | 7" | Capitol | CL14333 | 1955 | £1.50 | £4 | |
| Herd From Mars Vol. 1 | 7" EP | London | REP1001 | 1954 | £2 | £5 | |
| Herd From Mars Vol. 2 | 7" EP | London | REP1002 | 1955 | £2 | £5 | |
| Herd Rides Again | LP | Top Rank | 35038 | 1959 | £5 | £12 | |
| Here's Herman | 10" LP | Columbia | 33S1060 | 1955 | £8 | £20 | |
| Hush | 7" | Chess | CRS8095 | 1969 | £1.50 | £4 | |
| Jackpot! | LP | Capitol | T748 | 1956 | £6 | £15 | |
| Jazz – The Utmost! | LP | Columbia | 33CX10129 | 1959 | £8 | £20 | |
| Men From Mars | 10" LP | London | HAPB1018 | 1954 | £8 | £20 | |
| Mexican Hat Trick | 7" | Capitol | CL14231 | 1955 | £1.50 | £4 | |
| Moody Woody | LP | Top Rank | BUY009 | 1960 | £5 | £12 | |
| Music For Tired Lovers | LP | Philips | BBL7056 | 1955 | £6 | £15 | ... with Erroll Garner |
| Muskrat Ramble | 7" | Capitol | CL14183 | 1954 | £2.50 | £6 | |
| Sequence In Jazz | 10" LP | Columbia | 33S1068 | 1955 | £8 | £20 | |
| Sorry 'Bout The Whole Darned Thing | 7" | London | HL8122 | 1955 | £6 | £12 | |
| Stomping At The Savoy | 10" LP | London | HAPB1014 | 1953 | £8 | £20 | |
| Summer Sequence | 10" LP | Fontana | TFR6015 | 1958 | £6 | £15 | |
| Three Herds | LP | Philips | BBL7123 | 1958 | £6 | £15 | |
| Thundering Herds Vol. 1 | LP | CBS | BPG62158 | 1964 | £4 | £10 | |
| Thundering Herds Vol. 2 | LP | CBS | BPG62159 | 1964 | £4 | £10 | |
| Thundering Herds Vol. 3 | LP | CBS | BPG62160 | 1964 | £4 | £10 | |
| Twelve Shades Of Blue | LP | Philips | BBL7124 | 1957 | £6 | £15 | |
| Woodchopper's Ball | LP | Brunswick | LAT8092 | 1956 | £6 | £15 | |
| Woody Herman | LP | HMV | CLP1130 | 1957 | £6 | £15 | |
| Woody Herman Band | 10" LP | Capitol | LCT6014 | 1955 | £8 | £20 | |
| Wooftie | 7" | London | HL8013 | 1954 | £7.50 | £15 | |

## HERMAN'S HERMITS
| | | | | | | | |
|---|---|---|---|---|---|---|---|
| Best Of Herman's Hermits | LP | Columbia | SCXC27 | 196– | £6 | £15 | export |
| Best Of Herman's Hermits Vol. 2 | LP | Columbia | SCXC32 | 1966 | £6 | £15 | export |
| Blaze | LP | Columbia | SCXC35 | 196– | £8 | £20 | export |
| Both Sides Of Herman's Hermits | LP | Columbia | SX6084 | 1966 | £5 | £12 | |
| Dandy | 7" EP | Columbia | SEG8520 | 1967 | £5 | £10 | |
| Herman's Hermits | LP | Columbia | 33SX1727 | 1965 | £5 | £12 | |
| Herman's Hermits | LP | Regal | SREG1117 | 196– | £5 | £12 | export |
| Herman's Hermits' Hits | 7" EP | Columbia | SEG8442 | 1965 | £4 | £8 | |
| Hermania | 7" EP | Columbia | SEG8380 | 1965 | £5 | £10 | |
| Hold On – Soundtrack Songs | 7" EP | Columbia | SEG8503 | 1966 | £5 | £10 | |
| I'm Henry VIII, I Am | 7" EP | Columbia | ESRF1707 | 1965 | £5 | £10 | French |
| I'm Into Something Good | 7" EP | Columbia | ESRF1615 | 1964 | £5 | £10 | French |
| Je suis anglais | 7" EP | Columbia | ESRF1750 | 1966 | £7.50 | £15 | French |
| London Look | 7" EP | Yardley | SLE15 | 1967 | £7.50 | £15 | French, promo |
| Mrs. Brown You've Got A Lovely Daughter | LP | Columbia | SCX6303 | 1968 | £5 | £12 | |
| Mrs. Brown You've Got A Lovely Daughter | 7" EP | Columbia | ESRF1663 | 1965 | £5 | £10 | French |
| Mrs. Brown You've Got A Lovely Daughter | 7" EP | Columbia | SEG8440 | 1965 | £4 | £8 | |
| Museum | 7" EP | Columbia | ESRF1865 | 1967 | £5 | £10 | French |
| Must To Avoid | 7" EP | Columbia | SEG8477 | 1966 | £4 | £8 | |
| There's A Kind Of Hush | LP | Columbia | SCXC34 | 196– | £8 | £20 | export |
| There's A Kind Of Hush | LP | Columbia | SX/SCX6174 | 1967 | £5 | £12 | |
| There's A Kind Of Hush | 7" EP | Columbia | ESRF1846 | 1967 | £5 | £10 | French |
| Train | 7" | Buddah | BDS700 | 1974 | £10 | £20 | |

## HERO
| | | | | | | | |
|---|---|---|---|---|---|---|---|
| Hero | LP | Ariola | 87304 | 1973 | £30 | £60 | German |

## HEROLD, TED
| | | | | | | | |
|---|---|---|---|---|---|---|---|
| Ted Herold | LP | Polydor | 46754 | 1961 | £37.50 | £75 | German |

## HERON
| | | | | | | | |
|---|---|---|---|---|---|---|---|
| Bye And Bye | 7" | Dawn | DNX2509 | 1971 | £2 | £5 | picture sleeve |
| Heron | LP | Dawn | DNLS3010 | 1970 | £20 | £40 | |
| Take Me Back Home | 7" | Dawn | DNS1015 | 1970 | £1.50 | £4 | |
| Twice As Nice | LP | Dawn | DNLS3025 | 1972 | £20 | £40 | double |

## HERON, MIKE
| | | | | | | | |
|---|---|---|---|---|---|---|---|
| Diamond Of Dream | LP | Bronze | ILPS9460 | 1977 | £4 | £10 | |
| Mike Heron | LP | Casablanca | NBLP7186 | 1980 | £5 | £12 | US |
| Mike Heron's Reputation | LP | Neighborhood | NBH80637 | 1975 | £4 | £10 | |
| Smiling Men With Bad Reputations | LP | Island | ILPS9146 | 1971 | £4 | £10 | |

## HERSANG, JIMMY JAMES
| | | | | | | | |
|---|---|---|---|---|---|---|---|
| Bewildered And Blue | 7" | Dice | CC4 | 1962 | £5 | £10 | |

## HERVEY, PAT & ART SNIDER
| | | | | | | | |
|---|---|---|---|---|---|---|---|
| Can't Get You Out Of My Mind | 7" | President | PT110 | 1967 | £1.50 | £4 | |

## HESITATIONS
| | | | | | | | |
|---|---|---|---|---|---|---|---|
| Born Free | 7" | London | HLR10180 | 1968 | £2.50 | £6 | |
| Impossible Dream | 7" | London | HLR10198 | 1968 | £2 | £5 | |
| New Born Free | LP | London | HAR/SHR8360 | 1968 | £4 | £10 | |

## HESTER, CAROLYN
| | | | | | | | |
|---|---|---|---|---|---|---|---|
| At Town Hall | LP | Dot | DLP3649 | 1966 | £4 | £10 | |
| Carolyn Hester | LP | CBS | (S)BPG62033 | 1966 | £4 | £10 | |
| Carolyn Hester | LP | Columbia | CL1796/CS8596 | 1962 | £5 | £12 | US |
| Carolyn Hester Coalition | LP | Pye | NSPL28121 | 1969 | £4 | £10 | |
| That's My Song | LP | Dot | DLP3604/25604 | 1964 | £4 | £10 | US |
| This Is My Living | LP | Columbia | CL2031/CS8831 | 1963 | £4 | £10 | US |
| This Life I'm Living | LP | Realm | RM2338 | 1967 | £4 | £10 | |

## HEWETT SISTERS
| | | | | | | | |
|---|---|---|---|---|---|---|---|
| Baby-O | 7" | HMV | POP567 | 1959 | £4 | £8 | |

## HEWITT, BEN
| | | | | | | | |
|---|---|---|---|---|---|---|---|
| Break It Up | 7" EP | Mercury | ZEP10035 | 1959 | £50 | £100 | |
| For Quite A While | 7" | Mercury | AMT1055 | 1959 | £6 | £12 | |
| I Want A Girl | 7" | Mercury | AMT1084 | 1960 | £10 | £20 | |
| You Break Me Up | 7" | Mercury | AMT1041 | 1959 | £20 | £40 | |

## HEYWOOD, ANNE
| | | | | | | | |
|---|---|---|---|---|---|---|---|
| I'd Rather Have Roses | 7" | Top Rank | JAR130 | 1959 | £1.50 | £4 | |

## HEYWOOD, EDDIE
| | | | | | | | |
|---|---|---|---|---|---|---|---|
| Soft Summer Breeze | 7" | Mercury | 7MT131 | 1957 | £1.50 | £4 | |

## HI FI FOUR
| | | | | | | | |
|---|---|---|---|---|---|---|---|
| Davy You Upset My Life | 7" | Parlophone | MSP6210 | 1956 | £62.50 | £125 | |

## HI FI'S
| | | | | | | | |
|---|---|---|---|---|---|---|---|
| Baby's In Black | 7" | Pye | 7N15788 | 1965 | £2.50 | £6 | |
| I Keep Forgettin' | 7" | Pye | 7N15710 | 1964 | £7.50 | £15 | |
| It's Gonna Be Morning | 7" | Alp | 595010 | 1966 | £12.50 | £25 | |
| Snakes And Hi Fi's | LP | Star Club | STY158035 | 1967 | £25 | £50 | German |
| Take Me Or Leave Me | 7" | Piccadilly | 7N35130 | 1963 | £1.50 | £4 | |
| Will Ya Won't Ya | 7" | Pye | 7N15635 | 1964 | £1.50 | £4 | |

## HI LITERS
| | | | | | | | |
|---|---|---|---|---|---|---|---|
| Dance Me To Death | 7" | Mercury | AMT1011 | 1958 | £37.50 | £75 | |
| For Your Precious Love | LP | Dandee | DLP206 | 195– | £6 | £15 | US |

## HI-LO'S
| | | | | | | | |
|---|---|---|---|---|---|---|---|
| All Over The Place | LP | Philips | SBBL589 | 1960 | £4 | £10 | stereo |
| All That Jazz | LP | Columbia | CL1259/CS8077 | 1959 | £4 | £10 | US |
| Broadway Playbill | LP | Columbia | CL1416/CS8213 | 1959 | £4 | £10 | US |
| Hi-Lo's | LP | Kapp | KL1027 | 195– | £4 | £10 | US |
| Hi-Lo's, I Presume | LP | Starlite | 7007 | 195– | £5 | £12 | US |
| In Stereo | LP | Omega | 11 | 195– | £4 | £10 | US |
| Listen To The Hi-Lo's | LP | Starlite | 7006 | 195– | £5 | £12 | US |
| Love Nest | LP | Philips | BBL7235 | 1958 | £4 | £10 | |
| Now Hear This | LP | Philips | BBL7177 | 1957 | £4 | £10 | |
| On Hand | LP | Kapp | KL1194 | 195– | £4 | £10 | US |
| On Hand | LP | Starlite | 7008 | 195– | £5 | £12 | US |
| Suddenly It's The Hi-Lo's | LP | Philips | BBL7154 | 1957 | £4 | £10 | |
| They Didn't Believe Me | 7" EP | London | REU1110 | 1958 | £2.50 | £6 | |
| Under Glass | LP | London | HAU2026 | 1957 | £5 | £12 | |
| Under Glass | 7" EP | London | REU1077 | 1957 | £2.50 | £6 | |

## HI-NUMBERS
| | | | | | | | |
|---|---|---|---|---|---|---|---|
| Heart Of Stone | 7" | Decca | F12233 | 1965 | £12.50 | £25 | |

## HI-SPOTS
| | | | | | | | |
|---|---|---|---|---|---|---|---|
| Lend Me Your Comb | 7" | Melodisc | 1457 | 1958 | £5 | £10 | |
| Secretly | 7" | Melodisc | 1473 | 1958 | £2.50 | £6 | |

## HI-TENSION
| | | | | | | | |
|---|---|---|---|---|---|---|---|
| Hi-Tension | 12" | Island | IPR2007 | 1977 | £2.50 | £6 | |
| There's A Reason | 12" | Island | 12WIP6493 | 1979 | £3 | £8 | |

## HI-TONES
| | | | | | | | |
|---|---|---|---|---|---|---|---|
| Ten Virgins | 7" | Island | WI086 | 1963 | £5 | £10 | |

| | | | | | | | |
|---|---|---|---|---|---|---|---|
| You Hold The Key | 7" | R&B | JB123 | 1963 | £5 | £10 | Don Drummond B side |

## HIATT, JOHN
| | | | | | | | |
|---|---|---|---|---|---|---|---|
| Hanging Round The Observatory | LP | Epic | KE32688 | 1974 | £5 | £12 | US |
| Overcoats | LP | Epic | 33190 | 1975 | £4 | £10 | US |

## HIBBLER, AL
| | | | | | | | |
|---|---|---|---|---|---|---|---|
| After The Lights Go Down Low | 7" | Brunswick | 05552 | 1956 | £1.50 | £4 | |
| Around The Corner From The Blues | 7" | Brunswick | 05703 | 1957 | £1.50 | £4 | |
| Danny Boy | 7" | London | HL7086 | 1959 | £1.50 | £4 | export |
| Eleventh Hour Melody | 7" | Brunswick | 05523 | 1956 | £1.50 | £4 | |
| He | 7" | Brunswick | 05492 | 1955 | £1.50 | £4 | |
| Now I Lay Me Down To Dream | 7" | London | HL8184 | 1955 | £6 | £12 | |
| They Say You're Laughing At Me | 7" | Brunswick | 05454 | 1955 | £4 | £8 | |
| Unchained Melody | 7" | Brunswick | 05420 | 1955 | £5 | £10 | |

## HICKEY, EDDIE
| | | | | | | | |
|---|---|---|---|---|---|---|---|
| Another Sleepless NIght | 7" | Decca | F11241 | 1960 | £1.50 | £4 | |

## HICKEY, ERSEL
| | | | | | | | |
|---|---|---|---|---|---|---|---|
| Don't Be Afraid Of Love | 7" | Fontana | H198 | 1959 | £20 | £40 | |

## HICKMAN, DWAYNE
| | | | | | | | |
|---|---|---|---|---|---|---|---|
| I'm A Lover Not A Fighter | 7" | Capitol | CL15164 | 1960 | £2 | £5 | |

## HICKORY
| | | | | | | | |
|---|---|---|---|---|---|---|---|
| Green Light | 7" | CBS | 3963 | 1969 | £10 | £20 | |

## HICKORY STIX
| | | | | | | | |
|---|---|---|---|---|---|---|---|
| Hello My Darling | 7" | Oak | RGJ149 | 1964 | £50 | £100 | |

## HICKORY WIND
| | | | | | | | |
|---|---|---|---|---|---|---|---|
| Hickory Wind | LP | Gigantic | | 1969 | £700 | £1000 | US |

## HICKS, COLIN & THE CABIN BOYS
| | | | | | | | |
|---|---|---|---|---|---|---|---|
| La Dee Dah | 7" | Pye | 7N15125 | 1958 | £2 | £5 | |
| Little Boy Blue | 7" | Pye | 7N15163 | 1958 | £2.50 | £6 | |
| Wild Eyes And Tender Lips | 7" | Pye | 7N15114 | 1957 | £5 | £10 | |

## HIDEAWAYS
| | | | | | | | |
|---|---|---|---|---|---|---|---|
| Hideout | 7" | Action | ACT4544 | 1969 | £1.50 | £4 | |

## HIFIS
| | | | | | | | |
|---|---|---|---|---|---|---|---|
| Snakes And Hifis | LP | Starclub | 158035STY | 1967 | £25 | £50 | German |

## HIGGINS, CHUCK
| | | | | | | | |
|---|---|---|---|---|---|---|---|
| Pachuko Hop | LP | Combo | LP300 | 1960 | £20 | £40 | US, Higgins cover |
| Pachuko Hop | LP | Combo | LP300 | 1960 | £50 | £100 | US, nude cover |

## HIGGINS, GARY
| | | | | | | | |
|---|---|---|---|---|---|---|---|
| Red Hash | LP | Nufusmoon | WM13673 | 1973 | £8 | £20 | |

## HIGGINS, LIZZIE
| | | | | | | | |
|---|---|---|---|---|---|---|---|
| Up And Awa Wi The Laverock | LP | Topic | 12TS260 | 1975 | £4 | £10 | |

## HIGGS, JOE
| | | | | | | | |
|---|---|---|---|---|---|---|---|
| I Am The Song | 7" | Island | WI3026 | 1967 | £5 | £10 | |
| Life Of Contradiction | LP | Grounation | GROL508 | 1975 | £6 | £15 | |
| Neighbour Neighbour | 7" | Coxsone | CS7004 | 1967 | £5 | £10 | Melodians B side |
| Unity Is Power | LP | Island | ILPS9535 | 1979 | £5 | £12 | |
| You Hurt My Soul | 7" | Island | WI3131 | 1968 | £5 | £10 | Lyn Taitt B side |

## HIGGS & WILSON
| | | | | | | | |
|---|---|---|---|---|---|---|---|
| Come On Home | 7" | Starlite | ST45042 | 1961 | £5 | £10 | |
| How Can I Be Sure | 7" | Blue Beat | BB95 | 1962 | £6 | £12 | |
| If You Want Pardon | 7" | Blue Beat | BB190 | 1963 | £6 | £12 | Baba Brooks B side |
| It Is The Day | 7" | Starlite | ST45036 | 1961 | £5 | £10 | |
| Lazy Saturday Night | 7" | Island | WI081 | 1963 | £5 | £10 | Prince Buster B side |
| Let Me Know | 7" | R&B | JB109 | 1963 | £5 | £10 | |
| Love Is Not For Me | 7" | Rio | R29 | 1964 | £5 | £10 | |
| Pretty Baby | 7" | Starlite | ST45035 | 1961 | £5 | £10 | |
| Sha Ba Ba | 7" | Starlite | ST45053 | 1961 | £5 | £10 | |
| When You Tell Me | 7" | Blue Beat | BB3 | 1960 | £6 | £12 | |

## HIGH
| | | | | | | | |
|---|---|---|---|---|---|---|---|
| Long Live The High | 7" | CBS | 4164 | 1969 | £2 | £5 | |

## HIGH & MIGHTY
| | | | | | | | |
|---|---|---|---|---|---|---|---|
| Tryin' To Stop Cryin' | 7" | HMV | POP1548 | 1966 | £10 | £20 | |

## HIGH BROOM
| | | | | | | | |
|---|---|---|---|---|---|---|---|
| Dancing In The Moonlight | 7" | Island | WIP6088 | 1970 | £5 | £10 | |

## HIGH KEYS
| | | | | | | | |
|---|---|---|---|---|---|---|---|
| Que Sera Sera | 7" | London | HLK9768 | 1963 | £5 | £10 | |

## HIGH LEVEL RANTERS
| | | | | | | | |
|---|---|---|---|---|---|---|---|
| Bonny Pit Laddie | LP | Topic | 212TS271/2 | 1975 £5 | £12 | double |
| English Sporting Ballads | LP | Broadside | BRO128 | 1977 £10 | £25 | side 2 by Martin Wyndham-Read |
| Four In A Bar | LP | Topic | 12TS388 | 1979 £4 | £10 | |
| High Level | LP | Trailer | LER2030 | 1971 £4 | £10 | |
| Keep Your Feet Still Geordie Hinnie | LP | Trailer | LER2020 | 1970 £4 | £10 | |
| Lads Of Northumbria | LP | Trailer | LER2007 | 1969 £4 | £10 | |
| Mile To Ride | LP | Trailer | LER2037 | 1972 £4 | £10 | |
| Northumberland For Ever | LP | Topic | 12TS186 | 1968 £5 | £12 | |
| Northumberland For Ever | LP | Topic | 12TS186 | 197– £4 | £10 | reissue with different cover |

## HIGH NUMBERS
'I'm The Face' is one of the most celebrated single rarities. The High Numbers was, of course, the original name of the Who. The group also recorded a version of 'The Kids Are Alright' before the name change, but this was only ever available as an acetate.

| | | | | | | |
|---|---|---|---|---|---|---|
| I'm The Face | 7" | Back Door | DOOR4 | 1980 £5 | £10 | picture sleeve |
| I'm The Face | 7" | Fontana | TF480 | 1964 £210 | £300 | best auctioned |

## HIGH SOCIETY
Graham Gouldman was the leader of High Society, which changed its name to the Manchester Mob for the next release.

| | | | | | |
|---|---|---|---|---|---|
| People Passing By | 7" | Fontana | TF771 | 1966 £5 | £10 |

## HIGH STREET EAST
| | | | | | |
|---|---|---|---|---|---|
| Newcastle Brown | 7" | Rubber | RUBBERONE | 1970 £5 | £10 |

## HIGH TIDE
High Tide were a heavy group from the time when the heavy metal style was not so rigidly set as to preclude a more experimental approach like this. A heavily distorted guitar is here partnered by an electric violin (courtesy of Simon House, who was later to join Hawkwind) and the two instruments manage to create an extraordinary maelstrom of sound. The singer, meanwhile, is a Jim Morrison sound-alike, the slightly doom-laden voice sounding very effective in this context.

| | | | | | |
|---|---|---|---|---|---|
| High Tide | LP | Liberty | LBS83294 | 1970 £15 | £30 |
| High Tide | LP | Psycho | PSYCHO27 | 1984 £4 | £10 |
| Sea Shanties | LP | Liberty | LBS83264 | 1969 £15 | £30 |
| Sea Shanties | LP | Psycho | PSYCHO26 | 1984 £4 | £10 |

## HIGH TIDE (2)
| | | | | | |
|---|---|---|---|---|---|
| Baby Dancing | 7" | Sunday Morning | | 1981 £2.50 | £6 | no picture sleeve |

## HIGH TREASON
| | | | | | | |
|---|---|---|---|---|---|---|
| High Treason | LP | Abbott | ABS1209 | 1968 £30 | £60 | US |

## HIGHTOWER, DEAN
| | | | | | |
|---|---|---|---|---|---|
| Twangy – With A Beat | LP | HMV | CLP1360 | 1960 £6 | £15 |

## HIGHTOWER, DONNA
| | | | | | |
|---|---|---|---|---|---|
| Take One | LP | Capitol | T1133 | 1959 £5 | £12 |

## HIGHTOWER, ROSETTA
| | | | | | |
|---|---|---|---|---|---|
| Hightower | LP | CBS | 64201 | 1971 £4 | £10 |

## HIGHWAYMEN
| | | | | | |
|---|---|---|---|---|---|
| Highwaymen | LP | HMV | CLP1510 | 1961 £4 | £10 |

## HIGNEY, KENNETH
| | | | | | | |
|---|---|---|---|---|---|---|
| Attic Demonstration | LP | Kebrutney | | 1976 £30 | £60 | US |

## HILARY HILARY
| | | | | | |
|---|---|---|---|---|---|
| How Come You're So Dumb | 7" | Modern | STP2 | 1980 £12.50 | £25 |

## HILDEBRAND, DIANE
| | | | | | |
|---|---|---|---|---|---|
| Early Morning Blues And Greens | LP | Elektra | EKS74031 | 1969 £4 | £10 |

## HILL, ANDREW
| | | | | | |
|---|---|---|---|---|---|
| Andrew!!! | LP | Blue Note | BLP/BST84203 | 1965 £10 | £25 |
| Black Fire | LP | Blue Note | BLP/BST84151 | 1963 £10 | £25 |
| Compulsion | LP | Blue Note | BLP/BST84217 | 1965 £8 | £20 |
| Grass Roots | LP | Blue Note | BST84303 | 1968 £5 | £12 |
| Judgement | LP | Blue Note | BLP/BST84159 | 1964 £8 | £20 |
| Lift Every Voice | LP | Blue Note | BST84330 | 1969 £5 | £12 |
| Point Of Departure | LP | Blue Note | BLP/BST84167 | 1964 £10 | £25 |
| Smoke Stack | LP | Blue Note | BLP/BST84160 | 1964 £10 | £25 |

## HILL, BENNY
| | | | | | |
|---|---|---|---|---|---|
| I Can't Tell A Waltz From A Tango | 7" | Decca | F10442 | 1955 £2 | £5 |
| Who Done It | 7" | Columbia | SCM5238 | 1956 £1.50 | £4 |

## HILL, BUNKER
| | | | | | |
|---|---|---|---|---|---|
| Hide And Go Seek | 7" | Stateside | SS135 | 1962 £2.50 | £6 |

## HILL, DAVID
| | | | | | |
|---|---|---|---|---|---|
| All Shook Up | 7" | Vogue | V9076 | 1957 £62.50 | £125 |

| That's Love | 7" | RCA | RCA1041 | 1958 £87.50 £175 | |

## HILL, JESSE
| Ooh Poo Pah Doo | 7" | London | HLU9117 | 1960 £5 £10 | |

## HILL, Z. Z.
| Brand New Z. Z. Hill | LP | Mojo | 2916013 | 1972 £4 £10 | |
| Gimme Gimme | 7" EP | Sue | IEP711 | 1966 £50 £100 | |
| I Keep On Loving You | 7" | United Artists | UP35727 | 1975 £1.50 £4 | |
| Make Me Yours | 7" | Action | ACT4532 | 1969 £5 £10 | |
| Someone To Love | 7" | R&B | MRB5005 | 1965 £7.50 £15 | |
| Whole Lot Of Soul | LP | Action | ACLP6004 | 1969 £8 £20 | |

## HILLAGE, STEVE
| Rainbow Dome Musick | LP | Virgin | VR1 | 1979 £5 £12 | clear vinyl |

## HILLERY, JANE
| You've Got A Hold On Me | 7" | Columbia | DB7918 | 1966 £5 £10 | |

## HILLMEN
| Hillmen | LP | Together | STT1012 | 1970 £6 £15 | US |

## HILLOW HAMMET
| Hammer | LP | House Of Fox | LP2 | 1968 £50 £100 | US |

## HILLSIDERS
| Our Country | LP | Polydor | 2460203 | 1973 £6 £15 | |

## HILLTOPPERS
| Alone | 7" | London | HLD9038 | 1960 £1.50 £4 | |
| Do The Bop | 7" | London | HLD8278 | 1956 £25 £50 | |
| Fallen Star | 7" | London | HLD8455 | 1957 £6 £12 | |
| From The Vine Came The Grape | 7" | London | HL8026 | 1954 £12.50 £25 | |
| Hilltoppers | LP | Dot | DLP3073 | 1958 £10 £25 | US |
| Hilltoppers Vol. 2 | 7" EP | London | RED1030 | 1955 £7.50 £15 | |
| Hilltoppers Vol. 3 | 7" EP | London | RED1099 | 1957 £7.50 £15 | |
| I'm Serious | 7" | London | HLD8441 | 1957 £6 £12 | |
| If I Didn't Care | 7" | London | HL8092 | 1954 £10 £20 | |
| Joker | 7" | London | HLD8528 | 1957 £7.50 £15 | |
| Kentuckian Song | 7" | London | HLD8168 | 1955 £10 £20 | |
| Marianne | 7" | London | HLD8381 | 1957 £7.50 £15 | |
| My Treasure | 7" | London | HLD8255 | 1956 £10 £20 | |
| Only You | 7" | London | HLD8221 | 1956 £10 £20 | |
| Poor Butterfly | 7" | London | HL8070 | 1954 £10 £20 | |
| Presenting The Hilltoppers | 7" EP | London | RED1012 | 1955 £7.50 £15 | |
| Searching | 7" | London | HLD8208 | 1955 £10 £20 | |
| So Tired | 7" | London | HLD8333 | 1956 £7.50 £15 | |
| Tops In Pops | LP | London | HAD2071 | 1957 £10 £25 | |
| Towering Hilltoppers | LP | London | HAD2029 | 1957 £10 £25 | |
| Tryin' | 7" | London | HLD8298 | 1956 £7.50 £15 | |
| Will You Remember | 7" | London | HL8081 | 1954 £20 £40 | |
| You Sure Look Good To Me | 7" | London | HLD8603 | 1958 £4 £8 | |
| You Try Somebody Else | 7" | London | HL8116 | 1955 £10 £20 | |

## HILTON, RONNIE
| Always | 7" EP | HMV | 7EG8121 | 1955 £2 £5 | |
| Around The World | 7" | HMV | POP338 | 1957 £1.50 £4 | |
| Blossom Fell | 7" | HMV | 7M285 | 1955 £4 £8 | |
| By The Fireside | 10" LP | HMV | DLP1109 | 1955 £6 £15 | |
| For Those In Love | 7" EP | HMV | 7EG8198 | 1957 £2 £5 | |
| For Those In Love No. 2 | 7" EP | HMV | 7EG8202 | 1957 £2 £5 | |
| For Those In Love No. 3 | 7" EP | HMV | 7EG8270 | 1957 £2 £5 | |
| He | 7" | HMV | 7M336 | 1955 £2.50 £6 | |
| Here Comes My Love | 7" | HMV | 7M382 | 1956 £2 £5 | |
| Hey There | 7" EP | HMV | 7EG8149 | 1955 £2 £5 | |
| Hit Parade | 7" EP | HMV | 7EG8446 | 1957 £2 £5 | |
| I'm Beginning To See The Light | LP | HMV | CLP1295 | 1959 £4 £10 | |
| My Loving Hands | 7" | HMV | 7M303 | 1955 £2.50 £6 | |
| No Other Love | 7" | HMV | 7M390 | 1956 £10 £20 | |
| Song For You | 7" EP | HMV | 7EG8375 | 1957 £2 £5 | |
| Two Different Worlds | 7" | HMV | POP274 | 1956 £4 £8 | |
| Who Are We | 7" | HMV | 7M413 | 1956 £4 £8 | |
| Wisdom Of A Fool | 7" | HMV | POP291 | 1957 £1.50 £4 | |
| Woman In Love | 7" | HMV | POP248 | 1956 £4 £8 | |
| Wonderful Wonderful | 7" | HMV | POP364 | 1957 £1.50 £4 | |
| Young And Foolish | 7" | HMV | 7M358 | 1956 £4 £8 | |

## HILTONAIRES
| Best Of The Hiltonaires | LP | Coxsone | CSL8004 | 1967 £50 £100 | |

## HIM & OTHERS
| I Mean It | 7" | Parlophone | R5510 | 1966 £250 £400 | best auctioned |

## HINDS, JUSTIN
| Botheration | 7" | Island | WI171 | 1965 £5 £10 | |
| Botheration | 7" | Treasure Isle | TI7063 | 1971 £1.50 £4 | Vincent Hinds B side |
| Carry Go Bring Come | 7" | Treasure Isle | TI7005 | 1967 £5 £10 | |
| Drink Milk | 7" | Duke | DU67 | 1970 £1.50 £4 | |

| | | | | | | | |
|---|---|---|---|---|---|---|---|
| Here I Stand | 7" | Treasure Isle | TI7002 | 1967 | £5 | £10 | |
| Higher The Monkey Climbs | 7" | Doctor Bird | DB1048 | 1966 | £5 | £10 | |
| Jordan River | 7" | Ska Beat | JB176 | 1964 | £5 | £10 | |
| Jump Out Of Frying Pan | 7" | Island | WI174 | 1965 | £5 | £10 | |
| Mighty Redeemer | 7" | Treasure Isle | TI7068 | 1971 | £1.50 | £4 | |
| Never Too Young | 7" | Island | WI244 | 1965 | £5 | £10 | *Skatalites B side* |
| On A Saturday Night | 7" | Island | WI3048 | 1967 | £5 | £10 | |
| On A Saturday Night | 7" | Treasure Isle | TI7014 | 1967 | £5 | £10 | |
| Once A Man | 7" | Treasure Isle | TI7017 | 1967 | £5 | £10 | *Tommy McCook B side* |
| Peace And Love | 7" | Island | WI236 | 1965 | £5 | £10 | *Skatalites B side* |
| Rub Up, Push Up | 7" | Island | WI194 | 1965 | £5 | £10 | |
| Say Me Say | 7" | Duke Reid | DR2511 | 1970 | £1.50 | £4 | |
| Turn Them Back | 7" | Island | WI232 | 1965 | £5 | £10 | *Tommy McCook B side* |
| You Should've Known Better | 7" | Trojan | TR652 | 1969 | £1.50 | £4 | *Tommy McCook B side* |

## HINDS, NEVILLE

| | | | | | | | |
|---|---|---|---|---|---|---|---|
| Black Man's Time | 7" | Upsetter | US384 | 1971 | £1.50 | £4 | *Upsetters B side* |
| Sunday Gravy | 7" | Duke Reid | DR2503 | 1970 | £1.50 | £4 | *John Holt B side* |

## HINE, RUPERT

| | | | | | | |
|---|---|---|---|---|---|---|
| Pick Up A Bone | LP | Purple | TPSA7502 | 1971 | £15 | £30 |

## HINES, EARL

| | | | | | | | |
|---|---|---|---|---|---|---|---|
| Blues In Thirds | LP | Fontana | SFJL902 | 1967 | £4 | £10 | |
| Earl 'Father' Hines | LP | Philips | BBL7185 | 1957 | £8 | £20 | |
| Earl Hines And His All Stars | 10" LP | Mercury | MG25018 | 1954 | £25 | £50 | |
| Earl Hines And His Orchestra | 7" EP | HMV | 7EG8114 | 1955 | £2 | £5 | |
| Earl's Backroom And Cozy's Caravan | LP | Felsted | FAJ7002 | 1958 | £6 | £15 | *with Cozy Cole* |
| Earl's Pearls | LP | MGM | C833 | 1960 | £5 | £12 | |
| Fatha Plays Fats | LP | Vogue | LAE12067 | 1957 | £5 | £12 | |
| Fats Waller Songs | 10" LP | Vogue Coral | LRA10031 | 1955 | £20 | £40 | |
| Grand Terrace Swing | 10" LP | HMV | DLP1132 | 1957 | £15 | £30 | |
| Jazz Means Hines | LP | Fontana | TL5378 | 1967 | £4 | £10 | |
| Midnight In New Orleans | 7" EP | MGM | MGMEP573 | 1956 | £2 | £5 | |
| Paris One Night Stand | LP | Philips | BBL7222 | 1958 | £6 | £15 | |
| Piano Moods | 10" LP | Columbia | 33S1063 | 1955 | £20 | £40 | |
| Spontaneous Explorations | LP | Stateside | SL10116 | 1965 | £5 | £12 | |

## HINES, FRAZER

| | | | | | | |
|---|---|---|---|---|---|---|
| Who Is Dr. Who | 7" | Major Minor | MM579 | 1968 | £10 | £20 |

## HINGE

| | | | | | | |
|---|---|---|---|---|---|---|
| Village Postman | 7" | RCA | RCA1721 | 1968 | £6 | £12 |

## HINTON, JOE

| | | | | | | | |
|---|---|---|---|---|---|---|---|
| Funny How Time Slips Away | LP | Backbeat | B60 | 1965 | £8 | £20 | *US* |
| Funny How Time Slips Away | 7" | Vocalion | VP9224 | 1964 | £5 | £10 | |
| Just A Kid Named Joe | 7" | Vocalion | VP9258 | 1966 | £2 | £5 | |

## HINTON, MILT

| | | | | | | |
|---|---|---|---|---|---|---|
| Milt Hinton Band | LP | London | LTZN15001 | 1956 | £8 | £20 |

## HIPPY BOYS

| | | | | | | |
|---|---|---|---|---|---|---|
| Doctor No Go | 7" | High Note | HS021 | 1969 | £1.50 | £4 |
| Love | 7" | Trojan | TR668 | 1969 | £1.50 | £4 |
| Michael Row The Boat Ashore | 7" | Trojan | TR669 | 1969 | £1.50 | £4 |
| Reggae Pressure | 7" | High Note | HS035 | 1969 | £1.50 | £4 |
| Reggae With The Hippy Boys | LP | Big Shot | BSLP5005 | 1969 | £10 | £25 |

## HIPSTER IMAGE

| | | | | | | |
|---|---|---|---|---|---|---|
| Can't Let You Go | 7" | Decca | F12137 | 1965 | £12.50 | £25 |

## HIRT, AL

| | | | | | | |
|---|---|---|---|---|---|---|
| Swingin' Dixie | LP | Audio Fidelity | AFLP1877/ AFSD5877 | 1960 | £6 | £15 |

## HIS NAME IS ALIVE

| | | | | | | | |
|---|---|---|---|---|---|---|---|
| How Ghosts Affect Relationships | 7" | 4AD | HNIA1 | 1990 | £2 | £5 | *promo* |

## HIT PACK

| | | | | | | |
|---|---|---|---|---|---|---|
| Never Say No To Your Baby | 7" | Tamla Motown | TMG513 | 1965 | £25 | £50 |

## HIT PARADE

| | | | | | | | |
|---|---|---|---|---|---|---|---|
| Forever | 7" | JSH | JSH1 | 1984 | £2 | £5 | |
| My Favourite Girl | 7" | JSH | JSH2 | 1984 | £1.50 | £4 | |
| Wax On The Melt | 12" | Eastern Bloc | EASTERN01 | 1988 | £25 | £50 | *promo* |

## HITCHCOCK, ALFRED

| | | | | | | | |
|---|---|---|---|---|---|---|---|
| Music To Be Murdered By | LP | London | HAP2130 | 1958 | £10 | £25 | |
| Music To Be Murdered By | LP | London | SHP6012 | 1959 | £15 | £30 | *stereo* |

## HITCHCOCK, ROBYN

| | | | | | | | |
|---|---|---|---|---|---|---|---|
| Man Who Invented Himself | 7" | Armageddon | AS008 | 1981 | £1.50 | £4 | |
| Man Who Invented Himself | 7" | Armageddon | AS008 | 1981 | £4 | £8 | *with flexi (4SPURT1)* |

## H.M.S. BOUNTY

| | | | | | | | | |
|---|---|---|---|---|---|---|---|---|
| Things | LP | Shamley | SS701 | 1968 | £37.50 | £75 | | US |
| Things | LP | Time Stood Still | TSSLP2 | 1985 | £5 | £12 | | US |

## HOBBIT

| | | | | | | | |
|---|---|---|---|---|---|---|---|
| First And Last | LP | Deroy | | 197– | £37.50 | £75 | |

## HOBBITS

| | | | | | | | | |
|---|---|---|---|---|---|---|---|---|
| Back From Middle Earth | LP | Perception | PLP10 | 1969 | £8 | £20 | | US |
| Daffodil Days | 7" | MCA | MU1002 | 1968 | £1.50 | £4 | | |
| Down To Middle Earth | LP | MCA | MUP301 | 1967 | £8 | £20 | | |
| Men And Doors | LP | Decca | DL75009 | 1968 | £8 | £20 | | US |

## HOBBS, CHRISTOPHER, JOHN ADAMS & GAVIN BRYARS

| | | | | | | |
|---|---|---|---|---|---|---|
| Ensemble Pieces | LP | Obscure | OBS2 | 1975 | £4 | £10 |

## HOBOKEN

| | | | | | | |
|---|---|---|---|---|---|---|
| Hoboken | LP | Oak | no number | 1973 | £330 | £500 |

## HOCKRIDGE, EDMUND

| | | | | | | |
|---|---|---|---|---|---|---|
| By The Fountains Of Rome | 7" EP | Pye | NEP24026 | 1957 | £2 | £5 |
| Edmund Hockridge | 7" EP | Pye | NEP24019 | 1956 | £2 | £5 |

## HODES, ART

| | | | | | | |
|---|---|---|---|---|---|---|
| Funky Piano | LP | Blue Note | B6502 | 1969 | £4 | £10 |
| Sittin' In Vol. 1 | LP | Blue Note | B6508 | 1969 | £4 | £10 |

## HODGE, CHRIS

| | | | | | | | |
|---|---|---|---|---|---|---|---|
| We're On Our Way | 7" | Apple | 43 | 1972 | £7.50 | £15 | picture sleeve |

## HODGES, CHARLES

| | | | | | | |
|---|---|---|---|---|---|---|
| Try A Little Love | 7" | Major Minor | MM654 | 1969 | £5 | £10 |

## HODGES, EDDIE

| | | | | | | |
|---|---|---|---|---|---|---|
| Bandit Of My Dreams | 7" | London | HLA9305 | 1962 | £2.50 | £6 |
| Eddie Hodges | 7" EP | London | REA1353 | 1963 | £15 | £30 |
| I'm Gonna Knock On Your Door | 7" | London | HLA9369 | 1961 | £2 | £5 |
| Love Minus Zero: No Limit | 7" | Stateside | SS469 | 1965 | £1.50 | £4 |
| Made To Love | 7" | London | HLA9576 | 1962 | £1.50 | £4 |

## HODGES, JOHNNY

| | | | | | | | |
|---|---|---|---|---|---|---|---|
| Big Sound | LP | Columbia | 33CX10136 | 1959 | £8 | £20 | |
| Blues-A-Plenty | LP | HMV | CLP1430 | 1961 | £6 | £15 | |
| Ellingtonia '56 | LP | Columbia | 33CX10055 | 1956 | £8 | £20 | |
| In A Tender Mood | LP | Columbia | 33C9051 | 1957 | £15 | £30 | |
| Johnny Hodges With The Ellington All Stars | LP | Columbia | 33CX10098 | 1958 | £6 | £15 | |
| Memories Of Ellington | LP | Columbia | 33CX10013 | 1955 | £20 | £40 | |
| Wings And Things | LP | Verve | (S)VLP9117 | 1965 | £4 | £10 | with Wild Bill Davis |
| With The Ellingtonians | 10" LP | Vogue | LDE011 | 1952 | £20 | £40 | |

## HOELDERLIN

| | | | | | | | |
|---|---|---|---|---|---|---|---|
| Clown And Clouds | LP | Spiegelei | 266056U | 1976 | £8 | £20 | German |
| Hoelderlin | LP | Spiegelei | 160601 | 1975 | £8 | £20 | German |
| Hoelderlin Traum | LP | Pilz | 20213145 | 1972 | £37.50 | £75 | German |
| Live Traumstadt | LP | Spiegelei | 180602 | 1978 | £6 | £15 | German double |
| Rare Birds | LP | Spiegelei | 160608 | 1977 | £5 | £12 | German |

## HOGAN, ANNIE

| | | | | | | |
|---|---|---|---|---|---|---|
| Plays Kickabye | 12" | Doublevision | DVR9 | 1985 | £2.50 | £6 |

## HOGAN, SILAS

| | | | | | | |
|---|---|---|---|---|---|---|
| Trouble At Home | LP | Blue Horizon | 2431008 | 1971 | £20 | £40 |

## HOGG, SMOKEY

| | | | | | | | |
|---|---|---|---|---|---|---|---|
| I'm So Lonely | LP | Realm | RM197 | 1964 | £6 | £15 | |
| Sings The Blues | LP | Ember | EMB3405 | 1971 | £4 | £10 | |
| Smokey Hogg | LP | Time | 6 | 1962 | £8 | £20 | US |

## HOGS

'Blues Theme' is collectable on two counts – the B side is a Frank Zappa production, while the Hogs afterwards changed their name to the Chocolate Watch Band.

| | | | | | | | |
|---|---|---|---|---|---|---|---|
| Blues Theme | 7" | HBR | 511 | 1966 | £75 | £150 | US |

## HOKUS POKE

| | | | | | | | |
|---|---|---|---|---|---|---|---|
| Earth Harmony | LP | Vertigo | 6360064 | 1972 | £25 | £50 | spiral label |

## HOLDE FEE

| | | | | | | | |
|---|---|---|---|---|---|---|---|
| Malaga | LP | private | 1383001 | 1975 | £4 | £10 | German |

## HOLDEN, RANDY

| | | | | | | | |
|---|---|---|---|---|---|---|---|
| Population II | LP | Hobbit | HB5002 | 1969 | £50 | £100 | US |

## HOLDEN, RON
| | | | | | | | |
|---|---|---|---|---|---|---|---|
| I Love You So | LP | Donna | DLP(S)2111 | 1960 | £15 | £30 | US |
| Love You So | 7" | London | HLU9116 | 1960 | £15 | £30 | |

## HOLDER, RAM BROTHERS
| | | | | | | |
|---|---|---|---|---|---|---|
| Ram Blues | 7" | Parlophone | R5471 | 1966 | £4 | £8 |

## HOLDER, RAM JOHN
| | | | | | | |
|---|---|---|---|---|---|---|
| Black London Blues | LP | Beacon | BEAS2 | 1974 | £10 | £25 |
| Bootleg Blues | LP | Beacon | BEAS17 | 1974 | £6 | £15 |
| You Simply Are | LP | Fresh Air | 9299470 | 1975 | £5 | £12 |

## HOLDSWORTH, ALLAN
| | | | | | | |
|---|---|---|---|---|---|---|
| Velvet Darkness | LP | CTI | 6068 | 1977 | £10 | £25 |

## HOLE IN THE WALL
| | | | | | | | |
|---|---|---|---|---|---|---|---|
| Hole In The Wall | LP | Sonet | SLP1420 | 1972 | £30 | £60 | Norwegian |

## HOLIDAY, BILLIE
| | | | | | | |
|---|---|---|---|---|---|---|
| An Evening With Billie Holiday | 7" EP | Columbia | SEB10035 | 1956 | £2 | £5 |
| At Jazz At The Philharmonic | 10" LP | Columbia | 33C9023 | 1956 | £25 | £50 |
| Billie Holiday | LP | Fontana | TL5287 | 1966 | £5 | £12 |
| Billie Holiday | LP | MGM | C792 | 1959 | £6 | £15 |
| Billie Holiday | LP | Stateside | SL10007 | 1962 | £6 | £15 |
| Billie Holiday | 7" EP | Columbia | SEB10009 | 1955 | £2 | £5 |
| Billie Holiday | 7" EP | Vogue | EPV1128 | 1956 | £2 | £5 |
| Billie Holiday | 10" LP | Columbia | 33S1034 | 1954 | £25 | £50 |
| Billie Holiday Memorial | LP | Fontana | TFL5106 | 1960 | £6 | £15 |
| Billie Holiday Sings | 7" EP | Columbia | SEB10048 | 1956 | £2 | £5 |
| Blue | 7" EP | Fontana | TFE17026 | 1960 | £2 | £5 |
| Detour Ahead | 7" | Vogue | V2408 | 1956 | £1.50 | £4 |
| Don't Worry 'Bout Me | 7" | MGM | MGM1033 | 1959 | £1.50 | £4 |
| Embraceable You | 7" EP | Melodisc | EPM7125 | 195— | £2 | £5 |
| Favourites | 10" LP | Philips | BBR8032 | 1955 | £20 | £40 |
| Lady Day | 7" EP | Fontana | TFE17010 | 1959 | £2 | £5 |
| Lady Day Vol. 1 | 7" EP | Brunswick | OE9172 | 1955 | £2 | £5 |
| Lady Day Vol. 2 | 7" EP | Brunswick | OE9199 | 1956 | £2 | £5 |
| Lady Day Vol. 3 | 7" EP | Brunswick | OE9251 | 1956 | £2 | £5 |
| Lady In Satin | LP | Fontana | TFL5032 | 1959 | £8 | £20 |
| Lady Sings The Blues | LP | Columbia | 33CX10092 | 1957 | £15 | £30 |
| Last Live Recording | LP | Island | ILP929 | 1966 | £6 | £15 |
| Lover Man | 10" LP | Brunswick | LA8676 | 1954 | £20 | £40 |
| Music For Torching | LP | Columbia | 33CX10019 | 1956 | £20 | £40 |
| Once Upon A Time | LP | Fontana | TL5262 | 1965 | £5 | £12 |
| Solitude | LP | Columbia | 33CX10076 | 1957 | £15 | £30 |
| Songs For Distingue Lovers | LP | Columbia | 33CX10145 | 1959 | £8 | £20 |
| Unforgettable Lady Day | LP | HMV | CLP1414 | 1960 | £6 | £15 |
| Velvet Moods | LP | Columbia | 33CX10064 | 1957 | £15 | £30 |

## HOLIDAY, CHICO
| | | | | | | |
|---|---|---|---|---|---|---|
| Chico Holiday | 7" EP | RCA | RCX171 | 1959 | £10 | £20 |
| God, Country And My Baby | 7" | Coral | Q72443 | 1961 | £1.50 | £4 |
| Young Ideas | 7" | RCA | RCA1117 | 1959 | £2 | £5 |

## HOLIDAY, JIMMY
| | | | | | | |
|---|---|---|---|---|---|---|
| Baby I Love You | 7" | Liberty | LIB12040 | 1966 | £4 | £8 |
| Everybody Needs Help | 7" | Liberty | LIB12053 | 1967 | £2 | £5 |
| Give Me Your Love | 7" | Liberty | LIB12048 | 1967 | £4 | £8 |
| Give Me Your Love | 7" | Minit | MLF11008 | 1968 | £2.50 | £6 |
| How Can I Forget | 7" | Vocalion | V9206 | 1963 | £7.50 | £15 |
| I Lied | 7" | London | HLY9868 | 1964 | £1.50 | £4 |

## HOLIDAY, JIMMY & CLYDIE KING
| | | | | | | |
|---|---|---|---|---|---|---|
| Oh Darling How I Miss You | 7" | Polydor | 56035 | 1965 | £4 | £8 |
| One Man In My Life | 7" | Polydor | 56166 | 1967 | £4 | £8 |
| Ready Willing And Able | 7" | Liberty | LIB12058 | 1967 | £7.50 | £15 |

## HOLIDAY, JOE
| | | | | | | |
|---|---|---|---|---|---|---|
| Joe Holiday Rhythm | 10" LP | Esquire | 20027 | 1954 | £20 | £40 |

## HOLIDAY, JOHNNY
| | | | | | | |
|---|---|---|---|---|---|---|
| Holiday For Romance | 7" EP | London | RED1227 | 1959 | £2 | £5 |
| Sentimental Holiday | 7" EP | London | RED1226 | 1959 | £2 | £5 |

## HOLIDAYS
| | | | | | | |
|---|---|---|---|---|---|---|
| I'll Love You Forever | 7" | Polydor | 56720 | 1966 | £30 | £60 |

## HOLIEN, DANNY
| | | | | | | |
|---|---|---|---|---|---|---|
| Danny Holien | LP | Tumbleweed | TW3503 | 1972 | £6 | £15 |

## HOLLAND, DAVE
| | | | | | | |
|---|---|---|---|---|---|---|
| Conference Of The Birds | LP | ECM | ECM1027ST | 1973 | £5 | £12 |
| Music From Two Basses | LP | ECM | ECM1011ST | 1971 | £8 | £20 |

## HOLLAND, EDDIE
| | | | | | | | |
|---|---|---|---|---|---|---|---|
| Eddie Holland | LP | Motown | 604 | 1963 | £25 | £50 | US |
| If It's Love | 7" | Oriole | CBA1808 | 1963 | £180 | £300 | best auctioned |

| | | | | | | |
|---|---|---|---|---|---|---|
| Jamie | 7" | Fontana | H387 | 1962 £150 | £250 | *best auctioned* |

## HOLLAND, TONY

| | | | | | | |
|---|---|---|---|---|---|---|
| Sidewalk | 7" | HMV | POP1135 | 1963 £7.50 | £15 | |

## HOLLAND & DOZIER

| | | | | | | |
|---|---|---|---|---|---|---|
| Why Can't We Be Lovers | 7" | Invictus | INV525 | 1972 £2 | £5 | |

## HOLLIDAY, BRENDA

| | | | | | | |
|---|---|---|---|---|---|---|
| Hurt A Little Everyday | 7" | Tamla Motown | TMG581 | 1966 £37.50 | £75 | *demo only* |

## HOLLIDAY, MICHAEL

| | | | | | | |
|---|---|---|---|---|---|---|
| All Of You | 7" | Columbia | DB3973 | 1957 £2.50 | £6 | |
| All Time Favourites | 7" EP | Columbia | SEG7761 | 1958 £2 | £5 | |
| Best Of Michael Holliday | LP | Columbia | 33SX1586 | 1964 £4 | £10 | |
| Four Feather Falls | 7" EP | Columbia | SEG7986/ESG7793 | 1960 £6 | £12 | |
| Gal With The Yaller Shoes | 7" | Columbia | SCM5273 | 1956 £4 | £8 | |
| Happy Holliday | LP | Columbia | 33SX1354 | 1961 £4 | £10 | |
| Happy Holliday | 7" EP | Columbia | SEG8161 | 1962 £2 | £5 | |
| Hi! | 10" LP | Columbia | 33S1114 | 1958 £8 | £20 | |
| Holliday Mixture | LP | Columbia | 33SX1262/SCX3331 | 1960 £4 | £10 | |
| In A Sentimental Mood | 7" EP | Columbia | ESG7864 | 1961 £2.50 | £6 | *stereo* |
| In A Sentimental Mood | 7" EP | Columbia | SEG8115 | 1961 £2 | £5 | |
| Melody Mike | 7" EP | Columbia | SEG7818 | 1958 £2.50 | £6 | |
| Memories Of Mike | 7" EP | Columbia | SEG8373 | 1964 £2 | £5 | |
| Mike | LP | Columbia | 33SX1170 | 1959 £4 | £10 | |
| Mike And The Other Fella | 7" EP | Columbia | SEG7892 | 1959 £2 | £5 | |
| Mike No. 1 | 7" EP | Columbia | ESG7784 | 1960 £2.50 | £6 | *stereo* |
| Mike No. 1 | 7" EP | Columbia | SEG7972 | 1960 £2 | £5 | |
| Mike No. 2 | 7" EP | Columbia | ESG7803 | 1960 £2.50 | £6 | *stereo* |
| Mike No. 2 | 7" EP | Columbia | SEG7996 | 1960 £2 | £5 | |
| Mike No. 3 | 7" EP | Columbia | ESG7842 | 1961 £2.50 | £6 | *stereo* |
| Mike No. 3 | 7" EP | Columbia | SEG8074 | 1961 £2 | £5 | |
| Mike Sings Country And Western Style | 7" EP | Columbia | SEG8242 | 1963 £2 | £5 | |
| Mike Sings Ragtime | 7" EP | Columbia | ESG7856 | 1961 £2.50 | £6 | *stereo* |
| Mike Sings Ragtime | 7" EP | Columbia | SEG8101 | 1961 £2 | £5 | |
| More Happy Holliday | 7" EP | Columbia | SEG8186 | 1962 £2 | £5 | |
| Music With Mike | 7" EP | Columbia | SEG7683 | 1957 £2.50 | £6 | |
| My Guitar And Me | 7" EP | Columbia | SEG7638 | 1956 £2 | £5 | |
| My House Is Your House | 7" | Columbia | DB3919 | 1957 £2 | £5 | |
| Nothin' To Do | 7" | Columbia | SCM5252 | 1956 £4 | £8 | |
| Old Cape Cod | 7" | Columbia | DB3992 | 1957 £1.50 | £4 | |
| Relax With Mike | 7" EP | Columbia | SEG7752 | 1958 £2 | £5 | |
| Sentimental Journey | 7" EP | Columbia | SEG7836 | 1958 £2 | £5 | |
| Sixteen Tons | 7" | Columbia | SCM5221 | 1956 £5 | £10 | |
| Story Of My Life | 7" | Columbia | DB4058 | 1958 £1.50 | £4 | |
| Ten Thousand Miles | 7" | Columbia | DB3813 | 1956 £5 | £10 | |
| To Bing From Mike | LP | Columbia | 33SX1425/SCX3441 | 1962 £4 | £10 | |
| Wringle Wrangle | 7" | Columbia | DB3948 | 1957 £2 | £5 | |
| Yaller Yaller Gold | 7" | Columbia | DB3871 | 1957 £2 | £5 | |

## HOLLIDAY, SUSAN

| | | | | | | |
|---|---|---|---|---|---|---|
| Any Day Now | 7" | Columbia | DB7403 | 1964 £4 | £8 | |
| I Wanna Say Hello | LP | Columbia | SX6067 | 1966 £37.50 | £75 | |
| Sometimes | 7" | Columbia | DB7616 | 1965 £2.50 | £6 | |

## HOLLIER, TIM

| | | | | | | |
|---|---|---|---|---|---|---|
| Message To A Harlequin | LP | United Artists | (S)ULP1211 | 1968 £6 | £15 | |
| Sky Sail | LP | Philips | 6308044 | 1971 £5 | £12 | |

## HOLLIES

The Hollies were easily one of the most successful of the first wave of British beat groups to emerge in the sixties and yet they seldom seem to receive much credit for the fact. Inevitably they tended to labour in the shadow of the Beatles and their records show a similar pattern of development. *Butterfly* is a kind of Lance-Corporal Pepper – it uses the same kind of inventive arranging and is one of the more interesting albums of the period. One is inclined to believe that it is actually much more of a psychedelic classic than celebrated rarities like those of Kaleidoscope.

| | | | | | | |
|---|---|---|---|---|---|---|
| After The Fox | 7" | United Artists | UP1152 | 1966 £10 | £20 | *with Peter Sellers* |
| Ain't That Just Like Me | 7" | Parlophone | R5030 | 1963 £2.50 | £6 | |
| Air That I Breathe | CD-s | EMI | CDEM80 | 1988 £2 | £5 | |
| Bus Stop | LP | Imperial | LP9330/12330 | 1966 £10 | £25 | *US* |
| Bus Stop | 7" EP | Odeon | MEO125 | 1966 £37.50 | £75 | *French, sleeve with group picture* |
| Bus Stop | 7" EP | Odeon | MEO125 | 1966 £12.50 | £25 | *French, sleeve with titles only* |
| Bus Stop | 7" | Parlophone | R5469 | 1966 £1.50 | £4 | |
| Butterfly | LP | Parlophone | PCS7039 | 1967 £10 | £25 | *stereo* |
| Butterfly | LP | Parlophone | PMC7039 | 1967 £10 | £30 | *mono* |
| Carrie Anne | 7" EP | Fontana | 460211 | 1967 £12.50 | £25 | *French* |
| Carrie Anne | 7" | Parlophone | R5602 | 1967 £1.50 | £4 | |
| Confessions Of The Mind | LP | Parlophone | PCS7116 | 1970 £5 | £12 | |
| Days | LP | Odeon | SMO74315 | 1965 £30 | £60 | *German* |
| Distant Light | LP | Parlophone | PAS10005 | 1971 £4 | £10 | |
| Everything You Wanted To Hear | LP | Epic | AS138 | 1972 £10 | £25 | *US promo* |
| Evolution | LP | Parlophone | PMC/PCS7022 | 1967 £10 | £25 | |

| Title | Format | Label | Catalogue | Year | Price | Price | Notes |
|---|---|---|---|---|---|---|---|
| For Certain Because | LP | Parlophone | PMC/PCS7011 | 1966 | £15 | £30 | |
| Gasoline Alley Bred | 7" | Parlophone | R5862 | 1970 | £1.50 | £4 | |
| He Ain't Heavy He's My Brother | CD-s | EMI | CDEM74 | 1988 | £2 | £5 | |
| He Ain't Heavy He's My Brother | 7" | Parlophone | R5806 | 1969 | £1.50 | £4 | |
| Hear! Here! | LP | Imperial | LP9299/12299 | 1965 | £15 | £30 | US |
| Here I Go Again | LP | Imperial | LP9265/12265 | 1964 | £20 | £40 | US |
| Here I Go Again | 7" EP | Parlophone | GEP8915 | 1964 | £12.50 | £25 | |
| Here I Go Again | 7" | Parlophone | R5137 | 1964 | £1.50 | £4 | |
| Hey Willy | 7" | Parlophone | R5905 | 1971 | £1.50 | £4 | |
| Hollies | LP | Parlophone | PMC1261 | 1965 | £15 | £30 | |
| Hollies | LP | Regal | SREG2024 | 1967 | £15 | £30 | export |
| Hollies | 7" EP | Parlophone | GEP8909 | 1964 | £10 | £20 | |
| Hollies – Beat Group | LP | Imperial | LP9312/12312 | 1966 | £10 | £25 | US |
| Hollies Greatest | LP | Parlophone | PMC/PCS7057 | 1968 | £5 | £12 | |
| I Can't Let Go | 7" EP | Parlophone | GEP8951 | 1966 | £12.50 | £25 | |
| I Can't Let Go | 7" | Parlophone | R5409 | 1966 | £1.50 | £4 | |
| I Can't Tell The Bottom From The Top | 7" | Parlophone | R5837 | 1970 | £1.50 | £4 | |
| I'm Alive | 7" EP | Odeon | SOE3770 | 1965 | £20 | £40 | French |
| I'm Alive | 7" EP | Parlophone | GEP8942 | 1965 | £12.50 | £25 | |
| I'm Alive | 7" | Parlophone | R5287 | 1965 | £1.50 | £4 | |
| If I Needed Someone | 7" EP | Odeon | MEO101 | 1965 | £20 | £40 | French |
| If I Needed Someone | 7" | Parlophone | R5392 | 1965 | £1.50 | £4 | |
| In The Hollies Style | LP | Parlophone | PMC1235 | 1965 | £20 | £40 | |
| In The Hollies Style | 7" EP | Parlophone | GEP8934 | 1965 | £12.50 | £25 | |
| Jennifer Eccles | 7" | Parlophone | R5680 | 1968 | £1.50 | £4 | |
| Jesus Was A Crossmaker | 7" | Epic | 510989 | 1973 | £4 | £8 | US |
| Just One Look | 7" EP | Parlophone | GEP8911 | 1964 | £10 | £20 | |
| Just One Look | 7" | Parlophone | R5104 | 1964 | £1.50 | £4 | |
| Kill Me Quick | 7" | Parlophon | QMSP16410 | 1967 | £15 | £30 | Italian |
| King Midas In Reverse | 7" | Parlophone | R5637 | 1967 | £1.50 | £4 | |
| Like Every Time Before | 7" | Hansa | 14093 | 1968 | £5 | £10 | German |
| Listen To Me | 7" | Parlophone | R5733 | 1968 | £1.50 | £4 | |
| Long Cool Woman In A Black Dress | 7" | Parlophone | R5939 | 1972 | £1.50 | £4 | |
| Look Through Any Window | 7" EP | Odeon | SOE3773 | 1965 | £20 | £40 | French |
| Look Through Any Window | 7" | Parlophone | R5322 | 1965 | £1.50 | £4 | |
| Maker – Would You Believe | 7" EP | Fontana | 460249 | 1968 | £15 | £30 | French |
| Music For 5am | 7" | Mercury | YARD002 | 196– | £5 | £10 | with other artists |
| Non Prego Per Me | 7" | Parlophone | QMSP16402 | 1967 | £15 | £30 | Italian |
| On A Carousel | 7" EP | Fontana | 460201 | 1967 | £15 | £30 | French |
| On A Carousel | 7" | Parlophone | R5562 | 1967 | £1.50 | £4 | |
| Out On The Road | LP | Hansa | 87119 | 1973 | £10 | £25 | German |
| Romany | LP | Polydor | 2383144 | 1972 | £4 | £10 | |
| Searchin' | 7" | Parlophone | R5052 | 1963 | £1.50 | £4 | |
| Sing Dylan | LP | Parlophone | PMC/PCS7078 | 1969 | £8 | £20 | |
| Sing Hollies | LP | Parlophone | PCS7092 | 1969 | £8 | £20 | |
| Sorry Suzanne | 7" | Parlophone | R5765 | 1969 | £1.50 | £4 | |
| Stay | 7" EP | Odeon | SOE3749 | 1963 | £20 | £40 | French |
| Stay | 7" | Parlophone | R5077 | 1963 | £1.50 | £4 | |
| Stay With The Hollies | LP | Parlophone | PCS3054 | 1964 | £25 | £50 | stereo |
| Stay With The Hollies | LP | Parlophone | PMC1220 | 1964 | £15 | £30 | |
| Stay With The Hollies | LP | World Records | ST1035 | 1968 | £8 | £20 | |
| Stop Stop Stop | LP | Imperial | LP9339/12339 | 1967 | £10 | £25 | US |
| Stop Stop Stop | 7" | Parlophone | R5508 | 1966 | £1.50 | £4 | |
| Tell Me To My Face | 7" EP | Odeon | MEO144 | 1967 | £20 | £40 | French |
| Twenty Golden Hits | CD | Mobile Fidelity | UDCD521 | 1989 | £6 | £15 | US audiophile |
| Up Front | LP | St. Michael | 21020101 | 1978 | £15 | £30 | |
| Vintage Hollies | LP | World Records | ST979 | 1967 | £8 | £20 | |
| We're Through | 7" EP | Parlophone | GEP8927 | 1964 | £12.50 | £25 | |
| We're Through | 7" | Parlophone | R5178 | 1964 | £1.50 | £4 | |
| Would You Believe | LP | Parlophone | PCS7008 | 1966 | £20 | £40 | stereo |
| Would You Believe | LP | Parlophone | PMC7008 | 1966 | £15 | £30 | |
| Yes I Will | 7" | Parlophone | R5232 | 1965 | £1.50 | £4 | |

## HOLLOW MEN

| Title | Format | Label | Catalogue | Year | Price | Price | Notes |
|---|---|---|---|---|---|---|---|
| Circa | CD-s | Arista | 260978 | 1990 | £2 | £5 | |
| Drowning Man | 12" | Blind Eye | BE007 | 1989 | £2.50 | £6 | fully autographed |
| Gold And Ivory | 12" | Evensong | EVE212 | 1987 | £2.50 | £6 | with postcard |
| Late Flowering Lust | 7" | Evensong | EVE107 | 1985 | £4 | £8 | |
| Man Who Would Be King | CD | Dead Man's Curve | VIVIDONE | 1988 | £5 | £12 | |
| Moon's A Balloon | CD-s | Arista | 663508 | 1990 | £2 | £5 | |
| Pink Panther | CD-s | Arista | 664026 | 1991 | £2 | £5 | |
| Thanks To The Rolling Sea | CD-s | Arista | 663167 | 1990 | £2 | £5 | |
| White Train | CD-s | Arista | 662695 | 1989 | £2 | £5 | |
| White Train | 7" | Gigantic | GI101 | 1988 | £2.50 | £6 | promo |

## HOLLOWAY, BRENDA

| Title | Format | Label | Catalogue | Year | Price | Price | Notes |
|---|---|---|---|---|---|---|---|
| Artistry Of Brenda Holloway | LP | Tamla Motown | (S)TML11083 | 1968 | £37.50 | £75 | |
| Every Little Bit Hurts | LP | Tamla | 257 | 1965 | £25 | £50 | US |
| Every Little Bit Hurts | 7" | Stateside | SS307 | 1964 | £15 | £30 | |
| Hurt A Little Everyday | 7" | Tamla Motown | TMG581 | 1966 | £12.50 | £25 | |
| Just Look What I've Done | 7" | Tamla Motown | TMG608 | 1967 | £7.50 | £15 | |
| Just Look What You've Done | 7" | Tamla Motown | TMG700 | 1969 | £2 | £5 | |
| Operator | 7" | Tamla Motown | TMG519 | 1965 | £20 | £40 | |
| Together Till The End Of Time | 7" | Tamla Motown | TMG556 | 1966 | £15 | £30 | |
| When I'm Gone | 7" | Tamla Motown | TMG508 | 1965 | £30 | £60 | |
| You've Made Me So Very Happy | 7" | Tamla Motown | TMG622 | 1967 | £7.50 | £15 | |

## HOLLOWAY, PATRICE

| Love And Desire | 7" | Capitol | CL15484 | 1966 | £20 | £40 | |

## HOLLOWAY, STANLEY

| 'Ere's 'Olloway | LP | Philips | BBL7237 | 1958 | £4 | £10 | |
| Famous Adventures With Old Sam And The Ramsbottoms | 10" LP | Columbia | 33S1093 | 1956 | £4 | £10 | |

## HOLLY

| Hobo Joe | 7" | Erics | ERICS007 | 1979 | £4 | £8 | |
| Yankee Rose | 7" | Erics | ERICS003 | 1979 | £2.50 | £6 | |

## HOLLY, BUDDY

There is a strong case for viewing Buddy Holly as the true father of the music we call rock. It was Buddy Holly and the Crickets who set the pattern for the line-up that is still considered as the classic one for a rock group – lead and rhythm guitars, bass guitar and drums. His songs too, based on blues chord progressions but with bright, major tonalities, defined a style that has been revisited by songwriters from Lennon and McCartney to Costello to Gallagher and all points in between. It should be noted, incidentally, that while most of Holly's records were credited to him by name, a few were credited merely to the Crickets. All, however, are listed here.

| Baby I Don't Care | 7" | Coral | Q72432 | 1961 | £1.50 | £4 | |
| Best Of Buddy Holly | LP | Coral | CX(S)B8 | 1966 | £8 | £20 | US |
| Blue Days Black Nights | 7" | Brunswick | 05581 | 1956 | £330 | £500 | best auctioned |
| Bo Diddley | 7" | Coral | Q72463 | 1963 | £1.50 | £4 | |
| Brown Eyed Handsome Man | 7" | Coral | Q72459 | 1963 | £1.50 | £4 | |
| Buddy By Request | 7" EP | Coral | FEP2065 | 1964 | £10 | £20 | |
| Buddy Holly | LP | Coral | CRL57210 | 1958 | £87.50 | £175 | US |
| Buddy Holly | LP | Coral | LVA9085 | 1958 | £10 | £25 | |
| Buddy Holly | LP | Vogue Coral | LVA9085 | 1958 | £25 | £50 | |
| Buddy Holly | 7" EP | Coral | FEP2032 | 1959 | £10 | £20 | tri-centre |
| Buddy Holly And The Crickets | LP | Coral | CRL(7)57405 | 1962 | £20 | £40 | US |
| Buddy Holly No. 1 | 7" EP | Brunswick | OE9456 | 1959 | £20 | £40 | tri-centre |
| Buddy Holly No. 2 | 7" EP | Brunswick | OE9457 | 1959 | £20 | £40 | tri-centre |
| Buddy Holly Sings | 7" EP | Coral | FEP2070 | 1965 | £15 | £30 | |
| Buddy Holly Story | LP | Coral | CRL57279 | 1959 | £37.50 | £75 | US |
| Buddy Holly Story | LP | Coral | LVA9105 | 1959 | £6 | £15 | |
| Buddy Holly Story | LP | World Records | SM301-5 | 1975 | £10 | £25 | 5 LPs, boxed |
| Buddy Holly Story 2 | LP | Coral | LVA9127 | 1960 | £5 | £12 | |
| Buddy Holly Story Vol. 2 | LP | Coral | CRL57326 | 1959 | £30 | £60 | US |
| Chirping Crickets | LP | Brunswick | BL54038 | 1957 | £150 | £250 | US |
| Chirping Crickets | LP | Coral | LVA9081 | 1958 | £15 | £30 | |
| Chirping Crickets | LP | Vogue Coral | LVA9081 | 1958 | £25 | £50 | |
| Complete Buddy Holly | LP | MCA | CDSP807 | 1978 | £15 | £30 | ... 6 LPs, book, boxed |
| Early In The Morning | 78 | Coral | Q72333 | 1958 | £5 | £10 | |
| Early In The Morning | 7" | Coral | Q72333 | 1958 | £5 | £10 | |
| Four More | 7" EP | Coral | FEP2060 | 1960 | £10 | £20 | |
| Good Rockin' | LP | Vocalion | VL73923 | 1971 | £25 | £50 | US |
| Great Buddy Holly | LP | Vocalion | VL(7)3811 | 1967 | £8 | £20 | US |
| Greatest Hits | LP | Coral | CRL(7)57492 | 1967 | £8 | £20 | US |
| Heartbeat | LP | Marks & Spencer | IMP114 | 1978 | £15 | £30 | |
| Heartbeat | 78 | Coral | Q72346 | 1958 | £7.50 | £15 | |
| Heartbeat | 78 | Coral | Q72392 | 1960 | £10 | £20 | |
| Heartbeat | 7" EP | Coral | FEP2015 | 1959 | £10 | £20 | |
| Heartbeat | 7" | Coral | Q72346 | 1958 | £5 | £10 | |
| Holly In The Hills | LP | Coral | CRL(7)57463 | 1965 | £15 | £30 | US |
| Holly In The Hills | LP | Coral | LVA9227 | 1965 | £15 | £30 | .... with 'Reminiscing' |
| Holly In The Hills | LP | Coral | LVA9227 | 1965 | £10 | £25 | ......... with 'Wishing' |
| It Doesn't Matter Anymore | 78 | Coral | Q72360 | 1958 | £7.50 | £15 | |
| It Doesn't Matter Anymore | 7" | Coral | Q72360 | 1958 | £2 | £5 | |
| It's So Easy | 78 | Coral | Q72343 | 1958 | £6 | £12 | |
| It's So Easy | 7" EP | Coral | FEP2014 | 1959 | £10 | £20 | |
| It's So Easy | 7" | Coral | Q72343 | 1958 | £5 | £10 | |
| Late Great Buddy Holly | 7" EP | Coral | FEP2044 | 1960 | £12.50 | £25 | tri-centre |
| Learning The Game | 78 | Coral | Q72411 | 1960 | £37.50 | £75 | |
| Learning The Game | 7" | Coral | Q72411 | 1960 | £2 | £5 | |
| Listen To Me | 78 | Coral | Q72288 | 1958 | £5 | £10 | |
| Listen To Me | 7" EP | Coral | FEP2002 | 1958 | £12.50 | £25 | |
| Listen To Me | 7" EP | Coral | FEP2002 | 1958 | £87.50 | £175 | ......... no glasses cover |
| Listen To Me | 7" | Coral | Q72288 | 1958 | £6 | £12 | |
| Listen To Me | 7" | Coral | Q72449 | 1962 | £1.50 | £4 | |
| Look At Me | 7" | Coral | Q72445 | 1961 | £1.50 | £4 | |
| Love's Made A Fool Of You | 7" | Coral | Q72475 | 1964 | £2 | £5 | |
| Maybe Baby | 78 | Coral | Q72307 | 1958 | £2.50 | £6 | |
| Maybe Baby | 7" | Coral | Q72307 | 1958 | £6 | £12 | |
| Maybe Baby | 7" | Coral | Q72483 | 1966 | £5 | £10 | |
| Midnight Shift | 78 | Brunswick | 05800 | 1959 | £12.50 | £25 | |
| Midnight Shift | 7" | Brunswick | 05800 | 1959 | £15 | £30 | |
| Oh Boy | CD-s | MCA | DMCAT1368 | 1989 | £4 | £10 | |
| Oh Boy | 78 | Coral | Q72298 | 1957 | £2.50 | £6 | |
| Oh Boy | 7" | Coral | Q72298 | 1957 | £6 | £12 | |
| Oh Boy | 7" | Decca | AD1012 | 1968 | £5 | £10 | export |
| Peggy Sue | CD-s | Old Gold | OG6154 | 1990 | £4 | £10 | |
| Peggy Sue | 78 | Vogue Coral | Q72293 | 1957 | £3 | £8 | |
| Peggy Sue | 7" | Coral | Q72293 | 1958 | £5 | £10 | |
| Peggy Sue | 7" | Vogue Coral | Q72293 | 1957 | £7.50 | £15 | |
| Peggy Sue Got Married | 78 | Coral | Q72376 | 1959 | £20 | £40 | |

| | | | | | | | |
|---|---|---|---|---|---|---|---|
| Peggy Sue Got Married | 7" | Coral | Q72376 | 1959 | £4 | £8 | |
| Rave On | 78 | Coral | Q72325 | 1958 | £5 | £10 | |
| Rave On | 7" EP | Coral | FEP2005 | 1958 | £10 | £20 | |
| Rave On | 7" | Coral | Q72325 | 1958 | £5 | £10 | |
| Rave On | 7" | Decca | AD1009 | 1968 | £5 | £10 | export |
| Reminiscing | LP | Coral | LVA9212 | 1963 | £6 | £15 | |
| Reminiscing | 7" | Coral | Q72455 | 1962 | £1.50 | £4 | |
| Rock & Roll Collection | LP | Decca | DXSE7207 | 1972 | £4 | £10 | US |
| Showcase | LP | Coral | LVA9222 | 1964 | £8 | £20 | |
| Showcase Vol. 1 | 7" EP | Coral | FEP2068 | 1964 | £20 | £40 | |
| Showcase Vol. 2 | 7" EP | Coral | FEP2069 | 1964 | £20 | £40 | |
| Sound Of The Crickets | 7" EP | Coral | FEP2003 | 1958 | £10 | £20 | |
| That Tex Mex Sound | 7" EP | Coral | FEP2066 | 1964 | £20 | £40 | |
| That'll Be The Day | LP | Ace Of Hearts | AH3 | 1961 | £5 | £12 | |
| That'll Be The Day | LP | Decca | DL8707 | 1958 | £250 | £400 | US |
| That'll Be The Day | CD-s | Old Gold | OG6147 | 1989 | £4 | £10 | |
| That'll Be The Day | 78 | Vogue Coral | Q72279 | 1957 | £3 | £8 | |
| That'll Be The Day | 7" EP | Coral | FEP2062 | 1960 | £10 | £20 | |
| That'll Be The Day | 7" | Coral | Q72279 | 1957 | £5 | £10 | |
| That'll Be The Day | 7" | Vogue Coral | Q72279 | 1957 | £7.50 | £15 | |
| Think It Over | 78 | Coral | Q72329 | 1958 | £5 | £10 | |
| Think It Over | 7" | Coral | Q72329 | 1958 | £6 | £12 | |
| True Love Ways | CD-s | MCA | DMCA1302 | 1988 | £4 | £10 | |
| True Love Ways | 78 | Coral | Q72397 | 1960 | £20 | £40 | |
| True Love Ways | 7" | Coral | Q72397 | 1960 | £1.50 | £4 | |
| What To Do | 7" | Coral | Q72419 | 1961 | £1.50 | £4 | |
| What To Do | 7" | Coral | Q72469 | 1963 | £1.50 | £4 | |
| Wishing | 7" EP | Coral | FEP2067 | 1964 | £12.50 | £25 | |
| Wishing | 7" | Coral | Q72466 | 1963 | £1.50 | £4 | |
| You've Got Love | 7" | Coral | Q72472 | 1964 | £2 | £5 | |

## HOLLY, STEVE

| | | | | | | | |
|---|---|---|---|---|---|---|---|
| Strange World | 7" | Planet | PLF107 | 1966 | £5 | £10 | |

## HOLLYWOOD, KENNY

'Magic Star' is a considerable novelty, being nothing other than the Tornados' huge hit 'Telstar' with added vocals.

| | | | | | | | |
|---|---|---|---|---|---|---|---|
| Magic Star | 7" | Decca | F11546 | 1962 | £7.50 | £15 | |

## HOLLYWOOD ARGYLES

| | | | | | | | |
|---|---|---|---|---|---|---|---|
| Alley Oop | LP | Lute | L9001 | 1960 | £75 | £150 | US |
| Alley Oop | 7" | London | HLU9146 | 1960 | £5 | £10 | |
| Gun Totin' Critter Called Jack | 7" | Top Rank | JAR530 | 1960 | £2 | £5 | |

## HOLLYWOOD FLAMES

| | | | | | | | |
|---|---|---|---|---|---|---|---|
| Buzz Buzz Buzz | 7" | London | HL7030 | 1957 | £10 | £20 | export |
| Buzz Buzz Buzz | 7" | London | HL8545 | 1958 | £15 | £30 | |
| If I Thought You Needed Me | 7" | London | HLE9071 | 1960 | £6 | £12 | |
| Much Too Much | 7" | London | HLW8955 | 1959 | £12.50 | £25 | |

## HOLLYWOOD PERSUADERS

The B side of 'Tijuana' was written by Frank Zappa, who also played guitar on the song.

| | | | | | | | |
|---|---|---|---|---|---|---|---|
| Tijuana | 7" | Original Sound | 39 | 1963 | £75 | £150 | US |

## HOLLYWOOD VINES

| | | | | | | | |
|---|---|---|---|---|---|---|---|
| When Johnny Comes Sliding Home | 7" | Capitol | CL15191 | 1961 | £2 | £5 | |

## HOLMAN, BILL

| | | | | | | | |
|---|---|---|---|---|---|---|---|
| Bill Holman Octet | 10" LP | Capitol | KPL101 | 1954 | £15 | £30 | |
| Fabulous Bill Holman | LP | Coral | LVA9088 | 1958 | £10 | £25 | |
| In A Jazz Orbit | LP | HMV | CLP1289 | 1959 | £6 | £15 | |

## HOLMAN, EDDIE

| | | | | | | | |
|---|---|---|---|---|---|---|---|
| Hey There Lonely Girl | 7" | Stateside | SS2159 | 1970 | £2 | £5 | |
| I Surrender | 7" | Action | ACT4547 | 1969 | £12.50 | £25 | |
| Since I Don't Have You | 7" | Stateside | SS2170 | 1970 | £2.50 | £6 | |
| This Can't Be True | 7" | Cameo Parkway | P960 | 1965 | £12.50 | £25 | |
| This Could Be A Night To Remember | 7" | Salsoul | SZ2026 | 1977 | £1.50 | £4 | |

## HOLMES, JAKE

| | | | | | | | |
|---|---|---|---|---|---|---|---|
| Above Ground Sound | LP | Tower | ST5079 | 1967 | £5 | £12 | US |

## HOLMES, JOE & LEN GRAHAM

| | | | | | | | |
|---|---|---|---|---|---|---|---|
| After Dawning | LP | Topic | 12TS401 | 1979 | £4 | £10 | |
| Chaste Muses, Bards And Sages | LP | Free Reed | FRR007 | 1976 | £5 | £12 | |

## HOLMES, RICHARD 'GROOVE'

| | | | | | | | |
|---|---|---|---|---|---|---|---|
| Comin' On Home | LP | Blue Note | BST84372 | 1970 | £5 | £12 | |
| Spicy | LP | Transatlantic | PR7493 | 1968 | £6 | £15 | |

## HOLOCAUST

| | | | | | | | |
|---|---|---|---|---|---|---|---|
| Comin' Through | 12" | Phoenix | 12PSP4 | 1982 | £2.50 | £6 | |
| Heavy Metal Mania | 12" | Phoenix | 12PSP1 | 1980 | £3 | £8 | |
| Lovin' Feelin' Danger | 7" | Phoenix | PSP3 | 1981 | £2.50 | £6 | |
| Nightcomers | LP | Phoenix | PSLP1 | 1981 | £4 | £10 | |

| Smokin' Valves | 12" | Phoenix | 12PSP2 | 1980 £3 £8 |
|---|---|---|---|---|

## HOLT, JOHN

| | | | | | |
|---|---|---|---|---|---|
| Ali Baba | 7" | Trojan | TR661 | 1969 £1.50 £4 | |
| Come Out Of My Bed | 7" | Duke Reid | DR2506 | 1970 £1.50 £4 | *Winston Wright B side* |
| Greatest Hits | LP | Melodisc | MLP12170 | 197– £5 £12 | |
| Have Sympathy | 7" | Trojan | TR694 | 1969 £1.50 £4 | *Harry J B side* |
| Holt | LP | Trojan | TRL(S)43 | 1972 £4 £10 | |
| I Cried A Tear | 7" | Island | WI041 | 1963 £5 £10 | |
| John Holt And Friends | LP | Melodisc | MLP12191 | 197– £5 £12 | |
| Let's Build Our Dreams | 7" | Treasure Isle | TI7061 | 1971 £1.50 £4 | *Tommy McCook B side* |
| Love I Can Feel | LP | Bamboo | BDLPS210 | 1970 £15 £30 | |
| OK Fred | LP | Melodisc | MLP12180 | 197– £5 £12 | |
| One Thousand Volts Of Holt | LP | Trojan | TRLS75 | 1973 £4 £10 | |
| Paragons Medley | 7" | Treasure Isle | TI7066 | 1971 £1.50 £4 | *Tommy McCook B side* |
| Sea Cruise | 7" | Unity | UN549 | 1970 £1.50 £4 | |
| Sister Big Stuff | 7" | Treasure Isle | TI7065 | 1971 £1.50 £4 | *Tommy McCook B side* |
| Still In Chains | LP | Trojan | TRL(S)37 | 1972 £4 £10 | |
| Time Is The Master | LP | Creole | CTLP109 | 1974 £4 £10 | |
| Tonight | 7" | Trojan | TR643 | 1968 £4 £8 | |
| What You Gonna Do Now | 7" | Trojan | TR674 | 1969 £1.50 £4 | |
| Wooden Heart | 7" | Trojan | TR7702 | 1969 £1.50 £4 | |

## HOLTS, ROOSEVELT

| Presenting The Country Blues | LP | Blue Horizon | 763201 | 1968 £15 £30 | |
|---|---|---|---|---|---|

## HOLY GHOST RECEPTION COMMITTEE

| Songs For Liturgical Worship | LP | Paulist | | 1968 £50 £100 | *US* |
|---|---|---|---|---|---|
| Torchbearers | LP | Paulist | P04436 | 1969 £50 £100 | *US* |

## HOLY MACKEREL

| Holy Mackerel | LP | CBS | 65297 | 1972 £6 £15 | |
|---|---|---|---|---|---|

## HOLY MODAL ROUNDERS

| | | | | | |
|---|---|---|---|---|---|
| Alleged In Their Own Time | LP | Rounder | 3004 | 1975 £6 £15 | *US* |
| Good Taste Is Timeless | LP | Metromedia | MD1039 | 1971 £6 £15 | *US* |
| Holy Modal Rounders | LP | Prestige | PR7410 | 1965 £8 £20 | *US* |
| Holy Modal Rounders | LP | Transatlantic | TRA7451 | 1970 £6 £15 | |
| Holy Modal Rounders 2 | LP | Prestige | PRS7451 | 1967 £8 £20 | *US* |
| Indian War Whoop | LP | ESP-Disk | 1068 | 1967 £15 £30 | *US* |
| Last Round | LP | Adelphi | AD1030 | 1978 £6 £15 | *US* |
| Moray Eels Eat The Holy Modal Rounders | LP | Elektra | EKL4026 | 1968 £6 £15 | |
| Peter Stampfel & Steve Weber | LP | Rounder | | 1981 £6 £15 | *US* |
| Stampfel And Weber | LP | Fantasy | F24711 | 1972 £8 £20 | *US double* |

## HOMBRES

| Let It All Hang Out | 7" | Verve | VS1510 | 1967 £4 £8 | |
|---|---|---|---|---|---|
| Let It Out | LP | Verve | FT(S)3036 | 1967 £5 £12 | *US* |

## HOME

| Home | LP | CBS | 64752 | 1972 £4 £10 | |
|---|---|---|---|---|---|
| Pause For A Hoarse Horse | LP | CBS | 64365 | 1971 £8 £20 | |
| unreleased album | LP | CBS | | 197– £50 £100 | *test pressing* |

## HOME SERVICE

| Alright Jack | LP | Making Waves | SPIN119 | 1986 £4 £10 | |
|---|---|---|---|---|---|
| Mysteries | LP | Coda | NAT001 | 1984 £5 £12 | |

## HOMER

| Grown In The USA | LP | United Recording Artist | URA101 | 1970 £75 £150 | *US* |
|---|---|---|---|---|---|

## HOMER & JETHRO

| | | | | | |
|---|---|---|---|---|---|
| Barefoot Ballads | LP | RCA | LPM1412 | 1957 £6 £15 | *US* |
| Homer & Jethro Fracture Frank Loesser | 10" LP | RCA | LPM3112 | 1953 £10 £25 | *US* |
| Life Can Be Miserable | LP | RCA | LPM/LSP1880 | 1958 £5 £12 | *US* |
| Musical Madness | LP | Audio Lab | AL1513 | 1958 £10 £25 | *US* |
| Swappin' Partners | 7" | HMV | 7M211 | 1954 £2 £5 | |
| They Sure Are Corny | LP | KIng | 639 | 1959 £6 £15 | *US* |
| Wanted For Murder Of The Standards | 7" EP | Parlophone | GEP8791 | 1959 £2 £5 | |
| Worst Of Homer And Jethro | LP | RCA | LPM1560 | 1957 £6 £15 | *US* |

## HONDA, MINAKO

| Cancel | LP | Eastworld | WTP90433 | 1986 £8 £20 | *Japanese, with Brian May* |
|---|---|---|---|---|---|
| Golden Days | 7" | Columbia | DB9153 | 1987 £10 £20 | *with Brian May* |

## HONDELLS

| | | | | | |
|---|---|---|---|---|---|
| Cheryl's Going Home | 7" | Mercury | MF967 | 1967 £2.50 £6 | |
| Go Little Honda | LP | Mercury | MG2/SR.60940 | 1964 £10 £25 | *US* |
| Hondells | LP | Mercury | MG2/SR.60982 | 1965 £10 £25 | *US* |
| Little Honda | 7" | Mercury | MF834 | 1964 £2 £5 | |
| Younger Girl | 7" | Mercury | MF925 | 1965 £1.50 £4 | |

## HONEST MEN
Cherie ................................................... 7" ...... Tamla Motown  TMG706 ................ 1969 £5 .......... £10 ..................

## HONEY CONE
Honey Cone ........................................ LP ..... Hot Wax ........ SHW5002 .............. 1969 £4 .......... £10 ..................

## HONEY DREAMERS
Sing Gershwin ...................................... 7" EP . Vogue ............. VE170124 ............. 1958 £2 .......... £5 ..................

## HONEYBUS
Readers of small print on record labels will see the songwriting credit Dello on the B sides of the first two singles by the Applejacks and will be instantly transported to a field where a girl and her packet of Nimble bread hang suspended from a balloon. It was Pete Dello, who as leader of the Honeybus, wrote and sang the memorable 'I Can't Let Maggie Go', a song which provided the group's only hit and was later used in the well-known bread advert on television. The Honeybus gave up trying in mid 1969, following Pete Dello's decision to leave. These days, Dello owns a string of garages, bought, no doubt, out of the proceeds from the one classic hit.

| | | | | | | | |
|---|---|---|---|---|---|---|---|
| Delighted To See You ........................... | 7" | ...... Deram | ............ | DM131 | ................ | 1967 £1.50 ...... £4 | .................. |
| Do I Still Figure In Your Life .................. | 7" | ...... Deram | ............ | DM152 | ................ | 1967 £2 .......... £5 | .................. |
| Girl Of Independent Means .................. | 7" | ...... Deram | ............ | DM207 | ................ | 1968 £1.50 ...... £4 | .................. |
| I Can't Let Maggie Go ......................... | 7" | ...... Deram | ............ | DM182 | ................ | 1968 £1.50 ...... £4 | .................. |
| Recital ............................................... | LP | ..... Warner Bros .... | K46248 | ........... | 1973 £75 ........ £150 | .................. |
| She Sold Blackpool Rock ...................... | 7" | ...... Deram | ............ | DM254 | ................ | 1969 £2 .......... £5 | .................. |
| Story ................................................. | LP | ..... Deram | ............ | SML1056 | .............. | 1970 £20 ........ £40 | .................. |
| Story ................................................. | 7" | ...... Deram | ............ | DM289 | ................ | 1970 £1.50 ...... £4 | .................. |

## HONEYCOMBS
| | | | | | | |
|---|---|---|---|---|---|---|
| All Systems Go .................................... | LP ..... Pye | .................. | NPL18132 | ........... | 1965 £37.50 .... £75 | |
| Colour Slide ...................................... | 7" EP . Pye | .................. | PNV24126 | ........... | 1964 £15 ........ £30 | ......................... French |
| Don't Love You No More .................... | 7" ...... Pye | .................. | 7N15781 | .......... | 1965 £12.50 .... £25 | |
| Eyes ................................................... | 7" ...... Pye | .................. | 7N15736 | .......... | 1964 £1.50 ...... £4 | |
| Have I The Right ................................. | 7" EP . Pye | .................. | PNV24122 | ........... | 1964 £15 ........ £30 | . French, B side by the Kinks |
| Have I The Right ................................. | 7" ...... Pye | .................. | 7N15664 | .......... | 1964 £1.50 ...... £4 | |
| Honeycombs ...................................... | LP ..... Golden Guinea | GGL0350 | .......... | 1965 £6 .......... £15 | |
| Honeycombs ...................................... | LP ..... Pye | .................. | NPL18097 | ........... | 1964 £15 ........ £30 | |
| In Tokyo ............................................ | LP ..... Pye | .................. | PS1277Y | .......... | 1965 £75 ........ £150 | .................. Japanese |
| Is It Because ...................................... | 7" ...... Pye | .................. | 7N15705 | .......... | 1964 £1.50 ...... £4 | |
| It's So Hard ....................................... | 7" ...... Pye | .................. | 7N17138 | .......... | 1966 £1.50 ...... £4 | |
| Something Better Beginning ................ | 7" ...... Pye | .................. | 7N15827 | .......... | 1965 £1.50 ...... £4 | |
| That Loving Feeling ............................ | 7" ...... Pye | .................. | 7N17173 | .......... | 1966 £2.50 ...... £6 | |
| That's The Way ................................... | 7" EP . Pye | .................. | NEP24230 | ........... | 1965 £10 ........ £20 | |
| That's The Way ................................... | 7" ...... Pye | .................. | 7N15890 | .......... | 1965 £1.50 ...... £4 | |
| This Year Next Year ............................. | 7" ...... Pye | .................. | 7N15979 | .......... | 1965 £1.50 ...... £4 | |
| Who Is Sylvia ..................................... | 7" ...... Pye | .................. | 7N17059 | .......... | 1966 £2 .......... £5 | |

## HONEYCRACK
Honeycrack's rediscovery of the delights of tightly harmonized, high-tension power pop was one of the many highlights of a period that is proving to be a new golden age in the history of rock – the mid nineties. In addition to their own sparkling material, the group also turned in a definitive rendering of a forgotten Beatles song, 'Hey Bulldog'. Honeycrack's one rarity so far, however, is a single pressed as a benefit for fans at the early gigs.

| | | | | | |
|---|---|---|---|---|---|
| King Of Misery .................................... | CD-s .. Sony | ............... | PPPCD1 | ............... | 1995 £12.50 .... £25 |
| King Of Misery .................................... | 7" ...... Sony | ............... | PPP1 | ................. | 1995 £12.50 .... £25 |

## HONEYDEW
Honeydew ........................................... LP ..... Argo ............... ZFB15 ................... 1971 £4 .......... £10 ..................

## HONEYS
The Honeys consisted of Brian Wilson's wife Marilyn, her sister Diane Rovell, and their cousin Ginger Blake. Their records were produced by Brian Wilson, who applied the same imagination and innovation as he did on his own records with the Beach Boys.

| | | | | | | |
|---|---|---|---|---|---|---|
| He's A Doll ......................................... | 7" ...... Warner Bros .... | 5430 | ................... | 1964 £75 ........ £150 | ...................... US |
| One You Can't Have ............................ | 7" ...... Capitol | ......... | 5093 | .................. | 1963 £37.50 .... £75 | ...................... US |
| Pray For Surf ...................................... | 7" ...... Capitol | ......... | 5034 | .................. | 1963 £37.50 .... £75 | ...................... US |
| Shoot The Curl ................................... | 7" ...... Capitol | ......... | 4952 | .................. | 1963 £25 ........ £50 | ...................... US |
| Surfing Down The Swanee River ........... | 7" ...... Capitol | ......... | CL15299 | ......... | 1963 £15 ........ £30 | ...................... US |
| Tonight You Belong To Me .................. | 7" ...... Capitol | ......... | 2454 | .................. | 1969 £15 ........ £30 | ...................... US |

## HONEYTONES
Don't Look Now But ............................ 7" ...... London .......... HLX8671 ............... 1958 £12.50 .... £25 ..................

## HONEYTREE
| | | | | | |
|---|---|---|---|---|---|
| Marantha Marathon ............................. | LP ..... Myrrh | ............. | MYR1086 | ............. | 1979 £6 .......... £15 |
| Way I Feel ......................................... | LP ..... Myrrh | ............. | MYR1018 | ............. | 1974 £15 ........ £30 |

## HOOK
| | | | | | | |
|---|---|---|---|---|---|---|
| Hooked .............................................. | LP ..... Uni | ............ | 73038 | ................. | 1968 £15 ........ £30 | ...................... US |
| Show You The Way ............................. | 7" ...... Uni | ............ | UN507 | ............... | 1969 £2 .......... £5 | |
| Will Grab You ..................................... | LP ..... Uni | ............ | 73023 | ................. | 1968 £15 ........ £30 | ...................... US |

## HOOKER, EARL
| | | | | | | |
|---|---|---|---|---|---|---|
| Boogie Don't Blot ............................... | 7" ...... Blue Horizon .... | 573166 | ............. | 1969 £5 .......... £10 | |
| Don't Have To Worry ......................... | LP ..... Stateside | ......... | SSL10298 | ............. | 1969 £6 .......... £15 | |
| Sweet Black Angel ............................... | LP ..... Blue Horizon ... | 763850 | ............. | 1970 £20 ........ £40 | |

## HOOKER, JOHN LEE

| | | | | | | | |
|---|---|---|---|---|---|---|---|
| Big Maceo Merriweather & John Lee Hooker | LP | Fortune | 3002 | 196– | £8 | £20 | US |
| Blue! | LP | Fontana | FJL119 | 1965 | £6 | £15 | |
| Blues Of John Lee Hooker | 7" EP | Stateside | SE1019 | 1964 | £5 | £10 | |
| Boom Boom | 7" | Stateside | SS203 | 1963 | £2.50 | £6 | |
| Burning Hell | LP | Riverside | RLP008 | 1965 | £6 | £15 | |
| Coast To Coast Blues Band | LP | United Artists | UAS29235 | 1971 | £4 | £10 | |
| Democrat Man | 7" EP | Riverside | REP3207 | 1960 | £2.50 | £6 | |
| Dimples | 7" | Stateside | SS297 | 1964 | £1.50 | £4 | |
| Don't Turn Me From Your Door | LP | London | HAK8097 | 1963 | £8 | £20 | |
| Down At The Landing | 7" EP | Chess | CRE6000 | 1965 | £5 | £10 | |
| Driftin' Blues | LP | Atlantic | 590003 | 1967 | £4 | £10 | |
| Driftin' Through The Blues | LP | Ember | (ST)EMB3371 | 1966 | £4 | £10 | |
| Folk Blues | LP | Fontana | 688700ZL | 1964 | £6 | £15 | |
| Folk Blues | LP | RIverside | RLP12838 | 1962 | £6 | £15 | |
| Folklore Of John Lee Hooker | LP | Stateside | SL10014 | 1962 | £8 | £20 | |
| High Priced Woman | 7" | Pye | 7N25255 | 1964 | £1.50 | £4 | |
| House Of The Blues | LP | Pye | NPL28042 | 1964 | £8 | £20 | |
| I Love You Honey | 7" | Stateside | SS341 | 1964 | £2 | £5 | |
| I Want To Shout The Blues | LP | Stateside | SL10074 | 1964 | £6 | £15 | |
| I'm In The Mood | 7" | Sue | WI361 | 1965 | £6 | £12 | |
| I'm John Lee Hooker | LP | Vee Jay | LP1007 | 1959 | £15 | £30 | US |
| I'm John Lee Hooker | 7" EP | Stateside | SE1023 | 1964 | £5 | £10 | |
| If You Miss 'Im I Got 'Im | LP | Probe | SPB1016 | 1971 | £4 | £10 | with Earl Hooker |
| It Serves You Right To Suffer | LP | HMV | CLP5032/CSD3542 | 1966 | £8 | £20 | |
| John Lee Hooker | LP | XTRA | XTRA114 | 1971 | £4 | £10 | |
| John Lee Hooker | 7" EP | Atlantic | AET6010 | 1965 | £4 | £8 | |
| John Lee Hooker Sings The Blues | LP | King | 727 | 1961 | £15 | £30 | US |
| Johnny Lee | LP | Green Bottle | GN4002 | 1973 | £4 | £10 | |
| Journey | 7" EP | Chess | CRE6014 | 1966 | £5 | £10 | |
| Let's Go Out Tonight | 7" | Chess | CRS8039 | 1966 | £2.50 | £10 | |
| Live At Café Au Go-Go | LP | HMV | CLP/CSD3612 | 1966 | £6 | £15 | |
| Love Blues | 7" EP | Pye | NEP44034 | 1964 | £6 | £12 | |
| Mai Lee | 7" | Planet | PLF114 | 1966 | £7.50 | £15 | |
| Need Somebody | 78 | London | HL8037 | 1954 | £10 | £20 | |
| On Campus | LP | Vee Jay | LP/SR1066 | 1963 | £6 | £15 | US |
| Plays And Sings The Blues | LP | Chess | CRL4500 | 1965 | £5 | £12 | |
| Preachin' The Blues | LP | Stateside | SL10053 | 1964 | £8 | £20 | |
| Real Folk Blues | LP | Chess | CRL4527 | 1966 | £4 | £10 | |
| Real Folk Blues Vol. 3 | 7" EP | Chess | CRE6021 | 1966 | £5 | £10 | |
| Rhythm And Blues | 7" EP | Stateside | SE1008 | 1962 | £5 | £10 | with Jimmy Reed |
| Serves You Right To Suffer | 7" EP | Impulse | 9103 | 1973 | £2.50 | £6 | |
| Shake It Baby | 7" | Polydor | NH52930 | 1964 | £2.50 | £6 | |
| Simply The Truth | LP | Stateside | (S)SL10280 | 1969 | £4 | £10 | |
| Sings The Blues | LP | Ember | EMB3356 | 1965 | £4 | £10 | |
| That's Where It's At | LP | Stax | SXATS1025 | 1970 | £4 | £10 | |
| Thinking Blues | 7" EP | Ember | EMBEP4561 | 1964 | £5 | £10 | |
| Tupelo Blues | LP | Storyville | 673020 | 1970 | £4 | £10 | |
| Urban Blues | LP | Stateside | (S)SL10246 | 1968 | £4 | £10 | |
| Walking The Boogie | 7" EP | Chess | CRE6007 | 1966 | £5 | £10 | |
| Wednesday Evening | 7" EP | Riverside | REP3202 | 1960 | £2.50 | £6 | |
| Whistlin' And Moanin' Blues | 78 | Vogue | V2102 | 1952 | £10 | £20 | |
| You're Leavin' Me Baby | LP | Storyville | 673005 | 1970 | £4 | £10 | |

## HOOKER, JOHN LEE & CANNED HEAT

| | | | | | | | |
|---|---|---|---|---|---|---|---|
| Hooker And Heat | LP | Liberty | LPS103/4 | 1971 | £8 | £20 | double |

## HOOKFOOT

| | | | | | | | |
|---|---|---|---|---|---|---|---|
| Hookfoot | LP | DJM | DJLPS413 | 1971 | £4 | £10 | |

## HOOKS, MARSHALL & CO.

| | | | | | | |
|---|---|---|---|---|---|---|
| I Want The Same Thing Tomorrow | 7" | Blue Horizon | 2096002 | 1971 | £2 | £5 |
| Marshall Hooks & Co. | LP | Blue Horizon | 2431003 | 1971 | £15 | £30 |

## HOOTCH

| | | | | | | | |
|---|---|---|---|---|---|---|---|
| Hootch | LP | Progress | PRS4844 | 1974 | £180 | £300 | US |

## HOOTENANNY SINGERS

This Swedish group had the future Abba star, Björn Ulvaeus, as singer and songwriter.

| | | | | | | | |
|---|---|---|---|---|---|---|---|
| Basta | LP | Polar | POLL101 | 1967 | £6 | £15 | Swedish |
| Bellman Pa Vart Satt | LP | Polar | POLS214 | 196– | £6 | £15 | Swedish |
| Civila | LP | Polar | POLS211 | 196– | £6 | £15 | Swedish |
| Dan Andersson Pa Vart Satt | LP | Polar | POLS249 | 197– | £6 | £15 | Swedish |
| De Basta Med & Bjorn Ulvaeus | LP | Polar | POLL103 | 196– | £6 | £15 | Swedish |
| Evert Taube | LP | Polar | POLS204 | 196– | £6 | £15 | Swedish |
| Evert Taube Pa Vart Satt | LP | Polar | POLS260 | 1974 | £6 | £15 | Swedish |
| Frogg | 7" EP | Pathe | EGF794 | 1964 | £10 | £20 | French |
| Gabriella | 7" | United Artists | UP1082 | 1965 | £7.50 | £15 | |
| Hootenanny Singers | LP | Polar | POLS201 | 196– | £6 | £15 | Swedish |
| International | LP | Polar | POLP206 | 1965 | £6 | £15 | Swedish |
| Manga Ansikten | LP | Polar | POLP209 | 196– | £6 | £15 | Swedish |
| No Time | 7" EP | Pathe | EGF880 | 1965 | £10 | £20 | French |
| Skillingtryck | LP | Polar | POLS225 | 1970 | £6 | £15 | Swedish |
| Vara Backraste Visor | LP | Polar | POLS229 | 197– | £6 | £15 | Swedish |

| | | | | | | | | |
|---|---|---|---|---|---|---|---|---|
| Vara Backraste Visor 2 | LP | Polar | POLS236 | 197– | £6 | £15 | | *Swedish* |

## HOPE, BOB
| | | | | | | | | |
|---|---|---|---|---|---|---|---|---|
| Paris Holiday | 7" | London | HLU8593 | 1958 | £1.50 | £4 | | *with Bing Crosby* |

## HOPE, ELMO
| | | | | | | | |
|---|---|---|---|---|---|---|---|
| Informal Jazz | LP | Esquire | 32039 | 1958 | £20 | £40 | |
| With Frank Butler And James Bond | LP | Vocalion | LAEH590 | 1966 | £5 | £12 | |

## HOPE, LYNN
| | | | | | | | |
|---|---|---|---|---|---|---|---|
| Blue Moon | 7" | Vogue | V9081 | 1957 | £7.50 | £15 | |
| Eleven Till Two | 7" | Vogue | V9082 | 1957 | £7.50 | £15 | |
| Lynn Hope | LP | Aladdin | 820 | 195– | £30 | £60 | *US* |
| Lynn Hope & His Tenor Sax | 7" EP | Vogue | VE170103 | 1957 | £20 | £40 | |
| Lynn Hope & His Tenor Sax | 7" EP | Vogue | VE170146 | 1960 | £20 | £40 | |
| Lynn Hope And His Tenor Sax | 10" LP | Aladdin | 707 | 195– | £50 | £100 | *US* |
| Shocking | 7" | Blue Beat | BB21 | 1960 | £6 | £12 | |
| Temptation | 7" | Vogue | V9115 | 1958 | £5 | £10 | |
| Tenderly | LP | Score | LP4015 | 1957 | £20 | £40 | *US* |

## HOPETOWN & GLENMORE
| | | | | | | | |
|---|---|---|---|---|---|---|---|
| Skinny Leg Girl | 7" | Fab | FAB43 | 1968 | £4 | £8 | |

## HOPKIN, MARY
| | | | | | | | |
|---|---|---|---|---|---|---|---|
| Earth Song/Ocean Song | LP | Apple | SAPCOR21 | 1971 | £6 | £15 | |
| Knock Knock Who's There | 7" | Apple | 26 | 1970 | £1.50 | £4 | *picture sleeve* |
| Let My Name Be Sorrow | 7" | Apple | 34 | 1971 | £5 | £10 | *picture sleeve* |
| Llais Swynol Mary Hopkin | 7" EP | Cambrian | CEP414 | 1968 | £4 | £8 | |
| Lontana Dagli Occhi | 7" | Apple | 7 | 1969 | £2.50 | £6 | *European* |
| Mary Ac Edward | 7" EP | Cambrian | CEP420 | 1969 | £4 | £8 | |
| Postcard | LP | Apple | APCOR5 | 1969 | £5 | £12 | *mono* |
| Postcard | LP | Apple | SAPCOR5 | 1969 | £4 | £10 | |
| Prince En Avignon | 7" | Apple | 9 | 1969 | £2.50 | £6 | *European* |
| Que Sera Sera | 7" | Apple | 27 | 1970 | £2.50 | £6 | *European* |
| Temma Harbour | 7" | Apple | 22 | 1970 | £1.50 | £4 | *picture sleeve* |
| Think About Your Children | 7" | Apple | 30 | 1970 | £2 | £5 | *picture sleeve* |
| Those Were The Days | LP | Apple | SAPCOR23 | 1972 | £30 | £60 | |
| Water, Paper And Clay | 7" | Apple | 39 | 1971 | £7.50 | £15 | *picture sleeve* |

## HOPKINS, LIGHTNIN'
| | | | | | | | |
|---|---|---|---|---|---|---|---|
| Autobiography In Blues | LP | Tradition | TLP1040 | 1960 | £10 | £25 | *US* |
| Blue Bird Blues | LP | Fontana | 688803ZL | 1966 | £4 | £10 | |
| Blues From East Texas | LP | Heritage | H1000 | 1960 | £15 | £30 | *with Joel Hopkins* |
| Blues In The Bottle | LP | XTRA | XTRA5036 | 1968 | £5 | £12 | |
| Blues/Folk | LP | Time | 1 | 1962 | £6 | £15 | *US* |
| Blues/Folk Vol. 2 | LP | Time | 3 | 1962 | £6 | £15 | *US* |
| Burnin' In L.A. | LP | Fontana | 688801ZL | 1965 | £4 | £10 | |
| California Mudslide And Earthquake | LP | Liberty | LBS83293 | 1970 | £4 | £10 | |
| Country Blues | LP | Tradition | TLP1035 | 1960 | £10 | £25 | *US* |
| Dirty House Blues | LP | Realm | RM171 | 1964 | £4 | £10 | |
| Down Home Blues | LP | Stateside | SL10155 | 1965 | £6 | £15 | |
| Earth Blues | LP | Minit | MLL/MLS40006 | 1968 | £6 | £15 | |
| Fast Life Woman | LP | Verve | V8453 | 1962 | £8 | £20 | *US* |
| Free Form Patterns | LP | International Artists | 6 | 1968 | £37.50 | £75 | *US* |
| Goin' Away | LP | Bluesville | BV1073 | 1964 | £6 | £15 | *US* |
| Got To Move Your Baby | LP | XTRA | XTRA5044 | 1968 | £4 | £10 | |
| His Greatest Hits | LP | Bluesville | BV1084 | 1964 | £6 | £15 | *US* |
| Hootin' The Blues | LP | Stateside | SL10110 | 1965 | £6 | £15 | |
| King Of Dowling Street | LP | Liberty | LBL83254 | 1969 | £6 | £15 | |
| Last Night Blues | LP | Bluesville | BV1029 | 1961 | £8 | £20 | *US* |
| Last Night Blues | LP | Fontana | 688301ZL | 1964 | £4 | £10 | |
| Last Of The Great Blues Singers | LP | Time | 70004 | 1960 | £8 | £20 | *US* |
| Let's Work Awhile | LP | Blue Horizon | 2431005 | 1971 | £20 | £40 | |
| Lightnin' | LP | Bluesville | BV1019 | 1961 | £8 | £20 | *US* |
| Lightnin' | LP | Poppy | 60002 | 1969 | £4 | £10 | *US* |
| Lightnin' And The Blues | LP | Herald | 1012 | 1960 | £75 | £150 | *US* |
| Lightnin' Hopkins | LP | 77 | LA121 | 1960 | £8 | £20 | |
| Lightnin' Hopkins | LP | Folkways | FS3822 | 1961 | £8 | £20 | *US* |
| Lightnin' Hopkins | LP | Fontana | 688807ZL | 1966 | £4 | £10 | |
| Lightnin' Hopkins | LP | Vee Jay | LP1044 | 1962 | £10 | £25 | *US* |
| Lightnin' Hopkins And The Blues | LP | Imperial | LP9211/12211 | 1962 | £8 | £20 | *US* |
| Lightnin' Hopkins On Stage | LP | Imperial | LP9180 | 1962 | £8 | £20 | *US* |
| Lightnin' Hopkins Strums The Blues | LP | Score | 4022 | 1960 | £37.50 | £75 | *US* |
| Lightnin' Strikes | LP | A&M | AMLB40001/2 | 1971 | £5 | £12 | *double* |
| Lightnin' Strikes | LP | Stateside | SL10031 | 1963 | £6 | £15 | |
| Lightnin' Strikes | LP | Verve | (S)VLP5014 | 1966 | £4 | £10 | |
| Lonesome Lightnin' | LP | Polydor | 2941005 | 1972 | £4 | £10 | |
| Mojo Hand | LP | Fire | 104 | 1962 | £25 | £50 | *US* |
| My Life In The Blues | LP | Prestige | PR7370 | 1965 | £6 | £15 | *US* |
| Nothin' But The Blues | LP | Mount Vernon | 104 | 196– | £6 | £15 | *US* |
| Roots Of Hopkins | LP | Verve | (S)VLP5003 | 1966 | £4 | £10 | |
| Roots Of Lightnin' Hopkins | LP | XTRA | XTRA1127 | 1971 | £5 | £12 | |
| Sings The Blues | LP | Realm | RM128 | 1963 | £4 | £10 | |
| Smokes Like Lightnin' | LP | Bluesville | BV1070 | 1963 | £6 | £15 | *US* |
| Something Blue | LP | Verve | FV(S)3013 | 1967 | £6 | £15 | *US* |
| Soul Blues | LP | Prestige | PR(S)7377 | 1966 | £6 | £15 | *US* |
| There's Good Rockin' Tonight | LP | Storyville | 616001 | 1970 | £6 | £15 | |

| | | | | | | | |
|---|---|---|---|---|---|---|---|
| Time For Blues | LP | Ember | EMB3389 | 1967 | £4 | £10 | |
| Walkin' This Road By Myself | LP | Bluesville | BV1057 | 1961 | £8 | £20 | US |

## HOPKINS, LIGHTNIN' & JOHN LEE HOOKER

| | | | | | | | |
|---|---|---|---|---|---|---|---|
| Lightnin' Hopkins And John Lee Hooker | LP | Storyville | SLP174 | 1965 | £6 | £15 | |

## HOPKINS, LIGHTNIN', SONNY TERRY & BROWNIE MCGHEE

| | | | | | | |
|---|---|---|---|---|---|---|
| Blues Hoot | LP | Stateside | SL10076 | 1964 | £6 | £15 |

## HOPKINS, LINDA

| | | | | | | |
|---|---|---|---|---|---|---|
| I Diddle Dum Dum | 7" | Coral | Q72423 | 1961 | £7.50 | £15 |
| Mama's Doing The Twist | 7" | Coral | Q72448 | 1962 | £5 | £10 |

## HOPKINS, NICKY

| | | | | | | | |
|---|---|---|---|---|---|---|---|
| High On A Hill | 7" | Fontana | TF906 | 1968 | £1.50 | £4 | actually Nigel Hopkins |
| Mr. Big | 7" | CBS | 202055 | 1966 | £2.50 | £6 | |
| Mr. Pleasant | 7" | Polydor | 56175 | 1967 | £4 | £8 | |
| Revolutionary Piano | LP | CBS | 62679 | 1966 | £8 | £20 | |
| Tin Man Was A Dreamer | LP | CBS | 65416 | 1973 | £4 | £10 | |

## HOPPER, HUGH

Although Hugh Hopper's fuzz bass guitar lines seemed like the element most rooted to rock in Soft Machine's rapid espousal of a jazz approach, it is Hopper who has actually continued to work mostly in a jazz context, while his former colleagues Mike Ratledge and Karl Jenkins have opted for a more commercial approach.

| | | | | | | | |
|---|---|---|---|---|---|---|---|
| 1984 | LP | CBS | 65466 | 1973 | £4 | £10 | |
| Cruel But Fair | LP | Compendium | FIDARDO4 | 1976 | £4 | £10 | |
| Hopper Tunity Box | LP | Compendium | FIDARDO7 | 1977 | £4 | £10 | |
| Monster Band | LP | Atmosphere | IRI5003 | 1979 | £4 | £10 | |
| Rogue Element | LP | Ogun | OG527 | 1978 | £5 | £12 | ...with Elton Dean, Alan Gowen, Dave Sheen |

## HOPSCOTCH

| | | | | | | |
|---|---|---|---|---|---|---|
| Long Black Veil | 7" | United Artists | UP35022 | 1969 | £1.50 | £4 |
| Look At The Lights Go Up | 7" | United Artists | UP2231 | 1969 | £2.50 | £6 |

## HORACE & THE IMPERIALS

| | | | | | | |
|---|---|---|---|---|---|---|
| Young Love | 7" | Nu Beat | NB012 | 1968 | £2.50 | £6 |

## HORDE CATALYTIQUE POUR LA FIN

| | | | | | | | |
|---|---|---|---|---|---|---|---|
| Gestation sonore | LP | Futura | SON003 | 1971 | £5 | £12 | French |

## HORDEN RAIKES

| | | | | | | |
|---|---|---|---|---|---|---|
| Horden Raikes | LP | Folk Heritage | FHR026 | 1972 | £5 | £12 |
| King Cotton | LP | Folk Heritage | FHR042 | 1972 | £5 | £12 |

## HORIZON

| | | | | | | |
|---|---|---|---|---|---|---|
| Stage Struck | 7" | SRT | SRTS81432 | 1981 | £2.50 | £6 |

## HORN, PAUL

| | | | | | | | |
|---|---|---|---|---|---|---|---|
| In Kashmir | LP | Liberty | LBL83084 | 1968 | £4 | £10 | |
| Inside | LP | Epic | EPC65201 | 1969 | £4 | £10 | |
| Inside Two | LP | Epic | 31600 | 1973 | £4 | £10 | US |
| Special Edition | LP | Island | ISLD6 | 1974 | £5 | £12 | double |
| Visions | LP | Epic | 32837 | 1974 | £4 | £10 | US |

## HORNE, KENNETH & OTHERS

| | | | | | | |
|---|---|---|---|---|---|---|
| Beyond Our Ken | LP | Parlophone | PMC1238 | 1964 | £4 | £10 |

## HORNE, LENA

| | | | | | | | |
|---|---|---|---|---|---|---|---|
| It's All Right With Me | 7" | HMV | 7M319 | 1955 | £1.50 | £4 | |
| It's Love | LP | RCA | LPM1148 | 1955 | £8 | £20 | US |
| Lena Horne | 7" EP | MGM | MGMEP503 | 1954 | £2 | £5 | |
| Let's Put Out The Lights | 7" EP | RCA | SRC7012 | 1959 | £2 | £5 | stereo |
| Love Me Or Leave Me | 7" | HMV | 7M309 | 1955 | £1.50 | £4 | |
| Stormy Weather | LP | RCA | LPM1375 | 1956 | £8 | £20 | US |

## HORNETS

| | | | | | | | |
|---|---|---|---|---|---|---|---|
| Motorcycles USA | LP | Liberty | LST7348 | 1964 | £6 | £15 | US |

## HORNSBY, BRUCE

| | | | | | | |
|---|---|---|---|---|---|---|
| Defenders Of The Flag | CD-s | RCA | PD49512 | 1988 | £2 | £5 |
| Look Out Any Window | CD-s | RCA | PD49534 | 1988 | £2 | £5 |
| Valley Road | CD-s | RCA | PD49562 | 1988 | £2 | £5 |

## HORNSEY AT WAR

| | | | | | | |
|---|---|---|---|---|---|---|
| Dead Beat Revival | 7" | War | WAR001 | 197– | £2 | £5 |

## HORRORCOMIC

| | | | | | | |
|---|---|---|---|---|---|---|
| Jesus Christ | 7" | B&C | BCS18 | 1979 | £2.50 | £6 |

## HORSE

| | | | | | | |
|---|---|---|---|---|---|---|
| Horse | LP | RCA | SF8109 | 1970 | £62.50 | £125 |

## HORSES

| | | | | | | | |
|---|---|---|---|---|---|---|---|
| Album No. 1 | LP | White Whale | WW7121 | 1969 | £10 | £25 | US |

## HORSLIPS

Horslips were employing traditional musical elements from their native Ireland long before the Pogues and the Waterboys made it fashionable. Their first LP, *Happy To Meet*, comes within an intricate package that is designed to look like a concertina and which is not often found in mint condition.

| | | | | | | | |
|---|---|---|---|---|---|---|---|
| Drive The Cold Winter Away | LP | Oats | MOO9 | 1976 | £4 | £10 | |
| Happy To Meet Sorry To Part | LP | Oats | MOO3 | 1972 | £8 | £20 | ... octagonal cover with booklet |
| Live | LP | Oats | MOO10 | 1976 | £6 | £15 | Irish double |
| Tain | LP | Oats | MOO5 | 1973 | £4 | £10 | |

## HORTON, JOHNNY

| | | | | | | | |
|---|---|---|---|---|---|---|---|
| All Grown Up | 7" | CBS | AAG132 | 1963 | £1.50 | £4 | |
| Battle Of New Orleans | 7" | Philips | PB932 | 1959 | £1.50 | £4 | |
| Country And Western Aces | 7" EP | Mercury | 10008MCE | 1964 | £10 | £20 | |
| Done Rovin' | LP | Briar | 104 | 195– | £30 | £60 | US |
| Done Rovin' | LP | London | HAU8096 | 1963 | £15 | £30 | |
| Fantastic | LP | Mercury | MG20478 | 1959 | £15 | £30 | US |
| Fantastic Johnny Horton | 7" EP | Mercury | ZEP10074 | 1960 | £12.50 | £25 | |
| Free And Easy Songs | LP | SESAC | 1201 | 1959 | £37.50 | £75 | US |
| Greatest Hits | LP | Columbia | CL1596/CS8396 | 1961 | £6 | £15 | US |
| Honky Tonk Man | LP | Philips | BBL7536 | 1961 | £8 | £20 | |
| I Can't Forget You | LP | Columbia | CL2299/CS9099 | 1965 | £4 | £10 | US |
| Johnny Horton | LP | Dot | DLP3221 | 1962 | £8 | £20 | US |
| Johnny Horton Makes History | LP | Columbia | CL1478/CS8269 | 1960 | £6 | £15 | US |
| Johnny Reb | 7" | Philips | PB951 | 1959 | £2 | £5 | |
| Mr. Moonlight | 7" | Philips | PB1130 | 1961 | £1.50 | £4 | |
| North to Alaska | 7" | Philips | PB1062 | 1960 | £1.50 | £4 | |
| Ole Slew Foot | 7" | Philips | PB1170 | 1961 | £1.50 | £4 | |
| Sink The Bismarck | 7" | Philips | PB995 | 1960 | £2 | £5 | |
| Sleepy Eyed John | 7" | Philips | PB1132 | 1961 | £1.50 | £4 | |
| Spectacular Johnny Horton | LP | Philips | BBL7464 | 1960 | £8 | £20 | |
| Take Me Like I Am | 7" | Philips | PB976 | 1959 | £1.50 | £4 | |
| Voice Of Johnny Horton | LP | Fontana | FJL306 | 1965 | £4 | £10 | |
| Words | 7" | Philips | PB1226 | 1962 | £2 | £5 | |

## HORTON, SHAKEY

| | | | | | | | |
|---|---|---|---|---|---|---|---|
| Soul Of Blues Harmonica | LP | Argo | 4037 | 1964 | £20 | £40 | US |

## HOST

| | | | | | | | |
|---|---|---|---|---|---|---|---|
| Pa Sterke Vinger | LP | Philips | 6317601 | 1974 | £50 | £100 | Norwegian |

## HOT CHOCOLATE BAND

| | | | | | | | |
|---|---|---|---|---|---|---|---|
| Give Peace A Chance | 7" | Apple | 18 | 1969 | £10 | £20 | |

## HOT DOGGERS

| | | | | | | | |
|---|---|---|---|---|---|---|---|
| Surfin' USA | LP | Epic | LN24/BN26054 | 1963 | £15 | £30 | US |

## HOT POOP

| | | | | | | | |
|---|---|---|---|---|---|---|---|
| Does Their Own Stuff | LP | Hot Poop | HPS3072 | 1967 | £30 | £60 | US |

## HOT POTATO

| | | | | | | | |
|---|---|---|---|---|---|---|---|
| Hot Potato | LP | private | PMTB1 | 1973 | £37.50 | £75 | |

## HOT SOUP

| | | | | | | | |
|---|---|---|---|---|---|---|---|
| Openers | LP | Rama Rama | RR78 | 1969 | £8 | £20 | US |

## HOT SPRINGS

| | | | | | | | |
|---|---|---|---|---|---|---|---|
| It's All Right | 7" | Columbia | DB7821 | 1966 | £2 | £5 | |

## HOT TODDYS

| | | | | | | | |
|---|---|---|---|---|---|---|---|
| Shakin' And Stompin' | 7" | Pye | 7N25020 | 1959 | £5 | £10 | |

## HOT TUNA

| | | | | | | | |
|---|---|---|---|---|---|---|---|
| America's Choice | LP | Grunt | BFD10820 | 1975 | £4 | £10 | US quad |
| Yellow Fever | LP | Grunt | BFD11238 | 1975 | £4 | £10 | US quad |

## HOT VULTURES

| | | | | | | | |
|---|---|---|---|---|---|---|---|
| Carrion On | LP | Red Rag | RRR005 | 1976 | £5 | £12 | |
| East Street Shakes | LP | Red Rag | RRR015 | 1978 | £4 | £10 | |

## HOTHOUSE FLOWERS

| | | | | | | | |
|---|---|---|---|---|---|---|---|
| Don't Go | CD-s | London | LONCD174 | 1988 | £2 | £5 | |
| Don't Go | CD-s | Polygram | 0804822 | 1988 | £4 | £10 | CD video |
| Easier In The Morning | CD-s | London | LONCD186 | 1988 | £2 | £5 | |
| Home | CD | London | 8281972 | 1990 | £20 | £40 | ... promo box set, with cassette and video |
| I'm Sorry | CD-s | London | LONCD187 | 1988 | £2 | £5 | |

## HOTLEGS

Hotlegs were not the one-hit wonders they might appear to be. The group who scored with a novelty recording, 'Neanderthal Man', were only waiting for successful songwriter Graham Gouldman to join them before starting to make records as Ten cc.

| | | | | | | | |
|---|---|---|---|---|---|---|---|
| Songs | LP | Philips | 6308080 | 1971 | £4 | £10 | |
| Thinks School Stinks | LP | Philips | 6308057 | 1971 | £4 | £10 | |

## HOTRODS
I Don't Love You No More................... 7".......Columbia........DB7693.................1965 £12.50....£25 ................................

## HOTZENPLOTZ
Songs Aus Der Schau..............................LP......Ho................1001....................1972 £8...........£20 ................German

## HOU-LOPS
69 ...................................................LP.....Canusa............33110...................1969 £6............£15 ................Canadian
Off.................................................LP.....Apex...............APL1591................1967 £6............£15 ................Canadian
Palamares.........................................LP.....Trans-...............916.....................1968 £25...........£50 ................Canadian
                                                        Canadian.........

## HOUND DOGS
Respect .............................................LP.....Profi...............LP3....................1966 £25...........£50 ................German
Twist Festival 1964.............................LP.....Philips............48063..................1964 £30...........£60 ................German

## HOUND HEAD HENRY & FRANKIE JAXON
Male Blues Vol. 6 ...............................7" EP . Collector........JEL10.................1960 £5...........£10 ................................

## HOUNDS
Lion Sleeps Tonight..............................LP.....Gazell............GMG1207...........1967 £8............£20 ................Swedish
My World Fell Down............................7" EP . Pathe.............EGF983................1966 £5............£10 ................French

## HOURGLASS
Hourglass...........................................LP ,.....Liberty............LBL/LBS83219......1968 £5...........£12 ................................
Hourglass...........................................LP.....United Artists...USD303/4...........1973 £5............£12 ................double
Power Of Love ...................................LP.....Liberty............LST7555...............1968 £6............£15 ................US

## HOUSE, SON
Father Of The Folk Blues......................LP.....CBS...............(S)BPG62604.........1966 £4...........£10 ................................
John The Revelator .............................LP.....Liberty............LBS83391.............1970 £6............£15 ................................
Vocal Intensity ...................................LP.....Saydisc............SL504 .................196– £4...........£10 ................................

## HOUSE, SON & J. D. SHORT
Son House And J. D. Short ..................LP.....XTRA...............XTRA1080............1969 £6............£15 ................................

## HOUSE OF LORDS
In The Land Of Dreams........................7".....B&C...............CB112.................1969 £2.50......£6 ................................

## HOUSE OF LOVE
Beatles And The Stones.........................CD-s ..Fontana...........HOLCD422..........1990 £2...........£5 ................................
Christine ............................................CD-s ..Creation...........CRESCD53 ........1991 £2...........£5 ................................
Christine ............................................7"....Creation...........CRE053..............1988 £2.50......£6 ................................
Christine ............................................12"....Creation...........CRE053T.............1988 £5............£12 ................................
Destroy The Heart ..............................CD-s ..Creation...........CRESCD57 ........1990 £2...........£5 ................................
Destroy The Heart ..............................7"....Creation...........CRE057..............1988 £2...........£5 ................................
House Of Love ...................................LP.....Creation...........CRELP034 .........1988 £4...........£10 ................with 7"
                                                                                                                (CREFRE01)
House Of Love ...................................CD.....Fontana...........................1989 £6............£15 ..US promo black disc
I Don't Know Why I Love You..............CD-s ..Fontana...........HOLCD2 ...........1989 £2...........£5 ................................
Live Cabaret Metro, Chicago 2-6-90........CD.....Fontana...........SACD189............1990 £6............£15 ................US promo
Never.................................................CD-s ..Fontana...........HOLCD1 ...........1989 £2...........£5 ................................
Real Animal.......................................12"....Creation...........CRE044T.............1987 £10...........£20 ................................
Shine On............................................CD-s ..Fontana...........HOLCD3 ...........1990 £2...........£5 ................................
Shine On............................................7"....Creation...........CREFRE5 ...........1988 £2.50......£6 ................flexi
Shine On............................................12"....Creation...........CRE043T.............1987 £10...........£20 ................................

## HOUSEHOLD
Guess I'll Learn How To Fly ...................7".......United Artists ..UP1190...............1967 £1.50.....£4 ................................
Twenty-First Summer............................7".......United Artists ..UP2210.................1968 £1.50.....£4 ................................

## HOUSEMARTINS
There Is Always Something There To........CD-s ..Go! Discs ........GODCD22 ............1988 £2...........£5 ................................
    Remind Me ....................................

## HOUSTON, CISCO
Cisco Special.......................................LP.....Top Rank .......30028..................1960 £25...........£50 ................................

## HOUSTON, CISSY
Cissy Houston .....................................LP......Janus...............6310205...............1971 £4...........£10 ................................
I Just Don't Know What To Do With........7"....Pye.................7N25537...............1970 £5...........£10 ................................
    Myself...........................................
Presenting Cissy Houston.........................LP.....Major Minor ...SMLP80................1970 £4...........£10 ................................

## HOUSTON, DAVID
Blue Prelude ......................................7".....London............HL8147................1955 £10...........£20 ................................

## HOUSTON, JOE
Joe Houston Blows All Night Long..........LP.....Modern.........LMP1206.............1956 £8...........£20 ................US
Rockin' At The Drive-In.........................LP.....Combo ..........LP400..................1960 £25...........£50 ................US
Where Is Joe?......................................LP.....Combo ..........LP100..................1960 £25...........£50 ................US

## HOUSTON, SAM
My Mother's Eyes ...............................7".......Island ............WI172.................1965 £2.50......£6 ................................

## HOUSTON, THELMA
Black California ..................................7".......Mowest..........MW3004 .............1973 £2.50......£6 ................demo only

| Title | Format | Label | Cat. No. | Year | | | Notes |
|---|---|---|---|---|---|---|---|
| I've Got The Music In Me | LP | Sheffield Lab | 2 | 1974 | £4 | £10 | US audiophile |
| Sunshower | LP | Stateside | SSL5010 | 1969 | £4 | £10 | |

## HOUSTON, WHITNEY

| Title | Format | Label | Cat. No. | Year | | | Notes |
|---|---|---|---|---|---|---|---|
| Didn't We Almost Have It All | CD-s | Arista | RISCD31 | 1987 | £2.50 | £6 | |
| I Wanna Dance With Somebody | CD-s | Arista | RISCD1 | 1987 | £2.50 | £6 | |
| It Isn't, It Wasn't, It Ain't Never Gonna Be | CD-s | Arista | 662545 | 1989 | £2 | £5 | |
| Love Will Save The Day | CD-s | Arista | 661516 | 1988 | £4 | £10 | picture disc |
| Love Will Save The Day | 7" | Arista | 111516P | 1988 | £1.50 | £4 | picture disc |
| One Moment In Time | CD-s | Arista | 661613 | 1988 | £2 | £5 | |
| So Emotional | CD-s | Arista | RISCD43 | 1987 | £2 | £5 | |
| Whitney Houston | LP | Arista | WHIT1 | 1986 | £4 | £10 | with cards, book, calendar, boxed |

## HOWARD, BRIAN & THE SILHOUETTES

| Title | Format | Label | Cat. No. | Year | | | Notes |
|---|---|---|---|---|---|---|---|
| Back In The USA | 7" | Fontana | TF464 | 1964 | £4 | £8 | |
| Somebody Help Me | 7" | Columbia | DB4914 | 1962 | £5 | £10 | |
| Worrying Kind | 7" | Columbia | DB7067 | 1963 | £4 | £8 | |

## HOWARD, HARLAN

| Title | Format | Label | Cat. No. | Year | | | Notes |
|---|---|---|---|---|---|---|---|
| All-Time Favorite Country Songwriter | LP | Monument | MLP/SLP18038 | 1965 | £5 | £12 | US |
| Harlan Howard Sings Harlan Howard | LP | Capitol | (S)T1631 | 1961 | £5 | £12 | US |

## HOWARD, JAN

| Title | Format | Label | Cat. No. | Year | | | Notes |
|---|---|---|---|---|---|---|---|
| One You Slip Around With | 7" | London | HL7088 | 1960 | £2 | £5 | export |

## HOWE, CATHERINE

| Title | Format | Label | Cat. No. | Year | | | Notes |
|---|---|---|---|---|---|---|---|
| What A Beautiful Place | LP | Reflection | REFL11 | 1971 | £50 | £100 | |

## HOWELL, EDDIE

| Title | Format | Label | Cat. No. | Year | | | Notes |
|---|---|---|---|---|---|---|---|
| Man From Manhattan | 7" | Warner Bros | K16701 | 1976 | £12.50 | £25 | with Queen |

## HOWERD, FRANKIE

| Title | Format | Label | Cat. No. | Year | | | Notes |
|---|---|---|---|---|---|---|---|
| At The Establishment | LP | Decca | LK4556 | 1963 | £4 | £10 | |
| It's All Right With Me | 7" | Columbia | DB4230 | 1958 | £1.50 | £4 | |
| Kiddy Geddin | 7" | Decca | F10420 | 1954 | £2.50 | £6 | |

## HOWLAND, CHRIS

| Title | Format | Label | Cat. No. | Year | | | Notes |
|---|---|---|---|---|---|---|---|
| Ma He's Making Eyes At Me | 7" | Columbia | DB4114 | 1958 | £1.50 | £4 | |
| Susie Darlin' | 7" | Columbia | DB4194 | 1959 | £1.50 | £4 | |

## HOWLIN' WOLF

| Title | Format | Label | Cat. No. | Year | | | Notes |
|---|---|---|---|---|---|---|---|
| AKA Chester Burnett | LP | Chess | 60016 | 1972 | £5 | £12 | US double |
| Back Door Wolf | LP | Chess | CH50045 | 1974 | £5 | £12 | US |
| Big City Blues | LP | Ember | EMB3370 | 1966 | £5 | £12 | |
| Down In The Bottom | 7" | Pye | 7N25101 | 1961 | £4 | £8 | |
| Evil | 7" | Chess | LP1540 | 1969 | £15 | £30 | US |
| Evil | 7" | Chess | CRS8097 | 1969 | £2 | £5 | |
| Howlin' Wolf | LP | Chess | LP1469 | 1962 | £20 | £40 | US |
| Howlin' Wolf | LP | Python | PLP13 | 1971 | £8 | £20 | |
| Howlin' Wolf Album | LP | Chess | CRLS4543 | 1969 | £20 | £40 | |
| Just Like I Treat You | 7" | Pye | 7N25192 | 1963 | £2.50 | £6 | |
| Killing Floor | 7" | Chess | CRS8010 | 1965 | £2.50 | £6 | |
| Little Girl | 7" | Pye | 7N25269 | 1964 | £2.50 | £6 | |
| London Sessions | LP | Rolling Stones | COC49101 | 1971 | £4 | £10 | |
| Love Me Darling | 7" | Pye | 7N25283 | 1964 | £2.50 | £6 | |
| Message To The Young | LP | Chess | 6310108 | 1971 | £4 | £10 | |
| Moanin' In The Moonlight | LP | Chess | LP1434 | 1958 | £25 | £50 | US |
| Moaning In The Moonlight | LP | Chess | CRL4006 | 1964 | £8 | £20 | |
| More Real Folk Blues | LP | Chess | LP1512 | 1966 | £8 | £20 | US |
| Ooh Baby | 7" | Chess | CRS8016 | 1965 | £2.50 | £6 | |
| Poor Boy | LP | Chess | CRL4508 | 1965 | £6 | £15 | |
| Real Folk Blues | LP | Chess | LP1502 | 1966 | £8 | £20 | US |
| Real Folk Blues Vol. 1 | 7" EP | Chess | CRE6017 | 1966 | £6 | £12 | |
| Rhythm & Blues With Howlin' Wolf | 7" EP | London | REU1072 | 1956 | £37.50 | £75 | |
| Smokestack Lightning | 7" EP | Pye | NEP44015 | 1963 | £6 | £12 | |
| Smokestack Lightning | 7" | Pye | 7N25244 | 1964 | £2 | £5 | |
| Tell Me | 7" EP | Pye | NEP44032 | 1964 | £ | £12 | |
| This Is Howlin' Wolf's New Album | LP | Cadet | 319 | 1969 | £20 | £40 | US |

## HOWLIN' WOLF, JUNIOR PARKER, & BOBBY BLAND

| Title | Format | Label | Cat. No. | Year | | | Notes |
|---|---|---|---|---|---|---|---|
| Blues For Mr. Crump | LP | Polydor | 2383257 | 1974 | £4 | £10 | |

## HOYLE, LINDA

Linda Hoyle was the singer with Affinity and her jazz-inflected tones on that group's album suggested that she could make a good jazz record. Her solo LP, recorded with members of Nucleus, is exactly that.

| Title | Format | Label | Cat. No. | Year | | | Notes |
|---|---|---|---|---|---|---|---|
| Pieces Of Me | LP | Vertigo | 6360060 | 1971 | £62.50 | £125 | spiral label |

## HU & THE HILLTOPS

| Title | Format | Label | Cat. No. | Year | | | Notes |
|---|---|---|---|---|---|---|---|
| I'll Follow You | LP | Polydor | 736033 | 1966 | £8 | £20 | Dutch |

## HUBBARD, FREDDIE

| Title | Format | Label | Cat. No. | Year | | | Notes |
|---|---|---|---|---|---|---|---|
| Backlash | LP | Atlantic | SD1477 | 1967 | £6 | £15 | US |
| Black Angel | LP | Atlantic | SD1549 | 1970 | £6 | £15 | US |
| Blue Spirits | LP | Blue Note | BLP/BST84196 | 1965 | £8 | £20 | |
| Breaking Point | LP | Blue Note | BLP/BST84172 | 1964 | £8 | £20 | |

| | | | | | | | |
|---|---|---|---|---|---|---|---|
| Goin' Up | LP | Blue Note | BLP/BST84056 | 1960 | £10 | £25 | |
| Groovy! | LP | Fontana | FJL136 | 1968 | £5 | £12 | |
| High Blues Pressure | LP | Atlantic | SD1501 | 1969 | £6 | £15 | US |
| Hub Cap | LP | Blue Note | BLP/BST84073 | 1961 | £15 | £30 | |
| Hub-Tones | LP | Blue Note | BLP/BST84115 | 1962 | £8 | £20 | |
| Night Of The Cookers Vol. 1 | LP | Blue Note | BLP/BST84207 | 1965 | £8 | £20 | |
| Night Of The Cookers Vol. 2 | LP | Blue Note | BLP/BST84208 | 1965 | £8 | £20 | |
| Open Sesame | LP | Blue Note | BLP/BST84040 | 1960 | £15 | £30 | |
| Ready For Freddie | LP | Blue Note | BLP/BST84085 | 1961 | £8 | £20 | |
| Sing Me A Song Of Songmy | LP | Atlantic | SD1576 | 1971 | £5 | £12 | US |

## HUCKNALL, MICK

| | | | | | | | |
|---|---|---|---|---|---|---|---|
| Early Years | LP | TJM | TJM101 | 1987 | £6 | £15 | |

## HUDSON, JOHNNY

| | | | | | | | |
|---|---|---|---|---|---|---|---|
| Makin' Up Is Hard To Do | 7" | Decca | F11679 | 1963 | £1.50 | £4 | |

## HUDSON, KEITH

| | | | | | | | |
|---|---|---|---|---|---|---|---|
| Flesh Of My Skin | LP | Mamba | 001 | 1974 | £6 | £15 | |
| Rasta Communication | LP | Greensleeves | GREL5 | 1979 | £5 | £12 | |
| Tambourine Man | 7" | Big Shot | BI528 | 1969 | £1.50 | £4 | |
| Too Expensive | LP | Virgin | V2056 | 1976 | £5 | £12 | |
| Torch Of Freedom | LP | Atra | 1001 | 1975 | £6 | £15 | |

## HUDSON, ROCK

| | | | | | | | |
|---|---|---|---|---|---|---|---|
| Rock Gently | LP | Stanyan | 10014 | 1971 | £5 | £12 | US |

## HUDSON PEOPLE

| | | | | | | | |
|---|---|---|---|---|---|---|---|
| Trip To Your Mind | 12" | Hithouse | HIT1 | 197– | £10 | £20 | |

## HUE & CRY

| | | | | | | | |
|---|---|---|---|---|---|---|---|
| Here Come Everybody | 12" | Stampede | STAMP2 | 1986 | £5 | £12 | |
| I Refuse | CD-s | Circa | YRCD8 | 1988 | £2 | £5 | |
| Looking For Linda | CD-s | Circa | YRCD24 | 1989 | £2 | £5 | |
| Ordinary Angel | CD-s | Circa | YRCD18 | 1988 | £2 | £5 | |
| Peaceful Face | CD-s | Circa | YRCD41 | 1989 | £2 | £5 | |
| Sweet Invisibility | CD-s | Circa | YRCD37 | 1989 | £2 | £5 | |
| Violently | CD-s | Circa | YRCD29 | 1989 | £2 | £5 | |

## HUEYS

| | | | | | | | |
|---|---|---|---|---|---|---|---|
| Coo Coo Over You | 7" | London | HLU10264 | 1969 | £2 | £5 | |

## HUGG, MIKE

| | | | | | | | |
|---|---|---|---|---|---|---|---|
| Somewhere | LP | Polydor | 2383140 | 1972 | £4 | £10 | |
| Stress And Strain | LP | Polydor | 2383213 | 1973 | £4 | £10 | |

## HUGGETT FAMILY

| | | | | | | | |
|---|---|---|---|---|---|---|---|
| Huggett Family | LP | Pye | NSPL18407 | 1973 | £20 | £40 | |

## HUGHES, DANNY

| | | | | | | | |
|---|---|---|---|---|---|---|---|
| Hi Ho Silver Lining | 7" | Pye | 7N17750 | 1969 | £2 | £5 | |

## HUGHES, FRED

| | | | | | | | |
|---|---|---|---|---|---|---|---|
| Oo Wee Baby I Love You | 7" | Fontana | TF583 | 1965 | £7.50 | £15 | |
| Send My Baby Back | LP | Wand | WD(S)664 | 1965 | £6 | £15 | US |

## HUGHES, JIMMY

| | | | | | | | |
|---|---|---|---|---|---|---|---|
| Chains Of Love | 7" | Stax | STAX126 | 1969 | £1.50 | £4 | |
| Goodbye My Love | 7" | Sue | WI4006 | 1966 | £5 | £10 | |
| Hi Heel Sneakers | 7" | Atlantic | 584135 | 1967 | £2 | £5 | |
| I'm Qualified | 7" | London | HL9680 | 1963 | £5 | £10 | |
| Neighbour Neighbour | 7" | Atlantic | 584017 | 1966 | £2 | £5 | |
| Steal Away | LP | Vee Jay | (SR)1102 | 1965 | £6 | £15 | US |
| Steal Away | 7" | Pye | 7N25254 | 1964 | £2 | £5 | |
| Sweet Things You Do | 7" | Stax | STAX117 | 1969 | £1.50 | £4 | |
| Why Not Tonight | LP | Atco | (SD)33209 | 1967 | £6 | £15 | US |

## HUGO & LUIGI

| | | | | | | | |
|---|---|---|---|---|---|---|---|
| La Plume De Ma Tante | 7" | RCA | RCA1127 | 1959 | £1.50 | £4 | |
| Shenandoah Rose | 7" | Columbia | DB3978 | 1957 | £2.50 | £6 | |
| Twilight In Tennessee | 7" | Columbia | DB4156 | 1958 | £1.50 | £4 | |

## HULL, ALAN

| | | | | | | | |
|---|---|---|---|---|---|---|---|
| We Can Sing Together | 7" | Transatlantic | BIG129 | 1970 | £2.50 | £6 | |

## HULLABALOOS

| | | | | | | | |
|---|---|---|---|---|---|---|---|
| Did You Ever | 7" EP | Roulette | VREX65033 | 1965 | £15 | £30 | French |
| Don't Stop | 7" | Columbia | DB7626 | 1965 | £1.50 | £4 | |
| England's Newest Singing Sensations | LP | Roulette | (S)R25297 | 1965 | £6 | £15 | US |
| Hullabaloos On Hullabaloo | LP | Roulette | (S)R25310 | 1965 | £6 | £15 | US |
| I'll Show You How To Love | 7" | Columbia | DB7558 | 1965 | £1.50 | £4 | |
| I'm Gonna Love You Too | 7" EP | Roulette | VREX65024 | 1964 | £15 | £30 | French |
| I'm Gonna Love You Too | 7" | Columbia | DB7392 | 1964 | £1.50 | £4 | |

## HULTGREEN, GEORG

| | | | | | | | |
|---|---|---|---|---|---|---|---|
| Say Hello | 7" | Warner Bros | WB8017 | 1970 | £1.50 | £4 | |

## HUMAN BEANS
Morning Dew.................................... 7" ...... Columbia ........ DB8230 ................ 1967 £20 ........ £40

## HUMAN BEAST
Human Beast Vol. 1 ................................ LP ..... Decca ............ SKL5053 ............... 1970 £62.50 .. £125

## HUMAN BEINZ
| | | | | | | |
|---|---|---|---|---|---|---|
| Evolution ........................................... | LP ..... | Capitol ........... | ST2926 ........... | 1968 | £20 ..... | £40 .................. US |
| Human Beinz/Mammals ........................ | LP ..... | Gateway ......... | GLP3012 ......... | 1968 | £15 ..... | £30 .................. US |
| Nobody But Me .................................... | LP ..... | Capitol ........... | ST2906 ........... | 1968 | £10 ..... | £25 .................. US |
| Nobody But Me .................................... | 7" ...... | Capitol ........... | CL15529 ......... | 1968 | £7.50 ... | £15 |
| Turn On Your Lovelight ....................... | 7" ...... | Capitol ........... | CL15542 ......... | 1968 | £6 ........ | £12 |

## HUMAN INSTINCT
| | | | | | | |
|---|---|---|---|---|---|---|
| Burning Up Years ................................ | LP ..... | | | 1969 | £180 ... | £300 ............ New Zealand |
| Can't Stop Loving You ........................ | 7" ...... | Mercury ......... | MF951 ............ | 1965 | £10 ..... | £20 |
| Day In My Mind's Mind ....................... | 7" ...... | Deram ............ | DM167 ............ | 1967 | £12.50 .. | £25 |
| Go Go ................................................. | 7" ...... | Mercury ......... | MF990 ............ | 1966 | £10 ..... | £20 |
| Pins In It ............................................ | LP ..... | Pye ................. | | 1971 | £180 ... | £300 ............ New Zealand |
| Renaissance Fair .................................. | 7" ...... | Deram ............ | DM177 ............ | 1968 | £10 ..... | £20 |
| Rich Man ............................................. | 7" ...... | Mercury ......... | MF972 ............ | 1966 | £12.50 .. | £25 |
| Stoned Guitars ..................................... | LP ..... | Allied ............. | ARBS107 ......... | 1970 | £210 ... | £350 ......... New Zealand |

## HUMAN LEAGUE
| | | | | | | |
|---|---|---|---|---|---|---|
| Empire State Human ............................. | 7" ...... | Virgin ............. | VS351 ............. | 1980 | £2 ........ | £5 ................... double |
| Greatest Hits ....................................... | CD .... | Virgin ............. | CDHLP1 .......... | 1988 | £5 ........ | £12 ........... picture disc |
| Hard Times/Love Action ....................... | CD-s .. | Virgin ............. | CDT6 .............. | 1988 | £2 ........ | £5 ............... 3" single |
| Holiday '80 .......................................... | 7" ...... | Virgin ............. | SV105 ............. | 1980 | £2.50 ... | £6 ........ double, purple & blue label |
| Holiday '80 .......................................... | 12" .... | Virgin ............. | SV105 ............. | 1980 | £4 ........ | £10 |
| Human League Interview ...................... | CD .... | East West ....... | PRCD91852 ...... | 1995 | £6 ........ | £15 ... US interview promo |
| Keep Feeling Fascination ...................... | CD-s .. | Virgin ............. | CDT24 ............ | 1988 | £2.50 ... | £6 ............... 3" single |
| Love Action .......................................... | CD-s .. | Virgin ............. | | 1988 | £2.50 ... | £6 |
| Love Is All That Matters ....................... | CD-s .. | Virgin ............. | VSCD1025 ....... | 1988 | £2 ........ | £5 |
| Soundtrack To A Generation ................. | CD-s .. | Virgin ............. | VSCDT1303 ...... | 1990 | £2.50 ... | £6 |
| Soundtrack To A Generation ................. | CD-s .. | Virgin ............. | VSCDX1303 ...... | 1990 | £4 ........ | £10 |

## HUMAN ZOO
Human Zoo .............................................. LP ...... Accent ............ ACS5055 ........... 1969 £10 ........ £25 ............... US

## HUMBLE PIE
| | | | | | | |
|---|---|---|---|---|---|---|
| As Safe As Yesterday Is ....................... | LP ..... | Immediate ...... | IMSP025 ......... | 1969 | £5 ........ | £12 |
| Eat It ................................................... | LP ..... | A&M ............... | AMLS6004 ....... | 1973 | £4 ........ | £10 |
| Humble Pie .......................................... | LP ..... | A&M ............... | AMLS986 ......... | 1970 | £4 ........ | £10 |
| Performance: Rockin' The Fillmore ........ | LP ..... | A&M ............... | AMLH63506 ..... | 1971 | £5 ........ | £12 ............... double |
| Rock On .............................................. | LP ..... | A&M ............... | AMLS2013 ....... | 1971 | £4 ........ | £10 |
| Smokin' ............................................... | LP ..... | A&M ............... | AMLS64342 ..... | 1972 | £4 ........ | £10 |
| Street Rats ........................................... | LP ..... | A&M ............... | AMLS68282 ..... | 1975 | £4 ........ | £10 |
| Thunderbox .......................................... | LP ..... | A&M ............... | AMLH63611 ..... | 1974 | £5 ........ | £12 ............... double |
| Town And Country ............................... | LP ..... | Immediate ...... | IMSP027 ......... | 1969 | £5 ........ | £12 |

## HUMBLEBUMS
'He's humble . . . ,' Billy Connolly used to quip when explaining the origin of his group's name. Originally a folk duo featuring Connolly and fellow Glaswegian Tam Harvey, the Humblebums broadened their appeal a little when Harvey was replaced by singer-songwriter Gerry Rafferty. Some of Rafferty's songs with the group are amongst the best that Paul McCartney never wrote, although both Rafferty and Connolly have become rather more famous since.

| | | | | | | |
|---|---|---|---|---|---|---|
| Complete ............................................. | LP ..... | Transatlantic ... | TRAT288 ......... | 1974 | £8 ........ | £20 ................. 3 LP set |
| First Collection .................................... | LP ..... | Transatlantic ... | TRA186 ........... | 1969 | £4 ........ | £10 |
| Humblebums ........................................ | LP ..... | Transatlantic ... | TRA201 ........... | 1969 | £4 ........ | £10 |
| Open Up The Door ............................... | LP ..... | Transatlantic ... | TRA218 ........... | 1970 | £4 ........ | £10 |

## HUMES, HELEN
| | | | | | | |
|---|---|---|---|---|---|---|
| Helen Humes And The Benny Carter All Stars .................................................. | LP ..... | Contemporary . | LAC12245 ........ | 1961 | £5 ........ | £12 |
| If I Could Be With You ......................... | 7" ...... | Vogue ............. | V2048 ............. | 1956 | £1.50 ... | £4 |
| When The Saints Come Marching In ...... | 7" ...... | Contemporary . | CV2415 ........... | 1959 | £1.50 ... | £4 |

## HUMPHREY, BOBBI
Flute-In ................................................... LP ..... Blue Note ...... BST84379 ......... 1970 £4 ........ £10

## HUMPHREY, DELLA
Don't Make The Good Girls So Bad ......... 7" ...... Action ............ ACT4525 .......... 1969 £1.50 ... £4

## HUNGER
| | | | | | | |
|---|---|---|---|---|---|---|
| Strickly From Hunger ........................... | LP ..... | Psycho .......... | PSYCHO14 ....... | 1984 | £6 ........ | £15 |
| Strickly From Hunger ........................... | LP ..... | Public ............ | 1006 .............. | 1969 | £250 ... | £400 .................. US |

## HUNGRY WOLF
Hungry Wolf ............................................ LP ..... Philips ............ 6308009 ........... 1970 £30 ........ £60

## HUNT, GERALDINE
Never Never Leave Me .............................. 7" ...... Roulette ......... RO515 .............. 1969 £2 ........ £5

## HUNT, MARSHA
Desdemona ............................................... 7" ...... Track ............... 604034 ............. 1969 £2.50 ... £6

417

| Title | Format | Label | Cat. No. | Year | Price | Price | Notes |
|---|---|---|---|---|---|---|---|
| Walk On Gilded Splinters | 7" | Track | 604030 | 1969 | £1.50 | £4 | |
| Woman Child | LP | Track | 2410101 | 1971 | £8 | £20 | |

## HUNT, MICHAEL

| | | | | | | | |
|---|---|---|---|---|---|---|---|
| Waters Of The Tyne | LP | Decca | LK4902 | 1967 | £15 | £30 | |

## HUNT, PEE WEE

| | | | | | | | |
|---|---|---|---|---|---|---|---|
| Dixieland Detour | 10" LP | Capitol | LC6608 | 1953 | £8 | £20 | |
| It's Never Too Late To Fall In Love | 7" | Capitol | CL14225 | 1955 | £1.50 | £4 | |
| Save Your Love For Me | 7" | Capitol | CL14286 | 1955 | £1.50 | £4 | |
| Swingin' Around | 10" LP | Capitol | LC6671 | 1954 | £8 | £20 | |

## HUNT, TOMMY

| | | | | | | | |
|---|---|---|---|---|---|---|---|
| Greatest Hits | LP | Dynamo | 8001 | 1967 | £6 | £15 | US |
| I Just Don't Know What To Do With Myself | LP | Scepter | (S)S506 | 1962 | £6 | £15 | US |
| I'm Wondering | 7" | Top Rank | JAR605 | 1962 | £2.50 | £6 | |

## HUNT, WILLIE AMOS

| | | | | | | | |
|---|---|---|---|---|---|---|---|
| Would You Believe | 7" | Camp | 602003 | 1967 | £12.50 | £25 | |

## HUNT & TURNER

| | | | | | | | |
|---|---|---|---|---|---|---|---|
| Magic Landscape | LP | Village Thing | VTS11 | 1972 | £5 | £12 | |

## HUNTER

| | | | | | | | |
|---|---|---|---|---|---|---|---|
| Some Time For Thinking | 7" | RCA | RCA1995 | 1970 | £4 | £8 | |

## HUNTER, DANNY

| | | | | | | | |
|---|---|---|---|---|---|---|---|
| Lost Weekend | 7" | Fontana | H300 | 1961 | £2 | £5 | |
| Make It Up | 7" | HMV | POP722 | 1960 | £4 | £8 | |
| Who's Gonna Walk Ya Home? | 7" | HMV | POP775 | 1960 | £4 | £8 | |

## HUNTER, DAVE

| | | | | | | | |
|---|---|---|---|---|---|---|---|
| She's A Heartbreaker | 7" | RCA | RCA1766 | 1968 | £2 | £5 | |

## HUNTER, GREG

| | | | | | | | |
|---|---|---|---|---|---|---|---|
| Five O'Clock World | 7" | Parlophone | R5483 | 1966 | £1.50 | £4 | |

## HUNTER, IAN

| | | | | | | | |
|---|---|---|---|---|---|---|---|
| American Music | CD-s | Mercury | MERCD315 | 1990 | £2 | £5 | with Mick Ronson |
| You're Never Alone With A Schizophrenic | CD | Chrysalis | CD25CR03 | 1994 | £5 | £12 | Chrysalis 25 pack |
| Yui Orta | CD | Mercury | 8389732 | 1990 | £5 | £12 | with Mick Ronson |

## HUNTER, IVORY JOE

| | | | | | | | |
|---|---|---|---|---|---|---|---|
| Fabulous Ivory Joe Hunter | LP | Goldisc | 403 | 1961 | £10 | £25 | US |
| Golden Hits | LP | Smash | MGS2/SRS67037 | 1963 | £6 | £15 | US |
| I Almost Lost My Mind | 78 | MGM | MGM271 | 1950 | £6 | £12 | |
| I Get That Lonesome Feeling | LP | MGM | E3488 | 1957 | £37.50 | £75 | US |
| I'm Hooked | 7" | Capitol | CL15220 | 1961 | £2.50 | £6 | |
| Ivory Joe Hunter | LP | Atlantic | 8008 | 1958 | £37.50 | £75 | US |
| Ivory Joe Hunter | LP | Sage | 603 | 1959 | £25 | £50 | US |
| Ivory Joe Hunter | LP | Sound | 603 | 1957 | £37.50 | £75 | US |
| Love's A Hurting Game | 7" | London | HLE8486 | 1957 | £37.50 | £75 | |
| May The Best Man Win | 7" | Capitol | CL15226 | 1961 | £2.50 | £6 | |
| Since I Met You Baby | 7" | Columbia | DB3872 | 1957 | £50 | £100 | |
| Sings The Old And The New | LP | Atlantic | 8015 | 1958 | £37.50 | £75 | US |
| Sixteen Of His Greatest Hits | LP | King | 605 | 1958 | £50 | £100 | US |
| Tear Fell | 7" | London | HLE8261 | 1956 | £100 | £200 | best auctioned |
| This Is Ivory Joe Hunter | LP | Dot | DLP3569/25569 | 1964 | £6 | £15 | US |

## HUNTER, ROBERT

| | | | | | | | |
|---|---|---|---|---|---|---|---|
| Amagamalin Street | LP | Relix | RRLP2003 | 1984 | £6 | £15 | US double |
| Tales Of Great Rum Runners | LP | Round | RX101 | 1974 | £6 | £15 | US |

## HUNTER, TAB

| | | | | | | | |
|---|---|---|---|---|---|---|---|
| Don't Let It Get Around | 7" | London | HLD8535 | 1958 | £5 | £10 | |
| I Can't Stop Loving You | 7" | London | HLD9559 | 1962 | £2 | £5 | |
| My Only Love | 7" | Warner Bros | WB8 | 1960 | £1.50 | £4 | |
| Ninety-Nine Ways | 7" | London | HLD8410 | 1957 | £4 | £8 | |
| R.F.D. Tab Hunter | LP | Warner Bros | W(S)1367 | 1960 | £8 | £20 | US |
| Tab Hunter | LP | Warner Bros | WM4008 | 1960 | £8 | £20 | mono |
| Tab Hunter | LP | Warner Bros | WS8008 | 1960 | £10 | £25 | stereo |
| Tab Hunter | 7" EP | Warner Bros | WSEP2023 | 1961 | £6 | £12 | stereo |
| Tab Hunter | 7" EP | Warner Bros | WEP6023 | 1961 | £5 | £10 | |
| Waitin' For The Fall | 7" | Warner Bros | WB20 | 1960 | £1.50 | £4 | |
| When I Fall In Love | LP | Warner Bros | W(S)1292 | 1959 | £8 | £20 | US |
| Wild Side Of Life | 7" | London | HLD9381 | 1961 | £2.50 | £6 | |
| Young Love | LP | London | HAD2401 | 1961 | £10 | £25 | |
| Young Love | LP | London | SAHG6201 | 1961 | £15 | £30 | stereo |
| Young Love | 7" EP | London | RED1134 | 1958 | £7.50 | £15 | |
| Young Love | 7" | London | HLD8380 | 1957 | £10 | £20 | |

## HUNTER MUSKETT

| | | | | | | | |
|---|---|---|---|---|---|---|---|
| Every Time You Move | LP | Nova | SDN20 | 1970 | £50 | £100 | |
| Hunter Muskett | LP | Bradley | BRADL1003 | 1973 | £8 | £20 | |

## HUNTERS

| | | | | | | | |
|---|---|---|---|---|---|---|---|
| Golden Earrings | 7" | Fontana | H303 | 1961 | £1.50 | £4 | |

| | | | | | | | |
|---|---|---|---|---|---|---|---|
| Hits From The Hunters | LP | Fontana | TFL5175/STFL572 | 1962 | £15 | £30 | |
| Storm | 7" | Fontana | H323 | 1961 | £1.50 | £4 | |
| Teen Scene | LP | Fontana | TFL5140/STFL561 | 1961 | £15 | £30 | |
| Teen Scene | 7" | Fontana | H276 | 1960 | £2 | £5 | |
| Teen Scene | 7" | Fontana | TF514 | 1964 | £1.50 | £4 | |

## HUNTERS (2)

| | | | | | | | |
|---|---|---|---|---|---|---|---|
| Russian Spy And I | 7" | RCA | RCA1541 | 1966 | £4 | £8 | |

## HURDY GURDY

| | | | | | | | |
|---|---|---|---|---|---|---|---|
| Hurdy Gurdy | LP | CBS | 64781 | 1971 | £75 | £150 | Danish |

## HURT, MISSISSIPPI JOHN

| | | | | | | | |
|---|---|---|---|---|---|---|---|
| Immortal | LP | Vanguard | VRS/VSD79248 | 1967 | £5 | £12 | US |
| Mississippi John Hurt | LP | Fontana | TFL6079 | 1967 | £6 | £15 | |
| Mississippi John Hurt | LP | Vanguard | VSD19/20 | 1973 | £5 | £12 | double |
| Original 1928 Recordings | LP | Spookane | SPL1001 | 1971 | £15 | £30 | |
| Today | LP | Vanguard | VRS/VSD79220 | 1966 | £6 | £15 | US |

## HURVITZ, SANDY

| | | | | | | | |
|---|---|---|---|---|---|---|---|
| Sandy's Album Is Here | LP | Bizarre | 5064 | 1968 | £8 | £20 | US |

## HUSH

| | | | | | | | |
|---|---|---|---|---|---|---|---|
| Grey | 7" | Fontana | TF944 | 1968 | £75 | £150 | |

## HUSKER DU

| | | | | | | | |
|---|---|---|---|---|---|---|---|
| Amusement | 7" | Reflex | 38285 | 1980 | £20 | £40 | US |
| Could You Be The One | 12" | Warner Bros | W8456T | 1987 | £2.50 | £6 | |
| Do You Remember | CD | Warner Bros | PROCD6853 | 1993 | £10 | £25 | US promo compilation |
| Don't Want To Know If You're Lonely | 12" | Warner Bros | W8746T | 1986 | £2.50 | £6 | |
| Eight Miles HIgh | CD-s | SST | SST025CD | 1988 | £2 | £5 | |
| Everything Falls Apart | LP | Reflex | REFLEXD | 1982 | £10 | £25 | US |
| Ice Cold Ice | 12" | Warner Bros | W8276T | 1987 | £2.50 | £6 | |
| In A Free Land | 7" | New Alliance | NAR010 | 1982 | £20 | £40 | US |
| Makes No Sense At All | CD-s | SST | SST051CD | 1988 | £2 | £5 | |
| Sorry Somehow | 7" | WEA | W8612F | 1986 | £2.50 | £6 | double |
| Sorry Somehow | 12" | Warner Bros | W8612T | 1986 | £2.50 | £6 | |

## HUSKY, FERLIN

| | | | | | | | |
|---|---|---|---|---|---|---|---|
| Born To Lose | LP | Capitol | T1204 | 1959 | £6 | £15 | US |
| Boulevard Of Broken Dreams | LP | Capitol | T880 | 1957 | £6 | £15 | US |
| Country Music Holiday | 7" EP | Capitol | EAP1921 | 1957 | £2.50 | £6 | |
| Country Round Up | 7" EP | Parlophone | GEP8795 | 1959 | £7.50 | £15 | |
| Country Tunes Sung From The Heart | LP | King | 647 | 1959 | £6 | £15 | US |
| Easy Livin' | LP | King | 728 | 1960 | £6 | £15 | US |
| Fallen Star | 7" | Capitol | CL14753 | 1957 | £6 | £12 | |
| Ferlin Husky Hits | 7" EP | Capitol | EAP1837 | 1957 | £2.50 | £6 | |
| Ferlin's Favorites | LP | Capitol | T1280 | 1960 | £6 | £15 | US |
| Ferlin's Favourites Part 1 | 7" EP | Capitol | EAP11280 | 1960 | £2.50 | £6 | |
| Ferlin's Favourites Part 2 | 7" EP | Capitol | EAP21280 | 1960 | £2.50 | £6 | |
| Ferlin's Favourites Part 3 | 7" EP | Capitol | EAP31280 | 1960 | £2.50 | £6 | |
| Gone | LP | Capitol | T1383 | 1960 | £6 | £15 | US |
| Gone | 7" | Capitol | CL14702 | 1957 | £4 | £8 | |
| I Feel That Old Heartache Again | 7" | Capitol | CL14916 | 1958 | £2 | £5 | |
| Kingdom Of Love | 7" | Capitol | CL14922 | 1958 | £1.50 | £4 | |
| Make Me Live Again | 7" | Capitol | CL14785 | 1957 | £1.50 | £4 | |
| Sittin' On A Rainbow | LP | Capitol | T976 | 1959 | £6 | £15 | US |
| Slow Down Brother | 7" | Capitol | CL14883 | 1958 | £4 | £8 | |
| Songs Of The Home And Heart | LP | Capitol | T718 | 1956 | £8 | £20 | US |
| Songs Of The Home And Heart | 7" EP | Capitol | EAP1718 | 1957 | £2.50 | £6 | |
| Wang Dang Do | 7" | Capitol | CL14824 | 1958 | £5 | £10 | |

## HUSTLER

| | | | | | | | |
|---|---|---|---|---|---|---|---|
| High Street | LP | A&M | AMLS68276 | 1974 | £4 | £10 | |
| Play Loud | LP | A&M | AMLH33001 | 1975 | £4 | £10 | |

## HUSTLERS

| | | | | | | | |
|---|---|---|---|---|---|---|---|
| Gimme What I Want | 7" | Philips | BF1275 | 1963 | £1.50 | £4 | |
| Sick Of Giving | 7" | Mercury | MF817 | 1964 | £5 | £10 | |
| You Can't Sit Down | 7" | Mercury | MF807 | 1964 | £1.50 | £4 | |

## HUTCHERSON, BOBBY

| | | | | | | | |
|---|---|---|---|---|---|---|---|
| Components | LP | Blue Note | BLP/BST84213 | 1965 | £6 | £15 | |
| Dialogue | LP | Blue Note | BLP/BST84198 | 1965 | £6 | £15 | |
| Happenings | LP | Blue Note | BLP/BST84231 | 1966 | £5 | £12 | |
| Head On | LP | Blue Note | BST84376 | 1970 | £4 | £10 | |
| Now | LP | Blue Note | BST84333 | 1969 | £4 | £10 | |
| San Francisco | LP | Blue Note | BST84362 | 1970 | £4 | £10 | |
| Stick-Up | LP | Blue Note | BLP/BST84244 | 1966 | £5 | £12 | |
| Total Eclipse | LP | Blue Note | BST84291 | 1968 | £4 | £10 | |

## HUTCHINGS, ASHLEY

| | | | | | | | |
|---|---|---|---|---|---|---|---|
| Compleat Dancing Master | LP | Island | HELP17 | 1974 | £4 | £10 | |
| Hour With Cecil Sharp And Ashley Hutchings | LP | Dambusters | DAM014 | 1986 | £8 | £20 | |
| Kickin' Up The Sawdust | LP | Harvest | SHSP4073 | 1977 | £20 | £40 | |
| Morris On | LP | Island | HELP5 | 1972 | £4 | £10 | |
| Rattlebone & Ploughjack | LP | Island | HELP24 | 1976 | £10 | £25 | |

| | | | | | | |
|---|---|---|---|---|---|---|
| Son Of Morris On | LP | Harvest | SHSM2012 | 1976 £4 | £10 | |

## HUTCHINS, HUTCH
| | | | | | | |
|---|---|---|---|---|---|---|
| Feels Like Rain | LP | Goodwood | GM12324 | 197– £25 | £50 | |

## HUTCHINS, SAM
| | | | | | | |
|---|---|---|---|---|---|---|
| Dang Me | 7" | Bell | BLL1044 | 1969 £1.50 | £4 | |

## HUTSON, LEROY
| | | | | | | |
|---|---|---|---|---|---|---|
| All Because Of You | 7" | Warner Bros | K16536 | 1975 £2 | £5 | |
| Leroy Hutson | LP | Warner Bros | K56139 | 1975 £20 | £40 | |
| Man | LP | Buddah | BDLP4013 | 1974 £4 | £10 | |

## HUTTO, J. B.
| | | | | | | |
|---|---|---|---|---|---|---|
| Hawk Squat | LP | Delmark | DS617 | 1970 £4 | £10 | |

## HUTTON, BETTY
| | | | | | | |
|---|---|---|---|---|---|---|
| Capitol Presents | 10" LP | Capitol | LC6639 | 1954 £4 | £10 | |
| Somebody Loves Me | 7" | HMV | 7M103 | 1953 £1.50 | £4 | |

## HUTTON SISTERS
| | | | | | | |
|---|---|---|---|---|---|---|
| Ko Ko Mo | 7" | Capitol | CL14250 | 1955 £6 | £12 | |

## HYATT, CHARLIE
| | | | | | | |
|---|---|---|---|---|---|---|
| Kiss Me Neck | LP | Island | ILP932 | 1966 £15 | £30 | |
| Rass! | 7" EP | Island | IEP707 | 1966 £4 | £8 | with Bam |

## HYGRADES
| | | | | | | |
|---|---|---|---|---|---|---|
| She Cared | 7" | Columbia | DB7734 | 1965 £1.50 | £4 | |

## HYLAND, BRIAN
| | | | | | | |
|---|---|---|---|---|---|---|
| Bashful Blonde | LP | London | HAR2289 | 1961 £25 | £50 | |
| Country Meets Folk | LP | HMV | CLP1759 | 1963 £10 | £25 | |
| Four Little Heels | 7" | London | HLR9203 | 1960 £1.50 | £4 | |
| Get The Message | 7" | Philips | BF1601 | 1967 £1.50 | £4 | |
| Ginny Come Lately | 7" | HMV | POP1013 | 1962 £1.50 | £4 | |
| Here's To Our Love | LP | Philips | PHM2/PHS600136 | 1964 £8 | £20 | US |
| Hung Up In Your Eyes | 7" | Philips | BF1555 | 1967 £1.50 | £4 | |
| I Gotta Go | 7" | London | HLR9262 | 1961 £1.50 | £4 | |
| I May Not Live To See Tomorrow | 7" | HMV | POP1113 | 1963 £1.50 | £4 | |
| I'm Afraid To Go Home | 7" | HMV | POP1188 | 1963 £1.50 | £4 | |
| If Mary's There | 7" | HMV | POP1143 | 1963 £1.50 | £4 | |
| Itsy Bitsy Teeny Weeny | 7" | London | HLR9161 | 1960 £1.50 | £4 | |
| Joker Went Wild | LP | Philips | BL7762 | 1966 £6 | £15 | |
| Joker Went Wild | 7" | Philips | BF1508 | 1966 £1.50 | £4 | |
| Let Me Belong To You | LP | HMV | CLP1553 | 1962 £20 | £40 | |
| Let Me Belong To You | 7" | HMV | POP915 | 1961 £1.50 | £4 | |
| Let Us Make Our Own Mistakes | 7" | HMV | POP1237 | 1963 £1.50 | £4 | |
| Night I Cried | 7" | HMV | POP955 | 1961 £1.50 | £4 | |
| Rockin' Folk | LP | Philips | PHM2/PHS600158 | 1965 £6 | £15 | US |
| Rosemary | 7" | London | HLR9113 | 1960 £5 | £10 | |
| Run, Run, Look And See | 7" | Philips | BF1528 | 1966 £1.50 | £4 | |
| Sealed With A Kiss | LP | ABC-Paramount | (S)431 | 1962 £10 | £25 | US |
| Sealed With A Kiss | 7" EP | HMV | 7EG8780 | 1962 £10 | £20 | |
| Sealed With A Kiss | 7" | HMV | POP1051 | 1962 £1.50 | £4 | |
| Somewhere In The Night | 7" | HMV | POP1169 | 1963 £1.50 | £4 | |
| Stay Away From Her | 7" | Philips | BF1429 | 1965 £1.50 | £4 | |
| Three Thousand Miles | 7" | Philips | BF1486 | 1965 £1.50 | £4 | |
| Warmed Over Kisses | 7" | HMV | POP1079 | 1962 £1.50 | £4 | |

## HYMAN, C.
| | | | | | | |
|---|---|---|---|---|---|---|
| Ska Is Movin' On | 7" | Ska Beat | JB200 | 1965 £5 | £10 | |

## HYMAN, DICK
| | | | | | | |
|---|---|---|---|---|---|---|
| Age Of Electronics | LP | Command | SCMD946 | 1970 £15 | £30 | |
| Electrics | LP | Command | 9383 | 1968 £20 | £40 | US |
| Moog | LP | Command | SCMD508 | 1969 £8 | £20 | |
| Swings | 7" EP | MGM | MGMEP646 | 1958 £2 | £5 | |
| Threepenny Opera Theme | 7" | MGM | SP1164 | 1956 £1.50 | £4 | |

# I

### I D COMPANY
I D Company.................................... LP...... Hor Zu........... SHZE801BL........... 1970 £6.......... £15 ................ German

### I DRIVE
I Drive .......................................... LP...... Metronome ..... 15420.................. 1972 £20...... £40 ................ German

### I JAH MAN
Haile I Hymn.................................. LP...... Island............. ILPS9521 ........... 1978 £4.......... £10 ................ ....

### I LIFE
Kiss You Gave ............................... 7"...... R&B ............ JB140................ 1964 £5.......... £10 ................ ....

### I LUV WIGHT
Let The World Wash In.................... 7"...... Philips............ 6006043 ............. 1970 £7.50...... £15 ................ ....
Let The World Wash In.................... 7"...... Philips............ 6006043 ............. 1970 £30.......... £60 ......... picture sleeve

### IAN, JANIS
For All The Seasons Of Your Mind........... LP...... Verve............ (S)VLP6003........... 1968 £4.......... £10 ................ ....
Janis Ian....................................... LP...... Verve............ (S)VLP6001 ........... 1967 £4.......... £10 ................ ....
Secret Life Of Eddie Fink.................. LP...... Verve............ FTS3048.............. 1968 £4.......... £10 ................ US
Society's Child ............................... 7"...... Verve............ VS1503............... 1967 £1.50...... £4 ................ ....
Society's Child ............................... 7"...... Verve............ VS1506............... 1967 £1.50...... £4 ................ ....
Sunflakes Fall, Snowrays Call .................. 7"...... Verve............ VS1513............... 1968 £2.......... £5 ................ ....
Who Really Cares ........................... LP...... Verve............ FTS3063.............. 1969 £4.......... £10 ................ US

### IAN & BELINDA
Who Wants To Live Forever ................ 7"...... Odeon ............ ODO112 .......... 1989 £2.......... £5 ...... with Brian May
Who Wants To Live Forever.................. 12"..... Odeon ............ 12ODO112 .......... 1989 £6.......... £15 ........ with Brian May

### IAN & SYLVIA
Best Of Ian And Sylvia ..................... LP...... Vanguard ........ SVRL19004........... 1968 £4.......... £10 ................ ....
Early Morning Rain ......................... LP...... Fontana.......... TF6053 ............. 1965 £4.......... £10 ................ ....
Four Strong Winds .......................... LP...... Vanguard ........ VSD2149 ........... 1964 £4.......... £10 ................ US
Ian And Sylvia ............................... LP...... Vanguard ........ VSD2113 ........... 1962 £4.......... £10 ................ US
Northern Journey ............................ LP...... Vanguard ........ VSD79154........... 1964 £4.......... £10 ................ US
Play One More ............................... LP...... Vanguard ........ VSD79215........... 1966 £4.......... £10 ................ US

### IAN & THE ZODIACS
Beechwood 45789............................ 7"...... Oriole............ CB1849 ............. 1963 £10.......... £20 ................ ....
Gear Again – 12 Hits ....................... LP...... Wing ........... WL1074.............. 1965 £15.......... £30 ................ ....
Ian And The Zodiacs ........................ LP...... Philips............ PHM200176/........ 1966 £20.......... £40 ................ US
                                                                    PHS600176 ...........
Just Listen To.................................. LP...... Starclub .......... 158020STY ........... 1966 £50.......... £100 ................ German
Just The Little Things I Like................ 7"...... Fontana.......... TF548................ 1965 £6.......... £12 ................ ....
Locomotive! ................................... LP...... Starclub .......... 158029STY ........... 1966 £50.......... £100 ................ German
No Money, No Honey.......................... 7"...... Fontana.......... TF708................ 1966 £6.......... £12 ................ ....
Starclub Show 7 .............................. LP...... Starclub .......... 158007STY ........... 1965 £30.......... £60 ................ German
Wade In The Water ........................... 7"...... Fontana.......... TF753................ 1966 £12.50.... £25 ................ ....

### IBIS
Ibis.............................................. LP...... Polydor........... 2448036 ................. 1975 £15.......... £30 ................ Italian

### IBLISS
Supernova...................................... LP...... Spiegelei.......... 285015U .............. 1972 £6.......... £15 ................ German

### ICARUS
Devil Rides Out................................ 7"...... Spark ............ SRL1012............. 1969 £4.......... £8 ................ ....
Marvel World .................................. LP...... Pye ............... NSPL28161 ........... 1971 £50.......... £100 ................ ....

### ICE
Anniversary Of Love........................... 7"...... Decca ............ F12680................ 1967 £20.......... £40 ................ ....
Ice Man......................................... 7"...... Decca ............ F12749................ 1968 £20.......... £40 ................ ....

### ICE (2)
Saga Of The Ice King ....................... LP...... Storm ............. SR3307................ 1979 £50.......... £100 ....... with blue booklet

### ICECROSS
First ............................................ LP...... Icecross ........ IC534753 ........... 1973 £62.50.. £125 ................ Icelandic

### ICEHOUSE
Crazy ........................................... CD-s .. Chrysalis ........ CHSCD3156......... 1988 £2.......... £5 ................ ....
Electric Blue .................................. CD-s .. Chrysalis ........ CHSCD3239.......... 1988 £2.......... £5 ................ ....
Full Circle ..................................... CD..... Chrysalis ........ ........................ ........ £10.......... £25 import double CD set

421

| | | | | | | | |
|---|---|---|---|---|---|---|---|
| Measure For Measure | CD | Chrysalis | CCD1527 | 1986 | £5 | £12 | |
| Touch The Fire | CD-s | Chrysalis | CHSCD3472 | 1989 | £2 | £5 | |

## ICICLE WORKS

| | | | | | | | |
|---|---|---|---|---|---|---|---|
| Ascending | cass | private | | 198– | £6 | £15 | |
| Birds Fly | 7" | Situation 2 | SIT22 | 1983 | £1.50 | £4 | |
| Birds Fly | 12" | Situation 2 | SIT22T | 1983 | £3 | £8 | |
| I Still Want You | CD-s | Epic | WORKSC102 | 1990 | £2 | £5 | |
| Kiss Off | CD-s | Beggars Banquet | IW1CD | 1988 | £2 | £5 | |
| Little Girl Lost | CD-s | Beggars Banquet | BEG215CD | 1988 | £4 | £10 | picture disc |
| Love Is A Wonderful Colour | 7" | Beggars Banquet | BEG99 | 1983 | £1.50 | £4 | double |
| Love Is A Wonderful Colour | 7" | Beggars Banquet | BEG99P | 1983 | £2 | £5 | picture disc |
| Melanie Still Hurts | CD-s | Epic | WORKSC101 | 1990 | £2 | £5 | |
| Motorcycle Rider | CD-s | Epic | WORKSC100 | 1990 | £2 | £5 | |
| Nirvana | 7" | Troll Kitchen | WORKS1 | 1983 | £4 | £8 | |
| Rapids | 12" | Beggars Banquet | BEG154T | 1986 | £3 | £8 | autographed promo |

## ID

| | | | | | | | |
|---|---|---|---|---|---|---|---|
| Inner Sounds Of The Id | LP | RCA | LPM/LSP3805 | 1967 | £20 | £40 | US |

## ID (2)

| | | | | | | | |
|---|---|---|---|---|---|---|---|
| Where Are We Going | LP | Aurora | AR1000 | 1975 | £30 | £60 | US |
| Where Are We Going? | LP | Aura | 1000 | 1976 | £10 | £25 | US |

## IDEALS

| | | | | | | | |
|---|---|---|---|---|---|---|---|
| Knee Socks | 7" | Pye | 7N25103 | 1961 | £7.50 | £15 | |

## IDEM DITO

| | | | | | | | |
|---|---|---|---|---|---|---|---|
| Facing Aquarius | LP | Audio Art | | 1985 | £8 | £20 | Dutch |

## IDES OF MARCH

| | | | | | | | |
|---|---|---|---|---|---|---|---|
| Hole In My Soul | 7" | London | HLU10183 | 1968 | £1.50 | £4 | |
| You Wouldn't Listen | 7" | London | HLU10058 | 1966 | £1.50 | £4 | |

## IDLE FLOWERS

| | | | | | | | |
|---|---|---|---|---|---|---|---|
| All I Want Is You | 7" | Miles Ahead | AHEAD1 | 1984 | £5 | £10 | |

## IDLE RACE

The Idle Race produced intelligent pop music with occasional touches of psychedelia (most notably in the single 'Imposters Of Life's Magazine'). The group's records displayed a degree of production skill and craftsmanship unusual in a little-known pop act of the time, but then the group's leader was Jeff Lynne.

| | | | | | | | |
|---|---|---|---|---|---|---|---|
| Birthday Party | LP | Liberty | LBL/LBS83132 | 1968 | £10 | £25 | |
| Birthday Party | LP | Sunset | SLS50381 | 1976 | £4 | £10 | |
| Come With Me | 7" | Liberty | LBF15242 | 1969 | £7.50 | £15 | |
| Dancing Flower | 7" | Regal Zonophone | RZ3036 | 1971 | £7.50 | £15 | |
| Days Of Broken Arrows | 7" | Liberty | LBF15218 | 1969 | £7.50 | £15 | |
| End Of The Road | 7" | Liberty | LBF15101 | 1968 | £7.50 | £15 | |
| I Like My Toys | 7" | Liberty | LBF15129 | 1968 | £15 | £30 | |
| Idle Race | LP | Liberty | LBS83211 | 1969 | £15 | £30 | demo |
| Imposters Of Life's Magazine | 7" | Liberty | LBF15026 | 1967 | £12.50 | £25 | |
| On With The Show | LP | Sunset | SLS50354 | 1973 | £4 | £10 | |
| Skeleton And The Roundabout | 7" | Liberty | LBF15054 | 1968 | £7.50 | £15 | |
| Time Is | LP | Regal Zonophone | SLRZ1017 | 1971 | £30 | £60 | |

## IDOL, BILLY

| | | | | | | | |
|---|---|---|---|---|---|---|---|
| Catch My Fall | CD-s | Chrysalis | IDOLCD13 | 1988 | £2 | £5 | |
| Cradle Of Love | CD-s | Chrysalis | IDOLCD14 | 1990 | £2 | £5 | |
| Hot In The City | CD-s | Chrysalis | IDOLCD12 | 1987 | £2 | £5 | |
| Hot In The City | 7" | Chrysalis | CHS2625 | 1982 | £1.50 | £4 | picture disc |
| L.A. Woman | CD-s | Chrysalis | IDOLCD15 | 1990 | £2 | £5 | |
| Prodigal Blues | CD-s | Chrysalis | IDOLCD16 | 1990 | £2 | £5 | |
| Rebel Yell | 7" | Chrysalis | IDOLP2 | 1984 | £1.50 | £4 | square picture disc |
| Whiplash Smile | CD | Chrysalis | CCD1514 | 1986 | £5 | £12 | |

## IF

If was a jazz-rock group formed by the previously mainstream jazz players Dick Morrissey and Terry Smith (saxophone and guitar respectively). It was interesting as a group formed from the jazz side of the jazz-rock divide, but was ultimately less convincing than the likes of Colosseum or Manfred Mann Chapter Three. Morrissey reappeared later as co-leader of the successful fusion group, Morrissey-Mullen.

| | | | | | | | |
|---|---|---|---|---|---|---|---|
| Double Diamond | LP | Brain | 201035 | 1973 | £8 | £20 | German |
| Goldenrock | LP | Brain | 201103 | 1974 | £6 | £15 | German |
| If | LP | Island | ILPS9129 | 1970 | £8 | £20 | pink label |
| If 2 | LP | Island | ILPS9137 | 1970 | £8 | £20 | |
| If 3 | LP | United Artists | UAG29158 | 1971 | £6 | £15 | |
| If 4 | LP | United Artists | UAG29315 | 1972 | £6 | £15 | |
| Raise The Level Of Your Conscious Mind | 7" | Island | WIP6083 | 1970 | £1.50 | £4 | |
| This Is If | LP | Brain | 201005 | 1973 | £6 | £15 | German |

## IGGINBOTTOM

The LP by Igginbottom marks the recording debut of the guitarists' guitarist, Allan Holdsworth, in a surprisingly understated context.

| | | | | | | | |
|---|---|---|---|---|---|---|---|
| Igginbottom's Wrench | LP | Deram | DML1051 | 1969 | £62.50 | £125 | mono |
| Igginbottom's Wrench | LP | Deram | SML1051 | 1969 | £50 | £100 | |

## IGUANA

| | | | | | | |
|---|---|---|---|---|---|---|
| Iguana | LP | Polydor | 2383108 | 1972 | £5 | £12 |

## IGUANAS

| | | | | | | |
|---|---|---|---|---|---|---|
| This Is What I Was Made For | 7" | RCA | RCA1484 | 1965 | £2.50 | £6 |

## IHRE KINDER

| | | | | | | | |
|---|---|---|---|---|---|---|---|
| 2375004 | LP | Kuckuck | 2375004 | 1970 | £8 | £20 | German |
| Anfang Ohne Ende | LP | Kuckuck | 2375016 | 1972 | £6 | £15 | German |
| Empty Hands | LP | Kuckuck | 2371165 | 1971 | £8 | £20 | German |
| Ihre Kinder | LP | Philips | 844393 | 1969 | £15 | £30 | German |
| Leere Hände | LP | Kuckuck | 2375001 | 1970 | £15 | £30 | German |
| Werdohl | LP | Kuckuck | 2375013 | 1971 | £8 | £20 | German |

## IKARUS

| | | | | | | | |
|---|---|---|---|---|---|---|---|
| Ikarus | LP | Plus | 4 | 1971 | £6 | £15 | German |

## IKETTES

| | | | | | | | |
|---|---|---|---|---|---|---|---|
| Fine Fine Fine | 7" EP | Stateside | SE1033 | 1965 | £15 | £30 | |
| Fine Fine Fine | 7" | Stateside | SS434 | 1965 | £2.50 | £6 | |
| I'm Blue | 7" | London | HLK9508 | 1962 | £2.50 | £6 | |
| I'm So Thankful | 7" | Polydor | 56506 | 1970 | £2 | £5 | |
| Never More Lonely For You | 7" | Polydor | 56516 | 1970 | £1.50 | £4 | |
| Peaches 'n' Cream | 7" | Stateside | SS407 | 1965 | £4 | £8 | |
| Prisoner Of Love | 7" | Sue | WI389 | 1965 | £7.50 | £15 | |
| Soul Hits | LP | Modern | M(ST)102 | 1965 | £10 | £25 | US |
| Whatcha Gonna Do | 7" | London | HLU10081 | 1966 | £2.50 | £6 | |

## ILANIT

| | | | | | | |
|---|---|---|---|---|---|---|
| I'm No One | 7" | Pye | 7N25739 | 1977 | £2.50 | £6 |

## ILL WIND

| | | | | | | | |
|---|---|---|---|---|---|---|---|
| Flashes | LP | ABC | S641 | 1968 | £37.50 | £75 | US |

## ILLINOIS SPEED PRESS

| | | | | | | | |
|---|---|---|---|---|---|---|---|
| Duet | LP | CBS | CS9976 | 1970 | £6 | £15 | US |
| Illinois Speed Press | LP | CBS | CS9792 | 1969 | £8 | £20 | US |

## ILLSLEY, JOHN

| | | | | | | |
|---|---|---|---|---|---|---|
| I Want To See The Moon | CD-s | Vertigo | VERCD39 | 1988 | £2 | £5 |

## ILLUSION

| | | | | | | |
|---|---|---|---|---|---|---|
| Did You See Her Eyes | 7" | Dot | 122 | 1969 | £1.50 | £4 |
| If It's So | LP | Paramount | SPFL264 | 1970 | £5 | £12 |
| Illusion | LP | Dot | (S)LPD531 | 1969 | £5 | £12 |
| Together | LP | Dot | SLPD537 | 1970 | £5 | £12 |

## ILLUSIVE DREAM

| | | | | | | |
|---|---|---|---|---|---|---|
| Electric Garden | 7" | RCA | RCA1791 | 1969 | £2.50 | £6 |

## ILLUSTRATION

| | | | | | | | |
|---|---|---|---|---|---|---|---|
| Illustration | LP | Janus | JLS3010 | 1969 | £10 | £25 | US |

## ILMO SMOKEHOUSE

| | | | | | | | |
|---|---|---|---|---|---|---|---|
| Ilmo Smokehouse | LP | Beautiful Sound | 3002 | 1971 | £6 | £15 | US |

## ILORI, SOLOMON

| | | | | | | |
|---|---|---|---|---|---|---|
| African High Life | LP | Blue Note | BLP/BST84136 | 1963 | £15 | £30 |

## IMAGE

Guitarist with the Image was Dave Edmunds, who subsequently achieved considerable success in his own right.

| | | | | | | |
|---|---|---|---|---|---|---|
| Come To The Party | 7" | Parlophone | R5281 | 1965 | £10 | £20 |
| Home Is Anywhere | 7" | Parlophone | R5352 | 1965 | £12.50 | £25 |
| I Can't Stop Myself | 7" | Parlophone | R5442 | 1966 | £7.50 | £15 |

## IMAGES

| | | | | | | |
|---|---|---|---|---|---|---|
| I Only Have Myself To Blame | 7" | Polydor | BM56011 | 1965 | £5 | £10 |

## IMAN CALIFATO INDEPENDIENTE

| | | | | | | | |
|---|---|---|---|---|---|---|---|
| Camuno Del Aguila | LP | CBS | 84277 | 1978 | £8 | £20 | Spanish |

## IMLACH, HAMISH

| | | | | | | |
|---|---|---|---|---|---|---|
| Ballads Of Booze | LP | XTRA | XTRA1094 | 1970 | £4 | £10 |
| Before And After | LP | XTRA | XTRA1059 | 1967 | £4 | £10 |
| Fine Old English Tory Times | LP | XTRA | XTRA1128 | 1972 | £4 | £10 |
| Murdered Ballads | LP | XTRA | XTRA1131 | 1973 | £4 | £10 |
| Old Rarity | LP | XTRA | XTRA1121 | 1971 | £4 | £10 |
| Two Sides Of Hamish Imlach | LP | XTRA | XTRA1069 | 1968 | £4 | £10 |

## IMMORTALS

| | | | | | | | |
|---|---|---|---|---|---|---|---|
| No Turning Back | 7" | MCA | MCA1057 | 1986 | £12.50 | £25 | |
| No Turning Back | 12" | MCA | MCAT1057 | 1986 | £15 | £30 | |

## IMORTALS

| | | | | | | | |
|---|---|---|---|---|---|---|---|
| Ultimate Warlord | 7" | Excaliber | EXC517 | 1982 | £10 | £20 | |
| Ultimate Warlord | 12" | Excaliber | EXC517 | 1982 | £10 | £25 | |

## IMPAC

| | | | | | | | |
|---|---|---|---|---|---|---|---|
| Too Far Out | 7" | CBS | 202402 | 1966 | £15 | £30 | |

## IMPACS

| | | | | | | | |
|---|---|---|---|---|---|---|---|
| Impact! | LP | King | (KS)886 | 1964 | £8 | £20 | US |
| Weekend With The Impacs | LP | King | (KS)916 | 1964 | £8 | £20 | US |

## IMP-ACTS

| | | | | | | | |
|---|---|---|---|---|---|---|---|
| Dum Dum Song | 7" EP | Pye | PNV24152 | 1965 | £5 | £10 | French, B side by Kenny Bernard |

## IMPACTS

| | | | | | | | |
|---|---|---|---|---|---|---|---|
| Wipe Out | LP | Del-Fi | DFLP/DFS1234 | 1963 | £6 | £15 | US |

## IMPALA SYNDROME

| | | | | | | | |
|---|---|---|---|---|---|---|---|
| Impala Syndrome | LP | Parallax | P4002 | 1969 | £15 | £30 | US |

## IMPALAS

| | | | | | | | |
|---|---|---|---|---|---|---|---|
| Oh What A Fool | 7" | MGM | MGM1031 | 1959 | £4 | £8 | |
| Peggy Darling | 7" | MGM | MGM1068 | 1960 | £2 | £5 | |
| Sorry | 7" EP | MGM | MGMEP696 | 1959 | £50 | £100 | |
| Sorry | 7" | MGM | MGM1015 | 1959 | £6 | £12 | |
| Sorry I Ran All The Way Home | LP | Cub | (S)8003 | 1959 | £50 | £100 | US |

## IMPERSONATORS

| | | | | | | | |
|---|---|---|---|---|---|---|---|
| Make It Easy On Yourself | 7" | Big Shot | BI524 | 1969 | £1.50 | £4 | |

## IMPOSSIBLE DREAMERS

| | | | | | | | |
|---|---|---|---|---|---|---|---|
| Books Books Books | 7" | Merciful Release | MR1 | 1980 | £4 | £8 | |
| Life On Earth | 12" | One Hundred Things | MR5 | 1982 | £2.50 | £6 | |

## IMPOSTERS

| | | | | | | | |
|---|---|---|---|---|---|---|---|
| Apache '69 | 7" | Mercury | MF1080 | 1969 | £4 | £8 | |

## IMPRESSIONS

| | | | | | | | |
|---|---|---|---|---|---|---|---|
| Amen | LP | Buddah | 2359009 | 1970 | £4 | £10 | |
| Amen | 7" | HMV | POP1492 | 1965 | £1.50 | £4 | |
| Big 16 | LP | HMV | CLP1935/CSD1642 | 1965 | £8 | £20 | |
| Big 16 Vol. 2 | LP | Stateside | (S)SL10279 | 1969 | £4 | £10 | |
| Can't Satisfy | 7" | HMV | POP1545 | 1966 | £5 | £10 | |
| Can't Satisfy | 7" | Stateside | SS2139 | 1969 | £1.50 | £4 | |
| Check Out Your Mind | LP | Buddah | 2318017 | 1971 | £4 | £10 | |
| Fabulous Impressions | LP | HMV | CLP/CSD3631 | 1967 | £6 | £15 | |
| Gypsy Woman | 7" | HMV | POP961 | 1961 | £7.50 | £15 | |
| I Need You | 7" | HMV | POP1472 | 1965 | £1.50 | £4 | |
| I'm So Proud | 7" | HMV | POP1295 | 1964 | £2 | £5 | |
| I'm The One Who Loves You | 7" | HMV | POP1129 | 1963 | £2 | £5 | |
| Impressions | LP | ABC | (S)450 | 1963 | £10 | £25 | US |
| It's All Right | 7" EP | HMV | 7EG8896 | 1965 | £7.50 | £15 | |
| It's All Right | 7" | HMV | POP1226 | 1963 | £2.50 | £6 | |
| Keep On Pushing | LP | ABC | (S)493 | 1964 | £8 | £20 | US |
| Keep On Pushing | 7" | HMV | POP1317 | 1964 | £2 | £5 | |
| Meeting Over Yonder | 7" | HMV | POP1446 | 1965 | £2 | £5 | |
| Mighty Mighty Spade And Whitey | 7" | Buddah | 201062 | 1969 | £1.50 | £4 | |
| Never Ending Impressions | LP | HMV | CLP1743 | 1964 | £8 | £20 | |
| One By One | LP | ABC | (S)523 | 1965 | £8 | £20 | US |
| People Get Ready | LP | ABC | (S)505 | 1965 | £8 | £20 | US |
| People Get Ready | 7" | HMV | POP1408 | 1965 | £1.50 | £4 | |
| Ridin' High | LP | HMV | CLP/CSD3548 | 1966 | £6 | £15 | |
| Since I Lost The One I Love | 7" | HMV | POP1516 | 1966 | £1.50 | £4 | |
| Soulfully | 7" EP | HMV | 7EG8954 | 1966 | £7.50 | £15 | |
| Talking About My Baby | 7" | HMV | POP1262 | 1964 | £2 | £5 | |
| This Is My Country | LP | Buddah | 203012 | 1969 | £4 | £10 | |
| Too Slow | 7" | HMV | POP1526 | 1966 | £2 | £5 | |
| We're A Winner | LP | Stateside | (S)SL10239 | 1968 | £4 | £10 | |
| We're A Winner | 7" | Stateside | SS2083 | 1968 | £1.50 | £4 | |
| Woman's Got Soul | 7" | HMV | POP1429 | 1965 | £2.50 | £6 | |
| You Always Hurt Me | 7" | HMV | POP1581 | 1967 | £1.50 | £4 | |
| You Must Believe Me | 7" | HMV | POP1343 | 1964 | £2 | £5 | |
| You've Been Cheating | 7" | HMV | POP1498 | 1966 | £4 | £8 | |
| Young Mod's Forgotten Story | LP | Buddah | 2359003 | 1970 | £4 | £10 | |

## IMPROVED SOUND LIMITED

| | | | | | | | |
|---|---|---|---|---|---|---|---|
| Improved Sound Limited | LP | Liberty | LBS83505/6 | 1971 | £8 | £20 | German double |

## IMPROVISORS' SYMPOSIUM

| | | | | | | | |
|---|---|---|---|---|---|---|---|
| Pisa 1980 | LP | Incus | INCUS37 | 1981 | £5 | £12 | |

## IMPS
Dim Dumb Blonde................................... 7" ...... Parlophone...... R4398 .................. 1958 £2.50........£6 ...............................

## IN BETWEENS
The In Betweens' sole single, a version of the Young Rascals' American hit, 'You Better Run', was produced by the legendary Kim Fowley. Success did not come to the group until a few years later, however, when it had changed its name to Slade.

Take A Heart............................................ 7" EP . Barclay............ 2017 .................... 1966 £180.....£300 *French, best auctioned*
Take A Heart............................................ 7" EP . Barclay............ 70907 .................. 1965 £180.....£300 *French, best auctioned*
You Better Run........................................ 7" ...... Columbia ........ DB8080 .............. 1966 £180.....£300 ...........*best auctioned*

## IN CAMERA
Die Laughing........................................... 7" ...... 4AD .............. AD8 .................... 1980 £1.50......£4
Fin.......................................................... 12" ...... 4AD .............. BAD205................ 1982 £2.50......£6
IV Songs................................................. 12" ...... 4AD .............. BAD19 ............... 1980 £2.50......£6

## IN CROWD
The soul singles of the In Crowd gave no indication that the group would ever evolve into that cornerstone of psychedelia, Tomorrow. 'That's How Strong My Love Is' was recorded before Steve Howe joined the group, but the other singles all feature his guitar playing, in behind Keith West's singing.

Stop! Wait A Minute ............................... 7" ...... Parlophone...... R5328 .................. 1965 £20.....£40
That's How Strong My Love Is................. 7" ...... Parlophone...... R5276 .................. 1965 £37.50...£75
Why Must They Criticise.......................... 7" ...... Parlophone...... R5364 .................. 1965 £20.....£40

## IN CROWD (2)
Where In The World................................. 7" ...... Deram .............. DM272 ............... 1969 £4.............£8

## IN THE NURSERY
Sonority – A Strength............................... 12" ...... New European BADVC55 ............. 1985 £3.............£8
When Cherished Dreams Come True ....... LP ...... Paragon .......... VIRTUE2............ 1983 £6.............£15
Witness To A Scream .............................. 7" ...... Paragon .......... VIRTUE5............ 1984 £6.............£12

## IN TWO A CIRCLE
Rise ....................................................... 12" ...... Arcadia .......... ARC001 ............. 1986 £3.............£8

## INADEQUATES
Audie...................................................... 7" ...... Capitol............ CL15051 .............. 1959 £1.50........£4

## INCA
Satya Sai – Maitreya Kali ........................ LP ...... private............... .................... £700 ...£1000 ............................*US*

## INCAS
I'll Keep Holding On................................ 7" ...... Parlophone...... R5551 .................. 1966 £10.............£20
Keele Rag Record.................................... 7" EP . Lyntone ......... LYN765/6 ........ 196– £15.............£30 ........ *with other artists*

## INCOGNITO
Parisienne Girl ........................................ 12" ...... Ensign............ ENY4412............ 1980 £2.50......£6

## INCREDIBLE BONGO BAND
Bongo Rock............................................ LP ...... DJM .............. 20452 ............... 1976 £5.............£12

## INCREDIBLE HOG
Volume One............................................ LP ...... Dart.............. 65372 ............... 1973 £50........£100

## INCREDIBLE STRING BAND
5000 Spirits Or The Layers Of The Onion . LP ...... Elektra ............ EUK/EUKS7257 ... 1967 £6.............£15
Be Glad For The Song Has No Ending....... LP ...... Island ............ ILPS9140 .......... 1970 £4.............£10
Big Huge................................................ LP ...... Elektra ............ EKL/EKS74037 .... 1968 £6.............£15
Big Ted.................................................. 7" ...... Elektra ............ EKSN45074 ........... 1969 £1.50.....£4
Changing Horses ..................................... LP ...... Elektra ............ EKS74057 .......... 1969 £6.............£15
Earthspan............................................... LP ...... Island ............ ILPS9211 .......... 1972 £4.............£10
Hangman's Beautiful Daughter ................. LP ...... Elektra ............ EKL/EKS74022 .... 1968 £6.............£15
Hangman's Beautiful Daughter ................. LP ...... Elektra ............ EUK/EUKS7258 ... 1968 £6.............£15
Hard Rope & Silken Twine ...................... LP ...... Island ............ ILPS9270 .......... 1974 £4.............£10
I Looked Up ........................................... LP ...... Elektra ............ EKS74061 .......... 1970 £6.............£15
Incredible String Band ........................... LP ...... Elektra ............ EKL322 ............. 1966 £20.....£40
Incredible String Band ........................... LP ...... Elektra ............ EUK254............ 1966 £20.....£40
Incredible String Band ........................... LP ...... Elektra ............ EUK254............ 1966 £25.....£50 .....*white Elektra label*
Liquid Acrobat As Regards The Air ......... LP ...... Island ............ ILPS9172 .......... 1971 £4.............£10
No Ruinous Feud ..................................... LP ...... Island ............ ILPS9229 .......... 1973 £4.............£10
Painting Box........................................... 7" ...... Elektra ............ EKSN45028 ......... 1967 £1.50.....£4
Seasons They Change ............................. LP ...... Island ............ ISLD9 ............... 1976 £5.............£12 .................. *double*
This Moment........................................... 7" ...... Elektra ............ 2101003 ............ 1970 £1.50.....£4
U............................................................ LP ...... Elektra ............ 2665001 ............ 1970 £6.............£15 .................. *double*
Wee Tam ............................................... LP ...... Elektra ............ EKL/EKS74036 .... 1968 £6.............£15
Wee Tam/The Big Huge.......................... LP ...... Elektra ............ EKL/EKS74036/7... 1968 £10.....£25 .................. *double*

## INCREDIBLES
There's Nothing Else To Say ................... 7" ...... Stateside .......... SS2053 .............. 1967 £25.....£50

## INCROWD
I'll Be Free ............................................ LP ...... Polydor .......... 736042................ 1966 £8...........£20 .................*Dutch*

## IND, PETER
Improvisation.......................................... LP ...... Wave .............. LP3..................... 1970 £6...........£15

| Title | Format | Label | Catalogue | Year | | | Notes |
|---|---|---|---|---|---|---|---|
| Jazz At The 1969 Richmond Festival | LP | Wave | LP5 | 1970 | £6 | £15 | |
| Looking Out | LP | Esquire | 32159 | 1962 | £8 | £20 | |
| Looking Out | LP | Wave | LP1 | 1970 | £6 | £15 | |
| Time For Improvisation | LP | Wave | LP4 | 1970 | £6 | £15 | |

## INDEPENDENT FOLK

| Title | Format | Label | Catalogue | Year | | | Notes |
|---|---|---|---|---|---|---|---|
| Independent Folk | LP | Great Western | DM015 | 1977 | £50 | £100 | |

## INDEX

| Title | Format | Label | Catalogue | Year | | | Notes |
|---|---|---|---|---|---|---|---|
| Index | LP | DC | | 1968 | £875 | £1250 | US |
| Index | LP | private | | 1967 | £700 | £1000 | US |

## INDIAN SUMMER

| Title | Format | Label | Catalogue | Year | | | Notes |
|---|---|---|---|---|---|---|---|
| Indian Summer | LP | Neon | NE3 | 1971 | £15 | £30 | |

## INDO JAZZMEN

| Title | Format | Label | Catalogue | Year | | | Notes |
|---|---|---|---|---|---|---|---|
| Ragas Reflections | LP | Saga | EROS2145 | 1968 | £10 | £25 | |

## INDO-BRITISH ENSEMBLE

| Title | Format | Label | Catalogue | Year | | | Notes |
|---|---|---|---|---|---|---|---|
| Curried Jazz | LP | MFP | 1307 | 197– | £4 | £10 | |

## INFANTES JUBILATE

| Title | Format | Label | Catalogue | Year | | | Notes |
|---|---|---|---|---|---|---|---|
| Exploding Galaxy | LP | Music Factory | CUB5 | 1968 | £12.50 | £25 | |

## INFESTED

| Title | Format | Label | Catalogue | Year | | | Notes |
|---|---|---|---|---|---|---|---|
| Flies | 7" | Dead City | | 197– | £50 | £100 | existence doubtful |
| No But I've Got A Dark Brown Overcoat | 7" | Great Disaster | | 197– | £50 | £100 | existence doubtful |

## INFLUENCE

| Title | Format | Label | Catalogue | Year | | | Notes |
|---|---|---|---|---|---|---|---|
| I Want To Live | 7" | Orange | OAS201 | 1969 | £2.50 | £6 | |
| Influence | LP | ABC | ABCS630 | 1968 | £15 | £30 | US |

## INFORMATION

| Title | Format | Label | Catalogue | Year | | | Notes |
|---|---|---|---|---|---|---|---|
| Face To The Sun | 7" | Evolution | E24615 | 1970 | £2 | £5 | |
| Orphan | 7" | Beacon | BEA3121 | 1968 | £1.50 | £4 | |

## INGLE, RED

| Title | Format | Label | Catalogue | Year | | | Notes |
|---|---|---|---|---|---|---|---|
| Cigareets,Whuskey,& Wild Wild Women | 7" EP | Capitol | EAP20052 | 1959 | £5 | £10 | |

## INGMANN, JORGEN

| Title | Format | Label | Catalogue | Year | | | Notes |
|---|---|---|---|---|---|---|---|
| Apache | LP | Atco | (SD)33130 | 1961 | £8 | £20 | US |
| Drina | 7" EP | Columbia | SEG8340 | 1964 | £4 | £8 | |
| Many Guitars Of Jorgen Ingmann | LP | Atco | (SD)33139 | 1962 | £6 | £15 | US |
| Swinging Guitar | LP | Mercury | MG20200 | 1956 | £8 | £20 | US |

## INGOES

Although the only record made by the Ingoes is this rather uninspiring and obscure French EP, the group is, in fact, an early version of the Blossom Toes, featuring both guitarists and the bass player.

| Title | Format | Label | Catalogue | Year | | | Notes |
|---|---|---|---|---|---|---|---|
| Dansez Le Monkiss | 7" EP | Riviera | 231141 | 1966 | £12.50 | £25 | French |

## INGRAM, LUTHER

| Title | Format | Label | Catalogue | Year | | | Notes |
|---|---|---|---|---|---|---|---|
| Home Don't Seem Like A Home | 7" | Stax | STAX148 | 1970 | £1.50 | £4 | |
| My Honey And Me | 7" | Stax | STAX142 | 1970 | £1.50 | £4 | |

## INITIALS

| Title | Format | Label | Catalogue | Year | | | Notes |
|---|---|---|---|---|---|---|---|
| School Days | 7" | London | HLR9860 | 1964 | £2.50 | £6 | |

## INJAROC

| Title | Format | Label | Catalogue | Year | | | Notes |
|---|---|---|---|---|---|---|---|
| Halen Y Ddaer! | LP | Sain | 1094M | 1977 | £8 | £20 | |

## INKER, DAVE

| Title | Format | Label | Catalogue | Year | | | Notes |
|---|---|---|---|---|---|---|---|
| Profile | LP | Ariola | 27297 | 1976 | £10 | £25 | German |

## INKSPOTS

| Title | Format | Label | Catalogue | Year | | | Notes |
|---|---|---|---|---|---|---|---|
| Charlie Fuqua's Inkspots | 7" EP | HMV | 7EG8410 | 1957 | £2.50 | £6 | |
| Ebb Tide | 7" | Parlophone | MSP6074 | 1954 | £5 | £10 | |
| Here In My Lonely Room | 7" | Parlophone | MSP6063 | 1954 | £5 | £10 | |
| Inkspots | 10" LP | Britone | LP1003 | 195– | £6 | £15 | |
| Melody Of Love | 7" | Parlophone | MSP6152 | 1955 | £4 | £8 | |
| Souvenir | 10" LP | Brunswick | LA8590 | 1953 | £6 | £15 | |
| Street Of Dreams | 10" LP | Brunswick | LA8710 | 1955 | £6 | £15 | |
| Swing High Swing Low Vol. 1 | 7" EP | Brunswick | OE9158 | 1955 | £2.50 | £6 | |
| Yesterdays | 7" EP | Parlophone | GEP8673 | 1957 | £2.50 | £6 | |
| Yesterdays | 7" | Parlophone | MSP6126 | 1954 | £5 | £10 | |

## INNES, NEIL

| Title | Format | Label | Catalogue | Year | | | Notes |
|---|---|---|---|---|---|---|---|
| How Sweet To Be An Idiot | LP | United Artists | UAG29492 | 1973 | £5 | £12 | |
| Rutland Times | LP | BBC | REB233 | 1976 | £4 | £10 | |

## INNOCENCE

| Title | Format | Label | Catalogue | Year | | | Notes |
|---|---|---|---|---|---|---|---|
| Mairzy Doats | 7" EP | Kama Sutra | 617107 | 1967 | £4 | £8 | French |

## INNOCENCE MISSION

| Title | Format | Label | Catalogue | Year | | | Notes |
|---|---|---|---|---|---|---|---|
| Black Sheep Wall | CD-s | A&M | AMCD563 | 1990 | £2 | £5 | |
| Wonder Of Birds | CD-s | A&M | AMCD543 | 1990 | £2 | £5 | |

## INNOCENTS

| | | | | | | | |
|---|---|---|---|---|---|---|---|
| Gee Whiz | 7" | Top Rank | JAR541 | 1961 | £5 | £10 | |
| Honest I Do | 7" | Top Rank | JAR508 | 1960 | £5 | £10 | |

## INNOCENTS (2)

| | | | | | | | |
|---|---|---|---|---|---|---|---|
| Fine Fine Bird | 7" | Columbia | DB7173 | 1963 | £1.50 | £4 | |
| Medley | 7" | Regal Zonophone | RZ502 | 1964 | £1.50 | £4 | with the Leroys |
| Stepping Stones | 7" | Columbia | DB7098 | 1963 | £1.50 | £4 | |
| Stick With Me Baby | 7" | Columbia | DB7314 | 1964 | £1.50 | £4 | |

## INNOCENTS (3)

| | | | | | | | |
|---|---|---|---|---|---|---|---|
| One Way Love | 7" | Kingdom | KV8010 | 1980 | £2.50 | £6 | |

## IN-SECT

| | | | | | | | |
|---|---|---|---|---|---|---|---|
| Introducing | LP | Camden | CAL909 | 1965 | £8 | £20 | US |

## INSECT TRUST

At a time when rock was blossoming with new approaches and unusual instruments, the Insect Trust still managed to sound unique. They are like a folk group, with a strong female lead singer, into which a couple of avant-garde jazz saxophonists have unaccountably wandered. The combination still sounds fresh today.

| | | | | | | | |
|---|---|---|---|---|---|---|---|
| Hoboken Saturday Night | LP | Atco | SD33313 | 1970 | £8 | £20 | US |
| Insect Trust | LP | Capitol | EST109 | 1968 | £10 | £25 | |

## INSIDE OUT

| | | | | | | | |
|---|---|---|---|---|---|---|---|
| Bringing It All Back | LP | Fredlo | 6834 | 1968 | £50 | £100 | US |

## INSPIRAL CARPETS

| | | | | | | | |
|---|---|---|---|---|---|---|---|
| Butterfly | 7" | Playtime | AMUSE4 | 1988 | £2 | £5 | promo only |
| Cow | cass | private | | 198– | £5 | £12 | |
| Find Out Why | CD-s | Cow | DUNG5CD | 1989 | £2 | £5 | |
| Find Out Why | 12" | Cow | DUNG5T | 1989 | £4 | £10 | signed, with newsletter |
| Garage Full Of Flowers | 7" | Debris | DEB06 | 1987 | £2 | £5 | flexi |
| Keep The Circle Around | cass-s | Cow | DUNG4 | 1989 | £4 | £10 | demo |
| Keep The Circle Around | 7" | Playtime | AMUSE2 | 1988 | £10 | £20 | |
| Keep The Circle Around | 12" | Cow | MOO1 | 1989 | £4 | £10 | test pressing |
| Keep The Circle Around | 12" | Playtime | AMUSE2T | 1988 | £10 | £25 | |
| Move | CD-s | Cow | DUNG6CD | 1989 | £2 | £5 | |
| Move | 7" | Cow | DUNG6X | 1989 | £1.50 | £4 | with badge |
| Peel Sessions | CD-s | Strange Fruit | SFPSCD072 | 1989 | £2 | £5 | |
| Please Be Cruel | CD-s | Cow | DUNG15CD | 1991 | £2 | £5 | |
| Songs Of Shallow Intensity | cass | private | | 198– | £6 | £15 | |
| Train Surfing | 12" | Cow | MOO2 | 1989 | £2.50 | £6 | |
| Train Surfing | 12" | Playtime | AMUSE4T | 1988 | £10 | £25 | promo |
| Waiting For Ours | cass | private | | 198– | £6 | £15 | |

## INSPIRATIONS

| | | | | | | | |
|---|---|---|---|---|---|---|---|
| Touch Me,Hold Me,Kiss Me | 7" | Polydor | 56730 | 1967 | £30 | £60 | |

## INSPIRATIONS (2)

| | | | | | | | |
|---|---|---|---|---|---|---|---|
| Reggae Fever | LP | Trojan | TTL27 | 1970 | £6 | £15 | |

## INSTANT SUNSHINE

| | | | | | | | |
|---|---|---|---|---|---|---|---|
| Here We Go Again | 7" | Page One | POF085 | 1968 | £1.50 | £4 | |
| Live At Tiddy Dols | LP | Page One | POL007 | 1968 | £10 | £25 | |

## INTERCONTINENTAL EXPRESS

| | | | | | | | |
|---|---|---|---|---|---|---|---|
| London | LP | Compendium | FIDARDO8 | 1976 | £4 | £10 | |

## INTERLUDE

| | | | | | | | |
|---|---|---|---|---|---|---|---|
| Dunskey Castle | LP | Seagull | | 1982 | £10 | £25 | Dutch |
| Interlude | LP | VR | | 1979 | £10 | £25 | Dutch |

## INTERNATIONAL SUBMARINE BAND

The International Submarine Band, led by Gram Parsons, is often credited with making the first country-rock LP, for Safe At Home pre-dates the Byrds' Sweetheart Of The Rodeo; in which Parsons was also involved.

| | | | | | | | |
|---|---|---|---|---|---|---|---|
| Safe At Home | LP | LHI | LHI12001 | 1968 | £30 | £60 | US, coloured label |
| Safe At Home | LP | Shiloh | RI4088 | 1979 | £4 | £10 | US |

## INTERNS

| | | | | | | | |
|---|---|---|---|---|---|---|---|
| Cry To Me | 7" | Philips | BF1345 | 1964 | £2.50 | £6 | |
| Don't You Dare | 7" | Philips | BF1320 | 1964 | £2 | £5 | |
| Is It Really What You Want | 7" | Parlophone | R5479 | 1966 | £10 | £20 | |
| Please Say Something Nice | 7" | Parlophone | R5586 | 1967 | £1.50 | £4 | |

## INTERWEAVE

| | | | | | | | |
|---|---|---|---|---|---|---|---|
| Interweave | LP | Silver Dragon | | 1986 | £37.50 | £75 | Dutch |

## INTRA VEIN

| | | | | | | | |
|---|---|---|---|---|---|---|---|
| Speed Of The City | 7" | Bum | FP001 | 1979 | £2.50 | £6 | PVC sleeve |

## INTRIGUES

| | | | | | | | |
|---|---|---|---|---|---|---|---|
| In A Moment | LP | Yew | YS777 | 1970 | £6 | £15 | US |
| In A Moment | 7" | London | HL10293 | 1969 | £2.50 | £6 | |

## INTRUDERS

| | | | | | | | |
|---|---|---|---|---|---|---|---|
| Cowboys To Girls | LP | Gamble | KZ5004 | 1968 | £8 | £20 | US |
| Intruders Are Together | LP | Gamble | (KZ)5001 | 1967 | £8 | £20 | US |
| Slow Drag | 7" | Action | ACT4523 | 1969 | £4 | £8 | |
| United | 7" | London | HL10069 | 1966 | £10 | £20 | |

## INVADERS

| | | | | | | | |
|---|---|---|---|---|---|---|---|
| Limbo Girl | 7" | Columbia | DB105 | 1967 | £2 | £5 | |
| Soulful Music | 7" | Studio One | SO2044 | 1968 | £6 | £12 | Soul Vendors B side |
| Stop Teasing | 7" | Columbia | DB109 | 1968 | £2 | £5 | |

## INVADERS (2)

| | | | | | | | |
|---|---|---|---|---|---|---|---|
| On The Right Track | LP | Justice | JLP125 | 1967 | £75 | £150 | US |

## INVICTAS

| | | | | | | | |
|---|---|---|---|---|---|---|---|
| A Go-Go | LP | Sahara | 101 | 1965 | £37.50 | £75 | US |

## INVITATIONS

| | | | | | | | |
|---|---|---|---|---|---|---|---|
| Hallelujah | 7" | Stateside | SS453 | 1965 | £2.50 | £6 | |
| What's Wrong With Me Baby | 7" | Stateside | SS478 | 1965 | £20 | £40 | |

## INXS

| | | | | | | | |
|---|---|---|---|---|---|---|---|
| Bitter Tears | CD-s | Mercury | INXCD17 | 1991 | £2 | £5 | |
| By My Side | CD-s | Mercury | INXCD16 | 1991 | £2 | £5 | |
| Devil Inside | CD-s | Mercury | INXCD10 | 1988 | £3 | £8 | |
| Disappear | CD-s | Mercury | INXCD15 | 1990 | £2 | £5 | |
| Don't Change | 7" | Mercury | INXS1 | 1983 | £2.50 | £6 | |
| Don't Change | 12" | Mercury | INXS121 | 1983 | £5 | £12 | |
| Gift | CD-s | Mercury | INXCD25 | 1993 | £2 | £5 | with tour pass |
| Good Times | CD-s | East West | A7751CD | 1991 | £2 | £5 | with Jimmy Barnes |
| Greatest Hits | CD | Mercury | 5262292 | 1994 | £6 | £15 | double |
| Inxs | CD | Atlantic | PR34162 | 1990 | £8 | £20 | US promo compilation |
| Just Keep Walking | 7" | RCA | RCA89 | 1981 | £12.50 | £25 | picture sleeve |
| Kick | LP | Mercury | MERHP114 | 1987 | £4 | £10 | picture disc |
| Listen Like Thieves | LP | Mercury | MERH82 | 1986 | £5 | £12 | with LP The Swing |
| Listen Like Thieves | 7" | Mercury | INXSP6 | 1986 | £2 | £5 | shaped picture disc |
| Mystify | CD-s | Mercury | 0808762 | 1989 | £10 | £20 | CD video |
| Mystify | CD-s | Mercury | INXCD13 | 1989 | £2 | £5 | |
| Need You Tonight | CD-s | Mercury | 0803942 | 1988 | £10 | £20 | CD video |
| Need You Tonight | CD-s | Mercury | INXCD8 | 1987 | £2.50 | £6 | |
| Need You Tonight | 12" | Mercury | INXS812 | 1987 | £2.50 | £6 | |
| Never Tear Us Apart | CD-s | Mercury | 0803962 | 1988 | £10 | £20 | CD video |
| Never Tear Us Apart | CD-s | Mercury | INXCD11 | 1988 | £2 | £5 | |
| New Sensation | CD-s | Mercury | INXCD9 | 1987 | £2 | £5 | |
| New Sensation | CD | Atlantic | PR2575 | 1989 | £15 | £30 | US promo double |
| One Thing | 7" | Mercury | INXS2 | 1983 | £2 | £5 | |
| One Thing | 12" | Mercury | INXS2i2 | 1983 | £5 | £12 | 2 tracks |
| One Thing | 12" | Mercury | INXS222 | 1983 | £4 | £10 | 3 tracks |
| Original Sin | 7" | Mercury | INXS3 | 1984 | £4 | £8 | |
| Original Sin | 12" | Mercury | INXS312 | 1984 | £5 | £12 | |
| Profiled! | CD | Atlantic | PRCD36752 | 1991 | £8 | £20 | US promo |
| Shining Star | CD-s | Mercury | INXCD18 | 1991 | £2 | £5 | |
| Suicide Blonde | CD-s | Mercury | INXCD14 | 1990 | £2 | £5 | |
| This Time | 7" | Mercury | INXSD4 | 1986 | £2 | £5 | double |
| What You Need | 12" | Mercury | INXSD512 | 1986 | £3 | £8 | double |

## IONA

| | | | | | | | |
|---|---|---|---|---|---|---|---|
| Cuckoo | LP | Silverscales | KOO13913 | 1978 | £25 | £50 | |
| Iona | LP | Celtic Music | CM001 | 1978 | £15 | £30 | |

## IPSISSIMUS

| | | | | | | | |
|---|---|---|---|---|---|---|---|
| Hold On | 7" | Parlophone | R5774 | 1969 | £10 | £20 | |

## IQ

| | | | | | | | |
|---|---|---|---|---|---|---|---|
| Awake And Nervous | 12" | Jim White | IQPROMO101 | 1984 | £15 | £30 | |
| Barbell Is In | 7" | Sahara | IQ1002 | 1984 | £2.50 | £6 | |
| Barbell Is In | 12" | Sahara | IQ121002 | 1984 | £4 | £10 | |
| Beef In A Box | 7" | Lyntone | LYN12028/9 | 1982 | £2 | £5 | with other artists |
| Corners | 7" | Sahara | IQ1003 | 1985 | £2.50 | £6 | |
| Corners | 12" | Sahara | IQ121003 | 1985 | £4 | £10 | |
| Different Magic Roundabout | 7" | fan club | ONEMORE-BOXER1 | 1988 | £5 | £10 | |
| Fascination | 7" | fan club | ANOTHER-BOXER1 | 1987 | £7.50 | £15 | |
| Hollow Afternoon | 7" | IQ | IQFREEB1 | 1984 | £15 | £30 | |
| It All Stops Here | 7" | Samurai | IQSD1 | 1986 | £7.50 | £15 | shaped picture disc |
| Living Proof | CD | Samurai | SAMRCD045 | 1986 | £5 | £12 | |
| Nine In A Pond Is Here | LP | fan club | BOXER1 | 1985 | £15 | £30 | double |
| Nomzamo | 7" | fan club | OTHERBOXER1 | 1986 | £7.50 | £15 | |
| Promises | 12" | Squawk | VERX34 | 1987 | £3 | £8 | |
| Sold On You | CD-s | Squawk | VERCD42 | 1989 | £2.50 | £6 | |
| Tales From The Lush Attic | LP | COSL | MAJ1001 | 1984 | £4 | £10 | brown sleeve |
| Tales From The Lush Attic | LP | MJL | MAJ1001 | 1983 | £6 | £15 | blue sleeve |
| Tales From The Lush Attic | CD | Samurai | SAMRCD1001 | 1986 | £5 | £12 | |
| Wake | LP | Sahara | SAH136 | 1985 | £4 | £10 | |

## IRELAND, TONY

| | | | | | | | |
|---|---|---|---|---|---|---|---|
| Johny O'Cockley's Well | LP | Peak | 3581 | 1983 | £4 | £10 | German |

## IRISH COFFEE

| | | | | | | | |
|---|---|---|---|---|---|---|---|
| Irish Coffee | LP | Triangle | BE920321 | 1971 | £210 | £350 | Belgian |

## IRISH RAMBLERS

| | | | | | | | |
|---|---|---|---|---|---|---|---|
| Patriot Game | LP | Golden Guinea | GGL0269 | 1963 | £4 | £10 | |

## IROLT KATTEKWAN

| | | | | | | | |
|---|---|---|---|---|---|---|---|
| Irolt Kattekwan | LP | Philips | | 1977 | £15 | £30 | Dutch |

## IRON BUTTERFLY

| | | | | | | | |
|---|---|---|---|---|---|---|---|
| Ball | LP | Atlantic | 228011 | 1969 | £6 | £15 | |
| Heavy | LP | Atco | 2465015 | 1970 | £6 | £15 | |
| In-A-Gadda-Da-Vida | LP | Atco | 588166 | 1968 | £6 | £15 | |
| Live | LP | Atlantic | 2400014 | 1970 | £5 | £12 | |
| Metamorphosis | LP | Atlantic | 2401003 | 1970 | £5 | £12 | |
| Possession | 7" | Atlantic | 584188 | 1968 | £1.50 | £4 | |
| Soul Experience | 7" | Atlantic | 584254 | 1969 | £1.50 | £4 | |

## IRON MAIDEN

Iron Maiden's striking death mascot has found particularly effective use as a recurring theme on the group's record covers and picture discs. Many of these are now very collectable, as befits a group that is probably the most successful of the New Wave of British Heavy Metal (though Def Leppard might argue the point).

| | | | | | | | |
|---|---|---|---|---|---|---|---|
| Aces High | 12" | EMI | 12EMIP5502 | 1984 | £5 | £12 | picture disc |
| Best Of The Beast | CD | EMI | | 1996 | £50 | £100 | promo box set with interview CD & video |
| Bring Your Daughter To The Slaughter | CD-s | EMI | CDEM171 | 1990 | £2 | £5 | |
| Bring Your Daughter To Your Slaughter | 7" | EMI | EMPD171 | 1990 | £1.50 | £4 | picture disc |
| Can I Play With Madness | CD-s | EMI | CDEM49 | 1988 | £3 | £8 | |
| Can I Play With Madness | 7" | EMI | EMP49 | 1988 | £1.50 | £4 | shaped picture disc |
| Can I Play With Madness/The Evil That Men Do | CD-s | EMI | CDIRN9 | 1990 | £2 | £5 | |
| Clairvoyant | CD-s | EMI | CDEM79 | 1988 | £2 | £5 | |
| Clairvoyant | 7" | EMI | EMP79 | 1988 | £2 | £5 | shaped picture disc |
| Clairvoyant/Infinite Dreams | CD-s | EMI | CDIRN10 | 1990 | £2 | £5 | |
| Evil That Men Do | CD-s | EMI | CDEM64 | 1988 | £2 | £5 | |
| Evil That Men Do | 7" | EMI | EMP64 | 1988 | £1.50 | £4 | shaped picture disc |
| Fear Of The Dark | 7" | EMI | EMPD263 | 1992 | £2.50 | £6 | shaped picture disc, B side plays Tailgunner |
| First Ten Years | CD-s | EMI | CDIRN1-10 | 1990 | £30 | £60 | 10 CDs, boxed |
| First Ten Years | 12" | EMI | IRN1-10 | 1990 | £20 | £40 | 10 double records, boxed |
| Flight Of Icarus | cass-s | EMI | TCIM4 | 1983 | £2.50 | £6 | |
| Flight Of Icarus | 12" | EMI | 12EMIP5378 | 1983 | £4 | £10 | picture disc |
| Flight Of Icarus/The Trooper | CD-s | EMI | CDIRN5 | 1990 | £2 | £5 | |
| Holy Smoke | CD-s | EMI | CDEM153 | 1990 | £2 | £5 | |
| Infinite Dreams | CD-s | EMI | CDEM117 | 1989 | £2 | £5 | |
| Infinite Dreams | 7" | EMI | EMPD117 | 1989 | £1.50 | £4 | shaped picture disc |
| Killers | LP | EMI | EMC3357 | 1981 | £20 | £40 | cover over-printed with Boom Town Rats cover design! |
| Live After Death | CD | EMI | CZ123 | 1986 | £5 | £12 | |
| Maiden England | CD | EMI | | 1994 | £30 | £60 | box set with video |
| Maiden Japan | 12" | EMI | 12EMI5219 | 1981 | £3 | £8 | |
| No Prayer 1991 Tour CD | CD | Epic | ESK73695 | 1991 | £10 | £25 | US promo |
| No Prayer For The Dying | LP | EMI | EMDPD1017 | 1990 | £6 | £15 | picture disc |
| No Prayer For The Dying | 10" | EMI | | 1990 | £20 | £40 | boxed promo |
| Number Of The Beast | LP | EMI | EMCP3400 | 1982 | £15 | £30 | picture disc |
| Number Of The Beast | 7" | EMI | EMI5287 | 1982 | £4 | £8 | red vinyl |
| Piece Of Mind | LP | Capitol | | 1983 | £15 | £30 | US picture disc |
| Powerslave | LP | EMI | POWERP1 | 1984 | £10 | £25 | picture disc |
| Powerslave | CD | EMI | CZ81 | 1984 | £5 | £12 | |
| Purgatory | 7" | EMI | EMI5184 | 1981 | £10 | £20 | |
| Purgatory/Maiden Japan | CD-s | EMI | CDIRN3 | 1990 | £2 | £5 | |
| Run To The Hills | 7" | EMI | EMI5263 | 1982 | £2 | £5 | |
| Run To The Hills | 7" | EMI | EMIP5263 | 1982 | £5 | £10 | picture disc |
| Run To The Hills | 7" | EMI | EMIP5263 | 1982 | £20 | £40 | picture disc, band photo on both sides |
| Run To The Hills | 12" | EMI | 12EMIP5542 | 1985 | £3 | £8 | picture disc |
| Run To The Hills (Live) | 7" | EMI | EMI5542 | 1985 | £2 | £5 | with Christmas card |
| Run To The Hills/The Number Of The Beast | CD-s | EMI | CDIRN4 | 1990 | £2 | £5 | |
| Running Free | 7" | EMI | EMI5032 | 1980 | £6 | £12 | |
| Running Free | 7" | EMI | EMI5532 | 1985 | £2 | £5 | poster sleeve |
| Running Free | 12" | EMI | 12EMIP5532 | 1985 | £4 | £10 | picture disc |
| Running Free/Run To The Hills | CD-s | EMI | CDIRN7 | 1990 | £2 | £5 | |
| Running Free/Sanctuary | CD-s | EMI | CDIRN1 | 1990 | £2 | £5 | |
| Sanctuary | 7" | EMI | EMI5065 | 1980 | £5 | £10 | censored picture sleeve |
| Sanctuary | 7" | EMI | EMI5065 | 1980 | £7.50 | £15 | uncensored picture sleeve |
| Seventh Son Of A Seventh Son | LP | EMI | EMDP1006 | 1988 | £4 | £10 | picture disc, banner |
| Somewhere In Time | CD | EMI | CZ120 | 1986 | £5 | £12 | |
| Soundhouse Tapes | 7" EP | Rock Hard | ROK1 | 1979 | £25 | £50 | |

| | | | | | | | |
|---|---|---|---|---|---|---|---|
| Stranger In A Strange Land | 7" | EMI | EMI5589 | 1986 £2 | £5 | poster sleeve |
| Stranger In A Strange Land | 12" | EMI | 12EMIP5589 | 1986 £3 | £8 | picture disc |
| Trooper | 7" | EMI | EMIP5397 | 1983 £7.50 | £15 | shaped picture disc |
| Twilight Zone | 7" | EMI | EMI5145 | 1981 £4 | £8 | |
| Twilight Zone | 7" | EMI | EMI5145 | 1981 £50 | £100 | brown vinyl mispress |
| Twilight Zone | 7" | EMI | EMI5145 | 1981 £10 | £20 | red or clear vinyl |
| Two Minutes To Midnight | 12" | EMI | 12EMIP5489 | 1984 £3 | £8 | picture disc |
| Two Minutes To Midnight/Aces High | CD | EMI | CDIRN6 | 1990 £2 | £5 | |
| Wasted Years | 7" | EMI | EMIP5583 | 1986 £5 | £10 | shaped picture disc |
| Wasted Years/Stranger In A Strange Land | CD | EMI | CDIRN8 | 1990 £2 | £5 | |
| Women In Uniform | 7" | EMI | EMI5105 | 1980 £4 | £8 | |
| Women In Uniform | 12" | EMI | 12EMI5105 | 1980 £3 | £8 | |
| Women In Uniform/Twilight Zone | CD | EMI | CDIRN2 | 1990 £2 | £5 | |

## IRON MAIDEN (2)

| | | | | | | |
|---|---|---|---|---|---|---|
| Falling | 7" | Gemini | GMS006 | 1971 £5 | £10 | |

## IRVINE, ANDY & PAUL BRADY

| | | | | | | |
|---|---|---|---|---|---|---|
| Andy Irvine And Paul Brady | LP | Mulligan | LUN008 | 1976 £4 | £10 | Irish |

## IRVING, LONNIE

| | | | | | | |
|---|---|---|---|---|---|---|
| Pinball Machine | 7" | Melodisc | 1546 | 1960 £5 | £10 | |

## IRWIN, BIG DEE

| | | | | | | |
|---|---|---|---|---|---|---|
| Donkey Walk | 7" | Stateside | SS261 | 1964 £2 | £5 | |
| I Can't Stand The Pain | 7" | Minit | MLF11013 | 1969 £1.50 | £4 | |
| You Satisfy My Needs | 7" | Stateside | SS450 | 1965 £12.50 | £25 | |

## IRWIN, BIG DEE & LITTLE EVA

| | | | | | | |
|---|---|---|---|---|---|---|
| Swinging On A Star | 7" EP | Colpix | PXE301 | 1963 £5 | £10 | |

## IRWIN, PEE WEE

| | | | | | | |
|---|---|---|---|---|---|---|
| Dixieland Band | LP | London | HAA2009 | 1956 £4 | £10 | |

## ISAACS, DAVID

| | | | | | | |
|---|---|---|---|---|---|---|
| Good Father | 7" | Upsetter | US302 | 1969 £1.50 | £4 | Slim Smith B side |
| He'll Have To Go | 7" | Upsetter | US311 | 1969 £1.50 | £4 | |
| I Can't Take It Anymore | 7" | Punch | PH6 | 1969 £1.50 | £4 | Lloyd Douglas B side |
| I'd Rather Be Lonely | 7" | Island | WI261 | 1966 £4 | £8 | |
| I've Got Memories | 7" | Upsetter | US305 | 1969 £1.50 | £4 | |
| Place In The Sun | 7" | Trojan | TR616 | 1968 £2.50 | £6 | Upsetters B side |
| Who To Tell | 7" | Upsetter | US319 | 1969 £1.50 | £4 | Busty Brown B side |

## ISAACS, GREGORY

| | | | | | | |
|---|---|---|---|---|---|---|
| All I Have Is Love | LP | Trojan | TRLS121 | 1976 £5 | £12 | |
| Cool Ruler | LP | Front Line | FL1020 | 1978 £5 | £12 | |
| Extra Classic | LP | Conflict | COLP2002 | 1978 £5 | £12 | |
| In Person | LP | Trojan | TRLS102 | 1975 £5 | £12 | |
| Mr. Issacs | LP | Deb | DEBLP04 | 1978 £5 | £12 | |
| Soon Forward | LP | Front Line | FL1044 | 1979 £4 | £10 | |

## ISAAK, CHRIS

| | | | | | | |
|---|---|---|---|---|---|---|
| San Francisco Days | CD | Reprise | 45116DJ | 1993 £6 | £15 | US promo picture disc |

## ISAIAH

| | | | | | | |
|---|---|---|---|---|---|---|
| Isaiah | LP | CBS | 80843 | 1975 £20 | £40 | Austrian |

## ISCA FAYRE

| | | | | | | |
|---|---|---|---|---|---|---|
| Then Around Me Young And Old | LP | Candle | | 1976 £25 | £50 | |

## ISHERWOOD, JOHN

| | | | | | | |
|---|---|---|---|---|---|---|
| Laughing Cry | LP | Decca | LK/SKL5051 | 1970 £15 | £30 | |

## ISKRA 1903

| | | | | | | |
|---|---|---|---|---|---|---|
| Free Improvisation | LP | Deutsche Grammophon | 2563298/299/300 | 1974 £25 | £50 | 3 LP set – with New Phonic Art & Wired |
| Iskra 1903 | LP | Incus | INCUS3/4 | 1972 £15 | £30 | double |

## ISLAND BOYS

| | | | | | | |
|---|---|---|---|---|---|---|
| Go Calypso No. 1 | 7" EP | London | RER1122 | 1958 £2 | £5 | |
| Go Calypso No. 2 | 7" EP | London | RER1123 | 1958 £2 | £5 | |
| Go Calypso No. 3 | 7" EP | London | RER1124 | 1958 £2 | £5 | |

## ISLE, JIMMY

| | | | | | | |
|---|---|---|---|---|---|---|
| Billy Boy | 7" | Top Rank | JAR274 | 1960 £1.50 | £4 | |
| Diamond Ring | 7" | London | HLS8832 | 1959 £20 | £40 | |

## ISLEY BROTHERS

| | | | | | | |
|---|---|---|---|---|---|---|
| Behind A Painted Smile | LP | Tamla Motown | (S)TML11112 | 1969 £6 | £15 | |
| Behind A Painted Smile | 7" | Tamla Motown | TMG693 | 1969 £1.50 | £4 | |
| Brothers Isley | LP | Stateside | SSL10300 | 1970 £5 | £12 | |
| Got To Have You Back | 7" | Tamla Motown | TMG606 | 1967 £2.50 | £6 | |
| How Deep Is The Ocean | 7" | RCA | RCA1190 | 1960 £4 | £8 | |
| I Guess I'll Always Love You | 7" | Tamla Motown | TMG572 | 1966 £5 | £10 | |
| I Guess I'll Always Love You | 7" | Tamla Motown | TMG683 | 1969 £1.50 | £4 | |
| Isley Brothers | 7" EP | RCA | RCX7149 | 1964 £15 | £30 | |
| It's Our Thing | LP | Major Minor | SMLP59 | 1969 £5 | £12 | |
| It's Your Thing | 7" | Major Minor | MM621 | 1969 £1.50 | £4 | |

| | | | | | | | |
|---|---|---|---|---|---|---|---|
| Last Lost Girl | 7" | Atlantic | AT4010 | 1964 | £4 | £8 | |
| Nobody But Me | 7" | Stateside | SS218 | 1963 | £2.50 | £6 | |
| Respectable | 7" | RCA | RCA1172 | 1960 | £5 | £10 | |
| Shake It With Me Baby | 7" | United Artists | UP1050 | 1964 | £2 | £5 | |
| Shout | LP | RCA | RD27165/SF7055 | 1960 | £15 | £30 | |
| Shout | 7" | RCA | RCA1149 | 1959 | £5 | £10 | |
| Soul On The Rocks | LP | Tamla Motown | (S)TML11066 | 1968 | £6 | £15 | |
| Take Me In Your Arms | 7" | Tamla Motown | TMG652 | 1968 | £4 | £8 | |
| Take Some Time Out | LP | Scepter | SC(S)552 | 1966 | £4 | £10 | US |
| Take Some Time Out For Love | 7" | Tamla Motown | TMG566 | 1966 | £5 | £10 | |
| Tango | 7" | United Artists | UP1034 | 1963 | £2 | £5 | |
| Tell Me Who | 7" | RCA | RCA1213 | 1960 | £4 | £8 | |
| This Old Heart Of Mine | LP | Tamla Motown | STML11034 | 1966 | £5 | £12 | |
| This Old Heart Of Mine | 7" | Tamla Motown | TMG555 | 1966 | £1.50 | £4 | |
| Twist And Shout | LP | Wand | WD(S)653 | 1962 | £8 | £20 | US |
| Twist And Shout | 7" | Stateside | SS112 | 1962 | £2.50 | £6 | |
| Twisting And Shouting | LP | United Artists | ULP1064 | 1964 | £6 | £15 | |
| Twisting With Linda | 7" | Stateside | SS132 | 1962 | £2 | £5 | |
| Warpath | 7" | Stateside | SS2188 | 1971 | £1.50 | £4 | |

## ISLEY, TEX & GRAY CRAIG

| | | | | | | | |
|---|---|---|---|---|---|---|---|
| North Carolina Boys | LP | Leader | LEA4040 | 1972 | £5 | £12 | |

## ISOLATION

| | | | | | | | |
|---|---|---|---|---|---|---|---|
| Isolation | LP | Riverside | HASLP2083 | 1973 | £500 | £750 | |

## ISRAEL VIBRATION

| | | | | | | | |
|---|---|---|---|---|---|---|---|
| Same Song | LP | Harvest | SHSP4099 | 1979 | £4 | £10 | |

## IT BITES

| | | | | | | | |
|---|---|---|---|---|---|---|---|
| Calling All The Heroes | 7" | Virgin | VSD872 | 1986 | £2.50 | £6 | double |
| Calling All The Heroes | 7" | Virgin | VSY872 | 1986 | £2 | £5 | picture disc |
| Eat Me In St. Louis | CD | Virgin | CDVX2591 | 1989 | £5 | £12 | ... with bonus 3" CD |
| Kiss Like Judas | CD-s | Virgin | CDEP21 | 1988 | £2 | £5 | |
| Midnight | CD-s | Virgin | VSCD1065 | 1988 | £2 | £5 | |
| Midnight | 7" | Virgin | VSS1065 | 1988 | £2.50 | £6 | square picture disc |
| Old Man And The Angel | CD-s | Virgin | MIKE94112 | 1987 | £2 | £5 | |
| Sister Sarah | CD-s | Virgin | VSCD1202 | 1989 | £2 | £5 | |
| Still Too Young To Remember | CD-s | Virgin | VSCD1184 | 1989 | £2 | £5 | 3 versions |
| Underneath Your Pillow | CD-s | Virgin | VSCD1215 | 1989 | £2 | £5 | 3" single |
| Whole New World | 7" | Virgin | VSD896 | 1986 | £2.50 | £6 | double |

## ITALS

| | | | | | | | |
|---|---|---|---|---|---|---|---|
| Don't Throw It Away | 7" | Giant | GN12 | 1967 | £2 | £5 | Caribbeats B side |
| New Loving | 7" | Giant | GN8 | 1967 | £2 | £5 | Soul Brothers B side |

## ITHACA

| | | | | | | | |
|---|---|---|---|---|---|---|---|
| Game For All Who Know | LP | Merlin | HF6 | 1972 | £400 | £600 | |

## IT'S A BEAUTIFUL DAY

| | | | | | | | |
|---|---|---|---|---|---|---|---|
| Choice Quality Stuff | LP | CBS | 64314 | 1971 | £4 | £10 | |
| It's A Beautiful Day | LP | CBS | 63722 | 1969 | £5 | £12 | |
| It's A Beautiful Day | LP | Columbia | CS9768 | 1969 | £20 | £40 | US, topless girl on cover |
| It's A Beautiful Day | LP | San Francisco Sound | 11790 | 1985 | £5 | £12 | US audiophile |
| Live At Carnegie Hall | LP | CBS | 64929 | 1972 | £4 | £10 | |
| Marrying Maiden | LP | CBS | 64065 | 1970 | £4 | £10 | |
| White Bird | 7" | CBS | 4457 | 1969 | £2 | £5 | |

## IT'S ALL MEAT

| | | | | | | | |
|---|---|---|---|---|---|---|---|
| It's All Meat | LP | Columbia | ELS374 | 1970 | £30 | £60 | Canadian |

## IVAN

The rare single by Ivan is a Buddy Holly collectable, as the label credit actually masks the identity of Crickets drummer Jerry Allison and Holly himself.

| | | | | | | | |
|---|---|---|---|---|---|---|---|
| Real Wild Child | 7" | Coral | Q72341 | 1958 | £100 | £200 | best auctioned |

## IVAN'S MEADS

| | | | | | | | |
|---|---|---|---|---|---|---|---|
| Sins Of A Family | 7" | Parlophone | R5342 | 1965 | £5 | £10 | |
| We'll Talk About It Tomorrow | 7" | Parlophone | R5503 | 1966 | £5 | £10 | |

## IVES, BURL

| | | | | | | | |
|---|---|---|---|---|---|---|---|
| Australian Folk Songs | 10" LP | Brunswick | LA8739 | 1956 | £4 | £10 | |
| Ballads And Folk Songs Vol. 1 | 10" LP | Brunswick | LA8583 | 1953 | £4 | £10 | |
| Burl Ives | 10" LP | Brunswick | LA8552 | 1953 | £4 | £10 | |
| Down To The Sea In Ships | LP | Brunswick | LAT8142 | 1956 | £4 | £10 | |
| Dying Stockman | 7" | Brunswick | 05551 | 1956 | £1.50 | £4 | |
| Folk Songs – Dramatic And Humorous | 10" LP | Brunswick | LA8633 | 1954 | £4 | £10 | |
| Goober Peas | 7" | Brunswick | 05510 | 1956 | £1.50 | £4 | |
| Women | 10" LP | Brunswick | LA8641 | 1954 | £4 | £10 | |

## IVEYS

The Iveys was the original name for the group Badfinger. The album *Maybe Tomorrow* received a limited release in Europe, but the British and American issues were cancelled. (A UK cover for the album, however, was sold at auction in 1988.) Counterfeits of the European issue exist, but they do not have the Apple labels of the originals.

| Dear Angie | | 7" | Apple | 14 | 1969 | £75 | £150 | European |
|---|---|---|---|---|---|---|---|---|
| Maybe Tomorrow | LP | | Apple | SAPCOR8 | 1969 | £150 | £250 | European |
| Maybe Tomorrow | | 7" | Apple | 5 | 1968 | £10 | £20 | |

## IVORY, JACK

| Hi Heeled Sneakers | | 7" | Atlantic | AT4075 | 1966 | £2.50 | £6 | |
|---|---|---|---|---|---|---|---|---|
| Soul Discovery | LP | | Atco | (SD)33178 | 1965 | £6 | £15 | US |

## IVY LEAGUE

| Funny How Love Can Be | | 7" EP | Piccadilly | NEP34038 | 1965 | £5 | £10 | |
|---|---|---|---|---|---|---|---|---|
| Holly And The Ivy League | | 7" EP | Piccadilly | NEP34046 | 1965 | £6 | £12 | |
| Our Love Is Slipping Away | | 7" EP | Piccadilly | NEP34048 | 1966 | £7.50 | £15 | |
| Sounds Of The Ivy League | LP | | Marble Arch | MAL741 | 1967 | £4 | £10 | |
| That's Why I'm Crying | | 7" EP | Pye | PNV24143 | 1965 | £7.50 | £15 | French |
| This Is The Ivy League | LP | | Piccadilly | NPL38015 | 1965 | £8 | £20 | |
| Tomorrow Is Another Day | LP | | Marble Arch | MAL821 | 1968 | £4 | £10 | |
| Tossing And Turning | | 7" EP | Piccadilly | NEP34042 | 1965 | £5 | £10 | |
| What More Do You Want | | 7" | Piccadilly | 7N35200 | 1964 | £1.50 | £4 | |

## IVY THREE

| Yogi | | 7" | London | HLW9178 | 1960 | £1.50 | £4 | |
|---|---|---|---|---|---|---|---|---|

## IWAN, DAFYDD

| Myn Duw, Mi A Wn Y Daw! | | 7" EP | Sain | SAIN2 | 1969 | £4 | £8 | |
|---|---|---|---|---|---|---|---|---|
| Pam Fod Eira Yn Wyn? | | 7" EP | Sain | SAIN18 | 1971 | £2.50 | £6 | |

# J

### J, HARRY ALL STARS
| | | | | | | |
|---|---|---|---|---|---|---|
| Liquidator | LP | Trojan | TBL104 | 1970 | £4 | £10 |
| Liquidator | 7" | Trojan | TR675 | 1969 | £1.50 | £4 |

### J. J. ALLSTARS
| | | | | | | |
|---|---|---|---|---|---|---|
| Memphis Underground | 7" | Trojan | TR691 | 1969 | £1.50 | £4 |

### JACK
| | | | | | | |
|---|---|---|---|---|---|---|
| Kid Stardust | 7" | Too Pure | PURE49 | 1995 | £7.50 | £15 |

### JACKAL
| | | | | | | | |
|---|---|---|---|---|---|---|---|
| Awake | LP | Periwinkle | PER7309 | 1973 | £30 | £60 | Canadian |
| Underneath The Arches | 12" | Criminal Damage | CRI12134 | 1986 | £2.50 | £6 | |

### JACKIE & BRIDIE
| | | | | | | |
|---|---|---|---|---|---|---|
| Folk World Of Jackie And Bridie | LP | Concord | CONS1002 | 1970 | £10 | £25 |

### JACKIE & DOREEN
| | | | | | | |
|---|---|---|---|---|---|---|
| Adorable You | 7" | Ska Beat | JB209 | 1965 | £5 | £10 |

### JACKIE & MILLIE
| | | | | | | | |
|---|---|---|---|---|---|---|---|
| In A Dream | 7" | Island | WIP6012 | 1967 | £2.50 | £6 | |
| My Desire | 7" | Island | WI265 | 1966 | £5 | £10 | |
| This Is My Story | 7" | Island | WI253 | 1965 | £5 | £10 | Sound System B side |

### JACKIE & ROY
| | | | | | | |
|---|---|---|---|---|---|---|
| You Smell So Good | 7" | Vogue | V9101 | 1958 | £30 | £60 |

### JACKPOTS
| | | | | | | |
|---|---|---|---|---|---|---|
| Jack In The Box | LP | Sonet | SLP68 | 1968 | £8 | £20 |

### JACKS
| | | | | | | | |
|---|---|---|---|---|---|---|---|
| Jacks | LP | Crown | CLP5021 | 1957 | £10 | £25 | US |
| Jumpin' With The Jacks | LP | RPM | LRP3006 | 195– | £50 | £100 | US |

### JACK'S ANGELS
| | | | | | | | |
|---|---|---|---|---|---|---|---|
| Our Fantasy's Kingdom | LP | Amadeo | 9224 | 1968 | £8 | £20 | Austrian |

### JACKSON, ALEXANDER & THE TURNKEYS
| | | | | | | |
|---|---|---|---|---|---|---|
| Whip | 7" | Sue | WI386 | 1965 | £10 | £20 |

### JACKSON, BO WEEVIL
| | | | | | | |
|---|---|---|---|---|---|---|
| Some Scream High Yellow | 7" | Jazz Collector | JDL81 | 1959 | £2.50 | £6 |

### JACKSON, BULL MOOSE
| | | | | | | | |
|---|---|---|---|---|---|---|---|
| Bull Moose Jackson | LP | Audio Lab | AL1524 | 1959 | £25 | £50 | US |
| Nosey Joe | 78 | Vogue | V2129 | 1952 | £3 | £8 | |

### JACKSON, CALVIN
| | | | | | | |
|---|---|---|---|---|---|---|
| Calvin Jackson Quartet | LP | Philips | BBL7084 | 1956 | £4 | £10 |
| Rave Notice | LP | Philips | BBL7107 | 1958 | £4 | £10 |

### JACKSON, CHRIS
| | | | | | | | |
|---|---|---|---|---|---|---|---|
| I'll Never Forget You | 7" | Soul City | SC112 | 1969 | £6 | £12 | |
| Since There's No Doubt | 7" | Soul City | SC120 | 1969 | £25 | £50 | test pressing |

### JACKSON, CHUCK
| | | | | | | | |
|---|---|---|---|---|---|---|---|
| Any Day Now | LP | Wand | LP/WDS654 | 1962 | £8 | £20 | US |
| Any Day Now | 7" | Pye | 7N25276 | 1964 | £2 | £5 | |
| Any Day Now | 7" | Stateside | SS102 | 1962 | £4 | £8 | |
| Beg Me | 7" | Pye | 7N25247 | 1964 | £2 | £5 | |
| Breaking Point | 7" | Top Rank | JAR607 | 1962 | £5 | £10 | |
| Chains Of Love | 7" | Pye | 7N25384 | 1966 | £12.50 | £25 | |
| Chuck Jackson Arrives | LP | Tamla Motown | (S)TML11071 | 1968 | £10 | £25 | |
| Dedicated To The King | LP | Wand | LP/WDS680 | 1966 | £8 | £20 | US |
| Encore | LP | Wand | LP/WDS655 | 1963 | £8 | £20 | US |
| Girls Girls Girls | 7" | Tamla Motown | TMG651 | 1968 | £4 | £8 | |
| Goin' Back To Chuck Jackson | LP | Tamla Motown | (S)TML11117 | 1969 | £8 | £20 | |
| Greatest Hits | LP | Wand | LP/WDS683 | 1967 | £6 | £15 | US |
| Honey Come Back | 7" | Tamla Motown | TMG729 | 1970 | £2 | £5 | |
| I Don't Want To Cry | LP | Wand | LP/WDS650 | 1961 | £8 | £20 | US |
| I Don't Want To Cry | 7" | Top Rank | JAR564 | 1961 | £7.50 | £15 | |

| | | | | | | | |
|---|---|---|---|---|---|---|---|
| I Keep Forgettin' | 7" | Stateside | SS127 | 1962 | £2.50 | £6 | |
| I Need You | 7" | Pye | 7N25301 | 1965 | £1.50 | £4 | |
| If I Didn't Love You | 7" | Pye | 7N25321 | 1965 | £2 | £5 | |
| Mr. Everything | LP | Wand | LP/WDS667 | 1965 | £8 | £20 | US |
| On Tour | LP | Wand | LP/WDS658 | 1964 | £8 | £20 | US |
| Shame On Me | 7" | Pye | 7N25439 | 1967 | £1.50 | £4 | |
| Since I Don't Have You | 7" | Pye | 7N25287 | 1965 | £12.50 | £25 | |
| Tell Him I'm Not Home | 7" | Stateside | SS171 | 1963 | £2.50 | £6 | |
| Through All Times | LP | Probe | SPB1084 | 1972 | £4 | £10 | |
| Tribute To Rhythm And Blues | LP | Pye | NPL28082 | 1967 | £8 | £20 | |
| Tribute To Rhythm And Blues Vol. 2 | LP | Wand | LP/WDS676 | 1966 | £8 | £20 | US |

### JACKSON, CHUCK & MAXINE BROWN

| | | | | | | | |
|---|---|---|---|---|---|---|---|
| Hold On, We're Coming | LP | Wand | LP/WDS678 | 1966 | £6 | £15 | US |
| Saying Something | LP | Pye | NPL28091 | 1967 | £5 | £12 | |
| Something You Got | 7" | Pye | 7N25308 | 1965 | £2 | £5 | |

### JACKSON, CHUCK & TAMMI TERRELL

| | | | | | | | |
|---|---|---|---|---|---|---|---|
| Early Show | LP | Wand | LP/WDS682 | 1967 | £6 | £15 | US |

### JACKSON, DEON

| | | | | | | | |
|---|---|---|---|---|---|---|---|
| Love Makes The World Go Around | 7" | Atlantic | AT4070 | 1966 | £5 | £10 | |
| Love Makes The World Go Round | LP | Atco | (SD)33188 | 1966 | £6 | £15 | US |
| Love Takes A Long Time Growing | 7" | Atlantic | 584012 | 1966 | £4 | £8 | |
| Ooh Baby | 7" | Atlantic | 584159 | 1968 | £2.50 | £6 | |

### JACKSON, FRED

| | | | | | | | |
|---|---|---|---|---|---|---|---|
| Hootin' 'n Tootin' | LP | Blue Note | BLP/BST84094 | 1962 | £20 | £40 | |

### JACKSON, GEORGE

| | | | | | | | |
|---|---|---|---|---|---|---|---|
| Find 'Em, Fool 'Em And Forget 'Em | 7" | Capitol | CL15605 | 1969 | £2 | £5 | |
| Let 'Em Know You Care | 7" | London | HLU10413 | 1973 | £2.50 | £6 | |

### JACKSON, GORDON

| | | | | | | | |
|---|---|---|---|---|---|---|---|
| Me And My Zoo | 7" | Marmalade | 598010 | 1969 | £1.50 | £4 | |
| Song For Freedom | 7" | Marmalade | 598021 | 1969 | £1.50 | £4 | |
| Thinking Back | LP | Marmalade | 608012 | 1969 | £8 | £20 | |

### JACKSON, HAROLD & THE TORNADOES

| | | | | | | | |
|---|---|---|---|---|---|---|---|
| Move It On Down The Line | 7" | Vogue | V9105 | 1958 | £15 | £30 | |

### JACKSON, J. J.

Although he called his group The Greatest Little Soul Band, the music that J. J. Jackson played was actually jazz-rock. Indeed, the soul band description was probably a marketing mistake. Fans of Colosseum and Manfred Mann Chapter Three would have loved this, but they looked no further than the cover. More precise is the comparison with the group If, whose leaders Dick Morrissey and Terry Smith both played with Jackson. The sleeve notes to the MCA album end with the words: 'go and see the band and you'll realise that if they aren't the biggest thing in the country in six months, there's no justice'. Sadly, there was none.

| | | | | | | | |
|---|---|---|---|---|---|---|---|
| And Proud Of It | LP | Perception | PLP12 | | £6 | £15 | US |
| But It's Alright | LP | Calla | C(S)1101 | 1967 | £6 | £15 | US |
| Come See Me | 7" | Strike | JH329 | 1967 | £2 | £5 | |
| Do The Boogaloo | 7" | Polydor | 56718 | 1966 | £2 | £5 | |
| Great J. J. Jackson | LP | Warner Bros | WS1797 | 1969 | £6 | £15 | US |
| Greatest Little Soul Band | LP | MCA | SKA100 | 1969 | £5 | £12 | |
| J. J. Jackson's Dilemma | LP | RCA | SF8093 | 1970 | £5 | £12 | |
| Sho Nuff | 7" | Warner Bros | WB2082 | 1967 | £1.50 | £4 | |
| With The Greatest Little Soul Band | LP | Strike | JHL104 | 1967 | £6 | £15 | |

### JACKSON, JANET

| | | | | | | | |
|---|---|---|---|---|---|---|---|
| Design Of A Decade 1986/1996 | CD | A&M | 5404222 | 1995 | £6 | £15 | double |
| Janet | CD | Virgin | CDVX2720 | 1993 | £5 | £12 | with bonus remix CD |
| Rhythm Nation | CD | A&M | AMAD3920 | 1989 | £5 | £12 | picture disc, numbered sleeve, poster |
| Two To The Power Of Love | 7" | A&M | AM210 | 1984 | £1.50 | £4 | .....with Cliff Richard |
| Two To The Power Of Love | 12" | A&M | AMX210 | 1984 | £2.50 | £6 | .....with Cliff Richard |

### JACKSON, JERRY

| | | | | | | | |
|---|---|---|---|---|---|---|---|
| Gypsy Eyes | 7" | London | HLR9689 | 1963 | £5 | £10 | |
| It's Rough Out There | 7" | Cameo Parkway | P100 | 1962 | £37.50 | £75 | |

### JACKSON, JIM

| | | | | | | | |
|---|---|---|---|---|---|---|---|
| RCA Victor Race Series Vol. 7 | 7" EP | RCA | RCX7182 | 1966 | £4 | £8 | |

### JACKSON, JIMMY

| | | | | | | | |
|---|---|---|---|---|---|---|---|
| Country And Blues | 7" EP | Columbia | SEG7768 | 1958 | £12.50 | £25 | |
| I Shall Not Be Moved | 7" | Columbia | DB3898 | 1957 | £5 | £10 | |
| Love A Love A Love A | 7" | Columbia | DB4085 | 1958 | £2 | £5 | |
| River Line | 7" | Columbia | DB3957 | 1957 | £4 | £8 | |
| Rock 'n' Skiffle | 7" EP | Columbia | SEG7750 | 1958 | £10 | £20 | |
| Sitting In The Balcony | 7" | Columbia | DB3937 | 1957 | £7.50 | £15 | |
| This Little Light Of Mine | 7" | Columbia | DB4153 | 1958 | £2 | £5 | |
| White Silver Sands | 7" | Columbia | DB3988 | 1957 | £2 | £5 | |

### JACKSON, JOE

| | | | | | | | |
|---|---|---|---|---|---|---|---|
| I'm The Man | 7" | A&M | SP1800 | 1980 | £5 | £10 | ... US 5 x 7", poster, boxed |

| Night And Day | CD.... | Mobile Fidelity | UDCD539 | 1991 | £6 | £15 | US audiophile |
|---|---|---|---|---|---|---|---|
| Will Power | CD..... | Mobile Fidelity | UDCD503 | 1988 | £6 | £15 | US audiophile |

## JACKSON, LEVI

| This Beautiful Day | 7".... | Columbia | DB8807 | 1971 | £15 | £30 | |
|---|---|---|---|---|---|---|---|

## JACKSON, LIL' SON

| Rockin' And Rollin' | LP..... | Imperial | 9142 | 1961 | £30 | £60 | US |
|---|---|---|---|---|---|---|---|

## JACKSON, MAHALIA

| Great Gettin' Up Morning | LP | Philips | BBL7362 | 1960 | £4 | £10 | |
|---|---|---|---|---|---|---|---|
| I Believe | LP | Philips | BBL7456/SBBL610. | 1961 | £4 | £10 | |
| Just As I Am | LP | Top Rank | 30006 | 1960 | £4 | £10 | |
| Mahalia Jackson | 10" LP | Vogue | LDE005 | 1952 | £4 | £10 | |
| Newport 1958 | LP | Philips | BBL7289/SBBL547. | 1959 | £5 | £12 | |
| Power And The Glory | LP | Philips | BBL7391/SBBL576. | 1960 | £4 | £10 | |

## JACKSON, MICHAEL

Michael Jackson has made the two biggest-selling albums ever, and has in the process acquired a legion of fans keen to collect anything they can find. Within the collectors' market, Jackson has joined the select few stars for whom there are dealers specializing exclusively in his music. The *Dangerous* picture disc is a distinct oddity, in that it does not actually play Michael Jackson's music at all. Copies were produced for promo and test purposes before it was realized that the vinyl release was going to be a double. A commercial picture disc was never produced in consequence (although double-album picture discs, such as Frankie Goes To Hollywood's *Welcome To The Pleasure Dome*, have been issued in the past). The Michael Jackson Megamix 12" was withdrawn and half the original thousand copies were destroyed. Counterfeits exist of the remainder, but these are identifiable by the fact that they play at 33 rpm, whereas the real thing plays at 45 rpm (despite the label stating that it is actually 33 rpm).

| Another Part Of Me | CD-s .. | Epic | 6530042 | 1988 | £4 | £10 | |
|---|---|---|---|---|---|---|---|
| Another Part Of Me | CD-s ... | Epic | 6530042 | 1988 | £10 | £20 | picture disc |
| Another Part Of Me | 7" .... | Epic | 4528449 | 1988 | £2.50 | £6 | with tour pass |
| Another Part Of Me | 7" .... | Epic | 6528440 | 1988 | £2.50 | £6 | poster picture sleeve |
| Bad | LP .... | Epic | 4502900 | 1987 | £4 | £10 | picture disc |
| Bad | CD.... | Epic | EPC4502909 | 1987 | £5 | £12 | picture disc |
| Bad | cass.... | Epic | 450290 | 1987 | £6 | £15 | with note pad, pen, calendar |
| Bad | 7" .... | Epic | MJ5 | 1988 | £7.50 | £15 | 5 picture discs |
| Bad | 12".... | Epic | 6511006 | 1987 | £5 | £12 | red vinyl |
| Bad Mixes | CD .... | Epic | ESK1215MC | 1988 | £100 | £200 | US promo |
| Billie Jean (Meanjean Mix) | CD-s .. | Epic | | 198– | £20 | £40 | |
| Black Or White | CD-s .. | Epic | 6575982 | 1991 | £2 | £5 | |
| Black Or White (Clivilles & Cole Remixes) | CD-s .. | Epic | 6577312 | 1992 | £2 | £5 | |
| Dangerous | LP ..... | Epic | | 1991 | £700 | £1000 | US sample picture disc – plays Richard Clayderman! |
| Dangerous | CD..... | Epic | | 1992 | £10 | £25 | Australian double, with remix disc |
| Dangerous | CD..... | Epic | 4658029 | 1992 | £6 | £15 | 10"-square pop-up pack |
| Dirty Diana | CD-s .. | Epic | 6515469 | 1988 | £6 | £15 | |
| Dirty Diana | 12".... | Epic | 6528646 | 1988 | £5 | £12 | poster picture sleeve |
| ET | LP ..... | MCA | MCA70000 | 1982 | £37.50 | £75 | with book and poster, boxed |
| ET | cass..... | MCA | CAC70000 | 1982 | £6 | £15 | with book & poster, boxed |
| Got To Be There | CD-s .. | Motown | ZD41951 | 1989 | £2 | £5 | |
| Happy | 7" .... | Tamla Motown | TMG986 | 1983 | £2.50 | £6 | picture disc |
| Happy | 7" .... | Tamla Motown | TMG986 | 1983 | £4 | £8 | poster picture sleeve |
| Heal The World | CD-s .. | Epic | 6584885 | 1992 | £2.50 | £6 | picture disc |
| History Begins | CD .... | Epic | XPCD656 | 1995 | £20 | £40 | promo |
| I Just Can't Stop Loving You | 7" .... | Epic | 6502020 | 1987 | £2.50 | £6 | poster picture sleeve |
| I Just Can't Stop Loving You | 12".... | Epic | 6502026 | 1987 | £3 | £8 | with poster |
| In The Closet | 12".... | Epic | E2S4467 | 1992 | £6 | £15 | US promo double |
| Jam | CD-s .. | Epic | 6583602 | 1992 | £2.50 | £6 | |
| Jam | 12".... | Epic | E2S4581 | 1992 | £10 | £20 | US promo double |
| Leave Me Alone | CD-s .. | Epic | 6546722 | 1989 | £4 | £10 | |
| Leave Me Alone | 7" .... | Epic | 6546720 | 1989 | £5 | £10 | pop-up sleeve |
| Liberian Girl | CD-s .. | Epic | 6549472 | 1989 | £4 | £10 | |
| Liberian Girl | 7" .... | Epic | 6549479 | 1989 | £2.50 | £6 | mobile pack |
| Man In THe Mirror | CD-s .. | Epic | 6513882 | 1988 | £6 | £15 | |
| Man In The Mirror | 7" .... | Epic | EPC6513889 | 1988 | £2.50 | £6 | shaped picture disc |
| Megamix | 12".... | Epic | XPR1242 | 1984 | £30 | £60 | |
| Off The Wall | LP ..... | Epic | EPC83458 | 1980 | £8 | £20 | with 7" picture disc |
| Off The Wall | LP ..... | Epic | HE47545 | 1980 | £5 | £12 | US audiophile |
| Remember The Time | 12".... | Epic | | 1992 | £10 | £20 | US promo double |
| Scream | 12".... | Epic | XPR2184 | 1995 | £12.50 | £25 | promo double |
| Singles Pack | 7" .... | Epic | MJ1 | 1983 | £20 | £40 | 9 x red vinyl |
| Smooth Criminal | CD-s .. | Epic | 6530263 | 1987 | £4 | £10 | |
| Smooth Criminal | 7" .... | Epic | 6530260 | 1987 | £2.50 | £6 | boxed with postcards |
| Smooth Criminal | 12".... | Epic | 6530261 | 1987 | £4 | £10 | with advent calendar |
| Smooth Criminal (Funkin' Smooth Mix) | 12".... | Epic | | 1988 | £15 | £30 | |
| Smooth Criminal (Smokin' Gun Mix) | 12".... | Epic | | 1988 | £20 | £40 | |
| Smooth Criminal (Vancouver Feetbeat) | 12".... | Epic | | 1988 | £15 | £30 | |
| Thriller | LP ..... | Epic | EPC1185930 | 1982 | £15 | £30 | picture disc |
| Thriller | LP ..... | Epic | HE48112 | 1982 | £6 | £15 | US audiophile |
| Thriller | 7" .... | Epic | EPCA3643 | 1983 | £4 | £8 | poster sleeve |
| Thriller | 12".... | Epic | TA3643 | 1983 | £20 | £40 | calendar sleeve |
| Tour Souvenir Pack | CD-s .. | Epic | 65828114(MJ4) | 1992 | £15 | £30 | 4 picture disc box set |

| | | | | | | | |
|---|---|---|---|---|---|---|---|
| Way You Make Me Feel | CD-s | Epic | 6512759 | 1987 | £4 | £10 | |
| Way You Make Me Feel | 12" | Epic | 6512753 | 1987 | £5 | £12 | double groove |
| Who Is It | 12" | Epic | | 1993 | £10 | £20 | US promo double |
| You Can't Win | CD-s | Epic | 6516613 | 1988 | £2 | £5 | |
| You Can't Win | 7" | Epic | EPC7135 | 1979 | £4 | £8 | picture disc |

## JACKSON, MICHAEL & PAUL McCARTNEY
| | | | | | | | |
|---|---|---|---|---|---|---|---|
| Girl Is Mine | 7" | Epic | EPCA112729 | 1982 | £10 | £20 | picture disc |

## JACKSON, MILLIE
| | | | | | | | |
|---|---|---|---|---|---|---|---|
| It Hurts So Good | LP | Polydor | 2391091 | 1972 | £4 | £10 | |
| Millie | LP | Spring | 6701 | 1973 | £4 | £10 | US |
| Millie Jackson | LP | Polydor | 2391025 | 1972 | £4 | £10 | |

## JACKSON, MILT
| | | | | | | | |
|---|---|---|---|---|---|---|---|
| At The Museum Of Modern Art | LP | Mercury | LML/SML4016 | 1965 | £4 | £10 | |
| Bags And Flutes | LP | London | LTZK15177 | 1960 | £5 | £12 | |
| Bags Meets Wes | LP | Riverside | RLP(9)407 | 1962 | £5 | £12 | with Wes Montgomery |
| Bags' Opus | LP | London | LTZK15172/SAHT6049 | 1959 | £5 | £12 | |
| Ballad Artistry | LP | London | LTZK15220/SAHK6163 | 1961 | £5 | £12 | |
| Ballad Artistry | 7" EP | London | REK1315 | 1962 | £2 | £5 | |
| Ballads And Blues | LP | London | LTZK15064 | 1957 | £8 | £20 | |
| Bean Bags | LP | London | LTZK15196/SAHK6095 | 1960 | £5 | £12 | with Coleman Hawkins |
| Born Free | LP | Mercury | LML/SML4028 | 1966 | £4 | £10 | |
| In A New Setting | LP | Mercury | LML/SML4008 | 1965 | £4 | £10 | |
| Jackson Ville | LP | London | LTZK15091 | 1957 | £8 | £20 | |
| Jackson's Ville | LP | London | LTZC15091 | 1957 | £8 | £20 | |
| Jazz Skyline | LP | London | LTZC15074 | 1957 | £8 | £20 | |
| Jazz Skyline | LP | London | LTZK15074 | 1957 | £8 | £20 | |
| Milt Jackson | LP | Blue Note | BLP/BST81509 | 1962 | £10 | £25 | with Thelonious Monk |
| Milt Jackson | LP | Philips | BBL7459 | 1961 | £5 | £12 | |
| Milt Jackson And His New Group | 10" LP | Vogue | LDE044 | 1954 | £25 | £50 | |
| Milt Jackson Quartet | LP | Esquire | 32009 | 1955 | £10 | £25 | |
| Milt Jackson Quartet | LP | Realm | RM119 | 1963 | £5 | £12 | |
| Milt Jackson Quartet | 10" LP | London | LZC14006 | 1955 | £15 | £30 | |
| Milt Jackson Quintet | 10" LP | Esquire | 20042 | 1955 | £20 | £40 | |
| Milt Jackson Septet | 7" EP | London | EZC19004 | 195– | £2 | £5 | |
| Modern Jazz Quartet/Quintet | LP | Esquire | 32134 | 1962 | £5 | £12 | |
| Opus De Jazz | LP | London | LTZC15026 | 1957 | £10 | £25 | |
| Plenty, Plenty Soul | LP | London | LTZK15141 | 1959 | £6 | £15 | |
| Statements | LP | HMV | CLP1589/CSD1455 | 1963 | £5 | £12 | |
| Vibrations | LP | Atlantic | ATL/SAL5012 | 1964 | £5 | £12 | |
| Wizard Of The Vibes | LP | Vogue | LAE12046 | 1957 | £6 | £15 | |

## JACKSON, PAPA CHARLIE
| | | | | | | | |
|---|---|---|---|---|---|---|---|
| Long Gone Lost John | 78 | Tempo | R30 | 1950 | £2.50 | £6 | |
| Papa Charlie Jackson | 7" EP | Heritage | R100 | 1960 | £7.50 | £15 | |

## JACKSON, PYTHON LEE
| | | | | | | | |
|---|---|---|---|---|---|---|---|
| In A Broken Dream | 7" EP | Young Blood | YEP89 | 1985 | £2.50 | £6 | promo |

## JACKSON, SHIRLEY
| | | | | | | | |
|---|---|---|---|---|---|---|---|
| Broken Home | 7" | Decca | F11788 | 1963 | £1.50 | £4 | |

## JACKSON, SHOVELVILLE K.
| | | | | | | | |
|---|---|---|---|---|---|---|---|
| Be Careful Of Stones That You Throw | 7" | Melodisc | 1683 | 196– | £2.50 | £6 | |

## JACKSON, SIMONE
| | | | | | | | |
|---|---|---|---|---|---|---|---|
| Doing What You Know Is Wrong | 7" EP | Pye | PNV24111 | 1963 | £2.50 | £6 | French |

## JACKSON, STONEWALL
| | | | | | | | |
|---|---|---|---|---|---|---|---|
| Dynamic Stonewall Jackson | LP | Columbia | CL1391/CS8186 | 1959 | £6 | £15 | US |
| Greatest Hits | LP | CBS | BPG62587 | 1965 | £4 | £10 | |
| I'm Gonna Find You | 7" | Philips | PB1073 | 1960 | £1.50 | £4 | |
| Sadness In A Song | LP | Columbia | CL1770/CS8570 | 1962 | £6 | £15 | US |
| Waterloo | 7" | Philips | PB941 | 1959 | £2.50 | £6 | |

## JACKSON, TONY

It must have seemed a good idea to Tony Jackson, as the lead singer of the Searchers, to strike out on his own. Unfortunately, it turned out that his personal following was only a fraction of the following enjoyed by the Searchers as a group. None of Tony Jackson's singles got anywhere at all, while the remaining Searchers enjoyed a further two-year run of chart success.

| | | | | | | | |
|---|---|---|---|---|---|---|---|
| Anything Else You Want | 7" | CBS | 202408 | 1966 | £10 | £20 | |
| Bye Bye Baby | 7" | Pye | 7N15685 | 1964 | £4 | £8 | |
| Follow Me | 7" | CBS | 202297 | 1966 | £12.50 | £25 | |
| Love Potion No. 9 | 7" | Pye | 7N15766 | 1965 | £10 | £20 | |
| Never Leave Your Baby's Side | 7" | CBS | 202069 | 1966 | £10 | £20 | |
| Stage Door | 7" | Pye | 7N15876 | 1965 | £4 | £8 | |
| This Little Girl Of Mine | 7" | Pye | 7N15745 | 1964 | £5 | £10 | |
| Tony Jackson Group | 7" EP | Estudio | | 1967 | £100 | £200 | Portuguese, best auctioned |
| You're My Number One | 7" EP | CBS | 5726 | 1966 | £75 | £150 | French |
| You're My Number One | 7" | CBS | 202039 | 1966 | £10 | £20 | |

436

## JACKSON, WALTER
| | | | | | | | |
|---|---|---|---|---|---|---|---|
| Corner In The Sun | 7" | Columbia | DB8054 | 1966 | £2.50 | £6 | |
| It's An Uphill Climb To The Bottom | 7" | Columbia | DB7949 | 1966 | £5 | £10 | |
| Speak Her Name | 7" | Columbia | DB8154 | 1967 | £2.50 | £6 | |
| Welcome Home | 7" | Columbia | DB7620 | 1965 | £2.50 | £6 | |

## JACKSON, WANDA

Wanda Jackson was one of the best female rock 'n' roll singers, although her competition was rather limited. Adopting the same rasping tones as Brenda Lee on her up-tempo material, Wanda Jackson's older voice had a greater depth and hence rather more power. In common with most of the American singers of her generation, she took the country route once the initial rock 'n' roll years were over.

| | | | | | | | |
|---|---|---|---|---|---|---|---|
| Blues In My Heart | LP | Capitol | (S)T2306 | 1964 | £5 | £12 | |
| If I Cried Every Time You Hurt Me | 7" | Capitol | CL15249 | 1962 | £2.50 | £6 | |
| In The Middle Of A Heartache | 7" | Capitol | CL15234 | 1962 | £2.50 | £6 | |
| Let's Have A Party | 7" EP | Capitol | EAP11041 | 1959 | £25 | £50 | |
| Let's Have A Party | 7" | Capitol | CL15147 | 1960 | £6 | £12 | |
| Little Bitty Tear | 7" EP | Capitol | EAP120353 | 1962 | £15 | £30 | |
| Love Me Forever | LP | Capitol | (S)T1911 | 1963 | £5 | £12 | US |
| Lovin' Country Style | LP | Decca | DL4224 | 1962 | £8 | £20 | US |
| Mean Mean Man | 7" | Capitol | CL15176 | 1961 | £6 | £12 | |
| Reaching | 7" | Capitol | CL15090 | 1959 | £5 | £10 | |
| Right Or Wrong | LP | Capitol | T1596 | 1961 | £20 | £40 | |
| Right Or Wrong | 7" | Capitol | CL15223 | 1961 | £2 | £5 | |
| Rockin' With Wanda | LP | Capitol | T1384 | 1960 | £37.50 | £75 | |
| There's A Party Goin' On | LP | Capitol | T1511 | 1961 | £30 | £60 | |
| Two Sides Of Wanda Jackson | LP | Capitol | (S)T2030 | 1964 | £8 | £20 | |
| Wanda Jackson | LP | Capitol | T1041 | 1958 | £50 | £100 | US |
| Wonderful Wanda | LP | Capitol | T1776 | 1962 | £8 | £20 | |
| You're The One For Me | 7" | Capitol | CL15033 | 1959 | £5 | £10 | |

## JACKSON & SMITH
| | | | | | | | |
|---|---|---|---|---|---|---|---|
| Ain't That Loving You Baby | 7" | Polydor | BM56051 | 1965 | £2.50 | £6 | |
| Party '66 | 7" | Polydor | BM56086 | 1966 | £2 | £5 | |

## JACKSON BROTHERS
| | | | | | | | |
|---|---|---|---|---|---|---|---|
| Tell Him No | 7" | London | HLX8845 | 1959 | £7.50 | £15 | |

## JACKSON FIVE
| | | | | | | | |
|---|---|---|---|---|---|---|---|
| ABC | 7" | Tamla Motown | TMB738 | 1970 | £25 | £50 | ... demo, picture sleeve |
| Goin' Places | LP | Epic | PAL348351G | 1978 | £4 | £10 | US picture disc |
| Jacksons | LP | CBS | AL34229 | 1977 | £4 | £10 | US picture disc |
| Looking Through The Windows | 7" | Tamla Motown | TMG833 | 1972 | £6 | £12 | demo, picture sleeve |
| Moving Violations | LP | Tamla Motown | STML11290 | 1975 | £4 | £10 | |
| Skywriter | 7" | Tamla Motown | TMG865 | 1973 | £5 | £10 | demo, picture sleeve |
| Talk And Sing To Valentine Readers | 7" | Lyntone | LYN2639 | 1974 | £2 | £5 | flexi |

## JACKSON HEIGHTS
| | | | | | | | |
|---|---|---|---|---|---|---|---|
| Bump And Grind | LP | Vertigo | 6360092 | 1973 | £5 | £12 | |
| Fifth Avenue Bus | LP | Vertigo | 6360067 | 1972 | £8 | £20 | spiral label |
| King Progress | LP | Charisma | CAS1018 | 1970 | £4 | £10 | |
| Ragamuffin's Fool | LP | Vertigo | 6360077 | 1973 | £8 | £20 | spiral label |

## JACKSON SISTERS
| | | | | | | | |
|---|---|---|---|---|---|---|---|
| I Believe In Miracles | 7" | Mums | MUM1829 | 1973 | £7.50 | £15 | |

## JACOB, DIRK
| | | | | | | | |
|---|---|---|---|---|---|---|---|
| Yes Till Death | LP | Blowin' Brains | VSATL112 | 1969 | £50 | £100 | US |

## JACOBS, DICK
| | | | | | | | |
|---|---|---|---|---|---|---|---|
| Big Beat | 7" | Vogue Coral | Q72245 | 1957 | £2.50 | £6 | |
| Rock-a-Billy Gal | 7" | Vogue Coral | Q72260 | 1957 | £1.50 | £4 | |
| Skiffle Sound | LP | Coral | LVA9076 | 1957 | £8 | £20 | |

## JACOBS, HANK
| | | | | | | | |
|---|---|---|---|---|---|---|---|
| Monkey Hips And Rice | 7" | Sue | WI313 | 1964 | £7.50 | £15 | |
| So Far Away | LP | Sue | 1023 | 1964 | £8 | £20 | US |

## JACQUES, BRIAN & BRIGANTINE
| | | | | | | | |
|---|---|---|---|---|---|---|---|
| Gig Wid Brig | LP | Sweet Folk & Country | SFAO11 | 1974 | £4 | £10 | |

## JACQUET, ILLINOIS
| | | | | | | | |
|---|---|---|---|---|---|---|---|
| Blow Illinois Blow | 7" | Vogue | V2387 | 1956 | £1.50 | £4 | |
| Groovin' With Jacquet | LP | Columbia | 33CX10085 | 1957 | £20 | £40 | |
| Illinois Jacquet | 10" LP | Columbia | 33C9018 | 1956 | £20 | £40 | |
| Illinois Jacquet | 10" LP | Vogue | LDE026 | 1953 | £25 | £50 | |

## JACQUI & BRIDIE
| | | | | | | | |
|---|---|---|---|---|---|---|---|
| Next Time Around | LP | Galliard | GAL4019 | | £20 | £40 | |

## JADE WARRIOR

Jade Warrior was essentially a duo – Tony Duhig and Jon Field – whose music is perfectly described by the album covers. Mostly instrumental, with a hint of the Orient and an emphasis on a gentle textural beauty, Jade Warrior's music laid down the ground rules for much of what is defined as 'new age'.

| | | | | | | | |
|---|---|---|---|---|---|---|---|
| Demon Trucker | 7" | Vertigo | 6059069 | 1972 | £2 | £5 | |

| | | | | | | | |
|---|---|---|---|---|---|---|---|
| Eclipse | LP | Vertigo | | 1973 | £100 | £200 | *promo only* |
| Floating World | LP | Island | ILPS9290 | 1974 | £4 | £10 | |
| Jade Warrior | LP | Vertigo | 6360033 | 1971 | £15 | £30 | *spiral label* |
| Kites | LP | Island | ILPS9393 | 1976 | £4 | £10 | |
| Last Autumn's Dream | LP | Vertigo | 6360079 | 1972 | £15 | £30 | *spiral label* |
| Reflections | LP | Butt | BUTT001 | 1979 | £4 | £10 | |
| Released | LP | Vertigo | 6360062 | 1971 | £20 | £40 | *spiral label* |
| Waves | LP | Island | ILPS9318 | 1975 | £4 | £10 | |
| Way Of The Sun | LP | Island | ILPS9552 | 1978 | £4 | £10 | |

## JADE

| | | | | | | | |
|---|---|---|---|---|---|---|---|
| Fly On Strange Wings | LP | DJM | DJLPS407 | 1970 | £15 | £30 | |

## JADE (2)

| | | | | | | | |
|---|---|---|---|---|---|---|---|
| Faces Of Jade | LP | General American Records | GAR11311 | 1968 | £30 | £60 | *US* |

## JADES

Both sides of the rare single by the Jades were written by a sixteen-year-old Lou Reed, who also played rhythm guitar. This is his recording debut.

| | | | | | | | |
|---|---|---|---|---|---|---|---|
| Leave Her For Me | 7" | Time | 1002 | 1957 | £100 | £200 | *US* |

## JAFFRAY

| | | | | | | |
|---|---|---|---|---|---|---|
| Seven Sided Dice | LP | private | | 1978 | £150 | £250 | |

## JAGGER, MICK

| | | | | | | | |
|---|---|---|---|---|---|---|---|
| Memo From Turner | 7" | Decca | F13067 | 1970 | £1.50 | £4 | |
| Memo From Turner | 7" | Decca | F13067 | 1970 | £12.50 | £25 | *.. export, picture sleeve* |
| Ned Kelly | LP | United Artists | UAS5213 | 1970 | £6 | £15 | *with other artists* |
| Performance | LP | Warner Bros | WS2554 | 1970 | £4 | £10 | *with other artists* |
| Throwaway | CD-s | CBS | THROWC1 | 1987 | £2 | £5 | |
| Wandering Spirit | CD | Atlantic | PRCD5002 | 1993 | £20 | £40 | *US interview promo* |

## JAGS

| | | | | | | | |
|---|---|---|---|---|---|---|---|
| Cry Wolf | 7" | Decca | F11397 | 1961 | £1.50 | £4 | |

## JAGUAR

| | | | | | | | |
|---|---|---|---|---|---|---|---|
| Axe Crazy | 7" | Neat | NEAT16 | 1982 | £4 | £8 | |
| Back Street Woman | 7" | Heavy Metal | HEAVY10 | 1981 | £2 | £5 | |

## JAGUARS

| | | | | | | | |
|---|---|---|---|---|---|---|---|
| Opus To Spring | 7" | Impression | IMP101 | 1963 | £7.50 | £15 | |
| We'll Live On Happily | 7" | Contest | RGJ152 | 1965 | £75 | £150 | |

## JAH LION

| | | | | | | | |
|---|---|---|---|---|---|---|---|
| Colombia Colly | LP | Island | ILPS9386 | 1976 | £5 | £12 | |

## JAH WHOOSH

| | | | | | | | |
|---|---|---|---|---|---|---|---|
| Dreadlocks Affair | LP | Trojan | TRLS113 | 1976 | £5 | £12 | |
| Jah Jah Dey Dey | LP | Cactus | CTLP116 | 1976 | £5 | £12 | |
| Jah Whoosh | LP | Cactus | CTLP103 | 1974 | £6 | £15 | |
| Religious Dread | LP | Trojan | TRLS157 | 1978 | £4 | £10 | |

## JAIM

| | | | | | | | |
|---|---|---|---|---|---|---|---|
| Prophesy Fulfilled | LP | Ethereal | 1001 | 1970 | £8 | £20 | *US* |

## JAKLIN

| | | | | | | | |
|---|---|---|---|---|---|---|---|
| Jaklin | LP | Stable | SLE8003 | 1969 | £100 | £200 | |

## JAM

| | | | | | | | |
|---|---|---|---|---|---|---|---|
| Beat Surrender | 7" | Polydor | PODJ540 | 1982 | £62.50 | £125 | *... autographed double, handwritten lyrics* |
| Beat Surrender | 7" | Polydor | PODJ540 | 1982 | £2.50 | £6 | *promo, censored version* |
| Beat Surrender | 12" | Polydor | POSP540X | 1982 | £10 | £20 | *mispressed B side* |
| Compact Snap! | CD | Polydor | 8217122 | 1983 | £5 | £12 | |
| Funeral Pyre | 7" | Fan Club | | 1982 | £7.50 | £15 | *flexi* |
| Going Underground | 7" | Polydor | POSPJ113/2816024 | 1980 | £2 | £5 | *double* |
| In The City | 7" | Polydor | 2058866 | 1977 | £2 | £5 | |
| News Of The World | 7" | Polydor | 2058995 | 1978 | £10 | £20 | *mispress with 2 B sides* |
| Peel Sessions | CD-s | Strange Fruit | SFPSCD080 | 1990 | £2 | £5 | |
| Snap! | LP | Polydor | SNAP1 | 1983 | £5 | £12 | *double, with 7" (SNAP45)* |
| Snap! Medley | 7" | Polydor | LEE1 | 1983 | £7.50 | £15 | *promo* |
| Tales From The Riverbank | 7" | Fan Club | no number | 1982 | £7.50 | £15 | *flexi* |
| That's Entertainment | CD-s | Polydor | PZCD155 | 1991 | £2 | £5 | |
| When You're Young | 7" | Fan Club | no number | 1981 | £7.50 | £15 | *flexi* |
| When You're Young | 7" | Polydor | POSP69 | 1979 | £10 | £20 | *mispress with 2 B sides* |

## JAM (2)

| | | | | | | | |
|---|---|---|---|---|---|---|---|
| From The Road | LP | private | | 1976 | £330 | £500 | *Dutch* |

## JAMAICAN SHADOWS

| | | | | | | | |
|---|---|---|---|---|---|---|---|
| Dirty Dozen | 7" | Upsetter | US320 | 1969 | £1.50 | £4 | |
| Have Mercy | 7" | Coxsone | CS7005 | 1967 | £5 | £10 | |

## JAMAICANS

| | | | | | | | |
|---|---|---|---|---|---|---|---|
| Bab Boom | 7" | Treasure Isle | TI7012 | 1967 | £5 | £10 | Tommy McCook B side |
| Cool Night | 7" | Doctor Bird | DB1109 | 1967 | £5 | £10 | |
| Dedicated To You | 7" | Trojan | TR007 | 1967 | £5 | £10 | |
| Early In The Morning | 7" | Escort | ES806 | 1969 | £1.50 | £4 | |
| Peace And Love | 7" | Treasure Isle | TI7037 | 1968 | £5 | £10 | |
| Things You Say You Love | 7" | Treasure Isle | TI7007 | 1967 | £5 | £10 | |

## JAMAL, AHMAD

| | | | | | | | |
|---|---|---|---|---|---|---|---|
| Ahmad Jamal | LP | London | LTZM15170 | 1959 | £6 | £15 | |
| Alhambra | LP | Pye | NJL38 | 1962 | £5 | £12 | |
| At The Top | LP | Impulse | SIPL521 | 1970 | £5 | £12 | |
| But Not For Me | LP | London | LTZM15162 | 1959 | £6 | £15 | |
| Cry Young | LP | Chess | CRL4532 | 1968 | £5 | £12 | |
| Macanudo | LP | Pye | NJL50 | 1963 | £5 | £12 | |
| Standard-Eyes | LP | Chess | CRL4530 | 1968 | £5 | £12 | |

## JAMES

| | | | | | | | |
|---|---|---|---|---|---|---|---|
| Chain Mail | 7" | Blanco Y Negro | JIM3 | 1986 | £2 | £5 | |
| Chain Mail | 12" | Blanco Y Negro | JIM3T | 1986 | £4 | £10 | |
| Come Home | CD-s | Fontana | JIMCD6 | 1990 | £2 | £5 | |
| Come Home | CD-s | Rough Trade | RTT245CD | 1989 | £2.50 | £6 | |
| How Was It For You | CD-s | Fontana | JIMCD5 | 1990 | £2 | £5 | |
| James II | 7" | Factory | FAC119 | 1985 | £2.50 | £6 | |
| Jimone | 7" | Factory | FAC78 | 1984 | £4 | £8 | |
| Lose Control | CD-s | Fontana | JIMCD7 | 1990 | £2 | £5 | |
| One Man Clapping | CD-s | Rough Trade | ONEMAN001CD | 1989 | £2 | £5 | |
| Sit Down | CD-s | Fontana | JIMCD8 | 1991 | £2 | £5 | |
| Sit Down | CD-s | Rough Trade | RTT225CD | 1989 | £3 | £8 | 3" single |
| Sit Down | 7" | Rough Trade | RT225 | 1989 | £1.50 | £4 | |
| Sit Down | 12" | Rough Trade | RTT225 | 1989 | £3 | £8 | |
| So Many Ways | 7" | Blanco Y Negro | JIM4 | 1986 | £2 | £5 | |
| So Many Ways | 12" | Blanco Y Negro | JIM4T | 1986 | £4 | £10 | |
| Sound | CD-s | Fontana | JIMCD9 | 1991 | £2 | £5 | |
| What For | 12" | Blanco Y Negro | NEG31T | 1988 | £3 | £8 | |
| Yaho | 12" | Blanco Y Negro | NEG26T | 1988 | £3 | £8 | |

## JAMES, CALVIN

| | | | | | | | |
|---|---|---|---|---|---|---|---|
| Some Things You Never Get Used To | 7" | Columbia | DB7516 | 1965 | £2.50 | £6 | |

## JAMES, DICK

| | | | | | | | |
|---|---|---|---|---|---|---|---|
| Garden Of Eden | 7" | Parlophone | R4255 | 1957 | £2.50 | £6 | |
| He | 7" | Parlophone | MSP6190 | 1955 | £2 | £5 | |
| I Only Know I Love You | 7" | Parlophone | R4220 | 1956 | £1.50 | £4 | |
| Joker | 7" | Parlophone | MSP6047 | 1953 | £2 | £5 | |
| Mother Nature And Father Time | 7" | Parlophone | MSP6039 | 1953 | £2 | £5 | |
| Robin Hood | 7" | Parlophone | MSP6199 | 1956 | £5 | £10 | |
| Skiffling Sing Song | 7" | Parlophone | R4375 | 1957 | £1.50 | £4 | |
| Unchained Melody | 7" | Parlophone | MSP6170 | 1955 | £2.50 | £6 | |
| Westward Ho The Wagons | 7" | Parlophone | R4314 | 1957 | £1.50 | £4 | |

## JAMES, ELMORE

As one of the major influences on the British blues boom, Elmore James both defined electric blues slide guitar playing and created the style's test piece, 'Dust My Blues' (a.k.a. 'Dust My Broom'). The high stabbing chord, with the slide chattering at the twelfth, octave fret, that sets the pattern for the song was re-worked for numerous other songs by James, who knew a good thing when he heard it, and also by his many followers. Fleetwood Mac's Jeremy Spencer, for example, based his entire blues career on being an Elmore James sound-alike and reworked the slide guitar figure for several of his contributions to the group's Blue Horizon albums. The slide guitar solo that James created for the original song, moreover, became so quickly assimilated into the blues vocabulary that Jesse Davis was able to quote it directly, and thereby sound traditional, on Taj Mahal's triumphant reclaiming of the blues for black America, 'Statesboro' Blues'.

| | | | | | | | |
|---|---|---|---|---|---|---|---|
| Anthology Of The Blues Legend | LP | Kent | KLP9001 | 196– | £6 | £15 | US |
| Best Of Elmore James | LP | Sue | ILP918 | 1965 | £15 | £30 | |
| Blues After Hours | LP | Crown | CLP5168 | 1961 | £15 | £30 | US |
| Calling The Blues | 7" | Sue | WI392 | 1965 | £25 | £50 | |
| Dust My Blues | 7" | Sue | WI335 | 1964 | £6 | £12 | |
| I Need You | LP | Sphere Sound | 7008 | 1964 | £8 | £20 | US |
| I Need You | 7" | Sue | WI4007 | 1966 | £6 | £12 | |
| It Hurts Me Too | 7" | Sue | WI383 | 1965 | £6 | £12 | |
| Late Fantastically Great Elmore James | LP | Ember | EMB3397 | 1968 | £4 | £10 | |
| Legend Of Elmore James | LP | United Artists | UAS29109 | 1970 | £6 | £15 | |
| Memorial Album | LP | Sue | ILP927 | 1965 | £15 | £30 | |
| Original Folk Blues | LP | Kent | KLP5022 | 1964 | £10 | £25 | US |
| Resurrection Of Elmore James | LP | Kent | KLP9010 | 196– | £6 | £15 | US |
| Sky Is Crying | LP | Sphere Sound | 7002 | 1964 | £8 | £20 | US |
| Something Inside Of Me | LP | Bell | MBLL/SBLL104 | 1968 | £8 | £20 | |
| To Know A Man | LP | Blue Horizon | 766230 | 1969 | £20 | £40 | double |
| Tough | LP | Blue Horizon | 763204 | 1968 | £15 | £30 | with John Brim |
| Whose Muddy Shoes | LP | Chess | 1537 | 1969 | £6 | £15 | US |

## JAMES, ETTA

| | | | | | | | |
|---|---|---|---|---|---|---|---|
| All I Could Do Was Cry | 7" | London | HLM9139 | 1960 | £7.50 | £15 | |
| Anything To Say You're Mine | 7" | Pye | 7N25080 | 1961 | £2.50 | £6 | |
| At Last | LP | Argo | (S)4003 | 1961 | £8 | £20 | US |
| At Last | LP | Chess | CRL4524 | 1967 | £4 | £10 | |
| At Last | 7" | Pye | 7N25079 | 1961 | £2.50 | £6 | |
| Etta James | LP | Argo | (S)4013 | 1962 | £6 | £15 | US |
| Etta James Sings For Lovers | LP | Argo | (S)4018 | 1962 | £6 | £15 | US |
| Fool That I Am | 7" | Pye | 7N25113 | 1961 | £2.50 | £6 | |
| I Got You Babe | 7" | Chess | CRS8076 | 1968 | £2 | £5 | |
| I Prefer You | 7" | Chess | CRS8052 | 1967 | £2.50 | £6 | |
| Miss Etta James | LP | Kent | 3002 | 196- | £6 | £15 | US |
| Miss Etta James | LP | Kent | 3002 | 196- | £8 | £20 | US, red vinyl |
| My Dearest Darling | 7" | London | HLM9234 | 1960 | £5 | £10 | |
| Pushover | 7" | Pye | 7N25205 | 1963 | £2.50 | £6 | |
| Queen Of Soul | LP | Argo | (S)4040 | 1965 | £4 | £10 | US |
| Rock With Me Henry | 7" | Sue | WI359 | 1965 | £6 | £12 | |
| Rocks The House | LP | Chess | CRL4502 | 1963 | £4 | £10 | |
| Second Time Around | LP | Argo | (S)4011 | 1961 | £6 | £15 | US |
| Security | 7" | Chess | CRS8069 | 1967 | £2 | £5 | |
| Something's Got A Hold Of Me | 7" | Pye | 7N25131 | 1962 | £2.50 | £6 | |
| Soul Of Etta James | LP | Ember | EMB3390 | 1968 | £4 | £10 | |
| Stop The Wedding | 7" | Pye | 7N25162 | 1962 | £2.50 | £6 | |
| Tell Mama | LP | Chess | CRL4536 | 1968 | £4 | £10 | |
| Tell Mama | 7" | Chess | CRS8063 | 1967 | £2.50 | £6 | |
| Top Ten | LP | Argo | (S)4025 | 1963 | £6 | £15 | US |
| You Got It | 7" | Chess | CRS8082 | 1968 | £1.50 | £4 | |

## JAMES, ETTA & SUGAR PIE DESANTO

| | | | | | | | |
|---|---|---|---|---|---|---|---|
| Do I Make Myself Clear | 7" | Chess | CRS8025 | 1965 | £4 | £8 | |

## JAMES, HARRY

| | | | | | | | |
|---|---|---|---|---|---|---|---|
| Harry James | LP | Capitol | LCT6107 | 1956 | £5 | £12 | |
| Harry James Orchestra | LP | Philips | BBL7036 | 1955 | £6 | £15 | |
| Wild About Harry | LP | Capitol | LCT6146 | 1957 | £5 | £12 | |

## JAMES, HOMESICK

| | | | | | | | |
|---|---|---|---|---|---|---|---|
| Crossroads | 7" | Sue | WI319 | 1964 | £5 | £10 | |
| Set A Date | 7" | Sue | WI330 | 1965 | £6 | £12 | |

## JAMES, HOMESICK & SNOOKY PRIOR

| | | | | | | | |
|---|---|---|---|---|---|---|---|
| Homesick James And Snooky Prior | LP | Caroline | C1502 | 1974 | £4 | £10 | |

## JAMES, JASON

| | | | | | | | |
|---|---|---|---|---|---|---|---|
| Miss Pilkington's Maid | 7" | CBS | 2705 | 1967 | £5 | £10 | |

## JAMES, JESSE

| | | | | | | | |
|---|---|---|---|---|---|---|---|
| Lonesome Day Blues | 78 | Vocalion | V1037 | 1954 | £3 | £8 | |

## JAMES, JIMMY

| | | | | | | | |
|---|---|---|---|---|---|---|---|
| Ain't Love Good | 7" | Piccadilly | 7N35349 | 1966 | £2.50 | £6 | |
| Ain't Love Good Ain't Love Proud | 7" EP | Pye | PNV24183 | 1966 | £10 | £20 | French |
| Help Yourself | 7" | Trojan | TR7806 | 1970 | £4 | £8 | |
| Hi Diddley Dee Dum Dum | 7" | Piccadilly | 7N35320 | 1966 | £2 | £5 | |
| I Can't Get Back Home To My Baby | 7" | Piccadilly | 7N35360 | 1967 | £2.50 | £6 | |
| I Feel Alright | 7" | Piccadilly | 7N35298 | 1966 | £2 | £5 | |
| Jimmy James & The Vagabonds | 7" EP | Piccadilly | NEP34053 | 1966 | £10 | £20 | |
| Jump Children | 7" | R&B | JB112 | 1963 | £2.50 | £6 | |
| New Religion | LP | Piccadilly | NPL38027 | 1966 | £5 | £12 | |
| New Religion | 7" EP | Pye | PNV24188 | 1967 | £10 | £20 | French |
| No Good To Cry | 7" EP | Pye | PNV24193 | 1967 | £10 | £20 | French |
| No Good To Cry | 7" | Piccadilly | 7N35374 | 1967 | £2 | £5 | |
| Open Up Your Soul | LP | Pye | N(S)PL18231 | 1968 | £5 | £12 | |
| Shoo Be Doo You're Mine | 7" | Columbia | DB7653 | 1965 | £2 | £6 | |
| Thinking Of You | 7" | Black Swan | WI437 | 1964 | £2 | £5 | |
| This Heart Of Mine | 7" | Piccadilly | 7N35331 | 1966 | £2.50 | £6 | |
| You Don't Stand A Chance | LP | Pye | NSPL18457 | 1975 | £4 | £10 | |
| Your Love | 7" | Ska Beat | JB242 | 1966 | £2 | £5 | |

## JAMES, JOHN

| | | | | | | | |
|---|---|---|---|---|---|---|---|
| Acoustica Eclectica | LP | Stoptime | STOP101 | 1984 | £4 | £10 | |
| Descriptive Guitar Instrumentals | LP | Kicking Mule | SNKF128 | 1976 | £4 | £10 | |
| Head In The Clouds | LP | Transatlantic | TRA305 | 1975 | £5 | £12 | |
| John James | LP | Transatlantic | TRA242 | 1971 | £5 | £12 | |
| Live In Concert | LP | Kicking Mule | SNKF136 | 1978 | £4 | £10 | |
| Morning Brings The Light | LP | Transatlantic | TRA219 | 1970 | £5 | £12 | |
| Sky In My Pie | LP | Transatlantic | TRA250 | 1971 | £5 | £12 | ...with Pete Berryman |

## JAMES, JONI

| | | | | | | | |
|---|---|---|---|---|---|---|---|
| After Hours | LP | MGM | C933 | 1963 | £4 | £10 | |
| Almost Always | 7" | MGM | SP1041 | 1953 | £4 | £8 | |
| Am I In Love | 7" | MGM | SP1089 | 1954 | £2.50 | £6 | |
| At Carnegie Hall | LP | MGM | (S)E3800 | 1959 | £4 | £10 | US |
| Award Winning Album | LP | MGM | E3346 | 1956 | £6 | £15 | US |
| Award Winning Album | 10" LP | MGM | E234 | 195- | £8 | £20 | US |
| Country Girl Style | LP | MGM | (S)E4101 | 1962 | £4 | £10 | US |

| | | | | | | |
|---|---|---|---|---|---|---|
| Give Us This Day | LP | MGM | E3528 | 1958 £6 | £15 | *US* |
| Give Us This Day | 7" | MGM | MGM918 | 1957 £1.50 | £4 | |
| Have You Heart | 7" | MGM | SP1025 | 1953 £2.50 | £6 | |
| How Important Can It Be | 7" | MGM | SP1125 | 1955 £2 | £5 | |
| Hundred Strings And Joni In Hollywood | LP | MGM | C839/CS6015 | 1961 £4 | £10 | |
| I Feel A Song Comin' On | LP | MGM | (S)E4053 | 1962 £4 | £10 | *US* |
| I Love You | 7" EP | MGM | MGMEP651 | 1958 £2 | £5 | |
| I Need You Now | 7" | MGM | SP1081 | 1954 £2 | £5 | |
| I'll Never Stand In Your Way | 7" | MGM | SP1064 | 1954 £4 | £8 | |
| I'm Your Girl | LP | MGM | (S)E4054 | 1962 £4 | £10 | *US* |
| In A Garden Of Roses | 7" | MGM | SP1100 | 1954 £2 | £5 | |
| In The Still Of The Night | LP | MGM | E3328 | 1956 £6 | £15 | *US* |
| Is This The End Of The Line | 7" | MGM | SP1135 | 1955 £2 | £5 | |
| Joni James | 7" EP | MGM | MGMEP504 | 1954 £2.50 | £6 | |
| Joni James Sings To You | 7" EP | MGM | MGMEP518 | 1955 £2.50 | £6 | |
| Let There Be Love | 10" LP | MGM | D127 | 1954 £8 | £20 | |
| Little Girl Blue | 7" EP | MGM | MGMEP530 | 1956 £2.50 | £6 | |
| Love Letters | 7" EP | MGM | MGMEP558 | 1956 £2 | £5 | |
| Mama Don't Cry At My Wedding | 7" | MGM | SP1105 | 1954 £2 | £5 | |
| Merry Christmas From Joni | LP | MGM | E3468 | 1957 £6 | £15 | *US* |
| Mood Is Blue | LP | MGM | (S)E3991 | 1961 £4 | £10 | *US* |
| Mood Is Romance | LP | MGM | (S)E3990 | 1961 £4 | £10 | *US* |
| Mood Is Swinging | LP | MGM | (S)E3987 | 1961 £4 | £10 | *US* |
| One Hundred Strings And Joni | LP | MGM | C777 | 1959 £4 | £10 | |
| Only Trust Your Heart | 7" | MGM | MGM954 | 1957 £1.50 | £4 | |
| Sings Irish Favourites | LP | MGM | C823/CS6005 | 1960 £4 | £10 | |
| Songs Of Hank Williams | LP | MGM | C785 | 1959 £4 | £10 | |
| Songs Of Hank Williams | 7" EP | MGM | ES3501 | 1960 £4 | £8 | *stereo* |
| Songs Of Hank Williams | 7" EP | MGM | MGMEP728 | 1960 £2.50 | £6 | |
| Stage Songs | 7" EP | MGM | MGMEP595 | 1957 £2 | £5 | |
| Swings Sweet | LP | MGM | C825 | 1960 £4 | £10 | |
| There Must Be A Way | 7" | MGM | MGM1002 | 1959 £1.50 | £4 | |
| Ti Voglio Bene | LP | MGM | C809 | 1960 £4 | £10 | |
| Why Don't You Believe Me? | 7" | MGM | SP1013 | 1953 £4 | £8 | |
| You Are My Love | 7" | MGM | SP1149 | 1956 £2 | £5 | |
| You're My Everything | 7" | MGM | SP1094 | 1954 £2 | £5 | |
| Your Cheatin' Heart | 7" | MGM | SP1026 | 1953 £4 | £8 | |

## JAMES, LEONARD

| | | | | | | |
|---|---|---|---|---|---|---|
| Boppin' And A-Strollin' | LP | Decca | DL8772 | 1958 £8 | £20 | *US* |

## JAMES, NICKY

| | | | | | | |
|---|---|---|---|---|---|---|
| Stagger Lee | 7" | Columbia | DB7747 | 1965 £5 | £10 | |
| Would You Believe | 7" | Philips | BF1635 | 1968 £4 | £8 | |

## JAMES, RICKY

| | | | | | | |
|---|---|---|---|---|---|---|
| Knee Deep In The Blues | 7" | HMV | POP306 | 1957 £6 | £12 | |
| Party Doll | 7" | HMV | POP334 | 1957 £7.50 | £15 | |

## JAMES, ROGER FOUR

| | | | | | |
|---|---|---|---|---|---|
| Better Than Here | 7" | Columbia | DB7813 | 1966 £2 | £5 |

## JAMES, RUBY

| | | | | | |
|---|---|---|---|---|---|
| Getting Mighty Crowded | 7" | Fontana | TF1051 | 1969 £2 | £5 |

## JAMES, SKIP

| | | | | | |
|---|---|---|---|---|---|
| Devil Got My Woman | LP | Vanguard | VSD79273 | 1968 £5 | £12 |
| Greatest Of The Delta Blues Singers | LP | Storyville | 670185 | 1967 £5 | £12 |
| Original 1930-31 Recordings | LP | Spokane | SPL1003 | 1970 £15 | £30 |
| Skip James Today | LP | Vanguard | VSD79219 | 1965 £5 | £12 |

## JAMES, SONNY

| | | | | | | |
|---|---|---|---|---|---|---|
| Are You Mine | 7" | Capitol | CL14879 | 1958 £1.50 | £4 | |
| Cat Came Back | 7" | Capitol | CL14635 | 1956 £5 | £10 | |
| Dear Love | 7" | Capitol | CL14742 | 1957 £2 | £5 | |
| First Date, First Kiss, First Love | 7" | Capitol | CL14708 | 1957 £2.50 | £6 | |
| Honey | LP | Capitol | T988 | 1958 £8 | £20 | |
| I Can See It In Your Eyes | 7" | Capitol | CL14915 | 1958 £1.50 | £4 | |
| Jenny Lou | 7" | London | HL9132 | 1960 £2 | £5 | |
| Kathleen | 7" | Capitol | CL14848 | 1958 £2 | £5 | |
| Mighty Lovable Man | 7" | Capitol | CL14788 | 1957 £5 | £10 | |
| Sonny | LP | Capitol | T867 | 1957 £10 | £25 | |
| Southern Gentleman | LP | Capitol | T779 | 1957 £10 | £25 | |
| This Is Sonny James | LP | Capitol | T1178 | 1959 £8 | £20 | *US* |
| Twenty Feet Of Muddy Water | 7" | Capitol | CL14664 | 1956 £4 | £8 | |
| Uh Uh Umm | 7" | Capitol | CL14814 | 1957 £5 | £10 | |
| Yo-Yo | 7" | Capitol | CL14991 | 1959 £2.50 | £6 | |
| You're The Only World I Know | 7" EP | Capitol | EAP120654 | 1964 £5 | £10 | |
| Young Love | LP | London | HAD8049 | 1963 £20 | £40 | |
| Young Love | 7" EP | Capitol | EAP1827 | 1957 £7.50 | £15 | |
| Young Love | 7" | Capitol | CL14683 | 1957 £4 | £8 | |

## JAMES, SULLIVAN BAND

| | | | | | |
|---|---|---|---|---|---|
| Goodbye Mr. Heartache | 7" | Parlophone | R5465 | 1966 £1.50 | £4 |

## JAMES, TOMMY & THE SHONDELLS

Tommy James and the Shondells produced a kind of basic guitar pop whose closest British equivalent was perhaps the Troggs. Records like 'Hanky Panky', 'Mony Mony' and 'I Think We're Alone Now' were enormous American hits and have proved to be a considerable influence on the kind of straightforward teenage rock typified by the likes of the Ramones and the Runaways.

| | | | | | | | |
|---|---|---|---|---|---|---|---|
| Best Of Tommy James And The Shondelles | LP | Roulette | SR42040 | 1970 | £4 | £10 | US |
| Cellophane Symphony | LP | Roulette | R/SRLP3 | 1969 | £4 | £10 | |
| Crimson And Clover | LP | Roulette | R/SRLP2 | 1968 | £4 | £10 | |
| Crimson And Clover | 7" | Roulette | RO502 | 1968 | £1.50 | £4 | |
| Getting Together | LP | Roulette | SR25357 | 1968 | £5 | £12 | US |
| Hanky Panky | LP | Roulette | (S)R25336 | 1966 | £5 | £12 | US |
| Hanky Panky | 7" EP | Roulette | VREX65044 | 1966 | £7.50 | £15 | French, B side by Dave Baby Cortez |
| Hanky Panky | 7" | Roulette | RK7000 | 1966 | £2 | £5 | |
| I Think We're Alone Now | LP | Roulette | (S)R25353 | 1967 | £5 | £12 | US |
| I Think We're Alone Now | 7" EP | Roulette | VREX65049 | 1967 | £7.50 | £15 | French |
| I Think We're Alone Now | 7" | Major Minor | MM511 | 1967 | £1.50 | £4 | |
| It's Only Love | LP | Roulette | (S)R25344 | 1967 | £5 | £12 | US |
| It's Only Love | 7" EP | Roulette | VREX65048 | 1966 | £7.50 | £15 | French |
| It's Only Love | 7" | Pye | 7N25398 | 1966 | £1.50 | £4 | |
| Mirage | 7" EP | Roulette | VREX65051 | 1967 | £7.50 | £15 | French |
| Mony Mony | LP | Roulette | R/SRLP1 | 1968 | £4 | £10 | |
| Mony Mony | 7" | Major Minor | MM567 | 1968 | £1.50 | £4 | |
| Say I Am | 7" EP | Roulette | VREX65045 | 1966 | £7.50 | £15 | French |
| Something Special | LP | Major Minor | M/SMLP27 | 1968 | £5 | £12 | |
| Wish It Were You | 7" | Major Minor | MM558 | 1968 | £1.50 | £4 | |

## JAMES BOYS
| | | | | | | |
|---|---|---|---|---|---|---|
| Mule | 7" | Direction | 583721 | 1968 | £1.50 | £4 |

## JAMES BROTHERS
| | | | | | | |
|---|---|---|---|---|---|---|
| Does It Have To Be Me | 7" | Page One | POF088 | 1968 | £1.50 | £4 |
| I Forgot To Give You Love | 7" | Page One | POF077 | 1968 | £1.50 | £4 |

## JAMES GANG
| | | | | | | | |
|---|---|---|---|---|---|---|---|
| Miami | LP | Atco | QD36102 | 1974 | £4 | £10 | US quad |
| Stop | 7" | Stateside | SS2173 | 1970 | £2 | £5 | |
| Yer Album | LP | Stateside | SSL10295 | 1969 | £4 | £10 | |

## JAMESON, BOBBY
| | | | | | | |
|---|---|---|---|---|---|---|
| All I Want Is My Baby | 7" | Decca | F12032 | 1964 | £6 | £12 |
| Rum-Pum | 7" | Brit | WI1001 | 1965 | £4 | £8 |

## JAMESON, BOBBY (2)
'Gotta Find My Roogalator' was arranged by Frank Zappa.

| | | | | | | | |
|---|---|---|---|---|---|---|---|
| Gotta Find My Roogalator | 7" | Penthouse | 503 | 1962 | £75 | £150 | US |
| I Wanna Love You | 7" | London | HL9921 | 1964 | £6 | £12 | |

## JAMESON, STEPHEN
| | | | | | | |
|---|---|---|---|---|---|---|
| Stephen Jameson | LP | Dawn | DNLS3044 | 1973 | £4 | £10 |

## JAMESON RAID
| | | | | | | |
|---|---|---|---|---|---|---|
| Hypnotist | 7" | Blackbird | BRAID001 | 1980 | £2.50 | £6 |
| Seven Days Of Splendour | 7" | GBH | GRC1 | 1979 | £4 | £8 |

## JAMIE WEDNESDAY
Jim Morrison and Leslie Carter – later to be known as Jim Bob and Fruitbat when trading as Carter the Unstoppable Sex Machine – led the five-piece Jamie Wednesday, before deciding to try and make it as a duo.

| | | | | | | | |
|---|---|---|---|---|---|---|---|
| Vote For Love | 7" | Pink | 7PINKY6 | 1985 | £1.50 | £4 | no picture sleeve |
| Vote For Love | 12" | Pink | PINKY6 | 1985 | £2.50 | £6 | |
| We Three Kings Of Orient Aren't | 7" | Pink | 7PINKY10 | 1986 | £1.50 | £4 | no picture sleeve |
| We Three Kings Of Orient Aren't | 12" | Pink | PINKY10 | 1986 | £2.50 | £6 | |

## JAMIES
| | | | | | | |
|---|---|---|---|---|---|---|
| Summertime Summertime | 7" | Columbia | DB4885 | 1962 | £4 | £8 |
| Summertime Summertime | 7" | Fontana | H153 | 1958 | £7.50 | £15 |

## JAMIE'S AGENT ORANGE
| | | | | | | |
|---|---|---|---|---|---|---|
| Losing My Way | 7" | Emma | EC002 | 1990 | £2 | £5 |

## JAMME
| | | | | | | |
|---|---|---|---|---|---|---|
| Jamme | LP | Stateside | SSL5024 | 1970 | £4 | £10 |

## JAMMER, JOE
| | | | | | | |
|---|---|---|---|---|---|---|
| Bad News | LP | Regal Zonophone | SRZA8515 | 1973 | £6 | £15 |

## JAN & ARNIE
| | | | | | | |
|---|---|---|---|---|---|---|
| Jennie Lee | 7" | London | HL8653 | 1958 | £20 | £40 |

## JAN & DEAN
| | | | | | | | |
|---|---|---|---|---|---|---|---|
| Baby Talk | 7" | London | HLN8936 | 1959 | £6 | £12 | |
| Batman | 7" | Liberty | LIB55860 | 1966 | £2.50 | £6 | |
| Clementine | 7" | London | HLU9063 | 1960 | £5 | £10 | |
| Command Performance | LP | Liberty | LRP3403/LST7403 | 1965 | £6 | £15 | US |
| Dead Man's Curve | 7" | Liberty | LIB55672 | 1964 | £1.50 | £4 | |
| Dead Man's Curve/New Girl In School | LP | Liberty | LBY1220 | 1964 | £5 | £12 | |

| Title | Format | Label | Catalogue | Year | Price 1 | Price 2 | Notes |
|---|---|---|---|---|---|---|---|
| Drag City | LP | Liberty | LRP3339/LST7339. | 1963 | £6 | £15 | US |
| Drag City | 7" EP | Liberty | LEP2155 | 1964 | £7.50 | £15 | French |
| Drag City | 7" | Liberty | LIB55641 | 1964 | £1.50 | £4 | |
| Filet Of Soul | LP | Liberty | LBY1339 | 1966 | £5 | £12 | |
| Folk And Roll | LP | Liberty | LBY1304 | 1965 | £5 | £12 | |
| From All Over The World | 7" | Liberty | LIB55766 | 1965 | £2 | £5 | |
| Golden Hits | LP | Liberty | LBL/LBS83016 | 1967 | £4 | £10 | |
| Golden Hits | LP | Liberty | LBY1279 | 1962 | £6 | £15 | |
| Golden Hits Vol. 2 | LP | Liberty | LRP3417/LST7417. | 1965 | £4 | £10 | US |
| Golden Hits Vol. 3 | LP | Liberty | LRP3460/LST7460. | 1966 | £4 | £10 | US |
| Heart And Soul | 7" | London | HLH9395 | 1961 | £4 | £8 | |
| Honolulu Lulu | 7" | Liberty | LIB55613 | 1963 | £1.50 | £4 | |
| I Found A Girl | 7" | Liberty | LIB55833 | 1965 | £1.50 | £4 | |
| Jan & Dean | LP | Dore | 101 | 1960 | £37.50 | £75 | US with photo |
| Linda | 7" | Liberty | LIB55531 | 1963 | £1.50 | £4 | |
| Little Old Lady From Pasadena | LP | Liberty | LRP3377/LST7377. | 1964 | £6 | £15 | US |
| Little Old Lady From Pasadena | 7" EP | Liberty | LEP2189 | 1964 | £7.50 | £15 | French |
| Little Old Lady From Pasadena | 7" | Liberty | LIB55704 | 1964 | £1.50 | £4 | |
| Meet Batman | 7" | Liberty | LBY1309 | 1966 | £6 | £15 | |
| Norwegian Wood | 7" | Liberty | LIB10225 | 1966 | £2.50 | £6 | |
| Pop Symphony No. 1 | LP | Liberty | LRP3414/LST7414. | 1965 | £6 | £15 | US |
| Popsicle | LP | Liberty | LRP3458/LST7458. | 1966 | £6 | £15 | US |
| Popsicle | 7" | Liberty | LIB10244 | 1966 | £2 | £5 | |
| Ride The Wild Surf | LP | Liberty | LBY1229 | 1964 | £6 | £15 | |
| Ride The Wild Surf | 7" | Liberty | LIB55724 | 1964 | £1.50 | £4 | |
| Save For A Rainy Day | LP | J&D | 101 | 1967 | £37.50 | £75 | US |
| Sidewalk Surfin' | 7" | Liberty | LIB55727 | 1965 | £1.50 | £4 | |
| Sunday Kind Of Love | 7" | Liberty | LIB55397 | 1962 | £1.50 | £4 | |
| Surf 'n' Drag Hits | 7" EP | Liberty | LEP2213 | 1965 | £6 | £12 | |
| Surf City | LP | Liberty | LBY1163 | 1963 | £6 | £15 | |
| Surf City | 7" EP | Liberty | LEP2112 | 1963 | £7.50 | £15 | French |
| Surf City | 7" | Liberty | LIB55580 | 1963 | £1.50 | £4 | |
| Take Linda Surfing | LP | Liberty | LRP3294/LST7294. | 1963 | £8 | £20 | US, with Beach Boys |
| Tennessee | 7" | Liberty | LIB10252 | 1966 | £4 | £8 | |
| There's A Girl | 7" | London | HLU8990 | 1959 | £6 | £12 | |
| Titanic Twosome | 7" EP | Liberty | LEP2258 | 1966 | £6 | £12 | |
| Yellow Balloon | 7" | CBS | 202630 | 1967 | £2.50 | £6 | |
| You Really Know How To Hurt A Guy | 7" | Liberty | LIB55792 | 1964 | £2 | £5 | |

## JAN & KELLY

| Title | Format | Label | Catalogue | Year | Price 1 | Price 2 | Notes |
|---|---|---|---|---|---|---|---|
| And Then He Kicked Me | 7" | Philips | BF1323 | 1964 | £1.50 | £4 | |
| Time For A Laugh | 7" EP | Philips | BE12536 | 1963 | £2.50 | £6 | |

## JAN & KJELD

| Title | Format | Label | Catalogue | Year | Price 1 | Price 2 | Notes |
|---|---|---|---|---|---|---|---|
| Goldener Löwe Fur | LP | Ariola | 70586IT | 1964 | £10 | £25 | German |
| Jan Und Kjeld | LP | Ariola | 31023 | 1964 | £8 | £20 | German |
| Kids From Copenhagen | LP | Ember | EMB3312 | 1960 | £6 | £15 | |
| Les Banjo Boys à Paris | 10" LP | Vogue | KV26 | 1960 | £8 | £20 | French |
| With A Banjo On My Knee | LP | Ariola | 31231 | 1965 | £8 | £20 | German |

## JAN & LORRAINE

| Title | Format | Label | Catalogue | Year | Price 1 | Price 2 | Notes |
|---|---|---|---|---|---|---|---|
| Gypsy People | LP | ABC | ABCS691 | 1969 | £8 | £20 | US |

## JAN DUKES DE GREY

| Title | Format | Label | Catalogue | Year | Price 1 | Price 2 | Notes |
|---|---|---|---|---|---|---|---|
| Mice & Rats In The Loft | LP | Transatlantic | TRA234 | 1971 | £25 | £50 | |
| Sorcerers | LP | Nova | SDN8 | 1970 | £10 | £25 | |

## JANE

| Title | Format | Label | Catalogue | Year | Price 1 | Price 2 | Notes |
|---|---|---|---|---|---|---|---|
| Fire, Water, Earth And Air | LP | Brain | 1084 | 1975 | £6 | £15 | German |
| Here We Are | LP | Brain | 1032 | 1973 | £6 | £15 | German |
| Lady | LP | Brain | 1066 | 1975 | £6 | £15 | German |
| Three | LP | Brain | 1048 | 1974 | £6 | £15 | German |
| Together | LP | Brain | 1002 | 1972 | £8 | £20 | German |

## JANES, PETER

| Title | Format | Label | Catalogue | Year | Price 1 | Price 2 | Notes |
|---|---|---|---|---|---|---|---|
| Do You Believe | 7" | CBS | 3299 | 1968 | £2 | £5 | |
| Emperors And Armies | 7" | CBS | 3004 | 1967 | £1.50 | £4 | |

## JANE'S ADDICTION

| Title | Format | Label | Catalogue | Year | Price 1 | Price 2 | Notes |
|---|---|---|---|---|---|---|---|
| Been Caught Stealing | CD-s | WEA | W0011CD | 1991 | £2 | £5 | |
| Classic Girl | CD-s | WEA | W0031CD | 1991 | £2 | £5 | |
| Three Days | CD-s | WEA | W9584CD | 1990 | £2 | £5 | |

## JANIE

| Title | Format | Label | Catalogue | Year | Price 1 | Price 2 | Notes |
|---|---|---|---|---|---|---|---|
| You Better Not Do That | 7" | Capitol | CL15180 | 1961 | £1.50 | £4 | |

## JANIS, CONRAD

| Title | Format | Label | Catalogue | Year | Price 1 | Price 2 | Notes |
|---|---|---|---|---|---|---|---|
| Dixieland Jam Session | LP | London | LTZU15095 | 1957 | £5 | £12 | |

## JANIS, JOHNNY

| Title | Format | Label | Catalogue | Year | Price 1 | Price 2 | Notes |
|---|---|---|---|---|---|---|---|
| Better To Love You | 7" | London | HLU8650 | 1958 | £2.50 | £6 | |
| For The First Time | LP | ABC-Paramount | LP140 | 1957 | £10 | £25 | US |

## JANSCH, BERT

With Davy Graham maintaining a deliberately low profile, it was left to Bert Jansch to define the sound and style of folk guitar playing in the sixties. His serviceable folk-singer's voice gives added interest to his records, but the guitar is the real focus – beginning with a faultless version of Graham's difficult 'Angie' and moving onwards from there.

| | | | | | | | |
|---|---|---|---|---|---|---|---|
| Avocet | LP | Charisma | CLASS6 | 1979 | £4 | £10 | |
| Bert Jansch | LP | Transatlantic | TRA125 | 1965 | £6 | £15 | |
| Bert Jansch | 7" EP | Transatlantic | TRAEP145 | 1966 | £5 | £10 | |
| Birthday Blues | LP | Transatlantic | TRA179 | 1968 | £6 | £15 | |
| Black Birds Of Brittany | 7" | Streetsong | 1 | 1978 | £2 | £5 | ... picture sleeve, with Richard Harvey |
| From The Outside | LP | Konexion | KOMA788006 | 1985 | £4 | £10 | |
| Heartbreak | LP | Logo | LOGO1035 | 1982 | £4 | £10 | |
| It Don't Bother Me | LP | Transatlantic | TRA132 | 1965 | £6 | £15 | |
| Jack Orion | LP | Transatlantic | TRA143 | 1966 | £6 | £15 | |
| L.A. Turnaround | LP | Charisma | CAS1090 | 1974 | £4 | £10 | |
| Life Depends On Love | 7" | Transatlantic | BIG102 | 1968 | £2 | £5 | |
| Live At La Foret | LP | Columbia | YX7273AK | 1980 | £6 | £15 | Japanese |
| Lucky Thirteen | LP | Vanguard | VSD79212 | 1966 | £6 | £15 | US |
| Moonshine | LP | Reprise | K44225 | 1973 | £4 | £10 | |
| Nicola | LP | Transatlantic | TRA157 | 1967 | £6 | £15 | |
| Rare Conundrum | LP | Charisma | CAS1111 | 1977 | £4 | £10 | |
| Rosemary Lane | LP | Transatlantic | TRA235 | 1971 | £5 | £12 | |
| Thirteen Down | LP | Sonet | SNKF162 | 1980 | £4 | £10 | |

## JANSCH, BERT & JOHN RENBOURN

| | | | | | | | |
|---|---|---|---|---|---|---|---|
| Bert & John | LP | Transatlantic | TRA144 | 1966 | £6 | £15 | |
| Stepping Stones | LP | Vanguard | VSD6506 | 1969 | £5 | £12 | US (As 'Bert & John' with 2 extra tracks) |

## JANUS

| | | | | | | | |
|---|---|---|---|---|---|---|---|
| Gravedigger | LP | Harvest | IC06229433 | 1972 | £37.50 | £75 | German |

## JAPAN

The pretty-boy posing of Japan was an unlikely environment for intelligent, questing music to be produced, and yet with each record release, the group became more and more of a vital force. Peaking with the refreshingly innovative *Ghosts*, it was perhaps inevitable that David Sylvian would then wish to continue the quest on his own.

| | | | | | | | |
|---|---|---|---|---|---|---|---|
| Don't Rain On My Parade | 7" | Ariola | AHA510 | 1978 | £5 | £10 | |
| Gentlemen Take Polaroids | CD-s | Virgin | CDT32 | 1988 | £2 | £5 | 3" single |
| Ghosts | CD-s | Virgin | CDT11 | 1988 | £2 | £5 | 3" single |
| Ghosts | 7" | Virgin | VSY472 | 1982 | £1.50 | £4 | picture disc |
| I Second That Emotion | 7" | Ariola | AHA559 | 1980 | £2 | £5 | red vinyl |
| Interview Album | LP | Ariola | | 1979 | £5 | £12 | US promo |
| Life In Tokyo | 12" | Ariola | AHAD540 | 1979 | £2.50 | £6 | red vinyl |
| Sometimes I Feel So Low | 7" | Ariola | AHA529 | 1978 | £2 | £5 | |
| Sometimes I Feel So Low | 7" | Ariola | AHA529 | 1978 | £4 | £8 | blue vinyl |
| Unconventional | 7" | Ariola | AHA525 | 1978 | £6 | £12 | picture sleeve |

## JARMAN, JOSEPH

| | | | | | | | |
|---|---|---|---|---|---|---|---|
| As If It Were Seasons | LP | Delmark | DS417 | 1969 | £5 | £12 | |
| Song For | LP | Delmark | DL410/DS9410 | 1967 | £5 | £12 | |
| Together Alone | LP | Delmark | DS428 | 1974 | £5 | £12 | with Anthony Braxton |

## JARMELS

| | | | | | | | |
|---|---|---|---|---|---|---|---|
| Little Bit Of Soap | 7" | Top Rank | JAR580 | 1961 | £10 | £20 | |
| She Loves To Dance | 7" | Top Rank | JAR560 | 1961 | £5 | £10 | |

## JARRE, JEAN-MICHEL

There is no rarer record than Jean-Michel Jarre's *Music For Supermarkets* – the LP was issued in a limited edition of just one copy and auctioned for charity in 1983, when it fetched a sum of the order of £10,000. Meanwhile, there are a couple of other rare Jarre albums which the keen collector does stand a reasonable chance of obtaining, although at a considerable price none the less, for the early soundtracks have never had a UK issue and are scarce even in their countries of origin.

| | | | | | | | |
|---|---|---|---|---|---|---|---|
| Calypso | CD-s | Polydor | PZCD84 | 1990 | £10 | £20 | |
| Cartolina | 7" | Labrador | LA4050 | 1973 | £15 | £30 | French |
| Chronologie 4 | 7" | Dreyfus | JMJ0693 | 1993 | £10 | £20 | French |
| Deserted Palace | LP | Sam Fox | SF1029 | 1972 | £330 | £500 | US promo |
| Equinoxe 4 (remix) | 12" | Polydor | JM1 | 1979 | £5 | £12 | promo |
| Equinoxe 5 | 7" | Polydor | POSP20 | 1978 | £2 | £5 | etched autograph |
| Equinoxe 7 (live) | 7" | Polydor | 2001968 | 1980 | £4 | £8 | |
| Hong Kong | CD-s | Dreyfus | FDM37521 | 1994 | £25 | £50 | French |
| Hypnose | 7" | Motors | MT4043 | 1973 | £37.50 | £75 | French |
| La Cage | 7" | Pathe | C00611739 | 1971 | £180 | £300 | French, best auctioned |
| Les Granges brûlées | LP | Eden Roc | ER62502 | 1973 | £100 | £200 | French |
| Les Granges brûlées | LP | Gamma | GS177 | 1973 | £100 | £200 | French |
| Les Granges brûlées | 7" | Eden Roc | ER62002 | 1973 | £30 | £60 | French |
| London Kid | CD-s | Polydor | PZCD32 | 1988 | £10 | £20 | |
| Magnetic Fields 4 (remix) | 7" | Polydor | POSP363 | 1981 | £2.50 | £6 | |
| Orient Express | 7" | Polydor | POSP430 | 1982 | £2.50 | £6 | |
| Orient Express | 12" | Polydor | POSPX430DJ | 1982 | £10 | £25 | promo |
| Oxygène | LP | Polydor | C8813 | 1988 | £4 | £10 | HMV box set |
| Oxygène | CD | Mobile Fidelity | UDCD613 | 1994 | £6 | £15 | US audiophile |
| Oxygène | CD | Polydor | C8813 | 1988 | £6 | £15 | HMV box set |
| Oxygène 4 | CD-s | Polydor | PZCD55 | 1989 | £6 | £15 | |
| Pop Corn | 7" | Motors | MT4028 | 1971 | £37.50 | £75 | French |
| Rendezvous 4 (remix) | 12" | Polydor | POSPX788 | 1986 | £10 | £20 | 2 different sleeves |
| Revolutions | CD-s | Polydor | PZCD25 | 1988 | £10 | £20 | |
| Tenth Anniversary | CD | Polydor | 8337372 | 1987 | £20 | £40 | boxed set |

| Une Alarme qui swingue | 7" | Dreyfus | JMJ1001 | 1991 | £15 | £30 | French |
| Zig Zag | 7" | Motors | MT4032 | 1973 | £10 | £20 | French |
| Zoolook (remix) | 12" | Polydor | POSPX718 | 1984 | £6 | £15 | |
| Zoolookologie (remix) | 7" | Polydor | POSPG740 | 1985 | £6 | £12 | double |
| Zoolookologie (remix) | 12" | Polydor | POSPX740 | 1985 | £6 | £15 | |

## JARRETT, KEITH

| Arbour Zena | LP | ECM | ECM1070ST | 1975 | £5 | £12 | |
| Backhand | LP | Impulse | AS9305 | 1975 | £6 | £15 | US |
| Belonging | LP | ECM | ECM1050ST | 1974 | £5 | £12 | |
| Birth | LP | Atlantic | SD1612 | 197– | £6 | £15 | US |
| Byablue | LP | Impulse | AS9331 | 1976 | £5 | £12 | US |
| Death And The Flower | LP | Impulse | IMPL8006 | 1975 | £6 | £15 | |
| El Juicio | LP | Atlantic | SD1673 | 1975 | £6 | £15 | US |
| Facing You | LP | ECM | ECM1017ST | 1971 | £5 | £12 | |
| Fort Yawuh | LP | Impulse | AS9240 | 1973 | £6 | £15 | US |
| Hymns/Spheres | LP | ECM | ECM1086/7ST | 1976 | £6 | £15 | double |
| In The Light | LP | ECM | ECM1033/4ST | 1973 | £6 | £15 | double |
| Koln Concert | LP | ECM | ECM1064/5ST | 1975 | £6 | £15 | double |
| Luminessence | LP | ECM | ECM1049ST | 1974 | £5 | £12 | |
| Mourning Of A Star | LP | Atlantic | K40309 | 1972 | £6 | £15 | |
| Mysteries | LP | Impulse | AS9315 | 1976 | £5 | £12 | US |
| Ruta And Daitya | LP | ECM | ECM1021ST | 1972 | £5 | £12 | with Jack DeJohnette |
| Shades | LP | Impulse | ASD9322 | 1976 | £5 | £12 | US |
| Solo Concerts – Bremen/Lausanne | LP | ECM | ECM1035/6/7ST | 1973 | £10 | £25 | triple |
| Staircase | LP | ECM | ECM1090/1ST | 1976 | £6 | £15 | double |
| Sun Bear Concerts | LP | ECM | ECM1100ST | 1976 | £50 | £100 | 10 LP set |
| Survivors' Suite | LP | ECM | ECM1085ST | 1976 | £4 | £10 | |
| Treasure Island | LP | Impulse | AS9274 | 1974 | £6 | £15 | US |

## JARVIS STREET REVUE

| Mr. Oil Man | LP | Columbia | 90020 | 1970 | £62.50 | £125 | Canadian |

## JASMIN T

| Some Other Guy | 7" | Tangerine | DP0013 | 1969 | £2 | £5 | |

## JASMINE MINKS

| Think | 7" | Creation | CRE004 | 1984 | £5 | £10 | |
| What's Happening | 7" | Creation | CRE018 | 1985 | £2 | £5 | |
| Where The Traffic Goes | 7" | Creation | CRE008 | 1984 | £4 | £8 | |

## JASON CREST

| Black Mass | 7" | Philips | BF1809 | 1969 | £50 | £100 | |
| Juliano The Bull | 7" | Philips | BF1650 | 1968 | £12.50 | £25 | |
| Lemon Tree | 7" | Philips | BF1687 | 1968 | £12.50 | £25 | |
| Turquoise Tandem Cycle | 7" | Philips | BF1633 | 1968 | £15 | £30 | |
| Waterloo Road | 7" | Philips | BF1752 | 1969 | £12.50 | £25 | |

## JASON'S GENERATION

| It's Up To You | 7" | Polydor | 56042 | 1966 | £15 | £30 | |

## JASPAR, BOBBY

| Bobby Jaspar | LP | London | LTZU15128 | 1958 | £10 | £25 | |
| Bobby Jaspar And His All Stars | LP | Felsted | PDL85017 | 1956 | £10 | £25 | |
| New Jazz Group | 10" LP | Vogue | LDE167 | 1956 | £10 | £25 | |
| New Jazz Vol. 1 | 10" LP | Vogue | LDE125 | 1955 | £20 | £40 | |
| New Sounds From Europe Vol. 4 | 10" LP | Vogue | LDE041 | 1954 | £20 | £40 | |

## JASPER

| Liberation | LP | Spark | SRLP103 | 1969 | £150 | £250 | |

## JASPER WRATH

| Jasper Wrath | LP | Sunflower | SNF5003 | 1971 | £30 | £60 | US |

## JAVALINS

| For Twen | LP | Columbia | SMC83880 | 1984 | £10 | £25 | German |

## JAWBONE

| Gotta Go | 7" | B&C. | CB190 | 1972 | £1.50 | £4 | |
| How's Ya Pa | 7" | Carnaby | CNS4007 | 1970 | £2.50 | £6 | |
| Jawbone | LP | Carnaby | CNLS6004 | 1970 | £30 | £60 | |
| Way Way Down | 7" | Carnaby | CNS4020 | 1971 | £2.50 | £6 | |

## JAXON, BOB

| Ali Baba | 7" | London | HL8156 | 1955 | £10 | £20 | |
| Beach Party | 7" | RCA | RCA1019 | 1957 | £30 | £60 | |

## JAXON, FRANKIE

| Male Blues Vol. 6 | 7" EP | Collector | JE110 | 1959 | £4 | £8 | |

## JAY

| I Rise, I Fall | 7" | Coral | Q72471 | 1964 | £5 | £10 | |

## JAY, DAVID & RENE HALKETT

| Nothing | 7" | 4AD | AD112 | 1981 | £2.50 | £6 | with lyric sheet |

## JAY, LAURIE COMBO

| Song Called Soul | 7" | Decca | F12083 | 1965 | £7.50 | £15 | |

| | | | | | | | |
|---|---|---|---|---|---|---|---|
| Teenage Idol | 7" | HMV | POP1234 | 1963 | £1.50 | £4 | |

## JAY, PETER & THE BLUEMEN

| | | | | | | | |
|---|---|---|---|---|---|---|---|
| Just Too Late | 7" | Triumph | RGM1000 | 1960 | £7.50 | £15 | |
| Paradise Garden | 7" | Pye | 7N15290 | 1960 | £10 | £20 | |

## JAY, PETER & THE JAYWALKERS

| | | | | | | | |
|---|---|---|---|---|---|---|---|
| Before The Beginning | 7" | Piccadilly | 7N35325 | 1966 | £2.50 | £6 | |
| Can Can '62 | 7" | Decca | F11531 | 1962 | £1.50 | £4 | |
| Parade Of Tin Soldiers | 7" | Decca | F11757 | 1963 | £1.50 | £4 | |
| Parchman Farm | 7" | Piccadilly | 7N35220 | 1965 | £4 | £8 | |
| Poet And Peasant | 7" | Decca | F11659 | 1963 | £1.50 | £4 | |
| Tonight You're Gonna Fall | 7" | Piccadilly | 7N35212 | 1964 | £1.50 | £4 | |
| Totem Pole | 7" | Decca | F11593 | 1963 | £1.50 | £4 | |
| Where Did Our Love Go | 7" | Piccadilly | 7N35199 | 1964 | £2 | £5 | |
| You Girl | 7" | Decca | F11840 | 1964 | £1.50 | £4 | |

## JAY & JOYA

| | | | | | | | |
|---|---|---|---|---|---|---|---|
| I'll Be Lonely | 7" | Trojan | TR633 | 1968 | £2 | £5 | Supersonics B side |

## JAY & THE AMERICANS

| | | | | | | | |
|---|---|---|---|---|---|---|---|
| At The Cafe Wha | LP | United Artists | UAL3300/ UAS6300 | 1963 | £6 | £15 | US |
| Blockbusters | LP | United Artists | UAL3417/ UAS6417 | 1965 | £6 | £15 | US |
| Cara Mia | 7" | United Artists | UP1094 | 1965 | £1.50 | £4 | |
| Come A Little Bit Closer | LP | United Artists | UAL3407/ UAS6407 | 1964 | £6 | £15 | US |
| Come A Little Bit Closer | 7" EP | United Artists | 36054 | 1964 | £7.50 | £15 | French |
| Come A Little Bit Closer | 7" EP | United Artists | UEP1003 | 1965 | £6 | £12 | |
| Come A Little Closer | 7" | United Artists | UP1069 | 1964 | £1.50 | £4 | |
| Come Dance With Me | 7" | United Artists | UP1039 | 1964 | £1.50 | £4 | |
| Crying | 7" | United Artists | UP1132 | 1966 | £1.50 | £4 | |
| En français | 7" EP | United Artists | 36102 | 1966 | £10 | £20 | French |
| Got Hung Up Along The Way | 7" | United Artists | UP1191 | 1967 | £10 | £20 | |
| Greatest Hits | LP | United Artists | UAL3453/ UAS6453 | 1965 | £6 | £15 | US |
| Greatest Hits Vol. 2 | LP | United Artists | UAL3555/ UAS6555 | 1966 | £6 | £15 | US |
| Jay And The Americans | LP | United Artists | ULP1117 | 1966 | £5 | £12 | |
| Kansas City | 7" EP | United Artists | 36027 | 1963 | £7.50 | £15 | French |
| Let's Lock The Door | 7" | United Artists | UP1075 | 1965 | £1.50 | £4 | |
| Livin' Above Your Head | LP | United Artists | UAL3534/ UAS6534 | 1966 | £6 | £15 | US |
| Living Above Your Head | 7" | United Artists | UP1142 | 1966 | £5 | £10 | |
| Living With Jay & The Americans | 7" EP | United Artists | UEP1017 | 1966 | £7.50 | £15 | |
| Raining In My Sunshine | 7" | United Artists | UP1162 | 1966 | £1.50 | £4 | |
| She Cried | LP | United Artists | UAL3222/ UAS6222 | 1962 | £6 | £15 | US |
| She Cried | 7" EP | HMV | POP1009 | 1962 | £2.50 | £6 | |
| Some Enchanted Evening | 7" EP | United Artists | 36065 | 1965 | £7.50 | £15 | French |
| Some Enchanted Evening | 7" | United Artists | UP1108 | 1965 | £1.50 | £4 | |
| Strangers Tomorrow | 7" | United Artists | UP1018 | 1963 | £1.50 | £4 | |
| Sunday And Me | LP | United Artists | UAL3474/ UAS6474 | 1966 | £6 | £15 | US |
| Sunday And Me | 7" EP | United Artists | 36074 | 1965 | £7.50 | £15 | French |
| Sunday And Me | 7" | United Artists | UP1119 | 1966 | £1.50 | £4 | |
| Think Of The Good Times | 7" | United Artists | UP1088 | 1965 | £1.50 | £4 | |
| This Is It | 7" | United Artists | UP1002 | 1964 | £1.50 | £4 | |
| Tonight | 7" EP | United Artists | 36018 | 1962 | £7.50 | £15 | French |
| Try Some Of This | LP | United Artists | UAL3562/ UAS6562 | 1967 | £6 | £15 | US |
| Why Can't You Bring Me Home | 7" | United Artists | UP1129 | 1966 | £1.50 | £4 | |

## JAY & THE TECHNIQUES

| | | | | | | | |
|---|---|---|---|---|---|---|---|
| Apples, Peaches, Pumpkin Pie | LP | Philips | (S)BL7834 | 1967 | £4 | £10 | |
| Apples, Peaches, Pumpkin Pie | 7" | Philips | BF1597 | 1967 | £2 | £5 | |
| Baby Make Your Own Sweet Music | 7" | Mercury | MF1034 | 1968 | £2 | £5 | |
| Keep The Ball Rolling | 7" | Philips | BF1618 | 1967 | £1.50 | £4 | |
| Strawberry Shortcake | 7" | Philips | BF1644 | 1968 | £1.50 | £4 | |

## JAY BEE FOUR

| | | | | | | | |
|---|---|---|---|---|---|---|---|
| Lucille | 7" EP | Barclay | 70751 | 1965 | £4 | £8 | French |

## JAY BOYS

| | | | | | | | |
|---|---|---|---|---|---|---|---|
| Splendour Splash | 7" | Trojan | TR665 | 1969 | £1.50 | £4 | Trevor Shield B side |

## JAY JAYS

| | | | | | | | |
|---|---|---|---|---|---|---|---|
| Jay Jays | LP | Philips | 625819 | 1966 | £75 | £150 | Dutch |

## JAYBIRDS

Although these singles conform to the Embassy label's policy of issuing sound-alike versions of current chart hits, the fact that the Jaybirds later became Ten Years After gives them a modest collectability. (It should be noted, however, that Alvin Lee has denied his involvement with the Embassy group.)

| | | | | | | | |
|---|---|---|---|---|---|---|---|
| All Day And All Of The Night | 7" | Embassy | WB663 | 1964 | £2 | £5 | |
| Juliet | 7" | Embassy | WB635 | 1964 | £1.50 | £4 | |

| | | | | | | | |
|---|---|---|---|---|---|---|---|
| Tell Me When | 7" | Embassy | WB624 | 1964 | £1.50 | £4 | |

**JAYBIRDS (2)**
| | | | | | | |
|---|---|---|---|---|---|---|
| Somebody Help Me | 7" | Sue | WI4013 | 1966 | £6 | £12 |

**JAYE, JERRY**
| | | | | | | |
|---|---|---|---|---|---|---|
| My Girl Josephine | 7" | London | HLU10128 | 1967 | £7.50 | £15 |

**JAYE SISTERS**
| | | | | | | |
|---|---|---|---|---|---|---|
| Sure Fire Love | 7" | London | HLT9011 | 1959 | £10 | £20 |

**JAYHAWKS**
| | | | | | | | |
|---|---|---|---|---|---|---|---|
| Stranded In The Jungle | 7" | Parlophone | R4228 | 1956 | £150 | £250 | best auctioned |

**JAYNETTS**
| | | | | | | | |
|---|---|---|---|---|---|---|---|
| Sally Go Round The Roses | LP | Tuff | LP13 | 1963 | £25 | £50 | US |
| Sally Go Round The Roses | 7" | Stateside | SS227 | 1963 | £2 | £5 | |

**JAZZ AT STORYVILLE**
| | | | | | | |
|---|---|---|---|---|---|---|
| Jazz At Storyville | LP | London | LTZC15061 | 1957 | £6 | £15 |

**JAZZ AT THE PHILHARMONIC**
| | | | | | | |
|---|---|---|---|---|---|---|
| 1955 Vol. 1 | LP | Columbia | 33CX10078 | 1957 | £6 | £15 |
| 1955 Vol. 2 | LP | Columbia | 33CX10079 | 1957 | £6 | £15 |
| Jam Concert No. 1 | LP | Columbia | 33CX10059 | 1956 | £6 | £15 |
| Jam Session | LP | Columbia | 33CX10030 | 1956 | £6 | £15 |
| Jam Session | LP | Emarcy | EJL103 | 1956 | £6 | £15 |
| Jam Session Group | LP | Columbia | 33CX10043 | 1956 | £6 | £15 |
| Jam Session No. 2 | LP | Columbia | 33CX10021 | 1956 | £6 | £15 |
| Jam Session No. 5 | LP | Columbia | 33CX10067 | 1957 | £6 | £15 |
| Midnight Jazz At Carnegie Hall | LP | Columbia | 33CX10020 | 1956 | £8 | £20 |
| New Vol. 1 | LP | Columbia | 33CX10032 | 1956 | £6 | £15 |
| New Vol. 2 | LP | Columbia | 33CX10033 | 1956 | £6 | £15 |
| New Vol. 3 | LP | Columbia | 33CX10034 | 1956 | £6 | £15 |
| New Vol. 4 | LP | Columbia | 33CX10035 | 1956 | £6 | £15 |
| New Vol. 5 | LP | Columbia | 33CX10036 | 1956 | £6 | £15 |
| New Vol. 7 | LP | Columbia | 33CX10037 | 1956 | £6 | £15 |
| Volume 1 | LP | Columbia | 33CX10009 | 1955 | £8 | £20 |
| Volume 2 | LP | Columbia | 33CX10010 | 1955 | £8 | £20 |
| Volume 3 | LP | Columbia | 33CX10011 | 1955 | £8 | £20 |

**JAZZ BUTCHER**
| | | | | | | | |
|---|---|---|---|---|---|---|---|
| Christmas With The Pygmies | 7" | Glass | HMMM001 | 1986 | £2.50 | £6 | promo |
| Girl Go | CD-s | Creation | CRE77CD | 1990 | £2 | £5 | |

**JAZZ CITY WORKSHOP**
| | | | | | | |
|---|---|---|---|---|---|---|
| Jazz City Workshop | LP | London | LTZN15037 | 1957 | £5 | £12 |

**JAZZ COURIERS**
| | | | | | | |
|---|---|---|---|---|---|---|
| Couriers Of Jazz | LP | London | LTZL15188 | 1960 | £50 | £100 |
| In Concert | LP | MFP | MFP1072 | 1966 | £6 | £15 |
| In Concert | LP | Tempo | TAP22 | 1958 | £50 | £100 |
| Jazz Couriers | LP | Tempo | TAP15 | 1957 | £50 | £100 |
| Jazz Couriers | 7" EP | Tempo | EXA75 | 1957 | £10 | £20 |
| Jazz Couriers | 7" EP | Tempo | EXA87 | 1958 | £10 | £20 |
| Last Word | LP | Tempo | TAP26 | 1959 | £50 | £100 |

**JAZZ CRUSADERS**
| | | | | | | |
|---|---|---|---|---|---|---|
| Thing | LP | Fontana | 688149ZL | 1966 | £5 | £12 |

**JAZZ GIANTS**
| | | | | | | |
|---|---|---|---|---|---|---|
| Jazz Giants | 10" LP | Emarcy | EJT751 | 1957 | £6 | £15 |

**JAZZ IN A STABLE GROUP**
| | | | | | | |
|---|---|---|---|---|---|---|
| Jazz In A Stable | LP | Esquire | 32018 | 1956 | £6 | £15 |

**JAZZ MESSAGE GROUP**
| | | | | | | |
|---|---|---|---|---|---|---|
| Jazz Message | LP | London | LTZC15028 | 1957 | £5 | £12 |

**JAZZ MODES**
| | | | | | | |
|---|---|---|---|---|---|---|
| Jazz Modes | LP | London | LTZK15203/ SAHK6117 | 1961 | £10 | £25 |
| Most Happy Fella | LP | London | LTZK15191 | 1960 | £10 | £25 |

**JAZZ ROCK EXPERIENCE**
| | | | | | | |
|---|---|---|---|---|---|---|
| Jazz Rock Experience | LP | Nova | SDN19 | 1970 | £6 | £15 |

**JAZZ STUDIO FOUR GROUP**
| | | | | | | |
|---|---|---|---|---|---|---|
| Jazz Studio Four | LP | Brunswick | LAT8098 | 1956 | £5 | £12 |

**JAZZ TODAY UNIT**
| | | | | | | |
|---|---|---|---|---|---|---|
| Jam Session | 10" LP | Polygon | JTL1 | 1955 | £5 | £12 |

**JAZZ WAVE LTD.**
| | | | | | | |
|---|---|---|---|---|---|---|
| On Tour | LP | Blue Note | BST89905 | 1970 | £4 | £10 |

**JB'S**
| | | | | | | |
|---|---|---|---|---|---|---|
| Breakin' Bread | LP | Polydor | 2391161 | 1975 | £10 | £25 |

| Title | Format | Label | Catalog | Year | | | Notes |
|---|---|---|---|---|---|---|---|
| Damn Right I Am Somebody | LP | Polydor | 2391125 | 1974 | £15 | £30 | |
| Doing It To Death | LP | Polydor | 2391087 | 1974 | £20 | £40 | |
| Doing It To Death | 7" | Polydor | 2066322 | 1973 | £1.50 | £4 | |
| Food For Thought | LP | Polydor | 2391034 | 1972 | £15 | £30 | |
| Gimme Some More | 7" | Mojo | 2093007 | 1974 | £2 | £5 | |
| Givin' Up Food For Funk | 7" | Mojo | 2093021 | 1974 | £2 | £5 | |
| Giving Up Food For Funk | LP | Polydor | 2391204 | 1976 | £15 | £30 | |
| Grunt | 7" | Mojo | 2027002 | 1971 | £2 | £5 | |
| Hot Pants Road | 7" | Mojo | 2093016 | 1974 | £2 | £5 | |
| Hustle With Speed | LP | Polydor | 2391194 | 1975 | £10 | £25 | |
| JB Shout | 7" | Mojo | 2093025 | 1974 | £1.50 | £4 | |
| Pass The Peas | LP | Polydor | 2918004 | 1972 | £15 | £30 | |
| These Are The JB's | 7" | Polydor | 2001115 | 1971 | £2 | £5 | |

## JEAN, CATHY & THE ROOMATES

| Title | Format | Label | Catalog | Year | | |
|---|---|---|---|---|---|---|
| Please Love Me | 7" | Parlophone | R4764 | 1961 | £7.50 | £15 |

## JEAN, EARL

| Title | Format | Label | Catalog | Year | | |
|---|---|---|---|---|---|---|
| I'm Into Something Good | 7" | Colpix | PX729 | 1964 | £5 | £10 |
| Randy | 7" | Colpix | PX748 | 1964 | £5 | £10 |

## JEAN, LANA

| Title | Format | Label | Catalog | Year | | |
|---|---|---|---|---|---|---|
| It Hurts To be Sixteen | 7" | Pye | 7N25214 | 1963 | £4 | £8 |

## JEAN & THE STATESIDERS

| Title | Format | Label | Catalog | Year | | |
|---|---|---|---|---|---|---|
| Putty In Your Hands | 7" | Columbia | DB7287 | 1964 | £2 | £5 |
| You Won't Forget Me | 7" | Columbia | DB7439 | 1965 | £2 | £5 |
| Mama Didn't Lie | 7" | Columbia | DB7651 | 1965 | £2 | £5 |

## JEANNIE

| Title | Format | Label | Catalog | Year | | |
|---|---|---|---|---|---|---|
| Don't Lie To Me | 7" | Piccadilly | 7N35147 | 1963 | £1.50 | £4 |
| I Want You | 7" | Piccadilly | 7N35164 | 1964 | £1.50 | £4 |

## JEANS, AUDREY

| Title | Format | Label | Catalog | Year | | |
|---|---|---|---|---|---|---|
| Ticky Ticky Tick | 7" | Decca | F10768 | 1956 | £2 | £5 |

## JEEPS

| Title | Format | Label | Catalog | Year | | |
|---|---|---|---|---|---|---|
| He Saw Eesaw | 7" | Strike | JH308 | 1966 | £1.50 | £4 |

## JEFFERSON, BLIND LEMON

| Title | Format | Label | Catalog | Year | | | Notes |
|---|---|---|---|---|---|---|---|
| Blind Lemon | LP | Riverside | 126 | | £8 | £20 | US |
| Blind Lemon Jefferson | 10" LP | Poydras | 99 | 195– | £6 | £15 | |
| Blind Lemon Jefferson & Rambling Thomas | LP | Heritage | HLP1007 | 195– | £20 | £40 | |
| Blind Lemon Jefferson/Willard 'Ramblin' Thomas | LP | Collector's Classics | CC5 | 196– | £5 | £12 | |
| Folk Blues | 10" LP | London | AL3508 | 1953 | £10 | £25 | |
| Folk Blues Classics | LP | Riverside | 125 | | £8 | £20 | US |
| Immortal | LP | CBS | 63738 | 1969 | £5 | £12 | |
| Male Blues Vol. 5 | 7" EP | Collector | JEL8 | 1960 | £2.50 | £6 | with Buddy Boy Hawkins |
| Male Blues Vol. 8 | 7" EP | Collector | JEL24 | 1964 | £2.50 | £6 | with Leadbelly |
| Masters Of The Blues Vol. 1 | LP | Collector's Classics | CC22 | 196– | £5 | £12 | |
| Penitentiary Blues | 10" LP | London | AL3546 | 1955 | £10 | £25 | |
| Sings The Blues | 10" LP | London | AL3564 | 1957 | £10 | £25 | |

## JEFFERSON, BLIND LEMON & ED BELL

| Title | Format | Label | Catalog | Year | | |
|---|---|---|---|---|---|---|
| Male Blues Vol. 7 | 7" EP | Collector | JEL13 | 1961 | £2.50 | £6 |

## JEFFERSON, EDDIE

| Title | Format | Label | Catalog | Year | | |
|---|---|---|---|---|---|---|
| Some Other Time | 7" | Stateside | SS591 | 1967 | £1.50 | £4 |

## JEFFERSON, GEORGE PAUL

| Title | Format | Label | Catalog | Year | | |
|---|---|---|---|---|---|---|
| Looking For My Mind | 7" | Fontana | TF923 | 1968 | £4 | £8 |

## JEFFERSON AIRPLANE

Jefferson Airplane were the premier Californian group, and the records they made in the sixties are the most impressive and essential of the West Coast genre – a fact that the inferior records made by various later editions of Jefferson Airplane and Jefferson Starship should never be allowed to obscure. The group was not well served by RCA in Britain, however. The UK version of *Surrealistic Pillow* is actually a compilation drawn from the first two American LPs and manages to leave out two of the most powerful and essential tracks – 'White Rabbit' and 'Plastic Fantastic Lover'. Original copies of the first US album, *Takes Off*, included the B side of the group's debut American single, 'Runnin' Round This World', but this was withdrawn due to a drug reference.

| Title | Format | Label | Catalog | Year | | | Notes |
|---|---|---|---|---|---|---|---|
| 2400 Fulton Street | CD | RCA | ND90036 | 1987 | £5 | £12 | |
| After Bathing At Baxters | LP | RCA | RD/SF7926 | 1967 | £8 | £20 | black label |
| Ballad Of You And Me And Pooneil | 7" | RCA | RCA1647 | 1967 | £1.50 | £4 | |
| Bless Its Pointed Little Head | LP | RCA | | 1969 | £15 | £30 | US interview promo |
| Bless Its Pointed Little Head | LP | RCA | RD/SF8019 | 1969 | £6 | £15 | |
| Crown Of Creation | LP | RCA | RD/SF7976 | 1968 | £6 | £15 | black label |
| Crown Of Creation | CD | Mobile Fidelity | UDCD523 | 1989 | £6 | £15 | US audiophile |
| Crown Of Creation | CD | RCA | ND83797 | 1991 | £5 | £12 | |
| Greasy Heart | 7" | RCA | RCA1711 | 1968 | £1.50 | £4 | |
| If You Feel Like China Breaking | 7" | RCA | RCA1736 | 1968 | £1.50 | £4 | |
| Jefferson Airplane Love You | CD | RCA | RDJ661132 | 1992 | £8 | £20 | US promo sampler |
| Somebody To Love | 7" | RCA | RCA1594 | 1967 | £1.50 | £4 | |
| Surrealistic Pillow | LP | RCA | LPM/LSP3766 | 1967 | £8 | £20 | US |

| | | | | | | |
|---|---|---|---|---|---|---|
| Surrealistic Pillow | LP | RCA | RD/SF7889 | 1967 £8 | £20 | *black label* |
| Surrealistic Pillow | CD | RCA | PD83766 | 1984 £5 | £12 | |
| Surrealistic Pillow | 7" EP | RCA | 86560 | 1967 £12.50 | £25 | *French* |
| Takes Off | LP | RCA | INT1476 | 1974 £5 | £12 | |
| Takes Off | LP | RCA | LPM/LSP3584 | 1966 £10 | £25 | *US* |
| Takes Off | LP | RCA | LPM/LSP3584 | 1966 £150 | £250 | *US with 'Runnin' Round This World'* |
| Takes Off | LP | RCA | SF8195 | 1971 £8 | £20 | |
| Volunteers | LP | RCA | APD10320 | 1973 £15 | £30 | *US quad* |
| Volunteers | LP | RCA | SF8076 | 1969 £6 | £15 | |
| Volunteers | 7" | RCA | RCA1933 | 1970 £1.50 | £4 | |
| White Rabbit | CD-s | RCA | PD46463 | 1989 £2 | £5 | |
| White Rabbit | 7" | RCA | RCA1631 | 1967 £2 | £5 | |
| White Rabbit | 7" | RCA | RCA1964 | 1970 £1.50 | £4 | |

## JEFFERSON STARSHIP

| | | | | | | |
|---|---|---|---|---|---|---|
| Dragonfly | LP | Grunt | BFD10717 | 1974 £4 | £10 | *US quad* |
| Gold | LP | Grunt | DJL13363 | 1978 £5 | £12 | *US promo picture disc* |
| Nothing's Gonna Stop Us Now | CD-s | RCA | PD49451 | 1989 £2 | £5 | |
| Red Octopus | LP | Grunt | BFD10999 | 1975 £4 | £10 | *US quad* |
| Spitfire | LP | Grunt | BFD11557 | 1976 £4 | £10 | *US quad* |

## JELLY BEAN BANDITS

| | | | | | | |
|---|---|---|---|---|---|---|
| Jelly Bean Bandits | LP | Mainstream | S6103 | 1967 £37.50 | £75 | *US* |

## JELLY BEANS

| | | | | | | |
|---|---|---|---|---|---|---|
| Baby Be Mine | 7" | Red Bird | RB10011 | 1964 £2.50 | £6 | |
| I Wanna Love Him So Bad | 7" | Pye | 7N25252 | 1964 £2.50 | £6 | |
| You Don't Mean Me No Good | 7" | Right On | R102 | 1975 £2.50 | £6 | |

## JELLYBREAD

Jellybread have the distinction of being perhaps the least collectable of the Blue Horizon roster. Pete Wingfield, pianist and leader of the band, would suggest that the reason for this lies in the records not being very good! In fact, the group's blend of soul and blues has worn remarkably well. The lack of guitar histrionics no doubt makes the group sound unexciting to fans of their British blues contemporaries, but it also helps to give Jellybread a distinctive sound that makes their music much less tied to its era. A scarce privately pressed album (theoretically limited to 99 copies, but actually more in the region of 500) predates the Blue Horizon material and is the most vital music recorded by the group.

| | | | | | | |
|---|---|---|---|---|---|---|
| 65 Parkway | LP | Blue Horizon | 2431002 | 1970 £8 | £20 | |
| 65 Parkway | LP | Blue Horizon | 763866 | 1970 £10 | £25 | |
| Back To Begin Again | LP | Blue Horizon | 2931004 | 1972 £25 | £50 | |
| Chairman Mao's Boogaloo | 7" | Blue Horizon | 573162 | 1969 £1.50 | £4 | |
| Down Along The Cove | 7" | Blue Horizon | 2096006 | 1971 £1.50 | £4 | |
| First Slice | LP | Blue Horizon | 763853 | 1969 £8 | £20 | |
| Jellybread | LP | Liphook | IBC/LP/3627 | 1969 £62.50 | £125 | |

## JELLYFISH

| | | | | | | |
|---|---|---|---|---|---|---|
| Baby's Coming Back | CD-s | Charisma | CUSCD2 | 1991 £2 | £5 | |
| Belly Button | CD | Charisma | | 1991 £8 | £20 | *US promo with pop-up cover* |
| Bellybutton | CD | Charisma | CDCUX3 | 1991 £5 | £12 | *with extra tracks* |
| King Is Half Undressed | CD-s | Charisma | CUSCD1 | 1991 £2 | £5 | *2 versions* |

## JENGHIZ KHAN

| | | | | | | |
|---|---|---|---|---|---|---|
| Well Cut | LP | Barclay | 920313T | 1971 £30 | £60 | *French* |

## JENKINS, JOHNNY

| | | | | | | |
|---|---|---|---|---|---|---|
| Ton Ton Macoute | LP | Atlantic | 2400033 | 1970 £4 | £10 | |

## JENKINS, KARL & MIKE RATLEDGE

| | | | | | | |
|---|---|---|---|---|---|---|
| Push Button | LP | De Wolfe | DWSLP3414 | 1979 £6 | £15 | |

## JENKINS, MARTIN

| | | | | | | |
|---|---|---|---|---|---|---|
| Carry Your Smile | LP | Oblivion | OBL002 | 1984 £5 | £12 | |

## JENNIFERS

Gaz Coombes, front-man for Supergrass, had his first single released while still in his last year at school. The Jennifers included drummer Danny Goffrey as well, who also became a member of Supergrass.

| | | | | | | |
|---|---|---|---|---|---|---|
| Just Got Back Today | CD-s | Nude | NUD2CD | 1992 £6 | £15 | |
| Just Got Back Today | 12" | Nude | NUD2T | 1992 £4 | £10 | |

## JENNINGS, WAYLON

Waylon Jennings is one of the best known of country artists and as a pioneer of the 'outlaw' sound, reflecting a deliberate move away from the showbiz concerns of the Grand Ole Opry, he has been enormously influential on the modern breed of rock-inflected country singers. The reason for the inclusion here of the American single, 'Jole Blon', however, lies in the identity of the song's producer and guitarist. This is Buddy Holly, in whose group at the time Jennings played bass.

| | | | | | | |
|---|---|---|---|---|---|---|
| At JD's | LP | Sounds | 1001 | 1964 £37.50 | £75 | *US* |
| Folk Country | LP | RCA | LPM/LSP3523 | 1966 £5 | £12 | *US* |
| Hangin' On | LP | RCA | LSP3918 | 1968 £4 | £10 | *US* |
| Jole Blon | 7" | Brunswick | 955130 | 1959 £50 | £100 | *US* |
| Leavin' Town | LP | RCA | LPM/LSP3620 | 1966 £5 | £12 | *US* |
| Love Of The Common People | LP | RCA | LPM/LSP3825 | 1967 £4 | £10 | *US* |
| Only The Greatest | LP | RCA | SF8003 | 1968 £4 | £10 | *US* |
| Waylon Sings Ol' Harlan | LP | RCA | LPM/LSP3660 | 1967 £5 | £12 | *US* |

## JENSEN, KRIS

| | | | | | | | |
|---|---|---|---|---|---|---|---|
| Claudette | 7" | Fontana | 267267TF | 1963 | £2.50 | £6 | |
| Come Back To Me | 7" | Hickory | 451256 | 1964 | £1.50 | £4 | |
| Donna Donna | 7" | Hickory | 451224 | 1964 | £2 | £5 | |
| Introducing Kris Jensen And Sue Thompson | 7" EP | Hickory | LPE1507 | 1965 | £4 | £8 | 2 tracks by Sue Thompson |
| Looking For Love | 7" | Hickory | 451243 | 1964 | £1.50 | £4 | |
| Somebody's Smiling | 7" | Hickory | 451285 | 1965 | £2 | £5 | |
| That's A Whole Lotta Love | 7" | Hickory | 451311 | 1965 | £2 | £5 | |
| Torture | LP | Hickory | MH110 | 1962 | £8 | £20 | US |
| Torture | 7" | Fontana | 267241TF | 1962 | £2 | £5 | |

## JENSENS

| | | | | | | | |
|---|---|---|---|---|---|---|---|
| Deep Thinking | 7" | Philips | BF1686 | 1968 | £2.50 | £6 | |

## JEREMY & THE SATYRS

Jeremy and the Satyrs, led by flautist Jeremy Steig, were one of the first American groups to bring jazz skills and sounds to rock. This was fledgling jazz-rock, with the two halves meeting on equal terms (unlike Blood, Sweat and Tears, for example, where the jazz content was no more than superficial). The Satyrs' experiment only lasted for one album, but each member has been a familiar session name ever since – Eddie Gomez, Donald McDonald, Warren Bernhardt and Adrian Guillory.

| | | | | | | | |
|---|---|---|---|---|---|---|---|
| Jeremy & The Satyrs | LP | Reprise | RS6282 | 1968 | £10 | £25 | US |

## JERICHO ( JONES )

| | | | | | | | |
|---|---|---|---|---|---|---|---|
| Don't You Let Me Down | 7" | A&M | AMS883 | 1972 | £7.50 | £15 | |
| Hey Man | 7" | A&M | AMS70 | 1972 | £7.50 | £15 | |
| Jericho | LP | A&M | AMLS68079 | 1972 | £30 | £60 | |
| Junkies, Monkeys, & Donkeys | LP | A&M | AMLH68050 | 1971 | £37.50 | £75 | |
| Mama's Gonna Take You Home | 7" | A&M | AMS7037 | 1972 | £6 | £12 | |
| Time is Now | 7" | A&M | AMS833 | 1971 | £7.50 | £15 | |

## JERMZ

| | | | | | | | |
|---|---|---|---|---|---|---|---|
| Power Cut | 7" | One Way | EFP1 | 1985 | £2 | £5 | |

## JERONIMO

| | | | | | | | |
|---|---|---|---|---|---|---|---|
| Cosmic Blues | LP | Bellaphon | BI1530 | 1970 | £10 | £25 | German |
| Jeronimo | LP | Bellaphon | BLPS19044 | 1971 | £62.50 | £125 | German |
| Time Ride | LP | Bellaphon | BLPS19095 | 1972 | £8 | £20 | German |

## JERUSALEM

| | | | | | | | |
|---|---|---|---|---|---|---|---|
| Jerusalem | LP | Deram | SDL6 | 1972 | £30 | £60 | |
| Kamakazi Moth | 7" | Deram | DMS358 | 1972 | £2 | £5 | |

## JESS & JAMES

| | | | | | | | |
|---|---|---|---|---|---|---|---|
| Something For Nothing | 7" | MGM | MGM1420 | 1968 | £1.50 | £4 | |

## JESTERS

| | | | | | | | |
|---|---|---|---|---|---|---|---|
| Casa Pedro | 7" | R&L | RL15/16 | 196– | £2 | £5 | |

## JESUS & MARY CHAIN

| | | | | | | | |
|---|---|---|---|---|---|---|---|
| Automatic | CD | Blanco Y Negro | SAM589 | 1989 | £6 | £15 | promo picture disc |
| Blues From A Gun | CD-s | Blanco Y Negro | NEG41CD | 1989 | £2 | £5 | |
| Blues From A Gun | 10" | Blanco Y Negro | NEGTE41 | 1989 | £5 | £12 | |
| Darklands | CD-s | Blanco Y Negro | NEGCD29 | 1987 | £2 | £5 | |
| Happy When It Rains | 7" | Blanco Y Negro | NEGB025 | 1987 | £2 | £5 | boxed, cards |
| Head On | CD-s | Blanco Y Negro | NEG42CD | 1989 | £2 | £5 | |
| Head On | 7" | Blanco Y Negro | NEG42 | 1989 | £7.50 | £15 | 4 x 7" boxed set |
| Just Like Honey | 7" | Blanco Y Negro | NEGF017 | 1985 | £2.50 | £6 | double |
| Never Understand | 7" | Blanco Y Negro | NEG008 | 1985 | £1.50 | £4 | |
| Never Understand | 12" | Blanco Y Negro | NEG8T | 1985 | £3 | £8 | |
| Rollercoaster EP | CD-s | Blanco Y Negro | NEG45CD | 1990 | £2 | £5 | |
| Some Candy Talking | 7" | Blanco Y Negro | NEGF019 | 1986 | £1.50 | £4 | double |
| Some Candy Talking | 12" | Blanco Y Negro | NEG19T | 1986 | £2.50 | £6 | with poster |
| Ten Smash Hits | CD | Def American | PROCD5336 | 1992 | £8 | £20 | US promo |
| Upside Down | 7" | Creation | CRE012 | 1984 | £5 | £10 | black, red & white picture sleeve |
| Upside Down | 7" | Creation | CRE012 | 1984 | £2.50 | £6 | pink, blue, or yellow picture sleeve |
| Upside Down | 12" | Creation | CRE012T | 1984 | £25 | £50 | demo only |
| You Trip Me Up | 12" | Blanco Y Negro | NEG13T | 1985 | £2.50 | £6 | |

## JESUS JONES

A prediction – Jesus Jones' *Liquidiser* album will, in years to come, be seen as one of the major rock music milestones. Its sophisticated blend of high energy guitar rock with modern sampling technology works so well and so seamlessly that it is easy to pass over what has been achieved here. But when, in addition, the songs themselves are so well crafted and memorable, the result is so obviously a masterpiece that it becomes astonishing that the group is not more highly rated that it seems to be!

| | | | | | | |
|---|---|---|---|---|---|---|
| Bring It On Down | CD-s .. | Food | CDFOOD22 | 1989 £2 | £5 | |
| Bring It On Down (Liquidiser Mix) | 12" .. | Food | 12FOODDJ22 | 1989 £2.50 | £6 | promo |
| Info Freako | CD-s .. | Food | CDFOOD18 | 1989 £2.50 | £6 | |
| Info Freako (Dance Extravaganza) | 12" .. | Food | 12FOODX18 | 1989 £2.50 | £6 | |
| International Bright Young Thing | CD-s .. | Food | CDFOOD27 | 1990 £2 | £5 | |
| Never Enough | CD-s .. | Food | CDFOOD21 | 1989 £2 | £5 | |
| Real Real Real | CD-s .. | Food | CDFOOD24 | 1990 £2 | £5 | |
| Right Here, Right Now | CD-s .. | Food | CDFOOD25 | 1990 £2 | £5 | |

## JESUS LOVES YOU

| | | | | | | |
|---|---|---|---|---|---|---|
| After The Love | CD-s .. | More Protein... | PROCD2 | 1990 £2 | £5 | 3" single |
| After The Love | 12" .. | More Protein... | PRTX12 | 1989 £4 | £10 | |
| One On One | 12" .. | More Protein... | PROT712 | 1990 £6 | £15 | promo |

## JET SET

| | | | | | | |
|---|---|---|---|---|---|---|
| VC10 | 7" | Delta | DW5001 | 1962 £2.50 | £6 | picture sleeve |
| You Got Me Hooked | 7" | Parlophone | R5199 | 1964 £2 | £5 | |

## JETHRO TULL

The first record made by Jethro Tull, the MGM single 'Sunshine Day', was mistakenly credited to 'Jethro Toe'. Both sides of the record – less bluesy than the music on *This Was*, but easily recognizable as the same group – were subsequently made available on the Polydor compilation *Rare Tracks*, but the single hardly sold at all and is extremely scarce. Copies that correct the spelling of the group's name on the label are counterfeits, this being emphasized by their having American-style large centre holes on what is supposed to be a UK release.

| | | | | | | |
|---|---|---|---|---|---|---|
| 1982 Tour Sampler | LP | Chrysalis | 47PDJ | 1982 £6 | £15 | US promo |
| Another Christmas Song | CD-s .. | Chrysalis | TULLCD5 | 1989 £2 | £5 | |
| Aqualung | LP | Chrysalis | CH41044 | 1973 £10 | £25 | US quad |
| Aqualung | LP | Chrysalis | CHR1044/ ILPS9145 : | 1971 £4 | £10 | |
| Aqualung | LP | Mobile Fidelity | MFSL1061 | 1980 £15 | £30 | US audiophile |
| Aqualung | CD | Chrysalis | CD25CR08 | 1994 £5 | £12 | Chrysalis 25 pack |
| Benefit | LP | Chrysalis | ILPS9123 | 1970 £4 | £10 | |
| Benefit | LP | Island | 6339009 | 1970 £6 | £15 | German, gatefold sleeve, poster |
| Benefit | LP | Island | ILPS9123 | 1970 £10 | £25 | pink label |
| Broadsword | 7" | Chrysalis | CHSP2619 | 1982 £2.50 | £6 | picture disc |
| Broadsword & The Beast | LP | Mobile Fidelity | MFSL1092 | 1982 £5 | £12 | US audiophile |
| Coronach | 12" | Chrysalis | TULLX2 | 1986 £6 | £15 | |
| Home | 7" | Chrysalis | CHS2394 | 1979 £4 | £8 | |
| Inside | 7" | Chrysalis | WIP6081 | 1970 £2.50 | £6 | |
| Jethro Tull Radio Show | LP | Chrysalis | PRO622 | 1976 £8 | £20 | US promo |
| Living In The Past | LP | Chrysalis | CJT1 | 1972 £100 | £200 | double, leather cover |
| Living In The Past | LP | Chrysalis | CJT1 | 1972 £6 | £15 | hard cover double |
| Living In The Past | 7" | Island | WIP6056 | 1969 £1.50 | £4 | |
| Living In The (Slightly More Recent) Past.. | CD-s .. | Chrysalis | 23970/1 | 1993 £2.50 | £6 | 2 CD set |
| Love Story | 7" | Island | WIP6048 | 1968 £1.50 | £4 | |
| Love Story | 7" | Island | WIP6048 | 1968 £2.50 | £6 | 'Henderson' song-writing credit |
| Moths/Beltane | 7" | Chrysalis | CHS2214 | 1978 £10 | £20 | |
| North Sea Oil | 7" | Chrysalis | CHS2378 | 1979 £2 | £5 | |
| Part Of The Machine | CD-s .. | Chrysalis | TULLPCD1 | 1988 £4 | £10 | picture disc |
| Passion Play | 7" | Chrysalis | CHS2012 | 1973 £25 | £50 | |
| Ring Out Solstice Bells | 7" | Chrysalis | CHS2443 | 1979 £1.50 | £4 | |
| Ring Out Solstice Bells | 7" | Chrysalis | CXP2 | 1976 £1.50 | £4 | picture sleeve |
| Rocks On The Road | CD-s .. | Chrysalis | TULLCD7 | 1992 £2.50 | £6 | boxed double |
| Rocks On The Road | 12" .. | Chrysalis | TULLX7 | 1992 £2.50 | £6 | picture disc |
| Said She Was A Dancer | CD-s .. | Chrysalis | TULLCD4 | 1987 £3 | £8 | |
| Said She Was A Dancer | 7" | Chrysalis | TULLP4 | 1988 £2.50 | £6 | shaped picture disc |
| Song For Jeffrey | 7" | Island | WIP6043 | 1968 £7.50 | £15 | |
| Stand Up | LP | Island | ILPS9103 | 1969 £6 | £15 | pink label |
| Stand Up | CD | Mobile Fidelity | UDCD524 | 1989 £6 | £15 | US audiophile |
| Stitch In Time | 7" | Chrysalis | CHS2260 | 1978 £2 | £5 | |
| Sunshine Day | 7" | MGM | MGM1384 | 1968 £62.50 | £125 | credited to Jethro Toe |
| Thick As A Brick | LP | Chrysalis | CHR1003 | 1972 £5 | £12 | newspaper sleeve |
| Thick As A Brick | CD | Mobile Fidelity | UDCD510 | 1988 £6 | £15 | US audiophile |
| This Is Not Love | CD-s .. | Chrysalis | TULLCD6 | 1991 £2 | £5 | |
| This Was | LP | Island | ILP985 | 1968 £15 | £30 | mono, pink label |
| This Was | LP | Island | ILPS9085 | 1968 £8 | £20 | pink label |
| Under Wraps | LP | Chrysalis | CDLP1461 | 1984 £4 | £10 | picture disc |
| War Child | LP | Chrysalis | CH41067 | 1974 £8 | £20 | US quad |
| Whistler | 7" | Chrysalis | CHS2135 | 1977 £1.50 | £4 | |

## JETSTREAMS

| | | | | | |
|---|---|---|---|---|---|
| Bongo Rock | 7" | Decca | F11149 | 1959 £4 | £8 |

## JEWELS

| | | | | | |
|---|---|---|---|---|---|
| But I Do | 7" | Colpix | PX11048 | 1965 £5 | £10 |
| Opportunity | 7" | Colpix | PX11034 | 1964 £5 | £10 |

## JIGSAW

| | | | | | | |
|---|---|---|---|---|---|---|
| Aurora Borealis | LP | Philips | 6308072 | 1971 £15 | £30 | |
| Broken Hearted | LP | BASF | BAG22291065 | 1973 £5 | £12 | |
| I've Seen The Film | LP | BASF | BAP5051 | 1974 £5 | £12 | |
| Jesu Joy Of Man's Desiring | 7" | Philips | 6006131 | 1971 £1.50 | £4 | |
| Keeping My Head Above Water | 7" | Philips | 6006182 | 1971 £1.50 | £4 | |
| Let Me Go Home | 7" | Music Factory | CUB6 | 1968 £20 | £40 | |
| Letherslade Farm | LP | Philips | 6309033 | 1970 £25 | £50 | |
| Lollipop And Goody Man | 7" | Fontana | 6007017 | 1970 £4 | £8 | |
| One Way Street | 7" | Philips | 6006112 | 1970 £2.50 | £6 | |

## JILL & THE BOULEVARDS

| | | | | | | |
|---|---|---|---|---|---|---|
| Eugene | 7" | Columbia | DB4823 | 1962 £2 | £5 | |

## JILL & THE Y'VERNS

| | | | | | | |
|---|---|---|---|---|---|---|
| My Soulful Dress | 7" | Oak | RGJ503 | 196– £10 | £20 | |

## JIM & JEAN

| | | | | | | |
|---|---|---|---|---|---|---|
| Changes | 7" EP | Verve | 519901 | 1967 £4 | £8 | French |

## JIM & JOE

| | | | | | | |
|---|---|---|---|---|---|---|
| Fireball Mail | 7" | London | HL9831 | 1964 £4 | £8 | |

## JIM & MONICA

| | | | | | | |
|---|---|---|---|---|---|---|
| Slippin' And Slidin' | 7" | Stateside | SS266 | 1964 £5 | £10 | |

## JIMMIE & THE NIGHT HOPPERS

| | | | | | | |
|---|---|---|---|---|---|---|
| Night Hop | 7" | London | HLP8830 | 1959 £7.50 | £15 | |

## JIMMY & THE RACKETS

| | | | | | | |
|---|---|---|---|---|---|---|
| Jimmy And The Rackets | LP | Elite | SOLP30039 | 1965 £15 | £30 | German |

## JIV-A-TONES

| | | | | | | |
|---|---|---|---|---|---|---|
| Flirty Gertie | 7" | Felsted | AF101 | 1958 £75 | £150 | |

## JIVE FIVE

| | | | | | | |
|---|---|---|---|---|---|---|
| I'm A Happy Man | 7" | United Artists | UP1106 | 1965 £10 | £20 | |
| Jive Five | LP | United Artists | UAL3455/ UAS6455 | 1965 £10 | £25 | US |
| My True Story | 7" | Parlophone | R4822 | 1961 £50 | £100 | |
| What Time Is It | 7" | Stateside | SS133 | 1962 £20 | £40 | |

## JIVERS

| | | | | | | |
|---|---|---|---|---|---|---|
| Little Mama | 7" | Vogue | V9060 | 1956 £180 | £300 | best auctioned |
| Ray Pearl | 7" | Vogue | V9068 | 1957 £180 | £300 | best auctioned |

## JIVERS (2)

| | | | | | | |
|---|---|---|---|---|---|---|
| Wear My Crown | 7" | Trojan | TR604 | 1968 £1.50 | £4 | |

## JIVING JUNIORS

| | | | | | | |
|---|---|---|---|---|---|---|
| Don't Leave Me | 7" | Island | WI027 | 1962 £5 | £10 | |
| Lollipop Girl | 7" | Blue Beat | BB4 | 1960 £6 | £12 | |
| My Heart's Desire | 7" | Blue Beat | BB5 | 1960 £6 | £12 | |
| Over The River | 7" | Blue Beat | BB36 | 1961 £6 | £12 | |
| Slop And Mash | 7" | Starlite | ST45049 | 1961 £5 | £10 | |
| Sugar Dandy | 7" | Island | WI003 | 1962 £5 | £10 | |
| Sugar Dandy | 7" | Island | WI129 | 1963 £5 | £10 | |
| Tu Woo Up Tu Woo | 7" | Starlite | ST45028 | 1960 £5 | £10 | |

## JO, DAMITA

| | | | | | | |
|---|---|---|---|---|---|---|
| I'd Do It Again | 7" | HMV | JO390 | 1954 £2 | £5 | export |
| I'll Save The Last Dance For You | 7" EP | Mercury | ZEP10118 | 1961 £4 | £8 | |

## JO JO GUNNE

| | | | | | | |
|---|---|---|---|---|---|---|
| Beggin' You Baby | 7" | Decca | F12906 | 1969 £1.50 | £4 | |
| Every Story Has An End | 7" | Decca | F12807 | 1968 £1.50 | £4 | |

## JODIMARS

| | | | | | | |
|---|---|---|---|---|---|---|
| Cloud Ninety-nine | 7" | Capitol | CL14700 | 1957 £15 | £30 | |
| Dance To The Bop | 7" | Capitol | CL14642 | 1956 £15 | £30 | |
| Lotsa Love | 7" | Capitol | CL14627 | 1956 £15 | £30 | |
| Midnight | 7" | Capitol | CL14663 | 1956 £15 | £30 | |
| Rattle Shaking Daddy | 7" | Capitol | CL14641 | 1956 £15 | £30 | |
| Well Now Dig This | LP | Ember | SPE6608 | 196– £6 | £15 | |
| Well Now Dig This | 7" | Capitol | CL14518 | 1956 £20 | £40 | |

## JODOROWSKY, ALEXANDRO

| | | | | | | |
|---|---|---|---|---|---|---|
| El Topo | LP | Apple | SWAO3388 | 1971 £6 | £15 | US |

## JODY GRIND

| | | | | | | |
|---|---|---|---|---|---|---|
| Far Canal | LP | Transatlantic | TRA221 | 1970 £8 | £20 | |
| One Step On | LP | Transatlantic | TRA210 | 1969 £8 | £20 | |

## JOE, AL T.

| | | | | | | |
|---|---|---|---|---|---|---|
| Fatso | 7" | Blue Beat | BB169 | 1963 £6 | £12 | |
| Goodbye Dreamboat | 7" | Blue Beat | BB166 | 1963 £6 | £12 | |
| I'm On My Own | 7" | Dice | CC9 | 1962 £5 | £10 | |

| | | | | | | | |
|---|---|---|---|---|---|---|---|
| Jacqueline | 7" | Blue Beat | BB368 | 1966 | £6 | £12 | |
| You Cheated On Me | 7" | Blue Beat | BB126 | 1962 | £6 | £12 | |

## JOE & ANN
| | | | | | | | |
|---|---|---|---|---|---|---|---|
| Gee Baby | 7" | Black Swan | WI468 | 1965 | £5 | £10 | |

## JOE & EDDIE
| | | | | | | | |
|---|---|---|---|---|---|---|---|
| Walkin' Down The Line | 7" | Vocalion | VP9250 | 1965 | £2 | £5 | |

## JOE SOAP
| | | | | | | | |
|---|---|---|---|---|---|---|---|
| Keep It Clean | LP | Polydor | 2383233 | 1973 | £4 | £10 | |

## JOE'S ALLSTARS
| | | | | | | | |
|---|---|---|---|---|---|---|---|
| Battle Cry Of Biafra | 7" | Joe | DU28 | 1969 | £1.50 | £4 | |
| Hey Jude | 7" | Joe | DU24 | 1969 | £1.50 | £4 | |
| Tony B's Theme | 7" | Joe | JRS9 | 1970 | £1.50 | £4 | |

## JOEL, BILLY
| | | | | | | | |
|---|---|---|---|---|---|---|---|
| 52nd Street | LP | Columbia | HC45609 | 1981 | £4 | £10 | US audiophile |
| Ballad Of Billy The Kid | 7" | Philips | 6078018 | 1973 | £10 | £20 | |
| Billy Joel | LP | Columbia | ABS1 | 1978 | £37.50 | £75 | US promo, 5 LPs, boxed |
| Cold Spring Harbour | LP | Philips | 6369150 | 1972 | £4 | £10 | recorded too fast |
| Entertainer | 7" | Philips | | 1973 | £12.50 | £25 | |
| Honesty | 7" | CBS | 7150 | 1979 | £7.50 | £15 | |
| Interchords | LP | Columbia | AS402 | 1976 | £5 | £12 | US interview promo |
| Leningrad | CD-s | CBS | JOELC3 | 1989 | £2 | £5 | 3" single |
| Now Playing | LP | CBS | BJ1 | 1978 | £5 | £12 | promo |
| Piano Man | LP | Columbia | CQ32544 | 1974 | £4 | £10 | US quad |
| Piano Man | LP | Philips | 6369160 | 1973 | £10 | £25 | |
| She's Got A Way | 7" | Philips | 6078001 | 1972 | £1.50 | £4 | |
| Songs From The Attic | LP | Columbia | AS1343 | 1981 | £6 | £15 | US sampler & interview promo |
| Souvenir | LP | Columbia | AS326 | 1974 | £6 | £15 | US 1 sided live promo |
| Stranger | LP | Columbia | HC34987 | 1980 | £4 | £10 | US audiophile |
| Streetlife Serenade | LP | Columbia | PCQ33146 | 1974 | £4 | £10 | US quad |
| That's Not Her Style – The Storm Front Tour CD | CD | Columbia | | 1990 | £8 | £20 | US promo |
| Turnstiles | LP | Columbia | PCQ33848 | 1976 | £4 | £10 | US quad |
| We Didn't Start The Fire | CD-s | CBS | JOELC1 | 1989 | £2 | £5 | |

## JOEY & THE CONTINENTALS
| | | | | | | | |
|---|---|---|---|---|---|---|---|
| She Rides With Me | 7" | Polydor | 56520 | 1970 | £1.50 | £4 | |

## JOEY & THE GENTLEMEN
| | | | | | | | |
|---|---|---|---|---|---|---|---|
| Like I Love You | 7" | Fontana | TF444 | 1964 | £2 | £5 | |

## JOHANNES
| | | | | | | | |
|---|---|---|---|---|---|---|---|
| First Album | LP | Pallas | HF100 | 1971 | £37.50 | £75 | German |

## JOHN, ANDREW
| | | | | | | | |
|---|---|---|---|---|---|---|---|
| Machine Stops | LP | CBS | 64835 | 1971 | £6 | £15 | |

## JOHN, DAVID & THE MOOD
| | | | | | | | |
|---|---|---|---|---|---|---|---|
| Bring It To Jerome | 7" | Parlophone | R5255 | 1965 | £75 | £150 | |
| Diggin' For Gold | 7" | Parlophone | R5301 | 1965 | £87.50 | £175 | |
| Pretty Thing | 7" | Vocalion | V9220 | 1964 | £100 | £200 | |

## JOHN, ELTON
| | | | | | | | |
|---|---|---|---|---|---|---|---|
| Border Song | 7" | DJM | DJS217 | 1970 | £1.50 | £4 | |
| Candle In The Wind | LP | St. Michael | 20940102 | 1978 | £10 | £25 | |
| Candle In The Wind | CD-s | Rocket | EJSCD15 | 1987 | £3 | £8 | |
| Captain Fantastic | LP | DJM | DJLPX1 | 1975 | £20 | £40 | brown vinyl |
| Captain Fantastic | LP | DJM | DJLPX1 | 1975 | £37.50 | £75 | brown vinyl, autographed cover |
| Captain Fantastic | LP | DJM | DJV2300 | 1978 | £4 | £10 | picture disc |
| Club At The End Of The Street | CD-s | Rocket | EJSCD21 | 1990 | £12.50 | £25 | with 'Give Peace A Chance' |
| Club At The End Of The Street | CD-s | Rocket | EJSCD23 | 1990 | £2 | £5 | |
| Don't Let The Sun Go Down On Me | CD-s | Rocket | EJSCD26 | 1991 | £2 | £5 | |
| Duets | CD | Rocket | | 1993 | £37.50 | £75 | promo box set of 16 CD singles |
| Duets | CD | Rocket | DUINT1 | 1994 | £8 | £20 | interview promo |
| Easier To Walk Away | CD-s | Rocket | EJSCD25 | 1990 | £2 | £5 | |
| Elton John | LP | DJM | DJM14512 | 1978 | £10 | £25 | 5 LPs, boxed |
| Elton John And Bernie Taupin Collection | CD | Polygram | PIPCD002 | 1990 | £25 | £50 | US promo double compilation |
| Empty Garden | 7" | Rocket | XPPIC77 | 1982 | £1.50 | £4 | picture disc |
| Empty Sky | LP | DJM | DJLPM403 | 1969 | £5 | £12 | mono |
| Excerpts From To Be Continued | CD | MCA | | 1990 | £8 | £20 | Canadian promo sampler |
| Fishing Trip | CD | Happenstance | HAPP001 | 1993 | £100 | £200 | 4 CD set, private pressing |
| Friends | 7" | DJM | DJS244 | 1971 | £1.50 | £4 | |
| Games | LP | Viking | 105 | 1970 | £37.50 | £75 | US, with other artists |
| Gli Opera | 7" | Rocket | | 1977 | £4 | £8 | sung in Italian |
| Goaldigger Song | 7" | Rocket | GOALD1 | 1977 | £37.50 | £75 | |
| Goodbye Yellow Brick Road | LP | DJM | DJE29001 | 1976 | £5 | £12 | yellow vinyl double |

| Title | Format | Label | Cat. No. | Year | | | Notes |
|---|---|---|---|---|---|---|---|
| Goodbye Yellow Brick Road | LP | Nautilus | 10003 | 1980 | £10 | £25 | US audiophile |
| Goodbye Yellow Brick Road | LP | Superdisk | SD216614 | 1982 | £6 | £15 | audiophile |
| Goodbye Yellow Brick Road | CD | Mobile Fidelity | UDCD526 | 1990 | £6 | £15 | US audiophile |
| Greatest Hits | CD | DCC | GZS1071 | 1994 | £6 | £15 | US audiophile |
| Greatest Hits Volume One | LP | Nautilus | | 1981 | £4 | £10 | US audiophile |
| Healing Hands | CD-s | Rocket | EJSCD19 | 1989 | £2 | £5 | |
| Honky Chateau | CD | Mobile Fidelity | UDCD536 | 1990 | £6 | £15 | US audiophile |
| I Don't Want To Go On With You Like That | CD-s | Polygram | 0805242 | 1988 | £4 | £10 | CD video |
| I Don't Want To Go On With You Like That | CD-s | Rocket | EJSCD16 | 1988 | £2 | £5 | |
| I'm Still Standing | 7" | Rocket | EJPIC1 | 1983 | £2.50 | £6 | shaped picture disc |
| I've Been Loving You | 7" | Philips | BF1643 | 1968 | £150 | £250 | best auctioned |
| Ice On Fire | CD | Rocket | 8262132 | 1985 | £5 | £12 | |
| It's Me That You Need | 7" | DJM | DJS205 | 1969 | £7.50 | £15 | |
| It's Me That You Need | 7" | DJM | DJS205 | 1969 | £25 | £50 | picture sleeve |
| Je veux de la tendresse | 7" | Rocket | 6000675 | 1980 | £2.50 | £6 | sung in French |
| Jump Up | CD | Rocket | 8000372 | 1983 | £5 | £12 | |
| Lady Samantha | 7" | Philips | BF1739 | 1969 | £12.50 | £25 | |
| Live In Australia With The Melbourne S.O. | LP | Rocket | EJBXL1 | 1987 | £5 | £12 | double |
| Live In Australia With The Melbourne Symphony Orchestra | CD | | | 1987 | £20 | £40 | gold double boxed set |
| Madman Across The Water | CD | Mobile Fidelity | UDCD516 | 1989 | £6 | £15 | US audiophile |
| Mama Can't Buy You Love | 7" | Rocket | XPRES20 | 1979 | £7.50 | £15 | |
| Nikita | CD-s | Polygram | 0802722 | 1988 | £4 | £10 | CD video |
| Nikita | 7" | Rocket | EJSD9 | 1985 | £2 | £5 | double, pop-up picture sleeve |
| Plays The Siran | CD | Happenstance | | 1993 | £50 | £100 | private pressing |
| Rock And Roll Madonna | 7" | DJM | DJS222 | 1970 | £2.50 | £6 | |
| Rocket Man | 7" | DJM | DJX501 | 1972 | £5 | £10 | gatefold picture sleeve |
| Sacrifice | CD-s | Rocket | EJSCD20 | 1989 | £2 | £5 | |
| Sacrifice | CD-s | Rocket | EJSCD22 | 1990 | £2 | £5 | |
| Sad Songs | 7" | Rocket | PHPIC7 | 1984 | £2.50 | £6 | shaped picture disc |
| Single Man | LP | MCA | MCAP14591 | 1979 | £4 | £10 | US picture disc |
| Singles Collection | 7" | DJM | EJBOX12 | 1978 | £20 | £40 | 12 singles, boxed |
| Superior Sound Of Elton John | CD | DJM | 8100622 | 1983 | £8 | £20 | remix compilation |
| Town Of Plenty | CD-s | Rocket | EJSCD17 | 1988 | £2 | £5 | |
| Tumbleweed Connection | CD | Mobile Fidelity | UDCD543 | 1991 | £6 | £15 | US audiophile |
| Twenty-Five Years On | CD | Rocket | DJMDJ1 | 1995 | £10 | £25 | promo compilation |
| Two Rooms – The Interview | CD | Mercury | | 1991 | £8 | £20 | promo |
| Warlock Sampler | LP | Warlock Music | WMM101/2 | 1970 | £330 | £500 | demo only, with Linda Peters (Thompson), best auctioned |
| Word In Spanish | CD-s | Rocket | EJSCD18 | 1988 | £3 | £8 | |
| World | CD | Rocket | EJCD89 | 1989 | £8 | £20 | promo sampler |
| Wrap Her Up | 7" | Rocket | EJPIC10 | 1985 | £2.50 | £6 | shaped picture disc, with George Michael |
| Wrap Her Up | 7" | Rocket | EJSC10 | 1985 | £1.50 | £4 | cube bag sleeve, with George Michael |
| Wrap Her Up | 7" | Rocket | EJSP10 | 1985 | £1.50 | £4 | with George Michael, shaped picture disc |
| You Gotta Love Someone | CD-s | Rocket | EJSCD24 | 1990 | £2 | £5 | |

## JOHN, ELTON & CLIFF RICHARD

| Title | Format | Label | Cat. No. | Year | | | Notes |
|---|---|---|---|---|---|---|---|
| Slow Rivers | 7" | Rocket | EJSP13 | 1986 | £1.50 | £4 | picture disc |

## JOHN, ELTON & FRANCE GALL

| Title | Format | Label | Cat. No. | Year | | | Notes |
|---|---|---|---|---|---|---|---|
| Les Areuse | 7" | | | 1981 | £1.50 | £4 | sung in French |
| Les Areuse | 12" | | | 1981 | £2.50 | £6 | sung in French |

## JOHN, ELTON & JOHN LENNON

| Title | Format | Label | Cat. No. | Year | | | Notes |
|---|---|---|---|---|---|---|---|
| I Saw Her Standing There | 7" | DJM | DJS10965 | 1981 | £1.50 | £4 | |
| I Saw Her Standing There | 7" | DJM | DJS354 | 1975 | £1.50 | £4 | picture sleeve |

## JOHN, LITTLE WILLIE

| Title | Format | Label | Cat. No. | Year | | | Notes |
|---|---|---|---|---|---|---|---|
| Action | LP | King | 691 | 1960 | £25 | £50 | US |
| Come On And Join Little Willie John | LP | London | HA8126 | 1964 | £20 | £40 | US |
| Fever | LP | King | 395564 | 1956 | £37.50 | £75 | US |
| Fever | 7" | Parlophone | R4209 | 1956 | £15 | £30 | |
| Free At Last | LP | King | KS1081 | 1970 | £8 | £20 | US |
| Heartbreak | 7" | Parlophone | R4674 | 1960 | £7.50 | £15 | |
| Leave My Kitten Alone | 7" | Parlophone | R4571 | 1959 | £7.50 | £15 | |
| Let's Rock While The Rocking's Good | 7" | Parlophone | R4472 | 1958 | £12.50 | £25 | |
| Little Willie Sings All Originals | LP | King | K(S)949 | 1966 | £10 | £25 | US |
| Mr. Little Willie John | LP | King | 603 | 1958 | £30 | £60 | US |
| Sleep | 7" | Parlophone | R4699 | 1960 | £6 | £12 | |
| Sure Things | LP | Parlophone | PMC1163 | 1959 | £37.50 | £75 | |
| Sweet, The Hot, The Teenage Beat | LP | King | 767 | 1961 | £15 | £30 | US |
| Talk To Me | LP | King | 395596 | 1958 | £30 | £60 | US |
| Talk To Me | 7" | Parlophone | R4432 | 1958 | £10 | £20 | |
| These Are My Favorite Songs | LP | King | 895 | 1964 | £15 | £30 | US |
| Uh Uh Baby | 7" | Parlophone | R4396 | 1958 | £10 | £20 | |

## JOHN, MABLE

| Title | Format | Label | Cat. No. | Year | | | Notes |
|---|---|---|---|---|---|---|---|
| Able Mable | 7" | Stax | 601034 | 1968 | £1.50 | £4 | |
| It's Catching | 7" | Atlantic | 584022 | 1966 | £2 | £5 | |
| Same Time Same Place | 7" | Stax | 601010 | 1967 | £2.50 | £6 | |

## JOHN & PAUL
People Say .................................................. 7" ...... London .......... HLU9997 .............. 1965 £2.50 ...... £6 ..............................................

## JOHN & SANDRA
John And Sandra ..................................... LP ..... Argo ............. ZFB2 .............. 1970 £4 .......... £10 ..............................................

## JOHN BULL BREED
I'm A Man ................................................ 7" ...... Polydor ......... 56065 .............. 1966 £75 ..... £150 ..............................................

## JOHN THE POSTMAN
Psychedelic Rock 'n' Roll 5 Skinners ........ 12" ..... Bent .......... BIGBENT4 ........ 1978 £3 ........ £8 ..............................................
Puerile.................................................... 12" ..... Bent .......... BIGBENT2 ........ 1978 £3 ........ £8 ..............................................

## JOHN THE REVELATOR
Wild Blues................................................ LP ..... Decca ............ 6419002 .............. 1970 £15 ......... £30 ..................... Dutch

## JOHN'S CHILDREN
The collectability of John's Children derives mainly from the fact that Marc Bolan played with the group for a short time. 'Desdemona' is a Bolan song, as is the withdrawn and extremely scarce 'Midsummer Night's Scene'. (Other unreleased Marc Bolan contributions were included on his LP *Beginning Of Doves*.) Many of the other John's Children recordings were actually made by session musicians (including Jeff Beck on the B side of 'Just What You Want'), as the group were too incompetent to do the job themselves.

Come And Play With Me In The Garden... 7" ...... Track .......... 604005 .......... 1967 £15 ...... £30 ..............................................
Come And Play With Me In The Garden... 7" ...... Track .......... 604005 .......... 1967 £50 ...... £100 ...... picture sleeve
Desdemona.............................................. 7" ...... Track .......... 604003 .......... 1967 £15 ...... £30 ..............................................
Desdemona.............................................. 7" ...... Track .......... 604003 .......... 1967 £50 ...... £100 ...... picture sleeve
Go Go Girl .............................................. 7" ...... Track .......... 604010 .......... 1967 £20 ...... £40 ..............................................
Just What You Want ............................... 7" ...... Columbia ...... DB8124 ......... 1967 £37.50 ... £75 ..............................................
Love I Thought I'd Found ....................... 7" ...... Columbia ...... DB8030 ......... 1966 £37.50 ... £75 ..............................................
Love I Thought I'd Found ....................... 7" ...... Columbia ...... DB8030 ......... 1966 £100 ...... £200 ...... picture sleeve, best auctioned
Midsummer Night's Scene ...................... 7" ...... Track .......... 604005 .......... 1967 £875 ... £1250 ... test pressing, best auctioned
Orgasm ................................................... LP ..... White Whale ... WW7128 .............. 1967 £37.50 .... £75 ..................... US

## JOHNNIE & JOE
Over the Mountain Across The Sea........... 7" ...... London .......... HLM8682 .............. 1958 £100 ..... £200 ...... best auctioned

## JOHNNY & CHAS & THE GUNNERS
Bobby ...................................................... 7" ...... Decca ............ F11365 .............. 1961 £7.50 ... £15 ..............................................

## JOHNNY & JACK
Hits .......................................................... LP ..... RCA ............. LPM2017 .............. 1959 £5 .......... £12 ..................... US
Honey I Need You ................................... 7" ...... HMV............. 7MC21 .............. 1954 £1.50 ... £4 ..................... export
Tennessee Mountain Boys........................ LP ..... RCA ............. LPM1587 .............. 1957 £5 .......... £12 ..................... US

## JOHNNY & JOHN
Bumper To Bumper ................................ 7" ...... Polydor .......... BM56087 .............. 1966 £4 .......... £8 ..............................................

## JOHNNY & JUDY
Bother Me Baby ...................................... 7" ...... Vogue............. V9128 .............. 1959 £100 ..... £200 ............ best auctioned

## JOHNNY & THE ATTRACTIONS
Young Wings Can Fly .............................. 7" ...... Doctor Bird..... DB1118 .............. 1967 £5 .......... £10 ... Dudley Williamson B side

## JOHNNY & THE BLUEBEATS
Shame ..................................................... 7" ...... Blue Beat ........ BB229 .............. 1964 £6 .......... £12 ..............................................

## JOHNNY & THE COPYCATS
I'm A Hog For You Baby ........................ 7" ...... Narco ............ AB102 .............. 196– £20 ...... £40 ..............................................

## JOHNNY & THE HURRICANES
Beatnik Fly .............................................. 7" ...... London .......... HLI9072 .............. 1959 £1.50 ... £4 ..............................................
Big Sound................................................ LP ..... London .......... HAX2322 .............. 1960 £10 ...... £25 ..............................................
Crossfire .................................................. 7" ...... London .......... HL8899 .............. 1959 £10 ...... £20 ..................... tri-centre
Down Yonder .......................................... 7" ...... London .......... HLX9134 .............. 1960 £1.50 ... £4 ..............................................
Greens And Jeans..................................... 7" ...... London .......... HLX9660 .............. 1963 £1.50 ... £4 ..............................................
Hep Canary ............................................. 7" ...... London .......... HL7099 .............. 1960 £12.50 ... £25 ..................... export
Ja-Da....................................................... 7" ...... London .......... HLX9289 .............. 1961 £1.50 ... £4 ..............................................
Johnny & The Hurricanes ....................... LP ..... Warwick ..... W(ST)2007 .............. 1959 £25 ...... £50 ..................... US
Johnny & The Hurricanes ....................... 7" EP. London .......... REX1347 .............. 1962 £7.50 ... £15 ..............................................
Johnny & The Hurricanes Vol. 2 ............. 7" EP. London .......... REX1414 .............. 1964 £10 ...... £20 ..............................................
Live At The Star Club .............................. LP ..... Atila .......... 1030 .............. 1962 £20 ...... £40 ..................... US
Minnesota Fats ........................................ 7" ...... London .......... HLX9617 .............. 1962 £1.50 ... £4 ..............................................
Money Honey .......................................... 7" ...... Stateside ......... SS347 .............. 1964 £2 ...... £5 ..............................................
Old Smokey ............................................ 7" ...... London .......... HLX9378 .............. 1961 £1.50 ... £4 ..............................................
Red River Rock ....................................... LP ..... London .......... HA2227 .............. 196– £4 ...... £10 ..................... black label
Red River Rock ....................................... LP ..... London .......... HA2227 .............. 1960 £15 ...... £30 ..................... plum label
Red River Rock ....................................... 7" ...... London .......... HL8948 .............. 1959 £2 ...... £5 ..................... tri-centre
Reveille Rock........................................... 7" ...... London .......... HL9017 .............. 1959 £2.50 ... £6 ..................... tri-centre
Rocking Goose ........................................ 7" EP. London .......... REX1284 .............. 1961 £10 ...... £20 ..............................................
Rocking Goose ........................................ 7" ...... London .......... HLX9190 .............. 1960 £1.50 ... £4 ..............................................
Salvation.................................................. 7" ...... London .......... HLX9536 .............. 1962 £2 ...... £5 ..............................................
Stormsville .............................................. LP ..... London .......... HA12269 .............. 1960 £10 ...... £25 ..............................................
Traffic Jam............................................... 7" ...... London .......... HLX9491 .............. 1962 £1.50 ... £4 ..............................................

You Are My Sunshine .............................. 7" ...... London .......... HLX7116 ................. 1962 £7.50 ...... £15 ..................... export

## JOHNNY & THE SELF ABUSERS

It is unlikely that Johnny and the Self Abusers would have become international stars if they had retained that name. Fortunately they decided to change it to Simple Minds . . .

Saints And Sinners .................................... 7" ...... Chiswick ........ NS22 ...................... 1977 £5 ........... £10 ........... picture sleeve

## JOHNNY & THE VIBRATIONS
Bird Stompin' ............................................. 7" ...... Warner Bros .... WB107 ................. 1963 £1.50 ........ £4

## JOHNNY'S BOYS
Sleepwalk ................................................... 7" ...... Decca ............ F11156 .................... 1959 £1.50 ........ £4

## JOHNNY'S JAZZ
R.J. Boogie .................................................. 7" ...... Decca ............ FJ10663 ................. 1956 £1.50 ........ £4

## JOHNS, GLYN
I'll Follow The Sun ..................................... 7" ...... Pye ............... 7N15818 ................ 1965 £1.50 ........ £4
January Blues ............................................. 7" ...... Decca ............ F11478 .................... 1962 £1.50 ........ £4
Mary Anne .................................................. 7" ...... Immediate .... IM013 .................... 1965 £4 ............. £8
Today You're Gone ..................................... 7" ...... Lyntone ........ LYN827/8 ............... 196– £1.50 ........ £4

## JOHNS, GLYNIS
I Can't Resist Men ..................................... 7" ...... Columbia ....... SCM5149 ............... 1954 £1.50 ........ £4

## JOHNSON, BETTY
1492 ........................................................... 7" ...... London ......... HLU8432 .............. 1957 £12.50 ...... £25
Betty Johnson ............................................ LP ..... Atlantic ........ 8017 ...................... 1958 £15 ............ £30 ............................... US
Does Your Heart Beat For Me ..................... 7" ...... London ......... HLE8839 .............. 1959 £10 ............ £20
Dream ........................................................ 7" EP . London ......... REE1221 .............. 1959 £15 ............ £30
Dream ........................................................ 7" ...... London ......... HLE8678 .............. 1958 £6 .............. £12
Honky Tonk Rock ....................................... 7" ...... London ......... HLU8326 .............. 1956 £50 ............ £100
Hoopa Hula ................................................ 7" ...... London ......... HLE8725 .............. 1958 £12.50 ...... £25
I Dreamed ................................................... 7" ...... London ......... HLU8365 .............. 1957 £15 ............ £30
I'll Wait ...................................................... 7" ...... London ......... HLU8307 .............. 1956 £15 ............ £30
Little Blue Man .......................................... 7" ...... London ......... HLE8557 .............. 1958 £12.50 ...... £25
Songs You Heard When You Fell In Love .. LP .... London ......... HAE2163 .............. 1959 £15 ............ £30
There's Never Been A Night ....................... 7" ...... London ......... HLE8701 .............. 1958 £15 ............ £30

## JOHNSON, BLIND WILLIE
Blind Willie Johnson .................................. LP ..... Folkways ....... 10 .......................... 1965 £5 .............. £12 ............................. US
Blind Willie Johnson .................................. LP ..... XTRA ............ XTRA1098 ............. 1970 £4 .............. £10
Blues .......................................................... LP ..... Folkways ....... 3585 ...................... 1957 £8 .............. £20 ............................. US
Treasures Of North American Negro Music  7" EP . Fontana .......... TFE17052 .............. 1958 £2.50 ......... £6
No. 2 ..........................................................

## JOHNSON, BOBBY & THE ATOMS
Do It Again A Little Bit Slower ................... 7" ...... Ember ............ EMBS245 .............. 1967 £2 ............... £5

## JOHNSON, BRYAN
Looking High .............................................. 7" EP . Decca ............ DFE6664 ............... 1961 £4 ............... £8

## JOHNSON, BUBBER
Come Home ................................................ LP ..... King .............. 395569 .................... 1957 £20 ............ £40 ............................. US
Confidential ............................................... 7" ...... Parlophone .... R4259 .................... 1957 £7.50 ......... £15
Sings Sweet Love Songs ............................ LP ..... King .............. 624 ....................... 1959 £15 ............ £30 ............................. US

## JOHNSON, BUDD
Blues A La Mode ......................................... LP ..... Felsted .......... FAJ7007/SJA2007 ... 1959 £10 ............ £25

## JOHNSON, BUDDY & ELLA
Buddy Johnson Wails .................................. LP ..... Mercury ......... MG20072 .............. 1958 £15 ............ £30 ............................. US
Buddy Johnson Wails .................................. 7" EP . Mercury ......... ZEP10009 ............. 1959 £20 ............ £40
Go Ahead And Rock And Roll ...................... LP ..... Roulette ......... (S)R25085 ............ 1959 £15 ............ £30 ............................. US
Rock And Roll ............................................. 10" LP Mercury ......... MPT7515 .............. 1957 £37.50 ...... £75
Rock 'n' Roll .............................................. LP ..... Mercury ......... MG20209 .............. 1956 £15 ............ £30 ............................. US
Rock 'n' Roll Stage Show ............................ LP ..... Wing ............. MGW12005 ........... 1956 £15 ............ £30 ............................. US
Swing Me .................................................... LP ..... Mercury ......... MG20347 .............. 1958 £15 ............ £30 ............................. US
Walkin' ....................................................... LP ..... Mercury ......... MG20322 .............. 1958 £15 ............ £30 ............................. US

## JOHNSON, BUNK
Bunk And Lu .............................................. LP ..... Good Time ..... LAG12121 ............. 1958 £5 .............. £12 ....... with Lu Watters
                                                                            Jazz ..............
Bunk Johnson And His New Orleans Band. LP ..... Columbia ....... 33SX1015 ............. 1954 £6 .............. £15
Bunk Johnson And His Superior Jazz Band . LP ..... Goodtime Jazz . LAG545 ................. 1963 £5 .............. £12
Bunk Johnson And The Yerba Buena Jazz    10" LP Goodtime Jazz . LDG110 ................. 1955 £8 .............. £20
Band ..........................................................
Bunk Johnson's Band 1944 .......................... LP ..... Storyville ....... SLP152 .................. 1964 £5 .............. £12
One You Love .............................................. 7" EP . Melodisc ........ EPM752 ................. 1955 £2 ............... £5

## JOHNSON, DANIEL
Come On My People .................................... 7" ...... Island ............ WI250 .................... 1965 £2 ............... £5

## JOHNSON, DICK
Dick Johnson Quartet .................................. LP ..... Emarcy .......... EJT753 ................... 1957 £10 ............ £25

## JOHNSON, DUNCAN
| | | | | | | | |
|---|---|---|---|---|---|---|---|
| Big Architect | 7" | Spark | SLR1022 | 1969 | £1.50 | £4 | |

## JOHNSON, J. J.
| | | | | | | | |
|---|---|---|---|---|---|---|---|
| Blue Trombone | LP | Fontana | TFL5137 | 1961 | £5 | £12 | |
| Boneology | LP | Realm | RM195 | 1964 | £5 | £12 | |
| Dial JJ5 | LP | Fontana | TFL5021 | 1958 | £5 | £12 | |
| First Place | LP | Fontana | TFL5005 | 1958 | £5 | £12 | |
| J Is For Jazz | LP | Philips | BBL7143 | 1957 | £8 | £20 | |
| J. J. In Person | LP | Fontana | TFL5041/STFL512 | 1960 | £5 | £12 | |
| J. J. Johnson Quintet | 10" LP | Vogue | LDE162 | 1955 | £25 | £50 | |
| J. J. Johnson Sextet | 10" LP | Vogue | LDE124 | 1955 | £25 | £50 | |
| Jay & Kai Plus Six | LP | Fontana | TFL5022 | 1958 | £5 | £12 | with Kai Winding |
| Jay Jay Johnson Vol. 1 | LP | Blue Note | BLP/BST81505 | 196– | £10 | £25 | |
| Jay Jay Johnson Vol. 2 | LP | Blue Note | BLP/BST81506 | 196– | £10 | £25 | |

## JOHNSON, JAMES P.
| | | | | | | | |
|---|---|---|---|---|---|---|---|
| Daddy Of The Piano | 10" LP | Brunswick | LA8548 | 1952 | £4 | £10 | |
| Early Harlem Piano | 10" LP | London | AL3511 | 1954 | £8 | £20 | |
| Fats Waller Favourites | 10" LP | Brunswick | LA8622 | 1953 | £8 | £20 | |
| Feeling Blue | 7" | Columbia | SCM5127 | 1954 | £2 | £5 | |
| Harlem Party Piano | 10" LP | London | HBU1057 | 1956 | £8 | £20 | .:.... B side by Luckey Roberts |
| James P. Johnson | 7" EP | HMV | 7EG8164 | 1956 | £2.50 | £6 | |
| James P. Johnson | 7" EP | Tempo | EXA65 | 1957 | £2.50 | £6 | |
| James P. Johnson | 10" LP | London | AL3540 | 1955 | £8 | £20 | |
| Jimmy Johnson And Joe Sullivan | 7" EP | Fontana | TFE17246 | 1960 | £2 | £5 | |
| Louisiana Sugar Babies | 7" EP | HMV | 7EG8215 | 1957 | £4 | £8 | with Fats Waller |

## JOHNSON, JIMMY
| | | | | | | | |
|---|---|---|---|---|---|---|---|
| Don't Answer The Door | 7" | Sue | WI387 | 1965 | £6 | £12 | |

## JOHNSON, JOHNNY & THE BANDWAGON
| | | | | | | | |
|---|---|---|---|---|---|---|---|
| Breaking Down The Walls Of Heartache | 7" | Direction | 583670 | 1968 | £1.50 | £4 | |
| Johnny Johnson And The Bandwagon | LP | Direction | 863500 | 1968 | £4 | £10 | |

## JOHNSON, JUD!
| | | | | | | | |
|---|---|---|---|---|---|---|---|
| How Many Times | 7" | HMV | POP1399 | 1965 | £1.50 | £4 | |

## JOHNSON, KENNY & NORTHWIND
| | | | | | | | |
|---|---|---|---|---|---|---|---|
| Lakeside Highway | LP | NWG | 76103 | 1976 | £6 | £15 | |

## JOHNSON, LARRY
| | | | | | | | |
|---|---|---|---|---|---|---|---|
| Presenting The Country Blues | LP | Blue Horizon | 763851 | 1970 | £15 | £30 | |

## JOHNSON, LAURIE
| | | | | | | | |
|---|---|---|---|---|---|---|---|
| Avengers | LP | HBR | 8/9506 | 1966 | £15 | £30 | US |
| Avengers | LP | Marble Arch | MAL695 | 1967 | £8 | £20 | |
| Avengers | 7" | Pye | 7N17015 | 1965 | £2.50 | £6 | |
| Avengers | 7" | Pye | 7N17015 | 1965 | £7.50 | £15 | picture sleeve |
| Brass Band Swinging | LP | Columbia | 33SX1231 | 1960 | £5 | £12 | |
| New Avengers Theme | 7" | EMI | EMI2562 | 1976 | £2 | £5 | picture sleeve |
| Synthesis | LP | Columbia | SCX6412 | 1970 | £8 | £20 | |

## JOHNSON, LINTON KWESI
| | | | | | | | |
|---|---|---|---|---|---|---|---|
| Dread Beat And Blood | LP | Front Line | FL1017 | 1978 | £5 | £12 | credited to Poet & The Roots |
| Forces Of Victory | LP | Island | ILPS9566 | 1979 | £4 | £10 | |

## JOHNSON, LONNIE
| | | | | | | | |
|---|---|---|---|---|---|---|---|
| Another Night To Cry | LP | Bluesville | BV1062 | 1963 | £6 | £15 | US |
| Blues And Ballads | LP | Bluesville | BV1011 | 1960 | £8 | £20 | US |
| Blues By Lonnie Johnson | LP | Bluesville | BV1007 | 1960 | £8 | £20 | US |
| Blues For Everybody | 78 | Melodisc | 1186 | 1951 | £3 | £8 | |
| Idle Hours | LP | Bluesville | BV1044 | 1961 | £8 | £20 | US |
| Jelly Roll Baker | 78 | Vogue | V2015 | 1951 | £3 | £8 | |
| Keep What You Got | 78 | Melodisc | 1221 | 1952 | £3 | £8 | |
| Little Rockin' Chair | 78 | Vogue | V2079 | 1951 | £3 | £8 | |
| Lonesome Road | LP | King | 395520 | 195– | £30 | £60 | US |
| Lonesome Road | 7" EP | Parlophone | GEP8635 | 1957 | £7.50 | £15 | |
| Lonnie Johnson | LP | Storyville | 616010 | 1969 | £4 | £10 | |
| Lonnie Johnson | LP | XTRA | XTRA1037 | 1966 | £6 | £15 | |
| Lonnie's Blues | 7" EP | Parlophone | GEP8663 | 1957 | £7.50 | £15 | |
| Lonnie's Blues No. 2 | 7" EP | Parlophone | GEP8693 | 1958 | £7.50 | £15 | |
| Losing Game | LP | Bluesville | BV1024 | 1961 | £8 | £20 | US |
| Masters Of The Blues Vol. 6 | LP | Collector's Classics | CC30 | 196– | £5 | £12 | |
| Portraits In Blues Vol. 6 | LP | Storyville | SLP162 | 1964 | £4 | £10 | |
| Sings 24 Twelve Bar Blues | LP | King | K(S)958 | 1966 | £5 | £12 | US |
| Solid Blues | 78 | Melodisc | 1138 | 1951 | £3 | £8 | |
| Woman Blues | LP | Bluesville | BV1054 | 1963 | £6 | £15 | US |

## JOHNSON, LOU
| | | | | | | | |
|---|---|---|---|---|---|---|---|
| Always Something There To Remind Me | 7" | London | HLX10269 | 1969 | £1.50 | £4 | |
| Always Something There To Remind Me | 7" | London | HLX9917 | 1964 | £6 | £12 | |
| Magic Potion | 7" | London | HLX9805 | 1963 | £7.50 | £15 | |
| Magic Potion Of Lou Johnson | 7" EP | London | REX1438 | 1964 | £20 | £40 | |

| Message To Martha | 7" | London | HLX9929 | 1964 | £2.50 | £6 | |
| Please Stop The Wedding | 7" | London | HLX9965 | 1965 | £2 | £5 | |
| Unsatisfied | 7" | London | HLX9994 | 1965 | £10 | £20 | |

## JOHNSON, LUTHER

| With The Muddy Waters Blues Band | LP | Transatlantic | TRA188 | 1968 | £4 | £10 | |

## JOHNSON, MARV

| Ain't Gonna Be That Way | 7" | London | HLT9165 | 1960 | £5 | £10 | |
| Come To Me | 7" | London | HLT8856 | 1959 | £25 | £50 | |
| Happy Days | 7" | London | HLT9265 | 1961 | £5 | £10 | |
| I Believe | LP | United Artists | UAL3187/ UAS6187 | 1962 | £15 | £30 | US |
| I Love The Way You Love | 7" | London | HL7095 | 1960 | £5 | £10 | export |
| I Love The Way You Love Me | 7" | London | HLT9109 | 1960 | £5 | £10 | |
| I'll Pick A Rose For My Rose | LP | Tamla Motown | (S)TML11111 | 1969 | £6 | £15 | |
| I'll Pick A Rose For My Rose | 7" | Tamla Motown | TMG680 | 1969 | £1.50 | £4 | |
| Marvellous Marv | LP | London | HAT2271 | 1960 | £25 | £50 | |
| Merry-Go-Round | 7" | London | HLT9311 | 1961 | £7.50 | £15 | |
| More Marv Johnson | LP | United Artists | UAL3118/ UAS6118 | 1960 | £20 | £40 | US |
| Move Two Mountains | 7" | London | HLT9187 | 1960 | £5 | £10 | |
| Why Do You Want To Let Me Go | 7" | Tamla Motown | TMG525 | 1965 | £25 | £50 | |
| You Got What It Takes | 7" | London | HLT9013 | 1959 | £4 | £8 | |

## JOHNSON, MATT

| Burning Blue Soul | LP | 4AD | CAD113 | 1981 | £6 | £15 | ..psychedelic eye sleeve |

## JOHNSON, MIRRIAM

| Lonesome Road | 7" | London | HLW9337 | 1961 | £2.50 | £6 | |

## JOHNSON, NORMAN

| Take It Baby | 7" | Action | ACT4545 | 1969 | £5 | £10 | |
| You're Everything | 7" | Action | ACT4529 | 1969 | £5 | £10 | |
| You're Everything | 7" | Action | ACT4601 | 1971 | £2.50 | £6 | |

## JOHNSON, PETE

| Boogie Woogie Mood | LP | Vogue Coral | LRA10016 | 1955 | £6 | £15 | |
| J.J.Boogie | 7" | Vogue | V2007 | 1956 | £10 | £20 | |
| Pete Johnson | 7" EP | Vogue | EPV1039 | 1955 | £7.50 | £15 | |
| Pete Johnson | 10" LP | London | AL3549 | 1955 | £10 | £25 | |
| Pete's Blues | LP | Savoy | MG14018 | 195– | £10 | £25 | US |
| Roll Em Boy | 7" EP | Top Rank | JKR8009 | 1959 | £4 | £8 | |
| Swanee River Boogie | 7" | Vogue | V2008 | 1956 | £10 | £20 | |

## JOHNSON, PETE & ALBERT AMMONS

| Eight To The Bar | 10" LP | HMV | DLP1011 | 1953 | £15 | £30 | |

## JOHNSON, PLAS

| Big Twist | 7" | Capitol | CL14772 | 1957 | £4 | £8 | |
| Bop Me Daddy | 10" LP | London | HBU1078 | 1957 | £10 | £25 | |
| Dinah | 7" | Capitol | CL14903 | 1958 | £4 | £8 | |
| Popcorn | 7" | Capitol | CL14836 | 1958 | £4 | £8 | |
| Robbins Nest Cha Cha | 7" | Capitol | CL14973 | 1959 | £1.50 | £4 | |
| You Send Me | 7" | Capitol | CL14816 | 1957 | £4 | £8 | |

## JOHNSON, PROFESSOR GOSPEL SINGERS

| Where Shall I Be | 7" EP | Brunswick | OE9352 | 1958 | £4 | £8 | |

## JOHNSON, RAY

| Calypso Blues | 7" | Vogue | V9093 | 1958 | £10 | £20 | |
| If You Don't Want Me Baby | 7" | Vogue | V9073 | 1957 | £12.50 | £25 | |

## JOHNSON, ROBERT

According to legend, bluesman Robert Johnson met the devil at the crossroads and sold his soul in exchange for prowess on the guitar. In any event, the twenty-nine songs that Johnson recorded in 1936 and 1937 have come to be regarded as the finest and most influential country blues recordings of all. The majority of Johnson's songs have been covered by blues performers in later years, and the British blues boom of the late sixties would have been almost impossible without Johnson's work to draw on. Not that this does Johnson himself any good at all, for he was murdered by a jealous husband just one year after his last recording session.

| Blues Legend 1936-7 | LP | Smokestack | SSLP1 | 196– | £8 | £20 | |
| King Of The Delta Blues Singers | LP | CBS | BPG62456 | 1963 | £4 | £10 | |
| King Of The Delta Blues Singers Vol. 2 | LP | CBS | 64102 | 1970 | £4 | £10 | |
| Robert Johnson | LP | Kokomo | K1000 | 1967 | £8 | £20 | |
| Robert Johnson | LP | Philips | BBL7539 | 1962 | £10 | £25 | |

## JOHNSON, ROY LEE

| So Anna Just Love Me | 7" | Action | ACT4518 | 1969 | £1.50 | £4 | |

## JOHNSON, RUBY

| If I Ever Needed Love | 7" | Stax | 601020 | 1967 | £1.50 | £4 | |

## JOHNSON, TEDDY & PEARL CARR

| Meet Teddy And Pearl | 7" EP | Pye | NEP24112 | 1959 | £2 | £5 | |

## JOHNSON, THEO

| Masters Of War | 7" | Island | WI604 | 1965 | £2 | £5 | |

## JOHNSTON, ADRIENNE

| | | | | | | | |
|---|---|---|---|---|---|---|---|
| Adrienne Of The Johnstons | LP | RCA | SF8416 | 1975 | £4 | £10 | |

## JOHNSTON, BRUCE

| | | | | | | | |
|---|---|---|---|---|---|---|---|
| Original Surfer Stomp | 7" | London | HL9780 | 1963 | £7.50 | £15 | |
| Surfer's Pajama Party | LP | Del-Fi | DFLP/DFST1228 | 1963 | £20 | £40 | US |
| Surfin' Round The World | LP | Columbia | CL2057/CS8857 | 1963 | £25 | £50 | US |

## JOHNSTON BROTHERS

| | | | | | | |
|---|---|---|---|---|---|---|
| Bandit | 7" | Decca | F10302 | 1954 | £1.50 | £4 |
| Chee Chee-oo Chee | 7" | Decca | F10513 | 1955 | £1.50 | £4 |
| Creep | 7" | Decca | F10234 | 1954 | £2 | £5 |
| Dreamboat | 7" | Decca | F10526 | 1955 | £1.50 | £4 |
| Give Her My Love | 7" | Decca | F10828 | 1956 | £2 | £5 |
| Heart | 7" | Decca | F10860 | 1957 | £1.50 | £4 |
| Hernando's Hideaway | 7" | Decca | F10608 | 1955 | £4 | £8 |
| How Little We Know | 7" | Decca | F10747 | 1956 | £1.50 | £4 |
| I Get So Lonely | 7" | Decca | F10286 | 1954 | £1.50 | £4 |
| I Like Music – You Like Music | 7" | Decca | F10939 | 1957 | £1.50 | £4 |
| In The Middle Of The House | 7" | Decca | F10781 | 1956 | £4 | £8 |
| Join In And Sing | 7" | Decca | F10414 | 1954 | £1.50 | £4 |
| Join In And Sing Again | 7" | Decca | F10636 | 1955 | £2 | £5 |
| Join In And Sing No. 3 | 7" | Decca | F10814 | 1956 | £2 | £5 |
| Majorca | 7" | Decca | F10451 | 1955 | £1.50 | £4 |
| Mambo In The Moonlight | 7" | Decca | F10401 | 1954 | £1.50 | £4 |
| No Other Love | 7" | Decca | F10721 | 1956 | £2 | £5 |
| Right To Be Wrong | 7" | Decca | F10490 | 1955 | £1.50 | £4 |
| Sh'boom | 7" | Decca | F10364 | 1954 | £4 | £8 |

## JOHNSTONS

| | | | | | | |
|---|---|---|---|---|---|---|
| Alamo | 7" | Pye | 7N17205 | 1966 | £1.50 | £4 |
| Barley Corn | LP | Transatlantic | TRA185 | 1969 | £6 | £15 |
| Bitter Green | LP | Transatlantic | TRA211 | 1969 | £6 | £15 |
| Both Sides Now | 7" | Transatlantic | BIG113 | 1968 | £1.50 | £4 |
| Colours Of The Dawn | LP | Transatlantic | TRA231 | 1971 | £5 | £12 |
| Curragh Of Kildare | 7" | Pye | 7N17315 | 1967 | £1.50 | £4 |
| Give A Damn | LP | Transatlantic | TRA184 | 1968 | £6 | £15 |
| Give A Damn | 7" | Transatlantic | BIG116 | 1968 | £1.50 | £4 |
| Going Home | 7" | Pye | 7N17144 | 1966 | £1.50 | £4 |
| I Never Will Marry | 7" | Pye | 7N17430 | 1967 | £1.50 | £4 |
| If I Sang My Sang | LP | Transatlantic | TRA251 | 1972 | £5 | £12 |
| Johnstons | LP | Transatlantic | TRA169 | 1968 | £10 | £25 |
| Johnstons Sampler | LP | Transatlantic | TRASAM16 | 1970 | £4 | £10 |
| My House | 7" | Transatlantic | BIG121 | 1969 | £1.50 | £4 |
| Streets Of London | 7" | Transatlantic | BIG132 | 1970 | £1.50 | £4 |
| They'll Never Get Their Man | 7" | Transatlantic | TRASP17 | 1967 | £1.50 | £4 |
| Travelling People | LP | Hallmark | HMA237 | 1967 | £10 | £25 |
| Travelling People | LP | Marble Arch | MAL808 | 1967 | £10 | £25 |

## JOINER, ARKANSAS, JUNIOR HIGH SCHOOL BAND

| | | | | | | |
|---|---|---|---|---|---|---|
| National City | 7" | London | HLG9147 | 1960 | £1.50 | £4 |

## JOINT EFFORT

| | | | | | | | |
|---|---|---|---|---|---|---|---|
| Cannabis | LP | Amphion Seahorse | AS8100 | 1972 | £30 | £60 | US |

## JOKERS

| | | | | | | |
|---|---|---|---|---|---|---|
| Dogfight | 7" | Salvo | SLO1806 | 1962 | £5 | £10 |

## JOKERS WILD

The ultra-collectability of the Jokers Wild's privately pressed record derives not so much from the fact that the drummer, Willie Wilson, was later in Quiver, nor from the fact that the bassist, Ricky Wills, was later in Cochise and the re-formed Small Faces, but from the presence of the lead guitarist, who is David Gilmour – subsequently to be found playing within the ranks of Pink Floyd.

| | | | | | | | |
|---|---|---|---|---|---|---|---|
| Don't Ask Me Why | 7" | Regent Sound | RSR0031 | 1966 | £330 | £500 | best auctioned |
| Jokers Wild | LP | Regent Sound | | 1966 | £700 | £1000 | 1 sided |

## JOLLIVER ARKANSAW

| | | | | | | |
|---|---|---|---|---|---|---|
| Home | LP | Bell | SBLL119 | 1969 | £10 | £25 |

## JOLSON, AL

| | | | | | | |
|---|---|---|---|---|---|---|
| Al Jolson | 7" EP | Fontana | TFE17024 | 1958 | £2 | £5 |
| Jolson Memories | 10" LP | Brunswick | LA8512 | 1951 | £4 | £10 |
| Jolson Sings Again | 10" LP | Brunswick | LA8502 | 1950 | £4 | £10 |
| Souvenir | 10" LP | Brunswick | LA8509 | 1951 | £4 | £10 |
| They Sold A Million No. 2 | 7" EP | Brunswick | OE9418 | 1959 | £2 | £5 |
| They Sold A Million No. 3 | 7" EP | Brunswick | OE9419 | 1959 | £2 | £5 |

## JON

| | | | | | | | |
|---|---|---|---|---|---|---|---|
| Is It Love | 7" | Columbia | DB8249 | 1967 | £12.50 | £25 | |
| So Much For Mary | 7" | Parlophone | R5604 | 1967 | £2.50 | £6 | |
| So Much For Mary | 7" | Parlophone | R5604 | 1967 | £6 | £12 | picture sleeve |

## JON & ALUN

| | | | | | | |
|---|---|---|---|---|---|---|
| Relax Your Mind | LP | Decca | LK/SKL4547 | 1963 | £15 | £30 |

## JON & ROBIN & THE IN CROWD
| | | | | | | | |
|---|---|---|---|---|---|---|---|
| Do It Again A Little Bit Slower | 7" | Stateside | SS2027 | 1967 | £1.50 | £4 | |
| Do It Again A Little Bit Slower | 7" EP | Barclay | 071178 | 1967 | £4 | £8 | French |

## JONAS PALM
| | | | | | | | |
|---|---|---|---|---|---|---|---|
| Ze Wormnest | LP | Piglet | PR1002 | 1980 | £6 | £15 | German |

## JONATHAN & CHARLES
| | | | | | | |
|---|---|---|---|---|---|---|
| Another Week To Go | LP | Herald | LLR566 | 1969 | £150 | £250 |

## JONES, AL
| | | | | | | |
|---|---|---|---|---|---|---|
| Mad Mad World | 7" | HMV | POP451 | 1958 | £37.50 | £75 |

## JONES, ALUN
| | | | | | | |
|---|---|---|---|---|---|---|
| Alun Ashworth Jones | LP | Parlophone | PMC/PCS7081 | 1969 | £8 | £20 |
| Jonesville | LP | Village Thing | VTS19 | 1972 | £6 | £15 |

## JONES, BEVERLY
| | | | | | | |
|---|---|---|---|---|---|---|
| Boy I Saw With You | 7" | HMV | POP1109 | 1963 | £1.50 | £4 |
| Heatwave | 7" | Parlophone | R5189 | 1964 | £2 | £5 |
| Wait Until My Bobby Gets Home | 7" | HMV | POP1201 | 1963 | £1.50 | £4 |
| Why Do Lovers Break Each Others' Hearts | 7" | HMV | POP1140 | 1963 | £1.50 | £4 |

## JONES, BRIAN
The one record credited to Brian Jones comes from the brief period between his leaving the Rolling Stones and his death, but it actually does not feature him at all. His decision to sponsor an ethnic band, however, is entirely symptomatic of his questing, open-minded approach at the time – the same approach as made the Stones' *Their Satanic Majesties Request* into one of the high points of sixties psychedelia, whatever the contrary views of modern critics may say. The Joujouka pipers, incidentally, turn up again in an intriguing meeting with saxophonist Ornette Coleman, on his album, *Dancing In Your Head*.

| | | | | | | |
|---|---|---|---|---|---|---|
| Pipes Of Pan At Joujouka | LP | Rolling Stones | COC49100 | 1971 | £20 | £40 |

## JONES, CAROL
| | | | | | | |
|---|---|---|---|---|---|---|
| Boys With Eyes Of Blue | 7" | Triumph | RGM1012 | 1960 | £25 | £50 |

## JONES, CASEY & THE ENGINEERS
| | | | | | | |
|---|---|---|---|---|---|---|
| One Way Ticket | 7" | Columbia | DB7083 | 1963 | £10 | £20 |

## JONES, CASEY & THE GOVERNORS
| | | | | | | | |
|---|---|---|---|---|---|---|---|
| Beat Hits Vol. 2 | LP | Bellaphon | BWS305 | 1965 | £15 | £30 | German |
| Casey Jones And The Governors | LP | Golden | 12LP108 | 1965 | £15 | £30 | German |
| Don't Ha Ha | LP | Golden | 12LP106 | 1964 | £20 | £40 | German |
| Don't Ha Ha | 7" EP | President | 425 | 1964 | £30 | £60 | French |
| Don't Ha Ha | 7" EP | Riviera | 231087 | 1965 | £20 | £40 | French |

## JONES, CURTIS
| | | | | | | |
|---|---|---|---|---|---|---|
| In London | LP | Decca | LK4587 | 1964 | £8 | £20 |
| Now Resident In Europe | LP | Blue Horizon | 763207 | 1968 | £15 | £30 |
| RCA Victor Race series Vol. 9 | 7" EP | RCA | RCX7184 | 1966 | £4 | £8 |

## JONES, DAVY
The Davy Jones whose records are listed here is the actor who became a member of the Monkees. Just to confuse matters, another Davy Jones also had records issued on the Pye label, but from 1960 to 1962. He has no connection with the Monkees whatsoever. A third Davy Jones made records with the Lower Third and the King Bees on the Vocalion and Parlophone labels. These are rare, but are listed in the guide under the name used by Jones later on – David Bowie. A David Jones who made one single for Philips in 1965 does not appear to have any connection with either the Monkees or David Bowie.

| | | | | | | | |
|---|---|---|---|---|---|---|---|
| Davy Jones | LP | Bell | 6067 | 1971 | £4 | £10 | US |
| Davy Jones | LP | Pye | NPL18178 | 1967 | £6 | £15 | |
| It Ain't Me Babe | 7" EP | Pye | PNV24189 | 1967 | £10 | £20 | French |
| It Ain't Me Babe | 7" | Pye | 7N17302 | 1967 | £2.50 | £6 | picture sleeve |
| Theme For A New Love | 7" | Pye | 7N17380 | 1967 | £2.50 | £6 | picture sleeve |
| Theme For A New Love | 7" | Pye | 7N25432 | 1967 | £1.50 | £4 | |
| What Are We Going To Do | 7" | Colpix | PX784 | 1965 | £1.50 | £4 | |

## JONES, DILL
| | | | | | | |
|---|---|---|---|---|---|---|
| Jones The Jazz | LP | Columbia | 33SX1336 | 1961 | £4 | £10 |
| Piano Moods Vol. 2 | 7" EP | Polygon | JTE104 | 1956 | £2 | £5 |
| Piano Moods Vol. 5 | 7" EP | Pye | NJE1024 | 1956 | £2 | £5 |

## JONES, ELVIN
| | | | | | | | |
|---|---|---|---|---|---|---|---|
| Coalition | LP | Blue Note | BST84361 | 1970 | £4 | £10 | |
| Elvin Jones | LP | Blue Note | BST84414 | 1970 | £4 | £10 | |
| Genesis | LP | Blue Note | BST84369 | 1970 | £4 | £10 | |
| Heavy Sounds | LP | Impulse | MIPL/SIPL513 | 1969 | £5 | £12 | |
| Live | LP | P.M.Records | PMR004 | 1975 | £5 | £12 | US |
| Live At The Lighthouse | LP | Blue Note | BNLA015 | 1973 | £6 | £15 | double |
| Midnight Walk | LP | Atlantic | 1485 | 1968 | £5 | £12 | |
| On The Mountain | LP | P.M.Records | PMR005 | 1975 | £5 | £12 | US |
| Poly-Currents | LP | Blue Note | BST84331 | 1969 | £5 | £12 | |
| Puttin' It Together | LP | Blue Note | BST84282 | 1968 | £5 | £12 | |
| Ultimate | LP | Blue Note | BST84305 | 1968 | £5 | £12 | |

## JONES, ETTA
| | | | | | | | |
|---|---|---|---|---|---|---|---|
| Don't Go To Strangers | LP | Prestige | PRLP7186 | 1960 | £5 | £12 | US |
| From The Heart | LP | Prestige | PRLP7214 | 1962 | £5 | £12 | US |

| Title | Format | Label | Catalog | Year | | | Notes |
|---|---|---|---|---|---|---|---|
| Holler | LP | Prestige | PRLP7284 | 1963 | £5 | £12 | US |
| Lonely And Blue | LP | Prestige | PRLP7241 | 1962 | £5 | £12 | US |
| Love Shout | LP | Prestige | PRLP7272 | 1963 | £5 | £12 | US |
| Sings | LP | King | 544 | 1958 | £10 | £25 | US |
| Sings | LP | King | 707 | 1961 | £8 | £20 | US |
| So Warm | LP | Prestige | PRLP7204 | 1961 | £5 | £12 | US |
| Something Nice | LP | Prestige | PRLP7194 | 1961 | £5 | £12 | US |

## JONES, GEORGE

| Title | Format | Label | Catalog | Year | | | Notes |
|---|---|---|---|---|---|---|---|
| Accidentally On Purpose | 7" | Mercury | AMT1100 | 1960 | £2.50 | £6 | |
| Ballad Side Of George Jones | LP | Mercury | MG2/SR60836 | 1963 | £5 | £12 | US |
| Best Of American Country Music Vol. 4 | 7" EP | Ember | EMBEP4548 | 1964 | £2 | £5 | |
| Big Harlen Taylor | 7" | Mercury | AMT1078 | 1959 | £2.50 | £6 | |
| Blue And Lonesome | LP | Mercury | MG2/SR60906 | 1964 | £5 | £12 | US |
| Blue Grass Hootenanny | LP | United Artists | ULP1077 | 1965 | £4 | £10 | with Melba Montgomery |
| Blue Moon Of Kentucky | LP | United Artists | (S)ULP1137 | 1966 | £4 | £10 | with Melba Montgomery |
| C & W Aces | 7" EP | Mercury | 10009MCE | 1964 | £4 | £8 | |
| Candy Hearts | 7" | Mercury | AMT1124 | 1961 | £2.50 | £6 | |
| Country & Western £1 Male Singer | LP | Mercury | MG2/SR60937 | 1964 | £5 | £12 | US |
| Country And Western | 7" EP | Mercury | ZEP10012 | 1959 | £10 | £20 | with Jimmie Skinner |
| Country And Western Hits | LP | Mercury | MG2/SR60624 | 1961 | £5 | £12 | US |
| Country And Western Winners | LP | Mercury | SMWL21003 | 1968 | £4 | £10 | |
| Country Church Time | LP | Mercury | MG20462 | 1959 | £8 | £20 | US |
| Country Heart | LP | Musicor | P2(S)5094 | 1966 | £4 | £10 | US |
| Country Song Hits | 7" EP | Melodisc | EPM7109 | 195– | £10 | £20 | |
| Crown Prince Of Country Music | LP | Ember | CW101 | 1963 | £4 | £10 | |
| Crown Prince Of Country Music | LP | Starday | SLP125 | 1960 | £6 | £15 | US |
| Duets Country Style | LP | Mercury | MG2/SR60747 | 1962 | £5 | £12 | US, with Margie Singleton |
| Fabulous Country Music Sound | LP | Ember | CW109 | 1964 | £4 | £10 | |
| Fabulous Country Music Sound | LP | Starday | SLP151 | 1962 | £6 | £15 | US |
| Fourteen Country Favourites | LP | Mercury | MG20306 | 1958 | £8 | £20 | US |
| From The Heart | LP | Mercury | MG2/SR60694 | 1962 | £5 | £12 | US |
| George Jones | LP | London | HAB8259 | 1966 | £6 | £15 | |
| George Jones | 7" EP | Mercury | ZEP10036 | 1959 | £25 | £50 | |
| George Jones And Gene Pitney | LP | Stateside | SL10147 | 1965 | £4 | £10 | with Gene Pitney |
| George Jones Salutes Hank Williams | LP | Mercury | MG20257/SR60257 | 1958 | £5 | £12 | US |
| George Jones Song Book | LP | London | HAB8340 | 1967 | £6 | £15 | |
| George Jones Story | LP | Starday | SLP366 | 1966 | £6 | £15 | US |
| Grand Ole Opry's New Star | LP | Starday | SLP101 | 1958 | £25 | £50 | US |
| Great George Jones | LP | United Artists | (S)ULP1136 | 1966 | £4 | £10 | |
| Greatest Hits | LP | London | HAB8125 | 1964 | £5 | £12 | |
| Greatest Hits | LP | Mercury | SMCL20107 | 1967 | £4 | £10 | |
| Heartaches And Tears | LP | Mercury | MG2/SR60990 | 1965 | £5 | £12 | US |
| Hits Of His Country Cousins | LP | United Artists | ULP1037 | 1963 | £4 | £10 | |
| I Get Lonely In A Hurry | LP | United Artists | ULP1091 | 1965 | £4 | £10 | |
| I Saw Me | 7" | United Artists | UP1015 | 1963 | £2 | £5 | |
| I Wish Tonight Would Never End | LP | United Artists | ULP1050 | 1964 | £4 | £10 | |
| If My Heart Had Windows | 7" | Stateside | SS2145 | 1969 | £1.50 | £4 | |
| It's Country Time Again | LP | Stateside | SL10173 | 1966 | £4 | £10 | with Gene Pitney |
| Love Bug | LP | Stateside | (S)SL10184 | 1966 | £4 | £10 | |
| More New Favourites | LP | United Artists | ULP1074 | 1964 | £4 | £10 | |
| Mr. Country And Western Music | LP | Stateside | SL10157 | 1965 | £4 | £10 | |
| Musical Loves, Life And Sorrows | LP | Musicor | MS3159 | 1968 | £4 | £10 | US |
| My Favourites Of Hank Williams | LP | United Artists | ULP1014 | 1963 | £4 | £10 | |
| New Favourites | LP | United Artists | ULP1007 | 1962 | £4 | £10 | |
| Novelty Side Of George Jones | LP | Mercury | MG2/SR60793 | 1963 | £6 | £15 | US |
| Race Is On | 7" | United Artists | UP1080 | 1965 | £2 | £5 | |
| She Thinks I Still Care | 7" | HMV | POP1037 | 1962 | £2.50 | £6 | |
| Singing The Blues | LP | Mercury | MG2/SR61029 | 1965 | £5 | £12 | US |
| Sings Like The Dickens | LP | United Artists | ULP1082 | 1965 | £4 | £10 | |
| Sings The Songs Of Dallas Frazier | LP | Stateside | (S)SL10236 | 1968 | £4 | £10 | |
| Song Book And Picture Album | LP | Starday | SLP401 | 1967 | £6 | £15 | US |
| Treasure Of Love | 7" | Mercury | AMT1021 | 1959 | £5 | £10 | |
| Trouble In Mind | LP | United Artists | ULP1101 | 1965 | £4 | £10 | |
| Variety Is The Spice | LP | Stateside | (S)SL10215 | 1967 | £4 | £10 | |
| We Found Heaven Right Here On Earth | LP | Stateside | (S)SL10195 | 1967 | £4 | £10 | |
| What's In Our Hearts | LP | United Artists | ULP1070 | 1964 | £4 | £10 | with Melba Montgomery |
| White Lightning | 7" | Mercury | AMT1036 | 1959 | £12.50 | £25 | |
| White Lightning And Other Favorites | LP | Mercury | MG20477 | 1959 | £8 | £20 | US |
| Who Shot Sam | 7" | Mercury | AMT1058 | 1959 | £6 | £12 | |

## JONES, GLORIA

| Title | Format | Label | Catalog | Year | | | Notes |
|---|---|---|---|---|---|---|---|
| Finders Keepers | 7" | Stateside | SS555 | 1966 | £7.50 | £15 | |
| Heartbeat | 7" | Capitol | CL15429 | 1966 | £5 | £10 | |

## JONES, GRACE

| Title | Format | Label | Catalog | Year | | | Notes |
|---|---|---|---|---|---|---|---|
| La Vie en rose | 12" | Island | IPR2004 | 1986 | £2.50 | £6 | promo |

## JONES, GRANDPA

| Title | Format | Label | Catalog | Year | | | Notes |
|---|---|---|---|---|---|---|---|
| Country And Western | 7" EP | Parlophone | GEP8766 | 1958 | £7.50 | £15 | |
| Country Round Up | 7" EP | Parlophone | GEP8781 | 1959 | £6 | £12 | |
| Dark As A Dungeon | 7" | Brunswick | 05676 | 1957 | £10 | £20 | |
| Do You Remember? | LP | King | 845 | 1963 | £8 | £20 | US |
| Evening With Grandpa Jones | LP | Decca | DL4364 | 1963 | £8 | £20 | US |

| | | | | | | | |
|---|---|---|---|---|---|---|---|
| Grandpa Sings Jimmie Rodgers | 7" EP | London | REU1417 | 1964 | £7.50 | £15 | |
| Greatest Hits | LP | King | 554 | 1958 | £8 | £20 | US |
| Make The Rafters Ring | LP | London | HAU/SHU8010 | 1962 | £8 | £20 | |
| Meet Grandpa Jones | 7" EP | Parlophone | GEP8666 | 1957 | £6 | £12 | |
| Mountain Music Vol. 3 | 7" EP | Brunswick | OE9455 | 1959 | £5 | £10 | |
| Other Side Of Grandpa Jones | LP | King | 888 | 1964 | £8 | £20 | US |
| Rollin' Along | LP | King | 809 | 1963 | £8 | £20 | US |
| Sixteen Sacred Gospel Songs | LP | King | 822 | 1963 | £8 | £20 | US |
| Strictly Country Tunes | LP | King | 625 | 1959 | £8 | £20 | US |
| Yodelling Hits | LP | London | HAU/SHU8119 | 1964 | £8 | £20 | |

## JONES, HANK

| | | | | | | | |
|---|---|---|---|---|---|---|---|
| Hank Jones Quartet | LP | London | LTZC15118 | 1958 | £8 | £20 | |
| Hank Jones Quartet/Quintet | LP | London | LTZC15014 | 1956 | £10 | £25 | |
| Have You Met Hank Jones? | LP | London | LTZC15079 | 1958 | £10 | £25 | |

## JONES, HEATHER

| | | | | | | | |
|---|---|---|---|---|---|---|---|
| Jiawl! | LP | Sain | 1047M | 1976 | £8 | £20 | |
| Mae'r Olwyn Yn Troi | LP | Sain | 1008M | 1973 | £10 | £25 | |

## JONES, HUW

| | | | | | | | |
|---|---|---|---|---|---|---|---|
| Dwr | 7" | Sain | SAIN1 | 1969 | £5 | £10 | picture sleeve |

## JONES, JANET

| | | | | | | | |
|---|---|---|---|---|---|---|---|
| Janet Jones | LP | Midas | | 1974 | £150 | £250 | |
| Sing To Me Lady | LP | Midas | MR005 | 1974 | £150 | £250 | |

## JONES, JANIE

| | | | | | | | |
|---|---|---|---|---|---|---|---|
| Back On My Feet Again | 7" | President | PT309 | 1970 | £1.50 | £4 | |
| Charlie Smith | 7" | Pye | 7N17550 | 1968 | £1.50 | £4 | |
| Girl's Song | 7" | Major Minor | MM577 | 1968 | £1.50 | £4 | |
| Gunning For You | 7" | HMV | POP1514 | 1966 | £4 | £8 | |
| Tickle Me Tootsie Wootsies | 7" | Columbia | DB8173 | 1967 | £1.50 | £4 | |
| Witches Brew | 7" | HMV | POP1495 | 1965 | £5 | £10 | |

## JONES, JERRY

| | | | | | | | |
|---|---|---|---|---|---|---|---|
| Live At The Kingston Hotel, Jamaica | LP | Bamboo | BALPS213 | 1971 | £10 | £25 | |

## JONES, JIMMY

| | | | | | | | |
|---|---|---|---|---|---|---|---|
| 39-21-46 | 7" | Stateside | SS2041 | 1967 | £1.50 | £4 | |
| Good Timin' | LP | MGM | C832 | 1960 | £15 | £30 | |
| Good Timin' | 7" | MGM | MGM1078 | 1960 | £1.50 | £4 | |
| Handy Man | 7" | MGM | MGM1051 | 1960 | £1.50 | £4 | |
| I Just Go For You | 7" | MGM | MGM1091 | 1960 | £1.50 | £4 | |
| I Say Love | 7" | MGM | MGM1133 | 1961 | £1.50 | £4 | |
| I Told You So | 7" | MGM | MGM1123 | 1961 | £1.50 | £4 | |
| Jimmy Handyman Jones | 7" EP | MGM | MGMEP745 | 1960 | £12.50 | £25 | |
| Mister Music Man | 7" | MGM | MGM1146 | 1961 | £1.50 | £4 | |
| Ready For Love | 7" | MGM | MGM1103 | 1960 | £1.50 | £4 | |
| Walkin' | 7" | Columbia | DB7592 | 1965 | £7.50 | £15 | |
| You're Much Too Young | 7" | MGM | MGM1168 | 1962 | £1.50 | £4 | |

## JONES, JO

| | | | | | | | |
|---|---|---|---|---|---|---|---|
| Jo Jones | LP | Top Rank | 25039 | 1959 | £4 | £10 | |
| Jo Jones Special | LP | Vanguard | PPL11002 | 1956 | £6 | £15 | |
| Jo Jones Trio | LP | Top Rank | 35039 | 1960 | £4 | £10 | |

## JONES, JOE

| | | | | | | | |
|---|---|---|---|---|---|---|---|
| You Talk Too Much | LP | Roulette | (S)R25143 | 1961 | £8 | £20 | US |
| You Talk Too Much | 7" | Columbia | DB4533 | 1960 | £2.50 | £6 | |

## JONES, JOHN PAUL

| | | | | | | | |
|---|---|---|---|---|---|---|---|
| Baja | 7" | Pye | 7N15637 | 1964 | £25 | £50 | |

## JONES, JONAH

| | | | | | | | |
|---|---|---|---|---|---|---|---|
| I Dig Chicks | LP | Capitol | T1193 | 1959 | £4 | £10 | |
| Jonah Jones Sextet | 10" LP | London | LZN14003 | 1955 | £8 | £20 | |
| Jonah Jones-Alix Combelle Sextet | 10" LP | Vogue | LDE145 | 1955 | £8 | £20 | |
| Jumpin' With Jonah | LP | Capitol | (S)T1039 | 1959 | £4 | £10 | |
| Swinging At The Cinema | LP | Capitol | T1083 | 1959 | £4 | £10 | |

## JONES, LINDA

| | | | | | | | |
|---|---|---|---|---|---|---|---|
| Hypnotised | LP | Loma | 5907 | 1967 | £10 | £25 | US |
| Hypnotised | 7" | Warner Bros | WB2070 | 1967 | £12.50 | £25 | |
| I Just Can't Live My Life | 7" | Warner Bros | K16621 | 1975 | £2 | £5 | |
| Your Precious Love | LP | Turbo | 7007 | 1973 | £5 | £12 | US |

## JONES, MAGGIE

| | | | | | | | |
|---|---|---|---|---|---|---|---|
| Columbia Recordings In Chronological Order Vol. 1 | LP | VJM | VLP23 | 1970 | £4 | £10 | |
| Columbia Recordings In Chronological Order Vol. 2 | LP | VJM | VLP25 | 1970 | £4 | £10 | |

## JONES, NIC

| | | | | | | | |
|---|---|---|---|---|---|---|---|
| Ballads And Songs | LP | Trailer | LER2014 | 1970 | £10 | £25 | |
| From The Devil To A Stranger | LP | Transatlantic | TRA507 | 1978 | £6 | £15 | |
| Nic Jones | LP | Trailer | LER2027 | 1971 | £8 | £20 | |
| Noah's Ark Trap | LP | Trailer | LER2091 | 1977 | £10 | £25 | |

## JONES, NIGEL MAZLYN

| | | | | | | | |
|---|---|---|---|---|---|---|---|
| Breaking Cover | LP | Isle Of Light | IOL0230 | 1982 | £6 | £15 | |
| Sentinel | LP | Avada | AVA105 | 1978 | £10 | £25 | |
| Ship To Shore | LP | Isle Of Light | IOL666/1 | 1976 | £20 | £40 | |

## JONES, PALMER

| | | | | | | | |
|---|---|---|---|---|---|---|---|
| Great Magic Of Love | 7" | Direction | 583603 | 1968 | £1.50 | £4 | |

## JONES, PAUL

| | | | | | | | |
|---|---|---|---|---|---|---|---|
| And The Sun Will Shine | 7" | Columbia | DB8379 | 1968 | £6 | £12 | |
| Come Into My Music Box | LP | Columbia | SCX6347 | 1969 | £8 | £20 | |
| Crucifix In A Horseshoe | LP | Vertigo | 6360059 | 1971 | £10 | £25 | spiral label |
| High Time | 7" EP | Pathe | EGF952 | 1966 | £6 | £12 | French |
| High Time | 7" | HMV | POP1554 | 1966 | £1.50 | £4 | |
| I've Been A Bad Bad Boy | 7" EP | Pathe | EGF965 | 1966 | £6 | £12 | French |
| I've Been A Bad Bad Boy | 7" | HMV | POP1576 | 1967 | £1.50 | £4 | |
| Love Me Love My Friends | LP | HMV | CLP/CSD3602 | 1967 | £6 | £15 | |
| My Way | LP | HMV | CLP/CSD3586 | 1966 | £6 | £15 | |
| Privilege | LP | HMV | CLP3523 | 1966 | £6 | £15 | |
| Privilege | 7" EP | HMV | 7EG8974 | 1966 | £5 | £10 | |
| Privilege | 7" EP | Pathe | EGF982 | 1966 | £6 | £12 | French |
| When I Was Six Years Old | 7" | Columbia | DB8417 | 1968 | £1.50 | £4 | |

## JONES, QUINCY

| | | | | | | | |
|---|---|---|---|---|---|---|---|
| Around The World | LP | Mercury | MMC14098/ CMS18064 | 1962 | £4 | £10 | |
| Big Band Bash | 7" EP | Mercury | ZEP10047 | 1960 | £2 | £5 | |
| Birth Of A Band | LP | Mercury | MMC14038/ CMS18026 | 1960 | £5 | £12 | |
| Birth Of A Band | 7" EP | Mercury | ZEP10109/ SEZ19017 | 1961 | £2 | £5 | |
| Birth Of A Band Part 2 | 7" EP | Mercury | ZEP10119/ SEZ19021 | 1961 | £2 | £5 | |
| Double Six Meet Quincy Jones | 7" EP | Columbia | SEG8088 | 1961 | £2 | £5 | |
| Go West, Man | LP | HMV | CLP1157 | 1958 | £6 | £15 | |
| Great Wide World Of Quincy Jones | LP | Mercury | MMC14046/ CMS18031 | 1960 | £5 | £12 | |
| I Dig Dancers | LP | Mercury | MMC14080/ CMS18055 | 1961 | £4 | £10 | |
| Plays Hip Hits | LP | Mercury | MMC14128 | 1963 | £4 | £10 | |
| Quintessence | LP | HMV | CLP1581/CSD1452 | 1962 | £5 | £12 | |
| Soul Bossa Nova | 7" | Mercury | AMT1195 | 1962 | £2 | £5 | |
| This Is How I Feel About Jazz | LP | HMV | CLP1162 | 1958 | £6 | £15 | |
| Walking In Space | LP | A&M | AMLS961 | 1969 | £4 | £10 | |

## JONES, RICK

| | | | | | | | |
|---|---|---|---|---|---|---|---|
| Twixt You And Me | LP | Argo | ZFB27 | 1971 | £4 | £10 | |

## JONES, RONNIE

| | | | | | | | |
|---|---|---|---|---|---|---|---|
| Anyone Who Knows What Love Is | 7" | Decca | F12146 | 1965 | £2.50 | £6 | |
| I Need Your Loving | 7" | Decca | F12012 | 1964 | £2.50 | £6 | |
| I'm So Clean | 7" | Parlophone | R5326 | 1965 | £10 | £20 | |
| In My Love Mind | 7" | Polydor | 56222 | 1967 | £2 | £5 | |
| Little Bitty Pretty One | 7" | CBS | 2699 | 1967 | £1.50 | £4 | |
| Little Bitty Pretty One | 7" | CBS | 3304 | 1968 | £1.50 | £4 | |
| My Love | 7" | Decca | F12066 | 1965 | £4 | £8 | |

## JONES, SAMANTHA

| | | | | | | | |
|---|---|---|---|---|---|---|---|
| And Suddenly | 7" | United Artists | UP2258 | 1968 | £4 | £8 | |
| It's All Because Of You | 7" | United Artists | UP1072 | 1965 | £1.50 | £4 | |
| Surrounded By A Ray Of Sunshine | 7" | United Artists | UP1185 | 1967 | £12.50 | £25 | |

## JONES, SANDIE

| | | | | | | | |
|---|---|---|---|---|---|---|---|
| Music Of Love | 7" | Polydor | 2058223 | 1972 | £5 | £10 | |

## JONES, SPIKE

| | | | | | | | |
|---|---|---|---|---|---|---|---|
| Deep Purple | 7" | HMV | 7MC3 | 1954 | £1.50 | £4 | export |
| Fun In Hi Fi | 7" EP | HMV | 7EG8286 | 1957 | £2 | £5 | |
| Hot Lips | 7" | HMV | 7M121 | 1953 | £4 | £8 | |
| I Saw Mommy Kissing Santa Claus | 7" | HMV | 7M160 | 1953 | £2 | £5 | |
| I Wanna Go Back To West Virginia | 7" | HMV | 7MC17 | 1954 | £1.50 | £4 | export |
| Omnibust TV Schedule | LP | London | HAG2270/ SHG6090 | 1960 | £4 | £10 | |
| Secret Love | 7" | HMV | 7M324 | 1955 | £2 | £5 | |
| Sixty Years Of Music America Hates Best | LP | London | HAG2298/ SHG6109 | 1961 | £4 | £10 | |
| Spike Jones In Hi Fi | 7" EP | Warner Bros | WEP6044 | 1961 | £2 | £5 | |
| Spike Jones In Stereo | 7" EP | Warner Bros | WSEP2044 | 1961 | £2.50 | £6 | |
| Spike Jones No. 1 | 7" EP | RCA | RCX1030 | 1959 | £2 | £5 | |
| Spike Jones No. 2 | 7" EP | RCA | RCX1037 | 1959 | £2 | £5 | |
| Spooktacular Sound | LP | Warner Bros | WB4004/WS8004 | 1960 | £4 | £10 | |

## JONES, STEVE

| | | | | | | | |
|---|---|---|---|---|---|---|---|
| Live | CD | MCA | CD4518179 | 1990 | £5 | £12 | promo only |

## JONES, THAD

| | | | | | | | |
|---|---|---|---|---|---|---|---|
| Leonard Feather Presents Mad Thad | LP | Nixa | NJL13 | 1957 | £20 | £40 | |

| | | | | | | | |
|---|---|---|---|---|---|---|---|
| Thad Jones | LP | Vogue | LDE172 | 1956 £20 | £40 | |

## JONES, THAD & MEL LEWIS JAZZ ORCHESTRA
| | | | | | | |
|---|---|---|---|---|---|---|
| Central Park North | LP | United Artists | UAS29058 | 1969 £4 | £10 | |
| Consummation | LP | Blue Note | BST84346 | 1970 £4 | £10 | |
| Live At The Village Vanguard | LP | United Artists | USS7008 | 1967 £5 | £12 | |
| Monday Night | LP | United Artists | UAS29016 | 1968 £5 | £12 | |
| Presenting Thad Jones–Mel Lewis & The Jazz Orchestra | LP | United Artists | SULP1169 | 1967 £5 | £12 | |

## JONES, THELMA
| | | | | | | |
|---|---|---|---|---|---|---|
| House That Jack Built | 7" | Soul City | SC110 | 1969 £4 | £8 | |
| Stranger | 7" | Sue | WI4047 | 1968 £5 | £10 | |

## JONES, TOM
| | | | | | | |
|---|---|---|---|---|---|---|
| Bama Lama Bama Loo | 7" EP | Decca | 457078 | 1965 £5 | £10 | French |
| Carrying A Torch | CD-s | Dover | ROJCD12 | 1991 £2 | £5 | ...with Van Morrison |
| Chills And Fever | 7" | Decca | F11966 | 1964 £5 | £10 | |
| Detroit City | 7" EP | Decca | 457141 | 1967 £4 | £8 | French |
| Detroit City | 7" | Decca | F22563 | 1967 £2.50 | £6 | export |
| Green Green Grass Of Home | 7" EP | Decca | 457134 | 1967 £4 | £8 | French |
| Green Green Grass Of Home | 7" | Decca | F12516 | 1966 £2.50 | £6 | export |
| It's Not Unusual | 7" EP | Decca | 457065 | 1965 £4 | £8 | French |
| Little Lonely One | 7" EP | Columbia | ESRF1684 | 1965 £5 | £10 | French, B side by Beau Brummel |
| Little Lonely One | 7" | Columbia | DB7566 | 1965 £4 | £8 | |
| Lonely Joe | 7" | Columbia | DB7733 | 1965 £2.50 | £6 | |
| Not Responsible | 7" EP | Decca | 457118 | 1966 £4 | £8 | French |
| On Stage | 7" EP | Decca | DFE8617 | 1965 £2.50 | £6 | |
| Stop Breaking My Heart | 7" EP | Decca | 457107 | 1966 £4 | £8 | French |
| Stop Breaking My Heart | 7" | Decca | F12349 | 1966 £2 | £5 | |
| Thunderball | 7" | Decca | F12292 | 1966 £1.50 | £4 | |
| Till | 7" | Decca | FR13237 | 1971 £2 | £5 | export |
| To Make A Big Man Cry | 7" | Decca | F12315 | 1966 £2.50 | £6 | export |
| Tom Jones | 7" EP | Columbia | SEG8464 | 1965 £6 | £12 | |
| What A Party | 7" EP | Decca | 457127 | 1966 £4 | £8 | French |
| What A Party | 7" EP | Decca | DFE8668 | 1965 £2.50 | £6 | |
| What's New Pussycat | 7" EP | Decca | 457088 | 1965 £4 | £8 | French |
| With These Hands | 7" EP | Decca | 457082 | 1965 £4 | £8 | French |

## JONES, WIZZ
| | | | | | | |
|---|---|---|---|---|---|---|
| Ballad Of Hollis Brown | 7" | Columbia | DB7776 | 1965 £4 | £8 | with Pete Stanley |
| Legendary Me | LP | Village Thing | VTS4 | 1970 £10 | £25 | |
| Magical Flight | LP | Plant Life | PLR009 | 1977 £4 | £10 | |
| Right Now | LP | CBS | 64809 | 1971 £20 | £40 | |
| Roll On River | LP | Folk Freak | FF4006 | 1981 £5 | £12 | German, with Werner Lammerhirt |
| Sixteen Tons Of Bluegrass | LP | Columbia | SX6083 | 1966 £62.50 | £125 | with Pete Stanley |
| Solo Flight | LP | Autogram | FLLP507 | 1973 £15 | £30 | with EP, German |
| When I Leave Berlin | LP | Village Thing | VTS24 | 1974 £6 | £15 | |
| Wizz Jones | LP | United Artists | (S)ULP1209 | 1969 £62.50 | £125 | |

## JONESY
Alan Bown's R&B band was a significant part of the sixties rock scene in Britain, even if it never managed to break through into the first division. Part of the problem was no doubt due to the difficulty Bown himself faced in finding a strong image when he was neither a singer nor a guitarist, but a trumpet player. Within Jonesy, Bown finally dealt with the problem by relegating himself to the status of band member rather than leader, but it is his trumpet playing that gives the band's slant on jazz-rock such a distinctive edge. If the electric-period Miles Davis had ever decided to play within a song-based band, it might have sounded something like this.

| | | | | | | |
|---|---|---|---|---|---|---|
| Growing | LP | Dawn | DNLS3055 | 1973 £6 | £15 | |
| Keeping Up | LP | Dawn | DNLS3048 | 1973 £6 | £15 | |
| No Alternative | LP | Dawn | DNLS3042 | 1972 £10 | £25 | |

## JONNS, HARLEM RESHUFFLE
| | | | | | | |
|---|---|---|---|---|---|---|
| Everything Under The Sun | 7" | Fontana | TF1004 | 1969 £1.50 | £4 | |
| Harlem Jonns Reshuffle | LP | Fontana | STL5509 | 1969 £4 | £10 | |
| You Are The One I Love | 7" | Fontana | TF970 | 1968 £2 | £5 | |

## JONSTON MCPHILBRY
| | | | | | | |
|---|---|---|---|---|---|---|
| She's Gone | 7" | Fontana | TF663 | 1966 £37.50 | £75 | |

## JOPLIN, JANIS
| | | | | | | |
|---|---|---|---|---|---|---|
| Cheap Thrills | CD | CBS | CD63392 | 1984 £5 | £12 | with Big Brother & The Holding Co. |
| I Got Dem Ol' Kozmic Blues Again | LP | CBS | 63546 | 1969 £4 | £10 | |
| In Concert | LP | CBS | 67241 | 1972 £5 | £12 | double |
| Janis | LP | CBS | 88115 | 1974 £5 | £12 | double |
| Move Over | 7" | CBS | 9136 | 1971 £1.50 | £4 | |
| Pearl | LP | CBS | 64188 | 1971 £4 | £10 | |
| Pearl | LP | CBS | Q64188 | 1974 £5 | £12 | quad |

## JORDAN, CHRISTOPHER
| | | | | | | |
|---|---|---|---|---|---|---|
| Knack | 7" EP | United Artists | 36075 | 1965 £4 | £8 | French |

## JORDAN, DICK
| | | | | | | |
|---|---|---|---|---|---|---|
| Hallelujah I Love Her So | 7" | Oriole | CB1534 | 1960 £1.50 | £4 | |
| Little Christine | 7" | Oriole | CB1548 | 1960 £1.50 | £4 | |

## JORDAN, DUKE

| | | | | | | | |
|---|---|---|---|---|---|---|---|
| Duke Jordan | 10" LP | Vogue | LDE099 | 1954 | £20 | £40 | |
| Flight To Jordan | LP | Blue Note | BLP/BST84046 | 196– | £25 | £50 | |

## JORDAN, FRED

| | | | | | | | |
|---|---|---|---|---|---|---|---|
| Songs Of A Shropshire Farm Worker | LP | Topic | 12T150 | 1966 | £5 | £12 | |
| When The Frost Is On The Pumpkin | LP | Topic | 12TS233 | 1974 | £4 | £10 | |

## JORDAN, LOUIS

| | | | | | | | |
|---|---|---|---|---|---|---|---|
| Dad Gum Ya Hide Boy | 78 | Melodisc | 1031 | 1954 | £3 | £8 | |
| Go Blow Your Horn | LP | Score | 4007 | 195– | £25 | £50 | US |
| Greatest Hits | LP | Decca | DL5035 | 1967 | £4 | £10 | US |
| Is You Is Or Is You Ain't My Baby | 7" | Melodisc | 1616 | 196– | £2 | £5 | with Chris Barber |
| Let The Good Times Roll | LP | Ace Of Hearts | AH85 | 1965 | £5 | £12 | |
| Let The Good Times Roll | LP | Coral | CP59 | 1970 | £4 | £10 | |
| Let The Good Times Roll | LP | Decca | DL8551 | 1958 | £10 | £25 | US |
| Louis Jordan | 7" EP | Melodisc | EPM766 | 1956 | £15 | £30 | |
| Man, We're Wailin' | LP | Mercury | MPL6541 | 1958 | £10 | £25 | |
| Messy Bessy | 78 | Melodisc | 1349 | 1956 | £3 | £8 | |
| Ooo Wee | 7" | Downbeat | CHA3 | 1960 | £6 | £12 | |
| Saturday Night Fish Fry | 78 | Brunswick | 04402 | 1950 | £2.50 | £6 | |
| Somebody Up There Digs Me | LP | Mercury | MG20242 | 1957 | £15 | £30 | US |
| Somebody Up There Digs Me | 10" LP | Mercury | MPT7521 | 1957 | £15 | £30 | |

## JORDAN, SHEILA

| | | | | | | | |
|---|---|---|---|---|---|---|---|
| Portrait | LP | Blue Note | BLP/BST89002 | 1962 | £20 | £40 | |

## JORDAN BROTHERS

| | | | | | | | |
|---|---|---|---|---|---|---|---|
| Never Never | 7" | London | HLW8908 | 1959 | £7.50 | £15 | |
| No Wings On My Angel | 7" | London | HLW9308 | 1961 | £2 | £5 | |
| Things I Didn't Say | 7" | London | HLW9235 | 1960 | £2.50 | £6 | |

## JORDANAIRES

| | | | | | | | |
|---|---|---|---|---|---|---|---|
| Beautiful City | 10" LP | RCA | LPM3081 | 1953 | £15 | £30 | US |
| Don't Be Cruel | 7" | Capitol | CL15281 | 1963 | £2.50 | £6 | |
| Gloryland | LP | Capitol | T1167 | 1959 | £10 | £25 | US |
| Heavenly Spirit | LP | Capitol | T1011 | 1958 | £10 | £25 | US |
| Little Miss Ruby | 7" | Capitol | CL14921 | 1958 | £2.50 | £6 | |
| Peace In The Valley | LP | Decca | DL8681 | 1957 | £10 | £25 | US |
| Spotlight On The Jordanaires | LP | Capitol | T1742 | 1962 | £10 | £25 | |
| Sugaree | 7" | Capitol | CL14687 | 1957 | £12.50 | £25 | |
| Summer Vacation | 7" | Capitol | CL14773 | 1957 | £2.50 | £6 | |

## JOSEF K

| | | | | | | | |
|---|---|---|---|---|---|---|---|
| Chance Meeting | 7" | Absolute | ABS1 | 1980 | £10 | £20 | |
| Chance Meeting | 7" | Postcard | 81-5 | 1981 | £2 | £5 | with postcard |
| It's Kinda Funny | 7" | Postcard | 80-5 | 1980 | £1.50 | £4 | |
| It's Kinda Funny | 7" | Postcard | 80-5 | 1980 | £4 | £8 | colour insert in bag |
| Only Fun In Town | LP | Postcard | 81-7 | 1981 | £5 | £12 | |
| Radio Drill Time | 7" | Postcard | 80-3 | 1980 | £2 | £5 | |
| Radio Drill Time | 7" | Postcard | 80-3 | 1980 | £5 | £10 | with poster |
| Sorry For Laughing | LP | Postcard | 81-1 | 1981 | £50 | £100 | test pressing |
| Sorry For Laughing | LP | Postcard | 81-1 | 1981 | £100 | £200 | test pressing with proof sleeve |

## JOSEFUS

| | | | | | | | |
|---|---|---|---|---|---|---|---|
| Dead Man | LP | Hookah | 330 | 1970 | £75 | £150 | US |
| Josefus | LP | Mainstream | 6127 | 1970 | £37.50 | £75 | US |

## JOSHUA

| | | | | | | | |
|---|---|---|---|---|---|---|---|
| Joshua | LP | Key | KL014 | 1973 | £37.50 | £75 | |

## JOSHUA FOX

| | | | | | | | |
|---|---|---|---|---|---|---|---|
| Joshua Fox | LP | Tetragrammaton | 125 | 1968 | £15 | £30 | US |

## JOSIE, MARVA

| | | | | | | | |
|---|---|---|---|---|---|---|---|
| Crazy Stockings | 7" | Polydor | 56711 | 1966 | £2 | £5 | |

## JOURNEY

| | | | | | | | |
|---|---|---|---|---|---|---|---|
| Departure | LP | Columbia | HC46339 | 1981 | £4 | £10 | US audiophile |
| Departure | CD | CBS | CD84101 | 1986 | £5 | £12 | |
| Dream After Dream | LP | Columbia | HC47998 | 1982 | £4 | £10 | US audiophile |
| Escape | LP | Columbia | HC47408 | 1981 | £4 | £10 | US audiophile |
| Escape | LP | Mobile Fidelity | MFSL1144 | 1981 | £6 | £15 | US audiophile |
| Infinity | LP | Columbia | HC4912 | 1981 | £4 | £10 | US audiophile |
| Who's Crying Now | CD-s | CBS | 6545412 | 1989 | £2 | £5 | |

## JOURNEYMEN

| | | | | | | | |
|---|---|---|---|---|---|---|---|
| Introducing The Journeymen | LP | Ember | EMB3382 | 1967 | £5 | £12 | |
| Journeymen | LP | Capitol | (S)T1629 | 1961 | £6 | £15 | US |
| Live | LP | Capitol | 1770 | 1962 | £10 | £25 | US |
| New Directions In Folk Music | LP | Capitol | (S)T1951 | 1963 | £6 | £15 | US |

## JOY, CARL & THE JOYBOYS

| | | | | | | | |
|---|---|---|---|---|---|---|---|
| Be My Girl | 7" | Top Rank | JAR529 | 1961 | £2 | £5 | |
| Bye Bye Baby Goodbye | 7" | Brunswick | 05806 | 1959 | £2 | £5 | |

## JOY, RODDIE
| Come Back Baby | 7" | Red Bird | RB021 | 1965 | £15 | £30 | |

## JOY & DAVID
| Joe's Been A Gitting There | 7" | Parlophone | R4855 | 1961 | £6 | £12 | |
| Let's Go See Grandma | 7" | Triumph | RGM1002 | 1960 | £10 | £20 | |
| My Very Good Friend The Milkman | 7" | Decca | F11291 | 1960 | £6 | £12 | |
| Rocking Away The Blues | 7" | Decca | F11123 | 1959 | £7.50 | £15 | |
| Whoopee | 7" | Parlophone | R4477 | 1958 | £7.50 | £15 | |

## JOY DIVISION
| Atmosphere | CD-s | Factory | FACD213 | 1988 | £2 | £5 | |
| Atmosphere | 7" | Sordide Sentimentale | SS33002 | 1980 | £20 | £40 | A4 folder |
| Earcom 2 | 12" | Fast Products | FAST9 | 1979 | £5 | £12 | with other artists |
| Factory Sample | 7" EP | Factory | FAC2 | 1979 | £15 | £30 | double, 5 stickers, with other artists |
| Ideal Beginning | 7" | Enigma | PSS138 | 1981 | £5 | £10 | |
| Ideal For Living | 7" | Enigma | PSS139 | 1978 | £37.50 | £75 | picture sleeve |
| Ideal For Living | 12" | Anonymous | ANON1 | 1978 | £25 | £50 | |
| Peel Sessions | CD-s | Strange Fruit | SFPSCD013 | 1988 | £2 | £5 | |
| Peel Sessions II | CD-s | Strange Fruit | SFPSCD033 | 1988 | £2 | £5 | |
| Still | LP | Factory | FACT40 | 1981 | £6 | £15 | double, hard cloth cover |

## JOY UNLIMITED
| Minne | LP | BASF | 1222331 | 1975 | £5 | £12 | German |
| Overground | LP | Polydor | 2371050 | 1970 | £8 | £20 | German |
| Reflections | LP | BASF | 20216861 | 1973 | £6 | £15 | German |
| Schmetterlinge | LP | Pilz | 2021090/1 | 1971 | £10 | £25 | German |
| Turbulence | LP | Page One | POLS028 | 1970 | £10 | £25 | |

## JOYCE'S ANGELS
| Flowers For My Friend | 7" | Major Minor | MM526 | 1967 | £1.50 | £4 | |

## JOYRIDE
| Friend Sound | LP | RCA | LSP4114 | 1969 | £20 | £40 | US |

## JSD BAND
| Country Of The Blind | LP | Regal Zonophone | SLRZ1018 | 1971 | £15 | £30 | |
| JSD Band | LP | Fly | HIFLY11 | 1972 | £4 | £10 | |
| Story So Far | 7" | Regal Zonophone | JSD1 | 1971 | £5 | £10 | promo with release sheet & photo |

## JUAN & JUNIOR
| To Girls | 7" | CBS | 3223 | 1968 | £2 | £5 | |

## JUBALAIRES
| King's Highway | 7" EP | Brunswick | OE9198 | 1955 | £2 | £5 | |

## JUDAS JUMP
| Run For Your Life | 7" | Parlophone | R5828 | 1969 | £1.50 | £4 | |
| Scorch | LP | Parlophone | PAS10001 | 1970 | £6 | £15 | |
| This Feelin' We Feel | 7" | Parlophone | R5838 | 1970 | £1.50 | £4 | |

## JUDAS PRIEST
| Defenders Of The Faith | CD | CBS | CD25713 | 1984 | £5 | £12 | |
| Painkiller | CD-s | CBS | 6562732 | 1990 | £2 | £5 | |
| Touch Of Evil | CD-s | CBS | 6565892 | 1991 | £2 | £5 | |
| Tyrant | 12" | Gull | GULS7612 | 1983 | £3 | £8 | white vinyl |

## JUDD
| Judd | LP | Penny Farthing | PELS504 | 1970 | £10 | £25 | |

## JUDGE HAPPINESS
| Hey Judge | 7" | Mynah | SCS8501 | 1985 | £10 | £20 | |
| Hey Judge | 7" | Mynah | SCS8501 | 1985 | £25 | £50 | picture sleeve |

## JUDGE, TERRY & THE BARRISTERS
| Come With Me And Love Me | 7" | Fontana | TF599 | 1965 | £2 | £5 | |
| Hey Look At Her | 7" | Oriole | CB1896 | 1963 | £2.50 | £6 | |
| I Don't Care | 7" | Oriole | CB1938 | 1964 | £2.50 | £6 | |

## JUG TRUST
| Cat And Mouse | 7" | Parlophone | R5825 | 1970 | £1.50 | £4 | |

## JUGGERNAUTS
| Come Throw Yourself | 7" | Supreme | 842 | 1984 | £2 | £5 | |

## JUICY LUCY
| Juicy Lucy | LP | Vertigo | VO2 | 1969 | £6 | £15 | spiral label |
| Lie Back & Enjoy It | LP | Vertigo | 6360014 | 1970 | £5 | £12 | spiral label |
| Who Do You Love | 7" | Vertigo | V1 | 1970 | £1.50 | £4 | |

## JULIAN
| Sue Saturday | 7" | Pye | 7N15236 | 1959 | £5 | £10 | |

## JULIAN, DON
Greatest Oldies......................................... LP ...... Amazon .......... 1009 .................... 1963 £10......... £25 ...................... US

## JULIAN'S TREATMENT
Phantom City ........................................ 7" ...... Youngblood .... YB1009................. 1972 £2......... £5 ..............................
Time Before This ................................... LP ...... Youngblood .... SYB2 .................... 1972 £37.50.... £75 .................. double

## JULY
The LP by July is a typical piece of psychedelia from 1968 – full of interesting ideas and sounds, but definitely a formative record for the musicians involved. These include Tony Duhig and Jon Field, who went on to form Jade Warrior, and Tom Newman, later a solo artist and also studio engineer for Virgin records.

Dandelion Seeds...................................... LP ...... Bam Caruso...... KIRI097 ................... 1987 £4......... £10 ..............................
Hello Who's There ................................. 7" ...... Major Minor ... MM580................... 1968 £25......... £50 ..............................
July .................................................... LP ...... Epic .............. BN26416 ............... 1969 £37.50.... £75 ...................... US
July .................................................... LP ...... Major Minor ... MMLP/SMLP29... 1968 £180..... £300 ..............................
My Clown ............................................ 7" ...... Major Minor ... MM568................... 1968 £30......... £60 ..............................

## JUMBLE LANE
Jumble Lane.......................................... LP ...... Holyground..... HG115.................. 1971 £250..... £400 ..............................

## JUMPIN' JACKS
Tried And Tested ................................... 7" ...... HMV.............. POP440 ................ 1958 £5......... £10 ..............................
Lady Play Your Mandolin ........................ 7" ...... Capitol........... CL14597 ............... 1956 £1.50......... £4 ..............................

## JUNCO PARTNERS
As Long As I Have You .......................... 7" ...... Columbia ........ DB7665 ................ 1965 £25......... £50 ..............................
Junco Partners ...................................... LP ...... Philips ............ 6308032 ............... 1971 £15......... £30 ..............................

## JUNCO PARTNERS (2)
Swinging Sixties Boys ............................. 7" ...... Rigid .............. JUNK1028 ............ 1979 £1.50......... £4 ..............................

## JUNCTION 32
Junction 32 .......................................... LP ...... Holyground..... HG119.................. 1975 £180..... £300 ..............................

## JUNE, ROSANNE
Charge Of The Light Brigade ................... 7" ...... London .......... HLU8352 ............... 1956 £6 ......... £12 ..............................

## JUNE, ROSEMARY
I'll Always Be In Love With You .............. 7" ...... Fontana.......... H141 .................... 1958 £1.50......... £4 ..............................
I'll Be With You In Apple Blossom Time ... 7" ...... Pye ................ 7N25005 ............... 1959 £1.50......... £4 ..............................

## JUNE BRIDES
Every Conversation ................................ 7" ...... Pink.............. PINKY2 ................. 1984 £1.50......... £4 ..............................
In The Rain........................................... 7" ...... Pink.............. PINKY1 ................. 1984 £5......... £10 ..............................

## JUNIORS
Both guitarist Mick Taylor and bass-player John Glascock (later with Jethro Tull) were members of the Juniors – an appropriate name indeed for Taylor, as he was barely fifteen when he made his recording debut on the band's single.

There's A Pretty Girl ............................. 7" ...... Columbia ........ DB7339 ............... 1964 £12.50.... £25 ..............................

## JUNIOR'S EYES
Battersea Power Station........................... LP ...... Regal           SLRZ1008 ............ 1969 £15......... £30 ..............................
                                                    Zonophone .....
Mr. Golden Trumpet Player ..................... 7" ...... Regal           RZ3009 ............... 1968 £4......... £8 ..............................
                                                    Zonophone .....
Star Child ............................................ 7" ...... Regal           RZ3023 ............... 1969 £2.50.... £6 ..............................
                                                    Zonophone .....
Woman Love ......................................... 7" ...... Regal           RZ3018 ............... 1969 £2.50.... £6 ..............................
                                                    Zonophone .....
Woman Love/White Light Part 2 .............. 7" ...... Regal           RZ3018 ............... 1969 £4......... £8 ..............................
                                                    Zonophone .....

## JUNIPHER GREEN
Friendship............................................ LP ...... Sonet ............. SLP1413/4 ............ 1971 £75......... £150 ..... Norwegian double

## JUNOFF, LENA
Yesterday Has Gone ............................... 7" ...... Olga ............. 008 .................... 1968 £5......... £10 ..............................

## JUPP, ERIC ORCHESTRA
Eric Jupp & His Orchestra....................... 7" EP . Columbia ........ SEG7589 ............... 1955 £4......... £8 ..............................
Perfect Combination............................... 7" EP . Columbia ........ SEG7621 ............... 1956 £2......... £5 ..............................
Rhythm And Blues.................................. 7" EP . Columbia ........ SEG7603 ............... 1956 £4......... £8 ..............................

## JUST FOUR MEN
Don't Come Any Closer .......................... 7" ...... Parlophone ..... R5241 .................. 1965 £20......... £40 ..............................
That's My Baby ..................................... 7" ...... Parlophone ..... R5208 .................. 1964 £20......... £40 ..............................

## JUST PLAIN JONES
Crazy Crazy.......................................... 7" ...... CBS.............. 7480 .................... 1971 £1.50......... £4 ..............................

## JUST PLAIN SMITH
February's Child..................................... 7" ...... Sunshine ......... SUN7702............... 1969 £62.50.. £125 ..............................

## JUST US
What Are We Gonna Do .......................... 7" EP . Kapp ................ KEV13036 ............. 1966 £5 .......... £10 .................. *French*

## JUST WILLIAM
I Don't Care ................................. 7" ...... Spark ............. SRL1018 ............... 1970 £5 .......... £10 ................

## JUSTE, SAMANTHA
No One Needs My Love Today ................ 7" ...... Go .............. AJ11402 ................ 1966 £2 .......... £5 ...............

## JUSTICE, JIMMY
| | | | | | |
|---|---|---|---|---|---|
| I Understand Just How You Feel .......... | 7" ...... | Pye ........... | 7N15301 ............ | 1960 £4 .......... | £8 |
| I'm Past Forgetting ...................... | 7" ...... | RCA .......... | RCA1681 ............ | 1968 £5 .......... | £10 |
| Jimmy Justice Hit Parade ................. | 7" EP . | Pye ........... | NEP24159 .......... | 1962 £6 .......... | £12 |
| Little Bit Of Soap ....................... | 7" ...... | Pye ........... | 7N15376 ............ | 1961 £2 .......... | £5 |
| Little Cracked Bell ...................... | 7" ...... | Pye ........... | 7N15509 ............ | 1963 £1.50 ....... | £4 |
| Smash Hits .............................. | LP ...... | Pye ........... | NPL18085 .......... | 1962 £8 .......... | £20 |
| Teacher ................................. | 7" ...... | Pye ........... | 7N15351 ............ | 1961 £2.50 ....... | £6 |
| Two Sides Of Jimmy Justice .............. | LP ...... | Pye ........... | NPL18080 .......... | 1962 £10 .......... | £25 |
| When My Little Girl Is Smiling .......... | 7" ...... | Pye ........... | 7N15421 ............ | 1962 £1.50 ....... | £4 |

## JUSTIFIED ANCIENTS OF MU MU

*1987* is an entirely brilliant example of the art of disc-jockey-as-producer, consisting of a kaleidoscope of bits of other people's records welded together into an inspired whole. Unfortunately, some of these other people – Benny Andersson and Björn Ulvaeus of Abba to be precise – took exception to their music being used in this way and obtained a court order for the recall of all remaining copies of the record. In a way, the JAMM were able to have the last laugh, for they later successfully advertised 'the last remaining five copies' of the record at £1000 each. Collectors do not have to pay as much as this, however – £60 is enough to acquire one of the copies that appears on the market from time to time.

| | | | | | |
|---|---|---|---|---|---|
| 1987 ................................... | LP ..... | KLF ............... | JAMSLP1 ............ | 1987 £30 .......... | £60 |
| 1987 ................................... | cass .... | KLF ............... | JAMSCLP1 ........... | 1987 £20 .......... | £40 |
| 1987 – The 45 Edits .................... | 12" ...... | KLF ............... | JAMS25T ............ | 1987 £4 .......... | £10 |
| All You Need Is Love ................... | 7" ...... | KLF ............... | JAMS23 ............ | 1987 £7.50 ....... | £15 |
| All You Need Is Love ................... | 12" ...... | KLF ............... | JAMS23 ............ | 1987 £10 .......... | £20 ....... *1 sided promo* |
| All You Need Is Love ................... | 12" ...... | KLF ............... | JAMS23T ............ | 1987 £6 .......... | £15 |
| Burn The Beat .......................... | 12" ...... | KLF ............... | JAMS26T ............ | 1988 £5 .......... | £12 |
| Down Town .............................. | 7" ...... | KLF ............... | JAMS27 ............ | 1987 £1.50 ....... | £4 ........ *no picture sleeve* |
| Down Town .............................. | 12" ...... | KLF ............... | JAMS27 ............ | 1987 £5 .......... | £12 ......... *1 sided promo* |
| Down Town .............................. | 12" ...... | KLF ............... | JAMS27T ............ | 1987 £4 .......... | £10 |
| It's Grim Up North ..................... | 12" ...... | KLF ............... | JAMS28T ............ | 1988 £30 .......... | £60 ... *1 sided, grey vinyl* |
| Made In Wales (Who Killed The Jams)...... | LP ...... | KLF ............... | JAMSLP2 ............ | 1988 £4 .......... | £10 |
| Whitney Joins The J.A.M.S .............. | 12" ...... | KLF ............... | JAMS24T ............ | 1987 £5 .......... | £12 |

## JUSTIN, JAY
I Sell Summertime ........................ 7" ...... Columbia ...... DB8439 ................ 1968 £1.50 ....... £4 ..............

## JUSTIN & KARLSSON
Somewhere They Can't Find Me ............. 7" ...... Piccadilly ...... 7N35295 ................ 1966 £5 .......... £10 .................

## JUSTINE
Justine .................................. LP ...... Uni ............. UNLS111 ................ 1970 £4 .......... £10 ................

## JUSTIS, BILL
| | | | | | |
|---|---|---|---|---|---|
| Cloud Nine .............................. | LP ..... | Philips ......... | 1950 ................ | 1959 £50 ....... | £100 .................. *US* |
| College Man ............................. | 7" ..... | London .......... | HLS8614 ............ | 1958 £5 .......... | £10 |
| I'm Gonna Learn To Dance ................ | 7" ..... | Mercury ......... | AMT1201 ............ | 1963 £1.50 ....... | £4 |
| Raunchy ................................. | 7" ..... | London .......... | HLS8517 ............ | 1957 £5 .......... | £10 |

## JUVENILES
Bo Diddley .............................. 7" ...... Pye ................ 7N25349 ................ 1966 £30 .......... £60 .............

## JYNX
How ..................................... 7" ...... Columbia ....... DB7304 ................ 1964 £10 .......... £20 .............

# K

### K, MOSES & THE PROPHETS
I Went Out With My Baby Tonight .......... 7" ...... Decca ............ F12244 ................... 1965 £4 ............ £8 ...................................

### K9'S
K9 Hassle ............................................... 7" ...... Dog Breath...... WOOF1 .................. 1985 £4 ............ £8

### KAIPA
Inget Nytt Unders Solen .......................... LP ...... Decca ............ SKL5260 ................ 1976 £15 ........ £30 ................... Swedish
Kaipa .................................................... LP ...... Decca ............ SKL5221 ................ 1975 £15 ........ £30 ................... Swedish
Solo ...................................................... LP ...... Decca ............ SKL5293 ................ 1978 £10 ........ £25 ................... Swedish

### KAK
Kak ...................................................... LP ...... Epic .............. BN26429 ................ 1969 £50 ....... £100 ........................ US

### KALA
Kala ...................................................... LP ...... Bradley .......... BRADL1002 ......... 1973 £6 .......... £15 ...................................

### KALACAKRA
Crawling To Lhasa ................................. LP ...... private ............. .............................. 1974 £30 ........ £60 ..................... German

### KALAMARIS
Staldfroes ............................................. LP ...... Scanfolk ......... 3 ........................... 1974 £20 ........ £40 ..................... Danish

### KALASANDRO
Chi Chi .................................................. 7" ...... Warner Bros .... WB13 .................... 1960 £1.50 ....... £4 .....................................

### KALB, DANNY & STEFAN GROSSMAN
Crosscurrents ........................................ LP ...... Cotillion .......... SD9007 ................... 1969 £5 .......... £12 ........................ US

### KALEIDOSCOPE
The two LPs made by Kaleidoscope were among the first of the more obscure psychedelic records to attract the attention of collectors. Accordingly, they reached the £100 mark some time before other similar records, but then stayed there while more recent discoveries leap-frogged ahead. In truth, the records are interesting, but lack the finesse of the established classics of the period (like *Music From A Doll's House* or *Dear Mr Fantasy*). They have the kudos of rarity, but, as is usually the case, their lack of renown is not without reason.

Balloon .................................................. 7" ...... Fontana ............ TF1048 ...... 1969 £37.50 .... £75 ...................................
Do It Again For Jeffrey ........................... 7" ...... Fontana ............ TF1002 ...... 1969 £12.50 .... £25 ...................................
Dream For Julie ..................................... 7" ...... Fontana ............ TF895 ........ 1968 £15 ........ £30 ...................................
Faintly Blowing ...................................... LP ...... 5 Hours Back ... TOCK006 .... 1987 £5 .......... £12 ...................................
Faintly Blowing ...................................... LP ...... Fontana ............ STL5491 ..... 1969 £75 ........ £150 ...................................
Flight From Ashiya .................................. 7" ...... Fontana ............ TF863 ........ 1967 £12.50 .... £25 ...................................
Flight From Ashiya .................................. 7" ...... Fontana ............ TF863 ........ 1967 £25 ........ £50 ........ picture sleeve
Jenny Artichoke ..................................... 7" ...... Fontana ............ TF964 ........ 1968 £12.50 .... £25 ...................................
Tangerine Dream .................................... LP ...... 5 Hours Back ... TOCK005 .... 1987 £5 .......... £12 ...................................
Tangerine Dream .................................... LP ...... Fontana ............ (S)TL5448 ... 1967 £75 ........ £150 ...................................

### KALEIDOSCOPE (US)
The American Kaleidoscope had a sound like no other group of the time. Over the course of three LPs (a fourth, *Bernice* is an unfortunate fall from grace; *When Scopes Collide* is a later attempt at a reunion) and culminating with the magnificent *Incredible*, which entirely lives up to its name, the group maintained a questing, innovative approach. A key factor was their fascination with Middle Eastern music, which gives some of Kaleidoscope's material a world music flavour very much ahead of its time. Both Chris Darrow and David Lindley have recorded much music since Kaleidoscope's demise, although little of it has been in the same league.

Beacon From Mars .................................. LP ...... Epic .............. LN24/BN26333 ..... 1968 £25 ........ £50 ......................... US
Bernice ................................................. LP ...... CBS ............... 64005 .................... 1970 £4 .......... £10 ...................................
Incredible .............................................. LP ...... Epic .............. BN26467 ............... 1969 £10 ........ £25 ......................... US
Side Trips .............................................. LP ...... Epic .............. LN24/BN26305 ..... 1967 £20 ........ £40 ......................... US
When Scopes Collide ............................. LP ...... Island ............. ILPS9462 .............. 1976 £4 .......... £10 ...................................

### KALEIDOSKOP
Kaleidoskop ........................................... LP ...... Lava ............... TCH0002 ............... 1974 £8 .......... £20 ..................... German

### KALIN TWINS
Chicken Thief .......................................... 7" ...... Brunswick ....... 05826 .................... 1960 £1.50 ...... £4 ...................................
Cool ...................................................... 7" ...... Brunswick ....... 05797 .................... 1959 £1.50 ...... £4 ...................................
Forget Me Not ......................................... 7" ...... Brunswick ....... 05759 .................... 1958 £1.50 ...... £4 ...................................
Kalin Twins ............................................. LP ...... Decca ............. DL8812 .................. 1958 £15 ........ £30 ......................... US
Kalin Twins ............................................. 7" EP . Brunswick ....... OE9449 ................. 1959 £10 ........ £20 ...................................
Meaning Of The Blues ............................. 7" ...... Brunswick ....... 05814 .................... 1959 £1.50 ...... £4 ...................................
Momma Poppa ........................................ 7" ...... Brunswick ....... 05848 .................... 1961 £1.50 ...... £4 ...................................
Oh My Goodness ..................................... 7" ...... Brunswick ....... 05775 .................... 1959 £2 .......... £5 ...................................
One More Time ........................................ 7" ...... Brunswick ....... 05862 .................... 1961 £1.50 ...... £4 ...................................

| | | | | | | | |
|---|---|---|---|---|---|---|---|
| Sweet Sugar Lips | 7" | Brunswick | 05803 | 1959 | £1.50 | £4 | |
| When | 7" EP | Brunswick | OE9383 | 1958 | £10 | £20 | |
| When | 7" | Brunswick | 05751 | 1958 | £1.50 | £4 | |
| Zing Went The Strings Of My Heart | 7" | Brunswick | 05844 | 1960 | £1.50 | £4 | |

## KALLABASH CORP
| | | | | | | | |
|---|---|---|---|---|---|---|---|
| Kallabash Corp | LP | Uncle Bill | 311 | 1970 | £30 | £60 | US |

## KALLEN, KITTY
| | | | | | | | |
|---|---|---|---|---|---|---|---|
| Forgive Me | 7" | Brunswick | 05447 | 1955 | £1.50 | £4 | |
| Go On With The Wedding | 7" | Brunswick | 05536 | 1956 | £2 | £5 | |
| How Lonely Can I Get | 7" | Brunswick | 05494 | 1955 | £1.50 | £4 | |
| I'm A Lonely Little Petunia | 7" | Brunswick | 05402 | 1955 | £1.50 | £4 | |
| In The Chapel In The Moonlight | 7" | Brunswick | 05261 | 1954 | £4 | £8 | |
| It's A Lonesome Old Town | LP | Decca | DL8397 | 1958 | £6 | £15 | US |
| Kiddy Geddin | 7" | Brunswick | 05359 | 1954 | £2.50 | £6 | |
| Kitty Who? | 7" | Brunswick | 05431 | 1955 | £1.50 | £4 | |
| Let's Make The Most Of Tonight | 7" | Brunswick | 05475 | 1955 | £1.50 | £4 | |
| Little Lie | 7" | Brunswick | 05394 | 1955 | £2 | £5 | |
| Little Things Mean A Lot | LP | Vocalion | VL3679 | 1959 | £5 | £12 | US |
| Little Things Mean A Lot | 7" | Brunswick | 05287 | 1954 | £12.50 | £25 | |
| Long Lonely Nights | 7" | Brunswick | 05705 | 1957 | £1.50 | £4 | |
| Pretty Kitty Kalen Sings | 10" LP | Mercury | MG25206 | 195– | £8 | £20 | US |
| Spirit Of Christmas | 7" | Brunswick | 05357 | 1954 | £2.50 | £6 | |
| True Love | 7" | Brunswick | 05612 | 1956 | £1.50 | £4 | |

## KALPANA IMPROVISATIONS
| | | | | | | | |
|---|---|---|---|---|---|---|---|
| Instrumental And Dance Music Of India | LP | Polydor | 184172 | 1968 | £4 | £10 | |

## KANE, AMORY
| | | | | | | | |
|---|---|---|---|---|---|---|---|
| Just To Be There | LP | CBS | 63849 | 1970 | £6 | £15 | |
| Memories Of Time Unwound | LP | MCA | MUP(S)348 | 1968 | £8 | £20 | |

## KANE, EDEN
| | | | | | | | |
|---|---|---|---|---|---|---|---|
| Come Back | 7" | Fontana | TF413 | 1963 | £1.50 | £4 | |
| Eden Kane | LP | Ace Of Clubs | ACL1133 | 1962 | £8 | £20 | |
| Eden Kane Hits | 7" EP | Decca | DFE8503 | 1962 | £7.50 | £15 | |
| Hot Chocolate Crazy | 7" | Pye | 7N15284 | 1960 | £5 | £10 | |
| It's Eden | LP | Fontana | TL5211 | 1964 | £15 | £30 | |
| It's Eden | 7" EP | Fontana | TFE17424 | 1964 | £6 | £12 | |
| Magic Town | 7" | Decca | F12342 | 1966 | £4 | £8 | |
| Six Great New Swingers | 7" EP | Decca | DFE8567 | 1964 | £7.50 | £15 | |
| Smoke Gets In Your Eyes | LP | Wing | WL1218 | 1966 | £5 | £12 | |
| Tomorrow Night | 7" | Fontana | TF398 | 1963 | £2 | £5 | picture sleeve |
| Well I Ask You | 7" EP | Decca | DFE6696 | 1962 | £7.50 | £15 | |

## KANE, LEE
| | | | | | | | |
|---|---|---|---|---|---|---|---|
| Around And Around | 7" | Capitol | CL14328 | 1955 | £1.50 | £4 | |
| Every Day | 7" | Capitol | CL14297 | 1955 | £1.50 | £4 | |

## KANE, PAUL
Paul Kane was one of the names tried by Paul Simon during the early years of his career.

| | | | | | | | |
|---|---|---|---|---|---|---|---|
| He Was My Brother | 7" | Tribute | 128 | 196– | £25 | £50 | US |

## KANE'S COUSINS
| | | | | | | | |
|---|---|---|---|---|---|---|---|
| Undergum Bubbleground | LP | Shove Love | ST9827 | 1968 | £5 | £12 | US |

## KANGAROO
| | | | | | | | |
|---|---|---|---|---|---|---|---|
| Kangaroo | LP | MGM | SE4586 | 1968 | £15 | £30 | US |

## KANSAS
Strange how all the groups called after place names seem to have the same sound. Regardless of the musical content, however, the LP *Point Of Know Return* by Kansas has a particularly striking cover, showing a galleon in full sail, just about to fall over the edge of the world. The record is available as a picture disc, which shows off the artwork even more dramatically, but this was unfortunately issued as an American promotional release only and is scarce.

| | | | | | | | |
|---|---|---|---|---|---|---|---|
| Leftoverture | LP | Kirshner | HZ44224 | 1981 | £5 | £12 | US audiophile |
| Point Of Know Return | LP | Kirshner | HZ44929 | 1981 | £5 | £12 | US audiophile |
| Point Of Know Return | LP | Kirshner | JZ34929 | 1977 | £10 | £25 | US promo picture disc |
| Vinyl Confessions | LP | Kirshner | HZ48002 | 1982 | £5 | £12 | US audiophile |

## KANSAS CITY MELROSE & CASINO SIMPSON
| | | | | | | | |
|---|---|---|---|---|---|---|---|
| Kansas City Melrose And Casino Simpson | LP | Chicago Piano | 12001 | 1972 | £4 | £10 | |

## KANTNER, PAUL
| | | | | | | | |
|---|---|---|---|---|---|---|---|
| Blows Against The Empire | LP | RCA | LSP4448 | 1970 | £30 | £60 | US clear vinyl |
| Blows Against The Empire | LP | RCA | SF8163 | 1970 | £4 | £10 | with booklet |
| Sunfighter | LP | Grunt | FTR1002 | 1971 | £4 | £10 | with booklet |

## KAPUTTER HAMSTER
| | | | | | | | |
|---|---|---|---|---|---|---|---|
| Kaputter Hamster | LP | e-Pa Records | 102009 | 1974 | £75 | £150 | German |

## KARAS, ANTON
| | | | | | | | |
|---|---|---|---|---|---|---|---|
| Harry Lime Theme | 7" | Decca | F9235 | 1960 | £2 | £5 | |

## KARAT
Karat ..................................................... LP ..... Amiga ............ 855573 ................. 1977 £4 .......... £10 .......... *East German*

## KARLOFF, BORIS
Evening With Karloff And His Friends ...... LP ..... Decca ............ DL(7)4833 .............. 1967 £5 .......... £12 .................. *US*
How The Grinch Stole Christmas ............. LP ..... MGM ............ (S)E901 ................. 1966 £5 .......... £12 .................. *US*
Tales Of The Frightened Vol. 1 ................. LP ..... MGM ............ MG2/SR60815 ...... 1963 £8 .......... £20 .................. *US*
Tales Of The Frightened Vol. 2 ................. LP ..... MGM ............ MG2/SR60816 ...... 1963 £8 .......... £20 .................. *US*

## KARTHAGO
Karthago .............................................. LP ..... BASF ............. 20211851 ............. 1971 £4 .......... £10 .......... *German*

## KASENATZ-KATZ SINGING ORCHESTRAL CIRCUS
Kasenatz-Katz Singing Orchestral Circus ..... LP ..... Pye ................. NSPL28119 ............ 1968 £4 .......... £10

## KASHMIR
Stay Calm ............................................. LP ..... private .......................................... 1986 £10 .......... £25

## KATCH 22
100,000 Years ....................................... 7" ..... Fontana ........... TF984 .................. 1968 £2 .......... £5
Major Catastrophe ................................. 7" ..... Fontana ........... TF768 .................. 1966 £10 .......... £20
Makin' Up My Mind ............................... 7" ..... Fontana ........... TF874 .................. 1967 £2 .......... £5
Out Of My Life ...................................... 7" ..... Fontana ........... TF1005 ................ 1969 £2 .......... £5
World's Getting Smaller ........................... 7" ..... Fontana ........... TF930 .................. 1968 £2 .......... £5

## KATE
Hold Me Now ........................................ 7" ..... CBS ................. 3815 .................... 1968 £5 .......... £10
Shout It ............................................... 7" ..... CBS ................. 4123 .................... 1969 £5 .......... £10
Strange Girl .......................................... 7" ..... CBS ................. 3631 .................... 1968 £5 .......... £10

## KATMANDU
Katmandu ............................................. LP ..... Mainstream ..... S6131 .................. 1971 £30 .......... £60 .................. *US*

## KATTONG
Gitarre Vor'm Bauch ............................... LP ..... Schwann ......... AMS515 .............. 1971 £10 .......... £25 .......... *German*
Stiehl Dem Volk Die Geduld ..................... LP ..... Schwann ......... AMS519 .............. 1972 £10 .......... £25 .......... *German*

## KATZ, DICK
Kool For Katz ....................................... 10" LP Pye ............... NPT19033 ............ 1959 £5 .......... £12

## KATZ, MICKEY
David Crockett ....................................... 7" ..... Capitol ............ CL14579 .............. 1956 £1.50 .......... £4
Poiple Kishke Eater ................................ 7" ..... Capitol ............ CL14926 .............. 1958 £1.50 .......... £4

## KAUFMANN, BOB
Trip Through A Blown Mind ..................... LP ..... LHI ................. 12002 .................. 1967 £8 .......... £20 .................. *US*

## KAY, ARTHUR ORIGINALS
Ska Wars .............................................. 7" ...... Red Admiral ... NYMPH1 ............. 1980 £1.50 .......... £4

## KAY, JOHN
John Kay And The Sparrows ..................... LP ..... Columbia ......... CS9758 ............... 1970 £5 .......... £12 .................. *US*

## KAY, KATHIE
House With Love In It ............................. 7" ..... HMV ............... POP265 .............. 1956 £1.50 .......... £4
Jimmy Unknown .................................... 7" ..... HMV ............... 7M363 ............... 1956 £2 .......... £5
Suddenly There's A Valley ........................ 7" ..... HMV ............... 7M335 ............... 1955 £2 .......... £5

## KAYAK
Kayak .................................................. LP ..... Harvest ......... SHSP4036 ........... 1974 £4 .......... £10
Phantom Of The Night ............................ LP ..... Janus ............ JXS7039 .............. 1978 £8 .......... £20 .......... *US picture disc*
Royal Bed Bouncer ................................. LP ..... Vertigo .......... 6360530 .............. 1975 £4 .......... £10
See See The Sun .................................... LP ..... Harvest ......... SHSP4033 ........... 1973 £4 .......... £10

## KAYE, DANNY
At The Palace ....................................... 10" LP Brunswick ...... LA8660 ............... 1954 £4 .......... £10
Children's Favourites .............................. 7" EP . Brunswick ...... OE9022 .............. 1954 £2 .......... £5
Danny Kaye .......................................... 10" LP Brunswick ...... LA8507 ............... 1951 £4 .......... £10
Hans Christian Andersen .......................... 10" LP Brunswick ...... LA8572 ............... 1953 £4 .......... £10
Knock On Wood .................................... 10" LP Brunswick ...... LA8668 ............... 1954 £4 .......... £10

## KAYE, DAVE
Fool Such As I ...................................... 7" ...... Decca ............ F11866 ............... 1964 £6 .......... £12
In My Way ........................................... 7" ...... Decca ............ F12073 ............... 1965 £6 .......... £12
Yesterday When I Was Young ..................... 7" ...... Major Minor ... MM641 ............... 1969 £2.50 .......... £6

## KAYE, LINDA
I Can't Stop Thinking About You ............. 7" ...... Columbia ......... DB7915 ............... 1966 £6 .......... £12

## KAYE, SHIRLEY
Make Me Yours ..................................... 7" ...... Trojan ............ TR015 ................. 1968 £5 .......... £10

## KAYE SISTERS
Are You Ready Freddy? ........................... 7" ...... Philips ............ PB806 ................. 1958 £2.50 .......... £6
At The Colony ...................................... 7" EP . Philips ............ BBE12256 ............ 1959 £5 .......... £10
Favourites ............................................ 7" EP . Philips ............ BBE12392 ............ 1960 £4 .......... £8
Ivory Tower .......................................... 7" ...... HMV ............... 7M401 ............... 1956 £5 .......... £10

| | | | | | | | | |
|---|---|---|---|---|---|---|---|---|
| Kaye Sisters | 7" EP | Philips | BBE12166 | 1957 | £4 | £8 | |
| Lay Down Your Arms | 7" | HMV | POP251 | 1956 | £4 | £8 | |
| Stroll Me | 7" | Philips | PB832 | 1958 | £1.50 | £4 | |

## KEANE, DOLORES
| | | | | | | | | |
|---|---|---|---|---|---|---|---|---|
| There Was A Maid | LP | Claddagh | CC23 | 1978 | £4 | £10 | *Irish* |

## KEANE, DOLORES & JOHN FAULKNER
| | | | | | | | | |
|---|---|---|---|---|---|---|---|---|
| Broken Hearted I'll Wander | LP | Mulligan | LUN033 | 1979 | £4 | £10 | *Irish* |

## KEANE, SHAKE
| | | | | | | | | |
|---|---|---|---|---|---|---|---|---|
| That's The Voice | LP | Ace Of Clubs | ACL1219 | 1967 | £4 | £10 | |
| With The Keating Sound | LP | Decca | SKL4720 | 1965 | £5 | £12 | |

## KEATING, JOHNNY
| | | | | | | | | |
|---|---|---|---|---|---|---|---|---|
| Swinging Scots | LP | London | LTZD15122 | 1958 | £6 | £15 | |
| Z Cars | 7" EP | Piccadilly | NEP34011 | 1962 | £2 | £5 | |

## KEBNEKAISE
| | | | | | | | | |
|---|---|---|---|---|---|---|---|---|
| III | LP | Silence | SRS4629 | 1975 | £4 | £10 | *Swedish* |
| Kebnekaise | LP | Silence | SRS4618 | 1973 | £6 | £15 | *Swedish* |
| Resa Mot Okant Mal | LP | Silence | SRS4605 | 1971 | £6 | £15 | *Swedish* |

## KEENAN, PADDY
| | | | | | | | | |
|---|---|---|---|---|---|---|---|---|
| Paddy Keenan | LP | Gael Linn | CEF045 | 1975 | £5 | £12 | *Irish* |

## KEENE, REX
| | | | | | | | | |
|---|---|---|---|---|---|---|---|---|
| Happy Texas Ranger | 7" | Columbia | DB3831 | 1956 | £2 | £5 | |

## KEFFORD, ACE STAND
| | | | | | | | | |
|---|---|---|---|---|---|---|---|---|
| For Your Love | 7" | Atlantic | 584260 | 1969 | £10 | £20 | |

## KEITH
| | | | | | | | | |
|---|---|---|---|---|---|---|---|---|
| 98.6 | LP | Mercury | 20103MCL | 1967 | £4 | £10 | |
| 98.6 | 7" | Mercury | MF955 | 1967 | £1.50 | £4 | |
| Daylight Saving Time | 7" | Mercury | MF989 | 1966 | £1.50 | £4 | |
| Tell It To My Face | 7" EP | Mercury | 126220 | 1967 | £5 | £10 | *French* |

## KEITH, BRIAN
| | | | | | | | | |
|---|---|---|---|---|---|---|---|---|
| When The First Tear Shows | 7" | Page One | POF103 | 1968 | £1.50 | £4 | |

## KEITH, BRYAN
| | | | | | | | | |
|---|---|---|---|---|---|---|---|---|
| Mean Mama | 7" | London | HLU9707 | 1963 | £2.50 | £6 | |

## KEITH, RON
| | | | | | | | | |
|---|---|---|---|---|---|---|---|---|
| Party Music | 7" | A&M | AMS7217 | 1976 | £10 | £20 | |

## KEITH & ENID
| | | | | | | | | |
|---|---|---|---|---|---|---|---|---|
| Just A Closer Walk | 7" | Dice | CC20 | 1963 | £5 | £10 | |
| Keith And Enid Sing | LP | Island | ILP901 | 1963 | £25 | £50 | |
| Lost My Love | 7" | Island | WI429 | 1964 | £5 | £10 | |
| Never Leave My Throne | 7" | Starlite | ST45047 | 1961 | £5 | £10 | |
| Sacred Vow | 7" | Dice | CC14 | 1963 | £5 | £10 | |
| Send Me | 7" | Blue Beat | BB11 | 1960 | £6 | £12 | *Trenton Spence B side* |
| Sing | LP | Trojan | TBL154 | 1970 | £4 | £10 | |
| Sing | LP | Trojan | TTL37 | 1970 | £5 | £12 | |
| When It's Spring | 7" | Blue Beat | BB125 | 1962 | £6 | £12 | |
| Worried Over You | 7" | Blue Beat | BB6 | 1960 | £6 | £12 | |
| You're Gonna Break My Heart | 7" | Starlite | ST45067 | 1961 | £5 | £10 | |

## KEITH & KEN
| | | | | | | | | |
|---|---|---|---|---|---|---|---|---|
| You'll Love Jamaica | LP | London | HAR/SHR8229 | 1965 | £8 | £20 | |

## KEITH & TEX
| | | | | | | | | |
|---|---|---|---|---|---|---|---|---|
| Hypnotizing Eyes | 7" | Island | WI3137 | 1968 | £5 | £10 | |
| Tighten Up Your Gird | 7" | Explosion | EX2008 | 1969 | £1.50 | £4 | |
| Tonight | 7" | Island | WI3085 | 1967 | £5 | £10 | *Lyn Taitt B side* |

## KELLER, JERRY
| | | | | | | | | |
|---|---|---|---|---|---|---|---|---|
| Here Comes Jerry Keller | LP | London | HAR2261/ SAHR.6083 | 1960 | £15 | £30 | |
| If I Had A Girl | 7" | London | HLR8980 | 1959 | £1.50 | £4 | |
| Now Now Now | 7" | London | HLR9106 | 1960 | £1.50 | £4 | |

## KELLEY, PETER
| | | | | | | | | |
|---|---|---|---|---|---|---|---|---|
| Path Of The Wave | LP | London | SHK8402 | 1969 | £8 | £20 | |

## KELLUM, MURRAY
| | | | | | | | | |
|---|---|---|---|---|---|---|---|---|
| Long Tall Texan | 7" | London | HLU9830 | 1964 | £4 | £8 | *Glen Sutton B side* |

## KELLY
| | | | | | | | | |
|---|---|---|---|---|---|---|---|---|
| Mary Mary | 7" | Deram | DM277 | 1969 | £4 | £8 | |

## KELLY, CHARLIE
| | | | | | | | | |
|---|---|---|---|---|---|---|---|---|
| So Nice Like Rice | 7" | Island | WI3155 | 1968 | £5 | £10 | *Stranger Cole B side* |

## KELLY, DAVE
Blues guitarist Dave Kelly was a significant figure within the British blues boom. In addition to the collectable solo albums listed below,

he also recorded with Tramp and the John Dummer Blues Band. Later he was a founder member of the Blues Band with Paul Jones, the success of which has kept his career alive through into the nineties, without him ever having to compromise his love of the blues.

| | | | | | | | |
|---|---|---|---|---|---|---|---|
| Black Blue Kelly | LP | Mercury | 6310001 | 1971 | £62.50 | £125 | |
| Keeps It In The Family | LP | Mercury | SMCL20151 | 1969 | £37.50 | £75 | |

## KELLY, GENE

| | | | | | | | |
|---|---|---|---|---|---|---|---|
| Singin' In The Rain | 7" | MGM | SP1012 | 1953 | £2.50 | £6 | |
| Song And Dance Man | 10" LP | MGM | D117 | 1953 | £4 | £10 | |
| S'Wonderful | 7" | MGM | SP1015 | 1953 | £1.50 | £4 | |
| S'Wonderful | 10" LP | MGM | D133 | 1955 | £4 | £10 | |

## KELLY, JO-ANN

Jo-Ann Kelly had a voice to rival that of blues power-house Bessie Smith, although she was English, white, and at the time of her debut EP, just twenty years old. In addition to the collectable records listed, she also appeared on the various artists EP, *New Sounds In Folk*, and on records by her brother Dave Kelly, Tony McPhee, John Dummer, the Brunning Hall Sunflower Blues Band, Tramp, and Chilli Willi and the Red Hot Peppers. She last performed live in 1990, but died that year of a brain tumour.

| | | | | | | | |
|---|---|---|---|---|---|---|---|
| Blues And Gospel | 7" EP | GW | EP1 | 1964 | £50 | £100 | |
| Do It | LP | Red Rag | RRR006 | 1976 | £15 | £30 | with Peter Emery |
| Jo Ann Kelly | LP | CBS | 63841 | 1969 | £50 | £100 | |
| Jo-Ann Kelly Meets Dick Wellstood | LP | BBC Radioplay | TSRP7726 | 197– | £100 | £200 | |
| Same Thing On Their Minds | LP | Sunset | SLS50209 | 1971 | £15 | £30 | with Tony McPhee |
| With Fahey, Mann, & Miller | LP | Blue Goose | 2009 | 1972 | £15 | £30 | US |

## KELLY, JOHN

| | | | | | | | |
|---|---|---|---|---|---|---|---|
| Fiddle And Concertina Player | LP | Free Reed | FRS504 | 1975 | £4 | £10 | |

## KELLY, JONATHAN

| | | | | | | | |
|---|---|---|---|---|---|---|---|
| Don't You Believe It | 7" | Parlophone | R5851 | 1970 | £1.50 | £4 | |
| Jonathan Kelly | LP | Parlophone | PCS7114 | 1970 | £8 | £20 | |

## KELLY, KEITH

| | | | | | | | |
|---|---|---|---|---|---|---|---|
| Cold White And Beautiful | 7" | Parlophone | R4797 | 1961 | £1.50 | £4 | |
| Listen Little Girl | 7" | Parlophone | R4676 | 1960 | £2 | £5 | |
| Save Your Love For Me | 7" | CBS | 201794 | 1965 | £1.50 | £4 | |
| Tease Me | 7" | Parlophone | R4640 | 1960 | £2 | £5 | |
| With You | 7" | Parlophone | R4713 | 1960 | £1.50 | £4 | |

## KELLY, PAT

| | | | | | | | |
|---|---|---|---|---|---|---|---|
| Cool Breezing | LP | Pama | PMLP2013 | 1971 | £15 | £30 | |
| How Long Will It Take | 7" | Gas | GAS115 | 1969 | £1.50 | £4 | |
| Little Boy Blue | 7" | Giant | GN37 | 1968 | £2 | £5 | |
| Sings | LP | Pama | PMLP12 | 1969 | £10 | £25 | |
| Somebody's Baby | 7" | Island | WI3121 | 1968 | £5 | £10 | Beverley Simmons B side |
| Workman Song | 7" | Gas | GAS110 | 1969 | £1.50 | £4 | |

## KELLY, PAUL

| | | | | | | | |
|---|---|---|---|---|---|---|---|
| Chills And Fever | 7" | Atlantic | AT4053 | 1965 | £5 | £10 | |
| Sweet Sweet Lovin' | 7" | Philips | BF1591 | 1967 | £2.50 | £6 | |

## KELLY, PETE SOULUTION

| | | | | | | | |
|---|---|---|---|---|---|---|---|
| Midnight Confessions | 7" | Decca | F12755 | 1968 | £4 | £8 | |

## KELLY, STAN

| | | | | | | | |
|---|---|---|---|---|---|---|---|
| Ballad Of Armagh Jail | 7" | Transatlantic | TRASP21 | 1968 | £1.50 | £4 | |
| Liverpool Packet | 7" EP | Topic | TOP27 | 1960 | £2 | £5 | |
| Songs For Swinging Landlords | 7" EP | Topic | TOP60 | 1961 | £2 | £5 | |

## KELLY, WYNTON

| | | | | | | | |
|---|---|---|---|---|---|---|---|
| Kelly Great | LP | Top Rank | 35107 | 1961 | £6 | £15 | |

## KELLY BROTHERS

| | | | | | | | |
|---|---|---|---|---|---|---|---|
| Falling In Love Again | 7" | Sue | WI4034 | 1967 | £12.50 | £25 | |
| Sweet Soul | LP | President | PTL1019 | 1968 | £6 | £15 | |
| That's What You Mean To Me | 7" | Blue Horizon | 573177 | 1970 | £2.50 | £6 | |
| You Put Your Touch On Me | 7" | President | PT143 | 1968 | £1.50 | £4 | |

## KELSEY, REV. SAMUEL

| | | | | | | | |
|---|---|---|---|---|---|---|---|
| Rev. Kelsey | 7" EP | Brunswick | OE9256 | 1956 | £5 | £10 | |
| Wedding Ceremony Of Sister R. Tharpe | 78 | Vocalion | V1014 | 1952 | £3 | £8 | |

## KEMP, LINDSAY

| | | | | | | | |
|---|---|---|---|---|---|---|---|
| Reality From Dream | LP | private | | | £75 | £150 | with the Grimsby Folk Group |

## KEMP, WAYNE

| | | | | | | | |
|---|---|---|---|---|---|---|---|
| Little Home Wrecker | 7" | Atlantic | 584006 | 1966 | £15 | £30 | |

## KEMPION

| | | | | | | | |
|---|---|---|---|---|---|---|---|
| Cam Ye O'er Frae France | LP | Sweet Folk & Country | SFA044 | 1977 | £6 | £15 | |
| Kempion | LP | Broadside | BRO123 | 1977 | £4 | £10 | |

## KENDALL, JOHNNY & THE HERALDS
St. James Infirmary .......................... 7" ..... RCA ............ RCA1416 .............. 1964 £5 ........ £10 ..........................
On The Move ................................. LP ..... RCA ............ CAL10041 ............ 1965 £25 ..... £50 ................. German

## KENDALL SISTERS
Won't You Be My Baby ...................... 7" ..... London ......... HLM8622 .............. 1958 £15 ........ £30

## KENDRICK, GRAHAM
Bright Side Up ............................... LP ..... Key ............ KL016 ................ 1973 £8 ........ £20
Footsteps On The Sea ........................ LP ..... Key ............ KL011 ................ 1973 £8 ........ £20
Paid On The Nail ............................ LP ..... Key ............ KL024 ................ 1974 £4 ........ £10 ....... with Peter Roe

## KENDRICK, LINDA
Friend Of Mine ............................... 7" ..... Polydor ....... 56146 ................ 1966 £1.50 ....... £4
It's The Little Things ........................ 7" ..... Polydor ....... 56076 ................ 1966 £7.50 ....... £15

## KENDRICK, NAT & THE SWANS
Dish Rag ...................................... 7" ..... Top Rank ..... JAR387 ............... 1960 £2 ........ £5
Mashed Potato ................................ 7" ..... Top Rank ..... JAR351 ............... 1960 £2.50 ....... £6

## KENNEDY, JERRY
Dancing Guitars Rock Elvis' Hits ............ LP ..... Smash ........ MGS2/SRS67004 ... 1962 £5 ........ £12 ............... US

## KENNEDY, NORMAN
Scots Songs And Ballads ..................... LP ..... Topic ......... 12T178 ............... 1968 £6 ........ £15

## KENNER, CHRIS
I Like It Like That ........................... 7" ..... London ......... HLU9410 .............. 1961 £4 ........ £8
Land Of A Thousand Dances ................. LP ..... Atlantic ....... 587008 ............... 1966 £6 ........ £15
Land Of A Thousand Dances ................. 7" ..... Sue ............ WI351 ............... 1965 £7.50 ....... £15

## KENNY & CASH
Knees ......................................... 7" ..... Decca ......... F12283 ............... 1965 £2.50 ....... £6

## KENNY & CORKY
Nuttin' For Christmas ....................... 7" ..... London ......... HLX9002 .............. 1959 £1.50 ....... £4

## KENNY & THE CADETS
The single by Kenny and the Cadets is an early spin-off from the Beach Boys, as the record features both Brian and Carl Wilson (together with their mother).

Barbie ........................................ 7" ..... Randy ......... 422 .................. 1962 £62.50 .. £125 ................... US

## KENNY & THE KASUALS
Garage Kings ................................. LP ..... Mark .......... 7000 ................. 1969 £10 ....... £25 ................... US
Live At The Studio Club ..................... LP ..... Mark .......... 5000 ................. 1966 £150 ..... £250 ................... US
Teen Dreams .................................. LP ..... Mark .......... 6000 ................. 1968 £50 ....... £100 ......... US, red vinyl

## KENNY & THE WRANGLERS
Doobie Doo ................................... 7" ..... Parlophone .... R5275 ................ 1965 £2.50 ....... £6
Somebody Help Me ........................... 7" ..... Parlophone .... R5224 ................ 1964 £2.50 ....... £6

## KENSINGTON MARKET
Aardvark ..................................... LP ..... Warner Bros ... WS1780 .............. 1969 £4 ........ £10 ................... US
Avenue Road ................................. LP ..... Warner Bros ... WS1754 .............. 1968 £4 ........ £10 ................... US

## KENT, AL
You Gotta Pay The Price ..................... 7" ..... Mojo .......... 2092015 ............. 1971 £4 ........ £8 ....... demo only
You Gotta Pay The Price ..................... 7" ..... Track ......... 604016 .............. 1967 £12.50 .... £25

## KENT, ENOCH
Sings The Butcher Boy And Other Ballads .. 7" EP . Topic ......... TOP81 ............... 1962 £2 ........ £5

## KENT, PAUL
P.C. Kent ..................................... LP ..... RCA ........... SF8083 ............... 1970 £6 ........ £15
Paul Kent ..................................... LP ..... B&C ........... CAS1044 ............. 1971 £6 ........ £15

## KENT, RICHARD STYLE
Crocodile Tears ............................... 7" ..... MCA ........... MU1032 .............. 1968 £10 ....... £20
Little Bit O' Soul ............................ 7" ..... Mercury ....... MF1090 .............. 1969 £10 ....... £20
Marching Off To War ........................ 7" ..... Columbia ...... DB8182 .............. 1967 £15 ....... £30
No Matter What You Do ..................... 7" ..... Columbia ...... DB7964 .............. 1966 £37.50 .... £75
You Can't Put Me Down ..................... 7" ..... Columbia ...... DB8051 .............. 1966 £15 ....... £30

## KENT, SHIRLEY
Sings For Charec 67 .......................... 7" ..... Keele ......... 103 .................. 1966 £7.50 ...... £15 ....... with The Master
                                                     University                                                                Singers

## KENT & DIMPLE
Day Is Done .................................. 7" ..... Island ......... WI046 ............... 1963 £5 ........ £10

## KENT & JEANIE
Daddy ........................................ 7" ..... Blue Beat ..... BB98 ................ 1962 £6 ........ £12

## KENTIGERN
Kentigern .................................... LP ..... Topic ......... 12TS394 ............. 1979 £4 ........ £10

## KENTON, STAN

| | | | | | | |
|---|---|---|---|---|---|---|
| A-Ting-A-Ling | 7" | Capitol | CL14259 | 1955 £1.50 | £4 | |
| Artistry In Rhythm | 10" LP | Capitol | LC6545 | 1952 £10 | £25 | |
| Back To Balboa | LP | Capitol | T995 | 1958 £6 | £15 | |
| Ballad Style | LP | Capitol | (S)T1068 | 1959 £5 | £12 | |
| City Of Glass | 10" LP | Capitol | LC6577 | 1953 £10 | £25 | |
| Classics | 10" LP | Capitol | LC6676 | 1954 £10 | £25 | |
| Concert In Progressive Jazz | 10" LP | Capitol | LC6546 | 1952 £10 | £25 | |
| Cuban Fire | LP | Capitol | LCT6118 | 1956 £8 | £20 | |
| Encores | 10" LP | Capitol | LC6523 | 1951 £10 | £25 | |
| Formative Years | LP | Brunswick | LAT8122 | 1956 £6 | £15 | |
| In Hi-Fi | LP | Capitol | LCT6109 | 1956 £6 | £15 | |
| Innovations In Modern Music | LP | Capitol | LCT6006 | 1954 £10 | £25 | |
| Kenton Era Vol. 1 | LP | Capitol | LCT6157 | 1958 £6 | £15 | |
| Kenton Era Vol. 2 | LP | Capitol | LCT6158 | 1958 £6 | £15 | |
| Kenton Era Vol. 3 | LP | Capitol | LCT6159 | 1958 £6 | £15 | |
| Kenton Era Vol. 4 | LP | Capitol | LCT6160 | 1958 £6 | £15 | |
| Kenton Showcase | LP | Capitol | LCT6009 | 1955 £8 | £20 | |
| Kenton Sidemen | LP | Vogue | LAE12028 | 1957 £6 | £15 | |
| Kenton With Voices | LP | Capitol | LCT6138 | 1957 £6 | £15 | |
| Lush Interlude | LP | Capitol | T1130 | 1959 £5 | £12 | |
| Milestones | 10" LP | Capitol | LC6517 | 1951 £10 | £25 | |
| New Concepts Of Artistry In Rhythm | 10" LP | Capitol | LC6595 | 1953 £10 | £25 | |
| Portraits On Standards | 10" LP | Capitol | LC6697 | 1955 £10 | £25 | |
| Presents | 10" LP | Capitol | LC6548 | 1952 £10 | £25 | |
| Rendezvous With Kenton | LP | Capitol | (S)T932 | 1958 £6 | £15 | |
| Road Show Vol. 1 | LP | Capitol | (S)T11327 | 1961 £4 | £10 | |
| Road Show Vol. 2 | LP | Capitol | (S)T21327 | 1961 £4 | £10 | |
| Sketches On Standards | 10" LP | Capitol | LC6602 | 1953 £10 | £25 | |
| Stage Door Swings | LP | Capitol | (S)T1166 | 1959 £5 | £12 | |
| Standards In Silhouette | LP | Capitol | (S)T1394 | 1961 £4 | £10 | |
| This Modern World | 10" LP | Capitol | LC6667 | 1954 £10 | £25 | |
| West Side Story | LP | Capitol | (S)T1609 | 1961 £4 | £10 | |

## KEN-TONES

| | | | | | | |
|---|---|---|---|---|---|---|
| Get With It | 7" | Parlophone | MSP6229 | 1956 £1.50 | £4 | |
| I Saw Esau | 7" | Parlophone | R4257 | 1957 £1.50 | £4 | |

## KENTUCKY BOYS

| | | | | | | |
|---|---|---|---|---|---|---|
| Don't Fetch It | 7" | HMV | 7M312 | 1955 £1.50 | £4 | |

## KENTUCKY COLONELS

| | | | | | | |
|---|---|---|---|---|---|---|
| Appalachian Swing | LP | World Pacific | (S)T1821 | 1964 £8 | £20 | US |
| Kentucky Colonels | LP | United Artists | UAS29514 | 1974 £4 | £10 | |
| New Sound Of Bluegrass | LP | Briar | M109 | 1963 £8 | £20 | US |

## KENWRIGHT, BILL

| | | | | | | |
|---|---|---|---|---|---|---|
| I Want To Go Back There Again | 7" | Columbia | DB8239 | 1967 £1.50 | £4 | |

## KENYATTA, ROBIN

| | | | | | | |
|---|---|---|---|---|---|---|
| Girl From Martinique | LP | ECM | ECM1008ST | 1971 £8 | £20 | |

## KERNOCHAN, SARAH

| | | | | | | |
|---|---|---|---|---|---|---|
| House Of Pain | LP | RCA | 0598 | 1974 £6 | £15 | |

## KEROUAC, JACK

| | | | | | | |
|---|---|---|---|---|---|---|
| Blues And Haikus | LP | Hanover | HML5006 | 1959 £25 | £50 | US |
| Poetry For The Beat Generation | LP | Dot | DLP3154 | 1959 £37.50 | £75 | US |
| Poetry For The Beat Generation | LP | Hanover | HML5000 | 1959 £25 | £50 | US |
| Readings On The Beat Generation | LP | Verve | MGV15005 | 1959 £25 | £50 | US |

## KERR, ANITA QUARTET

| | | | | | | |
|---|---|---|---|---|---|---|
| Anita Kerr Quartet | 7" EP | RCA | RCX7164 | 1964 £2 | £5 | |

## KERR, MOIRA

| | | | | | | |
|---|---|---|---|---|---|---|
| Folk Warm And Gentle | LP | Beltona | SBE102 | 1969 £25 | £50 | |

## KERR, PATRICK

| | | | | | | |
|---|---|---|---|---|---|---|
| Magic Potion | 7" | Decca | F12069 | 1965 £2.50 | £6 | |

## KERR, RICHARD

| | | | | | | |
|---|---|---|---|---|---|---|
| From Now Until Then | LP | Warner Bros | K46206 | 1972 £5 | £12 | |

## KERRIES

| | | | | | | |
|---|---|---|---|---|---|---|
| Kerries | LP | Major Minor | MMLP/SMLP9 | 1967 £6 | £15 | |

## KERRY, CHRIS

| | | | | | | |
|---|---|---|---|---|---|---|
| Seven Deadly Sins | 7" | Mercury | MF957 | 1965 £4 | £8 | |
| Watermelon Man | 7" | Mercury | MF985 | 1966 £4 | £8 | |

## KESEY, KEN & THE GRATEFUL DEAD

| | | | | | | |
|---|---|---|---|---|---|---|
| Acid Test | LP | Psycho | PSYCHO4 | 1983 £10 | £25 | |
| Acid Test | LP | Sound City | EX27690 | 1967 £50 | £100 | US |

## KESSEL, BARNEY

| | | | | | | |
|---|---|---|---|---|---|---|
| Barney Kessel | 10" LP | Vogue | LDE085 | 1954 £15 | £30 | |
| Barney Kessel Vol. 2 | 10" LP | Contemporary | LDC153 | 1955 £15 | £30 | |

| Title | Format | Label | Catalog | Year | | | Notes |
|---|---|---|---|---|---|---|---|
| Easy Like | LP | Contemporary | LAC12082 | 1958 | £10 | £25 | |
| Music To Listen To Barney Kessel By | LP | Contemporary | LAC12068/ SCA5002 | 1958 | £6 | £15 | |
| Plays Carmen | LP | Contemporary | LAC12214 | 1960 | £5 | £12 | |
| Plays Standards | LP | Contemporary | LAC12098 | 1959 | £5 | £12 | |
| Poll Winners | LP | Contemporary | LAC12122 | 1959 | £6 | £15 | |
| Poll Winners Ride Again | LP | Vogue | LAC12186 | 1959 | £5 | £12 | ... with Ray Brown & Shelly Manne |
| Poll Winners Three | LP | Contemporary | LAC12237 | 1960 | £4 | £10 | ... with Ray Brown & Shelly Manne |
| Slow Burn | LP | Phil Spector | 2307011 | 1977 | £4 | £10 | |
| Some Like It Hot | LP | Contemporary | LAC12206 | 1960 | £5 | £12 | |
| To Swing Or Not To Swing | LP | Contemporary | LAC12058 | 1958 | £6 | £15 | |

## KESTREL

| Title | Format | Label | Catalog | Year | | | Notes |
|---|---|---|---|---|---|---|---|
| Kestrel | LP | Cube | HIFLY19 | 1975 | £62.50 | £125 | |

## KESTRELS

| Title | Format | Label | Catalog | Year | | | Notes |
|---|---|---|---|---|---|---|---|
| I Can't Say Goodbye | 7" | Pye | 7N15248 | 1960 | £1.50 | £4 | |
| Kestrels | LP | Donegall | MAU500 | 1958 | £6 | £15 | |
| Smash Hits | LP | Piccadilly | NPL38009 | 1963 | £8 | £20 | |
| There Comes A Time | 7" | Pye | 7N15234 | 1959 | £1.50 | £4 | |

## KESTY

| Title | Format | Label | Catalog | Year | | | Notes |
|---|---|---|---|---|---|---|---|
| Only Fools And Fiddles | LP | private | | 1979 | £8 | £20 | |

## KETTELS

| Title | Format | Label | Catalog | Year | | | Notes |
|---|---|---|---|---|---|---|---|
| Overflight | LP | Karussell | 635081 | 1968 | £6 | £15 | German |

## KEY LARGO

| Title | Format | Label | Catalog | Year | | | Notes |
|---|---|---|---|---|---|---|---|
| Key Largo | LP | Blue Horizon | 763859 | 1970 | £6 | £15 | |
| Voodoo Rhythm | 7" | Blue Horizon | 573178 | 1971 | £4 | £8 | |

## KEYES, EBONY

| Title | Format | Label | Catalog | Year | | | Notes |
|---|---|---|---|---|---|---|---|
| Sitting In The Ring | 7" | Piccadilly | 7N35358 | 1966 | £1.50 | £4 | |

## KEYES, KAROL

| Title | Format | Label | Catalog | Year | | | Notes |
|---|---|---|---|---|---|---|---|
| Can't You Hear The Music | 7" | Fontana | TF846 | 1967 | £1.50 | £4 | |
| Fool In Love | 7" | Columbia | DB7899 | 1966 | £1.50 | £4 | |
| One In A Million | 7" | Columbia | DB8001 | 1966 | £12.50 | £25 | |
| You Beat Me To The Punch | 7" | Fontana | TF517 | 1964 | £2 | £5 | |

## KEYES, TROY

| Title | Format | Label | Catalog | Year | | | Notes |
|---|---|---|---|---|---|---|---|
| Love Explosions | 7" | Stateside | SS2087 | 1968 | £2.50 | £6 | |
| Love Explosions | 7" | Stateside | SS2149 | 1969 | £1.50 | £4 | |

## KEYMEN

| Title | Format | Label | Catalog | Year | | | Notes |
|---|---|---|---|---|---|---|---|
| Gazackstahagen | 7" | HMV | POP584 | 1959 | £1.50 | £4 | |

## KEYNOTES

| Title | Format | Label | Catalog | Year | | | Notes |
|---|---|---|---|---|---|---|---|
| Dime And A Dollar | 7" | Decca | F10302 | 1954 | £1.50 | £4 | Johnston Brothers B side |
| Steam Heat | 7" | Decca | F10643 | 1955 | £2.50 | £6 | |

## KHAN

| Title | Format | Label | Catalog | Year | | | Notes |
|---|---|---|---|---|---|---|---|
| Space Shanty | LP | Deram | SDLR11 | 1972 | £8 | £20 | |

## KHAN, ASHISH

| Title | Format | Label | Catalog | Year | | | Notes |
|---|---|---|---|---|---|---|---|
| Ashish Khan | LP | Liberty | LBL83083E | 1968 | £4 | £10 | |

## KHAN, USTAD ALI AKBAR

| Title | Format | Label | Catalog | Year | | | Notes |
|---|---|---|---|---|---|---|---|
| Dhun Palas Kafi | LP | Transatlantic | TRA183 | 1969 | £4 | £10 | |
| Music From India No. 5 | LP | HMV | ASD2367 | 1969 | £4 | £10 | |
| Peaceful Music | LP | Mushroom | 100MR14 | 1971 | £20 | £40 | |

## KHAN, USTAD VILAYAT

| Title | Format | Label | Catalog | Year | | | Notes |
|---|---|---|---|---|---|---|---|
| Duets | LP | HMV | ALP/ASD2295 | 1967 | £4 | £10 | |
| Music Of India | LP | HMV | ALP1946/ASD498 | 1962 | £5 | £12 | |
| Raga Tilakkamod | LP | Transatlantic | TRA239 | 1970 | £4 | £10 | |
| Ustad Vilayat Khan | LP | Track | | 1971 | £4 | £10 | |

## KHANDARS

| Title | Format | Label | Catalog | Year | | | Notes |
|---|---|---|---|---|---|---|---|
| Don't Dig A Hole For Me | 7" | Blue Beat | BB332 | 1965 | £6 | £12 | Buster's Allstars B side |

## KHANS

| Title | Format | Label | Catalog | Year | | | Notes |
|---|---|---|---|---|---|---|---|
| New Orleans 2am | 7" | London | HLU9555 | 1962 | £2.50 | £6 | |

## KHARTOMB

| Title | Format | Label | Catalog | Year | | | Notes |
|---|---|---|---|---|---|---|---|
| Swahili Lullaby | 7" | Whaam! | WHAAM14 | 1983 | £1.50 | £4 | |

## KHAZAD DOOM

| Title | Format | Label | Catalog | Year | | | Notes |
|---|---|---|---|---|---|---|---|
| Level Six And A Half | LP | LPL | LPL892 | 1970 | £700 | £1000 | US |

## KICKSTANDS

| Title | Format | Label | Catalog | Year | | | Notes |
|---|---|---|---|---|---|---|---|
| Black Boots And Bikes | LP | Capitol | (S)T2078 | 1964 | £5 | £12 | US |

## KIDD, JOHNNY & THE PIRATES

| | | | | | | | |
|---|---|---|---|---|---|---|---|
| Always And Ever | 7" | HMV | POP1269 | 1964 | £1.50 | £4 | |
| Birds And The Bees | 7" | HMV | POP1397 | 1965 | £1.50 | £4 | |
| Hungry For Love | 7" | HMV | POP1228 | 1963 | £1.50 | £4 | |
| Hurry On Back To Love | 7" | HMV | POP978 | 1962 | £2 | £5 | |
| I'll Never Get Over You | 7" | HMV | POP1173 | 1963 | £1.50 | £4 | |
| If You Were The Only Girl | 7" | HMV | POP674 | 1959 | £4 | £8 | |
| It's Got To Be You | 7" | HMV | POP1520 | 1965 | £4 | £8 | |
| Jealous Girl | 7" | HMV | POP1309 | 1964 | £1.50 | £4 | |
| Johnny Kidd & The Pirates | 7" EP. | HMV | 7EG8834 | 1964 | £12.50 | £25 | |
| Linda Lu | 7" | HMV | POP853 | 1961 | £2.50 | £6 | |
| Please Don't Bring Me Down | 7" | HMV | POP919 | 1961 | £2.50 | £6 | |
| Please Don't Touch | 7" | HMV | POP615 | 1959 | £4 | £8 | |
| Restless | 7" | HMV | POP790 | 1960 | £2 | £5 | |
| Send For That Girl | 7" | HMV | POP1559 | 1966 | £4 | £8 | |
| Shakin' All Over | LP | Starline | SRS5100 | 1971 | £4 | £10 | |
| Shakin' All Over | 7" EP. | HMV | 7EG8628 | 1960 | £12.50 | £25 | |
| Shakin' All Over | 7" EP. | Pathe | EGF813 | 1965 | £30 | £60 | French |
| Shaking All Over | 7" | HMV | POP753 | 1960 | £4 | £8 | |
| Shaking All Over '65 | 7" | HMV | POP1424 | 1965 | £2 | £5 | |
| Shot Of Rhythm And Blues | 7" | HMV | POP1088 | 1962 | £1.50 | £4 | |
| Whole Lotta Woman | 7" | HMV | POP1353 | 1964 | £1.50 | £4 | |
| You've Got What It Takes | 7" | HMV | POP698 | 1960 | £2 | £5 | |

## KIDS NEXT DOOR

| | | | | | | | |
|---|---|---|---|---|---|---|---|
| Inky Dinky Spider | 7" | London | HLR9993 | 1965 | £1.50 | £4 | |
| What's It All About? | 7" | Warner Bros | K17492 | 1979 | £2 | £5 | |

## KIESEWETTER, KNUT

| | | | | | | | |
|---|---|---|---|---|---|---|---|
| That's Me | LP | Starclub | 158033STY | 1967 | £25 | £50 | German |

## KILDAIRE, ROY

| | | | | | | | |
|---|---|---|---|---|---|---|---|
| What About It | 7" | Blue Beat | BB226 | 1964 | £6 | £12 | |

## KILEEN, JUDY

| | | | | | | | |
|---|---|---|---|---|---|---|---|
| Just Walking In The Rain | 7" | London | HLU8328 | 1956 | £7.50 | £15 | |

## KILFENORA CEILI BAND

| | | | | | | | |
|---|---|---|---|---|---|---|---|
| Kilfenora Ceili Band | LP | Transatlantic | TRS108 | 1974 | £5 | £12 | |

## KILGORE, MERLE

| | | | | | | | |
|---|---|---|---|---|---|---|---|
| Dear Mama | 7" | Melodisc | 1545 | 1960 | £4 | £8 | |
| Ernie | 7" | London | HLP8392 | 1957 | £75 | £150 | |
| Forty Two In Chicago | 7" | Mercury | AMT1193 | 1962 | £2.50 | £6 | |
| It Can't Rain All The Time | 7" | London | HL8103 | 1954 | £50 | £100 | |

## KILGORE, THEOLA

| | | | | | | | |
|---|---|---|---|---|---|---|---|
| I'll Keep Trying | 7" | Sue | WI4035 | 1967 | £5 | £10 | |

## KILLEN, LOU & SALLY

| | | | | | | | |
|---|---|---|---|---|---|---|---|
| Bright Shining Morning | LP | Front Hall | FHR06 | 1975 | £8 | £20 | US |

## KILLEN, LOUIS

| | | | | | | | |
|---|---|---|---|---|---|---|---|
| Ballads And Broadsides | LP | Topic | 12T126 | 1965 | £10 | £25 | |
| Northumbrian Garland | 7" EP. | Topic | TOP75 | 1962 | £7.50 | £15 | |

## KILLEN, LOUIS & JOHNNY HANDLE

| | | | | | | | |
|---|---|---|---|---|---|---|---|
| Collier's Rant | 7" EP. | Topic | TOP74 | 1962 | £7.50 | £15 | |

## KILLEN, LOUIS, JOHNNY HANDLE, COLIN ROSS

| | | | | | | | |
|---|---|---|---|---|---|---|---|
| Along The Coaly Tyne | LP | Topic | 12T189 | 1969 | £10 | £25 | |

## KILLEN, LOUIS, TOM GILFELLON, JOHNNY HANDLE, COLIN ROSS

| | | | | | | | |
|---|---|---|---|---|---|---|---|
| Tommy Armstrong Of Tyneside | LP | Topic | 12T122 | 1965 | £5 | £12 | |

## KILLERMETERS

| | | | | | | | |
|---|---|---|---|---|---|---|---|
| Twisted Wheel | 7" | Gem | GEMS22 | 1980 | £5 | £10 | |
| Why Should It Happen To Me | 7" | Psycho | P2620 | 1979 | £7.50 | £15 | no picture sleeve |
| Why Should It Happen To Me | 7" | Psycho | P2620 | 1979 | £15 | £30 | picture sleeve |

## KILLIGREW, JOHN

| | | | | | | | |
|---|---|---|---|---|---|---|---|
| John Killigrew | LP | Penny Farthing | PELS513 | 1971 | £4 | £10 | |

## KILLING FLOOR

| | | | | | | | |
|---|---|---|---|---|---|---|---|
| Call For The Politicians | 7" | Penny Farthing | PEN745 | 1970 | £5 | £10 | |
| Killing Floor | LP | Spark | SRLP102 | 1970 | £75 | £150 | |
| Original Killing Floor | LP | Spark | SRLM2004 | 1973 | £25 | £50 | |
| Out Of Uranus | LP | Penny Farthing | PELS511 | 1970 | £50 | £100 | |

## KILLING JOKE

| | | | | | | | |
|---|---|---|---|---|---|---|---|
| America | CD-s | Editions EG | EGOCD40 | 1988 | £2 | £5 | |
| Kings And Queens | 12" | Editions EG | EGOY21 | 1985 | £2.50 | £6 | |
| Love Like Blood | 12" | Editions EG | EGOY20 | 1985 | £2.50 | £6 | |
| Me Or You | 12" | Editions EG | EGOXD14 | 1983 | £4 | £10 | double |
| Money Is Not Our God | CD-s | Noise | AG0543 | 1990 | £2 | £5 | |
| Nervous System | 12" | Island | WIP6550 | 1981 | £2.50 | £6 | |
| Nervous System | 10" | Malicious | MD410 | 1979 | £4 | £10 | with 5 inserts |

| | | | | | | | |
|---|---|---|---|---|---|---|---|
| Requiem | 12" | Damage..........<br>Malicious | EGMDX100 | 1980 | £2.50 | £6 | |
| Revelations | CD | Editions EG | EGCD59 | 1987 | £5 | £12 | |
| Sanity | 7" | Editions EG | EGO30 | 1986 | £4 | £8 | with Wardance cassette |
| Wardance | 7" | Malicious<br>Damage.......... | MD540 | 1980 | £1.50 | £4 | with insert |

## KILOWATTS
| | | | | | | |
|---|---|---|---|---|---|---|
| Bring It On Home | 7" | Doctor Bird | DB1140 | 1968 | £5 | £10 |

## KILTIES
| | | | | | | |
|---|---|---|---|---|---|---|
| Teach You To Rock | 7" | Beltona | BL2666 | 1956 | £4 | £8 |

## KIMBER, BILL & THE COURIERS
| | | | | | | | |
|---|---|---|---|---|---|---|---|
| Shakin' Up A Storm | LP | Renown | NLP248 | 1965 | £50 | £100 | South African |
| Swinging Fashion | LP | Renown | NLP262 | 1965 | £50 | £100 | South African |

## KIMBER, WILLIAM
| | | | | | | |
|---|---|---|---|---|---|---|
| Art Of William Kimber | LP | Topic | 12T249 | 1974 | £4 | £10 |
| William Kimber | LP | EFSDS | LP1001 | 197– | £5 | £12 |

## KIMBER, WILLIAM E.
| | | | | | | |
|---|---|---|---|---|---|---|
| Kilburn Towers | 7" | Parlophone | R5735 | 1968 | £1.50 | £4 |

## KIMBLE, STEVIE
| | | | | | | |
|---|---|---|---|---|---|---|
| Some Things Take A Little Time | 7" | Decca | F12378 | 1966 | £5 | £10 |

## KIMMEL, JOHN J.
| | | | | | | |
|---|---|---|---|---|---|---|
| Early Recordings Of Irish Traditional<br>Dance Music | LP | Leader | LEO2060 | 1977 | £5 | £12 |

## KIN PING MEH
| | | | | | | | |
|---|---|---|---|---|---|---|---|
| Kin Ping Meh | LP | Polydor | 2371259 | 1971 | £50 | £100 | German |
| Kin Ping Meh 2 | LP | Zebra | 2949005 | 1972 | £6 | £15 | German |
| Kin Ping Meh 3 | LP | Zebra | 2949011 | 1973 | £6 | £15 | German |

## KINETIC
| | | | | | | | |
|---|---|---|---|---|---|---|---|
| Live Your Life | LP | Vogue | CLVLX148 | 1966 | £50 | £100 | French |
| Live Your Life | 7" EP | Vogue | EPL8544 | 1967 | £10 | £20 | French |
| Suddenly Tomorrow | 7" EP | Vogue | EPL8520 | 1967 | £10 | £20 | French |

## KING, AL
| | | | | | | |
|---|---|---|---|---|---|---|
| Think Twice Before You Speak | 7" | Sue | WI4045 | 1968 | £7.50 | £15 |

## KING, ALBERT
| | | | | | | | |
|---|---|---|---|---|---|---|---|
| Big Blues | LP | King | 852 | 1962 | £20 | £40 | US |
| Born Under A Bad Sign | LP | Stax | 723 | 1967 | £6 | £15 | US |
| Born Under A Bad Sign | 7" | Stax | 601015 | 1967 | £1.50 | £4 | |
| Cold Feet | 7" | Stax | 601029 | 1968 | £1.50 | £4 | |
| Crosscut Saw | 7" | Atlantic | 584099 | 1967 | £2.50 | £6 | |
| Does The King's Things | LP | Stax | SXATS1017 | 1968 | £5 | £12 | |
| King Of The Blues Guitar | LP | Atlantic | 588173 | 1969 | £4 | £10 | |
| Live Wire Blues Power | LP | Stax | (S)XATS1002 | 1968 | £4 | £10 | |
| Lucy | 7" | Stax | 601042 | 1968 | £1.50 | £4 | |
| Travelling To California | LP | Polydor | 2343026 | 1967 | £5 | £12 | |
| Years Gone By | LP | Stax | SXATS1022 | 1970 | £4 | £10 | |

## KING, ALBERT & OTIS RUSH
| | | | | | | | |
|---|---|---|---|---|---|---|---|
| Door To Door | LP | Chess | 1538 | 1969 | £5 | £12 | US |

## KING, ANNA
| | | | | | | | |
|---|---|---|---|---|---|---|---|
| Baby Baby Baby | 7" | Philips | BF1402 | 1965 | £2 | £5 | with Bobby Byrd |
| Back To Soul | LP | Philips | (S)BL7655 | 1965 | £20 | £40 | |
| Back To Soul | 7" EP | Philips | BE12584 | 1965 | £6 | £12 | |

## KING, B. B.
| | | | | | | | |
|---|---|---|---|---|---|---|---|
| Ain't Nobody Home | 7" | Probe | PRO546 | 1971 | £1.50 | £4 | |
| B. B. King | LP | Crown | CLP5359 | 1963 | £6 | £15 | US |
| B. B. King Sings Spirituals | LP | Crown | CLP5119/CST152 | 1960 | £6 | £15 | US |
| B. B. King Sings Spirituals | LP | Crown | CST152 | 1960 | £8 | £20 | US, red vinyl |
| B. B. King Story Vol. 1 | LP | Blue Horizon | 763216 | 1968 | £15 | £30 | |
| B. B. King Story Vol. 2 | LP | Blue Horizon | 763226 | 1969 | £15 | £30 | |
| B. B. King Wails | LP | Crown | CLP5115/CST147 | 1960 | £6 | £15 | US |
| B. B. King Wails | LP | Crown | CST147 | 1960 | £8 | £20 | US, red vinyl |
| Best Of B. B. King | LP | Galaxy | 202 | 1963 | £6 | £15 | US |
| Blues | LP | Crown | CLP5063 | 1960 | £6 | £15 | US |
| Blues In My Heart | LP | Crown | CLP5309 | 1962 | £6 | £15 | US |
| Blues Is King | LP | HMV | CLP3608 | 1967 | £6 | £15 | |
| Blues On Top Of Blues | LP | Stateside | (S)SL10238 | 1968 | £6 | £15 | |
| Completely Well | LP | Stateside | SSL10299 | 1970 | £6 | £15 | |
| Confessin' The Blues | LP | HMV | CLP3514 | 1966 | £6 | £15 | |
| Don't Answer The Door | 7" | HMV | POP1568 | 1966 | £2 | £5 | |
| Don't Waste My Time | LP | Stateside | SS2141 | 1969 | £1.50 | £4 | |
| Easy Listening Blues | LP | Crown | CLP5286 | 1962 | £6 | £15 | US |
| Electric B. B. King | LP | Stateside | SSL10284 | 1969 | £6 | £15 | |
| Every Day I Have The Blues | 7" | Blue Horizon | 573161 | 1969 | £2.50 | £6 | |
| Great B. B. King | LP | Crown | CLP5143 | 1961 | £6 | £15 | US |

| | | | | | | | |
|---|---|---|---|---|---|---|---|
| Hummingbird | 7" | Stateside | SS2176 | 1970 | £1.50 | £4 | |
| In London | LP | Probe | SPB1041 | 1971 | £4 | £10 | |
| Indianola Mississippi Seed | LP | Probe | SPBA6255 | 1970 | £4 | £10 | |
| Jungle | 7" | Polydor | 56735 | 1967 | £1.50 | £4 | |
| King Of The Blues | LP | Crown | CLP5167/CST195 | 1961 | £6 | £15 | US |
| King Of The Blues | LP | Crown | CST195 | 1961 | £8 | £20 | US, red vinyl |
| Live And Well | LP | Stateside | SSL10297 | 1970 | £6 | £15 | |
| Live At Cook County Jail | LP | Probe | SPB1032 | 1971 | £4 | £10 | |
| Live At The Regal | LP | HMV | CLP1870 | 1965 | £8 | £20 | |
| Lucille | LP | Stateside | (S)SL10272 | 1969 | £6 | £15 | |
| Mr. Blues | LP | ABC | (S)456 | 1963 | £6 | £15 | US |
| My Kind Of Blues | LP | Crown | CLP5188 | 1961 | £6 | £15 | US |
| Night Life | 7" | HMV | POP1580 | 1967 | £1.50 | £4 | |
| Paying The Cost To Be The Boss | 7" | Stateside | SS2112 | 1968 | £1.50 | £4 | |
| R&B And Soul | LP | Ember | EMB3379 | 1967 | £4 | £10 | |
| Rock Me Baby | 7" | Ember | EMBS196 | 1964 | £4 | £8 | |
| So Excited | 7" | Stateside | SS2169 | 1970 | £1.50 | £4 | |
| Take A Swing With Me | LP | Blue Horizon | 2431004 | 1970 | £20 | £40 | |
| Think It Over | 7" | HMV | POP1594 | 1967 | £1.50 | £4 | |
| Thrill Is Gone | 7" | Stateside | SS2161 | 1970 | £1.50 | £4 | |
| Tomorrow Night | 7" | HMV | POP1101 | 1962 | £4 | £8 | |
| Twist With B. B. King | LP | Crown | CLP5248 | 1962 | £6 | £15 | US |
| Woman I Love | 7" | Blue Horizon | 573144 | 1968 | £4 | £8 | |
| You Never Know | 7" | Sue | WI358 | 1965 | £4 | £8 | |

## KING, B. B. & BOBBY BLAND

| | | | | | | | |
|---|---|---|---|---|---|---|---|
| Together For The First Time | LP | ABC | ABCD605 | 1974 | £5 | £12 | double |

## KING, BEN E.

| | | | | | | | |
|---|---|---|---|---|---|---|---|
| Amor Amor | 7" | London | HLK9416 | 1961 | £1.50 | £4 | |
| Cry No More | 7" | Atlantic | AT4043 | 1965 | £4 | £8 | |
| Don't Play That Song | LP | London | HAK8012 | 1962 | £8 | £20 | |
| Don't Play That Song | 7" | London | HLK9544 | 1962 | £1.50 | £4 | |
| Don't Take Your Love From Me | 7" | Atlantic | 584184 | 1968 | £5 | £10 | |
| Goodnight My Love, Pleasant Dreams | 7" | Atlantic | AT4065 | 1966 | £1.50 | £4 | |
| Greatest Hits | LP | Atco | SD33165 | 1964 | £6 | £15 | US |
| Grooving | 7" | London | HLK9840 | 1964 | £1.50 | £4 | |
| Here Comes The Night | 7" | London | HLK9457 | 1961 | £2 | £5 | |
| How Can I Forget | 7" EP | London | REK1361 | 1963 | £7.50 | £15 | |
| How Can I Forget | 7" | London | HLK9691 | 1963 | £1.50 | £4 | |
| I (Who Have Nothing) | 7" | London | HLK9778 | 1963 | £1.50 | £4 | |
| I Could Have Danced All Night | 7" | London | HLK9819 | 1963 | £1.50 | £4 | |
| I'm Standing By | 7" EP | London | REK1386 | 1963 | £7.50 | £15 | |
| I'm Standing By | 7" | London | HLK9631 | 1962 | £1.50 | £4 | |
| Let The Water Run Down | 7" | Atlantic | AT4007 | 1964 | £1.50 | £4 | |
| Record | 7" | Atlantic | AT4025 | 1965 | £2 | £5 | |
| Seven Letters | LP | Atlantic | 588125 | 1968 | £4 | £10 | |
| Seven Letters | 7" | Atlantic | 584149 | 1968 | £1.50 | £4 | |
| Seven Letters | 7" | Atlantic | AT4018 | 1965 | £2 | £5 | |
| Songs For Soulful Lovers | LP | Atlantic | 587/588055 | 1966 | £4 | £10 | |
| Songs For Soulful Lovers | LP | London | HAK/SHK8026 | 1963 | £8 | £20 | |
| Spanish Harlem | LP | London | HAK2395/ SAHK6195 | 1961 | £10 | £25 | US |
| Spanish Harlem | LP | Atlantic | 590001 | 1967 | £4 | £10 | |
| Spanish Harlem | 7" | London | HLK9258 | 1961 | £2 | £5 | |
| Stand By Me | 7" | London | HLK9358 | 1961 | £2 | £5 | |
| Too Bad | 7" | London | HLK9586 | 1962 | £1.50 | £4 | |
| What Is Soul | 7" | Atlantic | 584069 | 1967 | £1.50 | £4 | |
| What Is Soul? | LP | Atlantic | 587072 | 1967 | £5 | £12 | |
| What Now My Love | 7" EP | Atlantic | AET6004 | 1964 | £6 | £12 | |
| Yes | 7" | London | HLK9517 | 1962 | £1.50 | £4 | |

## KING, BOB

| | | | | | | | |
|---|---|---|---|---|---|---|---|
| Hey Honey | 7" | Oriole | CB1497 | 1959 | £30 | £60 | |

## KING, BUZZY

| | | | | | | | |
|---|---|---|---|---|---|---|---|
| Schoolboy Blues | 7" | Top Rank | JAR278 | 1960 | £2 | £5 | |

## KING, CARL

| | | | | | | | |
|---|---|---|---|---|---|---|---|
| Out Of My Depth | 7" | CBS | 202407 | 1966 | £2.50 | £6 | |

## KING, CAROLE

| | | | | | | | |
|---|---|---|---|---|---|---|---|
| It Might As Well Rain Until September | 7" | London | HLU9591 | 1962 | £1.50 | £4 | |
| Music | LP | Ode | SQ88013 | 1971 | £4 | £10 | US quad |
| Road To Nowhere | 7" | London | HLU10036 | 1966 | £1.50 | £4 | |
| Tapestry | LP | Epic/Ode | HE44946 | 1980 | £5 | £12 | US audiophile |

## KING, CLAUDE

| | | | | | | | |
|---|---|---|---|---|---|---|---|
| Burning Of Atlanta | 7" | CBS | AAG119 | 1962 | £1.50 | £4 | |
| Commancheros | 7" | Philips | BF1199 | 1961 | £1.50 | £4 | |
| Sweet Loving | 7" | Philips | BF1173 | 1961 | £1.50 | £4 | |
| Tiger Woman | 7" EP | CBS | EP6067 | 1965 | £5 | £10 | |
| Wolverton Mountain | 7" | CBS | AAG108 | 1962 | £2 | £5 | |

## KING, CLYDIE

| | | | | | | | |
|---|---|---|---|---|---|---|---|
| One Part Two Part | 7" | Minit | MLF11014 | 1969 | £2 | £5 | |

## KING, DANNY & MAYFAIR SET

| | | | | | | | |
|---|---|---|---|---|---|---|---|
| Amen | 7" | Columbia | DB7792 | 1965 | £5 | £10 | |
| Pretty Things | 7" | Columbia | DB7456 | 1965 | £10 | £20 | |
| Tossing And Turning | 7" | Columbia | DB7276 | 1964 | £6 | £12 | |

## KING, DAVE

| | | | | | | | |
|---|---|---|---|---|---|---|---|
| Birds And The Bees | 7" | Decca | F10741 | 1956 | £1.50 | £4 | |
| Christmas And You | 7" | Decca | F10791 | 1956 | £1.50 | £4 | |
| Memories Are Made Of This | 7" | Decca | F10684 | 1956 | £2.50 | £6 | |
| No. 2 | 7" EP | Decca | DFE6514 | 1958 | £4 | £8 | |
| Selection | 7" EP | Decca | DFE6385 | 1956 | £4 | £8 | |
| Shake Me I Rattle | 7" | Decca | F10947 | 1957 | £1.50 | £4 | |
| Story Of My Life | 7" | Decca | F10973 | 1958 | £1.50 | £4 | |
| You Can't Be True To Two | 7" | Decca | F10720 | 1956 | £2 | £5 | |

## KING, DEE

| | | | | | | | |
|---|---|---|---|---|---|---|---|
| Sally Go Round The Roses | 7" | Piccadilly | 7N35316 | 1966 | £1.50 | £4 | |

## KING, FREDDIE

| | | | | | | | |
|---|---|---|---|---|---|---|---|
| Bonanza Of Instrumentals | LP | King | (S)928 | 1965 | £6 | £15 | US |
| Bossa Nova And Blues | LP | King | 821 | 1962 | £15 | £30 | US |
| Boy-Girl-Boy | LP | King | 777 | 1962 | £15 | £30 | US |
| Driving Sideways | 7" | Sue | WI349 | 1965 | £7.50 | £15 | |
| Freddie King Goes Surfin' | LP | King | (S)856 | 1963 | £10 | £25 | US |
| Freddie King Is A Blues Master | LP | Atlantic | 588186 | 1969 | £8 | £20 | |
| Freddie King Sings The Blues | LP | King | 762 | 1961 | £20 | £40 | US |
| Getting Ready | LP | A&M | AMLS65004 | 1971 | £4 | £10 | |
| Hide Away | LP | King | KS1059 | 1969 | £6 | £15 | US |
| Hideaway | 7" | Parlophone | R4777 | 1961 | £7.50 | £15 | |
| His Early Years | LP | Polydor | 2343047 | 1971 | £4 | £10 | |
| King Of R&B Vol. 2 | LP | Polydor | 2343009 | 1969 | £5 | £12 | |
| Let's Hide Away And Dance Away | LP | King | 773 | 1961 | £20 | £40 | US |
| Live Performances Volume 1 | LP | Black Bear | 904 | 1972 | £6 | £15 | |
| Live Performances Volume 2 | LP | Black Bear | 905 | 1972 | £6 | £15 | |
| Play It Cool | 7" | Atlantic | 584235 | 1969 | £1.50 | £4 | |
| Twenty-Four Vocals And Instrumentals | LP | King | 964 | 1966 | £6 | £15 | US |
| Volume 1 | LP | Python | KM5 | 1969 | £8 | £20 | |
| Volume 2 | LP | Python | KM7 | 1969 | £8 | £20 | |

## KING, HANK

| | | | | | | | |
|---|---|---|---|---|---|---|---|
| Country And Western | 7" EP | Starlite | GRK510 | 1966 | £2.50 | £6 | |
| Country And Western | 7" EP | Starlite | STEP41 | 1963 | £5 | £10 | |

## KING, JAY W.

| | | | | | | | |
|---|---|---|---|---|---|---|---|
| I'm So Afraid | 7" | Stateside | SS505 | 1966 | £5 | £10 | |

## KING, JONATHAN

| | | | | | | | |
|---|---|---|---|---|---|---|---|
| Everyone's Gone To The Moon | 7" EP | Decca | 457090 | 1965 | £5 | £10 | French |
| Or Then Again | LP | Decca | LK/SKL4908 | 1967 | £4 | £10 | |

## KING, MARK

| | | | | | | | |
|---|---|---|---|---|---|---|---|
| Clocks Go Forward | 12" | Polydor | MKX2DJ | 1984 | £4 | £10 | promo |
| I Feel Free | 7" | Polydor | MK1 | 1984 | £2 | £5 | |

## KING, MARTIN LUTHER

| | | | | | | | |
|---|---|---|---|---|---|---|---|
| Great March To Freedom | LP | Tamla Motown | TML11076 | 1968 | £50 | £100 | |
| I Have A Dream | 7" | Pama | PM732 | 1968 | £2.50 | £6 | |
| In The Struggle For Freedom | LP | Hallmark | CHM631 | 1968 | £5 | £12 | |

## KING, PAUL

| | | | | | | | |
|---|---|---|---|---|---|---|---|
| Been In The Pen Too Long | LP | Dawn | DNLS3035 | 1972 | £4 | £10 | |

## KING, PEE WEE

| | | | | | | | |
|---|---|---|---|---|---|---|---|
| Bimbo | 7" | HMV | 7MC14 | 1954 | £2 | £5 | export |

## KING, RAMONA

| | | | | | | | |
|---|---|---|---|---|---|---|---|
| It's In His Kiss | 7" | Warner Bros | WB125 | 1964 | £1.50 | £4 | |

## KING, REG

| | | | | | | | |
|---|---|---|---|---|---|---|---|
| Reg King | LP | United Artists | UAS29157 | 1971 | £25 | £50 | |

## KING, SAMMY

| | | | | | | | |
|---|---|---|---|---|---|---|---|
| Great Balls Of Fire | 7" | HMV | POP1285 | 1964 | £1.50 | £4 | |

## KING, SID & THE FIVE STRINGS

| | | | | | | | |
|---|---|---|---|---|---|---|---|
| Booger Red | 78 | Philips | PB589 | 1956 | £7.50 | £15 | |

## KING, SOLOMON

| | | | | | | | |
|---|---|---|---|---|---|---|---|
| She Wears My Ring | LP | Columbia | SX/SCX6250 | 1968 | £4 | £10 | |
| She Wears My Ring | 7" | Columbia | DB8306 | 1967 | £2 | £5 | |
| This Beautiful Day | 7" | Columbia | DB8676 | 1970 | £15 | £30 | |

## KING, TEDDI

| | | | | | | | |
|---|---|---|---|---|---|---|---|
| Miss Teddi King With Ruby Braff | 10" LP | Vogue | LDE142 | 1955 | £25 | £50 | |
| Now In Vogue | LP | Vogue | VA160109 | 1957 | £20 | £40 | |

## KING, TEDDY
| | | | | | | | |
|---|---|---|---|---|---|---|---|
| Mexican Divorce | 7" | Fab | FAB27 | 1967 | £4 | £8 | Soul Tops B side |

## KING, WENDY
| | | | | | | | |
|---|---|---|---|---|---|---|---|
| Wendy Experience | LP | Look | LKLP6355 | 1979 | £6 | £15 | |

## KING BEES
| | | | | | | | |
|---|---|---|---|---|---|---|---|
| On Your Way Down The Drain | 7" EP | RCA | 86521 | 1966 | £7.50 | £15 | French |

## KING BEES (2)
The rare single 'Liza Jane' is listed in the guide under the name later used by the group's lead singer – David Bowie.

## KING BISCUIT BOY
| | | | | | | |
|---|---|---|---|---|---|---|
| Gooduns | LP | Paramount | SPFA7001 | 1971 | £4 | £10 |
| Official Music | LP | Paramount | SPFL270 | 1971 | £4 | £10 |

## KING BROTHERS
| | | | | | | |
|---|---|---|---|---|---|---|
| Harmony Kings | 7" EP | Parlophone | GEP8638 | 1957 | £2 | £5 |
| Hop, Skip And Jump | 7" | Parlophone | R4554 | 1959 | £2 | £5 |
| In The Middle Of An Island | 7" | Parlophone | R4338 | 1957 | £1.50 | £4 |
| King Brothers | LP | Parlophone | PMC1060 | 1958 | £4 | £10 |
| King Size Hits | 7" EP | Parlophone | GEP8838 | 1961 | £2 | £5 |
| Kings Of Song | 7" EP | Parlophone | GEP8760 | 1958 | £2 | £5 |
| Little By Little | 7" | Parlophone | R4288 | 1957 | £2 | £5 |
| Put A Light In The Window | 7" | Parlophone | R4389 | 1958 | £1.50 | £4 |
| Six Five Jive | 7" | Parlophone | R4410 | 1958 | £2 | £5 |
| Torero | 7" | Parlophone | R4438 | 1958 | £1.50 | £4 |
| Wake Up Little Susie | 7" | Parlophone | R4367 | 1957 | £1.50 | £4 |
| White Sports Coat | 7" | Parlophone | R4310 | 1957 | £1.50 | £4 |

## KING CANNON
| | | | | | | | |
|---|---|---|---|---|---|---|---|
| Soul Pipe | 7" | Duke | DU13 | 1969 | £1.50 | £4 | |
| Soul Scorcher | 7" | Trojan | TR663 | 1969 | £1.50 | £4 | |
| Thunderstorm | 7" | Trojan | TR636 | 1968 | £1.50 | £4 | Burt Walters B side |

## KING CRIMSON
It is difficult today to convey the sense of excitement of the new that was apparent at King Crimson's early concerts. The one LP that exists of the original line-up is a frustrating affair in so far as it fails to display all the facets of a remarkable group. *In The Court Of The Crimson King* is, nevertheless, the progressive rock textbook, its vital place in the music being finally recognized by a noticeable rise in the value of original copies. The novel eccentricity apparent in the subsequent 'Catfood' single gives a hint of what might have followed. Unfortunately, the original line-up came apart after an American tour. Both *In The Wake Of Poseidon* and *McDonald And Giles* contain material that had been destined for the real, unheard second King Crimson album. With later King Crimson albums being essentially the work of Robert Fripp, rather than the co-operative unit that was there at the start, it is rather as though the Beatles had gone their separate ways immediately after making *Revolver*.

| | | | | | | | |
|---|---|---|---|---|---|---|---|
| Cat Food | 7" | Island | WIP6080 | 1970 | £10 | £20 | picture sleeve |
| Court Of The Crimson King | 7" | Island | WIP6071 | 1969 | £4 | £8 | |
| Earthbound | LP | Island | HELP6 | 1972 | £6 | £15 | |
| In The Court Of The Crimson King | LP | Island | ILPS9111 | 1969 | £20 | £40 | pink label |
| In The Court Of The Crimson King | LP | Mobile Fidelity | MFSL1075 | 1980 | £10 | £25 | US audiophile |
| In The Court Of The Crimson King | CD | Polydor | 8000302 | 1983 | £5 | £12 | |
| In The Wake Of Poseidon | LP | Island | ILPS9127 | 1970 | £10 | £25 | pink label |
| In The Wake Of Poseidon | CD | Editions EG | EGCD2 | 1987 | £5 | £12 | |
| Islands | LP | Island | ILPS9175 | 1971 | £6 | £15 | |
| Islands | CD | Editions EG | EGCD5 | 1987 | £5 | £12 | |
| Larks' Tongues In Aspic | CD | Editions EG | EGCD7 | 1987 | £5 | £12 | |
| Lizard | LP | Island | ILPS9141 | 1970 | £6 | £15 | |
| Return Of King Crimson | LP | Editions EG | | 1981 | £6 | £15 | interview promo |
| Thela Hun Ginjeet | 12" | Editions EG | KCX001 | 1981 | £2.50 | £6 | promo |
| Three Of A Perfect Pair | CD | Editions EG | 8178822 | 1984 | £5 | £12 | |
| Twenty-First Century Schizoid Man | 7" | Island | WIP6274 | 1976 | £7.50 | £15 | picture sleeve |

## KING EARL BOOGIE BAND
| | | | | | | |
|---|---|---|---|---|---|---|
| Trouble At Mill | LP | Dawn | DNLS3040 | 1972 | £4 | £10 |

## KING FIGHTER
| | | | | | | |
|---|---|---|---|---|---|---|
| People Will Talk | 7" | Jump Up | JU518 | 1967 | £1.50 | £4 |

## KING GEORGE
| | | | | | | |
|---|---|---|---|---|---|---|
| I'm Gonna Be Somebody | 7" | RCA | RCA1573 | 1967 | £4 | £8 |

## KING KURT
| | | | | | | | |
|---|---|---|---|---|---|---|---|
| America | 7" | Polydor | KURTP1 | 1986 | £1.50 | £4 | shaped picture disc |
| Banana Banana | 7" | Stiff | BUY206 | 1984 | £2 | £5 | shaped picture disc |
| Destination Zululand | 7" | Stiff | BUY189 | 1983 | £2.50 | £6 | shaped picture disc |
| Mack The Knife | 7" | Stiff | BUY199 | 1984 | £1.50 | £4 | picture disc |
| Mack The Knife | 7" | Stiff | PBUY199 | 1984 | £2 | £5 | shaped picture disc |
| Zulu Beat | 7" | Thin Sliced | TSR2 | 1982 | £2.50 | £6 | 60 coloured vinyl/ sleeve combinations! |

## KING OF MONTEGO BAY
| | | | | | | |
|---|---|---|---|---|---|---|
| Burn | 7" | Blue Beat | BB322 | 1965 | £6 | £12 |

## KING OF THE SLUMS
| | | | | | | |
|---|---|---|---|---|---|---|
| Spider Psychiatry | 7" | SLR | SLR001 | 1986 | £5 | £10 |

## KING PING MEH
| | | | | | | | | |
|---|---|---|---|---|---|---|---|---|
| Concrete | LP | Nova | 628370 | 1975 | £4 | £10 | | German |
| King Ping Meh 6 | LP | Bacillus | BAC2046 | 1977 | £4 | £10 | | German |
| Virtues And Sins | LP | Nova | 622015 | 1974 | £4 | £10 | | German |

## KING ROCKY
| | | | | | | | |
|---|---|---|---|---|---|---|---|
| King Is Back | 7" | Studio One | SO2045 | 1968 | £6 | £12 | Three Tops B side |

## KING SPORTY
| | | | | | | | |
|---|---|---|---|---|---|---|---|
| D.J. Special | 7" | Banana | BA323 | 1970 | £1.50 | £4 | Richard & Mad B side |
| Inspiration | 7" | Banana | BA321 | 1970 | £1.50 | £4 | |
| Lover's Version | 7" | Banana | BA322 | 1970 | £1.50 | £4 | . Dudley Sibley B side |

## KING STITT
| | | | | | | | |
|---|---|---|---|---|---|---|---|
| Back Out Version | 7" | Banana | BA332 | 1971 | £1.50 | £4 | Vegetables B side |
| Herbsman Shuffle | 7" | Clandisc | CLA207 | 1969 | £1.50 | £4 | Higgs & Wilson B side |
| King Of Kings | 7" | Clandisc | CLA223 | 1970 | £1.50 | £4 | Dynamites B side |
| On The Street | 7" | Clandisc | CLA203 | 1969 | £1.50 | £4 | Cynthia Richards B side |
| Rhyming Time | 7" | Banana | BA334 | 1971 | £1.50 | £4 | |
| Vigerton Two | 7" | Clandisc | CLA202 | 1969 | £1.50 | £4 | |

## KINGBEES
| | | | | | | | |
|---|---|---|---|---|---|---|---|
| I'm A Kingbee | 7" | Tempo | TPO103 | 1966 | £75 | £150 | picture sleeve |

## KINGDOM
| | | | | | | | |
|---|---|---|---|---|---|---|---|
| Kingdom | LP | Speciality | SPS2135 | 1970 | £37.50 | £75 | US |

## KINGDOM COME
| | | | | | | | |
|---|---|---|---|---|---|---|---|
| Galactic Zoo Dossier | LP | Polydor | 2310130 | 1971 | £8 | £20 | |
| Journey | LP | Polydor | 2310254 | 1973 | £6 | £15 | |
| Kingdom Come | LP | Polydor | 2310178 | 1973 | £8 | £20 | |
| Lost Ears | LP | Gull | GUD2003/4 | 1977 | £5 | £12 | double |

## KINGDOMS
The record credited to Kingdoms marks the recording debut of Guy Chadwick, who was later to find much more success with his band the House Of Love.

| | | | | | | | |
|---|---|---|---|---|---|---|---|
| Heartland | 7" | Regard | RG114 | 1984 | £2 | £5 | |
| Heartland | 12" | Regard | RG114 | 1984 | £3 | £8 | |

## KINGLY BAND
| | | | | | | | |
|---|---|---|---|---|---|---|---|
| Bitter And The Sweet | 7" | Decca | F12926 | 1969 | £1.50 | £4 | |

## KINGMAKER
| | | | | | | | |
|---|---|---|---|---|---|---|---|
| Celebrated Working Man | 7" | Sacred Heart | NONE1 | 1991 | £5 | £10 | promo |

## KINGPINS
| | | | | | | | |
|---|---|---|---|---|---|---|---|
| It Won't Be This Way Always | LP | King | 865 | 1963 | £8 | £20 | US |
| Ungaua | 7" | London | HLU8658 | 1958 | £5 | £10 | |

## KINGPINS (2)
| | | | | | | | |
|---|---|---|---|---|---|---|---|
| Two Right Feet | 7" | Oriole | CB1986 | 1965 | £5 | £10 | |

## KINGS IV
| | | | | | | | |
|---|---|---|---|---|---|---|---|
| Some Like It Hot | 7" | London | HLT8914 | 1959 | £2 | £5 | |

## KING'S GALLIARD
| | | | | | | | |
|---|---|---|---|---|---|---|---|
| Morning Dew | LP | Dolphin | DOLM5014 | 1976 | £4 | £10 | Irish |

## KING'S HENCHMEN
| | | | | | | | |
|---|---|---|---|---|---|---|---|
| Alan Freed Presents Vol. 1 | 7" EP | Coral | FEP2025 | 1959 | £37.50 | £75 | |

## KINGSLEY, CHARLES CREATION
| | | | | | | | |
|---|---|---|---|---|---|---|---|
| Summer Without Sun | 7" | Columbia | DB7758 | 1965 | £12.50 | £25 | |

## KINGSMEN
| | | | | | | | |
|---|---|---|---|---|---|---|---|
| 15 Great Hits | LP | Wand | WD(S)674 | 1966 | £4 | £10 | US |
| Annie Fanny | 7" | Pye | 7N25322 | 1965 | £1.50 | £4 | |
| Climb | 7" EP | Vogue | INT18015 | 1965 | £7.50 | £15 | French |
| Climb | 7" | Pye | 7N25311 | 1965 | £1.50 | £4 | |
| Daytime Shadows | 7" | Pye | 7N25406 | 1967 | £2 | £5 | |
| Death Of An Angel | 7" | Pye | 7N25273 | 1964 | £2 | £5 | |
| Fever | 7" EP | Pye | NEP44063 | 1966 | £5 | £10 | |
| Gamma Goochee | 7" EP | Vogue | INT18065 | 1966 | £7.50 | £15 | French |
| Greatest Hits | LP | Marble Arch | MAL829 | 1968 | £4 | £10 | |
| How To Stuff A Wild Bikini | 7" EP | Vogue | INT18025 | 1965 | £7.50 | £15 | French |
| In Person | LP | Pye | NPL28050 | 1964 | £6 | £15 | |
| Jolly Green Giant | 7" | Pye | 7N25292 | 1965 | £2 | £5 | |
| Killer Joe | 7" | Pye | 7N25370 | 1966 | £2.50 | £6 | |
| Kingsmen | 7" EP | Pye | NEP44023 | 1964 | £6 | £12 | |
| Little Latin Lupe Lu | 7" EP | Vogue | EPL8273 | 1964 | £7.50 | £15 | French |
| Little Latin Lupe Lu | 7" | Pye | 7N25262 | 1964 | £1.50 | £4 | |
| Louie Louie | 7" EP | Vogue | EPL8172 | 1963 | £7.50 | £15 | French, B side by Jocko Henderson |

| | | | | | | |
|---|---|---|---|---|---|---|
| Louie Louie | 7" | Pye | 7N25231 | 1963 £4 | £8 | |
| Louie Louie | 7" | Pye | 7N25366 | 1966 £1.50 | £4 | |
| Mojo Workout | 7" EP | Pye | NEP44040 | 1965 £6 | £12 | |
| Money | 7" EP | Vogue | EPL8209 | 1964 £7.50 | £15 | French |
| On Campus | LP | Pye | NPL28068 | 1965 £6 | £15 | |
| Volume II | LP | Pye | NPL28054 | 1964 £6 | £15 | |
| Volume III | LP | Wand | WD(S)662 | 1965 £4 | £10 | US |

## KINGSMEN (2)

| | | | | | | |
|---|---|---|---|---|---|---|
| Better Believe It | 7" | London | HLE8735 | 1958 £7.50 | £15 | |
| Conga Rock | 7" | London | HLE8812 | 1959 £10 | £20 | |
| Weekend | 7" EP | London | REE1211 | 1959 £25 | £50 | |

## KINGSTON, JOE

| | | | | | | |
|---|---|---|---|---|---|---|
| Time Is On My Friends | 7" | Blue Beat | BB253 | 1964 £6 | £12 | |

## KINGSTON PETE

| | | | | | | |
|---|---|---|---|---|---|---|
| Little Boy Blue | 7" | Blue Beat | BB403 | 1967 £6 | £12 | |

## KINGSTON TRIO

The Kingston Trio were enormously popular in America, their harmonized approach to folk music inspiring many future rock stars to begin their careers in music. The line of influence leads from the Kingston Trio to Haight-Ashbury, to the music of Jefferson Airplane and the Grateful Dead, and from there to the entire sound of modern AOR. John Stewart was a member of the Kingston Trio on the later releases.

| | | | | | | |
|---|---|---|---|---|---|---|
| Aspen Gold | LP | Nautilus | NR2 | 1979 £5 | £12 | US audiophile |
| Encores | LP | Capitol | (S)T1612 | 1961 £4 | £10 | |
| Folk Era | LP | Capitol | (S)T2180 | 1964 £4 | £10 | |
| From The Hungry i | LP | Capitol | T1107 | 1959 £4 | £10 | |
| Goin' Places | LP | Capitol | (S)T1564 | 1961 £4 | £10 | |
| Greenback Dollar | 7" EP | Capitol | EAP120460 | 1963 £2 | £5 | |
| Greenback Dollar | 7" | Capitol | CL15287 | 1963 £1.50 | £4 | |
| Here We Go Again Part 1 | 7" EP | Capitol | EAP11258 | 1960 £2 | £5 | |
| Here We Go Again Part 2 | 7" EP | Capitol | EAP21258 | 1960 £2 | £5 | |
| Here We Go Again Part 3 | 7" EP | Capitol | EAP31258 | 1960 £2 | £5 | |
| Kingston Trio | LP | Capitol | T996 | 1958 £5 | £12 | |
| Kingston Trio | 7" EP | Brunswick | OE9511 | 1965 £2 | £5 | |
| Lemon Tree | 7" EP | Capitol | EAP120655 | 1964 £2 | £5 | |
| M.T.A. | 7" EP | Capitol | EAP11119 | 1959 £2 | £5 | |
| Make Way! | LP | Capitol | (S)T1474 | 1961 £4 | £10 | |
| Raspberries Strawberries | 7" EP | Capitol | EAP11182 | 1959 £2 | £5 | |
| Scarlet Ribbons | 7" | Capitol | CL14918 | 1958 £1.50 | £4 | |
| Stereo Concert | LP | Capitol | ST1183 | 1959 £5 | £12 | |
| String Along | LP | Capitol | (S)T1397 | 1960 £4 | £10 | |
| Time To Think | 7" EP | Capitol | EAP42011 | 1962 £2 | £5 | |
| Tom Dooley | 7" EP | Capitol | EAP11136 | 1959 £2 | £5 | |
| Tom Dooley | 7" | Capitol | CL14951 | 1958 £1.50 | £4 | |
| Worried Man | 7" EP | Capitol | EAP11322 | 1960 £2 | £5 | |

## KINGSTONIANS

| | | | | | | |
|---|---|---|---|---|---|---|
| Fun Galore | 7" | Doctor Bird | DB1126 | 1968 £5 | £10 | |
| I Need You | 7" | Trojan | TR770 | 1969 £1.50 | £4 | |
| Mix It Up | 7" | Trojan | TR627 | 1968 £1.50 | £4 | |
| Mother Miserable | 7" | Coxsone | CS7066 | 1968 £5 | £10 | |
| Mummy And Daddy | 7" | Doctor Bird | DB1123 | 1968 £5 | £10 | |
| Nice Nice | 7" | Big Shot | BI526 | 1969 £1.50 | £4 | |
| Put Down Your Fire | 7" | Doctor Bird | DB1120 | 1968 £5 | £10 | |
| Sufferer | LP | Trojan | TBL113 | 1970 £4 | £10 | |
| Sufferer | 7" | Big Shot | BI508 | 1968 £2.50 | £6 | |
| Winey Winey | 7" | Rio | R140 | 1967 £4 | £8 | |

## KINKS

The Kinks' long career is shot through with many collectors' items, although the majority of these come from the early, hit-making years. All the original Pye albums are becoming increasingly scarce, although their value is held down by the Kinks being seemingly irredeemably out of fashion. The original pressing of *Village Green Preservation Society* was withdrawn and replaced with a version containing more tracks, but the shorter album does contain one or two different mixes. The American compilations, *Kink Kronikles* and *The Great Lost Kinks Album*, are highly sought-after in the UK as they contain many tracks that are not otherwise available. Meanwhile, no Kinks records have sold as few copies as the first two singles, 'Long Tall Sally' and 'You Still Want Me' – most copies appearing on the market are likely, therefore, to be demos.

| | | | | | | |
|---|---|---|---|---|---|---|
| All Day And All Of The Night | 7" EP | Pye | PNV24127 | 1964 £12.50 | £25 | French |
| All Day And All Of The Night | 7" | Pye | 7N15714 | 1964 £1.50 | £4 | |
| All The Good Times | LP | Pye | IIPP100 | 1973 £20 | £40 | 4 LPs, boxed |
| Apeman | 7" | Pye | 7N45016 | 1970 £1.50 | £4 | |
| Arthur | LP | Pye | NPL18317 | 1969 £8 | £20 | mono |
| Arthur | LP | Pye | NSPL18317 | 1969 £6 | £15 | |
| Autumn Almanac | 7" | Pye | 7N17400 | 1967 £1.50 | £4 | |
| Autumn Almanac/David Watts | 7" | Pye | 7N17405 | 1967 £20 | £40 | export |
| Celluloid Heroes | 7" | RCA | RCA2299 | 1972 £1.50 | £4 | |
| Dandy | 7" EP | Pye | PNV24177 | 1966 £10 | £20 | French |
| Days | 7" | Pye | 7N17573 | 1968 £1.50 | £4 | |
| Dead End Street | 7" EP | Pye | PNV24184 | 1966 £10 | £20 | French |
| Dead End Street | 7" | Pye | 7N17222 | 1966 £1.50 | £4 | |
| Dedicated Follower Of Fashion | 7" EP | Pye | PNV24167 | 1966 £10 | £20 | French |
| Dedicated Follower Of Fashion | 7" | Pye | 7N17064 | 1966 £1.50 | £4 | |
| Dedicated Kinks | 7" EP | Pye | NEP24258 | 1966 £20 | £40 | |
| Down All The Days | CD-s | London | LONCD239 | 1989 £2 | £5 | |

| Title | Format | Label | Catalogue | Year | | | Notes |
|---|---|---|---|---|---|---|---|
| Drivin' | 7" | Pye | 7N17776 | 1969 | £1.50 | £4 | |
| Ducks On The Wall | 7" | RCA | RCA2546 | 1975 | £1.50 | £4 | |
| Everybody's Gonna Be Happy | 7" | Pye | 7N15813 | 1965 | £1.50 | £4 | |
| Everybody's In Showbiz | LP | RCA | DPS2035 | 1972 | £5 | £12 | double |
| Face To Face | LP | Pye | NPL18149 | 1966 | £8 | £20 | |
| Face To Face | LP | Pye | NSPL18149 | 1966 | £20 | £40 | stereo |
| Give The People What They Want | LP | Arista | AL9567 | 1981 | £4 | £10 | US, different mixes |
| Give The People What They Want | LP | Arista | SPART1171 | 1981 | £8 | £20 | test pressing, US mix |
| God's Children | 7" | Pye | 7N8001 | 1971 | £7.50 | £15 | export |
| Got Love If You Want It | 7" EP | Pye | PNV24131 | 1964 | £30 | £60 | French |
| Great Lost Kinks Album | LP | Reprise | MS2172 | 1973 | £20 | £40 | US |
| Greatest Hits | LP | PRT | KINK1 | 1983 | £5 | £12 | with 10" LP (Dead End Street) |
| Greatest Hits | LP | Reprise | R(S)6217 | 1966 | £6 | £15 | US |
| Greatest Hits | CD | PRT | KINKCD7251 | 1984 | £6 | £15 | misplaced cue codes |
| Holiday Romance | 7" | RCA | RCA2478 | 1974 | £1.50 | £4 | |
| How Are You | 7" | Music Week | | 1986 | £1.50 | £4 | promo |
| How Do I Get Close | CD-s | London | LONCD250 | 1990 | £2 | £5 | |
| In Germany | LP | Vogue | LDVS17077 | 1965 | £50 | £100 | German |
| Kinda Kinks | LP | Pye | NPL18112 | 1965 | £8 | £20 | |
| Kinda Kinks | LP | Pye | NSPL18112 | 1965 | £37.50 | £75 | stereo, export |
| Kink Kronikles | LP | Reprise | RS6454 | 1972 | £15 | £30 | US |
| Kinks | LP | Golden Guinea | GSGL10357 | 1967 | £8 | £20 | stereo |
| Kinks | LP | Pye | NPL18096 | 1964 | £8 | £20 | |
| Kinks | LP | Pye | NPL18326 | 1970 | £6 | £15 | double |
| Kinks | LP | Pye | NSPL83021 | 1964 | £37.50 | £75 | stereo, export |
| Kinks | 7" EP | Pye | AMEP1001 | 1975 | £2.50 | £6 | export, red or blue vinyl |
| Kinks | 7" EP | Pye | NEP5039 | 1964 | £250 | £500 | export, best auctioned |
| Kinks Kontroversy | LP | Pye | NPL18131 | 1966 | £8 | £20 | |
| Kinks Kontroversy | LP | Pye | NSPL18131 | 1966 | £37.50 | £75 | stereo, export |
| Kinks' Kinkdom | LP | Reprise | R(S)6185 | 1965 | £8 | £20 | US |
| Kinksize | LP | Reprise | R(S)6158 | 1965 | £8 | £20 | US |
| Kinksize Hits | 7" EP | Pye | NEP24203 | 1964 | £5 | £10 | |
| Kinksize Session | 7" EP | Pye | NEP24200 | 1964 | £5 | £10 | |
| Kwyet Kinks | 7" EP | Pye | NEP24221 | 1965 | £5 | £10 | |
| Live At Kelvin Hall | LP | Pye | NPL18191 | 1967 | £8 | £20 | |
| Live At Kelvin Hall | LP | Pye | NSPL18191 | 1967 | £20 | £40 | stereo |
| Lola | 7" | Pye | 7N17961 | 1970 | £1.50 | £4 | |
| Long Tall Sally | 7" | Pye | 7N15611 | 1964 | £20 | £40 | |
| Low Budget Interview | LP | Arista | SP69 | 1979 | £6 | £15 | US promo |
| Mirror Of Love | 7" | RCA | RCA5015 | 1974 | £1.50 | £4 | |
| Mirror Of Love | 7" | RCA | RCA5042 | 1974 | £1.50 | £4 | |
| Mister Pleasant | 7" EP | Pye | PNV24191 | 1967 | £10 | £20 | French |
| Mr. Pleasant | 7" | Pye | 7N17314 | 1967 | £20 | £40 | export |
| Muswell Hillbillies | LP | RCA | SF8423 | 1971 | £4 | £10 | |
| No More Looking Back | 7" | RCA | RCM1 | 1976 | £1.50 | £4 | |
| Percy | LP | Pye | NSPL18365 | 1971 | £4 | £10 | |
| Percy | 7" | Pye | 7NX8001 | 1971 | £1.50 | £4 | |
| Percy | 7" | Pye | 7NX8001 | 1971 | £2 | £5 | picture sleeve |
| Plastic Man | 7" | Pye | 7N17724 | 1969 | £1.50 | £4 | |
| Predictable | 7" | Arista | ARIPD426 | 1981 | £1.50 | £4 | picture disc |
| Preservation Act 1 | LP | RCA | SF8392 | 1973 | £4 | £10 | |
| Preservation Act 2 | LP | RCA | 5040 | 1974 | £5 | £12 | double |
| Road | CD | London | 8280782 | 1988 | £5 | £12 | |
| See My Friend | 7" | Pye | 7N15919 | 1965 | £1.50 | £4 | |
| Set Me Free | 7" | Pye | 7N15854 | 1965 | £1.50 | £4 | |
| Shangri-La | 7" | Pye | 7N17812 | 1969 | £1.50 | £4 | |
| Shangri-La/Last Of The Steam Powered Trains | 7" | Pye | 7N17812 | 1969 | £37.50 | £75 | demo |
| Sitting In The Midday Sun | 7" | RCA | RCA2387 | 1973 | £1.50 | £4 | |
| Something Else | LP | Pye | NPL18193 | 1967 | £10 | £25 | |
| Something Else | LP | Pye | NSPL18193 | 1967 | £20 | £40 | stereo |
| Something Else | 7" EP | Pye | NEP24296 | 1968 | £150 | £250 | with 'David Watts' |
| Sunny Afternoon | 7" EP | Pye | PNV24173 | 1966 | £10 | £20 | French, R.Davies, Quaife facing left on sleeve |
| Sunny Afternoon | 7" EP | Pye | PNV24173 | 1966 | £12.50 | £25 | French, R.Davies, Quaife facing right on sleeve |
| Sunny Afternoon | 7" | Pye | 7N17125 | 1966 | £1.50 | £4 | |
| Supersonic Rocket Ship | 7" | RCA | RCA2211 | 1972 | £1.50 | £4 | |
| Sweet Lady Genevieve | 7" | RCA | RCA2418 | 1973 | £1.50 | £4 | |
| Then, Now And In Between | LP | Reprise | PRO328 | 1969 | £100 | £200 | US, boxed with various items of memorabilia |
| Think Visual | CD | London | 8280302 | 1986 | £5 | £12 | |
| Till The End Of The Day | 7" EP | Pye | PNV24160 | 1965 | £10 | £20 | French |
| Till The End Of The Day | 7" | Pye | 7N15981 | 1965 | £1.50 | £4 | |
| Tired Of Waiting For You | 7" EP | Pye | PNV24132 | 1965 | £15 | £30 | French |
| Tired Of Waiting For You | 7" | Pye | 7N15759 | 1965 | £1.50 | £4 | |
| Ultimate Collection | CD | Castle | CTVCD001 | 1990 | £8 | £20 | promo with leather pouch |
| Victoria | 7" | Pye | 7N17865 | 1969 | £1.50 | £4 | |
| Village Green Preservation Society | LP | Pye | N(S)PL18233 | 1967 | £150 | £250 | 12 track test pressing |
| Village Green Preservation Society | LP | Pye | N(S)PL18233 | 1968 | £6 | £15 | |
| Vol. 5 | 7" EP | Pye | PNV24140 | 1965 | £12.50 | £25 | French |
| Waterloo Sunset | 7" EP | Pye | PNV24194 | 1967 | £10 | £20 | French |

| | | | | | | |
|---|---|---|---|---|---|---|
| Waterloo Sunset | 7" | Pye | 7N17321 | 1967 £1.50 | £4 | |
| Well Respected Man | 7" EP | Pye | PNV24151 | 1965 £10 | £20 | French |
| Well Respected Man | 7" | Pye | 7N17100 | 1966 £20 | £40 | export |
| Wonderboy | 7" | Pye | 7N17468 | 1968 £1.50 | £4 | |
| Word Of Mouth | CD | Arista | 259047 | 1988 £5 | £12 | |
| You Can't Stop The Music | 7" | RCA | RCA2567 | 1975 £1.50 | £4 | |
| You Really Got Me | LP | Reprise | R(S)6143 | 1965 £8 | £20 | US |
| You Really Got Me | 7" | PRT | KBD1 | 1983 £2 | £5 | picture disc |
| You Really Got Me | 7" | Pye | 7N15673 | 1964 £1.50 | £4 | |
| You Still Want Me | 7" | Pye | 7N15636 | 1964 £30 | £60 | |

## KINSEY, TONY

| | | | | | | |
|---|---|---|---|---|---|---|
| Foursome | 7" EP | Parlophone | SGE2008 | 195– £2 | £5 | |
| How To Succeed | LP | Decca | LK4534 | 1963 £8 | £20 | |
| Jazz At The Flamingo Session | LP | Decca | LK4207 | 1957 £15 | £30 | |
| Presenting The Tony Kinsey Quartet No. 1 | 7" EP | Decca | DFE6282 | 1956 £2 | £5 | |
| Presenting The Tony Kinsey Quartet No. 2 | 7" EP | Decca | DFE6283 | 1956 £2 | £5 | |
| Red Bird – Jazz And Poetry | 7" EP | Parlophone | SGE2004 | 195– £2 | £5 | |
| Red Bird Jazz And Poetry | 7" EP | Parlophone | GEP8765 | 1958 £2 | £5 | with Christopher Logue |
| Time Gentlemen Please | LP | Decca | LK4274 | 1959 £6 | £15 | |
| Tony Kinsey Quintet | LP | Decca | LK4186 | 1957 £10 | £25 | |

## KINSMEN

| | | | | | |
|---|---|---|---|---|---|
| Glasshouse Green Splinter Red | 7" | Decca | F22724 | 1968 £4 | £8 |
| It's Good To See You | 7" | Decca | F22777 | 1968 £2.50 | £6 |

## KIPPINGTON LODGE

The career of Nick Lowe begins here, as singer and bass player for the group that was later renamed after the guitarist, Brinsley Schwarz.

| | | | | | |
|---|---|---|---|---|---|
| In My Life | 7" | Parlophone | R5776 | 1969 £7.50 | £15 |
| Kippington Lodge | 7" EP | EMI | NUT2894 | 1978 £2 | £5 |
| Rumours | 7" | Parlophone | R5677 | 1968 £7.50 | £15 |
| Shy Boy | 7" | Parlophone | R5645 | 1967 £7.50 | £15 |
| Tell Me A Story | 7" | Parlophone | R5717 | 1968 £7.50 | £15 |
| Tomorrow Today | 7" | Parlophone | R5750 | 1968 £7.50 | £15 |

## KIRBY

| | | | | | |
|---|---|---|---|---|---|
| Bottom Line | 7" | Hot Wax | WAX1 | 1978 £2.50 | £6 |
| Composition | LP | Hot Wax | HW2 | 1978 £30 | £60 |
| Love Letters | 7" | Anchor | ANC1031 | 1976 £4 | £8 |

## KIRBY, KATHY

| | | | | | |
|---|---|---|---|---|---|
| Best Of Kathy Kirby | LP | Ace Of Clubs | ACL1235 | 1968 £4 | £10 |
| Come Back Here With My Heart | 7" | Columbia | DB8521 | 1969 £1.50 | £4 |
| Do You Really Have A Heart | 7" | Columbia | DB8910 | 1972 £2 | £5 |
| I Almost Called Your Name | 7" | Columbia | DB8400 | 1968 £1.50 | £4 |
| I'll Catch The Sun | 7" | Columbia | DB8559 | 1969 £1.50 | £4 |
| In All The World | 7" | Columbia | DB8192 | 1967 £1.50 | £4 |
| Is That All There Is? | 7" | Columbia | DB8634 | 1969 £1.50 | £4 |
| Kathy Kirby | 7" EP | Decca | DFE8547 | 1963 £2 | £5 |
| Kathy Kirby Vol. 2 | 7" EP | Decca | DFE8596 | 1965 £2 | £5 |
| Little Song For You | 7" | Columbia | DB8965 | 1973 £2 | £5 |
| Love Can Be | 7" | Pye | 7N15313 | 1960 £2 | £5 |
| Make Someone Happy | LP | Decca | LK4746 | 1966 £5 | £12 |
| My Thanks To You | LP | Columbia | SX/SCX6259 | 1968 £30 | £60 |
| My Way | 7" | Columbia | DB8721 | 1970 £2 | £5 |
| No One's Gonna Hurt You Any More | 7" | Columbia | DB8139 | 1967 £1.50 | £4 |
| Singer With The Band | 7" | Orange | OAS216 | 1973 £1.50 | £4 |
| Sings Sixteen Hits From Stars And Garters | LP | Decca | LK4575 | 1963 £4 | £10 |
| So Here I Go | 7" | Columbia | DB8795 | 1971 £2 | £5 |
| Song For Europe | 7" EP | Decca | DFE8611 | 1965 £4 | £8 |
| Turn Around | 7" | Columbia | DB8302 | 1967 £1.50 | £4 |
| Wheel Of Fortune | 7" | Columbia | DB8682 | 1969 £1.50 | £4 |

## KIRCHIN, BASIL

| | | | | | |
|---|---|---|---|---|---|
| World Within Worlds (parts 1 & 2) | LP | Columbia | SCX6463 | 1971 £5 | £12 |
| World Within Worlds (parts 3 & 4) | LP | Island | HELP18 | 1974 £4 | £10 |

## KIRCHIN BAND

| | | | | | |
|---|---|---|---|---|---|
| Ivor & Basil Kirchin Band | 7" EP | Parlophone | GEP8569 | 1956 £2.50 | £6 |
| Kirchin Bandbox | 7" EP | Parlophone | GEP8531 | 1955 £2 | £5 |
| Mambo Macoco | 7" | Parlophone | MSP6144 | 1954 £1.50 | £4 |
| Mother Goose Jumps | 7" | Decca | F10434 | 1955 £4 | £8 |
| Rock Around The World | 7" | Parlophone | R4266 | 1957 £2 | £5 |
| Rockin' And Rollin' | 7" | Parlophone | R4237 | 1956 £2.50 | £6 |
| Roller | 7" | Parlophone | R4222 | 1956 £1.50 | £4 |

## KIRK, DEE

| | | | | | |
|---|---|---|---|---|---|
| I'll Cry | 7" | Salvo | SLO1809 | 1962 £5 | £10 |

## KIRK, ROLAND

| | | | | | |
|---|---|---|---|---|---|
| Blacknuss | LP | Atlantic | K40358 | 1972 £6 | £15 |
| Bright Moments | LP | Atlantic | K60077 | 1973 £6 | £15 |
| Case Of The Three Sided Dream In Audio Colour | LP | Atlantic | SD1674 | 1975 £6 | £15 | ...US double (3 sides) |
| Domino | LP | Mercury | MCL20045 | 1965 £8 | £20 |

| Title | Format | Label | Catalogue | Year | | | Notes |
|---|---|---|---|---|---|---|---|
| Gifts And Messages | LP | Mercury | SMWL21020 | 1969 | £6 | £15 | |
| Here Comes The Whistleman | LP | Atlantic | SD3007 | 1968 | £6 | £15 | US |
| Hip! | LP | Fontana | FJL114 | 1965 | £6 | £15 | |
| I Talk With The Spirits | LP | Mercury | (S)LML4005 | 1966 | £8 | £20 | |
| Inflated Tear | LP | Atlantic | SD1502 | 1969 | £8 | £20 | US |
| Kirk In Copenhagen | LP | Mercury | MCL20021 | 1964 | £8 | £20 | |
| Kirk's Work | LP | Esquire | 32164 | 1962 | £8 | £20 | ... with Jack McDuff |
| Left And Right | LP | Atlantic | 588178 | 1969 | £6 | £15 | |
| Meeting Of The Times | LP | Atlantic | K40457 | 1973 | £6 | £15 | ...... with Al Hibbler |
| Meets The Benny Golson Orchestra | LP | Mercury | 20002MCL | 1964 | £8 | £20 | |
| Meets The Benny Golson Orchestra | 7" EP | Mercury | 10015MCE | 1964 | £2 | £5 | |
| Natural Black Inventions: Root Strata | LP | Atlantic | 2400164 | 1971 | £6 | £15 | |
| Now Please Don't You Cry, Beautiful Edith | LP | Verve | (S)VLP9193 | 1968 | £8 | £20 | |
| Other Folk's Music | LP | Atlantic | SD1686 | 1976 | £5 | £12 | US |
| Prepare Thyself To Deal | LP | Atlantic | SD1640 | 197– | £6 | £15 | US |
| Rahsaan Rahsaan | LP | Atlantic | SD1575 | 197– | £6 | £15 | US |
| Rip, Rig And Panic | LP | Mercury | (S)LML4015 | 1965 | £8 | £20 | |
| Roland Speaks | 7" EP | Mercury | 10016MCE | 1965 | £2 | £5 | |
| Slightly Latin | LP | Mercury | (S)LML4019 | 1967 | £6 | £15 | |
| Volunteered Slavery | LP | Atlantic | 588207 | 1970 | £6 | £15 | |
| We Free Kings | LP | Mercury | MCL20037 | 1965 | £6 | £15 | |
| We Free Kings | LP | Mercury | MMC14126 | 1963 | £8 | £20 | |

## KIRKBYS

| Title | Format | Label | Catalogue | Year | | | |
|---|---|---|---|---|---|---|---|
| It's A Crime | 7" | RCA | RCA1542 | 1966 | £20 | £40 | |

## KIRKPATRICK, JOHN

| Title | Format | Label | Catalogue | Year | | | |
|---|---|---|---|---|---|---|---|
| Plain Capers | LP | Free Reed | FRR010 | 1976 | £4 | £10 | |

## KIRKPATRICK, JOHN & SUE HARRIS

| Title | Format | Label | Catalogue | Year | | | |
|---|---|---|---|---|---|---|---|
| Among The Attractions | LP | Topic | 12TS295 | 1976 | £4 | £10 | |
| Jump At The Sun | LP | Trailer | LER2033 | 1972 | £6 | £15 | |
| Rose Of Britain's Isle | LP | Topic | 12TS247 | 1974 | £4 | £10 | |

## KIRSCH, JULIAN

| Title | Format | Label | Catalogue | Year | | | |
|---|---|---|---|---|---|---|---|
| Clever Little Man | 7" | Columbia | DB8541 | 1969 | £2 | £5 | |

## KISS

Kiss's cartoon approach to heavy metal – turning the music into an affectionate parody of itself – is made into a perfect piece of pop art by their adoption of over-the-top stage costumes and elaborate character-defining make-up. The group's decision to abandon the grease-paint in the eighties had the effect of turning them into just another hard rock group; the reunion tour in 1996 of the original line-up, with the original stage clothes and faces, was a belated, though none the less gratifying acknowledgement of the fact. For this reason, the most essential Kiss records are those that play games with the image: the solo singles with their cardboard cut-out masks; the album *Unmasked*, with its cartoon story cover; or any of the many picture disc releases.

| Title | Format | Label | Catalogue | Year | | | Notes |
|---|---|---|---|---|---|---|---|
| 2000 Man | 7" | Casablanca | NB1001 | 1980 | £5 | £10 | no picture sleeve |
| 2000 Man | 12" | Casablanca | NBL1001 | 1980 | £3 | £8 | no picture sleeve |
| Alive | LP | Casablanca | CALD5001 | 1977 | £20 | £40 | red vinyl double |
| Alive | LP | Casablanca | CBC4011/2 | 1976 | £5 | £12 | double |
| Alive Vol. II | LP | Casablanca | CALD5004 | 1977 | £20 | £40 | red vinyl double |
| Alive Vol. II | LP | Casablanca | CALD5004 | 1977 | £5 | £12 | double |
| Alive Vol. II | LP | Casablanca | CALD5004 | 1977 | £6 | £15 | double, with booklet |
| Animalize | LP | Phonogram | PIC8224951 | 1984 | £4 | £10 | picture disc |
| Asylum | LP | Mercury | PIC8260991 | 1989 | £4 | £10 | picture disc |
| Beth | 7" | Casablanca | CBX519 | 1976 | £6 | £12 | |
| Crazy Crazy Nights | CD-s | Polygram | 0802322 | 1988 | £10 | £20 | gold CD video |
| Creatures Of The Night | LP | Casablanca | PIC6302219 | 1982 | £4 | £10 | picture disc |
| Creatures Of The Night | 7" | Casablanca | KISS4 | 1983 | £1.50 | £4 | |
| Creatures Of The Night | 12" | Casablanca | KISS412 | 1982 | £4 | £10 | |
| Creatures Of The Night | 12" | Casablanca | KISSD4 | 1982 | £6 | £15 | 1 sided, double groove, etched autographs |
| Destroyer | LP | Casablanca | CAL2009 | 1977 | £15 | £30 | red vinyl |
| Destroyer | LP | Casablanca | PIC6399064 | 1982 | £4 | £10 | picture disc |
| Double Platinum | LP | Casablanca | CALD5005 | 1978 | £5 | £12 | double |
| Dressed To Kill | LP | Casablanca | CAL2008 | 1977 | £15 | £30 | red vinyl |
| Dressed To Kill | LP | Casablanca | CBC4004 | 1975 | £4 | £10 | |
| Dynasty | LP | Casablanca | CALH2051 | 1979 | £20 | £40 | red vinyl |
| Dynasty | LP | Casablanca | PIC9128024 | 1982 | £4 | £10 | picture disc |
| Elder | LP | Casablanca | PIC6302163 | 1981 | £4 | £10 | picture disc |
| Elder | CD | Casablanca | 8251532 | 1989 | £5 | £12 | |
| Forever (remix) | CD-s | Vertigo | KISCD11 | 1990 | £2 | £5 | |
| God Gave Rock 'n' Roll To You II | CD-s | East West | 88696CD | 1991 | £2 | £5 | |
| Hard Luck Woman | 7" | Casablanca | CAN102 | 1977 | £6 | £12 | picture sleeve |
| Hide Your Heart | CD-s | Vertigo | KISCD10 | 1989 | £2 | £5 | |
| Hot In The Shade | CD | Fontana | 8389132 | 1989 | £5 | £12 | |
| Hotter Than Hell | LP | Casablanca | CAL2007 | 1977 | £15 | £30 | red vinyl |
| Hotter Than Hell | LP | Casablanca | PIC6399058 | 1982 | £4 | £10 | picture disc |
| I Was Made For Lovin' You | 7" | Casablanca | CAN152 | 1979 | £1.50 | £4 | |
| I Was Made For Lovin' You | 12" | Casablanca | CANL152 | 1979 | £5 | £12 | |
| Killer | 7" | Casablanca | KISS3 | 1982 | £2 | £5 | |
| Killer | 12" | Casablanca | KISS312 | 1982 | £5 | £12 | |
| Killers | LP | Casablanca | PIC6302193 | 1982 | £4 | £10 | picture disc |
| Kiss | LP | Casablanca | CAL2006 | 1977 | £15 | £30 | red vinyl |
| Kiss | LP | Casablanca | CBC4003 | 1975 | £4 | £10 | |
| Kiss | LP | Casablanca | PIC6399057 | 1982 | £4 | £10 | picture disc |
| Let's Put The X In Sex | 12" | Vertigo | KIZZA2 | 1988 | £2.50 | £6 | promo |

| Title | Format | Label | Cat. No. | Year | | | Notes |
|---|---|---|---|---|---|---|---|
| Lick It Up | LP | Mercury | PIC8142971 | 1989 | £4 | £10 | picture disc |
| Lick It Up | 7" | Vertigo | KISSP5 | 1983 | £2.50 | £6 | poster sleeve |
| Lick It Up | 7" | Vertigo | KPIC5 | 1983 | £10 | £20 | shaped picture disc |
| Love Gun | LP | Casablanca | CALH2017 | 1977 | £15 | £30 | red vinyl |
| Love Gun | LP | Casablanca | CALH2017 | 1977 | £4 | £10 | with card gun and inner sleeve |
| Love Gun | LP | Casablanca | PIC6399063 | 1982 | £4 | £10 | picture disc |
| Nothin' To Lose | 7" | Casablanca | CBX503 | 1975 | £7.50 | £15 | |
| Originals | LP | Casablanca | NBLP7032 | 1976 | £25 | £50 | US, 3 LP set with inserts |
| Reason To Live | CD-s | Vertigo | KISCD8 | 1987 | £2 | £5 | |
| Rock And Roll All Nite | 7" | Casablanca | CAN126 | 1978 | £6 | £12 | picture sleeve |
| Rock And Roll All Nite | 7" | Casablanca | CBX510 | 1975 | £6 | £12 | |
| Rock And Roll Over | LP | Casablanca | CALH2001 | 1977 | £15 | £30 | red vinyl |
| Rock and Roll Over | LP | Casablanca | PIC6399060 | 1982 | £4 | £10 | picture disc |
| Rocket Ride | 7" | Casablanca | CAN117 | 1978 | £2 | £5 | |
| Rocket Ride | 12" | Casablanca | CANL117 | 1977 | £2.50 | £6 | |
| Shout It Out Loud | 7" | Casablanca | CBX516 | 1976 | £4 | £8 | |
| Smashes, Thrashes And Hits | LP | Mercury | 8368871 | 1988 | £4 | £10 | US picture disc, gatefold sleeve |
| Talk To Me | 7" | Mercury | MER19 | 1980 | £2.50 | £6 | |
| Tears Are Falling | CD-s | Polygram | 0800582 | 1989 | £6 | £15 | CD video |
| Then She Kissed Me | 7" | Casablanca | CAN110 | 1977 | £4 | £8 | |
| Then She Kissed Me | 12" | Casablanca | CANL110 | 1977 | £3 | £8 | |
| Turn On The Night | CD-s | Vertigo | KISCD9 | 1988 | £2 | £5 | |
| Unholy | CD-s | Vertigo | KISCD12 | 1992 | £2 | £5 | |
| Unmasked | LP | Mercury | PIC6302032 | 1980 | £4 | £10 | picture disc |
| What Makes The World Go Round | 7" | Mercury | KISS1 | 1980 | £2.50 | £6 | |
| World Without Heroes | 7" | Casablanca | KISSP2 | 1982 | £2.50 | £6 | picture disc |

## KISS – ACE FREHLEY

| Title | Format | Label | Cat. No. | Year | | | Notes |
|---|---|---|---|---|---|---|---|
| Ace Frehley | LP | Casablanca | NBLP7121 | 1978 | £6 | £15 | US with poster & paper |
| Ace Frehley | LP | Casablanca | NBPIX7121 | 1978 | £8 | £20 | picture disc |
| New York Groove | 7" | Casablanca | CAN135 | 1979 | £4 | £8 | |
| New York Groove | 7" | Casablanca | CAN135 | 1979 | £12.50 | £25 | with mask, blue vinyl |

## KISS – GENE SIMMONS

| Title | Format | Label | Cat. No. | Year | | | Notes |
|---|---|---|---|---|---|---|---|
| Gene Simmons | LP | Casablanca | NBLP7120 | 1978 | £6 | £15 | US with poster & paper |
| Radioactive | 7" | Casablanca | CAN134 | 1979 | £4 | £8 | |
| Radioactive | 7" | Casablanca | CAN134 | 1979 | £7.50 | £15 | with mask, red vinyl |
| To Ace, Paul & Peter | LP | Casablanca | NBPIX7120 | 1978 | £8 | £20 | picture disc |

## KISS – PAUL STANLEY

| Title | Format | Label | Cat. No. | Year | | | Notes |
|---|---|---|---|---|---|---|---|
| Hold Me Touch Me | 7" | Casablanca | CAN140 | 1979 | £4 | £8 | |
| Hold Me, Touch Me | 7" | Casablanca | CAN140 | 1979 | £7.50 | £15 | with mask, purple vinyl |
| Paul Stanley | LP | Casablanca | NBLP7123 | 1978 | £6 | £15 | US with poster & paper |
| To Ace, Gene & Peter | LP | Casablanca | NBPIX7123 | 1978 | £8 | £20 | picture disc |

## KISS – PETER CRISS

| Title | Format | Label | Cat. No. | Year | | | Notes |
|---|---|---|---|---|---|---|---|
| Peter Criss | LP | Casablanca | NBLP7122 | 1978 | £6 | £15 | US with poster & paper |
| To Ace, Paul & Gene | LP | Casablanca | NBPIX7122 | 1978 | £8 | £20 | picture disc |
| You Matter To Me | 7" | Casablanca | CAN139 | 1979 | £7.50 | £15 | with mask, green vinyl |

## KIT KATS

| Title | Format | Label | Cat. No. | Year | | | Notes |
|---|---|---|---|---|---|---|---|
| Do Their Thing Live | LP | Jamie | LPM/LPS3032 | 1967 | £6 | £15 | US |
| It's Just A Matter Of Time | LP | Jamie | LPM/LPS3029 | 1966 | £6 | £15 | US |
| That's The Way | 7" | London | HLW10075 | 1966 | £1.50 | £4 | |

## KITCHEN CINQ

| Title | Format | Label | Cat. No. | Year | | | Notes |
|---|---|---|---|---|---|---|---|
| Everything But | LP | LHI | 12000 | 1967 | £15 | £30 | US |

## KITCHENS OF DISTINCTION

| Title | Format | Label | Cat. No. | Year | | | Notes |
|---|---|---|---|---|---|---|---|
| Last Gasp Death Shuffle | 7" | Gold Rush | GRR3 | 1987 | £4 | £8 | |

## KITT, EARTHA

| Title | Format | Label | Cat. No. | Year | | | Notes |
|---|---|---|---|---|---|---|---|
| Bad But Beautiful | LP | MGM | C878 | 1962 | £4 | £10 | |
| Bad But Beautiful No. 1 | 7" EP | MGM | MGMEP772 | 1963 | £2 | £5 | |
| Bad But Beautiful No. 2 | 7" EP | MGM | MGMEP774 | 1963 | £2 | £5 | |
| Bad But Beautiful No. 3 | 7" EP | MGM | MGMEP777 | 1963 | £2 | £5 | |
| C'est si bon | 7" | HMV | 7M288 | 1955 | £2 | £5 | |
| Down To Eartha | LP | RCA | RD27084 | 1958 | £4 | £10 | |
| Down To Eartha | 10" LP | HMV | DLP1087 | 1955 | £5 | £12 | |
| Eartha Kitt | 7" EP | HMV | 7EG8258 | 1957 | £2 | £5 | |
| Eartha Kitt Revisited | 7" EP | London | RER1266 | 1960 | £2 | £5 | |
| Easy Does It | 7" | HMV | 7M246 | 1954 | £2 | £5 | |
| Fabulous | LP | London | HAR2207/SHR6058 | 1960 | £4 | £10 | |
| Honolulu Rock-a-Roll-a | 7" | HMV | 7M422 | 1956 | £6 | £12 | |
| I Want To Be Evil | 7" | RCA | RCA1093 | 1958 | £1.50 | £4 | |
| Just An Old Fashioned Girl | 7" | HMV | POP309 | 1957 | £2 | £5 | |
| Just An Old Fashioned Girl | 7" | RCA | RCA1087 | 1958 | £1.50 | £4 | |
| Let's Do It | 7" | HMV | 7M234 | 1954 | £2 | £5 | |
| Love Is A Gamble | 7" | London | HLR8969 | 1959 | £1.50 | £4 | |

| | | | | | | |
|---|---|---|---|---|---|---|
| Monotonous | 7" | HMV | 7M282 | 1955 £2 | £5 | |
| Revisited | LP | London | HAR2296/ SHR6107 | 1960 £4 | £10 | |
| Saint Louis Blues | 7" EP | RCA | SRC7009 | 1959 £2.50 | £6 | |
| Somebody Bad Stole De Wedding Bell | 7" | HMV | 7M198 | 1954 £2 | £5 | |
| St. Louis Blues | LP | RCA | RD27076 | 1958 £4 | £10 | |
| That Bad Eartha | LP | RCA | RD27067 | 1958 £4 | £10 | |
| That Bad Eartha | 10" LP | HMV | DLP1067 | 1955 £5 | £12 | |
| That Blue Eartha | 7" EP | RCA | SRC7015 | 1959 £2.50 | £6 | |
| That's The Way | 7" | London | HL7119 | 1963 £2 | £5 | export |
| There Is No Cure For L'Amour | 7" | HMV | POP346 | 1957 £1.50 | £4 | |
| Thursday's Child | LP | HMV | CLP1104 | 1957 £5 | £12 | |
| Thursday's Child | LP | RCA | RD27099 | 1959 £4 | £10 | |
| Under The Bridges Of Paris | 7" | HMV | 7M191 | 1954 £4 | £8 | |

## KITTENS

| | | | | | | |
|---|---|---|---|---|---|---|
| Round About Way | 7" | Decca | F12036 | 1964 £1.50 | £4 | |

## KLAN

| | | | | | | |
|---|---|---|---|---|---|---|
| Fify The Fly | 7" EP | Palette | 22029 | 1967 £5 | £10 | French |
| Stop Little Girl | 7" EP | Palette | 22024 | 1967 £5 | £10 | French |

## KLEIN, ALAN

| | | | | | | |
|---|---|---|---|---|---|---|
| Striped Purple Shirt | 7" | Oriole | CB1719 | 1962 £5 | £10 | |
| Three Coins In The Sewer | 7" | Oriole | CB1737 | 1962 £5 | £10 | |

## KLEINOW, SNEAKY PETE

| | | | | | | |
|---|---|---|---|---|---|---|
| Sneaky Pete | LP | Shiloh | SLP4086 | 1970 £4 | £10 | US |

## KLEMMER, JOHN

| | | | | | | |
|---|---|---|---|---|---|---|
| Barefoot Ballet | LP | ABC | D950 | 1976 £5 | £12 | US |
| Intensity | LP | Impulse | AS9244 | 1973 £6 | £15 | US |
| Waterfalls | LP | Impulse | AS9220 | 1973 £6 | £15 | US |

## KLEPTOMANIA

| | | | | | | |
|---|---|---|---|---|---|---|
| Elephants Lost | LP | Flame | FLP03 | 1979 £15 | £30 | Dutch |

## KLF

| | | | | | | |
|---|---|---|---|---|---|---|
| 3 a.m. Eternal | CD-s | KLF | KLF005CD | 1991 £2 | £5 | |
| 3 am Eternal (Live At The S.S.L.) | 12" | KLF | KLF005S | 1991 £2.50 | £6 | white label |
| 3 am Eternal (Xmas Top Of The Pops Version) | 12" | KLF | KLF005TOTP | 1992 £20 | £40 | |
| America | 7" | KLF | PUB1 | 1991 £7.50 | £15 | promo |
| America: What Time Is January | 12" | KLF | 92PROMO2 | 1992 £20 | £40 | 1 sided white label |
| Burn The Beat II | 12" | KLF | KLF002T | 1988 £5 | £12 | |
| Chill Out | LP | KLF | JAMSLP5 | 1989 £6 | £15 | |
| Chill Out | CD | KLF | JAMSCD5 | 1989 £10 | £25 | |
| Justified And Ancient | CD-s | KLF | KLF99CD | 1991 £2 | £5 | with Tammy Wynette |
| Justified And Ancient | 12" | KLF | USA4X | 1992 £15 | £30 | picture disc |
| Justified And Ancient (All Bound For Mu Mu Land) | 12" | KLF | CHOICE1 | 1991 £4 | £10 | white label |
| Justified And Ancient (Anti-Acapella Version) | 12" | KLF | CHOICE3 | 1991 £20 | £40 | 1 sided white label |
| Justified And Ancient (Stand By The JAMS) | 12" | KLF | CHOICE2 | 1991 £4 | £10 | white label |
| Kylie In A Trance | 12" | KLF | KLF010RR | 1989 £15 | £30 | |
| Kylie Said To Jason | CD-s | KLF | KLF010CD | 1989 £15 | £30 | |
| Kylie Said To Jason | 12" | KLF | KLF010P | 1989 £3 | £8 | with poster |
| Kylie Said To Jason (Trance Kylie Express) | 12" | KLF | KLF010R | 1989 £6 | £15 | |
| Last Train To Trancentral (Remixes) | 12" | KLF | KLF008R | 1989 £10 | £20 | |
| Make It Rain | 12" | KLF | LPPROMO1 | 1988 £5 | £12 | promo |
| What Time Is Love ('89 Primal Remix) | 12" | KLF | KLF004R | 1989 £5 | £12 | |
| What Time Is Love (Live At Trancentral) | 12" | KLF | KLF004P | 1989 £15 | £30 | promo |
| What Time Is Love (Trance Mix) | 12" | KLF | KLF004T | 1989 £4 | £10 | |
| What Time Is Love Story | LP | KLF | JAMSLP4 | 1989 £10 | £25 | |
| What Time Is Love Story | CD | KLF | JAMSCD4 | 1989 £15 | £30 | |
| What Time Is Love? | CD-s | KLF | KLF004CD | 1990 £2.50 | £6 | |
| What Time Is Love? (Live At Trancentral) | 12" | KLF | KLF004X | 1990 £6 | £15 | |
| White Room | LP | KLF | JAMSLP6 | 1989 £4 | £10 | |
| White Room | CD | KLF | JAMSCD6 | 1989 £6 | £15 | |

## KLINGER, TONY & MICHAEL LYONS

| | | | | | | |
|---|---|---|---|---|---|---|
| Extreems | LP | Deram | SML1095 | 1971 £6 | £15 | |

## KLINT, PETER

| | | | | | | |
|---|---|---|---|---|---|---|
| Walkin' Proud | 7" | Mercury | MF997 | 1966 £4 | £8 | |

## KLOCKWERK ORANGE

| | | | | | | |
|---|---|---|---|---|---|---|
| Abracadabra | LP | CBS | 81119 | 1975 £62.50 | £125 | Austrian |

## KLOOGER, ANNETTE

| | | | | | | |
|---|---|---|---|---|---|---|
| Magic Touch | 7" | Decca | F10733 | 1956 £1.50 | £4 | |
| Mama Teach Me To Dance | 7" | Decca | F10776 | 1956 £1.50 | £4 | |
| Rock And Roll Waltz | 7" | Decca | F10701 | 1956 £2 | £5 | |
| Why Do Fools Fall In Love | 7" | Decca | F10738 | 1956 £2 | £5 | |
| Wisdom Of A Fool | 7" | Decca | F10844 | 1957 £1.50 | £4 | |

## KNACK

| | | | | | | | |
|---|---|---|---|---|---|---|---|
| Did You Ever Have To Make Up Your Mind | 7" | Piccadilly | 7N35315 | 1966 | £2 | £5 | |
| I'm Aware | 7" EP | Capitol | EAP120923 | 1966 | £5 | £10 | *French* |
| It's Love Baby | 7" | Decca | F12278 | 1965 | £10 | £20 | |
| Marriage Guidance And Advice Bureau | 7" | Piccadilly | 7N35367 | 1967 | £2 | £5 | |
| Save All My Love For Joey | 7" | Piccadilly | 7N35347 | 1966 | £2 | £5 | |
| Stop! | 7" | Piccadilly | 7N35322 | 1966 | £2 | £5 | |
| Who'll Be The Next In Line | 7" | Decca | F12234 | 1965 | £10 | £20 | |

## KNACKS

| | | | | | | | |
|---|---|---|---|---|---|---|---|
| Baby | 7" EP | Barclay | 70857 | 1965 | £5 | £10 | *French* |

## KNEF, HILDEGARD

| | | | | | | | |
|---|---|---|---|---|---|---|---|
| Das Mädchen Aus Hamburg | 7" EP | Fontana | 460592 | 1958 | £50 | £100 | *German* |
| From Here On It Gets Rough | LP | London | PS596 | 1966 | £6 | £15 | *US* |
| Grand Gala | LP | Decca | 6376101 | 1969 | £10 | £25 | *Dutch* |
| Love For Sale | LP | Decca | SKL4992 | 1969 | £4 | £10 | |
| Man I Love | LP | Decca | 25090 | 1964 | £30 | £60 | *German* |
| Worum Geht's Hier | LP | Decca | 25160 | 1965 | £50 | £100 | *German* |

## KNICKERBOCKERS

The Knickerbockers' 'Lies' is a near-perfect copy of the Beatles, let down only by a guitar solo much weaker than anything George Harrison might have produced. The single was a top twenty hit in America and is really the only recording for which the group is much remembered, although the other material listed below is actually well worth seeking out.

| | | | | | | | |
|---|---|---|---|---|---|---|---|
| Can You Help Me | 7" | London | HLH10102 | 1967 | £4 | £8 | |
| Fabulous Knickerbockers | LP | London | HA8294 | 1966 | £25 | £50 | |
| High On Love | 7" | London | HLH10061 | 1966 | £4 | £8 | |
| Jerk & Twine Time | LP | Challenge | LP621 | 1965 | £37.50 | £75 | *US* |
| Lies | 7" EP | London | RE10178 | 1966 | £30 | £60 | *French* |
| Lies | 7" | London | HLH10013 | 1966 | £4 | £8 | |
| Lloyd Thaxton Presents | LP | Challenge | LP1264 | 1965 | £37.50 | £75 | *US* |
| One Track Mind | 7" | London | HLH10035 | 1966 | £4 | £8 | |
| Rumours, Gossip, Words Untrue | 7" | London | HLH10093 | 1966 | £4 | £8 | |

## KNIGHT, BAKER

| | | | | | | | |
|---|---|---|---|---|---|---|---|
| Would You Believe It | 7" | Reprise | RS20465 | 1966 | £2 | £5 | |

## KNIGHT, CURTIS

| | | | | | | | |
|---|---|---|---|---|---|---|---|
| Fancy Meeting You Here | 7" | RCA | RCA1888 | 1969 | £2 | £5 | |
| Second Coming | LP | Dawn | DNLS3060 | 1974 | £4 | £10 | |

## KNIGHT, GLADYS

| | | | | | | | |
|---|---|---|---|---|---|---|---|
| Tastiest Hits | LP | Bell | MBLL103 | 1968 | £4 | £10 | |

## KNIGHT, GLADYS & THE PIPS

| | | | | | | | |
|---|---|---|---|---|---|---|---|
| End Of Our Road | 7" | Tamla Motown | TMG645 | 1968 | £1.50 | £4 | |
| Everybody Needs Love | LP | Tamla Motown | (S)TML11058 | 1968 | £4 | £10 | |
| Everybody Needs Love | 7" | Tamla Motown | TMG619 | 1967 | £1.50 | £4 | |
| Everybody Needs Love/ Stepping Closer To Your Heart | 7" | Tamla Motown | TMG619 | 1967 | £15 | £30 | *demo* |
| Feelin' Bluesy | LP | Tamla Motown | (S)TML11080 | 1968 | £4 | £10 | |
| Giving Up | 7" | Stateside | SS318 | 1964 | £4 | £8 | |
| Gladys Knight & The Pips | LP | Maxx | 3000 | 1964 | £8 | £20 | *US* |
| Gladys Knight & The Pips | LP | Sphere Sound | 7006 | 1964 | £8 | £20 | *US* |
| I Heard It Through The Grapevine | 7" | Tamla Motown | TMG629 | 1967 | £2.50 | £6 | |
| I Wish It Would Rain | 7" | Tamla Motown | TMG674 | 1968 | £1.50 | £4 | |
| It Should Have Been Me | 7" | Tamla Motown | TMG660 | 1968 | £1.50 | £4 | |
| Just Walk In My Shoes | 7" | Tamla Motown | TMG576 | 1966 | £12.50 | £25 | |
| Letter Full Of Tears | LP | Fury | 1003 | 1962 | £25 | £50 | *US* |
| Letter Full Of Tears | 7" | Sue | WI394 | 1965 | £6 | £12 | |
| Lovers Always Forgive | 7" | Stateside | SS352 | 1964 | £4 | £8 | |
| Nitty Gritty | LP | Tamla Motown | TML11135 | 1970 | £4 | £10 | *mono* |
| Silk 'n' Soul | LP | Tamla Motown | (S)TML11100 | 1969 | £4 | £10 | |
| Take Me In Your Arms And Love Me | 7" | Tamla Motown | TMG604 | 1967 | £2 | £5 | |

## KNIGHT, JASON

| | | | | | | | |
|---|---|---|---|---|---|---|---|
| Our Love Is Getting Stronger | 7" | Pye | 7N17399 | 1967 | £12.50 | £25 | |

## KNIGHT, MARIE

| | | | | | | | |
|---|---|---|---|---|---|---|---|
| Come Tomorrow | 7" | Fontana | H354 | 1962 | £2 | £5 | |
| Cry Me A River | 7" | Stateside | SS419 | 1965 | £1.50 | £4 | |

## KNIGHT, ROBERT

| | | | | | | | |
|---|---|---|---|---|---|---|---|
| Everlasting Love | LP | Monument | (S)LMO5015 | 1968 | £4 | £10 | |
| Everlasting Love | 7" | Monument | MON1008 | 1968 | £1.50 | £4 | |
| Free Me | 7" | London | HLD9496 | 1962 | £2.50 | £6 | |
| Love On A Mountain Top | 7" | Monument | MON1017 | 1968 | £2 | £5 | |

## KNIGHT, SONNY

| | | | | | | | |
|---|---|---|---|---|---|---|---|
| But Officer | 7" | Vogue | V9134 | 1959 | £37.50 | £75 | |
| Confidential | 7" | London | HL7016 | 1957 | £25 | £50 | *export* |
| Confidential | 7" | London | HLD8362 | 1957 | £100 | £200 | *gold label* |
| If You Want This Love | LP | Aura | AR/AS3001 | 1964 | £5 | £12 | *US* |

# KNIGHT, TERRY & THE PACK

This group contains the roots of the popular heavy-metal-by-numbers seventies band, Grand Funk Railroad. Knight (real name Terry Knapp) was the more famous group's non-playing mastermind, while Pack members Don Brewer and Mark Farner were responsible for whatever funk the group could muster.

| Title | Format | Label | Cat. no. | Year | | | Notes |
|---|---|---|---|---|---|---|---|
| I (Who Have Nothing) | 7" | Cameo Parkway | C102 | 1966 | £20 | £40 | |
| Reflections | LP | Cameo | C2007 | 1967 | £10 | £25 | US |
| Terry Knight & The Pack | LP | Lucky Eleven | (S)8000 | 1966 | £20 | £40 | US |

# KNIGHT, TONY

Tony Knight's Chessmen included saxophonist Lol Coxhill in their line-up, a man happy to play music in any company, even if his best preference is for free improvisation.

| Title | Format | Label | Cat. no. | Year | | | |
|---|---|---|---|---|---|---|---|
| Did You Ever Hear The Sound | 7" | Decca | F11989 | 1964 | £7.50 | £15 | |
| How Sweet | 7" | Decca | F12109 | 1965 | £7.50 | £15 | |

# KNIGHT BROTHERS

| Title | Format | Label | Cat. no. | Year | | | |
|---|---|---|---|---|---|---|---|
| Temptation 'Bout To Get Me | 7" | Chess | CRS8015 | 1965 | £2 | £5 | |
| That'll Get It | 7" | Chess | CRS8046 | 1966 | £4 | £8 | |

# KNIGHTS

| Title | Format | Label | Cat. no. | Year | | | |
|---|---|---|---|---|---|---|---|
| Hot Rod High | LP | Capitol | (S)T2189 | 1964 | £10 | £25 | US |

# KNIGHTS (2)

| Title | Format | Label | Cat. no. | Year | | | |
|---|---|---|---|---|---|---|---|
| Across The Board | LP | Ace | MG200854 | 1966 | £250 | £400 | US |
| Cold Days Hot Nights | LP | Ace Recording | 4763 | 196– | £250 | £400 | US |
| Knights 1967 | LP | Ace | MG201303 | 1967 | £250 | £400 | US |
| Off Campus | LP | Co | 1269 | 1965 | £250 | £400 | US |

# KNOCKER JUNGLE

| Title | Format | Label | Cat. no. | Year | | | |
|---|---|---|---|---|---|---|---|
| Knocker Jungle | LP | Ember | NR5052 | 1970 | £20 | £40 | |

# KNOCKOUTS

| Title | Format | Label | Cat. no. | Year | | | |
|---|---|---|---|---|---|---|---|
| Darling Lorraine | 7" | Top Rank | JAR279 | 1960 | £7.50 | £15 | |
| Go Ape With The Knockouts | LP | Tribute | 1202 | 1964 | £10 | £25 | US |

# KNOPFLER, DAVID

| Title | Format | Label | Cat. no. | Year | | | |
|---|---|---|---|---|---|---|---|
| Soul Kissing | 7" | Peach River | BBPR7 | 1983 | £2 | £5 | |

# KNOPFLER, MARK

Arguably, the instantly memorable theme that he wrote for the film *Local Hero* is the best piece of music that Mark Knopfler has ever produced.

| Title | Format | Label | Cat. no. | Year | | | Notes |
|---|---|---|---|---|---|---|---|
| Comfort And Joy | 12" | Vertigo | MARK1 | 1984 | £10 | £25 | 1 sided promo |
| Going Home | 12" | Vertigo | DSTR412 | 1983 | £2.50 | £6 | |
| Joy | 7" | Vertigo | DSDJ7 | 1984 | £10 | £20 | promo only |
| Joy | 12" | Vertigo | DSTR712 | 1984 | £10 | £25 | |
| Storybook Love | CD-s | Vertigo | VERCD37 | 1988 | £6 | £15 | |

# KNOX, BUDDY

| Title | Format | Label | Cat. no. | Year | | | Notes |
|---|---|---|---|---|---|---|---|
| All Time Loser | 7" | Liberty | LIB55694 | 1964 | £1.50 | £4 | |
| Buddy Knox | LP | Roulette | R25003 | 1957 | £37.50 | £75 | US |
| Buddy Knox And Jimmy Bowen | LP | Roulette | R25048 | 1957 | £62.50 | £125 | US, with Jimmy Bowen |
| C'mon Baby | 7" | Columbia | DB4180 | 1958 | £7.50 | £15 | |
| Chi-Hua-Hua | 7" | Liberty | LIB55411 | 1962 | £2 | £5 | |
| Devil Woman | 7" | Columbia | DB4014 | 1957 | £10 | £20 | |
| God Knows I Love You | 7" | United Artists | UP35019 | 1969 | £2 | £5 | |
| Golden Hits | LP | Liberty | LBY1114 | 1962 | £10 | £25 | |
| Gypsy Man | LP | United Artists | UAS6689 | 1969 | £5 | £12 | US |
| I Think I'm Gonna Kill Myself | 7" | Columbia | DB4302 | 1959 | £7.50 | £15 | |
| Ling Ting Tong | 7" | London | HLG9331 | 1961 | £2.50 | £6 | |
| Lovey Dovey | 7" | London | HLG9268 | 1961 | £5 | £10 | |
| Party Doll | 7" | Columbia | DB3914 | 1957 | £50 | £100 | gold label |
| Rock A Buddy Knox | 7" EP | Columbia | SEG7732 | 1957 | £30 | £60 | |
| Rock Reflections | LP | Sunset | SLS50206 | 1971 | £4 | £10 | |
| Rock Your Little Baby To Sleep | 7" | Columbia | DB3952 | 1957 | £15 | £30 | gold label |
| Shadaroom | 7" | Liberty | LIB55592 | 1963 | £1.50 | £4 | |
| She's Gone | 7" | Liberty | LIB55473 | 1962 | £2 | £5 | |
| Swinging Daddy | 7" | Columbia | DB4077 | 1958 | £10 | £20 | |
| Three Eyed Man | 7" | London | HLG9472 | 1961 | £2.50 | £6 | |

# KOALA

| Title | Format | Label | Cat. no. | Year | | | |
|---|---|---|---|---|---|---|---|
| Koala | LP | Capitol | 176 | 1969 | £6 | £15 | US |

# KOCH, MARIZA

| Title | Format | Label | Cat. no. | Year | | | |
|---|---|---|---|---|---|---|---|
| Arabas | LP | Minos | | 1972 | £37.50 | £75 | Greek |

# KODAKS

| Title | Format | Label | Cat. no. | Year | | | |
|---|---|---|---|---|---|---|---|
| Kodaks Vs. The Starlites | LP | Sphere Sound | LP7005 | 1964 | £25 | £50 | US |

# KODIAKS

| Title | Format | Label | Cat. no. | Year | | | |
|---|---|---|---|---|---|---|---|
| Tell Me Rhonda | 7" | Decca | F12942 | 1969 | £2 | £5 | |

## KOERNER, RAY & GLOVER

| Title | Format | Label | Catalogue | Year | | | Notes |
|---|---|---|---|---|---|---|---|
| Blues, Rags And Hollers | LP | Audiophile | AP78 | 1963 | £8 | £20 | US |
| Lots More Blues, Rags And Hollers | LP | Elektra | EKL/EKS7267 | 1964 | £8 | £20 | US |
| Return Of Koerner, Ray And Glover | LP | Elektra | EKL/EKS7305 | 1966 | £6 | £15 | US |

## KOERNER, SPIDER JOHN

| Title | Format | Label | Catalogue | Year | | | Notes |
|---|---|---|---|---|---|---|---|
| Spider Blues | LP | Elektra | EKL/EKS7290 | 1965 | £6 | £15 | US |
| Won't You Give Me Some Love | 7" | Elektra | EKSN45005 | 1967 | £2 | £5 | |

## KOERNER, SPIDER JOHN & WILLIE MURPHY

| Title | Format | Label | Catalogue | Year | | | |
|---|---|---|---|---|---|---|---|
| Friends And Lovers | 7" | Elektra | EKSN45063 | 1969 | £2 | £5 | |
| Running Jumping Standing Still | LP | Elektra | EKL/EKS74041 | 1968 | £8 | £20 | |
| Running Jumping Standing Still | LP | Elektra | K42026 | 1971 | £4 | £10 | |

## KOFFMAN, MOE

| Title | Format | Label | Catalogue | Year | | | |
|---|---|---|---|---|---|---|---|
| Little Pixie | 7" EP | London | REJ1163 | 1958 | £4 | £8 | |
| Little Pixie | 7" | London | HLJ8633 | 1958 | £1.50 | £4 | |
| Mighty Peculiar | 7" | CBS | 3544 | 1968 | £1.50 | £4 | |
| Shepherd's Cha-Cha | 7" | London | HLJ8813 | 1959 | £1.50 | £4 | |
| Swingin' Shepherd Blues | 7" | London | HLJ8549 | 1958 | £2 | £5 | |

## KOLETTES

| Title | Format | Label | Catalogue | Year | | | |
|---|---|---|---|---|---|---|---|
| Who's That Guy | 7" | Pye | 7N25278 | 1964 | £4 | £8 | |

## KOLINDA

| Title | Format | Label | Catalogue | Year | | | Notes |
|---|---|---|---|---|---|---|---|
| 1514 | LP | Hexagone | 883017 | 1978 | £8 | £20 | French |
| Kolinda | LP | Hexagone | 883006 | 1975 | £8 | £20 | French |

## KOLLEKTIV

| Title | Format | Label | Catalogue | Year | | | Notes |
|---|---|---|---|---|---|---|---|
| Kollektiv | LP | Brain | 1034 | 1973 | £6 | £15 | German |

## KOMACK, JIMMIE

| Title | Format | Label | Catalogue | Year | | | |
|---|---|---|---|---|---|---|---|
| Cold Summer Blues | 7" | Vogue Coral | Q2031 | 1954 | £2.50 | £6 | |
| Rock-A-Bye Your Baby With A Dixie Melody | 7" | Vogue Coral | Q72087 | 1955 | £1.50 | £4 | |
| Wabash 47473 | 7" | Vogue Coral | Q72061 | 1955 | £2 | £5 | |

## KOMKOL

| Title | Format | Label | Catalogue | Year | | | Notes |
|---|---|---|---|---|---|---|---|
| Index | LP | Kanal | LEUB25 | 1972 | £6 | £15 | German |

## KONGOS, JOHN

| Title | Format | Label | Catalogue | Year | | | Notes |
|---|---|---|---|---|---|---|---|
| Confusions About Goldfish | LP | Dawn | DNLS3002 | 1969 | £4 | £10 | |
| He's Gonna Step On You Again | 7" | Fly | BUG8 | 1971 | £1.50 | £4 | picture sleeve |
| I Love Mary | 7" | Piccadilly | 7N35341 | 1966 | £1.50 | £4 | |

## KONITZ, LEE

| Title | Format | Label | Catalogue | Year | | | Notes |
|---|---|---|---|---|---|---|---|
| Abstraction | LP | Atlantic | 590020 | 1968 | £5 | £12 | |
| Inside Hi-Fi | LP | Atlantic | 590027 | 1969 | £5 | £12 | |
| Inside Hi-Fi | LP | London | LTZK15092 | 1957 | £8 | £20 | |
| Lee Konitz | 10" LP | Vogue | LDE060 | 1954 | £25 | £50 | |
| Lee Konitz | 10" LP | Vogue | LDE129 | 1955 | £25 | £50 | |
| Lee Konitz | 10" LP | Vogue | LDE154 | 1955 | £25 | £50 | |
| Lee Konitz Collates | LP | Esquire | | 195– | £8 | £20 | |
| Lee Konitz With The Gerry Mulligan Quartet | LP | Vogue | LAE12181 | 1959 | £8 | £20 | |
| Lee Konitz With Warne Marsh | LP | London | LTZK15025 | 1957 | £10 | £25 | |
| Real Lee Konitz | LP | London | LTZK15147 | 1959 | £8 | £20 | |
| Subconscious-Lee | LP | XTRA | XTRA5049 | 1968 | £5 | £12 | with Lennie Tristano |
| Very Cool | LP | Columbia | 33CX10119 | 1958 | £8 | £20 | |
| You And Lee | LP | HMV | CLP1406/CSD1331 | 1960 | £6 | £15 | |

## KONRADS

| Title | Format | Label | Catalogue | Year | | | |
|---|---|---|---|---|---|---|---|
| Baby It's Too Late Now | 7" | CBS | 201812 | 1965 | £1.50 | £4 | |

## KONSTRUKTIVITS

| Title | Format | Label | Catalogue | Year | | | |
|---|---|---|---|---|---|---|---|
| Glenacaul | LP | Sterile | SR10 | 1986 | £6 | £15 | |
| Psyko Genetika | LP | Third Mind | TM02 | 198– | £6 | £15 | |

## KOOBAS

| Title | Format | Label | Catalogue | Year | | | |
|---|---|---|---|---|---|---|---|
| First Cut Is The Deepest | 7" | Columbia | DB8419 | 1968 | £15 | £30 | |
| Gypsy Fred | 7" | Columbia | DB8187 | 1967 | £15 | £30 | |
| Koobas | LP | Columbia | SX/SCX6271 | 1969 | £250 | £400 | |
| Sally | 7" | Columbia | DB8103 | 1967 | £15 | £30 | |
| Sweet Music | 7" | Columbia | DB7988 | 1966 | £15 | £30 | |
| Take Me For A Little While | 7" | Pye | 7N17012 | 1965 | £15 | £30 | |
| You'd Better Make Up Your Mind | 7" | Pye | 7N17087 | 1966 | £15 | £30 | |

## KOOL & THE GANG

| Title | Format | Label | Catalogue | Year | | | |
|---|---|---|---|---|---|---|---|
| Best Of Kool And The Gang | LP | Polydor | 2347002 | 1974 | £20 | £40 | |
| Funky Man | 7" | Mojo | 2027005 | 1971 | £1.50 | £4 | |
| Kool And The Gang | 7" | London | HLZ10308 | 1970 | £1.50 | £4 | |
| Light Of Worlds | LP | Polydor | 2310357 | 1974 | £4 | £10 | |
| Live At P.J.'s | LP | Polydor | 2347001 | 1974 | £25 | £50 | |
| Live At The Sex Machine | LP | Polydor | 2343083 | 1976 | £4 | £10 | |
| Live At The Sex Machine | LP | Polydor | 2347003 | 1974 | £6 | £15 | |
| Love The Life You Live | 7" | Mojo | 2027006 | 1972 | £1.50 | £4 | |
| Music Is The Message | LP | Polydor | 2347004 | 1974 | £8 | £20 | |

| | | | | | | | |
|---|---|---|---|---|---|---|---|
| Spirit Of The Boogie | LP | Polydor | 2310416 | 1975 £4 | £10 | |
| Wild And Peaceful | LP | Polydor | 2310299 | 1974 £4 | £10 | |

## KOOPER, AL

| | | | | | | | |
|---|---|---|---|---|---|---|---|
| Easy Does It | LP | CBS | 66252 | 1970 £5 | £12 | double |
| Hey Western Union Man | 7" | CBS | 4160 | 1969 £2 | £5 | |
| Kooper Session | LP | CBS | 63797 | 1970 £4 | £10 | with Shuggie Otis |
| Parchman Farm | 7" | Mercury | MF885 | 1965 £2.50 | £6 | |
| You Never Know Who Your Friends Are | 7" | CBS | 4011 | 1969 £1.50 | £4 | |

## KOOPER, AL & STEPHEN STILLS

| | | | | | | |
|---|---|---|---|---|---|---|
| Season Of The Witch | 7" | CBS | 3770 | 1968 £1.50 | £4 | |

## KOOPER, AL, MIKE BLOOMFIELD & STEVE STILLS

| | | | | | | | |
|---|---|---|---|---|---|---|---|
| Super Session | LP | CBS | 63396 | 1968 £5 | £12 | |
| Super Session | LP | CBS | Q63396 | 1973 £6 | £15 | quad |
| Super Session | LP | Mobile Fidelity | MFSL1178 | 1984 £4 | £10 | US audiophile |

## KOOYMANS, GEORGE

| | | | | | | |
|---|---|---|---|---|---|---|
| Jo Jo | LP | Polydor | 2925004 | 1971 £10 | £25 | Dutch |

## KOPPEL, ANDERS

| | | | | | | |
|---|---|---|---|---|---|---|
| Aftenlandet | LP | Demos | 38 | 1977 £8 | £20 | Danish |

## KOPPYCATS (IAN & THE ZODIACS)

| | | | | | | | |
|---|---|---|---|---|---|---|---|
| Beatles Best | LP | Fontana | SFL13052-3 | 1968 £8 | £20 | double |
| Beatles Best | LP | Fontana | 200153WGL | 1966 £4 | £10 | Dutch mono |
| Beatles Best | LP | Fontana | 700153 | 1966 £6 | £15 | Dutch stereo |
| More Beatles Best | LP | Fontana | 701543 | 1967 £8 | £20 | Dutch stereo |
| More Beatles Best | LP | Fontana | 701543WPY | 1967 £6 | £15 | Dutch mono |

## KORAN, TAMARA & PERCEPTION

| | | | | | | |
|---|---|---|---|---|---|---|
| Veils Of Morning Lace | 7" | Domain | D7 | 1968 £5 | £10 | |

## KORBERG, TOMMY

| | | | | | | |
|---|---|---|---|---|---|---|
| Dear Mrs. Jones | 7" | Sonet | SON2005 | 1969 £2 | £5 | |

## KORDA, PAUL

| | | | | | | |
|---|---|---|---|---|---|---|
| Go On Home | 7" | Columbia | DB7994 | 1966 £5 | £10 | |
| Passing Strangers | LP | MAM | MAM1003 | 1971 £5 | £12 | |

## KORNER, ALEXIS

Somewhat like John Mayall, Alexis Korner's importance within the development of rock music had more to do with the musicians he managed to discover than with what he actually played himself. *R&B From The Marquee*, viewed as being of crucial significance at the time, today sounds rather thin and ineffectual, and an unlikely base from which to begin a rock revolution. In truth, musicians like Charlie Watts, Jack Bruce and Robert Plant achieved far more after they left Korner than they ever did with him. Nevertheless, Alexis Korner was an important catalyst – a position best demonstrated on the double LP *Bootleg Him*, which provides a useful survey of his career via a well-chosen selection of out-takes and otherwise unreleased tracks.

| | | | | | | | |
|---|---|---|---|---|---|---|---|
| Accidentally Born In New Orleans | LP | Transatlantic | TRA269 | 1973 £8 | £20 | |
| Alexis | LP | RAK | SRAK501 | 1971 £8 | £20 | |
| Alexis Korner | LP | Polydor | 2374109 | 1974 £6 | £15 | German |
| Alexis Korner Blues Incorporated | 7" EP | Tempo | EXA102 | 1958 £25 | £50 | |
| All Stars Blues Inc | LP | Transatlantic | TRASAM7 | 1969 £5 | £12 | |
| At The Cavern | LP | Oriole | PS40058 | 1964 £50 | £100 | |
| Blues At The Roundhouse | LP | 77 | | 1957 £100 | £200 | |
| Blues From The Roundhouse Vol. 1 | 7" EP | Tempo | EXA76 | 1957 £25 | £50 | |
| Blues Incorporated | LP | Ace Of Clubs | ACL1187 | 1965 £25 | £50 | |
| Blues Incorporated | LP | Polydor | 236206 | 1967 £25 | £50 | |
| Bootleg Him | LP | RAK | SRAKSP51 | 1972 £10 | £25 | double |
| Both Sides | LP | Metronome | MLP15364 | 1969 £15 | £30 | German |
| C. C. Rider | 7" | King | KG1017 | 1965 £5 | £10 | |
| County Jail | 7" | Tempo | A166 | 1957 £25 | £50 | |
| Get Off My Cloud | LP | CBS | 69155 | 1975 £5 | £12 | |
| I Need Your Loving | 7" | Parlophone | R5206 | 1963 £5 | £10 | |
| I Wonder Who | LP | Fontana | STL5381 | 1967 £30 | £60 | |
| Just Easy | LP | Intercord | INT60099 | 1978 £5 | £12 | German |
| Little Baby | 7" | Parlophone | R5247 | 1965 £5 | £10 | |
| Me | LP | Jeton | 1003305 | 1979 £10 | £25 | German |
| Mr. Blues | LP | Mushroom | 35434 | 1974 £8 | £20 | German |
| New Church | LP | Metronome | | 1970 £15 | £30 | German |
| New Generation Of Blues | LP | Liberty | LBL/LBS83147 | 1968 £15 | £30 | |
| Party LP | LP | Intercord | 170000 | 1980 £6 | £15 | German double |
| R&B At The Marquee | LP | Ace Of Clubs | ACL1130 | 1962 £15 | £30 | |
| Red Hot From Alex | LP | Transatlantic | TRA117 | 1964 £50 | £100 | |
| River's Invitation | 7" | Fontana | TF706 | 1966 £5 | £10 | |
| Rosie | 7" | Fontana | TF817 | 1967 £5 | £10 | |
| Sky High | 7" | Spot | JW551 | 1965 £330 | £500 | |
| Snape Live On Tour | LP | Brain | 21039 | 1974 £8 | £20 | German double |
| Up-Town | 7" | Lyntone | LYN299 | 196- £10 | £20 | flexi |
| What's That Sound I Hear | LP | Sunset | SLS50245 | 1971 £4 | £10 | |

## KORNFELD, ARTIE TREE

| | | | | | | |
|---|---|---|---|---|---|---|
| Time To Remember | LP | Probe | SPB1022 | 1970 £4 | £10 | |

## KOSSOFF, PAUL

| | | | | | | |
|---|---|---|---|---|---|---|
| Back Street Crawler | LP | Island | ILPS9264 | 1973 £4 | £10 | |

| Title | Format | Label | Catalog# | Year | | | Notes |
|---|---|---|---|---|---|---|---|
| Croydon June 15th 1975 | LP | Street Tones | STLP1002 | 1983 | £6 | £15 | double |
| Mr. Big/Blue Soul | LP | Street Tones | SDLP0012PD | 1983 | £5 | £12 | picture disc |

## KOSSOFF, KIRKE, TETSU & RABBIT

| Title | Format | Label | Catalog# | Year | | | Notes |
|---|---|---|---|---|---|---|---|
| Kossoff, Kirke, Tetsu & Rabbit | LP | Island | ILPS9188 | 1971 | £15 | £30 | |

## KOTHARI, CHIM

| Title | Format | Label | Catalog# | Year | | | Notes |
|---|---|---|---|---|---|---|---|
| Sitar And Spice | 7" | Deram | DM108 | 1966 | £2.50 | £6 | |
| Sound Of The Sitar | LP | Deram | DML1002 | 1966 | £15 | £30 | |

## KOTTKE, LEO

| Title | Format | Label | Catalog# | Year | | | Notes |
|---|---|---|---|---|---|---|---|
| Circle Around The Sun | LP | Symposium | 2001 | 1970 | £4 | £10 | US |
| Live At The Scholar Coffee House | LP | Oblivion | S1A | 1968 | £8 | £20 | US |

## KOVAC, ROLAND SET

| Title | Format | Label | Catalog# | Year | | | Notes |
|---|---|---|---|---|---|---|---|
| Roland Kovac Set | LP | private | | | £180 | £300 | |

## KRAAN

| Title | Format | Label | Catalog# | Year | | | Notes |
|---|---|---|---|---|---|---|---|
| Kraan | LP | Speigelei | 28778/9 | 1973 | £8 | £20 | German |
| Winthrup | LP | Speigelei | 28523/9 | 1972 | £8 | £20 | German |

## KRACKER

| Title | Format | Label | Catalog# | Year | | | Notes |
|---|---|---|---|---|---|---|---|
| Kracker Brand | LP | Rolling Stones | COC49102 | 1973 | £5 | £12 | test pressing only |

## KRACQ

| Title | Format | Label | Catalog# | Year | | | Notes |
|---|---|---|---|---|---|---|---|
| Circumvision | LP | Unidentified Artist Productions | UAP1 | 1978 | £37.50 | £75 | Dutch |

## KRAFTWERK

| Title | Format | Label | Catalog# | Year | | | Notes |
|---|---|---|---|---|---|---|---|
| Comet Melody 2 | 7" | Vertigo | 6147015 | 1975 | £1.50 | £4 | |
| Computer Welt | LP | Kling Klang | 06264311 | 1981 | £4 | £10 | sung in German |
| Das Model | 12" | Kling Klang | 06245176 | 1978 | £3 | £8 | sung in German |
| Die Mensch Maschine | LP | Kling Klang | 05832843 | 1978 | £75 | £150 | German, red vinyl |
| Die Mensch Maschine | LP | Kling Klang | 05832843 | 1978 | £4 | £10 | sung in German |
| Electric Café | CD | EMI | CDP7464162 | 1986 | £5 | £12 | |
| Kraftwerk | LP | Vertigo | 6641077 | 1973 | £30 | £60 | spiral label double |
| Kraftwerk 1 | LP | Philips | 6305058 | 1971 | £30 | £60 | German |
| Kraftwerk 2 | LP | Philips | 6305117 | 1972 | £30 | £60 | German |
| Musique Non Stop | 12" | EMI | 12EMI5588 | 1986 | £2.50 | £6 | |
| Neon Lights | 12" | Capitol | CL15998 | 1978 | £4 | £10 | luminous vinyl |
| Pocket Calculator | cass-s | EMI | TCEMI5175 | 1981 | £4 | £10 | |
| Pocket Calculator | 7" | EMI | | 1981 | £1.50 | £4 | promo, English German versions |
| Pocket Calculator | 12" | EMI | 12EMI5175 | 1981 | £2.50 | £6 | |
| Radioactivity | CD-s | EMI | CDEM201 | 1991 | £2 | £5 | |
| Radioactivity | CD | EMI | CDP7464742 | 1987 | £5 | £12 | |
| Radioaktivität | LP | Kling Klang | 06282087 | 1975 | £4 | £10 | sung in German |
| Ralf And Florian | LP | Vertigo | 6360616 | 1973 | £8 | £20 | |
| Ralf And Florian | LP | Vertigo | 6360616 | 1973 | £15 | £30 | with poster |
| Robotronik | CD-s | EMI | CDEM192 | 1991 | £2 | £5 | |
| Robots (edited version) | 7" | Capitol | CL15981 | 1978 | £6 | £12 | picture sleeve |
| Showroom Dummies | 12" | Capitol | CL16098 | 1979 | £2.50 | £6 | |
| Showroom Dummies | 12" | Capitol | CLX104 | 1977 | £2.50 | £6 | |
| Technopop | LP | EMI | EMC3407 | 1983 | £330 | £500 | |
| Telephone Call | 12" | EMI | 12EMI5602 | 1987 | £2.50 | £6 | |
| Tour de France | 12" | EMI | 12EMI5413 | 1984 | £4 | £10 | |
| Trans Europa Express | LP | Kling Klang | 06482306 | 1977 | £4 | £10 | sung in German |
| Trans-Europe Express | CD | EMI | CDP7464732 | 1987 | £5 | £12 | |

## KRAMER, BILLY J.

| Title | Format | Label | Catalog# | Year | | | Notes |
|---|---|---|---|---|---|---|---|
| Colour Of My Love | 7" | MGM | MGM1474 | 1969 | £1.50 | £4 | |
| Town Of Tuxley Toymaker | 7" | Reaction | 591014 | 1967 | £6 | £12 | |

## KRAMER, BILLY J. & THE DAKOTAS

| Title | Format | Label | Catalog# | Year | | | Notes |
|---|---|---|---|---|---|---|---|
| Bad To Me | 7" EP | Odeon | SOE3743 | 1963 | £10 | £20 | French, B side by the Dakotas |
| Billy J. Plays The States | 7" EP | Parlophone | GEP8928 | 1965 | £10 | £20 | |
| Billy J. Kramer | LP | Regal | REG1057 | 196– | £5 | £12 | export |
| Do You Want To Know A Secret | CD-s | EMI | CDEM174 | 1991 | £2 | £5 | |
| From A Window | 7" EP | Parlophone | GEP8921 | 1964 | £10 | £20 | |
| I'll Keep You Satisfied | LP | Imperial | LP9273/12273 | 1964 | £8 | £20 | US |
| I'll Keep You Satisfied | 7" EP | Parlophone | GEP8895 | 1964 | £6 | £12 | |
| Kramer Hits | 7" EP | Parlophone | GEP8885 | 1963 | £6 | £12 | |
| Listen | LP | Parlophone | PCS3047 | 1963 | £6 | £15 | stereo |
| Listen | LP | Parlophone | PMC1209 | 1963 | £5 | £12 | |
| Little Children | LP | Imperial | LP9267/12267 | 1964 | £8 | £20 | US |
| Little Children | 7" EP | Odeon | SOE3753 | 1964 | £10 | £20 | French |
| Little Children | 7" EP | Parlophone | GEP8907 | 1964 | £7.50 | £15 | |
| Trains And Boats And Planes | LP | Imperial | LP9291/12291 | 1965 | £8 | £20 | US |
| We're Doing Fine | 7" | Parlophone | R5408 | 1966 | £1.50 | £4 | |
| You Make Me Feel Like Someone | 7" | Parlophone | R5482 | 1966 | £1.50 | £4 | |

## KRAUS, PETER

| Title | Format | Label | Catalog# | Year | | | Notes |
|---|---|---|---|---|---|---|---|
| Bella Italia | LP | Polydor | 46753/237253 | 1961 | £20 | £40 | German |
| Bossa Nova | LP | Polydor | 237130 | 1961 | £20 | £40 | German stereo |
| Bossa Nova | LP | Polydor | 46630 | 1961 | £37.50 | £75 | German mono |
| Das Haben Die Mädchen Gerne | LP | Polydor | 46812 | 1963 | £10 | £25 | German |

| | | | | | | | | |
|---|---|---|---|---|---|---|---|---|
| Liebelei | 7" EP | Polydor | 20330 | 1958 | £6 | £15 | | *German* |
| Peter Kraus | 10" LP | Polydor | 45197LPH | 1958 | £30 | £60 | | *German* |
| Seine Grossen Erfolge | LP | Polydor | 46770 | 1962 | £15 | £30 | | *German* |
| Singt Evergreens | LP | Polydor | 46535/237035 | 1961 | £20 | £40 | | *German* |
| Teenager Evergreens | LP | Polydor | 46857 | 1964 | £15 | £30 | | *German* |

## KRAUT
| | | | | | | | |
|---|---|---|---|---|---|---|---|
| Unemployed | 7" | Cabbage | K0002 | 1982 | £7.50 | £15 | |

## KRAVETZ, JEAN-JACQUES
| | | | | | | | |
|---|---|---|---|---|---|---|---|
| Kravetz | LP | Vertigo | 6360605 | 1972 | £8 | £20 | *German* |

## KRAVITZ, LENNY
| | | | | | | | |
|---|---|---|---|---|---|---|---|
| Always On The Run | CD-s | Virgin | VUSCD34 | 1991 | £2 | £5 | |
| I Build This Garden For Us | CD-s | Virgin | VUSCD17 | 1990 | £5 | £12 | |
| It Ain't Over 'Til It's Over | CD-s | Virgin | VUSCD43 | 1991 | £2 | £5 | |
| Let Love Rule | CD-s | Virgin | VUSCD10 | 1989 | £3 | £8 | *3" single* |
| Let Love Rule | CD-s | Virgin | VUSCD26 | 1990 | £3 | £8 | |
| Live In Amsterdam | LP | Virgin | LENNY1 | 1990 | £15 | £30 | *promo* |
| Mr. Cabdriver | CD-s | Virgin | VUSCD20 | 1990 | £2 | £5 | |
| Stand By My Woman | CD-s | Virgin | VUSCX45 | 1991 | £3 | £8 | |

## KRAY CHERUBS
| | | | | | | | |
|---|---|---|---|---|---|---|---|
| No | 7" | Fierce | FRIGHT014 | 1988 | £5 | £10 | *1 sided* |

## KRAZY KATS
| | | | | | | | |
|---|---|---|---|---|---|---|---|
| Movin' Out | LP | Damon | 12478 | | £6 | £15 | *US* |

## KREED
| | | | | | | | |
|---|---|---|---|---|---|---|---|
| Kreed! | LP | Visions Of Sound | 7156 | 1971 | £700 | £1000 | *US* |

## KRENZ, BILL RAGTIMERS
| | | | | | | | |
|---|---|---|---|---|---|---|---|
| Goofus | 7" | London | HLU8258 | 1956 | £6 | £12 | |

## KREW
| | | | | | | | |
|---|---|---|---|---|---|---|---|
| Everything Is Alright | 7" EP | Riviera | 231214 | 1966 | £5 | £10 | *French* |

## KREW KATS
| | | | | | | | |
|---|---|---|---|---|---|---|---|
| Samovar | 7" | HMV | POP894 | 1961 | £2.50 | £6 | |
| Trambone | 7" | HMV | POP840 | 1961 | £2.50 | £6 | |

## KRIEGEL, VOLKER
| | | | | | | | |
|---|---|---|---|---|---|---|---|
| Lift | LP | MPS | 21217531 | 1973 | £4 | £10 | *German* |
| Mild Maniac | LP | MPS | 21220206 | 1974 | £4 | £10 | *German* |
| Missing Link | LP | MPS | 33214311 | 1972 | £5 | £12 | *German double* |
| Spectrum | LP | MPS | 2120874 | 1971 | £5 | £12 | *German* |

## KRISTINA, SONJA
| | | | | | | | |
|---|---|---|---|---|---|---|---|
| Let The Sunshine In | 7" | Polydor | 56299 | 1968 | £2 | £5 | |
| Sonja Kristina | LP | Chopper | CHOPE5 | 1980 | £15 | £30 | |

## KRISTYL
| | | | | | | | |
|---|---|---|---|---|---|---|---|
| Kristyl | LP | private | | 1975 | £100 | £200 | *US* |

## KROKODIL
| | | | | | | | |
|---|---|---|---|---|---|---|---|
| Getting Up For The Morning | LP | Bellaphon | BLPS19117 | 1972 | £8 | £20 | *German* |
| Invisible World Revealed | LP | United Artists | UAS29250 | 1971 | £10 | £25 | *German* |
| Krokodil | LP | Liberty | LBS83306 | 1969 | £10 | £25 | |
| Musik | LP | United Artists | UAS293971 | 1971 | £8 | £20 | *German* |
| Swamp | LP | Liberty | LBS83417 | 1970 | £10 | £25 | |
| Sweat And Swim | LP | Bellaphon | 7502 | 1973 | £10 | £25 | *German double* |

## KRUG, MANFRED
| | | | | | | | |
|---|---|---|---|---|---|---|---|
| And Modern Jazz Big Band '65 | LP | Amiga | 850057 | 1965 | £10 | £25 | *East German* |

## KRUGER, JEFF
| | | | | | | | |
|---|---|---|---|---|---|---|---|
| Jazz At The Flamingo | LP | Tempo | TAP5 | 1956 | £15 | £30 | |

## KRUPA, GENE
| | | | | | | | |
|---|---|---|---|---|---|---|---|
| Collates | 10" LP | Columbia | 33C9000 | 1955 | £8 | £20 | |
| Drummin' Man | 10" LP | Columbia | 33S1051 | 1955 | £8 | £20 | |
| Gene Krupa And Buddy Rich | LP | Columbia | 33CX10040 | 1956 | £6 | £15 | |
| Gene Krupa Orchestra | LP | HMV | CLP1087 | 1956 | £6 | £15 | |
| Jazz At The Philharmonic | LP | Columbia | 33CX10015 | 1955 | £10 | £25 | |
| Krupa Rocks | LP | Columbia | 33CX10133 | 1959 | £6 | £15 | |
| Plays Gerry Mulligan Arrangements | LP | HMV | CLP1281 | 1959 | £6 | £15 | |
| Rhythm Parade | 10" LP | Columbia | 33S1064 | 1955 | £8 | £20 | |
| Rockin' Mr. Krupa | 10" LP | Columbia | 33C9032 | 1957 | £8 | £20 | |
| Selections From The Benny Goodman Story | LP | Columbia | 33CX10027 | 1956 | £8 | £20 | *with Lionel Hampton & Teddy Wilson* |

## KRYSTALS
| | | | | | | | |
|---|---|---|---|---|---|---|---|
| Krystals | LP | Fourmost | 8943 | 1967 | £15 | £30 | *Canadian* |

## KUBAN, BOB & THE IN MEN
| | | | | | | | |
|---|---|---|---|---|---|---|---|
| Cheater | 7" EP | Columbia | ESRF1761 | 1966 | £10 | £20 | *French* |
| Cheater | 7" | Bell | BLL1027 | 1968 | £1.50 | £4 | |

| | | | | | | |
|---|---|---|---|---|---|---|
| Cheater | 7" | Stateside | SS488 | 1966 £**7.50** | £**15** | |
| Look Out For The Cheater | LP | Musicland | (SLP)3500 | 1966 £**8** | £**20** | US |
| Teaser | 7" | Stateside | SS514 | 1966 £**4** | £**8** | |

## KUBAS
| | | | | | | |
|---|---|---|---|---|---|---|
| I Love Her | 7" | Columbia | DB7451 | 1965 £**7.50** | £**15** | |

## KUBINEC, DAVE
| | | | | | | |
|---|---|---|---|---|---|---|
| Schopi | 7" | Parlophone | R5762 | 1969 £**1.50** | £**4** | |

## KUFF LINX
| | | | | | | |
|---|---|---|---|---|---|---|
| So Tough | 7" | London | HLU8583 | 1958 £**62.50** | £**125** | |

## KUHN, ROLF
| | | | | | | |
|---|---|---|---|---|---|---|
| Streamline | LP | Vanguard | PPL11009 | 1958 £**4** | £**10** | |

## KUHN, STEVE
| | | | | | | |
|---|---|---|---|---|---|---|
| Ecstasy | LP | ECM | ECM1058ST | 1975 £**5** | £**12** | |
| Trance | LP | ECM | ECM1052ST | 1975 £**6** | £**15** | |

## KULA SHAKER
Kula Shaker's recasting of hippy psychedelia for the nineties pushed the group rapidly to the top in 1996, media interest being happily kindled by the fact of photogenic lead singer Crispian Mills being the son of actress Hayley Mills. 'Grateful When You're Dead' is, of course, a tribute to Jerry Garcia, the late-lamented lead guitarist with the Grateful Dead.

| | | | | | | |
|---|---|---|---|---|---|---|
| Grateful When You're Dead/Jerry Was There | CD-s | Columbia | KULACD2 | 1996 £**3** | £**8** | |
| Tattva | CD-s | Columbia | KULACD3 | 1996 £**2** | £**5** | with poster |
| Tattva (Lucky 13 Mix) | CD-s | Columbia | KULACD1 | 1995 £**15** | £**30** | |
| Tattva (Lucky 13 Mix) | 7" | Columbia | KULA71 | 1995 £**15** | £**30** | |

## KULT
| | | | | | | |
|---|---|---|---|---|---|---|
| No Home Today | 7" | CBS | 4276 | 1969 £**37.50** | £**75** | |

## KUPFERBERG, TULI
| | | | | | | |
|---|---|---|---|---|---|---|
| No Deposit No Return | LP | ESP-Disk | 1035 | 1966 £**6** | £**15** | US |
| No Deposit No Return | LP | ESP-Disk | 1035 | 1966 £**8** | £**20** | US, gold vinyl |

## KUSTOM KINGS
| | | | | | | |
|---|---|---|---|---|---|---|
| Kustom City, USA | LP | Smash | MGS2/SRS67051 | 1964 £**8** | £**20** | US |

## KUTI, FELA RANSOME
| | | | | | | |
|---|---|---|---|---|---|---|
| Afrodisiac | LP | Regal Zonophone | SLRZ1034 | 1973 £**8** | £**20** | |
| Black President | LP | Arista | SPART1167 | 1981 £**4** | £**10** | |
| Everything Scatter | LP | Creole | CRLP509 | 1979 £**5** | £**12** | |
| Gentlemen | LP | Creole | CRLP502 | 1979 £**5** | £**12** | |
| Shakara | LP | Creole | CRLP501 | 1975 £**6** | £**15** | |
| Yellow Fever | LP | Decca | PFS4412 | 1978 £**5** | £**12** | |
| Zombie | LP | Creole | CRLP511 | 1977 £**5** | £**12** | |

## KWESKIN, JIM JUG BAND
| | | | | | | |
|---|---|---|---|---|---|---|
| American Aviator | LP | Reprise | 6353 | 1969 £**4** | £**10** | US |
| Garden Of Joy | LP | Reprise | R(S)6266 | 1967 £**4** | £**10** | US |
| Greatest Hits | LP | Vanguard | VSD13/14 | 1973 £**6** | £**15** | US double |
| Jim Kweskin Jug Band | LP | Fontana | TFL6036 | 1964 £**4** | £**10** | |
| Jug Band Music | LP | Vanguard | VRS/VSD79163 | 1966 £**4** | £**10** | US |
| Jump For Joy | LP | Vanguard | VSD79243 | 1967 £**4** | £**10** | US |
| Relax Your Mind | LP | Vanguard | VSD79188 | 1966 £**6** | £**15** | US |
| See Reverse Side For Title | LP | Fontana | (S)TFL6080 | 1967 £**4** | £**10** | |
| Unblushing Brassiness | LP | Vanguard | VSD2158 | 1963 £**8** | £**20** | US |
| Whatever Happened To Those Good Old Days | LP | Vanguard | SVRL19046 | 1968 £**4** | £**10** | |

## KYTES
| | | | | | | |
|---|---|---|---|---|---|---|
| Blessed | 7" | Pye | 7N17136 | 1966 £**1.50** | £**4** | |
| Frosted Panes | 7" | Pye | 7N17179 | 1966 £**5** | £**10** | |
| Running In The Water | 7" | Island | WI6027 | 1968 £**12.50** | £**25** | |

# L

## L7
Hungry For Stink .......................... CD..... Slash ............. ..................... 1994 £5.......... £12  *Australian with bonus 4 track live CD*

## LA BAMBOCHE
| | | | | | | | | |
|---|---|---|---|---|---|---|---|---|
| La Bamboche | LP | Hexagone | 883003 | 1974 | £8 | £20 | | French |
| La Saison des amours | LP | Ballon Noir | 13007 | 197– | £8 | £20 | | French |
| Née de la lune | LP | Hexagone | 883037 | 1980 | £8 | £20 | | French |
| Quitte Paris | LP | Hexagone | 883012 | 1976 | £8 | £20 | | French |

## LA CHIFFONNIE
| | | | | | | | | |
|---|---|---|---|---|---|---|---|---|
| Au dessus du pont | LP | Hexagone | 883022 | 1979 | £10 | £25 | | French |
| La Chiffonnie | LP | Hexagone | 883008 | 1976 | £10 | £25 | | French |

## LA DE DA BAND
Come Together ................................. 7".... Parlophone.... R5810 ............. 1969 £1.50..... £4

## LA DE DAS
| | | | | | | | | |
|---|---|---|---|---|---|---|---|---|
| Happy Prince | LP | Columbia | SCXM7899 | 1969 | £30 | £60 | | New Zealand |
| Legend | LP | EMI | EMA309 | 1975 | £6 | £15 | | Australian |
| Rock And Roll Sandwich | LP | EMI | EMC2504 | 1973 | £20 | £40 | | Australian |

## LA PERVERSITA
La Perversita ..................................... LP..... Invisible ......... 10005.................... 1979 £4.......... £10 .................... French

## LA PESTE
Better Off Dead ............................... 7".... Backlash ......... CB711 ................ 1978 £5.......... £10

## LA ROCA, PETE
Basra ................................................. LP..... Blue Note ...... BLP/BST84205 ...... 1965 £15........ £30

## LA ROSA, JULIUS
| | | | | | | | |
|---|---|---|---|---|---|---|---|
| Domani | 7" | London | HLA8170 | 1955 | £6 | £12 | |
| Jingle Bells | 7" | London | HLA8353 | 1956 | £4 | £8 | |
| Julius La Rosa Sings | LP | London | HAA2031 | 1957 | £10 | £25 | |
| Julius La Rosa Sings | 7" EP | London | REP1005 | 1954 | £7.50 | £15 | |
| Lipstick And Candy And Rubber Sole Shoe | 7" | HMV | 7M384 | 1956 | £1.50 | £4 | |
| Mobile | 7" | London | HL8154 | 1955 | £6 | £12 | |
| No Other Love | 7" | London | HLA8272 | 1956 | £4 | £8 | |
| Suddenly There's A Valley | 7" | London | HLA8193 | 1955 | £6 | £12 | |
| Torero | 7" | RCA | RCA1063 | 1958 | £1.50 | £4 | |

## LABELLE, PATTI & THE BLUEBELLES
| | | | | | | | | |
|---|---|---|---|---|---|---|---|---|
| All Or Nothing | 7" | Atlantic | AT4055 | 1965 | £2.50 | £6 | | |
| Apollo Presents The Bluebelles | LP | Newtown | 631 | 1963 | £10 | £25 | | US |
| Danny Boy | 7" | Cameo Parkway | P935 | 1965 | £2.50 | £6 | | |
| Down The Aisle | 7" | Sue | WI324 | 1964 | £5 | £10 | | |
| Dreamer | LP | Atlantic | (SD)8101 | 1965 | £6 | £15 | | US |
| I Sold My Heart To The Junkman | 7" | HMV | POP1029 | 1962 | £4 | £8 | | |
| On Stage | LP | Parkway | 7043 | 1965 | £8 | £20 | | US |
| Over The Rainbow | LP | Atlantic | 587001 | 1966 | £5 | £12 | | |
| Over The Rainbow | 7" | Atlantic | AT4064 | 1966 | £1.50 | £4 | | |
| Patti's Prayer | 7" | Atlantic | 584007 | 1966 | £1.50 | £4 | | |
| Sleigh Bells, Jingle Bells And Bluebelles | LP | Newtown | 632 | 1963 | £8 | £20 | | US |
| Take Me For A Little While | 7" | Atlantic | 584072 | 1967 | £1.50 | £4 | | |

## LACE
| | | | | | | | |
|---|---|---|---|---|---|---|---|
| I'm A Gambler | 7" | Page One | POF135 | 1969 | £2 | £5 | |
| People People | 7" | Columbia | DB8499 | 1968 | £5 | £10 | |

## LACEWING
Lacewing................................... LP..... Mainstream ..... S6132.................... 1970 £30........ £60 .................... US

## LACEY, DAVE & THE CORVETTES
That's What They All Say .............. 7"..... Philips............. BF1419 ............. 1965 £1.50..... £4

## LACKEY & SWEENEY
Junk Store Songs For Sale.......... LP..... Village Thing... VTS23 ............. 1973 £6.......... £15

## LACY, STEVE
| | | | | | | | |
|---|---|---|---|---|---|---|---|
| Crust | LP | Emanem | 304 | 1975 | £6 | £15 | |
| Forest And The Zoo | LP | Fontana | SFJL932 | 1970 | £8 | £20 | |

| | | | | | | | |
|---|---|---|---|---|---|---|---|
| Gap | LP | America | 30AM6125 | 1973 | £6 | £15 | |
| Scraps | LP | Saravah | SH10049 | 1974 | £6 | £15 | |
| Solo – In Concert At Théâtre du Chêne Noir | LP | Emanem | 301 | 1974 | £6 | £15 | |

## LADDERS
| | | | | | | |
|---|---|---|---|---|---|---|
| Gotta See Jane | 12" | Statik | TAK212 | 1983 | £2.50 | £6 |

## LADD'S BLACK ACES
| | | | | | | |
|---|---|---|---|---|---|---|
| Ladd's Black Aces | 10" LP | London | AL3556 | 1956 | £4 | £10 |

## LADNIER, TOMMY
| | | | | | | |
|---|---|---|---|---|---|---|
| Blues And Stomps Vol. 1 | 10" LP | London | AL3524 | 1954 | £8 | £20 |
| Plays The Blues With Ma Rainey & Edmonia Henderson | 10" LP | London | AL3548 | 1955 | £8 | £20 |

## LADY
| | | | | | | | |
|---|---|---|---|---|---|---|---|
| Lady | LP | Vertigo | 6360636 | 1976 | £5 | £12 | German |

## LADY JUNE
| | | | | | | |
|---|---|---|---|---|---|---|
| Linguistic Leprosy | LP | Caroline | C1509 | 1974 | £6 | £15 |

## LADY LAKE
| | | | | | | | |
|---|---|---|---|---|---|---|---|
| No Pictures | LP | Q Records | BW1001 | 1978 | £10 | £25 | Dutch |

## LAFAYETTES
| | | | | | | | |
|---|---|---|---|---|---|---|---|
| Nobody But You | 7" EP | RCA | 75724 | 1962 | £5 | £10 | French |
| Nobody But You | 7" | RCA | RCA1299 | 1962 | £1.50 | £4 | |

## LAGGAN
| | | | | | | |
|---|---|---|---|---|---|---|
| I Am The Common Man | LP | Scottish Klub | | 1978 | £20 | £40 |
| Scottish Folk Songs | LP | Arfolk | | 1975 | £30 | £60 |

## LAGIN, NED
Despite bearing a list of musician credits featuring many of the stars of West Coast rock, *Seastones* is actually an electronic work having more in common with the classical avant-garde than rock music of any kind. The record label (though not the cover) has a co-credit to Phil Lesh – and the record is often misleadingly listed under his name. The Grateful Dead have actually been frequent sponsors of modern classical works, *Seastones* merely being the first of these.

| | | | | | | | |
|---|---|---|---|---|---|---|---|
| Seastones | LP | Round | RX106 | 1975 | £10 | £25 | US |

## LAGRIMA
| | | | | | | | |
|---|---|---|---|---|---|---|---|
| Lagrima | LP | Hexagone | | 1978 | £15 | £30 | French |

## LAIBACH
| | | | | | | | |
|---|---|---|---|---|---|---|---|
| Across The Universe | CD-s | Mute | CDMUTE91 | 1988 | £2 | £5 | 3" single |
| Die Liebe | CD-s | Cherry Red | CDCHERRY91 | 1985 | £2 | £5 | |
| Panorama | 12" | East West | 12EWS3 | 1984 | £2.50 | £6 | |
| Sympathy For The Devil | CD-s | Mute | MUTE80CD | 1988 | £2 | £5 | |

## LAINE, CLEO
| | | | | | | |
|---|---|---|---|---|---|---|
| All About Me | LP | Fontana | 680992TL | 1962 | £4 | £10 |
| Cleo Laine | 10" LP | Esquire | 15007 | 1955 | £6 | £15 |
| Cleo's Choice | 10" LP | Pye | NPT19024 | 1958 | £5 | £12 |
| Shakespeare And All That Jazz | LP | Fontana | STL5209 | 1964 | £4 | £10 |
| She's The Tops | LP | MGM | C765 | 1958 | £4 | £10 |

## LAINE, DENNY
The singles released by Denny Laine on the Deram label represented a bold experiment by the former Moody Blue and future Wing. Abandoning the usual rock group line-up, Laine surrounded himself with a small group of amplified violins and cellos – the Electric String Band – and thereby anticipated some of what was later achieved by the Electric Light Orchestra. Sadly, Laine's innovations found little public support and he never again attempted anything similar.

| | | | | | | |
|---|---|---|---|---|---|---|
| Say You Don't Mind | 7" | Deram | DM122 | 1967 | £1.50 | £4 |
| Say You Don't Mind | 7" | Deram | DM227 | 1971 | £1.50 | £4 |
| Too Much In Love | 7" | Deram | DM171 | 1968 | £2.50 | £6 |

## LAINE, FRANKIE
| | | | | | | | |
|---|---|---|---|---|---|---|---|
| All Of Me | 7" EP | Mercury | MEP9500 | 1956 | £5 | £10 | |
| All Time Hits | 7" EP | Mercury | ZEP10062 | 1960 | £4 | £8 | |
| Annabel Lee | 7" | Philips | PB797 | 1958 | £1.50 | £4 | |
| Autumn Leaves | 7" EP | Philips | BBE12216 | 1958 | £5 | £10 | |
| Balladeer | LP | Philips | BBL7357 | 1960 | £4 | £10 | |
| Call Of The Wild | LP | CBS | (S)BPG62082 | 1962 | £4 | £10 | |
| Command Performance | LP | Columbia | CL625 | 1956 | £8 | £20 | US |
| Concert Date | LP | Mercury | MG20085 | 1955 | £8 | £20 | US |
| Cry Of The Wild Goose | 10" LP | Mercury | MPT7007 | 1956 | £6 | £15 | |
| Deuces Wild | LP | Philips | BBL7535/SBBL663 | 1962 | £4 | £10 | |
| Deuces Wild No. 1 | 7" EP | CBS | AGG20003 | 1962 | £2 | £5 | |
| Deuces Wild No. 2 | 7" EP | CBS | AGG20007 | 1962 | £2 | £5 | |
| Deuces Wild No. 3 | 7" EP | CBS | AGG20011 | 1962 | £2 | £5 | |
| Favorites | 10" LP | Mercury | MG25007 | 195– | £10 | £25 | US |
| Foreign Affair | LP | Philips | BBL7238 | 1958 | £4 | £10 | |
| Frankie And Johnnie | 7" EP | Philips | BBE12153 | 1957 | £5 | £10 | with Johnnie Ray |
| Frankie Laine | 7" EP | Columbia | SEG7505 | 1954 | £5 | £10 | |
| Frankie Laine Songs | 10" LP | Mercury | MG10002 | 1952 | £15 | £30 | |
| Georgia On My Mind | 7" EP | Mercury | MEP9000 | 1956 | £5 | £10 | |

| Golden Hits | LP | Mercury | MG20587 | 1960 | £5 | £12 | US |
|---|---|---|---|---|---|---|---|
| Good Evening Friends | 7" | Philips | JK1026 | 1957 | £6 | £12 | ......with Johnnie Ray |
| Greater Sin | 7" | Philips | JK1032 | 1957 | £4 | £8 | |
| Greatest Hits | LP | Columbia | CL1231 | 1959 | £6 | £15 | US |
| Guys And Dolls | 10" LP | Columbia | CL2567 | 195- | £10 | £25 | US |
| Hell Bent For Leather | LP | Philips | BBL7468/SBBL616 | 1961 | £4 | £10 | |
| I Believe | 7" EP | Philips | BBE12005 | 1955 | £5 | £10 | |
| I'd Give My Life | 7" | Columbia | SCM5085 | 1954 | £5 | £10 | |
| I'm Just A Poor Bachelor | 7" | Columbia | SCM5031 | 1953 | £6 | £12 | |
| Jazz Spectacular | LP | Philips | BBL7080 | 1956 | £5 | £12 | |
| Jealousy | 7" | Columbia | SCM5017 | 1953 | £10 | £20 | |
| Juba Juba Jubilee | LP | Philips | BBL7111 | 1957 | £6 | £15 | |
| Juba Juba Jubilee | 7" EP | Philips | BBE12103 | 1956 | £4 | £8 | |
| Love Is A Golden Ring | 7" | Philips | JK1009 | 1957 | £4 | £8 | |
| Lover's Laine | 10" LP | Columbia | CL2504 | 195- | £10 | £25 | US |
| Lovin' Up A Storm | 7" | Philips | PB836 | 1958 | £1.50 | £4 | |
| Moby Dick | 7" EP | Philips | BBE12087 | 1956 | £5 | £10 | |
| Moonlight Gambler | 7" EP | Philips | BBE12130 | 1957 | £5 | £10 | |
| Moonlight Gambler | 7" | Philips | JK1000 | 1956 | £4 | £8 | |
| Mr. Rhythm | 10" LP | Philips | BBR8068 | 1955 | £8 | £20 | |
| Mr. Rhythm Sings | 10" LP | Mercury | MG10001 | 1952 | £15 | £30 | |
| Mr. Rhythm Sings | 10" LP | Mercury | MG25097 | 1954 | £10 | £25 | |
| My Gal And A Prayer | 7" | Philips | PB821 | 1958 | £1.50 | £4 | |
| One For My Baby | 10" LP | Columbia | CL2548 | 195- | £10 | £25 | US |
| Rawhide | 7" | Philips | PB965 | 1959 | £1.50 | £4 | |
| Reunion In Rhythm | LP | Philips | BBL7294/SBBL541 | 1959 | £4 | £10 | |
| Rockin' | LP | Philips | BBL7155 | 1957 | £5 | £12 | |
| Ruby And The Pearl | 7" | Columbia | SCM5016 | 1953 | £6 | £12 | |
| Showcase Of Hits | LP | Philips | BBL7263 | 1958 | £6 | £15 | |
| Sings | 10" LP | Columbia | 33S1047 | 1954 | £10 | £25 | |
| Sings For Us | LP | Mercury | MG20083 | 1955 | £8 | £20 | US |
| Song Of The Open Road | 7" EP | CBS | AGG20036 | 1963 | £2 | £5 | |
| Songs By Frankie Laine | LP | Mercury | MG20069 | 1955 | £8 | £20 | US |
| Songs By Frankie Laine | 10" LP | Mercury | MG25098 | 1954 | £10 | £25 | |
| Stay As Sweet As You Are | 7" EP | Mercury | MEP9520 | 1957 | £5 | £10 | |
| Swan Song | 7" | Columbia | SCM5073 | 1953 | £5 | £10 | |
| That's My Desire | LP | Mercury | MG20080 | 1955 | £8 | £20 | US |
| That's My Desire | 10" LP | Mercury | MPT7513 | 1957 | £6 | £15 | |
| Torching | LP | Philips | BBL7260 | 1958 | £4 | £10 | |
| Voice Of Your Choice | 10" LP | Philips | BBR8014 | 1954 | £10 | £25 | |
| Wanderlust | LP | CBS | (S)BPG62126 | 1963 | £4 | £10 | |
| Western Favourites | 7" EP | Philips | BBE12447 | 1960 | £5 | £10 | |
| With All My Heart | LP | Mercury | MG20105 | 1955 | £8 | £20 | US |
| Without Him | 7" | Philips | JK1017 | 1957 | £4 | £8 | |

## LAINE, LINDA & THE SINNERS

| Don't Say It Baby | 7" | Columbia | DB7549 | 1965 | £2 | £5 | |
|---|---|---|---|---|---|---|---|
| Doncha Know | 7" | Columbia | DB7204 | 1964 | £1.50 | £4 | |
| Low Grades And High Fever | 7" | Columbia | DB7370 | 1964 | £1.50 | £4 | |

## LAITY, PETE

| Rash Adventure | LP | Oblivion | OBL004 | 1984 | £4 | £10 | |
|---|---|---|---|---|---|---|---|
| True Dare Kiss Or Promise | LP | Accolade | OBL006 | 1986 | £4 | £10 | |

## LAKE, BONNIE & HER BEAUX

| Miracle Of Love | 7" | Brunswick | 05622 | 1956 | £5 | £10 | |
|---|---|---|---|---|---|---|---|

## LAMAR, LEE

| Sophia | 7" | London | HLB8508 | 1957 | £15 | £30 | |
|---|---|---|---|---|---|---|---|

## LAMB, KEVIN

| Sailing Down The Years | LP | Arista | AB4166 | 1978 | £5 | £12 | |
|---|---|---|---|---|---|---|---|
| Who Is The Hero | LP | Birth | RAB4 | 1971 | £8 | £20 | |

## LAMBE, JEANNIE

| Miss Disc | 7" | CBS | 202636 | 1967 | £5 | £10 | |
|---|---|---|---|---|---|---|---|

## LAMBERT, HENDRICKS & ROSS

| Hottest New Group In Jazz | LP | Philips | BBL7368/SBBL562 | 1960 | £5 | £12 | |
|---|---|---|---|---|---|---|---|
| Sing A Song Of Basie | LP | HMV | CLP1203 | 1958 | £8 | £20 | |
| Swingers | LP | Vogue | LAE12219 | 1960 | £8 | £20 | |

## LAMEGO, DANNY & HIS JUMPIN' JACKS

| Big Weekend | LP | Forget-Me-Not | 105A | 1964 | £8 | £20 | US |
|---|---|---|---|---|---|---|---|

## LAMERS, JOHN

| Crazy Love | LP | CNR | 5050 | 1962 | £10 | £25 | Dutch |
|---|---|---|---|---|---|---|---|

## LAMP SISTERS

| Woman With The Blues | 7" | Sue | WI4048 | 1968 | £10 | £20 | |
|---|---|---|---|---|---|---|---|

## LANA SISTERS

The Lana Sisters were not actually related to each other, but did include the young Mary O'Brien, who had yet to assume her better-known stage name of Dusty Springfield.

| Buzzin' | 7" | Fontana | H176 | 1959 | £5 | £10 | |
|---|---|---|---|---|---|---|---|
| Mister Dee-Jay | 7" | Fontana | H190 | 1959 | £5 | £10 | |

| Title | Format | Label | Catalog | Year | Price1 | Price2 | Note |
|---|---|---|---|---|---|---|---|
| Ring-a My Phone | 7" | Fontana | H148 | 1958 | £6 | £12 | |
| Sitting In The Back Seat | 7" | Fontana | H221 | 1959 | £2.50 | £6 | |
| Someone Loves You, Joe | 7" | Fontana | H252 | 1960 | £1.50 | £4 | |
| Twosome | 7" | Fontana | H283 | 1960 | £1.50 | £4 | |
| You've Got What It Takes | 7" | Fontana | H235 | 1960 | £2 | £5 | |

## LANCASHIRE FAYRE
| Title | Format | Label | Catalog | Year | Price1 | Price2 | Note |
|---|---|---|---|---|---|---|---|
| Not Easily Forgotten | LP | Fellside | FE045 | 1985 | £4 | £10 | |

## LANCASTER, PETER
| Title | Format | Label | Catalog | Year | Price1 | Price2 | Note |
|---|---|---|---|---|---|---|---|
| Rhythm 'n' Blues Show | LP | Polydor | 249105 | 1967 | £15 | £30 | German |

## LANCASTRIANS
| Title | Format | Label | Catalog | Year | Price1 | Price2 | Note |
|---|---|---|---|---|---|---|---|
| Let's Lock The Door | 7" | Pye | 7N15791 | 1965 | £1.50 | £4 | |
| Lonely Man | 7" | Pye | 7N15927 | 1965 | £1.50 | £4 | |
| There'll Be No More Goodbyes | 7" | Pye | 7N15846 | 1965 | £1.50 | £4 | |
| This World Keeps Going Round | 7" | Pye | 7N17043 | 1966 | £5 | £10 | |
| We'll Sing In The Sunshine | 7" | Pye | 7N15732 | 1964 | £1.50 | £4 | |

## LANCE, MAJOR
| Title | Format | Label | Catalog | Year | Price1 | Price2 | Note |
|---|---|---|---|---|---|---|---|
| Ain't No Soul | 7" | Columbia | DB8122 | 1967 | £12.50 | £25 | |
| Beat | 7" | Soul City | SC114 | 1969 | £1.50 | £4 | |
| Best Of Major Lance | LP | Epic | EPC81519 | 1976 | £4 | £10 | |
| Come See | 7" | Columbia | DB7527 | 1965 | £2.50 | £6 | |
| Everybody Loves A Good Time | 7" | Columbia | DB7787 | 1965 | £4 | £8 | |
| Follow That Leader | 7" | Atlantic | 584277 | 1969 | £1.50 | £4 | |
| Greatest Hits | LP | OKeh | OKM12110/ OKS14110 | 1965 | £10 | £25 | US |
| Hey Little Girl | 7" | Columbia | DB7168 | 1963 | £4 | £8 | |
| I Wanna Make Up | 7" | Stax | 2025124 | 1973 | £1.50 | £4 | |
| I'm So Lost | 7" | Columbia | DB7463 | 1965 | £2.50 | £6 | |
| Investigate | 7" | Columbia | DB7967 | 1966 | £12.50 | £25 | |
| Live At The Torch | LP | Contempo | COLP1001 | 1973 | £5 | £12 | |
| Matador | 7" | Columbia | DB7271 | 1964 | £4 | £8 | |
| Monkey Time | LP | OKeh | OKM12105/ OKS14105 | 1963 | £20 | £40 | US |
| Monkey Time | 7" | Columbia | DB7099 | 1963 | £10 | £20 | |
| Pride And Joy | 7" | Columbia | DB7609 | 1965 | £4 | £8 | |
| Rhythm | 7" | Columbia | DB7365 | 1964 | £5 | £10 | |
| Rhythm Of Major Lance | LP | Columbia | 33SX1728 | 1965 | £30 | £60 | |
| Sweeter As The Days Go By | 7" | Atlantic | 584302 | 1969 | £1.50 | £4 | |
| Too Hot To Hold | 7" | Columbia | DB7688 | 1965 | £5 | £10 | |
| Um Um Um Um Um Um | LP | OKeh | OKM12106/ OKS14106 | 1964 | £25 | £50 | US |
| Um Um Um Um Um Um | 7" EP | Columbia | SEG8318 | 1964 | £20 | £40 | |
| Um Um Um Um Um Um | 7" | Columbia | DB7205 | 1964 | £2.50 | £6 | |

## LANCELOT, RICK & THE SEVEN KNIGHTS
| Title | Format | Label | Catalog | Year | Price1 | Price2 | Note |
|---|---|---|---|---|---|---|---|
| Say Girl | 7" | RCA | RCA1502 | 1966 | £1.50 | £4 | |

## LANCERS
| Title | Format | Label | Catalog | Year | Price1 | Price2 | Note |
|---|---|---|---|---|---|---|---|
| Alphabet Rock | 7" | Vogue Coral | Q72128 | 1956 | £7.50 | £15 | |
| First Travelling Saleslady | 7" | Vogue Coral | Q72183 | 1956 | £1.50 | £4 | |
| Get Out Of The Car | 7" | Vogue Coral | Q72081 | 1955 | £4 | £8 | |
| Jo-Ann | 7" | Vogue Coral | Q72100 | 1955 | £2.50 | £6 | |
| Man Is As Good As His Word | 7" | Vogue Coral | Q72157 | 1956 | £2 | £5 | |
| Mister Sandman | 7" | Vogue Coral | Q2038 | 1954 | £5 | £10 | |
| Never Leave Me | 7" | Vogue Coral | Q72220 | 1957 | £1.50 | £4 | |
| Oh Sweet Mama | 10" LP | London | HAPB1029 | 1954 | £8 | £20 | |
| Presenting The Lancers | 7" EP | London | REP1027 | 1955 | £7.50 | £15 | |
| So High So Low So Wide | 7" | London | HL8079 | 1954 | £12.50 | £25 | |
| Stop Chasing Me Baby | 7" | London | HL8027 | 1954 | £12.50 | £25 | |
| Stroll | 7" | Coral | Q72300 | 1958 | £1.50 | £4 | |
| Timberjack | 7" | Vogue Coral | Q72062 | 1955 | £2.50 | £6 | |

## LAND, HAROLD
| Title | Format | Label | Catalog | Year | Price1 | Price2 | Note |
|---|---|---|---|---|---|---|---|
| Fox | LP | Vogue | LAE12269 | 1961 | £8 | £20 | |
| Harold In The Land Of Jazz | LP | Contemporary | LAC12178 | 1959 | £8 | £20 | |

## LANDER, BOB & THE SPOTNICKS
| Title | Format | Label | Catalog | Year | Price1 | Price2 | Note |
|---|---|---|---|---|---|---|---|
| Midnight Special | 7" | Oriole | CB1784 | 1962 | £2.50 | £6 | |
| My Old Kentucky Home | 7" | Oriole | CB1756 | 1962 | £6 | £12 | |

## LANDIS, BILL & BRETT
| Title | Format | Label | Catalog | Year | Price1 | Price2 | Note |
|---|---|---|---|---|---|---|---|
| Baby Talk | 7" | Parlophone | R4570 | 1959 | £1.50 | £4 | |

## LANDIS, JERRY

Jerry Landis was one of the many pseudonyms adopted by Paul Simon in the years before he discovered folk music. In America, the 'He Was My Brother' single was issued under the name Paul Kane.

| Title | Format | Label | Catalog | Year | Price1 | Price2 | Note |
|---|---|---|---|---|---|---|---|
| Anna Belle | 7" | MGM | 12822 | 1959 | £10 | £20 | US |
| He Was My Brother | 7" | Oriole | CB1390 | 1962 | £7.50 | £15 | US |
| I'm Lonely | 7" | Canadian American | 130 | 1961 | £10 | £20 | US |
| Just A Boy | 7" | Warwick | 552 | 1960 | £10 | £20 | US |
| Just A Boy | 7" | Warwick | 588 | 1960 | £10 | £20 | US |
| Lisa | 7" | Amy | 875 | 1962 | £12.50 | £25 | US |

Play Me A Sad Song .................................... 7" ...... Warwick ......... 616 ..................... 1961 £10 .......... £20 ...................... US

## LANDIS, JOYA
Kansas City ................................................ 7" ..... Trojan ............ TR620 .................. 1968 £4 .......... £8 ...............................
Moonlight Lover .......................................... 7" ..... Trojan ............ TR641 .................. 1968 £4 .......... £8 ...............................

## LANDON, NEIL
I Still Love You ........................................... 7" ..... Decca ............. F12451 ................. 1966 £1.50 .......... £4 ...............................
Waiting Here For Someone ......................... 7" ..... Decca ............. F12330 ................. 1966 £1.50 .......... £4 ...............................

## LANDS, HOAGY
I'm Yours ................................................... 7" ..... Stateside ......... SS2085 ................. 1968 £1.50 .......... £4 ...............................
Next In Line ............................................... 7" ..... Stateside ......... SS2030 ................. 1967 £50 ....... £100 ...............................
Why Didn't You Let Me Know ................. 7" ..... Action ............. ACT4605 .............. 1972 £1.50 .......... £4 ...............................

## LANDSLIDE
Two Sided Fantasy ..................................... LP ..... Capitol............. ST11006 ................ 1972 £20 .......... £40 ...................... US

## LANE, DES
Moonbird .................................................... 7" ..... Top Rank ........ JAR203 ................. 1959 £1.50 .......... £4 ...............................
Penny-Whistle Rock .................................... 7" ..... Decca ............. F10821 ................. 1956 £2 .......... £5 ...............................
Rock Mister Piper ....................................... 7" ..... Decca ............. F10847 ................. 1957 £2.50 .......... £6 ...............................

## LANE, MICKEY LEE
Hey Sah-lo-ney ........................................... 7" ..... Stateside ......... SS456 ................... 1965 £10 .......... £20 ...............................
Shaggy Dog ................................................ 7" ..... Stateside ......... SS354 ................... 1964 £1.50 .......... £4 ...............................

## LANE, TONY & THE DELTONES
It's Great .................................................... 7" ..... Sabre ............. SA455 .................. 1964 £1.50 .......... £4 ...............................

## LANE BROTHERS
Mimi........................................................... 7" ..... London ........... HLR9150 .............. 1960 £5 .......... £10 ...............................

## LANG, DON
Come Go With Me ...................................... 7" ..... HMV .............. POP335 ................. 1957 £7.50 .......... £15 ...............................
Don't Open That Door ............................... 7" ..... HMV .............. POP805 ................. 1960 £1.50 .......... £4 ...............................
Four Brothers ............................................. 7" ..... HMV .............. 7M354 .................. 1956 £7.50 .......... £15 ...............................
Hand Jive .................................................... 10" LP HMV .............. DLP1179 .............. 1958 £37.50 .......... £75 ...............................
Hey Daddy ................................................. 7" ..... HMV .............. POP510 ................. 1958 £1.50 .......... £4 ...............................
Hoot And A Holler ..................................... 7" ..... HMV .............. POP649 ................. 1959 £1.50 .......... £4 ...............................
Percy Green ............................................... 7" ..... HMV .............. POP623 ................. 1959 £1.50 .......... £4 ...............................
Queen Of The Hop ..................................... 7" ..... HMV .............. POP547 ................. 1958 £2.50 .......... £6 ...............................
Red Planet Rock .......................................... 7" ..... HMV .............. POP414 ................. 1957 £7.50 .......... £15 ...............................
Reveille Rock ............................................. 7" ..... HMV .............. POP682 ................. 1959 £1.50 .......... £4 ...............................
Rock 'n' Roll .............................................. 7" EP . HMV .............. 7EG8208 .............. 1957 £20 .......... £40 ...............................
Rock And Roll Blues ................................... 7" ..... HMV .............. 7M416 .................. 1956 £7.50 .......... £15 ...............................
Rock Around The Islands ............................ 7" ..... HMV .............. 7M381 .................. 1956 £7.50 .......... £15 ...............................
Rock Mister Piper ...................................... 7" ..... HMV .............. POP289 ................. 1957 £7.50 .......... £15 ...............................
Sink The Bismarck ..................................... 7" ..... HMV .............. POP714 ................. 1960 £2.50 .......... £6 ...............................
Six Five Hand Jive ...................................... 7" ..... HMV .............. POP434 ................. 1958 £6 .......... £12 ...............................
Six Five Special ........................................... 7" ..... HMV .............. POP350 ................. 1957 £6 .......... £12 ...............................
Skiffle Special ............................................ 10" LP HMV .............. DLP1151 .............. 1957 £25 .......... £50 ...............................
Sweet Sue ................................................... 7" ..... HMV .............. POP260 ................. 1956 £4 .......... £8 ...............................
Tequila ....................................................... 7" ..... HMV .............. POP465 ................. 1958 £4 .......... £8 ...............................
Twenty Top Twenty Twists.......................... LP ..... Ace Of Clubs .. ACL1111 ............... 1962 £6 .......... £15 ...............................
White Silver Sands...................................... 7" ..... HMV .............. POP382 ................. 1957 £2.50 .......... £6 ...............................
Wicked Women ........................................... 7" ..... Decca ............. F11483 ................. 1962 £1.50 .......... £4 ...............................
Wiggle Wiggle ........................................... 7" ..... HMV .............. POP585 ................. 1959 £1.50 .......... £4 ...............................
Witch Doctor .............................................. 7" ..... HMV .............. POP488 ................. 1958 £2 .......... £5 ...............................

## LANG, EDDIE & LONNIE JOHNSON
Blue Guitars................................................ LP ..... Parlophone..... PMC7019 ............ 1967 £10 .......... £25 ...............................
Blue Guitars Vol. 2 ..................................... LP ..... Parlophone..... PMC7106 ............ 1970 £10 .......... £25 ...............................

## LANG, kd
Blue Bayou ................................................. CD-s .. Virgin ............ VSCD1193 .......... 1989 £2.50 .......... £6 ..... with Roy Orbison
Blue Bayou ................................................. 12" ... Virgin ............ VST1193 ............. 1989 £2.50 .......... £6 ..... with Roy Orbison
Constant Craving ......................................... CD-s .. Sire ................ W0100CD ............ 1992 £4 .......... £10 ...............................
Constant Craving ......................................... CD-s .. Sire ................ W0157CD ............ 1993 £2 .......... £5 ...............................
Constant Craving (live) ................................ CD-s .. Sire ................ W0157CDX .......... 1993 £2.50 .......... £6 ...............................
Crying........................................................ CD-s .. Virgin ............ VSCD1166 .......... 1989 £3 .......... £8 ..... with Roy Orbison
Crying........................................................ CD-s .. Virgin ............ VSCD1173 .......... 1989 £2.50 .......... £6 ..... with Roy Orbison
Crying........................................................ CD-s .. Virgin ............ VUSCD63 ........... 1992 £2 .......... £5 ..... with Roy Orbison
Crying........................................................ CD-s .. Virgin ............ VUSCX63 ............ 1992 £2 .......... £5 ..... 2 different tracks
Crying........................................................ 12" ... Virgin ............ VST1166 ............. 1989 £4 .......... £10 ..... with Roy Orbison
Crying........................................................ 12" ... Virgin ............ VST1173 ............. 1989 £2.50 .......... £6 ..... with Roy Orbison
Damned Old Dog ........................................ 7" ..... Bumstead ....... ......................... 1983 £50 ....... £100 ..... Canadian
Making Of Shadowland ............................... CD .... Sire ................ PROCD3120 ........ 1988 £8 .......... £20 ...... US promo
Miss Chatelaine .......................................... CD-s .. Sire ................ W0135CD ............ 1992 £2 .......... £5 ...............................
Miss Chatelaine .......................................... CD-s .. Sire ................ W0181CDX .......... 1993 £2 .......... £5 ..... with 3 cards
Miss Chatelaine .......................................... 12" ... Sire ................ W0135TW ............ 1992 £3 .......... £8 ......with poster
Our Day Will Come ..................................... 7" ..... Sire ................ W7697 ................. 1988 £7.50 .......... £15 ...............................
Our Day Will Come ..................................... 12" ... Sire ................ W7697T ............... 1988 £25 .......... £50 ...............................
Ridin' The Rails .......................................... 7" ..... Warner Bros ... W9535 ................. 1990 £5 .......... £10 .. Darlene Love B side
Sugar Moon ................................................ 7" ..... Sire ................ W7841 ................. 1988 £7.50 .......... £15 ...............................
Sugar Moon ................................................ 12" ... Sire ................ W7841T ............... 1988 £20 .......... £40 ...............................

## LANG, RAY
Last Train .............................................. 7" ...... Brunswick ....... 05683 .................... 1957 £1.50 ........ £4 ................................

## LANGE, STEVIE
Remember My Name........................... 7" ...... Jive .............. JIVE23 ............. : ....... 1983 £2 ......... £5 ......... no picture sleeve
Remember My Name........................... 7" ...... RCA .............. LIM1 ................... 1981 £2 ......... £5 ................................
Remember My Name........................... 7" ...... RCA .............. RCA152 ............... 1981 £4 ......... £8 ................................

## LANGHORN, GORDON
Give A Fool A Chance ........................... 7" ...... Decca ............ F10591 ........ : ........ 1955 £1.50 ........ £4 ................................

## LANGLEY, PERPETUAL
So Sad ..................................................... 7" ...... Planet ........... PLF110 ................ 1966 £5 ....... £10 ................................
Surrender ................................................ 7" ...... Planet ........... PLF115 ................ 1966 £5 ....... £10 ................................

## LANG'SYNE
Lang'Syne ............................................... LP ..... Dusselton ........ TS2737 ................. 1976 £500 ..... £750 ................. German

## LANGTON, PHIL TRIO
Phil Langton Trio .................................... LP ..... Holyground ..... ................ 196– £6 ....... £15 ................................

## LANSON, SNOOKY
It's Almost Tomorrow ......................... 7" ..... London ........ HLD8223 ............. 1956 £37.50 ... £75 ................................
Last Minute Love .................................. 7" ..... London ........ HLD8236 ............. 1956 £62.50 .. £125 ................................
Seven Days ............................................ 7" ..... London ........ HL7005 ............... 1956 £15 ....... £30 ................ export
Seven Days ............................................ 7" ..... London ........ HLD8249 .............. 1956 £62.50 .. £125 ................................

## LANZA, MARIO
Great Caruso .......................................... LP ..... HMV ........ ALP1071 ............... 1953 £4 ....... £10 ................................
On Broadway ......................................... 10" LP HMV ........ BLP1091 ............... 1957 £4 ....... £10 ................................
Operatic Arias ....................................... LP ..... HMV ........ ALP1202 ............... 1954 £4 ....... £10 ................................
Songs Of Romance ................................ 10" LP HMV ........ BLP1071 ............... 1955 £4 ....... £10 ................................
Touch Of Your Hand ............................. 10" LP HMV ........ BLP1094 ............... 1957 £4 ....... £10 ................................

## LANZON & HUSBAND
Nostalgia ................................................ LP ..... Bradleys ......... BRADL1007 ........ 1974 £37.50 ... £75 ................................

## LAPERA
L'Acqua Purificatrice ........................... LP ..... Durium ......... MSA77360 ............. 1975 £8 ....... £20 ................ Italian

## LARD FREE
I'm Around About Midnight ................. LP ..... Vamp ......... VP59502 ............... 1975 £5 ....... £12 ................ French
Lard Free ............................................... LP ..... Cobra ......... 37007 ................... 1977 £4 ....... £10 ................ French
Lard Free ............................................... LP ..... Vamp ......... VP59500 ............... 1973 £10 ....... £25 ................ French

## LARKINS, ELLIS
Manhattan At Midnight ........................ LP ..... Brunswick ...... LAT8189 .............. 1957 £6 ....... £15 ................................
Melodies Of Harold Arlen ..................... 10" LP Brunswick ...... LA8694 ................ 1955 £8 ....... £20 ................................

## LARKS
Jerk ....................................................... LP ..... Money ......... LP1102 ............... 1965 £15 ....... £30 ................ US
Jerk ....................................................... 7" ..... Pye ............. 7N25284 ............. 1964 £5 ....... £10 ................ US
Soul Kaleidoscope ................................ LP ..... Money ......... LP/MS1107 ......... 1966 £8 ....... £20 ................ US
Superslick ............................................. LP ..... Money ......... MY/MS1110 ......... 1967 £8 ....... £20 ................ US

## LARNER, SAM
Garland For Sam .................................... LP ..... Topic ........... 12T244 ............... 1974 £4 ....... £10 ................................
Now Is The Time For Fishing ................... LP ..... Folkways ......... FG3507 ............... 1961 £6 ....... £15 ................................

## LARRY & ALVIN
Can't You Understand ........................... 7" ..... Studio One ...... SO2067 ............... 1968 £6 ....... £12 ................................
Lonely Room ......................................... 7" ..... Studio One ...... SO2080 ............... 1969 £6 ....... £12 ................................
Love Got Me .......................................... 7" ..... Coxsone .......... CS7081 ............... 1968 £5 ....... £10 ...... Bob Andy B side

## LARRY & JOHNNY
An attempt on the part of Larry Williams and Johnny Guitar Watson to cash in on the success of the Beatles produced considerably less income than did the fact that the Beatles themselves covered some of Williams's songs: 'Slow Down', 'Bad Boy' and 'Dizzy Miss Lizzy'.

Beatle Time .......................................... 7" ...... Outasite .......... 45501 ................... 1965 £15 ....... £30 ................................

## LARRY & TOMMY
You've Gotta Bend A Little ...................... 7" ...... Polydor ........... 56741 .................. 1968 £2 ......... £5 ................................

## LA'S
Feelin' ................................................... CD-s .. Go! Discs ....... LASCD6 ................ 1991 £2 ......... £5 ................................
La's ....................................................... LP ..... Go! Discs ....... 8282021 ............... 1990 £5 ....... £12 ................................
There She Goes ...................................... CD-s ... Go! Discs ....... LASCD2 ............... 1988 £2 ......... £5 ................................
Way Out ................................................. 7" ..... Go! Discs ....... GOLAS1 ............... 1987 £1.50 ....... £4 ................................
Way Out ................................................. 12" ..... Go! Discs ....... GOLAR112 ........... 1987 £4 ....... £10 ................................
Way Out ................................................. 12" ..... Go! Discs ....... GOLAS112 ........... 1987 £2.50 ....... £6 ................................

## LASSIES
Sleepy Head .......................................... 7" ...... Brunswick ....... 05571 .................. 1956 £1.50 ........ £4 ................................

## LAST CHANT
Run Of The Dove ................................... 7" ...... Chicken Jazz .... JAZZ4 ................... 1981 £2.50 ........ £6 ................................

## LAST EXIT

Last Exit was a rock group formed from within the ranks of the Newcastle Big Band, and like its parent organization, played in pubs and clubs around Newcastle. The singer/bass player was Gordon Sumner – better known as Sting – and it is he that can be heard on the group's locally produced single. (The Last Exit that recorded in the eighties has nothing to do with Sting, although, as it happens, the group's music is rather fine – an exhilarating brand of improvised noise-funk that makes virtually any other music sound tame.)

| | | | | | | | |
|---|---|---|---|---|---|---|---|
| Whispering Voices | 7" | Wudwink | WUD01 | 1975 | £12.50 | £25 | |

## LAST FLIGHT

| | | | | | | | |
|---|---|---|---|---|---|---|---|
| Dance To The Music | 7" | Heavy Metal | HEAVY5 | 1981 | £2 | £5 | |

## LAST POETS

The sound of Black Power. The Last Poets deliver their angry, razor-sharp rants over a percussion backing – and if that sounds like a description of rap music, then that is exactly what it is. The rhythms are 1971 rhythms (no drum machines), but the style and the stance is the same.

| | | | | | | | |
|---|---|---|---|---|---|---|---|
| Chastisement | LP | Blue Thumb | 539 | 1972 | £6 | £15 | US |
| Last Poets | LP | Douglas | Z30811 | 1971 | £6 | £15 | US |
| Right On | LP | Juggernaut | 8802 | 1971 | £6 | £15 | US |
| This Is Madness | LP | Douglas | DGL69012 | 1971 | £6 | £15 | |

## LAST RESORT

| | | | | | | | |
|---|---|---|---|---|---|---|---|
| Having Fun? | 7" | Red Meat | RMRS01 | 1978 | £2 | £5 | |

## LATCHES

| | | | | | | | |
|---|---|---|---|---|---|---|---|
| Long Tall Sally | LP | Northern Productions | | 1973 | £10 | £25 | Dutch |

## LATEEF, YUSEF

| | | | | | | | |
|---|---|---|---|---|---|---|---|
| Before Dawn | LP | Columbia | 33CX10124 | 1958 | £10 | £25 | |
| Blue Lateef | LP | Atlantic | SD1508 | 1969 | £6 | £15 | US |
| Cry! Tender | LP | Esquire | | 1961 | £8 | £20 | |
| Cry! Tender | LP | XTRA | XTRA5040 | 1968 | £6 | £15 | |
| Eastern Sounds | LP | Fontana | 688202ZL | 1964 | £8 | £20 | |
| Gentle Giant | LP | Atlantic | K50051 | 1973 | £6 | £15 | |
| Hush 'n' Thunder | LP | Atlantic | SD1635 | 1973 | £6 | £15 | US |
| Live At Pep's | LP | HMV | CLP3547 | 1964 | £8 | £20 | |
| Sounds Of Yusef | LP | Esquire | 32069 | 1958 | £10 | £25 | |
| Suite Sixteen | LP | Atlantic | SD1563 | 197– | £6 | £15 | US |
| Yusef Lateef – Donald Byrd | LP | Delmark | DL407 | 1967 | £6 | £15 | |

## LATTER, GENE

| | | | | | | | |
|---|---|---|---|---|---|---|---|
| Always | 7" | CBS | 202655 | 1967 | £1.50 | £4 | |
| Little Piece Of Leather | 7" | CBS | 2843 | 1967 | £2.50 | £6 | |
| Mother's Little Helper | 7" | Decca | F12397 | 1966 | £2.50 | £6 | |
| Sign On The Dotted Line | 7" | Spark | SRL1022 | 1970 | £2 | £5 | |
| With A Child's Heart | 7" | CBS | 2986 | 1967 | £1.50 | £4 | |

## LAUER, MARTIN

| | | | | | | | |
|---|---|---|---|---|---|---|---|
| Wenn Ich Ein Cowboy War | LP | Polydor | 46777/237277 | 1963 | £8 | £20 | German |

## LAUGHING APPLE

| | | | | | | | |
|---|---|---|---|---|---|---|---|
| Ha-Ha He-He | 7" | Autonomy | AUT001 | 1981 | £2.50 | £6 | |
| Participate | 7" | Autonomy | AUT002 | 1981 | £2 | £5 | |
| Precious Feeling | 7" | Essential | ESS001 | 1982 | £2.50 | £6 | |

## LAUGHING GRAVY

This Beach Boys cover was actually co-produced by Brian Wilson and features Dean Torrence of Jan and Dean on vocals.

| | | | | | | | |
|---|---|---|---|---|---|---|---|
| Vegetables | 7" | White Whale | 261 | 1967 | £30 | £60 | US |

## LAUGHING WIND

| | | | | | | | |
|---|---|---|---|---|---|---|---|
| Laughing Wind | LP | Tower | | 1967 | £15 | £30 | US |

## LAUPER, CYNDI

| | | | | | | | |
|---|---|---|---|---|---|---|---|
| Heading West | CD-s | Epic | CYNC6 | 1989 | £2 | £5 | picture disc |
| Hole In My Heart | CD-s | Epic | CYNC3 | 1988 | £2 | £5 | |
| I Drove All Night | CD-s | Epic | CYNC4 | 1989 | £2 | £5 | 2 versions |
| Money Changes Everything | 12" | Portrait | TA6009 | 1985 | £2.50 | £6 | |
| My First Night Without You | CD-s | Epic | CYNC5/6550911 | 1989 | £2 | £5 | 4 versions |
| She Bop | 7" | Portrait | WA4620 | 1984 | £2 | £5 | picture disc |
| Time After Time | 7" | Portrait | WA4290 | 1984 | £2 | £5 | picture disc |
| What's Going On | 7" | Portrait | CYNP1 | 1987 | £1.50 | £4 | picture disc |

## LAURENCE, ZACK

| | | | | | | | |
|---|---|---|---|---|---|---|---|
| Beatle Concerto | 7" EP | HMV | 7EG8968 | 1966 | £2 | £5 | |

## LAURENZ, JOHN

| | | | | | | | |
|---|---|---|---|---|---|---|---|
| Goodbye Stranger Goodbye | 7" | London | HL8138 | 1955 | £7.50 | £15 | |

## LAURIE

| | | | | | | | |
|---|---|---|---|---|---|---|---|
| I Love Onions | 7" | Decca | F12424 | 1966 | £1.50 | £4 | |

## LAURIE, CY

| | | | | | | | |
|---|---|---|---|---|---|---|---|
| Cy Laurie Jazz Band | LP | Esquire | 32008 | 1955 | £4 | £10 | |
| Cy Laurie Jazz Band | 10" LP | Esquire | 20037 | 1955 | £5 | £12 | |

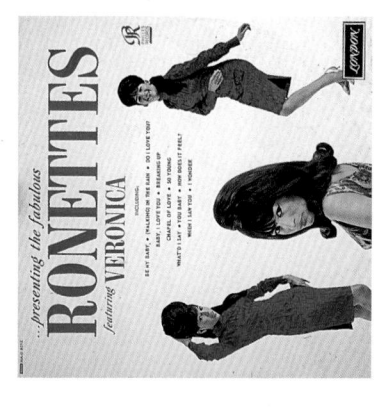

**Ronettes**
*Presenting The Fabulous Ronettes*
£75

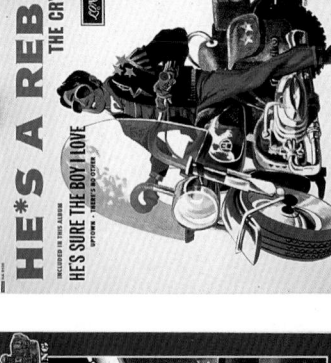

**Crystals**
*He's A Rebel*
£75

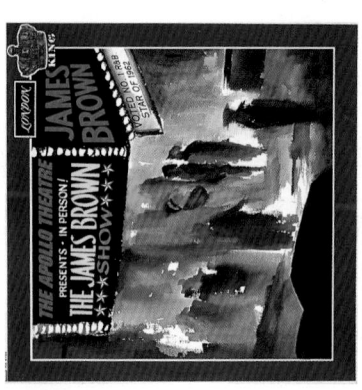
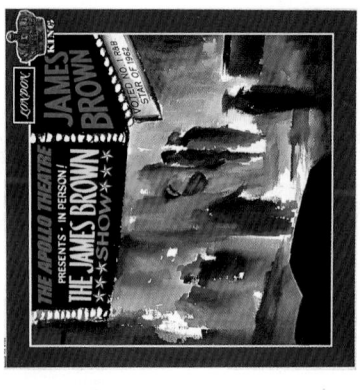

**James Brown**
*At The Apollo*
£30

**Gene Vincent**
*Crazy Times*
£40

**Buddy Holly**
*Chirping Crickets*
£30

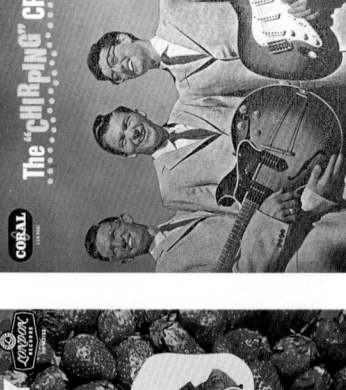

**Chuck Berry**
*One Dozen Berrys*
£60

**Elvis Presley**
*Rock'n'Roll No.2*
£200

**Coasters**
*Greatest Hits*
£40

**Cyril Davies**
*Sound Of Cyril Davies*
EP £40

**Move**
*Something Else From The Move*
EP £25

**Big Three**
*At The Cavern*
EP £12

**Lavern Baker**
*Best Of Lavern Baker*
EP £40

**Eyes**
*Arrival Of The Eyes*
EP £400

**Wayne Fontana & the Mindbenders**
*Road Runner*
EP £25

**Johnny Kidd**
*Shakin' All Over*
EP £25

**Kinks**
*Dedicated Kinks*
EP £40

**Billy Fury**
*Hits*
EP £15

**Marty Wilde**
*More Of Marty*
EP £20

**Downliners Sect**
*Sect Sing Sick Songs*
EP £50

**Byrds**
*Eight Miles High*
EP £15

**Eddie Cochran**
*C'mon Everybody*
EP £60

**Bob Dylan**
*Blowin' In The Wind*
French EP £40

**Spencer Davis Group**
*Every Little Bit Hurts*
EP £15

**Bill Haley**
*Rock'n'Roll*
EP £15

**Beatles**
*Volume 3*
French EP £100

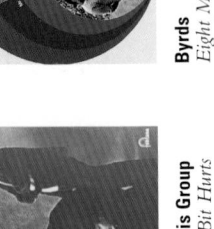

**Everly Brothers**
*Everly Brothers*
EP £15

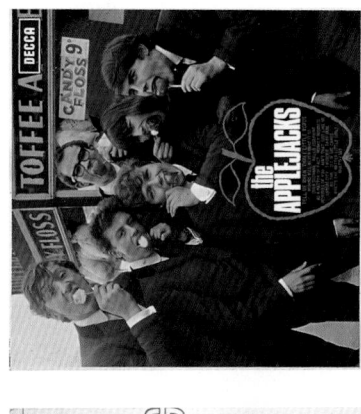

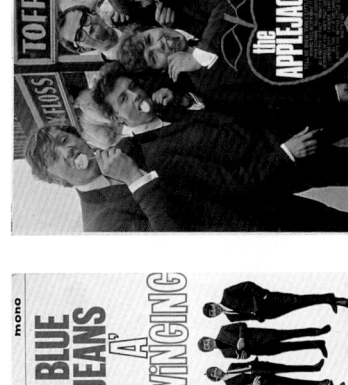

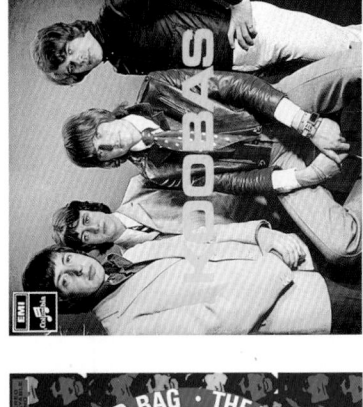

**Applejacks**
*Applejacks*
£75

**Swinging Blue Jeans**
*Blue Jeans A'Swinging*
£40

**Koobas**
*Koobas*
£400

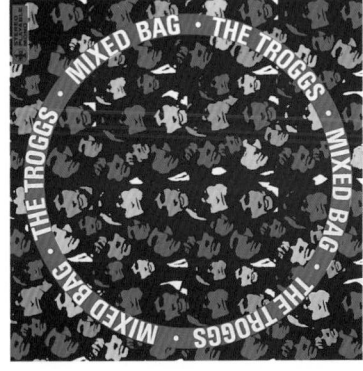

**Beatles**
*Yesterday And Today*
£3000

**Hollies**
*Would You Believe*
£40

**Troggs**
*Mixed Bag*
£75

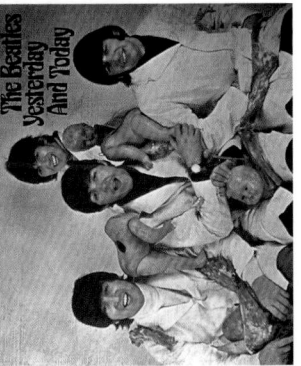

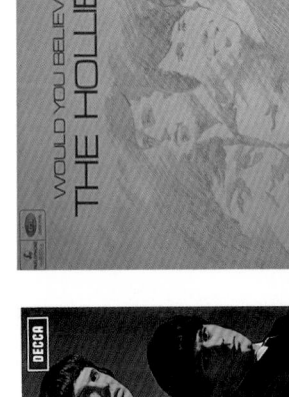

**Outlaws**
*Dream Of The West*
£100

**Zombies**
*Begin Here*
£125

**Graham Bond**
*There's A Bond Between Us*
£60

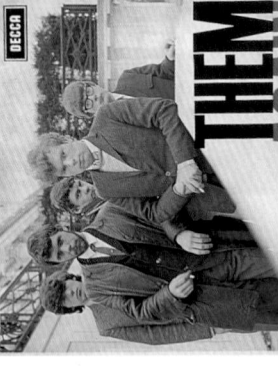

**Manfred Mann**
*As Is*
£100

**Zoot Money**
*It Should Have Been Me*
£60

**Them**
*Them Again*
£60

**Long John Baldry**
*Long John's Blues*
£40

**Pretty Things**
*Get The Picture*
£40

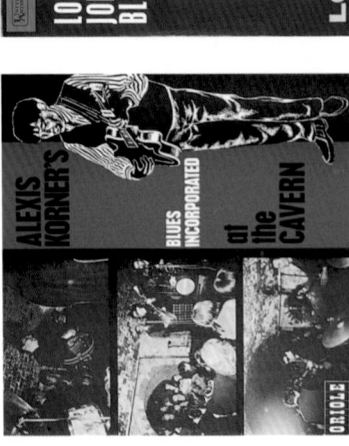

**Alexis Korner**
*At the Cavern*
£100

**Rolling Stones**
*Have You Seen Your Mother Live!*
£100

**Sorrows**
*Take A Heart*
£100

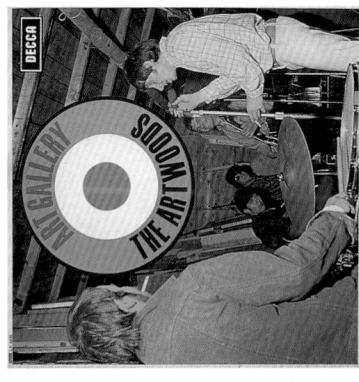

**Easybeats**
*Good Friday*
£60

**Who**
*My Generation*
£75

**Creation**
*We Are Paintermen*
£100

**Shamrocks**
*Smoke Rings*
£75

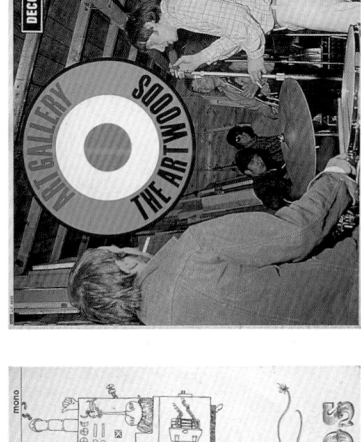

**Artwoods**
*Art Gallery*
£300

**Rattles**
*Twist At The Star Club Hamburg*
£75

**Yardbirds**
*Yardbirds*
£40

**Robert Parker**
*Barefootin'*
£25

**Dave Kelly**
*Black Blue Kelly*
£125

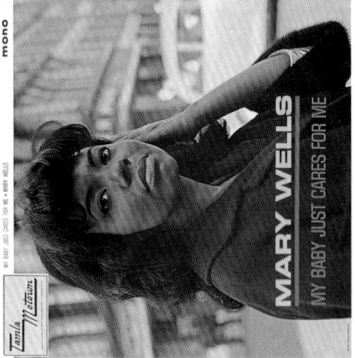

**Mary Wells**
*My Baby Just Cares For Me*
£25

**Chicken Shack**
*40 Blue Fingers*
£30

**Marvin Gaye**
*Moods Of Marvin Gaye*
£30

**John Mayall**
*Bluesbreakers*
£20

**Millie**
*More Millie*
£25

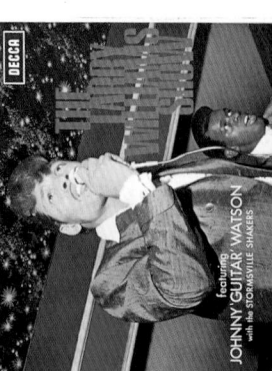
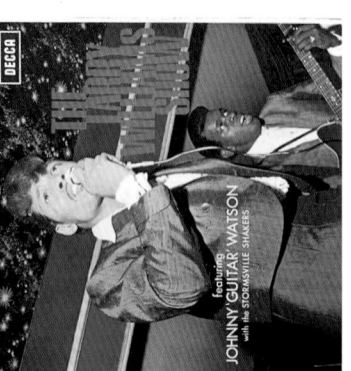

**Larry Williams**
*Larry Williams Show*
£30

**Rainbow Ffolly**
*Sallies Fforth*
£200

**Small Faces**
*Ogden's Nut Gone Flake*
£75

**Nirvana**
*Simon Simopath*
£40

**Blossom Toes**
*We Are Ever So Clean*
£50

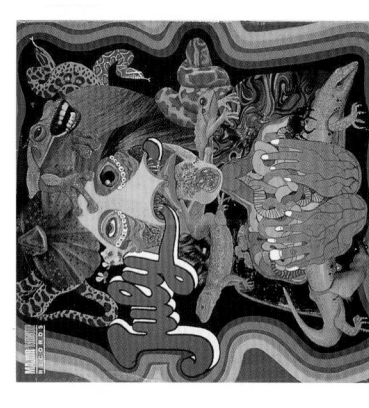

**Tomorrow**
*Tomorrow*
£100

**Pink Floyd**
*Saucerful Of Secrets*
£40 stereo / £75 mono

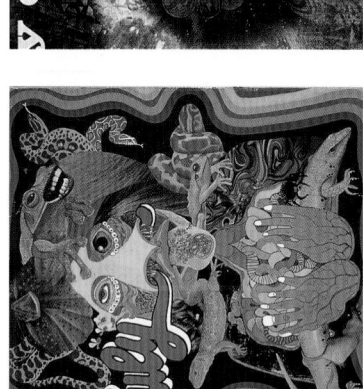

**July**
*July*
£300

**Art**
*Supernatural Fairy Tales*
£60

**Moving Sidewalks**
*Flash*
£200

**SRC**
*Traveller's Tale*
£40

**Ultimate Spinach**
*Behold And See*
£50

**Lothar And The Hand People**
*Space Hymn*
£40

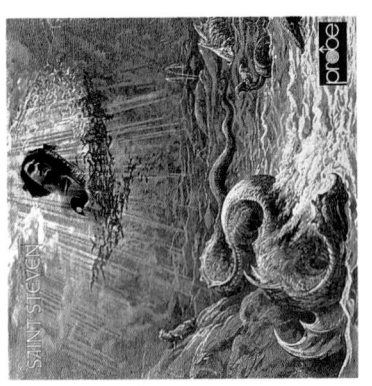

**Saint Steven**
*Saint Steven*
£75

**Thirteenth Floor Elevators**
*Bull Of The Woods*
£60

**Grateful Dead**
*Grateful Dead*
£30

**H.P. Lovecraft**
*H.P. Lovecraft*
£40

**Horace Silver**
*Song For My Father*
£25

**AMM**
*AMMMusic*
£100

**Gil Melle Quintet**
*Gil Melle Quintet*
10" LP  £50

**Sun Ra**
*Heliocentric Worlds Vol. 1*
£25

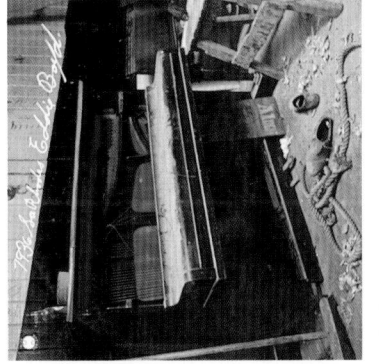

**Eddie Boyd**
*7936 South Rhodes*
£60

**Archie Shepp**
*Fire Music*
£25

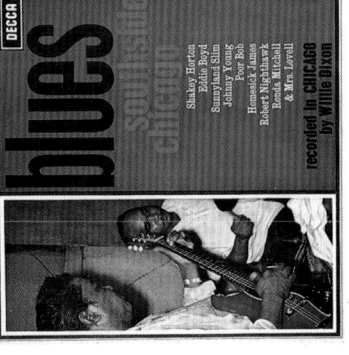

**Various**
*Blues Southside Chicago*
£40

**Ornette Coleman**
*Free Jazz*
£25

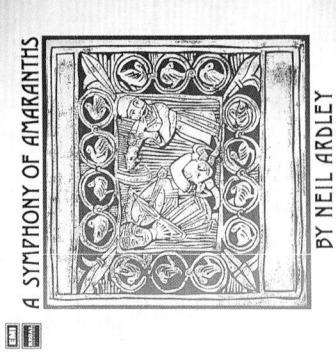

**Neil Ardley**
*Symphony Of Amaranths*
£100

**Jimi Hendrix**
*Band Of Gypsys*
£40

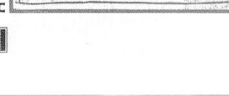

**Michael Garrick**
*Heart Is A Lotus*
£50

**Igginbottom**
*Igginbottom's Wrench*
£100 stereo / £125 mono

**Mike Westbrook**
*Love Songs*
£75

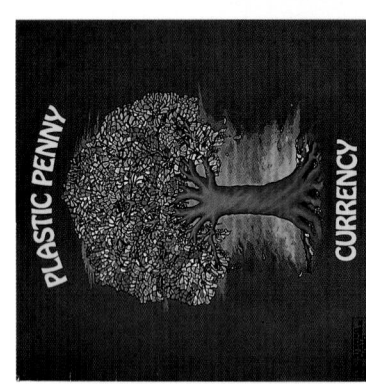
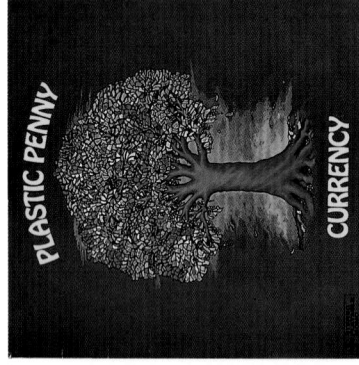

**Plastic Penny**
*Currency*
£40

**Keith Tippett**
*You Are Here I Am There*
£50

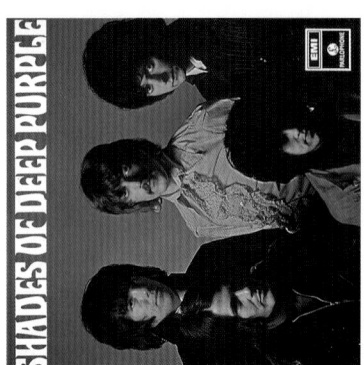

**Deep Purple**
*Shades Of Deep Purple*
£40 stereo / £75 mono

**Faust**
*Faust*
£30

**Mighty Baby**
*Mighty Baby*
£40

**Group 1850**
*Agemo's Trip To Mother Earth*
£75

**Audience**
*Audience*
£60

**065**
*Afghanistan*
£100

**Sandrose**
*Sandrose*
£125

**Amon Düül II**
*Phallus Dei*
£30

**Culpeper's Orchard**
*Second Sight*
£60

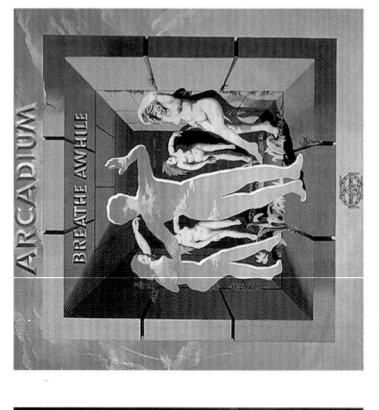

**Arcadium**
*Breathe Awhile*
£250

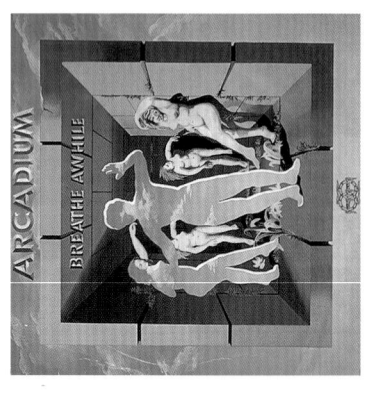

**Velvet Opera**
*Ride A Hustler's Dream*
£40

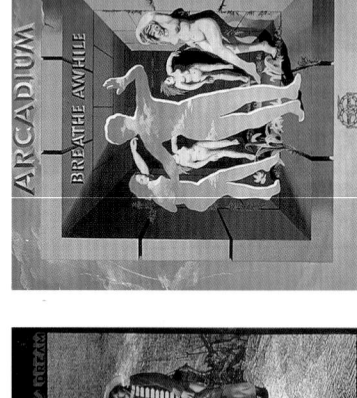

**Bakerloo**
*Bakerloo*
£60

**End**
*Introspection*
£75

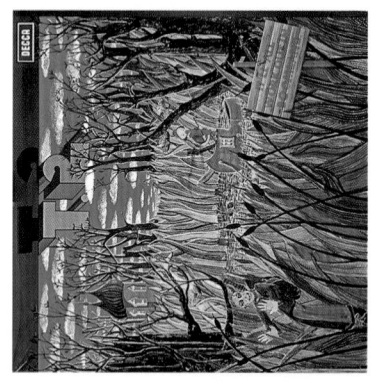

**Killing Floor**
*Out of Uranus*
£100

**T2**
*It'll All Work Out In Boomland*
£50

**Twink**
*Think Pink*
£60 / £150 pink vinyl

**Fire**
*Magic Shoemaker*
£200

**Open Mind**
*Open Mind*
£500

**Sandy Coast**
*From The Stereo Workshop*
£125

**Pete Brown**
*Art School Dance Goes On For Ever*
£50

**Spring**
*Spring*
£100

**Tea And Symphony**
*Asylum For The Musically Insane*
£60

**Fresh Maggots**
*Fresh Maggots*
£125

**Motherlight**
*Bobak, Jons, Malone*
£100

**Octopus**
*Restless Nights*
£150

**Megaton**
*Megaton*
£250

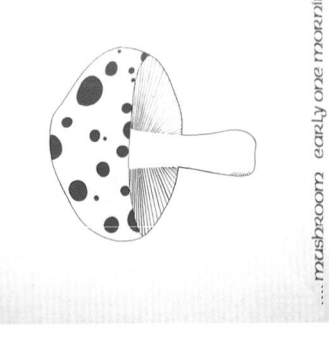

......mushroom  early one morning

**Mushroom**
*Early One Morning*
£250 / £350 with poster

**Comus**
*First Utterance*
£60

**Dark**
*Round The Edges*
£1250

**Junco Partners**
*Junco Partners*
£30

**Mellow Candle**
*Swaddling Songs*
£500

**Jade Warrior**
*Released*
£40

**Norman Haines Band**
*Den Of Iniquity*
£400

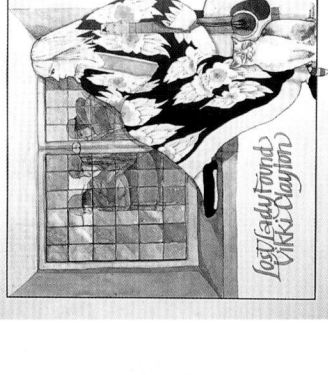

**Copper Family**
*Song For Every Season*
£100

**Halliard**
*It's The Irish In Me*
£50

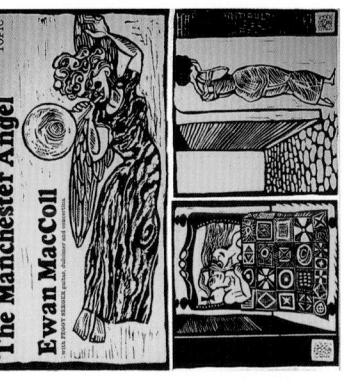

**Ewan MacColl and Peggy Seeger**
*Manchester Angel*
£30

**Various**
*Jug Of Punch*
£40

**Vikki Clayton**
*Lost Lady Found*
£100

**Oddsocks**
*Men Of The Moment*
£50

**Nick Drake**
*Bryter Layter*
£25

**Giles Farnaby's Dream Band**
*Giles Farnaby's Dream Band*
£100

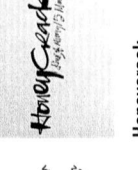

**Honeycrack**
'King Of Misery'
CD single £25

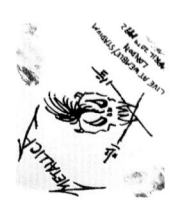

**Metallica**
'Enter Sandman'
CD single £20

**Madonna**
'Who's That Girl'
12" picture disc £30

**Queen**
'Breakthru'
Uncut shaped picture disc £25

**Christian Marclay**
*Record Without A Cover*
£50

DO NOT STORE IN A PROTECTIVE PACKAGE · 33 RPM · RECORD WITHOUT A COVER · CHRISTIAN MARCLAY

*Live at the White Bear*

**Dave Swarbrick & Simon Nicol**
*Live At The White Bear*
£25

T A L K   T A L K

**Talk Talk**
*Laughing Stock*
CD boxed set £50

**Ragged Heroes**
*Annual*
£200

**Def Leppard**
*Adrenalize*
CD boxed set
£150 / £200 special edition

## LAURIE, LINDA
| | | | | | | |
|---|---|---|---|---|---|---|
| All Winter Long | 7" | Top Rank | JAR277 | 1960 | £1.50 | £4 |
| Ambrose | 7" | London | HL8807 | 1959 | £1.50 | £4 |

## LAVA
| | | | | | | |
|---|---|---|---|---|---|---|
| Tears Are Going Home | LP | Brain | 1031 | 1973 | £6 | £15 .......... German |

## LAVERN, ROGER & THE MICRONS
| | | | | | | |
|---|---|---|---|---|---|---|
| Christmas Stocking | 7" | Decca | F11791 | 1963 | £10 | £20 |

## LAVETTE, BETTY
| | | | | | | |
|---|---|---|---|---|---|---|
| Doin' The Best I Can | 7" | Atlantic | K11198 | 1978 | £1.50 | £4 |
| He Made A Woman Out Of Me | 7" | Polydor | 56786 | 1969 | £2 | £5 |
| I Feel Good All Over | 7" | Pama | PM748 | 1968 | £2.50 | £6 |
| I Feel Good All Over | 7" | Stateside | SS2015 | 1967 | £2.50 | £6 |
| Your Turn To Cry | 7" | Atlantic | K10299 | 1973 | £1.50 | £4 |

## LAWRENCE, AZAR
| | | | | | | |
|---|---|---|---|---|---|---|
| Bridge Into The New Age | LP | Prestige | P10086 | 1975 | £5 | £12 ........ US |
| Summer Solstice | LP | Prestige | P10097 | 1976 | £5 | £12 ........ US |

## LAWRENCE, AZIE
| | | | | | | |
|---|---|---|---|---|---|---|
| Jamaica Blues | 7" | Melodisc | 1563 | 1960 | £1.50 | £4 |
| No Dice | 7" | Starlite | ST45041 | 1961 | £1.50 | £4 |
| Palms Of Victory | 7" | Blue Beat | BB71 | 1961 | £6 | £12 |
| Pempelem | 7" | Blue Beat | BB222 | 1964 | £6 | £12 |
| West Indians In England | 7" | Starlite | ST45022 | 1960 | £1.50 | £4 |
| You Didn't Want To Know | 7" | Melodisc | 1572 | 1960 | £1.50 | £4 |

## LAWRENCE, DIANE
| | | | | | | |
|---|---|---|---|---|---|---|
| I Won't Hang Around Like A Hound Dog | 7" | Doctor Bird | DB1075 | 1967 | £5 | £10 |
| Treat Me Nice | 7" | Jolly | JY005 | 1968 | £1.50 | £4 |

## LAWRENCE, ELLIOT
| | | | | | | |
|---|---|---|---|---|---|---|
| Gerry Mulligan Arrangements | LP | Vogue | LAE12057 | 1957 | £4 | £10 |
| Plays Tiny Kahn & Johnny Mandel Arrangements | LP | Vogue | LAE12101 | 1958 | £4 | £10 |
| Swinging At The Steel Pier | LP | Vogue | LAE12071 | 1958 | £4 | £10 |

## LAWRENCE, LARRY
| | | | | | | |
|---|---|---|---|---|---|---|
| Goofin' Off | 7" | Pye | 7N25042 | 1959 | £1.50 | £4 |
| Jug-a-Roo | 7" | Ember | EMBS106 | 1960 | £1.50 | £4 |

## LAWRENCE, LEE
| | | | | | | |
|---|---|---|---|---|---|---|
| Beyond The Stars | 7" | Columbia | SCM5175 | 1955 | £1.50 | £4 |
| By You By You By You | 7" | Columbia | DB3885 | 1957 | £1.50 | £4 |
| Chapel Of The Roses | 7" | Columbia | DB3922 | 1957 | £1.50 | £4 |
| Don't Tell Me Not To Love You | 7" | Columbia | SCM5228 | 1956 | £1.50 | £4 |
| High Upon A Mountain | 7" | Columbia | DB3830 | 1956 | £2.50 | £6 |
| Lee Lawrence | 7" EP | Columbia | SEG7780 | 1958 | £5 | £10 |
| Lights Of Paris | 7" | Decca | F10438 | 1955 | £1.50 | £4 |
| Little Mustard Seed | 7" | Decca | F10285 | 1954 | £2 | £5 |
| Lonely Ballerina | 7" | Columbia | DB3981 | 1957 | £1.50 | £4 |
| More Than A Millionaire | 7" | Columbia | SCM5190 | 1955 | £1.50 | £4 |
| My Own True Love | 7" | Decca | F10422 | 1955 | £1.50 | £4 |
| My World Stood Still | 7" | Columbia | SCM5181 | 1955 | £1.50 | £4 |
| Presenting Lee Lawrence | 10" LP | Decca | LF1132 | 1953 | £6 | £15 |
| Rock 'n' Roll Opera | 7" | Columbia | DB3855 | 1956 | £6 | £12 |
| Story Of Tina | 7" | Decca | F10367 | 1954 | £2 | £5 |
| Suddenly There's A Valley | 7" | Columbia | SCM5201 | 1955 | £4 | £8 |
| Things I Didn't Do | 7" | Decca | F10408 | 1954 | £1.50 | £4 |
| Valley Valparaiso | 7" | Columbia | SCM5283 | 1956 | £1.50 | £4 |
| We Believe In Love | 7" | Columbia | SCM5254 | 1956 | £1.50 | £4 |
| Will You Be Mine Alone? | 7" | Decca | F10485 | 1955 | £1.50 | £4 |

## LAWRENCE, STEVE
| | | | | | | |
|---|---|---|---|---|---|---|
| Banana Boat Song | 7" | Vogue Coral | Q72228 | 1957 | £2 | £5 |
| Fabulous | 7" | Vogue Coral | Q72264 | 1957 | £2 | £5 |
| Footsteps | 7" | HMV | POP726 | 1960 | £1.50 | £4 |
| Fräulein | 7" | Vogue Coral | Q72281 | 1957 | £2 | £5 |
| Here's Steve Lawrence No. 1 | 7" EP | Coral | FEP2010 | 1959 | £2.50 | £6 |
| Here's Steve Lawrence No. 2 | 7" EP | Coral | FEP2012 | 1959 | £2.50 | £6 |
| Never Mind | 7" | Vogue Coral | Q72286 | 1957 | £1.50 | £4 |
| Open Up The Gates Of Mercy | 7" | Vogue Coral | Q72114 | 1955 | £2 | £5 |
| Party Doll | 7" | Vogue Coral | Q72243 | 1957 | £2 | £5 |
| Pretty Blue Eyes | 7" | HMV | POP689 | 1960 | £1.50 | £4 |
| Speedo | 7" | Vogue Coral | Q72133 | 1956 | £4 | £8 |
| This Night | 7" | Parlophone | MSP6038 | 1953 | £2.50 | £6 |
| Too Little Time | 7" | Parlophone | MSP6080 | 1954 | £2.50 | £6 |
| You Can't Hold A Memory In Your Arms | 7" | Parlophone | MSP6106 | 1954 | £2.50 | £6 |

## LAWRIE, BILLY
| | | | | | | |
|---|---|---|---|---|---|---|
| Roll Over Beethoven | 7" | Polydor | 56363 | 1969 | £10 | £20 |

## LAWS, RONNIE
| | | | | | | |
|---|---|---|---|---|---|---|
| Pressure Sensitive | LP | Blue Note | BNLA452 | 1975 | £4 | £10 |

## LAWSON, JULIET
Boo................................................................ LP ...... Sovereign ........... SVNA7257 .............. 1972 £10 .......... £25 ...............................

## LAWSON, SHIRLEY
Star ................................................................ 7" ...... Soul City .......... SC108 ................ 1969 £7.50 ....... £15 ...............................

## LAWSON-HAGGART JAZZ BAND
| | | | | | | |
|---|---|---|---|---|---|---|
| Blues On The River ................................. | 10" LP | Brunswick ...... | LA8580 ............. | 1953 | £5 .......... | £12 |
| Jelly Roll's Jazz ...................................... | 10" LP | Brunswick ...... | LA8576 ............. | 1953 | £5 .......... | £12 |
| King Oliver's Jazz ................................... | 10" LP | Brunswick ...... | LA8593 ............. | 1953 | £5 .......... | £12 |
| Louis' Hot 5's And 7"s ........................... | 10" LP | Brunswick ...... | LA8698 ............. | 1955 | £5 .......... | £12 |
| Ragtime Jamboree .................................. | 10" LP | Brunswick ...... | LA8635 ............. | 1954 | £5 .......... | £12 |
| South Of The Mason-Dixon Line ............. | 10" LP | Brunswick ...... | LA8703 ............. | 1955 | £5 .......... | £12 |
| Windy City Jazz ..................................... | 10" LP | Brunswick ...... | LA8639 ............. | 1954 | £5 .......... | £12 |

## LAWSON-HAGGART ROCKIN' BAND
Boppin' At The Hop ........................ LP ...... Brunswick ...... LAT8288/STA3010 1959 £10 ...... £25
Boppin' At The Hop ........................ 7" EP . Brunswick ...... OE9451 .............. 1959 £10 ...... £20

## LAWTON, LOU
Doin' The Philly Dog ........................ 7" ...... Ember .......... EMBS232 ............. 1967 £6 .......... £12
I'm Just A Fool ............................... 7" ...... Speciality ........ SPE1005 .............. 1967 £6 .......... £12

## LAY, SAM
In Bluesland .................................... LP ...... Blue Thumb .... BTS8814 ............. 1969 £4 .......... £10 .................................. US

## LAYNE, OSSIE
Come Back ....................................... 7" ...... R&B ............. MRB5006 ............ 1965 £2.50 ...... £6

## LAYTON, EDDIE
Doodles .......................................... 7" ...... Mercury .......... AMT1064 ............. 1959 £1.50 ...... £4

## LAZY LESTER
I'm A Lover Not A Fighter ................... 7" ...... Stateside ........ SS277 ................ 1964 £2.50 ...... £6
Made Up My Mind ............................. LP ...... Blue Horizon ... 2431007 .............. 1971 £30 ....... £60

## LAZY SMOKE
Corridor Of Faces ............................. LP ...... Onyx ............. ES6903 ................ 1967 £700 .... £1000 ............................ US

## LE BON, SIMON
Grey Lady Of The Sea ........................ CD-s .. Parlophone ...... DT0001 ................... £30 .......... £60 ...................... promo

## LE CHEILE
Airis .............................................. LP ...... Inchecronin ...... INC7423 ............. 1978 £5 .......... £12
Lord Mayo ....................................... LP ...... Inchecronin ...... INC7424 ............. 1978 £5 .......... £12

## LE FORGE, JACK
Our Crazy Affair ............................... 7" ...... Stateside ........ SS444 ................ 1965 £1.50 ...... £4

## LE MAT
Waltz Of The Fool ............................. 7" ...... Whaam! .......... WHAAM8 ............ 1982 £1.50 ...... £4

## LE ORME
| | | | | | | | |
|---|---|---|---|---|---|---|---|
| Collage ................................ | LP ...... | Philips ............. | 6323007 .......... | 1971 | £5 .......... | £12 | ...... Italian |
| Contrappunti ......................... | LP ...... | Philips ............. | 6323035 .......... | 1974 | £4 .......... | £10 | ...... Italian |
| Felona And Serona ................. | LP ...... | Charisma ......... | CAS1072 .......... | 1973 | £5 .......... | £12 | ...... Italian |
| Florian ................................. | LP ...... | Philips ............. | 6323086 .......... | 1979 | £4 .......... | £10 | ...... Italian |
| In Concert ............................ | LP ...... | Philips ............. | 6323028 .......... | 1974 | £5 .......... | £12 | ...... Italian |
| Piccola Rapsodie Dell Ape ....... | LP ...... | Philips ............. | 6323102 .......... | 1980 | £4 .......... | £10 | ...... Italian |
| Italian Smogmagica ................. | LP ...... | Philips ............. | 6323041 .......... | 1975 | £5 .......... | £12 | ...... Italian |
| Storia O Leggenda ................. | LP ...... | Philips ............. | 6323052 .......... | 1977 | £4 .......... | £10 | ...... Italian |
| Uomo Di Pezza ..................... | LP ...... | Philips ............. | 6323013 .......... | 1972 | £5 .......... | £12 | ...... Italian |
| Venerdi ................................ | LP ...... | Polydor ........... | 2393341 .......... | 1982 | £4 .......... | £10 | ...... Italian |
| Verita Nascoste ..................... | LP ...... | Philips ............. | 6323045 .......... | 1976 | £5 .......... | £12 | ...... Italian |

## LE RÊVE DU DIABLE
Le Rêve du diable ............................. LP ...... Escargot ......... ESC352 ............. 1977 £8 .......... £20 ...................... French

## LE SAGE, BILL
Bill's Recipes ................................... LP ...... Saga ............. STM6019 ............. 1959 £5 .......... £12

## LEA VALLEY SKIFFLE GROUP
Lea Valley Skiffle Group ..................... 7" EP . Esquire .......... EP163 ................. 1958 £10 ...... £20

## LEADBELLY
| | | | | | | | |
|---|---|---|---|---|---|---|---|
| Alabama Bound ................... | 7" ...... | HMV ............. | MH190 .......... | 1955 | £5 .......... | £10 | ..... with Golden Gate Quartet |
| Backwater Blues ................. | 78 ...... | Capitol ........... | CL13282 .......... | 1950 | £3 .......... | £8 | |
| Classics In Jazz ................. | 10" LP | Capitol ........... | LC6597 .......... | 1953 | £8 .......... | £20 | |
| Demon Of A Man ................ | LP ...... | Storyville ......... | SLP124 .......... | 1964 | £4 .......... | £10 | |
| From The Last Sessions ....... | LP ...... | Folkways ......... | 3019 .............. | 1967 | £4 .......... | £10 | ...... US |
| Good Morning Blues ............ | LP ...... | RCA ............. | RD7567 .......... | 1963 | £4 .......... | £10 | |
| His Guitar, His Voice, His Piano | LP ...... | Capitol ........... | T1821 ............. | 1963 | £4 .......... | £10 | |
| How Long Blues ................. | 7" EP . | Melodisc ........ | EPM763 .......... | 1956 | £5 .......... | £10 | |
| Huddie Ledbetter ................ | 10" LP | Folkways ......... | 2013 ............. | 1960 | £8 .......... | £20 | ...... US |
| Keep Your Hands Off Her ..... | LP ...... | Verve ............. | (S)VLP5011 ...... | 1967 | £4 .......... | £10 | |
| Last Sessions Vol. 1 ........... | LP ...... | Melodisc ......... | MLP12113 ........ | 1959 | £6 .......... | £15 | |

| | | | | | | | | |
|---|---|---|---|---|---|---|---|---|
| Last Sessions Vol. 2 | LP | Melodisc | MLP12114 | 1959 | £6 | £15 | |
| Leadbelly | 7" EP | Capitol | EAP120111 | 1961 | £2.50 | £6 | |
| Leadbelly | 7" EP | Melodisc | EPM777 | 1958 | £5 | £10 | |
| Leadbelly | 7" EP | Storyville | SEP337 | 196– | £2.50 | £6 | |
| Leadbelly | 10" LP | Capitol | H369 | 195– | £37.50 | £75 | US |
| Leadbelly | 10" LP | Folkways | 14 | 1960 | £5 | £12 | US |
| Leadbelly | 10" LP | Folkways | 24 | 1960 | £5 | £12 | US |
| Leadbelly | 10" LP | Folkways | 4 | 1960 | £5 | £12 | US |
| Leadbelly | 10" LP | Folkways | 43 | 1960 | £5 | £12 | US |
| Leadbelly 2 | LP | Storyville | SLP139 | 1964 | £4 | £10 | |
| Leadbelly Box | LP | XTRA | XTRA1017 | 1965 | £6 | £15 | double |
| Leadbelly Vol. 1 | 10" LP | Melodisc | MLP511 | 1957 | £6 | £15 | |
| Leadbelly Vol. 2 | 10" LP | Melodisc | MLP512 | 1957 | £6 | £15 | |
| Leadbelly Vol. 3 | 10" LP | Melodisc | MLP515 | 1958 | £6 | £15 | |
| Ledbetter's Best | 7" EP | Capitol | EAP11821 | 1961 | £2.50 | £6 | |
| Ledbetter's Best | 7" EP | Capitol | EAP41821 | 1961 | £4 | £8 | |
| Library Of Congress Recordings | LP | Elektra | EKL301/2 | 1966 | £10 | £25 | 3 LPs, boxed |
| Memorial Vol. 3 | LP | Stinson | SLP48 | 1962 | £6 | £15 | US, red vinyl |
| Midnight Special | LP | RCA | LPV505 | 1964 | £4 | £10 | US |
| Party Plays And Songs | 7" EP | Melodisc | EPM787 | 1959 | £4 | £8 | |
| Plays Party Songs | 10" LP | Melodisc | MLP517 | 1958 | £6 | £15 | |
| Rock Island Line | 7" EP | RCA | RCX146 | 1959 | £2.50 | £6 | |
| Rock Island Line | 10" LP | Folkways | 2014 | 1960 | £8 | £20 | US |
| Saga Of Leadbelly | LP | Melodisc | MLP12107 | 1958 | £6 | £15 | |
| See See Rider | 7" EP | Melodisc | EPM782 | 1958 | £5 | £10 | |
| Shout On | LP | XTRA | XTRA1126 | 1971 | £6 | £15 | |
| Sinful Songs | 10" LP | Allegro | 4027 | 195– | £15 | £30 | US |
| Sings And Plays | LP | Society | SOC994 | 1965 | £4 | £10 | |
| Sings Folk Songs | LP | XTRA | XTRA1046 | 1966 | £6 | £15 | |
| Storyville Blues Anthology Vol. 7 | 7" EP | Storyville | SEP387 | 1963 | £2.50 | £6 | |
| Take This Hammer | LP | Verve | (S)VLP5002 | 1965 | £4 | £10 | |

## LEADERS

| | | | | | | | |
|---|---|---|---|---|---|---|---|
| Night People | 7" | Fontana | TF602 | 1965 | £1.50 | £4 | |

## LEADERS (2)

| | | | | | | | |
|---|---|---|---|---|---|---|---|
| Tit For Tat | 7" | Amalgamated | AMG804 | 1968 | £4 | £8 | Marvetts B side |

## LEADING FIGURES

| | | | | | | | |
|---|---|---|---|---|---|---|---|
| Oscillation '67 | LP | Deram | DML/SML1006 | 1967 | £6 | £15 | |
| Sound And Movement | LP | Ace Of Clubs | SCL1225 | 1967 | £15 | £30 | |

## LEAFHOUND

Some records gain a reputation within the collectors' market out of all proportion to their musical worth. The Leafhound LP is very much a case in point – the cover and its title imply some kind of psychedelic masterpiece, whereas the music is actually rather ordinary hard rock, with a singer who would love to be Robert Plant, but who sadly is not. The singer, Pete French, actually managed to sustain a surprisingly lengthy rock career, including stints with Brunning Hall Sunflower Blues Band and Black Cat Bones (a group that effectively evolved directly into Leafhound) before making *Growers Of Mushrooms*, and with Big Bertha, Atomic Rooster, Cactus and Randy Pie afterwards.

| | | | | | | | |
|---|---|---|---|---|---|---|---|
| Growers Of Mushrooms | LP | Decca | SKLR5094 | 1971 | £400 | £600 | |
| Growers Of Mushrooms | LP | Discwasher | TP396 | 1978 | £25 | £50 | US, with poster |
| Leafhound | LP | Telefunken | SLE14604 | 1970 | £30 | £60 | German |

## LEAGUE OF GENTLEMEN

| | | | | | | | |
|---|---|---|---|---|---|---|---|
| Each Little Falling Tear | 7" | Columbia | DB7666 | 1965 | £15 | £30 | |
| How Can You Tell | 7" | Planet | PLF109 | 1966 | £15 | £30 | |

## LEAPER, BOB

| | | | | | | | |
|---|---|---|---|---|---|---|---|
| High Wire | 7" | Pye | 7N15700 | 1965 | £7.50 | £15 | |

## LEAPERS CREEPERS SLEEPERS

| | | | | | | | |
|---|---|---|---|---|---|---|---|
| Ba Boo | 7" | Island | WI275 | 1966 | £2.50 | £6 | |

## LEAR, KEVIN 'KING'

| | | | | | | | |
|---|---|---|---|---|---|---|---|
| Count Me Out | 7" | Polydor | BM56203 | 1967 | £5 | £10 | |
| Cry Me A River | 7" | Page One | POF109 | 1968 | £4 | £8 | |
| Power Of Love | 7" | Page One | POF087 | 1968 | £1.50 | £4 | |
| Snake | 7" | Page One | POF132 | 1969 | £2.50 | £6 | |

## LEARY, TIMOTHY

| | | | | | | | |
|---|---|---|---|---|---|---|---|
| L.S.D. | LP | Pixie | CA1069 | 1966 | £37.50 | £75 | US |
| Turn On, Tune In, Drop Out | LP | ESP-Disk | 1027 | 1966 | £10 | £25 | US |
| Turn On, Tune In, Drop Out | LP | Mercury | MG2/SR61131 | 1967 | £8 | £20 | US |
| You Can Be Anyone This Time Around | LP | Douglas | 1 | 196– | £15 | £30 | US |

## LEATHER COATED MINDS

The album by the Leather Coated Minds contains the recording debut of J. J. Cale, although those seeking the roots of his inimitable sleepy guitar and singing style will be disappointed. Instead the music is exactly the kind of fare that bad sixties films included in their soundtracks whenever a party was shown. As is often the case in the record collectors' market, a high price tag is no guarantee of musical quality.

| | | | | | | | |
|---|---|---|---|---|---|---|---|
| Trip Down Sunset Strip | LP | Fontana | (S)TL5412 | 1967 | £20 | £40 | |

## LEATHER NUN

| | | | | | | | |
|---|---|---|---|---|---|---|---|
| Slow Death | 7" | Industrial | IR0006 | 1979 | £4 | £8 | |

## LEAVES

| | | | | | | | |
|---|---|---|---|---|---|---|---|
| All The Good That's Happening | LP | Capitol | (S)T2638 | 1967 | £37.50 | £75 | US |

| | | | | | | | |
|---|---|---|---|---|---|---|---|
| Hey Joe | LP | Mira | LP(S)3005 | 1966 | £20 | £40 | US |
| Hey Joe | 7" | Fontana | TF713 | 1966 | £7.50 | £15 | |

## LED ZEPPELIN

Original pressings of the Led Zeppelin LPs I–IV are easily identified by their purple and red Atlantic labels and pre-Kinney catalogue numbers, but for the very first LP, it is possible to identify which copies were issued during the few weeks following its release. These all have covers on which the title and company name are printed in turquoise, instead of the orange which has been used on every copy since. Similarly, the very first copies of the third LP are identifiable by the message 'Do what thou wilt' scratched in the vinyl, although there are many more copies like this than some collectors imagine. The rarest Led Zeppelin records are the early UK singles, which exist in demonstration form only due to the group's constant refusal to allow their full commercial release.

| | | | | | | | |
|---|---|---|---|---|---|---|---|
| Black Dog | 7" | Atlantic | 2849 | 1971 | £2 | £5 | US |
| Collector's Item | CD-s | Atlantic | PRCD27 | 1995 | £25 | £50 | 4 track German promo |
| Communication Breakdown | 7" | Atlantic | 584269 | 1969 | £250 | £400 | .. demo, best auctioned |
| D'yer Maker | 7" | Atlantic | 2986 | 1973 | £2 | £5 | US |
| D'yer Maker | 7" | Atlantic | K10296 | 1973 | £62.50 | £125 | demo |
| Dazed And Confused | 7" EP | Atlantic | 1019 | 1969 | £150 | £250 | US |
| Good Times Bad Times | 7" | Atlantic | 2613 | 1969 | £5 | £10 | US |
| Houses Of THe Holy | 7" EP | Atlantic | PR213 | 1973 | £37.50 | £75 | US promo |
| Immigrant Song | 7" | Atlantic | 2777 | 1970 | £4 | £8 | US |
| In Through The Out Door | LP | Swansong | SSK59410 | 1979 | £37.50 | £75 | set of 6 LPs in different sleeves A–F |
| Led Zeppelin | LP | Atlantic | 588171 | 1969 | £8 | £20 | |
| Led Zeppelin | LP | Atlantic | 588171 | 1969 | £37.50 | £75 | .. turquoise lettering on cover |
| Led Zeppelin | 7" EP | Atlantic | 171 | 1970 | £50 | £100 | US |
| Led Zeppelin 2 | LP | Atlantic | 588198 | 1969 | £6 | £15 | |
| Led Zeppelin 2 | LP | Mobile Fidelity | MFSL1065 | 1980 | £10 | £25 | US audiophile |
| Led Zeppelin 3 | LP | Atlantic | 2401002 | 1970 | £6 | £15 | |
| Led Zeppelin 3 | LP | Atlantic | 2401012 | 1970 | £75 | £150 | test pressing with alternate mixes |
| Led Zeppelin 3 | LP | Atlantic | SD7201 | 1971 | £25 | £50 | US mono promo |
| Led Zeppelin 4 | LP | Atlantic | 2401012 | 1971 | £6 | £15 | |
| Led Zeppelin 4 | LP | Atlantic | K50008 | 1978 | £15 | £30 | lilac vinyl |
| Led Zeppelin 4 | LP | Atlantic | K50008/C8814 | 1988 | £6 | £15 | HMV boxed set |
| Led Zeppelin IV | CD | Atlantic | K50008/C8814 | 1988 | £8 | £20 | HMV boxed set |
| Over The Hills And Far Away | 7" | Atlantic | 2970 | 1973 | £2 | £5 | US |
| Profiled! | CD | Atlantic | PRCD36292 | 1990 | £20 | £40 | US promo |
| Remasters | CD-s | Atlantic | CDLZ1 | 1990 | £12.50 | £25 | 4 track promo |
| Remasters | 10" | Atlantic | LZ2 | 1990 | £10 | £20 | 4 track promo |
| Rock And Roll | 7" | Atlantic | 2865 | 1972 | £2 | £5 | US |
| Stairway To Heaven | 7" EP | Atlantic | PR175 | 1973 | £50 | £100 | US promo, picture sleeve |
| Stairway To Heaven | 7" EP | Atlantic | PR269 | 1973 | £20 | £40 | US promo |
| Stairway To Heaven | 7" | Atlantic | LZ3 | 1990 | £50 | £100 | promo with letter |
| Stairway To Heaven | 7" | Atlantic | LZ3LC | 1990 | £6 | £12 | jukebox issue |
| Trampled Underfoot | 7" | Swan Song | DC1 | 1979 | £5 | £10 | custom sleeve |
| Whole Lotta Love | 7" | Atlantic | 2690 | 1969 | £2 | £5 | US |
| Whole Lotta Love | 7" | Atlantic | 584309 | 1969 | £250 | £400 | .. demo, best auctioned |

## LED ZEPPELIN & DUSTY SPRINGFIELD

| | | | | | | | |
|---|---|---|---|---|---|---|---|
| Climb Aboard Led Zeppelin/Dusty In Memphis | LP | Atlantic | TLST135 | 1969 | £25 | £50 | US promo |

## LEE, ARTHUR

| | | | | | | | |
|---|---|---|---|---|---|---|---|
| Ninth Wave | 7" | Capitol | 4980 | 1964 | £15 | £30 | US |
| Vindicator | LP | A&M | AMLS64356 | 1972 | £5 | £12 | |

## LEE, BENNY

| | | | | | | | |
|---|---|---|---|---|---|---|---|
| Love Plays The Strings Of My Banjo | 7" | Parlophone | MSP6214 | 1956 | £1.50 | £4 | |
| Rock 'n' Rollin' Santa Claus | 7" | Parlophone | R4245 | 1956 | £6 | £12 | |
| Sweet Heartaches | 7" | Parlophone | MSP6252 | 1956 | £1.50 | £4 | |

## LEE, BRENDA

| | | | | | | | |
|---|---|---|---|---|---|---|---|
| Ain't Gonna Cry No More | 7" | Brunswick | 05963 | 1966 | £1.50 | £4 | |
| Ain't That Love | 7" | Brunswick | 05720 | 1957 | £37.50 | £75 | |
| All Alone Am I | LP | Brunswick | LAT/STA8530 | 1962 | £5 | £12 | |
| All Alone Am I | 7" EP | Brunswick | OE9492 | 1963 | £10 | £20 | |
| All Alone Am I | 7" | Brunswick | 05882 | 1963 | £1.50 | £4 | |
| All The Way | LP | Brunswick | LAT8383/STA3048 | 1961 | £6 | £15 | |
| Alone With You | 7" | Brunswick | 05911 | 1964 | £1.50 | £4 | |
| As Usual | 7" | Brunswick | 05899 | 1964 | £1.50 | £4 | |
| Bill Bailey | 7" | Brunswick | 05780 | 1959 | £5 | £10 | tri-centre |
| Break It To Me Gently | 7" | Brunswick | 05864 | 1962 | £1.50 | £4 | |
| By Request | LP | Brunswick | LAT/STA8576 | 1964 | £6 | £15 | |
| Bye Bye Blues | LP | Brunswick | LAT/STA8649 | 1966 | £4 | £10 | |
| Call Me | LP | MCA | MUP(S)321 | 1968 | £4 | £10 | |
| Christmas Will Be Just Another Lonely Day | 7" | Brunswick | 05921 | 1964 | £1.50 | £4 | |
| Coming On Strong | LP | Brunswick | LAT/STA8672 | 1967 | £6 | £15 | |
| Coming On Strong | 7" | Brunswick | 05967 | 1966 | £1.50 | £4 | |
| Dum Dum | 7" | Brunswick | 05854 | 1961 | £1.50 | £4 | |
| Emotions | LP | Brunswick | LAT8376/STA3044 | 1961 | £6 | £15 | |
| Emotions | 7" | Brunswick | 05847 | 1961 | £1.50 | £4 | |
| Fairyland | 7" | Decca | BM31186 | 1958 | £20 | £40 | export |
| Fool Number One | 7" | Brunswick | 05860 | 1961 | £1.50 | £4 | |
| For The First Time | LP | MCA | MUP(S)332 | 1968 | £4 | £10 | with Pete Fountain |
| Four From Sixty Four | 7" EP | Brunswick | OE9510 | 1965 | £10 | £20 | |

| Title | Format | Label | Cat. No. | Year | | | Notes |
|---|---|---|---|---|---|---|---|
| Good Life | LP | MCA | MUP(S)322 | 1968 | £4 | £10 | |
| Grandma What Great Songs | LP | Brunswick | LAT8319 | 1958 | £15 | £30 | |
| Here Comes That Feeling | 7" | Brunswick | 05871 | 1962 | £1.50 | £4 | |
| I Want To Be Wanted | 7" | Brunswick | 05839 | 1960 | £1.50 | £4 | |
| I Wonder | 7" | Brunswick | 05891 | 1963 | £1.50 | £4 | |
| I'm Gonna Lassoo Santa Claus | 7" | Brunswick | 05628 | 1956 | £62.50 | £125 | |
| I'm Sorry | 7" | Brunswick | 05833 | 1960 | £2 | £5 | |
| Is It True | 7" | Brunswick | 05915 | 1964 | £1.50 | £4 | |
| It Started All Over Again | 7" | Brunswick | 05876 | 1962 | £1.50 | £4 | |
| Johnny One Time | LP | MCA | MUP(S)396 | 1970 | £4 | £10 | |
| Let Me Sing | LP | Brunswick | LAT/STA8548 | 1963 | £6 | £15 | |
| Let's Jump The Broomstick | 7" | Brunswick | 05823 | 1960 | £1.50 | £4 | |
| Losing You | 7" | Brunswick | 05886 | 1963 | £1.50 | £4 | |
| Love You | LP | Ace Of Hearts | AH59 | 1963 | £6 | £15 | |
| Love You Till I Die | 7" | Brunswick | 05685 | 1957 | £37.50 | £75 | |
| Merry Christmas | LP | MCA | MUP(S)330 | 1968 | £4 | £10 | |
| Merry Christmas From Brenda | LP | Brunswick | LAT/STA8590 | 1964 | £6 | £15 | |
| Miss Dynamite | LP | Brunswick | LAT8347 | 1959 | £10 | £25 | |
| Pretend | 7" EP | Brunswick | OE9482 | 1962 | £12.50 | £25 | |
| Reflections In Blue | LP | MCA | MUP(S)306 | 1968 | £4 | £10 | |
| Ride Ride Ride | 7" | Brunswick | 05970 | 1967 | £1.50 | £4 | |
| Ring A My Phone | 7" | Brunswick | 05755 | 1958 | £37.50 | £75 | |
| Rock The Bop | 7" EP | Brunswick | OE9462 | 1959 | £15 | £30 | tri-centre |
| Rockin' Around The Christmas Tree | 7" | Brunswick | 05880 | 1962 | £1.50 | £4 | |
| Rusty Bells | 7" | Brunswick | 05943 | 1965 | £1.50 | £4 | |
| Show For Christmas Seals | LP | Decca | MG(7)9226 | 1962 | £6 | £15 | US |
| Sincerely | LP | Brunswick | LAT8396/STA3056 | 1961 | £6 | £15 | |
| Speak To Me Pretty | 7" EP | Brunswick | OE9488 | 1962 | £10 | £20 | |
| Speak To Me Pretty | 7" | Brunswick | 05867 | 1962 | £1.50 | £4 | |
| Sweet Impossible You | 7" | Brunswick | 05896 | 1963 | £1.50 | £4 | |
| Sweet Nothings | 7" | Brunswick | 05819 | 1960 | £7.50 | £15 | tri-centre |
| Ten Golden Years | LP | Decca | DL(7)4757 | 1966 | £5 | £12 | US, gatefold |
| Thanks A Lot | 7" | Brunswick | 05927 | 1965 | £1.50 | £4 | |
| That's All | LP | Brunswick | LAT/STA8516 | 1962 | £6 | £15 | |
| That's All Right | 7" | Decca | AD1003 | 1968 | | £8 | export |
| Think | 7" | Brunswick | 05903 | 1964 | £1.50 | £4 | |
| This Is Brenda Lee | LP | Brunswick | LAT8360 | 1960 | £6 | £15 | |
| Too Little Time | 7" | Brunswick | 05957 | 1966 | £1.50 | £4 | |
| Too Many Rivers | LP | Brunswick | LAT/STA8622 | 1965 | £6 | £15 | |
| Too Many Rivers | 7" | Brunswick | 05936 | 1965 | £1.50 | £4 | |
| Top Teen Hits | LP | Brunswick | LAT/STA8603 | 1965 | £6 | £15 | |
| Tribute To Al Jolson | 7" EP | Brunswick | OE9499 | 1964 | £10 | £20 | |
| Truly Truly True | 7" | Brunswick | 05933 | 1965 | £1.50 | £4 | |
| Versatile Brenda Lee | LP | Brunswick | LAT8614 | 1965 | £4 | £10 | |
| Where's The Melody | 7" | Brunswick | 05976 | 1967 | £1.50 | £4 | |
| You Can Depend On Me | 7" | Brunswick | 05849 | 1961 | £1.50 | £4 | |

## LEE, BUNNY ALL STARS

| Title | Format | Label | Cat. No. | Year | | | Notes |
|---|---|---|---|---|---|---|---|
| Leaping With Mr. Lee | LP | Island | ILP986 | 1968 | £30 | £60 | pink label |

## LEE, BYRON

| Title | Format | Label | Cat. No. | Year | | | Notes |
|---|---|---|---|---|---|---|---|
| Caribbean Jungle | LP | Island | ILP905 | 1964 | £20 | £40 | |
| Dumplings | 7" | Blue Beat | BB2 | 1960 | £6 | £12 | Buddy Davidson B side |
| Every Day Will Be Like A Holiday | 7" | Major Minor | MM615 | 1969 | £1.50 | £4 | |
| Jamaica Ska | 7" | Parlophone | R5182 | 1964 | £2 | £5 | |
| Joy Ride | 7" | Starlite | ST45045 | 1961 | £2 | £5 | |
| Mash Mr. Lee | 7" | Blue Beat | BB28 | 1961 | £6 | £12 | Keith Lynn B side |
| Mr. Walker | 7" | Trojan | TR631 | 1968 | £1.50 | £4 | |
| My Sweet Lord | 7" | Dynamic | DYN409 | 1971 | £1.50 | £4 | |
| Night Train From Jamaica | 7" | MGM | MGM1256 | 1964 | £2 | £5 | |
| Reggae | LP | Trojan | TRLS18 | 1972 | £4 | £10 | |
| Reggae Blast Off | LP | Trojan | TBL110 | 1970 | £4 | £10 | |
| Reggae Hot Cool Easy | LP | Trojan | TRLS40 | 1972 | £4 | £10 | |
| Reggae Splash Down | LP | Trojan | TRLS28 | 1972 | £4 | £10 | |
| River Bank | 7" | Parlophone | R5124 | 1964 | £2 | £5 | |
| Rocksteady Explosion | LP | Trojan | TTL5 | 1969 | £4 | £10 | |
| Say Bye Bye | 7" | Parlophone | R5140 | 1964 | £2 | £5 | |
| Ska Time | 7" EP | Atlantic | AET6014 | 1965 | £12.50 | £25 | |
| Sloopy | 7" | Doctor Bird | DB1003 | 1966 | £5 | £10 | |
| Sloopy | 7" | Pyramid | PYR6015 | 1967 | £1.50 | £4 | |
| Soul Limbo | 7" | Trojan | TR624 | 1968 | £1.50 | £4 | |
| Soul Serenade | 7" | Duke | DU39 | 1969 | £1.50 | £4 | |
| Sound Of Jamaica | LP | Tower Hall | LP006 | 1970 | £10 | £25 | US |
| Sour Apples | 7" | Parlophone | R5125 | 1964 | £2 | £5 | |
| Too Late | 7" | Parlophone | R5177 | 1964 | £2 | £5 | |
| Walk Like A Dragon | 7" | Island | WI220 | 1965 | £5 | £10 | Ken Lazarus B side |
| Way Back Home | 7" | Dynamic | DYN414 | 1971 | £1.50 | £4 | |

## LEE, CURTIS

| Title | Format | Label | Cat. No. | Year | | | Notes |
|---|---|---|---|---|---|---|---|
| Get My Bag | 7" | CBS | 2717 | 1967 | £7.50 | £15 | |
| Night At Daddy Gees | 7" | London | HLX9533 | 1962 | £4 | £8 | |
| Pledge Of Love | 7" | London | HLX9313 | 1961 | £4 | £8 | |
| Pretty Little Angel Eyes | 7" | London | HLX9397 | 1961 | £4 | £8 | |
| Under The Moon Of Love | 7" | London | HLX9445 | 1961 | £4 | £8 | |
| With All My Heart | 7" | Top Rank | JAR317 | 1960 | £12.50 | £25 | |

## LEE, DAVE
Adam Adamant ....................................... 7" ...... Fontana ........... TF723 .................... 1966 £1.50 ........ £4 ................................
Take Four ............................................... 7" ...... Decca ............. F11600 .................... 1963 £1.50 ........ £4 ................................

## LEE, DEREK
Girl ....................................................... 7" ...... Parlophone ...... R5468 ................... 1966 £1.50 ........ £4

## LEE, DICKIE
I Saw Linda Yesterday ............................. 7" ...... Mercury ......... AMT1196 .............. 1962 £2 ............. £5
Patches ................................................. 7" ...... Mercury ......... AMT1190 .............. 1962 £1.50 ........ £4
Penny A Kiss, A Penny A Hug ................. 7" ...... MGM ............ MGM1013 .............. 1959 £10 .......... £20

## LEE, DINAH
I Can't Believe What You Say .................. 7" ...... Aladdin .......... WI608 ................... 1965 £2.50 ........ £6
I'll Forgive You Then Forget You ............. 7" ...... Aladdin .......... WI606 ................... 1965 £2 ............. £5

## LEE, DON TONY
It's Reggae Time ..................................... 7" ...... Big Shot ......... BI504 ................... 1968 £2.50 ........ £6 .Errol Dunkley B side
It's Reggae Time ..................................... 7" ...... Island ............. WI3160 ................. 1968 £5 ............. £10 .Errol Dunkley B side
Lee's Special .......................................... 7" ...... Doctor Bird ..... DB1106 ............... 1967 £5 ............. £10 Lloyd & The Groovers
                                                                                                                                                        B side

## LEE, FREDDIE FINGERS
Bossy Boss ............................................ 7" ...... Columbia ........ DB8002 ............... 1966 £1.50 ........ £4
Friendly Undertaker ................................ 7" ...... Fontana ........... TF619 .................. 1965 £5 ............. £10
I'm Gonna Buy Me A Dog ...................... 7" ...... Fontana ........... TF655 .................. 1966 £4 ............. £8

## LEE, JACKIE
Duck ..................................................... LP ..... London ........... HAM8336 ............. 1967 £5 ............. £12
Duck ..................................................... LP ..... Mirwood .......... SW7000 .............. 1966 £8 ............. £20 ................................ US
Duck ..................................................... 7" ...... Fontana ........... TF646 .................. 1965 £5 ............. £10
Duck ..................................................... 7" ...... London ........... HLM10233 ........... 1968 £1.50 ........ £4
Whether It's Right Or Wrong ................... 7" ...... B&C ............... CB105 ................. 1969 £1.50 ........ £4 .....with Delores Hall

## LEE, JACKIE (2)
Rancho ................................................. 7" ...... Top Rank ........ JAR286 ................ 1960 £1.50 ........ £4
Town I Live In ...................................... 7" ...... Columbia ........ DB8052 ............... 1966 £1.50 ........ £4

## LEE, JACKIE (3)
Lonely Clown ........................................ 7" ...... Columbia ........ DB7685 ............... 1965 £1.50 ........ £4

## LEE, JAMIE & THE ATLANTICS
In The Night ......................................... 7" ...... Decca ............. F11571 ................. 1963 £7.50 ........ £15

## LEE, JIMMY
All My Life ............................................ 7" ...... Starlite ............ ST45059 ............... 1961 £6 ............. £12

## LEE, JOHNNIE
Kiss Tomorrow Goodbye .......................... 7" ...... CBS ............... 202591 ................. 1967 £1.50 ........ £4

## LEE, JULIA
Party Time ............................................ LP ..... Capitol ........... T228 .................... 1955 £15 .......... £30 ................................ US
Party Time ............................................ 10" LP Capitol ........... LC6535 ................ 1952 £15 .......... £30

## LEE, LADY
When Love Comes Along ......................... 7" ...... Decca ............. F11961 ................. 1964 £1.50 ........ £4

## LEE, LAURA
As Long As I Got You ............................. 7" ...... Chess ............. CRS8070 ............. 1968 £1.50 ........ £4
Dirty Man ............................................. 7" ...... Chess ............. CRS8062 ............. 1967 £1.50 ........ £4
Two Sides Of Laura Lee ......................... LP ..... Hot Wax ......... SHW5009 ............ 1972 £5 ............. £12
Woman's Love Rights .............................. LP ..... Hot Wax ......... SHW5006 ............ 1972 £5 ............. £12

## LEE, LAURA (2)
Brand New Heartbeat .............................. 7" ...... Decca ............. F11513 ................. 1962 £2 ............. £5
Tell Tommy I Miss Him .......................... 7" ...... Triumph .......... RGM1030 ............. 1960 £7.50 ........ £15

## LEE, LEAPY
Although comedian Lee Graham made a large number of singles and scored a top five hit with one of them ('Little Arrows'), his sole collectors' item is sought after because Ray Davies wrote and produced the A side, using members of the Kinks to provide the musical backing.

King Of The Whole Wide World ............... 7" ...... Decca ............. F12369 ................. 1966 £10 .......... £20

## LEE, NICKIE
And Black Is Beautiful ............................ 7" ...... Deep Soul ....... DS9103 ................ 1970 £1.50 ........ £4

## LEE, PEGGY
All Aglow Again ..................................... LP ..... Capitol ........... T1366 .................. 1961 £4 ............. £10
Alright Okay You Win ............................ 7" EP . Capitol ........... EAP11213 ............ 1959 £2 ............. £5
Basin Street East Presents ........................ LP ..... Capitol ........... (S)T1520 .............. 1962 £4 ............. £10
Baubles, Bangles And Beads .................... 7" ...... Brunswick ....... 05421 .................. 1955 £1.50 ........ £4
Beauty And The Beat .............................. LP ..... Capitol ........... (S)T1219 .............. 1960 £4 ............. £10 .with George Shearing
Beauty And The Beat Pt. 1 ...................... 7" EP . Capitol ........... EAP71219 ............ 1960 £2 ............. £5 .with George Shearing
Beauty And The Beat Pt. 2 ...................... 7" EP . Capitol ........... EAP81219 ............ 1960 £2 ............. £5 .with George Shearing
Beauty And The Beat Pt. 3 ...................... 7" EP . Capitol ........... EAP91219 ............ 1960 £2 ............. £5 .with George Shearing

| Title | Format | Label | Cat. No. | Year | | | Notes |
|---|---|---|---|---|---|---|---|
| Bella Notte | 7" | Brunswick | 05483 | 1955 | £1.50 | £4 | |
| Black Coffee | LP | Ace Of Hearts | AH5 | 1961 | £4 | £10 | |
| Black Coffee | LP | Decca | DL8358 | 1956 | £6 | £15 | US |
| Black Coffee | 10" LP | Brunswick | LA8629 | 1953 | £6 | £15 | |
| Blues Cross Country | LP | Capitol | (S)T1671 | 1962 | £4 | £10 | |
| Capitol Presents Peggy Lee | 10" LP | Capitol | LC6584 | 1953 | £6 | £15 | |
| Christmas Carousel | LP | Capitol | (S)T1423 | 1961 | £4 | £10 | |
| Dream Street | LP | Brunswick | LAT8171 | 1957 | £5 | £12 | |
| Favourites | 7" EP | Capitol | EAP120074 | 1961 | £2 | £5 | |
| Fever | 7" EP | Capitol | EAP11052 | 1959 | £2 | £5 | |
| Fever | 7" | Capitol | CL14902 | 1958 | £1.50 | £4 | |
| He Needs Me | 7" | Brunswick | 05472 | 1955 | £1.50 | £4 | |
| He's A Tramp | 7" | Brunswick | 05482 | 1955 | £2.50 | £6 | |
| I Belong To You | 7" | Brunswick | 05435 | 1955 | £1.50 | £4 | |
| I Go To Sleep | 7" | Capitol | CL15413 | 1965 | £1.50 | £4 | |
| I Like Men | LP | Capitol | (S)T1131 | 1959 | £4 | £10 | |
| I'm A Woman | 7" EP | Capitol | EAP41857 | 1961 | £2 | £5 | |
| If You Go | LP | Capitol | (S)T1630 | 1962 | £4 | £10 | |
| In The Name Of Love | 7" EP | Capitol | EAP42096 | 1963 | £2 | £5 | |
| Is That All There Is? | LP | Capitol | T386 | 1956 | £5 | £12 | US |
| Johnny Guitar | 7" | Brunswick | 05286 | 1954 | £2.50 | £6 | |
| Jump For Joy | LP | Capitol | (S)T979 | 1957 | £4 | £10 | |
| Jump For Joy | 7" EP | Capitol | EAP1979 | 1958 | £2 | £5 | |
| Lady And The Tramp | 10" LP | Brunswick | LA8731 | 1956 | £6 | £15 | |
| Latin à la Lee | LP | Capitol | (S)T1290 | 1960 | £4 | £10 | |
| Latin à la Lee Pt. 1 | 7" EP | Capitol | SEP51290 | 1961 | £2 | £5 | stereo |
| Latin à la Lee Pt. 2 | 7" EP | Capitol | SEP61290 | 1961 | £2 | £5 | stereo |
| Latin à la Lee Pt. 3 | 7" EP | Capitol | SEP71290 | 1961 | £2 | £5 | stereo |
| Let Me Go Lover | 7" | Brunswick | 05360 | 1955 | £2.50 | £6 | |
| Man I Love | LP | Capitol | T864 | 1956 | £4 | £10 | |
| Mink Jazz | LP | Capitol | (S)T1850 | 1964 | £4 | £10 | |
| Miss Wonderful | LP | Brunswick | LAT8287 | 1959 | £4 | £10 | |
| Mr. Wonderful | 7" | Brunswick | 05671 | 1957 | £1.50 | £4 | |
| My Best To You | 10" LP | Capitol | H204 | 1952 | £8 | £20 | US |
| My Best To You | 10" LP | Capitol | LC6817 | 1956 | £6 | £15 | |
| Ole à la Lee | LP | Capitol | (S)T1475 | 1966 | £4 | £10 | |
| Ole à la Lee Pt. 1 | 7" EP | Capitol | SEP11475 | 1961 | £2 | £5 | stereo |
| Ole à la Lee Pt. 2 | 7" EP | Capitol | SEP21475 | 1961 | £2 | £5 | stereo |
| Ooh That Kiss | 7" | Brunswick | 05461 | 1955 | £1.50 | £4 | |
| Peggy With Benny | 7" EP | Philips | BBE12172 | 1958 | £2 | £5 | with Benny Goodman |
| Pete Kelly's Blues | LP | Brunswick | LAT8078 | 1955 | £5 | £12 | |
| Pete Kelly's Blues No. 1 | 7" EP | Brunswick | OE9153 | 1955 | £2 | £5 | |
| Pete Kelly's Blues No. 2 | 7" EP | Brunswick | OE9154 | 1955 | £2 | £5 | |
| Presenting Peggy Lee | 7" EP | Brunswick | OE9282 | 1956 | £2 | £5 | |
| Pretty Eyes | LP | Capitol | (S)T1401 | 1960 | £4 | £10 | |
| Rendezvous | 10" LP | Capitol | H155 | 1952 | £8 | £20 | US |
| Sea Shells | LP | Brunswick | LAT8266 | 1958 | £5 | £12 | |
| Sisters | 7" | Brunswick | 05345 | 1954 | £2 | £5 | |
| Songs In An Intimate Style | 10" LP | Brunswick | LA8717 | 1955 | £6 | £15 | |
| Songs In Intimate Style | 10" LP | Decca | DL5539 | 1953 | £8 | £20 | US |
| Straight Ahead | 7" | Brunswick | 05368 | 1955 | £2 | £5 | |
| Sugar | 7" | Brunswick | 05471 | 1955 | £1.50 | £4 | |
| Sugar And Spice | 7" EP | Capitol | EAP11772 | 1961 | £2 | £5 | |
| Things Are Swingin' | LP | Capitol | T1049 | 1959 | £4 | £10 | |
| Things Are Swingin' | 7" EP | Capitol | EAP11049 | 1959 | £2 | £5 | |
| Three Cheers For Mister Magoo | 7" | Brunswick | 05549 | 1956 | £1.50 | £4 | |

## LEE, ROBERTA

| Title | Format | Label | Cat. No. | Year | | | Notes |
|---|---|---|---|---|---|---|---|
| Ridin' To Tennessee | 7" | Brunswick | 05388 | 1955 | £1.50 | £4 | |
| True Love And Tender Care | 7" | HMV | 7M261 | 1954 | £1.50 | £4 | |

## LEE, ROBIN

| Title | Format | Label | Cat. No. | Year | | | Notes |
|---|---|---|---|---|---|---|---|
| Gamblin' Man | 7" | Reprise | R20068 | 1962 | £2.50 | £6 | |

## LEE, VINNY & THE RIDERS

| Title | Format | Label | Cat. No. | Year | | | Notes |
|---|---|---|---|---|---|---|---|
| Gamblers Guitar | 7" | HMV | POP856 | 1961 | £2 | £5 | |

## LEE KINGS

| Title | Format | Label | Cat. No. | Year | | | Notes |
|---|---|---|---|---|---|---|---|
| Bingo | LP | RCA | 10106 | 1966 | £15 | £30 | Swedish |

## LEEMAN, MARK FIVE

| Title | Format | Label | Cat. No. | Year | | | Notes |
|---|---|---|---|---|---|---|---|
| Blow My Blues Away | 7" | Columbia | DB7648 | 1965 | £7.50 | £15 | |
| Follow Me | 7" | Columbia | DB7955 | 1966 | £5 | £10 | |
| Forbidden Fruit | 7" | Columbia | DB7812 | 1966 | £5 | £10 | |
| Portland Town | 7" | Columbia | DB7452 | 1965 | £5 | £10 | |

## LEER, THOMAS

| Title | Format | Label | Cat. No. | Year | | | Notes |
|---|---|---|---|---|---|---|---|
| Private Plane | 7" | Oblique | ER101 | 1978 | £2.50 | £6 | |

## LEES, JOHN

| Title | Format | Label | Cat. No. | Year | | | Notes |
|---|---|---|---|---|---|---|---|
| Best Of My Love | 7" | Polydor | 2058513 | 1974 | £2.50 | £6 | |

## LEESIDERS

| Title | Format | Label | Cat. No. | Year | | | Notes |
|---|---|---|---|---|---|---|---|
| Leesiders | LP | Ash | ALP105S | 1970 | £25 | £50 | |

## LEFEVRE, RAYMOND

| Title | Format | Label | Cat. No. | Year | | | Notes |
|---|---|---|---|---|---|---|---|
| Soul Coaxing | 7" | Major Minor | MM559 | 1968 | £1.50 | £4 | |

## LEFT BANKE

The delicate chamber and pop music made by the Left Banke is one of the overlooked delights of the sixties. Songs like 'Walk Away Renee' (covered by the Four Tops), 'Pretty Ballerina' and 'Desiree' are distinctive – beautiful even – and they were hits in America, but not Britain. The group's creative centre was pianist Michael Brown, but he rather squandered his talents by continual indecision as to whether he actually wanted to be in a group. The Left Banke duly floundered and Brown's attempts to relaunch himself via the groups Montage, Stories and the Beckies were not at all successful.

| | | | | | | | |
|---|---|---|---|---|---|---|---|
| Desiree | 7" | Philips | BF1614 | 1967 | £2 | £5 | |
| Desiree | 7" | Philips | BF1614 | 1967 | £4 | £8 | picture sleeve |
| Ivy Ivy | 7" | Philips | BF1575 | 1967 | £2 | £5 | |
| Pretty Ballerina | 7" | Philips | BF1540 | 1967 | £2 | £5 | |
| Too | LP | Smash | SRS67113 | 1968 | £20 | £40 | US |
| Walk Away Renee | LP | Philips | (S)BL7773 | 1967 | £15 | £30 | |
| Walk Away Renee | 7" | Philips | BF1517 | 1966 | £2 | £5 | |

## LEFT END

| | | | | | | | |
|---|---|---|---|---|---|---|---|
| Spoiled Rotten | LP | Polydor | PD6022 | 1975 | £8 | £20 | US |

## LEFT HANDED MARRIAGE

Brian May, the guitarist with Queen, was briefly a member of the Left Handed Marriage, but he does not play on the group's ultra-rare private pressing.

| | | | | | | | |
|---|---|---|---|---|---|---|---|
| On The Right Side Of The Left Handed Marriage | LP | private | | 1967 | £400 | £600 | |

## LEGAY

| | | | | | | | |
|---|---|---|---|---|---|---|---|
| No One | 7" | Fontana | TF904 | 1969 | £37.50 | £75 | |

## LEGEND

| | | | | | | | |
|---|---|---|---|---|---|---|---|
| Don't You Know | 7" | Vertigo | 6059036 | 1971 | £2 | £5 | |
| Georgia George | 7" | Bell | BLL1082 | 1970 | £2 | £5 | |
| Legend | LP | Bell | MBLL/SBLL115 | 1969 | £25 | £50 | |
| Life | 7" | Vertigo | 6059021 | 1971 | £2 | £5 | |
| Moonshine | LP | Vertigo | 6360063 | 1972 | £25 | £50 | spiral label |
| National Gas | 7" | Bell | BLL1048 | 1969 | £2.50 | £6 | |
| Red Boot Album | LP | Vertigo | 6360019 | 1971 | £25 | £50 | spiral label |

## LEGEND (2)

| | | | | | | | |
|---|---|---|---|---|---|---|---|
| 73 In '83 | 7" | Creation | CRE001 | 1983 | £2.50 | £6 | |
| 73 In '83 | 7" | Creation | CRE001 | 1983 | £5 | £10 | ...with flexi (by Pastels Laughing Apple) |
| Destroys The Blues | 7" | Creation | CRE010 | 1984 | £2.50 | £6 | |

## LEGEND (3)

| | | | | | | | |
|---|---|---|---|---|---|---|---|
| Death In The Nursey | LP | Workshop | WR3477 | 1982 | £4 | £10 | |
| Legend | LP | Workshop | WR3478 | 1980 | £4 | £10 | |

## LEGEND (4)

| | | | | | | | |
|---|---|---|---|---|---|---|---|
| Legend | LP | Megaphone | 101 | 1968 | £30 | £60 | US |

## LEGENDS

| | | | | | | | |
|---|---|---|---|---|---|---|---|
| I've Found Her | 7" | Pye | 7N15904 | 1965 | £2 | £5 | |
| Tomorrows's Gonna Be Another Day | 7" | Parlophone | R5581 | 1967 | £7.50 | £15 | |
| Under The Sky | 7" | Parlophone | R5613 | 1967 | £4 | £8 | |

## LEGENDS (2)

| | | | | | | | |
|---|---|---|---|---|---|---|---|
| Let Loose | LP | Capitol | (S)T1925 | 1963 | £8 | £20 | US |
| Let Loose | LP | Ermine | 101 | 1963 | £15 | £30 | US |

## LEGRAND, MICHEL

| | | | | | | | |
|---|---|---|---|---|---|---|---|
| Legrand Jazz | LP | Philips | BBL7328/SBBL510. | 1959 | £5 | £12 | |
| Legrand Piano | LP | Philips | BBL7378/SBBL572. | 1960 | £5 | £12 | |
| Never Say Never Again | LP | Seven Seas | K28P4122 | 1983 | £25 | £50 | Japanese |

## LEGRAND, MICHEL & GIL ASKEY

| | | | | | | | |
|---|---|---|---|---|---|---|---|
| Love Theme From Lady Sings The Blues | 7" | Tamla Motown | TMG848 | 1973 | £5 | £10 | ... demo, picture sleeve |

## LEGS DIAMOND

| | | | | | | | |
|---|---|---|---|---|---|---|---|
| Diamond Is A Hard Rock | LP | Mercury | SRM11191 | 1979 | £6 | £15 | US |
| Legs Diamond | LP | Mercury | SRM11136 | 1978 | £6 | £15 | US |

## LEHRER, TOM

| | | | | | | | |
|---|---|---|---|---|---|---|---|
| Evening Wasted | LP | Decca | LK4332/SKL4097 | 1960 | £4 | £10 | |
| More Of Tom Lehrer | 10" LP | Decca | LF1323 | 1959 | £4 | £10 | |
| Poisoning Pigeons In The Park | 7" | Decca | F11243 | 1960 | £1.50 | £4 | picture sleeve |
| Songs By Tom Lehrer | 10" LP | Decca | LF1311 | 1958 | £4 | £10 | |
| Tom Lehrer Revisited | LP | Decca | LK4375 | 1960 | £4 | £10 | |

## LEIBER, JERRY

| | | | | | | | |
|---|---|---|---|---|---|---|---|
| Scooby-Doo | LP | Kapp | KL1127 | 1959 | £10 | £25 | US |

## LEIBER STOLLER ORCHESTRA

| | | | | | | | |
|---|---|---|---|---|---|---|---|
| Blue Baion | 7" | HMV | POP1050 | 1962 | £2.50 | £6 | |
| Yakety Yak | LP | Atlantic | (SD)847 | 1960 | £8 | £20 | US |

## LEIBSTANDARTE SS
| | | | | | | | |
|---|---|---|---|---|---|---|---|
| Triumph Of The Will | LP | Come Organisation | | 1981 | £30 | £60 | |
| Weltanschauung | LP | Come Organisation | | 198– | £20 | £40 | |

## LEIGH, ANDY
| | | | | | | | |
|---|---|---|---|---|---|---|---|
| Magician | LP | Polydor | 2343034 | 1970 | £4 | £10 | |

## LELAND
| | | | | | | | |
|---|---|---|---|---|---|---|---|
| This Is My World | LP | Contempt | R2954 | 1978 | £8 | £20 | US |

## LEMER, PETE
| | | | | | | | |
|---|---|---|---|---|---|---|---|
| Local Colour | LP | ESP-Disk | 1057 | 1968 | £25 | £50 | US |

## LEMMINGS
| | | | | | | | |
|---|---|---|---|---|---|---|---|
| Out Of My Mind | 7" | Pye | 7N15837 | 1965 | £2 | £5 | |
| You Can't Blame Me For Trying | 7" | Pye | 7N15899 | 1965 | £2 | £5 | |

## LEMON DIPS
| | | | | | | | |
|---|---|---|---|---|---|---|---|
| Who's Gonna Buy? | LP | De Wolfe | DWLP3114 | 1969 | £37.50 | £75 | |

## LEMON KITTENS
| | | | | | | | |
|---|---|---|---|---|---|---|---|
| Big Dentist | LP | Illuminated | JAMS131 | 1982 | £15 | £30 | |
| Cake Beast | 12" | United Dairies | UD07 | 1981 | £10 | £20 | |
| Spoonfed And Writhing | 7" | Step Forward | SF10 | 1979 | £5 | £10 | |
| We Buy A Hammer For Daddy | LP | United Dairies | UD02 | 1980 | £20 | £40 | |

## LEMON PIPERS
| | | | | | | | |
|---|---|---|---|---|---|---|---|
| Green Tambourine | LP | Buddah | 2349006 | 1970 | £4 | £10 | |
| Green Tambourine | LP | Pye | NPL28112 | 1968 | £5 | £12 | |
| Green Tambourine | 7" | Pye | 7N25444 | 1968 | £1.50 | £4 | |
| Jelly Jungle | 7" | Pye | 7N25464 | 1968 | £2.50 | £6 | |
| Jungle Marmalade | LP | Pye | NSPL28118 | 1969 | £4 | £10 | |
| Rice Is Nice | 7" | Pye | 7N25454 | 1968 | £1.50 | £4 | |

## LEMON PIPERS & NINETEEN TEN FRUITGUM COMPANY
| | | | | | | | |
|---|---|---|---|---|---|---|---|
| Presenting | 7" EP | Pye | NEP44091 | 1968 | £2.50 | £6 | |

## LEMON TREE
| | | | | | | | |
|---|---|---|---|---|---|---|---|
| It's So Nice To Come Home | 7" | Parlophone | R5739 | 1968 | £2.50 | £6 | |
| William Chalker's Time Machine | 7" | Parlophone | R5671 | 1968 | £5 | £10 | |

## LEMONHEADS
| | | | | | | | |
|---|---|---|---|---|---|---|---|
| Car Button Cloth | CD | Atlantic | PROP214 | 1996 | £12.50 | £25 | promo with extra track |
| Different Drum | CD-s | Roughneck | HYPE3CD | 1990 | £2 | £5 | |
| Gonna Get Along Without Ya Now | 7" | Atlantic | A7709 | 1991 | £2 | £5 | |
| Hate Your Friends | LP | Taang! | T15 | 1987 | £6 | £15 | US, yellow label and sleeve lettering |
| Hate Your Friends | LP | Taang! | T15 | 1987 | £5 | £12 | US, yellow label, sleeve lettering, vinyl |
| Laughing All The Way To The Cleaners | 7" | Armory Arms | 1/2/Huh-Bag1 | 1986 | £37.50 | £75 | US |
| Lick | CD | World Service | SERV007 | 1989 | £5 | £12 | |
| Luka | CD-s | World Service | SERVS010CD | 1989 | £2 | £5 | |
| Luka | 7" | Taang | TAANG031 | 1989 | £2 | £5 | |

## LENNON, FREDDIE

John Lennon's father was one of the many people who tried to divert a little piece of Beatlemania in his own direction, but with no more success than most of the others.

| | | | | | | | |
|---|---|---|---|---|---|---|---|
| That's My Life | 7" EP | Pye | PNV24172 | 1966 | £25 | £50 | French, B side by Brian Diamond & The Cutters |
| That's My Life | 7" | Piccadilly | 7N35290 | 1966 | £15 | £30 | |

## LENNON, JIMMY & THE ATLANTICS
| | | | | | | | |
|---|---|---|---|---|---|---|---|
| I Learned To Yodel | 7" | Decca | F11825 | 1964 | £7.50 | £15 | |

## LENNON, JOHN

The expensive albums recorded by John Lennon and Yoko Ono together are rare because, at the height of the Beatles influence and popularity, even John Lennon could not sell records of a foetal heartbeat, inconsequential chatter, ambient noises, and the like. Later Lennon–Ono collaborations include some excellent and underrated pieces of rock avant-garde, such as the superbly cathartic 'Open Your Box', but the early records are strictly for the completist. The American *Roots* album is not a bootleg (although bootleg copies of the Adam VIII original do exist). The owner of the label claimed that Lennon had assigned the album to him and began an intensive TV advertising campaign for it. Lennon disagreed, however, and won a court injunction for the record's withdrawal. *Roots* is of particular interest to collectors because it consists of the original version of the LP that became *Rock 'n' Roll* – all the tracks are Phil Spector productions and the selection of songs is slightly different. The rare version of the 'Cold Turkey' single picture sleeve differs from the regular commercial UK issue in having the X-ray skulls together on the front, rather than one on each side. A French issue duplicates the rare design, but with a green and black sleeve, and it is rather more common (selling for £30).

| | | | | | | | |
|---|---|---|---|---|---|---|---|
| Cold Turkey | 7" | Apple | 1001 | 1969 | £5 | £10 | picture sleeve |
| Cold Turkey | 7" | Apple | 1001 | 1969 | £100 | £200 | two skulls (on one side) picture sleeve, Dutch or promo |
| Double Fantasy | LP | Nautilus | NR47 | 1980 | £10 | £25 | US audiophile, poster, with Yoko Ono |

| Title | Format | Label | Catalogue | Year | | | Notes |
|---|---|---|---|---|---|---|---|
| Double Fantasy | CD | Geffen | 299131 | 1983 | £5 | £12 | with Yoko Ono |
| Double Fantasy | CD | Mobile Fidelity | UDCD600 | 1991 | £6 | £15 | US audiophile, with Yoko Ono |
| Give Peace A Chance | 7" | Apple | 13 | 1969 | £2.50 | £6 | picture sleeve |
| Give Peace A Chance | 7" | Apple | R5795 | 1969 | £7.50 | £15 | |
| Happy First Birthday Capital Radio | 7" | Warner Bros | SAM20 | 1974 | £15 | £30 | promo |
| Happy Xmas (War Is Over) | 7" | Apple | R5970 | 1972 | £2 | £5 | picture sleeve, green vinyl, with Yoko Ono |
| Imagine | LP | Apple | PAS10004 | 1971 | £4 | £10 | inner, postcard |
| Imagine | LP | Apple | Q4PAS10004 | 1974 | £50 | £100 | quad |
| Imagine | LP | Mobile Fidelity | MFSL1153 | 1984 | £6 | £15 | US audiophile |
| Imagine | CD-s | Parlophone | CDR6199 | 1988 | £2 | £5 | |
| Imagine | 7" | Apple | R6009 | 1975 | £2.50 | £6 | picture sleeve |
| Imagine | 7" | Parlophone | RP6199 | 1988 | £1.50 | £4 | picture disc |
| Instant Karma | 7" | Apple | 1003 | 1970 | £2.50 | £6 | picture sleeve |
| John Lennon | LP | Parlophone | JLB8 | 1981 | £30 | £60 | 8 LP boxed set |
| John Lennon Collection | LP | Geffen | LS2023 | 1982 | £6 | £15 | US audiophile promo |
| John Lennon Collection | CD | Parlophone | CDEMTV37 | 1989 | £6 | £15 | with promo edit of 'Number Nine Dream' |
| John Lennon On Ronnie Hawkins | 7" | Atlantic | PRO104 | 1970 | £25 | £50 | US promo |
| John Lennon On Ronnie Hawkins | 7" | Cotillion | PR105 | 1970 | £15 | £30 | US promo |
| KYA Peace Talk | LP | Capitol | KYA1969 | 1969 | £25 | £50 | US promo, with Yoko Ono |
| Live Peace In Toronto | LP | Apple | CORE2001 | 1969 | £25 | £50 | with calendar, with Yoko Ono |
| Live Peace In Toronto | CD | Parlophone | CDP7904282 | 1989 | £5 | £12 | with Yoko Ono |
| Milk And Honey | LP | Polydor | POLHP5 | 1984 | £8 | £20 | picture disc, thick |
| Milk And Honey | CD | Polydor | 8171602 | 1990 | £5 | £12 | with Yoko Ono |
| Mind Games | 7" | Apple | R5994 | 1973 | £2 | £5 | picture sleeve |
| Number Nine Dream (2 versions) | 7" | Apple | R6003DJ | 1974 | £15 | £30 | promo |
| Power To The People | 7" | Apple | R5892 | 1971 | £4 | £8 | picture sleeve |
| Roots | LP | Adam VIII | LP8018 | 1975 | £100 | £200 | US |
| Sometime In New York City | CD | Parlophone | CDS7467828 | 1987 | £10 | £25 | double, with Yoko Ono |
| Unfinished Music No. 1: Two Virgins | LP | Apple | APCOR2 | 1968 | £500 | £750 | mono, with Yoko Ono |
| Unfinished Music No. 1: Two Virgins | LP | Apple | SAPCOR2 | 1968 | £100 | £200 | stereo, with Yoko Ono |
| Unfinished Music No. 2: Life With The Lions | LP | Apple | ZAPPLE1 | 1969 | £37.50 | £75 | card insert, with Yoko Ono |
| Unfinished Music No. 2: Life With The Lions | LP | Apple | ZAPPLE1 | 1969 | £30 | £60 | with Yoko Ono |
| Wedding Album | LP | Apple | SAPCOR11 | 1969 | £62.50 | £125 | boxed, inserts, with Yoko Ono |
| Whatever Gets You Thru The Night | 7" | EMI | PSR369 | 1974 | £75 | £150 | interview promo |
| Woman Is The Nigger Of The World | 7" | Apple | R5953 | 1972 | £100 | £200 | demo only, best auctioned |
| You Know My Name | 7" | Apple | 1002 | 1969 | £1050 | £1500 | test pressing, best auctioned |

## LENNON, JULIAN

| Title | Format | Label | Catalogue | Year | | | Notes |
|---|---|---|---|---|---|---|---|
| Too Late For Goodbyes | 7" | Charisma | JLY1 | 1984 | £2 | £5 | picture disc |
| Valotte | 7" | Charisma | JLS2 | 1984 | £2.50 | £6 | shaped picture disc |

## LENNON SISTERS

| Title | Format | Label | Catalogue | Year | | | Notes |
|---|---|---|---|---|---|---|---|
| Graduation Day | 7" | Vogue Coral | Q72176 | 1956 | £1.50 | £4 | |
| Shake Me I Rattle | 7" | Vogue Coral | Q72285 | 1957 | £2 | £5 | |
| Young And In Love | 7" | Vogue Coral | Q72259 | 1957 | £1.50 | £4 | |

## LENNOX, ANNIE

| Title | Format | Label | Catalogue | Year | | | Notes |
|---|---|---|---|---|---|---|---|
| Diva | CD | Arista | | 1992 | £10 | £25 | US promo with bonus interview disc |

## LENOIR, J. B.

| Title | Format | Label | Catalogue | Year | | | Notes |
|---|---|---|---|---|---|---|---|
| Alabama Blues | LP | CBS | 62593 | 1966 | £8 | £20 | |
| Crusade | LP | Polydor | 2482014 | 1970 | £4 | £10 | |
| I Sing The Way I Feel | 7" | Sue | WI339 | 1965 | £5 | £10 | |
| J. B. Lenoir | LP | Python | PLP25 | 1972 | £8 | £20 | |
| J. B. Lenoir | LP | Rarity | LP2 | 1975 | £6 | £15 | |
| Man Watch Your Woman | 7" | Bootleg | 503 | 1965 | £10 | £20 | |
| Mojo Boogie | 7" | Blue Horizon | 451004 | 1966 | £50 | £100 | |
| Natural Man | LP | Chess | 1410 | 1963 | £8 | £20 | US |

## LENT, ROBIN

| Title | Format | Label | Catalogue | Year | | | Notes |
|---|---|---|---|---|---|---|---|
| Scarecrow's Journey | LP | Nepentha | 6437002 | 1971 | £8 | £20 | |

## LENTILMAS

The Lentilmas flexi-disc was a promotional release given away to journalists as a 1977 Christmas present. The record is supposed to include Christmas carols sung by the Sex Pistols.

| Title | Format | Label | Catalogue | Year | | | Notes |
|---|---|---|---|---|---|---|---|
| Lentilmas | 7" | Virgin | no number | 1977 | £62.50 | £125 | flexi |

## LENTON, VAL

| Title | Format | Label | Catalogue | Year | | | Notes |
|---|---|---|---|---|---|---|---|
| You Don't Care | 7" | Immediate | IM008 | 1965 | £5 | £10 | |

## LEONARD, DEKE

| Title | Format | Label | Catalogue | Year | | | Notes |
|---|---|---|---|---|---|---|---|
| Nothing Is Happening | 7" | United Artists | UP35556 | 1973 | £2 | £5 | demo |

## LEONETTI, TOMMY
| | | | | | | | |
|---|---|---|---|---|---|---|---|
| Dream Lover | 7" | RCA | RCA1107 | 1959 | £1.50 | £4 | |
| Ever Since You Went Away | 7" | Capitol | CL14272 | 1955 | £1.50 | £4 | |
| That's What You Made Me | 7" | Capitol | CL14199 | 1954 | £1.50 | £4 | |

## LEO'S SUNSHIPP
| | | | | | | | |
|---|---|---|---|---|---|---|---|
| Give Me The Sunshine | 12" | Grapevine | REDC3 | 1979 | £4 | £10 | |

## LEROY & ROCKY
| | | | | | | | |
|---|---|---|---|---|---|---|---|
| Love Me Girl | 7" | Studio One | SO2042 | 1968 | £6 | £12 | *Wrigglers B side* |

## LEROYS
| | | | | | | | |
|---|---|---|---|---|---|---|---|
| Chills | 7" | HMV | POP1312 | 1964 | £2 | £5 | |
| Don't Cry Baby | 7" | HMV | POP1274 | 1964 | £1.50 | £4 | |
| Money | 7" | Lyntone | LYN504 | 1963 | £2 | £5 | *flexi* |

## LES COMPAGNONS DE LA CHANSON
| | | | | | | | |
|---|---|---|---|---|---|---|---|
| Galley Slave | 7" | Columbia | SCM5056 | 1953 | £4 | £8 | |
| Song Successes In English | 7" EP | Columbia | SEG7829 | 1958 | £2 | £5 | |
| Three Bells | 7" | Columbia | SCM5005 | 1953 | £5 | £10 | |

## LES COPAINS
| | | | | | | | |
|---|---|---|---|---|---|---|---|
| Les Croulants | LP | Symco | 100 | 1963 | £8 | £20 | *French* |

## LES CRUCHES
| | | | | | | | |
|---|---|---|---|---|---|---|---|
| Live | LP | CBS | 52499 | 1968 | £10 | £25 | *Dutch* |

## LES FLAMBEAUX
| | | | | | | | |
|---|---|---|---|---|---|---|---|
| Les Flambeaux | LP | Mushroom | 100MR13 | 1971 | £15 | £30 | |

## LES GOSSES
| | | | | | | | |
|---|---|---|---|---|---|---|---|
| 1 April 1963 – 31 Mei 1971 | LP | private | | 1971 | £500 | £750 | *Dutch* |

## LES HABITS JAUNES
| | | | | | | | |
|---|---|---|---|---|---|---|---|
| Canada Beat! | LP | Laval | 4202 | 1964 | £6 | £15 | *Canadian* |

## LES HOBEAUX
| | | | | | | | |
|---|---|---|---|---|---|---|---|
| Dynamo | 7" | HMV | POP444 | 1958 | £5 | £10 | |
| Mama Don't Allow | 7" | HMV | POP403 | 1957 | £5 | £10 | |
| Oh Mary Don't You Weep | 7" | HMV | POP377 | 1957 | £5 | £10 | |
| Soho Skiffle | 7" EP | HMV | 7EG8297 | 1957 | £10 | £20 | |

## LES MISSILES
| | | | | | | | |
|---|---|---|---|---|---|---|---|
| Les Missiles de France | 7" EP | Columbia | SEG8371 | 1964 | £2 | £5 | |

## LES NAPOLEONS
| | | | | | | | |
|---|---|---|---|---|---|---|---|
| A Go Go | LP | Passe Temps | 17 | 1965 | £30 | £60 | *Canadian* |

## LES PLAYERS
| | | | | | | | |
|---|---|---|---|---|---|---|---|
| Les Players | 7" EP | Polydor | EPH27129 | 1965 | £2 | £5 | |

## LES RITA MITSOUKO
| | | | | | | | |
|---|---|---|---|---|---|---|---|
| Singing In The Shower | CD-s | Virgin | VSCD1163 | 1989 | £4 | £10 | |

## LES SAUTERELLES
| | | | | | | | |
|---|---|---|---|---|---|---|---|
| Heavenly Club | 7" | Decca | F22824 | 1968 | £12.50 | £25 | |

## LES ZARJAZ
| | | | | | | | |
|---|---|---|---|---|---|---|---|
| One Charming Nyte | 7" | Creation | CRE013 | 1985 | £2 | £5 | |

## LESLEY, LORNE
| | | | | | | | |
|---|---|---|---|---|---|---|---|
| So High So Low | 7" | Parlophone | R4581 | 1959 | £1.50 | £4 | |
| We're Gonna Dance | 7" | Polydor | NH66956 | 1960 | £2 | £5 | |

## LESLEY, MICHAEL
| | | | | | | | |
|---|---|---|---|---|---|---|---|
| Make Up Or Break Up | 7" | Pye | 7N15959 | 1965 | £2.50 | £6 | |

## LESLIE, JOHN & CHRIS
| | | | | | | | |
|---|---|---|---|---|---|---|---|
| Ship Of Time | LP | Cottage | COT901 | 1976 | £6 | £15 | |

## LESTER, KETTY
| | | | | | | | |
|---|---|---|---|---|---|---|---|
| Ketty Lester | 7" EP | London | REN1348 | 1962 | £6 | £12 | |
| Love Letters | LP | Era | EL/ES108 | 1963 | £8 | £20 | *US* |
| Love Letters | 7" | London | HLN9527 | 1962 | £1.50 | £4 | |
| Roses Grow With Thorns | 7" | RCA | RCA1403 | 1964 | £6 | £12 | |
| Some Things Are Better Left Unsaid | 7" | RCA | RCA1394 | 1964 | £12.50 | £25 | |
| Soul Of Me | LP | RCA | RD7669 | 1964 | £5 | £12 | |
| West Coast | 7" | Capitol | CL15427 | 1965 | £5 | £10 | |
| Where Is Love | LP | RCA | RD7712 | 1965 | £5 | £12 | |

## LETHE
| | | | | | | | |
|---|---|---|---|---|---|---|---|
| Lethe | LP | M.M.P. | | 1981 | £50 | £100 | *Dutch* |

## LETTERMEN
| | | | | | | | |
|---|---|---|---|---|---|---|---|
| Lettermen | 7" EP | Capitol | EAP41669 | 1961 | £2 | £5 | |

## LETTERMEN (2)
First Class .......................................... LP ..... Stag ................ SG10075 ................ 1974 £87.50 .. £175 ..............................

## LETTS, DON & JAH WOBBLE
Steel Leg: Stratetime And The Wide Man... 7" ...... Virgin ............ VS239 .................... 1979 £2.50 ....... £6 ..............................

## LEVEE BREAKERS
Baby I'm Leaving You .............................. 7" ...... Parlophone ... R5291 .................... 1965 £7.50 ....... £15 ..............................

## LEVEE CAMP MOAN
Levee Camp Moan ................................. LP ..... County .......... no number ............ 1969 £330 ..... £500 ..............................
Peacock Farm ...................................... LP ..... County .......... no number ............ 1969 £250 ..... £400 ..............................

## LEVEL 42
Children Say .......................................... 7" ...... Polydor ......... POSPP911 ............ 1987 £1.50 ...... £4 ........... picture disc
Children Say (Extended Remix) ........... CD-s .. Polydor ......... POCD911 ............ 1987 £2 .......... £5 ........... card sleeve
Chinese Way .......................................... 12" .... Polydor ......... POSPPX538 .......... 1983 £3 .......... £8 ........... double
Chinese Way .......................................... 12" .... Polydor ......... POSPX538 ........... 1983 £6 .......... £15 ...... yellow vinyl
Family Of Five ....................................... CD-s .. Polygram ...... 0802769 ............. 1988 £4 .......... £10 ...... CD video
Guaranteed ........................................... CD-s .. RCA ............. PD44746 ............. 1991 £2 .......... £5 ..............................
Guaranteed ........................................... CD .... RCA ............. PD75005 ............. 1991 £10 ......... £25 ... promo box set with
cassette
Heaven In My Hands.............................. CD-s .. Polydor ......... PZCD14 ............... 1988 £2 .......... £5 ..............................
Heaven In My Hands.............................. CD-s .. Polygram ...... 0805022 ............. 1988 £4 .......... £10 ...... CD video
Hot Water ............................................. 12" .... Polydor ......... POSPA697 ........... 1986 £10 ......... £20 ..............................
It's Over................................................ CD-s .. Polygram ...... 0801562 ............. 1989 £4 .......... £10 ...... CD video
Leaving Me Now .................................... CD-s .. Polygram ...... 0802182 ............. 1988 £4 .......... £10 ...... CD video
Leaving Me Now .................................... 10" .... Polydor ......... POSPT776 ........... 1985 £2.50 ...... £6 ..............................
Lessons In Love ..................................... CD-s .. Polygram ...... 0800042 ............. 1988 £4 .......... £10 ...... CD video
Love Meeting Love ................................ 12" .... Elite ............... DAZZ5 ................. 1980 £15 ......... £30 ...... no picture sleeve
Love Meeting Love ................................ 12" .... Polydor ......... POSPX170 ........... 1980 £4 .......... £10 ...... no picture sleeve
Micro-Kid ............................................. 12" .... Polydor ......... POSPX643 ........... 1983 £10 ......... £20 ...... double
Out Of Sight Out Of Mind..................... 7" ...... Polydor ......... POSPP570 ........... 1983 £2 .......... £5 ........... picture disc
Out Of Sight Out Of Mind..................... 12" .... Polydor ......... POSPP570 ........... 1984 £2.50 ...... £6 ........... picture disc
Out Of Sight Out Of Mind..................... 12" .... Polydor ......... POSPX570 ........... 1984 £2.50 ...... £6 ..............................
Overtime................................................ CD-s .. RCA ............. PD44998 ............. 1991 £2 .......... £5 ..............................
Running In The Family ........................... CD-s .. Polygram ...... 0800002 ............. 1988 £4 .......... £10 ...... CD video
Running In The Family (Platinum Edition) CD .... Polydor ......... 8836892 ............. 1987 £5 .......... £12 .... with extra remixes
Sandstorm............................................. 12" .... Elite ............... DAZZ4................. 1980 £50 ......... £100 ...... promo
Something About You............................ 10" .... Polydor ......... POSPT759 ........... 1985 £2.50 ...... £6 ..............................
Strategy ............................................... LP ..... Elite ............... LEVLP1 ............... 1981 £250 ..... £400 ...... test pressing only
Take A Look .......................................... CD-s .. Polydor ......... PZCD24 ............... 1988 £2 .......... £5 ..............................
Take A Look .......................................... CD-s .. Polygram ...... 0805762 ............. 1989 £4 .......... £10 ...... CD video
Take Care Of Yourself............................ CD-s .. Polydor ......... PZCD58 ............... 1989 £2 .......... £5 ..............................
To Be With You Again ........................... 7" ...... Polydor ......... POSPP855 ........... 1987 £1.50 ...... £4 ........... picture disc
Tracie................................................... CD-s .. Polydor ......... PZCD34 ............... 1989 £2 .......... £5 ..............................
Wings Of Love ...................................... 7" ...... Polydor ......... POSP200 ............. 1980 £1.50 ...... £4 ........ no picture sleeve
Wings Of Love ...................................... 12" .... Polydor ......... POSPX200 ........... 1980 £4 .......... £10 ...... no picture sleeve
Wings Of Love (Remix) .......................... 12" .... Polydor ......... POSPX200 ........... 1981 £6 .......... £15 ...... no picture sleeve
You Can't Blame Louis............................ 12" .... Polydor ......... POSPX500 ........... 1982 £15 ......... £30 ...... test pressing, no
picture sleeve

## LEVELLERS
Agreement Of The People ...................... cass ..... private................ ...................... 1989 £6 .......... £15 ..............................
All The Free Commons Of England........... cass ... private................ ...................... 1988 £6 .......... £15 ..............................
Big Friday............................................. CD-s .. Probe Plus ...... PP25CD ............. 1990 £2 .......... £5 ..............................
Carry Me.............................................. 12" .... Hag ............... HAG005 ............. 1989 £6 .......... £15 ... Brighton address on
sleeve
Far From Home ..................................... CD-s .. China ............ WOKCD2010 ...... 1991 £2 .......... £5 ..............................
Live 1992 ............................................. LP ..... On The Fiddle.. OTFLP2 ............. 1992 £4 .......... £10 ..............................
One Way............................................... CD-s .. China ............ WOKCD2008 ...... 1991 £2 .......... £5 ..............................
Outside Inside ...................................... 7" ...... Hag ............... HAG006 ............. 1989 £5 .......... £10 ...... promo only
Peel Sessions ....................................... CD-s .. Strange Fruit.... SFPSCD083 ........... 1991 £2 .......... £5 ..............................

## LEVENE, GERRY & THE AVENGERS
Doctor Feelgood ................................... 7" ...... Decca ............. F11815 ............... 1964 £10 ......... £20 ..............................

## LEVEY, STAN
Grand Stan ........................................... LP ..... London .......... LTZN15100........... 1957 £6 .......... £15 ..............................
This Time The Drum's On Me ................. LP ...... Parlophone ...... PMC1086 ............ 1959 £6 .......... £15 ..............................

## LEVIATHAN
Flames................................................. 7" ...... Elektra ............ EKSN45075 ......... 1969 £10 ...... £20 ..............................
Remember The Times.............................. 7" ...... Elektra ............ EKSN45052 ......... 1968 £10 ...... £20 ..............................
War Machine ......................................... 7" ...... Elektra ............ EKSN45057 ......... 1969 £10 ...... £20 ..............................

## LEVINE, HANK
Image.................................................. 7" ...... HMV............... POP947 .............. 1961 £2.50 ...... £6 ..............................

## LEVITATION
Need For Not......................................... LP ..... Rough Trade... R2861 ................. 1992 £4 ........... £10 ...with 7" (LEV001)
and etching

## LEVON & THE HAWKS
Go Go, Lisa Jane ................................... 7" ...... Atco ............... 6625 ............... 1968 £10 ...... £20 ..............................US
Stones I Throw ...................................... 7" ...... Atlantic ........... AT4054................. 1965 £10 ......... £20 ..............................

## LEVY, BEN
| | | | | | | | |
|---|---|---|---|---|---|---|---|
| Doren | 7" | Ska Beat | JB245 | 1966 | £5 | £10 | |
| I'll Make You Glad | 7" | Ska Beat | JB255 | 1966 | £5 | £10 | |

## LEVY, KEN & THE PHANTOMS
| | | | | | | | |
|---|---|---|---|---|---|---|---|
| Ken Levy And The Phantoms | LP | Nashville | NSLP30102 | 1965 | £37.50 | £75 | |
| Swedish Wow! | LP | Nashville | NSLP30101 | 1964 | £50 | £100 | Swedish |

## LEWIS, ALVA
| | | | | | | | |
|---|---|---|---|---|---|---|---|
| Return Home | 7" | Caltone | TONE111 | 1967 | £4 | £8 | King Rock B side |

## LEWIS, BARBARA
| | | | | | | | |
|---|---|---|---|---|---|---|---|
| Baby I'm Yours | LP | Atlantic | ATL5042 | 1966 | £6 | £15 | |
| Baby I'm Yours | 7" | Atlantic | AT4031 | 1965 | £2.50 | £6 | |
| Baby What Do You Want Me To Do | 7" | Atlantic | 584061 | 1967 | £7.50 | £15 | |
| Don't Forget About Me | 7" | Atlantic | AT4068 | 1966 | £2.50 | £6 | |
| Hello Stranger | LP | Atlantic | (SD)8086 | 1963 | £10 | £25 | US |
| Hello Stranger | 7" | Atlantic | 584153 | 1968 | £2 | £5 | |
| Hello Stranger | 7" | London | HLK9724 | 1963 | £4 | £8 | |
| It's Magic | LP | Atlantic | 587002 | 1966 | £6 | £15 | |
| Make Me Belong To You | 7" | Atlantic | 584037 | 1966 | £1.50 | £4 | |
| Make Me Your Baby | 7" | Atlantic | AT4041 | 1965 | £2.50 | £6 | |
| Pushing A Good Thing Too Far | 7" | Atlantic | AT4013 | 1964 | £2.50 | £6 | |
| Sho-Nuff | 7" | Atlantic | 584174 | 1968 | £1.50 | £4 | |
| Snap Your Fingers | LP | Atlantic | (SD)8090 | 1964 | £10 | £25 | US |
| Snap Your Fingers | 7" EP | Atlantic | AET6015 | 1965 | £10 | £20 | |
| Snap Your Fingers | 7" | London | HLK9832 | 1964 | £4 | £8 | |
| Some Day We're Gonna Love Again | 7" | Atlantic | 2091143 | 1971 | £1.50 | £4 | |
| Straighten Up Your Heart | 7" | London | HLK9779 | 1963 | £4 | £8 | |
| Workin' On A Groovy Thing | LP | Atlantic | SD8173 | 1968 | £6 | £15 | US |

## LEWIS, BOBBY
| | | | | | | | |
|---|---|---|---|---|---|---|---|
| I'm Tossing And Turning Again | 7" | Stateside | SS126 | 1962 | £4 | £8 | |
| One Track Mind | 7" | Parlophone | R4831 | 1961 | £4 | £8 | |
| Tossing And Turning | LP | Beltone | 4000 | 1961 | £25 | £50 | US |
| Tossing And Turning | 7" | Parlophone | R4794 | 1961 | £5 | £10 | |

## LEWIS, DAVE
| | | | | | | | |
|---|---|---|---|---|---|---|---|
| Giving Gas | 7" EP | Pye | NEP44057 | 1966 | £5 | £10 | |

## LEWIS, DAVID
| | | | | | | | |
|---|---|---|---|---|---|---|---|
| Songs Of David Lewis | LP | private | AX1 | 1970 | £210 | £350 | |

## LEWIS, FURRY
| | | | | | | | |
|---|---|---|---|---|---|---|---|
| Back On My Feet Again | LP | Bluesville | BV(S)1036 | 1961 | £10 | £25 | US |
| Early Years 1927–9 | LP | Spookane | SPL1004 | 1971 | £10 | £25 | |
| Furry Lewis | LP | Folkways | FS3823 | 1961 | £10 | £25 | |
| Furry Lewis | LP | Xtra | XTRA116 | 1971 | £4 | £10 | |
| In Memphis | LP | Saydisc | SDR190 | 1970 | £4 | £10 | |
| Presenting The Country Blues | LP | Blue Horizon | 763228 | 1969 | £20 | £40 | |

## LEWIS, GARY & THE PLAYBOYS
| | | | | | | | |
|---|---|---|---|---|---|---|---|
| Count Me In | 7" EP | Liberty | LEP2236 | 1965 | £7.50 | £15 | French |
| Count Me In | 7" | Liberty | LIB55778 | 1965 | £2.50 | £6 | |
| Everybody Loves A Clown | LP | Liberty | LRP3428/LST7428 | 1965 | £6 | £15 | US |
| Everybody Loves A Clown | 7" EP | Liberty | LEP2241 | 1965 | £7.50 | £15 | French |
| Everybody Loves A Clown | 7" | Liberty | LIB55818 | 1965 | £1.50 | £4 | |
| Girls In Love | 7" | Liberty | LIB55971 | 1967 | £1.50 | £4 | |
| Golden Greats | LP | Liberty | LRP3468/LST7468 | 1966 | £6 | £15 | US |
| Green Grass | 7" | Liberty | LIB55880 | 1966 | £1.50 | £4 | |
| Hits Again | LP | Liberty | LRP3452/LST7452 | 1966 | £6 | £15 | US |
| Jill | 7" | Liberty | LBF15025 | 1967 | £2 | £5 | |
| Just Our Style | LP | Liberty | LBY1322 | 1966 | £4 | £10 | |
| Listen | LP | Liberty | LRP3524/LST7524 | 1967 | £4 | £10 | US |
| Loser | 7" | Liberty | LIB55949 | 1967 | £1.50 | £4 | |
| My Heart's Symphony | 7" | Liberty | LIB55898 | 1966 | £2.50 | £6 | |
| New Directions | LP | Liberty | LRP3519/LST7519 | 1967 | £4 | £10 | US |
| Paint Me A Picture | 7" | Liberty | LIB55914 | 1966 | £1.50 | £4 | |
| Save Your Heart For Me | 7" | Liberty | LIB55809 | 1965 | £1.50 | £4 | |
| Sealed With A Kiss | 7" | Liberty | LBF15131 | 1968 | £1.50 | £4 | |
| Session With Gary Lewis | LP | Liberty | LRP3419/LST7419 | 1965 | £6 | £15 | US |
| She's Just My Style | LP | Liberty | LRP3435/LST7435 | 1966 | £6 | £15 | US |
| She's Just My Style | 7" | Liberty | LIB55846 | 1966 | £1.50 | £4 | |
| Sure Gonna Miss Her | 7" | Liberty | LIB55865 | 1966 | £1.50 | £4 | |
| This Diamond Ring | LP | Liberty | LBY1259 | 1965 | £8 | £20 | |
| This Diamond Ring | 7" EP | Liberty | LEP2216 | 1965 | £7.50 | £15 | French |
| This Diamond Ring | 7" | Liberty | LIB10187 | 1965 | £1.50 | £4 | |
| Where Will The Words Come From | 7" EP | Liberty | LEP2270 | 1967 | £7.50 | £15 | French |
| Where Will The Words Come From | 7" | Liberty | LIB55933 | 1967 | £1.50 | £4 | |
| You Don't Have To Paint Me A Picture | LP | Liberty | LRP3487/LST7487 | 1967 | £4 | £10 | US |

## LEWIS, GEORGE
| | | | | | | | |
|---|---|---|---|---|---|---|---|
| Blues From The Bayou | LP | HMV | CLP1371/CSD1309 | 1960 | £6 | £15 | |
| Concert | LP | Blue Note | BLP/BST81208 | 196– | £8 | £20 | |
| Dallas Blues | 7" EP | Storyville | SEP504 | 196– | £2 | £5 | |
| Doctor Jazz | LP | HMV | CLP1413/CSD1337 | 1961 | £6 | £15 | |
| George Lewis | 7" EP | Tempo | EXA101 | 1959 | £2 | £5 | |

| | | | | | | |
|---|---|---|---|---|---|---|
| George Lewis | 7" EP . Tempo | EXA62 | 1957 £2 | £5 | |
| George Lewis | 7" EP . Tempo | EXA66 | 1957 £2 | £5 | |
| George Lewis | 7" EP . Tempo | EXA97 | 1958 £2 | £5 | |
| George Lewis And His New Orleans Allstars | 10" LP Vogue | LDE012 | 1952 £8 | £20 | |
| George Lewis And His New Orleans Ragtime Band | 10" LP Esquire | 20086 | 1957 £6 | £15 | |
| George Lewis And His New Orleans Stompers | LP ..... Vogue | LAE12005 | 1955 £8 | £20 | |
| George Lewis And His New Orleans Stompers | 7" EP . Tempo | EXA15 | 1956 £2 | £5 | |
| George Lewis And His New Orleans Stompers | 7" EP . Vogue | EPV1066 | 1955 £2 | £5 | |
| George Lewis And His New Orleans Stompers | 7" EP . Vogue | EPV1081 | 1956 £2 | £5 | |
| George Lewis In Hi Fi | 7" EP . Vogue | EPV1220 | 1959 £2 | £5 | |
| George Lewis In Hi Fi | 7" EP . Vogue | EPV1252 | 1959 £2 | £5 | |
| George Lewis Jam Session | 10" LP Vogue | LDE082 | 1954 £8 | £20 | |
| George Lewis Ragtime Band | LP ..... Tempo | TAP13 | 1957 £10 | £25 | |
| George Lewis Ragtime Band | 10" LP Esquire | 20067 | 1956 £8 | £20 | |
| George Lewis Ragtime Band | 10" LP Esquire | 20073 | 1956 £8 | £20 | |
| George Lewis Vol. 1 | LP ..... Blue Note | BLP/BST81205 | 196– £8 | £20 | |
| George Lewis Vol. 2 | LP ..... Blue Note | BLP/BST81206 | 196– £8 | £20 | |
| George Lewis' Ragtime Band | 7" EP . Tempo | EXA70 | 1957 £2 | £5 | |
| High Society | 7" EP . Storyville | SEP503 | 196– £2 | £5 | |
| Ice Cream | 7" EP . Storyville | SEP315 | 195– £2 | £5 | |
| Isle Of Capri | 7" EP . Storyville | SEP365 | 1961 £2 | £5 | |
| Jazz At Preservation Hall Vol. 4 | LP ..... London | HAK/SHK8165 | 1964 £6 | £15 | |
| Jazz At Vespers | LP ..... London | LTZU15112 | 1958 £6 | £15 | |
| Jazz From New Orleans | 7" EP . Storyville | SEP349 | 1960 £2 | £5 | |
| Louisiana | 7" EP . Storyville | SEP322 | 195– £2 | £5 | |
| Muskrat Ramble | 7" EP . Storyville | SEP369 | 1961 £2 | £5 | |
| New Orleans Music | 7" EP . Good Time Jazz | EPG1182 | 195– £2 | £5 | |
| New Orleans Ragtime Band Vol. 1 | 7" EP . Esquire | EP125 | 1957 £2 | £5 | |
| New Orleans Ragtime Band Vol. 2 | 7" EP . Esquire | EP135 | 1957 £2 | £5 | |
| New Orleans Ragtime Band Vol. 3 | 7" EP . Esquire | EP155 | 1957 £2 | £5 | |
| New Orleans Ragtime Band Vol. 4 | 7" EP . Esquire | EP175 | 1958 £2 | £5 | |
| New Orleans Ragtime Band Vol. 5 | 7" EP . Esquire | EP209 | 1959 £2 | £5 | |
| New Orleans Ragtime Band Vol. 6 | 7" EP . Esquire | EP211 | 1959 £2 | £5 | |
| New Orleans Ragtime Band Vol. 7 | 7" EP . Esquire | EP215 | 1959 £2 | £5 | |
| New Orleans Ragtime Band Vol. 8 | 7" EP . Esquire | EP219 | 1959 £2 | £5 | |
| New Orleans Ragtime Band Vol. 9 | 7" EP . Esquire | EP225 | 1960 £2 | £5 | |
| Newport Jazz Festival 1957 | LP ..... Columbia | 33CX10099 | 1958 £6 | £15 | ...... side 2 by Turk Murphy |
| Panama | 7" EP . Storyville | SEP321 | 195– £2 | £5 | |
| Perennial George Lewis | LP ..... Columbia | 33CX10131 | 1959 £6 | £15 | |
| Raggin' And Stompin' | 10" LP Columbia | 33C9042 | 1959 £6 | £15 | |
| Smile Darn Ya Smile | LP ..... 77 | LA1228 | 1964 £6 | £15 | |
| Sounds Of New Orleans | 7" EP . HMV | 7EG8540 | 1960 £2 | £5 | |
| Till We Meet Again | 7" EP . Storyville | SEP361 | 1961 £2 | £5 | |
| Vol. 1 Jazz Band | 10" LP London | HAPB1041 | 1955 £8 | £20 | |
| Vol. 2 All Stars | 10" LP London | HBU1045 | 1956 £8 | £20 | |
| Willie The Weeper | 7" EP . Storyville | SEP325 | 195– £2 | £5 | |

## LEWIS, HOPETON

| | | | | | | |
|---|---|---|---|---|---|---|
| Boom Shacka Lacka | 7" ...... Duke Reid | DR2505 | 1970 £1.50 | £4 | ...... Tommy McCook B side |
| Everybody Rocking | 7" ...... Island | WI3076 | 1968 £5 | £10 | |
| Grooving Out On Life | LP ..... Trojan | TRL36 | 1971 £4 | £10 | |
| Judgement Day | 7" ...... Treasure Isle | TI7071 | 1972 £1.50 | £4 | ...... Earl Lindo B side |
| Let Me Come On Home | 7" ...... Island | WI3056 | 1967 £5 | £10 | |
| Let The Little Girl Dance | 7" ...... Island | WI3059 | 1967 £5 | £10 | |
| Rock A Shacka | 7" ...... Island | WI3068 | 1967 £5 | £10 | |
| Rock Steady | 7" ...... Island | WI3054 | 1967 £5 | £10 | |
| Run Down | 7" ...... Island | WI3057 | 1967 £5 | £10 | |
| Take It Easy | LP ..... Island | ILP957 | 1967 £50 | £100 | ............... pink label |
| Testify | 7" ...... Duke Reid | DR2516 | 1970 £1.50 | £4 | ...... Tommy McCook B side |
| To The Other Man | 7" ...... Treasure Isle | TI7060 | 1971 £1.50 | £4 | ...... Tommy McCook B side |

## LEWIS, JERRY

| | | | | | |
|---|---|---|---|---|---|
| Rock-a-bye Your Baby With A Dixie Melody | 7" ...... Brunswick | 05636 | 1957 £1.50 | £4 | |

## LEWIS, JERRY LEE

| | | | | | |
|---|---|---|---|---|---|
| Another Place, Another Time | 7" ...... Mercury | MF1020 | 1968 £1.50 | £4 | |
| Another Time, Another Place | LP ..... Mercury | SMWL21011 | 1969 £4 | £10 | |
| Baby Baby Bye Bye | 7" ...... London | HLS9131 | 1960 £4 | £8 | |
| Baby Hold Me Close | 7" ...... Philips | BF1407 | 1965 £1.50 | £4 | |
| Break Up | 7" ...... London | HLS8700 | 1958 £5 | £10 | |
| Breathless | LP ..... London | HAS8323 | 1966 £10 | £25 | |
| Breathless | 7" ...... London | HLS8592 | 1958 £5 | £10 | |
| By Request – More Greatest Live Show On Earth | LP ..... Philips | (S)BL7746 | 1967 £4 | £10 | |
| Carry Me Back To Old Virginia | 7" ...... London | HLS9980 | 1965 £2 | £5 | |
| Country Songs For City Folks | LP ..... Philips | BL7688 | 1965 £4 | £10 | |

516

| | | | | | | | |
|---|---|---|---|---|---|---|---|
| Country Style | 7" EP | Philips | BE12599 | 1966 | £4 | £8 | |
| Fabulous Jerry Lee Lewis Vol. 1 | 7" EP | Sun | JLLEP001 | 197– | £4 | £8 | |
| Fabulous Jerry Lee Lewis Vol. 2 | 7" EP | Sun | JLLEP002 | 197– | £4 | £8 | |
| Four More From Jerry Lee Lewis | 7" EP | London | RES1378 | 1963 | £10 | £20 | |
| Golden Hits | LP | Philips | BL7622 | 1964 | £4 | £10 | |
| Good Golly Miss Molly | 7" | London | HL7120 | 1963 | £5 | £10 | export |
| Good Golly Miss Molly | 7" | London | HLS9688 | 1963 | £1.50 | £4 | |
| Got You On My Mind | LP | Fontana | SFJL964 | 1968 | £4 | £10 | |
| Great Balls Of Fire | 7" | London | HLS8529 | 1957 | £10 | £20 | |
| Great Balls Of Fire | 7" | Mercury | MF1110 | 1969 | £1.50 | £4 | |
| Greatest Live Show On Earth | LP | Philips | (S)BL7650 | 1964 | £4 | £10 | |
| Hang Up My Rock & Roll Shoes | 7" | London | HLS9202 | 1960 | £2 | £4 | |
| High School Confidential | 7" | London | HL7050 | 1958 | £6 | £12 | export |
| High School Confidential | 7" | London | HLS8780 | 1959 | £7.50 | £15 | |
| Hit The Road Jack | 7" | Mercury | AMT1216 | 1963 | £1.50 | £4 | |
| I'll Sail My Ship Alone | 7" | London | HLS9083 | 1960 | £2 | £5 | |
| I'm On Fire | LP | Mercury | SMCL20156 | 1969 | £4 | £10 | |
| I'm On Fire | 7" | Philips | BF1324 | 1964 | £2 | £5 | |
| In The Mood | 7" | London | HL7123 | 1963 | £12.50 | £25 | export |
| It Won't Happen With Me | 7" | London | HLS9414 | 1961 | £1.50 | £4 | |
| It's A Hang Up Baby | 7" | Philips | BF1594 | 1967 | £1.50 | £4 | |
| Jerry Lee Lewis | LP | London | HAS2138 | 1959 | £15 | £30 | |
| Jerry Lee Lewis | LP | Sun | SLP1230 | 1958 | £37.50 | £75 | US |
| Jerry Lee Lewis No. 1 | 7" EP | London | RES1140 | 1958 | £12.50 | £25 | tri-centre |
| Jerry Lee Lewis No. 2 | 7" EP | London | RES1186 | 1959 | £15 | £30 | tri-centre |
| Jerry Lee Lewis No. 3 | 7" EP | London | RES1187 | 1959 | £15 | £30 | tri-centre |
| Jerry Lee Lewis No. 4 | 7" EP | London | RES1296 | 1961 | £10 | £20 | |
| Jerry Lee Lewis No. 5 | 7" EP | London | RES1336 | 1962 | £7.50 | £15 | |
| Jerry Lee Lewis No. 6 | 7" EP | London | RES1351 | 1963 | £7.50 | £15 | |
| Jerry Lee Lewis Vol. 2 | LP | London | HAS2440 | 1962 | £10 | £25 | |
| Jerry Lee's Greatest | LP | Sun | SLP1265 | 1961 | £37.50 | £75 | US |
| Let's Talk About Us | 7" | London | HLS8941 | 1959 | £2.50 | £6 | tri-centre |
| Lewis Boogie | 7" | London | HLS9867 | 1964 | £2.50 | £6 | |
| Little Queenie | 7" | London | HLS8993 | 1959 | £4 | £8 | tri-centre |
| Live At The Star Club Hamburg | LP | Philips | BL7646 | 1965 | £5 | £12 | ... with The Nashville Teens |
| Long Tall Sally | 7" | Mercury | MF1105 | 1969 | £1.50 | £4 | |
| Loving Up A Storm | 7" | London | HLS8840 | 1959 | £6 | £15 | |
| Memphis Beat | LP | Philips | (S)BL7706 | 1967 | £4 | £10 | |
| Memphis Beat | 7" | Philips | BF1521 | 1966 | £1.50 | £4 | |
| Rambling Rose | 7" | London | HLS9526 | 1962 | £1.50 | £4 | |
| Return Of Rock | LP | Philips | (S)BL7668 | 1967 | £4 | £10 | |
| Rocking Pneumonia | 7" | Philips | BF1425 | 1965 | £1.50 | £4 | |
| Save The Last Dance For Me | 7" | London | HL7117 | 1962 | £12.50 | £25 | export |
| She Still Comes Around | LP | Mercury | SMCL21047 | 1969 | £4 | £10 | |
| Shotgun Man | 7" | Philips | BF1615 | 1967 | £1.50 | £4 | |
| Soul My Way | LP | Mercury | 20117MCL | 1968 | £4 | £10 | |
| Sunstroke | LP | Ember | NR5038 | 1966 | £4 | £10 | .... with Carl Perkins |
| Sweet Little Sixteen | 7" | London | HLS9584 | 1962 | £1.50 | £4 | |
| Teenage Letter | 7" | London | HLS9722 | 1963 | £2 | £5 | |
| Together | LP | Mercury | SMCL20172 | 1970 | £4 | £10 | with Linda Gail Lewis |
| What'd I Say | 7" | London | HLS9335 | 1961 | £1.50 | £4 | |
| When I Get Paid | 7" | London | HLS9446 | 1961 | £1.50 | £4 | |
| Whole Lotta Shaking Goin' On | LP | London | HAS8251 | 1965 | £10 | £25 | |
| Whole Lotta Shaking Going On | 7" | London | HLS8457 | 1957 | £12.50 | £25 | |
| You Win Again | 7" | London | HLS8559 | 1958 | £10 | £20 | |

## LEWIS, JIMMY

| | | | | | | | |
|---|---|---|---|---|---|---|---|
| Girl From Texas | 7" | Minit | MLF11002 | 1968 | £5 | £10 | |

## LEWIS, JOHN

| | | | | | | | |
|---|---|---|---|---|---|---|---|
| Afternoon In Paris | LP | Oriole | MG20036 | 1960 | £5 | £12 | ......with Sacha Distel |
| Cool! | LP | Fontana | FJL106 | 1964 | £4 | £10 | |
| Golden Striker | LP | London | LTZK15218 | 1961 | £6 | £15 | |
| Grand Encounter | LP | Vogue | LAE12065 | 1958 | £10 | £25 | ......with Bill Perkins |
| Improvised Meditations And Excursions | LP | London | LTZK15186 | 1960 | £6 | £15 | |
| Odds Against Tomorrow | LP | London | HAT2220 | 1960 | £6 | £15 | |
| Wonderful World Of Jazz | LP | London | LTZK15237 | 1961 | £6 | £15 | |

## LEWIS, LINDA

| | | | | | | | |
|---|---|---|---|---|---|---|---|
| You Turn My Bitter Into Sweet | 7" | Polydor | 56173 | 1967 | £20 | £40 | |

## LEWIS, MARGARET

| | | | | | | | |
|---|---|---|---|---|---|---|---|
| Something's Wrong Baby | 7" | Starlite | ST45081 | 1962 | £4 | £8 | |

## LEWIS, MEADE LUX

| | | | | | | | |
|---|---|---|---|---|---|---|---|
| Barrel House Piano | LP | Tops | L1533 | | £8 | £20 | US |
| Blues Piano Artistry | LP | Riverside | 9402 | | £8 | £20 | US |
| Boogie Woogie And Blues | 7" EP | Melodisc | EPM7107 | 1956 | £10 | £20 | |
| Boogie Woogie Piano And Drums No. 1 | 7" EP | Columbia | SEB10030 | 1956 | £5 | £10 | |
| Boogie Woogie Piano And Drums No. 2 | 7" EP | Columbia | SEB10052 | 1957 | £5 | £10 | |
| House Party | LP | Philips | 652014BL | 1962 | £6 | £15 | |
| Jazz At The Philharmonic | 10" LP | Columbia | 33C9021 | 1956 | £6 | £15 | .... with Slim Gaillard |
| Meade Lux Lewis | 7" EP | Vogue | EPV1065 | 1955 | £10 | £20 | |
| Out Of The Roaring Twenties | 10" LP | HMV | DLP1176 | 1958 | £6 | £15 | |
| Yancey's Last Ride | LP | Columbia | 33CX10094 | 1957 | £8 | £20 | |

## LEWIS, MIA
Nothing Lasts Forever ............................ 7" ...... Parlophone ...... R5526 .................... 1966 £4 ............ £8 ....................................

## LEWIS, NEIL
Profile .............................................. LP ..... Swamp .......... WAM680 ........... 1980 £8 .......... £20

## LEWIS, PETER
Sing Life Sing Lore ............................. LP ..... Quest ............. QLP539 ............... 1974 £8 .......... £20

## LEWIS, RAMSEY
| At The Bohemian Caverns | LP | Pye | NJL55 | 1965 | £4 | £10 | |
|---|---|---|---|---|---|---|---|
| Dancin' In The Street | LP | Chess | CRL(S)4533 | 1968 | £4 | £10 | |
| Function At The Junction | 7" | Chess | CRS8058 | 1967 | £1.50 | £4 | |
| Girl Talk | 7" | Chess | CRS8061 | 1967 | £1.50 | £4 | |
| Hang On Ramsey | LP | Chess | CRL4517 | 1966 | £4 | £10 | |
| Hang On Sloopy | 7" | Chess | CRS8024 | 1965 | £1.50 | £4 | |
| Hard Day's Night | 7" EP | Chess | CRE6019 | 1966 | £4 | £8 | |
| Hard Day's Night | 7" | Chess | CRS8029 | 1966 | £1.50 | £4 | |
| Hi Heel Sneakers | 7" | Chess | CRS8031 | 1966 | £1.50 | £4 | |
| Hour With | LP | Cadet | 645 | 1959 | £4 | £10 | US |
| In Crowd | LP | Chess | CRL4511 | 1965 | £4 | £10 | |
| In Crowd | 7" | Chess | CRS8020 | 1965 | £1.50 | £4 | |
| More Music From Soul | LP | Cadet | 680 | 1962 | £4 | £10 | US |
| Movie Album | LP | Chess | CRL4531 | 1967 | £4 | £10 | |
| Never On Sunday | LP | Cadet | 686 | 1962 | £4 | £10 | US |
| Stretchin' Out | LP | Cadet | 665 | 1962 | £4 | £10 | US |
| Uptight | 7" | Chess | CRS8044 | 1966 | £1.50 | £4 | |
| Wade In The Water | LP | Chess | CRL4522 | 1966 | £4 | £10 | |
| Wade In The Water | 7" | Chess | CRS8041 | 1966 | £1.50 | £4 | |

## LEWIS, RICHARD
Hey Little Girl ................................... 7" ...... Downbeat ....... CHA1 ................. 1960 £6 .......... £12

## LEWIS, SMILEY
| Big Mamou | 78 | London | L1189 | 1953 | £25 | £50 | |
|---|---|---|---|---|---|---|---|
| Don't Be That Way | 7" | London | HLU8337 | 1956 | £250 | £400 | best auctioned |
| I Hear You Knocking | LP | Imperial | LP9141 | 1961 | £62.50 | £125 | US |
| I Hear You Knocking | 7" | Liberty | LBF15337 | 1970 | £1.50 | £4 | |
| One Night | 7" | London | HLU8312 | 1956 | £250 | £400 | best auctioned |
| Shame Shame Shame | 7" | London | HLP8367 | 1957 | £180 | £300 | best auctioned |
| Shame, Shame, Shame | LP | Liberty | LBS83308 | 1970 | £5 | £12 | |

## LEWIS, STEVIE
Take Me For A Little While ................... 7" ...... Mercury ........ MF871 ............... 1965 £4 .......... £8

## LEWIS, TINY
Too Much Rocking ............................... 7" ...... Parlophone ...... R4617 ................. 1959 £37.50 .... £75

## LEWIS SISTERS
You Need Me ..................................... 7" ...... Tamla Motown TMG536 .............. 1965 £20 .......... £40

## LEYTON, JOHN
| All I Want Is You | 7" | HMV | POP1374 | 1964 | £2 | £5 | ... with Mike Sarne & Grazina Frame |
|---|---|---|---|---|---|---|---|
| Always Yours | LP | HMV | CLP1664 | 1962 | £25 | £50 | |
| Beautiful Dreamer | 7" EP | HMV | 7EG8843 | 1964 | £12.50 | £25 | |
| Beautiful Dreamer | 7" | HMV | POP1230 | 1963 | £1.50 | £4 | |
| Cupboard Love | 7" | HMV | POP1122 | 1963 | £1.50 | £4 | |
| Dancing In The Graveyard | 7" | York | SYK551 | 1973 | £1.50 | £4 | |
| Don't Let Her Go Away | 7" | HMV | POP1338 | 1964 | £2 | £5 | |
| Down The River Nile | 7" | HMV | POP1054 | 1962 | £1.50 | £4 | |
| Girl On The Floor Above | 7" | HMV | POP798 | 1960 | £25 | £50 | |
| I'll Cut Your Tail Off | 7" | HMV | POP1175 | 1963 | £1.50 | £4 | |
| John Leyton | LP | York | FYK416 | 1973 | £6 | £15 | |
| John Leyton | 7" EP | Top Rank | JKP3016 | 1962 | £12.50 | £25 | |
| John Leyton Hit Parade | 7" EP | HMV | 7EG8747 | 1962 | £10 | £20 | |
| Johnny Remember Me | 7" | Top Rank | JAR577 | 1961 | £1.50 | £4 | |
| Lone Rider | 7" | HMV | POP992 | 1962 | £2.50 | £6 | |
| Lonely City | 7" | HMV | POP1014 | 1962 | £1.50 | £4 | |
| Lonely Johnny | 7" | HMV | POP1076 | 1962 | £1.50 | £4 | |
| Make Love To Me | 7" | HMV | POP1264 | 1964 | £1.50 | £4 | |
| On Lovers' Hill | 7" | HMV | POP1204 | 1963 | £1.50 | £4 | |
| Rock 'n' Roll | 7" | York | YR210 | 1974 | £1.50 | £4 | |
| Son This Is She | 7" | HMV | POP956 | 1961 | £1.50 | £4 | |
| Tell Laura I Love Her | 7" EP | HMV | 7EG8854 | 1964 | £15 | £30 | |
| Tell Laura I Love Her | 7" | Top Rank | JAR426 | 1960 | £20 | £40 | |
| Two Sides Of John Leyton | LP | HMV | CLP1497 | 1961 | £15 | £30 | |
| Wild Wind | 7" | Top Rank | JAR585 | 1961 | £1.50 | £4 | |

## LIBERACE
I Don't Care ..................................... 7" ...... Columbia ........ DB4834 ................. 1956 £1.50 .... £4

## LIBERATORS
It Hurts So Much ............................... 7" ...... Stateside ......... SS424 ............. 1965 £1.50 .... £4

## LIBERMAN, JEFF
Synergy ............................................ LP ...... Librah ............. 12157 .................... 1978 £50 ....... £100 ................. US

## LIBERMAN, JEFFREY
| | | | | | | |
|---|---|---|---|---|---|---|
| Jeffrey Liberman | LP | Librah | 1545 | 1975 £**75** | £**150** | US |
| Solitude Within | LP | Librah | 6969 | 1975 £**75** | £**150** | US |

## LIEBMAN, DAVE
| | | | | | | |
|---|---|---|---|---|---|---|
| Drum Ode | LP | ECM | ECM1046ST | 1975 £**8** | £**20** | |
| Lookout Farm | LP | ECM | ECM1039ST | 1974 £**8** | £**20** | |
| Sweet Hands | LP | Horizon | SP702 | 1975 £**5** | £**12** | US |

## LIED DES TEUFELS
| | | | | | | |
|---|---|---|---|---|---|---|
| Lied Des Teufels | LP | Kuckuck | 2375019 | 1973 £**4** | £**10** | German |

## LIEUTENANT PIGEON
| | | | | | | |
|---|---|---|---|---|---|---|
| World Of Lieutenant Pigeon | LP | Decca | SPA414 | 1976 £**5** | £**12** | test pressing only |

## LIFE
| | | | | | | |
|---|---|---|---|---|---|---|
| Hands Of The Clock | 7" | Polydor | 56778 | 1969 £**1.50** | £**4** | |
| Life | LP | Columbia | C06234264 | 1970 £**50** | £**100** | Swedish |
| Life After Death | LP | Polydor | 2383295 | 1974 £**15** | £**30** | |

## LIFE (2)
| | | | | | | |
|---|---|---|---|---|---|---|
| Cats' Eyes | 7" | Philips | 6006280 | 1973 £**4** | £**8** | blue paper label |

## LIFE AFTER LIFE
| | | | | | | |
|---|---|---|---|---|---|---|
| Life After Life | LP | Time Track | | 1985 £**100** | £**200** | |

## LIFE 'n' SOUL
| | | | | | | |
|---|---|---|---|---|---|---|
| Here Comes Yesterday Again | 7" | Decca | F12851 | 1968 £**1.50** | £**4** | |
| Peacefully Asleep | 7" | Decca | F12659 | 1967 £**5** | £**10** | |

## LIGGINS, JOE & THE HONEYDRIPPERS
| | | | | | | |
|---|---|---|---|---|---|---|
| I've Got A Right To Cry | 78 | Parlophone | R3309 | 1950 £**6** | £**12** | |

## LIGHT
| | | | | | | |
|---|---|---|---|---|---|---|
| Story Of Moses | LP | Brain | 1013 | 1972 £**6** | £**15** | German |

## LIGHT FANTASIC
| | | | | | | |
|---|---|---|---|---|---|---|
| Jeanie | 7" | RCA | RCA2331 | 1973 £**6** | £**12** | |

## LIGHT OF DARKNESS
| | | | | | | |
|---|---|---|---|---|---|---|
| Light Of Darkness | LP | Philips | 6305062 | 1970 £**50** | £**100** | German |

## LIGHTBEARERS
| | | | | | | |
|---|---|---|---|---|---|---|
| Going Dutch | LP | Dovetail | DOVE22 | 1975 £**10** | £**25** | |

## LIGHTCRUST DOUGHBOYS
| | | | | | | |
|---|---|---|---|---|---|---|
| Lightcrust Doughboys | LP | Audio Lab | AL1525 | 1959 £**15** | £**30** | US |

## LIGHTFOOT, GORDON
| | | | | | | |
|---|---|---|---|---|---|---|
| Back Here On Earth | LP | United Artists | SULP1239 | 1969 £**4** | £**10** | |
| Day Before Yesterday | 7" | Fontana | TF405 | 1963 £**1.50** | £**4** | |
| Did She Mention My Name | LP | United Artists | SULP1199 | 1968 £**4** | £**10** | |
| Early Lightfoot | LP | United Artists | UAS29012 | 1969 £**4** | £**10** | |
| I'm The One | 7" | Decca | F11527 | 1962 £**1.50** | £**4** | |
| Just Like Tom Thumb's Blues | 7" | United Artists | UP1109 | 1965 £**1.50** | £**4** | |
| Lightfoot | LP | United Artists | UAL3487/ UAS6487 | 1965 £**4** | £**10** | US |
| Negotiations | 7" | Fontana | 267275 | 1963 £**1.50** | £**4** | |
| Sunday Concert | LP | United Artists | UAS29040 | 1969 £**4** | £**10** | |
| Way I Feel | LP | United Artists | UAL3587/ UAS6587 | 1967 £**4** | £**10** | US |

## LIGHTFOOT, PAPA GEORGE
| | | | | | | |
|---|---|---|---|---|---|---|
| Natchez Trace | LP | Liberty | LBS83353 | 1969 £**4** | £**10** | |

## LIGHTFOOT, TERRY
| | | | | | | |
|---|---|---|---|---|---|---|
| Alleycat | LP | Columbia | 33SX1721 | 1965 £**4** | £**10** | |
| Jazz Gumbo Vol. 1 | 10" LP | Nixa | NJT503 | 1956 £**5** | £**12** | |
| Trad Parade | LP | Columbia | 33SX1290/ SCX3354 | 1961 £**5** | £**12** | |
| Tradition In Colour | LP | Columbia | 33SX1073 | 1958 £**5** | £**12** | |

## LIGHTHOUSE
| | | | | | | |
|---|---|---|---|---|---|---|
| Eight Miles High | 7" | RCA | RCA1884 | 1969 £**1.50** | £**4** | |
| Lighthouse | LP | RCA | LSP4173 | 1969 £**5** | £**12** | US |
| One Fine Morning | LP | Vertigo | 6342010 | 1971 £**8** | £**20** | spiral label |
| Peacing It All Together | LP | RCA | SF8121 | 1970 £**4** | £**10** | |
| Suite Feeling | LP | RCA | SF8103 | 1970 £**4** | £**10** | |
| Thoughts Of Moving On | LP | Vertigo | 6342011 | 1971 £**8** | £**20** | spiral label |

## LIGHTNIN' ROD
| | | | | | | |
|---|---|---|---|---|---|---|
| Hustler's Convention | LP | United Artists | UALA156F | 1973 £**5** | £**12** | US |

## LIGHTNIN' ROD & JIMI HENDRIX
'Doriella Du Fontane' is one of the more overlooked records involving Jimi Hendrix. Although released in 1984, and featuring Hendrix in the unaccustomed role of providing rhythmic support to a rapper, the record is not the result of an eighties remixing project. Lightnin' Rod was a member of the Last Poets, whose blend of street poetry and percussion anticipates the work of artists like Public Enemy by some

years. His collaboration with Jimi Hendrix was recorded during the guitarist's lifetime and represents an important reminder of Hendrix's occasional wish to reaffirm his blackness.

| | | | | | | | |
|---|---|---|---|---|---|---|---|
| Doriella Du Fontane | 12" | Celluloid | CRT332 | 1984 | £5 | £10 | |

## LIGHTNIN' SLIM

| | | | | | | | |
|---|---|---|---|---|---|---|---|
| Bell Ringer | LP | Excello | (S)8004 | 1965 | £8 | £20 | US |
| Downhome Blues Part 1 | LP | Python | PLP8 | 1969 | £8 | £20 | |
| Just A Little Bit | 7" | Blue Horizon | 2096013 | 1972 | £5 | £10 | |
| London Gumbo | LP | Blue Horizon | 2931005 | 1972 | £20 | £40 | |
| Rooster Blues | LP | Blue Horizon | 763863 | 1970 | £15 | £30 | |
| Rooster Blues | LP | Excello | 8000 | 1960 | £15 | £30 | US |

## LIGHTNING

| | | | | | | | |
|---|---|---|---|---|---|---|---|
| Lightning | LP | P.I.P. | PP6807 | 1969 | £15 | £30 | US |

## LIGHTNING RAIDERS

| | | | | | | | |
|---|---|---|---|---|---|---|---|
| Criminal World | 7" | Revenge | REVS200 | 1981 | £4 | £8 | |

## LIGHTNING SEEDS

| | | | | | | | |
|---|---|---|---|---|---|---|---|
| All I Want | CD-s | Ghetto | CDGTG9 | 1990 | £2 | £5 | |
| Jollification | CD | Epic | 4772379 | 1994 | £5 | £12 | strawberry scented packaging, pic disc |
| Joy | CD-s | Ghetto | CDGTG6 | 1989 | £2 | £5 | |
| Pure | CD-s | Ghetto | CDGTG4 | 1989 | £2 | £5 | |
| Sweet Dreams | CD-s | Ghetto | CDGTG8 | 1990 | £2 | £5 | |
| Upside Down | CD-s | Ghetto | CDGTG7 | 1989 | £2 | £5 | |

## LIGHTSHINE

| | | | | | | | |
|---|---|---|---|---|---|---|---|
| Feeling | LP | Trefiton | HS1049ST | 1973 | £50 | £100 | German |

## LILAC ANGELS

| | | | | | | | |
|---|---|---|---|---|---|---|---|
| I'm Not Afraid To Say Yes | LP | Dingerland | 09490211 | 1973 | £4 | £10 | German |

## LILAC TIME

| | | | | | | | |
|---|---|---|---|---|---|---|---|
| All For Love And Love For All | CD-s | Fontana | LILCD8 | 1990 | £2 | £5 | |
| American Eyes | CD-s | Fontana | LILCD5 | 1989 | £2 | £5 | |
| And Love For All | CD | Fontana | 8461902 | 1990 | £5 | £12 | |
| Black Velvet | CD-s | Fontana | LILCD4 | 1988 | £2 | £5 | |
| Days Of The Week | CD-s | Fontana | LILCD6 | 1989 | £2 | £5 | |
| Girl Who Waves At Trains | CD-s | Fontana | LILCD7 | 1989 | £2 | £5 | |
| It'll End In Tears | CD-s | Fontana | LILCD10 | 1990 | £2 | £5 | |
| Laundry | CD-s | Fontana | LILCD9 | 1990 | £2 | £5 | |
| Lilac Time | CD | Fontana | 8348352 | 1988 | £6 | £15 | |
| Lilac Time | CD | Swordfish | SWFCD6 | 1988 | £8 | £20 | |
| Paradise Circus | CD | Fontana | 8386412 | 1989 | £6 | £15 | |
| Return To Yesterday | CD-s | Fontana | LILCD2 | 1988 | £2 | £5 | |
| Return To Yesterday | CD-s | Polygram | 0804602 | 1988 | £4 | £10 | CD video |
| Return To Yesterday | 7" | Swordfish | LILAC1 | 1988 | £2 | £5 | no picture sleeve |
| Return To Yesterday | 12" | Swordfish | 12LILAC1 | 1988 | £3 | £8 | |
| You've Got To Love | CD-s | Fontana | LILCD3 | 1988 | £2 | £5 | |

## LIMBUS

| | | | | | | | |
|---|---|---|---|---|---|---|---|
| Cosmic Music Experience | LP | CPM | LPS001 | 1969 | £62.50 | £125 | German |
| Mandalas | LP | Ohr | OMM56001 | 1970 | £6 | £15 | German |
| New Atlantis | LP | private | | 1976 | £62.50 | £125 | German |

## LIMELIGHT

| | | | | | | | |
|---|---|---|---|---|---|---|---|
| Ashes To Ashes | 7" | Future Earth | FER010 | 1982 | £2 | £5 | |
| Limelight | LP | Avatar | AALP5005 | 1981 | £10 | £25 | with 7" |
| Limelight | LP | Future Earth | FER008 | 1980 | £10 | £25 | |
| Metal Man | 7" | Future Earth | FER006 | 1980 | £2 | £5 | |

## LIMELIGHT (BRINSLEY SCHWARZ)

| | | | | | | | |
|---|---|---|---|---|---|---|---|
| I Should Have Known Better | 7" | United Artists | UP35779 | 1975 | £2.50 | £6 | |

## LIMELITERS

| | | | | | | | |
|---|---|---|---|---|---|---|---|
| Four Folk Songs | 7" EP | RCA | RCX7151 | 1964 | £2 | £5 | |
| Fun And Folk | 7" EP | RCA | RCX7126 | 1963 | £2 | £5 | |
| Limeliters | LP | Elektra | EKL180 | 1961 | £4 | £10 | US |

## LIMEYS

| | | | | | | | |
|---|---|---|---|---|---|---|---|
| Cara Lin | 7" | Decca | F12382 | 1966 | £10 | £20 | |
| I Can't Find My Way Through | 7" | Pye | 7N15820 | 1965 | £1.50 | £4 | |
| Mountain's High | 7" | Decca | F12466 | 1966 | £1.50 | £4 | |
| Some Tears Fall Dry | 7" | Pye | 7N15909 | 1965 | £1.50 | £4 | |

## LINCOLN, PETER

| | | | | | | | |
|---|---|---|---|---|---|---|---|
| In The Day Of My Youth | 7" | Major Minor | MM520 | 1967 | £2 | £5 | |

## LINCOLN, PHILAMORE

| | | | | | | | |
|---|---|---|---|---|---|---|---|
| North Wind Blew South | LP | Epic | BN26497 | 1967 | £5 | £12 | US |
| Running By The River | 7" | Nems | 563711 | 1968 | £1.50 | £4 | |

## LINCOLN STREET EXIT

| | | | | | | | |
|---|---|---|---|---|---|---|---|
| Drive It | LP | London | SHAU122 | 1970 | £30 | £60 | German |

## LINCOLNS
Tribute To Elvis................................... LP...... Attic .............. TCA70 .................. 1977 £10.........£25 .................Canadian

## LIND, BOB
Don't Be Concerned ............................ LP...... Fontana........... (S)TL5340 .............. 1966 £4..........£10 ................................
Elusive Butterfly................................. 7"...... Fontana........... TF670 .................. 1966 £1.50........£4 ................................

## LINDEN, KATHY
Billy..................................................... 7"...... Felsted ........... AF102 ................. 1958 £1.50........£4 ................................
Goodbye Jimmy Goodbye...................... 7"...... Felsted ........... AF122 ................. 1959 £1.50........£4 ................................
Kathy .................................................. 7" EP. Felsted ........... GEP1001............. 1959 £6............£12 ................................
Kathy In Love Vol. 1 ........................... 7" EP. Felsted ........... GEP1002............. 1959 £6............£12 ................................
Kathy In Love Vol. 2 ........................... 7" EP. Felsted ........... GEP1004............. 1959 £6............£12 ................................
Kissin' Conversation ............................ 7"...... Felsted ........... AF111 ................. 1958 £1.50........£4 ................................
Mary Lou Wilson And Johnny Brown....... 7"...... Felsted ........... AF130 ................. 1960 £1.50........£4 ................................
Oh Johnny Oh Johnny Oh..................... 7"...... Felsted ........... AF108 ................. 1958 £1.50........£4 ................................
That Certain Boy ................................. LP...... Felsted ........... 7501 ................... 195– £10..........£25 ..........................US
You Don't Know Girls .......................... 7"...... Felsted ........... AF124 ................. 1959 £1.50........£4 ................................
You'd Be Surprised............................... 7"...... Felsted ........... AF105 ................. 1958 £1.50........£4 ................................

## LINDENBERG, UDO
Daumen Im Wind.................................. LP...... Telefunken...... SLE14679.............. 1972 £4..........£10 .................... German
Lindenberg .......................................... LP...... Telefunken...... SLE14637.............. 1971 £4..........£10 .................... German

## LINDH, BJORN J:SON
Cous Cous ........................................... LP...... Metronome ..... MLP15450 ............ 1972 £4..........£10 ................... Swedish
Fran Storsted Till Grodspad ................... LP...... SR.................. RELP1135 ............. 1971 £5..........£12 ................... Swedish

## LINDISFARNE
Lindisfarne became quite popular in their day, achieving the remarkable feat, for a group marketed as being 'progressive', of gaining a pair of top ten single hits. Today, their cheery, sing-along folk-rock is not highly regarded and even the fact that their earliest albums are on the collectable Charisma pink label does not appear to be enough to give them a collectors' value.

Clear White Light ................................ 7"...... Charisma......... CB137 ................. 1970 £2.50........£6 ................................
Dingly Dell .......................................... CD..... Charisma......... CASCD1057 .......... 1988 £5............£12 ................................
Lady Eleanor 88 .................................. CD-s .. Virgin ............. LADYD1 ............... 1988 £2............£5 ...............3" single
Peel Sessions ....................................... CD-s .. Strange Fruit... SFPSCD059 ........... 1988 £2............£5 ................................

## LINDYS
Boy With The Eyes Of Blue ................... 7"...... Decca ............. F11272 ................. 1960 £4............£8 ................................
Train Of Love....................................... 7"...... Decca ............. F11253 ................. 1960 £2.50........£6 ................................

## LINN, ELMO
Sam Houston ....................................... 7"...... Starlite ........... ST45101 ............... 1963 £2.50........£6 ................................

## LINN COUNTY
Fever Shot ........................................... LP...... Mercury.......... SMCL20165 .......... 1969 £4..........£10 ................................
Proud Flesh Soothseer........................... LP...... Mercury.......... SMCL20142 .......... 1968 £4..........£10 ................................
Till The Break Of Dawn......................... LP...... Philips............. SBL7923............... 1970 £4..........£10 ................................

## LION, JOHNNY
Johnny Lion And The Jumping Jewels........ LP...... Philips............. 12902................... 1963 £10.........£25 .....................Dutch

## LION TAMERS
Speak Your Mind.................................. 7"...... Polydor ........... 56283................... 1968 £1.50........£4 ................................

## LIONS OF JUDAH
Our Love's A Growin' Thing.................... 7"...... Fontana........... TF1016 ................ 1969 £2............£5 ................................

## LIP MOVES
Guest .................................................. 7"...... Tichonderoga .. HP1 .................... 1979 £2............£5 ................................

## LIPSCOMB, MANCE
Trouble In Mind.................................... LP...... Reprise ........... R(9)2012............... 1961 £5............£12 ..........................US

## LIQUID SMOKE
Liquid Smoke ....................................... LP...... Avco................ 33005................... 1969 £25.........£50 ..........................US

## LISTEN
The lead singer of Listen was Robert Plant and he is, in fact, the only member of the group to appear on the single credited to them.

You Better Run ..................................... 7"...... CBS................. 202456.................. 1965 £75.......£150 ................................

## LISTENING
Listening............................................... LP...... Vanguard ........ VSD6504 .............. 1969 £30.........£60 ..........................US

## LITE STORM
Warning................................................ LP...... Beverly Hills.... BHS1135 .............. 1973 £30.........£60 ..........................US

## LITTER
$100 Fine ............................................ LP...... Hexagon ......... HX681 ................. 1969 £150.....£250 ..........................US
Distortions............................................ LP...... Warick............. 671 ..................... 1968 £180.....£300 ..........................US
Emerge ................................................ LP...... Probe .............. CLPS4504 ............ 1969 £10..........£25 ................................

## LITTLE, BIG TINY
School Day ........................................... 7"...... Vogue Coral.... Q72263................. 1957 £10..........£20 ................................

## LITTLE, MARIE
| | | | | | | | |
|---|---|---|---|---|---|---|---|
| Factory Girl | LP | Argo | ZFB19 | 1971 | £50 | £100 | |
| Marie Little | LP | Trailer | LER2084 | 1973 | £30 | £60 | |

## LITTLE ANGELS
| | | | | | | | |
|---|---|---|---|---|---|---|---|
| '87 EP | 12" | Song Management | LAN001 | 1987 | £10 | £25 | |
| Big Bad EP | CD-s | Polydor | LTLCD2 | 1989 | £2.50 | £6 | |
| Big Bad EP | 12" | Polydor | LTLEP2 | 1989 | £2.50 | £6 | |
| Do You Wanna Riot | CD-s | Polydor | LTLCD3 | 1989 | £2 | £5 | |
| Don't Prey For Me | CD-s | Polydor | LTLCD4 | 1989 | £2 | £5 | |
| I Ain't Gonna Cry | CD-s | Polydor | LTLCD11 | 1991 | £2 | £5 | |
| Kicking Up Dust | CD-s | Polydor | LTLCD15 | 1990 | £2 | £5 | |
| Ninety Degrees In The Shade | 7" | Polydor | LTLD1 | 1988 | £4 | £8 | poster sleeve |
| Ninety Degrees In The Shade | 12" | Polydor | LTLX1 | 1988 | £2.50 | £6 | |
| Ninety Degrees In The Shade | 12" | Polydor | LTLXP1 | 1988 | £4 | £10 | shaped picture disc |
| Product Of The Working Class | CD-s | Polydor | LTCDB9 | 1991 | £3 | £8 | CD set |
| Too Posh To Mosh | LP | Powerstation | AMP14 | 1987 | £10 | £25 | |
| Young Gods | CD-s | Polydor | LTLCD10 | 1991 | £4 | £10 | with booklet |

## LITTLE ANTHONY & THE IMPERIALS
| | | | | | | | |
|---|---|---|---|---|---|---|---|
| Bayou Bayou Baby | 7" | Top Rank | JAR366 | 1960 | £5 | £10 | |
| Best Of Little Anthony And The Imperials | LP | DCP | DC3809/DS6809 | 1966 | £8 | £20 | US |
| Better Use Your Head | 7" | United Artists | UP1137 | 1966 | £10 | £20 | |
| Goin' Out Of My Head | LP | United Artists | ULP1100 | 1966 | £15 | £30 | |
| Goin' Out Of My Head | 7" | United Artists | UP1073 | 1964 | £1.50 | £4 | |
| Gonna Fix You Good | 7" | United Artists | UP1151 | 1966 | £12.50 | £25 | |
| Hurt | 7" | United Artists | UP1126 | 1966 | £1.50 | £4 | |
| Hurt So Bad | 7" | United Artists | UP1083 | 1965 | £2.50 | £6 | |
| I Miss You So | 7" | United Artists | UP1112 | 1965 | £1.50 | £4 | |
| I'm On The Outside Lookin' In | LP | United Artists | ULP1089 | 1964 | £25 | £50 | |
| I'm On The Outside Looking In | 7" | United Artists | UP1065 | 1964 | £2 | £5 | |
| Little Anthony And The Imperials | 7" EP | United Artists | UEP1004 | 1965 | £20 | £40 | |
| Oh Yeah | 7" | London | HL8848 | 1959 | £10 | £20 | |
| Shades Of The 40s | LP | End | 311 | 1960 | £20 | £40 | US |
| Shimmy Shimmy Ko Ko Bop | 7" | Top Rank | JAR256 | 1959 | £6 | £12 | |
| Take Me Back | 7" | United Artists | UP1098 | 1965 | £1.50 | £4 | |
| Tears On My Pillow | 7" | London | HLH8704 | 1958 | £25 | £50 | |
| We Are Little Anthony & The Imperials | LP | End | 303 | 1960 | £30 | £60 | US |

## LITTLE BEVERLEY
| | | | | | | | |
|---|---|---|---|---|---|---|---|
| What A Guy | 7" | Pama | PM731 | 1968 | £1.50 | £4 | |

## LITTLE BILL & THE BLUENOTES
| | | | | | | | |
|---|---|---|---|---|---|---|---|
| I Love An Angel | 7" | Top Rank | JAR176 | 1959 | £2 | £5 | |

## LITTLE BOY BLUE
| | | | | | | | |
|---|---|---|---|---|---|---|---|
| Dark End Of The Street | 7" | Jackpot | JP701 | 1969 | £1.50 | £4 | |
| Since You Are Gone | 7" | Jackpot | JP705 | 1969 | £1.50 | £4 | |

## LITTLE BOY BLUES
| | | | | | | | |
|---|---|---|---|---|---|---|---|
| In The Woodland Of Weir | LP | Fontana | MGF2/SRF67578 | 1967 | £8 | £20 | US |

## LITTLE CAESAR & THE ROMANS
| | | | | | | | |
|---|---|---|---|---|---|---|---|
| Memories Of Those Oldies But Goodies | LP | Del-Fi | DFLP1218 | 1961 | £10 | £25 | US |

## LITTLE DARLINGS
| | | | | | | | |
|---|---|---|---|---|---|---|---|
| Little Bit Of Soul | 7" | Fontana | TF539 | 1965 | £20 | £40 | |

## LITTLE DIPPERS
| | | | | | | | |
|---|---|---|---|---|---|---|---|
| Forever | 7" | Pye | 7N25051 | 1960 | £1.50 | £4 | |
| Lonely | 7" | London | HLG9269 | 1961 | £4 | £8 | |

## LITTLE EVA
| | | | | | | | |
|---|---|---|---|---|---|---|---|
| Keep Your Hands Off My Baby | 7" | London | HLU9633 | 1962 | £1.50 | £4 | |
| Let's Turkey Trot | 7" | London | HLU9687 | 1963 | £1.50 | £4 | |
| Llllocomotion | LP | London | HAU8036 | 1963 | £10 | £25 | |
| Locomotion | 7" | London | HL9581 | 1962 | £1.50 | £4 | |
| Please Hurt Me | 7" | Colpix | PX11119 | 1963 | £1.50 | £4 | |
| Run To Her | 7" | Colpix | PX11035 | 1964 | £1.50 | £4 | |
| Stand By Me | 7" | Stateside | SS477 | 1965 | £2.50 | £6 | |
| Trouble With Boys | 7" | Colpix | PX11013 | 1963 | £1.50 | £4 | |

## LITTLE FEAT
| | | | | | | | |
|---|---|---|---|---|---|---|---|
| Feats Don't Fail Me Now | LP | Warner Bros | K56030 | 198– | £4 | £10 | Nimbus supercut |
| Sailin' Shoes | CD | Atlantic | K46156CD | 1988 | £5 | £12 | |
| Waiting For Columbus | LP | Mobile Fidelity | MFSL2013 | 1978 | £6 | £15 | US audiophile double |

## LITTLE FRANKIE
| | | | | | | | |
|---|---|---|---|---|---|---|---|
| It Doesn't Matter Any More | 7" | Columbia | DB7681 | 1965 | £1.50 | £4 | |

## LITTLE FREE ROCK
| | | | | | | | |
|---|---|---|---|---|---|---|---|
| Little Free Rock | LP | Transatlantic | TRA608 | 1969 | £25 | £50 | |

## LITTLE GEORGE
| | | | | | | | |
|---|---|---|---|---|---|---|---|
| Mary Anne | 7" | Rio | R45 | 1964 | £5 | £10 | Edward's Allstars B side |

## LITTLE HANK

| Title | Format | Label | Catalog | Year | | | Notes |
|---|---|---|---|---|---|---|---|
| Mr. Bang Bang Man | 7" | London | HLU10090 | 1966 | £15 | £30 | |
| Mr. Bang Bang Man | 7" | Monument | MON1045 | 1970 | £2 | £5 | |

## LITTLE JOE

| Title | Format | Label | Catalog | Year | | | Notes |
|---|---|---|---|---|---|---|---|
| Stay | 7" | Fontana | H281 | 1960 | £5 | £10 | |

## LITTLE JOEY & THE FLIPS

| Title | Format | Label | Catalog | Year | | | Notes |
|---|---|---|---|---|---|---|---|
| Bongo Stomp | 7" | Pye | 7N25152 | 1962 | £1.50 | £4 | |

## LITTLE JOHNNY & THE THREE TEENAGERS

| Title | Format | Label | Catalog | Year | | | Notes |
|---|---|---|---|---|---|---|---|
| Baby Lover | 7" | Decca | F10990 | 1958 | £2.50 | £6 | |

## LITTLE LUMAN

| Title | Format | Label | Catalog | Year | | | Notes |
|---|---|---|---|---|---|---|---|
| Hurry Harry | 7" | Rio | R44 | 1964 | £5 | £10 | Roland Alphonso B side |

## LITTLE LUTHER

| Title | Format | Label | Catalog | Year | | | Notes |
|---|---|---|---|---|---|---|---|
| Eenie Meenie Minie Mo | 7" | Pye | 7N25266 | 1964 | £12.50 | £25 | |

## LITTLE MAC & THE BOSS SOUNDS

| Title | Format | Label | Catalog | Year | | | Notes |
|---|---|---|---|---|---|---|---|
| In The Midnight Hour | 7" | Atlantic | 584031 | 1966 | £1.50 | £4 | |

## LITTLE MILTON

Little Milton is a fine blues singer and an even finer blues guitarist – very much in the manner of B. B. King on both counts – but most of his releases are soul records, where he is rather more ordinary. The *Grits Ain't Groceries* LP provides a reasonable balance between the styles, with the outstanding track being a smouldering version of 'I Can't Quit You Baby' (also the B side of the 'Grits Ain't Groceries' single).

| Title | Format | Label | Catalog | Year | | | Notes |
|---|---|---|---|---|---|---|---|
| Blindman | 7" | Pye | 7N25289 | 1965 | £2 | £5 | |
| Early In The Morning | 7" | Sue | W14021 | 1966 | £7.50 | £15 | |
| Grits Ain't Groceries | LP | Chess | CRLS4552 | 1969 | £5 | £12 | |
| Grits Ain't Groceries | 7" | Chess | CRS8087 | 1969 | £2.50 | £6 | |
| Let's Get Together | 7" | Chess | CRS8101 | 1969 | £2.50 | £6 | |
| Little Milton Sings Big Blues | LP | Checker | 3002 | 1966 | £6 | £15 | US |
| We're Gonna Make It | LP | Checker | 2995 | 1965 | £15 | £30 | US |
| We're Gonna Make It | 7" | Chess | CRS8013 | 1965 | £2.50 | £6 | |
| Who's Cheating Who | 7" | Chess | CRS8018 | 1965 | £4 | £8 | |

## LITTLE MR. LEE & THE CHEROKEES

| Title | Format | Label | Catalog | Year | | | Notes |
|---|---|---|---|---|---|---|---|
| Young Lover | 7" | Vocalion | VP9268 | 1966 | £7.50 | £15 | |

## LITTLE NORMA

| Title | Format | Label | Catalog | Year | | | Notes |
|---|---|---|---|---|---|---|---|
| Ten Commandments Of Woman | 7" | Dice | CC26 | 1964 | £5 | £10 | |

## LITTLE RAY

'I Been Trying' is an early example of Arthur Lee's songwriting, although Lee (later the leader of the group Love) does not appear to be otherwise involved in the record.

| Title | Format | Label | Catalog | Year | | | Notes |
|---|---|---|---|---|---|---|---|
| I Been Trying | 7" | Donna | 1404 | 1964 | £25 | £50 | US |

## LITTLE RICHARD

| Title | Format | Label | Catalog | Year | | | Notes |
|---|---|---|---|---|---|---|---|
| Baby Face | 7" | London | HL7056 | 1958 | £2 | £5 | export |
| Baby Face | 7" | London | HLU8770 | 1958 | £2.50 | £6 | |
| Baby What You Want Me To Do | 7" | Action | ACT4528 | 1969 | £2 | £5 | |
| Bama Lama Bama Loo | 7" | London | HL9896 | 1964 | £2 | £5 | |
| Blueberry Hill | 7" | Fontana | TF519 | 1964 | £2 | £5 | |
| By The Light Of The Silvery Moon | 7" | London | HL7079 | 1959 | £4 | £8 | export |
| By The Light Of The Silvery Moon | 7" | London | HLU8831 | 1959 | £2.50 | £6 | |
| Coming Home | LP | Coral | LVA9220 | 1964 | £6 | £15 | |
| Crying In The Chapel | 7" | London | HLK9708 | 1963 | £2 | £5 | |
| Do You Feel It | 7" EP | Stateside | SE1042 | 1966 | £6 | £12 | |
| Explosive Little Richard | LP | Columbia | SX/SCX6136 | 1967 | £6 | £15 | |
| Fabulous Little Richard | LP | London | HAU2193 | 1959 | £10 | £25 | |
| Four Dynamic Numbers | 7" EP | Summit | LSE2049 | 1963 | £2.50 | £6 | with Brock Peters |
| Get Down And Get With It | 7" | Columbia | DB8116 | 1967 | £7.50 | £15 | |
| Girl Can't Help It | 7" | London | HLO8382 | 1957 | £37.50 | £75 | gold label |
| Good Golly Miss Molly | 7" | London | HLU8560 | 1958 | £10 | £20 | |
| Great Hits | LP | Fontana | TL5314 | 1966 | £4 | £10 | |
| He Got What He Wanted | 7" | Mercury | AMT1189 | 1962 | £1.50 | £4 | |
| He's Back | 7" EP | London | REK1400 | 1963 | £7.50 | £15 | |
| Here's Little Richard | LP | London | HAO2055 | 1957 | £10 | £25 | |
| Here's Little Richard | LP | London | HAO2055 | 1957 | £20 | £40 | glossy red rear sleeve |
| Here's Little Richard | LP | Speciality | 100 | 1957 | £75 | £150 | US |
| Holy Mackrel | 7" | Stateside | SS508 | 1966 | £2 | £5 | |
| I Don't Know What You've Got | 7" | Fontana | TF652 | 1966 | £2 | £5 | |
| I Don't Wanna Discuss It | 7" | Columbia | DB8263 | 1967 | £6 | £12 | |
| I Got It | 7" | London | HLU9065 | 1960 | £2.50 | £6 | |
| I Need Love | 7" | Columbia | DB8058 | 1966 | £4 | £8 | |
| It Ain't What You Do | 7" | Sue | WI4015 | 1966 | £6 | £12 | |
| It's Real | LP | Mercury | MCL20036 | 1965 | £5 | £12 | |
| It's Real | LP | Mercury | MG2/SR60656 | 1961 | £8 | £20 | US |
| Jenny Jenny | 7" | London | HL7022 | 1957 | £6 | £12 | export |
| Jenny Jenny | 7" | London | HLO8470 | 1957 | £10 | £20 | |
| Joy Joy Joy | 7" | Mercury | AMT1165 | 1961 | £1.50 | £4 | |
| Kansas City | 7" | London | HLU8868 | 1959 | £4 | £8 | |
| Keep A Knocking | 7" | London | HLO8509 | 1957 | £10 | £20 | |

| | | | | | | |
|---|---|---|---|---|---|---|
| Little Bit Of Something | 7" | Columbia | DB8240 | 1967 £12.50 | £25 | |
| Little Richard | LP | Camden | CAL420 | 1956 £25 | £50 | US |
| Little Richard | LP | Camden | CDN125 | 1959 £6 | £15 | some tracks by Buck Ram Orchestra |
| Little Richard | LP | Speciality | SP2103 | 1957 £15 | £30 | US |
| Little Richard & His Band Vol. 1 | 7" EP | London | REO1071 | 1957 £7.50 | £15 | gold label |
| Little Richard & His Band Vol. 2 | 7" EP | London | REO1074 | 1957 £7.50 | £15 | gold label |
| Little Richard & His Band Vol. 3 | 7" EP | London | REO1103 | 1957 £7.50 | £15 | |
| Little Richard & His Band Vol. 4 | 7" EP | London | REO1106 | 1957 £7.50 | £15 | |
| Little Richard & His Band Vol. 5 | 7" EP | London | REU1208 | 1959 £7.50 | £15 | |
| Little Richard & His Band Vol. 6 | 7" EP | London | REU1234 | 1960 £7.50 | £15 | |
| Little Richard & His Band Vol. 7 | 7" EP | London | REU1235 | 1960 £7.50 | £15 | |
| Little Richard 2 | LP | London | HAU2126 | 1958 £10 | £25 | |
| Little Richard Is Back | LP | Fontana | TL5235 | 1965 £4 | £10 | |
| Little Richard Sings Freedom Songs | LP | Egmont | EGM9207 | 1963 £4 | £10 | |
| Little Richard/Memphis Slim | 7" EP | Vocalion | VEP170155 | 1964 £15 | £30 | with Memphis Slim |
| Long Tall Sally | 7" | London | HLO8366 | 1957 £37.50 | £75 | gold label |
| Lucille | 7" | London | HLO8446 | 1957 £10 | £20 | |
| Ooh My Soul | 7" | London | HL7049 | 1958 £4 | £8 | export |
| Ooh My Soul | 7" | London | HLO8647 | 1958 £6 | £12 | |
| Poor Dog | 7" | Columbia | DB7974 | 1966 £6 | £12 | |
| Pray Along With Little Richard | LP | Egmont | EGM9270 | 1963 £4 | £10 | |
| Pray Along With Little Richard Vol. 1 | LP | Top Rank | 25025 | 1960 £15 | £30 | plain white sleeve |
| Pray Along With Little Richard Vol. 2 | LP | Top Rank | 25026 | 1960 £25 | £50 | plain white sleeve |
| Rip It Up | 7" | London | HLO8336 | 1956 £37.50 | £75 | gold label |
| She Knows How To Rock | 7" | London | HL7074 | 1959 £5 | £10 | export |
| She's Together | 7" | Decca | AD1006 | 1968 £5 | £10 | export |
| Sings Gospel | LP | Stateside | SL10054 | 1964 £6 | £15 | |
| Travelling Shoes | 7" | London | HLK9756 | 1963 £2 | £5 | |
| Whole Lotta Shakin' Goin' On | 7" | London | HL7085 | 1959 £10 | £20 | export |
| Whole Lotta Shaking Going On | 7" | Stateside | SS340 | 1964 £2 | £5 | |
| Without Love | 7" | Sue | WI4001 | 1966 £6 | £12 | |

## LITTLE ROYS

| | | | | | | |
|---|---|---|---|---|---|---|
| Bongonyah | 7" | Camel | CA36 | 1969 £1.50 | £4 | |

## LITTLE TONY & HIS BROTHERS

| | | | | | | |
|---|---|---|---|---|---|---|
| Four And Twenty Thousand Kisses | 7" | Durium | DC16657 | 1961 £1.50 | £4 | |
| Hippy Hippy Shake | 7" | Decca | F11169 | 1959 £2 | £5 | |
| I Can't Help It | 7" | Decca | F11164 | 1959 £1.50 | £4 | |
| I Love You | 7" | Decca | F21218 | 1960 £1.50 | £4 | |
| Let Her Go | 7" | Durium | DRS54008 | 1958 £1.50 | £4 | |
| Let Her Go | LP | Durium | DRL50020 | 1966 £8 | £20 | |
| Little Tony | LP | Durium | DRL50006 | 195- £8 | £20 | |
| Non E Normale | 7" EP | Durium | DRE52012 | 1966 £7.50 | £15 | |
| Presenting Little Tony | 7" EP | Durium | U20058 | 1958 £15 | £30 | |
| Princess | 7" | Decca | F21223 | 1960 £1.50 | £4 | |
| Teddy Girl | 7" | Decca | F21247 | 1960 £2 | £5 | |
| Too Good | 7" | Decca | F11190 | 1959 £1.50 | £4 | |
| Who's That Knocking | 7" | Durium | DC16639 | 1959 £4 | £8 | |

## LITTLE WALTER

| | | | | | | |
|---|---|---|---|---|---|---|
| Best Of Little Walter | LP | Chess | LP1428 | 1958 £15 | £30 | US |
| Little Walter | LP | Pye | NPL28043 | 1964 £8 | £20 | |
| Little Walter & His Jukes | 7" EP | London | REU1061 | 1956 £37.50 | £75 | |
| Little Walter And His Dukes | LP | Python | PLPKM20 | 1969 £8 | £20 | |
| My Babe | 7" | London | HLM9175 | 1960 £10 | £20 | |
| My Babe | 7" | Pye | 7N25263 | 1964 £2.50 | £6 | |

## LITTLE WILBUR

Records credited to Little Wilbur are listed in this guide under the name Wilbur Whitfield.

## LIVELY ONES

| | | | | | | |
|---|---|---|---|---|---|---|
| Great Surf Hits | LP | Del-Fi | DFLP/DFST1238 | 1963 £8 | £20 | US |
| Surf Drums | LP | London | HA8082 | 1963 £8 | £20 | |
| Surf Rider | LP | London | HA8107 | 1963 £8 | £20 | |
| Surfin' South Of The Border | LP | Del-Fi | DFLP/DFST1240 | 1964 £8 | £20 | US |
| This Is Surf City | LP | Del-Fi | DFLP/DFST1237 | 1963 £8 | £20 | US |

## LIVERBIRDS

| | | | | | | |
|---|---|---|---|---|---|---|
| More Of | LP | Starclub | 158020STY | 1966 £50 | £100 | German |
| Star Club Show 4 | LP | Starclub | 148003STL/ 158003STY | 1965 £37.50 | £75 | German |

## LIVERPOOL BEATS

| | | | | | | |
|---|---|---|---|---|---|---|
| New Merseyside Sound | LP | Rondo | 2026 | 1964 £20 | £40 | US |
| This Is Liverpool | LP | Vogue | 17005 | 1964 £25 | £50 | German |

## LIVERPOOL FISHERMEN

| | | | | | | |
|---|---|---|---|---|---|---|
| Swallow The Anchor | LP | Mushroom | 150MR9 | 1971 £50 | £100 | |

## LIVERPOOL FIVE

| | | | | | | |
|---|---|---|---|---|---|---|
| Arrive | LP | RCA | LPM/LSP3583 | 1966 £8 | £20 | US |
| Heart | 7" EP | RCA | 86493 | 1965 £7.50 | £15 | French |
| Out Of Sight | LP | RCA | LPM/LSP3682 | 1967 £8 | £20 | US |

## LIVERPOOL KIDS
Beatle Mash .......................................... LP ...... Palace ............. 777 ....................... 1964 £8 .......... £20 ...................... US

## LIVERPOOL SCENE _____

The first Liverpool Scene consisted of the three poets Roger McGough, Brian Patten and Adrian Henri, with music supplied by guitarist Andy Roberts. The group that performs on the RCA records is more of a regular rock group, although it is still one that tends to act as an umbrella for the individual talents beneath – Henri and Roberts as before, with poet/saxophonist Mike Evans and singer/guitarist Mike Hart also making telling contributions. Each LP is tremendously varied, encompassing rock, jazz and folk; poetry, comedy and drama – a real pot-pourri, in fact, but it worked.

Amazing Adventures Of ............................ LP ...... RCA .............. SF7995 ................... 1968 £6 .......... £15 ......................
Bread On The Night .................................. LP ...... RCA .............. SF8057 ................... 1969 £6 .......... £15 ......................
Heirloon ................................................. LP ...... RCA .............. SF8134 ................... 1970 £5 .......... £12 ......................
Incredible New Liverpool Scene ................ LP ...... CBS .............. 63045 ..................... 1967 £15 .......... £30 ......................
St. Adrian Co. Broadway & 3rd ................ LP ...... RCA .............. SF8100 ................... 1970 £6 .......... £15 ......................

## LIVERPOOLS
Beatle-Mania In The USA ......................... LP ...... Wyncote ...... 9001 ................... 1964 £6 .......... £15 ...................... US
Hit Sounds From England ......................... LP ...... Wyncote ...... 9061 ................... 1965 £6 .......... £15 ...................... US

## LIVIN' BLUES
Bamboozle ............................................... LP ...... Philips ............ 6413024 ............. 1971 £4 .......... £10 ....................Dutch
Dutch Treat ............................................ LP ...... Dwarf ............ 2003 ................. 1971 £5 .......... £12 ....................US
Hell's Session ......................................... LP ...... Philips ............ 6440315 ............. 1969 £4 .......... £10 ....................Dutch
Rockin' At The Tweedmill ........................ LP ...... Philips ............ 6423052 ............. 1972 £4 .......... £10 ....................German
Wang Dang Doodle ................................. LP ...... Philips ............ 6440125 ............. 1970 £4 .......... £10 ....................Dutch

## LIVING COLOUR
Cult Of Personality ................................. CD-s .. Epic .............. CDLCL3 .............. 1988 £3 .......... £8
Cult Of Personality ................................. CD-s .. Epic .............. CDLCL5 .............. 1989 £2 .......... £5
Glamour Boys .......................................... CD-s .. Epic .............. CDLCL2 .............. 1988 £2 .......... £5
Glamour Boys (remix) .............................. CD-s .. Epic .............. CDLCL6 .............. 1989 £2 .......... £5
Love Rears Its Ugly Head ......................... CD-s .. Epic .............. 6565935 .............. 1991 £2 .......... £5 ....................picture disc
Middle Man ............................................. CD-s .. Epic .............. CDLCL1 .............. 1988 £2 .......... £5
Open Letter (To A Landlord) .................... CD-s .. Epic .............. CDLCL4 .............. 1989 £2 .......... £5
Solace Of You .......................................... CD-s .. Epic .............. 6569089 .............. 1991 £2 .......... £5
Type ....................................................... CD-s .. Epic .............. CDLCL7 .............. 1990 £2 .......... £5

## LIVING DAYLIGHTS
Always With Him ..................................... 7" ...... Philips ............ BF1613 ................ 1967 £10 .......... £20
Let's Live For Today ................................ 7" EP . Fontana ........... 460234 ............... 1967 £12.50 .. £25 ....................French
Let's Live For Today ................................ 7" ...... Philips ............ BF1561 ................ 1967 £5 .......... £10

## LIVING IN TEXAS
And David Cried ...................................... 7" ...... Rhythmic ....... RMNS2 ............... 1983 £2 .......... £5

## LIVINGSTONES
In Concert .............................................. LP ...... Waverley ........ (S)ZLP2105 ........... 1968 £6 .......... £15

## LIZA & THE JET SET
How Can I Know? ................................... 7" ...... Parlophone .... R5248 ................. 1965 £2 .......... £5

## LLAN
Realise .................................................... 7" ...... CBS .............. 202405 ................. 1966 £7.50 .. £15

## LLOYD, A. L.
Australian Bush Songs ............................. LP ...... Riverside ........ RLP12606 ............. 196– £8 .......... £20 ...................... US
Best Of A. L. Lloyd ................................ LP ...... XTRA ............ XTRA5023 ........... 1966 £10 .......... £25
Bird In The Bush ..................................... LP ...... Topic ............ 12T135 ............... 1965 £30 .......... £60 .. with Anne Briggs & Frankie Armstrong
England And Her Folk Songs ................... 7" EP . Collector ......... JEB8 ..................... 1962 £10 .......... £20
English And Scottish Folk Ballads ............ LP ...... Topic ......... 12T103 ............... 1964 £10 .......... £25 .. with Ewan MacColl
English Drinking Songs ............................ LP ...... Riverside ........ RLP12618 ............. 196– £8 .......... £20 ...................... US
English Street Songs ................................ LP ...... Riverside ........ RLP12614 ............. 196– £8 .......... £20 ...................... US
First Person ............................................ LP ...... Topic ............ 12T118 ............... 1965 £10 .......... £25
Great Australian Legend ........................... LP ...... Topic ............ 12TS203 ............... 1971 £37.50 .. £75 ..... with Trevor Lucas
Leviathan! ............................................... LP ...... Topic ............ 12T174 ............... 1967 £10 .......... £25
Outback Ballads ...................................... LP ...... Topic ............ 12T51 ................. 1960 £10 .......... £25
Selection From The Penguin Book Of ....... LP ...... Collector ......... JGB5001 ............... 1961 £20 .......... £40
  English Folk Songs ..............................

## LLOYD, CHARLES _____

In tune with the questing spirit of the times, jazz saxophonist Charles Lloyd's group in the late sixties was marketed as though it was a rock band, with appearances at venues like the Fillmore, album titles like *Love-In*, and stage dress that included kaftans and beads. Such tactics undoubtedly gave Lloyd's music more prominence than it would otherwise have achieved, but the group did also contain two musicians who subsequently played with Miles Davis, before embarking on highly successful solo careers – drummer Jack DeJohnette and pianist Keith Jarrett.

Dream Weaver .......................................... LP ...... Atlantic ........... 587025 ............... 1966 £8 .......... £20
Flowering Of The Original Charles Lloyd  LP ...... Atlantic ........... 2400165 ................ 1971 £6 .......... £15
  Quartet ..............................................
Forest Flower ......................................... LP ...... Atlantic ........... SD1473 ............... 1967 £8 .......... £20 ...................... US
In Europe .............................................. LP ...... Atlantic ........... 588108 ............... 1968 £8 .......... £20
Journey Within ....................................... LP ...... Atlantic ........... 587/588101 ............. 1968 £8 .......... £20
Love-In .................................................. LP ...... Atlantic ........... 587/588077 ............. 1967 £8 .......... £20

| Soundtrack | LP | Atlantic | SD1519 | 1969 £6 | £15 | US |
| Waves | LP | A&M | SP3044 | 1972 £6 | £15 | US |

## LLOYD, JIMMY
| Call On Me | 7" | Philips | 326568BF | 1963 £1.50 | £4 | |
| Prince Of Players | 7" | Philips | PB795 | 1958 £1.50 | £4 | |
| Teenage Sonata | 7" | Philips | PB1010 | 1960 £1.50 | £4 | |
| Witch Doctor | 7" | Philips | PB827 | 1958 £2 | £5 | |

## LLOYD, PEGGY
| Dixieland Honky Tonk | 7" EP | London | REP1017 | 1955 £4 | £8 | |

## LLOYD & CECIL
| Come Over Here | 7" | Blue Beat | BB49 | 1961 £6 | £12 | C. Byrd B side |

## LLOYD & DEVON
| Love Is The Key | 7" | Punch | PH14 | 1967 £2 | £5 | Virtues B side |
| Out Of The Fire | 7" | Blue Cat | BS151 | 1968 £2.50 | £6 | |

## LLOYD & GLEN
| Keep On Pushing | 7" | Doctor Bird | DB1071 | 1967 £5 | £10 | Bobby Aitken B side |
| That Girl | 7" | Coxsone | CS7011 | 1967 £5 | £10 | |

## LLOYD & JOHNNY
| My Argument | 7" | Island | WI3158 | 1968 £5 | £10 | George Dekker B side |

## LLOYD & THE GROOVERS
| Do It To Me Baby | 7" | Caltone | TONE108 | 1967 £4 | £8 | Diplomats B side |
| Listen To The Music | 7" | Caltone | TONE112 | 1968 £4 | £8 | Diplomats B side |
| My Heart My Soul | 7" | Caltone | TONE109 | 1967 £4 | £8 | Diplomats B side |

## LLOYDIE & THE LOWBITES
| Censored | LP | Lowbite | LOW1 | 1971 £6 | £15 | |

## LLOYD'S ALLSTARS
| Love Kiss Blue | 7" | Doctor Bird | DB1178 | 1969 £5 | £10 | Uniques B side |

## LLYGOD FFYRNIG
| N.C.B. | 7" | Pwdwr | PWDWR1 | 1978 £6 | £12 | |

## LOADER, DICKIE
| Heatwave | 7" | Palette | PG9015 | 1961 £5 | £10 | |

## LOADING ZONE
| Loading Zone | LP | RCA | LSP3959 | 1968 £8 | £20 | US |
| One For All | LP | Umbrella | US101 | 1968 £15 | £30 | US |

## LOADSTONE
| Loadstone | LP | Barnaby | 21235004 | 1969 £8 | £20 | US |

## LOCHLIN, HANK
| Best Of Hank Lochlin | LP | King | 672 | 1961 £6 | £15 | US |
| Country Guitar Vol. 3 | 7" EP | RCA | RCX115 | 1958 £2.50 | £6 | |
| Encores | LP | King | 738 | 1961 £6 | £15 | US |
| Encores | 7" EP | Parlophone | GEP8875 | 1963 £4 | £8 | |
| Foreign Love | LP | RCA | LPM1673 | 1958 £6 | £15 | US |
| Happy Journey | LP | RCA | LPM/LSP2464 | 1962 £5 | £12 | US |
| Irish Songs Country Style | 7" EP | RCA | RCX7150 | 1964 £2 | £5 | |
| Please Help Me, I'm Falling | LP | RCA | RD27201 | 1961 £4 | £10 | |
| Seven Days | 7" EP | RCA | RCX217 | 1962 £2.50 | £6 | |
| Tribute To Roy Acuff | LP | RCA | LPM/LSP2597 | 1962 £5 | £12 | US |
| Waltz Of The Wind | 7" EP | RCA | RCX7116 | 1963 £2.50 | £6 | |
| Ways Of Love | LP | RCA | LPM/LSP2680 | 1963 £5 | £12 | US |

## LOCKETS
| Doncha Know | 7" | Pye | 7N25232 | 1963 £2.50 | £6 | |

## LOCKJAW
| Journalist Jive | 7" | Raw | RAW19 | 1978 £1.50 | £4 | |

## LOCKRAN, GERRY
| Blues At Sunrise | LP | Saga | FID2165 | 1969 £4 | £10 | |
| Blues Vendetta | LP | Waverley | ZLP2091 | 1968 £6 | £15 | |
| Essential | LP | Spark | SRLP104 | 1969 £5 | £12 | |
| Hold On I'm Coming | LP | Planet | PLL1002 | 1967 £20 | £40 | |

## LOCKYER, MALCOLM
| Eccentric Dr. Who | 7" | Columbia | DB7663 | 1965 £10 | £20 | |

## LOCOMOTIVE
| Mr. Armageddan | 7" | Parlophone | R5758 | 1969 £2 | £5 | |
| Roll Over Mary | 7" | Parlophone | R5835 | 1970 £2 | £5 | |
| Rudi's In Love | 7" | Parlophone | R5718 | 1968 £1.50 | £4 | |
| Rudi's In Love | 7" | Parlophone | R5915 | 1971 £1.50 | £4 | |
| Rudy A Message To You | 7" | Direction | 583114 | 1967 £1.50 | £4 | |
| We Are Everything You See | LP | Parlophone | PCS7093 | 1969 £62.50 | £125 | |
| You Must Be Joking | 7" | Parlophone | R5801 | 1969 £2.50 | £6 | |

## LODGE, JOHN
Natural Avenue .......................................... CD ..... London ........... 8204642 ................ 1987 £5 .......... £12 ..................................

## LOFGREN, NILS
Back It Up ............................................... LP ..... A&M .......... SP8362 ............. 1975 £5 .......... £12 .......... *US promo*

## LOFT
Up The Hill And Down The Slope ........... 7" ...... Creation ......... CRE015 ......... 1985 £4 .......... £8 ..................................
Why Does The Rain Fall ...................... 7" ...... Creation ........ CRE009 ............. 1984 £5 .......... £10 ................................

## LOFTON, CRIPPLE CLARENCE
Blues Pianist .......................................... 10" LP Vogue ........... LDE122 ......... 1955 £10 .......... £25 ........................
Cripple Clarence Lofton ...................... 7" EP . Vogue ........... EPV1209 ............ 1959 £10 .......... £20 ........................
Lost Recording Date .............................. 10" LP London ........... AL3531 ........... 1954 £10 .......... £25 ........................

## LOLLIPOP SHOPPE
Just Colour ............................................ LP ...... Uni ............... 73019 .............. 1968 £25 .......... £50 .................... *US*

## LOMAN, LAURIE
Whither Thou Goest ............................. 7" ...... London .......... HL8101 ............ 1954 £10 .......... £20 ..................................

## LOMAX, ALAN
Alan Lomax Sings ................................. 7" EP . Pye ................. NJE1055 ........... 1957 £4 .......... £8 ..................................
Blues In The Mississippi Night ............. LP ...... Pye ................. NJL8 .................. 1957 £4 .......... £10 ................................
Dirty Old Town ..................................... 7" ...... Decca ............ F10787 ............... 1956 £2 .......... £5 ................................
Great American Ballads ......................... LP ...... HMV ............. CLP1192 ............ 1958 £4 .......... £10 ................................
Oh Lula .............................................. 7" EP . Decca ............ DFE6367 ............ 1956 £2 .......... £5 ..............................
Presents American Song Train ............... LP ...... Pye ................. NPL18013 ......... 1958 £4 .......... £10 ..............................
Songs From Texas ................................ 7" EP . Melodisc ........ EPM788 ............. 1959 £2.50 .......... £6 ..............................
Sounds Of The South ........................... LP ...... Atlantic ......... 590033 ............... 1969 £4 .......... £10 ..............................

## LOMAX, JACKIE
Genuine Imitation Life .......................... 7" ...... CBS ............... 2554 .................. 1968 £2 .......... £5 ..............................
How The Web Was Woven ..................... 7" ...... Apple ............. 23 ..................... 1970 £5 .......... £10 .......... *picture sleeve*
Interview With Jackie Lomax ................. LP ...... Warner Bros . PRO520 ............. 1972 £6 .......... £15 .......... *US promo*
Is This What You Want .......................... LP ...... Apple ............. APCOR6 ........... 1969 £15 .......... £30 .......... *mono*
Is This What You Want .......................... LP ...... Apple ............. SAPCOR6 .......... 1969 £6 .......... £15 .......... *stereo*
New Day ............................................... 7" ...... Apple ............. 11 ..................... 1969 £5 .......... £10 ..............................
Sour Milk Sea ...................................... 7" ...... Apple ............. 3 ...................... 1968 £4 .......... £8 ..............................

## LOMAX ALLIANCE
Try As You May ................................... 7" ...... CBS ............... 2729 .................. 1967 £2 .......... £5 ..............................

## LOMBARDO, GUY
Cherry Pink And Apple Blossom White ..... 7" ...... Brunswick ....... 05443 ................ 1955 £1.50 .......... £4 ..............................

## LOMBARDY, AL
Blues ................................................... 7" ...... London .......... HL8076 ............ 1954 £10 .......... £20 ..............................
In A Little Spanish Town ....................... 7" ...... London .......... HL8127 ............ 1955 £10 .......... £20 ..............................

## LONDON, JIMMY
Bridge Over Troubled Waters ................ LP ...... Trojan ............ TRL39 ............... 1972 £5 .......... £12 ..............................

## LONDON, JOE
It Might Have Been .............................. 7" ...... London .......... HLW9008 ......... 1959 £1.50 .......... £4 ..............................

## LONDON, JULIE
About The Blues ................................... LP ...... London .......... HAU2091 ......... 1958 £8 .......... £20 ..............................
All Through The Night .......................... LP ...... Liberty .......... (S)LBY1300 ....... 1966 £4 .......... £10 ..............................
All Through The Night .......................... 7" EP . Liberty .......... LEP2260 ............ 1966 £4 .......... £8 ..............................
Around Midnight .................................. LP ...... London .......... HAG2299 ......... 1961 £5 .......... £12 ..............................
Baby Baby All The Time ........................ 7" ...... London .......... HLU8279 ......... 1956 £10 .......... £20 .......... *gold label*
Best Of Julie London ........................... LP ...... Liberty .......... LBY1023 ........... 1962 £4 .......... £10 ..............................
Boy On A Dolphin ................................. 7" ...... London .......... HLU8414 ......... 1957 £4 .......... £8 ..............................
Calendar Girl ....................................... LP ...... London .......... HAU2038 ......... 1957 £8 .......... £20 ..............................
Cry Me A River ..................................... 7" ...... London .......... HLU8240 ......... 1956 £15 .......... £30 .......... *gold label*
Desafinado ........................................... 7" EP . Liberty .......... LEP2103 ............ 1963 £4 .......... £8 ..............................
End Of The World ................................. LP ...... Liberty .......... LRP3300/LST7300. 1963 £4 .......... £10 .......... *US*
Feeling Good ........................................ LP ...... Liberty .......... (S)LBY1281 ....... 1966 £4 .......... £10 ..............................
For The Night People ............................ LP ...... Liberty .......... (S)LBY1334 ....... 1967 £4 .......... £10 ..............................
Great Performances .............................. LP ...... Liberty .......... LBL/LBS83049 ... 1968 £4 .......... £10 ..............................
I'm Coming Back To You ....................... 7" ...... Liberty .......... LIB55605 .......... 1963 £2 .......... £5 ..............................
In Person At The Americana ................. LP ...... Liberty .......... LBY1222 ........... 1965 £4 .......... £10 ..............................
Julie ................................................... LP ...... London .......... HAU2112 ......... 1958 £8 .......... £20 ..............................
Julie At Home ...................................... LP ...... London .......... HAG2280/ ........ 1960 £5 .......... £12 ..............................
                                                                            SAHG6097 .........
Julie Is Her Name ................................ LP ...... Liberty .......... LST7027 ............ 1957 £20 .......... £40 .......... *US, blue vinyl*
Julie Is Her Name ................................ LP ...... London .......... HAU2005 ......... 1956 £10 .......... £25 ..............................
Julie Is Her Name Vol. 2 ....................... LP ...... London .......... HAU2186/ ......... 1959 £8 .......... £20 ..............................
                                                                            SAHU6042 .........
Julie London ........................................ LP ...... Liberty .......... LRP3342/LST7342. 1964 £4 .......... £10 .......... *US*
Julie Part 1 .......................................... 7" EP . London .......... REU1180 ........... 1959 £5 .......... £10 ..............................
Julie Part 2 .......................................... 7" EP . London .......... REU1181 ........... 1959 £5 .......... £10 ..............................
Julie Part 3 .......................................... 7" EP . London .......... REU1182 ........... 1959 £5 .......... £10 ..............................
Latin In A Satin Mood .......................... LP ...... Liberty .......... (S)LBY1136 ....... 1963 £4 .......... £10 ..............................
London By Night ................................... LP ...... London .......... HAU2171 ......... 1959 £6 .......... £15 ..............................
London's Girl Friends Vol. 1 ................. 7" EP . London .......... REN1092 .......... 1957 £6 .......... £12 ..............................

| | | | | | | | |
|---|---|---|---|---|---|---|---|
| Lonely Girl | LP | Liberty | LRP3012 | 1956 | £10 | £25 | US |
| Love Letters | LP | Liberty | (S)LBY1083 | 1962 | £4 | £10 | |
| Love On The Rocks | LP | Liberty | (S)LBY1113 | 1963 | £4 | £10 | |
| Make Love To Me | LP | London | HAU2083 | 1958 | £8 | £20 | |
| Make Love To Me Part 1 | 7" EP | London | REU1151 | 1958 | £5 | £10 | |
| Make Love To Me Part 2 | 7" EP | London | REU1152 | 1958 | £5 | £10 | |
| Make Love To Me Part 3 | 7" EP | London | REU1153 | 1958 | £5 | £10 | |
| Man Of The West | 7" | London | HLU8769 | 1958 | £1.50 | £4 | |
| Meaning Of The Blues | 7" | London | HLU8394 | 1957 | £7.50 | £15 | gold label |
| Must Be Catchin' | 7" | London | HLU8891 | 1959 | £2.50 | £6 | |
| My Strange Affair | 7" | London | HLU8657 | 1958 | £2 | £5 | |
| Nice Girls Don't Stay For Breakfast | LP | Liberty | (S)LBY1364 | 1967 | £4 | £10 | |
| Our Fair Lady | LP | Liberty | (S)LBY1251 | 1965 | £4 | £10 | |
| Saddle The Wind | 7" | London | HLU8602 | 1958 | £2.50 | £6 | |
| Sanctuary | 7" | London | HLG9360 | 1961 | £1.50 | £4 | |
| Send For Me | LP | London | HAG2353/ SAHG6154 | 1961 | £5 | £12 | |
| Sings Film Songs | 7" EP | London | REU1076 | 1957 | £6 | £12 | gold label |
| Sophisticated Lady | LP | Liberty | LRP3203/LST7203 | 1962 | £4 | £10 | US |
| Swing Me An Old Song | LP | London | HAW2225 | 1960 | £5 | £12 | |
| Whatever Julie Wants | LP | London | HAG2405/ SAHG6205 | 1962 | £5 | £12 | |
| Wonderful World Of Julie London | LP | Liberty | (S)LBY1185 | 1964 | £4 | £10 | |
| Your Number Please | LP | London | HAW2229 | 1960 | £5 | £12 | |
| Yummy Yummy Yummy | LP | Liberty | LBL/LBS83183 | 1969 | £4 | £10 | |

## LONDON, LAURIE

| | | | | | | | |
|---|---|---|---|---|---|---|---|
| He's Got The Whole World In His Hands | 7" | Parlophone | R4359 | 1957 | £1.50 | £4 | |
| Laurie London | LP | Capitol | T1016 | 1958 | £8 | £20 | US |
| Laurie London | 7" EP | Parlophone | GEP8664 | 1957 | £6 | £12 | |
| Little Laurie London No. 2 | 7" EP | Parlophone | GEP8689 | 1958 | £6 | £12 | |

## LONDON, MARK

| | | | | | | | |
|---|---|---|---|---|---|---|---|
| Stranger In The World | 7" | Pye | 7N15825 | 1965 | £2.50 | £6 | |

## LONDON, PETER

| | | | | | | | |
|---|---|---|---|---|---|---|---|
| Bless You | 7" | Pye | 7N15957 | 1965 | £7.50 | £15 | |

## LONDON & BRIDGES

| | | | | | | | |
|---|---|---|---|---|---|---|---|
| It Just Ain't Right | 7" | CBS | 202056 | 1966 | £10 | £20 | |

## LONDON BEATS

| | | | | | | | |
|---|---|---|---|---|---|---|---|
| London Beats | LP | Pronit | XL0278 | 1964 | £25 | £50 | Polish |

## LONDON JAZZ FOUR

| | | | | | | | |
|---|---|---|---|---|---|---|---|
| Norwegian Wood | 7" | Polydor | BM56092 | 1966 | £2 | £5 | |
| Take A New Look At The Beatles | LP | Polydor | 582005 | 1967 | £10 | £25 | |

## LONDON JAZZ QUARTET

| | | | | | | | |
|---|---|---|---|---|---|---|---|
| London Jazz Quartet | LP | Tempo | TAP28 | 1960 | £20 | £40 | |

## LONDON WAITS

| | | | | | | | |
|---|---|---|---|---|---|---|---|
| Serenadio | 7" | Immediate | IM030 | 1966 | £5 | £10 | |

## LONDON'S GENTLEMEN OF JAZZ

Although there are no musician credits on the album, this is actually the work of the Phil Seamen Trio. Rated by many as Britain's best jazz drummer (and Ginger Baker named him as a major influence), Seamen made few records. This one is not one of his best, but is nevertheless an essential purchase for his fans.

| | | | | | | | |
|---|---|---|---|---|---|---|---|
| Fiddler On The Roof – Sweet Charity | LP | Ace Of Clubs | ACL/SCL1254 | 1969 | £8 | £20 | |

## LONE RANGER

| | | | | | | | |
|---|---|---|---|---|---|---|---|
| Adventures Of The Lone Ranger | LP | Decca | DL8578 | | £10 | £25 | US |
| Lone Ranger No. 1 | 7" EP | Brunswick | OE9394 | 1959 | £2 | £5 | |
| Lone Ranger No. 2 | 7" EP | Brunswick | OE9395 | 1959 | £2 | £5 | |
| Lone Ranger No. 3 | 7" EP | Brunswick | OE9396 | 1959 | £2 | £5 | |

## LONESOME, JOHNNY

| | | | | | | | |
|---|---|---|---|---|---|---|---|
| Marie Marie | 7" | HMV | POP837 | 1961 | £1.50 | £4 | |

## LONESOME STONE

| | | | | | | | |
|---|---|---|---|---|---|---|---|
| Lonesome Stone | LP | Reflection | RL306 | 1973 | £10 | £25 | |

## LONESOME SUNDOWN

| | | | | | | | |
|---|---|---|---|---|---|---|---|
| Lonesome Lonely Blues | LP | Blue Horizon | 763864 | 1970 | £25 | £50 | |

## LONESOME TRAVELLERS

| | | | | | | | |
|---|---|---|---|---|---|---|---|
| Lonesome Travellers | LP | Tradition | TSR004 | 1970 | £10 | £25 | |
| Lost Children | LP | Nebula | NEB100 | 1971 | £15 | £30 | |

## LONG, SHORTY

| | | | | | | | |
|---|---|---|---|---|---|---|---|
| Chantilly Lace | 7" | Tamla Motown | TMG600 | 1967 | £2.50 | £6 | |
| Function At The Junction | 7" | Tamla Motown | TMG573 | 1966 | £6 | £12 | |
| Here Comes The Judge | LP | Tamla Motown | (S)TML11086 | 1968 | £6 | £15 | |
| Here Comes The Judge | 7" | Tamla Motown | TMG663 | 1968 | £1.50 | £4 | |
| Night Fo' Last | 7" | Tamla Motown | TMG644 | 1968 | £2.50 | £6 | |
| Out To Get You | 7" | Tamla Motown | TMG512 | 1965 | £20 | £40 | |

| | | | | | | |
|---|---|---|---|---|---|---|
| Prime Of Shorty Long | LP | Tamla Motown | (S)TML11144 | 1970 £6 | £15 | |

## LONG & THE SHORT
| | | | | | | |
|---|---|---|---|---|---|---|
| Choc Ice | 7" | Decca | F12043 | 1964 £4 | £8 | |
| Letter | 7" | Decca | F11964 | 1964 £4 | £8 | |

## LONG TALL SHORTY
| | | | | | | |
|---|---|---|---|---|---|---|
| By Your Love | 7" | Warner Bros | K17491 | 1979 £10 | £20 | |
| If I Was You | 7" | Dr. Creation | LYN9904 | 1981 £1.50 | £4 | flexi |
| On The Streets Again | 7" | Diamond | DIA002 | 1985 £2 | £5 | with poster |
| Win Or Lose | 7" | Ramkup | CAC007 | 1981 £12.50 | £25 | |

## LONGBOATMEN
| | | | | | | |
|---|---|---|---|---|---|---|
| Take Her Any Time | 7" | Polydor | 56115 | 1966 £180 | £300 | best auctioned |

## LONGBRANCH PENNYWHISTLE

Longbranch Pennywhistle was a duo comprising J. D. Souther and Glenn Frey, both of whom have been familiar faces within the American country-rock scene ever since – Frey being a member of the Eagles.

| | | | | | | |
|---|---|---|---|---|---|---|
| Longbranch Pennywhistle | LP | Amos | AAS7007 | 1969 £8 | £20 | US |

## LONGET, CLAUDINE
| | | | | | | |
|---|---|---|---|---|---|---|
| Colours | LP | A&M | AMLS929 | 1968 £4 | £10 | with Randy Newman |

## LONGMAN, BRENDA & IAN
| | | | | | | |
|---|---|---|---|---|---|---|
| No Royalties | LP | Private | PLP1081 | 1977 £15 | £30 | |

## LONGPIGS
| | | | | | | |
|---|---|---|---|---|---|---|
| She Said | 12" | Elektra | | 1993 £20 | £40 | promo only |

## LOOP
| | | | | | | |
|---|---|---|---|---|---|---|
| Arc-Lite | CD-s | Situation 2 | SIT64CD | 1989 £2 | £5 | |
| Collision | 7" | Chapter 22 | LCHAP27 | 1988 £1.50 | £4 | |
| Fade Out | LP | Chapter 22 | CHAPLLP34 | 1988 £4 | £10 | .2 45rpm discs, signed |
| Gilded Eternity | CD | Situation 2 | SITU27CD | 1990 £5 | £12 | |
| Sixteen Dreams | 12" | Head | HEAD5 | 1987 £4 | £10 | |
| Soundhead | 7" | Cheree | CHEREE1 | 1988 £2.50 | £6 | flexi, B side by The Telescopes |
| Spinning | 7" | Head | HEADL7 | 1987 £2 | £5 | no picture sleeve |
| Spinning | 12" | Head | HEAD7 | 1987 £4 | £10 | |

## LOOSE ENDS
| | | | | | | |
|---|---|---|---|---|---|---|
| Send The People Away | 7" | Decca | F12437 | 1966 £4 | £8 | |
| Taxman | 7" | Decca | F12476 | 1966 £4 | £8 | |

## LOOSE TUBES
| | | | | | | |
|---|---|---|---|---|---|---|
| Open Letter | CD | Editions EG | EEGCD55 | 1988 £5 | £12 | |

## LOOT
| | | | | | | |
|---|---|---|---|---|---|---|
| Baby Come Closer | 7" EP | Fontana | 460206 | 1967 £12.50 | £25 | French |
| Baby Come Closer | 7" | Page One | POF013 | 1966 £2 | £5 | |
| Don't Turn Around | 7" | CBS | 3231 | 1968 £1.50 | £4 | |
| I've Just Gotta Love You | 7" | Page One | POF026 | 1967 £5 | £10 | |
| She's A Winner | 7" | Page One | POF095 | 1968 £6 | £12 | 2 different B sides |
| Try To Keep It Secret | 7" | Page One | POF115 | 1969 £7.50 | £15 | |
| Whenever You're Ready | 7" EP | Palette | 22021 | 1967 £12.50 | £25 | French |
| Whenever You're Ready | 7" | CBS | 2938 | 1967 £2.50 | £6 | |

## LOPEZ, TRINI
| | | | | | | |
|---|---|---|---|---|---|---|
| If I Had A Hammer | 7" | Reprise | R20198 | 1963 £1.50 | £4 | |
| Jean Marie | 7" | London | HL9808 | 1963 £1.50 | £4 | |
| More Of Trini Lopez | LP | London | HA8160 | 1964 £4 | £10 | |
| Teenage Love Songs | LP | London | HA8132 | 1964 £6 | £15 | |

## LOR, DENISE
| | | | | | | |
|---|---|---|---|---|---|---|
| If I Give My Heart To You | 7" | Parlophone | MSP6120 | 1954 £1.50 | £4 | |

## LORAN, KENNY
| | | | | | | |
|---|---|---|---|---|---|---|
| Mama's Little Baby | 7" | Capitol | CL15081 | 1959 £10 | £20 | |

## L'ORANGE MECHANIK
| | | | | | | |
|---|---|---|---|---|---|---|
| Symphony | 7" | Artpop | POP44 | 1985 £2 | £5 | |

## LORD, BRIAN & THE MIDNIGHTERS

The Brian Lord single features both Frank Zappa and his colleague in the Mothers of Invention, Ray Collins.

| | | | | | | |
|---|---|---|---|---|---|---|
| Big Surfer | 7" | Capitol | 4981 | 1963 £50 | £100 | US |
| Big Surfer | 7" | Vigah | 001 | 1963 £100 | £200 | US |

## LORD, TONY
| | | | | | | |
|---|---|---|---|---|---|---|
| World's Champion | 7" | Planet | PLF102 | 1966 £5 | £10 | |

## LORD BEGINNER
| | | | | | | |
|---|---|---|---|---|---|---|
| Victory Test Match | 7" | Melodisc | CAL1 | 1963 £1.50 | £4 | |

## LORD BRISCO
| | | | | | | |
|---|---|---|---|---|---|---|
| Jonah | 7" | Island | WI187 | 1965 £5 | £10 | |

| | | | | | | |
|---|---|---|---|---|---|---|
| My Love Has Come | 7" | Black Swan | WI450 | 1964 £5 | £10 | ... *Baba Brooks B side* |
| Spiritual Mambo | 7" | Black Swan | WI447 | 1964 £5 | £10 | ... *Baba Brooks B side* |
| Trojan | 7" | Black Swan | WI454 | 1964 £5 | £10 | |

## LORD BRYNNER
| | | | | | |
|---|---|---|---|---|---|
| Congo War | 7" | Island | WI266 | 1966 £5 | £10 | |

## LORD BUCKLEY
| | | | | | | |
|---|---|---|---|---|---|---|
| Bad Rapping The Marquis De Sade | LP | World Pacific | WPS21889 | 1969 £6 | £15 | US |
| Best Of Lord Buckley | LP | Crestview | CRV(7)801 | 1963 £6 | £15 | US |
| Best Of Lord Buckley | LP | Elektra | EKS74047 | 1969 £4 | £10 | US |
| Blowing His Mind And Yours Too | LP | World Pacific | WP1849 | 1966 £6 | £15 | US |
| Buckley's Best | LP | Liberty | LBS83191 | 1968 £6 | £15 | US |
| Hipsters, Flipsters, & Finger Poppin' Daddies | 10" LP | RCA | LPM3246 | 195– £25 | £50 | US |
| In Concert | LP | World Pacific | WP1815 | 1964 £6 | £15 | US |
| Lord Buckley | LP | Bizarre | RS6389 | 1970 £6 | £15 | US |
| Most Immaculately Hip Autocrat | LP | Straight | STS1054 | 1970 £6 | £15 | US |
| Way Out Humor Of Lord Buckley | LP | World Pacific | WP1279 | 1959 £8 | £20 | US |

## LORD BURGESS & HIS SUN ISLANDERS
| | | | | | |
|---|---|---|---|---|---|
| Calypso Au Go-Go | LP | Pye | NPL28109 | 1968 £4 | £10 | |

## LORD CREATOR
| | | | | | | |
|---|---|---|---|---|---|---|
| Big Bamboo | 7" | Jump Up | JU524 | 1967 £1.50 | £4 | |
| Drive With Care | 7" | National Calypso | NC2001 | 1964 £1.50 | £4 | |
| Evening News | 7" | Blue Beat | BB292 | 1965 £6 | £12 | |
| Independent Jamaica | 7" | Island | WI001 | 1962 £6 | £12 | |
| Jamaica Jump Up | 7" | Jump Up | JU503 | 1967 £1.50 | £4 | |
| Jamaica's Anniversary | 7" | Port-O-Jam | PJ4119 | 1964 £5 | £10 | |
| Obeah Wedding | 7" | Doctor Bird | DB1029 | 1966 £5 | £10 | *Bertram Ennis B side* |
| Peeping Tom | 7" | Kalypso | XX24 | 1963 £1.50 | £4 | |
| Rhythm Of The Blues | 7" | Port-O-Jam | PJ4005 | 1964 £5 | £10 | |
| We Will Be Lovers | 7" | Island | WI105 | 1963 £5 | £10 | |
| Wicked Lady | 7" | Black Swan | WI463 | 1965 £5 | £10 | *Maytals B side* |

## LORD INVADER
| | | | | | |
|---|---|---|---|---|---|
| Kings Of Calypso Vol. 2 | 7" EP | Pye | NEP24038 | 1957 £2 | £5 | |

## LORD IVANHOE
| | | | | | |
|---|---|---|---|---|---|
| Kings Of Calypso Vol. 6 | 7" EP | Pye | NEP24087 | 1958 £2 | £5 | |

## LORD KITCHENER
| | | | | | | |
|---|---|---|---|---|---|---|
| Black Pudding | 7" | Melodisc | 1498 | 1959 £1.50 | £4 | |
| Calypsos Too Hot To Handle | LP | Melodisc | 12129 | 196– £6 | £15 | |
| Calypsos Too Hot To Handle | LP | Melodisc | 12199 | 196– £6 | £15 | *extra tracks* |
| Calypsos Too Hot To Handle Vol. 2 | LP | Melodisc | 12130 | 196– £6 | £15 | |
| Calypsos Too Hot To Handle Vol. 2 | LP | Melodisc | 12200 | 196– £6 | £15 | *extra tracks* |
| Dr. Kitch | 7" | Aladdin | WI612 | 1965 £1.50 | £4 | |
| If You're Brown | 7" | Melodisc | 1531 | 1959 £1.50 | £4 | |
| Jamaica Turkey | 7" | Melodisc | 1577 | 1960 £1.50 | £4 | |
| Kitch – King Of Calypso | 10" LP | Melodisc | MLP500 | 1955 £6 | £15 | |

## LORD LEBBY
| | | | | | |
|---|---|---|---|---|---|
| Caledonia | 7" | Starlite | ST45018 | 1960 £20 | £40 | |
| Sweet Jamaica | 7" | Kalypso | XX05 | 1960 £1.50 | £4 | |

## LORD NELSON
| | | | | | |
|---|---|---|---|---|---|
| Proud West Indian | 7" EP | Stateside | SE1024 | 1964 £2.50 | £6 | |

## LORD NELSON & HIS CREW
| | | | | | |
|---|---|---|---|---|---|
| Return Of Rock | LP | Metronome | HLP10213 | 1968 £8 | £20 | *German* |

## LORD POWER
| | | | | | |
|---|---|---|---|---|---|
| Temptation | 7" | Coxsone | CS7079 | 1968 £5 | £10 | *Al & Vibrators B side* |

## LORD ROCKINGHAM'S XI
| | | | | | | |
|---|---|---|---|---|---|---|
| Hoots Mon | 7" | Decca | F11059 | 1958 £1.50 | £4 | |
| Oh Boy | 7" EP | Decca | DFE6555 | 1958 £10 | £20 | |
| Ra Ra Rockingham | 7" | Decca | F11139 | 1959 £1.50 | £4 | |
| Return Of Lord Rockingham's XI | LP | Columbia | SCX6291 | 1968 £6 | £15 | |
| Rockingham Twist | 7" | Decca | F11426 | 1962 £1.50 | £4 | |
| Squelch | 7" | Decca | F11024 | 1958 £2 | £5 | |
| Wee Tom | 7" | Decca | F11104 | 1959 £2 | £5 | |

## LORD SITAR
Suggestions that the name Lord Sitar hides the identity of George Harrison have given the album whatever collectability it has. It is actually extremely unlikely that Harrison would ever have considered recording a set of cover versions like this – even more so that he could then have kept the matter quiet for thirty years.

| | | | | | |
|---|---|---|---|---|---|
| Lord Sitar | LP | Columbia | SCX6256 | 1968 £8 | £20 | |

## LORD TANAMO
| | | | | | | |
|---|---|---|---|---|---|---|
| Come Down | 7" | Island | WI108 | 1963 £5 | £10 | |
| I Had A Dream | 7" | Rio | R21 | 1964 £5 | £10 | ... *Osbourne Graham B side* |

| | | | | | | | |
|---|---|---|---|---|---|---|---|
| I Love You Truly | 7" | Caribou | CRC3 | 196– | £4 | £8 | |
| I'm In The Mood For Ska | 7" | Ska Beat | JB224 | 1965 | £5 | £10 | |
| Mothers Love | 7" | Ska Beat | JB243 | 1966 | £5 | £10 | |
| Sweet Dreaming | 7" | Kalypso | XX20 | 1960 | £2.50 | £6 | |

## LORDAN, JERRY

| | | | | | | | |
|---|---|---|---|---|---|---|---|
| All My Own Work | LP | Parlophone | PCS3014 | 1961 | £37.50 | £75 | *stereo* |
| All My Own Work | LP | Parlophone | PMC1133 | 1961 | £25 | £50 | *mono* |
| I'll Stay Single | 7" | Parlophone | R4588 | 1959 | £1.50 | £4 | |
| Let's Try Again | 7" | Parlophone | R4748 | 1961 | £1.50 | £4 | |
| One Good Solid 24 Carat Reason | 7" | Parlophone | R4903 | 1962 | £1.50 | £4 | |
| Ring, Write, Or Call | 7" | Parlophone | R4695 | 1960 | £1.50 | £4 | |
| Sing Like An Angel | 7" | Parlophone | R4653 | 1960 | £1.50 | £4 | |
| Who Could Be Bluer | 7" | Parlophone | R4627 | 1960 | £1.50 | £4 | |

## LORDS

| | | | | | | | |
|---|---|---|---|---|---|---|---|
| Best Of The Lords | LP | Columbia | 29783 | 1971 | £6 | £15 | *German* |
| Don't Mince Matters | 7" | Columbia | DB8121 | 1967 | £20 | £40 | |
| Gloryland | 7" | Columbia | DB8367 | 1968 | £2.50 | £6 | |
| Good Side Of June | LP | Columbia | 74244 | 1968 | £10 | £25 | *German* |
| Hey Baby | 7" EP | Columbia | ESRF1656 | 1965 | £20 | £40 | *French* |
| In Black And White | LP | Columbia | 83859 | 1965 | £20 | £40 | *German* |
| Inside Out | LP | Columbia | 1C06228887 | 1971 | £6 | £15 | *German* |
| Lords | LP | Columbia | 31972 | 1974 | £4 | £10 | *German* |
| Lords 2 | LP | Columbia | 84013 | 1966 | £15 | £30 | *German* |
| Shakin' All Over '70 | LP | Columbia | 1C06228478 | 1970 | £6 | £15 | *German* |
| Some Folks | LP | Hor Zu | SHZT174 | 1967 | £15 | £30 | *German* |
| Ulleogamaxbe | LP | Columbia | SMC74343 | 1969 | £15 | £30 | *German* |

## LORDS OF THE NEW CHURCH

| | | | | | | | |
|---|---|---|---|---|---|---|---|
| Dance With Me | 12" | Illegal | PFSX1022 | 1983 | £2.50 | £6 | *picture disc* |
| Russian Roulette | 7" | Illegal | ILSP0033 | 1983 | £1.50 | £4 | *picture disc* |

## LOREN, SOPHIA

| | | | | | | | |
|---|---|---|---|---|---|---|---|
| In Rome | LP | Columbia | OL6310/OS2710 | 1964 | £15 | £30 | *. US, with John Barry* |

## LORRIE, MYRNA

| | | | | | | | |
|---|---|---|---|---|---|---|---|
| Life's Changing Scene | 7" | London | HLU8294 | 1956 | £7.50 | £15 | |
| Underway | 7" | London | HLU8187 | 1955 | £12.50 | £25 | |

## LORY, DICK

| | | | | | | | |
|---|---|---|---|---|---|---|---|
| Cool It Baby | 7" | London | HLD8348 | 1956 | £180 | £300 | *best auctioned* |
| I Got Over You | 7" | Liberty | LIB55529 | 1963 | £1.50 | £4 | |
| My Last Date | 7" | London | HLG9284 | 1961 | £6 | £12 | |
| Pain Is Here | 7" | Liberty | LIB55415 | 1962 | £1.50 | £4 | |

## LOS BRAVOS

| | | | | | | | |
|---|---|---|---|---|---|---|---|
| Black Is Black | LP | Decca | LK4822 | 1966 | £6 | £15 | |
| Black Is Black | 7" EP | Barclay | 071050 | 1966 | £6 | £12 | *French* |
| Going Nowhere | 7" EP | Barclay | 071091 | 1966 | £5 | £10 | *French, 2 different sleeves* |
| Los Bravos | LP | Decca | LK/SKL4905 | 1968 | £5 | £12 | |
| Los Bravos | LP | Eclipse | ECJR2026 | 1970 | £4 | £10 | |

## LOS BRINCOS

| | | | | | | | |
|---|---|---|---|---|---|---|---|
| Lola | 7" | Page One | POF023 | 1967 | £12.50 | £25 | *picture sleeve* |
| Nobody Wants You Now | 7" | Page One | POF031 | 1967 | £2.50 | £6 | |

## LOS CANARIOS

| | | | | | | | |
|---|---|---|---|---|---|---|---|
| Get On Your Knees | 7" | Major Minor | MM532 | 1967 | £2.50 | £6 | |

## LOS LOBOS

| | | | | | | | |
|---|---|---|---|---|---|---|---|
| Just Another Band From East LA | LP | New Vista | 1001 | 1978 | £37.50 | £75 | *US* |
| Si Se Puede! | LP | Pan American | 101 | 1976 | £25 | £50 | *US* |

## LOSS, JOE

| | | | | | | | |
|---|---|---|---|---|---|---|---|
| Thunderbirds | 7" | HMV | POP1500 | 1966 | £5 | £10 | |

## LOST & FOUND

| | | | | | | | |
|---|---|---|---|---|---|---|---|
| Everybody's Here | LP | International Artists | IALP3 | 1967 | £20 | £40 | *US* |

## LOST JOCKEY

| | | | | | | | |
|---|---|---|---|---|---|---|---|
| Professor Slack | 7" | Operation Twilight | OPT11 | 1982 | £2 | £5 | |

## LOTHAR & THE HAND PEOPLE

| | | | | | | | |
|---|---|---|---|---|---|---|---|
| Presenting | LP | Capitol | ST2997 | 1968 | £20 | £40 | *US* |
| Sdrawkcab | 7" | Capitol | CL15610 | 1969 | £4 | £8 | |
| Space Hymn | LP | Capitol | ST247 | 1969 | £20 | £40 | *US* |

## LOTIS, DENNIS

| | | | | | | | |
|---|---|---|---|---|---|---|---|
| Bidin' My Time | LP | Columbia | 33SX1089 | 1958 | £5 | £12 | |
| Chain Reaction | 7" | Decca | F10471 | 1955 | £1.50 | £4 | |
| Face Of An Angel, Heart Of A Devil | 7" | Decca | F10469 | 1955 | £1.50 | £4 | |
| Honey Love | 7" | Decca | F10392 | 1954 | £2 | £5 | |
| How About You | LP | Pye | NPL18002 | 1957 | £6 | £15 | |
| Such A Night | 7" | Decca | F10287 | 1954 | £2.50 | £6 | |

## LOTUS

| | | | | | | | |
|---|---|---|---|---|---|---|---|
| Lotus | LP | | SMA1 | 1974 | £25 | £50 | Swedish |
| Second | LP | | SMA16 | 1975 | £25 | £50 | Swedish |

## LOU, BONNIE

| | | | | | | | |
|---|---|---|---|---|---|---|---|
| Barnyard Hop | 7" | Parlophone | MSP6178 | 1955 | £4 | £8 | |
| Blue Tennessee Rain | 7" | Parlophone | MSP6117 | 1954 | £5 | £10 | |
| Bo Weevil | 7" | Parlophone | MSP6234 | 1956 | £4 | £8 | |
| Dancin' In My Socks | 7" | Parlophone | MSP6188 | 1955 | £6 | £12 | |
| Don't Stop Kissing Me Goodnight | 7" | Parlophone | MSP6095 | 1954 | £5 | £10 | |
| Drop Me A Line | 7" | Parlophone | MSP6173 | 1955 | £4 | £8 | |
| Hand-Me-Down Heart | 7" | Parlophone | MSP6036 | 1953 | £12.50 | £25 | |
| Huckleberry Pie | 7" | Parlophone | MSP6108 | 1954 | £5 | £10 | |
| I'm Available | 7" | Parlophone | DP545 | 195– | £7.50 | £15 | export |
| La Dee Dah | 7" | Parlophone | R.4409 | 1958 | £20 | £40 | with Rusty York |
| Lonesome Lover | 7" | Parlophone | MSP6253 | 1956 | £6 | £12 | |
| Miss The Love | 7" | Parlophone | MSP6223 | 1956 | £2.50 | £6 | |
| No Rock 'n' Roll Tonight | 7" | Parlophone | R4215 | 1956 | £4 | £8 | |
| Papaya Mama | 7" | Parlophone | MSP6051 | 1953 | £10 | £20 | |
| Runnin' Away | 7" | Parlophone | R4350 | 1957 | £4 | £8 | |
| Seven Lonely Days | 7" | Parlophone | MSP6021 | 1953 | £12.50 | £25 | |
| Tennessee Mambo | 7" | Parlophone | MSP6151 | 1955 | £5 | £10 | |
| Tennessee Wig Walk | 7" | Parlophone | MSP6048 | 1953 | £12.50 | £25 | |
| Texas Polka | 7" | Parlophone | MSP6072 | 1954 | £5 | £10 | |
| Tweedle Dee | 7" | Parlophone | MSP6157 | 1955 | £6 | £12 | |
| Two Step Side Step | 7" | Parlophone | MSP6132 | 1954 | £5 | £10 | |

## LOUDERMILK, JOHN D.

| | | | | | | | |
|---|---|---|---|---|---|---|---|
| Angela Jones | 7" | RCA | RCA1323 | 1962 | £2 | £5 | |
| Language Of Love | LP | RCA | RD27248/SF5123 | 1962 | £6 | £15 | |
| Sidewalks | 7" | RCA | RCA1761 | 1968 | £1.50 | £4 | |
| Sings A Bizarre Collection | LP | RCA | RD/SF7890 | 1967 | £4 | £10 | |
| Suburban Attitudes In Country Verse | LP | RCA | LPM/LSP3807 | 1967 | £4 | £10 | US |
| Twelve Sides Of John D. Loudermilk | LP | RCA | RD/SF7515 | 1962 | £6 | £15 | |

## LOUDEST WHISPER

| | | | | | | | |
|---|---|---|---|---|---|---|---|
| Children Of Lir | LP | Polydor | | 197– | £250 | £400 | Irish |
| Hard Times | LP | Fiona | O11 | 1983 | £62.50 | £125 | Irish |
| Loudest Whisper | LP | Polydor | 2908043 | 1981 | £62.50 | £125 | Irish |
| Name Of The Game | 7" | Polydor | 2078113 | 1980 | £10 | £20 | Irish |

## LOUIS, JOE HILL

| | | | | | | | |
|---|---|---|---|---|---|---|---|
| Blues In The Morning | LP | Polydor | 2383214 | 1974 | £4 | £10 | |
| Heartache Baby | 7" | Bootleg | 502 | 1965 | £10 | £20 | |

## LOUISIANA RED

| | | | | | | | |
|---|---|---|---|---|---|---|---|
| I Done Woke Up | 7" | Sue | WI337 | 1964 | £5 | £10 | |
| Keep Your Hands Of My Woman | 7" | Columbia | DB7270 | 1964 | £2.50 | £6 | |
| Lowdown Back Porch Blues | LP | Columbia | 33SX1612 | 1964 | £10 | £25 | |
| Seventh Son | LP | Polydor | 2941002 | 1972 | £4 | £10 | |

## LOUNGE LIZARDS

| | | | | | | | |
|---|---|---|---|---|---|---|---|
| No Pain For Cakes | CD | Antilles | ANCD8714 | 1987 | £5 | £12 | |

## LOUSSIER, JACQUES

| | | | | | | | |
|---|---|---|---|---|---|---|---|
| Air On A G String | 7" | Decca | F22383 | 1966 | £1.50 | £4 | |
| Air On A G String | 7" | Decca | F22876 | 1969 | £1.50 | £4 | |
| Play Bach | LP | London | GLB1002 | 1962 | £4 | £10 | |
| Play Bach No. 2 | LP | London | GLB1004 | 1963 | £4 | £10 | |

## LOUVIN, CHARLIE

| | | | | | | | |
|---|---|---|---|---|---|---|---|
| I Forgot To Cry | LP | Capitol | (S)T2787 | 1967 | £5 | £12 | US |
| I'll Remember Always | LP | Capitol | (S)T2689 | 1967 | £5 | £12 | US |
| Less And Less | LP | Capitol | (S)T2208 | 1965 | £5 | £12 | US |
| Lonesome Is Me | LP | Capitol | (S)T2482 | 1966 | £5 | £12 | US |
| Many Moods Of Charlie Louvin | LP | Capitol | (S)T2437 | 1966 | £5 | £12 | US |
| Will You Visit Me On Sundays | LP | Capitol | ST2958 | 1968 | £4 | £10 | US |

## LOUVIN, IRA

| | | | | | | | |
|---|---|---|---|---|---|---|---|
| Unforgettable Ira Louvin | LP | Capitol | (S)T2413 | 1965 | £5 | £12 | US |

## LOUVIN BROTHERS

| | | | | | | | |
|---|---|---|---|---|---|---|---|
| Country Christmas | LP | Capitol | (S)T1616 | 1961 | £5 | £12 | US |
| Country Love Ballads | LP | Capitol | T1106 | 1959 | £10 | £25 | US |
| Country Love Ballads | 7" EP | Capitol | EAP11106 | 1959 | £4 | £8 | |
| Encore | LP | Capitol | T1547 | 1961 | £5 | £12 | US |
| Family Who Prays | LP | Capitol | T1061 | 1958 | £10 | £25 | US |
| Ira And Charlie | LP | Capitol | T910 | 1958 | £20 | £40 | US |
| Ira And Charlie | 7" EP | Capitol | EAP1910 | 1957 | £5 | £10 | |
| Keep Your Eyes On Jesus | LP | Capitol | (S)T1834 | 1963 | £5 | £12 | US |
| Knoxville Girl | 7" | Capitol | CL14989 | 1959 | £1.50 | £4 | |
| Louvin Brothers | LP | MGM | E3426 | 1956 | £50 | £100 | US |
| My Baby's Gone | LP | Capitol | T1385 | 1960 | £10 | £25 | US |
| Nearer My God To Thee | LP | Capitol | T825 | 1957 | £20 | £40 | US |
| Satan Is Real | LP | Capitol | T1277 | 1960 | £10 | £25 | US |
| Sing And Play Their Current Hits | LP | Capitol | (S)T2091 | 1964 | £5 | £12 | US |
| Tragic Songs Of Life | LP | Capitol | T769 | 1957 | £25 | £50 | US |

| | | | | | | | |
|---|---|---|---|---|---|---|---|
| Tragic Songs Of Life | 7" EP | Capitol | EAP1769 | 1957 | £5 | £10 | |
| Tribute To The Delmore Brothers | LP | Capitol | T1449 | 1960 | £8 | £20 | US |
| Weapon Of Prayer | LP | Capitol | (S)T1721 | 1962 | £5 | £12 | US |
| You're Learning | 7" | Capitol | CL15078 | 1959 | £1.50 | £4 | |

## LOVABLES

| | | | | | | | |
|---|---|---|---|---|---|---|---|
| You're The Cause Of It | 7" | Stateside | SS2108 | 1968 | £4 | £8 | |

## LOVE

The personnel of Love varies from album to album, but the group always revolves around the singing and writing talents of Arthur Lee. His is an inconsistent talent, but at his best he is little short of brilliant. All of Love's albums (except perhaps the first, on which the group have barely emerged from their garage punk beginnings) contain moments of pure magic, although none is entirely flawless. The critics' favourite is *Forever Changes*, whose largely gentle sound is enhanced by modest orchestration, but the heavier, guitar-centred *Four Sail* actually has songs of greater distinction. It is a very fine, and very underrated record. The first side of *Da Capo* has some excellent songs too, but the album as a whole is let down by the extended jam on side two, which does not really work. *Out Here* and *False Start* are similar in sound to *Four Sail*, though overall neither is in the same league. Each contains one masterpiece, however – 'The Everlasting First' is a collaboration with Jimi Hendrix, who makes a typically fine contribution to an unusually structured song; while 'Love Is More Than Words' is dominated by a long, highly charged guitar solo that turns the track into one of the classic pieces of rock improvisation.

| | | | | | | | |
|---|---|---|---|---|---|---|---|
| Alone Again Or | 7" | Elektra | EKSN45024 | 1968 | £1.50 | £4 | |
| Andmoreagain | 7" | Elektra | EKSN45026 | 1968 | £2 | £5 | |
| Da Capo | LP | Elektra | EKL4005/ EKS74005 | 1967 | £8 | £20 | |
| Do The Merlin | 7" | LSD | 1009 | 1966 | £150 | £250 | US, best auctioned |
| Everlasting First | 7" | Harvest | HAR5030 | 1970 | £2 | £5 | with Jimi Hendrix |
| False Start | LP | Harvest | SHVL787 | 1971 | £8 | £20 | |
| Forever Changes | LP | Elektra | EKL4013 | 1967 | £8 | £20 | mono |
| Forever Changes | LP | Elektra | EKS74013 | 1967 | £6 | £15 | |
| Forever Changes | LP | Elektra | EKS74013 | 1970 | £4 | £10 | red label |
| Four Sail | LP | Elektra | EKS74049 | 1969 | £6 | £15 | |
| Four Sail | LP | Elektra | K42030 | 1976 | £4 | £10 | |
| I'm With You | 7" | Elektra | EKSN45086 | 1970 | £1.50 | £4 | |
| Laughing Stock | 7" | Elektra | EKSN45038 | 1968 | £2.50 | £6 | |
| Love | LP | Elektra | EKL/EKS74001 | 1966 | £8 | £20 | |
| Love | LP | Elektra | K42068 | 1972 | £4 | £10 | |
| Love Revisited | LP | Elektra | 2469009 | 1970 | £4 | £10 | |
| My Little Red Book | 7" EP | Vogue | INT18072 | 1966 | £37.50 | £75 | French |
| My Little Red Book | 7" | London | HLZ10053 | 1966 | £5 | £10 | |
| Out Here | LP | Harvest | SHDW3/4 | 1970 | £8 | £20 | double |
| Reel To Real | LP | RSO | 2394145 | 1974 | £4 | £10 | |
| Seven And Seven Is | 7" EP | Vogue | INT18095 | 1966 | £50 | £100 | French |
| Seven And Seven Is | 7" | London | HLZ10073 | 1966 | £5 | £10 | |
| She Comes In Colours | 7" | Elektra | EKSN45010 | 1967 | £2.50 | £6 | |
| Softly To Me | 7" | Elektra | EKSN45016 | 1967 | £2 | £5 | |
| Stand Out | 7" | Harvest | HAR5014 | 1970 | £1.50 | £4 | |

## LOVE, CHRISTOPHER

| | | | | | | | |
|---|---|---|---|---|---|---|---|
| Curse Goes On | 7" | London | HLU10263 | 1969 | £2 | £5 | |

## LOVE, DARLENE

| | | | | | | | |
|---|---|---|---|---|---|---|---|
| Boy I'm Gonna Marry | 7" | London | HLU9725 | 1963 | £5 | £10 | |
| Fine Fine Boy | 7" | London | HLU9815 | 1963 | £5 | £10 | |
| Wait Till My Bobby Gets Home | 7" EP | London | REU1411 | 1964 | £50 | £100 | |
| Wait Till My Bobby Gets Home | 7" | London | HLU10244 | 1969 | £2.50 | £6 | |
| Wait Till My Bobby Gets Home | 7" | London | HLU9765 | 1963 | £5 | £10 | |

## LOVE, GARFIELD & JIMMY SPRUILL

| | | | | | | | |
|---|---|---|---|---|---|---|---|
| Next Time You See Me | 7" | Blue Horizon | 573150 | 1969 | £5 | £10 | |

## LOVE, MARY

| | | | | | | | |
|---|---|---|---|---|---|---|---|
| Hurt is Just Beginning | 7" | Stateside | SS2135 | 1969 | £5 | £10 | |
| Lay This Burden Down | 7" | Stateside | SS2009 | 1967 | £12.50 | £25 | |
| You Turned My Bitter Into Sweet | 7" | King | KG1024 | 1965 | £25 | £50 | |

## LOVE, RONNIE

| | | | | | | | |
|---|---|---|---|---|---|---|---|
| Chills And Fever | 7" | London | HLD9272 | 1961 | £6 | £12 | |

## LOVE, WILLIE & WILLIE NIX

| | | | | | | | |
|---|---|---|---|---|---|---|---|
| Two Willies From Memphis | LP | Highway 51 | H700 | 1966 | £20 | £40 | |

## LOVE & TEARS

| | | | | | | | |
|---|---|---|---|---|---|---|---|
| Love And Tears | LP | Polydor | 2371334 | 1972 | £6 | £15 | German |

## LOVE AFFAIR

| | | | | | | | |
|---|---|---|---|---|---|---|---|
| Everlasting Love Affair | LP | CBS | 63416 | 1969 | £5 | £12 | |
| New Day | LP | CBS | 64109 | 1970 | £4 | £10 | |
| Rainbow Valley | 7" | CBS | 3366 | 1968 | £1.50 | £4 | picture sleeve |
| She Smiled Sweetly | 7" | Decca | F12558 | 1967 | £7.50 | £15 | |

## LOVE CHILDREN

| | | | | | | | |
|---|---|---|---|---|---|---|---|
| Paper Chase | 7" | Deram | DM303 | 1970 | £1.50 | £4 | |

## LOVE GENERATION

| | | | | | | | |
|---|---|---|---|---|---|---|---|
| She Touched Me | 7" | Liberty | LBF15018 | 1967 | £1.50 | £4 | |

## LOVE SCULPTURE

Love Sculpture evolved from the Human Beans as a blues group and showcase for the flashy guitar playing of Dave Edmunds. The success of their version of Khachaturian's 'Sabre Dance' led them to try another classical reworking, but due to copyright problems, 'Mars' was only made available on the US version of *Forms And Feelings* and has not been reissued since.

| | | | | | | | |
|---|---|---|---|---|---|---|---|
| Blues Helping | LP | Parlophone | PCS7059 | 1968 | £8 | £20 | |
| Blues Helping | LP | Parlophone | PMC7059 | 1968 | £10 | £25 | *mono* |
| Forms And Feelings | LP | Parlophone | PCS7090 | 1969 | £10 | £25 | |
| Forms And Feelings | LP | Parrot | PAS71035 | 1969 | £15 | £30 | *US* |
| In The Land Of The Few | 7" | Parlophone | R5831 | 1970 | £2 | £5 | |
| River To Another Day | 7" | Parlophone | R5664 | 1968 | £5 | £10 | |
| Sabre Dance | 7" | Parlophone | R5744 | 1968 | £1.50 | £4 | |
| Seagull | 7" | Parlophone | R5807 | 1969 | £2 | £5 | |
| Wang Dang Doodle | 7" | Parlophone | R5731 | 1968 | £4 | £8 | |

## LOVECRAFT

| | | | | | | | |
|---|---|---|---|---|---|---|---|
| Valley Of The Moon | LP | Reprise | RS6419 | 1970 | £4 | £10 | *US* |

## LOVECUT D. B.

| | | | | | | | |
|---|---|---|---|---|---|---|---|
| Heartspin | 12" | Suburbs Of Hell | SOH009EP | 1991 | £2.50 | £6 | |

## LOVED ONES

| | | | | | | | |
|---|---|---|---|---|---|---|---|
| Loved One | 7" EP | Festival | 1528 | 196– | £5 | £10 | *French* |
| Magic Box | LP | Astor | WG5127 | 1967 | £10 | £25 | *US* |

## LOVERS

| | | | | | | | |
|---|---|---|---|---|---|---|---|
| Let's Elope | 7" | Vogue | V9111 | 1958 | £150 | £250 | *best auctioned* |

## LOVICH, LENE

| | | | | | | | |
|---|---|---|---|---|---|---|---|
| I Saw Mommy Kissing Santa Claus | 7" | Polydor | 2058812 | 1976 | £5 | £10 | |
| I Think We're Alone Now (Japanese) | 7" | Stiff | BUYJ32 | 1978 | £2.50 | £6 | |

## LOVIN'

| | | | | | | | |
|---|---|---|---|---|---|---|---|
| All You've Got | 7" | Page One | POF041 | 1967 | £12.50 | £25 | |
| Keep On Believing | 7" | Page One | POF035 | 1967 | £10 | £20 | |

## LOVIN' SPOONFUL

| | | | | | | | |
|---|---|---|---|---|---|---|---|
| Almost Grown | 7" EP | Vogue | INT18032 | 1965 | £6 | £12 | *French* |
| Darling Be Home Soon | 7" EP | Kama Sutra | 617108 | 1967 | £5 | £10 | *French* |
| Day Blues | 7" EP | Kama Sutra | KEP303 | 1967 | £5 | £10 | |
| Daydream | LP | Pye | NPL28078 | 1966 | £4 | £10 | |
| Daydream | 7" EP | Kama Sutra | 617102 | 1966 | £5 | £10 | *French* |
| Did You Ever Have To Make Up Your Mind | 7" EP | Kama Sutra | KEP300 | 1966 | £4 | £8 | |
| Do You Believe In Magic | LP | Pye | NPL28069 | 1965 | £4 | £10 | |
| Do You Believe In Magic | 7" EP | Kama Sutra | 617101 | 1965 | £5 | £10 | *French* |
| Do You Believe In Magic | 7" EP | Kama Sutra | KEP306 | 1967 | £5 | £10 | |
| Do You Believe In Magic | 7" | Pye | 7N25327 | 1965 | £1.50 | £4 | |
| Everything Playing | LP | Kama Sutra | KLP404 | 1968 | £4 | £10 | |
| Hums Of The Lovin' Spoonful | LP | Kama Sutra | KLP401 | 1967 | £4 | £10 | |
| Jug Band Music | 7" EP | Kama Sutra | KEP301 | 1966 | £5 | £10 | |
| Loving You | 7" EP | Kama Sutra | KEP305 | 1967 | £5 | £10 | |
| Nashville Cats | 7" EP | Kama Sutra | 617106 | 1967 | £5 | £10 | *French* |
| Nashville Cats | 7" EP | Kama Sutra | KEP304 | 1967 | £5 | £10 | |
| Never Going Back | 7" | Kama Sutra | KAS213 | 1967 | £1.50 | £4 | |
| Rain On The Roof | 7" EP | Kama Sutra | 617105 | 1966 | £5 | £10 | *French* |
| Revelation Revolution '69 | LP | Kama Sutra | KLP406 | 1969 | £4 | £10 | |
| Six O'Clock | 7" EP | Kama Sutra | 617110 | 1967 | £5 | £10 | *French* |
| Summer In The City | CD-s | Special Edition | CD311 | 1988 | £2 | £5 | *3" single* |
| Summer In The City | 7" EP | Kama Sutra | 617103 | 1966 | £5 | £10 | *French* |
| Summer In The City | 7" EP | Kama Sutra | KEP302 | 1966 | £5 | £10 | |
| You Didn't Have To Be So Nice | 7" | Pye | 7N25344 | 1966 | £1.50 | £4 | |
| You're A Big Boy Now | LP | Kama Sutra | KLP402 | 1967 | £4 | £10 | |

## LOVING KIND

| | | | | | | | |
|---|---|---|---|---|---|---|---|
| Accidental Love | 7" | Piccadilly | 7N35299 | 1966 | £2.50 | £6 | |
| Ain't That Peculiar | 7" | Piccadilly | 7N35342 | 1966 | £5 | £10 | |
| I Love The Things You Do | 7" | Piccadilly | 7N35318 | 1966 | £4 | £8 | |

## LOW, BRUCE

| | | | | | | | |
|---|---|---|---|---|---|---|---|
| Just Walking In The Rain | 7" | HMV | JO464 | 1956 | £2 | £5 | *export* |

## LOWE, JEZ

| | | | | | | | |
|---|---|---|---|---|---|---|---|
| Galloways | LP | Fellside | FE049 | 1985 | £4 | £10 | |
| Old Durham Road | LP | Fellside | FE034 | 1983 | £4 | £10 | |

## LOWE, JIM

| | | | | | | | |
|---|---|---|---|---|---|---|---|
| Blue Suede Shoes | 7" | London | HLD8276 | 1956 | £25 | £50 | |
| By You By You By You | 7" | London | HLD8368 | 1957 | £10 | £20 | *gold label* |
| Close The Door | 7" | London | HLD8171 | 1955 | £15 | £30 | *gold label* |
| Door Of Fame | LP | Mercury | MG20246 | 1957 | £15 | £30 | *US* |
| Four Walls | 7" | London | HLD8431 | 1957 | £7.50 | £15 | |
| Green Door | 7" | London | HLD8317 | 1956 | £12.50 | £25 | *gold label* |
| He'll Have To Go | 7" | London | HLD9043 | 1960 | £4 | £8 | |
| Love Is A $64,000 Question | 7" | London | HLD8288 | 1956 | £15 | £30 | *gold label* |
| Rock A Chicka | 7" | London | HLD8538 | 1958 | £37.50 | £75 | |
| Songs They Sing Behind The Green Door | LP | London | HAD2108 | 1958 | £15 | £30 | |
| Wicked Women | LP | London | HAD2146 | 1959 | £8 | £20 | |

## LOWE, MUNDELL

| Title | Format | Label | Cat. No. | Year | | | Notes |
|---|---|---|---|---|---|---|---|
| Mundell Lowe Quartet | LP | London | LTZU15020 | 1957 | £8 | £20 | |
| Mundell Lowe Quintet | 10" LP | HMV | DLP1084 | 1955 | £8 | £20 | |

## LOWE, NICK

Nick Lowe's response to David Bowie releasing an album called *Low*, was to make a record called *Bowi*, although this was unfortunately only a four-track single, rather than an album. The humour of the concept is enough to make one listen fondly to the music regardless (actually the songs are quite memorable), but not quite enough to make the record into a collectors' item.

| Title | Format | Label | Cat. No. | Year | | | Notes |
|---|---|---|---|---|---|---|---|
| Bowi | 12" | Stiff | LAST1 | 1977 | £4 | £10 | promo |
| Live At The El Mocambo | 7" | Columbia | | 1978 | £4 | £8 | Canadian promo |

## LOWE, PETER

| Title | Format | Label | Cat. No. | Year | | | Notes |
|---|---|---|---|---|---|---|---|
| Banana Boat Song | 7" | Parlophone | R4270 | 1957 | £1.50 | £4 | |
| Hear My Song Of Love | 7" | Parlophone | R4199 | 1956 | £1.50 | £4 | |

## LOWTHER, HENRY

Henry Lowther is a classically trained violinist who took up the trumpet in order to play jazz and plays both instruments as a session musician on numerous LP releases. He played on the fringes of jazz as a member of Manfred Mann, John Mayall's Bluesbreakers, and the Keef Hartley Band, and he is featured on several of the British jazz albums to be made during the late sixties and early seventies. His own moment came with the LP *Child Song*, which is as fresh and sparkling as British jazz gets. The record is also, unfortunately, as rare as British jazz gets, and commands a correspondingly high price.

| Title | Format | Label | Cat. No. | Year | | | Notes |
|---|---|---|---|---|---|---|---|
| Child Song | LP | Deram | SML1070 | 1970 | £37.50 | £75 | |

## LOYD, MARK

| Title | Format | Label | Cat. No. | Year | | | Notes |
|---|---|---|---|---|---|---|---|
| When Evening Falls | 7" | Parlophone | R5423 | 1966 | £15 | £30 | |

## LUCAS, BUDDY

| Title | Format | Label | Cat. No. | Year | | | Notes |
|---|---|---|---|---|---|---|---|
| I Want To Know | 7" | Pye | 7N25045 | 1960 | £1.50 | £4 | |

## LUCAS, TREVOR

Singer/guitarist Trevor Lucas became well known as a member of Fairport Convention, following stints with the Eclection and Fotheringay – he was also the partner of singer Sandy Denny. Originally from Australia, Lucas recorded a folk album there, but *Overlander* is extremely hard to find now.

| Title | Format | Label | Cat. No. | Year | | | Notes |
|---|---|---|---|---|---|---|---|
| Overlander | LP | Reality | RY1002 | 1966 | £180 | £300 | |
| Waltzing Matilda | 7" | Reality | RE505 | 1966 | £10 | £20 | |

## LUCAS & THE MIKE COTTON SOUND

| Title | Format | Label | Cat. No. | Year | | | Notes |
|---|---|---|---|---|---|---|---|
| Mother In Law | 7" | MGM | MGM1427 | 1968 | £1.50 | £4 | |
| Step Out Of Line | 7" | Pye | 7N17313 | 1967 | £5 | £10 | |
| We Got A Thing Going Baby | 7" | MGM | MGM1398 | 1968 | £5 | £10 | |

## LUCIEN, JON

| Title | Format | Label | Cat. No. | Year | | | Notes |
|---|---|---|---|---|---|---|---|
| Premonition | LP | Columbia | PC34255 | 1976 | £6 | £15 | US |
| Rashida | LP | RCA | AFL10161 | 1973 | £10 | £25 | US |
| Rashida | LP | RCA | AYL13820 | 197– | £8 | £20 | US |
| Song For My Lady | LP | Columbia | | 1975 | £6 | £15 | US |

## LUCIFER

| Title | Format | Label | Cat. No. | Year | | | Notes |
|---|---|---|---|---|---|---|---|
| Big Gun | LP | private | LLP1 | 1972 | £30 | £60 | |
| Don't Care | LP | private | L001/002 | 1971 | £2 | £5 | |
| Exit | LP | private | LLP2 | 1972 | £30 | £60 | |
| Fuck You | 7" | private | L003/004 | 1972 | £2 | £5 | |
| Prick | 7" | Lucifer | L005/006 | 1972 | £2 | £5 | |

## LUCIFER'S FRIEND

| Title | Format | Label | Cat. No. | Year | | | Notes |
|---|---|---|---|---|---|---|---|
| Lucifer's Friend | LP | Philips | 6305068 | 1971 | £5 | £12 | German |
| Ride The Sky | 7" | Philips | 6003092 | 1971 | £1.50 | £4 | |
| Where The Groupies Killed The Blues | LP | Vertigo | 6360602 | 1973 | £4 | £10 | German |

## LUDLOWS

| Title | Format | Label | Cat. No. | Year | | | Notes |
|---|---|---|---|---|---|---|---|
| Wind And The Sea | LP | Pye | NPL18150 | 1966 | £4 | £10 | |

## LUDUS

| Title | Format | Label | Cat. No. | Year | | | Notes |
|---|---|---|---|---|---|---|---|
| Seduction | 12" | New Hormones | ORG16 | 1981 | £3 | £8 | double |

## LUKE, ROBIN

| Title | Format | Label | Cat. No. | Year | | | Notes |
|---|---|---|---|---|---|---|---|
| Chicka Chicka Honey | 7" | London | HLD8771 | 1958 | £4 | £8 | |
| Robin Luke | 7" EP | London | RED1222 | 1959 | £20 | £40 | |
| Susie Darling | 7" | London | HLD8676 | 1958 | £2 | £5 | |

## LULU

| Title | Format | Label | Cat. No. | Year | | | Notes |
|---|---|---|---|---|---|---|---|
| Boom Bang-A-Bang | 7" EP | Columbia | | 1969 | £4 | £8 | French |
| Can't Hear You No More | 7" | Decca | F11965 | 1964 | £1.50 | £4 | |
| Chocolate Ice | 7" EP | Decca | 457099 | 1966 | £5 | £10 | French |
| Love Loves To Love Lulu | LP | Columbia | SX/SCX6201 | 1968 | £4 | £10 | |
| Lulu | LP | Ace Of Clubs | ACL1232 | 1967 | £4 | £10 | |
| Lulu | 7" EP | Decca | DFE8597 | 1965 | £6 | £12 | |
| Lulu's Album | LP | Columbia | SX/SCX6365 | 1969 | £4 | £10 | |
| Man With The Golden Gun | 7" | Chelsea | 2005015 | 1974 | £1.50 | £4 | |
| Satisfied | 7" EP | Decca | 457084 | 1965 | £5 | £10 | French |
| Satisfied | 7" | Decca | F12128 | 1965 | £1.50 | £4 | |
| Shout | 7" EP | Decca | 457045 | 1964 | £7.50 | £15 | French |

| | | | | | | | |
|---|---|---|---|---|---|---|---|
| Shout | 7" | Decca | F11884 | 1964 | £1.50 | £4 | |
| Something To Shout About | LP | Decca | LK4719 | 1965 | £8 | £20 | |
| That's Really Some Good | 7" EP | Decca | 457052 | 1964 | £5 | £10 | French |
| To Sir With Love | LP | Fontana | STL5446 | 1967 | £6 | £15 | with The Mindbenders |
| What A Wonderful Feeling | 7" EP | Decca | 457132 | 1966 | £5 | £10 | French |

## LUMAN, BOB

| | | | | | | | |
|---|---|---|---|---|---|---|---|
| Ain't Got Time To Be Unhappy | 7" | CBS | 3602 | 1968 | £4 | £8 | |
| Bad Bad Day | 7" | Hickory | 451289 | 1965 | £2 | £5 | |
| Bigger Men Than I | 7" | Hickory | 451238 | 1964 | £1.50 | £4 | |
| Come On And Sing | 7" | Hickory | 451410 | 1965 | £1.50 | £4 | |
| Dreamy Doll | 7" | Warner Bros | WB12 | 1960 | £1.50 | £4 | |
| Great Snowman | 7" | Warner Bros | WB37 | 1961 | £1.50 | £4 | |
| Hey Joe | 7" | Warner Bros | WB75 | 1962 | £1.50 | £4 | |
| Hickory Showcase Vol. 2 | 7" EP | Hickory | LPE1501 | 1964 | £2.50 | £6 | side 2 by Bobby Lord |
| Hickory Showcase Vol. 3 | 7" EP | Hickory | LPE1504 | 1964 | £2.50 | £6 | side 2 by Bobby Lord |
| I Like Your Kind Of Love | 7" | Hickory | 451221 | 1964 | £1.50 | £4 | |
| Let's Think About Living | LP | Warner Bros | WS8025 | 1960 | £25 | £50 | stereo |
| Let's Think About Living | LP | Warner Bros | WM4025 | 1960 | £20 | £40 | |
| Let's Think About Living | 7" EP | Warner Bros | WEP6046 | 1961 | £10 | £20 | |
| Let's Think About Living | 7" EP | Warner Bros | WSEP2046 | 1961 | £15 | £30 | stereo |
| Let's Think About Living | 7" | Warner Bros | WB18 | 1960 | £1.50 | £4 | |
| Let's Think About Living No. 2 | 7" EP | Warner Bros | WEP6055 | 1962 | £10 | £20 | |
| Let's Think About Living No. 2 | 7" EP | Warner Bros | WSEP2055 | 1962 | £15 | £30 | stereo |
| Let's Think About Living No. 3 | 7" EP | Warner Bros | WEP6102 | 1962 | £10 | £20 | |
| Let's Think About Living No. 3 | 7" EP | Warner Bros | WSE6102 | 1962 | £15 | £30 | stereo |
| Livin' Lovin' Sounds | LP | Hickory | LPM124 | 1964 | £6 | £15 | |
| Old George Dickie | 7" | Hickory | 451277 | 1964 | £1.50 | £4 | |
| Private Eye | 7" | Warner Bros | WB49 | 1961 | £1.50 | £4 | |
| Run On Home Baby Brother | 7" | Hickory | 451266 | 1964 | £1.50 | £4 | |
| Why Why Bye Bye | 7" | Warner Bros | WB28 | 1960 | £1.50 | £4 | |

## LUMAN, BOB & BOBBY LORD

| | | | | | | | |
|---|---|---|---|---|---|---|---|
| Can't Take The Country From The Boys | LP | Hickory | LPM121 | 1964 | £4 | £10 | |

## LUMBLE

| | | | | | | | |
|---|---|---|---|---|---|---|---|
| Overdose | LP | Radnor | R2003 | 1970 | £30 | £60 | US |

## LUMLEY, RUFUS

| | | | | | | | |
|---|---|---|---|---|---|---|---|
| I'm Standing | 7" | Stateside | SS516 | 1966 | £25 | £50 | |

## LUNAR TWO

| | | | | | | | |
|---|---|---|---|---|---|---|---|
| Get It, Take It | 7" | Spot | JWS551 | 196– | £1.50 | £4 | |

## LUNCEFORD, JIMMIE

| | | | | | | | |
|---|---|---|---|---|---|---|---|
| For Dancer's Only | 10" LP | Brunswick | LA8738 | 1956 | £8 | £20 | |
| Jimmie Lunceford Orchestra | LP | Brunswick | LAT8027 | 1954 | £6 | £15 | |
| Lunceford Special | LP | Philips | BBL7037 | 1955 | £6 | £15 | |

## LUNCH, LYDIA

| | | | | | | | |
|---|---|---|---|---|---|---|---|
| Stinkfist | CD-s | Widowspeak | WSP020 | 1989 | £2 | £5 | with Jim Thirwell |

## LUND, GARRETT

| | | | | | | | |
|---|---|---|---|---|---|---|---|
| Almost Grown | LP | private | 5113 | 1975 | £330 | £500 | US |

## LUREX, LARRY

Larry Lurex is Freddie Mercury, and his single, issued just before the start of Queen's career is sought-after in both its UK and US incarnations. The latter, however, turns up suspiciously often and it is likely that many copies are actually counterfeits.

| | | | | | | | |
|---|---|---|---|---|---|---|---|
| I Can Hear Music | 7" | Anthem | 104 | 1973 | £25 | £50 | US |
| I Can Hear Music | 7" | EMI | EMI2030 | 1973 | £50 | £100 | |

## LURKERS

| | | | | | | | |
|---|---|---|---|---|---|---|---|
| Shadow | 7" | Beggars Banquet | BEG1 | 1978 | £2 | £5 | red, blue, or white vinyl |

## LUSH

| | | | | | | | |
|---|---|---|---|---|---|---|---|
| Black Spring | CD-s | 4AD | ADBAD1016 | 1991 | £2 | £5 | |
| Mad Love | CD-s | 4AD | BAD0003CD | 1990 | £2 | £5 | |
| Scar | CD-s | 4AD | JAD911CD | 1989 | £2 | £5 | |
| Sweetness And Light | CD-s | 4AD | BAD0013CD | 1990 | £2 | £5 | |

## LUSHER, DON

| | | | | | | | |
|---|---|---|---|---|---|---|---|
| Rock 'n' Roll | 7" | Decca | F10560 | 1955 | £1.50 | £4 | |

## LUSTMORD

| | | | | | | | |
|---|---|---|---|---|---|---|---|
| Lustmord | LP | Sterile | SR3 | 1982 | £20 | £40 | |

## LUTCHER, NELLIE

| | | | | | | | |
|---|---|---|---|---|---|---|---|
| Blues In The Night | 7" | Brunswick | 05352 | 1954 | £2.50 | £6 | |
| It's Been Said | 7" | Brunswick | 05437 | 1955 | £1.50 | £4 | |
| Nellie Lutcher | 7" EP | Philips | BBE12045 | 1956 | £7.50 | £15 | |
| Our New Nellie | LP | London | HAU2036 | 1957 | £6 | £15 | |
| Real Gone | LP | Capitol | T232 | 195– | £8 | £20 | US |
| Real Gone | 7" EP | Capitol | EAP20066 | 1960 | £12.50 | £25 | |
| Real Gone | 10" LP | Capitol | LC6506 | 1951 | £20 | £40 | |
| Whee! Nellie | 10" LP | Epic | 1108 | 195– | £10 | £25 | US |

| | | | | | | |
|---|---|---|---|---|---|---|
| Whose Honey Are You | 7" | Brunswick | 05497 | 1955 | £1.50 | £4 |

## LUTHA

| | | | | | | |
|---|---|---|---|---|---|---|
| | LP | | | | £100 | £200 | *New Zealand* |

## LUTHER

| | | | | | | |
|---|---|---|---|---|---|---|
| It's Good For The Soul | 7" | Atlantic | K10781 | 1976 | £7.50 | £15 |

## LUTHER, FRANK

While few people will be familiar with the name of Frank Luther, everyone who ever listened to *Children's Favourites* with Uncle Mac will know Luther's classic children's song. Now, after me, 'I'm a troll, foll-de-roll!'

| | | | | | | |
|---|---|---|---|---|---|---|
| Three Billygoats Gruff | 7" | Decca | F9051 | 1954 | £4 | £10 |

## LUTHER & LITTLE EVA

| | | | | | | |
|---|---|---|---|---|---|---|
| Ain't Got No Home | 7" | Parlophone | R4292 | 1957 | £100 | £200 | *best auctioned* |

## LUV BUG

| | | | | | | |
|---|---|---|---|---|---|---|
| You Can Count On Me | 7" | Roxy-Ritz | TEASE2 | 1986 | £1.50 | £4 |

## LUV MACHINE

| | | | | | | |
|---|---|---|---|---|---|---|
| Luv Machine | LP | Polydor | 2460102 | 1971 | £50 | £100 |

## LUVVERS

| | | | | | | |
|---|---|---|---|---|---|---|
| House On The Hill | 7" | Parlophone | R5459 | 1966 | £10 | £20 |

## LUZIFER

| | | | | | | |
|---|---|---|---|---|---|---|
| Black Mass | LP | RCA | UNI73111 | 1971 | £8 | £20 | US |

## L-VOAG

| | | | | | | |
|---|---|---|---|---|---|---|
| Move | 7" | Sesame Songs | MOVE1 | 1979 | £4 | £8 |
| Way Out | LP | Axis | No. 9 | 1979 | £4 | £10 |

## LYMON, FRANKIE & THE TEENAGERS

| | | | | | | |
|---|---|---|---|---|---|---|
| ABC's In Love | 7" | Columbia | DB3858 | 1956 | £10 | £20 |
| At The London Palladium | 10" LP | Columbia | 33S1127 | 1958 | £50 | £100 |
| Frankie Lymon & The Teenagers | 7" EP | Columbia | SEG7734 | 1957 | £20 | £40 |
| Goody Goody | 7" | Columbia | DB3983 | 1957 | £4 | £8 |
| I Promise To Remember | 7" | Columbia | DB3819 | 1956 | £10 | £20 |
| I Want You To Be My Girl | 7" | Columbia | SCM5285 | 1956 | £12.50 | £25 |
| I'm Not A Juvenile Delinquent | 7" EP | Columbia | SEG7694 | 1957 | £15 | £30 |
| I'm Not A Juvenile Delinquent | 7" | Columbia | DB3878 | 1957 | £10 | £20 |
| Jerry Blavatt Presents The Teenagers | LP | Roulette | R25250 | 1964 | £25 | £50 | US |
| Little Bitty Pretty One | 7" | Columbia | DB4499 | 1960 | £7.50 | £15 |
| Mama Don't Allow It | 7" | Columbia | DB4134 | 1958 | £4 | £8 |
| My Girl | 7" | Columbia | DB4028 | 1957 | £6 | £12 |
| No Matter What You've Done | 7" | Columbia | DB4295 | 1959 | £5 | £10 |
| Only Way To Love | 7" | Columbia | DB4245 | 1959 | £2.50 | £6 |
| Out In The Cold Again | 7" | Columbia | DB3942 | 1957 | £10 | £20 |
| Rock And Roll | LP | Roulette | R25036 | 1958 | £50 | £100 | US |
| Rockin' With Frankie | 10" LP | Columbia | 33S1134 | 1957 | £250 | £400 |
| Teenage Love | 7" | Columbia | DB3910 | 1957 | £10 | £20 |
| Teenage Rock | 7" EP | Columbia | SEG7662 | 1957 | £15 | £30 |
| Teenagers | LP | Gee | GLP701 | 1957 | £100 | £200 | *US red label* |
| Teenagers | LP | Gee | GLP701 | 1961 | £30 | £60 | *US grey label* |
| Teenagers At The London Palladium | LP | Roulette | R25013 | 1958 | £50 | £100 | US |
| Thumb Thumb | 7" | Columbia | DB4073 | 1958 | £5 | £10 |
| Why Do Fools Fall In Love | 7" | Columbia | SCM5265 | 1956 | £15 | £30 |
| Why Do Fools Fall In Love? | 7" | King | KG1043 | 1966 | £2 | £5 |

## LYMON, LEWIS

| | | | | | | |
|---|---|---|---|---|---|---|
| Too Young | 7" | Oriole | CB1419 | 1958 | £180 | £300 | *best auctioned* |

## LYNCH, DERMOTT

| | | | | | | |
|---|---|---|---|---|---|---|
| Adults Only | 7" | Doctor Bird | DB1115 | 1967 | £5 | £10 |
| Hot Shot | 7" | Blue Cat | BS101 | 1968 | £4 | £8 |
| I Got Everything | 7" | Blue Cat | BS122 | 1968 | £4 | £8 |
| Something Is Worrying Me | 7" | Blue Cat | BS129 | 1968 | £4 | £8 | *Trevor B side* |
| You Went Away | 7" | Blue Cat | BS130 | 1968 | £4 | £8 | *Trevor B side* |

## LYNCH, KENNY

| | | | | | | |
|---|---|---|---|---|---|---|
| Drifter | 7" | Columbia | DB8599 | 1969 | £1.50 | £4 |
| Hey Girl | 7" EP | HMV | 7EG8820 | 1963 | £6 | £12 |
| It's Too Late | 7" | HMV | POP1577 | 1967 | £1.50 | £4 |
| Kenny Lynch | 7" EP | HMV | 7EG8855 | 1964 | £6 | £12 |
| Misery | 7" | HMV | POP1136 | 1963 | £1.50 | £4 |
| Mountain Of Love | 7" | HMV | POP751 | 1960 | £1.50 | £4 |
| Movin' Away | 7" | HMV | POP1604 | 1967 | £2.50 | £6 |
| My Own Two Feet | 7" | HMV | POP1367 | 1964 | £2.50 | £6 |
| Up On The Roof | LP | HMV | CLP1635 | 1963 | £10 | £25 | *mono* |
| Up On The Roof | LP | HMV | CSD1489 | 1963 | £20 | £40 | *stereo* |
| We Like Kenny | LP | MFP | MFP1022 | 1966 | £4 | £10 |
| What Am I To You | 7" EP | HMV | 7EG8881 | 1965 | £6 | £12 |

## LYNDELL, LINDA

| | | | | | | |
|---|---|---|---|---|---|---|
| Bring Your Love Back To Me | 7" | Stax | 601041 | 1968 | £7.50 | £15 |

## LYNGSTAD, ANNI-FRID

Anni-Frid Lyngstad has achieved some success as a solo artist (some of the records are credited to 'Frida') both before and after being a member of Abba.

| | | | | | | | |
|---|---|---|---|---|---|---|---|
| Anni-Frid Lyngstad | LP | Columbia | 04851017 | 197– | £6 | £15 | Swedish |
| Frida | LP | Columbia | 06234380 | 1971 | £25 | £50 | Swedish |
| Frida | LP | Columbia | E05434549 | 1971 | £5 | £12 | Swedish |
| Frida Ensam | LP | Polar | POLS265 | 1976 | £5 | £12 | Swedish |
| Something's Going On | CD | CBS | CDCBS85966 | 1988 | £5 | £12 | |

## LYNN, BARBARA

| | | | | | | | |
|---|---|---|---|---|---|---|---|
| Barbara Lynn Story | LP | Sue | ILP949 | 1967 | £20 | £40 | |
| Here Is Barbara Lynn | LP | Atlantic | SD8171 | 1968 | £8 | £20 | US |
| Letter To Mommy And Daddy | 7" | Sue | WI4028 | 1967 | £5 | £10 | |
| Oh Baby | 7" | London | HLW9918 | 1964 | £2 | £5 | |
| Sister Of Soul | LP | Jamie | JLP(S)3026 | 1964 | £8 | £20 | US |
| Until Then I Suffer | 7" | Atlantic | 2091133 | 1971 | £2 | £5 | |
| You Can't Buy Me Love | 7" | Immediate | IM011 | 1965 | £7.50 | £15 | |
| You Left The Water Running | 7" | London | HLU10094 | 1966 | £4 | £8 | |
| You'll Lose A Good Thing | LP | Jamie | JLP(S70)3023 | 1962 | £8 | £20 | US |
| You'll Lose A Good Thing | 7" | Sue | WI4038 | 1967 | £5 | £10 | |

## LYNN, BOBBY

| | | | | | | | |
|---|---|---|---|---|---|---|---|
| Earthquake | 7" | Bell | BLL1168 | 1971 | £1.50 | £4 | |
| Earthquake | 7" | Stateside | SS2088 | 1968 | £7.50 | £15 | |

## LYNN, KARI

| | | | | | | | |
|---|---|---|---|---|---|---|---|
| Lonesome And Sorry | 7" | Oriole | CB1644 | 1961 | £1.50 | £4 | |
| Yo Yo | 7" | Oriole | CB1632 | 1961 | £1.50 | £4 | |

## LYNN, LORETTA

| | | | | | | | |
|---|---|---|---|---|---|---|---|
| Before I'm Over You | LP | Decca | DL(7)4541 | 1964 | £6 | £15 | US |
| Blue Kentucky Girl | LP | Decca | DL(7)4665 | 1965 | £6 | £15 | US |
| Country Christmas | LP | Decca | DL(7)4817 | 1966 | £5 | £12 | US |
| Hymns | LP | Decca | DL(7)4695 | 1965 | £5 | £12 | US |
| I Like 'Em Country | LP | Decca | DL(7)4744 | 1966 | £5 | £12 | US |
| Loretta Lynn Sings | LP | Decca | DL(7)4457 | 1963 | £8 | £20 | US |
| Mr. & Mrs. Used To Be | LP | Decca | DL(7)4639 | 1965 | £5 | £12 | US, with Ernest Tubb |
| Songs From My Heart | LP | Decca | DL(7)4620 | 1965 | £6 | £15 | US |
| You Ain't Woman Enough | LP | Decca | DL(7)4783 | 1966 | £5 | £12 | US |

## LYNN, PATTI

| | | | | | | | |
|---|---|---|---|---|---|---|---|
| Patti | 7" EP | Fontana | TFE17392 | 1962 | £10 | £20 | |

## LYNN, TAMMI

| | | | | | | | |
|---|---|---|---|---|---|---|---|
| I'm Gonna Run Away From You | 7" | Atlantic | AT4071 | 1966 | £12.50 | £25 | |

## LYNN, VERA

| | | | | | | | |
|---|---|---|---|---|---|---|---|
| Auf Wiederseh'n Sweetheart | 7" | Decca | F9927 | 1959 | £1.50 | £4 | |
| Faithful Hussar | 7" | Decca | F10846 | 1957 | £1.50 | £4 | |
| House With Love In It | 7" | Decca | F10799 | 1956 | £1.50 | £4 | |
| My Son My Son | 7" | Decca | F10372 | 1954 | £5 | £10 | |
| Travellin' Home | 7" | Decca | F10903 | 1957 | £1.50 | £4 | |
| Who Are We? | 7" | Decca | F10715 | 1956 | £1.50 | £4 | |

## LYNNE, SUE

| | | | | | | | |
|---|---|---|---|---|---|---|---|
| Don't Pity Me | 7" | RCA | RCA1822 | 1969 | £25 | £50 | |

## LYNOTT, PHIL

| | | | | | | | |
|---|---|---|---|---|---|---|---|
| Solo In Soho | LP | Vertigo | PHIL1 | 1980 | £4 | £10 | picture disc |

## LYNTON, JACKIE

The backing group on the A side of 'All Of Me' is called the Jury. The bass player is Pat Donaldson – kept busy on a variety of sessions following his stints with Zoot Money and with Fotheringay – while the guitarist is Albert Lee, here making his first recording.

| | | | | | | | |
|---|---|---|---|---|---|---|---|
| All Of Me | 7" | Piccadilly | 7N35064 | 1962 | £2 | £5 | |

## LYNYRD SKYNYRD

| | | | | | | | |
|---|---|---|---|---|---|---|---|
| Free Bird | 7" | MCA | MCA251 | 1976 | £1.50 | £4 | picture sleeve |
| Free Bird | 7" | MCA | MCA275 | 1976 | £1.50 | £4 | picture sleeve |
| Freebird | CD-s | MCA | DMCA1315 | 1989 | £2 | £5 | |
| Freebird | 12" | MCA | MCATP251 | 1982 | £2.50 | £6 | picture disc |
| Ten From The Swamp | CD | MCA | CD332033 | 1991 | £8 | £20 | US promo sampler |
| Travis Tritt Interviews Lynyrd Skynyrd | CD | Atlantic | PRCD50782 | 1993 | £6 | £15 | US promo |

## LYON, BARBARA

| | | | | | | | |
|---|---|---|---|---|---|---|---|
| Band Of Gold | 7" | Columbia | SCM5232 | 1956 | £1.50 | £4 | |
| Birds And The Bees | 7" | Columbia | SCM5276 | 1956 | £1.50 | £4 | |
| It's Better In The Dark | 7" | Columbia | DB3826 | 1956 | £1.50 | £4 | |
| Letter To A Soldier | 7" | Columbia | DB3865 | 1956 | £2 | £5 | |
| My Charlie | 7" | Triumph | RGM1027 | 1960 | £10 | £20 | |
| My Four Friends | 7" EP | Columbia | SEG7640 | 1956 | £5 | £10 | |
| Whisper | 7" | Columbia | SCM5207 | 1955 | £1.50 | £4 | |
| Yes You Are | 7" | Columbia | SCM5186 | 1955 | £1.50 | £4 | |

## LYONESSE

| | | | | | | | | |
|---|---|---|---|---|---|---|---|---|
| Cantrique | LP | PDU | PLDA6029 | 1975 | £37.50 | £75 | | Italian |
| Lyonesse | LP | PDU | PLDA5093 | 1974 | £37.50 | £75 | | Italian |

## LYONS, JOHN

| | | | | | | | |
|---|---|---|---|---|---|---|---|
| May Morning Dew | LP | Topic | 12TS248 | 1974 | £5 | £12 | |

## LYONS, TIM

| | | | | | | | |
|---|---|---|---|---|---|---|---|
| Easter Snow | LP | Innisfree | SIF1014 | 1978 | £4 | £10 | US |
| Green Linnet | LP | Trailer | LER3036 | 1972 | £4 | £10 | |

## LYRICS

| | | | | | | | |
|---|---|---|---|---|---|---|---|
| A Get It | 7" | Coxsone | CS7003 | 1967 | £5 | £10 | Ken Parker B side |
| Music Like Dirt | 7" | Coxsone | CS7067 | 1968 | £5 | £10 | |

## LYTELL, JIMMY

| | | | | | | | |
|---|---|---|---|---|---|---|---|
| Hot Cargo | 7" | London | HL8873 | 1959 | £1.50 | £4 | |

## LYTLE, JOHNNY

| | | | | | | | |
|---|---|---|---|---|---|---|---|
| Blue Vibes | LP | Jazzland | JLP22 | 1960 | £4 | £10 | |

## LYTTELTON, HUMPHREY

| | | | | | | | |
|---|---|---|---|---|---|---|---|
| Bad Penny Blues | 7" | Parlophone | CMSP41 | 1958 | £10 | £20 | |
| Blues In The Night | LP | Columbia | 33SX1239/ SCX3316 | 1960 | £5 | £12 | |
| East Coast Trot | 7" | Parlophone | MSP6076 | 1954 | £1.50 | £4 | |
| Here's Humph | 10" LP | Parlophone | PMD1049 | 1957 | £6 | £15 | |
| Humph At The Conway | LP | Parlophone | PMC1012 | 1954 | £6 | £15 | |
| Humph In Perspective | LP | Parlophone | PMC1070 | 1958 | £5 | £12 | |
| Humph Swings Out | 10" LP | Parlophone | PMD1044 | 1956 | £6 | £15 | |
| Humph's Blues No. 2 | 7" EP | Parlophone | GEP8645 | 1957 | £2.50 | £6 | |
| Humphrey Lyttelton And His Band | LP | Esquire | 32007 | 1955 | £5 | £12 | |
| I Play As I Please | LP | Decca | LK4276 | 1958 | £5 | £12 | |
| Jazz At The Royal Festival Hall | 10" LP | Parlophone | PMD1032 | 1955 | £5 | £12 | |
| Jazz Concert | 10" LP | Parlophone | PMD1006 | 1953 | £6 | £15 | |
| Jazz Session With Humph | 10" LP | Parlophone | PMD1035 | 1956 | £6 | £15 | |
| Just Once For All Time | 7" | Parlophone | MSP6093 | 1954 | £1.50 | £4 | |
| Kater Street Rag | 7" | Parlophone | MSP6045 | 1953 | £1.50 | £4 | |
| Kath Meets Humph | 10" LP | Parlophone | PMD1052 | 1958 | £6 | £15 | with Kathy Stobart |
| Love Love Love | 7" | Parlophone | R4212 | 1956 | £1.50 | £4 | |
| Mainly Traditional | 7" | Parlophone | MSP6097 | 1954 | £1.50 | £4 | |
| Martiniquen Song | 7" | Parlophone | MSP6061 | 1953 | £1.50 | £4 | |
| Maryland My Maryland | 7" | Parlophone | MSP6033 | 1953 | £1.50 | £4 | |
| Mezzy's Tune | 7" | Parlophone | MSP6128 | 1954 | £1.50 | £4 | |
| Muskrat Ramble | 7" | Parlophone | MSP6023 | 1953 | £1.50 | £4 | |
| Out Of The Gallion | 7" | Parlophone | MSP6001 | 1953 | £1.50 | £4 | |
| Shake It And Break It | 7" | Parlophone | MSP6034 | 1953 | £1.50 | £4 | |
| Triple Exposure | LP | Parlophone | PMC1110 | 1959 | £5 | £12 | |
| When The Saints Go Marching In | 7" | Tempo | A10 | 1956 | £1.50 | £4 | |

## LYTTLE, JOHNNY

| | | | | | | | |
|---|---|---|---|---|---|---|---|
| Gonna Get That Boat | 7" | Minit | MLF11006 | 1968 | £2 | £5 | |

# M

**M**

| | | | | | | |
|---|---|---|---|---|---|---|
| Pop Musik (1989 remix) | CD-s .. | Freestyle | FRSCD1 | 1989 £2 | £5 | |

## MAAJUN
| | | | | | | |
|---|---|---|---|---|---|---|
| Vivre la mort du vieux monde | LP | Vogue | SLVX545 | 1971 £25 | £50 | French |

## MABLE JOY
| | | | | | | |
|---|---|---|---|---|---|---|
| Mable Joy | LP | Real | RR2004 | 1975 £15 | £30 | |

## MABON, WILLIE
| | | | | | | |
|---|---|---|---|---|---|---|
| Got To Have Some | 7" | Sue | WI320 | 1964 £5 | £10 | |
| I'm The Fixer | 7" | Sue | WI382 | 1965 £5 | £10 | |
| Just Got Some | 7" | Sue | WI331 | 1965 £5 | £10 | |
| Willie Mabon | LP | Chess | 1439 | 195- £20 | £40 | US |

## MACCOLL, EWAN
| | | | | | | |
|---|---|---|---|---|---|---|
| As We Were A-Sailing | LP | Argo | ZDA137 | 1970 £6 | £15 | with other artists |
| Bad Lads And Hard Cases | LP | Riverside | RLP12632 | 196- £8 | £20 | US |
| Barrack Room Ballads | 10" LP | Topic | 10T26 | 1958 £15 | £30 | |
| Best Of Ewan MacColl | LP | PRE | 13004 | 1961 £10 | £25 | |
| Blow Boys Blow | LP | XTRA | XTRA1052 | 1967 £5 | £12 | with A. L. Lloyd |
| Bundook Ballads | LP | Topic | 12T130 | 1965 £10 | £25 | |
| English And Scottish Popular Ballads | LP | Folkways | FG3509 | 1961 £6 | £15 | US |
| English And Scottish Popular Ballads Vol. 1 | LP | Riverside | RLP12621/2 | 196- £15 | £30 | US double, with A. L. Lloyd |
| English And Scottish Popular Ballads Vol. 2 | LP | Folkways | FG3510 | 1961 £6 | £15 | US |
| English And Scottish Popular Ballads Vol. 2 | LP | Riverside | RLP12623/4 | 196- £15 | £30 | US double, with A. L. Lloyd |
| English And Scottish Popular Ballads Vol. 3 | LP | Riverside | RLP12625/6 | 196- £15 | £30 | US double, with A. L. Lloyd |
| English And Scottish Popular Ballads Vol. 4 | LP | Riverside | RLP12627/8 | 196- £15 | £30 | US double, with A. L. Lloyd |
| English And Scottish Popular Ballads Vol. 5 | LP | Riverside | RLP12629 | 196- £8 | £20 | US, with A. L. Lloyd |
| Popular Scottish Songs | LP | Folkways | FW8757 | 1960 £6 | £15 | US |
| Scots Drinking Songs | LP | Riverside | RLP12605 | 196- £8 | £20 | US |
| Scots Folk Songs | LP | Riverside | RLP12609 | 196- £8 | £20 | US |
| Scots Street Songs | LP | Riverside | RLP12612 | 196- £8 | £20 | US |
| Second Shift | 10" LP | Topic | 10T25 | 1958 £15 | £30 | |
| Shuttle And Cage | 10" LP | Topic | 10T13 | 1958 £15 | £30 | |
| Solo Flight | LP | Argo | ZFB12 | 1972 £6 | £15 | |
| Songs Of Robert Burns | LP | Folkways | FW8758 | 1959 £8 | £20 | US |
| Still I Love Him | 10" LP | Topic | 10T50 | 1960 £20 | £40 | with Isla Cameron |
| Streets Of Song | LP | Topic | 12T41 | 1960 £10 | £25 | with Dominic Behan |
| Thar She Blows! | LP | Riverside | RLP12635 | 196- £8 | £20 | US, with A. L. Lloyd |

## MACCOLL, EWAN & PEGGY SEEGER
| | | | | | | |
|---|---|---|---|---|---|---|
| Amorous Muse | LP | Argo | (Z)DA84 | 1968 £6 | £15 | |
| Amorous Muse | LP | Argo | ZFB66 | 1972 £6 | £15 | |
| Angry Muse | LP | Argo | (Z)DA83 | 1968 £6 | £15 | |
| Angry Muse | LP | Argo | ZFB65 | 1972 £6 | £15 | |
| Bothy Ballads Of Scotland | LP | Folkways | FW8759 | 1961 £6 | £15 | US |
| Chorus From The Gallows | LP | Topic | 12T16 | 1960 £15 | £30 | |
| Folkways Record Of Contemporary Songs | LP | Folkways | FW8736 | 1973 £5 | £12 | US |
| Jacobite Rebellions | LP | Topic | 12T79 | 1962 £10 | £25 | |
| Long Harvest Vol. 1 | LP | Argo | (Z)DA66 | 1967 £6 | £15 | |
| Long Harvest Vol. 2 | LP | Argo | (Z)DA67 | 1967 £6 | £15 | |
| Long Harvest Vol. 3 | LP | Argo | (Z)DA68 | 1967 £6 | £15 | |
| Long Harvest Vol. 4 | LP | Argo | (Z)DA69 | 1967 £6 | £15 | |
| Long Harvest Vol. 5 | LP | Argo | (Z)DA70 | 1967 £6 | £15 | |
| Long Harvest Vol. 6 | LP | Argo | (Z)DA71 | 1967 £6 | £15 | |
| Long Harvest Vol. 7 | LP | Argo | (Z)DA72 | 1967 £6 | £15 | |
| Long Harvest Vol. 8 | LP | Argo | (Z)DA73 | 1967 £6 | £15 | |
| Long Harvest Vol. 9 | LP | Argo | (Z)DA74 | 1967 £6 | £15 | |
| Long Harvest Vol. 10 | LP | Argo | (Z)DA75 | 1967 £6 | £15 | |
| Manchester Angel | LP | Topic | 12T147 | 1966 £15 | £30 | |
| New Briton Gazette | LP | Folkways | FW8734 | 1973 £6 | £15 | US |
| Paper Stage Vol. 1 | LP | Argo | (Z)DA98 | 1969 £6 | £15 | |
| Paper Stage Vol. 2 | LP | Argo | (Z)DA99 | 1969 £6 | £15 | |
| Songs Of Two Rebellions | LP | Folkways | FW8756 | 1960 £6 | £15 | US |
| Steam Whistle Ballads | LP | Topic | 12T104 | 1964 £8 | £20 | |
| Traditional Songs And Ballads | LP | Folkways | FW8760 | 1964 £6 | £15 | US |
| Two Way Trip | LP | Folkways | FW8755 | 1961 £6 | £15 | US |
| Wanton Muse | LP | Argo | (Z)DA85 | 1968 £6 | £15 | |

| | | | | | | |
|---|---|---|---|---|---|---|
| Wanton Muse | LP | Argo | ZFB67 | 1972 | £6 | £15 |
| We Are The Engineers | 7" | AUEW | AUEW1 | 196– | £1.50 | £4 |
| World Of Ewan MacColl And Peggy Seeger | LP | Argo | SPA102 | 1970 | £5 | £12 |
| World Of Ewan MacColl And Peggy Seeger Vol. 2 | LP | Argo | SPA216 | 1972 | £4 | £10 |

## MACCOLL, EWAN, PEGGY SEEGER & CHARLES PARKER

| | | | | | | |
|---|---|---|---|---|---|---|
| Ballad Of John Axon | LP | Argo | DA139 | 1971 | £10 | £25 |
| Ballad Of John Axon | LP | Argo | RG474 | 1965 | £10 | £25 |
| Big Hewer | LP | Argo | DA140 | 1971 | £8 | £20 |
| Big Hewer | LP | Argo | RG– | 1967 | £10 | £25 |
| Fight Game | LP | Argo | DA141 | 1971 | £6 | £15 |
| Fight Game | LP | Argo | RG539 | 1968 | £10 | £25 |
| On The Edge | LP | Argo | DA136 | 1971 | £6 | £15 |
| On The Edge | LP | Argo | RG– | 196– | £10 | £25 |
| Singing The Fishing | LP | Argo | DA142 | 1971 | £6 | £15 |
| Singing The Fishing | LP | Argo | RG– | 196– | £10 | £25 |
| Travelling People | LP | Argo | DA133 | 1970 | £15 | £30 |

## MACCOLL, KIRSTY

The daughter of traditional folk master Ewan MacColl is one of our most underrated singer-songwriters. She scored an early success with the witty 'There's A Guy Works Down The Chip Shop Swears He's Elvis', but she is otherwise best known for her cover versions of Billy Bragg's 'New England' and Ray Davies's 'Days'. Despite her relative lack of success, however, she continues to deliver classy collections of her clever and imaginative material. Her recording debut was as a young teenager with the family – Peggy Seeger's 'Penelope Isn't Waiting Any More'.

| | | | | | | | |
|---|---|---|---|---|---|---|---|
| Days | CD-s | Virgin | KMACDX2 | 1989 | £2 | £5 | 3" single |
| Free World | CD-s | Virgin | KMACD1 | 1989 | £2 | £5 | 3" single |
| Innocence | CD-s | Virgin | KMACD3 | 1989 | £2 | £5 | 3" single |
| You Caught Me Out | 7" | Stiff | BUY57 | 1979 | £2.50 | £6 | demo |

## MACEO & ALL THE KING'S MEN

It is extraordinary how the same musicians that formed James Brown's band in the late sixties lack a significant percentage of their drive and rhythmic power when Brown is not there. Here is the proof that James Brown is indeed the master of his own music.

| | | | | | | |
|---|---|---|---|---|---|---|
| Funky Music Machine | LP | Contempo | CRM114 | 1975 | £10 | £25 |
| Funky Music Machine | LP | Mojo | 2916017 | 1972 | £25 | £50 |
| Got To Get 'Cha | 7" | Pye | 7N25571 | 1972 | £2 | £5 |

## MACEO & THE MACKS

| | | | | | | |
|---|---|---|---|---|---|---|
| Cross The Tracks | 12" | Urban | URBX1 | 1987 | £3 | £8 |
| Us | LP | Polydor | 2391122 | 1974 | £10 | £25 |
| Us | LP | Urban | URBLP8 | 1988 | £4 | £10 |

## MACERO, TEO

The CBS staff producer who is perhaps best known as the man who worked on Miles Davis's ground-breaking albums on the label is also a talented alto saxophonist and composer in his own right – which is probably why he is such an effective producer.

| | | | | | | |
|---|---|---|---|---|---|---|
| Teo | LP | Esquire | 32113 | 1961 | £10 | £25 |

## MACGREGOR, MARY

| | | | | | | |
|---|---|---|---|---|---|---|
| Torn Between Two Lovers | LP | Eurodisc | 913119 | 1980 | £4 | £10 |

## MACHINE

| | | | | | | | |
|---|---|---|---|---|---|---|---|
| Machine | LP | Polydor | 2441020 | 1980 | £8 | £20 | Dutch |

## MACHITO

| | | | | | | |
|---|---|---|---|---|---|---|
| Kenya | LP | Columbia | 33SX1103 | 1958 | £8 | £20 |

## MACK, JOHNNY

| | | | | | | |
|---|---|---|---|---|---|---|
| Reggae All Night Long | 7" | Columbia | DB116 | 1970 | £1.50 | £4 |

## MACK, LONNIE

| | | | | | | |
|---|---|---|---|---|---|---|
| For Collectors Only | LP | Elektra | 2410007 | 1970 | £5 | £12 |
| Glad I'm In The Band | LP | Elektra | EKL/EKS74040 | 1969 | £4 | £10 |
| Hills Of Indiana | LP | Elektra | K42097 | 1972 | £4 | £10 |
| Lonnie On The Move | 7" | Stateside | SS312 | 1964 | £1.50 | £4 |
| Memphis | 7" | Elektra | EKSN45044 | 1969 | £1.50 | £4 |
| Memphis | 7" | Stateside | SS207 | 1963 | £2 | £5 |
| Sa-Ba-Hoola | 7" | Stateside | SS393 | 1965 | £4 | £8 |
| Save Your Money | 7" | Elektra | EKSN45060 | 1969 | £1.50 | £4 |
| Save Your Money | 7" | President | PT142 | 1967 | £1.50 | £4 |
| Soul Express | 7" | President | PT198 | 1968 | £1.50 | £4 |
| Wham | 7" | Stateside | SS226 | 1963 | £2.50 | £6 |
| Wham Of The Memphis Man | LP | President | PTL1004 | 1967 | £6 | £15 |
| Whatever's Right | LP | Elektra | EKS74050 | 1969 | £4 | £10 |
| Where There's A Will | 7" | President | PT127 | 1967 | £1.50 | £4 |

## MACK, WARNER

| | | | | | | |
|---|---|---|---|---|---|---|
| Country Touch | LP | Brunswick | LAT8658 | 1966 | £5 | £12 |
| Drifting Apart | LP | Brunswick | LAT8684 | 1967 | £4 | £10 |
| Golden Country Hits | LP | London | HAR/SHR.8002 | 1962 | £5 | £12 |
| Golden Country Hits Vol. 2 | LP | London | HAR/SHR.8025 | 1963 | £5 | £12 |
| Rock A Chicka | 7" | Brunswick | 05728 | 1958 | £37.50 | £75 |

## MACK SISTERS
Long Range Love.................................... 7" ...... London .......... HLU8331............... 1956 £10........£20 .....................................

## MACKAY, MAHNA
Mah Na Mah Na..................................... 7" ...... Parlophone ...... R5808 ................... 1969 £1.50........£4 ................................

## MACKENZIE THEORY
Out Of The Blue ..................................... LP ...... Mushroom ...... L34925................... 1973 £6..........£15 .............. Australian

## MACKINTOSH, KEN
Applejack................................................ 7" ...... HMV ......... POP300 ............... 1957 £4...........£8 ....................
Big Guitar............................................... 7" ...... HMV ......... POP464 ............... 1958 £1.50....£4 ....................
Keep It Moving....................................... 7" ...... HMV ......... POP358 ............... 1957 £1.50....£4 ....................
Ken Mackintosh ...................................... 10" LP HMV ......... DLP1093.............. 1955 £4..........£10 ....................
One Night Stand ..................................... 10" LP HMV ......... DLP1178.............. 1958 £4..........£10 ....................
Raunchy ................................................. 7" ...... HMV ......... POP426 ............... 1957 £1.50....£4 ....................
Regimental Rock ..................................... 7" ...... HMV ......... POP287 ............... 1957 £2..........£5 ....................
Rock Man Rock ...................................... 7" ...... HMV ......... POP327 ............... 1957 £4...........£8 ....................
Six Five Blues ........................................ 7" ...... HMV ......... POP396 ............... 1957 £1.50....£4 ....................
Swinging Shepherd Blues ........................ 7" ...... HMV ......... POP441 ............... 1958 £1.50....£4 ....................
Teenager's Special .................................. 7" EP . HMV ......... 7EG8170.............. 1956 £4...........£8 ....................

## MACLAINE, PETE & CLAN
U.S. Mail................................................ 7" ...... Decca ............. F11699................... 1963 £2..........£5 ....................

## MACLEAN, DOUGIE
Snaigow ................................................. LP ...... Plant Life........ PLR022 ................ 1980 £5..........£12 ....................

## MACLENNAN, DOLINA & ROBIN GRAY
By Mormond Braes .................................. 7" EP . Topic ............. TOP68 ................. 1964 £2..........£5 ....................

## MACLEOD, JOHN FIRST XI
Don't Shoot The Ref ............................... 7" ...... Fontana ......... TF696................... 1966 £1.50....£4 ....................

## MACLISE, ANGUS
Trance.................................................... 7" ...... Fierce ............ FRIGHT010 .......... 1987 £2.50....£6 ....................

## MACMAHON, DOLLY
Dolly...................................................... LP ...... Claddagh ....... CC3 ..................... 1966 £4..........£10 .................. Irish

## MACON, UNCLE DAVE
Uncle Dave Macon No. 1 ........................ 7" EP . RCA ............. RCX7112 ............. 1963 £4...........£8 ....................
Uncle Dave Macon No. 2 ........................ 7" EP . RCA ............. RCX7113 .............. 1963 £4...........£8 ....................

## MACRAE, GORDON
Bella Notte ............................................ 7" ...... Capitol........... CL14361 .............. 1955 £2..........£5 ....................
C'est Magnifique .................................... 7" ...... Capitol........... CL14168 .............. 1954 £2..........£5 ....................
Count Your Blessings Instead Of Sheep...... 7" ...... Capitol........... CL14193 .............. 1954 £2..........£5 ....................
Here's What I'm Here For ........................ 7" ...... Capitol........... CL14222 .............. 1955 £2..........£5 ....................
Jim Bowie .............................................. 7" ...... Capitol........... CL14334 .............. 1955 £2..........£5 ....................
Stranger In Paradise ............................... 7" ...... Capitol........... CL14276 .............. 1955 £2..........£5 ....................
You Forgot............................................. 7" ...... Capitol........... CL14293 .............. 1955 £2..........£5 ....................

## MACRAE, JOSH
Messing About On The River .................... 7" ...... Pye................. 7N15319 .............. 1960 £1.50....£4 ....................
Talking Army Blues................................. 7" ...... Top Rank ...... JAR290............... 1960 £1.50....£4 ....................
Walking Talking Singing.......................... 7" EP . Pye................. NEP24131........... 1960 £2.50....£6 ....................
Wild Side Of Life ................................... 7" ...... Pye................. 7N15308 .............. 1960 £1.50....£4 ....................

## MACREEL
Step It Out ............................................ LP ...... JMR.............. ............................ 1984 £50........£100 ................Dutch

## MAD CATS
Losing You............................................. 7" ...... Coxsone.......... CS7099 ................. 1969 £5..........£10 ........ Winston Jarrett

## MAD LADS
Don't Have To Shop Around .................... 7" ...... Atlantic .......... AT4051 .............. 1965 £2.50....£6 ....................
I Want Someone ..................................... 7" ...... Atlantic .......... AT4083................ 1966 £2.50....£6 ....................
Mad Lads In Action ................................ LP ...... Volt................ 414 ..................... 1966 £6..........£15 ....................US
Sugar Sugar............................................ 7" ...... Atlantic .......... 584038................. 1966 £2..........£5 ....................

## MAD MAGAZINE
Fink Along With Mad .............................. LP ...... Big Top ......... 1206 .................... 196– £6..........£15 ....................US
Mad Twists Rock 'n' Roll........................ LP ...... Big Top ......... 1305 .................... 1963 £6..........£15 ....................US

## MAD RIVER
The first album made by Mad River is a superior example of West Coast rock in the same style, and at least as impressive as the early albums by the Grateful Dead and Quicksilver Messenger Service. As it happens, the album was cut at the wrong speed, so that the music on the original pressings is higher and faster than it should be. The eighties reissue of the album on Edsel corrects this fault. *Paradise Bar And Grill* has more of a country-rock emphasis and is rather less remarkable. A very rare EP predates both albums and includes early versions of two of the first album songs.

Mad River............................................. LP ...... Capitol........... ST2985 ................ 1968 £10........£25 ....................US
Paradise Bar & Grill ............................... LP ...... Capitol........... ST185 ................. 1969 £15........£30 ....................US
Wind Chimes ......................................... 7" EP . Wee .............. 10021 ................. 1967 £180.....£300 .... US, best auctioned

## MAD ROY

| | | | | | | | |
|---|---|---|---|---|---|---|---|
| Home Version | 7" | Banana | BA326 | 1971 | £1.50 | £4 | |
| Nannie Goat Version | 7" | Banana | BA324 | 1970 | £1.50 | £4 | |
| Universal Love | 7" | Banana | BA327 | 1971 | £1.50 | £4 | *Roland Alphonso B side* |

## MADARA, JOHNNY

| | | | | | | | |
|---|---|---|---|---|---|---|---|
| Be My Girl | 7" | HMV | POP389 | 1957 | £1.50 | £4 | |

## MADDEN, TOM & FRANK WARREN

| | | | | | | | |
|---|---|---|---|---|---|---|---|
| Little Thatched Cabin | LP | Inchecronin | INC7727 | 1977 | £6 | £15 | |

## MADDER LAKE

| | | | | | | | |
|---|---|---|---|---|---|---|---|
| Still Point | LP | Mushroom | L34915 | 1973 | £10 | £25 | *Australian* |

## MADDOX, JOHNNY

| | | | | | | | |
|---|---|---|---|---|---|---|---|
| Crazy Otto Medley | 7" | London | HL8134 | 1955 | £6 | £12 | |
| Dixieland Band | 7" | London | HLD8347 | 1956 | £4 | £8 | |
| Dixieland Blues | LP | London | HAD2175/ SHD6022 | 1959 | £4 | £10 | |
| Do Do Do | 7" | London | HLD8203 | 1955 | £6 | £12 | |
| Hands Off | 7" | London | HLD8277 | 1956 | £6 | £12 | |
| Honky Tonk Jazz | 7" EP | London | RED1150 | 1958 | £2 | £5 | |
| My Old Flames | LP | London | HAD2101 | 1958 | £4 | £10 | |
| Old Fashioned Love | 7" EP | London | RED1270 | 1961 | £2 | £5 | |
| Plays | 10" LP | London | HBD1060 | 1956 | £4 | £10 | |
| Presenting Johnny Maddox | 7" EP | London | REP1020 | 1955 | £2 | £5 | |
| Presenting Johnny Maddox No. 2 | 7" EP | London | REP1040 | 1955 | £2 | £5 | |
| Yellow Dog Blues | 7" | London | HLD8540 | 1958 | £1.50 | £4 | |

## MADDOX, ROSE

| | | | | | | | |
|---|---|---|---|---|---|---|---|
| Alone With You | LP | Capitol | (S)T1993 | 1963 | £5 | £12 | US |
| Big Bouquet Of Roses | LP | Capitol | (S)T1548 | 1961 | £5 | £12 | US |
| Gambler's Love | 7" | Capitol | CL15023 | 1959 | £1.50 | £4 | US |
| Glorybound Train | LP | Capitol | (S)T1437 | 1960 | £5 | £12 | US |
| One Rose | LP | Capitol | (S)T1312 | 1960 | £5 | £12 | US |
| Precious Memories | LP | Columbia | CL1159 | 1958 | £8 | £20 | US |
| Rose Maddox Sings Bluegrass | LP | Capitol | (S)T1779 | 1962 | £5 | £12 | US |

## MADDOX BROTHERS & ROSE

| | | | | | | | |
|---|---|---|---|---|---|---|---|
| Collection Of Standard Sacred Songs | LP | King | 669 | 1960 | £15 | £30 | US |
| I'll Write Your Name In The Sand | LP | King | 752 | 1961 | £10 | £25 | US |
| Maddox Brothers And Rose | LP | King | 677 | 1961 | £10 | £25 | US |

## MADE IN SHEFFIELD

| | | | | | | | |
|---|---|---|---|---|---|---|---|
| Amelia Jane | 7" | Fontana | TF871 | 1967 | £6 | £12 | |

## MADE IN SWEDEN

| | | | | | | | |
|---|---|---|---|---|---|---|---|
| Live At The Golden Circle | LP | Sonet | SLP2506 | 1970 | £4 | £10 | |
| Mad River | LP | Sonet | SNTF621 | 1971 | £4 | £10 | |
| Made In England | LP | Sonet | SLP2512 | 1970 | £4 | £10 | |
| Made In Sweden | LP | Sonet | SLP71 | 1969 | £4 | £10 | |
| Snakes In A Hole | LP | Sonet | SLP2504 | 1969 | £4 | £10 | |

## MADISON DYKE

| | | | | | | | |
|---|---|---|---|---|---|---|---|
| Zeitmaschine | LP | Racket Records | RRK15001 | 1977 | £6 | £15 | *German* |

## MADNESS

| | | | | | | | |
|---|---|---|---|---|---|---|---|
| Absolutely | LP | Stiff | STIFF29 | 1980 | £10 | £25 | *different cover pose* |
| Carols On 45 | 7" | Lyntone | LYN10719 | 1982 | £1.50 | £4 | *flexi* |
| I Pronounce You | CD-s | Virgin | VSCD1054 | 1988 | £2 | £5 | |
| Madness Pack | 7" | Stiff | GRAB1 | 1982 | £10 | £20 | *6 x 7" in plastic wallet* |
| Peel Sessions | CD-s | Strange Fruit | SFPSCD007 | 1988 | £2 | £5 | |
| Prince | 7" | 2-Tone | TT3 | 1979 | £2.50 | £6 | *paper labels, no picture sleeve* |
| Return Of The Los Palmas 7 | 7" | Stiff | BUYIT108 | 1981 | £5 | £10 | *with comic* |
| Swan Lake | 12" | Stiff | MAD1 | 1979 | £10 | £20 | *promo* |
| Sweetest Girl | 7" | Zarjazz | JAZZD8 | 1986 | £1.50 | £4 | *double* |
| Take It Or Leave It | 7" | Lyntone | LYN10353 | 1982 | £2 | £5 | *flexi* |
| Uno Paso Adalante | 7" | Stiff | MO1922 | 1980 | £2.50 | £6 | *sung in Spanish* |
| Yesterday's Men | 7" | Zarjazz | JAZZD5 | 1985 | £2 | £5 | *picture disc double pack* |

## MADONNA

Astute marketing has kept Madonna at the top for far longer than seemed likely when her pictures first started to appear on teenage bedroom walls. Virtually everything she has released is now a collectors' item of some kind, with particular interest being generated by the series of picture disc releases. The value of many of these is much higher than can be explained merely by their rarity, although the early 'Crazy For You' is reckoned to be one of the scarcest commercially released picture discs of all. More valuable still, by quite a long way, is the withdrawn picture disc release of 'Erotica'.

| | | | | | | | |
|---|---|---|---|---|---|---|---|
| Angel | 7" | Sire | W8881P | 1985 | £6 | £12 | *shaped picture disc* |
| Angel | 7" | Sire | W8881P | 1985 | £10 | £20 | *shaped picture disc, plinth* |
| Bedtime Stories | CD | Maverick | 9457672 | 1994 | £20 | £40 | *US promo, velvet digipak* |

| Title | Format | Label | Cat. No. | Year | | | Notes |
|---|---|---|---|---|---|---|---|
| Borderline | 7" | Sire | W9260F | 1984 | £30 | £60 | double |
| Borderline | 7" | Sire | W9260P | 1986 | £15 | £30 | shaped picture disc |
| Causing A Commotion | 7" | Sire | W8224 | 1987 | £15 | £30 | with badge |
| Causing A Commotion (Silver Screen Mix) | 12" | Sire | W8224TP | 1987 | £6 | £15 | picture disc |
| Cherish | CD-s | Sire | W2883CD | 1989 | £2 | £5 | 3" single |
| Cherish | 12" | Sire | W2883TP | 1989 | £4 | £10 | picture disc |
| Crazy For You | CD-s | Sire | W0008CD | 1991 | £2 | £5 | picture disc |
| Crazy For You | 7" | Geffen | WA6323 | 1985 | £25 | £50 | shaped picture disc |
| Crazy For You (Remix) | 7" | Sire | W0008P | 1991 | £1.50 | £4 | shaped picture disc, plinth |
| Dear Jessie | CD-s | Sire | W2668CD | 1989 | £20 | £40 | picture disc |
| Dear Jessie | 12" | Sire | W2668T | 1989 | £2.50 | £6 | poster sleeve |
| Dear Jessie | 12" | Sire | W2668TP | 1989 | £2.50 | £6 | picture disc |
| Deeper And Deeper | 12" | Sire | W0146TP | 1992 | £2.50 | £6 | picture disc |
| Dress You Up | 7" | Sire | W8848P | 1985 | £10 | £20 | shaped picture disc |
| Dress You Up (Formal Mix) | 12" | Sire | W8848T | 1985 | £6 | £15 | poster sleeve |
| Erotica | CD | Sire | | 1992 | £15 | £30 | Australian, fold-out cover |
| Erotica | 12" | Sire | W0138TP | 1992 | £330 | £500 | picture disc, gold insert |
| Everybody | 7" | Sire | W9899 | 1982 | £50 | £100 | |
| Everybody | 12" | Sire | W9899T | 1982 | £37.50 | £75 | no picture sleeve |
| Express Yourself | CD-s | Sire | W2948CD | 1989 | £2 | £5 | |
| Express Yourself | 7" | Sire | W2948W | 1989 | £7.50 | £15 | zipper sleeve |
| Express Yourself | 7" | Sire | W2948X | 1989 | £6 | £12 | poster sleeve |
| Express Yourself (Non-Stop Express Mix) | 12" | Sire | W2948TP | 1989 | £10 | £20 | picture disc |
| Gambler | 7" | Geffen | QA6585 | 1985 | £6 | £12 | poster sleeve |
| Gambler | 12" | Geffen | A6585TA | 1985 | £4 | £10 | |
| Hanky Panky | CD-s | Sire | W9789CD | 1990 | £2 | £5 | |
| Hanky Panky | 12" | Sire | W9789TP | 1990 | £5 | £12 | picture disc |
| Holiday | 12" | Sire | W0037TP | 1991 | £2.50 | £6 | picture disc, insert |
| Holiday (Edit) | 7" | Sire | W9405 | 1983 | £1.50 | £4 | train picture sleeve |
| Holiday (Full Length Version) | 12" | Sire | W9405P | 1985 | £10 | £20 | picture disc |
| Holiday (Full Length Version) | 12" | Sire | W9405T | 1983 | £4 | £10 | train picture sleeve |
| Holiday Collection | CD-s | Sire | W0037CD | 1991 | £2 | £5 | |
| I'm Breathless | CD | Sire | 2620942DJ | 1990 | £10 | £25 | US promo picture disc |
| I'm Breathless | CD | Sire | 7599262092 | 1990 | £25 | £50 | promo box set with video |
| Into The Groove | 7" | Sire | W8934P | 1985 | £10 | £20 | shaped picture disc |
| Into The Groove | 12" | Sire | W8934T | 1985 | £4 | £10 | with poster |
| Justify My Love | CD-s | Sire | W9000CD | 1990 | £2 | £5 | |
| Justify My Love | 12" | Sire | W9000TP | 1990 | £2.50 | £6 | picture disc, insert |
| La Isla Bonita (Extended Remix) | 12" | Sire | W8378TP | 1987 | £6 | £15 | picture disc |
| Like A Prayer | CD-s | Sire | W7539CD | 1989 | £2 | £5 | |
| Like A Prayer | CD | Sire | | 1989 | £10 | £25 | US promo gold picture disc |
| Like A Prayer | CD | Sire | K9258442 | 1989 | £100 | £200 | promo box set with cassette, slides, badge, photos, biog |
| Like A Prayer (3 mixes) | 12" | Sire | W7539TX | 1989 | £3 | £8 | |
| Like A Prayer (Extended Remix) | 12" | Sire | W7539TP | 1989 | £3 | £8 | picture disc |
| Like A Virgin | LP | Sire | | 1984 | £25 | £50 | US, white vinyl |
| Like A Virgin | LP | Sire | WX20P | 1985 | £15 | £30 | picture disc |
| Like A Virgin (US Dance Remix) | 12" | Sire | W9210T | 1984 | £6 | £15 | with poster |
| Live To Tell | 12" | Sire | W8717T | 1986 | £4 | £10 | with poster |
| Look Of Love | 12" | Sire | W8115TP | 1987 | £6 | £15 | picture disc |
| Love Don't Live Here Anymore | 12" | Warner Bros | SAM1880 | 1996 | £15 | £30 | promo only |
| Lucky Star | 7" | Sire | W9522 | 1983 | £62.50 | £125 | sunglasses picture sleeve |
| Lucky Star (full length version) | 12" | Sire | W9522T | 1983 | £15 | £30 | sunglasses picture sleeve |
| Lucky Star (full length version) | 12" | Sire | W9522T | 1983 | £4 | £10 | TV screen picture sleeve |
| Lucky Star (full length version) | 12" | Sire | W9522T | 1983 | £10 | £25 | TV screen picture sleeve, poster |
| Lucky Star (US Remix) | 12" | Sire | W9522TV | 1983 | £20 | £40 | plain sleeve |
| Material Girl | 7" | Sire | W9083 | 1985 | £50 | £100 | poster sleeve |
| Material Girl (Jellybean Dance Remix) | 12" | Sire | W9083T | 1985 | £6 | £15 | with poster |
| Open Your Heart (Extended Version) | 12" | Sire | W8480TP | 1986 | £6 | £15 | picture disc |
| Papa Don't Preach (Extended Remix) | 12" | Sire | W8636TP | 1986 | £10 | £20 | picture disc |
| Papa Don't Preach (Extended Version) | 12" | Sire | W8636T | 1986 | £4 | £10 | with poster |
| Rescue Me | CD-s | Sire | W0024CD | 1991 | £2 | £5 | |
| Royal Box (Immaculate Collection) | CD | Sire | 7599264642 | 1990 | £25 | £50 | CD, video, poster, cards – boxed |
| Secret | 7" | Maverick | W0268P | 1994 | £2.50 | £6 | picture disc, insert |
| True Blue | LP | Sire | | 1986 | £20 | £40 | US picture disc |
| True Blue | LP | Sire | WX54 | 1986 | £20 | £40 | blue vinyl, poster |
| True Blue | LP | Sire | WX54 | 1986 | £20 | £40 | clear vinyl |
| True Blue (Extended Dance Version) | 12" | Sire | W8550TP | 1986 | £6 | £15 | picture disc |
| Vogue | CD-s | Sire | W9851CD | 1990 | £2 | £5 | |
| Vogue | 7" | Sire | W9851P | 1990 | £1.50 | £4 | picture disc |
| Vogue | 12" | Sire | W9851TP | 1990 | £4 | £10 | picture disc |
| Vogue | 12" | Sire | W9851TX | 1990 | £2.50 | £6 | with poster |
| Who's That Girl (Extended Version) | 12" | Sire | W8341TP | 1987 | £15 | £30 | picture disc |
| You Can Dance | LP | Sire | PROMAD1 | 1987 | £30 | £60 | promo picture disc |
| You Can Dance – Radio Edits | CD | Sire | PROCD2892 | 1987 | £10 | £25 | US promo |

## MADRIGAL

| Title | Format | Label | Cat. No. | Year | | | Notes |
|---|---|---|---|---|---|---|---|
| Beneath The Greenwood Tree | LP | private | MAD100 | 1973 | £25 | £50 | |

## MADURA
Madura.................................................. LP...... CBS.............. 67222.................... 1971 £8........... £20 ........... *Italian double*

## MAESTRO, JOHNNY
Before I Loved Her ................................ 7"...... United Artists .. UP1004................. 1964 £4.............£8 ..................
Johnny Maestro Story ............................. LP...... Buddah ......... BDS5091........... 1971 £6...........£15 .................. *US*
Mr. Happiness........................................ 7"...... HMV............. POP909 ............. 1961 £7.50.....£15 ...............
What A Surprise...................................... 7"...... HMV............. POP875 ............. 1961 £7.50.....£15 ...............

## MAGENTA
Canterbury Moon .................................. LP...... Cottage ......... ................... 1978 £30.........£60 ..................
Wot's Next Then?.................................... LP...... private........... ................... 1983 £50.......£100 ..................

## MAGI
Win Or Lose.......................................... LP...... Uncle Dirty's... 6102N13 ............. 1972 £180.....£300 ...................... *US*

## MAGIC
Enclosed................................................ LP...... Armadillo........ 8031 ................. 1969 £250....£400 ...................... *US*

## MAGIC CARPET
The Magic Carpet album is a delightful period piece, mixing oriental sonorities with contemporary folk music to create a sound that epitomizes the interests of the hippy movement. Sitar player Clem Alford made three albums subsequently (one under the name Sagram), while singer Alisha Sufit waited until the nineties before recording her own solo album. She is often to be found at record fairs, selling copies of this and also reissues of the Magic Carpet album.

Magic Carpet ........................................ LP...... Mushroom ...... 200MR20 ............. 1972 £50........£100 ..................

## MAGIC CHRISTIANS
If You Want It........................................ 7"...... Major Minor ... MM673................. 1970 £2.............£5 ..................

## MAGIC LANTERNS
Auntie Grizelda...................................... 7"...... CBS.............. 202637............ 1967 £1.50......£4 ...............
Excuse Me Baby...................................... 7" EP . CBS.............. 5798................ 1966 £10.......£20 ............... *French*
Excuse Me Baby...................................... 7" . CBS.............. 202094............ 1966 £1.50......£4 ...............
Haymarket Square.................................. LP...... Chaparral ...... CRM201 ........... 1966 £20.......£40 ............... *US*
Knight In Rusty Armour......................... 7"...... CBS.............. 202459............ 1967 £1.50......£4 ...............
Lit Up With The Magic Lanterns............ 7"...... CBS.............. 62935.............. 1969 £4.......£10 ...............
Melt All Your Troubles Away ................. 7"...... Camp............ 602009............ 1969 £1.50......£4 ...............
Rumplestiltskin...................................... 7"...... CBS.............. 202250............ 1966 £7.50....£15 ...............
Shame Shame.......................................... LP...... Atlantic ......... SD8217............ 1969 £5.......£12 ............... *US*
Shame Shame.......................................... 7"...... Camp............ 602007............ 1969 £1.50......£4 ...............

## MAGIC MIXTURE
This Is Magic Mixture ........................... LP...... Saga.............. FID2125.............. 1968 £25........£50 ..................

## MAGIC MUSHROOM BAND
Politics Of Ecstasy ................................ LP...... Pagan............. PM003.............. 1986 £25.........£50 ............ *with poster*
Process Of Illumination.......................... LP...... Fungus........... FUN003 .............. 1990 £6..........£15 ............ *with comic*
Spaced Out ............................................ LP...... Fungus........... FUN005 ............. 1991 £4..........£10 ............ *with booklet*

## MAGIC NOTES
Album Of Memory ............................... 7"...... Blue Beat ....... BB9................. 1960 £6...........£12 ..................

## MAGIC SAM
Black Magic........................................... LP...... Delmark........ DS620............. 1971 £5...........£12 ..................
Magic Sam 1937–69 .............................. LP...... Blue Horizon.. 763223............ 1969 £25.........£50 ..................
Mean Mistreater .................................... 7" EP . Rooster.......... 707................. 1969 £2.............£5 ..................
Twenty-One Days In Jail ........................ 7"...... Python........... PEN701 ........... 1969 £10.........£20 ..................
West Side Soul........................................ LP...... Delmark........ DS615............. 1970 £5...........£12 ..................

## MAGIC VALLEY
Taking The Heart Out Of Love................ 7"...... Penny Farthing PEN701 ........... 1969 £2.............£5 ..................

## MAGICAL RING
Light Flight........................................... LP...... Chicago ......... 2000900152............ 1977 £25.........£50 .................. *French*

## MAGICIANS
Liars...................................................... 7"...... Decca ............. F12374................ 1966 £1.50......£4 ..................
Tarzan March ........................................ 7"...... Decca ............. F12602 ............. 1967 £1.50......£4 ..................

## MAGISTRATES
After The Fox ........................................ 7"...... MGM............. MGM1437 ........ 1968 £1.50......£4 ..................
Here Comes The Judge............................ 7"...... MGM............. MGM1425 ......... 1968 £1.50......£4 ..................

## MAGMA
French group Magma acquired a certain notoriety in recent times when snooker player Steve Davis – himself something of an avid record collector – decided to indulge his love of their music and organized a tour for them. Magma have always been the brainchild of drummer Christian Vander, whose distinctive music combines science fiction imagery, jazz-rock solos (virtuoso violinist Didier Lockwood was a member for a time) and operatic vocals, within an overall progressive rock framework. Uniquely, Vander's chosen language for the songs is a Germanic tongue of his own invention. As these elements will suggest, Magma's music is not quite like that of any other group, although values of original album issues have been kept low by the frequent availability of reissue copies.

1001° Centigrade .................................... LP...... Philips.......... 6397031 ............. 1971 £6...........£15 ..................
Inedits .................................................. LP...... Tapioca........... TP10001 ............... 1977 £5...........£12 .................. *French*
Kohntarkosz.......................................... LP...... A&M............. AMLH68260 ...... 1974 £5...........£12 ..................
Live ...................................................... LP...... Utopia........... DUTS001 ............. 1975 £6..........£15 .................. *double*

| | | | | | | | | |
|---|---|---|---|---|---|---|---|---|
| Magma | LP | Philips | 635951/2 | 1970 | £6 | £15 | double |
| Mekanik Destruktiw Kommandoh | LP | A&M | AMLH64397 | 1973 | £4 | £10 | |
| Mekanik Machine | 7" | A&M | AMS7119 | 1974 | £1.50 | £4 | |

## MAGNA CARTA

| | | | | | | | |
|---|---|---|---|---|---|---|---|
| In Concert | LP | Vertigo | 6360068 | 1972 | £4 | £10 | spiral label |
| Lord Of The Ages | LP | Vertigo | 6360093 | 1973 | £4 | £10 | |
| Magna Carta | LP | Mercury | SMCL20166 | 1969 | £10 | £25 | |
| Mid Winter | 7" | Mercury | MF1096 | 1969 | £2 | £5 | |
| Romeo Jack | 7" | Fontana | TF1060 | 1969 | £2 | £5 | |
| Seasons | LP | Vertigo | 6360003 | 1970 | £4 | £10 | spiral label |
| Songs From Wasties Orchard | LP | Vertigo | 6360040 | 1971 | £6 | £15 | spiral label |

## MAGNIFICENT MEN

| | | | | | | | |
|---|---|---|---|---|---|---|---|
| Peace Of Mind | 7" | Capitol | CL15462 | 1966 | £6 | £12 | |
| Save The Country | 7" | Capitol | CL15570 | 1968 | £1.50 | £4 | |

## MAGNUM

| | | | | | | | |
|---|---|---|---|---|---|---|---|
| Days Of No Trust | CD-s | Polydor | POCD910 | 1988 | £2 | £5 | |
| Heartbroke And Busted | CD-s | Polydor | PZCDT94 | 1990 | £2 | £5 | in tin |
| It Must Have Been Love | CD-s | Polydor | POCD930 | 1988 | £2 | £5 | |
| Magnum | CD-s | Special Edition | CD37 | 1988 | £2 | £5 | 3" single |
| Marauder | CD | Castle | CLACD124 | 1986 | £5 | £12 | |
| On The Wings Of Heaven | CD-s | Polygram | 0803881 | 1988 | £4 | £10 | CD video |
| Rockin' Chair | CD-s | Polydor | PZCD88 | 1990 | £2 | £5 | |
| Start Talking Love | CD-s | Polydor | POCD920 | 1988 | £4 | £10 | card sleeve |
| Start Talking Love | CD-s | Polygram | 0804062 | 1988 | £4 | £10 | CD video |

## MAGPIES

| | | | | | | | |
|---|---|---|---|---|---|---|---|
| Blue Boy | 7" | Doctor Bird | DB1132 | 1968 | £5 | £10 | |
| Lulu | 7" | Doctor Bird | DB1129 | 1968 | £5 | £10 | |

## MAGUIRE, JOHN

| | | | | | | | |
|---|---|---|---|---|---|---|---|
| Come Day, Go Day, God Send Sunday | LP | Leader | LEE4062 | 1973 | £4 | £10 | |

## MAGUS

| | | | | | | | |
|---|---|---|---|---|---|---|---|
| Breezin' Away | LP | Northern Sound | NSR200 | 1980 | £50 | £100 | |

## MAHAL, TAJ

Taj Mahal is in many ways the black equivalent of Ry Cooder. He has an archivist's approach to his musical culture, rediscovering old songs and presenting them as fresh pieces of music in order to encourage his audience to delve further. His earliest records are exclusively concerned with the blues, but he has ranged more widely since. In fact, Ry Cooder and Taj Mahal were both members of the cult sixties group the Rising Sons and Cooder is also a member of the band on the first Taj Mahal LP.

| | | | | | | | |
|---|---|---|---|---|---|---|---|
| Eezee Rider | 7" | Direction | 584044 | 1969 | £1.50 | £4 | |
| Everybody's Got To Change Sometime | 7" | Direction | 583547 | 1968 | £1.50 | £4 | |
| Giant Step/De Ole Folks | LP | CBS | 66226 | 1969 | £6 | £15 | double |
| Natch'l Blues | LP | Direction | 863397 | 1968 | £4 | £10 | |
| Real Thing | LP | CBS | 66288 | 1971 | £5 | £12 | double |
| Taj Mahal | LP | Direction | 863279 | 1967 | £6 | £15 | |

## MAHJUN

| | | | | | | | |
|---|---|---|---|---|---|---|---|
| Happy French Band | LP | Gratte-Ciel | ZL37049 | 1977 | £4 | £10 | French |
| Mahjun | LP | Saravah | SH10040 | 1973 | £15 | £30 | French |
| Mahjun | LP | Saravah | SH10047 | 1974 | £15 | £30 | French |

## MAHOGANY RUSH

| | | | | | | | |
|---|---|---|---|---|---|---|---|
| Child Of The Novelty | LP | 20th Century | S451 | 1973 | £4 | £10 | US |
| Maxoom | LP | 20th Century | S463 | 1975 | £4 | £10 | US |
| Maxoom | LP | Nine | 936 | 1972 | £10 | £25 | US |

## MAIN ATTRACTION

| | | | | | | | |
|---|---|---|---|---|---|---|---|
| And Now | LP | Tower | ST5117 | 1968 | £4 | £10 | US |

## MAINEEAXE

| | | | | | | | |
|---|---|---|---|---|---|---|---|
| Gonna Make You Rock | 7" | Powerstation | OHM6 | 1984 | £1.50 | £4 | |

## MAINHORSE

| | | | | | | | |
|---|---|---|---|---|---|---|---|
| Mainhorse | LP | Polydor | 2383049 | 1971 | £4 | £10 | |

## MAINLAND

| | | | | | | | |
|---|---|---|---|---|---|---|---|
| Exposure | LP | Christy | ACML0200 | 1979 | £5 | £12 | |

## MAINLINE

| | | | | | | | |
|---|---|---|---|---|---|---|---|
| Canada Our Home | LP | GRT | 92301011 | 1971 | £6 | £15 | Canada |

## MAJAMOOD

| | | | | | | | |
|---|---|---|---|---|---|---|---|
| Two Hundred Million Red Ants | 7" | Doctor Bird | DB1052 | 1966 | £5 | £10 | |

## MAJIC SHIP

| | | | | | | | |
|---|---|---|---|---|---|---|---|
| Majic Ship | LP | Bel Ami | BA711 | 1968 | £330 | £500 | US |

## MAJOR ACCIDENT

| | | | | | | | |
|---|---|---|---|---|---|---|---|
| Warboots | 7" | Massacred Melodies | MAME1001 | 1982 | £6 | £12 | test pressing |

## MAJOR SURGERY
First Cut .................................. LP ...... Next ................ NEXT1 ................. 1977 £6 .......... £15 ..................................

## MAJORITY
Little Bit Of Sunlight ............................. 7" ...... Decca ............ F12271 ................ 1965 £1.50 ......... £4
Running Away With My Baby ................. 7" ...... Decca ............ F12638 ................ 1967 £7.50 ..... £15
Simplified .................................. 7" ...... Decca ............ F12453 ................ 1966 £7.50 ..... £15

## MAJORS
Meet The Majors .............................. LP ...... London .......... HAP8068 ........ 1963 £37.50 .... £75
Meet The Majors .............................. 7" EP . London .......... REP1358 ........ 1963 £30 ...... £60
Ooh Wee Baby .................................. 7" ...... Liberty ........... LIB66009 ............. 1964 £6 ...... £12
She's A Troublemaker ......................... 7" ...... London .......... HLP9627 .......... 1962 £5 ...... £10
What In The World ............................ 7" ...... London .......... HLP9693 ............. 1963 £4 ........ £8
Wonderful Dream .............................. 7" ...... London .......... HLP9602 ........... 1962 £4 ...... £8

## MAKEBA, MIRIAM
Click Song.................................. 7" ...... London .......... HL9747 .............. 1963 £1.50 ...... £4
In Concert.................................. LP ...... Reprise ........... RLP6253 ............... 1967 £4 ...... £10
Keep Me In Mind ............................. LP ...... Reprise ........... RSLP6381 ........... 1970 £4 ...... £10
Makeba! .................................. LP ...... Reprise ........... R(S)LP6310 ........... 1968 £4 ...... £10
Miriam Makeba .............................. LP ...... London .......... HA2332 ............. 1961 £4 ...... £10

## MAKEM, SARAH
Ulster Ballad Singer ........................... LP ...... Topic ............. 12T185 ............ 1969 £5 ......... £12

## MAKEM, TOMMY
Bard Of Armagh.............................. LP ...... CBS ............. 64001 .............. 1970 £4 ...... £10
Ever The Winds .............................. LP ...... Polydor .......... 2383328 ............ 1975 £4 ...... £10
In The Dark Green Woods .................... LP ...... Polydor .......... 2383280 ............ 1974 £4 ...... £10
It's Tommy Makem .......................... LP ...... Emerald .......... MLD20 ............. 1967 £5 ...... £12
Sings Tommy Makem ....................... LP ...... CBS ............. 63112 .............. 1967 £5 ...... £12

## MAKEM, TOMMY & LIAM CLANCY
Makem And Clancy Concert .................. LP ...... CBS ............. 88302 .............. 1977 £5 ...... £12 .................. double
Tommy Makem And Liam Clancy ............. LP ...... Epic ............. EPC82081 ........ 1976 £4 ...... £10

## MAL & THE PRIMITIVES
Every Minute Of Every Day .................. 7" ...... Pye ............... 7N15915 ............ 1965 £20 ...... £40
Mal Dei Primitives ........................... LP ...... RCA ............. PSL10442 ........... 1967 £15 ...... £30 .................. Italian
Sua Eccelenza................................ LP ...... RCA ............. PSL10439 ........... 1967 £25 ...... £50 .................. Italian

## MALCOLM, CARLOS
Bonanza Ska ................................ 7" ...... Island ............ WI173 .............. 1965 £5 ...... £10

## MALCOLM, GEORGE
Bach Goes To Town .......................... 7" ...... Parlophone ...... MSP6058 .............. 1953 £1.50 ...... £4

## MALCOLM, HUGH
Good Time Rock............................... 7" ...... Amalgamated ... AMG827 ................ 1968 £4 ...... £8 ....... Lyn Taitt B side

## MALCOLM & ALWYN
Fool's Wisdom............................... LP ...... Pye ............... NSPL18404 ......... 1973 £5 ...... £12
Wildwall.................................. LP ...... Key ............... K1022 ............. 1974 £10 ...... £25

## MALE
Zensur Zensur............................... LP ...... Modell Music .. ROCKON1 ........... 1978 £6 .......... £15 ............. German

## MALICORNE
Almanach .................................. LP ...... Hexagone ....... 883007 ............ 1976 £6 .......... £15 .................. French
En public .................................. LP ...... Ballon Noire... BAL13010 ............ 1978 £4 ...... £10 .................. French
L'Extraordinaire ............................. LP ...... Ballon Noire... BAL13006 ............ 1978 £4 ...... £10 .................. French
Le Bestiaire................................ LP ...... Ballon Noire... BAL13012 ............ 1979 £4 ...... £10 .................. French
Malicorne .................................. LP ...... Hexagone ....... 883004 ............ 1974 £6 .......... £15 .................. French
Malicorne II................................ LP ...... Hexagone ....... 883005 ............ 1975 £6 .......... £15 .................. French
Malicorne IV............................... LP ...... Hexagone ....... 883015 ............ 1976 £6 .......... £15 .................. French
Quintessence ............................... LP ...... Hexagone ....... 883018 ............ 1979 £6 .......... £15 .................. French

## MALLARD
Mallard was the group formed by members of Captain Beefheart's Magic Band and its music has much of the same flavour as albums like *Strictly Personal*. The first album is quite common and no longer merits inclusion in the guide, but *In A Different Climate* is much harder to find, despite its value remaining low.

In A Different Climate .......................... LP ...... Virgin ............ V2077 ................. 1977 £4 ...... £10

## MALON
Rebellion .................................. LP ...... Philips ............ 6397032 .............. 1971 £6 .......... £15 .................. French

## MALONE, WIL
Wil Malone ................................ LP ...... Fontana .......... STL5541 ............. 1970 £25 ......... £50

## MALTBY, RICHARD
Rat Race.................................. 7" ...... Columbia ........ DB4606 ............. 1961 £4 ...... £8

## MAMAS & PAPAS
California Dreamin'.............................. LP ...... St. Michael ...... MO101225............. 1979 £4 ...... £10

California Dreamin' ............................... 7" EP . RCA ............. 86902.................... 1966 £6.......... £12 ...................... French
California Dreaming ............................. 7" ..... RCA ............. RCA1503 .......... 1966 £1.50...... £4
Cass, John, Michelle, & Denny ................. LP ..... RCA ............. RD/SF7834 .......... 1966 £4.......... £10
Dedicated To The One I Love ................. 7" EP . RCA ............. 86911.................... 1967 £5.......... £10 ...................... French
Deliver ................................................. LP ..... RCA ............. RD/SF7880 .......... 1967 £4.......... £10
Gathering Of Flowers ........................... LP ..... Probe ........... SPB1003/4 .......... 1970 £5.......... £12 ...................... double
I Saw Her Again ................................... 7" EP . RCA ............. 86907.................... 1966 £5.......... £10 ...................... French
If You Can Believe Your Eyes And Ears ..... LP ..... RCA ............. RD7803 .............. 1966 £4.......... £10
Look Through My Window...................... 7" EP . RCA ............. 86910.................... 1966 £5.......... £10 ...................... French
Look Through My Window...................... 7" ..... RCA ............. RCA1551 .......... 1966 £1.50...... £4
Monday Monday ................................... 7" EP . RCA ............. 86905.................... 1966 £5.......... £10 ...................... French
Monterey Pop Festival ........................... LP ..... Dunhill ......... DS50100 .......... 1971 £5.......... £12 ...................... US
Papas And Mamas ................................ LP ..... RCA ............. RD/SF7960 .......... 1968 £4.......... £10
You've Got To Hide Your Love Away ...... 7" ..... RCA ............. RCA1525 .......... 1966 £2.50...... £6 Barry McGuire B side

## MAMA'S BOYS
Silence Is Out Of Fashion ...................... 7" ..... Pussy ........... 1981 £4.......... £8
Turn It Up/Too Little Of You To Love .... LP ..... Spartan .......... SPLP001 .......... 1983 £6.......... £15 ...................... double

## MAMMUT
Mammut ............................................. LP ..... Mouse............ TTM5022 .......... 1971 £180..... £300 ...................... German

## MAN
2oz Of Plastic With A Hole In The Middle LP ..... Dawn.............. DNLS3003 .......... 1969 £6.......... £15 ...................... orange label
Bananas ............................................... 7" EP . United Artists .. REM408............ 1976 £2.......... £5
Be Good To Yourself ............................ LP ..... United Artists .. UAG29417.......... 1972 £4.......... £10 ...map of Wales cover
Christmas At The Patti............................ 10" LP United Artists .. UDX205/6 .......... 1973 £6.......... £15 ...................... double
Daughter Of The Fireplace ..................... 7" ..... Liberty .......... LBF15448 .......... 1971 £2.50...... £6
Do You Like It Here .............................. LP ..... United Artists .. UAG29236.......... 1971 £4.......... £10
Don't Go Away ..................................... 7" ..... United Artists .. UP35643............ 1974 £6.......... £12
Live At The Padget Rooms ..................... LP ..... United Artists .. USP100.............. 1972 £8.......... £20
Man ................................................... LP ..... Liberty .......... LBS83464.......... 1970 £4.......... £10
Revelation ........................................... LP ..... Pye ............... N(S)PL18275.......... 1969 £6.......... £15
Sudden Life ......................................... 7" ..... Pye ............... 7N17684............ 1969 £4.......... £8

## MAN FROM DELMONTE
Drive Drive Drive ................................. 7" ..... Ugly Man....... UGLY3............ 1987 £2.......... £5
Water In My Eyes ................................. 7" ..... Ugly Man....... UGLY5............ 1987 £1.50...... £4
Water In My Eyes ................................. 12" .... Ugly Man....... UGLY5T............ 1987 £3.......... £8

## MAN FROM U.N.C.L.E.
Music associated with the sixties cult TV series, *The Man From U.N.C.L.E.*, can be found in the guide under the names of Hugo Montenegro (who was responsible for the main theme), the Challengers and the Gallants – with a late entry from 1982 by Moskow. Meanwhile, David McCallum, who starred as agent Illya Kuryakin in the programmes, took the opportunity to record a pair of moderately collectable albums.

## MANASSAS
Manassas was the group formed by Steve Stills in the wake of the first disbanding of Crosby, Stills and Nash. It was something of a supergroup itself, with various ex-members of the CSN rhythm section and of the Flying Burrito Brothers being involved. Steve Stills, however, remains firmly in control and the Manassas albums are very much a showcase for his talents. They include some of Stills' best songs.

Manassas................................................. LP ..... Atlantic ........... K60021 ................. 1972 £5........... £12 ................... double

## MANCE, JUNIOR
At The Village Vanguard.......................... LP ..... Jazzland ........ JLP41 ................ 1961 £6.......... £15
Big Chief............................................. LP ..... Jazzland ........ JLP(9)53 ................ 1961 £6.......... £15
Harlem Lullaby ..................................... LP ..... Atlantic ......... 1479 ................. 1968 £5.......... £12
Junior Mance And His Swinging Piano....... LP ..... HMV ............ CLP1342 .......... 1959 £6.......... £15
Soulful Piano ....................................... LP ..... Jazzland ........ JLP30 .............. 1960 £6.......... £15

## MANCHESTER MEKON
No Forgetting....................................... 7" ...... Newmarket ..... NEW102 .......... 1979 £2.......... £5

## MANCHESTER MOB
Although future Ten cc star, Graham Gouldman, was successful at creating hits for the likes of the Hollies, the Yardbirds and Herman's Hermits, he had no luck with any of the groups that he fronted during the sixties – the Manchester Mob being one.

Bony Maronie At The Hop....................... 7" ...... Parlophone ...... R5552 ................. 1967 £20.......... £40

## MANCHESTER PLAYBOYS
I Feel So Good....................................... 7" ...... Fontana........... TF745.............. 1966 £12.50...... £25
Wooly Bully ......................................... 7" EP . Barclay............ 70852................ 1965 £25.......... £50 ...................... French

## MANCHESTERS
Tribute To The Beatles........................... LP ..... Ember............ FA2029 ............. 1966 £6.......... £15

## MANCINI, HENRY
Music From Peter Gunn ......................... LP ..... RCA ............. RD27123/SF5033... 1959 £6.......... £15
Peter Gunn Theme ................................ 7" ...... RCA ............. RCA1134 .......... 1959 £1.50...... £4
Pink Panther ......................................... 7" EP . RCA ............. RCX7136 ............. 1964 £2.50...... £6

## MANCUSO, GUS
Introducing Gus Mancuso ....................... LP ..... Vogue ............ LAE12069 .......... 1958 £5.......... £12

## MANDEL, HARVEY
Baby Batter........................................... LP ..... Dawn.............. DNLS3015 ............ 1971 £4.......... £10
Cristo Redentor ..................................... LP ..... Philips............ SBL7873 ............ 1968 £5.......... £12
Cristo Redentor ..................................... CD..... Editions EG..... EEGCD62............ 1989 £5.......... £12

| | | | | | | | | |
|---|---|---|---|---|---|---|---|---|
| Games Guitars Play | LP | Philips | SBL7915 | 1970 £4 | £10 | |
| Righteous | LP | Philips | SBL7904 | 1969 £4 | £10 | |

## MANDINGO
| | | | | | | | |
|---|---|---|---|---|---|---|---|
| Fever Pitch | 7" | EMI | EMI2062 | 1973 £1.50 | £4 | |
| Medicine Man | 7" | EMI | EMI2014 | 1973 £1.50 | £4 | |

## MANDRAKE MEMORIAL
| | | | | | | | |
|---|---|---|---|---|---|---|---|
| Mandrake Memorial | LP | Poppy | PYS40002 | 1968 £10 | £25 | US |
| Medium | LP | RCA | SF8028 | 1969 £10 | £25 | |
| Puzzle | LP | Poppy | PYS11003 | 1970 £20 | £40 | US |

## MANDRAKE PADDLE STEAMER
| | | | | | | | |
|---|---|---|---|---|---|---|---|
| Strange Walking Man | 7" | Parlophone | R5780 | 1969 £25 | £50 | |

## MANDRILL
| | | | | | | | |
|---|---|---|---|---|---|---|---|
| Composite Truth | LP | Polydor | 2391061 | 1973 £5 | £12 | |
| Just Outside Of Town | LP | Polydor | 2391092 | 1973 £5 | £12 | |
| Mandrill | LP | Polydor | 2489028 | 1970 £5 | £12 | |
| Mandrill Is | LP | Polydor | 2391030 | 1972 £5 | £12 | |

## MANEATERS
| | | | | | | | |
|---|---|---|---|---|---|---|---|
| Nine To Five | 7" | Editions EG | EGO8 | 1982 £12.50 | £25 | Adam & Toyah picture sleeve |

## MANHATTAN JAZZ SEPTET
| | | | | | | | |
|---|---|---|---|---|---|---|---|
| Manhattan Jaz Septet | LP | Vogue Coral | LVA9053 | 1957 £10 | £25 | |

## MANHATTANS
| | | | | | | | |
|---|---|---|---|---|---|---|---|
| Baby I Need You | 7" | Carnival | CAR100 | 1966 £2.50 | £6 | |
| I Wanna Be Your Everything | 7" | Sue | WI384 | 1965 £4 | £8 | |
| That New Girl | 7" | Carnival | CAR101 | 1966 £2.50 | £6 | |

## MANIAX
| | | | | | | | |
|---|---|---|---|---|---|---|---|
| Out Of Reach | 7" | White Label | WLR101/2 | 1966 £2.50 | £6 | |

## MANIC STREET PREACHERS
| | | | | | | | |
|---|---|---|---|---|---|---|---|
| Feminine Is Beautiful | 7" | Caff | 15 | 1991 £7.50 | £15 | |
| Generation Terrorists | LP | Columbia | 4710609 | 1992 £5 | £12 | double picture disc |
| Generation Terrorists | CD | Columbia | 4710600 | 1992 £5 | £12 | picture disc |
| Love's Sweet Exile | CD-s | CBS | 6575822 | 1991 £2 | £5 | |
| Motown Junk | CD-s | Heavenly | HVN8CD | 1991 £6 | £15 | |
| Motown Junk | 12" | Heavenly | HVN812 | 1991 £5 | £12 | |
| New Art Riot | CD-s | Damaged Goods | YUBB4CD | 1992 £2 | £5 | picture disc |
| New Art Riot EP | 12" | Damaged Goods | YUBB004 | 1990 £2.50 | £6 | black & white label |
| New Art Riot EP | 12" | Damaged Goods | YUBB004P | 1990 £3 | £8 | pink vinyl |
| Stay Beautiful | CD-s | CBS | 6573372 | 1991 £2 | £5 | |
| Suicide Alley | 7" | SBS | 002 | 1989 £25 | £50 | no picture sleeve |
| Suicide Alley | 7" | SBS | 002 | 1989 £50 | £100 | picture sleeve |
| UK Channel Boredom | 7" | Hopelessly Devoted | 1 | 1990 £2 | £5 | flexi |
| You Love Us | CD-s | Heavenly | HVN10CD | 1991 £5 | £12 | |

## MANISH BOYS

The rare single by the Manish Boys, 'I Pity The Fool', is listed in the guide under the name later used by the group's lead singer – David Bowie.

## MANN, BARRY
| | | | | | | | |
|---|---|---|---|---|---|---|---|
| Angelica | 7" | Capitol | CL15463 | 1966 £1.50 | £4 | |
| Bless You | 7" | HMV | POP1108 | 1963 £1.50 | £4 | |
| Hey Baby I'm Dancing | 7" | HMV | POP1084 | 1962 £1.50 | £4 | |
| Little Miss USA | 7" | HMV | POP949 | 1961 £1.50 | £4 | |
| Talk To Me Baby | 7" | Colpix | PX776 | 1964 £1.50 | £4 | |
| Who Put The Bomp | LP | HMV | CLP1559 | 1963 £62.50 | £125 | |
| Who Put The Bomp | 7" | HMV | POP911 | 1961 £5 | £10 | |
| Young Electric Psychedelic Hippy | 7" | Capitol | CL15538 | 1968 £1.50 | £4 | |

## MANN, CARL
| | | | | | | | |
|---|---|---|---|---|---|---|---|
| Like Mann | LP | London | HAS2277 | 1960 £50 | £100 | |
| Like Mann | LP | Philips | 1960 | 1960 £180 | £300 | US |
| Mona Lisa | 7" | London | HLS8935 | 1959 £7.50 | £15 | |
| Pretend | 7" | London | HLS9006 | 1959 £7.50 | £15 | |
| South Of The Border | 7" | London | HLS9170 | 1960 £6 | £12 | |

## MANN, GLORIA
| | | | | | | | |
|---|---|---|---|---|---|---|---|
| It Happened Again | 7" | Brunswick | 05610 | 1956 £1.50 | £4 | |
| Why Do Fools Fall In Love | 7" | Brunswick | 05569 | 1956 £4 | £8 | |

## MANN, HERBIE
| | | | | | | | |
|---|---|---|---|---|---|---|---|
| At Newport | LP | Atlantic | ATL5008 | 1964 £6 | £15 | |
| At The Village Gate | LP | Atlantic | 587/588054 | 1967 £6 | £15 | |
| East Coast Jazz No. 4 Part 1 | 7" EP | London | EZN19006 | 1956 £2 | £5 | |
| Evolution Of Mann | LP | Atlantic | K60020 | 1972 £6 | £15 | double |
| Flute Fraternity | 10" LP | Top Rank | 25015 | 1960 £6 | £15 | ...with Buddy Colette |

| Free For All | LP | Atlantic | 590013 | 1968 | £5 | £12 | |
| Herbie Mann | 7" EP | Fontana | TFE17113 | 1958 | £2 | £5 | |
| Herbie Mann-Sam Most Quintet | LP | London | LTZN15049 | 1957 | £8 | £20 | |
| Hold On I'm Comin' | LP | Atlantic | K40467 | 1973 | £5 | £12 | |
| Inspiration I Feel | LP | Atlantic | 588156 | 1969 | £5 | £12 | |
| Latin Mann | LP | CBS | (S)BPG62585 | 1966 | £5 | £12 | |
| Live At Newport | LP | Atlantic | SD1413 | 1965 | £6 | £15 | US |
| Magic Flute Of Herbie Mann | 7" EP | Columbia | SEB10102 | 1959 | £2 | £5 | |
| Memphis Two-Step | LP | Atlantic | 2400121 | 1971 | £4 | £10 | |
| Memphis Underground | LP | Atlantic | 588200 | 1969 | £5 | £12 | |
| Mississippi Gambler | LP | Atlantic | K40385 | 1972 | £5 | £12 | |
| Monday Night At The Village Gate | LP | Atlantic | 587/588003 | 1966 | £6 | £15 | |
| Muscle Shoals Nitty Gritty | LP | Atlantic | K40096 | 1970 | £5 | £12 | |
| Nirvana | LP | Atlantic | 587/588028 | 1966 | £6 | £15 | with Bill Evans |
| Philly Dog | 7" | Atlantic | 584052 | 1966 | £2.50 | £6 | Dave Pike B side |
| Returns To The Village Gate | LP | Atlantic | SD1407 | 1963 | £6 | £15 | US |
| Right Now | LP | London | HAK/SHK8043 | 1963 | £6 | £15 | |
| Roar Of The Grease Paint | LP | Atlantic | ATL/SAL5035 | 1965 | £5 | £12 | |
| Salute To The Flute | LP | Fontana | TFL5013 | 1958 | £6 | £15 | |
| Standing Ovation At Newport | LP | Atlantic | ATL/SAL5038 | 1966 | £6 | £15 | |
| Stone Flute | LP | Atlantic | 2465088 | 1970 | £5 | £12 | |

## MANN, JOHNNY SINGERS

| Ballads Of The King | 7" EP | London | REG1325 | 1961 | £2 | £5 | |

## MANN, MANFRED

When Manfred Mann decided to call a halt to his pop career, the result was one of the best albums of all to emerge from the interface between jazz and rock. Essentially the work of a big band, *Manfred Mann Chapter Three* showcased some fine playing – most notably from saxophonist Bernie Living, formerly with the Mike Westbrook band – and also demonstrated the excellence of the Mann-Hugg writing team. 'Travelling Lady' was an update of 'A B Side' – to be found on the reverse of the single 'Ragamuffin Man' and itself the same piece of music as that used in a TV advert. The powerful brass riff that drives 'Time', meanwhile, was adopted as the theme tune for a radio jazz programme. Manfred Mann had earlier indicated that he might have something like this up his sleeve when he released the *Instrumental Asylum* EP (whose tracks are also to be found on the LP *Soul Of Mann*). Paul Jones had just left the group, so the others took advantage of their singerless condition to make a record of sparkling jazz versions of a few well-known rock tunes. The presence of Jack Bruce on bass, together with trumpeter Henry Lowther and saxophonist Lyn Dobson, was a distinct bonus. *Instrumental Assassination* attempted to repeat the formula, but somewhat less successfully, as new member Klaus Voorman was no substitute, in this kind of music, for the three jazzers he replaced.

| 5-4-3-2-1 | 7" | HMV | POP1252 | 1964 | £1.50 | £4 | |
| As Is | LP | Fontana | (S)TL5377 | 1966 | £6 | £15 | |
| As Is | LP | Fontana | (S)TL5377 | 1966 | £50 | £100 | train cover |
| As Was | 7" EP | HMV | 7EG8962 | 1966 | £6 | £12 | |
| Cock A Hoop | 7" | HMV | POP1225 | 1963 | £4 | £8 | |
| Come Tomorrow | 7" | Electrola | E22892 | 1965 | £6 | £12 | sung in German |
| Come Tomorrow | 7" | HMV | POP1381 | 1965 | £1.50 | £4 | |
| Do Wah Diddy Diddy | 7" EP | Pathe | EGF747 | 1964 | £7.50 | £15 | French |
| Do Wah Diddy Diddy | 7" | HMV | POP1320 | 1964 | £1.50 | £4 | |
| Five Faces Of Manfred Mann | LP | HMV | CLP1731 | 1964 | £6 | £15 | |
| Fox On The Run | 7" | Fontana | TF985 | 1968 | £1.50 | £4 | |
| Greatest Hits | LP | United Artists | UAL3551/ UAS6551 | 1966 | £4 | £10 | US |
| Grooving With Manfred Mann | 7" EP | HMV | 7EG8876 | 1965 | £4 | £8 | |
| Ha Ha Said The Clown | 7" EP | Fontana | 465376 | 1966 | £7.50 | £15 | French |
| Ha Ha Said The Clown | 7" | Fontana | TF812 | 1967 | £1.50 | £4 | |
| Ha Ha Said The Clown | 7" | Fontana | TF812 | 1967 | £2 | £5 | picture sleeve |
| Hits Of Manfred Mann | cass-s | Philips | MCF5002 | 1968 | £4 | £10 | |
| Hits Of Manfred Mann & DDDBM&T | cass-s | Philips | MCF5005 | 1968 | £4 | £10 | |
| Hubble Bubble | 7" | HMV | POP1282 | 1964 | £1.50 | £4 | |
| If You Gotta Go, Go Now | 7" EP | Pathe | EGF853 | 1965 | £7.50 | £15 | French |
| If You Gotta Go, Go Now | 7" | HMV | POP1466 | 1965 | £1.50 | £4 | |
| Instrumental Assassination | 7" EP | Fontana | TE17483 | 1966 | £2.50 | £6 | |
| Instrumental Asylum | 7" EP | HMV | 7EG8949 | 1966 | £5 | £10 | |
| Just Like A Woman | 7" EP | Fontana | 465320 | 1966 | £7.50 | £15 | French |
| Just Like A Woman | 7" | Fontana | TF730 | 1966 | £1.50 | £4 | |
| Machines | 7" EP | HMV | 7EG8942 | 1966 | £5 | £10 | |
| Manfred Mann | 7" EP | HMV | 7EG8848 | 1964 | £6 | £12 | |
| Manfred Mann Album | LP | Ascot | ALM13015/ ALS16015 | 1964 | £6 | £15 | US |
| Mann Made | LP | Electrola | SME84039 | 1965 | £37.50 | £75 | German, white and gold label |
| Mann Made | LP | HMV | CLP1911/CSD1628 | 1964 | £8 | £20 | |
| Mann Made Hits | LP | HMV | CLP3559 | 1966 | £8 | £20 | |
| Maxwell House Shake | 7" | Lyntone | LYN1981 | 1970 | £1.50 | £4 | flexi |
| Michelin Theme | 7" | Michelin | MIC1 | 1971 | £4 | £8 | gatefold sleeve |
| Mighty Garvey | LP | Fontana | (S)TL5470 | 1968 | £5 | £12 | |
| Mighty Quinn | LP | Mercury | SR61168 | 1968 | £4 | £10 | US |
| Mighty Quinn | 7" | Fontana | TF897 | 1968 | £1.50 | £4 | |
| My Little Red Book Of Winners | LP | Ascot | ALM13021/ ALS16021 | 1965 | £15 | £30 | US |
| My Name Is Jack | 7" | Fontana | TF943 | 1968 | £1.50 | £4 | |
| No Living Without Loving | 7" EP | HMV | 7EG8922 | 1965 | £4 | £8 | |
| Oh No Not My Baby | 7" | HMV | POP1413 | 1965 | £1.50 | £4 | |
| One In The Middle | 7" EP | HMV | 7EG8908 | 1965 | £4 | £8 | |
| Pretty Flamingo | LP | United Artists | UAL3549/ UAS6549 | 1966 | £4 | £10 | US |
| Pretty Flamingo | 7" EP | Pathe | EGF901 | 1966 | £7.50 | £15 | French |
| Pretty Flamingo | 7" | HMV | POP1523 | 1966 | £1.50 | £4 | |

| | | | | | | | |
|---|---|---|---|---|---|---|---|
| Ragamuffin Man | 7" | Fontana | TF1013 | 1969 | £1.50 | £4 | |
| Semi-Detached Suburban Mr. James | 7" | Fontana | TF757 | 1966 | £1.50 | £4 | |
| Semi-Detached, Suburban Mr. James | 7" EP | Fontana | 465341 | 1966 | £7.50 | £15 | French |
| Sha La La | 7" EP | Pathe | EGF781 | 1964 | £7.50 | £15 | French |
| Sha La La | 7" | HMV | POP1346 | 1964 | £1.50 | £4 | |
| Ski 'Full-Of-Fitness' Theme | 7" | Ski | SKI01 | 1971 | £1.50 | £4 | |
| Ski 'Full-Of-Fitness' Theme | 7" | Ski | SKI01 | 1971 | £5 | £10 | picture sleeve |
| So Long Dad | 7" | Fontana | TF862 | 1967 | £1.50 | £4 | |
| Soul Of Mann | LP | HMV | CLP/CSD3594 | 1967 | £8 | £20 | |
| Sweet Pea | 7" | Fontana | TF828 | 1967 | £1.50 | £4 | |
| There's No Living Without Your Loving | 7" | HMV | 7XEA22017/8 | 1965 | £5 | £10 | promo |
| Up The Junction | LP | Fontana | (S)TL5460 | 1968 | £6 | £15 | |
| Up The Junction | 7" | Fontana | TF908 | 1968 | £1.50 | £4 | |
| Up The Junction | 7" | Fontana | TF908 | 1968 | £2.50 | £6 | picture sleeve |
| What A Man | LP | Fontana | SFL13003 | 1968 | £5 | £12 | |
| Why Should We Not | 7" | HMV | POP1189 | 1963 | £5 | £10 | |
| You Gave Me Somebody To Love | 7" | HMV | POP1541 | 1966 | £2 | £5 | |

## MANN, MANFRED CHAPTER THREE

| | | | | | | | |
|---|---|---|---|---|---|---|---|
| Happy Being Me | 7" | Vertigo | 6059012 | 1970 | £1.50 | £4 | |
| Manfred Mann Chapter Three | LP | Vertigo | VO3 | 1969 | £8 | £20 | spiral label |
| Manfred Mann Chapter Three Vol. 2 | LP | Vertigo | 6360012 | 1970 | £10 | £25 | spiral label |

## MANN, SHADOW

| | | | | | | | |
|---|---|---|---|---|---|---|---|
| Come Live With Me | 7" | Roulette | RO504 | 1968 | £1.50 | £4 | |
| Shadow Mann | LP | Tomorrow Productions | | 1968 | £6 | £15 | US |

## MANNE, SHELLY

| | | | | | | | |
|---|---|---|---|---|---|---|---|
| 2, 3, 4 | LP | HMV | CLP1625 | 1962 | £5 | £12 | |
| At The Black Hawk Vol. 1 | LP | Contemporary | LAC12250/ SCA5015 | 1961 | £5 | £12 | |
| At The Black Hawk Vol. 2 | LP | Contemporary | LAC12255/ SCA5016 | 1961 | £5 | £12 | |
| At The Black Hawk Vol. 3 | LP | Contemporary | LAC12260/ SCA5017 | 1961 | £5 | £12 | |
| At The Black Hawk Vol. 4 | LP | Contemporary | LAC12265/ SCA5018 | 1961 | £5 | £12 | |
| Bells Are Ringing | LP | Contemporary | LAC12212 | 1960 | £4 | £10 | |
| My Fair Lady | LP | Contemporary | LAC12100 | 1958 | £5 | £12 | |
| Peter Gunne | LP | Contemporary | LAC12193 | 1959 | £5 | £12 | |
| Shelly Manne | 10" LP | London | LZC14019 | 1955 | £20 | £40 | |
| Shelly Manne And Co. | LP | Stateside | SL10125 | 1965 | £4 | £10 | |
| Shelly Manne And His Friends | LP | Contemporary | LAC12075 | 1958 | £6 | £15 | |
| Shelly Manne And His Men Vol. 1 | LP | Contemporary | LAC12138 | 1959 | £6 | £15 | |
| Shelly Manne And His Men Vol. 1 | 10" LP | Vogue | LDE072 | 1954 | £20 | £40 | |
| Shelly Manne And His Men Vol. 2 | LP | Contemporary | LAC12148 | 1959 | £6 | £15 | |
| Shelly Manne And His Men Vol. 2 | 10" LP | Contemporary | LDC143 | 1955 | £20 | £40 | |
| Shelly Manne And Russ Freeman | 10" LP | Contemporary | LDC192 | 1956 | £20 | £40 | |
| Son Of Gunn | LP | Contemporary | LAC12220 | 1960 | £5 | £12 | |
| Songs Fom Li'l Abner | LP | Contemporary | LAC12130 | 1958 | £5 | £12 | |
| Three | 10" LP | Contemporary | LDC190 | 1956 | £20 | £40 | with Shorty Rogers and Jimmy Giuffre |
| Three And The Two | LP | Contemporary | LAC12276 | 1961 | £5 | £12 | |
| Vol. 4 | LP | Contemporary | LAC12062 | 1957 | £6 | £15 | |
| Vol. 7 – The Gambit | LP | Vogue | LAC12241 | 1961 | £5 | £12 | |
| Volume 6 | LP | Contemporary | LAC12232 | 1960 | £4 | £10 | |

## MANNIN FOLK

| | | | | | | | |
|---|---|---|---|---|---|---|---|
| King Of The Sea | LP | Kelly | MAN2 | 1976 | £20 | £40 | |

## MANNING, BOB

| | | | | | | | |
|---|---|---|---|---|---|---|---|
| It's All Right With Me | 7" | Capitol | CL14190 | 1954 | £1.50 | £4 | |
| Majorca | 7" | Capitol | CL14256 | 1955 | £1.50 | £4 | |
| Mission San Michel | 7" | Capitol | CL14288 | 1955 | £1.50 | £4 | |
| My Love Song To You | 7" | Capitol | CL14234 | 1955 | £1.50 | £4 | |
| Very Thought Of You | 7" | Capitol | CL14220 | 1955 | £1.50 | £4 | |
| What A Wonderful Way To Die | 7" | Capitol | CL14318 | 1955 | £1.50 | £4 | |

## MANNING, MARTY & THE CHEETAHS

| | | | | | | | |
|---|---|---|---|---|---|---|---|
| Tarzan March | 7" | CBS | 2721 | 1967 | £1.50 | £4 | |

## MANNION, EDDIE

| | | | | | | | |
|---|---|---|---|---|---|---|---|
| Just Driftin' | 7" | HMV | POP804 | 1960 | £1.50 | £4 | |

## MANONE, WINGY

| | | | | | | | |
|---|---|---|---|---|---|---|---|
| Go-Group | LP | London | HBU1063 | 1956 | £6 | £15 | |
| Party Doll | 7" | Brunswick | 05655 | 1957 | £4 | £8 | |
| Trumpet On The Wing | LP | Brunswick | LAT8236 | 1958 | £6 | £15 | |

## MANSANO, JOE

| | | | | | | | |
|---|---|---|---|---|---|---|---|
| Life On Reggae Planet | 7" | Blue Cat | BS150 | 1968 | £4 | £8 | Rico B side |

## MANSFIELD, JAYNE

| | | | | | | | |
|---|---|---|---|---|---|---|---|
| As Clouds Drift By | 7" | London | HL10147 | 1967 | £6 | £12 | Jimi Hendrix plays on B side |
| Busts Up Las Vegas | LP | 20th Century | | | £8 | £20 | US |
| Shakespeare, Tchaikovsky And Me | LP | MGM | (S)E4204 | 1964 | £5 | £12 | US |

## MANSON, CHARLES
| | | | | | | |
|---|---|---|---|---|---|---|
| It's Comin' Down Fast | 7" | Fierce | FRIGHT012 | 1988 £4 £8 | |
| Lie | LP | Awareness | 22145 | 1970 £30 £60 | US |
| Love And Terror Cult | LP | Fierce | FRIGHT001 | 1986 £10 £25 | |
| Rise | 7" | Fierce | FRIGHT006 | 1986 £4 £8 | |

## MANSUN
| | | | | | |
|---|---|---|---|---|---|
| Take It Easy Chicken | 7" | Sci Fi Hi Fi | MANSON1 | 1995 £2.50 £6 | |

## MANTELL, JOHN
| | | | | | |
|---|---|---|---|---|---|
| Remember Child | 7" | CBS | 201783 | 1965 £7.50 £15 | |

## MANTLER, MIKE
| | | | | | |
|---|---|---|---|---|---|
| Jazz Composers' Orchestra | LP | Virgin | JD3001 | 1974 £6 £15 | double |

## MANUEL, IAN
| | | | | | |
|---|---|---|---|---|---|
| Frosty Ploughshare | LP | Topic | 12TS220 | 1972 £4 £10 | |

## MANUELA & DRAFI
| | | | | | |
|---|---|---|---|---|---|
| Im Duett | LP | Hor Zu | SHZE536 | 1966 £20 £40 | German |

## MAPHIA
| | | | | | |
|---|---|---|---|---|---|
| Hans Im Gluck | LP | Alco | ALC80541 | 1974 £6 £15 | German |

## MAPHIS, JOE
| | | | | | |
|---|---|---|---|---|---|
| Fire On The Strings | LP | Columbia | CL1005 | 1957 £10 £25 | US |

## MAPHIS, JOE & ROSE LEE
| | | | | | |
|---|---|---|---|---|---|
| Mr. And Mrs. Country Music | LP | Starday | SLP286 | 1964 £4 £10 | US |
| With The Blue Ridge Mountain Boys | LP | Capitol | (S)T1778 | 1962 £5 £12 | US |

## MAPLE OAK
| | | | | | |
|---|---|---|---|---|---|
| Maple Oak | LP | Decca | SKL5085 | 1971 £100 £200 | |
| Son Of A Gun | 7" | Decca | F13008 | 1970 £5 £10 | |

## MAPP, LUCILLE
| | | | | | |
|---|---|---|---|---|---|
| I'm Available | 7" | Columbia | DB4040 | 1957 £1.50 £4 | |
| Mangos | 7" | Columbia | DB3916 | 1957 £1.50 £4 | |

## MAQUINA
| | | | | | |
|---|---|---|---|---|---|
| Why | LP | White Diablo | 1003 | 1971 £50 £100 | Spanish |

## MARA, TOMMY
| | | | | | |
|---|---|---|---|---|---|
| Pledging My Love | 7" | MGM | SP1128 | 1955 £1.50 £4 | |
| Where The Blues Of The Night | 7" | Felsted | AF109 | 1958 £1.50 £4 | |

## MARAKESH
| | | | | | |
|---|---|---|---|---|---|
| Marakesh | LP | Mirasound | | 1976 £50 £100 | Dutch |

## MARATHONS
| | | | | | |
|---|---|---|---|---|---|
| Peanut Butter | LP | Arvee | A428 | 1961 £25 £50 | US |
| Peanut Butter | 7" | Pye | 7N25088 | 1961 £2.50 £6 | |
| Peanut Butter | 7" | Vogue | V9185 | 1961 £5 £10 | |

## MARAUDERS
| | | | | | |
|---|---|---|---|---|---|
| Baby | 7" | Fontana | TF609 | 1965 £1.50 £4 | |
| Check In | LP | no label | | 196– £20 £40 | US |
| Heart Full Of Tears | 7" | Decca | F11748 | 1963 £1.50 £4 | |
| Little Egypt | 7" | Decca | F11836 | 1964 £1.50 £4 | |
| That's What I Want | 7" | Decca | F11695 | 1963 £1.50 £4 | |

## MARBLE PHROGG
| | | | | | |
|---|---|---|---|---|---|
| Marble Phrogg | LP | Derrick | 8868 | 1968 £700 £1000 | US |
| Marble Phrogg | LP | Derrick | 8868 | 1992 £6 £15 | US |

## MARBLES
| | | | | | |
|---|---|---|---|---|---|
| Marbles | LP | Cotillion | SD9029 | 1970 £5 £12 | US |

## MARC & THE MAMBAS
| | | | | | |
|---|---|---|---|---|---|
| Big Louise | 12" | Some Bizarre | BZS1512 | 1982 £10 £25 | |
| Bite Black And Blues | LP | Gutterheart | GH1 | 1984 £8 £20 | fan club only |
| Black Heart | 7" | Some Bizarre | BZS19 | 1983 £1.50 £4 | with card |
| Black Heart | 12" | Some Bizarre | BZS1912 | 1983 £3 £8 | |
| Discipline | 7" | Lyntone | LYN12505 | 1982 £2 £5 | flexi |
| Sleaze | 12" | Some Bizarre | BZS512 | 1982 £6 £15 | fan club |
| Torment | 12" | Some Bizarre | BZS2112 | 1983 £5 £12 | |

## MARCEL
| | | | | | |
|---|---|---|---|---|---|
| Dream Consumed | LP | BASF | 20210944 | 1971 £5 £12 | German |

## MARCELLE, LYDIA
| | | | | | |
|---|---|---|---|---|---|
| Another Kind Of Fellow | 7" | Sue | WI4025 | 1966 £7.50 £15 | |

## MARCELLINO, MUZZY
| | | | | | |
|---|---|---|---|---|---|
| Mary Lou | 7" | London | HLU8355 | 1956 £7.50 £15 | Mr. Ford & Mr. Goon-Bones B side |

## MARCELS

| Title | Format | Label | Cat# | Year | | | Notes |
|---|---|---|---|---|---|---|---|
| Blue Moon | LP | Pye | NPL28016 | 1961 | £37.50 | £75 | |
| Blue Moon | 7" | Pye | 7N25073 | 1961 | £1.50 | £4 | |
| Heartaches | 7" | Pye | 7N25114 | 1961 | £2.50 | £6 | |
| I Wanna Be The Leader | 7" | Pye | 7N25201 | 1963 | £1.50 | £4 | |
| My Melancholy Baby | 7" | Pye | 7N25124 | 1962 | £2 | £5 | |
| Summertime | 7" | Pye | 7N25083 | 1961 | £1.50 | £4 | |
| You Are My Sunshine | 7" | Pye | 7N25105 | 1961 | £2 | £5 | |

## MARCH, GLORIA

| Title | Format | Label | Cat# | Year | | | Notes |
|---|---|---|---|---|---|---|---|
| Baby Of Mine | 7" | London | HLB8568 | 1958 | £4 | £8 | |

## MARCH, HAL

| Title | Format | Label | Cat# | Year | | | Notes |
|---|---|---|---|---|---|---|---|
| Hear Me Good | 7" | London | HLD8534 | 1958 | £7.50 | £15 | |

## MARCH, JO

| Title | Format | Label | Cat# | Year | | | Notes |
|---|---|---|---|---|---|---|---|
| Dormi, Dormi, Dormi | 7" | London | HLR8696 | 1958 | £1.50 | £4 | |
| Virgin Mary Had One Son | 7" | London | HLR8763 | 1958 | £1.50 | £4 | |

## MARCH, PEGGY

| Title | Format | Label | Cat# | Year | | | Notes |
|---|---|---|---|---|---|---|---|
| I Will Follow Him | LP | RCA | LPM/LSP2732 | 1963 | £6 | £15 | US |
| If You Loved Me | 7" | RCA | RCA1687 | 1968 | £10 | £20 | |
| In Our Fashion | LP | RCA | LPM/LSP3408 | 1965 | £6 | £15 | US |
| Let Her Go | 7" | RCA | RCA1472 | 1965 | £1.50 | £4 | |
| No Foolin' | LP | RCA | LSP3883 | 1968 | £5 | £12 | US |
| Watch What You Do With My Baby | 7" | RCA | RCA1426 | 1964 | £1.50 | £4 | |

## MARCH HARE

The two singles made by March Hare both feature Peter Skellern as lead singer.

| Title | Format | Label | Cat# | Year | | | Notes |
|---|---|---|---|---|---|---|---|
| Cry My Heart | 7" | Chapter One | CH101 | 1968 | £1.50 | £4 | |
| I Could Make It There With You | 7" | Deram | DM258 | 1969 | £1.50 | £4 | |

## MARCH VIOLETS

| Title | Format | Label | Cat# | Year | | | Notes |
|---|---|---|---|---|---|---|---|
| Grooving In Green | 7" | Merciful Release | MR017 | 1982 | £4 | £8 | |
| Religious As Hell | 7" | Merciful Release | MR013 | 1982 | £4 | £8 | |

## MARCHAN, BOBBY

| Title | Format | Label | Cat# | Year | | | Notes |
|---|---|---|---|---|---|---|---|
| There's Something On Your Mind | LP | Sphere Sound | SSR7004 | 1964 | £10 | £25 | US |

## MARCLAY, CHRISTIAN

Christian Marclay is a scratch-mixer, a virtuoso player of record turntables, yet he chooses not to work in the dance music field. A frequent contributor to the records of John Zorn and other members of the contemporary New York avant-garde, Marclay has also found time for a couple of records of his own. *More Encores* is made up entirely of extracts from other people's records, teased and manipulated by Marclay until they begin to take on meanings entirely different from those intended by the original artists. Just as extraordinary is *Record Without A Cover*, a description intended to be taken entirely literally – any resultant scratches fitting naturally into the collage of clicks and scratch sounds already present in the grooves.

| Title | Format | Label | Cat# | Year | | | Notes |
|---|---|---|---|---|---|---|---|
| More Encores | 10" LP | No Man's Land | NML8816 | 1989 | £10 | £25 | German |
| Record Without A Cover | LP | Recycled | no number | 1985 | £25 | £50 | US |

## MARCUS

| Title | Format | Label | Cat# | Year | | | Notes |
|---|---|---|---|---|---|---|---|
| Marcus | LP | United Artists | UAS30000 | 1976 | £6 | £15 | |

## MARDEN, JANIE

| Title | Format | Label | Cat# | Year | | | Notes |
|---|---|---|---|---|---|---|---|
| Soldier Boy | 7" | Decca | F10600 | 1955 | £1.50 | £4 | |
| You Are My Love | 7" | Decca | F10673 | 1955 | £1.50 | £4 | |

## MARESCA, ERNIE

| Title | Format | Label | Cat# | Year | | | Notes |
|---|---|---|---|---|---|---|---|
| Love Express | 7" | London | HLU9720 | 1963 | £2.50 | £6 | |
| Mary Jane | 7" | London | HLU9579 | 1962 | £4 | £8 | |
| Rockin' Boulevard Street | 7" | Stateside | SS560 | 1966 | £2.50 | £6 | |
| Rovin' Kind | 7" | London | HLU9834 | 1964 | £2 | £5 | |
| Shout Shout | 7" | London | HLU9531 | 1962 | £4 | £8 | |
| Shout! Shout! Knock Yourself Out | LP | Seville | SV7/87001 | 1962 | £10 | £25 | US |

## MARGO & THE MARVETTES

| Title | Format | Label | Cat# | Year | | | Notes |
|---|---|---|---|---|---|---|---|
| Cherry Pie | 7" | Parlophone | R5154 | 1964 | £2 | £5 | |
| When Love Slips Away | 7" | Pye | 7N17423 | 1967 | £1.50 | £4 | |

## MARGRET, ANN-

| Title | Format | Label | Cat# | Year | | | Notes |
|---|---|---|---|---|---|---|---|
| And Here She Is | LP | RCA | RD27239/SF5116 | 1962 | £6 | £15 | |
| Ann Margret | LP | RCA | RD/SF7691 | 1964 | £5 | £12 | |
| Bachelors' Paradise | LP | RCA | RD/SF7649 | 1964 | £5 | £12 | |
| Beauty And The Beard | LP | RCA | RD/SF7632 | 1964 | £5 | £12 | with Al Hirt |
| Bye Bye Birdie | LP | RCA | RD/SF7580 | 1963 | £5 | £12 | |
| On The Way Up | LP | RCA | RD/SF7503 | 1962 | £5 | £12 | |
| Vivacious One | 7" EP | RCA | RCX7148 | 1964 | £10 | £20 | |

## MARGUERITA

| Title | Format | Label | Cat# | Year | | | Notes |
|---|---|---|---|---|---|---|---|
| Woman Come | 7" | Black Swan | WI431 | 1964 | £5 | £10 | Eric Morris B side |

## MARGULIS, CHARLIE

| Title | Format | Label | Cat# | Year | | | Notes |
|---|---|---|---|---|---|---|---|
| Gigi | 7" | London | HLL8774 | 1959 | £1.50 | £4 | |

## MARIANE
| | | | | | | |
|---|---|---|---|---|---|---|
| You Know My Name | 7" | Columbia | DB8420 | 1968 | £1.50 | £4 |
| You'd Better Change Your Evil Ways | 7" | Columbia | DB8456 | 1968 | £1.50 | £4 |

## MARIANI
| | | | | | | |
|---|---|---|---|---|---|---|
| Perpetuum Mobile | LP | Sonobeat | 1004 | 197– | £1050 . £1500 | US |

## MARIANO, CHARLIE
| | | | | | | |
|---|---|---|---|---|---|---|
| Beauties Of 1918 | LP | Vogue | LAE12166 | 1959 | £6 £15 | with Jerry Dodgion |
| Charlie Mariano Quartet/Septet | LP | Parlophone | PMC1094 | 1959 | £6 £15 | |
| Charlie Mariano Sextet | LP | London | LTZN15031 | 1957 | £15 £30 | |
| Charlie Mariano Sextet | 10" LP | London | LZN14032 | 1956 | £25 £50 | |

## MARIAS, A. C.
| | | | | | | |
|---|---|---|---|---|---|---|
| Drop | 7" | Dome | DOM451 | 1981 | £2 £5 | |

## MARIE CELESTE
| | | | | | | |
|---|---|---|---|---|---|---|
| And Then Perhaps | LP | private | | 1971 | £180 £300 | |

## MARILLION

The considerable success of an 'old-fashioned' progressive group was one of the more surprising aspects of rock music in the eighties. Marillion achieved this, however, by gigging hard up and down the country and building a sizeable following before making any records at all. In common with other stars of the eighties, Marillion's recording career has been highlighted by a succession of picture disc releases, and it is these that now form the central axis of a Marillion collection.

| | | | | | | |
|---|---|---|---|---|---|---|
| Assassing | 12" | EMI | 12MARILP2 | 1984 | £4 £10 | picture disc |
| Clutching At Straws | LP | EMI | EMDP1002 | 1987 | £4 £10 | picture disc |
| Cover My Eyes | CD-s | EMI | CDMARIL13 | 1991 | £2 £5 | |
| Dry Land | CD-s | EMI | CDMARIL15 | 1991 | £2 £5 | |
| Easter | CD-s | EMI | CDMARIL12 | 1990 | £2 £5 | |
| Freaks | 7" | EMI | MARILP9 | 1988 | £2.50 £6 | shaped picture disc |
| Freaks Live | CD-s | EMI | CDMARIL9 | 1988 | £2 £5 | |
| Fugazi | LP | EMI | MRLP1 | 1984 | £6 £15 | picture disc |
| Garden Party | 7" | EMI | EMIP5393 | 1983 | £5 £10 | shaped picture disc |
| Garden Party | 12" | EMI | 12EMIS5393 | 1983 | £3 £8 | with poster |
| Heart Of Lothian | 12" | EMI | 12MARILP5 | 1985 | £2.50 £6 | picture disc |
| Hooks In You | CD-s | EMI | CDMARIL10 | 1989 | £2 £5 | |
| Incommunicado | CD-s | EMI | CDMARIL6 | 1987 | £3 £8 | |
| Kayleigh | 7" | EMI | MARILP3 | 1985 | £2.50 £6 | picture disc |
| Kayleigh | 12" | EMI | 12MARILP3 | 1985 | £3 £8 | picture disc |
| Lavender Blue | 12" | EMI | 12MARILP4 | 1985 | £2.50 £6 | picture disc |
| Market Square Heroes | 12" | EMI | 12EMIP5351 | 1983 | £15 £30 | picture disc |
| Misplaced Childhood | LP | EMI | MRLP2 | 1985 | £4 £10 | picture disc |
| No One Can | CD-s | EMI | CDMARIL14 | 1991 | £2 £5 | |
| Punch And Judy | 12" | EMI | 12MARILP1 | 1984 | £4 £10 | picture disc |
| Real To Reel | LP | EMI | JESTP1 | 1984 | £4 £10 | picture disc |
| Script For A Jester's Tear | LP | EMI | EMCP3429 | 1984 | £8 £20 | picture disc |
| Sugar Mice | CD-s | EMI | CDMARIL7 | 1987 | £3 £8 | |
| Sugar Mice | 7" | EMI | MARILP7 | 1987 | £2 £5 | picture disc with poster |
| Sugar Mice | 12" | EMI | 12MARILP7 | 1987 | £3 £8 | picture disc |
| Uninvited Guest | CD-s | EMI | CDMARIL11 | 1989 | £2 £5 | |
| Warm Wet Circles | CD-s | EMI | CDMARIL8 | 1987 | £2 £5 | |
| Warm Wet Circles | 12" | EMI | 12MARILP8 | 1987 | £2.50 £6 | picture disc |

## MARINE GIRLS
| | | | | | | |
|---|---|---|---|---|---|---|
| Beach Party | LP | Whaam! | COD1 | 1981 | £4 £10 | |
| On My Mind | 7" | In Phaze | COD2 | 1982 | £4 £8 | |

## MARINERS
| | | | | | | |
|---|---|---|---|---|---|---|
| I Love You Fair Dinkum | 7" | London | HLA8201 | 1955 | £7.50 £15 | |
| Spirituals | LP | London | HAA2007 | 1956 | £4 £10 | |

## MARINI, MARINO
| | | | | | | |
|---|---|---|---|---|---|---|
| Ciao Ciao Bambina | 7" | Durium | DC16636 | 1959 | £1.50 £4 | |
| Come Prima | 7" | Durium | DC16632 | 1958 | £1.50 £4 | |
| Guitar Boogie | 7" | Durium | DC16631 | 1958 | £1.50 £4 | |
| Stella Stella | 7" | Durium | DC16635 | 1958 | £1.50 £4 | |

## MARION
| | | | | | | |
|---|---|---|---|---|---|---|
| Sleep | CD-s | London | LONCD360 | 1995 | £3 £8 | |
| Toys For Boys | CD-s | London | LONCD366 | 1995 | £2.50 £6 | |
| Violent Men | CD-s | Rough Trade | RT3193 | 1994 | £4 £10 | |
| Violent Men | 7" | Rough Trade | RT3193 | 1994 | £5 £12 | |

## MARIONETTES
| | | | | | | |
|---|---|---|---|---|---|---|
| Like A Man | 7" | Parlophone | R5416 | 1966 | £1.50 £4 | |
| Raining It's Pouring | 7" | Parlophone | R5356 | 1965 | £1.50 £4 | |

## MARK II
| | | | | | | |
|---|---|---|---|---|---|---|
| Night Theme | 7" | Columbia | DB4549 | 1960 | £1.50 £4 | |

## MARK IV
| | | | | | | |
|---|---|---|---|---|---|---|
| I Got A Wife | 7" | Mercury | AMT1025 | 1959 | £2.50 £6 | |
| Move Over Rover | 7" | Mercury | AMT1045 | 1959 | £2 £5 | |
| Ring Ring Ring Those Bells | 7" | Mercury | AMT1060 | 1959 | £1.50 £4 | |

## MARK ALMOND

Mark Almond ........................................ LP ...... Harvest ........... SHSP4011 .............. 1971 £4 ........... £10 ...............................

## MARK FIVE

Baby What's Wrong ............................... 7" ...... Fontana ........... TF513 ................... 1964 £12.50 .... £25 ...............................

## MARK FOUR

The Mark Four who recorded singles for Decca and Fontana were an early line-up of the Creation. The bass player was John Dalton, later a member of the Kinks.

| | | | | | | | |
|---|---|---|---|---|---|---|---|
| Crazy Country Hop ......................... | 7" | Mercury ......... | MF825 ............. | 1964 | £10 | £20 | |
| Hurt Me If You Will ...................... | 7" | Decca ........... | F12204 ............. | 1965 | £20 | £40 | |
| Live At The Beat Scene Club ............ | 7" | Bam Caruso ..... | OPRA037 ......... | 1985 | £2.50 | £6 | |
| Rock Around The Clock .................. | 7" | Mercury ......... | MF815 ............. | 1964 | £10 | £20 | |
| Work All Day ............................. | 7" | Fontana ......... | TF664 ............. | 1966 | £20 | £40 | |

## MARKETTS

| | | | | | | | |
|---|---|---|---|---|---|---|---|
| Balbao Blue ............................. | 7" | Liberty ........... | LIB55443 ............... | 1962 | £1.50 | £4 | |
| Batman ................................. | LP | Warner Bros .... | W1642 ............. | 1966 | £5 | £12 | |
| Batman Theme ......................... | 7" | Warner Bros .... | WB5696 ............. | 1966 | £2 | £5 | |
| Out Of Limits .......................... | LP | Warner Bros .... | (S)T1537 ............. | 1964 | £6 | £15 | US |
| Out Of Limits .......................... | 7" | Warner Bros .... | WB120 ............. | 1964 | £2.50 | £6 | |
| Surfer Stomp ........................... | LP | Liberty ........... | LRP3226/LST7226. | 1962 | £8 | £20 | US |
| Surfer Stomp ........................... | 7" | Liberty ........... | LIB55401 ............. | 1962 | £2 | £5 | |
| Surfing Scene .......................... | LP | Liberty ........... | LRP3326/LST7326. | 1963 | £6 | £15 | US |
| Take To Wheels ........................ | LP | Warner Bros .... | WM8140 ............. | 1963 | £6 | £15 | |
| Tarzan's March ......................... | 7" | Warner Bros .... | WB5847 ............. | 1967 | £12.50 | £25 | |

## MARKEYS

| | | | | | | | |
|---|---|---|---|---|---|---|---|
| Damifiknow ............................. | LP | Stax ........... | STS2025 ............. | 1969 | £4 | £10 | US |
| Do The Pop-Eye ........................ | LP | London ........... | HAK8011 ............. | 1962 | £8 | £20 | |
| Foxy ................................... | 7" | London ........... | HLK9510 ............. | 1962 | £1.50 | £4 | |
| Great Memphis Sound ................... | LP | Atlantic ......... | 587/588024 ........... | 1966 | £5 | £12 | |
| Last Night .............................. | LP | Atlantic ......... | (SD)8055 ............. | 1961 | £8 | £20 | US |
| Last Night .............................. | 7" | Atlantic ......... | 584074 ............... | 1967 | £1.50 | £4 | |
| Last Night .............................. | 7" | London ........... | HLK9399 ............. | 1961 | £2 | £5 | |
| Mellow Jelly ............................ | LP | Atlantic ......... | 587/588135 ........... | 1968 | £5 | £12 | |
| Morning After .......................... | 7" | London ........... | HLK9449 ............. | 1961 | £1.50 | £4 | |
| Philly Dog .............................. | 7" | Atlantic ......... | AT4079 ............. | 1966 | £2 | £5 | |

## MARKHAM, PIGMEAT

Pigmeat Markham was a black American comedian who might well be described as the James Brown of comedy for the way in which he kept his art in the ghetto, even when he himself had moved out of it. Markham invented the 'Here Comes The Judge' by-line which featured on the TV show *Rowan And Martin's Laugh-In*, although the song built around it was commandeered by Shorty Long for Tamla Motown.

| | | | | | | | |
|---|---|---|---|---|---|---|---|
| Here Come The Judge ................... | LP | Chess ............. | LPS1523 ............... | 1968 | £6 | £15 | US |
| Here Comes The Judge .................. | 7" | Chess ............. | CRS8077 ............... | 1968 | £1.50 | £4 | |

## MARKLEY

Markley: A Group ...................... LP ...... Forward ........... STF1007 ............... 1969 £15 ......... £30 ..................... US

## MARKSMEN

Smersh ................................... 7" ...... Parlophone ........ R5075 ................... 1963 £4 ........... £8 ...............................

## MARLEY, BOB

During the late sixties and early seventies, reggae music was considered to be virtually worthless by a majority of rock fans – an opinion that was hardly ameliorated by the fact that most reggae albums of the time seemed to be bargain priced compilations with tacky covers. Bob Marley put an end to all that. The influential rock magazine *Let It Rock* ran a feature on Marley's music at the time of the release of the first Island LP, *Catch A Fire*. Every reader thereby encouraged to give the record a listen found music that was as exciting as it was sophisticated, producer Chris Blackwell having consciously enhanced its appeal for the rock audience in the UK by remixing the Jamaican version of the music with additional keyboard and lead guitar parts (as well as issuing the record in an attractive cover made with a hinged top like a giant cigarette lighter). When Eric Clapton decided to record a version of 'I Shot The Sheriff' and when Marley himself managed to produce a performance as magnificent as the live 'No Woman No Cry', his rise to the position of reggae's first international star seemed inevitable. Marley's recording career stretched back as far as the beginning of the sixties, records not listed below being found in this guide under the name of the Wailers.

| | | | | | | | |
|---|---|---|---|---|---|---|---|
| African Herbsman ....................... | LP | Trojan ........... | TRLS62 ............. | 1973 | £8 | £20 | |
| African Herbsman ....................... | 7" | Upsetter ......... | US392 ............. | 1972 | £5 | £10 | |
| Baby We've Got A Date ................. | 7" | Blue Mountain | 1021 .............. | 1973 | £2 | £5 | |
| Babylon By Bus ........................ | LP | Island ............. | ISLD11 ............. | 1978 | £5 | £12 | with 12" (IPR2026) |
| Burial ................................... | 7" | Fab ............. | FAB41 ............. | 1968 | £37.50 | £75 | test pressing |
| Burnin' ................................. | LP | Island ............. | ILPS9256 ............. | 1973 | £5 | £12 | |
| Catch A Fire ........................... | LP | Island ............. | ILPS9241 ............. | 1972 | £8 | £20 | lighter cover |
| Confrontation .......................... | LP | Island ............. | PILPS9760 ............. | 1983 | £8 | £20 | picture disc |
| Confrontation .......................... | CD | Mango ............. | CID9760 ............. | 1988 | £5 | £12 | |
| Could You Be Loved ................... | 7" | Island ............. | ISP210 ............. | 1984 | £1.50 | £4 | picture disc |
| Duppy Conqueror ...................... | 7" | Unity ............. | UN562 ............. | 1972 | £5 | £10 | Upsetters B side |
| Duppy Conqueror ...................... | 7" | Upsetter ......... | US348 ............. | 1971 | £5 | £10 | Upsetters B side |
| Exodus ................................. | LP | Island ............. | ILPS9498 ............. | 1977 | £4 | £10 | |
| Exodus ................................. | CD | Mobile Fidelity | | 1995 | £6 | £15 | US audiophile |
| Freedom Train .......................... | LP | Summit ........... | SUM8530 ............. | 1971 | £5 | £10 | |
| Get Up Stand Up ....................... | 7" | Island ............. | BMRM1 ............. | 1973 | £2 | £5 | 1 sided promo |
| Guava Jelly ............................. | 7" | Green Door ...... | GD4025 ............. | 1972 | £5 | £10 | |
| Have Faith In The Lord ................. | 7" | Studio One ...... | SO2010 ............. | 1967 | £20 | £40 | Joe Higgs B side |

| | | | | | | | |
|---|---|---|---|---|---|---|---|
| I Like It Like This | 7" | Supreme | SUP216 | 1973 | £15 | £30 | |
| I Shot The Sheriff | 7" | Island | IDJ2 | 1974 | £2 | £5 | *promo* |
| Jah Live | 7" | Island | WIP6265 | 1974 | £1.50 | £4 | |
| Johnny Was | 7" | Island | WIP6296 | 1975 | £1.50 | £4 | |
| Judge Not | 7" | Island | WI088 | 1963 | £75 | £150 | |
| Kaya | 7" | Upsetter | US356 | 1971 | £5 | £10 | *Upsetters B side* |
| Legend | LP | Island | PBMW1 | 1984 | £4 | £10 | *picture disc* |
| Lick Samba | 7" | Bullet | BU493 | 1971 | £6 | £12 | |
| Live | LP | Island | ILPS9376 | 1975 | £5 | £12 | *with poster* |
| Lively Up Yourself | 7" | Green Door | GD4002 | 1971 | £6 | £12 | *Tommy McCook B side* |
| Lively Up Yourself | 7" | Punch | PH102 | 1973 | £5 | £10 | *Tommy McCook B side* |
| More Axe | 7" | Upsetter | US369 | 1971 | £5 | £10 | *Upsetters B side* |
| More Axe | 7" | Upsetter | US372 | 1971 | £5 | £10 | *Upsetters B side* |
| Mr. Brown | 7" | Trojan | TR7926 | 1974 | £1.50 | £4 | |
| Mr. Brown | 7" | Upsetter | US354 | 1971 | £5 | £10 | *Upsetters B side* |
| My Cup | 7" | Upsetter | US340 | 1970 | £6 | £12 | *Lee Perry B side* |
| Natty Dread | LP | Island | ILPS9281 | 1975 | £4 | £10 | |
| Natty Dread | 7" | Island | WIP6212 | 1974 | £1.50 | £4 | |
| Oh My Darling | 7" | Coxsone | CS7021 | 1967 | £20 | £40 | *Hamlins B side* |
| One Cup Of Coffee | 7" | Island | WI128 | 1963 | £50 | £100 | *Ernest Ranglin B side* |
| One Love | 12" | Island | 12ISP169 | 1984 | £2.50 | £6 | *picture disc* |
| One Love – People Get Ready | CD-s | Tuff Gong | TGXCD1 | 1991 | £2 | £5 | |
| Radio Sampler | LP | Island | ISS3 | 197– | £20 | £40 | |
| Rasta Revolution | LP | Trojan | TRLS89 | 1974 | £6 | £15 | |
| Rastaman Vibration | LP | Island | ILPS9383 | 1976 | £4 | £10 | |
| Roots Rock Reggae | 7" | Island | WIP6309 | 1976 | £1.50 | £4 | |
| Run For Cover | 7" | Escort | ERT842 | 1970 | £6 | £12 | |
| Screw Face | 7" | Punch | PH101 | 1973 | £5 | £10 | |
| Small Axe | 7" | Punch | PH69 | 1971 | £6 | £12 | *Dave Barker B side* |
| Small Axe | 7" | Upsetter | US357 | 1971 | £5 | £10 | |
| Soul Rebel | LP | Trojan | TBL126 | 1971 | £10 | £25 | |
| Soul Shake Down Party | 7" | Trojan | TR7759 | 1970 | £6 | £12 | *Beverly Allstars B side* |
| Soul Shake Down Party | 7" | Trojan | TR7911 | 1974 | £1.50 | £4 | |
| Soultown | 7" | Bullet | BU464 | 1971 | £5 | £10 | |
| Stir It Up | 7" | Island | WIP6478 | 1976 | £5 | £10 | *demo* |
| Stir It Up | 7" | Trojan | TR617 | 1968 | £20 | £40 | |
| Trenchtown Rock | 7" | Green Door | GD4005 | 1971 | £6 | £12 | |
| Trenchtown Rock | 7" | Island | IDJ7 | 1974 | £2 | £5 | *promo* |

## MARLEY, BOB & ROBERT PALMER

| | | | | | | | |
|---|---|---|---|---|---|---|---|
| Record Shop Sampler | LP | Island | RSS1 | 197– | £10 | £25 | *promo* |

## MARLEY, RITA

| | | | | | | | |
|---|---|---|---|---|---|---|---|
| Come To Me | 7" | Island | WI3052 | 1967 | £5 | £10 | *Soul Boys B side* |
| Pied Piper | 7" | Rio | R108 | 1966 | £4 | £8 | |
| You Lied | 7" | Rio | R118 | 1966 | £4 | £8 | *Soul Brothers B side* |

## MARLO, MICKI

| | | | | | | | |
|---|---|---|---|---|---|---|---|
| Prize Of Gold | 7" | Capitol | CL14271 | 1955 | £2 | £5 | |
| That's Right | 7" | London | HL8481 | 1957 | £7.50 | £15 | *B side with Paul Anka* |

## MARLOWE, MARION

| | | | | | | | |
|---|---|---|---|---|---|---|---|
| Hands Of Time | 7" | London | HLA8306 | 1956 | £20 | £40 | |

## MARMALADE

The Marmalade were frequent visitors to the charts at the end of the sixties, but their good-humoured harmony pop is not the kind of thing to appeal to many collectors today. Nevertheless, the group's early single, 'I See The Rain' is well worth hearing for the combination of harmony singing with a much heavier guitar sound than was the group's normal practice.

| | | | | | | | |
|---|---|---|---|---|---|---|---|
| I See The Rain | 7" | CBS | 2948 | 1967 | £2 | £5 | |

## MARQUIS OF KENSINGTON

| | | | | | | | |
|---|---|---|---|---|---|---|---|
| Changing Of The Guards | 7" | Immediate | IM052 | 1967 | £5 | £10 | |

## MARR, HANK

| | | | | | | | |
|---|---|---|---|---|---|---|---|
| Tonk Game | 7" | Blue Beat | BB26 | 1960 | £6 | £12 | |

## MARRIOT, MIKE

| | | | | | | | |
|---|---|---|---|---|---|---|---|
| Buskin' | LP | Top Line | TOP1LP | 1982 | £8 | £20 | |

## MARRIOTT, STEVE

| | | | | | | | |
|---|---|---|---|---|---|---|---|
| Give Her My Regards | 7" | Decca | F11619 | 1963 | £37.50 | £75 | |
| Marriott | LP | A&M | AMLH64572 | 1976 | £4 | £10 | |

## MARS, JOHNNY

| | | | | | | | |
|---|---|---|---|---|---|---|---|
| Blues From Mars | LP | Polydor | 2460168 | 1972 | £4 | £10 | |

## MARSDEN, BERYL

| | | | | | | | |
|---|---|---|---|---|---|---|---|
| I Know | 7" | Decca | F11707 | 1963 | £1.50 | £4 | |
| Music Talk | 7" | Columbia | DB7797 | 1965 | £2 | £5 | |
| What's She Got | 7" | Columbia | DB7888 | 1966 | £2 | £5 | |
| When The Lovelight Starts | 7" | Decca | F11819 | 1964 | £2 | £5 | |
| Who You Gonna Hurt | 7" | Columbia | DB7718 | 1965 | £2 | £5 | |

## MARSDEN, GERRY

In addition to the hunks of raw rock 'n' roll, 'You'll Never Walk Alone' and 'Ferry Cross The Mersey', that he recorded with Gerry and the Pacemakers, the man who saw fit to lampoon Cliff Richard for his lack of rock 'n' roll credibility (his filmed comments are included in the *Compleat Beatles* video), was also responsible for such roots classics as 'I've Got My Ukelele' (not included here) and the B side of 'Liverpool', which features a collaboration with that rock music giant, Derek Nimmo.

| | | | | | | | |
|---|---|---|---|---|---|---|---|
| Ferry Cross The Mersey | CD-s | PWL | PWCD41 | 1989 | £2 | £5 | with Paul McCartney |
| Gilbert Green | 7" | CBS | 2946 | 1967 | £2 | £5 | |
| Liverpool | 7" | CBS | 3575 | 1968 | £2 | £5 | B side with Derek Nimmo |
| Please Let Them Be | 7" | CBS | 2784 | 1967 | £2 | £5 | |

## MARSH, STEVIE

| | | | | | | | |
|---|---|---|---|---|---|---|---|
| If You Were The Only Boy In The World | 7" | Decca | F11181 | 1959 | £1.50 | £4 | |

## MARSH, WARNE

| | | | | | | | |
|---|---|---|---|---|---|---|---|
| Jazz Of Two Cities | LP | London | LTZP15080 | 1957 | £15 | £30 | |
| Warne Marsh | LP | Wave | LP6 | 1970 | £6 | £15 | |

## MARSHALL, JACK

| | | | | | | | |
|---|---|---|---|---|---|---|---|
| Eighteenth Century Jazz | LP | Capitol | T1108 | 1959 | £4 | £10 | |
| Soundsville | LP | Capitol | (S)T1194 | 1961 | £4 | £10 | |
| Thunder Road Chase | 7" | Capitol | CL14888 | 1958 | £2.50 | £6 | |

## MARSHALL, LARRY

| | | | | | | | |
|---|---|---|---|---|---|---|---|
| Move Your Feet | 7" | Blue Beat | BB374 | 1967 | £6 | £12 | |
| No One To Give Me Love | 7" | Caltone | TONE126 | 1968 | £4 | £8 | Phil Pratt B side |
| Suspicion | 7" | Blue Beat | BB380 | 1967 | £6 | £12 | |

## MARSHMALLOW WAY

| | | | | | | | |
|---|---|---|---|---|---|---|---|
| Marshmallow Way | LP | United Artists | UAS6708 | 1970 | £6 | £15 | US |

## MARSON, STUART

| | | | | | | | |
|---|---|---|---|---|---|---|---|
| Night Falls On The Orchestra | LP | Sweet Folk And Country | SFA012 | 1974 | £4 | £10 | |

## MARSUPILAMI

| | | | | | | | |
|---|---|---|---|---|---|---|---|
| Arena | LP | Transatlantic | TRA230 | 1971 | £15 | £30 | |
| Marsupilami | LP | Transatlantic | TRA213 | 1970 | £15 | £30 | |

## MARTELLS

| | | | | | | | |
|---|---|---|---|---|---|---|---|
| Time To Say Goodnight | 7" | Decca | F12463 | 1966 | £1.50 | £4 | |

## MARTERIE, RALPH

| | | | | | | | |
|---|---|---|---|---|---|---|---|
| Cha-Hua-Hua | 7" | Mercury | 7MT232 | 1958 | £1.50 | £4 | |
| Guaglione | 7" | Mercury | 7MT138 | 1957 | £1.50 | £4 | |
| Music For A Private Eye | 7" EP | Mercury | ZEP10068 | 1960 | £2 | £5 | |
| Night Stroll | 7" | Mercury | 7MT213 | 1958 | £1.50 | £4 | |
| Presenting | 7" EP | Mercury | MEP9517 | 1957 | £5 | £10 | |
| Shish-kebab | 7" | Mercury | 7MT158 | 1958 | £1.50 | £4 | |
| Swinging Sound | 7" EP | Mercury | ZEP10040 | 1959 | £2 | £5 | |
| Tequila | 7" | Mercury | 7MT204 | 1958 | £1.50 | £4 | |

## MARTERIE, RALPH & QUINCY JONES ORCHESTRAS

| | | | | | | | |
|---|---|---|---|---|---|---|---|
| Big Band Sound | 7" EP | Mercury | ZEP10024 | 1959 | £2 | £5 | |

## MARTHA & THE VANDELLAS

| | | | | | | | |
|---|---|---|---|---|---|---|---|
| Come And Get These Memories | LP | Oriole | PS40052 | 1963 | £75 | £150 | |
| Come And Get These Memories | 7" | Oriole | CBA1819 | 1963 | £62.50 | £125 | |
| Dance Party | LP | Tamla Motown | TML11013 | 1965 | £20 | £40 | |
| Dancing In The Street | LP | Tamla Motown | (S)TML11099 | 1969 | £4 | £10 | |
| Dancing In The Street | 7" | Stateside | SS345 | 1964 | £5 | £10 | |
| Dancing In The Street | 7" | Tamla Motown | TMG684 | 1969 | £1.50 | £4 | |
| Greatest Hits | LP | Tamla Motown | (S)TML11040 | 1967 | £5 | £12 | |
| Heat Wave | 7" | Stateside | SS228 | 1963 | £12.50 | £25 | |
| Heatwave | LP | Tamla Motown | TML11005 | 1965 | £15 | £30 | |
| Hitting | 7" EP | Tamla Motown | TME2017 | 1966 | £30 | £60 | |
| Honey Chile | 7" | Tamla Motown | TMG636 | 1968 | £2.50 | £6 | |
| I Can't Dance To The Music You're Playing | 7" | Tamla Motown | TMG669 | 1968 | £2 | £5 | |
| I Promise To Wait My Love | 7" | Tamla Motown | TMG657 | 1968 | £1.50 | £4 | |
| I'll Have To Let Him Go | 7" | Oriole | CBA1814 | 1963 | £180 | £300 | best auctioned |
| I'm Ready For Love | 7" | Tamla Motown | TMG582 | 1966 | £1.50 | £4 | |
| In My Lonely Room | 7" | Stateside | SS305 | 1964 | £15 | £30 | |
| Jimmy Mack | 7" | Tamla Motown | TMG599 | 1967 | £1.50 | £4 | |
| Live | LP | Gordy | (GS)925 | 1967 | £6 | £15 | US |
| Live Wire | 7" | Stateside | SS272 | 1964 | £12.50 | £25 | |
| Love Bug Leave My Heart Alone | 7" | Tamla Motown | TMG621 | 1967 | £2 | £5 | |
| Martha & The Vandellas | 7" EP | Tamla Motown | TME2009 | 1965 | £25 | £50 | |
| My Baby Loves Me | 7" | Tamla Motown | TMG549 | 1966 | £4 | £8 | |
| Nowhere to Run | 7" | Tamla Motown | TMG502 | 1965 | £2.50 | £6 | |
| Nowhere To Run | 7" | Tamla Motown | TMG694 | 1969 | £1.50 | £4 | |
| Quicksand | 7" | Stateside | SS250 | 1964 | £12.50 | £25 | |
| Ridin' High | LP | Tamla Motown | (S)TML11078 | 1968 | £5 | £12 | |
| Watch Out | LP | Tamla Motown | (S)TML11051 | 1967 | £8 | £20 | |
| What Am I Going To Do | 7" | Tamla Motown | TMG567 | 1966 | £2.50 | £6 | |

| | | | | | | |
|---|---|---|---|---|---|---|
| Wild One | 7" | Stateside | SS383 | 1965 £10 | £20 | |
| You've Been In Love Too Long | 7" | Tamla Motown | TMG530 | 1965 £6 | £12 | |

Martin

## MARTIN, ALAN

| | | | | | | |
|---|---|---|---|---|---|---|
| Days Are Lonely | 7" | Rio | R94 | 1966 £2.50 | £6 | |
| Mother Brother | 7" | Rio | R10 | 1963 £5 | £10 | |
| Must Know I Love You | 7" | Rio | R66 | 1965 £5 | £10 | Vic Brown B side |
| Party | 7" | Rio | R3 | 1963 £5 | £10 | |
| Rome Wasn't Built In A Day | 7" | Rio | R96 | 1966 £2.50 | £6 | |
| Secretly | 7" | Rio | R9 | 1963 £5 | £10 | |
| Since I Married Dorothy | 7" | Rio | R74 | 1965 £5 | £10 | |
| Sweet Rosemarie | 7" | Rio | R67 | 1965 £5 | £10 | Honey Duckers B side |
| Why Must I Cry | 7" | Rio | R68 | 1965 £5 | £10 | |
| You Came Late | 7" | Rio | R6 | 1963 £5 | £10 | |

## MARTIN, DAVE

| | | | | | | |
|---|---|---|---|---|---|---|
| All My Dreams | 7" | Port-O-Jam | PJ4115 | 1964 £5 | £10 | |
| Let Them Fight | 7" | Port-O-Jam | PJ4112 | 1964 £5 | £10 | |

## MARTIN, DEAN

| | | | | | | |
|---|---|---|---|---|---|---|
| Belle From Barcelona | 7" | Capitol | CL14253 | 1955 £4 | £8 | |
| Capitol Presents | 10" LP | Capitol | LC6590 | 1953 £15 | £30 | |
| Cha Cha D'Amor | 7" EP | Capitol | EAP71702 | 1961 £2 | £5 | |
| Chee Chhe-oo Chee | 7" | Capitol | CL14311 | 1955 £4 | £8 | |
| Dean Martin | 7" EP | Capitol | EAP19123 | 1955 £5 | £10 | |
| Dean Martin And Jerry Lewis | 7" EP | Capitol | EAP1033 | 1956 £2 | £5 | with Jerry Lewis |
| Dean Martin Sings, Nicolini Lucchesi Plays. | 10" LP | Britone | LP1002 | 1956 £20 | £40 | |
| Everybody Loves Somebody | 7" EP | Reprise | R30034 | 1964 £2 | £5 | |
| Hey Brother Pour The Wine | 7" | Capitol | CL14123 | 1954 £5 | £10 | |
| Hollywood Or Bust | 7" EP | Capitol | EAP1806 | 1957 £2 | £5 | |
| How Do You Speak To An Angel? | 7" | Capitol | CL14150 | 1954 £4 | £8 | |
| I'm Yours | 7" EP | Capitol | EAP120152 | 1961 £2.50 | £6 | |
| If I Could Sing Like Bing | 7" | Capitol | CL14180 | 1954 £4 | £8 | |
| In Movieland | 7" EP | Capitol | EAP120124 | 1961 £2.50 | £6 | |
| In Napoli | 7" | Capitol | CL14370 | 1955 £4 | £8 | |
| Innamorata | 7" | Capitol | CL14507 | 1956 £2 | £5 | |
| Let Me Go Lover | 7" | Capitol | CL14226 | 1955 £5 | £10 | |
| Line And Dino | 7" EP | Capitol | EAP120060 | 1961 £2 | £5 | with Line Renaud |
| Mambo Italiano | 7" | Capitol | CL14227 | 1955 £5 | £10 | |
| Man Who Plays The Mandolino | 7" | Capitol | CL14690 | 1957 £1.50 | £4 | |
| Memories Are Made Of This | 7" | Capitol | CL14523 | 1956 £4 | £8 | |
| Open Up The Doghouse | 7" | Capitol | CL14215 | 1955 £5 | £10 | |
| Peddler Man | 7" | Capitol | CL14170 | 1954 £4 | £8 | |
| Pretty Baby | LP | Capitol | T849 | 1957 £4 | £10 | |
| Relax-ay-voo | 7" | Capitol | CL14356 | 1955 £4 | £8 | |
| Relaxing With Dean Martin | 7" EP | Capitol | EAP120072 | 1961 £2 | £5 | |
| Return To Me | 7" EP | Capitol | EAP1939 | 1957 £2 | £5 | |
| Return To Me | 7" | Capitol | CL14844 | 1958 £1.50 | £4 | |
| Rio Bravo | 7" | Capitol | CL15015 | 1959 £1.50 | £4 | |
| Simpatico | 7" | Capitol | CL14367 | 1955 £4 | £8 | |
| Somebody Loves You | 7" EP | Capitol | EAP61702 | 1961 £2 | £5 | |
| Sunny Italy | 7" EP | Capitol | EAP1481 | 1955 £2.50 | £6 | |
| Sway | 7" | Capitol | CL14138 | 1954 £6 | £12 | |
| Swinging Down Yonder No. 1 | 7" EP | Capitol | EAP1007 | 1956 £2 | £5 | |
| Swinging Down Yonder No. 2 | 7" EP | Capitol | EAP1022 | 1956 £2 | £5 | |
| Swinging Down Yonder No. 3 | 7" EP | Capitol | EAP1037 | 1956 £2 | £5 | |
| Ten Thousand Bedrooms | 7" EP | Capitol | EAP1840 | 1957 £2 | £5 | |
| This Is Dean Martin | LP | Capitol | T1047 | 1958 £4 | £10 | |
| Under The Bridges Of Paris | 7" | Capitol | CL14255 | 1955 £4 | £8 | |
| Volare | 7" EP | Capitol | EAP11027 | 1958 £2 | £5 | |
| Volare | 7" | Capitol | CL14910 | 1958 £1.50 | £4 | |
| Watching The World Go By | 7" | Capitol | CL14586 | 1956 £1.50 | £4 | |
| When You Pretend | 7" | Capitol | CL14505 | 1956 £1.50 | £4 | |
| Winter Romance Pt. 1 | 7" EP | Capitol | EAP11285 | 1960 £2 | £5 | |
| Winter Romance Pt. 2 | 7" EP | Capitol | EAP21285 | 1960 £2 | £5 | |
| Winter Romance Pt. 3 | 7" EP | Capitol | EAP31285 | 1960 £2 | £5 | |
| Young And Foolish | 7" | Capitol | CL14519 | 1956 £2 | £5 | |

## MARTIN, DEAN (TEX)

| | | | | | | |
|---|---|---|---|---|---|---|
| Country Star | LP | Reprise | R6061 | 1963 £4 | £10 | |
| Rides Again | LP | Reprise | R6085 | 1964 £4 | £10 | |

## MARTIN, DEREK

| | | | | | | |
|---|---|---|---|---|---|---|
| Daddy Rolling Stone | 7" | Sue | WI308 | 1964 £6 | £12 | credited to Derak Martin |
| Soul Power | 7" | Stax | 601039 | 1968 £5 | £10 | |
| You Better Go | 7" | Columbia | DB7694 | 1965 £6 | £12 | |

## MARTIN, DEWEY

| | | | | | | |
|---|---|---|---|---|---|---|
| Dewey Martin And Medicine Ball | LP | Uni | 73088 | 1970 £5 | £12 | US |

## MARTIN, DON & DANDY

| | | | | | | |
|---|---|---|---|---|---|---|
| Got A Feelin' | 7" | Giant | GN6 | 1967 £1.50 | £4 | |
| Keep On Fighting | 7" | Giant | GN24 | 1968 £1.50 | £4 | |

## MARTIN, GEORGE

| | | | | | | |
|---|---|---|---|---|---|---|
| All My Loving | 7" | Parlophone | R5135 | 1964 £1.50 | £4 | |

| And I Love Her | LP | Studio Two | TWO141 | 1966 | £5 | £12 | |
| Beatles To Bond And Bach | LP | St. Michael | IMP105 | 1978 | £6 | £15 | |
| British Maid | LP | United Artists | (S)ULP1196 | 1968 | £4 | £10 | |
| I Feel Fine | 7" | Parlophone | R5256 | 1965 | £1.50 | £4 | |
| Instrumentally Salutes Beatles Girls | LP | United Artists | (S)ULP1157 | 1966 | £6 | £15 | |
| Love In The Open Air | 7" | United Artists | UP1165 | 1966 | £6 | £12 | |
| Music From A Hard Day's Night | 7" EP | Parlophone | GEP8930 | 1965 | £6 | £12 | |
| Off The Beatles Track | LP | Parlophone | PMC1227/ PCS3057 | 1964 | £8 | £20 | |
| Plays Help | LP | Columbia | SX1775/TWO102 | 1965 | £5 | £12 | |
| Ringo's Theme | 7" | Parlophone | R5166 | 1964 | £2 | £5 | |
| Theme One | 7" | United Artists | UP1194 | 1967 | £2.50 | £6 | |
| Yesterday | 7" | Parlophone | R5375 | 1965 | £2.50 | £6 | |

## MARTIN, GRADY SLEW FOOT FIVE
| Nashville | 7" | Brunswick | 05535 | 1956 | £4 | £8 | |

## MARTIN, JANIS
| Here Today & Gone Tomorrow Love | 7" | Palette | PG9000 | 1960 | £10 | £20 | |

## MARTIN, JEAN
| Ain't Gonna Kiss Ya | 7" | Decca | F11751 | 1963 | £1.50 | £4 | |
| Will You Still Love Me Tomorrow | 7" | Decca | F11897 | 1964 | £1.50 | £4 | |

## MARTIN, KERRY
| Stroll Me | 7" | Parlophone | R4449 | 1958 | £1.50 | £4 | |

## MARTIN, LUCIA
| Big Jim | 7" | Parlophone | R4915 | 1962 | £2.50 | £6 | |

## MARTIN, MARK
| Extraordinary Girl | 7" | Page One | POF020 | 1967 | £1.50 | £4 | |

## MARTIN, MILES FOLK GROUP
| Miles Martin Folk Group | LP | Amber | | 1971 | £50 | £100 | |

## MARTIN, PAUL
| Snake In The Grass | 7" | Sue | WI4041 | 1967 | £6 | £12 | |

## MARTIN, RAY
| Blue Tango | 7" | Columbia | SCM5001 | 1953 | £2 | £5 | |
| Carousel Waltz | 7" | Columbia | SCM5264 | 1956 | £1.50 | £4 | |
| Swedish Rhapsody | 7" | Columbia | SCM5063 | 1953 | £2 | £5 | |
| Waltzing Cat | 7" | Columbia | SCM5002 | 1953 | £1.50 | £4 | |

## MARTIN, RICKY & THE TYME MACHINE
| Something Else | 7" | Olga | OLE4 | 1968 | £1.50 | £4 | |

## MARTIN, RODGE
| When She Touches Me | 7" | Polydor | 56725 | 1967 | £2 | £5 | |

## MARTIN, RON
| Give Your Love To Me | 7" | Doctor Bird | DB1151 | 1968 | £5 | £10 | |

## MARTIN, SETH
| Another Day Goes By | 7" | Page One | POF073 | 1968 | £1.50 | £4 | |

## MARTIN, SHANE
| You're So Young | 7" | CBS | 3894 | 1969 | £50 | £100 | |

## MARTIN, STEVE
| Only You | 7" | Columbia | SCM5212 | 1956 | £1.50 | £4 | |

## MARTIN, TONY
| All Of You | 7" | HMV | POP282 | 1957 | £1.50 | £4 | |
| Bigger Your Heart Is | 7" | Tamla Motown | TMG537 | 1965 | £20 | £40 | |
| Dream Music | 10" LP | Mercury | MPT7516 | 1957 | £6 | £15 | |
| Favourites | 10" LP | Mercury | MPT7005 | 1956 | £6 | £15 | |
| Golden Years | 7" | HMV | 7M136 | 1953 | £2 | £5 | |
| I Could Write A Book | 7" | HMV | 7M203 | 1954 | £1.50 | £4 | |
| I Love Paris | 7" | HMV | 7M258 | 1954 | £1.50 | £4 | |
| It's Better In The Dark | 7" | HMV | POP257 | 1956 | £1.50 | £4 | |
| Love You Funny Thing | 7" | HMV | 7M376 | 1956 | £1.50 | £4 | |
| My Bambina | 7" | HMV | 7M283 | 1955 | £1.50 | £4 | |
| Please Please | 7" | HMV | 7M137 | 1953 | £2 | £5 | |
| Sorta On The Border | 7" | HMV | 7M158 | 1953 | £2 | £5 | |
| Speak To Me Of Love | 10" LP | HMV | DLP1137 | 1957 | £4 | £10 | |
| Stranger In Paradise | 7" | HMV | 7M302 | 1955 | £4 | £8 | |
| Talkin' To Your Picture | 7" | Stateside | SS394 | 1965 | £25 | £50 | |
| Tenement Symphony | 7" | HMV | 7M105 | 1953 | £2.50 | £6 | |
| That's What A Rainy Day Is For | 7" | HMV | 7M210 | 1954 | £1.50 | £4 | |
| Tony Martin Sings Vol. 1 | 10" LP | Brunswick | LA8713 | 1955 | £6 | £15 | |
| Uno | 7" | HMV | 7M254 | 1954 | £1.50 | £4 | |
| Walk Hand In Hand | 7" | HMV | 7M414 | 1956 | £2 | £5 | |
| Walk Hand In Hand | 7" | HMV | 7MC41 | 1956 | £2.50 | £6 | *export* |
| What's The Time In Nicaragua | 7" | HMV | 7M320 | 1955 | £1.50 | £4 | |

## MARTIN, TRADE
Hula Hula Dancin' Doll ............................ 7" ...... London .......... HL9662 ................. 1963 £1.50 ...... £4 .............................

## MARTIN, VINCE & THE TARRIERS
Cindy Oh Cindy ..................................... 7" ...... London .......... HLN8340 .............. 1956 £10 ........ £20 ...........................

## MARTIN & FINLEY
It's Another Sunday .............................. 7" ...... Tamla Motown TMG867 ................ 1973 £20 ........ £40 ..................... demo

## MARTINDALE, WINK
| | | | | | | | |
|---|---|---|---|---|---|---|---|
| Black Land Farmer | 7" | | London | HLD9419 | 1961 | £1.50 | £4 |
| Deck Of Cards | 7" | EP | Dot | DEP20000 | 1965 | £2 | £5 |
| Deck Of Cards | 7" | EP | London | RED1370 | 1963 | £5 | £10 |
| Deck Of Cards | 7" | | London | HLD8962 | 1959 | £1.50 | £4 |
| Life Gets Teejus Don't It? | 7" | | London | HLD9042 | 1960 | £1.50 | £4 |
| Wink Martindale | LP | | London | HAD2240 | 1960 | £8 | £20 |

## MARTINO, AL
| | | | | | | | |
|---|---|---|---|---|---|---|---|
| Al Martino Sings | 7" | EP | Capitol | EAP1405 | 1955 | £6 | £12 |
| Come Close To Me | 7" | | Capitol | CL14379 | 1955 | £5 | £10 |
| Darling I Love You | 7" | EP | Ember | EMBEP4528 | 1963 | £2.50 | £6 |
| Darling I Love You | 7" | | Top Rank | JAR187 | 1959 | £2 | £5 |
| Don't Go To Strangers | 7" | | Capitol | CL14224 | 1955 | £6 | £12 |
| Girl I Left In Rome | 7" | | Capitol | CL14614 | 1956 | £2.50 | £6 |
| Give Me Something To Go On With | 7" | | Capitol | CL14148 | 1954 | £7.50 | £15 |
| I Can't Get You Out Of My Heart | 7" | | Top Rank | JAR108 | 1959 | £2 | £5 |
| I Still Believe | 7" | | Capitol | CL14192 | 1954 | £6 | £12 |
| I'm Sorry | 7" | | Capitol | CL14680 | 1957 | £2.50 | £6 |
| Journey's End | 7" | | Capitol | CL14550 | 1956 | £2.50 | £6 |
| Losing You | 7" | EP | Capitol | EAP120590 | 1964 | £2 | £5 |
| Mama | 7" | | Top Rank | JAR337 | 1960 | £1.50 | £4 |
| Man From Laramie | 7" | | Capitol | CL14343 | 1955 | £7.50 | £15 |
| Not As A Stranger | 7" | | Capitol | CL14202 | 1954 | £6 | £12 |
| Sings Of Love | 7" | EP | Capitol | EAP42107 | 1963 | £2 | £5 |
| Snowy Snowy Mountains | 7" | | Capitol | CL14284 | 1955 | £6 | £12 |
| Story Of Tina | 7" | | Capitol | CL14163 | 1954 | £7.50 | £15 |
| Summertime | 7" | | Top Rank | JAR312 | 1960 | £1.50 | £4 |
| To Please My Lady | 7" | EP | Capitol | EAP120153 | 1961 | £2.50 | £6 |
| Wanted | 7" | | Capitol | CL14128 | 1954 | £7.50 | £15 |

## MARTIN'S MAGIC SOUNDS
Martin's Magic Sounds ............................ LP ...... Deram .......... DML/SML1014 ...... 1968 £4 ........ £10 ....... credited to Irving Martin

## MARTYN, JOHN
John Martyn's first two albums are fairly conventional folk affairs, but his marriage to singer Beverley seemed to make him decide to experiment a little. The two LPs recorded by John and Beverley together are wonderful pieces of folk-rock with the strongly melodic, distinctive songs being enhanced by sympathetic playing from some well-known session names. Thereafter, John Martyn began to explore the sonic possibilities of the amplified guitar, coaxing a range of exciting and unusual sounds from his effects pedals, but without ever abandoning his love of melody. In live performance he was particularly impressive, as a dense wash of echoplexed sound would fill the hall – emanating from a man apparently playing nothing more than an acoustic guitar! This is brilliantly captured on the mock-bootleg *Live At Leeds*, which was available in some European record shops, but could only be obtained by mail order from John Martyn himself in the UK.

| | | | | | | | |
|---|---|---|---|---|---|---|---|
| Bless The Weather | LP | | Island | ILPS9167 | 1971 | £4 | £10 |
| Classic John Martyn | CD-s | | Island | CID265 | 1986 | £6 | £15 |
| Johnny Too Bad | 12" | | Island | IPR2046 | 1981 | £2.50 | £5 |
| Live At Leeds | LP | | Island | ILPS9343 | 1975 | £8 | £20 |
| Live At Leeds | LP | | Island | ILPS9343 | 1975 | £15 | £30 | autographed |
| London Conversation | LP | | Island | ILP952 | 1967 | £6 | £15 | pink label |
| May You Never | 7" | | Island | WIP6116 | 1971 | £1.50 | £4 |
| Philentropy | LP | | Body Swerve | JMLP001 | 1983 | £4 | £10 |
| Tumbler | LP | | Island | ILP991/ILPS9091 | 1968 | £6 | £15 | pink label |

## MARTYN, JOHN & BEVERLEY
| | | | | | | | |
|---|---|---|---|---|---|---|---|
| John The Baptist | 7" | | Island | WIP6076 | 1969 | £1.50 | £4 |
| Road To Ruin | LP | | Island | ILPS9133 | 1970 | £5 | £12 |
| Road To Ruin | LP | | Island | ILPS9133 | 1970 | £8 | £20 | pink label |
| Stormbringer | LP | | Island | ILPS9113 | 1970 | £6 | £15 | pink label |

## MARTYN, KID
In New Orleans With Kid Sheik's Band ..... LP ...... 77 ................. LA1220 ................ 1962 £5 ........ £12

## MARVELETTES
| | | | | | | | |
|---|---|---|---|---|---|---|---|
| As Long As I Know He's Mine | 7" | | Stateside | SS251 | 1964 | £15 | £30 |
| Beechwood 45789 | 7" | | Oriole | CBA1764 | 1962 | £30 | £60 |
| Danger Heartbreak Dead Ahead | 7" | | Tamla Motown | TMG535 | 1965 | £7.50 | £15 |
| Don't Mess With Bill | 7" | | Tamla Motown | TMG546 | 1966 | £7.50 | £15 |
| Finders Keepers, Losers Weepers | 7" | | Tamla Motown | TMG1000 | 1975 | £5 | £10 | Kim Weston B side |
| He's A Good Guy | 7" | | Stateside | SS273 | 1964 | £15 | £30 |
| Here I Am Baby | 7" | | Tamla Motown | TMG659 | 1968 | £4 | £8 |
| Hunter Gets Captured By The Game | 7" | | Tamla Motown | TMG594 | 1967 | £5 | £10 |
| I'll Keep Holding On | 7" | | Tamla Motown | TMG518 | 1965 | £12.50 | £25 |
| In Full Bloom | LP | | Tamla Motown | (S)TML11145 | 1970 | £6 | £15 |
| Locking Up My Heart | 7" | | Oriole | CBA1817 | 1963 | £180 | £300 | best auctioned |
| Marvelettes | LP | | Tamla Motown | (S)TML11052 | 1967 | £10 | £25 |
| Marvelettes | 7" | EP | Tamla Motown | TME2003 | 1965 | £30 | £60 |

| | | | | | | | |
|---|---|---|---|---|---|---|---|
| Marvellous Marvelettes | LP | Tamla Motown | TML11008 | 1965 | £62.50 | £125 | |
| My Baby Must Be A Magician | 7" | Tamla Motown | TMG639 | 1968 | £4 | £8 | |
| Please Mr. Postman | 7" | Fontana | H355 | 1961 | £15 | £30 | |
| Reaching For Something I Can't Have | 7" | Tamla Motown | TMG701 | 1969 | £1.50 | £4 | |
| Reaching For Something I Can't Have/ Magician | 7" | Tamla Motown | TMG860 | 1973 | £12.50 | £25 | demo |
| Sophisticated Soul | LP | Tamla Motown | (S)TML11090 | 1969 | £8 | £20 | |
| Too Many Fish In The Sea | 7" | Stateside | SS369 | 1965 | £10 | £20 | |
| Twisting Postman | 7" | Fontana | H386 | 1962 | £20 | £40 | |
| When You're Young And In Love | 7" | Tamla Motown | TMG609 | 1967 | £2 | £5 | |
| You're My Remedy | 7" | Stateside | SS334 | 1964 | £12.50 | £25 | |
| You're The One | 7" | Tamla Motown | TMG562 | 1966 | £6 | £12 | |

## MARVELOWS
| | | | | | | |
|---|---|---|---|---|---|---|
| I Do | 7" | HMV | POP1433 | 1965 | £5 | £10 |

## MARVELS
| | | | | | | |
|---|---|---|---|---|---|---|
| Keep On Searching | 7" | Columbia | DB8341 | 1968 | £2 | £5 |

## MARVELS (2)
| | | | | | | |
|---|---|---|---|---|---|---|
| Angelo | 7" | Dice | CC8 | 1962 | £5 | £10 |
| Don't Cry My Love | 7" | Dice | CC17 | 1963 | £5 | £10 |
| Sonia | 7" | Blue Beat | BB191 | 1963 | £6 | £12 |

## MARVETTES
| | | | | | | |
|---|---|---|---|---|---|---|
| I Want A Revival | 7" | Tabernacle | TS1001 | 1968 | £1.50 | £4 |
| It's Revival Time | LP | Coxsone | TLP1002 | 196– | £50 | £100 |
| Sweet Jesus | 7" | Tabernacle | TS1003 | 1968 | £1.50 | £4 |

## MARVIN, BRETT & THE THUNDERBOLTS
| | | | | | | |
|---|---|---|---|---|---|---|
| Brett Marvin & The Thunderbolts | LP | Sonet | SNTF616 | 1970 | £4 | £10 |

## MARVIN, HANK
| | | | | | | | |
|---|---|---|---|---|---|---|---|
| Break Another Dawn | 7" | Columbia | DB8693 | 1970 | £2 | £5 | |
| Break Another Dawn/Would You Believe It? | 7" | Columbia | DB8693 | 1970 | £37.50 | £75 | demo |
| Goodnight Dick | 7" | Columbia | DB8552 | 1969 | £2 | £5 | |
| Hank Marvin | LP | Columbia | SCX6352 | 1969 | £4 | £10 | |
| Hank Marvin | LP | Columbia | SX6352 | 1969 | £6 | £15 | mono |
| London's Not Too Far | 7" | Columbia | DB8326 | 1968 | £2 | £5 | Shadows B side |
| Midnight Cowboy | 7" | Columbia | DB8628 | 1969 | £2.50 | £6 | Shadows B side |
| Sacha | 7" | Columbia | DB8601 | 1969 | £2 | £5 | |

## MARVIN & FARRAR
| | | | | | | |
|---|---|---|---|---|---|---|
| Marvin & Farrar | LP | EMI | EMA755 | 1973 | £4 | £10 |
| Music Makes My Day | 7" | EMI | EMI2044 | 1973 | £2 | £5 |
| Small And Lonely Light | 7" | EMI | EMI2335 | 1975 | £1.50 | £4 |

## MARVIN & JOHNNY
| | | | | | | | |
|---|---|---|---|---|---|---|---|
| Cherry Pie | 7" | Black Swan | WI467 | 1965 | £5 | £10 | |
| Smack Smack | 7" | Vogue | V9099 | 1958 | £87.50 | £175 | |
| Yak Yak | 7" | Vogue | V9074 | 1957 | £150 | £250 | best auctioned |

## MARVIN, WELCH & FARRAR
| | | | | | | | |
|---|---|---|---|---|---|---|---|
| Faithful | 7" | Regal Zonophone | RZ3030 | 1971 | £1.50 | £4 | |
| Lady Of The Morning | 7" | Regal Zonophone | RZ3035 | 1971 | £1.50 | £4 | |
| Marmaduke | 7" | Regal Zonophone | RZ3048 | 1972 | £1.50 | £4 | |
| Marvin, Welch & Farrar | LP | Regal Zonophone | SRZA8502 | 1971 | £4 | £10 | |
| Second Opinion | LP | Regal Zonophone | 4SRZA8504 | 1971 | £6 | £15 | quad |
| Second Opinion | LP | Regal Zonophone | SRZA8504 | 1971 | £5 | £12 | |

## MARX, ANDY
| | | | | | | | |
|---|---|---|---|---|---|---|---|
| Circle | LP | Spiegelei | 285171U | 1973 | £6 | £15 | German |

## MARX, GROUCHO
| | | | | | | | |
|---|---|---|---|---|---|---|---|
| Evening With Groucho Marx | LP | A&M | PR3515 | 1972 | £10 | £25 | US picture disc |
| Hooray For Captain Spaulding | LP | Decca | DL5405 | 1968 | £15 | £30 | US |

## MARY BUTTERWORTH
| | | | | | | | |
|---|---|---|---|---|---|---|---|
| Mary Butterworth | LP | Custom Fidelity | CFS2092 | 1969 | £250 | £400 | US |

## MARZ, RAINER
| | | | | | | | |
|---|---|---|---|---|---|---|---|
| Drean Is Over | LP | Bacillus | BLPS19094 | 1972 | £5 | £12 | German |

## MARZ & EPERJESSY
| | | | | | | | |
|---|---|---|---|---|---|---|---|
| Marz And Eperjessy | LP | Bacillus | 6494009 | 1971 | £4 | £10 | German |

## MASAI
| | | | | | | |
|---|---|---|---|---|---|---|
| Across The Tracks | 7" | Contempo | CS2007 | 1974 | £2.50 | £6 |

## MASCOTS
Hey Little Angel.......................................... 7" ...... Pye ................. 7N25189 ................ 1963 £1.50 ...... £4 .............................

## MASEKELA, HUGH
Alive And Well At The Whiskey ............... LP ...... Uni.................. UNL(S)101 ............ 1968 £4 .......... £10 ...........................
And The Union Of South Africa ............... LP ...... Rare Earth ...... SRE3002 .............. 1971 £4 .......... £10 ...........................
Hugh Masekela ........................................ LP ...... Fontana ........... SFL13056 .............. 1969 £4 .......... £10 ...........................

## MASKED MARAUDERS
By 1969, if rock music was supposed to have matured into an art form, and its exponents were to be taken as serious musicians, then it went with the territory that the members of various star groups should, in the manner of jazz musicians, start playing on each other's albums. Al Kooper had shown the way by inviting Mike Bloomfield and Steve Stills to participate in the making of his *Super Session* album; Bloomfield had jammed on record with Moby Grape; and groups like Blind Faith and Crosby, Stills and Nash had been set up as a meeting-place for star performers. It was against this background that *Rolling Stone* magazine printed a review of an album by the 'Masked Marauders', a title that was apparently a thinly disguised cover for a collaboration between the Beatles, Mick Jagger and Bob Dylan. The album really exists, too. Whether a joke on *Rolling Stone*'s part inspired someone to actually make the record, or whether the magazine was simply happy to go along with a record company joke, is no longer clear. The album, however, is an interesting novelty, even if it becomes obvious fairly quickly that it is the work of impersonators. Despite this, the concept of such a stellar gathering being directed, amongst other tellingly inappropriate choices, towards the production of a version of 'I Am The Japanese Sandman' is so delicious, that the record becomes an essential purchase despite itself!

Masked Marauders ................................. LP ...... Reprise ........... RS6378 .................. 1969 £5 .......... £12 ........................ US

## MASKERS
Beat Meets Rhythm & Blues .................... LP ...... Artone ............. PDR552 ................ 1966 £10 ........ £25 ..................... Dutch
Sensations In Sound ................................ LP ...... Artone ............. PDS510 ................ 1966 £4 .......... £10 ..................... Dutch

## MASON
Mason ...................................................... LP ...... Dawn.............. DNLS3050 .............. 1974 £4 .......... £10 .............................

## MASON (2)
Harbour .................................................... LP ...... Eleventh Hour. 1001 ...................... 1971 £37.50 .... £75 ........................ US

## MASON, BARBARA
Oh How It Hurts ...................................... LP ...... Action ............ ACLP6002 ............ 1969 £6 .......... £15 .............................
Oh How It Hurts ...................................... 7" ...... Direction ........ 583382 .................. 1968 £2 ............ £5 .............................
Slipping Away ........................................... 7" ...... Action............. ACT4542 .............. 1969 £4 ............ £8 .............................
Yes I'm Ready ........................................... 7" ...... London ........... HL9977 ................ 1965 £7.50 ...... £15 .............................

## MASON, BARRY
Over The Hills & Far Away ...................... 7" ....... Deram .............. DM104 ................ 1966 £15 ......... £30 .............................

## MASON, BONNIE JO
Cher recorded her tribute to Ringo Starr under this pseudonym.

Ringo, I Love You ..................................... 7" ....... Annette ........... 1000 ...................... 1964 £30 ......... £60 ........................ US

## MASON, DAVE
Alone Together ......................................... LP ...... Blue Thumb .... BTS19 ................. 1970 £5 .......... £12 ..... US, marbled vinyl
Alone Together ......................................... CD ..... Mobile Fidelity UDCD573 ............ 1992 £6 .......... £15 .......... US audiophile
Little Woman ........................................... 7" ...... Island .............. WIP6032.............. 1968 £4 ............ £8 .............................
Only You Know And I Know ................... 7" ...... Harvest ........... HAR5024 ............ 1970 £1.50 ...... £4 .............................
World In Changes .................................... 7" ...... Harvest ........... HAR5017 ............ 1970 £1.50 ...... £4 .............................

## MASON, GLEN
Battle Of New Orleans ............................ 7" ...... Parlophone ...... R4562 ................. 1959 £1.50 ...... £4 .............................
Don't Forbid Me ...................................... 7" ...... Parlophone ...... R4271 ................. 1957 £1.50 ...... £4 .............................
Glendora .................................................. 7" ...... Parlophone ...... R4203 ................. 1956 £2 ............ £5 .............................
Green Door ............................................... 7" ...... Parlophone ...... R4244 ................. 1956 £2 ............ £5 .............................
Hot Diggity .............................................. 7" ...... Parlophone ...... MSP6240 ............ 1956 £2.50 ...... £6 .............................
I May Never Pass This Way Again ............ 7" ...... Parlophone ...... R4415 ................. 1958 £1.50 ...... £4 .............................
Round And Round .................................... 7" ...... Parlophone ...... R4291 ................. 1957 £1.50 ...... £4 .............................
You Got What It Takes ............................ 7" ...... Parlophone ...... R4626 ................. 1960 £1.50 ...... £4 .............................

## MASON, JAMES
Tell Tale Heart.......................................... 7" EP . Brunswick ....... OE9444 ............... 1959 £2 ............ £5 .............................

## MASON, MARLIN
Don't Throw My Love Away .................... 7" ...... Vogue Coral .... Q72168 ................ 1956 £1.50 ...... £4 .............................

## MASON, SPENCER
Flugel In Carnaby Street........................... 7" ...... Parlophone ...... R5555 ................. 1967 £1.50 ...... £4 .............................

## MASON PROFFIT
Moving Towards Happiness ...................... LP ...... Happy Tiger .... 1019 ...................... 1970 £5 .......... £12 ........................ US
Wanted ..................................................... LP ...... Happy Tiger .... 1009 ...................... 1969 £5 .......... £12 ........................ US

## MASS
Labour Of Love ........................................ LP ...... 4AD ................ CAD107 ............... 1981 £4 .......... £10 .............................
You And I ................................................. 7" ...... 4AD ................ AD14 .................... 1980 £2 ............ £5 ............... with poster

## MASSED ALBERTS
Goodbye Dolly .......................................... 7" ...... Parlophone ...... R5159 ................. 1964 £1.50 ...... £4 .............................

## MASSIVE ATTACK
Daydreaming ........................................... CD-s .. Wild Bunch ..... WBRX1 .............. 1990 £2 ............ £5 .............................

| | | | | | | | |
|---|---|---|---|---|---|---|---|
| Safe From Harm | CD-s | Wild Bunch | WBRX3 | 1991 £2 | £5 | | |
| Unfinished Symphony | CD-s | Wild Bunch | WBRX2 | 1991 £2 | £5 | | |

## MASTERBOY
| | | | | | | |
|---|---|---|---|---|---|---|
| Shake It Up And Dance | CD-s | Polydor | CIOCD2 | 1991 £2 | £5 | |

## MASTERMINDS
| | | | | | | |
|---|---|---|---|---|---|---|
| She Belongs To Me | 7" | Immediate | IM005 | 1965 £5 | £10 | |

## MASTERS

'Breaktime' was co-written by Frank Zappa.

| | | | | | | |
|---|---|---|---|---|---|---|
| Breaktime | 7" | Emmy | 10082 | 1962 £75 | £150 | US |

## MASTERS, SAMMY
| | | | | | | |
|---|---|---|---|---|---|---|
| Big Man Cried | 7" | London | HLR9949 | 1965 £2.50 | £6 | |
| Rocking Red Wing | 7" | Warner Bros | WB10 | 1960 £7.50 | £15 | |

## MASTERS, VALERIE
| | | | | | | |
|---|---|---|---|---|---|---|
| Christmas Calling | 7" | Columbia | DB7426 | 1964 £10 | £20 | |
| Cow Cow Boogie | 7" | Fontana | H253 | 1960 £1.50 | £4 | |

## MASTER'S APPRENTICES
| | | | | | | |
|---|---|---|---|---|---|---|
| Best Of | LP | EMI | EMC2517 | 1972 £8 | £20 | Australian |
| Choice Cuts | LP | Columbia | SCX07903 | 1971 £25 | £50 | Australian |
| I'm Your Satisfier | 7" | Regal Zonophone | RZ3031 | 1971 £6 | £12 | |
| Master's Apprentices | LP | Regal Zonophone | SLRZ1016 | 1970 £50 | £100 | |
| Masterpiece | LP | Columbia | SCX07915 | 1972 £25 | £50 | Australian |
| Nickelodeon | LP | Columbia | 7992 | 1972 £62.50 | £125 | Australian |
| Toast To Panama Red | LP | Regal Zonophone | SLRZ1022 | 1971 £50 | £100 | |

## MASTERS OF DECEIT
| | | | | | | |
|---|---|---|---|---|---|---|
| Hensley's Electric Jazz Band And Synthetic Symphonette | LP | Vanguard | 6522 | 1969 £15 | £30 | US |

## MASTERSOUNDS
| | | | | | | |
|---|---|---|---|---|---|---|
| Ballads And Blues | LP | Vogue | LAE12223 | 1960 £4 | £10 | |
| In Concert | LP | Vogue | LAE12226 | 1960 £4 | £10 | |

## MATATA
| | | | | | | |
|---|---|---|---|---|---|---|
| Good Good Understanding | 7" | President | PT438 | 1975 £1.50 | £4 | |
| I Feel Funky | 7" | President | PT406 | 1973 £2.50 | £6 | |
| I Wanna Do My Thing | 7" | President | PT380 | 1972 £1.50 | £4 | |
| Independence | LP | President | PTLS1057 | 1975 £10 | £25 | |
| Matata | LP | President | PTLS1052 | 1974 £4 | £10 | |

## MATCHING MOLE
| | | | | | | |
|---|---|---|---|---|---|---|
| Little Red Record | LP | CBS | 65260 | 1973 £4 | £10 | |
| Matching Mole | LP | CBS | 64850 | 1972 £4 | £10 | |
| O Caroline | 7" | CBS | 8101 | 1972 £1.50 | £4 | |

## MATHETAI
| | | | | | | |
|---|---|---|---|---|---|---|
| Knowing | LP | CAUS | | 1977 £62.50 | £125 | |

## MATHEWS, WILSON, DOONAN
| | | | | | | |
|---|---|---|---|---|---|---|
| Mathews, Wilson, Doonan | LP | Rola | R009 | 1981 £4 | £10 | |

## MATHIS, COUNTRY JOHNNY
| | | | | | | |
|---|---|---|---|---|---|---|
| Country And Western Express No. 5 | 7" EP | Top Rank | JKP2064 | 1960 £7.50 | £15 | |

## MATHIS, JOHNNY
| | | | | | | |
|---|---|---|---|---|---|---|
| Ave Maria | 7" EP | Fontana | TFE17064 | 1958 £2 | £5 | |
| Away From Home | LP | HMV | CSD1638 | 1966 £15 | £30 | stereo |
| Certain Smile | LP | Columbia | CL1194 | 1958 £8 | £20 | US |
| Certain Smile | 7" | Fontana | H142 | 1958 £1.50 | £4 | |
| Chances Are | 7" | Philips | JK1029 | 1957 £5 | £10 | |
| Christmas With Johnny Mathis | 7" EP | Fontana | TFE17162 | 1958 £2 | £5 | |
| Come To Me | 7" EP | Fontana | TFE17039 | 1958 £2 | £5 | |
| Eli Eli | 7" EP | Fontana | TFE17282 | 1960 £2 | £5 | |
| Faithfully | LP | Fontana | STFL522 | 1960 £6 | £15 | stereo |
| Faithfully | LP | Fontana | TFL5084 | 1960 £4 | £10 | |
| Four Hits | 7" EP | Fontana | TFE17275 | 1960 £2 | £5 | |
| Gina | 7" | CBS | AAG117 | 1962 £1.50 | £4 | picture insert |
| Good Night Dear Lord | LP | Columbia | CL1119 | 1958 £8 | £20 | US |
| Greatest Hits | LP | Fontana | TFL5058 | 1959 £4 | £10 | |
| Handful Of Stars | 7" EP | Fontana | TFE17091 | 1958 £2 | £5 | |
| Heavenly | LP | Fontana | TFL5023 | 1958 £5 | £12 | |
| I'll Be Seeing You | 7" EP | Fontana | TFE17283 | 1960 £2 | £5 | |
| I'll Buy You A Star | LP | Fontana | TFL5134/STFL557 | 1961 £4 | £10 | |
| It's De Lovely | 7" EP | Fontana | STFE8001 | 1960 £2.50 | £6 | stereo |
| It's De Lovely | 7" EP | Fontana | TFE17194 | 1959 £2 | £5 | |
| Johnny Mathis | LP | Fontana | TFL5011 | 1957 £6 | £15 | |
| Johnny Mathis | 7" EP | Fontana | TFE17011 | 1958 £2 | £5 | |
| Johnny Mathis | 7" EP | Philips | BBE12156 | 1957 £2.50 | £6 | |

| | | | | | | | |
|---|---|---|---|---|---|---|---|
| Johnny's Moods | LP | Fontana | TFL5117/STFL545 | 1961 | £4 | £10 | |
| Let Me Love You | 7" EP | Fontana | TFE17025 | 1958 | £2 | £5 | |
| Like Someone In Love | 7" EP | Fontana | STFE8018 | 1960 | £2 | £5 | stereo |
| Like Someone In Love | 7" EP | Fontana | TFE17285 | 1960 | £2 | £5 | |
| Love Is Everything | LP | HMV | CLP/CSD3522 | 1966 | £4 | £10 | |
| Meet Mister Mathis | 7" EP | Fontana | TFE17177 | 1959 | £2 | £5 | |
| Merry Christmas | LP | Fontana | TFL5031/STFL506 | 1958 | £5 | £12 | |
| More Greatest Hits | LP | Fontana | STFL517 | 1960 | £6 | £15 | stereo |
| More Greatest Hits | LP | Fontana | TFL5083 | 1960 | £4 | £10 | |
| My Love For You | 7" | Fontana | H267 | 1960 | £1.50 | £4 | picture sleeve |
| Ole | LP | HMV | CSD1578 | 1965 | £20 | £40 | stereo |
| Open Fire, Two Guitars | LP | Fontana | TFL5050/STFL515 | 1959 | £5 | £12 | |
| Portrait Of Johnny | LP | Fontana | TFL5153/STFL571 | 1961 | £4 | £10 | |
| Rhythms And Ballads Of Broadway | LP | Fontana | SET(S)101 | 1960 | £6 | £15 | double |
| Ride On A Rainbow | LP | Fontana | STFL516 | 1960 | £6 | £15 | stereo |
| Ride On A Rainbow | LP | Fontana | TFL5061 | 1960 | £4 | £10 | |
| Shadow Of Your Smile | LP | HMV | CLP/CSD3556 | 1966 | £4 | £10 | |
| So Nice | 7" EP | Fontana | STFE8000 | 1960 | £2.50 | £6 | stereo |
| So Nice | 7" EP | Fontana | TFE17215 | 1960 | £2 | £5 | |
| Swing Low | 7" EP | Fontana | TFE17089 | 1958 | £2 | £5 | |
| Swing Softly | LP | Fontana | TFL5039/STFL500 | 1959 | £5 | £12 | |
| Teacher Teacher | 7" | Fontana | H130 | 1958 | £1.50 | £4 | |
| Tender Is The Night | LP | HMV | CSD1535 | 1964 | £4 | £10 | stereo |
| Tenderly | 7" EP | Fontana | TFE17281 | 1960 | £2 | £5 | |
| There Goes My Heart | 7" EP | Fontana | TFE17088 | 1958 | £2 | £5 | |
| This Is Love | LP | HMV | CSD1600 | 1965 | £6 | £15 | stereo |
| Twelfth Of Never | 7" EP | Fontana | TFE17056 | 1958 | £2 | £5 | |
| Warm | LP | Fontana | TFL5015/STFL510 | 1958 | £5 | £12 | |
| While We're Young | 7" EP | Fontana | TFE17047 | 1958 | £2 | £5 | |
| Wild Is The Wind | LP | Columbia | CL1090 | 1957 | £15 | £30 | US |
| Wild Is The Wind | 7" | Fontana | H103 | 1957 | £1.50 | £4 | |
| Wonderful Wonderful | LP | Fontana | TFL5003 | 1957 | £6 | £15 | |
| Wonderful World Of Make Believe | LP | HMV | CSD1553 | 1965 | £8 | £20 | stereo |
| Your Teenage Dreams | 7" | HMV | POP1217 | 1963 | £2.50 | £6 | export, picture sleeve |

## MATTHEWS, IAN

| | | | | | | | |
|---|---|---|---|---|---|---|---|
| If You Saw Through My Eyes | LP | Vertigo | 6360034 | 1971 | £5 | £12 | spiral label |
| Matthews Southern Comfort | LP | Uni | UNLS108 | 1970 | £5 | £12 | |
| Some Days You Eat The Bear | LP | Elektra | K42160 | 1974 | £4 | £10 | |
| Tigers Will Survive | LP | Vertigo | 6360056 | 1972 | £5 | £12 | spiral label |
| Valley Hi | LP | Elektra | K42144 | 1973 | £4 | £10 | |

## MATTHEWS, JOE

| | | | | | | | |
|---|---|---|---|---|---|---|---|
| Sorry Ain't Good Enough | 7" | Sue | WI4046 | 1968 | £12.50 | £25 | |

## MATTHEWS, WINSTON

| | | | | | | | |
|---|---|---|---|---|---|---|---|
| Sun Is Shining | 7" | Banana | BA329 | 1971 | £1.50 | £4 | Inn Keepers B side |

## MATTHEWS' SOUTHERN COMFORT

| | | | | | | | |
|---|---|---|---|---|---|---|---|
| Second Spring | LP | Uni | UNLS112 | 1970 | £4 | £10 | |
| Woodstock | CD-s | MCA | 2574542 | 1989 | £2 | £5 | |

## MATUMBI

| | | | | | | | |
|---|---|---|---|---|---|---|---|
| Seven Seals | LP | Harvest | SHSP4090 | 1978 | £4 | £10 | |

## MATUSOW, HARVEY JEWS HARP BAND

| | | | | | | | |
|---|---|---|---|---|---|---|---|
| Afghan Red | 7" | Head | HEAD4004 | 1969 | £1.50 | £4 | |
| War Between The Fats And The Thins | LP | Head | HDLS6001 | 1969 | £10 | £25 | |

## MAUDS

| | | | | | | | |
|---|---|---|---|---|---|---|---|
| Hold On | LP | Mercury | MG2/SR61135 | 1967 | £5 | £12 | US |
| Hold On | 7" | Mercury | MF1000 | 1967 | £2 | £5 | |
| Soul Drippin' | 7" | Mercury | MF1062 | 1968 | £1.50 | £4 | |

## MAUGHAN, SUSAN

| | | | | | | | |
|---|---|---|---|---|---|---|---|
| Bobby's Girl | 7" | Philips | 326544BF | 1962 | £1.50 | £4 | |
| Cable Car For Two | 7" | Philips | BF1713 | 1968 | £1.50 | £4 | |
| Come And Get It | 7" | Philips | BF1495 | 1966 | £1.50 | £4 | |
| Don't Go Home | 7" | Philips | BF1564 | 1967 | £1.50 | £4 | |
| Effervescent Miss Maughan | 7" EP | Philips | 433621BE | 1962 | £5 | £10 | |
| Four Beaux And A Belle | 7" EP | Philips | BE12549 | 1963 | £6 | £12 | |
| Hand A Handkerchief To Helen | 7" | Philips | 326562BF | 1963 | £1.50 | £4 | |
| Hey Look Me Over | LP | Fontana | SFL13135 | 1969 | £4 | £10 | |
| Hey Lover | 7" | Philips | BF1301 | 1964 | £1.50 | £4 | |
| Hi I'm Susan Maughan & I Sing | 7" EP | Philips | BBE12525 | 1962 | £5 | £10 | |
| I Can't Make You Love Me | 7" | Spark | SRL1049 | 1971 | £1.50 | £4 | |
| I Didn't Mean What I Said | 7" | Philips | 326533BF | 1962 | £1.50 | £4 | |
| I Remember Loving You | 7" | Philips | BF1679 | 1968 | £1.50 | £4 | |
| I Wanna Be Bobby's Girl But | LP | Philips | 632300BL | 1963 | £10 | £25 | |
| Kiss Me Sailor | 7" | Philips | BF1336 | 1964 | £1.50 | £4 | |
| Make Him Mine | 7" | Philips | BF1382 | 1964 | £1.50 | £4 | |
| Mama Do The Twist | 7" | Philips | BF1216 | 1961 | £1.50 | £4 | |
| More Of Susan Maughan | 7" EP | Philips | 433641BE | 1963 | £6 | £12 | |
| Poor Boy | 7" | Philips | BF1445 | 1965 | £1.50 | £4 | |
| Sentimental Susan | 7" | Philips | BL7637 | 1965 | £6 | £15 | |
| She's New To You | 7" | Philips | 326586BF | 1963 | £1.50 | £4 | |
| Some Of These Days | 7" | Philips | BF1236 | 1961 | £1.50 | £4 | |
| Swingin' Susan | LP | Philips | BL7577 | 1964 | £6 | £15 | |

| | | | | | | | |
|---|---|---|---|---|---|---|---|
| That Other Place | 7" | Philips | BF1363 | 1964 | £5 | £10 | |
| To Him | 7" | Philips | BF1619 | 1967 | £1.50 | £4 | |
| Verdict Is Guilty | 7" | Philips | BF1266 | 1963 | £1.50 | £4 | |
| We Really Go Together | 7" | Philips | BF1824 | 1969 | £1.50 | £4 | |
| When She Walks Away | 7" | Philips | BF1417 | 1965 | £1.50 | £4 | |
| Where The Bullets Fly | 7" | Philips | BF1518 | 1966 | £1.50 | £4 | |
| You Can Never Get Away From Me | 7" | Philips | BF1399 | 1965 | £1.50 | £4 | |

## MAUPIN, BENNIE

| | | | | | | | |
|---|---|---|---|---|---|---|---|
| Jewel In The Lotus | LP | ECM | ECM1043ST | 1974 | £8 | £20 | |

## MAUREENY WISHFUL

| | | | | | | | |
|---|---|---|---|---|---|---|---|
| Maureeny Wishful | LP | Moonshine | WO2388 | 1968 | £50 | £100 | |

## MAURICE & MAC

| | | | | | | | |
|---|---|---|---|---|---|---|---|
| Why Don't You Try Me | 7" | Chess | CRS8081 | 1968 | £2 | £5 | |
| You Left The Water Running | 7" | Chess | CRS8074 | 1968 | £1.50 | £4 | |

## MAXI

| | | | | | | | |
|---|---|---|---|---|---|---|---|
| Do I Dream | 7" | Decca | F13394 | 1973 | £2 | £5 | |

## MAXIMILIAN

| | | | | | | | |
|---|---|---|---|---|---|---|---|
| Snake | 7" | London | HLX9356 | 1961 | £12.50 | £25 | |

## MAXIMILIAN (2)

| | | | | | | | |
|---|---|---|---|---|---|---|---|
| Maximilian | LP | ABC | ABCS696 | 1969 | £30 | £60 | US |

## MAXIM'S TRASH

| | | | | | | | |
|---|---|---|---|---|---|---|---|
| Disco Girls | 7" | Gimp | GIMP1 | 1979 | £15 | £30 | |

## MAXIMUM BAND

| | | | | | | | |
|---|---|---|---|---|---|---|---|
| Cupid | 7" | Fab | FAB51 | 1968 | £1.50 | £4 | |

## MAXWELL, DIANE

| | | | | | | | |
|---|---|---|---|---|---|---|---|
| Almost Seventeen | LP | Challenge | CHL607/CHS2501 | 1959 | £5 | £12 | US |

## MAY, BILLY

| | | | | | | | |
|---|---|---|---|---|---|---|---|
| Arthur Murray Cha Cha Mambos Pt. 1 | 7" EP | Capitol | EAP1578 | 1955 | £2 | £5 | |
| Arthur Murray Cha Cha Mambos Pt. 2 | 7" EP | Capitol | EAP2578 | 1955 | £2 | £5 | |
| Dixieland Band | 7" EP | Tempo | EXA4 | 1955 | £2 | £5 | |
| Hernando's Hideaway | 7" | Capitol | CL14353 | 1955 | £1.50 | £4 | |
| How Important Can It Be? | 7" | Capitol | CL14266 | 1955 | £1.50 | £4 | |
| It's Billy May Time | 7" EP | Capitol | EAP1013 | 1956 | £2 | £5 | |
| Making Whoopee | 7" EP | Capitol | EAP20064 | 1960 | £2 | £5 | |
| Man With The Golden Arm | 7" | Capitol | CL14551 | 1956 | £1.50 | £4 | |
| More May | 7" EP | Capitol | EAP1536 | 1955 | £2 | £5 | |
| Nightmare | 7" | Capitol | CL14609 | 1956 | £2 | £5 | |
| Rudolph The Red Nosed Reindeer Mambo | 7" | Capitol | CL14210 | 1954 | £1.50 | £4 | |
| Shaner Maidel | 7" | Capitol | CL14308 | 1955 | £1.50 | £4 | |
| Sorta Dixie No. 1 | 7" EP | Capitol | EAP1677 | 1957 | £2 | £5 | |
| Sorta Dixie No. 2 | 7" EP | Capitol | EAP2677 | 1957 | £2 | £5 | |
| Sorta Dixie No. 3 | 7" EP | Capitol | EAP3677 | 1957 | £2 | £5 | |
| Sorta May Pt. 1 | 7" EP | Capitol | EAP1562 | 1955 | £2 | £5 | |
| Sorta May Pt. 2 | 7" EP | Capitol | EAP2562 | 1955 | £2 | £5 | |
| Sorta May Pt. 3 | 7" EP | Capitol | EAP3562 | 1955 | £2 | £5 | |

## MAY, BRIAN

| | | | | | | | |
|---|---|---|---|---|---|---|---|
| Back To The Light | CD-s | Parlophone | CDRX6329 | 1992 | £2 | £5 | 2 versions |
| Driven By You | CD-s | Parlophone | | 1991 | £12.50 | £25 | 4 track promo |
| Resurrection | CD-s | EMI | CDRS6351 | 1993 | £6 | £15 | 2 single set |
| Starfleet | CD | Collectors' Pipeline | | 1992 | £10 | £25 | US |
| Starfleet | 7" | EMI | EMI5436 | 1983 | £2 | £5 | |
| Starfleet Project | LP | EMI | SFLT1078061 | 1983 | £4 | £10 | |
| Too Much Love Will Kill You | CD-s | Parlophone | CDRS6320 | 1992 | £10 | £20 | round card sleeve |

## MAY, PHIL

| | | | | | | | |
|---|---|---|---|---|---|---|---|
| Phil May & The Fallen Angels | LP | Philips | 6410969 | 1978 | £4 | £10 | Dutch |

## MAY BLITZ

| | | | | | | | |
|---|---|---|---|---|---|---|---|
| May Blitz | LP | Vertigo | 6360007 | 1970 | £15 | £30 | spiral label |
| Second Of May | LP | Vertigo | 6360037 | 1971 | £30 | £60 | spiral label |

## MAYALL, JOHN

The various editions of the Bluesbreakers that John Mayall led during the sixties were an extraordinary training-ground for many of the more influential musicians of that time. Cream, Fleetwood Mac, the Aynsley Dunbar Retaliation, the Keef Hartley Band, Colosseum, Free, Mark-Almond, Stone the Crows and even the Rolling Stones were all staffed by Mayall alumni. By placing a premium on instrumental prowess, but at the same time managing to place many of his albums among the best-sellers, John Mayall was of crucial importance in the growing maturity of rock music generally. He was never really a singles artist, however, and his original 45 rpm releases have become quite scarce. All the songs are actually available on LP, but it should be noted that the version of 'Double Trouble' included on the stereo pressing of *Looking Back* lacks the echo that helps to make the lead guitar part on the single into one of Peter Green's finest performances. (The mono *Looking Back* retains the echo in all its glory.)

| | | | | | | | |
|---|---|---|---|---|---|---|---|
| Back To The Roots | LP | Polydor | 2657005 | 1971 | £6 | £15 | double |
| Banquet In Blues | LP | ABC | ABCL5187 | 1976 | £4 | £10 | |
| Bare Wires | LP | Decca | LK/SKL4945 | 1968 | £6 | £15 | |

| | | | | | | | |
|---|---|---|---|---|---|---|---|
| Bear | 7" | Decca | F12846 | 1968 | £1.50 | £4 | |
| Blues Alone | LP | Ace Of Clubs | ACL/SCL1243 | 1967 | £4 | £10 | |
| Blues From Laurel Canyon | LP | Decca | LK/SKL4972 | 1969 | £6 | £15 | |
| Bluesbreakers | LP | Decca | LK4804 | 1966 | £8 | £20 | |
| Bluesbreakers | LP | Decca | SKL4804 | 1969 | £10 | £25 | stereo, unboxed Decca logo |
| Bluesbreakers | LP | Teldec | HZ630122 | 1981 | £37.50 | £75 | German, 12 LP box set |
| Bluesbreakers With Eric Clapton | CD | Mobile Fidelity | UDCD616 | 1994 | £6 | £15 | US audiophile |
| Crawling Up A Hill | 7" | Decca | F11900 | 1964 | £10 | £20 | |
| Crocodile Walk | 7" | Decca | F12120 | 1965 | £7.50 | £15 | |
| Crusade | LP | Decca | LK/SKL4890 | 1967 | £6 | £15 | |
| Diary Of A Band Vol. 1 | LP | Decca | LK/SKL4918 | 1968 | £6 | £15 | |
| Diary Of A Band Vol. 2 | LP | Decca | LK/SKL4919 | 1968 | £6 | £15 | |
| Don't Waste My Time | 7" | Polydor | 56544 | 1970 | £2 | £5 | |
| Double Trouble | 7" | Decca | F12621 | 1967 | £2 | £5 | |
| Empty Rooms | LP | Polydor | 583580 | 1970 | £4 | £10 | |
| Hard Road | LP | Decca | LK/SKL4853 | 1967 | £8 | £20 | |
| I'm Your Witchdoctor | 7" | Immediate | IM012 | 1965 | £10 | £20 | |
| I'm Your Witchdoctor | 7" | Immediate | IM051 | 1967 | £7.50 | £15 | |
| Jazz Blues Fusion | LP | Polydor | 2425103 | 1972 | £4 | £10 | |
| Jenny | 7" | Decca | F12732 | 1968 | £2 | £5 | |
| John Mayall Plays John Mayall | LP | Decca | LK4680 | 1965 | £10 | £25 | |
| John Mayall's Bluesbreakers With Paul Butterfield | 7" EP | Decca | DFER8673 | 1967 | £5 | £10 | |
| Lonely Years | 7" | Purdah | 453502 | 1966 | £37.50 | £75 | |
| Looking Back | LP | Decca | LK/SKL5010 | 1970 | £5 | £12 | |
| Looking Back | 7" EP | Decca | 457030 | 1964 | £12.50 | £25 | French |
| Looking Back | 7" | Decca | F12506 | 1966 | £2 | £5 | |
| Memories | LP | Polydor | 2425085 | 1971 | £4 | £10 | |
| No Reply | 7" | Decca | F12792 | 1968 | £1.50 | £4 | |
| Parchman Farm | 7" | Decca | F12490 | 1966 | £2.50 | £6 | |
| Sitting In The Rain | 7" | Decca | F12545 | 1967 | £2 | £5 | |
| So Many Roads | LP | Decca | SLK16590P | 1970 | £8 | £20 | German |
| Suspicions | 7" | Decca | F12684 | 1967 | £2 | £5 | |
| Thinking Of My Woman | 7" | Polydor | 2066021 | 1971 | £2 | £5 | |
| Through The Years | LP | Decca | SKL5086 | 1971 | £4 | £10 | |
| Turning Point | LP | Polydor | 583571 | 1970 | £4 | £10 | |
| USA Union | LP | Polydor | 2425020 | 1970 | £4 | £10 | |

## MAYER, JOHN

| | | | | | | | |
|---|---|---|---|---|---|---|---|
| Acka Raga | 7" | Columbia | DB8037 | 1966 | £1.50 | £4 | |
| Etudes | LP | Sonet | SNTF603 | 1969 | £8 | £20 | |
| Indo-Jazz Fusions | LP | Columbia | SX/SCX6122 | 1967 | £20 | £40 | with Joe Harriott |
| Indo-Jazz Fusions | LP | Double-Up | DUO123 | 197– | £6 | £15 | double |
| Indo-Jazz Fusions II | LP | Columbia | SX/SCX6215 | 1968 | £20 | £40 | with Joe Harriott |
| Radha Krishna | LP | Columbia | SCX6462 | 1971 | £20 | £40 | |

## MAYER, NATHANIEL

| | | | | | | | |
|---|---|---|---|---|---|---|---|
| Going Back To The Village Of Love | LP | Fortune | 8014 | 1964 | £8 | £20 | US |
| Village Of Love | 7" | HMV | POP1041 | 1962 | £7.50 | £15 | |

## MAYFIELD, CURTIS

| | | | | | | | |
|---|---|---|---|---|---|---|---|
| Back To The World | LP | Buddah | 2318085 | 1973 | £4 | £10 | |
| Curtis | LP | Buddah | 2318015 | 1971 | £6 | £15 | |
| Curtis Live | LP | Buddah | 2659005 | 1971 | £6 | £15 | double |
| Curtis Live | LP | Buddah | BDLP2001 | 1974 | £5 | £12 | double |
| If There's A Hell Below | 7" | Buddah | 2011055 | 1970 | £1.50 | £4 | |
| Move On Up | 7" | Buddah | 2011080 | 1971 | £1.50 | £4 | |
| Roots | LP | Buddah | 2318045 | 1972 | £4 | £10 | |
| Superfly | LP | Buddah | 2318065 | 1972 | £4 | £10 | |
| Sweet Exorcist | LP | Buddah | 2318099 | 1974 | £4 | £10 | |
| We Got To Have Peace | 7" | Buddah | 2011101 | 1971 | £1.50 | £4 | |

## MAYFIELD, PERCY

| | | | | | | | |
|---|---|---|---|---|---|---|---|
| Bought Blues | LP | Tangerine | TRC1510 | 1969 | £4 | £10 | |
| My Jug And I | LP | HMV | CLP/CSD3572 | 1967 | £4 | £10 | |
| Percy Mayfield | LP | Tangerine | TRC1505 | 1969 | £4 | £10 | |
| River's Invitation | 7" | HMV | POP1185 | 1963 | £1.50 | £4 | |

## MAYFIELD'S MULE

Mayfield's Mule included Andy Scott who was later a member of the Sweet.

| | | | | | | | |
|---|---|---|---|---|---|---|---|
| Double Dealing Woman | 7" | Parlophone | R5817 | 1969 | £5 | £10 | |
| I See A River | 7" | Parlophone | R5843 | 1970 | £5 | £10 | |
| We Go Rollin' | 7" | Parlophone | R5858 | 1970 | £2 | £5 | |

## MAYHEM

| | | | | | | | |
|---|---|---|---|---|---|---|---|
| Bloodrush | 12" | Vigilante | VIG1T | 1985 | £2.50 | £6 | |

## MAYL, GENE

| | | | | | | | |
|---|---|---|---|---|---|---|---|
| Dixieland Rhythm Kings | LP | London | LTZU15069 | 1957 | £6 | £15 | |
| Dixieland Rhythm Kings | 10" LP | London | HAPB1037 | 1955 | £6 | £15 | |

## MAYPOLE

| | | | | | | | |
|---|---|---|---|---|---|---|---|
| Maypole | LP | Colossus | CS1007 | 1970 | £30 | £60 | US |

# MAYTALS

| Title | Format | Label | Cat. No. | Year | | | Notes |
|---|---|---|---|---|---|---|---|
| 54–46 Was My Number | 7" | Pyramid | PYR6030 | 1968 | £4 | £8 | Roland Alphonso B side |
| 54–46, That's My Number | 7" | Trojan | TR7726 | 1969 | £1.50 | £4 | |
| Aldina | 7" | Pyramid | PYR6070 | 1969 | £2 | £5 | |
| Another Chance | 7" | R&B | JB141 | 1964 | £5 | £10 | Frankie Anderson B side |
| Bam Bam | 7" | Doctor Bird | DB1038 | 1966 | £5 | £10 | |
| Bim Today Bam Tomorrow | 7" | Pyramid | PYR6050 | 1968 | £4 | £8 | |
| Bla Bla Bla | 7" | Trojan | TR7741 | 1970 | £1.50 | £4 | |
| Christmas Feelings | 7" | Ska Beat | JB174 | 1964 | £5 | £10 | |
| Country Road | 7" | Dragon | DRA1013 | 1973 | £1.50 | £4 | |
| Do The Reggay | 7" | Pyramid | PYR6057 | 1968 | £4 | £8 | Beverley's Allstars B side |
| Dog War | 7" | Blue Beat | BB231 | 1964 | £6 | £12 | Rico B side |
| Don't Trouble Trouble | 7" | Pyramid | PYR6066 | 1969 | £1.50 | £4 | |
| Don't Trouble Trouble | 7" | Pyramid | PYR6066 | 1969 | £4 | £8 | Beverley's Allstars B side |
| Everytime | 7" | Island | WI102 | 1963 | £5 | £10 | Tommy McCook B side |
| Fever | 7" | Dragon | DRA1021 | 1974 | £1.50 | £4 | |
| From The Roots | LP | Trojan | TRLS65 | 1973 | £6 | £15 | |
| Funky Kingston | LP | Dragon | DRLS5002 | 1973 | £4 | £10 | |
| Funky Kingston | LP | Island | ILPS9186 | 1973 | £4 | £10 | |
| Give Me Your Love | 7" | R&B | JB153 | 1964 | £5 | £10 | |
| Hallelujah | 7" | Blue Beat | BB176 | 1963 | £6 | £12 | |
| He Is Real | 7" | Blue Beat | BB215 | 1964 | £6 | £12 | |
| Hurry Up | 7" | R&B | JB130 | 1963 | £5 | £10 | |
| I've Got A Pain | 7" | Blue Beat | BB220 | 1964 | £6 | £12 | Buster's Allstars B side |
| In The Dark | LP | Dragon | DRLS5004 | 1974 | £4 | £10 | |
| In The Dark | LP | Island | ILPS9231 | 1974 | £4 | £10 | |
| In The Dark | 7" | Dragon | DRA1016 | 1973 | £1.50 | £4 | |
| John And James | 7" | Black Swan | WI464 | 1965 | £4 | £8 | Theo Beckford B side |
| Joy And Jean | 7" | Ska Beat | JB202 | 1965 | £5 | £10 | |
| Judgement Day | 7" | Blue Beat | BB255 | 1964 | £6 | £12 | |
| Just Tell Me | 7" | Pyramid | PYR6048 | 1968 | £4 | £8 | |
| Light Of The World | 7" | Blue Beat | BB299 | 1965 | £6 | £12 | |
| Little Flea | 7" | Blue Beat | BB245 | 1964 | £6 | £12 | |
| Looking Down The Street | 7" | Blue Beat | BB281 | 1965 | £6 | £12 | Buster's Allstars B side |
| Louie Louie | 7" | Trojan | TR7865 | 1972 | £1.50 | £4 | |
| Man Who Knows | 7" | R&B | JB161 | 1964 | £5 | £10 | |
| Marching On | 7" | Banana | BA340 | 1971 | £1.50 | £4 | Roland Alphonso B side |
| Marching On | 7" | R&B | JB150 | 1964 | £5 | £10 | Lester Sterling B side |
| Matthew Mark | 7" | R&B | JB103 | 1963 | £5 | £10 | Don Drummond B side |
| Millie | 7" | Blue Beat | BB221 | 1964 | £6 | £12 | |
| Monkey Man | LP | Trojan | TBL107 | 1970 | £8 | £20 | |
| Monkey Man | 7" | Trojan | TR7711 | 1969 | £1.50 | £4 | |
| My Darling | 7" | Ska Beat | JB237 | 1966 | £5 | £10 | Charmers B side |
| My New Name | 7" | Island | WI213 | 1965 | £5 | £10 | |
| Never Grow Old | LP | R&B | JBL1113 | 1964 | £50 | £100 | |
| Never You Change | 7" | Island | WI200 | 1965 | £5 | £10 | |
| Original Golden Oldies Vol. 3 | LP | Prince Buster | PB11 | 1974 | £6 | £15 | |
| Peeping Tom | 7" | Summit | SUM8510 | 1970 | £1.50 | £4 | Beverley's Allstars B side |
| Pressure Drop | 7" | Pyramid | PYR6073 | 1969 | £2 | £5 | Beverley's Allstars B side |
| Pressure Drop | 7" | Trojan | TR7709 | 1969 | £1.50 | £4 | Beverley's Allstars B side |
| Redemption Song | 7" | Dynamic | DYN438 | 1972 | £1.50 | £4 | |
| Sailing On | 7" | Dragon | DRA1026 | 1974 | £1.50 | £4 | |
| Scare Him | 7" | Pyramid | PYR6064 | 1969 | £2.50 | £6 | |
| Schooldays | 7" | Pyramid | PYR6055 | 1968 | £4 | £8 | |
| Sensational Maytals | LP | Doctor Bird | DLM5003 | 1966 | £50 | £100 | |
| She's My Scorcher | 7" | Trojan | TR7757 | 1970 | £1.50 | £4 | |
| Shining Light | 7" | R&B | JB155 | 1964 | £5 | £10 | Lester Sterling B side |
| Sit Right Down | 7" | Dragon | DRA1007 | 1973 | £1.50 | £4 | |
| Ska War | 7" | Blue Beat | BB306 | 1965 | £6 | £12 | Skatalites B side |
| Struggle | 7" | Pyramid | PYR6043 | 1968 | £4 | £8 | Roland Alphonso B side |
| Sun, Moon And Stars | 7" | Trojan | TR7768 | 1970 | £1.50 | £4 | |
| Sweet And Dandy | 7" | Pyramid | PYR6074 | 1969 | £2 | £5 | |
| Tell Me The Reason | 7" | Island | WI219 | 1965 | £5 | £10 | Philip James B side |
| Time Tough | 7" | Dragon | DRA1024 | 1974 | £1.50 | £4 | |
| We Shall Overcome | 7" | Pyramid | PYR6052 | 1968 | £4 | £8 | Desmond Dekker B side |
| You Got Me Spinning | 7" | Blue Beat | BB270 | 1964 | £6 | £12 | |

# MAYTONES

| Title | Format | Label | Cat. No. | Year | | | Notes |
|---|---|---|---|---|---|---|---|
| Billy Goat | 7" | Blue Cat | BS149 | 1968 | £2.50 | £6 | |
| Botheration | 7" | Blue Cat | BS165 | 1969 | £2.50 | £6 | GG Rhythm Section B side |
| Copper Girl | 7" | Blue Cat | BS166 | 1969 | £2.50 | £6 | |
| Loving Reggae | 7" | Blue Cat | BS152 | 1969 | £2.50 | £6 | |

| Mi Nah Tek You Lick | 7" | Blue Cat | BS173 | 1969 | £2.50 | £6 | |

## MAZE

Ian Paice and Roger Evans of Maze were soon to experience a considerable change of fortune (albeit short-lived in the case of Evans), as they were recruited by Ritchie Blackmore as founder members of Deep Purple.

| Catari Catari | 7" | MGM | MGM1368 | 1967 | £20 | £40 | |
| Hello Stranger | 7" | Reaction | 591009 | 1966 | £37.50 | £75 | |
| In Special Danse Discotheque | 7" EP | Vogue | INT18136 | 1967 | £180 | £300 | *French, best auctioned* |

## MAZE (2)
| Armageddon | LP | MTA | 5012 | 1968 | £50 | £100 | US |
| Armageddon | LP | MTA | MTS5012 | 1969 | £37.50 | £75 | US |

## MC5

The revolutionary political stance of the MC5 (for Motor City 5) was backed up by the fact that the group's manager was John Sinclair, the leader of the White Panthers and hero of a John Lennon song, and by the music, which on the crucial first LP was aggressive and rowdy to an extent unprecedented in 1969. The group were the centre of controversy almost immediately – the live introduction to the music on the first album has singer Rob Tyner swearing at the audience, with the result that at least one US record shop chain refused to stock the record. In retaliation, the MC5 took out a press advertisement in which they encouraged fans to boycott the shops – and included an Elektra logo to suggest that the record company was behind the action. The MC5 were promptly dropped from the label and the album withdrawn – to be replaced by a version including the more acceptable replacement line, 'Kick out the jams, brothers and sisters!' Guitarists Wayne Kramer and the late Fred 'Sonic' Smith (husband of Patti Smith) have been frequent guests on a variety of albums since, their status as major influences on late seventies punk undisputed.

| Back In The USA | LP | Atlantic | 2400016 | 1970 | £8 | £20 | |
| Back In The USA | LP | Atlantic | K50346 | 1977 | £4 | £10 | |
| High Time | LP | Atlantic | K40223 | 1971 | £6 | £15 | |
| I Can Only Give You Everything | 7" | AMG | 1001 | 1966 | £15 | £30 | US |
| Kick Out The Jams | LP | Elektra | EKL74042 | 1969 | £20 | £40 | *mono* |
| Kick Out The Jams | LP | Elektra | EKS74042 | 1969 | £15 | £30 | |
| Kick Out The Jams | LP | Elektra | EKS74042 | 1969 | £37.50 | £75 | *. US, uncensored intro* |
| Kick Out The Jams | LP | Elektra | K42027 | 1977 | £4 | £10 | |
| Kick Out The Jams | 7" | Elektra | EKSN45056 | 1968 | £5 | £10 | |
| Looking At You | 7" | A-Square | 333 | 1967 | £15 | £30 | US |
| Ramblin' Rose | 7" | Elektra | EKSN45067 | 1969 | £5 | £10 | |

## MCALOON, SEAN & JOHN REA
| Drops Of Brandy | LP | Topic | 12TS287 | 1976 | £4 | £10 | |

## MCARTHUR, NEIL

Immediately after the demise of the Zombies, lead singer Colin Blunstone adopted a new stage name, Neil McArthur, and recorded a new version of the Zombies' best-known song, 'She's Not There'. The new interpretation is dramatically different from the original, even while keeping the same tempo. Few people were fooled by the name change, however, for Blunstone's breathy singing voice is very distinctive. Before long he was back using his own name.

| Don't Try To Explain | 7" | Deram | DM262 | 1969 | £1.50 | £4 | |
| It's Not Easy | 7" | Deram | DM275 | 1969 | £1.50 | £4 | |
| She's Not There | 7" | Deram | DM225 | 1969 | £1.50 | £4 | |

## MCAULEY, JACKIE
| Jackie McAuley | LP | Dawn | DNLS3023 | 1971 | £10 | £25 | |
| Rocking Shoes | 7" | Dawn | DNS1020 | 1971 | £1.50 | £4 | |

## MCAULIFF, LEON
| Cozy Inn | LP | ABC | (S)394 | 1961 | £6 | £15 | US |
| Take Off | LP | Dot | DLP3139 | 1958 | £6 | £15 | US |

## MCBEATH, JIMMY
| Come A'Ye Tramps And Hawkers | 7" EP | Collector | JES10 | 1961 | £2 | £5 | |
| Wild Rover No More | LP | Topic | 12T173 | 1967 | £4 | £10 | |

## MCBRIDE, OWEN
| Owen McBride | LP | Philo | 1005 | 1973 | £5 | £12 | US |

## MCCAIN, JERRY
| Homogenised Love | 7" | Python | P02 | 1969 | £10 | £20 | |

## MCCALL, CASH
| Anytime | 7" | Ember | EMBS173 | 1963 | £2.50 | £6 | |
| It's Wonderful | 7" | Chess | CRS8056 | 1967 | £2 | £5 | |
| Many Are The Words | 7" | Ember | EMBS204 | 1965 | £2.50 | £6 | |

## MCCALL, DARRELL
| My Kind Of Lovin' | 7" | Capitol | CL15196 | 1961 | £1.50 | £4 | |

## MCCALL, TOUSSAINT
| Nothing Takes The Place Of You | 7" | Pye | 7N25420 | 1967 | £4 | £8 | |

## MCCALLUM, DAVID
| Communication | 7" | Capitol | CL15439 | 1966 | £1.50 | £4 | |
| Music A Bit More Of Me | LP | Capitol | (S)T2498 | 1966 | £4 | £10 | |
| Music A Part Of Me | LP | Capitol | (S)T2432 | 1966 | £4 | £10 | |

## MCCALMANS
| Audience With The McCalmans | LP | RCA | LSA3179 | 1973 | £4 | £10 | |
| McCalmans Folk | LP | One Up | OU2161 | 1968 | £4 | £10 | |

| | | | | | | |
|---|---|---|---|---|---|---|
| Turn Again | LP | CBS | 64145 | 1970 £5 | £12 | |

## MCCALMON, IAN FOLK GROUP
| | | | | | | |
|---|---|---|---|---|---|---|
| All In One Hand | LP | Waverley | (S)ZLP2103 | 1968 £6 | £15 | |

## MCCANN, JIM
| | | | | | | |
|---|---|---|---|---|---|---|
| McCanned! | LP | Polydor | 2489053 | 1973 £20 | £40 | |

## MCCANN, LES
| | | | | | | |
|---|---|---|---|---|---|---|
| Bucket O'Grease | 7" | Mercury | MF973 | 1966 £2 | £5 | |
| Comment | LP | Atlantic | SD1547 | 1970 £6 | £15 | US |
| Invitation To Openness | LP | Atlantic | SD1603 | 1972 £6 | £15 | US |
| Live At Montreux | LP | Atlantic | SD2312 | 197– £6 | £15 | US double |
| Much Les | LP | Atlantic | 588176 | 1969 £6 | £15 | |
| Talk To The People | LP | Atlantic | SD1619 | 1973 £6 | £15 | US |
| Truth | LP | Vogue | LAE12238 | 1960 £6 | £15 | |

## MCCARTHY
| | | | | | | |
|---|---|---|---|---|---|---|
| In Purgatory | 7" | Wall Of Salmon | MAC001 | 1986 £6 | £12 | |

## MCCARTHY, KEITH
| | | | | | | |
|---|---|---|---|---|---|---|
| Everybody Rude Now | 7" | Coxsone | CS7014 | 1967 £5 | £10 | |

## MCCARTHY, LYN & GRAHAM
| | | | | | | |
|---|---|---|---|---|---|---|
| I Think It's Going To Rain | 7" | Columbia | DB8422 | 1968 £1.50 | £4 | |

## MCCARTHY, MARY
| | | | | | | |
|---|---|---|---|---|---|---|
| Easy Kind Of Love | 7" | CBS | 2832 | 1967 £1.50 | £4 | |

## MCCARTNEY, CECIL
| | | | | | | |
|---|---|---|---|---|---|---|
| Om | LP | Columbia | SX/SCX6283 | 1968 £5 | £12 | |

## MCCARTNEY, PAUL

Some of Paul McCartney's more unusual records have been released under pseudonyms – The Country Hams, Suzy and the Redstripes, Percy 'Thrills' Thrillington, and the Fireman. Rarities issued under his own name include a series of lavish packages promoting various of his album releases. Most collectable of these is the picture disc version of *Back To The Egg*, which has acquired legendary status. (The regular issue of the album is, of course, quite common and not at all collectable.) The rare version of the Apple single R5999, it should be mentioned, has 'Sally G' as the A side; there is nothing special about copies with 'Junior's Farm' on the A side. The first edition of the *Price Guide* included the LP *CHOBA B CCCP* in its McCartney section. This was a collection of rock 'n' roll cover versions that Paul McCartney decided to issue in Russia only. The first copies to be seen in the UK were eagerly snapped up by collectors at a much higher price than they were worth. Over the succeeding months more and more copies turned up and the prices took a nose-dive – today one can hardly give copies of the record away. The album has now been issued in the UK, but on CD only.

| | | | | | | |
|---|---|---|---|---|---|---|
| All My Trials | CD-s | Parlophone | CDRX6278 | 1990 £2 | £5 | |
| Back To The Egg | LP | Parlophone | PCTC257 | 1979 £100 | £200 | promo, boxed |
| Back To The Egg | LP | Parlophone | PCTCP257 | 1979 £875 | £1250 | promo picture disc |
| Band On The Run | LP | Apple | | 197– £10 | £25 | yellow vinyl |
| Band On The Run | LP | Capitol | SEAX11901 | 1978 £15 | £30 | US picture disc |
| Band On The Run | LP | Columbia | HC36482 | 1981 £8 | £20 | US audiophile |
| Band On The Run Interview Album | LP | Apple | SPRO2955/6 | 1974 £20 | £40 | US promo |
| Biker Like An Icon | CD-s | Parlophone | CDRDJ6347 | 1993 £25 | £50 | promo only |
| Birthday | CD-s | Parlophone | CDR6271 | 1990 £2 | £5 | |
| Boxed Set Of 9 Promo Singles | 7" | Parlophone | PMBOX1 | 1986 £75 | £150 | numbered and signed |
| Brung To Ewe By Ram | LP | Apple | SPRO6210 | 1971 £15 | £30 | US 1 sided interview promo |
| C'mon People | CD-s | Parlophone | CDRDJ6338 | 1993 £6 | £15 | promo only |
| Family Way | LP | Decca | LK/SKL4847 | 1966 £50 | £100 | with George Martin |
| Figure Of Eight | CD-s | Parlophone | CD3R6235 | 1989 £2 | £5 | 3" single, card sleeve |
| Figure Of Eight | CD-s | Parlophone | CDRS6235 | 1989 £2 | £5 | card sleeve |
| Flowers In The Dirt | CD | Parlophone | CDPCSD106 | 1989 £20 | £40 | promo in A4 box |
| Flowers In The Dirt | CD | Parlophone | CDPCSDX106 | 1989 £20 | £40 | with 3" CD, postcards, poster |
| Getting Closer | 7" | Parlophone | R6027 | 1979 £2.50 | £6 | picture sleeve |
| Give Ireland Back To The Irish | 7" | Apple | R5936 | 1972 £2.50 | £6 | shamrock sleeve |
| Good Sign | 12" | Parlophone | GOOD1 | 1989 £20 | £40 | promo |
| I've Had Enough | 7" | Parlophone | R6020 | 1978 £2.50 | £6 | picture sleeve |
| Mary Had A Little Lamb | 7" | Apple | R5949 | 1972 £2 | £5 | picture sleeve |
| McCartney | r-reel | Apple | TAPMC7102 | 1970 £20 | £40 | mono |
| McCartney | r-reel | Apple | TDPCS7102 | 1970 £8 | £20 | stereo |
| McCartney | LP | Apple | PCS7102 | 1970 £20 | £40 | promo with interview sheets |
| McCartney | CD | DCC | GZS1029 | 1992 £6 | £15 | US audiophile |
| McCartney Interview | LP | Columbia | A2S821 | 1980 £50 | £100 | US promo double with book |
| McCartney Rocks | CD | Capitol | DPRO79987 | 1990 £25 | £50 | US promo |
| Mull Of Kintyre | 7" | Capitol | R6018 | 1977 £6 | £12 | blue vinyl test pressing |
| My Brave Face | CD-s | Parlophone | CDR6213 | 1989 £2 | £5 | |
| No More Lonely Nights | 12" | Parlophone | 12PR6080 | 1984 £2.50 | £6 | picture disc |
| No More Lonely Nights (Arthur Baker Remix) | 12" | Parlophone | 12RA6080 | 1984 £10 | £25 | |
| No More Lonely Nights (Mole Mix) | 12" | Parlophone | 12R6080DJ | 1984 £50 | £100 | 1 sided promo |
| Off The Ground | CD | Parlophone | CDPCSD125 | 1992 £20 | £40 | promo box set, with cassette and press kit |
| Off The Ground Complete Works | CD | EMI | | 1993 £10 | £25 | German double CD |
| Old Siam, Sir | 7" | Parlophone | R6026 | 1979 £2.50 | £6 | picture sleeve |
| Once Upon A Long Ago | CD-s | Parlophone | | 1987 £30 | £60 | promo, different sleeve |

| Title | Format | Label | Catalog | Year | | | Notes |
|---|---|---|---|---|---|---|---|
| One Upon A Long Ago | CD-s | Parlophone | CDR6170 | 1987 | £3 | £8 | |
| One Upon A Long Ago (Extended Version) | 12" | Parlophone | 12RX6170 | 1987 | £2.50 | £6 | |
| Party | 12" | Parlophone | 12RDJ6238 | 1989 | £15 | £30 | promo |
| Paul Is Live | CD | Parlophone | PMLIVE1 | 1993 | £25 | £50 | 5 track sampler, promo only |
| Paul McCartney & Bob Harris Talk About Buddy Holly | LP | MCA | BH1 | 1983 | £10 | £25 | US promo |
| Paul McCartney Collection | CD | Parlophone | CDPMCOLDJ1 | 1993 | £20 | £40 | 18 track sampler, promo only |
| Press | 10" | Parlophone | 10R6133 | 1986 | £3 | £8 | |
| Put It There | CD-s | Parlophone | CDR6246 | 1990 | £2 | £5 | |
| Sally G | 7" | Apple | R5999 | 1975 | £50 | £100 | .. demo, Junior's Farm on B side |
| Spies Like Us | 7" | Parlophone | RP6118 | 1985 | £5 | £10 | shaped picture disc |
| Spies Like Us | 12" | Parlophone | 12RP6118 | 1985 | £2.50 | £6 | picture disc |
| Temporary Secretary | 7" | Parlophone | R6039 | 1980 | £10 | £20 | demo only |
| Temporary Secretary | 12" | Parlophone | 12R6039 | 1980 | £5 | £12 | |
| This One | CD-s | Parlophone | CDR6223 | 1989 | £2 | £5 | |
| This One | 7" | Parlophone | RX6223 | 1989 | £2 | £5 | envelope pack with 6 cards |
| Tripping The Live Fantastic | CD | Parlophone | | 1990 | £15 | £30 | French double with bonus birthday CD single |
| Tug Of War | LP | Parlophone | PCTC259 | 1982 | £50 | £100 | promo, press pack, cassette interview |
| Venus And Mars | CD | DCC | GZS1067 | 1994 | £6 | £15 | US audiophile |
| We All Stand Together | 7" | Parlophone | RP6086 | 1984 | £4 | £8 | shaped picture disc |
| Wings Over America | LP | Capitol | SWCO11593 | 1977 | £30 | £60 | US promo, red, white and blue vinyl |
| Wonderful Christmastime | 7" | Parlophone | R6029 | 1979 | £2.50 | £6 | picture sleeve |

## MCCHURCH SOUNDROOM

| Title | Format | Label | Catalog | Year | | | Notes |
|---|---|---|---|---|---|---|---|
| Delusion | LP | Pilz | 20211037 | 1971 | £15 | £30 | German |

## MCCLINTON, DELBERT

| Title | Format | Label | Catalog | Year | | | Notes |
|---|---|---|---|---|---|---|---|
| Hully Gully | 7" | Decca | F11541 | 1962 | £2 | £5 | |

## MCCLURE, BOBBY

| Title | Format | Label | Catalog | Year | | | Notes |
|---|---|---|---|---|---|---|---|
| Peak Of Love | 7" | Chess | CRS8048 | 1966 | £7.50 | £15 | |

## MCCLURE, CHRIS

| Title | Format | Label | Catalog | Year | | | Notes |
|---|---|---|---|---|---|---|---|
| Hazy People | 7" | Polydor | 56227 | 1968 | £2 | £5 | |

## MCCONNELL, CATHAL

| Title | Format | Label | Catalog | Year | | | Notes |
|---|---|---|---|---|---|---|---|
| Irish Jubilee | LP | Topic | 12TS290 | 1976 | £4 | £10 | with Robin Morton |
| On Lough Ernie's Shore | LP | Topic | 12TS377 | 1978 | £4 | £10 | |

## MCCOOK, TOMMY

| Title | Format | Label | Catalog | Year | | | Notes |
|---|---|---|---|---|---|---|---|
| Avengers | 7" | Unity | UN506 | 1969 | £1.50 | £4 | . Laurel Aitken B side |
| Black Coffee | 7" | Trojan | TR7706 | 1969 | £1.50 | £4 | Vic Taylor B side |
| Bridge View | 7" | R&B | JB163 | 1964 | £5 | £10 | .. Naomi & Co B side |
| Buck And The Preacher | 7" | Pyramid | PYR7002 | 1973 | £1.50 | £4 | |
| Exodus | 7" | Port-O-Jam | PJ4001 | 1964 | £5 | £10 | Lee Perry B side |
| Indian Love Call | 7" | Doctor Bird | DB1053 | 1966 | £5 | £10 | Owen & Leon B side |
| Jam Session | 7" | Doctor Bird | DB1058 | 1966 | £5 | £10 | Lloyd & Glen B side |
| Jerk Time | 7" | Rio | R100 | 1966 | £4 | £8 | Uniques B side |
| Junior Jive | 7" | Island | WI124 | 1963 | £5 | £10 | . Horace Seaton B side |
| Lock Jaw | 7" | Trojan | TR7717 | 1969 | £1.50 | £4 | Yardbrooms B side |
| Love Is A Treasure | 7" | Duke | DU161 | 1973 | £1.50 | £4 | |
| Moving | 7" | Treasure Isle | TI7042 | 1968 | £5 | £10 | Silvertones B side |
| Music Is My Occupation | 7" | Ska Beat | JB179 | 1965 | £5 | £10 | Mellodites B side |
| My Business | 7" | Ska Beat | JB178 | 1965 | £5 | £10 | Don Drummond B side |
| One Two Three | 7" | Island | WI3047 | 1967 | £5 | £10 | Treasure Isle Boys B side |
| Our Man Flint | 7" | Treasure Isle | TI7039 | 1968 | £5 | £10 | Silvertones B side |
| Out Of Space | 7" | Rio | R101 | 1966 | £4 | £8 | Uniques B side |
| Rub It Down | 7" | Technique | TE927 | 1973 | £1.50 | £4 | |
| Saboo | 7" | Island | WI3049 | 1967 | £5 | £10 | Movin Brothers B side |
| Saboo | 7" | Treasure Isle | TI7018 | 1967 | £5 | £10 | Moving Brothers B side |
| Saints | 7" | Trojan | TR657 | 1969 | £1.50 | £4 | Soul Ofrous B side |
| Sampson | 7" | R&B | JB139 | 1964 | £5 | £10 | Roy & Annette B side |
| Ska Jam | 7" | Rio | R103 | 1966 | £4 | £8 | |
| Two For One | 7" | Black Swan | WI422 | 1964 | £5 | £10 | Lascelles Perkins B side |
| Venus | 7" | Treasure Isle | TI7032 | 1968 | £5 | £10 | |

## MCCOOK, TOMMY & STRANGER COLE

| Title | Format | Label | Catalog | Year | | | Notes |
|---|---|---|---|---|---|---|---|
| Last Flight To Reggae City | 7" | Unity | UN501 | 1968 | £2.50 | £6 | Junior Smith B side |

## MCCORMICK, GAYLE

| Title | Format | Label | Catalog | Year | | | Notes |
|---|---|---|---|---|---|---|---|
| Flesh And Blood | LP | MCA | MUPS482 | 1972 | £6 | £15 | |

## MCCORMICK BROTHERS

| Title | Format | Label | Catalog | Year | | | Notes |
|---|---|---|---|---|---|---|---|
| Authentic Bluegrass Hits | 7" EP | Hickory | LPE1509 | 1966 | £4 | £8 | |
| Red Hen Boogie | 7" | Polydor | NH66986 | 1963 | £15 | £30 | |

## MCCOY, BUDD
| | | | | | | | |
|---|---|---|---|---|---|---|---|
| Hiawatha | 7" | RCA | RCA1106 | 1959 | £1.50 | £4 | |

## MCCOY, CLYDE
| | | | | | | | |
|---|---|---|---|---|---|---|---|
| Dancing To The Blues | 7" EP | Mercury | MEP9513 | 1957 | £2.50 | £6 | |

## MCCOY, JOE
| | | | | | | | |
|---|---|---|---|---|---|---|---|
| One In A Hundred | 7" | Collector | JDL81 | 1959 | £10 | £20 | |

## MCCOY, VIOLA
| | | | | | | | |
|---|---|---|---|---|---|---|---|
| 1923–1927 | 10" LP | Ristic | LP27 | 195– | £20 | £40 | |

## MCCOYS
| | | | | | | | |
|---|---|---|---|---|---|---|---|
| Beat The Clock | 7" EP | Bang | 770005 | 1966 | £10 | £20 | French |
| Don't Worry Mother | 7" | Immediate | IM028 | 1966 | £1.50 | £4 | |
| Fever | 7" EP | Atlantic | 750007 | 1965 | £10 | £20 | French |
| Fever | 7" | Immediate | IM021 | 1965 | £1.50 | £4 | |
| Hang On Sloopy | LP | Immediate | IMLP001 | 1965 | £10 | £25 | |
| Hang On Sloopy | 7" EP | Barclay | 70864 | 1965 | £12.50 | £25 | French, B side by Strangeloves |
| Hang On Sloopy | 7" EP | Barclay | 70864 | 1965 | £15 | £30 | French, embossed sleeve, B side by Strangeloves |
| Hang On Sloopy | 7" | Immediate | IM001 | 1965 | £1.50 | £4 | |
| Human Ball | LP | Mercury | SR61207 | 1969 | £5 | £12 | US |
| I Got To Go Back | 7" | Immediate | IM046 | 1967 | £2 | £5 | |
| Infinite McCoys | LP | Mercury | SR61163 | 1968 | £6 | £15 | US |
| Jesse Brady | 7" | Mercury | MF1067 | 1968 | £1.50 | £4 | |
| McCoys Vol. 1 | 7" EP | Immediate | IMEP002 | 1966 | £7.50 | £15 | |
| McCoys Vol. 2 | 7" EP | Immediate | IMEP003 | 1966 | £7.50 | £15 | |
| Runaway | 7" | Immediate | IM034 | 1966 | £1.50 | £4 | |
| Say Those Magic Words | 7" | London | HLZ10154 | 1967 | £6 | £12 | |
| So Good | 7" | Immediate | IM037 | 1966 | £1.50 | £4 | |
| Up And Down | 7" | Immediate | IM029 | 1966 | £1.50 | £4 | |
| You Make Me Feel So Good | LP | Bang | BLP(S)213 | 1966 | £15 | £30 | US |

## MCCRACKLIN, JIMMY
| | | | | | | | |
|---|---|---|---|---|---|---|---|
| Christmas Time | 7" | Outasite | 45120 | 1966 | £10 | £20 | |
| Every Night Every Day | 7" | Liberty | LIB66094 | 1965 | £1.50 | £4 | |
| Every Night, Every Day | LP | Imperial | LP9285/12285 | 1965 | £5 | £12 | US |
| How Do You Like Your Love | 7" | Minit | MLF11003 | 1968 | £2 | £5 | |
| I Got Eyes For You | 7" | R&B | MRB5001 | 1965 | £5 | £10 | |
| I Just Gotta Know | LP | Stax | 8506 | 1963 | £10 | £25 | US |
| Jimmy McCracklin | 7" EP | Vocalion | VEP170160 | 1965 | £25 | £50 | |
| Jimmy McCracklin Sings | LP | Chess | 1464 | 1961 | £15 | £30 | US |
| Just Got To Know | 7" | Top Rank | JAR617 | 1962 | £5 | £10 | |
| My Answer | LP | Imperial | LP9306/12306 | 1966 | £5 | £12 | US |
| New Soul | LP | Imperial | LP9316/12316 | 1966 | £5 | £12 | US |
| Pretty Little Sweet Thing | 7" | Minit | MLF11009 | 1968 | £2 | £5 | |
| Think | LP | Imperial | LP9297/12297 | 1965 | £5 | £12 | US |
| Think | 7" | Liberty | LIB66129 | 1966 | £1.50 | £4 | |
| Walk | 7" | London | HL7035 | 1958 | £10 | £20 | export |
| Walk | 7" | London | HLM8598 | 1958 | £20 | £40 | |

## MCCULLOCH, DANNY
| | | | | | | | |
|---|---|---|---|---|---|---|---|
| Wings Of A Man | LP | Capitol | E(S)T174 | 1969 | £6 | £15 | |

## MCCULLOCH, GORDEANNA & THE CLUTHA
| | | | | | | | |
|---|---|---|---|---|---|---|---|
| Sheath And Knife | LP | Topic | 12TS370 | 1978 | £4 | £10 | |

## MCCULLOCH, IAN
| | | | | | | | |
|---|---|---|---|---|---|---|---|
| Unravelled | CD | Sire | | 1992 | £8 | £20 | US promo compilation |

## MCCURDY, ED
| | | | | | | | |
|---|---|---|---|---|---|---|---|
| Box Of Dalliance | LP | Transatlantic | XTRA1048 | 1966 | £10 | £25 | 2 LP boxed set |

## MCCURN, GEORGE
| | | | | | | | |
|---|---|---|---|---|---|---|---|
| I'm Just A Country Boy | 7" | London | HLH9705 | 1963 | £1.50 | £4 | |

## MCCUTCHEON, JOHN
| | | | | | | | |
|---|---|---|---|---|---|---|---|
| Wind That Shakes The Barley | LP | June Appal | JA014 | 1977 | £4 | £10 | US |

## MCDANIEL, MAISIE
| | | | | | | | |
|---|---|---|---|---|---|---|---|
| Country Style | 7" EP | Fontana | TFE17398 | 1962 | £2 | £5 | |
| Meet Maisie McDaniel | 7" EP | Fontana | TE17397 | 1963 | £2 | £5 | |

## MCDANIELS, GENE
| | | | | | | | |
|---|---|---|---|---|---|---|---|
| Change Of Mood | 7" EP | Liberty | LEP2054 | 1962 | £7.50 | £15 | |
| Chip Chip | 7" | Liberty | LIB55405 | 1962 | £1.50 | £4 | |
| Gene McDaniels | 7" EP | London | REG1298 | 1961 | £15 | £30 | |
| Gene McDaniels Sings Movie Memories | LP | Liberty | LRP3204/LST7204 | 1962 | £8 | £20 | US |
| Hit After Hit | LP | Liberty | LRP3258/LST7258 | 1962 | £8 | £20 | US |
| Hundred Pounds Of Clay | LP | London | HAG2384/ SAHG6184 | 1961 | £15 | £30 | |
| Hundred Pounds Of Clay | 7" | London | HLG9319 | 1961 | £1.50 | £4 | |
| In Times Like These | LP | Liberty | LRP3146/LST7146 | 1960 | £10 | £25 | US |
| In Times Like These | 7" | Liberty | LIB55723 | 1964 | £2 | £5 | |

| | | | | | | | |
|---|---|---|---|---|---|---|---|
| It's A Lonely Town | 7" | Liberty | LIB55597 | 1963 | £2 | £5 | |
| Point Of No Return | 7" | Liberty | LIB55480 | 1962 | £1.50 | £4 | |
| Sometimes I'm Happy | LP | Liberty | LBY1003 | 1962 | £8 | £20 | |
| Spanish Lace | LP | Liberty | (S)LBY1128 | 1963 | £8 | £20 | |
| Tear | 7" | London | HLG9396 | 1961 | £1.50 | £4 | |
| Tower Of Strength | LP | Liberty | LBY1021 | 1962 | £8 | £20 | |
| Tower Of Strength | 7" | London | HLG9448 | 1961 | £1.50 | £4 | |
| Walk With A Winner | 7" | Liberty | LIB55805 | 1965 | £20 | £40 | |
| Wonderful World Of Gene McDaniels | LP | Liberty | LRP3311/LST7311 | 1963 | £6 | £15 | US |

## MCDEVITT, CHAS

| | | | | | | | |
|---|---|---|---|---|---|---|---|
| Across The Bridge | 7" | Oriole | CB1405 | 1958 | £2 | £5 | |
| Face In The Rain | 7" | Oriole | CB1386 | 1957 | £2 | £5 | |
| Forever | 7" | Top Rank | JAR338 | 1960 | £1.50 | £4 | |
| It Takes A Worried Man | 7" | Oriole | CB1357 | 1957 | £2.50 | £6 | |
| Johnny O | 7" | Oriole | CB1403 | 1958 | £2 | £5 | |
| Juke Box Jumble | 7" | Oriole | CB1457 | 1958 | £2 | £5 | |
| Naughty But Nice | 7" EP | Columbia | SEG8471 | 1965 | £2 | £5 | |
| Sing Sing Sing | 7" | Oriole | CB1395 | 1957 | £2 | £5 | |
| Six Big Folk Hits | 7" EP | Columbia | SEG8468 | 1965 | £2 | £5 | |
| Teenage Letter | 7" | Oriole | CB1511 | 1959 | £1.50 | £4 | Shirley Douglas B side |

## MCDEVITT, CHAS & NANCY WHISKEY

| | | | | | | | |
|---|---|---|---|---|---|---|---|
| Chas And Nancy | 7" EP | Oriole | EP7002 | 1957 | £6 | £12 | |
| Freight Train | 7" | Oriole | CB1352 | 1957 | £4 | £8 | |
| Greenback Dollar | 7" | Oriole | CB1371 | 1957 | £4 | £8 | |

## MCDONALD, ALISTAIR

| | | | | | | | |
|---|---|---|---|---|---|---|---|
| Battle Ballads | LP | Major Minor | MMLP51 | 1969 | £4 | £10 | |

## MCDONALD, COUNTRY JOE

| | | | | | | | |
|---|---|---|---|---|---|---|---|
| Joe McDonald | LP | Custom Fidelity | | 1965 | £700 | £1000 | US, plain sleeve, best auctioned |

## MCDONALD, GAVIN

| | | | | | | | |
|---|---|---|---|---|---|---|---|
| Lines | LP | Regal Zonophone | SLRZ1027 | 1972 | £4 | £10 | |

## MCDONALD, SHELAGH

| | | | | | | | |
|---|---|---|---|---|---|---|---|
| Shelagh McDonald | LP | B&C | CAS1019 | 1970 | £8 | £20 | |
| Stargazer | LP | B&C | CAS1043 | 1971 | £10 | £25 | |

## MCDONALD, SKEETS

| | | | | | | | |
|---|---|---|---|---|---|---|---|
| Country's Best | LP | Capitol | T1179 | 1959 | £8 | £20 | US |
| Fallen Angel | 7" | Capitol | CL14566 | 1956 | £10 | £20 | |
| Going Steady With The Blues | LP | Capitol | T1040 | 1958 | £15 | £30 | US |
| Going Steady With The Blues | 7" EP | Capitol | EAP11040 | 1959 | £15 | £30 | |

## MCDONALD & GILES

| | | | | | | | |
|---|---|---|---|---|---|---|---|
| McDonald & Giles | LP | Island | ILPS9126 | 1970 | £8 | £20 | pink label |

## MCDOWELL, MISSISSIPPI FRED

| | | | | | | | |
|---|---|---|---|---|---|---|---|
| 1904–72 | LP | Xtra | XTRA1136 | 1974 | £4 | £10 | |
| Going Down South | LP | Polydor | 236278 | 1969 | £4 | £10 | |
| I Do Not Play No Rock 'n' Roll | LP | Capitol | EST409 | 1970 | £5 | £12 | |
| Long Way From Home | LP | CBS | 63735 | 1970 | £4 | £10 | |
| Mississippi Delta Blues | LP | Fontana | 688806ZL | 1966 | £4 | £10 | |
| My Home Is In The Delta | LP | Bounty | BY6022 | 1966 | £4 | £10 | |

## MCDUFF, BROTHER JACK

| | | | | | | | |
|---|---|---|---|---|---|---|---|
| Change Is Gonna Come | LP | Atlantic | 587030 | 1966 | £6 | £15 | |
| Concert McDuff | LP | Stateside | SL10165 | 1966 | £6 | £15 | |
| Double Barrelled Soul | LP | Atlantic | SD1498 | 1968 | £6 | £15 | US, with David Newman |
| Down Home Style | LP | Blue Note | BST84322 | 1969 | £5 | £12 | |
| Dynamic! | LP | Stateside | SL10101 | 1964 | £6 | £15 | |
| Live At The Jazz Workshop | LP | Stateside | SL10121 | 1965 | £6 | £15 | |
| Live At The Jazz Workshop | LP | Transatlantic | PR7286 | 1968 | £5 | £12 | |
| Live! | LP | Stateside | SL10060 | 1964 | £6 | £15 | |
| Moon Rappin' | LP | Blue Note | BST84334 | 1969 | £5 | £12 | |
| Prelude | LP | Stateside | SL10142 | 1965 | £6 | £15 | |
| Screamin' | LP | Transatlantic | PR7259 | 1967 | £6 | £15 | |
| Silk And Soul | LP | Transatlantic | PR7404 | 1967 | £6 | £15 | |
| To Seek A New Home | LP | Blue Note | BST84348 | 1970 | £4 | £10 | |
| Who Knows What Tomorrow Brings | LP | Blue Note | BST84358 | 1970 | £4 | £10 | |

## MCELROY, WILLIE

| | | | | | | | |
|---|---|---|---|---|---|---|---|
| Fair Of Enniskillen | LP | Outlet | OAS3001 | 1977 | £5 | £12 | Irish |

## MCEVOY, JOHNNY

| | | | | | | | |
|---|---|---|---|---|---|---|---|
| Sounds Like Johnny McEvoy | LP | Halpix | 117 | 197– | £6 | £15 | |

## MCEWEN, RORY & ALEX & ISLA CAMERON

| | | | | | | | |
|---|---|---|---|---|---|---|---|
| Folksong Jubilee | LP | HMV | CLP1220 | 1958 | £30 | £60 | |

## MCFADDEN, BOB

| | | | | | | | |
|---|---|---|---|---|---|---|---|
| Beat Generation | 7" | Coral | Q72378 | 1959 | £1.50 | £4 | |

## MCGARRITY, LOU
Salute To Louis ........................................ 10" LP Parlophone ...... PMD1063 .............. 1958 £4 .......... £10 ...............................

## MCGEAR, MIKE
After various jokey performances as a member of the Scaffold and of Grimms, the solo recordings by Mike McGear find him in a relatively serious singer-songwriting mode. *McGear* is of considerable interest to Paul McCartney collectors as the album is virtually a Wings album with Mike McGear as guest star. McGear and McCartney are, of course, brothers.

McGear ........................................... LP ...... Centre Labs ..... ........................... 198– £10 ......... £25 . 6 tracks, numbered & autographed

## MCGEEGAN, PAT
Chance Of A Lifetime .......................... 7" ...... Emerald .......... MD1096 ................ 1968 £1.50 ........ £4 ..............................

## MCGHEE, BROWNIE
| | | | | | | | | |
|---|---|---|---|---|---|---|---|---|
| At The Bunkhouse | LP | Smash | MGS27067 | 1965 | £5 | £12 | | US |
| Black Country Blues | LP | London | LTZC15144 | 1958 | £8 | £20 | | |
| Blues | 10" LP | Folkways | 2030 | 1955 | £6 | £15 | | US |
| Bluest | 7" EP. | Pye | NJE1060 | 1957 | £2 | £5 | with Dave Lee | |
| Brownie McGhee | LP | Sharp | 2003 | | £10 | £25 | | US |
| Me And My Dog | 78 | Melodisc | 1127 | 1951 | £3 | £8 | | |

## MCGHEE, HOWARD
| | | | | | | | | |
|---|---|---|---|---|---|---|---|---|
| Howard McGhee And Milt Jackson | LP | London | LTZC15062 | 1957 | £10 | £25 | | |
| Howard McGhee Sextet | 10" LP | Vogue | LDE008 | 1952 | £37.50 | £75 | | |
| Jazz Concert West Coast | LP | London | LTZC15045 | 1957 | £8 | £20 | | |
| Maggie's Back In Town | LP | Contemporary | LAC12303 | 1961 | £5 | £12 | | |
| Return Of Howard McGhee | LP | London | LTZN15011 | 1956 | £15 | £30 | | |
| Together Again! | LP | Contemporary | LAC12291 | 1961 | £6 | £15 | with Teddy Edwards | |
| With The Frank Hunter Orchestra | LP | London | HAN2033 | 1957 | £15 | £30 | | |

## MCGHEE, STICKS & JOHN LEE HOOKER
Highway Of Blues ............................ LP ...... Audio Lab ....... AL1520 ................ 1959 £20 ......... £40 ...................... US

## MCGINN, MATT
| | | | | | | | | |
|---|---|---|---|---|---|---|---|---|
| Little Ticks Of Time | LP | XTRA | XTRA1078 | 1969 | £4 | £10 | | |
| Matt McGinn Again | LP | XTRA | XTRA1057 | 1968 | £5 | £12 | | |

## MCGOUGH, ROGER
Summer With Monika ............................ LP ...... Island .............. ILPS9551 ............ 1978 £4 ......... £10 ...............................

## MCGOUGH, ROGER & BRIAN PATTEN
British Poets Of Our Time ...................... LP ...... Argo .............. ZPL1190 ........... 1975 £8 ......... £20 ...............................

## MCGOUGH & MCGEAR
It would be pleasing to imagine that the high value of the album recorded by two-thirds of the Scaffold was in some way a tribute to the songwriting of Mike McGear or the inimitable poetic talents of Roger McGough. Sadly, the value has more to do with the cast of supporting musicians used on this poor-selling album, which includes Jimi Hendrix.

| | | | | | | | | |
|---|---|---|---|---|---|---|---|---|
| McGough & McGear | LP | Parlophone | PCS7047 | 1968 | £100 | £200 | | |
| McGough & McGear | LP | Parlophone | PMC7047 | 1968 | £150 | £250 | mono | |
| McGough & McGear | CD | Parlophone | CDP7918772 | 1990 | £5 | £12 | | |

## MCGRATH, BAT
Introducing ............................................. LP ...... Epic ................. 26499 ................ 1969 £5 ......... £12 ...................... US

## MCGREGOR, CHRIS
The rare *South African Cold Castle Jazz Festival* is the earliest recording to feature the musicians who came to Britain with pianist Chris McGregor, but playing in different groups. After the festival McGregor invited them to join his own Blue Notes. The music played by these South African exiles (who were unable to function as a mixed-race group in their home country) is an exciting blend of modern jazz and kwela. It is heard to best effect on the big band Brotherhood of Breath recordings, but much of the distinctive sound is intact on the small group records. In addition to those listed below, there are also listings of collectable records by other members of McGregor's Blue Notes – Dudu Pukwana, Mongezi Feza, and Louis Moholo.

| | | | | | | | | |
|---|---|---|---|---|---|---|---|---|
| African Sound | LP | Gallotone | | 1963 | £75 | £150 | South African | |
| Brotherhood | LP | RCA | SF8269 | 1972 | £15 | £30 | | |
| Brotherhood Of Breath | LP | Neon | NE2 | 1971 | £20 | £40 | | |
| Cold Castle National Jazz Festival | LP | Gallotone | NSL1010 | 1963 | £75 | £150 | South African, with other artists | |
| In His Good Time | LP | Ogun | OG521 | 1979 | £5 | £12 | | |
| Kwela | LP | 77 | | 1968 | £50 | £100 | | |
| Live At Willisau | LP | Ogun | OG100 | 1974 | £6 | £15 | | |
| Up To Earth | LP | Polydor | 583072 | 1968 | £100 | £200 | test pressing | |
| Very Urgent | LP | Polydor | 184137 | 1968 | £25 | £50 | | |

## MCGRIFF, EDNA
Edna McGriff 's The Name .................. 7" EP. Gala ................ 45XP1014 .............. 196– £2.50 ........ £6 ...............................

## MCGRIFF, JIMMY
| | | | | | | | | |
|---|---|---|---|---|---|---|---|---|
| All About My Girl | 7" | Sue | WI303 | 1963 | £6 | £12 | | |
| At The Apollo | LP | London | HAC8242 | 1966 | £8 | £20 | | |
| Bag Full Of Soul | LP | United Artists | (S)ULP1158 | 1966 | £5 | £12 | | |
| Big Band | LP | United Artists | (S)ULP1170 | 1968 | £5 | £12 | | |
| Black Pearl | LP | Blue Note | BST84374 | 1970 | £4 | £10 | | |
| Blues For Mr. Jimmy | LP | London | HAC8247 | 1966 | £8 | £20 | | |
| Electric Funk | LP | Blue Note | BST84350 | 1970 | £6 | £15 | | |

| | | | | | | | |
|---|---|---|---|---|---|---|---|
| Gospel Time | LP | Sue | ILP908 | 1964 £15 | £30 | |
| Greatest Organ Hits | LP | United Artists | UAS29010 | 1969 £5 | £12 | |
| I've Got A Woman | LP | Sue | ILP907 | 1964 £15 | £30 | |
| I've Got A Woman | 7" | Sue | WI317 | 1964 £6 | £12 | |
| Last Minute | 7" | Sue | WI310 | 1964 £6 | £12 | |
| Round Midnight | 7" | Sue | WI333 | 1964 £5 | £10 | |
| See See Rider | 7" | United Artists | UP1170 | 1966 £1.50 | £4 | |
| Something To Listen To | LP | Blue Note | BST84364 | 1970 £4 | £10 | |
| Worm | LP | United Artists | UAS29004 | 1968 £5 | £12 | |
| Worm | 7" | United Artists | UP35025 | 1969 £2 | £5 | |

## MCGUFFIE, BILL

| | | | | | | |
|---|---|---|---|---|---|---|
| Concerto For Boogie | 7" | Parlophone | MSP6040 | 1953 £1.50 | £4 | |
| Fugue For Thought (Daleks:Invasion Earth) | 7" | Philips | BF1550 | 1967 £10 | £20 | |
| Latin Overtones | LP | Philips | LPS16001 | 1968 £8 | £20 | |

## MCGUINN, ROGER

| | | | | | | |
|---|---|---|---|---|---|---|
| Airplay Anthology | LP | Columbia | AS353 | 1975 £6 | £15 | US promo |

## MCGUINNESS FLINT

| | | | | | | |
|---|---|---|---|---|---|---|
| McGuinness Flint | LP | Capitol | EAST22625 | 1970 £4 | £10 | |

## MCGUIRE, BARRY

| | | | | | | |
|---|---|---|---|---|---|---|
| Eve Of Destruction | LP | RCA | RD7751 | 1965 £4 | £10 | |
| Eve Of Destruction | 7" EP | RCA | 86900 | 1965 £6 | £12 | French |
| Eve Of Destruction | 7" | RCA | RCA1469 | 1965 £1.50 | £4 | |
| Masters Of War | 7" | RCA | RCA1638 | 1967 £1.50 | £4 | |
| This Precious Time | LP | Dunhill | D50005 | 1966 £6 | £15 | .. US, with Mamas & Papas |
| This Precious Time | 7" EP | RCA | 86904 | 1966 £4 | £8 | French |
| World's Last Private Citizen | LP | Dunhill | D50033 | 1968 £4 | £10 | US |

## MCGUIRE SISTERS

| | | | | | | |
|---|---|---|---|---|---|---|
| Beginning To Miss You | 7" | Vogue Coral | Q72265 | 1957 £1.50 | £4 | |
| By Request | 10" LP | Coral | CRL56123 | 1955 £8 | £20 | US |
| Children's Holiday | LP | Vogue Coral | LVA9072 | 1957 £6 | £15 | |
| Delilah Jones | 7" | Vogue Coral | Q72161 | 1956 £2.50 | £6 | |
| Ding Dong | 7" | Vogue Coral | Q72327 | 1958 £1.50 | £4 | |
| Do You Remember When? | LP | Vogue Coral | LVA9024 | 1956 £6 | £15 | |
| Endless | 7" | Vogue Coral | Q72201 | 1956 £1.50 | £4 | |
| Forgive Me | 7" | Vogue Coral | Q72296 | 1957 £1.50 | £4 | |
| Goodnight My Love, Pleasant Dreams | 7" | Vogue Coral | Q72216 | 1957 £1.50 | £4 | |
| Greetings | LP | Coral | CRL57225 | 1958 £6 | £15 | US |
| He | LP | Coral | CRL57033 | 195– £6 | £15 | US |
| He | 7" | Vogue Coral | Q72108 | 1955 £1.50 | £4 | |
| Heart | 7" | Vogue Coral | Q72238 | 1957 £1.50 | £4 | |
| His And Hers | LP | Coral | LVA9140 | 1961 £4 | £10 | |
| In The Alps | 7" | Vogue Coral | Q72188 | 1956 £1.50 | £4 | |
| Interlude | 7" | Vogue Coral | Q72272 | 1957 £1.50 | £4 | |
| Lonesome Polecat | 7" | Vogue Coral | Q2028 | 1954 £2 | £5 | |
| May You Always | LP | Coral | LVA9115 | 1959 £6 | £15 | |
| May You Always | 7" EP | Coral | FEP2033 | 1959 £5 | £10 | |
| McGuire Sisters | 7" EP | Coral | FEP2001 | 1958 £5 | £10 | |
| Melody Of Love | 7" | Vogue Coral | Q72052 | 1955 £1.50 | £4 | |
| Missing | 7" | Vogue Coral | Q72145 | 1956 £1.50 | £4 | |
| Musical Magic | LP | Coral | CRL57180 | 1957 £6 | £15 | US |
| No More | 7" | Vogue Coral | Q72050 | 1955 £4 | £8 | |
| Our Golden Favorites | LP | Coral | LVA9133 | 1960 £4 | £10 | |
| Sincerely | LP | Coral | CRL57052 | 195– £6 | £15 | US |
| Something's Gotta Give | 7" | Vogue Coral | Q72082 | 1955 £1.50 | £4 | |
| Sugartime | LP | Coral | CRL57217 | 1958 £6 | £15 | US |
| Sugartime | 7" | Coral | Q72305 | 1958 £2 | £5 | |
| Teenage Party | LP | Coral | LVA9073 | 1957 £6 | £15 | |
| Tip Toe Through The Tulips | 7" | Vogue Coral | Q72209 | 1956 £1.50 | £4 | |
| Volare | 7" EP | Coral | FEP2006 | 1958 £5 | £10 | |
| When The Lights Are Low | LP | Coral | LVA9082 | 1958 £4 | £10 | |
| Without Him | 7" | Vogue Coral | Q72249 | 1957 £1.50 | £4 | |
| Young And Foolish | 7" | Vogue Coral | Q72117 | 1956 £1.50 | £4 | |

## MCKAY, FREDDIE

| | | | | | | |
|---|---|---|---|---|---|---|
| Picture On The Wall | LP | Attack | ATLP1013 | 1973 £5 | £12 | |
| Picture On The Wall | LP | Banana | BALPS01 | 1971 £20 | £40 | |

## MCKAY, SCOTT

| | | | | | | |
|---|---|---|---|---|---|---|
| Cold Cold Heart | 7" | London | HLU9885 | 1964 £1.50 | £4 | |
| I Can't Make Your Way | 7" | Columbia | DB8147 | 1967 £10 | £20 | |

## MCKAY, TONY

| | | | | | | |
|---|---|---|---|---|---|---|
| Nobody's Perfect | 7" | Polydor | BM56513 | 1966 £12.50 | £25 | |

## MCKENNA, VAL

| | | | | | | |
|---|---|---|---|---|---|---|
| Mixed Up Shook Up Girl | 7" | Piccadilly | 7N35256 | 1965 £1.50 | £4 | |

## MCKENNA MENDELSON MAINLINE

| | | | | | | |
|---|---|---|---|---|---|---|
| Better Watch Out | 7" | Liberty | LBF15235 | 1969 £1.50 | £4 | |
| Blues | LP | Paragon | No. 15 | 1968 £25 | £50 | Canadian |
| Stink | LP | Liberty | LBS83251 | 1969 £6 | £15 | |

## MCKENZIE, DOUG & BOB
Take Off .................................................. 7" ...... Mercury .......... HOSER1 .............. 1982 £5 ......... £10 ................................

## MCKENZIE, JUDY
Judy ...................................................... LP ...... Key .............. KL005 ................. 1970 £6 ......... £15 .......................
Peace And Love And Freedom ................. LP ...... Key .............. KL009 ................. 1971 £6 ......... £15 .......................

## MCKENZIE, MARLENE
Left Me For Another .............................. 7" ...... Double D ...... DD106 ................. 1968 £2.50 ........ £6 ...*Bobby Aitken B side*

## MCKENZIE, SCOTT
San Francisco ........................................ 7" ...... CBS .............. 2816 ................... 1967 £1.50 ........ £4 ........................
Voice Of Scott McKenzie ........................ LP ...... CBS .............. (S)BPG63157 ...... 1967 £4 ......... £10 ........................

## MCKINLEY, RAY & JOE MARSALA
Dixieland Jazz Battle ................................ 10" LP Brunswick ....... LA8545 .............. 1952 £5 ......... £12 ........................

## MCKINLEYS
Give Him My Love .................................. 7" ...... Columbia ....... DB7583 ............ 1965 £4 ......... £8 ........................
Someone Cares For Me .......................... 7" ...... Columbia ....... DB7230 ............ 1964 £2.50 ........ £6 ......................•...
Sweet And Tender Romance .................... 7" ...... Parlophone ..... R5211 ................. 1964 £1.50 ........ £4 ........................
When He Comes Along ........................... 7" ...... Columbia ....... DB7310 ............ 1964 £1.50 ........ £4 ........................

## MCKUEN, ROD
Happy Is A Boy Named Me ..................... 7" ...... London .......... HLU8390 ......... 1957 £10 ......... £20 ........................
Summer Love ......................................... LP ...... Decca ........... DL8714 .............. 1958 £8 ......... £20 ........................*US*
Two Brothers ......................................... 7" ...... Brunswick ....... 05828 ................. 1960 £4 ......... £8 ........................

## MCKUSICK, HAL
East Coast Jazz ...................................... LP ...... London .......... LTZN15006 ...... 1956 £20 ......... £40 ........................
Hal McKusick Quartet ............................. LP ...... Parlophone ..... PMC1093 ......... 1959 £8 ......... £20 ........................
Hal McKusick Quintet .............................. LP ...... Voge Coral .... LVA9062 ......... 1957 £10 ......... £25 ........................
Jazz At The Academy .............................. LP ...... Vogue Coral ... LVA9054 ......... 1957 £10 ......... £25 ........................

## MCLAIN, TOMMY
Sweet Dreams ........................................ 7" ...... London .......... HL10065 ......... 1966 £2.50 ........ £6 ........................
Think It Over .......................................... 7" ...... London .......... HL10091 ......... 1966 £2 ......... £5 ........................

## MCLAREN, MALCOLM
Madame Butterfly.................................... CD-s .. Virgin ........... CDT30 ............... 1988 £2 ......... £5 ................*3" single*

## MCLAUGHLIN, DINNY
Rake O'Reels And A Clatter Of Jigs .......... LP ...... Robin ............ ROBALM027 ........ 1971 £8 ......... £20 ................*Irish*

## MCLAUGHLIN, JOHN

John McLaughlin apparently spent much of the sixties driving a van for an amplification company, while playing his guitar wherever and whenever he could. He was given the chance to make an album for the Marmalade label, but while *Extrapolation* is an above-average British jazz record of the period, it was almost immediately eclipsed by McLaughlin's good fortune in being invited to play with Miles Davis. As a player on the key albums to start electric jazz, it was therefore John McLaughlin who made highly amplified guitar respectable in jazz (although he had to work up to it – the tone on both *In A Silent Way* and *Bitches Brew* is quite mild).

Devotion ................................................ LP ...... Douglas .......... DGL65075 ............ 1972 £4 ......... £10 ........................
Extrapolation ......................................... LP ...... Marmalade ...... 608007 ................. 1969 £6 ......... £15 ........................
Extrapolation ......................................... LP ...... Polydor .......... 2343012 ............... 1970 £4 ......... £10 ........................
My Goal's Beyond ................................... LP ...... Douglas .......... DGL69014 ........... 1972 £4 ......... £10 ........................
Where Fortune Smiles ............................ LP ...... Dawn ............. DNLS3018 ............ 1971 £8 ......... £20 *with John Surman and others*

## MCLEAN, DON
American Pie .......................................... CD-s .. Liberty ........... CDEMCT3 ........... 1991 £2 ......... £5 ........................

## MCLEAN, JACKIE
'Bout Soul ............................................. LP ...... Blue Note ...... BST84284 .......... 1968 £6 ......... £15 ........................
Action Action Action .............................. LP ...... Blue Note ...... BLP/BST84218 .... 1965 £15 ......... £30 ........................
Bluesnik ................................................ LP ...... Blue Note ...... BLP/BST84067 .... 196– £10 ......... £25 ........................
Capuchin Swing ..................................... LP ...... Blue Note ...... BLP/BST84038 .... 196– £10 ......... £25 ........................
Demon's Dance ..................................... LP ...... Blue Note ...... BST84345 .......... 1969 £6 ......... £15 ........................
Destination Out ...................................... LP ...... Blue Note ...... BLP/BST84165 .... 1964 £10 ......... £25 ........................
Fickle Sonance ...................................... LP ...... Blue Note ...... BLP/BST84089 .... 1961 £20 ......... £40 ........................
It's Time! .............................................. LP ...... Blue Note ...... BLP/BST84179 .... 1964 £15 ......... £30 ........................
Jackie's Bag .......................................... LP ...... Blue Note ...... BLP/BST84051 .... 196– £20 ......... £40 ........................
Jackie's Pal ........................................... LP ...... Esquire .......... 32111 ................. 1960 £10 ......... £25 ........................
Let Freedom Ring ................................... LP ...... Blue Note ...... BLP/BST84106 .... 1962 £10 ......... £25 ........................
Lights Out ............................................. LP ...... Esquire .......... 32041 ................. 1958 £15 ......... £30 ........................
New And Old Gospel ............................... LP ...... Blue Note ...... BLP/BST84262 .... 1967 £10 ......... £25 ........................
One Step Beyond .................................... LP ...... Blue Note ...... BLP/BST84137 .... 1963 £10 ......... £25 ........................
Right Now! ............................................ LP ...... Blue Note ...... BLP/BST84215 .... 1965 £15 ......... £30 ........................

## MCLEAN, PHIL
Big Mouth Bill ........................................ 7" ...... Top Rank ....... JAR613 ............... 1962 £1.50 ........ £4 ........................
Small Sad Sam ....................................... 7" ...... Top Rank ....... JAR597 ............... 1961 £1.50 ........ £4 ........................

## MCLOLLIE, OSCAR HONEYJUMPERS
Love Me Tonight ..................................... 7" ...... London .......... HL8130 ............... 1955 £75 ......... £150 ........................

## MCLUHAN, MARSHALL
Medium Is The Message ......................... LP ..... Columbia ........ CL2701/CS9501 ..... 1967 £8 ......... £20 ......................... US

## MCLYNNS
Old Market Street ................................... LP ..... CBS ............... 63836 ................ 1970 £37.50 .... £75

## MCMILLAN, RODDY
McPherson's Rant ................................... 7" EP . Beltona ........... SEP83 ................ 1960 £2 ......... £5

## MCNABB, IAN
Great Dreams Of Heaven ......................... CD-s .. WayCool ....... 14CD ................ 1991 £2 ......... £5
Merseybeast ........................................... CD ..... Island ............. 5242402 ............. 1996 £6 ......... £15 ................. double
These Are The Days ............................... CD-s .. Fat Cat ........... FC001CD ............ 1991 £2 ......... £5

## MCNAIR, BARBARA
Here I Am .............................................. LP ..... Motown ........ (S)644 ................ 1966 £8 ......... £20 ...................... US
I Enjoy Being A Girl ............................... LP ..... Warner Bros .. W(S)1541 ............ 1964 £6 ......... £15 ...................... US
I Enjoy Being A Girl ............................... 7" EP . Warner Bros .. WEP6129 ............ 1964 £5 ......... £10
Livin' End ............................................. LP ..... Warner Bros .. W(S)1570 ............ 1964 £6 ......... £15 ...................... US
Real Barbara McNair .............................. LP ..... Motown ........ S680 ................ 1969 £8 ......... £20 ...................... US
You're Gonna Love My Baby ................... 7" ...... Tamla Motown  TMG544 ............ 1966 £100 ......... £200

## MCNAIR, HAROLD
Affectionate Fink ................................... LP ..... Island ........... ILP926 ................ 1965 £25 ......... £50
Fence .................................................... LP ..... B&C ............. CAS1016 ............. 1970 £15 ......... £30
Flute And Nut ....................................... LP ..... RCA ............. INTS1096 ............ 1970 £15 ......... £30
Harold McNair ...................................... LP ..... B&C ............. CAS1045 ............. 1971 £15 ......... £30
Harold McNair ...................................... LP ..... RCA ............. SF7969 ............... 1968 £20 ......... £40
Hipster ................................................. 7" ...... RCA ............. RCA1742 ............ 1968 £2.50 ......... £6

## MCNEELY, BIG JAY
Big Jay McNeely .................................... LP ..... Warner Bros .. W(S)1523 ............ 1963 £6 ......... £15 ...................... US
Big Jay McNeely .................................... 10" LP Federal ......... 29596 ................ 1954 £50 ......... £100 ...................... US
Big Jay McNeely In 3-D .......................... LP ..... Federal ......... 395530 ............... 1956 £37.50 ......... £75 ...................... US
Big Jay McNeely In 3-D .......................... LP ..... King ............. 650 ................... 1959 £20 ......... £40 ...................... US
Big Jay's Party ....................................... LP ..... Warner Bros .. WM8143 ............ 1964 £6 ......... £15
Rhythm And Blues Concert ..................... 10" LP Savoy ........... MG15045 ............ 1955 £37.50 ......... £75 ...................... US
Something On Your Mind ........................ 7" ...... Sue ............... WI373 ................ 1965 £6 ......... £12
Something On Your Mind ........................ 7" ...... Top Rank ...... JAR169 ............... 1959 £4 ......... £8

## MCNEIL, DAVID
Don't Let Your Chance Go By ................. 7" ...... President ........ PT212 ................ 1968 £4 ......... £8

## MCNEIL, PAUL
Contemporary Folk ................................ LP ..... Decca ........... LK4699 ............... 1965 £10 ......... £25
Traditionally At The Troubadour .............. LP ..... Decca ........... LK4803 ............... 1966 £20 ......... £40

## MCNEIL, PAUL & LINDA PETERS
You Ain't Goin' Nowhere ....................... 7" ...... MGM ........... MGM1408 ........... 1968 £2.50 ......... £6

## MCOIL
All Our Hopes ...................................... LP ..... private ........... 2066 ................ 1979 £50 ......... £100 ................. German

## MCPARTLAND, JIMMY
Dixieland At Carnegie Hall ..................... LP ..... Columbia ....... 33SX1122 ............. 1959 £5 ......... £12
Shades Of Bix ....................................... 10" LP Vogue Coral .... LRA10006 ........... 1954 £6 ......... £15

## MCPARTLAND, MARIAN
Marian McPartland ................................ LP ..... Capitol .......... LCT6017 .............. 1955 £5 ......... £12
Marian McPartland ................................ 10" LP Capitol .......... LC6828 ............... 1956 £6 ......... £15
Marian McPartland Trio ......................... LP ..... Capitol .......... T785 ................ 1957 £5 ......... £12
With You In Mind .................................. LP ..... Capitol .......... T895 ................ 1958 £5 ......... £12

## MCPEAKE FAMILY
At Home With The McPeakes ................... LP ..... Fontana ......... (S)TL5258 ............ 1965 £10 ......... £25
Delightful McPeakes ............................... LP ..... Philips ........... 6856017 .............. 1967 £10 ......... £25
Irish Folk! ............................................. LP ..... Fontana ......... TL5214 ............... 1964 £10 ......... £25
Irish To Be Sure ................................... LP ..... Windmill ........ WMD151 ............ 1972 £10 ......... £25
McPeake ............................................... LP ..... Evolution ....... Z1002 ............... 1969 £30 ......... £60
McPeake Family ..................................... LP ..... Topic ............. 12T87 ............... 1963 £20 ......... £40
McPeake Family Of Belfast ...................... LP ..... Transatlantic ... XTRA5012 ........... 1966 £6 ......... £15
Pleasant And Delightful ........................... LP ..... Fontana ......... (S)TL5433 ............ 1967 £10 ......... £25

## MCPHATTER, CLYDE
Best Of Clyde McPhatter ......................... LP ..... Atlantic .......... ATL5001 .............. 1964 £15 ......... £30
Clyde .................................................... LP ..... Atlantic .......... 8031 ................ 1959 £50 ......... £100 ...................... US
Clyde McPhatter .................................... 7" EP . London .......... REE1202 ............. 1959 £87.50 .... £175 ........ best auctioned
Come What May .................................... 7" ...... London .......... HLE8707 ............. 1958 £20 ......... £40
Everybody's Somebody's Fool .................. 7" ...... Stateside ........ SS487 ................ 1966 £1.50 ......... £4
Golden Blues Hits .................................. LP ..... Mercury ......... MG2/SR60655 ..... 1962 £8 ......... £20 ...................... US
Greatest Hits ......................................... LP ..... Mercury ......... MG2/SR60783 ..... 1963 £8 ......... £20 ...................... US
Greatest Hits ......................................... LP ..... MGM ........... (S)E3866 ............ 1960 £10 ......... £25 ...................... US
Just Give Me A Ring .............................. 7" ...... London .......... HLE9079 ............. 1960 £10 ......... £20
Just To Hold Your Hand ......................... 7" ...... London .......... HLE8462 ............. 1957 £50 ......... £100
Lavender Lace ....................................... 7" ...... Stateside ........ SS592 ................ 1967 £2 ......... £5
Let's Start Over Again ............................ LP ..... MGM ........... (S)E3775 ............ 1959 £15 ......... £30 ...................... US
Let's Try Again ...................................... 7" ...... MGM ........... MGM1048 ........... 1959 £5 ......... £10

| | | | | | | | | |
|---|---|---|---|---|---|---|---|---|
| Little Bitty Pretty One | 7" | Mercury | AMT1181 | 1962 | £4 | £8 | |
| Live At The Apollo | LP | Mercury | MG2/SR60915 | 1964 | £8 | £20 | US |
| Long Lonely Nights | 7" | London | HLE8476 | 1957 | £30 | £60 | |
| Love Ballads | LP | Atlantic | 8024 | 1958 | £62.50 | £125 | US |
| Lover Please | LP | Mercury | MMC14120 | 1963 | £20 | £40 | |
| Lover Please | 7" | Mercury | AMT1174 | 1962 | £5 | £10 | |
| Lover's Question | 7" | London | HLE8755 | 1958 | £12.50 | £25 | |
| Lovey Dovey | 7" | London | HLE8878 | 1959 | £10 | £20 | |
| Masquerade Is Over | 7" | MGM | MGM1014 | 1959 | £5 | £10 | |
| McPhatter & Wilson Meet the Dominoes | LP | Ember | NR5001 | 1962 | £50 | £100 | with Jackie Wilson |
| Rhythm And Soul | LP | Mercury | MG2/SR60750 | 1962 | £15 | £30 | US |
| Rock And Cry | 7" | London | HLE8525 | 1957 | £30 | £60 | |
| Seven Days | 7" | London | HL7006 | 1956 | £37.50 | £75 | export |
| Seven Days | 7" | London | HLE8250 | 1956 | £150 | £250 | best auctioned |
| Shot Of Rhythm & Blues | 7" | Pama | PM775 | 1969 | £1.50 | £4 | |
| Shot Of Rhythm & Blues | 7" | Stateside | SS567 | 1966 | £2 | £5 | |
| Since You've Been Gone | 7" | London | HLE8906 | 1959 | £12.50 | £25 | |
| Songs Of The Big City | LP | Mercury | MG2/SR60902 | 1964 | £8 | £20 | US |
| Ta Ta | 7" | Mercury | MG2/SR60597 | 1960 | £15 | £30 | US |
| Ta Ta | 7" | Mercury | AMT1108 | 1960 | £2.50 | £6 | |
| Think Me A Kiss | 7" | MGM | MGM1061 | 1960 | £4 | £8 | |
| This Is Not Goodbye | 7" EP | MGM | MGMEP739 | 1960 | £37.50 | £75 | |
| Tomorrow Is A-Comin' | 7" | Mercury | AMT1136 | 1961 | £2.50 | £6 | |
| Treasure Of Love | 7" | London | HLE8293 | 1956 | £87.50 | £175 | |
| Tribute | LP | Atlantic | K30033 | 1973 | £4 | £10 | |
| Twice As Nice | 7" EP | MGM | MGMEP705 | 1959 | £37.50 | £75 | |
| Twice As Nice | 7" | MGM | MGM1040 | 1959 | £5 | £10 | |
| You Went Back On Your Word | 7" | London | HLE9000 | 1959 | £15 | £30 | |
| You're For Me | 7" | Mercury | AMT1120 | 1960 | £2.50 | £6 | |

## MCPHEE, TONY

The lead guitarist of the Groundhogs has also made a number of solo recordings. He continues to play live to this day, though without issuing any more records.

| | | | | | | | | |
|---|---|---|---|---|---|---|---|---|
| I Asked For Water But She Gave Me Gasoline | LP | Liberty | LBS83252 | 1969 | £30 | £60 | with other artists |
| Me & The Devil | LP | Liberty | LBL/LBS83190 | 1968 | £25 | £50 | |
| Someone To Love Me | 7" | Purdah | 453501 | 1966 | £37.50 | £75 | |
| Time Of Action | 7" | Tony McPhee | TS001 | 198– | £2.50 | £6 | |
| Two Sides Of Tony McPhee | LP | WWA | WWA001 | 1973 | £6 | £15 | |

## MCPHERSON, CHARLES

| | | | | | | | |
|---|---|---|---|---|---|---|---|
| Bebop Revisited | LP | Stateside | SL10151 | 1965 | £5 | £12 | |

## MCPHERSON, GILLIAN

| | | | | | | | |
|---|---|---|---|---|---|---|---|
| Poets And Painters And Performers Of Blues | LP | RCA | SF8220 | 1971 | £4 | £10 | |

## MCQUAID, JOHN

| | | | | | | | | |
|---|---|---|---|---|---|---|---|---|
| Stations In The Sky | LP | Royalty | RR101085201 | 1985 | £4 | £10 | US |

## MCRAE, CARMEN

| | | | | | | | |
|---|---|---|---|---|---|---|---|
| Afterglow | LP | Brunswick | LAT8257 | 1958 | £4 | £10 | |
| Blue Moon | LP | Brunswick | LAT8147 | 1956 | £4 | £10 | |
| Book Of Ballads | LP | London | HAR2185 | 1959 | £4 | £10 | |
| By Special Request | LP | Brunswick | LAT8104 | 1956 | £4 | £10 | |
| London's Girl Friends No. 3 | 7" EP | London | REN1094 | 1957 | £4 | £8 | |
| Love Is Here To Stay | 7" | Brunswick | 05502 | 1955 | £1.50 | £4 | |
| Play For Keeps | 7" | London | HLR8837 | 1959 | £2 | £5 | |
| So Much | 7" EP | Mercury | ZEP10132 | 1962 | £2 | £5 | |
| Torchy | LP | Brunswick | LAT8133 | 1956 | £4 | £10 | |
| Whatever Lola Wants | 7" | Brunswick | 05652 | 1957 | £1.50 | £4 | |

## MCSHANN, JAY

| | | | | | | | |
|---|---|---|---|---|---|---|---|
| Kansas City Memories | 10" LP | Brunswick | LA8735 | 1956 | £20 | £40 | |

## MCTELL, BLIND WILLIE

| | | | | | | | |
|---|---|---|---|---|---|---|---|
| Atlanta Twelve String Guitar | LP | Atlantic | K40400 | 1973 | £4 | £10 | |
| Blind Willie McTell | LP | Storyville | 670186 | 1967 | £5 | £12 | |

## MCTELL, RALPH

| | | | | | | | |
|---|---|---|---|---|---|---|---|
| 8 Frames A Second | LP | Transatlantic | TRA165 | 1968 | £4 | £10 | |
| My Side Of Your Window | LP | Transatlantic | TRA209 | 1969 | £4 | £10 | |
| Spiral Staircase | LP | Transatlantic | TRA177 | 1969 | £4 | £10 | |
| You, Well Meaning, Brought Me Here | LP | Famous | SFMA5753 | 1971 | £4 | £10 | |

## MCVAY, RAY

| | | | | | | | |
|---|---|---|---|---|---|---|---|
| Genesis | 7" | Parlophone | R5460 | 1966 | £1.50 | £4 | |
| Kinda Kinky | 7" | Pye | 7N15816 | 1965 | £5 | £10 | |
| Revenge | 7" | Pye | 7N15777 | 1965 | £10 | £20 | |

## MCVIE, CHRISTINE

| | | | | | | | |
|---|---|---|---|---|---|---|---|
| Christine McVie | CD | WEA | 9250592 | 1984 | £5 | £12 | |

## MCVOY, CARL

| | | | | | | | |
|---|---|---|---|---|---|---|---|
| Tootsie | 7" | London | HLU8617 | 1958 | £75 | £150 | |

## MCWILLIAMS, DAVID

*The Days Of Pearly Spencer* by David McWilliams, with its megaphone vocals and fountaining strings, was heavily promoted by the pirate radio stations and is, in consequence, particularly redolent of that era. The song is something of an oddity within McWilliams's recordings, however, as none of his other, folky material makes any attempt to match the inventiveness of *Pearly Spencer*'s arrangement.

| | | | | | | |
|---|---|---|---|---|---|---|
| David McWilliams Vol. 2 | LP | Major Minor | MMLP10 | 1967 | £4 | £10 |
| David McWilliams Vol. 3 | LP | Major Minor | MMLP11 | 1968 | £4 | £10 |
| Days Of Pearly Spencer | 7" | Major Minor | MM533 | 1968 | £2.50 | £6 |
| Days Of Pearly Spencer | 7" | Parlophone | R5886 | 1971 | £1.50 | £4 |
| God And My Country | 7" | CBS | 202348 | 1966 | £1.50 | £4 |
| Singing Songs By David McWilliams | LP | Major Minor | MMLP2 | 1967 | £5 | £12 |
| Stranger | 7" | Major Minor | MM592 | 1969 | £1.50 | £4 |

## ME & THEM

| | | | | | | |
|---|---|---|---|---|---|---|
| Everything I Do Is Wrong | 7" | Pye | 7N15631 | 1964 | £1.50 | £4 |
| Feel So Good | 7" | Pye | 7N15596 | 1964 | £2 | £5 |
| Getaway | 7" | Pye | 7N15683 | 1964 | £1.50 | £4 |

## MEAN STREET DEALERS

| | | | | | | |
|---|---|---|---|---|---|---|
| Bent Needles | LP | Graduate | GRADLP1 | 1979 | £6 | £15 |
| Japanese Motorbikes | 7" | Graduate | GRAD5 | 1980 | £1.50 | £4 |

## MEASLES

| | | | | | | |
|---|---|---|---|---|---|---|
| Casting My Spell | 7" | Columbia | DB7531 | 1965 | £7.50 | £15 |
| Kicks | 7" | Columbia | DB7875 | 1966 | £6 | £12 |
| Night People | 7" | Columbia | DB7673 | 1965 | £6 | £12 |
| Walking In | 7" | Columbia | DB8029 | 1966 | £6 | £12 |

## MEAT PUPPETS

| | | | | | | |
|---|---|---|---|---|---|---|
| In A Car | CD-s | SST | SST044CD | 1988 | £2 | £5 |

## MEAT WHIPLASH

| | | | | | | | |
|---|---|---|---|---|---|---|---|
| Don't Slip Up | 7" | Creation | CRE020 | 1985 | £4 | £8 | ...sleeve photo of band by fence |
| Don't Slip Up | 7" | Creation | CRE020 | 1985 | £2 | £5 | ...sleeve photo of band in field |

## MEATBEAT MANIFESTO

| | | | | | | |
|---|---|---|---|---|---|---|
| I Got The Fear | 12" | Sweatbox | SOX023R | 1988 | £2.50 | £6 |
| Suck Hard | 12" | Sweatbox | SOX023 | 1987 | £3 | £8 |

## MEATLOAF

| | | | | | | | |
|---|---|---|---|---|---|---|---|
| Bat Out Of Hell | LP | Epic | EPC1182419 | 1982 | £6 | £15 | picture disc |
| Bat Out Of Hell | CD | Epic | 4677322 | 1990 | £5 | £12 | picture disc |
| Dead Ringer For Love | CD-s | Epic | 6569822 | 1991 | £2 | £5 | |
| Live At Father's Place | LP | Epic | AS409 | 1978 | £6 | £15 | US promo |
| Live At The El Mocambo | LP | CBS | CDN9 | 1978 | £6 | £15 | Canadian promo |
| Modern Girl | 7" | Arista | ARISDP585 | 1984 | £1.50 | £4 | shaped picture disc, poster & plinth |
| More Than You Deserve | 7" | RSO | RS407 | 1974 | £10 | £20 | US |
| Special Girl | CD-s | Arista | RISCD14 | 1987 | £2 | £5 | |
| Stand By Me | 7" | Ode | ODS66304 | 1975 | £15 | £30 | |
| Stoney & Meatloaf | LP | Rare Earth | SRE3005 | 1972 | £5 | £12 | |
| What You See Is What You Get | 7" | Rare Earth | RES103 | 1971 | £4 | £8 | Stoney And Meatloaf credit |

## MEATLOAF & BRIAN MAY

| | | | | | | | |
|---|---|---|---|---|---|---|---|
| Time For Heroes | CD-s | Orpheum | 060187D | 1987 | £20 | £40 | US, Tangerine Dream B side |
| Time For Heroes | 7" | Orpheum | 060187 | 1987 | £20 | £40 | US, Tangerine Dream B side |
| Time For Heroes | 12" | Orpheum | 012387 | 1987 | £20 | £40 | US, Tangerine Dream B side |

## MEC OP SINGERS

| | | | | | | | |
|---|---|---|---|---|---|---|---|
| Dies Irae | 7" EP | DiscAZ | 1071 | 1967 | £4 | £8 | French |

## MECKENBURG ZINC

| | | | | | | |
|---|---|---|---|---|---|---|
| Hard Working Woman | 7" | Orange | OAS205 | 1970 | £1.50 | £4 |

## MECKI MARK MEN

| | | | | | | | |
|---|---|---|---|---|---|---|---|
| Marathon | LP | Sonet | SLP2521 | 1971 | £5 | £12 | Swedish |
| Mecki Mark Band | LP | Limelight | 86054 | 1968 | £6 | £15 | US |
| Running In The Summernight | LP | Limelight | 86068 | 1969 | £6 | £15 | US |

## MEDDY EVILS

| | | | | | | |
|---|---|---|---|---|---|---|
| Find Somebody To Love | 7" | Pye | 7N15941 | 1965 | £37.50 | £75 |
| Ma's Place | 7" | Pye | 7N17091 | 1966 | £37.50 | £75 |

## MEDICINE HEAD

| | | | | | | |
|---|---|---|---|---|---|---|
| Coast To Coast | 7" | Dandelion | 5075 | 1970 | £1.50 | £4 |
| Dark Side Of The Moon | LP | Polydor | 2310166 | 1971 | £4 | £10 |
| Heavy On The Drum | LP | Dandelion | DAN8005 | 1971 | £6 | £15 |
| His Guiding Hand | 7" | Dandelion | 4661 | 1970 | £2.50 | £6 |
| New Bottles Old Medicine | LP | Dandelion | 63757 | 1970 | £6 | £15 |

## MEDITATIONS
Transcendental Meditation ......................... 7" ...... Liberty ............ LBF15045 ............... 1968 £1.50 ....... £4 ...............................

## MEDIUM
Edward Never Lies ...................................... 7" ...... CBS ............ 3404 .................... 1968 £2.50 ....... £6 ...............................
Medium ................................................... LP ..... Gamma ....... GS503 .................... 1969 £6 ......... £15 ................................. US

## MEDLEY, BILL
Peace Brother Peace .................................. 7" ...... MGM ............ MGM1456 .............. 1968 £1.50 ....... £4 ...............................

## MEDLIN, JOE
I Kneel At Your Throne ............................. 7" ...... Mercury ......... AMT1032 ............... 1959 £1.50 ....... £4 ...............................

## MEDWIN, MICHAEL
Army Game ............................................... 7" ...... HMV ............. POP490 ................ 1958 £1.50 ....... £4 ...............................

## MEEHAN, KEITH
Darkness Of My Life .................................. 7" ...... Marmalade ..... 598016 ................. 1969 £2.50 ........ £6 . *Tony Meehan B side*

## MEEHAN, TONY
Song Of Mexico ......................................... 7"-s .. Decca ............. F11801 .................. 1964 £1.50 ....... £4 ...............................

## MEEK, JOE ORCHESTRA
Kennedy March .......................................... 7" ...... Decca ............. F11796 .................. 1963 £10 ......... £20 ...............................

## MEGA CITY FOUR
Miles Apart .............................................. 7" ...... Primitive ....... PRIME009 ............. 1988 £5 ........... £10 ...............................

## MEGADETH
Anarchy In The UK .................................. 7" ...... Capitol .......... CLP480 ................ 1988 £1.50 ....... £4 ................. *picture disc*
Hangar 18 ................................................. CD-s . Capitol .......... CDCL604 .............. 1991 £2 ............ £5 ...............................
Holy Wars The Punishment Due .............. CD-s . Capitol .......... CDCL588 .............. 1990 £2 ............ £5 ...............................
No More Mr. Nice Guy .............................. CD-s . SBK ............... CDSBK4 ............... 1989 £2 ............ £5 ...............................
Peace Sells But Who's Buying? ................ LP .... Capitol .......... ESTP2022 ............. 1986 £4 ........... £10 ................. *picture disc*
Skin O' My Teeth ..................................... CD-s . Capitol .......... CDCL669 .............. 1992 £2 ............ £5 ................. *picture disc*
Symphony For Destruction ....................... CD-s . Capitol .......... CDCL662 .............. 1992 £2 ............ £5 ...............................
Wake Up Dead .......................................... 7" ...... Capitol .......... CLP476 ................ 1987 £2.50 ........ £6 ................. *picture disc*
Youthanasia ............................................. CD .... Capitol .......... 724383273928 ....... 1996 £6 ........... £15 .................... *double*

## MEGATON
Megaton ................................................... LP ..... Decca ............. SLK16690P .......... 1971 £25 ........ £50 .................... *German*
Megaton ................................................... LP ..... Deram ........... SMLR1086 .......... 1971 £150 ... £250 ...............................
Out Of Your Own Little World ................. 7" ...... Deram ........... DM331 ................. 1971 £10 ........ £20 ...............................

## MEGATONS
Shimmy Shimmy Walk ............................ 7" ...... Sue ................ WI325 .................. 1965 £6 ............ £12 ...............................

## MEGATRONS
Velvet Waters ........................................... 7" ...... Top Rank ...... JAR146 ................ 1959 £1.50 ....... £4 ...............................
Whispering Winds ..................................... 7" ...... Top Rank ...... JAR236 ................ 1959 £1.50 ....... £4 ...............................

## MEHEGAN, JOHN
First Mehegan Vol. 1 ............................... 7" EP . London ........... EZC19005 ............ 1956 £2 ............ £5 ...............................
First Mehegan Vol. 2 ............................... 7" EP . London ........... EZC19015 ............ 1956 £2 ............ £5 ...............................

## MEID, LOTHAR
Mensch Dieser Klaus ................................. LP ..... Philips ........... 6305283 ............... 1975 £4 ........... £10 .................... *German*

## MEIGHAN, BOB
Dancer ..................................................... LP ..... Capitol .......... ST11555 ............... 1976 £6 ........... £15 ...................... US
Me'hun .................................................... LP ..... Capitol .......... ST11686 ............... 1977 £6 ........... £15 ...................... US

## MEINERT, CARSTEN
Musictrain ............................................... LP ..... Spectator ......... SL1007 ................ 1970 £5 ........... £12 .................... *Danish*
To You .................................................... LP ..... Spectator ......... SL1001 ................ 1969 £20 ......... £40 .................... *Danish*

## MEISENFLOO
Meisenfloo .............................................. LP ..... Lagua .............. 60723 .................. 1972 £25 ......... £50 .................... *German*

## MEKONS
Amnesia .................................................. CD-s .. Blast First ........ BFFP53CD ........... 1989 £2 ........... £5 ...............................

## MELACHRINO ORCHESTRA
Autumn Concerto ..................................... 7" ...... HMV ............. B10958 ................ 1956 £2 ............ £5 ...............................

## MELANIE
Affectionately .......................................... LP ..... Buddah ........... 203028 ................. 1969 £4 ........... £10 ...............................
All The Right Noises ................................ LP ..... Buddah ........... 2318034 ............... 1971 £4 ........... £10 ...............................
Born To Be .............................................. LP ..... Buddah ........... 203019 ................. 1969 £4 ........... £10 ...............................
Candles In The Rain ................................ LP ..... Buddah ........... 2318009 ............... 1970 £4 ........... £10 ...............................
Four Sides Of Melanie .............................. LP ..... Buddah ........... 26590013 ............. 1974 £5 ........... £12 .................... *double*
Garden In The City .................................. LP ..... Buddah ........... 2318054 ............... 1972 £4 ........... £10 .. *scratch & sniff sleeve*
Gather Me ............................................... LP ..... Buddah ........... 2322002 ............... 1971 £4 ........... £10 ...............................
Good Book ............................................... LP ..... Buddah ........... 2322001 ............... 1971 £4 ........... £10 ...............................
Leftover Wine .......................................... LP ..... Buddah ........... 2318011 ............... 1970 £4 ........... £10 ...............................
Ruby Tuesday ........................................... CD-s .. Silvertone ........ CDYUM117 ........... 1989 £2 ........... £5 ...............................

| | | | | | | | |
|---|---|---|---|---|---|---|---|
| Stoneground Words | LP | Neighborhood | NHTC251 | 1972 | £4 | £10 | |
| Tuning My Guitar | 7" | Buddah | 201063 | 1969 | £4 | £8 | |

## MELLE, GIL

| | | | | | | | |
|---|---|---|---|---|---|---|---|
| Gil Melle Quintet | 10" LP | Vogue | LDE141 | 1955 | £25 | £50 | |

## MELLEN, SUSAN

| | | | | | | | |
|---|---|---|---|---|---|---|---|
| Mellen Bird | LP | Mam | MAMAS1014 | 1975 | £8 | £20 | |

## MELLENCAMP, JOHN

| | | | | | | | |
|---|---|---|---|---|---|---|---|
| Mr. Happy Go Lucky | CD | Mercury | 3145328962 | 1996 | £37.50 | £75 | *US promo pack, with interview CD & book* |

## MELLOKINGS

| | | | | | | | |
|---|---|---|---|---|---|---|---|
| Tonight Tonight | LP | Herald | H1013 | 1960 | £50 | £100 | *US* |

## MELLO-LARKS

| | | | | | | | |
|---|---|---|---|---|---|---|---|
| Just For A Lark | LP | Camden | CAL530 | 1959 | £8 | £20 | *US* |

## MELLOTONES

| | | | | | | | |
|---|---|---|---|---|---|---|---|
| Facts Of Life | 7" | Camel | CA18 | 1969 | £1.50 | £4 | *Termites B side* |
| Fat Girl In Red | 7" | Amalgamated | AMG812 | 1968 | £4 | £8 | *Versatiles B side* |
| Feel Good | 7" | Amalgamated | AMG817 | 1968 | £4 | £8 | |
| Let's Join Together | 7" | Pyramid | PYR6060 | 1969 | £2.50 | £6 | *Beverley's Allstars B side* |
| None Such | 7" | Doctor Bird | DB1136 | 1968 | £5 | £10 | *Val Bennett B side* |
| Uncle Charlie | 7" | Trojan | TR612 | 1968 | £4 | £8 | |

## MELLOW CANDLE

The rarest album on the Deram label contains folk-rock with two good female singers and is certainly strong enough to have sold very much better than it did. Several band members turned up on later albums by a range of artists including Mike Oldfield, Jade Warrior, Amazing Blondel, Paul Kossoff and Gary Moore, but for Mellow Candle themselves, sadly one failure was all they were allowed to have.

| | | | | | | | |
|---|---|---|---|---|---|---|---|
| Dan The Wing | 7" | Deram | DM357 | 1972 | £20 | £40 | |
| Feeling High | 7" | SNB | 553645 | 1968 | £20 | £40 | |
| Swaddling Songs | LP | Deram | SDL7 | 1972 | £330 | £500 | |

## MELLOW CATS

| | | | | | | | |
|---|---|---|---|---|---|---|---|
| Another Moses | 7" | Blue Beat | BB54 | 1961 | £6 | £12 | |
| Rock A Man Soul | 7" | Blue Beat | BB68 | 1961 | £6 | £12 | *Monto & The Cyclones B side* |

## MELLOW LARKS

| | | | | | | | |
|---|---|---|---|---|---|---|---|
| Love You Baby | 7" | Blue Beat | BB16 | 1960 | £6 | £12 | |

## MELLY, GEORGE

| | | | | | | | |
|---|---|---|---|---|---|---|---|
| Abdul Abulbul Amir | 7" EP | Decca | DFE6557 | 1958 | £2 | £5 | |
| Black Bottom | 7" | Decca | FJ10840 | 1957 | £1.50 | £4 | |
| Cemetery Blues | 7" | Tempo | A147 | 1956 | £1.50 | £4 | |
| Frankie And Johnny | 7" | Decca | F10457 | 1955 | £1.50 | £4 | |
| George Melly | 7" EP | Tempo | EXA47 | 1957 | £2.50 | £6 | |
| Heebie Jeebies | 7" | Decca | FJ10806 | 1956 | £1.50 | £4 | |
| Jenny's Ball | 7" | Tempo | A144 | 1956 | £1.50 | £4 | |
| Kingdom Come | 7" | Decca | F10763 | 1956 | £1.50 | £4 | |
| Michigan Water Blues | 7" EP | Decca | DFE6552 | 1958 | £2 | £5 | |
| Psychological Significance | 7" EP | Columbia | SEG8093 | 1961 | £2 | £5 | |
| Waiting For A Train | 7" | Decca | FJ10779 | 1956 | £1.50 | £4 | |
| With Mick Mulligan's Jazz Band | 7" EP | Tempo | EXA41 | 1957 | £2.50 | £6 | |

## MELODIANS

| | | | | | | | |
|---|---|---|---|---|---|---|---|
| Come On Little Girl | 7" | Treasure Isle | TI7028 | 1968 | £5 | £10 | *Tommy McCook B side* |
| Everbody Bawlin' | 7" | Trojan | TR660 | 1969 | £1.50 | £4 | *Tommy McCook B side* |
| Last Train To Expo '67 | 7" | Treasure Isle | TI7023 | 1967 | £5 | £10 | *Tommy McCook B side* |
| Lay It On | 7" | Island | WI3014 | 1966 | £5 | £10 | |
| Let's Join Together | 7" | Studio One | SO2013 | 1967 | £6 | £12 | *Gaylads B side* |
| Little Nut Tree | 7" | Doctor Bird | DB1125 | 1968 | £5 | £10 | |
| Rivers Of Babylon | 7" | Summit | SUM8508 | 1970 | £1.50 | £4 | |
| Sweet Rose | 7" | Fab | FAB61 | 1968 | £4 | £8 | |
| Sweet Sensation | LP | Trojan | | 1970 | £5 | £12 | |
| Sweet Sensation | 7" | Trojan | TR695 | 1969 | £1.50 | £4 | |
| Swing And Dine | 7" | Doctor Bird | DB1139 | 1968 | £5 | £10 | |
| You Don't Need Me | 7" | Treasure Isle | TI7006 | 1967 | £5 | £10 | |
| You Have Caught Me | 7" | Treasure Isle | TI7022 | 1967 | £5 | £10 | |

## MELODY ENCHANTERS

| | | | | | | | |
|---|---|---|---|---|---|---|---|
| Blueberry Hill | 7" | R&B | JB117 | 1963 | £5 | £10 | |
| Enchanter's Ball | 7" | Island | WI049 | 1963 | £5 | £10 | |

## MELODY FAIR

| | | | | | | | |
|---|---|---|---|---|---|---|---|
| Something Happened To Me | 7" | Decca | F12801 | 1968 | £1.50 | £4 | |

## MELODY MAKER ALL STARS

| | | | | | | | |
|---|---|---|---|---|---|---|---|
| Melody Maker All Stars | 10" LP | Esquire | 20001 | 1952 | £15 | £30 | |

| Artist / Title | Format | Label | Catalogue | Year | Price 1 | Price 2 | Notes |
|---|---|---|---|---|---|---|---|
| Melody Maker All Stars | 10" LP | Esquire | 20008 | 1953 | £15 | £30 | |
| Melody Maker All Stars | 10" LP | Esquire | 20031 | 1954 | £15 | £30 | |

## MELODY MAKER JAZZ POLL WINNERS

| Title | Format | Label | Catalogue | Year | Price 1 | Price 2 | Notes |
|---|---|---|---|---|---|---|---|
| All The Winners | 10" LP | Pye | NJT518 | 1959 | £6 | £15 | |

## MELODY MAKER MODERN GROUP

| Title | Format | Label | Catalogue | Year | Price 1 | Price 2 | Notes |
|---|---|---|---|---|---|---|---|
| Melody Maker Modern Group | 10" LP | Esquire | 20030 | 1954 | £15 | £30 | |

## MELSON, JOE

| Title | Format | Label | Catalogue | Year | Price 1 | Price 2 | Notes |
|---|---|---|---|---|---|---|---|
| Hey Mister Cupid | 7" | Polydor | NH66961 | 1961 | £15 | £30 | |
| Oh Yeah | 7" | Polydor | NH66959 | 1961 | £15 | £30 | |

## MELTING BEER

| Title | Format | Label | Catalogue | Year | Price 1 | Price 2 | Notes |
|---|---|---|---|---|---|---|---|
| It Makes No Difference | 7" | Beggars Banquet | BEG144 | 1985 | £2.50 | £6 | test pressing |

## MELTON, BARRY

| Title | Format | Label | Catalogue | Year | Price 1 | Price 2 | Notes |
|---|---|---|---|---|---|---|---|
| We Are Like The Ocean | LP | Music Is Medicine | MIM9007 | 1977 | £8 | £20 | US |

## MELTON CONSTABLE

| Title | Format | Label | Catalogue | Year | Price 1 | Price 2 | Notes |
|---|---|---|---|---|---|---|---|
| Melton Constable | LP | SIS | | 197– | £180 | £300 | |

## MELTZER, TINA & DAVID

| Title | Format | Label | Catalogue | Year | Price 1 | Price 2 | Notes |
|---|---|---|---|---|---|---|---|
| Poet Song | LP | Vanguard | 6519 | 1968 | £37.50 | £75 | US |

## MEMBERS

| Title | Format | Label | Catalogue | Year | Price 1 | Price 2 | Notes |
|---|---|---|---|---|---|---|---|
| Fear On The Streets | 7" | XS | | 1977 | £2.50 | £6 | |
| Offshore Banking Business | 7" | Stiff | OFF3 | 1978 | £1.50 | £4 | |

## MEMOS

| Title | Format | Label | Catalogue | Year | Price 1 | Price 2 | Notes |
|---|---|---|---|---|---|---|---|
| My Type Of Girl | 7" | Parlophone | R4616 | 1959 | £25 | £50 | |

## MEMPHIS BEND

| Title | Format | Label | Catalogue | Year | Price 1 | Price 2 | Notes |
|---|---|---|---|---|---|---|---|
| Ubangi Stomp | 7" | United Artists | UP36132 | 1976 | £2 | £5 | |

## MEMPHIS JUG BAND

| Title | Format | Label | Catalogue | Year | Price 1 | Price 2 | Notes |
|---|---|---|---|---|---|---|---|
| Memphis Jug Band | LP | Saydisc | RL33 | 1970 | £4 | £10 | |
| Memphis Jug Band | 7" EP | HMV | 7EG8073 | 1955 | £25 | £50 | |
| Memphis Jug Band Vol. 2 | LP | Saydisc | RL337 | 1971 | £4 | £10 | |

## MEMPHIS MINNIE

| Title | Format | Label | Catalogue | Year | Price 1 | Price 2 | Notes |
|---|---|---|---|---|---|---|---|
| 1934–1936 | LP | Limited Edition | no number | 1969 | £8 | £20 | |
| 1934–1941 | LP | Limited Edition | no number | 1969 | £8 | £20 | |
| 1941–1949 | LP | Sunflower | ET1400 | 1969 | £8 | £20 | |
| Memphis Minnie | 7" EP | Heritage | H103 | 1964 | £7.50 | £15 | |

## MEMPHIS SLIM

| Title | Format | Label | Catalogue | Year | Price 1 | Price 2 | Notes |
|---|---|---|---|---|---|---|---|
| All Kinds Of Blues | LP | Bluesville | BV(S)1053 | 1963 | £5 | £12 | US |
| All Kinds Of Blues | LP | XTRA | XTRA5063 | 1970 | £4 | £10 | |
| Alone With My Friends | LP | Battle | BM6118 | 1963 | £5 | £12 | US |
| And The Real Honky Tonk | LP | Folkways | FG3535 | 1961 | £6 | £15 | US |
| At The Gate Of Horn | LP | Vee Jay | VJLP1012 | 1959 | £15 | £30 | US |
| Big City Girl | 7" | Storyville | A45055 | 1962 | £2.50 | £6 | |
| Blue Memphis | LP | Barclay | 920214 | 1972 | £25 | £50 | with Peter Green |
| Blues In Europe | LP | Storyville | SLP188 | 1966 | £4 | £10 | |
| Bluesingly Yours | LP | Polydor | 623263 | 1968 | £4 | £10 | |
| Boogie Woogie & The Blues | 7" EP | Storyville | SEP385 | 1962 | £4 | £8 | |
| Boogie Woogie Piano | LP | CBS | 63470 | 1961 | £6 | £15 | |
| Broken Soul Blues | LP | United Artists | ULP1042 | 1963 | £6 | £15 | |
| Chicago Blues | LP | Folkways | FG3536 | 1961 | £6 | £15 | US |
| Chicago Blues | LP | XTRA | XTRA1085 | 1969 | £4 | £10 | |
| Clap Your Hands | LP | Fontana | TL5254 | 1965 | £4 | £10 | |
| Frisco Bay Blues | LP | Fontana | 688315ZL | 1964 | £6 | £15 | |
| Going To Kansas City | 7" EP | Collector | JEN5 | 1961 | £4 | £8 | |
| Just Blues | LP | Bluesville | BV(S)1018 | 1961 | £6 | £15 | US |
| Memphis Slim | LP | Chess | LP1455 | 1961 | £10 | £25 | US |
| Memphis Slim | LP | Collector | JGN1004 | 1961 | £6 | £15 | |
| Memphis Slim | LP | King | LP885 | 1964 | £6 | £15 | US |
| Memphis Slim | LP | World Record Club | T394 | 1962 | £4 | £10 | |
| Memphis Slim | LP | XTRA | XTRA1008 | 1965 | £5 | £12 | |
| Memphis Slim Vol. 2 | LP | Collector | JGN1005 | 1961 | £6 | £15 | |
| Memphis Slim, USA | LP | Candid | 9024 | 1962 | £8 | £20 | US |
| No Strain | LP | Fontana | 688302ZL | 1964 | £6 | £15 | |
| Pinetop Blues | 7" | Collector | JDN102 | 1960 | £1.50 | £4 | |
| Pinetop's Blues | LP | Polydor | 623211 | 1967 | £4 | £10 | |
| Real Folk Blues | LP | Chess | 1510 | 1966 | £8 | £20 | US |
| Self Portrait | LP | Scepter | SM535 | 1966 | £5 | £12 | US |
| Steady Rollin' Blues | LP | Bluesville | BV(S)1075 | 1964 | £6 | £15 | US |
| Travellin' With The Blues | LP | Storyville | SLP118 | 1964 | £4 | £10 | |
| Tribute To Big Bill Broonzy | LP | Candid | 9023 | 1961 | £8 | £20 | US |
| World's Foremost Blues Singer | 7" EP | Summit | LSE2041 | 1963 | £2 | £5 | |

## MEN

One of the Men was thinking of growing his hair long on one side only; the others were still working out how to get the best out of their new synthesizers. This was, in fact, the Human League.

| | | | | | | | |
|---|---|---|---|---|---|---|---|
| I Don't Depend On You | 7" | Virgin | VS269 | 1979 | £2.50 | £6 | |
| I Don't Depend On You | 12" | Virgin | VS26912 | 1979 | £2.50 | £6 | |

## MEN AT WORK

| | | | | | | | |
|---|---|---|---|---|---|---|---|
| Down Under | 7" | Epic | EPCA1980 | 1983 | £1.50 | £4 | shaped picture disc |

## MENDES, CARLOS

| | | | | | | | |
|---|---|---|---|---|---|---|---|
| Shadows | 7" | Pye | 7N25581 | 1972 | £2 | £5 | |

## MENDES PREY

| | | | | | | | |
|---|---|---|---|---|---|---|---|
| Wonderland | 7" | Wag | WAG2 | 1986 | £2 | £5 | |

## MENSWEAR

| | | | | | | | |
|---|---|---|---|---|---|---|---|
| Day Dreamer | 7" | Laurel | LAU5 | 1995 | £1.50 | £4 | |
| Day Dreamer | 10" | Laurel | LAUXDJ5 | 1995 | £10 | £20 | promo |
| I'll Manage Somehow | CD-s | Laurel | LAU4 | 1995 | £10 | £20 | |
| I'll Manage Somehow | 7" | Laurel | LAU4 | 1995 | £10 | £20 | |

## MENZIES, IAN

| | | | | | | | |
|---|---|---|---|---|---|---|---|
| Have Tartan, Will Trad | LP | Pye | NJL23 | 1960 | £4 | £10 | |
| Melody Maker All Stars | 7" EP | Pye | NJE1049 | 1958 | £2 | £5 | |

## MERCER, MARY MAE

| | | | | | | | |
|---|---|---|---|---|---|---|---|
| Mary Mae Mercer | 7" EP | Decca | DFE8599 | 1965 | £4 | £8 | |

## MERCHANT, NATALIE

| | | | | | | | |
|---|---|---|---|---|---|---|---|
| Companion To Tigerlily | CD | East West | NATPRO1 | 1996 | £8 | £20 | US promo picture disc |

## MERCHANTS OF DREAM

| | | | | | | | |
|---|---|---|---|---|---|---|---|
| Strange Night Voyage | LP | A&M | SP4199 | 1967 | £6 | £15 | US |

## MERCURY, FREDDIE

| | | | | | | | |
|---|---|---|---|---|---|---|---|
| Barcelona | CD-s | Polydor | POCD887 | 1987 | £3 | £8 | |
| Barcelona | CD-s | Polydor | POCD887 | 1987 | £30 | £60 | signed |
| Barcelona | CD-s | Polygram | 0805482 | 1989 | £12.50 | £25 | CD video |
| Barcelona | 7" | Polydor | POSP887 | 1987 | £1.50 | £4 | with Montserrat Caballé |
| Barcelona | 12" | Polydor | POSPP887 | 1987 | £20 | £40 | with Montserrat Caballé, picture disc |
| Barcelona | 12" | Polydor | POSPX887 | 1987 | £4 | £10 | with Montserrat Caballé, gatefold sleeve |
| Freddie Mercury Album | CD | EMI | CDPCSDX124 | 1992 | £5 | £12 | boxed with 5 photos |
| Golden Boy | CD-s | Polydor | POCD23 | 1988 | £12.50 | £25 | |
| Golden Boy | 7" | Polydor | PO23 | 1988 | £1.50 | £4 | with Montserrat Caballé |
| Golden Boy | 12" | Polydor | POSPX23 | 1988 | £4 | £10 | with Montserrat Caballé |
| Great Pretender | CD-s | EMI | CDR6336 | 1993 | £2 | £5 | |
| Great Pretender | 7" | Parlophone | R6151 | 1987 | £1.50 | £4 | |
| Great Pretender | 7" | Parlophone | RP6151 | 1987 | £20 | £40 | shaped picture disc & plinth |
| Great Pretender | 12" | Parlophone | 12R6151 | 1987 | £5 | £12 | |
| Great Pretender | 10" | Parlophone | 10R6151 | 1987 | £20 | £40 | promo |
| How Can I Go On | CD-s | Polydor | PZCD29 | 1989 | £3 | £8 | with Montserrat Caballé |
| How Can I Go On | 7" | Polydor | POSX29 | 1988 | £20 | £40 | with Montserrat Caballé, picture disc |
| How Can I Go On | 12" | Polydor | POSPX29 | 1989 | £4 | £10 | with Montserrat Caballé |
| I Was Born To Love You | 7" | CBS | A6019 | 1985 | £1.50 | £4 | |
| I Was Born To Love You | 7" | CBS | DA6019 | 1985 | £12.50 | £25 | double |
| I Was Born To Love You | 12" | CBS | TA6019 | 1985 | £4 | £10 | |
| In My Defence | CD-s | EMI | CDR6331 | 1992 | £2 | £5 | 2 versons |
| Living On My Own | CD-s | EMI | CDR6355 | 1993 | £2 | £5 | |
| Living On My Own | 7" | CBS | A6555 | 1985 | £1.50 | £4 | |
| Living On My Own | 12" | CBS | GTA6555 | 1985 | £10 | £20 | gatefold sleeve |
| Living On My Own | 12" | CBS | TA6555 | 1985 | £3 | £8 | |
| Love Kills | 7" | CBS | A4735 | 1984 | £2 | £5 | Giorgio Moroder B side |
| Love Kills | 7" | CBS | WA4735 | 1984 | £20 | £40 | Giorgio Moroder B side, picture disc |
| Love Kills | 12" | CBS | TA4735 | 1984 | £5 | £12 | Giorgio Moroder B side |
| Love Me Like There's No Tomorrow | 12" | CBS | TA6725 | 1985 | £10 | £20 | |
| Made In Heaven | 7" | CBS | A6413 | 1985 | £2 | £5 | |
| Made In Heaven | 7" | CBS | WA6413 | 1985 | £20 | £40 | shaped picture disc |
| Made In Heaven | 12" | CBS | TA6413 | 1985 | £5 | £12 | |
| Mr. Bad Guy | LP | CBS | 86312 | 1985 | £4 | £10 | |
| Mr. Bad Guy | CD | CBS | CD86312 | 1985 | £6 | £15 | |
| Mr. Bad Guy | CD | CBS | CD86312 | 1985 | £75 | £150 | 14 tracks |
| Time | 12" | EMI | 12EMI5559 | 1986 | £4 | £10 | |

| | | | | | | | |
|---|---|---|---|---|---|---|---|
| Zabou | LP | EMI | 1C06642407281 | 1986 | £25 | £50 | *... German, with other artists* |
| Zabou | CD | EMI | 5647466092 | 1986 | £30 | £60 | *... German, with other artists* |

## MERCURY REV

| | | | | | | | |
|---|---|---|---|---|---|---|---|
| Yerself Is Steam/Lego My Ego | CD | Beggars Banquet | BBQCD125 | 1995 | £6 | £15 | *double* |

## MERION

| | | | | | | |
|---|---|---|---|---|---|---|
| I Go To Sleep | 7" | Page One | POF041 | 1967 | £1.50 | £4 | |

## MERKIN

| | | | | | | | |
|---|---|---|---|---|---|---|---|
| Music From Merkin Manor | LP | Windi | 1005 | 1969 | £150 | £250 | *US* |

## MERMAN, ETHEL

| | | | | | | |
|---|---|---|---|---|---|---|
| Husband A Wife | 7" | Brunswick | 05346 | 1954 | £1.50 | £4 |
| There's No Business Like Show Business | 7" | Brunswick | 05381 | 1955 | £1.50 | £4 |

## MERRELL, RAY

| | | | | | | |
|---|---|---|---|---|---|---|
| Tears Of Joy | 7" | Jayboy | BOY22 | 1970 | £50 | £100 |

## MERRICK, TONY

| | | | | | | |
|---|---|---|---|---|---|---|
| Lady Jane | 7" | Columbia | DB7913 | 1966 | £1.50 | £4 |

## MERRILL, BOB

| | | | | | | |
|---|---|---|---|---|---|---|
| Nairobi | 7" | Columbia | DB4086 | 1958 | £1.50 | £4 |

## MERRILL, BUDDY

| | | | | | | |
|---|---|---|---|---|---|---|
| Sweet September | 7" | Vocalion | VN9261 | 1966 | £2.50 | £6 |

## MERRILL, HELEN

| | | | | | | |
|---|---|---|---|---|---|---|
| Date With The Blues | 7" EP | MGM | MGMEP699 | 1959 | £2 | £5 |
| Nearness Of You | LP | Mercury | MMB12000 | 1959 | £6 | £15 |

## MERRY-GO-ROUND

| | | | | | | | |
|---|---|---|---|---|---|---|---|
| Merry-Go-Round | LP | A&M | (SP)4132 | 1967 | £5 | £12 | *US* |

## MERRYMEN

| | | | | | | | |
|---|---|---|---|---|---|---|---|
| Big Bamboo | 7" | Doctor Bird | DB1004 | 1966 | £5 | £10 | |
| Caribbean Treasure Chest | LP | Island | ILP984 | 1968 | £15 | £30 | *pink label* |

## MERRYWEATHER, BIG MACEO

| | | | | | | | |
|---|---|---|---|---|---|---|---|
| Big Maceo Merryweather And John Lee Hooker | LP | Fortune | 3002 | | £10 | £25 | *US* |

## MERRYWEATHER, NEIL

| | | | | | | | |
|---|---|---|---|---|---|---|---|
| Word Of Mouth | LP | Capitol | STBB278 | 1969 | £8 | £20 | *US double* |

## MERSEYBEATS

| | | | | | | | |
|---|---|---|---|---|---|---|---|
| Don't Let It Happen To Us | 7" | Fontana | TF568 | 1965 | £1.50 | £4 | |
| England's Best Sellers | LP | ARC International | 834 | 1964 | £15 | £30 | *US* |
| I Love You, Yes I Do | 7" | Fontana | TF607 | 1965 | £1.50 | £4 | |
| I Stand Accused | 7" | Fontana | TF645 | 1965 | £1.50 | £4 | |
| I Think Of You | 7" EP | Fontana | 465328 | 1966 | £12.50 | £25 | *French* |
| I Think Of You | 7" EP | Fontana | TE17423 | 1964 | £10 | £20 | |
| It's Love That Really Counts | 7" | Fontana | TF412 | 1963 | £1.50 | £4 | |
| Last Night | 7" | Fontana | TF504 | 1964 | £1.50 | £4 | |
| Merseybeats | LP | Fontana | TL5210 | 1964 | £30 | £60 | |
| Merseybeats | LP | Wing | WL1163 | 1965 | £8 | £20 | |
| Merseybeats On Stage | 7" EP | Fontana | TE17422 | 1964 | £7.50 | £15 | |
| Wishin' And Hopin' | 7" EP | Fontana | TE17432 | 1964 | £7.50 | £15 | |

## MERSEYBOYS

| | | | | | | |
|---|---|---|---|---|---|---|
| Fifteen Greatest Songs Of The Beatles | LP | Ace Of Clubs | ACL1169 | 1964 | £4 | £10 |

## MERSEYS

| | | | | | | | |
|---|---|---|---|---|---|---|---|
| Cat | 7" | Fontana | TF845 | 1967 | £1.50 | £4 | |
| Lovely Loretta | 7" | Fontana | TF955 | 1968 | £1.50 | £4 | |
| Penny In My Pocket | 7" | Fontana | TF916 | 1968 | £1.50 | £4 | |
| Rhythm Of Love | 7" EP | Fontana | 465356 | 1966 | £12.50 | £25 | *French* |
| Rhythm Of Love | 7" | Fontana | TF776 | 1966 | £1.50 | £4 | |
| So Sad About Us | 7" | Fontana | TF732 | 1966 | £1.50 | £4 | |
| Sorrow | 7" | Fontana | TF694 | 1966 | £1.50 | £4 | |

## MERSEYSIPPI JAZZ BAND

| | | | | | | |
|---|---|---|---|---|---|---|
| Any Old Rags | 10" LP | Esquire | 20093 | 1958 | £4 | £10 |
| Merseysippi Jazz Band | 10" LP | Esquire | 20063 | 1956 | £4 | £10 |
| Merseysippi Jazz Band | 10" LP | Esquire | 20083 | 1957 | £4 | £10 |
| Merseysippi Jazz Band | 10" LP | Esquire | 20088 | 1957 | £4 | £10 |

## MERTON PARKAS

| | | | | | | |
|---|---|---|---|---|---|---|
| Flat Nineteen | 7" | Well Suspect | BLAM002 | 1983 | £2 | £5 |

## MESMERIZING EYE
Psychedelia .......................................... LP ...... Smash ............. MGS27090 ............. 1967 £6 .......... £15 ....................... US

## MESSAGE
Dawn Anew Is Coming ........................... LP ...... Bacillus ........... BLPS19081 ............. 1972 £5 .......... £12 ................ German

## MESSENGER
Oy I Value Elation ................................... 7" ...... Anagram ........ A001 ..................... 1967 £5 .......... £10 .............

## MESSINA, JIM
Dragsters .................................................. LP ...... Audio Fidelity.. DF(S)7037 ............. 1964 £10 ..... £25 ................... US
Jim Messina And The Jesters ................... LP ...... Thimble ......... 3 ............................. 196– £8 ...... £20 ................... US

## METABOLIST
Dromm ..................................................... 7" ...... Dromm ........... DRO1 ..................... 1979 £2.50 ..... £6 .............
Identity ................................................... 7" ...... Dromm ........... DRO3 ..................... 1979 £2 .......... £5 .............

## METALLICA
| Title | Format | Label | Cat no | Year | | | Notes |
|---|---|---|---|---|---|---|---|
| Creeping Death | 12" | Music For Nations | CV12KUT112 | 1987 | £2.50 | £6 | blue vinyl |
| Creeping Death | 12" | Music For Nations | CV12KUT112 | 1987 | £15 | £30 | green or red vinyl |
| Creeping Death | 12" | Music For Nations | GV12KUT112 | 1987 | £5 | £12 | gold vinyl |
| Creeping Death | 12" | Music For Nations | P12KUT112 | 1984 | £3 | £8 | picture disc |
| Enter Sandman | CD-s | Vertigo | 8687332 | 1991 | £2 | £5 | |
| Enter Sandman | CD-s | Vertigo | METCD7 | 1991 | £2 | £5 | |
| Enter Sandman | CD-s | Vertigo | METCD7 | 1991 | £20 | £40 | boxed set |
| Enter Sandman | 7" | Vertigo | METAL7 | 1991 | £2.50 | £6 | picture disc |
| Enter Sandman | 12" | Vertigo | METBX712 | 1991 | £3 | £8 | boxed with 4 prints |
| Eye Of The Beholder | 12" | Vertigo | | 1988 | £10 | £20 | promo |
| Fifteen Pieces Of Live Shit | CD | Elektra | PRCD88792 | 1993 | £20 | £40 | US double promo |
| Good, The Bad And The Live | 12" | Vertigo | 8754871 | 1990 | £15 | £30 | 6 x 12" plus EP |
| Harvester Of Sorrow | CD-s | Vertigo | METCD2 | 1988 | £15 | £30 | |
| Harvester Of Sorrow | 7" | Vertigo | METAL2 | 1988 | £10 | £20 | promo, special sleeve |
| Harvester Of Sorrow | 12" | Vertigo | METAL212 | 1988 | £6 | £15 | promo, special sleeve |
| Jump in The Fire | 7" | Music For Nations | PKUT105 | 1986 | £6 | £12 | shaped picture disc |
| Jump In The Fire | 12" | Music For Nations | 12KUT105 | 1984 | £5 | £12 | red or gold vinyl |
| Kill 'Em All | LP | Music For Nations | MFN7P | 1986 | £5 | £12 | picture disc |
| Mandatory Metallica | CD | Elektra | PRCD8020 | 1988 | £10 | £25 | US promo |
| Master Of Puppets | LP | Music For Nations | MFN60P | 1986 | £5 | £12 | picture disc |
| Nothing Else Matters | CD-s | Vertigo | METCD10 | 1992 | £10 | £20 | |
| Nothing Else Matters – Live | CD-s | Vertigo | METCL10 | 1992 | £12.50 | £25 | |
| One | CD-s | Vertigo | METCD5 | 1989 | £2 | £5 | |
| One | 7" | Vertigo | MET5 | 1989 | £12.50 | £25 | promo, special sleeve |
| One | 10" | Vertigo | METPD510 | 1989 | £4 | £10 | picture disc |
| One (Demo Version) | 12" | Vertigo | METALG512 | 1989 | £3 | £8 | gatefold picture sleeve |
| Ride The Lightning | LP | Music For Nations | MFN27 | 1984 | £30 | £60 | green or blue vinyl |
| Ride The Lightning | LP | Music For Nations | MFN27P | 1986 | £5 | £12 | picture disc |
| Sad But True | CD-s | Vertigo | METCH11 | 1993 | £6 | £15 | picture disc |
| Unforgiven | CD-s | Vertigo | 8661392 | 1991 | £2 | £5 | |
| Unforgiven | CD-s | Vertigo | METCD8 | 1991 | £2 | £5 | |
| Wherever I May Roam | CD-s | Vertigo | METCD9 | 1992 | £4 | £10 | picture disc |
| Whiplash | 12" | Megaforce | MRS04P | 1987 | £10 | £20 | picture disc |
| Whiplash Sampler | CD-s | Vertigo | METCD100 | 1988 | £20 | £40 | promo |

## METEORS
| Title | Format | Label | Cat no | Year | | | Notes |
|---|---|---|---|---|---|---|---|
| Crazed | 7" | Lost Soul | LOST101 | 1981 | £2 | £5 | |
| Johnny Remember Me | 7" | ID | EYE1P | 1983 | £1.50 | £4 | picture disc |
| Meteor Madness | 7" | Ace | SW65 | 1981 | £2 | £5 | blue vinyl |
| Meteor Madness | 10" | Ace | SWT65 | 1981 | £10 | £20 | test pressing |
| Radioactive Kid | 7" | Ace | NS74 | 1981 | £1.50 | £4 | clear vinyl |

## METERS
| Title | Format | Label | Cat no | Year | | | Notes |
|---|---|---|---|---|---|---|---|
| Cabbage Alley | LP | Reprise | K33242 | 1972 | £4 | £10 | |
| Cissy Strut | LP | Island | ILPS9250 | 1974 | £6 | £15 | |
| Fire On The Bayou | LP | Reprise | K54044 | 1975 | £6 | £15 | |
| Look A Py-Py | 7" | Direction | 584751 | 1970 | £1.50 | £4 | |
| Look-ka Py Py | LP | Josie | JOS4011 | 1970 | £6 | £15 | US |
| Meters | LP | Josie | JOS4010 | 1969 | £6 | £15 | US |
| Rejuvenation | LP | Reprise | K54027 | 1974 | £6 | £15 | |
| Sophisticated Cissy | 7" | Stateside | SS2140 | 1969 | £2 | £5 | |
| Struttin' | LP | Josie | JOS4012 | 1970 | £6 | £15 | US |
| Trick Bag | LP | Reprise | K54078 | 1976 | £6 | £15 | |

## METHENY, PAT
| Title | Format | Label | Cat no | Year | | | Notes |
|---|---|---|---|---|---|---|---|
| Bright Size Life | LP | ECM | ECM1073ST | 1975 | £5 | £12 | |
| Watercolors | LP | ECM | ECM1097T | 1976 | £4 | £10 | |

## METHUSELAH
Matthew, Mark, Luke, & John.................. LP ..... Elektra ............ EKS74052 .............. 1969 £20......... £40 .....................US

## METIS, FRANK
Show Business.................................. 7" EP . London .......... REN1048 .............. 1956 £2........... £5 ...............................

## METROPHASE
In Black................................. 7" ...... Neo London.... MS01 .................... 1979 £2........... £5 ...............................
New Age................................. 7" ...... Neo London.... MS02 .................... 1979 £2........... £5 ...............................

## METROTONES
Tops In Rock And Roll......................... 10" LP Columbia ........ 6341 .................... 1955 £50....... £100 .....................US

## MEZA, LEE
If It Happens................................. 7" ...... Stateside ......... SS589.................... 1967 £15......... £30 ...............................

## MEZZROW, MEZZ
At The Schola Cantorum, Paris.............. 10" LP Ducretet- ....... TKL93092 .............. 1956 £8........... £20 ...............................
 .......................................................... Thomson .......
King Jazz Story............................. 7" EP . Storyville ....... SEP394 .................... 1962 £2........... £5 ...............................
Mezzrow-Bechet Quintet ...................... LP ..... Vogue............ LAE12017 ........... 1956 £6........... £15 ...............................
Pleyel Concert ................................ LP ..... Vogue............ LAE12007 .............. 1955 £6........... £15 ...............................

## MGM STUDIO ORCHESTRA
Rock Around The Clock........................ 7" ...... MGM ........... SP1144.................... 1955 £1.50........ £4 ...............................

## MICHAEL, GEORGE
Careless Whisper ............................. 7" ...... Epic ........... A4603 .................... 1984 £5........... £10 .... poster picture sleeve
Careless Whisper ............................ 12" .... Epic ........... WA4603 .............. 1984 £10......... £25 ........................picture disc
Careless Whisper (Wexler mix)................ 12" .... Epic ........... QTA4603................ 1984 £15......... £30 ...............................
Cowboys And Angels ......................... CD-s .. Epic ........... 6567742 .................. 1991 £3........... £8 ...............................
Don't Let The Sun Go Down On Me........ CD-s .. Epic ........... 6576462 .................. 1991 £2........... £5 ...... with Elton John
Faith ............................................. LP ..... Epic ........... ........................ 1987 £15......... £30 Australian picture disc
Faith ............................................. CD-s .. Epic ........... CDEMU3 ......... 1987 £6........... £15 ...............................
Faith ............................................. CD ..... Columbia ....... CSK2850 ......... 1987 £8........... £20 ..US promo, hologram
 .......................................................................................................................................................... cover
Faith ............................................. CD ..... Epic ........... 4600009 ......... 1987 £5........... £12 .....................picture disc
Faith ............................................. 12" .... Epic ........... EMUP3 .......... 1987 £2.50........ £6 ....................picture disc
Father Figure ................................ CD-s .. Epic ........... CDEMU4 ......... 1988 £4........... £10 ...............................
Father Figure ................................ 7" ...... Epic ........... EMUP4 .......... 1988 £2.50........ £6 ..... shaped picture disc
Freedom ....................................... CD-s .. Epic ........... GEOC3 .......... 1990 £2........... £5 ...............................
Heal The Pain ............................... CD-s .. Epic ........... 6566475 ......... 1991 £2.50........ £6 ..................... 2 versions
I Want Your Sex............................. CD-s .. Epic ........... CDLUST1 ......... 1987 £2.50........ £6 ...............................
I Want Your Sex............................. 12" .... Epic ........... QT1 .............. 1987 £2.50........ £6 ...............................
Kissing A Fool ............................... CD-s .. Epic ........... CDEMU7 ......... 1988 £2........... £5 ...............................
Listen Without Prejudice .................. LP ..... Epic ........... ........................ 1990 £20......... £40 ..Brazilian picture disc
Listen Without Prejudice .................. CD ..... Epic ........... 4672959 ......... 1990 £5........... £12 .....................picture disc
Listen Without Prejudice-An Interview ..... CD ..... Columbia ....... CSK72226 ......... 1990 £8........... £20 .................US promo
Monkey ........................................ CD-s .. Epic ........... CDEMU6 ......... 1988 £2.50........ £6 ...............................
Older ........................................... CD ..... Virgin ............ CDV2802.......... 1996 £20......... £40 .. Press pack with CD
 ........................................................................................................................................................ and cassette
One More Try ................................ CD-s .. Epic ........... CPEMU5......... 1988 £4........... £10 .....................picture disc
One More Try ................................ CD-s .. Epic ........... EPC6515322 ....... £5........... £12 ...........................3" single
Praying For Time ........................... CD-s .. Epic ........... GEOC1 .......... 1990 £2.50........ £6 ..................... 2 versions
Too Funky .................................... CD-s .. Epic ........... 6580582 ......... 1992 £2........... £5 ...............................
Waiting For That Day........................ CD-s .. Epic ........... CDGEO2.......... 1990 £2........... £5 ...............................
Wembley........................................ cass ..... Epic ........... XPC4060 .......... 1991 £6........... £15 ...............................

## MICHAELS, MARILYN
Tell Tommy I Miss Him....................... 7" ...... RCA ............. RCA1208 ......... 1960 £2........... £5 ...............................

## MICHIGAN RAG
Don't Run Away ............................. 7" ...... Blue Horizon... 2096009 ................ 1972 £2.50........ £6 ...............................

## MICKEY & KITTY
Buttercup ...................................... 7" ...... London .......... HLE9054 .............. 1960 £4........... £8 ...............................

## MICKEY & SYLVIA
Bewildered .................................... 7" ...... RCA ............. RCA1064 ......... 1958 £10......... £20 ...............................
Love Is Strange.............................. LP ..... RCA ............. CDN5133 ......... 1965 £37.50..... £75 ...............................
Love Is Strange.............................. 7" ...... HMV............ POP331 .......... 1957 £87.50..... £175 ...............................
Love Is Strange.............................. 7" ...... RCA ............. RCA1487 ......... 1965 £7.50....... £15 ...............................
New Sounds ................................... LP ..... Vik ............. LX1102............ 1958 £50......... £100 .....................US
Sweeter As The Day Goes By.................. 7" ...... RCA ............. RCA1206 ......... 1960 £5........... £10 ...............................

## MICKEY FINN
Garden Of My Mind ......................... 7" ...... Direction ........ 583086............ 1967 £37.50..... £75 ...............................
If I Had You Baby............................ 7" ...... Polydor.......... 56719............ 1966 £37.50..... £75 ...............................
Sporting Life .................................. 7" ...... Columbia ....... DB7510 .......... 1965 £37.50..... £75 ...............................

## MIDDLETON, TONY
Don't Ever Leave Me ........................ 7" ...... Polydor.......... 56704............ 1966 £150..... £250 .......... best auctioned
My Little Red Book .......................... 7" ...... London .......... HLR9983.............. 1965 £6........... £12 .. with Burt Bacharach

## MIDKNIGHTS
Midknights .................................... 7" EP . E.R.S............ MN1/MEP101 ...... 1963 £50......... £100 ...............................

## MIDNIGHT AT NIXA GROUP
Midnight At Nixa ..................................... LP ...... Nixa .............. NJL3 ....................... ....... £4 .......... £10 .......................

## MIDNIGHT CIRCUS
Midnight Circus ........................... LP ...... Bellaphon ....... ...................... 1972 £50 ....... £100 .......................

## MIDNIGHT OIL
| | | | | | | | |
|---|---|---|---|---|---|---|---|
| Beds Are Burning | CD-s | CBS | CDOIL1 | 1988 | £2 | £5 | |
| Beds Are Burning | CD-s | CBS | CDOIL3 | 1989 | £2 | £5 | |
| Blue Sky Mining | CD-s | CBS | CDOIL5 | 1990 | £2 | £5 | |
| Dead Heart | CD-s | CBS | CDOIL2 | 1988 | £2 | £5 | |
| Dead Heart | CD-s | CBS | CDOIL4 | 1989 | £2 | £5 | |
| Earth And Sun And Moon | CD | CBS | 4736052 | 1993 | £10 | £25 | *embossed green fold-out envelope* |
| Forgotten Years | CD-s | CBS | CDOIL6 | 1990 | £2 | £5 | |

## MIDNIGHT RAGS
| | | | | | | |
|---|---|---|---|---|---|---|
| Cars That Ate New York | 7" | Velvet Moon | VM1 | 1980 | £2.50 | £6 |
| Public Enemy | 7" | Ace | ACE005 | 1980 | £2 | £5 |

## MIDNIGHT SHIFT
'Saturday Jump' was the theme for the long-running *Saturday Club* programme on BBC radio.

Saturday Jump ................................. 7" ...... Decca ............ F12487 .................... 1966 £2.50 ......... £6 .......................

## MIDNIGHT SUN
| | | | | | | | |
|---|---|---|---|---|---|---|---|
| Dansk Beat | LP | Sonet | SLP2411 | 1975 | £6 | £15 | *Danish* |
| Midnight Dream | LP | Sonet | SLPS1547 | 1973 | £5 | £12 | *Danish* |
| Midnight Sun | LP | MCA | MCF2687 | 1973 | £4 | £10 | |
| Midnight Sun | LP | MCA | MKPS2019 | 1972 | £6 | £15 | |
| Rainbow Band | LP | Sonet | SLPS1523 | 1970 | £25 | £50 | |
| Rainbow Band | LP | Sonet | SLPS1523A | 1971 | £6 | £15 | *different vocals* |
| Walking Circles | LP | MCA | MCF2691 | 1973 | £4 | £10 | |
| Walking Circles | LP | MCA | MKPS2024 | 1972 | £6 | £15 | |
| Walking Circles | LP | Sonet | SLPS1536 | 1972 | £6 | £15 | |

## MIDNIGHTS
Show Me Around ...................... 7" ...... Ember .......... EMBS220 ......... 1966 £1.50 ......... £4 .......................

## M.I.FIVE
Deep Purple's drummer, Ian Paice, first appeared on record with M.I.Five, as did the original singer with the more famous group, Rod Evans.

You'll Never Stop Me Loving You ........... 7" ...... Parlophone ...... R5486 ................... 1966 £20 ......... £40 .......................

## MIGHTY AVENGERS
| | | | | | | |
|---|---|---|---|---|---|---|
| Blue Turns To Grey | 7" | Decca | F12085 | 1965 | £5 | £10 |
| Hide Your Pride | 7" | Decca | F11891 | 1964 | £2.50 | £6 |
| Sleepy City | 7" | Decca | F12198 | 1965 | £5 | £10 |
| So Much In Love | 7" | Decca | F11962 | 1964 | £2.50 | £6 |

## MIGHTY BABY
The group evolved out of the Action, but their music sounded little like that of the earlier group. With late arrivals Martin Stone (playing impressive lead guitar) and Ian Whiteman (keyboards and woodwinds) dominating the proceedings, Mighty Baby produced a floating, melodic kind of progressive rock that is amongst the most memorable of the genre. Remarkably, the best songs of all remained as forgotten out-takes until issued by Castle in 1985 (*Action Speaks Louder Than . . .*). Although credited to the Action, these five songs are actually the work of Mighty Baby and, despite their somewhat unsophisticated production, they emerge as classic recordings. (These tracks are also included on the CD reissue of the *Mighty Baby* album.)

| | | | | | | |
|---|---|---|---|---|---|---|
| Devil's Whisper | 7" | Blue Horizon | 2096003 | 1971 | £20 | £40 |
| Egyptian Tomb | LP | Psycho | PSYCHO31 | 1985 | £4 | £10 |
| Jug Of Love | LP | Blue Horizon | 2931001 | 1971 | £37.50 | £75 |
| Mighty Baby | LP | Head | HDLS6002 | 1969 | £20 | £40 |

## MIGHTY DIAMONDS
| | | | | | | |
|---|---|---|---|---|---|---|
| Deeper Roots | LP | Front Line | FL8001 | 1979 | £5 | £12 |
| Ice In Fire | LP | Virgin | V2078 | 1977 | £5 | £12 |
| Planet Earth | LP | Virgin | V2102 | 1978 | £5 | £12 |
| Right Time | LP | Virgin | V2052 | 1976 | £5 | £12 |

## MIGHTY MEN
No Way Out ............................ 7" ...... Salvo .............. SLO1804 ............... 1962 £4 .......... £8 .......................

## MIGHTY SAM
| | | | | | | |
|---|---|---|---|---|---|---|
| Fannie Mae | 7" | Stateside | SS544 | 1966 | £2 | £5 |
| Mighty Soul | LP | Soul City | SCM004 | 1970 | £15 | £30 |
| Papa True Love | 7" | Soul City | SC115 | 1969 | £2 | £5 |
| Sweet Dreams | 7" | Stateside | SS534 | 1966 | £2 | £5 |
| When She Touches Me | 7" | Stateside | SS2076 | 1968 | £1.50 | £4 |

## MIGHTY TERROR
| | | | | | | |
|---|---|---|---|---|---|---|
| Kings Of Calypso No. 1 | 7" EP | Pye | NEP24009 | 1956 | £2 | £5 |
| Kings Of Calypso No. 5 | 7" EP | Pye | NEP24086 | 1958 | £2 | £5 |

## MIGHTY VIKINGS
Do Re Mi ........................... 7" ...... Island .............. WI3060 .............. 1967 £4 .............. £8 .......................

Rockitty Fockitty .................................... 7" ...... Island .............. WI3074 ................. 1967 £4 ............. £8 ...............................

## MIGIL FIVE
Meet The Migil Five ............................. 7" EP . Pye ................. NEP24191 ........... 1964 £5 ...... £10 ................................
Mocking Bird Hill ................................ 7" ...... Pye ................. 7N15597 ............ 1964 £1.50 ...... £4 ...............................
Mockingbird Hill .................................. LP ..... Pye ................. NPL18093 ............ 1964 £6 ...... £15 ...............................
Together ........................................... 7" ...... Columbia ........ DB8196 ............... 1967 £4 ............. £8 ...............................
Maybe .............................................. 7" ...... Pye ................. 7N15572 ............ 1963 £1.50 ...... £4 ...............................

## MIKE & THE MECHANICS
All I Need Is A Miracle .......................... 12" ..... WEA ............. U8765TP ............ 1985 £2.50 ...... £6 ..................... picture disc
Everybody Gets A Second Chance ............ CD-s .. Virgin ............ VSCDX1396 ....... 1992 £2 ............. £5 ......... with sheet music
Get Up ............................................. CD-s .. Virgin ............ VSCDG1359 ........ 1991 £2 ............. £5 ...............................
Living Years ...................................... CD-s .. WEA ............. U7717CD ............ 1988 £2 ............. £5 ..................... 3" single
Nobody Knows ................................... CD-s .. WEA ............. U7602CD ............ 1989 £2 ............. £5 ...............................
Nobody's Perfect ................................ CD-s .. WEA ............. U7789CD ............ 1988 £2 ............. £5 ..................... 3" single
Silent Running ................................... 7" ...... WEA ............. U8908P ............... 1985 £2.50 ...... £6 ..... shaped picture disc
Time And Place .................................. CD-s .. Virgin ............ VSCDX1351 ....... 1991 £2 ............. £5 ............ with 5 prints
Word Of Mouth .................................. CD-s .. Virgin ............ VSCD1345 .......... 1991 £2 ............. £5 ...............................
Word Of Mouth .................................. CD-s .. Virgin ............ VSCDX1345 ....... 1991 £2.50 ...... £6 . numbered picture disc

## MIKE & THE MODIFIERS
I Found Myself A Brand New Baby .......... 7" ...... Oriole ............. CB1775 ............... 1962 £400 ..... £600 ........... best auctioned

## MIKLAGARD
Miklagard ......................................... LP ..... Edge ............... 791 ................... 1979 £10 ......... £25 ................. Swedish

## MILANO, BOBBY
If Tears Could Bring You Back ................ 7" ...... Capitol ........... CL14309 ............. 1955 £1.50 ...... £4 ...............................
King Or A Slave .................................. 7" ...... Capitol .......... CL14252 ............. 1955 £1.50 ...... £4 ...............................

## MILBURN, AMOS
Blues Boss ......................................... LP ..... Motown .......... 608 ................... 1963 £75 ...... £150 .................... US
Every Day Of The Week ........................ 7" ...... Vogue ............ V9064 ............... 1957 £50 ...... £100 ............ tri-centre
Let's Have A Party ............................... LP ..... Score .............. LP4012 .............. 1957 £50 ...... £100 .................... US
Million Sellers ................................... LP ..... Imperial .......... A9176 ............... 1962 £25 ............ £50 .................... US
One Scotch One Bourbon One Beer ......... 7" ...... Vogue ............ V9163 ............... 1960 £37.50 ...... £75 ...............................
Rock And Roll .................................... 7" EP . Vogue ............ VE170102 ........... 1957 £75 ...... £100 ...............................
Rockin' The Boogie .............................. LP ..... Aladdin ........... 810 ................... 1958 £62.50 ...... £125 .................... US
Rockin' The Boogie .............................. 10" LP Aladdin ........... 704 ................... 1956 £100 ...... £200 .................... US
Rockin' The Boogie .............................. 10" LP Aladdin ........... 704 ................... 1956 £150 ...... £250 ...... US, red vinyl
Rum And Coca Cola ............................. 7" ...... Vogue ............ V9069 ............... 1957 £50 ...... £100 ...............................
Thinking Of You Baby ......................... 7" ...... Vogue ............ V9080 ............... 1957 £50 ...... £100 ...............................

## MILBURN, AMOS JR.
Gloria .............................................. 7" ...... London ........... HLU9795 ............ 1963 £4 ............. £8 ...............................

## MILEM, PERCY
Crying Baby, Baby, Baby ....................... 7" ...... Stateside ......... SS566 ................ 1966 £2.50 ...... £6 ...............................

## MILES, BUDDY
*Expressway To Your Skull* is exciting and dynamic big-band jazz-rock and it deserves to be very much more widely appreciated than it seems to be. This is the music that the Electric Flag were trying to create, without ever quite getting there – here Buddy Miles manages it without guitarist Mike Bloomfield's help. The sleeve notes to the album are by Jimi Hendrix, who knew a good thing when he heard it, although he does not play on the record. It is possible that he does play on the follow-up, *Electric Church*, but in a surprisingly understated manner, if it is he.

Electric Church ................................... LP ..... Mercury .......... SMCL20163 ........... 1969 £4 ............. £10 ...............................
Expressway To Your Skull ..................... LP ..... Mercury .......... SMCL20137 ........... 1968 £6 ............. £15 ...............................
Them Changes .................................... LP ..... Mercury .......... 6338016 ............... 1970 £4 ............. £10 ...............................
Train ............................................... 7" ...... Mercury .......... MF1065 ............... 1968 £1.50 ...... £4 ...............................
With Carlos Santana ............................ LP ..... Columbia ........ CQ31308 ............... 1974 £4 ............. £10 ............... US quad

## MILES, DICK
Cheating The Tide .............................. LP ..... Greenwich       GVR227 ................ 1984 £4 ............. £10 ...............................
                                                      Village ............

## MILES, GARRY
Look For A Star .................................. 7" ...... London ........... HLG9155 ............. 1960 £2.50 ...... £6 ...............................
Looking For A Star .............................. 7" EP . London ........... REG1264 ............. 1960 £12.50 ...... £25 ...............................

## MILES, JOSIE
Josie Miles ........................................ 7" EP . Poydras ........... 103 ................... 196– £2 ............. £5 ...............................

## MILES, LENNY
Don't Believe Him Donna ...................... 7" ...... Top Rank ....... JAR546 .............. 1961 £2.50 ...... £6 ...............................

## MILES, LIZZIE
Blues They Sang .................................. 7" EP . HMV ............ 7EG8178 ............ 1956 £6 ............. £12 ..... side 2 by Billy Young
Clambake On Bourbon Street ................. LP ..... Cook .............. 1185 ................. 1957 £6 ............. £15 .................... US
Hot Songs ......................................... LP ..... Cook .............. 1183 ................. 1956 £6 ............. £15 .................... US
Jazz ................................................. 10" LP Nixa ............... SLPY150 ............. 1954 £6 ............. £15 ...............................
Lizzie Miles New Orleans Boys ............... 7" EP . Melodisc .......... EPM755 .............. 1955 £6 ............. £12 ...............................
Moans And Blues ................................ LP ..... Cook .............. 1182 ................. 1956 £6 ............. £15 .................... US
Torchy Lullabies ................................. LP ..... Cook .............. 1184 ................. 1956 £6 ............. £15 .................... US

## MILESTONES
Milestones ................................................. LP ..... Bellaphon ........ 3311 .................... 1971 £6 .......... £15 ................. *German*

## MILKSHAKES
Please Don't Tell My Baby ...................... 7" ...... Bilko .............. BILK0 ................... 1982 £1.50 ..... £4 ...........................

## MILKWOOD
Many of the groups to emerge as 'new wave' at the end of the seventies were not as new as all that. The Cars evolved from a group called Milkwood, who released a typically countryish mainstream rock LP as early as 1973.

How's The Weather ................................ LP ..... Paramount ...... PAS6046 ............... 1972 £10 ......... £25 .................... *US*

## MILKWOOD TAPESTRY
Milkwood Tapestry .............................. LP ..... Metromedia ..... MD1007 ............... 1969 £15 ......... £30 .................... *US*

## MILLENNIUM
Begin ...................................................... LP ..... Columbia ........ CS9663 ............... 1968 £4 .......... £10 .................... *US*

## MILLER
Baby I Got News For You ...................... 7" ...... Columbia ........ DB7735 ............... 1965 £62.50.. £125 ...........................
Baby I Got News For You ...................... 7" ...... Oak ................. RGJ190 ............... 1965 £62.50.. £125 ...........................

## MILLER, BOB & THE MILLERMEN
Uptown And Downtown ......................... 7" ...... Mercury .......... MF947 ............... 1965 £1.50 ..... £4 ...........................

## MILLER, BOBBIE
Everywhere I Go ..................................... 7" ...... Decca ............. F12354 ............... 1966 £20 ......... £40 ..... *Ian Stewart B side*
What A Guy ............................................ 7" ...... Decca ............. F12064 ............... 1965 £12.50 .. £25 ...........................

## MILLER, CHUCK
Auctioneer .............................................. 7" ...... Mercury .......... 7MT153 ............... 1958 £7.50 ... £15 ...........................
Auctioneer .............................................. 7" ...... Mercury .......... AMT1026 ............ 1959 £4 .......... £8 ...........................
Down The Road Apiece ......................... 7" ...... Mercury .......... 7MT215 ............... 1958 £15 ......... £30 ...........................
Going Going Gone ................................. 7" EP . Mercury .......... ZEP10058 ........... 1960 £15 ......... £30 ...........................
No Baby Like You ................................... 7" ...... Capitol ........... CL14543 ............... 1956 £4 .......... £8 ...........................

## MILLER, FRANKIE
Country Music ........................................ 7" EP . Top Rank ........ JKP3013 ............... 1962 £7.50 ... £15 ...........................
Popping Johnnie ..................................... 7" ...... Melodisc ......... 1529 ................... 1959 £2 .......... £5 ...........................
Rain Rain ............................................... 7" ...... Melodisc ......... 1552 ................... 1960 £2 .......... £5 ...........................
True Blue ................................................ 7" ...... Melodisc ......... 1519 ................... 1959 £4 .......... £8 ...........................

## MILLER, GARY
Gary Miller Hit Parade Vol. 1 ............... 7" EP . Pye ................. NEP24047 ........... 1957 £5 .......... £10 ...........................
Gary Miller Hit Parade Vol. 2 ............... 7" EP . Pye ................. NEP24072 ........... 1958 £4 .......... £8 ...........................
Gary On The Ball .................................. LP ..... Pye ................. NPL18059 ............ 1961 £4 .......... £10 ...........................
Lollipop ................................................. 7" ...... Pye ................. 7N15136 .............. 1958 £1.50 ..... £4 ...........................
Meet Mister Miller Pt. 1 ...................... 7" EP . Pye ................. NEP24057 ........... 1957 £2.50 ... £6 ...........................
Meet Mister Miller Pt. 2 ...................... 7" EP . Pye ................. NEP24058 ........... 1957 £2.50 ... £6 ...........................
Meet Mister Miller Pt. 3 ...................... 7" EP . Pye ................. NEP24059 ........... 1957 £2.50 ... £6 ...........................
Meet Mr. Miller ..................................... LP ..... Pye ................. NPL18008 ............ 1957 £6 .......... £15 ...........................
Stingray ................................................. 7" ...... Pye ................. 7N15698 .............. 1964 £4 .......... £8 ...........................
Story Of My Life ................................... 7" ...... Pye ................. 7N15120 .............. 1958 £1.50 ..... £4 ...........................
Yellow Rose Of Texas ........................... 7" EP . Pye ................. NEP24013 ........... 1956 £6 .......... £12 ...........................

## MILLER, GLEN
Rocksteady Party .................................... 7" ...... Doctor Bird .... DB1128 ............... 1968 £5 .......... £10 ...........................
Where Is The Love ................................ 7" ...... Doctor Bird .... DB1089 ............... 1967 £5 .......... £10 ...........................

## MILLER, GLENN
Army Airforce Band ............................... LP ..... HMV .............. RLS637 ............... 1956 £25 ......... £50 ................. *5 LP set*
Concert Vol. 1 ....................................... 10" LP HMV .............. DLP1012 ............. 1953 £6 .......... £15 ...........................
Concert Vol. 2 ....................................... 10" LP HMV .............. DLP1013 ............. 1953 £6 .......... £15 ...........................
Concert Vol. 3 ....................................... 10" LP HMV .............. DLP1021 ............. 1953 £6 .......... £15 ...........................
Concert Vol. 4 ....................................... 10" LP HMV .............. DLP1081 ............. 1955 £4 .......... £10 ...........................
Glenn Miller .......................................... 10" LP Philips ........... BBR8072 ............. 1955 £4 .......... £10 ...........................
Glenn Miller .......................................... 10" LP Philips ........... BBR8092 ............. 1956 £4 .......... £10 ...........................
Glenn Miller Story ................................. 10" LP HMV .............. DLP1024 ............. 1954 £4 .......... £10 ...........................
I Got Rhythm ........................................ 7" ...... Columbia ........ SCM5086 ............ 1954 £2 .......... £5 ...........................
Limited Edition ...................................... LP ..... HMV .............. RLS598 ............... 1954 £25 ......... £50 ................. *5 LP set*
Limited Edition Vol. 2 .......................... LP ..... HMV .............. RLS599 ............... 1956 £25 ......... £50 ................. *5 LP set*
Little Brown Jug .................................... 7" ...... HMV .............. 7M195 ............... 1954 £4 .......... £8 ...........................
Miller Magic .......................................... 10" LP HMV .............. DLP1122 ............. 1956 £4 .......... £10 ...........................
Orchestra Wives ..................................... 10" LP HMV .............. DLP1059 ............. 1954 £4 .......... £10 ...........................
Polka Dots And Moonbeams .................. 10" LP HMV .............. DLP1145 ............. 1957 £4 .......... £10 ...........................
Sun Valley Serenade .............................. 10" LP HMV .............. DLP1104 ............. 1955 £4 .......... £10 ...........................
Sunrise Serenade ................................... 10" LP HMV .............. DLP1062 ............. 1955 £4 .......... £10 ...........................
Time For Melody ................................... 10" LP HMV .............. DLP1049 ............. 1954 £4 .......... £10 ...........................

## MILLER, HARRY
Berlin Bones ........................................... LP ..... FMP ............... SAJ930 ............... 1981 £5 .......... £12 ................. *German*
Bracknell Breakdown ............................. LP ..... Ogun .............. OG320 ............... 1978 £5 .......... £12 ...........................
Children At Play ..................................... LP ..... Ogun .............. OG200 ............... 1974 £6 .......... £15 ...........................
Down South ........................................... LP ..... Vera Jazz ........ 4213 ................... 1984 £5 .......... £12 ...........................
Family Affair .......................................... LP ..... Ogun .............. OG310 ............... 1977 £5 .......... £12 ...........................
In Conference ........................................ LP ..... Ogun .............. OG523 ............... 1978 £5 .......... £12 ...........................

| | | | | | | | |
|---|---|---|---|---|---|---|---|
| Opened But Hardly Touched | LP | FMP | SAJ848/50 | 1980 | £8 | £20 | German double |
| Sweeter The Meat | LP | FMP | SAJ690 | 1979 | £5 | £12 | German |
| Zweckngal | LP | FMP | SAJ34 | 1980 | £5 | £12 | German |

## MILLER, JIMMY BARBECUES

| | | | | | | |
|---|---|---|---|---|---|---|
| Jelly Baby | 7" | Columbia | DB4081 | 1958 | £15 | £30 |
| Sizzling Hot | 7" | Columbia | DB4006 | 1957 | £20 | £40 |

## MILLER, JODY

| | | | | | | |
|---|---|---|---|---|---|---|
| Home Of The Brave | 7" | Capitol | CL15415 | 1965 | £1.50 | £4 |
| If You Were A Carpenter | 7" | Capitol | CL15482 | 1966 | £1.50 | £4 |

## MILLER, KENNY

| | | | | | | |
|---|---|---|---|---|---|---|
| Take My Tip | 7" | Stateside | SS405 | 1965 | £10 | £20 |

## MILLER, MANDY

| | | | | | | |
|---|---|---|---|---|---|---|
| Children's Choice | 7" EP | Parlophone | GEP8776 | 1958 | £2 | £5 |
| Nellie The Elephant | 7" EP | Parlophone | R4219 | 1956 | £2 | £5 |

## MILLER, MAX

| | | | | | | |
|---|---|---|---|---|---|---|
| Cheeky Chappie | 7" EP | HMV | 7EG8558 | 1959 | £2 | £5 |
| Max At The Met | 7" EP | Pye | NEP24154 | 1961 | £2 | £5 |
| Max At The Met Vol. 2 | 7" EP | Pye | NEP24162 | 1962 | £2 | £5 |

## MILLER, MITCH

| | | | | | | |
|---|---|---|---|---|---|---|
| Lisbon Antigua | 7" EP | Philips | BBE12043 | 1956 | £2 | £5 |

## MILLER, NED

| | | | | | | | |
|---|---|---|---|---|---|---|---|
| Do What You Do Do Well | 7" | London | HL9937 | 1964 | £1.50 | £4 | |
| From A Jack To A King | LP | Fabor | FLP1001 | 1963 | £20 | £40 | US, coloured vinyl |
| From A Jack To A King | LP | London | HA8072 | 1963 | £8 | £20 | |
| Go On Back, You Fool | 7" | Capitol | CL15301 | 1963 | £1.50 | £4 | |
| Ned Miller | 7" EP | Capitol | EAP120492 | 1963 | £5 | £10 | |
| Ned Miller | 7" EP | London | RE1382 | 1963 | £5 | £10 | |

## MILLER, ROGER

| | | | | | | |
|---|---|---|---|---|---|---|
| King Of The Road | 7" EP | Philips | BE12578 | 1965 | £2 | £5 |

## MILLER, RUSS

| | | | | | | |
|---|---|---|---|---|---|---|
| I Sit In My Window | 7" | HMV | POP391 | 1957 | £10 | £20 |

## MILLER, STEVE BAND

Steve Miller could never quite decide whether he wanted to lead a progressive rock outfit or a blues band – so for much of the time the group's early records are both. Boz Scaggs was a member long enough to appear on the first two albums, while 'My Dark Hour' features a rare guest appearance from Paul McCartney, on bass, drums, and backing vocals, at a time when he was still technically a member of the Beatles.

| | | | | | | | |
|---|---|---|---|---|---|---|---|
| Anthology | LP | Capitol | ESTSP12 | 1972 | £5 | £12 | double |
| Children Of The Future | LP | Capitol | (S)T2920 | 1968 | £4 | £10 | |
| Fly Like An Eagle | LP | Mobile Fidelity | MFSL1021 | 1978 | £5 | £12 | US audiophile |
| Going To The Country | 7" | Capitol | CL15656 | 1970 | £1.50 | £4 | |
| Joker | CD-s | Capitol | CDCL583 | 1990 | £2 | £5 | |
| Little Girl | 7" | Capitol | CL15618 | 1969 | £1.50 | £4 | |
| Living In The USA | 7" | Capitol | CL15564 | 1968 | £1.50 | £4 | |
| My Dark Hour | 7" | Capitol | CL15604 | 1969 | £1.50 | £4 | |
| Revolution | LP | United Artists | UAS5185 | 1968 | £4 | £10 | US, with other artists |
| Sailor | LP | Capitol | (S)T2984 | 1969 | £4 | £10 | |
| Sittin' In Circles | 7" | Capitol | CL15539 | 1968 | £1.50 | £4 | |

## MILLER, SUZI

| | | | | | | | |
|---|---|---|---|---|---|---|---|
| Ay Ay Senores | 7" | Decca | F10677 | 1956 | £1.50 | £4 | |
| Banjo's Back In Town | 7" | Decca | F10593 | 1955 | £1.50 | £4 | |
| Dance With Me Henry | 7" | Decca | F10512 | 1955 | £2 | £5 | |
| Get Up Get Up | 7" | Decca | F10722 | 1956 | £1.50 | £4 | |
| Happy Days And Lonely Nights | 7" | Decca | F10389 | 1954 | £4 | £8 | with The Johnston Brothers |
| I Love My Baby | 7" | Decca | F10848 | 1957 | £1.50 | £4 | |
| Tweedle Dee | 7" | Decca | F10475 | 1955 | £2.50 | £6 | |
| Two Step Side Step | 7" | Decca | F10423 | 1954 | £1.50 | £4 | with The Johnston Brothers |

## MILLERS THUMB

| | | | | | | |
|---|---|---|---|---|---|---|
| Sitting On The Right Side | LP | Tradition | TSC3 | 1976 | £50 | £100 |

## MILLIE

| | | | | | | | |
|---|---|---|---|---|---|---|---|
| Best Of Jackie & Millie Vol. 2 | LP | Trojan | TTL52 | 1970 | £6 | £15 | |
| Best Of Millie Small | LP | Island | ILP953 | 1967 | £20 | £40 | pink label |
| Best Of Millie Small | LP | Trojan | TTL49 | 1969 | £6 | £15 | |
| Bloodshot Eyes | 7" | Fontana | TF617 | 1965 | £4 | £8 | |
| Bournvita Song | 7" | Cadbury's | BNVT01 | 1964 | £7.50 | £15 | picture sleeve |
| Chicken Feed | 7" | Fontana | TF796 | 1967 | £1.50 | £4 | |
| Don't You Know | 7" | Fontana | TF425 | 1963 | £1.50 | £4 | |
| How Can I Be Sure | 7" | Blue Beat | BB96 | 1962 | £6 | £12 | with Owen Gray |
| I Love The Way You Love | 7" | Fontana | TF502 | 1964 | £1.50 | £4 | |
| I've Fallen In Love With A Snowman | 7" | Fontana | TF515 | 1965 | £1.50 | £4 | |
| Killer Joe | 7" | Fontana | TF740 | 1966 | £1.50 | £4 | |
| Millie | 7" EP | Bluebeat | BBEP302 | 1961 | £37.50 | £75 | |

| | | | | | | | |
|---|---|---|---|---|---|---|---|
| Millie & Her Boyfriends | LP | Trojan | TTL17 | 1969 | £6 | £15 | |
| Millie And Her Boyfriends | 7" EP | Island | IEP705 | 1966 | £15 | £30 | |
| Millie Sings Fats Domino | LP | Fontana | TL5276 | 1965 | £15 | £30 | |
| More Millie | LP | Fontana | (S)TL5220 | 1964 | £10 | £25 | |
| My Boy Lollipop | LP | Smash | MGS27055 | 1964 | £10 | £25 | US |
| My Boy Lollipop | 7" EP | Fontana | TE17425 | 1964 | £7.50 | £15 | |
| My Boy Lollipop | 7" | Fontana | TF449 | 1964 | £1.50 | £4 | |
| My Love And I | 7" | Pyramid | PYR6080 | 1970 | £1.50 | £4 | |
| My Street | 7" | Brit | WI1002 | 1965 | £5 | £10 | |
| My Street | 7" | Fontana | TF591 | 1965 | £1.50 | £4 | |
| Pledging My Love | LP | Trojan | TTL47 | 1970 | £6 | £15 | with Jackie Edwards |
| Readin' Writin' Arithmetic | 7" | Decca | F12948 | 1969 | £1.50 | £4 | |
| See You Later Alligator | 7" | Fontana | TF529 | 1965 | £1.50 | £4 | |
| Sugar Plum | 7" | Island | WI014 | 1962 | £5 | £10 | with Owen Gray |
| Sweet William | 7" | Fontana | TF479 | 1964 | £1.50 | £4 | |
| This World | 7" | Island | WI050 | 1962 | £5 | £10 | with Roy Panton |
| Time Will Tell | LP | Trojan | TBL108 | 1970 | £6 | £15 | |
| When I Dance With You | 7" | Fontana | TF948 | 1968 | £1.50 | £4 | |
| You Better Forget | 7" | Island | WIP6021 | 1967 | £1.50 | £4 | |

### MILLIGAN, SPIKE

| | | | | | | | |
|---|---|---|---|---|---|---|---|
| Milligan Preserved | LP | Parlophone | PMC1148 | 1961 | £4 | £10 | |
| Muses With Milligan | LP | Decca | LK4701 | 1965 | £4 | £10 | |
| World Of Beachcomber | LP | Pye | NPL18271 | 1969 | £4 | £10 | |

### MILLINDER, LUCKY

| | | | | | | | |
|---|---|---|---|---|---|---|---|
| Grape Vine | 78 | Vogue | V9021 | 1951 | £3 | £8 | |
| I'm Waiting Just For You | 78 | Vogue | V9007 | 1951 | £3 | £8 | |
| Ram Bunk Shush | 78 | Vogue | V2138 | 1952 | £3 | £8 | |

### MILLINS, PAUL

| | | | | | | | |
|---|---|---|---|---|---|---|---|
| Paul Millins | LP | Fresh Air | 6370505 | 1975 | £15 | £30 | with Jo-Ann Kelly |

### MILLIONAIRES

| | | | | | | | |
|---|---|---|---|---|---|---|---|
| Chatterbox | 7" | Decca | F12468 | 1966 | £12.50 | £25 | |

### MILLIONAIRES (2)

| | | | | | | | |
|---|---|---|---|---|---|---|---|
| Never For Me | 7" | Mercury | 6052301 | 1973 | £1.50 | £4 | black label |

### MILLS, BARBARA

| | | | | | | | |
|---|---|---|---|---|---|---|---|
| Queen Of Fools | 7" | Hickory | 451323 | 1965 | £37.50 | £75 | |
| Queen Of Fools | 7" | London | HLE10491 | 1975 | £2 | £5 | |
| Try | 7" | Hickory | 451392 | 1965 | £4 | £8 | |

### MILLS, GARY

| | | | | | | | |
|---|---|---|---|---|---|---|---|
| Bless You | 7" | Decca | F11383 | 1961 | £1.50 | £4 | |
| Comin' Down With Love | 7" | Top Rank | JAR393 | 1960 | £1.50 | £4 | |
| Hey Baby | 7" | Top Rank | JAR119 | 1959 | £2.50 | £6 | |
| I'll Step Down | 7" | Decca | F11358 | 1961 | £1.50 | £4 | |
| Look For A Star | 7" | Top Rank | JAR336 | 1960 | £1.50 | £4 | |
| Looking For A Star | 7" EP | Top Rank | JKP3001 | 1961 | £10 | £20 | |
| Sad Little Girl | 7" | Decca | F11415 | 1961 | £1.50 | £4 | |
| Save A Dream For Me | 7" | Decca | F11471 | 1962 | £1.50 | £4 | |
| Top Teen Baby | 7" | Top Rank | JAR500 | 1960 | £1.50 | £4 | |
| Top Teen Baby | 7" | Top Rank | JAR500 | 1960 | £2.50 | £6 | picture sleeve |

### MILLS, HAYLEY

| | | | | | | | |
|---|---|---|---|---|---|---|---|
| Gypsy Girl | LP | Mainstream | 6090 | 1966 | £4 | £10 | US stereo |
| In Search Of The Castaways | LP | Disneyland | ST3916 | 1962 | £5 | £12 | US stereo |
| Let's Get Together | LP | Buena Vista | STER3311 | 1962 | £4 | £10 | US stereo |
| Let's Get Together | 7" | Decca | F21396 | 1961 | £1.50 | £4 | |
| Parent Trap | LP | Buena Vista | STER3309 | 1961 | £5 | £12 | US stereo |
| Pollyanna | LP | Disneyland | ST1960 | 1960 | £5 | £12 | US |
| Summer Magic | LP | MGM | (S)E4025 | 1963 | £5 | £12 | US |

### MILLS, MAUDE

| | | | | | | | |
|---|---|---|---|---|---|---|---|
| Maude Mills | 7" EP | Vintage Jazz | VEP34 | 196– | £4 | £8 | |

### MILLS, RUDY

| | | | | | | | |
|---|---|---|---|---|---|---|---|
| John Jones | 7" | Big Shot | BI509 | 1968 | £2.50 | £6 | |
| Lemi Li | 7" | Explosion | EX2007 | 1969 | £2 | £5 | |
| Reggae Hits | LP | Pama | SECO12 | 1969 | £10 | £25 | |

### MILLS, STEPHANIE

| | | | | | | | |
|---|---|---|---|---|---|---|---|
| This Empty Place/I See You For The First Time | 7" | Tamla Motown | TMG1020 | 1976 | £10 | £20 | demo |

### MILLS BROTHERS

| | | | | | | | |
|---|---|---|---|---|---|---|---|
| Barber Shop Harmony | LP | Decca | DL8890 | 195– | £5 | £12 | US |
| Best Of The Mills Brothers | LP | Decca | DXB193/ DXSB7193 | 195– | £5 | £12 | US |
| Dream Of You | 7" | Brunswick | 05550 | 1956 | £1.50 | £4 | |
| End Of The World | LP | London | HAD/SAHD8092 | 1963 | £4 | £10 | |
| Four Boys And A Guitar | 10" LP | Brunswick | LA8702 | 1955 | £4 | £10 | |
| Get A Job | 7" | London | HLD8553 | 1958 | £5 | £10 | |
| Glow | LP | Decca | DL8827 | 195– | £5 | £12 | US |
| Greatest Hits | LP | London | HAD2192/ SHD6046 | 1959 | £4 | £10 | |

| Title | Format | Label | Catalogue | Year | | | Notes |
|---|---|---|---|---|---|---|---|
| Greatest Hits | LP | London | HAD2319 | 1961 | £4 | £10 | |
| Gum Drop | 7" | Brunswick | 05487 | 1955 | £6 | £12 | |
| Harmonizin' | LP | Decca | DL8892 | 195– | £5 | £12 | US |
| How Blue? | 7" | Brunswick | 05325 | 1954 | £2.50 | £6 | |
| I've Changed My Mind A Thousand Times | 7" | Brunswick | 05522 | 1956 | £2 | £5 | |
| In Hi-Fi | LP | Decca | DL8664 | 195– | £5 | £12 | US |
| Louis Armstrong And The Mills Brothers | 10" LP | Brunswick | LA8681 | 1954 | £5 | £12 | |
| Meet The Mills Brothers | 10" LP | Brunswick | LA8664 | 1954 | £6 | £15 | |
| Memory Lane | LP | Decca | DL8219 | 195– | £5 | £12 | US |
| Mills Brothers | 7" EP | London | RED1215 | 1959 | £2.50 | £6 | |
| Mills Brothers No. 2 | 7" EP | Brunswick | OE9060 | 1955 | £2 | £5 | |
| Ninety-Eight Cents | 7" | Brunswick | 05600 | 1956 | £1.50 | £4 | |
| One Dozen Roses | LP | Decca | DL8491 | 195– | £5 | £12 | US |
| Paper Valentine | 7" | Brunswick | 05390 | 1955 | £2 | £5 | |
| Presenting | 7" EP | Brunswick | OE9014 | 1954 | £4 | £8 | |
| San Antonio Rose | LP | London | HAD2383/ SAHD6183 | 1961 | £4 | £10 | |
| Sing | LP | London | HAD2250/ SHD6074 | 1960 | £4 | £10 | |
| Singin' And Swingin' | LP | Decca | DL8209 | 195– | £5 | £12 | US |
| Singing And Swinging Pt. 1 | 7" EP | Brunswick | OE9239 | 1956 | £2 | £5 | |
| Smack Dab In The Middle | 7" | Brunswick | 05439 | 1955 | £4 | £8 | |
| Souvenir Album | LP | Decca | DL8148 | 195– | £5 | £12 | US |
| Souvenir Album | 10" LP | Decca | DL5102 | 195– | £8 | £20 | US |
| Suddenly There's A Valley | 7" | Brunswick | 05488 | 1955 | £2 | £5 | |
| That's Right | 7" | Brunswick | 05606 | 1956 | £2 | £5 | |
| Wonderful Words | 10" LP | Decca | DL5337 | 195– | £8 | £20 | US |
| Yes You Are | 7" | Brunswick | 05452 | 1955 | £2 | £5 | |

## MILLSTONE GRIT

| Title | Format | Label | Catalogue | Year | | | |
|---|---|---|---|---|---|---|---|
| Millstone Grit | LP | Box | 488 | 1980 | £5 | £12 | |

## MILLTOWN BROTHERS

| Title | Format | Label | Catalogue | Year | | | |
|---|---|---|---|---|---|---|---|
| Applegreen | CD-s | A&M | AMCD704 | 1990 | £2 | £5 | |
| Coming From The Mill | CD-s | Big Round | BIGR101CD | 1989 | £4 | £10 | |
| Coming From The Mill | 12" | Big Round | BIGR101T | 1989 | £4 | £10 | |
| Roses | 7" | Big Round | BIGR101 | 1989 | £2.50 | £6 | |
| Which Way Should I Jump | 12" | Big Round | BIGR104T | 1989 | £2.50 | £6 | |

## MILSAP, RONNIE

| Title | Format | Label | Catalogue | Year | | | Notes |
|---|---|---|---|---|---|---|---|
| Ain't No Sole Left In These Ole Shoes | 7" | Pye | 7N25392 | 1966 | £7.50 | £15 | |
| Soul Sensations | 7" EP | Pye | NEP44078 | 1966 | £5 | £10 | with Roscoe Robinson |

## MILTON, JOHNNY & THE CONDORS

| Title | Format | Label | Catalogue | Year | | | |
|---|---|---|---|---|---|---|---|
| Somethin' Else | 7" | Decca | F11862 | 1964 | £1.50 | £4 | |

## MILTON, ROY

| Title | Format | Label | Catalogue | Year | | | Notes |
|---|---|---|---|---|---|---|---|
| Great Roy Milton | LP | Kent | 554 | 1963 | £10 | £25 | US |

## MILTON, ROY & CHUCK HIGGINS

| Title | Format | Label | Catalogue | Year | | | Notes |
|---|---|---|---|---|---|---|---|
| Rock 'n' Roll Versus Rhythm And Blues | LP | Dooto | DL223 | 1959 | £25 | £50 | US |

## MIMMS, GARNETT

| Title | Format | Label | Catalogue | Year | | | Notes |
|---|---|---|---|---|---|---|---|
| All About Love | 7" | United Artists | UP1172 | 1966 | £2.50 | £6 | |
| As Long As I Have You | LP | United Artists | UAL3396/ UAS6396 | 1965 | £10 | £25 | US |
| As Long As I Love You | 7" | United Artists | UP1186 | 1967 | £2 | £5 | |
| Cry Baby | LP | United Artists | ULP1067 | 1963 | £15 | £30 | |
| Cry Baby | 7" | United Artists | UP1033 | 1963 | £2 | £5 | |
| For Your Precious Love | 7" | United Artists | UP1038 | 1963 | £2 | £5 | |
| I Can Hear My Baby Crying | 7" | Verve | VS569 | 1968 | £2 | £5 | |
| I'll Take Good Care Of You | LP | United Artists | UAL3498/ UAS6498 | 1965 | £10 | £25 | US |
| I'll Take Good Care Of You | 7" | United Artists | UP1130 | 1966 | £25 | £50 | |
| It Was Easier To Hurt Her | 7" | United Artists | UP1090 | 1965 | £4 | £8 | |
| It's Been Such A Long Way Home | 7" | United Artists | UP1147 | 1966 | £2.50 | £6 | |
| Live | LP | United Artists | (S)ULP1174 | 1967 | £10 | £25 | |
| My Baby | 7" | United Artists | UP1153 | 1966 | £1.50 | £4 | |
| Roll With The Punches | 7" | United Artists | UP1181 | 1967 | £2.50 | £6 | |
| Tell Me Baby | 7" | United Artists | UP1048 | 1964 | £2 | £5 | |
| Warm And Soulful | LP | United Artists | (S)ULP1145 | 1966 | £10 | £25 | |
| We Can Find That Love | 7" | Verve | VS574 | 1968 | £2 | £5 | |

## MIND EXPANDERS

| Title | Format | Label | Catalogue | Year | | | Notes |
|---|---|---|---|---|---|---|---|
| What's Happening | LP | Dot | DLP25773 | 1967 | £10 | £25 | US, stereo |
| What's Happening | LP | Dot | DLP3773 | 1967 | £30 | £60 | US, mono |

## MINDBENDERS

| Title | Format | Label | Catalogue | Year | | | Notes |
|---|---|---|---|---|---|---|---|
| Ashes To Ashes | 7" EP | Fontana | 465322 | 1966 | £7.50 | £15 | French |
| Ashes To Ashes | 7" | Fontana | TF731 | 1966 | £1.50 | £4 | |
| Blessed Are The Lonely | 7" | Fontana | TF910 | 1968 | £1.50 | £4 | |
| Can't Live With You | 7" | Fontana | TF697 | 1966 | £1.50 | £4 | |
| Groovy Kind Of Love | LP | Fontana | MGF2/SRF67554 | 1966 | £8 | £20 | US |
| I Want Her, She Wants Me | 7" | Fontana | TF780 | 1966 | £1.50 | £4 | |
| Letter | 7" | Fontana | TF869 | 1967 | £1.50 | £4 | |
| Mindbenders | LP | Fontana | (S)TL5324 | 1966 | £10 | £25 | |
| Mindbenders | LP | Fontana | SFL13045 | 1968 | £6 | £15 | |
| Schoolgirl | 7" | Fontana | TF877 | 1967 | £1.50 | £4 | |

| | | | | | | |
|---|---|---|---|---|---|---|
| Uncle Joe The Ice Cream Man | 7" | Fontana | TF961 | 1968 £1.50 | £4 | |
| We'll Talk About It Tomorrow | 7" EP | Fontana | 465378 | 1967 £7.50 | £15 | *French* |
| We'll Talk About It Tomorrow | 7" | Fontana | TF806 | 1967 £1.50 | £4 | |
| With Woman In Mind | LP | Fontana | (S)TL5403 | 1967 £25 | £50 | |

## MINEO, SAL

| | | | | | | |
|---|---|---|---|---|---|---|
| Aladdin | LP | Columbia | CL1117 | 1958 £20 | £40 | *US* |
| Cutting In | 7" | Fontana | H118 | 1958 £10 | £20 | |
| Sal | LP | Fontana | TFL5004 | 1958 £20 | £40 | |
| Seven Steps To Love | 7" | Fontana | H135 | 1958 £6 | £12 | |
| Start Moving | 7" | Philips | JK1024 | 1958 £10 | £20 | |

## MINGUS, CHARLES

Although he was an impressive player of the double bass, Charles Mingus is increasingly remembered as the leader of some particularly inspiring line-ups and as the finest jazz composer since Duke Ellington. In the sixties, Mingus's music was the first port of call for rock fans wishing to develop an interest in jazz. His pieces were recorded by groups as diverse as the Pentangle, East of Eden, and Alexis Korner. Mingus returned the favour to the rock world when he collaborated with Joni Mitchell on her exploration of the man's music on the album *Mingus*. Of Mingus's own albums, *Mingus Ah Um*, *Oh Yeah*, *The Black Saint And The Sinner Lady* and all the recordings featuring saxophonist Eric Dolphy are rightly regarded as classics of modern jazz.

| | | | | | | |
|---|---|---|---|---|---|---|
| Black Saint And The Sinner Lady | LP | HMV | CLP1694 | 1963 £8 | £20 | |
| Blues And Roots | LP | London | LTZK15194/ SAHK6087 | 1960 £10 | £25 | |
| Charles Mingus | 7" EP | Philips | BBE12399 | 1960 £2 | £5 | |
| Charles Mingus Presents Charles Mingus | LP | Atlantic | SD8005 | 1962 £8 | £20 | |
| Charlie Mingus | LP | Atlantic | ATL/SAL5019 | 1965 £8 | £20 | |
| Charlie Mingus Quintet With Max Roach | LP | Vocalion | LAEF/SEAF591 | 1965 £8 | £20 | |
| Chazz | LP | Vocalion | LAE543 | 1963 £8 | £20 | |
| Clown | LP | London | LTZK15164 | 1959 £10 | £25 | |
| Duke's Choice | LP | Atlantic | 545111 | 1970 £6 | £15 | |
| East Coasting | LP | Parlophone | PMC1092 | 1959 £10 | £25 | |
| East Coasting | LP | Polydor | 623215 | 1968 £6 | £15 | |
| Great Concert Of Charles Mingus | LP | America | 30AM003/4/5 | 1971 £10 | £25 | *French triple* |
| Jazz Composers Workshop | LP | Realm | RM211 | 1966 £8 | £20 | |
| Jazz Experiments | LP | London | LTZN15087 | 1957 £10 | £25 | |
| Jazz Makers | 7" EP | Mercury | 10021MCE | 1965 £2 | £5 | |
| Jazz Portraits | LP | United Artists | ULP1004 | 1962 £8 | £20 | |
| Jazz Workshop Vol. 2 | 10" LP | Vogue | LDE178 | 1956 £20 | £40 | |
| Let My Children Hear Music | LP | CBS | 64715 | 1972 £5 | £12 | |
| Mingus Ah Um | LP | CBS | 52346 | 1969 £6 | £15 | |
| Mingus Ah Um | LP | Philips | BBL7352 | 1960 £8 | £20 | |
| Mingus At Monterey | LP | Liberty | LDS84002 | 1969 £8 | £20 | *double* |
| Mingus Dynasty | LP | CBS | (S)BPG62261 | 1966 £8 | £20 | |
| Mingus Dynasty | 7" EP | Philips | BBE12451/ SBBE9050 | 1961 £2 | £5 | |
| Mingus Mingus Mingus | LP | HMV | CLP1742/CSD1545 | 1965 £8 | £20 | |
| Mingus Plays Piano | LP | HMV | CLP1796 | 1964 £8 | £20 | |
| Mingus Revisited | LP | Mercury | SMWL21056 | 1969 £6 | £15 | |
| My Favourite Quintet | LP | Liberty | LBS83346 | 1970 £6 | £15 | |
| Oh Yeah | LP | London | HAK/SHK8007 | 1962 £8 | £20 | |
| Pithecanthropus Erectus | LP | Atlantic | 587131 | 1968 £6 | £15 | |
| Pithecanthropus Erectus | LP | London | LTZK15052 | 1957 £10 | £25 | |
| Reincarnation Of A Lovebird | LP | Atlantic | 587166 | 1969 £6 | £15 | |
| Scenes In The City | 7" EP | Parlophone | GEP8786 | 1963 £2 | £5 | |
| Things Ain't What They Used To Be | 7" EP | Philips | BBE12453/ SBBE9052 | 1961 £2 | £5 | |
| Tijuana Moods | LP | RCA | RD/SF7514 | 1962 £8 | £20 | |
| Tonight At Noon | LP | Atlantic | SD1416 | 196– £8 | £20 | *US* |
| Town Hall Concert | LP | United Artists | ULP1068 | 1965 £8 | £20 | |
| Trio | LP | London | LTZJ15129 | 1958 £10 | £25 | |

## MINIM

| | | | | | | |
|---|---|---|---|---|---|---|
| Wrapped In A Union Jack | LP | Polydor | 582011 | 1967 £30 | £60 | |

## MINISTRY

| | | | | | | |
|---|---|---|---|---|---|---|
| Cold Life | 12" | Situation 2 | SIT17T | 1982 £2.50 | £6 | |
| Work For Love | 7" | Arista | ARIST510 | 1983 £1.50 | £4 | *with cassette* |

## MINISTRY OF SOUND

| | | | | | | |
|---|---|---|---|---|---|---|
| White Collar Worker | 7" | Decca | F12449 | 1966 £4 | £8 | |

## MINNELLI, LIZA

| | | | | | | |
|---|---|---|---|---|---|---|
| Don't Drop Bombs | CD-s | Epic | ZEEC2 | 1989 £3 | £8 | |
| Losing My Mind | CD-s | Epic | ZEEC1 | 1989 £3 | £8 | |
| Love Pains | CD-s | Epic | CDZEE4 | 1990 £3 | £8 | |
| Middle Of The Street | 7" | Capitol | CL15483 | 1966 £1.50 | £4 | |
| So Sorry, I Said | CD-s | Epic | ZEEC3 | 1989 £3 | £8 | *2 versions* |

## MINOGUE, KYLIE

| | | | | | | |
|---|---|---|---|---|---|---|
| Better The Devil You Know | CD-s | PWL | PWLCD56 | 1990 £5 | £12 | |
| Especially For You | CD-s | PWL | PWCD24 | 1988 £10 | £20 | |
| Got To Be Certain | CD-s | PWL | PWCD12 | 1988 £6 | £15 | |
| Got To Be Certain (Extra Beat Boys Mix) | 12" | PWL | PWLT12R | 1988 £5 | £12 | |
| Hand On Your Heart (Heartache Mix) | 12" | PWL | PWLT35R | 1989 £15 | £30 | |
| I Should Be So Lucky | CD-s | PWL | | £20 | £40 | *German or Dutch* |
| I Should Be So Lucky (Bicentennial Mix) | 12" | PWL | PWLT8R | 1988 £5 | £12 | |

| Title | Format | Label | Catalog | Year | | | Notes |
|---|---|---|---|---|---|---|---|
| If You Were With Me Now | CD-s | PWL | PWCD208 | 1991 | £2 | £5 | with Keith Washington |
| Je ne sais pas pourquoi | CD-s | PWL | PWCD21 | 1988 | £10 | £20 | |
| Je ne sais pas pourquoi | 7" | PWL | PWLP21 | 1988 | £10 | £20 | poster picture sleeve |
| Je ne sais pas pourquoi | 12" | PWL | PWLT21R | 1988 | £5 | £12 | |
| Keep On Pumpin' It | CD-s | PWL | PWCD207 | 1991 | £6 | £15 | |
| Kylie Minogue | CD | Deconstruction | KM001 | 1994 | £15 | £30 | promo in fold-out sleeve |
| Locomotion (Sankie Mix) | 12" | PWL | PWLT14R | 1988 | £2.50 | £6 | |
| Never Too Late | CD-s | PWL | PWCD45 | 1989 | £6 | £15 | |
| Shocked | CD-s | PWL | PWCD81 | 1991 | £5 | £12 | |
| Step Back In Time | CD-s | PWL | PWCD64 | 1990 | £6 | £15 | |
| Tears On My Pillow | CD-s | PWL | PWCD47 | 1989 | £10 | £20 | |
| What Do I Have To Do | CD-s | PWL | PWCD72 | 1991 | £6 | £15 | |
| Where Is The Feeling | 12" | RCA | FEEL1 | 1994 | £3 | £8 | promo |
| Where Is The Feeling | 12" | RCA | FEEL2 | 1994 | £10 | £20 | promo |
| Where Is The Feeling | 12" | RCA | FEEL3 | 1994 | £37.50 | £75 | promo |
| Where Is The Feeling | 12" | RCA | FEEL4 | 1994 | £6 | £15 | promo |
| Word Is Out | CD-s | PWL | PWCD204 | 1991 | £2 | £5 | |
| Wouldn't Change A Thing | CD-s | PWL | PWLCD42 | 1989 | £2 | £5 | |
| Wouldn't Change A Thing (Espagna Mix) | 12" | PWL | PWLT42R | 1989 | £3 | £8 | |

## MINOR THREAT
| | | | | | | | |
|---|---|---|---|---|---|---|---|
| Out Of Step | LP | Discord | | 198– | £10 | £25 | US |

## MINORBOPS
| | | | | | | | |
|---|---|---|---|---|---|---|---|
| Need You Tonight | 7" | Vogue | V9110 | 1958 | £150 | £250 | best auctioned |

## MINOTAURUS
| | | | | | | | |
|---|---|---|---|---|---|---|---|
| Fly Away | LP | private | 1010 | 1971 | £25 | £50 | German |
| Rain Over Thessalia | LP | Thorofon | ATH112 | 1970 | £25 | £50 | German |

## MINSTRELS
| | | | | | | | |
|---|---|---|---|---|---|---|---|
| Miss Highty Tighty | 7" | Studio One | SO2050 | 1968 | £6 | £12 | Westmorelites B side |

## MINT
| | | | | | | | |
|---|---|---|---|---|---|---|---|
| Luv | 7" | Tangerine | DP14 | 1969 | £1.50 | £4 | |

## MINUTE MEN
| | | | | | | | |
|---|---|---|---|---|---|---|---|
| Yankee Diddle | 7" | Capitol | CL15206 | 1961 | £1.50 | £4 | |
| Buzz Or Howl Under The Influence Of The Heat | 12" | SST | SST016 | 1984 | £2.50 | £6 | |
| Paranoid Time | 7" | SST | SST002 | 1983 | £2.50 | £6 | |

## MIRACLES
| | | | | | | | |
|---|---|---|---|---|---|---|---|
| Ain't It Baby | 7" | London | HL9366 | 1961 | £30 | £60 | |
| Away We A Go Go | LP | Tamla Motown | (S)TML11044 | 1967 | £10 | £25 | |
| Christmas With The Miracles | LP | Tamla | 236 | 1963 | £50 | £100 | US |
| Come On Do The Jerk | 7" | Stateside | SS377 | 1965 | £10 | £20 | |
| Cookin' With The Miracles | LP | Tamla | 223 | 1962 | £50 | £100 | US |
| Doin' Mickey's Monkey | LP | Tamla | 245 | 1963 | £25 | £50 | US, mono |
| Doin' Mickey's Monkey | LP | Tamla | T2245 | 1963 | £50 | £100 | US, stereo |
| Fabulous Miracles | LP | Stateside | SL10099 | 1964 | £37.50 | £75 | |
| From The Beginning | LP | Tamla Motown | (S)TML11031 | 1966 | £15 | £30 | |
| Going To A Go Go | LP | Tamla Motown | TML11024 | 1966 | £15 | £30 | |
| Going To A Go-Go | 7" | Tamla Motown | TMG547 | 1966 | £2.50 | £6 | |
| Hi We're The Miracles | LP | Oriole | PS40044 | 1963 | £50 | £100 | |
| Hi We're The Miracles | LP | Tamla | 220 | 1961 | £62.50 | £125 | US |
| I Gotta Dance To Keep From Crying | 7" | Stateside | SS263 | 1964 | £15 | £30 | |
| I Like It Like That | LP | Tamla Motown | TML11003 | 1965 | £20 | £40 | |
| I Like It Like That | 7" | Stateside | SS324 | 1964 | £10 | £20 | |
| I'll Try Something New | LP | Tamla | 230 | 1962 | £50 | £100 | US |
| I'm The One You Need | 7" | Tamla Motown | TMG584 | 1966 | £2.50 | £6 | |
| Man In You | 7" | Stateside | SS282 | 1964 | £10 | £20 | |
| Mickey's Monkey | 7" | Oriole | CBA1863 | 1963 | £20 | £40 | |
| My Girl Has Gone | 7" | Tamla Motown | TMG540 | 1965 | £6 | £12 | |
| Nothing But A Man | LP | Motown | MT/S630 | 1965 | £10 | £25 | US, with other artists |
| On Stage | LP | Tamla | 241 | 1963 | £25 | £50 | US |
| Ooh Baby Baby | 7" | Tamla Motown | TMG503 | 1965 | £10 | £20 | |
| Shop Around | LP | Tamla | 224 | 1962 | £50 | £100 | US |
| Shop Around | 7" EP | London | RE1295 | 1961 | £37.50 | £75 | |
| Shop Around | 7" | London | HL9276 | 1961 | £20 | £40 | |
| That's What Love Is Made Of | 7" | Stateside | SS353 | 1964 | £10 | £20 | |
| Tracks Of My Tears | 7" | Tamla Motown | TMG522 | 1965 | £12.50 | £25 | |
| What's So Good About Goodbye | 7" | Fontana | H384 | 1962 | £37.50 | £75 | |
| Whole Lotta Shakin' In My Heart | 7" | Tamla Motown | TMG569 | 1966 | £6 | £12 | |
| You've Really Got A Hold On Me | 7" | Oriole | CBA1795 | 1963 | £30 | £60 | |

## MIRAGE
| | | | | | | | |
|---|---|---|---|---|---|---|---|
| Carolyn | 7" | Page One | POF111 | 1969 | £1.50 | £4 | |
| Go Away | 7" | CBS | 202007 | 1965 | £5 | £10 | |
| Hold On | 7" | Philips | BF1554 | 1967 | £2.50 | £6 | |
| It's In Her Kiss | 7" | CBS | 201772 | 1965 | £5 | £10 | |
| Mystery Lady | 7" | Page One | POF078 | 1968 | £1.50 | £4 | |
| Tomorrow Never Knows | 7" | Philips | BF1534 | 1966 | £10 | £20 | |
| Wedding Of Ramona Blair | 7" | Philips | BF1571 | 1967 | £7.50 | £15 | |

## MIRKWOOD
| Mirkwood | LP | Flams Ltd | PR1067 | 1973 | £330 | £500 | |

## MIRROR
| Daybreak | LP | TLP | TLP7623 | 1976 | £50 | £100 | Dutch |
| Gingerbread Man | 7" | Philips | BF1666 | 1968 | £20 | £40 | |

## MISFITS
| Beware | 12" | Cherry Red | PLP9 | 1981 | £25 | £50 | |
| Horror Business | 7" | Plan 9 | PL1009 | 198– | £25 | £50 | |
| Night Of The Living Dead | 7" | Plan 9 | | 1980 | £25 | £50 | |

## MISFITS (2)
| You Won't See Me | 7" | Aberdeen Students | PRI101 | 1966 | £2.50 | £6 | |

## MISS JANE
| Bad Mind People | 7" | Pama | PM704 | 1968 | £2 | £5 | |

## MISS LAVELL
| Everybody's Got Somebody | 7" | Vocalion | VP9236 | 1965 | £4 | £8 | |

## MISS X
| Christine | 7" | Ember | EMBS175 | 1963 | £1.50 | £4 | |

## MISSING LINK
| Nevergreen | LP | United Artists | UAS29439 | 1972 | £8 | £20 | German |

## MISSING SCIENTISTS
| Big City Bright Lights | 7" | Rough Trade | RT057 | 1980 | £2.50 | £6 | |

## MISSION
| Beyond The Pale (Armageddon Mix) | CD-s | Mercury | MTHCD62 | 1988 | £2.50 | £6 | |
| Butterfly On A Wheel | CD-s | Mercury | MYCDB8 | 1990 | £2 | £5 | 12" box |
| Carved In Sand | CD | Mercury | 8422512 | 1990 | £20 | £40 | promo box set, with sampler CD and cassette, video, single, biog |
| Deliverance | CD-s | Mercury | MTHCD9 | 1990 | £2 | £5 | 2 versions |
| Deliverance Tour 1990 Sampler | CD | Mercury | SACD166 | 1990 | £8 | £20 | US promo, with the Wonderstuff |
| Garden Of Delight | 12" | Chapter 22 | | 1986 | £5 | £12 | promo |
| Hands Across The Ocean | CD-s | Mercury | MTHCD11 | 1990 | £2 | £5 | |
| Into The Blue | CD-s | Mercury | MTHCD10 | 1990 | £2 | £5 | |
| Kingdom Come | 12" | Mercury | MYTHX7 | 1988 | £6 | £15 | promo |
| Like A Hurricane | 12" | Chapter 22 | L12CHAP7 | 1986 | £4 | £10 | autographed |
| Stay With Me | 7" | Mercury | MYSG1 | 1986 | £2 | £5 | autographed, gatefold picture sleeve |
| Tower Of Strength | CD-s | Mercury | MTHCD4 | 1988 | £2 | £5 | |
| Tower Of Strength | CD-s | Polygram | 0805262 | 1988 | £4 | £10 | CD video |
| Wasteland | CD-s | Polygram | 0801202 | 1988 | £4 | £10 | CD video |
| Wasteland | 7" | Mercury | MYTHB2 | 1987 | £2 | £5 | 2 singles, 5 photos, boxed |
| Wasteland | 12" | Mercury | MYTHX22DJ | 1987 | £2.50 | £6 | promo with poster |
| Wasteland (Anniversay Mix) | 12" | Mercury | MYTHX22 | 1987 | £2.50 | £6 | |
| Words Upon The Sand | CD | Mercury | CDP169 | 1990 | £8 | £20 | US promo |

## MISSION BELLES
| Sincerely | 7" | Decca | F12154 | 1965 | £1.50 | £4 | |

## MISSOURI
| Missouri | LP | Panama | PRS1022 | 1978 | £10 | £25 | US |

## MISSUS BEASTLY
| Dr. Aftershave And The Mixed Pickles | LP | April | 001 | 1976 | £4 | £10 | German |
| Missus Beastly | LP | Nova | 622030 | 1974 | £6 | £15 | German |
| Nara Asst Incense | LP | Opp | 532 | 1970 | £15 | £30 | German |

## MISTY
| Misty | LP | Cottage | COT511 | 1977 | £15 | £30 | |

## MISUNDERSTOOD
| Children Of The Sun | 7" | Fontana | TF998 | 1969 | £10 | £20 | |
| I Can Take You To The Sun | 7" | Fontana | TF777 | 1966 | £10 | £20 | |
| Never Had A Girl Like You | 7" | Fontana | TF1041 | 1969 | £10 | £20 | |
| You're Tuff Enough | 7" | Fontana | TF1028 | 1969 | £7.50 | £15 | |
| You're Tuff Enough | 7" | Fontana | TF1028 | 1969 | £12.50 | £25 | picture sleeve |

## MITCHELL, BLUE
| Bantu Village | LP | Blue Note | BST84324 | 1969 | £6 | £15 | |
| Blue's Blues | LP | Mainstream | MRL374 | 1973 | £4 | £10 | US |
| Boss Horn | LP | Blue Note | BLP/BST84257 | 1967 | £10 | £25 | |
| Bring It Home To Me | LP | Blue Note | BLP/BST84228 | 1966 | £10 | £25 | |
| Collision In Black | LP | Blue Note | BST84300 | 1968 | £6 | £15 | |
| Down With It | LP | Blue Note | BLP/BST84214 | 1965 | £10 | £25 | |
| Heads Up! | LP | Blue Note | BST84272 | 1968 | £10 | £25 | |
| Smooth As The Wind | LP | Riverside | RLP367 | 1961 | £6 | £15 | |

Thing To Do ........................................... LP ..... Blue Note ....... BLP/BST84178 ...... 1964  £6 .......... £15 ...........................

## MITCHELL, CHAD TRIO
Dona Dona Dona ...................................... 7" EP . Kapp ............. KEV13015 .............. 1965 £5 ......... £10 ..................... *French*
Paddy ...................................................... 7" EP . Colpix ............ CPS855 ................. 1965 £4 ................ £8 ...... *French, no picture sleeve*

## MITCHELL, GUY
| | | | | | | | |
|---|---|---|---|---|---|---|---|
| Best Of Guy Mitchell | LP | Realm | RM52336 | 1966 | £4 | £10 | |
| C'mon Let's Go | 7" | Philips | PB766 | 1958 | £2 | £5 | |
| Call Rosie On The Phone | 7" | Philips | JK1027 | 1957 | £4 | £8 | |
| Feet Up | 7" | Columbia | SCM5018 | 1952 | £7.50 | £15 | |
| Go Tiger Go | 7" | Pye | 7N25179 | 1963 | £4 | £8 | |
| Guy In Love | LP | Philips | BBL7246 | 1958 | £8 | £20 | |
| Guy Mitchell | 7" EP | Columbia | SEG7513 | 1954 | £4 | £8 | |
| Guy Mitchell Sings | 10" LP | Columbia | 33S1028 | 1954 | £15 | £30 | |
| Hangin' Around | 7" | Philips | PB830 | 1958 | £1.50 | £4 | |
| Knee Deep In The Blues | 7" | Philips | JK1005 | 1957 | £6 | £12 | |
| Let It Shine, Let It Shine | 7" | Philips | PB858 | 1958 | £1.50 | £4 | |
| My Heart Cries For You | 7" | Philips | PB885 | 1958 | £1.50 | £4 | |
| My Shoes Keep Walking Back To You | 7" | Philips | PB1050 | 1960 | £1.50 | £4 | |
| Pennies From Heaven | 7" EP | Philips | BBE12215 | 1958 | £5 | £10 | |
| Pretty Little Black Eyed Susie | 7" | Columbia | SCM5037 | 1953 | £7.50 | £15 | |
| Pride O' Dixie | 7" | Philips | PB915 | 1959 | £1.50 | £4 | |
| Rock-a-Billy | 7" | Philips | JK1015 | 1957 | £6 | £12 | |
| She Wears Red Feathers | 7" | Columbia | SCM5032 | 1953 | £7.50 | £15 | |
| Showcase Of Hits | LP | Philips | BBL7265 | 1958 | £8 | £20 | |
| Singing The Blues | 7" EP | Philips | BBE12112 | 1957 | £5 | £10 | |
| Singing The Blues | 7" | CBS | 202238 | 1966 | £4 | £8 | |
| Singing The Blues | 7" | Philips | JK1001 | 1956 | £7.50 | £15 | |
| Sings No. 1 | 7" EP | Philips | BBE12008 | 1955 | £4 | £8 | |
| Sings No. 2 | 7" EP | Philips | BBE12093 | 1956 | £5 | £10 | |
| Successes | 7" EP | Columbia | SEG7598 | 1955 | £4 | £8 | |
| Sunshine Guitar | LP | Philips | BBL7465 | 1961 | £8 | £20 | |
| Sweet Stuff | 7" | Philips | JK1023 | 1957 | £4 | £8 | |
| Train Of Love | 7" | Columbia | SCM5022 | 1953 | £6 | £12 | |
| Travelling Shoes | LP | London | HAB/SHB8364 | 1968 | £4 | £10 | |
| Voice Of Your Choice | 10" LP | Philips | BBR8031 | 1955 | £10 | £25 | |
| Wonderful Guy | 7" EP | Columbia | SEG7581 | 1955 | £4 | £8 | |
| Wonderin' And Worryin' | 7" | Philips | PB798 | 1958 | £1.50 | £4 | |

## MITCHELL, JONI
Joni Mitchell's way with words, combined with an ear for an unusual melody, a love of musical change and adventure, and above all, a beautiful voice, has made her into one of the world's dozen or so truly essential rock artists. This guide persists in listing her first LP as *Song To A Seagull*, since although the label has only the more prosaic *Joni Mitchell*, the cover has the more interesting title spelled out by seagulls, painted, as the majority of her album sleeves are, by Joni Mitchell herself.

| | | | | | | | |
|---|---|---|---|---|---|---|---|
| Blue | CD | Reprise | CD8811 | 1988 | £6 | £15 | ................ *box set* |
| Chalk Mark In A Rain Storm – Inside Information | CD | Geffen | | 1988 | £20 | £40 | ... *promo box set, with cassette, photo, biog* |
| Chelsea Morning | 7" | Reprise | RS23402 | 1969 | £1.50 | £4 | |
| Chinese Cafe | 7" | Geffen | DA3122 | 1983 | £1.50 | £4 | ...... *with interview 7"* |
| Clouds | LP | Reprise | RSLP6341 | 1969 | £5 | £12 | |
| Come In From The Cold | CD-s | Geffen | GFSTD4 | 1991 | £2 | £5 | |
| Conversation With Joni Mitchell | CD | Geffen | PROCD3076 | 1988 | £10 | £25 | ................ *US promo* |
| Court And Spark | LP | Asylum | EQ10001 | 1974 | £6 | £15 | ............... *US quad* |
| Court And Spark | LP | Nautilus | NR11 | 1981 | £5 | £12 | ......... *US audiophile* |
| Hissing Of Summer Lawns | LP | Asylum | EQ1051 | 1975 | £6 | £15 | ............... *US quad* |
| Hissing Of Summer Lawns | LP | Nimbus/ Asylum | K53018 | 1982 | £5 | £12 | ......... *audiophile* |
| Ladies Of The Canyon | LP | Reprise | RSLP6376 | 1970 | £5 | £12 | |
| Night In The City | 7" | Reprise | RS20694 | 1968 | £1.50 | £4 | |
| Night Ride Home | CD-s | Geffen | GFSTD2 | 1991 | £2 | £5 | |
| Night Ride Home Radio Program | CD | Geffen | GEFD9143 | 1991 | £20 | £40 | ......... *US promo* |
| Song To A Seagull | LP | Reprise | RSLP6293 | 1968 | £5 | £12 | |
| Wild Things Run Fast | LP | Geffen | GHS2019 | 1982 | £10 | £25 | . *US audiophile promo* |
| You Turn Me On I'm A Radio | 7" | Asylum | AYM511 | 1972 | £1.50 | £4 | |

## MITCHELL, KEVIN
Free And Easy ......................................... LP ..... Topic ............. 12TS314 .............. 1977 £5 ......... £12 .............................

## MITCHELL, PAT
Uillean Pipes ........................................... LP ..... Topic ............. 12TS294 .............. 1976 £4 ......... £10 .............................

## MITCHELL, RED
Presenting Red Mitchell ........................... LP ..... Contemporary . LAC12155 ............. 1959 £8 ......... £20 ..........................
Red Mitchell ............................................ LP ..... London ........... LTZN15041 ........... 1957 £8 ......... £20 ..........................

## MITCHELL, RONNIE
How Many Times ..................................... 7" ..... London ........... HLU9220 .............. 1960 £1.50 ......... £4 ..........................

## MITCHELL, ROSCOE
Sound ..................................................... LP ..... Delmark ......... DL408/DS9408 ...... 1967 £5 ......... £12 ..........................

## MITCHELL, SINX
Weird Sensation ....................................... 7" ..... Hickory .......... 451248 ................. 1964 £2 ......... £5 ..........................

## MITCHELL, WARREN
| | | | | | | | |
|---|---|---|---|---|---|---|---|
| Alf Garnett – Sex And Other Thoughts | LP | Pye | NPL18192 | 1968 | £4 | £10 | |
| Till Death Us Do Part | LP | Pye | NPL18154 | 1966 | £4 | £10 | *with other artists* |

## MITCHELL, WILLIE
| | | | | | | | |
|---|---|---|---|---|---|---|---|
| 20–75 | 7" | London | HLU9926 | 1964 | £1.50 | £4 | |
| Bad Eye | 7" | London | HLU10039 | 1966 | £1.50 | £4 | |
| Everything Is Gonna Be Alright | 7" | London | HLU10004 | 1965 | £4 | £8 | |
| Hit Sound Of Willie Mitchell | LP | London | HAU8319 | 1967 | £4 | £10 | |
| Live | LP | London | HAU/SHU8368 | 1968 | £4 | £10 | |
| Mercy | 7" | London | HLU10085 | 1966 | £1.50 | £4 | |
| On Top | LP | London | HAU/SHU8388 | 1969 | £4 | £10 | |
| Solid Soul | LP | London | HAU/SHU8372 | 1969 | £4 | £10 | |
| Soul Bag | LP | London | HAU/SHU8408 | 1970 | £4 | £10 | |
| Soul Serenade | LP | London | HAU/SHU8365 | 1968 | £4 | £10 | |
| Sunrise Serenade | LP | Hi | (S)HL32010 | 1963 | £4 | £10 | *US* |

## MITCHELLS
| | | | | | | | |
|---|---|---|---|---|---|---|---|
| Get Those Elephants Outa Here | LP | MGM | C803 | 1960 | £8 | £20 | |

## MITCHUM, ROBERT
| | | | | | | | |
|---|---|---|---|---|---|---|---|
| Calypso Is Like So | LP | Capitol | T853 | | £10 | £25 | *US* |
| Rachel And The Stranger | 7" EP | Brunswick | OE9197 | 1955 | £4 | £8 | |
| What Is This Generation Coming To? | 7" | Capitol | CL14701 | 1957 | £1.50 | £4 | |

## MITHRANDIR
| | | | | | | | |
|---|---|---|---|---|---|---|---|
| For You The Old Women | LP | private | | 1976 | £20 | £40 | *US* |

## MITTOO, JACKIE
| | | | | | | | |
|---|---|---|---|---|---|---|---|
| Ba Ba Boom | 7" | Coxsone | CS7009 | 1967 | £5 | £10 | *Slim Smith B side* |
| Can I Change My Mind | 7" | Bamboo | BAM31 | 1970 | £1.50 | £4 | *Brentford Allstars B side* |
| Clean Up | 7" | Bamboo | BAM15 | 1969 | £1.50 | £4 | |
| Dancing Groove | 7" | Bamboo | BAM51 | 1970 | £1.50 | £4 | *Black & George B side* |
| Dark Of The Moon | 7" | Bamboo | BAM17 | 1970 | £1.50 | £4 | |
| Dark Of The Sun | 7" | Doctor Bird | DB1177 | 1969 | £5 | £10 | *Matador Allstars B side* |
| Evening Time | LP | Coxsone | CSL8014 | 1968 | £50 | £100 | |
| Gold Dust | 7" | Bamboo | BAM20 | 1970 | £1.50 | £4 | *Supertones B side* |
| Holy Holy | 7" | Bamboo | BAM315 | 1970 | £1.50 | £4 | *Larry Marshall B side* |
| In London | LP | Coxsone | CSL8009 | 1967 | £50 | £100 | |
| Keep On Dancing | LP | Coxsone | CSL8020 | 1969 | £50 | £100 | |
| Killer Diller | 7" | Island | WI293 | 1966 | £5 | £10 | *Patrick Hytton B side* |
| Man Pon Spot | 7" | Coxsone | CS7046 | 1968 | £5 | £10 | *Bop & The Beltones B side* |
| Mission Impossible | 7" | Coxsone | CS7075 | 1968 | £5 | £10 | *Heptones B side* |
| Napoleon Solo | 7" | Coxsone | CS7050 | 1968 | £5 | £10 | *Cannonball Bryan B side* |
| Norwegian Wood | 7" | Coxsone | CS7040 | 1968 | £5 | £10 | *Gaylads B side* |
| Now | LP | Bamboo | BDLPS209 | 1970 | £15 | £30 | |
| Our Thing | 7" | Bamboo | BAM6 | 1969 | £1.50 | £4 | *C. Marshall B side* |
| Peenie Wallie | 7" | Bamboo | BAM320 | 1970 | £1.50 | £4 | *Roy Richards B side* |
| Put It On | 7" | Studio One | SO2043 | 1968 | £6 | £12 | *Soul Vendors B side* |
| Ram Jam | 7" | Coxsone | CS7019 | 1967 | £5 | £10 | *Summertaires B side* |
| Somebody Help Me | 7" | Coxsone | CS7002 | 1967 | £5 | £10 | *Gaylads B side* |
| Somethin' Stupid | 7" | Coxsone | CS7026 | 1967 | £5 | £10 | *Lyrics B side* |
| Songbird | 7" | Coxsone | CS7070 | 1968 | £5 | £10 | |
| Sure Shot | 7" | Coxsone | CS7042 | 1968 | £5 | £10 | *Octaves B side* |

## MIXTURE
| | | | | | | | |
|---|---|---|---|---|---|---|---|
| Sad Old Song | 7" | Parlophone | R5755 | 1969 | £1.50 | £4 | |

## MIXTURES
| | | | | | | | |
|---|---|---|---|---|---|---|---|
| Stompin' At The Rainbow | LP | Linda | 3301 | 1962 | £8 | £20 | *US* |

## MIZZY, VIC
| | | | | | | | |
|---|---|---|---|---|---|---|---|
| Addams Family Main Theme | 7" | RCA | RCA1440 | 1965 | £5 | £10 | |

## MNEMONISTS
| | | | | | | | |
|---|---|---|---|---|---|---|---|
| Gyromancy | LP | Dys | DYS10 | 1985 | £5 | £12 | *US* |
| Mnemonist Orchestra | 7" | Recommended | REX84 | 1984 | £4 | £8 | |

## MO & CO
| | | | | | | | |
|---|---|---|---|---|---|---|---|
| You've Got A Friend | LP | Cottage | COT131 | 1979 | £5 | £12 | |

## MO & STEVE
| | | | | | | | |
|---|---|---|---|---|---|---|---|
| Oh What A Day It's Going To Be | 7" | Pye | 7N17175 | 1966 | £1.50 | £4 | |

## MOBLEY, HANK
| | | | | | | | |
|---|---|---|---|---|---|---|---|
| All Stars | LP | Blue Note | BLP/BST81544 | 196– | £15 | £30 | |
| Caddy For Daddy | LP | Blue Note | BLP/BST84230 | 1966 | £8 | £20 | |
| Dippin' | LP | Blue Note | BLP/BST84209 | 1965 | £15 | £30 | |
| Flip | LP | Blue Note | BST84329 | 1969 | £5 | £12 | |
| Hi Voltage | LP | Blue Note | BST84273 | 1968 | £8 | £20 | |
| Jazz Message No. 2 | LP | London | LTZC15099 | 1957 | £15 | £30 | |
| Mobley's Message | LP | Esquire | 32029 | 1957 | £15 | £30 | |
| No Room For Squares | LP | Blue Note | BLP/BST84149 | 1963 | £10 | £25 | |

| | | | | | | | | |
|---|---|---|---|---|---|---|---|---|
| Reach Out!. | LP | Blue Note | BST84288 | 1968 | £6 | £15 | |
| Roll Call | LP | Blue Note | BLP/BST84058 | 1961 | £15 | £30 | |
| Soul Station | LP | Blue Note | BLP/BST84031 | 196– | £20 | £40 | |
| Turnaround! | LP | Blue Note | BLP/BST84186 | 1964 | £15 | £30 | |
| Workout | LP | Blue Note | BLP/BST84080 | 1961 | £15 | £30 | |

## MOBY

| | | | | | | | | |
|---|---|---|---|---|---|---|---|---|
| Everything Is Wrong | CD | Mute | CDSTUMM130 | 1995 | £6 | £15 | double |
| Go | CD-s | Outer Rhythm | FOOT015CD | 1991 | £2 | £5 | |

## MOBY GRAPE

When Columbia records in America decided to try the marketing device of simultaneously releasing every track from Moby Grape's first LP on five singles, this was certainly recognition of the fact that every track is distinctive enough to withstand the treatment. The LP is frequently held up as San Francisco's best, an assessment that is not far from the truth. Thereafter, Moby Grape's career was one of decline, although *Wow* has its moments. The *Grape Jam* record that accompanied the US release is a wasted opportunity, however. Acquiring the services of a master guitarist like Mike Bloomfield and then sitting him in front of a piano is simply daft.

| | | | | | | | | |
|---|---|---|---|---|---|---|---|---|
| Can't Be So Bad | 7" | CBS | 3555 | 1968 | £1.50 | £4 | |
| Moby Grape | LP | CBS | (S)BPG63090 | 1967 | £6 | £15 | |
| Moby Grape | LP | San Francisco Sound | 04805 | 1983 | £4 | £10 | US audiophile |
| Moby Grape '69 | LP | CBS | 63430 | 1969 | £4 | £10 | |
| Omaha | 7" | CBS | 2935 | 1967 | £2 | £5 | |
| Trucking Man | 7" | CBS | 3945 | 1969 | £1.50 | £4 | |
| Truly Fine Citizen | LP | CBS | 63698 | 1970 | £4 | £10 | |
| Wow | LP | CBS | 63271 | 1968 | £6 | £15 | |
| Wow/Grape Jam | LP | Columbia | CS9613 | 1968 | £8 | £20 | US double |
| Wow/Grape Jam | LP | San Francisco Sound | 04801 | 1983 | £8 | £20 | US audiophile double |

## MOCK TURTLES

| | | | | | | | |
|---|---|---|---|---|---|---|---|
| And Then She Smiles | 12" | Mirage | 015 | 1989 | £2.50 | £6 | |
| Pomona | 12" | Mirage | 003 | 1987 | £5 | £12 | |
| Wicker Man | 12" | Mirage | 009 | 1989 | £3 | £8 | |

## MOCKINGBIRDS

Kevin Godley and Graham Gouldman of Ten CC were both members of the Mockingbirds, while the Immediate single also featured Julie Driscoll on backing vocals.

| | | | | | | | |
|---|---|---|---|---|---|---|---|
| How To Find A Lover | 7" | Decca | F12510 | 1966 | £20 | £40 | |
| I Can Feel We're Parting | 7" | Columbia | DB7565 | 1965 | £25 | £50 | |
| One By One | 7" | Decca | F12434 | 1966 | £20 | £40 | |
| That's How It's Gonna Stay | 7" | Columbia | DB7480 | 1965 | £25 | £50 | |
| You Stole My Love | 7" | Immediate | IM015 | 1965 | £50 | £100 | |

## M.O.D.

| | | | | | | | |
|---|---|---|---|---|---|---|---|
| M.O.D. | 7" | Vertigo | 6059233 | 1979 | £2 | £5 | |

## MODE

| | | | | | | | |
|---|---|---|---|---|---|---|---|
| Mode | 7" EP | private | | 1967 | £100 | £200 | best auctioned |

## MODERN ART

| | | | | | | | |
|---|---|---|---|---|---|---|---|
| Dreams To Live | 7" | Color Disc | COLORS1 | 1985 | £10 | £20 | |
| Penny Valentine | 7" | Color Disc | COLORS5 | 198– | £4 | £8 | |
| Stereoland | LP | Color Disc | COLOR3 | 1987 | £20 | £40 | |

## MODERN ENGLISH

| | | | | | | | |
|---|---|---|---|---|---|---|---|
| Drowning Man | 7" | Limp | LMP2 | 1979 | £6 | £12 | |
| Gathering Dust | 7" | 4AD | AD15 | 1980 | £2 | £5 | |
| Smiles And Laughter | 7" | 4AD | AD110 | 1981 | £1.50 | £4 | |
| Swans On Glass | 7" | 4AD | AD6 | 1980 | £2 | £5 | |

## MODERN EON

| | | | | | | | |
|---|---|---|---|---|---|---|---|
| Euthenics | 7" | Inevitable | INEV003 | 1981 | £2 | £5 | |
| Pieces | 7" | Modern Eon | EON001 | 1980 | £6 | £12 | |

## MODERN FOLK QUARTET

| | | | | | | | |
|---|---|---|---|---|---|---|---|
| Changes | LP | Warner Bros | WM8157 | 1964 | £4 | £10 | |
| Modern Folk Quartet | LP | Warner Bros | WM/WS8135 | 1963 | £4 | £10 | |
| Night Time Girl | 7" | RCA | RCA1514 | 1966 | £4 | £8 | |
| Palm Springs Weekend | LP | Warner Bros | W(S)1519 | 1963 | £5 | £12 | US, with Connie Stevens |

## MODERN JAZZ QUARTET

| | | | | | | | |
|---|---|---|---|---|---|---|---|
| All Of You | 7" EP | Fontana | 469204TE | 195– | £2 | £5 | |
| At Music Inn | LP | London | LTZK15085 | 1957 | £6 | £15 | |
| At Music Inn | LP | London | LTZK15173/ SAHK6050 | 1959 | £6 | £15 | |
| At Music Inn | 7" EP | London | REK1320 | 1961 | £2 | £5 | |
| At The Opera House | LP | Columbia | 33CX10128 | 1958 | £8 | £20 | with Oscar Peterson |
| Best Of The Modern Jazz Quartet | LP | Stateside | SL10141 | 1965 | £5 | £12 | |
| Blues At Carnegie Hall | LP | Atlantic | SD1468 | 1967 | £5 | £12 | US |
| Collaboration | LP | Atlantic | SD1429 | 1966 | £5 | £12 | US |
| Comedy Suite | LP | London | HAK/SHK8046 | 1963 | £5 | £12 | |
| Concorde | LP | Transatlantic | PR7005 | 196– | £4 | £10 | |
| European Concert | 7" EP | London | REK1319 | 1961 | £2 | £5 | |
| Five Ways Of Playing La Ronde | 7" EP | Esquire | EP166 | 1958 | £2 | £5 | |

| Title | Format | Label | Catalogue | Year | | | Notes |
|---|---|---|---|---|---|---|---|
| Fontessa | LP | London | LTZK15022/ SAHK6031 | 1957 | £6 | £15 | |
| Gershwin Ballad Medley | 7" EP | Esquire | EP116 | 195– | £2 | £5 | |
| Jazz Dialogue | LP | Atlantic | SD1449 | 1966 | £5 | £12 | US |
| Legendary Profile | LP | Atlantic | K40421 | 1973 | £4 | £10 | |
| Live At The Lighthouse | LP | Atlantic | SD1486 | 1967 | £5 | £12 | US |
| Lonely Woman | LP | London | HAK/SHK8016 | 1963 | £5 | £12 | |
| Looking Back | LP | Esquire | 32124 | 1961 | £6 | £15 | |
| Modern Jazz Quartet | LP | London | LTZK15136 | 1958 | £6 | £15 | |
| Modern Jazz Quartet | 7" EP | Esquire | EP106 | 195– | £2 | £5 | |
| Modern Jazz Quartet | 7" EP | Esquire | EP109 | 195– | £2 | £5 | |
| Modern Jazz Quartet | 7" EP | London | EZK19047 | 1959 | £2 | £5 | |
| Modern Jazz Quartet | 7" EP | London | REK1314 | 1961 | £2 | £5 | |
| Modern Jazz Quartet | 10" LP | Esquire | 20038 | 1955 | £20 | £40 | |
| Modern Jazz Quartet And Orchestra | LP | Atlantic | SD1359 | 1961 | £6 | £15 | US |
| Modern Jazz Quartet Vol. 2 (Concorde) | 10" LP | Esquire | 20069 | 1956 | £20 | £40 | |
| No Sun In Venice | LP | Atlantic | SD1284 | 1958 | £6 | £15 | US |
| Odds Against Tomorrow | LP | London | LTZT15181 | 1960 | £6 | £15 | |
| One Never Knows | LP | London | LTZK15140/ SAHK6029 | 1958 | £6 | £15 | |
| One Never Knows | 7" EP | London | EZK19046 | 1959 | £2 | £5 | |
| Plastic Dreams | LP | Atlantic | K40318 | 1972 | £4 | £10 | |
| Porgy And Bess | LP | Atlantic | SD1440 | 1966 | £5 | £12 | US |
| Pyramid | LP | London | LTZK15193/ SAHK6086 | 1960 | £6 | £15 | |
| Quartet | 7" EP | London | EZC19019 | 1957 | £2 | £5 | |
| Quartet Is A Quartet Is A Quartet | LP | Atlantic | 587044 | 1966 | £5 | £12 | |
| Sheriff | LP | London | HAK/SHK8161 | 1964 | £5 | £12 | |
| Space | LP | Apple | SAPCOR10 | 1969 | £15 | £30 | single or gatefold sleeve |
| Stockholm Concert | LP | Atlantic | 590012 | 1968 | £5 | £12 | |
| Sun Dance | LP | Atlantic | 588126 | 1968 | £5 | £12 | |
| Third Stream Music | LP | London | LTZK15207/ SAHK6124 | 1961 | £6 | £15 | |
| Under The Jasmine Tree | LP | Apple | APCOR4 | 1968 | £20 | £40 | mono |
| Under The Jasmine Tree | LP | Apple | SAPCOR4 | 1968 | £15 | £30 | stereo |

## MODERN JAZZ SEXTET

| | | | | | | | |
|---|---|---|---|---|---|---|---|
| Modern Jazz Sextet | LP | Columbia | 33CX10048 | 1956 | £20 | £40 | |

## MODERN JAZZ SOCIETY

| | | | | | | | |
|---|---|---|---|---|---|---|---|
| Concert Of Contemporary Music | LP | Columbia | 33CX10038 | 1956 | £20 | £40 | |

## MODERNAIRES

| | | | | | | | |
|---|---|---|---|---|---|---|---|
| At My Front Door | 7" | Vogue Coral | Q72112 | 1955 | £2.50 | £6 | |
| Birds And Puppies And Tropical Fish | 7" | Vogue Coral | Q72069 | 1955 | £2 | £5 | |
| Go On With The Wedding | 7" | Vogue Coral | Q72158 | 1956 | £1.50 | £4 | |
| Here Comes The Modernaires | LP | Coral | LVA9080 | 1958 | £4 | £10 | |
| Let's Dance | 7" | Vogue Coral | Q72135 | 1956 | £1.50 | £4 | |
| Mood Indigo | 7" | Vogue Coral | Q2024 | 1954 | £2 | £5 | |
| New Juke Box Saturday Night | 7" | Vogue Coral | Q2035 | 1954 | £2 | £5 | |
| Sluefoot | 7" | Vogue Coral | Q72084 | 1955 | £2 | £5 | |
| Stop, Look And Listen | 10" LP | Vogue Coral | LVC10012 | 1955 | £6 | £15 | |

## MODS

| | | | | | | | |
|---|---|---|---|---|---|---|---|
| Something On My Mind | 7" | RCA | RCA1399 | 1964 | £1.50 | £4 | |

## MODUGNO, DOMENICO

| | | | | | | | |
|---|---|---|---|---|---|---|---|
| Ciao Ciao Bambina | 7" | Oriole | CB1489 | 1959 | £1.50 | £4 | |
| Volare | 7" | Oriole | CB1460 | 1958 | £1.50 | £4 | |
| Volare | 7" | Oriole | CB5000 | 1958 | £1.50 | £4 | |

## MOFFAT ALLSTARS

| | | | | | | | |
|---|---|---|---|---|---|---|---|
| Riot | 7" | Jackpot | JP719 | 1969 | £1.50 | £4 | .. Impersonators B side |

## MOGUL THRASH

| | | | | | | | |
|---|---|---|---|---|---|---|---|
| Mogul Thrash | LP | RCA | SF8156 | 1971 | £6 | £15 | |
| Sleeping In The Kitchen | 7" | RCA | RCA2030 | 1970 | £1.50 | £4 | |

## MOHAWK, ESSRA

| | | | | | | | |
|---|---|---|---|---|---|---|---|
| Essra Mohawk | LP | Mooncrest | CREST24 | 1975 | £4 | £10 | |

## MOHAWKS

| | | | | | | | |
|---|---|---|---|---|---|---|---|
| Baby Hold On | 7" | Pama | PM739 | 1968 | £2 | £5 | |
| Champ | LP | Pama | PMLP5 | 1968 | £20 | £40 | |
| Champ | 7" | Pama | PM719 | 1968 | £4 | £8 | |
| Mony Mony | 7" | Pama | PM757 | 1968 | £2 | £5 | |
| Ride Your Pony | 7" | Pama | PM758 | 1968 | £2 | £5 | |
| Sweet Soul Music | 7" | Pama | PM751 | 1968 | £2 | £5 | |

## MOHOLO, LOUIS

| | | | | | | | |
|---|---|---|---|---|---|---|---|
| Spirits Rejoice! | LP | Ogun | OG520 | 1978 | £6 | £15 | |

## MOJO BLUESBAND

| | | | | | | | |
|---|---|---|---|---|---|---|---|
| Hey Bartender | LP | Ex Libris | 12387 | 1970 | £15 | £30 | Swiss |

## MOJO HANNAH

| | | | | | | | |
|---|---|---|---|---|---|---|---|
| Six Days On The Road | LP | Kingdom | KVL9001 | 1972 | £6 | £15 | |

## MOJO MEN
| | | | | | | | |
|---|---|---|---|---|---|---|---|
| Dance With Me | 7" EP | Vogue | INT18050 | 1965 | £30 | £60 | French |
| Dance With Me | 7" | Pye | 7N25336 | 1965 | £2 | £5 | |
| Hanky Panky | 7" | Reprise | RS20486 | 1966 | £10 | £20 | |
| Me About You | 7" | Reprise | RS20580 | 1967 | £2.50 | £6 | |
| Sit Down I Think I Love You | 7" | Reprise | RS20539 | 1967 | £2 | £5 | |

## MOJOS
| | | | | | | | |
|---|---|---|---|---|---|---|---|
| Comin' On To Cry | 7" | Decca | F12127 | 1965 | £2 | £5 | |
| Everything's Alright | 7" | Decca | F11853 | 1964 | £1.50 | £4 | |
| Forever | 7" | Decca | F11732 | 1963 | £1.50 | £4 | |
| Goodbye Dolly Gray | 7" | Decca | F12557 | 1967 | £2 | £5 | |
| Mojos | 7" EP | Decca | DFE8591 | 1964 | £20 | £40 | |
| Seven Daffodils | 7" | Decca | F11959 | 1964 | £1.50 | £4 | |
| Until My Baby Comes Home | 7" | Liberty | LBF15097 | 1968 | £10 | £20 | |
| Wait A Minute | 7" | Decca | F12231 | 1965 | £5 | £10 | Stu James credit |
| Why Not Tonight | 7" | Decca | F11918 | 1964 | £1.50 | £4 | |

## MOLES
Noting that the Moles' single was on the Parlophone label, and that it had moreover been produced by George Martin, many observers concluded that it must be a Beatles performance. In fact, 'the Moles' was indeed a pseudonym, but for the rather less exciting Simon Dupree and the Big Sound.

| | | | | | | | |
|---|---|---|---|---|---|---|---|
| We Are The Moles | 7" | Parlophone | R5743 | 1968 | £10 | £20 | |

## MOLLOY, MATT
| | | | | | | | |
|---|---|---|---|---|---|---|---|
| Heathery Breeze | LP | Polydor | 2904018 | 1981 | £4 | £10 | Irish |
| Matt Molloy | LP | Mulligan | LUN004 | 1976 | £4 | £10 | Irish |

## MOLLOY, MATT, PAUL BRADY, TOMMY PEOPLES
| | | | | | | | |
|---|---|---|---|---|---|---|---|
| Matt Molloy, Paul Brady, Tommy Peoples | LP | Mulligan | LUN017 | 1978 | £4 | £10 | Irish |

## MOLLY HATCHET
| | | | | | | | |
|---|---|---|---|---|---|---|---|
| Beatin' The Odds | LP | Epic | AS99844 | 1980 | £10 | £25 | US promo picture disc |
| Flirtin' With Disaster | LP | CBS | AL36110 | 1979 | £10 | £25 | US picture disc |
| Molly Hatchet | LP | Epic | 35347 | 1978 | £10 | £25 | US picture disc |
| Take No Prisoners | LP | Epic | AS991320 | 1981 | £10 | £25 | US promo picture disc |

## MOLOCH
| | | | | | | | |
|---|---|---|---|---|---|---|---|
| Moloch | LP | Enterprise | ENS1002 | 1972 | £8 | £20 | US |

## MOLONEY, MICK
| | | | | | | | |
|---|---|---|---|---|---|---|---|
| We Have Met Together | LP | Transatlantic | TRA263 | 1973 | £5 | £12 | |

## MOLONEY, PADDY & SEAN POTTS
| | | | | | | | |
|---|---|---|---|---|---|---|---|
| Tin Whistles | LP | Claddagh | CC15 | 1974 | £5 | £12 | Irish |

## MOMENTS
| | | | | | | | |
|---|---|---|---|---|---|---|---|
| Walk Right In | 7" | London | HLN9656 | 1963 | £1.50 | £4 | |

## MON DYH
| | | | | | | | |
|---|---|---|---|---|---|---|---|
| Murderer | LP | Elgenprod | 6622192 | 1981 | £4 | £10 | German |

## MONARCHS
| | | | | | | | |
|---|---|---|---|---|---|---|---|
| Look Homeward Angel | 7" | London | HLU9862 | 1964 | £6 | £12 | |

## MONCUR III, GRACHAN
| | | | | | | | |
|---|---|---|---|---|---|---|---|
| Evolution | LP | Blue Note | BLP/BST84153 | 1963 | £8 | £20 | |
| Some Other Stuff | LP | Blue Note | BLP/BST84177 | 1964 | £8 | £20 | |

## MONDAY, PAUL
Paul Monday was one of several names used by the man who found success as Gary Glitter.

| | | | | | | | |
|---|---|---|---|---|---|---|---|
| Here Comes The Sun | 7" | MCA | MK5008 | 1969 | £5 | £10 | |
| Musical Man | 7" | MCA | MU1024 | 1968 | £5 | £10 | |

## MONEY, ZOOT
| | | | | | | | |
|---|---|---|---|---|---|---|---|
| Big Time Operator | 7" EP | Columbia | ESRF1801 | 1966 | £50 | £100 | French |
| Big Time Operator | 7" EP | Columbia | SEG8519 | 1966 | £62.50 | £125 | |
| Big Time Operator | 7" | Columbia | DB7975 | 1966 | £7.50 | £15 | |
| Good | 7" | Columbia | DB7518 | 1965 | £7.50 | £15 | |
| It Should Have Been Me | LP | Columbia | SX1734 | 1965 | £30 | £60 | |
| Let's Run For Cover | 7" | Columbia | DB7876 | 1966 | £7.50 | £15 | |
| Nick Knack | 7" EP | Columbia | ESRF1874 | 1967 | £50 | £100 | French |
| Nick Nack | 7" | Columbia | DB8172 | 1967 | £7.50 | £15 | |
| No One But You | 7" | Polydor | 2058020 | 1970 | £5 | £10 | |
| Please Stay | 7" EP | Columbia | ESRF1766 | 1966 | £50 | £100 | French |
| Please Stay | 7" | Columbia | DB7600 | 1965 | £7.50 | £15 | |
| Something Is Worrying Me | 7" | Columbia | DB7697 | 1965 | £7.50 | £15 | |
| Star Of the Show | 7" | Columbia | DB8090 | 1966 | £7.50 | £15 | |
| Transition | LP | Direction | 863231 | 1968 | £10 | £25 | |
| Uncle Willie | 7" | Decca | F11954 | 1964 | £12.50 | £25 | |
| Welcome To My Head | LP | Capitol | 318 | 1969 | £8 | £20 | US |
| Zoot | LP | Columbia | SX/SCX6075 | 1966 | £10 | £25 | |
| Zoot Money | LP | Polydor | 2482019 | 1970 | £6 | £15 | |

## MONGREL

| | | | | | | | |
|---|---|---|---|---|---|---|---|
| Get Your Teeth Into This | LP | Polydor | 2383182 | 1973 | £6 | £15 | |

## MONGRELS

| | | | | | | | |
|---|---|---|---|---|---|---|---|
| I Long To Hear | 7" | Decca | F12003 | 1964 | £10 | £20 | |
| My Love For You | 7" | Decca | F12086 | 1965 | £10 | £20 | |

## MONITORS

| | | | | | | | |
|---|---|---|---|---|---|---|---|
| Greetings We're The Monitors | LP | Tamla Motown | (S)TML11108 | 1969 | £20 | £40 | |

## MONK, THELONIOUS

| | | | | | | | |
|---|---|---|---|---|---|---|---|
| Alone In San Francisco | LP | Riverside | RLP312 | 1965 | £5 | £12 | |
| Blue Monk | 7" EP | Esquire | EP246 | 1962 | £2 | £5 | |
| Brilliant Corners | LP | London | LTZU15097 | 1957 | £10 | £25 | |
| Brilliant Corners | LP | Riverside | RLP12226 | 1961 | £8 | £20 | |
| Criss-Cross | LP | CBS | (S)BPG62173 | 1964 | £5 | £12 | |
| Five By Monk By Five | LP | Riverside | RLP305 | 1965 | £5 | £12 | |
| Genius Of Modern Music Vol. 1 | LP | Blue Note | BLP/BST81510 | 1964 | £10 | £25 | |
| Genius Of Modern Music Vol. 2 | LP | Blue Note | BLP/BST81511 | 1964 | £10 | £25 | |
| Golden Monk | LP | Stateside | SL10152 | 1965 | £5 | £12 | |
| In Europe Vol. 1 | LP | Riverside | RLP002 | 1964 | £5 | £12 | |
| In Europe Vol. 2 | LP | Riverside | RLP003 | 1965 | £5 | £12 | |
| In Europe Vol. 3 | LP | Riverside | RLP004 | 1966 | £5 | £12 | |
| It's Monk's Time | LP | CBS | (S)BPG62391 | 1965 | £5 | £12 | |
| Misterioso | LP | CBS | (S)BPG62620 | 1966 | £5 | £12 | |
| Misterioso | LP | Riverside | RLP279 | 1964 | £5 | £12 | |
| Monk | LP | CBS | (S)BPG62497 | 1965 | £5 | £12 | |
| Monk's Blues | LP | CBS | 63609 | 1969 | £4 | £10 | |
| Monk's Dream | LP | CBS | (S)BPG62135 | 1963 | £5 | £12 | |
| Monk's Moods | LP | Esquire | 32119 | 1961 | £10 | £25 | |
| Monk's Moods | LP | Transatlantic | PR7159 | 1967 | £4 | £10 | |
| Monk's Music | LP | Riverside | RLP12242 | 1962 | £6 | £15 | |
| Nica's Tempo | LP | Realm | RM52223 | 1965 | £4 | £10 | |
| Nutty | 7" EP | Riverside | REP3214 | 196– | £2 | £5 | ...with John Coltrane |
| Nutty Monk | 7" EP | Esquire | EP236 | 1961 | £2 | £5 | |
| Quartet Plus Two At The Black Hawk | LP | Riverside | RLP12323 | 1962 | £6 | £15 | |
| Ruby My Dear | 7" EP | Riverside | REP3217 | 196– | £2 | £5 | ...with John Coltrane |
| Solo | LP | CBS | (S)BPG62549 | 1965 | £5 | £12 | |
| Straight, No Chaser | LP | CBS | (S)BPG63009 | 1967 | £5 | £12 | |
| Thelonious Himself | LP | London | LTZU15120 | 1958 | £10 | £25 | |
| Thelonious Himself | LP | Riverside | RLP12235 | 1963 | £6 | £15 | |
| Thelonious In Action | LP | Riverside | RLP12262 | 1961 | £6 | £15 | |
| Thelonious Monk | LP | CBS | (S)BPG62248 | 1964 | £5 | £12 | |
| Thelonious Monk | 7" EP | Vogue | EPV1115 | 1956 | £2 | £5 | |
| Thelonious Monk | 10" LP | Esquire | 20049 | 1955 | £25 | £50 | |
| Thelonious Monk Orchestra At Town Hall | LP | Riverside | RLP12300 | 1962 | £6 | £15 | |
| Thelonious Monk Plays | 10" LP | Esquire | 20075 | 1956 | £25 | £50 | |
| Thelonious Monk Plays Duke Ellington | LP | London | LTZU15019 | 1957 | £10 | £25 | |
| Thelonious Monk Plays Duke Ellington | LP | Riverside | RLP12201 | 1961 | £8 | £20 | |
| Thelonious Monk Quintet | 10" LP | Esquire | 20039 | 1955 | £25 | £50 | |
| Thelonious Monk Quintets | LP | Esquire | 32109 | 1960 | £10 | £25 | |
| Thelonious Monk Trio | 7" EP | Esquire | EP75 | 195– | £2 | £5 | |
| Thelonious Monk Vol. 1 | LP | Philips | BBL1510 | 1961 | £6 | £15 | |
| Thelonious Monk Vol. 2 | LP | Philips | BBL1511 | 1962 | £6 | £15 | |
| Thelonious Monk With John Coltrane | LP | Riverside | JLP(9)46 | 1963 | £5 | £12 | |
| Unique Thelonious | LP | London | LTXU15071 | 1957 | £10 | £25 | |
| Way Out! | LP | Fontana | FJL113 | 1965 | £4 | £10 | |
| Work | LP | Esquire | 32115 | 1961 | £10 | £25 | |
| Work | LP | Transatlantic | PR7169 | 1967 | £5 | £12 | |

## MONKEES

Just because the Monkees were a manufactured group, put together by businessmen keen to create a facsimile of the Beatles' *A Hard Day's Night* and *Help* films to turn into a TV series, it does not follow automatically that the group's music was worthless. In fact, some real craftsman-songwriters were drafted in to write the songs (Neil Diamond, John Stewart and Carole King among them) and a set of crack session musicians were employed to do the actual playing. All the Monkees had to do on the records was sing. The result, in 'I'm A Believer', 'A Little Bit Me, A Little Bit You' and the rest, was some of the decade's most sparkling pop singles. When the Monkees had become sufficiently entrenched in the pop market place to be able to start dictating their own terms, the result was some worthy self-produced material, but an inevitable decline in sales. These later Monkees releases are now the most sought after (the early albums are still very common, though they are not often found in excellent condition). Most desirable is the soundtrack album, *Head*, to the film that is either an extraordinary psychedelic masterpiece or a self-indulgent mess, depending on the critic's point of view. One song from it, however, 'Porpoise Song', is rightly acclaimed for its aching beauty and its floating ambience as a period classic.

| | | | | | | | |
|---|---|---|---|---|---|---|---|
| Alternate Title | 7" EP | RCA | 86956 | 1967 | £7.50 | £15 | French |
| Barrel Full Of Monkees | LP | Colgems | SCOS1001 | 1971 | £8 | £20 | US |
| Birds, The Bees And The Monkees | LP | RCA | RD/SF7948 | 1968 | £4 | £10 | |
| Changes | LP | Colgems | COS119 | 1970 | £10 | £25 | US |
| Daydream Believer | CD-s | Arista | 662157 | 1989 | £2 | £5 | |
| Golden Hits | LP | RCA | PRS329 | 1972 | £8 | £20 | US |
| Good Clean Fun | 7" | RCA | RCA1887 | 1969 | £1.50 | £4 | |
| Greatest Hits | LP | Colgems | COS115 | 1969 | £6 | £15 | US |
| Head | LP | RCA | RD/SF8051 | 1969 | £20 | £40 | |
| Headquarters | LP | Colgems | COM/COS103 | 1967 | £6 | £15 | US, photo of 2 bearded Monkees |
| Headquarters | LP | RCA | RD/SF7886 | 1967 | £4 | £10 | |
| Hey Hey It's The Monkees – 20 Smash Hits | CD | Platinum | PLATCD05 | 1988 | £5 | £12 | |

| | | | | | | | | |
|---|---|---|---|---|---|---|---|---|
| I'm A Believer | 7" EP | RCA | 86952 | 1966 | £7.50 | £15 | | *French* |
| Instant Replay | LP | RCA | RD/SF8016 | 1969 | £6 | £15 | | |
| Last Train To Clarksville | CD-s | Arista | 662158 | 1989 | £2 | £5 | | *2 versions* |
| Last Train To Clarksville | 7" EP | RCA | 86950 | 1966 | £7.50 | £15 | | *French* |
| Last Train To Clarksville | 7" | RCA | RCA1547 | 1966 | £1.50 | £4 | | |
| Listen To The Band | 7" | RCA | RCA1824 | 1969 | £1.50 | £4 | | |
| Little Bit Me, A Little Bit You | 7" EP | RCA | 86955 | 1967 | £7.50 | £15 | | *French* |
| Monkees | LP | RCA | RD/SF7844 | 1967 | £4 | £10 | | |
| Monkees | CD | Arista | 258773 | 1985 | £5 | £12 | | |
| Monkees Present | LP | Colgems | COS117 | 1969 | £10 | £25 | | *US* |
| Monkees Vol. 2 | CD-s | Arista | 112158 | 1989 | £2 | £5 | | |
| More Of The Monkees | LP | RCA | RD/SF7868 | 1967 | £4 | £10 | | |
| Oh My My | 7" | RCA | RCA1958 | 1970 | £2 | £5 | | |
| Pisces, Aquarius, Capricorn And Jones Ltd. | LP | RCA | RD/SF7912 | 1967 | £4 | £10 | | |
| Porpoise Song | 7" | RCA | RCA1862 | 1969 | £2 | £5 | | |
| Re-Focus | LP | Bell | 6081 | 1973 | £15 | £30 | | *US* |
| Teardrop City | 7" | RCA | RCA1802 | 1969 | £1.50 | £4 | | |
| Tema Dei Monkees | 7" | RCA | 1546 | 1967 | £6 | £12 | | *sung in Italian* |

## MONKS
| | | | | | | | | |
|---|---|---|---|---|---|---|---|---|
| It's Black Monk Time | LP | Polydor | 249900 | 1966 | £50 | £100 | | *German* |

## MONOGRAMS
| | | | | | | | |
|---|---|---|---|---|---|---|---|
| Juke Box Cha Cha | 7" | Parlophone | R4515 | 1959 | £1.50 | £4 | |

## MONOPOLY
| | | | | | | | |
|---|---|---|---|---|---|---|---|
| House Of Lords | 7" | Polydor | 56164 | 1967 | £1.50 | £4 | |
| We Belong Together | 7" | Pye | 7N17940 | 1970 | £1.50 | £4 | |
| We're All Going To The Seaside | 7" | Polydor | 56188 | 1967 | £1.50 | £4 | |

## MONOTONES
| | | | | | | | |
|---|---|---|---|---|---|---|---|
| Book Of Love | 7" | London | HLM8625 | 1958 | £20 | £40 | |

## MONOTONES (2)
| | | | | | | | |
|---|---|---|---|---|---|---|---|
| What Would I Do | 7" | Pye | 7N15608 | 1964 | £1.50 | £4 | |

## MONRO, MATT
| | | | | | | | |
|---|---|---|---|---|---|---|---|
| Blue And Sentimental | 10" LP | Decca | LF1276 | 1957 | £8 | £20 | |
| Everybody Falls In Love With Someone | 7" | Decca | F10816 | 1956 | £4 | £8 | |
| From Russia With Love | 7" EP | Parlophone | GEP8889 | 1963 | £4 | £8 | |
| Garden Of Eden | 7" | Decca | F10845 | 1957 | £4 | £8 | |
| My House Is Your House | 7" | Decca | F10870 | 1957 | £4 | £8 | |
| Prisoner Of Love | 7" | Fontana | H167 | 1958 | £2.50 | £6 | |
| Story Of Ireland | 7" | Fontana | H122 | 1958 | £2.50 | £6 | |

## MONROE, BARRY
| | | | | | | | |
|---|---|---|---|---|---|---|---|
| Never Again | 7" | Polydor | 56088 | 1966 | £1.50 | £4 | |

## MONROE, BILL
| | | | | | | | | |
|---|---|---|---|---|---|---|---|---|
| Bluegrass Ramble | LP | Brunswick | LAT/STA8511 | 1963 | £4 | £10 | | |
| Bluegrass Special | LP | Brunswick | LAT/STA8579 | 1965 | £4 | £10 | | |
| Country Date | 7" EP | Brunswick | OE9160 | 1955 | £5 | £10 | | |
| Country Waltz | 7" EP | Brunswick | OE9195 | 1955 | £5 | £10 | | |
| Early Bluegrass | LP | Camden | CAL774 | 1963 | £4 | £10 | | *US* |
| Father Of Bluegrass Music | LP | Camden | CAL719 | 1962 | £4 | £10 | | *US* |
| Four Walls | 7" | Brunswick | 05681 | 1957 | £2 | £5 | | |
| Gotta Travel On | 7" | Brunswick | 05776 | 1959 | £2 | £5 | | |
| Great Bill Monroe | LP | Harmony | HL7290 | 1961 | £4 | £10 | | *US* |
| I Saw The Light | LP | Brunswick | LAT8338 | 1961 | £4 | £10 | | |
| I Saw The Light | LP | Decca | DL(7)8769 | 1959 | £6 | £15 | | *US* |
| Knee Deep In Bluegrass | LP | Decca | DL(7)8731 | 1958 | £6 | £15 | | *US* |
| Mr. Bluegrass | LP | Decca | DL(7)4080 | 1960 | £6 | £15 | | *US* |
| My All Time Country Favorites | LP | Decca | DL(7)4327 | 1962 | £4 | £10 | | *US* |
| New John Henry Blues | 7" | Brunswick | 05567 | 1956 | £2 | £5 | | |

## MONROE, MARILYN
| | | | | | | | | |
|---|---|---|---|---|---|---|---|---|
| Gentlemen Prefer Blondes | LP | MGM | E3231 | 1955 | £15 | £30 | | *US* |
| Gentlemen Prefer Blondes | 10" LP | MGM | D116 | 1953 | £25 | £50 | | |
| Heat Wave | 78 | HMV | B10847 | 1955 | £6 | £12 | | |
| I Wanna Be Loved By You | 7" | London | HLT8862 | 1959 | £6 | £12 | | |
| I'm Gonna File My Claim | 7" | HMV | 7M232 | 1954 | £7.50 | £15 | | |
| Let's Make Love | LP | Philips | BBL7414/SBBL592 | 1960 | £10 | £25 | | |
| Let's Make Love | 7" EP | Philips | BBE12414 | 1960 | £6 | £12 | | |
| Let's Make Love | 7" EP | Philips | SBBE9031 | 1961 | £10 | £20 | | *stereo* |
| Marilyn | LP | 20th Century | FXG/SXG5000 | 1959 | £25 | £50 | | *US, with poster* |
| Marilyn | LP | Stateside | (S)SL10048 | 1963 | £10 | £25 | | |
| Marilyn Monroe | LP | Ascot | ALM13008/ ALS16008 | 1964 | £10 | £25 | | *US* |
| Some Like It Hot | LP | London | HAT2176/ SHT6040 | 1959 | £20 | £40 | | |
| Some Like It Hot | 7" EP | London | RET1231 | 1960 | £20 | £40 | | *tri-centre* |
| There's No Business Like Show Business | 7" EP | HMV | 7EG8090 | 1955 | £10 | £20 | | |
| Unforgettable | LP | Movietone | 72016 | 1967 | £6 | £15 | | *US* |

## MONROE, VAUGHN
| | | | | | | | |
|---|---|---|---|---|---|---|---|
| Black Denim Trousers And Motorcycle Boots | 7" | HMV | 7M332 | 1955 | £6 | £12 | |
| Butterscotch Mop | 7" | HMV | 7M287 | 1955 | £1.50 | £4 | |

| | | | | | | | |
|---|---|---|---|---|---|---|---|
| Fiesta | 7" | HMV | 7M165 | 1953 | £1.50 | £4 | |
| Greatest Hits | 7" EP | RCA | RCX1043 | 1959 | £4 | £8 | |
| Less Than Tomorrow | 7" | HMV | 7M144 | 1953 | £1.50 | £4 | |
| Small World | 7" | HMV | 7M148 | 1953 | £1.50 | £4 | |
| They Were Doin' The Mambo | 7" | HMV | 7M247 | 1954 | £1.50 | £4 | |

## MONROE BROTHERS

| | | | | | | | |
|---|---|---|---|---|---|---|---|
| Country Guitar Vol. 14 | 7" EP | RCA | RCX7103 | 1963 | £2.50 | £6 | |
| Country Guitar Vol. 15 | 7" EP | RCA | RCX7104 | 1963 | £2.50 | £6 | |
| Country Guitar Vol. 16 | 7" EP | RCA | RCX7105 | 1963 | £2 | £5 | ...... with Bill Monroe |

## MONSTERAS BLUESBAND

| | | | | | | | |
|---|---|---|---|---|---|---|---|
| Mixture | LP | Frog Music | LFK03 | 1978 | £20 | £40 | Swedish |

## MONTANA SLIM

| | | | | | | | |
|---|---|---|---|---|---|---|---|
| Dynamite Trail | LP | Decca | DL4092 | 1960 | £8 | £20 | US |
| I'm Ragged But I'm Right | LP | Decca | DL8917 | 1959 | £8 | £20 | US |
| Wilf Carter As Montana Slim | LP | Starday | SLP300 | 1964 | £4 | £10 | US |
| Wilf Carter/Montana Slim | LP | Camden | CAL527 | 1959 | £5 | £12 | US |

## MONTANAS

| | | | | | | | |
|---|---|---|---|---|---|---|---|
| All That Is Mine Can Be Yours | 7" | Piccadilly | 7N35262 | 1965 | £2 | £5 | |
| Ciao Baby | 7" | Pye | 7N17282 | 1967 | £1.50 | £4 | |
| Roundabout | 7" | Pye | 7N17697 | 1969 | £2 | £5 | |
| Step In The Right Direction | 7" | Pye | 7N17499 | 1968 | £2 | £5 | |
| Take My Hand | 7" | Pye | 7N17338 | 1967 | £2 | £5 | |
| That's When Happiness Began | 7" EP | Pye | PNV24179 | 1966 | £50 | £100 | French |
| That's When Happiness Began | 7" | Pye | 7N17183 | 1966 | £12.50 | £25 | |
| You're Making A Big Mistake | 7" | Pye | 7N17597 | 1968 | £2 | £5 | |
| You've Got To Be Loved | 7" | Pye | 7N17394 | 1967 | £2 | £5 | |

## MONTCLAIRS

| | | | | | | | |
|---|---|---|---|---|---|---|---|
| Hung Up On Your Love | 7" | Contempo | CS2036 | 1975 | £2 | £5 | |

## MONTE, LOU

| | | | | | | | |
|---|---|---|---|---|---|---|---|
| Darktwon Strutters' Ball | 7" | HMV | 7M190 | 1954 | £1.50 | £4 | |

## MONTE, VINNIE

| | | | | | | | |
|---|---|---|---|---|---|---|---|
| Joannie Don't Be Angry | 7" | Stateside | SS156 | 1963 | £1.50 | £4 | |
| Summer Spree | 7" | London | HL8947 | 1959 | £2.50 | £6 | |

## MONTENEGRO, HUGO

| | | | | | | | |
|---|---|---|---|---|---|---|---|
| Get Off The Moon | 7" | Oriole | CBA1792 | 1963 | £7.50 | £15 | |
| Man From UNCLE | LP | RCA | RD7758 | 1966 | £15 | £30 | |
| More Music From The Man From UNCLE | LP | RCA | RD7832 | 1966 | £15 | £30 | |

## MONTEZ, CHRIS

| | | | | | | | |
|---|---|---|---|---|---|---|---|
| Chris Montez | 7" EP | Pye | NEP44080 | 1966 | £4 | £8 | |
| Let's Dance | 7" EP | London | REU1392 | 1963 | £10 | £20 | |
| Let's Dance | 7" | London | HLU9596 | 1962 | £1.50 | £4 | |
| Let's Dance And Have Some Kinda Fun | LP | London | HAU8079 | 1963 | £10 | £25 | |
| More I See You | LP | Pye | NPL23080 | 1966 | £4 | £10 | |
| More I See You | 7" EP | Pye | NEP44071 | 1966 | £5 | £10 | |
| More I See You | 7" | Pye | 7N25369 | 1966 | £1.50 | £4 | |
| My Baby Loves To Dance | 7" | London | HLU9764 | 1963 | £1.50 | £4 | |
| Some Kinda Fun | 7" | London | HLU9650 | 1963 | £1.50 | £4 | |
| Time After Time | LP | Pye | N(S)PL28187 | 1967 | £4 | £10 | |

## MONTGOMERY, LITTLE BROTHER

| | | | | | | | |
|---|---|---|---|---|---|---|---|
| 1930–1969 | LP | Saydisc | SDR213 | 1971 | £4 | £10 | |
| Chicago Blues Session | LP | 77 | LA1221 | 1963 | £5 | £12 | .with Sunnyland Slim |
| Little Brother Montgomery | LP | Columbia | 33SX1289 | 1960 | £6 | £15 | |
| Little Brother Montgomery | LP | Decca | LK4664 | 1965 | £5 | £12 | |
| Pinetop's Boogie Woogie | 7" | Columbia | DB4595 | 1961 | £4 | £8 | |
| Southside Blues | LP | Riverside | 403 | 1960 | £6 | £15 | US |

## MONTGOMERY, MARIAN

| | | | | | | | |
|---|---|---|---|---|---|---|---|
| Love Makes Two People Sing | 7" | Reaction | 591018 | 1967 | £2 | £5 | |

## MONTGOMERY, WES

| | | | | | | | |
|---|---|---|---|---|---|---|---|
| Full House | LP | Riverside | RLP434 | 1962 | £4 | £10 | |
| Go! | LP | Fontana | FJL109 | 1965 | £4 | £10 | |
| Groove Yard | LP | Riverside | RLP12362 | 1961 | £5 | £12 | . with Buddy & Monk Montgomery |
| Incredible Jazz Guitar | LP | Riverside | RLP12320 | 1960 | £5 | £12 | |
| Movin' Along | LP | Riverside | RLP12342 | 1960 | £4 | £10 | |
| Wes Montgomery Trio | LP | Riverside | RLP12310 | 1959 | £5 | £12 | |

## MONTGOMERY BROTHERS

| | | | | | | | |
|---|---|---|---|---|---|---|---|
| Montgomery Brothers Plus Five Others | LP | Vogue | LAE12137 | 1959 | £8 | £20 | |
| Montgomeryland | LP | Vogue | LAE12246 | 1961 | £5 | £12 | |

## MONTROSE, JACK

| | | | | | | | |
|---|---|---|---|---|---|---|---|
| Blues And Vanilla | LP | RCA | RD27023 | 1958 | £6 | £15 | |
| Jack Montrose Sextet | LP | Vogue | LAE12042 | 1957 | £10 | £25 | |
| Jack Montrose With Bob Gordon | LP | London | LTZK15043 | 1957 | £10 | £25 | |

## MONTY & ROY
Tra La La Boogie...................................... 7" ...... Blue Beat ........ BB61 .................... 1961 £6.........£12 ..............................

## MONTY PYTHON
Always Look On The Bright Side Of Life... CD-s .. Virgin ............ PYTHD1 ............... 1991 £2...........£5 ..............................
Brian ....................................................... 7" ...... Warner Bros.... K17495PRO ......... 1980 £1.50........£4 ..........bleeped promo
Flying Sheep ........................................... 7" ...... BBC ................................... 1970 £6...........£12 ..............................
Live At The City Center, April 1976......... LP ..... Arista ............ AL4073................. 1976 £4............£10 .......................US
Python On Song ...................................... 7" ...... Charisma ....... MP001 ............... 1975 £2...........£5 .......................double

## MONUMENT
First Monument ...................................... LP ..... Beacon .......... BEAS15 ............... 1971 £25.........£50 ..............................

## MOOCHE
Hot Smoke And Sasafrass ......................... 7" ...... Pye ................. 7N17735 ............ 1969 £7.50......£15 ..............................

## MOOD MOSAIC
Chinese Chequers ................................... 7" ...... Columbia ........ DB8149 .............. 1967 £2...........£5 ..............................
Mood Mosaic............................................ LP ..... Columbia ........ SX6153/TWO160 .. 1967 £10.........£25 ..............................
Touch Of Velvet, A Sting Of Brass ........... 7" ...... Columbia ........ DB7801 .............. 1966 £2.50.......£6 ..............................
Touch Of Velvet, A Sting Of Brass ........... 7" ...... Columbia ........ DB8618 .............. 1969 £1.50.......£4 ..............................

## MOOD OF HAMILTON
Why Can't There Be More Love?............. 7" ...... Columbia ........ DB8304 .............. 1967 £5...........£10 ..............................

## MOOD SIX
She's Too Far............................................ 7" ...... EMI............... EMI5336............... 1982 £10.........£20 ........ test pressing

## MOODIE, AMEIL
Mello Reggae ......................................... 7" ...... Blue Cat......... BS143 ................ 1968 £2.50.......£6 ..............................
Ratchet Knife .......................................... 7" ...... Blue Cat......... BS164 ................ 1969 £2.50.......£6 ..............................

## MOODS
Duckwalk ................................................ 7" ...... Starlite ........... ST45098 ............. 1963 £5...........£10 ..............................

## MOODY, CLYDE
Best Of Clyde Moody............................. LP ..... King .............. 891 ...................... 1964 £6............£15 .......................US

## MOODY, JAMES
James Moody ........................................... 10" LP Esquire .......... 20035................. 1955 £25.........£50 ..............................
James Moody ........................................... 10" LP Esquire .......... 20036................. 1955 £25.........£50 ..............................
James Moody ........................................... 10" LP Esquire .......... 20071................. 1956 £20.........£40 ..............................
James Moody ........................................... 10" LP Esquire .......... 20077................. 1956 £20.........£40 ..............................
Moody's Workshop .................................. LP ..... XTRA ............ XTRA5017 .......... 1966 £6............£15 ..............................

## MOODY, JAMES & GEORGE WALLINGTON
Beginning And End Of Bop .................... LP ..... Blue Note ....... B6503 ................. 1969 £8............£20 ..............................

## MOODY BLUES
Boulevard De La Madelaine...................... 7" ...... Decca ............ F12498................. 1966 £1.50........£4 ..............................
Boulevard De La Madeleine ..................... 7" EP . Decca ............ 457117................. 1966 £7.50......£15 .......................French
Bye Bye Bird ........................................... 7" EP . Decca ............ 457098................. 1966 £7.50......£15 .......................French
Days Of Future Passed ............................ LP ..... Deram ........... DML707 .............. 1968 £4............£10 .......................mono
Days Of Future Passed ............................ LP ..... Mobile Fidelity MFSL1042 ........... 1980 £4............£10 ........US audiophile
Days Of Future Passed ............................ CD .... Mobile Fidelity UDCD512 ............ 1988 £6............£15 ........US audiophile
Every Good Boy Deserves Favour.............. CD .... Mobile Fidelity ........................... 1995 £6............£15 ........US audiophile
Everyday ................................................ 7" ...... Decca ............ F12266................. 1965 £1.50........£4 ..............................
Fly Me High ........................................... 7" ...... Decca ............ F12607................. 1967 £2.50........£6 ..............................
From The Bottom Of My Heart.................. 7" ...... Decca ............ F12166................. 1965 £1.50........£4 ..............................
Go Now..................................................... 7" EP . Decca ............ 457057................. 1964 £7.50......£15 .......................French
Go Now..................................................... 7" ...... Decca ............ F12022................. 1964 £1.50........£4 ..............................
I Don't Want To Go On Without You ...... 7" ...... Decca ............ F12095................. 1965 £1.50........£4 ..............................
I Know You're Out There Somewhere ...... CD-s .. Polydor .......... POCD921 ............ 1988 £2...........£5 ..............................
In Search Of The Lost Chord .................... LP ..... Deram ........... DML717 .............. 1968 £5............£12 .......................mono
Life's Not Life ........................................ 7" ...... Decca ............ F12543................. 1967 £15.........£30 ..............................
Lose Your Money .................................... 7" ...... Decca ............ F11971................. 1964 £10.........£20 ..............................
Love And Beauty ..................................... 7" ...... Decca ............ F12670................. 1967 £2.50.......£6 ..............................
Magnificent Moodies .............................. LP :..... Decca ............ LK4711 .............. 1966 £4............£10 ..............................
Moody Blues ........................................... 7" EP . Decca ............ DFE8622.............. 1965 £5............£10 ..............................
Moody Blues ........................................... 7" EP . Decca ............ DFE8622.............. 1968 £2...........£5 .........boxed Decca logo
Octave ..................................................... LP ..... Decca ............ TXS129 .............. 1978 £4............£10 .......................blue vinyl
Octave ..................................................... CD .... Decca ............ 8203292 .............. 1986 £5............£12 ..............................
On The Threshold Of A Dream ................ LP ..... Deram ........... DML1035 ............ 1968 £5............£12 .......................mono
On The Threshold Of A Dream ................ LP ..... Nautilus ......... NR21 ................. 1981 £6............£15 ........US audiophile
On The Threshold Of A Dream ................ CD .... Mobile Fidelity UDCD612 ............ 1994 £6............£15 ........US audiophile
Question Of Balance .............................. CD .... Decca ............ 8202112 .............. 1986 £5............£12 ..............................
Ride My See-Saw ..................................... 7" ...... Deram ........... DM213 ............... 1968 £1.50........£4 ..............................
Say It With Love...................................... CD-s .. Polydor .......... PZCD153 ............ 1991 £2...........£5 ..............................
Seventh Sojourn ..................................... LP ..... Mobile Fidelity MFSL1151 ........... 1984 £4............£10 ........US audiophile
Talking Out Of Turn .............................. 7" ...... Threshold........ THPD29 ............ 1981 £2...........£5 .........picture disc
To Our Children's Children's Children ...... LP ..... Threshold........ THM1 ................ 1969 £6............£15 .......................mono
Watching And Waiting ........................... 7" ...... Threshold........ TH1 ................... 1969 £1.50........£4 ..............................

## MOOLAH
Woe Ye Demons ...................................... LP ..... Annuit Coeptis M1 ...................... 1969 £62.50.. £125 .......................US

## MOON
| | | | | | | | | |
|---|---|---|---|---|---|---|---|---|
| Without Earth | LP | Liberty | LBL/LBS83146 | 1968 | £5 | £12 | |

## MOON, KEITH
| | | | | | | | |
|---|---|---|---|---|---|---|---|
| Two Sides Of The Moon | LP | Polydor | 2442134 | 1975 | £5 | £12 | |

## MOONDOG
Louis T. Hardin is a New York street musician and composer, who has never let the fact that he is blind get in the way of his full-time career as an eccentric. His infrequent recordings contain idiosyncratic instrumental works, which blend a classical approach with elements of jazz and rock. He successfully sued DJ Alan Freed in the fifties, forcing him to change the name of his programme, *Moondog's Rock and Roll Party*.

| | | | | | | | |
|---|---|---|---|---|---|---|---|
| H'art Songs | LP | Kopf | RRF33016 | 1978 | £5 | £12 | German |
| Moondog | LP | CBS | 63906 | 1969 | £8 | £20 | |
| Moondog | LP | Esquire | 32055 | 1958 | £20 | £40 | US |
| Moondog 2 | LP | CBS | 30897 | 1971 | £8 | £20 | US |
| Moondog In Europe | LP | Kopf | RRF33014 | 1978 | £8 | £20 | German |
| On The Streets Of New York | 7" EP | London | REP1010 | 1954 | £12.50 | £25 | |

## MOONEY, ART
| | | | | | | | |
|---|---|---|---|---|---|---|---|
| Giant | 7" | MGM | MGM943 | 1957 | £2.50 | £6 | |
| Rebel Without A Cause Theme | 7" | MGM | MGM923 | 1957 | £2.50 | £6 | |
| Rock And Roll Tumbleweed | 7" | MGM | MGM951 | 1957 | £6 | £12 | |

## MOONGLOWS
| | | | | | | | |
|---|---|---|---|---|---|---|---|
| Best Of Bobby Lester & The Moonglows | LP | Chess | LP1471 | 1962 | £30 | £60 | US |
| Collectors Showcase | LP | Constellation | CS2 | 1964 | £6 | £15 | US |
| I Knew From The Start | 7" | London | HLN8374 | 1957 | £180 | £300 | best auctioned |
| Look It's The Moonglows | LP | Chess | LP1430 | 1958 | £50 | £100 | US |

## MOONGOONERS
This is a name used by Scott Walker in two of his many attempts to find success in the days before the Walker Brothers – this time in a duo with his fellow 'brother', John Maus.

| | | | | | | | |
|---|---|---|---|---|---|---|---|
| Moongoon Stomp | 7" | Candix | 335 | 1962 | £10 | £20 | US |
| Moongoon Twist | 7" | Donna | 1373 | 1962 | £7.50 | £15 | US |
| Moongoon Twist | 7" | Essar | 1007 | 1962 | £10 | £20 | US |

## MOONKYTE
| | | | | | | | |
|---|---|---|---|---|---|---|---|
| Count Me Out | LP | Mother | SMOT1 | 1971 | £50 | £100 | |

## MOONLIGHTERS
| | | | | | | | |
|---|---|---|---|---|---|---|---|
| Going Out | 7" | Island | WI043 | 1963 | £5 | £10 | |

## MOONRAKERS
| | | | | | | | |
|---|---|---|---|---|---|---|---|
| Together With Him | LP | Shamley | SS704 | 1968 | £8 | £20 | US |

## MOON'S TRAIN
| | | | | | | | |
|---|---|---|---|---|---|---|---|
| Deed I Do | 7" | MGM | MGM1333 | 1967 | £2.50 | £6 | |

## MOONSHINE, MICKEY
| | | | | | | | |
|---|---|---|---|---|---|---|---|
| Baby Blue | 7" | Decca | F13555 | 1974 | £1.50 | £4 | |

## MOONSHINERS
| | | | | | | | |
|---|---|---|---|---|---|---|---|
| Hold Up | LP | Page One | POLS004 | 1967 | £6 | £15 | |

## MOONTREKKERS
| | | | | | | | |
|---|---|---|---|---|---|---|---|
| Moondust | 7" | Decca | F11714 | 1963 | £2.50 | £6 | |
| Night Of The Vampire | 7" | Parlophone | R4814 | 1961 | £5 | £10 | |
| There's Something At The Bottom | 7" | Parlophone | R4888 | 1962 | £6 | £12 | |

## MOORCOCK, MICHAEL
| | | | | | | | |
|---|---|---|---|---|---|---|---|
| Brothel In Rosenstrasse | 7" | Flicknife | EJSP9831 | 1982 | £12.50 | £25 | with lyric sheet |
| Dodgem Dude | 7" | Flicknife | FLEP200 | 1980 | £2 | £5 | |
| New World's Fair | LP | United Artists | UAG29732 | 1975 | £20 | £40 | with Deep Fix |

## MOORE, ALAN & DAVID J
| | | | | | | | |
|---|---|---|---|---|---|---|---|
| V For Vendetta | 12" | Glass | 12032 | 1984 | £2.50 | £6 | cartoon strip insert |

## MOORE, ANTHONY
| | | | | | | | |
|---|---|---|---|---|---|---|---|
| Flying Doesn't Help | LP | Quango | HMG98 | 1979 | £4 | £10 | |
| Pieces From The Cloudland Ballroom | LP | Polydor | 2310162 | 1971 | £15 | £30 | |
| Secrets Of The Blue Bag | LP | Polydor | 2310179 | 1972 | £15 | £30 | |

## MOORE, BARRY
| | | | | | | | |
|---|---|---|---|---|---|---|---|
| Treaty Stone | LP | Mulligan | LUN022 | 1978 | £8 | £20 | Irish |

## MOORE, BOB
| | | | | | | | |
|---|---|---|---|---|---|---|---|
| Viva | LP | Hickory | 131 | 1968 | £25 | £50 | US |

## MOORE, BOBBY
| | | | | | | | |
|---|---|---|---|---|---|---|---|
| Searching For My Love | LP | Chess | CRL4521 | 1966 | £6 | £15 | |
| Searching For My Love | 7" | Chess | CRS8033 | 1966 | £2 | £5 | |

## MOORE, BREW
| | | | | | | | |
|---|---|---|---|---|---|---|---|
| Quartet And Quintet | LP | Vocalion | LAE564 | 1964 | £5 | £12 | |

## MOORE, BUTCH
Walking The Streets In The Rain ............. 7" ...... Pye ................ 7N15832 ................ 1965 £1.50 ........ £4 ..............................

## MOORE, CHRISTY
Anti Nuclear ........................................ 12" ..... Alt ................. 101 ...................... 1978 £10 ........ £20 .. with Barry Moore &
*The Early Grave*
*Band*

Christy Moore ...................................... LP ..... Polydor ........... 2383426 ........... 1976 £5 ......... £12 ..............................
Iron Behind The Velvet ...................... LP ..... Tara ................. 2002 ................ 1978 £4 ......... £10 ........................ *Irish*
Paddy On The Road ............................ LP ..... Mercury ........... 20170SMCL ........... 1969 £75 ......... £150 ..............................
Prosperous ......................................... LP ..... Trailer ............. LER3035 ............... 1972 £10 ......... £25 ..............................
Whatever Tickles Your Fancy ................ LP ..... Polydor ........... 2383344 ........... 1975 £8 ......... £20 ..............................

## MOORE, CHRISTY, DONAL LUNNY & JIMMY FAULKNER
Live In Dublin ................................... LP ..... Tara ................. 2005 ................ 1978 £4 ......... £10 ........................ *Irish*

## MOORE, DUDLEY
Dudley Moore Trio ............................ LP ..... Decca ............ LK/SKL4976 ......... 1969 £8 ......... £20 ..............................
Music Of Dudley Moore ...................... LP ..... Decca ............ LK/SKL4980 ......... 1969 £5 ......... £12 ..............................

## MOORE, GARY
After The War ..................................... CD-s .. Virgin ........... GMSCD1 ............ 1989 £2 ......... £5 ..............................
After The War ..................................... CD-s .. Virgin ........... VSCD1153 ............ 1988 £2 ......... £5 ..............................
Always Gonna Love You ...................... 7" ...... Virgin ........... VSY528 .......... 1982 £1.50 ......... £4 ...................... *picture disc*
Back On The Streets ............................ 7" ...... MCA ........... MCA386 .......... 1978 £7.50 ......... £15 ...................... *picture sleeve*
Empty Rooms ....................................... CD-s .. Virgin ........... CDT35 .............. 1988 £2 ......... £5 ........................... *3" single*
Falling In Love With You ...................... 7" ...... Virgin ........... VSY564 .......... 1983 £1.50 ......... £4 ...................... *picture disc*
Friday On My Mind .............................. CD-s .. 10 ............... KERRY164 .......... 1987 £3 ......... £8 ..............................
Gary Moore EP .................................... CD-s .. Special Edition. CD34 ............... 1988 £2 ......... £5 ..............................
Grinding Stone ................................... LP ..... Columbia ........ 65527 .............. 1973 £4 ......... £10 ..............................
Hold On To Your Love ......................... 7" ...... 10 ............... TENS13 ............ 1984 £2.50 ........ £6 ..... *shaped picture disc*
Oh Pretty Woman .............................. CD-s .. Virgin ........... VSCDT1233 ......... 1990 £2 ......... £5 ..............................
Over The Hills And Far Away ................ CD-s .. 10 ............... TENCD134 ......... 1988 £2 ......... £5 ..............................
Over The Hills And Far Away ................ 7" ...... 10 ............... TENS134 .......... 1986 £2 ......... £5 ..... *shaped picture disc*
Parisienne Walkways ............................ 7" ...... MCA ........... MCA419 .......... 1979 £2.50 ........ £6 ...................... *picture sleeve*
Ready For Love .................................... CD-s .. Virgin ........... GMSCD2 ............ 1989 £2 ......... £5 ........................... *2 versions*
Separate Ways ..................................... CD-s .. Virgin ........... VSCDX1437 ....... 1992 £3 ......... £8 ... *boxed with booklet*
Shapes Of Things ................................ 7" ...... 10 ............... TENS19 ............ 1984 £2.50 ........ £6 ..... *shaped picture disc*
Spanish Guitar ..................................... 7" ...... MCA ........... MCA534 .......... 1979 £2.50 ........ £6 ...................... *picture sleeve*
Still Got The Blues .............................. CD-s .. Virgin ........... VSCDT1267 ......... 1990 £2 ......... £5 ........................... *2 versions*
Too Tired ............................................ CD-s .. Virgin ........... VSCD1306 .......... 1990 £2 ......... £5 ........................... *2 versions*
Walking By Myself ............................... CD-s .. Virgin ........... VSCDT1281 ......... 1990 £2 ......... £5 ..............................
Wild Frontier ...................................... CD-s .. 10 ............... KERRY159 .......... 1987 £3 ......... £8 ..............................

## MOORE, GARY & PHIL LYNOTT
Out In The Fields ................................ 7" ...... 10 ............... TENS49 ............ 1985 £4 ......... £8 . *shaped picture disc (2
different)*

## MOORE, GATEMOUTH
I'm A Fool To Care ............................. LP ..... King .............. 684 ................ 1960 £180 ..... £300 ...................... *US*

## MOORE, JOHNNY
Big Big Boss ........................................ 7" ...... Doctor Bird ..... DB1180 ................ 1969 £5 ......... £10 ..... *Carl Bryan B side*

## MOORE, LATTIE
Best Of Lattie Moore ........................... LP ..... Audio Lab ....... AL1555 ............ 1960 £10 ......... £25 ...................... *US*
Country Side ....................................... LP ..... Audio Lab ....... AL1573 ............ 1962 £10 ......... £25 ...................... *US*

## MOORE, MERRILL
Bellyfull Of Blue Thunder ................... LP ..... Ember ........... EMB3392 ........... 1967 £4 ......... £10 ..............................
Down The Road A-Piece ...................... 7" ...... Ember ........... EMBS253 ........... 1968 £4 ......... £8 ..............................
Hard Top Race .................................... 7" ...... Capitol ........... CL14369 .......... 1955 £37.50 ... £75 ..............................
Rough House 88 ................................... LP ..... Ember ........... EMB3394 ........... 1968 £4 ......... £10 ..............................
Sweet Mama ........................................ 7" ...... B&C ............. CB100 ............. 1969 £1.50 ........ £4 ..............................

## MOORE, OSCAR
Oscar Moore Trio ................................ 10" LP London ........... HAPB1035 ............. 1955 £10 ......... £25 ..............................

## MOORE, PHIL
Moore's Tour – An American In England... LP ..... MGM ............ C790 ................ 1959 £5 ......... £12 ..............................

## MOORE, R. STEVIE
R. Stevie Moore is one of rock music's eccentrics, preferring to issue his records through his own mail order scheme than to tangle with record companies who would doubtless attempt to compromise Moore's quirky approach. The original issue of his first album, *Phonography*, was produced in an edition of just ninety-nine copies and long ago sold out. The Zappa household has one, and so did UK collector, the late Michael Gerzon, whose copy is likely to be the only one in the country.

Delicate Tension .................................. LP ..... HP Music ........ HPS30735 ........... 1979 £8 ......... £20 ...................... *US*
Phonography ....................................... LP ..... HP Music ........ HPS30734 ........... 1978 £8 ......... £20 ...................... *US*
Phonography ....................................... LP ..... Vital .............. VS0001 ................ 1976 £100 ..... £200 ...................... *US*

## MOORE, SCOTTY
Guitar That Changed The World ............ LP ..... Columbia ........ 33SX1680 ........... 1964 £20 ......... £40 ..............................

## MOORE, THURSTON, KIM GORDON, EPIC SOUNDTRACKS
Sitting On A Barbed Wire Fence ............. 7" ...... Imaginary ........ FREE003 ............... 1992 £2 ......... £5 ...................... *promo*

## MOORE, WHISTLING ALEX
Whistling Alex Moore .............................. LP ...... 77 .................. LA126 .................... 1961 £8 .......... £20 ...............................

## MOORS MURDERERS

The Moors Murderers, a punk group of which Steve Strange and Chrissie Hynde were both members, were supposed to have released a single called 'Free Myra Hindley'. Although acetates have turned up, however, it seems unlikely that regular vinyl copies exist.

Free Myra Hindley .................................. 7" ...... Pop Corn ....... ........................... 1978 £700 ... £1000 ..... existence doubtful

## MOOSKNUKKL GROOVBAND
Moosknukkl Groovband ........................ LP ...... Spiegelei .......... 285163V ............... 1972 £25 .......... £50 .................... German

## MOPED, JOHNNY
Basically The Original Johnny Moped Tape  7" ...... Chiswick ........ PROMO3 ............ 1976 £2.50 ...... £6 .......................... promo

## MOPEDS
Whiskey And Soda ................................. 7" ...... Columbia ...... DB108 .................. 1968 £1.50 ...... £4 .......................

## MOQUETTES
Right String But Wrong Yo Yo ............... 7" ...... Columbia ..... DB7315 ............... 1964 £12.50 .... £25 .........................

## MORECAMBE & WISE
Boom Oo Yatta-Ta-Ta ........................... 7" ...... HMV ............. POP1240 ............. 1963 £1.50 ...... £4 ...........................
Mr. Morecambe Meets Mr. Wise ............... LP ...... HMV ............. CLP1682/CSD1522 1964 £4 .......... £10 .......................

## MOREL, TERRY
Songs Of A Woman In Love ..................... LP ...... Bethlehem ....... 47 ........................ 1955 £8 .......... £20 .............................. US

## MORGAN
Nova Solis .......................................... LP ...... RCA ............. SF8321 ................... 1972 £10 .......... £25 .......................

## MORGAN, AL
Jealous Heart ....................................... 7" ...... London ......... HLU8741 ............... 1958 £2 .......... £5 ...........................
Jealous Heart ....................................... 10" LP London .......... HAPB1001 ............ 1951 £4 .......... £10 ...........................
Little Red Book .................................... 10" LP London .......... HAPB1003 ............ 1951 £4 .......... £10 ...........................

## MORGAN, DAVY
Tomorrow I'll Be Gone .......................... 7" ...... Columbia ...... DB7624 ............... 1965 £7.50 ...... £15 ...........................
True To Life ........................................ 7" ...... Parlophone ...... R5692 ................. 1968 £2.50 ...... £6 ...........................

## MORGAN, DERRICK
Amelita ............................................... 7" ...... Island ......... WI289 .................. 1966 £5 .......... £10 ...........................
Angel With Blue Eyes ........................... 7" ...... Island ......... WI1080 ................. 1963 £5 .......... £10 ...........................
Are You Going To Marry Me? .................. 7" ...... Blue Beat ...... BB110 ................. 1962 £6 .......... £12 ...... with Patsy Todd
Around The Corner ............................... 7" ...... Ska Beat ........ JB188 ................. 1965 £5 .......... £10 ...........................
Baby Please Don't Leave Me ................... 7" ...... Blue Beat ...... BB65 .................. 1961 £6 .......... £12 ...... with Patsy Todd
Balzing Fire ......................................... 7" ...... Rio ............... R1 ..................... 1963 £5 .......... £10 ...........................
Be Still ............................................... 7" ...... Blue Beat ...... BB76 .................. 1962 £6 .......... £12 ...........................
Ben Johnson Day .................................. 7" ...... Pyramid ........ PYR6056 .......... 1968 £4 .......... £8 ...... Maytals B side
Best Of Derrick Morgan ........................ LP ...... Doctor Bird.... DLMB5014 ......... 1969 £50 .......... £100 ...........................
Blazing Fire ......................................... 7" ...... Island ......... WI051 ................. 1962 £5 .......... £10 ...........................
Call My Name ...................................... 7" ...... Blue Beat ...... BB171 ................. 1963 £6 .......... £12 ...... with Patsy Todd
Cherry Home ....................................... 7" ...... Island ......... WI013 ................. 1962 £5 .......... £10 ...........................
Cherry Pie ........................................... 7" ...... Black Swan.... WI425 ................. 1964 £5 .......... £10 ...........................
Come Back My Love .............................. 7" ...... Blue Beat ...... BB121 ................. 1962 £6 .......... £12 ...........................
Come On ............................................. 7" ...... Island ......... WI024 ................. 1962 £5 .......... £10 .... Monty & Cyclones
                                                                                                                                                 B side
Come On Over ..................................... 7" ...... Blue Beat ...... BB85 .................. 1962 £6 .......... £12 ...........................
Conquering Ruler .................................. 7" ...... Island ......... WI3094 ............... 1967 £5 .......... £10 Lloyd & Devon B side
Contented Wife .................................... 7" ...... Blue Beat ...... BB261 ................. 1964 £6 .......... £12 ...........................
Cool Off Rudies .................................... 7" ...... Rio ............... R122 .................. 1966 £4 .......... £8 ...........................
Copy Cat ............................................. 7" ...... Bullet .......... BU419 ................ 1969 £1.50 ...... £4 ...........................
Court Dismiss ...................................... 7" ...... Pyramid ........ PYR6014 .......... 1967 £4 .......... £8 ...... Frederick McLean
                                                                                                                                                 B side
Derrick Morgan And His Friends .............. LP ...... Island ......... ILP990 ............... 1969 £30 .......... £60 .......... pink label
Derrick Top The Pop ............................. 7" ...... Unity ........... UN540 ................ 1969 £1.50 ...... £4 ...........................
Do The Beng Beng ................................ 7" ...... Pyramid ........ PYR6025 .......... 1968 £4 .......... £8 ...........................
Don't Cry ............................................ 7" ...... Blue Beat ...... BB12 .................. 1960 £6 .......... £12 ...........................
Don't Say ............................................ 7" ...... Pyramid ........ PYR6063 .......... 1969 £2.50 ...... £6 ...........................
Don't You Know Little Girl .................... 7" ...... Blue Beat ...... BB82 .................. 1962 £6 .......... £12 Basil Gabbidon B side
Eternity .............................................. 7" ...... Blue Beat ...... BB318 ................. 1965 £6 .......... £12 ...... with Patsy Todd
Fat Man .............................................. 7" ...... Blue Beat ...... BB7 ................... 1960 £6 .......... £12 ...........................
Feel So Fine ........................................ 7" ...... Blue Beat ...... BB57 .................. 1961 £6 .......... £12 ...... with Patsy Todd,
                                                                                                                                            Roland Alphonso
                                                                                                                                                 B side
Forward March ..................................... LP ...... Island ......... ILP903 ............... 1963 £50 .......... £100 ...........................
Forward March ..................................... LP ...... Trojan .......... TTL38 ................. 1970 £6 .......... £15 ...........................
Gather Together .................................... 7" ...... Island ......... WI3010 ............... 1966 £5 .......... £10 ...........................
Gimme Back ........................................ 7" ...... Island ......... WI3101 ............... 1967 £5 .......... £10 ...... Viceroys B side
Give You My Love ................................ 7" ...... Nu Beat ........ NB027 ................ 1969 £2 .......... £5 ...........................
Greedy Gal ......................................... 7" ...... Pyramid ........ PYR6013 .......... 1967 £4 .......... £8 .. Soul Brothers B side
Heart Of Stone .................................... 7" ...... Ska Beat ........ JB185 ................. 1965 £5 .......... £10 with Naomi Campbell
Hey Boy, Hey Girl ................................ 7" ...... Nu Beat ........ NB008 ................ 1968 £2.50 ...... £6 ...... with Patsy Todd
Hold You Jack ..................................... 7" ...... Island ......... WI3159 ............... 1968 £5 .......... £10 ...........................
Hop ................................................... 7" ...... Island ......... WI006 ................. 1962 £5 .......... £10 ...........................
Housewive's Choice ............................... 7" ...... Island ......... WI018 ................. 1962 £5 .......... £10 ...... with Patsy Todd

| I Am The Ruler | 7" | Pyramid | PYR6029 | 1968 | £4 | £8 | |
| I Found A Queen | 7" | Island | WI288 | 1966 | £5 | £10 | |
| I Love You | 7" | Nu Beat | NB016 | 1968 | £1.50 | £4 | *Junior Smith B side* |
| I Want A Lover | 7" | Island | WI193 | 1965 | £5 | £10 | *with Naomi Campbell* |
| I'm Sending This Message | 7" | Island | WI091 | 1963 | £5 | £10 | *Larry Lawrence B side* |
| In London | LP | Pama | ECO10 | 1969 | £15 | £30 | |
| In My Heart | 7" | Blue Beat | BB100 | 1962 | £6 | £12 | *..., Bell's Group B side* |
| It's Alright | 7" | Island | WI277 | 1966 | £5 | £10 | |
| Jezebel | 7" | Blue Beat | BB148 | 1963 | £6 | £12 | |
| Johnny Grove | 7" | Blue Beat | BB283 | 1965 | £6 | £12 | *Buster's AllstarsB side* |
| Joybells | 7" | Blue Beat | BB141 | 1962 | £6 | £12 | |
| Judge Dread In Court | 7" | Pyramid | PYR6019 | 1967 | £4 | £8 | |
| Katy Katy | 7" | Blue Beat | BB268 | 1964 | £6 | £12 | |
| Kill Me Dead | 7" | Pyramid | PYR6021 | 1967 | £4 | £8 | |
| King For Tonight | 7" | Pyramid | PYR6046 | 1968 | £4 | £8 | |
| Leave Earth | 7" | Blue Beat | BB35 | 1961 | £6 | £12 | |
| Leave Her Alone | 7" | Island | WI037 | 1962 | £5 | £10 | |
| Let Them Talk | 7" | Blue Beat | BB233 | 1964 | £6 | £12 | |
| Little Brown Girl | 7" | Blue Beat | BB152 | 1963 | £6 | £12 | *with Patsy Todd* |
| Look Before You Leap | 7" | Island | WI055 | 1962 | £5 | £10 | *with Patsy Todd* |
| Love And Leave Me | 7" | Blue Beat | BB135 | 1962 | £6 | £12 | *with Lloyd Clarke* |
| Love Not To Brag | 7" | Blue Beat | BB97 | 1962 | £6 | £12 | *Drumbago B side* |
| Lover Boy | 7" | Blue Beat | BB18 | 1960 | £6 | £12 | |
| Lover Boy | 7" | Blue Beat | BB207 | 1964 | £6 | £12 | *with Patsy Todd* |
| Me Naw Give Up | 7" | Pyramid | PYR6053 | 1968 | £4 | £8 | *Beverley's Allstars B side* |
| Meekly Wait | 7" | Blue Beat | BB94 | 1962 | £6 | £12 | *with Yvonne Harrison* |
| Millie Girl | 7" | Blue Beat | BB91 | 1962 | £6 | £12 | |
| Miss Lulu | 7" | Blue Beat | BB239 | 1964 | £6 | £12 | *with Patsy Todd* |
| Moon Hop | LP | Pama | PSP1006 | 1969 | £15 | £30 | |
| Moon Hop | 7" | Crab | CRAB21 | 1970 | £1.50 | £4 | |
| National Dance | 7" | Island | WI224 | 1965 | £5 | £10 | *with Patsy Todd, Desmond Dekker B side* |
| Never Give Up | 7" | Smash | SMA2339 | 1973 | £1.50 | £4 | |
| No Dice | 7" | Pyramid | PYR6024 | 1968 | £4 | £8 | |
| No Raise, No Praise | 7" | Island | WI053 | 1962 | £5 | £10 | |
| Now We Know | 7" | Blue Beat | BB31 | 1961 | £6 | £12 | |
| Oh My Love | 7" | Blue Beat | BB123 | 1962 | £6 | £12 | *with Patsy Todd* |
| Oh Shirley | 7" | Blue Beat | BB106 | 1962 | £6 | £12 | *with Patsy Todd* |
| Patricia My Dear | 7" | Blue Beat | BB177 | 1963 | £6 | £12 | |
| Please Don't Talk About Me (with Eric Morris) | 7" | Island | WI011 | 1962 | £5 | £10 | |
| River To The Bank | 7" | Crab | CRAB3 | 1968 | £2 | £5 | *Peter King B side* |
| Send Me Some Loving | 7" | Crab | CRAB23 | 1970 | £1.50 | £4 | |
| Seven Letters | LP | Trojan | TTL5 | 1969 | £8 | £20 | |
| Seven Letters | 7" | Crab | CRAB8 | 1969 | £1.50 | £4 | *Tartans B side* |
| Shake A Leg | 7" | Blue Beat | BB62 | 1961 | £6 | £12 | *with Drumbago* |
| Should Be Ashamed | 7" | Blue Beat | BB130 | 1962 | £6 | £12 | |
| Shower Of Rain | 7" | Big Shot | BI506 | 1968 | £2.50 | £6 | *Val Bennett B side* |
| Someone | 7" | Island | WI3079 | 1967 | £5 | £10 | |
| Starvation | 7" | Island | WI225 | 1965 | £5 | £10 | |
| Steal Away | 7" | Blue Beat | BB224 | 1964 | £6 | £12 | *with Patsy Todd* |
| Stir The Pot | 7" | Blue Beat | BB280 | 1965 | £6 | £12 | |
| Street Girl | 7" | Black Swan | WI402 | 1964 | £5 | £10 | |
| Sweeter Than Honey | 7" | Blue Beat | BB329 | 1965 | £6 | £12 | |
| Tears On My Pillow | 7" | Blue Beat | BB187 | 1963 | £6 | £12 | |
| Telephone | 7" | Blue Beat | BB196 | 1963 | £6 | £12 | |
| Throw Them Away | 7" | Blue Beat | BB311 | 1965 | £6 | £12 | |
| Times Are Going | 7" | Blue Beat | BB48 | 1961 | £6 | £12 | |
| Tougher Than Tough | 7" | Pyramid | PYR6010 | 1967 | £4 | £8 | *Roland Alphonso B side* |
| Travel On | 7" | Island | WI004 | 1962 | £5 | £10 | |
| Troubles | 7" | Blue Beat | BB247 | 1964 | £6 | £12 | *with Patsy Todd* |
| Try Me | 7" | Pyramid | PYR6045 | 1968 | £4 | £8 | |
| Trying To Make You Mine | 7" | Blue Beat | BB160 | 1963 | £6 | £12 | |
| Want More | 7" | Pyramid | PYR6040 | 1968 | £4 | £8 | *Roland Alphonso B side* |
| Weep No More | 7" | Blue Beat | BB276 | 1965 | £6 | £12 | |
| Woman A Grumble | 7" | Pyramid | PYR6039 | 1968 | £4 | £8 | |
| You I Love | 7" | Blue Beat | BB291 | 1965 | £6 | £12 | *with Patsy Todd* |
| You Never Miss Your Water | 7" | Pyramid | PYR6027 | 1968 | £4 | £8 | |

## MORGAN, FRANK

| Frank Morgan | LP | Vogue | LAE12012 | 1956 | £15 | £30 | |

## MORGAN, FREDDY

| Side Saddle | 7" | London | HL7077 | 1959 | £2 | £5 | *export* |

## MORGAN, GEORGE

| Morgan, By George | LP | Columbia | CL1044 | 1957 | £6 | £15 | *US* |

## MORGAN, JANE

| All The Way | LP | London | HAR2110 | 1958 | £6 | £15 | |
| All The Way Part 1 | 7" EP | London | RER1161 | 1958 | £5 | £10 | |
| All The Way Part 2 | 7" EP | London | RER1162 | 1958 | £5 | £10 | |
| Around The World | 7" | London | HLR8436 | 1957 | £4 | £8 | |
| At The Coconut Grove | LP | London | HAR2430/ | 1962 | £5 | £12 | |

|  |  |  | SAHR6226 ............ |  |  |  |  |
|---|---|---|---|---|---|---|---|
| Ballads Of Lady Jane | LP | London | HAR2316 | 1960 | £5 | £12 |  |
| Day The Rains Came | LP | London | HAR2158 | 1959 | £6 | £15 |  |
| Day The Rains Came | 7" EP | London | RER1204 | 1959 | £5 | £10 |  |
| Day The Rains Came | 7" | London | HL7064 | 1958 | £2.50 | £6 | *export* |
| Day The Rains Came | 7" | London | HLR8751 | 1958 | £1.50 | £4 |  |
| Enchanted Island | 7" | London | HLR8649 | 1958 | £2 | £5 |  |
| Fascination | LP | London | HAR2086 | 1957 | £6 | £15 |  |
| Fascination | 7" | London | HLR8468 | 1957 | £2.50 | £6 |  |
| From The First Hello | 7" | London | HLR8395 | 1957 | £7.50 | £15 |  |
| Great Songs From The Great Shows Vol. 1. | LP | London | HAR2136 | 1959 | £5 | £12 |  |
| Great Songs From The Great Shows Vol. 2. | LP | London | HAR2137 | 1959 | £5 | £12 |  |
| I'm New At The Game Of Romance | 7" | London | HLR8539 | 1958 | £2.50 | £6 |  |
| I've Got Bells On My Heart | 7" | London | HLR8611 | 1958 | £2.50 | £6 |  |
| If I Could Only Live My Life Again | 7" | London | HLR8810 | 1959 | £1.50 | £4 |  |
| In My Style | LP | Columbia | SX6010 | 1965 | £4 | £10 |  |
| Jane In Spain | LP | London | HAR2244 | 1960 | £5 | £12 |  |
| Jane Morgan | LP | Kapp | KL1023 | 195– | £6 | £15 | *US* |
| Jane Morgan | LP | Kapp | KL1098 | 1958 | £6 | £15 | *US* |
| Jane Morgan | 7" EP | London | RER1331 | 1961 | £6 | £12 |  |
| Jane Morgan Time | LP | London | HAR2371 | 1961 | £5 | £12 |  |
| Love Makes The World Go Around | LP | London | HAR/SHR.8069 | 1963 | £5 | £12 |  |
| Second Time Around | LP | London | HAR2377/ | 1961 | £5 | £12 |  |
|  |  |  | SAHR6177 ............ |  |  |  |  |
| Serenades The Victors | LP | Colpix | PXL460 | 1963 | £4 | £10 |  |
| Something Old, Something New | LP | London | HAR2133 | 1958 | £6 | £15 |  |
| What Now My Love | LP | London | HAR/SHR.8042 | 1962 | £5 | £12 |  |
| Why Oh Why | 7" | London | HL8148 | 1955 | £10 | £20 |  |

## MORGAN, JAYE P.

|  |  |  |  |  |  |  |  |
|---|---|---|---|---|---|---|---|
| Are You Lonesome Tonight? | 7" | MGM | MGM1005 | 1959 | £1.50 | £4 |  |
| Have You Ever Been Lonely | 7" | Brunswick | 05519 | 1956 | £2 | £5 |  |
| Jaye P Sings | 7" EP | London | REP1013 | 1954 | £5 | £10 |  |
| Longest Walk | 7" | HMV | 7M327 | 1955 | £1.50 | £4 |  |
| Not One Goodbye | 7" | HMV | 7M365 | 1956 | £1.50 | £4 |  |
| Pepper Hot Baby | 7" | HMV | 7M348 | 1955 | £6 | £12 |  |

## MORGAN, JOHN

Records credited in the name of pianist John Morgan are listed in this guide along with those by his group, Spirit of John Morgan.

## MORGAN, LEE

|  |  |  |  |  |  |  |  |
|---|---|---|---|---|---|---|---|
| Another Monday Night At Birdland | LP | Columbia | 33SX1181 | 1959 | £6 | £15 | *all star band* |
| Birdland Story Vol. 1 | LP | Columbia | 33SX1399 | 1961 | £6 | £15 |  |
| Capra Black | LP | Blue Note | BST84901 | 1973 | £5 | £12 |  |
| Caramba | LP | Blue Note | BST84289 | 1968 | £5 | £12 |  |
| Charisma | LP | Blue Note | BST84312 | 1969 | £5 | £12 |  |
| Cooker | LP | Blue Note | BLP/BST81578 | 196– | £10 | £25 |  |
| Cornbread | LP | Blue Note | BLP/BST84222 | 1965 | £8 | £20 |  |
| Delightfulee Morgan | LP | Blue Note | BLP/BST84243 | 1966 | £10 | £25 |  |
| Expoobident | LP | Stateside | SL10016 | 1962 | £6 | £15 |  |
| Gigolo | LP | Blue Note | BLP/BST84212 | 1965 | £8 | £20 |  |
| Introducing Lee Morgan | LP | London | LTZC15101 | 1958 | £20 | £40 |  |
| Lee Morgan | LP | Blue Note | BST84381 | 1970 | £5 | £12 |  |
| Leeway | LP | Blue Note | BLP/BST84034 | 1965 | £15 | £30 |  |
| Live At The Lighthouse | LP | Blue Note | BST89906 | 1970 | £5 | £12 |  |
| Monday Night At Birdland | LP | Columbia | 33SX1160 | 1959 | £6 | £15 | *all star band* |
| Rumproller | LP | Blue Note | BLP/BST84199 | 1966 | £10 | £25 |  |
| Search For The New Land | LP | Blue Note | BLP/BST84169 | 1966 | £10 | £25 |  |
| Sidewinder | LP | Blue Note | BLP/BST84157 | 1965 | £10 | £25 |  |
| Sixth Sense | LP | Blue Note | BST84335 | 1969 | £5 | £12 |  |

## MORGAN, MACE THUNDERBIRDS

|  |  |  |  |  |  |  |
|---|---|---|---|---|---|---|
| Shake And Swing | 7" EP | Starlite | STEP36 | 1963 | £7.50 | £15 |

## MORGAN, PC ALEXANDER

|  |  |  |  |  |  |  |
|---|---|---|---|---|---|---|
| Sussex By The Sea | 7" | Columbia | DB8095 | 1966 | £2.50 | £6 |

## MORGAN, RUSS

|  |  |  |  |  |  |  |
|---|---|---|---|---|---|---|
| Moonlight Music | 7" EP | Brunswick | OE9068 | 1955 | £2 | £5 |

## MORGAN & MARK SEVEN

|  |  |  |  |  |  |  |
|---|---|---|---|---|---|---|
| I'm Gonna Turn My Life Around | 7" | Polydor | BM56083 | 1966 | £1.50 | £4 |

## MORGAN BROTHERS

|  |  |  |  |  |  |  |
|---|---|---|---|---|---|---|
| Kissin' On The Red Light | 7" | MGM | MGM1026 | 1959 | £1.50 | £4 |
| Nola | 7" | MGM | MGM1007 | 1959 | £2 | £5 |

## MORGAN TWINS

|  |  |  |  |  |  |  |
|---|---|---|---|---|---|---|
| Let's Get Going | 7" | RCA | RCA1083 | 1958 | £30 | £60 |

## MORGEN, STEVE

|  |  |  |  |  |  |  |  |
|---|---|---|---|---|---|---|---|
| Morgen | LP | Probe | CPLP4507 | 1969 | £37.50 | £75 | *US* |

## MORIN & WILSON

|  |  |  |  |  |  |  |
|---|---|---|---|---|---|---|
| Peaceful Company | LP | Sovereign | SVNA7252 | 1972 | £8 | £20 |

608

## MORISETTE, JOHNNY
Meet Me At The Twisting Place ................ 7" ...... Stateside .......... SS107 .................... 1962 £1.50 ..... £4 ...............................

## MORISSETTE, ALANIS
Alanis ..................................................... CD .... MCA ............. MCAD10253 ......... 1991 £20 ........ £40 ................ Canadian
Alanis ..................................................... CD .... MCA ............. MCBBD10253 ..... 1991 £15 ........ £30 ................ Canadian
Fate Stay With Me ................................. 7" ...... Lamor ............ ....................... 1985 £50 ..... £100 ........ Canadian, best
auctioned
Now Is The Time ................................... CD .... MCA ............. MCAD10731 ......... 1992 £20 ........ £40 ................ Canadian

## MORLY GREY
Only Truth ............................................. LP ..... Starshine ........ ....................... 1969 £20 ........ £40 ........................... US

## MORMOS
Ça doit être bien .................................... LP ..... CBS ............ 64558 .................. 1973 £15 ........ £30 ........................... French
Great Wall Of China .............................. LP ..... CBS ............ 64430 .................. 1971 £37.50 ... £75 ........................... German
Magic Spell Of Mother's Wrath ............. LP ..... CBS ............ 64979 .................. 1972 £50 ........ £100 ........................... French

## MORNING
Morning .................................................. LP ..... Liberty ........... LBS83463 ......... 1970 £4 .......... £10 ...............................

## MORNING DEW
Morning Dew .......................................... LP ..... Roulette ........ R(S)41045 ......... 1967 £37.50 ... £75 ........................... US

## MORNING GLORY
Morning Glory ........................................ LP ..... Island .......... ILPS9237 ............. 1973 £5 .......... £12 ...............................

## MORPHEUS
Rabenteuer ............................................. LP ..... private ......... 34705 .................. 1976 £15 ........ £30 ........................... German

## MORRIS, DERRICK
What's Your Grouse ............................... 7" ...... Pyramid .......... PYR6061 ............. 1969 £1.50 ..... £4 ..... Beverley's Allstars

## MORRIS, ERIC
By The Sea ............................................. 7" ...... Rio ............... R72 ...................... 1965 £5 .......... £10 ...............................
Children Of Today ................................. 7" ...... Island ............ WI234 ................. 1965 £5 .......... £10 ... Baba Brooks B side
Country Girl .......................................... 7" ...... Blue Beat ...... BB184 ................. 1963 £6 .......... £12 ...............................
Fast Mouth ........................................... 7" ...... Island ............ WI199 ................. 1965 £5 .......... £10 ...............................
G.I. Lady .............................................. 7" ...... Blue Beat ...... BB115 ................. 1962 £6 .......... £12 ...............................
Home Sweet Home ................................. 7" ...... Black Swan .... WI445 ................. 1965 £5 .......... £10 . Lester Sterling B side
Humpty Dumpty ..................................... 7" ...... Blue Beat ...... BB53 ................... 1961 £6 .......... £12 ...............................
If I Didn't Love You ............................ 7" ...... Doctor Bird .... DB1056 ............... 1966 £5 .......... £10 ........... Tommy McCook
B side
Little District ......................................... 7" ...... Rio ............... R39 ...................... 1964 £5 .......... £10 ...............................
Live As A Man ...................................... 7" ...... Rio ............... R48 ...................... 1964 £5 .......... £10 ...............................
Lonely Blue Boy .................................... 7" ...... Blue Beat ...... BB153 ................. 1963 £6 .......... £12 ... Prince Buster B side
Love Can Break A Man .......................... 7" ...... Blue Beat ...... BB218 ................. 1964 £6 .......... £12 ...............................
Love Can Make A Mansion .................... 7" ...... Island ............ WI183 ................. 1965 £5 .......... £10 ...............................
Mama No Fret ....................................... 7" ...... Island ............ WI147 ................. 1964 £5 .......... £10 ...... Frankie Anderson
B side
Miss Peggy's Grandmother .................... 7" ...... Blue Beat ...... BB137 ................. 1962 £6 .......... £12 ...... Buster's Allstars
B side
Money Can't Buy Life ............................ 7" ...... Blue Beat ...... BB83 ................... 1962 £6 .......... £12 ... Alton Ellis B side
My Forty-Five ........................................ 7" ...... Blue Beat ...... BB74 ................... 1962 £6 .......... £12 ...............................
Oh My Dear .......................................... 7" ...... Port-O-Jam .... PJ4006 ............... 1964 £5 .......... £10 ...............................
Over The Hills ....................................... 7" ...... Blue Beat ...... BB128 ................. 1962 £6 .......... £12 ...............................
Pack Up Your Troubles .......................... 7" ...... Blue Beat ...... BB105 ................. 1962 £6 .......... £12 ...............................
Penny Reel ............................................ 7" ...... Island ............ WI142 ................. 1964 £5 .......... £10 ....... Dotty & Bonnie
B side
River Come Down ................................... 7" ...... Black Swan .... WI439 ................. 1964 £5 .......... £10 ...............................
Search The World .................................. 7" ...... Starlite .......... ST45052 ............. 1961 £5 .......... £10 Buster's Group B side
Seven Long Years ................................... 7" ...... Blue Beat ...... BB140 ................. 1962 £6 .......... £12 ...............................
Sinners Repent And Pray ....................... 7" ...... Blue Beat ...... BB81 ................... 1962 £6 .......... £12 ... Alton Ellis B side
So You Shot Reds ................................... 7" ...... Blue Beat ...... BB193 ................. 1963 £6 .......... £12 ...............................
Solomon Grundie .................................... 7" ...... Black Swan .... WI414 ................. 1964 £5 .......... £10 .. Baba Brooks B side
Stitch In Time ....................................... 7" ...... Blue Beat ...... BB273 ................. 1964 £6 .......... £12 ...............................
Suddenly ................................................ 7" ...... Island ............ WI185 ................. 1965 £5 .......... £10 ...............................
Supper In The Gutter ............................ 7" ...... Black Swan .... WI433 ................. 1964 £5 .......... £10 ...............................
What A Man Doeth ................................ 7" ...... Island ............ WI151 ................. 1964 £5 .......... £10 ..... Duke Reid B side

## MORRIS, HEMSLEY
Love Is Strange ...................................... 7" ...... Caltone ........... TONE104 ........... 1967 £2.50 ..... £6 ... Don Drummond Jr.
B side

## MORRIS, JOE
Just Your Way Baby ............................... 78 ...... London ........... HL8088 ............... 1954 £15 ........ £30 ...............................
Travelin' Man ........................................ 78 ...... London ........... HL8098 ............... 1954 £3 .......... £8 ...............................

## MORRIS, LIBBY
When Liberace Winked At Me ................ 7" ...... Parlophone ...... R4225 ................. 1956 £1.50 ..... £4 ...............................

## MORRIS, MILTON
No Bread And Butter .............................. 7" ...... Upsetter .......... US318 ................. 1969 £1.50 ..... £4 ....... Upsetters B side

## MORRIS, MONTY
Can't Get No Peace ............................... 7" ...... Camel ............ CA12 ................... 1969 £1.50 ..... £4 ........ Upsetters B side
Deportation ........................................... 7" ...... Big Shot ......... BI513 .................. 1969 £1.50 ..... £4 ...............................

| | | | | | | | |
|---|---|---|---|---|---|---|---|
| Last Laugh | 7" | Doctor Bird | DB1162 | 1968 | £5 | £10 | |
| Same Face | 7" | Doctor Bird | DB1176 | 1969 | £5 | £10 | |
| Say What You're Saying | 7" | Pama | PM721 | 1968 | £1.50 | £4 | |

## MORRIS, ROGER

| | | | | | | | |
|---|---|---|---|---|---|---|---|
| First Album | LP | Regal Zonophone | SRZA8509 | 1972 | £8 | £20 | |

## MORRIS, RUSSELL

| | | | | | | | |
|---|---|---|---|---|---|---|---|
| Real Thing | 7" | Decca | F22964 | 1969 | £12.50 | £25 | |

## MORRIS, VICTOR

| | | | | | | | |
|---|---|---|---|---|---|---|---|
| Now I'm Alone | 7" | Amalgamated | AMG813 | 1968 | £2 | £5 | |

## MORRIS & MITCH

| | | | | | | | |
|---|---|---|---|---|---|---|---|
| Cumberland Gap | 7" | Decca | F10900 | 1957 | £2 | £5 | |
| Highway Patrol | 7" | Decca | F11086 | 1958 | £2 | £5 | |
| Six Five Nothing Special | 7" EP | Decca | DFE6486 | 1958 | £5 | £10 | |
| What Is A Skiffler? | 7" | Decca | F10929 | 1957 | £2 | £5 | |

## MORRIS & THE MINORS

| | | | | | | | |
|---|---|---|---|---|---|---|---|
| State The Obvious | 7" | Round | MOR1 | 1980 | £2 | £5 | |

## MORRISEY, PAT

| | | | | | | | |
|---|---|---|---|---|---|---|---|
| I'm Pat Morrisey, I Sing | LP | Mercury | MG20197 | 1956 | £8 | £20 | US |

## MORRISON, CURLEY JIM

| | | | | | | | |
|---|---|---|---|---|---|---|---|
| Air Force Blues | 7" | Starlite | ST45065 | 1961 | £37.50 | £75 | |

## MORRISON, JAMES

| | | | | | | | |
|---|---|---|---|---|---|---|---|
| Pure Genius Of James Morrison | LP | Shanachie | 33004 | 1978 | £4 | £10 | US |

## MORRISON, JAMES & TOM ENNIS

| | | | | | | | |
|---|---|---|---|---|---|---|---|
| James Morrison And Tom Ennis | LP | Topic | 12T390 | 1980 | £4 | £10 | |

## MORRISON, TOM

| | | | | | | | |
|---|---|---|---|---|---|---|---|
| Adventures Of Mighty Mouse & His Pals | 7" EP | MGM | MGMEP709 | 1960 | £2 | £5 | |

## MORRISON, VAN

| | | | | | | | |
|---|---|---|---|---|---|---|---|
| Astral Weeks | LP | Warner Bros | WS1768 | 1968 | £4 | £10 | |
| Avalon Sunset | CD | Polydor | AST1 | 1989 | £25 | £50 | promo box set, with cassette, biog, photo, slides, pen |
| Blowin' Your Mind | LP | London | HAZ8346 | 1967 | £8 | £20 | |
| Brown Eyed Girl | 7" | London | HLZ10150 | 1967 | £5 | £10 | |
| Caldonia | 7" | Warner Bros | K16392 | 1974 | £1.50 | £4 | |
| Coney Island | CD-s | Polydor | VANCD4 | 1990 | £2 | £5 | |
| Enlightenment | CD-s | Polydor | VANCD8 | 1991 | £2 | £5 | |
| Excerpts From Van | CD | Polydor | VANCD001 | 1990 | £8 | £20 | promo |
| Gloria | CD-s | Polydor | VANCD5 | 1990 | £2 | £5 | |
| Have I Told You Lately | CD-s | Polydor | VANCD1 | 1989 | £2 | £5 | |
| His Band And Street Choir | LP | Warner Bros | WS1884 | 1970 | £4 | £10 | |
| I Can't Stop Loving You | CD-s | Polydor | VANCD9 | 1991 | £2 | £5 | with the Chieftains |
| I'll Tell Me Ma | CD-s | Mercury | MERCD262 | 1988 | £2 | £5 | with the Chieftains |
| In The Days Before Rock 'n' Roll | CD-s | Polydor | VANCD7 | 1990 | £2 | £5 | |
| Live At The Roxy | LP | Warner Bros | WBMS102 | 1978 | £15 | £30 | US promo |
| Moondance | LP | Nautilus | SD110 | 1981 | £5 | £12 | US audiophile |
| Moondance | LP | Warner Bros | WS1835 | 1970 | £4 | £10 | |
| Moondance | CD | Warner Bros | C88110 | 1988 | £6 | £15 | box set |
| Orangefield | CD-s | Polydor | VANCD3 | 1989 | £2 | £5 | |
| Real Real Gone | CD-s | Polydor | VANCD6 | 1990 | £2 | £5 | |
| Sense Of Wonder | LP | Mercury | MERH54 | 1985 | £15 | £30 | test pressing with 'Crazy Jane On God' |
| Tupelo Honey | LP | Warner Bros | WS1950 | 1971 | £4 | £10 | |
| Whenever God Shines His Light | CD-s | Polydor | VANCD2 | 1989 | £2 | £5 | with Cliff Richard |
| Why Must I Always Explain? | CD-s | Polydor | VANCD10 | 1991 | £2 | £5 | |

## MORRISSEY

| | | | | | | | |
|---|---|---|---|---|---|---|---|
| Certain People I Know | CD-s | HMV | CDPOP1631 | 1992 | £2 | £5 | |
| Education In Reverse | LP | HMV | | 1988 | £6 | £15 | Australian |
| Every Day Is Like Sunday | CD-s | HMV | CDPOP1619 | 1988 | £3 | £8 | |
| Interesting Drug | CD-s | HMV | CDPOP1621 | 1989 | £3 | £8 | |
| Jack The Ripper (live) | CD-s | HMV | POPDJ1632 | 1993 | £3 | £8 | promo only |
| Last Of The Famous International Playboys | CD-s | HMV | CDPOP1620 | 1989 | £5 | £12 | |
| My Love Life | CD-s | HMV | CDPOP1628 | 1991 | £2 | £5 | |
| November Spawned A Monster | CD-s | HMV | CDPOP1623 | 1990 | £4 | £10 | |
| Now My Heart Is Full | CD | Sire | PROCD6778 | 1994 | £10 | £25 | US promo compilation |
| Ouija Board, Ouija Board | CD-s | HMV | CDPOP1622 | 1989 | £6 | £15 | |
| Our Frank | CD-s | HMV | CDPOP1625 | 1991 | £2 | £5 | |
| Piccadilly Palare | CD-s | HMV | CDPOP1624 | 1990 | £2.50 | £6 | |
| Pregnant For The Last Time | CD-s | HMV | CDPOP1627 | 1991 | £2 | £5 | |
| Sing Your Life | CD-s | HMV | CDPOP1626 | 1991 | £5 | £12 | |
| Suedehead | CD-s | HMV | CDPOP1618 | 1988 | £3 | £8 | |
| Viva Hate! | CD | HMV | CDCSD3787 | 1988 | £15 | £30 | promo boxed set |
| You're The One For Me, Fatty | CD-s | HMV | CDPOP1630 | 1992 | £2 | £5 | |

## MORROW, BUDDY

| | | | | | | | |
|---|---|---|---|---|---|---|---|
| Buddy Morrow And His Orchestra | 7" EP | HMV | 7EG8076 | 1955 | £2 | £5 | |

| Dragnet | 7" | HMV | 7M162 | 1953 | £1.50 | £4 | |
| Impact | 7" EP | RCA | RCX174 | 1959 | £2 | £5 | |
| Knock On Wood | 7" | HMV | 7M216 | 1954 | £1.50 | £4 | |
| Staccato's Theme | 7" | RCA | RCA1167 | 1960 | £1.50 | £4 | |

## MORSE, ELLA MAE

| Barrelhouse Boogie And The Blues | LP | Capitol | T513 | 1956 | £15 | £30 | US |
| Barrelhouse Boogie And The Blues | 7" EP | Capitol | EAP1513 | 1955 | £15 | £30 | |
| Barrelhouse Boogie And The Blues | 10" LP | Capitol | LC6687 | 1954 | £25 | £50 | |
| Birmingham | 7" | Capitol | CL14376 | 1955 | £10 | £20 | |
| Bring Back My Baby To Me | 7" | Capitol | CL14223 | 1955 | £15 | £30 | |
| Down In Mexico | 7" | Capitol | CL14572 | 1956 | £10 | £20 | |
| Heart Full Of Hope | 7" | Capitol | CL14332 | 1955 | £10 | £20 | |
| Hits Of Ella Mae Morse & Freddie Slack | LP | Capitol | T1802 | 1962 | £8 | £20 | US |
| I'm Gone | 7" | Capitol | CL14760 | 1957 | £4 | £8 | |
| Morse Code | LP | Capitol | T898 | 1957 | £10 | £25 | US |
| Razzle Dazzle | 7" | Capitol | CL14341 | 1955 | £25 | £50 | |
| Seventeen | 7" | Capitol | CL14362 | 1955 | £15 | £30 | |
| Smack Dab In The Middle | 7" | Capitol | CL14303 | 1955 | £10 | £20 | |
| What Good'll It Do Me | 7" | Capitol | CL14726 | 1957 | £4 | £8 | |
| When Boy Kiss Girl | 7" | Capitol | CL14508 | 1956 | £5 | £10 | |

## MORTIFEE, ANN

| Baptism | LP | EMI | EMC3094 | 1975 | £10 | £25 | |

## MORTIMER, AZIE

| Lips | 7" | London | HLX9237 | 1960 | £2.50 | £6 | |

## MORTON, JELLY ROLL

| Burnin' The Iceberg | 7" | HMV | 7M256 | 1954 | £2 | £5 | |
| Classic Jazz Piano Vol. 1 | 10" LP | London | AL3534 | 1954 | £10 | £25 | |
| Classic Jazz Piano Vol. 2 | 10" LP | London | AL3559 | 1956 | £10 | £25 | |
| Classic Piano Solos | LP | Riverside | RLP12111 | 1962 | £6 | £15 | |
| Fat Frances | 7" | HMV | 7M178 | 1954 | £2 | £5 | |
| Jazz Originators Vol. 3 | 7" EP | Collector | JE120 | 1959 | £2 | £5 | |
| Jelly Roll Morton | LP | Fontana | TL5261 | 1965 | £4 | £10 | |
| Jelly Roll Morton | 7" EP | RCA | RCX168 | 1955 | £2 | £5 | |
| Jelly Roll Morton | 7" EP | Storyville | SEP379 | 1961 | £2 | £5 | |
| Jelly Roll Morton | 7" EP | Vogue | EPV1126 | 1956 | £2 | £5 | |
| Jelly Roll Morton & His Red Hot Peppers | 10" LP | HMV | DLP1016 | 1953 | £10 | £25 | |
| Jelly Roll Morton No. 2 | 7" EP | RCA | RCX207 | 1960 | £2 | £5 | |
| Jungle Blues | 7" | HMV | 7M207 | 1954 | £2 | £5 | |
| King Of New Orleans Jazz | LP | RCA | RD27113 | 1959 | £8 | £20 | |
| King Of New Orleans Jazz Vol. 2 | LP | RCA | RD27184 | 1961 | £8 | £20 | |
| Kings Of Jazz | 10" LP | London | AL3520 | 1954 | £10 | £25 | |
| Morton Sixes And Sevens | LP | Fontana | TL5415 | 1967 | £4 | £10 | |
| Morton's Red Hot Peppers | 10" LP | HMV | DLP1044 | 1954 | £10 | £25 | |
| Morton's Red Hot Peppers No. 3 | 10" LP | HMV | DLP1071 | 1955 | £10 | £25 | |
| Mr. Jelly Lord | LP | Riverside | RLP12132 | 1961 | £6 | £15 | |
| New Orleans Memories | 10" LP | Vogue | LDE080 | 1954 | £10 | £25 | |
| Smoke House Blues | 7" | HMV | 7M187 | 1954 | £2 | £5 | |
| Solos | 10" LP | London | AL3519 | 1954 | £10 | £25 | |
| Tank Town Bump | 7" | HMV | 7M132 | 1953 | £2 | £5 | |
| Treasures Of North American Negro Music Vol. 4 | 7" EP | Fontana | TFE17263 | 1960 | £2 | £5 | |

## MORTON, MANDY

| Magic Lady | LP | Banshee | BAN1011 | 1978 | £180 | £300 | blue vinyl |
| Magic Lady | LP | Banshee | BAN1011 | 1978 | £100 | £200 | with Spriguns |
| Sea Of Storms | LP | Polydor | 2382101 | 1980 | £6 | £15 | German |
| Song For Me (Music Prince) | 7" | Banshee | BANS791 | 1979 | £5 | £10 | with Spriguns |
| Valley Of Light | LP | Banshee | | 1983 | £15 | £30 | |

## MORTON, ROBIN & CATHAL MCCONNEL

| Irish Jubilee | LP | Mercier | IRL10 | 1970 | £10 | £25 | Irish |

## MOSAICS

| Let's Go Drag Racing | 7" | Columbia | DB7990 | 1966 | £4 | £8 | |

## MOSCA, SAL

| At The Den | LP | Wave | LP2 | 1970 | £6 | £15 | with Peter Ind |
| At The Piano | LP | Wave | LP8 | 1970 | £6 | £15 | |

## MOSELEY, REVEREND

| Treasures Of North American Negro Music Vol. 6 | 7" EP | Fontana | TFE17265 | 1960 | £2 | £5 | |

## MOSES

| Changes | LP | Spectator | 2037 | 1971 | £50 | £100 | Danish |

## MOSES & JOSHUA

| Get Out Of My Heart | 7" | Bell | BLL1018 | 1968 | £1.50 | £4 | |

## MOSKOW

| Man From UNCLE | 7" | Moskow | SRS2103 | 1982 | £2 | £5 | |

## MOSS, BUDDY

| Georgia Blues Vol. 2 | LP | Kokomo | K1003 | 196– | £20 | £40 | |

## MOSS, GENE & THE MONSTERS
Dracula's Greatest Hits.............................. LP ..... RCA ............. LSP2977.................. 1964 £10........ £25 ....................... US

## MOSS, JENNY
Hobbies...................................................... 7" ..... Columbia ....... DB7061 ................. 1963 £15........ £30 ..............................

## MOST, ABE OCTET
Presenting The Abe Most Octet................. 7" EP . London .......... REP1028 .............. 1955 £2.50........ £6 ..............................

## MOST, MICKIE
Big Beat Ball............................................... LP ..... Rave ............. RMG1157............... 1963 £50..... £100 ............ South African
Feminine Look............................................ 7" ..... Columbia ....... DB7117 ................ 1963 £2.50........ £6 ..............................
Hear The Most ........................................... LP ..... Rave ............. RMG1139............... 1962 £50..... £100 ............ South African
Mickie Most ............................................... LP ..... Rave ............. RMG1151............... 1962 £50..... £100 ............ South African
Money Honey .............................................. 7" ..... Columbia ....... DB7245 ................ 1964 £4............ £8 ..............................
Sea Cruise................................................... 7" ..... Columbia ....... DB7180 ................ 1963 £2.50........ £6 ..............................
That's Alright.............................................. 7" EP . Columbia ....... ESRF1588.............. 1964 £12.50.... £25 .................... French
Yes Indeed I Do......................................... 7" ..... Decca ............ F11664.................. 1963 £5........... £10 ..............................

## MOST, SAM
Plays Bird, Bud, Monk And Miles............ LP ..... Parlophone ..... PMC1087 ............... 1959 £8........... £20 ..............................
Sam Most .................................................... LP ..... London ........... LTZN15063............ 1957 £8........... £20 ..............................
Sam Most Sextet.......................................... 10" LP Vanguard ....... PPT12009 ............. 1956 £8........... £20 ..............................

## MOST BROTHERS
Dottie......................................................... 7" ..... Decca ............ F11040.................. 1958 £1.50........ £4 ..............................
Teen Angel.................................................. 7" ..... Decca ............ F10998.................. 1958 £2.50........ £6 ..............................
Whistle Bait ............................................... 7" ..... Decca ............ F10968.................. 1957 £2.50........ £6 ..............................

## MOTEN, BENNY
Plays Kay-Cee Jazz ..................................... 10" LP HMV.............. DLP1057 ............... 1954 £8........... £20 ..............................

## MOTHER EARTH
I Did My Part............................................. 7" ..... Mercury......... MF1081 ................. 1969 £2............ £5 ..............................
Living With The Animals........................... LP ..... Mercury......... SMCL20143 ............ 1968 £5........... £12 ..............................
Make A Joyful Noise .................................. LP ..... Mercury......... SMCL20173 ............ 1969 £5........... £12 ..............................
Satisfied ..................................................... LP ..... Mercury......... 6338023 ................. 1970 £5........... £12 ..............................
Tracy Nelson Country................................. LP ..... Mercury......... SMCL20179 ............ 1969 £5........... £12 ..............................

## MOTHER MALLARD'S PORTABLE MASTERPIECE COMPANY
Like A Duck To Water............................... LP ..... Earthquack ...... 0002 ...................... 1973 £8........... £20 ....................... US
Mother Mallard's Portable Masterpiece ..... LP ..... Earthquack ...... 0001 ...................... 1973 £8........... £20 ....................... US
Company ..............

## MOTHER TUCKER'S YELLOW DUCK
Home Grown Stuff........................................ LP ..... Capitol............ ............................... 1969 £20......... £40 ................... Canadian
Starting A New Day ................................... LP ..... Capitol............ ............................... 197– £20......... £40 ................... Canadian

## MOTHERHOOD
I Feel So Free............................................. LP ..... United Artists .. UAS69173.............. 1969 £6........... £15 ................. German

## MOTHERLIGHT
Bobak, Jons, Malone.................................. LP ..... Morgan Blue .... BT5003................. 1969 £50......... £100 ..............................
............................................................... ..... Town .............

## MOTHER'S LOVE
Take One .................................................... LP ..... Havoc.............. IHLP3A ................ 1967 £37.50.... £75 .................... Dutch

## MOTHER'S RUIN
Say It's Not True....................................... 7" ..... Spectra ............ SPC7 ..................... 1982 £2............ £5 ..............................
Street Lights............................................... 7" ..... Spectra ............ SPC6 ..................... 1982 £2............ £5 ..............................

## MOTHMEN
Show Me Your House And Car ................ 7" ..... Do It .............. DUN12 .................. 1981 £2............ £5 ..............................
Show Me Your House And Car ................ 12" ..... Do It .............. DUNIT12................ 1981 £2.50........ £6 ..............................

## MOTHS
Moths ........................................................ LP ..... Deroy ............. no number ............ 1969 £250..... £400 ..............................

## MOTIAN, PAUL
Conception Vessel...................................... LP ..... ECM .............. ECM1028ST .......... 1974 £4........... £10 ..............................
Tribute........................................................ LP ..... ECM .............. ECM1048ST .......... 1975 £4........... £10 ..............................

## MOTIONS
Electric Baby.............................................. LP ..... Philips............ PHS600317 ............ 1970 £8........... £20 ....................... US
Every Step I Take...................................... 7" EP . Vogue............. INT18097 .............. 1966 £5........... £10 .................... French
I've Waited So Long................................... 7" EP . Vogue............. INT18017 .............. 1965 £5........... £10 .................... French
Impressions Of Wonderful......................... LP ..... Negram.......... CD1103 ................. 1968 £8........... £20 ....................... US
Introducing................................................. LP ..... Negram.......... NJH2 ..................... 1965 £20......... £40 .................... Dutch
Live ............................................................ LP ..... Marble Arch ... MALH201.............. 1968 £6........... £15 ....................... US
Song Book.................................................. LP ..... Teenbeat ......... APLP101................. 1967 £8........... £20 .................... Dutch
Their Own Way ......................................... LP ..... Negram.......... IHLP2.................... 1968 £8........... £20 .................... Dutch
Wasted Words............................................. 7" EP . Vogue............. INT18069 .............. 1966 £5........... £10 .................... French

## MOTIVATION
Come On Down........................................... 7" ..... Direction ........ 583248.................... 1968 £1.50........ £4 ..............................

## MOTLEY CRUE

| Title | Format | Label | Catalog | Year | | | Notes |
|---|---|---|---|---|---|---|---|
| Dr. Feelgood | 7" | Elektra | EKR97P | 1989 | £2.50 | £6 | shaped picture disc |
| Girls Girls Girls | 7" | Elektra | EKR59 | 1987 | £2 | £5 | X-rated picture sleeve |
| Girls Girls Girls | 7" | Elektra | EKR59P | 1987 | £2 | £5 | poster sleeve |
| Girls Girls Girls | 12" | Elektra | EKR59TB | 1987 | £3 | £8 | with patch, boxed |
| Girls Girls Girls | 12" | Elektra | EKR59TP | 1987 | £3 | £8 | picture disc |
| Helter Skelter | 12" | Elektra | | 198– | £10 | £20 | US promo picture disc, poster |
| Looks That Kill | 7" | Elektra | E9756 | 1984 | £2.50 | £6 | |
| Looks That Kill | 12" | Elektra | E9756T | 1984 | £3 | £8 | with transfer |
| Looks That Kill | 12" | Elektra | E9756TP | 1984 | £6 | £15 | picture disc |
| Primal Scream | CD-s | Elektra | EKR133CD | 1991 | £2 | £5 | |
| Shout At The Devil | LP | Elektra | 9602891 | 1983 | £6 | £15 | picture disc, poster |
| Smokin' In The Boys' Room | 7" | Elektra | EKR16TP | 1986 | £7.50 | £15 | mask shaped picture disc |
| Smokin' In The Boys' Room | 7" | Elektra | EKR33PA/PB | 1986 | £7.50 | £15 | 2 interlocking shaped picture discs |
| Smokin' In The Boys' Room | 12" | Elektra | EKR33T | 1986 | £3 | £8 | with patch & poster |
| Too Fast For Love | LP | Leathur | LR123 | 1981 | £30 | £60 | US |
| Too Young To Fall In Love | 7" | Elektra | E9732 | 1984 | £2.50 | £6 | |
| Too Young To Fall In Love | 12" | Elektra | E9732T | 1984 | £3 | £8 | with poster |
| You're All I Need | 12" | Elektra | EKR65TB | 1988 | £2.50 | £6 | with patch & poster, boxed |
| You're All I Need | 12" | Elektra | EKR65TP | 1988 | £2.50 | £6 | picture disc |

## MOTORHEAD

When Lemmy left Hawkwind, he covered over the psychedelic designs on his equipment with black paint and thereby defined the image for his new group. Motorhead managed to become popular among fans of punk at a time when heavy metal was distinctly out of fashion. Of course, the group's approach to heavy metal was a bit different – short pieces played very fast, the emphasis being on energy rather than on displays of virtuosity – and they very much anticipated the thrash metal style of the late eighties. The first edition of the *Price Guide* gave the information that only ten copies of the 'Motorhead' single on white vinyl exist – information that has since been repeated elsewhere. In fact, it turns out that the single was not at all limited – and the author was inundated with phone calls from collectors telling him so!

| Title | Format | Label | Catalog | Year | | | Notes |
|---|---|---|---|---|---|---|---|
| 1916 | CD | Epic | 4674819 | 1991 | £5 | £12 | picture disc |
| Ace Of Spades | LP | Bronze | BRON531 | 1980 | £4 | £10 | gold vinyl |
| Ace Of Spades | 7" | GWR | GWR15 | 1988 | £5 | £10 | |
| Ace Of Spades | 12" | Bronze | BROX106 | 1980 | £2.50 | £6 | |
| Beerdrinkers And Hellraisers | 12" | Big Beat | SWT61 | 1980 | £2.50 | £6 | orange vinyl |
| Bomber | LP | Bronze | BRON523 | 1979 | £4 | £10 | blue vinyl |
| Bomber | 7" | Bronze | BRO85 | 1979 | £2 | £5 | blue vinyl |
| Iron Fist | 7" | Bronze | BRO146 | 1982 | £2 | £5 | blue vinyl |
| Killed By Death | 7" | Bronze | BROP185 | 1984 | £5 | £10 | shaped picture disc |
| Motorhead | LP | Chiswick | WIK2 | 1977 | £10 | £25 | silver sleeve |
| Motorhead | CD-s | Castle Communications | CD310 | 1988 | £2 | £5 | |
| Motorhead | 7" | Big Beat | NSP13 | 1980 | £2 | £5 | picture disc (2 versions) |
| Motorhead | 12" | Chiswick | S13 | 1977 | £2.50 | £6 | |
| Motorhead (Live) | 7" | Bronze | BROP124 | 1981 | £2.50 | £6 | picture disc |
| No Remorse | LP | Bronze | PROLP5 | 1984 | £5 | £12 | double, 'leather' sleeve |
| No Remorse | CD | Castle Communications | CLACD121 | 1986 | £5 | £12 | leather sleeve |
| No Sleep Till Hammersmith | LP | Bronze | BRON535 | 1981 | £4 | £10 | gold vinyl |
| One To Sing The Blues | CD-s | Epic | 6565782 | 1990 | £2 | £5 | |
| Orgasmatron | CD | GWR | GWCD1 | 1986 | £25 | £50 | mispressing – plays Beatles Please Please Me |
| Overkill | LP | Bronze | BRON515 | 1979 | £4 | £10 | green vinyl |
| Overkill | 7" | Bronze | BRO67 | 1979 | £1.50 | £4 | with badge |
| Overkill | 12" | Bronze | 12BRO67 | 1979 | £2.50 | £6 | |
| White Line Fever | 7" | Stiff | BUY9 | 1977 | £5 | £10 | picture sleeve |

## MOTORHEAD & GIRLSCHOOL

| Title | Format | Label | Catalog | Year | | | Notes |
|---|---|---|---|---|---|---|---|
| St. Valentine's Massacre EP | 10" | Bronze | BROX116 | 1981 | £2.50 | £6 | |

## MOTOWNS

| Title | Format | Label | Catalog | Year | | | Notes |
|---|---|---|---|---|---|---|---|
| Si, Proprio I Motowns! | LP | RCA | S14 | 1967 | £25 | £50 | Italian |

## MOTT THE HOOPLE

| Title | Format | Label | Catalog | Year | | | Notes |
|---|---|---|---|---|---|---|---|
| All The Young Dudes | CD-s | CBS | 6581772 | 1992 | £2 | £5 | |
| Brain Capers | LP | Island | ILPS9178 | 1971 | £4 | £10 | |
| Downtown | 7" | Island | WIP6112 | 1971 | £2 | £5 | |
| Mad Shadows | LP | Island | ILPS9119 | 1970 | £4 | £10 | pink label |
| Midnight Lady | 7" | Island | WIP6105 | 1971 | £2 | £5 | picture sleeve |
| Mott The Hoople | LP | Island | ILPS9108 | 1969 | £6 | £15 | pink label |
| Mott The Hoople | LP | Island | ILPS9108 | 1969 | £15 | £30 | with 'Road To Birmingham', pink label |
| Rock And Roll Queen | 7" | Island | WIP6072 | 1969 | £4 | £8 | |
| The Hoople | LP | Columbia | PCQ32871 | 1974 | £4 | £10 | US quad |
| Wild Life | LP | Island | ILPS9144 | 1971 | £4 | £10 | |

## MOULD, BOB

| Title | Format | Label | Catalog | Year | | | Notes |
|---|---|---|---|---|---|---|---|
| See A Little Light | CD-s | Virgin | VUSCD2 | 1989 | £2 | £5 | |
| Workbook | CD | Virgin | PRCDBOB | 1989 | £8 | £20 | US promo picture disc, cloth cover |

## MOULE, KEN

| | | | | | | |
|---|---|---|---|---|---|---|
| Jazz At Toad Hall | LP | Decca | LK4261/SKL4042 | 1958 | £8 | £20 |
| Ken Moule | LP | Decca | LK4192 | 1957 | £10 | £25 |

## MOULTRIE, MATTIE

| | | | | | | |
|---|---|---|---|---|---|---|
| That's How Strong My Love Is | 7" | CBS | 202547 | 1967 | £1.50 | £4 |

## MOUND CITY BLUE BLOWERS

| | | | | | | |
|---|---|---|---|---|---|---|
| Blues Blowing Jazz Vol. 1 | 7" EP | Collector | JEL1 | 1959 | £2 | £5 |
| Mound City Blue Blowers | 7" EP | HMV | 7EG8096 | 1955 | £2 | £5 |

## MOUNT RUSHMORE

| | | | | | | |
|---|---|---|---|---|---|---|
| Stone Free | 7" | Dot | 115 | 1968 | £1.50 | £4 |

## MOUNTAIN

Mountain was formed by Felix Pappalardi in a deliberate attempt to capture some of the market that had been opened up by Cream. Pappalardi had, of course, worked with Cream on both *Disraeli Gears* and *Wheels Of Fire*. Guitarist Leslie West was not in Eric Clapton's league, but Mountain nevertheless had its moments – most notably on *Nantucket Sleighride*, a section of which was made familiar to Sunday TV viewers in the London area as the theme tune to *Weekend World*.

| | | | | | | | |
|---|---|---|---|---|---|---|---|
| Avalanche | LP | Columbia | CQ33088 | 1974 | £4 | £10 | US quad |
| Best Of Mountain | LP | Columbia | CQ32079 | 1973 | £4 | £10 | US quad |
| Dreams Of Milk And Honey | 7" | Bell | BLL1078 | 1970 | £2 | £5 | |
| Flowers Of Evil | LP | Island | ILPS9179 | 1971 | £4 | £10 | |
| Mountain Climbing | LP | Bell | SBLL133 | 1970 | £5 | £12 | |
| Nantucket Sleighride | LP | Island | ILPS9148 | 1971 | £5 | £12 | |
| Road Goes Ever On | LP | Island | ILPS9199 | 1972 | £4 | £10 | |
| Twin Peaks | LP | CBS | 88095 | 1974 | £5 | £12 | double |

## MOUNTAIN, VALERIE

| | | | | | | |
|---|---|---|---|---|---|---|
| Go It Alone | 7" | Columbia | DB4660 | 1961 | £1.50 | £4 |

## MOUNTAIN, VALERIE & THE EAGLES

| | | | | | | |
|---|---|---|---|---|---|---|
| Some People | 7" EP | Pye | NEP24158 | 1962 | £2.50 | £6 |

## MOUNTAIN ASH

| | | | | | | |
|---|---|---|---|---|---|---|
| Hermit | LP | Witches Bane | LKLP6036 | 1975 | £75 | £150 |

## MOUNTAIN BUS

| | | | | | | | |
|---|---|---|---|---|---|---|---|
| Sundance | LP | Good | 101 | 1971 | £37.50 | £75 | US |

## MOURNING PHASE

| | | | | | | |
|---|---|---|---|---|---|---|
| Mourning Phase | LP | private | | 1971 | £330 | £500 |

## MOUSE

| | | | | | | |
|---|---|---|---|---|---|---|
| All The Fallen Teen Angels | 7" | Sovereign | SOV127 | 1974 | £5 | £10 |
| Lady Killer | LP | Sovereign | SVNA7262 | 1974 | £62.50 | £125 |
| We Can Make It | 7" | Sovereign | SOV122 | 1973 | £5 | £10 |

## MOUSE & THE TRAPS

| | | | | | | |
|---|---|---|---|---|---|---|
| L.O.V.E. | 7" | President | PT174 | 1968 | £5 | £10 |
| Sometimes You Just Can't Win | 7" | President | PT210 | 1968 | £2.50 | £6 |

## MOUSEFOLK

| | | | | | | | |
|---|---|---|---|---|---|---|---|
| Don't Let It Slip Away | 7" | Tea Time<br>Surf's Up | 01 | 1988 | £2.50 | £6 | flexi, picture sleeve |

## MOVE

The Move could never quite decide whether they wished to become part of the burgeoning progressive rock scene or whether they just wanted to be a pop group. In the event, much of the group's music is an uneasy compromise between the two, with the series of hit singles receiving the most care and invention in their construction. The most interesting Move release is possibly the live EP *Something Else*, where the group powers its way through an assortment of dynamic cover versions. They turn Spooky Tooth's 'Sunshine Help Me' into something of a showcase for Roy Wood's squally lead guitar, but the fact that the melodic bass playing is given at least as much prominence in the mix makes the music sound remarkably fresh.

| | | | | | | | |
|---|---|---|---|---|---|---|---|
| Blackberry Way | 7" | Regal Zonophone | RZ3015 | 1969 | £1.50 | £4 | |
| Brontosaurus | 7" | Regal Zonophone | RZ3026 | 1970 | £1.50 | £4 | |
| Cherry Blossom Clinic | 7" | Regal Zonophone | | 1968 | £25 | £50 | test pressing |
| Curly | 7" | Regal Zonophone | RZ3021 | 1969 | £1.50 | £4 | |
| Fire Brigade | 7" | MagniFly | ECHO104 | 1972 | £1.50 | £4 | picture sleeve |
| Fire Brigade | 7" | Regal Zonophone | RZ3005 | 1968 | £1.50 | £4 | |
| Flowers In The Rain | 7" | Regal Zonophone | RZ3001 | 1967 | £1.50 | £4 | |
| I Can Hear The Grass Grow | 7" EP | Deram | 15002 | 1967 | £12.50 | £25 | French |
| I Can Hear The Grass Grow | 7" | Deram | DM117 | 1967 | £1.50 | £4 | |
| Looking On | LP | Fly | FLY1 | 1971 | £4 | £10 | |
| Message From The Country | LP | Harvest | SHSP4013 | 1971 | £4 | £10 | |
| Move | LP | Regal Zonophone | (S)LRZ1002 | 1968 | £8 | £20 | |
| Night Of Fear | 7" | Deram | DM109 | 1966 | £1.50 | £4 | |

| Title | Format | Label | Cat. No. | Year | | | Notes |
|---|---|---|---|---|---|---|---|
| Shazam | LP | Regal Zonophone | SLRZ1012 | 1970 | £6 | £15 | |
| Something Else | 7" EP | Regal Zonophone | TRZ2001 | 1968 | £12.50 | £25 | |
| Something Else From The Move | 7" | EMI | PSRS315 | 1968 | £12.50 | £25 | 1 sided promo sampler |
| Wild Tiger Woman | 7" | Regal Zonophone | RZ3012 | 1968 | £1.50 | £4 | |

## MOVEMENT

| Title | Format | Label | Cat. No. | Year | | | |
|---|---|---|---|---|---|---|---|
| Head For The Sun | 7" | Transatlantic | BIG112 | 1968 | £20 | £40 | |
| Something You've Got | 7" | Pye | 7N17443 | 1968 | £37.50 | £75 | |

## MOVING FINGER

| Title | Format | Label | Cat. No. | Year | | | |
|---|---|---|---|---|---|---|---|
| Higher And Higher | 7" | Mercury | MF1077 | 1969 | £1.50 | £4 | |
| Jeremy The Lamp | 7" | Mercury | MF1051 | 1968 | £5 | £10 | |
| So Many People | 7" | Decca | F13406 | 1973 | £1.50 | £4 | |

## MOVING GELATINE PLATES

| Title | Format | Label | Cat. No. | Year | | | Notes |
|---|---|---|---|---|---|---|---|
| Moving Gelatine Plates | LP | CBS | 64399 | 1971 | £37.50 | £75 | French |
| World Of Genius Hans | LP | CBS | 64146 | 1972 | £37.50 | £75 | French |

## MOVING HEARTS

| Title | Format | Label | Cat. No. | Year | | | |
|---|---|---|---|---|---|---|---|
| Live Hearts | LP | WEA | IR0203 | 1983 | £4 | £10 | |
| Moving Hearts | LP | WEA | K583387 | 1981 | £4 | £10 | |

## MOVING SIDEWALKS

| Title | Format | Label | Cat. No. | Year | | | Notes |
|---|---|---|---|---|---|---|---|
| Flash | LP | Tantara | TYS6919 | 1968 | £100 | £200 | US |

## MOYET, ALISON

| Title | Format | Label | Cat. No. | Year | | | |
|---|---|---|---|---|---|---|---|
| Love Letters | CD-s | CBS | MOYETC5 | 1987 | £2 | £5 | |

## MOZART, MICKEY

| Title | Format | Label | Cat. No. | Year | | | |
|---|---|---|---|---|---|---|---|
| Little Dipper | 7" | Columbia | DB4308 | 1959 | £1.50 | £4 | |

## MR. BIG

| Title | Format | Label | Cat. No. | Year | | | |
|---|---|---|---|---|---|---|---|
| Drill Song | CD-s | Atlantic | A7712CD | 1991 | £2 | £5 | |
| Green Tinted Sixties Mind | CD-s | Atlantic | A7702CD | 1991 | £2 | £5 | |
| Just Take My Heart | CD-s | East West | A7490CD | 1992 | £2 | £5 | |
| To Be With You | CD-s | Atlantic | A7514CD | 1992 | £2 | £5 | |

## MR. BROWN

| Title | Format | Label | Cat. No. | Year | | | Notes |
|---|---|---|---|---|---|---|---|
| Mellan Tre Ogon | LP | Fly Khan | 0177 | 1977 | £15 | £30 | Swedish |

## MR. CLEAN

Both sides of the Mr. Clean single are the work of Frank Zappa, who wrote and produced the songs and played guitar on them.

| Title | Format | Label | Cat. No. | Year | | | Notes |
|---|---|---|---|---|---|---|---|
| Mr. Clean | 7" | Original Sound | 40 | 1964 | £75 | £150 | US |

## MR. DYNAMITE

| Title | Format | Label | Cat. No. | Year | | | |
|---|---|---|---|---|---|---|---|
| Sh'mon | 7" | Sue | WI4027 | 1967 | £10 | £20 | |

## MR. FLOOD'S PARTY

| Title | Format | Label | Cat. No. | Year | | | Notes |
|---|---|---|---|---|---|---|---|
| Compared To What | 7" | Bulldog | BD6 | 1975 | £2 | £5 | |
| Compared To What | 7" | Ember | EMBS312 | 1970 | £4 | £8 | |
| Mr. Flood's Party | LP | Cotillion | 9003 | 1969 | £8 | £20 | US |

## MR. FOUNDATION

| Title | Format | Label | Cat. No. | Year | | | Notes |
|---|---|---|---|---|---|---|---|
| Time-oh | 7" | Studio One | SO2061 | 1968 | £6 | £12 | Dudley Sibley & Peter Austin B side |

## MR. FOX

| Title | Format | Label | Cat. No. | Year | | | Notes |
|---|---|---|---|---|---|---|---|
| Complete Mr. Fox | LP | Transatlantic | TRA303 | 1975 | £10 | £25 | double |
| Gypsy | LP | Transatlantic | TRA236 | 1971 | £15 | £30 | |
| Little Woman | 7" | Transatlantic | BIG135 | 1970 | £1.50 | £4 | |
| Mr. Fox | LP | Transatlantic | TRA226 | 1970 | £10 | £25 | |

## MR. GASSER & THE WEIRDOS

| Title | Format | Label | Cat. No. | Year | | | Notes |
|---|---|---|---|---|---|---|---|
| Hot Rod Hootenanny | LP | Capitol | (S)T2010 | 1963 | £6 | £15 | US |
| Rods 'n' Ratfinks | LP | Capitol | (S)T2057 | 1963 | £6 | £15 | US |
| Surfink! | LP | Capitol | (S)T2114 | 1964 | £8 | £20 | US |

## MR. MISTER

| Title | Format | Label | Cat. No. | Year | | | |
|---|---|---|---|---|---|---|---|
| Broken Wings | CD-s | RCA | PD49449 | 1989 | £2 | £5 | |

## MR. MO'S MESSENGERS

| Title | Format | Label | Cat. No. | Year | | | |
|---|---|---|---|---|---|---|---|
| Feelin' Good | 7" | Columbia | DB8133 | 1967 | £2 | £5 | |

## MTUME UMOJA ENSEMBLE

*Alkebu-Lan* is an uncompromising celebration of black culture, mixing avant-garde and modal jazz with poetry and chanting in a heady brew. Much of the music is similar to that of pianist McCoy Tyner and in fact some of the musicians here did also play with Tyner. Mtume himself was percussionist in Miles Davis's seventies band, but later moved into considerably more commercial areas, scoring a sizeable US hit with 'Juicy Fruit' and producing several tracks for Madonna.

| Title | Format | Label | Cat. No. | Year | | | Notes |
|---|---|---|---|---|---|---|---|
| Alkebu-Lan | LP | Strata-East | SES19724 | 1972 | £15 | £30 | US double |

## M.U. (MENTALLY UNFIT)
Motion In Tune ....................................... LP ..... Backstreet/    BBR010 ................ 1981 £**30** ........ £**60** ..................... *Dutch*
               Backlash .........

## MU
Last Album ............................................. LP ..... Appaloosa........ AP017 ............... 1981 £6 ........ £**15** ................ *Italian*
Lemurian Music .................................... LP ..... United Artists .. UAG29709 ....... 1975 £**15** ...... £**30** ...............
Mu ......................................................... LP ..... RTV ............. 300 ..................... 1971 £**18** ..... £**300** .................... *US*

## MUCKRAM WAKES
Map Of Derbyshire................................. LP ..... Trailer............ LER2085 ......... 1973 £8 ....... £**20**
Muckram Wakes .................................... LP ..... Trailer............ LER2093 ......... 1976 £5 ....... £**12**
Warbles, Jangles And Reeds..................... LP ..... Highway ........ SHY7009 ........... 1980 £5 ....... £**12**

## MUD
Flower Power ........................................ 7" ..... CBS............. 203002 ............. 1967 £5 ......... £**10**
Flower Power ........................................ 7" ..... CBS............. 203002 ............. 1967 £**10** ...... £**20** ......... *picture sleeve*
Jumping Jehosaphat ............................. 7" ..... Philips........... 6006022 ............ 1970 £2 ......... £5
Shangri-La ............................................ 7" ..... Philips........... BF1775 ............ 1969 £4 ........ £8
Up The Airy Mountain ......................... 7" ..... CBS............. 3355 .................. 1968 £4 ........ £8

## MUDCRUTCH
The songs issued by Mudcrutch are the earliest recordings to feature Tom Petty.

Depot Street .......................................... 7" ...... Shelter ......... 40357 ............... 1975 £**7.50** ...... £**15** ..................... *US*
Up In Mississippi ................................. 7" ...... Pepper ........... 9449 .................. 1971 £**100** ..... £**200** .... *US, best auctioned*

## MUDLARKS
Book Of Love ........................................ 7" ...... Columbia ....... DB4133 ............ 1958 £2 ......... £5
Lollipop................................................ 7" ...... Columbia ....... DB4099 ............ 1958 £2 ......... £5
Love Game ............................................ 7" ...... Columbia ....... DB4250 ............ 1959 £**1.50** ...... £4
Mudlarks .............................................. 7" EP . Columbia ....... SEG7854 .......... 1958 £6 ........ £**12**
New Love .............................................. 7" ...... Columbia ....... DB4064 ............ 1958 £**1.50** ...... £4
There's Never Been A Night ................... 7" ...... Columbia ....... DB4190 ............ 1958 £**1.50** ...... £4
Which Witch Doctor............................. 7" ...... Columbia ....... DB4210 ............ 1958 £**1.50** ...... £4

## MUGWUMPS
I Don't Wanna Know ............................ 7" ...... Warner Bros.... WB144 ............ 1964 £2 ......... £5
Mugwumps ........................................... LP ..... Warner Bros.... W1697 ............. 1967 £6 ........ £**15**

## MUIR, BOBBY
Baby What You Done Me Wrong ............. 7" ...... Blue Beat ....... BB20 ............... 1960 £6 ........ £**12**
Spanish Town Twist .............................. 7" ...... Blue Beat ....... BB77 ............... 1962 £6 ........ £**12**
That's My Girl ....................................... 7" ...... Blue Beat ....... BB44 ............... 1961 £6 ........ £**12**

## MULCAYS
Harbour Lights...................................... 7" ...... London .......... HLF8188............ 1955 £**7.50** ...... £**15**
Harmonics By The Mulcays ................... 7" EP . London .......... REF1046 .......... 1956 £6 ........ £**12**
Merry Christmas ................................... 7" EP . London .......... REP1016 .......... 1954 £6 ........ £**12**

## MULDAUR, GEOFF
Geoff Muldaur ...................................... LP ..... Prestige ......... 14004 ............... 1964 £6 ........ £**15** ..................... *US*
Sleepy Man Blues .................................. LP ..... Prestige ......... 7727 .................. 1965 £6 ........ £**15** ..................... *US*

## MULDAUR, GEOFF & MARIA
Pottery Pie............................................ LP ..... Reprise .......... RS6350 ............ 1970 £4 ........ £**10** ..................... *US*
Sweet Potatoes ...................................... LP ..... Warner Bros.... MS2073 ............ 1972 £4 ........ £**10** ..................... *US*

## MULDOONS
I'm Lost Without You ........................... 7" ...... Decca ........... F12164............. 1965 £**10** ........ £**20**

## MULESKINNERS
Back Door Man ..................................... 7" ...... Fontana........... TF527 ............... 1965 £**30** ...... £**60** ...............
Muleskinners........................................ 7" EP . Keepoint ....... KEEEP7104 ........... 196– £**330** ..... £**500** ........... *best auctioned*

## MULLICAN, MOON
Cherokee Boogie ................................... 78...... Vogue........... V9013 ............... 1951 £6 ........ £**12**
Country Round Up ............................... 7" EP . Parlophone...... GEP8794........... 1959 £**15** ...... £**30**
His All-Time Greatest Hits...................... LP ..... King ............. 555 .................... 1958 £**25** ...... £**50** ..................... *US*
I'll Sail My Ship Alone .......................... LP ..... Sterling ......... ST601 ............... 196– £**10** ...... £**25** ..................... *US*
Instrumentals........................................ LP ..... Audio Lab ....... AL1568 ............ 1962 £**20** ...... £**40** ..................... *US*
Many Moods Of Moon Mullican ........... LP ..... King ............. 681 .................... 1960 £**25** ...... £**50** ..................... *US*
Moon Over Mullican.............................. LP ..... Coral ........... CRL57235 ......... 1958 £**75** ..... £**150** ..................... *US*
Mr. Piano Man ...................................... LP ..... Starday .......... SLP267 ............ 1964 £6 ........ £**15** ..................... *US*
Piano Breakdown ................................. 7" EP . Parlophone...... CGEP15 ........... 195– £**10** ...... £**20** ..................... *export*
Seven Nights To Rock ........................... 7" ...... Parlophone...... MSP6254 .......... 1956 £**180** ..... £**300** ... *with Boyd Bennett,*
                                                 *best auctioned*
Sixteen Of His Favorite Tunes ................ LP ..... King ............. 628 .................... 1959 £**25** ...... £**50** ..................... *US*
Twenty-Four Of His Favorite Tunes......... LP ..... King ............. 937 .................... 1965 £5 ....... £**12** ..................... *US*
Unforgettable Moon Mullican ............... LP ..... Starday .......... SLP398 ............ 1967 £4 ........ £**10** ..................... *US*

## MULLIGAN, GERRY
At The Village Vanguard........................ LP ..... HMV........... CLP1488/CSD1396 1962 £6 ........ £**15**
Concert In Jazz ..................................... LP ..... HMV........... CLP1549/CSD1432 1962 £5 ....... £**12**
Concert Jazz Band ................................. LP ..... HMV........... CLP1432/CSD1351 1961 £6 ........ £**15**
Concert Jazz Band ................................. LP ..... Verve ........... VLP9037 ............... 1963 £5 ....... £**12**

| Title | Format | Label | Catalogue | Year | | | Notes |
|---|---|---|---|---|---|---|---|
| Genius Of Gerry Mulligan | LP | Vocalion | LAE12268 | 1960 | £6 | £15 | |
| Gerry Mulligan Allstars | LP | Esquire | 32014 | 1956 | £10 | £25 | |
| Gerry Mulligan Allstars | 10" LP | Esquire | 20032 | 1954 | £25 | £50 | |
| Gerry Mulligan And Paul Desmond Quartet | LP | Columbia | 33CX10113 | 1958 | £6 | £15 | |
| Gerry Mulligan Meets Ben Webster | LP | HMV | CLP1373 | 1960 | £6 | £15 | |
| Gerry Mulligan Meets Johnny Hodges | LP | HMV | CLP1465/CSD1372 | 1962 | £6 | £15 | |
| Gerry Mulligan Quartet | LP | Vogue | LAE12006 | 1956 | £10 | £25 | |
| Gerry Mulligan Quartet | LP | Vogue | LAE12015 | 1956 | £10 | £25 | |
| Gerry Mulligan Quartet | LP | Vogue | LAE12050 | 1957 | £8 | £20 | |
| Gerry Mulligan Quartet | LP | Vogue | LAE12080 | 1958 | £8 | £20 | |
| Gerry Mulligan Quartet | 10" LP | Vogue | LDE075 | 1954 | £25 | £50 | |
| Gerry Mulligan Quartet Vol. 1 | 10" LP | Vogue | LDE029 | 1953 | £25 | £50 | |
| Gerry Mulligan Quartet Vol. 2 | 10" LP | Vogue | LDE030 | 1953 | £25 | £50 | |
| Gerry Mulligan Quartet Vol. 3 | 10" LP | Vogue | LDE031 | 1953 | £25 | £50 | |
| Gerry Mulligan Quartet Vol. 4 | 10" LP | Vogue | LDE083 | 1954 | £25 | £50 | |
| Gerry Mulligan Quartet With Lee Konitz | 10" LP | Vogue | LDE156 | 1955 | £25 | £50 | |
| Gerry Mulligan Tentette | 10" LP | Capitol | LC6621 | 1953 | £25 | £50 | |
| Getz Meets Mulligan In Hi-Fi | LP | Columbia | 33CX10120 | 1958 | £6 | £15 | with Stan Getz |
| I Want To Live | LP | London | LTZT15161/ SAHT6023 | 1959 | £6 | £15 | with Shelly Manne |
| Mainstream Of Jazz | LP | Emarcy | EJL1259 | 1957 | £10 | £25 | |
| Mainstream Vol. 1 | 7" EP | Emarcy | ERE1574 | 1958 | £2 | £5 | |
| Mainstream Vol. 2 | 7" EP | Emarcy | ERE1575 | 1958 | £2 | £5 | |
| Mulligan Mania | 7" EP | Mercury | ZEP10071 | 1960 | £2 | £5 | |
| Mulligan Meets Monk | LP | London | LTZU15127 | 1958 | £8 | £20 | with Thelonious Monk |
| Mulligan Meets Monk | LP | Riverside | RLP12247 | 1962 | £6 | £15 | |
| On Tour | LP | HMV | CLP1585 | 1962 | £5 | £12 | with Zoot Sims |
| Phil Sunkel's Jazz Concerto Grosso | LP | HMV | CLP1204 | 1958 | £8 | £20 | with Bob Brookmeyer |
| Presenting Gerry Mulligan & His Tentette | 7" EP | Capitol | EAP1439 | 1955 | £2 | £5 | |
| Presenting Gerry Mulligan & His Tentette | 7" EP | Capitol | EAP2439 | 1955 | £2 | £5 | |
| Presenting The Gerry Mulligan Sextet | LP | Emarcy | EJL101 | 1956 | £10 | £25 | |
| Presenting The Gerry Mulligan Sextet | 7" EP | Emarcy | ERE1553 | 1958 | £2 | £5 | |
| Presenting The Gerry Mulligan Sextet Vol. 2 | 7" EP | Emarcy | ERE1556 | 1958 | £2 | £5 | |
| Presenting The Gerry Mulligan Sextet Vol. 3 | 7" EP | Emarcy | ERE1560 | 1958 | £2 | £5 | |
| Relax | LP | Fontana | FJL105 | 1964 | £4 | £10 | |
| Reunion With Chet Baker | LP | Vogue | LAE12185/ SEA5007 | 1959 | £8 | £20 | |
| Songbook Vol. 1 | LP | Vogue | LAE12128/ SEA5006 | 1959 | £10 | £25 | |
| What Is There To Say? | LP | Philips | BBL7320 | 1959 | £4 | £10 | |
| What Is There To Say? | LP | Philips | SBBL552 | 1959 | £5 | £12 | |

## MULLIGAN, MICK

| Title | Format | Label | Catalogue | Year | | | Notes |
|---|---|---|---|---|---|---|---|
| Jazz At The Railway Arms | LP | Tempo | TAP14 | 1957 | £10 | £25 | with George Melly |
| Meet Mick Mulligan | LP | Pye | NJL21 | 1959 | £5 | £12 | |
| Mick Mulligan's Jazz Band | 7" EP | Tempo | EXA25 | 1955 | £2.50 | £6 | |
| Saints Meet The Sinners | LP | Parlophone | PMC1103/ PCS3005 | 1959 | £5 | £12 | with George Melly |

## MUMFORD, GENE

| Title | Format | Label | Catalogue | Year | | | Notes |
|---|---|---|---|---|---|---|---|
| More Than You Know | 7" | Philips | PB862 | 1958 | £1.50 | £4 | |

## MUMPS

| Title | Format | Label | Catalogue | Year | | | Notes |
|---|---|---|---|---|---|---|---|
| Matter Of Taste | LP | MPS | 0068169 | 1977 | £6 | £15 | German |

## MUNRO, HAL

| Title | Format | Label | Catalogue | Year | | | Notes |
|---|---|---|---|---|---|---|---|
| Breathless | 7" | Embassy | WB284 | 1958 | £1.50 | £4 | |
| C'mon Everybody | 7" | Embassy | WB336 | 1959 | £1.50 | £4 | |

## MUNSTERS

| Title | Format | Label | Catalogue | Year | | | Notes |
|---|---|---|---|---|---|---|---|
| Munsters | LP | Decca | DL4588 | 1964 | £8 | £20 | US |

## MURE, BILLY

| Title | Format | Label | Catalogue | Year | | | Notes |
|---|---|---|---|---|---|---|---|
| Supersonics In Flight | 7" EP | RCA | RCX158/SRC7032 | 1959 | £5 | £10 | |
| Versatile Billy Mure | 7" EP | Felsted | GEP1006 | 1959 | £2 | £5 | |

## MURGATROYD BAND

| Title | Format | Label | Catalogue | Year | | | Notes |
|---|---|---|---|---|---|---|---|
| Magpie | 7" | Decca | F13256 | 1972 | £1.50 | £4 | |

## MURMAIDS

| Title | Format | Label | Catalogue | Year | | | Notes |
|---|---|---|---|---|---|---|---|
| Popsicles And Icicles | 7" EP | Columbia | ESRF1487 | 1964 | £4 | £8 | French |
| Popsicles And Icicles | 7" | Stateside | SS247 | 1963 | £1.50 | £4 | |

## MURPHEY, MICHAEL

| Title | Format | Label | Catalogue | Year | | | Notes |
|---|---|---|---|---|---|---|---|
| Geronimo's Cadillac | LP | Regal Zonophone | SRZA8512 | 1972 | £4 | £10 | |

## MURPHY, DENIS & JULIA CLIFFORD

| Title | Format | Label | Catalogue | Year | | | Notes |
|---|---|---|---|---|---|---|---|
| Star Above The Garter | LP | Claddagh | CC5 | 1969 | £4 | £10 | Irish |

## MURPHY, MARK

| Title | Format | Label | Catalogue | Year | | | Notes |
|---|---|---|---|---|---|---|---|
| Hit Parade | LP | Capitol | (S)T5011 | 1960 | £4 | £10 | |
| Mark Time! | LP | Fontana | (S)TL5217 | 1964 | £4 | £10 | |
| Meet Mark Murphy | LP | Brunswick | LAT8172 | 1957 | £4 | £10 | |
| This Could Be The Start Of Something | LP | Capitol | T1177 | 1959 | £4 | £10 | |

| | | | | | | | |
|---|---|---|---|---|---|---|---|
| Who Can I Turn To | LP | Immediate | IMLP/IMSP004 | 1966 | £15 | £30 | |

## MURPHY, NOEL

| | | | | | | | |
|---|---|---|---|---|---|---|---|
| Another Round | LP | Fontana | STL5496 | 1969 | £4 | £10 | |
| Murf | LP | Village Thing | VTS25 | 1973 | £4 | £10 | |
| Nya-a-a-a-h! | LP | Fontana | (S)TL5450 | 1967 | £5 | £12 | |

## MURPHY, ROSE

| | | | | | | | |
|---|---|---|---|---|---|---|---|
| Songs By Rose Murphy | 10" LP | Mercury | MG10004 | 1953 | £4 | £10 | |

## MURPHY, TURK

| | | | | | | | |
|---|---|---|---|---|---|---|---|
| Music Of Jelly Roll Morton | LP | Philips | BBL7051 | 1955 | £5 | £12 | |
| New Orleans Shuffle | LP | Philips | BBL7145 | 1957 | £4 | £10 | |
| Turk Murphy Jazz Band | LP | Philips | BBL7088 | 1956 | £5 | £12 | |
| Turk Murphy Jazz Band | LP | Philips | BBL7095 | 1956 | £5 | £12 | |
| Turk Murphy Jazz Band | 10" LP | Good Time Jazz | LDG037 | 1954 | £5 | £12 | |
| Turk Murphy Jazz Band | 10" LP | Good Time Jazz | LDG078 | 1954 | £5 | £12 | |
| Turk Murphy Jazz Band | 10" LP | Good Time Jazz | LDG180 | 1956 | £5 | £12 | |
| Turk Murphy Jazz Band | 10" LP | Good Time Jazz | LDG186 | 1956 | £5 | £12 | |

## MURPHY BLEND

| | | | | | | | |
|---|---|---|---|---|---|---|---|
| First Loss | LP | Kuckuck | 2375005 | 1970 | £50 | £100 | German |

## MURRAY, ALEX

| | | | | | | | |
|---|---|---|---|---|---|---|---|
| Teen Angel | 7" | Decca | F11203 | 1960 | £1.50 | £4 | |

## MURRAY, LARRY

| | | | | | | | |
|---|---|---|---|---|---|---|---|
| Sweet Country Suite | LP | Verve | FTS3090 | 1969 | £15 | £30 | US |

## MURRAY, MISTER

| | | | | | | | |
|---|---|---|---|---|---|---|---|
| Down Came The Rain | 7" | Fontana | TF623 | 1965 | £1.50 | £4 | |

## MURRAY, MITCH CLAN

| | | | | | | | |
|---|---|---|---|---|---|---|---|
| Skyliner | 7" | Clan | 597001 | 1966 | £1.50 | £4 | |

## MURRAY, PETE/PASCAL FRUITS

| | | | | | | | |
|---|---|---|---|---|---|---|---|
| TV Themes | 7" EP | ATV | ATV1 | 1969 | £2.50 | £6 | |

## MURRAY, RUBY

| | | | | | | | |
|---|---|---|---|---|---|---|---|
| Ain't That A Grand And Glorious Feeling | 7" | Columbia | DB4042 | 1957 | £1.50 | £4 | |
| Endearing Young Charms | 7" EP | Columbia | SEG7952 | 1959 | £2 | £5 | |
| Endearing Young Charms | 10" LP | Columbia | 33S1135 | 1958 | £8 | £20 | |
| Evermore | 7" | Columbia | SCM5180 | 1955 | £4 | £8 | |
| Everybody's Sweetheart No. 1 | 7" EP | Columbia | SEG7620 | 1956 | £2 | £5 | |
| Everybody's Sweetheart No. 2 | 7" EP | Columbia | SEG7631 | 1956 | £2 | £5 | |
| Everybody's Sweetheart No. 3 | 7" EP | Columbia | SEG7636 | 1956 | £2.50 | £6 | |
| Forgive Me My Darling | 7" | Columbia | DB4075 | 1958 | £1.50 | £4 | |
| From The First Hello | 7" | Columbia | DB3911 | 1957 | £2 | £5 | |
| Goodbye Jimmy Goodbye | 7" | Columbia | DB4305 | 1959 | £1.50 | £4 | |
| If Anyone Finds This, I Love You | 7" | Columbia | SCM5169 | 1955 | £4 | £8 | |
| In Love | 7" | Columbia | DB3852 | 1956 | £2 | £5 | |
| In My Life | 7" | Columbia | DB4108 | 1958 | £1.50 | £4 | |
| It Only Hurts For A Little While | 7" | Columbia | DB3810 | 1956 | £2.50 | £6 | |
| Little White Lies | 7" | Columbia | DB3994 | 1957 | £1.50 | £4 | |
| Love's Old Sweet Song | 7" EP | Columbia | ESG7830 | 1960 | £4 | £8 | stereo |
| Love's Old Sweet Song | 7" EP | Columbia | SEG8052 | 1960 | £2 | £5 | |
| Mr. Wonderful | 7" | Columbia | DB3933 | 1957 | £2 | £5 | |
| Oh Please Make Him Jealous | 7" | Columbia | SCM5225 | 1956 | £2.50 | £6 | |
| Real Love | 7" | Columbia | DB4192 | 1958 | £1.50 | £4 | |
| Ruby | LP | Columbia | 33SX1201/ SCX3289 | 1960 | £4 | £10 | |
| Ruby Is A Gem | 7" EP | Columbia | SEG7588 | 1955 | £5 | £10 | |
| Scarlet Ribbons | 7" | Columbia | DB3955 | 1957 | £2 | £5 | |
| Softly Softly | 7" | Columbia | SCM5162 | 1955 | £6 | £12 | |
| True Love | 7" | Columbia | DB3849 | 1956 | £2 | £5 | |
| When Irish Eyes Are Smiling | 10" LP | Columbia | 33S1079 | 1955 | £6 | £15 | |

## MUSHROOM

| | | | | | | | |
|---|---|---|---|---|---|---|---|
| Devil Amongst The Tailors | 7" | Hawk | HASP320 | 1973 | £10 | £20 | |
| Early One Morning | LP | Hawk | HALPX116 | 1973 | £150 | £250 | |
| Early One Morning | LP | Hawk | HALPX116 | 1973 | £210 | £350 | with poster |
| Kings And Queens | 7" | Hawk | HASP340 | 1974 | £10 | £20 | |

## MUSHROOM SOUP

In the first edition of this *Price Guide* (1991), an album was listed by a group called Mushroom Soup. For long a feature within the wants lists of a few dealers, the record's details were so delightful (Mushroom Soup: *And Other Recipes* on the Roll and Butter label, catalogue number PAT1) that one longed for it to be real, despite the almost certain knowledge that it was not! (As was said in the first edition.) Of course, the record was a fiction – but as such, it joins a fairly long catalogue of imaginary records, some of which have had collectors scouring the specialist shops and record fairs far and wide in an increasingly frantic and fruitless quest. One collectors' shop always used to head its wants list with an intriguing reference to an album called *Where's Mutley?*; others are more mischievous, slipping in a tantalizing reference to a twelve-inch version of a record one was certain only existed as a seven inch, or else advertising a previously undiscovered picture disc (such records have always 'just been sold', of course). It was Greil Marcus who started a tradition of joke references within otherwise sensible discographies, with the 'Zurvans: *Close The Book* (End)' entry at the end of his desert island anthology, *Stranded*. It is not Marcus's fault if his quiet wit has been worn a little thin in the work of other authors who have repeated the joke to the point of exhaustion.

From time to time, the rock press has put its own slant on the process by reviewing records of its own invention – some of which have subsequently turned out to be real after all. Examples can be found in this guide under the headings 'Heavy Jelly' and 'Masked Marauders'. As for Mushroom Soup, their discography has miraculously expanded of late, if we are to believe the entry in a limited-edition *Rare Record Guide* published in 1994. An imaginary band that has managed to produce nine separate collectors' items (including three made by some kind of spin-off unit) is clearly a force to be reckoned with. Perhaps the band could be persuaded to re-form for some kind of imaginary tour – the support slot to the Beatles reunion is still vacant, so far as we know!

## MUSIC BOX
Songs Of Sunshine.................................... LP ...... Westwood....... MRS013 ............... 1972 £6.......... £15

## MUSIC DOCTORS
Reggae In The Summertime .................... LP ...... Trojan............. TBL117 ................ 1970 £4.......... £10

## MUSIC EMPORIUM
Music Emporium ..................................... LP ...... Psycho ........... PSYCHO11 .......... 1983 £8.......... £20 ..............................
Music Emporium ..................................... LP ...... Sentinel........... 100 ...................... 1969 £1400 . £2000 .................... US

## MUSIC EXPLOSION
Little Bit O' Soul..................................... LP ...... London .......... HAP/SHP8352....... 1967 £5.......... £12 ..............................
Little Bit O' Soul..................................... 7" EP . Vogue............. INT18140 ........... 1967 £10.......... £20 .................... French
Little Bit O' Soul..................................... 7" ...... Stateside .......... SS2028 ............... 1967 £1.50........ £4 ..............................
Little Black Egg....................................... 7" ...... Philips ............. BF1547 ................ 1967 £1.50........ £4 ..............................

## MUSIC IMPROVISATION COMPANY
1968–70 .................................................. LP ...... Incus ............. INCUS17............. 1976 £5.......... £12 ..............................
Packaged Eel............................................ LP ...... ECM .............. ECM1005ST ....... 1971 £8.......... £20 ..............................

## MUSIC MACHINE
Bonniwell Music Machine....................... LP ...... Warner Bros .... WS1732 .............. 1967 £15.......... £30 ..................... US
People In Me ........................................... 7" ...... Pye ................. 7N25414 ............ 1967 £7.50.... £15 .................... demo
Talk Talk ................................................. 7" EP . Vogue............. INT18121 ............ 1967 £75.......... £150 .................... French
Talk Talk ................................................. 7" ...... Pye ................. 7N25407 ............ 1967 £10.......... £20 ..............................
Turn On The Music Machine .................. LP ...... Original Sound 5015/8875.......... 1966 £20.......... £40 ..................... US

## MUSICA ELETTRONICA VIVA
Although based in Rome, the members of MEV were American. Using the most advanced technology available to them at the time, MEV performed free electronic improvisations. Only AMM was working in anything like the same area, so it was appropriate that one LP release devoted a side to each group (it is listed under AMM in this guide). Alvin Curran, Frederic Rzewski, and Richard Teitelbaum have all composed and recorded electronic works since, while Teitelbaum also worked as an improvisor with saxophonist Anthony Braxton.

Leave The City ........................................ LP ...... Byg................. 529335 ............... 1970 £10.......... £25 .................... French
Musica Elettronica Viva .......................... LP ...... Polydor........... 583769 ................ 1969 £10.......... £25 ..............................

## MUSICA URBANA
Musica Urbana......................................... LP ...... Edigsa ............. UM2033 ............. 1976 £6.......... £15 ................ Spanish

## MUSKETEER GRIPWEED
The single credited to Musketeer Gripweed is taken from the soundtrack of the film *How I Won The War* and is an often overlooked rarity from the oeuvre of the man who played the character in the film – John Lennon. As it happens, Lennon's contribution to the record is fairly minimal. His role in the film was not a singing one and on the record he merely contributes a fragment of speech to a basically instrumental piece.

How I Won The War............................... 7" ...... United Artists .. UP1196................ 1966 £30.......... £60 ..............................

## MUSSELWHITE, CHARLIE
Charlie Musselwhite ................................ LP ...... Vanguard ........ VSD79287............ 1968 £5.......... £12 ..................... US
Stand Back, Here Comes Charlie ........... LP ...... Vanguard ........ VSD79232............ 1967 £5.......... £12 ..................... US
  Musslewhite .........................................
Stone Blues ............................................. LP ...... Vanguard ........ SVRL19012........... 1968 £5.......... £12 ..............................
Tennessee Woman .................................. LP ...... Vanguard ........ VSD6528 ............ 1969 £4.......... £10 ..................... US

## MUSSULLI, BOOTS
Diga Diga Doo.......................................... 7" ...... Capitol............. KC65002 ............. 1954 £1.50........ £4 ..............................
Kenton Presents Jazz ............................... 10" LP Capitol............. KPL106................ 1955 £10.......... £25 ..............................

## MUSTANG
Why .......................................................... 7" ...... Parlophone ...... R5579 ................ 1967 £7.50...... £15 ..............................

## MUSTANGS
Dartell Stomp............................................ LP ...... Providence ...... PLP001 .............. 1963 £8.......... £20 ..................... US
Liverpool Beat .......................................... LP ...... Ariola ............. 72251.................. 1966 £15.......... £30 .................... German
Mustangs ................................................... LP ...... Ariola ............. 71741IT .............. 1965 £25.......... £50 .................... German

## MUSTWANGS
Rock Lomond ............................................ 7" ...... Mercury.......... AMT1140 ............. 1961 £2.......... £5

## MUTANTES
Ao Vivo ..................................................... LP ...... Som Livre ....... 4036097 ............. 1976 £6.......... £15 .................... Brazilian
E Seus Cometas No Pais Do Baurets ......... LP ...... Polydor........... ........................ 1972 £15.......... £30 .................... Brazilian
Mutantes ................................................... LP ...... Polydor........... 2451002 ................ 1971 £20.......... £40 .................... Brazilian

## MUTE DRIVERS
Mute Drivers ............................................. LP ...... Mute Drivers ... MD001 ................ 198– £4.......... £10 ..............................

## MUTT 'n' JEFF
Don't Nag Me Ma...................................... 7" ...... Decca ............. F12335.................. 1966 £1.50........ £4 ..............................

## MUTZIE

| | | | | | | | |
|---|---|---|---|---|---|---|---|
| Light Of Your Shadow | LP | Sussex | 7001 | 1970 | £15 | £30 | US |

## MY BLOODY VALENTINE

After a shaky start (as represented by many of their early collectable records), My Bloody Valentine achieved greatness with the release of their *Isn't Anything* album. Decades after the invention of the electric guitar, they managed to find entirely new ways of making it sound – and added this to a melodic strength in a combination that is frequently exhilarating.

| | | | | | | | |
|---|---|---|---|---|---|---|---|
| Ecstasy | LP | Lazy | LAZY08 | 1987 | £10 | £25 | |
| Feed Me With Your Kiss | CD-s | Creation | CRE061CD | 1990 | £2 | £5 | |
| Feed Me With Your Kiss | 7" | Creation | CRE061 | 1988 | £1.50 | £4 | |
| Geek! | 12" | Fever | FEV5 | 1986 | £6 | £15 | |
| Glider EP | CD-s | Creation | CRECD73 | 1990 | £2 | £5 | |
| Isn't Anything | LP | Creation | CRELP040 | 1988 | £4 | £10 | with 7" (CREFRE4) |
| New Record By My Bloody Valentine | 12" | Kaleidoscope Sound | KS101 | 1986 | £10 | £20 | |
| No Place To Go | 7" | Fever | FEV5X | 1986 | £4 | £8 | |
| Strawberry Wine | 12" | Lazy | LAZY07T | 1987 | £6 | £15 | |
| Sunny Sundae Smile | 7" | Lazy | LAZY04 | 1987 | £6 | £12 | |
| Sunny Sundae Smile | 12" | Lazy | LAZY04T | 1987 | £6 | £15 | |
| This Is Your Bloody Valentine | mini LP | Tycoon | ST7501 | 1985 | £25 | £50 | German |
| Tremolo | CD-s | Creation | CRESCD085 | 1991 | £2 | £5 | |
| You Made Me Realise | CD-s | Creation | CRECD055 | 1990 | £2 | £5 | |
| You Made Me Realise | 7" | Creation | CRE055 | 1988 | £1.50 | £4 | |

## MY CAPTAINS

| | | | | | | |
|---|---|---|---|---|---|---|
| History | 7" | 4AD | AD103 | 1981 | £1.50 | £4 |

## MY DEAR WATSON

| | | | | | | |
|---|---|---|---|---|---|---|
| Elusive Face | 7" | Parlophone | R5687 | 1968 | £5 | £10 |
| Have You Seen Your Saviour | 7" | DJM | DJS224 | 1970 | £2 | £5 |
| Stop Stop I'll Be There | 7" | Parlophone | R5737 | 1968 | £5 | £10 |

## MY LIFE STORY

| | | | | | | | |
|---|---|---|---|---|---|---|---|
| 17 Reasons Why | 12" | Parlophone | | 1996 | £10 | £20 | promo |
| Girl A, Girl B, Boy C | CD-s | Mother Tongue | MOTHER2CD | 1993 | £4 | £10 | |
| Girl A, Girl B, Boy C | 7" | Mother Tongue | MOTHER27 | 1993 | £2 | £5 | |
| Girl A, Girl B, Boy C | 12" | Mother Tongue | MOTHER212 | 1993 | £3 | £8 | |

## MY LORDE SHERIFFE'S COMPLAINTE

| | | | | | | |
|---|---|---|---|---|---|---|
| My Lorde Sheriffe's Complainte | LP | Frog | FROG1 | 1979 | £10 | £25 |

## MY SOLID GROUND

| | | | | | | | |
|---|---|---|---|---|---|---|---|
| My Solid Ground | LP | Bacillus | 6494008 | 1971 | £50 | £100 | German |

## MYERS, DAVE

| | | | | | | | |
|---|---|---|---|---|---|---|---|
| Greatest Racing Themes | LP | Carole | CAR(S)8002 | 1967 | £5 | £12 | US |
| Hangin' Twenty | LP | Del-Fi | DFLP/DFST1239 | 1963 | £6 | £15 | US |

## MYLES, BILLY

| | | | | | | | |
|---|---|---|---|---|---|---|---|
| Joker | 7" | HMV | POP423 | 1957 | £7.50 | £15 | |

## MYNEDIAD AM DDIM

| | | | | | | |
|---|---|---|---|---|---|---|
| Mae'r Grwp Yn Talu | LP | Sain | 1064M | 1976 | £6 | £15 |
| Mynediad Am Ddim | LP | Sain | 1021M | 1975 | £10 | £25 |
| Rhwng Saith Stol | LP | Sain | 1083M | 1977 | £6 | £15 |
| Torth O Fara | LP | Sain | 1137M | 1978 | £5 | £12 |

## MYRTELLES

| | | | | | | |
|---|---|---|---|---|---|---|
| Don't Wanna Cry Again | 7" | Oriole | CB1805 | 1963 | £1.50 | £4 |

## MYSTERIES

| | | | | | | |
|---|---|---|---|---|---|---|
| Give Me Rhythm And Blues | 7" | Decca | F11919 | 1964 | £7.50 | £15 |

## MYSTERY MAKER

| | | | | | | |
|---|---|---|---|---|---|---|
| Mystery Maker | LP | Caves | UHC3 | 1977 | £50 | £100 |

## MYSTIC ASTROLOGICAL CRYSTAL BAND

| | | | | | | | |
|---|---|---|---|---|---|---|---|
| Clip Out, Put On Book | LP | Carole | S8003 | 1968 | £15 | £30 | US |
| Mystic Astrological Crystal Band | LP | Carole | (S)8001 | 1967 | £15 | £30 | US |

## MYSTIC MOODS ORCHESTRA

| | | | | | | | |
|---|---|---|---|---|---|---|---|
| Cosmic Force | LP | Mobile Fidelity | 1002 | 1981 | £6 | £15 | US audiophile |
| Emotions | LP | Mobile Fidelity | 1001 | 1981 | £6 | £15 | US audiophile |
| Stormy Weekend | LP | Mobile Fidelity | 1003 | 1981 | £6 | £15 | US audiophile |

## MYSTIC SIVA

| | | | | | | | |
|---|---|---|---|---|---|---|---|
| Mystic Siva | LP | Vo | 19713 | 1972 | £330 | £500 | US |

## MYSTICS

| | | | | | | | |
|---|---|---|---|---|---|---|---|
| Adam And Eve | 7" | HMV | POP646 | 1959 | £15 | £30 | |
| Don't Take The Stars | 7" | Top Rank | JAR243 | 1959 | £6 | £12 | |

## MYTHOS

| | | | | | | | |
|---|---|---|---|---|---|---|---|
| Dreamlab | LP | Kosmische | KM58016 | 1975 | £8 | £20 | German |
| Mythos | LP | Ohr | OMM556019 | 1972 | £15 | £30 | German |
| Strange Guys | LP | Venus | MYF1003 | 1977 | £6 | £15 | German |

## MYTHRA

| | | | | | | | |
|---|---|---|---|---|---|---|---|
| Death And Destiny | 7" | Streetbeat | LAMP2 | 1980 | £2.50 | £6 | |
| Killer | 12" | Streetbeat | LAMP2T | 1980 | £10 | £25 | |

# N

## NA FILI
| | | | | | | | |
|---|---|---|---|---|---|---|---|
| Chanter's Tune | LP | Transatlantic | TRA353 | 1977 | £4 | £10 | |
| Farewell To Connacht | LP | Outlet | SOLP1010 | 1971 | £5 | £12 | *Irish* |
| Kindly Welcome | LP | Dolphin | DOL1008 | 1974 | £4 | £10 | *Irish* |
| Na Fili 3 | LP | Outlet | SOLP1017 | 1973 | £5 | £12 | *Irish* |
| One Day For Recreation (with Sean O Se) | LP | Circa | 003 | 1980 | £4 | £10 | *Irish* |

## NADIR, RIKKI
The records credited to Rikki Nadir are actually by Peter Hammill, in a back-to-basic rock 'n' roll mood, and are listed in this guide along with his other solo work.

## NAMYSLOWSKI, ZBIGNIEW
| | | | | | | | |
|---|---|---|---|---|---|---|---|
| Lola | LP | Decca | LK4644 | 1964 | £5 | £12 | |

## NANETTE
| | | | | | | | |
|---|---|---|---|---|---|---|---|
| Nanette | LP | Columbia | SCX6398 | 1970 | £6 | £15 | |

## NANGLE, ED
| | | | | | | | |
|---|---|---|---|---|---|---|---|
| Whipping The Prince | 7" | Coxsone | CS7038 | 1968 | £5 | £10 | *Heptones B side* |

## NANTOS, NICK & THE FIREBALLERS
| | | | | | | | |
|---|---|---|---|---|---|---|---|
| Guitars On Fire | 7" EP | Summit | LSE2042 | 1963 | £2 | £5 | |

## NAPALM DEATH
| | | | | | | | |
|---|---|---|---|---|---|---|---|
| Mentally Murdered | CD-s | Earache | MOSH14CD | 1989 | £2 | £5 | |
| Peel Sessions | CD-s | Strange Fruit | SFPDCD049 | 1989 | £2 | £5 | |
| Suffer The Children | CD-s | Earache | MOSH24CD | 1990 | £2 | £5 | |

## NAPOLEON XIV
This was a pseudonym adopted by recording engineer Jerry Samuels for his zany novelty hit 'They're Coming To Take Me Away Ha Ha'. The record was hardly a suitable basis for a lengthy rock career, however, especially when Samuels allowed Richard Stern to take his place in public appearances and when rock maverick Kim Fowley also tried to cast himself in the role.

| | | | | | | | |
|---|---|---|---|---|---|---|---|
| I'm In Love With My Little Red Tricycle | 7" | Warner Bros | WB5853 | 1966 | £2.50 | £6 | |
| They're Coming To Take Me Away | LP | Warner Bros | W(S)1661 | 1966 | £25 | £50 | *US* |
| They're Coming To Take Me Away | 7" EP | Warner Bros | WB108 | 1966 | £10 | £20 | *French* |
| They're Coming To Take Me Away Ha Ha | 7" | Warner Bros | WB5831 | 1966 | £1.50 | £4 | |

## NARNIA
| | | | | | | | |
|---|---|---|---|---|---|---|---|
| Narnia | LP | Myrrh | MYR1007 | 1974 | £50 | £100 | |

## NASCIMBENE, MARIO
| | | | | | | | |
|---|---|---|---|---|---|---|---|
| Solomon And Sheba | LP | United Artists | UASF5051 | 1965 | £20 | £40 | *French* |

## NASH, GENE
| | | | | | | | |
|---|---|---|---|---|---|---|---|
| Ja Ja Ja | 7" | Capitol | CL15042 | 1959 | £4 | £8 | |

## NASH, JOHNNY
| | | | | | | | |
|---|---|---|---|---|---|---|---|
| Glad You're My Baby | 7" | MGM | MGM1480 | 1969 | £2.50 | £6 | |
| I Got Rhythm | LP | HMV | CLP1325/CSD1288 | 1960 | £5 | £12 | |
| Johnny Nash | LP | HMV | CLP1251 | 1959 | £6 | £15 | |
| Johnny Nash And Kim Weston | LP | Major Minor | MMLP/SMLP54 | 1969 | £4 | £10 | |
| Ladder Of Love | 7" | HMV | POP402 | 1957 | £1.50 | £4 | |
| Love Ain't Nothing | 7" | Pye | 7N25250 | 1964 | £4 | £8 | |
| Presenting Johnny Nash | 7" EP | RCA | RCX7163 | 1964 | £15 | £30 | |
| Quiet Hour | LP | HMV | CLP1299 | 1959 | £6 | £15 | |
| Strange Feeling | 7" | Chess | CRS.8005 | 1965 | £2 | £5 | |

## NASHVILLE FIVE
| | | | | | | | |
|---|---|---|---|---|---|---|---|
| Like Nashville | 7" EP | Decca | DFE6706 | 1962 | £7.50 | £15 | |

## NASHVILLE TEENS
| | | | | | | | |
|---|---|---|---|---|---|---|---|
| All Along The Watchtower | 7" | Decca | F12754 | 1968 | £1.50 | £4 | |
| Biggest Night Of Her Life | 7" | Decca | F12657 | 1967 | £1.50 | £5 | |
| Ella James | 7" | Parlophone | R5925 | 1971 | £2 | £5 | |
| Find My Way Back Home | 7" EP | Decca | 457074 | 1965 | £30 | £60 | *French* |
| Find My Way Back Home | 7" | Decca | F12089 | 1965 | £1.50 | £4 | |
| Forbidden Fruit | 7" | Decca | F12458 | 1966 | £2 | £5 | |
| Google Eye | 7" | Decca | F12000 | 1964 | £1.50 | £4 | |
| Hard Way | 7" | Decca | F12316 | 1966 | £1.50 | £4 | |
| I'm Coming Home | 7" | Decca | F12580 | 1967 | £1.50 | £4 | |

| | | | | | | |
|---|---|---|---|---|---|---|
| Lament Of The Cherokee Reservation Indian | 7" | Major Minor | MM599 | 1969 £2 | £5 | |
| Nashville Teens | LP | New World | NW6002 | 1975 £10 | £25 | |
| Nashville Teens | 7" EP | Decca | DFE8600 | 1965 £15 | £30 | |
| Soon Forgotten | 7" | Decca | F12255 | 1965 £1.50 | £4 | |
| That's My Woman | 7" | Decca | F12542 | 1966 £2 | £5 | |
| This Little Bird | 7" | Decca | F12143 | 1965 £1.50 | £4 | |
| Tobacco Road | LP | London | LL3407/PS407 | 1964 £25 | £50 | US |
| Tobacco Road | 7" EP | Decca | 457047 | 1964 £20 | £40 | French |
| Tobacco Road | 7" | Decca | F11930 | 1964 £1.50 | £4 | |

## NATIONAL HEAD BAND
| | | | | | | |
|---|---|---|---|---|---|---|
| Albert One | LP | Warner Bros | K46094 | 1971 £4 | £10 | |

## NATIONAL PINION POLE
| | | | | | | |
|---|---|---|---|---|---|---|
| Make Your Mark Little Mark | 7" | Planet | PLF111 | 1966 £5 | £10 | |

## NATURAL ACOUSTIC BAND
| | | | | | | |
|---|---|---|---|---|---|---|
| Branching In | LP | RCA | SF8314 | 1972 £4 | £10 | |
| Learning To Live | LP | RCA | SF8272 | 1972 £4 | £10 | |

## NATURALS
| | | | | | | |
|---|---|---|---|---|---|---|
| Blue Roses | 7" | Parlophone | R5257 | 1965 £2 | £5 | |
| Daisy Chain | 7" | Parlophone | R5116 | 1964 £1.50 | £4 | |
| I Should Have Known Better | 7" | Parlophone | R5165 | 1964 £1.50 | £4 | |
| It Was You | 7" | Parlophone | R5202 | 1964 £1.50 | £4 | |

## NAURA, MICHAEL
| | | | | | | |
|---|---|---|---|---|---|---|
| Vanessa | LP | ECM | ECM1053ST | 1975 £5 | £12 | |

## NAVARRO, FATS
| | | | | | | |
|---|---|---|---|---|---|---|
| Memorial | 10" LP | London | LZC14015 | 1955 £25 | £50 | |
| Memorial Vol. 1 | LP | Realm | RM52192 | 1965 £4 | £10 | |
| Memorial Vol. 2 | LP | Realm | RM52208 | 1965 £4 | £10 | |
| Trumpet Giants | LP | Stateside | SL10103 | 1964 £4 | £10 | with tracks by Miles Davis & Dizzy Gillespie |

## NAYLOR, JERRY
| | | | | | | |
|---|---|---|---|---|---|---|
| Stop Your Crying | 7" | Top Rank | JAR591 | 1961 £4 | £8 | |

## NAYLOR, SHEL
The collectability of 'One Fine Day' derives not so much from Naylor's vocal performance, but rather from the fine Jimmy Page guitar solo, together with the fact that the song is a Dave Davies composition never recorded by the Kinks themselves. Naylor, whose real name was Robert Woodward, later achieved a number one hit as a member and prime mover of the novelty group Lieutenant Pigeon.

| | | | | | | |
|---|---|---|---|---|---|---|
| How Deep Is The Ocean | 7" | Decca | F11776 | 1963 £4 | £8 | |
| One Fine Day | 7" | Decca | F11856 | 1964 £50 | £100 | |

## NAZARETH
| | | | | | | |
|---|---|---|---|---|---|---|
| Bad Bad Boy | 7" | Mooncrest | MOON9 | 1973 £2 | £5 | picture sleeve |
| Dear John | 7" | Pegasus | PGS2 | 1972 £6 | £12 | |
| Exercises | LP | Pegasus | PEG14 | 1972 £4 | £10 | |
| If You See My Baby | 7" | Pegasus | PGS5 | 1972 £7.50 | £15 | |
| Morning Dew | 7" | Pegasus | PGS4 | 1972 £7.50 | £15 | |
| Nazareth | LP | Pegasus | PEG10 | 1971 £6 | £15 | |
| Nazareth EP | CD-s | Special Edition | CD317 | 1988 £2 | £5 | |
| Whatever You Want Babe | 7" | Mountain | NAZ4 | 1979 £2.50 | £6 | purple vinyl, picture sleeve |

## NAZZ
The Nazz were responsible for a classic psychedelic single, 'Open My Eyes' (included on the first album), that by some miraculous means entirely failed to become a hit. Leader of the group was Todd Rundgren, who has managed to maintain a successful solo career ever since.

| | | | | | | |
|---|---|---|---|---|---|---|
| Hello It's Me | 7" | Screen Gems | SGC219002 | 1969 £2 | £5 | |
| Nazz | LP | Screen Gems | SGC22001 | 1968 £20 | £40 | |
| Nazz 3 | LP | Screen Gems | SGC5004 | 1969 £20 | £40 | US |
| Nazz 3 | LP | Screen Gems | SGC5004 | 1969 £25 | £50 | US, green vinyl |
| Nazz Nazz | LP | Screen Gems | SGC5002 | 1969 £37.50 | £75 | US |
| Nazz Nazz | LP | Screen Gems | SGC5002 | 1969 £37.50 | £75 | US, red vinyl |
| Not Wrong Long | 7" | Screen Gems | SGC219003 | 1969 £2.50 | £6 | |
| Open My Eyes | 7" | Atlantic | 584224 | 1968 £20 | £40 | demo |
| Open My Eyes | 7" | Screen Gems | SGC219001 | 1968 £2.50 | £6 | |

## NAZZ (2)
Presumably to avoid confusion with Todd Rundgren's slightly more successful group, this Nazz subsequently changed its name to Alice Cooper.

| | | | | | | |
|---|---|---|---|---|---|---|
| Lay Down And Die, Goodbye | 7" | Very | 001 | 1967 £330 | £500 | US, best auctioned |

## NEAL, JOHNNY & THE STARLINERS
| | | | | | | |
|---|---|---|---|---|---|---|
| And I Will Love You | 7" | Pye | 7N15388 | 1961 £20 | £40 | |

## NEAL, TOMMY
| | | | | | | |
|---|---|---|---|---|---|---|
| Goin' To A Happening | 7" | Vocalion | VP9290 | 1968 £2.50 | £6 | |

## NEAT CHANGE
Guitarist with this group was Peter Banks, who became part of the first line-up of Yes.

| | | | | | | | |
|---|---|---|---|---|---|---|---|
| I Lied To Auntie May | 7" | Decca | F12809 | 1968 £5 | £10 | | |

## NECROMANDUS
| | | | | | | |
|---|---|---|---|---|---|---|
| Quicksand Dream | LP | Reflection | MM09 | 1990 £4 | £10 | |

## NECROMONICON
| | | | | | | |
|---|---|---|---|---|---|---|
| Tips Zum Selbstmord | LP | Best Prehodi | F60634 | 1972 £330 | £500 | German |

## NED & NELDA
This typically irreverent parody was the work of Frank Zappa and Ray Collins.

| | | | | | | |
|---|---|---|---|---|---|---|
| Hey Nelda | 7" | Vigah | 002 | 1963 £75 | £150 | US |

## NEE, BERNIE
| | | | | | | |
|---|---|---|---|---|---|---|
| Medal Of Honour | 7" | Philips | PB794 | 1958 £4 | £8 | |

## NEEFS, LOUIS
| | | | | | | |
|---|---|---|---|---|---|---|
| Jennifer Jennings | 7" | Columbia | DB8561 | 1969 £5 | £10 | |

## NEELY, ELGIN
| | | | | | | |
|---|---|---|---|---|---|---|
| Four Walls | 7" | Vogue | V9240 | 1965 £1.50 | £4 | |

## NEIGHB'RHOOD CHILDR'N
| | | | | | | |
|---|---|---|---|---|---|---|
| Neighb'rhood Childr'n | LP | Acta | 38005 | 1968 £37.50 | £75 | US |

## NEIL, FRED
| | | | | | | |
|---|---|---|---|---|---|---|
| Bleecker & MacDonald | LP | Elektra | EKL/EKS7293 | 1965 £8 | £20 | US |
| Candy Man | 7" | Elektra | EKSN45036 | 1968 £1.50 | £4 | US |
| Everybody's Talkin' | LP | Capitol | ST2665 | 1969 £6 | £15 | US |
| Everybody's Talkin' | 7" | Capitol | CL15616 | 1969 £1.50 | £4 | US |
| Hootenanny Live At The Bitter End | LP | FM | FM309 | 1964 £8 | £20 | US |
| Little Bit Of Rain | LP | Elektra | EKS74073 | 1970 £6 | £15 | US |
| Other Side Of This Life | LP | Capitol | ST657 | 1971 £4 | £10 | US |
| Sessions | LP | Capitol | ST2862 | 1971 £4 | £10 | US |
| Tear Down The Walls | LP | Elektra | EKL/EKS7248 | 1964 £8 | £20 | US |
| World Of Folk Music | LP | FM | FM319 | 1964 £8 | £20 | US |

## NEIL & JACK
Neil Diamond began his recording career here.

| | | | | | | |
|---|---|---|---|---|---|---|
| I'm Afraid | 7" | Duel | 517 | 1961 £75 | £150 | US |
| You Are My Love At Last | 7" | Duel | 508 | 1960 £75 | £150 | US |

## NEKROPOLIS
| | | | | | | |
|---|---|---|---|---|---|---|
| Suite Til Sommeren | LP | private | | 1976 £75 | £150 | |

## NEKTAR
| | | | | | | |
|---|---|---|---|---|---|---|
| Down To Earth | LP | United Artists | UAG29680 | 1974 £4 | £10 | |
| Journey To The Centre Of The Eye | LP | Bellaphon | BLPS19064 | 1972 £4 | £10 | German |
| Live At The Roundhouse | LP | Bellaphon | BLPS19182 | 1974 £4 | £10 | German |
| Nektar | LP | Bellaphon | BLPS19224 | 1976 £4 | £10 | German |
| Remember The Future | LP | United Artists | UAS29545 | 1973 £4 | £10 | |
| Sounds Like This | LP | United Artists | UAD60041/2 | 1973 £5 | £12 | double |
| Tab In The Ocean | LP | United Artists | UAS29499 | 1972 £4 | £10 | |

## NELSON, BILL
| | | | | | | |
|---|---|---|---|---|---|---|
| Northern Dream | LP | Smile | LAF2182 | 1971 £10 | £25 | with booklet |

## NELSON, DAVID
| | | | | | | |
|---|---|---|---|---|---|---|
| Somebody Loves Me | 7" | Philips | BF1321 | 1964 £2 | £5 | |

## NELSON, EARL
| | | | | | | |
|---|---|---|---|---|---|---|
| No Time To Cry | 7" | London | HLW8950 | 1959 £2.50 | £6 | |

## NELSON, OLIVER
| | | | | | | |
|---|---|---|---|---|---|---|
| Blues And The Abstract Truth | LP | HMV | CLP1528 | 1961 £8 | £20 | |
| Live From Los Angeles | LP | Impulse | MIPL/SIPL510 | 1968 £5 | £12 | |
| More Blues And The Abstract Truth | LP | HMV | CLP1868/CSD1604 | 1965 £6 | £15 | |

## NELSON, OZZIE & HARRIET
| | | | | | | |
|---|---|---|---|---|---|---|
| Ozzie And Harriet Nelson | LP | London | HAP2145 | 1959 £8 | £20 | |

## NELSON, RICK
| | | | | | | |
|---|---|---|---|---|---|---|
| Album Seven | LP | London | HAP2445 | 1962 £10 | £25 | mono |
| Album Seven | LP | London | SAHP6236 | 1962 £15 | £30 | stereo |
| Another Side Of Rick | LP | MCA | MUP(S)302 | 1968 £4 | £10 | |
| Be Bop Baby | 7" | London | HLP8499 | 1957 £10 | £20 | |
| Believe What You Say | 7" | London | HLP8594 | 1958 £6 | £12 | |
| Best Always | LP | Brunswick | LAT/STA8615 | 1965 £8 | £20 | |
| Bright Lights,Country Music | LP | Brunswick | LAT/STA8657 | 1966 £8 | £20 | |
| Come Out Dancin' | 7" | Brunswick | 05939 | 1965 £2 | £5 | |
| Country Fever | LP | Brunswick | LAT/STA8680 | 1967 £10 | £25 | |
| Everlovin' | 7" | London | HLP9440 | 1961 £1.50 | £4 | |

| Title | Format | Label | Cat. No. | Year | Price | Price | Notes |
|---|---|---|---|---|---|---|---|
| Fools Rush In | 7" | Brunswick | 05895 | 1963 | £1.50 | £4 | |
| For You | 7" | Brunswick | 05900 | 1964 | £1.50 | £4 | |
| For Your Sweet Love | LP | Brunswick | LAT8545 | 1963 | £8 | £20 | mono |
| For Your Sweet Love | LP | Brunswick | STA8545 | 1963 | £10 | £25 | stereo |
| Happy Guy | 7" EP | Brunswick | OE9512 | 1965 | £7.50 | £15 | |
| Happy Guy | 7" | Brunswick | 05924 | 1964 | £1.50 | £4 | |
| Hello Mary Lou | 7" | London | HLP9347 | 1961 | £1.50 | £4 | |
| I Got A Feeling | 7" EP | London | REP1238 | 1960 | £10 | £20 | |
| I Got A Woman | 7" | Brunswick | 05885 | 1963 | £1.50 | £4 | |
| I Wanna Be Loved | 7" | London | HLP9021 | 1960 | £1.50 | £4 | |
| I'm In Love Again | 7" EP | Liberty | LEP4028 | 1965 | £12.50 | £25 | |
| I'm Walking | 7" | HMV | POP355 | 1957 | £50 | £100 | gold label |
| In Concert | LP | MCA | MUPS409 | 1970 | £4 | £10 | |
| It's A Young World | 7" EP | London | REP1339 | 1962 | £7.50 | £15 | |
| It's Up To You | LP | London | HAP8066 | 1963 | £10 | £25 | |
| It's Up To You | 7" EP | London | REP1362 | 1963 | £7.50 | £15 | |
| It's Up To You | 7" | London | HLP9648 | 1963 | £1.50 | £4 | |
| Just A Little Too Much | 7" | London | HLP8927 | 1959 | £1.50 | £4 | |
| Lonely Corner | 7" | Brunswick | 05918 | 1964 | £1.50 | £4 | |
| Long Vacation | LP | Imperial | LP9244/12244 | 1963 | £10 | £25 | US |
| Love And Kisses | LP | Brunswick | LAT/STA8630 | 1965 | £8 | £20 | |
| Milkcow Blues | 7" | London | HLP9260 | 1961 | £2.50 | £6 | |
| Million Sellers | LP | Liberty | LBY3027 | 1963 | £6 | £15 | |
| More Songs By Ricky | LP | Imperial | LP12059 | 1960 | £75 | £150 | US, blue vinyl |
| More Songs By Ricky | LP | London | HAP2290 | 1960 | £10 | £25 | mono |
| More Songs By Ricky | LP | London | SAHP6102 | 1960 | £15 | £30 | stereo |
| My Babe | 7" | London | HLP8738 | 1958 | £2.50 | £6 | |
| Never Be Anyone Else But You | 7" | London | HLP8817 | 1959 | £2 | £5 | |
| On The Flip Side | LP | Decca | DL(7)4836 | 1967 | £8 | £20 | US, with Joanie Sommers |
| One Boy Too Late | 7" EP | Brunswick | OE9502 | 1963 | £7.50 | £15 | |
| Perspective | LP | Decca | DL75014 | 1968 | £6 | £15 | US |
| Poor Little Fool | 7" | London | HLP8670 | 1958 | £2 | £5 | |
| Rick Is 21 | LP | London | HAP2379 | 1961 | £10 | £25 | mono |
| Rick Is 21 | LP | London | SAHP6179 | 1961 | £15 | £30 | stereo |
| Rick Nelson Country | LP | MCA | 24004 | 1973 | £4 | £10 | US |
| Ricky | LP | London | HAP2080 | 1957 | £20 | £40 | |
| Ricky Nelson | LP | London | HAP2119 | 1958 | £15 | £30 | |
| Ricky Nelson No. 1 | 7" EP | London | REP1168 | 1959 | £10 | £20 | |
| Ricky Nelson No. 2 | 7" EP | London | REP1169 | 1959 | £10 | £20 | |
| Ricky Nelson No. 3 | 7" EP | London | REP1170 | 1959 | £10 | £20 | |
| Ricky Nelson No. 4 | 7" EP | London | REP1300 | 1961 | £12.50 | £25 | |
| Ricky No. 1 | 7" EP | London | REP1141 | 1958 | £10 | £20 | |
| Ricky No. 2 | 7" EP | London | REP1142 | 1958 | £10 | £20 | |
| Ricky No. 3 | 7" EP | London | REP1143 | 1958 | £10 | £20 | |
| Ricky No. 4 | 7" EP | London | REP1144 | 1958 | £10 | £20 | |
| Ricky Sings Again | LP | London | HAP2159 | 1959 | £15 | £30 | |
| Ricky Sings Again Pt. 1 | 7" EP | London | REP1200 | 1959 | £10 | £20 | |
| Ricky Sings Again Pt. 2 | 7" EP | London | REP1201 | 1959 | £10 | £20 | |
| Ricky Sings Spirituals | 7" EP | London | REP1249 | 1960 | £7.50 | £15 | |
| Sings For You | LP | Brunswick | LAT8562 | 1964 | £8 | £20 | mono |
| Sings For You | LP | Brunswick | STA8562 | 1964 | £10 | £25 | stereo |
| Sings For You | 7" EP | Liberty | LEP4001 | 1964 | £7.50 | £15 | |
| Someday | 7" | London | HLP8732 | 1958 | £1.50 | £4 | |
| Songs By Ricky | LP | London | HAP2206 | 1959 | £15 | £30 | |
| Spotlight On Rick | LP | Brunswick | LAT/STA8596 | 1964 | £8 | £20 | |
| Stood Up | 7" | London | HLP8542 | 1958 | £6 | £12 | |
| String Along | 7" | Brunswick | 05889 | 1963 | £1.50 | £4 | |
| Teen Time | LP | Verve | V2083 | 1957 | £75 | £150 | US |
| Teenage Idol | 7" | London | HLP9583 | 1962 | £1.50 | £4 | |
| That's All | 7" EP | Liberty | LEP4019 | 1964 | £12.50 | £25 | |
| Today's Teardrops | 7" | Liberty | LIB66004 | 1964 | £2 | £5 | |
| Very Thought Of You | LP | Brunswick | LAT/STA8581 | 1964 | £8 | £20 | |
| Very Thought Of You | 7" | Brunswick | 05908 | 1964 | £1.50 | £4 | |
| Yes Sir That's My Baby | 7" | London | HLP9188 | 1960 | £1.50 | £4 | |
| You Are My One And Only Love | 7" | HMV | POP390 | 1957 | £30 | £60 | Barney Kessel B side |
| You Can't Just Quit | 7" | Brunswick | 05964 | 1966 | £2.50 | £6 | |
| Young Emotions | 7" | London | HLP9121 | 1960 | £1.50 | £4 | |
| Young World | 7" | London | HLP9524 | 1962 | £1.50 | £4 | |

## NELSON, SANDY

| Title | Format | Label | Cat. No. | Year | Price | Price | Notes |
|---|---|---|---|---|---|---|---|
| And Then There Were Drums | 7" | London | HLP9612 | 1962 | £1.50 | £4 | |
| Bouncy | 7" | London | HLP9214 | 1960 | £1.50 | £4 | |
| Compelling Percussion | LP | London | HAP/SHP8029 | 1963 | £4 | £10 | |
| Drum Party | 7" | London | HLP9015 | 1959 | £2 | £5 | |
| Drummin' Up A Storm | LP | London | HAP/SHP8009 | 1962 | £6 | £15 | |
| Drummin' Up A Storm | 7" | London | HLP9558 | 1962 | £1.50 | £4 | |
| Drums A Go-go | LP | Liberty | LBY3061 | 1965 | £4 | £10 | |
| Get With It | 7" | London | HLP9377 | 1961 | £1.50 | £4 | |
| In The Mood | 7" EP | London | REP1371 | 1963 | £5 | £10 | |
| Let There Be Drums | LP | London | HAP2425/ SAHP6221 | 1961 | £6 | £15 | |
| Let There Be Drums | 7" EP | London | REP1337 | 1962 | £5 | £10 | |
| Live In Las Vegas | LP | Liberty | LBY3035 | 1965 | £4 | £10 | |
| Ooh Poo Pah Doo | 7" | London | HLP9717 | 1963 | £1.50 | £4 | |
| Rushing For Percussion | 7" EP | Top Rank | JKP2060 | 1960 | £7.50 | £15 | 2 tracks by Preston Epps |
| Sandy Nelson Plays | LP | Liberty | LBY3007 | 1964 | £4 | £10 | |

| | | | | | | | | |
|---|---|---|---|---|---|---|---|---|
| Sandy Nelson Plays | 7" EP | Liberty | LEP4033 | 1965 | £4 | £8 | |
| Superdrums | LP | Liberty | (S)LBY3080 | 1967 | £4 | £10 | |
| Teen Beat | LP | London | HAP2260/ SAHP6082 | 1960 | £6 | £15 | |
| Teen Beat | 7" | Top Rank | JAR197 | 1959 | £1.50 | £4 | |
| Teenage House Party | LP | London | HAP/SHP8051 | 1963 | £6 | £15 | |

## NELSON, TERRY

| | | | | | | | |
|---|---|---|---|---|---|---|---|
| Bulldog Push | 7" | Dice | CC25 | 1964 | £5 | £10 | |
| Love On Saturday Night | 7" | Dice | CC22 | 1963 | £5 | £10 | |
| My Blue Eyed Baby | 7" | Dice | CC27 | 1964 | £5 | £10 | |
| Run Baby Run | 7" | Dice | CC23 | 1963 | £5 | £10 | |

## NELSON, WILLIE

| | | | | | | | |
|---|---|---|---|---|---|---|---|
| And Then I Wrote | LP | Liberty | (S)LBY1240 | 1966 | £4 | £10 | |
| And Then I Wrote | LP | Liberty | LRP3238/LST7238 | 1962 | £6 | £15 | US |
| Country Willie | LP | RCA | RD7749 | 1965 | £4 | £10 | |
| Half A Man | 7" | Liberty | LIB55532 | 1963 | £1.50 | £4 | |
| Here's Willie Nelson | LP | Liberty | LRP3308/LST7308 | 1963 | £6 | £15 | US |
| River Boy | 7" | Liberty | LIB55697 | 1964 | £1.50 | £4 | |
| Texas In My Soul | LP | RCA | RD7997 | 1969 | £4 | £10 | |

## NELSON TRIO

| | | | | | | | |
|---|---|---|---|---|---|---|---|
| All In Good Time | 7" | London | HLL9019 | 1960 | £1.50 | £4 | |
| Tear It Up | 7" | Oriole | CB1360 | 1957 | £1.50 | £4 | |

## NENA

| | | | | | | | |
|---|---|---|---|---|---|---|---|
| It's All In The Game | LP | Sony | 303P686 | 1985 | £37.50 | £75 | ...Japanese picture disc |

## NEO MAYA

| | | | | | | | |
|---|---|---|---|---|---|---|---|
| I Won't Hurt You | 7" | Pye | 7N17371 | 1967 | £15 | £30 | |

## NEOGY, CHIITRA

| | | | | | | | |
|---|---|---|---|---|---|---|---|
| Perfumed Garden | LP | Gemini | GMX5030 | 1970 | £4 | £10 | |
| Perfumed Garden | LP | Morgan | M1003L | 1968 | £6 | £15 | |

## NEON HEARTS

| | | | | | | | |
|---|---|---|---|---|---|---|---|
| Regulations | 7" | Neon Hearts | NEON1 | 1977 | £2 | £5 | |

## NEON ROSE

| | | | | | | | |
|---|---|---|---|---|---|---|---|
| Dream Of Glory And Pride | LP | Vertigo | 6316250 | 1974 | £8 | £20 | Swedish |
| Reload | LP | Vertigo | 6316252 | 1975 | £8 | £20 | Swedish |
| Two | LP | Vertigo | 6316251 | 1974 | £8 | £20 | Swedish |

## NEP-TUNES

| | | | | | | | |
|---|---|---|---|---|---|---|---|
| Surfer's Holiday | LP | Family | (S)FLP552 | 1963 | £6 | £15 | US |

## NEPTUNE'S EMPIRE

| | | | | | | | |
|---|---|---|---|---|---|---|---|
| Neptune's Empire | LP | Polymax | PXX01 | 1971 | £37.50 | £75 | |

## NERO & THE GLADIATORS

| | | | | | | | |
|---|---|---|---|---|---|---|---|
| Czardas | 7" | Decca | F11413 | 1961 | £2.50 | £6 | |
| Entry Of The Gladiators | 7" | Decca | F11329 | 1961 | £2.50 | £6 | |
| In The Hall Of The Mountain King | 7" | Decca | F11367 | 1961 | £2.50 | £6 | |

## NERVE

| | | | | | | | |
|---|---|---|---|---|---|---|---|
| It Is | 7" | Page One | POF081 | 1968 | £4 | £8 | |
| Magic Spectacles | 7" | Page One | POF055 | 1968 | £4 | £8 | |
| Piece By Piece | 7" | Page One | POF097 | 1968 | £2 | £5 | |
| Ten Downing Street | 7" | Page One | POF019 | 1967 | £1.50 | £4 | |

## NERVOUS NORVUS

| | | | | | | | |
|---|---|---|---|---|---|---|---|
| Ape Call | 7" | London | HLD8338 | 1956 | £30 | £60 | gold label |
| Bullfrog Hop | 7" | London | HLD8383 | 1957 | £37.50 | £75 | gold label |
| Does A Chinese Chicken Have A Pigtail | 7" | Salvo | SLO1812 | 1962 | £7.50 | £15 | Rod Barton B side |

## NESMITH, MICHAEL

| | | | | | | | |
|---|---|---|---|---|---|---|---|
| And The First National Band | 7" EP | Island | IEP4 | 1976 | £2 | £5 | |
| And The Hits Just Keep On Coming | LP | RCA | LSP4695 | 1972 | £4 | £10 | US |
| Just A Little Love | 7" | Edan | 1001 | 197- | £25 | £50 | US |
| Loose Salute | LP | RCA | LSP4415 | 1970 | £4 | £10 | US |
| Magnetic South | LP | RCA | SF8136 | 1970 | £4 | £10 | |
| Mike Nesmith Radio Special | LP | Pacific Arts | PAC71300 | 1976 | £6 | £15 | US promo |
| Nevada Fighter | LP | RCA | SF8209 | 1971 | £4 | £10 | |
| Pretty Much Your Standard Ranch Stash | LP | RCA | APL10164 | 1973 | £4 | £10 | US |
| Prison | LP | Pacific Arts | PAC7101 | 1975 | £6 | £15 | US, boxed with booklet |
| Tantamount To Treason | LP | RCA | SF8276 | 1972 | £4 | £10 | |
| Wichita Train Whistle Sings | LP | Dot | (S)LDP516 | 1968 | £8 | £20 | |

## NEU

The increasingly collectable work of the German electronic group Neu is closely related to that of Kraftwerk. Klaus Dinger and Thomas Homann were members of the parent group on the first album, *Kraftwerk 1*, before deciding that they could achieve more on their own.

| | | | | | | | |
|---|---|---|---|---|---|---|---|
| Neu | LP | United Artists | UAS29396 | 1972 | £15 | £30 | |
| Neu 2 | LP | United Artists | UAS29500 | 1973 | £10 | £25 | |
| Neu '75 | LP | United Artists | UAS29782 | 1975 | £10 | £25 | |

## NEURONIUM

| | | | | | | | |
|---|---|---|---|---|---|---|---|
| Quasar 2C361 | LP | Harvest | 21442 | 1977 | £4 | £10 | Spanish |
| Vuelo Quinico | LP | Harvest | 21523 | 1978 | £4 | £10 | Spanish |

## NEVILLE, AARON

| | | | | | | | |
|---|---|---|---|---|---|---|---|
| Here 'Tis | LP | Liberty | LBY3089 | 1967 | £6 | £15 | |
| Tell It Like It Is | LP | Par-Lo | LP1 | 1967 | £8 | £20 | US |
| Tell It Like It Is | 7" | B&C | CB107 | 1969 | £1.50 | £4 | |
| Tell It Like It Is | 7" | Stateside | SS584 | 1967 | £4 | £8 | |

## NEW AGE STEPPERS

| | | | | | | | |
|---|---|---|---|---|---|---|---|
| Fade Away | 7" | ONU Sound | ONU1 | 1980 | £1.50 | £4 | B side by The London Underground |

## NEW BREED

| | | | | | | | |
|---|---|---|---|---|---|---|---|
| Friends And Lovers Forever | 7" | Decca | F12295 | 1965 | £7.50 | £15 | |

## NEW CHRISTY MINSTRELS

| | | | | | | | |
|---|---|---|---|---|---|---|---|
| Green Green | 7" | CBS | AAG160 | 1963 | £1.50 | £4 | |
| Three Wheels On My Wagon | 7" EP | CBS | EP6057 | 1965 | £2 | £5 | |
| Three Wheels On My Wagon | 7" | CBS | 201328 | 1965 | £1.50 | £4 | |

## NEW COLONY SIX

| | | | | | | | |
|---|---|---|---|---|---|---|---|
| At The River's Edge | 7" | Stateside | SS522 | 1966 | £25 | £50 | |
| Attacking A Strawman | LP | Mercury | SR61228 | 1970 | £6 | £15 | US |
| Breakthrough | LP | Sentar | LP101 | 1966 | £150 | £250 | US |
| Colonization | LP | Sentar | (S)ST3001 | 1967 | £25 | £50 | US |
| I Confess | 7" | London | HLZ10033 | 1966 | £12.50 | £25 | |
| I Will Always | 7" | Mercury | MF1030 | 1968 | £1.50 | £4 | |
| Revelations | LP | Mercury | SR61165 | 1969 | £4 | £10 | US |
| Things I'd Like To Say | 7" | Mercury | MF1086 | 1969 | £1.50 | £4 | |

## NEW DAWN

| | | | | | | | |
|---|---|---|---|---|---|---|---|
| There's A New Dawn | LP | Hoot/Garland | 704569 | 1970 | £250 | £400 | US |

## NEW DEAL STRING BAND

| | | | | | | | |
|---|---|---|---|---|---|---|---|
| New Deal String Band | LP | Argo | ZDA104 | 1969 | £6 | £15 | |

## NEW DIMENSIONS

| | | | | | | | |
|---|---|---|---|---|---|---|---|
| Deuces And Eights | LP | Sutton | (SSU)331 | 1963 | £5 | £12 | US |
| Soul Surf | LP | Sutton | (SSU)336 | 1964 | £5 | £12 | US |
| Surf 'n' Bongos | LP | Sutton | (SSU)332 | 1963 | £5 | £12 | US |

## NEW FORMULA

| | | | | | | | |
|---|---|---|---|---|---|---|---|
| My Baby's Coming Home | 7" | Pye | 7N17552 | 1968 | £1.50 | £4 | |
| Stay Indoors | 7" | Pye | 7N17818 | 1969 | £7.50 | £15 | |

## NEW GENERATION

This was the first version of the Sutherland Brothers, who made several records in the seventies, both on their own and with the group Quiver. Gavin Sutherland had the good fortune to see one of his songs turned into a major hit by Rod Stewart – 'Sailing'.

| | | | | | | | |
|---|---|---|---|---|---|---|---|
| Police Is Here | 7" | Spark | SRL1019 | 1970 | £1.50 | £4 | |
| Sadie And Her Magic Mr. Garland | 7" | Spark | SRL1000 | 1969 | £1.50 | £4 | |
| Smokey Blues Away | 7" | Spark | SRL1007 | 1969 | £2 | £5 | |

## NEW HEAVENLY BLUE

| | | | | | | | |
|---|---|---|---|---|---|---|---|
| Educated Homegrown | LP | RCA | SF8189 | 1971 | £4 | £10 | |
| New Heavenly Blue | LP | Atlantic | SD7247 | 1972 | £5 | £12 | US |

## NEW JAZZ ORCHESTRA

The LPs credited to the New Jazz Orchestra are listed under the name of the orchestra's leader, Neil Ardley.

## NEW LORDS

| | | | | | | | |
|---|---|---|---|---|---|---|---|
| New Lords | LP | Columbia | 1C06229429 | 1971 | £4 | £10 | German |

## NEW MODEL

| | | | | | | | |
|---|---|---|---|---|---|---|---|
| Chilean Warning | 7" | Mr. Clean | MRC1 | 1983 | £2 | £5 | in folder |

## NEW MODEL ARMY

| | | | | | | | |
|---|---|---|---|---|---|---|---|
| Aries Enterprises | cass | private | | 1981 | £8 | £20 | with other artists |
| Better Than Them | 7" | EMI | NMAD2 | 1985 | £2 | £5 | double |
| Better Than Them | 12" | EMI | 12NMA2 | 1985 | £3 | £8 | |
| Bittersweet | 7" | Quiet! | QS002 | 1983 | £5 | £10 | with flexi |
| Brave New World | 12" | EMI | 12NMAD3 | 1985 | £4 | £10 | double |
| Fifty-First State | 12" | EMI | 12NMAD4 | 1986 | £4 | £10 | double |
| Great Expectations | 7" | Abstract | ABS0020 | 1983 | £7.50 | £15 | |
| Green And Grey | CD-s | EMI | CDNMA9 | 1989 | £2 | £5 | |
| Never Mind The Jacksons, Here's The Pollocks | 12" | Abstract | 12ABS030 | 1985 | £2.50 | £6 | with tracks by other artists |
| No Rest | 12" | EMI | 12NMAD1 | 1985 | £4 | £10 | double |
| Poison Street | 7" | EMI | NMA5 | 1987 | £7.50 | £15 | red vinyl |
| Poison Street | 12" | EMI | 12NMAD5 | 1987 | £4 | £10 | double |
| Price | 7" | Abstract | ABS0028 | 1984 | £2.50 | £6 | |
| White Coats | 7" | EMI | NMA6 | 1987 | £5 | £10 | red vinyl |

## NEW ORDER

| | | | | | | | |
|---|---|---|---|---|---|---|---|
| Best Of New Order | CD and cass | London | 8285802 | 1995 | £20 | £40 | promo boxed set |
| Blue Monday | CD- s | Factory | FACDV73R | 1988 | £6 | £12 | CD video |
| Brotherhood | CD | Factory | FACD150SP | 1987 | £6 | £15 | metallic box |
| Brotherhood | CD | Factory | FACD150SP | 1987 | £5 | £12 | with 'State Of The Nation' |
| Gatefold Substance | LP | Factory | FACT200S | 1987 | £8 | £20 | numbered gatefold sleeve |
| Hacienda Christmas Flexi | 7" | Factory | FAC51B | 1982 | £2.50 | £6 | flexi |
| Peel Sessions | CD-s | Strange Fruit | SFPSCD001 | 1988 | £2 | £5 | |
| Peel Sessions II | CD-s | Strange Fruit | SFPSCD039 | 1988 | £2 | £5 | |
| Power, Corruption And Lies | LP | Factory | | 1983 | £37.50 | £75 | German, multi-coloured vinyl |
| Round And Round | CD-s | Factory | FACD263R | 1989 | £2 | £5 | 3" single |
| Round And Round (Ben Grosse remix) | 12" | Factory | FAC263DJ | 1989 | £2.50 | £6 | promo |
| Run 2 | 12" | Factory | FAC273 | 1989 | £3 | £8 | |
| Substance | cass | Factory | FACT200C | 1987 | £6 | £15 | box set |
| Touched By The Hand Of God | CD-s | Factory | FACD193 | 1989 | £6 | £15 | gatefold card sleeve |
| True Faith | CD-s | Factory | FACDV183 | 1989 | £4 | £10 | CD video |

## NEW ORDER (2)

| | | | | | | | |
|---|---|---|---|---|---|---|---|
| Bradford Red Light District | LP | Come | CARA12 | 1981 | £6 | £15 | |

## NEW ORDER (3)

| | | | | | | | |
|---|---|---|---|---|---|---|---|
| You've Got Me High | 7" EP | Warner Bros | WB113 | 1966 | £6 | £12 | French |

## NEW ORLEANS ALL STAR JAZZ BAND

| | | | | | | | |
|---|---|---|---|---|---|---|---|
| New Orleans All Star Jazz Band | LP | Vogue | LAE12013 | 1956 | £5 | £12 | |

## NEW ORLEANS BOOTBLACKS

| | | | | | | | |
|---|---|---|---|---|---|---|---|
| Flat Foot | 7" | Columbia | SCM5090 | 1954 | £1.50 | £4 | |

## NEW ORLEANS RHYTHM KINGS

| | | | | | | | |
|---|---|---|---|---|---|---|---|
| New Orleans Rhythm Kings | 10" LP | London | AL3552 | 1956 | £6 | £15 | |

## NEW TROLLS

| | | | | | | | |
|---|---|---|---|---|---|---|---|
| Concerto Grosso | LP | Fonit Cetra | LPX8 | 1972 | £4 | £10 | Italian |
| Searching For A Land | LP | Fonit Cetra | DPU70 | 1973 | £5 | £12 | Italian double |
| Senza Oravio Senza Bandiera | LP | Fonit Cetra | LPX3 | 1971 | £4 | £10 | Italian |
| Ut | LP | Fonit Cetra | LPX20 | 1972 | £4 | £10 | Italian |

## NEW TWEEDY BROTHERS

| | | | | | | | |
|---|---|---|---|---|---|---|---|
| New Tweedy Brothers | LP | private | | 1992 | £6 | £15 | US |
| New Tweedy Brothers | LP | Ridon | 234 | 1966 | £700 | £1000 | US |

## NEW VAUDEVILLE BAND

| | | | | | | | |
|---|---|---|---|---|---|---|---|
| Finchley Central | LP | Fontana | (S)TL5430 | 1967 | £4 | £10 | |
| Finchley Central | 7" EP | Fontana | 465381 | 1967 | £2.50 | £6 | French |
| New Vaudeville Band | 7" EP | Fontana | TFE17497 | 1968 | £2 | £5 | |
| Peek-A-Boo | 7" EP | Fontana | 465362 | 1966 | £2.50 | £6 | French |
| Winchester Cathedral | LP | Fontana | 886408TY | 1966 | £4 | £10 | |
| Winchester Cathedral | 7" EP | Fontana | 465342 | 1966 | £2.50 | £6 | French |

## NEW VICTORY BAND

| | | | | | | | |
|---|---|---|---|---|---|---|---|
| One More Dance And Then | LP | Topic | 12TS382 | 1978 | £5 | £12 | |

## NEW YORK ART QUARTET

| | | | | | | | |
|---|---|---|---|---|---|---|---|
| Mohawk | LP | Fontana | 681009ZL | 1967 | £8 | £20 | |
| New York Art Quartet | LP | ESP-Disk | 1004 | 1965 | £10 | £25 | US |

## NEW YORK BLONDES

The 'Madam X' featured on the New York Blondes' single is Debbie Harry, who was highly annoyed at the record's release. She had in fact recorded her vocal part purely as a demo for US DJ Rodney Bigenheimer to follow when making his own record (and the single's B side is indeed by him).

| | | | | | | | |
|---|---|---|---|---|---|---|---|
| Little GTO | 7" | London | HL10574 | 1979 | £2 | £5 | picture sleeve |

## NEW YORK DOLLS

| | | | | | | | |
|---|---|---|---|---|---|---|---|
| Jet Boy | 7" | Mercury | 6052402 | 1973 | £1.50 | £4 | |
| New York Dolls | LP | Mercury | 6338270 | 1973 | £4 | £10 | |
| New York Dolls | CD-s | Counterpoint | CDEP14C | 1988 | £2 | £5 | |
| Personality Crisis | CD-s | See For Miles | SEACD3 | 1990 | £2 | £5 | |
| Stranded In The Jungle | 7" | Mercury | 6052615 | 1974 | £1.50 | £4 | |
| Too Much Too Soon | LP | Mercury | 6338498 | 1974 | £4 | £10 | |

## NEW YORK PUBLIC LIBRARY

| | | | | | | | |
|---|---|---|---|---|---|---|---|
| Got To Get Away | 7" | MCA | MU1025 | 1968 | £2 | £5 | |
| I Ain't Gonna Eat Out My Heart Anymore | 7" | Columbia | DB7948 | 1966 | £7.50 | £15 | |
| Love Me Two Times | 7" | MCA | MU1045 | 1968 | £2 | £5 | |

## NEW YORK ROCK & ROLL ENSEMBLE

| | | | | | | | |
|---|---|---|---|---|---|---|---|
| Faithful Friends | LP | Atco | 228032 | 1969 | £4 | £10 | |
| New York Rock & Roll Ensemble | LP | Atco | 33240 | 1968 | £5 | £12 | US |
| Reflections | LP | Atco | 33312 | 1970 | £4 | £10 | US |

## NEWBEATS

| | | | | | | | | |
|---|---|---|---|---|---|---|---|---|
| Ain't That Lovin' You Baby | 7" EP | Hickory | LPE1506 | 1965 | £4 | £8 | |
| Big Beat Sounds | LP | Hickory | LP(S)122 | 1965 | £6 | £15 | US |
| Birds Are For The Bees | 7" EP | CBS | 6095 | 1965 | £5 | £10 | French |
| Bread And Butter | LP | Hickory | LPM120 | 1965 | £6 | £15 | |
| Bread And Butter | 7" EP | CBS | 5916 | 1964 | £5 | £10 | French |
| Bread And Butter | 7" | Hickory | 451269 | 1964 | £1.50 | £4 | |
| Crying My Heart Out | 7" | Hickory | 451387 | 1965 | £5 | £10 | |
| My Yesterday Love | 7" | Hickory | 451422 | 1965 | £1.50 | £4 | |
| Newbeats | 7" EP | Hickory | LPE1503 | 1964 | £4 | £8 | |
| Oh Girls Girls | 7" EP | Hickory | LPE1510 | 1966 | £5 | £10 | |
| Run Baby Run | LP | Hickory | LP(S)128 | 1965 | £6 | £15 | US |
| Run Baby Run | 7" EP | CBS | 6209 | 1965 | £5 | £10 | French |
| Run Baby Run | 7" | Hickory | 451332 | 1965 | £1.50 | £4 | |
| Too Sweet To Be Forgotten | 7" | Hickory | 451366 | 1965 | £2.50 | £6 | |

## NEWBORN, PHINEAS

| | | | | | | |
|---|---|---|---|---|---|---|
| Phineas Newborn | LP | London | LTZK15057 | 1957 | £8 | £20 |

## NEWCASTLE BIG BAND

The Newcastle Big Band was a semi-professional sixteen-piece jazz band whose privately produced LP would mean little to anyone who had not actually seen the band live, were it not for the fact that the bass player just happened to go by the name of Sting.

| | | | | | | |
|---|---|---|---|---|---|---|
| Newcastle Big Band | LP | Impulse | ISSNBB106 | 1972 | £180 | £300 |

## NEWLEY, ANTHONY

| | | | | | | |
|---|---|---|---|---|---|---|
| Can Heironymus Merkin Ever Forget Mercy Humppe | LP | MCA | MUPS380 | 1969 | £4 | £10 |
| I've Waited So Long | 7" | Decca | F11127 | 1959 | £1.50 | £4 |
| Idle On Parade | 7" EP | Decca | DFE6566 | 1959 | £4 | £8 |
| Idle On Parade | 7" | Decca | F11137 | 1959 | £2 | £5 |
| In My Solitude | LP | Decca | LK4600 | 1964 | £4 | £10 |
| Love Is A Now And Then Thing | LP | Decca | LK4343 | 1960 | £4 | £10 |
| More Hits From Tony | 7" EP | Decca | DFE6655 | 1960 | £2 | £5 |
| Newley Delivered | LP | Decca | LK4654 | 1965 | £4 | £10 |
| Newley Recorded | LP | RCA | RD/SF7837 | 1967 | £4 | £10 |
| Personality | 7" | Decca | F11142 | 1959 | £1.50 | £4 |
| Stop The World – I Want To Get Off | LP | Decca | LK4408 | 1961 | £4 | £10 |
| This Time The Dream's On Me | 7" EP | Decca | DFE6687 | 1961 | £2 | £5 |
| Tony | LP | Decca | LK4406 | 1961 | £4 | £10 |
| Tony's Hits | 7" EP | Decca | DFE6629 | 1960 | £2 | £5 |
| Who Can I Turn To | LP | RCA | RD/SF7737 | 1966 | £4 | £10 |

## NEWLEY, ANTHONY, PETER SELLERS & JOAN COLLINS

| | | | | | | |
|---|---|---|---|---|---|---|
| Fool Brittania | 7" EP | Ember | EMBEP4530 | 1963 | £2 | £5 |

## NEWMAN, ANDY

| | | | | | | |
|---|---|---|---|---|---|---|
| Rainbow | LP | Track | 2406103 | 1971 | £4 | £10 |

## NEWMAN, BRAD

| | | | | | | |
|---|---|---|---|---|---|---|
| Somebody To Love | 7" | Fontana | H357 | 1962 | £1.50 | £4 |

## NEWMAN, COLIN

| | | | | | | |
|---|---|---|---|---|---|---|
| We Means We Starts | 7" | 4AD | AD209 | 1982 | £1.50 | £4 |

## NEWMAN, JIMMY

| | | | | | | |
|---|---|---|---|---|---|---|
| Fallen Star | 7" | London | HLD8460 | 1957 | £7.50 | £15 |
| Grin And Bear It | 7" EP | MGM | MGMEP706 | 1959 | £10 | £20 |
| Grin And Bear It | 7" | MGM | MGM1037 | 1959 | £1.50 | £4 |
| What About Me | 7" | MGM | MGM1085 | 1960 | £1.50 | £4 |
| Whatcha Gonna Do | 7" | MGM | MGM1009 | 1959 | £2 | £5 |

## NEWMAN, JOE

| | | | | | | | |
|---|---|---|---|---|---|---|---|
| I Feel Like A Newman | LP | Vogue | LAE12049 | 1957 | £15 | £30 | |
| Joe Newman And His Band | 10" LP | Vanguard | PPT12001 | 1955 | £20 | £40 | |
| Joe Newman And The Boys In The Band | 10" LP | Vogue | LDE126 | 1955 | £20 | £40 | |
| Joe Newman Octet | 10" LP | HMV | DLP1114 | 1956 | £15 | £30 | |
| Joe Newman Sextet | LP | Vogue Coral | LVA9052 | 1957 | £8 | £20 | |
| Locking Horns | LP | Columbia | 33SX1064 | 1957 | £6 | £15 | with Zoot Sims |
| Soft Swingin' Jazz | LP | Coral | LVA9106 | 1959 | £8 | £20 | with Shirley Scott |
| With Woodwinds | LP | Columbia | 33SX1143 | 1959 | £6 | £15 | |

## NEWMAN, LIONEL ORCHESTRA

| | | | | | | |
|---|---|---|---|---|---|---|
| Hey Eula | 7" | Columbia | DB4150 | 1958 | £1.50 | £4 |

## NEWMAN, PAUL

| | | | | | | |
|---|---|---|---|---|---|---|
| Ain't You Got A Heart | 7" | Mercury | MF969 | 1966 | £4 | £8 |

## NEWMAN, RANDY

| | | | | | | | |
|---|---|---|---|---|---|---|---|
| 12 Songs | LP | Reprise | RSLP6373 | 1970 | £4 | £10 | |
| Creates Something New Under The Sun | LP | Reprise | R(S)LP6286 | 1968 | £5 | £12 | |
| Good Old Boys | LP | Reprise | MS42193 | 1974 | £4 | £10 | US quad |
| I Think It's Gonna Rain Today | 78 | Reprise | 0284 | 1968 | £5 | £10 | US promo |

## NEWMAN, TOM

| | | | | | | |
|---|---|---|---|---|---|---|
| Faerie Symphony | LP | Decca | TXS123 | 1977 | £6 | £15 |

| | | | | | | |
|---|---|---|---|---|---|---|
| Fine Old Tom | LP | Virgin | V2022 | 1975 £4 | £10 | |
| Live At The Argonaut | LP | Virgin | V2042 | 1975 £37.50 | £75 | test pressing only |

## NEWMAN, TONY
| | | | | | |
|---|---|---|---|---|---|
| Soul Thing | 7" | Decca | F12795 | 1968 £2 | £5 |
| Soul Thing | 7" | Decca | F13041 | 1970 £1.50 | £4 |

## NEWPORT JAZZ FESTIVAL ALL STARS
| | | | | | |
|---|---|---|---|---|---|
| Newport Jazz Festival All Stars | LP | London | LTZK15202 | 1961 £4 | £10 |

## NEWPORTERS
Having achieved little success as the Moongooners, Scott Engel and John Maus next tried the name Newporters.

| | | | | | |
|---|---|---|---|---|---|
| Adventures In Paradise | 7" | Scotchtown | 500 | 1963 £15 | £30 | US |

## NEWS
| | | | | | |
|---|---|---|---|---|---|
| Entertainer | 7" | Decca | F12356 | 1966 £1.50 | £4 |
| This Is The Moment | 7" | Decca | F12477 | 1966 £2.50 | £6 |

## NEWTON-JOHN, OLIVIA
| | | | | | |
|---|---|---|---|---|---|
| If Not For You | LP | Polydor | 2310136 | 1976 £5 | £12 | German |
| If Not For You | LP | Uni | UNLS73117 | 1971 £10 | £25 | US |
| Magic | 7" | Jet | P196 | 1980 £1.50 | £4 | picture disc |
| Olivia Newton-John | LP | Pye | NSPL28155 | 1971 £4 | £10 |
| Rumour | CD-s | Mercury | MERCD272 | 1988 £2 | £5 |
| Till You Say You'll Be Mine | 7" | Decca | F12396 | 1966 £50 | £100 |
| Totally Hot | LP | EMI | EMAP789 | 1978 £6 | £15 | picture disc |
| Xanadu | 10" | Jet | 10185 | 1980 £6 | £15 | pink vinyl, with E.L.O. |

## NEWTOWN NEUROTICS
| | | | | | |
|---|---|---|---|---|---|
| Hypocrite | 7" | No Wonder | SRTS79CUS363 | 1979 £2.50 | £6 |
| When The Oil Runs Out | 7" | No Wonder | NOW4 | 1980 £2 | £5 | with insert |

## NI DHOMHNAILL, MAIREAD
| | | | | | |
|---|---|---|---|---|---|
| Mairead Ni Dhomhnaill | LP | Gael-Linn | CEF055 | 1976 £4 | £10 | Irish |

## NI DHOMHNAILL, TRIONA
| | | | | | |
|---|---|---|---|---|---|
| Triona | LP | Gael Linn | CEF043 | 1975 £4 | £10 | Irish |

## NI GHUAIRIM, SORCHA
| | | | | | |
|---|---|---|---|---|---|
| Sings Traditional Irish Songs | LP | Folkways | FW6861 | 1966 £5 | £12 | US |

## NIAGARA
| | | | | | |
|---|---|---|---|---|---|
| Niagara | LP | United Artists | UAS29232 | 1971 £4 | £10 | German |
| S.U.B. | LP | United Artists | UAS29343 | 1972 £4 | £10 | German |

## NICE
| | | | | | |
|---|---|---|---|---|---|
| America | 7" | Immediate | IM068 | 1968 £2.50 | £6 | picture sleeve |
| Ars Longa Vita Brevis | LP | Immediate | IMSP020 | 1968 £4 | £10 |
| Nice | LP | Immediate | IMSP026 | 1969 £4 | £10 |
| She Belongs To Me | 7" | Immediate | AS4 | 1969 £7.50 | £15 | promo |
| Thoughts Of Emerlist Davjack | LP | Immediate | IMLP/IMSP016 | 1967 £4 | £10 |
| Thoughts Of Emerlist Davjack | 7" | Immediate | AS2 | 1967 £12.50 | £25 | promo with John Peel interview |
| Thoughts Of Emerlist Davjack | 7" | Immediate | IM059 | 1967 £1.50 | £4 |

## NICELY, NICK
| | | | | | |
|---|---|---|---|---|---|
| DCT Dreams | 7" | Voxette | VOX1001 | 1980 £2 | £5 |
| Hillyfields (1892) | 7" | EMI | EMI5256 | 1982 £2 | £5 |

## NICHOLAS, PAUL
| | | | | | |
|---|---|---|---|---|---|
| Freedom City | 7" | Polydor | 56374 | 1970 £1.50 | £4 |
| Where Do I Go | 7" | Polydor | 56285 | 1968 £1.50 | £4 |
| Who Can I Turn To | 7" | Polydor | 56322 | 1969 £1.50 | £4 |

## NICHOLLS, BILLY
| | | | | | |
|---|---|---|---|---|---|
| Forever's No Time At All | 7" | Track | 2094109 | 1973 £2 | £5 | with Pete Townshend |
| Would You Believe | LP | Immediate | IMLP009 | 1967 £500 | £750 |
| Would You Believe | 7" | Immediate | IM063 | 1968 £10 | £20 |

## NICHOLLS, JANICE
Janice Nicholls was a regular member of the teenage panel called upon every week to mark selected new singles out of five on TV's *Thank Your Lucky Stars*. In those innocent days, a Birmingham accent was considered a novelty on TV, and Ms Nicholls's cry of 'Oi'll give it foive' was greeted with enthusiastic applause.

| | | | | | |
|---|---|---|---|---|---|
| Oi'll Give It Five | 7" | Decca | F11586 | 1963 £2.50 | £6 |

## NICHOLLS, SUE
Sue Nicholls achieved a minor hit with her first single release, but she is much better known these days for her role in TV's *Coronation Street*, as Audrey Roberts.

| | | | | | |
|---|---|---|---|---|---|
| All The Way To Heaven | 7" | Pye | 7N17674 | 1969 £1.50 | £4 |
| Where Will You Be | 7" | Pye | 7N17565 | 1968 £1.50 | £4 |

## NICHOLS, RED
| | | | | | |
|---|---|---|---|---|---|
| Jazz Time | 10" LP | Capitol | LC6534 | 1951 £8 | £20 |

## NICHOLSON, LEA
Horsemusic.................................................. LP ...... Trailer............. LER3010 ............... 1971 £8.........£20 ...................................

## NICHOLSON, ROGER
Gentle Sound Of The Dulcimer ............... LP ...... Argo ............. ZDA204.................... 1974 £4.........£10 ...................................

## NICHOLSON, ROGER, JAKE WALTON, ANDREW CRONSHAW
Times And Traditions For Dulcimer .......... LP ...... Trailer............. LER2094.................... 1976 £4.........£10 ...................................

## NICKELSON
Sitting On A Fence................................... 7" ...... Decca ........... F13328.................... 1972 £1.50........£4 ...................................

## NICKS, STEVIE
Bella Donna............................................. LP ...... Mobile Fidelity MFSL1121 ........... 1982 £4.........£10 .......... US audiophile
I Can't Wait............................................ CD-s .. EMI............... CDEM214 ............ 1991 £2.........£5 ...................................
I Can't Wait............................................ 12" .... Parlophone ..... 12R6110 ............. 1986 £2.50......£6 ...................................
Long Way To Go..................................... CD-s .. EMI............... CDEM97 .............. 1989 £2.........£5 .............. 3" single
Other Side Of The Mirror ....................... CD ..... EMI............... CDEMC1008 ........ 1989 £5.........£12 ......... hologram cover
Reflections: The Other Side Of The .......... CD ..... Modern .......... PR2881 ............... 1989 £8.........£20 ...US interview promo
  Mirror ..................................................
Rock A Little........................................... CD ..... Parlophone ..... CZ80 .................. 1986 £5.........£12 ...................................
Rooms On Fire (Extended)....................... CD-s .. EMI............... CDEM90 .............. 1989 £2.........£5 ...................................
Sometimes It's A Bitch............................. CD-s .. EMI............... CDEM203 ............ 1991 £2.........£5 ...................................
Stand Back.............................................. 12" .... WEA .............. U9870T .............. 1983 £3.........£8 ...................................
Whole Lotta Trouble ............................... CD-s .. EMI............... CDEM114 ............ 1989 £2.........£5 ...................................

## NICO
Chelsea Girl ............................................ LP ...... MGM ............. 2353025 .............. 1971 £6.........£15 ...................................
Desert Shore ........................................... LP ...... Reprise ........... RSLP6424............. 1971 £6.........£15 ...................................
End ....................................................... LP ...... Island ............. ILPS9311 ............. 1974 £4.........£10 ...................................
I'm Not Saying ....................................... 7" ...... Immediate ...... IM003................. 1965 £10.......£20 ...................................
Marble Index .......................................... LP ...... Elektra ........... EKL/EKS74029 .... 1968 £8.........£20 ...................................
Peel Sessions .......................................... CD-s .. Strange Fruit.... SFPSCD064 ......... 1988 £2.........£5 ...................................
Vegas .................................................... 7" ...... Flicknife ......... FLS206 ............... 1981 £2.........£5 ...................................

## NICODEMUS
Back Street Orange.................................. LP ...... Zedikiah ......... 1070 ................... 1978 £15........£30 ...................... US

## NICOL, JIMMY ──────────────────────────────────
Drummer Jimmy Nicol was briefly a member of the Beatles when he deputized for a sick Ringo Starr during the group's world tour in 1964. In a recent interview he declared the experience to have been the worst in his life, although this would seem to be more a reaction to the confounding of his subsequent expectations than to anything that actually happened on the tour. For, sadly, Nicol's fame was short-lived and none of the records he made afterwards was at all successful.

Baby Please Don't Go ............................. 7" ...... Pye ................ 7N15699 .............. 1964 £7.50......£15 ...................................
Clementine............................................. 7" ...... Decca ............. F12107................ 1965 £2.50......£6 ...................................
Humpty Dumpty...................................... 7" ...... Pye ................ 7N15623 .............. 1964 £4.........£8 ...................................
Husky .................................................... 7" ...... Pye ................ 7N15666 .............. 1964 £2.50......£6 ...................................

## NICOLL, WATT
Nice To Be Nice...................................... LP ...... XTRA ............. XTRA1122 ............ 1971 £4.........£10 ...................................

## NIEHAUS, LENNIE
Lennie Niehaus ....................................... 10" LP Contemporary . LDC150............... 1955 £20.......£40 ...................................
Lennie Niehaus Quintet............................ LP ...... Contemporary . LDC120............... 1955 £20.......£40 ...................................
Vol. 1 The Quintet.................................. LP ...... Vogue ............ LAC12167............ 1960 £8.........£20 ...................................
Vol. 3 – The Octet No. 2 ......................... LP ...... Contemporary . LAC12054............ 1957 £10.......£25 ...................................
Vol. 5 The Sextet .................................... LP ...... Contemporary . LAC12151............ 1959 £8.........£20 ...................................
Zounds!.................................................. LP ...... Contemporary . LAC12222............ 1960 £8.........£20 ...................................

## NIGHT OWLS
Twisting The Oldies.................................. LP ...... Valmor............ 79 ..................... 1962 £8.........£20 ...................... US

## NIGHT SUN
Mournin'................................................ LP ...... Zebra ............. 2949004 .............. 1972 £6.........£15 ................ German

## NIGHTBIRDS
Cat On A Hot Tin Roof............................ 7" ...... Oriole ............ CB1490 ............... 1959 £1.50......£4 ...................................

## NIGHTBLOOMS
Crystal Eyes ........................................... 7" ...... Fierce ............ FRIGHT041 .......... 1990 £4.........£8 ...................................

## NIGHTCAPS
Wine Wine Wine...................................... LP ...... Vandan .......... VRLP8124............ 1961 £20.......£40 ...................... US

## NIGHTCRAWLERS
Little Black Egg....................................... LP ...... Kapp .............. KL1520/KS3520 ..... 1967 £30.......£60 ...................... US
Little Black Egg....................................... 7" ...... London ........... HLR10109............ 1967 £7.50......£15 ...................................

## NIGHTHAWK, ROBERT
Robert Nighthawk .................................. 7" EP . XX ................ MIN718 ............... 196– £2.........£5 ...................................

## NIGHTHAWKS
Rock And Roll ........................................ LP ...... Aladdin ........... 101 ................... 195– £37.50....£75 ...................... US

## NIGHTINGALE, MAXINE
Don't Push Me Baby ........................................ 7" ...... Pye ................. 7N17798 ............... 1969 £**1.50** ........ £4 .................................

## NIGHTINGALES
This Package .................................................... 7" ...... Vindaloo ......... VILP2X ................. 1985 £**4** ......... £8 .................................

## NIGHTMARES IN WAX
Birth Of A Nation ........................................... 7" ...... Inevitable ....... INEV002 ............... 1979 £**6** ........ £12 .................................
Black Leather ................................................. 12" ..... KY ................. KY9 ................... 1984 £**5** ........ £12 ................................. 2 tracks
Black Leather ................................................. 12" ..... KY ................. KY91/2 ................ 1985 £**5** ........ £12 ................................. 3 tracks

## NIGHTRIDERS
It's Only The Dog ............................................ 7" ...... Polydor ........... 56116 ................ 1966 £**37.50** .... £75 .................................
Love Me Right Now .......................................... 7" ...... Polydor ........... ..................... 1966 £**37.50** .... £75 ................................. demo

## NIGHTROCKERS
Dance To The Rock .......................................... 7" EP . Golf Drouot .... 71014 ................. 1967 £**4** ......... £8 ................................. French
I Can Tell ...................................................... 7" EP . Golf Drouot .... 71013 ................. 1967 £**4** ......... £8 ................................. French

## NIGHTSHADOWS
Invasion Of The Acid Eaters .............................. LP ..... Hottrax ........... ..................... 1982 £**6** ........ £15 ................................. US
Live At The Spot ............................................. LP ..... Hottrax ........... ST1430 ............... 1981 £**6** ........ £15 ................................. US
Square Root Of Two ......................................... LP ..... Hottrax ........... ST1414 ............... 1978 £**15** ....... £30 ................................. US
Square Root Of Two ......................................... LP ..... Spectrum ......... ..................... 1968 £**700** ... £**1000** ........................... US
                                                                    Sounds ............

## NIGHTSHIFT
Corrine Corrina .............................................. 7" ...... Piccadilly ......... 7N35243 .............. 1965 £**4** ......... £8 .................................
That's My Story .............................................. 7" ...... Piccadilly ......... 7N35264 .............. 1965 £**4** ......... £8 .................................

## NIGHTSHIFT (2)
Nightshift ..................................................... LP ..... private ............ ..................... 1980 £**25** ....... £50 ................................. Dutch

## NIGHT-TIMERS
Music Played On .............................................. 7" ...... Parlophone ..... R5355 ................. 1965 £**7.50** ...... £15 .................................

## NIGHTWINGS
Grande Randonnee ........................................... LP ..... Crossroad ........ ..................... 1981 £**50** ....... £100 ................................. Dutch

## NIHILIST SPASM BAND
IX – X = X ..................................................... LP ..... United Dairies . UD016 ................. 1985 £**4** ......... £10 .................................

## NILES, JOHN JACOB
Folk Balladeer ................................................ LP ..... RCA .............. RD7729 ............... 1965 £**5** ........ £12 .................................

## NILSSON, HARRY
Nilsson Schmilsson .......................................... CD ..... Mobile Fidelity .. UDCD541 ............ 1990 £**6** ........ £15 ........... US audiophile
Scatalogue ..................................................... LP ..... RCA .............. SP33567 .............. 1974 £**5** ........ £12 US promo compilation
Spotlight On Nilsson ........................................ LP ..... Tower ............. (D)T5095 .............. 1967 £**5** ........ £12 ................................. US

## NILSSON, HARRY & JOHN LENNON
Pussy Cats ...................................................... LP ..... RCA .............. APD10570 ............ 1974 £**4** ......... £10 ................................. US quad

## NIMOY, LEONARD
Mr. Spock's Music From Outer Space ........ LP ..... Dot .............. DLP3794/25794 ..... 1967 £**10** ....... £25 ................................. US
New World Of Leonard Nimoy ............... LP ..... Dot .............. DLP25966 ............. 1969 £**6** ........ £15 ................................. US
Outer Space/Inner Mind ........................ LP ..... Paramount ....... 1030 .................. 197– £**8** ........ £20 ................................. US
Touch Of Leonard Nimoy ....................... LP ..... Dot .............. DLP25910 ............. 1969 £**6** ........ £15 ................................. US
Two Sides Of Leonard Nimoy .................. LP ..... Dot .............. DLP25835 ............. 1968 £**6** ........ £15 ................................. US
Way I Feel ...................................................... LP ..... Dot .............. DLP25883 ............. 1968 £**6** ........ £15 ................................. US

## NINA
Do You Know How Christmas Trees Are 7" ...... CBS ............... 4681 .................. 1970 £**4** ......... £8 .................................
    Grown? ....................................................

## NINE DAYS WONDER
Nine Days Wonder ............................................ LP ..... Harvest .......... SHSP4014 ............. 1971 £**10** ....... £25 .................................
Only The Dancers ............................................ LP ..... Bacillus .......... BLPS19200 ........... 1975 £**4** ......... £10 ................................. German
Sonnet To Billy Frost ....................................... LP ..... Bacillus .......... BLPS19234 ........... 1975 £**4** ......... £10 ................................. German
We Never Lost Control ...................................... LP ..... Bacillus .......... BLPS19163 ........... 1973 £**4** ......... £10 ................................. German

## NINE INCH NAILS
Down In It ..................................................... CD–s .. Island ............ CID482 ................ 1990 £**4** ......... £10 ................................. 6 tracks

## NINE NINE NINE
I'm Alive ....................................................... 7" ...... Labritian .......... LAB999 ............... 1977 £**2** ......... £5 .................................
Nasty Nasty .................................................... 78...... United Artists .. FREE7 ................. 1977 £**10** ....... £20 ................................. promo

## NINE SENSE
Oh! For The Edge ............................................ LP ..... Ogun ............. OG900 ................. 1976 £**5** ........ £12 .................................

## NINETEEN EIGHTY-FOUR
Got To Have Your Love ...................................... 7" ...... Transatlantic .... BIG120 ............... 1969 £**1.50** ........ £4 .................................
Little Girl ...................................................... 7" ...... Decca ............. F23159 ................ 1971 £**1.50** ........ £4 .................................
This Little Boy ................................................ 7" ...... Transatlantic .... BIG117 ............... 1969 £**1.50** ........ £4 .................................

## NINE-THIRTY FLY

| | | | | | | | |
|---|---|---|---|---|---|---|---|
| Nine-Thirty Fly | LP | Ember | NR5062 | 1972 | £50 | £100 | |

## NING

| | | | | | | | |
|---|---|---|---|---|---|---|---|
| Machine | 7" | Decca | F23114 | 1971 | £1.50 | £4 | |

## NINO & THE EBBTIDES

| | | | | | | | |
|---|---|---|---|---|---|---|---|
| Those Oldies But Goodies | 7" | Top Rank | JAR572 | 1961 | £12.50 | £25 | |

## NINTH CREATION

| | | | | | | | |
|---|---|---|---|---|---|---|---|
| Bubble Gum | LP | Rite Track | RKA01M | 1969 | £8 | £20 | US |

## NIPPLE ERECTORS

The Pogues' Shane MacGowan began his recording career with the punk Nipple Erectors, later abbreviated to the less controversial Nips.

| | | | | | | | |
|---|---|---|---|---|---|---|---|
| King Of The Bop | 7" | Soho | SH1 | 1978 | £5 | £10 | glossy picture sleeve |
| King Of The Bop | 7" | Soho | SH1 | 1978 | £4 | £8 | matt picture sleeve |

## NIPS

| | | | | | | | |
|---|---|---|---|---|---|---|---|
| All The Time In The World | 7" | Soho | SH4 | 1978 | £6 | £12 | |
| Gabrielle | 7" | Chiswick | CHIS119 | 1979 | £2.50 | £6 | |
| Gabrielle | 7" | Soho | SH9 | 1979 | £2 | £5 | |
| Gabrielle | 7" | Soho | SH9 | 1980 | £10 | £20 | 'licensed to cool' stamp |
| Happy Song | 7" | Burning Rome | TP5 | 1981 | £5 | £10 | |
| Only At The End Of The Beginning | LP | Soho | HOHO1 | 1980 | £6 | £15 | |

## NIRVANA

The original Nirvana had long since ceased recording when Kurt Cobain arrived on the scene with a band of the same name, but it was clearly very much in Patrick Campbell-Lyons's interest to claim copyright infringement. He received an out-of-court financial settlement, although there is little possibility of confusion between the adventurous psychedelic pop of Campbell-Lyons's band and the agonized guitar mayhem of the American newcomers.

| | | | | | | | |
|---|---|---|---|---|---|---|---|
| All Of Us | LP | Island | ILP987/ILPS9087 | 1968 | £15 | £30 | pink label |
| All Of Us | 7" | Island | WIP6045 | 1968 | £2.50 | £6 | |
| Dedicated To Markos III | LP | Pye | NSPL28132 | 1970 | £25 | £50 | |
| Girl In The Park | 7" | Island | WIP6038 | 1968 | £2.50 | £6 | |
| Local Anaesthetic | LP | Vertigo | 6360031 | 1971 | £15 | £30 | spiral label |
| Nirvana | LP | Metromedia | 1018 | 1970 | £10 | £25 | US |
| Oh! What A Performance | 7" | Island | WIP6057 | 1969 | £2.50 | £6 | |
| Pentecost Hotel | 7" EP | Fontana | 460236 | 1967 | £10 | £20 | French |
| Pentecost Hotel | 7" | Island | WIP6020 | 1967 | £2.50 | £6 | |
| Pentecost Hotel | 7" | Philips | 6006127 | 1971 | £1.50 | £4 | |
| Rainbow Chaser | 7" | Island | WIP6029 | 1968 | £2.50 | £6 | |
| Rainbow Chaser | 7" | Philips | 6006129 | 1972 | £1.50 | £4 | |
| Saddest Day Of My Life | 7" | Vertigo | 6059035 | 1970 | £2.50 | £6 | |
| Simon Simopath | LP | Island | ILP959/ILPS9059 | 1967 | £20 | £40 | pink label |
| Songs Of Love And Praise | LP | Philips | 6308089 | 1972 | £15 | £30 | |
| Stadium | 7" | Philips | 6006166 | 1972 | £1.50 | £4 | |
| Tiny Goddess | 7" | Island | WIP6016 | 1967 | £4 | £8 | |
| Wings Of Love | 7" | Island | WIP6052 | 1968 | £2.50 | £6 | |
| World Is Cold Without You | 7" | Pye | 7N25525 | 1970 | £4 | £8 | |

## NIRVANA (2)

Although his approach to music was not very similar, Kurt Cobain became a Jimi Hendrix for the nineties rock generation when he chose the ultimate escape from the unwelcome pressures of stardom. It may well be the case that Nirvana had already passed their best – but sadly, we shall never know. It remains the case, however, that *Nevermind* seems more like one of the all-time classic rock albums with every month that passes.

| | | | | | | | |
|---|---|---|---|---|---|---|---|
| Bleach | LP | Sub Pop | SP34 | 1989 | £20 | £40 | US, white vinyl |
| Bleach | LP | Sub Pop | SP34 | 1989 | £6 | £15 | US, with poster |
| Bleach | LP | Tupelo | TUPLP6 | 1989 | £15 | £30 | green vinyl |
| Bleach | LP | Tupelo | TUPLP6 | 1989 | £30 | £60 | white vinyl |
| Bleach | CD | Tupelo | TUPCD6 | 1989 | £5 | £12 | |
| Blew | CD-s | Tupelo | TUPCD8 | 1989 | £4 | £10 | |
| Blew | 12" | Tupelo | TUPEP8 | 1989 | £6 | £15 | |
| Come As You Are | CD-s | MCA | DGCTD7 | 1992 | £2 | £5 | |
| Come As You Are | 12" | Geffen | DGCTP7 | 1992 | £2.50 | £6 | picture disc |
| Grunge Is Dead | CD-s | Geffen | | 199– | £37.50 | £75 | 12" boxed set – 6 CD singles, T shirt, poster, photo |
| Hormoaning | LP | Geffen | GEF21711 | 1991 | £8 | £20 | burgundy vinyl |
| In Bloom | CD-s | BMG | GFSTD34 | 1992 | £2 | £5 | |
| In Bloom | 12" | Geffen | GFSTP34 | 1992 | £2.50 | £6 | picture disc |
| In Utero | LP | Geffen | GEF24536 | 1993 | £6 | £15 | clear vinyl |
| Lithium | 12" | Geffen | DGCTP9 | 1992 | £2.50 | £6 | picture disc |
| Love Buzz | 7" | Sub Pop | SP23 | 1988 | £50 | £100 | US, 'Guitars' matrix message |
| Molly's Lips | 7" | Sub Pop | SP97 | 1991 | £10 | £20 | US, black vinyl |
| Molly's Lips | 7" | Sub Pop | SP97 | 1991 | £15 | £30 | US, green vinyl |
| Nevermind It's An Interview | CD | DGC | PROCD4382 | 1991 | £10 | £25 | US promo |
| Oh The Guilt | CD-s | Touch & Go | TG83CD | 1993 | £2 | £5 | with track by Jesus Lizard |
| Oh, The Guilt | 7" | Touch & Go | TG83 | 1993 | £1.50 | £4 | blue vinyl |
| Oh, The Guilt | 7" | Touch & Go | TG83 | 1993 | £2.50 | £6 | blue vinyl, with poster |
| Sliver | CD-s | Tupelo | TUPCD25 | 1991 | £2 | £5 | |

| | | | | | | |
|---|---|---|---|---|---|---|
| Sliver | 7" | Sub Pop | SP73 | 1990 £7.50 | £15 | US, blue vinyl, foldover picture sleeve |
| Sliver | 7" | Tupelo | TUP25 | 1991 £7.50 | £15 | green vinyl |
| Smells Like Teen Spirit | CD-s | Geffen | DGCTD5 | 1991 £2.50 | £6 | |
| Smells Like Teen Spirit | 12" | Geffen | DGCTP5 | 1991 £3 | £8 | picture disc |

## NITE PEOPLE

| | | | | | | |
|---|---|---|---|---|---|---|
| Is This A Dream | 7" | Page One | POF159 | 1969 £1.50 | £4 | |
| Love, Love, Love | 7" | Page One | POF149 | 1969 £2.50 | £6 | with insert |
| Morning Sun | 7" | Fontana | TF919 | 1968 £4 | £8 | |
| P.M. | LP | Page One | POLS025 | 1969 £100 | £200 | |
| Season Of The Rain | 7" | Page One | POF174 | 1970 £1.50 | £4 | |
| Summertime Blues | 7" | Fontana | TF885 | 1967 £12.50 | £25 | |
| Sweet Tasting Wine | 7" | Fontana | TF747 | 1966 £2.50 | £6 | |
| Trying To Find Another Man | 7" | Fontana | TF808 | 1967 £2 | £5 | |

## NITE ROCKERS

| | | | | | | |
|---|---|---|---|---|---|---|
| Ooh Baby | 7" | RCA | RCA1079 | 1958 £30 | £60 | |

## NITESHADES

| | | | | | | |
|---|---|---|---|---|---|---|
| Be My Guest | 7" | CBS | 201763 | 1965 £1.50 | £4 | |
| Fell So Fast | 7" | CBS | 201817 | 1965 £1.50 | £4 | |

## NITTY GRITTY DIRT BAND

| | | | | | | |
|---|---|---|---|---|---|---|
| Alive | LP | Liberty | LST7615 | 1969 £4 | £10 | US |
| Buy For Me The Rain | 7" EP | Liberty | LEP2279 | 1967 £7.50 | £15 | French |
| Dead And Alive | LP | Liberty | LBS83286 | 1969 £4 | £10 | |
| Nitty Gritty Dirt Band | LP | Liberty | LRP3501/LST7501 | 1967 £4 | £10 | US |
| Pure Dirt | LP | Liberty | LBL/LBS83122 | 1968 £4 | £10 | |
| Rare Junk | LP | Liberty | LST7611 | 1967 £4 | £10 | US |
| Ricochet | LP | Liberty | LRP3516/LST7516 | 1967 £4 | £10 | US |
| Will The Circle Be Unbroken | LP | United Artists | UAS9801 | 1973 £10 | £25 | US triple |

## NITZER EBB

| | | | | | | |
|---|---|---|---|---|---|---|
| Warsaw Ghetto | 12" | Power Of Voice Com- munications | NEP/NEBX2 | 1986 £4 | £10 | double |

## NITZSCHE, JACK

Jack Nitzsche was Phil Spector's arranger during the sixties and hence due as much credit as Spector himself for the invention of the 'wall of sound' that is so characteristic of Spector's productions. Nitzsche made a number of instrumental records in a series of attempts to take advantage of contemporary music fads, but his masterpiece is St Giles Cripplegate, recorded in 1972. This is a suite of short pieces scored for a small group of strings and is essentially a classical work made contemporary by its use of acid harmonies.

| | | | | | | |
|---|---|---|---|---|---|---|
| Chopin '66 | LP | Reprise | R(S)6200 | 1966 £6 | £15 | US |
| Hits Of The Beatles | LP | Reprise | R(S)6115 | 1964 £8 | £20 | US |
| Lonely Surfer | LP | Reprise | R(S)6101 | 1963 £8 | £20 | US |
| Lonely Surfer | 7" EP | Reprise | RVEP60036 | 1963 £10 | £20 | French |
| Lonely Surfer | 7" | Reprise | R20202 | 1963 £2.50 | £6 | |
| Night Walker | 7" | Reprise | R20337 | 1964 £1.50 | £4 | |
| St. Giles Cripplegate | LP | Reprise | K41211 | 1972 £4 | £10 | |

## NIVENS

| | | | | | | |
|---|---|---|---|---|---|---|
| Let Loose Of My Knee | 7" | Woosh | WOOSH1 | 1988 £2.50 | £6 | flexi, B side by Holidaymakers |

## NIX NOMADS

| | | | | | | |
|---|---|---|---|---|---|---|
| You're Nobody Till Somebody Loves You | 7" | HMV | POP1354 | 1964 £25 | £50 | |

## NO INTRODUCTION

| | | | | | | |
|---|---|---|---|---|---|---|
| No Introduction | LP | Spark | | 1968 £8 | £20 | |

## NO MAN

| | | | | | | |
|---|---|---|---|---|---|---|
| Colours | 7" | Hidden Art | HA4 | 1990 £4 | £8 | |
| Colours | 12" | Probe Plus | PP27T | 1990 £3 | £8 | |
| Girl From Missouri | 12" | Plastic Head | PLASS012 | 1989 £2.50 | £6 | |

## NO QUARTER

| | | | | | | |
|---|---|---|---|---|---|---|
| Survivors | 12" | Reel | REEL1 | 1983 £2.50 | £6 | |

## NOAKES, RAB

| | | | | | | |
|---|---|---|---|---|---|---|
| Do You See The Light | LP | Decca | SKL5061 | 1970 £6 | £15 | |
| Never Too Late | LP | Warner Bros | K56114 | 1975 £4 | £10 | |
| Rab Noakes | LP | A&M | AMLS68119 | 1972 £4 | £10 | |
| Red Pump Special | LP | Warner Bros | K46284 | 1974 £4 | £10 | |
| Restless | LP | Ring O | 2339201 | 1978 £4 | £10 | |

## NOBLE, PATSY ANN

| | | | | | | |
|---|---|---|---|---|---|---|
| Don't You Ever Change Your Mind | 7" | Columbia | DB4956 | 1963 £1.50 | £4 | |

## NOBLE, STEVE & ALEX MAGUIRE

| | | | | | | |
|---|---|---|---|---|---|---|
| Live At Oscars | LP | Incus | INCUS52 | 1986 £5 | £12 | |

## NOBLEMEN

| | | | | | | |
|---|---|---|---|---|---|---|
| Thunder Wagon | 7" | Top Rank | JAR155 | 1959 £2 | £5 | |

## NOBLES, CLIFF
| | | | | | | |
|---|---|---|---|---|---|---|
| Horse | LP | Direction | 863477 | 1969 | £4 | £10 |

## NOCTURNAL EMISSIONS
| | | | | | | | |
|---|---|---|---|---|---|---|---|
| Befehlsnotstand | LP | Sterile | SR5 | 1984 | £20 | £40 | |
| Beyond Logic | LP | Earthly Delights | EARTH05 | 1989 | £4 | £10 | |
| Chaos – Live At The Ritzy | LP | CFC | LP2 | 1984 | £20 | £40 | |
| Drowning In A Sea Of Bliss | LP | Sterile | SR4 | 1984 | £25 | £50 | |
| Fruiting Body | LP | Sterile | ION2 | 1984 | £20 | £40 | |
| Mouth Of The Babes | LP | Earthly Delights | EARTH06 | 1990 | £4 | £10 | |
| No Sacrifice | 12" | Sterile | SR6 | 1984 | £4 | £10 | |
| Shake Those Chains, Rattle Those Cages | LP | Sterile | SR9 | 1986 | £4 | £10 | |
| Songs Of Love And Revolution | LP | Sterile | SR7 | 1985 | £6 | £15 | |
| Spiritflesh | LP | Earthly Delights | EARTH04 | 1988 | £8 | £20 | |
| Tissue Of Lies | LP | Sterile | EMISS001 | 1984 | £15 | £30 | |
| Tissue Of Lies | LP | Sterile | EMISS001 | 1984 | £30 | £60 | numbered |
| Viral Shedding | LP | Illuminated | JAMSLP33 | 1984 | £6 | £15 | |
| World Is My Womb | LP | Earthly Delights | EARTH02 | 1987 | £6 | £15 | |

## NOCTURNS
| | | | | | | |
|---|---|---|---|---|---|---|
| Carrying On | 7" | Decca | F12002 | 1964 | £1.50 | £4 |

## NOCTURNES
| | | | | | | |
|---|---|---|---|---|---|---|
| Troilka | 7" | Solar | SRP102 | 1964 | £5 | £10 |

## NOCTURNES (2)
| | | | | | | |
|---|---|---|---|---|---|---|
| Nocturnes | LP | Columbia | SX/SCX6223 | 1968 | £4 | £10 |
| Wanted Alive | LP | Columbia | SX/SCX6315 | 1968 | £5 | £12 |

## NOEL, DICK
| | | | | | | |
|---|---|---|---|---|---|---|
| Birds And The Bees | 7" | London | HLH8295 | 1956 | £7.50 | £15 |

## NOIR
| | | | | | | |
|---|---|---|---|---|---|---|
| We Had To Let You Have It | LP | Dawn | DNLS3029 | 1971 | £6 | £15 |

## NOLAN SISTERS
| | | | | | | | |
|---|---|---|---|---|---|---|---|
| Blackpool | 7" | Nevis | NEVS007 | 1972 | £5 | £10 | |
| But I Do | 7" | EMI | EMI2209 | 1974 | £4 | £8 | |
| Medley | 7" | Target | SAM84 | 1978 | £2 | £5 | promo |
| Nolan Sisters | LP | Hanover Grand | HG19751 | 1977 | £10 | £25 | |
| Silent Night | 7" EP | Nevis | NEVEP005 | 1972 | £2 | £5 | |
| Singing Nolans | LP | Nevis | NEVR009 | 1972 | £6 | £15 | |

## NOLAND, TERRY
| | | | | | | | |
|---|---|---|---|---|---|---|---|
| Oh Baby Look At Me | 7" | Coral | Q72311 | 1958 | £37.50 | £75 | |
| Terry Noland | LP | Brunswick | BL54041 | 1958 | £75 | £150 | US |

## NOMADI
| | | | | | | | |
|---|---|---|---|---|---|---|---|
| Interpretano | LP | Columbia | 06417990 | 1974 | £4 | £10 | Italian |

## NOONE, JIMMY
| | | | | | | |
|---|---|---|---|---|---|---|
| Jimmy Noone Orchestra | 10" LP | Vogue Coral | LRA10026 | 1955 | £5 | £12 |

## NORDINE, KEN
| | | | | | | | |
|---|---|---|---|---|---|---|---|
| Classic Collection | LP | Dot | DLP25880 | 1968 | £6 | £15 | US |
| Colors | LP | Philips | 2/600224 | 196– | £6 | £15 | US |
| Concert In The Sky | LP | Decca | DL8550 | 1957 | £10 | £25 | US |
| Ken Nordine Reads | 7" EP | London | RED1091 | 1957 | £10 | £20 | |
| Love Words | LP | Dot | DLP3115/ DLP25115 | 1958 | £6 | £15 | US |
| My Baby | LP | Dot | DLP3142/ DLP25142 | 1958 | £6 | £15 | US |
| Next! | LP | Dot | DLP3196/ DLP25196 | 1959 | £6 | £15 | US |
| Shifting Whispering Sands | 7" | London | HLD8205 | 1955 | £5 | £10 | gold label |
| Ship That Never Sailed | 7" | London | HLD8417 | 1957 | £1.50 | £4 | |
| Son Of Word Jazz | LP | London | LTZD15145 | 1959 | £8 | £20 | |
| Twink | LP | Philips | 2/600258 | 196– | £6 | £15 | US |
| Word Jazz | LP | London | LTZD15131 | 1958 | £10 | £25 | |
| Word Jazz | 7" EP | London | EZD19040 | 1959 | £5 | £10 | |
| Word Jazz Vol. 2 | LP | Dot | DLP3301/25301 | 1960 | £6 | £15 | US |

## NORMAN, LARRY
| | | | | | | | |
|---|---|---|---|---|---|---|---|
| So Long Ago/The Garden | LP | MGM | SE4942 | 1973 | £5 | £12 | US |
| Upon This Rock | LP | Key | DOVE6 | 1969 | £4 | £10 | |

## NORMAN, MONTY
| | | | | | | | |
|---|---|---|---|---|---|---|---|
| Dr. No | LP | United Artists | SULP1097 | 1965 | £6 | £15 | |
| Dr. No | LP | United Artists | ULP1097 | 1965 | £4 | £10 | mono |
| Dr. No | 7" EP | United Artists | UEP1010 | 1965 | £6 | £12 | |
| Garden Of Eden | 7" | HMV | POP281 | 1957 | £2 | £5 | |

## NORMAN, OLIVER
Down In The Basement............................ 7" ...... Polydor............ 56176.................... 1967 £1.50........ £4 ..............................

## NORMAN & THE INVADERS
Night Train To Surbiton.......................... 7" ...... United Artists .. UP1077.................. 1965 £4................. £8 ........................

## NORMAN CONQUEST
Two People........................................ 7" ...... MGM ............. MGM1376 ............. 1968 £25........ £50 .......................

## NORTH, ROY
Blues In Three ................................... 7" ...... Oak ............... RGJ107.................. 1963 £10......... £20 ...................

## NORTH STARS
She's So Far Out She's In ........................ 7" ...... Fontana........... TF726.................... 1966 £4................ £8 ......................

## NORTHERN LIGHTS
The singles credited to Northern Lights were actually by the Hootenanny Singers and are therefore of considerable interest to Abba collectors.

No Time........................................... 7" ...... United Artists .. UP1123................. 1966 £10......... £20 ...................
Through Darkness Light ........................... 7" ...... United Artists .. UP1161................. 1966 £10......... £20 ...................

## NORTHWIND
Sister Brother Lover.................................. LP ..... Regal            SLRZ1020 ............. 1971 £75....... £150 .......................
                                                               Zonophone .....

## NORVO, RED
Ad Lib............................................ LP ..... London............ LTZD15116 ........... 1958 £5........... £12 .....................
Hi-Five .......................................... LP ..... RCA ............. RD27013............... 1957 £5........... £12 .....................
Move! ........................................... LP ..... Realm............ RM158................. 1964 £5........... £12 .....................
Red Norvo........................................ 10" LP ... London............ LZU14039 .......... 1957 £10......... £25 .....................
Red Norvo All Stars .............................. LP ..... Philips............ BBL7077 ............. 1956 £8........... £20 .....................
Red Norvo Nine .................................. 10" LP ... Vogue.............. LDE061 ............. 1954 £20......... £40 .....................
Red Norvo Trio .................................. 10" LP ... Brunswick ...... LA8718 ............. 1955 £20......... £40 .....................
Red Norvo Trio .................................. 10" LP ... Vogue............. LDE115 ............. 1955 £20......... £40 .....................
Windjammer City Style ............................ LP ..... London............ HAD2134 ............ 1958 £4........... £10 .....................

## NOSEY PARKER
Nosey Parker ..................................... LP ..... private ...          ........................ 1975 £100..... £200 .................. US

## NOSFERATU
Nosferatu......................................... LP ..... Vogue............. LDVS17178........... 1970 £100..... £200 .................. German

## NOSMO
Goodbye (Nothing To Say)......................... 7" ...... Pye ............... 7N45383 ............. 1974 £2................ £5 .......................

## NOSTRADAMUS
Nostradamus ...................................... LP ..... Zodiac ...........    ........................ 1972 £100..... £200 .................. Greek

## NOTATIONS
Need Your Love ................................... 7" ...... Chapter One ... SCH174.................. 1974 £4................ £8 ........................

## NOTATIONS (2)
Notations......................................... LP ..... Curtom........... K56212 ................ 1976 £8........... £20 .......................

## NOTES, FREDDIE & THE RUDIES
Montego Bay ..................................... LP ..... Trojan............ TBL152 ............... 1970 £6............ £15 ......................
Montego Bay ..................................... 7" ...... Trojan............ TR7791 .............. 1970 £1.50........ £4 ........................
Unity ........................................... LP ..... Trojan............ TBL109 ............... 1970 £6............ £15 ......................

## NOTHINGS
At Times Like This................................ 7" ...... CBS............... 201779 ............... 1965 £1.50........ £4 ........................

## NOTSENSIBLES
Margaret Thatcher................................ 7" ...... Redball ........... RR021 ................ 1979 £2................ £5 .......................

## NOTTING HILLBILLIES
Feel Like Going Home ............................ CD-s .. Vertigo .......... NHBCD2 ............. 1990 £2................ £5 .......................
Will You Miss Me................................. CD-s .. Vertigo .......... NHBCD3 ............. 1990 £2................ £5 .......................
Your Own Sweet Way ............................ CD-s .. Vertigo .......... NHBCD1 ............. 1990 £2................ £5 .......................

## NOTTS ALLIANCE
Cheerful 'Orn .................................... LP ..... Tradition.......... TSR011 .............. 1972 £4................ £10 .......................

## NOVA LOCAL
Nova 1 ........................................... LP ..... MCA............. MUPS377 ............. 1968 £15......... £30 .......................

## NOVAC
Novac ........................................... LP ..... Hor Zu .......... SHZE804............. 1970 £8........... £20 .................. German

## NOVALIS
Banished Bridge .................................. LP ..... Brain ............ 1029 ................. 1973 £6............ £15 .................. German
Novalis.......................................... LP ..... Brain ............ 1070 ................. 1975 £5............ £12 .................. German
Sommerabend ..................................... LP ..... Brain ............ 1087 ................. 1976 £5............ £12 .................. German

## NOVAS
Push A Little Harder............................. 7" ...... RCA .............. RCA1360 ............... 1963 £1.50........£4 ...............................

## NOVAS (2)
Crusher ................................................. 7" ...... London .......... HLU9940............. 1965 £7.50......£15 ...............................

## NOVELLS
Happening (That Did It) .......................... LP ..... Mothers .......... MRS73 ................. 1968 £15 ........£30 ........................... US

## NOVEMBER
16 E November ........................................ LP ..... Sonet .............. SLP2530........... 1972 £5 ............£12 ..................... Swedish
En Hy Tid Ar Nar.................................... LP ..... Sonet .............. SLP2509........... 1970 £6 ............£15 ..................... Swedish
Zia.......................................................... LP ..... Sonet .............. SLP2520........... 1971 £15 ..........£30 ..................... Swedish

## NOW
Development Corporations ..................... 7" ...... Ultimate.......... ULT401 ............. 1978 £2.50........£6 ......blue vinyl, picture
sleeve

## NOW (2)
Marcia .................................................... 7" ...... NEMS ........... 564125 ............... 1969 £1.50.....£4 ...............................

## NOWY, RALF
Escalation .............................................. LP ..... Atlantic .......... K40556 ............. 1974 £4 ............£10 ..................... German
Lucifer's Dream...................................... LP ..... Intercord ........ 260158 .............. 1973 £5 ............£12 ..................... German
Nowy 2................................................... LP ..... Atlantic .......... ATL50205 .......... 1975 £4 ............£10 ..................... German

## NOYS OF US
He's Alright Jill ..................................... 7" ...... KRS .............. KRS502 ............. 196– £12.50 ... £25 ...............................

## NRBQ
NRBQ..................................................... LP ..... CBS................ 63653 ............... 1969 £4 ............£10 ...............................

## NSU
Turn On Or Turn Me Down.................... LP ..... Stable .............. SLE8002 ........... 1969 £50 .......£100 ...............................

## NU NOTES
Hall Of Mirrors...................................... 7" ...... HMV.............. POP1232 ........... 1963 £12.50 ... £25 ...............................
Kathy ..................................................... 7" ...... HMV.............. POP1311 ........... 1964 £2.50........£6 ...............................

## NU TORNADOS
Philadelphia USA ................................... 7" ...... London .......... HLU8756............. 1958 £4 ............£8 ...............................

## NUBBIT, GUITAR
Guitar Nubbit ........................................ 7" EP . XX ................ MIN705................ 196– £2 ............£5 ...............................

## NUCLEUS
Alley Cat ................................................ LP ..... Vertigo .......... 6360 124 ........... 1977 £5 ............£12 ...............................
Awakening .............................................. LP ..... Mood ............ 24000............... 1980 £8 ............£20 ...............................
Belladonna.............................................. LP ..... Vertigo .......... 6360076 ............ 1972 £8 ............£20 ..................... spiral label
Belladonna.............................................. LP ..... Vertigo .......... 6360076 ............ 1973 £5 ............£12 ...............................
Elastic Rock............................................ LP ..... Vertigo .......... 6360008 ............ 1970 £8 ............£20 ..................... spiral label
Elastic Rock............................................ LP ..... Vertigo .......... 6360008 ............ 1973 £4 ............£10 ...............................
Labyrinth ................................................ LP ..... Vertigo .......... 6360091 ............ 1973 £5 ............£12 ...............................
Roots...................................................... LP ..... Vertigo .......... 6360 100 ........... 1973 £5 ............£12 ...............................
Snake Hips Etcetera ................................ LP ..... Vertigo .......... 6360 119 ........... 1975 £5 ............£12 ...............................
Solar Plexus ............................................ LP ..... Vertigo .......... 6360039 ............ 1971 £8 ............£20 ..................... spiral label
Solar Plexus ............................................ LP ..... Vertigo .......... 6360039 ............ 1973 £4 ............£10 ...............................
Under The Sun ....................................... LP ..... Vertigo .......... 6360 110 ........... 1974 £5 ............£12 ...............................
We'll Talk About It Later........................ LP ..... Vertigo .......... 6360027 ............ 1970 £8 ............£20 ..................... spiral label
We'll Talk About It Later........................ LP ..... Vertigo .......... 6360027 ............ 1973 £4 ............£10 ...............................

## NUCLEUS (2)
Nucleus................................................... LP ..... Mainstream ..... 6120 ..................... 1967 £30 .........£60 ........................ US

## NUGENT, TED
State Of Shock........................................ LP ..... Epic................ AS99607 ............. 1979 £4 ............£10 ......... US picture disc

## NUGGETS
Quirl Up In My Arms.............................. 7" ...... Capitol............ CL14216 ............ 1955 £6 ............£12 ...............................
Shtiggy Boom .......................................... 7" ...... Capitol............ CL14267 ............ 1955 £5 ............£10 ...............................

## NUMAN, GARY
America................................................... CD-s .. IRS .............. ILSCD1004 ............ 1988 £2 ............£5 ...............................
America................................................... 7" ...... IRS .............. ILPD1004 ............ 1988 £1.50.....£4 ..................... picture disc
America................................................... 7" ...... IRS .............. ILPD1004 ............ 1988 £7.50.....£15 ..picture disc, Gary on
both sides
Cars ....................................................... 12" ..... Intercord......... INT126502 ......... 1979 £5 ............£12 ..................... German
Cars ('93 Sprint) .................................... CD-s .. Beggars ......... BEG264CD........... 1993 £3 ............£8
Banquet ...........
Cars (E Reg Model) ............................... 7" ...... Beggars ......... BEG199P ........... 1987 £1.50.....£4 ..................... picture disc
Banquet ...........
Emotion................................................. CD-s .. Numa ............ NUCD22............. 1991 £2 ............£5 ...............................
Fury........................................................ LP ..... Numa ............ NUMAP1003......... 1986 £10 .........£25 ...... picture disc, Your
Fascination picture
Fury........................................................ CD .... Numa ............ CDNUMA1003...... 1986 £10 .........£25 ...............................
Ghost ..................................................... LP ..... Numa ............ NUMAD1007 ........ 1987 £6 ............£15 ........................ double
Heart....................................................... CD-s .. IRS ................ NUMANCD1........ 1991 £2 ............£5 ...............................

| | | | | | | |
|---|---|---|---|---|---|---|
| I Die: You Die | 7" | Beggars Banquet | BEG26A1 | 1980 £7.50 | £15 | test pressing, different mix |
| Images Five And Six | LP | Fan Club | GNFCDA3 | 1987 £6 | £15 | double |
| Images Nine And Ten | LP | Fan Club | GNFCDA5 | 1989 £5 | £12 | double |
| Images One And Two | LP | Fan Club | GNFCDA1 | 1986 £8 | £20 | double |
| Images Seven And Eight | LP | Fan Club | GNFCDA4 | 1987 £6 | £15 | double |
| Images Three And Four | LP | Fan Club | GNFCDA2 | 1987 £8 | £20 | double |
| Machine And Soul | CD | Numa | NUMACDX1009 | 1993 £5 | £12 | 9 tracks |
| Metal Rhythm | LP | IRS | ILPX035 | 1988 £4 | £10 | picture disc |
| New Anger | CD-s | IRS | ILSCD1003 | 1988 £3 | £8 | |
| Peel Sessions | CD-s | Strange Fruit | SFPMACD202 | 1989 £2 | £5 | |
| Photograph | LP | Intercord | INT146606 | 1981 £30 | £60 | German |
| Plan | LP | Beggars Banquet | BEGA55P | 1985 £4 | £10 | picture disc |
| Remember I Was Vapour | 12" | Intercord | INT126600 | 1980 £4 | £10 | German |
| Strange Charm | CD | Numa | CDNUMA1005 | 1986 £20 | £40 | |
| Telekon | LP | Beggar's Banquet | BEGA19 | 1980 £5 | £12 | green vinyl |
| Telekon | LP | Beggars Banquet | BEGA19 | 1980 £20 | £40 | clear or white vinyl |
| Telekon | LP | Beggars Banquet | BEGA19 | 1980 £8 | £20 | red, yellow, blue, or orange vinyl |
| This Is Love | 12" | Numa | NUMX16 | 1986 £2.50 | £6 | double |
| Warriors | 7" | Beggars Banquet | BEG95P | 1983 £7.50 | £15 | shaped picture disc |
| Your Fascination | 7" | Numa | NUP9 | 1985 £1.50 | £4 | picture disc |
| Your Fascination | 12" | Numa | NUMP9 | 1985 £2.50 | £6 | picture disc |

## NUMBER NINE BREAD STREET

| | | | | | | |
|---|---|---|---|---|---|---|
| Number Nine Bread Street | LP | Holyground | HG112 | 1967 £180 | £300 | |

## NURSE WITH WOUND

| | | | | | | |
|---|---|---|---|---|---|---|
| Alas The Madonna Does Not Function | 12" | United Dairies | UD027 | 1986 £3 | £8 | |
| Automating Vol. 1 | LP | United Dairies | UD019 | 1986 £4 | £10 | |
| Automating Vol. 2 | LP | United Dairies | UD030 | 1989 £4 | £10 | |
| Chance Meeting On A Dissecting Table | LP | United Dairies | UD1 | 1979 £37.50 | £75 | |
| Crank | 7" | Wisewound | WW01 | 1987 £2.50 | £6 | B side by Termite Queen |
| Drunk With The Old Man Of The Mountains | LP | United Dairies | UD025 | 1987 £20 | £40 | |
| Faith's Favourites | 12" | Yankhi | YANKHI02 | 1988 £2.50 | £6 | B side by Current 93 |
| Homotopy To Marie | LP | United Dairies | UD013 | 1985 £10 | £25 | |
| Insect And Individual Silenced | LP | United Dairies | UD08 | 1981 £20 | £40 | |
| Merzbild Schwet | LP | United Dairies | UD04 | 1980 £30 | £60 | |
| Missing Sense | LP | United Dairies | UD020 | 1986 £4 | £10 | B side by Organum |
| Ostranenie 1913 | LP | Third Mind | YMR03 | 1984 £10 | £25 | |
| Soliloquy For Lilith | LP | Idle Hole | MIRRORONE | 1988 £15 | £30 | 3 LPs, boxed |
| Soresucker | CD-s | United Dairies | UD031CD | 1990 £2 | £5 | |
| Spiral Insana | LP | Torso | 33016 | 1986 £4 | £10 | Dutch |
| To The Quiet Man From A Tiny Girl | LP | United Dairies | UD03 | 1980 £30 | £60 | |

## NUTRONS

| | | | | | | |
|---|---|---|---|---|---|---|
| Very Best Things | 7" | Melodisc | 1593 | 1964 £5 | £10 | |

## NUTTER, MAY'F

| | | | | | | |
|---|---|---|---|---|---|---|
| Head Shrinker | 7" | Vocalion | VP9282 | 1966 £1.50 | £4 | |

## NUTTY SQUIRRELS

| | | | | | | |
|---|---|---|---|---|---|---|
| Uh! Oh! | 7" | Pye | 7N25044 | 1959 £1.50 | £4 | |

## NYL

| | | | | | | |
|---|---|---|---|---|---|---|
| Nyl | LP | Urus | 000013 | 1976 £5 | £12 | French |

## NYMAN, MICHAEL

| | | | | | | |
|---|---|---|---|---|---|---|
| Decay Music | LP | Obscure | OBS6 | 1976 £4 | £10 | |

## NYRO, LAURA

Laura Nyro was a singer-songwriter with soul – and it is that quality that makes her records so distinctive. The trilogy begun by *Eli And The Thirteenth Confession* represents her best work, with *Eli* perhaps having the edge. Any album that can take the listener from the bleakest despair ('Poverty Train'), through the wistfully romantic ('Emmie'), to uplifting joy ('Eli's Comin'') can only be described as special.

| | | | | | | |
|---|---|---|---|---|---|---|
| Christmas & The Beads Of Sweat | LP | CBS | 64157 | 1970 £4 | £10 | |
| Eli & The 13th Confession | LP | CBS | 63346 | 1968 £4 | £10 | |
| First Songs | LP | CBS | 64991 | 1973 £4 | £10 | |
| First Songs | LP | Verve | SVLP6022 | 1969 £6 | £15 | |
| Gonna Take A Miracle | LP | CBS | 64770 | 1971 £4 | £10 | |
| More Than A New Discovery | LP | Verve | FTS3020 | 1966 £8 | £20 | US |
| New York Tendaberry | LP | CBS | 63510 | 1969 £4 | £10 | |

# O

## O LEVEL
| | | | | | | | |
|---|---|---|---|---|---|---|---|
| East Sheen | 7" | Psycho | PSYCHO1 | 1978 | £7.50 | £15 | *2 picture sleeves* |
| Malcolm McLaren | 7" | King's Road | KR002 | 1978 | £4 | £8 | *2 picture sleeves* |

## O'BRIEN, ANNE
| | | | | | | |
|---|---|---|---|---|---|---|
| Anne O'Brien | LP | Spin | | | £30 | £60 |

## O'BRIEN, HUGH
| | | | | | | | |
|---|---|---|---|---|---|---|---|
| Wyatt Earp Sings | LP | ABC | 203 | 1957 | £10 | £25 | *US* |

## O'CONNOR, DES
| | | | | | | |
|---|---|---|---|---|---|---|
| Moonlight Swim | 7" | Columbia | DB4011 | 1957 | £1.50 | £4 |

## O'CONNOR, HAZEL
| | | | | | | |
|---|---|---|---|---|---|---|
| Compact Hits | CD-s | A&M | AMCD902 | 1988 | £2 | £5 |

## O'CONNOR, SINEAD
| | | | | | | | |
|---|---|---|---|---|---|---|---|
| Emperor's New Clothes | CD-s | Ensign | ENYCD633 | 1990 | £2 | £5 | |
| I Do Not Want What I Have Not Got | CD | Chrysalis | CCD1759 | 1994 | £5 | £12 | *Chrysalis 25 pack* |
| I Want Your Hands On Me | CD-s | Ensign | ENYCD613 | 1988 | £2 | £5 | |
| Jump In The River | CD-s | Ensign | ENYCD618 | 1988 | £2 | £5 | |
| Mandinka | CD-s | Ensign | ENYCD611 | 1987 | £3 | £8 | |
| Mandinka ( Jake's Remix) | 12" | Ensign | ENYXR611 | 1987 | £2.50 | £6 | |
| My Special Child | CD-s | Ensign | ENYCD646 | 1991 | £2 | £5 | |
| Nothing Compares 2U | CD-s | Ensign | ENYCD630 | 1990 | £2 | £5 | |
| Silent Night | CD-s | Ensign | ENYCD652 | 1991 | £2 | £5 | |
| Three Babies | CD-s | Ensign | ENYCD635 | 1990 | £2 | £5 | |

## O'CONNOR, SINEAD & THE EDGE
| | | | | | | |
|---|---|---|---|---|---|---|
| Heroine | 12" | Virgin | VS89712 | 1986 | £3 | £8 |

## O'DAY, ANITA
| | | | | | | |
|---|---|---|---|---|---|---|
| And Billy May Swing Rodgers And Hart | LP | HMV | CLP1436/CSD1354 | 1961 | £6 | £15 |
| Anita | LP | HMV | CLP1085 | 1956 | £6 | £15 |
| Anita O'Day Collates | 10" LP | Columbia | 33C9020 | 1956 | £15 | £30 |
| Anita Sings The Most | LP | Columbia | 33CX10125 | 1958 | £6 | £15 |
| At Mister Kelly's | 10" LP | HMV | DLP1203 | 1959 | £6 | £15 |
| Evening With Anita O'Day | LP | Columbia | 33CX10068 | 1957 | £10 | £25 |
| PIck Yourself Up | 10" LP | HMV | DLP1169 | 1958 | £6 | £15 |
| Swings Cole Porter With Billy May | LP | HMV | CLP1332 | 1960 | £6 | £15 |

## O'DAY, PAT
| | | | | | | |
|---|---|---|---|---|---|---|
| Earth Angel | 7" | MGM | SP1129 | 1955 | £5 | £10 |
| Soldier Boy | 7" | MGM | SP1142 | 1955 | £2.50 | £6 |

## O'DELL, MAC
| | | | | | | | |
|---|---|---|---|---|---|---|---|
| Hymns For The Country Folk | LP | Audio Lab | AL1544 | 1960 | £10 | £25 | *US* |
| Stone Has Rolled Away | 7" | Parlophone | CMSP25 | 1954 | £2.50 | £6 | *export* |

## O'DELL, RONNIE
| | | | | | | |
|---|---|---|---|---|---|---|
| Melody Of Napoli | 7" | London | HLD8439 | 1957 | £2.50 | £6 |

## O'DONNELL, AL
| | | | | | | |
|---|---|---|---|---|---|---|
| Al O'Donnell | LP | Trailer | LER2073 | 1972 | £10 | £25 |
| Al O'Donnell 2 | LP | Transatlantic | LTRA501 | 1978 | £4 | £10 |

## O'DONNELL, JOE
| | | | | | | |
|---|---|---|---|---|---|---|
| Gaodhal's Vision | LP | Polydor | 2383465 | 1977 | £8 | £20 |

## O'DOORS, PATTI
| | | | | | | |
|---|---|---|---|---|---|---|
| World Turned Upside Down | LP | MEK | MEK002 | 1985 | £6 | £15 |

## O'HALLORAN BROTHERS
| | | | | | | |
|---|---|---|---|---|---|---|
| Men Of The Island | LP | Topic | 12TS305 | 1976 | £5 | £12 |

## O'HARA'S PLAYBOYS
| | | | | | | | |
|---|---|---|---|---|---|---|---|
| Get Ready | LP | Fontana | (S)TL5461 | 1968 | £8 | £20 | |
| Party No. 1 | LP | Decca | SKL16295P | 1964 | £25 | £50 | *German* |

## O'JAYS
| | | | | | | | |
|---|---|---|---|---|---|---|---|
| Back On Top | LP | Bell | 6014 | 1968 | £6 | £15 | *US* |
| Comin' Through | LP | Imperial | LP9290/12290 | 1965 | £6 | £15 | *US* |
| I'll Be Sweeter Tomorrow | 7" | Stateside | SS2073 | 1967 | £15 | £30 | |

| Lipstick Traces | 7" | Liberty | LIB66102 | 1965 | £12.50 | £25 | |
| Look Over Your Shoulder | 7" | Bell | BLL1020 | 1968 | £2 | £5 | |
| Soul Sounds | LP | Minit | LP40008 | 1967 | £6 | £15 | US |
| Stand In For Love | 7" | Liberty | LIB66197 | 1966 | £4 | £8 | |

## O'KEEFE, JOHNNY

| Real Wild Child | 7" | Coral | Q72330 | 1958 | £50 | £100 | |
| Tell the Blues So Long | 7" | Zodiac | ZR0016 | 196– | £6 | £12 | |

## O'KEEFE, PADRAIG, DENIS MURPHY, JULIA CLIFFORD

| Kerry Fiddles | LP | Topic | 12T309 | 1977 | £4 | £10 | |

## O'LEARY, JOHN

| Music For The Set | LP | Topic | 12TS357 | 1977 | £4 | £10 | |

## O'NEIL, MATTY

| Don't Sell Daddy Any More Whisky | 7" | London | L1037 | 1954 | £12.50 | £25 | gold label |

## O'NEILL, JOHNNY

| Wagon Train | 7" | RCA | RCA1114 | 1959 | £1.50 | £4 | |

## O'QUIN, GENE

| Boogie Woogie Fever | 78 | Capitol | CL13600 | 1951 | £2.50 | £6 | |

## O'RIADA, SEAN

| Ceol Na Nuasal | LP | Gael Linn | CEF015 | 1967 | £5 | £12 | Irish |
| O'Riada's Farewell | LP | Claddagh | CC12 | 1972 | £4 | £10 | Irish |
| Reacaireacht An Riadaigh | LP | Gael Linn | CEF010 | 1965 | £5 | £12 | Irish |

## O'SULLIVAN, BERNARD & TOMMY MCMAHON

| Play Irish Traditional Music From County Clare | LP | Free Reed | FRS505 | 1976 | £4 | £10 | |

## OAK

| Welcome To Our Fair | LP | Topic | 12TS212 | 1971 | £37.50 | £75 | |

## OAKENSHIELD

| Across The Narrow Seas | LP | Acorn | OAK1 | 1983 | £6 | £15 | |
| Against The Grain | LP | Acorn | OAK2 | 1985 | £6 | £15 | |

## OASIS

Oasis have achieved far greater success than predecessors like the Stone Roses or the Charlatans, partly because the Gallagher brothers have proved themselves to be experts at handling the media. On the premise that no publicity is bad publicity, they have ensured their continual presence in the public notice through real or contrived drug escapades, public squabbling and generally loutish behaviour. By the end of 1996, the group's hold on the popular media was so secure that Liam Gallagher managed to get himself front page coverage by the simple device of getting his hair cut! The actual music struggles to be worthy of the resultant attention, but it is suitably robust – if not at all innovative – and many of the tunes are genuinely memorable.

| Acquiesce | CD-s | Creation | CCD204P | 1995 | £62.50 | £125 | promo |
| Acquiesce | 12" | Creation | CTP204 | 1995 | £50 | £100 | promo |
| Cigarettes And Alcohol | 12" | Creation | CRE190TP | 1994 | £20 | £40 | promo |
| Columbia | 12" | Creation | CTP8 | 1993 | £150 | £250 | 1 sided promo only |
| Cum On Feel The Noize | 12" | Creation | CTP221X | 1996 | £30 | £60 | promo |
| Cum On Feel The Noize | CD-s | Creation | CCD221 | 1996 | £50 | £100 | promo |
| Definitely, Maybe | CD | Sony | SAMP369 | 1994 | £8 | £20 | French or Australian, with bonus CD-s |
| I Am The Walrus | 12" | Creation | CTP190 | 1994 | £180 | £300 | promo only |
| It's Good To Be Free | 12" | Creation | CTP195 | 1994 | £30 | £60 | promo |
| Live At The Metro, Chicago | CD | Sony | ESK6805 | 1995 | £25 | £50 | US promo only |
| Live Forever | 12" | Creation | CRE185TP | 1994 | £15 | £30 | promo |
| Roll With It | 12" | Creation | CTP212 | 1996 | £20 | £40 | promo |
| Round Are Way | 12" | Creation | CTP215 | 1995 | £30 | £60 | promo |
| Singles Collection | CD-s | Sony | HES6611112 | 1995 | £37.50 | £75 | French 5 disc set |
| Slide Away | CD-s | Creation | CCD169 | 1995 | £20 | £40 | promo |
| Some Might Say | CD-s | Creation | CCD204 | 1995 | £25 | £50 | 1 track promo |
| Supersonic | 12" | Creation | CRE176TP | 1994 | £20 | £40 | promo |
| Supersonic | CD-s | Creation | CRESCD176P | 1994 | £7.50 | £15 | promo |
| What's The Story Morning Glory | CD | Creation | CRECD189P | 1995 | £30 | £60 | promo with extra track |
| What's The Story Morning Glory? | CD | Sony | | 1995 | £8 | £20 | Australian, with bonus CD-s |
| Whatever | 12" | Creation | CRE195TP | 1994 | £20 | £40 | promo |

## OBELISQUE

| How Time Flies | LP | Ultimate Record Label | | 1978 | £100 | £200 | Dutch |

## OBERON

| Midsummer Night's Dream | LP | Acorn | no number | 1971 | £500 | £750 | |

## OCCASIONAL WORD ENSEMBLE

| Year Of The Great Leap Sideways | LP | Dandelion | 63753 | 1969 | £6 | £15 | |

## OCCULT CHEMISTRY

| Water Earth Fire Air | 7" | Bikini Girl | | 1980 | £2.50 | £6 | clear flexi |

## OCEAN COLOUR SCENE

Ocean Colour Scene's reinvention of themselves, encouraged by the experience gained by two of their members playing in Paul Weller's backing group, resulted in their second album being a near perfect re-creation of the early seventies progressive hard rock style, and a massive commercial success. *Moseley Shoals* files easily alongside such overlooked classics as *Andromeda* and T2's *It'll All Work Out In Boomland* and proves that there is still much that can be done with the progressive guitar formula. Inevitably, the acclaim generated by *Moseley Shoals* has caused considerable interest in the group's earlier releases.

| | | | | | | |
|---|---|---|---|---|---|---|
| Do Yourself A Favour | CD-s | Fontana | OCSCD3 | 1992 | £2 ......... £5 | |
| Giving It All Away | CD-s | Fontana | OCSCD2 | 1992 | £2 ......... £5 | |
| One Of Those Days | 7" | Phffft | WAVE1P | 1990 | £15 ......... £30 | |
| One Of Those Days | 12" | Phffft | WAVE1 | 1990 | £12.50 ......... £25 | |
| Sway | CD-s | Fontana | OCSCD1 | 1992 | £2 ......... £5 | |
| Sway | CD-s | Phffft | FITCD1 | 1990 | £4 ......... £10 | |
| Sway | 12" | Phffft | FITX001 | 1990 | £3 ......... £8 | |
| Yesterday Today | CD-s | Phffft | FITCD2 | 1991 | £3 ......... £8 | |

## OCHS, PHIL

| | | | | | | |
|---|---|---|---|---|---|---|
| All The News That's Fit To Sing | LP | Elektra | EKL269 | 1964 | £8 ......... £20 | |
| Chords Of Fame | LP | A&M | AMLM64599 | 1974 | £6 ......... £15 | double |
| Greatest Hits | LP | A&M | AMLS973 | 1970 | £6 ......... £15 | |
| Gunfight At Carnegie Hall | LP | A&M | SP9010 | 1971 | £6 ......... £15 | Canadian |
| I Ain't Marchin' Anymore | LP | Elektra | EKL287 | 1965 | £8 ......... £20 | |
| I Ain't Marching Anymore | 7" | Elektra | EKSN45002 | 1965 | £2 ......... £5 | |
| In Concert | LP | Elektra | EKL310 | 1966 | £8 ......... £20 | |
| Interviews With Phil Ochs | LP | Folkways | FB5321 | 1971 | £6 ......... £15 | US |
| Pleasures Of The Harbour | LP | A&M | AML(S)913 | 1967 | £6 ......... £15 | |
| Rehearsals For Retirement | LP | A&M | AMLS934 | 1969 | £6 ......... £15 | |
| Small Circle Of Friends | 7" | A&M | AMS716 | 1968 | £1.50 ......... £4 | |
| Tape From California | LP | A&M | AMLS919 | 1968 | £6 ......... £15 | |

## OCTOBER, JOHNNY

| | | | | | | |
|---|---|---|---|---|---|---|
| Growin' Prettier | 7" | Capitol | CL15070 | 1959 | £1.50 ......... £4 | |
| There'll Always Be A Feeling | 7" | Capitol | CL15121 | 1960 | £1.50 ......... £4 | |

## OCTOBRE

| | | | | | | |
|---|---|---|---|---|---|---|
| Octobre | LP | PGP | 13001 | 1973 | £20 ......... £40 | Canadian |

## OCTOPUS

| | | | | | | |
|---|---|---|---|---|---|---|
| Hey Na Na | 7" | Mooncrest | MOON7 | 1973 | £1.50 ......... £4 | |
| Laugh At The Poor Man | 7" | Penny Farthing | PEN705 | 1969 | £6 ......... £12 | |
| Restless Nights | LP | Penny Farthing | PELS508 | 1970 | £75 ......... £150 | |
| River | 7" | Penny Farthing | PEN716 | 1970 | £5 ......... £10 | |

## OCTOPUS (2)

| | | | | | | |
|---|---|---|---|---|---|---|
| Octopus | LP | ESP-Disk | 2000 | 1969 | £15 ......... £30 | US |

## OCTOPUS (3)

| | | | | | | |
|---|---|---|---|---|---|---|
| Keep Smiling | 7" EP | Vogue | EPL8167 | 1963 | £4 ......... £8 | French |

## ODA

| | | | | | | |
|---|---|---|---|---|---|---|
| Oda | LP | Loud | 80011 | 1973 | £50 ......... £100 | US |

## ODD PERSONS

| | | | | | | |
|---|---|---|---|---|---|---|
| Odd Persons | LP | Somerset | 658 | 1966 | £15 ......... £30 | German |

## ODDSOCKS

Gerald Claridge, whose tape-only *Staggering* album from 1990 is well worth investigating as a set of intriguing contemporary folk songs, is also central to the one album made by Oddsocks. Also in the group is Nick Saloman, later to issue a series of albums under the name of Bevis Frond.

| | | | | | | |
|---|---|---|---|---|---|---|
| Men Of The Moment | LP | Sweet Folk & Country | SFA030 | 1975 | £25 ......... £50 | |

## ODELL, ANN

| | | | | | | |
|---|---|---|---|---|---|---|
| A Little Taste | LP | DJM | DJLPS434 | 1973 | £6 ......... £15 | |

## ODIN

| | | | | | | |
|---|---|---|---|---|---|---|
| Odin | LP | Vertigo | 6360608 | 1972 | £8 ......... £20 | German |

## ODYSSEY

| | | | | | | |
|---|---|---|---|---|---|---|
| Setting Forth | LP | private | | | £1050 ......... £1500 | US |
| Setting Forth | LP | Trip | T1000 | 1990 | £5 ......... £12 | US |

## ODYSSEY (2)

| | | | | | | |
|---|---|---|---|---|---|---|
| Beware | 7" EP | Jag | 232001 | 1967 | £6 ......... £12 | French, B side by Jimmy Powell |

## ODYSSEY (3)

| | | | | | | |
|---|---|---|---|---|---|---|
| Odyssey | LP | Mowest | MWS7002 | 1973 | £8 ......... £20 | |

## ODYSSEY (4)

| | | | | | | |
|---|---|---|---|---|---|---|
| How Long Is Time | 7" | Strike | JH312 | 1966 | £1.50 ......... £4 | |

## OHIO EXPRESS

| | | | | | | |
|---|---|---|---|---|---|---|
| Beg Borrow & Steal | LP | Cameo | CS20000 | 1968 | £5 ......... £12 | US |

## OISIN

| | | | | | | |
|---|---|---|---|---|---|---|
| Bealoideas | LP | ID | IDLP2011 | 1979 | £4 ......... £10 | Irish |
| Jeannie C | LP | Tara | 2013 | 1982 | £4 ......... £10 | Irish |

| | | | | | | | |
|---|---|---|---|---|---|---|---|
| Oisin | LP | ID | IDLP2006 | 1976 | £4 | £10 | Irish |
| Over The Moor To Maggie | LP | Tara | 2012 | 1980 | £4 | £10 | Irish |

## OKAYSIONS
| | | | | | | | |
|---|---|---|---|---|---|---|---|
| Girl Watcher | 7" | Stateside | SS2126 | 1969 | £7.50 | £15 | |

## OKEEFENOKEE JUG BAND
| | | | | | | | |
|---|---|---|---|---|---|---|---|
| Okeefenokee Jug Band | 7" EP | Vogue | EPV1188 | 1958 | £2 | £5 | |

## OKIN, EARL
| | | | | | | | |
|---|---|---|---|---|---|---|---|
| Stop And You'll Become Aware | 7" | CBS | 4495 | 1968 | £2 | £5 | |

## OKKO
| | | | | | | | |
|---|---|---|---|---|---|---|---|
| Sitar And Electronics | LP | BASF | 20211177 | 1971 | £4 | £10 | German |

## OKTOBER
| | | | | | | | |
|---|---|---|---|---|---|---|---|
| Uhrsprung | LP | Trikont | US0024 | 1976 | £4 | £10 | German |

## OLA & THE JANGLERS
| | | | | | | | |
|---|---|---|---|---|---|---|---|
| Alex Is The Man | 7" EP | Pathe | EGF975 | 1966 | £10 | £20 | French |
| Happily Together | LP | Sonet | GMG1217 | 1969 | £8 | £20 | Swedish |
| I Can Wait | 7" | Decca | F12646 | 1967 | £2 | £5 | |
| Let's Dance | LP | Sonet | GMG1214 | 1968 | £8 | £20 | Swedish |
| Limelight | LP | Sonet | GMG1205 | 1967 | £8 | £20 | Swedish |
| Patterns | LP | Sonet | GMG1204 | 1967 | £8 | £20 | Swedish |
| Pictures And Sounds | LP | Sonet | GMG1208 | 1967 | £8 | £20 | Swedish |
| Surprise Surprise | LP | Sonet | GP9928 | 1968 | £8 | £20 | Swedish |
| That's When | 7" EP | Pathe | EGF924 | 1966 | £10 | £20 | French |
| Twelve Big Hits | LP | Sonet | GP9939 | 1969 | £6 | £15 | Swedish |
| Underground | LP | Sonet | GMG1211 | 1968 | £8 | £20 | Swedish |
| What A Way To Die | 7" | Transatlantic | BIG108 | 1968 | £1.50 | £4 | |

## OLD MAN & THE SEA
| | | | | | | | |
|---|---|---|---|---|---|---|---|
| Old Man & The Sea | LP | Sonet | SLPS1539 | 1972 | £150 | £250 | Danish |

## OLD PULL & PUSH
| | | | | | | | |
|---|---|---|---|---|---|---|---|
| Velocipede | LP | Druid | DR1A | 1980 | £4 | £10 | |

## OLD SWAN BAND
| | | | | | | | |
|---|---|---|---|---|---|---|---|
| No Reels | LP | Free Reed | FRR011 | 1976 | £5 | £12 | |
| Old Swan Band | LP | Free Reed | FRR028 | 1978 | £6 | £15 | |

## OLDFIELD, MIKE

Interesting variations exist with regard to the quadrophonic version of Mike Oldfield's *Tubular Bells*. All copies of the picture disc are a stereo remix of the quadrophonic version, the same as first appeared in the four-album *Boxed* compilation. The first 40,000 copies of the black vinyl edition are not a true quadrophonic recording at all, but merely a doctored version of the stereo issue. Thereafter, the records are a true quadrophonic mix, but there is no indication on the cover or label of the record that the substitution has been made.

| | | | | | | | |
|---|---|---|---|---|---|---|---|
| Amarok | CD | Virgin | CDVG2640 | 1991 | £6 | £15 | Australian gold CD |
| Amarok X-Trax | CD-s | Virgin | AMACD1 | 1990 | £5 | £12 | 3" single |
| Don Alfonso | 7" | Virgin | VS117 | 1975 | £4 | £8 | picture sleeve |
| Earth Moving | CD-s | Virgin | VSCD1189 | 1989 | £2 | £5 | |
| Family Man | 7" | Virgin | VSY489 | 1982 | £1.50 | £4 | picture disc |
| Five Miles Out | 7" | Virgin | VSY464 | 1982 | £1.50 | £4 | picture disc |
| Heaven's Open | CD-s | Virgin | VSCDT1341 | 1991 | £2 | £5 | |
| Hergest Ridge | LP | Virgin | QV2013 | 1975 | £6 | £15 | quad |
| Hergest Ridge | 7" | Virgin | | 1974 | £4 | £8 | 1 sided promo sampler |
| Impressions | LP | Tellydisc | TEL4 | 1979 | £8 | £20 | |
| Impressions | cass | Tellydisc | TEL4 | 1979 | £6 | £15 | |
| Innocent | CD-s | Virgin | VSCD1214 | 1989 | £2 | £5 | |
| Islands | CD-s | Virgin | CDEP6 | 1988 | £2 | £5 | |
| Mike Oldfield's Single | 7" | Virgin | VS101 | 1974 | £2 | £5 | picture sleeve |
| Mistake | 7" | Virgin | VSY541 | 1982 | £1.50 | £4 | picture disc |
| Moonlight Shadow | CD-s | Virgin | CDT7 | 1988 | £2 | £5 | 3" single |
| Moonlight Shadow | 7" | Virgin | VSY586 | 1983 | £2.50 | £6 | picture disc |
| Ommadawn | LP | Virgin | QV2043 | 1976 | £6 | £15 | quad |
| Ommadawn | 12" | Virgin | VDJ9 | 1975 | £10 | £20 | promo sampler |
| Orchestral Tubular Bells | 7" | Virgin | VDJ1 | 1975 | £4 | £8 | promo sampler |
| Shine | 7" | Virgin | VSS863 | 1986 | £4 | £8 | shaped picture disc |
| Songs Of Distant Earth | CD | WEA | SAM1477 | 1995 | £20 | £40 | promo in tin box |
| Spanish Tune | 7" | Virgin | VS112 | 1974 | £20 | £40 | promo |
| Tubular Bells | LP | Virgin | QV2001 | 1974 | £5 | £12 | quad |
| Tubular Bells | LP | Virgin | VP2001 | 1978 | £4 | £10 | picture disc |
| Tubular Bells | CD | Virgin | CDVG2001 | 1991 | £6 | £15 | Australian gold CD |
| Virgin Compilation | CD | Virgin | PRCD2113 | 1987 | £20 | £40 | US promo |

## OLDHAM, ANDREW ORCHESTRA
| | | | | | | | |
|---|---|---|---|---|---|---|---|
| 16 Hip Hits | LP | Ace Of Clubs | ACL1180 | 1964 | £15 | £30 | |
| 365 Rolling Stones | 7" | Decca | F11878 | 1964 | £6 | £12 | |
| East Meets West | LP | Parrot | PA6/PAS71003 | 1965 | £15 | £30 | US |
| Funky And Fleopatra | 7" | Decca | F11829 | 1964 | £7.50 | £15 | B side by Jeannie & Her Redheads |
| Maggie May | LP | Decca | LK4636 | 1964 | £6 | £15 | |
| Right Of Way | 7" | Decca | F11987 | 1964 | £6 | £12 | |
| Rolling Stones Songbook | LP | Decca | LK/SKL4796 | 1966 | £20 | £40 | |
| There Are But Five Rolling Stones | 7" | Decca | F11817 | 1964 | £6 | £12 | B side by Cleo |

## OLDHAM TINKERS

| | | | | | | |
|---|---|---|---|---|---|---|
| Best O'T Bunch | LP | Topic | 12TS237 | 1974 | £4 | £10 |
| For Old Time's Sake | LP | Topic | 12TS276 | 1975 | £5 | £12 |
| Oldham's Burning Sands | LP | Topic | 12TS206 | 1971 | £5 | £12 |
| Sit Thee Down | LP | Topic | 12TS323 | 1977 | £5 | £12 |
| That Lancashire Band | LP | Topic | 12TS399 | 1979 | £5 | £12 |

## OLENN, JOHNNY

| | | | | | | | |
|---|---|---|---|---|---|---|---|
| Born Reckless | 7" | Mercury | AMT1050 | 1959 | £20 | £40 | |
| Just Rollin' | LP | LIberty | LRP3029 | 1958 | £75 | £150 | US |
| My Idea Of Love | 7" | London | HLU8388 | 1957 | £100 | £200 | |

## OLIVER

| | | | | | | |
|---|---|---|---|---|---|---|
| Standing Stone | LP | private | OL1 | 1974 | £100 | £200 |

## OLIVER, JOHNNY

| | | | | | | |
|---|---|---|---|---|---|---|
| Chain Gang | 7" | MGM | SP1165 | 1956 | £2 | £5 |
| What A Kiss Won't Do | 7" | Mercury | AMT1095 | 1960 | £1.50 | £4 |

## OLIVER, KING

| | | | | | | |
|---|---|---|---|---|---|---|
| Creole Jazz Band | 10" LP | London | AL3504 | 1954 | £10 | £25 |
| In Harlem | 10" LP | HMV | DLP1609 | 1955 | £10 | £25 |
| King Oliver | LP | Philips | BBL7181 | 1957 | £6 | £15 |
| King Oliver Jazz Band | 10" LP | Columbia | 33S1065 | 1955 | £10 | £25 |
| Louis Armstrong 1923 | LP | Riverside | RLP12122 | 1961 | £4 | £10 |
| Oliver Dixie Syncopators | 10" LP | Vogue Coral | LRA10020 | 1955 | £10 | £25 |
| Plays The Blues | 10" LP | London | AL3510 | 1954 | £10 | £25 |

## OLIVER, PAUL

| | | | | | | |
|---|---|---|---|---|---|---|
| Conversation With The Blues | LP | Decca | LK4664 | 1965 | £15 | £30 |

## OLIVER & THE TWISTERS

| | | | | | | | |
|---|---|---|---|---|---|---|---|
| Look Who's Twistin' Everybody | LP | Colpix | CP423 | 1961 | £8 | £20 | US |

## OLLIE & THE NIGHTINGALES

| | | | | | | |
|---|---|---|---|---|---|---|
| You're Leaving Me | 7" | Stax | STAX109 | 1969 | £2 | £5 |

## OLSSON, NIGEL

| | | | | | | |
|---|---|---|---|---|---|---|
| Drum Orchestra And Chorus | LP | DJM | DJLPS417 | 1972 | £4 | £10 |

## OLYMPICS

| | | | | | | | |
|---|---|---|---|---|---|---|---|
| Baby Do The Philly Dog | 7" | Action | ACT4539 | 1969 | £2 | £5 | |
| Baby Do The Philly Dog | 7" | Fontana | TF778 | 1966 | £4 | £8 | |
| Baby It's Hot | 7" | Vogue | V9204 | 1962 | £2.50 | £6 | |
| Dance By The Light Of The Moon | LP | Vocalion | VAH8059 | 1961 | £15 | £30 | |
| Dance With A Dolly | 7" | Vogue | V9181 | 1961 | £2.50 | £6 | |
| Dance With The Teacher | 7" | HMV | POP564 | 1958 | £5 | £10 | |
| Do The Bounce | LP | Tri-Disc | 1001 | 1963 | £10 | £25 | US |
| Doin' The Hully Gully | LP | Arvee | A423 | 1960 | £30 | £60 | US |
| Good Lovin' | 7" | Warner Bros | WB157 | 1965 | £4 | £8 | |
| I Wish I Could Shimmy | 7" | Vogue | V9174 | 1960 | £2.50 | £6 | |
| I'll Do A Little Bit More | 7" | Action | ACT4556 | 1969 | £1.50 | £4 | |
| Little Pedro | 7" | Vogue | V9184 | 1961 | £4 | £8 | .. B side Cappy Lewis |
| Nothing | 7" | HMV | POP1155 | 1963 | £1.50 | £4 | |
| Party Time | LP | Arvee | A429 | 1961 | £25 | £50 | US |
| Private Eye | 7" | Columbia | DB4346 | 1959 | £5 | £10 | |
| Something Old, Something New | LP | Fontana | TL5407 | 1967 | £6 | £15 | |
| Stomp | 7" | Vogue | V9198 | 1962 | £2.50 | £6 | |
| The Bounce | 7" | Sue | WI348 | 1964 | £6 | £12 | |
| Twist | 7" | Vogue | V9196 | 1962 | £2.50 | £6 | |
| We Go Together | 7" | Fontana | TF678 | 1966 | £4 | £8 | |
| Western Movies | 7" | HMV | POP528 | 1958 | £4 | £8 | |

## O.M.D.

The rarest Orchestral Manoeuvres in the Dark record is not one that a collector of the group's music is ever likely to find. As a mispressing, however, it is arguably only of interest to the completist in any case – the song 'Souvenir' replaces 'Love Action' as the A side on forty copies of the Human League single. Thirty-five of these were destroyed, which leaves a grand total of five copies available for collectors. In the circumstances, it is not realistic to quote a price for these.

| | | | | | | | |
|---|---|---|---|---|---|---|---|
| Call My Name | CD-s | Virgin | VSCDG1380 | 1991 | £2.50 | £6 | digipak |
| Constructive Conversation With OMD | LP | Epic | AS1408 | 1982 | £5 | £12 | US promo |
| Dreaming | CD-s | Virgin | TRICD4 | 1988 | £2.50 | £6 | 3" single |
| Dreaming | CD-s | Virgin | VSCDX987 | 1988 | £5 | £12 | |
| Electricity | 7" | Factory | FAC6 | 1979 | £5 | £10 | |
| La Femme Accident | 7" | Virgin | VSS811 | 1985 | £1.50 | £4 | square picture disc |
| Locomotion | CD-s | Virgin | CDT12 | 1988 | £4 | £10 | 3" single |
| Locomotion | 7" | Virgin | VSY660 | 1984 | £1.50 | £4 | shaped picture disc |
| Maid Of Orleans | CD-s | Virgin | CDT27 | 1988 | £2 | £5 | 3" single |
| Never Turn Away | 7" | Virgin | VSY727 | 1984 | £1.50 | £4 | picture disc |
| Pandora's Box | CD-s | Virgin | VSCDX1331 | 1991 | £4 | £10 | in black wooden box |
| Sailing On The Seven Seas | CD-s | Virgin | VSCDT1310 | 1991 | £3 | £8 | |
| Sailing On The Seven Seas | CD-s | Virgin | VSCDX1310 | 1991 | £10 | £20 | triple CD set |
| Shame | CD-s | Virgin | MIKE93812 | 1987 | £3 | £8 | |
| Talking Loud And Clear | 7" | Virgin | VSY685 | 1984 | £1.50 | £4 | picture disc |
| We Love You | 7" | Virgin | VSC911 | 1986 | £2 | £5 | with cassette |

## OMEGA

| | | | | | | | |
|---|---|---|---|---|---|---|---|
| Csillagok Utjaa | LP | Pepita | SLPX17570 | 1978 £6 | £15 | Hungarian |
| Elo | LP | Pepita | SLPX17447 | 1972 £6 | £15 | Hungarian |
| Five | LP | Pepita | SLPX17457 | 1974 £6 | £15 | Hungarian |
| Idorablo | LP | Pepita | SLPX17523 | 1977 £6 | £15 | Hungarian |
| Omega | LP | Bellaphon | BLPS19147 | 1973 £6 | £15 | German |
| Omega III | LP | Bellaphon | BLPS19191 | 1974 £6 | £15 | German |
| Red Star | LP | Decca | SKL/LK4974 | 1968 £20 | £40 | |
| Trombitas Fredi | LP | Pepita | SLPX17390 | 1968 £10 | £25 | Hungarian |
| Two Hundred Years After The Last War | LP | Bellaphon | BLPS19175 | 1974 £6 | £15 | German |

## OMEGA (2)

| | | | | | | | |
|---|---|---|---|---|---|---|---|
| Prophet | LP | Rock Machine. | MACH1 | 1985 £6 | £15 | |

## ON THE SEVENTH DAY

| | | | | | | | |
|---|---|---|---|---|---|---|---|
| On The Seventh Day | LP | Mercury | SR61248 | 1972 £6 | £15 | US |

## ONE

| | | | | | | | |
|---|---|---|---|---|---|---|---|
| One | LP | Fontana | STL5539 | 1969 £25 | £50 | |

## ONE IN A MILLION

Guitarist Jimmy McCulloch must have been no more than fourteen when recording for the first time with One in a Million. He later played with Thunderclap Newman, Stone the Crows and Paul McCartney's Wings.

| | | | | | | | |
|---|---|---|---|---|---|---|---|
| Fredereek Hernando | 7" | MGM | MGM1370 | 1968 £250 | £400 | best auctioned |
| Use Your Imagination | 7" | CBS | 202513 | 1967 £30 | £60 | |

## ONE THOUSAND MEXICANS

| | | | | | | | |
|---|---|---|---|---|---|---|---|
| Art Of Love | 7" | Whaam! | WHAAM12 | 1983 £1.50 | £4 | |

## ONE THOUSAND VIOLINS

| | | | | | | | |
|---|---|---|---|---|---|---|---|
| Halcyon Days | 12" | Dreamworld | DREAM2 | 1985 £2.50 | £6 | |

## ONE TWO & THREE

| | | | | | | | |
|---|---|---|---|---|---|---|---|
| Black Pearl | 7" | Decca | F12093 | 1965 £2 | £5 | |
| Black Pearls And Green Diamonds | LP | Decca | LK4682 | 1965 £37.50 | £75 | |

## ONE-O-ONERS

| | | | | | | | |
|---|---|---|---|---|---|---|---|
| Elgin Avenue Breakdown | LP | Andalucia | AND101 | 1981 £4 | £10 | |
| Key To Your Heart | 7" | Chiswick | S3 | 1976 £2.50 | £6 | picture sleeve |

## ONES

The lead guitarist with the Ones was Edgar Froese, later to play in an entirely different style as leader of Tangerine Dream.

| | | | | | | | |
|---|---|---|---|---|---|---|---|
| Lady Greengrass | 7" | Star Club | 148593STF | 1966 £100 | £200 | German, best auctioned |

## ONES (2)

| | | | | | | | |
|---|---|---|---|---|---|---|---|
| Ones | LP | Ashwood House | 1105 | 1966 £250 | £400 | US |

## ONE-TWO-SIX

| | | | | | | | |
|---|---|---|---|---|---|---|---|
| Curtains Falling | LP | RCA | 10156 | 1967 £10 | £25 | German |

## ONLOOKERS

| | | | | | | | |
|---|---|---|---|---|---|---|---|
| You And I | 7" | Demon | D1012 | 1982 £5 | £10 | |

## ONLY ONES

Many of the punk musicians to emerge in the late seventies were far from being the brash youngsters they were painted. Skulking at the back of the Only Ones' line-up was the familiar face of Mike Kellie, formerly the drummer with Spooky Tooth. The pedigree of the group's bass player went back even further – he was a member of Scottish beat group, the Beatstalkers. This experience was no doubt the reason the Only Ones were able to deliver such convincing interpretations of Peter Perrett's material. *Another Girl Another Planet* in particular is a classic rock recording by any standard.

| | | | | | | | |
|---|---|---|---|---|---|---|---|
| Another Girl Another Planet | CD-s | CBS | 6577502 | 1992 £2 | £5 | with track by Psychedelic Furs |
| Another Girl, Another Planet | 7" | CBS | 6228 | 1978 £2.50 | £6 | picture sleeve |
| Another Girl, Another Planet | 7" | CBS | 6576 | 1978 £2.50 | £6 | demo |
| Another Girl, Another Planet | 12" | CBS | 126576 | 1978 £2.50 | £6 | |
| Lovers Of Today | 7" | Vengeance | VEN001 | 1977 £2.50 | £6 | |
| Lovers Of Today | 12" | Vengeance | VEN001 | 1977 £3 | £8 | |
| Out There In The Night | 7" | CBS | 7285 | 1979 £1.50 | £4 | |
| Trouble In The World | 7" | CBS | 7963 | 1979 £25 | £50 | black & red picture sleeve |

## ONO, YOKO

| | | | | | | | |
|---|---|---|---|---|---|---|---|
| Approximately Infinite Universe | LP | Apple | SAPDO1001 | 1973 £6 | £15 | double |
| Death Of Samantha | 7" | Apple | 47 | 1973 £6 | £12 | |
| Feeling The Space | LP | Apple | SAPCOR26 | 1973 £15 | £30 | |
| Fly | LP | Apple | SPTU101/2 | 1971 £15 | £30 | double |
| Mind Train | 7" | Apple | 41 | 1972 £2 | £5 | |
| Mind Train | 7" | Apple | 41 | 1972 £7.50 | £15 | picture sleeve |
| Mrs. Lennon | 7" | Apple | 38 | 1971 £4 | £8 | |
| Plastic Ono Band | LP | Apple | SAPCOR17 | 1970 £10 | £25 | |
| Run Run Run | 7" | Apple | 48 | 1973 £6 | £12 | |
| Walking On Thin Ice | 12" | WEA | PROA934 | 1981 £6 | £15 | promo |

| Welcome (The Many Sides Of Yoko Ono). | LP | Apple | PRP18026 | 1974 £150 | £250 | *Japanese promo* |

## ONYX

| Air | 7" | Parlophone | R5888 | 1971 £2 | £5 | |
| My Son John | 7" | Pye | 7N17622 | 1968 £2.50 | £6 | |
| Next Stop Is Mine | 7" | Parlophone | R5906 | 1971 £2 | £5 | |
| Tamaris Khan | 7" | Pye | 7N17668 | 1969 £10 | £20 | |
| Time Off | 7" | CBS | 4635 | 1969 £5 | £10 | |
| You've Gotta Be With Me | 7" | Pye | 7N17477 | 1968 £2.50 | £6 | |

## 004'S

| It's Alright | LP | CBS | ALD6911 | 1966 £50 | £100 | *South African* |

## OPAL BUTTERFLY

Ian 'Lemmy' Kilminster was the guitarist on the third Opal Butterfly single, while his colleague in Hawkwind, Simon King, was the group's drummer.

| Beautiful Beige | 7" | CBS | 3576 | 1968 £7.50 | £15 | |
| Mary Anne With The Shakey Hand | 7" | CBS | 3921 | 1969 £20 | £40 | |
| You're A Groupie Girl | 7" | Polydor | 2058041 | 1970 £5 | £10 | |

## OPEL, JACKIE

| Cry Me A River | 7" | King | KG1011 | 1965 £5 | £10 | |
| Done With A Friend | 7" | Ska Beat | JB190 | 1965 £5 | £10 | |
| Go Whey | 7" | Island | WI209 | 1965 £5 | £10 | |
| I Am What I Am | 7" | Rio | R117 | 1966 £4 | £8 | *...Jackie Mittoo B side* |
| Little More | 7" | Ska Beat | JB227 | 1965 £5 | £10 | |
| Old Rockin' Chair | 7" | Island | WI227 | 1965 £5 | £10 | *Skatalites B side* |
| Pity The Fool | 7" | R&B | JB160 | 1964 £5 | £10 | |
| Solid Rock | 7" | R&B | JB138 | 1964 £5 | £10 | |
| TV In Jamaica | 7" | Jump Up | JU512 | 1967 £2.50 | £6 | |
| Wipe Those Tears | 7" | Island | WI203 | 1965 £5 | £10 | |
| You're No Good | 7" | Black Swan | WI421 | 1964 £5 | £10 | |

## OPEN MIND

| Horses And Chariots | 7" | Philips | BF1790 | 1969 £20 | £40 | |
| Magic Potion | 7" | Philips | BF1805 | 1969 £62.50 | £125 | |
| Open Mind | LP | Antar | ANTAR2 | 1986 £5 | £12 | |
| Open Mind | LP | Philips | SBL7893 | 1969 £330 | £500 | |

## OPEN ROAD

| Swamp Fever | 7" | Greenwich | GSS102 | 1972 £1.50 | £4 | |
| Windy Daze | LP | Greenwich | GSLP1001 | 1971 £10 | £25 | |

## OPEN SKY

| Open Sky | LP | P.M.Records | PMR001 | 1975 £6 | £15 | *US* |
| Spirit In The Sky | LP | P.M.Records | PMR003 | 1975 £6 | £15 | *US* |

## O.P.M.C.

| Amalgamation | LP | Pink Elephant | PE877001 | 1970 £6 | £15 | *Dutch* |
| Product Of Pisces And Capricorn | LP | Pink Elephant | PEL877006 | 1970 £10 | £25 | *Dutch* |

## OPO

| Fallen Asleep Just Like Papa | LP | Spoof | | 1975 £37.50 | £75 | *Dutch* |
| Opo 2 | LP | Spoof | | 1977 £30 | £60 | *Dutch* |

## OPUS

| Baby Come On | 7" | Columbia | DB8675 | 1970 £5 | £10 | |

## OPUS 5

| Contre Courant | LP | Celebration | 1929 | 1976 £10 | £25 | *Canadian* |

## ORA

| Ora | LP | Tangerine | DPLP002S | 1969 £100 | £200 | |

## ORANG UTAN

| Orang Utan | LP | Bell | 6054 | 1971 £15 | £30 | *US* |

## ORANGE BICYCLE

| Carry That Weight | 7" | Parlophone | R5811 | 1969 £2 | £5 | |
| Early Pearly Morning | 7" | Columbia | DB8352 | 1968 £5 | £10 | |
| Goodbye Stranger | 7" | Regal Zonophone | RZ3029 | 1971 £2.50 | £6 | |
| Hyacinth Threads | 7" EP | Impact | 200013 | 1967 £25 | £50 | *French* |
| Hyacinth Threads | 7" | Columbia | DB8259 | 1967 £5 | £10 | |
| Jelly On The Bread | 7" | Parlophone | R5854 | 1970 £2 | £5 | |
| Jenskadajka | 7" | Columbia | DB8413 | 1968 £5 | £10 | |
| Laura's Garden | 7" | Columbia | DB8311 | 1967 £5 | £10 | |
| Orange Bicycle | LP | Parlophone | PCS7108 | 1970 £30 | £60 | |
| Sing This All Together | 7" | Columbia | DB8483 | 1968 £5 | £10 | |
| Take Me To The Pilot | 7" | Parlophone | R5827 | 1970 £2 | £5 | |
| Tonight I'll Be Staying Here | 7" | Parlophone | R5789 | 1969 £2 | £5 | |

## ORANGE JUICE

One feature of the punk explosion was the emergence of a number of independently run record labels. Only a lucky few have survived, but one of the most fondly regarded of those that have not is Postcard records. Much of this regard has to do with the label's sponsoring of Orange Juice. The group's series of sparkling singles are amongst the delights of the immediate post-punk years and they possess a drive and a liveliness somewhat lacking in the new versions of the same songs recorded for the first Polydor LP. These singles are rightly highly prized.

| | | | | | | | | |
|---|---|---|---|---|---|---|---|---|
| Blue Boy | 7" | Postcard | 80-2 | 1980 | £7.50 | £15 | ... hand coloured sleeve |
| Blue Boy | 7" | Postcard | 80-2 | 1980 | £2 | £5 | . white or brown sleeve |
| Falling And Laughing | 7" | Postcard | 80-0 | 1980 | £20 | £40 | picture in bag, Felicity flexi |
| Falling And Laughing | 7" | Postcard | 80-0 | 1980 | £25 | £50 | picture in bag, Felicity flexi, postcard |
| Poor Old Soul | 7" | Postcard | 81-2 | 1981 | £1.50 | £4 | |
| Poor Old Soul | 7" | Postcard | 81-2 | 1981 | £2.50 | £6 | ...with postcard |
| Simply Thrilled Honey | 7" | Postcard | 80-6 | 1980 | £1.50 | £4 | |
| Simply Thrilled Honey | 7" | Postcard | 80-6 | 1980 | £6 | £12 | ....colour insert in bag |

## ORANGE MACHINE

| | | | | | | | |
|---|---|---|---|---|---|---|---|
| Three Jolly Little Dwarfs | 7" | Pye | 7N17559 | 1968 | £20 | £40 | |
| You Can All Join In | 7" | Pye | 7N17680 | 1969 | £20 | £40 | |

## ORANGE PEEL

| | | | | | | | |
|---|---|---|---|---|---|---|---|
| I Got No Time | 7" | Reflection | R55 | 1970 | £2.50 | £6 | |
| Orange Peel | LP | Bellaphon | BLPS19036 | 1972 | £50 | £100 | German |

## ORANGE SEAWEED

| | | | | | | | |
|---|---|---|---|---|---|---|---|
| Stay Awhile | 7" | Pye | 7N17515 | 1968 | £7.50 | £15 | |

## ORANGE WEDGE

| | | | | | | | |
|---|---|---|---|---|---|---|---|
| No One Left But Me | LP | private | | 1974 | £330 | £500 | US |
| Wedge | LP | private | | 1972 | £330 | £500 | US |

## ORB

The success of the Orb was achieved despite (or because of?) breaking so many of the rules governing the methods of most rock artists that it becomes impossible not to be fascinated by their career. Within a critical climate that still reviled the progressive rock of the seventies, the Orb nevertheless managed to achieve acclaim by working within an approach that is indistinguishable from one of the major progressive strands (emphasized by the Orb's use of Pink Floyd quotes and imagery, and the collaborations with Steve Hillage). At the same time, the Orb managed to persuade people that a music based on texture and sound-sculpture – music that seems to call for its listeners to be sitting or lying down in a blissed-out condition – is actually a kind of dance music. Along the way, the Orb have sold a large number of records, including several multiple-album sets and singles playing for vastly longer than the norm. One of the group's biggest hits is 'Blue Room', a single playing at just two seconds under the forty-minute time-span ruled by Gallup to be the maximum length for an item to qualify for inclusion in the singles charts.

| | | | | | | | |
|---|---|---|---|---|---|---|---|
| Adventures Beyond The Underworld | LP | Big Life | BLRDLP5 | 1991 | £5 | £12 | double |
| Assassin | CD-s | Big Life | ORBPROMOCD5 | 1992 | £2.50 | £6 | promo |
| Assassin | 12" | Big Life | ORBPROMO5 | 1992 | £3 | £8 | promo, turquoise vinyl |
| Aubrey Mixes: The Ultraworld Excursions | LP | Big Life | BLRLP14 | 1991 | £5 | £12 | |
| Aubrey Mixes: The Ultraworld Excursions | CD | Big Life | BLRCD14 | 1991 | £8 | £20 | |
| Blue Room | CD-s | Big Life | BLRDA75 | 1992 | £2.50 | £6 | with postcard |
| Blue Room | 7" | Big Life | BLR81D | 1992 | £5 | £10 | jukebox issue |
| Huge Ever Growing Pulsating Brain | CD-s | Big Life | BLR27CD | 1990 | £6 | £15 | |
| Huge Ever Growing Pulsating Brain | 12" | Big Life | BLR27T | 1990 | £6 | £15 | |
| Huge Ever Growing Pulsating Brain | 12" | Wau! Mr. Modo | MWS017T | 1990 | £10 | £20 | |
| | 12" | Wau! Mr. Modo | MWS017R | 1990 | £15 | £30 | |
| Huge Ever Growing Pulsating Brain (remixes) | CD-s | Big Life | BLR27CD | 1990 | £10 | £20 | |
| Huge Ever Growing Pulsating Brain (remixes) | 12" | Big Life | BLR27T | 1990 | £10 | £20 | |
| Huge Ever Growing Pulsating Remix | 12" | Big Life | ORBPROMO1 | 1990 | £4 | £10 | promo |
| Huge Ever Growing Pulsating Remix | 12" | Wau! Mr. Modo | MWS017T | 1990 | £20 | £40 | promo |
| Kiss | 12" | Wau! Mr. Modo | MWS010T | 1989 | £15 | £30 | |
| Little Fluffy Clouds | CD-s | Big Life | BLR33CD | 1990 | £4 | £10 | |
| Little Fluffy Clouds | 12" | Big Life | BLR33T | 1990 | £4 | £10 | |
| Little Fluffy Clouds (Dance Mix) | 12" | Big Life | ORBPROMO2 | 1990 | £4 | £10 | promo |
| Little Fluffy Clouds (Drums And Vox Version) | 12" | Big Life | BLR33R | 1990 | £6 | £15 | |
| Orb In Dub | 12" | Big Life | BLRR46 | 1991 | £10 | £20 | |
| Orbis Terrarum | CD | Island | CID8037 | 1995 | £5 | £12 | ... card sleeve in plastic wallet |
| Perpetual Dawn | CD-s | Big Life | BLR46CD | 1991 | £3 | £8 | |
| Perpetual Dawn | 12" | Big Life | BLRT46 | 1991 | £3 | £8 | |
| Perpetual Dawn: Ultrabass | 12" | Big Life | ORBPROMO3 | 1991 | £4 | £10 | promo |
| Perpetual Dawn: Ultrabass II | 12" | Big Life | ORBPICTURE3 | 1991 | £10 | £20 | promo picture disc |
| Perpetual Dawn: Ultrabass II | 12" | Big Life | ORBPICTURE3 | 1991 | £15 | £30 | promo picture disc – plays Towers Of Dub |
| UFOrb | LP | Big Life | BLRLP18 | 1992 | £5 | £12 | double |
| UFOrb | LP | Big Life | BLRLP18 | 1992 | £8 | £20 | triple |

## ORBIDOIG

| | | | | | | | |
|---|---|---|---|---|---|---|---|
| Nocturnal Operation | 7" | Situation 2 | SIT15 | 1981 | £2 | £5 | |

## ORBISON, ROY

Although the thousands of fans who bought the hits for which Roy Orbison is best known would doubtless disagree, the aching purity of Orbison's high tenor voice was seldom displayed to best advantage on his sixties material. The pathos of 'It's Over', the tranquillity of 'Blue Bayou', even the raunch of 'Pretty Woman' are all undermined by trite, poppy arrangements, conceived without any long-term view of the singer's art. Collectors, it would seem, are inclined to agree, for the values of the sixties records remain stubbornly unspectacular. The recordings made near the end of Roy Orbison's life are another matter altogether – the robust country-rock of both the Traveling Wilburys and Orbison's own *Mystery Girl* album sounds like the music that Orbison had waited all his life to make.

| Title | Format | Label | Cat. No. | Year | | | Notes |
|---|---|---|---|---|---|---|---|
| At The Rockhouse | LP | Sun | LP1260 | 1961 | £50 | £100 | US |
| Big O | LP | London | HAU/SHU8406 | 1970 | £5 | £12 | |
| Black And White Night | CD | Virgin | PRCDPOLAROY | 1989 | £8 | £20 | US promo |
| Blue Angel | 7" | London | HLU9207 | 1960 | £1.50 | £4 | |
| Break My Mind | 7" | London | HLU10294 | 1969 | £1.50 | £4 | |
| Classic | LP | London | HAU/SHU8297 | 1966 | £8 | £20 | |
| Cry Softly Lonely One | LP | London | HAU/SHU8357 | 1968 | £6 | £15 | |
| Crying | LP | London | HAU2437/ SHU6229 | 1962 | £8 | £20 | |
| Devil Doll | 7" EP | Ember | EMBEP4570 | 1965 | £15 | £30 | |
| Early Orbison | LP | Monument | LMO/SMO5013 | 1967 | £4 | £10 | |
| Exciting Sounds | LP | Ember | NR5013 | 1964 | £4 | £10 | |
| Fastest Guitar Alive | LP | London | HAU/SHU8358 | 1968 | £8 | £20 | |
| God Loves You | 7" | London | HLU10358 | 1972 | £1.50 | £4 | |
| Hank Williams The Roy Orbison Way | LP | MGM | SE4683 | 1970 | £4 | £10 | US |
| Heartache | 7" | London | HLU10222 | 1968 | £1.50 | £4 | |
| Hillbilly Rock | 7" EP | London | RES1089 | 1957 | £37.50 | £75 | gold label |
| I'm Hurtin' | 7" | London | HLU7108 | 1961 | £5 | £10 | export |
| I'm Hurtin' | 7" | London | HLU9307 | 1961 | £1.50 | £4 | |
| In Dreams | LP | London | HAU/SHU8108 | 1963 | £8 | £20 | |
| In Dreams | CD | Virgin | VDGCD3514 | 1991 | £6 | £15 | Australian gold CD |
| In Dreams | 7" EP | London | REU1373 | 1963 | £5 | £10 | |
| It's Over | 7" EP | London | REU1435 | 1964 | £5 | £10 | |
| Last Night | 7" | London | HLU10339 | 1971 | £1.50 | £4 | |
| Lonely And Blue | LP | London | HAU2342 | 1961 | £8 | £20 | |
| Love Hurts | 7" EP | London | REU1440 | 1965 | £6 | £12 | |
| Memphis | LP | London | SHU8445 | 1973 | £5 | £12 | |
| Memphis Tennessee | 7" | London | HLU10388 | 1972 | £2.50 | £6 | |
| My Friend | 7" | London | HLU10261 | 1969 | £1.50 | £4 | |
| Mystery Girl | CD | Virgin | CDVG2576 | 1991 | £6 | £15 | Australian gold CD |
| Mystery Girl | CD | Virgin | PROCDROY | 1989 | £8 | £20 | US promo in cloth cover |
| Oh Pretty Woman | LP | London | HAU8207 | 1964 | £6 | £15 | |
| Oh Pretty Woman | CD-s | Virgin | VSCD1224 | 1989 | £2 | £5 | 3" single |
| Oh Pretty Woman | 7" EP | London | REU1437 | 1964 | £5 | £10 | |
| Only The Lonely | 78 | London | HLU9149 | 1960 | £50 | £100 | |
| Only The Lonely | 7" EP | London | REU1274 | 1960 | £5 | £10 | |
| Only The Lonely | 7" | London | HLU9149 | 1960 | £1.50 | £4 | |
| Orbison Way | LP | London | HAU/SHU8279 | 1966 | £8 | £20 | |
| Orbisongs | LP | Monument | LMO/SMO5004 | 1966 | £5 | £12 | |
| Penny Arcade | 7" | London | HLU10285 | 1969 | £5 | £10 | |
| Roy Orbison Sings | LP | London | SHU8435 | 1972 | £4 | £10 | |
| Roy Orbison's Stage Show Hits | 7" EP | London | REU1439 | 1965 | £6 | £12 | |
| Sings Don Gibson | LP | London | HAU/SHU8318 | 1967 | £6 | £15 | |
| So Young | 7" | London | HLU10310 | 1970 | £1.50 | £4 | |
| Special Delivery | LP | Camden | CAL820 | 1964 | £5 | £12 | US |
| Sweet And Easy To Love | 7" EP | Ember | EMBEP4546 | 1964 | £15 | £30 | |
| Sweet And Easy To Love | 7" | Ember | EMBS209 | 1965 | £5 | £10 | |
| Sweet And Easy To Love | 7" | Ember | EMBS209 | 1965 | £4 | £8 | picture sleeve |
| There Is Only One | LP | London | HAU/SHU8252 | 1965 | £6 | £15 | |
| This Kind Of Love | 7" | Ember | EMBS200 | 1964 | £1.50 | £4 | |
| This Kind Of Love | 7" | Ember | EMBS200 | 1964 | £4 | £8 | picture sleeve |
| Trying To Get To You | 7" EP | Ember | EMBEP4563 | 1964 | £15 | £30 | |
| Uptown | 7" EP | London | REU1354 | 1963 | £5 | £10 | |
| Walk On | 7" | London | HLU10206 | 1968 | £1.50 | £4 | |
| Wild Hearts | 7" | ZTT | DZTAS9 | 1985 | £7.50 | £15 | double |
| Workin' For The Man | 7" | London | HLU9607 | 1962 | £1.50 | £4 | |
| You're My Baby | 7" | Ember | EMBS197 | 1964 | £1.50 | £4 | |

## ORBIT FIVE

| Title | Format | Label | Cat. No. | Year | | | Notes |
|---|---|---|---|---|---|---|---|
| I Wanna Go To Heaven | 7" | Decca | F12799 | 1968 | £10 | £20 | |
| I Wanna Go To Heaven | 7" | Decca | F12799 | 1968 | £10 | £20 | picture sleeve |

## ORBITAL

| Title | Format | Label | Cat. No. | Year | | | Notes |
|---|---|---|---|---|---|---|---|
| Chimes | CD-s | FFRR | FCD135 | 1990 | £2 | £5 | |
| Midnight | CD-s | FFRR | FCD163 | 1991 | £2 | £5 | |
| Omen | CD-s | FFRR | FCD145 | 1990 | £2 | £5 | |
| Satan | CD-s | FFRR | FCD149 | 1991 | £2 | £5 | |

## ORCHIDS

| Title | Format | Label | Cat. No. | Year | | | Notes |
|---|---|---|---|---|---|---|---|
| Gonna Make Him Mine | 7" | Decca | F11743 | 1963 | £4 | £8 | |
| I've Got That Feeling | 7" | Decca | F11861 | 1964 | £4 | £8 | |
| Love Hit Me | 7" | Decca | F11785 | 1963 | £4 | £8 | |

## ORCHIDS (2)

| Title | Format | Label | Cat. No. | Year | | | Notes |
|---|---|---|---|---|---|---|---|
| From This Day | 7" | Sha La La | 005 | 1988 | £2 | £5 | flexi, B side by Sea Urchins |
| I've Got A Habit | 7" | Sarah | 002 | 1988 | £5 | £10 | with poster |

## ORE

| Title | Format | Label | Cat. No. | Year | | | Notes |
|---|---|---|---|---|---|---|---|
| Halcyon Days | LP | Akashic | | 1979 | £10 | £25 | US picture disc |
| Your Time Will Come | 7" | Bandit | BR003 | 1982 | £6 | £12 | |

## OREGON

| | | | | | | | |
|---|---|---|---|---|---|---|---|
| Distant Hills | LP | Vanguard | VSD79341 | 1974 | £5 | £12 | |
| In Concert | LP | Vanguard | VSD79358 | 1976 | £5 | £12 | US |
| Music Of Another Present Era | LP | Vanguard | VSD79326 | 1974 | £5 | £12 | |
| Winter Light | LP | Vanguard | VSD79350 | 1975 | £5 | £12 | |

## ORGANAIRE, CHARLES

| | | | | | | | |
|---|---|---|---|---|---|---|---|
| Little Village | 7" | R&B | JB149 | 1964 | £5 | £10 | |
| Little Village | 7" | Rio | R28 | 1964 | £5 | £10 | |

## ORGANGRINDERS

| | | | | | | | |
|---|---|---|---|---|---|---|---|
| Out Of The Egg | LP | Mercury | SR.61282 | 1970 | £15 | £30 | US |

## ORGANISATION

Ralf Hutter and Florian Schneider-Esleban, the creative centre of Kraftwerk, recorded an earlier album as Organisation. Like Tangerine Dream's *Electronic Meditation*, *Tone Float* is the work of a unit trying to create an electronic soundscape with acoustic instruments and essentially biding time until the invention of a usable synthesizer. Objectively, the music is not really very impressive, although its historical importance is undeniable.

| | | | | | | | |
|---|---|---|---|---|---|---|---|
| Tone Float | LP | RCA | SF8111 | 1970 | £75 | £150 | |

## ORGANISERS

| | | | | | | | |
|---|---|---|---|---|---|---|---|
| Lonesome Road | 7" | Pye | 7N17022 | 1966 | £25 | £50 | |

## ORGANUM

| | | | | | | | |
|---|---|---|---|---|---|---|---|
| Pulp | 7" | Aeroplane | AR7 | 198– | £10 | £20 | |

## ORIENT EXPRESS

| | | | | | | | |
|---|---|---|---|---|---|---|---|
| Orient Express | LP | Mainstream | S6117 | 1969 | £37.50 | £75 | US |

## ORIENTAL SUNSHINE

| | | | | | | | |
|---|---|---|---|---|---|---|---|
| Dedicated To The Bird We Love | LP | Fontana | | 1971 | £180 | £300 | Swedish |

## ORIGINAL BARNSTORMERS SPASM BAND

| | | | | | | | |
|---|---|---|---|---|---|---|---|
| That's All There Is | 7" | Tempo | A168 | 195– | £1.50 | £4 | |

## ORIGINAL CHECKMATES

| | | | | | | | |
|---|---|---|---|---|---|---|---|
| Checkmate Twist | 7" | Pye | 7N15442 | 1962 | £2.50 | £6 | |
| Hot Toddy | 7" | Pye | 7N15428 | 1962 | £2 | £5 | |
| Union Pacific | 7" | Decca | F11688 | 1963 | £7.50 | £15 | |

## ORIGINAL DIXIELAND JAZZ BAND

| | | | | | | | |
|---|---|---|---|---|---|---|---|
| Historic Records Of The First Recorded Jazz | 10" LP | HMV | DLP1065 | 1955 | £8 | £20 | |
| In England | 10" LP | Columbia | 33S1087 | 1956 | £8 | £20 | |
| In England No. 2 | 10" LP | Columbia | 33S1133 | 1957 | £8 | £20 | |

## ORIGINAL DOWNTOWN SYNCOPATORS

| | | | | | | | |
|---|---|---|---|---|---|---|---|
| It's Jass | 7" EP | Columbia | SEG8293 | 1964 | £2 | £5 | |
| Original Downtown Syncopators | 7" EP | VJM | VEP14 | 1962 | £2 | £5 | |

## ORIGINAL DYAKS

| | | | | | | | |
|---|---|---|---|---|---|---|---|
| Gotta Get A Good Thing Going | 7" | Columbia | DB8184 | 1967 | £2 | £5 | |

## ORIGINAL FIVE BLIND BOYS

| | | | | | | | |
|---|---|---|---|---|---|---|---|
| Original Five Blind Boys | 7" EP | Vogue | EPV1159 | 1957 | £4 | £8 | |

## ORIGINAL NEW ORLEANS RHYTHM KINGS

| | | | | | | | |
|---|---|---|---|---|---|---|---|
| Golden Leaf Strut | 7" | Columbia | SCM5113 | 1954 | £1.50 | £4 | |

## ORIGINAL TORNADOES

| | | | | | | | |
|---|---|---|---|---|---|---|---|
| Telstar | 7" | SRT | SRTS75350 | 1975 | £2 | £5 | |

## ORIGINALS

| | | | | | | | |
|---|---|---|---|---|---|---|---|
| Baby I'm For Real | 7" | Tamla Motown | TMG733 | 1970 | £1.50 | £4 | |
| Down To Love Town | 12" | Tamla Motown | TMGT1038 | 1976 | £2.50 | £6 | |
| Good Night Irene | 7" | Tamla Motown | TMG592 | 1967 | £12.50 | £25 | |
| Green Grow The Lilacs | LP | Tamla Motown | (S)TML11116 | 1969 | £5 | £12 | |
| Green Grow The Lilacs | 7" | Tamla Motown | TMG702 | 1969 | £1.50 | £4 | |

## ORIGINALS (2)

| | | | | | | | |
|---|---|---|---|---|---|---|---|
| Gimme A Little Kiss Will Ya | 7" | Top Rank | JAR600 | 1962 | £4 | £8 | |

## ORIGINELLS

| | | | | | | | |
|---|---|---|---|---|---|---|---|
| My Girl | 7" | Columbia | DB7259 | 1964 | £2.50 | £6 | |
| Nights | 7" | Columbia | DB7388 | 1964 | £2 | £5 | |

## ORIOLES

| | | | | | | | |
|---|---|---|---|---|---|---|---|
| Crying In The Chapel | 78 | London | L1201 | 1953 | £25 | £50 | |
| Hold Me, Thrill Me, Kiss Me | 78 | London | L1180 | 1953 | £25 | £50 | |
| In The Mission Of St. Augustine | 78 | London | HL8001 | 1954 | £25 | £50 | |

## ORION, P. J. & THE MAGNATES

| | | | | | | | |
|---|---|---|---|---|---|---|---|
| P. J.Orion & The Magnates | LP | Magnate | 122459 | 1961 | £15 | £30 | US |

## ORION THE HUNTER
Orion The Hunter ..................................... CD..... Portrait ........... PRT25906 ............. 1984 £10.........£25 ...........................

## ORLANDO
Am I The Same Guy ................................. 7"...... NEMS .......... 564159 ................. 1969 £1.50.........£4

## ORLANDO, TONY
| | | | | | | | |
|---|---|---|---|---|---|---|---|
| Beautiful Dreamer | 7" | Columbia | DB4954 | 1963 | £1.50 | £4 | |
| Bless You | LP | Fontana | STFL582 | 1963 | £20 | £40 | stereo |
| Bless You | LP | Fontana | TFL5167 | 1963 | £15 | £30 | mono |
| Bless You | 7" EP | Columbia | SEG8238 | 1963 | £20 | £40 | |
| Bless You | 7" | Fontana | H330 | 1961 | £1.50 | £4 | |
| Chills | 7" | Columbia | DB4871 | 1962 | £1.50 | £4 | |
| Halfway To Paradise | 7" | Fontana | H308 | 1961 | £2.50 | £6 | |
| Happy Times | 7" | Fontana | H350 | 1961 | £1.50 | £4 | |
| Joannie | 7" | Columbia | DB4991 | 1963 | £1.50 | £4 | |
| Talking About You | 7" | Fontana | H366 | 1962 | £1.50 | £4 | |
| Tell Me What I Can Do | 7" | Columbia | DB7288 | 1964 | £1.50 | £4 | |

## ORLONS
| | | | | | | | |
|---|---|---|---|---|---|---|---|
| All The Hits | LP | Cameo Parkway | C1033 | 1962 | £10 | £25 | |
| Biggest Hits | LP | Cameo Parkway | C1061 | 1963 | £8 | £20 | |
| Bon Doo Wah | 7" | Cameo Parkway | C287 | 1963 | £2.50 | £6 | |
| Crossfire | 7" | Cameo Parkway | C273 | 1963 | £2 | £5 | |
| Don't Hang Up | 7" | Cameo Parkway | C231 | 1962 | £2 | £5 | |
| Down Memory Lane | LP | Cameo | C1073 | 1963 | £8 | £20 | US |
| Knock Knock | 7" | Cameo Parkway | C332 | 1964 | £2.50 | £6 | |
| Not Me | LP | Cameo | C1054 | 1963 | £8 | £20 | US |
| Not Me | 7" | Cameo Parkway | C257 | 1963 | £1.50 | £4 | |
| Rules Of Love | 7" | Cameo Parkway | C319 | 1964 | £2.50 | £6 | |
| Shimmy Shimmy | 7" | Cameo Parkway | C295 | 1963 | £1.50 | £4 | |
| South Street | LP | Cameo | C1041 | 1963 | £10 | £25 | US |
| South Street | 7" | Cameo Parkway | C243 | 1963 | £1.50 | £4 | |
| Spinning Top | 7" | Mojo | 2092029 | 1972 | £1.50 | £4 | |
| Spinning Top | 7" | Planet | PLF117 | 1966 | £20 | £40 | |
| Wah Watusi | LP | Cameo | C1020 | 1962 | £10 | £25 | US |
| Wah Watusi | 7" | Columbia | DB4865 | 1962 | £2.50 | £6 | |

## ORLONS & DOVELLS
Golden Hits ................................... LP ..... Cameo ........... C1067 ............... 1963 £8.........£20 ........... US

## ORNANDEL, CYRIL
King Of Kings ................................ 7" ..... MGM ............ SP 1141 .......... 1955 £1.50.........£4

## ORPHAN EGG
Orphan Egg ................................... LP ..... Carole ............ CARS8004 ......... 1968 £15.........£30 ........... US

## ORPHEUS
My Life ....................................... 7" ..... Red Bird........ RB10041 ............... 1966 £4.........£8

## ORPHEUS (2)
| | | | | | | | |
|---|---|---|---|---|---|---|---|
| Orpheus | LP | Bell | 6061 | 1968 | £6 | £15 | US, different tracks |
| Orpheus | LP | MGM | C(S)8072 | 1968 | £6 | £15 | |

## ORY, KID
| | | | | | | | |
|---|---|---|---|---|---|---|---|
| Dance With Kid Ory – Or Just Listen | LP | HMV | CLP1395/CSD1325 | 1960 | £5 | £12 | |
| In The Beginning | 7" EP | Collector | JE117 | 1960 | £2 | £5 | |
| In The Mood | LP | HMV | CLP1329 | 1960 | £5 | £12 | |
| Kid From New Orleans | LP | HMV | CLP1303 | 1959 | £6 | £15 | |
| Kid Ory | 7" EP | Philips | BBE12275 | 1959 | £2 | £5 | |
| Kid Ory | 7" EP | Storyville | SEP317 | 195– | £2 | £5 | |
| Kid Ory In Europe | LP | Columbia | 33CX10116 | 1958 | £6 | £15 | |
| Kid Ory Plays W.C.Handy | LP | HMV | CLP1364 | 1960 | £5 | £12 | |
| Kid Ory's Creole Jazz Band | LP | Good Time Jazz | LAG12064 | 1957 | £6 | £15 | |
| Kid Ory's Creole Jazz Band | LP | Good Time Jazz | LAG12104 | 1958 | £5 | £12 | |
| Kid Ory's Creole Jazz Band | 7" EP | Good Time Jazz | EPG1006 | 195– | £2 | £5 | |
| Kid Ory's Creole Jazz Band | 7" EP | Tempo | EXA5 | 1955 | £2 | £5 | |
| Kid Ory's Creole Jazz Band | 7" EP | Vogue | EPV1035 | 1955 | £2 | £5 | |
| Kid Ory's Creole Jazz Band | 10" LP | Philips | BBR8088 | 1956 | £5 | £12 | |
| Kid Ory's Creole Jazz Band 1944–1945 | 10" LP | Goodtime Jazz | LDG055 | 1954 | £6 | £15 | |
| Kid Ory's Creole Jazz Band 1944–1945 Vol. 2 | 10" LP | Goodtime Jazz | LDG093 | 1954 | £6 | £15 | |
| Kid Ory's Creole Jazz Band 1944–1945 Vol. 3 | 10" LP | Goodtime Jazz | LDG184 | 1956 | £6 | £15 | |

| | | | | | | | |
|---|---|---|---|---|---|---|---|
| Kid Ory's Creole Jazz Band 1954 | LP | Good Time Jazz | LAG12004 | 1955 | £5 | £12 | |
| Legendary Kid 1956 | LP | Good Time Jazz | LAG12084 | 1958 | £5 | £12 | |
| Song Of The Wanderer | LP | Columbia | 33CX10134 | 1959 | £6 | £15 | |
| We've Got Rhythm | LP | HMV | CLP1422/CSD1342 | 1961 | £6 | £15 | *with Henry Allen* |

## OS MUNDI

| | | | | | | | |
|---|---|---|---|---|---|---|---|
| 43 Minuten | LP | Brain | 1015 | 1972 | £10 | £25 | *German* |
| Latin Mass | LP | Metronome | 15381 | 1970 | £10 | £25 | *German* |

## OSAMU

| | | | | | | | |
|---|---|---|---|---|---|---|---|
| Banzaiten | LP | Island | ILPS80580 | 1976 | £6 | £15 | *Japanese* |

## OSANNA

| | | | | | | | |
|---|---|---|---|---|---|---|---|
| L'Uomo | LP | Fonit | LPX10 | 1971 | £8 | £20 | *Italian* |
| Landscape Of Life | LP | Fonit | LPX32 | 1974 | £6 | £15 | *Italian* |
| Milano Calibro 9 | LP | Fonit | LPX14 | 1972 | £6 | £15 | *Italian* |
| Palepoli | LP | Fonit | LPX19 | 1972 | £6 | £15 | *Italian* |
| Uno | LP | Fonit | LPX26 | 1974 | £6 | £15 | *Italian* |

## OSBORNE, MIKE

| | | | | | | | |
|---|---|---|---|---|---|---|---|
| All Night Long | LP | Ogun | OG700 | 1975 | £8 | £20 | |
| Border Crossing | LP | Ogun | OG300 | 1974 | £8 | £20 | |
| Marcel's Muse | LP | Ogun | OG810 | 1977 | £8 | £20 | |
| Original | LP | Cadillac | SGC1002 | 1974 | £8 | £20 | *with Stan Tracy* |
| Outback | LP | Turtle | TUR300 | 1971 | £25 | £50 | |
| Tandem | LP | Ogun | OG210 | 1976 | £8 | £20 | *with Stan Tracy* |

## OSBORNE BROTHERS

| | | | | | | | |
|---|---|---|---|---|---|---|---|
| Banjo Boys | 7" | MGM | MGM1184 | 1962 | £2 | £5 | |
| Country Picking & Hillside Singing | 7" EP | MGM | MGMEP691 | 1959 | £7.50 | £15 | |

## OSBOURNE, JOHNNY

| | | | | | | | |
|---|---|---|---|---|---|---|---|
| Come Back Darling | LP | Trojan | TTL29 | 1970 | £6 | £15 | |

## OSBOURNE, OZZY

| | | | | | | | |
|---|---|---|---|---|---|---|---|
| Bark At The Moon | 12" | Epic | TA3915 | 1983 | £6 | £15 | *silver vinyl* |
| Bark At The Moon | 12" | Epic | WA3915 | 1983 | £5 | £12 | *picture disc* |
| Diary Of A Madman | LP | Jet | | 1981 | £15 | £30 | *US promo picture disc* |
| Just Say Ozzy | CD | Epic | 4659402 | 1993 | £5 | £12 | |
| Mama I'm Coming Home | CD-s | Epic | 6576179 | 1991 | £2 | £5 | |
| Miracle Man | CD-s | Epic | 6530632 | 1988 | £2 | £5 | |
| Miracle Man | 7" | Epic | 6530639 | 1988 | £2 | £5 | *shaped picture disc* |
| Mr. Crowley | 7" | Jet | JET7003 | 1980 | £2 | £5 | |
| Mr. Crowley | 12" | Jet | JETP12003 | 1980 | £5 | £12 | *picture disc* |
| No More Tears | CD-s | Epic | 6574402 | 1991 | £2 | £5 | *wallet sleeve* |
| So Tired | 12" | Epic | WA4452 | 1984 | £3 | £8 | *gold vinyl* |
| Symptom Of The Universe | 7" | Jet | JETP7030 | 1982 | £2.50 | £6 | *picture disc* |
| Tribute | CD | Columbia | ASK2695 | 1987 | £10 | £25 | *US promo sampler* |
| Ultimate Sin | LP | Epic | 1126404 | 1986 | £4 | £10 | *picture disc* |
| Ultimate Sin | CD-s | Epic | 6528752 | 1988 | £2 | £5 | |

## OSBURN, BOB

| | | | | | | | |
|---|---|---|---|---|---|---|---|
| Bound To Happen | 7" | London | HLD9869 | 1964 | £4 | £8 | |

## OSCAR

Oscar (Beuselinck) is the real name of the singer and actor who has found far greater success under the name of Paul Nicholas. 'Over The Wall We Go' has the extra attraction of being an early David Bowie production (with Bowie himself making a cameo appearance), while 'Join My Gang' is a Pete Townshend song that the Who never recorded themselves.

| | | | | | | | |
|---|---|---|---|---|---|---|---|
| Club Of Lights | 7" | Reaction | 591003 | 1966 | £6 | £12 | |
| Holiday | 7" | Reaction | 591016 | 1967 | £6 | £12 | |
| Join My Gang | 7" | Reaction | 591006 | 1966 | £7.50 | £15 | |
| Open Up The Skies | 7" | Polydor | 56257 | 1968 | £6 | £12 | |
| Over The Wall We Go | 7" | Reaction | 591012 | 1967 | £7.50 | £15 | |

## OSCAR BICYCLE

| | | | | | | | |
|---|---|---|---|---|---|---|---|
| On A Quiet Night | 7" | CBS | 3237 | 1968 | £7.50 | £15 | |

## OSIBISA

| | | | | | | | |
|---|---|---|---|---|---|---|---|
| Osibisa | LP | MCA | MDKS8001 | 1971 | £4 | £10 | |
| Woyaya | LP | MCA | MDKS8005 | 1971 | £4 | £10 | |

## OSWALD, JOHN

*Plunderphonic* is constructed entirely from other people's records, which John Oswald manipulates, chops and changes with all the skill of a surgeon. The result is a masterpiece to be filed alongside Christian Marclay's *More Encores* and the KLF's *1987*. Unfortunately, like the KLF album, *Plunderphonic* managed to offend one of the original copyright holders. Despite being conceived as a totally non-profit making album – original copies were given away rather than sold – Michael Jackson's management objected to the unauthorized sampling of 'Bad' and were able to order the destruction of all remaining copies of the CD. One suspects, however, that the real source of outrage was the cover picture, created as a visual parallel to the sound aesthetics inside, and showing Jackson in half-naked 'Bad' pose, the body clearly revealed as being female.

| | | | | | | | |
|---|---|---|---|---|---|---|---|
| Plunderphonic | CD | Mystery Lab | no number | 1989 | £25 | £50 | *Canadian* |

## OSWALD, LEE HARVEY

| | | | | | | | |
|---|---|---|---|---|---|---|---|
| Self Portrait In Red | LP | Inca | 1001 | 1967 | £6 | £15 | *US* |

| | | | | | | | |
|---|---|---|---|---|---|---|---|
| Speaks | LP | Truth | 2265 | 1967 £6 | £15 | US |

## OTHER BROTHERS
| | | | | | | | |
|---|---|---|---|---|---|---|---|
| Let's Get Together | 7" | Pama | PM785 | 1969 £1.50 | £4 | |

## OTHER HALF
Guitarist with the Other Half was Randy Holden, who subsequently became a member of Blue Cheer.

| | | | | | | | |
|---|---|---|---|---|---|---|---|
| Mr. Pharmacist | 7" EP | Vogue | INT18112 | 1966 £50 | £100 | French |
| Other Half | LP | Acta | A38004 | 1968 £20 | £40 | US |

## OTHER HALF (2)
| | | | | | | | |
|---|---|---|---|---|---|---|---|
| Other Half | LP | 7/2 Records | HS12 | 1966 £875 | £1250 | US |
| Other Half | LP | Resurrection | CX1266 | 1984 £5 | £12 | US |

## OTHER TWO
| | | | | | | | |
|---|---|---|---|---|---|---|---|
| Don't You Wanna Love Me | 7" | RCA | RCA1465 | 1965 £1.50 | £4 | |
| I Wanna Be With You | 7" | Decca | F11911 | 1964 £2 | £5 | |
| I'll Never Let You Go | 7" | RCA | RCA1531 | 1966 £1.50 | £4 | |

## OTHERS
| | | | | | | | |
|---|---|---|---|---|---|---|---|
| Oh Yeah | 7" | Fontana | TF501 | 1964 £20 | £40 | |

## OTIS, JOHNNY
| | | | | | | | |
|---|---|---|---|---|---|---|---|
| All I Want Is Your Love | 7" | Capitol | CL14837 | 1958 £2 | £5 | |
| Bye Bye Baby | 7" | Capitol | CL14817 | 1958 £4 | £8 | |
| Casting My Spell | 7" | Capitol | CL15018 | 1959 £2.50 | £6 | |
| Crazy Country Hop | 7" | Capitol | CL14941 | 1958 £5 | £10 | |
| Cuttin' Up | LP | Epic | BN26524 | 1970 £4 | £10 | US |
| Formidable | LP | Ember | SPE6604 | 196– £5 | £12 | |
| Harlem Nocturne | 78 | Parlophone | R3291 | 1950 £10 | £20 | ..B side Slim Gaillard |
| Johnny Otis | 7" EP | Vocalion | VEP170162 | 1965 £30 | £60 | |
| Johnny Otis Show | LP | Capitol | T940 | 1958 £15 | £30 | |
| Johnny Otis Show | 7" EP | Capitol | EAP11134 | 1959 £20 | £40 | |
| Ma He's Making Eyes At Me | 7" | Capitol | CL14794 | 1957 £2 | £5 | |
| Mumbling Mosie | 7" | Capitol | CL15112 | 1960 £2 | £5 | |
| Pioneers Of Rock Vol. 3 | LP | Starline | SRS5129 | 1973 £4 | £10 | |
| Ring A Ling | 7" | Capitol | CL14875 | 1958 £5 | £10 | |
| Rock And Roll Hit Parade Vol. 1 | LP | Dig | 104 | 1957 £50 | £100 | US |
| Three Girls Named Molly | 7" | Capitol | CL15057 | 1959 £2 | £5 | |
| Well Well Well Well | 7" | Capitol | CL14854 | 1958 £2 | £5 | |
| You | 7" | Capitol | CL15008 | 1959 £2 | £5 | |

## OTIS, SHUGGIE
| | | | | | | | |
|---|---|---|---|---|---|---|---|
| Here Comes Shuggie Otis | LP | CBS | 63996 | 1970 £4 | £10 | |

## OTWAY, JOHN
| | | | | | | | |
|---|---|---|---|---|---|---|---|
| Beware Of The Flowers | 7" | Viking | no number | 1975 £7.50 | £15 | |
| Deep And Meaningless | LP | Polydor | 2383501 | 1978 £4 | £10 | with 7" (OT1) |
| Gypsy | 7" | County | COUN215 | 1972 £7.50 | £15 | |

## OTWAY, JOHN & WILD WILLY BARRETT
| | | | | | | | |
|---|---|---|---|---|---|---|---|
| John Otway & Wild Willie Barrett | LP | Extracted | ELP1 | 1977 £4 | £10 | |
| Murder Man | 7" | Track | 2094111 | 1973 £1.50 | £4 | |

## OUGENWEIDE
| | | | | | | | |
|---|---|---|---|---|---|---|---|
| All Die Weill Ich Mag | LP | Polydor | 2371517 | 1974 £6 | £15 | German |
| Eulenspiegel | LP | Polydor | 2371714 | 1976 £5 | £12 | German |
| Fryheit | LP | Polydor | 2437576 | 1978 £5 | £12 | German |
| Ohrenschmaus | LP | Polydor | 2371700 | 1975 £5 | £12 | German |
| Ougenweide | LP | Polydor | 2371678 | 1974 £6 | £15 | German |
| Ougenweide | LP | Zebra | 2949009 | 1973 £6 | £15 | German |
| Ungezwungen | LP | Polydor | 2634091 | 1977 £6 | £15 | German double |

## OUR PLASTIC DREAM
| | | | | | | | |
|---|---|---|---|---|---|---|---|
| Little Bit Of Shangrila | 7" | Go | AJ11411 | 1967 £37.50 | £75 | |

## OUT OF DARKNESS
| | | | | | | | |
|---|---|---|---|---|---|---|---|
| Out Of Darkness | LP | Key | KL006 | 1970 £100 | £200 | |

## OUT OF FOCUS
| | | | | | | | |
|---|---|---|---|---|---|---|---|
| Four Letter Monday Afternoon | LP | Kuckuck | 2640101 | 1972 £20 | £40 | German double |
| Out Of Focus | LP | Kuckuck | 2375010 | 1972 £15 | £30 | German |
| Wake Up | LP | Kuckuck | 2375006 | 1971 £10 | £25 | German |

## OUTCASTS
| | | | | | | | |
|---|---|---|---|---|---|---|---|
| Frustration | 7" | It | IT4 | 1978 £2.50 | £6 | |
| Just Another Teenage Rebel | 7" | Good Vibrations | GOT3 | 1978 £2 | £5 | 2 different picture sleeves |

## OUTER LIMITS
| | | | | | | | |
|---|---|---|---|---|---|---|---|
| Dark Side Of The Moon | 7" | Decca | F13176 | 1971 £2 | £5 | |
| Great Train Robbery | 7" | Instant | IN001 | 1968 £6 | £12 | |
| Just One More Chance | 7" | Deram | DM125 | 1967 £5 | £10 | |
| When The Work Is Thru' | 7" | Elephant | LUR100 | 1967 £15 | £30 | ..5 Man Cargo B side |

## OUTLAW BLUES BAND

| | | | | | | |
|---|---|---|---|---|---|---|
| Breaking In | LP | Stateside | SSL10290 | 1969 £4 | £10 | |
| Outlaw Blues Band | LP | Bluesway | BLS6021 | 1968 £4 | £10 | US |

## OUTLAWS

The Outlaws were employed as session men by producer Joe Meek and therefore appear on records by the likes of Mike Berry, John Leyton and Heinz. Between October 1962 and April 1964 the lead guitarist was Ritchie Blackmore. He can be heard on the four Outlaws singles issued in 1963–4, but not on the Outlaws album. This record, which contains cowboy-oriented instrumentals, has been highly sought-after since the early days of record collecting.

| | | | | | |
|---|---|---|---|---|---|
| Ambush | 7" | HMV | POP877 | 1961 £2.50 | £6 |
| Dream Of The West | LP | HMV | CLP1484 | 1961 £50 | £100 |
| Keep A Knocking | 7" | HMV | POP1277 | 1964 £10 | £20 |
| Last Stage West | 7" | HMV | POP990 | 1962 £4 | £8 |
| Law And Order | 7" | HMV | POP1241 | 1963 £4 | £8 |
| Return Of The Outlaws | 7" | HMV | POP1124 | 1963 £2.50 | £6 |
| Sioux Serenade | 7" | HMV | POP1074 | 1962 £4 | £8 |
| Swinging Low | 7" | HMV | POP844 | 1961 £2.50 | £6 |
| That Set The Wild West Free | 7" | HMV | POP1195 | 1963 £4 | £8 |
| Valley Of The Sioux | 7" | HMV | POP927 | 1961 £4 | £8 |

## OUTRIGGERS

| | | | | | | |
|---|---|---|---|---|---|---|
| Surrender | 7" EP | Warner Bros | WSEP2027 | 1961 £2 | £5 | stereo |

## OUTSIDERS

| | | | | | | |
|---|---|---|---|---|---|---|
| Album No. 2 | LP | Capitol | (S)T2568 | 1966 £8 | £20 | US |
| Girl In Love | 7" | Capitol | CL15450 | 1966 £5 | £10 | |
| Happening Live | LP | Capitol | (S)T2745 | 1967 £8 | £20 | US |
| Help Me Girl | 7" EP | Capitol | EAP120879 | 1966 £15 | £30 | French |
| Help Me Girl | 7" | Capitol | CL15480 | 1966 £2.50 | £6 | |
| I'll Give You Time | 7" EP | Capitol | EAP120948 | 1967 £15 | £30 | French |
| I'll Give You Time | 7" | Capitol | CL15495 | 1967 £4 | £8 | |
| Outsiders In | LP | Capitol | (S)T2636 | 1967 £8 | £20 | US |
| Respectable | 7" | Capitol | CL15468 | 1966 £5 | £10 | |
| Time Won't Let Me | LP | Capitol | (S)T2501 | 1966 £8 | £20 | US |
| Time Won't Let Me | 7" EP | Capitol | EAP120804 | 1966 £15 | £30 | French |
| Time Won't Let Me | 7" | Capitol | CL15435 | 1966 £6 | £12 | |

## OUTSIDERS (2)

| | | | | | |
|---|---|---|---|---|---|
| Calling On Youth | LP | Raw Edge | RER001 | 1977 £4 | £10 |
| Close Up | LP | Raw Edge | RER003 | 1978 £4 | £10 |
| One To Infinity | 7" | Raw Edge | RER002 | 1977 £2 | £5 |
| Vital Hours | 7" | Xciting Plastic | | 1978 £5 | £10 |

## OUTSIDERS (3)

| | | | | | | |
|---|---|---|---|---|---|---|
| CQ | LP | Polydor | 236803 | 1972 £50 | £100 | Dutch |
| Outsiders | LP | Relax | 30007 | 1964 £30 | £60 | Dutch |
| Outsiders Or Insiders | LP | CNR | GA5501 | 1966 £37.50 | £75 | Dutch |

## OUTSIDERS (4)

| | | | | | |
|---|---|---|---|---|---|
| Keep On Doing It | 7" | Decca | F12213 | 1965 £4 | £8 |

## OUTSKIRTS OF INFINITY

| | | | | | |
|---|---|---|---|---|---|
| Lord Of The Dark Skies | LP | Woronzow | WOO7 | 1987 £4 | £10 |

## OVARY LODGE

| | | | | | |
|---|---|---|---|---|---|
| Ovary Lodge | LP | Ogun | OG600 | 1976 £5 | £12 |
| Ovary Lodge | LP | RCA | SF8372 | 1973 £15 | £30 |

## OVERLANDERS

| | | | | | | |
|---|---|---|---|---|---|---|
| Don't It Make You Feel Good | 7" EP | Pye | PNV24124 | 1964 £7.50 | £15 | French |
| Michelle | LP | Pye | NPL18138 | 1966 £10 | £25 | |
| Michelle | 7" EP | Pye | NEP24245 | 1966 £7.50 | £15 | |
| Michelle | 7" EP | Pye | PNV24161 | 1966 £7.50 | £15 | French |

## OVERTAKERS

| | | | | | |
|---|---|---|---|---|---|
| That's The Way You Like It | 7" | Amalgamated | AMG803 | 1968 £4 | £8 |

## OWEN, RAY

| | | | | | |
|---|---|---|---|---|---|
| Ray Owen's Moon | LP | Polydor | 2325061 | 1971 £5 | £12 |

## OWEN, REG

| | | | | | |
|---|---|---|---|---|---|
| Manhattan Spiritual | 7" | Pye | 7N25009 | 1959 £1.50 | £4 |

## OWEN & LEON

| | | | | | | |
|---|---|---|---|---|---|---|
| Fits Is On Me | 7" | Island | WI164 | 1964 £5 | £10 | Skatalites B side |
| My Love For You | 7" | Island | WI163 | 1964 £5 | £10 | |
| Running Around | 7" | Island | WI165 | 1964 £5 | £10 | Skatalites B side |

## OWEN-B

| | | | | | | |
|---|---|---|---|---|---|---|
| Owen-B | LP | Musicol | 101209/10 | 1970 £37.50 | £75 | US |

## OWENS, BUCK

| | | | | | |
|---|---|---|---|---|---|
| Act Naturally | 7" EP | Capitol | EAP120602 | 1964 £4 | £8 |
| Before You Go | LP | Capitol | (S)T2353 | 1966 £4 | £10 |
| Best Of Buck Owens | LP | Capitol | (S)T2105 | 1964 £4 | £10 |

| | | | | | | | |
|---|---|---|---|---|---|---|---|
| Buck Owens Sings Harlan Howard | LP | Capitol | (S)T1482 | 1961 | £5 | £12 | US |
| Carnegie Hall Concert | LP | Capitol | (S)T2556 | 1967 | £4 | £10 | |
| Everlasting Love | 7" | Capitol | CL15009 | 1959 | £1.50 | £4 | |
| Fabulous Country Music Sound | LP | Starday | SLP172 | 1962 | £4 | £10 | US |
| Foolin' Around | 7" EP | Capitol | EAP11550 | 1961 | £4 | £8 | |
| I've Got A Tiger By The Tail | LP | Capitol | (S)T2283 | 1966 | £4 | £10 | |
| It Takes People Like You To Make People Like Me | LP | Capitol | (S)T2841 | 1968 | £4 | £10 | |
| Roll Out The Red Carpet | LP | Capitol | (S)T2443 | 1966 | £4 | £10 | |
| Together Again | LP | Capitol | T2135 | 1965 | £4 | £10 | |
| Under Your Spell Again | LP | Capitol | (D)T1489 | 1961 | £5 | £12 | US |
| Your Tender Loving Care | LP | Capitol | (S)T2760 | 1968 | £4 | £10 | |
| Yours, Country Style | LP | Capitol | (S)T20861 | 1966 | £4 | £10 | |

## OWENS, DONNIE

| | | | | | | | |
|---|---|---|---|---|---|---|---|
| Need You | 7" | London | HL8747 | 1958 | £6 | £12 | |

## OWL

| | | | | | | | |
|---|---|---|---|---|---|---|---|
| Run To The Sun | 7" | United Artists | UP2240 | 1968 | £5 | £10 | |

## OXFORDS

| | | | | | | | |
|---|---|---|---|---|---|---|---|
| Flying Up Through The Sky | LP | Union Jac | LH6497 | 1970 | £15 | £30 | US |

## OXLEY, TONY

| | | | | | | | |
|---|---|---|---|---|---|---|---|
| Ach Was? | LP | FMP | 0871 | 1981 | £5 | £12 | German |
| Baptised Traveller | LP | CBS | 52664 | 1969 | £20 | £40 | |
| Duo | LP | ADMW | 005 | 197– | £6 | £15 | with Davie Alan |
| February Papers | LP | Incus | INCUS18 | 1976 | £6 | £15 | |
| Four Compositions For Sextet | LP | CBS | 64071 | 1970 | £20 | £40 | |
| Ichnos | LP | RCA | SF8215 | 1971 | £20 | £40 | |
| Quartet – Dedications | LP | Knonnex | ST5002 | 1983 | £5 | £12 | |
| Ronnie's Lament | LP | View | VS0018 | 1981 | £5 | £12 | German |
| SOH | LP | Ego | 4011 | 1979 | £6 | £15 | |
| Tomorrow Is Here | LP | Dossier | ST7507 | 1986 | £5 | £12 | |
| Tony Oxley | LP | Incus | INCUS8 | 1975 | £8 | £20 | |

## OXYM

| | | | | | | | |
|---|---|---|---|---|---|---|---|
| Music Power | 7" | Cargo | CRS3 | 1981 | £2.50 | £6 | |

## OYSTER BAND

| | | | | | | | |
|---|---|---|---|---|---|---|---|
| English Rock And Roll The Early Years (1800–1850) | LP | Pukka | YOP1 | 1982 | £20 | £40 | |
| Jack's Alive | LP | Dingles | DIN309 | 1980 | £15 | £30 | credited to Oyster Ceilidh Band |
| Liberty Hall | LP | Pukka | YOP7 | 1985 | £20 | £40 | |
| Lie Back And Think Of England | LP | Pukka | YOP6 | 1985 | £20 | £40 | |
| Twenty Golden Tie Slackeners | LP | Pukka | YOP06 | 1984 | £20 | £40 | |

## OZ KNOZZ

| | | | | | | | |
|---|---|---|---|---|---|---|---|
| Ruff Mix | LP | Ozone | OZ1000 | 1975 | £180 | £300 | US |

## OZO

| | | | | | | | |
|---|---|---|---|---|---|---|---|
| Listen To The Buddah | LP | DJM | DJF20488 | 1970 | £8 | £20 | |

## OZZ II

| | | | | | | | |
|---|---|---|---|---|---|---|---|
| Assassin | LP | Zebra | ZEB2 | 1984 | £6 | £15 | |

# P

## PABLO, AUGUSTUS

| | | | | | | | |
|---|---|---|---|---|---|---|---|
| East Of The River Nile | 7" | Big Shot | BI579 | 1971 | £1.50 | £4 | Herman B side |
| Ital Dub | LP | Trojan | TRLS115 | 1976 | £6 | £15 | |
| King Tubby Meets Rockers Uptown | LP | Yard Music | DSR8225 | 197– | £6 | £15 | |
| Original Rockers | LP | Greensleeves | GREL8 | 1979 | £5 | £12 | |
| Reggae In The Fields | 7" | Duke | DU122 | 1971 | £1.50 | £4 | ... Tommy McCook B side |
| Snowball And Pudding | 7" | Ackee | ACK138 | 1971 | £1.50 | £4 | Aquarians B side |
| Still Yet | 7" | Ackee | ACK134 | 1971 | £1.50 | £4 | Aquarians B side |
| This Is Augustus Pablo | LP | Tropical | TROPS101 | 1974 | £6 | £15 | |

## PACIFIC DRIFT

| | | | | | | | |
|---|---|---|---|---|---|---|---|
| Feelin' Free | LP | Nova | (S)DN13 | 1970 | £8 | £20 | |
| Water Woman | 7" | Deram | DM304 | 1970 | £1.50 | £4 | |

## PACIFIC GAS & ELECTRIC

| | | | | | | | |
|---|---|---|---|---|---|---|---|
| Get It On | LP | B&C | CAS1003 | 1969 | £4 | £10 | |
| Pacific Gas & Electric | LP | CBS | 63822 | 1969 | £4 | £10 | |

## PACIFIC SOUND

| | | | | | | | |
|---|---|---|---|---|---|---|---|
| Forget Your Dream | LP | Splendid | 50104 | 1972 | £250 | £400 | Swiss |

## PACK

| | | | | | | | |
|---|---|---|---|---|---|---|---|
| Do You Believe In Magic | 7" | Columbia | DB7702 | 1965 | £10 | £20 | |

## PACK (2)

| | | | | | | | |
|---|---|---|---|---|---|---|---|
| Brave New Soldiers | 7" | SS | PAK1 | 1979 | £4 | £8 | |
| King Of Kings | 7" | Rough Trade | RT025 | 1979 | £2.50 | £6 | |
| Kirk Brandon And The Pack Of Lies | 7" | SS | SS1N2/SS2N1 | 1980 | £5 | £10 | |
| Long Live The Past | 7" | Cyclops | CYCLOPS1 | 1982 | £1.50 | £4 | |

## PACKABEATS

| | | | | | | | |
|---|---|---|---|---|---|---|---|
| Dream Lover | 7" | Pye | 7N15549 | 1963 | £5 | £10 | |
| Evening In Paris | 7" | Pye | 7N15480 | 1962 | £5 | £10 | |
| Gypsy Beat | 7" | Parlophone | R4729 | 1961 | £2.50 | £6 | |

## PACKERS

| | | | | | | | |
|---|---|---|---|---|---|---|---|
| Hole In The Wall | LP | Soul City | SCM003 | 1970 | £8 | £20 | |
| Hole In The Wall | 7" | Pye | 7N25343 | 1966 | £4 | £8 | |
| Hole In The Wall | 7" | Soul City | SC111 | 1969 | £2 | £5 | |

## PAC-KEYS

| | | | | | | | |
|---|---|---|---|---|---|---|---|
| Stone Fox | 7" | Speciality | SPE1003 | 1967 | £2 | £5 | |

## PADDY, KLAUS & GIBSON

| | | | | | | | |
|---|---|---|---|---|---|---|---|
| I Wanna Know | 7" | Pye | 7N15906 | 1965 | £4 | £8 | |
| No Good Without You Baby | 7" | Pye | 7N17060 | 1966 | £7.50 | £15 | |
| Teresa | 7" | Pye | 7N17112 | 1966 | £4 | £8 | |

## PAESE DEI BOLOCCHI

| | | | | | | | |
|---|---|---|---|---|---|---|---|
| Paese Dei Bolocchi | LP | CGD | FGL5115 | 1972 | £20 | £40 | Italian |

## PAGE, HAL & THE WHALERS

| | | | | | | | |
|---|---|---|---|---|---|---|---|
| Going Back To My Home Town | 7" | Melodisc | 1553 | 1960 | £10 | £20 | |

## PAGE, JIMMY

| | | | | | | | |
|---|---|---|---|---|---|---|---|
| Interview With Jimmy Page | CD | Geffen | PROCD3099 | 1988 | £10 | £25 | US promo |
| Outrider | CD | Geffen | | 1988 | £10 | £25 | US promo sampler with interview |
| Outrider | CD | Geffen | 9241882 | 1988 | £20 | £40 | promo box set, with cassette, interview CD, video, photo |
| She Just Satisfies | CD-s | Fontana | TFCD533 | 1991 | £2.50 | £6 | Led Zeppelin pack |
| She Just Satisfies | 7" | Fontana | TF533 | 1965 | £180 | £300 | best auctioned |
| Wasting My Time | 7" | Geffen | GEF41 | 1988 | £2 | £5 | |

## PAGE, JIMMY & ROBERT PLANT

| | | | | | | | |
|---|---|---|---|---|---|---|---|
| Conversations With Jimmy Page And Robert Plant | CD | Atlantic | PRCD59872 | 1994 | £10 | £25 | US promo |
| Gallows Pole | CD-s | Fontana | PPDD2 | 1994 | £2.50 | £6 | |
| No Quarter – Unledded Radio Special | CD | Fontana | PPID1 | 1995 | £37.50 | £75 | interview promo |
| Songwriting Legacy | CD | Atlantic | PRCD60952 | 1995 | £20 | £40 | US promo only 'Greatest Hits' |

## PAGE, LARRY
| | | | | | | |
|---|---|---|---|---|---|---|
| Big Blon' Baby | 7" | Saga | SAG452902 | 1959 | £2.50 | £6 |
| Cool Shake | 7" | Columbia | DB3965 | 1957 | £5 | £10 |
| How Am I Doing, Hey, Hey | 7" | Saga | SAG452903 | 1959 | £2 | £5 |
| Kinky Music | LP | Decca | LK4692 | 1965 | £25 | £50 |
| Sings His Personal Choice | 7" EP | Saga | STP1024 | 1963 | £2 | £5 |
| That'll Be The Day | 7" | Columbia | DB4012 | 1957 | £5 | £10 |
| Under Control | 7" | Columbia | DB4080 | 1958 | £4 | £8 |

## PAGE, MALLY
| | | | | | | |
|---|---|---|---|---|---|---|
| Life And Soul Of The Party | 7" | Pye | 7N17105 | 1966 | £1.50 | £4 |

## PAGE, PATTI
| | | | | | | | |
|---|---|---|---|---|---|---|---|
| Christmas With Patti Page | 10" LP | Mercury | MPT7510 | 1956 | £5 | £12 | |
| Folk Song Favourites | 10" LP | Mercury | MG25101 | 1954 | £5 | £12 | |
| I'm Getting Sentimental Over You | 10" LP | Mercury | MPT7531 | 1957 | £5 | £12 | |
| In The Land Of Hi-Fi | LP | Emarcy | EJL1252 | 1957 | £4 | £10 | |
| Lady Is A Tramp | 7" EP | Mercury | SEZ19008 | 1961 | £2 | £5 | stereo |
| Left Right Out Of Your Heart | 7" | Mercury | 7MT223 | 1958 | £1.50 | £4 | |
| My Kinda Love | 7" EP | Mercury | SEZ19020 | 1961 | £2 | £5 | stereo |
| Patti Page | 7" EP | Mercury | MEP9502 | 1956 | £2 | £5 | |
| Patti Page No. 1 | 7" EP | Mercury | ZEP10006 | 1959 | £2 | £5 | |
| Patti Page No. 2 | 7" EP | Mercury | ZEP10017 | 1959 | £2 | £5 | |
| Patti Page No. 3 | 7" EP | Mercury | ZEP10032 | 1959 | £2 | £5 | |
| Patti Page No. 4 | 7" EP | Mercury | ZEP10045 | 1959 | £2 | £5 | |
| Patti's Songs | 10" LP | Mercury | MG25197 | 1955 | £5 | £12 | |
| Patti's Songs | 10" LP | Mercury | MPT7535 | 1957 | £4 | £10 | |

## PAGE BOYS
| | | | | | | |
|---|---|---|---|---|---|---|
| You're My Kind Of Girl | 7" | Whaam! | WHAAM10 | 1983 | £2 | £5 |

## PAGE FIVE
| | | | | | | |
|---|---|---|---|---|---|---|
| Let Sleeping Dogs Lie | 7" | Parlophone | R5426 | 1966 | £7.50 | £15 |

## PAGE TEN
| | | | | | | |
|---|---|---|---|---|---|---|
| Boutique | 7" | Decca | F12248 | 1965 | £2.50 | £6 |

## PAICH, MARTY
| | | | | | | |
|---|---|---|---|---|---|---|
| Marty Paich Quartet | 10" LP | London | LZU14040 | 1957 | £8 | £20 |

## PAIGE, JOEY
| | | | | | | |
|---|---|---|---|---|---|---|
| Cause I'm In Love With You | 7" | Fontana | TF554 | 1965 | £5 | £10 |

## PAIGE, ROSALIND
| | | | | | | |
|---|---|---|---|---|---|---|
| Love, Oh Careless Love | 7" | MGM | MGM937 | 1957 | £1.50 | £4 |
| When The Saints | 7" | London | HL8120 | 1955 | £7.50 | £15 |

## PAINTED SHIP
| | | | | | | |
|---|---|---|---|---|---|---|
| Frustration | 7" | Mercury | MF988 | 1967 | £15 | £30 |

## PAISLEYS
| | | | | | | | |
|---|---|---|---|---|---|---|---|
| Cosmic Mind At Play | LP | Audio City | 94452809 | 1968 | £50 | £100 | US |
| Cosmic Mind At Play | LP | Peace | 70P1 | 1970 | £30 | £60 | US |
| Cosmic Mind At Play | LP | Psycho | PSYCHO7 | 1983 | £6 | £15 | |

## PALADIN
| | | | | | | |
|---|---|---|---|---|---|---|
| Charge | LP | Bronze | ILPS9190 | 1972 | £8 | £20 |
| Paladin | LP | Bronze | ILPS9150 | 1971 | £6 | £15 |

## PALE SAINTS
| | | | | | | | |
|---|---|---|---|---|---|---|---|
| Children Break | 7" | Panic | | 198– | £5 | £10 | flexi, B side by Savlons & Kerry Fiddles |

## PALEY, TOM
| | | | | | | |
|---|---|---|---|---|---|---|
| Sue Cow | LP | Argo | ZFB3 | 1969 | £5 | £12 |

## PALEY, TOM & PEGGY SEEGER
| | | | | | | |
|---|---|---|---|---|---|---|
| Who's Going To Shoe Your Pretty Little Foot? | LP | Topic | 12T113 | 1964 | £10 | £25 |

## PALLAS
| | | | | | | | |
|---|---|---|---|---|---|---|---|
| Arrive Alive | LP | Cool King | CKLP002 | 1983 | £4 | £10 | |
| Arrive Alive | 7" | Granite Wax | GWS1 | 1982 | £12.50 | £25 | |
| Knightmoves | 12" | Harvest | 12PLSD3 | 1985 | £6 | £15 | with Mad Machine 7" |
| Pallas | 7" | Suicide | PAL101 | 1978 | £20 | £40 | |
| Paris Is Burning | 12" | Cool King | 12CK010 | 1983 | £2.50 | £6 | |

## PALMEIRA
| | | | | | | | |
|---|---|---|---|---|---|---|---|
| Palmeira | LP | ANS | | 1983 | £5 | £12 | Dutch |

## PALMER, BRUCE
| | | | | | | | |
|---|---|---|---|---|---|---|---|
| Cycle Is Complete | LP | Verve | VRF3086 | 1971 | £10 | £25 | US |

## PALMER, CLIVE
| | | | | | | | |
|---|---|---|---|---|---|---|---|
| Just Me | LP | Autogram | ALLP258 | 1979 | £25 | £50 | German |

## PALMER, EARL
| | | | | | | | |
|---|---|---|---|---|---|---|---|
| Drum Village | 7" | Capitol | CL14859 | 1958 | £2 | £5 | |
| Swingin' Drums | 7" EP | Capitol | EAP11026 | 1958 | £2 | £5 | ...... with Billy May |

## PALMER, ROBERT
| | | | | | | | |
|---|---|---|---|---|---|---|---|
| Bad Case Of Lovin' You | CD-s | Island | CID438 | 1989 | £2 | £5 | |
| Change His Ways | CD-s | EMI | CDEM85 | 1989 | £2 | £5 | |
| I Didn't Mean To Turn You On | CD-s | Island | CID283 | 1986 | £15 | £30 | |
| It Could Happen To You | CD-s | EMI | CDEM99 | 1989 | £2 | £5 | |
| Live In Boston | LP | Warner Bros | WBMS111 | 1979 | £8 | £20 | US promo |
| Secrets | LP | Island | PROA819 | 1979 | £8 | £20 | US promo picture disc |
| She Makes My Day | CD-s | EMI | CDEM65 | 1988 | £2 | £5 | |
| Simply Irresistible | CD-s | EMI | CDEM61 | 1988 | £2 | £5 | |

## PALMER, ROY & THE STATE STREET RAMBLERS
| | | | | | | | |
|---|---|---|---|---|---|---|---|
| Chicago Skiffle Session | 10" LP | London | AL3518 | 1954 | £8 | £20 | |

## PALMETTO KINGS
| | | | | | | | |
|---|---|---|---|---|---|---|---|
| Ten Rum Bottles | 7" | Starlite | ST45021 | 1960 | £1.50 | £4 | |

## PAN
| | | | | | | | |
|---|---|---|---|---|---|---|---|
| Pan | LP | Sonet | SLPS1518 | 1970 | £100 | £200 | |

## PAN (2)
| | | | | | | | |
|---|---|---|---|---|---|---|---|
| Pan | LP | Columbia | KC32062 | 1973 | £8 | £20 | US |

## PANAMA LTD. JUG BAND
| | | | | | | | |
|---|---|---|---|---|---|---|---|
| Indian Summer | LP | Harvest | SHVL779 | 1970 | £20 | £40 | |
| Lady Of Shallott | 7" | Harvest | HAR5010 | 1969 | £2 | £5 | |
| Panama Ltd. Jug Band | LP | Harvest | SHVL753 | 1969 | £15 | £30 | |
| Round And Round | 7" | Harvest | HAR5022 | 1970 | £2 | £5 | |

## PANCAKE
| | | | | | | | |
|---|---|---|---|---|---|---|---|
| Roxy Elephant | LP | Offers | OMP7602 | 1975 | £4 | £10 | German |

## PANCHO, GENE
| | | | | | | | |
|---|---|---|---|---|---|---|---|
| I Like Sweet Music | 7" | Giant | GN21 | 1968 | £1.50 | £4 | |

## PANDAMONIUM
| | | | | | | | |
|---|---|---|---|---|---|---|---|
| Chocolate Buster Dan | 7" | CBS | 3451 | 1968 | £20 | £40 | |
| No Presents For Me | 7" | CBS | 2664 | 1967 | £30 | £60 | |
| Season Of The Witch | 7" | CBS | 202462 | 1967 | £20 | £40 | |

## PANDORRA ENSEMBLE
| | | | | | | | |
|---|---|---|---|---|---|---|---|
| III | LP | Disaster Electronics | | 1978 | £50 | £100 | Dutch |

## PANHANDLE
| | | | | | | | |
|---|---|---|---|---|---|---|---|
| Panhandle | LP | Decca | SKL5105 | 1972 | £6 | £15 | |

## PANIC, JOHNNY & THE BIBLE OF DREAMS
| | | | | | | | |
|---|---|---|---|---|---|---|---|
| Johnny Panic | CD-s | Fontana | PANCD1 | 1991 | £2.50 | £6 | |
| Johnny Panic | 12" | Fontana | PANIC112 | 1991 | £2.50 | £6 | |

## PANTA RHEI
| | | | | | | | |
|---|---|---|---|---|---|---|---|
| Panta Rhei | LP | Amiga | 855318 | 1973 | £20 | £40 | East German |

## PANTER, JAN
| | | | | | | | |
|---|---|---|---|---|---|---|---|
| Scratch My Back | 7" | Pye | 7N17097 | 1966 | £7.50 | £15 | |

## PANTHEON
| | | | | | | | |
|---|---|---|---|---|---|---|---|
| Orion | LP | Vertigo | 6360850 | 1973 | £30 | £60 | Dutch |

## PANTHER
| | | | | | | | |
|---|---|---|---|---|---|---|---|
| Wir Wollen Alles | LP | Panther | 2667 | 1974 | £15 | £30 | German |

## PANTHERS
| | | | | | | | |
|---|---|---|---|---|---|---|---|
| Baby | 7" EP | Polydor | 60118 | 196– | £25 | £50 | French |

## PANTON, DAVE
| | | | | | | | |
|---|---|---|---|---|---|---|---|
| One Music | LP | Nondo | HTLP1370 | 1973 | £10 | £25 | |

## PANTON, DAVID
| | | | | | | | |
|---|---|---|---|---|---|---|---|
| One Music Ensemble | LP | Nodo | 001 | | £6 | £15 | |

## PANTON, ROY
| | | | | | | | |
|---|---|---|---|---|---|---|---|
| Cherita | 7" | Rio | R19 | 1964 | £5 | £10 | |
| Forty Four | 7" | Blue Beat | BB117 | 1962 | £6 | £12 | Leon & Owen B side |
| Hell Gate | 7" | Blue Beat | BB219 | 1964 | £6 | £12 | |
| Mighty Ruler | 7" | Blue Beat | BB182 | 1963 | £6 | £12 | |
| You Don't Know Me | 7" | Rio | R33 | 1964 | £5 | £10 | Edward's Allstars B side |

## PANTRY, JOHN
| | | | | | | | |
|---|---|---|---|---|---|---|---|
| John Pantry | LP | Philips | 6308129 | 1972 | £4 | £10 | |
| Long White Trail | LP | Philips | 6308138 | 1973 | £4 | £10 | |

## PANZA DIVISION
We'll Rock The World.............................. 7" ....... Panza Trax ...... PTO1 .................... 1982 £4.........£8 ..............................

## PAOLA
Bonjour Bonjour ...................................... 7" ...... Decca ............ F22916 ................. 1969 £1.50 ........ £4 ..............................

## PAPAS, NIKKI
By The River ........................................... 7" ...... Parlophone..... R4652 .................. 1960 £2.50 ........ £6 ..............................
Forty-Nine State Rock .......................... 7" ...... Parlophone...... R4590 .................. 1959 £5 .......... £10 ..............................

## PAPER BLITZ TISSUE
Boy Meets Girl........................................ 7" ...... RCA ............ RCA1652 ............. 1967 £50 ........ £100 ..............................

## PAPER BUBBLE
Scenery ................................................... LP ..... Deram ........... DML/SML1059...... 1970 £6 .......... £15 ..............................

## PAPER DOLLS
Paper Doll's House ................................. LP ..... Pye ............... N(S)PL18226 .......... 1968 £4 .......... £10 ..............................

## PAPER GARDEN
Paper Garden .......................................... LP ..... Musicor .......... MS3175 ................. 1968 £20 ......... £40 ................................. US

## PAPER WINGED DREAMS
Paper Winged Dreams ............................ LP ..... Brimstone ........................................ 1970 £20 ......... £40 ................................. US

## PARADIS, VANESSA
Be My Baby............................................ CD-s .. Polydor ....... PZCDD235............. 1992 £2 ............ £5 ......... picture insert
Coupe Coupe .......................................... 7" ...... Polydor ....... 8719427 ............... 1989 £4............ £8 ............... French
Joe Le Taxi ............................................. CD-s .. Polydor ....... 0804662 ............... 1987 £15 ......... £30 ................. CD video
Joe Le Taxi ............................................. 7" ...... Polydor ....... POSPG902 .......... 1988 £7.50 ...... £15 ... poster picture sleeve
Just As Long As You Are There ............. CD-s .. Polydor ....... PZCDD272 ............ 1993 £2 ............ £5 ............ with 2 pics
La Magie des surprises parties ............. 7" ...... Polydor ..................................... 1985 £75 ......... £150 ............... French
Manolo Manolete .................................... CD-s .. Polydor ....... 8873082 ............... 1988 £20 ......... £40 ............... French
Manolo Manolete .................................... 7" ...... Polydor ....... 8872657 ............... 1988 £7.50 ...... £15 ............... French
Manolo Manolete .................................... 12".... Polydor ....... 8872651 ............... 1988 £15 ......... £30 ............... French
Marilyn And John .................................. CD-s .. Polygram ........................................ 1988 £15 ......... £30 ................. CD video
Marilyn And John .................................. 7" ...... Polydor ....... PO16 .................... 1988 £1.50 ...... £4 ..............................
Marilyn And John .................................. 12".... Polydor ....... PZ16 ..................... 1988 £2.50 ...... £6 ..............................
Maxou .................................................... CD-s .. Polydor ....... 8712252 ............... 1989 £2 ............ £5 ..............................
Maxou .................................................... 7" ...... Polydor ....... PO38 .................... 1988 £1.50 ...... £4 ..............................
Maxou .................................................... 12".... Polydor ....... PZ38 ..................... 1988 £4 ............ £10 ..............................
Mosquito ................................................ 7" ...... Polydor ....... 8730747 ............... 1989 £4 ............ £8 ............... French
Sunday Mondays ................................... CD-s .. Polydor ....... PZCDD251............. 1992 £2 ............ £5 ......... with poster
Tandem .................................................. 7" ...... Polydor ....... 8773027 ............... 1990 £4 ............ £8 ............... French
Tandem .................................................. 12".... Polydor ....... 8773022 ............... 1990 £6 ............ £15 ............... French
Tandem (remix) ..................................... CD-s .. Polydor ..................................... 1990 £25 ......... £50 ............... French
Tandem (remix) ..................................... 12".... Polydor ....... 8773031 ............... 1990 £10 ......... £25 ............... French
Variations sur le même t'aime .............. LP ..... Polydor ..................................... 1990 £8 ............ £20 ............... French
Works ..................................................... CD..... Polydor ....... DCI3106 ............... 1994 £50 ......... £100 .......... Japanese promo
                                                                                                                                                   compilation

## PARADONS
Diamonds And Pearls.............................. 7" ...... Top Rank ...... JAR514.................. 1960 £37.50 .... £75 ..............................

## PARADOX
Ring The Changes ................................... 7" ...... Polydor ........ 56275 ................... 1968 £30 ......... £60 ..............................

## PARAGON
Looking For You ..................................... LP ..... Delta Music ................................ 1982 £15 ......... £30 .............Dutch
                                                            Corporation ....

## PARAGONS
Paragons Meet The Jesters...................... LP ..... Jubilee .......... JLP1098 ................ 1959 £330 ...... £60 .............................. US
Paragons Meet The Jesters...................... LP ..... Jubilee .......... JLP1098 ................ 1959 £50 ....... £100 .... US, coloured vinyl
Paragons Vs.The Harptones ................... LP ..... Musicnote ....... M8001 .................. 1964 £10 ......... £25 .............................. US

## PARAGONS (2)
Happy Go Lucky Girl ............................. 7" ...... Doctor Bird..... DB1060 ............... 1966 £5 ........... £10 ..............................
Have You Ever Been In Love................... 7" ...... Studio One..... SO2081................ 1969 £6 ........... £12 ..............................
Left With A Broken Heart ..................... 7" ...... Duke ......... DU7 .................... 1968 £4 ........... £8 ..............................
Memories By The Score ......................... 7" ...... Island ......... WI3138................ 1968 £5 ........... £10 ..............................
Mercy Mercy Mercy................................ 7" ...... Treasure Isle .... TI7011................. 1967 £5 ........... £10 ..............................
On The Beach ........................................ LP ..... Doctor Bird..... DLM5010 ............. 1967 £50 ......... £100 ..............................
On The Beach ........................................ 7" ...... Island ......... WI3045................ 1967 £5 ........... £10 ..... Tommy McCook
                                                                                                                                                   B side
Same Song ............................................. 7" ...... Treasure Isle .... TI7013................. 1967 £5 ........... £10 ..... Tommy McCook
                                                                                                                                                   B side
Silver Bird ............................................. 7" ...... Treasure Isle .... TI7034................. 1968 £5 ........... £10 ..............................
So Depressed .......................................... 7" ...... Island ......... WI3093................ 1967 £5 ........... £10 ..............................
Talking Love .......................................... 7" ...... Island ......... WI3067................ 1967 £5 ........... £10 ..............................
Tide Is High .......................................... 7" ...... Treasure Isle ... TI7009................. 1967 £5 ........... £10 ..............................
Wear You To The Ball............................. 7" ...... Treasure Isle .... TI7025................. 1967 £5 ........... £10 ..............................

## PARAMOR, NORRIE ORCHESTRA
Dance Of The Warriors ......................... 7" ...... Columbia ....... DB7446 ............... 1965 £1.50 ....... £4 ..............................
Randall And Hopkirk (Deceased)............. 7" ...... Polydor ........... 56375 .................. 1970 £10 ......... £20 ..............................
Z Cars .................................................... 7" ...... Columbia ....... DB4789 ............... 1962 £1.50 ...... £4 ..............................

## PARAMOUNTS

The Paramounts were yet another R&B group who gigged hard through the sixties without ever gaining very much success and who made several singles that essentially serve to emphasize why this was. Arguably, however, the group was capable of very much more, for the handful of unreleased tracks included on the Edsel compilation of the Paramounts singles are easily the most impressive. And later, the original line-up of the group made two LPs which do much more to realize its potential – but these, *Home* and *Broken Barricades*, came out under a different name – that of Procol Harum.

| | | | | | | | |
|---|---|---|---|---|---|---|---|
| Bad Blood | 7" | Parlophone | R5187 | 1964 | £4 | £8 | |
| Blue Ribbons | 7" | Parlophone | R5272 | 1965 | £5 | £10 | |
| Draw Me Closer | 7" EP | Odeon | SOE3774 | 1965 | £150 | £250 | *French* |
| I'm The One Who Loves You | 7" | Parlophone | R5155 | 1964 | £5 | £10 | |
| Little Bitty Pretty One | 7" | Parlophone | R5107 | 1964 | £5 | £10 | |
| Paramounts | 7" EP | Parlophone | GEP8908 | 1964 | £150 | £250 | *best auctioned* |
| Poison Ivy | 7" | Parlophone | R5093 | 1963 | £4 | £8 | |
| You've Never Had It So Good | 7" | Parlophone | R5351 | 1965 | £5 | £10 | |

## PARCEL OF FOLK

| | | | | | | | |
|---|---|---|---|---|---|---|---|
| Parcel Of Rogues And The Villagers | LP | Deroy | | | £100 | £200 | *insert, no sleeve* |

## PARCHMENT

| | | | | | | | |
|---|---|---|---|---|---|---|---|
| Hollywood Sunset | LP | Pye | NSPL18409 | 1973 | £6 | £15 | |
| Light Up The Fire | LP | Pye | NSPL18388 | 1972 | £5 | £12 | |
| Rehearsal For A Reunion | LP | Pilgrim | 106 | 1977 | £6 | £15 | |
| Shamblejam | LP | Myrrh | MYR1028 | 1975 | £8 | £20 | |

## PARENTI, TONY

| | | | | | | | |
|---|---|---|---|---|---|---|---|
| Ragtime | LP | London | LTZU15072 | 1957 | £6 | £15 | |

## PARFITT, PAULA

| | | | | | | | |
|---|---|---|---|---|---|---|---|
| I'm Gonna Give Back Your Ring | 7" | Beacon | BEA135 | 1969 | £15 | £30 | |

## PARIS, BOBBY

| | | | | | | | |
|---|---|---|---|---|---|---|---|
| Personally | 7" | Polydor | 56747 | 1968 | £20 | £40 | |

## PARIS, MICA

After 4th & Broadway had sent out 200 promotional copies of Mica Paris's *A Stand 4 Love* EP, they discovered that they had inadvertently included Prince's original demo of 'If I Love U 2 Nite' on the record. The DJs who had received it were asked to return the offending article, but one wonders how many actually did.

| | | | | | | | |
|---|---|---|---|---|---|---|---|
| If I Love U 2 Nite | 12" | 4th & Broadway | 12BRWDJ207 | 1991 | £30 | £60 | *promo* |

## PARIS SISTERS

| | | | | | | | |
|---|---|---|---|---|---|---|---|
| Dream Lover | 7" | MGM | MGM1240 | 1964 | £7.50 | £15 | |
| I Love How You Love Me | 7" | Top Rank | JAR588 | 1961 | £20 | £40 | |

## PARISH HALL

| | | | | | | | |
|---|---|---|---|---|---|---|---|
| Parish Hall | LP | Liberty | LBS83374 | 1970 | £4 | £10 | |

## PARKER, BENNY & THE DYNAMICS

| | | | | | | | |
|---|---|---|---|---|---|---|---|
| Boys And Girls | 7" | Decca | F11944 | 1964 | £10 | £20 | |

## PARKER, BOBBY

| | | | | | | | |
|---|---|---|---|---|---|---|---|
| It's Hard But It's Fair | 7" | Blue Horizon | 573151 | 1969 | £7.50 | £15 | |
| Watch Your Step | 7" | London | HLU9393 | 1961 | £6 | £12 | |
| Watch Your Step | 7" | Sue | WI340 | 1964 | £6 | £12 | |

## PARKER, CHARLIE

| | | | | | | | |
|---|---|---|---|---|---|---|---|
| All Star Quintet/Sextet | 7" EP | Vogue | EPV1264 | 1960 | £2 | £5 | |
| April In Paris | LP | Columbia | 33CX10081 | 1957 | £25 | £50 | |
| Bird And Diz | 10" LP | Columbia | 33C9026 | 1956 | £37.50 | £75 | *.with Dizzy Gillespie* |
| Bird At St. Nick's | LP | Melodisc | MLP12105 | 1955 | £20 | £40 | |
| Bird Is Free | LP | Esquire | 32157 | 1962 | £6 | £15 | |
| Charlie Parker Big Band | LP | Columbia | 33CX10004 | 1955 | £37.50 | £75 | |
| Charlie Parker Big Band | 7" EP | HMV | 7EG8626 | 1960 | £2 | £5 | |
| Charlie Parker Plays | 7" EP | Vogue | EPV1011 | 1955 | £2 | £5 | |
| Charlie Parker Plays Cole Porter | LP | Columbia | 33CX10089 | 1957 | £20 | £40 | |
| Charlie Parker Quintet | 7" EP | Esquire | EP57 | 195– | £2 | £5 | |
| Charlie Parker Vol. 1 | 10" LP | Vogue | LDE004 | 1952 | £50 | £100 | |
| Charlie Parker Vol. 2 | 10" LP | Vogue | LDE016 | 1953 | £50 | £100 | |
| Essential Charlie Parker | LP | HMV | CLP1538 | 1961 | £5 | £12 | |
| Immortal Charlie Parker Vol. 1 | LP | London | LTZC15104 | 1958 | £10 | £25 | |
| Immortal Charlie Parker Vol. 2 | LP | London | LTZC15105 | 1958 | £10 | £25 | |
| Immortal Charlie Parker Vol. 3 | LP | London | LTZC15106 | 1958 | £10 | £25 | |
| Immortal Charlie Parker Vol. 4 | LP | London | LTZC15107 | 1958 | £10 | £25 | |
| Immortal Charlie Parker Vol. 5 | LP | London | LTZC15108 | 1958 | £10 | £25 | |
| In Sweden | LP | Collector | JGN1002 | 1960 | £6 | £15 | |
| In Sweden 1950 | LP | Storyville | SLP27 | 1962 | £5 | £12 | |
| Jazz Perennial | LP | Columbia | 33CX10117 | 1958 | £10 | £25 | |
| Magnificent Charlie Parker No. 1 | 7" EP | Columbia | SEB10002 | 1955 | £2 | £5 | |
| Magnificent Charlie Parker No. 2 | 7" EP | Columbia | SEB10038 | 1956 | £2 | £5 | |
| Magnificent Charlie Parker No. 3 | 7" EP | Columbia | SEB10053 | 1957 | £2 | £5 | |
| Now's The Time | 7" EP | Columbia | SEB10026 | 1956 | £2 | £5 | |
| Parker's Mood | 7" EP | Realm | REP4008 | 1964 | £2 | £5 | |
| Plays South Of The Border | 7" EP | Columbia | SEB10032 | 1956 | £2 | £5 | |
| Portrait Of The Bird | LP | Columbia | 33SX1555 | 1963 | £4 | £10 | |

## PARKER, CHET
Hammer Dulcimer ................................ LP ..... Folkways ......... FA2381 ................ 1966 £4 ......... £10 ........................ US

## PARKER, DAVID
David Parker ...................................... LP ..... Polydor ............ 2460101 ............... 1971 £20 ........ £40

## PARKER, DEAN & THE REDCAPS
Stormy Evening ...................................... 7" ...... Decca ............. F11555 .............. 1962 £10 ........ £20

## PARKER, DYON
Out On The Highway ............................ LP ..... Marble Arch .... MAL787 ................ 1968 £4 ......... £10

## PARKER, EULA
Silhouettes ............................................ 7" ...... Oriole ............. CB1411 ................ 1957 £5 ......... £10

## PARKER, EVAN
At The Unity Theatre ............................ LP ..... Incus ..... INCUS14 .............. 197– £5 ......... £12 ...... with Paul Lytton
Circadian Rhythm ................................ LP ..... Incus ..... INCUS33 ............. 1979 £5 ......... £12 ....... with other artists
Collective Calls .................................... LP ..... Incus ..... INCUS5 ............... 197– £10 ....... £25 ...... with Paul Lytton
From Saxophone And Trombone ............. LP ..... Incus ..... INCUS35 ............. 1980 £5 ......... £12 .... with George Lewis
Hook, Line And Shuffle ......................... LP ..... Incus ..... INCUS45 ............. 1985 £5 ......... £12
Monoceros ............................................ LP ..... Incus ..... INCUS27 ............. 1978 £5 ......... £12
Saxophone Solos .................................... LP ..... Incus ..... INCUS19 ............. 1976 £5 ......... £12
Six Of One ............................................ LP ..... Incus ..... INCUS39 ............. 1982 £5 ......... £12
Snake Decides ........................................ LP ..... Incus ..... INCUS49 ............. 1986 £5 ......... £12
Topography Of The Lungs ...................... LP ..... Incus ..... INCUS1 ............... 1970 £15 ....... £30 . with Derek Bailey & Han Bennink
Tracks .................................................. LP ..... Incus ..... INCUS42 ............. 1983 £5 ......... £12 .... with Barry Guy & Paul Lytton

## PARKER, FESS
Wringle Wrangle .................................... 7" ...... Oriole ............. CB1378 ............... 1957 £1.50 ...... £4

## PARKER, GRAHAM
Live At Marble Arch ............................. LP ..... Vertigo ..... GP1 ................... 1977 £4 ......... £10 ...................... promo
Live Sparks .......................................... LP ..... Arista ............. SP63 ................... 1979 £4 ......... £10 ............... US promo

## PARKER, JIMMY
We Gonna .............................................. 7" ...... Top Rank ...... JAR608 ............. 1962 £1.50 ...... £4

## PARKER, JUNIOR
Annie Get Your Yo Yo ........................... 7" ...... Vogue ............ V9193 ............... 1962 £5 ......... £12
Driving Wheel ...................................... LP ..... Duke ............. DLP76 ............... 1962 £15 ....... £30 ........................ US
Goodbye Little Girl ............................... 7" ...... Vocalion ........ VP9275 ............. 1966 £2.50 ...... £6
Like It Is ............................................. LP ..... Mercury ........ SMCL20097 ...... 1967 £5 ......... £12
Stand By Me ........................................ 7" ...... Vogue ............ V9179 ............... 1961 £6 ......... £12
These Kind Of Blues ............................. 7" ...... Vocalion ....... VP9256 ............. 1966 £5 ......... £10

## PARKER, KEN
Change Is Gonna Come ........................... 7" ...... Giant ............. GN34 ................ 1968 £4 ......... £8 .... Val Bennett B side
Down Low ............................................ 7" ...... Island ............. WI3096 ............. 1967 £5 ......... £10
Help Me Make It Through The Night ....... 7" ...... Treasure Isle .... TI7073 .............. 1972 £1.50 ...... £4 ....... Tommy McCook B side
I Can't Hide ......................................... 7" ...... Duke ............. DU79 ................ 1970 £1.50 ...... £4 ....... Tommy McCook B side
It's Alright ............................................ 7" ...... Amalgamated ... AMG847 ............ 1969 £2.50 ...... £6 ............ Cobbs B side
Jimmy Brown ........................................ LP ..... Trojan ............ TRLS80 ............. 1974 £4 ......... £10
Jimmy Brown ........................................ 7" ...... Duke Reid ....... DR2521 ............. 1971 £1.50 ...... £4
Lonely Man ........................................... 7" ...... Island ............. WI3105 ............. 1967 £5 ......... £10 .Erol Dunkley B side
My Whole World Is Falling Down ............. 7" ...... Bamboo ......... BAM1 ............... 1969 £1.50 ...... £4
Only Yesterday ...................................... 7" ...... Amalgamated ... AMG853 ............ 1969 £2.50 ...... £6 ............ Cobbs B side
See Them A Come ................................. 7" ...... Studio One ...... SO2001 ............. 1967 £6 ......... £12 Mr. Foundation B side

## PARKER, KNOCKY
Knocky Parker ...................................... LP ..... London ........... HAU2008 .............. 1956 £5 ......... £12
Knocky Parker Trio ................................ 10" LP London ............ HBU1044 .............. 1956 £5 ......... £12

## PARKER, LEO
Let Me Tell You 'Bout It ......................... LP ..... Blue Note ....... BLP/BST84087 ...... 1961 £20 ....... £40

## PARKER, RAY
Ghostbusters ........................................ 12" .... Arista .............. ARIPD12580 ......... 1984 £3 ......... £8 .. luminous picture disc

## PARKER, RAYMOND
Ring Around The Roses ........................... 7" ...... Sue .................. WI4024 ................. 1966 £6 ......... £12

## PARKER, ROBERT
Barefootin' ........................................... LP ..... Island ............. ILP942 .............. 1966 £10 ....... £25
Barefootin' ........................................... 7" ...... Island ............. WI286 ............... 1966 £2 ......... £5
Happy Feet ........................................... 7" ...... Island ............. WI3008 .............. 1966 £4 ......... £8

## PARKER, SONNY
My Soul's On Fire ................................. 7" ...... Vogue ............ V2392 ............... 1956 £87.50 .. £175

## PARKING LOT
World Spinning Sadly ............................. 7" ...... Parlophone ...... R5779 ............... 1969 £10 ......... £20

## PARKINSON, JIMMY

| | | | | | | | |
|---|---|---|---|---|---|---|---|
| Great Pretender | 7" | Columbia | SCM5236 | 1956 £5 | £10 | |
| In The Middle Of The House | 7" | Columbia | DB3833 | 1956 £4 | £8 | |
| Lover's Quarrel | 7" | Columbia | DB3808 | 1956 £4 | £8 | |
| Solo | 10" LP | Columbia | 33S1109 | 1957 £6 | £15 | |
| Walk Hand In Hand | 7" | Columbia | SCM5267 | 1956 £4 | £8 | |

## PARKS, BERNICE

| | | | | | | | |
|---|---|---|---|---|---|---|---|
| Only Love Me | 7" | Vogue Coral | Q72056 | 1955 £2.50 | £6 | |

## PARKS, SONNY

| | | | | | | | |
|---|---|---|---|---|---|---|---|
| New Boy In Town | 7" | Warner Bros | WB100 | 1963 £1.50 | £4 | |

## PARKS, VAN DYKE

| | | | | | | | |
|---|---|---|---|---|---|---|---|
| Song Cycle | LP | Warner Bros | WS1727 | 1968 £5 | £12 | US |

## PARLAN, HORACE

| | | | | | | | |
|---|---|---|---|---|---|---|---|
| Headin' South | LP | Blue Note | BLP/BST84062 | 1961 £20 | £40 | |
| Movin' & Groovin' | LP | Blue Note | BLP/BST84028 | 196– £25 | £50 | |
| On The Spur Of The Moment | LP | Blue Note | BLP/BST84074 | 1961 £20 | £40 | |
| Speakin' My Piece | LP | Blue Note | BLP/BST84043 | 196– £20 | £40 | |
| Up And Down | LP | Blue Note | BLP/BST84082 | 1961 £15 | £30 | |
| Us Three | LP | Blue Note | BLP/BST84037 | 196– £20 | £40 | |

## PARLET

The album credited to Parlet is one of several spin-off projects undertaken by George Clinton of Parliament and Funkadelic fame – this time his female backing singers are given the star billing.

| | | | | | | | |
|---|---|---|---|---|---|---|---|
| Invasion Of The Booty Snatchers | LP | Casablanca | CAL2052 | 1979 £6 | £15 | |

## PARLIAMENT

George Clinton takes the uncompromising stance of James Brown, the ultra-hip posing of Sly Stewart, and the electric-warrior/sky-gypsy combination that was Jimi Hendrix and reaches wider still. He pulls in the most colourful black dialect, with his own variations; comic book science fiction; updated psychedelia; and a considerable amount of pure lunacy. Above all, he is obsessed with funk, reminding us, though with tongue firmly in cheek, that the term has a euphemistic meaning that goes hand in hand with its musical one. All this becomes apparent from Clinton's album covers alone. Songs are given titles like 'Dr Funkenstein', 'The Landing Of The Holy Mothership' and 'Lunchmeataphobia'; there are credits for 'extra-singing clones' and 'bass thumpasaurians'; and the artwork incorporates underground-style cartoons or else photographs of band members in fantastic costumes. There are, in fact, several different, overlapping recording outlets used by George Clinton – Parliament, ostensibly a vocal group, with roots in the more conventional sixties approach of Clinton's Parliaments; Funkadelic, a band devoted more to instrumental prowess; and Bootsy's Rubber Band, led by Clinton's bass guitarist, Bootsy Collins – as well as more recent recordings in Clinton's own name and minor projects like Parlet, the Brides of Funkenstein, and the Horny Horns – all united under the banner of P-Funk.

| | | | | | | | |
|---|---|---|---|---|---|---|---|
| Chocolate City | LP | Casablanca | CAL2012 | 1976 £5 | £12 | |
| Chocolate City | LP | Casablanca | NBLP7014 | 1975 £6 | £15 | |
| Clones Of Dr. Funkenstein | LP | Casablanca | CAL2003 | 1976 £5 | £12 | |
| Come In Out Of The Rain | 7" | Invictus | INV522 | 1972 £2 | £5 | |
| Funkentelechy Vs. The Placebo Syndrome | LP | Casablanca | CALH2021 | 1978 £5 | £12 | |
| Gloryhallastoopid | LP | Casablanca | NBLP7195 | 1979 £4 | £10 | US |
| Live/Funk Earth Tour | LP | Casablanca | CALD5002 | 1977 £6 | £15 | double |
| Mothership Connection | LP | Casablanca | CAL2013 | 1977 £4 | £10 | |
| Mothership Connection | LP | Casablanca | CBC4009 | 1976 £5 | £12 | |
| Motor Booty Affair | LP | Casablanca | CALN2044 | 1979 £5 | £12 | |
| Motor Booty Affair | LP | Casablanca | NBPIX7125 | 1978 £5 | £12 | US picture disc |
| Osmium | LP | Invictus | SVT1004 | 1971 £25 | £50 | |
| Silent Boatman | 7" | Invictus | INV513 | 1971 £2 | £5 | |
| Trombipulation | LP | Casablanca | NBLP7294 | 1981 £4 | £10 | US |
| Up For The Down Stroke | LP | Casablanca | CAL2011 | 1976 £5 | £12 | |
| Up For The Down Stroke | LP | Casablanca | NBLP7002 | 1974 £8 | £20 | |

## PARLIAMENTS

| | | | | | | | |
|---|---|---|---|---|---|---|---|
| I Wanna Testify | 7" | Track | 604013 | 1967 £5 | £10 | |
| I Wanna Testify | 7" | Track | 604032 | 1969 £1.50 | £4 | |

## PARLOPHONE POPS ORCHESTRA

| | | | | | | | |
|---|---|---|---|---|---|---|---|
| Rock Around The Clock | 7" | Parlophone | R4250 | 1956 £1.50 | £4 | |

## PARLOUR BAND

| | | | | | | | |
|---|---|---|---|---|---|---|---|
| Is A Friend | LP | Deram | SDL10 | 1972 £50 | £100 | |

## PARNELL, JACK

| | | | | | | | |
|---|---|---|---|---|---|---|---|
| Jack Parnell And His Orchestra | 7" EP | Parlophone | GEP8532 | 1955 £2 | £5 | |
| Jack Parnell Quartet | 10" LP | Decca | LF1065 | 1952 £4 | £10 | |
| Night Train | 7" | Parlophone | MSP6031 | 1953 £1.50 | £4 | |
| Trip To Mars | 10" LP | Parlophone | PMD1053 | 1958 £4 | £10 | |
| Waltzing The Blues | 7" | Parlophone | MSP6009 | 1953 £1.50 | £4 | |

## PARR, CATHERINE

| | | | | | | | |
|---|---|---|---|---|---|---|---|
| You Belong To Me | 7" | Decca | F12210 | 1965 £2 | £5 | |

## PARRALELE

| | | | | | | | |
|---|---|---|---|---|---|---|---|
| Parralele | LP | Barclay | 920389 | 1971 £8 | £20 | French |

## PARRISH, DEAN

| | | | | | | | |
|---|---|---|---|---|---|---|---|
| Determination | 7" | Stateside | SS550 | 1966 £15 | £30 | |
| Skate | 7" | Stateside | SS580 | 1967 £7.50 | £15 | |

Tell Her .................................................. 7" ...... Stateside .......... SS531 ..................... 1966 £10 ........ £20 ...............................

# PARRISH & GURVITZ
Parrish & Gurvitz ...................................... LP ..... Regal         SRZA8506 ............. 1971 £4 ........... £10
                                                         Zonophone .....

# PARRY, SAM
If Sadness Could Sing ............................. LP ..... Argo .............. ZDA155 ................. 1972 £20 ........ £40

# PARSONS, ALAN PROJECT
Best Of The Alan Parsons Project .............. LP ..... Mobile Fidelity MFSL1175 ............. 1984 £4 ........... £10 .......... *US audiophile*
Gaudi ..................................................... CD .... Arista .......... 2580842 ................ 1987 £5 ........... £12
I, Robot ................................................. LP ..... Mobile Fidelity MFSL1084 ............. 1982 £4 ........... £10 .......... *US audiophile*
I, Robot ................................................. LP ..... Mobile Fidelity MFSL1084 ............. 1982 £5 ........... £12 .......... *US audiophile*
                                                                                                                          *(UHQR)*
Stereotomy ............................................. CD .... Arista .......... 610581 ................. 1985 £5 ........... £12
Turn Of A Friendly Card .......................... LP ..... Arista ........................................ 1980 £4 ........... £10 ............ *audiophile*
Vulture Culture ....................................... LP ..... Arista ........................................ 1984 £5 ........... £12 *US promo picture disc*

# PARSONS, BILL
All American Boy ..................................... 7" ...... London .......... HL8798 ............... 1959 £4 ........... £8 ................................

# PARSONS, GRAM
G.P. ....................................................... LP ..... Reprise .......... K44228 ........... 1973 £4 ........... £10
Grievous Angel ........................................ LP ..... Reprise .......... K54018 ........... 1974 £4 ........... £10

# PARTISANS
Partisans ................................................ 7" EP . Eaglestone                             1963 £50 ....... £100 ...............................
                                                         Recording
                                                         Service ............

# PARTON, DOLLY
Hello I'm Dolly ........................................ LP ..... Monument ...... MLP8085/        1967 £5 ........... £12 ........................ *US*
                                                                          SLP18085 ...............

# PARTON, DOLLY & GEORGE JONES
Dolly Parton And George Jones ................ LP ..... Starday ........... SLP429 ............. 1968 £4 ........... £10 ........................ *US*

# PARTRIDGE, DON
Don Partridge ......................................... LP ..... Columbia ........ SX/SCX6280 ........ 1968 £5 ........... £12
Singing Soho Style .................................. 7" EP . CFP .............. CFP001/002 ........... 196– £4 ........... £8

# PARZIVAL
Barock .................................................... LP ..... Telefunken ...... SLE14685 ............. 1972 £25 ........ £50 ................ *German*
Legend ................................................... LP ..... Teldec ........... 14635 .................... 1971 £6 ........... £15 ................ *German*

# PASCALIS, MARIANNA, ROBERT & BESSY
Music Lesson .......................................... 7" ...... Power          PX254 .............. 1977 £2 .............. £5 .................................
                                                         Exchange ........

# PASHA
Although suggestions of this kind are often proved to be misplaced, the rumour that Pasha was actually the Searchers in disguise has yet to
be refuted.

Someone Shot The Lollipop Man .............. 7" ...... Liberty ............ LBF15199 ............. 1968 £37.50 .... £75 ...............................

# PASSING FANCY
Passing Fancy .......................................... LP ..... Boo ............... 6801 .................... 196– £37.50 .... £75 ........................ *US*

# PASSIONS
I Only Want You ...................................... 7" ...... Top Rank ....... JAR313 ................ 1960 £10 ........ £20 ...............................
Jackie Brown ........................................... 7" ...... Capitol ........... CL14874 ............... 1958 £7.50 .... £15 ...............................
Just To Be With You ............................... 7" ...... Top Rank ....... JAR224 ................ 1959 £10 ........ £20 ...............................

# PASSPORT
Passport ................................................. LP ..... Reprise .......... K44243 ............. 1973 £5 ........... £12 ...............................

# PAST SEVEN DAYS
Raindance ............................................... 7" ...... 4AD .............. AD102 ............... 1981 £1.50 ...... £4 ................................

# PASTEL SIX
Cinnamon Cinder ..................................... LP ..... Zen ............... 1001 ..................... 1963 £8 ........... £20 ........................ *US*
Cinnamon Cinder ..................................... 7" ...... London .......... HLU9651 ............... 1963 £1.50 ...... £4
Golden Oldies .......................................... LP ..... Mark56 .......... MLP511 ............... 1963 £6 ........... £15 ........................ *US*

# PASTELS
Heavens Above ........................................ 7" ...... Villa 21 ......... VILLA3 ............... 1985 £10 ........ £20
Heavens Above ........................................ 7" ...... Whaam! ......... WHAAM5 ............ 1982 £7.50 .... £15
I Wonder Why ........................................ 7" ...... Rough Trade .. RT137 ................ 1983 £6 ........... £12
I'm Alright With You ............................... 12" ... Creation ........ CRE023T ............ 1985 £2.50 ...... £6
Something Going On ................................ 7" ...... Creation ........ CRE005 .............. 1984 £6 ........... £12
Truck Train Tractor ................................ 12" ... Glass .............. PASTEL001 ........ 1987 £2.50 ...... £6 ................. *double*

# PASTIES & CREAM
Pasties & Cream ...................................... LP ..... Sentinel ........................................ 1971 £5 ........... £12 ...............................

## PASTORAL SYMPHONY
Love Machine.................................... 7" ...... President ......... PT202................ 1968 £1.50........£4 ..............................

## PASTORIUS, JACO
Jaco Pastorius .................................. LP ..... Epic............ PE33949 ............... 1976 £6..........£15 ...................... US

## PAT & MARIE
I Try Not To Tell You .................... 7" ...... Ska Beat .... JB234............... 1966 £5........£10 ..............................
You're Really Leaving ..................... 7" ...... Ska Beat .... JB235............... 1966 £5........£10 ..............................

## PAT & ROXIE
Sing To Me ...................................... 7" ...... Caribou ...... CRC2................. 1965 £1.50........£4 ..............................

## PATCHES
Living In America .......................... 7" ...... Warner Bros.... K16201 ................ 1972 £2..........£5 ..............................

## PATCHWORK
Patchwork ....................................... LP ..... Canon............ ........ £50.......£100 ..............................

## PATE, JOHNNY
Jazz Goes Ivy League ...................... 10" LP Parlophone...... PMD1057 ............ 1958 £10.......£25 ..............................
Swingin' Flute................................. 10" LP Parlophone...... PMD1072 ............ 1959 £10.......£25 ..............................

## PATERNOSTER
Paternoster....................................... LP ..... CBS............... 64958 ............... 1972 £25 .......£50 ............... Austrian

## PATERSON, BOBBY & THE CAMP CREEK BOYS
Virginia Reel .................................. LP ..... Leader............ LED2053................ 1973 £4..........£10 ..............................

## PATHETIX
Aleister Crowley ............................. 7" ...... No Records .... 001 ...................... 1978 £1.50........£4 ..............................

## PATHFINDERS
I Love You Caroline......................... 7" ...... Decca ............. F12038................. 1964 £1.50........£4 ..............................

## PATHFINDERS (2)
Don't You Believe It........................ 7" ...... Parlophone...... R5372 ................. 1965 £1.50........£4 ..............................

## PATHFINDERS (3)
What'd I Say................................... 7" ...... Hayton ........ SP138/9............... 1964 £10 .......£20 ..............................

## PATHWAY TO YOUR MIND
Preparing The Mind And Body For .... LP ..... Major Minor ... MM/SMLP19........ 1968 £10 .......£25 ..............................
  Meditation ................................

## PATIENCE & PRUDENCE
Dreamers' Bay.................................. 7" ...... London .......... HLU8425............... 1957 £4..........£8 ..............................
Gonna Get Alomg Without Ya Now ........ 7" ...... London .......... HL7017................. 1957 £2..........£5 ............export
Gonna Get Along Without You Now ....... 7" ...... London ......... HLU8369.............. 1957 £6..........£12 ..............................
Smile And A Song............................ 7" EP . London .......... REU1087............. 1957 £10 .......£20 ..............................
Tom Thumb's Tune........................... 7" ...... London .......... HLU8773............. 1958 £2..........£5 ..............................
Tonight You Belong To Me ................ 7" ...... London .......... HLU8321............. 1956 £7.50.....£15 ..............................
You Tattletale.................................. 7" ...... London .......... HLU8493............. 1957 £2.50......£6 ..............................

## PATRICK, BOBBY BIG SIX
Monkey Time................................... 7" ...... Decca ............ F12030................. 1964 £5..........£10 ..............................
Shake It Easy Baby ......................... 7" ...... Decca ............ F11898................. 1964 £6..........£12 ..............................
Tenbeat From Star Club Hamburg............. 7" EP . Decca ............ DFE8570............. 1964 £30 .......£60 ..............................

## PATRICK, DAN
Tiger Lee ........................................ 7" ...... Stateside ......... SS2004................. 1967 £2..........£5 ..............................

## PATRICK, KENTRICK
Don't Stay Out Late........................ 7" ...... Island ............ WI079................. 1963 £5..........£10 ..............................
End Of The World........................... 7" ...... Island ............ WI104................. 1963 £5..........£10 ..............................
Golden Love.................................... 7" ...... Island ............ WI119................. 1963 £5..........£10 ..............................
Goodbye Peggy Darling..................... 7" ...... Island ............ WI137................. 1964 £5..........£10 ... Baba Brooks B side
I Am Wasting Time .......................... 7" ...... Island ............ WI140................. 1964 £5..........£10 ..............................
Man To Man ................................... 7" ...... Island ............ WI066................. 1963 £5..........£10 ..............................
Take Me To The Party...................... 7" ...... Island ............ WI132................. 1963 £5..........£10 ..............................

## PATRIOTS
Prophet .......................................... 7" ...... Fontana........... TF650.................. 1966 £2..........£5 ..............................

## PATRON OF THE ARTS
Eleanor Rigby.................................. 7" ...... Page One ........ POF012................. 1966 £6..........£12 ..............................

## PATSY
Little Flea ...................................... 7" ...... Doctor Bird..... DB1122 ................ 1968 £5..........£10 ..............................

## PATTEN, BRIAN
Brian Patten.................................... LP ...... Caedmon ........ TC1300 ............... 1970 £10 .......£25 ..............................
Sly Cormorant ................................ LP ...... Argo ............... ZSW607 ............... 1977 £6..........£15 ..............................
Vanishing Trick .............................. LP ...... Tangent .......... TGS116 ............... 1971 £20 .......£40 ..............................

## PATTERN PEOPLE
Take A Walk In The Sun...................... 7" ...... MGM ............ MGM1429 ............. 1968 £1.50........£4 ...............................

## PATTERSON, BOBBY
Broadway Ain't Funky No More ............. 7" ...... Pama ............. PM735 ................ 1968 £1.50........£4 ...............................
I'm In Love With You.......................... 7" ...... Action............ ACT4604................. 1972 £2.50........£6 ...............................
T.C.B. Or T.Y.A. ............................... 7" ...... Pama ............. PM763 ................. 1969 £2 ..........£5 ...............................

## PATTERSON, OTTILIE
3000 Years With Ottilie........................... LP ..... Marmalade ...... 608011.................... 1969 £6............£15 ...............................
Baby Please Don't Go............................ 7" ...... Columbia ....... DB7208 ................ 1964 £7.50.....£15 ...............................
Bitterness Of Death ............................ 7" ...... Marmalade ...... 598020.................... 1969 £1.50........£4 ...............................
Blues .............................................. 7" EP . Decca ............. DFE6303............... 1956 £2 ..........£5 ...............................
Ottilie ............................................ 7" EP . Columbia ........ SEG7915 ............... 1959 £2 ..........£5 ...............................
That Patterson Girl............................ 7" EP . Polygon ......... JTE102 ................. 1956 £4 ..........£8 ...............................
That Patterson Girl ............................ 7" EP . Pye................. NJE1012 ............... 1956 £2 ..........£5 ...............................
That Patterson Girl Vol. 2 .................... 7" EP . Pye................. NJE1023 ............... 1956 £2 ..........£5 ...............................

## PATTERSON'S PEOPLE
Shake Hands With The Devil................... 7" ...... Mercury.......... MF913 ................. 1966 £4............£8 ...............................

## PATTO
Patto's original take on jazz-rock never quite managed to achieve the wide acclaim that it deserved, despite the band having a singer (Mike Patto) possessing one of the classic rock voices and a guitarist (Ollie Halsall) whose blend of technical expertise and imagination made him into the kind of player that other guitarists looked up to. The album *Hold Your Fire* is an oddity in that it exists with two different versions of the A side. The songs are the same, but on one they have a much rougher, rawer sound than on the other. There do not appear to be any visual differences between the two versions of the album, unfortunately.

Hold Your Fire ................................... LP ..... Vertigo .......... 6360032 ............... 1971 £50.......£100 ............... *spiral label*
Patto ............................................. LP ..... Vertigo .......... 6360016 ............... 1970 £15.......£30 ............... *spiral label*
Roll Em Smoke Em .............................. LP ..... Island ............. ILPS9210 .............. 1972 £8............£20 ...............................

## PATTO, MIKE
Can't Stop Talking About My Baby .......... 7" ...... Columbia ....... DB8091 ............... 1966 £30........£60 ...............................

## PATTON, ALEXANDER
Li'l Lovin' Sometimes........................... 7" ...... Capitol............ CL15461 ............... 1966 £30........£60 ...............................

## PATTON, CHARLIE
Charlie Patton.................................... 7" EP . Heritage .......... REU4 ................ 195– £7.50......£15 ...............................

## PATTON, JIMMY
Blue Darlin'....................................... LP ..... Sims............... 127 .................... 1965 £8............£20 ............................... US
Make Room For The Blues...................... LP ...... Moon ............. 101 .................... 196– £8............£20 ............................... US

## PATTON, JOHN
Accent On The Blues ............................ LP ..... Blue Note ....... BST84340 ............. 1969 £10.........£25 ...............................
Along Came John................................ LP ..... Blue Note ....... BLP/BST84130 ...... 1963 £20.........£40 ...............................
Got A Good Thing Goin' ....................... LP ..... Blue Note ....... BLP/BST84229 ...... 1966 £15.........£30 ...............................
Let 'Em Roll....................................... LP ..... Blue Note ....... BLP/BST84239 ...... 1966 £15.........£30 ...............................
Oh Baby!.......................................... LP ..... Blue Note ....... BLP/BST84192 ...... 1964 £25.........£50 ...............................
That Certain Feeling............................ LP ..... Blue Note ....... BST84281 ............. 1968 £10.........£25 ...............................
Understanding.................................... LP ..... Blue Note ....... BST84306 ............. 1968 £10.........£25 ...............................
Way I Feel......................................... LP ..... Blue Note ....... BLP/BST84174 ...... 1964 £15.........£30 ...............................

## PATTY & THE EMBLEMS
Mixed Up Shook Up Girl ....................... 7" ...... Stateside .......... SS322................... 1964 £7.50......£15 ...............................

## PAUL
Will You Follow Me .............................. 7" ...... Polydor........... BM56045 .............. 1965 £37.50.....£75 ...............................

## PAUL, BUNNY
Lovey Dovey ...................................... 7" ...... Columbia ........ SCM5131............ 1954 £2 ..........£5 ...............................
New Love .......................................... 7" ...... Columbia ........ SCM5102............ 1954 £1.50........£4 ...............................
Please Have Mercy .............................. 7" ...... Capitol............ CL14279 .............. 1955 £2 ..........£5 ...............................
Song Of The Dreamer........................... 7" ...... Capitol............ CL14368 .............. 1955 £1.50........£4 ...............................
Such A Night...................................... 7" ...... Columbia ........ SCM5112............ 1954 £2.50........£6 ...............................
Two Castanets ................................... 7" ...... Capitol............ CL14304 .............. 1955 £1.50........£4 ...............................
You Came A Long Way From St. Louis ..... 7" ...... Columbia ........ SCM5151............ 1954 £1.50........£4 ...............................

## PAUL, DARLENE
Act Like Nothing Happened .................... 7" ...... Capitol............ CL15344 .............. 1964 £2.50........£6 ...............................

## PAUL, JOHN E.
I Wanna Know ................................... 7" ...... Decca ............. F12685................. 1967 £10........£20 ...............................

## PAUL, LES & MARY FORD
Although guitarist Les Paul gained his many hits by playing a bouncy, light pop with his singer wife, Mary Ford, he has an importance in the history of rock that entirely transcends the actual sound of his music. He was a fearless experimentalist in the studio, pioneering the use of multiple over-dubbing and speeded-up tape effects and building the first eight-track tape recorder as early as 1954. And if that was not enough, he also designed the electric guitar that still bears his name and which has played such a major role in the development of blues and heavy rock – persuading the Gibson company to begin mass production of the instrument at a time when the only other commercially available electric guitar was the Fender Telecaster.

Amukiriki......................................... 7" ...... Capitol............ CL14521 .............. 1956 £2 ..........£5 ...............................
At The Save A Penny Super Store............. 7" ...... Philips............. PB906................... 1959 £1.50........£4 ...............................

| | | | | | | |
|---|---|---|---|---|---|---|
| Bewitched | 7" | Capitol | CL14839 | 1958 | £1.50 | £4 |
| Bye Bye Blues | LP | Capitol | T356 | 1953 | £8 | £20 ............ US |
| Bye Bye Blues | 10" LP | Capitol | LC6806 | 1956 | £6 | £15 |
| Cimarron | 7" | Capitol | CL14593 | 1956 | £1.50 | £4 |
| Cinco Robles | 7" | Capitol | CL14710 | 1957 | £1.50 | £4 |
| Genuine Love | 7" | Capitol | CL14300 | 1955 | £5 | £10 |
| Hitmakers | LP | Capitol | T416 | 195– | £5 | £12 |
| Hits Of Les And Mary | LP | Capitol | T1476 | 1960 | £4 | £10 |
| Hummin' And Waltzin' | 7" | Capitol | CL14738 | 1957 | £1.50 | £4 |
| Hummingbird | 7" | Capitol | CL14342 | 1955 | £5 | £10 |
| Jazz Me Blues | 7" EP | Capitol | EAP120740 | 1965 | £2.50 | £6 |
| Jealous Heart | 7" | Philips | PB882 | 1959 | £1.50 | £4 |
| Les And Mary | LP | Capitol | T577 | 195– | £5 | £12 ............ US |
| Les And Mary | 10" LP | Capitol | LC6704 | 1955 | £8 | £20 |
| Les Paul And Mary Ford | 10" LP | Capitol | LC6701 | 1955 | £8 | £20 |
| Lover | LP | Capitol | T1276 | 1959 | £4 | £10 |
| Lover's Luau | LP | Philips | BBL7306 | 1959 | £4 | £10 |
| Mandolino | 7" | Capitol | CL14185 | 1954 | £5 | £10 |
| Mister Sandman | 7" | Capitol | CL14212 | 1954 | £10 | £20 |
| Mr. And Mrs. Music | 7" EP | Capitol | EAP20048 | 1959 | £4 | £8 |
| New Sound Vol. 1 | LP | Capitol | T226 | 195– | £8 | £20 ............ US |
| New Sound Vol. 1 | 10" LP | Capitol | LC6514 | 1951 | £8 | £20 |
| New Sound Vol. 2 | LP | Capitol | T286 | 195– | £8 | £20 ............ US |
| New Sound Vol. 2 | 10" LP | Capitol | LC6581 | 1953 | £8 | £20 |
| Nola | 7" EP | Capitol | EAP120145 | 1961 | £2 | £5 |
| Pair Of Fools | 7" | Capitol | CL14809 | 1957 | £2 | £5 |
| Presenting Les Paul And Mary Ford | 7" EP | Capitol | EAP19121 | 1955 | £2.50 | £6 |
| Put A Ring On My Finger | 7" | Philips | PB873 | 1958 | £4 | £8 |
| Runnin' Wild | 7" | Capitol | CL14665 | 1956 | £2 | £5 |
| Say The Words I Love To Hear | 7" | Capitol | CL14577 | 1956 | £1.50 | £4 |
| Sitting On Top Of The World | 7" EP | Capitol | EAP1540 | 1955 | £4 | £8 |
| Small Island | 7" | Capitol | CL14858 | 1958 | £1.50 | £4 |
| Song In Blue | 7" | Capitol | CL14233 | 1955 | £5 | £10 |
| Strollin' Blues | 7" | Capitol | CL14776 | 1957 | £2 | £5 |
| Texas Lady | 7" | Capitol | CL14502 | 1956 | £2.50 | £6 |
| Theme From The Threepenny Opera | 7" | Capitol | CL14534 | 1956 | £2 | £5 |
| Time To Dream | LP | Capitol | T802 | 1957 | £5 | £12 |

## PAUL & PAULA

| | | | | | | |
|---|---|---|---|---|---|---|
| First Day Back At School | 7" | Philips | BF1281 | 1963 | £1.50 | £4 |
| First Quarrel | 7" | Philips | BF1256 | 1963 | £1.50 | £4 |
| Hey Paula | 7" | Philips | 304012BF | 1963 | £1.50 | £4 |
| Holiday For Teens | LP | Philips | BL7587 | 1964 | £6 | £15 |
| No Other Baby | 7" | Philips | BF1380 | 1964 | £1.50 | £4 |
| Sing For Young Lovers | LP | Philips | 652026BL | 1963 | £10 | £25 |
| Something Old Something New | 7" | Philips | BF1269 | 1963 | £1.50 | £4 |
| We Go Together | LP | Philips | BL7573 | 1963 | £6 | £15 |
| Young Lovers | 7" EP | Philips | BBE12539 | 1963 | £7.50 | £15 |
| Young Lovers | 7" | Philips | 304016BF | 1963 | £1.50 | £4 |

## PAUL & RITCHIE & THE CRYIN' SHAMES

| | | | | | | |
|---|---|---|---|---|---|---|
| C'mon Back | 7" | Decca | F12483 | 1966 | £62.50 | £125 |

## PAUL & THE JETLINERS

| | | | | | | |
|---|---|---|---|---|---|---|
| Great Pretender | 7" | Rainbow | RAI102 | 1966 | £2 | £5 |
| Something On My Mind | 7" | Rainbow | RAI105 | 1966 | £1.50 | £4 |

## PAULETTE SISTERS

| | | | | | | |
|---|---|---|---|---|---|---|
| Dream Boat | 7" | Capitol | CL14294 | 1955 | £4 | £8 |
| Ring-A-Dang-A-Do | 7" | Capitol | CL14310 | 1955 | £4 | £8 |
| You Win Again | 7" | Capitol | CL14347 | 1955 | £4 | £8 |

## PAUL'S DISCIPLES

| | | | | | | |
|---|---|---|---|---|---|---|
| See That My Grave Is Kept Clean | 7" | Decca | F12081 | 1965 | £7.50 | £15 |

## PAUL'S TROUBLES

| | | | | | | |
|---|---|---|---|---|---|---|
| You'll Find Out | 7" | Ember | EMBS233 | 1967 | £7.50 | £15 |

## PAUPERS

| | | | | | | |
|---|---|---|---|---|---|---|
| Ellis Island | LP | Verve | SVLP6017 | 1968 | £4 | £10 |
| Magic People | LP | Verve | 3026 | 1967 | £5 | £12 ............ US |

## PAVILION, PERCY (CAPTAIN SENSIBLE)

| | | | | | | |
|---|---|---|---|---|---|---|
| Cricket EP | 7" | Pavilioned In Splendour | PIS1 | 1983 | £1.50 | £4 |

## PAVLOV'S DOG

| | | | | | | |
|---|---|---|---|---|---|---|
| Pampered Menial | LP | CBS | 80872 | 1975 | £4 | £10 |
| Sound Of The Bell | LP | CBS | 81163 | 1976 | £4 | £10 |
| St. Louis Hounds | LP | private | | 197– | £37.50 | £75 ............ US |

## PAX ETERNAL

| | | | | | | |
|---|---|---|---|---|---|---|
| Second Chance Mr. Jones | 7" | Decca | F13167 | 1971 | £1.50 | £4 |

## PAXTON, TOM

| | | | | | | |
|---|---|---|---|---|---|---|
| Ain't That News | LP | Elektra | EKL/EKS7289 | 1965 | £5 | £12 |
| Jennifer's Rabbit | 7" | Elektra | EKSN45021 | 1967 | £1.50 | £4 |
| Last Thing On My Mind | 7" | Elektra | EKSN45001 | 1965 | £1.50 | £4 |

| | | | | | | |
|---|---|---|---|---|---|---|
| Leaving London | 7" | Elektra | EKSN45006 | 1967 £1.50 | £4 | |
| Morning Again | LP | Elektra | EKL/EKS74019 | 1968 £5 | £12 | |
| Number Six | LP | Elektra | EKS74066 | 1970 £4 | £10 | |
| One Time And One Time Only | 7" | Elektra | EKSN45003 | 1967 £1.50 | £4 | |
| Outward Bound | LP | Elektra | EKL/EKS7317 | 1966 £5 | £12 | |
| Ramblin' Boy | LP | Elektra | EKL/EKS7277 | 1965 £5 | £12 | |
| Things I Notice Now | LP | Elektra | EKS74043 | 1969 £5 | £12 | |
| Tom Paxton | 7" EP | Elektra | EPK802 | 1967 £2 | £5 | |

## PAYNE, BENNY
| Sunny Side Up | LP | London | LTZR15103 | 1957 £10 | £25 | |

## PAYNE, CECIL
| Connection | LP | Summit | AJS16 | 1962 £8 | £20 | |

## PAYNE, FREDA
| Band Of Gold | LP | Invictus | SVT1001 | 1971 £4 | £10 | |
| Band Of Gold | 7" | Invictus | INV533 | 1973 £2 | £5 | |
| Contact | LP | Invictus | SVT1005 | 1972 £4 | £10 | |
| He Who Laughs Last | 7" | HMV | POP1091 | 1962 £2.50 | £6 | |

## PAYNE, GORDON
| Gordon Payne | LP | A&M | SP4725 | 1978 £8 | £20 | US |

## PAYNE, LEON
| Americana | LP | Starday | SLP236 | 1963 £5 | £12 | US |
| Leon Payne | LP | Starday | SLP231 | 1963 £5 | £12 | US |

## PAZ
| Live At Chichester | LP | Magnus | 2 | 1978 £6 | £15 | |
| Look Inside | LP | Paradin | PALP001 | 1983 £5 | £12 | |
| Paz Are Back | LP | Spotlight | SPJ518 | 1980 £5 | £12 | |

## PEABODY, DAVE
| Peabody Hotel | LP | Village Thing | VTS22 | 1973 £5 | £12 | |

## PEACE, DAVE QUARTET
| Good Morning Mr. Blues | LP | Saga | FID2155 | 1969 £6 | £15 | |

## PEACE, JOE
| Finding Peace Of Mind | LP | Rite | 29917 | 1972 £75 | £150 | US |

## PEACEFUL COMPANY
| Peaceful Company | LP | Sovereign | SVNA7252 | 1973 £8 | £20 | |

## PEACHES & HERB
| Close Your Eyes | 7" | CBS | 2711 | 1967 £1.50 | £4 | |
| For Your Love | LP | CBS | 63119 | 1967 £4 | £10 | |
| For Your Love | 7" | CBS | 2866 | 1967 £2.50 | £6 | |
| Golden Duets | LP | Direction | 863263 | 1968 £4 | £10 | |
| Let's Fall In Love | LP | CBS | 62966 | 1967 £4 | £10 | |
| Let's Fall In Love | 7" | CBS | 202509 | 1967 £2.50 | £6 | |
| Soothe Me With Your Love | 7" | Direction | 585249 | 1970 £2 | £5 | |

## PEACOCK, ANNETTE
Singer Annette Peacock was championed by jazz pianist Paul Bley, who recorded many of her compositions on his albums from the late sixties. In the seventies they toured together, pioneering the use of synthesizers as live improvising tools – the collectable albums they made in the style are listed under Bley's name in this guide. *I'm The One*, however, is Peacock's masterpiece. As much a rock album as jazz, the record demonstrates her impressive ability to direct electronic technology towards her own creative ends, using her voice as a sound-source to be shaped by the synthesizers.

| I'm The One | LP | RCA | LSP4578 | 1972 £5 | £12 | US, metallic cover |
| I'm The One | LP | RCA | SF8255 | 1972 £4 | £10 | |
| Live In Paris | LP | Aura | 0060476 | 1981 £25 | £50 | |

## PEAK FOLK
| Peak Folk | LP | Folk Heritage | | 197– £6 | £15 | |

## PEANUT
Peanut was a teenage American girl singer (at least she sounds like a teenager – she features in no rock reference books) whose version of 'Home Of The Brave' was played on the radio a few times without becoming a chart hit. Nevertheless, her singing conveys such a sense of angst, of youthful hopes and wishes and love – and frustration in the face of blind adult unreason – that the song is an absolute classic, even if an unheralded one. (It has since been suggested elsewhere that Peanut is Katie Kissoon, who has appeared on numerous recordings as a backing singer, including some by Van Morrison, as well as scoring a number of seventies chart hits as half of the duo Mac and Katie Kissoon.)

| Home Of The Brave | 7" | Pye | 7N15963 | 1965 £2.50 | £6 | |
| I Didn't Love Him Anyway | 7" | Columbia | DB8104 | 1967 £2.50 | £6 | |
| I'm Waiting For The Day | 7" | Columbia | DB8032 | 1966 £2.50 | £6 | |
| Thank You For The Rain | 7" | Pye | 7N15901 | 1965 £1.50 | £4 | |

## PEANUT BUTTER CONSPIRACY
The Peanut Butter Conspiracy added Mamas-and-Papas-style harmony vocals on to the instrumental sound of Jefferson Airplane. The combination works brilliantly and the group's best songs are quite delightful, although somehow the group failed to find the success that they should have.

| Back In L.A. | 7" | London | HLH10290 | 1969 £1.50 | £4 | |

| | | | | | | | | |
|---|---|---|---|---|---|---|---|---|
| For Children Of All Ages | LP | Challenge | 2000 | 1968 | £8 | £20 | US |
| Great Conspiracy | LP | CBS | 63277 | 1968 | £10 | £25 | |
| Is Spreading | LP | Columbia | CL2654/CS9495 | 1967 | £10 | £25 | US |
| It's A Happening Thing | 7" | CBS | 2981 | 1967 | £2.50 | £6 | |
| Turn On A Friend | 7" | CBS | 3543 | 1968 | £2.50 | £6 | |

## PEARCE, BOB BLUES BAND
| | | | | | | | |
|---|---|---|---|---|---|---|---|
| Blues Crusade | LP | Avenue | BEV1054 | 1968 | £4 | £10 | |

## PEARL JAM
| | | | | | | | |
|---|---|---|---|---|---|---|---|
| Jeremy | CD-s | Epic | 6582582 | 1992 | £2 | £5 | picture disc |
| Pearl Jam Live – KROQ | CD | private | no number | 1994 | £25 | £50 | US promo |
| Rarified And Live | CD | Epic | SAMP656 | 1995 | £180 | £300 | Australian double promo |
| Ten | LP | Epic | 4688840 | 1992 | £4 | £10 | picture disc |
| Ten | CD | Epic | 4688845 | 1992 | £5 | £12 | metallic yellow pack |

## PEARLS BEFORE SWINE
| | | | | | | | |
|---|---|---|---|---|---|---|---|
| Balaklava | LP | Fontana | STL5503 | 1968 | £8 | £20 | |
| Beautiful Lies You Could Live | LP | Reprise | RSLP6467 | 1971 | £4 | £10 | |
| City Of Gold | LP | Reprise | RSLP6442 | 1971 | £4 | £10 | |
| One Nation Underground | LP | Fontana | STL5505 | 1967 | £8 | £20 | |
| These Things Too | LP | Reprise | RSLP6364 | 1969 | £4 | £10 | |
| Use Of Ashes | LP | Reprise | RSLP6405 | 1970 | £4 | £10 | |

## PEARSE, JOHN
| | | | | | | | |
|---|---|---|---|---|---|---|---|
| John Pearse | LP | XTRA | XTRA1056 | 1968 | £4 | £10 | |
| Teach Yourself Folk Guitar | LP | Saga | XID5503 | 1963 | £4 | £10 | |

## PEARSON, DUKE
| | | | | | | | |
|---|---|---|---|---|---|---|---|
| How Insensitive | LP | Blue Note | BST84344 | 1969 | £5 | £12 | |
| Introducing Duke Pearson's Big Band | LP | Blue Note | BST84276 | 1968 | £6 | £15 | |
| Merry Ole Soul | LP | Blue Note | BST84323 | 1969 | £6 | £15 | |
| Now Hear This | LP | Blue Note | BST84308 | 1969 | £5 | £12 | |
| Phantom | LP | Blue Note | BST84293 | 1968 | £5 | £12 | |
| Right Touch | LP | Blue Note | BST84267 | 1968 | £6 | £15 | |
| Sweet Honey Bee | LP | Blue Note | BLP/BST84252 | 1967 | £10 | £25 | |
| Tender Feelin's | LP | Blue Note | BLP/BST84035 | 196– | £20 | £40 | |
| Wahoo | LP | Blue Note | BLP/BST84191 | 1965 | £10 | £25 | |

## PEARSON, JOHNNY
| | | | | | | | |
|---|---|---|---|---|---|---|---|
| Rat Catcher's Theme | 7" | Columbia | DB7851 | 1966 | £2.50 | £6 | |

## PEARSON, RONNIE
| | | | | | | | |
|---|---|---|---|---|---|---|---|
| Teenage Fancy | 7" | HMV | POP489 | 1958 | £250 | £400 | best auctioned |

## PEASANTS
| | | | | | | | |
|---|---|---|---|---|---|---|---|
| Got Some Lovin' For You Baby | 7" | Columbia | DB7642 | 1965 | £100 | £200 | best auctioned |

## PEBBLES
| | | | | | | | |
|---|---|---|---|---|---|---|---|
| Incredible George | 7" | Decca | F22944 | 1969 | £1.50 | £4 | |

## PEBBLES (2)
| | | | | | | | |
|---|---|---|---|---|---|---|---|
| Huma La La La La | 7" EP | President | PRC512 | 196– | £4 | £8 | French |

## PEDDLERS
| | | | | | | | |
|---|---|---|---|---|---|---|---|
| Birthday | LP | CBS | 63682 | 1969 | £4 | £10 | |
| Fantastic Peddlers | LP | Fontana | SFL13016 | 1968 | £4 | £10 | |
| Freewheelers | LP | CBS | (S)BPG63183 | 1968 | £4 | £10 | |
| Georgia On My Mind | LP | Philips | 6386066 | 1971 | £4 | £10 | |
| Live At The Pickwick | LP | Philips | (S)BL7768 | 1967 | £6 | £15 | |
| Suite London | LP | Philips | 6308102 | 1972 | £4 | £10 | |
| Three For All | LP | Philips | 6308028 | 1970 | £4 | £10 | |
| Three In A Cell | LP | CBS | 63411 | 1968 | £4 | £10 | |

## PEDECIN, MIKE QUINTET
| | | | | | | | |
|---|---|---|---|---|---|---|---|
| Musical Medicine | LP | Apollo | LP484 | 1957 | £25 | £50 | US |

## PEDRICKS, BOBBY
| | | | | | | | |
|---|---|---|---|---|---|---|---|
| White Bucks And Saddle Shoes | 7" | London | HLX8740 | 1958 | £12.50 | £25 | |

## PEEBLES, ANN
| | | | | | | | |
|---|---|---|---|---|---|---|---|
| I Can't Stand The Rain | LP | London | SHU8468 | 1974 | £4 | £10 | |
| Part Time Love | LP | Hi | HL32059 | 1971 | £5 | £12 | US |
| Straight From The Heart | LP | London | SHU8434 | 1972 | £4 | £10 | |
| Tellin' It | LP | London | SHU8490 | 1976 | £4 | £10 | |
| This Is | LP | Hi | HL32053 | 1969 | £5 | £12 | US |

## PEEL, DAVID & LOWER EAST SIDE
| | | | | | | | |
|---|---|---|---|---|---|---|---|
| American Revolution | LP | Elektra | EKS74069 | 1970 | £5 | £12 | |
| American Revolution | LP | Elektra | K42074 | 1972 | £4 | £10 | |
| Have A Marijuana | LP | Elektra | EKL/EKS74032 | 1968 | £6 | £15 | |
| Pope Smokes Dope | LP | Apple | SW3391 | 1972 | £6 | £15 | US |

## PEEL, JOHN
John Peel has made many cameo appearances on other people's records – the odd spoken line, the occasional burst of jew's harp – but *Archive Things*, which is credited to him, contains not a single sound of Peel. Instead, the record is a compilation of short world music

extracts that were included in John Peel's wide-ranging *Night Ride* radio programme. There are some fascinating noises to be heard here and, as a sixties artefact, the record is almost as essential as *Sgt Pepper*, if rather less celebrated.

| | | | | | | | |
|---|---|---|---|---|---|---|---|
| Archive Things | LP | BBC | REC68M | 1970 | £8 | £20 | |

## PEELERS
| | | | | | | | |
|---|---|---|---|---|---|---|---|
| Banished Misfortune | LP | Polydor | 2460165 | 1972 | £100 | £200 | |

## PEELS
| | | | | | | | |
|---|---|---|---|---|---|---|---|
| Juanita Banana | LP | Karate | 5402 | 1966 | £8 | £20 | US |
| Time Marches On | 7" | Audio Fidelity | AFSP527 | 1966 | £4 | £8 | |

## PEENUTS
| | | | | | | | |
|---|---|---|---|---|---|---|---|
| Theme From The Monkees | 7" | Ember | EMBS242 | 1967 | £1.50 | £4 | |

## PEEP SHOW
| | | | | | | | |
|---|---|---|---|---|---|---|---|
| Esprit De Corps | 7" | Polydor | BM52226 | 1968 | £5 | £10 | |
| Mazy | 7" | Polydor | 56196 | 1967 | £50 | £100 | |

## PEEPS
| | | | | | | | |
|---|---|---|---|---|---|---|---|
| Gotta Get A Move On | 7" | Philips | BF1478 | 1966 | £1.50 | £4 | |
| Now Is The Time | 7" | Philips | BF1421 | 1965 | £2 | £5 | |
| Tra La La | 7" | Philips | BF1509 | 1966 | £1.50 | £4 | |
| What Can I Say | 7" | Philips | BF1443 | 1965 | £2.50 | £6 | |

## PEG LEG SAM
| | | | | | | | |
|---|---|---|---|---|---|---|---|
| Last Medicine Show | LP | Flyright | LP507/8 | 1974 | £5 | £12 | double |

## PEGASUS
| | | | | | | | |
|---|---|---|---|---|---|---|---|
| Seems A Long Time Gone | LP | private | CPK175 | 1975 | £8 | £20 | German |

## PEGASUS (2)
| | | | | | | | |
|---|---|---|---|---|---|---|---|
| Pegasus | LP | Univers | | 1979 | £15 | £30 | Dutch |

## PEGG, BOB
| | | | | | | | |
|---|---|---|---|---|---|---|---|
| Ancient Maps | LP | Transatlantic | TRA299 | 1975 | £5 | £12 | |
| Bob Pegg & Nick Strutt | LP | Transatlantic | TRA265 | 1973 | £5 | £12 | |
| Shipbuilder | LP | Transatlantic | TRA280 | 1974 | £5 | £12 | |

## PEGG, BOB & CAROLANNE
| | | | | | | | |
|---|---|---|---|---|---|---|---|
| He Came From The Mountains | LP | Trailer | LER3016 | 1971 | £6 | £15 | |

## PEGG, CAROLANNE
| | | | | | | | |
|---|---|---|---|---|---|---|---|
| Carolanne Pegg | LP | Transatlantic | TRA266 | 1973 | £30 | £60 | |

## PEGGY'S LEG
| | | | | | | | |
|---|---|---|---|---|---|---|---|
| Grinilla | LP | Bunch | BAN2001 | 1973 | £180 | £300 | |
| William Tell Overture | 7" | Bunch | no number | 1973 | £10 | £20 | |

## PEIFFER, BERNARD
| | | | | | | | |
|---|---|---|---|---|---|---|---|
| Bernard Peiffer | LP | Felsted | PDL85022 | 1956 | £5 | £12 | |
| Bernard Peiffer Trio | LP | Top Rank | 30025 | 1960 | £4 | £10 | |
| Bernard Peiffer Trio | 10" LP | Felsted | EDL87016 | 1955 | £10 | £25 | |
| Orchestra | 10" LP | Felsted | EDL87011 | 1955 | £10 | £25 | |
| Piano A La Mood | LP | Brunswick | LAT8262 | 1958 | £5 | £12 | |
| Trio | 10" LP | Felsted | EDL87013 | 1955 | £10 | £25 | |

## PELL, DAVE
| | | | | | | | |
|---|---|---|---|---|---|---|---|
| Dave Pell Octet | LP | London | HAK2021 | 1957 | £5 | £12 | |
| I Had The Craziest Dream | LP | Capitol | T925 | 1958 | £4 | £10 | |
| Irving Berlin Gallery | 10" LP | London | HAPB1020 | 1954 | £20 | £40 | |
| Love Story | LP | London | LTZK15082 | 1957 | £10 | £25 | |
| Rodgers And Hart Gallery | 10" LP | London | HAPB1034 | 1955 | £15 | £30 | |

## PELL MELL
| | | | | | | | |
|---|---|---|---|---|---|---|---|
| From The New World | LP | Philips | 6305193 | 1975 | £4 | £10 | German |
| Marburg | LP | Bacillus | BLPS19090 | 1972 | £5 | £12 | German |
| Rhapsody | LP | Venus | VB761PMAB | 1976 | £4 | £10 | German |

## PEMBROKE, JIM
| | | | | | | | |
|---|---|---|---|---|---|---|---|
| Corporal Cauliflower's Mental Functions | LP | Love | LRLP214 | 1977 | £6 | £15 | Swedish |
| Hot Thumbs O'Riley | LP | Charisma | CAS1071 | 1973 | £6 | £15 | |
| Pigworm | LP | Love | LRLP103 | 1974 | £6 | £15 | Swedish |
| Wicked Ivory | LP | Love | LRLP52 | 1972 | £6 | £15 | Swedish |

## PENDARVIS, TRACY
| | | | | | | | |
|---|---|---|---|---|---|---|---|
| South Bound Line | 7" | London | HLS9213 | 1960 | £5 | £10 | |
| Thousand Guitars | 7" | London | HLS9059 | 1960 | £5 | £10 | |

## PENDLEFOLK
| | | | | | | | |
|---|---|---|---|---|---|---|---|
| Pendlefolk | LP | Folk Heritage | FHR007 | 1970 | £6 | £15 | |

## PENETRATION
| | | | | | | | |
|---|---|---|---|---|---|---|---|
| Aquarian Symphony | LP | Higher Key | 33071 | 1974 | £30 | £60 | US |

## PENGUIN CAFE ORCHESTRA
| | | | | | | | |
|---|---|---|---|---|---|---|---|
| Broadcasting From Home | LP | Editions EG | EGED38 | 1984 | £5 | £12 | |

| | | | | | | |
|---|---|---|---|---|---|---|
| Mini Album | LP | Editions EG | EGMLP2 | 1983 £8 | £20 | |
| Music From The Penguin Café | LP | Editions EG | EGED27 | 1984 £4 | £10 | |
| Music From The Penguin Café | LP | Obscure | OBS7 | 1976 £8 | £20 | |
| Penguin Café Orchestra | LP | Editions EG | EGED11 | 1983 £6 | £15 | |

## PENGUINS

The Penguins' 'Earth Angel' is arguably the definitive doo-wop performance, although the UK sales of the original issue were minimal. In consequence, this is now one of the most valuable London recordings of all. The later 'Memories Of El Monte' is collectable largely on account of its having been written by Frank Zappa and Ray Collins.

| | | | | | | |
|---|---|---|---|---|---|---|
| Best Vocal Groups: Rhythm And Blues | LP | DooTone | DTL204 | 195– £125 | £250 | US, with other artists |
| Best Vocal Groups: Rhythm And Blues | LP | DooTone | DTL204 | 195– £1050 | £1500 | US, with other artists, red vinyl |
| Cool Cool Penguins | LP | Dooto | DTL242 | 1959 £150 | £300 | US |
| Earth Angel | 7" | London | HL8114 | 1955 £700 | £1000 | gold label, best auctioned |
| Memories Of El Monte | 7" | Original Sound | 27 | 1962 £75 | £150 | US |

## PENN, DAWN

| | | | | | | |
|---|---|---|---|---|---|---|
| Long Days, Short Nights | 7" | Rio | R113 | 1967 £4 | £8 | |
| You Don't Love Me | 7" | Studio One | SO2030 | 1967 £6 | £12 | |

## PENN, TONY

| | | | | | | |
|---|---|---|---|---|---|---|
| That's What I Like | 7" | Starlite | ST45083 | 1962 £10 | £20 | |

## PENNINES

| | | | | | | |
|---|---|---|---|---|---|---|
| Manchester Morning | LP | Penny Farthing | PELS514 | 1971 £50 | £100 | |

## PENNY, HANK

| | | | | | | |
|---|---|---|---|---|---|---|
| Bloodshot Eyes | 7" | Parlophone | MSP6202 | 1956 £15 | £30 | |

## PENNY PEEPS

| | | | | | | |
|---|---|---|---|---|---|---|
| I See The Morning | 7" | Liberty | LBF15114 | 1968 £2.50 | £6 | |
| Model Village | 7" | Liberty | LBF15053 | 1968 £15 | £30 | |

## PENROSE, CHARLES

| | | | | | | |
|---|---|---|---|---|---|---|
| Adventures Of A Laughing Policeman | 7" EP | Columbia | SEG7743 | 1957 £2 | £5 | |
| Laughing Policeman | 7" | Columbia | DB8959 | 1972 £1.50 | £4 | |

## PENTAD

| | | | | | | |
|---|---|---|---|---|---|---|
| Don't Throw It All Away | 7" | Parlophone | R5368 | 1965 £2 | £5 | |
| It Better Be Me | 7" | Parlophone | R5424 | 1966 £2 | £5 | |
| Silver Dagger | 7" | Parlophone | R5288 | 1965 £5 | £10 | |

## PENTAGONS

| | | | | | | |
|---|---|---|---|---|---|---|
| To Be Loved | 7" | London | HLU9333 | 1961 £20 | £40 | |

## PENTANGLE

The Pentangle were a kind of folk super-group, formed when the influential solo guitarists Bert Jansch and John Renbourn decided to join forces with the current rhythm section from Alexis Korner's Blues Incorporated and with folk singer Jacqui McShee. The group's approach was more of a folk-jazz synthesis than anything to do with what is normally conceived as rock music, but it proved to be enormously popular. 'Light Flight', a television theme (for *Take Three Girls*) that is probably better known than the series it was designed to introduce, is included on the group's best-known album, *Basket Of Light*.

| | | | | | | |
|---|---|---|---|---|---|---|
| Basket Of Light | LP | Transatlantic | TRA205 | 1969 £4 | £10 | |
| Cruel Sister | LP | Transatlantic | TRA228 | 1970 £4 | £10 | gatefold sleeve |
| Pentangle | LP | Transatlantic | TRA162 | 1968 £5 | £12 | |
| Reflection | LP | Transatlantic | TRA240 | 1971 £4 | £10 | gatefold sleeve |
| Solomon's Seal | LP | Reprise | K44197 | 1972 £10 | £25 | |
| Sweet Child | LP | Transatlantic | TRA178 | 1968 £8 | £20 | double |
| Travellin' Song | 7" | Transatlantic | BIG109 | 1968 £1.50 | £4 | |

## PEOPLE

| | | | | | | |
|---|---|---|---|---|---|---|
| Both Sides Of People | LP | Capitol | ST151 | 1969 £10 | £25 | US |
| I Love You | LP | Capitol | ST2924 | 1968 £10 | £25 | US |
| Somebody Tell Me My Name | 7" | Capitol | CL15553 | 1968 £2 | £5 | |
| There Are People And There Are People | LP | Paramount | PAS5013 | 1970 £6 | £15 | US |
| Ulla | 7" | Capitol | CL15599 | 1969 £1.50 | £4 | |

## PEOPLE (2)

| | | | | | | |
|---|---|---|---|---|---|---|
| In Ancient Times | 7" | Deram | DM346 | 1971 £1.50 | £4 | |

## PEOPLE BAND

| | | | | | | |
|---|---|---|---|---|---|---|
| People Band | LP | Transatlantic | TRA214 | 1970 £8 | £20 | |

## PEOPLES, TOMMY

| | | | | | | |
|---|---|---|---|---|---|---|
| Tommy Peoples | LP | Eireann | CL13 | 1976 £6 | £15 | |

## PEOPLES, TOMMY & DAITHI SPROULE

| | | | | | | |
|---|---|---|---|---|---|---|
| Iron Man | LP | Shanachie | 79044 | 1985 £4 | £10 | US |

## PEOPLES, TOMMY & PAUL BRADY

| | | | | | | |
|---|---|---|---|---|---|---|
| High Part Of The Road | LP | Shanachie | 29003 | 1976 £4 | £10 | US |

## PEOPLE'S CHOICE

| | | | | | | |
|---|---|---|---|---|---|---|
| I Like To Do It | 7" | Mojo | 2092024 | 1971 £2 | £5 | |

## PEPPER
| | | | | | | |
|---|---|---|---|---|---|---|
| We'll Make It Together | 7" | Pye | 7N17569 | 1968 £2 | £5 | |

## PEPPER, ART
| | | | | | |
|---|---|---|---|---|---|
| Art Pepper Quartet | LP | London | LZU14038 | 1956 £15 | £30 |
| Art Pepper Quartet | 10" LP | Vogue | LDE067 | 1954 £25 | £50 |
| Gettin' Together | LP | Contemporary | LAC12262 | 1961 £8 | £20 |
| Meets The Rhythm Section | LP | Contemporary | LAC12066 | 1958 £8 | £20 |
| Modern Jazz Classics | LP | Contemporary | LAC12229 | 1960 £8 | £20 |

## PEPPER, JIM
| | | | | | |
|---|---|---|---|---|---|
| Pepper's Pow Wow | LP | Atlantic | 2400149 | 1971 £6 | £15 |

## PEPPERMINT, DANNY
| | | | | | |
|---|---|---|---|---|---|
| Maybe Tomorrow | 7" | London | HLL9614 | 1962 £1.50 | £4 |
| One More Time | 7" | London | HLL9516 | 1962 £1.50 | £4 |
| Peppermint Twist | 7" | London | HLL9478 | 1961 £1.50 | £4 |
| Twist With Danny Peppermint | LP | London | HAL2438 | 1962 £6 | £15 |

## PEPPERMINT CIRCUS
| | | | | | |
|---|---|---|---|---|---|
| All The King's Horses | 7" | Olga | OLE007 | 1967 £1.50 | £4 |

## PEPPERMINT TROLLEY COMPANY
| | | | | | | |
|---|---|---|---|---|---|---|
| Peppermint Trolley Company | LP | Acta | A38007 | 1968 £8 | £20 | US |

## PEPPI
| | | | | | |
|---|---|---|---|---|---|
| I Never Danced Before | 7" | Decca | F11638 | 1963 £1.50 | £4 |
| Pistol Packin' Mama | 7" | Decca | F11991 | 1964 £1.50 | £4 |
| Skip | 7" | Decca | F12055 | 1965 £1.50 | £4 |

## PERCEWOOD'S ONAGRAM
| | | | | | | |
|---|---|---|---|---|---|---|
| Ameurope | LP | Onagram | PO1004 | 1974 £6 | £15 | German |
| Lessons For Virgins | LP | Virgin | AR6601 | 1971 £6 | £15 | German |
| Percewood's Onagram | LP | Virgin | PO1 | 1970 £4 | £10 | German |
| Tropical Brainforest | LP | Virgin | AR6602 | 1972 £4 | £10 | German |

## PERE UBU
| | | | | | | |
|---|---|---|---|---|---|---|
| Breath | CD-s | Fontana | UBUCD4 | 1989 £2 | £5 | |
| Fabulous Sequel | 7" | Chrysalis | CHS2372 | 1979 £2 | £5 | |
| I Hear They Smoke The Barbeque | CD-s | Fontana | UBUCD5 | 1990 £2 | £5 | |
| Love Love Love | CD-s | Fontana | UBUCD3 | 1989 £2 | £5 | |
| Love Love Love | CD-s | Fontana | UBUCD33 | 1989 £2 | £5 | |
| Modern Dance | LP | Fontana | SFLP3 | 1988 £4 | £10 | |
| Modern Dance | LP | Mercury | 9100052 | 1978 £4 | £10 | |
| Modern Dance | CD | Fontana | 8342672 | 1988 £5 | £12 | numbered ltd edn |
| Tenement Year | CD | Fontana | 8345372 | 1988 £5 | £12 | |
| Waiting For Mary | CD-s | Fontana | UBUCD2 | 1989 £2 | £5 | |
| We Have The Technology | CD-s | Fontana | UBUCD1 | 1988 £2 | £5 | |

## PEREGRINE
| | | | | | |
|---|---|---|---|---|---|
| Songs Of Mine | LP | Westwood | WRS016 | 1972 £25 | £50 |

## PERFECT, CHRISTINE

Christine Perfect was pianist and vocalist with Chicken Shack and since the songs that she led were always the best that the group produced, it is not surprising that her solo LP is a particularly good example of British blues. When Peter Green left Fleetwood Mac, Christine Perfect was drafted in as his replacement, when she began to use her married name, Christine McVie.

| | | | | | |
|---|---|---|---|---|---|
| Christine Perfect | LP | Blue Horizon | 763860 | 1970 £15 | £30 |
| I'm Too Far Gone | 7" | Blue Horizon | 573172 | 1970 £2 | £5 |
| When You Say | 7" | Blue Horizon | 573165 | 1969 £1.50 | £4 |

## PERFECT PEOPLE
| | | | | | |
|---|---|---|---|---|---|
| House In The Country | 7" | MCA | MU1079 | 1969 £2.50 | £6 |

## PERFORMERS
| | | | | | |
|---|---|---|---|---|---|
| I Can't Stop You | 7" | Action | ACT4552 | 1969 £2 | £5 |

## PERIGEO
| | | | | | | |
|---|---|---|---|---|---|---|
| Abbiamo Tutti Un Blues Da Piangere | LP | RCA | DPSL10609 | 1973 £6 | £15 | Italian |
| Attraverso Il Parigeo | LP | RCA | NL33039 | 1977 £5 | £12 | Italian |
| Azimut | LP | RCA | DPSL10555 | 1972 £6 | £15 | Italian |
| Genealogia | LP | RCA | TPL11080 | 1974 £6 | £15 | Italian |
| La Valle Del Tepli | LP | RCA | TPL11175 | 1975 £6 | £15 | Italian |
| Non E Poi Cosi Lontano | LP | RCA | | 1976 £6 | £15 | Italian |

## PERISHERS
| | | | | | |
|---|---|---|---|---|---|
| How Does It Feel | 7" | Fontana | TF965 | 1968 £7.50 | £15 |

## PERKINS, BILL
| | | | | | |
|---|---|---|---|---|---|
| Just Friends | LP | Vogue | LAE12088 | 1958 £10 | £25 |
| On Stage | LP | Vogue | LAE12078 | 1958 £8 | £20 |

## PERKINS, CARL
| | | | | | | |
|---|---|---|---|---|---|---|
| Any Way The Wind Blows | 7" | Philips | PB1179 | 1961 £4 | £8 | |
| Big Bad Blues | 7" | Brunswick | 05909 | 1964 £1.50 | £4 | ... with The Nashville Teens |

| Title | Format | Label | Cat. No. | Year | Price | Price | Notes |
|---|---|---|---|---|---|---|---|
| Blue Suede Shoes | 7" | London | HLS10192 | 1968 | £1.50 | £4 | |
| Blue Suede Shoes | 7" | London | HLU8271 | 1956 | £50 | £100 | |
| Boppin' The Blues | LP | CBS | 63826 | 1970 | £4 | £10 | with NRBQ |
| Country Boy's Dream | LP | London | HAP/SHP8366 | 1968 | £4 | £10 | |
| Country Boy's Dream | 7" | London | HLP7125 | 1968 | £5 | £10 | export |
| Country Boy's Dream | 7" | Stateside | SS599 | 1967 | £2 | £5 | |
| Dance Album | LP | Sun | LP1225 | 1957 | £150 | £250 | US |
| Dance Album (Teen Beat) | LP | London | HAS2202 | 1959 | £30 | £60 | |
| Dixie Fried | 7" | London | HLS10192 | 1968 | £30 | £60 | demo |
| Glad All Over | 7" | London | HLS8527 | 1957 | £37.50 | £75 | |
| Gone, Gone, Sone | 7" | Sun | 224 | 1955 | £25 | £50 | US |
| Help Me Find My Baby | 7" | Brunswick | 05905 | 1964 | £2 | £5 | |
| King Of Rock | LP | CBS | 63309 | 1968 | £4 | £10 | |
| Lake County Cotton Country | 7" | Spark | SRL1009 | 1968 | £2 | £5 | |
| Matchbox | 7" | London | HLS8408 | 1957 | £50 | £100 | |
| Monkeyshine | 7" | Brunswick | 05923 | 1964 | £2.50 | £6 | |
| Movie Magg | 7" | Flip | 501 | 1955 | £150 | £250 | US, best auctioned |
| One Ticket To Loneliness | 7" | Philips | PB983 | 1959 | £4 | £8 | |
| Restless | 7" | CBS | 3932 | 1969 | £1.50 | £4 | |
| Teen Beat | LP | Sun | LP1225 | 1961 | £75 | £150 | US |
| That's Right | 7" | London | HLS8608 | 1958 | £37.50 | £75 | |
| Whole Lotta Carl Perkins | LP | CBS | 52305 | 1962 | £4 | £10 | |
| Whole Lotta Shakin' | LP | Columbia | CL1234 | 1958 | £50 | £100 | US |

## PERKINS, LASCELLES

| Title | Format | Label | Cat. No. | Year | Price | Price | Notes |
|---|---|---|---|---|---|---|---|
| Creation | 7" | Blue Beat | BB41 | 1961 | £6 | £12 | |
| I'm So Grateful | 7" | Ska Beat | JB175 | 1964 | £5 | £10 | |
| Tango Lips | 7" | Island | WI038 | 1963 | £5 | £10 | |
| Tell It All Brothers | 7" | Banana | BA317 | 1970 | £1.50 | £4 | Sound Dimension B side |

## PERKINS, POLLY

| Title | Format | Label | Cat. No. | Year | Price | Price | Notes |
|---|---|---|---|---|---|---|---|
| Girls Are At It Again | 7" | Decca | F11583 | 1963 | £1.50 | £4 | |

## PERLINPINPIN FOLO

| Title | Format | Label | Cat. No. | Year | Price | Price | Notes |
|---|---|---|---|---|---|---|---|
| Al Biule | LP | Auvidis | AV4520 | 1985 | £8 | £20 | French |

## PERRIN, PAT

| Title | Format | Label | Cat. No. | Year | Price | Price | Notes |
|---|---|---|---|---|---|---|---|
| Over You | 7" | Island | WI3115 | 1968 | £5 | £10 | Lloyd Terrell B side |

## PERRINE, PEP

| Title | Format | Label | Cat. No. | Year | Price | Price | Notes |
|---|---|---|---|---|---|---|---|
| Live And In Person | LP | Hideout | 1004 | 1968 | £50 | £100 | US |

## PERRI'S

| Title | Format | Label | Cat. No. | Year | Price | Price | Notes |
|---|---|---|---|---|---|---|---|
| Jerri-Lee | 7" | Oriole | CB1481 | 1959 | £1.50 | £4 | |

## PERRY, JEFF

| Title | Format | Label | Cat. No. | Year | Price | Price | Notes |
|---|---|---|---|---|---|---|---|
| Love Don't Come No Stronger | 7" | Arista | ARIST51 | 1976 | £1.50 | £4 | |

## PERRY, LEE

| Title | Format | Label | Cat. No. | Year | Price | Price | Notes |
|---|---|---|---|---|---|---|---|
| Africa's Blood | LP | Trojan | TBL166 | 1980 | £5 | £12 | |
| Bad Minded People | 7" | Port-O-Jam | PJ4003 | 1964 | £5 | £10 | Tommy McCook B side |
| Chatty Chatty Woman | 7" | Port-O-Jam | PJ4010 | 1964 | £5 | £10 | Tommy McCook B side |
| Country Girl | 7" | Island | WI223 | 1965 | £5 | £10 | |
| Doctor Dick | 7" | Island | WI292 | 1966 | £6 | £12 | Soul Brothers B side |
| Just Keep It Up | 7" | Island | WI259 | 1965 | £6 | £12 | Roland Alphonso B side |
| Kill Them All | 7" | Upsetter | US325 | 1970 | £1.50 | £4 | |
| King Tubby Meets The Upsetter | LP | Fay | FMLP304 | 1975 | £8 | £20 | |
| Man And Wife | 7" | R&B | JB106 | 1963 | £6 | £12 | |
| Never Get Weary | 7" | Island | WI118 | 1963 | £6 | £12 | Tommy McCook B side |
| Old For New | 7" | R&B | JB104 | 1963 | £6 | £12 | |
| Open Up | 7" | Ska Beat | JB215 | 1965 | £5 | £10 | Roland Alphonso B side |
| People Funny Boy | 7" | Doctor Bird | DB1146 | 1968 | £5 | £10 | Burt Walters B side |
| Please Don't Go | 7" | Island | WI210 | 1965 | £5 | £10 | |
| Prince In The Dark | 7" | R&B | JB102 | 1963 | £6 | £12 | |
| Revolution Dub | LP | Cactus | CTLP112 | 1979 | £5 | £12 | |
| Roast Duck | 7" | Ska Beat | JB201 | 1965 | £5 | £10 | |
| Royalty | 7" | R&B | JB135 | 1964 | £6 | £12 | |
| Rub And Squeeze | 7" | Island | WI298 | 1966 | £5 | £10 | Soul Brothers B side |
| Run For Cover | 7" | Doctor Bird | DB1073 | 1967 | £5 | £10 | |
| Scratch On The Wire | LP | Island | ILPS9583 | 1979 | £5 | £12 | |
| Super Ape | LP | Island | ILPS9417 | 1976 | £8 | £20 | orange label |
| Trial And Crosses | 7" | Ska Beat | JB203 | 1965 | £5 | £10 | |
| Uncle Desmond | 7" | Trojan | TR644 | 1968 | £4 | £8 | |
| Upsetter | LP | Trojan | TTL13 | 1969 | £8 | £20 | |
| Upsetter | 7" | Amalgamated | AMG808 | 1968 | £4 | £8 | |
| Upsetter Again | LP | Trojan | TTL28 | 1970 | £8 | £20 | |
| Whop Whop Man | 7" | Doctor Bird | DB1098 | 1967 | £5 | £10 | |
| Wishes Of The Wicked | 7" | Ska Beat | JB212 | 1965 | £5 | £10 | |
| Woodman | 7" | Ska Beat | JB251 | 1966 | £5 | £10 | |
| Yakety Yak | 7" | Upsetter | US324 | 1969 | £1.50 | £4 | |

## PERRY SISTERS
Willie Boy ............................................... 7" ...... Brunswick ....... 05802 .................... 1959 £**7.50** ...... £**15** .........................................

## PERSEPHONE, BILLY
Billy Persephone ........................................ LP ..... Orion ............. ............................ 1972 £**10** ........ £**25** ...................*US*

## PERSEPHONY
To Those Who Loved Us ........................ LP ..... Unidentified  UAP3 ................... 1979 £**37.50** .... £**75** ...................*Dutch*
Artist
Productions .....

## PERSIMMON'S PECULIAR SHADES
Watchmaker ............................................. 7" ...... Major Minor ... MM554 ................. 1968 £**6** .......... £**12** .........................................

## PERSONALITIES
Hey Little Girl ......................................... 7" ...... Ska Beat ....... JB222 ................. 1965 £**5** .......... £**10** .........................................
Push It Down .......................................... 7" ...... Blue Beat ...... BB354 ................. 1966 £**6** .......... £**12** .........................................
Suffering ................................................. 7" ...... Dice ............. CC30 ................. 1965 £**5** .......... £**10** .........................................

## PERSUADERS
Surfer's Nightmare ...................................... LP ..... Saturn ............ SAT(S)5000 ........... 1963 £**20** ........ £**40** ...................*US*

## PERSUASIONS
Acappella ................................................ LP ..... Straight .......... STS1062 ......... 1970 £**10** ........ £**25** .........................................
Party In The Woods ................................ 7" ...... Minit ............ MLF11017 ......... 1969 £**2** .......... £**5** .........................................
Street Corner Symphony ........................... LP ..... Island .......... ILPS9201 ......... 1972 £**4** .......... £**10** .........................................
We Came To Play ................................... LP ..... Capitol ........... ST791 ......... 1971 £**4** .......... £**10** ...................*US*

## PERSUASIONS (2)
Big Brother ............................................. 7" ...... Columbia ....... DB7700 ......... 1965 £**7.50** ...... £**15** .........................................
I'll Go Crazy ........................................... 7" ...... Columbia ....... DB7560 ......... 1965 £**5** .......... £**10** .........................................
La La La La La ......................................... 7" ...... Columbia ....... DB7859 ......... 1966 £**7.50** ...... £**15** .........................................

## PERT, MORRIS
Book Of Love/Fragmenti I/Ultimate ......... LP ..... Chantry .......... CHT007 ......... 1982 £**25** ........ £**50** .........................................
 Decay .................................................
Contemporary Clarinet Vol. 2 .................. LP ..... Chantry .......... ABM25 ......... 1978 £**25** ........ £**50** *with Georgina Dobree*
*& works by John*
*Mayer & Elisabeth*
*Lutyens*
Contemporary Clarinet Vol. 2 .................. LP ..... Chantry .......... CHT005 ......... 198– £**20** ........ £**40** *with Georgina Dobree*
*& works by John*
*Mayer & Elisabeth*
*Lutyens*
Luminos/Chromosphere/4 Japanese Verses. LP ...... Chantry ......... ABM21 ......... 1975 £**30** ........ £**60** *with Georgina Dobree,*
*Veronica Hayward &*
*Suntreader*
Luminos/Chromosphere/4 Japanese Verses. LP ...... Chantry ......... CHT001 ......... 198– £**25** ........ £**50** *with Georgina Dobree,*
*Veronica Hayward &*
*Suntreader*

## PERTH COUNTY CONSPIRACY
Does Not Exist ....................................... LP ..... Columbia ....... ELS375 ......... 1969 £**10** ........ £**25** ...............*Canadian*

## PERTWEE, JON
Who Is The Doctor? ................................ 7" ...... Purple ............. PUR111 ............... 1972 £**2.50** ..... £**6** .........................................

## PESKY GEE
Exclamation Mark .................................... LP ..... Pye ................. NSPL18293 ........... 1969 £**20** ........ £**40** .........................................
Where Is My Mind .................................. 7" ...... Pye ................ 7N17708 ............... 1969 £**5** .......... £**10** .........................................

## PET SHOP BOYS
Actually .................................................. LP ..... Parlophone ..... PCSD104 ......... 1987 £**25** ........ £**50** .................*blue vinyl*
Actually .................................................. LP ..... Parlophone ..... PCSD104 ......... 1987 £**20** ........ £**40** .................*clear vinyl*
Actually .................................................. CD .... Parlophone ..... CDPCSDX104 ....... 1987 £**6** .......... £**15** .......*with US CD-s*
*'Always On My*
*Mind'*
Always On My Mind (Dance Mix) ............ CD-s .. Parlophone ..... CDR6171 ......... 1987 £**3** .......... £**8** .........................................
Always On My Mind (Dance Mix) ............ 12" .... Parlophone ..... 12RS6171 ......... 1987 £**4** .......... £**10** ..*gatefold picture sleeve*
Always On My Mind (Phil Harding ........... 12" .... Parlophone ..... 12RX6171 ......... 1987 £**4** .......... £**10** .........................................
 Remix) .................................................
Behaviour ............................................... CD .... Parlophone ..... CDPCSD113 ........... 1990 £**25** ........ £**50** *promo box set with*
*cassette*
Being Boring ........................................... CD-s .. Parlophone ..... CDR6275 ......... 1990 £**2** .......... £**5** .........................................
Bilingual ................................................. CD .... Parlophone ..... 724385310225 ........ 1996 £**30** ........ £**60** ...........*promo pack*
Disco 2 ................................................... CD .... EMI .............. E230852 .............. 1994 £**10** ........ £**25** .... *US double pack –*
*bonus 5 track CD*
*including 'Euroboy'*
Discography ............................................ CD .... Parlophone ..... CDPSBDJ1 ........... 1991 £**15** ........ £**30** .... *promo with spoken*
*intros*
DJ Culturemix ........................................ CD-s .. Parlophone ..... CDRX6301 ......... 1991 £**5** .......... £**12** .........................................
Domino Dancing ..................................... CD-s .. Parlophone ..... CDR6190 ......... 1988 £**4** .......... £**10** .........................................
Domino Dancing (Remix) ......................... 12" .... Parlophone ..... 12RX6190 ......... 1988 £**4** .......... £**10** .........................................
Heart ...................................................... CD-s .. Parlophone ..... CDR6177 ......... 1988 £**4** .......... £**10** .........................................
Heart ( Julian Mendelsohn Remix) ............. 12" .... Parlophone ...... 12RX6177 ............ 1988 £**4** .......... £**10** .........................................

| Title | Format | Label | Catalogue | Year | | | Notes |
|---|---|---|---|---|---|---|---|
| Hit Music | CD | Parlophone | | 1991 | £25 | £50 | French promo of original version of Discography |
| It's A Sin | CD-s | Parlophone | CDR6158 | 1987 | £4 | £10 | |
| It's A Sin | cass-s | Parlophone | TCR6158 | 1987 | £2.50 | £6 | |
| It's A Sin | 12" | Parlophone | 12R6158 | 1987 | £3 | £8 | double sleeve |
| It's A Sin (Ian Levine Remix) | 12" | Parlophone | 12RX6158 | 1987 | £4 | £10 | |
| It's Alright | CD-s | Parlophone | CDR6220 | 1989 | £4 | £10 | |
| It's Alright | 10" | Parlophone | 10R6220 | 1989 | £2.50 | £6 | with poster |
| Jealousy | CD-s | Parlophone | CDR6283 | 1991 | £2 | £5 | |
| Jealousy | CD-s | Parlophone | CDRS6283 | 1991 | £5 | £12 | digipak |
| Left To My Own Devices | CD-s | Parlophone | CDR6198 | 1988 | £4 | £10 | |
| Love Comes Quickly | 10" | Parlophone | 10R6116 | 1986 | £30 | £60 | with poster |
| Love Comes Quickly (Dance Mix) | 12" | Parlophone | 12R6116 | 1986 | £2.50 | £6 | |
| Love Comes Quickly (Dance Mix) | 12" | Parlophone | 12R6116 | 1986 | £4 | £10 | cut-out sleeve |
| Megamix | CD-s | ZYX | ZYX95995 | 1988 | £2 | £5 | |
| Opportunities | 7" | Parlophone | R6097 | 1985 | £7.50 | £15 | 2 different mixes |
| Opportunities | 12" | Parlophone | 12R6097 | 1985 | £10 | £20 | |
| Opportunities (Version Latina) | 12" | Parlophone | 12RA6097 | 1985 | £15 | £30 | |
| Paninaro | 12" | Parlophone | 2015626 | 1987 | £15 | £30 | Italian |
| Pet Shop Boys Compiled | CD | Abbey Road | | 1993 | £150 | £250 | promo CD-R, autographed |
| Rent | CD-s | Parlophone | CDR6168 | 1987 | £3 | £8 | |
| So Hard | CD-s | Parlophone | CDR6269 | 1990 | £3 | £8 | |
| Suburbia | cass-s | Parlophone | TCR6140 | 1986 | £2.50 | £6 | 2 versions |
| Suburbia | 7" | Parlophone | RD6140 | 1986 | £4 | £8 | double |
| Suburbia | 12" | Parlophone | 12R6140 | 1986 | £3 | £8 | double sleeve |
| Very Relentless | CD | Parlophone | CDPCSDX143 | 1993 | £6 | £15 | with 6 track bonus CD |
| Was It Worth It | CD-s | Parlophone | CDR6306 | 1991 | £2 | £5 | |
| West End – Sunglasses | CD-s | ZYX | ZYX85196 | 1988 | £2 | £5 | |
| West End Girls | 7" | Epic | A4292 | 1984 | £12.50 | £25 | |
| West End Girls | 12" | Epic | TA4292 | 1984 | £20 | £40 | |
| West End Girls (Dance Mix) | 12" | Parlophone | 12R6115 | 1985 | £3 | £8 | cut-out sleeve, picture labels |
| West End Girls (Shep Pettibone Mastermix) | 12" | Parlophone | 12RA6115 | 1986 | £4 | £10 | 2 sleeves |
| West End Girls (Untitled Remix) | 10" | Parlophone | 10R6115 | 1985 | £30 | £60 | round sleeve |
| What Have I Done To Deserve This | CD-s | Parlophone | CDR6163 | 1987 | £3 | £8 | with Dusty Springfield |
| Where The Streets Have No Name | CD-s | Parlophone | CDR6285 | 1991 | £2 | £5 | |

## PETARDS

| Title | Format | Label | Catalogue | Year | | | Notes |
|---|---|---|---|---|---|---|---|
| Deeper Blue | LP | Europa | E313 | 1968 | £10 | £25 | German |
| Hits | LP | Sunset | SLS50143 | 1971 | £10 | £20 | German |
| Hitshock | LP | Liberty | LBS83325 | 1969 | £10 | £25 | German |
| Pet Arts | LP | Liberty | LBS83481/2 | 1971 | £10 | £25 | German double |
| Petards | LP | Liberty | LBS83204 | 1969 | £10 | £25 | German |

## PETER, PAUL & MARY

| Title | Format | Label | Catalogue | Year | | | Notes |
|---|---|---|---|---|---|---|---|
| In Concert | LP | Warner Bros | (W)W21555 | 1964 | £5 | £12 | double |
| In The Wind | LP | Warner Bros | (W)W1507 | 1963 | £4 | £10 | |
| In The Wind Vol. 1 | 7" EP | Warner Bros | WEP6135 | 1964 | £2 | £5 | |
| In The Wind Vol. 2 | 7" EP | Warner Bros | WEP6137 | 1964 | £2 | £5 | |
| Moving | LP | Warner Bros | (W)W1473 | 1962 | £4 | £10 | |
| Moving | 7" EP | Warner Bros | WEP6119 | 1964 | £2 | £5 | |
| Peter, Paul & Mary | LP | Warner Bros | (W)W1449 | 1962 | £4 | £10 | |
| Peter, Paul & Mary | 7" EP | Warner Bros | WEP6114 | 1963 | £2 | £5 | |
| Peter, Paul & Mary | 7" EP | Warner Bros | WEP6122 | 1964 | £2 | £5 | |

## PETER & GORDON

| Title | Format | Label | Catalogue | Year | | | Notes |
|---|---|---|---|---|---|---|---|
| Chantent en français | 7" EP | Columbia | ESRF1726 | 1965 | £10 | £20 | French |
| Hits Of Nashville | LP | Capitol | (S)T2430 | 1966 | £4 | £10 | US |
| Hot, Cold & Custard | LP | Capitol | (S)T2882 | 1968 | £4 | £10 | US |
| Hurtin' 'n' Lovin' | LP | Columbia | 33SX1761/ SCX3565 | 1965 | £5 | £12 | |
| I Don't Want To See You Again | LP | Capitol | (S)T2220 | 1964 | £4 | £10 | US |
| I Don't Want To See You Again (Cilla Black B side) | 7" | Capitol | PRO2720 | 1964 | £15 | £30 | US promo – Paul McCartney & John Lennon intros |
| I Go To Pieces | LP | Capitol | (S)T2324 | 1965 | £4 | £10 | US |
| I Go To Pieces | LP | Columbia | SCXC25 | 1965 | £8 | £20 | export |
| I Go To Pieces | 7" EP | Columbia | ESRF1677 | 1965 | £5 | £10 | French |
| In London For Tea | LP | Capitol | (S)T2747 | 1967 | £4 | £10 | US |
| In Touch | LP | Columbia | 33SX1660/ SCX3532 | 1964 | £5 | £12 | |
| Knight In Rusty Armour | LP | Capitol | (S)T2729 | 1967 | £4 | £10 | US |
| Lady Godiva | LP | Capitol | (S)T2664 | 1967 | £4 | £10 | US |
| Lady Godiva | LP | Columbia | SCXC33 | 1966 | £8 | £20 | export |
| Lady Godiva | 7" EP | Columbia | ESRF1824 | 1966 | £5 | £10 | French |
| Nobody I Know | 7" EP | Columbia | ESRF1566 | 1964 | £5 | £10 | French |
| Nobody I Know | 7" EP | Columbia | SEG8348 | 1964 | £6 | £12 | |
| Peter & Gordon | LP | Columbia | 33SX1630/ SCX3518 | 1964 | £5 | £12 | |
| Peter & Gordon | LP | Columbia | SX/SCX6045 | 1966 | £6 | £15 | |
| Somewhere | LP | Columbia | SX/SCX6097 | 1966 | £5 | £12 | |
| Sunday For Tea | 7" EP | Columbia | ESRF1858 | 1967 | £5 | £10 | French |
| True Love Ways | LP | Capitol | (S)T2368 | 1965 | £4 | £10 | US |
| Woman | LP | Capitol | (S)T2477 | 1966 | £4 | £10 | US |
| Woman | LP | Columbia | SCXC29 | 1965 | £8 | £20 | export |

| World Without Love | LP | Capitol | (S)T2115 | 1964 £4 | £10 | US |
|---|---|---|---|---|---|---|
| World Without Love | 7" EP | Columbia | ESRF1533 | 1964 £5 | £10 | French |

## PETER & PAUL
| Schoolgirl | 7" | Blue Beat | BB364 | 1966 £6 | £12 | |
|---|---|---|---|---|---|---|

## PETER & THE HEADLINES
| Don't Cry Little Girl | 7" | Decca | F11980 | 1964 £4 | £8 | |
|---|---|---|---|---|---|---|
| I've Got My Reasons | 7" | Decca | F12035 | 1964 £4 | £8 | |

## PETER & THE PERSUADERS
| Wanderer | 7" EP | Oak | RGJ197 | 1965 £12.50 | £25 | |
|---|---|---|---|---|---|---|

## PETER & THE WOLVES
| Lanternlight | 7" | MGM | MGM1374 | 1968 £1.50 | £4 | |
|---|---|---|---|---|---|---|
| Little Girl Lost And Found | 7" | MGM | MGM1352 | 1967 £1.50 | £4 | |

## PETER B'S
Each member of this instrumental group went on to further success. Initially, they all formed the backing group for Shotgun Express; later bassist Dave Ambrose joined the Brian Auger Trinity, organist Peter Bardens formed Camel, while guitarist Peter Green and drummer Mick Fleetwood became half of Fleetwood Mac.

| If You Wanna Be Happy | 7" | Columbia | DB7862 | 1966 £15 | £30 | |
|---|---|---|---|---|---|---|

## PETERS, JANICE
| This Little Girl's Gone Rocking | 7" | Columbia | DB4222 | 1958 £7.50 | £15 | |
|---|---|---|---|---|---|---|
| You're The One | 7" | Columbia | DB4276 | 1959 £5 | £10 | |

## PETERS, JENNY
| This Is Jenny Peters | LP | Redball | RR031 | 1980 £25 | £50 | |
|---|---|---|---|---|---|---|

## PETERS, MARK
| Cindy's Gonna Cry | 7" | Oriole | CB1909 | 1964 £5 | £10 | |
|---|---|---|---|---|---|---|
| Don't Cry For Me | 7" | Piccadilly | 7N35207 | 1964 £1.50 | £4 | |
| Janie | 7" | Oriole | CB1836 | 1963 £5 | £10 | |

## PETERS, WENDY
| Morning Dew | 7" | Saga | OPP1 | 1968 £4 | £8 | |
|---|---|---|---|---|---|---|

## PETER'S FACES
| Wait | 7" | Piccadilly | 7N35205 | 1964 £2 | £5 | |
|---|---|---|---|---|---|---|

## PETERSEN, PAUL
| She Can't Find Her Keys | 7" | Pye | 7N25133 | 1962 £1.50 | £4 | ..with Shelley Fabares |
|---|---|---|---|---|---|---|

## PETERSON, BOBBY
| Hunch | 7" | Top Rank | JAR232 | 1959 £5 | £10 | |
|---|---|---|---|---|---|---|
| Piano Rock | 7" | Sue | WI346 | 1965 £5 | £10 | |
| Rocking Charlie | 7" | Sue | WI342 | 1964 £5 | £10 | |

## PETERSON, OSCAR
| At The Cocertgebouw | LP | HMV | CLP1317 | 1959 £6 | £15 | |
|---|---|---|---|---|---|---|
| In Romantic Mood | LP | HMV | CLP1086 | 1956 £6 | £15 | |
| Jazz Soul | LP | HMV | CLP1429 | 1961 £6 | £15 | |
| Keyboard | LP | Columbia | 33CX10062 | 1957 £6 | £15 | |
| My Fair Lady | LP | HMV | CLP1278 | 1959 £6 | £15 | |
| Newport Jazz Frestival 1957 ..' | LP | Columbia | 33CX10109 | 1958 £6 | £15 | |
| Night On The Town | LP | Columbia | 33CX10135 | 1959 £6 | £15 | |
| Night Train | LP | Verve | VLP9052 | 1963 £4 | £10 | |
| O Lady Be Good | 10" LP | Columbia | 33C9025 | 1956 £10 | £25 | |
| Oscar Peterson | LP | Columbia | 33CX10024 | 1956 £8 | £20 | |
| Oscar Peterson | 7" EP | Columbia | SEB10005 | 1955 £2 | £5 | |
| Oscar Peterson No. 2 | 7" EP | Columbia | SEB10022 | 1956 £2 | £5 | |
| Oscar Peterson Quartet | 10" LP | Columbia | 33C1038 | 1955 £20 | £40 | |
| Oscar Peterson Quartet | 10" LP | Columbia | 33C9013 | 1955 £15 | £30 | |
| Oscar Peterson Sings | 10" LP | Columbia | 33C1039 | 1955 £20 | £40 | |
| Oscar Peterson Sings | 10" LP | Columbia | 33C9014 | 1955 £15 | £30 | |
| Plays Cole Porter | LP | Columbia | 33CX10016 | 1955 £10 | £25 | |
| Plays Count Basie | LP | Columbia | 33CX10039 | 1956 £10 | £25 | |
| Plays Duke Ellington | LP | Columbia | 33CX10012 | 1955 £10 | £25 | |
| Plays Harold Arlen | LP | Columbia | 33CX10073 | 1957 £6 | £15 | |
| Plays Pretty | 10" LP | Columbia | 33C1037 | 1955 £20 | £40 | |
| Plays Pretty | 10" LP | Columbia | 33C9012 | 1955 £15 | £30 | |
| Plays Richard Rogers | LP | Columbia | 33CX10028 | 1956 £10 | £25 | |
| Stratford | LP | Columbia | 33CX10096 | 1958 £6 | £15 | |
| Swinging Brass | LP | HMV | CLP1403/CSD1326 | 1960 £6 | £15 | |

## PETERSON, PAUL
| Little Bit Of Sandy | 7" | Tamla Motown | TMG670 | 1968 £5 | £10 | |
|---|---|---|---|---|---|---|

## PETERSON, RAY
| Answer Me | 7" | RCA | RCA1175 | 1960 £2 | £5 | |
|---|---|---|---|---|---|---|
| Corrine Corrina | 7" EP | London | REX1293 | 1961 £15 | £30 | |
| Corrine Corrina | 7" | London | HLX9246 | 1960 £2.50 | £6 | |
| Give Us Your Blessing | 7" | London | HLX9746 | 1963 £2 | £5 | |
| I Could Have Loved You So Well | 7" | London | HLX9489 | 1962 £2 | £5 | |
| Other Side Of Ray Peterson | LP | MGM | (S)E4277 | 1965 £6 | £15 | US |

| Title | Format | Label | Cat. No. | Year | | | Notes |
|---|---|---|---|---|---|---|---|
| Shirley Purly | 7" | RCA | RCA1154 | 1959 | £2.50 | £6 | |
| Sweet Little Kathy | 7" | London | HLX9332 | 1961 | £2 | £5 | |
| Tell Laura I Love Her | LP | RCA | LPM/LSP2297 | 1960 | £20 | £40 | US |
| Tell Laura I Love Her | 7" | RCA | RCA1195 | 1960 | £2 | £5 | |
| Very Best Of Ray Peterson | LP | MGM | (S)E4250 | 1964 | £10 | £25 | US |
| Wonder Of You | 7" | RCA | RCA1131 | 1959 | £2.50 | £6 | |
| You Didn't Care | 7" | London | HLX9569 | 1962 | £1.50 | £4 | |
| You Thrill Me | 7" | London | HLX9379 | 1961 | £1.50 | £4 | |

## PETITES
| Title | Format | Label | Cat. No. | Year | | | Notes |
|---|---|---|---|---|---|---|---|
| Get Your Daddy's Car Tonight | 7" | Philips | PB1035 | 1960 | £1.50 | £4 | |

## PETS
| Title | Format | Label | Cat. No. | Year | | | Notes |
|---|---|---|---|---|---|---|---|
| Beyond The Sea | 7" | Pye | 7N25004 | 1959 | £1.50 | £4 | |
| Cha Hua Hua | 7" | London | HL8652 | 1958 | £7.50 | £15 | |

## PETTI, MARY
| Title | Format | Label | Cat. No. | Year | | | Notes |
|---|---|---|---|---|---|---|---|
| Hey Lawdy Lawdy | 7" | RCA | RCA1239 | 1961 | £7.50 | £15 | |

## PETTIFORD, OSCAR
| Title | Format | Label | Cat. No. | Year | | | Notes |
|---|---|---|---|---|---|---|---|
| In Hi Fi No. 2 | 10" LP | HMV | DLP1197 | 1958 | £15 | £30 | |
| Oscar Pettiford Group | LP | London | LTZN15035 | 1957 | £15 | £30 | |
| Oscar Pettiford Group | 10" LP | London | LZN14023 | 1956 | £20 | £40 | |
| Oscar Pettiford Orchestra | LP | HMV | CLP1171 | 1958 | £15 | £30 | |
| Oscar Pettiford Sextet | 10" LP | Vogue | LDE098 | 1954 | £37.50 | £75 | |

## PETTY, NORMAN
| Title | Format | Label | Cat. No. | Year | | | Notes |
|---|---|---|---|---|---|---|---|
| Corsage | LP | Vik | 1073 | 1959 | £10 | £25 | US |
| Mood Indigo | 7" | HMV | 7M274 | 1954 | £4 | £8 | |
| Moondreams | LP | Columbia | CL1092 | 1958 | £30 | £60 | US |
| Petty For Your Thoughts | LP | Top Rank | RS639 | 1960 | £8 | £20 | US |

## PETTY, TOM
| Title | Format | Label | Cat. No. | Year | | | Notes |
|---|---|---|---|---|---|---|---|
| 1991 Into The Great Wide Open | CD | MCA | | 1991 | £8 | £20 | ...US interview promo |
| Damn The Torpedoes | LP | MCA | MCA5105 | 1980 | £4 | £10 | ..Canadian audiophile |
| Free Fallin' | CD-s | MCA | DMCAX1381 | 1989 | £2 | £5 | . boxed with biography |
| Full Moon Fever | CD | MCA | 6253P | 1990 | £8 | £20 | US promo with bonus live track |
| Gone Gator Sampler | CD | Gone Gator | CD331478 | 1991 | £8 | £20 | ...US promo |
| Hard Promises | LP | MCA | BSR5162 | 1981 | £4 | £10 | ..Canadian audiophile |
| Hard Promises | CD | Mobile Fidelity | UDCD565 | 1991 | £6 | £15 | US audiophile |
| I Won't Back Down | CD-s | MCA | DMCAT1334 | 1989 | £2 | £5 | 2 versions |
| Official Bootleg | LP | Shelter | IDJ24 | 1977 | £4 | £10 | ...promo |
| Runnin' Down A Dream | CD-s | MCA | DMCAX1359 | 1989 | £2 | £5 | |
| Tom Petty Interview | CD | MCA | TOM1 | 1989 | £8 | £20 | ...German promo |

## PFM
| Title | Format | Label | Cat. No. | Year | | | Notes |
|---|---|---|---|---|---|---|---|
| Chocolate Kings | CD | Great Expectations | PIPCD009 | 1990 | £5 | £12 | |
| Per Un Amico | LP | Numero Uno | ZSLN55155 | 1972 | £4 | £10 | Italian |
| Per Un Amico | CD | Great Expectations | PIPCD012 | 1990 | £5 | £12 | |
| Photos Of Ghosts | CD | Great Expectations | PIPCD010 | 1990 | £5 | £12 | |
| Storia Di Un Minoto | LP | Numero Uno | ZSLN55055 | 1972 | £4 | £10 | Italian |
| Storia Di Un Minuto | CD | Great Expectations | PIPCD011 | 1990 | £5 | £12 | |

## PHAFNER
| Title | Format | Label | Cat. No. | Year | | | Notes |
|---|---|---|---|---|---|---|---|
| Overdrive | LP | Dragon | no number | 1971 | £1050 | £1500 | US |

## PHANTOM
| Title | Format | Label | Cat. No. | Year | | | Notes |
|---|---|---|---|---|---|---|---|
| Phantom's Divine Comedy Part One | LP | Capitol | ST11313 | 1974 | £37.50 | £75 | US |

## PHANTOMS
| Title | Format | Label | Cat. No. | Year | | | Notes |
|---|---|---|---|---|---|---|---|
| Great Guitar Hits | LP | Arc | 655 | 1964 | £15 | £30 | |
| Ken Levy And The Phantoms | LP | Nashville | NSPL30102 | 1964 | £30 | £60 | Swedish |
| Phantom Guitar | 7" | Palette | PG9014 | 1961 | £4 | £8 | |
| Phantoms | LP | Metronome | MLP10057 | 1965 | £15 | £30 | German |

## PHAROAHS
| Title | Format | Label | Cat. No. | Year | | | Notes |
|---|---|---|---|---|---|---|---|
| Pharoahs | 7" EP | Decca | DFE6522 | 1958 | £180 | £300 | ...best auctioned |

## PHASE FOUR
| Title | Format | Label | Cat. No. | Year | | | Notes |
|---|---|---|---|---|---|---|---|
| Man Am I Worried? | 7" | Fab | FAB6 | 1967 | £10 | £20 | |
| What Do You Say About That | 7" | Decca | F12327 | 1966 | £2 | £5 | |
| What Do You Say About That | 7" | Fab | FAB1 | 1966 | £2 | £5 | |

## PHEASANT PLUCKERS
| Title | Format | Label | Cat. No. | Year | | | Notes |
|---|---|---|---|---|---|---|---|
| Live At The Plume Of Feathers | LP | Sentinel | SENP506 | 1973 | £10 | £25 | |

## PHELPS, JAMES
| Title | Format | Label | Cat. No. | Year | | | Notes |
|---|---|---|---|---|---|---|---|
| Check Yourself | 7" | Paramount | 3019 | 1971 | £2 | £5 | |

## PHEW
| Title | Format | Label | Cat. No. | Year | | | Notes |
|---|---|---|---|---|---|---|---|
| Phew | LP | Pass | 3F28002 | 1981 | £6 | £15 | Japanese |

## PHILLIPS, ANTHONY

Anthony Phillips was an original member of Genesis, playing guitar on both the debut album and its follow-up, *Trespass* – his successor was Steve Hackett.

| | | | | | | |
|---|---|---|---|---|---|---|
| Anthem From Tarka | CD-s .. | PRT | PYD18 | 1988 £4 | £10 | |
| Anthem From Tarka | 7" | PRT | PYS18 | 1988 £2.50 | £6 | |
| Collections | 7" | Philips | 6837406 | 1977 £7.50 | £15 | picture sleeve |
| Prelude '84 | 7" | RCA | RCA102 | 1981 £2 | £5 | picture sleeve |
| Private Parts And Pieces | LP | Arista | AFLP1 | 1979 £4 | £10 | |
| Um And Aargh | 7" | Arista | ARIST252 | 1978 £2 | £5 | picture sleeve |
| We're All As We Lie | 7" | Arista | ARIST192 | 1978 £2.50 | £6 | |
| Wise After The Event | LP | Passport | PB9828 | 1978 £4 | £10 | US picture disc |

## PHILLIPS, BARRE

| | | | | | | |
|---|---|---|---|---|---|---|
| For All It Is | LP | Japo | 60003 | 1973 £6 | £15 | |
| Unaccompanied Barre | LP | Music Man | SMLS601 | 1970 £6 | £15 | |

## PHILLIPS, CONFREY

| | | | | | | |
|---|---|---|---|---|---|---|
| Shotgun Rock And Roll | 7" | Decca | F10866 | 1957 £2.50 | £6 | |

## PHILLIPS, ESTHER

| | | | | | | |
|---|---|---|---|---|---|---|
| Am I That Easy To Forget | 7" | Ember | EMBS174 | 1963 £1.50 | £4 | |
| And I Love Him | LP | Atlantic | (SD)8102 | 1965 £6 | £15 | US |
| And I Love Him | 7" | Atlantic | AT4028 | 1965 £1.50 | £4 | |
| Chains | 7" | Sue | WI395 | 1965 £5 | £10 | |
| Country Side Of Esther Phillips | LP | Atlantic | (SD)8130 | 1966 £5 | £12 | US |
| Esther | LP | Atlantic | (SD)8122 | 1966 £5 | £12 | US |
| From A Whisper To A Scream | LP | Kudu | KUL2 | 1973 £6 | £15 | |
| Home Is Where The Hatred Is | 7" | Kudu | KUS4000 | 1973 £2 | £5 | |
| I Could Have Told You | 7" | Atlantic | AT4077 | 1966 £7.50 | £15 | |
| Let Me Know When It's Over | 7" | Atlantic | AT4048 | 1965 £1.50 | £4 | |
| Memory Lane | LP | King | LP622 | 1956 £400 | £600 | US |
| Reflections Of Great Country And Western Standards | LP | Ember | CW103 | 1963 £4 | £10 | |
| Release Me | LP | Lenox | 227 | 1962 £10 | £25 | US |
| Release Me | 7" | Ember | EMBS221 | 1966 £1.50 | £4 | |
| Release Me | 7" | Stateside | SS140 | 1962 £1.50 | £4 | |
| Sings | LP | Atlantic | 587/588010 | 1966 £4 | £10 | |

## PHILLIPS, FLIP

| | | | | | | |
|---|---|---|---|---|---|---|
| Flip Phillips | 10" LP | Columbia | 33C9003 | 1955 £25 | £50 | |

## PHILLIPS, GREGORY

| | | | | | | |
|---|---|---|---|---|---|---|
| Down In The Boondocks | 7" | Immediate | IM004 | 1965 £2.50 | £6 | |

## PHILLIPS, JOHN

| | | | | | | |
|---|---|---|---|---|---|---|
| Wolfking Of L.A. | LP | Stateside | SSL5027 | 1970 £4 | £10 | |

## PHILLIPS, PHIL

| | | | | | | |
|---|---|---|---|---|---|---|
| I Love To Love You | 7" | Mercury | AMT1139 | 1961 £5 | £10 | |
| Sea Of Love | 7" | Mercury | AMT1059 | 1959 £12.50 | £25 | |
| Take This Heart | 7" | Mercury | AMT1072 | 1960 £2.50 | £6 | |
| Your True Love Once More | 7" | Mercury | AMT1093 | 1960 £4 | £8 | |

## PHILLIPS, SHAWN

| | | | | | | |
|---|---|---|---|---|---|---|
| I'm A Loner | LP | Columbia | 33SX1748 | 1965 £37.50 | £75 | |
| Little Tin Soldier | 7" | Columbia | DB7789 | 1965 £1.50 | £4 | |
| Nobody Listens | 7" | Columbia | DB7699 | 1965 £2 | £5 | |
| Shawn | LP | Columbia | SCX6006 | 1966 £30 | £60 | |
| Solitude | 7" | Columbia | DB7611 | 1965 £2 | £5 | |
| Stargazer | 7" | Parlophone | R5606 | 1967 £7.50 | £15 | |
| Summer Came | 7" | Columbia | DB7956 | 1966 £1.50 | £4 | |

## PHILLIPS, STU

| | | | | | | |
|---|---|---|---|---|---|---|
| Champlain & St. Lawrence Line | 7" | London | HL8673 | 1958 £2 | £5 | |
| Strangers When We Meet | 7" | Pye | 7N25062 | 1960 £1.50 | £4 | Bob Mersey Orchestra B side |

## PHILLIPS, TEDDY

| | | | | | | |
|---|---|---|---|---|---|---|
| Ridin' To Tennessee | 7" | London | HL8032 | 1954 £10 | £20 | |

## PHILLIPS, TOM, GAVIN BRYARS & FRED ORTON

| | | | | | | |
|---|---|---|---|---|---|---|
| Irma | LP | Obscure | OBS9 | 1978 £4 | £10 | |

## PHILLIPS, WARREN & THE ROCKETS (SAVOY BROWN)

| | | | | | | |
|---|---|---|---|---|---|---|
| World Of Rock And Roll | LP | Decca | (S)PA43 | 1969 £6 | £15 | |

## PHILOSOPHERS

| | | | | | | |
|---|---|---|---|---|---|---|
| After Sundown | LP | PS | 1001 | 1969 £50 | £100 | US |

## PHILPOTT, VINCE & THE DRAGS

| | | | | | | |
|---|---|---|---|---|---|---|
| Cramp | 7" | Decca | F11997 | 1964 £5 | £10 | |

## PHILWIT & PEGASUS

| | | | | | | |
|---|---|---|---|---|---|---|
| Philwit & Pegasus | LP | Chapter One | CHS805 | 1970 £10 | £25 | |

## PHLUPH
| Phluph | | LP | Verve | V65054 | 1968 | £5 | £12 | | US |

## PHOENIX, PAT
| Rovers Chorus | | 7" | HMV | POP1030 | 1962 | £2 | £5 | |

## PHOTOGRAPHED BY LIGHTNING
| Sleeps Terminator | | 7" | Fierce | FRIGHT008 | 1986 | £10 | £20 | |

## PIAF, EDITH
| Great Piaf | | 7" EP | Columbia | SEG8220 | 1963 | £2 | £5 | |
| Non je ne regrette rien | | 7" EP | Columbia | SEG8308 | 1964 | £2 | £5 | |
| Qu'il était triste | | 7" EP | Columbia | SEG8387 | 1965 | £2 | £5 | |

## PIANO RED
| Bouncin' With Red | | 78 | HMV | B10316 | 1952 | £10 | £20 | |
| Hey Good Lookin' | | 78 | HMV | B10246 | 1952 | £10 | £20 | |
| In Concert | | LP | Groove | 1002 | 1964 | £50 | £100 | US |
| Jump Man Jump | | LP | Groove | 1001 | 1964 | £50 | £100 | US |
| Rhythm & Blues Vol. 2 | | 7" EP | RCA | RCX7138 | 1964 | £10 | £20 | |
| Rocking With Red | | 7" | HMV | 7M108 | 1953 | £62.50 | £125 | |

## PIC & BILL
| All I Want Is You | | 7" | Page One | POF024 | 1967 | £2 | £5 | |
| Sad World Without You | | 7" | Page One | POF052 | 1968 | £2.50 | £6 | |

## PICCADILLY LINE
| At The Third Stroke | | 7" | CBS | 2785 | 1967 | £2 | £5 | |
| Emily Small | | 7" | CBS | 2958 | 1967 | £2 | £5 | |
| Evenings With Corrina | | 7" | CBS | 3743 | 1968 | £1.50 | £4 | |
| Huge World Of Emily Small | | LP | CBS | (S)BPG63129 | 1967 | £10 | £25 | |
| Yellow Rainbow | | 7" | CBS | 3595 | 1968 | £1.50 | £4 | |

## PICKENS, BUSTER
| Texas Piano | | LP | Heritage | HLP1008 | 196– | £15 | £30 | |

## PICKETT, BOBBY & THE CRYPT KICKERS
| Monster Mash | | LP | Garpax | (S)GP67001 | 1962 | £10 | £25 | US |
| Monster Mash | | 7" | London | HLU9597 | 1962 | £2.50 | £6 | |

## PICKETT, DAN
| Dan Pickett | | 7" EP | XX | MIN710 | 196– | £2 | £5 | |

## PICKETT, KENNY
| Got A Gun | | 7" | F-Beat | PRO2 | 1980 | £2.50 | £6 | promo |

## PICKETT, NICK
| Silversleeves | | LP | Reprise | K44172 | 1972 | £6 | £15 | |

## PICKETT, WILSON
| 634-5789 | | 7" | Atlantic | AT4072 | 1966 | £1.50 | £4 | |
| 99 & A Half Won't Do | | 7" | Atlantic | 584023 | 1966 | £1.50 | £4 | |
| Best Of Wilson Pickett | | LP | Atlantic | 587/588092 | 1968 | £4 | £10 | |
| Don't Fight It | | 7" | Atlantic | AT4052 | 1965 | £1.50 | £4 | |
| Engine No. 9 | | LP | Atlantic | 2400026 | 1971 | £4 | £10 | |
| Engine No. 9 | | 7" | Atlantic | 2091032 | 1970 | £1.50 | £4 | |
| Everybody Needs Somebody To Love | | 7" | Atlantic | 584101 | 1967 | £1.50 | £4 | |
| Exciting Wilson Pickett | | LP | Atlantic | 587/588029 | 1966 | £5 | £12 | |
| Funky Broadway | | 7" | Atlantic | 584130 | 1967 | £1.50 | £4 | |
| Hey Joe | | 7" | Atlantic | 584281 | 1969 | £1.50 | £4 | |
| Hey Jude | | LP | Atlantic | 588170 | 1969 | £4 | £10 | |
| Hey Jude | | 7" | Atlantic | 584236 | 1969 | £1.50 | £4 | |
| I Found A True Love | | 7" | Atlantic | 584221 | 1968 | £1.50 | £4 | |
| I'm A Midnight Mover | | 7" | Atlantic | 584203 | 1968 | £1.50 | £4 | |
| I'm In Love | | LP | Atlantic | 587/588107 | 1968 | £4 | £10 | |
| In The Midnight Hour | | LP | Atlantic | 587032 | 1966 | £5 | £12 | |
| In The Midnight Hour | | LP | Atlantic | ATL5037 | 1965 | £6 | £15 | |
| In The Midnight Hour | | 7" | Atlantic | 584150 | 1968 | £1.50 | £4 | |
| In The Midnight Hour | | 7" | Atlantic | AT4036 | 1965 | £2 | £5 | |
| It's Too Late | | LP | Double-L | DL2300/SDL8300 | 1963 | £10 | £25 | US |
| It's Too Late | | 7" | Liberty | LIB10115 | 1963 | £5 | £10 | |
| Land Of 1000 Dances | | 7" | Atlantic | 584039 | 1966 | £1.50 | £4 | |
| Midnight Mover | | LP | Atlantic | 587/588111 | 1968 | £4 | £10 | |
| Mini-Skirt Minnie | | 7" | Atlantic | 584261 | 1969 | £1.50 | £4 | |
| Mustang Sally | | 7" | Atlantic | 584066 | 1966 | £1.50 | £4 | |
| My Heart Belongs To You | | 7" | MGM | MGM1286 | 1965 | £10 | £20 | |
| New Orleans | | 7" | Atlantic | 584107 | 1967 | £1.50 | £4 | |
| She's Looking Good | | 7" | Atlantic | 584183 | 1968 | £1.50 | £4 | |
| Sound Of Wilson Pickett | | LP | Atlantic | 587/588080 | 1967 | £5 | £12 | |
| Stag-o-lee | | 7" | Atlantic | 584142 | 1967 | £1.50 | £4 | |
| Sugar Sugar | | 7" | Atlantic | 2091005 | 1970 | £1.50 | £4 | |
| That Kind Of Love | | 7" | Atlantic | 584173 | 1968 | £1.50 | £4 | |
| Wicked Pickett | | LP | Atlantic | 587/588057 | 1967 | £5 | £12 | |
| You Keep Me Hanging On | | 7" | Atlantic | 584313 | 1970 | £1.50 | £4 | |

## PICKFORD, ED
| Facing The Crowd | | LP | Rip Off | ROF002 | 1982 | £4 | £10 | |

| | | | | | | |
|---|---|---|---|---|---|---|
| Songwriter | LP | Rip Off | ROF001 | 1976 £5 | £12 | |

## PICKFORD-HOPKINS, GARY
| | | | | | | |
|---|---|---|---|---|---|---|
| Why? | 7" | Spartan | SP143 | 1983 £4 | £8 | |
| Why? | 12" | Spartan | SP143T | 1983 £4 | £10 | |

## PICKUPS
| | | | | | | |
|---|---|---|---|---|---|---|
| Keep On Dancing | LP | Metronome | MLP10058 | 1967 £8 | £20 | German |
| Keep On Dancing Vol. 2 | LP | Metronome | MLP10084 | 1967 £6 | £15 | German |

## PICKWICKS
| | | | | | | |
|---|---|---|---|---|---|---|
| Apple Blossom Time | 7" | Decca | F11901 | 1964 £2 | £5 | |
| Little By Little | 7" | Warner Bros | WB151 | 1965 £20 | £40 | |
| You're Old Enough | 7" | Decca | F11957 | 1964 £2 | £5 | |

## PIED PIPERS
| | | | | | | |
|---|---|---|---|---|---|---|
| Kissin' Drive Rock | 7" | Parlophone | CMSP21 | 1954 £4 | £8 | export |
| Ragamuffin | 7" | Columbia | DB7883 | 1966 £1.50 | £4 | |

## PIERCE, BILLY & DEDE
| | | | | | | |
|---|---|---|---|---|---|---|
| Jazz At Preservation Hall Vol. 2 | LP | London | HAK/SHK8163 | 1964 £5 | £12 | |

## PIERCE, NAT
| | | | | | | |
|---|---|---|---|---|---|---|
| Chamber Music For Moderns | LP | Vogue Coral | LVA9060 | 1957 £5 | £12 | |
| Kansas City Memories | LP | Vogue Coral | LVA9050 | 1957 £5 | £12 | |

## PIERCE, WEBB
| | | | | | | |
|---|---|---|---|---|---|---|
| Bound For The Kingdom | LP | Decca | DL(7)8889 | 1959 £6 | £15 | US |
| Bye Bye Love | 7" | Brunswick | 05682 | 1957 £10 | £20 | |
| Country & Western Favourites Vol. 1 | 7" EP | Ember | EMBEP4520 | 1962 £2 | £5 | |
| Country Round Up | 7" EP | Parlophone | GEP8792 | 1959 £7.50 | £15 | |
| Cross Country | LP | Brunswick | LAT8551 | 1965 £4 | £10 | |
| Drifting Texas Sands | 7" | Brunswick | 05842 | 1960 £2 | £5 | |
| Hideaway Heart | LP | Brunswick | LAT8540 | 1965 £6 | £15 | |
| I Ain't Never | 7" | Brunswick | 05809 | 1959 £2.50 | £6 | |
| In The Jailhouse Now | LP | MCA | MUPS364 | 1969 £4 | £10 | |
| Just Imagination | LP | Decca | DL8728 | 1957 £8 | £20 | US |
| No Love Have I | 7" | Brunswick | 05820 | 1960 £2 | £5 | |
| One And Only Webb Pierce | LP | King | 648 | 1959 £6 | £15 | US |
| Teenage Boogie | 7" | Brunswick | 05630 | 1956 £62.50 | £125 | |
| That Wondering Boy | LP | Decca | DL8295 | 1956 £8 | £20 | US |
| That Wondering Boy | 10" LP | Brunswick | LA8716 | 1955 £10 | £25 | |
| Webb | LP | Brunswick | LAT8324 | 1959 £6 | £15 | |
| Webb Pierce | LP | Decca | DL8129 | 1955 £8 | £20 | US |
| Webb Pierce Pt. 1 | 7" EP | Brunswick | OE9253 | 1956 £5 | £10 | |
| Webb Pierce Pt. 2 | 7" EP | Brunswick | OE9254 | 1956 £5 | £10 | |
| Webb Pierce Pt. 3 | 7" EP | Brunswick | OE9255 | 1956 £5 | £10 | |
| Webb Pierce Story | LP | Decca | DX(S)B(7)181 | 1964 £6 | £15 | US, with booklet |

## PIERROT LUNAIRE
| | | | | | | |
|---|---|---|---|---|---|---|
| Patrice | LP | RCA | NL74114 | 1984 £8 | £20 | Italian |

## PIGG, BILLY
| | | | | | | |
|---|---|---|---|---|---|---|
| Border Minstrel | LP | Leader | LEA4006 | 1971 £5 | £12 | |

## PIGGLESWICK FOLK
| | | | | | | |
|---|---|---|---|---|---|---|
| Pig In The Middle | LP | Acorn | CF256 | 197– £6 | £15 | |

## PIGSTY HILL LIGHT ORCHESTRA
| | | | | | | |
|---|---|---|---|---|---|---|
| Cushion Foot Stomp | LP | Village Thing | VTS1 | 1970 £8 | £20 | |
| Piggery Jokery | LP | Village Thing | VTS8 | 1971 £8 | £20 | |
| Pigsty Hill Light Orchestra | LP | PHLO | 001 | 1976 £10 | £25 | |

## PIIRPAUKE
| | | | | | | |
|---|---|---|---|---|---|---|
| Live | LP | Love | LRLP251 | 1977 £6 | £15 | Swedish |
| Piirpauke I | LP | Love | LRLP148 | 1975 £8 | £20 | Swedish |
| Piirpauke II | LP | Love | LRLP192 | 1976 £8 | £20 | Swedish |

## PIKEMEN
| | | | | | | |
|---|---|---|---|---|---|---|
| Lonesome Boatmen | LP | Emerald | GES1185 | 1978 £8 | £20 | |

## PILTDOWN MEN
| | | | | | | |
|---|---|---|---|---|---|---|
| Gargantua | 7" | Capitol | CL15211 | 1961 £2.50 | £6 | |
| Goodnight Mrs. Flintstone | 7" | Capitol | CL15186 | 1961 £1.50 | £4 | |
| Goodnight Mrs. Flintstone/Piltdown Rides Again | 7" EP | Capitol | EAP120155 | 1961 £10 | £20 | |
| McDonald's Cave | 7" | Capitol | CL15149 | 1960 £1.50 | £4 | |
| Piltdown Rides Again | 7" | Capitol | CL15175 | 1961 £1.50 | £4 | |
| Pretty Girl Is Like A Melody | 7" | Capitol | CL15245 | 1962 £2 | £5 | |

## PIMM, SIR HUBERT
| | | | | | | |
|---|---|---|---|---|---|---|
| Goodnight And Cheerio | 7" | London | HL8155 | 1955 £12.50 | £25 | |
| Pimm's Party | 7" EP | London | REU1032 | 1955 £10 | £20 | |

## PINDER, MICHAEL
| | | | | | | |
|---|---|---|---|---|---|---|
| Promise | CD | Threshold | 8207762 | 1989 £5 | £12 | |

## PINEAPPLE BOYS
Fabulous .................. LP ..... Moon ............ 23001 ................... 1983 £20 ...... £40 ................. *Japanese*

## PINEAPPLE CHUNKS
Drive My Car .................................... 7" ..... Mercury .......... MF922 ................ 1965 £2 ......... £5

## PINEWOOD TOM & TALL TOM
Male Blues Vol. 4 ................................ 7" EP . Collector ........ JEL5 ............... 1959 £4 ......... £8 ...........

## PINGUIN
Der Grosse Rote Vogel ........................... LP ..... Zebra ............ 2949001 ................ 1971 £8 ....... £20 .............. *German*

## PINHAS, RICHARD
Chronolyse .................................... LP ..... Cobra ...... COB37015 ............ 1978 £4 ........ £10 ............. *French*
East West .................................... LP ..... Pulse ...... 003 ................. 1980 £4 ........ £10 ...........
Iceland .................................... LP ..... Polydor ...... 2393254 ............ 1979 £4 ........ £10 .............. *French*
L'Ethique .................................... LP ..... Pulse ...... 006 ................. 1982 £4 ........ £10 ...........
Rhizosphere .................................... LP ..... Cobra ...... COB37005 ............ 1977 £4 ........ £10 .............. *French*

## PINK FAIRIES
Kings Of Oblivion ............................ LP ..... Polydor ...... 2383212 ............ 1973 £6 ........ £15 ...*with cardboard poster*
Never Never Land ............................ LP ..... Polydor ...... 2383045 ............ 1971 £4 ........ £10 ...........
Never Never Land ............................ LP ..... Polydor ...... 2383045 ............ 1971 £10 ........ £25 ............. *plastic cover*
Never Never Land ............................ LP ..... Polydor ...... 2383045 ............ 1971 £75 ........ £150 ........ *red vinyl*
Snake .................................... 7" ...... Polydor ...... 2058089 ............ 1970 £5 ........ £10 ...........
Well Well Well .................................... 7" ...... Polydor ...... 2058302 ............ 1972 £2.50 ........ £6 ...........

## PINK FLOYD

In their early days, Pink Floyd epitomized what British psychedelic music was all about and their first two albums are rightly prized as crucially important documents of the period. Like many LPs recorded in the second half of the sixties, there are many differences between the mono and stereo versions, this being particularly noticeable on the often densely arranged *Saucerful Of Secrets* record. The Columbia singles are also much in demand, especially since the only vinyl reissue of the last three consists of a German compilation LP. Promotional copies of the 1967 singles were issued in picture sleeves, which are extremely scarce today.

Animals .................................... LP ..... Columbia ...... PCQ34474 ............ 1977 £10 ........ £25 .............. *US quad*
Another Brick In The Wall Pt. 2 (live) ...... 12" ..... EMI ............ 12PF1 ............. 1988 £4 ........ £10 ......... *promo only*
Apples And Oranges .......................... 7" ..... Columbia ...... DB8310 ............ 1967 £12.50 ..... £25 ...........
Apples And Oranges .......................... 7" ..... Columbia ...... DB8310 ............ 1967 £250 ..... £400 . *promo, picture sleeve, best auctioned*
Arnold Layne .................................... 7" EP . Columbia ...... ESRF1857 ............ 1967 £180 ..... £300 *French, best auctioned*
Arnold Layne .................................... 7" ..... Columbia ...... DB8156 ............ 1967 £10 ........ £20 ...........
Arnold Layne .................................... 7" ..... Columbia ...... DB8156 ............ 1967 £250 ..... £400 . *promo, picture sleeve, best auctioned*
Atom Heart Mother ........................... LP ..... Harvest ...... Q4SHVL781 ............ 1973 £10 ........ £25 .............. *quad*
Atom Heart Mother ........................... CD .... Mobile Fidelity UDCD584 ............ 1993 £6 ........ £15 ......... *US audiophile*
Collection Of Great Dance Songs ........... LP ..... Columbia ...... HC47680 ............ 1983 £8 ........ £20 ......... *US audiophile*
Dark Side Of The Moon ..................... LP ..... Capitol ...... SEAX11902 ............ 1978 £8 ........ £20 ......... *US picture disc*
Dark Side Of The Moon ..................... LP ..... Harvest ...... Q4SHVL804 ............ 1973 £10 ........ £25 .............. *quad*
Dark Side Of The Moon ..................... LP ..... Mobile Fidelity MFSL1017 ............ 1978 £8 ........ £20 ......... *US audiophile*
Dark Side Of The Moon ..................... LP ..... Mobile Fidelity UHQR1017 ............ 1982 £75 ........ £150 ......... *US audiophile, numbered box set*
Dark Side Of The Moon ..................... CD .... EMI ............ 077778147923 ........ 1993 £5 ........ £12 ......... *20th Anniversary Edition, in cardboard box with 5 cards*
Dark Side Of The Moon ..................... CD .... EMI ............ PCDDSOM20 ........ 1993 £20 ........ £40 ..... *promo with slides, photos, biog*
Dark Side Of The Moon ..................... CD .... Mobile Fidelity UDCD517 ............ 1988 £6 ........ £15 ......... *US audiophile*
Delicate Sound Of Thunder ................... CD .... PMI ............ PMCD4912752 ....... 1995 £10 ........ £25 ..... *double CD video, initial pressings gave black lines across the screen*
Division Bell ................... CD .... EMI ............ 8289842 ................ 1994 £50 ....... £100 . *French promo box set with cassette, booklet*
First XI ................... LP ..... Harvest ...... PF11 ............ 1979 £100 ..... £200 ... *9LPs plus 2 picture discs, boxed*
High Hopes ................... CD-s . EMI ............ CDEMS342 ............ 1994 £2 ........ £5 ..... *card packet with 7 cards*
It Would Be So Nice ................... 7" ..... Columbia ...... DB8401 ............ 1968 £12.50 .... £25 ...........
Learning To Fly ................... CD-s . EMI ............ CDEM26 ............ 1987 £2 ........ £5 ...........
Learning To Fly ................... 7" ..... EMI ............ EMP26 ............ 1987 £1.50 ..... £4 ......... *pink vinyl*
Meddle ................... CD .... Harvest ...... CDP7460342 ......... 1987 £25 ........ £50 ... *mispressing – plays With The Beatles*
Meddle ................... CD .... Mobile Fidelity UDCD518 ............ 1989 £6 ........ £15 ......... *US audiophile*
Momentary Lapse Of Reason Official Tour CD .... Columbia ...... CSK1100 ............ 1987 £15 ........ £30 ......... *US promo*
CD ...........
Money ................... 7" ..... Harvest ...... HAR5217 ............ 1981 £7.50 ..... £15 ............. *pink vinyl*
More ................... LP ..... Columbia ...... SCX6346 ............ 1969 £5 ........ £12 ......... *green rear sleeve*
Nice Pair ................... LP ..... Harvest ...... SHDW403 ............ 1973 £5 ........ £12 ... *double, Mr. Phang sleeve*
Off The Wall ................... LP ..... Columbia ...... AS756 ............ 1979 £8 ........ £20 ....*US promo sampler*
On The Turning Away ................... CD-s . EMI ............ CDEM34 ............ 1987 £2 ........ £5 ...........
One Slip ................... CD-s . EMI ............ CDEM52 ............ 1988 £2 ........ £5 ...........
Piper At The Gates Of Dawn ................... LP ..... Columbia ...... SCX6157 ............ 1967 £20 ........ £40 ...........*stereo*
Piper At The Gates Of Dawn ................... LP ..... Columbia ...... SX6157 ............ 1967 £37.50 .... £75 ...........*mono*
Point Me At The Sky ................... 7" ..... Columbia ...... DB8511 ............ 1968 £15 ........ £30 ...........
Pulse ................... LP ..... EMI ............ EMD578 ............ 1995 £15 ........ £30 ........ *4 LP boxed set*

678

| | | | | | | | |
|---|---|---|---|---|---|---|---|
| Saucerful Of Secrets | LP | Columbia | SCX6258 | 1968 | £20 | £40 | stereo |
| Saucerful Of Secrets | LP | Columbia | SX6258 | 1968 | £37.50 | £75 | mono |
| See Emily Play | 7" | Columbia | DB8214 | 1967 | £10 | £20 | |
| See Emily Play | 7" | Columbia | DB8214 | 1967 | £250 | £400 | . promo, picture sleeve, best auctioned |
| Selected Tracks From Shine On | CD | EMI | SHINE1 | 1992 | £15 | £30 | promo |
| Tonight Let's All Make Love In London | LP | Instant | INLP002 | 1968 | £30 | £60 | with other artists |
| Tonite Let's All Make Love In London | CD-s | See For Miles | SEACD4 | 1991 | £2 | £5 | |
| Tonite Let's All Make Love In London | CD | See For Miles | SFM2 | 1993 | £4 | £10 | promo sampler |
| Tour '75 | LP | Capitol | SPRO8116/7 | 1975 | £15 | £30 | US promo compilation |
| Wall | LP | Columbia | H2C46183 | 1983 | £25 | £50 | US audiophile |
| Wall | CD | Harvest | CDS7460368 | 1988 | £25 | £50 | mispressing – plays Beatles Past Masters I on 1 disc |
| Wall | CD | Mobile Fidelity | UDCD2537 | 1990 | £10 | £25 | US audiophile |
| Wall In Store | LP | Columbia | XDAP93012 | 1979 | £30 | £60 | US promo |
| Wish You Were Here | LP | Columbia | HC43453 | 1982 | £8 | £20 | US audiophile |
| Wish You Were Here | LP | Harvest | Q4SHVL814 | 1976 | £15 | £30 | quad |
| Zabriskie Point | LP | MGM | 2315002 | 1970 | £6 | £15 | with other artists |
| Zabriskie Point | LP | MGM | 2354040 | 197– | £4 | £10 | with other artists |
| Zabriskie Point | LP | MGM | CS8120 | 1970 | £6 | £15 | with other artists |

## PINK MICE

| | | | | | | | |
|---|---|---|---|---|---|---|---|
| In Action | LP | Europa | E456 | 1971 | £4 | £10 | German |
| In Synthesizer | LP | Europa | E1011 | 1973 | £4 | £10 | German |

## PINK MILITARY

| | | | | | | |
|---|---|---|---|---|---|---|
| Buddha Waking Disney Sleeping | 7" | Last Trumpet | LT001 | 1979 | £2 | £5 |

## PINK PEOPLE

| | | | | | | | |
|---|---|---|---|---|---|---|---|
| Indian Hate Call | 7" | Philips | BF1356 | 1964 | £5 | £10 | |
| Psychologically Unsound | 7" | Philips | BF1355 | 1964 | £10 | £20 | |

## PINKERTON'S ASSORTED COLOURS

| | | | | | | | |
|---|---|---|---|---|---|---|---|
| Magic Rocking Horse | 7" | Decca | F12493 | 1966 | £4 | £8 | |
| Mirror Mirror | 7" EP | Decca | 457113 | 1966 | £10 | £20 | French |
| Mirror Mirror | 7" | Decca | F12307 | 1966 | £1.50 | £4 | |

## PINKY

| | | | | | | |
|---|---|---|---|---|---|---|
| All Cried Out | 7" | Polydor | BM56009 | 1965 | £1.50 | £4 |

## PINNACLE

| | | | | | | |
|---|---|---|---|---|---|---|
| Assassin | LP | Stag | HP125 | 1974 | £50 | £100 |

## PIONEERS

| | | | | | | | |
|---|---|---|---|---|---|---|---|
| Alli Button | 7" | Amalgamated | AMG850 | 1969 | £4 | £8 | Hippy Boys B side |
| Bad To Be Good | 7" | Trojan | TR7897 | 1973 | £1.50 | £4 | |
| Battle Of The Giants | LP | Trojan | TBL139 | 1970 | £5 | £12 | |
| Black Bud | 7" | Trojan | TR685 | 1969 | £1.50 | £4 | |
| Catch The Beat | 7" | Amalgamated | AMG828 | 1968 | £4 | £8 | Sir Gibbs' Allstars B side |
| Don't You Know | 7" | Amalgamated | AMG833 | 1969 | £4 | £8 | |
| Easy Come Easy Go | 7" | Pyramid | PYR6062 | 1969 | £2.50 | £6 | Beverley's Allstars B side |
| Freedom Feeling | LP | Trojan | TRLS64 | 1973 | £4 | £10 | |
| Give And Take | 7" | Trojan | TR7846 | 1972 | £1.50 | £4 | |
| Give It To Me | 7" | Blue Cat | BS103 | 1968 | £4 | £8 | Leaders B side |
| Give Me A Little Loving | 7" | Amalgamated | AMG811 | 1968 | £4 | £8 | |
| Give Up | 7" | Rio | R106 | 1966 | £4 | £8 | |
| Good Nannie | 7" | Rio | R102 | 1966 | £4 | £8 | |
| Greetings From The Pioneers | LP | Amalgamated | AMGLP2003 | 1968 | £30 | £60 | |
| Honey Bee | 7" | Trojan | TR7923 | 1974 | £1.50 | £4 | |
| I Believe In Love | LP | Trojan | TRLS48 | 1972 | £4 | £10 | |
| I Love No Other Girl | 7" | Caltone | TONE119 | 1968 | £4 | £8 | Milton Boothe B side |
| Jackpot | 7" | Amalgamated | AMG821 | 1968 | £4 | £8 | Creators B side |
| Let Your Yeah Be Yeah | 7" | Trojan | TR7825 | 1971 | £1.50 | £4 | |
| Long Shot | 7" | Amalgamated | AMG814 | 1968 | £4 | £8 | |
| Long Shot Kick The Bucket | 7" | Trojan | TR672 | 1969 | £1.50 | £4 | Rico B side |
| Longshot | LP | Trojan | TBL103 | 1969 | £5 | £12 | |
| Love Love Every Day | 7" | Amalgamated | AMG846 | 1969 | £4 | £8 | Moon Boys B side |
| Mama Look Deh | 7" | Amalgamated | AMG835 | 1969 | £4 | £8 | Blenders B side |
| No Dope Me Pony | 7" | Amalgamated | AMG823 | 1968 | £4 | £8 | Lord Salmons B side |
| Pee Pee Cluck Cluck | 7" | Pyramid | PYR6065 | 1969 | £2.50 | £6 | Beverley's Allstars B side |
| Poor Rameses | 7" | Trojan | TR698 | 1969 | £1.50 | £4 | Beverley's Allstars B side |
| Reggae Beat | 7" | Blue Cat | BS139 | 1968 | £4 | £8 | |
| Shake It Up | 7" | Blue Cat | BS100 | 1968 | £4 | £8 | |
| Sweet Dreams | 7" | Amalgamated | AMG830 | 1968 | £4 | £8 | Don Drummond Jr. B side |
| Tickle Me For Days | 7" | Amalgamated | AMG826 | 1968 | £4 | £8 | Versatiles B side |
| Whip Them | 7" | Blue Cat | BS105 | 1968 | £4 | £8 | |
| Who The Cap Fits | 7" | Amalgamated | AMG840 | 1969 | £4 | £8 | |
| Yeah | LP | Trojan | TRL24 | 1971 | £4 | £10 | |

## PIPS

| | | | | | | |
|---|---|---|---|---|---|---|
| Every Beat Of My Heart | 7" | Top Rank | JAR574 | 1961 | £5 | £10 |

## PIRANHAS
| | | | | | | |
|---|---|---|---|---|---|---|
| Somethin' Fishy | LP | Custom Fidelity | 1452 | 1969 | £37.50 £75 | US |

## PIRATES
| | | | | | |
|---|---|---|---|---|---|
| My Babe | 7" | HMV | POP1250 | 1964 | £5 £10 |
| Shades Of Blue | 7" | Polydor | 56712 | 1966 | £7.50 £15 |

## PISCES
| | | | | | |
|---|---|---|---|---|---|
| Pisces | LP | Trailer | LER2025 | 1971 | £8 £20 |

## PITNEY, GENE
| | | | | | | |
|---|---|---|---|---|---|---|
| Backstage | 7" EP | Stateside | SE1040 | 1966 | £2 £5 | |
| Big Sixteen | LP | United Artists | ULP1073 | 1964 | £6 £15 | |
| Blue Gene | LP | United Artists | ULP1061 | 1964 | £4 £10 | |
| Every Breath I Take | 7" | HMV | POP933 | 1961 | £4 £8 | |
| Gene Italiano | 7" EP | Stateside | SE1032 | 1965 | £2.50 £6 | |
| Gene Pitney Sings Just For You | 7" EP | Stateside | SE1036 | 1966 | £2 £5 | |
| I Must Be Seeing Things | 7" EP | Stateside | SE1030 | 1965 | £2 £5 | |
| I Wanna Love My Life Away | 7" | London | HL9270 | 1961 | £2.50 £6 | |
| Man Who Shot Liberty Valance | 7" | HMV | POP1018 | 1962 | £2.50 £6 | |
| Many Sides Of Gene Pitney | LP | HMV | CLP1566 | 1961 | £8 £20 | |
| Meets The Fair Young Ladies Of Folkland | LP | United Artists | ULP1064 | 1964 | £4 £10 | |
| Only Love Can Break A Heart | LP | United Artists | (S)ULP1028 | 1963 | £5 £12 | |
| Pitney Sings Just For You | LP | United Artists | ULP1043 | 1963 | £4 £10 | |
| San Remo Winners And Others | 7" EP | Stateside | SE1041 | 1967 | £2 £5 | |
| That Girl Belongs To Yesterday | 7" EP | Stateside | SE1028 | 1965 | £2 £5 | |
| That Girl Belongs To Yesterday | 7" EP | United Artists | UEP1002 | 1964 | £2.50 £6 | |
| There's No Living Without Your Love | 7" EP | Stateside | SE1045 | 1967 | £2 £5 | |
| Town Without Pity | 7" EP | HMV | 7EG8832 | 1963 | £12.50 £25 | |
| Town Without Pity | 7" | HMV | POP952 | 1962 | £2.50 £6 | |
| Twenty Four Hours From Tulsa | 7" EP | Stateside | SE1027 | 1965 | £4 £8 | |
| Twenty Four Hours From Tulsa | 7" EP | United Artists | UEP1001 | 1964 | £2.50 £6 | |

## PIXIES
| | | | | | | |
|---|---|---|---|---|---|---|
| Dig For Fire | CD-s | 4AD | BAD0014CD | 1990 | £2 £5 | |
| Gigantic | CD-s | 4AD | BAD805CD | 1988 | £2 £5 | |
| Here Comes Your Man | CD-s | 4AD | BAD909CD | 1989 | £2 £5 | |
| Live | LP | 4AD | | 1989 | £15 £30 | promo |
| Planet Of Sound | CD-s | 4AD | BAD1008CD | 1991 | £2 £5 | |
| This Monkey's Gone To Heaven | CD-s | 4AD | BAD904CD | 1989 | £2 £5 | |
| Velouria | CD-s | 4AD | BADCD0009 | 1990 | £2 £5 | |

## PIXIES THREE
| | | | | | | |
|---|---|---|---|---|---|---|
| Birthday Party | 7" | Mercury | AMT1214 | 1963 | £1.50 £4 | |
| Party With The Pixies Three | LP | Mercury | MG2/SR60912 | 1964 | £20 £40 | US |

## PLAGUE
| | | | | | |
|---|---|---|---|---|---|
| Looking For The Sun | 7" | Decca | F12730 | 1968 | £25 £50 |

## PLAIN JANE
| | | | | | | |
|---|---|---|---|---|---|---|
| Plain Jane | LP | Hobbit | HB5000 | 1969 | £15 £30 | US |

## PLAINSONG
| | | | | | | |
|---|---|---|---|---|---|---|
| In Search Of Amelia Earhart | LP | Elektra | K42120 | 1972 | £5 £12 | |
| Plainsong II | LP | Elektra | K42136 | 1973 | £37.50 £75 | demo only |

## PLANETARIUM
| | | | | | | |
|---|---|---|---|---|---|---|
| Infinity | LP | Victory | RCA10051 | 1971 | £75 £150 | Italian |

## PLANETEN SIT IN
| | | | | | | |
|---|---|---|---|---|---|---|
| Planeten Sit In | LP | Kosmische | KM58011 | 1974 | £8 £20 | German |

## PLANETS
| | | | | | | |
|---|---|---|---|---|---|---|
| Chunky | 7" | HMV | POP818 | 1960 | £1.50 £4 | |
| Jam Roll | 7" | HMV | POP832 | 1961 | £2 £5 | |
| Jungle Street | 7" | HMV | POP895 | 1961 | £2.50 £6 | |
| Like Party | 7" | Palette | PG9008 | 1960 | £2.50 £6 | |
| Like Party | 7" | Palette | PG9008 | 1960 | £5 £10 | picture sleeve |

## PLANT, RICHARD
| | | | | | |
|---|---|---|---|---|---|
| Better Be Sane | LP | Tradition | TSR022 | 1975 | £4 £10 |

## PLANT, ROBERT
| | | | | | | |
|---|---|---|---|---|---|---|
| Heaven Knows | CD-s | Es Paranza | A9373CD | 1988 | £2 £5 | 3" single |
| Long Time Coming | 7" | CBS | 202858 | 1966 | £50 £100 | |
| Manic Nirvana | CD | Es Paranza | WX339CD | 1990 | £20 £40 | promo box set |
| Our Song | 7" | CBS | 202656 | 1966 | £50 £100 | |
| Pictures At Eleven | LP | Swan Song | SAM154 | 1982 | £4 £10 | interview promo |
| Principal Of Moments | LP | Es Paranza | SAM169 | 1983 | £4 £10 | interview promo |
| Profiled! | CD | Es Paranza | PRCD32972 | 1990 | £10 £25 | US promo |
| Ship Of Fools | CD-s | Es Paranza | A9281CDB | 1988 | £2 £5 | 3" single, inserts |
| Your Ma Said You Cried In Your Sleep Last Night | CD-s | East West | A8945CD | 1990 | £2 £5 | |

## PLANXTY
| | | | | | | |
|---|---|---|---|---|---|---|
| After The Break | LP | Tara | 3001 | 1979 | £4 £10 | Irish |

| | | | | | | | |
|---|---|---|---|---|---|---|---|
| Aris | LP | Polydor | 8152291 | 1984 | £4 | £10 | *Irish* |
| Cold Blow And Rainy Night | LP | Polydor | 2383301 | 1974 | £5 | £12 | |
| Planxty | LP | Polydor | 2383186 | 1973 | £5 | £12 | |
| Planxty Collection | LP | Polydor | 2383397 | 1974 | £4 | £10 | |
| Time Dance | 12" | WEA | IR28207 | 1981 | £10 | £25 | *Irish* |
| Well Below The Valley | LP | Polydor | 2383232 | 1973 | £5 | £12 | |
| Woman I Loved So Well | LP | Tara | 3005 | 1980 | £4 | £10 | *Irish* |
| Words And Music | LP | WEA | 2401011 | 1983 | £4 | £10 | *Irish* |

## PLASTIC CLOUD
| | | | | | | | |
|---|---|---|---|---|---|---|---|
| Plastic Cloud | LP | Allied | 10 | 1968 | £75 | £150 | *Canadian* |

## PLASTIC GANGSTERS
| | | | | | | | |
|---|---|---|---|---|---|---|---|
| Plastic Gangsters | 7" | Secret | SHH144 | 1983 | £10 | £20 | *promo* |

## PLASTIC PENNY
| | | | | | | | |
|---|---|---|---|---|---|---|---|
| Currency | LP | Page One | POLS014 | 1969 | £20 | £40 | |
| Heads I Win, Tails You Lose | LP | Page One | POLS611 | 1970 | £20 | £40 | |
| Two Sides Of Plastic Penny | LP | Page One | POL(S)005 | 1968 | £20 | £40 | |

## PLASTIC PEOPLE OF THE UNIVERSE
| | | | | | | | |
|---|---|---|---|---|---|---|---|
| Egon Bondy's Happy Hearts Club Banned | LP | Invisible | SCOPA10001 | 1979 | £5 | £12 | *French* |

## PLATFORM SIX
| | | | | | | | |
|---|---|---|---|---|---|---|---|
| Girl Down Town | 7" | Piccadilly | 7N35255 | 1965 | £5 | £10 | |

## PLATTERS
| | | | | | | | |
|---|---|---|---|---|---|---|---|
| Are You Sincere | 7" | Mercury | 7MT205 | 1958 | £7.50 | £15 | |
| Around The World | LP | Mercury | MMC14009 | 1959 | £10 | £25 | |
| Ebb Tide | 7" | Mercury | AMT1098 | 1960 | £1.50 | £4 | |
| Enchanted | 7" | Mercury | AMT1039 | 1959 | £1.50 | £4 | |
| Fabulous Platters | 7" EP | Mercury | MEP9504 | 1956 | £4 | £8 | |
| Fabulous Platters Vol. 2 | 7" EP | Mercury | MEP9514 | 1957 | £5 | £10 | |
| Fabulous Platters Vol. 3 | 7" EP | Mercury | MEP9524 | 1957 | £5 | £10 | |
| Flying Platters | LP | Mercury | MPL6528 | 1957 | £10 | £25 | |
| Flying Platters | 7" EP | Mercury | MEP9526 | 1958 | £5 | £10 | |
| Flying Platters No. 2 | 7" EP | Mercury | MEP9528 | 1958 | £5 | £10 | |
| Golden Hits | LP | Mercury | MMC14091 | 1962 | £4 | £10 | |
| Great Pretender | 7" | Mercury | MT117 | 1956 | £10 | £20 | *export* |
| Harbour Lights | 7" EP | Mercury | ZEP10112 | 1961 | £5 | £10 | |
| Harbour Lights | 7" | Mercury | AMT1081 | 1960 | £1.50 | £4 | |
| Helpless | 7" | Mercury | 7MT197 | 1958 | £12.50 | £25 | |
| I Love You A Thousand Times | 7" | Stateside | SS511 | 1966 | £4 | £8 | |
| I Wish | 7" | Mercury | AMT1001 | 1958 | £4 | £8 | |
| I'll Be Home | 7" | Stateside | SS568 | 1966 | £1.50 | £4 | |
| I'll Never Smile | 7" | Mercury | AMT1154 | 1961 | £1.50 | £4 | |
| If I Didn't Care | 7" | Mercury | AMT1128 | 1961 | £1.50 | £4 | |
| Life Is Just A Bowl Of Cherries | LP | Mercury | MMC14072 | 1961 | £6 | £15 | |
| Magic Touch | 78 | Mercury | MT107 | 1956 | £3 | £8 | |
| My Blue Heaven | 7" | Mercury | AMT1066 | 1959 | £1.50 | £4 | |
| My Secret | 7" | Mercury | AMT1076 | 1960 | £1.50 | £4 | |
| Only You | 7" | Ember | JBS701 | 1962 | £62.50 | £125 | |
| Pick Of The Platters No. 1 | 7" EP | Mercury | ZEP10000 | 1959 | £5 | £10 | |
| Pick Of The Platters No. 2 | 7" EP | Mercury | ZEP10008 | 1959 | £5 | £10 | |
| Pick Of The Platters No. 3 | 7" EP | Mercury | ZEP10025 | 1959 | £5 | £10 | |
| Pick Of The Platters No. 4 | 7" EP | Mercury | ZEP10031 | 1959 | £5 | £10 | |
| Pick Of The Platters No. 5 | 7" EP | Mercury | ZEP10042 | 1959 | £5 | £10 | |
| Pick Of The Platters No. 6 | 7" EP | Mercury | ZEP10056 | 1960 | £6 | £12 | |
| Pick Of The Platters No. 7 | 7" EP | Mercury | ZEP10070 | 1960 | £6 | £12 | |
| Platters | LP | Federal | 395549 | 1955 | £180 | £300 | *US* |
| Platters | LP | King | LP549 | 1956 | £100 | £200 | *US* |
| Platters | LP | Mercury | MPL6504 | 1956 | £15 | £30 | |
| Platters | 7" EP | Mercury | MEP9537 | 1958 | £5 | £10 | |
| Platters | 10" LP | Parlophone | PMD1058 | 1958 | £62.50 | £125 | |
| Platters On A Platter | 7" EP | Mercury | ZEP10126 | 1962 | £7.50 | £15 | |
| Platters On Parade | LP | Mercury | MMC14010 | 1959 | £10 | £25 | |
| Platters Vol. 2 | LP | Mercury | MPL6511 | 1957 | £15 | £30 | |
| Red Sails In The Sunset | 7" | Mercury | AMT1106 | 1960 | £1.50 | £4 | |
| Reflections | LP | Mercury | MMC14045 | 1960 | £6 | £15 | |
| Remember When | LP | Mercury | MMC14014 | 1959 | £8 | £20 | |
| Remember When | 7" | Mercury | AMT1053 | 1959 | £1.50 | £4 | |
| Smoke Gets In Your Eyes | 7" | Mercury | AMT1016 | 1958 | £2 | £5 | |
| Sweet Sweet Lovin' | 7" | Stateside | SS2067 | 1967 | £2.50 | £6 | |
| To Each His Own | 7" | Mercury | AMT1118 | 1960 | £1.50 | £4 | |
| Twilight Time | 7" | Mercury | 7MT214 | 1958 | £4 | £8 | |
| Washed Ashore | 7" | Stateside | SS2042 | 1967 | £2 | £5 | |
| With This Ring | 7" | Stateside | SS2007 | 1967 | £2 | £5 | |
| You're Making A Mistake | 7" | Mercury | 7MT227 | 1958 | £5 | £10 | |

## PLAY DEAD
| | | | | | | | |
|---|---|---|---|---|---|---|---|
| Poison Takes A Hold | 7" | Fresh | FRESH29 | 1981 | £1.50 | £4 | |
| This Side Of Heaven | 7" | Tanz | TANZ1 | 1985 | £2 | £5 | *promo only* |
| TV Eye | 7" | Fresh | FRESH38 | 1981 | £1.50 | £4 | |

## PLAYBOYS
| | | | | | | | |
|---|---|---|---|---|---|---|---|
| Over The Weekend | 7" | London | HLU8681 | 1958 | £12.50 | £25 | |

## PLAYBOYS (2)
Playboys ............................................. 10" LP Electrocord...... EDD1115 ............... 1965 £50 ....... £100 ............... *Romanian*

## PLAYBOYS OF EDINBURGH
Up Through The Spiral ........................... LP ..... Uni ................. 73099 ................... 1971 £6 .......... £15 ...................... *US*

## PLAYERS
Mockingbird .......................................... 7" ...... Oriole ............. CB1861 ................. 1963 £2.50 ....... £6 ....................

## PLAYGIRLS
Hey Sport .............................................. 7" ...... RCA ............. RCA1133 ............. 1959 £2.50 ....... £6 ...................

## PLAYGIRLS (2)
Looks Are Deceiving ............................... 7" ...... Black Swan ...... WI456 ................. 1965 £5 .......... £10 ..................

## PLAYGROUND
At The Zoo .......................................... 7" ...... MGM ............ MGM1351 ............. 1967 £1.50 ......... £4 .................

## PLAYMATES
At Play With The Playmates ...................... 7" EP . Columbia ....... SEG7864 ........ 1958 £2 ........... £5 ...........
Barefoot Girl ........................................ 7" ...... Columbia ....... DB3941 ......... 1957 £1.50 ....... £4 ........
Beep Beep ............................................ 7" ...... Columbia ....... DB4224 ......... 1958 £1.50 ....... £4 ........
Darling It's Wonderful ............................ 7" ...... Columbia ....... DB4033 ......... 1957 £1.50 ....... £4 ........
Day I Died ........................................... 7" ...... Columbia ....... DB4207 ......... 1958 £1.50 ....... £4 ........
Don't Go Home ..................................... 7" ...... Columbia ....... DB4151 ......... 1958 £1.50 ....... £4 ........
Jo-Ann ................................................ 7" ...... Columbia ....... DB4084 ......... 1958 £1.50 ....... £4 ........
Let's Be Lovers ...................................... 7" ...... Columbia ....... DB4127 ......... 1958 £1.50 ....... £4 ........
Party Playmates ..................................... 7" EP . Columbia ....... SEG7949 ......... 1959 £2 ........... £5 ........
Party Playmates No. 2 ............................ 7" EP . Columbia ....... SEG7966 ......... 1960 £2 ........... £5 ........
Star Love ............................................. 7" ...... Columbia ....... DB4288 ......... 1959 £1.50 ....... £4 ........
What Is Love ......................................... 7" ...... Columbia ....... DB4338 ......... 1959 £2 ........... £5 ........

## PLAYTHINGS
Stop What You're Doing To Me .............. 7" ...... Pye ........... 7N45212 ......... 1970 £1.50 ....... £4 ........
Surrounded By A Ray Of Sunshine ........... 7" ...... Pye ........... 7N45399 ......... 1974 £1.50 ....... £4 ........

## PLEASE, BOBBY
Your Driver's License Please ..................... 7" ...... London ........... HLB8507 ............... 1957 £100 ..... £200 ...................... *demo*

## PLEASURE, KING
Golden Days ......................................... LP ..... Vogue ........... LAE12258 ......... 1961 £5 ........... £12 ........
King Pleasure ........................................ 7" EP . Vocalion ........... EPVH1285 ........... 1964 £2 ........... £5 ........
King Pleasure ........................................ 10" LP Esquire ........... 20066 ............... 1956 £25 .......... £50 ........

## PLEASURE SEEKERS
Suzi Quatro was just fifteen when she formed the Pleasure Seekers – an all-girl group that also included her sister Patti, who later turned up as a member of Fanny.

Good Kind Of Hurt ............................... 7" ...... Mercury .......... 72800 ................ 1968 £7.50 ....... £15 ............... *US*
Never Thought You'd Leave Me .............. 7" ...... Hideout .......... 1006 ..................... 1967 £30 .......... £60 ............... *US*

## PLEASURES
Music City ............................................ 7" ...... Sue ................. WI357 ................. 1965 £5 ........... £10 ........

## PLEBS
Bad Blood .......................................... 7" ...... Decca ........... F12006 ................ 1964 £12.50 ..... £25 ........
Plebs ................................................. LP ..... Oak ............. ................ 196– £250 ..... £400 ............... *1 sided*

## PLEXUS
Life Up The Creek ................................. LP ..... Hill And Dale .. HD4004 ................ 1979 £25 .......... £50 ........
Plexus ................................................. LP ..... Look ............. LKLP6175 ............. 1978 £25 .......... £50 ........

## PLUM, JON
Alice ................................................... 7" ...... SNB ............. SS3971 ................ 1969 £1.50 ......... £4 ........

## PLUM NELLY
Deceptive Lines ..................................... LP ..... Capitol ............ ST692 ............... 1971 £15 .......... £30 ............... *US*

## PLUMMERS
Litle Stars ............................................ 7" ...... Blue Beat ....... BB260 ................ 1964 £6 ........... £12 ........

## PLUS
Seven Deadly Sins ................................. LP ..... Probe ............. SPB1009 ............. 1970 £6 ........... £15 ........

## PLUTO
I Really Want It ..................................... 7" ...... Dawn ............ DNS1026 ............. 1972 £5 ........... £10 ........
Pluto ................................................... LP ..... Dawn ............ DNLS3030 ......... 1972 £37.50 ...... £75 ........
Rag A Bone Joe ..................................... 7" ...... Dawn ............ DNS1017 ............. 1971 £5 ........... £10 ........

## PNEUMONIA
I Can See Your Face ............................... 7" ...... Oak ............. RGJ625 ................. 1968 £50 .......... £100 ........

## POACHER, CYRIL
Broomfield Wager ................................. LP ..... Topic ............. 12TS252 ............. 1975 £4 ........... £10 ........

## POCHETTE NOIRE
Fais que ton rêve soit plus long .................. LP ...... Reprise ........... 540009 ................... 1971 £25 ......... £50 ................... *French*

## POCO
| | | | | | | | |
|---|---|---|---|---|---|---|---|
| Cantamos | LP | Epic | PEQ33192 | 1974 | £4 | £10 | *US quad* |
| Crazy Eyes | LP | Epic | EQ32354 | 1973 | £4 | £10 | *US quad* |
| Deliverin' | LP | Epic | EQ30209 | 1971 | £4 | £10 | *US quad* |
| Legend | LP | Mobile Fidelity | MFSL1020 | 1978 | £4 | £10 | *US audiophile* |

## POET & THE ONE MAN BAND
Poet and the One Man Band featured neither a poet nor a one-man band, but instead was the home for some subsequently well-known musicians – notably guitarists Albert Lee and Jerry Donahue and bass player Pat Donaldson. The group was not able to survive the collapse of its record company, but eventually metamorphosed into Heads, Hands and Feet.

Poet & The One Man Band ...................... LP ...... Verve ............ SVLP6012 ............. 1969 £15 ......... £30

## POETS
| | | | | | | | |
|---|---|---|---|---|---|---|---|
| Alone Am I | 7" | Pye | 7N17668 | 1968 | £62.50 | £125 | |
| Baby Don't You Do It | 7" | Immediate | IM024 | 1966 | £37.50 | £75 | |
| Call Again | 7" | Immediate | IM006 | 1965 | £37.50 | £75 | |
| Heyla Hola | 7" | Strike Cola | RSA1 | 1971 | £15 | £30 | |
| I Am So Blue | 7" | Decca | F12195 | 1965 | £15 | £30 | |
| Now We're Thru | 7" | Decca | F11995 | 1964 | £7.50 | £15 | |
| That's The Way It's Got To Be | 7" | Decca | F12074 | 1965 | £25 | £50 | |
| Wooden Spoon | 7" | Decca | F12569 | 1967 | £62.50 | £125 | |

## POGUE MAHONE
Dark Streets Of London ........................... 7" ..... Rough Trade... PM1 .............. 1984 £2 ............. £5 ........ *no picture sleeve*

## POGUES
| | | | | | | | |
|---|---|---|---|---|---|---|---|
| Boys From The County Hell | 7" | Stiff | BUY212 | 1984 | £4 | £8 | |
| Dark Streets Of London | 7" | Stiff | BUY207 | 1984 | £2 | £5 | *no picture sleeve* |
| Dirty Old Town | 7" | Stiff | PBUY229 | 1985 | £2 | £5 | *picture disc* |
| Dirty Old Town | 12" | Stiff | BUYIT229 | 1985 | £4 | £10 | |
| Dirty Old Town | 12" | Stiff | BUYIT229 | 1985 | £6 | £15 | *with poster* |
| Dirty Old Town | 12" | Stiff | MAIL3 | 1985 | £4 | £10 | *mail order* |
| Fairytale Of New York | CD-s | Pogue Mahone | CDNY1 | 1987 | £2 | £5 | *..with Kirsty MacColl* |
| Haunted | 12" | MCA | MCAT1084 | 1986 | £2.50 | £6 | *with poster* |
| If I Should Fall From Grace With God | CD-s | Stiff | CDFG1 | 1988 | £2 | £5 | |
| Jack's Heroes | CD-s | WEA | YZ500CD | 1990 | £2 | £5 | *... with The Dubliners* |
| Miss Otis Regrets | CD-s | Chrysalis | CHSCD3629 | 1990 | £2 | £5 | *..with Kirsty MacColl* |
| Misty Morning | CD-s | WEA | YZ407CD | 1989 | £5 | £12 | *3" single* |
| Pair Of Brown Eyes | 7" | Stiff | DBUY220 | 1985 | £2 | £10 | *picture disc* |
| Pair Of Brown Eyes | 12" | Stiff | BUYIT220 | 1985 | £4 | £10 | |
| Poguetry In Motion | 7" | Stiff | PBUY243 | 1986 | £1.50 | £4 | *picture disc* |
| Sally MacLennane | 7" | Stiff | BUY224 | 1985 | £2.50 | £6 | *green vinyl, wraparound picture sleeve* |
| Sally MacLennane | 7" | Stiff | DBUY224 | 1985 | £4 | £8 | *... shaped picture disc* |
| Sally MacLennane | 12" | Stiff | BUYIT224 | 1985 | £3 | £8 | |
| White City | CD-s | WEA | YZ409CD | 1989 | £2 | £5 | *3" single* |

## POHJOLA, PEKKA
| | | | | | | | |
|---|---|---|---|---|---|---|---|
| Group | LP | Dig It | LP1 | 1978 | £5 | £12 | *Finnish* |
| Katkavaaran Lohikaarme | LP | Dig It | LP12 | 1980 | £5 | £12 | *Finnish* |
| Pihkasilma Kaarnakorva | LP | Love | LRLP71 | 1972 | £8 | £20 | *Swedish* |
| Visitation | LP | Dig It | LP4 | 1980 | £5 | £12 | *Finnish* |

## POISON
| | | | | | | | |
|---|---|---|---|---|---|---|---|
| Every Rose Has Its Thorn | CD-s | Capitol | CDCL520 | 1989 | £2 | £5 | |
| Nothin' But A Good Time | CD-s | Capitol | CDCL539 | 1989 | £2 | £5 | |
| Your Mama Don't Dance | CD-s | Capitol | CDCL523 | 1989 | £4 | £10 | |

## POLICE
In addition to the various coloured vinyl releases, picture discs, and other limited edition rarities issued by the Police, there is an American version of *Ghost In The Machine* too rare to be given a realistic value. This is a picture disc, with red LED lights set into the vinyl, along with the (small!) batteries to operate them. Whether it was ever intended to issue this commercially is not clear, but in the event only ten copies were actually produced.

| | | | | | | | |
|---|---|---|---|---|---|---|---|
| Can't Stand Losing You | 7" | A&M | AM214 | 1979 | £7.50 | £15 | *US badge shaped picture disc* |
| Can't Stand Losing You | 7" | A&M | AMS7381 | 1978 | £4 | £8 | *....red, yellow or green vinyl* |
| Can't Stand Losing You | 7" | A&M | AMS7381 | 1979 | £2.50 | £6 | *white vinyl* |
| Compact Hits | CD-s | A&M | AMCD905 | 1988 | £2 | £5 | |
| Don't Stand So Close To Me | 7" | A&M | SP3720 | 1981 | £7.50 | £15 | *US star-shaped picture disc* |
| Every Breath You Take | 7" | A&M | AM117 | 1983 | £4 | £8 | *double* |
| Every Breath You Take | 7" | A&M | AMSP117 | 1983 | £2 | £5 | *picture disc* |
| Fall Out | 7" | Illegal | IL001 | 1977 | £4 | £8 | *black & white picture sleeve* |
| Ghost In The Machine | LP | Nautilus | NR40 | 1982 | £5 | £12 | *US audiophile* |
| Message In A Bottle | 7" | A&M | | 1979 | £7.50 | £15 | *US badge shaped picture disc* |
| Message In A Bottle | 7" | A&M | PR4400 | 1980 | £7.50 | £15 | *US star shaped picture disc* |

| | | | | | | |
|---|---|---|---|---|---|---|
| Outlandos D'Amour | LP | A&M | AMLH68502 | 1978 £5 | £12 | blue vinyl |
| Police Enquiry | LP | A&M | SAMP13 | 1981 £4 | £10 | interview promo |
| Police Pack | 7" | A&M | AMPP6001 | 1980 £7.50 | £15 | 6 x 7", blue vinyl |
| Regatta De Blanc | 10" LP | A&M | AMLT64792 | 1979 £5 | £12 | double |
| Roxanne | 7" | A&M | 2096/2147 | 1979 £7.50 | £15 | US badge-shaped picture disc |
| Roxanne | 7" | A&M | AMS7348 | 1978 £1.50 | £4 | telephone picture sleeve |
| Roxanne | 12" | A&M | AMS7348 | 1978 £4 | £10 | telephone picture sleeve |
| Selections From Message In A Box | CD | A&M | 8044 | 1993 £10 | £25 | US promo |
| Spirits In The Material World | 7" | A&M | AMS8194 | 1981 £2 | £5 | poster sleeve, badge |
| Syncronicity | CD | Mobile Fidelity | UDCD511 | 1988 £6 | £15 | US audiophile |
| Wrapped Around Your Finger | 7" | A&M | AMP127 | 1983 £2.50 | £6 | picture disc (Stewart or Andy) |
| Wrapped Around Your Finger | 7" | A&M | AMP127 | 1983 £1.50 | £4 | picture disc (Sting) |
| Zenyatta Mondatta | LP | Nautilus | NR19 | 1981 £5 | £12 | US audiophile |

## POLIPHONY

| | | | | | | |
|---|---|---|---|---|---|---|
| Poliphony | LP | Zella | no number | 1973 £75 | £150 | |

## POLITICIANS

| | | | | | | |
|---|---|---|---|---|---|---|
| Politicians | LP | Hot Wax | SHW5007 | 1972 £4 | £10 | |

## POLK, FRANK

| | | | | | | |
|---|---|---|---|---|---|---|
| Trying To Keep Up With The Joneses | 7" | Capitol | CL15389 | 1965 £7.50 | £15 | |

## POLLACK, BEN

| | | | | | | |
|---|---|---|---|---|---|---|
| Dixieland | LP | London | LTZC15081 | 1957 £5 | £12 | |

## POLLARD, RAY

| | | | | | | |
|---|---|---|---|---|---|---|
| Drifter | 7" | United Artists | UP1111 | 1965 £50 | £100 | |
| It's A Sad Thing | 7" | United Artists | UP1133 | 1966 £25 | £50 | |

## POLLEN

| | | | | | | |
|---|---|---|---|---|---|---|
| Pollen | LP | Kebec | 908 | 1976 £6 | £15 | Canadian |

## POLYPHONY

| | | | | | | |
|---|---|---|---|---|---|---|
| Polyphony | LP | Zella | | 1973 £75 | £150 | |

## POLYROCK

Polyrock's attractively brittle songs – exploring a similar territory to that of Talking Heads on its first albums – have yet to be discovered by serious collectors. It is interesting, however, to find composer Philip Glass taking the Brian Eno role here and establishing an early, yet generally unremarked connection with rock music.

| | | | | | | |
|---|---|---|---|---|---|---|
| Polyrock | LP | RCA | PL43502 | 1980 £4 | £10 | |

## POMEROY, HERB

| | | | | | | |
|---|---|---|---|---|---|---|
| Life Is A Many-Splendoured Gig | LP | Columbia | 33SX1091 | 1958 £10 | £25 | |

## PONI-TAILS

| | | | | | | |
|---|---|---|---|---|---|---|
| Born Too Late | 7" | HMV | POP516 | 1958 £2.50 | £6 | |
| Close Friends | 7" | HMV | POP558 | 1958 £1.50 | £4 | |
| Early To Bed | 7" | HMV | POP596 | 1959 £2 | £5 | |
| I'll Be Seeing You | 7" | HMV | POP663 | 1959 £1.50 | £4 | |
| Moody | 7" | HMV | POP644 | 1959 £1.50 | £4 | |
| Poni-Tails | 7" EP | HMV | 7EG8427 | 1957 £30 | £60 | |

## PONTY, JEAN-LUC

Ponty is a rather fine jazz violinist, who during the course of a long career has played with both Frank Zappa and John McLaughlin (and managed to annoy both of them, apparently). The *King Kong* album is effectively part of Frank Zappa's oeuvre – he produced the record and plays guitar on the one track he did not actually write.

| | | | | | | |
|---|---|---|---|---|---|---|
| Astrorama | LP | Far East | 65016 | 1970 £4 | £10 | |
| Electric Connection | LP | Liberty | LBL/LBS83262 | 1969 £5 | £12 | |
| Experience | LP | Pacific Jazz | PJ20168 | 1969 £5 | £12 | US |
| King Kong | LP | Liberty | LBS83375 | 1970 £4 | £10 | |
| Open Strings | LP | BASF | 21288 | 1972 £4 | £10 | German |
| Sunday Walk | LP | BASF | 20645 | 197– £4 | £10 | German |
| Sunday Walk | LP | MPS | 15045 | 1967 £5 | £12 | German |

## POOGY

| | | | | | | |
|---|---|---|---|---|---|---|
| She Looked Me In The Eye | 7" | EMI | EMI2136 | 1974 £5 | £10 | |

## POOH STICKS

| | | | | | | |
|---|---|---|---|---|---|---|
| 1-2-3 Red Light | 7" | Fierce | FRIGHT021 | 1988 £6 | £12 | |
| Alan McGee | CD-s | Fierce | FRIGHT026 | 1988 £5 | £12 | |
| Alan McGee | CD-s | Fierce | FRIGHT026 | 1988 £6 | £15 | boxed, booklet |
| Dying For It | 7" | Fierce | FRIGHT034 | 1989 £6 | £12 | |
| Dying For It | 7" | Fierce | FRIGHT034 | 1989 £5 | £10 | 1 sided |
| Dying For It | 7" | Fierce | FRIGHT034 | 1989 £7.50 | £15 | autographed |
| Fierce Box Set | 7" | Fierce | FRIGHT021-025 | 1988 £25 | £50 | 5 one-sided singles |
| Go Go Girl | 7" | Cheree | 3 | 1989 £1.50 | £4 | flexi |
| Hard On Love | 7" | Woosh | WOOSH7 | 1989 £4 | £8 | yellow flexi with fanzine |
| Million Seller | 7" | Fierce | FRIGHT42 | 1992 £2.50 | £6 | 1 sided |
| On Tape | 7" | Fierce | FRIGHT011 | 1988 £20 | £40 | |
| Orgasm | LP | 53rd & 3rd | AGAMC5 | 1989 £8 | £20 | pink vinyl |
| Pooh Sticks | LP | Fierce | FRIGHT025 | 1989 £4 | £10 | |

Trade Mark Of Quality.................................. LP...... Fierce ............. FRIGHT035 .......... 1990 £8.......... £20 ......................

## POOLE, BRIAN
Everything I Touch Turns To Tears.......... 7"..... CBS................ 202349 .................... 1966 £2.......... £5 ......................
Just How Loud................................... 7"..... CBS................ 3005 ..................... 1967 £2.......... £5 ......................

## POOLE, BRIAN & THE TREMELOES
This was the group that Decca elected to sign rather than the Beatles, a decision that might not have appeared too disastrous at first, as Poole and his group managed to achieve eight chart hits, including a number one with 'Do You Love Me'. When Poole decided to go solo in 1966, it must have been rather galling to see his former backing group go on to achieve considerably greater success without him. In the long run, moreover, he risks being known merely as the father of Karen and Shellie, who at the time of writing are collecting critical plaudits for their group, Alisha's Attic.

After A While ......................................... 7"..... Decca ............ F12124................. 1965 £1.50...... £4 ......................
Big Hits Of 1962 .................................... LP...... Ace Of Clubs .. ACL1146 .............. 1963 £15...... £30 ......................
Brian Poole & The Tremeloes ................ 7" EP . Decca ........... DFE8566.............. 1964 £10...... £20 ......................
Brian Poole & The Tremeloes Vol. 2 ....... 7" EP . Decca ........... DFE8610.............. 1965 £10...... £20 ......................
Brian Poole Is Here .............................. LP...... Audio Fidelity.. 2151/6151 ......... 1966 £10...... £25 .................. US
Candy Man.......................................... 7" EP . Decca ........... 457027................ 1964 £10...... £20 .............. French
Do You Love Me................................... 7" EP . Decca ........... 457017................ 1963 £10...... £20 .............. French
Good Lovin' ........................................ 7"..... Decca ........... F12274................ 1965 £1.50...... £4 ......................
I Can Dance ........................................ 7"..... Decca ........... F11771................ 1963 £1.50...... £4 ......................
I Want Candy ....................................... 7"..... Decca ........... F12197................ 1965 £1.50...... £4 ......................
It's About Time..................................... LP...... Decca ........... LK4685 .............. 1965 £15...... £30 ......................
Keep On Dancing .................................. 7"..... Decca ........... F11616................ 1963 £1.50...... £4 ......................
Meet Me Where We Used To Meet ......... 7"..... Decca ........... F11567................ 1963 £1.50...... £4 ......................
That Ain't Right .................................... 7"..... Decca ........... F11515................ 1962 £1.50...... £4 ......................
Time Is On My Side ............................... 7" EP . Decca ........... 457064................ 1965 £10...... £20 .............. French
Tremeloes Are Here .............................. LP...... Audio Fidelity.. 2177/6177.......... 1967 £8...... £20 .................. US
Twelve Steps To Love ........................... 7"..... Decca ........... F11951................ 1964 £1.50...... £4 ......................
Twenty Miles ....................................... 7" EP . Decca ........... 457034................ 1964 £10...... £20 .............. French
Twist And Shout ................................... LP...... Decca ........... LK4550 .............. 1963 £15...... £30 ......................
Twist Little Sister ................................. 7"..... Decca ........... F11455................ 1962 £2.50...... £6 ......................

## POOLE, LOU & LAURA
Only You And I Know.............................. 7"..... Jay Boy .......... BOY63 ................ 1972 £1.50...... £4 ......................

## POOR SOULS
Love Me.............................................. 7"..... Alp ............... 595004................ 1966 £12.50...... £25 ......................
When My Baby Cries .............................. 7"..... Decca ........... F12183................ 1965 £2.50...... £6 ......................

## POP, IGGY
Candy ................................................ CD-s . Virgin ............ VUSCD29 ........... 1990 £2...... £5 ...... with Kate Pierson
Compact Hits........................................ CD-s . A&M.............. AMCD909 ........... 1988 £2...... £5 ......................
Five Foot One ...................................... 7"..... Arista ............ ARIST274 ........... 1979 £1.50...... £4 ............ picture disc
Fun House........................................... LP...... Elektra ........... 2410009 ............. 1970 £5...... £12 ...... with the Stooges
Fun House........................................... LP...... Elektra ........... EKS74071 ........... 1970 £10...... £25 ...... with the Stooges
Fun House........................................... LP...... Elektra ........... K42051 .............. 1971 £4...... £10 ...... with the Stooges
Home ................................................ CD-s . Virgin ............ VUSCD22 ........... 1990 £2...... £5 ......................
I Got Nothing....................................... CD-s . Skydog........... 622332............... 1990 £2...... £5 ...... with the Stooges
Live At The Channel 7-19-88 .................. CD..... A&M.............. SP17641 ............. 1988 £15...... £30 ........ US promo
Livin' On The Edge Of The Night ............ CD-s . Virgin ............ VUSCD18 ........... 1990 £2...... £5 ............ 3" single
Metallic K.O. ...................................... LP...... Skydog........... SGIS008............. 1976 £4...... £10 ...... French, with the Stooges
Raw Power .......................................... LP...... CBS............... 65586................. 1973 £5...... £12 ...... inner sleeve, with the Stooges
Raw Trax............................................. CD..... Virgin ............ PRCD3365 .......... 1991 £15...... £30 ...US demos compilation
Stooges.............................................. LP...... Elektra ........... EKS74051 ........... 1969 £15...... £30 ...... with the Stooges
Stooges.............................................. LP...... Elektra ........... K42032 .............. 1971 £4...... £10 ...... with the Stooges

## POP GROUP
Y....................................................... LP...... Radar ............ RAD20 .............. 1979 £4...... £10 .............. with poster

## POP RIVITS
Empty Sounds From Anarchy Ranch ........ LP...... Hipocrite ........ HIP0 ................. 1979 £6...... £15 ......................
Fun In The UK..................................... 7"..... Hypocrite........ JIM1 ................. 1979 £4...... £8 .............. double
Greatest Hits....................................... LP...... Hipocrite ........ HIP007 .............. 1979 £4...... £10 ......................
Pop Rivits ........................................... 7"..... Hypocrite........ HEP002 .............. 1979 £1.50...... £4 ......................
Pop Rivits EP ...................................... 7"..... Hypocrite........ HEP001 .............. 1979 £2...... £5 ......................

## POP TOPS
Oh Lord, Why Lord ............................... 7" EP . Princess ......... 745001............... 196– £4...... £8 .............. French

## POP WILL EAT ITSELF
Beaver Patrol ...................................... 7"..... Chapter 22 ...... LCHAP16 ............ 1987 £2...... £5 ...... pink or clear vinyl
Can U Dig It ........................................ CD-s . RCA .............. PD42620.............. 1989 £2...... £5 ......................
Def Con One ....................................... CD-s . Chapter 22 ...... PWEICD001 .......... 1988 £2.50...... £6 ......................
Def Con One ....................................... CD-s . RCA .............. PD42884.............. 1989 £2...... £5 ......................
Love Missile F1-11 (Designer Grebo Mix) .. 12"..... Chapter 22 ...... L12CHAP13 .......... 1987 £2.50...... £6 ......................
Poppies Say Grrr .................................. 7"..... Desperate ....... DAN1................. 1986 £1.50...... £4 ...... orange sleeve
Poppies Say Grrr .................................. 7"..... Desperate ....... SRT1................. 1986 £7.50...... £15 ... brown paper sleeve
There Is No Love Between Us Anymore ... 12"..... Chapter 22 ...... L12CHAP20 .......... 1988 £2.50...... £6 ......................
There Is No Love Between Us Anymore ... 12"..... Chapter 22 ...... CLUBCHAP20 ...... 1988 £3...... £8 ......................
   (High Mix)......................................
Wise Up Sucker .................................... CD-s . RCA .............. PD42762.............. 1989 £2...... £5 ......................

## POPCORN BLIZZARD

The 'Once Upon A Time' single marks the recording debut of Marvin Aday, better known by his stage name, Meat Loaf.

| | | | | | | | |
|---|---|---|---|---|---|---|---|
| Once Upon A Time | 7" | Magenta | | 1967 | £15 | £30 | US |

## POPE, TIM

| | | | | | | | |
|---|---|---|---|---|---|---|---|
| I Want To Be A Tree | 7" | Fiction | FICS21 | 1984 | £7.50 | £15 | |
| I Want To Be A Tree | 12" | Fiction | FICSX21 | 1984 | £10 | £20 | |

## POPOL VUH

| | | | | | | | |
|---|---|---|---|---|---|---|---|
| Affenstunde | LP | Liberty | LBS83460 | 1971 | £10 | £25 | German |
| Aguirre | LP | Barclay | 840103 | 1975 | £6 | £15 | French |
| Bruder Des Schattens | LP | Brain | 0060167 | 1978 | £5 | £12 | German |
| Coeur de verre | LP | Egg | 900536 | 1977 | £6 | £15 | French |
| Das Hohelied Salomos | LP | United Artists | UAS29781 | 1975 | £6 | £15 | German |
| Discover Cosmic | LP | Ohr | 940119/20 | 1976 | £10 | £25 | French double |
| Einsjäger Und Siebenjäger | LP | Komische | KM58017 | 1975 | £8 | £20 | German |
| Herz Aus Glas | LP | Brain | 0060079 | 1977 | £5 | £12 | German |
| Hosianna Mantra | LP | Pilz | 20291431 | 1973 | £10 | £25 | German |
| In Den Garten Pharaos | LP | Pilz | 20212769 | 1971 | £10 | £25 | German |
| Letzte Tage Letzte Nächte | LP | United Artists | UAS29916 | 1976 | £6 | £15 | German |
| Nosferatu | LP | Egg | 900573 | 1978 | £5 | £12 | French |
| Perlenklanged | LP | PDU | 6073 | 1977 | £5 | £12 | Italian |
| Seligpreisung | LP | Komische | KM58009 | 1974 | £8 | £20 | German |
| Tantric Songs | LP | Brain | 0060242 | 1979 | £5 | £12 | German |
| Yoga | LP | PDU | 6060 | 1976 | £8 | £20 | Italian |

## POPOL VUH (2)

| | | | | | | | |
|---|---|---|---|---|---|---|---|
| Popol Vuh | LP | Polydor | 2923009 | 1972 | £8 | £20 | Norwegian |
| Quiche Maya | LP | Polydor | 2382038 | 1973 | £8 | £20 | Norwegian |

## POPPIES

| | | | | | | | |
|---|---|---|---|---|---|---|---|
| Lullaby Of Love | 7" | Columbia | DB7879 | 1966 | £5 | £10 | |

## POPPYHEADS

| | | | | | | | |
|---|---|---|---|---|---|---|---|
| Cremation Town | 7" | Sarah | 006 | 1988 | £2 | £5 | with poster |
| Postcard For Flossy | 7" | Sha La La | 004 | 1988 | £2 | £5 | flexi |

## POPULAR FIVE

| | | | | | | | |
|---|---|---|---|---|---|---|---|
| I'm A Lovemaker | 7" | Minit | MLF11011 | 1968 | £2.50 | £6 | |

## PORCUPINE TREE

| | | | | | | | |
|---|---|---|---|---|---|---|---|
| Radioactive EP | CD-s | Delerium | DELECPROMO-CD1 | 1993 | £10 | £20 | promo |
| Voyage 34 Phase 1 | CD-s | Delerium | DELECCDEP010 | 1992 | £4 | £10 | |
| Voyage 34 Phase 1 | 12" | Delerium | DELECEP010 | 1992 | £4 | £10 | |
| Voyage 34 Remix Phase 3 | 12" | Delerium | DELECEP007 | 1993 | £2.50 | £6 | |
| Yellow Hedgerow Dreamscape | CD | Magic Gnome | MG4299325 | 1994 | £20 | £40 | |

## PORTER, NOLAN

| | | | | | | | |
|---|---|---|---|---|---|---|---|
| If I Could Only Be Sure | 7" | Probe | PRO580 | 1972 | £2 | £5 | |

## PORTION CONTROL

| | | | | | | | |
|---|---|---|---|---|---|---|---|
| Hit The Pulse | LP | In Phaze | EZ2 | 1983 | £4 | £10 | |
| Raise The Pulse | 12" | Illuminated | ILL2612 | 1984 | £2.50 | £6 | |
| Rough Justice | 12" | Illuminated | ILL3212 | 1984 | £2.50 | £6 | |
| Surface And Be Seen | 12" | In Phaze | PORCON006 | 1982 | £4 | £10 | |

## PORTOBELLO EXPLOSION

| | | | | | | | |
|---|---|---|---|---|---|---|---|
| We Can Fly | 7" | Carnaby | CNS4001 | 1969 | £10 | £20 | |

## POSEIDON

| | | | | | | | |
|---|---|---|---|---|---|---|---|
| Found My Way | LP | private | Z33010 | 1975 | £8 | £20 | German |

## POSEY, SANDY

| | | | | | | | |
|---|---|---|---|---|---|---|---|
| Best Of Sandy Posey | LP | MGM | CS8060 | 1968 | £4 | £10 | |
| Born A Woman | LP | MGM | C(S)8035 | 1967 | £5 | £12 | |
| Born A Woman | 7" | MGM | MGM1321 | 1966 | £1.50 | £4 | |
| Looking At You | LP | MGM | C(S)8073 | 1968 | £4 | £10 | |
| Sandy Posey | LP | MGM | C(S)8051 | 1968 | £4 | £10 | |
| Single Girl | LP | MGM | C(S)8042 | 1967 | £4 | £10 | |
| Single Girl | 7" | MGM | MGM1330 | 1966 | £1.50 | £4 | |

## POSITIVELY THIRTEEN O'CLOCK

| | | | | | | | |
|---|---|---|---|---|---|---|---|
| Psychotic Reaction | 7" EP | Vogue | INT18099 | 1966 | £30 | £60 | French, B side by TV & The Tribesmen |

## POST, HOWIE & THE SWIFTIES

| | | | | | | | |
|---|---|---|---|---|---|---|---|
| Tom Swift | 7" | Fontana | TF421 | 1963 | £2 | £5 | |

## POSTER, ADRIENNE

| | | | | | | | |
|---|---|---|---|---|---|---|---|
| He Doesn't Love Me | 7" | Decca | F12079 | 1965 | £4 | £8 | |
| Only Fifteen | 7" | Decca | F11797 | 1963 | £2.50 | £6 | |
| Only Fifteen | 7" | Oriole | CB1890 | 1963 | £4 | £8 | |
| Shang A Doo Lang | 7" | Decca | F11864 | 1964 | £4 | £8 | |
| Something Beautiful | 7" | Decca | F12329 | 1966 | £2 | £5 | |

| | | | | | | | |
|---|---|---|---|---|---|---|---|
| Winds That Blow | 7" | Decca | F12181 | 1965 £2.50 | £6 | |

## POTEMKINE
| | | | | | | | |
|---|---|---|---|---|---|---|---|
| Foetus | LP | Tapioca | TP10008 | 1976 £6 | £15 | French |
| Nicolas II | LP | Phaeton | 7801 | 1978 £4 | £10 | French |
| Triton | LP | Phaeton | VST7162 | 1977 £4 | £10 | French |

## POTLIQUOR
| | | | | | | | |
|---|---|---|---|---|---|---|---|
| First Taste | LP | Dawn | DNLS3016 | 1971 £30 | £60 | |
| Levee Blues | LP | Janus | JLS3033 | 1971 £8 | £20 | US |
| Louisiana Rock 'n' Roll | LP | Janus | JLS3036 | 1971 £8 | £20 | US |

## POTTER, PHIL
| | | | | | | | |
|---|---|---|---|---|---|---|---|
| My Song Is Love Unknown | LP | Genesis | GEN10 | 197– £8 | £20 | |
| Restorer | LP | Dove | DOVE61 | 1979 £4 | £10 | |

## POUND
| | | | | | | | |
|---|---|---|---|---|---|---|---|
| Odd Man Out | LP | AMS | 74840 | 1974 £30 | £60 | US |

## POUND HOUNDS
| | | | | | | | |
|---|---|---|---|---|---|---|---|
| Home Sweet Home | 7" | Brunswick | 05484 | 1955 £1.50 | £4 | Mellomen B side |

## POUNDS, ALAN GET RICH
| | | | | | | | |
|---|---|---|---|---|---|---|---|
| Searching In The Wilderness | 7" | Parlophone | R5532 | 1966 £180 | £300 | best auctioned |

## POWELL, BOBBY
| | | | | | | | |
|---|---|---|---|---|---|---|---|
| Peace Begins Within | 7" | Mojo | 2092034 | 1972 £2 | £5 | |

## POWELL, BUD
| | | | | | | | |
|---|---|---|---|---|---|---|---|
| Amazing Bud Powell Vol. 1 | LP | Blue Note | BLP/BST81503 | 1963 £10 | £25 | |
| Amazing Bud Powell Vol. 2 | LP | Blue Note | BLP/BST81504 | 1964 £10 | £25 | |
| At The Blue Note Cafe | LP | Fontana | SFJL924 | 1969 £4 | £10 | |
| Blues For Bouffemont | LP | Fontana | SFJL901 | 1968 £4 | £10 | |
| Blues For Bud | LP | Columbia | 33CX10123 | 1958 £10 | £25 | |
| Bouncing With Bud | LP | XTRA | XTRA1011 | 1965 £4 | £10 | |
| Bud Powell | 7" EP | Columbia | SEB10013 | 1955 £2 | £5 | |
| Bud Powell Trio | 7" EP | Vogue | EPV1030 | 1955 £2 | £5 | |
| Bud Powell Trio | 7" EP | Vogue | EPV1036 | 1955 £2 | £5 | |
| Bud Powell Trio | 10" LP | Columbia | 33C9016 | 1956 £20 | £40 | |
| Bud Powell Trio | 10" LP | Vogue | LDE010 | 1952 £30 | £60 | |
| Bud Powell Trio Featuring Max Roach | LP | Columbia | 33SX1575 | 1963 £6 | £15 | |
| Bud Powell's Modernists | 7" EP | Vogue | EPV1033 | 1955 £2 | £5 | |
| Genius Of Bud Powell | 7" EP | Columbia | SEB10074 | 1957 £2 | £5 | |
| Genius Of Bud Powell No. 2 | 7" EP | Columbia | SEB10094 | 1958 £2 | £5 | |
| Jazz At Massey Hall | LP | Vogue | LAE558 | 1964 £6 | £15 | |
| Jazz Original | LP | Columbia | 33CX10069 | 1957 £20 | £40 | |
| Lonely One | LP | HMV | CLP1294 | 1959 £8 | £20 | |
| Return Of Bud Powell | LP | Columbia | 33SX1700 | 1965 £5 | £12 | |
| Scene Changes | LP | Blue Note | BLP/BST84009 | 196– £10 | £25 | |
| Time Waits | LP | Blue Note | BLP/BST81598 | 196– £10 | £25 | |
| Vintage Years | LP | Verve | VLP9075 | 1964 £4 | £10 | |

## POWELL, JANE
| | | | | | | | |
|---|---|---|---|---|---|---|---|
| Jane Powell | LP | HMV | CLP1131 | 1957 £5 | £12 | |
| Jane Powell Sings | 7" EP | MGM | MGMEP701 | 1959 £5 | £10 | |
| King And I | 7" EP | MGM | MGMEP584 | 1957 £2 | £5 | |
| Three Sailors And A Girl | 10" LP | Capitol | LC6665 | 1954 £5 | £12 | |
| True Love | 7" | HMV | POP267 | 1956 £1.50 | £4 | |

## POWELL, JIMMY
| | | | | | | | |
|---|---|---|---|---|---|---|---|
| I Can Go Down | 7" | Strike | JH309 | 1966 £2 | £5 | |
| I Just Can't Get Over You | 7" | Decca | F12751 | 1968 £1.50 | £4 | |
| Remember Then | 7" | Decca | F11570 | 1963 £1.50 | £4 | |
| Sugar Babe | 7" | Decca | F11447 | 1962 £1.50 | £4 | |
| Sugar Babe | 7" | Decca | F12793 | 1968 £1.50 | £4 | |
| Sugar Babe | 7" | Pye | 7N15735 | 1964 £5 | £10 | |
| That's Alright | 7" | Pye | 7N15663 | 1964 £12.50 | £25 | |
| Tom Hark | 7" | Decca | F11544 | 1962 £1.50 | £4 | |
| Unexpected Mirrors | 7" | Decca | F12664 | 1967 £1.50 | £4 | |

## POWELL, KEITH
| | | | | | | | |
|---|---|---|---|---|---|---|---|
| Answer Is No | 7" | Columbia | DB7116 | 1963 £2 | £5 | |
| I Should Know Better | 7" | Columbia | DB7366 | 1964 £7.50 | £15 | |
| It Keeps Rainin' | 7" | Piccadilly | 7N35353 | 1966 £1.50 | £4 | |
| Tore Up | 7" | Columbia | DB7229 | 1964 £2.50 | £6 | |

## POWELL, KEITH & BILLIE DAVIS
| | | | | | | | |
|---|---|---|---|---|---|---|---|
| You Don't Know Like I Know | 7" | Piccadilly | 7N35321 | 1966 £2 | £5 | |

## POWELL, MARILYN
| | | | | | | | |
|---|---|---|---|---|---|---|---|
| All My Loving | 7" | Fontana | TF448 | 1964 £1.50 | £4 | |

## POWELL, MEL
| | | | | | | | |
|---|---|---|---|---|---|---|---|
| Borderline | LP | Vanguard | PPL11001 | 1956 £6 | £15 | |
| Thingamagig | LP | Vanguard | PPL11000 | 1956 £6 | £15 | |

## POWELL, SELDON
| | | | | | | | |
|---|---|---|---|---|---|---|---|
| Seldon Powell Plays | LP | Vogue | LAE12184 | 1959 £6 | £15 | |

| | | | | | | | | |
|---|---|---|---|---|---|---|---|---|
| Seldon Powell Sextet | LP | Vogue | LAE12201 | 1959 | £8 | £20 | | |

## POWELL, SPECS
| | | | | | | | |
|---|---|---|---|---|---|---|---|
| Movin' In | LP | Columbia | 33SX1083 | 1958 | £5 | £12 | |

## POWER, DUFFY
| | | | | | | | |
|---|---|---|---|---|---|---|---|
| Davy O'Brien | 7" | Parlophone | R5631 | 1967 | £5 | £10 | |
| Dream Lover | 7" | Fontana | H194 | 1959 | £4 | £8 | |
| Duffy Power | LP | GSF | GS502 | 1973 | £5 | £12 | |
| Duffy Power | LP | Spark | SRLM2005 | 1973 | £6 | £15 | |
| Hell Hound | 7" | CBS | 5176 | 1970 | £2.50 | £6 | |
| Hey Girl | 7" | Parlophone | R5059 | 1963 | £2.50 | £6 | |
| I Saw Her Standing There | 7" | Parlophone | R5024 | 1963 | £10 | £20 | |
| I've Got Nobody | 7" | Fontana | H302 | 1961 | £5 | £10 | |
| Innovations | LP | Transatlantic | TRA229 | 1971 | £10 | £20 | |
| It Ain't Necessarily So | 7" | Parlophone | R4992 | 1963 | £4 | £8 | |
| Kissing Time | 7" | Fontana | H214 | 1959 | £4 | £8 | |
| No Other Love | 7" | Fontana | H344 | 1961 | £2.50 | £6 | |
| Starry Eyed | 7" | Fontana | H230 | 1959 | £2.50 | £6 | |
| Tired Broke And Busted | 7" | Parlophone | R5111 | 1964 | £4 | £8 | |
| Where Am I | 7" | Parlophone | R5169 | 1964 | £2.50 | £6 | |
| Whole Lotta Shaking Going On | 7" | Fontana | H279 | 1960 | £5 | £10 | |

## POWER, JIMMY
| | | | | | | | |
|---|---|---|---|---|---|---|---|
| Irish Fiddle Player | LP | Topic | 12TS306 | 1976 | £4 | £10 | |

## POWERHOUSE
| | | | | | | | |
|---|---|---|---|---|---|---|---|
| Chain Gang | 7" | Decca | F12471 | 1966 | £4 | £8 | |
| Raindrops | 7" | Decca | F12507 | 1966 | £1.50 | £4 | |

## POWERPACK
| | | | | | | | |
|---|---|---|---|---|---|---|---|
| Hannibal Brooks | 7" | Polydor | 56311 | 1969 | £1.50 | £4 | |
| I'll Be Anything For You | 7" | CBS | 202551 | 1967 | £2 | £5 | |
| It Hurts Me So | 7" | CBS | 202335 | 1966 | £7.50 | £15 | |
| Oh Calcutta | 7" | Polydor | 2001077 | 1970 | £1.50 | £4 | |

## POWERS, JOEY
| | | | | | | | |
|---|---|---|---|---|---|---|---|
| Midnight Mary | 7" | Stateside | SS236 | 1963 | £1.50 | £4 | |

## PRADO, PEREZ
| | | | | | | | |
|---|---|---|---|---|---|---|---|
| Cherry Pink And Apple Blossom White | 7" | HMV | 7M295 | 1955 | £2 | £5 | |
| Patricia | 7" | RCA | RCA1067 | 1958 | £1.50 | £4 | |

## PRALINS
| | | | | | | | |
|---|---|---|---|---|---|---|---|
| Beat Beat Beat | LP | Popular | 21003 | 1966 | £15 | £30 | German |
| Beat With The Pralins | LP | Popular | 21004 | 1966 | £6 | £15 | German |

## PRANNATH, PANDIT
| | | | | | | | |
|---|---|---|---|---|---|---|---|
| Earth Groove | LP | Transatlantic | TRA193 | 1969 | £6 | £15 | |

## PRATT, GRAHAM & EILEEN
| | | | | | | | |
|---|---|---|---|---|---|---|---|
| Clear Air Of The Day | LP | Cottage | 811 | 1977 | £8 | £20 | |

## PRATT, PHIL
| | | | | | | | |
|---|---|---|---|---|---|---|---|
| Sweet Song | 7" | Jolly | JY008 | 1968 | £4 | £8 | Thrillers B side |

## PRAYING MANTIS
| | | | | | | | |
|---|---|---|---|---|---|---|---|
| All Day And All Of The Night | 7" | Arista | ARIST397 | 1981 | £2 | £5 | |
| Soundhouse Tapes | 7" EP | Ripper | HAR5201 | 1980 | £4 | £8 | |
| Tell Me The Nightmare's Wrong | 7" | Jet | JET7026 | 1982 | £1.50 | £4 | |
| Time Tells No Lies | LP | Arista | SPART1153 | 1981 | £6 | £15 | |

## PREACHERS
| | | | | | | | |
|---|---|---|---|---|---|---|---|
| Hole In My Soul | 7" | Columbia | DB7680 | 1965 | £15 | £30 | |
| Zeke | 7" EP | Barclay | 70890 | 1965 | £50 | £100 | French |

## PRECISIONS
| | | | | | | | |
|---|---|---|---|---|---|---|---|
| If This Is Love | 7" | Track | 604014 | 1967 | £2.50 | £6 | |

## PREFAB SPROUT
| | | | | | | | |
|---|---|---|---|---|---|---|---|
| Cars And Girls | CD-s | Kitchenware | CDDSK35 | 1988 | £2 | £5 | picture disc |
| Golden Calf | CD-s | Kitchenware | CDSK41 | 1989 | £2 | £5 | |
| Hey Manhattan | CD-s | Kitchenware | CDSK38 | 1988 | £2 | £5 | |
| Jordan – The Comeback | CD | Kitchenware | KWCDX14 | 1990 | £5 | £12 | picture disc |
| King Of Rock And Roll | CD-s | Kitchenware | CDSK37 | 1988 | £2 | £5 | |
| Lions In My Own Garden | 7" | Candle | 1 | 1982 | £7.50 | £15 | no picture sleeve |
| Lions In My Own Garden | 7" | Kitchenware | SK4 | 1983 | £2 | £5 | |
| Looking For Atlantis | CD-s | Kitchenware | SKQ47 | 1990 | £2 | £5 | |
| Nightingales | CD-s | Kitchenware | CDSK39 | 1988 | £2 | £5 | |

## PREGNANT INSOMNIA
| | | | | | | | |
|---|---|---|---|---|---|---|---|
| Wallpaper | 7" | Direction | 583132 | 1967 | £15 | £30 | |

## PRELUDE
| | | | | | | | |
|---|---|---|---|---|---|---|---|
| Prelude | LP | Crochet | no number | 197– | £25 | £50 | |

## PREMIERS
| | | | | | | | |
|---|---|---|---|---|---|---|---|
| Farmer John | LP | Warner Bros | W(S)1565 | 1964 | £25 | £50 | US |

| Farmer John | 7" EP | Warner Bros | WEP1437 | 1964 | £20 | £40 | French |
| Farmer John | 7" | Warner Bros | WB134 | 1964 | £2.50 | £6 | |

## PREMO & HOPETON
| Your Safekeep | 7" | Rio | R139 | 1967 | £4 | £8 | |

## PRESELI FOLK
| Preseli Folk | LP | private | PRE001 | 1979 | £20 | £40 | |

## PRESENCE
| In Wonder | CD-s | Reality | LOLCD1 | 1991 | £2 | £5 | |

## PRESIDENTS
| Candy Man | 7" | Decca | F11826 | 1964 | £10 | £20 | |

## PRESLEY, ELVIS

Elvis Presley's position as the most popular rock solo artist ever is indisputable and the list of collectable records made by him is correspondingly long. Although American singles are generally outside the scope of the present volume, Presley's Sun singles were felt to be of such historical importance that they have been included. For the same reason, the legendary *Elvis And Janis* South African release is also included. As far as Presley's earliest records in the UK are concerned, the HMV issues are not that rare: they were all enormous sellers at the time of their release. What are rare, however, are copies in anything like mint condition. The values quoted are for these rarities. For records in less than mint condition, the drop in value with deteriorating condition is dramatic – one of the HMV albums, with its cover torn and repaired with Selotape and with its playing surface displaying an impressive network of scratches and scars, would be worth a nominal few pounds only, if anything at all. Meanwhile, it should be noted that, with the exception of the last issued records whose sales were quite small in the format, 78 rpm releases are worth considerably less than their 45 rpm equivalents. Of course, not everything by Elvis Presley is automatically valuable – one example that is not, despite appearances to the contrary, is the double hits compilation, *Elvis's 40 Greatest*, pressed on pink vinyl. The record cover proclaims 'special pink pressing', but in fact most copies are like this, and the set is very common. Other non-rarities include the picture disc versions of the *Legendary Performer* albums, which are attractive items but not valuable, and any of the vast number of Elvis repackages on RCA's cheap Camden label.

| Ain't That Lovin' You Baby | 7" | RCA | RCA1422 | 1964 | £1.50 | £4 | |
| All Shook Up | 78 | HMV | POP359 | 1957 | £6 | £12 | |
| All Shook Up | 78 | RCA | RCA1088 | 1958 | £15 | £30 | |
| All Shook Up | 7" | HMV | JO473 | 1957 | £75 | £150 | export |
| All Shook Up | 7" | HMV | POP359 | 1957 | £37.50 | £75 | gold label |
| All Shook Up | 7" | HMV | POP359 | 1957 | £10 | £20 | silver label |
| All Shook Up | 7" | RCA | RCA1088 | 1958 | £10 | £20 | tri-centre |
| All That I Am | 7" | RCA | RCA1545 | 1966 | £1.50 | £4 | |
| Aloha From Hawaii Via Satellite | LP | RCA | DPS2040 | 1973 | £5 | £12 | double |
| Aloha From Hawaii Via Satellite | LP | RCA | R4P5035 | 1973 | £8 | £20 | quad double |
| Aloha From Hawaii Via Satellite | LP | RCA | VPSX6089 | 1973 | £500 | £750 | US, with 'Chicken of the Sea' sticker |
| Amazing Grace | CD | RCA | RDJ66512 | 1994 | £15 | £30 | US promo sampler |
| Are You Lonesome Tonight | 7" | RCA | RCA1216 | 1961 | £1.50 | £4 | |
| Are You Lonesome Tonight (Laughing Version) | CD-s | RCA | PD49178 | 1991 | £2 | £5 | |
| Baby I Don't Care | 7" | RCA | RCAP332 | 1983 | £1.50 | £4 | picture disc |
| Best Of Elvis | 10" LP | HMV | DLP1159 | 1956 | £100 | £200 | |
| Big Boss Man | 7" | RCA | RCA1642 | 1967 | £2 | £5 | |
| Big Hunk Of Love | 78 | RCA | RCA1136 | 1959 | £15 | £30 | |
| Big Hunk Of Love | 7" | RCA | RCA1136 | 1959 | £4 | £8 | tri-centre |
| Blue Christmas | 7" | RCA | RCA1430 | 1964 | £1.50 | £4 | |
| Blue Hawaii | LP | RCA | LPM2426 | 1961 | £8 | £20 | US, black label, 'Long 3⅓ Play' |
| Blue Hawaii | LP | RCA | LPM2426 | 1961 | £20 | £40 | US, black label, 'Long 33⅓ Play', 'Contains The Twist Special' |
| Blue Hawaii | LP | RCA | LSP2426 | 1961 | £15 | £30 | US, black label, 'Living Stereo' |
| Blue Hawaii | LP | RCA | LSP2426 | 1961 | £25 | £50 | US, black label, 'Living Stereo', 'Contains The Twist Special' |
| Blue Hawaii | LP | RCA | RD27238 | 1961 | £4 | £10 | mono |
| Blue Hawaii | LP | RCA | SF5115 | 1961 | £8 | £20 | stereo |
| Blue Moon | 78 | HMV | POP272 | 1956 | £6 | £12 | |
| Blue Moon | 7" | HMV | POP272 | 1956 | £75 | £150 | gold label |
| Blue Moon | 7" | HMV | POP272 | 1956 | £50 | £100 | silver label |
| Blue Moon | 7" | RCA | RCA2601 | 1975 | £2 | £5 | |
| Blue River | 7" | RCA | RCA1504 | 1966 | £1.50 | £4 | |
| Blue Suede Shoes | 78 | HMV | POP213 | 1956 | £7.50 | £15 | |
| Blue Suede Shoes | 7" | HMV | 7M405 | 1956 | £75 | £150 | gold label |
| Blue Suede Shoes | 7" | HMV | 7M405 | 1956 | £50 | £100 | silver label |
| Bossa Nova Baby | 7" | RCA | RCA1374 | 1963 | £1.50 | £4 | |
| Californian Holiday | LP | RCA | RD7820 | 1966 | £5 | £12 | mono |
| Californian Holiday | LP | RCA | SF7820 | 1966 | £6 | £15 | stereo |
| Canadian Tribute | LP | RCA | KKL17065 | 1978 | £4 | £10 | US, yellow vinyl |
| Christmas Album | LP | RCA | LOC1035 | 1957 | £150 | £250 | US, black label, 'Long 33⅓ Play' |
| Christmas Album | LP | RCA | LPM1951 | 1958 | £25 | £50 | US, black label, 'Long 33⅓ Play' |
| Christmas Album | LP | RCA | RD27052 | 1957 | £30 | £60 | glossy cover |
| Christmas Album | LP | RCA | RD27052 | 1958 | £20 | £40 | matt cover |
| Clambake | LP | RCA | LPM3893 | 1967 | £37.50 | £75 | US, black label, 'Monaural' |
| Clambake | LP | RCA | LPM3893 | 1967 | £50 | £100 | US, black label, 'Monaural', with photo |

| Title | Format | Label | Catalogue | Year | Price | Price | Notes |
|---|---|---|---|---|---|---|---|
| Clambake | LP | RCA | LSP3893 | 1967 | £8 | £20 | US, black label, 'Stereo' |
| Clambake | LP | RCA | LSP3893 | 1967 | £20 | £40 | US, black label, 'Stereo', with photo |
| Clambake | LP | RCA | RD7917 | 1967 | £4 | £10 | mono |
| Clambake | LP | RCA | SF7917 | 1967 | £6 | £15 | stereo |
| Clean Up Your Own Backyard | 7" | RCA | RCA1869 | 1969 | £1.50 | £4 | |
| Collectors' Gold | 7" EP | RCA | RCX3 | 1983 | £2.50 | £6 | |
| Crying In The Chapel | 7" | RCA | RCA1455 | 1965 | £1.50 | £4 | |
| Date With Elvis | LP | RCA | LPM2011 | 1959 | £25 | £50 | US, black label, 'Long 33⅓ Play' |
| Date With Elvis | LP | RCA | LPM2011 | 1959 | £50 | £100 | US, black label, 'Long 33⅓ Play', titles on sticker |
| Date With Elvis | LP | RCA | RD27128 | 1959 | £15 | £30 | |
| Devil In Disguise | 7" | RCA | RCA1355 | 1963 | £1.50 | £4 | |
| Do The Clam | 7" | RCA | RCA1443 | 1965 | £1.50 | £4 | |
| Don't | 78 | RCA | RCA1043 | 1958 | £6 | £12 | |
| Don't | 7" | RCA | RCA1043 | 1958 | £4 | £8 | tri-centre |
| Don't Be Cruel | CD-s | RCA | 74321110612 | 1992 | £2 | £5 | |
| Don't Cry Daddy | 7" | RCA | RCA1916 | 1970 | £1.50 | £4 | picture sleeve |
| Double Trouble | LP | RCA | LPM/LSP3787 | 1967 | £20 | £40 | US, black label, with photo |
| Double Trouble | LP | RCA | LPM3787 | 1967 | £10 | £25 | US, black label, 'Monaural' |
| Double Trouble | LP | RCA | LSP3787 | 1967 | £8 | £20 | US, black label, 'Stereo' |
| Double Trouble | LP | RCA | RD7892 | 1967 | £4 | £10 | mono |
| Double Trouble | LP | RCA | SF7892 | 1967 | £6 | £15 | stereo |
| Easy Come Easy Go | 7" EP | RCA | RCX7187 | 1967 | £12.50 | £25 | |
| Elvis | LP | RCA | LPM1382 | 1956 | £25 | £50 | US, black label, 'Long 33⅓ Play' |
| Elvis | LP | RCA | LPM1382 | 1956 | £37.50 | £75 | US, black label, 'Long 33⅓ Play', album ads on cover |
| Elvis | LP | RCA | LPM1382 | 1956 | £500 | £750 | US, black label, 'Long 33⅓ Play', alternate 'Old Shep' |
| Elvis | LP | RCA | LPM1382 | 1956 | £75 | £150 | US, black label, 'Long 33⅓ Play', tracks listed as 'band' |
| Elvis | LP | RCA | LPM1382 | 1957 | £100 | £200 | US mispress – same song 6 times on one side |
| Elvis | LP | RCA | LPM1382 | 1957 | £100 | £200 | US mispress – unbanded |
| Elvis | LP | RCA | RD8011 | 1968 | £4 | £10 | mono |
| Elvis | LP | RCA | SF8378 | 1973 | £4 | £10 | |
| Elvis – A Golden Celebration | LP | RCA | PL85172 | 1985 | £10 | £25 | 6 LPs, boxed |
| Elvis – For LP Fans Only | LP | RCA | RD27120 | 1959 | £15 | £30 | |
| Elvis Aaron Presley | LP | RCA | CPL83699 | 1980 | £20 | £40 | 8 LPs, booklet, boxed |
| Elvis Aaron Presley Radio Station Sampler | LP | RCA | DJL13781 | 1980 | £8 | £20 | promo |
| Elvis Aaron Presley Sampler | LP | RCA | DJL13729 | 1980 | £8 | £20 | promo |
| Elvis For Everyone | LP | RCA | LPM3450 | 1965 | £8 | £20 | US, black label, 'Monaural' |
| Elvis For Everyone | LP | RCA | LSP3450 | 1965 | £10 | £25 | US, black label, 'Stereo' |
| Elvis For Everyone | LP | RCA | RD7752 | 1965 | £4 | £10 | mono |
| Elvis For Everyone | LP | RCA | SF7752 | 1965 | £6 | £15 | stereo |
| Elvis For You Vol. 1 | 7" EP | RCA | RCX7142 | 1964 | £12.50 | £25 | |
| Elvis For You Vol. 2 | 7" EP | RCA | RCX7143 | 1964 | £12.50 | £25 | |
| Elvis In Tender Mood | 7" EP | RCA | RCX135 | 1959 | £7.50 | £15 | tri-centre |
| Elvis Is Back | LP | RCA | LPM2231 | 1960 | £20 | £40 | US, black label, 'Long 33⅓ Play' |
| Elvis Is Back | LP | RCA | LPM2231 | 1960 | £30 | £60 | US, black label, 'Long 33⅓ Play', titles on sticker |
| Elvis Is Back | LP | RCA | LSP2231 | 1960 | £25 | £50 | US, black label, 'Living Stereo' |
| Elvis Is Back | LP | RCA | LSP2231 | 1960 | £37.50 | £75 | US, black label, 'Living Stereo', song titles on sticker |
| Elvis Is Back | LP | RCA | RD27171 | 1960 | £6 | £15 | gatefold mono |
| Elvis Is Back | LP | RCA | SF5060 | 1960 | £10 | £25 | gatefold stereo |
| Elvis Now | LP | RCA | SF8266 | 1972 | £4 | £10 | |
| Elvis Presley | LP | RCA | LPM1254 | 1956 | £25 | £50 | US, black label, 'Long 33⅓ Play', dark pink 'Elvis' on cover |
| Elvis Presley | LP | RCA | LPM1254 | 1956 | £37.50 | £75 | US, black label, 'Long 33⅓ Play', light pink 'Elvis' on cover |
| Elvis Presley | LP | St. Michael | IMP113 | 1978 | £10 | £25 | |
| Elvis Presley | 7" EP | RCA | RCX104 | 1957 | £7.50 | £15 | tri-centre |
| Elvis Presley Interview Record | LP | RCA | PL80835 | | £8 | £20 | promo |
| Elvis Presley Story | LP | Watermark Inc | EPS1A13B | 1977 | £330 | £500 | promo 13 LP boxed set |
| Elvis Sails | 7" EP | RCA | RCX131 | 1959 | £10 | £20 | tri-centre |

| Title | Format | Label | Catalogue | Year | Price | Price | Notes |
|---|---|---|---|---|---|---|---|
| Elvis Sings Christmas Songs | 7" EP | RCA | RCX121 | 1958 | £30 | £60 | . round centre, gatefold sleeve |
| Elvis Sings Christmas Songs | 7" EP | RCA | RCX121 | 1958 | £10 | £20 | tri-centre |
| Elvis Today | LP | RCA | APD11039 | 1975 | £20 | £40 | .US quad (black label) |
| Elvis Today | LP | RCA | APD11039 | 1975 | £37.50 | £75 | US quad (orange label) |
| EP Collection | 7" EP | RCA | EP1 | 1982 | £25 | £50 | 11 EP set |
| EP Collection Vol. 2 | 7" EP | RCA | EP2 | 1983 | £25 | £50 | 11 EP set |
| Flaming Star & Summer Kisses | LP | RCA | RD7723 | 1965 | £10 | £25 | |
| Follow That Dream | 7" EP | RCA | RCX211 | 1962 | £4 | £8 | |
| Follow That Dream | 7" EP | RCA | RCX211 | 1962 | £37.50 | £75 | ... mispressed 2nd side |
| Fool Such As I | 78 | RCA | RCA1113 | 1959 | £12.50 | £25 | |
| Fool Such As I | 7" | RCA | RCA1113 | 1959 | £4 | £8 | tri-centre |
| For LP Fans Only | LP | RCA | LPM1990 | 1959 | £37.50 | £75 | US, black label, 'Long 33⅓ Play' |
| For The Asking | CD | RCA | ND90513 | 1990 | £5 | £12 | |
| Four Double Features | CD | RCA | | 1993 | £37.50 | £75 | US 4 picture disc set in film cannister |
| Frankie And Johnny | LP | RCA | LPM/LSP3553 | 1966 | £20 | £40 | . US, black label, with photo |
| Frankie And Johnny | LP | RCA | LPM3553 | 1966 | £8 | £20 | US, black label, 'Monaural' |
| Frankie And Johnny | LP | RCA | LSP3553 | 1966 | £8 | £20 | US, black label, 'Stereo' |
| Frankie And Johnny | LP | RCA | RD7793 | 1966 | £4 | £10 | mono |
| Frankie And Johnny | LP | RCA | SF7793 | 1966 | £6 | £15 | stereo |
| Frankie And Johnny | 7" | RCA | RCA1509 | 1966 | £1.50 | £4 | |
| From Elvis In Memphis | LP | Mobile Fidelity | MFSL1059 | 1980 | £4 | £10 | US audiophile |
| From Elvis In Memphis | LP | RCA | RD8029 | 1969 | £5 | £12 | mono |
| From Elvis In Memphis | LP | RCA | SF8029 | 1969 | £4 | £10 | stereo |
| From Memphis To Vegas – From Vegas To Memphis | LP | RCA | SF8080/1 | 1970 | £5 | £12 | double |
| Fun In Acapulco | LP | RCA | LPM2756 | 1963 | £8 | £20 | US, black label, 'Mono' |
| Fun In Acapulco | LP | RCA | LSP2756 | 1963 | £10 | £25 | US, black label, 'Living Stereo' |
| Fun In Acapulco | LP | RCA | RD7609 | 1963 | £4 | £10 | mono |
| Fun In Acapulco | LP | RCA | SF7609 | 1963 | £6 | £15 | stereo |
| G.I. Blues | LP | RCA | LPM2256 | 1960 | £8 | £20 | US, black label, 'Long 33⅓ Play' |
| G.I. Blues | LP | RCA | LSP2256 | 1960 | £15 | £30 | US, black label, 'Living Stereo' |
| G.I. Blues | LP | RCA | RD27192 | 1960 | £4 | £10 | mono |
| G.I. Blues | LP | RCA | SF5078 | 1960 | £10 | £25 | stereo |
| G.I. Blues: The Alternate Takes | 7" EP | RCA | RCX1 | 1982 | £4 | £8 | |
| G.I. Blues: The Alternate Takes Vol. 2 | 7" EP | RCA | RCX2 | 1982 | £2.50 | £6 | |
| Girl Happy | LP | RCA | LPM3338 | 1965 | £8 | £20 | US, black label, 'Monaural' |
| Girl Happy | LP | RCA | LSP3338 | 1965 | £10 | £25 | US, black label, 'Stereo' |
| Girl Happy | LP | RCA | RD7714 | 1965 | £4 | £10 | mono |
| Girl Happy | LP | RCA | SF7714 | 1965 | £6 | £15 | stereo |
| Girl Of My Best Friend | 78 | RCA | RCA1194 | 1960 | £180 | £300 | |
| Girl Of My Best Friend | 7" | RCA | RCA1194 | 1960 | £1.50 | £4 | |
| Girls Girls Girls | LP | RCA | LPM2621 | 1962 | £8 | £20 | US, black label, 'Long 33⅓ Play' |
| Girls Girls Girls | LP | RCA | LPM2621 | 1962 | £30 | £60 | US, black label, 'Long 33⅓ Play', with calendar |
| Girls Girls Girls | LP | RCA | LSP2621 | 1962 | £15 | £30 | US, black label, 'Living Stereo' |
| Girls Girls Girls | LP | RCA | LSP2621 | 1962 | £37.50 | £75 | US, black label, 'Living Stereo', with calendar |
| Girls Girls Girls | LP | RCA | RD7534 | 1963 | £4 | £10 | mono |
| Girls Girls Girls | LP | RCA | SF7534 | 1963 | £6 | £15 | stereo |
| Gold 16 Series | 7" | RCA | RCA2694-2709 | 1977 | £20 | £40 | . 16 x 7" in cardboard carrier |
| Gold Records Volume Two | CD | RCA | PCD15197 | 1984 | £75 | £150 | US promo picture disc |
| Golden Boy Elvis | LP | Hor Zu | SHZT521 | 1965 | £62.50 | £125 | German |
| Golden Boy Elvis | LP | RCA | 25037 | 1965 | £500 | £750 | Swiss |
| Golden Records | LP | RCA | LPM1707 | 1958 | £30 | £60 | US, black label, 'Long 33⅓ Play', title in blue print |
| Golden Records | LP | RCA | RB16069 | 1958 | £25 | £50 | gatefold sleeve, 4 photo pages |
| Golden Records | LP | RCA | RB16069 | 1958 | £10 | £25 | gatefold sleeve, 2 photo pages |
| Golden Records | LP | RCA | RB16069 | 1958 | £6 | £15 | no photo pages |
| Golden Records Vol. 2 | LP | RCA | LPM2075 | 1960 | £25 | £50 | US, black label, 'Long 33⅓ Play' |
| Golden Records Vol. 2 | LP | RCA | RD27159 | 1959 | £10 | £25 | |
| Golden Records Vol. 3 | LP | RCA | LPM/LSP2765 | 1963 | £25 | £50 | . US, black label, with book |
| Golden Records Vol. 3 | LP | RCA | LPM2765 | 1963 | £8 | £20 | US, black label, 'Mono' |
| Golden Records Vol. 3 | LP | RCA | LSP2765 | 1963 | £10 | £25 | US, black label, 'Living Stereo' |

| Title | Format | Label | Catalogue | Year | Price | Price | Notes |
|---|---|---|---|---|---|---|---|
| Golden Records Vol. 3 | LP | RCA | RD7630 | 1964 | £4 | £10 | mono |
| Golden Records Vol. 3 | LP | RCA | SF7630 | 1964 | £6 | £15 | stereo |
| Golden Records Vol. 4 | LP | RCA | LPM3921 | 1968 | £180 | £300 | US, black label, 'Monaural' |
| Golden Records Vol. 4 | LP | RCA | LPM3921 | 1968 | £210 | £350 | US, black label, 'Monaural', with photo |
| Golden Records Vol. 4 | LP | RCA | LSP3921 | 1968 | £8 | £20 | US, black label, 'Stereo' |
| Golden Records Vol. 4 | LP | RCA | LSP3921 | 1968 | £37.50 | £75 | US, black label, 'Stereo', with photo |
| Golden Records Vol. 4 | LP | RCA | RD/SF7924 | 1968 | £6 | £15 | |
| Golden Records Vol. 4 | LP | RCA | RD/SF7924 | 1968 | £10 | £25 | Never Ending listed on sleeve |
| Golden Records Vol. 5 | CD | RCA | PD84941 | 1986 | £5 | £12 | |
| Good Luck Charm | 7" | RCA | RCA1280 | 1962 | £1.50 | £4 | |
| Good Rockin' Tonight | 78 | Sun | 210 | 1954 | £100 | £200 | US, best auctioned |
| Good Rockin' Tonight | 7" EP | HMV | 7EG8256 | 1957 | £50 | £100 | |
| Good Rockin' Tonight | 7" | Sun | 210 | 1954 | £330 | £500 | US, best auctioned |
| Good Times | LP | RCA | APL10475 | 1974 | £4 | £10 | |
| Got A Lot Of Living To Do | 78 | RCA | RCA1020 | 1957 | £6 | £12 | |
| Got A Lot Of Living To Do | 7" | RCA | RCA1020 | 1957 | £4 | £8 | tri-centre |
| Greatest Hits | LP | RCA/Readers Digest | GELV6A | 1975 | £10 | £25 | 7 LPs, booklet, boxed |
| Guitar Man | 7" | RCA | RCA1663 | 1968 | £1.50 | £4 | |
| Hard Headed Woman | 78 | RCA | RCA1070 | 1958 | £7.50 | £15 | |
| Hard Headed Woman | 7" | RCA | RCA1070 | 1958 | £4 | £8 | tri-centre |
| Harem Holiday | LP | RCA | RD7767 | 1965 | £4 | £10 | mono |
| Harum Holiday | LP | RCA | SF7767 | 1965 | £6 | £15 | stereo |
| Harum Scarum | LP | RCA | LPM/LSP3468 | 1965 | £20 | £40 | US, black label, with photo |
| Harum Scarum | LP | RCA | LPM3468 | 1965 | £8 | £20 | US, black label, 'Monaural' |
| Harum Scarum | LP | RCA | LSP3468 | 1965 | £8 | £20 | US, black label, 'Stereo' |
| Having Fun On Stage | LP | Boxcar | | 1974 | £37.50 | £75 | US |
| Having Fun On Stage | LP | RCA | APM10818 | 1974 | £4 | £10 | |
| He Touched Me | LP | RCA | SF8275 | 1972 | £4 | £10 | |
| Heartbreak Hotel | CD-s | RCA | PD49467 | 1989 | £2 | £5 | |
| Heartbreak Hotel | 78 | HMV | POP182 | 1956 | £6 | £12 | |
| Heartbreak Hotel | 7" | HMV | 7M385 | 1956 | £75 | £150 | gold label |
| Heartbreak Hotel | 7" | HMV | 7M385 | 1956 | £50 | £100 | silver label |
| His Hand In Mine | LP | RCA | LPM2328 | 1961 | £10 | £25 | US, black label, 'Long 33⅓ Play' |
| His Hand In Mine | LP | RCA | LSP2328 | 1961 | £20 | £40 | US, black label, 'Living Stereo' |
| His Hand In Mine | LP | RCA | RD27211 | 1960 | £6 | £15 | mono |
| His Hand In Mine | LP | RCA | SF5094 | 1960 | £10 | £25 | stereo |
| His Latest Flame | 7" | RCA | RCA1258 | 1961 | £1.50 | £4 | |
| Honeymoon Companion | CD | RCA | RDJ661242 | 1992 | £20 | £40 | US promo |
| Hound Dog | 78 | HMV | POP249 | 1956 | £6 | £12 | |
| Hound Dog | 78 | RCA | RCA1095 | 1958 | £25 | £50 | |
| Hound Dog | 7" | HMV | 7MC50 | 1957 | £100 | £200 | export |
| Hound Dog | 7" | HMV | POP249 | 1956 | £75 | £100 | gold label |
| Hound Dog | 7" | HMV | POP249 | 1956 | £50 | £100 | silver label |
| Hound Dog | 7" | RCA | RCA1095 | 1958 | £12.50 | £25 | tri-centre |
| How Great Thou Art | LP | RCA | LPM3758 | 1967 | £10 | £25 | US, black label, 'Monaural' |
| How Great Thou Art | LP | RCA | LSP3758 | 1967 | £8 | £20 | US, black label, 'Stereo' |
| How Great Thou Art | LP | RCA | RD/SF7867 | 1967 | £6 | £15 | |
| I Want You I Need You I Love You | 78 | HMV | POP235 | 1956 | £6 | £12 | |
| I Want You I Need You I Love You | 7" | HMV | 7M424 | 1956 | £75 | £150 | gold label |
| I Want You I Need You I Love You | 7" | HMV | 7M424 | 1956 | £50 | £100 | silver label |
| I Want You I Need You I Love You | 7" | HMV | 7MC45 | 1957 | £100 | £200 | export |
| I'm Left You're Right She's Gone | 78 | HMV | POP428 | 1958 | £6 | £12 | |
| I'm Left You're Right She's Gone | 78 | Sun | 217 | 1955 | £100 | £200 | US, best auctioned |
| I'm Left You're Right She's Gone | 7" | HMV | POP428 | 1957 | £25 | £50 | |
| I'm Left You're Right She's Gone | 7" | Sun | 217 | 1955 | £330 | £500 | US, best auctioned |
| If Every Day Was Like Christmas | 7" | RCA | RCA1557 | 1966 | £1.50 | £4 | |
| If I Can Dream | 7" | RCA | RCA1795 | 1969 | £1.50 | £4 | |
| In The Ghetto | 7" | RCA | RCA1831 | 1969 | £1.50 | £4 | |
| Indescribably Blue | 7" | RCA | RCA1565 | 1967 | £1.50 | £4 | |
| International Hotel, Las Vegas, Presents Elvis Presley | LP | RCA | LSP6020 | 1970 | £330 | £500 | US double LP, 7", various inserts, boxed |
| It Happened At The World's Fair | LP | RCA | LPM2697 | 1963 | £10 | £25 | US, black label, 'Long 33⅓ Play' |
| It Happened At The World's Fair | LP | RCA | LPM2697 | 1963 | £50 | £100 | US, black label, 'Long 33⅓ Play', with photo |
| It Happened At The World's Fair | LP | RCA | LSP2697 | 1963 | £15 | £30 | US, black label, 'Living Stereo' |
| It Happened At The World's Fair | LP | RCA | LSP2697 | 1963 | £62.50 | £125 | US, black label, 'Living Stereo', with photo |
| It Happened At The World's Fair | LP | RCA | RD7565 | 1963 | £4 | £10 | mono |
| It Happened At The World's Fair | LP | RCA | SF7565 | 1963 | £6 | £15 | stereo |
| It's Now Or Never | 7" | RCA | RCA1207 | 1960 | £1.50 | £4 | |

| Title | Format | Label | Cat. No. | Year | Low | High | Notes |
|---|---|---|---|---|---|---|---|
| Jailhouse Rock | LP | MGM | | 1957 | £50 | £100 | ... US red vinyl promo with Leiber & Stoller interview |
| Jailhouse Rock | 78 | RCA | RCA1028 | 1958 | £6 | £12 | |
| Jailhouse Rock | 7" EP | RCA | RCX106 | 1958 | £5 | £10 | ... tri-centre |
| Jailhouse Rock | 7" | RCA | RCA1028 | 1958 | £4 | £8 | ... tri-centre |
| Jailhouse Rock | 7" | RCA | RCAMAXI2153 | 1971 | £1.50 | £4 | |
| Jailhouse Rock | 7" | RCA | RCAP1028 | 1983 | £1.50 | £4 | ...picture disc |
| Jailhouse Rock | 7" | RCA | RCAP1028 | 1983 | £2 | £5 | ....picture disc, B side credits 'Hound Dog' |
| Jailhouse Rock (B side not Elvis) | 78 | Decca | | 1958 | £37.50 | £75 | ...promo |
| Kentucky Rain | 7" | RCA | RCA1949 | 1970 | £1.50 | £4 | ... picture sleeve |
| Kid Galahad | 7" EP | RCA | RCX7106 | 1963 | £5 | £10 | |
| King Creole | LP | RCA | LPM1884 | 1958 | £30 | £60 | US, black label, 'Long 33⅓ Play' |
| King Creole | LP | RCA | LPM1884 | 1958 | £62.50 | £125 | US, black label, 'Long 33⅓ Play', with bonus photo |
| King Creole | LP | RCA | RD27088 | 1958 | £10 | £25 | ....................mono |
| King Creole | 78 | RCA | RCA1081 | 1958 | £7.50 | £15 | |
| King Creole | 7" | RCA | RCA1081 | 1958 | £5 | £10 | ............ tri-centre |
| King Creole Vol. 1 | 7" EP | RCA | RCX117 | 1958 | £5 | £10 | .. tri-centre, black label |
| King Creole Vol. 1 | 7" EP | RCA | RCX117 | 1969 | £2.50 | £6 | ........orange label |
| King Creole Vol. 2 | 7" EP | RCA | RCX118 | 1958 | £5 | £10 | ............ tri-centre |
| King Of Rock And Roll – Instore Sampler | CD | RCA | KCDP51096 | 1992 | £20 | £40 | ..... Canadian promo |
| Kiss Me Quick | 7" | RCA | RCA1375 | 1963 | £1.50 | £4 | |
| Kissin' Cousins | LP | RCA | LPM/LSP2894 | 1964 | £25 | £50 | US, black label, no photo on cover |
| Kissin' Cousins | LP | RCA | LPM2894 | 1964 | £8 | £20 | US, black label, 'Mono', with photo on cover |
| Kissin' Cousins | LP | RCA | LSP2894 | 1964 | £10 | £25 | US, black label, 'Living Stereo', photo on cover |
| Kissin' Cousins | LP | RCA | RD7645 | 1964 | £4 | £10 | ....................mono |
| Kissin' Cousins | LP | RCA | SF7645 | 1964 | £6 | £15 | ....................stereo |
| Kissin' Cousins | 7" | RCA | RCA1404 | 1964 | £1.50 | £4 | |
| Lawdy Miss Clawdy | 78 | HMV | POP408 | 1957 | £7.50 | £15 | |
| Lawdy Miss Clawdy | 7" | HMV | POP408 | 1957 | £20 | £40 | |
| Legend | CD | RCA | PD89000 | 1983 | £87.50 | £175 | ... 3 gold discs, boxed |
| Legend | CD | RCA | PD89000 | 1983 | £25 | £50 | ... 3 silver discs, boxed |
| Little Less Conversation | 7" | RCA | RCA1768 | 1968 | £2 | £5 | |
| Long Legged Girl | 7" | RCA | RCA1616 | 1967 | £2 | £5 | |
| Love In Las Vegas | 7" EP | RCA | RCX7141 | 1964 | £5 | £10 | |
| Love Letters | 7" | RCA | RCA1526 | 1966 | £1.50 | £4 | |
| Love Letters From Elvis | LP | RCA | SF8202 | 1971 | £4 | £10 | |
| Love Machine | 7" | RCA | RCA1593 | 1967 | £2 | £5 | |
| Love Me Tender | 78 | HMV | POP253 | 1956 | £6 | £12 | |
| Love Me Tender | 7" EP | HMV | 7EG8199 | 1957 | £37.50 | £75 | |
| Love Me Tender | 7" | HMV | JO465 | 1957 | £100 | £200 | ............export |
| Love Me Tender | 7" | HMV | POP253 | 1956 | £75 | £100 | ............gold label |
| Love Me Tender | 7" | HMV | POP253 | 1956 | £50 | £100 | ........ silver label |
| Loving You | LP | RCA | LPM1515 | 1957 | £30 | £60 | US, black label, 'Long 33⅓ Play' |
| Loving You | 78 | RCA | RCA1013 | 1957 | £6 | £12 | |
| Loving You | 7" | RCA | RCA1013 | 1957 | £5 | £10 | ............ tri-centre |
| Loving You | 10" LP | RCA | RC24001 | 1957 | £20 | £40 | |
| Mean Woman Blues | CD-s | RCA | PD49474 | 1989 | £2 | £5 | |
| Milkcow Blues Boogie | 78 | Sun | 215 | 1955 | £100 | £200 | ... US, best auctioned |
| Milkcow Blues Boogie | 7" | Sun | 215 | 1955 | £330 | £500 | ... US, best auctioned |
| Moody Blue | LP | RCA | AFL12428 | 1977 | £50 | £100 | ... US, black vinyl |
| Mystery Train | 78 | HMV | POP295 | 1957 | £10 | £20 | |
| Mystery Train | 78 | Sun | 223 | 1955 | £100 | £200 | ... US, best auctioned |
| Mystery Train | 7" | HMV | 7MC42 | 1957 | £100 | £200 | ..................export |
| Mystery Train | 7" | HMV | POP295 | 1957 | £75 | £150 | ............gold label |
| Mystery Train | 7" | HMV | POP295 | 1957 | £50 | £100 | ........ silver label |
| Mystery Train | 7" | Sun | 223 | 1955 | £250 | £400 | ... US, best auctioned |
| O Sole Mio | 7" | RCA | 479314 | 1961 | £7.50 | £15 | .........sung in Italian |
| On Stage February 1970 | LP | RCA | SF8128 | 1970 | £4 | £10 | |
| One Broken Heart For Sale | 7" | RCA | RCA1337 | 1963 | £1.50 | £4 | |
| One Night | 78 | RCA | RCA1100 | 1959 | £7.50 | £15 | |
| One Night | 7" | RCA | RCA1100 | 1959 | £2 | £5 | ............ tri-centre |
| Paradise Hawaiian Style | LP | RCA | LPM3643 | 1966 | £8 | £20 | US, black label, 'Monaural' |
| Paradise Hawaiian Style | LP | RCA | LSP3643 | 1966 | £8 | £20 | US, black label, 'Stereo' |
| Paradise Hawaiian Style | LP | RCA | RD7810 | 1966 | £4 | £10 | ....................mono |
| Paradise Hawaiian Style | LP | RCA | SF7810 | 1966 | £6 | £15 | ....................stereo |
| Paralyzed | 78 | HMV | POP378 | 1957 | £6 | £12 | |
| Paralyzed | 7" | HMV | POP378 | 1957 | £30 | £60 | ............gold label |
| Paralyzed | 7" | HMV | POP378 | 1957 | £25 | £50 | ........ silver label |
| Peace In The Valley | 7" EP | RCA | RCX101 | 1957 | £10 | £20 | ............ tri-centre |
| Pot Luck | LP | RCA | RD27265 | 1962 | £4 | £10 | ....................mono |
| Pot Luck | LP | RCA | SF5135 | 1962 | £8 | £20 | ....................stereo |
| Pot Luck With Elvis | LP | RCA | LPM2523 | 1962 | £15 | £30 | US, black label, 'Long 33⅓ Play' |
| Pot Luck With Elvis | LP | RCA | LSP2523 | 1962 | £20 | £40 | US, black label, 'Living Stereo' |

| Title | Format | Label | Catalogue | Year | Price | Price | Notes |
|---|---|---|---|---|---|---|---|
| Promised Land | LP | RCA | APD10873 | 1974 | £20 | £40 | US quad (black label) |
| Promised Land | LP | RCA | APD10873 | 1974 | £37.50 | £75 | US quad (orange label) |
| Promised Land | LP | RCA | APL10873 | 1975 | £4 | £10 | |
| Pure Elvis | LP | RCA | DJL13455 | 1980 | £100 | £200 | US promo |
| Radio Special | CD | RCA | RDJ661212 | 1992 | £20 | £40 | US promo |
| Rags To Riches | 7" | RCA | RCA2084 | 1971 | £1.50 | £4 | picture sleeve |
| Raised On Rock | LP | RCA | APL10388 | 1973 | £50 | £100 | UK pressing in US sleeve |
| Recorded Live On Stage In Memphis | LP | RCA | APD10606 | 1974 | £62.50 | £125 | US quad |
| Return To Sender | 7" | RCA | RCA1320 | 1962 | £1.50 | £4 | |
| Rip It Up | 78 | HMV | POP305 | 1957 | £12.50 | £25 | |
| Rip It Up | 7" | HMV | POP305 | 1957 | £75 | £150 | gold label |
| Rip It Up | 7" | HMV | POP305 | 1957 | £50 | £100 | silver label |
| Rock 'n' Roll | LP | HMV | CLP1093 | 1956 | £100 | £200 | |
| Rock 'n' Roll No. 2 | LP | HMV | CLP1105 | 1956 | £100 | £200 | |
| Rock 'n' Roll No. 2 | LP | RCA | RD7528 | 1962 | £5 | £12 | mono |
| Rock 'n' Roll No. 2 | LP | RCA | SF7528 | 1962 | £8 | £20 | stereo |
| Rock-A-Hula Baby | 7" | RCA | RCA1270 | 1962 | £1.50 | £4 | |
| Rocker Elvis | CD | RCA | PD85182 | 1985 | £5 | £12 | |
| Roustabout | LP | RCA | LPM/LSP2999 | 1964 | £10 | £25 | US, black label |
| Roustabout | LP | RCA | LSP2999 | 1964 | £150 | £250 | US, black label, 'Living Stereo' |
| Roustabout | LP | RCA | RD7678 | 1965 | £4 | £10 | mono |
| Roustabout | LP | RCA | SF7678 | 1965 | £6 | £15 | stereo |
| Santa Bring My Baby Back | 78 | RCA | RCA1025 | 1957 | £6 | £12 | |
| Santa Bring My Baby Back | 7" | RCA | RCA1025 | 1957 | £7.50 | £15 | tri-centre |
| Shake Rattle And Roll – 18 Number One Hits | CD | RCA | 6382RDJ | 1992 | £20 | £40 | US promo |
| She's Not You | 7" | RCA | RCA1303 | 1962 | £1.50 | £4 | |
| Singer Presents Elvis | LP | RCA | PRS279 | 1968 | £6 | £15 | US promo |
| Singer Presents Elvis | LP | RCA | PRS279 | 1968 | £8 | £20 | US, with photo |
| Sings The Wonderful World Of Christmas | LP | RCA | SF8221 | 1971 | £4 | £10 | |
| Sings The Wonderful World Of Christmas | CD | RCA | ND81936 | 1990 | £5 | £12 | |
| Something For Everybody | LP | RCA | LPM2370 | 1961 | £10 | £25 | US, black label, 'Long 33⅓ Play' |
| Something For Everybody | LP | RCA | LSP2370 | 1961 | £20 | £40 | US, black label, 'Living Stereo' |
| Something For Everybody | LP | RCA | RD27244 | 1961 | £5 | £12 | mono |
| Something For Everybody | LP | RCA | SF5106 | 1961 | £8 | £20 | stereo |
| Sound Of Your Cry | 7" | RCA | RCAP232 | 1982 | £1.50 | £4 | picture disc |
| Special Palm Sunday Programme | LP | RCA | SP33461 | 1967 | £400 | £600 | US promo |
| Speedway | LP | RCA | LPM3989 | 1968 | £250 | £400 | US, black label, 'Monaural' |
| Speedway | LP | RCA | LSP3989 | 1968 | £8 | £20 | US, black label, 'Stereo' |
| Speedway | LP | RCA | LSP3989 | 1968 | £25 | £50 | US, black label, 'Stereo', with photo |
| Speedway | LP | RCA | RD7957 | 1968 | £6 | £15 | mono |
| Speedway | LP | RCA | SF7957 | 1968 | £8 | £20 | stereo |
| Spinout | LP | RCA | LPM/LSP3702 | 1966 | £20 | £40 | US, black label, with photo |
| Spinout | LP | RCA | LPM3702 | 1966 | £8 | £20 | US, black label, 'Monaural' |
| Spinout | LP | RCA | LSP3702 | 1966 | £8 | £20 | US, black label, 'Stereo' |
| Strictly Elvis | 7" EP | RCA | RCX175 | 1959 | £6 | £12 | tri-centre |
| Stuck On You | CD-s | RCA | PD49596 | 1989 | £2 | £5 | |
| Stuck On You | 78 | RCA | RCA1187 | 1960 | £50 | £100 | |
| Stuck On You | 7" | RCA | RCA1187 | 1960 | £1.50 | £4 | |
| Such A Night | 7" EP | RCA | RCX190 | 1960 | £5 | £10 | |
| Such A Night | 7" | RCA | RCA1411 | 1964 | £1.50 | £4 | |
| Sun Sessions | CD | RCA | C8812 | 1988 | £8 | £20 | box set |
| Surrender | 7" | RCA | RCA1227 | 1961 | £1.50 | £4 | |
| Suspicious Minds | 7" | RCA | RCA1900 | 1969 | £1.50 | £4 | picture sleeve |
| Take Good Care Of Her | 7" | RCA | APBO0196 | 1974 | £50 | £100 | |
| Tell Me Why | 7" | RCA | RCA1489 | 1965 | £2 | £5 | |
| That's All Right | 78 | Sun | 209 | 1954 | £150 | £250 | US |
| That's All Right | 7" | Sun | 209 | 1954 | £330 | £500 | US, best auctioned |
| That's The Way It Is | CD | Mobile Fidelity | UDCD560 | 1993 | £6 | £15 | US audiophile |
| There Goes My Everything | 7" | RCA | RCA2060 | 1971 | £1.50 | £4 | picture sleeve |
| There's Always Me | 7" | RCA | RCA1628 | 1967 | £10 | £20 | |
| Tickle Me Vol. 1 | 7" EP | RCA | RCX7173 | 1965 | £5 | £10 | |
| Tickle Me Vol. 2 | 7" EP | RCA | RCX7174 | 1965 | £5 | £10 | |
| Today | LP | RCA | RS1011 | 1975 | £4 | £10 | |
| Too Much | 78 | HMV | POP330 | 1957 | £6 | £12 | |
| Too Much | 7" | HMV | JO466 | 1957 | £100 | £200 | export |
| Too Much | 7" | HMV | POP330 | 1957 | £50 | £100 | gold label |
| Too Much | 7" | HMV | POP330 | 1957 | £37.50 | £75 | silver label |
| Torna A Surrento | 7" | RCA | 1160 | 1960 | £7.50 | £15 | sung in Italian |
| Touch Of Gold | 7" EP | RCA | RCX1045 | 1959 | £7.50 | £15 | tri-centre |
| Touch Of Gold Vol. 2 | 7" EP | RCA | RCX1048 | 1960 | £20 | £40 | tri-centre |
| Truth About Me | 78 | Weekend Mail | | 1957 | £50 | £100 | cardboard folder |
| TV Guide Presents Elvis Presley | 7" | RCA | GBMW8705 | 1956 | £2500 | £4000 | promo, best auctioned |
| U.S. Male | 7" | RCA | RCA1688 | 1968 | £2 | £4 | |
| Until It's Time For You To Go | 7" | RCA | RCA2188 | 1972 | £1.50 | £4 | picture sleeve |
| Viva Las Vegas | 7" | RCA | RCA1390 | 1964 | £1.50 | £4 | |
| Wear My Ring Around Your Neck | 78 | RCA | RCA1058 | 1958 | £6 | £12 | |
| Wear My Ring Around Your Neck | 7" | RCA | RCA1058 | 1958 | £4 | £8 | tri-centre |

694

| Title | Format | Label | Catalog | Year | | | Notes |
|---|---|---|---|---|---|---|---|
| Wild In The Country | 7" | RCA | RCA1244 | 1961 | £1.50 | £4 | |
| Wonderful World Of Elvis Presley | LP | St. Michael | IMP204 | 1978 | £20 | £40 | |
| Wooden Heart | 7" | RCA | RCA1226 | 1961 | £1.50 | £4 | |
| Worldwide Gold Award Hits Vol. 1 | LP | RCA | LPM6401 | 1970 | £10 | £25 | 4 LPs, booklet, boxed |
| Worldwide Gold Award Hits Vol. 2 | LP | RCA | LPM6402 | 1971 | £15 | £30 | 4 LPs, piece of cloth, boxed |
| You'll Never Walk Alone | 7" | RCA | RCA1747 | 1968 | £2 | £5 | |
| Your Time Hasn't Come Yet Baby | 7" | RCA | RCA1714 | 1968 | £1.50 | £4 | |

## PRESLEY, ELVIS & JANIS MARTIN

| Title | Format | Label | Catalog | Year | | | Notes |
|---|---|---|---|---|---|---|---|
| Elvis And Janis | 10" LP | Teal | T31077 | 1958 | £1050 | £1500 | South African |

## PRESLEY, REG

| Title | Format | Label | Catalog | Year | | | Notes |
|---|---|---|---|---|---|---|---|
| It's Down To You Marianne | 7" | CBS | 1478 | 1973 | £2.50 | £6 | |
| Lucinda Lee | 7" | Page One | POF131 | 1969 | £2.50 | £6 | |

## PRESLEY, SID EXPERIENCE

| Title | Format | Label | Catalog | Year | | | Notes |
|---|---|---|---|---|---|---|---|
| Cold Turkey | 12" | Sid Presley Experience | SPE41 | 1984 | £2.50 | £6 | |
| Hup 234 | 7" | I.D. | EYE4 | 1984 | £2 | £5 | |

## PRESS GANG

| Title | Format | Label | Catalog | Year | | | Notes |
|---|---|---|---|---|---|---|---|
| Press Gang | LP | Hawk | HALP135 | 1976 | £5 | £12 | Irish |

## PRESTIGE BLUES SWINGERS

| Title | Format | Label | Catalog | Year | | | Notes |
|---|---|---|---|---|---|---|---|
| Outskirts Of Town | LP | Esquire | 32110 | 1961 | £8 | £20 | |

## PRESTON, BILLY

| Title | Format | Label | Catalog | Year | | | Notes |
|---|---|---|---|---|---|---|---|
| All That I've Got | 7" | Apple | 21 | 1970 | £1.50 | £4 | |
| All That I've Got | 7" | Apple | 21 | 1970 | £7.50 | £15 | picture sleeve |
| Billy's Bag | 7" | President | PT263 | 1969 | £1.50 | £4 | |
| Billy's Bag | 7" | Sue | WI4012 | 1966 | £4 | £8 | |
| Encouraging Words | LP | Apple | SAPCOR14 | 1969 | £8 | £20 | |
| Greazee | 7" | Soul City | SC107 | 1969 | £2.50 | £6 | |
| In The Midnight Hour | 7" | Capitol | CL15458 | 1966 | £1.50 | £4 | |
| Most Exciting Organ Ever | LP | Sue | ILP935 | 1966 | £15 | £30 | |
| Sunny | 7" | Capitol | CL15471 | 1966 | £1.50 | £4 | |
| That's The Way God Planned It | LP | Apple | SAPCOR9 | 1969 | £6 | £15 | |
| That's The Way God Planned It | LP | Apple | ST3359 | 1969 | £10 | £25 | US, face close-up on cover |
| That's The Way God Planned It | LP | Apple | ST3359 | 1969 | £4 | £10 | US, multiple Prestons on cover |
| That's The Way God Planned It | 7" | Apple | 12 | 1969 | £1.50 | £4 | |
| That's The Way God Planned It | 7" | Apple | 12 | 1969 | £2.50 | £6 | picture sleeve |
| Wildest Organ In Town | LP | Capitol | (S)T2532 | 1966 | £4 | £10 | |

## PRESTON, DON

| Title | Format | Label | Catalog | Year | | | Notes |
|---|---|---|---|---|---|---|---|
| Bluse | LP | A&M | SP4155 | 1969 | £6 | £15 | US |

## PRESTON, EARL

| Title | Format | Label | Catalog | Year | | | Notes |
|---|---|---|---|---|---|---|---|
| That's For Sure | 7" | Fontana | TF481 | 1964 | £4 | £8 | |
| Watch Your Step | 7" | Fontana | TF406 | 1963 | £4 | £8 | |

## PRESTON, JOHNNY

| Title | Format | Label | Catalog | Year | | | Notes |
|---|---|---|---|---|---|---|---|
| Big Chief Heartache | 7" | Mercury | AMT1145 | 1961 | £2.50 | £6 | |
| Charming Billy | 7" | Mercury | AMT1114 | 1960 | £1.50 | £4 | |
| Come Rock With Me | LP | Mercury | MG2/SR60609 | 1961 | £15 | £30 | US |
| Cradle Of Love | 7" | Mercury | AMT1092 | 1960 | £1.50 | £4 | |
| Free Me | 7" | Mercury | AMT1167 | 1961 | £2.50 | £6 | |
| I'm Starting To Go Steady | 7" | Mercury | AMT1104 | 1960 | £2 | £5 | |
| Leave My Kitten Alone | 7" | Mercury | AMT1129 | 1961 | £4 | £8 | |
| Ring Tail Tooter | 7" EP | Mercury | ZEP10098 | 1960 | £25 | £50 | |
| Rock And Roll Guitar | 7" | Mercury | AMT1164 | 1961 | £2.50 | £6 | |
| Running Bear | LP | Mercury | MMC14051 | 1960 | £25 | £50 | |
| Running Bear | 7" EP | Mercury | ZEP10078 | 1960 | £15 | £30 | |
| Running Bear | 7" | Mercury | AMT1079 | 1960 | £1.50 | £4 | |
| Token Of Love | 7" EP | Mercury | ZEP10116 | 1961 | £37.50 | £75 | |

## PRESTON, MIKE

| Title | Format | Label | Catalog | Year | | | Notes |
|---|---|---|---|---|---|---|---|
| Four Songs By Ray Noble | 7" EP | Decca | DFE6635 | 1960 | £2.50 | £6 | |
| Girl Like You | 7" | Decca | F11222 | 1960 | £1.50 | £4 | |
| I'd Do Anything | 7" | Decca | F11255 | 1960 | £1.50 | £4 | |
| In Surabaya | 7" | Decca | F11120 | 1959 | £1.50 | £4 | |
| Marry Me | 7" EP | Decca | DFE6679 | 1961 | £2.50 | £6 | |
| Marry Me | 7" | Decca | F11335 | 1961 | £1.50 | £4 | |
| Mr. Blue | 7" | Decca | F11167 | 1959 | £1.50 | £4 | |
| My Lucky Love | 7" | Decca | F11053 | 1958 | £2.50 | £6 | |
| Togetherness | 7" | Decca | F11287 | 1960 | £1.50 | £4 | |
| Why Why Why | 7" | Decca | F11087 | 1958 | £1.50 | £4 | |

## PRETENDERS

| Title | Format | Label | Catalog | Year | | | Notes |
|---|---|---|---|---|---|---|---|
| Adultress | 7" | Real | | 1981 | £2 | £5 | promo only |
| Packed! | CD | Sire | 262192 | 1990 | £15 | £30 | US promo in mini-crate |
| Packed! | CD | WEA | WX346CD | 1990 | £20 | £40 | promo with cassette in attache case |
| Pretenders | LP | Nautilus | NR38 | 1981 | £5 | £12 | US audiophile |
| Pretenders | LP | Real | RAL3 | 1980 | £6 | £15 | autographed |

## PRETTY THINGS

The Pretty Things always seemed to suffer from too much labouring in the shadow of the Rolling Stones (Dick Taylor had, of course, been an early member of the Stones), but they nevertheless achieved a fair degree of success and, despite numerous comings and goings on the part of various of the group's members, they are still around and playing. *S.F. Sorrow* has received a fair amount of acclaim for being a kind of rock opera pre-dating the Who's *Tommy*, but the group's best work has always been found on their singles. The early Fontana singles are tough, gritty R&B that easily stand comparison with the likes of Them, or even the Rolling Stones. Later, the Columbia singles 'Defecting Grey' and 'Talkin' About The Good Times' are superb pieces of psychedelia and should definitely be included on any list of the essential recordings of the period.

| Title | Format | Label | Cat# | Year | | | Notes |
|---|---|---|---|---|---|---|---|
| Children | 7" | Fontana | TF829 | 1967 | £2.50 | £6 | |
| Come See Me | 7" | Fontana | TF688 | 1966 | £2 | £5 | |
| Cry To Me | 7" | Fontana | TF585 | 1965 | £1.50 | £4 | |
| Defecting Grey | 7" | Columbia | DB8300 | 1967 | £15 | £30 | |
| Don't Bring Me Down | 7" EP | Fontana | 465253 | 1964 | £20 | £40 | French |
| Don't Bring Me Down | 7" | Fontana | TF503 | 1964 | £1.50 | £4 | |
| Emotions | LP | Fontana | (S)TL5425 | 1967 | £15 | £30 | |
| Emotions | LP | Fontana | SFL13140 | 1969 | £5 | £12 | |
| Get The Picture | LP | Fontana | TL5280 | 1965 | £20 | £40 | |
| Good Mr. Square | 7" | Harvest | HAR5016 | 1970 | £1.50 | £4 | |
| Honey I Need | 7" | Fontana | TF537 | 1965 | £1.50 | £4 | |
| House In The Country | 7" | Fontana | TF722 | 1966 | £2 | £5 | |
| I Can Never Say | 7" EP | Fontana | 465296 | 1965 | £20 | £40 | French |
| Midnight To Six Man | 7" EP | Fontana | 465310 | 1966 | £20 | £40 | French |
| Midnight To Six Man | 7" | Fontana | TF647 | 1965 | £2 | £5 | |
| October 26 | 7" | Harvest | HAR5031 | 1970 | £1.50 | £4 | |
| On Film | 7" EP | Fontana | TE17472 | 1966 | £37.50 | £75 | |
| Parachute | LP | Harvest | SHVL774 | 1970 | £6 | £15 | |
| Pretty Things | LP | Fontana | TL5239 | 1965 | £20 | £40 | |
| Pretty Things | LP | Wing | WL1167 | 1967 | £5 | £12 | |
| Pretty Things | 7" EP | Fontana | TE17434 | 1964 | £12.50 | £25 | |
| Private Sorrow | 7" | Columbia | DB8494 | 1968 | £5 | £10 | |
| Progress | 7" EP | Fontana | 465353 | 1966 | £20 | £40 | French |
| Progress | 7" | Fontana | TF773 | 1966 | £2 | £5 | |
| Raining In My Heart | 7" EP | Fontana | TE17442 | 1965 | £12.50 | £25 | |
| Rosalyn | 7" | Fontana | TF469 | 1964 | £4 | £8 | |
| S.F. Sorrow | LP | Columbia | SCX6306 | 1968 | £10 | £25 | |
| S.F. Sorrow/Parachute | LP | Harvest | SHDW406 | 1975 | £5 | £12 | double |
| Stone Hearted Mama | 7" | Harvest | HAR5037 | 1971 | £1.50 | £4 | |
| Talkin' About The Good Times | 7" | Columbia | DB8353 | 1968 | £10 | £20 | |
| We'll Be Together | LP | Fontana | QL626000 | 1966 | £20 | £40 | Dutch |

## PREVIN, ANDRE

| Title | Format | Label | Cat# | Year | | | Notes |
|---|---|---|---|---|---|---|---|
| André Previn | LP | Brunswick | LAT8093 | 1956 | £6 | £15 | |
| Double Play | LP | Contemporary | LAC12142/ SCA5004 | 1959 | £6 | £15 | ... with Russ Freeman |
| Modern Jazz Performances Of Songs From Gigi | LP | Contemporary | LAC12144 | 1959 | £4 | £10 | |
| Pal Joey | LP | Contemporary | LAC12126 | 1958 | £4 | £10 | |

## PREVIN, DORY

| Title | Format | Label | Cat# | Year | | | Notes |
|---|---|---|---|---|---|---|---|
| Dory Previn | LP | Warner Bros | K56066 | 1974 | £4 | £10 | |
| Live At Carnegie Hall | LP | United Artists | UAD60045 | 1973 | £5 | £12 | double |
| Mary C. Brown And The Hollywood Sign | LP | United Artists | UAG29435 | 1972 | £4 | £10 | |
| On My Way To Where | LP | United Artists | UAG29176 | 1973 | £4 | £10 | |
| Reflections In A Mud Puddle | LP | United Artists | UAG29346 | 1972 | £4 | £10 | |
| We're Children Of Coincidence | LP | Warner Bros | K56213 | 1976 | £4 | £10 | |

## PREVOST, EDDIE

| Title | Format | Label | Cat# | Year | | | Notes |
|---|---|---|---|---|---|---|---|
| Live Vol. 1 | LP | Matchless | MR1 | 1978 | £5 | £12 | |
| Live Vol. 2 | LP | Matchless | MR2 | 197– | £5 | £12 | |

## PRICE, ALAN

| Title | Format | Label | Cat# | Year | | | Notes |
|---|---|---|---|---|---|---|---|
| Amazing Alan Price | 7" EP | Decca | DFE8677 | 1967 | £6 | £12 | |
| Barefootin' | 7" EP | Decca | 457129 | 1966 | £6 | £12 | French |
| I Put A Spell On You | 7" EP | Decca | 457109 | 1966 | £6 | £12 | French |
| Price Is Right | LP | Parrot | PAS71018 | 1968 | £4 | £10 | US |
| Price On His Head | LP | Decca | LK/SKL4907 | 1967 | £4 | £10 | |
| Price To Pay | LP | Decca | LK4839 | 1966 | £6 | £15 | |
| Simon Smith And The Amazing Dancing Bear | 7" EP | Decca | 457143 | 1967 | £6 | £12 | French |

## PRICE, LLOYD

| Title | Format | Label | Cat# | Year | | | Notes |
|---|---|---|---|---|---|---|---|
| Another Fairy Tale | 7" | HMV | POP983 | 1962 | £1.50 | £4 | |
| Boo-Hoo | 7" | HMV | POP926 | 1961 | £1.50 | £4 | |
| Come Into My Heart | 7" | HMV | POP672 | 1959 | £1.50 | £4 | |
| Cookin' | LP | HMV | CLP1519 | 1962 | £8 | £20 | mono |
| Cookin' | LP | HMV | CSD1413 | 1962 | £15 | £30 | stereo |
| Exciting Lloyd Price | LP | HMV | CLP1285 | 1959 | £15 | £30 | |
| Exciting Lloyd Price | 7" EP | HMV | 7EG8538 | 1959 | £15 | £30 | |
| Exciting Lloyd Price | 7" EP | HMV | GES5784 | 1959 | £20 | £40 | stereo |
| Fantastic Lloyd Price | LP | HMV | CLP1393 | 1960 | £8 | £20 | mono |
| Fantastic Lloyd Price | LP | HMV | CSD1323 | 1960 | £15 | £30 | stereo |
| I'm Gonna Get Married | 7" | HMV | POP650 | 1959 | £1.50 | £4 | |
| Just Because | 7" | London | HL8438 | 1957 | £37.50 | £75 | |
| Just Call Me | 7" | HMV | POP799 | 1960 | £1.50 | £4 | |

| | | | | | | |
|---|---|---|---|---|---|---|
| Know What You're Doing | 7" | HMV | POP826 | 1961 £1.50 | £4 | |
| Lady Luck | 7" | HMV | POP712 | 1960 £1.50 | £4 | |
| Lloyd Price | LP | London | HAU2213 | 1960 £15 | £30 | |
| Lloyd Price Now | LP | Major Minor | SMLP57 | 1969 £4 | £10 | |
| Lloyd Price Orchestra | LP | Double-L | D2301/SDL8301 | 1963 £8 | £20 | US |
| Lloyd Swings For Sammy | LP | Monument | MLP8032/ SMP18032 | 1965 £5 | £12 | US |
| Love Music | 7" | GSF | GSZ5 | 1973 £1.50 | £4 | |
| Misty | LP | Double-L | D2303/SDL8303 | 1963 £8 | £20 | US |
| Mr. Personality | LP | HMV | CLP1314 | 1959 £10 | £25 | |
| Mr. Personality Sings The Blues | LP | HMV | CLP1361 | 1960 £8 | £20 | |
| Mr. Personality's Big 15 | LP | ABC | (S)324 | 1960 £8 | £20 | US |
| No Ifs No Ands | 7" | HMV | POP741 | 1960 £1.50 | £4 | |
| Personality | 7" | HMV | POP626 | 1959 £1.50 | £4 | |
| Question | 7" | HMV | POP772 | 1960 £1.50 | £4 | |
| Sings The Million Dollar Sellers | LP | Encore | ENC2004 | 1963 £5 | £12 | |
| Stagger Lee | 7" | HMV | POP580 | 1959 £2 | £5 | |
| Under Your Spell Again | 7" | HMV | POP1100 | 1962 £1.50 | £4 | |
| Where Were You On Our Wedding Day | 7" | HMV | POP598 | 1959 £1.50 | £4 | |

## PRICE, MALCOLM

| | | | | | | |
|---|---|---|---|---|---|---|
| Country Session | LP | Decca | LK4627 | 1964 £4 | £10 | |
| Pickin' On The Country Strings | 7" EP | Oak | RGJ106 | 196– £7.50 | £15 | |
| Then We All Got Up And Walked Away | LP | Sweet Folk And Country | SFA017 | 1975 £4 | £10 | |
| Way Down Town | LP | Decca | LK4665 | 1965 £4 | £10 | |

## PRICE, RAY

| | | | | | | |
|---|---|---|---|---|---|---|
| Greatest Hits | LP | Columbia | CL1566 | 1961 £6 | £15 | US |
| Ray Price | 7" EP | Philips | BBE12137 | 1957 £4 | £8 | |
| Ray Price Sings Heart Songs | LP | Columbia | CL1015 | 1957 £8 | £20 | US |
| Talk To Your Heart | LP | Columbia | CL1148 | 1958 £6 | £15 | US |

## PRICE, RED

| | | | | | | |
|---|---|---|---|---|---|---|
| Danger Man | 7" | Parlophone | R4789 | 1961 £4 | £8 | |
| Rocky Mountain Gal | 7" | Decca | F10822 | 1956 £1.50 | £4 | |
| Weekend | 7" | Pye | 7N15169 | 1958 £1.50 | £4 | |
| Wow | 7" | Pye | 7N15262 | 1960 £1.50 | £4 | |

## PRICE, RED (2)

| | | | | | | |
|---|---|---|---|---|---|---|
| Blue Beat's Over | 7" | Blue Beat | BB209 | 1964 £6 | £12 | |

## PRICE, RICK

| | | | | | | |
|---|---|---|---|---|---|---|
| Talking To The Flowers | LP | Gemini | GME1017 | 1971 £4 | £10 | |

## PRICE, RIKKI

| | | | | | | |
|---|---|---|---|---|---|---|
| Rikki Price | 7" EP | Fontana | TFE17100 | 1958 £5 | £10 | |

## PRICE, SAMMY

| | | | | | | |
|---|---|---|---|---|---|---|
| Blues Ain't Nothin' | LP | London | LTZR15240/ SAHR6234 | 1962 £10 | £25 | |
| Boogieing With Big Sid | 7" | Storyville | A45068 | 196– £7.50 | £15 | |
| Original Sammy Blues | 7" EP | Columbia | SEG7679 | 1957 £5 | £10 | |
| Sammy Price | 7" EP | Vogue | EPV1146 | 1956 £20 | £40 | |
| Sammy Price's Bluesicians | 7" EP | Vogue | EPV1151 | 1956 £20 | £40 | |
| Swingin' Paris Style | LP | Vogue | LAE12027 | 1957 £6 | £15 | |

## PRICE, VINCENT

| | | | | | | |
|---|---|---|---|---|---|---|
| Vincent Price | LP | Columbia | 33SX1141 | 1959 £5 | £12 | |

## PRIDE

| | | | | | | |
|---|---|---|---|---|---|---|
| Pride | LP | Warner Bros | 1848 | 1970 £15 | £30 | US |

## PRIDE, DICKIE

| | | | | | | |
|---|---|---|---|---|---|---|
| Betty Betty | 7" | Columbia | DB4403 | 1960 £2.50 | £6 | |
| Midnight Oil | 7" | Columbia | DB4296 | 1959 £4 | £8 | |
| Pride Without Prejudice | LP | Columbia | 33SX1307 | 1960 £30 | £60 | |
| Pride Without Prejudice | LP | Columbia | SCX3369 | 1961 £37.50 | £75 | stereo |
| Primrose Lane | 7" | Columbia | DB4340 | 1959 £6 | £12 | |
| Sheik Of Shake | 7" EP | Columbia | SEG7937 | 1959 £50 | £100 | |
| Slipping And Sliding | 7" | Columbia | DB4283 | 1959 £10 | £20 | |
| You're Singing Our Love Song | 7" | Columbia | DB4451 | 1960 £1.50 | £4 | |

## PRIESTER, JULIAN

| | | | | | | |
|---|---|---|---|---|---|---|
| Love, Love | LP | ECM | ECM1044ST | 1974 £6 | £15 | |

## PRIMA, LOUIS

| | | | | | | |
|---|---|---|---|---|---|---|
| Buona Sera | 7" | Capitol | CL14821 | 1958 £4 | £8 | |
| Call Of The Wildest | LP | Capitol | T836 | 1958 £6 | £15 | |
| Doin' The Twist | LP | Dot | DLP3410/25410 | 1961 £5 | £12 | US |
| Five Months, Two Weeks, Two Days | 7" | Capitol | CL14669 | 1956 £10 | £20 | |
| Fun With Louis Prima | 7" EP | Philips | BBE12290 | 1959 £2 | £5 | |
| Louis Prima | LP | Rondo | 842 | 1959 £8 | £20 | US |
| Ol' Man Moses | 7" | London | HLD9230 | 1960 £2 | £5 | |
| Strictly Prima | LP | Capitol | T1132 | 1959 £6 | £15 | |
| Strictly Prima | 7" EP | Capitol | EAP11132 | 1959 £2 | £5 | |
| Wildest | LP | Capitol | T755 | 1957 £6 | £15 | |
| Wildest Comes Home | LP | Capitol | (S)T1723 | 1962 £5 | £12 | US |

| Wonderland By Night | LP | Dot | DLP3352/25352 | 1960 | £5 | £12 | US |

## PRIMA, LOUIS & KEELY SMITH

| Bei Mir Bist Du Schon | 7" | London | HLD8923 | 1959 | £1.50 | £4 | |
| I'm Confessin' | 7" | London | HLD9084 | 1960 | £1.50 | £4 | |
| Las Vegas Prima Style | LP | Capitol | T1010 | 1958 | £4 | £10 | |
| Louis And Keely | LP | London | HAD2243 | 1960 | £4 | £10 | |
| On Stage | LP | London | HAD2350/ | 1961 | £4 | £10 | |
| | | | SAHD6149 | | | | |
| Take A Little Walk Around The Block | 7" | Columbia | SCM5092 | 1954 | £4 | £8 | |

## PRIMAL SCREAM

| All Fall Down | 7" | Creation | CRE17 | 1985 | £6 | £12 | |
| Crystal Crescent | 7" | Creation | CRE26 | 1986 | £2.50 | £6 | |
| Gentle Tuesday | 12" | Elevation | ACID3T | 1987 | £3 | £8 | |
| Gentle Tuesday/Imperial | 7" | Elevation | | 1987 | £5 | £10 | promo |
| Higher Than The Sun | CD-s | Creation | CRESCD096 | 1991 | £2 | £5 | |
| Imperial | 12" | Elevation | ACIDT5 | 1987 | £3 | £8 | poster sleeve |
| Ivy Ivy Ivy | CD-s | Creation | CRE067CD | 1989 | £2 | £5 | |
| Loaded | CD-s | Creation | CRESCD070 | 1990 | £2 | £5 | |
| Primal Scream | LP | Creation | CRELP054 | 1989 | £4 | £10 | ..with 7" (Split Wide Open) |

## PRIMARY INDUSTRY

| At Gunpoint | 7" | Temps Modernes | CSBTVV | 1986 | £4 | £8 | |

## PRIMETTES

*Looking Back With The Primettes* consists of early material recorded by the Supremes under their original name. Only one US single was actually released prior to the group signing with Tamla records.

| Looking Back With The Primettes | LP | Ember | EMBS3398 | 1968 | £15 | £30 | |
| Roots Of Diana Ross | LP | Windmill | WMD192 | 1973 | £4 | £10 | |
| Tears Of Sorrow | 7" | Lupine | 120 | 1960 | £50 | £100 | US |

## PRIMEVIL

| Smokin' Bats At Campton's | LP | 700 West | 740105 | 1974 | £37.50 | £75 | US |

## PRIMITIVES

| Blow Up | LP | Arc | SA22 | 1967 | £75 | £150 | Italian |
| Help Me | 7" | Pye | 7N15721 | 1964 | £75 | £150 | |
| Ho Mary | 7" EP | Vogue | INT18093 | 1966 | £75 | £150 | French |
| You Said | 7" | Pye | 7N15755 | 1965 | £75 | £150 | |

## PRIMITIVES (2)

| Ocean Blue | 7" | Lazy | LAZY5 | 1987 | £2.50 | £6 | no picture sleeve |
| Out Of Reach | CD-s | RCA | PD42012 | 1988 | £2 | £5 | |
| Really Stupid | 7" | Lazy | LAZY2 | 1986 | £1.50 | £4 | |
| Really Stupid | 12" | Lazy | LAZYT2 | 1986 | £3 | £8 | |
| Secrets | CD-s | RCA | PD43174 | 1989 | £2 | £5 | |
| Sick Of It | CD-s | RCA | PD42948 | 1989 | £2 | £5 | |
| Stop Killing Me | 7" | Lazy | LAZY3 | 1986 | £2 | £5 | with badge |
| Stop Killing Me | 12" | Lazy | LAZYT3 | 1986 | £2.50 | £6 | |
| Thru The Flowers | 12" | Head | HEAD010 | 1986 | £10 | £25 | test pressing |
| Thru The Flowers | 12" | Lazy | LAZY1 | 1986 | £4 | £10 | |

## PRIMITIVES (3)

During 1964, Lou Reed was employed as a songwriter and performer by a company specializing in quick cash-in records. 'The Ostrich' was one of these, but it managed to gain sufficient attention for an invitation to be made to appear on Dick Clark's TV show. The group put together for the purpose was almost a prototype Velvet Underground, consisting of Lou Reed, John Cale and fellow avant-garde enthusiast Tony Conrad.

| Ostrich | 7" | Pickwick | 1001 | 1964 | £30 | £60 | US |

## PRINCE

All the major stars of the eighties have had their recording careers boosted by a proliferation of picture disc and other limited-edition releases, and Prince is no exception. Most critics would have it that the legendary *Black Album* contains music of unparalleled splendour and that its last minute withdrawal was an act of typically idiosyncratic and wilful behaviour on the part of its maker. Original copies are rare (though not as rare as to justify some of the extreme prices that are quoted on occasion – the thousand pound figure quoted here is a maximum), but bootleg versions, with a variety of cover designs, are in common circulation, while an official release was finally made in 1994 (effectively this is a reissue). These enable anyone not overawed by the record's reputation to hear that the *Black Album* lacks entirely the sense of surprise that is present in the best of Prince's work.

| 1999 | LP | WEA | 9238091 | 1983 | £4 | £10 | single LP |
| 1999 | 7" | WEA | W9896 | 1983 | £2 | £5 | |
| 1999 | 7" | WEA | W9896C | 1983 | £7.50 | £15 | with cassette |
| 1999 | 12" | WEA | W9896T | 1983 | £6 | £15 | |
| Alphabet Street | CD-s | WEA | W7900CD | 1988 | £5 | £12 | 3" single |
| Anotherloverholenyohead | 7" | WEA | W8521W | 1986 | £2 | £5 | poster sleeve |
| Anotherloverholenyohead | 7" | WEA | W8521F | 1986 | £4 | £8 | double |
| Anotherloverholenyohead | 12" | WEA | W8521T | 1986 | £4 | £10 | poster sleeve |
| Arms Of Orion | CD-s | WEA | W2757CDX | 1989 | £2.50 | £6 | tri-fold sleeve |
| Batdance | CD-s | WEA | W2924CD | 1989 | £2 | £5 | |
| Batdance | CD-s | WEA | W2924CDX | 1989 | £3 | £8 | batpack box, 3" single |
| Batdance | 12" | WEA | W2924TP | 1989 | £3 | £8 | picture disc |
| Batman | LP | WEA | WX281P | 1989 | £6 | £15 | picture disc |

| | | | | | | | |
|---|---|---|---|---|---|---|---|
| Black Album | LP or CD | Paisley Park | WX147 | 1988 | £700 | £1000 | promo only |
| Black Album | LP | Warner Bros | 145793 | 1995 | £50 | £100 | US promo, white or multicoloured vinyl |
| Controversy | 7" | WEA | K17866 | 1981 | £10 | £20 | |
| Controversy | 12" | WEA | K17866T | 1981 | £15 | £30 | |
| Crown Jewels | CD | WEA | SAM1037 | 1992 | £25 | £50 | promo |
| D.M.S.R. | 12" | WEA | SAM172 | 1983 | £20 | £40 | promo |
| Diamonds And Pearls | CD | Paisley Park | 253792DJ | 1991 | £10 | £25 | US promo picture disc |
| Diamonds And Pearls | CD | Paisley Park | 7599253792 | 1991 | £6 | £15 | hologram cover |
| Do It All Night | 7" | WEA | K17768 | 1981 | £7.50 | £15 | no picture sleeve |
| Do It All Night | 12" | WEA | K17768T | 1981 | £20 | £40 | no picture sleeve |
| Girls And Boys | 7" | WEA | W8586F | 1986 | £4 | £8 | double |
| Girls And Boys | 7" | WEA | W8586P | 1986 | £20 | £40 | shaped picture disc |
| Girls And Boys | 12" | WEA | W8586T | 1986 | £4 | £10 | with poster |
| Glam Slam | CD-s | WEA | W7806CD | 1988 | £5 | £12 | 3" single |
| Gotta Stop Messin' About | 7" | WEA | K17819 | 1981 | £30 | £60 | 2 different B sides |
| Gotta Stop Messin' About | 12" | WEA | LV47 | 1981 | £50 | £100 | 2 different B sides |
| Graffiti Bridge | CD | Paisley Park | 274932DJ | 1990 | £10 | £25 | US promo picture disc |
| Hits Sampler | CD | Warner Bros | PRCD2 | 1993 | £15 | £30 | promo |
| I Could Never Take The Place Of Your Man | 12" | WEA | W8288TP | 1987 | £6 | £15 | picture disc |
| I Wanna Be Your Lover | 7" | WEA | K17537 | 1979 | £2.50 | £6 | no picture sleeve |
| I Wanna Be Your Lover | 12" | WEA | K17527T | 1979 | £6 | £15 | no picture sleeve |
| I Wish U Heaven | CD-s | WEA | W7745CD | 1988 | £5 | £12 | 3" single |
| I Wish U Heaven | 7" | WEA | W7745 | 1988 | £2 | £5 | poster sleeve |
| I Would Die 4 U (US Remix) | 12" | WEA | W9121TE | 1984 | £10 | £25 | |
| If I Was Your Girlfriend | 7" | WEA | W8334E | 1987 | £4 | £8 | peach vinyl, cards & stickers |
| If I Was Your Girlfriend | 7" | WEA | W8334W | 1987 | £2 | £5 | poster sleeve |
| If I Was Your Girlfriend | 12" | WEA | W8334TP | 1987 | £10 | £20 | picture disc |
| Kiss | 7" | WEA | W8751TP | 1986 | £5 | £10 | shaped picture disc |
| Kiss | 7" | WEA | W8751TP | 1986 | £10 | £20 | shaped picture disc, plinth |
| Kiss | 12" | WEA | W8751T | 1986 | £4 | £10 | with poster |
| Let's Go Crazy | 12" | WEA | W2000T | 1985 | £2.50 | £6 | with poster & sticker |
| Let's Work | 7" | WEA | K17922 | 1982 | £12.50 | £25 | |
| Let's Work | 12" | WEA | K17922T | 1982 | £50 | £100 | |
| Little Red Corvette | 7" | WEA | W9436 | 1983 | £12.50 | £25 | poster sleeve |
| Little Red Corvette | 7" | WEA | W9688 | 1983 | £2.50 | £6 | |
| Little Red Corvette | 12" | WEA | W9436T | 1983 | £15 | £30 | |
| Little Red Corvette | 12" | WEA | W9436T | 1983 | £37.50 | £75 | with calendar |
| Little Red Corvette | 12" | WEA | W9436T | 1983 | £25 | £50 | with poster |
| Little Red Corvette | 12" | WEA | W9688T | 1983 | £10 | £20 | |
| Little Red Corvette | 12" | WEA | W9688T | 1983 | £15 | £30 | with poster & sticker |
| Little Red Corvette/1999 | 7" | Warner Bros | 201290 | 1983 | £7.50 | £15 | US picture disc |
| Mountains | 12" | WEA | W8711T | 1986 | £4 | £10 | with poster |
| Mountains | 10" | WEA | W8711TW | 1986 | £15 | £30 | white vinyl |
| New Power Generation | CD-s | Paisley Park | W9525CD | 1990 | £2 | £5 | |
| Paisley Park | 7" | WEA | W9052P | 1985 | £12.50 | £25 | shaped picture disc |
| Paisley Park | 12" | WEA | W9052T | 1985 | £2.50 | £6 | |
| Paisley Park | 12" | WEA | W9052TP | 1985 | £4 | £10 | with poster |
| Parade | LP | WEA | WX39P | 1986 | £10 | £25 | picture disc |
| Partyman | CD-s | Paisley Park | W2814CDX | 1989 | £2 | £5 | hexagonal sleeve |
| Partyman | 12" | WEA | W2814TP | 1989 | £4 | £10 | picture disc |
| Pop Life | 12" | WEA | W8858T | 1985 | £3 | £8 | |
| Purple Rain | LP | WEA | 9251101 | 1984 | £10 | £25 | purple vinyl, poster |
| Purple Rain | CD | Warner Bros | 251102 | 1984 | £10 | £25 | US, special cardboard cover |
| Purple Rain | 7" | WEA | W9174P | 1984 | £20 | £40 | shaped picture disc |
| Purple Rain | 12" | WEA | W9174T | 1984 | £2.50 | £6 | |
| Purple Rain | 12" | WEA | W9174T | 1984 | £4 | £10 | with poster |
| Raspberry Beret | 12" | WEA | W8929T | 1985 | £2.50 | £6 | |
| Sexy Dancer | 7" | WEA | K17590 | 1980 | £7.50 | £15 | no picture sleeve |
| Sexy Dancer | 12" | WEA | K17590T | 1980 | £20 | £40 | no picture sleeve |
| Sexy MF | 12" | Paisley Park | W0123P | 1992 | £2.50 | £6 | picture disc |
| Sign O The Times | 12" | WEA | W8399TP | 1987 | £12.50 | £25 | picture disc |
| Symbol | CD | Paisley Park | 9451212 | 1992 | £8 | £20 | gold cardboard box |
| Thieves In The Temple | CD-s | WEA | W9751CD | 1990 | £2 | £5 | |
| Thieves In The Temple | 12" | Paisley Park | W9751TP | 1990 | £3 | £8 | picture disc |
| U Got The Look | 12" | WEA | W8289TP | 1987 | £6 | £15 | picture disc |
| Undertaker | CD | no label | 930902H | 1995 | £100 | £200 | no cover |
| When Doves Cry/1999 | 12" | WEA | W9296T | 1984 | £10 | £20 | shrinkwrapped double |

## PRINCE, VIV

| | | | | | | | |
|---|---|---|---|---|---|---|---|
| Light Of The Charge Brigade | 7" | Columbia | DB7960 | 1966 | £7.50 | £15 | |

## PRINCE & PRINCESS

| | | | | | | | |
|---|---|---|---|---|---|---|---|
| Ready Steady Go | 7" | Island | WI609 | 1965 | £5 | £10 | |

## PRINCE BUSTER

| | | | | | | | |
|---|---|---|---|---|---|---|---|
| Aguar Fumar | 7" | Blue Beat | BB293 | 1965 | £6 | £12 | |
| Al Capone | 7" | Blue Beat | BB324 | 1965 | £6 | £12 | |
| All My Loving | 7" | Fab | FAB35 | 1968 | £4 | £8 | |
| All On My Mind | 7" | Blue Beat | BB400 | 1967 | £6 | £12 | |
| Ambition | 7" | Blue Beat | BB328 | 1965 | £6 | £12 | Ivanhoe Martin B side |
| Baldhead Pum Pum | 7" | Prince Buster | PB47 | 1972 | £1.50 | £4 | |
| Big Fight | 7" | Blue Beat | BB282 | 1965 | £6 | £12 | |

| Title | Format | Label | Catalogue | Year | Price | Price | Notes |
|---|---|---|---|---|---|---|---|
| Big Fight | 7" | Blue Beat | BB338 | 1966 | £6 | £12 | |
| Big Five | LP | Melodisc | MLP12157 | 1972 | £5 | £12 | |
| Big Five | 7" | Fab | FAB150 | 1970 | £1.50 | £4 | |
| Big Five | 7" | Prince Buster | PB1 | 1970 | £2 | £5 | |
| Big Sister Stuff | 7" | Prince Buster | PB14 | 1972 | £1.50 | £4 | |
| Black Organ | 7" | Fab | FAB141 | 1970 | £1.50 | £4 | |
| Black Soul | 7" | Fab | FAB102 | 1969 | £2.50 | £6 | ...Caledonians B side |
| Blackhead Chinaman | 7" | Dice | CC11 | 1963 | £5 | £10 | |
| Blood Pressure | 7" | Blue Beat | BB278 | 1965 | £6 | £12 | |
| Blue Beat Spirit | 7" | Blue Beat | BB211 | 1964 | £6 | £12 | |
| Bonanza | 7" | Blue Beat | BB307 | 1965 | £6 | £12 | |
| Bull Buck | 7" | Fab | FAB118 | 1969 | £2.50 | £6 | ...Roland Alphonso B side |
| Burning Creation | 7" | Blue Beat | BB173 | 1963 | £6 | £12 | |
| Bye Bye Baby | 7" | Fab | FAB16 | 1967 | £4 | £8 | |
| Captain Burke | 7" | Blue Beat | BB333 | 1965 | £6 | £12 | |
| Cincinatti Kid | 7" | Blue Beat | BB342 | 1966 | £6 | £12 | |
| Come And Do It With Me | 7" | Fab | FAB32 | 1968 | £4 | £8 | |
| Come Home | 7" | Blue Beat | BB317 | 1965 | £6 | £12 | |
| Congo Revolution | 7" | Blue Beat | BB325 | 1965 | £6 | £12 | ...Little Darling B side |
| Dallas Texas | 7" | Fab | FAB37 | 1968 | £4 | £8 | |
| Dallas, Texas | 7" | Blue Beat | BB266 | 1964 | £6 | £12 | |
| Dance Cleopatra | 7" | Blue Beat | BB388 | 1967 | £6 | £12 | |
| Dark End Of The Street | 7" | Blue Beat | BB377 | 1967 | £6 | £12 | |
| Doctor Rodney | 7" | Fab | FAB82 | 1969 | £2.50 | £6 | |
| Don't Throw Stones | 7" | Blue Beat | BB343 | 1966 | £6 | £12 | |
| Drunkard's Psalm | 7" | Blue Beat | BB378 | 1967 | £6 | £12 | |
| Everybody Ska | 7" | Stateside | SS335 | 1964 | £5 | £10 | |
| Everybody Yeah Yeah | 7" | Blue Beat | BB313 | 1965 | £6 | £12 | |
| Eye For An Eye | 7" | Blue Beat | BB294 | 1965 | £6 | £12 | |
| Fabulous Greatest Hits | LP | Melodisc | MS1 | 1968 | £4 | £10 | |
| Fishey | 7" | Prince Buster | PB4 | 1971 | £1.50 | £4 | |
| Float Like A Butterfly | 7" | Blue Beat | BB314 | 1965 | £6 | £12 | |
| Fowl Thief | 7" | Blue Beat | BB186 | 1963 | £6 | £12 | |
| Free Love | 7" | Fab | FAB38 | 1968 | £4 | £8 | ...Daltons B side |
| Ganja Plant | 7" | Fab | FAB132 | 1970 | £1.50 | £4 | |
| Glory Of Love | 7" | Fab | FAB36 | 1968 | £4 | £8 | |
| Glory Of Love | 7" | Fab | FAB49 | 1968 | £4 | £8 | |
| Going To Ethiopia | 7" | Fab | FAB47 | 1968 | £4 | £8 | |
| Going To The River | 7" | Fab | FAB26 | 1967 | £4 | £8 | |
| Going West | 7" | Blue Beat | BB277 | 1965 | £6 | £12 | |
| Green Green Grass Of Home | 7" | Fab | FAB57 | 1968 | £4 | £8 | Soul Makers B side |
| Here Comes The Bride | 7" | Blue Beat | BB309 | 1965 | £6 | £12 | |
| Hey Jude | 7" | Fab | FAB94 | 1969 | £2.50 | £6 | |
| Hit Me Back | 7" | Fab | FAB140 | 1970 | £1.50 | £4 | |
| Hypocrite | 7" | Fab | FAB80 | 1968 | £4 | £8 | |
| I Feel The Spirit | LP | Blue Beat | BBLP802 | 1963 | £50 | £100 | |
| I Feel The Spirit | LP | Fab | MS2 | 1970 | £5 | £12 | |
| I May Never Love You Again | 7" | Blue Beat | BB274 | 1964 | £6 | £12 | |
| I Wish Your Picture Was You | 7" | Prince Buster | PB7 | 1971 | £1.50 | £4 | |
| I Won't Let You Cry | 7" | Blue Beat | BB357 | 1966 | £6 | £12 | |
| Independence Day | 7" | Blue Beat | BB116 | 1962 | £6 | £12 | |
| Intensified Dirt | 7" | Fab | FAB56 | 1968 | £4 | £8 | |
| It's Burke's Law | LP | Blue Beat | BBLP806 | 1965 | £50 | £100 | |
| It's Too Late | 7" | Blue Beat | BB352 | 1966 | £6 | £12 | |
| Jealous | 7" | Blue Beat | BB243 | 1964 | £6 | £12 | |
| Johnny Cool | 7" | Fab | FAB11 | 1967 | £5 | £10 | |
| Johnny Dark | 7" | Blue Beat | BB290 | 1965 | £6 | £12 | ...Owen Gray B side |
| Johnny Dollar | 7" | Blue Beat | BB326 | 1965 | £6 | £12 | ..Terry Nelson B side |
| Judge Dread | LP | Blue Beat | BBLP809 | 1967 | £37.50 | £75 | |
| Judge Dread | 7" | Blue Beat | BB387 | 1967 | £6 | £12 | ..Fitzroy Campbell B side |
| King Duke Sir | 7" | Blue Beat | BB163 | 1963 | £6 | £12 | |
| Kings Of Old | 7" | Fab | FAB31 | 1968 | £4 | £8 | |
| Knock On Wood | 7" | Blue Beat | BB373 | 1967 | £6 | £12 | |
| Land Of Imagination | 7" | Blue Beat | BB391 | 1967 | £6 | £12 | |
| Ling Ting Tang | 7" | Blue Beat | BB302 | 1965 | £6 | £12 | |
| Love Each Other | 7" | Rainbow | RAI110 | 1966 | £4 | £8 | |
| Madness | 7" | Blue Beat | BB170 | 1963 | £6 | £12 | |
| Medley | 7" | Prince Buster | PB19 | 1972 | £1.50 | £4 | |
| Money | 7" | Blue Beat | BB162 | 1963 | £6 | £12 | ...School Boys B side |
| Mules Mules Mules | 7" | Blue Beat | BB279 | 1965 | £6 | £12 | ...Charmers B side |
| My Girl | 7" | Blue Beat | BB321 | 1965 | £6 | £12 | |
| My Happiness | 7" | Prince Buster | PB9 | 1971 | £1.50 | £4 | |
| My Heart Is Gone | 7" | Prince Buster | PB16 | 1972 | £1.50 | £4 | |
| Nice Nice | 7" | Fab | FAB64 | 1968 | £4 | £8 | |
| No Knowledge In College | 7" | Blue Beat | BB271 | 1964 | £6 | £12 | |
| Ob La Di Ob La Da | 7" | Fab | FAB93 | 1969 | £2.50 | £6 | |
| Old Lady | 7" | Blue Beat | BB262 | 1964 | £6 | £12 | |
| One Hand Washes The Other | 7" | Blue Beat | BB138 | 1962 | £6 | £12 | |
| Open Up Bartender | 7" | Blue Beat | BB158 | 1963 | £6 | £12 | |
| Original Golden Oldies Vol. 1 | LP | Prince Buster | PB9 | 1973 | £4 | £10 | |
| Outlaw | LP | Blue Beat | BBLP822 | 1969 | £20 | £40 | |
| Pharaoh House Crash | 7" | Fab | FAB92 | 1969 | £2.50 | £6 | |
| Picket Line | 7" | Blue Beat | BB349 | 1966 | £6 | £12 | ...Eric Morris B side |
| Police Trim Rasta | 7" | Fab | FAB176 | 1971 | £1.50 | £4 | |
| Prince Buster On Tour | LP | Blue Beat | BBLP808 | 1967 | £37.50 | £75 | |
| Prince Royal | 7" | Blue Beat | BB244 | 1964 | £6 | £12 | ...Cosmo B side |

700

| Title | Format | Label | Cat. No. | Year | Price | Price | Notes |
|---|---|---|---|---|---|---|---|
| Prophet | 7" | Blue Beat | BB359 | 1966 | £6 | £12 | |
| Protection | 7" | Prince Buster | PB15 | 1972 | £1.50 | £4 | |
| Pum Pum A Go Kill You | 7" | Fab | FAB101 | 1969 | £2.50 | £6 | |
| Quiet Place | 7" | Blue Beat | BB393 | 1967 | £6 | £12 | |
| Rat Trap | 7" | Fab | FAB142 | 1970 | £1.50 | £4 | |
| Rat Trap | 7" | Prince Buster | PB2 | 1971 | £1.50 | £4 | |
| Rebel | 7" | Fab | FAB124 | 1969 | £1.50 | £4 | |
| Repect | 7" | Blue Beat | BB335 | 1965 | £6 | £12 | |
| Rock And Shake | 7" | Fab | FAB20 | 1967 | £4 | £8 | Hortense Ellis B side |
| Rolling Stones | 7" | Blue Beat | BB192 | 1963 | £6 | £12 | Rico B side |
| Rough Rider | 7" | Fab | FAB40 | 1968 | £4 | £8 | |
| Rum And Coca Cola | 7" | Blue Beat | BB330 | 1965 | £6 | £12 | |
| Run Man Run | 7" | Blue Beat | BB150 | 1963 | £6 | £12 | |
| Shakin' Up Orange Street | 7" | Fab | FAB10 | 1967 | £5 | £10 | |
| Shanty Town Get Scanty | 7" | Blue Beat | BB370 | 1967 | £6 | £12 | |
| She Loves You | 7" | Blue Beat | BB234 | 1964 | £6 | £12 | |
| She Pon Top | 7" | Blue Beat | BB232 | 1964 | £6 | £12 | |
| She Was A Rough Rider | LP | Blue Beat | BBLP820 | 1969 | £25 | £50 | |
| Shepherd Beng | 7" | Fab | FAB41 | 1968 | £4 | £8 | with Teddy King |
| Sister's Big Stuff | LP | Melodisc | MLP12156 | 1972 | £6 | £15 | |
| Sit And Wonder | 7" | Blue Beat | BB382 | 1967 | £6 | £12 | Roland Alphonso B side |
| Sit Down And Cry | 7" | Blue Beat | BB389 | 1967 | £6 | £12 | |
| Ska-Lip-Soul | LP | Blue Beat | BBLP805 | 1965 | £50 | £100 | |
| Sons Of Zion | 7" | Prince Buster | PB8 | 1971 | £1.50 | £4 | Ansell Collins B side |
| Soul Dance | 7" | Blue Beat | BB398 | 1967 | £6 | £12 | |
| Soul Serenade | 7" | Blue Beat | BB390 | 1967 | £6 | £12 | |
| Sounds And Pressure | 7" | Blue Beat | BB372 | 1967 | £6 | £12 | |
| South Of The Border | 7" | Prince Buster | PB36 | 1972 | £1.50 | £4 | |
| Spider And The Fly | 7" | Blue Beat | BB199 | 1963 | £6 | £12 | |
| Stand Up | 7" | Fab | FAB122 | 1969 | £1.50 | £4 | |
| Still | 7" | Prince Buster | PB32 | 1972 | £1.50 | £4 | |
| Sugar Pop | 7" | Blue Beat | BB316 | 1965 | £6 | £12 | |
| Take It Easy | 7" | Blue Beat | BB384 | 1967 | £6 | £12 | |
| Talkin' 'Bout My Girl | 7" | Blue Beat | BB355 | 1966 | £6 | £12 | |
| Ten Commandments | LP | RCA | LPM/LSP3792 | 1967 | £8 | £20 | US |
| Ten Commandments | 7" | Blue Beat | BB167 | 1963 | £6 | £12 | |
| Ten Commandments | 7" | Blue Beat | BB334 | 1965 | £6 | £12 | |
| Ten Commandments | 7" | Philips | BF1552 | 1967 | £5 | £10 | |
| That's All | 7" | Fab | FAB131 | 1970 | £1.50 | £4 | |
| They Got To Come | 7" | Dice | CC6 | 1962 | £5 | £10 | |
| They Got To Go | 7" | Blue Beat | BB101 | 1962 | £6 | £12 | |
| Thirty Pieces Of Silver | 7" | Blue Beat | BB248 | 1964 | £6 | £12 | |
| Thirty Pieces Of Silver | 7" | Unity | UN522 | 1969 | £1.50 | £4 | |
| This Gun For Hire | 7" | Blue Beat | BB395 | 1967 | £6 | £12 | |
| Three Blind Mice | 7" | Blue Beat | BB225 | 1964 | £6 | £12 | |
| Three More Rivers To Cross | 7" | Blue Beat | BB180 | 1963 | £6 | £12 | Raymond Harper B side |
| Tickler | 7" | Blue Beat | BB269 | 1964 | £6 | £12 | Cosmo B side |
| Tie The Donkey's Tail | 7" | Fab | FAB119 | 1969 | £2.50 | £6 | |
| Time Longer Than Rope | 7" | Blue Beat | BB133 | 1962 | £6 | £12 | |
| To Be Loved | 7" | Blue Beat | BB362 | 1966 | £6 | £12 | |
| Train To Girls Town | 7" | Fab | FAB25 | 1967 | £4 | £8 | |
| Tutti Frutti | LP | Fab | MS6 | 1970 | £6 | £15 | |
| Under Arrest | 7" | Blue Beat | BB339 | 1966 | £6 | £12 | |
| Vagabond | 7" | Blue Beat | BB402 | 1967 | £6 | £12 | |
| Wash All Your Troubles Away | 7" | Blue Beat | BB200 | 1963 | £6 | £12 | Rico B side |
| Wash All Your Troubles Away | 7" | Blue Beat | BB210 | 1964 | £6 | £12 | Rico B side |
| Watch It Blackhead | 7" | Blue Beat | BB189 | 1963 | £6 | £12 | |
| We Shall Overcome | 7" | Fab | FAB58 | 1968 | £4 | £8 | |
| Welcome To Jamaica | LP | Blue Beat | BBLP821 | 1969 | £15 | £30 | |
| What A Hard Man Fe Dead | LP | Blue Beat | BBLP807 | 1967 | £50 | £100 | |
| What A World | 7" | Blue Beat | BB144 | 1962 | £6 | £12 | |
| Window Shopping | 7" | Blue Beat | BB197 | 1963 | £6 | £12 | |
| Wine And Grind | 7" | Fab | FAB108 | 1969 | £2.50 | £6 | |
| Wine And Grind | 7" | Fab | FAB81 | 1968 | £4 | £8 | |
| Wings Of A Dove | 7" | Blue Beat | BB254 | 1964 | £6 | £12 | Maytals B side |
| World Peace | 7" | Dice | CC18 | 1963 | £5 | £10 | |
| You'll Be Lonely And Blue | 7" | Blue Beat | BB383 | 1967 | £6 | £12 | |
| You're Mine | 7" | Blue Beat | BB216 | 1964 | £6 | £12 | |
| Young Gifted And Black | 7" | Fab | FAB127 | 1970 | £1.50 | £4 | |
| Your Turn | 7" | Rainbow | RAI107 | 1966 | £4 | £8 | |

## PRINCE CHARLIE

| Title | Format | Label | Cat. No. | Year | Price | Price |
|---|---|---|---|---|---|---|
| Hit And Run | 7" | Coxsone | CS7101 | 1969 | £5 | £10 |

## PRINCE FAR I

| Title | Format | Label | Cat. No. | Year | Price | Price |
|---|---|---|---|---|---|---|
| Cry Tuff Dub Encounter Part Two | LP | Front Line | FL4002 | 1979 | £5 | £12 |
| Free From Sin | LP | Trojan | TRLS175 | 1979 | £4 | £10 |
| Long Life | LP | Front Line | FL1021 | 1978 | £5 | £12 |
| Message From The King | LP | Front Line | FL1013 | 1978 | £5 | £12 |

## PRINCE HAROLD

| Title | Format | Label | Cat. No. | Year | Price | Price |
|---|---|---|---|---|---|---|
| Forget About Me | 7" | Mercury | MF952 | 1966 | £2.50 | £6 |

## PRINCE MOHAMMED

| Title | Format | Label | Cat. No. | Year | Price | Price |
|---|---|---|---|---|---|---|
| African Roots | LP | Burning Sounds | BR1005 | 1979 | £4 | £10 |

| People Are You Ready | | LP | Ballistic | UAS30192 | 1978 £4 | £10 | |
|---|---|---|---|---|---|---|---|

## PRINCE OF DARKNESS
| Burial Of Longshot | 7" | Down Town | DT441 | 1969 £1.50 | £4 |
|---|---|---|---|---|---|

## PRINCE PATO EXPEDITION
| Firebird | LP | Beacon | BEAS18 | 197– £8 | £20 |
|---|---|---|---|---|---|

## PRINCESS & THE SWINEHERD
| Princess And The Swineherd | LP | Oak | RGJ633 | 1968 £10 | £25 |
|---|---|---|---|---|---|

## PRINCIPAL EDWARD'S MAGIC THEATRE

Principal Edward's Magic Theatre was the first, and perhaps the only group ever to receive an Arts Council Grant. It was a large organization, incorporating dancers and light-show operators as well as musicians, so that the records do not entirely succeed in conveying what the group did. *Soundtrack*, however, is an interesting record, crossing folk with rock and poetry so well that one is never quite sure what is coming next. The music also features a cameo appearance from John Peel, who delivers one spoken line (in the role of a child). The second album, meanwhile, includes a welcome antidote to all those hymns of praise to various American cities, in the form of a song dedicated to the town of Kettering.

| Asmoto Running Band | LP | Dandelion | DAN8002 | 1971 £5 | £12 | |
|---|---|---|---|---|---|---|
| Ballad Of The Big Girl Now | 7" | Dandelion | K4405 | 1970 £1.50 | £4 | |
| Round One | LP | Deram | SML1108 | 1974 £5 | £12 | |
| Soundtrack | LP | Dandelion | 63752 | 1969 £6 | £15 | |

## PRIOR, MADDY
| Changing Winds | LP | Chrysalis | CHR1203 | 1978 £5 | £12 | |
|---|---|---|---|---|---|---|
| Woman In The Wings | LP | Chrysalis | CHR1185 | 1978 £5 | £12 | |

## PRIOR, MADDY & JUNE TABOR
| Silly Sisters | LP | Chrysalis | CHR1101 | 1976 £4 | £10 | |
|---|---|---|---|---|---|---|

## PRISMA
| Prisma | LP | Prisma | | 1983 £10 | £25 | *Dutch* |
|---|---|---|---|---|---|---|

## PRISONAIRES
| Just Walkin' In The Rain | 7" | Sun | 186 | 1953 £30 | £60 | *US* |
|---|---|---|---|---|---|---|
| My God Is Real | 7" | Sun | 189 | 1953 £50 | £100 | *US* |
| Prisoner's Prayer | 7" | Sun | 191 | 1953 £30 | £60 | *US* |
| There Is Love In You | 7" | Sun | 207 | 1954 £2100 | £3000 | *US, best auctioned* |

## PROBY, P. J.

All four members of Led Zeppelin appear on one track of the P. J. Proby album *Three Week Hero*, and the record has long been a collectors' item for this reason. Proby's career is dotted with moments like this: he was the lucky recipient of an unreleased Beatles song (although his mannered voice is not actually ideal for making the best of 'That Means A Lot'); he managed to land the starring role in the *Elvis* stage show (and is accordingly central in the collectable album that was only ever available at the theatre); and was later to be found recording in an unlikely partnership with the group Focus. (The resulting album is listed within their entry. Cynics should resist making too much of its title, however, for *Focus Con Proby* is Italian in origin!)

| Believe It Or Not | LP | Liberty | LBL/LBS83087 | 1968 £6 | £15 | |
|---|---|---|---|---|---|---|
| California License | LP | Liberty | LBL83320 | 1969 £20 | £40 | *..credited to Jet Powers* |
| Christmas With P. J. Proby | 7" EP | Liberty | LEP2239 | 1965 £5 | £10 | |
| Day That Lorraine Came Down | 7" | Liberty | LIB15152 | 1968 £2.50 | £6 | |
| Elvis | LP | Astoria | 1 | 1978 £10 | £25 | *with other artists* |
| Enigma | LP | Liberty | LBL/LBS83032 | 1967 £4 | £10 | |
| Enigma | LP | Liberty | LBY1361 | 1966 £6 | £15 | |
| Go Go P. J. Proby | LP | Liberty | LRP3406/LST7406 | 1965 £6 | £15 | *US* |
| Hanging From Your Loving Tree | 7" | Liberty | LIB15245 | 1969 £2.50 | £6 | |
| Hero | LP | Palm | 7007 | 1981 £6 | £15 | *with other artists* |
| Hold Me | 7" EP | Decca | 457044 | 1964 £7.50 | £15 | *French* |
| I Am P. J. Proby | LP | Liberty | LBY1235 | 1964 £6 | £15 | |
| I Can't Make It Alone | 7" EP | Liberty | LEP2274 | 1967 £7.50 | £15 | *French* |
| I Can't Make It Alone | 7" | Liberty | LIB10250 | 1966 £1.50 | £4 | |
| It's Goodbye | 7" | Liberty | LIB15386 | 1970 £2.50 | £6 | |
| Let The Water Run Down | 7" | Liberty | LIB10206 | 1965 £1.50 | £4 | |
| My Prayer | 7" EP | Liberty | LEP2253 | 1966 £6 | £12 | *French* |
| Niki Hoeky | 7" | Liberty | LBS55936 | 1967 £1.50 | £4 | |
| P. J. Proby | LP | Liberty | LBY1264 | 1965 £6 | £15 | |
| P. J. Proby | 7" EP | Liberty | LEP2192 | 1965 £4 | £8 | |
| P. J. Proby Again | 7" EP | Liberty | LEP2267 | 1966 £7.50 | £15 | |
| P. J. Proby Hits | 7" EP | Liberty | LEP2251 | 1966 £7.50 | £15 | |
| P. J. Proby's In Town | LP | Liberty | LBL/LBS83018 | 1967 £4 | £10 | |
| P. J. Proby's In Town | LP | Liberty | LBY1291 | 1965 £5 | £12 | |
| Phenomenon | LP | Liberty | LBL/LBS83045 | 1967 £6 | £15 | |
| Somewhere | 7" EP | Liberty | LEP2220 | 1965 £5 | £10 | *French* |
| Somewhere | 7" EP | Liberty | LEP2229 | 1965 £4 | £8 | |
| That Means A Lot | 7" EP | Liberty | LEP2240 | 1965 £10 | £20 | *French* |
| That Means A Lot | 7" | Liberty | LIB10215 | 1965 £2 | £5 | |
| Three Week Hero | LP | Liberty | LBS83219 | 1969 £20 | £40 | |
| Today I Killed A Man | 7" | Liberty | LIB15280 | 1970 £2.50 | £6 | |
| Try To Forget Her | 7" | Liberty | LIB55367 | 1964 £2 | £5 | |
| What's Wrong With My World | LP | Liberty | LST7561 | 1968 £4 | £10 | *US* |
| What's Wrong With My World | 7" | Liberty | LIB15085 | 1968 £1.50 | £4 | |
| Work With Me Annie | 7" | Liberty | LIB55974 | 1967 £2 | £5 | |
| You Got Me Cryin' | 7" | Melodisc | FAB2 | 1966 £1.50 | £4 | |
| You Got Me Cryin' | 7" | Melodisc | FAB2 | 1966 £2.50 | £6 | *picture sleeve* |

## PROCESSION

| | | | | | | | |
|---|---|---|---|---|---|---|---|
| Every American Citizen | 7" | Mercury | MF1053 | 1968 | £1.50 | £4 | |

## PROCLAIMERS

| | | | | | | | |
|---|---|---|---|---|---|---|---|
| I'm On My Way | CD-s | Chrysalis | CLAMCD4 | 1989 | £2 | £5 | |
| Sunshine On Leith | CD-s | Chrysalis | CLAMCD3 | 1988 | £2 | £5 | |

## PROCOL HARUM

When R&B veterans the Paramounts changed their name to Procol Harum and started wearing brightly coloured kaftans, they were almost ahead of their time. The music press berated the group for choosing to stand still on stage and simply play – an approach that became standard not long afterwards as the progressive rock movement developed. 'A Whiter Shade Of Pale' was one of those records destined to shoot to the top of the charts as soon as it was heard on the radio, but to some extent it became a millstone for the band, which never managed to make quite as much impact again. There is nevertheless much fine music to be found on the group's albums, particularly on *Shine On Brightly* and *A Salty Dog*, where Robin Trower's Hendrix-inspired guitar collides with Gary Brooker's dead-pan vocals and lyricist Keith Reid's finely crafted sense of the absurd. The hit single is not listed below – the record sold so many copies that it is quite common today.

| | | | | | | | |
|---|---|---|---|---|---|---|---|
| Broken Barricades | LP | Chrysalis | ILPS9158 | 1971 | £4 | £10 | |
| Homburg | 7" | Regal Zonophone | RZ3003 | 1967 | £1.50 | £4 | |
| Home | LP | Regal Zonophone | SLRZ1014 | 1970 | £4 | £10 | |
| Home | CD | Mobile Fidelity | MFCD793 | 1989 | £6 | £15 | *US audiophile* |
| Il Tuo Diamente | 7" | IL | IL9005 | 1969 | £4 | £8 | *sung in Italian* |
| Live With The Edmonton Symphony Orchestra | CD | Mobile Fidelity | MFCD788 | 1989 | £6 | £15 | *US audiophile* |
| Lives | LP | A&M | SP8053 | 1972 | £6 | £15 | *...US interview promo* |
| Procol Harum | LP | Regal Zonophone | LRZ1001 | 1967 | £5 | £12 | |
| Prodigal Stranger | CD | Zoo | | 1991 | £20 | £40 | *.. US promo double in cloth cover* |
| Quite Rightly So | 7" | Regal Zonophone | RZ3007 | 1968 | £1.50 | £4 | |
| Salty Dog | LP | Regal Zonophone | SLRZ1009 | 1969 | £5 | £12 | |
| Salty Dog | CD | Mobile Fidelity | MFCD823 | 1985 | £6 | £15 | *US audiophile* |
| Salty Dog | 7" | Regal Zonophone | RZ3019 | 1969 | £1.50 | £4 | |
| Shine On Brightly | LP | Regal Zonophone | (S)LRZ1004 | 1968 | £5 | £12 | |

## PROCOPE, RUSSELL

| | | | | | | | |
|---|---|---|---|---|---|---|---|
| Persuasive Sax | LP | London | HAD2013 | 1956 | £5 | £12 | |

## PROCTOR, JUDD

| | | | | | | | |
|---|---|---|---|---|---|---|---|
| Better Late | 7" | Parlophone | R5126 | 1964 | £1.50 | £4 | |
| Guitars Galore | LP | Morgan | MR103P | 196– | £5 | £12 | |
| It's Bluesy | 7" | Parlophone | R4920 | 1962 | £1.50 | £4 | |
| Nola | 7" | Parlophone | R4809 | 1961 | £1.50 | £4 | |
| Plainsman | 7" | Parlophone | R4769 | 1961 | £1.50 | £4 | |
| Speakeasy | 7" | Parlophone | R4841 | 1961 | £1.50 | £4 | |
| Turk | 7" | Parlophone | R4885 | 1962 | £1.50 | £4 | |

## PROCTOR, MIKE

| | | | | | | | |
|---|---|---|---|---|---|---|---|
| Mr. Commuter | 7" | Columbia | DB8254 | 1967 | £12.50 | £25 | |

## PRODIGY

| | | | | | | | |
|---|---|---|---|---|---|---|---|
| Charly | CD-s | XL | XLS21 | 1991 | £2 | £5 | |
| Firestarter | CD | XL | XLS70CDP | 1996 | £8 | £20 | *promo sampler* |
| Minefields | cass | XL | XLS76 | 1996 | £12.50 | £25 | *promo only* |
| Minefields | 12" | XL | XLT76 | 1996 | £50 | £100 | *test pressing only* |
| What Evil Lurks | 12" | XL | XLT17 | 1991 | £15 | £30 | |

## PROFESSOR LONGHAIR

| | | | | | | | |
|---|---|---|---|---|---|---|---|
| Baby Let Me Hold Your Hand | 7" | Sue | WI397 | 1965 | £7.50 | £15 | |
| Live On The Queen Mary | LP | Harvest | SHSP4086 | 1978 | £4 | £10 | |
| New Orleans 88 | 10" LP | Speakeasy | 1078 | 1972 | £15 | £30 | |
| New Orleans Piano | LP | Atlantic | K40402 | 1972 | £6 | £15 | |
| Professor Longhair | 7" EP | XX | MIN708 | 196– | £4 | £8 | |

## PROFESSOR WOLFF

| | | | | | | | |
|---|---|---|---|---|---|---|---|
| Professor Wolff | LP | Metronome | MLP15422 | 1972 | £50 | £100 | *German* |

## PROFILE

| | | | | | | | |
|---|---|---|---|---|---|---|---|
| Got To Find A Way | 7" | Mercury | MF891 | 1965 | £1.50 | £4 | |
| Haven't They Got Better Things To Do | 7" | Mercury | MF875 | 1965 | £1.50 | £4 | |

## PROJECTION COMPANY

| | | | | | | | |
|---|---|---|---|---|---|---|---|
| Give Me Some Lovin' | LP | Custom | | 1966 | £15 | £30 | *US* |

## PROLES

| | | | | | | | |
|---|---|---|---|---|---|---|---|
| Proles Go To The Seaside | 7" | Can't Play | | 1978 | £6 | £12 | |

## PROPAGANDA

| | | | | | | | |
|---|---|---|---|---|---|---|---|
| 13th Life Of Dr. Mabuse | 12" | ZTT | 12ZTAS2 (2A2U) | 1985 | £5 | £12 | |
| Bejewelled Duel | 12" | ZTT | 12ZTAS8 | 1985 | £2.50 | £6 | *white label promo* |

| | | | | | | | |
|---|---|---|---|---|---|---|---|
| Complete Machinery | cass-s | ZTT | CTIS12 | 1985 £4 | £10 | |
| Das Testaments Des Mabuse | cass-s | ZTT | CTIS101 | 1985 £3 | £8 | |
| Das Testaments Des Mabuse | 12" | ZTT | 12ZTAS2 | 1985 £3 | £8 | 2 different picture sleeves |
| Dr. Mabuse (Remix) | 12" | ZTT | 12ZTAS2DJ | 1985 £4 | £10 | promo |
| Duel | CD-s | ZTT | CTIS108 | 1985 £4 | £10 | |
| Duel | 7" | ZTT | DUAL1 | 1985 £2 | £5 | double |
| Duel | 7" | ZTT | PZTAS8 | 1985 £2 | £5 | shaped picture disc |
| Heaven Give Me Words | CD-s | Virgin | VSCDX1245 | 1990 £2 | £5 | boxed |
| Only One Word | CD-s | Virgin | CSCDT1271 | 1990 £2 | £5 | |
| P Machinery (Beta) | 12" | ZTT | 12XZTAS12 | 1985 £4 | £10 | |
| P Machinery (Beta) | 12" | ZTT | 12ZTAST12 | 1985 £2.50 | £6 | double |
| P Machinery (Polish) | 12" | ZTT | 12PZTAS12 | 1985 £2.50 | £6 | clear vinyl |
| Secret Wish | CD | ZTT | CID126 | 1985 £5 | £12 | |
| Wishful Thinking | CD | ZTT | ZCIDQ20 | 1985 £15 | £30 | |

## PROPAGATION
| | | | | | | |
|---|---|---|---|---|---|---|
| By Means Of Music | LP | Road | | 1983 £6 | £15 | Dutch |

## PROPELLER
| | | | | | | |
|---|---|---|---|---|---|---|
| Let Us Live Together | LP | Philips | 6305114 | 1971 £5 | £12 | German |

## PROPHET, ORVAL
| | | | | | | |
|---|---|---|---|---|---|---|
| Run Run Run | 7" | London | HLL9729 | 1963 £2 | £5 | |

## PROPHET, REX
| | | | | | | |
|---|---|---|---|---|---|---|
| Canadian Plowboy | 7" EP | Brunswick | OE9144 | 1955 £2.50 | £6 | |

## PROPHETS
| | | | | | | |
|---|---|---|---|---|---|---|
| I Got The Fever | 7" | Mercury | MF1097 | 1969 £5 | £10 | |

## PROTOS
| | | | | | | |
|---|---|---|---|---|---|---|
| One Day A New Horizon | LP | Airship | AP391 | 1982 £50 | £100 | |

## PROVIDENCE
| | | | | | | |
|---|---|---|---|---|---|---|
| Ever Sense The Dawn | LP | Threshold | THS9 | 1972 £8 | £20 | |

## PROVINE, DOROTHY
| | | | | | | |
|---|---|---|---|---|---|---|
| Don't Bring Lulu | 7" | Warner Bros | WB53 | 1961 £1.50 | £4 | |

## PROX
| | | | | | | |
|---|---|---|---|---|---|---|
| At Last | LP | Polydor | 2413122 | 1979 £8 | £20 | German |

## PRUDENCE
| | | | | | | |
|---|---|---|---|---|---|---|
| Drunk And Happy | LP | Polydor | 2382031 | 1973 £6 | £15 | Norwegian |

## PRYSOCK, ARTHUR
| | | | | | | |
|---|---|---|---|---|---|---|
| Again | 7" EP | CBS | EP6076 | 1966 £5 | £10 | |
| I Worry About You | LP | Old Town | LP102 | 1962 £6 | £15 | US |
| It's Too Late Baby Too Late | 7" | CBS | 201820 | 1965 £2 | £5 | |

## PRYSOCK, RED
| | | | | | | |
|---|---|---|---|---|---|---|
| Battle Royal | LP | Mercury | MG20106 | 1956 £15 | £30 | US |
| Beat | LP | Mercury | MPL6535 | 1958 £15 | £30 | |
| Blow Your Horn | 78 | Mercury | MB3158 | 1954 £7.50 | £15 | |
| Chop Suey | 7" | Mercury | AMT1028 | 1959 £2.50 | £6 | |
| First Rock 'n' Roll Party | 10" LP | Mercury | MPT7512 | 1957 £20 | £40 | |
| Fruit Boots | LP | Mercury | MPL6550 | 1958 £15 | £30 | |
| Jump Red, Jump | 10" LP | Mercury | MPT7517 | 1957 £20 | £40 | |
| Rock 'n' Roll | LP | Mercury | MG20088 | 1955 £20 | £40 | US |
| Swing Softly Red | LP | Mercury | MG20188 | 1956 £15 | £30 | US |
| Teen Age Rock | 78 | Mercury | MT154 | 1957 £5 | £10 | |

## PSYCHEDELIC FURS
| | | | | | | |
|---|---|---|---|---|---|---|
| All That Money Wants | CD-s | CBS | CDFURS4 | 1988 £2 | £5 | |
| Forever Now | CD | CBS | CD85909 | 1986 £5 | £12 | |
| House | CD-s | CBS | CDFURS5 | 1990 £2 | £5 | |
| Interchords | LP | Columbia | AS1296 | 1981 £6 | £15 | US interview promo |
| Talk Talk Talk | CD | CBS | CD32539 | 1989 £5 | £12 | |
| We Love You | 7" | Epic | 8005DJ | 1979 £2 | £5 | censored promo |

## PSYCHEDELIC PSOUL
| | | | | | | |
|---|---|---|---|---|---|---|
| Freak Scene | LP | Columbia | CS9456 | 1968 £4 | £10 | US |

## PSYCHIC TV

When Throbbing Gristle split, the pieces flew off into three directions, one of which led to the group Psychic TV. Genesis P. Orridge retained a similar record release policy to that of Throbbing Gristle, with a plethora of limited-edition issues that were inevitably destined to rise in value. The music is considerably more commercial on the whole, but with a sardonic streak reminiscent of Frank Zappa's irreverent approach.

| | | | | | | |
|---|---|---|---|---|---|---|
| Album Ten | LP | Temple | TOPY032 | 1988 £6 | £15 | picture disc |
| Allegory And Self | LP | Temple | TOPY038 | 1988 £4 | £10 | picture disc |
| Beyond The Infinite Beat | CD-s | Temple | TOPCD051 | 1990 £2 | £5 | |
| Dreams Less Sweet | LP | CBS | 25737 | 1983 £4 | £10 | with 12" |
| Force The Hand Of Chance | LP | Some Bizarre | PSY1 | 1982 £6 | £15 | double, with insert |
| Godstar | 12" | Temple | TOPIC009 | 1986 £2.50 | £6 | picture disc |
| Good Vibrations | 12" | Temple | TOPY023 | 1987 £2.50 | £6 | |

| | | | | | | |
|---|---|---|---|---|---|---|
| Jack The Tab | 12" | DC | DC23 | 1988 | **£2.50** ... **£6** | |
| Just Drifting | 7" | Some Bizarre | PTV1 | 1982 | **£2.50** ... **£6** | |
| Just Drifting | 12" | Some Bizarre | PTV1T | 1982 | **£5** ... **£12** | |
| Live At Thee Pyramid NYC 1988 | LP | Temple | TOPY047 | 1989 | **£4** ... **£10** | *picture disc* |
| Love War Riot | 10" | Temple | TOPY048T | 1989 | **£2.50** ... **£6** | |
| Magick Defends Itself | 12" | Temple | TOPY022 | 1987 | **£2.50** ... **£6** | |
| Mouth Of The Night | LP | Temple | TOPY010 | 1985 | **£4** ... **£10** | *picture disc* |
| Pagan Day | LP | Temple | TOPY003 | 1984 | **£6** ... **£15** | *picture disc* |
| Psychick TV Themes Vol. 2 | LP | Temple | TOPY004 | 1985 | **£4** ... **£10** | |
| Psychick TV Themes Vol. 3 | LP | Temple | TOPY008 | 1985 | **£4** ... **£10** | |
| Rev. Jim Jones | LP | | | | **£8** ... **£20** | *US picture disc* |
| Roman P. | 7" | Sordide Sentimental | SS33009 | 1984 | **£4** ... **£8** | |
| Unclean | 12" | Temple | TOPY001 | 1984 | **£3** ... **£8** | |

## PTOLOMY PSYCON
| | | | | | | |
|---|---|---|---|---|---|---|
| Loose Capacitor | 7" EP | private | | 197– | **£250** ... **£400** | *best auctioned* |

## PUBLIC ENEMY
| | | | | | | |
|---|---|---|---|---|---|---|
| Rebel Without A Pause | 7" | Def Jam | 6512450 | 1987 | **£2** ... **£5** | *picture disc* |

## PUBLIC FOOT THE ROMAN
| | | | | | | |
|---|---|---|---|---|---|---|
| Public Foot The Roman | LP | Sovereign | SVNA7259 | 1973 | **£10** ... **£25** | |

## PUBLIC IMAGE LTD.
| | | | | | | |
|---|---|---|---|---|---|---|
| Metal Box | LP | Virgin | METAL1 | 1979 | **£6** ... **£15** | *3 x 12" in can* |
| This Is Not A Love Song | CD-s | Virgin | CDT14 | 1988 | **£2** ... **£5** | *3" single* |

## PUCKETT, GARY & UNION GAP
| | | | | | | |
|---|---|---|---|---|---|---|
| Incredible | LP | CBS | 63429 | 1968 | **£4** ... **£10** | |
| Woman Woman | LP | Columbia | CS9612 | 1968 | **£4** ... **£10** | *US* |
| Young Girl | LP | CBS | 63342 | 1968 | **£4** ... **£10** | |

## PUDDING
| | | | | | | |
|---|---|---|---|---|---|---|
| Magic Bus | 7" | Decca | F12603 | 1967 | **£10** ... **£20** | |

## PUGSLEY MUNION
| | | | | | | |
|---|---|---|---|---|---|---|
| Just Like You | LP | J&S | SLP0001 | 1969 | **£37.50** ... **£75** | *US* |

## PUKWANA, DUDU
| | | | | | | |
|---|---|---|---|---|---|---|
| Flute Music | LP | Caroline | CA2005 | 1975 | **£5** ... **£12** | |
| In The Townships | LP | Caroline | C1504 | 1974 | **£5** ... **£12** | *with Spear* |

## PULLINS, LEROY
| | | | | | | |
|---|---|---|---|---|---|---|
| I'm A Nut | LP | Kapp | 1488 | 1969 | **£30** ... **£60** | *US* |
| I'm A Nut | 7" | London | HLR10056 | 1966 | **£4** ... **£8** | |

## PULP
Pulp's *His 'n' Hers* was one of the highlights of 1994, the confident swagger and sleaze of Jarvis Cocker's songwriting being matched by a scintillating performance from the whole group and recalling some of the best moments of an imaginary meeting between Soft Cell and David Bowie. An album as fresh as this might have been expected to be the group's debut but, in fact, Pulp had been around for nearly a dozen years, so that there are numerous early recordings for collectors to seek out (although none is in the same league as *His 'n' Hers* or its follow-up, *Different Class*). Unless Jarvis Cocker once performed under the name of Ann Bean, who is the singer on 'Low Flying Aircraft', then the 1979 Pulp is a different group.

| | | | | | | |
|---|---|---|---|---|---|---|
| Babies | CD-s | Gift | GIF3CD | 1992 | **£6** ... **£15** | |
| Countdown | CD-s | Fire | BLAZE51CD | 1991 | **£10** ... **£20** | |
| Countdown | 12" | Fire | BLAZE51T | 1991 | **£3** ... **£8** | |
| Dogs Are Everywhere | 12" | Fire | BLAZE10S | 1986 | **£10** ... **£20** | |
| Everybody's Problem | 7" | Red Rhino | RED37 | 1983 | **£10** ... **£20** | |
| Freaks | LP | Fire | FIRELP5 | 1987 | **£6** ... **£15** | |
| It | LP | Red Rhino | REDLP29 | 1984 | **£4** ... **£10** | |
| Lipgloss | CD-s | Island | CID567 | 1993 | **£4** ... **£10** | |
| Little Girl With Blue Eyes | 12" | Fire | FIRE5 | 1985 | **£10** ... **£20** | |
| Master Of The Universe | 7" | Fire | BLAZE21S | 1987 | **£5** ... **£10** | |
| Master Of The Universe | 12" | Fire | BLAZE21T | 1987 | **£10** ... **£20** | |
| My Legendary Girlfriend | 7" | Caff | CAFF17 | 1992 | **£20** ... **£40** | |
| My Legendary Girlfriend | 12" | Fire | BLAZE44T | 1991 | **£10** ... **£20** | |
| My Lighthouse | 7" | Red Rhino | RED32 | 1983 | **£15** ... **£30** | |
| O.U. | CD-s | Gift | GIF1CD | 1992 | **£10** ... **£20** | |
| Razzmatazz | CD-s | Gift | GIF6CD | 1993 | **£10** ... **£20** | |
| They Suffocate At Night | 7" | Fire | BLAZE17S | 1987 | **£7.50** ... **£15** | |
| They Suffocate At Night | 12" | Fire | BLAZE17T | 1987 | **£10** ... **£20** | |

## PULP (2)
| | | | | | | |
|---|---|---|---|---|---|---|
| Low Flying Aircraft | 7" | Pulp | PB1 | 1979 | **£2** ... **£5** | |

## PULSAR
| | | | | | | |
|---|---|---|---|---|---|---|
| Halloween | LP | CBS | 82477 | 1977 | **£5** ... **£12** | *French* |
| Pollen | LP | Decca | SKLR5228 | 1976 | **£6** ... **£15** | |
| Strands Of The Future | LP | Decca | TXS119 | 1976 | **£6** ... **£15** | |

## PULSE
| | | | | | | |
|---|---|---|---|---|---|---|
| Pulse | LP | Major Minor | SMLP64 | 1970 | **£25** ... **£50** | |

## PUMA, JOE
| | | | | | | |
|---|---|---|---|---|---|---|
| Joe Puma Quintet | 10" LP | London | LZN14033 | 1956 | **£25** ... **£50** | |

## PUMPKIN, PETER
Would You Believe A March ................... 7" ...... Page One ........ POF048 ................ 1968 £1.50 ........£4 ...........................

## PUMPKIN PIE
Down The Cut ................................. LP ..... Saydisc ........... SDL272 ................. 1976 £8 ...........£20 ...................................

## PUMPKINHEAD
Pumpkinhead ................................. LP ..... Mulligan ........ LUN001 ............. 1976 £5 ...........£12 ................. *Irish*

## PUNCHIN' JUDY
Punchin' Judy ................................. LP ..... Transatlantic .... TRA272 ............. 1973 £5 ...........£12 ..............................

## PUPILS
Cheaply made cover version LPs like *Tribute To The Rolling Stones* seldom attract much collectors' interest. The reason for this album being one of the few exceptions is that the group masquerading as the Pupils was actually the cult freakbeat band, the Eyes.

Tribute To The Rolling Stones ................ LP ..... Fontana ........... SFL13087 ............. 1969 £20 .........£40 ..............................
Tribute To The Rolling Stones ................ LP ..... Wing .............. WL1150 ................ 1966 £37.50 ....£75 ............................

## PUPPETS
Baby Don't Cry ............................... 7" ...... Pye .............. 7N15634 ............ 1964 £6 ...........£12 ..............................
Everybody's Talking ........................... 7" ...... Pye .............. 7N15556 ............ 1963 £6 ...........£12 ..............................
Shake With Me ............................... 7" ...... Pye .............. 7N15625 ............ 1964 £6 ...........£12 ..............................

## PURDIE, BERNARD 'PRETTY'
Soul Drums ..................................... LP ..... Direction ......... 863290 ................. 1968 £4 ...........£10 ..............................

## PURGE
Mayor Of Simpleton Hall ..................... 7" ...... Corn .............. CP101 .................. 1969 £37.50 ....£75 ............................

## PURIFY, JAMES & BOBBY
Do Unto Me .................................. 7" ...... Stateside ......... SS2093 ................. 1968 £1.50 ........£4 ...........................
Help Yourself To All My Lovin' ............... 7" ...... Bell .............. BLL1024 ............... 1968 £1.50 ........£4 ...........................
I Can't Remember ............................ 7" ...... Bell .............. BLL1008 ............... 1968 £1.50 ........£4 ...........................
I'm Your Puppet .............................. 7" ...... Stateside ......... SS547 ................. 1966 £1.50 ........£4 ...........................
James And Bobby Purify ....................... LP ..... Stateside ......... SL10206 ............... 1967 £5 ...........£12 ..............................
Let Love Come Between Us ..................... 7" ...... Stateside ......... SS2049 ................. 1967 £1.50 ........£4 ...........................
Pure Sound Of James And Bobby Purify ..... LP ..... Bell .............. MBLL/SBLL101 ..... 1967 £4 ...........£10 ..............................
Shake A Tail Feather .......................... 7" ...... Bell .............. BLL1056 ............... 1969 £1.50 ........£4 ...........................
Shake A Tail Feather .......................... 7" ...... Stateside ......... SS2016 ................. 1967 £2 ............£5 ...........................

## PURIM, FLORA
Butterfly Dreams .............................. LP ..... Milestone ........ M9052 ................. 1973 £5 ...........£12 ................. *US*
Five Hundred Miles High At Montreux ..... LP ..... Milestone ........ M9070 ................. 1976 £5 ...........£12 ................. *US*
Open Your Eyes You Can Fly ................. LP ..... Milestone ........ M9065 ................. 1976 £5 ...........£12 ................. *US*
Stories To Tell ................................ LP ..... Milestone ........ M9058 ................. 1974 £5 ...........£12 ................. *US*

## PURPLE BARRIER
Shapes And Sounds ........................... 7" ...... Eyemark .......... EMS1011 ............. 1968 £25 .........£50 ..............................

## PURPLE FOX
Tribute To Jimi Hendrix ...................... LP ..... Stereo Gold ...... MER340 ................ 1971 £4 ...........£10 ..............................
............................................................... Award ............

## PURPLE GANG
'Granny Takes A Trip' became a theme tune for the hippy movement in Britain – the title being adopted too by a Carnaby Street clothes shop – although the song is a good-time folk jugband performance and not at all psychedelic.

Granny Takes A Trip .......................... 7" ...... Transatlantic .... BIG101 ................. 1967 £1.50 ........£4 ...........................
Purple Gang Strikes ........................... LP ..... Transatlantic .... ...................... 1968 £10 .........£25 ..............................

## PUSSY
Plays ........................................... LP ..... Morgan Blue ...... BT5002 ................. 1969 £180 ..... £300 ..............................
............................................................... Town .............

## PUSSY (2)
Feline Woman .................................. 7" ...... Deram ............ DM368 ................. 1972 £5 ...........£10 ..............................

## PUSSYCATS
Mrrr Mrrr ..................................... LP ..... Polydor ........... 623020 ................. 1966 £10 .........£25 ................. *Swedish*
Psst Psst ....................................... LP ..... Polydor ........... 623013 ................. 1966 £10 .........£25 ................. *German*

## PUSSYFOOT
Freeloader ...................................... 7" ...... Decca ............ F12474 ................. 1966 £2.50 ........£6 ...........................
Good Times ................................... 7" ...... Pye .............. 7N17520 ............... 1968 £2.50 ........£6 ...........................
Mr. Hyde ...................................... 7" ...... Decca ............ F12561 ................. 1967 £2.50 ........£6 ...........................

## PUTHLI, ASHA
Asha Puthli ................................... LP ..... CBS ............... 65804 ................. 1973 £8 ...........£20 ..............................
Devil Is Loose ................................ LP ..... CBS ............... 81443 ................. 1976 £8 ...........£20 ..............................
She Loves To Hear The Music ................ LP ..... CBS ............... 80978 ................. 1975 £6 ...........£15 ..............................

## PUZZLE
Puzzle ......................................... LP ..... ABC ............... ABCS671 ............. 1969 £15 .........£30 ................. *US*

## PYNE, NATASHA
It's All In Your Head ................................ 7" ...... Polydor ........... 56713 .................... 1966 £1.50 ........ £4 .............................

## PYRAMID
The lead singer on the Pyramid's impressive Deram single was Ian Matthews, subsequently a member of Fairport Convention before embarking on a solo career.

Summer Of Last Year ................................ 7" ...... Deram ........... DM111 .................. 1966 £5 ......... £10 .............................

## PYRAMIDS
Penetration ............................................. LP ..... Best ............... LPM1001/ ........ 1964 £20 ........ £40 ........................ US
                                                          BRS36501 ..............
Penetration ............................................. 7" ...... London ........... HLU9847 .............. 1964 £7.50 ...... £15 .............................

## PYRAMIDS (2)
Pyramids ................................................ LP ..... President ........ PTL1021 ............... 1968 £6 ......... £15 .............................
Train Tour To Rainbow City ................... 7" ...... President ........ PT161 .................... 1967 £1.50 ........ £4 .............................

## PYRAMIDS (3)
Stay With Him ........................................ 7" ...... Doctor Bird ..... DB1307 ................ 1969 £5 ......... £10 .............................

## PYTHAGORAS
After The Silence .................................... LP ..... WEA ............. 58465 .................... 1981 £5 ......... £12 .................... Dutch
Journey To The Vast Unknown ................ LP ...... Syntone ........... ............................. 1981 £10 ......... £25 .................... Dutch

# Q

## Q65

| | | | | | | | |
|---|---|---|---|---|---|---|---|
| Afghanistan | LP | Negram | NELP075 | 1969 | £50 | £100 | Dutch |
| Greatest Hits | LP | Decca | 6454409 | 1969 | £25 | £50 | Dutch |
| Revival | LP | Decca | XBY846515 | 1969 | £62.50 | £125 | Dutch |
| Revolution | LP | Decca | QL625363 | 1966 | £30 | £60 | Dutch |
| We're Gonna Make It | LP | Negram | ELS914 | 1969 | £20 | £40 | Dutch |

## QUAITE, CHRISTINE

| | | | | | | | |
|---|---|---|---|---|---|---|---|
| Guilty Eyes | 7" | Oriole | CB1739 | 1962 | £1.50 | £4 | |
| Here She Comes | 7" | Oriole | CB1921 | 1963 | £1.50 | £4 | |
| If You've Got A Heart | 7" | Stateside | SS435 | 1965 | £1.50 | £4 | |
| In The Middle Of The Floor | 7" | Oriole | CB1876 | 1963 | £1.50 | £4 | |
| Long After Tonight Is All Over | 7" | Stateside | SS482 | 1966 | £5 | £10 | |
| Mister Heartache | 7" | Oriole | CB1845 | 1963 | £1.50 | £4 | |
| Will You Be The Same Tomorrow | 7" | Oriole | CB1945 | 1964 | £1.50 | £4 | |
| Your Nose Is Gonna Grow | 7" | Oriole | CB1772 | 1962 | £1.50 | £4 | |

## QUAKER CITY BOYS

| | | | | | | | |
|---|---|---|---|---|---|---|---|
| Teasin' | 7" | London | HLU8796 | 1959 | £2 | £5 | |

## QUAKERS

| | | | | | | | |
|---|---|---|---|---|---|---|---|
| I'm Ready | 7" | Oriole | CB1992 | 1965 | £62.50 | £125 | |
| She's Alright | 7" | Studio 36 | KSP109/110 | 1965 | £150 | £250 | best auctioned |

## QUARTER NOTES

| | | | | | | | |
|---|---|---|---|---|---|---|---|
| Ten Minutes To Midnight | 7" | Parlophone | R4365 | 1957 | £1.50 | £4 | |

## QUARTERMAN, JOE & FREE SOUL

| | | | | | | | |
|---|---|---|---|---|---|---|---|
| Joe Quarterman And Free Soul | LP | GSF | GS504 | 1973 | £20 | £40 | |

## QUARTZ

| | | | | | | | |
|---|---|---|---|---|---|---|---|
| Nantucket Sleighride | 7" | Reddingtons | DAN1 | 1980 | £2 | £5 | white vinyl |

## QUATERMASS

| | | | | | | | |
|---|---|---|---|---|---|---|---|
| Quatermass | LP | Harvest | SHVL775 | 1970 | £20 | £40 | |

## QUEBEC, IKE

| | | | | | | | |
|---|---|---|---|---|---|---|---|
| Blue And Sentimental | LP | Blue Note | BLP/BST84098 | 1963 | £10 | £25 | |
| Bossa Nova – Soul Samba | LP | Blue Note | BLP/BST84114 | 1964 | £10 | £25 | |
| Buzzard Lope | 7" | Blue Note | 451749 | 1964 | £1.50 | £4 | |
| Heavy Soul | LP | Blue Note | BLP/BST84093 | 1961 | £15 | £30 | |
| It Might As Well Be Spring | LP | Blue Note | BLP/BST84105 | 1964 | £10 | £25 | |

## QUEEN

When EMI were given the Queen's Award to Industry, they were in a position to make an appropriate memento of the occasion and, accordingly, they pressed up a small number of copies of the group Queen's 'Bohemian Rhapsody' on royal blue vinyl. The choice has become doubly appropriate since then, for Queen went on to become one of EMI's bestselling acts. Since Freddie Mercury's death in November 1991, the values of Queen rarities have inevitably increased rapidly, as indeed have the solo records made by all four members. In addition to those items listed below, there have been coloured vinyl pressings of several Queen LPs issued in various countries and selling for £40–£50. The red vinyl UK pressing of *Sheer Heart Attack* that appears on several dealers' and collectors' want lists, however, would appear never to have been released.

| | | | | | | | |
|---|---|---|---|---|---|---|---|
| Another One Bites The Dust | CD-s | Parlophone | QUECD8 | 1988 | £3 | £8 | 3" single |
| Another One Bites The Dust | 7" | EMI | EMI5102 | 1980 | £2 | £5 | picture sleeve |
| Back Chat | 7" | EMI | EMI5325 | 1982 | £2.50 | £6 | |
| Back Chat | 12" | EMI | 12EMI5325 | 1982 | £10 | £25 | |
| Bicycle Race | 7" | EMI | EMI2870 | 1978 | £4 | £8 | mispressed B side – plays Crystal Gale or Dollar |
| Bicycle Race | 7" | EMI | EMI2870 | 1978 | £1.50 | £4 | picture sleeve |
| Body Language | 7" | EMI | EMI5293 | 1982 | £1.50 | £4 | |
| Body Language | 12" | EMI | 12EMI5293 | 1982 | £6 | £15 | |
| Bohemian Rhapsody | CD-s | Parlophone | QUECD3 | 1988 | £3 | £8 | 3" single |
| Bohemian Rhapsody | 7" | EMI | EMI2375 | 1975 | £700 | £1000 | blue vinyl, picture sleeve |
| Bohemian Rhapsody | 7" | EMI | EMI2375 | 1975 | £12.50 | £25 | picture sleeve |
| Bohemian Rhapsody | 7" | EMI | EMI2378 | 1975 | £5 | £10 | misprinted number |
| Breakthru | CD-s | EMI | CDQUEEN11 | 1989 | £10 | £20 | |
| Breakthru | 7" | EMI | QUEENPD11 | 1989 | £12.50 | £25 | shaped picture disc |
| Breakthru' | 12" | Parlophone | 12QUEEN11 | 1989 | £2.50 | £6 | |
| Classic Queen | CD | Capitol | DPRO79591 | 1989 | £15 | £30 | US promo compilation |
| Complete Works | LP | EMI | QB1 | 1985 | £62.50 | £125 | 14 LP boxed set |

| Title | Format | Label | Cat. No. | Year | Price | Price | Notes |
|---|---|---|---|---|---|---|---|
| Complete Works | LP | EMI | QB1 | 1985 | £210 | £350 | 14 LP boxed set, autographed |
| Crazy Little Thing Called Love | CD-s | Parlophone | QUECD7 | 1988 | £3 | £8 | 3" single |
| Crazy Little Thing Called Love | 7" | EMI | EMI5001 | 1979 | £5 | £10 | mispressed with 2 B sides |
| Crazy Little Thing Called Love | 7" | EMI | EMI5001 | 1979 | £1.50 | £4 | picture sleeve |
| Digital Master Sampler | CD | EMI | CDDIG1 | 1994 | £37.50 | £75 | promo compilation |
| Don't Stop Me Now | 7" | EMI | EMI2910 | 1979 | £1.50 | £4 | picture sleeve |
| Flash | 7" | EMI | EMI5126 | 1980 | £1.50 | £4 | picture sleeve |
| Friends Will Be Friends | 7" | EMI | QUEEN8 | 1986 | £2 | £5 | |
| Friends Will Be Friends | 7" | EMI | QUEENP8 | 1986 | £15 | £30 | picture disc |
| Friends Will Be Friends | 12" | EMI | 12QUEEN8 | 1986 | £3 | £8 | |
| Game | CD | Mobile Fidelity | UDCD610 | 1994 | £6 | £15 | US audiophile |
| Greatest Hits | LP | EMI | EMTV30 | 1981 | £5 | £12 | mispress – side 2 plays Anne Murray |
| Greatest Hits Volume Two | CD | Parlophone | CDPCSD161 | 1991 | £50 | £100 | ... promo box set, with video, photos, booklet |
| Hammer To Fall | 7" | EMI | QUEEN4 | 1984 | £50 | £100 | live picture sleeve |
| Hammer To Fall | 7" | EMI | QUEEN4 | 1984 | £1.50 | £4 | red picture sleeve |
| Hammer To Fall (Headbangers Mix) | 12" | EMI | 12QUEEN4 | 1984 | £62.50 | £125 | live picture sleeve |
| Hammer To Fall (Headbangers Mix) | 12" | EMI | 12QUEEN4 | 1984 | £3 | £8 | red picture sleeve |
| Headlong | CD-s | EMI | CDQUEEN18 | 1991 | £3 | £8 | |
| Headlong | 12" | Parlophone | 12QUEENPD18 | 1991 | £6 | £15 | picture disc |
| Highlander | CDV | EMI | EMCDV2 | 1986 | £62.50 | £125 | |
| I Want It All | CD-s | Parlophone | CDQUEEN10 | 1989 | £10 | £20 | picture disc |
| I Want It All | 12" | Parlophone | 12QUEEN10 | 1989 | £2.50 | £6 | |
| I Want To Break Free | CD-s | Parlophone | QUECD11 | 1988 | £3 | £8 | 3" single |
| I Want To Break Free | 7" | EMI | QUEEN2 | 1984 | £2.50 | £6 | 4 different picture sleeves |
| I Want To Break Free | 12" | EMI | 12QUEEN2 | 1984 | £3 | £8 | |
| I'm Going Slightly Mad | CD-s | Parlophone | CDQUEEN17 | 1991 | £3 | £8 | |
| I'm Going Slightly Mad | 7" | Parlophone | QUEENPD17 | 1991 | £7.50 | £15 | shaped picture disc |
| I'm Going Slightly Mad | 12" | Parlophone | 12QUEENG17 | 1991 | £3 | £8 | gatefold picture sleeve |
| Innuendo | CD-s | Parlophone | CDQUEEN16 | 1991 | £2 | £5 | |
| Innuendo | CD | EMI | CDP7958870 | 1991 | £8 | £20 | German, with calendar |
| Innuendo | CD | Parlophone | CDPCSD115 | 1991 | £50 | £100 | ... promo box set, with cassette, single and calendar |
| Innuendo | 12" | Parlophone | 12QUEENPD16 | 1991 | £10 | £20 | picture disc |
| Invisible Man | CD-s | Parlophone | CDQUEEN12 | 1989 | £12.50 | £25 | |
| Invisible Man | 7" | Parlophone | QUEENX12 | 1989 | £5 | £10 | clear vinyl |
| Invisible Man | 12" | EMI | 12QUEENX12 | 1989 | £6 | £15 | clear vinyl |
| Invisible Man | 12" | Parlophone | 12QUEEN12 | 1989 | £2.50 | £6 | |
| It's A Hard Life | 7" | EMI | QUEEN3 | 1984 | £2 | £5 | |
| It's A Hard Life | 7" | EMI | QUEEN3 | 1984 | £25 | £50 | John Taylor's head superimposed on cover pic |
| It's A Hard Life | 12" | EMI | 12QUEEN3 | 1984 | £5 | £12 | no picture sleeve |
| It's A Hard Life | 12" | EMI | 12QUEENP3 | 1984 | £15 | £30 | picture disc |
| Jazz | LP | EMI | PIC3 | 1978 | £100 | £200 | French picture disc |
| Jealousy | 7" | EMI | | 1979 | £7.50 | £15 | promo |
| Keep Yourself Alive | 7" | EMI | EMI2036 | 1973 | £15 | £30 | |
| Killer Queen | CD-s | Parlophone | QUECD2 | 1988 | £3 | £8 | 3" single |
| Killer Queen | 7" | EMI | EMI2229 | 1974 | £1.50 | £4 | |
| Kind Of Magic | CD-s | Parlophone | QUECD12 | 1988 | £3 | £8 | 3" single |
| Kind Of Magic | 7" | EMI | QUEEN7 | 1986 | £1.50 | £4 | |
| Kind Of Magic | 12" | EMI | 12QUEEN7 | 1986 | £2.50 | £6 | |
| Kind Of Magic | 12" | EMI | 12QUEENP7 | 1986 | £25 | £50 | picture disc |
| Las Palabras De Amor | 7" | EMI | EMI5316 | 1982 | £5 | £10 | |
| Live At The BBC | LP | Hollywood | SPRO62005 | 1995 | £50 | £100 | US promo picture disc |
| Love Of My Life | 7" | EMI | EMI2959 | 1979 | £10 | £20 | |
| Miracle | CD-s | Parlophone | CDQUEEN15 | 1989 | £6 | £15 | |
| Miracle | CD | Parlophone | CDPCSD107 | 1989 | £37.50 | £75 | ... promo box set, with cassette sampler and booklet |
| Miracle | 7" | Parlophone | QUEEN15 | 1989 | £1.50 | £4 | |
| Miracle | 7" | Parlophone | QUEENH15 | 1989 | £5 | £10 | hologram picture sleeve |
| Miracle | 12" | Parlophone | 12QUEEN15 | 1989 | £2.50 | £6 | ... yellow picture sleeve |
| Miracle | 12" | Parlophone | 12QUEENP15 | 1989 | £6 | £15 | turquoise picture sleeve, insert |
| News Of The World | LP | EMI | EMA784 | 1977 | £75 | £150 | promo, boxed |
| Night At The Opera | LP | Mobile Fidelity | MFSL1067 | 1980 | £8 | £20 | US audiophile |
| Night At The Opera | CD | Mobile Fidelity | UDCD568 | 1992 | £6 | £15 | US audiophile |
| Now I'm Here | 7" | EMI | EMI2256 | 1975 | £1.50 | £4 | |
| One Vision | 7" | EMI | QUEEN6 | 1985 | £2.50 | £6 | lyric inner sleeve |
| One Vision | 12" | EMI | 12QUEEN6 | 1985 | £2.50 | £6 | |
| One Vision | 12" | EMI | 12QUEEN6 | 1985 | £10 | £25 | PVC cover, red inner |
| One Vision | 12" | EMI | 12QUEEN6 | 1985 | £4 | £10 | with inner sleeve |
| Play The Game | 7" | EMI | EMI5076 | 1980 | £5 | £10 | mispressed with 2 B sides |
| Play The Game | 7" | EMI | EMI5076 | 1980 | £1.50 | £4 | picture sleeve |
| Queen | LP | Elektra | EQ5064 | 1973 | £8 | £20 | US quad |
| Queen | LP | EMI | EMC3006 | 1973 | £25 | £50 | EMI conference copy, unfinished sleeve |
| Queen Rocks | CD | Hollywood | | 1991 | £75 | £150 | US promo 4 CD boxed set |
| Queen Rocks Volume Four | CD | Hollywood | PRCD82982 | 1991 | £15 | £30 | US promo sampler |
| Queen Rocks Volume One | CD | Hollywood | PRCD82632 | 1991 | £15 | £30 | US promo sampler |

| | | | | | | | |
|---|---|---|---|---|---|---|---|
| Queen Rocks Volume Three | CD | Hollywood | PRCD82972 | 1991 | £15 | £30 | *US promo sampler* |
| Queen Rocks Volume Two | CD | Hollywood | PRCD82962 | 1991 | £15 | £30 | *US promo sampler* |
| Queen Talks | CD | Hollywood | PRCD8674 | 1992 | £15 | £30 | *US promo* |
| Queen's First EP | CD-s | Parlophone | QUECD5 | 1988 | £3 | £8 | *3" single* |
| Queen's First EP | 7" EP | EMI | EMI2623 | 1977 | £4 | £8 | |
| Radio Ga Ga | CD-s | Parlophone | QUECD10 | 1988 | £3 | £8 | *3" single* |
| Radio Ga Ga | 12" | EMI | 12QUEEN1 | 1984 | £2.50 | £6 | |
| Sample Of Magic | CD | Parlophone | | 1991 | £10 | £25 | *promo* |
| Save Me | 7" | EMI | EMI5022 | 1980 | £1.50 | £4 | *picture sleeve* |
| Scandal | CD-s | Parlophone | CDQUEEN14 | 1989 | £10 | £20 | |
| Scandal | 7" | Parlophone | QUEENP14 | 1989 | £6 | £12 | *poster sleeve* |
| Scandal | 12" | Parlophone | 12QUEEN14 | 1989 | £2.50 | £6 | |
| Scandal | 12" | Parlophone | 12QUEENS14 | 1989 | £10 | £20 | *1 side etched with signatures* |
| Seven Seas Of Rhye | 7" | EMI | EMI2121 | 1974 | £2 | £5 | |
| Seven Seas Of Rye | CD-s | Parlophone | QUECD1 | 1988 | £3 | £8 | *3" single* |
| Show Must Go On | CD-s | Parlophone | CDQUEEN19 | 1991 | £3 | £8 | |
| Show Must Go On | CD-s | Parlophone | CDQUEENS19 | 1991 | £12.50 | £25 | *boxed with poster* |
| Show Must Go On | 12" | Parlophone | 12QUEENSG19 | 1991 | £6 | £15 | *1 side etched with signatures* |
| Somebody To Love | CD-s | Parlophone | QUECD4 | 1988 | £3 | £8 | *3" single* |
| Somebody To Love | 7" | EMI | EMI2565 | 1976 | £4 | £8 | *picture sleeve* |
| Spread Your Wings | 7" | EMI | EMI2757 | 1978 | £2.50 | £6 | *picture sleeve* |
| Thank God It's Christmas | 7" | EMI | QUEEN5 | 1984 | £2.50 | £6 | |
| Thank God It's Christmas | 12" | EMI | 12QUEEN5 | 1984 | £6 | £15 | |
| These Are The Days Of Our Lives | CD-s | Parlophone | CDQUEEN20 | 1991 | £2 | £5 | |
| Twelve Inch Collection | CD | Parlophone | CDQTEL0001 | 1992 | £50 | £100 | *boxed set with video, badge, patch, T-shirt, booklet, poster* |
| Under Pressure | CD-s | Parlophone | QUECD9 | 1988 | £3 | £8 | *3" single, with David Bowie* |
| Under Pressure (Live) | 7" | EMI | | 1986 | £10 | £20 | *promo* |
| We Are The Champions | CD-s | EMI | QUECD6 | 1988 | £3 | £8 | *3" single* |
| We Are The Champions | 7" | EMI | EMI2708 | 1977 | £1.50 | £4 | *picture sleeve* |
| Who Wants To Live Forever | 7" | EMI | QUEEN9 | 1986 | £2.50 | £6 | |
| Who Wants To Live Forever | 12" | EMI | 12QUEEN9 | 1986 | £10 | £20 | |
| Works | 7" | EMI | | 1984 | £2.50 | £6 | *promo flexi* |
| You Don't Fool Me (remixes) | 12" | Parlophone | 12RDJ6446 | 1996 | £20 | £40 | *orange vinyl promo* |
| You're My Best Friend | 7" | EMI | EMI2494 | 1976 | £12.50 | £25 | *picture sleeve* |

## QUEEN'S NECTARINE MACHINE

| | | | | | | | |
|---|---|---|---|---|---|---|---|
| Mystical Powers Of Roving Tarot Gamble | LP | ABC | ABCS666 | 1969 | £15 | £30 | *US* |

## QUEENSRYCHE

| | | | | | | | |
|---|---|---|---|---|---|---|---|
| Best I Can | CD-s | EMI | CDMT97 | 1991 | £2 | £5 | |
| Empire | CD-s | EMI | CDMT90 | 1990 | £2 | £5 | |
| Empire | 7" | EMI | MTPD90 | 1990 | £2.50 | £6 | *shaped picture disc* |
| Eyes Of A Stranger | CD-s | EMI | 2033492 | 1989 | £10 | £20 | |
| Eyes Of A Stranger | CD-s | EMI | CDMT65 | 1989 | £3 | £8 | |
| Eyes Of A Stranger | 12" | EMI | 12MTG65 | 1989 | £3 | £8 | *gatefold picture sleeve* |
| Gonna Get Close To You | 7" | EMI | EA22 | 1986 | £2 | £5 | |
| Gonna Get Close To You | 7" | EMI | EAD22 | 1986 | £5 | £10 | *double* |
| Gonna Get Close To You | 12" | EMI | 12EA22 | 1986 | £4 | £10 | |
| Jet City Woman | CD-s | EMI | CDMT98 | 1991 | £2 | £5 | |
| Operation Mindcrime | LP | EMI | SPRO04137 | 1988 | £10 | £25 | *US promo picture disc* |
| Overseeing The Operation | 10" | EMI | 10QR1 | 1988 | £3 | £8 | |
| Queen Of The Reich | 12" | EMI | 12EA162 | 1983 | £4 | £10 | |
| Silent Lucidity | CD-s | EMI | CDMT94 | 1991 | £2 | £5 | |
| Take Hold Of The Flame | 7" | EMI | EA183 | 1984 | £4 | £8 | |

## QUESTION MARK & THE MYSTERIANS

| | | | | | | | |
|---|---|---|---|---|---|---|---|
| 96 Tears | LP | Cameo | C(S)2004 | 1966 | £25 | £50 | *US* |
| 96 Tears | 7" EP | Columbia | ESRF1825 | 1966 | £20 | £40 | *French* |
| 96 Tears | 7" | Cameo Parkway | C428 | 1966 | £6 | £12 | |
| Action | LP | Cameo | C(S)2006 | 1966 | £25 | £50 | *US* |
| Can't Get Enough Of You baby | 7" EP | Stateside | FSE105 | 1967 | £15 | £30 | *French* |
| Can't Get Enough Of You Baby | 7" | Cameo Parkway | C467 | 1967 | £1.50 | £4 | |
| Do Something To Me | 7" | Cameo Parkway | C496 | 1967 | £1.50 | £4 | |
| Girl | 7" EP | Stateside | FSE1006 | 1967 | £15 | £30 | *French* |
| I Need Somebody | 7" | Cameo Parkway | C441 | 1966 | £5 | £10 | |
| You Captivate Me | 7" | Cameo Parkway | C479 | 1967 | £1.50 | £4 | |

## QUESTIONS

| | | | | | | | |
|---|---|---|---|---|---|---|---|
| We Got Love | 7" | Decca | F22740 | 1968 | £5 | £10 | |

## QUICK, BENNY & TWEN BAND

| | | | | | | | |
|---|---|---|---|---|---|---|---|
| Twens Top | LP | Columbia | 83874 | 1964 | £10 | £25 | *German* |

## QUICKLY, TOMMY

| | | | | | | | |
|---|---|---|---|---|---|---|---|
| Humpty Dumpty | 7" | Pye | 7N15748 | 1964 | £4 | £8 | |
| Tip Of My Tongue | 7" | Piccadilly | 7N35137 | 1963 | £10 | £20 | |
| Wild Side Of Life | 7" | Pye | 7N15708 | 1964 | £1.50 | £4 | |

## QUICKSAND
| | | | | | | | | |
|---|---|---|---|---|---|---|---|---|
| Home Is Where I Belong | LP | Dawn | DNLS3056 | 1974 | £20 | £40 | | |
| Passing By | 7" | Carnaby | CNS4015 | 1970 | £1.50 | £4 | | |
| Time To Live | 7" | Dawn | DNS1046 | 1973 | £1.50 | £4 | | |

## QUICKSILVER MESSENGER SERVICE
| | | | | | | | | |
|---|---|---|---|---|---|---|---|---|
| Comin' Thru' | LP | Capitol | ST11002 | 1972 | £4 | £10 | | |
| Happy Trails | LP | Capitol | E(S)T120 | 1969 | £6 | £15 | | |
| Just For Love | LP | Capitol | EAST498 | 1970 | £4 | £10 | | |
| Maiden Of The Cancer Moon | LP | Psycho | PSYCHO10 | 1983 | £10 | £25 | double |
| Quicksilver | LP | Capitol | SW819 | 1972 | £4 | £10 | | |
| Quicksilver Messenger Service | LP | Capitol | (S)T2904 | 1968 | £8 | £20 | | |
| Shady Grove | LP | Capitol | EST391 | 1969 | £4 | £10 | | |
| What About Me | LP | Capitol | EAST630 | 1971 | £4 | £10 | | |

## QUIET FIVE
| | | | | | | | |
|---|---|---|---|---|---|---|---|
| Homeward Bound | 7" | Parlophone | R5421 | 1966 | £1.50 | £4 | |
| I Am Waiting | 7" | Parlophone | R5470 | 1966 | £1.50 | £4 | |

## QUIET WORLD

Guitarist with Quiet World, prior to his joining Genesis, was the young Steve Hackett.

| | | | | | | | |
|---|---|---|---|---|---|---|---|
| Love Is Walking | 7" | Dawn | DNS1005 | 1970 | £5 | £10 | |
| Miss Whittington | 7" | Dawn | DNS1001 | 1969 | £5 | £10 | |
| Rest Comfortably | 7" | Pye | 7N45005 | 1970 | £4 | £8 | |
| Road | LP | Dawn | DNLS3007 | 1970 | £25 | £50 | |

## QUIK
| | | | | | | | |
|---|---|---|---|---|---|---|---|
| I Can't Sleep | 7" | Deram | DM155 | 1967 | £12.50 | £25 | |
| King Of The World | 7" | Deram | DM139 | 1967 | £5 | £10 | |
| Love Is A Beautiful Thing | 7" | Deram | DM121 | 1967 | £12.50 | £25 | |

## QUILL, GENE
| | | | | | | | |
|---|---|---|---|---|---|---|---|
| Three Bones And A Quill | LP | Vogue | LAE12204 | 1959 | £8 | £20 | |

## QUINCICASM
| | | | | | | | |
|---|---|---|---|---|---|---|---|
| Quincicasm | LP | Saydisc | SDL249 | 1973 | £5 | £12 | |

## QUINICHETTE, PAUL
| | | | | | | | |
|---|---|---|---|---|---|---|---|
| Basie Reunion | LP | Esquire | 32087 | 1960 | £8 | £20 | |
| For Basie | LP | Esquire | 32067 | 1959 | £10 | £25 | |

## QUINTESSENCE

Quintessence seemed to epitomize hippiedom – living communally, radiating peace and love, and above all being obsessed with Eastern religion and music. The group's albums are a smooth blend of Indian chanting and English electric guitar, the two being held together by Raja Ram's fluid, melodic flute playing. They are among the most successful attempts to fuse Eastern and Western musics, although the hippy context will inevitably make the music sound rather dated to modern listeners.

| | | | | | | | |
|---|---|---|---|---|---|---|---|
| Dive Deep | LP | Island | ILPS9143 | 1970 | £5 | £12 | |
| In Blissful Company | LP | Island | ILPS9110 | 1969 | £8 | £20 | pink label |
| Indweller | LP | RCA | SF8317 | 1972 | £4 | £10 | |
| Notting Hill Gate | 7" | Island | WIP6075 | 1970 | £1.50 | £4 | |
| Quintessence | LP | Island | ILPS9128 | 1970 | £8 | £20 | pink label |
| Self | LP | RCA | SF8273 | 1971 | £4 | £10 | |
| Sweet Jesus | 7" | Neon | NE1003 | 1971 | £1.50 | £4 | |
| Sweet Jesus | 7" | Neon | NE1003 | 1971 | £5 | £10 | picture sleeve |

## QUINTET OF THE YEAR
| | | | | | | | |
|---|---|---|---|---|---|---|---|
| Jazz At Massey Hall | LP | Vogue | LAE12031 | 1957 | £50 | £100 | |
| Jazz At Massey Hall Vol. 1 | 10" LP | Vogue | LDE040 | 1954 | £50 | £100 | |
| Jazz At Massey Hall Vol. 2 | 10" LP | Vogue | LDE053 | 1954 | £50 | £100 | |
| Jazz At Massey Hall Vol. 3 | 10" LP | Vogue | LDE087 | 1954 | £50 | £100 | |

## QUIREBOYS
| | | | | | | | |
|---|---|---|---|---|---|---|---|
| Hey You | CD-s | Parlophone | CDR6241 | 1989 | £2 | £5 | |
| Seven O'Clock | CD-s | Parlophone | CDR6230 | 1989 | £2 | £5 | |

## QUIST, DARYL
| | | | | | | | |
|---|---|---|---|---|---|---|---|
| Above And Beyond | 7" | Pye | 7N15605 | 1964 | £1.50 | £4 | |
| Thanks To You | 7" | Pye | 7N15538 | 1963 | £1.50 | £4 | picture sleeve |

## QUO VARDIS
| | | | | | | | |
|---|---|---|---|---|---|---|---|
| 100 Mph | 7" | Redball | RB001 | 1979 | £5 | £10 | |

## QUODLING'S DELIGHT
| | | | | | | | |
|---|---|---|---|---|---|---|---|
| Among The Leaves So Green | LP | Fanfare | FR2179 | 197– | £5 | £12 | |
| Among The Leaves So Green | LP | Volta | Q121 | 197– | £5 | £12 | |

## QUOTATIONS
| | | | | | | | |
|---|---|---|---|---|---|---|---|
| Imagination | 7" | HMV | POP975 | 1962 | £12.50 | £25 | |

## QUOTATIONS (2)
| | | | | | | | |
|---|---|---|---|---|---|---|---|
| Alright Baby | 7" | Decca | F11907 | 1964 | £2.50 | £6 | |
| Cool It | 7" | CBS | 3710 | 1968 | £1.50 | £4 | |

# R

### RA CAN ROW
Acid Rock For The Eighties.................... LP ..... Eye ................ 8107 ..................... 1982 £8 .......... £20 ....................... US

### RABBLE
Rabble ........................................ LP..... Roulette ........ SR42010 .............. 1969 £50....... £100 ....................... US
Rabble Album ............................... LP ..... Transworld...... 6700 ................ 1966 £50....... £100 ....................... US

### RABIN, MIKE
Head Over Heels........................... 7" ..... Columbia ........ DB7350 ............... 1964 £12.50.... £25 ..................
If I Were You ............................... 7" ..... Polydor .......... BM56007 .............. 1965 £5........... £10 ..................

### RACAILLE, JOSEPH
Six Petites Chansons ...................... 7" ...... Recommended RR16.5 ................. 1983 £4........... £8 .........clear vinyl

### RACHEL & THE REVOLVERS
'The Revo-Lution' is one of several early Brian Wilson productions.

Revo-Lution............................... 7" ..... Dot................ 16392.................... 1962 £150..... £250 .... US, best auctioned

### RACHELL, YANK TENNESSEE JUG BUSTERS
Mandolin Blues ............................ LP ..... 77 ............... LA1223 ................. 1964 £6........... £15 ..........................

### RADAVIQUE
B Sides ...................................... LP ..... Radavique ...... ................. 1984 £75....... £150 .................Dutch

### RADCLIFFE, JIMMY
Long After Tonight Is All Over ............ 7" ...... Stateside ....... SS374 ................ 1965 £10....... £20 ..................

### RADHA KRISHNA TEMPLE
Govinda ..................................... 7" ..... Apple ............ 25 ................. 1970 £5........... £10 ......... picture sleeve
Hare Krishna Mantra ...................... 7" ..... Apple ............ 15 ................. 1969 £2.50....... £6 ..................
Hare Krishna Mantra ...................... 7" ..... Apple ............ 15 ................. 1969 £6........... £12 ... picture sleeve, insert
Radha Krishna Temple .................... LP ..... Apple ............ SAPCOR18 .......... 1971 £15....... £30 ..................

### RADIANTS
Hold On ..................................... 7" ...... Chess ............. CRS8073 .............. 1968 £2........... £5 ..................
Voice Your Choice ........................ 7" ...... Chess ............. CRS8002 .............. 1965 £1.50....... £4 ..................

### RADIATORS FROM SPACE
Song Of The Faithful Departed............. 7" ..... Chiswick........ CHIS144............ 1979 £2........... £5 ....................Irish
Sunday World............................... 7" ..... CBS ............. 5572 ................ 1977 £10....... £20 ....................Irish
Teenager In Love .......................... 7" ..... Chiswick........ NS24 ................ 1978 £7.50....... £15 .......... test pressing
Walkin' Home Alone Again ............... 7" ..... Chiswick........ NS45 ................ 1979 £7.50....... £15 ...............test presing

### RADICE, MARK
Hey My Love ............................... 7" ...... Paramount....... PARA3024......... 1972 £1.50....... £4 ..................
New Day..................................... 7" ...... Paramount....... PARA3025......... 1972 £1.50....... £4 ..................

### RADIO ACTORS
Nuclear Waste............................... 7" ...... Charly............ CYS1058 ............. 1979 £1.50....... £4 ......... picture sleeve
Nuclear Waste............................... 7" ...... DB ............... DBS5................... 1979 £1.50....... £4 ......... picture sleeve

### RADIO BIRDMAN
Aloha Steve And Danno.................... 7" ...... Trafalgar....... TRS12............ 1978 £2.50....... £6 ..................
Alone In The Endzone .................... 7" ..... WEA ............. 100160.............. 1981 £25....... £50 ..................
Burn My Eye .............................. 7" ..... Trafalgar....... ME109 .............. 1976 £50....... £100 ..................
New Race .................................. 7" ..... Trafalgar....... TRS11............ 1977 £25....... £50 ..................
Radios Appear ............................ LP ..... Sire ............. 9103332 .............. 1978 £6........... £15 ..................
Radios Appear (Second Version)............ LP ..... Sire ............. SRK6050 .......... 1978 £4........... £10 ..................
What Gives? ............................... 7" ...... Sire ............. 6078617 .............. 1978 £2.50....... £6 ..................

### RADIO HEART
All Across The Nation ..................... CD-s .. NBR ............. CDNBR1 ............ 1987 £2.50....... £6 ..... shaped picture disc
London Times .............................. 7" ...... GFM ............ GFMX112........... 1987 £1.50....... £4 ..... shaped picture disc
Radio Heart................................. LP ..... NBR ............. NBRL1.............. 1987 £4........... £10 ..................
Radio Heart................................. CD ..... NBR ............. ................. 1987 £20....... £40 ...............European
Radio Heart................................. 7" ...... GFM ............ GFMG109........... 1987 £2.50....... £6 ..... shaped picture disc
Radio Heart................................. 7" ...... GFM ............ GFMX109........... 1987 £2.50....... £6 ............picture disc

### RADIOHEAD
Anyone Can Play Guitar .................... CD-s .. EMI ............. CDR6333 .......... 1993 £6........... £15 ..................
Anyone Can Play Guitar .................... 12" ..... Parlophone ..... 12R6333 .............. 1993 £3........... £8 ..................

| | | | | | | | |
|---|---|---|---|---|---|---|---|
| Creep | CD-s .. | Parlophone | CDR6078 | 1992 | £10 | £20 | |
| Creep | CD-s .. | Parlophone | CDR6359 | 1993 | £4 | £10 | digipak |
| Creep | 7" | Parlophone | RS6359 | 1993 | £1.50 | £4 | clear vinyl |
| Creep | 12" | Parlophone | 12R6078 | 1992 | £4 | £10 | |
| Creep | 12" | Parlophone | 12RG6359 | 1993 | £2.50 | £6 | |
| My Iron Lung | CD-s .. | Parlophone | CDR6394 | 1994 | £2 | £5 | |
| My Iron Lung | CD-s .. | Parlophone | CDRS6394 | 1994 | £2 | £5 | |
| Pop Is Dead | CD-s .. | EMI | CDR6345 | 1993 | £6 | £15 | |
| Pop Is Dead | 12" | Parlophone | 12R6345 | 1993 | £2.50 | £6 | |
| Prove Yourself (Drill EP) | CD-s .. | Parlophone | CDR6312 | 1992 | £12.50 | £25 | |
| Prove Yourself (Drill EP) | 12" | Parlophone | 12R6312 | 1992 | £10 | £20 | |

## RAEBURN, BOYD
| | | | | | | | |
|---|---|---|---|---|---|---|---|
| Teen Rock | LP | Columbia | CL1073 | 1957 | £10 | £25 | US |

## RAELETS
| | | | | | | | |
|---|---|---|---|---|---|---|---|
| One Hurt Deserves Another | 7" | HMV | POP1591 | 1967 | £1.50 | £4 | |

## RAFFERTY, GERRY
| | | | | | | | |
|---|---|---|---|---|---|---|---|
| Baker Street (remix) | CD-s .. | EMI | CDEM132 | 1990 | £2 | £5 | |

## RAG DOLLS
| | | | | | | | |
|---|---|---|---|---|---|---|---|
| Dusty | 7" | Stateside | SS398 | 1965 | £1.50 | £4 | |
| Society Girl | 7" | Cameo Parkway | P921 | 1964 | £1.50 | £4 | |

## RAG DOLLS (2)
| | | | | | | | |
|---|---|---|---|---|---|---|---|
| My Old Man's A Groovy Old Man | 7" | Columbia | DB8378 | 1968 | £1.50 | £4 | |
| Never Had So Much Loving | 7" | Columbia | DB8289 | 1967 | £1.50 | £4 | |

## RAGGED HEROES
| | | | | | | | |
|---|---|---|---|---|---|---|---|
| Ragged Heroes Annual | LP | Celtic Music | CM013 | 1983 | £100 | £200 | best auctioned |

## RAGING STORMS
| | | | | | | | |
|---|---|---|---|---|---|---|---|
| Dribble | 7" | London | HLU9556 | 1962 | £6 | £12 | |

## RAGLAND, LOU
| | | | | | | | |
|---|---|---|---|---|---|---|---|
| Since You Said You'd Be Mine | 7" | Warner Bros | K16312 | 1973 | £2 | £5 | |

## RAGNAROK
| | | | | | | | |
|---|---|---|---|---|---|---|---|
| Fata Morgana | LP | Silence | SRS4666 | 1981 | £5 | £12 | Swedish |
| Fjarliar I Magen | LP | Silence | SRS4655 | 1980 | £5 | £12 | Swedish |
| Ragnarok | LP | Silence | SRS4633 | 1977 | £6 | £15 | Swedish |
| Three Signs | LP | Silence | SRS126704 | 1984 | £4 | £10 | Swedish |
| Undertakers Circus | LP | Polydor | 2382025 | 1973 | £6 | £15 | Swedish |

## RAHMANN
| | | | | | | | |
|---|---|---|---|---|---|---|---|
| Rahmann | LP | Polydor | 2393252 | 1979 | £15 | £30 | French |

## RAILWAY CHILDREN
| | | | | | | | |
|---|---|---|---|---|---|---|---|
| Music From The East Zone | 7" | Gross Product | OBCT1 | 1983 | £2 | £5 | with tracks by other artists |

## RAIN
| | | | | | | | |
|---|---|---|---|---|---|---|---|
| Album | LP | Axe | 501 | 1976 | £8 | £20 | Canadian |

## RAIN (2)
| | | | | | | | |
|---|---|---|---|---|---|---|---|
| Live Xmas Night | LP | Whazoo! | USR3046 | 1968 | £50 | £100 | US |

## RAIN (3)
| | | | | | | | |
|---|---|---|---|---|---|---|---|
| Rain | LP | Project | 3 | 1972 | £6 | £15 | US |

## RAIN (4)
| | | | | | | | |
|---|---|---|---|---|---|---|---|
| Once | 7" | Jive Alive | JA002 | 1985 | £1.50 | £4 | |

## RAINBEAUS
| | | | | | | | |
|---|---|---|---|---|---|---|---|
| That's All I'm Asking Of You | 7" | Vogue | V9161 | 1960 | £2.50 | £6 | |

## RAINBOW
| | | | | | | | |
|---|---|---|---|---|---|---|---|
| Bent Out Of Shape | CD | Polydor | 8153052 | 1983 | £5 | £12 | |
| L.A. Connection | 7" | Polydor | 2066968 | 1978 | £2 | £5 | red vinyl |
| Ritchie Blackmore's Rainbow | CD | Polydor | 8250892 | 1988 | £5 | £12 | |
| Straight Between The Eyes | CD | Polydor | 8000282 | 1983 | £5 | £12 | |
| Street Of Dreams | 7" | Polydor | POSPP631 | 1983 | £2 | £5 | picture disc |

## RAINBOW (2)
| | | | | | | | |
|---|---|---|---|---|---|---|---|
| After The Storm | LP | Crescendo | GNPS2049 | 1968 | £20 | £40 | US |

## RAINBOW FFOLLY

*Sallies Fforth* is one of the great post-*Sgt Pepper* albums, which should be filed next to the first Blossom Toes LP by all those with any interest in the musical delights of the best late-sixties music. It was originally intended that the album should have a round sleeve, but the plan was abandoned when the release of Ogden's Nut Gone Flake showed that the Small Faces had come up with the idea first! I am informed by Mary Payne, whose husband was a founder member of Wycombe Hospital Radio, that the group also recorded a number of jingles for the station, although these never made it beyond the tape stage.

| | | | | | | | |
|---|---|---|---|---|---|---|---|
| Drive My Car | 7" | Parlophone | R5701 | 1968 | £7.50 | £15 | |
| Sallies Fforth | LP | Parlophone | PMC/PCS7050 | 1967 | £100 | £200 | |

## RAINBOW PEOPLE
| | | | | | | | |
|---|---|---|---|---|---|---|---|
| Dream Time | 7" | Pye | 7N17582 | 1968 | £2.50 | £6 | |
| Living In A Dream World | 7" | Pye | 7N17759 | 1969 | £1.50 | £4 | |

## RAINBOW PRESS
| | | | | | | | |
|---|---|---|---|---|---|---|---|
| Sunday Funnies | LP | Mr. G | 9004 | 1969 | £37.50 | £75 | US |
| There's A War On | LP | Mr. G | 9003 | 1968 | £37.50 | £75 | US |

## RAINBOW PROMISE
| | | | | | | | |
|---|---|---|---|---|---|---|---|
| Rainbow Promise | LP | Wine Press | LPS25901 | 1970 | £250 | £400 | US |

## RAINBOWS
| | | | | | | | |
|---|---|---|---|---|---|---|---|
| Rainbows | LP | CBS | 62625 | 1966 | £50 | £100 | German |

## RAINCHECKS
| | | | | | | | |
|---|---|---|---|---|---|---|---|
| How Are You Baby | 7" | R&B | MRB5002 | 1965 | £10 | £20 | |

## RAINDROPS
| | | | | | | | |
|---|---|---|---|---|---|---|---|
| Book Of Love | 7" | Fontana | TF463 | 1964 | £2.50 | £6 | |
| Kind Of Boy You Can't Forget | 7" | London | HL9769 | 1963 | £4 | £8 | |
| Raindrops | LP | London | HA8140 | 1964 | £15 | £30 | |
| That Boy John | 7" | London | HL9825 | 1964 | £4 | £8 | |
| What A Guy | 7" EP | London | RE1415 | 1964 | £20 | £40 | |
| What A Guy | 7" | London | HL9718 | 1963 | £5 | £10 | |

## RAINDROPS (2)
| | | | | | | | |
|---|---|---|---|---|---|---|---|
| Along Came Jones | 7" | Parlophone | R4559 | 1959 | £1.50 | £4 | |

## RAINE, LORRY
| | | | | | | | |
|---|---|---|---|---|---|---|---|
| Love Me Tonight | 7" | London | HL8132 | 1955 | £10 | £20 | |
| You Broke My Broken Heart | 7" | London | HL8043 | 1954 | £10 | £20 | |

## RAINEY, MA
| | | | | | | | |
|---|---|---|---|---|---|---|---|
| Female Blues Vol. 3 | 7" EP | Collector | JEL22 | 1964 | £4 | £8 | with Trixie Smith |
| Ma Rainey | 10" LP | Ristic | LP13 | 195– | £10 | £25 | |
| Ma Rainey | 10" LP | Ristic | LP19 | 195– | £10 | £25 | |
| Sings The Blues | LP | Riverside | RL12108 | 1962 | £6 | £15 | |
| Vol. 1 | 10" LP | London | AL3502 | 1953 | £8 | £20 | |
| Vol. 2 | 10" LP | London | AL3538 | 1955 | £8 | £20 | |
| Vol. 3 | 10" LP | London | AL3558 | 1956 | £8 | £20 | |

## RAINMAN
| | | | | | | | |
|---|---|---|---|---|---|---|---|
| Rainman | LP | Negram | NQ20038 | 1971 | £37.50 | £75 | Dutch |

## RAINWATER, MARVIN
| | | | | | | | |
|---|---|---|---|---|---|---|---|
| Country & Western Favourites Vol. 2 | 7" EP | Ember | EMBEP4521 | 1962 | £5 | £10 | |
| Dance Me Daddy | 7" | MGM | MGM988 | 1958 | £2.50 | £6 | |
| Gonna Find Me A Bluebird | LP | MGM | E4046 | 1962 | £15 | £30 | US |
| Gonna Find Me A Bluebird | 7" | MGM | MGM961 | 1957 | £5 | £10 | |
| Half Breed | 7" | MGM | MGM1030 | 1959 | £2 | £5 | |
| I Can't Forget | 7" | London | HLU9447 | 1961 | £37.50 | £75 | |
| I Dig You Baby | 7" | MGM | MGM980 | 1958 | £2 | £5 | |
| Marvin Rainwater | 7" EP | MGM | MGMEP685 | 1958 | £15 | £30 | |
| Meet Marvin Rainwater | 7" EP | MGM | MGMEP647 | 1958 | £12.50 | £25 | |
| Nothin' Needs Nothin' | 7" | MGM | MGM1052 | 1960 | £2.50 | £6 | |
| Songs By Marvin Rainwater | LP | MGM | E3534 | 1957 | £30 | £60 | US |
| Songs By Marvin Rainwater | 10" LP | MGM | D152 | 1957 | £30 | £60 | |
| Tennessee Hound Dog Yodel | 7" | MGM | SP1150 | 1955 | £15 | £30 | |
| What Am I Supposed To Do | 7" | MGM | MGM929 | 1956 | £7.50 | £15 | |
| Whole Lotta Marvin | 7" EP | MGM | MGMEP662 | 1958 | £15 | £30 | |
| Whole Lotta Woman | 7" | MGM | MGM974 | 1958 | £2 | £5 | |
| With A Heart, With A Beat | LP | MGM | E3721 | 1958 | £20 | £40 | US |

## RAINY DAY
| | | | | | | | |
|---|---|---|---|---|---|---|---|
| Painting Pictures | 7" | EMI | EMI5472 | 1984 | £4 | £8 | |

## RAINY DAZE
| | | | | | | | |
|---|---|---|---|---|---|---|---|
| Blood Of Oblivion | 7" | Polydor | BM56737 | 1968 | £7.50 | £15 | |
| That Acapulco Gold | LP | Uni | (7)3002 | 1967 | £25 | £50 | US |
| That Acapulco Gold | 7" | Polydor | 56731 | 1968 | £12.50 | £25 | |

## RAITT, BONNIE
| | | | | | | | |
|---|---|---|---|---|---|---|---|
| I Can't Make You Love Me | CD-s | Capitol | CDCLS639 | 1991 | £2 | £5 | boxed |
| Nick Of Time | CD-s | Capitol | CDCL530 | 1990 | £2 | £5 | |
| Thing Called Love | CD-s | Capitol | CDCL576 | 1990 | £2 | £5 | |

## RALLY ROUNDERS
'Bike Beat' is actually the work of the Outlaws, with Ritchie Blackmore on guitar.

| | | | | | | | |
|---|---|---|---|---|---|---|---|
| Bike Beat | 7" | Lyntone | LYN574 | 1964 | £20 | £40 | flexi |

## RAM
| | | | | | | | |
|---|---|---|---|---|---|---|---|
| Where? In Conclusion | LP | Polydor | POLD5013 | 1972 | £15 | £30 | US |

## RAM, BUCK
| | | | | | | | |
|---|---|---|---|---|---|---|---|
| Benfica | 7" | London | HLU9677 | 1963 | £2 | £5 | |

Magic Touch ............... LP ...... Mercury ...... MG2/SR60392 ....... 1960 £5 ......... £12 ..................... US

## RAM JAM BAND
Shake Shake Senora ..................... 7" ...... Columbia ........ DB7621 ................. 1965 £2 ......... £5

## RAMASES
Ballroom ................................. 7" ...... Philips............ 6113001 ................ 1971 £1.50 ..... £4
Glass Top Coffin ..................... LP ...... Vertigo .......... 6360115 ................ 1975 £5 ......... £12
Jesus Come Back........................ 7" ...... Philips............ 6113003 ................ 1972 £1.50 ..... £4
Space Hymns ............................ LP ...... Vertigo .......... 6360046 ............... 1971 £10 ....... £25 .................. spiral label
Space Hymns ............................ LP ...... Vertigo .......... 6360046 ............... 1973 £5 ......... £12

## RAMASES & SELEKA
Love You .................................. 7" ...... Major Minor ... MM704.............. 1970 £6 ......... £12
Crazy One ................................ 7" ...... CBS................ 3717 ................. 1968 £30 ....... £60

## RAMATAM
In April Came The Dawning.................... LP ...... Atlantic ........... SD7261 ............. 1973 £4 ......... £10 ..................... US

## RAMBLERS
Dodge City.............................. 7" ...... Decca ............. F11775 .............. 1963 £6 ......... £12

## RAMONES
Blitzkrieg Bop........................... 7" ...... Sire ........... 6078601 ............. 1976 £20 ....... £40 ...... picture sleeve
I Remember You ......................... 7" ...... Sire ........... 6078603 ............. 1977 £4 ......... £8 ...... picture sleeve
I Wanna Be Sedated ................... 7" ...... RSO ........... RSO70 .............. 1981 £2 ......... £5
Meltdown With The Ramones........ 7" ...... Sire ........... SREP1 .............. 1980 £1.50 ..... £4
Poison Heart ............................. CD-s .. Chrysalis ........ CDCHSS3917 ... 1992 £2 ......... £5
Ramones Leave Home.................... LP ...... Sire ........... 9103254 ............. 1977 £4 ......... £10 .....with 'Carbona Not Glue'
Rockaway Beach ........................ 12" ...... Sire ........... 6078611 ............. 1977 £2.50 ...... £6 ...... with poster
She's The One ............................ 7" ...... Sire ........... SIR4009............. 1979 £2 ......... £5
Sheena Is A Punk Rocker .......... 7" ...... Sire ........... 6078606 ............. 1977 £2 ......... £5
Sheena Is A Punk Rocker .......... 12" ...... Sire ........... 6078606 ............. 1977 £3 ......... £8
Swallow My Pride .................... 7" ...... Sire ........... 6078607 ............. 1977 £2 ......... £5
Time Has Come Today ............... 7" ...... Sire ........... W9606.............. 1983 £4 ......... £8
Time Has Come Today ............... 12" ...... Sire ........... WT9606.............. 1983 £4 ......... £10

## RAMPART STREET PARADERS
Rampart And Vine ..................... LP ...... Philips......... BBL7194 .......... 1958 £6 ......... £15
Rampart Street Paraders ........................ LP ...... Philips......... BBL7112 .......... 1957 £6 ......... £15

## RAMRODS
Loch Lomond Rock ................... 7" ...... London ......... HLU9355.......... 1961 £2 ......... £5
Riders In The Sky ................... 7" EP . London ......... REU1292.......... 1961 £25 ....... £50
Riders In The Sky ................... 7" ...... London ......... HLU9282.......... 1961 £1.50 ..... £4

## RAMRODS (2)
Overdrive................................. 7" ...... United Artists .. UP1113................ 1965 £2 ......... £5

## RAMSEY, BILL
Go Man Go ............................. 7" ...... Polydor........... NH66812 ........ 1962 £2 ......... £5

## RANALDO, LEE
From Here To Infinity........................... 12" ..... Blast First ........ BFFP9............... 1987 £2.50 ........ £6 ...............clear vinyl

## RANCHERS
American Sailor At The Cavern ................. 7" ...... Cavern Sound.. IMSTL2 ................ 1965 £2.50 ........ £6

## RANDALL, FREDDY
Dr. Jazz .................................. 10" LP Parlophone...... PMD1046 ............. 1957 £4 ......... £10

## RANDAZZO, TEDDY
Big Wide World ......................... LP ...... Colpix ........ CP445 ............ 1963 £15 ....... £30 ..................... US
Dance To The Locomotion............... 7" ...... HMV............ POP1062 ...... 1962 £1.50 ..... £4
Hey, Let's Twist......................... LP ...... Roulette ........ R25168 .......... 1962 £15 ....... £30 ..................... US
I'm Confessin'........................... LP ...... Vik ........... LX1121 .......... 1960 £15 ....... £30 ..................... US
Journey To Love ...................... LP ...... HMV............ CLP1527/CSD1421 1962 £15 ....... £30
Twists .................................... LP ...... HMV............ CLP1601 .......... 1963 £20 ....... £40

## RANDELL, LYNNE
Ciao Baby ................................. 7" ...... CBS................ 2847 ................. 1967 £50 ....... £100
That's A Hoe Down ................... 7" ...... CBS................ 2927 ................. 1967 £2.50 ...... £6

## RANDELLS
Martian Hop ............................. 7" ...... London ........... HLU9760.............. 1963 £7.50 ...... £15

## RANDI, DON
Live At The Discotheque ...................... 7" EP . Reprise ........... RVEP6102............ 1967 £2.50 ........ £6 ............... French

## RANDOLPH, BARBARA
I Got A Feeling........................... 7" ...... Tamla Motown TMG628 ........... 1967 £12.50 .... £25
I Got A Feeling........................... 7" ...... Tamla Motown TMG788 ........... 1971 £1.50 ..... £4

## RANDOLPH, BOOTS
Hey Mr. Sax Man...................... 7" ...... London ........... HLU9891.............. 1964 £1.50 ..... £4
More Yakety Sax......................... LP ...... London ........... HAU8280 ............. 1966 £5 ......... £12
These Boots Were Made For Walking........ 7" ...... London ........... HLU10028 ............. 1966 £1.50 ..... £4

715

| | | | | | | | |
|---|---|---|---|---|---|---|---|
| Yakety Sax | LP | London | HAU8106 | 1963 | £5 | £12 | |
| Yakety Sax | 7" | London | HLU9685 | 1963 | £2 | £5 | |
| Yakety Sax Of Boots Randolph | 7" EP | London | REU1365 | 1963 | £6 | £12 | |

## RANDOM BLUES BAND
| | | | | | | | |
|---|---|---|---|---|---|---|---|
| Winchester Cathedral | 7" EP | Vogue | INT18103 | 1966 | £2.50 | £6 | *French* |

## RANDY & THE RAINBOWS
| | | | | | | | |
|---|---|---|---|---|---|---|---|
| Denise | 7" | Stateside | SS214 | 1963 | £12.50 | £25 | |

## RANEE & RAJ
| | | | | | | | |
|---|---|---|---|---|---|---|---|
| Don't Tell Me I Must Go | 7" | Fontana | TF941 | 1968 | £1.50 | £4 | |
| Feel Like A Clown | 7" | Fontana | TF920 | 1968 | £2 | £5 | |

## RANEY, JIMMY
| | | | | | | | |
|---|---|---|---|---|---|---|---|
| In Three Attitudes | LP | HMV | CLP1264 | 1959 | £8 | £20 | |
| Jimmy Raney 1955 | 10" LP | Esquire | 20054 | 1955 | £20 | £40 | |
| Visits Paris | 10" LP | Vogue | LDE071 | 1954 | £20 | £40 | |
| Visits Paris Vol. 2 | 10" LP | Vogue | LDE097 | 1955 | £20 | £40 | |

## RANEY, SUE
| | | | | | | | |
|---|---|---|---|---|---|---|---|
| When Your Lover Has Gone | 7" EP | Capitol | EAP1964 | 1958 | £4 | £8 | |

## RANEY, WAYNE
| | | | | | | | |
|---|---|---|---|---|---|---|---|
| Adam | 7" | Parlophone | CSMP20 | 1954 | £6 | £12 | *export* |
| Country And Western | 7" EP | Parlophone | GEP8746 | 1958 | £10 | £20 | |

## RANGLERS
| | | | | | | | |
|---|---|---|---|---|---|---|---|
| You Never Said Goodbye | 7" | Trend | TRE1007 | 1968 | £5 | £10 | |

## RANGLIN, ERNEST
| | | | | | | | |
|---|---|---|---|---|---|---|---|
| Harmonica Twist | 7" | Island | WI015 | 1962 | £5 | £10 | |
| Reflections | LP | Island | ILP915 | 1964 | £20 | £40 | |
| Soho | 7" EP | Black Swan | IEP704 | 1966 | £10 | £20 | |
| Swing-A-Ling | 7" | Black Swan | WI417 | 1964 | £5 | £10 | |
| Wranglin' | LP | Island | ILP909 | 1964 | £20 | £40 | |

## RANKIN, KENNY
| | | | | | | | |
|---|---|---|---|---|---|---|---|
| Mind Dusters | LP | Mercury | 20145SMCL | 1968 | £4 | £10 | |

## RANKIN FILE
| | | | | | | | |
|---|---|---|---|---|---|---|---|
| Rankin File | LP | Circle | | 1971 | £25 | £50 | |

## RANSOME, PETER
| | | | | | | | |
|---|---|---|---|---|---|---|---|
| Peter Ransome | LP | York | FYK402 | 1972 | £4 | £10 | |

## RAPEMAN
| | | | | | | | |
|---|---|---|---|---|---|---|---|
| Hated Chinee | 7" | Fierce | FRIGHT031 | 1988 | £2 | £5 | |

## RAPHAEL, JOHNNY
| | | | | | | | |
|---|---|---|---|---|---|---|---|
| We're Only Young Once | 7" | Vogue | V9104 | 1958 | £25 | £50 | |

## RAPIERS
| | | | | | | | |
|---|---|---|---|---|---|---|---|
| Vol. 1 | 7" | Red Door | RA001 | 1983 | £2.50 | £6 | |
| Vol. 2 | 7" | Twang | RA002 | 1984 | £2 | £5 | |
| Vol. 3 | 7" | Twang | RA003 | 1985 | £1.50 | £4 | |

## RAPKIN, BRIAN & KELVIN JONES
| | | | | | | | |
|---|---|---|---|---|---|---|---|
| Dreams Of The Blue Beast | LP | MSR | | 197– | £6 | £15 | |

## RAPP, TOM
| | | | | | | | |
|---|---|---|---|---|---|---|---|
| Stardancer | LP | Blue Thumb | BTS44 | 1972 | £6 | £15 | US |
| Sunforest | LP | Blue Thumb | BTS56 | 1973 | £5 | £12 | US |
| Tom Rapp | LP | Reprise | MS2069 | 1972 | £6 | £15 | US |

## RARE AMBER
| | | | | | | | |
|---|---|---|---|---|---|---|---|
| Malfunction Of The Engine | 7" | Polydor | 56309 | 1969 | £2.50 | £6 | |
| Rare Amber | LP | Polydor | 583046 | 1969 | £50 | £100 | |

## RARE BIRD
| | | | | | | | |
|---|---|---|---|---|---|---|---|
| As Your Mind Flies By | LP | Charisma | CAS1011 | 1970 | £5 | £20 | |
| Epic Forest | LP | Polydor | 2442101 | 1972 | £8 | £20 | *.. with 7" (2814011)* |
| Rare Bird | LP | Charisma | CAS1005 | 1969 | £5 | £12 | |
| Sympathy | 7" | Charisma | CB179 | 1972 | £1.50 | £4 | *picture sleeve* |

## RARE BREED
| | | | | | | | |
|---|---|---|---|---|---|---|---|
| Beg Borrow And Steal | 7" | Strike | JH316 | 1966 | £6 | £12 | |

## RARE EARTH
| | | | | | | | |
|---|---|---|---|---|---|---|---|
| Ecology | LP | Tamla Motown | STML11180 | 1971 | £4 | £10 | |
| Get Ready | LP | Tamla Motown | STML11165 | 1970 | £4 | £10 | |
| Get Ready | 7" | Tamla Motown | TMG742 | 1970 | £1.50 | £4 | |

## RAS MICHAEL & THE SONS OF NEGUS
| | | | | | | | |
|---|---|---|---|---|---|---|---|
| Dadawah | LP | Trojan | TRLS103 | 1975 | £6 | £15 | |
| Nyahbinghi | LP | Trojan | TRS113 | 1975 | £5 | £12 | |
| Rastafari | LP | Grounation | GROL505 | 1976 | £6 | £15 | |
| Tribute To The Emperor | LP | Trojan | TRS132 | 1976 | £5 | £12 | |

## RASCALS

| Title | | Label | Cat No | Year | | | Notes |
|---|---|---|---|---|---|---|---|
| Beautiful Morning | 7" | Atlantic | 584182 | 1968 | £1.50 | £4 | |
| Carry Me Back | 7" | Atlantic | 584292 | 1969 | £1.50 | £4 | |
| Collection | LP | Atlantic | 587060 | 1967 | £6 | £15 | |
| Come On Up | 7" | Atlantic | 584050 | 1966 | £2.50 | £6 | |
| Freedom Suite | LP | Atlantic | 588183 | 1969 | £4 | £10 | |
| Freedom Suite Narration | LP | Atlantic | | 1969 | £5 | £12 | US promo |
| Girl Like You | 7" | Atlantic | 584128 | 1967 | £1.50 | £4 | |
| Good Lovin' | 7" EP | Atlantic | 750011 | 1966 | £6 | £12 | French |
| Good Lovin' | 7" | Atlantic | AT4082 | 1966 | £1.50 | £4 | |
| Greatest Hits | LP | Atlantic | 587/588120 | 1968 | £4 | £10 | |
| Groovin' | LP | Atlantic | 587/588074 | 1967 | £6 | £15 | |
| Groovin' | 7" | Atlantic | 584111 | 1967 | £1.50 | £4 | |
| Heaven | 7" | Atlantic | 584255 | 1969 | £1.50 | £4 | |
| Hold On | 7" | Atlantic | 584307 | 1970 | £1.50 | £4 | |
| How Can I Be Sure | 7" | Atlantic | 584138 | 1967 | £1.50 | £4 | |
| I Ain't Gonna Eat Out My Heart | 7" | Atlantic | 584085 | 1967 | £1.50 | £4 | |
| I Ain't Gonna Eat Out My Heart | 7" | Atlantic | AT4059 | 1965 | £2 | £5 | |
| I've Been Lonely Too Long | 7" EP | Atlantic | 750021 | 1967 | £6 | £12 | French |
| I've Been Lonely Too Long | 7" | Atlantic | 584081 | 1967 | £2.50 | £6 | |
| It's Wonderful | 7" | Atlantic | 584161 | 1968 | £1.50 | £4 | |
| Love Is A Beautiful Thing | 7" | Atlantic | 584024 | 1966 | £2.50 | £6 | |
| Once Upon A Dream | LP | Atlantic | 587/588098 | 1968 | £4 | £10 | |
| People Got To Be Free | 7" | Atlantic | 584210 | 1968 | £1.50 | £4 | |
| Search And Nearness | LP | Atlantic | 2400113 | 1971 | £4 | £10 | |
| See | LP | Atlantic | 588210 | 1969 | £4 | £10 | |
| See | 7" | Atlantic | 584274 | 1969 | £1.50 | £4 | |
| Sentirai La Pioggla | 7" | Atlantic | NP3124 | 1968 | £4 | £8 | sung in Italian |
| Sueno | 7" EP | Atlantic | 750027 | 1967 | £6 | £12 | French |
| Too Many Fish In The Sea | 7" | Atlantic | 584067 | 1966 | £1.50 | £4 | |
| Young Rascals | LP | Atlantic | 587012 | 1966 | £8 | £20 | |

## RASPUT & THE SEPOY MUTINY

| Title | | Label | Cat No | Year | | | Notes |
|---|---|---|---|---|---|---|---|
| Flower Power Sitar | LP | Design | SDLP280 | 1967 | £10 | £25 | US |

## RASPUTIN & THE MONKS

| Title | | Label | Cat No | Year | | | Notes |
|---|---|---|---|---|---|---|---|
| Rasputin & The Monks | LP | Resurrection | CX1227 | 198– | £6 | £15 | US, one sided |
| Sum Of My Soul | LP | Trans Radio | 200836 | 1965 | £250 | £400 | US, B side by the Octet |

## RAT, MIKE & THE RUNAWAYS

| Title | | Label | Cat No | Year | | | Notes |
|---|---|---|---|---|---|---|---|
| Live Recording From The Kaskade Beat Club | LP | Ariola | 72659IT | 1963 | £50 | £100 | German |

## RATIONALS

| Title | | Label | Cat No | Year | | | Notes |
|---|---|---|---|---|---|---|---|
| Rationals | LP | Crewe | 1334 | 1969 | £8 | £20 | US |

## RATIP, ARMAN

| Title | | Label | Cat No | Year | | | Notes |
|---|---|---|---|---|---|---|---|
| Introducing | LP | Columbia | SCX6432 | 1970 | £8 | £20 | |
| Spy From Istanbul | LP | Regal Zonophone | SLRZ1038 | 1973 | £15 | £30 | |

## RATS

The Rats, whose recording career had begun and ended a little earlier, were the group taken on by David Bowie and renamed the Spiders From Mars. The assumption is that Mick Ronson is to be heard playing on the singles, but in fact he did not join the Rats until the late sixties. His recording debut is therefore not to be found on any of the singles by the Rats, but on the 1969 album by Michael Chapman, *Fully Qualified Survivor*.

| Title | | Label | Cat No | Year | | | Notes |
|---|---|---|---|---|---|---|---|
| I Gotta See My Baby | 7" | Columbia | DB7607 | 1965 | £25 | £50 | |
| Spoonful | 7" | Columbia | DB7483 | 1965 | £37.50 | £75 | |
| Spoonful | 7" | Oak | RGJ145 | 1964 | £75 | £150 | 1 sided |

## RATS (2)

| Title | | Label | Cat No | Year | | | Notes |
|---|---|---|---|---|---|---|---|
| Parchman Farm | 7" | Oriole | CB1967 | 1964 | £20 | £40 | |
| Sack Of Woe | 7" | CBS | 201740 | 1965 | £15 | £30 | |

## RATT

| Title | | Label | Cat No | Year | | | Notes |
|---|---|---|---|---|---|---|---|
| Lay It Down | 7" | Atlantic | A9546P | 1985 | £1.50 | £4 | shaped picture disc |
| You're In Love | 7" | Atlantic | A9502P | 1986 | £2 | £5 | shaped picture disc |

## RATTLES

| Title | | Label | Cat No | Year | | | Notes |
|---|---|---|---|---|---|---|---|
| Au Star Club De Hambourg | 7" EP | Barclay | 70656 | 1964 | £30 | £60 | French |
| Bye Bye Johnny | 7" | Decca | F11873 | 1964 | £4 | £8 | |
| Come On And Sing | 7" | Fontana | TF618 | 1965 | £2 | £5 | |
| Gin Mill | LP | RCA | PPL14016 | 1974 | £5 | £12 | German |
| Greatest Hits | LP | Mercury | MG1127 | 1967 | £10 | £25 | |
| Hurra, Die Rattles Kommen | LP | Star Club | STY158013 | 1966 | £30 | £60 | German |
| Liverpool Beat Vol. 2 | LP | Ariola | 71741IT | 1965 | £25 | £50 | German |
| Rattles | LP | Decca | SKL5088 | 1971 | £8 | £20 | |
| Rattles Production | LP | Fontana | 885445ZY | 1968 | £10 | £25 | German |
| Remember Finale Ligure | LP | Star Club | STY158031 | 1967 | £37.50 | £75 | German |
| Say All Right | 7" | Fontana | TF724 | 1966 | £2 | £5 | |
| Sha-La-La-La-Lee | 7" EP | Fontana | 466030 | 1967 | £30 | £60 | French |
| Star Club Show 1 | LP | Starclub | STY158000 | 1965 | £30 | £60 | German |
| Stomp | 7" | Philips | BF1277 | 1963 | £2 | £5 | |
| Teenbeat From The Star Club Hamburg | 7" EP | Decca | DFE8568 | 1964 | £30 | £60 | |

| | | | | | | | |
|---|---|---|---|---|---|---|---|
| Tell Me What Can I Do | 7" | Decca | F11936 | 1964 | £2 | £5 | |
| Tonight Starring Edna | LP | Philips | 6305176 | 1972 | £4 | £10 | German |
| Twist At The Star Club | LP | Philips | BL7614 | 1964 | £37.50 | £75 | |
| Witch | LP | Philips | 6305072 | 1971 | £8 | £20 | German |

## RAVA, ENRICO
| | | | | | | | |
|---|---|---|---|---|---|---|---|
| Pilgrim And The Stars | LP | ECM | ECM1063ST | 1975 | £4 | £10 | |

## RAVEL, CHRIS & THE RAVERS

Chris Ravel was Chris Andrews, later a moderately successful solo artist and a more successful songwriter and producer – most notably for Sandie Shaw.

| | | | | | | |
|---|---|---|---|---|---|---|
| I Do | 7" | Decca | F11696 | 1963 | £2.50 | £6 |

## RAVEN
| | | | | | | | |
|---|---|---|---|---|---|---|---|
| Live At The Inferno | LP | Discovery | 36133 | 1967 | £6 | £15 | US |
| Raven | LP | Columbia | CS9903 | 1969 | £5 | £12 | US |

## RAVEN, JON
| | | | | | | |
|---|---|---|---|---|---|---|
| Ballad Of The Black Country | LP | Broadside | BRO116 | 1975 | £5 | £12 |
| Harvest | LP | Broadside | BRO117 | 1976 | £5 | £12 |

## RAVEN, JON, JOHN KIRKPATRICK, SUE HARRIS
| | | | | | | |
|---|---|---|---|---|---|---|
| English Canals | LP | Broadside | BRO118 | 1976 | £5 | £12 |

## RAVEN, JON, MIKE RAVEN, PETE SAGE, JEAN WARD
| | | | | | | |
|---|---|---|---|---|---|---|
| Kate Of Coalbrookdale | LP | Argo | ZFB29 | 1971 | £8 | £20 |

## RAVEN, JON, NIC JONES, TONY ROSE
| | | | | | | |
|---|---|---|---|---|---|---|
| Songs Of A Changing World | LP | Trailer | LER2083 | 1973 | £10 | £25 |

## RAVEN, MIKE

Mike Raven was a disc jockey on pirate radio and then on Radio One. He used to present a specialist programme of soul and blues and the two LPs listed here are to some extent re-creations of the blues part. The *Blues Show* provides a necessarily brief, but effective, history of the blues. Mike Raven introduces each track and his comments are relevant enough – and his voice soothing enough – to prevent the introductions becoming irritating on successive hearings. The *Blues Sampler* is similar, but attempts to show the range of blues styles rather than following a historical approach.

| | | | | | | |
|---|---|---|---|---|---|---|
| Mike Raven Blues Sampler | LP | Transatlantic | TRASAM5 | 1969 | £4 | £10 |
| Mike Raven Blues Show | LP | XTRA | XTRA1047 | 1966 | £5 | £12 |

## RAVEN, PAUL

It is astonishing to realize that the earliest record made by Gary Glitter dates from as early as 1960! The man who was born Paul Gadd adopted the Raven surname for most of the sixties, and has a starring role on the original *Jesus Christ Superstar* album under this name.

| | | | | | | |
|---|---|---|---|---|---|---|
| Soul Thing | 7" | MCA | MU1035 | 1968 | £2.50 | £6 |
| Stand | 7" | MCA | MKS5053 | 1970 | £2 | £5 |
| Too Proud | 7" | Decca | F11202 | 1960 | £7.50 | £15 |
| Tower Of Strength | 7" | Parlophone | R4842 | 1961 | £5 | £10 |
| Walk On Boy | 7" | Parlophone | R4812 | 1961 | £5 | £10 |

## RAVEN, SIMON
| | | | | | | |
|---|---|---|---|---|---|---|
| I Wonder If She Remembers Me | 7" | Piccadilly | 7N35301 | 1966 | £10 | £20 |

## RAVENS
| | | | | | | | |
|---|---|---|---|---|---|---|---|
| Begin The Beguine | 78 | Oriole | CB1149 | 1953 | £6 | £12 | |
| I Just Wanna Hear You Say | 7" | Oriole | CB1910 | 1964 | £2.50 | £6 | |
| Rock Me All Night Long | 78 | Oriole | CB1148 | 1953 | £6 | £12 | |
| Who'll Be The Fool? | 78 | Oriole | CB1258 | 1954 | £6 | £12 | |
| Write Me A Letter | LP | Regent | MG6062 | 195– | £30 | £60 | US |

## RAVERS
| | | | | | | | |
|---|---|---|---|---|---|---|---|
| Badam Bam | 7" | Upsetter | US312 | 1969 | £1.50 | £4 | Upsetters B side |

## RAW HERBS
| | | | | | | | |
|---|---|---|---|---|---|---|---|
| Old Joe | 7" | Medium Cool | MC002 | 1986 | £1.50 | £4 | flexi |

## RAW HOLLY
| | | | | | | | |
|---|---|---|---|---|---|---|---|
| Raw Holly | LP | MCA | MAPS4067 | 1971 | £8 | £20 | German |

## RAW MATERIAL
| | | | | | | |
|---|---|---|---|---|---|---|
| Hi There Allelujah | 7" | Evolution | E2445 | 1970 | £7.50 | £15 |
| Raw Material Album | LP | Evolution | Z1006 | 1970 | £75 | £150 |
| Ride On Pony | 7" | Neon | NE1002 | 1972 | £7.50 | £15 |
| Time And Illusion | 7" | Evolution | E2441 | 1969 | £7.50 | £15 |
| Time Is | LP | Neon | NE8 | 1971 | £150 | £250 |
| Traveller Man | 7" | Evolution | E24495 | 1970 | £10 | £20 |

## RAWLS, LOU
| | | | | | | |
|---|---|---|---|---|---|---|
| I Don't Love You Anymore | 7" | Capitol | CL15515 | 1967 | £1.50 | £4 |
| Lost And Looking | 7" EP | Capitol | EAP120646 | 1964 | £6 | £12 |
| Love Is A Hurting Thing | 7" | Capitol | CL15465 | 1966 | £1.50 | £4 |
| Soul Serenade | 7" | Capitol | CL15548 | 1968 | £1.50 | £4 |
| Yes It Hurts Doesn't It | 7" | Capitol | CL15499 | 1967 | £1.50 | £4 |
| You Can Bring Me All Your Heartaches | 7" | Capitol | CL15488 | 1967 | £1.50 | £4 |

## RAY, JAMES
| | | | | | | | |
|---|---|---|---|---|---|---|---|
| If You Gotta Make A Fool Of Somebody... | LP | Caprice | (S)LP1002 | 1962 | £10 | £25 | US |
| If You Gotta Make A Fool Of Somebody... | 7" | Pye | 7N25126 | 1962 | £4 | £8 | |
| Itty Bitty Pieces | 7" | Pye | 7N25147 | 1962 | £2.50 | £6 | |

## RAY, JAMES (2)
| | | | | | | |
|---|---|---|---|---|---|---|
| Another Million Dollars | CD-s | Merciful Release | MRAY99CD | 1989 | £2 | £5 |
| Mexican Sundown Blues | 7" | Merciful Release | MRAY52 | 1986 | £1.50 | £4 |
| Mexican Sundown Blues | 12" | Merciful Release | MRAY52 | 1986 | £2.50 | £6 |
| New Kind Of Assassin | CD-s | Merciful Release | MRAY89CD | 1989 | £2 | £5 |
| Without Conscience | CD-s | Merciful Release | MRAY101CD | 1990 | £2 | £5 |

## RAY, JOHNNIE
| | | | | | | | |
|---|---|---|---|---|---|---|---|
| At The London Palladium | 10" LP | Philips | BBR8001 | 1953 | £10 | £25 | |
| Best Of Johnnie Ray | LP | Realm | RM52317 | 1966 | £4 | £10 | |
| Big Beat | LP | Philips | BBL7148 | 1957 | £10 | £25 | |
| Build Your Love | 7" | Philips | JK1025 | 1957 | £6 | £12 | |
| Here And Now | 7" | Philips | PB918 | 1959 | £1.50 | £4 | |
| How Many Nights How Many Days | 7" | HMV | POP902 | 1961 | £2 | £5 | |
| I Believe | 7" | London | HLG9484 | 1962 | £2 | £5 | Timi Yuro B side |
| I'll Never Fall In Love Again | 7" | Philips | PB952 | 1959 | £1.50 | £4 | |
| I'm Just A Shadow Of Myself | 7" | Columbia | SCM5122 | 1954 | £7.50 | £15 | |
| In Las Vegas | LP | Philips | BBL7254 | 1958 | £10 | £25 | |
| In The Heart Of A Fool | 7" | London | HLA9216 | 1960 | £1.50 | £4 | |
| Johnnie Ray | LP | Liberty | LBY1020 | 1962 | £5 | £12 | |
| Johnnie Ray | 7" EP | Columbia | SEG7511 | 1954 | £5 | £10 | |
| Johnnie Ray | 7" EP | Philips | BBE12006 | 1955 | £5 | £10 | |
| Johnnie Ray | 7" EP | Philips | BBE12217 | 1958 | £2.50 | £6 | |
| Lonely For A Letter | 7" | Philips | PB829 | 1958 | £1.50 | £4 | |
| Look Homeward Angel | 7" | Philips | JK1004 | 1957 | £10 | £20 | |
| Miss Me Just A Little | 7" | Philips | PB785 | 1958 | £1.50 | £4 | |
| Nobody's Sweetheart | 7" | Columbia | SCM5111 | 1954 | £7.50 | £15 | |
| On The Trail | LP | Philips | BBL7363 | 1961 | £6 | £15 | |
| On The Trail | 7" EP | Philips | BBE12460 | 1961 | £4 | £8 | |
| Pink Sweater Angel | 7" | Philips | JK1033 | 1957 | £7.50 | £15 | |
| Please Don't Talk About Me | 7" | Columbia | SCM5074 | 1953 | £7.50 | £15 | |
| Showcase Of Hits | LP | Philips | BBL7264 | 1959 | £6 | £15 | |
| Sinner Man Am I | LP | Philips | BBL7348 | 1960 | £8 | £20 | |
| So Long | 7" | Philips | JK1011 | 1957 | £7.50 | £15 | |
| Strollin' Girl | 7" | Philips | PB808 | 1958 | £1.50 | £4 | |
| Tales From The Vienna Woods | LP | Ace Of Clubs | ACL1059 | 1961 | £4 | £10 | |
| Tell The Lady I Said Goodbye | 7" | Columbia | SCM5041 | 1953 | £7.50 | £15 | |
| Till Morning | LP | Philips | BBL7285/SBBL555 | 1959 | £6 | £15 | |
| Up Until Now | 7" | Philips | PB849 | 1958 | £1.50 | £4 | |
| Voice Of Your Choice | 10" LP | Philips | BBR8062 | 1955 | £10 | £25 | |
| Walkin' My Baby Back Home | 7" | Columbia | SCM5015 | 1953 | £10 | £20 | |
| Walking And Crying | 7" EP | Philips | BBE12115 | 1957 | £5 | £10 | |
| What More Can I Say | 7" | Philips | PB884 | 1958 | £1.50 | £4 | |
| When's Your Birthday Baby | 7" | Philips | PB901 | 1959 | £1.50 | £4 | |
| Yes Tonight Josephine | 7" EP | Philips | BBE12192 | 1958 | £5 | £10 | |
| Yes Tonight Josephine | 7" | Philips | JK1016 | 1957 | £7.50 | £15 | |

## RAY, RICARDO
| | | | | | | |
|---|---|---|---|---|---|---|
| Nitty Gritty | 7" | Roulette | RO501 | 1967 | £2.50 | £6 |

## RAY, WADE
| | | | | | | |
|---|---|---|---|---|---|---|
| Burning Desire | 7" | London | HL9700 | 1963 | £2.50 | £6 |

## RAYBURN, MARGIE
| | | | | | | |
|---|---|---|---|---|---|---|
| I Would | 7" | London | HLU8648 | 1958 | £4 | £8 |
| I'm Available | 7" | London | HLU8515 | 1957 | £4 | £8 |
| Wedding Song | 7" | Capitol | CL14532 | 1956 | £1.50 | £4 |

## RAYMOND, TONY
| | | | | | | |
|---|---|---|---|---|---|---|
| Infant King | 7" | Oriole | CB1777 | 1962 | £1.50 | £4 |

## RAYNOR, MARTIN & THE SECRETS
| | | | | | | |
|---|---|---|---|---|---|---|
| Candy To Me | 7" | Columbia | DB7563 | 1965 | £6 | £12 |

## RAYNOR, MIKE
| | | | | | | |
|---|---|---|---|---|---|---|
| Ob La Di Ob La Da | 7" | Decca | F22864 | 1969 | £1.50 | £4 |

## RAYS
| | | | | | | |
|---|---|---|---|---|---|---|
| Silhouettes | 7" | London | HLU8505 | 1957 | £15 | £30 |

## RAZORCUTS
| | | | | | | |
|---|---|---|---|---|---|---|
| Big Pink Cake | 7" | Subway Organisation | SUBWAY5 | 1986 | £2.50 | £6 |
| Sometimes I Worry About You | 7" | Caff | CAFF10 | 198– | £4 | £8 |

## REA, CHRIS
| | | | | | | |
|---|---|---|---|---|---|---|
| Bombolini | 12" | Magnet | MAGT259 | 1984 | £3 | £8 |

| Driving Home For Christmas | CD-s | WEA | YZ325CD | 1988 | £2 | £5 | *3" single* |
| I Can Hear Your Heart Beat | CD-s | WEA | YZ320CD | 1988 | £2 | £5 | |
| I Don't Know What It Is But I Love It | 12" | Magnet | MAGT255 | 1984 | £2.50 | £6 | |
| Josephine | 12" | Magnet | MAGT280 | 1985 | £2.50 | £6 | |
| Joys Of Christmas | CD-s | Magnet | CDMAG314 | 1987 | £2 | £5 | |
| Let It Loose | 12" | Magnet | 12MAG233 | 1982 | £3 | £8 | *.. with 7" (CHRIS1)* |
| Let's Dance | CD-s | Magnet | CDMAG299 | 1987 | £2 | £5 | |
| Let's Dance (Rea Mix) | 12" | Magnet | MAGT299R | 1987 | £2.50 | £6 | |
| On The Beach | CD-s | WEA | YZ195CD | 1988 | £2 | £5 | |
| Que Sera | CD-s | Magnet | CDMAG318 | 1988 | £2 | £5 | |
| Road To Hell | CD-s | WEA | YZ431CD | 1989 | £2 | £5 | |
| Road To Hell | CD | Geffen | 224276DJ | 1989 | £8 | £20 | *US promo picture disc* |
| Road To Hell | CD | Magnet | K2462852 | 1989 | £20 | £40 | *... promo box set, with cassette and booklet* |
| So Much Love | 7" | Magnet | MAG10 | 1974 | £10 | £20 | |
| That's What They Always Say | CD-s | WEA | YZ448CD | 1989 | £2 | £5 | |
| Working On It | CD-s | WEA | YZ350CD | 1989 | £2 | £5 | |

## REA, JOHN

| Traditional Music On The Hammer Dulcimer | LP | Topic | 12TS373 | 1978 | £4 | £10 | |

## REACTA

| Stop The World | 7" | Battery Operated | WAC1 | 1979 | £7.50 | £15 | |

## REACTION

| Oh Me Oh My | 7" | Columbia | DB119 | 1970 | £2 | £5 | *Rico B side* |

## REACTION (2)

| Reaction | LP | Polydor | 2371251 | 1972 | £37.50 | £75 | *German* |

## REACTION (3)

| I Can't Resist | 7" | Island | WIP6437 | 1978 | £2 | £5 | |

## READER, PAT

| Cha Cha On The Moon | 7" | Piccadilly | 7N35077 | 1962 | £15 | £30 | |
| Helpless | 7" | Oriole | CB1903 | 1963 | £1.50 | £4 | |
| Ricky | 7" | Triumph | RGM1024 | 1960 | £6 | £12 | |

## READING, BERTICE

| Jazz Train Girl | 7" EP | Parlophone | GEP8537 | 1955 | £2 | £5 | |
| My Big Best Shoes | 7" | Parlophone | R4487 | 1958 | £4 | £8 | |
| No Flowers By Request | 7" | Decca | F10965 | 1957 | £4 | £8 | |
| Rock Baby Rock | 7" | Parlophone | R4462 | 1958 | £7.50 | £15 | |

## REAL MCCOY

| This Is The Real McCoy | LP | Marble Arch | MAL1251 | 1970 | £8 | £20 | |

## REALITY FOLK

| Light Up My Life | LP | Profile | | | £62.50 | £125 | |

## REALITY FROM DREAM

| Reality From Dream | LP | private | | 1975 | £150 | £250 | |

## REALIZATION OF ETERNITY

| Beyond The End | LP | Narco | | 197– | £20 | £40 | *US* |

## REALLY RED

| Teaching You The Fear | LP | CIA | CIA006 | 1981 | £15 | £30 | |

## REALM

| Hard Time Loving You | 7" | CBS | 202044 | 1966 | £2.50 | £6 | |

## REAPERS

| No Greater Love | LP | Agra | BSS388 | 1979 | £10 | £25 | |

## REBECCA & THE SUNNYBROOK FARMERS

| Birth | LP | Musicor | MS3176 | 1967 | £20 | £40 | *US* |

## REBEL

| Beat Hits Vol. 3 | LP | Bellaphon | MWS308 | 1965 | £8 | £20 | *German* |

## REBEL ROUSERS

| Should I | 7" | Fontana | TF973 | 1968 | £5 | £10 | |

## REBELS

| Hard To Love You | 7" | Page One | POF017 | 1967 | £7.50 | £15 | |

## REBENNACK, MAC

Mac Rebennack achieved early notoriety as the only white musician to find employment on R&B sessions in New Orleans. Later he re-invented himself as the voodoo singer Dr John, although it is as Rebennack that he continues to play as a highly respected boogie pianist.

| Good Times | 7" | Ace | 611 | 1961 | £7.50 | £15 | *US* |
| Storm Warning | 7" | Rex | 1008 | 196– | £7.50 | £15 | *US* |

## REBIRTH
Rebirth ........................................... LP ...... Avantgarde ...... 135 ...................... 1968 £**25** ......... £**50** ........................ *US*

## REBOUNDS
Help Me......................................... 7" ...... Fontana............ TF461 .................... 1964 £**5**......... £**10** ........................

## REBS
Bunky ........................................... 7" ...... Capitol............ CL14932 ................ 1958 £**2**............. £**5** ........................

## REBS (2)
1968 A.D. Break Through ........................ LP ...... Fredlo ............ 6830 .................... 1968 £**180** ..... £**300** ........................ *US*

## RECO, EZZ
Rico Rodriguez, the legendary (and still recording) Rastafarian trombone player, had records issued under the names Reco, Ezo Reco and Ezz Reco, with and without the Launchers. Apart from the records below, all are listed under Rico in this guide.

## RECO, EZO & THE LAUNCHERS
Jamaica Blue Beat ........................... 7" EP . Columbia ...... SEG8326 .............. 1964 £**10** ......... £**20**
King Of Kings.................................... 7" ...... Columbia ...... DB7217 ............... 1964 £**2.50** ......... £**6**
Little Girl......................................... 7" ...... Columbia ...... DB7222 ............... 1964 £**2.50** ......... £**6**
Please Come Back ........................... 7" ...... Columbia ...... DB7290 ............... 1964 £**2.50** ......... £**6**

## RECREATION
Recreation ..................................... LP ...... Bellaphon ...... BLPS19006........ 1970 £**4** ......... £**10** ........................ *German*

## RED, SONNY
Out Of The Blue ............................. LP ...... Blue Note ...... BLP/BST84032 ...... 196– £**20** ......... £**40**

## RED BOX
Circle And The Square ....................... CD .... WEA ............ K2420372............ 1986 £**15** ......... £**30**
Train.............................................. CD-s .. East West ........ YZ531CD............. 1990 £**2** ......... £**5**

## RED CHAIR FADEAWAY
Any group choosing to name itself after a Bee Gees song is either impossibly naive or else uncaringly knowing – for the original 'Red Chair Fadeaway' is a classy piece of psychedelic pop, but from a group that is terminally unfashionable. Red Chair Fadeaway's music is proving to be unfashionable too. Despite being recorded in the nineties, the sound is that of a progressive folk group *circa* 1970, and for the album *Curiouser And Curiouser* there is packaging to match. Issued in a limited edition of a thousand copies, this is likely to be a very expensive collectors' item in the future.

Curiouser And Curiouser ........................ LP ...... Tangerine........ MM10 ................ 1991 £**10** ......... £**25**
Let It Happen ................................. 12" ...... Cosmic English CTA103.............. 1989 £**3** ......... £**8**
    Music ............
Mesmerised...................................... LP ...... Aural ............. AUR102 ............. 1993 £**6** ......... £**15**
Mr. Jones....................................... 12" ...... Cosmic English CTA105.............. 1989 £**3** ......... £**8**
    Music ............

## RED CRAYOLA
God Bless The Red Crayola ................... LP ...... International IALP7 .................... 1968 £**25** ......... £**50** ........................ *US*
    Artists ............
God Bless The Red Crayola ................... LP ...... Radar ............ RAD16................ 1978 £**4** ......... £**10** ........................
Parable Of Arable Land....................... LP ...... International IALP2 .................... 1967 £**30** ......... £**60** ........................ *US mono*
    Artists ............
Parable Of Arable Land ...................... LP ...... International IALP2 .................... 1967 £**25** ......... £**50** ........................ *US stereo*
    Artists ............
Parable Of Arable Land ...................... LP ...... Radar ............ RAD12................ 1978 £**4** ......... £**10**
Soldier Talk .................................... LP ...... Radar ............ RAD18................ 1979 £**4** ......... £**10**

## RED DIRT
Red Dirt ........................................ LP ...... Fontana............ STL5540 .......... 1970 £**330** ..... £**500**

## RED HASH
Red Hash ....................................... LP ...... Nufusmoon ..... 3673 .................... 1973 £**15** ......... £**30** ........................ *US*

## RED HOT CHILI PEPPERS
Abbey Road EP ............................... 12" ...... EMI............ 12MTPD41 ........ 1988 £**4** ......... £**10** ........................ *picture disc*
Fight Like A Brave ........................... 12"...... EMI............ 12EAP241 ......... 1988 £**4** ......... £**10** ........................ *picture disc*
Higher Ground ................................ CD-s .. EMI............ CDMT75........... 1989 £**2** ......... £**5**
Higher Ground ................................ CD-s .. EMI............ CDMT88........... 1990 £**2** ......... £**5**
Hollywood (Africa)............................ 7" ...... EMI............ EA205.............. 1985 £**2** ......... £**5**
Hollywood (Africa)............................ 12" ...... EMI............ 12EA205........... 1985 £**3** ......... £**8**
Knock Me Down ............................. CD-s .. EMI............ CDMT70........... 1989 £**2** ......... £**5**
Knock Me Down ............................. 7" ...... EMI............ MTPD70 ........... 1989 £**2.50** ......... £**6** ........................ *picture disc*
Taste The Pain ............................... CD-s .. EMI............ CDMT85........... 1990 £**2** ......... £**5**

## RED LIGHTS
Never Wanna Leave ........................... 7" ...... Free Range...... PF5 .................... 1978 £**1.50** ......... £**4**

## RED LORRY YELLOW LORRY
Beating My Head ............................. 7" ...... Red Rhino...... RED20................ 1982 £**4** ......... £**8**
He's Read........................................ 7" ...... Red Rhino..... RED39 ............... 1983 £**2** ......... £**5**
Take It All ...................................... 7" ...... Red Rhino..... RED28 ............... 1983 £**2.50** ......... £**6**

## RED ONION JAZZ BABIES
New Orleans Encore .............................. 10" LP London............ HAPB1025........ 1954 £**6** ......... £**15**

## RED ONION JAZZ BAND
Dance Off Both Your Shoes.................... LP ...... London ........... LTZU15138 ........... 1958 £6 ........... £15 .......................................

## RED SQUARES
It's Happening............................................ LP ...... Columbia ....... KSX6 ..................... 1967 £10 ....... £25 .................. *Danish*
Mountain's High ...................................... 7" ...... Columbia ....... DB8160 ............. 1967 £2 ........... £5
Red Squares...:........................................... LP ...... Columbia ....... KSX5 ..................... 1966 £10 ....... £25 .................. *Danish*
True Love Story ........................................ 7" ...... Columbia ....... DB8247 ............. 1967 £2 ........... £5

## RED TELEVISION
Red Television ........................................ LP ...... Brecht Times... ...................................... 1971 £100 ..... £200

## REDCAPS
Mighty Fine Girl ...................................... 7" ...... Decca ............. F11903 ................ 1964 £2 ........... £5
Shout ........................................................ 7" ...... Decca ............. F11716 ................ 1963 £2 ........... £5
Talking About You ................................... 7" ...... Decca ............. F11789 ................ 1963 £2.50 ....... £6

## REDD, FREDDIE
Get Happy.................................................. LP ...... Nixa ............... NJL19 ................... 1958 £8 ........... £20
Music From The Connection ................... LP ...... Blue Note ...... BLP/BST84027 .... 196– £15 ........... £30
Shades Of Redd ....................................... LP ...... Blue Note ...... BLP/BST84045 .... 196– £20 ........... £40

## REDD, GENE & THE GLOBE TROTTERS
Red River Valley Rock ............................. 7" ...... Parlophone ... R4584 ................... 1959 £4 ........... £8

## REDDING, OTIS
Champagne And Wine .............................. 7" ...... Atlantic ......... 584220 ................. 1968 £1.50 ....... £4
Come To Me.............................................. 7" ...... London .......... HLK9876 ............. 1964 £5 ........... £10
Day Tripper .............................................. 7" ...... Stax ............... 601005 ................. 1967 £1.50 ....... £4
Dictionary Of Soul .................................. LP ...... Atlantic ......... 587/588050 ......... 1967 £6 ........... £15
Dock Of The Bay ..................................... LP ...... Atco ............... 228022 ................. 1969 £4 ........... £10
Dock Of The Bay ..................................... LP ...... Stax ............... 230/231001 ........ 1968 £6 ........... £15
Dock Of The Bay ..................................... 7" ...... Atlantic ......... 2091112 .............. 1971 £1.50 ....... £4
Dock Of The Bay ..................................... 7" ...... Stax ............... 601031................. 1968 £1.50 ....... £4
Early Otis Redding .................................. 7" EP . Sue ............... IEP710................. 1966 £15 ........... £30
Fa Fa Fa Fa Fa Song................................ 7" ...... Atlantic ......... 584049 ................. 1966 £2 ........... £5
Free Me..................................................... 7" ...... Atco ............... 226002................. 1969 £1.50 ....... £4
Glory Of Love .......................................... 7" ...... Stax ............... 601017................. 1967 £2 ........... £5
Happy Song.............................................. 7" ...... Stax ............... 601040................. 1968 £1.50 ....... £4
Hard To Handle ....................................... 7" ...... Atlantic ......... 584199................. 1968 £1.50 ....... £4
History Of Otis Redding ......................... LP ...... Atco ............... 228001................. 1969 £4 ........... £10
History Of Otis Redding ......................... LP ...... Volt ............... 418 ....................... 1968 £6 ........... £15
I Can't Turn You Loose ........................... 7" ...... Atlantic ......... 584030................. 1966 £2 ........... £5
I've Been Loving You Too Long............... 7" ...... Atlantic ......... 2091062 .............. 1971 £1.50 ....... £4
I've Been Loving You Too Long............... 7" ...... Atlantic ......... AT4029................ 1965 £12.50 ... £25 ........... *demo only*
Immortal Otis Redding ........................... LP ...... Atlantic ......... 587/588113 ......... 1968 £6 ........... £15
In Person At The Whiskey ...................... LP ...... Atlantic ......... 587/588148 ......... 1968 £6 ........... £15
Let Me Come On Home ........................... 7" ...... Stax ............... 601007................. 1967 £1.50 ....... £4
Live In Europe ......................................... LP ...... Atco ............... 228017................. 1969 £4 ........... £10
Live In Europe ......................................... LP ...... Stax ............... 589016................. 1968 £6 ........... £15
Look At The Girl ...................................... 7" ...... Atco ............... 226012................. 1970 £1.50 ....... £4
Love Man .................................................. LP ...... Atco ............... 228025................. 1969 £5 ........... £12
Love Man .................................................. 7" ...... Atco ............... 226001................. 1969 £1.50 ....... £4
Lover's Question ...................................... 7" ...... Atlantic ......... 584249................. 1969 £1.50 ....... £4
Mr. Pitiful................................................. 7" ...... Atlantic ......... AT4024................ 1965 £2.50 ....... £6
My Girl ..................................................... 7" ...... Atlantic ......... 584092................. 1967 £2 ........... £5
My Girl ..................................................... 7" ...... Atlantic ......... AT4050................ 1965 £2.50 ....... £6
My Lover's Prayer .................................... 7" ...... Atlantic ......... 584019................. 1966 £2 ........... £5
Otis Blue .................................................. LP ...... Atlantic ......... 587/588036 ......... 1966 £5 ........... £12
Otis Blue .................................................. LP ...... Atlantic ......... ATL5041 ............. 1966 £6 ........... £15
Otis Blue .................................................. CD ..... Mobile Fidelity EUCD575............ 1992 £6 ........... £15 ........... *US audiophile*
Pain In My Heart ..................................... LP ...... Atlantic ......... 587042................. 1967 £6 ........... £15
Pain In My Heart ..................................... 7" ...... London .......... HLK9833 ............. 1964 £5 ........... £10
Papa's Got A Brand New Bag ................. 7" ...... Atlantic ......... 584234................. 1968 £1.50 ....... £4
Remembering............................................ LP ...... Atlantic ......... 2464003 .............. 1970 £4 ........... £10
Respect ..................................................... 7" ...... Atlantic ......... 584091................. 1967 £2 ........... £5
Respect ..................................................... 7" ...... Atlantic ......... AT4039................ 1965 £2.50 ....... £6
Satisfaction .............................................. 7" ...... Atlantic ......... AT4080................ 1966 £2 ........... £5
Satisfaction .............................................. 7" ...... Stax ............... 601027................. 1967 £1.50 ....... £4
Shake ....................................................... 7" ...... Stax ............... 601011................. 1967 £1.50 ....... £4
She's Alright ............................................ 7" ...... Evolution ....... E2442 ................... 1969 £2 ........... £5
She's Alright ............................................ 7" ...... Pye ................. 7N25463.............. 1968 £2 ........... £5
Shout Bamalama ...................................... 7" ...... Sue ................. WI362 .................. 1965 £7.50 ....... £15
Sings Soul Ballads .................................. LP ...... Atlantic ......... 587035................. 1966 £5 ........... £12
Sings Soul Ballads .................................. LP ...... Atlantic ......... ATL5029 ............. 1965 £6 ........... £15
Soul Album .............................................. LP ...... Atlantic ......... 587011................. 1966 £6 ........... £15
Tell The Truth........................................... LP ...... Atco ............... 2400018 .............. 1971 £4 ........... £10
Try A Little Tenderness ........................... 7" ...... Atlantic ......... 584070................. 1967 £2 ........... £5
Wonderful World ..................................... 7" ...... Atlantic ......... 2091020 .............. 1970 £1.50 ....... £4

## REDDING, OTIS & CARLA THOMAS
King And Queen....................................... LP ...... Atlantic ......... 589007................. 1967 £6 ........... £15
Knock On Wood ...................................... 7" ...... Stax ............... 601021................. 1967 £1.50 ....... £4
Lovey Dovey ............................................ 7" ...... Stax ............... 601033................. 1968 £1.50 ....... £4
Tramp....................................................... 7" ...... Stax ............... 601012................. 1967 £1.50 ....... £4

## REDDING, OTIS & JIMI HENDRIX

| | | | | | | | |
|---|---|---|---|---|---|---|---|
| Historic Performances Recorded At Monterey | LP | Reprise | MS2029 | 1970 | £5 | £12 | US, 1 side each artist |

## REDE, EMMA

| | | | | | | | |
|---|---|---|---|---|---|---|---|
| Just Like A Man | 7" | Columbia | DB8136 | 1967 | £4 | £8 | |

## REDELL, TEDDY

| | | | | | | | |
|---|---|---|---|---|---|---|---|
| Judy | 7" | London | HLK9140 | 1960 | £20 | £40 | |

## REDMAN, GEORGE

| | | | | | | | |
|---|---|---|---|---|---|---|---|
| George Redman Group | 10" LP | London | HAPB1036 | 1955 | £10 | £25 | |

## REDMOND, ROY

| | | | | | | | |
|---|---|---|---|---|---|---|---|
| Good Day Sunshine | 7" | Warner Bros | WB2075 | 1967 | £1.50 | £4 | |

## REDPATH, JEAN

| | | | | | | | |
|---|---|---|---|---|---|---|---|
| Ballad Folk | LP | BBC | REC293 | 1977 | £5 | £12 | |
| Love, Life And Laughter | LP | Clan Special | 233004 | 1969 | £5 | £12 | |
| Love, Lilt And Laughter | LP | Bounty | BY6004 | 1966 | £5 | £12 | |
| There Were Minstrels | LP | Trailer | LER2106 | 1977 | £4 | £10 | |

## REDSKINS

| | | | | | | | |
|---|---|---|---|---|---|---|---|
| Lev Bronstein | 7" | CNT | CNT007 | 1982 | £6 | £12 | |

## REDWAY, MIKE

| | | | | | | | |
|---|---|---|---|---|---|---|---|
| Have No Fear, Bond Is Here | 7" | Deram | DM124 | 1967 | £2 | £5 | |

## REDWOODS

| | | | | | | | |
|---|---|---|---|---|---|---|---|
| Please Mister Scientist | 7" | Columbia | DB4859 | 1962 | £2.50 | £6 | |

## REECE, DIZZY

| | | | | | | | |
|---|---|---|---|---|---|---|---|
| Dizzy/Deuchar | LP | Tempo | TAP4 | 1956 | £20 | £40 | ...with Jimmy Deuchar |
| Progress Report | LP | Tempo | TAP9 | 1957 | £20 | £40 | |
| Soundin' Off | LP | Blue Note | BLP/BST84033 | 196– | £15 | £30 | |

## REED, CHUCK

| | | | | | | | |
|---|---|---|---|---|---|---|---|
| Let's Put Our Hearts Together | 7" | Columbia | DB4113 | 1958 | £4 | £8 | |
| Whispering Heart | 7" | Brunswick | 05646 | 1957 | £2 | £5 | |

## REED, DENNY

| | | | | | | | |
|---|---|---|---|---|---|---|---|
| Teenager Feels It Too | 7" | London | HLK9274 | 1961 | £5 | £10 | |

## REED, FRED

| | | | | | | | |
|---|---|---|---|---|---|---|---|
| Northumbrian Voice | LP | White Meadow | 01 | 1978 | £4 | £10 | |

## REED, JERRY

| | | | | | | | |
|---|---|---|---|---|---|---|---|
| Bessie Baby | 7" | Capitol | CL14851 | 1958 | £75 | £150 | |

## REED, JIMMY

| | | | | | | | |
|---|---|---|---|---|---|---|---|
| At Carnegie Hall | LP | Stateside | SL10012 | 1962 | £8 | £20 | |
| At Soul City | LP | Vee Jay | LP1095 | 1964 | £8 | £20 | US |
| Baby What You Want Me To Do | 7" | Top Rank | JAR333 | 1960 | £4 | £8 | |
| Best Of Jimmy Reed | LP | Vee Jay | LP/SR1039 | 1962 | £8 | £20 | US |
| Big Boss Man | LP | BluesWay | BLS6013 | 1968 | £5 | £12 | US |
| Blues Of Jimmy Reed | 7" EP | Stateside | SE1016 | 1964 | £6 | £12 | |
| Boss Man Of The Blues | LP | Stateside | SL10091 | 1964 | £6 | £15 | |
| Down In Virginia | LP | Action | ACLP6011 | 1969 | £6 | £15 | |
| Found Love | LP | Vee Jay | LP1022 | 1960 | £10 | £25 | US |
| Found Love | 7" | Top Rank | JAR394 | 1960 | £2.50 | £6 | |
| Hush Hush | 7" | Top Rank | JAR533 | 1961 | £2.50 | £6 | |
| I'm Jimmy Reed | LP | Vee Jay | LP1004 | 1958 | £25 | £50 | US |
| I'm Jimmy Reed | 7" EP | Stateside | SE1026 | 1964 | £6 | £12 | |
| Jimmy Reed & Eddie Taylor | 7" EP | XX | MIN704 | 196– | £2 | £5 | with Eddie Taylor |
| Just Jimmy Reed | LP | Stateside | SL10055 | 1963 | £8 | £20 | |
| Legend, The Man | LP | Vee Jay | VJ(S)8501 | 1965 | £6 | £15 | US |
| More Of The Best Of Jimmy Reed | LP | Vee Jay | LP/SR1035 | 1964 | £6 | £15 | US |
| New Jimmy Reed | LP | HMV | CLP/CSD3611 | 1967 | £5 | £12 | |
| Now Appearing | LP | Vee Jay | LP1025 | 1960 | £10 | £25 | US |
| Odds And Ends | 7" | Sue | WI4004 | 1966 | £6 | £12 | |
| Plays 12 String Guitar Blues | LP | Stateside | SL10086 | 1964 | £6 | £15 | |
| Rockin' With Reed | LP | Vee Jay | LP1008 | 1959 | £20 | £40 | US |
| Shame Shame Shame | 7" | Stateside | SS205 | 1963 | £2 | £5 | |
| Shame Shame Shame | 7" | Stateside | SS330 | 1964 | £2 | £5 | |
| Sings The Best Of The Blues | LP | Stateside | SL10069 | 1964 | £6 | £15 | |
| Soulin' | LP | Stateside | (S)SL10221 | 1968 | £5 | £12 | |
| T'Ain't No Big Thing | LP | Vee Jay | LP1067 | 1963 | £8 | £20 | US |
| Things Ain't What They Used To Be | LP | Fontana | 688514ZL | 1965 | £5 | £12 | |
| Two Ways To Skin A Cat | 7" | HMV | POP1579 | 1967 | £2 | £5 | |

## REED, LOU

The battle of the formats was won by the compact disc the moment that a reissue of Lou Reed's *Metal Machine Music* was released on CD. The disturbing electronic hubbub that the album contains may be an interesting insight into Reed's early association with minimalist avant-garde composer La Monte Young, but it does not make for a listening experience that many Reed fans would wish to endure even once. It has been suggested that the album was Reed's ironic way of fulfilling a contract, but tapes exist of the Velvet Underground playing music not very dissimilar to this. More indicative of cynicism are the live recordings of the Velvet Underground's 1993 tour, which show

Reed to be performing some of the old material with an alarming lack of enthusiasm. (The shame of this being heightened all the more by the knowledge that much of Reed's solo material from recent years has been rather fine.)

| | | | | | | | |
|---|---|---|---|---|---|---|---|
| Blue Mask | LP | RCA | DJL14266 | 1981 | £4 | £10 | US interview promo |
| Magic And Loss | CD | Sire | | 1992 | £20 | £40 | US promo in metal box |
| Metal Machine Music | LP | RCA | CPD21101 | 1975 | £20 | £40 | US quad |
| Metal Machine Music | LP | RCA | CPL21101 | 1975 | £15 | £30 | |
| Mistrial | CD | RCA | PD87190 | 1986 | £5 | £12 | |
| New York | CD | Sire | | 1988 | £8 | £20 | US promo in metal box |
| No Money Down | 12" | RCA | | 1986 | £2.50 | £6 | promo, green vinyl |
| Rock 'n' Roll Animal | CD | RCA | ND83664 | 1988 | £5 | £12 | |
| Rock 'n' Roll Life | CD | Sire | PROCD3358 | 1989 | £15 | £30 | US promo double |
| Selections From Between Thought And Expression | CD | RCA | 62284RDJ | 1992 | £8 | £20 | US promo |
| Songs For Drella | CD | Sire | 9262052 | 1990 | £8 | £20 | US promo in velvet cover, with John Cale |
| Transformer | CD | RCA | C8819 | 1988 | £6 | £15 | box set |
| Walk On The Wild Side | CD-s | RCA | PD49453 | 1989 | £2 | £5 | |

## REED, LULU

| | | | | | | | |
|---|---|---|---|---|---|---|---|
| Blue And Moody | LP | King | 604 | 1959 | £100 | £200 | US |
| Troubles On Your Mind | 7" | Parlophone | CMSP34 | 1955 | £6 | £12 | export |

## REED, LULU & FREDDY KING

| | | | | | | | |
|---|---|---|---|---|---|---|---|
| Lulu Reed & Freddy King | 7" EP | Ember | EMBEP4536 | 1963 | £10 | £20 | |

## REED, LULU & SYL JOHNSON

| | | | | | | | |
|---|---|---|---|---|---|---|---|
| Lulu Reed & Syl Johnson | 7" EP | Ember | EMBEP4535 | 1963 | £12.50 | £25 | |

## REED, NEHEMIAH

| | | | | | | | |
|---|---|---|---|---|---|---|---|
| Family War | 7" | Island | WI3102 | 1968 | £5 | £10 | |

## REED, OLIVER

| | | | | | | | |
|---|---|---|---|---|---|---|---|
| Wild One | 7" | Decca | F11390 | 1961 | £2 | £5 | |

## REED, TAWNY

| | | | | | | | |
|---|---|---|---|---|---|---|---|
| Needle In A Haystack | 7" | Pye | 7N15935 | 1965 | £2.50 | £6 | |
| You Can't Take It Away | 7" | Pye | 7N17078 | 1966 | £2 | £5 | |

## REEGAN, VALA & THE VALARONS

| | | | | | | | |
|---|---|---|---|---|---|---|---|
| Fireman | 7" | Atlantic | 584009 | 1966 | £50 | £100 | |

## REESE, DELLA

| | | | | | | | |
|---|---|---|---|---|---|---|---|
| Della | LP | RCA | RD27167/SF5057 | 1960 | £4 | £10 | |
| Della Della Cha-Cha-Cha | LP | RCA | RD27208/SF5091 | 1961 | £4 | £10 | |
| I Cried For You | 7" | London | HL7024 | 1957 | £1.50 | £4 | export |
| On Stage | LP | RCA | RD/SF7508 | 1963 | £4 | £10 | |
| Sermonette | 7" | London | HLJ8814 | 1959 | £1.50 | £4 | |
| Special Delivery | LP | RCA | RD27234/SF5112 | 1962 | £4 | £10 | |
| Story Of The Blues | LP | London | LTZJ15163/ SAHJ6021 | 1959 | £5 | £12 | |
| You Gotta Love Everybody | 7" | London | HLJ8687 | 1958 | £1.50 | £4 | |

## REESE, PETER & THE PAGES

| | | | | | | | |
|---|---|---|---|---|---|---|---|
| Hippy Hippy Shake | LP | Philips | P48075L | 1964 | £10 | £25 | German |

## REEVES, EDDIE

| | | | | | | | |
|---|---|---|---|---|---|---|---|
| Cry Baby | 7" | London | HL9548 | 1962 | £2.50 | £6 | |

## REEVES, JIM

| | | | | | | | |
|---|---|---|---|---|---|---|---|
| Bimbo | LP | London | HAU8015 | 1962 | £6 | £15 | |
| Bimbo | 7" | London | HL8014 | 1954 | £62.50 | £125 | |
| Bimbo Boy | 7" EP | London | REP1015 | 1954 | £20 | £40 | |
| Bimbo Vol. 2 | 7" EP | London | REP1033 | 1955 | £20 | £40 | |
| Blue Boy | 7" | RCA | RCA1074 | 1958 | £5 | £10 | |
| Butterfly Love | 7" | London | HL8055 | 1954 | £50 | £100 | |
| Drinking Tequila | 7" | London | HL8159 | 1955 | £62.50 | £125 | |
| Echo Bonita | 7" | London | HL8064 | 1954 | £50 | £100 | |
| Four Walls | 7" | RCA | RCA1005 | 1957 | £10 | £20 | |
| Girls I Have Known | LP | RCA | LPM1685 | 1958 | £8 | £20 | US |
| God Be With You | LP | RCA | LPM/LSP1950 | 1958 | £5 | £12 | US |
| He'll Have To Go | LP | RCA | RD27176 | 1960 | £4 | £10 | |
| He'll Have To Go | 7" | RCA | RCA1168 | 1960 | £1.50 | £4 | |
| Intimate Jim Reeves | LP | RCA | RD27193/SF5079 | 1961 | £4 | £10 | |
| Jim Reeves | LP | RCA | LPM1576 | 1957 | £10 | £25 | US |
| Jim Reeves Sings | LP | Abbott | LP5001 | 1956 | £210 | £350 | US |
| Jimbo | LP | RCA | LPM1410 | 1957 | £15 | £30 | US |
| Mexican Joe | 7" | London | HL8030 | 1954 | £50 | £100 | |
| Padre Of Old San Antone | 7" | London | HL8105 | 1954 | £30 | £60 | |
| Partners | 7" | RCA | RCA1144 | 1959 | £2 | £5 | |
| Penny Candy | 7" | London | HL8118 | 1955 | £37.50 | £75 | |
| Singing Down The Lane | LP | RCA | LPM1256 | 1956 | £25 | £50 | US |
| Songs To Warm Your Heart | LP | RCA | LPM/LSP2001 | 1959 | £5 | £12 | US |
| Tahiti | 7" | London | HLU8185 | 1955 | £37.50 | £75 | |
| Talkin' To Your Heart | LP | RCA | LPM/LSP2339 | 1961 | £5 | £12 | US |

| | | | | | | | |
|---|---|---|---|---|---|---|---|
| Tall Tales And Short Tempers | LP | RCA | LPM/LSP2284 | 1961 | £5 | £12 | US |
| Wilder Your Heart Beats | 7" | London | HLU8351 | 1956 | £37.50 | £75 | |

## REFLECTION
| | | | | | | |
|---|---|---|---|---|---|---|
| Present Tense | LP | Reflection | RL3015 | 1968 | £10 | £25 |

## REFLECTIONS
| | | | | | | |
|---|---|---|---|---|---|---|
| Just Like Romeo And Juliet | LP | Golden World | LPM300 | 1964 | £20 | £40 | US |
| Just Like Romeo And Juliet | 7" | Stateside | SS294 | 1964 | £6 | £12 | |
| Poor Man's Son | 7" EP | Stateside | SE1034 | 1965 | £15 | £30 | |
| Poor Man's Son | 7" | Stateside | SS406 | 1965 | £2 | £5 | |

## REFUGEE
| | | | | | | |
|---|---|---|---|---|---|---|
| Refugee | LP | Charisma | CAS1087 | 1974 | £4 | £10 |

## REGAN, JOAN
| | | | | | | |
|---|---|---|---|---|---|---|
| Cross Of Gold | 7" | Decca | F10659 | 1956 | £4 | £8 |
| Danger Heartbreak Ahead | 7" | Decca | F10505 | 1955 | £2 | £5 |
| Don't Take Me For Granted | 7" | Decca | F10710 | 1956 | £1.50 | £4 |
| Don't Talk To Me About Love | 7" | CBS | 202100 | 1966 | £12.50 | £25 |
| Girl Next Door | 10" LP | Decca | LF1182 | 1954 | £8 | £20 |
| Gone | 7" | Decca | F10801 | 1956 | £1.50 | £4 |
| Honestly | 7" | Decca | F10742 | 1956 | £1.50 | £4 |
| If I Give My Heart To You | 7" | Decca | F10373 | 1954 | £4 | £8 |
| Just Joan | LP | Decca | LK4153 | 1956 | £4 | £10 |
| Just Say You Love Her | 7" | Decca | F10521 | 1955 | £2 | £5 |
| No One Beside You | 7" | CBS | 2657 | 1967 | £5 | £10 |
| Open Up Your Heart | 7" | Decca | F10474 | 1955 | £4 | £8 |
| Prize Of Gold | 7" | Decca | F10432 | 1955 | £4 | £8 |
| Shepherd Boy | 7" | Decca | F10598 | 1955 | £2 | £5 |
| Successes | 7" EP | Decca | DFE6235 | 1955 | £4 | £8 |
| Successes Vol. 2 | 7" EP | Decca | DFE6278 | 1956 | £5 | £10 |
| Sweet Heartaches | 7" | Decca | F10757 | 1956 | £1.50 | £4 |
| This Ole House | 7" | Decca | F10397 | 1954 | £5 | £10 |
| Wait For Me Darling | 7" | Decca | F10362 | 1954 | £4 | £8 |

## REGENTS
| | | | | | | |
|---|---|---|---|---|---|---|
| Barbara Ann | LP | Gee | (S)GLP708 | 1961 | £20 | £40 | US |
| Barbara Ann | 7" | Columbia | DB4666 | 1961 | £4 | £8 | |
| Live At The Am/Pm Discotheque | LP | Capitol | (S)KAO2153 | 1964 | £8 | £20 | US |
| Runaround | 7" | Columbia | DB4694 | 1961 | £4 | £8 | |

## REGENTS (2)
| | | | | | | |
|---|---|---|---|---|---|---|
| Bye Bye Johnny | 7" | Oriole | CB1912 | 1964 | £6 | £12 |

## REGENTS (3)
| | | | | | | |
|---|---|---|---|---|---|---|
| Words | 7" | CBS | 202247 | 1966 | £5 | £10 |

## REGENTS (4)
| | | | | | | |
|---|---|---|---|---|---|---|
| Seventeen | 7" | Rialto | TREB111 | 1979 | £2 | £5 |

## REGGAE BOYS
| | | | | | | |
|---|---|---|---|---|---|---|
| Me No Born Ya | 7" | Amalgamated | AMG841 | 1969 | £2.50 | £6 | |
| Pupa Live On Eye Top | 7" | Bullet | BU431 | 1970 | £1.50 | £4 | |
| Reggae Train | 7" | Amalgamated | AMG843 | 1969 | £2.50 | £6 | |
| Walk By Day Fly By Night | 7" | Pressure Beat | PB5503 | 1970 | £1.50 | £4 | Joe Gibbs B side |

## REICH, STEVE
| | | | | | | |
|---|---|---|---|---|---|---|
| Four Organs | LP | Angel | S36059 | | £4 | £10 | |
| Four Organs | LP | Shandar | 83511 | | £4 | £10 | |
| Live/Electronic Music | LP | Columbia | MS7265 | | £4 | £10 | US |
| New Sounds In Electronic Music | LP | Odyssey | 32160160 | | £4 | £10 | |

## REICHEL, ACHIM
| | | | | | | |
|---|---|---|---|---|---|---|
| A.R.3 | LP | Zebra | 2949006 | 1973 | £6 | £15 | German |
| A.R.4 | LP | Zebra | 2949008 | 1973 | £6 | £15 | German |
| Autovision | LP | Zebra | 2949016 | 1974 | £6 | £15 | German |
| Die Grüne Reise | LP | Polydor | 2371128 | 1971 | £8 | £20 | German |
| Echo | LP | Polydor | 2633003 | 1972 | £10 | £25 | German double |
| Erholung | LP | Brain | 1068 | 1975 | £5 | £12 | German |

## REID, BERYL
| | | | | | | |
|---|---|---|---|---|---|---|
| Love Makes The World Go Around | 7" | HMV | POP1489 | 1965 | £1.50 | £4 |

## REID, CARLTON
| | | | | | | |
|---|---|---|---|---|---|---|
| Leave Me To Cry | 7" | Blue Cat | BS162 | 1969 | £2.50 | £6 |
| Turn On The Lights | 7" | Ska Beat | JB254 | 1966 | £5 | £10 |

## REID, DUKE
| | | | | | | |
|---|---|---|---|---|---|---|
| Duke's Cookies | 7" | Blue Beat | BB24 | 1960 | £6 | £12 | Jiving Juniors B side |
| Hurt | 7" | Duke Reid | DR2522 | 1971 | £1.50 | £4 | |
| Mood I Am In | 7" | Blue Beat | BB165 | 1963 | £6 | £12 | Stranger Cole B side |
| True Confession | 7" | Doctor Bird | DB1028 | 1966 | £5 | £10 | Tommy McCook B side |

## REID, LEROY
| | | | | | | |
|---|---|---|---|---|---|---|
| Fiddler | 7" | Blue Cat | BS125 | 1968 | £2.50 | £6 | Lovelettes B side |

## REID, P.
| | | | | | | | |
|---|---|---|---|---|---|---|---|
| Redeemed | 7" | Ska Beat | JB197 | 1965 | £5 | £10 | |

## REID, TERRY
| | | | | | | | |
|---|---|---|---|---|---|---|---|
| Bang Bang, You're Terry Reid | LP | Epic | BN26427 | 1968 | £6 | £15 | US |
| Better By Far | 7" | Columbia | DB8409 | 1968 | £4 | £8 | |
| Hand Don't Fit The Glove | 7" | Columbia | DB8166 | 1967 | £2.50 | £6 | |
| River | LP | Warner Bros | K40340 | 1973 | £4 | £10 | |
| Superlungs | 7" | Columbia | PSR.S323 | 1969 | £5 | £10 | 1 sided demo |
| Terry Reid | LP | Columbia | SCX6370 | 1969 | £6 | £15 | |

## REIGN
| | | | | | | | |
|---|---|---|---|---|---|---|---|
| Line Of Least Resistance | 7" | Regal Zonophone | RZ3028 | 1970 | £20 | £40 | |

## REIGN GHOST
| | | | | | | | |
|---|---|---|---|---|---|---|---|
| Allied | LP | | | | £100 | £200 | Canadian |

## REILLY, JOHN
| | | | | | | | |
|---|---|---|---|---|---|---|---|
| Bonny Green Tree | LP | Topic | 12T359 | 1978 | £5 | £12 | |

## REILLY, PADDY
| | | | | | | | |
|---|---|---|---|---|---|---|---|
| At Home | LP | Dolphin | DOLM5006 | 1975 | £6 | £15 | Irish |
| Fields Of Athenry | LP | Dolphin | DLX9002 | | £6 | £15 | Irish |
| Life Of Paddy Reilly | LP | Dolphin | DOLM5001 | 1975 | £6 | £15 | Irish |
| Town I Loved So Well | LP | Dolphin | DOLM5010 | 1975 | £6 | £15 | Irish |

## REILLY, VINI
| | | | | | | | |
|---|---|---|---|---|---|---|---|
| Vini Reilly | CD | Factory | FACD244 | 1988 | £8 | £20 | with 3" CD by Reilly & Morrissey |

## REILLY, VINI & MORRISSEY
| | | | | | | | |
|---|---|---|---|---|---|---|---|
| I Know Very Well How I Got My Note Wrong | 7" | Factory | FACT244 | 1989 | £2 | £5 | |

## REINHARDT, DJANGO
| | | | | | | | |
|---|---|---|---|---|---|---|---|
| Art Of Django | LP | HMV | CLP1340 | 1960 | £6 | £15 | |
| Django | LP | HMV | CLP1249 | 1959 | £8 | £20 | |
| Django – The Unforgettable | 10" LP | Mercury | MG10019 | 1957 | £20 | £40 | |
| Django – The Unforgettable | LP | HMV | CLP1389 | 1960 | £6 | £15 | |
| Django Reinhardt | 7" EP | HMV | 7EG8132 | 1955 | £2 | £5 | |
| Django Reinhardt | 10" LP | HMV | DLP1045 | 1954 | £20 | £40 | |
| Django Reinhardt Vol. 1 | 10" LP | Vogue | LDE049 | 1954 | £20 | £40 | |
| Django Reinhardt Vol. 2 | 10" LP | Vogue | LDE084 | 1954 | £20 | £40 | |
| Django Reinhardt Vol. 3 | 10" LP | Vogue | LDE106 | 1954 | £20 | £40 | |
| Improvisation | 7" EP | Collector | JEN8 | 1962 | £2 | £5 | |
| Memorial | LP | Vogue | LAE12251 | 1961 | £4 | £10 | |
| Nuages | 10" LP | Felsted | EDL87005 | 1954 | £20 | £40 | |
| Requiem For A Jazzman | LP | Ember | CJS810 | 196– | £5 | £12 | |
| Swing From Paris | 10" LP | Decca | LF1139 | 1953 | £20 | £40 | |
| Swing Guitars | 7" EP | Collector | JEN6 | 1961 | £2 | £5 | |

## REIVERS
| | | | | | | | |
|---|---|---|---|---|---|---|---|
| Work Of The Reivers Vol. 2 | 7" EP | Top Rank | JKP2062 | 1960 | £2 | £5 | |

## RELEASE MUSIC ORCHESTRA
| | | | | | | | |
|---|---|---|---|---|---|---|---|
| Garuda | LP | Brain | 1072 | 1975 | £4 | £10 | German |
| Get The Ball | LP | Brain | 1083 | 1975 | £4 | £10 | German |
| Life | LP | Brain | 1056 | 1974 | £5 | £12 | German |

## RELF, JANE
| | | | | | | | |
|---|---|---|---|---|---|---|---|
| Without A Song From You | 7" | Decca | F13231 | 1971 | £5 | £10 | |

## RELF, KEITH
| | | | | | | | |
|---|---|---|---|---|---|---|---|
| Mr. Zero | 7" | Columbia | DB7920 | 1966 | £7.50 | £15 | |
| Shapes In My Mind | 7" | Columbia | DB8084 | 1966 | £15 | £30 | |

## R.E.M.

R.E.M. stand in the odd position of having signed a record-breaking 1996 contract with Warner Bros, making them in one sense the biggest rock group in the world, yet have achieved such little chart success in the UK that the casual listener is likely to be largely unaware of their music. Arguably, the group's eighties version of a Byrds–Band hybrid is a little too restrained, a little too dignified to be inspirational in the way that those sixties bands were. For this listener, R.E.M. never sounded so convincing as when they borrowed the vocal chords of Kate Pierson from the B52's, while Michael Stipe has produced his best work in a side-project, as a member of the Golden Palominos.

| | | | | | | | |
|---|---|---|---|---|---|---|---|
| Academy Fight Song | 7" | fan club | 122589 | 1989 | £37.50 | £75 | |
| AOR Staple | CD | IRS | IRSDSEVEN | 1987 | £15 | £30 | US promo compilation |
| Automatic For The People | CD | WEA | 9362450552 | 1992 | £10 | £25 | boxed with cards |
| Baby Baby | 7" | fan club | 122591 | 1991 | £25 | £50 | |
| Can't Get There From Here | 12" | IRS | IRT102 | 1985 | £3 | £8 | |
| Chronic Town | LP | IRS | SP70502 | 1982 | £8 | £20 | US, gargoyle label |
| Dead Letter Office | CD | IRS | CDA70054 | 1987 | £5 | £12 | |
| Document | CD | IRS | DMIRG1025 | 1987 | £5 | £12 | |
| Fables Of The Reconstruction | CD | IRS | DMIRF1003 | 1987 | £5 | £12 | |
| Fall On Me | 12" | IRS | IRMT121 | 1986 | £2.50 | £6 | |
| Femme Fatale | 7" | Evatone | REAL005 | 1986 | £7.50 | £15 | US flexi, picture sleeve |
| Finest Worksong | CD-s | IRS | DIRM161 | 1988 | £6 | £15 | 6" box |

| Title | Format | Label | Cat. No. | Year | | | Notes |
|---|---|---|---|---|---|---|---|
| Ghost Reindeer In The Sky | 7" | fan club | 122590 | 1990 | £25 | £50 | |
| Green | CD | Warner Bros | PROCD3292 | 1988 | £10 | £25 | US promo, cloth cover |
| It's The End Of The World As We Know It | CD-s | IRS | DIRMX180 | 1992 | £4 | £10 | 4 tracks |
| It's The End Of The World As We Know It | CD-s | MCA | DMIRT180 | 1991 | £2 | £5 | |
| Losing My Religion | CD-s | Warner Bros | W0015CDX | 1991 | £2.50 | £6 | with poster |
| Losing My Religion | CD-s | WEA | W0015CD | 1991 | £2 | £5 | |
| Murmur | CD | A&M | CDA7014 | 1988 | £5 | £12 | |
| One I Love | CD-s | IRS | DIRM146 | 1987 | £3 | £8 | |
| One I Love | CD-s | IRS | DIRM173 | 1988 | £2 | £5 | |
| One I Love | CD-s | MCA | DIRM178 | 1991 | £2 | £5 | |
| Orange Crush | CD-s | Warner Bros | W2960CD | 1989 | £2 | £5 | 3" single |
| Orange Crush | 7" | Warner Bros | W2960B | 1989 | £2 | £5 | boxed with poster |
| Our Price New Releases | CD | Our Price | no number | 1995 | £37.50 | £75 | promo |
| Out Of Time | CD | Warner Bros | 7599264962 | 1991 | £8 | £20 | ...black 'leather' cover, with 10 cards |
| Parade Of The Wooden Soldiers | 7" | fan club | U23528M | 1988 | £50 | £100 | green vinyl |
| Pop Songs 89–95 | CD | Warner Bros | SAM1558 | 1995 | £20 | £40 | promo compilation |
| Radio Free Europe | 7" | Hibtone | HT0001 | 1981 | £50 | £100 | US |
| Radio Free Europe | 7" | IRS | PFP1017 | 1983 | £12.50 | £25 | |
| Radio Song | CD-s | Warner Bros | W0072CDX | 1991 | £6 | £15 | in case for CD set |
| Rockville | 7" | IRS | IRS107 | 1984 | £6 | £12 | |
| Rockville | 12" | IRS | IRSX107 | 1984 | £6 | £15 | |
| Shall We Talk About The Weather | CD | Warner Bros | PROCD3377 | 1988 | £10 | £25 | US promo |
| Shiny Happy People | CD-s | WEA | W0027CD | 1991 | £2 | £5 | |
| Silver Bells | 7" | fan club | L41936X | 1993 | £10 | £25 | |
| South Central Rain | 7" | IRS | IRS105 | 1984 | £6 | £12 | |
| South Central Rain | 12" | IRS | IRSX105 | 1984 | £6 | £15 | |
| Stand | CD-s | Warner Bros | W2833CD | 1989 | £2 | £5 | |
| Stand | CD-s | Warner Bros | W2833CDX | 1989 | £2.50 | £6 | black sleeve in envelope |
| Stand | CD-s | Warner Bros | W7577CD | 1989 | £6 | £15 | ..3" single, maple leaf pack |
| Stand | CD-s | Warner Bros | W7577CDX | 1989 | £2 | £5 | 3" single |
| Talk About The Passion | 7" | IRS | PFP1026 | 1983 | £5 | £10 | promo only |
| Talk About The Passion | 12" | IRS | PFSX1026 | 1983 | £10 | £20 | |
| Tighten Up | 7" | Bucketfull Of Brains | BOB5 | 1985 | £2.50 | £6 | flexi |
| Wendell Gee | 7" | IRS | IRMD105 | 1985 | £5 | £10 | double |
| Wendell Gee | 12" | IRS | IRT105 | 1985 | £3 | £8 | |
| Where's Captain Kirk? | 7" | fan club | REM92 | 1992 | £20 | £40 | |
| Wolves Lower | 7" | Trouser Press | FLEXI112 | 1982 | £10 | £20 | US, flexi |

## REMAINS

| Title | Format | Label | Cat. No. | Year | | | Notes |
|---|---|---|---|---|---|---|---|
| Remains | LP | Epic | LN24214/BN26214 | 1967 | £37.50 | £75 | US |
| Remains | LP | Spoonfed | 3305 | 1978 | £6 | £15 | US |

## REMO FOUR

| Title | Format | Label | Cat. No. | Year | | | Notes |
|---|---|---|---|---|---|---|---|
| Attention | LP | Phonogram | 6434158 | 1973 | £8 | £20 | German |
| Live Like A Lady | 7" | Fontana | TF787 | 1967 | £15 | £30 | |
| Peter Gunn | 7" | Piccadilly | 7N35175 | 1964 | £5 | £10 | |
| Sally Go Round The Roses | 7" | Piccadilly | 7N35186 | 1964 | £5 | £10 | |
| Smile | LP | Starclub | STY158034 | 1967 | £50 | £100 | German |

## RENAISSANCE

The history of Renaissance is complicated by the fact that the name covers what, in effect, are two entirely different groups. The first eponymous LP was made by ex-Yardbirds Keith Relf and Jim McCarty and represented the results of a conscious attempt to broaden their music beyond the Yardbirds' blues-based material. It is Beethoven, rather than Jimmy Reed, who is the major influence here. While making the second LP, however (eventually given a limited release as *Illusion*), the group fell apart, with only pianist John Hawken prepared to carry on. He found a new group of musicians to complete the line-up, then decided to leave himself. The immediate result was a stage set consisting of songs from the first LP played by a set of musicians, none of whom had played on the record. Somewhat later, most of the original members got back together, but now had to issue their records under the name Illusion, as the second Renaissance had become quite successful in their own right during the intervening years.

| Title | Format | Label | Cat. No. | Year | | | Notes |
|---|---|---|---|---|---|---|---|
| Illusion | LP | Island | 6339017 | 1972 | £8 | £20 | German |
| Illusion | LP | Island | HELP27 | 1976 | £20 | £40 | test pressing only |
| Jekyll And Hyde | 7" | Sire | SIR4019 | 1979 | £5 | £10 | |
| Northern Lights | 7" | Sire | SRE1022 | 1978 | £5 | £10 | export picture disc |
| Prologue/Ashes Are Burning | LP | Sovereign | CAPACK3 | 1979 | £5 | £12 | double |
| Renaissance | LP | Island | ILPS9114 | 1969 | £6 | £15 | pink label |
| Scheherazade | LP | Mobile Fidelity | MFSL1099 | 1982 | £4 | £10 | US audiophile |
| Sea | 7" | Island | WIP6079 | 1970 | £1.50 | £4 | |

## RENAUD

| Title | Format | Label | Cat. No. | Year | | | Notes |
|---|---|---|---|---|---|---|---|
| Renaud | LP | Disjuncta | 000003 | 1975 | £6 | £15 | French |

## RENAUD, HENRI

| Title | Format | Label | Cat. No. | Year | | | Notes |
|---|---|---|---|---|---|---|---|
| Henri Renaud All Stars | 10" LP | Vogue | LDE088 | 1955 | £15 | £30 | |
| Henri Renaud Band | 10" LP | Vogue | LDE111 | 1955 | £15 | £30 | |
| Henri Renaud-Al Cohn Quartet | 10" LP | Vogue | LDE103 | 1954 | £15 | £30 | |
| Henri Renaud-Bobby Jaspar Quintet | 10" LP | Vogue | LDE096 | 1955 | £15 | £30 | |

## RENAUD, LINE

| Title | Format | Label | Cat. No. | Year | | | Notes |
|---|---|---|---|---|---|---|---|
| If I Love You | 7" | Capitol | CL14230 | 1955 | £4 | £8 | |

## RENAY, DIANE

| Title | Format | Label | Cat. No. | Year | | | Notes |
|---|---|---|---|---|---|---|---|
| Kiss Me Sailor | 7" | Stateside | SS290 | 1964 | £1.50 | £4 | |

| | | | | | | | |
|---|---|---|---|---|---|---|---|
| Navy Blue | LP | Twentieth Century | TF(S)3133 | 1964 | £5 | £12 | *US* |
| Unbelievable Guy | 7" | Stateside | SS270 | 1964 | £1.50 | £4 | |

## RENBOURN, JOHN

| | | | | | | |
|---|---|---|---|---|---|---|
| Another Monday | LP | Transatlantic | TRA149 | 1966 | £6 | £15 |
| Enchanted Garden | LP | Transatlantic | TRA356 | 1980 | £4 | £10 |
| Faro Annie | LP | Transatlantic | TRA247 | 1971 | £4 | £10 |
| Hermit | LP | Transatlantic | TRA336 | 1976 | £6 | £15 |
| John Renbourn | LP | Transatlantic | TRA135 | 1965 | £6 | £15 |
| Lady & The Unicorn | LP | Transatlantic | TRA224 | 1970 | £5 | £12 |
| Maid In Bedlam | LP | Transatlantic | TRA348 | 1977 | £4 | £10 |
| Sir John Alot Of Merrie England | LP | Transatlantic | TRA167 | 1968 | £5 | £12 |

## RENBOURN, JOHN & STEFAN GROSSMAN

| | | | | | | |
|---|---|---|---|---|---|---|
| John Renbourn And Stefan Grossman | LP | Sonet | SNTF139 | 1978 | £4 | £10 |

## RENDELL, DON

As one of the British jazz musicians to emerge after the War, saxophonist Don Rendell's earliest records are not especially remarkable. Unlike the majority of his contemporaries, however, Rendell was interested in the way jazz in America was moving forwards. *Roarin'* is a good hard bop recording which stands up well against the American competition. It also features the playing of a young Graham Bond on alto saxophone. Later Don Rendell formed a quintet with trumpeter Ian Carr and the pair proceeded to create an English version of what Miles Davis was doing in America. When Davis went electric, Ian Carr did the same, founding the group Nucleus. For Rendell, however, this was a step too far. His contribution to rock-influenced jazz is limited to membership of the jazz orchestra used on Neil Ardley's *Symphony Of Amaranths*.

| | | | | | | | |
|---|---|---|---|---|---|---|---|
| Don Rendell Jazz Six | 7" EP | Pye | NJE1044 | 1957 | £7.50 | £15 | |
| Don Rendell Presents The Jazz Six | LP | Nixa | NJL7 | 1957 | £20 | £40 | |
| Don Rendell Quartet | 7" EP | Tempo | EXA11 | 1955 | £7.50 | £15 | |
| Don Rendell Quintet | 7" EP | Tempo | EXA20 | 1956 | £7.50 | £15 | |
| Don Rendell Sextet | 7" EP | Tempo | EXA12 | 1955 | £7.50 | £15 | |
| Don Rendell Sextet | 7" EP | Tempo | EXA16 | 1955 | £7.50 | £15 | *...2 tracks by Damian Robinson* |
| In Paris | 10" LP | Vogue | LDE144 | 1955 | £25 | £50 | |
| Jazz At The Festival Hall | LP | Decca | LK4087 | 1954 | £37.50 | £75 | |
| Jazz Britannia | 7" EP | MGM | MGMEP615 | 1957 | £7.50 | £15 | *.........2 tracks by Joe Harriott* |
| Jazz Committee | 7" EP | Decca | DFE6587 | 1959 | £7.50 | £15 | |
| Meet Don Rendell | 10" LP | Tempo | LAP1 | 1955 | £27.50 | £75 | |
| Packet Of Blues | 7" EP | Decca | DFE6501 | 1958 | £7.50 | £15 | |
| Playtime | LP | Decca | LK4265 | 1958 | £20 | £40 | |
| Roarin' | LP | Jazzland | JLP51 | 1962 | £50 | £100 | |
| Spacewalk | LP | Columbia | SCX6491 | 1971 | £20 | £40 | |
| Tenorama | LP | Nixa | NJL4 | 1956 | £25 | £50 | |

## RENDELL, DON & IAN CARR QUINTET

| | | | | | | |
|---|---|---|---|---|---|---|
| Change Is | LP | Columbia | SCX6368 | 1969 | £37.50 | £75 |
| Dusk Fire | LP | Columbia | SX6064 | 1966 | £37.50 | £75 |
| Live | LP | Columbia | SX/SCX6316 | 1969 | £37.50 | £75 |
| Phase III | LP | Columbia | SX/SCX6214 | 1968 | £37.50 | £75 |
| Shades Of Blue | LP | Columbia | 33SX1733 | 1965 | £37.50 | £75 |

## RENE, GOOGIE

| | | | | | | |
|---|---|---|---|---|---|---|
| Chica Boo | 7" | Atlantic | 584015 | 1966 | £1.50 | £4 |
| Forever | 7" | London | HLY9056 | 1960 | £4 | £8 |
| Smokey Joe's Lala | 7" | Atlantic | AT4076 | 1966 | £7.50 | £15 |

## RENE & RENE

| | | | | | | |
|---|---|---|---|---|---|---|
| Loving You Could Hurt Me So | 7" | Island | WIP6001 | 1967 | £1.50 | £4 |

## RENE & THE ALLIGATORS

| | | | | | | | |
|---|---|---|---|---|---|---|---|
| Guitar Boogie | LP | Fontana | 826401 | 1967 | £15 | £30 | *Dutch* |
| She Broke My Heart | 7" | Decca | F22324 | 1966 | £1.50 | £4 | |

## RENEGADE SOUNDWAVE

| | | | | | | |
|---|---|---|---|---|---|---|
| Cocaine Sex | 12" | Rhythm King | LEFT20T | 1988 | £10 | £20 |
| Kray Twins | 12" | Rhythm King | LEFT8T | 1987 | £2.50 | £6 |

## RENEGADES

| | | | | | | | |
|---|---|---|---|---|---|---|---|
| Cadillac | LP | Ariola | 73368 | 1965 | £37.50 | £75 | *German* |
| Cadillac | LP | Artone | PSM041 | 1965 | £15 | £30 | *Dutch* |
| Cadillac | 7" EP | Riviera | 231113 | 1965 | £37.50 | £75 | *French* |
| Cadillac | 7" | Polydor | 56508 | 1970 | £7.50 | £15 | |
| Half And Half | LP | Ariston | AR0162 | 1967 | £30 | £60 | *Italian* |
| Have Beat, Will Travel | LP | Artone | PSM034 | 1965 | £15 | £30 | *Dutch* |
| No Man's Land | 7" | Columbia | DB8383 | 1968 | £5 | £10 | |
| Pop | LP | Artone | PSM007 | 1965 | £15 | £30 | *Dutch* |
| Take A Heart | LP | Ariola | 73956 | 1966 | £37.50 | £75 | *German* |
| Take A Message | 7" | Parlophone | R5592 | 1967 | £5 | £10 | |
| Thirteen Women | 7" | President | PT106 | 1968 | £20 | £40 | |

## RENIA

| | | | | | | |
|---|---|---|---|---|---|---|
| First Offenders | LP | Transatlantic | TRA261 | 1973 | £6 | £15 |

## RENNARD, JON

| | | | | | | |
|---|---|---|---|---|---|---|
| Brimbledon Fair | LP | Tradition | TSR003 | 1970 | £5 | £12 |
| Parting Glass | LP | Tradition | TSR010 | 1971 | £5 | £12 |

## RENO, DON & RED SMILEY
Country And Western ............................ 7" EP . Parlophone ...... GEP8777 ................ 1958 £7.50 ...... £15 ................................

## RENTAL, ROBERT
Bridge ................................................... LP ..... Industrial ........ IR0007 .................. 1979 £4 ........... £10 ..... with Thomas Leer
Paralysis ............................................... 7" ....... Regular ........... ER102 ................... 1978 £2 .......... £5 .................................

## REPARATA & THE DELRONS
Captain Of Your Ship ........................... 7" ...... Bell ............... BLL1002 ...... 1968 £1.50 ...... £4 ............................
Saturday Night It Didn't Happen ............. 7" ...... Bell ............... BLL1014 ...... 1968 £7.50 ...... £15 ..........................
Tommy .................................................. 7" ...... Stateside ......... SS414 ......... 1965 £2 ......... £5 ............................
Whenever A Teenager Cries ................... LP ...... World Artists .. 2/3006 ........ 1965 £10 ........ £25 ................... US
Whenever A Teenager Cries ................... 7" ...... Stateside ......... SS382 .......... 1965 £4 .......... £8 ...........................

## RESEARCH 1-6-12
1-6-12 In Research ................................. LP ...... Flick City ........ FC5001 ........ 1967 £30 ........... £60 .................. US

## RESIDENTS
The Residents' gimmick of keeping the individual members' identities completely secret has, amazingly, been successfully maintained since the early seventies. Their music is extremely eccentric, a quality that is emphasized by their record release policy. The proliferation of limited-edition cover designs, coloured vinyls and so forth listed here does not include such ultra-rarities as a one-sided clear vinyl 'Duck Stab' 12", of which just six copies were made.

Big Bubble .............................................. LP ...... Ralph ............. RZ8552 ......... 198– £25 ........... £50 US pink marbled vinyl
Blorp Esette ........................................... LP ...... LAFMS .......... 005 ............... 1975 £25 ........... £50 ................... US
Census Taker .......................................... LP ...... Episode .......... ED21 ............. 1985 £15 ........... £30 ................... US
Commercial Album ................................. LP ...... Pre ................ PREX2 ........... 1980 £4 ........... £10 ..........................
Commercial Single .................................. 7" ....... Pre ................ PRE009 .......... 1980 £4 .......... £8 ...........................
Diskomo ................................................ CD-s .. Torso ............ CD40021 ........ 1990 £2 .......... £5 ............................
Duck Stab/Buster And Glen .................... LP ...... Ralph ............. RR0278 .......... 1978 £4 .......... £10 .................. US
Eskimo ................................................... LP ...... Ralph ............. ESK7906 ........ 1979 £4 .......... £10 .................. US
Eskimo ................................................... LP ...... Ralph ............. ESK7906 ........ 1979 £10 ......... £25 ...... US, white vinyl
Eskimo ................................................... LP ...... Ralph ............. ESK7906 ........ 1983 £8 .......... £20 ...... US picture disc
Fingerprince .......................................... LP ...... Ralph ............. RR1276 .......... 1977 £25 ........... £50 ... US, brown sleeve
Fingerprince .......................................... LP ...... Ralph ............. RR1276 .......... 1978 £4 .......... £10 ... US, black & pink
                                                                                                                                          sleeve
Fingerprince .......................................... LP ...... Ralph ............. RR1276 .......... 1978 £8 .......... £20 ...... US, sienna sleeve
George And James ................................. LP ...... Korova ........... KODE9 ........... 1984 £4 .......... £10 ..........................
George And James ................................. LP ...... Ralph ............. RZ8402 ......... 1984 £10 ......... £25 ................... US
George And James ................................. LP ...... Ralph ............. RZ8402 ......... 1984 £25 ........... £50 ...... US, clear vinyl
Hit The Road Jack ................................. 7" ...... Torso ............ 70032 ............ 1987 £1.50 ...... £4 ............. picture disc
Intermission .......................................... LP ...... Ralph ............. RZ8522 ......... 1982 £4 .......... £10 .................. US
Intermission .......................................... 12" .... London ........... RALPH1 ......... 1983 £2.50 ...... £6 ...........................
Kaw-Liga ............................................... CD-s .. Torso ............ CD322 ........... 1988 £2 .......... £5 ............................
Mark Of The Mole ................................ LP ...... Ralph ............. RZ8152 ......... 1981 £4 .......... £10 .................. US
Mark Of The Mole ................................ LP ...... Ralph ............. RZ8152 ......... 1981 £10 ......... £25 ...... US, brown vinyl
Meet The Residents .............................. LP ...... Ralph ............. RR0274 .......... 1974 £37.50 .... £75 .................. US
Meet The Residents .............................. LP ...... Ralph ............. RR0677 .......... 1985 £8 .......... £20 ...... US picture disc
Meet The Residents (remixed) ............... LP ...... Ralph ............. RR0677 .......... 1977 £4 .......... £10 .................. US
Mole Show ............................................ LP ...... Ralph ............. RZ0001 .......... 1983 £6 .......... £15 .................. US
Mole Show ............................................ LP ...... Ralph ............. RZ0001 .......... 1983 £10 ......... £25 ...... US picture disc
Nibbles .................................................. LP ...... Virgin ............ VR3 ............... 1979 £4 .......... £10 ..........................
Not Available ........................................ LP ...... Ralph ............. RR1174 .......... 1978 £4 .......... £10 .................. US
Not Available ........................................ LP ...... Ralph ............. RR1174 .......... 1978 £25 ........... £50 ...... US, purple label
Pal TV LP ............................................. LP ...... Doublevision ... DVR17 ........... 1985 £4 .......... £10 ........... red vinyl
Please Do Not Steal It ........................... LP ...... Ralph ............. DJ7901 ........... 1979 £6 .......... £15 .................. US
Ralph Before '84 Vol. 1 .......................... LP ...... Korova ........... KODE10 ......... 1984 £4 .......... £10 ..........................
Ralph Before '84 Vol. 2 .......................... LP ...... Korova ........... KODE12 ......... 1985 £4 .......... £10 ..........................
Residents Radio Special ......................... LP ...... Ralph ............. 173 ............... 1977 £10 ......... £25 ............ US promo
Stars And Hank Forever ......................... LP ...... Ralph ............................. £25 ........... £50 ...... US green vinyl
Subterranean Modern ............................ LP ...... Ralph ............. SM7908 .......... 1979 £4 .......... £10 .................. US
Ten Years In Twenty Minutes ................. LP ...... Ralph ............. RR8205D ........ 198– £25 ........... £50 ...... US clear vinyl, 1
                                                                                                                                          sided, no sleeve
Third Reich And Roll ............................. LP ...... Ralph ............. RR1075 .......... 1975 £25 ........... £50 ...US, orange & green
                                                                                                                                          carrot on sleeve
Third Reich And Roll ............................. LP ...... Ralph ............. RR1075 .......... 1977 £4 .......... £10 .................. US
Third Reich And Roll ............................. LP ...... Ralph ............. RR1075 .......... 1977 £8 .......... £20 .... US, censored sleeve
Thirteenth Anniversary Edition ................ LP ...... Ralph ............. RZ8602 ......... 1986 £6 .......... £15 ...... US picture disc
Tunes Of Two Cities .............................. LP ...... Ralph ............. RR8202 .......... 1982 £4 .......... £10 .................. US
Vileness Fats .......................................... LP ...... Ralph ............. RZ8452 ......... 1984 £25 ........... £50 ...... US, red vinyl

## RESTIVO, JOHNNY
I Like Girls ............................................ 7" ...... RCA .............. RCA1159 ....... 1959 £4 .......... £8 ...........................
Oh Johnny ............................................. LP ...... RCA .............. LPM/LSP2149 ...... 1959 £15 ......... £30 ................... US
Shape I'm In .......................................... 7" ...... RCA .............. RCA1143 ....... 1959 £7.50 ...... £15 .............. tri-centre
Sweet Sweet Loving .............................. 7" ...... Ember ............ EMBS135 ........ 1961 £2 .......... £5 ............................

## RETREADS
Would You Listen Girl ........................... 7" ...... Eddi Cosmo .... EO101 ............ 1980 £4 .......... £8 ...........................

## REVALONS
Discotheque A Go Go ............................ LP ...... Fantastic ........ 1410 ............. 1964 £10 ......... £25 ............ Canadian

## REVELL, DIGGER & THE DENVER MEN
Surfside ................................................. 7" ...... Decca ............. F11657 ........... 1963 £2 .......... £5 ............................

## REVELLS
Mind Party ..................................... 7" ...... CBS............... 7050 .................... 1971 £2............ £5 ...............................

## REVELS
Midnight Stroll.......................................... 7" ...... Top Rank ....... JAR235.................. 1959 £7.50...... £15 .....................

## REVELS (2)
Revels On A Rampage .......................... LP ...... Impact ............ LPM1 ................... 1964 £25.......... £50 ........................ US

## REVERE, PAUL & THE RAIDERS
| | | | | | | | |
|---|---|---|---|---|---|---|---|
| Alias Pink Puzz ............................. | LP ..... | Columbia ...... | CS9905 ................... | 1969 | £4...... | £10 | ........ US |
| Christmas Past And Present .......... | LP ..... | Columbia ...... | CL2755/CS9555..... | 1967 | £15..... | £30 | ........ US |
| Cinderella Sunshine ...................... | 7" ...... | CBS................ | 3757 ....................... | 1968 | £1.50... | £4 | |
| Don't Take It So Hard..................... | 7" ...... | CBS................ | 3586 ....................... | 1968 | £1.50... | £4 | |
| Goin' To Memphis........................... | LP ..... | CBS................ | 63265...................... | 1968 | £4...... | £10 | |
| Good Thing..................................... | LP ..... | CBS................ | (S)BPG62963 ........ | 1969 | £4...... | £10 | |
| Good Thing..................................... | 7" ...... | CBS................ | 202502.................... | 1967 | £2...... | £5 | |
| Great Airplane Strike ..................... | 7" ...... | CBS................ | 202411.................... | 1966 | £2...... | £5 | |
| Greatest Hits ................................. | LP ..... | Columbia ...... | KCL2662/KCS9462 | 1967 | £4...... | £10 | ........ US |
| Hard 'n' Heavy ............................... | LP ..... | CBS................ | 63649...................... | 1969 | £4...... | £10 | |
| Here They Come ............................ | LP ..... | Columbia ...... | CL2307/CS9107.:.. | 1965 | £8...... | £20 | ........ US |
| Him Or Me – Who's It Gonna Be?.......... | 7" ...... | CBS................ | 2737 ....................... | 1967 | £2...... | £5 | |
| Hungry .......................................... | 7" ...... | CBS................ | 202253.................... | 1966 | £2...... | £5 | |
| In The Beginning........................... | LP ..... | Jerden ............ | JRL/JRS7004 ......... | 1966 | £37.50... | £75 | ........ US |
| Indian Reservation ......................... | LP ..... | Columbia ...... | CQ30768................ | 1973 | £4...... | £10 | ...... US quad |
| Just Like Me .................................. | 7" ...... | CBS................ | 202027.................... | 1966 | £1.50... | £4 | |
| Just Like Us ................................... | LP ..... | CBS................ | (S)BPG62406.......... | 1966 | £6...... | £15 | |
| Kicks ............................................. | 7" ...... | CBS................ | 202205.................... | 1966 | £2...... | £5 | |
| Let Me ........................................... | 7" ...... | CBS................ | 4260 ....................... | 1969 | £1.50... | £4 | |
| Like Long Hair............................... | LP ..... | Gardena ......... | G1000..................... | 1961 | £75... | £150 | ........ US |
| Like Long Hair............................... | 7" ...... | Sue ................. | WI344 .................... | 1966 | £4...... | £8 | |
| Like Long Hair............................... | 7" ...... | Top Rank ...... | JAR557................... | 1961 | £4...... | £8 | |
| Midnight Ride ................................ | LP ..... | CBS................ | (S)BPG62397.......... | 1966 | £4...... | £10 | |
| Moreen .......................................... | 7" ...... | CBS................ | 3186 ....................... | 1967 | £1.50... | £4 | |
| Paul Revere & The Raiders............. | LP ..... | Sande ............. | 1001 ....................... | 1962 | £100... | £200 | ........ US |
| Paul Revere & The Raiders............. | LP ..... | Sears .............. | SPS439................... | 1970 | £25... | £50 | ........ US |
| Revolution ..................................... | LP ..... | CBS................ | (S)BPG63095.......... | 1967 | £4...... | £10 | |
| Something Happening ..................... | LP ..... | Columbia ...... | CS9665................... | 1968 | £4...... | £10 | ........ US |
| Spirit Of '67.................................. | LP ..... | Columbia ...... | CL2595/CS9395..... | 1967 | £4...... | £10 | ........ US |
| Steppin' Out .................................. | 7" EP . | CBS................ | 5930 ....................... | 1966 | £15... | £30 | ........ French |
| Steppin' Out .................................. | 7" ...... | CBS................ | 202003.................... | 1965 | £1.50... | £4 | |
| Ups And Downs.............................. | 7" ...... | CBS................ | 202610.................... | 1967 | £2...... | £5 | ...............................|

## REVEREND BLACK & THE ROCKIN' VICARS
Zing Went The Strings Of My Heart ........ 7" ...... Decca ............ ............................ 1963 £25......... £50 ..................... Irish

## REVILLOS
Attack .......................................................... LP ...... Superville ........ SV4001 ................ 1982 £10......... £25 ................................

## REVOLUTION
Hallelujah ................................................... 7" ...... Piccadilly......... 7N35289 .............. 1966 £10......... £20 ................................

## REVOLUTIONARIES
| | | | | | | | |
|---|---|---|---|---|---|---|---|
| Black Ash ...................................... | LP ..... | Trojan............. | TRLS186 ............... | 1980 | £4...... | £10 | |
| Goldmine Dub ............................... | LP ..... | Greensleeves ... | GREL4 .................. | 1979 | £5...... | £12 | |
| Jonkanoo Dub................................ | LP ..... | Cha Cha ......... | CHALP005 ............ | 1978 | £5...... | £12 | |
| Negrea Love Dub ........................... | LP ..... | Trojan............. | TRLS153 ............... | 1979 | £5...... | £12 | |
| Outlaw Dub .................................... | LP ..... | Trojan............. | TRLS169 ............... | 1979 | £5...... | £12 | |
| Reaction In Dub ............................. | LP ..... | Cha Cha ......... | CHALP002 ............ | 1978 | £5...... | £12 | |
| Revolutionary Sounds Vol. 2............ | LP ..... | Ballistic .......... | UAS30237............. | 1978 | £5...... | £12 | |

## REVOLUTIONARY BLUES BAND
Revolutionary Blues Band...................... LP ...... MCA............. MUPS402 ............. 1970 £4.......... £10 ................................

## REVOLVER
Frisco Annie ............................................... 7" ...... Youngblood .... YB1006................. 1969 £5.......... £10 ................................

## REVOLVING PAINT DREAM
Flowers In The Sky .................................... 7" ...... Creation ......... CRE2 .................... 1984 £7.50...... £15 ................................

## REX & THE MINORS
Chicken Sax ............................................... 7" ...... Triumph ......... RGM1023............. 1960 £10......... £20 ................................

## REXROTH, KENNETH
Poetry And Jazz At The Blackhawk............ LP ...... Fantasy ........... 7008 ..................... 1958 £8.......... £20 ........................ US

## REY, ALVINO
Original Mama Blues.................................. 7" ...... London ........... HLD9431 .............. 1961 £1.50...... £4 ................................

## REY, LITTLE BOBBY
Rockin' J Bells............................................ 7" ...... Top Rank ....... JAR525................. 1960 £1.50...... £4 ................................

## REYNARD
Fresh From The Earth................................ LP ...... Pilgrim............ GRA102 ................ 1976 £15......... £30 ................................

## REYNOLDS, DEBBIE
Am I That Easy To Forget? ..................... LP ...... London ........... HAD2294/ ...........  1960 £5.......... £12 ................................

| | | | | | | | |
|---|---|---|---|---|---|---|---|
| | | | SAHD6106.............. | | | | |
| Athena ......................................... | LP ..... | Mercury......... | MG25202............ | 1954 | £25 ....... £50 | | US |
| Bundle Of Joy..................................... | LP .... | RCA ............. | LPM1339............ | 1956 | £15 ....... £30 | | US |
| Carolina In The Morning........................ | 7" ..... | MGM ............ | SP1127............. | 1955 | £2........ £5 | | |
| Debbie ............................................ | LP ..... | London ........... | HAD2200/ | 1959 | £5........ £12 | | |
| | | | SHD6051 .............. | | | | |
| Debbie Reynolds................................. | 7" EP . | MGM ............ | MGMEP670.......... | 1958 | £2.50.... £6 | | |
| Delightful ........................................ | 7" EP . | MGM ............ | MGMEP694.......... | 1959 | £2.50.... £6 | | |
| Fine And Dandy................................... | LP ..... | London ........... | HAD2326............ | 1961 | £4........ £10 | | |
| From Debbie With Love......................... | 7" EP . | MGM ............ | MGMEP725.......... | 1960 | £2.50.... £6 | | |
| Great Folk Hits .................................. | LP ..... | London ....... | HAD/SHD8075 ..... | 1963 | £4........ £10 | | |
| I Love Melvin .................................... | 10" LP | MGM ............ | D114............... | 1953 | £15....... £30 | | |
| Love Is The Tender Trap ....................... | 7" ..... | MGM ............ | SP1155............. | 1956 | £1.50..... £4 | | |
| Say One For Me................................... | LP ..... | Columbia ....... | CL1337/CS8137..... | 1959 | £6........ £15 | | US |
| Tammy ............................................ | LP ..... | Vogue Coral.... | LVA9070 .......... | 1957 | £10....... £25 | | |
| Tammy ............................................ | 7" ..... | Vogue Coral.... | Q72274............. | 1957 | £2.50.... £6 | | |
| This Happy Feeling .............................. | 7" ..... | Coral ............ | Q72324............. | 1958 | £1.50..... £4 | | |
| Two Weeks With Love ........................... | LP ..... | MGM ............ | E3233 .............. | 1955 | £6........ £15 | | US |
| Two Weeks With Love ........................... | 10" LP | MGM ............ | E530 ............... | 1950 | £10....... £25 | | US |

### REYNOLDS, JODY
| | | | | | | | |
|---|---|---|---|---|---|---|---|
| Endless Sleep.................... | 7" ...... | London ......... | HL8651 ......... | 1958 | £7.50..... £15 | | |

### REYNOLDS, TIMMY
| | | | | | | | |
|---|---|---|---|---|---|---|---|
| Lullaby Of Love ................................. | 7" ...... | Ember............ | EMBS133......... | 1962 | £1.50..... £4 | | B side Jeff Mills |

### REYS, RITA
| | | | | | | | |
|---|---|---|---|---|---|---|---|
| Cool Voice Of Rita Reys........................ | 10" LP | Philips............ | BBR8120 ......... | 1958 | £8........ £20 | | |

### REZILLOS
| | | | | | | | |
|---|---|---|---|---|---|---|---|
| Can't Stand My Baby............................ | 7" ...... | Sensible.......... | FAB1 ............ | 1977 | £1.50..... £4 | | picture sleeve |
| Can't Stand The Rezillos ....................... | LP ..... | Sire ............. | K56530 .......... | 1978 | £4........ £10 | | inner and card insert |
| Cold Wars ....................................... | 7" ..... | Sire ............. | SIR4014.......... | 1979 | £1.50..... £4 | | picture sleeve |
| Flying Saucer Attack ............................ | 7" ..... | Sensible.......... | FAB2 ............ | 1977 | £12.50.... £25 | | |
| Flying Saucer Attack ............................ | 7" ..... | Sire ............. | 6078612 ......... | 1977 | £1.50..... £4 | | picture sleeve |
| Top Of The Pops ................................ | 7" ..... | Sire ............. | SIR4001.......... | 1978 | £1.50..... £4 | | picture sleeve |

### RHESUS
| | | | | | | | |
|---|---|---|---|---|---|---|---|
| O– ................................................ | LP ..... | Epic ............. | EPC64560 ........ | 1971 | £10....... £25 | | French |

### RHINOCEROS
| | | | | | | | |
|---|---|---|---|---|---|---|---|
| Apricot Brandy................................... | 7" ...... | Elektra ........... | EKSN45051 ........ | 1968 | £1.50..... £4 | | |
| Rhinoceros ....................................... | LP ..... | Elektra ........... | EKL/EKS74030 ... | 1968 | £4........ £10 | | |

### RHODEN PAT
| | | | | | | | |
|---|---|---|---|---|---|---|---|
| Time is Tight..................................... | 7" ...... | Mary Lyn ....... | ML101 ............ | 1970 | £1.50..... £4 | | |
| Jezebel............................................ | 7" ..... | Ska Beat ........ | JB195 ............ | 1965 | £5........ £10 | | |
| Woman Is Greedy ............................... | 7" ..... | Trojan........... | TR606 ........... | 1968 | £1.50..... £4 | | |

### RHODEN, WINSTON
| | | | | | | | |
|---|---|---|---|---|---|---|---|
| Make Believe ..................................... | 7" ...... | Blue Beat ....... | BB360............ | 1966 | £6........ £12 | | |

### RHODES, TODD
| | | | | | | | |
|---|---|---|---|---|---|---|---|
| Specks ............................................ | 7" ...... | Parlophone ..... | MSP6171 ......... | 1955 | £5........ £10 | | |

### RHUBARB RHUBARB
| | | | | | | | |
|---|---|---|---|---|---|---|---|
| Rainmaker......................................... | 7" ...... | President ........ | PT229 ........... | 1968 | £7.50..... £15 | | |

### RHYTHM & BLUES INC.
| | | | | | | | |
|---|---|---|---|---|---|---|---|
| Honey Don't ...................................... | 7" ...... | Fontana ......... | TF524 ........... | 1965 | £12.50.... £25 | | |

### RHYTHM ACES
| | | | | | | | |
|---|---|---|---|---|---|---|---|
| Christmas ......................................... | 7" ...... | Island ........... | WI032 ........... | 1962 | £5........ £10 | | |
| I'll Be There ..................................... | 7" ..... | Blue Beat ....... | BB134............ | 1962 | £6........ £12 | | |
| Please Don't Go Away ........................... | 7" ..... | Starlite .......... | ST45066 ......... | 1961 | £5........ £10 | | |
| Thousand Teardrops.............................. | 7" ..... | Starlite .......... | ST45061 ......... | 1961 | £5........ £10 | | |

### RHYTHM KINGS
| | | | | | | | |
|---|---|---|---|---|---|---|---|
| Blue Soul.......................................... | 7" ...... | Vogue............ | V9212 ........... | 1963 | £4........ £8 | | |

### RHYTHM OF LIFE
| | | | | | | | |
|---|---|---|---|---|---|---|---|
| Soon .............................................. | 7" ...... | Rhythm Of Life.......... | RHYTHM001 ....... | 1982 | £1.50..... £4 | | |

### RHYTHM ROCKERS
| | | | | | | | |
|---|---|---|---|---|---|---|---|
| Soul Surfin'....................................... | LP ...... | Challenge........ | CHL617........... | 1963 | £6........ £15 | | US |

### RHYTHMETTES
| | | | | | | | |
|---|---|---|---|---|---|---|---|
| I'll Be With You In Apple Blossom Time... | 7" ...... | Coral ............ | Q72358........... | 1959 | £1.50..... £4 | | |

### RIBA, PAU
| | | | | | | | |
|---|---|---|---|---|---|---|---|
| Jo, La Donya I El Gripau........................ | LP ..... | Edigsa ........... | | 1971 | £30....... £60 | | US |

### RIBEIRO, CATHERINE & ALPES
| | | | | | | | |
|---|---|---|---|---|---|---|---|
| Le Rat débile et l'homme des champs........ | LP ..... | Philips........... | 9101003 ......... | 1974 | £6........ £15 | | French |
| Libertés? .......................................... | LP ..... | Fontana.......... | 9101501 ......... | 1975 | £6........ £15 | | French |
| Paix ............................................... | LP ..... | Philips........... | 6325019 ......... | 1974 | £6........ £15 | | French |
| Passions .......................................... | LP ..... | Philips........... | 9101270 ......... | 1979 | £4........ £10 | | French |

## RICE, TIM & THE WEBBER GROUP

| Title | Format | Label | Cat. No. | Year | | | Notes |
|---|---|---|---|---|---|---|---|
| Come Back Richard Your Country Needs You | 7" | RCA | RCA1895 | 1969 | £2 | £5 | |

## RICE-DAVIES, MANDY

| Title | Format | Label | Cat. No. | Year | | | Notes |
|---|---|---|---|---|---|---|---|
| Introducing Mandy | 7" EP | Ember | EMBEP4537 | 1963 | £7.50 | £15 | |

## RICH, BUDDY

| Title | Format | Label | Cat. No. | Year | | | Notes |
|---|---|---|---|---|---|---|---|
| Buddy And Sweets | LP | Columbia | 33CX10080 | 1957 | £6 | £15 | .... with Harry Edison |
| Buddy Rich | 7" EP | Columbia | SEB10024 | 195– | £2 | £5 | |
| In Miami | LP | Columbia | 33CX10138 | 1959 | £6 | £15 | |
| Just Sings | LP | HMV | CLP1185 | 1958 | £6 | £15 | |
| Rich Versus Roach | LP | Mercury | MMC14031 | 1960 | £6 | £15 | ...with Max Roach |
| Sings Johnny Mercer | LP | HMV | CLP1092 | 1956 | £6 | £15 | |
| Swinging Buddy Rich | 7" EP | Columbia | SEB10071 | 1957 | £2 | £5 | |
| This One's For Basie | LP | Columbia | 33CX10071 | 1957 | £6 | £15 | |
| Wailing Buddy Rich | LP | Columbia | 33CX10052 | 1956 | £6 | £15 | |

## RICH, CHARLIE

| Title | Format | Label | Cat. No. | Year | | | Notes |
|---|---|---|---|---|---|---|---|
| Big Boss Man | LP | RCA | LPM/LSP3537 | 1966 | £6 | £15 | US |
| Charlie Rich | LP | Groove | G(S)1000 | 1964 | £6 | £15 | US |
| Just A Little Bit Sweet | 7" | London | HLS9482 | 1962 | £7.50 | £15 | |
| Lonely Weekends | LP | Philips | 1970 | 1960 | £150 | £250 | US |
| Lonely Weekends | 7" | London | HLU9107 | 1960 | £10 | £20 | |
| Love Is After Me | 7" | London | HLU10104 | 1967 | £5 | £10 | |
| Many New Sides Of Charlie Rich | LP | Philips | BL7695 | 1966 | £6 | £15 | |
| Mohair Sam | 7" | Philips | BF1432 | 1965 | £1.50 | £4 | |
| That's Rich | LP | RCA | RD7719 | 1965 | £10 | £25 | |
| Too Many Teardrops | 7" | RCA | RCA1433 | 1965 | £1.50 | £4 | |

## RICH, DAVE

| Title | Format | Label | Cat. No. | Year | | | Notes |
|---|---|---|---|---|---|---|---|
| City Lights | 7" | RCA | RCA1092 | 1958 | £2 | £5 | |

## RICH, LEWIS

| Title | Format | Label | Cat. No. | Year | | | Notes |
|---|---|---|---|---|---|---|---|
| Everybody But Me | 7" | Parlophone | R5283 | 1965 | £1.50 | £4 | |
| I Don't Want To Hear It Anymore | 7" | Parlophone | R5434 | 1966 | £2 | £5 | |

## RICH MOUNTAIN TOWER

| Title | Format | Label | Cat. No. | Year | | | Notes |
|---|---|---|---|---|---|---|---|
| Rich Mountain Tower | LP | London | SHO8427 | 1972 | £4 | £10 | |

## RICHARD, CLIFF

Cliff Richard's first two LPs were issued in mono only and yet stereo mixes of some the tracks can be found on EPs. These are consequently much sought after. Cliff's 78 rpm releases are also scarce and break the usual maxim that 78s are much less valuable than their 45 rpm equivalents. Few of the religious records he has made over the years have sold particularly well and many of these now fetch quite high prices. Becoming increasingly hard to find, too, is the single 'Honky Tonk Angel', which was withdrawn at Cliff Richard's insistence, despite being a likely chart hit, after someone told him what a honky tonk angel actually was (a prostitute). The most desirable Cliff Richard collectors' item of all, however (apart from unreleased acetates which are too scarce to be a realistic collectors' goal for most people), is likely to be one of the complete film soundtrack albums that were presented to all the people involved in the making of *Summer Holiday* and *Wonderful Life*.

| Title | Format | Label | Cat. No. | Year | | | Notes |
|---|---|---|---|---|---|---|---|
| 21 Today | LP | Columbia | 33SX1368 | 1961 | £8 | £20 | mono |
| 21 Today | LP | Columbia | SCX3409 | 1961 | £20 | £40 | stereo |
| 31st Of February Street | LP | EMI | EMC3048 | 1974 | £8 | £20 | |
| 32 Minutes 17 Seconds | LP | Columbia | 33SX1431 | 1962 | £8 | £20 | mono |
| 32 Minutes 17 Seconds | LP | Columbia | SCX3436 | 1962 | £20 | £40 | stereo |
| About That Man | LP | Columbia | SCX6408 | 1970 | £50 | £100 | |
| Aladdin & His Wonderful Lamp | LP | Columbia | 33SX1676 | 1964 | £4 | £10 | mono |
| Aladdin & His Wonderful Lamp | LP | Columbia | SCX3522 | 1964 | £6 | £15 | stereo |
| All My Love | 7" | Columbia | DB8293 | 1967 | £1.50 | £4 | |
| Angel | 7" EP | Columbia | SEG8444 | 1965 | £7.50 | £15 | |
| Angel | 7" | Columbia | DC762 | 1965 | £20 | £40 | export |
| Best Of Cliff Richard | LP | Columbia | SX/SCX6343 | 1969 | £4 | £10 | |
| Best Of Cliff Richard And The Shadows | LP | Readers Digest | GRICA140 | 1984 | £25 | £50 | 8 LPs, boxed |
| Best Of Cliff Richard And The Shadows | 7" | Lyntone | LYN14745 | 197– | £2.50 | £6 | flexi |
| Best Of Me | CD-s | EMI | CDEM92 | 1989 | £2 | £5 | 2 versions |
| Big Ship | 7" | Columbia | DB8581 | 1969 | £1.50 | £4 | |
| Bin Verliebt | 7" | Columbia | C21703 | 1961 | £7.50 | £15 | sung in German |
| Blue Turns To Grey | 7" | Columbia | DB7866 | 1966 | £1.50 | £4 | |
| Boyfriend flexi | 7" | Boyfriend | | 196– | £7.50 | £15 | flexi |
| Brand New Song | 7" | Columbia | DB8957 | 1972 | £1.50 | £4 | |
| Carnival | 7" | Columbia | 23060 | 1965 | £7.50 | £15 | German import |
| Carol Singers | 7" EP | Columbia | SEG8533 | 1967 | £12.50 | £25 | |
| Carols | LP | Word | WRDR3034 | 1988 | £10 | £25 | |
| Cinderella | LP | Columbia | SX/SCX6103 | 1967 | £8 | £20 | |
| Cinderella | 7" EP | Columbia | SEG8527 | 1967 | £30 | £60 | |
| Cliff | LP | Columbia | 33SX1147 | 1959 | £8 | £20 | blue & black label |
| Cliff | LP | Columbia | 33SX1147 | 1959 | £15 | £30 | green label |
| Cliff | CD | EMI | CZ1 | 1987 | £5 | £12 | |
| Cliff En España | 7" EP | HMV | 7EPL13979 | 1963 | £15 | £30 | sung in Spanish |
| Cliff In Japan | LP | Columbia | SX/SCX6244 | 1968 | £10 | £25 | blue & black label |
| Cliff In Japan | LP | Columbia | SX/SCX6244 | 1968 | £6 | £15 | white & black label |
| Cliff No. 1 | 7" EP | Columbia | ESG7754 | 1959 | £20 | £40 | stereo |
| Cliff No. 1 | 7" EP | Columbia | SEG7903 | 1959 | £10 | £20 | |
| Cliff No. 2 | 7" EP | Columbia | ESG7769 | 1959 | £20 | £40 | stereo |
| Cliff No. 2 | 7" EP | Columbia | SEG7910 | 1959 | £10 | £20 | |
| Cliff Richard | LP | Columbia | 33SX1709 | 1965 | £10 | £25 | mono |

| Title | Format | Label | Catalogue | Year | Price | Price | Notes |
|---|---|---|---|---|---|---|---|
| Cliff Richard | LP | Columbia | SCX3546 | 1965 | £15 | £30 | stereo |
| Cliff Richard | LP | World Record Club | STP1051 | 1972 | £20 | £40 | |
| Cliff Richard | 7" EP | Columbia | SEG8151 | 1962 | £10 | £20 | |
| Cliff Richard In Spain | LP | Epic | LN24115/BN26115 | 1964 | £10 | £25 | US |
| Cliff Richard No. 2 | 7" EP | Columbia | SEG8168 | 1962 | £10 | £20 | |
| Cliff Richard Singles Sampler | LP | EMI | PSLP350 | 1982 | £10 | £25 | promo |
| Cliff Richard Songbook | LP | World Record Club | ALBUM26 | 1980 | £15 | £30 | 6 LPs, boxed |
| Cliff Richard Story | LP | World Record Club | SM255-260 | 1972 | £15 | £30 | 6 LPs, boxed |
| Cliff Richard Story | 7" | Lyntone | LYNSF1218 | 1973 | £1.50 | £4 | sampler flexi with interview |
| Cliff Sings | LP | ABC | (S)321 | 1960 | £15 | £30 | US |
| Cliff Sings | LP | Columbia | 33SX1192 | 1959 | £8 | £20 | blue & black label |
| Cliff Sings | LP | Columbia | 33SX1192 | 1959 | £15 | £30 | green label |
| Cliff Sings No. 1 | 7" EP | Columbia | ESG7788 | 1960 | £20 | £40 | stereo |
| Cliff Sings No. 1 | 7" EP | Columbia | SEG7979 | 1960 | £7.50 | £15 | |
| Cliff Sings No. 2 | 7" EP | Columbia | ESG7794 | 1960 | £20 | £40 | stereo |
| Cliff Sings No. 2 | 7" EP | Columbia | SEG7987 | 1960 | £7.50 | £15 | |
| Cliff Sings No. 3 | 7" EP | Columbia | ESG7808 | 1960 | £20 | £40 | stereo |
| Cliff Sings No. 3 | 7" EP | Columbia | SEG8005 | 1960 | £7.50 | £15 | |
| Cliff Sings No. 4 | 7" EP | Columbia | ESG7816 | 1960 | £20 | £40 | stereo |
| Cliff Sings No. 4 | 7" EP | Columbia | SEG8021 | 1960 | £10 | £20 | |
| Cliff's Hit Parade | 7" EP | Columbia | SEG8133 | 1962 | £5 | £10 | |
| Cliff's Hits | 7" EP | Columbia | SEG8203 | 1962 | £5 | £10 | |
| Cliff's Hits From Aladdin | 7" EP | Columbia | SEG8395 | 1965 | £5 | £10 | |
| Cliff's Lucky Lips | 7" EP | Columbia | SEG8269 | 1963 | £5 | £10 | |
| Cliff's Palladium Successes | 7" EP | Columbia | SEG8320 | 1964 | £7.50 | £15 | |
| Cliff's Rock Party | 7" | Serenade | | 196– | £7.50 | £15 | flexi |
| Cliff's Silver Discs | 7" EP | Columbia | SEG8050 | 1960 | £4 | £8 | |
| Congratulations | 7" EP | Columbia | SEG8540 | 1968 | £10 | £20 | |
| Das Glück Ist Rosarot | 7" | Columbia | C23371 | 1966 | £7.50 | £15 | German import |
| Das Ist Die Frage Aller Fragen | 7" | Columbia | C22811 | 1964 | £7.50 | £15 | German import |
| Don't Forget To Catch Me | 7" | Columbia | DB8503 | 1968 | £1.50 | £4 | |
| Don't Stop Me Now | LP | Columbia | SX/SCX6133 | 1967 | £8 | £20 | |
| Don't Talk To Him | 7" EP | Columbia | SEG8299 | 1964 | £7.50 | £15 | |
| Dream | 7" EP | Columbia | ESG7867 | 1961 | £12.50 | £25 | stereo |
| Dream | 7" EP | Columbia | SEG8119 | 1961 | £5 | £10 | |
| Du Bist Mein Erster Gedanke | 7" | Columbia | C23211 | 1967 | £7.50 | £15 | sung in German |
| Ein Girl Wie Du | 7" | Columbia | C23510 | 196– | £7.50 | £15 | sung in German |
| Es War Keine So Wunderbar Wie Du | 7" | Columbia | 22962 | 1964 | £7.50 | £15 | German import |
| Established 1958 | LP | Columbia | SX/SCX6282 | 1968 | £6 | £15 | |
| Every Face Tells A Story | 7" | EMI | PSR410 | 1977 | £10 | £20 | promo sampler |
| Expresso Bongo | 7" EP | Columbia | ESG7783 | 1960 | £15 | £30 | stereo |
| Expresso Bongo | 7" EP | Columbia | SEG7971 | 1960 | £7.50 | £15 | |
| Fall In Love With You | 7" | Columbia | DB4431 | 1960 | £1.50 | £4 | |
| Fall In Love With You | 7" | Columbia | DB4431 | 1960 | £4 | £8 | black label |
| Finders Keepers | LP | Columbia | SX/SCX6079 | 1966 | £5 | £12 | |
| Finders Keepers | 7" | EMI | PSR304 | 1967 | £5 | £10 | 1 sided promo |
| Flying Machine | 7" | Columbia | DB8797 | 1971 | £1.50 | £4 | |
| Forever Kind Of Love | 7" EP | Columbia | SEG8347 | 1964 | £7.50 | £15 | |
| Forty Greatest Hits | 7" | EMI | PSR414/5 | 1977 | £7.50 | £15 | double promo sampler |
| From A Distance | CD-s | EMI | CDEM155 | 1990 | £2 | £5 | |
| From A Distance | 7" | EMI | EMPD155 | 1990 | £1.50 | £4 | picture disc |
| From A Distance – The Event | CD | EMI | CDCRTV31 | 1990 | £15 | £30 | promo with bonus single |
| Gee Whiz It's You | 7" | Columbia | DC756 | 1961 | £2 | £5 | export |
| Girl Like You | 7" | Columbia | DB4667 | 1961 | £1.50 | £4 | |
| Girl Like You | 7" | Columbia | DB4667 | 1961 | £2.50 | £6 | black label |
| Good News | LP | Columbia | JSX6167 | 1967 | £15 | £30 | export |
| Good News | LP | Columbia | SX/SCX6167 | 1967 | £6 | £15 | |
| Good Times (Better Times) | 7" | Columbia | DB8548 | 1969 | £1.50 | £4 | |
| Green Light | 7" | EMI | EMI2920 | 1979 | £10 | £20 | picture sleeve |
| Gut Das Es Freunde Gibt | 7" | EMI | 1C00605315 | 196– | £7.50 | £15 | sung in German |
| Heart User | 12" | EMI | 12RICH2 | 1985 | £2.50 | £6 | poster picture sleeve |
| Help It Along | LP | EMI | EMA768 | 1974 | £6 | £15 | |
| Help It Along | 7" | EMI | EMI2022 | 1973 | £2.50 | £6 | picture sleeve |
| High Class Baby | 78 | Columbia | DB4203 | 1958 | £7.50 | £15 | |
| High Class Baby | 7" | Columbia | DB4203 | 1958 | £2.50 | £6 | |
| High Class Baby | 7" | Columbia | DB4203 | 1958 | £10 | £20 | black label |
| His Land | LP | Columbia | SCX6443 | 1970 | £25 | £50 | |
| Hit Album | LP | Columbia | 33SX1512 | 1963 | £4 | £10 | |
| Hits From Summer Holiday | 7" EP | Columbia | ESG7896 | 1963 | £12.50 | £25 | stereo |
| Hits From Summer Holiday | 7" EP | Columbia | SEG8250 | 1963 | £4 | £8 | |
| Hits From The Young Ones | 7" EP | Columbia | SEG8159 | 1962 | £4 | £8 | different mixes |
| Hits From When In Rome | 7" EP | Columbia | SEG8478 | 1966 | £20 | £40 | |
| Hits From Wonderful Life | 7" EP | Columbia | ESG7906 | 1964 | £15 | £30 | stereo |
| Hits From Wonderful Life | 7" EP | Columbia | SEG8376 | 1964 | £7.50 | £15 | |
| Holiday Carnival | 7" EP | Columbia | ESG7892 | 1963 | £12.50 | £25 | stereo |
| Holiday Carnival | 7" EP | Columbia | SEG8246 | 1963 | £5 | £10 | |
| Honky Tonk Angel | 7" | EMI | EMI2344 | 1975 | £10 | £20 | |
| How Wonderful To Know | LP | World Record Club | (S)T643 | 1964 | £8 | £20 | |
| Hymns And Inspirational Songs | LP | Word | WRDR3017 | 1986 | £10 | £25 | |
| I Ain't Got Time Anymore | 7" | Columbia | DB8708 | 1970 | £1.50 | £4 | |
| I Just Don't Have The Heart | CD-s | EMI | CDEM101 | 1989 | £2 | £5 | |
| I Just Don't Have The Heart | 12" | EMI | 12EMP101 | 1989 | £2.50 | £6 | picture disc |

| Title | Format | Label | Catalogue | Year | | | Notes |
|---|---|---|---|---|---|---|---|
| I Love You | 7" | Columbia | DB4547 | 1960 | £1.50 | £4 | |
| I Love You | 7" | Columbia | DB4547 | 1960 | £4 | £8 | *black label* |
| I'll Come Running | 7" | Columbia | DB8210 | 1967 | £1.50 | £4 | |
| I'll Love You Forever Today | 7" | Columbia | DB8437 | 1968 | £2 | £5 | |
| I'm Lookin' Out The Window | 7" | Columbia | DB4828 | 1962 | £2.50 | £6 | *black label* |
| I'm Looking Out The Window | 7" | Columbia | DB4828 | 1962 | £1.50 | £4 | |
| Ich Traume Deine Träume | 7" | Columbia | 1C00604706 | 1971 | £7.50 | £15 | *sung in German* |
| In The Country | 7" | Columbia | DB8094 | 1966 | £1.50 | £4 | |
| It'll Be Me | 7" | Columbia | DB4886 | 1962 | £1.50 | £4 | |
| It'll Be Me | 7" | Columbia | DB4886 | 1962 | £2.50 | £6 | *black label* |
| It's A Small World | LP | Myrrh | MYRR1209 | 1988 | £15 | £30 | |
| It's All In The Game | LP | Epic | LN24089/BN26089 | 1964 | £10 | £25 | *US* |
| It's All Over | 7" | Columbia | DB8150 | 1967 | £1.50 | £4 | |
| It's Only Me You've Left Behind | 7" | EMI | EMI2279 | 1975 | £4 | £8 | |
| Japan Tour 1974 | LP | EMI | EMS67037 | 1975 | £50 | £100 | *Japanese* |
| Jesus | 7" | Columbia | DB8864 | 1972 | £2 | £5 | |
| Kinda Latin | LP | Columbia | SCX6039 | 1966 | £15 | £30 | *stereo* |
| Kinda Latin | LP | Columbia | SX6039 | 1966 | £10 | £25 | *mono* |
| La La La La La | 7" EP | Columbia | SEG8517 | 1966 | £10 | £20 | |
| Lean On You | CD-s | EMI | CDEM105 | 1989 | £2 | £5 | |
| Lean On You | 7" | EMI | EMP105 | 1989 | £1.50 | £4 | *picture disc* |
| Leave My Woman Alone | 7" | Columbia | DB8657 | 1970 | £1.50 | £4 | *with Hank Marvin* |
| Listen To Cliff | LP | ABC | (S)391 | 1961 | £10 | £25 | *US* |
| Listen To Cliff | LP | Columbia | 33SX1320 | 1961 | £8 | £20 | *mono* |
| Listen To Cliff | LP | Columbia | SCX3375 | 1961 | £20 | £40 | *stereo* |
| Listen To Cliff No. 1 | 7" EP | Columbia | ESG7858 | 1961 | £15 | £30 | |
| Listen To Cliff No. 1 | 7" EP | Columbia | SEG8105 | 1961 | £7.50 | £15 | |
| Listen To Cliff No. 2 | 7" EP | Columbia | ESG7870 | 1961 | £15 | £30 | *stereo* |
| Listen To Cliff No. 2 | 7" EP | Columbia | SEG8126 | 1961 | £7.50 | £15 | |
| Little Town | 7" | EMI | EMIP5348 | 1982 | £1.50 | £4 | *picture disc* |
| Live In Japan '72 | LP | EMI | EOP930773B | 1972 | £62.50 | £125 | *Japanese* |
| Livin' Lovin' Doll | 78 | Columbia | DB4249 | 1959 | £15 | £30 | |
| Livin' Lovin' Doll | 7" | Columbia | DB4249 | 1959 | £7.50 | £15 | |
| Livin' Lovin' Doll | 7" | Columbia | DB4249 | 1959 | £12.50 | £25 | *black label* |
| Living Doll | 78 | Columbia | DB4306 | 1959 | £10 | £20 | |
| Living Doll | 7" | Columbia | DB4306 | 1959 | £1.50 | £4 | |
| Living Doll | 7" | Columbia | DB4306 | 1959 | £7.50 | £15 | *black label* |
| Look In My Eyes Maria | 7" EP | Columbia | SEG8405 | 1965 | £7.50 | £15 | |
| Love Is Forever | LP | Columbia | SX1769/SCX3569 | 1965 | £8 | £20 | |
| Love Is Forever | 7" EP | Columbia | SEG8488 | 1966 | £10 | £20 | |
| Love Songs | 7" EP | Columbia | ESG7900 | 1963 | £20 | £40 | *stereo* |
| Love Songs | 7" EP | Columbia | SEG8272 | 1963 | £5 | £10 | |
| Man Gratuliert Mir | 7" | Columbia | C23776 | 1968 | £7.50 | £15 | *sung in German* |
| Maria No Mas | 7" | Columbia | C22667 | 1964 | £7.50 | £15 | *sung in Spanish* |
| Marianne | 7" | Columbia | DB8476 | 1968 | £1.50 | £4 | |
| Me And My Shadows | LP | Columbia | 33SX1261 | 1960 | £8 | £20 | *mono* |
| Me And My Shadows | LP | Columbia | SCX3330 | 1960 | £20 | £40 | *stereo* |
| Me And My Shadows | LP | Regal | SREG1120 | 1960 | £25 | £50 | *export* |
| Me And My Shadows No. 1 | 7" EP | Columbia | ESG7837 | 1961 | £12.50 | £25 | *stereo* |
| Me And My Shadows No. 1 | 7" EP | Columbia | SEG8065 | 1961 | £7.50 | £15 | |
| Me And My Shadows No. 2 | 7" EP | Columbia | ESG7841 | 1961 | £12.50 | £25 | *stereo* |
| Me And My Shadows No. 2 | 7" EP | Columbia | SEG8071 | 1961 | £7.50 | £15 | |
| Me And My Shadows No. 3 | 7" EP | Columbia | ESG7843 | 1961 | £12.50 | £25 | *stereo* |
| Me And My Shadows No. 3 | 7" EP | Columbia | SEG8078 | 1961 | £7.50 | £15 | |
| Mean Streak | 78 | Columbia | DB4290 | 1959 | £15 | £30 | |
| Mean Streak | 7" | Columbia | DB4290 | 1959 | £2.50 | £6 | |
| Mean Streak | 7" | Columbia | DB4290 | 1959 | £10 | £20 | *black label* |
| Mistletoe And Wine | CD-s | EMI | CDEM78 | 1988 | £2 | £5 | *...with Christmas card* |
| Mistletoe And Wine | 12" | EMI | 12EMX78 | 1988 | £2.50 | £6 | *. with Advent calendar* |
| More Hits | LP | Columbia | SCX3555 | 1965 | £6 | £15 | *stereo* |
| More Hits | LP | Columbia | SX1737 | 1965 | £4 | £10 | *mono* |
| More Hits From Summer Holiday | 7" EP | Columbia | ESG7898 | 1963 | £12.50 | £25 | *stereo* |
| More Hits From Summer Holiday | 7" EP | Columbia | SEG8263 | 1963 | £7.50 | £15 | |
| More To Life | CD-s | EMI | CDEM205 | 1991 | £2 | £5 | |
| Move It | 78 | Columbia | DB4178 | 1958 | £7.50 | £15 | |
| Move It | 7" | Columbia | DB4178 | 1958 | £4 | £8 | |
| Move It | 7" | Columbia | DB4178 | 1958 | £10 | £20 | *black label* |
| Music And Life Of Cliff Richard | cass | EMI | TCEXSP1601 | 1974 | £8 | £20 | *6 tapes, boxed* |
| Music From America | 7" | Rainbow | | 196– | £7.50 | £15 | *flexi* |
| Nine Times Out Of Ten | 7" | Columbia | DB4506 | 1960 | £1.50 | £4 | |
| Nine Times Out Of Ten | 7" | Columbia | DB4506 | 1960 | £4 | £8 | *black label* |
| Non Dimenticare Chi Ti Ama | 7" | Columbia | SCMQ | 1968 | £7.50 | £15 | *sung in Italian* |
| Non L'Ascoltare | 7" | Columbia | SCMQ1860 | 196– | £7.50 | £15 | *sung in Italian* |
| Nothing To Remind Me | 7" | EMI | PSR368 | 1967 | £7.50 | £15 | *promo* |
| O Mio Signore | 7" EP | Columbia | SLEM2221 | 196– | £15 | £30 | *sung in Italian* |
| Original | 10" LP | Columbia | C60691 | 1959 | £62.50 | £125 | *German* |
| Per Un Bacio Di Amour | LP | Columbia | QPX8081 | 196– | £25 | £50 | *sung in Italian* |
| Personal Message To You | 7" | Serenade | | 1960 | £7.50 | £15 | *blue flexi* |
| Please Don't Tease | 7" | Columbia | DB4479 | 1960 | £1.50 | £4 | |
| Please Don't Tease | 7" | Columbia | DB4479 | 1960 | £4 | £8 | *black label* |
| Power To All Our Friends | 7" | EMI | 1J00605340 | 196– | £7.50 | £15 | *sung in Spanish* |
| Presentation | CD | EMI | CDP7913702 | 199– | £37.50 | £75 | *promo only commemorative picture CD* |
| Remember Me | CD-s | EMI | CDEM31 | 1987 | £2 | £5 | |
| Rote Lippen Soll Man Küssen | 7" | Columbia | C22563 | 196– | £7.50 | £15 | *sung in German* |
| Saviour's Day | CD-s | EMI | CDXMAS90 | 1990 | £2 | £5 | |
| Schön Wie Ein Traum | 7" | Columbia | C21843 | 196– | £7.50 | £15 | *sung in German* |

| Title | Format | Label | Cat No | Year | | | Notes |
|---|---|---|---|---|---|---|---|
| Serious Charge | 7" EP | Columbia | SEG7895 | 1959 | £10 | £20 | |
| Shooting From The Heart | 7" | EMI | RICHP1 | 1984 | £2.50 | £6 | ..... shaped picture disc |
| Silhouettes | CD-s | EMI | CDEM152 | 1990 | £2 | £5 | |
| Silver | CD | EMI | CDP7460082 | 1983 | £5 | £12 | |
| Silvery Rain | 7" | Columbia | DB8774 | 1971 | £2 | £5 | |
| Sincerely | LP | Columbia | SCX6357 | 1969 | £6 | £15 | ....................stereo |
| Sincerely | LP | Columbia | SX6357 | 1969 | £8 | £20 | ....................mono |
| Sing A Song Of Freedom | 7" | Columbia | DB8836 | 1971 | £1.50 | £4 | |
| Small Corners | LP | Word | WRDR3036 | 1988 | £10 | £25 | |
| Some People | 7" | EMI | EMP18 | 1987 | £1.50 | £4 | ..... shaped picture disc |
| Star Souvenir Greetings | 7" | New Spotlight | | 196– | £5 | £10 | ....................flexi |
| Stronger Than That | CD-s | EMI | CDEM129 | 1990 | £2 | £5 | |
| Summer Holiday | LP | Columbia | 33SX1472 | 1963 | £4 | £10 | ....................mono |
| Summer Holiday | LP | Columbia | SCX3462 | 1963 | £5 | £12 | .....blue & black label |
| Summer Holiday | LP | Columbia | SCX3462 | 1963 | £8 | £20 | ..... stereo, green label |
| Summer Holiday | LP | Elstree Studios | EMS1009 | 1963 | £330 | £500 | .....original soundtrack, double |
| Summer Holiday | LP | Epic | LN24063/BN26063 | 1963 | £10 | £25 | ....................US |
| Sunny Honey Girl | 7" | Columbia | DB8747 | 1971 | £1.50 | £4 | |
| Swinger's Paradise | LP | Epic | LN24145/BN26145 | 1965 | £10 | £25 | ....................US |
| Take Four | 7" EP | Columbia | SEG8450 | 1965 | £7.50 | £15 | |
| Take Me High | LP | EMI | EMC3016 | 1973 | £4 | £10 | |
| Take Me High | LP | EMI | EMC3016 | 1973 | £8 | £20 | .....with poster |
| Theme for A Dream | 7" | Columbia | DB4593 | 1961 | £1.50 | £4 | |
| Theme for A Dream | 7" | Columbia | DB4593 | 1961 | £8 | £8 | .............. black label |
| Thirtieth Anniversary Picture Record Collection | LP | EMI | SMPLC1 | 1989 | £10 | £25 | .....double picture disc |
| This Was My Special Day | 7" | Columbia | DB7435 | 1964 | £10 | £20 | ............. demo only |
| Throw Down A Line | 7" | Columbia | DB8615 | 1969 | £1.50 | £4 | .... with Hank Marvin |
| Thunderbirds Are Go | 7" EP | Columbia | SEG8510 | 1966 | £20 | £40 | |
| Time Drags By | 7" | Columbia | DB8017 | 1966 | £1.50 | £4 | |
| Time For Cliff And The Shadows | 7" EP | Columbia | ESG7887 | 1963 | £20 | £40 | ....................stereo |
| Time For Cliff And The Shadows | 7" EP | Columbia | SEG8228 | 1963 | £7.50 | £15 | |
| Time In Between | 7" | Columbia | DB7660 | 1965 | £1.50 | £4 | |
| To My Italian Friends | LP | Columbia | QPX8024 | 196– | £25 | £50 | |
| Tracks And Grooves | LP | Columbia | SCX6435 | 1970 | £8 | £20 | |
| Travellin' Light | 78 | Columbia | DB4351 | 1959 | £15 | £30 | |
| Travellin' Light | 7" | Columbia | DB4351 | 1959 | £1.50 | £4 | |
| Travellin' Light | 7" | Columbia | DB4351 | 1959 | £4 | £8 | .............. black label |
| Two A Penny | LP | Columbia | SX/SCX6262 | 1968 | £8 | £20 | .....blue & black label |
| Two A Penny | LP | Columbia | SX/SCX6262 | 1968 | £6 | £15 | ..... white & black label |
| Two Hearts | CD-s | EMI | CDEM42 | 1988 | £2 | £5 | |
| Two Hearts | 7" | EMI | EMP42 | 1987 | £1.50 | £4 | ..... shaped picture disc |
| Un Saludo De Cliff | 7" EP | HMV | 13955 | 196– | £15 | £30 | ..... sung in Spanish |
| Voice In The Wilderness | 78 | Columbia | DB4398 | 1960 | £15 | £30 | |
| Voice In The Wilderness | 7" | Columbia | DB4398 | 1960 | £1.50 | £4 | |
| Voice In The Wilderness | 7" | Columbia | DB4398 | 1960 | £4 | £8 | .............. black label |
| Walking In The Light | LP | Myrrh | MYR1176 | 1985 | £10 | £25 | |
| Walking In The Light | CD | Myrrh | MYRCD1176 | 1985 | £6 | £15 | |
| We Don't Talk Anymore | 7" | EMI | EMI2975 | 1979 | £4 | £8 | ......mispress – plays Queen's 'Bohemian Rhapsody' |
| We Don't Talk Anymore (2 versions) | 12" | EMI | SPRO9252 | 1979 | £4 | £10 | .....US promo |
| We Should Be Together | CD-s | EMI | CDXMAS91 | 1991 | £2 | £5 | |
| What'd I Say | 7" | Columbia | DC758 | 1963 | £100 | £200 | . export, best auctioned |
| When In France | LP | EMI | 4C06206234 | 1977 | £8 | £20 | ....................Belgian |
| When In France | 7" EP | Columbia | SEG8290 | 1964 | £6 | £12 | |
| When In Rome | LP | Columbia | SX1762 | 1965 | £10 | £25 | |
| When In Spain | LP | Columbia | 33SX1541 | 1963 | £6 | £15 | ....................mono |
| When In Spain | LP | Columbia | SCX3488 | 1963 | £10 | £25 | ....................stereo |
| When The Girl In Your Arms | 7" | Columbia | DB4716 | 1961 | £1.50 | £4 | |
| When The Girl In Your Arms | 7" | Columbia | DB4716 | 1961 | £2.50 | £6 | .............. black label |
| Why Don't They Understand | 7" EP | Columbia | SEG8384 | 1965 | £7.50 | £15 | |
| Wind Me Up | 7" EP | Columbia | SEG8474 | 1966 | £7.50 | £15 | |
| With The Eyes Of A Child | 7" | Columbia | DB8641 | 1969 | £1.50 | £4 | |
| Wonderful Life | LP | Columbia | 33SX1628 | 1964 | £4 | £10 | ....................mono |
| Wonderful Life | LP | Columbia | SCX3515 | 1964 | £8 | £20 | ....................stereo |
| Wonderful Life | LP | Elstree Studios | | 1963 | £330 | £500 | .....original soundtrack, double |
| Wonderful Life No. 1 | 7" EP | Columbia | ESG7902 | 1964 | £12.50 | £25 | ....................stereo |
| Wonderful Life No. 1 | 7" EP | Columbia | SEG8338 | 1964 | £5 | £10 | |
| Wonderful Life No. 2 | 7" EP | Columbia | ESG7903 | 1964 | £12.50 | £25 | ....................stereo |
| Wonderful Life No. 2 | 7" EP | Columbia | SEG8354 | 1964 | £6 | £12 | |
| Wonderful To Be Young | LP | Dot | DLP3474/25474 | 1962 | £10 | £25 | ....................US |
| Yes He Lives | 7" | EMI | EMI2730 | 1978 | £2 | £5 | |
| Young Ones | LP | Columbia | 33SX1384 | 1961 | £6 | £15 | ....................mono |
| Young Ones | LP | Columbia | SCX3397 | 1961 | £10 | £25 | ....................stereo |
| Young Ones | 7" | Columbia | DB4761 | 1962 | £1.50 | £4 | |
| Zuviel Allein | 7" | Columbia | C22707 | 1964 | £7.50 | £15 | ..... sung in German |

## RICHARD & THE YOUNG LIONS

| Title | Format | Label | Cat No | Year | | | |
|---|---|---|---|---|---|---|---|
| Open Up Your Door | 7" | Philips | BF1520 | 1966 | £20 | £40 | |

## RICHARDS, CYNTHIA

| Title | Format | Label | Cat No | Year | | | |
|---|---|---|---|---|---|---|---|
| Foolish Fool | LP | Trojan | TBL123 | 1970 | £5 | £12 | |

## RICHARDS, JOHNNY

| Title | Format | Label | Cat No | Year | | | |
|---|---|---|---|---|---|---|---|
| Experiments In Sound | LP | Capitol | T981 | 1959 | £4 | £10 | |

| | | | | | | | |
|---|---|---|---|---|---|---|---|
| Rites Of Diablo | LP | Esquire | 32076 | 1959 | £4 | £10 | |
| Something Else | LP | London | LTZN1511 | 1958 | £5 | £12 | |
| Walk Softly – Run Wild | LP | Coral | LVA9122 | 1960 | £4 | £10 | |
| Wide Range | LP | Capitol | T885 | 1958 | £5 | £12 | |

## RICHARDS, KEITH

| | | | | | | | |
|---|---|---|---|---|---|---|---|
| Before They Make Me Run | 7" | Rolling Stones | | 1979 | £2.50 | £6 | promo |
| Make No Mistake | CD-s | Virgin | VSCD1179 | 1989 | £2 | £5 | |
| Run Rudolph Run | 7" | Rolling Stones | RSR102 | 1979 | £5 | £10 | picture sleeve |
| Take It So Hard | CD-s | Virgin | VSCD1125 | 1988 | £2 | £5 | |
| Talk Is Cheap | LP | Virgin | | 1988 | £37.50 | £75 | promo album on 4 x 7 |
| Talk Is Cheap | CD | Mobile Fidelity | UDCD557 | 1992 | £6 | £15 | US audiophile |
| Talk Is Cheap | CD | Virgin | | 1988 | £15 | £30 | US interview promo |

## RICHARDS, LISA

| | | | | | | | |
|---|---|---|---|---|---|---|---|
| Mean Old World | 7" | Vocalion | VP9244 | 1965 | £7.50 | £15 | |

## RICHARDS, LLOYD

| | | | | | | | |
|---|---|---|---|---|---|---|---|
| Be Good | 7" | Port-O-Jam | PJ4004 | 1964 | £5 | £10 | |

## RICHARDS, ROY

| | | | | | | | |
|---|---|---|---|---|---|---|---|
| Contact | 7" | Doctor Bird | DB1012 | 1966 | £5 | £10 | |
| Double Trouble | 7" | Island | WI283 | 1966 | £5 | £10 | Fitzy & Freddy B side |
| Hopeful Village | 7" | Island | WI3037 | 1967 | £5 | £10 | Delroy Wilson B side |
| Rub-A-Dub | 7" | Island | WI3027 | 1967 | £5 | £10 | |
| South Vietnam | 7" | Island | WI3000 | 1966 | £5 | £10 | |
| Summertime | 7" | Coxsone | CS7061 | 1968 | £5 | £10 | Righteous Flames B side |
| Western Standard Time | 7" | Island | WI299 | 1966 | £5 | £10 | Eagles B side |

## RICHARDS, TRUDY

| | | | | | | | |
|---|---|---|---|---|---|---|---|
| Wishbone | 7" | Capitol | CL14728 | 1957 | £1.50 | £4 | |

## RICHARDS, WENDY & DIANA BERRY

| | | | | | | | |
|---|---|---|---|---|---|---|---|
| We Had A Dream | 7" | Decca | F11680 | 1963 | £1.50 | £4 | |

## RICHARDS, WINSTON

| | | | | | | | |
|---|---|---|---|---|---|---|---|
| Green Coolie | 7" | Island | WI297 | 1966 | £5 | £10 | Marcia Griffiths B side |
| Studio Blitz | 7" | Rio | R124 | 1967 | £4 | £8 | |

## RICHARDSON, WARREN S.

| | | | | | | | |
|---|---|---|---|---|---|---|---|
| Warren S.Richardson | LP | Cotillion | SD9013 | 1969 | £8 | £20 | German |

## RICHMOND

| | | | | | | | |
|---|---|---|---|---|---|---|---|
| Frightened | LP | Dart | ARTS65371 | 1973 | £8 | £20 | |

## RICK & THE KEENS

| | | | | | | | |
|---|---|---|---|---|---|---|---|
| Peanuts | 7" | Mercury | AMT1150 | 1961 | £7.50 | £15 | |

## RICKETTS, BERESFORD

| | | | | | | | |
|---|---|---|---|---|---|---|---|
| Baby Baby | 7" | Starlite | ST45029 | 1960 | £2 | £5 | |
| Cherry Baby | 7" | Starlite | ST45025 | 1960 | £5 | £10 | |
| I'm Going To Cry | 7" | Starlite | ST45079 | 1962 | £5 | £10 | |
| Jailer Bring Me Water | 7" | Blue Beat | BB350 | 1966 | £6 | £12 | |
| O Jean | 7" | Dice | CC12 | 1963 | £5 | £10 | |
| You Better Be Gone | 7" | Blue Beat | BB107 | 1962 | £6 | £12 | |

## RICKETTS & ROWE

| | | | | | | | |
|---|---|---|---|---|---|---|---|
| Hold Me Tight | 7" | Starlite | ST45048 | 1961 | £5 | £10 | |

## RICO

| | | | | | | | |
|---|---|---|---|---|---|---|---|
| Baby Face | 7" | Doctor Bird | DB1302 | 1969 | £5 | £10 | Rudies B side |
| Blow Your Horn | LP | Trojan | TTL12 | 1969 | £8 | £20 | |
| Blues From The Hills | 7" | Blue Beat | BB195 | 1963 | £6 | £12 | Stranger Cole B side |
| Bullet | 7" | Blue Cat | BS160 | 1969 | £2.50 | £6 | |
| In Reggae Land | LP | Pama | ECO14 | 1969 | £10 | £25 | |
| Jama | LP | Two Tone | TT5006 | 1982 | £4 | £10 | |
| Jingle Bells | 7" | Fab | FAB12 | 1967 | £2.50 | £6 | |
| Lion Speaks | 7" | Treasure Isle | TI7052 | 1969 | £2.50 | £6 | Andy Capp B side |
| Luke Lane Shuffle | 7" | Blue Beat | BB56 | 1961 | £6 | £12 | Prince Buster B side |
| Man From Wareika | LP | Island | ILPS9485 | 1977 | £5 | £12 | |
| Midnight In Ethiopia | LP | Island | ILPS9516 | 1978 | £5 | £12 | |
| Planet Rock | 7" | Planetone | RC4 | 197– | £1.50 | £4 | |
| Quando Quando | 7" | Downtown | DT417 | 1969 | £1.50 | £4 | |
| Reco's Farewell | 7" | Island | WI022 | 1962 | £5 | £10 | Bunny & Skitter B side |
| Soul Man | 7" | Pama | PM706 | 1968 | £2.50 | £6 | |
| Tender Foot Ska | 7" | Pama | PM715 | 1968 | £2.50 | £6 | |
| That Man Is Forward | LP | Two Tone | TT5005 | 1981 | £4 | £10 | |
| Tribute To Don Drummond | 7" | Bullet | BU407 | 1969 | £1.50 | £4 | |
| Youth Boogie | 7" | Planetone | RC5 | 197– | £1.50 | £4 | |

## RICOTTI, FRANK

| | | | | | | | |
|---|---|---|---|---|---|---|---|
| Our Point Of View | LP | CBS | 52668 | 1969 | £10 | £25 | |
| Ricotti And Albuquerque | LP | Pegasus | PEG2 | 1971 | £5 | £12 | |

## RIDDLE, NELSON
| | | | | | | | |
|---|---|---|---|---|---|---|---|
| Batman | LP | Stateside | (S)SL10179 | 1966 | £20 | £40 | |
| Pendulum Song | 7" | Capitol | CL14262 | 1955 | £1.50 | £4 | |
| Route Sixty-Six | 7" EP | Capitol | EAP41771 | 1961 | £2 | £5 | |
| Run For Cover | 7" | Capitol | CL14305 | 1955 | £1.50 | £4 | |
| Supercar | 7" | Capitol | CL15309 | 1963 | £2.50 | £6 | |
| Vera Cruz | 7" | Capitol | CL14241 | 1955 | £1.50 | £4 | |

## RIDDLERS
| | | | | | | | |
|---|---|---|---|---|---|---|---|
| Batman Theme | 7" | Polydor | 56716 | 1966 | £2.50 | £6 | |

## RIDE
| | | | | | | | |
|---|---|---|---|---|---|---|---|
| Fall EP | CD-s | Creation | CRE087CD | 1990 | £2 | £5 | |
| Play EP | CD-s | Creation | CRE075CD | 1990 | £2 | £5 | |
| Ride EP | CD-s | Creation | CRESCD072 | 1990 | £2 | £5 | |
| Taste | 7" | Creation | CRE087P | 1990 | £2 | £5 | 1 sided promo |
| Today Forever | CD-s | Creation | CRECD100T | 1991 | £2 | £5 | |

## RIFF RAFF
| | | | | | | | |
|---|---|---|---|---|---|---|---|
| Original Man | LP | RCA | LPL15023 | 1974 | £10 | £25 | |
| Riff Raff | LP | RCA | SF8351 | 1973 | £10 | £25 | |

## RIFFS
| | | | | | | | |
|---|---|---|---|---|---|---|---|
| Oh What A Feeling | 7" | Blue Beat | BB242 | 1964 | £6 | £12 | |

## RIFKIN
| | | | | | | | |
|---|---|---|---|---|---|---|---|
| Continental Hesitation | 7" | Page One | POF071 | 1968 | £15 | £30 | |

## RIFKIN, JOSHUA
| | | | | | | | |
|---|---|---|---|---|---|---|---|
| Baroque Beatles | LP | Elektra | | 1968 | £10 | £25 | US |

## RIGBY, ELEANOR
| | | | | | | | |
|---|---|---|---|---|---|---|---|
| I Want To Sleep With You | 7" | Waterloo Sunset | RUSS101 | 1985 | £4 | £8 | with condom & sticker |
| Take Another Shot Of My Heart | 7" | Waterloo Sunset | RUSS102 | 1985 | £2.50 | £6 | with signed story |

## RIGG, BRAM SET
| | | | | | | | |
|---|---|---|---|---|---|---|---|
| Take The Time To Be Yourself | 7" | Stateside | SS2020 | 1967 | £37.50 | £75 | |

## RIGG, DIANA
| | | | | | | | |
|---|---|---|---|---|---|---|---|
| Sentimental Journey | 7" | RCA | RCA2179 | 1972 | £2 | £5 | |

## RIGGS, JACKIE
| | | | | | | | |
|---|---|---|---|---|---|---|---|
| Great Pretender | 7" | London | HLF8244 | 1956 | £12.50 | £25 | |

## RIGHTEOUS BROTHERS
| | | | | | | | |
|---|---|---|---|---|---|---|---|
| Back To Back | LP | London | HA8278 | 1966 | £6 | £15 | |
| Ebb Tide | 7" EP | Barclay | 070915 | 1965 | £6 | £12 | French |
| Ebb Tide | 7" | London | HL10011 | 1965 | £1.50 | £4 | |
| In Action | LP | Sue | ILP937 | 1966 | £10 | £25 | |
| Just Once In My Life | LP | London | HA8245 | 1965 | £8 | £20 | |
| Just Once In My Life | 7" | London | HL9962 | 1965 | £20 | £40 | demo only |
| Little Latin Lupe Lu | 7" | London | HL9743 | 1963 | £1.50 | £4 | |
| My Babe | 7" | London | HL9814 | 1963 | £1.50 | £4 | |
| One For The Road | LP | Verve | (S)VLP9228 | 1968 | £4 | £10 | |
| Right Now | LP | Pye | NPL28059 | 1965 | £6 | £15 | |
| Righteous Brothers | 7" EP | Pye | NEP44043 | 1965 | £5 | £10 | |
| Righteous Brothers | 7" EP | Verve | VEP5024 | 1966 | £5 | £10 | |
| Some Blue Eyed Soul | LP | Pye | NPL28056 | 1965 | £6 | £15 | |
| Soul And Inspiration | LP | Verve | (S)VLP9131 | 1966 | £6 | £15 | |
| Soul And Inspiration | 7" EP | Verve | 26501 | 1966 | £6 | £12 | French |
| Soul And Inspiration | 7" | Verve | VS535 | 1966 | £1.50 | £4 | |
| Souled Out | LP | Verve | (S)VLP9190 | 1967 | £4 | £10 | |
| Unchained Melody | 7" EP | Barclay | 70860 | 1965 | £6 | £12 | French |
| Unchained Melody | 7" | London | HL9975 | 1965 | £1.50 | £4 | |
| You Can Have Her | 7" | Sue | WI4018 | 1966 | £2.50 | £6 | |
| You've Lost That Lovin' Feelin' | LP | London | HA8226 | 1965 | £8 | £20 | |
| You've Lost That Lovin' Feelin' | 7" | London | HL9943 | 1965 | £1.50 | £4 | |
| You've Lost That Lovin' Feeling | 7" EP | Barclay | 70766 | 1965 | £6 | £12 | French |

## RIGHTEOUS FLAMES
| | | | | | | | |
|---|---|---|---|---|---|---|---|
| Gimme Some Sign Girl | 7" | Fab | FAB18 | 1967 | £4 | £8 | |

## RIGHTEOUS TWINS
| | | | | | | | |
|---|---|---|---|---|---|---|---|
| If I Could Hear My Master | 7" | Blue Cat | BS174 | 1969 | £1.50 | £4 | |

## RIKKI & THE LAST DAYS OF EARTH
| | | | | | | | |
|---|---|---|---|---|---|---|---|
| City Of The Damned | 7" | DJM | DJS10814 | 1977 | £2 | £5 | |

## RILEY, BILLY LEE
| | | | | | | | |
|---|---|---|---|---|---|---|---|
| Harmonica Beatlemania | LP | Mercury | SR60974 | 1964 | £6 | £15 | US |
| I've Been Searchin' | 7" | King | KG1015 | 1965 | £2 | £5 | |

## RILEY, BOB
| | | | | | | | |
|---|---|---|---|---|---|---|---|
| Midnight Line | 7" | MGM | MGM977 | 1958 | £15 | £30 | |

## RILEY, HOWARD

| Title | Format | Label | Cat# | Year | | |
|---|---|---|---|---|---|---|
| Angle | LP | CBS | 52669 | 1969 | £10 | £25 |
| Day Will Come | LP | CBS | 64077 | 1970 | £8 | £20 |
| Discussions | LP | Opportunity | CP2500 | 1967 | £75 | £150 |
| Duality | LP | View | VS0020 | 1982 | £5 | £12 | *German* |
| Facets | LP | Impetus | 38002 | 1981 | £10 | £25 | *3 LP box set* |
| Flight | LP | Turtle | TUR301 | 1970 | £15 | £30 |
| For Four On Two Two | LP | Affinity | AFF110 | 1983 | £4 | £10 |
| In Focus | LP | Affinity | AFF137 | 1985 | £4 | £10 | *with Keith Tippett* |
| Intertwine | LP | Mosaic | GCM771 | 1977 | £5 | £12 |
| Other Side | LP | Spotlight | SPJ511 | 1979 | £5 | £12 |
| Shaped | LP | Mosaic | GCM781 | 1977 | £5 | £12 |
| Singleness | LP | Canon | | 197– | £6 | £15 |
| Solo Imprints | cass | Jaguar | JS3 | 1974 | £5 | £12 |
| Synopsis | LP | Incus | INCUS13 | 1973 | £6 | £15 |
| Turin Concert | LP | Vinyl | VS112 | 1977 | £5 | £12 |

## RILEY, ILLMAN

| Title | Format | Label | Cat# | Year | | |
|---|---|---|---|---|---|---|
| Gambler | LP | Tradition | TSR009 | 1971 | £8 | £20 |

## RILEY, JEANNIE C.

| Title | Format | Label | Cat# | Year | | |
|---|---|---|---|---|---|---|
| Harper Valley P.T.A. | 7" | Polydor | 56748 | 1968 | £1.50 | £4 |

## RILEY, TERRY

Composer Terry Riley pioneered the use of tape-loops to create a dense, meditational sound and was a direct influence on the Soft Machine school of rock music. His *Church Of Anthrax* is co-credited to John Cale, and the well-known ex-member of the Velvet Underground gets the star billing. Really, however, the music is all Riley's, with Cale essentially sitting at the feet of the master and following as best as he can.

| Title | Format | Label | Cat# | Year | | |
|---|---|---|---|---|---|---|
| Happy Ending | LP | Warner Bros | WB46125 | 1972 | £6 | £15 | *French* |
| In 'C' | LP | CBS | 64565 | 1970 | £4 | £10 |
| Keyboard Studies | LP | Byg | | 1969 | £15 | £30 | *French* |
| Le Secret de la vie | LP | Philips | 9120037 | 1975 | £4 | £10 |
| Persian Surgery Dervishes | LP | Shandar | 83501 | 1972 | £10 | £25 | *French double* |
| Rainbow In Curved Air | LP | CBS | 64564 | 1971 | £4 | £10 |
| Reed Streams | LP | Mass Art Inc | M131 | 1967 | £15 | £30 | *US* |

## RIMMER, SHANE

| Title | Format | Label | Cat# | Year | | |
|---|---|---|---|---|---|---|
| Three Bells | 7" | Columbia | DB4343 | 1959 | £1.50 | £4 |

## RINGS & THINGS

| Title | Format | Label | Cat# | Year | | |
|---|---|---|---|---|---|---|
| Strange Things Are Happening | 7" | Fontana | TF987 | 1968 | £20 | £40 |

## RINKY DINKS

| Title | Format | Label | Cat# | Year | | |
|---|---|---|---|---|---|---|
| Choo Choo Cha Cha | 7" | Capitol | CL14999 | 1959 | £2 | £5 |

## RIO, BOBBY

| Title | Format | Label | Cat# | Year | | |
|---|---|---|---|---|---|---|
| Boy Meets Girl | 7" | Pye | 7N15790 | 1965 | £7.50 | £15 |
| Everything In The Garden | 7" | Pye | 7N15897 | 1965 | £7.50 | £15 |
| Value For Love | 7" | Pye | 7N15958 | 1965 | £7.50 | £15 |

## RIO GRANDES

| Title | Format | Label | Cat# | Year | | |
|---|---|---|---|---|---|---|
| Soldiers Take Over | 7" | Pyramid | PYR6001 | 1966 | £2.50 | £6 |

## RIOT SQUAD

| Title | Format | Label | Cat# | Year | | |
|---|---|---|---|---|---|---|
| Any Time | 7" | Pye | 7N15752 | 1965 | £7.50 | £15 |
| Cry Cry Cry | 7" | Pye | 7N17041 | 1966 | £7.50 | £15 |
| Gotta Be A First Time | 7" | Pye | 7N17237 | 1967 | £7.50 | £15 |
| I Take It We're Through | 7" | Pye | 7N17092 | 1966 | £10 | £20 |
| I Wanna Talk About My Baby | 7" EP | Pye | PNV24134 | 1965 | £87.50 | £175 | *French* |
| I Wanna Talk About My Baby | 7" | Pye | 7N15817 | 1965 | £10 | £20 |
| It's Never Too Late to Forgive | 7" | Pye | 7N17130 | 1966 | £7.50 | £15 |
| Not A Great Talker | 7" | Pye | 7N15869 | 1965 | £7.50 | £15 |

## RIOTS

| Title | Format | Label | Cat# | Year | | |
|---|---|---|---|---|---|---|
| I Am In Love | 7" | Island | WI197 | 1965 | £5 | £10 |
| Telling Lies | 7" | Island | WI176 | 1965 | £5 | £10 |

## RIPCHORDS

| Title | Format | Label | Cat# | Year | | |
|---|---|---|---|---|---|---|
| Gone | 7" | CBS | AAG162 | 1963 | £2.50 | £6 |
| Here I Stand | 7" | CBS | AAG143 | 1963 | £2.50 | £6 |
| Hey Little Cobra | LP | CBS | BPG62228 | 1964 | £15 | £30 |
| Hey Little Cobra | 7" EP | CBS | 5682 | 1964 | £10 | £20 | *French* |
| Hey Little Cobra | 7" | CBS | AAG181 | 1964 | £5 | £10 |
| Three Window Coupe | LP | CBS | CL2216/CS9016 | 1965 | £10 | £25 | *US* |
| Three Window Coupe | 7" | CBS | AAG202 | 1964 | £5 | £10 |

## RIPPERS

| Title | Format | Label | Cat# | Year | | |
|---|---|---|---|---|---|---|
| Honestly | LP | Saga | FID2142 | 1968 | £6 | £15 |

## RISING MOON

| Title | Format | Label | Cat# | Year | | |
|---|---|---|---|---|---|---|
| Rising Moon | LP | Theatre Projects | | 1974 | £10 | £25 |

## RISING SONS

The bright blues-based music of the Rising Sons was gathered together on to CD in 1992. The result shows the band to be one of the great lost sixties units, with a timeless quality that allows the music to easily transcend its decade. The Rising Sons were driven by the combined talents of Taj Mahal and Ry Cooder, both of whose careers can be seen to proceed logically from this starting point.

| | | | | | | | |
|---|---|---|---|---|---|---|---|
| Candy Man | 7" | Columbia | 43534 | 1966 | £10 | £20 | US |
| Rising Sons | LP | Groucho | MARX48501 | | £20 | £40 | Italian |
| You're My Girl | 7" | Stateside | SS426 | 1965 | £5 | £10 | |

## RISING STORM

| | | | | | | | |
|---|---|---|---|---|---|---|---|
| Alive Again At Andover | LP | ARF | 007 | 1983 | £8 | £20 | US |
| Calm Before The Rising Storm | LP | Remnant | BBA3571 | 1966 | £700 | £1000 | US |

## RITA

| | | | | | | | |
|---|---|---|---|---|---|---|---|
| Erotica | 7" | Major Minor | MM6533 | 1969 | £2 | £5 | |

## RITCHIE, JEAN

| | | | | | | | |
|---|---|---|---|---|---|---|---|
| Child Ballads Vol. 1 | LP | Folkways | FA2301 | 1960 | £4 | £10 | US |
| Child Ballads Vol. 2 | LP | Folkways | FA2302 | 1961 | £4 | £10 | US |
| Songs From Kentucky | 10" LP | Argo | ARS1009 | 1953 | £8 | £20 | |

## RITTER, TEX

| | | | | | | | |
|---|---|---|---|---|---|---|---|
| Blood On The Saddle | LP | Capitol | (S)T1292 | 1960 | £4 | £10 | |
| Cowboy Favourites | 10" LP | Capitol | LC6552 | 1952 | £6 | £15 | |
| Deck Of Cards | 7" EP | Capitol | EAP11323 | 1960 | £2.50 | £6 | |
| Hillbilly Heaven | LP | Capitol | (S)T1623 | 1961 | £4 | £10 | US |
| Is There A Santa Claus? | 7" | Capitol | CL14175 | 1954 | £2 | £5 | |
| Last Frontier | 7" | Capitol | CL14536 | 1956 | £1.50 | £4 | |
| Last Wagon | 7" | Capitol | CL14660 | 1956 | £1.50 | £4 | |
| Lincoln Hymns | LP | Capitol | (S)W1562 | 1961 | £4 | £10 | US |
| Marshall Of Wichita | 7" | Capitol | CL14335 | 1955 | £2 | £5 | |
| Psalms | LP | Capitol | T1100 | 1959 | £4 | £10 | |
| Searchers | 7" | Capitol | CL14605 | 1956 | £1.50 | £4 | |
| Songs From The Western Screen | LP | Capitol | T971 | 1958 | £10 | £25 | US |
| Wayward Wind | 7" | Capitol | CL14581 | 1956 | £4 | £8 | |
| Whale Of A Tale | 7" | Capitol | CL14277 | 1955 | £2 | £5 | |

## RIVERS, BLUE & THE MAROONS

| | | | | | | | |
|---|---|---|---|---|---|---|---|
| Blue Beat In My Soul | LP | Columbia | SX6192 | 1967 | £30 | £60 | |
| Witchcraft Man | 7" | Columbia | DB103 | 1967 | £2 | £5 | |

## RIVERS, BOYD & CLIFF AUNGIER

| | | | | | | | |
|---|---|---|---|---|---|---|---|
| Wanderin' | LP | Decca | LK4696 | 1965 | £6 | £15 | |

## RIVERS, CLIFF

| | | | | | | | |
|---|---|---|---|---|---|---|---|
| True Lips | 7" | London | HLU9739 | 1963 | £6 | £12 | |

## RIVERS, DANNY

| | | | | | | | |
|---|---|---|---|---|---|---|---|
| Can't You Hear My Heart | 7" | Decca | F11294 | 1960 | £5 | £10 | |
| Hawk | 7" | Top Rank | JAR408 | 1960 | £5 | £10 | |
| Moving In | 7" | HMV | POP1000 | 1962 | £7.50 | £15 | |
| My Baby's Gone Away | 7" | Decca | F11357 | 1961 | £4 | £8 | |
| There Will Never Be Anyone | 7" | Decca | F11865 | 1964 | £1.50 | £4 | |

## RIVERS, DEKE

| | | | | | | | |
|---|---|---|---|---|---|---|---|
| Outsider | 7" | Oriole | CB1735 | 1962 | £2 | £5 | |

## RIVERS, JOHNNY

| | | | | | | | |
|---|---|---|---|---|---|---|---|
| And I Know You Wanna Dance | LP | Imperial | LP9307/12307 | 1966 | £4 | £10 | US |
| At The Whisky A Go Go | LP | Liberty | LBY3031 | 1964 | £5 | £12 | |
| Back At The Whisky | LP | Imperial | LP9284/12284 | 1965 | £4 | £10 | US |
| Blue Skies | 7" | Pye | 7N25118 | 1962 | £1.50 | £4 | |
| Changes | LP | Liberty | (S)LBY3087 | 1967 | £4 | £10 | |
| Go Johnny Go | LP | United Artists | UAL3386/ UAS6386 | 1964 | £4 | £10 | US |
| Golden Hits | LP | Imperial | LP9324/12324 | 1966 | £4 | £10 | US |
| Here We Go Go Again | LP | Liberty | LBY3036 | 1964 | £4 | £10 | |
| I Washed My Hands In Muddy Water | 7" | Liberty | LIB66175 | 1966 | £1.50 | £4 | |
| In Action | LP | Imperial | LP9280/12280 | 1965 | £4 | £10 | US |
| Maybellene | 7" | Liberty | LIB66056 | 1964 | £1.50 | £4 | |
| Meanwhile Back At The Whisky A Go-Go | LP | Liberty | LBY3056 | 1965 | £4 | £10 | |
| Memphis | 7" | Liberty | LIB66032 | 1964 | £1.50 | £4 | |
| Midnight Special | 7" | Liberty | LIB66087 | 1965 | £1.50 | £4 | |
| More Johnny Rivers | 7" EP | Liberty | LEP4049 | 1966 | £5 | £10 | |
| Mountain Of Love | 7" | Liberty | LIB66075 | 1964 | £1.50 | £4 | |
| Rocks The Folk | LP | Liberty | LBY3064 | 1965 | £4 | £10 | |
| Sensational Johnny Rivers | LP | Capitol | (S)T2161 | 1964 | £5 | £12 | US |
| Tom Dooley | 7" | Liberty | LIB12023 | 1965 | £1.50 | £4 | |
| Tracks Of My Tears | 7" | Liberty | LIB66244 | 1966 | £1.50 | £4 | |

## RIVERS, SAM

| | | | | | | | |
|---|---|---|---|---|---|---|---|
| Contours | LP | Blue Note | BLP/BST84206 | 1965 | £8 | £20 | |
| Fuchsia Swing Song | LP | Blue Note | BLP/BST84184 | 1964 | £8 | £20 | |
| New Conception | LP | Blue Note | BLP/BST84249 | 1966 | £8 | £20 | |
| Streams | LP | Impulse | AS9251 | 1973 | £6 | £15 | US |

## RIVERS, TONY & THE CASTAWAYS

| | | | | | | | |
|---|---|---|---|---|---|---|---|
| Come Back | 7" | Columbia | DB7536 | 1965 | £1.50 | £4 | |
| Girl Don't Tell Me | 7" | Immediate | IM027 | 1966 | £5 | £10 | |

| | | | | | | | |
|---|---|---|---|---|---|---|---|
| God Only Knows | 7" | Columbia | DB7971 | 1966 | £1.50 | £4 | |
| I Can Guarantee Your Love | 7" | Polydor | 56245 | 1968 | £1.50 | £4 | |
| I Love The Way You Walk | 7" | Columbia | DB7224 | 1964 | £2 | £5 | |
| Life's Too Short | 7" | Columbia | DB7336 | 1964 | £1.50 | £4 | |
| Nowhere Man | 7" | Parlophone | R5400 | 1966 | £1.50 | £4 | |
| Shake Shake Shake | 7" | Columbia | DB7135 | 1963 | £4 | £8 | |
| She | 7" | Columbia | DB7448 | 1965 | £1.50 | £4 | |

## RIVETS
| | | | | | | | |
|---|---|---|---|---|---|---|---|
| Yes It's Time | LP | Starclub | 158019STY | 1966 | £25 | £50 | *German* |

## RIVIERAS
| | | | | | | | |
|---|---|---|---|---|---|---|---|
| California Sun | LP | USA | 102 | 1967 | £8 | £20 | *US* |
| California Sun | 7" EP | Columbia | ESRF1523 | 1964 | £12.50 | £25 | *French* |
| California Sun | 7" | Pye | 7N25237 | 1964 | £5 | £10 | |
| Campus Party | LP | Riviera | 701 | 1964 | £15 | £30 | *US* |
| Let's Have A Party | LP | USA | 102 | 1964 | £10 | £25 | *US* |

## RIVIERAS (2)
| | | | | | | | |
|---|---|---|---|---|---|---|---|
| Blessings Of Love | 7" | HMV | POP773 | 1960 | £10 | £20 | |

## RIVINGTONS
| | | | | | | | |
|---|---|---|---|---|---|---|---|
| Bird's The Word | 7" | Liberty | LIB55553 | 1963 | £7.50 | £15 | |
| Doin' The Bird | LP | Liberty | LRP3282/LST7282 | 1963 | £15 | £30 | *US* |
| Pappa Oom Mow Mow | 7" | Liberty | LIB55427 | 1962 | £7.50 | £15 | |
| Rose Growing In The Ruins | 7" | CBS | 202088 | 1966 | £7.50 | £15 | |

## RO RO
| | | | | | | | |
|---|---|---|---|---|---|---|---|
| Blackbird | 7" | Regal Zonophone | RZ3076 | 1973 | £2.50 | £6 | |
| Down On The Road | 7" | Regal Zonophone | RZ3056 | 1972 | £2.50 | £6 | |
| Here I Go Again | 7" | Parlophone | R5920 | 1971 | £2.50 | £6 | |
| Meet At The Water | LP | Regal Zonophone | SRZA8510 | 1972 | £75 | £150 | |

## ROACH, FREDDIE
| | | | | | | | |
|---|---|---|---|---|---|---|---|
| All That's Good | LP | Blue Note | BLP/BST84190 | 1965 | £15 | £30 | |
| Brown Sugar | LP | Blue Note | BLP/BST84168 | 1964 | £15 | £30 | |
| Down To Earth | LP | Blue Note | BLP/BST84113 | 1962 | £15 | £30 | |
| Good Move | LP | Blue Note | BLP/BST84158 | 1964 | £15 | £30 | |
| Mo' Greens Please | LP | Blue Note | BLP/BST84128 | 1963 | £15 | £30 | |

## ROACH, MAX
| | | | | | | | |
|---|---|---|---|---|---|---|---|
| At Newport | LP | Emarcy | MMB12005 | 1959 | £8 | £20 | |
| Best Of Max Roach & Clifford Brown In Concert | LP | Vocalion | LAE12036 | 1957 | £15 | £30 | |
| I Remember Clifford | LP | Mercury | MMC14041 | 1960 | £6 | £15 | |
| Jazz In 3/4 Time | LP | Emarcy | EJL1282 | 1958 | £15 | £30 | |
| Max Roach And Clifford Brown | 7" EP | Vogue | EPV1074 | 1956 | £2 | £5 | |
| Max Roach And Clifford Brown | 7" EP | Vogue | EPV1083 | 1956 | £2 | £5 | |
| Max Roach And Clifford Brown | 7" EP | Vogue | EPV1091 | 1956 | £2 | £5 | |
| Max Roach And Clifford Brown In Concert Vol. 1 | 10" LP | Vogue | LDE117 | 1955 | £20 | £40 | |
| Max Roach And Clifford Brown In Concert Vol. 2 | 10" LP | Vogue | LDE128 | 1955 | £20 | £40 | |
| Max Roach Plus Four | LP | Emarcy | MMB12009 | 1959 | £10 | £25 | |
| Percussion Bitter Suite | LP | HMV | CLP1522 | 1962 | £5 | £12 | |
| Quiet As It's Kept | LP | Mercury | MMC14054 | 1961 | £8 | £20 | |

## ROAD
| | | | | | | | |
|---|---|---|---|---|---|---|---|
| Road | LP | Rare Earth | SRE3006 | 1972 | £4 | £10 | |

## ROADRUNNERS
| | | | | | | | |
|---|---|---|---|---|---|---|---|
| Pantomania | 7" EP | Cavern Sound | 2BSNL7 | 1965 | £20 | £40 | |
| Star Club Show 2 | LP | Starclub | 158001STY | 1965 | £37.50 | £75 | *German, with Shorty & Them* |
| Twist Time Im Star Club Hamburg 4 | LP | Ariola | 71224IT | 1964 | £50 | £100 | *German* |

## ROADSTERS
| | | | | | | | |
|---|---|---|---|---|---|---|---|
| Joy Ride | 7" | Stateside | SS293 | 1964 | £4 | £8 | |

## ROARING JELLY
| | | | | | | | |
|---|---|---|---|---|---|---|---|
| Golden Greats | LP | Free Reed | FRR013 | 1976 | £4 | £10 | |

## ROARING SIXTIES

Confusion as to the identity of the group who made this single in defence of the pirate radio stations has arisen from the fact that Leicester band the Farinas used the Roaring Sixties name for a while before changing to Family. In fact, however, the single was made by a different group, though one that subsequently also changed to a name that brought success – Ten Years After. (Information supplied by Harry Overnall, drummer with the Farinas and Family.)

| | | | | | | | |
|---|---|---|---|---|---|---|---|
| We Love The Pirates | 7" | Marmalade | 598001 | 1966 | £12.50 | £25 | |

## ROBAN'S SKIFFLE GROUP
| | | | | | | | |
|---|---|---|---|---|---|---|---|
| Careless Love | 7" | Storyville | A45062 | 1962 | £4 | £8 | |
| Roban's Skiffle Group | 7" EP | Storyville | SEP507 | 195– | £20 | £40 | |
| Roban's Skiffle Group | 7" EP | Storyville | SEP509 | 195– | £20 | £40 | |

Roban's Skiffle Group .............................. 7″ EP . Storyville.......... SEP511 .................. 195– £20......... £40 .......................

## ROBBINS, MARTY
Ballad Of The Alamo................................ 7″ ...... Fontana........... H270 ................ 1960 £1.50..... £4 ............ *picture sleeve*
Big Iron................................................. 7″ ...... Fontana........... H229 ................ 1959 £1.50..... £4
Carl, Lefty, & Marty ......................... 10″ LP Columbia ......... CL2544 ............ 1956 £50..... £100 ..................... US
Devil Woman ......................................... LP ..... CBS............... (S)BPG62113... 1963 £4.......... £10
Devil Woman ......................................... 7″ ...... CBS............... AAG114 ........... 1962 £1.50..... £4
El Paso ................................................. 7″ ...... Fontana........... H233 ................ 1959 £1.50..... £4
Greatest Hits ......................................... LP ..... Columbia ......... CL1325 ............ 1959 £6.......... £15 ..................... US
Gunfighter............................................. 7″ EP . Fontana........... TFE17224 ........ 1960 £2.50..... £6
Gunfighter Ballads And Trail Songs.......... LP ..... Fontana........... TFL5063 ........... 1959 £6.......... £15
Hanging Tree.......................................... 7″ ...... Fontana........... H184 ................ 1959 £1.50..... £4
Hawaii's Calling Me ................................ LP ..... CBS............... (S)BPG62169... 1963 £4.......... £10
Heart Of Marty Robbins .......................... LP ..... Columbia ......... STS2016 .......... 1969 £6.......... £15 ..................... US
Island Woman ........................................ LP ..... CBS............... (S)BPG62297... 1964 £4.......... £10
Just A Little Sentimental .......................... LP ..... Fontana........... TFL5162/STFL579 . 1961 £6.......... £15
Just A Little Sentimental .......................... 7″ EP . CBS............... AGG20004 ....... 1962 £2.......... £5
Just A Little Sentimental Vol. 2 ................. 7″ EP . CBS............... AGG20013 ....... 1962 £2.......... £5
Long Tall Sally ....................................... 78...... Philips........... PB590 .............. 1956 £2.50..... £6
Marty After Midnight .............................. LP ..... CBS............... (S)BPG62041... 1962 £4.......... £10
Marty Robbins ....................................... LP ..... Columbia ......... CL1189............ 1958 £8.......... £20 ..................... US
Marty Robbins ....................................... 7″ EP . CBS............... AGG20049 ....... 1964 £2.......... £5
Marty's Big Hits ..................................... 7″ EP . Fontana........... TFE17161 ........ 1959 £7.50..... £15
More Greatest Hits .................................. LP ..... Fontana........... TFL5145/STFL565 . 1961 £6.......... £12
More Gunfighter Ballads And Trail Songs... LP ..... Fontana........... TFL5113/STFL541 . 1961 £6.......... £15
Portrait Of Marty .................................... LP ..... Columbia ......... CL1855/CS8655... 1962 £5......... £12 ..................... US
R.F.D. ................................................... LP ..... CBS............... (S)BPG62437... 1965 £4.......... £10
Rock 'n' Roll 'n' Robbins ..................... 10″ LP Columbia ......... CL2601 ............ 1956 £210..... £350 ..................... US
Sittin' In A Tree House............................ 7″ ...... Fontana........... H150 ................ 1958 £2.50..... £6
Song Of Robbins .................................... LP ..... Columbia ......... CL2621/CS9421... 1967 £4.......... £10 ..................... US
Song Of Robbins .................................... LP ..... Columbia ......... CL976.............. 1957 £10.......... £25 ..................... US
Song Of The Islands ............................... LP ..... Columbia ......... CL1087............ 1957 £10.......... £25 ..................... US
Song Of The Islands ............................... LP ..... Columbia ......... CL2625 ............ 1967 £4.......... £10 ..................... US
Song Of The Islands ............................... 7″ EP . Columbia ......... TFE17167 ........ 1959 £2.......... £5 ..................... US
Stairway Of Love .................................... 7″ ...... Fontana........... H128 ................ 1958 £5.......... £10
Wedding Bells......................................... 7″ EP . Fontana........... TFE17168 ........ 1959 £2.......... £5
White Sports Coat................................... 7″ ...... Philips........... JK1019............. 1957 £10.......... £20

## ROBBINS, MEL
Save It.................................................. 7″ ...... London ............ HLM8966 ......... 1959 £180..... £300 ........... *tri-centre, best*
*auctioned*

## ROBBINS, SYLVIA
Frankie And Johnny................................ 7″ ...... London ............ HLJ9118 ........... 1960 £4.......... £8

## ROBBS
Robbs .................................................. LP ..... Mercury........... MG2/SR61130....... 1966 £10.......... £25 ..................... US

## ROBERTS, ANDY
Andy Roberts & The Great Stampede ........ LP ...... Elektra ............ K42151 ............ 1973 £4.......... £10
Home Grown .......................................... LP ..... RCA ............... SF8086............ 1970 £4.......... £10
Nina And The Dream Tree ........................ LP ..... Pegasus ........... PEG5............... 1971 £5.......... £12
Urban Cowboy ........................................ LP ..... Elektra ............ K42139 ............ 1973 £4.......... £10

## ROBERTS, BOB
Songs From The Sailing Barges................. LP ...... Topic.............. 12TS361 .......... 1978 £4.......... £10
Stormy Weather Boys.............................. 7″ EP . Collector......... JEB6 ............... 1961 £2.......... £5

## ROBERTS, HOWARD
Mr. Roberts Plays Guitar...................... 10″ LP Columbia........ 33C9038 .......... 1957 £6.......... £15

## ROBERTS, JOHN
I'll Forget About You .............................. 7″ ...... Action............. ACT4511 ............ 1968 £2.50..... £6
Sockin' 1, 2, 3, 4 ................................... 7″ ...... Sue ................ WI4042............. 1967 £4.......... £8

## ROBERTS, KEITH
Pier Of The Realm .................................. LP ..... Trailer............ LER3031 ........... 1972 £5.......... £12

## ROBERTS, KENNY
Run Like The Devil................................. 7″ ...... Pye ................ 7N17054 .......... 1966 £7.50..... £15

## ROBERTS, KIM
I'll Prove It ........................................... 7″ ...... Decca ............. F11813.............. 1964 £15.......... £30

## ROBERTS, LUCKEY
Harlem Piano Solos ................................ LP ..... Good Time ....... LAG12256............. 1960 £4.......... £10 .......*with Willie 'The*
Jazz................. *Lion' Smith*

## ROBERTSON, DON
Happy Whistler....................................... 7″ ...... Capitol............ CL14575 ............ 1956 £2.......... £5

## ROBERTSON, JEANNIE
Cuckoo's Nest & Other Scottish Folk ........ LP ..... XTRA............ XTRA5037 ............ 1968 £4.......... £10
Songs....................................................
Gallowa' Hills ........................................ 7″ EP . Collector......... JES1................. 1960 £2.......... £5
I Ken Where I'm Going............................ 7″ EP . Collector......... JES8................. 1960 £2.......... £5
I Ken Where I'm Going............................ 10″ LP Topic.............. 10T52............... 1960 £8.......... £20

| | | | | | | |
|---|---|---|---|---|---|---|
| Jeannie Robertson | LP | Topic | 12T96 | 1963 £6 | £15 | |
| Jeannie's Merry Muse | 7" EP | HMV | 7EG8534 | 1960 £2 | £5 | |
| Lord Donald | LP | Collector | JFS4001 | 1960 £6 | £15 | |
| Twa Brothers | 7" EP | Collector | JES4 | 1960 £2 | £5 | |

## ROBERTSON, ROBBIE

| | | | | | | |
|---|---|---|---|---|---|---|
| Robbie Robertson | CD | Mobile Fidelity | UDCD618 | 1994 £6 | £15 | US audiophile |

## ROBIC, IVO

| | | | | | |
|---|---|---|---|---|---|
| Morgen | 7" | Polydor | NH23923 | 1959 £1.50 | £4 |

## ROBIN, TINA

| | | | | | |
|---|---|---|---|---|---|
| Everyday | 7" | Vogue Coral | Q72309 | 1958 £2 | £5 |
| Get Out Of My Life | 7" | Mercury | AMT1199 | 1962 £1.50 | £4 |
| Lady Fair | 7" | Vogue Coral | Q72284 | 1957 £4 | £8 |
| Never In A Million Years | 7" | Vogue Coral | Q72294 | 1957 £2 | £5 |
| No School Tomorrow | 7" | Coral | Q72323 | 1958 £2.50 | £6 |

## ROBINS

| | | | | | | |
|---|---|---|---|---|---|---|
| Cherry Lips | 7" | Vogue | V9168 | 1960 £37.50 | £75 | |
| Just Like That | 7" | Vogue | V9173 | 1960 £30 | £60 | |
| Rock 'n' Roll With The Robins | LP | Whippet | WLP703 | 195– £75 | £150 | US |

## ROBINS, JIMMY

| | | | | | |
|---|---|---|---|---|---|
| I Can't Please You | 7" | President | PT118 | 1968 £10 | £20 |

## ROBINSON, ALVIN

| | | | | | |
|---|---|---|---|---|---|
| Down Home Girl | 7" | Red Bird | RB10010 | 1964 £4 | £8 |
| Something You Got | 7" | Pye | 7N25248 | 1964 £2.50 | £6 |
| You Brought My Heart Right Down | 7" | Strike | JH307 | 1966 £4 | £8 |

## ROBINSON, BROTHER CLEOPHUS

| | | | | | |
|---|---|---|---|---|---|
| Negro Spirituals | 7" EP | Vogue | EPV1196 | 1958 £5 | £10 |

## ROBINSON, FLOYD

| | | | | | |
|---|---|---|---|---|---|
| Floyd Robinson | LP | RCA | RD27166 | 1960 £10 | £25 |
| Makin' Love | 7" | RCA | RCA1146 | 1959 £1.50 | £4 |

## ROBINSON, JACKIE

| | | | | | | |
|---|---|---|---|---|---|---|
| Let The Little Girl Dance | 7" | Amalgamated | AMG824 | 1968 £2.50 | £6 | Derrick Morgan B side |
| Over And Over | 7" | Amalgamated | AMG819 | 1968 £4 | £8 | |

## ROBINSON, LLOYD

| | | | | | |
|---|---|---|---|---|---|
| Cuss Cuss | 7" | Duke | DU5 | 1968 £2.50 | £6 |
| When You Walk | 7" | Blue Beat | BB122 | 1962 £6 | £12 |
| Worm | 7" | Camel | CA41 | 1970 £1.50 | £4 |
| You Told Me | 7" | Blue Beat | BB159 | 1963 £6 | £12 |

## ROBINSON, M.

| | | | | | |
|---|---|---|---|---|---|
| Who Are You | 7" | Port-O-Jam | PJ4114 | 1964 £5 | £10 |

## ROBINSON, ROSCOE

| | | | | | |
|---|---|---|---|---|---|
| That's Enough | 7" | Pye | 7N25385 | 1966 £6 | £12 |

## ROBINSON, SMOKEY & THE MIRACLES

| | | | | | |
|---|---|---|---|---|---|
| Baby Baby Don't Cry | 7" | Tamla Motown | TMG687 | 1969 £1.50 | £4 |
| Greatest Hits | LP | Tamla Motown | (S)TML11072 | 1968 £4 | £10 |
| I Second That Emotion | 7" | Tamla Motown | TMG631 | 1967 £1.50 | £4 |
| If You Can Want | 7" | Tamla Motown | TMG648 | 1968 £2 | £5 |
| Love I Saw In You Was Just A Mirage | 7" | Tamla Motown | TMG598 | 1967 £5 | £10 |
| Make It Happen | LP | Tamla Motown | (S)TML11067 | 1968 £5 | £12 |
| More Love/Come Spy With Me | 7" | Tamla Motown | TMG614 | 1967 £30 | £60 |
| More Love/Swept For You Baby | 7" | Tamla Motown | TMG614 | 1967 £4 | £8 |
| Special Occasion | LP | Tamla Motown | (S)TML11089 | 1969 £4 | £10 |
| Special Occasion | 7" | Tamla Motown | TMG673 | 1968 £1.50 | £4 |
| Tears Of A Clown/Who's Gonna Take The Blame | 7" | Tamla Motown | TMG745 | 1970 £1.50 | £4 |
| Tears Of A Clown/You Must Be Love | 7" | Tamla Motown | TMG745 | 1970 £10 | £20 |
| Tracks Of My Tears | 7" | Tamla Motown | TMG696 | 1969 £1.50 | £4 |
| Yester-Love | 7" | Tamla Motown | TMG661 | 1968 £1.50 | £4 |

## ROBINSON, SUGAR CHILE

| | | | | | |
|---|---|---|---|---|---|
| Capitol Presents | 10" LP | Capitol | LC6586 | 1953 £15 | £30 |

## ROBINSON, TOM

| | | | | | | |
|---|---|---|---|---|---|---|
| All Right All Night | 7" | EMI | EMI2946 | 1978 £2.50 | £6 | demo |
| Good To Be Gay | 7" | Chebel | SRT/CUS015 | 1975 £7.50 | £15 | |
| Pre-Album Sampler | LP | Harvest | SPRO8791 | 1978 £5 | £12 | US |

## ROBISON, CARSON

| | | | | | |
|---|---|---|---|---|---|
| Eight Square Dances | 10" LP | MGM | D101 | 1952 £4 | £10 |
| Jitterbug | 7" | MGM | SP1004 | 1953 £4 | £8 |
| Lady Round | 7" | MGM | SP1004 | 1953 £2 | £5 |
| Life Gets Teejus | 7" EP | MGM | MGMEP669 | 1958 £4 | £8 |
| Square Dance – With Calls | 7" EP | MGM | MGMEP755 | 1961 £2.50 | £6 |

## ROBSON, NICKY

| | | | | | |
|---|---|---|---|---|---|
| Stars | 7" | Scratch | SCR6 | 1980 £6 | £12 |

Stars ................................................... 12" ...... Scratch ............ SCRT6 ................. 1980 £10 ......... £25 .............................................

## ROCCO, TONY
Keep A Walking .................................... 7" ...... Parlophone ...... R4886 ................. 1962 £2.50 ........ £6 ...................................

## ROCK, DICKIE
Come Back To Stay .............................. 7" ...... Pye ................. 7N17063 ............... 1965 £4 ......... £8 ...............................

## ROCK, JOHNNY
Johnny Rock ....................................... 7" EP . Vogue ............ VE170112 ......... 1958 £2 .............. £5 ...............................

## ROCK BROTHERS
Dungaree Doll ..................................... 7" ...... Parlophone ...... MSP6201 ............... 1956 £15 ........ £30 ..............................

## ROCK 'N' ROLL REVIVAL SHOW
Midnight Train .................................... 7" ...... Decca ............. F12752 ................. 1968 £1.50 ....... £4 ...............................

## ROCK SHOP
Rock Shop .......................................... LP ..... Lee ................. 1 ........................... 1969 £37.50 .... £75 ....................... US

## ROCK WORKSHOP
Rock Workshop .................................... LP ..... CBS ................ 64075 ................... 1970 £6 ......... £15 ..............................
Very Last Time .................................... LP ..... CBS ................ 64394 ................... 1971 £6 ......... £15 ..............................

## ROCK-A-TEENS
Woo Hoo ............................................ LP ..... Roulette .......... (S)R25109 ........... 1960 £25 ........ £50 ....................... US
Woo Hoo ............................................ 7" ...... Columbia ........ DB4361 ............... 1959 £7.50 ...... £15 ..............................

## ROCKERS
Get Cracking ...................................... 7" ...... Oriole ............. CB1501 ............... 1959 £2.50 ...... £6 ...............................

## ROCKETS
Gibraltar Rock ..................................... 7" ...... Philips ............ PB982 ................. 1959 £4 ......... £8 ...............................
Warrior ............................................... 7" ...... Zodiac ............ ZR0010 ............... 196– £5 ......... £10 ..............................

## ROCKETS (2)
Neil Young became friendly with the Rockets while still a member of Buffalo Springfield. When later he was looking for a permanent backing band, the Rockets were an obvious choice. Young renamed the group Crazy Horse, recording a 'Requiem For The Rockets' on the first album they made together (*Everybody Knows This Is Nowhere*).

Hole In My Pocket .............................. 7" ...... White Whale ... 270 ...................... 1967 £6 ......... £12 ....................... US
Rockets ............................................... LP ..... White Whale ... S7116 .................. 1968 £8 ......... £20 ....................... US

## ROCKETS (3)
Plasteroid ............................................ LP ..... Rockland ......... RKL20137 ............. 1977 £4 ......... £10 ..... *French picture disc*

## ROCKIN' BERRIES
Dawn Go Away .................................... 7" ...... Pye ................. 7N17411 ............... 1967 £2 .............. £5 ...............................
Happy To Be Blue ............................... 7" EP . Piccadilly ........ NEP34045 .......... 1965 £7.50 ...... £15 ..............................
He's In Town ...................................... 7" EP . Pye ................. PNV24128 .......... 1964 £10 ........ £20 ....................... French
I Could Make You Fall In Love ............... 7" ...... Piccadilly ........ 7N35304 ............. 1966 £1.50 ...... £4 ...............................
I Didn't Mean To Hurt You .................... 7" EP . Piccadilly ........ NEP34039 .......... 1965 £6 ......... £12 ..............................
I Didn't Mean To Hurt You .................... 7" ...... Piccadilly ........ 7N35197 ............. 1964 £1.50 ...... £4 ...............................
In Town ............................................. LP ..... Piccadilly ........ NPL38013 ........... 1964 £25 ........ £50 ..............................
Itty Bitty Pieces ................................... 7" ...... Decca ............. F11760 ................. 1963 £4 ......... £8 ...............................
Life Is Just A Bowl Of Berries ................ LP ..... Piccadilly ........ NPL38022 ........... 1964 £25 ........ £50 ..............................
Midnight Mary .................................... 7" ...... Piccadilly ........ 7N35327 ............. 1966 £1.50 ...... £4 ...............................
Mr. Blue ............................................ 7" ...... Pye ................. 7N17589 ............. 1968 £1.50 ...... £4 ...............................
New From The Berries ........................... 7" EP . Piccadilly ........ NEP34043 .......... 1965 £6 ......... £12 ..............................
Smiles ................................................ 7" ...... Piccadilly ........ 7N35400 ............. 1967 £2 .............. £5 ...............................
Sometimes ........................................... 7" ...... Piccadilly ........ 7N35373 ............. 1967 £1.50 ...... £4 ...............................
Wah Wah Woo ..................................... 7" ...... Decca ............. F11698 ................. 1963 £6 ......... £12 ..............................
Water Is Over My Head .......................... 7" ...... Piccadilly ........ 7N35270 ............. 1965 £1.50 ...... £4 ...............................
When I Reach The Top ........................... 7" ...... Pye ................. 7N17519 ............. 1968 £1.50 ...... £4 ...............................
You're My Girl ..................................... 7" ...... Piccadilly ........ 7N35254 ............. 1965 £1.50 ...... £4 ...............................

## ROCKIN' FOO
Rockin' Foo ........................................ LP ..... Stateside ......... SSL10303 ............. 1970 £4 ......... £10 ..............................

## ROCKIN' HORSE
Biggest Gossip In Town ......................... 7" ...... Philips ............ 6006156 ............... 1971 £1.50 ...... £4 ...............................
Julian The Hooligan ............................. 7" ...... Philips ............ 6006200 ............... 1972 £1.50 ...... £4 ...............................
Yes It Is ............................................. LP ..... Philips ............ 6308075 ............... 1970 £20 ........ £40 ..............................

## ROCKIN' RAMRODS
Don't Fool With Fu Manchu ................... 7" ...... Polydor ........... 56512 ................... 1970 £5 ......... £10 ..............................

## ROCKIN' REBELS
Rockin' Crickets ................................... 7" ...... Stateside ......... SS187 .................. 1963 £2.50 ...... £6 ...............................
Wild Weekend ..................................... LP ..... Swan ............... SLP509 ................ 1962 £25 ........ £50 ....................... US
Wild Weekend ..................................... 7" ...... Stateside ......... SS162 .................. 1963 £2.50 ...... £6 ...............................

## ROCKIN' R'S
Crazy Baby .......................................... 7" ...... London ............ HL8872 ............... 1959 £12.50 .... £25 ..............................

## ROCKIN' SAINTS
Cheat On Me Baby ................................ 7" ...... Brunswick ........ 05843 .................. 1960 £30 ........ £60 ..............................

## ROCKIN' VICKERS

| | | | | | | | |
|---|---|---|---|---|---|---|---|
| Dandy | 7" | CBS | 202241 | 1966 | £10 | £20 | |
| I Go Ape | 7" | Decca | F11993 | 1964 | £6 | £12 | |
| It's Alright | 7" | CBS | 202051 | 1966 | £15 | £30 | |

## ROCKING GHOSTS

| | | | | | | | |
|---|---|---|---|---|---|---|---|
| For Ghosts Only | LP | Metronome | MLP15230 | 1966 | £10 | £25 | German |
| Golden Pigtrad | LP | Metronome | HLP10559 | 1975 | £10 | £25 | Danish |
| Keep Rocking | LP | Metronome | MLP15192 | 1967 | £20 | £40 | German |
| Rocking Ghosts | LP | Metronome | MLP10052 | 1965 | £10 | £25 | German |
| Rocking Ghosts | LP | Metronome | MLP15166 | 1966 | £15 | £30 | German |
| Two Band Party | LP | Metronome | HLP10066 | 1965 | £10 | £25 | German, with the Matadors |

## ROCKSTEADYS

| | | | | | | | |
|---|---|---|---|---|---|---|---|
| Squeeze And Freeze | 7" | Giant | GN2 | 1967 | £2 | £5 | |

## ROCKY HORROR SHOW

| | | | | | | | |
|---|---|---|---|---|---|---|---|
| Rocky Horror Box Set | LP | Pacific | RHBX1 | 1983 | £10 | £25 | 2LPs, 1 double LP, poster, badge, confetti, boxed |
| Rocky Horror Picture Show | LP | Ode | ODE78332 | 1975 | £4 | £10 | |
| Rocky Horror Picture Show | CD | Ode | RHBXCD1 | 1990 | £20 | £40 | 4 CD boxed set |
| Rocky Horror Show | LP | UK | UKAL1015 | 1973 | £4 | £10 | |
| Rocky Horror Show (US Roxy Cast) | LP | Ode | ODE77026 | 1974 | £4 | £10 | |
| Rocky Horror Show (US Roxy Cast) | LP | Ode | OSVP77026 | 1983 | £4 | £10 | picture disc |
| Time Warp | 7" | Ode | ODS66305 | 1975 | £2 | £5 | |

## ROCKYFELLERS

| | | | | | | | |
|---|---|---|---|---|---|---|---|
| Ching A Ling Baby | 7" | Pye | 7N25225 | 1963 | £1.50 | £4 | |
| Killer Joe | LP | Scepter | SP(S)512 | 1963 | £6 | £15 | US |
| Killer Joe | 7" | Stateside | SS175 | 1963 | £1.50 | £4 | |
| Like The Big Guys Do | 7" | Stateside | SS212 | 1963 | £1.50 | £4 | |

## ROCOMARS

| | | | | | | | |
|---|---|---|---|---|---|---|---|
| All In Black Woman | 7" | King | KG1031 | 1965 | £7.50 | £15 | |

## ROD, KEN & THE CAVALIERS

| | | | | | | | |
|---|---|---|---|---|---|---|---|
| Magic Wheel | 7" | Triumph | RGM1001 | 1960 | £7.50 | £15 | |

## ROD & THE COBRAS

| | | | | | | | |
|---|---|---|---|---|---|---|---|
| At A Drag Race At Surf City | LP | Somerset | 20500 | 1963 | £5 | £12 | US |

## RODDENBERRY, GENE

| | | | | | | | |
|---|---|---|---|---|---|---|---|
| Star Trek Theme | 7" | CBS | 4692 | 1976 | £2 | £5 | |

## RODGERS, EILEEN

| | | | | | | | |
|---|---|---|---|---|---|---|---|
| Careful, Careful | 7" | Fontana | H136 | 1958 | £1.50 | £4 | |
| Sailor | 7" | London | HLR9271 | 1961 | £2.50 | £6 | |
| Treasure Of Your Love | 7" | Fontana | H156 | 1958 | £1.50 | £4 | |

## RODGERS, IKE

| | | | | | | | |
|---|---|---|---|---|---|---|---|
| Ike Rodgers | 10" LP | London | AL3512 | 1954 | £5 | £12 | |

## RODGERS, JIMMIE

| | | | | | | | |
|---|---|---|---|---|---|---|---|
| Best Of Jimmie Rodgers | LP | RCA | LPM3315 | 1965 | £5 | £12 | US |
| Country Music Hall Of Fame | LP | RCA | RD7505 | 1962 | £5 | £12 | US |
| Jimmie Rodgers | 7" EP | HMV | 7EG8163 | 1956 | £6 | £12 | |
| Jimmie The Kid | LP | RCA | RD27241 | 1961 | £4 | £10 | |
| Legendary Jimmie Rodgers | 7" EP | RCA | RCX1058 | 1960 | £5 | £10 | |
| Memorial Album Vol. 1 | 10" LP | RCA | LPT3037 | 1952 | £10 | £25 | US |
| Memorial Album Vol. 2 | 10" LP | RCA | LPT3038 | 1952 | £10 | £25 | US |
| Memorial Album Vol. 3 | 10" LP | RCA | LPT3039 | 1952 | £10 | £25 | US |
| My Rough And Rowdy Ways | LP | RCA | RD27203 | 1961 | £4 | £10 | |
| My Time Ain't Long | LP | RCA | RD7644 | 1964 | £4 | £10 | |
| Never No Mo' Blues | LP | RCA | RD27138 | 1960 | £5 | £12 | |
| Short But Brilliant Life Of Jimmie Rodgers | LP | RCA | RD7562 | 1963 | £4 | £10 | |
| Train Whistle Blues | LP | RCA | RD27110 | 1959 | £5 | £12 | |
| Travellin' Blues | 10" LP | RCA | LPT3073 | 1952 | £10 | £25 | US |

## RODGERS, JIMMIE (2)

| | | | | | | | |
|---|---|---|---|---|---|---|---|
| English Country Garden | 7" EP | Columbia | SEG8253 | 1963 | £2 | £5 | |
| English Country Garden | 7" EP | Dot | DEP20002 | 1965 | £2 | £5 | |
| Favourites | LP | Columbia | 33SX1176 | 1959 | £4 | £10 | |
| Folk Songs And Readings | LP | Roulette | R25020 | 1958 | £4 | £10 | US |
| His Golden Year | LP | Roulette | R25057 | 1959 | £4 | £10 | US |
| Honeycomb | 7" | Columbia | DB3986 | 1957 | £5 | £10 | |
| Jimmie Rodgers | LP | Columbia | 33SX1082 | 1958 | £6 | £15 | |
| Jimmie Rodgers | 7" EP | Columbia | SEG7770 | 1958 | £6 | £12 | |
| Jimmie Rodgers Favourites | 7" EP | Dot | DEP20007 | 1965 | £2 | £5 | |
| Jimmie Rodgers Sings | 7" EP | Columbia | SEG7811 | 1958 | £5 | £10 | |
| Kisses Sweeter Than Wine | 7" | Columbia | DB4052 | 1957 | £2 | £5 | |
| Long Hot Summer | LP | Roulette | R25026 | 1958 | £6 | £15 | US |
| Number One Ballads | LP | Columbia | 33SX1097 | 1958 | £4 | £10 | |
| Oh Oh, I'm Falling In Love Again | 7" | Columbia | DB4078 | 1958 | £2 | £5 | |
| Secretly | 7" | Columbia | DB4130 | 1958 | £1.50 | £4 | |

| | | | | | | | |
|---|---|---|---|---|---|---|---|
| Sings Folk Songs | LP | Columbia | 33SX1144 | 1959 | £4 | £10 | |
| Twilight On The Trail | LP | Columbia | 33SX1217/ SCX3302 | 1960 | £4 | £10 | |
| Wizard | 7" | Columbia | DB4175 | 1958 | £1.50 | £4 | |
| Woman From Liberia | 7" | Columbia | DB4206 | 1958 | £1.50 | £4 | |

## RODYS

| | | | | | | | |
|---|---|---|---|---|---|---|---|
| Earnest Vocation | LP | Philips | 855075XPY | 1968 | £8 | £20 | Dutch |
| Just Fancy | LP | Philips | 855034XPY | 1967 | £8 | £20 | Dutch |

## ROE, TOMMY

| | | | | | | | |
|---|---|---|---|---|---|---|---|
| Ballads And Beat | LP | HMV | CLP1860 | 1965 | £6 | £15 | |
| Dizzy | LP | Stateside | (S)SL10282 | 1969 | £4 | £10 | |
| Everybody Likes Tommy Roe | LP | HMV | CLP1074 | 1965 | £8 | £20 | |
| Folk Singer | 7" EP | HMV | 7EG8806 | 1963 | £10 | £20 | |
| Sheila | LP | HMV | CLP1614 | 1963 | £8 | £20 | |
| Sheila | 7" | HMV | POP1060 | 1962 | £1.50 | £4 | |
| Something For Everybody | LP | ABC | (S)467 | 1964 | £6 | £15 | US |
| Sweet Pea | LP | ABC | (S)575 | 1966 | £6 | £15 | US |
| Town Crier | 7" | HMV | POP1116 | 1963 | £4 | £8 | demo only |

## ROGERS, DEAN

| | | | | | | | |
|---|---|---|---|---|---|---|---|
| Keep The Miracle Going | 7" | Parlophone | R4732 | 1961 | £1.50 | £4 | |
| Timber | 7" | Parlophone | R4835 | 1961 | £1.50 | £4 | |

## ROGERS, JULIE

| | | | | | | | |
|---|---|---|---|---|---|---|---|
| Julie Rogers | 7" EP | Mercury | 10023MCE | 1964 | £2.50 | £6 | |
| Sound Of Julie | 7" EP | Mercury | 10028MCE | 1965 | £2.50 | £6 | |

## ROGERS, LINCOLN

| | | | | | | | |
|---|---|---|---|---|---|---|---|
| Let Love Come Between Us | 7" | Phoenix | NIX137 | 1973 | £2 | £5 | |

## ROGERS, MARK & THE MARKSMEN

| | | | | | | | |
|---|---|---|---|---|---|---|---|
| Hold It | 7" | Parlophone | R5045 | 1963 | £2.50 | £6 | |

## ROGERS, PAULINE

| | | | | | | | |
|---|---|---|---|---|---|---|---|
| Spinning The Blues | 7" | Columbia | SCM5106 | 1954 | £1.50 | £4 | |

## ROGERS, PIERCE & THE OVERLANDERS

| | | | | | | | |
|---|---|---|---|---|---|---|---|
| Do You Still Love Me? | 7" | Parlophone | R4838 | 1961 | £1.50 | £4 | |

## ROGERS, ROY

| | | | | | | | |
|---|---|---|---|---|---|---|---|
| Bible Tells Me So | LP | Capitol | (S)T1745 | 1962 | £5 | £12 | US |
| Christmas Is Always | LP | Capitol | (S)T2818 | 1967 | £4 | £10 | US |
| Happy Trails | 7" EP | HMV | 7EG8182 | 1956 | £5 | £10 | |
| Hymns Of Faith | 10" LP | RCA | LPT3168 | 1954 | £8 | £20 | US |
| Jesus Loves Me | LP | Bluebird | LBY1022 | 1959 | £5 | £12 | US |
| Roy Rogers | 7" EP | HMV | 7EG8145 | 1955 | £5 | £10 | |
| Souvenir Album | 10" LP | RCA | LPT3041 | 1952 | £10 | £25 | US |
| Sweet Hour Of Prayer | LP | RCA | LPM1439 | 1957 | £6 | £15 | US |

## ROGERS, SHORTY

| | | | | | | | |
|---|---|---|---|---|---|---|---|
| Chances Are It Swings | LP | RCA | RD27149/SF5048 | 1960 | £5 | £12 | |
| Cool And Crazy | 10" LP | HMV | DLP1030 | 1954 | £25 | £50 | |
| Courts The Count | LP | HMV | CLP1041 | 1955 | £10 | £25 | |
| Eight Shorty Rogers Numbers | 10" LP | HMV | DLP1058 | 1954 | £25 | £50 | |
| Modern Sounds | LP | Capitol | T2025 | 1963 | £5 | £12 | with Gerry Mulligan |
| Modern Sounds | 10" LP | Capitol | LC6549 | 1952 | £25 | £50 | |
| Shorty Rogers And His Giants | LP | London | LTZK15023 | 1957 | £10 | £25 | |
| Shorty Rogers And His Giants | LP | London | LTZK15056 | 1957 | £10 | £25 | |
| Shorty Rogers And His Orchestra | LP | MGM | C820 | 1960 | £4 | £10 | |
| Shorty Rogers And His Orchestra | 7" EP | HMV | 7EG8044 | 1954 | £2 | £5 | |
| Shorty Rogers Plays Richard Rodgers | LP | RCA | RD27018 | 1958 | £8 | £20 | |
| Swingin' Nutcracker | LP | RCA | RD27199/SF5084 | 1961 | £5 | £12 | |
| Way Up There | LP | London | LTZK15179 | 1960 | £6 | £15 | |
| Wherever The Five Winds Blow | LPL | HMV | CLP1129 | 1957 | £10 | £25 | |

## ROGERS, TIMMIE

| | | | | | | | |
|---|---|---|---|---|---|---|---|
| Back To School Again | 7" | London | HLU8510 | 1957 | £20 | £40 | |
| Take Me To Your Leader | 7" | London | HLU8601 | 1958 | £25 | £50 | |

## ROGERS, VERN & THE HI-FI'S

| | | | | | | | |
|---|---|---|---|---|---|---|---|
| I Will | 7" | Oriole | CB1885 | 1963 | £1.50 | £4 | |
| That Ain't Right | 7" | Oriole | CB1785 | 1962 | £1.50 | £4 | |

## ROGUES

| | | | | | | | |
|---|---|---|---|---|---|---|---|
| Memories Of Missy | 7" | Decca | F12718 | 1967 | £1.50 | £4 | |
| Rogue's Reef | 7" | CBS | 201731 | 1965 | £1.50 | £4 | |

## ROHDE, JAN

| | | | | | | | |
|---|---|---|---|---|---|---|---|
| Come Back Baby | 7" | Qualiton | PSP7128 | 1960 | £1.50 | £4 | |

## ROHDE, JAN & THE WILD ONES

| | | | | | | | |
|---|---|---|---|---|---|---|---|
| Play Let Kiss | LP | Metronome | MLP15194 | 1965 | £6 | £15 | German |

## ROKES

| | | | | | | | |
|---|---|---|---|---|---|---|---|
| Che Mondo Strano | LP | RCA | FPM185 | 1967 | £15 | £30 | US |
| Hold My Hand | 7" | RCA | RCA1646 | 1967 | £7.50 | £15 | |

| Title | Format | Label | Cat. No. | Year | Price | Price | Notes |
|---|---|---|---|---|---|---|---|
| Let's Live For Today | 7" EP | RCA | 86577 | 1967 | £15 | £30 | French |
| Let's Live For Today | 7" | RCA | RCA1587 | 1967 | £5 | £10 | |
| Rokes | LP | ARC | ALP11002 | 1965 | £25 | £50 | Italian |
| Rokes | LP | ARC | ALP11006 | 1968 | £15 | £30 | Italian |
| Rokes | LP | ARC | SA4 | 1965 | £25 | £50 | Italian |
| Rokes Vol. 2 | LP | ARC | SA8 | 1966 | £25 | £50 | Italian |
| These Were Beat | LP | RCA | 33037 | 1967 | £10 | £25 | Italian |
| When The Wind Arises | 7" | RCA | RCA1694 | 1968 | £15 | £30 | |

## ROLAND, CHERRY

| Title | Format | Label | Cat. No. | Year | Price | Price | Notes |
|---|---|---|---|---|---|---|---|
| Boys | 7" | Fontana | TF420 | 1963 | £1.50 | £4 | |
| Handy Sandy | 7" | Decca | F11579 | 1963 | £1.50 | £4 | |
| Just For Fun | 7" | Decca | F11648 | 1963 | £1.50 | £4 | |

## ROLAND, JOE

| Title | Format | Label | Cat. No. | Year | Price | Price | Notes |
|---|---|---|---|---|---|---|---|
| Joe Roland Quintet | LP | London | LTZN15005 | 1956 | £8 | £20 | |

## ROLAND, PAUL

| Title | Format | Label | Cat. No. | Year | Price | Price | Notes |
|---|---|---|---|---|---|---|---|
| Blades Of Battenburg | 12" | Aftermath | AEP12011 | 1983 | £2.50 | £6 | |
| Demon In A Glass Case | 7" | Imaginary | MIRAGE002 | 1986 | £1.50 | £4 | |

## ROLAND, WALTER & GEORGIA SLIM

| Title | Format | Label | Cat. No. | Year | Price | Price | Notes |
|---|---|---|---|---|---|---|---|
| Male Blues Vol. 1 | 7" EP | Collector | JEL2 | 1959 | £4 | £8 | |

## ROLL MOVEMENT

| Title | Format | Label | Cat. No. | Year | Price | Price | Notes |
|---|---|---|---|---|---|---|---|
| I'm Out On My Own | 7" | Go | AJ11410 | 1967 | £2.50 | £6 | |

## ROLLERS

| Title | Format | Label | Cat. No. | Year | Price | Price | Notes |
|---|---|---|---|---|---|---|---|
| Continental Walk | 7" | London | HLG9340 | 1961 | £4 | £8 | |

## ROLLING STONES

It is easily forgotten how the Rolling Stones had some of the role of tougher alter egos for the Beatles during the sixties. As the Beatles started to become more and more experimental in their approach, so the Rolling Stones did the same. When eventually the Beatles came up with *Sgt Pepper* and 'Strawberry Fields Forever', the Rolling Stones responded with *Their Satanic Majesties Request* and 'We Love You'. Critics do not like these records very much, seeing them as being apart from what the Rolling Stones are all about, but they quite clearly achieve everything that psychedelic music tried to do. The death of Brian Jones, who loved to experiment with different instruments, apparently robbed the Rolling Stones of their ambition, for little of what the group has played since has extended much beyond a diet of the blues and Chuck Berry. The mono pressing of *Satanic Majesties* attracts a premium, especially in America, but for once, the mix does not actually sound any different in detail from the stereo version. The LP *Sticky Fingers*, with its Andy Warhol zip cover, just scrapes into the collectors' list – this was not a limited edition and is very much more common than some people believe. Bootleg copies of the notorious 'Cocksucker Blues', recorded to fulfil the Stones' Decca contract, have long been available. The German Teldec boxed set is remarkable, however, for including a copy of the single as a bonus, issued for the first and only time as an official release.

| Title | Format | Label | Cat. No. | Year | Price | Price | Notes |
|---|---|---|---|---|---|---|---|
| 12 X 5 | LP | London | LL3402 | 1964 | £8 | £20 | US |
| 12 X 5 | LP | London | LL3402 | 1964 | £700 | £1000 | US, blue vinyl |
| 1963–1971 – A Selection Of No. 1 Singles | CD | London | ROLCD1 | 1995 | £15 | £30 | US promo compilation |
| 19th Nervous Breakdown | 7" EP | Decca | 450206 | 1966 | £75 | £150 | French |
| 19th Nervous Breakdown | 7" | Decca | F12331 | 1966 | £1.50 | £4 | |
| 19th Nervous Breakdown | 7" | Decca | F12331 | 1966 | £12.50 | £25 | export, Dutch picture sleeve |
| 2000 Light Years From Home | 7" | Decca | F22706 | 1967 | £10 | £20 | export |
| Aftermath | LP | Decca | LK/SKL4786 | 1966 | £10 | £25 | |
| Aftermath | LP | London | LL3476 | 1966 | £8 | £20 | US |
| Aftermath And Out Of Time | LP | Decca | H220 | 1967 | £50 | £100 | German Club pressing |
| Almost Hear You Sigh | CD-s | CBS | 6560652 | 1990 | £2 | £5 | 2 versions |
| Around And Around | LP | Decca | SLK16315P | 1965 | £15 | £30 | German |
| As Tears Go By | 7" EP | Decca | 457104 | 1966 | £10 | £20 | French |
| Beat Beat Beat | 10" LP | Decca | 60368 | 1964 | £50 | £100 | German Club pressing |
| Beggar's Banquet | LP | Decca | LK4955 | 1968 | £15 | £30 | mono |
| Beggar's Banquet | LP | Decca | SKL4955 | 1968 | £5 | £12 | |
| Best Of Beat | LP | Decca | 25035 | 1966 | £50 | £100 | Swiss Club pressing |
| Between The Buttons | LP | Decca | 6835207 | | £8 | £20 | Dutch, yellow vinyl |
| Between The Buttons | LP | Decca | LK/SKL4852 | 1967 | £8 | £20 | |
| Between The Buttons | LP | London | LL3499 | 1967 | £8 | £20 | US |
| Big Hits | LP | Decca | 78299 | 1969 | £25 | £50 | German Club pressing |
| Big Hits (High Tide And Green Grass) | LP | Decca | TXL/TXS101 | 1966 | £6 | £15 | picture booklet |
| Big Hits (High Tide And Green Grass) | LP | London | NP1 | 1966 | £8 | £20 | US |
| Black And Blue | LP | CBS | 4502032 | 1989 | £5 | £12 | |
| Bravo | LP | Hor Zu | SHZT531 | 1965 | £25 | £50 | German |
| Brown Sugar | 7" | Atlantic | K19107 | 1974 | £7.50 | £15 | |
| Brown Sugar | 7" | Rolling Stones | RS19100 | 1971 | £6 | £12 | picture sleeve |
| Brown Sugar | 7" | Rolling Stones | SUGARP1 | 1984 | £7.50 | £15 | shaped picture disc |
| Carol | 7" EP | Decca | 457036 | 1964 | £10 | £20 | French |
| Come On | 7" | Decca | F11675 | 1963 | £2.50 | £6 | |
| Complete Singles Collection – sampler | CD | ABKCO | 121831 | 1989 | £10 | £25 | US promo |
| Con Le Mie La Crime | 7" | Decca | F22270 | 1965 | £15 | £30 | sung in Italian |
| Could You Walk On The Waters | LP | Decca | | 1966 | £150 | £250 | |
| December's Children | LP | London | LL3451 | 1965 | £8 | £20 | US |
| Desert Island Survival Kit | CD | ABKCO | | 1994 | £20 | £40 | US promo compilation |
| Ed Rudy Interview Album | LP | INS Radio | 1003 | 1965 | £25 | £50 | US |
| Emotional Rescue | CD | CBS | 4502062 | 1989 | £5 | £12 | |
| Emotional Rescue | 7" | Rolling Stones | | 1980 | £2 | £5 | interview promo, blue flexi |
| Empty Heart | 7" | Decca | AT15035 | 1964 | £37.50 | £75 | export |
| Exile On Main Street | LP | Rolling Stones | COC69100 | 1972 | £6 | £15 | double, with postcards |
| Fan Club Single | 7" | Rolling Stones | R8370/1 | 1983 | £2 | £5 | interview disc |

| Title | Format | Label | Catalogue | Year | | | Notes |
|---|---|---|---|---|---|---|---|
| First Eight Studio Albums | LP | Decca | ROLL1 | 1983 | £100 | £200 | ... 8 LPs, book, boxed |
| Five By Five | 7" EP | Decca | DFE8590 | 1964 | £5 | £10 | |
| Flashpoint/Interview 1990 | CD | Sony | 4681359/4681352 | 1991 | £20 | £40 | double pack |
| Flowers | LP | Decca | 25084 | 1967 | £50 | £100 | ... Swiss Club pressing |
| Flowers | LP | Decca | LK/SKL4888 | 1967 | £50 | £100 | export |
| Flowers | LP | Decca | SKL4888 | 197– | £15 | £30 | boxed Decca logo |
| Flowers | LP | London | LL3509 | 1967 | £8 | £20 | US |
| Get Off My Cloud | 7" EP | Decca | 457092 | 1965 | £10 | £20 | French |
| Get Off My Cloud | 7" EP | Decca | 457092 | 1965 | £37.50 | £75 | ..French, picture sleeve on stage at Olympia |
| Get Off My Cloud | 7" | Decca | F12263 | 1965 | £1.50 | £4 | |
| Get Off My Cloud | 7" | Decca | F22265 | 1965 | £7.50 | £15 | export |
| Get Off My Cloud | 7" | Decca | F22265 | 1965 | £20 | £40 | .. export, picture sleeve |
| Get Yer Ya-Ya's Out | LP | Decca | SKL5065 | 1970 | £5 | £12 | |
| Gimme Shelter | LP | Decca | SKL5101 | 1971 | £4 | £10 | |
| Goats Head Soup | CD | CBS | 4502072 | 1989 | £5 | £12 | |
| Golden B Sides | LP | Decca | SKL5165 | 1973 | £330 | £500 | test pressing only |
| Got Live If You Want It | LP | London | LL3493 | 1966 | £8 | £20 | US |
| Got Live If You Want It | 7" EP | Decca | 457081 | 1965 | £6 | £12 | French |
| Got Live If You Want It | 7" EP | Decca | DFE8620 | 1965 | £5 | £10 | |
| Got Live If You Want It | 7" EP | Decca | DFE8620 | 1965 | £25 | £50 | export, red label |
| Got Live If You Want It | 7" EP | Decca | SDE7502 | 1965 | £20 | £40 | export |
| Great Years | LP | Reader's Digest | GROLA119 | 1983 | £15 | £30 | 4 LPs, boxed |
| Greatest Hits | LP | RCA | SP0268 | 1972 | £15 | £30 | US |
| Happy | 7" | Rolling Stones | SAM4 | 1971 | £10 | £20 | promo |
| Have You Seen Your Mother Baby | 7" | Decca | F12497 | 1966 | £1.50 | £4 | |
| Have You Seen Your Mother Live! | LP | Decca | SKL4838 | 197– | £15 | £30 | boxed Decca logo |
| Have You Seen Your Mother, Live | LP | Decca | LK/SKL4838 | 1966 | £50 | £100 | export |
| Heart Of Stone | 7" EP | Decca | 457066 | 1965 | £10 | £20 | French |
| Heart Of Stone | 7" | Decca | F22180 | 1965 | £10 | £20 | export |
| Heart Of Stone | 7" | Decca | F22180 | 1965 | £20 | £40 | .. export, picture sleeve |
| Highwire | CD-s | CBS | 6567562 | 1991 | £2 | £5 | |
| Highwire | CD-s | CBS | 6567565 | 1991 | £5 | £12 | gatefold card sleeve |
| History Of The Rolling Stones | LP | Decca | ZAL12996–13001 | 1975 | £500 | £750 | 3 LP test pressings |
| Hits Live | LP | Decca | SKL4495 | 1965 | £75 | £150 | export promo |
| Honky Tonk Women | 7" | Decca | F12952 | 1969 | £1.50 | £4 | |
| Honky Tonk Women | 7" | Decca | F12952 | 1969 | £12.50 | £25 | .. export, picture sleeve |
| Hot Rocks | CD | Decca | 8000832 | 1984 | £10 | £25 | |
| Hot Stuff | 12" | Rolling Stones | | 1976 | £10 | £20 | .. promo, black & blue vinyl |
| Hot Stuff | 12" | Rolling Stones | | 1976 | £10 | £25 | promo, clear vinyl |
| I Don't Know Why | 7" | Decca | F13584 | 1975 | £4 | £8 | Jagger/Richard writing credit |
| I Don't Know Why | 7" | Decca | F13584 | 1975 | £2 | £5 | Stevie Wonder writing credit |
| I Wanna Be Your Man | 7" EP | Decca | 457026 | 1963 | £25 | £50 | ..French, picture sleeve with 4 titles listed |
| I Wanna Be Your Man | 7" EP | Decca | 457026 | 1963 | £15 | £30 | ..French, picture sleeve with main title only |
| I Wanna Be Your Man | 7" | Decca | AT15005 | 1963 | £25 | £50 | export |
| I Wanna Be Your Man | 7" | Decca | F11764 | 1963 | £2.50 | £6 | |
| I Wanna Be Your Man/Stones | 7" | Decca | F11764 | 1963 | £4 | £8 | |
| If You Need Me | 7" EP | Decca | 457043 | 1964 | £10 | £20 | French |
| In Action | LP | S*R International | 74307 | 1966 | £75 | £150 | German Club pressing |
| Interview | CD | Rolling Stones | CSK1910 | 1989 | £20 | £40 | US promo |
| Interview With Mick Jagger By Tom Donahue | LP | Rolling Stones | PR164 | 1971 | £15 | £30 | US promo |
| It's All Over Now | 7" EP | Decca | 457039 | 1964 | £10 | £20 | French |
| It's All Over Now | 7" | Decca | F11934 | 1964 | £1.50 | £4 | |
| It's All Over Now | 7" | Decca | F13517 | 1974 | £37.50 | £75 | demo only |
| It's Only Rock 'n' Roll | CD | CBS | 4502022 | 1989 | £5 | £12 | |
| Jumpin' Jack Flash | 7" | Decca | F12782 | 1968 | £1.50 | £4 | |
| Last Time | 7" | Decca | F12104 | 1965 | £1.50 | £4 | |
| Last Time | 7" | Decca | F12104 | 1965 | £15 | £30 | . export, Dutch picture sleeve |
| Let It Bleed | LP | Decca | 6835204 | | £8 | £20 | Dutch, red vinyl |
| Let It Bleed | LP | Decca | LK5025 | 1969 | £10 | £25 | mono |
| Let It Bleed | LP | Decca | LK5025 | 1969 | £15 | £30 | mono, with sticker and poster |
| Let It Bleed | LP | Decca | SKL5025 | 1969 | £5 | £12 | with inner sleeve |
| Let It Bleed | LP | Decca | SKL5025 | 1969 | £10 | £25 | with sticker, inner sleeve and poster |
| Let's Spend The Night Together | 7" | Decca | F12546 | 1967 | £1.50 | £4 | |
| Let's Spend The Night Together | 7" | Decca | F12546 | 1967 | £15 | £30 | .. export, picture sleeve |
| Let's Spend The Night Together (live) | 7" | Rolling Stones | RSR112DJ | 1983 | £5 | £10 | promo only |
| Little Queenie | 7" | Decca | F13126 | 1971 | £5 | £10 | export |
| Little Queenie | 7" | Decca | F13126 | 1971 | £12.50 | £25 | .. export, picture sleeve |
| Little Red Rooster | 7" | Decca | AT15040 | 1965 | £37.50 | £75 | export |
| Little Red Rooster | 7" | Decca | F12014 | 1964 | £1.50 | £4 | |
| Love You Live | CD | CBS | 4502082 | 1989 | £5 | £12 | |
| Made In The Shade | CD | CBS | 4502012 | 1989 | £5 | £12 | |
| Mixed Emotions | CD-s | CBS | 6551935 | 1989 | £2 | £5 | |
| Mixed Emotions | CD-s | CBS | 6551935 | 1989 | £15 | £30 | in tin |
| Mixed Emotions | CD-s | CBS | 6552142 | 1989 | £15 | £30 | in tin |
| Mother's Little Helper | 7" EP | Decca | 457122 | 1966 | £10 | £20 | French |
| Not Fade Away | 7" EP | Decca | 457031 | 1964 | £15 | £30 | French |
| Not Fade Away | 7" | Decca | AT15008 | 1964 | £25 | £50 | export |

| Title | Format | Label | Catalogue | Year | Price 1 | Price 2 | Notes |
|---|---|---|---|---|---|---|---|
| Not Fade Away | 7" | Decca | F11845 | 1964 | £1.50 | £4 | |
| Original Master Records | LP | Mobile Fidelity | 01657 | 1984 | £87.50 | £175 | US 10 LP boxed set |
| Out Of Our Heads | LP | Decca | LK/SKL4725 | 1965 | £37.50 | £75 | export, US format |
| Out Of Our Heads | LP | Decca | LK4733 | 1965 | £10 | £25 | |
| Out Of Our Heads | LP | Decca | SKL4733 | 196– | £5 | £12 | boxed Decca logo |
| Out Of Our Heads | LP | Decca | SKL4733 | 1965 | £15 | £30 | stereo |
| Out Of Our Heads | LP | London | LL3429 | 1965 | £8 | £20 | US |
| Paint It Black | 7" | Decca | F12395 | 1966 | £1.50 | £4 | |
| Pleasure Of Pain | CD | Rolling Stones | XDDP930823 | 1990 | £330 | £500 | Japanese promo double |
| Poison Ivy | 7" | Decca | F11742 | 1963 | £250 | £400 | best auctioned |
| Promotional LP | LP | Decca | RSM1 | 1969 | £330 | £500 | promo compilation |
| Radio Sampler | CD | London | RSCD1 | 1990 | £15 | £30 | promo |
| Rest Of The Best Of The Rolling Stones | LP | Teldec | 630125FX | 1984 | £50 | £100 | 4 LPs, boxed, with 7", German |
| Rock And A Hard Place | CD-s | CBS | 6554222 | 1989 | £2 | £5 | |
| Rock And A Hard Place | CD-s | Rolling Stones | RSR6554482 | 1989 | £10 | £20 | boxed with poster |
| Rock And A Hard Place | CD-s | Rolling Stones | RSR6554485 | 1989 | £10 | £20 | tongue-shaped sleeve |
| Rock And Roll Circus | CD | Abkco | 12112 | 1996 | £15 | £30 | US promo |
| Rocks Off | 7" | Rolling Stones | SAM3 | 1971 | £10 | £20 | promo |
| Rolling Stones | LP | Decca | 25014 | 1965 | £100 | £200 | Swiss Club pressing |
| Rolling Stones | LP | Decca | LK4605 | 196– | £5 | £12 | red label, no flaps on rear sleeve |
| Rolling Stones | LP | Decca | LK4605 | 1964 | £10 | £25 | |
| Rolling Stones | LP | Decca | LK4605 | 1964 | £25 | £50 | with 2.52 version of 'Tell Me' |
| Rolling Stones | LP | London | LL3375 | 1964 | £8 | £20 | US |
| Rolling Stones | LP | London | LL3375 | 1964 | £50 | £100 | US, maroon label, 'London/ffrr' in box, bonus photo – advertised |
| Rolling Stones | CD | Rolling Stones | | 1986 | £20 | £40 | US promo compilation |
| Rolling Stones | 7" EP | Decca | DFE8560 | 1964 | £5 | £10 | |
| Rolling Stones | 7" EP | Decca | SDE7260 | 1964 | £25 | £50 | export |
| Rolling Stones | 7" EP | Decca | SDE7503 | 1966 | £37.50 | £75 | export |
| Rolling Stones No. 2 | LP | Decca | LK4661 | 1965 | £10 | £25 | |
| Rolling Stones No. 2 | LP | Decca | LK4661 | 1965 | £5 | £12 | red label, no flaps on rear sleeve |
| Rolling Stones Now! | LP | London | LL3420 | 1965 | £8 | £20 | US |
| Rolling Stones Story | LP | Decca | 630120 | 1980 | £37.50 | £75 | German 12 LP boxed set |
| Rolling Stones Vol. 2 | 7" EP | Decca | SDE7501 | 1964 | £20 | £40 | export |
| Rolling Stones/Living Colour | CD | Columbia | | 1989 | £15 | £30 | US promo |
| Ruby Tuesday (live) | CD-s | Epic | 6568922 | 1991 | £2 | £5 | |
| Sad Day | 7" | Decca | F13404 | 1973 | £1.50 | £4 | |
| Satisfaction | 7" EP | Decca | 457086 | 1965 | £10 | £20 | French, B. Jones in centre of group pic |
| Satisfaction | 7" EP | Decca | 457086 | 1965 | £37.50 | £75 | French, K. Richards in centre of group pic |
| Satisfaction | 7" | Decca | AT15043 | 1965 | £37.50 | £75 | export, picture sleeve |
| Satisfaction | 7" | Decca | F12220 | 1965 | £1.50 | £4 | |
| Satisfaction/Under Assistant West Coast ... | 7" | Decca | F12220 | 1965 | £5 | £10 | export |
| Satisfaction/Under Assistant West Coast ... | 7" | Decca | F12220 | 1965 | £12.50 | £25 | export, picture sleeve |
| Say Ahhh! | CD | Rolling Stones | CSK1827 | 1989 | £20 | £40 | US promo compilation |
| She Was Hot | 7" | Rolling Stones | RSRP114 | 1984 | £7.50 | £15 | shaped picture disc |
| Single Stones | 7" | Decca | STONE1-12 | 1981 | £20 | £40 | mail order box set with poster & badge |
| Some Girls | LP | Decca | DC2 | 1978 | £8 | £20 | French, red vinyl |
| Some Girls | LP | Mobile Fidelity | MFSL1087 | 1982 | £6 | £15 | US audiophile |
| Some Girls | CD | CBS | 4501972 | 1989 | £5 | £12 | |
| Songs Of The Rolling Stones | LP | ABKCO | MPD1 | 1973 | £50 | £100 | US promo |
| Songs Of The Rolling Stones Vol. 2 | LP | ABKCO | | 197– | £50 | £100 | US promo |
| Steel Wheels | CD | CBS | 4657522 | 1989 | £5 | £12 | |
| Steel Wheels | CD | CBS | 4657522 | 1990 | £62.50 | £125 | promo box set, with LP, cassette, T-shirt, 12", book |
| Steel Wheels | CD | Rolling Stones | CK46009 | 1989 | £10 | £25 | US, in steel case |
| Sticky Fingers | LP | Mobile Fidelity | MFSL1060 | 1980 | £8 | £20 | US audiophile |
| Sticky Fingers | LP | Rolling Stones | COC59100 | 1971 | £6 | £15 | zip sleeve, insert |
| Sticky Fingers | LP | Rolling Stones | HRSS59101 | 1971 | £30 | £60 | Spanish, treacle tin sleeve |
| Sticky Fingers | CD | CBS | 4501952 | 1989 | £5 | £12 | |
| Sticky Fingers | CD | Rolling Stones | 4501959 | 1990 | £8 | £20 | German, zip sleeve |
| Still Life | LP | Rolling Stones | CUNP39115 | 1982 | £4 | £10 | picture disc |
| Still Life | CD | CBS | 4502042 | 1989 | £5 | £12 | |
| Stones In The Park | CD | BMG | 781223 | 1992 | £10 | £25 | laser disc |
| Stones On CD | CD | CBS | SAMP1103 | 1987 | £37.50 | £75 | promo |
| Street Fighting Man | 7" | Decca | F13195 | 1971 | £1.50 | £4 | |
| Street Fighting Man | 7" | Decca | F13195 | 1971 | £10 | £20 | export, picture sleeve |
| Street Fighting Man | 7" | Decca | F13203 | 1971 | £5 | £10 | |
| Street Fighting Man | 7" | Decca | F13204 | 1971 | £5 | £10 | export |
| Street Fighting Man | 7" | Decca | F13204 | 1971 | £12.50 | £25 | export, picture sleeve |
| Street Fighting Man | 7" | Decca | F22825 | 1968 | £20 | £40 | export, picture sleeve |
| Stripped | CD | Virgin | IVDG2801 | 1996 | £50 | £100 | promo with bonus interview disc |
| Sucking In The Seventies | CD | CBS | 4502052 | 1989 | £5 | £12 | |
| Tattoo You | CD | CBS | 4501982 | 1989 | £5 | £12 | |

| Title | Format | Label | Catalogue | Year | | | Notes |
|---|---|---|---|---|---|---|---|
| Tell Me | 7" | Decca | AT15032 | 1964 | £37.50 | £75 | export |
| Terrifying | CD-s | CBS | 6561222 | 1990 | £2 | £5 | |
| Terrifying | CD-s | Rolling Stones | RSR6551225 | 1990 | £4 | £10 | card sleeve |
| Their Satanic Majesties Request | LP | Decca | 6835208 | | £8 | £20 | Dutch, white vinyl |
| Their Satanic Majesties Request | LP | Decca | TXL103 | 1967 | £20 | £40 | 3D Cover, mono |
| Their Satanic Majesties Request | LP | Decca | TXS103 | 1967 | £15 | £30 | 3D cover |
| Their Satanic Majesties Request | LP | Decca | TXS103 | 198– | £6 | £15 | reissue with 3D sleeve |
| Their Satanic Majesties Request | LP | London | NP2 | 1967 | £37.50 | £75 | US, mono |
| Through The Past Darkly | LP | Decca | LK5019 | 1969 | £8 | £20 | octagonal cover, mono |
| Through The Past Darkly | LP | Decca | SKL5019 | 1969 | £6 | £15 | octagonal cover |
| Time Is On My Side | 7" EP | Decca | 457050 | 1964 | £10 | £20 | French |
| Time Is On My Side | 7" | Decca | AT15039 | 1965 | £37.50 | £75 | export |
| Trident Mixes | LP | ABKCO | PR164 | 197– | £330 | £500 | US promo double |
| Under Cover | CD | CBS | 4502002 | 1989 | £5 | £12 | |
| Under Cover | CD | Rolling Stones | CDP7460242 | 1984 | £6 | £15 | |
| Urban Jungle Tour Special | CD | Rolling Stones | | 1990 | £50 | £100 | promo box set, with cassette, 12", biog |
| Voodoo Lounge | CD | Rolling Stones | | 1994 | £10 | £25 | Australian, in slipcase |
| We Love You | 7" | Decca | F12654 | 1967 | £1.50 | £4 | |
| We Love You | 7" | Decca | F12654 | 1967 | £15 | £30 | export, picture sleeve |

## ROLLINS, SONNY

| Title | Format | Label | Catalogue | Year | | | Notes |
|---|---|---|---|---|---|---|---|
| Alfie | LP | HMV | CLP/CSD3529 | 1967 | £8 | £20 | |
| At Music Inn | LP | MGM | C818 | 1960 | £8 | £20 | side 2 by Teddy Edwards |
| Blow! | LP | Fontana | FJL124 | 1965 | £5 | £12 | |
| Bridge | LP | RCA | RD/SF7504 | 1962 | £6 | £15 | |
| East Broadway Rundown | LP | HMV | CLP/CSD3610 | 1967 | £6 | £15 | |
| Freedom Suite | LP | Riverside | RLP12258 | 1962 | £8 | £20 | |
| Horn Culture | LP | Milestone | M9051 | 1973 | £6 | £15 | US |
| Movin' Out | LP | Esquire | 32155 | 1962 | £8 | £20 | |
| Newk's Time | LP | Blue Note | BLP/BST84001 | 1964 | £10 | £25 | |
| Next Album | LP | Milestone | MSP9042 | 1972 | £6 | £15 | US |
| Night At The Village Vanguard | LP | Blue Note | BLP/BST81581 | 1964 | £10 | £25 | |
| Now's The Time | LP | RCA | RD7670 | 1965 | £6 | £15 | |
| Nucleus | LP | Milestone | M9064 | 1975 | £6 | £15 | US |
| On Impulse | LP | HMV | CLP1915 | 1966 | £6 | £15 | |
| Our Man In Jazz | LP | RCA | RD/SF7546 | 1963 | £6 | £15 | |
| Perspectives | LP | Esquire | 32035 | 1957 | £10 | £25 | with MJQ |
| Rollins And Brownie | 7" EP | Esquire | EP238 | 1961 | £2 | £5 | with Clifford Brown |
| Saint Thomas | 7" EP | Esquire | EP248 | 1962 | £2 | £5 | |
| Saxophone Colossus | LP | Esquire | 32045 | 1958 | £10 | £25 | |
| Saxophone Colossus | LP | Stateside | SL10164 | 1966 | £5 | £12 | |
| Sonny Boy | LP | Esquire | 32175 | 1963 | £6 | £15 | |
| Sonny Meets Hawk | LP | RCA | RD/SF7593 | 1964 | £8 | £20 | with Coleman Hawkins |
| Sonny Rollins | LP | Blue Note | BLP/BST81542 | 1961 | £10 | £25 | |
| Sonny Rollins & Co. | LP | RCA | RD/SF7626 | 1964 | £6 | £15 | |
| Sonny Rollins And The Big Brass | LP | MGM | C776 | 1959 | £8 | £20 | |
| Sonny Rollins And The Contemporary Leaders | LP | Contemporary | LAC12213 | 1960 | £8 | £20 | |
| Sonny Rollins And The Contemporary Leaders | LP | Contemporary | SCA5013 | 1960 | £8 | £20 | |
| Sonny Rollins And The Modern Jazz Quartet | 7" EP | Esquire | EP94 | 195– | £2 | £5 | |
| Sonny Rollins Plus Four | LP | Esquire | 32025 | 1957 | £10 | £25 | |
| Sonny Rollins Quartet | LP | Esquire | 32038 | 1958 | £10 | £25 | |
| Sonny Rollins Quartet | 10" LP | Esquire | 20050 | 1955 | £25 | £50 | |
| Sonny Rollins Quintet | LP | Esquire | 32075 | 1959 | £10 | £25 | |
| Sonny Rollins Quintet | 10" LP | Esquire | 20080 | 1957 | £25 | £50 | |
| Sonny Rollins Vol. 2 | LP | Blue Note | BLP/BST81558 | 1961 | £10 | £25 | |
| Sonny Rollins With Thelonious Monk | 7" EP | Esquire | EP148 | 1957 | £2 | £5 | |
| Sound Of Sonny | LP | Riverside | RLP12241 | 1961 | £8 | £20 | |
| Standard Sonny Rollins | LP | RCA | RD/SF7736 | 1967 | £6 | £15 | |
| Tenor Madness | LP | Esquire | 32058 | 1958 | £10 | £25 | |
| Tour De Force | LP | Esquire | 32085 | 1959 | £10 | £25 | |
| Valse Hot | 7" EP | Esquire | EP228 | 1960 | £2 | £5 | |
| Wailing Mr. Rollins | 7" EP | Esquire | EP198 | 1958 | £2 | £5 | |
| Way I Feel | LP | Milestone | M9074 | 1976 | £5 | £12 | US |
| Way Out West | LP | Contemporary | LAC12118 | 1958 | £8 | £20 | |
| What's New | LP | RCA | RD/SF7524 | 1963 | £6 | £15 | |

## ROMAN, MURRAY

| Title | Format | Label | Catalogue | Year | | | Notes |
|---|---|---|---|---|---|---|---|
| Blind Man's Movie | LP | Track | 613015 | 1969 | £4 | £10 | |
| You Can't Beat People Up | LP | Track | 613007 | 1969 | £5 | £12 | |

## ROMAN, RON

'Love Of My Life' was written by Frank Zappa and was later recorded by him on the LP *Cruising With Ruben And The Jets*.

| Title | Format | Label | Catalogue | Year | | | Notes |
|---|---|---|---|---|---|---|---|
| Love Of My Life | 7" | Daani | 101 | 1963 | £75 | £150 | US |

## ROMAN, TONY

| Title | Format | Label | Catalogue | Year | | | Notes |
|---|---|---|---|---|---|---|---|
| Shadows On A Foggy Day | 7" EP | Festival | CEP19101 | 196– | £4 | £8 | French |

## ROMEO, MAX

| Title | Format | Label | Catalogue | Year | | | Notes |
|---|---|---|---|---|---|---|---|
| Belly Woman | 7" | Unity | UN507 | 1969 | £1.50 | £4 | Paulett & The Lovers B side |

| Title | Format | Label | Cat. No. | Year | | | Notes |
|---|---|---|---|---|---|---|---|
| Blowing In The Wind | 7" | Nu Beat | NB022 | 1969 | £2.50 | £6 | Larry Marshall B side |
| Clap Clap | 7" | Unity | UN545 | 1969 | £1.50 | £4 | |
| Don't Want To Let You Go | 7" | Caltone | TONE106 | 1967 | £4 | £8 | |
| Dream | LP | Pama | PMLP11 | 1969 | £8 | £20 | |
| It's Not The Way | 7" | Blue Cat | BS163 | 1969 | £2.50 | £6 | Al Reid B side |
| Let The Power Fall | LP | Pama | PMP2010 | 1971 | £8 | £20 | |
| Me Want Man | 7" | Blue Cat | BS161 | 1969 | £2.50 | £6 | |
| Put Me In The Mood | 7" | Island | WI3104 | 1968 | £5 | £10 | |
| Sweet Chariot | 7" | Trojan | TR656 | 1969 | £1.50 | £4 | |
| Twelfth Of Never | 7" | Island | WI3124 | 1967 | £5 | £10 | Val Bennett B side |
| Twelfth Of Never | 7" | Unity | UN511 | 1969 | £1.50 | £4 | Tartons B side |
| Walk Into The Room | 7" | Island | WI3111 | 1968 | £5 | £10 | Dawn Penn B side |
| War In A Babylon | 7" | Island | WIP6283 | 1976 | £1.50 | £4 | |
| Wet Dream | 7" | Unity | UN503 | 1969 | £1.50 | £4 | |
| Wine Her Goosie | 7" | Unity | UN516 | 1969 | £1.50 | £4 | King Cannon B side |

## ROMEOS
| Precious Memories | LP | Mark II | 1001 | 1967 | £5 | £12 | US |
|---|---|---|---|---|---|---|---|

## ROMERO, CHAN
| Hippy Hippy Shake | 7" | Columbia | DB4341 | 1959 | £30 | £60 | |
|---|---|---|---|---|---|---|---|
| My Little Ruby | 7" | Columbia | DB4405 | 1960 | £37.50 | £75 | |

## ROMNEY, HUGH 'WAVY GRAVY'
| Third Stream Humor | LP | World Pacific | WP1805 | 1962 | £6 | £15 | US |
|---|---|---|---|---|---|---|---|

## RONALD, TONY
| Tony Ronald | LP | Ariola | 86447IT | 1972 | £6 | £15 | German |
|---|---|---|---|---|---|---|---|
| Tony Ronald And His Kroners | LP | Imperial | NCLP1001 | 1966 | £30 | £60 | Dutch |

## RONALD & RUBY
| Lollipop | 7" | RCA | RCA1053 | 1958 | £6 | £12 | |
|---|---|---|---|---|---|---|---|

## RONALDE, RONNIE
| Ave Maria | 7" | Columbia | SCM5141 | 1954 | £1.50 | £4 | |
|---|---|---|---|---|---|---|---|
| Ballad Of Davy Crockett | 7" | Columbia | SCM5214 | 1956 | £2.50 | £6 | |
| Christmastide | 7" | Columbia | SCM5205 | 1955 | £1.50 | £4 | |
| Happy Whistler | 7" | Columbia | SCM5275 | 1956 | £1.50 | £4 | |
| In A Monastery Garden | 7" | Columbia | SCM5007 | 1953 | £2.50 | £6 | |
| My Starlight Lullaby | 7" | Columbia | SCM5116 | 1954 | £1.50 | £4 | |
| Robin Hood | 7" | Columbia | SCM5241 | 1956 | £2.50 | £6 | |
| Song Of The Mountains | 7" | Columbia | SCM5006 | 1953 | £2.50 | £6 | |
| We'll Always Remember | 7" | Columbia | SCM5101 | 1954 | £1.50 | £4 | |
| Yarmouth Song | 7" | Columbia | SCM5262 | 1956 | £1.50 | £4 | |

## RONDELLS
| Backbeat Number One | 7" | London | HLU9404 | 1961 | £5 | £10 | |
|---|---|---|---|---|---|---|---|
| Good Good | 7" | London | HLU8716 | 1958 | £37.50 | £75 | |

## RONDO, DON
| Blonde Bombshell | 7" | London | HLJ8641 | 1958 | £4 | £8 | |
|---|---|---|---|---|---|---|---|
| I've Got Bells On My Heart | 7" | London | HLJ8610 | 1958 | £2 | £5 | |
| Rondo Part One | 7" EP | London | REJ1154 | 1958 | £5 | £10 | |
| Rondo Part Two | 7" EP | London | REJ1155 | 1958 | £5 | £10 | |
| What A Shame | 7" | London | HLJ8567 | 1958 | £2.50 | £6 | |
| White Silver Sands | 7" | London | HLJ8466 | 1957 | £2 | £5 | |

## RONDO, GENE
| Ben Nevis | 7" | Giant | GN39 | 1968 | £1.50 | £4 | |
|---|---|---|---|---|---|---|---|

## RONETTES
| Baby I Love You | 7" | London | HLU9826 | 1964 | £1.50 | £4 | |
|---|---|---|---|---|---|---|---|
| Be My Baby | 7" | London | HLU9793 | 1963 | £1.50 | £4 | |
| Best Part Of Breaking Up | 7" | London | HLU9905 | 1964 | £2.50 | £6 | |
| Born To Be Together | 7" | London | HLU9952 | 1965 | £4 | £8 | |
| Do I Love You | 7" | London | HLU9922 | 1964 | £2 | £5 | |
| I Can Hear Music | 7" | London | HLU10087 | 1966 | £20 | £40 | |
| I'm Gonna Quit While I'm Ahead | 7" | Colpix | 646 | 1962 | £7.50 | £15 | US |
| Is This What I Get For Loving You | 7" | London | HLU9976 | 1965 | £4 | £8 | |
| Presenting The Fabulous Ronettes | LP | London | HAU8212 | 1964 | £15 | £30 | black label |
| Presenting The Fabulous Ronettes | LP | London | HAU8212 | 1964 | £37.50 | £75 | plum label |
| Presenting The Fabulous Ronettes | LP | Philles | PHLP4006 | 1964 | £37.50 | £75 | US, mono |
| Presenting The Fabulous Ronettes | LP | Philles | PHLPST4006 | 1964 | £50 | £100 | US, stereo |
| Ronettes | LP | Colpix | PXL486 | 1965 | £30 | £60 | |
| Walking In The Rain | 7" | London | HLU9931 | 1964 | £2 | £5 | |
| You Came You Saw You Conquered | 7" | A&M | AMS748 | 1969 | £1.50 | £4 | |

## RONNIE & ROY
| Big Fat Sally | 7" | Capitol | CL15028 | 1959 | £30 | £60 | |
|---|---|---|---|---|---|---|---|

## RONNIE & THE DEL AIRES
| Drag | 7" | Coral | Q72473 | 1964 | £2 | £5 | |
|---|---|---|---|---|---|---|---|

## RONNIE & THE HI-LITES
| Twistin' And Kissin' | 7" | Pye | 7N25140 | 1962 | £2.50 | £6 | |
|---|---|---|---|---|---|---|---|

## RONNIE & THE POMONA CASUALS

Interest in this group revolves around the fact that Arthur Lee sang lead vocal on the track 'Slow Jerk', which was also written by him. The music, however, bears no resemblance to that of any of the incarnations of Lee's better-known group, Love.

| | | | | | | | |
|---|---|---|---|---|---|---|---|
| Everybody Jerk | LP | Donna | 2112 | 1965 | £50 | £100 | US |

## RONNIE & THE RAINBOWS

| | | | | | | | |
|---|---|---|---|---|---|---|---|
| Loose Ends | 7" | London | HL9345 | 1961 | £2.50 | £6 | |

## RONNO

The single credited to Ronno was recorded by the musicians who featured on David Bowie's *Ziggy Stardust* album (led by much-missed guitarist Mick Ronson), with the former singer from the Rats, Benny Marshall.

| | | | | | | | |
|---|---|---|---|---|---|---|---|
| Fourth Hour Of My Sleep | 7" | Vertigo | 6059029 | 1970 | £7.50 | £15 | |

## RONNY & THE DAYTONAS

| | | | | | | | |
|---|---|---|---|---|---|---|---|
| Beach Boy | 7" | Stateside | SS432 | 1965 | £4 | £8 | |
| Bucket T | 7" EP | Columbia | ESRF1641 | 1964 | £10 | £20 | French |
| Bucket T | 7" | Stateside | SS391 | 1965 | £4 | £8 | |
| California Bound | 7" | Stateside | SS367 | 1964 | £1.50 | £4 | |
| GTO | LP | Mala | 4001 | 1964 | £15 | £30 | US |
| GTO | 7" | Stateside | SS333 | 1964 | £2.50 | £6 | |
| Sandy | LP | Mala | 4002(S) | 1964 | £10 | £25 | US |
| Sandy | 7" | Stateside | SS484 | 1966 | £2.50 | £6 | |

## RONSON, MICK

| | | | | | | | |
|---|---|---|---|---|---|---|---|
| Mick Ronson Primer | CD | Epic | ESK6076 | 1994 | £8 | £20 | US promo compilation |
| Mick Ronson Story – Heaven And Hull | CD | Epic | ESK6143 | 1994 | £8 | £20 | US promo |

## RONSTADT, LINDA

| | | | | | | | |
|---|---|---|---|---|---|---|---|
| Cry Like A Rainstorm, Howl Like The Wind | CD | Elektra | 9608722 | 1989 | £20 | £40 | ... promo box set, with cassette |

## ROOFTOP SINGERS

| | | | | | | | |
|---|---|---|---|---|---|---|---|
| Walk Right In | LP | Fontana | 680999TL | 1963 | £4 | £10 | |
| Walk Right In | 7" | Fontana | 271700TF | 1963 | £1.50 | £4 | |

## ROOM

| | | | | | | | |
|---|---|---|---|---|---|---|---|
| Pre-Flight | LP | Deram | SML1073 | 1970 | £180 | £300 | |

## ROOM 13

| | | | | | | | |
|---|---|---|---|---|---|---|---|
| Murder Mystery | 12" | Woronzow | WOO2 | 1982 | £10 | £20 | |

## ROOT BOYS

| | | | | | | | |
|---|---|---|---|---|---|---|---|
| Please Don't Stop The Wedding | 7" | Columbia | DB115 | 1970 | £2.50 | £6 | |

## ROSA, LISA

| | | | | | | | |
|---|---|---|---|---|---|---|---|
| Mama He Treats Your Daughter Mean | 7" | Ember | EMBS168 | 1963 | £1.50 | £4 | |

## ROSANO, ROSITA

| | | | | | | | |
|---|---|---|---|---|---|---|---|
| Queer Things | 7" | Melodisc | 1436 | 1957 | £1.50 | £4 | |

## ROSANOVA, JOE & THE VINEYARD

| | | | | | | | |
|---|---|---|---|---|---|---|---|
| In Dedication To The Ones We Love | LP | Astro Sonie | DAP4000 | 1968 | £30 | £60 | US |

## ROSE, ANDY

| | | | | | | | |
|---|---|---|---|---|---|---|---|
| Just Young | 7" | London | HLU8761 | 1958 | £7.50 | £15 | |

## ROSE, DUSTY

| | | | | | | | |
|---|---|---|---|---|---|---|---|
| Birds And The Bees | 7" | London | HLU8162 | 1955 | £15 | £30 | |
| Country Songs | 7" EP | London | REU1078 | 1957 | £20 | £40 | |

## ROSE, JOHNNY

| | | | | | | | |
|---|---|---|---|---|---|---|---|
| Linda Lea | 7" | Capitol | CL15166 | 1960 | £1.50 | £4 | |

## ROSE, TIM

| | | | | | | | |
|---|---|---|---|---|---|---|---|
| Love – A Kind Of Hate Story | LP | Capitol | ST673 | 1970 | £5 | £12 | US |
| Morning Dew | 7" | CBS | 202631 | 1967 | £1.50 | £4 | |
| Through Rose Coloured Glasses | LP | CBS | 63636 | 1969 | £5 | £12 | |
| Tim Rose | LP | CBS | (S)BPG63168 | 1967 | £6 | £15 | |
| Tim Rose | LP | Dawn | DNLS3062 | 1974 | £4 | £10 | |
| Tim Rose | LP | Playboy | PB101 | 1972 | £5 | £12 | US |

## ROSE, TONY

| | | | | | | | |
|---|---|---|---|---|---|---|---|
| On Banks Of Green Willow | LP | Trailer | LER2101 | 1976 | £4 | £10 | |
| Under The Greenwood Tree | LP | Trailer | LER2024 | 1971 | £4 | £10 | |
| Young Hunting | LP | Trailer | LER2013 | 1970 | £5 | £12 | |

## ROSE GARDEN

| | | | | | | | |
|---|---|---|---|---|---|---|---|
| Next Plane To London | 7" | Atlantic | 584163 | 1968 | £1.50 | £4 | |
| Rose Garden | LP | Atco | SD33225 | 1968 | £6 | £15 | US |

## ROSE OF AVALANCHE

| | | | | | | | |
|---|---|---|---|---|---|---|---|
| L.A. Rain | 12" | L.I.L. | 12LIL1 | 1985 | £2.50 | £6 | |
| Peace Inside | CD-s | Avalantic | AVE004CD | 1990 | £2 | £5 | |

## ROSENMAN, LEONARD
Lord Of The Rings ................................ LP ..... Fantasy ........... LORPD2 ............... 1978 £8 .......... £20 *US double picture disc*

## ROSIE
Lonely Blue Nights ................................. 7" ...... Coral ............. Q72426 .................. 1961 £4 ............ £8 ...............

## ROSIE & THE ORIGINALS
Angel Baby ........................................... 7" ...... London ........... HLU9266 ............... 1961 £10 ........ £20 ...............

## ROSOLINO, FRANK
I Play Trombone ..................................... LP ..... London ........... LTZN15067 ........... 1957 £8 .......... £20
That Old Black Magic ............................ 7" ...... Capitol .......... KC65001 ............... 1954 £1.50 ....... £4

## ROSS, ANNIE
Annie By Candlelight ............................ 10" LP Nixa ............. NJT504 ................ 1957 £8 .......... £20
Fish ....................................................... 7" ...... Decca ............ F10514 ............... 1955 £2.50 ...... £6
Gasser ................................................... LP ..... Vogue ............ LAE12233 ........... 1960 £8 .......... £20 ........ *with Zoot Sims*
Go To The Wall ..................................... 7" EP . Transatlantic .... TRAEP112 .......... 1964 £2 ............ £5
Nocturne For Vocalist ........................... 7" EP . Pye ............. NJE1035 .............. 1957 £2 ............ £5
Only You ............................................... 7" ...... Decca ............ F10680 ............... 1956 £2 ............ £5
Sings A Song With Mulligan .................. LP ..... Vogue ............ LAE12203 ........... 1959 £8 .......... £20 .. *with Gerry Mulligan*
With The Teacho Wiltshire Group ......... 7" EP . Esquire .......... EP1 ................... 1954 £2 ............ £5
With The Tony Crombie Fourtet ............ 7" EP . Pieces Of Eight PEP604 ................ 195– £2 ............ £5
With The Tony Kinsey Quintet ............. LP ..... XTRA ............ XTRA1049 .......... 1966 £4 .......... £10

## ROSS, ANNIE & PONY POINDEXTER
Annie Ross And Pony Poindexter ............... LP ..... Polydor ........... 583711 ................ 1968 £4 .......... £10

## ROSS, DIANA
Best Years Of My Life ........................... CD .... EMI ............. MIDEM94 ........... 1994 £15 ........ £30 ..... *promo picture disc*
Theme From Mahogany ........................ 7" ...... Tamla Motown TMG1010 ............. 1976 £2.50 ...... £6 ... *demo, picture sleeve*
Workin' Overtime .................................. CD .... Motown .......................................... 1989 £25 ....... £50 .. *US promo lunchbox, with cassette, video, biog*

## ROSS, DIANA & THE SUPREMES
Forever Came Today .............................. 7" ...... Tamla Motown TMG650 .............. 1968 £1.50 ....... £4
I'm Living In Shame ............................... 7" ...... Tamla Motown TMG695 .............. 1969 £1.50 ....... £4
In And Out of Love ................................ 7" ...... Tamla Motown TMG632 .............. 1967 £1.50 ....... £4
Live At The Talk Of The Town .............. LP ..... Tamla Motown (S)TML11070 ....... 1968 £4 .......... £10
Love Child ............................................. LP ..... Tamla Motown TML11095 ........... 1969 £4 .......... £10 ...............*mono*
Love Child ............................................. 7" ...... Tamla Motown TMG677 .............. 1968 £1.50 ....... £4
No Matter What Sign You Are ................ 7" ...... Tamla Motown TMG704 .............. 1969 £1.50 ....... £4
Reflections ............................................ LP ..... Tamla Motown (S)TML11073 ....... 1968 £4 .......... £10
Reflections ............................................ 7" ...... Tamla Motown TMG616 .............. 1967 £1.50 ....... £4
Sing And Perform Funny Girl ............... LP ..... Tamla Motown TML11088 ........... 1969 £4 .......... £10 ...............*mono*
Some Things You Never Get Used To ...... 7" ...... Tamla Motown TMG662 .............. 1968 £1.50 ....... £4

## ROSS, DIANA & THE SUPREMES & THE TEMPTATIONS
I'm Gonna Make You Love Me ................ 7" ...... Tamla Motown TMG685 .............. 1969 £1.50 ....... £4

## ROSS, Dr. ISAIAH
Call The Doctor ..................................... LP ..... Bounty ........... BY6020 ............... 1966 £5 .......... £12
Doctor Ross ........................................... LP ..... XTRA ........... XTRA1038 .......... 1966 £8 .......... £20
Flying Eagle .......................................... LP ..... Blue Horizon... LP1 .................... 1966 £400 .... £600
Live At Montreux .................................. LP ..... Polydor .......... 2460169 ............. 1972 £4 .......... £10

## ROSS, GENE
Endless Sleep ......................................... 7" ...... Parlophone ...... R4434 ................ 1958 £7.50 ..... £15 ...............

## ROSS, JACKIE
Jerk And Twine ..................................... 7" ...... Chess ............. CRS8003 .............. 1965 £5 .......... £10
Selfish One ............................................ 7" ...... Pye ............. 7N25259 .............. 1964 £10 ........ £20

## ROSS, RONNIE
Cleopatra's Needle ................................ LP ..... Fontana .......... SFJL915 .............. 1968 £8 .......... £20
Double Event ........................................ LP ..... Parlophone ...... PMC1079 ............. 1959 £10 ........ £25

## ROSSELSON, LEON
Palaces Of Gold ..................................... LP ..... Acorn ............ CF249 ................. 1975 £6 .......... £15

## ROSSELSON, LEON & ADRIAN MITCHELL
Laugh, A Song, And A Hand Grenade ........ LP ..... Transatlantic .... TRA171 ............... 1968 £5 .......... £12 ...............

## ROSSELSON, LEON & ROY BAILEY
That's Not The Way It's Got To Be .......... LP ..... Acorn ............ CF251 ................. 1975 £4 .......... £10

## ROSSELSON, LEON, ROY BAILEY, MARTIN CARTHY
Word Is Hugga Mugga Chugga Humbugga LP ..... Trailer ............ LER3015 ............... 1971 £4 .......... £10
Boom Chit .............................

## ROSSI, NITA
Here I Go Again ..................................... 7" ...... Piccadilly ........ 7N35307 .............. 1966 £5 .......... £10
Misty Blue ............................................ 7" ...... Piccadilly ........ 7N35384 .............. 1967 £1.50 ....... £4
Untrue Unfaithful .................................. 7" ...... Piccadilly ........ 7N35258 .............. 1965 £2.50 ...... £6

## ROSSI & FROST
| | | | | | | | |
|---|---|---|---|---|---|---|---|
| Jealousy | 12" | Vertigo | VERX24 | 1985 | £2.50 | £6 | |
| Modern Romance | 12" | Vertigo | VERX17 | 1985 | £3 | £8 | |

## ROSTILL, JOHN
| | | | | | | |
|---|---|---|---|---|---|---|
| Funny Old World | 7" | Columbia | DB8794 | 1971 | £20 | £40 |

## ROTARY CONNECTION
| | | | | | | |
|---|---|---|---|---|---|---|
| Aladdin | LP | Chess | CRLS4547 | 1969 | £4 | £10 |
| Rotary Connection | LP | Chess | CRL4538 | 1968 | £4 | £10 |
| Songs | LP | Chess | CRLS4551 | 1969 | £4 | £10 |

## ROTATIONS
'Heavies' is one of several early Frank Zappa productions.

| | | | | | | | |
|---|---|---|---|---|---|---|---|
| Heavies | 7" | Original Sound | 41 | 1964 | £75 | £150 | US |

## ROTH, DAVE LEE
| | | | | | | | |
|---|---|---|---|---|---|---|---|
| Yankee Rose | 7" | Warner Bros | W8656 | 1986 | £2 | £5 | ..... shaped picture disc |
| Sensible Shoes | 5" | Warner Bros | W0016P | 1991 | £2.50 | £6 | ..... shaped picture disc |
| Skyscraper | CD | Warner Bros | | 1988 | £8 | £20 | US promo picture disc |

## ROTHCHILDS
| | | | | | | |
|---|---|---|---|---|---|---|
| Artificial City | 7" | Decca | F12488 | 1966 | £2.50 | £6 |
| You've Made Your Choice | 7" | Decca | F12411 | 1966 | £2 | £5 |

## ROULETTES
The Roulettes were formed as a backing group for Adam Faith, when the singer attempted to meet the challenge of the Beatles head-on by adopting the beat style himself. The Roulettes tried very hard to establish an independent career for themselves as well, but little of the group's material was sufficiently distinctive. The closest they came to a hit was with 'Long Cigarette', which is a memorable song for all that it is closely modelled on a John Lennon performance, but a BBC ban put a stop to its progress up the charts. Guitarist Russ Ballard and drummer Bob Henrit were subsequently members of Argent.

| | | | | | | |
|---|---|---|---|---|---|---|
| Bad Time | 7" | Parlophone | R5110 | 1964 | £2 | £5 |
| Help Me Help Myself | 7" | Fontana | TF876 | 1967 | £2.50 | £6 |
| Hully Gully Slip And Slide | 7" | Pye | 7N15467 | 1962 | £2.50 | £6 |
| I Can't Stop | 7" | Oak | RGJ205 | 1965 | £20 | £40 |
| I Can't Stop | 7" | Parlophone | R5461 | 1966 | £2 | £5 |
| I Hope He Breaks Your Heart | 7" | Parlophone | R5278 | 1965 | £2 | £5 |
| I'll Remember Tonight | 7" | Parlophone | R5148 | 1964 | £2 | £5 |
| Long Cigarette | 7" | Parlophone | R5382 | 1965 | £2 | £5 |
| Rhyme Boy Rhyme | 7" | Fontana | TF822 | 1967 | £2.50 | £6 |
| Soon You'll Be Leaving | 7" | Parlophone | R5072 | 1963 | £2 | £5 |
| Stakes And Chips | LP | Parlophone | PMC1257 | 1965 | £250 | £400 |
| Stubborn Kind Of Fellow | 7" | Parlophone | R5218 | 1964 | £2 | £5 |
| Tracks Of My Tears | 7" | Parlophone | R5419 | 1966 | £2.50 | £6 |

## ROUND ROBIN
| | | | | | | |
|---|---|---|---|---|---|---|
| Kick That Little Foot Sally Ann | 7" | London | HLU9908 | 1964 | £10 | £20 |

## ROUSE, CHARLIE
| | | | | | | | |
|---|---|---|---|---|---|---|---|
| Bossa Nova Bacchanal | LP | Blue Note | BLP/BST84119 | 1962 | £10 | £25 | |
| Chase Is On | LP | Parlophone | PMC1090 | 1959 | £6 | £15 | with Paul Quinichette |
| Takin' Care Of Business | LP | Jazzland | JLP19 | 1960 | £8 | £20 | |

## ROUTERS
| | | | | | | | |
|---|---|---|---|---|---|---|---|
| A Ooga | 7" | Warner Bros | WB108 | 1963 | £1.50 | £4 | |
| Charge! | LP | Warner Bros | WM/WS8162 | 1964 | £8 | £20 | |
| Let's Go | 7" EP | Warner Bros | WEP1418 | 1962 | £7.50 | £15 | French |
| Let's Go | 7" | Warner Bros | WB77 | 1962 | £1.50 | £4 | |
| Let's Go With The Routers | LP | Warner Bros | WM/WS8126 | 1963 | £8 | £20 | |
| Make It Snappy | 7" | Warner Bros | WB91 | 1963 | £1.50 | £4 | |
| Play 1963's Great Instrumentals | LP | Warner Bros | WM/WS8144 | 1964 | £8 | £20 | |
| Stamp And Shake | 7" | Warner Bros | WB139 | 1964 | £1.50 | £4 | |
| Stingray | 7" | Warner Bros | WB97 | 1963 | £1.50 | £4 | |

## ROUTH, JONATHAN
| | | | | | | |
|---|---|---|---|---|---|---|
| Candid Mike | 7" EP | Pye | NEP24128 | 1960 | £2 | £5 |

## ROVERS
| | | | | | | |
|---|---|---|---|---|---|---|
| Ichi Bon Tami Dachi | 7" | Capitol | CL14283 | 1955 | £25 | £50 |

## ROWAN & MARTIN
| | | | | | | |
|---|---|---|---|---|---|---|
| Rowan & Martin's Laugh-In | LP | CBS | 63490 | 1969 | £4 | £10 |

## ROWDIES
| | | | | | | |
|---|---|---|---|---|---|---|
| She's No Angel | 7" | Teenage Depression | TD1/2 | 1979 | £1.50 | £4 |

## ROWE, NORMIE
| | | | | | | | |
|---|---|---|---|---|---|---|---|
| So Much Love | LP | Sunshine Festival | L32144 | 1966 | £8 | £20 | Australian |

## ROWELY, MAJOR
| | | | | | | |
|---|---|---|---|---|---|---|
| There's A Riot Going On | 7" | Stateside | SS438 | 1965 | £1.50 | £4 |

## ROWLAND, KEVIN
Tonight............................................ CD-s .. Mercury........... ROWCD1............. 1988 £2............ £5 ..............................

## ROWLAND, STEVE
So Sad............................................ 7" ..... Fontana........... TF844.................... 1967 £2............ £5 ..............................

## ROWSOME, LEO
Classics Of Irish Piping Vol. 1.................. LP ..... Topic............. 12T259 ............... 1976 £4............ £10 .............................
Classics Of Irish Piping Vol. 3.................. LP ..... Topic............. 12T322 ............... 1977 £4............ £10 .............................
Ri Na Bpiobari .................................. LP ..... Claddagh......... CC1 ................... 1959 £10.......... £25 ........................ Irish

## ROXETTE
Big L ............................................ CD-s .. EMI............... CDEM204 ............ 1991 £5............ £12 .............................
Church Of Your Heart ........................... CD-s .. EMI............... CDEM227 ............ 1992 £2............ £5 ............ 2 versions
Dance Passion ................................... LP ..... EMI............... 1362611 .............. 1987 £25.......... £50 .............. Swedish
Dressed For Success ............................. CD-s .. EMI............... CDEM162 ............ 1990 £10.......... £20 .............................
Dressed For Success ............................. CD-s .. EMI............... CDEM96 ............. 1989 £12.50..... £25 .............................
Dressed For Success ............................. 12" .... EMI............... 12EM96 .............. 1989 £2.50....... £6 .............................
Fading Like A Flower ............................ CD-s .. EMI............... CDEM190 ............ 1991 £5............ £12 .............................
How Do You Do .................................. CD-s .. EMI............... CDEM241 ............ 1992 £2............ £5 .............................
It Must Have Been Love .......................... CD-s .. EMI............... CDEM141 ............ 1990 £2.50....... £6 .............................
It Must Have Been Love .......................... CD-s .. EMI............... CDEM285 ............ 1993 £2............ £5 .............................
Joyride ......................................... CD-s .. EMI............... CDEM177 ............ 1991 £2............ £5 .............................
Listen To Your Heart ............................ CD-s .. EMI............... CDEM108 ............ 1990 £12.50..... £25 .............................
Listen To Your Heart ............................ CD-s .. EMI............... CDEM149 ............ 1990 £4............ £10 .............................
Listen To Your Heart ............................ 12" .... EMI............... 12EM108 ............ 1990 £2.50....... £6 .............................
Look ............................................ CD-s .. EMI............... CDEM87 ............. 1989 £12.50..... £25 .............................
Look ............................................ 7" ..... EMI............... EM87 ................ 1989 £15.......... £30 ............ red vinyl
Look ............................................ 12" .... EMI............... 12EM87 .............. 1989 £2.50....... £6 .............................
Look ............................................ 12" .... EMI............... 12EM87 .............. 1989 £25.......... £50 ............ red vinyl
Look Sharp ...................................... LP ..... EMI............................................ 1989 £50.......... £100 . European picture disc
Look Sharp ...................................... CD..... EMI............... CDEMC3557 ........ 1989 £50.......... £100 ....picture disc, special cover
Pearls Of Passion ............................... LP ..... EMI............... 1362451 .............. 1986 £20.......... £40 .............. Swedish
Pearls Of Passion ............................... CD..... EMI............... 7464592 .............. 1986 £37.50..... £75 .............. Swedish
Queen Of Rain................................... CD-s .. EMI............... CDEM253 ............ 1992 £2............ £5 ............ 2 versions
Spending My Time............................... CD-s .. EMI............... CDEM215 ............ 1991 £2............ £5 .............................

## ROXY MUSIC
Atlantic Years 1973–1980 ....................... CD..... Editions EG..... 8158492 .............. 1983 £5............ £12 .............................
Jealous Guy..................................... CD-s .. Virgin ........... CDT8.................. 1988 £2............ £5 ............ 3" single
Love Is The Drug ............................... CD-s .. Editions EG..... EGOCD55............ 1990 £2............ £5 .............................
Love Is The Drug ............................... 12" .... Editions EG..... EGOX26 .............. 1986 £3............ £8 ............... promo
Over You/Eight Miles High ...................... 12" .... Polydor........... POSPX93 ............. 1980 £3............ £8 ............... promo
Siren ........................................... CD..... Polydor........... 8230202 .............. 1984 £3............ £12 .............................
Trash ........................................... 12" .... Polydor........... POSPX32 ............. 1978 £3............ £8 ............... promo
Virginia Plain .................................. 7" ..... Island ........... WIP6144.............. 1972 £5............ £10 ......... picture sleeve

## ROY, I
Blackman Time................................... 7" ..... Downtown...... DT503 ................ 1973 £1.50....... £4 .............................
Can't Conquer Rasta ............................ LP ..... Justice ........... JUSTLP008 ........... 1977 £5............ £12 .............................
Cancer .......................................... LP ..... Front Line ....... 4001 ................. 1979 £5............ £12 .............................
Crisus Time ..................................... LP ..... Caroline ......... CA2011 .............. 1976 £5............ £12 .............................
Dread Baldhead ................................. LP ..... Klik ............. KLP9020 ............. 1976 £5............ £12 .............................
General ......................................... LP ..... Front Line ....... FLD6002.............. 1978 £6............ £15 .............. double
Godfather ....................................... LP ..... Third World ..... 930 .................. 1978 £4............ £10 .............................
Heart Of A Lion ................................ LP ..... Front Line ....... FL1001 .............. 1978 £5............ £12 .............................
Hell And Sorrow ................................ LP ..... Trojan........... TRLS71 .............. 1973 £6............ £15 .............................
I Roy ........................................... LP ..... Trojan........... TRLS91 .............. 1974 £6............ £15 .............................
Monkey Fashion................................. 7" ..... Technique....... TE930 ............... 1973 £1.50....... £4 .............................
Musical Drum Sound ............................ 7" ..... Harry J.......... HJ6655 .............. 1973 £1.50....... £4 .............................
Musical Shark Attack ........................... LP ..... Virgin ........... V2075 ............... 1977 £5............ £12 .............................
Outformer Parker ............................... 7" ..... Attack ........... ATT8102 ............ 1975 £1.50....... £4 .............................
Presenting I Roy ................................ LP ..... Trojan........... TRLS63 .............. 1973 £6............ £15 .............................
Ten Commandments ............................. LP ..... Front Line ....... FL1028 .............. 1978 £5............ £12 .............................
Welding ......................................... 7" ..... Philips........... 6006479 .............. 1975 £1.50....... £4 .............................
Whap'n Bap'n .................................. LP ..... Virgin ........... V2164 ............... 1980 £4............ £10 .............................
World On Fire ................................... LP ..... Front Line ....... FL1033 .............. 1978 £5............ £12 .............................
Yaha Ma Ride .................................. 7" ..... Atra ............. ATRA17 .............. 1974 £1.50....... £4 .............................

## ROY, LEE
Oh Ee Baby...................................... 7" ..... Island ........... WI251 ................ 1965 £5............ £10 .............................

## ROY, U
U Roy is the major pioneer where the art of Jamaican DJ music is concerned. It was U Roy who first scored a series of successes with singles that used the stripped-down backing tracks from other people's hits as a springboard for his spoken rants. This 'toasting' style rapidly became all-pervasive in reggae and was undoubtedly a significant influence on the later American rapping scene.

Dread In A Babylon.............................. LP ..... Virgin ........... V2048 ............... 1976 £5............ £12 .............................
Dreadlocks In Jamaica .......................... LP ..... Love And Live. LALP05 .............. 1978 £4............ £10 ... with other artists
Festival Wise .................................... 7" ..... Dynamic......... DYN448 ............. 1972 £1.50....... £4 .............................
Flashing My Whip ............................... 7" ..... Duke Reid ..... DR2519 .............. 1971 £2.50....... £6 .............................
Hard Feeling .................................... 7" ..... Gay Feet ....... GS210 ............... 1973 £1.50....... £4 .............................
Jah Son Of Africa ............................... LP ..... Live And Love. LALP08 .............. 1977 £5............ £12 .............................
Love I Tender................................... 7" ..... Duke ........... DU105............... 1970 £1.50....... £4 .....Joya Landis B side
Natty Rebel ..................................... LP ..... Virgin ........... V2059 ............... 1976 £5............ £12 .............................

| | | | | | | |
|---|---|---|---|---|---|---|
| Rasta Ambassador | LP | Virgin | V2092 | 1977 £5 | £12 | |
| Rule The Nation | 7" | Duke Reid | DR2510 | 1970 £2.50 | £6 | *Nora Dean B side* |
| Tom Drunk | 7" | Duke Reid | DR2517 | 1971 £2.50 | £6 | |
| True True | 7" | Duke Reid | DR2518 | 1971 £2.50 | £6 | |
| U Roy | LP | Attack | ATLP1006 | 1973 £6 | £15 | |
| Version Galore | LP | Front Line | FL1018 | 1978 £5 | £12 | |
| Version Galore | LP | Trojan | TBL161 | 1971 £6 | £15 | *with other artists* |
| Version Galore | 7" | Duke Reid | DR2515 | 1970 £2.50 | £6 | *Tommy McCook B side* |
| Wake The Town | 7" | Duke Reid | DR2509 | 1970 £2.50 | £6 | |
| Wear You To The Ball | 7" | Duke Reid | DR2513 | 1970 £2.50 | £6 | *Earl Lindo B side* |
| You'll Never Get Away | 7" | Duke Reid | DR2514 | 1970 £2.50 | £6 | *Tommy McCook B side* |

## ROY & ANNETTE
| | | | | | | |
|---|---|---|---|---|---|---|
| My Baby | 7" | R&B | JB107 | 1963 £5 | £10 | |

## ROY & ENID
| | | | | | | |
|---|---|---|---|---|---|---|
| He'll Have To Go | 7" | Coxsone | CS7069 | 1968 £5 | £10 | |
| Reggae For Days | 7" | Coxsone | CS7088 | 1969 £5 | £10 | |
| Rockin' Time | 7" | Coxsone | CS7063 | 1968 £5 | £10 | |

## ROY & MILLIE
| | | | | | | |
|---|---|---|---|---|---|---|
| Cherry I Love You | 7" | Black Swan | WI409 | 1964 £5 | £10 | |
| Oh Merna | 7" | Black Swan | WI410 | 1964 £5 | £10 | *Don Drummond B side* |
| Oh Shirley | 7" | Black Swan | WI427 | 1964 £5 | £10 | |
| Over And Over | 7" | Blue Beat | BB154 | 1963 £6 | £12 | |
| There'll Come A Day | 7" | Island | WI090 | 1963 £5 | £10 | |
| We'll Meet | 7" | Island | WI005 | 1962 £5 | £10 | *Roland Alphonso B side* |

## ROY & PATSY
| | | | | | | |
|---|---|---|---|---|---|---|
| In Your Arms Dear | 7" | Blue Beat | BB118 | 1962 £6 | £12 | |

## ROY & PAULINE
| | | | | | | |
|---|---|---|---|---|---|---|
| Have You Seen My Baby | 7" | Island | WI067 | 1963 £5 | £10 | |

## ROY & THE DUKE ALL STARS
| | | | | | | |
|---|---|---|---|---|---|---|
| Pretty Blue Eyes | 7" | Blue Cat | BS113 | 1968 £4 | £8 | |
| Train | 7" | Blue Cat | BS117 | 1968 £4 | £8 | |

## ROY & YVONNE
| | | | | | | |
|---|---|---|---|---|---|---|
| Little Girl | 7" | Blue Beat | BB258 | 1964 £6 | £12 | |
| Two Roads | 7" | Black Swan | WI436 | 1964 £5 | £10 | |

## ROYAL, BILLY JOE
| | | | | | | |
|---|---|---|---|---|---|---|
| Down In The Boondocks | 7" EP | CBS | 6206 | 1965 £5 | £10 | *French* |
| Down In The Boondocks | 7" | CBS | 201802 | 1965 £1.50 | £4 | |
| Heart's Desire | 7" | CBS | 202087 | 1966 £15 | £30 | |
| Introducing Billy Joe Royal | LP | CBS | BPG62590 | 1966 £4 | £10 | |
| Never In A Hundred Years | 7" | Oriole | CB1751 | 1962 £2.50 | £6 | |
| Yo Yo | 7" | CBS | 202548 | 1967 £1.50 | £4 | |

## ROYAL, JAMES
| | | | | | | |
|---|---|---|---|---|---|---|
| Call My Name | LP | CBS | 63780 | 1967 £4 | £10 | |
| Hey Little Boy | 7" | CBS | 3450 | 1968 £5 | £10 | |
| Light And Shade | LP | Carnaby | CNLS6008 | 1971 £8 | £20 | |
| Send Out Love | 7" | CBS | 4463 | 1969 £2.50 | £6 | |
| She's About A Mover | 7" | Parlophone | R5290 | 1965 £2.50 | £6 | |
| Woman Called Sorrow | 7" | CBS | 3624 | 1968 £2.50 | £6 | |
| Work Song | 7" | Parlophone | R5383 | 1965 £4 | £8 | |

## ROYAL, ROBBIE
| | | | | | | |
|---|---|---|---|---|---|---|
| Only Me | 7" | Mercury | MF923 | 1965 £2 | £5 | |

## ROYAL FLAIRS
| | | | | | | |
|---|---|---|---|---|---|---|
| Rare Recordings | LP | Unlimited Productions | UPLP1007 | 1988 £5 | £12 | US |

## ROYAL GUARDSMEN
| | | | | | | |
|---|---|---|---|---|---|---|
| Return Of The Red Baron | LP | London | HAP/SHP8351 | 1968 £5 | £12 | |
| Snoopy And His Friends | LP | Laurie | (S)LLP2042 | 1967 £5 | £12 | US |
| Snoopy For President | LP | Laurie | SLLP2046 | 1968 £5 | £12 | US |
| Snoopy Vs. The Red Baron | 7" EP | Vogue | INT18118 | 1967 £10 | £20 | French |
| Snoopy Vs. The Red Baron | 7" | Stateside | SS574 | 1967 £1.50 | £4 | |
| Snoopy Vs. The Red Baron | LP | Stateside | (S)SL10202 | 1967 £5 | £12 | |
| Wednesday | 7" | Stateside | SS2051 | 1967 £1.50 | £4 | |

## ROYAL HOLIDAYS
| | | | | | | |
|---|---|---|---|---|---|---|
| Margaret | 7" | London | HLU8722 | 1958 £25 | £50 | |

## ROYAL JOKERS
| | | | | | | |
|---|---|---|---|---|---|---|
| Rock And Roll Spectacular | LP | Dawn | 1119 | 195– £10 | £25 | US |

## ROYAL PLAYBOYS
| | | | | | | |
|---|---|---|---|---|---|---|
| Spirituals And Jubilees | 10" LP | Waldorf | 33136 | 195– £8 | £20 | US |

## ROYAL ROCKERS
Jet II .......................................... 7" ...... Top Rank ....... JAR329 ................. 1960 £2 ........ £5

## ROYAL SERVANTS
We ........................................... LP ..... Elite ............... PLPS30130 ............ 1969 £10 ........ £25 ................ German

## ROYAL TEENS
Little Cricket ........................... 7" ...... Capitol .......... CL15068 ................. 1959 £6 ........ £12
Music Gems ............................. LP ..... Tru–Gems ...... TG1001 ................... 1966 £8 ........ £20 ...................... US
Newies But Oldies ................... LP ..... Musicor .......... MS3186 .................. 1969 £10 ........ £25 ...................... US
Short Shorts ............................. 7" ...... HMV ............. POP454 .................. 1958 £10 ........ £20

## ROYALETTES
Elegant Sound Of The Royalettes ........... LP ..... MGM ............ C8028 ................. 1966 £10 ........ £25
I Want To Meet Him ................ 7" ...... MGM ............ MGM1292 ......... 1965 £2.50 ........ £6
It's A Big Mistake ..................... 7" ...... MGM ............ MGM1324 ......... 1966 £2.50 ........ £6
It's Gonna Take A Miracle ........ LP ..... MGM ............ (S)E4332 ............ 1965 £10 ........ £25 ...................... US
It's Gonna Take A Miracle ........ 7" ...... MGM ............ MGM1279 ......... 1965 £7.50 ........ £15
Poor Boy .................................. 7" ...... MGM ............ MGM1272 ......... 1965 £2.50 ........ £6
River Of Tears .......................... 7" ...... Transatlantic ... BIG106 ............... 1968 £1.50 ........ £4
You Bring Me Down .................. 7" ...... MGM ............ MGM1302 ......... 1966 £5 ........ £10

## ROYALS
Israel Be Wise .......................... LP ..... Ballistic .......... UAG30206 ........... 1978 £5 ........ £12
Never Gonna Give You Up ........ 7" ...... Duke ............ DU29 ................... 1969 £2 ........ £5
Never See Come See .................. 7" ...... Amalgamated ... AMG831 ............. 1968 £4 ........ £8 ... Cannonball Bryan
B side
Pick Out Me Eye ...................... 7" ...... Trojan ............ TR662 ............... 1969 £2.50 ........ £6
Pick Up The Pieces ................... LP ..... Magnum ......... DEAD1004 ........... 1977 £5 ........ £12
Save Mama ............................... 7" ...... Blue Beat ........ BB259 ................ 1964 £6 ........ £12
Ten Years After ........................ LP ..... United Artists .. UAS30189 .......... 1978 £5 ........ £12

## ROYALTONES
Flamingo Express ...................... 7" ...... London ........... HLU9296 ............. 1961 £4 ........ £8
Holy Smokes ............................ 7" ...... Stateside ........ SS309 ................ 1964 £2.50 ........ £6
Poor Boy .................................. 7" ...... London ........... HLJ8744 ............. 1958 £5 ........ £10

## ROYCE, EARL & THE OLYMPICS
Guess Things Happen That Way .............. 7" ...... Parlophone ..... R5261 ............... 1965 £4 ........ £8
Que Sera Sera ........................... 7" ...... Columbia ........ DB7433 .............. 1964 £4 ........ £8

## ROZA, LITA
Bell Bottom Blues ..................... 7" ...... Decca ............. F10269 .............. 1954 £2.50 ........ £6
Between The Devil And The Deep Blue LP ..... Decca ............. LK4218 .............. 1957 £6 ........ £15
Sea
Between The Devil And The Deep Blue 7" EP . Decca ............. DFE6443 ............ 1957 £2.50 ........ £6
Sea
But Love Me ............................. 7" ...... Decca ............. F10761 .............. 1956 £1.50 ........ £4
Changing Partners ..................... 7" ...... Decca ............. F10240 .............. 1954 £2 ........ £5
Heartbeat ................................. 7" ...... Decca ............. F10427 .............. 1954 £2 ........ £4
Hey There ................................ 7" ...... Decca ............. F10611 .............. 1955 £4 ........ £8
Innismore ................................ 7" ...... Decca ............. F10792 .............. 1956 £1.50 ........ £4
Jimmy Unknown ....................... 7" ...... Decca ............. F10679 .............. 1956 £4 ........ £8
Julie ......................................... 7" ...... Decca ............. F10830 .............. 1956 £1.50 ........ £4
Let Me Go Lover ...................... 7" ...... Decca ............. F10431 .............. 1955 £2 ........ £5
Listening In The After Hours ...... 10" LP Decca ............. LF1243 .............. 1956 £8 ........ £20
Lita Roza ................................. 7" EP . Decca ............. DFE6399 ............ 1957 £4 ........ £8
Love Is The Answer ................... LP ..... Decca ............. LK4171 .............. 1957 £6 ........ £15
Lucky Lips ................................ 7" ...... Decca ............. F10861 .............. 1957 £2 ........ £5
Mama Doll Song ....................... 7" ...... Decca ............. F10393 .............. 1954 £1.50 ........ £4
Man In The Raincoat ................ 7" ...... Decca ............. F10541 .............. 1955 £1.50 ........ £4
Me On A Carousel ..................... LP ..... Pye .............. NPL18020/ .......... 1958 £4 ........ £10
NSPL83003 ............
Presenting ................................ 10" LP Decca ............. LF1187 .............. 1954 £8 ........ £20
Secret Love .............................. 7" ...... Decca ............. F10277 .............. 1954 £2 ........ £5
Selection .................................. 7" EP . Decca ............. DFE6386 ............ 1956 £5 ........ £10
Tomorrow ................................ 7" ...... Decca ............. F10479 .............. 1955 £2 ........ £5
Tonight My Heart She Is Crying ............. 7" ...... Decca ............. F10884 .............. 1957 £1.50 ........ £4
Too Young To Go Steady ........... 7" ...... Decca ............. F10728 .............. 1956 £1.50 ........ £4
Two Hearts, Two Kisses ............. 7" ...... Decca ............. F10536 .............. 1955 £2 ........ £5

## RUB-A-DUBS
Without Love .......................... 7" ...... Blue Beat ........ BB304 ............... 1965 £6 ........ £12

## RUBBER BAND
Cream Song Book ...................... LP ..... Major Minor ... SMLP5045 ............ 1969 £4 ........ £10
Hendrix Song Book .................. LP ..... Major Minor ... SMLP5048 ............ 1969 £4 ........ £10

## RUBBER BOOTZ
Joy Ride ................................... 7" ...... Deram ............ DM134 ................. 1967 £2 ........ £5

## RUBBER BUCKET
The Rubber Bucket single is actually the work of Gary Glitter.

We Are Living In One Place ...................... 7" ...... MCA ............. MK5006 ................. 1969 £4 ........ £8

## RUBBER MEMORY

| | | | | | | | |
|---|---|---|---|---|---|---|---|
| Welcome | LP | RPC | 69401 | 1966 | £10 | £25 | US |

## RUBEN & THE JETS

| | | | | | | | |
|---|---|---|---|---|---|---|---|
| Con Safos | LP | Mercury | SRM1694 | 1973 | £5 | £12 | US |
| For Real | LP | Mercury | SRM1659 | 1973 | £6 | £15 | US |

## RUBY & THE ROMANTICS

| | | | | | | | |
|---|---|---|---|---|---|---|---|
| Baby Come Home | 7" | London | HLR9916 | 1964 | £2.50 | £6 | |
| Greatest Hits | LP | London | HAR8282 | 1966 | £10 | £25 | |
| Hey There Lonely Boy | 7" EP | London | RER1427 | 1964 | £15 | £30 | |
| Hey There Lonely Boy | 7" | London | HLR9771 | 1963 | £2 | £5 | |
| More Than Yesterday | LP | ABC | S638 | 1968 | £6 | £15 | US |
| My Summer Love | 7" | London | HLR9734 | 1963 | £2 | £5 | |
| Our Day Will Come | LP | London | HAR8078 | 1963 | £15 | £30 | |
| Our Day Will Come | 7" EP | London | RER1389 | 1963 | £15 | £30 | |
| Our Day Will Come | 7" | London | HLR9679 | 1963 | £1.50 | £4 | |
| Our Everlasting Love | 7" | London | HLR9881 | 1964 | £2 | £5 | |
| Ruby And The Romantics | LP | Kapp | KL1526/KS3526 | 1967 | £6 | £15 | US |
| Till Then | LP | Kapp | KL1341/KS3341 | 1963 | £10 | £25 | US |
| When You're Young And In Love | 7" | London | HLR9935 | 1964 | £2 | £5 | |
| Young Wings Can Fly | 7" | London | HLR9801 | 1963 | £2 | £5 | |
| Your Baby Doesn't Love You Anymore | 7" | London | HLR9972 | 1965 | £2 | £5 | |

## RUDE BOYS

| | | | | | | | |
|---|---|---|---|---|---|---|---|
| Rock Steady Massachusetts | 7" | Island | WI3088 | 1967 | £5 | £10 | |

## RUDIES

| | | | | | | | |
|---|---|---|---|---|---|---|---|
| 7-11 | 7" | Blue Cat | BS107 | 1968 | £4 | £8 | |
| Brixton Market | 7" | Fab | FAB104 | 1969 | £1.50 | £4 | |
| Cupid | 7" | Blue Cat | BS109 | 1968 | £4 | £8 | Rico B side |
| Engine 59 | 7" | Nu Beat | NB005 | 1968 | £1.50 | £4 | |
| Give Me The Rights | 7" | Fab | FAB70 | 1968 | £1.50 | £4 | |
| I Wanna Go Home | 7" | Fab | FAB46 | 1968 | £2 | £5 | |
| Mighty Meaty | 7" | Fab | FAB71 | 1968 | £1.50 | £4 | |
| Train To Vietnam | 7" | Nu Beat | NB001 | 1968 | £2 | £5 | |

## RUDIMENTARY PENI

| | | | | | | | |
|---|---|---|---|---|---|---|---|
| Media Person | 7" | Outer Himalayan | OH003 | 1981 | £2 | £5 | |

## RUDY & SKETTO

| | | | | | | | |
|---|---|---|---|---|---|---|---|
| ABC Boogie | 7" | Dice | CC2 | 1962 | £5 | £10 | |
| Hold The Fire | 7" | Dice | CC16 | 1963 | £5 | £10 | |
| Little Schoolgirl | 7" | Dice | CC7 | 1962 | £5 | £10 | |
| Minna | 7" | Blue Beat | BB252 | 1964 | £6 | £12 | |
| Mr. Postman | 7" | Dice | CC10 | 1963 | £5 | £10 | |
| Oh Dolly | 7" | Blue Beat | BB310 | 1965 | £6 | £12 | |
| See What You Done | 7" | Blue Beat | BB297 | 1965 | £6 | £12 | |
| Show Me The Way To Go Home | 7" | Blue Beat | BB208 | 1964 | £6 | £12 | |
| Summer Is Just Around The Corner | 7" | Dice | CC5 | 1962 | £5 | £10 | |
| Ten Thousand Miles From Home | 7" | Blue Beat | BB230 | 1964 | £6 | £12 | |
| Was It Me | 7" | Blue Beat | BB198 | 1963 | £6 | £12 | |
| We Are So Happy | 7" | Dice | CC19 | 1963 | £5 | £10 | |

## RUFF, RAY & THE CHECKMATES

| | | | | | | | |
|---|---|---|---|---|---|---|---|
| I Took A Liking To You | 7" | London | HLU9889 | 1964 | £5 | £10 | |

## RUFFIN, BRUCE

| | | | | | | | |
|---|---|---|---|---|---|---|---|
| Rain | LP | Trojan | TRL23 | 1971 | £4 | £10 | |

## RUFFIN, DAVID

| | | | | | | | |
|---|---|---|---|---|---|---|---|
| Feelin' Good | LP | Tamla Motown | (S)TML11139 | 1970 | £5 | £12 | |
| I've Lost Everything I Ever Loved | 7" | Tamla Motown | TMG711 | 1969 | £1.50 | £4 | |
| My Whole World Ended | LP | Tamla Motown | (S)TML11118 | 1969 | £5 | £12 | |
| Whole World Ended | 7" | Tamla Motown | TMG689 | 1969 | £1.50 | £4 | |

## RUFFIN, JIMMY

| | | | | | | | |
|---|---|---|---|---|---|---|---|
| Don't Let Him Take Your Love From Me | 7" | Tamla Motown | TMG664 | 1968 | £1.50 | £4 | |
| Don't You Miss Me A Little Bit Baby | 7" | Tamla Motown | TMG617 | 1967 | £2 | £5 | |
| Gonna Give Her All The Love I Got | 7" | Tamla Motown | TMG603 | 1967 | £1.50 | £4 | |
| I'll Say Forever My Love | 7" | Tamla Motown | TMG649 | 1968 | £1.50 | £4 | |
| I've Passed This Way Before | 7" | Tamla Motown | TMG593 | 1967 | £1.50 | £4 | |
| Jimmy Ruffin Way | LP | Tamla Motown | (S)TML11048 | 1967 | £6 | £15 | |
| Ruff 'n' Ready | LP | Tamla Motown | (S)TML11106 | 1969 | £6 | £15 | |
| What Becomes Of The Broken Hearted | 7" | Tamla Motown | TMG577 | 1966 | £1.50 | £4 | |

## RUFUS ZUPHALL

| | | | | | | | |
|---|---|---|---|---|---|---|---|
| Phallobst | LP | Pilz | 20210995 | 1971 | £10 | £25 | German |
| Weiss Der Teufel | LP | Good Will | GLS10001 | 1969 | £75 | £150 | German |

## RUGBYS

| | | | | | | | |
|---|---|---|---|---|---|---|---|
| Hot Cargo | LP | Amazon | 1000 | 1969 | £15 | £30 | US |

## RUGOLO, PETE

| | | | | | | | |
|---|---|---|---|---|---|---|---|
| Adventures In Rhythm | LP | Philips | BBL7035 | 1955 | £5 | £12 | |
| Behind Brigitte Bardot | LP | Warner Bros | WM4001/WS8001 | 1960 | £4 | £10 | |

| | | | | | | | |
|---|---|---|---|---|---|---|---|
| Music From Richard Diamond | LP | Mercury | MMC14034/<br>CMS18025 | 1960 | £5 | £12 | |
| Out On A Limb | LP | Emarcy | EJL1274 | 1958 | £4 | £10 | |
| Percussion At Work | LP | Mercury | MMB12004 | 1959 | £4 | £10 | |
| Pete Rugolo | LP | Philips | BBL7069 | 1956 | £5 | £12 | |
| Pete Rugolo And His Orchestra | 10" LP | Philips | BBR8024 | 1954 | £4 | £10 | |
| Pete Rugolo Orchestra | LP | Emarcy | EJL1254 | 1957 | £5 | £12 | |
| Reeds In Hi Fi | LP | Mercury | MMC14012 | 1959 | £4 | £10 | |
| Rugolo Plays Kenton | LP | Mercury | BMS17000 | 1959 | £6 | £15 | |
| Rugolo Plays Kenton | LP | Mercury | MMB12011 | 1959 | £4 | £10 | |

## RULERS

| | | | | | | | |
|---|---|---|---|---|---|---|---|
| Copasetic | 7" | Rio | R107 | 1966 | £5 | £10 | |
| Don't Be A Rude Boy | 7" | Rio | R105 | 1966 | £4 | £8 | |
| Got To Be Free | 7" | Trojan | TR696 | 1969 | £1.50 | £4 | |
| Well Covered | 7" | Rio | R135 | 1967 | £4 | £8 | Carl Dawkins B side |
| Wrong Embryo | 7" | Rio | R132 | 1967 | £4 | £8 | |

## RUMBLERS

| | | | | | | | |
|---|---|---|---|---|---|---|---|
| Boss | 7" | London | HLD9684 | 1963 | £6 | £12 | |
| Bossounds | LP | London | HAD/SHD8081 | 1963 | £25 | £50 | |
| Bossounds | 7" EP | London | RED1396 | 1963 | £30 | £60 | |
| Soulful Jerk | 7" | King | KG1021 | 1965 | £12.50 | £25 | |

## RUMPELSTILTSKIN

| | | | | | | | |
|---|---|---|---|---|---|---|---|
| Rumpelstiltskin | LP | Bell | 6047 | 1969 | £6 | £15 | US |

## RUMPO, SID

| | | | | | | | |
|---|---|---|---|---|---|---|---|
| First Offence | LP | Mushroom | 35109 | 1971 | £10 | £25 | Australian |

## RUMSEY, HOWARD

| | | | | | | | |
|---|---|---|---|---|---|---|---|
| Howard Rumsey's Lighthouse All Stars | LP | Contemporary | LAC12055 | 1957 | £8 | £20 | |
| Howard Rumsey's Lighthouse All Stars | 10" LP | Contemporary | LDC187 | 1956 | £10 | £25 | |
| Howard Rumsey's Lighthouse All-Stars | 10" LP | Vogue | EPC1175 | 1953 | £10 | £25 | |
| Jazz Rolls Royce | LP | Colrich | XSD5 | 1959 | £4 | £10 | |
| Lighthouse All Stars | 10" LP | Contemporary | LDC146 | 1955 | £10 | £25 | |
| Lighthouse All Stars | 10" LP | Contemporary | LDC152 | 1955 | £10 | £25 | |
| Lighthouse All Stars Vol. 3 | LP | Contemporary | LAC12182 | 1960 | £5 | £12 | |
| Lighthouse At Laguna | LP | Contemporary | LAC12125 | 1959 | £6 | £15 | |
| Music For Lighthousekeeping | LP | Contemporary | LAC12086 | 1958 | £6 | £15 | |
| Oboe – Flute | LP | Contemporary | LAC12146 | 1959 | £6 | £15 | |
| Sunday Jazz A La Lighthouse Vol. 1 | LP | Contemporary | LAC12120 | 1958 | £6 | £15 | |

## RUN 229

| | | | | | | | |
|---|---|---|---|---|---|---|---|
| Soho | 7" | MM | JR7040S | 1980 | £4 | £8 | |

## RUNAWAYS

| | | | | | | | |
|---|---|---|---|---|---|---|---|
| And Now The Runaways | LP | Cherry Red | ARED3 | 1979 | £4 | £10 | blue, orange, red or<br>yellow vinyl |
| And Now The Runaways | LP | Cherry Red | ARED38 | 1979 | £4 | £10 | blue vinyl |
| Little Lost Girls | LP | Rhino | RNDF250 | 1981 | £4 | £10 | US picture disc |
| Right Now | 7" | Cherry Red | CHERRY8 | 1979 | £2.50 | £6 | picture sleeve |
| Runaways | LP | Mercury | 9100029 | 1976 | £4 | £10 | orange vinyl |

## RUNDGREN, TODD

| | | | | | | | |
|---|---|---|---|---|---|---|---|
| Ballad Of Todd Rundgren | LP | Bearsville | K45506 | 1971 | £4 | £10 | |
| Oops! Wrong Planet | CD | Mobile Fidelity | | 1995 | £6 | £15 | US audiophile |
| Runt | LP | Bearsville | K45505 | 1970 | £4 | £10 | |
| Something Anything | LP | Bearsville | 2BR2066 | 1972 | £37.50 | £75 | US double promo, 1<br>red, 1 blue vinyl |
| Something/Anything | CD | Mobile Fidelity | UDCD2591 | 1994 | £6 | £15 | US audiophile |
| Todd Rundgren Radio Show | LP | Bearsville | PRO524 | 1972 | £15 | £30 | US promo |
| Todd Rundgren Radio Show | LP | Bearsville | PRO597 | 1974 | £10 | £25 | US promo |
| Wizard A True Star | LP | Bearsville | K45513 | 1973 | £4 | £10 | |

## RUNDGREN, TODD & PATTI SMITH

| | | | | | | | |
|---|---|---|---|---|---|---|---|
| Back To The Bars | LP | Bearsville | PROA788 | 1978 | £10 | £25 | US promo |

## RUNNING MAN

| | | | | | | | |
|---|---|---|---|---|---|---|---|
| Running Man | LP | Neon | NE11 | 1972 | £62.50 | £125 | |

## RUNRIG

| | | | | | | | |
|---|---|---|---|---|---|---|---|
| Alba | 7" | Ridge | RRS007 | 1987 | £7.50 | £15 | |
| Capture The Heart | 10" | Chrysalis | CHS103594 | 1990 | £4 | £10 | |
| Capture The Heart EP | CD-s | Chrysalis | CHSCD3594 | 1990 | £2 | £5 | |
| Cutter And The Clan | CD | Chrysalis | CD25CR17 | 1994 | £5 | £12 | Chrysalis 25 pack |
| Dance Called America | 7" | Simple | SIM4 | 1987 | £5 | £10 | |
| Dance Called America | 12" | Simple | 12SIM4 | 1987 | £10 | £20 | |
| Every River | CD-s | Chrysalis | CHSCD3451 | 1989 | £10 | £20 | |
| Flower Of The West | CD-s | Chrysalis | CHSCD3805 | 1991 | £2 | £5 | |
| Hearthammer | CD-s | Chrysalis | CHSGCD3754 | 1991 | £2 | £5 | |
| Highland Connection | LP | Ridge | RR001 | 1979 | £4 | £10 | |
| Loch Lomond | 7" | Ridge | RRS003 | 1982 | £4 | £8 | |
| News From Heaven | CD-s | Chrysalis | CHSCD3404 | 1989 | £10 | £20 | |
| News From Heaven | 12" | Chrysalis | CHS123404 | 1989 | £6 | £15 | picture disc |
| Protect And Survive | CD-s | Chrysalis | CHSCD3284 | 1990 | £10 | £20 | |
| Protect And Survive | 7" | Chrysalis | CHS3284 | 1988 | £5 | £10 | |
| Protect And Survive | 12" | Chrysalis | CHS123284 | 1988 | £6 | £15 | |

| | | | | | | | |
|---|---|---|---|---|---|---|---|
| Runrig Play Gaelic | LP | Neptune | NA105 | 1978 | £5 | £12 | |
| Skye | 7" | Simple | SIM8 | 1984 | £10 | £20 | |
| Work Song | 7" | Ridge | RRS006 | 1986 | £2 | £5 | |

## RUPERT'S PEOPLE

| | | | | | | | |
|---|---|---|---|---|---|---|---|
| I Can Show You | 7" | Columbia | DB8362 | 1968 | £12.50 | £25 | |
| Prologue To A Magic World | 7" | Columbia | DB8278 | 1967 | £12.50 | £25 | |
| Reflections Of Charles Brown | 7" | Columbia | DB8226 | 1967 | £7.50 | £15 | |

## RUSH

| | | | | | | | |
|---|---|---|---|---|---|---|---|
| 2112 | CD | Mobile Fidelity | UDCD590 | 1993 | £6 | £15 | US audiophile |
| All The World's A Stage | LP | Mercury | 6672015 | 1977 | £6 | £15 | double with photo page |
| Big Money | CD-s | Polygram | 0800842 | 1989 | £20 | £40 | CD video |
| Body Electric | 12" | Vertigo | RUSH1112 | 1984 | £10 | £20 | |
| Body Electric | 10" | Mercury | RUSH1110 | 1984 | £2.50 | £6 | red vinyl |
| Countdown | 7" | Mercury | RUSHP10 | 1982 | £6 | £12 | shaped picture disc |
| Everything You Always Wanted To Hear | LP | Mercury | MK32 | 1975 | £6 | £15 | US promo |
| Hemispheres | LP | Mercury | 9100059 | 1978 | £5 | £12 | picture disc |
| Moving Pictures | CD | Mobile Fidelity | UDCD569 | 1992 | £6 | £15 | US audiophile |
| Not Fade Away | 7" | Moon | MN001 | 1973 | £100 | £200 | Canadian, best auctioned |
| Power Windows | LP | Vertigo | VERHP31 | 1985 | £5 | £12 | picture disc |
| Prime Mover | CD-s | Vertigo | RUSHCD14 | 1988 | £2.50 | £6 | |
| Profiled! | CD | Atlantic | | 1990 | £8 | £20 | US promo |
| Rush | LP | Moon | | | £62.50 | £125 | Canadian |
| Rush 'n' Roulette | 12" | Mercury | | 1982 | £10 | £20 | US promo, 6 tracks running simultaneously |
| Rush Through Time | LP | Mercury | 001 | 1978 | £10 | £25 | US promo picture disc |
| Signals | CD | Mobile Fidelity | UDCD614 | 1994 | £6 | £15 | US audiophile |
| Subdivisions | 7" | Mercury | RUSHP9 | 1982 | £1.50 | £4 | picture disc |
| Time Stand Still | CD-s | Vertigo | RUSHCD13 | 1987 | £2 | £5 | |

## RUSH (2)

| | | | | | | | |
|---|---|---|---|---|---|---|---|
| Make Mine Music | 7" | Decca | F12635 | 1967 | £1.50 | £4 | |

## RUSH, OTIS

| | | | | | | | |
|---|---|---|---|---|---|---|---|
| All Your Love | 7" | Blue Horizon | 573159 | 1969 | £4 | £8 | |
| Groaning The Blues | LP | Python | KM3 | 1970 | £8 | £20 | |
| Homework | 7" | Vocalion | VP9260 | 1966 | £5 | £10 | |
| Mourning In The Morning | LP | Atlantic | 588188 | 1969 | £8 | £20 | |
| This One's A Good Un | LP | Blue Horizon | 763222 | 1968 | £20 | £40 | |

## RUSH, TOM

| | | | | | | | |
|---|---|---|---|---|---|---|---|
| At The Unicorn | LP | Ly Cornu | SA702 | 1962 | £25 | £50 | US |
| Blues And Folk | LP | XTRA | XTRA5024 | 1966 | £5 | £12 | |
| Circle Game | LP | Elektra | EKL/EKS74018 | 1968 | £5 | £12 | |
| Classic Rush | LP | Elektra | EKL/EKS74062 | 1969 | £4 | £10 | |
| I Got A Mind To Ramble | LP | XTRA | XTRA5053 | 1968 | £5 | £12 | |
| Long John | 7" EP | Vogue | INT18040 | 1965 | £5 | £10 | French |
| Mind Ramblin' | LP | Prestige | 14003 | 1963 | £6 | £15 | US |
| No Regrets | 7" | Elektra | EKSN45025 | 1968 | £1.50 | £4 | |
| On The Road Again | 7" | Elektra | EKSN45015 | 1967 | £1.50 | £4 | |
| Something In The Way She Moves Me | 7" | Elektra | EKSN45032 | 1968 | £1.50 | £4 | |
| Take A Little Walk With Me | LP | Elektra | EKL/EKS7308 | 1966 | £6 | £15 | |
| Tom Rush | LP | Elektra | EKL288 | 1965 | £5 | £12 | |
| Who Do You Love | 7" | Elektra | EKSN45005 | 1967 | £1.50 | £4 | |

## RUSHING, JIMMY

| | | | | | | | |
|---|---|---|---|---|---|---|---|
| And The Big Brass | LP | Philips | BBL7252/SBBL524 | 1958 | £6 | £15 | |
| Blues I Love To Sing | LP | Ace Of Hearts | AH119 | 1966 | £4 | £10 | |
| Cat Meets Chick | LP | Philips | BBL7105 | 1957 | £6 | £15 | with Ada Moore |
| Cat Meets Chick | 7" EP | Philips | BBE12150 | 1957 | £4 | £8 | with Ada Moore |
| Every Day I Have The Blues | LP | HMV | CLP/CSD3632 | 1967 | £4 | £10 | |
| If This Ain't The Blues | LP | Vanguard | PPL11008 | 1958 | £6 | £15 | |
| Jazz Odyssey | LP | Philips | BBL7166 | 1957 | £6 | £15 | |
| Jimmy Rushing | 7" EP | Ember | EMBEP4523 | 1962 | £2 | £5 | |
| Jimmy Rushing | 7" EP | Parlophone | GEP8597 | 1957 | £2.50 | £6 | |
| Listen To The Blues | LP | Fontana | FJL405 | 1967 | £4 | £10 | |
| Little Jimmy All Star Band | 7" EP | Vanguard | EPP14003 | 1957 | £2.50 | £6 | |
| Little Jimmy Rushing And The Big Brass | LP | Philips | BBL7252 | 1958 | £5 | £12 | |
| Rushing Lullabies | LP | Philips | BBL7360 | 1960 | £6 | £15 | |
| Showcase | 10" LP | Vanguard | PPT12016 | 1957 | £8 | £20 | |
| Sings The Blues | 10" LP | Vanguard | PPT12002 | 1955 | £10 | £25 | |
| Smith Girls – Bessie, Clara | LP | Philips | BBL7484/SBBL631 | 1961 | £6 | £15 | |
| Way I Feel | 7" EP | Parlophone | GEP8695 | 1958 | £2.50 | £6 | |

## RUSKIN, BARBARA

| | | | | | | | |
|---|---|---|---|---|---|---|---|
| Halfway To Paradise | 7" | Piccadilly | 7N35224 | 1965 | £1.50 | £4 | |

## RUSSAL, THANE

| | | | | | | | |
|---|---|---|---|---|---|---|---|
| Drop Everything And Run | 7" | CBS | 202403 | 1966 | £30 | £60 | |
| Security | 7" | CBS | 202049 | 1966 | £30 | £60 | |
| Security | 7" | CBS | 202049 | 1966 | £62.50 | £125 | picture sleeve |

## RUSSELL, CONNIE

| | | | | | | | |
|---|---|---|---|---|---|---|---|
| Ayuh Ayuh | 7" | Capitol | CL14236 | 1955 | £2.50 | £6 | |
| Farewell Farewell | 7" | Capitol | CL14268 | 1955 | £1.50 | £4 | |
| Foggy Night In San Francisco | 7" | Capitol | CL14214 | 1955 | £2 | £5 | |

| | | | | | | |
|---|---|---|---|---|---|---|
| Green Fire | 7" | Capitol | CL14246 | 1955 £**1.50** | £**4** | |
| Love Me | 7" | Capitol | CL14197 | 1954 £**2** | £**5** | |
| No One But You | 7" | Capitol | CL14171 | 1954 £**2.50** | £**6** | |

## RUSSELL, DOROTHY

| | | | | | | |
|---|---|---|---|---|---|---|
| You're The One I Love | 7" | Duke Reid | DR2524 | 1971 £**1.50** | £**4** | |

## RUSSELL, GEORGE

| | | | | | | |
|---|---|---|---|---|---|---|
| At Beethoven Hall | LP | Polydor | 583706 | 1965 £**5** | £**12** | |
| Ezz-thetics | LP | Riverside | RLP375 | 1961 £**6** | £**15** | |
| Jazz Workshop | LP | RCA | RD7511 | 1962 £**6** | £**15** | |
| New York, N.Y. | LP | Brunswick | LAT8333 | 1960 £**8** | £**20** | |
| Outer View | LP | Fontana | 688705ZL | 1964 £**5** | £**12** | |
| Stratus Seekers | LP | Riverside | RLP(9)412 | 1962 £**5** | £**12** | |

## RUSSELL, JANE

| | | | | | | |
|---|---|---|---|---|---|---|
| If You Wanna See Mamie Tonight | 7" | Capitol | CL14590 | 1956 £**2** | £**5** | |
| Jane Russell | 7" EP | MGM | MGMEP702 | 1959 £**7.50** | £**15** | |
| Please Do It Again | 7" | Columbia | SCM5043 | 1953 £**2.50** | £**6** | |

## RUSSELL, JOHNNY

| | | | | | | |
|---|---|---|---|---|---|---|
| Lonesome Boy | 7" | MGM | MGM1074 | 1960 £**1.50** | £**4** | |

## RUSSELL, LEON

| | | | | | | |
|---|---|---|---|---|---|---|
| Everybody's Talkin' 'Bout The Young | 7" | Pye | 7N16771 | 1965 £**2.50** | £**6** | |
| Leon Russell | LP | Shelter | SHE1001 | 1968 £**4** | £**10** | US, extra track |

## RUSSELL, RAY

| | | | | | | |
|---|---|---|---|---|---|---|
| Dragon Hill | LP | CBS | 52663 | 1969 £**10** | £**25** | |
| Illusions | LP | Music House | MHA4 | 197– £**6** | £**15** | |
| June 11th 1971 | LP | RCA | SF8214 | 1971 £**8** | £**20** | |
| Master Format | LP | JW Music Library | | 197– £**6** | £**15** | |
| Rites And Rituals | LP | CBS | 64271 | 1971 £**10** | £**25** | |
| Secret Asylum | LP | Black Lion | 2460207 | 1973 £**6** | £**15** | |
| Turn Circle | LP | CBS | 52586 | 1968 £**10** | £**25** | |

## RUSSELL, ROLAND

| | | | | | | |
|---|---|---|---|---|---|---|
| Rhythm Hips | 7" | Nu Beat | NB019 | 1968 £**1.50** | £**4** | |

## RUSSELL FAMILY

| | | | | | | |
|---|---|---|---|---|---|---|
| Of Doolin County Clare | LP | Topic | 12TS251 | 1975 £**4** | £**10** | |

## RUSSO, WILLIAM

| | | | | | | |
|---|---|---|---|---|---|---|
| Three Pieces For Blues Band & Symphony Orchestra | LP | Deutsche Grammophon | 2530309 | 197– £**6** | £**15** | ... with Siegel-Schwall Band |

## RUST

| | | | | | | |
|---|---|---|---|---|---|---|
| Come With Me | LP | Hor Zu | SHZEL59 | 1969 £**8** | £**20** | German |

## RUSTIKS

| | | | | | | |
|---|---|---|---|---|---|---|
| What A Memory Can Do | 7" | Decca | F11960 | 1964 £**1.50** | £**4** | |

## RUSTLERS

| | | | | | | |
|---|---|---|---|---|---|---|
| High Strung | 7" | Pye | 7N15398 | 1961 £**1.50** | £**4** | |

## RUSTY & DOUG

| | | | | | | |
|---|---|---|---|---|---|---|
| Cajun Joe | 7" | Fontana | 267238TF | 1962 £**4** | £**8** | |
| Hey Mae | 7" | Oriole | CB1510 | 1959 £**62.50** | £**125** | |
| Hey Mae | 7" | Polydor | NH66970 | 1962 £**10** | £**20** | |
| I Like You | 7" | London | HL8972 | 1959 £**7.50** | £**15** | |

## RUTHERFORD, MIKE

| | | | | | | |
|---|---|---|---|---|---|---|
| Time And Time Again/End Of The Day | 7" | Charisma | CB364 | 1980 £**2.50** | £**6** | picture sleeve |
| Time And Time Again/Overnight Job | 7" | Charisma | CB364 | 1980 £**2** | £**5** | picture sleeve |

## RUTLES

The Rutles album and its accompanying television programme is an affectionate parody by Neil Innes and Eric Idle of the career of the Beatles. The cover of the LP is almost better than the music inside – it displays numerous photographs of album sleeves and group portraits that exactly mirror originals featuring the Beatles. The music is cleverly constructed to be reminiscent of key songs by the Beatles, although ultimately Neil Innes's re-creations are rather less skilful than those put together by XTC on their Dukes of Stratosfear albums.

| | | | | | | |
|---|---|---|---|---|---|---|
| Rutles | LP | Warner Bros | K56459 | 1978 £**4** | £**10** | |
| Rutles Sampler | 12" | Warner Bros | PROA723 | 1978 £**4** | £**10** | US promo, yellow vinyl |

## RUTS

| | | | | | | |
|---|---|---|---|---|---|---|
| Stepping Bondage | 7" | Bohemian | BO4 | 1983 £**2.50** | £**6** | |

## RYAN, BARRY

| | | | | | | |
|---|---|---|---|---|---|---|
| Barry Ryan | LP | Polydor | 583067 | 1969 £**4** | £**10** | |
| Sings Paul Ryan | LP | MGM | CS8106 | 1968 £**5** | £**12** | |

## RYAN, CHARLIE

| | | | | | | |
|---|---|---|---|---|---|---|
| Hot Rod | LP | King | 751 | 1961 £**8** | £**20** | US |

## RYAN, KRIS & THE QUESTIONS

| Title | Format | | Label | Catalogue | Year | | | Notes |
|---|---|---|---|---|---|---|---|---|
| On The Right Track | 7" | EP | Mercury | 10024MCE | 1965 | £10 | £20 | |

## RYAN, MARION

| Title | Format | | Label | Catalogue | Year | | | Notes |
|---|---|---|---|---|---|---|---|---|
| Better Use Your Head | 7" | | Philips | BF1721 | 1968 | £2.50 | £6 | |
| Hit Parade | 7" | EP | Pye | NEP24079 | 1958 | £6 | £12 | |
| Jo-Jo The Dog Faced Boy | 7" | | Pye | 7N15200 | 1959 | £1.50 | £4 | |
| Lady Loves | LP | | Pye | NPL18030 | 1959 | £15 | £30 | mono |
| Lady Loves | LP | | Pye | NSPL18030 | 1959 | £20 | £40 | stereo |
| Love Me Forever | 7" | | Pye | 7N15121 | 1958 | £1.50 | £4 | |
| Oh Oh I'm Falling In Love Again | 7" | | Pye | 7N15130 | 1958 | £1.50 | £4 | |
| Stairway Of Love | 7" | | Pye | 7N15138 | 1958 | £1.50 | £4 | |
| That Ryan Gal | 7" | EP | Pye | NEP24041 | 1957 | £6 | £12 | |
| World Goes Around And Around | 7" | | Pye | 7NSR15157 | 1958 | £1.50 | £4 | stereo |

## RYAN, PAUL & BARRY

| Title | Format | Label | Catalogue | Year | | | |
|---|---|---|---|---|---|---|---|
| Paul And Barry Ryan | LP | MGM | C(S)8081 | 1968 | £5 | £12 | |
| Two Of A Kind | LP | Decca | LK4878 | 1967 | £6 | £15 | |

## RYAN, PHIL & THE CRESCENTS

| Title | Format | Label | Catalogue | Year | | | |
|---|---|---|---|---|---|---|---|
| Gypsy Woman | 7" | Columbia | DB7574 | 1965 | £4 | £8 | |
| Mary Don't You Weep | 7" | Columbia | DB7406 | 1964 | £1.50 | £4 | |

## RYDELL, BOBBY

| Title | Format | | Label | Catalogue | Year | | | Notes |
|---|---|---|---|---|---|---|---|---|
| All The Hits | LP | | Cameo Parkway | C1019 | 1962 | £5 | £12 | |
| All The Hits Vol. 2 | LP | | Cameo Parkway | C1040 | 1963 | £5 | £12 | |
| At The Copa | LP | | Columbia | 33SX1425 | 1962 | £20 | £40 | |
| Best Of Bobby Rydell | 7" | EP | Summit | LSE2036 | 1963 | £2.50 | £6 | |
| Biggest Hits | LP | | Cameo | C1009 | 1961 | £6 | £15 | US, gatefold |
| Biggest Hits Vol. 2 | LP | | Cameo | C1028 | 1962 | £4 | £10 | US |
| Bobby Rydell | 7" | EP | Cameo Parkway | CPE553 | 1963 | £6 | £12 | |
| Bye Bye Birdie | LP | | Cameo Parkway | C1043 | 1963 | £4 | £10 | |
| Forget Him | 7" | | Cameo Parkway | C108 | 1963 | £2 | £5 | picture sleeve |
| Kissin' Time | 7" | | Top Rank | JAR181 | 1959 | £2.50 | £6 | |
| Lovingest | 7" | EP | Top Rank | JKP2059 | 1960 | £10 | £20 | |
| Salutes The Great Ones | LP | | Columbia | 33SX1352 | 1961 | £5 | £12 | |
| Sings And Swings | LP | | Columbia | 33SX1308 | 1960 | £6 | £15 | |
| Somebody Loves You | LP | | Capitol | T2281 | 1965 | £4 | £10 | |
| Sway With Bobby Rydell | 7" | EP | Cameo Parkway | CPE551 | 1963 | £6 | £12 | |
| Swinging School | 7" | | Columbia | DB4471 | 1960 | £1.50 | £4 | |
| Volare | 7" | | Columbia | DB4495 | 1960 | £1.50 | £4 | |
| We Got Love | LP | | Cameo | C1006 | 1959 | £8 | £20 | US |
| We Got Love | 7" | | Top Rank | JAR227 | 1959 | £2 | £5 | |
| When I See That Girl Of Mine | 7" | | Capitol | CL15424 | 1965 | £1.50 | £4 | |
| Wild One | LP | | Columbia | 33SX1243 | 1960 | £15 | £30 | |
| Wild One | 7" | | Columbia | DB4429 | 1960 | £1.50 | £4 | |
| Wild (Wood) Days | LP | | Cameo | C1055 | 1963 | £5 | £12 | |

## RYDER, MAL

| Title | Format | Label | Catalogue | Year | | | |
|---|---|---|---|---|---|---|---|
| Cry Baby | 7" | Decca | F11669 | 1963 | £4 | £8 | |
| Lonely Room | 7" | Piccadilly | 7N35234 | 1965 | £5 | £10 | |
| See The Funny Little Clown | 7" | Vocalion | V9219 | 1964 | £20 | £40 | |
| Your Friend | 7" | Piccadilly | 7N35209 | 1964 | £7.50 | £15 | |

## RYDER, MITCH

| Title | Format | | Label | Catalogue | Year | | | Notes |
|---|---|---|---|---|---|---|---|---|
| All Mitch Ryder Hits! | LP | | Bell | MBLL/SBLL114 | 1968 | £4 | £10 | |
| Breakout | LP | | Stateside | (S)SL10189 | 1967 | £6 | £15 | |
| Breakout | 7" | | Stateside | SS521 | 1966 | £5 | £10 | |
| Devil With A Blue Dress On | 7" | | Stateside | SS549 | 1966 | £1.50 | £4 | |
| Jenny Take A Ride | 7" | EP | Columbia | ESRF1745 | 1966 | £7.50 | £15 | French |
| Jenny Take A Ride | 7" | | Stateside | SS481 | 1966 | £1.50 | £4 | |
| Little Latin Lupe Lu | 7" | EP | Columbia | ESRF1804 | 1966 | £7.50 | £15 | French |
| Little Latin Lupe Lu | 7" | | Stateside | SS498 | 1966 | £1.50 | £4 | |
| Mitch Ryder Sings The Hits | LP | | New Voice | S2005 | 1968 | £4 | £10 | US |
| Personality | 7" | | Stateside | SS2096 | 1968 | £1.50 | £4 | |
| Ridin' | 7" | EP | Stateside | SE1039 | 1966 | £7.50 | £15 | |
| Sock It To Me | LP | | Stateside | (S)SL10204 | 1967 | £6 | £15 | |
| Sock It To Me Baby | 7" | EP | Columbia | ESRF1849 | 1967 | £7.50 | £15 | French |
| Sock It To Me Baby | 7" | | Stateside | SS596 | 1967 | £1.50 | £4 | |
| Take A Ride | LP | | Stateside | (S)SL10178 | 1966 | £5 | £12 | |
| Too Many Fish In The Sea | 7" | EP | Stateside | FSE1005 | 1967 | £7.50 | £15 | French |
| Too Many Fish In The Sea | 7" | | Stateside | SS2023 | 1967 | £2 | £5 | |
| What Now My Love | LP | | Stateside | (S)SL10229 | 1967 | £4 | £10 | |
| What Now My Love | 7" | | Stateside | SS2063 | 1967 | £5 | £10 | |

## RYLES & DALLAS

| Title | Format | | Label | Catalogue | Year | | | Notes |
|---|---|---|---|---|---|---|---|---|
| Blowin' In The Wind | 7" | EP | Riviera | 231125 | 1965 | £4 | £8 | French |

## RYPDAL, TERJE

Terje Rypdal is one of the stars of the ECM label, having made a large number of albums in both the jazz and orchestral categories. As a guitarist, Rypdal is without question one of the great players, with an instantly recognizable sound based on the use of long sustain, frequently with no initial plectrum attack, and combined with a cavernous echo.

| | | | | | | | |
|---|---|---|---|---|---|---|---|
| After The Rain | LP | ECM | ECM1083ST | 1976 | £5 | £12 | |
| Bleak House | LP | Polydor | 2915053 | 1968 | £37.50 | £75 | Swedish |
| Odyssey | LP | ECM | ECM1067/8ST | 1975 | £8 | £20 | double |
| Rolling Stone | LP | Polydor | 2371618 | 1975 | £20 | £40 | German |
| Terje Rypdal | LP | ECM | ECM1016ST | 1971 | £8 | £20 | |
| Ved Soerevatn | LP | BASF | 15269 | 1969 | £25 | £50 | German |
| What Comes After | LP | ECM | ECM1031ST | 1974 | £5 | £12 | |
| Whenever I Seem To Be Far Away | LP | ECM | ECM1045ST | 1974 | £5 | £12 | |

# S

## SABLE, PARK & THE JUNGLE 'N' BEATS
Rave On ............................................. 7" ..... Fontana ........... TF457 ................. 1964 £10 ......... £20 .........................

## SABLES, BILL
Bill Sables ........................................ LP ..... Westwood ...... WRS027 ............... 1973 £15 ......... £30

## SABRE
Miracle Man ..................................... 7" ..... Neat ............. NEAT23 ............... 1983 £1.50 ....... £4 .........................

## SABRES
Roly Poly .......................................... 7" ..... Decca ............ F12528 ................ 1966 £2.50 ....... £6

## SACRED ALIEN
Legends ........................................... 7" ..... Neon ............. SADX1 ................ 1984 £4 .......... £8
Spiritual Planet ................................ 7" ..... Greenwood ..... GW1 .................. 198– £7.50 ..... £15

## SACRED MUSHROOMS
Sacred Mushrooms ........................... LP ..... Parallax .......... P4001 ................. 1969 £30 ......... £60 ................. US

## SACROS
Sacros ............................................. LP ..... IRT ................. ILS136 ............... 1973 £15 ......... £30 .............. Chilean

## SAD LOVERS & GIANTS
Colourless Dream ............................. 7" ..... Last Movement LM005 ................ 1981 £2.50 ....... £6
Imagination ..................................... 7" ..... Last Movement LM003 ................ 1981 £4 .......... £8
Lost In A Moment ............................. 7" ..... Midnight ....... DING1 ............... 1982 £1.50 ....... £4
Music .............

## SADI, FATS
Fats Sadi .......................................... 10" LP Vogue ............ LDE133 .............. 1955 £37.50 ..... £75
Fats Sadi-Martial Solal Quartet ........... LP ..... Vogue ............ LAE12043 ........... 1957 £10 ......... £25

## SAFARIS
Image Of A Girl ................................ 7" ..... Top Rank ....... JAR424 .............. 1960 £7.50 ..... £15
Summer Nights ................................. 7" ..... Top Rank ....... JAR528 .............. 1961 £1.50 ..... £4

## SAFT
Horn ............................................... LP ..... Polydor ........... 2923005 ............. 1971 £8 .......... £20 ............. Norwegian

## SAGA
To Whom It Concerns ....................... LP ..... Unidentified .. UAP4 ................ 1979 £25 ......... £50 .................. Dutch
Artist
Productions .....

## SAGAR, MIKE & THE CRESTERS
Deep Feeling ..................................... 7" ..... HMV ............. POP819 .............. 1960 £4 ........... £8

## SAGE
Going Strong .................................... LP ..... Redball .......... RR032 ............... 1980 £37.50 ..... £75

## SAGITTARIUS
Another Time ................................... 7" ..... CBS ................ 3276 .................. 1968 £2.50 ....... £6
Blue Marble ..................................... LP ..... Together ......... STT1002 ............ 1969 £20 ......... £40 .................. US
My World Fell Down .......................... 7" ..... CBS ................ 2867 .................. 1967 £4 .......... £8
Present Tense .................................... LP ..... Columbia ........ CS9644 .............. 1968 £20 ......... £40 .................. US

## SAGRAM
Pop Explosion Sitar Style .................... LP ..... Windmill ........ WMD118 ........... 1972 £10 ......... £25

## SAHARA
Sunrise ............................................ LP ..... Dawn ............. DNLS3068 .......... 1973 £4 .......... £10

## SAHM, DOUG
Return Of Doug Saldana ..................... LP ..... Philips ........... PHS600353 ......... 1971 £15 ......... £30 .................. US
Rough Edges ..................................... LP ..... Mercury ......... SRM1655 ........... 1973 £5 .......... £12 .................. US

## SAINT ETIENNE
I Love To Paint ................................. CD ..... Heavenly ........ HVNCD9 ............ 1995 £8 .......... £20
Kiss And Make Up ............................. CD-s .. Heavenly ........ HVN4CD ............ 1990 £3 .......... £8
Kiss And Make Up ............................. 12" ... Heavenly ........ HVN412R ........... 1990 £2.50 ....... £6
Nothing Can Stop Us .......................... CD-s .. Heavenly ........ HVN9CD ............ 1991 £2 .......... £5
Only Love Can Break Your Heart ......... 12" ... Heavenly ........ HVN212 ............. 1990 £2.50 ....... £6
Only Love Can Break Your Heart ......... 12" ... Heavenly ........ HVN212R ........... 1990 £3 .......... £8

Only Love Can Break Your Heart ............. CD-s .. Creation.......... HVN12CD ............ 1991 £2 ......... £5 .....................

## SAINT JUST
La Casa Del Lago...................................... LP ...... Harvest ......... .............................. 1974 £50 ...... £100 ................... *Italian*
Saint Just ................................................. LP ...... Harvest ......... .............................. 1973 £50 ...... £100 ................... *Italian*

## SAINT STEVEN
Over The Hills.......................................... LP ..... Probe............. SPB1005 ............... 1969 £37.50 .... £75 .......................

## SAINTE ANTHONY'S FYRE
Sainte Anthony's Fyre ............................. LP ...... Zonk ............. ZP001.................... 1971 £50 ...... £100 ........................... *US*

## SAINTE-MARIE, BUFFY
Fire, Fleet & Candle Light........................ LP ...... Vanguard ........ VSD79250............. 1967 £4 ......... £10 .......................
I'm Gonna Be A Country Girl Again ........ LP ...... Vanguard ........ VSD79280............. 1968 £4 ......... £10 .......................
Illuminations .......................................... LP ...... Vanguard ........ VSD79300............. 1969 £4 ......... £10 .......................
It's My Way............................................. LP ...... Fontana ........ TFL6040 ............. 1964 £5 ......... £12 .......................
It's My Way............................................. LP ...... Vanguard ........ VSD79142............. 1969 £4 ......... £10 .......................
Little Wheel Spin And Spin...................... LP ...... Fontana ........ (S)TFL6071 ........ 1966 £5 ......... £12 .......................
Little Wheel Spin And Spin...................... LP ...... Vanguard ........ SVRL19023........... 1969 £4 ......... £10 .......................
Many A Mile ........................................... LP ...... Fontana ........ TFL6047 ............. 1965 £5 ......... £12 .......................
Many A Mile ........................................... LP ...... Vanguard ........ SVRL19031........... 1969 £4 ......... £10 .......................
Sweet America ......................................... LP ...... ABC ............ ABCL5168 ............ 1976 £4 ......... £10 .......................

## SAINTS
I'm Stranded ........................................... 7" ...... Power ........ PX242 .................... 1976 £1.50 ........ £4 .......................
                                                   Exchange ........

## SAINTS (2)
Husky Team ............................................. 7" ...... Pye ............. 7N15582 ............... 1963 £6 ......... £12 .......................
Wipe Out ................................................ 7" ...... Pye ............. 7N15548 ............... 1963 £6 ......... £12 .......................

## SAINTS (3)
Alive ....................................................... LP ...... MJB ............. BEVLP127/8........... 1964 £330 ..... £500 .......................
Saints ..................................................... 10" LP MJB ............ BEV73/4............... 1964 £180 .... £300 .......................

## SAINTY, RUSS
Happy Go Lucky Me................................. 7" ...... Top Rank ..... JAR381................... 1960 £2 ......... £5 .......................
Race With The Devil ................................ 7" ...... Decca .......... F11270.................... 1960 £2 ......... £5 .......................

## SAKAMOTO, KYU
Sukiyaki ................................................. LP ...... Capitol........... (D)T10349 ............ 1963 £5 ......... £12 ........................... *US*

## SAKER
Foggy Tuesday.......................................... 7" ...... Parlophone ...... R5740 .................. 1968 £2 ......... £5 .......................
Hey Joe ................................................... 7" ...... Parlophone ...... R5752 .................. 1969 £2 ......... £5 .......................

## SALAD
Drink Me ................................................ CD ...... Island ........... CIRDX1002 ......... 1995 £5 ......... £12 ........ *boxed with book*

## SALAMANDER
Crystal Ball ............................................. 7" ...... CBS............. 5102 ..................... 1970 £5 ......... £10 .......................
Ten Commandments.................................. LP ...... Youngblood .... SSYB14.................. 1972 £62.50 .. £125 .......................

## SALEM MASS
Witch Burning.......................................... LP ...... Salem Mass...... SLP101 ................ 197– £75 ...... £150 ........................... *US*

## SALES, SOUPY
Mouse..................................................... 7" ...... HMV............ POP1432 ............. 1965 £1.50 ........ £4 .......................

## SALLY & THE ALLEYCATS
Is It Something I Said............................... 7" ...... Parlophone ...... R5183 ................. 1964 £1.50 ........ £4 .......................

## SALLYANGIE
The Sallyangie was a folky duo comprising Sally Oldfield and her young brother Michael. Their one LP was re-released in the seventies, in a vain attempt on the part of Transatlantic records to gain some spin-off benefit from the success of *Tubular Bells* and its successors. The new cover, however, is completely different to the original, which shows a close-up of the two Oldfields, so distinguishing the two versions is no problem.

Child Of Allah ......................................... 7" ...... Philips ........... 6006259 ............... 1972 £5 ......... £10 .......................
Children Of The Sun................................. LP ...... Transatlantic ... TRA176 ................ 1968 £20 ...... £40 .......................
Children Of The Sun................................. LP ...... Transatlantic ... TRA176 ................ 1973 £5 ......... £12 *reissue, different sleeve*
Two Ships ............................................... 7" ...... Transatlantic .... BIG126 ................ 1969 £5 ......... £10 .......................

## SALLY'S FRIENDS
Boys Of The Town .................................... LP ...... Cottage ........... COT231 ............... 1980 £15 ...... £30 .......................

## SALMONTAILS
Salmontails.............................................. LP ...... Oblivion ......... OBL001 ............... 1980 £8 ......... £20 .......................

## SALT & PEPPER
High Noon............................................... 7" ...... London ........... HLU9338.............. 1961 £1.50 ........ £4 .......................

## SALVADOR, SAL
Sal Salvador Quartet ................................. 10" LP Capitol............ KPL105................. 1955 £15 ...... £30 .......................

## SALVATION

| | | | | | | | | |
|---|---|---|---|---|---|---|---|---|
| Salvation | LP | United Artists | UAS29062 | 1969 | £5 | £12 | |

## SALVATION (2)

| | | | | | | | | |
|---|---|---|---|---|---|---|---|---|
| Girlsoul | 7" | Merciful Release | MR025 | 1983 | £2.50 | £6 | |
| Girlsoul | 12" | Merciful Release | MRX025 | 1983 | £3 | £8 | |

## SALVO, SAMMY

| | | | | | | | |
|---|---|---|---|---|---|---|---|
| Afraid | 7" | London | HLP8997 | 1959 | £2 | £5 | |
| Billy Blue | 7" | Polydor | NH66974 | 1962 | £2 | £5 | |
| Say Yeah | 7" | RCA | RCA1032 | 1958 | £6 | £12 | |

## SAM & BILL

| | | | | | | | |
|---|---|---|---|---|---|---|---|
| Fly Me To The Moon | 7" | Pye | 7N25355 | 1966 | £5 | £10 | |
| I Feel Like Tryin' | 7" | Brunswick | 05973 | 1967 | £7.50 | £15 | |

## SAM & DAVE

| | | | | | | | |
|---|---|---|---|---|---|---|---|
| Baby Baby Don't Stop Now | 7" | Atlantic | 584324 | 1970 | £1.50 | £4 | |
| Best Of Sam And Dave | LP | Atlantic | 587/588155 | 1969 | £4 | £10 | |
| Can't You Find Another Way | 7" | Atlantic | 584211 | 1968 | £1.50 | £4 | |
| Double Dynamite | LP | Atlantic | 588181 | 1969 | £5 | £12 | |
| Double Dynamite | LP | Stax | 589003 | 1967 | £6 | £15 | |
| Everybody Got To Believe | 7" | Atlantic | 584228 | 1968 | £1.50 | £4 | |
| Hold On I'm Comin' | LP | Atlantic | 587/588045 | 1966 | £6 | £15 | |
| Hold On I'm Comin' | 7" | Atlantic | 584003 | 1966 | £1.50 | £4 | |
| I Thank You | LP | Atlantic | 587/588154 | 1968 | £4 | £10 | |
| I Thank You | 7" | Stax | 601030 | 1968 | £1.50 | £4 | |
| If You Got The Loving | 7" | Atlantic | 584047 | 1966 | £1.50 | £4 | |
| No More Pain | 7" | King | KG1041 | 1966 | £2 | £5 | |
| Ooh Ooh Ooh | 7" | Atlantic | 584303 | 1969 | £1.50 | £4 | |
| Sam And Dave | LP | Major Minor | MCP5000 | 1968 | £4 | £10 | |
| Sam And Dave | LP | King | KGL4001 | 1966 | £8 | £20 | |
| Soothe Me | 7" | Stax | 601004 | 1967 | £1.50 | £4 | |
| Soul Man | 7" | Stax | 601023 | 1967 | £1.50 | £4 | |
| Soul Men | LP | Atlantic | 588185 | 1969 | £4 | £10 | |
| Soul Men | LP | Stax | 589015 | 1967 | £6 | £15 | |
| Soul Sister Brown Sugar | 7" | Atlantic | 584237 | 1969 | £1.50 | £4 | |
| When Something Is Wrong With My Baby | 7" | Stax | 601006 | 1967 | £1.50 | £4 | |
| You Don't Know Like I Know | 7" | Atlantic | 584086 | 1967 | £1.50 | £4 | |
| You Don't Know Like I Know | 7" | Atlantic | 584247 | 1969 | £1.50 | £4 | |
| You Don't Know Like I Know | 7" | Atlantic | AT4066 | 1966 | £2 | £5 | |
| You Don't Know What You Mean To Me | 7" | Atlantic | 584192 | 1968 | £1.50 | £4 | |
| You Got Me Hummin' | 7" | Atlantic | 584064 | 1967 | £1.50 | £4 | |

## SAM APPLE PIE

| | | | | | | | |
|---|---|---|---|---|---|---|---|
| East 17 | LP | DJM | DJLPS429 | 1973 | £6 | £15 | |
| Sam Apple Pie | LP | Decca | LKR/SKLR5005 | 1969 | £37.50 | £75 | |
| Sometime Girl | 7" | Decca | F22932 | 1969 | £2.50 | £6 | |

## SAM THE SHAM & THE PHARAOHS

| | | | | | | | |
|---|---|---|---|---|---|---|---|
| Best Of Sam The Sham | LP | MGM | (S)E4422 | 1967 | £6 | £15 | US |
| Hair On My Chinny Chin Chin | 7" EP | MGM | 63639 | 1966 | £10 | £20 | French |
| Ju Ju Hand | 7" EP | MGM | 63624 | 1965 | £10 | £20 | French |
| Ju Ju Hand | 7" | MGM | MGM1278 | 1965 | £1.50 | £4 | |
| Li'l Red Riding Hood | LP | MGM | C(S)8032 | 1966 | £6 | £15 | |
| Li'l Red Riding Hood | 7" | MGM | MGM1315 | 1966 | £1.50 | £4 | |
| Lil' Red Riding Hood | 7" EP | MGM | 63637 | 1966 | £10 | £20 | French |
| Nefertiti | LP | MGM | (S)E4479 | 1967 | £4 | £10 | US |
| On Tour | LP | MGM | (S)E4347 | 1966 | £6 | £15 | US |
| Red Hot | 7" | MGM | 63631 | 1966 | £10 | £20 | French |
| Red Hot | 7" EP | MGM | MGMEP794 | 1966 | £10 | £20 | |
| Red Hot | 7" | MGM | MGM1298 | 1966 | £2 | £5 | |
| Ring Dang Doo | 7" EP | MGM | 63626 | 1965 | £10 | £20 | French |
| Ring Dang Doo | 7" | MGM | MGM1285 | 1965 | £1.50 | £4 | |
| Ten Of Pentacles | LP | MGM | SE4526 | 1968 | £4 | £10 | US |
| Their Second Album | LP | MGM | (S)E4314 | 1965 | £6 | £15 | US |
| Wooly Bully | LP | MGM | C1007 | 1965 | £8 | £20 | |
| Wooly Bully | 7" EP | MGM | 63623 | 1965 | £12.50 | £25 | French, group picture sleeve |
| Wooly Bully | 7" EP | MGM | 63623 | 1965 | £10 | £20 | French, sphinx picture sleeve |
| Wooly Bully | 7" | MGM | MGM1269 | 1965 | £1.50 | £4 | |
| Yakety Yak | 7" | MGM | MGM1379 | 1968 | £1.50 | £4 | |

## SAMAIN

| | | | | | | | |
|---|---|---|---|---|---|---|---|
| Vibrations Of Doom | LP | Roadrunner | | | £37.50 | £75 | Canadian |

## SAME

| | | | | | | | |
|---|---|---|---|---|---|---|---|
| Wild About You | 7" | Wessex | WEX267 | 1979 | £1.50 | £4 | |

## SAMETI

| | | | | | | | |
|---|---|---|---|---|---|---|---|
| Hungry For Love | LP | Warner Bros | 56074 | 1974 | £4 | £10 | German |
| Sameti | LP | Brain | 1020 | 1972 | £6 | £15 | German |

## SAMLA MAMMAS MANNA

| | | | | | | | |
|---|---|---|---|---|---|---|---|
| Klossa Knapitatet | LP | Silence | SRS4627 | 1974 | £4 | £10 | Swedish |
| Maltid | LP | Silence | SRS4621 | 1973 | £5 | £12 | Swedish |
| Samla Mammas Manna | LP | Silence | SRS4604 | 1971 | £6 | £15 | Swedish |
| Schlagerns Mystik/For Aldre Nybegynnare | LP | Silence | SRS4640 | 1978 | £6 | £15 | Swedish double |
| Snorungarnas Symfoni | LP | Musiknatet Waxholm | MNW70 | 1976 | £4 | £10 | Swedish |

## SAMMY

| | | | | | | | |
|---|---|---|---|---|---|---|---|
| Sammy | LP | Philips | 6308136 | 1972 | £8 | £20 | |

## SAMPSON, DAVE & THE HUNTERS

| | | | | | | | |
|---|---|---|---|---|---|---|---|
| Dave | 7" EP | Columbia | ESG7853 | 1961 | £37.50 | £75 | stereo |
| Dave | 7" EP | Columbia | SEG8095 | 1961 | £30 | £60 | |
| Easy To Dream | 7" | Columbia | DB4625 | 1961 | £2.50 | £6 | |
| If You Need Me | 7" | Columbia | DB4502 | 1960 | £4 | £8 | |
| Sweet Dreams | 7" | Columbia | DB4449 | 1960 | £4 | £8 | |
| Why The Chicken | 7" | Columbia | DB4597 | 1961 | £2 | £5 | |
| Wide Wide World | 7" | Fontana | H361 | 1962 | £1.50 | £4 | |

## SAMPSON, EDGAR

| | | | | | | | |
|---|---|---|---|---|---|---|---|
| Swing Softly Sweet Sampson | LP | Vogue Coral | LVA9039 | 1957 | £6 | £15 | |

## SAMPSON, TOMMY & HIS STRONGMEN

| | | | | | | | |
|---|---|---|---|---|---|---|---|
| Rockin' | 7" | Melodisc | 1411 | 1958 | £5 | £10 | |

## SAMSON

| | | | | | | | |
|---|---|---|---|---|---|---|---|
| Are You Samson | LP | Instant | INSP004 | 1969 | £15 | £30 | |

## SAMSON (2)

| | | | | | | | |
|---|---|---|---|---|---|---|---|
| Riding With The Angels | 7" | RCA | RCA67 | 1981 | £1.50 | £4 | picture disc |
| Telephone | 7" | Lightning | GIL547 | 1978 | £7.50 | £15 | |
| Vice Versa | 7" | EMI | EMI5061 | 1980 | £7.50 | £15 | promo only |

## SAMSON (3)

| | | | | | | | |
|---|---|---|---|---|---|---|---|
| Venus | 7" | Parlophone | R5867 | 1970 | £1.50 | £4 | |

## SAMUEL PRODY

| | | | | | | | |
|---|---|---|---|---|---|---|---|
| Samuel Prody | LP | Global | 6306906 | 1974 | £75 | £150 | German |

## SAMUELS, JERRY

| | | | | | | | |
|---|---|---|---|---|---|---|---|
| Puppy Love | 7" | HMV | 7M411 | 1956 | £1.50 | £4 | |

## SAMUELS, WINSTON

| | | | | | | | |
|---|---|---|---|---|---|---|---|
| Be Prepared | 7" | Ska Beat | JB196 | 1965 | £5 | £10 | |
| Follow | 7" | Rio | R26 | 1964 | £5 | £10 | |
| Greatest | 7" | Island | WI3051 | 1967 | £5 | £10 | |
| I Won't Be Discouraged | 7" | Island | WI3053 | 1967 | £5 | £10 | |
| Luck Will Come My Way | 7" | Black Swan | WI419 | 1964 | £5 | £10 | Lloyd Brevitt B side |
| My Angel | 7" | Ska Beat | JB214 | 1965 | £5 | £10 | |
| Time Will Tell | 7" | Ska Beat | JB244 | 1966 | £5 | £10 | |
| Up And Down | 7" | Ska Beat | JB241 | 1966 | £5 | £10 | |
| What Have I Done | 7" | Ska Beat | JB238 | 1966 | £5 | £10 | |
| You Are The One | 7" | Black Swan | WI426 | 1964 | £5 | £10 | |
| You Are The One | 7" | Columbia | DB7405 | 1964 | £2.50 | £6 | |

## SAMURAI

| | | | | | | | |
|---|---|---|---|---|---|---|---|
| Samurai | LP | Greenwich | GSLP1003 | 1971 | £37.50 | £75 | |

## SAN FRANCISCO EARTHQUAKE

| | | | | | | | |
|---|---|---|---|---|---|---|---|
| Fairy Tales Can Come True | 7" | Mercury | MF1036 | 1968 | £2 | £5 | |

## SAN REMO STRINGS

| | | | | | | | |
|---|---|---|---|---|---|---|---|
| Festival Time | 7" | Tamla Motown | TMG795 | 1971 | £1.50 | £4 | |

## SANCTUS

| | | | | | | | |
|---|---|---|---|---|---|---|---|
| Sound Of Celebration | LP | Focus | F3326 | 1975 | £25 | £50 | |

## SAND

| | | | | | | | |
|---|---|---|---|---|---|---|---|
| Sand | LP | Barnaby | BR15006 | 1973 | £6 | £15 | US double |

## SANDELLS

| | | | | | | | |
|---|---|---|---|---|---|---|---|
| Scramblers | LP | World Pacific | (ST)1818 | 1964 | £5 | £12 | US |
| Scramblers | LP | World Pacific | ST1818 | 1964 | £10 | £25 | US red vinyl |

## SANDERS, ALEX

| | | | | | | | |
|---|---|---|---|---|---|---|---|
| Witch Is Born | LP | A&M | AMLS984 | 1970 | £15 | £30 | |

## SANDERS, GARY

| | | | | | | | |
|---|---|---|---|---|---|---|---|
| Ain't No Beatle | 7" | Warner Bros | WB5676 | 1966 | £1.50 | £4 | |

## SANDERS, PHAROAH

These days, Pharoah Sanders has matured into a tranquil elder statesman of jazz. Originally, however, he was the angry young saxophonist with the flame-thrower technique, who was brought in by John Coltrane to help push his own playing towards a new peak of intensity. Sanders's own first album on ESP has become very scarce, although the music represents the uneasy compromise that results when a fiery, avant-garde player is provided with a rhythm section whose idea of an appropriate support derives from a politer, earlier time.

| | | | | | | | |
|---|---|---|---|---|---|---|---|
| Black Unity | LP | Impulse | AS9219 | 1972 £15 | £30 | |
| Live At The East | LP | Impulse | AS9227 | 1973 £10 | £25 | |
| Pharoah | LP | ESP-Disk | 1003 | 1965 £30 | £60 | |
| Elevation | LP | Impulse | AS9261 | 1974 £10 | £25 | US |
| Izipho Zau | LP | Strata East | | 197– £25 | £50 | |
| Jewels Of Thought | LP | Impulse | AS9190 | 1969 £10 | £25 | US |
| Karma | LP | Impulse | AS9181 | 1969 £10 | £25 | US |
| Pharoah | LP | India Navigation | IN1027 | 1977 £25 | £50 | |
| Summun Bukmun Umyun | LP | Impulse | AS9199 | 1971 £15 | £30 | US |
| Tauhid | LP | Impulse | AS9138 | 1967 £15 | £30 | US |
| Thembi | LP | Impulse | AS9206 | 1971 £8 | £20 | US |
| Village Of The Pharoahs | LP | Impulse | AS9254 | 1973 £15 | £30 | US |
| Wisdom Through Music | LP | Impulse | AS9238 | 1973 £15 | £30 | US |

### SANDERS, RAY
| | | | | | | | |
|---|---|---|---|---|---|---|---|
| World So Full Of Love | 7" | London | HLG7106 | 1960 £2.50 | £6 | export |

### SANDON, JOHNNY
| | | | | | | | |
|---|---|---|---|---|---|---|---|
| Blizzard | 7" | Pye | 7N15717 | 1964 £1.50 | £4 | |
| Donna Means Heartbreak | 7" | Pye | 7N15665 | 1964 £1.50 | £4 | |
| Lies | 7" | Pye | 7N15542 | 1963 £1.50 | £4 | |
| Magic Potion | 7" | Pye | 7N15559 | 1963 £1.50 | £4 | |
| Sixteen Tons | 7" | Pye | 7N15602 | 1964 £1.50 | £4 | |

### SANDPEBBLES
| | | | | | | | |
|---|---|---|---|---|---|---|---|
| Love Power | 7" | Track | 604015 | 1967 £2 | £5 | |
| Love Power | 7" | Track | 604028 | 1969 £2 | £5 | |

### SANDPIPERS
| | | | | | | | |
|---|---|---|---|---|---|---|---|
| Guantanamera | 7" EP | Pye | NEP44081 | 1966 £2 | £5 | |

### SANDRA
| | | | | | | | |
|---|---|---|---|---|---|---|---|
| I'll Never Be Maria Magdalena | 12" | 10 | TENY7812 | 1986 £3 | £8 | picture disc |

### SANDROSE

The music on the one album made by Sandrose is superior progressive rock, occupying similar territory to that of Yes. Rose Podwojny is a terrific singer, with a voice like a slightly more fragile Grace Slick, while guitarist Jean-Pierre Alarcen, who is the leader of the group, manages to deliver a number of impressive solos without ever outstaying his welcome. The album was one of the first rare progressive records to cross the £100 barrier (although its value has remained static since due to the availability of a vinyl reissue) and, for once, the music is worth it.

| | | | | | | | |
|---|---|---|---|---|---|---|---|
| Sandrose | LP | Polydor | 2480137 | 1972 £62.50 | £125 | |

### SANDS

The Sands evolved out of an R&B group called the Others, who began playing while at grammar school in Middlesex. The single, 'Mrs Gillespie's Refrigerator', however, is not R&B but a novelty Bee Gees song that the Gibb brothers wisely decided not to record themselves. The single is very collectable, but for the sake of its B side, 'Listen To The Sky'. This starts fairly unpromisingly too, but then, without warning, the song gives way to the sounds of an air attack, simulated by multiple overdriven guitars. The song then ends with a section of Gustav Holst's 'Mars', played on guitars.

| | | | | | | | |
|---|---|---|---|---|---|---|---|
| Mrs. Gillespie's Refrigerator | 7" | Reaction | 591017 | 1967 £62.50 | £125 | |
| Venus | 7" | Major Minor | MM681 | 1970 £5 | £10 | |

### SANDS (2)
| | | | | | | | |
|---|---|---|---|---|---|---|---|
| Dance Dance Dance | 7" | Tribune | TRS122 | 1969 £2 | £5 | |
| Sand Doin's | LP | Tribune | TRLP1009 | 1969 £10 | £25 | |

### SANDS, CLIVE
| | | | | | | | |
|---|---|---|---|---|---|---|---|
| Witchi Tai To | 7" | SNB | 554431 | 1969 £2.50 | £6 | |

### SANDS, DAVEY & THE ESSEX
| | | | | | | | |
|---|---|---|---|---|---|---|---|
| Advertising Girl | 7" | CBS | 202620 | 1967 £2.50 | £6 | |
| Please Be Mine | 7" | Decca | F12170 | 1965 £4 | £8 | |

### SANDS, EVIE
| | | | | | | | |
|---|---|---|---|---|---|---|---|
| Picture Me Gone | 7" | Cameo Parkway | C413 | 1966 £20 | £40 | |
| Take Me For A Little While | 7" | Red Bird | BC118 | 1965 £7.50 | £15 | |

### SANDS, JODIE
| | | | | | | | |
|---|---|---|---|---|---|---|---|
| All I Ask Of You | 7" | Starlite | ST45005 | 1958 £1.50 | £4 | |
| Please Don't Tell Me | 7" | London | HL8530 | 1957 £1.50 | £4 | |
| Someday | 7" | HMV | POP533 | 1958 £1.50 | £4 | |
| With All My Heart | 7" | London | HL8456 | 1957 £1.50 | £4 | |

### SANDS, TOMMY
| | | | | | | | |
|---|---|---|---|---|---|---|---|
| Big Date | 7" | Capitol | CL14889 | 1958 £2 | £5 | |
| Blue Ribbon Baby | 7" | Capitol | CL14925 | 1958 £5 | £10 | |
| Connie | 7" | HMV | POP1193 | 1963 £1.50 | £4 | |
| Dream With Me | LP | Capitol | T1426 | 1961 £8 | £20 | |
| Going Steady | 7" | Capitol | CL14745 | 1957 £2.50 | £6 | |
| Hawaiian Rock | 7" | Capitol | CL14872 | 1958 £5 | £10 | |
| Is It Ever Gonna Happen | 7" | Capitol | CL15013 | 1959 £5 | £10 | |
| Let Me Be Loved | 7" | Capitol | CL14781 | 1957 £2 | £5 | |
| Love In A Goldfish Bowl | 7" | Capitol | CL15219 | 1961 £1.50 | £4 | |
| Man Like Wow | 7" | Capitol | CL14811 | 1957 £2.50 | £6 | |

| | | | | | | |
|---|---|---|---|---|---|---|
| Old Oaken Bucket | 7" | Capitol | CL15143 | 1960 £1.50 | £4 | |
| Only 'Cos I'm Lonely | 7" | HMV | POP1247 | 1963 £1.50 | £4 | |
| Ring A Ding Ding | 7" | Capitol | CL14724 | 1957 £4 | £8 | |
| Sands At The Sands | LP | Capitol | (S)T1364 | 1960 £8 | £20 | US |
| Sands Storm | LP | Capitol | T1081 | 1959 £10 | £25 | |
| Sands Storm Part 1 | 7" EP | Capitol | EAP11081 | 1959 £10 | £20 | |
| Sands Storm Part 2 | 7" EP | Capitol | EAP21081 | 1959 £12.50 | £25 | |
| Sands Storm Part 3 | 7" EP | Capitol | EAP31081 | 1959 £12.50 | £25 | |
| Sing Boy Sing | LP | Capitol | T929 | 1958 £15 | £30 | |
| Sing Boy Sing | 7" | Capitol | CL14834 | 1958 £2.50 | £6 | |
| Sinner Man | 7" | Capitol | CL15047 | 1959 £1.50 | £4 | |
| Statue | 7" | Liberty | LIB55842 | 1966 £7.50 | £15 | |
| Steady Date | LP | Capitol | T848 | 1957 £15 | £30 | |
| Steady Date Part 1 | 7" EP | Capitol | EAP1848 | 1957 £10 | £20 | |
| Steady Date Part 2 | 7" EP | Capitol | EAP2848 | 1957 £10 | £20 | |
| Steady Date Part 3 | 7" EP | Capitol | EAP3848 | 1957 £10 | £20 | |
| Teenage Crush | 7" EP | Capitol | EAP1851 | 1957 £10 | £20 | |
| Teenage Crush | 7" | Capitol | CL14695 | 1957 £5 | £10 | |
| Teenage Rock | LP | Capitol | T1109 | 1959 £8 | £20 | US |
| That's The Way I Am | 7" | Capitol | CL15071 | 1959 £1.50 | £4 | |
| This Thing Called Love | LP | Capitol | T1123 | 1959 £6 | £15 | |
| This Thing Called Love | 7" EP | Capitol | EAP11123 | 1959 £6 | £12 | |
| When I'm Thinking Of You | LP | Capitol | (S)T1239 | 1960 £6 | £15 | |
| Worrying Kind | 7" | Capitol | CL14971 | 1959 £6 | £12 | |
| You Hold The Future | 7" | Capitol | CL15109 | 1960 £1.50 | £4 | |

## SANDS, TONY & THE DRUMBEATS

| | | | | | | |
|---|---|---|---|---|---|---|
| Shame Shame Shame | 7" | Studio 36 | NSRSEP1/2 | 1964 £75 | £150 | |

## SANDS, WES

| | | | | | | |
|---|---|---|---|---|---|---|
| There's Lots More Where This Came From | 7" | Columbia | DB4996 | 1963 £7.50 | £15 | |

## SANDS FAMILY

| | | | | | | |
|---|---|---|---|---|---|---|
| First Day And Second Day | LP | Autogram | FLLP501 | 1974 £5 | £12 | German |
| Folk From The Mournes | LP | Outlet | OAS3004 | 1968 £5 | £12 | Irish |
| Real Irish Folk | LP | Emerald | GES1201 | 1979 £5 | £12 | |
| Third Day | LP | Autogram | ALLP233 | 1974 £5 | £12 | German |
| You'll Be Well Looked After | LP | Leaf | 7005 | 1975 £4 | £10 | Irish |

## SANDY COAST

| | | | | | | |
|---|---|---|---|---|---|---|
| Blackboard Jungle Lady | 7" | Polydor | 2001457 | 1973 £5 | £10 | |
| From The Stereo Workshop | LP | Page One | POLS020 | 1969 £62.50 | £125 | |
| Shipwreck | LP | Page One | MORS201 | 1969 £62.50 | £125 | |
| Stone Wall | LP | Polydor | 2310277 | 1973 £8 | £20 | |

## SANSOM, BOBBY

| | | | | | | |
|---|---|---|---|---|---|---|
| There's A Place | 7" | Oriole | CB1837 | 1963 £2 | £5 | |
| Where Have You Been | 7" | Oriole | CB1888 | 1963 £1.50 | £4 | |

## SANSON, VERONIQUE

French singer-songwriter Véronique Sanson composed 'Amoureuse', which was a big hit for Kiki Dee. Her own version is the lead track of an excellent album which was released in two versions, one with French lyrics and one with English. One would not have thought that it would make much difference, but the French version is far superior. The way in which Ms Sanson's voice takes on an attractive soft vibrato at the end of the lines is ideally matched to the soft endings of the French words. In English she sounds a little ordinary, but in French the record stands revealed as a superb example of the singer-songwriting genre. Veronique Sanson is a considerable star in France these days, but 'Amoureuse' remains her only success outside that country.

| | | | | | | |
|---|---|---|---|---|---|---|
| Amoureuse | LP | Elektra | K42106 | 1972 £4 | £10 | English vocals |
| Véronique Sanson | LP | Elektra | K42106 | 1972 £4 | £10 | French vocals |

## SANTAMARIA, MONGO

| | | | | | | |
|---|---|---|---|---|---|---|
| 25 Miles | 7" | Direction | 584430 | 1969 £1.50 | £4 | |
| Cloud Nine | 7" | Direction | 584086 | 1969 £1.50 | £4 | |
| El Pussycat | 7" | CBS | 201766 | 1965 £1.50 | £4 | |
| Sherry | 7" | Oriole | | 1963 £7.50 | £15 | |
| Watermelon Man | 7" | Riverside | RIF106909 | 1963 £2.50 | £6 | |
| Working On A Groovy Thing | LP | CBS | 63904 | 1971 £4 | £10 | |

## SANTANA

| | | | | | | |
|---|---|---|---|---|---|---|
| Abraxas | LP | CBS | Q64087 | 1974 £4 | £10 | quad |
| Abraxas | LP | Columbia | HC40130 | 1981 £4 | £10 | US audiophile |
| Abraxas | CD | Mobile Fidelity | UDCD552 | 1991 £6 | £15 | US audiophile |
| Amigos | LP | Columbia | PCQ33576 | 1975 £4 | £10 | US quad |
| Barboletta | LP | CBS | Q69084 | 1974 £4 | £10 | quad |
| Beyond Appearances | CD | CBS | CD86307 | 1986 £5 | £12 | |
| Blues For Salvador | CD | CBS | 4602582 | 1987 £5 | £12 | |
| Caravanserai | LP | CBS | Q65299 | 1974 £4 | £10 | quad |
| Festival | LP | Columbia | PCQ34423 | 1977 £4 | £10 | US quad |
| Freedom | CD | CBS | 4503942 | 1987 £5 | £12 | |
| Greatest Hits | LP | CBS | Q69081 | 1974 £4 | £10 | quad |
| Gypsy Woman | CD-s | CBS | 6560272 | 1990 £2 | £5 | |
| Havana Moon | CD | CBS | CD25350 | 1987 £5 | £12 | |
| Illuminations | LP | Columbia | PCQ32900 | 1974 £4 | £10 | US quad |
| Marathon | CD | CBS | CD86098 | 1987 £5 | £12 | |
| Mother Earth Tour | CD | Columbia | CSK2099 | 1990 £10 | £25 | US promo |
| Santana | LP | CBS | 63815 | 1970 £4 | £10 | laminated cover |
| Santana | LP | Columbia | PCQ32964 | 1974 £4 | £10 | US quad |

| | | | | | | | | |
|---|---|---|---|---|---|---|---|---|
| Santana III | LP | CBS | Q69015 | 1974 | £4 | £10 | quad |
| Solo Guitar Of Devadip Carlos Santana | LP | Columbia | AS573 | 1979 | £8 | £20 | US promo |
| Spirits Dancing In The Flesh | CD | CBS | 4669132 | 1990 | £5 | £12 | |
| Viva Santana – sampler | CD | Columbia | CSK1264 | 1988 | £8 | £20 | US promo |
| Welcome | LP | CBS | Q69040 | 1974 | £4 | £10 | quad |
| Zebop | LP | Columbia | HC47158 | 1981 | £4 | £10 | US audiophile |
| Zebop | CD | CBS | CD84946 | 1985 | £5 | £12 | |

## SANTELLS
| | | | | | | |
|---|---|---|---|---|---|---|
| So Fine | 7" | Sue | WI4020 | 1966 | £6 | £12 |

## SANTO & JOHNNY
| | | | | | | | |
|---|---|---|---|---|---|---|---|
| Beatles' Greatest Hits | LP | Canadian American | (S)1017 | 1964 | £8 | £20 | US |
| Birmingham | 7" | Parlophone | R4865 | 1962 | £1.50 | £4 | |
| Brilliant Guitar Sounds | LP | Imperial | LP9363/12363 | 1967 | £4 | £10 | US |
| Bullseye | 7" | Parlophone | R4844 | 1961 | £1.50 | £4 | |
| Caravan | 7" | Parlophone | R4644 | 1960 | £1.50 | £4 | |
| Come On In | LP | Canadian American | (S)1006 | 1962 | £6 | £15 | US |
| Come September | 7" | Pye | 7N25111 | 1961 | £1.50 | £4 | |
| Encore | LP | Canadian American | (S)1002 | 1960 | £6 | £15 | US |
| Golden Guitars | LP | Imperial | LP12366 | 1968 | £4 | £10 | US |
| Hawaii | LP | Stateside | (S)SL1008 | 1964 | £6 | £15 | |
| In The Still Of The Night | LP | Canadian American | (S)1014 | 1963 | £6 | £15 | US |
| Mona Lisa | LP | Philips | (S)BL7760 | 1967 | £4 | £10 | |
| Mucho | LP | Canadian American | (S)1018 | 1965 | £5 | £12 | US |
| Off Shore | LP | Canadian American | (S)1011 | 1963 | £6 | £15 | US |
| On The Road Again | LP | Imperial | LP12418 | 1968 | £4 | £10 | US |
| Pulcinella | LP | Philips | (S)BL7759 | 1967 | £4 | £10 | |
| Santo & Johnny No. 1 | 7" EP | Parlophone | GEP8806 | 1960 | £6 | £12 | |
| Santo & Johnny No. 2 | 7" EP | Parlophone | GEP8813 | 1960 | £6 | £12 | |
| Santo And Johnny | LP | Canadian American | 1001 | 1959 | £10 | £25 | US |
| Sleepwalk | 7" | Pye | 7N25037 | 1959 | £1.50 | £4 | |
| Spanish Harlem | 7" | Stateside | SS110 | 1962 | £1.50 | £4 | |
| Teardrop | 7" | Parlophone | R4619 | 1960 | £1.50 | £4 | |
| Wish You Were Here | LP | Canadian American | (S)1016 | 1964 | £6 | £15 | US |

## SANTORO, ANGELO NOCE
| | | | | | | | |
|---|---|---|---|---|---|---|---|
| For You | LP | ANS | | 1979 | £6 | £15 | Dutch |
| Land Of The Pharao | LP | ANS | | 1981 | £6 | £15 | Dutch |

## SAPPHIRE THINKERS
| | | | | | | | |
|---|---|---|---|---|---|---|---|
| From Within | LP | Hobbit | 5003 | 1969 | £20 | £40 | US |

## SAPPHIRES
| | | | | | | | |
|---|---|---|---|---|---|---|---|
| Evil One | 7" | HMV | POP1461 | 1965 | £37.50 | £75 | |
| Gotta Have Your Love | 7" | HMV | POP1441 | 1965 | £37.50 | £75 | |
| Who Do You Love | LP | Swan | LP513 | 1964 | £25 | £50 | US |
| Who Do You Love | 7" | Stateside | SS267 | 1964 | £10 | £20 | |
| Your True Love | 7" | Stateside | SS223 | 1963 | £10 | £20 | |

## SARABAND
| | | | | | | |
|---|---|---|---|---|---|---|
| Close To It All | LP | Folk Heritage | FHR050 | 1973 | £10 | £25 |

## SARACEN
| | | | | | | |
|---|---|---|---|---|---|---|
| Heroes Saints And Fools | LP | Nucleus | NEAT492 | 1982 | £6 | £15 |
| No More Lonely Nights | 7" | Nucleus | SAR1 | 1982 | £2 | £5 |
| We Have Arrived | 7" | Nucleus | NEAT30 | 1983 | £2 | £5 |

## SARGEANT, DEREK & HAZEL KING
| | | | | | | |
|---|---|---|---|---|---|---|
| Folk Matters | LP | Assembly | JP3012 | 1973 | £25 | £50 |
| Sings English Folk | LP | Joy | JS5001 | 1970 | £10 | £25 |

## SARGENT, DON
| | | | | | | |
|---|---|---|---|---|---|---|
| Gypsy Boots | 7" | Vogue | V9160 | 1960 | £75 | £150 |

## SARI & THE SHALIMARS
| | | | | | | |
|---|---|---|---|---|---|---|
| It's So Lonely Being Together | 7" | United Artists | UP2235 | 1968 | £4 | £8 |

## SARJEANT, DEREK
| | | | | | | |
|---|---|---|---|---|---|---|
| Derek Sarjeant Folk Trio | LP | Assembly | JP3001 | 1971 | £15 | £30 |
| Folk Songs | 7" EP | Oak | RGJ101 | 196– | £10 | £20 |
| Folk Songs Vol. 2 | 7" EP | Oak | RGJ105 | 196– | £10 | £20 |
| Man Of Kent | 7" EP | Oak | RGJ117 | 1963 | £10 | £20 |
| Songs We Like To Sing | 7" EP | Oak | RGJ103 | 196– | £7.50 | £15 |

## SARNE, MIKE
| | | | | | | | |
|---|---|---|---|---|---|---|---|
| Come Outside | LP | Parlophone | PMC1187 | 1962 | £10 | £25 | |
| Just Like Eddie | 7" | Parlophone | DP558 | 1963 | £20 | £40 | export |
| Love Me Please | 7" | Parlophone | R5170 | 1964 | £1.50 | £4 | |
| Mike Sarne Hit Parade | 7" EP | Parlophone | GEP8879 | 1963 | £7.50 | £15 | |

Out And About..................................... 7" ...... Parlophone...... R5129 ................. 1964 £1.50........£4 ..................................

## SAROFEEN & SMOKE
Do It........................................................ LP ...... Pye ................. NSPL28153 ...... 1971 £4...........£10

## SASSENACHS
That Don't Worry Me ........................... 7" ...... Fontana ............. TF518 ................. 1964 £4...........£8

## SATAN & THE DE-CIPLES
Underground ......................................... LP ...... Goldband ........ 7750 .................. 1969 £50........£100 ..................................... US

## SATANIC RITES
Live To Ride ......................................... 7" ...... Heavy Metal.... HEAVY8 ................. 1981 £4...........£8

## SATAN'S RATS
In My Love For You ............................ 7" ...... DJM ............. DJS10819 ............... 1977 £4...........£8
Year Of The Rats................................. 7" ...... DJM ............. DJS10821 ............... 1978 £4...........£8
You Make Me Sick ............................... 7" ...... DJM ............. DJS10840 ............... 1978 £4...........£8

## SATCHMO, PAT
Hello Dolly............................................ 7" ...... Upsetter ........... US316. ................. 1969 £1.50........£4

## SATIN BELLS
I Stand Accused.................................... 7" ...... Decca ............. F22937 ................. 1969 £1.50........£4

## SATIN WHALE
Desert Places........................................ LP ...... Brain ............. 0001049 ................. 1974 £4...........£10 ..................... German

## SATINS FOUR & THE CINNAMON ANGELS
Mixed Soul............................................ LP ...... B.T.Puppy ...... S1010................... 1970 £6...........£15 ..................................... US

## SATISFACTION
Satisfaction........................................... LP ...... Decca ............. SKL5075 ............... 1971 £5...........£12

## SATISFIERS
Where'll I Be Tomorrow Tonight? ............ 7" ...... Vogue Coral.... Q72247............... 1957 £4...........£8

## SATRIANI, JOE
Satch EP............................................... CD-s .. Relativity ...... 6589532................. 1991 £2...........£5
Surfing With The Alien ............................ LP ...... Food For ....... GRUB8P ............. 1987 £4...........£10 ..............picture disc
                                                              Thought..........

## SATTIN, LONNIE
Trapped.................................................. 7" ...... Capitol............ CL14552................. 1956 £1.50........£4

## SATURNALIA
Like the other early rock LP picture disc (Curved Air's *Airconditioning*), *Magical Love* looks rather better than it sounds, for only a few playings are enough to make the sound quality begin to deteriorate seriously. And unlike the situation with Curved Air, Saturnalia's record was never issued in the more conventional form. As a result, it is hard to be fair to the music: it sounds like third-division progressive fare – a bit like Principal Edward's Magic Theatre on an off day – but listening through the welter of background hiss one cannot be sure. To be complete, by the way, the record should come with a booklet, although few copies of this seem to have survived.

Magical Love ........................................ LP ...... Matrix............. TRIX1 ................. 1969 £10........£25 *picture disc with centre*
                                                                                                                    *pattern & booklet*
Magical Love ........................................ LP ...... Matrix............. TRIX1 ................. 1969 £25........£50 *..... test pressing, black*
                                                                                                                    *vinyl*

## SAUNDERS, LARRY
On The Real Side ................................. 7" ...... London ........... HLU10469 ............. 1974 £2...........£5

## SAUTER, JIM & DON DIETRICH
Bells Together....................................... LP ...... Agaric ............. AG1985 ............... 1985 £8...........£20 ..................................... US

## SAUTER-FINEGAN ORCHESTRA
Inside Sauter-Finegan............................ LP ...... HMV ............. CLP1027 ............... 1955 £10........£25
Memories Of Goodman And Miller .......... LP ...... RCA ............. RD27093/SF5029... 1959 £5...........£12

## SAUTERELLES
Les Sauterelles .................................... LP ...... Columbia ....... 10108................... 1968 £15........£30 ..................................... Swiss
View To Heaven.................................... LP ...... Decca ............. SLK16561 ............. 1968 £20........£40 ..................... German

## SAVAGE, EDNA
Arrivederci Darling................................ 7" ...... Parlophone...... MSP6189 ............. 1955 £4...........£8
Candlelight............................................ 7" ...... Parlophone...... MSP6181 ............. 1955 £2.50........£6
Let Me Be Loved .................................. 7" ...... Parlophone...... R4360 ................. 1957 £1.50........£4
Me Head's In De Barrel ........................ 7" ...... Parlophone...... R4301 ................. 1957 £1.50........£4
My Prayer.............................................. 7" ...... Parlophone...... R4226 ................. 1956 £2...........£5
Never Leave Me .................................... 7" ...... Parlophone...... R4253 ................. 1957 £1.50........£4
Please Hurry Home .............................. 7" ...... Parlophone...... MSP6217 ............. 1956 £2...........£5
Stars Shine In Your Eyes...................... 7" ...... Parlophone...... MSP6175 ............. 1955 £2.50........£6

## SAVAGE, JOAN
Five Oranges, Four Apples ................... 7" ...... Columbia ....... DB3929 ............... 1957 £1.50........£4
Left Right Out Of My Heart................... 7" ...... Columbia ....... DB4159 ............... 1958 £1.50........£4
Love Letters In The Sand ..................... 7" ...... Columbia ....... DB3968 ............... 1957 £1.50........£4
Shake Me I Rattle ................................. 7" ...... Columbia ....... DB4039 ............... 1957 £4...........£8

## SAVAGE RESURRECTION
| | | | | | | | |
|---|---|---|---|---|---|---|---|
| Savage Resurrection | LP | Mercury | SMCL20123 | 1968 | £10 | £25 | |
| Thing In E | 7" | Mercury | MF1027 | 1968 | £5 | £10 | |

## SAVAGE ROSE
| | | | | | | | |
|---|---|---|---|---|---|---|---|
| In The Plain | LP | Polydor | 46292 | 1968 | £4 | £10 | |
| Savage Rose | LP | Polydor | 184144 | 1968 | £4 | £10 | |
| Travellin' | LP | Polydor | 184316 | 1969 | £4 | £10 | |

## SAVAGES
| | | | | | | | |
|---|---|---|---|---|---|---|---|
| Everybody Surf | 7" EP | Decca | DFE8546 | 1963 | £100 | £200 | |
| Live 'n' Wild | LP | Resurrection | CX1330 | 1984 | £5 | £12 | US |
| Surfin' USA | 7" EP | Decca | 457020 | 1963 | £100 | £200 | French |

## SAVAGES (2)
| | | | | | | | |
|---|---|---|---|---|---|---|---|
| Live And Wild | LP | Duane | 1047 | 1966 | £180 | £300 | US |

## SAVARIN, JULIAN JAY
| | | | | | | | |
|---|---|---|---|---|---|---|---|
| I Am You | 7" | Lyntone | LYN3426 | 197– | £2.50 | £6 | |
| Waiters On The Dance | LP | Birth | RAB2 | 1971 | £50 | £100 | |

## SAVOY BROWN
Savoy Brown passed through numerous line-ups, in which the presence of guitarist Kim Simmonds was the only constant factor. Simmonds and his companions lacked the imagination to break very far out of the constraints of playing the blues, although they tried hardest on *Blue Matter*, which includes the memorable 'Train To Nowhere'.

| | | | | | | | |
|---|---|---|---|---|---|---|---|
| Blue Matter | LP | Decca | LK/SKL4994 | 1968 | £8 | £20 | |
| Boogie Brothers | LP | Decca | SKL5186 | 1974 | £4 | £10 | |
| Getting To The Point | LP | Decca | LK/SKL4925 | 1968 | £10 | £25 | |
| Hard Way To Go | 7" | Decca | F13019 | 1970 | £1.50 | £4 | |
| Hellbound Train | LP | Decca | TXS107 | 1972 | £4 | £10 | |
| I Tried | 7" | Purdah | 453503 | 1966 | £37.50 | £75 | |
| I'm Tired | 7" | Decca | F12978 | 1969 | £1.50 | £4 | |
| Jack The Toad | LP | Decca | TXS112 | 1973 | £4 | £10 | |
| Lion's Share | LP | Decca | SKL5152 | 1973 | £4 | £10 | |
| Looking In | LP | Decca | SKL5066 | 1970 | £5 | £12 | |
| Poor Girl | 7" | Decca | F13098 | 1970 | £1.50 | £4 | |
| Raw Sienna | LP | Decca | LK5030 | 1970 | £6 | £15 | mono |
| Raw Sienna | LP | Decca | SKL5030 | 1970 | £5 | £12 | stereo |
| Shake Down | LP | Decca | LK/SKL4883 | 1967 | £10 | £25 | |
| Skin 'n' Bone | LP | London | PS670 | 1976 | £4 | £10 | US |
| Step Further | LP | Decca | LK/SKL5013 | 1969 | £6 | £15 | |
| Street Corner Talking | LP | Decca | TXS104 | 1970 | £4 | £10 | |
| Taste And Try Before You Buy | 7" | Decca | F12702 | 1967 | £2.50 | £6 | |
| Tell Mama | 7" | Decca | F13247 | 1971 | £1.50 | £4 | |
| Train To Nowhere | 7" | Decca | F12843 | 1969 | £1.50 | £4 | |
| Walking By Myself | 7" | Decca | F12797 | 1968 | £1.50 | £4 | |
| Wire Fire | LP | London | PS659 | 1975 | £4 | £10 | US |

## SAXON
| | | | | | | | |
|---|---|---|---|---|---|---|---|
| And The Bands Played On | 7" | Carrere | CAR180P | 1981 | £1.50 | £4 | picture disc |
| Back On The Streets | 7" | Parlophone | RP6103 | 1985 | £1.50 | £4 | shaped picture disc |
| Power And The Glory | 7" | RCA | SAXONP1 | 1983 | £1.50 | £4 | signed picture disc |
| Ride Like The Wind | CD-s | EMI | CDEM43 | 1988 | £2 | £5 | |
| Rock The Nations | 7" | EMI | EMIP5587 | 1986 | £1.50 | £4 | shaped picture disc |

## SAXON, AL
| | | | | | | | |
|---|---|---|---|---|---|---|---|
| Battle Of The Sexes | 7" EP | Fontana | TFE17271 | 1960 | £4 | £8 | |
| Big Deal | 7" EP | Fontana | TFE17202 | 1959 | £4 | £8 | |
| Only Sixteen | 7" | Fontana | H205 | 1959 | £1.50 | £4 | |
| Those You've Never Heard | 7" EP | Fontana | TFE17014 | 1958 | £4 | £8 | |
| You're The Top Cha | 7" | Fontana | H164 | 1958 | £1.50 | £4 | |

## SAXON, SKY
| | | | | | | | |
|---|---|---|---|---|---|---|---|
| Dog=God | 7" | Fierce | FRIGHT029 | 1987 | £4 | £8 | various inserts |
| They Say | 7" | Conquest | 777 | 196– | £10 | £20 | US |

## SAXONS
| | | | | | | | |
|---|---|---|---|---|---|---|---|
| Meet The Saxons | LP | Ace Of Clubs | ACL1173 | 1963 | £37.50 | £75 | |
| Saxon War Cry | 7" | Decca | F12179 | 1965 | £12.50 | £25 | |

## SAXONS (2)
| | | | | | | | |
|---|---|---|---|---|---|---|---|
| Love Minus Zero | LP | Mirrosonic | AS1017 | 1966 | £10 | £25 | US |

## SAYLES, JOHNNY
| | | | | | | | |
|---|---|---|---|---|---|---|---|
| Deep Down In Your Heart | 7" | Liberty | LIB12042 | 1966 | £2.50 | £6 | |

## SCAFFOLD
| | | | | | | | |
|---|---|---|---|---|---|---|---|
| 2 Day's Monday | 7" | Parlophone | R5443 | 1966 | £1.50 | £4 | |
| Do You Remember? | 7" | Parlophone | R5679 | 1968 | £1.50 | £4 | |
| Evening With The Scaffold | LP | Parlophone | PMC/PCS7051 | 1968 | £5 | £12 | |
| Fresh Liver | LP | Island | ILPS9234 | 1973 | £4 | £10 | |
| Goodbat Nightman | 7" | Parlophone | R5548 | 1966 | £1.50 | £4 | |
| L The P | LP | Parlophone | PMC/PCS7077 | 1969 | £4 | £10 | |

## SCAGGS, BOZ

| | | | | | | | | |
|---|---|---|---|---|---|---|---|---|
| Boz | LP | Polydor | LPHM46253 | 1965 | £20 | £40 | | Swedish |
| Boz Scaggs | LP | Atlantic | 588205 | 1969 | £4 | £10 | | |
| Boz Scaggs | LP | Columbia | AS203 | 1974 | £6 | £15 | | US promo sampler |
| Silk Degrees | LP | Columbia | HC43920 | 1980 | £4 | £10 | | US audiophile |
| Still Falling For You | LP | Columbia | | 1978 | £6 | £15 | | US early version of 'Two Down Then Left' |

## SCALES, HARVEY & THE SOUND

| | | | | | | | |
|---|---|---|---|---|---|---|---|
| Get Down | 7" | Atlantic | 584146 | 1967 | £1.50 | £4 | |

## SCAMPS

| | | | | | | | |
|---|---|---|---|---|---|---|---|
| Petite Fleur | 7" | London | HLW8827 | 1959 | £1.50 | £4 | |

## SCAPA FLOW

| | | | | | | | |
|---|---|---|---|---|---|---|---|
| Uuteen Aikaan | LP | | KOLP22 | 1980 | £37.50 | £75 | Finnish |

## SCARECROW

| | | | | | | | |
|---|---|---|---|---|---|---|---|
| Scarecrow | LP | Spilt Milk | SMFM11278 | 1978 | £30 | £60 | numbered |

## SCENE

| | | | | | | | |
|---|---|---|---|---|---|---|---|
| Hey Girl | 7" | Hole In The Wall | HS1 | 1980 | £1.50 | £4 | |

## SCHAEFER, HAL ORCHESTRA

| | | | | | | | |
|---|---|---|---|---|---|---|---|
| March Of The Vikings | 7" | London | HLT8692 | 1958 | £1.50 | £4 | |

## SCHAUBROECK, ARMAND STEALS

| | | | | | | | |
|---|---|---|---|---|---|---|---|
| I Came To Visit | LP | Mirror | 3 | 1977 | £6 | £15 | US |
| Live At Holiday Inn | LP | Mirror | 4 | 1977 | £8 | £20 | US, with 12" |
| Lot Of People Would Like To See A. S. Dead | LP | Mirror | FPV42202/3/4 | 1977 | £10 | £25 | US triple |
| Ratfucker | LP | Mirror | 7 | 1978 | £6 | £15 | US |
| Shakin' Shakin' | LP | Mirror | 5 | 1978 | £6 | £15 | US |

## SCHICKERT, GUNTER

| | | | | | | | |
|---|---|---|---|---|---|---|---|
| Samtvogel | LP | Brain | 1080 | 1975 | £5 | £12 | German |
| Samtvogel | LP | SCH | 33003 | 1974 | £15 | £30 | German |

## SCHIFRIN, LALO

| | | | | | | | |
|---|---|---|---|---|---|---|---|
| Mission Impossible | LP | Dot | (S)LPD503 | 1968 | £10 | £25 | |
| Mission Impossible | 7" | Dot | DOT103 | 1968 | £2 | £5 | |
| More Mission Impossible | LP | Paramount | SPFL252 | 1969 | £15 | £30 | |

## SCHMETTERLINGE

| | | | | | | | |
|---|---|---|---|---|---|---|---|
| Boom Boom Boomerang | 7" | Pye | 7N25743 | 1977 | £2.50 | £6 | |

## SCHMIDT, ZAPPATA

| | | | | | | | |
|---|---|---|---|---|---|---|---|
| It's Gonna Get You | LP | President | PTLS1041 | 1971 | £4 | £10 | |

## SCHMITT, OLIVER LINDSEY

| | | | | | | | |
|---|---|---|---|---|---|---|---|
| Graffenstadden | LP | private | | 1972 | £20 | £40 | |

## SCHNITZLER, CONRAD

| | | | | | | | |
|---|---|---|---|---|---|---|---|
| Auf Dem Schwarzen Kanal | LP | RCA | 5908 | 1980 | £4 | £10 | German |
| Black Cassette | cass | private | | 1974 | £6 | £15 | German |
| Blau | LP | Block | KS1003 | 1972 | £8 | £20 | German |
| Con | LP | Paragon | 66052 | 1978 | £4 | £10 | German |
| Con 3 | LP | Sky | SKY061 | 1981 | £4 | £10 | German |
| Conal | LP | Uniton | U002 | 1981 | £4 | £10 | Norwegian |
| Conrad Und Sohn | LP | private | GS1001 | 1981 | £4 | £10 | German |
| Contempora | LP | private | CT1001 | 1981 | £4 | £10 | German |
| Control | LP | Dys | DYS04 | 1981 | £4 | £10 | US |
| Convex | LP | private | GS1002 | 1982 | £4 | £10 | German |
| Conzequenz | LP | Block | KS1004 | 1980 | £4 | £10 | German |
| Gelb | LP | Block | EB110 | 1983 | £4 | £10 | German |
| Grun | LP | Block | EB111 | 1983 | £4 | £10 | German |
| Red Cassette | cass | private | | 1974 | £6 | £15 | German |
| Rot | LP | Block | KS1002 | 1971 | £8 | £20 | German |
| Schwarz | LP | Block | KS1001 | 1971 | £8 | £20 | German |

## SCHOENER, EBERHARD

| | | | | | | | |
|---|---|---|---|---|---|---|---|
| Bali Agung | LP | Horzu | 29647 | 1976 | £4 | £10 | German |
| Bastien Und Bastienne | LP | EMI | 30231 | 1977 | £4 | £10 | German |
| Book | LP | Ariola | 28706 | 1978 | £4 | £10 | German |
| Day's Lullaby | LP | Reprise | REP44143 | 1971 | £4 | £10 | German |
| Der Schauspieldirektor | LP | EMI | 30230 | 1977 | £4 | £10 | German |
| Destruction Of Harmony | LP | Ariola | 808471U | 1971 | £5 | £12 | German |
| Die Schachtel | LP | Reprise | | 1971 | £10 | £25 | German |
| Events | LP | Harvest | 45879 | 1980 | £4 | £10 | German |
| Flash Back | LP | Harvest | 32839 | 1978 | £4 | £10 | German |
| Meditation | LP | Ariola | 87131 | 1974 | £4 | £10 | German |
| Spurensicherung | LP | Phonogram | 814167 | 1983 | £4 | £10 | German |
| Trance Formation | LP | Harvest | 32526 | 1977 | £4 | £10 | German |
| Video Magic | LP | Harvest | 45234 | 1978 | £4 | £10 | German |
| Windows | LP | EMI | 95634 | 1974 | £4 | £10 | German |

## SCHOOL BOYS

| | | | | | | |
|---|---|---|---|---|---|---|
| Dream Lover | 7" | Port-O-Jam | PJ4000 | 1964 | £5 | £10 |
| Little Dilly | 7" | Blue Beat | BB174 | 1963 | £6 | £12 ...Prince Buster B side |

## SCHOOL GIRLS

| | | | | | | |
|---|---|---|---|---|---|---|
| Last Time | 7" | Blue Beat | BB214 | 1964 | £6 | £12 |
| Live Up To Justice | 7" | Blue Beat | BB185 | 1963 | £6 | £12 |
| Love Another Love | 7" | Blue Beat | BB168 | 1963 | £6 | £12 |
| Never Let You Go | 7" | Blue Beat | BB263 | 1964 | £6 | £12 ...... Skatalites B side |

## SCHOOLBOYS

| | | | | | | |
|---|---|---|---|---|---|---|
| Beatle Mania | LP | Palace | 778 | 1964 | £8 | £20 ...... US |

## SCHROEDER, JOHN ORCHESTRA

| | | | | | | |
|---|---|---|---|---|---|---|
| Agent OO Soul | 7" | Piccadilly | 7N35271 | 1965 | £2.50 | £6 |
| Fugitive Theme | 7" | Piccadilly | 7N35240 | 1965 | £1.50 | £4 ...... picture sleeve |
| Hungry For Love | 7" | Piccadilly | 7N35285 | 1966 | £2 | £5 |
| Soul For Sale | 7" | Piccadilly | 7N35362 | 1967 | £4 | £8 |
| Virgin Soldiers March | 7" | Pye | 7N17862 | 1969 | £1.50 | £4 |
| Working In The Soulmine | LP | Piccadilly | N(S)PL38025 | 1966 | £5 | £12 |
| You've Lost That Lovin' Feeling | 7" | Piccadilly | 7N35253 | 1965 | £1.50 | £4 |

## SCHULLER, GUNTHER

| | | | | | | |
|---|---|---|---|---|---|---|
| Jazz Abstractions | LP | Atlantic | 587/588043 | 1966 | £6 | £15 |

## SCHULMAN, IVY & THE BOWTIES

| | | | | | | |
|---|---|---|---|---|---|---|
| Rock Pretty Baby | 7" | London | HLN8372 | 1957 | £20 | £40 |

## SCHULTZ, ERNST

| | | | | | | |
|---|---|---|---|---|---|---|
| Paranoia Picknick | LP | Kuckuck | 2375014 | 1972 | £10 | £25 ...... German |

## SCHULZE, KLAUS

Although Schulze started his recording career as a drummer with Tangerine Dream (he appears on the group's debut, *Electronic Meditation*), all his own albums, of which there are a large number, contain music performed by a bank of synthesizers. Schulze's music, which has a kinship with that of Tangerine Dream, tends nevertheless to sound starker and more experimental. His records vary considerably in their effectiveness, but at their best, they show Schulze to be the finest synthesizer artist of all. *Irrlicht* is available in two different versions – the one listed here has the added benefit of a real orchestra blended with the electronics.

| | | | | | | |
|---|---|---|---|---|---|---|
| Black Dance | LP | Brain | 1051 | 1974 | £6 | £15 ...... German |
| Cyborg | LP | Komische | KM258005 | 1973 | £8 | £20 ...... German double |
| Irrlicht | LP | Ohr | OMM556022 | 1972 | £6 | £15 ...... German |
| Picture Music | LP | Brain | 1067 | 1974 | £4 | £10 ...... German |

## SCHUMANN, WALTER

| | | | | | | |
|---|---|---|---|---|---|---|
| Haunted House | 7" | HMV | 7M229 | 1954 | £1.50 | £4 |
| Man From Laramie | 7" | HMV | 7M323 | 1955 | £1.50 | £4 |

## SCHUNGE

| | | | | | | |
|---|---|---|---|---|---|---|
| Ballad Of A Simple Love | LP | Regal Zonophone | SLRZ1033 | 1972 | £6 | £15 |
| Ballad Of A Simple Love | 7" | Regal Zonophone | RZ3077 | 1973 | £1.50 | £4 |
| Misty | 7" | Regal Zonophone | RZ3066 | 1972 | £1.50 | £4 |

## SCIENCE POPTION

| | | | | | | |
|---|---|---|---|---|---|---|
| You've Got Me High | 7" | Columbia | DB8106 | 1967 | £15 | £30 |

## SCIENTIST

| | | | | | | |
|---|---|---|---|---|---|---|
| Professor In Action | 7" | Amalgamated | AMG848 | 1969 | £2.50 | £6 |

## SCI-FI SEX STARS

| | | | | | | |
|---|---|---|---|---|---|---|
| Rock It Miss USA | 12" | Sputnicko | WMI001 | 1986 | £2.50 | £6 |

## SCOBEY, BOB

| | | | | | | |
|---|---|---|---|---|---|---|
| Bob Scobey Band | LP | Columbia | 33CX10058 | 1956 | £5 | £12 |
| Bob Scobey Band | 10" LP | Good Time Jazz | LDG155 | 1955 | £6 | £15 |
| Bob Scobey's Frisco Band | LP | Good Time Jazz | LAG12116 | 1958 | £6 | £15 |
| Bob Scobey's Frisco Band | LP | Good Time Jazz | LAG12180 | 1959 | £5 | £12 |
| Bob Scobey's Frisco Jazz Band | 10" LP | HMV | DLP1146 | 1957 | £5 | £12 |
| Scobey And Clancy | LP | Good Time Jazz | LAG12145 | 1959 | £5 | £12 ....with Clancy Hayes |
| Swingin' On The Golden Gate | LP | RCA | RD27031 | 1958 | £5 | £12 |

## SCORCHED EARTH

| | | | | | | |
|---|---|---|---|---|---|---|
| Tomorrow Never Comes | 7" | Carrere | CAR342 | 1985 | £4 | £8 |
| Tomorrow Never Comes | 12" | Carrere | CART342 | 1985 | £10 | £20 |

## SCORCHERS

| | | | | | | |
|---|---|---|---|---|---|---|
| Ugly Man | 7" | Doctor Bird | DB1170 | 1968 | £5 | £10 |

## SCORE

| | | | | | | |
|---|---|---|---|---|---|---|
| Please Please Me | 7" | Decca | F12527 | 1966 | £50 | £100 |

## SCORPIONS
| | | | | | | | |
|---|---|---|---|---|---|---|---|
| Fly To The Rainbow | CD | RCA | ND70084 | 1988 | £5 | £12 | |
| Lonesome Crow | LP | Brain | 1001 | 1972 | £4 | £10 | *German* |
| Lonesome Crow | LP | Heavy Metal | MHIPD2 | 1982 | £4 | £10 | *picture disc* |
| Passion Rules The Game | CD-s .. | Harvest | CDHAR5242 | 1989 | £2 | £5 | |

## SCORPIONS (2)
| | | | | | | | |
|---|---|---|---|---|---|---|---|
| Riders In The Sky | 7" | Parlophone | R4740 | 1961 | £4 | £8 | |
| Scorpio | 7" | Parlophone | R4768 | 1961 | £4 | £8 | |

## SCORPIONS (3)
| | | | | | | | |
|---|---|---|---|---|---|---|---|
| Scorpions | LP | Tower | ST5171 | 1969 | £8 | £20 | *US* |

## SCORPIONS (4)
| | | | | | | | |
|---|---|---|---|---|---|---|---|
| Climbing The Charts | LP | CNR | LPT35023 | 1965 | £50 | £100 | *Dutch* |
| Hello Josephine | LP | CNR | GA5000 | 1965 | £15 | £30 | *Dutch* |
| Keep In Touch | LP | CNR | SKLP4240 | 1966 | £50 | £100 | *Dutch* |
| Scorpions | LP | CNR | 385250 | 1965 | £15 | £30 | *Dutch* |
| Sweet And Lovely | LP | CNR | GA5027 | 1968 | £20 | £40 | *Dutch* |

## SCOTCH
| | | | | | | | |
|---|---|---|---|---|---|---|---|
| Scotch | LP | R.T.Club | LP25002 | 1966 | £150 | £250 | *Italian* |

## SCOTS OF ST. JAMES
| | | | | | | | |
|---|---|---|---|---|---|---|---|
| Gypsy | 7" | Go | AJ111404 | 1966 | £50 | £100 | |
| Timothy | 7" | Spot | JW1 | 1967 | £50 | £100 | |

## SCOTT, ANDY
| | | | | | | | |
|---|---|---|---|---|---|---|---|
| Invisible | 12" | Static | TAK3112 | 1984 | £2.50 | £6 | *clear vinyl* |
| Lady Starlight | 7" | RCA | RCA2629 | 1975 | £2.50 | £6 | |
| Let Her Dance | 7" | Static | TAK24 | 1984 | £2.50 | £6 | |
| Let Her Dance | 12" | Static | TAK2412 | 1984 | £2.50 | £6 | |

## SCOTT, BILLY
| | | | | | | | |
|---|---|---|---|---|---|---|---|
| You're The Greatest | 7" | London | HLU8565 | 1958 | £5 | £10 | |

## SCOTT, BOBBY
| | | | | | | | |
|---|---|---|---|---|---|---|---|
| Bobby Scott Trio | 7" EP | London | EZC19008 | 1956 | £2 | £5 | |
| Bobby Scott Trio | 10" LP | London | LZN14001 | 1955 | £10 | £25 | |
| Chain Gang | 7" | London | HL8254 | 1956 | £10 | £20 | |
| Compositions | 10" LP | London | LZN14018 | 1956 | £10 | £25 | |
| Great Scott | 10" LP | Bethlehem | 1004 | 1954 | £8 | £20 | *US* |

## SCOTT, CECIL
| | | | | | | | |
|---|---|---|---|---|---|---|---|
| Harlem Washboard | LP | Columbia | 33SX1232 | 1960 | £4 | £10 | |

## SCOTT, FREDDIE
| | | | | | | | |
|---|---|---|---|---|---|---|---|
| Am I Grooving You | 7" | London | HLZ10139 | 1967 | £1.50 | £4 | |
| Are You Lonely For Me | LP | Shout | SLP(S)501 | 1967 | £6 | £15 | *US* |
| Are You Lonely For Me | 7" | London | HLZ10103 | 1967 | £2 | £5 | |
| Cry To Me | 7" | London | HLZ10123 | 1967 | £1.50 | £4 | |
| Everything I Have Is Yours | LP | Columbia | CL2258/CS9058 | 1964 | £6 | £15 | *US* |
| Freddie Scott Sings | LP | Colpix | (S)CP461 | 1964 | £6 | £15 | *US* |
| Hey Girl | 7" | Colpix | PX692 | 1963 | £5 | £10 | |
| I Got A Woman | 7" | Colpix | PX709 | 1963 | £5 | £10 | |
| Lonely Man | LP | Columbia | CL2660/CS9460 | 1967 | £6 | £15 | *US* |

## SCOTT, HAZEL
| | | | | | | | |
|---|---|---|---|---|---|---|---|
| Late Show | 10" LP | Capitol | LC6607 | 1953 | £6 | £15 | |

## SCOTT, JACK
| | | | | | | | |
|---|---|---|---|---|---|---|---|
| All I See Is Blue | 7" | Capitol | CL15302 | 1963 | £4 | £8 | |
| Burning Bridges | LP | Capitol | (S)T2035 | 1964 | £20 | £40 | |
| Burning Bridges | 7" EP | Capitol | EAP20035 | 1959 | £50 | £100 | *demo* |
| Burning Bridges | 7" | Top Rank | JAR375 | 1960 | £1.50 | £4 | |
| Cool Water | 7" | Top Rank | JAR419 | 1960 | £2.50 | £6 | |
| Goodbye Baby | 7" | London | HLU8804 | 1959 | £6 | £12 | |
| I Can't Hold Your Letters In My Arms | 7" | Capitol | CL15261 | 1962 | £4 | £8 | |
| I Never Felt Like This | 7" | London | HLL8851 | 1959 | £6 | £12 | |
| I Remember Hank Williams | LP | Top Rank | BUY034 | 1960 | £15 | £30 | |
| I Remember Hank Williams | 7" EP | Top Rank | JKP3011 | 1961 | £10 | £20 | |
| Is There Something On Your Mind | 7" | Top Rank | JAR547 | 1961 | £2 | £5 | |
| Jack Scott | LP | London | HAL2156 | 1958 | £37.50 | £75 | |
| Little Feeling | 7" | Capitol | CL15200 | 1961 | £2 | £5 | |
| My Dream Come True | 7" | Capitol | CL15216 | 1961 | £2.50 | £6 | |
| My True Love | 7" EP | Capitol | REI1205 | 1959 | £30 | £60 | *tri-centre* |
| My True Love | 7" | London | HLU8626 | 1958 | £6 | £12 | |
| Patsy | 7" | Top Rank | JAR524 | 1960 | £2 | £5 | |
| Spirit Moves Me | LP | Top Rank | 35109 | 1961 | £20 | £40 | |
| Steps One And Two | 7" | Capitol | CL15236 | 1962 | £2.50 | £6 | |
| There Comes A Time | 7" | London | HLL8970 | 1959 | £5 | £10 | |
| Way I Walk | 7" | London | HLL8912 | 1959 | £7.50 | £15 | |
| What Am I Living For | LP | Carlton | (ST)LP12122 | 1958 | £37.50 | £75 | *US* |
| What In The World's Come Over You | LP | Top Rank | 25024 | 1960 | £25 | £50 | |
| What In The World's Come Over You | 7" EP | Top Rank | JKP3002 | 1961 | £15 | £30 | |
| What In The World's Come Over You | 7" | Top Rank | JAR280 | 1960 | £1.50 | £4 | |
| With Your Love | 7" | London | HLU8765 | 1958 | £7.50 | £15 | |

## SCOTT, JUDI

| | | | | | | |
|---|---|---|---|---|---|---|
| Billy Sunshine | 7" | Page One | POF066 | 1968 £2.50 | £6 | |

## SCOTT, LINDA

| | | | | | | |
|---|---|---|---|---|---|---|
| Great Scott | LP | Columbia | | 1961 £20 | £40 | |
| Greatest Hits | LP | Canadian American | (S)1007 | 1962 £10 | £25 | US |
| Hey Look At Me Now | LP | Kapp | KL1424/KS3424 | 1965 £6 | £15 | US |
| I've Told Every Little Star | 7" | Columbia | DB4638 | 1960 £1.50 | £4 | |
| It's All Because | 7" | Columbia | DB4748 | 1961 £1.50 | £4 | |
| Linda | LP | Congress | (S)3001 | 1962 £8 | £20 | US |
| Starlight, Starbright | LP | Columbia | 33SX1386 | 1961 £20 | £40 | |

## SCOTT, LINDA (2)

| | | | | | | |
|---|---|---|---|---|---|---|
| Composer | 7" | CBS | 4528 | 1969 £1.50 | £4 | |

## SCOTT, MIKE

| | | | | | | |
|---|---|---|---|---|---|---|
| I Am A Rock | 7" | Mercury | MF906 | 1965 £1.50 | £4 | |

## SCOTT, NICKY

| | | | | | | |
|---|---|---|---|---|---|---|
| Back Street Girl | 7" | Immediate | IM045 | 1967 £4 | £8 | |
| Big City | 7" | Immediate | IM044 | 1967 £7.50 | £15 | |

## SCOTT, PETE

| | | | | | | |
|---|---|---|---|---|---|---|
| Don't Panic | LP | Rubber | RUB003 | 1971 £10 | £25 | |
| Jimmy The Moonlight | LP | Rubber | RUB020 | 1976 £10 | £25 | |

## SCOTT, RAMBLIN' TOMMY

| | | | | | | |
|---|---|---|---|---|---|---|
| Ain't Love Grand | 7" | Parlophone | CMSP15 | 1954 £2 | £5 | export |

## SCOTT, ROBIN

| | | | | | | |
|---|---|---|---|---|---|---|
| Sailor | 7" | Head | HEAD4003 | 1969 £4 | £8 | |
| Woman From The Warm Grass | LP | Head | HDLS6003 | 1969 £50 | £100 | |

## SCOTT, RONNIE

| | | | | | | |
|---|---|---|---|---|---|---|
| At The Royal Festival Hall | 10" LP | Decca | LF1261 | 1956 £10 | £25 | |
| Live At Ronnie Scott's | LP | CBS | 52661 | 1969 £8 | £20 | |
| Night Is Scott And You're So Swingable | LP | Fontana | TL5332 | 1966 £5 | £12 | |
| Presenting The Ronnie Scott Sextet | LP | Philips | BBL7153 | 1957 £8 | £20 | |
| Ronnie Scott Jazz Club Vol. 1 | LP | Esquire | 32001 | 1954 £8 | £20 | |
| Ronnie Scott Jazz Club Vol. 2 | LP | Esquire | 32002 | 1954 £8 | £20 | |
| Ronnie Scott Jazz Club Vol. 3 | LP | Esquire | 32003 | 1954 £8 | £20 | |
| Ronnie Scott Jazz Club Vol. 4 | LP | Esquire | 32006 | 1954 £8 | £20 | |
| Ronnie Scott Quartet | 10" LP | Esquire | 20006 | 1953 £15 | £30 | |

## SCOTT, SHIRLEY

| | | | | | | |
|---|---|---|---|---|---|---|
| And The Soul Saxes | LP | Atlantic | SD1532 | 1970 £5 | £12 | US |

## SCOTT, SIMON & THE LEROYS

| | | | | | | |
|---|---|---|---|---|---|---|
| Move It Baby | 7" | Parlophone | R5164 | 1964 £1.50 | £4 | |
| My Baby's Got Soul | 7" | Parlophone | R5207 | 1964 £1.50 | £4 | |

## SCOTT, TERRY

| | | | | | | |
|---|---|---|---|---|---|---|
| My Brother | 7" | Parlophone | R4967 | 1962 £2.50 | £6 | |

## SCOTT, TONY

| | | | | | | |
|---|---|---|---|---|---|---|
| Fifty-Second Street Scene | LP | Coral | LVA9109 | 1959 £8 | £20 | |
| South Pacific Jazz | LP | HMV | CLP1190 | 1958 £5 | £12 | |
| Tony Scott Quartet | 10" LP | Vogue Coral | LRA10034 | 1955 £15 | £30 | |
| Tony Scott Quartet | 10" LP | Vogue Coral | LRA10037 | 1955 £15 | £30 | |

## SCOTT, WILLIE

| | | | | | | |
|---|---|---|---|---|---|---|
| Shepherd's Song – Border Ballads | LP | Topic | 12T183 | 1968 £6 | £15 | |

## SCOTT-HERON, GIL

Gil Scott-Heron's blending of street poetry with music that straddles the divide between funk and jazz has a crucial role in the development of rap. Indeed, when Scott-Heron took on the rap approach directly, on his savage attack against Ronald Reagan, 'B Movie', he managed to create one of the most powerful performances of all. All his records, with the possible exception of the hit single, 'Johannesburg', are now keenly sought after, especially the early albums issued only in the US.

| | | | | | | |
|---|---|---|---|---|---|---|
| 1980 | LP | Arista | AL9514 | 1980 £6 | £15 | US |
| B Movie | 7" | Arista | ARIST452 | 1981 £1.50 | £4 | |
| B Movie | 7" | Arista | ARIST573 | 1984 £1.50 | £4 | |
| B Movie | 12" | Arista | ARIST573 | 1984 £2.50 | £6 | |
| Best Of Gil Scott-Heron | LP | Arista | 206618 | 1984 £4 | £10 | |
| Bottle | LP | Audio Fidelity | 1017 | 1981 £6 | £15 | US |
| Bottle | 7" | Arista | ARIST169 | 1978 £1.50 | £4 | |
| Bottle | 7" | Inferno | HEAT23 | 1979 £1.50 | £4 | |
| Bottle | 12" | Arista | ARIST169 | 1978 £2.50 | £6 | |
| Bottle | 12" | Inferno | HEAT2312 | 1979 £2.50 | £6 | |
| Bridges | LP | Arista | SPARTY1031 | 1977 £6 | £15 | |
| First Minute Of A New Day | LP | Arista | ARTY106 | 1975 £10 | £25 | |
| Free Will | LP | Flying Dutchman | 10153 | 1972 £20 | £40 | US |
| From South Africa To South Carolina | LP | Arista | ARTY121 | 1976 £6 | £15 | |
| It's Your World | LP | Arista | DARTY1 | 1976 £15 | £30 | double |

| Lady Day And John Coltrane | 7" | Philips | 6073705 | 1971 | £1.50 | £4 | |
|---|---|---|---|---|---|---|---|
| Moving Targets | LP | Arista | 204921 | 1982 | £5 | £12 | |
| Pieces Of a Man | LP | Philips | 6369415 | 1973 | £15 | £30 | |
| Real Eyes | LP | Arista | AL9540 | 1980 | £6 | £15 | US |
| Reflections | LP | Arista | SPARTY1180 | 1981 | £5 | £12 | |
| Revolution Will Not Be Televised | LP | RCA | SF8428 | 1975 | £8 | £20 | |
| Secrets | LP | Arista | SPARTY1073 | 1978 | £6 | £15 | |
| Small Talk At 125th And Lennox | LP | Flying Dutchman | FDS131 | 1972 | £20 | £40 | US |
| Winter In America | LP | Strata East | 19742 | 1975 | £15 | £30 | US |

## SCOTTY
| Schooldays | LP | Trojan | TRL33 | 1971 | £8 | £20 | |
|---|---|---|---|---|---|---|---|

## SCRAMBLERS
| Cycle Psychos | LP | Crown | 384 | 1964 | £8 | £20 | US |
|---|---|---|---|---|---|---|---|

## SCREAMING GYPSY BANDITS
| In The Eye | LP | BRBQ | BRBQ3 | 1973 | £30 | £60 | US |
|---|---|---|---|---|---|---|---|

## SCRITTI POLITTI
| Absolute | 12" | Virgin | VSY68012 | 1984 | £2.50 | £6 | picture disc |
|---|---|---|---|---|---|---|---|
| First Boy In This Town | CD-s | Virgin | VSCD1082 | 1988 | £2 | £5 | |
| Oh Patti | CD-s | Virgin | CDEP17 | 1988 | £2 | £5 | |
| Skank Bloc | 7" | St. Pancras | SCRIT1 | 1978 | £2 | £5 | |
| Wood Beez | CD-s | Virgin | CDT34 | 1988 | £2 | £5 | 3" single |
| Word Girl | CD-s | Virgin | CDT13 | 1988 | £2 | £5 | 3" single |
| Work In Progress | 7" | Rough Trade | RT034 | 1979 | £1.50 | £4 | |

## SCROTUM POLES
| Revelation | 7" | Scrotum Poles | ERECT1 | 1980 | £1.50 | £4 | |
|---|---|---|---|---|---|---|---|

## SCRUGG
| I Wish I Was Five | 7" | Pye | 7N17451 | 1968 | £10 | £20 | |
|---|---|---|---|---|---|---|---|
| Lavender Popcorn | 7" | Pye | 7N17551 | 1968 | £10 | £20 | |
| Will The Real Geraldine Please Stand Up | 7" | Pye | 7N17656 | 1969 | £7.50 | £15 | |

## SEA URCHINS
| 30.10.88 | 7" | Fierce | FRIGHT032 | 1989 | £2.50 | £6 | |
|---|---|---|---|---|---|---|---|
| Pristine Christine | 7" | Sarah | 001 | 1987 | £7.50 | £15 | with poster |
| Solace | 7" | Sarah | 008 | 1988 | £2 | £5 | |

## SEA-DERS
| Sea-ders | 7" EP | Decca | DFER8674 | 1968 | £50 | £100 | export |
|---|---|---|---|---|---|---|---|
| Thanks A Lot | 7" | Decca | F22576 | 1967 | £12.50 | £25 | |

## SEAMEN, PHIL
| Meets Eddie Gomez | LP | Saga | OPP102 | 1968 | £20 | £40 | |
|---|---|---|---|---|---|---|---|
| Phil On Drums | LP | 77 | SEU1253 | 1974 | £15 | £30 | |
| Phil Seamen Now Live! | LP | Verve | (S)VLP9220 | 1968 | £20 | £40 | |
| Phil Seamen Story | LP | Decibel | BSN103 | 1973 | £20 | £40 | |

## SEARCH PARTY
| Montgomery's Chapel | LP | private | | 1969 | £1400 | £2000 | US |
|---|---|---|---|---|---|---|---|

## SEARCHERS

The Searchers filtered the R&B material of the day through vocal harmonies derived from the Everly Brothers and a noticeable country influence, emerging as the second most successful of the Merseybeat groups. Although the group's run of hit singles ran out towards the end of the sixties, they continued to tour with new material despite having no record contract for much of the seventies. They came close to managing a come-back in 1980 with a critically acclaimed album for Sire, but these days they are finally forced to ply the nostalgia circuit – sadly split by internal disagreement into two separate sets of Searchers. The group's collectable items from the sixties include their own privately pressed demo album and a live album recorded in Germany, neither of which turns up very often.

| Ain't Gonna Kiss Ya | 7" EP | Pye | NEP24177 | 1963 | £2.50 | £6 | |
|---|---|---|---|---|---|---|---|
| Bumble Bee | 7" EP | Pye | NEP24218 | 1965 | £4 | £8 | |
| Bumble Bee | 7" EP | Pye | PNV24137 | 1965 | £10 | £20 | French |
| Chantent en français | 7" EP | Pye | PNV24121 | 1964 | £50 | £100 | French |
| Desdemona | 7" | RCA | RCA2057 | 1971 | £5 | £10 | |
| Don't Make Promises | 7" | private | | 197– | £2.50 | £6 | |
| Don't Throw Your Love Away | 7" EP | Pye | PNV24120 | 1964 | £10 | £20 | French |
| Four By Four | 7" EP | Pye | NEP24228 | 1965 | £5 | £10 | |
| Four Strong Winds | 7" | private | | 197– | £2.50 | £6 | |
| He's Got No Love | 7" | Pye | 7N15878 | 1965 | £1.50 | £4 | |
| Hear Hear | LP | Mercury | MG2/SR60914 | 1964 | £10 | £25 | US |
| Hungry For Love | 7" EP | Pye | NEP24184 | 1964 | £2.50 | £6 | |
| It's The Searchers | LP | Pye | NPL18092 | 1964 | £6 | £15 | |
| It's Too Late | 7" | Sire | SIR4036 | 1980 | £1.50 | £4 | |
| Kinky Kathy Abernathy | 7" | Liberty | LBF15340 | 1969 | £10 | £20 | |
| Love Is Everywhere | 7" | RCA | RCA2139 | 1971 | £2 | £5 | |
| Meet The Searchers | LP | Kapp | KL1363/KS3363 | 1964 | £6 | £15 | US |
| Meet The Searchers | LP | Pye | NPL18086 | 1963 | £6 | £15 | |
| Needles And Pins | 7" EP | Pye | PNV24118 | 1964 | £10 | £20 | French |
| Needles And Pins | 7" | Ariola | | 1964 | £10 | £20 | sung in German |
| Needles And Pins | 7" | Pye | | 1964 | £10 | £20 | sung in French |
| New Searchers LP | LP | Kapp | KL1412/KS3412 | 1965 | £6 | £15 | US |
| Play The System | 7" EP | Pye | NEP24201 | 1964 | £4 | £8 | |
| Popcorn Double Feature | 7" | Pye | 7N17225 | 1967 | £2 | £5 | |

| | | | | | | | |
|---|---|---|---|---|---|---|---|
| Searchers | LP | private | | 1962 | £75 | £150 | |
| Searchers '65 | 7" EP | Pye | NEP24222 | 1965 | £5 | £10 | |
| Searchers Meet The Rattles | LP | Mercury | MG2/SR60994 | 1965 | £15 | £30 | US |
| Searchers No. 4 | LP | Kapp | KL1449/KS3449 | 1965 | £6 | £15 | US |
| Secondhand Dealer | 7" | Pye | 7N17424 | 1967 | £4 | £8 | |
| Sing Singer Sing | 7" | RCA | RCA2231 | 1972 | £2 | £5 | |
| Someday We're Gonna Love Again | 7" EP | Pye | PNV24123 | 1964 | £10 | £20 | French |
| Sounds Like The Searchers | LP | Pye | NPL18111 | 1964 | £6 | £15 | |
| Sub Ist Sie | 7" | Vogue | 14116 | 1963 | £10 | £20 | sung in German |
| Sugar And Spice | LP | Pye | NPL18089 | 1963 | £6 | £15 | |
| Surf Encore | 7" EP | Pye | PNV24114 | 1963 | £10 | £20 | French |
| Surfin' With The Searchers | 7" EP | Pye | PNV24112 | 1963 | £10 | £20 | French |
| Sweet Nothings | 7" | Philips | BF1274 | 1963 | £2 | £5 | |
| Sweets For My Sweet | 7" EP | Pye | NEP24183 | 1963 | £2 | £5 | |
| Sweets For My Sweet | 7" EP | Pye | PNV24108 | 1963 | £7.50 | £15 | French |
| Sweets For My Sweet – At The Starclub Hamburg | LP | Philips | 48052L | 1963 | £37.50 | £75 | German |
| Take It Or Leave It | 7" | Pye | 7N17094 | 1966 | £1.50 | £4 | |
| Take Me For What I'm Worth | LP | Pye | NPL18120 | 1965 | £6 | £15 | |
| Take Me For What I'm Worth | 7" EP | Pye | NEP24263 | 1966 | £30 | £60 | |
| Take Me For What I'm Worth | 7" | Pye | 7N15992 | 1965 | £10 | £20 | export picture sleeve |
| Tausend Nadelstiche | 7" | Vogue | 14130 | 1963 | £10 | £20 | sung in German |
| Umbrella Man | 7" | Liberty | LBF15159 | 1968 | £5 | £10 | |
| Verzeih My Love | 7" | Vogue | 14338 | 1965 | £10 | £20 | sung in German |
| Western Union | 7" | Pye | 7N17308 | 1967 | £2.50 | £6 | |
| When You Walk In The Room | 7" EP | Pye | NEP24204 | 1964 | £5 | £10 | |
| When You Walk In The Room | 7" | Pye | 7N15694 | 1964 | £1.50 | £4 | |

## SEASTONE

| | | | | | | | |
|---|---|---|---|---|---|---|---|
| Mirrored Dreams | LP | Plankton | PKN101 | 1978 | £50 | £100 | |

## SEATHROUGH

| | | | | | | | |
|---|---|---|---|---|---|---|---|
| Lala Lapla | LP | private | | 197– | £20 | £40 | |

## SEATON, B. B.

| | | | | | | | |
|---|---|---|---|---|---|---|---|
| Hold On | 7" | R&B | JB143 | 1964 | £5 | £10 | . Lester Sterling B side |
| I'm So Glad | 7" | Island | WI123 | 1963 | £5 | £10 | |
| Thin Line Between Love And Hate | LP | Trojan | TRLS59 | 1973 | £4 | £10 | |

## SEATRAIN

Seatrain evolved out of the Blues Project, following the departure of founder members Danny Kalb, Steve Katz and Al Kooper. The new sounds of violin and saxophone acquired a dominant role and for the first Seatrain LP the musicians are clearly inspired by the novelty of their new line-up. Unfortunately, this inspiration was short-lived and the two LPs that followed are rather ordinary.

| | | | | | | | |
|---|---|---|---|---|---|---|---|
| Seatrain | LP | A&M | AMLS941 | 1969 | £5 | £12 | |

## SEAWIND

| | | | | | | | |
|---|---|---|---|---|---|---|---|
| One Sweet Night | 7" | CTI | CTSP13 | 1978 | £4 | £8 | |

## SEBASTIAN, JOHN

| | | | | | | | |
|---|---|---|---|---|---|---|---|
| John B. Sebastian | LP | Reprise | RSLP6379 | 1970 | £4 | £10 | |
| Live | LP | MGM | SE4720 | 1970 | £5 | £12 | US |

## SEBASTIAN, JOHN (2)

| | | | | | | | |
|---|---|---|---|---|---|---|---|
| Inca Dance | 7" | London | HL8029 | 1954 | £10 | £20 | |
| Stranger In Paradise | 7" | London | HL8131 | 1955 | £7.50 | £15 | |

## SECOND CITY JAZZMEN

| | | | | | | | |
|---|---|---|---|---|---|---|---|
| Tribute To Madge | LP | Esquire | 32053 | 1958 | £4 | £10 | |

## SECOND COMING

| | | | | | | | |
|---|---|---|---|---|---|---|---|
| Second Coming | LP | Mercury | 6338030 | 1970 | £4 | £10 | |

## SECOND HAND

Second Hand revolved around keyboard virtuoso Ken Elliott and drummer Kieran O'Connor, who subsequently recorded as Seventh Wave. Their music is an interesting blend of classical and avant-garde influences within a sound that is nevertheless rock-based – rather like the better-known Egg, in fact. *Death May Be Your Santa Claus* is that rare thing, an expensive progressive album that is actually something of a forgotten masterpiece.

| | | | | | | | |
|---|---|---|---|---|---|---|---|
| Death May Be Your Santa Claus | LP | Mushroom | 200MR6 | 1972 | £50 | £100 | |
| Fairy Tale | 7" | Polydor | 56308 | 1969 | £2 | £5 | |
| Reality | LP | Polydor | 583045 | 1968 | £30 | £60 | |

## SECOND LAYER

| | | | | | | | |
|---|---|---|---|---|---|---|---|
| Flesh As Property | 7" | Fresh | FRESH5 | 1979 | £2.50 | £6 | |
| Flesh As Property | 7" | Tortch | TOR001 | 1979 | £4 | £8 | |
| State Of Emergency | 7" | Tortch | TOR006 | 1980 | £2 | £5 | |

## SECOND LIFE

| | | | | | | | |
|---|---|---|---|---|---|---|---|
| Second Life | LP | Metronome | MLP15409 | 1971 | £15 | £30 | German |

## SECOND MOVEMENT

| | | | | | | | |
|---|---|---|---|---|---|---|---|
| Blind Man's Mirror | LP | Castle | 1003 | 1976 | £5 | £12 | German |

## SECRET OYSTER

| | | | | | | | |
|---|---|---|---|---|---|---|---|
| Secret Oyster | LP | CBS | 65769 | 1973 | £6 | £15 | Danish |
| Vidunderlige Kalling | LP | CBS | 81044 | 1975 | £6 | £15 | Danish |

## SECRETS

| | | | | | | |
|---|---|---|---|---|---|---|
| Boy Next Door | 7" | Philips | BF1298 | 1964 | £2.50 | £6 |
| Other Side Of Town | 7" | Philips | BF1318 | 1964 | £2.50 | £6 |

## SECRETS (2)

| | | | | | | |
|---|---|---|---|---|---|---|
| I Intend To Please | 7" | CBS | 2818 | 1967 | £5 | £10 |
| Infatuation | 7" | CBS | 202585 | 1967 | £5 | £10 |
| Such A Pity | 7" | CBS | 202466 | 1967 | £5 | £10 |

## SEDAKA, NEIL

| | | | | | | | |
|---|---|---|---|---|---|---|---|
| Circulate | LP | RCA | RD27207/SF5090 | 1960 | £10 | £25 | |
| Greatest Hits | LP | RCA | LPM/LSP2627 | 1962 | £6 | £15 | US |
| I Go Ape | 7" | RCA | RCA1115 | 1959 | £2 | £5 | |
| Little Devil And His Other Hits | LP | RCA | LPM/LSP2421 | 1961 | £8 | £20 | US |
| Neil Sedaka | LP | RCA | RD27140 | 1959 | £25 | £50 | |
| Neil Sedaka | 7" EP | RCA | RCX166 | 1959 | £10 | £20 | |
| Neil Sedaka No. 2 | 7" EP | RCA | RCX186 | 1960 | £6 | £12 | |
| Neil Sedaka No. 3 | 7" EP | RCA | RCX212 | 1962 | £6 | £12 | |
| No Vacancy | 7" | RCA | RCA1099 | 1959 | £5 | £10 | |
| Oh Carol | 7" | RCA | RCA1152 | 1959 | £2.50 | £6 | tri-centre |
| Oh Delilah | 7" | Stateside | SS105 | 1962 | £2.50 | £6 | Marvels B side |
| Ring A Rocking | 7" | London | HLW8961 | 1959 | £12.50 | £25 | |
| Rock With Sedaka | LP | RCA | LPM/LSP2035 | 1959 | £20 | £40 | US |
| With The Tokens | LP | Vernon | 518 | 1963 | £6 | £15 | US |
| World Through A Tear | 7" | RCA | RCA1475 | 1965 | £1.50 | £4 | |
| You've Got To Learn Your Rhythm And Blues | 7" | RCA | RCA1130 | 1959 | £5 | £10 | |

## SEEDORF, RUDY

| | | | | | | |
|---|---|---|---|---|---|---|
| One Million Stars | 7" | Island | WI189 | 1965 | £5 | £10 |

## SEEDS

The Seeds, led by the eccentric Sky Saxon, were a garage punk band who achieved considerable success in their native California before being rendered obsolete by the more adventurous West Coast bands like Jefferson Airplane and Quicksilver Messenger Service. Some of their titles and visual imagery suggested that the group was heavily into psychedelia, but they are not really very convincing in this role.

| | | | | | | | |
|---|---|---|---|---|---|---|---|
| Can't Seem To Make You Mine | 7" | Vocalion | VN9287 | 1967 | £7.50 | £15 | |
| Farmer | 7" EP | Vogue | INT18125 | 1967 | £25 | £50 | French |
| Full Spoon Of Seedy Blues | LP | GNP Crescendo | (S)2040 | 1967 | £10 | £25 | US red label |
| Future | LP | Vocalion | VAN/SAVN8070 | 1967 | £10 | £25 | |
| Lover's Cosmic Voyage | LP | private | | 1977 | £75 | £150 | US |
| Merlin's Music Box | LP | GNP Crescendo | (S)2043 | 1967 | £10 | £25 | US red label |
| No Escape | 7" EP | Vogue | INT18022 | 1966 | £37.50 | £75 | French |
| Psych-Out | LP | Sidewalk | ST5913 | 1968 | £8 | £20 | US, with other artists |
| Pushin' Too Hard | 7" | Vocalion | VN9277 | 1966 | £10 | £20 | |
| Seeds | LP | GNP Crescendo | (S)2023 | 1966 | £15 | £30 | US red label |
| Try To Understand | 7" EP | Vogue | INT18077 | 1966 | £25 | £50 | French |
| Web Of Sound | LP | Vocalion | VAN8062 | 1966 | £15 | £30 | |

## SEEGER, MIKE

| | | | | | | |
|---|---|---|---|---|---|---|
| Mike Seeger | LP | Fontana | TFL6039 | 1965 | £8 | £20 |

## SEEGER, PEGGY

| | | | | | | |
|---|---|---|---|---|---|---|
| Best Of Peggy Seeger | LP | Pre | PRE13005 | 1961 | £8 | £20 |
| Early In The Spring | 7" EP | Topic | TOP73 | 1962 | £2 | £5 |
| Peggy Alone | LP | Argo | (Z)DA63 | 1969 | £8 | £20 |
| Pretty Little Baby | 7" | Decca | F12282 | 1965 | £1.50 | £4 |
| Troubled Love | 7" EP | Topic | TOP72 | 1962 | £2 | £5 |

## SEEGER, PEGGY & GUY CARAWAN

| | | | | | | |
|---|---|---|---|---|---|---|
| America At Play | LP | HMV | CLP1174 | 1958 | £8 | £20 |

## SEEGER, PEGGY & MIKE

| | | | | | | |
|---|---|---|---|---|---|---|
| Peggy 'n' Mike | LP | Argo | (Z)DA80 | 1968 | £8 | £20 |
| Peggy 'n' Mike | LP | Argo | ZFB62 | 1972 | £4 | £10 |

## SEEGER, PETE

| | | | | | | | |
|---|---|---|---|---|---|---|---|
| Careless Love | 7" | Top Rank | TR5020 | 1960 | £1.50 | £4 | B side by Leon Bibb |
| Guitar Guide For Folksingers | LP | Topic | 12T20 | 1958 | £8 | £20 | with booklet |
| In Concert | 7" EP | CBS | AGG20055 | 1964 | £2 | £5 | |
| Pete And Five Strings | 7" EP | Topic | TOP33 | 1959 | £4 | £8 | |
| Tribute To Leadbelly | 7" EP | Melodisc | EPM778 | 1958 | £2.50 | £6 | |
| We Shall Overcome | LP | CBS | (S)BPG62209 | 1963 | £5 | £12 | |

## SEEKERS

| | | | | | | |
|---|---|---|---|---|---|---|
| With A Swag On My Shoulder | 7" | Oriole | CB1935 | 1965 | £1.50 | £4 |

## SEEMON & MARIJKE

| | | | | | | | |
|---|---|---|---|---|---|---|---|
| Son Of America | LP | A&M | SP4309 | 1970 | £6 | £15 | US |

## SEFTONES

| | | | | | | |
|---|---|---|---|---|---|---|
| I Can See Through You | 7" | CBS | 202491 | 1966 | £5 | £10 |

## SEGAL, MARTIN & SILVER JADE
| | | | | | | | | |
|---|---|---|---|---|---|---|---|---|
| Fly On Strange Wings | LP | DJM | DJM9100 | 1970 | £10 | £25 | | |

## SEGER, BOB
| | | | | | | | | |
|---|---|---|---|---|---|---|---|---|
| Against The Wind | LP | Mobile Fidelity | MFSL1127 | 1983 | £4 | £10 | US audiophile |
| Bob Seger Story | LP | Capitol | | 1981 | £6 | £15 | US promo |
| Brand New Morning | LP | Capitol | ST731 | 1971 | £6 | £15 | US |
| Fire Inside | CD | Capitol | DPRO79227 | 1991 | £8 | £20 | US interview promo |
| Lucifer | 7" | Capitol | CL15642 | 1970 | £2 | £5 | |
| Mongrel | LP | Capitol | SKAO499 | 1970 | £4 | £10 | US gatefold |
| Night Moves | LP | Capitol | PST11557 | 1977 | £10 | £25 | US picture disc |
| Night Moves | LP | Mobile Fidelity | MFSL1034 | 1979 | £5 | £12 | US audiophile |
| Noah | LP | Capitol | ST236 | 1969 | £6 | £15 | US |
| Ramblin' Gamblin' Man | LP | Capitol | ST172 | 1969 | £5 | £12 | US |
| Ramblin' Gamblin' Man | 7" | Capitol | CL15574 | 1968 | £1.50 | £4 | |
| Seger Classics | LP | Capitol | PSLP271/2 | 1977 | £10 | £25 | promo double |
| Silver Seger Sampler | CD | Capitol | DPRO79622 | 1993 | £8 | £20 | US promo |
| Smokin' OP's | LP | Reprise | K44214 | 1972 | £4 | £10 | |
| Stranger In Town | LP | Capitol | SEAX11904 | 1978 | £4 | £10 | US picture disc |
| Stranger In Town | CD | DCC | | 1995 | £6 | £15 | US audiophile |

## SELAH JUBILEE QUARTET
| | | | | | | | | |
|---|---|---|---|---|---|---|---|---|
| Spirituals | 10" LP | Remington | 1023 | 195– | £10 | £25 | US |

## SELF, RONNIE
| | | | | | | | | |
|---|---|---|---|---|---|---|---|---|
| Bop-a-Lena | 78 | Philips | PB810 | 1958 | £12.50 | £25 | |

## SELLERS, BROTHER JOHN
| | | | | | | | | |
|---|---|---|---|---|---|---|---|---|
| Big Beat Up The River | LP | Monitor | 505 | | £8 | £20 | US |
| Blues & Spirituals | 7" EP | Columbia | SEG7740 | 1957 | £2 | £5 | |
| Blues & Spirituals | 7" EP | Vanguard | EPP14002 | 1956 | £2 | £5 | |
| In London | LP | Decca | LK4197 | 1957 | £6 | £15 | |
| In London | 7" EP | Decca | DFE6457 | 1957 | £2 | £5 | |
| Jack Of Diamonds | 10" LP | Vanguard | PPT12017 | 1957 | £4 | £10 | |
| Sings Blues And Folk Songs | 10" LP | Vanguard | PPT12008 | 1956 | £4 | £10 | |

## SELLERS, PETER
| | | | | | | | | |
|---|---|---|---|---|---|---|---|---|
| Any Old Iron | 7" | Parlophone | R4337 | 1957 | £1.50 | £4 | |
| Best Of Sellers | 7" EP | Parlophone | GEP8770 | 1958 | £2 | £5 | |
| Best Of Sellers | 10" LP | Parlophone | PMD1069 | 1958 | £4 | £10 | |
| Drop Of The Hard Stuff | 7" | Parlophone | R4491 | 1958 | £1.50 | £4 | |
| Putting on The Smile | 7" | Parlophone | R4605 | 1959 | £1.50 | £4 | |
| Songs For Swingin' Sellers | 7" EP | Parlophone | GEP8822 | 1960 | £2 | £5 | |
| Songs For Swingin' Sellers | 7" EP | Parlophone | SGE2013 | 1960 | £2 | £5 | stereo |
| Songs For Swingin' Sellers No. 2 | 7" EP | Parlophone | SGE2016 | 1960 | £2 | £5 | stereo |
| Songs For Swingin' Sellers No. 3 | 7" EP | Parlophone | SGE2019 | 1961 | £2 | £5 | stereo |
| Songs For Swingin' Sellers No. 4 | 7" EP | Parlophone | SGE2020 | 1961 | £2 | £5 | stereo |
| Unchained Melody | CD-s | EMI | CDEM146 | 1990 | £2 | £5 | with Spike Milligan |

## SELLERS, PETER & SOPHIA LOREN
| | | | | | | | | |
|---|---|---|---|---|---|---|---|---|
| Peter And Sophia | LP | Parlophone | PMC1131/ PCS3012 | 1960 | £4 | £10 | |
| Peter And Sophia No. 1 | 7" EP | Parlophone | SGE2021 | 1961 | £2 | £5 | |
| Peter And Sophia No. 2 | 7" EP | Parlophone | SGE2022 | 1961 | £2 | £5 | |
| Peter And Sophia No. 3 | 7" EP | Parlophone | SGE2023 | 1961 | £2 | £5 | |

## SELLERS, PETER, SPIKE MILLIGAN & HARRY SECOMBE
| | | | | | | | | |
|---|---|---|---|---|---|---|---|---|
| How To Win An Election | LP | Philips | AL3464 | 1964 | £4 | £10 | |

## SEMA FOUR
| | | | | | | | | |
|---|---|---|---|---|---|---|---|---|
| Four From Sema Four | 7" | Pollen | PBM022 | 1979 | £2 | £5 | |
| Up And Down | 7" | Pollen | PBM024 | 1979 | £2 | £5 | |

## SEMIRAMIS
| | | | | | | | | |
|---|---|---|---|---|---|---|---|---|
| Dedicato A Frazzo | LP | Trident | TRI1004 | | £8 | £20 | Italian |

## SEMOOL
| | | | | | | | | |
|---|---|---|---|---|---|---|---|---|
| Essais | LP | Futura | 005 | 1972 | £10 | £25 | French |

## SENATE
| | | | | | | | | |
|---|---|---|---|---|---|---|---|---|
| I Can't Stop | 7" | Columbia | DB8110 | 1967 | £2 | £5 | |
| Sock It To You One More Time | LP | United Artists | (S)ULP1180 | 1968 | £5 | £12 | |

## SENATOR BOBBY
| | | | | | | | | |
|---|---|---|---|---|---|---|---|---|
| Wild Thing | 7" | Cameo Parkway | P127 | 1962 | £1.50 | £4 | |

## SENATORS
| | | | | | | | | |
|---|---|---|---|---|---|---|---|---|
| Breakdown | 7" | Oriole | CB1957 | 1964 | £5 | £10 | |
| She's A Mod | 7" | Dial | DSP7001 | 1964 | £15 | £30 | |
| Tables Are Turning | 7" | CBS | 201768 | 1965 | £5 | £10 | |

## SENDIT, RAY & HIS ROCKY TEAM
| | | | | | | | | |
|---|---|---|---|---|---|---|---|---|
| Rocket 0869 | 7" | Felsted | SD80052 | 1957 | £1.50 | £4 | |

## SENSATION FIX
| | | | | | | | | |
|---|---|---|---|---|---|---|---|---|
| Boxes Paradise | LP | Polydor | 2448068 | 1977 | £5 | £12 | Italian |

| | | | | | | | |
|---|---|---|---|---|---|---|---|
| Finest Finger | LP | Polydor | 2448048 | 1976 £6 | £15 | | Italian |
| Flying Tapes | LP | Polydor | 2448074 | 1978 £5 | £12 | | Italian |
| Fragment Of Light | LP | Polydor | 2448023 | 1974 £6 | £15 | | Italian |
| Portable Madness | LP | Polydor | 2448034 | 1974 £6 | £15 | | Italian |
| Vision's Fugitives | LP | All Ears | SF11478 | 1977 £5 | £12 | | US |

## SENSATIONAL CREED

| | | | | | | | |
|---|---|---|---|---|---|---|---|
| Nocturnal Operations | 7" | Beggars Banquet | BEG125 | 1984 £2 | £5 | | |
| Nocturnal Operations | 12" | Beggars Banquet | BEG125T | 1984 £2.50 | £6 | | |

## SENSATIONS

| | | | | | | | |
|---|---|---|---|---|---|---|---|
| Let Me In | LP | Argo | LP4022 | 1963 £15 | £30 | | US |
| Let Me In | 7" | Pye | 7N25128 | 1962 £2.50 | £6 | | |
| Music Music Music | 7" | Pye | 7N25110 | 1961 £2.50 | £6 | | |

## SENSATIONS (2)

| | | | | | | | |
|---|---|---|---|---|---|---|---|
| Born To Love You | 7" | Doctor Bird | DB1102 | 1967 £5 | £10 | | |
| Right On Time | 7" | Doctor Bird | DB1100 | 1967 £5 | £10 | | |
| Thing Called Soul | 7" | Doctor Bird | DB1074 | 1967 £5 | £10 | | |
| Those Guys | 7" | Duke | DU2 | 1968 £4 | £8 | | |
| Warrior | 7" | Camel | CA31 | 1969 £1.50 | £4 | | |

## SENSATIONS (3)

| | | | | | | | |
|---|---|---|---|---|---|---|---|
| Look At My Baby | 7" | Decca | F12392 | 1966 £1.50 | £4 | | |

## SENSELESS THINGS

| | | | | | | | |
|---|---|---|---|---|---|---|---|
| Andi In A Karma | 12" | What Goes On | GOESON37 | 1990 £6 | £15 | | test pressing |
| Everybody's Gone | CD-s | Epic | 6569802 | 1991 £2 | £5 | | |
| Got It At The Delmar | CD-s | Epic | 6574492 | 1991 £2 | £5 | | |
| I'm Moving | 7" | Yo Jo Jo | 3 | 1988 £4 | £8 | | flexi |
| Up And Coming | CD-s | Way Cool | WC006CD | 1991 £4 | £10 | | |
| Up And Coming | 12" | Red | RED001T | 1988 £6 | £15 | | two versions |
| Up And Coming | 12" | Way Cool | WC006 | 1991 £3 | £8 | | |

## SENSORY SYSTEM

| | | | | | | | |
|---|---|---|---|---|---|---|---|
| Sensory System | LP | Hookfarm | HKS1 | 1973 £10 | £25 | | Danish |

## SENTINELS

| | | | | | | | |
|---|---|---|---|---|---|---|---|
| Big Surf | LP | Del-Fi | LP/ST1232 | 1963 £5 | £12 | | US |
| Surfer Girl | LP | Del-Fi | LP/ST1241 | 1963 £5 | £12 | | US |
| Vegas Go-Go | LP | Sutton | SU338 | 1964 £10 | £25 | | US |

## SEPULTURA

| | | | | | | | |
|---|---|---|---|---|---|---|---|
| Arise | LP | Roadracer | RO93288 | 1991 £4 | £10 | | picture disc |
| Bestial Devastation | LP | Gogumelo | 803248 | 1985 £20 | £40 | | Brazilian, B side by Overdose |

## SERENADE

| | | | | | | | |
|---|---|---|---|---|---|---|---|
| Serenade | LP | Negram | NQ20019 | 1972 £10 | £25 | | Dutch |

## SERENDIPITY

| | | | | | | | |
|---|---|---|---|---|---|---|---|
| Castles | 7" | CBS | 4428 | 1969 £25 | £50 | | |
| Through With You | 7" | CBS | 3733 | 1968 £37.50 | £75 | | |

## SERFS

| | | | | | | | |
|---|---|---|---|---|---|---|---|
| Early Bird Cafe | LP | Capitol | SKAO207 | 1969 £8 | £20 | | US |

## SERPENT POWER

| | | | | | | | |
|---|---|---|---|---|---|---|---|
| Serpent Power | LP | Vanguard | VSD79252 | 1967 £25 | £50 | | US |

## SETTLERS

| | | | | | | | |
|---|---|---|---|---|---|---|---|
| Alive | LP | Columbia | SCX6381 | 1969 £6 | £15 | | |
| Call Again | LP | Marble Arch | MAL1226 | 1969 £4 | £10 | | |
| Early Settlers | LP | Island | ILP947 | 1967 £8 | £20 | | |
| Lightning Tree | LP | York | FYK405 | 1972 £6 | £15 | | |
| Sing A New Song | LP | Myrrh | MST6507 | 1972 £4 | £10 | | |
| Sing Out | LP | Decca | LK4645 | 1964 £6 | £15 | | |

## SEVEN LETTERS

| | | | | | | | |
|---|---|---|---|---|---|---|---|
| Bam Bam Baji | 7" | Doctor Bird | DB1209 | 1969 £5 | £10 | | |
| Flour Dumpling | 7" | Doctor Bird | DB1195 | 1969 £5 | £10 | | |
| Fung Sure | 7" | Doctor Bird | DB1306 | 1969 £5 | £10 | | |
| La Bella Jig | 7" | Treasure Isle | TI7055 | 1969 £2.50 | £6 | | |
| Mama Me Want Girl | 7" | Doctor Bird | DB1206 | 1969 £5 | £10 | | |
| Parsons Corner | 7" | Treasure Isle | TI7054 | 1969 £2.50 | £6 | | |
| People Get Ready | 7" | Doctor Bird | DB1189 | 1969 £5 | £10 | | |
| Please Stay | 7" | Doctor Bird | DB1194 | 1969 £5 | £10 | | |
| Soul Crash | 7" | Doctor Bird | DB1207 | 1969 £5 | £10 | | |
| There Goes My Heart | 7" | Doctor Bird | DB1208 | 1969 £5 | £10 | | |

## SEVEN SECONDS

| | | | | | | | |
|---|---|---|---|---|---|---|---|
| Skins, Brains, And Guts | 7" | Alternative Tentacles | VIRUS15 | 1982 £1.50 | £4 | | |

## SEVENTEEN

| | | | | | | | |
|---|---|---|---|---|---|---|---|
| Don't Let Go | 7" | Vendetta | VD001 | 1980 £15 | £30 | | |

## SEVENTEEN-SEVENTY-SIX
1776....................................................... LP ...... Palladium ........ 1005 ...................... 1971 £10......... £25 ...................... US

## SEVENTH SONS
4.00am At Franks .................................. LP ...... ESP-Disk ....... 1078 ...................... 1968 £10......... £25 ...................... US

## SEVERIN
Chance In Time ...................................... 7" ...... CBS................ 7280 ...................... 1971 £2.............. £5

## SEVILLE, DAVID
Armen's Theme ....................................... 7" ...... London........... HLU8359.............. 1957 £5......... £10 ................gold label
Bird On My Head...................................... 7" ...... London........... HLU8659.............. 1958 £1.50........ £4
Bonjour Tristesse...................................... 7" ...... London........... HLU8582.............. 1958 £1.50........ £4
David Seville & His Orchestra ............. 7" EP . London........... REU1085.............. 1957 £5......... £10
Gift ......................................................... 7" ...... London........... HLU8411.............. 1957 £1.50........ £4
Got To Get To Your House .................... 7" ...... London........... HLU8485.............. 1957 £2............. £5
Witch Doctor .......................................... LP ...... London........... HAU2153.............. 1959 £5......... £12
Witch Doctor .......................................... 7" ...... London........... HLU8619.............. 1958 £1.50........ £4
Witch Doctor & His Friends ................... 7" EP . London........... REU1219.............. 1959 £5......... £10

## SEX
End Of My Life ...................................... LP ...... Trans-Canada .. 785 ...................... 1972 £6......... £15 ................Canadian
Sex.......................................................... LP ...... Trans-Canada .. 775 ...................... 1971 £15......... £30 ................Canadian

## SEX PISTOLS
What was revolutionary about the Sex Pistols was not so much their music or their image, but the way in which they (or rather their manager, Malcolm McLaren) saw rock music as an institution out of which it was possible to make a considerable amount of money. The strategy of signing to a label for a large advance, which was retained when the record company became too outraged by the group's behaviour to honour its side of the contract, worked supremely well. The Sex Pistols found themselves wealthy almost before they had recorded anything. Curiously, when Sigue Sigue Sputnik demonstrated a similarly mercenary attitude to music making, they found themselves vilified, rather than lauded as the Sex Pistols had been. Meanwhile, the Sex Pistols' early carryings-on have left us with one of the most valuable of modern collectors' items: the version of 'God Save The Queen' that was very briefly available on the A&M label.

Anarchie pour l'UK ................................ 7" ...... Barclay.......:... 640162................ 1979 £2......... £5 ...French, picture sleeve
Anarchy In The UK ................................ CD-s .. Virgin ........... CDT3................... 1988 £2......... £5 ................3" single
Anarchy In The UK ................................ 7" ...... Barclay........... 640112................ 1977 £2......... £5 ...French, picture sleeve
Anarchy In The UK ................................ 7" ...... EMI ............... EMI2566............. 1976 £7.50..... £15 ......... Chris Thomas production credit on B side
Anarchy In The UK ................................ 7" ...... EMI ............... EMI2566............. 1976 £2.50....... £6 ....... Dave Goodman production credit on B side
Anarchy In The UK ................................ 12".... Barclay........... 740501................ 1977 £2.50....... £6 ...................... French
Biggest Blow .......................................... 12".... Virgin ........... VS22012............. 1978 £2.50....... £6 ....... with interview
Filth And The Fury ................................ LP ...... McDonald Brothers........... JOCKBOX .......... 1987 £10......... £25 ...... 6 LP boxed set
Frigging In The Rigging.......................... 7" ...... Barclay........... 640159................ 1979 £4......... £8 ...French, picture sleeve
Frigging In The Rigging.......................... 7" ...... Virgin ........... VS240................. 1979 £5......... £10 mispress, A side plays 'Silly Thing'
God Save The Queen .............................. CD-s .. Virgin ........... CDT37................. 1988 £2......... £5 ................3" single
God Save The Queen .............................. 7" ...... A&M............. AMS7284.............. 1977 £700.. £1000
God Save The Queen .............................. 7" ...... Barclay........... 640106................ 1977 £2.50....... £6 ...French, picture sleeve
Great Rock 'n' Roll Swindle .................. 7" ...... Virgin ........... VS290................. 1979 £4......... £8 .with bonus 'telephone call' track
Heyday..................................................... cass .... Factory............ FACT30 .............. 1980 £4......... £10 satin pouch, Xmas card
Holidays In The Sun............................... 7" ...... Barclay........... 640116................ 1977 £2......... £5 ..French, picture sleeve
Holidays In The Sun............................... 7" ...... Virgin ........... VS191................. 1977 £2......... £5 ............ picture sleeve
Kiss This.................................................. CD ..... Virgin ........... CDVX2702.......... 1992 £8......... £20 .. double, with Live In Trondheim disc
My Way.................................................... 7" ...... Barclay........... 640154................ 1978 £2.50....... £6 ...French, picture sleeve
My Way.................................................... 7" ...... Virgin ........... VS220................. 1978 £5......... £10 .... mispress, other side plays The Motors
My Way.................................................... 12"..... Barclay........... 740509................ 1979 £3......... £8 ...................... French
Never Mind The Bollocks....................... LP ...... Virgin ........... V2086.................. 1977 £4......... £10 ......no track listing on sleeve
Never Mind The Bollocks....................... LP ...... Virgin ........... V2086.................. 1977 £10......... £25 . with poster & 1 sided 7" (VDJ24)
Never Mind The Bollocks....................... LP ...... Virgin ........... VP2086................ 1978 £8......... £20 ...............picture disc
Never Mind The Bollocks, Here's The Sex Pistols ... CD ..... Virgin ........... CDV2086............. 1986 £6......... £15 .... mispress – plays country music
Pistols Pack ............................................ 7" ...... Virgin ........... SEX1.................... 1980 £7.50..... £15 ... 6x7", plastic wallet
Pretty Vacant .......................................... 7" ...... Barclay........... 640109................ 1977 £2......... £5 ..French, picture sleeve
Stepping Stone ........................................ 7" ...... Virgin ........... VS339................. 1980 £4......... £8 mispress, plays Gillan
Submission............................................... 7" ...... Barclay........... 640137................ 1977 £2......... £5 ..French, picture sleeve
Submission............................................... 7" ...... Chaos............. DICK1................. 1985 £2.50....... £6 .. blue, pink, or yellow vinyl
Who Killed Bambi .................................. 7" ...... Barclay........... 640160................ 1979 £4......... £8 ..French, picture sleeve
You Need Hands ..................................... 7" ...... Barclay........... 640161................ 1979 £2......... £5 ..French, picture sleeve

## SEXY GIRLS
Pom-Pom Song ....................................... 7" ...... Fab ................. FAB100................ 1969 £1.50..... £4 ...... Little Joe B side

## SEYTON, DENNY & THE SABRES
It's The Gear (14 Hits) ........................... LP ...... Wing .............. WL1032.............. 1965 £8......... £20
Just A Kiss .............................................. 7" ...... Parlophone...... R5363 ................. 1965 £6......... £12
Short Fat Fanny....................................... 7" ...... Mercury........... MF814................. 1964 £5......... £10

| Title | Format | Label | Catalogue | Year | | | Notes |
|---|---|---|---|---|---|---|---|
| Tricky Dicky | 7" | Mercury | MF800 | 1964 | £4 | £8 | |
| Way You Look Tonight | 7" | Mercury | MF824 | 1964 | £10 | £20 | |

## SHACKLEFORDS
| Title | Format | Label | Catalogue | Year | | | Notes |
|---|---|---|---|---|---|---|---|
| Shacklefords | LP | Capitol | SMK74129 | 1966 | £6 | £15 | German |

## SHADE JOEY & THE NIGHT OWLS
| Title | Format | Label | Catalogue | Year | | | Notes |
|---|---|---|---|---|---|---|---|
| Blue Birds Over The Mountain | 7" | Parlophone | R5180 | 1964 | £15 | £30 | |

## SHADES
| Title | Format | Label | Catalogue | Year | | | Notes |
|---|---|---|---|---|---|---|---|
| Sun Glasses | 7" | London | HLX8713 | 1958 | £10 | £20 | B side Knott Sisters |

## SHADES (2)
| Title | Format | Label | Catalogue | Year | | | Notes |
|---|---|---|---|---|---|---|---|
| Weird Walk | 7" | Starlite | ST45074 | 1962 | £5 | £10 | |

## SHADES OF BLACK LIGHTNING SOUL
| Title | Format | Label | Catalogue | Year | | | Notes |
|---|---|---|---|---|---|---|---|
| Shades Of Black Lightning Soul | LP | Tower | | 1968 | £6 | £15 | US |

## SHADES OF BLUE
| Title | Format | Label | Catalogue | Year | | | Notes |
|---|---|---|---|---|---|---|---|
| Happiness Is The Shades Of Blue | LP | Impact | IM101/1001 | 1966 | £6 | £15 | US |
| Oh How Happy | 7" | Sue | WI4022 | 1966 | £5 | £10 | |

## SHADES OF BLUE (2)
| Title | Format | Label | Catalogue | Year | | | Notes |
|---|---|---|---|---|---|---|---|
| Voodoo Blues | 7" | Parlophone | R5270 | 1965 | £6 | £12 | |
| Where Did All The Good Times Go | 7" | Pye | 7N15988 | 1965 | £2.50 | £6 | |

## SHADES OF JOY
| Title | Format | Label | Catalogue | Year | | | Notes |
|---|---|---|---|---|---|---|---|
| Shades Of Joy | LP | Fontana | STL5498 | 1969 | £4 | £10 | |

## SHADOWS

The Shadows came together as a backing group for Cliff Richard (initially as the Drifters), but started to gain considerable success in their own right as soon as they realized that their strength lay in playing guitar instrumentals. Although only gaining very limited recognition in America (where the Ventures had an equivalent role), as far as UK listeners are concerned, when it comes to instrumental rock, the Shadows wrote the book. Several other groups attempted to copy the Shadows sound, but only the originals managed to achieve a string of chart hits – not least because their instrumental skills were probably unequalled in rock music during the early sixties.

| Title | Format | Label | Catalogue | Year | | | Notes |
|---|---|---|---|---|---|---|---|
| Alice In Sunderland | 7" EP | Columbia | SEG8445 | 1965 | £6 | £12 | |
| Apache | 7" | Columbia | DB4484 | 196– | £4 | £8 | black label |
| Apache | 7" | Columbia | DB4484 | 1960 | £1.50 | £4 | |
| Atlantis | 7" EP | Columbia | ESDF1480 | 1963 | £6 | £12 | French |
| Be Bop A Lula | 7" EP | Columbia | ESRF20002 | 196– | £6 | £12 | French |
| Boys | 7" EP | Columbia | ESG7881 | 1962 | £10 | £20 | stereo |
| Boys | 7" EP | Columbia | SEG8193 | 1962 | £2.50 | £6 | |
| Brilliant Shadows – Brilliant Songs | LP | Columbia | C83609 | 1963 | £8 | £20 | German mono |
| Brilliant Shadows – Brilliant Songs | LP | Columbia | SMC83609 | 1966 | £10 | £25 | German stereo |
| Chelsea Boot | 7" | Columbia | PSR310 | 1967 | £4 | £8 | promo |
| Dance On | 7" EP | Columbia | ESDF1457 | 1963 | £6 | £12 | French |
| Dance On With The Shadows | 7" EP | Columbia | SEG8233 | 1963 | £5 | £10 | |
| Dance With The Shadows | LP | Columbia | 33SX1619 | 1964 | £4 | £10 | |
| Dance With The Shadows | LP | Columbia | SCX3511 | 1964 | £5 | £12 | stereo |
| Dance With The Shadows No. 1 | 7" EP | Columbia | SEG8342 | 1964 | £5 | £10 | |
| Dance With The Shadows No. 2 | 7" EP | Columbia | SEG8375 | 1964 | £5 | £10 | |
| Dance With The Shadows No. 3 | 7" EP | Columbia | SEG8408 | 1965 | £6 | £12 | |
| Dear Old Mrs. Bell | 7" | Columbia | DB8372 | 1968 | £1.50 | £4 | |
| Don't Cry For Me Argentina | 12" | EMI | 12EMI2890 | 1978 | £2.50 | £6 | double groove |
| Don't Make My Baby Blue | 7" | Columbia | DB7650 | 1965 | £1.50 | £4 | |
| Dreams I Dream | 7" | Columbia | DB8034 | 1966 | £1.50 | £4 | |
| F.B.I. | 7" | Columbia | DB4580 | 196– | £4 | £8 | black label |
| F.B.I. | 7" | Columbia | DB4580 | 1961 | £1.50 | £4 | |
| Foot Tapping With The Shadows | 7" EP | Columbia | SEG8268 | 1963 | £5 | £10 | |
| Frightened City | 7" | Columbia | DB4637 | 196– | £4 | £8 | black label |
| Frightened City | 7" | Columbia | DB4637 | 1961 | £1.50 | £4 | |
| From Hank, Bruce, Brian, & John | LP | Columbia | SX/SCX6199 | 1967 | £4 | £10 | |
| Genie With The Light Brown Lamp | 7" | Columbia | DB7416 | 1964 | £1.50 | £4 | |
| Greatest Hits | LP | Columbia | 33SX1522 | 1963 | £4 | £10 | |
| Guitar Tango | 7" EP | Columbia | ESDF1437 | 1963 | £6 | £12 | French |
| Guitar Tango | 7" | Columbia | DB4870 | 196– | £4 | £8 | black label |
| Guitar Tango | 7" | Columbia | DB4870 | 1962 | £1.50 | £4 | |
| I Met A Girl | 7" | Columbia | DB7853 | 1966 | £1.50 | £4 | |
| In Japan | LP | Odeon | 8259 | 1967 | £87.50 | £175 | Japanese red vinyl |
| It'll Be Me Babe | 7" | EMI | EMI2461 | 1976 | £1.50 | £4 | |
| Jigsaw | LP | Columbia | SX/SCX6148 | 1967 | £4 | £10 | |
| Kon-Tiki | 7" | Columbia | DB4698 | 196– | £4 | £8 | black label |
| Kon-Tiki | 7" | Columbia | DB4698 | 1961 | £1.50 | £4 | |
| Little B | 7" EP | Columbia | ESDF1447 | 1963 | £6 | £12 | French |
| Los Shadows | 7" EP | Columbia | | 1964 | £10 | £20 | export |
| Los Shadows | 7" EP | Columbia | SEG8278 | 1963 | £5 | £10 | |
| Magical Mrs. Clamps | 7" | EMI | PSR316 | 1968 | £5 | £10 | promo, B side by Cliff Richard |
| Man Of Mystery | 7" | Columbia | DB4530 | 196– | £4 | £8 | black label |
| Man Of Mystery | 7" | Columbia | DB4530 | 1960 | £1.50 | £4 | |
| Maroc 7 | 7" | Columbia | DB8170 | 1967 | £1.50 | £4 | |
| Maroc 7 | 7" | Columbia | PSR304 | 1967 | £5 | £10 | promo, spoken intro |
| Mary Anne | 7" | Columbia | DB7476 | 1965 | £1.50 | £4 | |
| More Hits | LP | Columbia | 33SX1791/ SCX3578 | 1965 | £4 | £10 | |
| Mountains Of The Moon | CD-s | Polydor | PZCD47 | 1989 | £2 | £5 | |

| Title | Format | Label | Cat. No. | Year | | | Notes |
|---|---|---|---|---|---|---|---|
| Naughty Nippon Nights | 7" | Columbia | PSR313 | 1967 | £30 | £60 | promo |
| On Stage And Screen | 7" EP | Columbia | SEG8528 | 1967 | £7.50 | £15 | |
| Out Of The Shadows | LP | Columbia | 33SX1458 | 1962 | £4 | £10 | |
| Out Of The Shadows | LP | Columbia | SCX3449 | 1962 | £5 | £12 | stereo |
| Out Of The Shadows | 7" EP | Columbia | ESG7883 | 1963 | £10 | £20 | stereo |
| Out Of The Shadows | 7" EP | Columbia | SEG8218 | 1963 | £5 | £10 | |
| Out Of The Shadows | 10" LP | Columbia | FP1143 | 1962 | £20 | £40 | French |
| Out Of The Shadows No. 2 | 7" EP | Columbia | ESG7895 | 1963 | £10 | £20 | stereo |
| Out Of The Shadows No. 2 | 7" EP | Columbia | SEG8249 | 1963 | £4 | £8 | |
| Place In The Sun | 7" | Columbia | DB7952 | 1966 | £1.50 | £4 | |
| Rhythm And Greens | 7" EP | Columbia | ESG7904 | 1964 | £10 | £20 | stereo |
| Rhythm And Greens | 7" EP | Columbia | SEG8362 | 1964 | £5 | £10 | |
| Rhythm And Greens | 7" | Columbia | DB7342 | 1964 | £1.50 | £4 | |
| Rise And Fall Of Flingel Bunt | 7" | Columbia | DB7261 | 1964 | £2.50 | £6 | mispress, 2 A sides |
| Rockin' With Curly Leads | LP | EMI | EMA762 | 1973 | £4 | £10 | |
| Saturday Dance | 7" | Columbia | DB4387 | 1959 | £12.50 | £25 | |
| Savage | 7" | Columbia | DB4726 | 196– | £4 | £8 | black label |
| Savage | 7" | Columbia | DB4726 | 1961 | £1.50 | £4 | |
| Shadow Music | LP | Columbia | 33SX/SCX6041 | 1966 | £4 | £10 | |
| Shadowmix | CD-s | Polydor | PZCD61 | 1989 | £2 | £5 | |
| Shadows | LP | Columbia | 33SX1374 | 1962 | £4 | £10 | |
| Shadows | LP | Columbia | SCX3414 | 1962 | £8 | £20 | stereo |
| Shadows | LP | World Record Club | ALBUM72 | 1972 | £15 | £30 | 6 LPs, boxed |
| Shadows | 7" EP | Columbia | ESG7834 | 1961 | £10 | £20 | stereo |
| Shadows | 7" EP | Columbia | SEG8061 | 1961 | £4 | £8 | |
| Shadows Know | LP | Atlantic | (SD)8097 | 1964 | £10 | £25 | US |
| Shadows No. 2 | 7" EP | Columbia | SEG8148 | 1962 | £4 | £8 | |
| Shadows No. 3 | 7" EP | Columbia | SEG8166 | 1962 | £4 | £8 | |
| Shadows To The Fore | 7" EP | Columbia | SEG8094 | 1961 | £2.50 | £6 | |
| Shazam | 7" EP | Columbia | ESRF1402 | 1963 | £6 | £12 | French |
| Shindig | 7" | Columbia | DB7106 | 1963 | £1.50 | £4 | |
| Shindig With The Shadows | 7" EP | Columbia | SEG8286 | 1963 | £5 | £10 | |
| Sleepwalk | 7" EP | Columbia | ESDF1434 | 1963 | £6 | £12 | French |
| Sound Of The Shadows | LP | Columbia | 33SX1736 | 1965 | £4 | £10 | |
| Sound Of The Shadows | LP | Columbia | SCX3554 | 1965 | £5 | £12 | stereo |
| Sound Of The Shadows No. 1 | 7" EP | Columbia | SEG8459 | 1965 | £6 | £12 | |
| Sound Of The Shadows No. 2 | 7" EP | Columbia | SEG8473 | 1966 | £6 | £12 | |
| Sound Of The Shadows No. 3 | 7" EP | Columbia | SEG8494 | 1966 | £6 | £12 | |
| Spotlight On The Shadows | 7" EP | Columbia | SEG8135 | 1962 | £4 | £8 | |
| Stingray | 7" | Columbia | DB7588 | 1965 | £1.50 | £4 | |
| Surfing With The Shadows | LP | Atlantic | (SD)8089 | 1963 | £10 | £25 | US |
| Themes From Aladdin | 7" EP | Columbia | SEG8396 | 1965 | £5 | £10 | |
| Those Brilliant Shadows | 7" EP | Columbia | SEG8321 | 1964 | £5 | £10 | |
| Those Talented Shadows | 7" EP | Columbia | SEG8500 | 1966 | £6 | £12 | |
| Thunderbirds Are Go | 7" | EMI | PSR305 | 1967 | £30 | £60 | 1 sided promo |
| Tomorrow's Cancelled | 7" | Columbia | DB8264 | 1967 | £2.50 | £6 | |
| Twenty Golden Greats | 7" | EMI | | 1977 | £1.50 | £4 | promo sampler |
| Warlord | 7" | Columbia | DB7769 | 1965 | £1.50 | £4 | |
| Wonderful Land | 7" | Columbia | DB4726 | 196– | £2.50 | £6 | black label |
| Wonderful Land | 7" | Columbia | DB4790 | 1962 | £1.50 | £4 | |
| Wonderful Land Of The Shadows | 7" EP | Columbia | SEG8171 | 1962 | £4 | £8 | |

## SHADOWS (2)

| Title | Format | Label | Cat. No. | Year | | | Notes |
|---|---|---|---|---|---|---|---|
| Under Stars Of Love | 7" | HMV | POP563 | 1958 | £20 | £40 | |

## SHADOWS OF KNIGHT

| Title | Format | Label | Cat. No. | Year | | | Notes |
|---|---|---|---|---|---|---|---|
| Back Door Men | LP | Dunwich | (S)667 | 1966 | £25 | £50 | US |
| Bad Little Woman | 7" | Atlantic | 584045 | 1966 | £5 | £10 | |
| Gloria | LP | Dunwich | (S)666 | 1966 | £25 | £50 | US |
| Gloria | 7" | Atlantic | AT4085 | 1966 | £5 | £10 | |
| Oh Yeah | 7" EP | Atco | 113 | 1966 | £30 | £60 | French |
| Oh Yeah | 7" | Atlantic | 584021 | 1966 | £5 | £10 | |
| Shadows Of Knight | LP | Super K | SKS6002 | 1969 | £10 | £25 | US |
| Shake | 7" | Buddah | 201024 | 1968 | £2.50 | £6 | |
| Someone Like Me | 7" | Atlantic | 584136 | 1967 | £5 | £10 | |

## SHADRACK CHAMELEON

| Title | Format | Label | Cat. No. | Year | | | Notes |
|---|---|---|---|---|---|---|---|
| Shadrack Chameleon | LP | Iglus | 40515 | 1971 | £180 | £300 | US |

## SHADROCKS

| Title | Format | Label | Cat. No. | Year | | | Notes |
|---|---|---|---|---|---|---|---|
| Go Go Special | 7" | Island | WI3061 | 1967 | £4 | £8 | |

## SHAFTESBURY

| Title | Format | Label | Cat. No. | Year | | | Notes |
|---|---|---|---|---|---|---|---|
| Lull Before The Storm | LP | OK Records | OKA001 | 1980 | £15 | £30 | |
| We Are The Boys | LP | OK | OKO002 | 1981 | £6 | £15 | |

## SHAGGS

| Title | Format | Label | Cat. No. | Year | | | Notes |
|---|---|---|---|---|---|---|---|
| Philosophy Of The World | LP | Third World | 3001 | 1972 | £330 | £500 | US |

## SHAGGS (2)

| Title | Format | Label | Cat. No. | Year | | | Notes |
|---|---|---|---|---|---|---|---|
| Wink | LP | MCM | 6311 | 1967 | £700 | £1000 | US |
| Wink | LP | Resurrection | CX1295 | 1984 | £6 | £15 | US |

## SHAKEOUTS

| Title | Format | Label | Cat. No. | Year | | | Notes |
|---|---|---|---|---|---|---|---|
| Every Little Once In A While | 7" | Columbia | DB7613 | 1965 | £10 | £20 | |

## SHAKERS (KINGSIZE TAYLOR & THE DOMINOES)
Hippy Hippy Shake .................................... 7" ...... Polydor ........... NH52213 ................ 1963 £5 .......... £10 ...........................................
Hippy Hippy Shake .................................... 7" ...... Polydor ........... NH66991 ................ 1963 £5 .......... £10 ...........................................
Let's Do The Madison, Twist, Locomotion LP ..... Polydor ........... 46639/237139 ........ 1963 £30 ......... £60 .................. German
........................................................................
Memphis Tennessee .................................... 7" EP . Polydor ........... 50025 .................. 1963 £20 ......... £40 .................. French
Money ...................................................... 7" ...... Polydor ........... NH52158 ................ 1963 £5 .......... £10 ...........................................
Money ...................................................... 7" ...... Polydor ........... NH52258 ................ 1963 £5 .......... £10 ...........................................
Whole Lotta Loving .................................. 7" ...... Polydor ........... NH52272 ................ 1964 £5 .......... £10 ...........................................

## SHAKERS (2)
Break It All .............................................. LP ...... Audio Fidelity.. (S)2155 ................ 1966 £8 .......... £20 .................. US

## SHAKESPEAR
Stay ......................................................... LP ..... Real ............... RR2001 ............... 1975 £15 ......... £30

## SHAKESPEARE, CHRIS GLOBE SHOW
Ob La Di, Ob La Da ................................ 7" ...... Page One ....... POF113 ............... 1969 £5 .......... £10

## SHAKESPEARES
Something To Believe In ............................ 7" ...... RCA ............... RCA1695 ............ 1968 £20 ......... £40

## SHAKESPEARS
Give It To Me ......................................... LP ...... Philips............. QU625276 ............. 196– £150 ..... £250 .................. Dutch
Saint......................................................... 7" EP . Barclay ........... 070981 ............... 1966 £12.50 ... £25 .................. French
Summertime ............................................. 7" EP . Barclay ........... 071036 ............... 1966 £12.50 ... £25 .................. French

## SHAKEY JAKE
Further On Up The Road.......................... LP ...... Liberty ........... LBL83217E ........ 1969 £4 .......... £10

## SHAKEY VICK
Little Woman You're So Sweet ................. LP ...... Pye ................. NSPL18276 ......... 1969 £15 ......... £30

## SHAM, SAM
Drumbago's Dead....................................... 7" ...... Blue Cat........... BS157 .................. 1969 £2 ............. £5 .......... Sparters B side

## SHAM 69
I Don't Wanna.......................................... 7" ...... Step Forward ... SF4 ...................... 1977 £2 ............. £5 ...........................................
I Don't Wanna.......................................... 12" .... Step Forward ... SF4 ...................... 1977 £2.50 ........ £6 ...........................................
Sons Of The Streets ................................ 7" ...... no label ........... no number .......... 1977 £2 ............. £5 .................. 1 sided
What Have We Got ................................. 7" ...... Brick Wall ....... no number ........... 1978 £2.50 ........ £6 .................. 1 sided

## SHAME
Don't Go Away Little Girl ....................... 7" ...... MGM ............. MGM1349 ............ 1967 £30 ......... £60

## SHAME (2)
Real Tears ............................................... 7" ...... Fierce ............. FRIGHT003 ......... 1985 £10 ......... £20 ............ test pressing

## SHAMEN
Hyperreal ................................................ CD-s .. One Little ....... 48TP7CD .......... 1991 £2 ............. £5
.......................................................................... Indian .............
Jesus Loves Amerika ............................... CD-s .. Ediesta ........... CALCCD069 ........ 1988 £2 ............. £5
Make It Mine EP ..................................... CD-s .. One Little ....... 7TP46CD .......... 1990 £2 ............. £5
.......................................................................... Indian .............
Omega Amigo ......................................... CD-s .. One Little ....... 7TP30CD .......... 1989 £2 ............. £5
.......................................................................... Indian .............
Phorward.................................................. CD .... Moksha........... SOMACD3 ......... 1989 £4 ............. £10
Progen .................................................... CD-s .. One Little ....... 36TP7CD .......... 1990 £2 ............. £5
.......................................................................... Indian .............
Progen (C-Mix F) .................................... 12" .... One Little ....... 36TP12L ........... 1990 £3 ............. £8
.......................................................................... Indian .............
Strange Day Dreams ............................... CD .... Materiali ......... MASO90003 .......... 1990 £5 ............. £12
.......................................................................... Sonori.............
They May Be Right ................................. 12" .... One Big Guitar OBG003T ............. 1986 £3 ............. £8
Wayward Wednesday In May Affair ........... 7" ...... Skipping Kitten ........................... 1986 £2.50 ........ £6 .................. 1 sided flexi
You, Me And Everything .......................... CD-s .. Moksha........... SOMA6CD .......... 1989 £2 ............. £5
Young Till Yesterday................................. 7" ...... Moksha........... SOMA1 .............. 1986 £1.50 ........ £4
Young Till Yesterday................................. 12" .... Moksha........... SOMA1T ............ 1986 £2.50 ........ £6

## SHAMES
Greenburg Glickstein Charles ................... 7" ...... CBS................. 3820 ................... 1968 £1.50 ........ £4
I Wanna Meet You ................................. 7" ...... CBS................. 202450 ............... 1966 £1.50 ........ £4
Mr. Unreliable .......................................... 7" ...... CBS................. 2704 ................... 1967 £1.50 ........ £4
Sugar And Spice ...................................... 7" ...... CBS................. 202344 ............... 1966 £7.50 ........ £15

## SHAMPOO
Vol. One ................................................. LP ...... Motor ............. MT44009 ............. 1972 £6 ............. £15 .................. French

## SHAMROCKS
Cadillac ................................................... 7" EP . Polydor ........... 60122 .................. 196– £10 ......... £20 .................. French
Don't Say ................................................ 7" EP . Polydor ........... 60124 .................. 196– £12.50 ... £25 .................. French
In Paris ................................................... LP ...... Polydor ........... 658032 ............... 1966 £37.50 ... £75 .................. French
Shamrocks ................................................ LP ...... Ariola ............. 72151 .................. 1965 £37.50 ... £75 .................. German
Smoke Rings ............................................ LP ...... Polydor ........... 623015 ............... 1966 £37.50 ... £75 .................. German

## SHANE, VALERIE
One Billion Seven Million Thirty-Three .... 7" ...... Philips............. PB879 .................. 1958 £2 ............. £5

## SHANE & THE SHANE GANG
| | | | | | | |
|---|---|---|---|---|---|---|
| Whistle Stop | 7" | Pye | 7N15662 | 1964 | £2.50 | £6 |

## SHANES
| | | | | | | |
|---|---|---|---|---|---|---|
| I Don't Want Your Love | 7" | Columbia | DB7601 | 1965 | £15 | £30 |
| SSS–Shanes | LP | Columbia | 1026 | 1967 | £8 | £20 | Swedish |

## SHANGAANS
| | | | | | | |
|---|---|---|---|---|---|---|
| Jungle Drums | LP | Columbia | SMC74113 | 1965 | £6 | £15 | German |

## SHANGRI-LAS
| | | | | | | | |
|---|---|---|---|---|---|---|---|
| Give Him A Great Big Kiss | 7" EP | Red Bird | RBEV28007 | 1965 | £15 | £30 | French |
| Give Him A Great Big Kiss | 7" | Red Bird | RB10018 | 1965 | £2 | £5 | |
| Give Us Your Blessings | 7" | Red Bird | RB10030 | 1965 | £2.50 | £6 | |
| Golden Hits | LP | Mercury | MCL20096 | 1966 | £4 | £10 | |
| He Cried | 7" | Red Bird | RB10053 | 1966 | £2.50 | £6 | |
| I Can Never Go Home Any More | 7" EP | Red Bird | RB40004 | 1966 | £20 | £40 | demo |
| I Can Never Go Home Any More | 7" EP | Red Bird | RBEV28009 | 1966 | £15 | £30 | French |
| I Can Never Go Home Any More | 7" | Red Bird | RB10043 | 1966 | £2 | £5 | |
| I Can Never Go Home Anymore | LP | Red Bird | RB20104 | 1965 | £25 | £50 | US |
| Leader Of The Pack | LP | Red Bird | RB20101 | 1964 | £20 | £40 | |
| Leader Of The Pack | 7" EP | Red Bird | RBEV28005 | 1964 | £12.50 | £25 | French, B side by The Jelly Beans |
| Leader Of The Pack | 7" | Red Bird | RB10014 | 1964 | £1.50 | £4 | |
| Long Live Our Love | 7" | Red Bird | RB10048 | 1966 | £2.50 | £6 | |
| Maybe | 7" | Red Bird | RB10019 | 1965 | £6 | £12 | |
| Out In The Streets | 7" | Red Bird | RB10025 | 1965 | £2 | £5 | |
| Past Present And Future | 7" | Red Bird | RB10068 | 1966 | £5 | £10 | |
| Remember | 7" EP | Red Bird | RBEV28004 | 1964 | £12.50 | £25 | French, B side by The Butterflies |
| Remember Walking In The Sand | CD-s | Charly | CDS3 | 1989 | £2 | £5 | |
| Remember Walking In The Sand | 7" | Red Bird | RB10008 | 1964 | £1.50 | £4 | |
| Right Now And Not Later | 7" | Red Bird | RB10036 | 1965 | £6 | £12 | |
| Shangri-Las | 7" EP | Red Bird | RB40002 | 1965 | £15 | £30 | |
| Shangri-Las '65 | LP | Red Bird | RB20104 | 1965 | £20 | £40 | US |
| Shangri-Las Sing | LP | Post | 4000 | | £5 | £12 | US |
| Sweet Sound Of Summer | 7" | Mercury | MF962 | 1967 | £2 | £5 | |
| Take Your Time | 7" | Mercury | MF979 | 1967 | £2 | £5 | |

## SHANK, BUD
| | | | | | | | |
|---|---|---|---|---|---|---|---|
| Bud Shank Group | 10" LP | Vogue | LDE157 | 1955 | £15 | £30 | |
| Bud Shank Quartet | LP | Vogue | LAE12113 | 1958 | £10 | £25 | |
| Bud Shank Quintet | LP | Vogue | LAE12020 | 1956 | £10 | £25 | |
| Bud Shank-Bob Brookmeyer Group | 10" LP | Vogue | LDE181 | 1956 | £15 | £30 | |
| California Dreamin' | LP | Fontana | STL5371 | 1966 | £5 | £12 | with Chet Baker |
| Flute 'n Oboe | LP | Vogue | VA160124 | 1958 | £6 | £15 | with Bob Cooper |
| Holiday In Brazil | LP | Vogue | LAE12215 | 1960 | £6 | £15 | |
| Jazz At Cal-Tech | LP | Vogue | LAE12095 | 1958 | £8 | £20 | |
| Michelle | LP | Fontana | TL5326 | 1966 | £4 | £12 | with Chet Baker |
| New Groove | LP | Vogue | LAE12288 | 1961 | £5 | £12 | |
| Swing's To TV | LP | Vogue | VA160134 | 1959 | £8 | £20 | with Bob Cooper |

## SHANKAR, ANANDA
| | | | | | | |
|---|---|---|---|---|---|---|
| Ananda Shankar | LP | Reprise | K44082 | 1971 | £100 | £200 |
| Jumping Jack Flash | LP | Reprise | RSLP6398 | 1969 | £100 | £200 |

## SHANKAR, L.
| | | | | | | | |
|---|---|---|---|---|---|---|---|
| Touch Me There | LP | Zappa | SRZ11602 | 1979 | £4 | £10 | US |

## SHANKAR, RAVI
| | | | | | | | |
|---|---|---|---|---|---|---|---|
| At The Woodstock Festival | LP | United Artists | UAG29379 | 1970 | £5 | £12 | |
| Four Raga Moods | LP | Melodisc | 300ML8 | 1971 | £8 | £20 | double |
| Improvisations | LP | Liberty | LBS83076 | 1968 | £5 | £12 | |
| In Concert | LP | Liberty | LBS83077 | 1968 | £5 | £12 | |
| In Concert 1972 | LP | Apple | SAPDO1002 | 1973 | £50 | £100 | double |
| In New York | LP | Fontana | TL5424 | 1967 | £5 | £15 | |
| In San Francisco | LP | Columbia | SCX6382 | 1970 | £5 | £12 | |
| India's Master Musician | LP | Fontana | TL5253 | 1965 | £6 | £15 | |
| India's Master Musician | LP | Vogue | VA160156 | 1959 | £6 | £15 | |
| Joi Bangla | 7" | Apple | 37 | 1971 | £5 | £10 | picture sleeve |
| Live At The Monterey Pop Festival | LP | Columbia | SX/SCX6273 | 1968 | £5 | £12 | |
| Music Of India | LP | HMV | ASD463 | 1962 | £6 | £15 | |
| Portrait Of Genius | LP | Fontana | TL5285 | 1966 | £6 | £15 | |
| Raga | LP | Apple | SWAO3384 | 1971 | £8 | £20 | US |
| Sitar Recital | LP | Transatlantic | TRA182 | 1968 | £5 | £12 | |
| Song From The Hills | 7" | Fontana | TF712 | 1966 | £2 | £5 | |
| Sound Of The Sitar | LP | Fontana | TL5357 | 1966 | £6 | £15 | |

## SHANNON, CHICK
| | | | | | | |
|---|---|---|---|---|---|---|
| Tears On The Console | LP | Holyground | HG120 | 1975 | £100 | £200 |
| Tears On The Console | LP | Magic Mixture | MM3 | 1990 | £4 | £10 |

## SHANNON, DEAN
| | | | | | | |
|---|---|---|---|---|---|---|
| Jezebel | 7" | HMV | POP820 | 1960 | £4 | £8 |
| Ubangi Stomp | 7" | HMV | POP1103 | 1962 | £6 | £12 |

## SHANNON, DEL

The years between the decline of rock 'n' roll at the end of the fifties and the rise of the Beatles in 1963 are generally viewed as holding comparatively few delights for the rock historian. One definite exception, however, is the work of Del Shannon, whose powerful, ragged voice was linked to incisive material, much of it written by himself. When the Beatles did arrive, Shannon was one of the first people to see which way things were going and his version of 'From Me To You' was the first Beatles cover version to be issued in America. In the long term, however, Shannon found the decline in his fortunes too hard to take – sadly, he took his own life in 1990.

| | | | | | | |
|---|---|---|---|---|---|---|
| 1,661 Seconds | LP | Amy | S8006 | 1965 £20 | £40 | US, stereo |
| 1,661 Seconds | LP | Stateside | SL10140 | 1965 £8 | £20 | |
| Best Of Del Shannon | LP | Dot | DLP3834 | 1967 £4 | £10 | US |
| Big Hurt | 7" | Liberty | LIB55866 | 1966 £2 | £5 | |
| Break Up | 7" | Stateside | SS430 | 1965 £1.50 | £4 | |
| Comin' Back To Me | 7" | Stateside | SS8025 | 1969 £2 | £5 | |
| Cry Myself To Sleep | 7" | London | HLX9587 | 1962 £1.50 | £4 | |
| Del Shannon | 7" EP | London | REX1332 | 1962 £6 | £12 | |
| Del Shannon No. 2 | 7" EP | London | REX1346 | 1963 £6 | £12 | |
| Del Shannon's Hits | 7" EP | Stateside | SE1029 | 1965 £6 | £12 | |
| Del's Own Favourites | 7" EP | London | REX1383 | 1963 £6 | £12 | |
| Do You Want To Dance | 7" | Stateside | SS349 | 1964 £1.50 | £4 | |
| For A Little While | 7" | Liberty | LIB55889 | 1966 £2 | £5 | |
| From Del To You | 7" EP | London | REX1387 | 1963 £6 | £12 | |
| Further Adventures Of Charles Westover | LP | Liberty | LBL/LBS83114 | 1968 £6 | £15 | |
| Gemini | 7" | Liberty | LBF15079 | 1968 £2 | £5 | |
| Handy Man | LP | Stateside | SL10115 | 1965 £6 | £15 | |
| Handy Man | 7" | Stateside | SS317 | 1964 £1.50 | £4 | |
| Hats Off To Del Shannon | LP | London | HAX8071 | 1963 £8 | £20 | |
| Hats Off To Larry | 7" | London | HLX9402 | 1961 £1.50 | £4 | |
| I Can't Believe My Ears | 7" | Stateside | SS494 | 1966 £2 | £5 | |
| Little Town Flirt | LP | Big Top | S121308 | 1963 £25 | £50 | US, stereo |
| Little Town Flirt | LP | London | HAX8091 | 1963 £8 | £20 | |
| Little Town Flirt | 7" | London | HLX9653 | 1963 £1.50 | £4 | |
| Mary Jane | 7" | Stateside | SS269 | 1964 £1.50 | £4 | |
| Mind Over Matter | 7" | Liberty | LIB10277 | 1967 £1.50 | £4 | |
| Move It On Over | 7" | Stateside | SS452 | 1965 £2.50 | £6 | |
| New Del Shannon | 7" EP | Liberty | LEP2272 | 1967 £12.50 | £25 | |
| Runaway | LP | Big Top | 123003 | 1961 £20 | £40 | US, mono |
| Runaway | LP | Big Top | S123003 | 1961 £150 | £250 | US, stereo |
| Runaway | LP | London | HAX2402 | 1961 £10 | £25 | |
| Runaway | 7" | London | HLX9317 | 1961 £1.50 | £4 | |
| Runaway | 7" | London | HLX9317 | 1961 £5 | £10 | B side mispress – plays 'Snake' |
| Runaway '67 | 7" | Liberty | LBF15020 | 1967 £1.50 | £4 | |
| She | 7" | Liberty | LIB55939 | 1967 £2 | £5 | |
| Sings Hank Williams | LP | Stateside | SL10130 | 1965 £6 | £15 | |
| Sister Isabelle | 7" | Stateside | SS8040 | 1970 £2 | £5 | |
| Stranger In Town | 7" | Stateside | SS395 | 1965 £1.50 | £4 | |
| Sue's Gonna Be Mine | 7" | London | HLX9800 | 1963 £1.50 | £4 | |
| Swiss Maid | 7" | London | HLX9609 | 1962 £1.50 | £4 | |
| That's The Way Love Is | 7" | London | HLX9858 | 1964 £1.50 | £5 | |
| Thinkin' It Over | 7" | Liberty | LBF15061 | 1968 £2 | £5 | |
| This Is My Bag | LP | Liberty | (S)LBY1320 | 1966 £8 | £20 | |
| Total Commitment | LP | Liberty | (S)LBY1335 | 1966 £8 | £20 | |
| Two Kinds Of Teardrops | 7" | London | HLX9719 | 1963 £1.50 | £4 | |
| Two Silhouettes | 7" | London | HLX9761 | 1963 £1.50 | £4 | |
| What's A Matter Baby | 7" | United Artists | UP35460 | 1972 £1.50 | £4 | |

## SHANNON, HUGH

| | | | | | | |
|---|---|---|---|---|---|---|
| Hugh Shannon Sings | 10" LP | Atlantic | 406 | £8 | £20 | US |

## SHAPE OF THE RAIN

| | | | | | | |
|---|---|---|---|---|---|---|
| Riley, Riley, Wood & Waggett | LP | Neon | NE7 | 1971 £10 | £25 | |
| Woman | 7" | Neon | NE1901 | 1971 £2 | £5 | |

## SHAPIRO, HELEN

| | | | | | | |
|---|---|---|---|---|---|---|
| Don't Treat Me Like A Child | 7" | Columbia | DB4589 | 1961 £1.50 | £4 | |
| Even More Hits From Helen | 7" EP | Columbia | SEG8209 | 1962 £4 | £8 | |
| Fever | 7" | Columbia | DB7190 | 1964 £2.50 | £6 | |
| Forget About The Bad Things | 7" | Columbia | DB7810 | 1966 £1.50 | £4 | |
| He Knows How To Love Me | 7" | Columbia | DB7340 | 1964 £15 | £30 | |
| Helen | 7" EP | Columbia | ESG7872 | 1961 £5 | £10 | stereo |
| Helen | 7" EP | Columbia | SEG8128 | 1961 £2.50 | £6 | |
| Helen Hits Out | LP | Columbia | 33SX1661 | 1964 £6 | £15 | |
| Helen Hits Out | LP | Columbia | SCX3533 | 1964 £10 | £25 | stereo |
| Helen In Nashville | LP | Columbia | 33SX1561 | 1963 £8 | £20 | |
| Helen's Hit Parade | 7" EP | Columbia | SEG8136 | 1961 £2.50 | £6 | |
| Helen's Sixteen | LP | Columbia | 33SX1494 | 1963 £6 | £15 | |
| Helen's Sixteen | LP | Columbia | SCX3470 | 1963 £10 | £25 | stereo |
| Here In Your Arms | 7" | Columbia | DB7587 | 1965 £1.50 | £4 | |
| I Wish I'd Never Loved You | 7" | Columbia | DB7395 | 1964 £1.50 | £4 | |
| In My Calendar | 7" | Columbia | DB8073 | 1966 £1.50 | £4 | |
| Look Over Your Shoulder | 7" | Columbia | DB7266 | 1964 £1.50 | £4 | |
| Look Who It Is | 7" | Columbia | DB7130 | 1963 £1.50 | £4 | |
| Make Me Belong To You | 7" | Columbia | DB8148 | 1967 £1.50 | £4 | |
| More Hits From Helen | 7" EP | Columbia | SEG8174 | 1962 £2.50 | £6 | |
| Not Responsible | 7" | Columbia | DB7072 | 1963 £1.50 | £4 | |
| Something Wonderful | 7" | Columbia | DB7690 | 1965 £1.50 | £4 | |

| | | | | | | | |
|---|---|---|---|---|---|---|---|
| Stop & You'll Become Aware | 7" | Columbia | DB8256 | 1967 | £20 | £40 | |
| Take Down A Note Miss Smith | 7" | Pye | 7N17893 | 1970 | £1.50 | £4 | |
| Teenager In Love | LP | Epic | LN24/BN26075 | 1963 | £8 | £20 | US |
| Teenager Sings The Blues | 7" EP | Columbia | ESG7880 | 1962 | £6 | £12 | stereo |
| Teenager Sings The Blues | 7" EP | Columbia | SEG8170 | 1962 | £5 | £10 | |
| Today Has Been Cancelled | 7" | Pye | 7N17714 | 1969 | £1.50 | £4 | |
| Tomorrow Is Another Day | 7" | Columbia | DB7517 | 1965 | £1.50 | £4 | |
| Tops With Me | LP | Columbia | 33SX1397 | 1962 | £5 | £12 | |
| Tops With Me | LP | Columbia | SCX3428 | 1962 | £8 | £20 | stereo |
| Tops With Me No. 1 | 7" EP | Columbia | ESG7888 | 1962 | £12.50 | £25 | stereo |
| Tops With Me No. 1 | 7" EP | Columbia | SEG8229 | 1963 | £6 | £12 | |
| Tops With Me No. 2 | 7" EP | Columbia | ESG7891 | 1962 | £12.50 | £25 | stereo |
| Tops With Me No. 2 | 7" EP | Columbia | SEG8243 | 1963 | £6 | £12 | |
| Twelve Hits And A Miss | LP | Encore | ENC209 | 1967 | £5 | £12 | |
| Waiting On The Shores Of Nowhere | 7" | Pye | 7N17975 | 1970 | £1.50 | £4 | |
| You'll Get Me Loving You | 7" | Pye | 7N17600 | 1968 | £1.50 | £4 | |
| You've Guessed It | 7" | Pye | 7N17785 | 1969 | £2.50 | £6 | |

## SHARADES

| | | | | | | |
|---|---|---|---|---|---|---|
| Dumbhead | 7" | Decca | F11811 | 1964 | £25 | £50 |

## SHARAE, BILLY

| | | | | | | |
|---|---|---|---|---|---|---|
| Do It | 7" | Action | ACT4602 | 1971 | £1.50 | £4 |

## SHARKS

| | | | | | | |
|---|---|---|---|---|---|---|
| Goodbye Lorene | 7" | RCA | RCA1776 | 1968 | £1.50 | £4 |

## SHARON, RALPH

| | | | | | | |
|---|---|---|---|---|---|---|
| Around The World In Jazz | LP | Columbia | 33SX1090 | 1958 | £6 | £15 |

## SHARON, SUE & RALPH

| | | | | | | |
|---|---|---|---|---|---|---|
| Mr. And Mrs. Jazz | LP | London | LTZN15102 | 1958 | £5 | £12 |

## SHARON, MARIE

These songs were produced by Brian Wilson, who used the same tune for 'Thinkin' 'Bout You Baby' as for the later Beach Boys' song 'Darlin''.

| | | | | | | | |
|---|---|---|---|---|---|---|---|
| Run-Around Lover | 7" | Capitol | 5064 | 1963 | £30 | £60 | US |
| Thinkin' 'Bout You Baby | 7" | Capitol | 5195 | 1964 | £30 | £60 | US |

## SHARON PEOPLE

| | | | | | | | |
|---|---|---|---|---|---|---|---|
| Inside Looking Out | LP | Indigo | IRS5510 | 1974 | £100 | £200 | Irish |

## SHARONS

| | | | | | | |
|---|---|---|---|---|---|---|
| Someone To Turn To | LP | Emblem | JDR325 | 1970 | £37.50 | £75 |

## SHARP, DEE DEE

| | | | | | | | |
|---|---|---|---|---|---|---|---|
| All The Hits | LP | Cameo | (S)C1032 | 1962 | £8 | £20 | US |
| Biggest Hits | LP | Cameo | C1062 | 1963 | £6 | £15 | US |
| Do The Bird | LP | Cameo | (S)C1050 | 1963 | £8 | £20 | US |
| Do The Bird | 7" | Cameo Parkway | C244 | 1963 | £2.50 | £6 | |
| Down Memory Lane | LP | Cameo | C1074 | 1963 | £6 | £15 | US |
| Eighteen Golden Hits | LP | Cameo | (S)C2002 | 1966 | £6 | £15 | US |
| Gravy For My Mashed Potatoes | 7" | Columbia | DB4874 | 1962 | £2 | £5 | |
| I Really Love You | 7" | Cameo Parkway | C375 | 1965 | £15 | £30 | |
| It's A Funny Situation | 7" | Cameo Parkway | C382 | 1965 | £37.50 | £75 | demo |
| It's Mashed Potato Time | LP | Cameo | C1018 | 1962 | £8 | £20 | US |
| Mashed Potato Time | 7" | Columbia | DB4818 | 1962 | £2 | £5 | |
| My Best Friend's Man | 7" | Atlantic | 584056 | 1966 | £2.50 | £6 | |
| Ride | 7" | Cameo Parkway | C230 | 1962 | £1.50 | £4 | |
| Rock Me In The Cradle Of Love | 7" | Cameo Parkway | C260 | 1963 | £2 | £5 | |
| Songs Of Faith | LP | Cameo | C1022 | 1962 | £6 | £15 | US |
| What Kinda Lady | 7" | Action | ACT4522 | 1969 | £7.50 | £15 | |
| Wild | 7" | Cameo Parkway | C274 | 1963 | £1.50 | £4 | |

## SHARP, STEVIE & CLEANCUTS

| | | | | | | | |
|---|---|---|---|---|---|---|---|
| We Are The Mods | 7" | Happy Face | MM122 | 1980 | £15 | £30 | no picture sleeve |

## SHARPE, BILL

| | | | | | | | |
|---|---|---|---|---|---|---|---|
| Change Your Mind | 7" | Polydor | POSPP722 | 1985 | £2.50 | £6 | picture disc |
| Change Your Mind | 12" | Polydor | POPX722 | 1985 | £4 | £10 | picture disc |
| Famous People | CD | Polydor | 8254972 | 1985 | £5 | £12 | |

## SHARPE, RAY

| | | | | | | |
|---|---|---|---|---|---|---|
| Hey Little Girl | 7" | United Artists | UP1032 | 1963 | £5 | £10 |
| Linda Lu | 7" | London | HLW8932 | 1959 | £12.50 | £25 |

## SHARPE & NUMAN

| | | | | | | | |
|---|---|---|---|---|---|---|---|
| Automatic | CD | Polydor | 8395202 | 1989 | £5 | £12 | |
| I'm On Automatic | CD-s | Polydor | PVCD43 | 1989 | £2 | £5 | |
| New Thing From London Town | 12" | Numa | NUMP19 | 1986 | £2.50 | £6 | picture disc |

No More Lies ........................................... CD-s .. Polydor ........... POCD894............. 1988 £2............£5 .......................................

## SHARPEES
Tired Of Being Lonely............................... 7" ...... Stateside .......... SS495 ................... 1966 £15.........£30 ...................................

## SHARPLES, BOB
Hurricane Boogie ..................................... 7" ...... Decca ............. F10707 ............... 1956 £1.50......£4 ...................................

## SHARPS
Lock My Heart ......................................... 7" ...... Vogue............. V9086 ............... 1957 £100.....£200 ...........best auctioned
Shuffling.................................................. 7" ...... Vogue............. V9096 ............... 1958 £100.....£200 ...........best auctioned

## SHARROCK, SONNY
Paradise .................................................. LP ...... Atco ............... SD36121 ............... 1975 £6............£15 ......US, with Linda
Sharrock

## SHATNER, WILLIAM
Transformed Man...................................... LP ...... Decca ............. DL75043 ............... 1968 £8............£20 .......................US

## SHAVERS, CHARLIE
Charlie Shavers Quintet ............................ 10" LP London ........... LZN14009 ............ 1956 £10............£25 ...............................
Gershwin, Shavers And Strings ................. 10" LP London ........... HBU1053 ............ 1956 £8............£20 ...............................
With The Sy Oliver Orchestra................... 10" LP London ........... HBN1047 ............ 1956 £10............£25 ...............................

## SHAW, ARTIE
Any Old Time ......................................... LP ...... RCA ............. RD27065 ............... 1958 £6............£15 ...............................
Artie Shaw And His Gramercy Five ........... 10" LP Columbia ...... 33C9006 ............ 1955 £8............£20 ...............................
Speak To Me Of Love............................. 10" LP Brunswick ...... LA8677 ............... 1954 £8............£20 ...............................

## SHAW, ARVELL
Skin Tight And Cymbal Wise..................... LP ...... Columbia ......... 33SX1076 ............... 1958 £4............£10 ...............................

## SHAW, GEORGIE
Banjo Woogie.......................................... 7" ...... Brunswick ...... 05476 ............... 1955 £1.50......£4 ...............................

## SHAW, MARLENA
Mercy, Mercy, Mercy................................ 7" ...... Chess ............. CRS8054 ............... 1967 £2............£5 ...............................

## SHAW, NINA
Woven In My Soul.................................... 7" ...... CBS ............. 3239 ............... 1968 £1.50......£4 ...............................

## SHAW, RICKY
No Love But Your Love............................. 7" ...... London ......... HLU9606 ............... 1962 £1.50......£4 ...............................

## SHAW, ROLAND ORCHESTRA
James Bond In Action ............................... LP ...... Decca ............. LK4730 ............... 1965 £5............£12 ...............................
I Spy ....................................................... 7" EP . Decca ............. DFE8670 ............... 1966 £5............£10 ...............................

## SHAW, SANDIE
Always Something There To Remind Me .. 7" EP . Pye ............... NEP24208............ 1964 £2.50......£6 ...............................
As Long As You're Happy Baby ................. 7" ...... Pye ............... 7N15671 ............... 1964 £10............£20 ...............................
Hand In Glove ......................................... 12"..... Rough Trade... RTT130 ............ 1984 £2.50......£6 ...............................
Hello Angel ............................................. CD-s .. Rough Trade... ROUGHCD110... 1988 £2............£5 ...............................
Long Live Love ........................................ 7" EP . Pye ............... NEP24220............ 1965 £2.50......£6 ...............................
Love Me, Please Love Me .......................... LP ...... Pye ............... N(S)PL18205......... 1967 £4............£10 ...............................
Me.......................................................... LP ...... Pye ............... NPL18121 ............ 1965 £6............£15 ...............................
Message Understood................................... 7" EP . Pye ............... NEP24236............ 1966 £2.50......£6 ...............................
Nothing Comes Easy ................................. 7" EP . Pye ............... NEP24254............ 1966 £5............£10 ...............................
Nothing Less Than Brilliant....................... CD-s .. Rough Trade... RTT230CD ......... 1988 £2............£5 ...............................
Puppet On A String................................... LP ...... Pye ............... N(S)PL18182......... 1967 £4............£10 ...............................
Reviewing The Situation ........................... LP ...... Pye ............... N(S)PL18323......... 1970 £4............£10 ...............................
Run With Sandie Shaw ............................. 7" EP . Pye ............... NEP24264............ 1966 £5............£10 ...............................
Sandie ..................................................... LP ...... Pye ............... NPL18110 ............ 1965 £6............£15 ...............................
Sandie ..................................................... 7" EP . Pye ............... NEP24232............ 1965 £2.50......£6 ...............................
Sandie Shaw In French............................. 7" EP . Pye ............... NEP24271............ 1967 £7.50......£15 ...............................
Sandie Shaw In Italian.............................. 7" EP . Pye ............... NEP24273............ 1967 £7.50......£15 ...............................
Sandie Shaw Supplement........................... LP ...... Pye ............... N(S)PL18232......... 1968 £4............£10 ...............................
Tell The Boys .......................................... 7" EP . Pye ............... NEP24281............ 1967 £5............£10 ...............................
Tomorrow................................................. 7" EP . Pye ............... NEP24247............ 1966 £5............£10 ...............................

## SHAW, THOMAS
Thomas Shaw .......................................... LP ...... XTRA............. XTRA1132 ............ 1972 £4............£10 ...............................

## SHAW, TIMMY & THE STERNPHONES
Gonna Send You Back To Georgia ............. 7" ...... Pye ............... 7N25239 ............... 1964 £2.50......£6 ...............................

## SHE TRINITY
Across The Street ..................................... 7" ...... CBS............. 2819 ............... 1967 £1.50......£4 ...............................
Hair ........................................................ 7" ...... President ...... PT283 ............... 1969 £1.50......£4 ...............................
Have I Sinned .......................................... 7" ...... Columbia ........ DB7943 ............... 1966 £1.50......£4 ...............................
He Fought The Law .................................. 7" ...... Columbia ........ DB7874 ............... 1966 £1.50......£4 ...............................
Wild Flower ............................................. 7" ...... Columbia ........ DB7959 ............... 1966 £1.50......£4 ...............................
Yellow Submarine ..................................... 7" ...... Columbia ........ DB7992 ............... 1966 £1.50......£4 ...............................

## SHEARING, GEORGE
Black Satin ............................................. LP ...... Capitol............. (S)T858 ............... 1958 £4............£10 ...............................
Blue Chiffon............................................ LP ...... Capitol............. T1124 ............... 1959 £4............£10 ...............................
Burnished Brass ....................................... LP ...... Capitol............. T1038 ............... 1959 £4............£10 ...............................

| | | | | | | | |
|---|---|---|---|---|---|---|---|
| George Shearing And The Montgomery Brothers | LP | Jazzland | JLP55 | 1961 | £6 | £15 | |
| I Hear Music | 10" LP | MGM | D118 | 1953 | £6 | £15 | |
| In The Night | LP | Capitol | T1003 | 1959 | £5 | £12 | ...with Dakota Staton |
| Jazz Conception | LP | MGM | C769 | 1958 | £4 | £10 | |
| Latin Escapade | LP | Capitol | T737 | 1957 | £4 | £10 | |
| Latin Lace | LP | Capitol | (S)T1082 | 1959 | £4 | £10 | |
| Nearness Of You | 10" LP | Decca | LF1036 | 1951 | £6 | £15 | |
| On Stage | LP | Capitol | (S)T1187 | 1960 | £4 | £10 | |
| Shearing Caravan | LP | MGM | C767 | 1958 | £4 | £10 | |
| Shearing Piano | LP | Capitol | T909 | 1958 | £4 | £10 | |
| Shearing Spell | 10" LP | Capitol | LC6803 | 1956 | £6 | £15 | |
| Touch Of Genius | 10" LP | MGM | D129 | 1954 | £6 | £15 | |
| Velvet Carpet | LP | Capitol | T720 | 1956 | £4 | £10 | |
| Very First Session | 10" LP | Vogue | LDE188 | 1956 | £6 | £15 | |
| You're Hearing George Shearing | 10" LP | MGM | D103 | 1952 | £6 | £15 | |

## SHED SEVEN

| | | | | | | | |
|---|---|---|---|---|---|---|---|
| Maximum High | CD | Polydor | 5333772 | 1996 | £6 | £15 | double |

## SHEEN, BOBBY

| | | | | | | | |
|---|---|---|---|---|---|---|---|
| Dr. Love | 7" | Capitol | CL15455 | 1966 | £20 | £40 | |

## SHEEP

| | | | | | | | |
|---|---|---|---|---|---|---|---|
| Hide And Seek | 7" | Stateside | SS493 | 1966 | £4 | £8 | |

## SHEEP (2)

| | | | | | | | |
|---|---|---|---|---|---|---|---|
| Sheep | LP | Myrrh | MYR1000 | 1973 | £15 | £30 | |

## SHEFFIELDS

| | | | | | | | |
|---|---|---|---|---|---|---|---|
| Bag's Groove | 7" | Pye | 7N15767 | 1965 | £30 | £60 | |
| Got My Mojo Working | 7" | Pye | 7N15627 | 1964 | £25 | £50 | |
| It Must Be Love | 7" | Pye | 7N15600 | 1964 | £25 | £50 | |

## SHEIKS

| | | | | | | | |
|---|---|---|---|---|---|---|---|
| Missing You | 7" EP | Odeon | MEO123 | 1966 | £6 | £12 | French |
| Missing You | 7" | Parlophone | R5500 | 1966 | £1.50 | £4 | |
| Tears Are Coming | 7" EP | Odeon | MEO131 | 1966 | £6 | £12 | French |

## SHEIKS (2)

| | | | | | | | |
|---|---|---|---|---|---|---|---|
| Tres Chic | 7" | London | HLW9012 | 1959 | £1.50 | £4 | |

## SHELDON, DOUG

| | | | | | | | |
|---|---|---|---|---|---|---|---|
| Here I Stand | 7" EP | Decca | DFE8527 | 1963 | £15 | £30 | |
| Mickey's Monkey | 7" | Decca | F11790 | 1963 | £1.50 | £4 | |
| Take It Like A Man | 7" | Sue | WI332 | 1965 | £4 | £8 | |

## SHELL

| | | | | | | | |
|---|---|---|---|---|---|---|---|
| Goodbye Little Girl | 7" | Columbia | DB8082 | 1966 | £2 | £5 | |

## SHELLEY

| | | | | | | | |
|---|---|---|---|---|---|---|---|
| I Will Be Wishing | 7" | Pye | 7N15711 | 1964 | £2 | £5 | |

## SHELLEY, LIZ

| | | | | | | | |
|---|---|---|---|---|---|---|---|
| Make Me Your Baby | 7" | Brunswick | 05940 | 1965 | £1.50 | £4 | |

## SHELLEY, PETE

| | | | | | | | |
|---|---|---|---|---|---|---|---|
| Sky Yen | 12" | Groovy | STP2 | 1980 | £4 | £10 | |

## SHELLS

| | | | | | | | |
|---|---|---|---|---|---|---|---|
| Baby Oh Baby | 7" | London | HLU9288 | 1961 | £10 | £20 | |
| It's A Happy Holiday | 7" | London | HLU9644 | 1962 | £7.50 | £15 | |

## SHELLY, ALAN

| | | | | | | | |
|---|---|---|---|---|---|---|---|
| Lady Black Wife | 7" | Philips | BF1709 | 1969 | £4 | £8 | |

## SHELTON, ANNE

| | | | | | | | |
|---|---|---|---|---|---|---|---|
| Absent Friends | 7" | Philips | JK1012 | 1957 | £2 | £5 | |
| Anne Shelton | LP | Philips | BBL7188 | 1957 | £5 | £12 | |
| Anne Shelton | 7" EP | Philips | BBE12090 | 1956 | £5 | £10 | |
| Answer Me | 7" | HMV | 7M164 | 1953 | £2 | £5 | |
| Book | 7" | HMV | 7M186 | 1954 | £2 | £5 | |
| Cross Over The Bridge | 7" | HMV | 7M197 | 1954 | £2 | £5 | |
| Favourites | 10" LP | Decca | LF1023 | 1952 | £6 | £15 | |
| Favourites Vol. 2 | 10" LP | Decca | LF1106 | 1953 | £6 | £15 | |
| Four Standards | 7" EP | Decca | DFE6321 | 1956 | £2 | £5 | |
| Goodnight, Well It's Time To Go | 7" | HMV | 7M240 | 1954 | £2 | £5 | |
| My Gypsy Heart | 7" | HMV | 7M279 | 1954 | £2 | £5 | |
| Songs From The Heart | LP | Philips | BBL7291 | 1959 | £4 | £10 | |

## SHELTON, ROSCOE

| | | | | | | | |
|---|---|---|---|---|---|---|---|
| Question | 7" | Sue | WI354 | 1965 | £5 | £10 | |
| Roscoe Shelton | LP | Excello | 8002 | 1961 | £20 | £40 | US |

## SHENDERY, DEANNA

| | | | | | | | |
|---|---|---|---|---|---|---|---|
| Comin' Home Baby | 7" | Decca | F12090 | 1965 | £1.50 | £4 | |

## SHENLEY & ANNETTE
Million Dollar Baby ........................... 7" ...... Blue Beat ........ BB72 ..................... 1961 £6 .......... £12 .................

## SHENLEY & HYACINTH
World Is On A Wheel ........................... 7" ...... Rio ............... R80 ....................... 1966 £4 .......... £8

## SHEP & THE LIMELITES
Daddy's Home ..................................... 7" ...... Pye ............... 7N25090 ................. 1961 £25 .......... £50
Our Anniversary ................................ LP .... Hull ............... 1001 ..................... 1962 £100 .. £200 ............ US
Our Anniversary ................................ LP .... Roulette ........ R25350 ................. 1967 £10 .......... £25 ............ US
Ready For Your Love ........................... 7" ...... Pye ............... 7N25112 ................. 1961 £15 .......... £30

## SHEPARD, JEAN
Lonesome Love .................................. LP ..... Capitol ........... T1126 ................... 1959 £4 .......... £10 ............ US
Songs Of A Love Affair ..................... LP ..... Capitol ........... T728 .................... 1956 £8 .......... £20 ............ US

## SHEPARD, TOMMY
Shepard's Flock ................................ LP ..... Vogue Coral .... LVA9046 ............... 1957 £10 .......... £25

## SHEPHERD, BILL
Big Guitar ......................................... 7" ...... Pye ............... 7N15137 ................. 1958 £1.50 .......... £4
Whistling Sailor ................................. 7" ...... Island ............ WIP6013 ................. 1967 £1.50 .......... £4

## SHEPHERD BOYS
Teenage Love ..................................... 7" ...... Columbia ........ SCM5282 .............. 1956 £1.50 .......... £4

## SHEPHERD SISTERS
Alone .................................................. 7" ...... HMV .............. POP411 ................. 1957 £2 .......... £5
Dancing Baby ..................................... 7" ...... Mercury ......... AMT1005 .............. 1958 £1.50 .......... £4
Eating Pizza ....................................... 7" ...... Mercury ......... 7MT218 ................. 1958 £1.50 .......... £4
Gettin' Ready For Freddy .................... 7" ...... Mercury ......... 7MT196 ................. 1958 £2.50 .......... £6
Talk Is Cheap ..................................... 7" ...... London .......... HLK9758 ................. 1963 £2.50 .......... £6
What Makes Little Girls Cry ................ 7" ...... London .......... HLK9681 ................. 1963 £4 .......... £8

## SHEPLEY, TOM
How Do You Do? ................................ LP ..... Tradition ........ TSR031 ................. 1978 £4 .......... £10

## SHEPP, ARCHIE
And The New York Contemporary Five .... LP .... Delmark ........ DL409/DS9409 ...... 1967 £8 .......... £20
And The New York Contemporary Five .... LP .... Polydor ......... 623235 .................. 1967 £8 .......... £20
And The New York Contemporary Five .... LP .... Sonet ............. SLP36 .................. 1973 £5 .......... £12
And The New York Contemporary Five
  Vol. 2 .......................................... LP .... Delmark ........ DS412 .................. 1968 £8 .......... £20
And The New York Contemporary Five
  Vol. 2 .......................................... LP .... Polydor ......... 623267 .................. 1968 £8 .......... £20
Archie Shepp ..................................... LP ..... Impulse .......... AS71 ................... 1964 £15 .......... £30 ............ US
Attica Blues ....................................... LP ..... Impulse .......... AS9222 ............... 1972 £8 .......... £20 ............ US
Black Gypsy ....................................... LP ..... America .......... 30AM6099 ........... 1970 £8 .......... £20 ............ French
Cry Of My People ............................. LP ..... Impulse .......... AS9231 ............... 1973 £6 .......... £15 ............ US
Fire Music .......................................... LP ..... Impulse .......... AS86 ................... 1965 £10 .......... £25 ............ US
For Losers .......................................... LP ..... Impulse .......... AS9188 ............... 1969 £8 .......... £20 ............ US
Four For Trane ................................... LP ..... HMV .............. CLP/CSD3524 ...... 1966 £8 .......... £20
Live In San Francisco ........................ LP ..... HMV .............. CLP/CSD3600 ...... 1967 £8 .......... £20
Magic Of Ju-Ju ................................... LP ..... Impulse .......... MIPL/SIPL512 ...... 1969 £8 .......... £20
Mama Too Tight ................................. LP ..... Impulse .......... MIPL/SIPL508 ...... 1968 £8 .......... £20
New Africa .......................................... LP ..... Impulse .......... AS9262 ............... 1974 £6 .......... £15 ............ US
On This Night ..................................... LP ..... HMV .............. CLP/CSD3561 ...... 1966 £8 .......... £20
One For The Trane ............................. LP ..... Atlantic .......... 583732 .................. 1969 £8 .......... £20
Rufus ................................................... LP ..... Fontana ......... 681014ZL ............... 1967 £8 .......... £20
Three For A Quarter, One For A Dime ..... LP ..... Impulse .......... SIPL520 ............... 1969 £8 .......... £20
Way Ahead ......................................... LP ..... Impulse .......... MIPL/SIPL516 ...... 1969 £8 .......... £20

## SHEPPARDS
Sheppards ......................................... LP ..... Constellation ... CS4 ...................... 1964 £8 .......... £20 ............ US

## SHEPPERD, VIC & JOHN BOWDEN
Motty Down ....................................... LP ..... Burlington ...... BURL015 ............... 1982 £8 .......... £20

## SHEPPERTON FLAMES
Take Me For What I Am ...................... 7" ...... Deram ............ DM257 ................. 1969 £2 .......... £5

## SHERIDAN, DANI
Guess I'm Dumb ............................... 7" ...... Planet ............ PLF106 ................. 1966 £5 .......... £10

## SHERIDAN, MIKE & THE NIGHTRIDERS
Here I Stand ....................................... 7" ...... Columbia ........ DB7462 ................. 1965 £10 .......... £20
No Other Guy ..................................... 7" ...... Columbia ........ DB7141 ................. 1963 £12.50 .... £25
Please Mister Postman ........................ 7" ...... Columbia ........ DB7183 ................. 1963 £10 .......... £20
What A Sweet Thing That Was ............. 7" ...... Columbia ........ DB7302 ................. 1964 £10 .......... £20

## SHERIDAN, MIKE LOT
Don't Turn Your Back On Me .............. 7" ...... Columbia ........ DB7798 ................. 1966 £12.50 .... £25
Take My Hand .................................... 7" ...... Columbia ........ DB7677 ................. 1965 £12.50 .... £25

## SHERIDAN, TONY
Best Of Tony Sheridan ........................ LP ..... Polydor .......... 237640 .................. 1964 £62.50 . £125 ............ German
Foolish Little Girl .............................. LP ..... Scepter .......... 511 ...................... 1964 £8 .......... £20 ............ US

| | | | | | | | |
|---|---|---|---|---|---|---|---|
| Little Bit Of Tony Sheridan | LP | Polydor | 237629 | 1964 £15 | £30 | | German |
| Live In Der Deutschlandhalle | LP | Metronome | MLP15489 | 1973 £30 | £60 | | German |
| Skinnie Minnie | 7" EP | Polydor | 21978 | 1964 £20 | £40 | | French |
| Skinnie Minnie | 7" | Polydor | NH52927 | 1964 £4 | £8 | | |
| Tony Sheridan | LP | Polydor | 46612/237112 | 1963 £15 | £30 | | German |
| Will You Still Love Me Tomorrow | 7" | Polydor | NH52315 | 1964 £4 | £8 | | |

## SHERIDAN-PRICE

| | | | | | | |
|---|---|---|---|---|---|---|
| Sometimes I Wonder | 7" | Gemini | GMS009 | 1979 £2 | £5 | |
| This Is To Certify That | LP | Gemini | GME1002 | 1970 £4 | £10 | |

## SHERLOCK, ROGER

| | | | | | | |
|---|---|---|---|---|---|---|
| Memories Of Sligo | LP | Inchecronin | INC7419 | 1978 £5 | £12 | |

## SHERMAN, ALLAN

| | | | | | | |
|---|---|---|---|---|---|---|
| My Son The Nut Vol. 1 | 7" EP | Warner Bros | WSEP6120 | 1964 £2 | £5 | stereo |

## SHERRYS

| | | | | | | |
|---|---|---|---|---|---|---|
| At The Hop With The Sherrys | LP | Guyden | GLP503 | 1962 £25 | £50 | US |
| Do The Popeye | 7" EP | London | RE1363 | 1963 £25 | £50 | |
| Pop Pop Popeye | 7" | London | HLW9625 | 1962 £2 | £5 | |
| Slop Time | 7" | London | HL9686 | 1963 £2.50 | £6 | |

## SHERWOOD, BOBBY

| | | | | | | |
|---|---|---|---|---|---|---|
| Bobby Sherwood Orchestra | 10" LP | Capitol | LC6632 | 1954 £6 | £15 | |

## SHERWOOD, TONY

| | | | | | | |
|---|---|---|---|---|---|---|
| Piano Boogie Twist | 7" | Zodiac | ZR010 | 196– £2 | £5 | |

## SHERWOODS

| | | | | | | |
|---|---|---|---|---|---|---|
| El Scorpion | 7" | Pye | 7N25097 | 1961 £1.50 | £4 | |

## SHEVELLS

| | | | | | | |
|---|---|---|---|---|---|---|
| Big City Lights | 7" | Polydor | 56239 | 1968 £5 | £10 | |
| Come On Home | 7" | United Artists | UP1125 | 1966 £20 | £40 | |
| I Could Conquer The World | 7" | United Artists | UP1059 | 1964 £5 | £10 | |
| Ooh Poo Pah Do | 7" | Oriole | CB1915 | 1963 £2.50 | £6 | |
| Walking On The Edge | 7" | United Artists | UP1076 | 1965 £5 | £10 | |
| Watermelon Man | 7" | United Artists | UP1081 | 1965 £5 | £10 | |

## SHEVETON, TONY

| | | | | | | |
|---|---|---|---|---|---|---|
| Excuses | 7" | Oriole | CB1975 | 1964 £1.50 | £4 | |
| Hey Little Girl | 7" | Oriole | CB1766 | 1962 £1.50 | £4 | |
| Lonely Heart | 7" | Oriole | CB1726 | 1962 £1.50 | £4 | |
| Lullaby Of Love | 7" | Oriole | CB1705 | 1962 £1.50 | £4 | |
| Million Drums | 7" | Oriole | CB1895 | 1963 £1.50 | £4 | |
| Runaround Sue Is Getting Married | 7" | Oriole | CB1788 | 1963 £1.50 | £4 | |

## SHIDE & ACORN

| | | | | | | |
|---|---|---|---|---|---|---|
| Under The Tree | LP | private | | 1973 £330 | £500 | |

## SHIELD, TREVOR

| | | | | | | |
|---|---|---|---|---|---|---|
| Moon is Playing A Trick | 7" | Trojan | TR664 | 1969 £1.50 | £4 | |

## SHIELDS

| | | | | | | |
|---|---|---|---|---|---|---|
| You Cheated | 7" | London | HLD8706 | 1958 £15 | £30 | |

## SHIELDS, KEITH

| | | | | | | |
|---|---|---|---|---|---|---|
| Hey Gyp | 7" | Decca | F12572 | 1967 £12.50 | £25 | |
| So Hard Living Without You | 7" | Decca | F12666 | 1967 £4 | £8 | |
| Wonder Of You | 7" | Decca | F12609 | 1967 £2.50 | £6 | |

## SHIHAB, SAHIB

| | | | | | | |
|---|---|---|---|---|---|---|
| Seeds | LP | Youngblood | SSYB12 | 1970 £4 | £10 | |

## SHILOH

Shiloh was an early country-rock band and included several members who achieved later success. Pedal steel guitarist Al Perkins played with Stephen Stills and the Flying Burrito Brothers, keyboard player Jim Norman became string arranger for the Eagles, while drummer Don Henley followed his years as a member of the Eagles with a flourishing solo career.

| | | | | | | |
|---|---|---|---|---|---|---|
| Shiloh | LP | Amos | AAS7015 | 1970 £15 | £30 | US |

## SHINDIGS

| | | | | | | |
|---|---|---|---|---|---|---|
| Little While Back | 7" | Parlophone | R5377 | 1965 £10 | £20 | |
| One Little Letter | 7" | Parlophone | R5316 | 1965 £10 | £20 | |

## SHINDOGS

| | | | | | | |
|---|---|---|---|---|---|---|
| Who Do You Think You Are | 7" | Fontana | TF790 | 1967 £2 | £5 | |

## SHINES, JOHNNY

| | | | | | | |
|---|---|---|---|---|---|---|
| Country Blues | LP | XTRA | XTRA1142 | 1974 £4 | £10 | |
| Last Night's Dream | LP | Blue Horizon | 763212 | 1969 £25 | £50 | |

## SHINN, DON

| | | | | | | |
|---|---|---|---|---|---|---|
| Departures | LP | Columbia | SCX6355 | 1969 £6 | £15 | |
| Temples With Prophets | LP | Columbia | SX/SCX6319 | 1969 £10 | £25 | |

## SHIP

| | | | | | | | |
|---|---|---|---|---|---|---|---|
| Contemporary Folk Music Journey | LP | Elektra | 75036 | 1972 | £6 | £15 | US |

## SHIRALEE

| | | | | | | |
|---|---|---|---|---|---|---|
| I'll Stay By Your Side | 7" | Fontana | TF855 | 1967 | £2.50 | £6 |

## SHIRELLES

| | | | | | | | |
|---|---|---|---|---|---|---|---|
| Are You Still My Baby | 7" | Pye | 7N25288 | 1965 | £1.50 | £4 | |
| Baby It's You | LP | Stateside | SL10006 | 1962 | £20 | £40 | |
| Baby It's You | 7" | Top Rank | JAR601 | 1962 | £1.50 | £4 | |
| Big John | 7" | Top Rank | JAR590 | 1961 | £1.50 | £4 | |
| Dedicated To The One I Love | 7" | Top Rank | JAR549 | 1961 | £1.50 | £4 | |
| Don't Say Goodnight | 7" | Stateside | SS213 | 1963 | £1.50 | £4 | |
| Everybody Loves A Lover | 7" | Stateside | SS152 | 1963 | £1.50 | £4 | |
| Foolish Little Girl | LP | Scepter | S(PS)511 | 1963 | £15 | £30 | US |
| Foolish Little Girl | 7" | Stateside | SS181 | 1963 | £1.50 | £4 | |
| Greatest Hits | LP | Stateside | SL10041 | 1963 | £10 | £25 | |
| Greatest Hits Vol. 2 | LP | Scepter | S(PS)560 | 1967 | £6 | £15 | US |
| Here And Now | LP | Pricewise | P4002 | 197– | £5 | £12 | US |
| I Met Him On A Sunday | 7" | Brunswick | 05746 | 1958 | £15 | £30 | |
| It's A Mad, Mad, Mad, Mad World | LP | Scepter | S(PS)514 | 1963 | £10 | £25 | US |
| It's A Mad, Mad, Mad, Mad World | 7" | Pye | 7N25229 | 1963 | £1.50 | £4 | |
| It's Love That Really Counts | 7" | Stateside | SS129 | 1962 | £2 | £5 | |
| Mama Said | 7" | Top Rank | JAR567 | 1961 | £1.50 | £4 | |
| Maybe Tonight | 7" | Pye | 7N25279 | 1964 | £4 | £8 | |
| Sha La La | 7" | Pye | 7N25240 | 1964 | £1.50 | £4 | |
| Shades of Blue | 7" | Pye | 7N25386 | 1966 | £1.50 | £4 | |
| Shirelles Sing The Golden Oldies | LP | Scepter | S(PS)516 | 1964 | £8 | £20 | US |
| Shirelles Sound | 7" EP | Top Rank | JKP3012 | 1961 | £15 | £30 | |
| Sing To Trumpet & Strings | LP | Top Rank | 35115 | 1961 | £30 | £60 | |
| Soldier Boy | 7" | HMV | POP1019 | 1962 | £1.50 | £4 | |
| Spontaneous Combustion | LP | Scepter | S(PS)562 | 1967 | £6 | £15 | US |
| Swing The Most | LP | Pricewise | P4001 | 197– | £5 | £12 | US |
| There's A Storm Going On In My Heart | 7" | Mercury | MF1093 | 1969 | £4 | £8 | |
| Tonight You're Gonna Fall In Love | 7" | Pye | 7N25233 | 1964 | £1.50 | £4 | |
| Tonight's The Night | LP | Scepter | S(PS)501 | 1961 | £20 | £40 | US |
| Tonight's The Night | 7" | London | HL9233 | 1960 | £4 | £8 | |
| Too Much Of A Good Thing | 7" | Pye | 7N25425 | 1967 | £2.50 | £6 | |
| Twist Party | LP | Scepter | S(PS)505 | 1962 | £10 | £25 | US, with King Curtis |
| Welcome Home Baby | 7" | Stateside | SS119 | 1962 | £2 | £5 | |
| What A Difference A Day Made | 7" | Top Rank | JAR578 | 1961 | £1.50 | £4 | |
| What Does A Girl Do | 7" | Stateside | SS232 | 1963 | £1.50 | £4 | |
| Will You Still Love Me Tomorrow | 7" | Top Rank | JAR540 | 1960 | £1.50 | £4 | |

## SHIRLEY, DON

| | | | | | | | |
|---|---|---|---|---|---|---|---|
| Improvisations | LP | London | HAA2046 | 1957 | £4 | £10 | ... with Richard Davis |

## SHIRLEY, ROY

| | | | | | | | |
|---|---|---|---|---|---|---|---|
| Dance Arena | 7" | Giant | GN32 | 1968 | £4 | £8 | |
| Dance The Reggae | 7" | Doctor Bird | DB1168 | 1968 | £5 | £10 | |
| Facts Of Life | 7" | Island | WI3119 | 1968 | £5 | £10 | |
| Get On The Ball | 7" | Caltone | CAL101 | 1967 | £4 | £8 | Johnny Moore B side |
| Get On The Ball | 7" | Caltone | TONE101 | 1967 | £4 | £8 | Johnny Moore B side |
| Good Is Better Than Bad | 7" | Island | WI3118 | 1967 | £5 | £10 | |
| Hold Them | 7" | Doctor Bird | DB1068 | 1966 | £5 | £10 | |
| Hush A Bye | 7" | Doctor Bird | DB1165 | 1968 | £5 | £10 | |
| I'm The Winner | 7" | Doctor Bird | DB1079 | 1967 | £5 | £10 | |
| If I Did Know | 7" | Island | WI3125 | 1967 | £5 | £10 | |
| Life | 7" | Duke | DU18 | 1969 | £1.50 | £4 | |
| Million Dollar Baby | 7" | Island | WI3110 | 1967 | £5 | £10 | Sensations B side |
| Move All Day | 7" | Island | WI3108 | 1967 | £5 | £10 | |
| Musical Field | 7" | Doctor Bird | DB1093 | 1967 | £5 | £10 | Lee Perry B side |
| Musical War | 7" | Island | WI3071 | 1967 | £5 | £10 | |
| Paradise | 7" | Ska Beat | JB253 | 1966 | £5 | £10 | |
| Prophet | 7" | Doctor Bird | DB1088 | 1967 | £5 | £10 | |
| Thank You | 7" | Doctor Bird | DB1108 | 1967 | £5 | £10 | |
| Thank You | 7" | Island | WI3098 | 1967 | £5 | £10 | |
| Think About The Future | 7" | Fab | FAB54 | 1968 | £4 | £8 | |
| Warming Up The Scene | 7" | Giant | GN33 | 1968 | £4 | £8 | ... Glen Adams B side |
| World Needs Love | 7" | Amalgamated | AMG815 | 1968 | £4 | £8 | |

## SHIRLEY, SUSAN

| | | | | | | |
|---|---|---|---|---|---|---|
| Really Into Something Good | 7" | Philips | 6006037 | 1970 | £5 | £10 |

## SHIRLEY & LEE

| | | | | | | | |
|---|---|---|---|---|---|---|---|
| Come On And Have Your Fun | 7" | Vogue | V9129 | 1959 | £20 | £40 | |
| Everybody's Rocking | 7" | Vogue | V9118 | 1958 | £25 | £50 | |
| I Feel Good | 7" | Vogue | V9063 | 1957 | £25 | £50 | |
| I Want To Dance | 7" | Vogue | V9088 | 1957 | £20 | £40 | |
| I'll Do It | 7" | Vogue | V9137 | 1959 | £20 | £40 | |
| I'll Thrill You | 7" | Vogue | V9103 | 1958 | £20 | £40 | |
| I've Been Loved Before | 7" | London | HLI9186 | 1960 | £7.50 | £15 | |
| Legendary Masters | LP | United Artists | LA026G2 | 1974 | £5 | £12 | US |
| Let The Good Times Roll | LP | Aladdin | 807 | 1956 | £100 | £200 | US |
| Let The Good Times Roll | LP | Imperial | A9179 | 1962 | £25 | £50 | US |
| Let The Good Times Roll | LP | Score | SLP4023 | 1957 | £50 | £100 | US |
| Let The Good Times Roll | LP | Warwick | (WST)2028 | 1961 | £30 | £60 | US |

| | | | | | | | | | |
|---|---|---|---|---|---|---|---|---|---|
| Let The Good Times Roll | 7" | Island | WI257 | 1965 | £5 | £10 | |
| Let The Good Times Roll | 7" | London | HLI9209 | 1960 | £5 | £10 | |
| Let The Good Times Roll | 7" | Vogue | V9059 | 1956 | £30 | £60 | |
| Little Word | 7" | Vogue | V9135 | 1959 | £20 | £40 | |
| Rock 'n' Roll | 7" EP | Vogue | VE170101 | 1957 | £75 | £150 | |
| Rock All Nite | 7" | Vogue | V9072 | 1957 | £30 | £60 | |
| Rocking With The Clock | 7" | Vogue | V9084 | 1957 | £30 | £60 | |
| Shirley And Lee | 7" EP | Vogue | VE170145 | 1960 | £62.50 | £125 | |
| That's What I Wanna Do | 7" | Vogue | V9067 | 1957 | £25 | £50 | |
| True Love | 7" | Vogue | V9156 | 1959 | £20 | £40 | |
| You'd Be Thinking Of Me | 7" | Vogue | V9094 | 1957 | £25 | £50 | |

## SHIRLEY & THE RUDE BOYS

| | | | | | | | |
|---|---|---|---|---|---|---|---|
| Gently Set Me Free | 7" | Blue Beat | BB375 | 1967 | £6 | £12 | |

## SHIRLEY & THE SHIRELLES

| | | | | | | | |
|---|---|---|---|---|---|---|---|
| Look What You've Done | 7" | Bell | BLL1049 | 1969 | £1.50 | £4 | |

## SHIVA'S HEADBAND

| | | | | | | | |
|---|---|---|---|---|---|---|---|
| Coming To A Head | LP | Armadillo | NO001 | 1972 | £37.50 | £75 | US |
| Psychedelic Yesterday | LP | Ape | 1001 | 1977 | £8 | £20 | US |
| Take Me To The Mountains | LP | Capitol | ST538 | 1970 | £25 | £50 | US |

## SHIVEL, BUNNY

| | | | | | | | |
|---|---|---|---|---|---|---|---|
| You'll Never Find Another Love Like Mine | 7" | Capitol | CL15487 | 1967 | £2 | £5 | |

## SHIVER

| | | | | | | | |
|---|---|---|---|---|---|---|---|
| Walpurgis | LP | Maris | 20501 | 1969 | £62.50 | £125 | German |

## SHIVOO

| | | | | | | | |
|---|---|---|---|---|---|---|---|
| Shivoo | LP | private | | 1983 | £50 | £100 | Dutch |

## SHOCKING BLUE

With a lead singer who sounded not unlike Grace Slick, Shocking Blue would have loved to have been taken seriously as the Dutch Jefferson Airplane. Unfortunately, their material was cast a little too firmly in the light-weight pop mould, but this stood the group in good stead in the case of their hit single 'Venus', whose absurdly catchy melody and rhythm have made the song into a perennial favourite.

| | | | | | | | |
|---|---|---|---|---|---|---|---|
| At Home | LP | Penny Farthing | PELS500 | 1969 | £5 | £12 | |
| Scorpio's Dance | LP | Penny Farthing | PELS510 | 1970 | £5 | £12 | |

## SHOES

| | | | | | | | |
|---|---|---|---|---|---|---|---|
| Un dans Versailles | LP | private | | 1974 | £50 | £100 | US |

## SHONDELL, TROY

| | | | | | | | |
|---|---|---|---|---|---|---|---|
| I Got A Woman | 7" | London | HL9668 | 1963 | £2.50 | £6 | |
| Many Sides Of Troy Shondell | LP | London | HAY8128 | 1964 | £20 | £40 | |
| Tears From An Angel | 7" | Liberty | LIB55398 | 1962 | £1.50 | £4 | |
| This Time | 7" | London | HLG9432 | 1961 | £2 | £5 | |

## SHONDELLS

| | | | | | | | |
|---|---|---|---|---|---|---|---|
| At The Saturday Hop | LP | La Louisianne | 109 | 1964 | £20 | £40 | US |
| Don't Cry My Soldier Boy | 7" | Ember | EMBS191 | 1964 | £1.50 | £4 | |

## SHONEN KNIFE

| | | | | | | | |
|---|---|---|---|---|---|---|---|
| Get The Wow | CD-s | August | CAUG003CD | 1993 | £2 | £5 | 2 versions |
| Riding On The Rocket | CD-s | August | CAUG001CD | 1992 | £2 | £5 | |
| We Are Very Happy You Came | CD-s | August | RUST004CD | 1993 | £2 | £5 | |

## SHOOT

| | | | | | | | |
|---|---|---|---|---|---|---|---|
| On The Frontier | LP | EMI | EMA73 | 1973 | £8 | £20 | |

## SHOP ASSISTANTS

| | | | | | | | |
|---|---|---|---|---|---|---|---|
| All Day Long | 7" | Subway Organisation | SUBWAY1 | 1985 | £4 | £8 | red picture sleeve |
| Something To Do | 7" | Villa 21 | 002 | 1985 | £15 | £30 | |

## SHORE, DINAH

| | | | | | | | |
|---|---|---|---|---|---|---|---|
| Changing Partners | 7" | HMV | 7M183 | 1954 | £2 | £5 | |
| Come Back To My Arms | 7" | HMV | 7M221 | 1954 | £2 | £5 | |
| Holding Hands At Midnight | LP | RCA | RD27072 | 1958 | £4 | £10 | |
| If I Give My Heart To You | 7" | HMV | 7M250 | 1954 | £2.50 | £6 | |
| Keep It A Secret | 7" | HMV | 7M119 | 1953 | £4 | £8 | |
| Love And Marriage | 7" | HMV | 7M352 | 1956 | £1.50 | £4 | |
| Sweet Thing | 7" | HMV | 7M139 | 1953 | £2 | £5 | |
| Three Coins In The Fountain | 7" | HMV | 7M236 | 1954 | £2.50 | £6 | |

## SHORT, BOBBY

| | | | | | | | |
|---|---|---|---|---|---|---|---|
| Bobby Short | LP | London | HAK2123 | 1958 | £4 | £10 | |

## SHORT, BRIAN

| | | | | | | | |
|---|---|---|---|---|---|---|---|
| Anything For A Laugh | LP | Transatlantic | TRA245 | 1971 | £4 | £10 | |

## SHORT CROSS

| | | | | | | | |
|---|---|---|---|---|---|---|---|
| Arising | LP | Grizly | 16013 | 1970 | £100 | £200 | US |

## SHORTER, WAYNE

| | | | | | | | |
|---|---|---|---|---|---|---|---|
| Adam's Apple | LP | Blue Note | BLP/BST84232 | 1966 | £8 | £20 | |
| All Seeing Eye | LP | Blue Note | BLP/BST84219 | 1965 | £8 | £20 | |
| Ju Ju | LP | Blue Note | BLP/BST84182 | 1964 | £10 | £25 | |
| Moto Grosso Feio | LP | Blue Note | LA014G | 1974 | £6 | £15 | US |
| Native Dancer | LP | CBS | 80721 | 1975 | £5 | £12 | |
| Night Dreamer | LP | Blue Note | BLP/BST84173 | 1964 | £10 | £25 | |
| Schizophrenia | LP | Blue Note | BST84297 | 1968 | £8 | £20 | |
| Speak No Evil | LP | Blue Note | BLP/BST84194 | 1965 | £8 | £20 | |
| Super Nova | LP | Blue Note | BST84332 | 1969 | £6 | £15 | |

## SHORTKUTS

| | | | | | | | |
|---|---|---|---|---|---|---|---|
| Your Eyes May Shine | 7" | United Artists | UP2233 | 1968 | £4 | £8 | |

## SHORTY & THEM

| | | | | | | | |
|---|---|---|---|---|---|---|---|
| Pills | 7" | Fontana | TF460 | 1964 | £7.50 | £15 | |

## SHOTGUN EXPRESS

| | | | | | | | |
|---|---|---|---|---|---|---|---|
| Funny 'Cos Neither Could I | 7" | Columbia | DB8178 | 1967 | £7.50 | £15 | |
| I Could Feel The Whole World | 7" | Columbia | DB8025 | 1966 | £7.50 | £15 | |
| I Could Feel The Whole World Turn Round | 7" EP | Columbia | ESRF1864 | 1967 | £100 | £200 | French |

## SHOTS

| | | | | | | | |
|---|---|---|---|---|---|---|---|
| Keep A Hold Of What You've Got | 7" | Columbia | DB7713 | 1965 | £10 | £20 | |

## SHOUTERS

| | | | | | | | |
|---|---|---|---|---|---|---|---|
| Beat Party | LP | Eurocord | H997 | 1966 | £15 | £30 | German |

## SHOUTS

| | | | | | | | |
|---|---|---|---|---|---|---|---|
| She Was My Baby | 7" | React | EA101 | 1964 | £2.50 | £6 | |

## SHOWBIZ KIDS

| | | | | | | | |
|---|---|---|---|---|---|---|---|
| I Don't Want To Discuss That | 7" | Top Secret | CON1 | 198– | £5 | £10 | |

## SHOWMEN

| | | | | | | | |
|---|---|---|---|---|---|---|---|
| It Will Stand | 7" | London | HLP9481 | 1962 | £20 | £40 | |
| Wrong Girl | 7" | London | HLP9571 | 1962 | £30 | £60 | |

## SHOWSTOPPERS

| | | | | | | | |
|---|---|---|---|---|---|---|---|
| Ain't Nothing But A House Party | 7" | Beacon | 3100 | 1968 | £2 | £5 | |
| Ain't Nothing But A House Party | 7" | Beacon | BEA100 | 1968 | £1.50 | £4 | |

## SHOX

| | | | | | | | |
|---|---|---|---|---|---|---|---|
| No Turning Back | 7" | Axis | AXIS4 | 1980 | £4 | £8 | |
| No Turning Back | 7" | Beggars Banquet | BEG33 | 1980 | £2 | £5 | |

## SHRIEVE, MICHAEL

| | | | | | | | |
|---|---|---|---|---|---|---|---|
| Transfer Station Blue | LP | Fortuna | FOR023 | 1984 | £20 | £40 | US |

## SHUBERT

| | | | | | | | |
|---|---|---|---|---|---|---|---|
| Until The Rains Come | 7" | Fontana | TF942 | 1968 | £4 | £8 | |

## SHUMAN, MORT

| | | | | | | | |
|---|---|---|---|---|---|---|---|
| I'm A Man | 7" | Decca | F11184 | 1959 | £20 | £40 | tri-centre |
| Monday Monday | 7" | Immediate | IM048 | 1967 | £4 | £8 | |

## SHUSHA

| | | | | | | | |
|---|---|---|---|---|---|---|---|
| From East To West | LP | Tangent | TGS138 | 1978 | £4 | £10 | |
| Persian Love Songs And Mystic Chants | LP | Tangent | TGS108 | 1970 | £5 | £12 | |
| Shusha | LP | United Artists | UAS29575 | 1974 | £4 | £10 | |
| Song Of Long Time Lovers | LP | Tangent | TGS114 | 1972 | £4 | £10 | |

## SHUTDOWN DOUGLAS

| | | | | | | | |
|---|---|---|---|---|---|---|---|
| Twin Cut Outs | 7" EP | Capitol | EAP41997 | 1964 | £4 | £8 | French |

## SHUTDOWNS

| | | | | | | | |
|---|---|---|---|---|---|---|---|
| Four In The Floor | 7" | Colpix | PX11016 | 1963 | £5 | £10 | |

## SHY

| | | | | | | | |
|---|---|---|---|---|---|---|---|
| Once Bitten Twice Shy | LP | Ebony | EBON15 | 1983 | £6 | £15 | |

## SHY LIMBS

| | | | | | | | |
|---|---|---|---|---|---|---|---|
| Lady In Black | 7" | CBS | 4624 | 1969 | £15 | £30 | |
| Reputation | 7" | CBS | 4190 | 1969 | £20 | £40 | |

## SHY ONES

| | | | | | | | |
|---|---|---|---|---|---|---|---|
| La Route | 7" | Oriole | CB1924 | 1964 | £2 | £5 | |
| Nightcap | 7" | Oriole | CB1848 | 1963 | £2.50 | £6 | |

## SHYLOCK

| | | | | | | | |
|---|---|---|---|---|---|---|---|
| Ile de fièvre | LP | CBS | 82862 | 1978 | £6 | £15 | French |

## SHYSTER

The name Shyster conceals the identity of sixties cult group, the Fleur De Lys.

Tick Tock .................................................. 7" ...... Polydor ........... 56202.................... 1968 £50....... £100 ..................................

## SIBERRY, JANE
Walking .................................................. CD..... WEA ............. 9256782 ............. 1988 £5........... £12 ..................................

## SIBLEY, DUDLEY
Gun Man.................................................. 7" ...... Island .............. WI3034................. 1967 £5........... £10 ..................................
Run Boy Run.......................................... 7" ...... Coxsone .......... CS7010.................. 1967 £5........... £10 ..................................

## SIDEKICKS
The Sidekicks evolved into the highly rated British progressive pop band, Kaleidoscope.

Suspicions.............................................. 7" ...... RCA ............. RCA1538 ............. 1966 £4........... £10 ..................................

## SIDEKICKS (2)
Fifi The Flea ........................................... LP ...... RCA ............. 3712 .................... 1966 £6........... £15 ..................... US

## SIDEWINDERS
Sidewinders ............................................ LP ...... RCA ............. LSP4696................ 1972 £6........... £15 ..................... US

## SIEGEL-SCHWALL BAND
The Siegel-Schwall Band so accurately epitomizes the worst aspects of the late-sixties fascination with the blues on the part of white rock performers, that it is amazing how the group managed to make such a large number of albums. Each is characterized by an entirely routine approach to the blues in which the form is reproduced without any genuine understanding or feeling. Composer William Russo was able to use this to interesting effect, however, when he incorporated the group within his 'Three Pieces For Blues Band And Symphony Orchestra'. Here it is vital that the blues group play clichés, so that they can be subverted by the oblique lines superimposed by the orchestra. It is an unusual approach to the combination of rock and classical styles, but it works superbly well.

Say Siegel-Schwall ................................... LP ...... Vanguard ....... VRS/VSD79249.. 1967 £4........... £10 ..................... US
Shake ..................................................... LP ...... Vanguard ....... SVRL19044........... 1968 £4........... £10 ..................................
Siegel-Schwall '70 ................................... LP ...... Vanguard ....... VSD6562 ............ 1970 £4........... £10 ..................... US
Siegel-Schwall Band ............................... LP ...... RCA ............. SF8246................. 1971 £4........... £10 ..................................
Siegel-Schwall Band ............................... LP ...... Vanguard ....... VRS/VSD79235.... 1966 £4........... £10 ..................... US
Sleepy Hollow ........................................ LP ...... RCA ............. LSP10394........... 1972 £4........... £10 ..................................

## SIFFRE, LABI
Remember My Song .............................. LP ...... EMI.............. .............................. 197– £20........ £40 ..................................

## SIGHT & SOUND
Alley Alley.............................................. 7" ...... Fontana .......... TF982.................. 1968 £4........... £8 ..................................
Our Love Is In The Pocket ..................... 7" ...... Fontana .......... TF927.................. 1968 £4........... £8 ..................................

## SIGLER, BUNNY
Let The Good Times Roll........................ LP ...... Parkway .......... P(S)50000............. 1967 £6........... £15 ..................... US
Let The Good Times Roll........................ 7" ...... Cameo ............ P153 .................... 1967 £4........... £8 ..................................
                                                                 Parkway ..........

## SIGNATURES
Prepare To Flip ...................................... LP ...... Warner Bros.... W1353................. 1959 £5........... £12 ..................... US
Sing In ................................................... LP ...... Warner Bros.... W1250................. 1959 £5........... £12 ..................... US
Their Voices And Instruments ................. LP ...... Whippet.......... 702 ..................... 1957 £6........... £15 ..................... US

## SIGNS
Ain't You Got A Heart .......................... 7" ...... Decca ........... F12522................. 1966 £2.50...... £6 ..................................

## SILBERBART
Four Times Sound Razing ....................... LP ...... Philips............. 6305095 .............. 1971 £20........ £40 .................. German

## SILENT PARTNER
Hung By A Thread................................. LP ...... Lucky Boy ...... ............... £75....... £150 ..................... US

## SILHOUETTES
Get A Job.............................................. LP ...... Goodway ........ GLP100 ................ 195– £50....... £100 ..................... US
Get A Job.............................................. 7" ...... Parlophone...... R4407 .................. 1958 £12.50.... £25 ..................................
Heading For The Poorhouse ................... 7" ...... Parlophone...... R4425 .................. 1958 £15........... £30 ..................................

## SILK
Smooth As Raw Silk............................... LP ...... ABC.............. ABCS694 ............. 1969 £8........... £20 ..................... US

## SILK, ERIC
Silken Touch ......................................... 10" LP Esquire........... 20095................... 1958 £6........... £15 ..................................

## SILKIE
Born To Be With You ........................... 7" EP . Fontana........... 465306............ 1966 £6........... £12 ..................... French
Sing Dylan............................................. LP ...... Fontana........... TL5256 ............. 1965 £5........... £12 ..................................
You've Got To Hide Your Love Away ...... LP ...... Fontana........... MGF2/SRF67548... 1965 £8........... £20 ..................... US
You've Got To Hide Your Love Away ...... 7" EP . Fontana........... 465294............ 1965 £10........... £20 ..................... French
You've Got To Hide Your Love Away ...... 7" ...... Fontana........... TF603.................... 1965 £1.50........ £4 ..................................

## SILL, JUDEE
Heart Food ............................................ LP ...... Asylum .......... SYL9006 ............. 1973 £4........... £10 ..................................
Judee Sill .............................................. LP ...... Asylum .......... SYLA8751 ........... 1971 £4........... £10 ..................................

## SILLY SURFERS
Sounds Of The Silly Surfers...................... LP ...... Mercury.......... MG2/SR60977....... 1965 £8........... £20 ..................... US

## SILLY WIZARD

| | | | | | | | |
|---|---|---|---|---|---|---|---|
| Silly Wizard | LP | XTRA | XTRA1158 | 1976 | £5 | £12 | |

## SILOAH

| | | | | | | | |
|---|---|---|---|---|---|---|---|
| Saureadler | LP | Car | 1558015 | 1970 | £100 | £200 | German |
| Sukram Gurk | LP | German Blues | 1558025 | 1972 | £100 | £200 | German |

## SILVER

| | | | | | | | |
|---|---|---|---|---|---|---|---|
| Love Me Forever | 7" | Columbia | DB117 | 1970 | £1.50 | £4 | |
| Things | 7" | Jolly | JY012 | 1968 | £1.50 | £4 | |

## SILVER, ANDEE

| | | | | | | | |
|---|---|---|---|---|---|---|---|
| Boy I Used To Know | 7" | HMV | POP1344 | 1964 | £1.50 | £4 | |
| Handful Of Silver | LP | Decca | SKL5059 | 1970 | £4 | £10 | |
| Only Your Love Can Save Me | 7" | Fontana | TF666 | 1966 | £1.50 | £4 | |
| Too Young To Go Steady | 7" | HMV | POP1297 | 1964 | £1.50 | £4 | |

## SILVER, EDDIE

| | | | | | | | |
|---|---|---|---|---|---|---|---|
| Rockin' Robin | 7" | Parlophone | R4483 | 1958 | £2 | £5 | |
| Seven Steps To Love | 7" | Parlophone | R4439 | 1958 | £4 | £8 | |

## SILVER, HORACE

| | | | | | | | |
|---|---|---|---|---|---|---|---|
| Best Of Horace Silver | LP | Blue Note | BST84325 | 1969 | £5 | £12 | |
| Blowin' The Blues Away | LP | Blue Note | BLP/BST84017 | 196– | £15 | £30 | |
| Cape Verdean Blues | LP | Blue Note | BLP/BST84220 | 1965 | £10 | £25 | |
| Doin' The Thing At The Village Gate | LP | Blue Note | BLP/BST84076 | 196– | £15 | £30 | |
| Finger Poppin' | LP | Blue Note | BLP/BST84008 | 196– | £15 | £30 | |
| Horace Silver And The Jazz Messengers | LP | Blue Note | BLP/BST81518 | 196– | £10 | £25 | |
| Horace Silver Trio | 10" LP | Vogue | LDE065 | 1954 | £25 | £50 | |
| Horace-Scope | LP | Blue Note | BLP/BST84042 | 196– | £15 | £30 | |
| Jody Grind | LP | Blue Note | BLP/BST84250 | 1966 | £8 | £20 | |
| Let's Get To The Nitty Gritty | 7" | Blue Note | 451902 | 1963 | £2 | £5 | |
| Serenade To A Soul Sister | LP | Blue Note | BST84277 | 1968 | £8 | £20 | |
| Silver's Blue | LP | Philips | BBL7183 | 1957 | £10 | £25 | |
| Silver's Serenade | LP | Blue Note | BLP/BST84131 | 1963 | £15 | £30 | |
| Sister Sadie | 7" | Blue Note | 451750 | 1961 | £2 | £5 | |
| Six Pieces Of Silver | LP | Blue Note | BLP/BST81539 | 196– | £20 | £40 | |
| Song For My Father | LP | Blue Note | BLP/BST84185 | 1964 | £10 | £25 | |
| Stylings Of Silver | LP | Blue Note | BLP/BST81562 | 196– | £15 | £30 | |
| Sweet Sweetie Dee | 7" | Blue Note | 451903 | 1964 | £2 | £5 | |
| That Healin' Feelin' | LP | Blue Note | BST84352 | 1970 | £5 | £12 | |
| Tokyo Blues | LP | Blue Note | BLP/BST84110 | 1962 | £15 | £30 | |
| Too Much Sake | 7" | Blue Note | 451873 | 1963 | £2 | £5 | |
| United States Of Mind | LP | Blue Note | BST84368 | 1970 | £5 | £12 | |
| You Gotta Take A Little Love | LP | Blue Note | BST84309 | 1969 | £6 | £15 | |

## SILVER, LORRAINE

| | | | | | | | |
|---|---|---|---|---|---|---|---|
| Happy Faces | 7" | Pye | 7N17055 | 1966 | £12.50 | £25 | |
| Lost Summer Love | 7" | Pye | 7N15922 | 1965 | £25 | £50 | |

## SILVER APPLES

| | | | | | | | |
|---|---|---|---|---|---|---|---|
| Contact | LP | Kapp | KS3584 | 1969 | £20 | £40 | US |
| Silver Apples | LP | Kapp | KL/KS3562 | 1968 | £15 | £30 | US |

## SILVER BIRCH

| | | | | | | | |
|---|---|---|---|---|---|---|---|
| Silver Birch | LP | Brayford | BR02 | 1974 | £100 | £200 | |

## SILVER EAGLE

| | | | | | | | |
|---|---|---|---|---|---|---|---|
| Theodore | 7" | MGM | MGM1345 | 1967 | £5 | £10 | |

## SILVER METRE

| | | | | | | | |
|---|---|---|---|---|---|---|---|
| Silver Metre | LP | National General | NG2000 | 1969 | £4 | £10 | US |

## SILVER STARS STEEL BAND

| | | | | | | | |
|---|---|---|---|---|---|---|---|
| Silver Stars Steel Band | LP | Island | ILP904 | 1963 | £10 | £25 | |

## SILVERSTARS

| | | | | | | | |
|---|---|---|---|---|---|---|---|
| Old Man Say | 7" | Trojan | TR646 | 1968 | £2.50 | £6 | |

## SILVERSTEIN, SHEL

| | | | | | | | |
|---|---|---|---|---|---|---|---|
| Hairy Jazz | LP | Elektra | EKL/EKS7176 | 1959 | £6 | £15 | US |
| Inside Folk Songs | LP | Atlantic | (SD)8072 | 1963 | £4 | £10 | US |

## SILVERTONES

| | | | | | | | |
|---|---|---|---|---|---|---|---|
| Cool Down | 7" | Treasure Isle | TI7020 | 1967 | £5 | £10 | Tommy McCook B side |
| Intensified Change | 7" | Trojan | TR7705 | 1969 | £1.50 | £4 | |
| It's Real | 7" | Doctor Bird | DB1041 | 1966 | £5 | £10 | Lyn Taitt B side |
| Midnight Hour | 7" | Treasure Isle | TI7027 | 1968 | £5 | £10 | Tommy McCook B side |
| Silver Bullets | LP | Trojan | TRLS69 | 1971 | £5 | £12 | |

## SILVESTER, VICTOR

| | | | | | | | |
|---|---|---|---|---|---|---|---|
| Alligator Roll | 7" | Columbia | DB3907 | 1957 | £2 | £5 | |
| Rockin' Rhythm Roll | 7" | Columbia | DB3888 | 1957 | £2 | £5 | |

## SILVO, JOHNNY & DAVE MOSES
| | | | | | | | |
|---|---|---|---|---|---|---|---|
| Live From London | LP | Bus Stop | BUSLP5001 | 1973 | £4 | £10 | |

## SIMEON, OMER
| | | | | | | | |
|---|---|---|---|---|---|---|---|
| Omer Simeon | 10" LP | Vogue | LDE174 | 1956 | £25 | £50 | |

## SIMMONS, BEVERLEY
| | | | | | | | |
|---|---|---|---|---|---|---|---|
| Remember Otis | LP | Pama | PMLP/PMSP9 | 1969 | £6 | £15 | |
| Mr. Pitiful | 7" | Pama | PM716 | 1968 | £1.50 | £4 | |

## SIMMONS, JEFF

Simmons's brief membership of the Mothers of Invention and his ambitions to achieve solo success are described within Frank Zappa's film *200 Motels*. Zappa produced *Lucille Has Messed Up My Mind* and subsequently recorded the title track himself, but Simmons did not achieve the stardom he craved.

| | | | | | | | |
|---|---|---|---|---|---|---|---|
| Lucille Has Messed Up My Mind | LP | Reprise | RS6391 | 1969 | £20 | £40 | |
| Lucille Has Messed Up My Mind | LP | Straight | STS1057 | 1969 | £20 | £40 | |
| Naked Angels Soundtrack | LP | Straight | STS1056 | 1969 | £15 | £30 | US |

## SIMMONS, JUMPIN' GENE
| | | | | | | | |
|---|---|---|---|---|---|---|---|
| Haunted House | 7" | London | HLU9913 | 1964 | £4 | £8 | |
| Jump | 7" | London | HLU9933 | 1964 | £4 | £8 | |
| Jumpin' Gene Simmons | LP | Hi | (S)HL12018 | 1964 | £8 | £20 | US |

## SIMMONS, LITTLE MAC
| | | | | | | | |
|---|---|---|---|---|---|---|---|
| Blues From Chicago | 7" EP | Outasite | OSEP1 | 1966 | £50 | £100 | |

## SIMON, CARLY
| | | | | | | | |
|---|---|---|---|---|---|---|---|
| Coming Round Again | CD-s | Arista | ARISTCD687 | 1987 | £2 | £5 | |
| Coming Round Again | CD | Polygram | 0803781 | 1988 | £4 | £10 | CD video |
| Let The River Run | CD-s | Arista | 162124 | 1989 | £2 | £5 | |
| Nobody Does It Better (live) | CD-s | Arista | 661807 | 1988 | £2 | £5 | |
| You're So Vain | CD-s | Elektra | EKR123CD | 1991 | £2 | £5 | |

## SIMON, JOE
| | | | | | | | |
|---|---|---|---|---|---|---|---|
| My Special Prayer | 7" | Monument | MON1004 | 1967 | £1.50 | £4 | |
| Nine Pound Steel | 7" | Monument | MON1010 | 1968 | £1.50 | £4 | |
| Teenager's Prayer | 7" | London | HLU10057 | 1966 | £4 | £8 | |
| That's The Way I Want Our Love | 7" | Monument | MON1051 | 1970 | £2 | £5 | |

## SIMON, PAUL
| | | | | | | | |
|---|---|---|---|---|---|---|---|
| Early Songs | LP | Crest | EBM7172 | 196– | £15 | £30 | US promo |
| Greatest Hits, Etc. | LP | Columbia | HC45032 | 1981 | £5 | £12 | US audiophile |
| I Am A Rock | 7" EP | CBS | 6211 | 1965 | £6 | £12 | French, no picture sleeve |
| I Am A Rock | 7" | CBS | 201797 | 1965 | £5 | £10 | |
| Kodakchrome | 7" | CBS | 1545 | 1973 | £5 | £10 | |
| Mother And Child Reunion | CD-s | WEA | W7655CD | 1988 | £2 | £5 | |
| Obvious Child | CD-s | WEA | W9549CD | 1990 | £2 | £5 | |
| Paul Simon | LP | CBS | Q69007 | 1972 | £4 | £10 | quad |
| Paul Simon 1964–1993 Box Set Sampler | CD | Warner Bros | | 1993 | £10 | £25 | US promo |
| Paul Simon Plus | LP | MCP | 8027 | 1966 | £8 | £20 | US, with Neil Sedaka & 4 Seasons |
| Paul Simon Songbook | LP | CBS | (S)BPG62579 | 1965 | £5 | £12 | |
| Paul Simon Songbook | CD | WEA | 9255872 | 1987 | £5 | £12 | |
| Proof | CD-s | WEA | W0003CD | 1991 | £2 | £5 | |
| Rhythm Of The Saints | CD | Warner Bros | 9260982 | 1990 | £10 | £25 | US promo with ribbon, bead, feather, cloth cover |
| Still Crazy After All These Years | LP | CBS | Q86001 | 1975 | £4 | £10 | quad |
| Still Crazy After All These Years | LP | Columbia | HC43540 | 1981 | £5 | £12 | US audiophile |
| There Goes Rhymin' Simon | LP | CBS | Q69035 | 1973 | £4 | £10 | quad |

## SIMON, PLUG & GRIMES
| | | | | | | | |
|---|---|---|---|---|---|---|---|
| Is This A Dream? | 7" | Deram | DM296 | 1970 | £2 | £5 | |

## SIMON, TONY
| | | | | | | | |
|---|---|---|---|---|---|---|---|
| Gimme A Little Sign | 7" | Track | 604012 | 1967 | £2 | £5 | |

## SIMON & GARFUNKEL
| | | | | | | | |
|---|---|---|---|---|---|---|---|
| At The Zoo | 7" EP | CBS | 6339 | 1967 | £4 | £8 | French |
| At The Zoo | 7" | CBS | 202608 | 1967 | £2 | £5 | |
| Bridge Over Troubled Water | LP | CBS | Q63699 | 1973 | £5 | £12 | quad |
| Bridge Over Troubled Waters | LP | Columbia | HC49914 | 1981 | £5 | £12 | US audiophile |
| Bridge Over Troubled Waters | LP | Mobile Fidelity | MFSL1173 | 1981 | £5 | £12 | US audiophile |
| Dangling Conversation | 7" | CBS | 202285 | 1966 | £4 | £8 | |
| Fakin' It | 7" | CBS | 2911 | 1967 | £2 | £5 | |
| Feelin' Groovy | 7" EP | CBS | EP6360 | 1967 | £2.50 | £6 | |
| Greatest Hits | LP | Columbia | HC41350 | 1981 | £5 | £12 | US audiophile |
| Hazy Shade Of Winter | 7" | CBS | 202378 | 1966 | £1.50 | £4 | |
| Hit Sounds Of Simon And Garfunkel | LP | Pickwick | SPC3059 | 1966 | £6 | £15 | US |
| Homeward Bound | 7" | CBS | 202045 | 1966 | £1.50 | £4 | |
| I Am A Rock | 7" EP | CBS | EP6074 | 1966 | £2.50 | £6 | |
| I Am A Rock | 7" | CBS | 202303 | 1966 | £1.50 | £4 | |
| Mrs. Robinson | 7" EP | CBS | EP6400 | 1968 | £2.50 | £6 | |
| Seven O'Clock News | CD-s | CBS | 6576535 | 1991 | £2 | £5 | |

| | | | | | | | |
|---|---|---|---|---|---|---|---|
| Simon & Garfunkel | LP | Sears | SP435 | 1969 £6 | £15 | | US |
| Simon And Garfunkel | LP | Allegro | ALL836 | 1967 £6 | £15 | | |
| Sound Of Silence | 7" | CBS | 201977 | 1965 £1.50 | £4 | | |
| Sounds Of Silence | 7" EP | CBS | 5655 | 1965 £4 | £8 | | French |
| Wednesday Morning 3 a.m. | 7" EP | CBS | EP6053 | 1965 £2.50 | £6 | | |

## SIMON SISTERS

The Simon Sisters made a number of records of mainly children's songs, before sister Lucy got married and decided to leave the music business. Younger sister Carly carried on by herself and eventually became rather successful.

| | | | | | | | |
|---|---|---|---|---|---|---|---|
| Cuddlebug | LP | Kapp | KL1397/KS3397 | 1964 £6 | £15 | | US |
| Cuddlebug | 7" | London | HLR9984 | 1965 £1.50 | £4 | | |
| Lobster Quadrille | LP | Columbia | CS24506 | 1969 £4 | £10 | | US |
| Simon Sisters | LP | Kapp | KL1359/KS3359 | 1964 £6 | £15 | | US |
| Winkin' Blinkin' And Nod | 7" | London | HLR9893 | 1964 £2.50 | £6 | | |

## SIMONE, NINA

| | | | | | | | |
|---|---|---|---|---|---|---|---|
| Amazing | LP | Colpix | (S)CP407 | 1959 £4 | £10 | | US |
| And Her Friends | LP | Bethlehem | BCP6041 | 1959 £4 | £10 | | US |
| At Carnegie Hall | LP | Colpix | (S)CP455 | 1963 £4 | £10 | | US |
| At Newport | LP | Colpix | (S)CP412 | 1960 £4 | £10 | | US |
| At The Town Hall | LP | Pye | NPL28014 | 1962 £4 | £10 | | |
| At The Village Gate | LP | Colpix | PXL421 | 1965 £4 | £10 | | |
| Best Of Nina Simone | LP | Philips | SBL7895 | 1969 £4 | £10 | | |
| Broadway, Blues, Ballads | LP | Philips | BL7662 | 1965 £4 | £10 | | |
| Don't Let Me Be Misunderstood | 7" EP | Philips | BE12585 | 1965 £2 | £5 | | |
| Don't Let Me Be Misunderstood | 7" | Philips | BF1388 | 1965 £1.50 | £4 | | |
| Either Way I Lose | 7" | Philips | BF1465 | 1966 £2 | £5 | | |
| Exactly Like You | 7" | Colpix | PX799 | 1964 £1.50 | £4 | | |
| Fine And Mellow | 7" EP | Colpix | PXE303 | 1964 £2.50 | £6 | | |
| Folksy Nina | LP | Colpix | PXL465 | 1964 £4 | £10 | | |
| Forbidden Fruit | LP | Colpix | PXL419 | 1965 £4 | £10 | | |
| Forbidden Fruit | LP | Pye | NJL36 | 1961 £5 | £12 | | |
| High Priestess Of Soul | LP | Philips | BL7764 | 1967 £4 | £10 | | |
| I Love To Love | 7" EP | Colpix | PXE307 | 1966 £2.50 | £6 | | |
| I Loves You Porgy | 7" | Parlophone | R4583 | 1959 £1.50 | £4 | | |
| I Put A Spell On You | LP | Philips | BL7671 | 1965 £4 | £10 | | |
| I Put A Spell On You | 7" | Philips | BF1415 | 1965 £1.50 | £4 | | |
| In Concert | LP | Philips | BL7678 | 1965 £4 | £10 | | |
| Intimate Nina Simone | 7" EP | Parlophone | GEP8864 | 1962 £2.50 | £6 | | |
| Just Say I Love Him | 7" EP | Colpix | PXE306 | 1966 £2.50 | £6 | | |
| Let It All Out | LP | Philips | (S)BL7722 | 1966 £4 | £10 | | |
| Little Girl Blue | LP | Bethlehem | BCP6028 | 1959 £6 | £15 | | US |
| My Baby Just Cares For Me | CD-s | Charly | CDS1 | 1987 £2 | £5 | | |
| My Baby Just Cares For Me | 7" EP | Parlophone | GEP8844 | 1961 £4 | £8 | | |
| Nina Simone | LP | Polydor | 623214 | 1969 £4 | £10 | | |
| Nina With Strings | LP | Colpix | (S)CP496 | 1966 £4 | £10 | | US |
| Nina's Choice | LP | Colpix | (S)CP443 | 1963 £4 | £10 | | US |
| Nuff Said | LP | RCA | SF7979 | 1969 £4 | £10 | | |
| Original | LP | Bethlehem | BCP(S)6028 | 1961 £4 | £10 | | US |
| Pastel Blues | LP | Philips | BL7683 | 1966 £4 | £10 | | |
| Silk And Soul | LP | RCA | RD/SF7967 | 1968 £4 | £10 | | |
| Sings Ellington | LP | Colpix | (S)CP425 | 1962 £4 | £10 | | US |
| Sings The Blues | LP | RCA | RD/SF7883 | 1967 £4 | £10 | | |
| Solitaire | 7" | Pye | 7N25029 | 1959 £1.50 | £4 | | |
| Strange Fruit | 7" EP | Philips | BE12589 | 1965 £2 | £5 | | |
| Tell Me More | LP | Fontana | SFJL954 | 1968 £4 | £10 | | |
| Wild Is The Wind | LP | Philips | BL7726 | 1966 £4 | £10 | | |
| You Can Have Him | 7" | Colpix | PX200 | 1963 £1.50 | £4 | | |

## SIMONE, SUGAR

| | | | | | | | |
|---|---|---|---|---|---|---|---|
| Black Is Gold | 7" | Doctor Bird | DB1192 | 1969 £5 | £10 | | |
| Boom Biddy Boom | 7" | Fab | FAB106 | 1969 £1.50 | £4 | | Rudies B side |
| Come And Try | 7" | Doctor Bird | DB1201 | 1969 £5 | £10 | | |
| I Love My Baby | 7" | Rainbow | RAI114 | 1967 £4 | £8 | | |
| I Need A Witness | 7" | Fab | FAB107 | 1969 £1.50 | £4 | | |
| Is It Because | 7" | Rainbow | RAI103 | 1966 £4 | £8 | | |
| It's Alright | 7" | Go | AJ11409 | 1967 £2 | £5 | | |
| Squeeze Is On | 7" | Doctor Bird | DB1193 | 1969 £5 | £10 | | |
| Suddenly | 7" | Sue | WI4029 | 1967 £5 | £10 | | |
| Vow | 7" | CBS | 3250 | 1968 £1.50 | £4 | | |

## SIMON'S SECRETS

| | | | | | | | |
|---|---|---|---|---|---|---|---|
| I Know What Her Name Is | 7" | CBS | 3056 | 1967 £5 | £10 | | |
| Naughty Boy | 7" | CBS | 3406 | 1968 £5 | £10 | | |

## SIMPLE MINDS

| | | | | | | | |
|---|---|---|---|---|---|---|---|
| Amsterdam EP | CD-s | Virgin | SMXCD6 | 1989 £2 | £5 | | 3" single |
| Amsterdam EP | CD-s | Virgin | SMXX6 | 1989 £2 | £5 | | |
| Ballad Of The Streets | CD-s | Virgin | SMXCD3 | 1989 £2 | £5 | | 3" single |
| Celebrate | 7" | Arista | ARIST394 | 1981 £2 | £5 | | |
| Celebrate | 12" | Arista | ARIST12394 | 1981 £2.50 | £6 | | |
| Changeling | 7" | Zoom | ARIST325 | 1980 £2.50 | £6 | | |
| Chelsea Girl | 7" | Zoom | ZUM11 | 1979 £1.50 | £4 | | |
| Don't You Forget About Me | CD-s | Virgin | CDT2 | 1988 £2 | £5 | | 3" single |
| Don't You Forget About Me | 7" | Virgin | VSS749 | 1985 £7.50 | £15 | | shaped picture disc |
| Ghostdancing | CD-s | Virgin | MIKE90712 | 1986 £2.50 | £6 | | |

| | | | | | | | |
|---|---|---|---|---|---|---|---|
| I Travel | 7" | Arista | ARIST372 | 1980 £4 | £8 | .... with blue flexi 7" |
| I Travel | 12" | Arista | ARIST12372 | 1980 £2.50 | £6 | |
| Kick It In | CD-s | Virgin | SMXCD5 | 1989 £2 | £5 | |
| Let There Be Love | CD-s | Virgin | VSCDT1332 | 1991 £2 | £5 | |
| Life In A Day | 7" | Zoom | ZUM10 | 1979 £2 | £5 | |
| Live In The City Of Light | LP | Virgin | SMDL1 | 1987 £5 | £12 | .. double, booklet, gold embossed sleeve |
| Live In The City Of Light | CD | Virgin | CDSM1 | 1987 £20 | £40 | ... promo box set, with LP and cassette |
| Once Upon A Time | LP | Virgin | V2364 | 1985 £4 | £10 | ... picture disc |
| Real Life | CD-s | Virgin | VSCDG1382 | 1991 £2 | £5 | |
| Real Life | CD | A&M | | 1991 £10 | £25 | US promo with 2 CD singles |
| Real Life Tour | CD | Virgin | | 1991 £10 | £25 | .... Australian double |
| See The Lights | CD-s | Virgin | VSCDT1343 | 1991 £2 | £5 | |
| Someone Somewhere In Summertime | 7" | Virgin | VS538 | 1982 £2 | £5 | ... poster sleeve |
| Someone Somewhere In Summertime | 7" | Virgin | VSY538 | 1982 £2 | £5 | ... picture disc |
| Sons And Fascination/Sister Feelings Call | LP | Virgin | V2207 | 1981 £6 | £15 | ... double |
| Sparkle In The Rain | LP | Virgin | V2300 | 1984 £4 | £10 | ... white vinyl |
| Sparkle In The Rain | CD | Virgin | CDV2300 | 1986 £5 | £12 | |
| Speed Your Love To Me | 7" | Virgin | VSY649 | 1984 £2.50 | £6 | ... picture disc |
| Street Fighting Years | CD | Virgin | PMIND1 | 1991 £5 | £12 | ... picture disc |
| Street Fighting Years | CD | Virgin | SMBXD1 | 1989 £10 | £25 | ... boxed with book & interview cassettes |
| Street Fighting Years | cass | Virgin | SMBXC1 | 1989 £6 | £15 | ... boxed with book & interview cassettes |
| Themes Vol. 1 | CD-s | Virgin | SMTCD1 | 1990 £8 | £20 | ... 5 CD set |
| Themes Vol. 2 | CD-s | Virgin | SMTCD2 | 1990 £8 | £20 | ... 5 CD set |
| Themes Vol. 3 | CD-s | Virgin | SMTCD3 | 1990 £8 | £20 | ... 5 CD set |
| Themes Vol. 4 | CD-s | Virgin | SMTCD4 | 1990 £8 | £20 | ... 5 CD set |
| This Is Your Land | CD-s | Virgin | SMXCD4 | 1989 £2 | £5 | ... 3" single |
| Up On The Catwalk | 7" | Virgin | VSY661 | 1984 £2.50 | £6 | ... picture disc |

### SIMPLICITY

| | | | | | | |
|---|---|---|---|---|---|---|
| Any Minute Of Your Life | 7" | York | SYK501 | 1971 £1.50 | £4 | |

### SIMPLY RED

| | | | | | | |
|---|---|---|---|---|---|---|
| Come To My Aid | 12" | Elektra | EKR19TX | 1985 £2.50 | £6 | |
| Every Time We Say Goodbye | CD-s | WEA | YZ161CD | 1987 £3 | £8 | |
| Every Time We Say Goodbye | 12" | WEA | YZ161TW | 1987 £5 | £12 | ... with sheet music & 4 cards |
| Every Time We Say Goodbye | 10" | WEA | YZ161TE | 1987 £2.50 | £6 | |
| For Your Babies | CD-s | East West | YZ642CDX | 1992 £2 | £5 | ... holographic |
| Holding Back The Years | 7" | Elektra | EKR29F | 1985 £2.50 | £6 | gatefold picture sleeve, poster |
| Holding Back The Years | 7" | Elektra | EKR29P | 1985 £7.50 | £15 | ... shaped picture disc |
| Holding Back The Years | 12" | Elektra | EKR29T | 1985 £3 | £8 | |
| I Won't Feel Bad | CD-s | WEA | YZ172CD | 1988 £4 | £10 | ... 3" single |
| If You Don't Know Me By Now | CD-s | WEA | YZ377CD | 1989 £2 | £5 | ... 3" single |
| If You Don't Know Me By Now | CD-s | WEA | YZ377CDX | 1989 £3 | £8 | |
| If You Don't Know Me By Now | 10" | WEA | YZ377TE | 1989 £2.50 | £6 | |
| Infidelity | 12" | Elektra | YZ114TP | 1987 £3 | £8 | ... picture disc |
| It's Only Love | CD-s | WEA | YZ349CD | 1989 £2.50 | £6 | |
| It's Only Love | CD-s | WEA | YZ349CDX | 1989 £5 | £12 | ... 3" single |
| It's Only Love | 10" | WEA | YZ349TE | 1989 £2.50 | £6 | |
| Jericho | 7" | WEA | YZ63R | 1986 £1.50 | £4 | ... red vinyl |
| Let Me Take You Home | CD-s | Warner Bros | 9031728296 | 1990 £4 | £10 | ... CD video |
| Life | CD | East West | 0630120692 | 1995 £10 | £25 | .. promo in ring-binder |
| Maybe Someday | 12" | WEA | YZ141T | 1987 £2.50 | £6 | |
| Money's Too Tight To Mention | 7" | Elektra | EKR9P | 1985 £2 | £5 | ... picture disc |
| Money's Too Tight To Mention | 12" | Elektra | EKR9TX | 1985 £2.50 | £6 | |
| Montreux EP | CD-s | East West | YZ716CDX | 1992 £2 | £5 | ...digipak with booklet |
| New Flame | CD-s | WEA | YZ404CD | 1989 £2.50 | £6 | |
| New Flame | 10" | WEA | YZ404TE | 1989 £2.50 | £6 | |
| Open Up The Red Box | 7" | WEA | YZ75B | 1986 £2 | £5 | ... box sleeve |
| Open Up The Red Box | 7" | WEA | YZ75F | 1986 £2 | £5 | ... double |
| Open Up The Red Box – Remix | 12" | WEA | YZ75TF | 1986 £3 | £8 | ... double |
| Picture Book | LP | Elektra | EKT27P | 1985 £4 | £10 | ...picture disc |
| Right Thing | 7" | WEA | YZ103F | 1987 £2 | £5 | ... double |
| Right Thing | 12" | WEA | YZ103TP | 1987 £2.50 | £6 | ... picture disc |
| Something Got Me Started | CD-s | East West | YZ614CD | 1991 £2 | £5 | |
| Something's Burning | 7" | Lyntone | LYN15914 | 1985 £1.50 | £4 | flexi, 10000 Maniacs B side |
| Stars | CD-s | East West | YZ626CD | 1991 £2 | £5 | |
| You've Got It | CD-s | WEA | YZ424CD | 1989 £2 | £5 | |
| Your Mirror | CD-s | East West | YZ689CD | 1992 £2 | £5 | ... holographic |

### SIMPSON, DANNY

| | | | | | | |
|---|---|---|---|---|---|---|
| Outa Sight | 7" | Trojan | TR653 | 1969 £1.50 | £4 | |

### SIMPSON, FRANK

| | | | | | | |
|---|---|---|---|---|---|---|
| Four Star Hits | LP | Audio Lab | 1552 | 1960 £10 | £25 | ... US |

### SIMPSON, HOKE

| | | | | | | |
|---|---|---|---|---|---|---|
| I Finally Found You | 7" | HMV | POP442 | 1958 £1.50 | £4 | |

### SIMPSON, JEANETTE

| | | | | | | |
|---|---|---|---|---|---|---|
| My Baby Just Cares For Me | 7" | Giant | GN29 | 1968 £2.50 | £6 | |

| | | | | | | | |
|---|---|---|---|---|---|---|---|
| Rain | 7" | Giant | GN16 | 1967 | £2.50 | £6 | |
| Through Loving You | 7" | Giant | GN35 | 1968 | £2.50 | £6 | |

## SIMPSON, LEO

| | | | | | | | |
|---|---|---|---|---|---|---|---|
| I Love Her So | 7" | Blue Beat | BB351 | 1966 | £6 | £12 | |
| Waxy Doodle | 7" | Pyramid | PYR.7004 | 1973 | £1.50 | £4 | |

## SIMPSON, LIONEL

| | | | | | | | |
|---|---|---|---|---|---|---|---|
| Eight People | 7" | Ska Beat | JB221 | 1965 | £5 | £10 | |
| Give Over | 7" | Ska Beat | JB233 | 1966 | £5 | £10 | |
| Love Is A Game | 7" | Ska Beat | JB205 | 1965 | £5 | £10 | |

## SIMPSON, MARTIN

| | | | | | | | |
|---|---|---|---|---|---|---|---|
| Golden Vanity | LP | Trailer | LER.2099 | 1976 | £8 | £20 | |

## SIMS, CHUCK

| | | | | | | | |
|---|---|---|---|---|---|---|---|
| Little Pigeon | 7" | London | HLR.8577 | 1958 | £75 | £150 | |

## SIMS, ZOOT

| | | | | | | | |
|---|---|---|---|---|---|---|---|
| At Ronnie Scott's | LP | Fontana | TFL5176 | 1961 | £10 | £25 | |
| Choice | LP | Vogue | LAE12309 | 1961 | £10 | £25 | |
| Cookin! | LP | Fontana | FJL123 | 1965 | £5 | £12 | |
| Down Home | LP | Parlophone | PMC1169 | 1961 | £10 | £25 | |
| George Handy Compositions | LP | HMV | CLP1165 | 1958 | £15 | £30 | |
| Goes To Town | 10" LP | Vogue | LDE056 | 1954 | £25 | £50 | |
| Plays Four Altos | LP | HMV | CLP1188 | 1958 | £15 | £30 | |
| Solo For Zoot | LP | Phillips | 680982 | 196– | £10 | £25 | |
| Trotting | LP | XTRA | XTRA5001 | 1966 | £5 | £12 | |
| Waiting Game | LP | Impulse | MIPL/SIPL501 | 1968 | £5 | £12 | |
| You 'n' Me | LP | Mercury | MMC14071 | 1961 | £10 | £25 | with Al Cohn |
| Zoot Sims Allstars | 10" LP | Esquire | 20010 | 1953 | £25 | £50 | |
| Zoot Sims Quartet | LP | Jazzland | JLP2 | 195– | £25 | £50 | |
| Zoot Sims Quartet/Quintet | 10" LP | Esquire | 20002 | 1952 | £25 | £50 | |
| Zoot Sims Quartet/Quintet | 10" LP | Esquire | 20018 | 1953 | £25 | £50 | |
| Zoot Sims Quartet/Quintet | 10" LP | Esquire | 20040 | 1955 | £25 | £50 | |
| Zoot! | LP | London | LTZU15135 | 1958 | £15 | £30 | |

## SIMS, ZOOT (2)

| | | | | | | | |
|---|---|---|---|---|---|---|---|
| Please Don't Do It | 7" | Port-O-Jam | PJ4007 | 1964 | £5 | £10 | with Lloyd Robinson |
| Press Along | 7" | Blue Beat | BB183 | 1963 | £6 | £12 | Prince Buster B side |
| Searching | 7" | Blue Beat | BB143 | 1962 | £6 | £12 | with Lloyd Robinson |
| Tit For Tat | 7" | Coxsone | CS7095 | 1969 | £5 | £10 | |

## SIN SAY SHUNS

| | | | | | | | |
|---|---|---|---|---|---|---|---|
| I'll Be There | LP | Venett | VS940 | 1966 | £15 | £30 | US |

## SINATRA, FRANK

| | | | | | | | |
|---|---|---|---|---|---|---|---|
| Adventures Of The Heart | LP | Fontana | TFL5006 | 1958 | £6 | £15 | |
| All The Way | LP | Capitol | W(S)1538 | 1962 | £4 | £10 | |
| Among My Souvenirs | 7" EP | Fontana | TFE17272 | 1960 | £2 | £5 | |
| Anchors Aweigh | 7" EP | Fontana | TFE17043 | 1958 | £2 | £5 | |
| Birth Of The Blues | 7" | Columbia | SCM5052 | 1953 | £5 | £10 | |
| Broadway Kick | LP | Fontana | TFL5054 | 1959 | £6 | £15 | |
| Bye Baby | 7" EP | Fontana | TFE17273 | 1960 | £2 | £5 | |
| Capitol Years | CD | Capitol | DPRO79375 | 1990 | £8 | £20 | US promo |
| Christmas Dreaming | 10" LP | Philips | BBR8114 | 1957 | £6 | £15 | |
| Christmas Songs | 10" LP | Columbia | CL6019 | 195– | £6 | £15 | US |
| Christmas Waltz | 7" | Capitol | CL14174 | 1954 | £4 | £8 | |
| Close To You | LP | Capitol | LCT6130 | 1957 | £4 | £10 | |
| Come Back To Sorrento | LP | Fontana | TFL5082 | 1960 | £4 | £10 | |
| Come Dance With Me | LP | Capitol | (S)LCT6179 | 1959 | £4 | £10 | |
| Come Swing With Me | LP | Capitol | W(S)1594 | 1962 | £4 | £10 | |
| Complete Frank Sinatra Sampler | CD | Columbia | | 1993 | £8 | £20 | US promo |
| Conducts The Music Of Alex Wilder | 10" LP | Columbia | ML4271 | 195– | £6 | £15 | US |
| Conducts Tone Poems Of Colour | LP | Capitol | LCT6111 | 1956 | £4 | £10 | |
| Dedicated To You | 10" LP | Columbia | CL6096 | 195– | £6 | £15 | US |
| Don't Change Your Mind About Me | 7" | Capitol | CL14270 | 1955 | £4 | £8 | |
| Dream | 7" EP | Fontana | TFE17158 | 1959 | £2 | £5 | |
| Duets | CD | DCC | GZS1053 | 1994 | £6 | £15 | US audiophile |
| Duets II | CD | DCC | GZS1073 | 1994 | £6 | £15 | US audiophile |
| Embraceable You | 7" EP | Fontana | TFE17286 | 1960 | £2 | £5 | |
| Fabulous Frank | 10" LP | Philips | BBR8038 | 1955 | £6 | £15 | |
| Fairy Tale | 7" | Capitol | CL14373 | 1955 | £2.50 | £6 | |
| Five Minutes More | 7" EP | Fontana | TFE17280 | 1960 | £2 | £5 | |
| Flowers Mean Forgiveness | 7" | Capitol | CL14564 | 1956 | £1.50 | £4 | |
| Fools Rush In | 7" EP | Fontana | TFE17037 | 1958 | £2 | £5 | |
| Francis A.Sinatra And Edward K.Ellington | LP | Reprise | R(S)LP1024 | 1968 | £4 | £10 | |
| Frank Sinatra | 7" EP | Columbia | SEG7565 | 1955 | £2.50 | £6 | |
| Frank Sinatra | 7" EP | HMV | 7EG8070 | 1954 | £2 | £5 | |
| Frankie | LP | Philips | BBL7168 | 1957 | £6 | £15 | |
| Frankie | 7" EP | Fontana | TFE17182 | 1959 | £2 | £5 | |
| Frankie And Tommy (with Tommy Dorsey) | LP | RCA | RD27069 | 1958 | £6 | £15 | |
| Frankie's Favourites | 7" EP | Columbia | SEG7597 | 1955 | £2.50 | £6 | |
| Frankly Sentimental | 10" LP | Columbia | CL6059 | 195– | £6 | £15 | US |
| Gal That Got Away | 7" | Capitol | CL14221 | 1955 | £4 | £8 | |
| Great Years | LP | Capitol | W1/2/31762 | 1963 | £6 | £15 | triple |
| High Hopes | 7" EP | Capitol | EAP11224 | 1959 | £2 | £5 | |

| Title | Format | Label | Catalogue | Year | Price | Price | Notes |
|---|---|---|---|---|---|---|---|
| I Am Loved | 7" EP | Fontana | TFE17038 | 1958 | £2 | £5 | |
| I Dream Of You | 7" EP | Fontana | TFE17284 | 1960 | £2 | £5 | |
| I've Got A Crush On You | 7" EP | Fontana | TFE17254 | 1960 | £2 | £5 | |
| I've Got A Crush On You | 10" LP | Columbia | CL6290 | 195- | £6 | £15 | US |
| If I Forget You | 7" | Fontana | H140 | 1958 | £1.50 | £4 | |
| In The Wee Small Hours Of The Morning | 7" | Capitol | CL14360 | 1955 | £2.50 | £6 | |
| In The Wee Small Hours Vol. 1 | 10" LP | Capitol | LC6702 | 1955 | £5 | £12 | |
| In The Wee Small Hours Vol. 2 | 10" LP | Capitol | LC6705 | 1955 | £5 | £12 | |
| It's D-Lovely | 10" LP | HMV | DLP1123 | 1956 | £8 | £20 | ...with Tommy Dorsey |
| Jolly Christmas | LP | Capitol | LCT6144 | 1957 | £4 | £10 | |
| Learnin' The Blues | LP | Capitol | CL14296 | 1955 | £4 | £8 | |
| London By Night | LP | Capitol | T20389 | 1962 | £4 | £10 | |
| Look To Your Heart | LP | Capitol | LCT6181 | 1959 | £4 | £10 | |
| Love And Marriage | 7" | Capitol | CL14503 | 1956 | £2 | £5 | |
| Love Is A Kick | LP | Fontana | TFL5074 | 1960 | £4 | £10 | |
| Lover | 7" EP | Fontana | TFE17012 | 1958 | £2 | £5 | |
| Mad About You | 7" EP | Fontana | TFE17023 | 1958 | £2 | £5 | |
| Man And His Music | LP | Reprise | R(9)1016 | 1966 | £5 | £12 | double |
| Melancholy Baby | 7" EP | Fontana | TFE17274 | 1960 | £2 | £5 | |
| Melody Of Love | 7" EP | Capitol | EAP1590 | 1956 | £2 | £5 | |
| Melody Of Love | 7" | Capitol | CL14238 | 1955 | £4 | £8 | |
| Moonlight Sinatra | LP | Reprise | R(9)1018 | 1966 | £4 | £10 | |
| Moonlight Sinatra | 7" EP | HMV | 7EG8128 | 1955 | £2.50 | £6 | |
| My Funny Valentine | LP | Capitol | T20577 | 1964 | £4 | £10 | |
| My Funny Valentine | 7" | Capitol | CL14352 | 1955 | £2.50 | £6 | |
| Nearness Of You | 7" EP | Philips | BBE12182 | 1958 | £2 | £5 | |
| New Orleans (with Jo Stafford) | 10" LP | Columbia | CL6268 | 195- | £6 | £15 | US |
| Nice 'n' Easy | LP | Capitol | W(S)1417 | 1961 | £4 | £10 | |
| No One Cares | LP | Capitol | (S)LCT6185 | 1959 | £4 | £10 | |
| No One Cares | 7" EP | Capitol | SEP11221 | 1961 | £4 | £8 | stereo |
| No One Cares No. 2 | 7" EP | Capitol | SEP21221 | 1961 | £4 | £8 | stereo |
| No One Cares No. 3 | 7" EP | Capitol | SEP31221 | 1961 | £4 | £8 | stereo |
| Not As A Stranger | 7" | Capitol | CL14326 | 1955 | £4 | £8 | |
| Out Town | 7" EP | Capitol | EAP1025 | 1956 | £2 | £5 | |
| Pal Joey | LP | Capitol | LCT6148 | 1958 | £4 | £10 | |
| Point Of No Return | LP | Capitol | W(S)1676 | 1962 | £4 | £10 | |
| Put Your Dreams Away | LP | Fontana | TFL5048 | 1959 | £8 | £20 | |
| Reflections | LP | Fontana | TFL5107 | 1960 | £4 | £10 | |
| Reprise Collection | CD | Reprise | PROCD4540 | 1990 | £8 | £20 | US promo |
| Ring-A-Ding-Ding | LP | Reprise | R1001 | 1961 | £4 | £10 | |
| Robin And The Seven Hoods | LP | Reprise | R2021 | 1964 | £25 | £50 | |
| S'posin' | 7" | Columbia | SCM5167 | 1955 | £5 | £10 | |
| Santa Claus Is Comin' To Town | 7" | Columbia | SCM5076 | 1953 | £5 | £10 | |
| Session With Sinatra | 7" EP | Capitol | EAP1629 | 1956 | £2 | £5 | |
| Sinatra '65 | LP | Reprise | R(9)6167 | 1965 | £4 | £10 | |
| Sinatra And Strings | LP | Reprise | R(9)1004 | 1962 | £4 | £10 | |
| Sinatra Family Wish You A Happy Christmas | LP | Reprise | R(S)LP1026 | 1969 | £4 | £10 | |
| Sinatra Plus | LP | Fontana | SET303 | 1961 | £5 | £12 | double |
| Sinatra Serenade | 7" EP | Columbia | SEG7582 | 1955 | £2.50 | £6 | |
| Sinatra Souvenir | LP | Fontana | TFL5138 | 1961 | £4 | £10 | |
| Sinatra, Bailey & James (with Pearl Bailey & Harry James) | 7" EP | Fontana | TFE17028 | 1958 | £2 | £5 | |
| Sing And Dance | 10" LP | Philips | BBR8003 | 1954 | £8 | £20 | |
| Sing And Dance No. 1 | 7" EP | Philips | BBE12016 | 1956 | £2 | £5 | |
| Sing And Dance No. 2 | 7" EP | Philips | BBE12058 | 1956 | £2 | £5 | |
| Sings For Only The Lonely | LP | Capitol | (S)LCT6168 | 1958 | £4 | £10 | |
| Sings Great Songs From Great Britain | LP | Reprise | R1006 | 1962 | £8 | £20 | |
| Sings Great Songs From Great Britain | LP | Reprise | R91006 | 1962 | £15 | £30 | stereo |
| Sings Of Love And Things | LP | Capitol | W(S)1729 | 1963 | £4 | £10 | |
| Sings Rodgers And Hart | LP | Capitol | W1825 | 1963 | £4 | £10 | |
| Sings Songs From Carousel | 7" EP | Philips | BBE12152 | 1957 | £2 | £5 | |
| Song Is You | 7" EP | Fontana | TFE17253 | 1960 | £2 | £5 | |
| Songs By Sinatra Vol. 1 | 10" LP | Columbia | CL6087 | 195- | £6 | £15 | US |
| Songs For Swingin' Lovers | LP | Capitol | LCT6106 | 1956 | £4 | £10 | |
| Songs For Swinging Lovers | CD | Mobile Fidelity | UDCD538 | 1990 | £6 | £15 | US audiophile |
| Songs For Young Lovers | 10" LP | Capitol | LC6654 | 1954 | £6 | £15 | |
| Songs For Young Lovers No. 1 | 7" EP | Capitol | EAP1488 | 1955 | £2 | £5 | |
| Songs For Young Lovers No. 2 | 7" EP | Capitol | EAP2488 | 1955 | £2 | £5 | |
| Songs From Young At Heart | 7" EP | Capitol | EAP1571 | 1955 | £2 | £5 | |
| Story | LP | Fontana | TFL5030 | 1958 | £6 | £15 | |
| Summit | LP | Reprise | R5031 | 1966 | £25 | £50 | ... with Crosby, Davis Jr., Martin |
| Swing Easy | LP | Capitol | W587 | 1960 | £4 | £10 | |
| Swing Easy | 10" LP | Capitol | LC6689 | 1954 | £6 | £15 | |
| Swingin' Affair | LP | Capitol | LCT6135 | 1957 | £4 | £10 | |
| Swingin' Session | LP | Capitol | W(S)1491 | 1961 | £4 | £10 | |
| Tender Trap | 7" | Capitol | CL14511 | 1956 | £2 | £5 | |
| That Old Feeling | LP | Philips | BBL7180 | 1957 | £6 | £15 | |
| They Say It's Wonderful | 7" EP | Fontana | TFE17255 | 1960 | £2 | £5 | |
| This Is Sinatra | LP | Capitol | LCT6123 | 1957 | £4 | £10 | |
| This Is Sinatra Vol. 2 | LP | Capitol | LCT6155 | 1958 | £4 | £10 | |
| Three Coins In The Fountain | 7" | Capitol | CL14120 | 1954 | £5 | £10 | |
| Two Hearts, Two Kisses | 7" | Capitol | CL14292 | 1955 | £4 | £8 | |
| Voice | LP | Fontana | TFL5000 | 1958 | £6 | £15 | |
| Voice No. 1 – Four Star | 7" EP | Fontana | TFE17181 | 1959 | £2 | £5 | |
| Voice Of Sinatra | 10" LP | Columbia | CL6001 | 195- | £6 | £15 | US |
| Watertown | LP | Reprise | RSLP1031 | 1970 | £4 | £10 | |

| | | | | | | | |
|---|---|---|---|---|---|---|---|
| We're In Love | 7" EP | Fontana | TFE17042 | 1958 | £2 | £5 | |
| When I Stop Loving You | 7" | Capitol | CL14188 | 1954 | £4 | £8 | |
| Where Are You? | LP | Capitol | (S)LCT6152 | 1958 | £4 | £10 | stereo |
| Who Wants To Be A Millionaire | 7" | Capitol | CL14644 | 1956 | £1.50 | £4 | |
| You Do Something To Me | 7" | Columbia | SCM5060 | 1953 | £5 | £10 | |
| You Go To My Head | 7" EP | Fontana | TFE17256 | 1960 | £2 | £5 | |
| You My Love | 7" | Capitol | CL14240 | 1955 | £4 | £8 | |
| Young At Heart | 7" | Capitol | CL14064 | 1954 | £6 | £12 | |

## SINATRA, NANCY

| | | | | | | | |
|---|---|---|---|---|---|---|---|
| Boots | LP | Reprise | R(S)LP6202 | 1966 | £4 | £10 | |
| Country My Way | LP | Reprise | R(S)LP6251 | 1967 | £4 | £10 | |
| Cuff Links And A Tie Clip | 7" | Reprise | R20017 | 1961 | £2.50 | £6 | |
| Greatest Hits | LP | Reprise | RSLP6409 | 1970 | £4 | £10 | |
| How Does That Grab You? | LP | Reprise | R6207 | 1966 | £4 | £10 | |
| I Move Around | 7" EP | Reprise | REP30072 | 1966 | £4 | £8 | |
| Movin' With Nancy | LP | Reprise | R(S)LP6277 | 1968 | £4 | £10 | |
| Nancy | LP | Reprise | RSLP6333 | 1969 | £4 | £10 | |
| Nancy In London | LP | Reprise | R(S)LP6221 | 1966 | £4 | £10 | |
| Nashville Nancy | 7" EP | Reprise | REP30086 | 1967 | £2 | £5 | |
| Run For Your Life | 7" EP | Reprise | REP30069 | 1966 | £4 | £8 | |
| Something Stupid | 7" EP | Reprise | REP30082 | 1967 | £2 | £5 | |
| Sorry 'Bout That | 7" EP | Reprise | REP30080 | 1967 | £4 | £8 | |
| Sugar | LP | Reprise | RLP6239 | 1966 | £4 | £10 | |
| To Know Him Is To Love Him | 7" | Reprise | R20045 | 1962 | £2 | £5 | |
| Woman | LP | RCA | SF8331 | 1972 | £4 | £10 | |
| You Only Live Twice | 7" | Reprise | RS20595 | 1967 | £1.50 | £4 | |

## SINATRA, NANCY & LEE HAZELWOOD

| | | | | | | | |
|---|---|---|---|---|---|---|---|
| Jackson | 7" EP | Reprise | REP30083 | 1967 | £4 | £8 | |
| Nancy And Lee | LP | Reprise | R(S)LP6273 | 1968 | £4 | £10 | |
| Nancy And Lee Again | LP | RCA | LSP4645 | 1972 | £4 | £10 | US |
| Did You Ever? | LP | RCA | SF8240 | 1972 | £4 | £10 | |

## SINCLAIR, JIMMY

| | | | | | | | |
|---|---|---|---|---|---|---|---|
| Verona | 7" | Blue Beat | BB47 | 1961 | £6 | £12 | |

## SINDELFINGEN

| | | | | | | | |
|---|---|---|---|---|---|---|---|
| Odgipig | LP | Medway | no number | 1973 | £330 | £500 | |
| Odgipig/Triangle | LP | Cenotaph | CEN111 | 1990 | £10 | £25 | double |

## SINEWAVE

| | | | | | | | |
|---|---|---|---|---|---|---|---|
| Star Trek | 7" | Chapter One | CH172 | 1972 | £2 | £5 | |

## SINFIELD, PETE

| | | | | | | | |
|---|---|---|---|---|---|---|---|
| Still | LP | Manticore | K43501 | 1973 | £4 | £10 | |

## SINGER, RAY

| | | | | | | | |
|---|---|---|---|---|---|---|---|
| What's Been Done | 7" | Ember | EMBS231 | 1967 | £4 | £8 | |

## SINGER, SUSAN

| | | | | | | | |
|---|---|---|---|---|---|---|---|
| Autumn Leaves | 7" | Oriole | CB1778 | 1962 | £2.50 | £6 | |
| Hello First Love | 7" | Oriole | CB1703 | 1962 | £2.50 | £6 | |
| I Know | 7" | Oriole | CB1882 | 1963 | £2.50 | £6 | |
| Johnny Summertime | 7" | Oriole | CB1741 | 1962 | £6 | £12 | |
| Lock Your Heart Away | 7" | Oriole | CB1802 | 1963 | £2 | £6 | |

## SINGING BELLES

| | | | | | | | |
|---|---|---|---|---|---|---|---|
| Someone Loves You Joe | 7" | Top Rank | JAR350 | 1960 | £1.50 | £4 | |

## SINGING DOGS

| | | | | | | | |
|---|---|---|---|---|---|---|---|
| Singing Dogs | 7" EP | Pye | NEP24029 | 1957 | £5 | £10 | |

## SINGING FOLK

| | | | | | | | |
|---|---|---|---|---|---|---|---|
| I Was Wrong | 7" | Polydor | BM56018 | 1965 | £1.50 | £4 | |

## SINGING POSTMAN

| | | | | | | | |
|---|---|---|---|---|---|---|---|
| First Delivery | 7" EP | Parlophone | GEP8956 | 1966 | £2 | £5 | |

## SINGLETON, MARGIE

| | | | | | | | |
|---|---|---|---|---|---|---|---|
| Eyes Of Love | 7" | Melodisc | 1544 | 1960 | £1.50 | £4 | |
| Magic Star | 7" | Mercury | AMT1197 | 1962 | £2 | £5 | |

## SINISTER DUCKS

| | | | | | | | |
|---|---|---|---|---|---|---|---|
| March Of The Sinister Ducks | 7" | Situation 2 | SIT25 | 1983 | £5 | £10 | |

## SINK, EARL

| | | | | | | | |
|---|---|---|---|---|---|---|---|
| Little Suzie Parker | 7" | Warner Bros | WB51 | 1961 | £1.50 | £4 | |
| Looking For Love | 7" | Capitol | CL15310 | 1963 | £2 | £5 | |
| Supermarket | 7" | Warner Bros | WB38 | 1961 | £1.50 | £4 | |

## SINNERS

| | | | | | | | |
|---|---|---|---|---|---|---|---|
| I Can't Stand It | 7" | Columbia | DB7158 | 1963 | £2 | £5 | |
| It's So Exciting | 7" | Columbia | DB7295 | 1964 | £2 | £5 | |

## SINNERS (2)

| | | | | | | | |
|---|---|---|---|---|---|---|---|
| Sinnerisme | LP | Jupiter | JDY7009 | 1974 | £50 | £100 | Canadian |
| Sinners | LP | Transworld | TW6801 | 1968 | £20 | £40 | Canadian |

| | | | | | | | |
|---|---|---|---|---|---|---|---|
| Vox Populi | LP | | | 197– | £20 | £40 | Canadian |

## SIOUXSIE & THE BANSHEES

| | | | | | | | |
|---|---|---|---|---|---|---|---|
| Candyman | 7" | Wonderland | SHEDP10 | 1986 | £2 | £5 | double, gatefold picture sleeve |
| Head Cut | 7" | Fan Club | FILE1 | 1983 | £15 | £30 | |
| Hong Kong Garden | 7" | Polydor | 2059052 | 1978 | £4 | £8 | gatefold sleeve |
| Israel | 12" | Polydor | POSPX205 | 1980 | £3 | £8 | no picture sleeve |
| Killing Jar | CD-s | Wonderland | SHECD15 | 1988 | £2 | £5 | |
| Kiss Them For Me | CD-s | Wonderland | SHECD19 | 1991 | £2 | £5 | |
| Last Beat Of My Heart | CD-s | Wonderland | SHECD16 | 1988 | £2 | £5 | |
| Mittageisen | 7" | Polydor | 2059151 | 1979 | £2 | £5 | picture sleeve |
| Peek-A-Boo | CD-s | Polygram | 0803982 | 1988 | £4 | £10 | CD video |
| Peek-A-Boo | CD-s | Wonderland | SHECD14 | 1988 | £2 | £5 | |
| Peel Sessions | CD-s | Strange Fruit | SFPSCD012 | 1988 | £2 | £5 | |
| Peel Sessions II | CD-s | Strange Fruit | SFPSCD066 | 1989 | £2 | £5 | |
| Playground Twist | 7" | Polydor | POSP59 | 1979 | £1.50 | £4 | red paper label |
| Shadowtime | CD-s | Polydor | SHECD20 | 1991 | £2 | £5 | |
| Superstition | CD | Geffen | PROCD4260 | 1991 | £10 | £25 | US promo, round box set with cracked mirror front |
| This Wheel's On Fire | 7" | Wonderland | SHEG11 | 1987 | £2 | £5 | double, gatefold picture sleeve, numbered |
| Through The Looking Glass | LP | Wonderland | SHELP4 | 1987 | £5 | £12 | mispress, 1 side plays Jimi Hendrix |
| Through The Looking Glass | 7" | Wonderland | | 1987 | £6 | £12 | 3 x 7" in plastic wallet, promo |
| Voices | 7" | Wonderland | | 1984 | £2 | £5 | promo |

## SIR COLLINS BAND

| | | | | | | | |
|---|---|---|---|---|---|---|---|
| Collins And The Boys | 7" | Collins Downbeat | CR0011 | 1968 | £2 | £5 | |
| Soul Feelings | 7" | Collins Downbeat | CR0017 | 1968 | £2 | £5 | |

## SIR DOUGLAS QUINTET

| | | | | | | | |
|---|---|---|---|---|---|---|---|
| 1+1+1=4 | LP | Philips | PHS600344 | 1970 | £4 | £10 | US |
| Best Of The Sir Douglas Quintet | LP | London | HAU8311 | 1965 | £25 | £50 | |
| Best Of The Sir Douglas Quintet | LP | Tribe | 37001 | 1966 | £37.50 | £75 | US |
| Dynamite Woman | 7" | Mercury | MF1129 | 1969 | £1.50 | £4 | |
| Honky Blues | LP | Smash | SRS67108 | 1968 | £8 | £20 | US |
| Mendocino | LP | Mercury | SMCL20160 | 1969 | £4 | £10 | |
| Mendocino | 7" | Mercury | MF1079 | 1969 | £1.50 | £4 | |
| Rains Came | 7" | London | HLU10019 | 1966 | £1.50 | £4 | |
| She's About A Mover | 7" EP | London | REU10171 | 1965 | £12.50 | £25 | French |
| She's About A Mover | 7" | London | HLU9964 | 1965 | £1.50 | £4 | |
| Story Of John Hardy | 7" | London | HLU10001 | 1965 | £1.50 | £4 | |
| Together After Five | LP | Mercury | SMCL20186 | 1970 | £4 | £10 | |
| Tracker | 7" | London | HLU9982 | 1965 | £1.50 | £4 | |

## SIR HENRY & HIS BUTLERS

| | | | | | | | |
|---|---|---|---|---|---|---|---|
| Camp | LP | Columbia | SMC74562 | 1968 | £6 | £15 | German |
| H2O | LP | Columbia | 73006 | 1967 | £6 | £15 | German |
| Let's Go | LP | Polydor | 623003 | 1965 | £20 | £40 | German |
| Let's Go | 7" EP | Polydor | 60101 | 196– | £12.50 | £25 | French |
| Portrait | LP | Columbia | KSX4 | 1966 | £10 | £25 | Danish |
| Pretty Style | 7" | Columbia | DB8497 | 1968 | £4 | £8 | |
| Sir Henry & His Butlers Are Serving You | LP | Sonet | SLPS1211 | 1964 | £10 | £25 | Danish |
| Sir Henry And His Butlers | LP | Columbia | KSX2 | 1965 | £15 | £30 | Danish |

## SIR HORATIO

| | | | | | | | |
|---|---|---|---|---|---|---|---|
| Abracadubra | 12" | Rock Steady | MIX1T | 1982 | £3 | £8 | |

## SIR LORD COMIC

| | | | | | | | |
|---|---|---|---|---|---|---|---|
| Great Wuga Wuga | 7" | Doctor Bird | DB1070 | 1967 | £5 | £10 | |
| Jack Of My Trade | 7" | Pressure Beat | PB5506 | 1969 | £1.50 | £4 | Cynthia Richards B side |
| Rhythm Rebellion | 7" | Bamboo | BAM66 | 1970 | £1.50 | £4 | Roy Richards B side |
| Ska-ing West | 7" | Doctor Bird | DB1019 | 1966 | £5 | £10 | Maytals B side |

## SIREN

Originally named Coyne-Clague after the lead singer and guitarist, the group had settled on the rather more wieldy Siren by the time of their first recording for John Peel's Dandelion label. Kevin Coyne has made Siren's bluesy style into the basis of a still continuing solo career, gaining a considerable cult following, while Dave Clague has opted to temper his music-making with the financial security of being a teacher.

| | | | | | | | |
|---|---|---|---|---|---|---|---|
| Siren | LP | Dandelion | 63755 | 1969 | £6 | £15 | |
| Strange Locomotion | LP | Dandelion | DAN8001 | 1971 | £5 | £12 | |
| Strange Locomotion | 7" | Dandelion | DAN7002 | 1971 | £1.50 | £4 | |

## SISTER MARY GERTRUDE

| | | | | | | | |
|---|---|---|---|---|---|---|---|
| My Auld Killarney Hat | 7" | Pye | 7N15787 | 1965 | £1.50 | £4 | |

## SISTERS OF MERCY

| | | | | | | | |
|---|---|---|---|---|---|---|---|
| Alice | 7" | Merciful Release | MR015 | 1982 | £5 | £10 | white background |

| Title | Format | Label | Catalogue | Year | | | Notes |
|---|---|---|---|---|---|---|---|
| Body And Soul | 7" | Merciful Release | MR029 | 1984 | £2 | £5 | |
| Body Electric | 7" | CNT | 002 | 1982 | £20 | £40 | |
| Damage Done | 7" | Merciful Release | MR007 | 1980 | £37.50 | £75 | |
| Doctor Jeep | CD-s | Merciful Release | MR51CD | 1990 | £2 | £5 | |
| Doctor Jeep | 12" | Merciful Release | MR51TX | 1990 | £2.50 | £6 | 3 tracks |
| Dominion | CD-s | Merciful Release | MR43CD | 1988 | £10 | £20 | 3" single |
| First And Last And Always | LP | Merciful Release | MR337L | 1985 | £6 | £15 | gatefold sleeve |
| Floodland | CD | Merciful Release | 2422462 | 1987 | £20 | £40 | ... promo bag set, with video and T-shirt |
| Lucretia My Reflection | CD-s | Merciful Release | MR44CD | 1988 | £2 | £5 | |
| More | CD-s | Merciful Release | MR47CD | 1990 | £2 | £5 | |
| More | CD-s | Merciful Release | MR47CDX | 1990 | £2.50 | £6 | 12" sleeve |
| No Time To Cry | 7" | Merciful Release | MR035 | 1985 | £2 | £5 | |
| No Time To Cry | 12" | Merciful Release | MR035T | 1985 | £2.50 | £6 | |
| Reptile House | 12" | Merciful Release | MR023 | 1983 | £2.50 | £6 | with lyric sheet |
| Temple Of Love | CD-s | Merciful Release | MR53CD | 1992 | £2 | £5 | boxed |
| This Corrosion | CD-s | Merciful Release | MR039CD | 1987 | £2 | £5 | |
| This Corrosion | CD-s | Merciful Release | MR039CD | 1987 | £4 | £10 | no WEA logo on back |
| This Corrosion | 7" | Merciful Release | MR039 | 1987 | £2.50 | £6 | boxed with 3 postcards |
| This Corrosion | 12" | Merciful Release | MR039T | 1987 | £10 | £25 | promo with video |
| Tour Thing | CD | Elektra | | 1991 | £10 | £25 | US promo sampler |
| Walk Away | 7" | Merciful Release | MR033 | 1984 | £2 | £5 | |
| Walk Away | 7" | Merciful Release | MR033 | 1984 | £5 | £10 | with flexi |
| Walk Away | 12" | Merciful Release | MR033T | 1984 | £3 | £8 | with flexi (SAM218) |

## SITTING BULL

| Title | Format | Label | Catalogue | Year | | | Notes |
|---|---|---|---|---|---|---|---|
| Trip Away | LP | CBS | 64697 | 1971 | £5 | £12 | German |

## SITUATION

| Title | Format | Label | Catalogue | Year | | | Notes |
|---|---|---|---|---|---|---|---|
| Situation | 7" | CBS | 202392 | 1966 | £2 | £5 | |

## SIX

| Title | Format | Label | Catalogue | Year | | | Notes |
|---|---|---|---|---|---|---|---|
| Six | LP | London | LTZN15042 | 1957 | £10 | £25 | |
| Six | 10" LP | Columbia | 33C9028 | 1956 | £10 | £25 | |
| View From Jazzbo's Head | LP | London | LTZN15066 | 1957 | £10 | £25 | |

## SIX TEENS

| Title | Format | Label | Catalogue | Year | | | Notes |
|---|---|---|---|---|---|---|---|
| Casual Look | 7" | London | HLU8345 | 1956 | £180 | £300 | best auctioned |

## SIXPENCE

| Title | Format | Label | Catalogue | Year | | | Notes |
|---|---|---|---|---|---|---|---|
| You're The Love | 7" | London | HLJ10124 | 1967 | £2.50 | £6 | |

## SIXTY FOOT DOLLS

| Title | Format | Label | Catalogue | Year | | | Notes |
|---|---|---|---|---|---|---|---|
| Happy Shopper | 7" | Townhill | TIDY001 | 1994 | £6 | £12 | |

## SIXTY-NINE

| Title | Format | Label | Catalogue | Year | | | Notes |
|---|---|---|---|---|---|---|---|
| Circle Of The Crayfish | LP | Philips | 6305164 | 1972 | £5 | £12 | German |
| Live | LP | Philips | 6623046 | 1974 | £6 | £15 | German double |

## SKA CHAMPIONS

| Title | Format | Label | Catalogue | Year | | | Notes |
|---|---|---|---|---|---|---|---|
| My Tears | 7" | Blue Beat | BB305 | 1965 | £6 | £12 | |

## SKA KINGS

| Title | Format | Label | Catalogue | Year | | | Notes |
|---|---|---|---|---|---|---|---|
| Oil In My Lamp | 7" | Atlantic | AT4003 | 1964 | £4 | £8 | |
| Skasville | 7" | Parlophone | R5338 | 1965 | £2 | £5 | |

## SKATALITES

| Title | Format | Label | Catalogue | Year | | | Notes |
|---|---|---|---|---|---|---|---|
| Ball O' Fire | 7" | Island | WI207 | 1965 | £5 | £10 | Linval Sparker B side |
| Beardman Ska | 7" | Island | WI228 | 1965 | £5 | £10 | Bonnie & Rita B side |
| Confucius | LP | Doctor Bird | DLM5000 | 1966 | £50 | £100 | |
| Dick Tracy | 7" | Island | WI226 | 1965 | £5 | £10 | Soulettes B side |
| Dr. Kildare | 7" | Island | WI191 | 1965 | £5 | £10 | |
| Dragon Weapon | 7" | Island | WI175 | 1965 | £5 | £10 | Desmond Dekker B side |
| Guns Of Navarone | 7" | Island | WI168 | 1965 | £5 | £10 | |
| Latin Goes Ska | 7" | Ska Beat | JB177 | 1965 | £5 | £10 | Lord Tanamo B side |
| Ska Authentic | LP | Studio One | SOL9006 | 1967 | £50 | £100 | |
| Timothy | 7" | Ska Beat | JB206 | 1965 | £5 | £10 | King Scratch B side |

## SKATALITES (2)
| | | | | | | |
|---|---|---|---|---|---|---|
| Cos You're The One I Love | 7" | Spark | SRL1034 | 1971 | £2 | £5 |
| Don't Knock It | 7" | Decca | F12743 | 1968 | £1.50 | £4 |

## SKELETAL FAMILY
| | | | | | | |
|---|---|---|---|---|---|---|
| Night | 7" | Red Rhino | RED36 | 1983 | £2 | £5 |
| Trees | 7" | Luggage | RRP00724 | 1983 | £4 | £8 |

## SKI PATROL
| | | | | | | |
|---|---|---|---|---|---|---|
| Agent Orange | 7" | Malicious Damage | MD2 | 1980 | £2 | £5 |

## SKID ROW
A modern band calling itself Skid Row cannot detract from the fact that the name truly belongs to the Irish band with whom the seventeen-year-old Gary Moore made his first recordings.

| | | | | | | | |
|---|---|---|---|---|---|---|---|
| 34 Hours | LP | CBS | 64411 | 1971 | £4 | £10 | |
| New Places, Old Faces | 7" | Song | SO0002 | 1969 | £15 | £30 | Irish |
| Night Of The Warm Witch | 7" | CBS | 7181 | 1971 | £1.50 | £4 | |
| Sandie's Gone | 7" | CBS | 4893 | 1970 | £1.50 | £4 | |
| Saturday Morning Man | 7" | Song | SO0003 | 1969 | £15 | £30 | Irish |
| Skid | LP | CBS | 63965 | 1970 | £4 | £10 | |

## SKID ROW (2)
| | | | | | | | |
|---|---|---|---|---|---|---|---|
| Eighteen And Life | 7" | Atlantic | A8883P | 1990 | £1.50 | £4 | shaped picture disc |

## SKIDMORE, ALAN
| | | | | | | | |
|---|---|---|---|---|---|---|---|
| Jazz In Britain 1968–69 | LP | Decca | ECS2114 | 1972 | £10 | £25 | with other artists |
| Morning Rise | LP | Ego | 4006 | 1977 | £6 | £15 | |
| Once Upon A Time | LP | Nova | SDN11 | 1969 | £20 | £40 | |
| TCB | LP | Philips | 6308041 | 1970 | £20 | £40 | |

## SKIFS, BJORN
| | | | | | | |
|---|---|---|---|---|---|---|
| Haunted By A Dream | 7" | EMI | EMI5172 | 1981 | £2 | £5 |

## SKILLETS
| | | | | | | |
|---|---|---|---|---|---|---|
| Both Sides Now | LP | Panatonic | PAN6303 | 1970 | £15 | £30 |

## SKIN
| | | | | | | | |
|---|---|---|---|---|---|---|---|
| Skin | CD | Parlophone | 724383117727 | 1994 | £6 | £15 | double |

## SKIN ALLEY
| | | | | | | |
|---|---|---|---|---|---|---|
| Skin Alley | LP | CBS | 63847 | 1969 | £25 | £50 |
| Skintight | LP | Transatlantic | TRA273 | 1973 | £5 | £12 |
| To Pagham & Beyond | LP | CBS | 64140 | 1970 | £8 | £20 |
| Two Quid Deal | LP | Transatlantic | TRA260 | 1972 | £5 | £12 |

## SKIN, FLESH & BONES
| | | | | | | |
|---|---|---|---|---|---|---|
| Butter Te Fish | 7" | Pyramid | PYR7014 | 1974 | £1.50 | £4 |

## SKINNER, JIMMIE
| | | | | | | | |
|---|---|---|---|---|---|---|---|
| Country Singer | LP | Decca | DL(7)4132 | 1961 | £6 | £15 | US |
| John Wesley Hardin | 7" | Mercury | AMT1062 | 1959 | £1.50 | £4 | |
| Kentucky Colonel Vol. 1 | 7" EP | London | REB1421 | 1964 | £2.50 | £6 | |
| Kentucky Colonel Vol. 2 | 7" EP | London | REB1422 | 1964 | £2.50 | £6 | |
| Kentucky Colonel Vol. 3 | 7" EP | London | REB1423 | 1964 | £2.50 | £6 | |
| Songs That Make The Juke Box Play | LP | Mercury | MG20352 | 1957 | £8 | £20 | US |
| Walking My Blues Away | 7" | Mercury | AMT1030 | 1959 | £1.50 | £4 | |

## SKIP & FLIP
| | | | | | | |
|---|---|---|---|---|---|---|
| Cherry Pie | 7" | Top Rank | JAR358 | 1960 | £2 | £5 |
| Fancy Nancy | 7" | Top Rank | JAR248 | 1959 | £1.50 | £4 |
| It Was I | 7" | Top Rank | JAR156 | 1959 | £2 | £5 |

## SKIP & THE CREATIONS
| | | | | | | | |
|---|---|---|---|---|---|---|---|
| Mobam | LP | Justice | | 196– | £100 | £200 | US |

## SKIP BIFFERTY
The album made by Skip Bifferty is something of a forgotten sixties classic, to file next to the debut albums by Family and Traffic. The group never managed to build on its encouraging start, however. Four years later, the follow-up was finally made and issued under the name of Bell and Arc. Sadly, by this time, much of the group's inspiration seemed to have evaporated.

| | | | | | | | |
|---|---|---|---|---|---|---|---|
| Happy Land | 7" | RCA | RCA1648 | 1967 | £7.50 | £15 | |
| Man In Black | 7" | RCA | RCA1720 | 1968 | £7.50 | £15 | |
| On Love | 7" | RCA | RCA1621 | 1967 | £7.50 | £15 | |
| Skip Bifferty | LP | RCA | RD/SF7941 | 1968 | £37.50 | £75 | black label |
| Skip Bifferty | LP | RCA | RD/SF7941 | 1968 | £25 | £50 | orange label |

## SKREWDRIVER
| | | | | | | | |
|---|---|---|---|---|---|---|---|
| All Skrewed Up | LP | Chiswick | CH3 | 1977 | £4 | £10 | plays at 45rpm |
| Anti-Social | 7" | Chiswick | NS18 | 1977 | £2 | £5 | picture sleeve |
| Back With A Bang | 12" | Skrewdriver | SKREW1T | 1982 | £4 | £10 | |
| Built Up | 7" | TJM | TJM4 | 1980 | £6 | £12 | |
| Hards | 7" | White Noise | WN3 | 1983 | £7.50 | £15 | |
| Streetfight | 7" | Chiswick | NS28 | 1978 | £20 | £40 | test pressing |
| Voice Of Britain | 7" | White Noise | WN2 | 1983 | £6 | £12 | |

| Title | Format | Label | Cat No | Year | Price | Price | Notes |
|---|---|---|---|---|---|---|---|
| White Power | 7" | White Noise | WN1 | 1983 | £7.50 | £15 | |
| You're So Dumb | 7" | Chiswick | S11 | 1977 | £2 | £5 | picture sleeve |

## SKULLFLOWER

| Title | Format | Label | Cat No | Year | Price | Price | Notes |
|---|---|---|---|---|---|---|---|
| In The Bottomless Pit | 7" | Shock | SX001 | 1989 | £5 | £10 | |
| Rotten Sun | 7" | Toe Jam | | 1990 | £1.50 | £4 | |
| Xaman | 7" | Shock | SX008 | 1989 | £2.50 | £6 | |

## SKULLSNAPS

| Title | Format | Label | Cat No | Year | Price | Price | Notes |
|---|---|---|---|---|---|---|---|
| My Hang Up Is You | 7" | GSF | GSZ7 | 1973 | £4 | £8 | |

## SKUNK ANANSIE

| Title | Format | Label | Cat No | Year | Price | Price | Notes |
|---|---|---|---|---|---|---|---|
| Little Baby Swastikkka | 7" | One Little Indian | TPLP55PROMO | 1994 | £7.50 | £15 | promo |

## SKUNKS

| Title | Format | Label | Cat No | Year | Price | Price | Notes |
|---|---|---|---|---|---|---|---|
| Gettin' Started | LP | Teen Town | 101 | 1967 | £8 | £20 | US |

## SKY, PATRICK

| Title | Format | Label | Cat No | Year | Price | Price | Notes |
|---|---|---|---|---|---|---|---|
| Harvest Of Gentle Clang | LP | Vanguard | SVRL19054 | 1970 | £5 | £12 | |
| Patrick Sky | LP | Vanguard | VSD79179 | 1965 | £5 | £12 | |
| Photographs | LP | Verve | FTS3079 | 1969 | £5 | £12 | US |
| Reality Is Bad Enough | LP | Verve | FTS3052 | 1968 | £6 | £15 | US |

## SKYBIRD

| Title | Format | Label | Cat No | Year | Price | Price | Notes |
|---|---|---|---|---|---|---|---|
| Summer Of '73 | LP | Holyground | HGS118 | 1973 | £20 | £40 | |

## SKYLINERS

| Title | Format | Label | Cat No | Year | Price | Price | Notes |
|---|---|---|---|---|---|---|---|
| I'll Close My Eyes | 7" | Pye | 7N25091 | 1961 | £4 | £8 | |
| It Happened Today | 7" | London | HLU8971 | 1959 | £12.50 | £25 | |
| Pennies From Heaven | 7" | Polydor | NH66951 | 1960 | £4 | £8 | |
| Since I Don't Have You | LP | Original Sound | (S)8873 | 1963 | £15 | £30 | US |
| Since I Don't Have You | 7" | London | HLB8829 | 1959 | £75 | £150 | |
| Skyliners | LP | Calico | LP3000 | 1959 | £75 | £150 | US |
| This I Swear | 7" | London | HLU8924 | 1959 | £25 | £50 | |

## SKYLINERS (2)

| Title | Format | Label | Cat No | Year | Price | Price | Notes |
|---|---|---|---|---|---|---|---|
| | 7" | Studio 36 | | 1964 | £30 | £60 | |

## SLACK, FREDDIE

| Title | Format | Label | Cat No | Year | Price | Price | Notes |
|---|---|---|---|---|---|---|---|
| Boogie Woogie | 10" LP | Capitol | LC6529 | 1951 | £10 | £25 | |
| Boogie Woogie On The 88 | 10" LP | Wing | MGW60003 | | £8 | £20 | US |
| Boogie Woogie On The 88 | 10" LP | Wing | MGW60003 | 195– | £10 | £25 | US |

## SLADE

| Title | Format | Label | Cat No | Year | Price | Price | Notes |
|---|---|---|---|---|---|---|---|
| Alive At Reading '80 | 7" | Cheapskate | CHEAP5 | 1980 | £1.50 | £4 | |
| Alive Vol. 2 | LP | Barn | 2314106 | 1978 | £6 | £15 | |
| All Join Hands | 12" | RCA | RCAT455 | 1984 | £4 | £10 | |
| Bangin' Man | 7" | Polydor | 2058492 | 1974 | £10 | £20 | picture sleeve |
| Burning In The Heat Of Love | 7" | Barn | 2014106 | 1977 | £5 | £10 | |
| Cum On Feel The Noize | 12" | Polydor | POSPX399 | 1981 | £2.50 | £6 | |
| Do You Believe In Miracles | 7" | RCA | PB40449 | 1985 | £4 | £8 | double |
| Do You Believe In Miracles | 12" | RCA | PT40450D | 1985 | £4 | £10 | double |
| Do You Believe In Miracles | 12" | RCA | RCAPT40449D | 1985 | £3 | £8 | double |
| Far Far Away | 7" | Lyntone | LYN3156/7 | 1975 | £2.50 | £6 | flexi |
| Get Down And Get With It | 7" | Polydor | 2058112 | 1971 | £2 | £5 | |
| Ginny Ginny | 7" | Barn | 002 | 1979 | £10 | £20 | black vinyl promo |
| Ginny Ginny | 7" | Barn | 002 | 1979 | £4 | £8 | yellow vinyl |
| Hear Me Calling | 7" | Polydor | 2814008 | 1970 | £25 | £50 | promo |
| Hokey Cokey | 7" | Speed | SPEED201P | 1982 | £2 | £5 | picture disc |
| How Does It Feel | CD-s | Counterpoint | CDEP12C | 1988 | £2 | £5 | with tracks by Wizzard picture sleeve |
| In For A Penny | 7" | Polydor | 2058663 | 1975 | £2 | £5 | |
| Know Who You Are | 7" | Polydor | 2058054 | 1970 | £25 | £50 | |
| Knuckle Sandwich | 7" | Cheapskate | CHEAP24 | 1981 | £1.50 | £4 | |
| Let's Dance (1988 Remix) | CD-s | Cheapskate | BOYZCD3 | 1988 | £2 | £5 | 3" single |
| Merry Xmas Everybody | CD-s | Receiver | CDBOYZ4 | 1989 | £2 | £5 | |
| Merry Xmas Everybody | 7" | Cheapskate | CHEAP11 | 1980 | £2 | £5 | picture sleeve |
| Merry Xmas Everybody | 7" | Polydor | 2058422 | 1973 | £10 | £20 | picture sleeve |
| My Baby Left Me/That's Alright Mama | 7" | Barn | 2014114 | 1977 | £2.50 | £6 | picture sleeve |
| Myzsterious Mizster Jones | 7" | RCA | PB40027 | 1985 | £2 | £5 | picture disc |
| Night Starvation | 7" | S.O.T.B. | SUPER3 | 1980 | £10 | £20 | demo |
| Okey Cokey | 7" | Barn | 011 | 1979 | £2.50 | £6 | |
| Okey Cokey | 7" | Speed | SPEED201 | 1982 | £2.50 | £6 | no picture sleeve |
| Return To Base | LP | Barn | NARB003 | 1979 | £10 | £25 | |
| Rock 'n' Roll | 7" | Barn | 2014127 | 1978 | £4 | £8 | |
| Ruby Red | 7" | RCA | RCA191 | 1982 | £2.50 | £6 | |
| Ruby Red | 7" | RCA | RCAD191 | 1982 | £2 | £5 | double |
| Shape Of Things To Come | 7" | Fontana | TF1079 | 1970 | £20 | £40 | |
| Sign Of The Times | 7" | Barn | 010 | 1979 | £5 | £10 | |
| Six Of The Best | 12" | S.O.T.B. | SUPER453 | 1980 | £3 | £8 | |
| Slade Talk To 19 Readers | 7" | Lyntone | LYN2797 | 1973 | £2 | £5 | flexi |
| Slade Talk To Melanie Readers | 7" | Lyntone | LYN2645 | 1973 | £2 | £5 | flexi |
| Slade Talk To Melanie/19 Readers | 7" | Lyntone | LYN2645/2797 | 1975 | £4 | £8 | flexi |
| Still The Same | 7" | RCA | PB41147 | 1987 | £2.50 | £6 | double |
| Thanks For The Memory | 7" | Polydor | 2058585 | 1975 | £10 | £20 | promo, different lyrics |
| We'll Bring The House Down | 7" | Cheapskate | CHEAP16 | 1981 | £1.50 | £4 | |
| Whatever Happened To Slade | LP | Barn | 2314103 | 1977 | £6 | £15 | |

| | | | | | | | | |
|---|---|---|---|---|---|---|---|---|
| Wheels Ain't Comin' Down | 7" | Cheapskate | CHEAP21 | 1981 | £1.50 | £4 | |
| Whole World's Going Crazy | 7" | Polydor | SFI122 | 1972 | £2 | £5 | ...flexi, Mike Hugg B side |
| Wild Winds Are Blowing | 7" | Fontana | TF1056 | 1969 | £20 | £40 | |
| You Boyz Make Big Noize | 7" | Cheapskate | BOYZ1 | 1987 | £2 | £5 | |

## SLADE, PRENTIS
| | | | | | | | |
|---|---|---|---|---|---|---|---|
| I Can Tell | 7" | Parlophone | R4850 | 1961 | £1.50 | £4 | |

## SLAM CREEPERS
| | | | | | | | |
|---|---|---|---|---|---|---|---|
| Saturday | 7" | Olga | OLE009 | 1968 | £5 | £10 | |

## SLAPP HAPPY
| | | | | | | | |
|---|---|---|---|---|---|---|---|
| Acnalbasac Noom | LP | Recommended | RRFIVE | 1980 | £5 | £12 | ... 2 different covers |
| Casablanca Moon | 7" | Virgin | VS105 | 1974 | £1.50 | £4 | |
| Desperate Straights | LP | Virgin | V2024 | 1974 | £4 | £10 | ..... with Henry Cow |
| Johnny's Dead | 7" | Virgin | VS124 | 1975 | £2 | £5 | .......... picture sleeve |
| Slapp Happy | LP | Virgin | V2014 | 1974 | £4 | £10 | |
| Sort Of | LP | Polydor | 2310204 | 1972 | £50 | £100 | .............. with insert |

## SLAUGHTER & THE DOGS
| | | | | | | | |
|---|---|---|---|---|---|---|---|
| Do It Dog Style | LP | Decca | SKL5292 | 1978 | £6 | £15 | |

## SLAUGHTER JOE
| | | | | | | | |
|---|---|---|---|---|---|---|---|
| I'll Follow You Down | 7" | Creation | CRE019 | 1985 | £2.50 | £6 | |
| I'll Follow You Down | 12" | Creation | CRET019 | 1985 | £2.50 | £6 | |

## SLAY, FRANK ORCHESTRA
| | | | | | | | |
|---|---|---|---|---|---|---|---|
| Flying Circle | 7" | Top Rank | JAR599 | 1962 | £1.50 | £4 | |

## SLAYER
| | | | | | | | |
|---|---|---|---|---|---|---|---|
| Criminally Insane | 7" | London | LON133 | 1987 | £5 | £10 | ..cross sleeve, red vinyl |
| Decade Of Aggression | CD-s | Def American | 226792 | 1991 | £20 | £40 | ... US metal pack |
| Haunting The Chapel | CD-s | Road Runner | RR24442 | 1989 | £2 | £5 | |
| Seasons In The Abyss | CD-s | Def American | DEFAC9 | 1991 | £2 | £5 | |

## SLEDGE, F.
| | | | | | | | |
|---|---|---|---|---|---|---|---|
| Red Eye Girl | 7" | Blue Beat | BB386 | 1967 | £6 | £12 | |

## SLEDGE, PERCY
| | | | | | | | |
|---|---|---|---|---|---|---|---|
| Any Day Now | 7" | Atlantic | 584264 | 1969 | £1.50 | £4 | |
| Baby Help Me | 7" | Atlantic | 584080 | 1967 | £1.50 | £4 | |
| Best Of Percy Sledge | LP | Atlantic | 587/588153 | 1969 | £4 | £10 | |
| Come Softly To Me | 7" | Atlantic | 584225 | 1968 | £1.50 | £4 | |
| Heart Of A Child | 7" | Atlantic | 584055 | 1966 | £1.50 | £4 | |
| It Tears Me Up | 7" | Atlantic | 584071 | 1967 | £1.50 | £4 | |
| Kind Woman | 7" | Atlantic | 584286 | 1969 | £1.50 | £4 | |
| Out Of Left Field | 7" | Atlantic | 584108 | 1967 | £1.50 | £4 | |
| Percy Sledge Way | LP | Atlantic | 587/588081 | 1967 | £5 | £12 | |
| Pledging My Love | 7" | Atlantic | 584140 | 1967 | £1.50 | £4 | |
| Take Time To Know Her | LP | Atlantic | SD8180 | 1968 | £5 | £12 | US |
| Take Time To Love Her | 7" | Atlantic | 584177 | 1968 | £1.50 | £4 | |
| True Love Travels On A Gravel Road | 7" | Atlantic | 584300 | 1969 | £1.50 | £4 | |
| Warm And Tender Love | 7" | Atlantic | 584034 | 1966 | £1.50 | £4 | |
| Warm And Tender Soul | LP | Atlantic | 587/588048 | 1967 | £5 | £12 | |
| When A Man Loves A Woman | LP | Atlantic | 587/588105 | 1968 | £5 | £12 | |
| When A Man Loves A Woman | CD-s | Intertape | 500068 | 1987 | £2 | £5 | |
| When A Man Loves A Woman | 7" | Atlantic | 584001 | 1966 | £1.50 | £4 | |

## SLEDGEHAMMER
| | | | | | | | |
|---|---|---|---|---|---|---|---|
| In The Queue | 7" | Illuminated | ILL33 | 1985 | £5 | £10 | ..... shaped picture disc |
| Sledgehammer | 7" | Slammer | SRTS79/CUS395 | 1979 | £2 | £5 | |

## SLEEPER
| | | | | | | | |
|---|---|---|---|---|---|---|---|
| Alice In Vain | CD-s | Indolent | SLEEP001CD | 1993 | £2.50 | £6 | |
| Bucket And Spade | 7" | Indolent | SLEEP004 | 1994 | £5 | £10 | ..............green vinyl |
| Bucket And Spade | 7" | Indolent | SLEEP004CD | 1994 | £2.50 | £6 | |

## SLEEPWALKERS
| | | | | | | | |
|---|---|---|---|---|---|---|---|
| Sleepwalk | 7" | Parlophone | R4580 | 1959 | £1.50 | £4 | |

## SLEEPY
| | | | | | | | |
|---|---|---|---|---|---|---|---|
| Love's Immortal Fire | 7" | CBS | 3592 | 1968 | £5 | £10 | |
| Rosie Can't Fly | 7" | CBS | 3838 | 1968 | £5 | £10 | |

## SLENDER PLENTY
| | | | | | | | |
|---|---|---|---|---|---|---|---|
| Silver Tree Top School For Boys | 7" | Polydor | 56189 | 1967 | £7.50 | £15 | |

## SLEVIN, JIMI
| | | | | | | | |
|---|---|---|---|---|---|---|---|
| Freeflight | LP | Claddagh | CCF7 | 1982 | £37.50 | £75 | |

## SLICK, GRACE
| | | | | | | | |
|---|---|---|---|---|---|---|---|
| And Through The Hoop | LP | RCA | DJL13544 | 1979 | £5 | £12 | ...US interview promo |
| Welcome To The Wrecking Ball | LP | RCA | DJL13922 | 1981 | £5 | £12 | ...US interview promo |

## SLICKEE BOYS
| | | | | | | | |
|---|---|---|---|---|---|---|---|
| Separated Vegetables | LP | Dacoit | 1001 | 1977 | £50 | £100 | US |
| Separated Vegetables | LP | Limp | 10003 | 1980 | £37.50 | £75 | US |

## SLICKERS

| | | | | | | | |
|---|---|---|---|---|---|---|---|
| Frying Pan | 7" | Blue Cat | BS154 | 1969 | £2.50 | £6 | Rarfield Williams B side |
| Johnny Too Bad | 7" | Dynamic | DYN406 | 1970 | £1.50 | £4 | Roland Alphonso B side |
| Man Beware | 7" | Amalgamated | AMG852 | 1969 | £2.50 | £6 | |
| Money Reaper | 7" | Amalgamated | AMG866 | 1969 | £2.50 | £6 | |
| Nana | 7" | Blue Cat | BS134 | 1968 | £4 | £8 | Martin Riley B side |
| Run Fattie | 7" | Trojan | TR7719 | 1969 | £1.50 | £4 | |
| Wala Wala | 7" | Blue Cat | BS133 | 1968 | £4 | £8 | Lester Sterling B side |

## SLITS

| | | | | | | | |
|---|---|---|---|---|---|---|---|
| Peel Sessions | CD-s | Strange Fruit | SFPMACD207 | 1989 | £2 | £5 | |
| Return Of The Giant Slits | LP | CBS | 85269 | 1981 | £4 | £10 | with 7" (XPS125) |

## SLOAN, P. F.

| | | | | | | | |
|---|---|---|---|---|---|---|---|
| 12 More Times | LP | Dunhill | D50007 | 1966 | £4 | £10 | US |
| Man Behind The Red Balloon | 7" EP | RCA | 86903 | 1966 | £2.50 | £6 | French |
| Sins Of The Family | 7" EP | RCA | 86901 | 1965 | £2.50 | £6 | French |
| Songs Of Our Times | LP | Dunhill | D50004 | 1965 | £4 | £10 | US |

## SLOAN, SAMMI

| | | | | | | | |
|---|---|---|---|---|---|---|---|
| Yes I Would | 7" | Columbia | DB8480 | 1968 | £2 | £5 | |

## SLOWDIVE

| | | | | | | | |
|---|---|---|---|---|---|---|---|
| Catch The Breeze | CD-s | Creation | CRESCD112 | 1991 | £2 | £5 | |
| Morningrise | CD-s | Creation | CRESCD098 | 1991 | £2 | £5 | |
| Slowdive | CD-s | Creation | CRESCD93 | 1990 | £2 | £5 | |
| Souvlaki | CD | Creation | CRECD139/ CRECDX101 | 1993 | £6 | £15 | double |

## SLY & THE FAMILY STONE

| | | | | | | | |
|---|---|---|---|---|---|---|---|
| Dance To The Music | LP | Direction | 863412 | 1968 | £6 | £15 | |
| Dance To The Music | 7" | Columbia | DB8369 | 1968 | £10 | £20 | |
| Dance To The Music | 7" | Direction | 583568 | 1968 | £1.50 | £4 | |
| Everyday People | 7" | Direction | 583938 | 1969 | £1.50 | £4 | |
| Family Affair | 7" | Epic | EPC1148 | 1973 | £2 | £5 | picture sleeve |
| Family Affair | 7" | Epic | EPC7632 | 1971 | £1.50 | £4 | |
| Fresh | LP | Epic | EPC69039 | 1973 | £4 | £10 | |
| Greatest Hits | LP | CBS | Q69002 | 1973 | £5 | £12 | quad |
| Greatest Hits | LP | Epic | EPC69002 | 1970 | £4 | £10 | |
| High Energy | LP | Epic | EPC22004 | 1975 | £6 | £15 | double |
| High On You | LP | Epic | PEQ33835 | 1975 | £4 | £10 | US quad |
| Hot Fun In The Summertime | 7" | Direction | 584471 | 1969 | £1.50 | £4 | |
| I Want To Take You Higher | 7" | CBS | 5054 | 1970 | £1.50 | £4 | |
| Life | LP | Epic | BN26397 | 1968 | £6 | £15 | US |
| M'Lady | LP | Direction | 863461 | 1968 | £6 | £15 | |
| M'Lady | 7" | Direction | 583707 | 1968 | £1.50 | £4 | |
| Running Away | 7" | Epic | EPC7810 | 1972 | £1.50 | £4 | |
| Small Talk | LP | Epic | EPC69070 | 1974 | £4 | £10 | |
| Small Talk | LP | Epic | PEQ32930 | 1974 | £4 | £10 | US quad |
| Stand | LP | Direction | 863655 | 1969 | £6 | £15 | |
| Stand | 7" | Direction | 584279 | 1969 | £1.50 | £4 | |
| Thank You | 7" | Direction | 584782 | 1970 | £1.50 | £4 | |
| There's A Riot Going On | LP | Epic | EPC64613 | 1971 | £5 | £12 | |
| Whole New Thing | LP | Epic | LN24/BN26324 | 1967 | £6 | £15 | US |

## SMACK

| | | | | | | | |
|---|---|---|---|---|---|---|---|
| Smack | LP | Audio House | no number | 1967 | £700 | £1000 | US |

## SMALL, JOAN

| | | | | | | | |
|---|---|---|---|---|---|---|---|
| You Can't Say I Love You | 7" | Parlophone | R4269 | 1957 | £2 | £5 | |

## SMALL, KAREN

| | | | | | | | |
|---|---|---|---|---|---|---|---|
| To Get You Back Again | 7" | Vocalion | VP9281 | 1966 | £1.50 | £4 | |

## SMALL FACES

The music of the Small Faces seems to have grown in stature over the years, a fact that is reflected amongst collectors by substantial recent gains in value of the group's albums. As the only genuine mods to achieve success with their own music, the Small Faces stayed slightly apart from the rock mainstream in the sixties − a factor which stood them in good stead when British beat evolved into psychedelia. 'Itchycoo Park' is a great psychedelic single (with the first recorded use of phasing), at least in part because the Small Faces were making fun of the style, even while delivering a masterful example of it. The chaotic state of the group's reissue catalogue is a reflection of the fact that the Small Faces switched from Decca to Immediate half way through their career. Though too late to benefit the sadly missed Steve Marriott (who died in a house fire in 1991), drummer Kenny Jones won a lengthy legal battle in 1996 to retrieve substantial unpaid royalties.

| | | | | | | | |
|---|---|---|---|---|---|---|---|
| | 7" | Immediate | AS1 | 1967 | £15 | £30 | promo |
| Afterglow Of Your Love | 7" | Immediate | IM077 | 1969 | £1.50 | £4 | |
| Afterglow Of Your Love | 7" | Immediate | IM077 | 1969 | £15 | £30 | demo with demo mix B side |
| All Or Nothing | 7" EP | Decca | 457123 | 1966 | £25 | £50 | French |
| All Or Nothing | 7" | Decca | F12470 | 1966 | £1.50 | £4 | |
| Autumn Stone | LP | Immediate | IMA101/2 | 1969 | £37.50 | £75 | double |
| From The Beginning | LP | Decca | LK4879 | 1967 | £37.50 | £75 | |
| Here Come The Nice | 7" EP | Columbia | ESRF1876 | 1967 | £25 | £50 | French |
| Here Comes The Nice | 7" | Immediate | IM050 | 1967 | £1.50 | £4 | |
| Hey Girl | 7" | Decca | F12393 | 1966 | £1.50 | £4 | |

| Title | Format | Label | Cat. No. | Year | Price | Price | Notes |
|---|---|---|---|---|---|---|---|
| I Can't Make It | 7" EP | Decca | 457144 | 1967 | £25 | £50 | French |
| I Can't Make It | 7" | Decca | F12565 | 1967 | £1.50 | £4 | |
| I've Got Mine | 7" | Decca | F12276 | 1965 | £4 | £8 | |
| In Memoriam | LP | Immediate | IMSP022 | 1969 | £150 | £250 | |
| In Memoriam | LP | Immediate | IMSP022 | 1970 | £20 | £40 | German |
| Itchycoo Park | 7" EP | Columbia | ESRF1882 | 1967 | £25 | £50 | French |
| Itchycoo Park | 7" | Immediate | IM057 | 1967 | £1.50 | £4 | |
| Lazy Sunday | 7" | Immediate | IM064 | 1968 | £1.50 | £4 | |
| My Mind's Eye | 7" EP | Decca | 457133 | 1967 | £25 | £50 | French |
| My Mind's Eye | 7" | Decca | F12500 | 1967 | £1.50 | £4 | |
| My Mind's Eye | 7" | Decca | F12500 | 1966 | £20 | £40 | demo mix, matrix TI-IC |
| Ogden's Nut Gone Flake | LP | Immediate | IMLP/IMSP012 | 1967 | £37.50 | £75 | round cover |
| Ogden's Nut Gone Flake | CD | Castle | CLACT016 | 1991 | £8 | £20 | round tin |
| Patterns | 7" | Decca | F12619 | 1967 | £7.50 | £15 | |
| Sha-La-La-La-Lee | 7" EP | Decca | 457106 | 1966 | £25 | £50 | French |
| Sha-La-La-La-Lee | 7" | Decca | F12317 | 1966 | £1.50 | £4 | |
| Small Faces | LP | Decca | LK4790 | 1966 | £30 | £60 | |
| Small Faces | LP | Immediate | IMLP/IMSP008 | 1967 | £75 | £150 | |
| Small Faces EP | CD-s | Special Edition | CD39 | 1988 | £2 | £5 | |
| There Are But Four Small Faces | LP | Immediate | Z1252002 | 1968 | £25 | £50 | US |
| Tin Soldier | 7" | Immediate | IM062 | 1967 | £1.50 | £4 | |
| Tin Soldier | 7" | Immediate | IM062 | 1967 | £7.50 | £15 | picture sleeve |
| Universal | 7" | Immediate | IM069 | 1968 | £1.50 | £4 | |
| Whatcha Gonna Do About It | 7" EP | Decca | 457091 | 1965 | £25 | £50 | French |
| Whatcha Gonna Do About it | 7" | Decca | F12208 | 1965 | £1.50 | £4 | |

## SMALL HOURS
| Title | Format | Label | Cat. No. | Year | Price | Price | Notes |
|---|---|---|---|---|---|---|---|
| Kid | 7" | Automatic | K17708 | 1980 | £10 | £20 | |
| Kid | 10" | Automatic | K17708X | 1980 | £6 | £15 | |

## SMALL WORLD
| Title | Format | Label | Cat. No. | Year | Price | Price | Notes |
|---|---|---|---|---|---|---|---|
| Love Is Dead | 7" | Whaam! | WHAAM3 | 1982 | £6 | £12 | |

## SMASH
| Title | Format | Label | Cat. No. | Year | Price | Price | Notes |
|---|---|---|---|---|---|---|---|
| Vanguardia Y Pureza Del Flamenco | LP | Serdisco | 30112047 | 1989 | £10 | £25 | Spanish |
| We Come To Smash | LP | Philips | 4328044 | 1973 | £62.50 | £125 | Spanish |

## SMASHING PUMPKINS
| Title | Format | Label | Cat. No. | Year | Price | Price | Notes |
|---|---|---|---|---|---|---|---|
| Screen Raver | CD | | | 1995 | £10 | £25 | promo only Apple Mac CD ROM |

## SMILE
Smile included Brian May and Roger Taylor who, not long after the release of the group's only single, left in order to help found Queen. Red vinyl copies of the single, incidentally, are counterfeits.

| Title | Format | Label | Cat. No. | Year | Price | Price | Notes |
|---|---|---|---|---|---|---|---|
| Earth | 7" | Mercury | 72977 | 1969 | £50 | £100 | US, promo only (stamped matrix no.) |
| Smile | LP | Mercury | 18PP1 | 1982 | £20 | £40 | Japanese |

## SMILIN' JOE
| Title | Format | Label | Cat. No. | Year | Price | Price | Notes |
|---|---|---|---|---|---|---|---|
| ABC's | 78 | London | HL8106 | 1954 | £25 | £50 | |

## SMITH, ADAM
| Title | Format | Label | Cat. No. | Year | Price | Price | Notes |
|---|---|---|---|---|---|---|---|
| I Wonder Why | 7" | Island | WI057 | 1962 | £5 | £10 | |

## SMITH, ARTHUR 'GUITAR BOOGIE'
| Title | Format | Label | Cat. No. | Year | Price | Price | Notes |
|---|---|---|---|---|---|---|---|
| Arthur 'Guitar Boogie' Smith And His Crackerjacks | 7" EP | MGM | MGMEP510 | 1954 | £5 | £10 | |
| Arthur 'Guitar Boogie' Smith And His Crackerjacks | 7" EP | MGM | MGMEP695 | 1959 | £6 | £12 | |
| Express Boogie | 7" | MGM | SP1039 | 1953 | £6 | £12 | |
| Fingers On Fire | LP | MGM | E3525 | 1958 | £8 | £20 | US |
| Fingers On Fire | 10" LP | MGM | D111 | 1953 | £10 | £25 | |
| Five String Banjo Boogie | 7" | MGM | SP1021 | 1953 | £6 | £12 | |
| Foolish Questions | 10" LP | MGM | D131 | 1954 | £10 | £25 | |
| Guitar Boogie | 7" | MGM | SP1008 | 1953 | £10 | £20 | |
| Hi Lo Boogie | 7" | MGM | SP1122 | 1955 | £6 | £12 | |
| I Get So Lonely | 7" | MGM | SP1096 | 1954 | £6 | £12 | |
| Mister Guitar | 7" EP | Stateside | SE1005 | 1963 | £4 | £8 | |
| Original Guitar Boogie | LP | Dot | DLP5600 | 1964 | £4 | £10 | US |
| Red Headed Stranger | 7" | MGM | SP1110 | 1954 | £6 | £12 | |
| Specials | 10" LP | MGM | E3301 | 195– | £10 | £25 | US |

## SMITH, BARRY
| Title | Format | Label | Cat. No. | Year | Price | Price | Notes |
|---|---|---|---|---|---|---|---|
| Hold On To It | 7" | People | PEO119 | 1975 | £5 | £10 | |

## SMITH, BEASLEY
| Title | Format | Label | Cat. No. | Year | Price | Price | Notes |
|---|---|---|---|---|---|---|---|
| Goodnight Sweet Dreams | 7" | London | HLD8235 | 1956 | £10 | £20 | |
| My Foolish Heart | 7" | London | HLD8273 | 1956 | £10 | £20 | |

## SMITH, BESSIE
| Title | Format | Label | Cat. No. | Year | Price | Price | Notes |
|---|---|---|---|---|---|---|---|
| Any Woman's Blues | LP | CBS | 66262 | 1971 | £5 | £12 | double |
| Bessie Smith | 7" EP | Philips | BBE12360 | 1960 | £2 | £5 | |
| Bessie Smith Story Vol. 1 | LP | CBS | BPG62377 | 1966 | £5 | £12 | |
| Bessie Smith Story Vol. 1 | LP | Philips | BBL7019 | 1955 | £8 | £20 | |
| Bessie Smith Story Vol. 2 | LP | CBS | BPG62378 | 1966 | £5 | £12 | |

| | | | | | | |
|---|---|---|---|---|---|---|
| Bessie Smith Story Vol. 2 | LP | Philips | BBL7020 | 1955 £8 | £20 | |
| Bessie Smith Story Vol. 3 | LP | CBS | BPG62379 | 1966 £5 | £12 | |
| Bessie Smith Story Vol. 3 | LP | Philips | BBL7042 | 1955 £8 | £20 | |
| Bessie Smith Story Vol. 4 | LP | CBS | BPG62380 | 1966 £5 | £12 | |
| Bessie Smith Story Vol. 4 | LP | Philips | BBL7049 | 1955 £8 | £20 | |
| Bessie's Blues | LP | Philips | BBL7513 | 1962 £6 | £15 | |
| Empress | LP | CBS | 66264 | 1971 £5 | £12 | double |
| Empress Of The Blues | 7" EP. | Philips | BBE12202 | 1958 £2.50 | £6 | |
| Empress Of The Blues No. 2 | 7" EP. | Philips | BBE12231 | 1959 £2.50 | £6 | |
| Empress Of The Blues No. 3 | 7" EP. | Philips | BBE12233 | 1959 £2.50 | £6 | |
| Empty Bed Blues | LP | CBS | 66273 | 1971 £5 | £12 | double |
| Nobody's Blues But Mine | LP | CBS | 67232 | 1972 £5 | £12 | double |
| World's Greatest Blues Singer | LP | CBS | 66258 | 1971 £5 | £12 | double |

## SMITH, BETTY

| | | | | | | |
|---|---|---|---|---|---|---|
| Begin The Beguine | 7" | Decca | F11071 | 1958 £1.50 | £4 | |
| Betty Smith Quintet | 7" EP. | Decca | DFE6446 | 1957 £5 | £10 | |
| Betty's Blues | 7" | Decca | F11031 | 1958 £2 | £5 | |
| Bewitched | 7" | Decca | F10986 | 1958 £2 | £5 | |
| Song Of India | 7" | Decca | F11124 | 1959 £1.50 | £4 | |
| Sweet Georgia Brown | 7" | Tempo | A163 | 1957 £6 | £12 | |
| There's A Blue Ridge Mountain | 7" | Tempo | A162 | 1957 £4 | £8 | |

## SMITH, BOB

| | | | | | | |
|---|---|---|---|---|---|---|
| Visit | LP | Kent | KST551 | 1969 £37.50 | £75 | US |

## SMITH, BUSTER

| | | | | | | |
|---|---|---|---|---|---|---|
| Legendary Buster Smith | LP | London | LTZK15206 | 1960 £4 | £10 | |

## SMITH, CARL

| | | | | | | |
|---|---|---|---|---|---|---|
| Carl Smith | 10" LP | Columbia | HL2579 | 1956 £8 | £20 | US |
| Carl Smith Touch | LP | Philips | BBL7437 | 1960 £4 | £10 | |
| Let's Live A Little | LP | Columbia | CL1172 | 1958 £6 | £15 | US |
| Sentimental Songs | 10" LP | Columbia | HL9023 | 195– £8 | £20 | US |
| Smith's The Name | LP | Columbia | CL1022 | 1957 £6 | £15 | US |
| Softly And Tenderly | 10" LP | Columbia | HL9026 | 195– £8 | £20 | US |
| Sunday Down South | LP | Columbia | CL959 | 1957 £6 | £15 | US |
| Ten Thousand Drums | 7" | Philips | PB943 | 1959 £2 | £5 | |

## SMITH, CLARA

| | | | | | | |
|---|---|---|---|---|---|---|
| Blues | 7" EP. | Philips | BBE12491 | 1961 £4 | £8 | |
| Volume 1 | LP | VJM | VLP15 | 1969 £4 | £10 | |
| Volume 2 | LP | VJM | VLP16 | 1969 £4 | £10 | |
| Volume 3 | LP | VJM | VLP17 | 1969 £4 | £10 | |

## SMITH, DAVE & THE ASTRONAUTS

| | | | | | | |
|---|---|---|---|---|---|---|
| Lover Like You | 7" | Columbia | DB104 | 1967 £2 | £5 | |

## SMITH, EDDIE

| | | | | | | |
|---|---|---|---|---|---|---|
| Silver Star Stomp | 7" | Parlophone | MSP6186 | 1955 £4 | £8 | |
| Upturn | 7" | Top Rank | JAR285 | 1960 £2.50 | £6 | |

## SMITH, EDGEWOOD & FABULOUS TAILFEATHERS

| | | | | | | |
|---|---|---|---|---|---|---|
| Ain't That Lovin' You | 7" | Sue | WI4037 | 1967 £5 | £10 | |

## SMITH, EFFIE

| | | | | | | |
|---|---|---|---|---|---|---|
| Dial That Phone | 7" | Sue | WI4010 | 1966 £5 | £10 | |

## SMITH, ELSON

| | | | | | | |
|---|---|---|---|---|---|---|
| Flip Flop | 7" | Fontana | H291 | 1961 £5 | £10 | |

## SMITH, GEORGE HARMONICA

| | | | | | | |
|---|---|---|---|---|---|---|
| Arkansas Trap | LP | Deram | SML1082 | 1971 £15 | £30 | |
| Blues In The Dark | 7" | Blue Horizon... | 451002 | 1966 £50 | £100 | |
| Blues With A Feeling | LP | Liberty | LBS83218 | 1970 £5 | £12 | |
| No Time To Jive | LP | Blue Horizon | 763856 | 1970 £25 | £50 | |
| Someday You're Gonna Learn | 7" | Blue Horizon. | 573170 | 1970 £2.50 | £6 | |

## SMITH, GLORIA

| | | | | | | |
|---|---|---|---|---|---|---|
| Playmates | 7" | London | HLU8903 | 1959 £2 | £5 | |

## SMITH, GORDON

| | | | | | | |
|---|---|---|---|---|---|---|
| Long Overdue | LP | Blue Horizon... | 763211 | 1968 £20 | £40 | |
| Too Long | 7" | Blue Horizon... | 573156 | 1969 £2.50 | £6 | |

## SMITH, HOBART

| | | | | | | |
|---|---|---|---|---|---|---|
| Hobart Smith | LP | Topic | 12T187 | 1969 £6 | £15 | |

## SMITH, HUEY 'PIANO'

| | | | | | | |
|---|---|---|---|---|---|---|
| Don't You Know Yokomo | 7" | Top Rank | JAR282 | 1960 £7.50 | £15 | |
| For Dancing | LP | Ace | LP1015 | 1961 £30 | £60 | US |
| Having A Good Time | LP | Ace | LP1004 | 1959 £37.50 | £75 | US |
| High Blood Pressure | 7" | Columbia | DB4138 | 1958 £20 | £40 | |
| If It Ain't One Thing It's Another | 7" | Sue | WI364 | 1965 £6 | £12 | |
| Popeye | 7" | Top Rank | JAR614 | 1962 £5 | £10 | |
| Rock 'n' Roll Revival | LP | Ace | LP2021 | 196– £25 | £50 | US |
| Rockin' Pneumonia | 7" | Sue | WI380 | 1965 £6 | £12 | |

| | | | | | | |
|---|---|---|---|---|---|---|
| Rockin' Pneumonia And Boogie Woogie Flu | LP | Sue | ILP917 | 1965 £15 | £30 | |
| Twas The Night Before Christmas | LP | Ace | LP1027 | 1962 £25 | £50 | US |

## SMITH, JIMMY

| | | | | | | |
|---|---|---|---|---|---|---|
| Any Number Can Win | LP | Verve | VLP9057 | 1963 £4 | £10 | |
| At Club Baby Grand, Wilmington, Delaware Vol. 1 | LP | Blue Note | BLP/BST81528 | 1966 £10 | £25 | |
| At Club Baby Grand, Wilmington, Delaware Vol. 2 | LP | Blue Note | BLP/BST81529 | 1966 £10 | £25 | |
| At Small's Paradise Vol. 1 | LP | Blue Note | BLP/BST81585 | 196– £10 | £25 | |
| At Small's Paradise Vol. 2 | LP | Blue Note | BLP/BST81586 | 196– £10 | £25 | |
| At The Organ Vol. 1 | LP | Blue Note | BLP/BST81512 | 196– £10 | £25 | |
| At The Organ Vol. 2 | LP | Blue Note | BLP/BST81514 | 196– £10 | £25 | |
| Back At The Chicken Shack | LP | Blue Note | BLP/BST84117 | 1964 £10 | £25 | |
| Bashin' | LP | Verve | CLP1596/CSD1462 | 1962 £4 | £10 | |
| Bucket | LP | Blue Note | BLP/BST84235 | 1966 £6 | £15 | |
| Can Heat | 7" | Blue Note | 451905 | 1964 £2 | £5 | |
| Cat | LP | Verve | (S)VLP9079 | 1964 £4 | £10 | |
| Christmas Cookin' | LP | Verve | (S)VLP9231 | 1968 £4 | £10 | |
| Crazy Baby | LP | Blue Note | BLP/BST84030 | 1961 £10 | £25 | |
| Creeper | 7" EP | Verve | VEP5021 | 1965 £2 | £5 | |
| Date With Jimmy Smith Vol. 1 | LP | Blue Note | BLP/BST81547 | 196– £10 | £25 | |
| Date With Jimmy Smith Vol. 2 | LP | Blue Note | BLP/BST81548 | 196– £10 | £25 | |
| Dynamic Duo | LP | Verve | (S)VLP9160 | 1967 £4 | £10 | with Wes Montgomery |
| Further Adventures Of Jimmy And Wes | LP | Verve | (S)VLP9241 | 1969 £4 | £10 | with Wes Montgomery |
| Got My Mojo Working | LP | Verve | (S)VLP9123 | 1966 £4 | £10 | |
| Greatest Hits | LP | Blue Note | BST89901 | 1970 £4 | £10 | |
| Hobo Flats | LP | Verve | (S)VLP9039 | 1963 £4 | £10 | |
| Home Cookin' | LP | Blue Note | BLP/BST84050 | 1961 £10 | £25 | |
| Hoochie Coochie Man | LP | Verve | (S)VLP9142 | 1966 £4 | £10 | |
| House Party | LP | Blue Note | BLP/BST84002 | 1964 £10 | £25 | |
| I'm Movin' On | LP | Blue Note | BLP/BST84255 | 1967 £6 | £15 | |
| Incredible Jimmy Smith Vol. 1 | LP | Blue Note | BLP/BST81551 | 1964 £10 | £25 | |
| Incredible Jimmy Smith Vol. 2 | LP | Blue Note | BLP/BST81552 | 1965 £10 | £25 | |
| Jimmy Smith Vol. 3 | LP | Blue Note | BLP/BST81525 | 196– £10 | £25 | |
| Livin' It Up | LP | Verve | (S)VLP9227 | 1968 £4 | £10 | |
| Midnight Special | LP | Blue Note | BLP/BST84078 | 1962 £10 | £25 | |
| Monster | LP | Verve | (S)VLP9093 | 1965 £4 | £10 | |
| Open House | LP | Blue Note | BST84269 | 1968 £6 | £15 | |
| Organ Grinder Swing | LP | Verve | (S)VLP9108 | 1966 £4 | £10 | |
| Peter And The Wolf | LP | Verve | (S)VLP9159 | 1966 £4 | £10 | |
| Plain Talk | LP | Blue Note | BST84296 | 1968 £5 | £12 | |
| Plays Fats Waller | LP | Blue Note | BLP/BST84100 | 1964 £8 | £20 | |
| Plays Pretty For You | LP | Blue Note | BLP/BST81563 | 196– £10 | £25 | |
| Plays The Blues | 7" EP | Verve | VEP5016 | 1965 £2 | £5 | |
| Prayer Meetin' | LP | Blue Note | BLP/BST84164 | 1964 £10 | £25 | |
| Respect | LP | Verve | (S)VLP9182 | 1967 £4 | £10 | |
| Rockin' The Boat | LP | Blue Note | BLP/BST84141 | 1964 £8 | £20 | |
| Sermon | LP | Blue Note | BLP/BST84011 | 1966 £10 | £25 | |
| Sermon | 7" | Blue Note | 451879 | 1964 £2 | £5 | |
| Softly As A Summer Breeze | LP | Blue Note | BLP/BST84200 | 1966 £8 | £20 | |
| Sounds Of Jimmy Smith | LP | Blue Note | BLP/BST81556 | 196– £10 | £25 | |
| Stay Loose | LP | Verve | (S)VLP9218 | 1968 £4 | £10 | |
| Swinging With The Incredible Jimmy Smith | 7" EP | Verve | VEP5022 | 1965 £2 | £5 | |
| Walk On The Wild Side | 7" EP | Verve | VEP5008 | 1964 £2 | £5 | |
| When My Dreamboat Comes Home | 7" | Blue Note | 451904 | 1963 £2 | £5 | |
| Who's Afraid Of Virginia Woolf | LP | Verve | VLP9068 | 1964 £4 | £10 | |

## SMITH, JOEY & BABA BROOKS

| | | | | | | |
|---|---|---|---|---|---|---|
| Maybe Once | 7" | R&B | JB131 | 1964 £5 | £10 | |

## SMITH, JOHN

| | | | | | | |
|---|---|---|---|---|---|---|
| Rock 'n' Roll Again | LP | Vogue | 10160 | 1968 £6 | £15 | German |
| Rockin' With John Smith | LP | Pop | ZS10169 | 1968 £6 | £15 | German |

## SMITH, JOHNNY

| | | | | | | |
|---|---|---|---|---|---|---|
| Johnny Smith And His New Quartet | LP | Vogue | LAE12202 | 1960 £4 | £10 | |
| Johnny Smith Quartet | LP | Vogue | LAE12221 | 1960 £4 | £10 | |
| Moods | LP | Vogue | LAE12198 | 1961 £6 | £15 | |
| Moonlight In Vermont | LP | Vogue | LAE12189 | 1959 £8 | £20 | |
| Plays Jimmy Van Heusen | LP | Vogue | LAE12169 | 1959 £8 | £20 | |

## SMITH, JUDI

| | | | | | | |
|---|---|---|---|---|---|---|
| Leaves Come Tumbling Down | 7" | Decca | F12132 | 1965 £2.50 | £6 | |

## SMITH, JUNIOR

| | | | | | | |
|---|---|---|---|---|---|---|
| Come Cure Me | 7" | Giant | GN25 | 1968 £2 | £5 | |
| Cool Down Your Temper | 7" | Giant | GN1 | 1967 £2 | £5 | |
| I'm Gonna Leave You Girl | 7" | Giant | GN18 | 1968 £2 | £5 | |

## SMITH, KATHY

| | | | | | | |
|---|---|---|---|---|---|---|
| Some Songs I've Saved | LP | Polydor | 2310081 | 1970 £25 | £50 | |

## SMITH, KEELY

| | | | | | | |
|---|---|---|---|---|---|---|
| Don't Take Your Love From Me | 7" | Capitol | CL14994 | 1959 £1.50 | £4 | |
| Here In My Heart | 7" | London | HLD9240 | 1960 £1.50 | £4 | |

| | | | | | | |
|---|---|---|---|---|---|---|
| If I Knew I'd Find You | 7" | London | HLD8984 | 1959 £2 | £5 | |
| That Old Black Magic | 7" | Capitol | CL14948 | 1958 £1.50 | £4 | |

## SMITH, LONNIE
| | | | | | | |
|---|---|---|---|---|---|---|
| Drives | LP | Blue Note | BST84351 | 1970 £6 | £15 | |
| Move Your Hand | LP | Blue Note | BST84326 | 1969 £6 | £15 | |
| Think | LP | Blue Note | BST84290 | 1968 £6 | £15 | |
| Turning Point | LP | Blue Note | BST84313 | 1969 £6 | £15 | |

## SMITH, LONNIE LISTON

Lonnie Liston Smith is a jazz keyboard player who was briefly a part of the Miles Davis band during the time in the early seventies when the trumpeter was engaged in some of his most experimental work with densely constructed rhythms. Smith's own records contain a very much more commercial form of jazz-funk, the track 'Expansions' having acquired something of the status of a disco classic.

| | | | | | | |
|---|---|---|---|---|---|---|
| Expansions | LP | RCA | SF8434 | 1975 £6 | £15 | |
| Expansions | 12" | RCA | PC9450 | 1979 £3 | £8 | |

## SMITH, LORENZO
| | | | | | | |
|---|---|---|---|---|---|---|
| Firewater | 7" | Outasite | 45503 | 1966 £12.50 | £25 | |

## SMITH, MARVIN
| | | | | | | |
|---|---|---|---|---|---|---|
| Time Stopped | 7" | Coral | Q72486 | 1966 £7.50 | £15 | |

## SMITH, MEL
| | | | | | | |
|---|---|---|---|---|---|---|
| Mel Smith's Greatest Hits | 7" | Mercury | MEL1 | 1981 £1.50 | £4 | |

## SMITH, MICHAEL
| | | | | | | |
|---|---|---|---|---|---|---|
| Mi Cyaan Believe It | LP | Island | ILPS9717 | 1982 £4 | £10 | |

## SMITH, MICK
| | | | | | | |
|---|---|---|---|---|---|---|
| Somebody Nobody Knows | LP | Midas | MFHR078 | 1976 £30 | £60 | |
| Words And Music | LP | Alida Star | AS771 | 1977 £15 | £30 | |

## SMITH, O. C.
| | | | | | | |
|---|---|---|---|---|---|---|
| Dynamic O. C. Smith | LP | CBS | 63147 | 1968 £4 | £10 | |

## SMITH, OCIE
| | | | | | | |
|---|---|---|---|---|---|---|
| Lighthouse | 7" | London | HLA8480 | 1957 £25 | £50 | |

## SMITH, PATTI
| | | | | | | |
|---|---|---|---|---|---|---|
| Brian Jones | 7" | Fierce | FRIGHT017 | 1988 £5 | £10 | |
| Hey Joe | 7" | Mer | 601 | 1974 £37.50 | £75 | US |
| Horses | LP | Arista | S4066 | 1975 £6 | £15 | US grey vinyl |
| People Have The Power | CD-s | Arista | 659877 | 1988 £2 | £5 | |

## SMITH, PAUL
| | | | | | | |
|---|---|---|---|---|---|---|
| Big Men | LP | HMV | CLP1356 | 1960 £5 | £12 | |
| Delicate Jazz | LP | Capitol | T1017 | 1959 £5 | £12 | |
| Paul Smith | 10" LP | Capitol | LC6820 | 1956 £8 | £20 | |
| Paul Smith Quartet | 10" LP | Vogue | LDE168 | 1956 £8 | £20 | |

## SMITH, RAY
| | | | | | | |
|---|---|---|---|---|---|---|
| Best Of Ray Smith | LP | T | 56062 | 196– £8 | £20 | US |
| Greatest Hits | LP | Columbia | CL1937/CS8737 | 1963 £6 | £15 | US |
| Rocking Little Angel | 7" | London | HL9051 | 1960 £20 | £40 | |
| Travellin' With Ray | LP | Judd | JLPA701 | 1960 £50 | £100 | US |

## SMITH, SLIM
| | | | | | | |
|---|---|---|---|---|---|---|
| Everybody Needs Love | LP | Pama | ECO9 | 1969 £10 | £25 | |
| Greatest Hits | LP | Trojan | TBL198 | 1973 £4 | £10 | |
| I've Got Your Number | 7" | Island | WI3023 | 1966 £5 | £10 | |
| Just A Dream | LP | Trojan | TBL186 | 1972 £5 | £12 | |
| Rougher Yet | 7" | Coxsone | CS7034 | 1968 £5 | £10 | |
| Slim Smith | LP | Lord Koos | KLP1 | 197– £8 | £20 | |
| Watch This Sound | 7" | Trojan | TR619 | 1968 £1.50 | £4 | |

## SMITH, SOMETHIN' & THE REDHEADS
| | | | | | | |
|---|---|---|---|---|---|---|
| I Don't Want To Set The World On Fire | 7" | Fontana | H154 | 1958 £1.50 | £4 | |

## SMITH, STUFF
| | | | | | | |
|---|---|---|---|---|---|---|
| Stuff Smith | LP | Columbia | 33CX10093 | 1957 £6 | £15 | |

## SMITH, T. V. EXPLORERS
| | | | | | | |
|---|---|---|---|---|---|---|
| Servant | cass-s | Kaleidoscope | KRLA401162 | 1981 £10 | £20 | |

## SMITH, TAB
| | | | | | | |
|---|---|---|---|---|---|---|
| Jump Time | 7" | Vogue | V2410 | 1956 £4 | £8 | |
| Music Styled By Tab Smith | 10" LP | United | LP001 | 195– £25 | £50 | US |
| My Happiness Cha-Cha | 7" | London | HLM8801 | 1959 £1.50 | £4 | |
| Red Hot And Cool Blues | 10" LP | United | LP003 | 195– £25 | £50 | US |

## SMITH, TED
| | | | | | | |
|---|---|---|---|---|---|---|
| Requiem For A Nobody | LP | Light | LS7003 | 1973 £8 | £20 | |

## SMITH, TERRY
| | | | | | | |
|---|---|---|---|---|---|---|
| Fall Out | LP | Philips | SBL7871 | 1969 £20 | £40 | |
| Terry Smith | LP | Lambert | LAM002 | 1977 £15 | £30 | |

## SMITH, TRIXIE

| | | | | | | | |
|---|---|---|---|---|---|---|---|
| Freight Train Blues | 78 | Vocalion | V1006 | 1952 | £3 | £8 | |
| He Likes It Slow | 78 | Tempo | R42 | 1951 | £2.50 | £6 | |
| My Daddy Rocks Me | 78 | Vocalion | V1017 | 1952 | £3 | £8 | |
| Trixie Smith | 10" LP | Audubon | | 195– | £8 | £20 | |
| Trixie Smith | 10" EP | Poydras | 101 | 195– | £4 | £10 | |
| Trixie Smith | 10" EP | Ristic | 12 | 195– | £4 | £10 | |

## SMITH, TRULY

| | | | | | | | |
|---|---|---|---|---|---|---|---|
| I Wanna Go Back There Again | 7" | Decca | F12645 | 1967 | £1.50 | £4 | |
| Love Is Me Love Is You | 7" EP | Decca | 457115 | 1966 | £5 | £10 | French |
| My Smile Is Just A Frown Turned Upside Down | 7" | Decca | F12373 | 1966 | £7.50 | £15 | |
| This Is The First Time | 7" | MGM | MGM1431 | 1968 | £2 | £5 | |

## SMITH, VERDELLE

| | | | | | | | |
|---|---|---|---|---|---|---|---|
| I Don't Need Anything | 7" | Capitol | CL15481 | 1966 | £2.50 | £6 | |
| Tar And Cement | 7" | Capitol | CL15456 | 1966 | £1.50 | £4 | |
| There's So Much Love Around Me | 7" | Capitol | CL15514 | 1967 | £1.50 | £4 | |

## SMITH, WARREN

| | | | | | | | |
|---|---|---|---|---|---|---|---|
| First Country Collection | LP | Liberty | LRP3199/LST7199. | 1961 | £10 | £25 | US |
| I Don't Believe I'll Fall In Love | 7" | London | HL7101 | 1960 | £10 | £20 | export |
| Judge And Jury | 7" | Liberty | LIB55699 | 1964 | £2.50 | £6 | |
| Odds And Ends | 7" | London | HLG7110 | 1961 | £10 | £20 | |

## SMITH, WHISPERING

| | | | | | | | |
|---|---|---|---|---|---|---|---|
| Over Easy | LP | Blue Horizon | 2431015 | 1971 | £15 | £30 | |

## SMITH, WHISTLING JACK

Billy Moeller, brother of the Unit Four Plus Two singer, appeared on television miming to the novelty hit, 'I Was Kaiser Bill's Batman', although he had not been part of the studio team that put the record together. Dressed in an antique military costume to match the title of the tune, he became the unlikely inspiration for a Carnaby Street shop, selling exotic uniforms as fashion items from premises called I Was Kaiser Bill's Batman.

| | | | | | | | |
|---|---|---|---|---|---|---|---|
| Around The World | LP | Deram | DML1009 | 1967 | £4 | £10 | |
| Hey There Little Miss Mary | 7" EP | Deram | 15005 | 1967 | £4 | £8 | French |
| I Was Kaiser Bill's Batman | 7" EP | Deram | 15001 | 1967 | £2.50 | £6 | French |
| I Was Kaiser Bill's Batman | 7" | Deram | DM112 | 1967 | £1.50 | £4 | |

## SMITH, WILLIE

| | | | | | | | |
|---|---|---|---|---|---|---|---|
| And His Friends | 10" LP | Mercury | MG26000 | 1954 | £20 | £40 | |

## SMITH, WILLIE 'THE LION'

| | | | | | | | |
|---|---|---|---|---|---|---|---|
| Legend Of Willie 'The Lion' Smith | LP | Top Rank | RX3015 | 1959 | £6 | £15 | |
| Willie 'The Lion' Smith | 10" LP | London | HAPB1017 | 1954 | £10 | £25 | |
| Willie 'The Lion' Smith | 10" LP | Vogue | LDE177 | 1956 | £8 | £20 | |

## SMITHEREENS

| | | | | | | | |
|---|---|---|---|---|---|---|---|
| Beauty And Sadness | LP | Little Ricky | LR103 | 1983 | £6 | £15 | US |
| Blue Period | CD-s | Enigma | UNVCD21 | 1990 | £3 | £8 | with Belinda Carlisle |
| House We Used To Live In | CD-s | Enigma | ENVCD2 | 1988 | £2 | £5 | 3" single |

## SMITHFIELD MARKET

| | | | | | | | |
|---|---|---|---|---|---|---|---|
| After Shakespeare | LP | Gloucester | GLS0443 | 1974 | £100 | £200 | |
| London In 1665 | LP | Gloucester | GLS0435 | 1973 | £250 | £400 | |

## SMITHS

The Smiths remained with Rough Trade for the major part of their career and saw the record company's fortunes rise along with their own, so that there are no obscure early singles for the Smiths collector to seek out. The single 'This Charming Man', available in three versions, has, however, become quite scarce, despite gaining a respectable position in the lower reaches of the charts. The original cover of 'What Difference Does It Make', showing a film still of Terence Stamp in The Collector is not particularly rare. One suspects that its withdrawal in favour of a cover with Morrissey in identical pose was designed solely to illustrate the song's title.

| | | | | | | | |
|---|---|---|---|---|---|---|---|
| Ask | CD-s | Rough Trade | RT194CD | 1988 | £10 | £20 | |
| Ask | cass-s | Rough Trade | RT194C | 1986 | £2.50 | £6 | |
| Ask | 12" | Rough Trade | RTT194 | 1986 | £4 | £10 | clear vinyl |
| Barbarism Begins At Home | CD-s | Rough Trade | RTT171CD | 1988 | £6 | £15 | |
| Boy With The Thorn In His Side | CD-s | Rough Trade | RT191CD | 1988 | £6 | £15 | |
| Girlfriend In A Coma | cass-s | Rough Trade | RTT197C | 1987 | £2.50 | £6 | |
| Hand In Glove | 7" | Rough Trade | RT131 | 1983 | £2.50 | £6 | Rough Trade logo on label |
| Hand In Glove | 7" | Rough Trade | RT131 | 1987 | £20 | £40 | blue sleeve, silver photo |
| Hatful Of Hollow | CD | Rough Trade | ROUGHCD76 | 1988 | £6 | £15 | |
| Headmaster Ritual | CD-s | Rough Trade | RTT215CD | 1988 | £20 | £40 | |
| Heaven Knows I'm Miserable Now | CD-s | Rough Trade | RTT156CD | 1988 | £10 | £20 | |
| How Soon Is Now? | CD-s | WEA | YZ0002CD1/CD2. | 1992 | £5 | £12 | 2 single set |
| Last Night I Dreamt Somebody Loved Me | CD-s | Rough Trade | RT200CD | 1988 | £4 | £10 | |
| Louder Than Bombs | CD | Rough Trade | ROUGHCD255 | 1987 | £5 | £12 | |
| Meat Is Murder | CD | Rough Trade | ROUGHCD81 | 1985 | £5 | £12 | |
| Meat Is Murder | 7" | Rough Trade | RT186 | 1985 | £15 | £30 | test pressing |
| Meat Is Murder | 12" | Rough Trade | RTT186 | 1985 | £20 | £40 | test pressing |
| Panic | CD-s | Rough Trade | RT193CD | 1988 | £5 | £12 | |
| Panic | 7" | Rough Trade | RT193 | 1986 | £2.50 | £6 | 'Hang the DJ' stickers |

| | | | | | | | |
|---|---|---|---|---|---|---|---|
| Panic | 12" | Rough Trade | RTT193 | 1986 £3 | £8 | 'Hang the DJ' stickers |
| Panic | 12" | Rough Trade | RTT193 | 1986 £3 | £8 | blue vinyl |
| Peel Sessions | CD-s | Strange Fruit | SFPSCD055 | 1988 £2 | £5 | |
| Queen Is Dead | LP | Rough Trade | RTD36 | 1986 £8 | £20 | German, green vinyl |
| Queen Is Dead | CD | Rough Trade | ROUGHCD96 | 1986 £5 | £12 | |
| Reel Around The Fountain | 7" | Rough Trade | RT136 | 1983 £150 | £250 | test pressing |
| Shoplifters Of The World Unite | 12" | Rough Trade | RTT195 | 1987 £2.50 | £6 | with carrier bag |
| Smiths | LP | Rough Trade | RTD25 | 1984 £50 | £100 | German, multi-coloured vinyl |
| Smiths | CD | Rough Trade | ROUGHCD61 | 1986 £5 | £12 | |
| Still Ill | 7" | Rough Trade | RT161DJ | 1984 £5 | £10 | promo |
| Strangeways Here We Come | LP | Rough Trade | RTD60 | 1987 £6 | £15 | German, blue-grey vinyl |
| Strangeways Here We Come | CD | Rough Trade | ROUGHCD106 | 1987 £5 | £12 | |
| This Charming Man | 7" | Rough Trade | RT136 | 1983 £5 | £10 | |
| This Charming Man | 12" | Rough Trade | RTT136 | 1983 £5 | £12 | |
| This Charming Man (New York remix) | 12" | Rough Trade | RTT136NY | 1983 £6 | £15 | |
| What Difference Does It Make | 12" | Rough Trade | RTT146 | 1984 £2.50 | £6 | Terence Stamp sleeve |
| What Difference Does It Make? | CD-s | Rough Trade | RT146CD | 1988 £10 | £20 | |
| William, It Was Really Nothing | CD-s | Rough Trade | RT166CD | 1988 £6 | £15 | |
| William, It Was Really Nothing | 7" | Rough Trade | RT166 | 1984 £2.50 | £6 | |
| William, It Was Really Nothing | 12" | Rough Trade | RTT166 | 1984 £3 | £8 | |
| World Won't Listen | CD | Rough Trade | ROUGHCD101 | 1987 £5 | £12 | |
| You Just Haven't Earned It Yet Baby | 12" | Rough Trade | RTT195 | 1987 £20 | £40 | mispressing |

## SMOKE

The English Smoke managed to maintain a surprisingly long career (including making records under the name of Chords Five) for a group that was essentially a one-hit wonder. That one hit, however, 'My Friend Jack', is something of a psychedelic classic, driven by viciously reverbed and fuzzed guitars.

| | | | | | | | |
|---|---|---|---|---|---|---|---|
| Dreams Of Dreams | 7" | Revolution | REVP1002 | 1970 £10 | £20 | |
| If The Weather's Sunny | 7" | Columbia | DB8252 | 1967 £10 | £20 | |
| It Could Be Wonderful | 7" | Island | WIP6023 | 1967 £25 | £50 | |
| It's Just Your Way Of Lovin' | 7" EP | Impact | 200012 | 1967 £25 | £50 | French |
| It's Smoke Time | LP | Metronome | MLP15279 | 1967 £30 | £60 | German |
| My Friend Jack | 7" EP | Impact | 200010 | 1967 £25 | £50 | French |
| My Friend Jack | 7" | Columbia | DB8115 | 1966 £10 | £20 | |
| Ride Ride Ride | 7" | Pageant | SAM101 | 1971 £10 | £20 | |
| Sugar Man | 7" | Regal Zonophone | RZ3071 | 1972 £10 | £20 | |
| Utterly Simple | 7" | Island | WIP6031 | 1968 £100 | £200 | demo, best auctioned |

## SMOKE (2)

| | | | | | | | |
|---|---|---|---|---|---|---|---|
| Smoke | LP | Sidewalk | ST5912 | 1968 £10 | £25 | US |

## SMOKE (3)

| | | | | | | | |
|---|---|---|---|---|---|---|---|
| At George's Coffee Shop | LP | Uni | 73065 | 1970 £5 | £12 | US |
| Carry On Your Idea | LP | Uni | 73052 | 1969 £5 | £12 | US |

## SMOKESTACK LIGHTNIN'

Although the name would suggest a blues group, Smokestack Lightnin' actually played blue-eyed soul, though without very much ambition or even very much soulfulness. The long version of the song after which the group was named is used as a climax to the *Off The Wall* album. The piece becomes stretched out as each member delivers a solo on his instrument – but none is in the least memorable.

| | | | | | | | |
|---|---|---|---|---|---|---|---|
| Light In My Window | 7" | Bell | BLL1046 | 1969 £1.50 | £4 | |
| Off The Wall | LP | Bell | MBLL/SBLL116 | 1969 £6 | £15 | |

## SMOKEY BABE

| | | | | | | | |
|---|---|---|---|---|---|---|---|
| Smokey Babe And His Friends | LP | 77 | LA1212 | 1962 £6 | £15 | |

## SMOKEY CIRCLES

| | | | | | | | |
|---|---|---|---|---|---|---|---|
| Long, Long, Love | 7" | Carnaby | CNS4011 | 1970 £1.50 | £4 | |
| Smokey Circles' Album | LP | Carnaby | CNLS6006 | 1970 £25 | £50 | |

## SMOTHERS, SMOKEY

| | | | | | | | |
|---|---|---|---|---|---|---|---|
| Backporch Blues | LP | King | 779 | 1962 £50 | £100 | US |
| Driving Blues Of Smokey Smothers | LP | Polydor | 623239 | 1966 £20 | £40 | |

## SNAKEHIPS

| | | | | | | | |
|---|---|---|---|---|---|---|---|
| Snakehips Arnold And The King Of Boogie | LP | Spaceward | 3S2/EDENLP75 | 1975 £6 | £15 | |

## SNAPPERS

| | | | | | | | |
|---|---|---|---|---|---|---|---|
| If There Were | 7" | Top Rank | JAR167 | 1959 £2.50 | £6 | |

## SNAPPERS (2)

| | | | | | | | |
|---|---|---|---|---|---|---|---|
| Snappers | LP | Elite | PLPS30110 | 1967 £10 | £25 | German |
| Upside Down Inside Out | 7" | CBS | 2719 | 1967 £2.50 | £6 | |

## SNEAKERS

| | | | | | | | |
|---|---|---|---|---|---|---|---|
| In The Red | LP | Car | 0398 | 1978 £6 | £15 | US |

## SNEAKY PETES

| | | | | | | | |
|---|---|---|---|---|---|---|---|
| Savage | 7" | Decca | F11199 | 1960 £1.50 | £4 | |

## SNEEKERS

| | | | | | | | |
|---|---|---|---|---|---|---|---|
| I Just Can't Get To Sleep | 7" | Columbia | DB7385 | 1964 £20 | £40 | |

## SNIVELLING SHITS

| | | | | | | | |
|---|---|---|---|---|---|---|---|
| Isgodaman? | 7" | Damaged Goods | FNARR4B | 1989 | £1.50 | £4 | .... box set, pink vinyl |
| Terminal Stupid | 7" | Ghetto Rockers | PRE2 | 1977 | £4 | £8 | |

## SNOBS

| | | | | | | | |
|---|---|---|---|---|---|---|---|
| Buckle Shoe Stomp | 7" | Decca | F11867 | 1964 | £7.50 | £15 | |

## SNOOKY & MOODY

| | | | | | | | |
|---|---|---|---|---|---|---|---|
| Snooky And Moody's Blues | 7" | Blue Horizon | 451003 | 1966 | £50 | £100 | |

## SNOW, HANK

| | | | | | | | |
|---|---|---|---|---|---|---|---|
| Big Country Hits | LP | RCA | LPM/LSP2458 | 1961 | £6 | £15 | US |
| Country & Western Jamboree | LP | RCA | LPM1419 | 1957 | £10 | £25 | US |
| Country Classics | LP | RCA | LPM1233 | 1955 | £10 | £25 | US |
| Country Classics | 10" LP | RCA | LPT3026 | 1952 | £15 | £30 | US |
| Country Guitar No. 4 | 7" EP | RCA | RCX116 | 1958 | £2.50 | £6 | |
| Country Guitar No. 7 | 7" EP | RCA | RCX142 | 1959 | £4 | £8 | |
| Hank Snow Salutes Jimmie Rodgers | 10" LP | RCA | LPT3131 | 1953 | £15 | £30 | US |
| Hank Snow Sings | 10" LP | RCA | LPT3070 | 1952 | £15 | £30 | US |
| Hank Snow Sings Jimmie Rodgers Songs | LP | RCA | LPM/LSP2043 | 1959 | £6 | £15 | US |
| Hank Snow Sings Sacred Songs | LP | RCA | LPM1638 | 1958 | £8 | £20 | US |
| Hank Snow's Country Guitar | LP | RCA | LPM1435 | 1957 | £10 | £25 | US |
| Hank Snow's Country Guitar | 10" LP | RCA | LPT3267 | 1954 | £15 | £30 | US |
| Hits, Hits And More Hits | LP | RCA | LPM/LSP3965 | 1968 | £4 | £10 | US |
| Just Keep A-Movin' | LP | RCA | LPM1113 | 1955 | £10 | £25 | US |
| My Arabian Baby | 7" | HMV | 7MC24 | 1954 | £2 | £5 | export |
| My Religion's Not Old-Fashioned | 7" | HMV | 7MC25 | 1954 | £2 | £5 | export |
| Old Doc Brown | LP | RCA | LPM1156 | 1955 | £15 | £30 | US |
| Souvenirs | LP | RCA | LPM/LSP2285 | 1961 | £6 | £15 | US |
| Spanish Fireball | 7" | HMV | 7MC15 | 1954 | £2 | £5 | export |
| That Country Gentleman | 7" EP | RCA | RCX7154 | 1964 | £4 | £8 | |
| Together Again | LP | RCA | LPM/LSP2580 | 1962 | £5 | £12 | US |
| When Tragedy Struck | LP | RCA | RD27115 | 1959 | £5 | £12 | |
| When Tragedy Struck | 7" EP | RCA | RCX7125 | 1963 | £2 | £5 | |
| Why Do You Punish Me | 7" | HMV | 7MC7 | 1954 | £2 | £5 | export |
| Yellow Roses | 7" | HMV | 7MC31 | 1954 | £2 | £5 | export |

## SNYDER, BILL

| | | | | | | | |
|---|---|---|---|---|---|---|---|
| Bewitched | 7" EP | London | REP1011 | 1954 | £2 | £5 | |

## SOAR, MIKE

| | | | | | | | |
|---|---|---|---|---|---|---|---|
| Our Side Of The Bridge | LP | Westwood | WRS014 | 1972 | £10 | £25 | |

## SOCIALITES

| | | | | | | | |
|---|---|---|---|---|---|---|---|
| Jive Jimmy | 7" | Warner Bros | WB148 | 1964 | £5 | £10 | |

## SOCIETIE

| | | | | | | | |
|---|---|---|---|---|---|---|---|
| Bird Has Flown | 7" | Deram | DM162 | 1967 | £5 | £10 | |

## SOCOLOW, FRANK

| | | | | | | | |
|---|---|---|---|---|---|---|---|
| Sounds By Socolow | LP | London | LTZN15090 | 1957 | £10 | £25 | |

## SOCRATES

| | | | | | | | |
|---|---|---|---|---|---|---|---|
| On The Wings | LP | Peters | PILPS9002 | 1976 | £5 | £12 | US |
| Phos | LP | Peters | PILPS9013 | 1977 | £5 | £12 | US |

## SOFT BOYS

| | | | | | | | |
|---|---|---|---|---|---|---|---|
| Anglepoise Lamp | 7" | Radar | ADA8 | 1978 | £4 | £8 | picture sleeve |
| Can Of Bees | LP | Two Crabs | CLAW1001 | 1979 | £6 | £15 | white & black labels |
| Give It To The Soft Boys | 7" | Raw | RAW5 | 1977 | £6 | £12 | |
| He's A Reptile | 7" | Midnight Music | DING4 | 1983 | £1.50 | £4 | |
| I Wanna Destroy You | 7" | Armageddon | AS005 | 1980 | £2.50 | £6 | |
| Love Poisoning | 7" | Bucketfull Of Brains | BOB1 | 1982 | £1.50 | £4 | |
| Near The Soft Boys | 7" | Armageddon | AEP002 | 1980 | £4 | £8 | |
| Only The Stones Remain | 7" | Armageddon | AS029 | 1981 | £2 | £5 | |
| Wading Through The Ventilator | 12" | Delorean | SOFT1P | 1985 | £2.50 | £6 | picture disc |

## SOFT CELL

The combination of a singer with a limited, rather tuneless voice and a keyboard player still struggling with the opening chapter of his synthesizer instruction manual was an unlikely recipe for the creation of some of the finest single releases of the eighties. Soft Cell proved that rock music's perennial reliance on the inspired amateur can sometimes strike gold.

| | | | | | | | |
|---|---|---|---|---|---|---|---|
| 12" Singles | 12" | Some Bizarre | CELBX1 | 1982 | £30 | £60 | 6 x 12", boxed |
| A Man Can Get Lost | 7" | Some Bizarre | HARD1 | 1981 | £4 | £8 | |
| Down In The Subway (Remix) | 12" | Some Bizarre | BZSR2212 | 1984 | £5 | £12 | |
| Ghostrider (live) | 7" | fan club | | 1984 | £4 | £8 | flexi |
| Memorabilia | 12" | Some Bizarre | HARD12 | 1981 | £4 | £10 | |
| Mutant Moments | 7" | Big Frock | ABF1 | 1980 | £25 | £50 | with insert |
| Say Hello Wave Goodbye '91 | CD-s | Mercury | SOFCD1 | 1991 | £2 | £5 | |
| Say Hello Wave Goodbye '91 | CD-s | Mercury | SOFCP1 | 1991 | £2.50 | £6 | picture disc |
| Say Hello Wave Goodbye (live) | 7" | fan club | | 1983 | £5 | £10 | flexi |
| Soul Inside | 7" | Some Bizarre | BZS2020 | 1983 | £2 | £5 | double |

| | | | | | | | |
|---|---|---|---|---|---|---|---|
| Tainted Love | CD-s | Mercury | SOFCD2 | 1991 | £2 | £5 | |
| Tainted Love | CD-s | Mercury | SOFCD2 | 1991 | £4 | £10 | leather pouch |
| Tainted Love | CD-s | Mercury | SOFCP2 | 1991 | £2.50 | £6 | picture disc |

## SOFT MACHINE

| | | | | | | | |
|---|---|---|---|---|---|---|---|
| Alive And Well | LP | Harvest | SHSP4083 | 1978 | £4 | £10 | |
| Bundles | LP | Harvest | SHSP4044 | 1975 | £4 | £10 | |
| Fifth | LP | CBS | 64806 | 1972 | £4 | £10 | |
| Fourth | LP | CBS | 64280 | 1971 | £4 | £10 | |
| Love Makes Sweet Music | 7" | Polydor | 56151 | 1967 | £37.50 | £75 | |
| Seven | LP | CBS | 65799 | 1973 | £4 | £10 | |
| Six | LP | CBS | 68214 | 1973 | £6 | £15 | double |
| Soft Machine | LP | Probe | 4500 | 1968 | £8 | £20 | US, wheel cover |
| Softs | LP | Harvest | SHSP4056 | 1976 | £4 | £10 | |
| Third | LP | CBS | 66246 | 1970 | £5 | £12 | double |
| Triple Echo | LP | Harvest | SHTW800 | 1977 | £10 | £25 | triple |
| Volume 2 | LP | Probe | SPB1002 | 1969 | £6 | £15 | |
| Volumes 1 & 2 | LP | ABC | ABCL5004 | 1974 | £5 | £12 | double |

## SOFT SHOE

| | | | | | | | |
|---|---|---|---|---|---|---|---|
| For Those Alone | LP | Aardvark | AARD1 | 1978 | £37.50 | £75 | |

## SOFTLEY, MICK

| | | | | | | | |
|---|---|---|---|---|---|---|---|
| Am I The Red One | 7" | CBS | 202469 | 1967 | £12.50 | £25 | |
| Any Mother Doesn't Grumble | LP | CBS | 64841 | 1972 | £10 | £25 | |
| I'm So Confused | 7" | Immediate | IM014 | 1965 | £2.50 | £6 | |
| Songs For Swingin' Survivors | LP | Columbia | 33SX1781 | 1965 | £50 | £100 | |
| Street Singer | LP | CBS | 64395 | 1971 | £10 | £25 | |
| Sunrise | LP | CBS | 64098 | 1970 | £6 | £15 | |

## SOHO SKIFFLE GROUP

| | | | | | | | |
|---|---|---|---|---|---|---|---|
| Soho Skiffle Group | 7" EP | Melodisc | EPM772 | 1957 | £25 | £50 | |

## SOL INVICTUS

| | | | | | | | |
|---|---|---|---|---|---|---|---|
| Looking For Europe | 7" | World Serpent | WS7002 | 1991 | £2 | £5 | 1 sided |
| See The Dove Fall | 7" | Shock | SX016 | 1991 | £2 | £5 | |

## SOLAL, MARTIAL

| | | | | | | | |
|---|---|---|---|---|---|---|---|
| Martial Solal Trio | 10" LP | Vogue | LDE105 | 1954 | £10 | £25 | |

## SOLAR PLEXUS

| | | | | | | | |
|---|---|---|---|---|---|---|---|
| Concerto Grosso (English) | LP | Odeon | E15434684/5 | 1972 | £6 | £15 | Swedish double |
| Concerto Grosso (Swedish) | LP | Odeon | 34573/4 | 1972 | £6 | £15 | Swedish double |
| Det Er Inte Baten | LP | Harvest | 06234975 | 1974 | £4 | £10 | European |
| Hellrre Gycklare An Hycklare | LP | Harvest | 06235166 | 1975 | £4 | £10 | European |
| Solar Plexus | LP | Polydor | 2383222 | 1973 | £5 | £12 | |
| Solar Plexus 2 | LP | Odeon | 34797 | 1973 | £5 | £12 | Swedish |

## SOLDIER

| | | | | | | | |
|---|---|---|---|---|---|---|---|
| Sheralee | 7" | Heavy Metal | HEAVY12 | 1982 | £2 | £5 | |

## SOLEN SKINER

| | | | | | | | |
|---|---|---|---|---|---|---|---|
| Solen Skiner | LP | Silence | MNW60P | 1976 | £8 | £20 | Swedish |

## SOLID GOLD CADILLAC

In common with most British jazz musicians of the time, Mike Westbrook incorporated many elements of rock music within his compositions, while many of the members of his band were equally at home whether playing jazz, rock or somewhere in between. Solid Gold Cadillac was the closest that Westbrook came to leading a straight rock group, although the music is inevitably suffused with a jazz sensibility.

| | | | | | | | |
|---|---|---|---|---|---|---|---|
| Brain Damage | LP | RCA | SF8365 | 1973 | £5 | £12 | |
| Solid Gold Cadillac | LP | RCA | SF8311 | 1972 | £5 | £12 | |

## SOLITAIRES

| | | | | | | | |
|---|---|---|---|---|---|---|---|
| Walking Along | 7" | London | HLM8745 | 1958 | £50 | £100 | |

## SOLO

| | | | | | | | |
|---|---|---|---|---|---|---|---|
| Solo | LP | | | 197– | £25 | £50 | US |

## SOLSTICE

Marillion pulled off a considerable feat when they managed to get progressive rock into the album and singles charts at a time when the music was supposed to be deeply unfashionable. A number of other bands were actually working in the same area at the time, one of the best being Solstice – for all that they sounded strongly reminiscent of mid-seventies Yes. Bass player Mark Hawkins was invited to join Marillion in the early days – sadly, he turned the offer down on the grounds that Solstice were more likely to be successful.

| | | | | | | | |
|---|---|---|---|---|---|---|---|
| Silent Dance | LP | Equinox | EQRLP001 | 1984 | £10 | £25 | |

## SOME CHICKEN

| | | | | | | | |
|---|---|---|---|---|---|---|---|
| Arabian Daze | 7" | Raw | RAW13 | 1978 | £2 | £5 | picture sleeve |
| Arabian Daze | 7" | Raw | RAW13 | 1978 | £25 | £50 | picture sleeve, coloured vinyl |
| New Religion | 7" | Raw | RAW7 | 1977 | £1.50 | £4 | picture sleeve |

## SOMEONE'S BAND

| | | | | | | | |
|---|---|---|---|---|---|---|---|
| Someone's Band | LP | Deram | SML1068 | 1970 | £37.50 | £75 | |
| Story | 7" | Deram | DM313 | 1970 | £2.50 | £6 | |

## SOMERS, GORDON

| | | | | | | | |
|---|---|---|---|---|---|---|---|
| Sound Of The Beatles | 7" EP | Top Ten | TPSX101 | 1964 | £2 | £5 | |

## SOMERS, VIRGINIA

| | | | | | | | |
|---|---|---|---|---|---|---|---|
| Lovin' Spree | 7" | Decca | F10301 | 1954 | £1.50 | £4 | |

## SOMETHING HAPPENS!

| | | | | | | | |
|---|---|---|---|---|---|---|---|
| Burn Clear | 7" | Cooking Vinyl | WILD001 | 1986 | £4 | £8 | |

## SOMMERS, JOANNIE

| | | | | | | | |
|---|---|---|---|---|---|---|---|
| Behind Closed Doors | LP | Warner Bros | B1348 | 1960 | £6 | £15 | US, boxed with booklet |
| Come Alive | LP | Columbia | CL2495/CS9295 | 1966 | £4 | £10 | US |
| For Those Who Think Young | LP | Warner Bros | WM4062/WS8062 | 1962 | £6 | £15 | |
| Goodbye Joey | 7" | Warner Bros | WB85 | 1963 | £1.50 | £4 | |
| If You Love Him | 7" | Warner Bros | WB150 | 1965 | £1.50 | £4 | |
| Johnny Get Angry | LP | Warner Bros | WM/WS8107 | 1963 | £6 | £15 | |
| Johnny Get Angry | 7" | Warner Bros | WB71 | 1962 | £1.50 | £4 | |
| Johnny Get Angry Vol. 1 | 7" EP | Warner Bros | WEP6121 | 1964 | £4 | £8 | |
| Johnny Get Angry Vol. 1 | 7" EP | Warner Bros | WSEP6121 | 1964 | £7.50 | £15 | stereo |
| Johnny Get Angry Vol. 2 | 7" EP | Warner Bros | WEP6123 | 1964 | £4 | £8 | |
| Johnny Get Angry Vol. 2 | 7" EP | Warner Bros | WSEP6123 | 1964 | £7.50 | £15 | stereo |
| Let's Talk About Love | LP | Warner Bros | WM/WS8119 | 1964 | £4 | £10 | |
| Little Girl Bad | 7" | Warner Bros | WB105 | 1963 | £1.50 | £4 | |
| Lively Set | LP | Decca | DL(7)9119 | 1964 | £5 | £12 | US |
| Positively The Most | LP | Warner Bros | W(S)1346 | 1960 | £6 | £15 | US |
| Positively The Most | 7" EP | Warner Bros | WEP6013 | 1960 | £4 | £8 | |
| Positively The Most | 7" EP | Warner Bros | WSEP2013 | 1960 | £6 | £12 | stereo |
| Softly, The Brazilian Sound | LP | Warner Bros | W(S)1575 | 1965 | £5 | £12 | US |
| Sommers' Seasons | LP | Warner Bros | W(S)1504 | 1964 | £6 | £15 | US |
| Voice Of The Sixties | LP | Warner Bros | WM4045/WS8045 | 1961 | £6 | £15 | |
| Voice Of The Sixties | 7" EP | Warner Bros | WEP6047 | 1961 | £4 | £8 | |
| Voice Of The Sixties | 7" EP | Warner Bros | WSEP2047 | 1961 | £6 | £12 | stereo |

## SONG PEDDLERS

| | | | | | | | |
|---|---|---|---|---|---|---|---|
| Rose Marie | 7" | Philips | BF1352 | 1964 | £1.50 | £4 | |

## SONGSTERS

| | | | | | | | |
|---|---|---|---|---|---|---|---|
| Bahama Buggy Ride | 7" | London | HL8100 | 1954 | £10 | £20 | |

## SONIA

| | | | | | | | |
|---|---|---|---|---|---|---|---|
| Be Young, Be Foolish, Be Happy | CD-s | IQ | ZD44936 | 1991 | £2 | £5 | |
| Boogie Nights | CD-s | Arista | 74321113462 | 1992 | £2 | £5 | |
| Counting Every Minute | CD-s | Chrysalis | CHSCD3492 | 1990 | £2 | £5 | |
| End Of The World | CD-s | Chrysalis | CHSCD3557 | 1990 | £2 | £5 | |
| Listen To Your Heart | CD-s | Chrysalis | CHSCD3465 | 1989 | £2 | £5 | |
| Only Fools Never Fall In Love | CD-s | IQ | ZD44614 | 1991 | £2 | £5 | |
| You To Me Are Everything | CD-s | IQ | ZD45122 | 1991 | £2 | £5 | |
| You'll Never Stop Me From Loving You | CD-s | Chrysalis | CHSCD3385 | 1989 | £2 | £5 | |

## SONIC BOOM

Since the acrimonious split between Pete Kember and Jason Pierce put an end to the career of cult favourites Spacemen 3, Kember has worked under his solo identity, Sonic Boom. Sadly, his continuation of Spacemen 3's characteristic drone style seems very pedestrian in comparison with the flights of fancy created by Pierce's group, Spiritualised. Meanwhile, his attempts to forge a more avant-garde version of the approach lack the sense of excitement and power of the group that should be a major influence – Sonic Youth. (The impact of the guitar drones on 'Octaves' compares very poorly with Lee Ranaldo's earlier 'From Here To Infinity' experimental creation.)

| | | | | | | | |
|---|---|---|---|---|---|---|---|
| Angel | CD-s | Silvertone | ORECD11 | 1989 | £2 | £5 | |
| Octaves | 10" | Silvertone | SONIC1 | 1990 | £3 | £8 | orange vinyl |
| Soul Kiss (Glide Divine) | LP | Silvertone | OREZLP518 | 1992 | £6 | £15 | oil filled cover |
| Spectrum | LP | Silvertone | OREZLP506 | 1990 | £4 | £10 | rotating disc sleeve |
| To The Moon And Back | 7" | Silvertone | SONIC2 | 1991 | £2 | £5 | |
| To The Moon And Back | 7" | Silvertone | SONIC2 | 1991 | £4 | £8 | picture sleeve |

## SONIC YOUTH

Sonic Youth have never seemed able to make up their minds whether they want to be a rock group or an avant-garde assembly of noise explorers, with the result that they are frequently both. Guitarists Lee Ranaldo and Thurston Moore have both taken part in side-projects of an extremely listener unfriendly nature. Their love of extreme sound abrasion spills over too into their rock work, giving Sonic Youth a cutting-edge quality that has made them into one of the key shapers of modern rock.

| | | | | | | | |
|---|---|---|---|---|---|---|---|
| Daydream Nation | LP | Blast First | BFFP34 | 1988 | £5 | £12 | double, with signed poster |
| Dirty Boots EP | CD-s | Geffen | DGCD21634 | 1991 | £2 | £5 | |
| Flower | 7" | Blast First | BFFP3 | 1985 | £5 | £10 | promo |
| Flower | 12" | Blast First | BFFP3 | 1986 | £4 | £10 | yellow vinyl |
| Flower (censored version)/Rewolf | 12" | Blast First | BFFP3 | 1985 | £6 | £15 | promo |
| Kool Thing | CD-s | Geffen | GEF81CD | 1990 | £2 | £5 | |
| Savage Pencil | 12" | Blast First | BFFP3P | 1986 | £4 | £10 | |
| Savage Pencil | 12" | Blast First | BFFP3P | 1986 | £15 | £30 | signed by S. Pencil |
| Screaming Fields Of Sonic Love | CD | Geffen | PROCD4577 | 1994 | £8 | £20 | US promo compilation |
| Sonic Death | cass | Ecstatic Peace | | 1984 | £6 | £15 | US |
| Sonic Youth | LP | Neutral | ND01 | 1982 | £4 | £10 | US |
| Starpower | 7" | Blast First | BFFP7 | 1986 | £4 | £8 | with badge & poster |
| Stick Me Donna Magick Momma | 7" | Fierce | FRIGHT015/6 | 1988 | £5 | £10 | |
| Stick Me Donna Magick Momma | 7" | Fierce | FRIGHT015/6 | 1988 | £10 | £20 | 2 x 1 sided 7" |
| Walls Have Ears | LP | NOT | NOT1 | 1986 | £25 | £50 | double |

## SONICS

| | | | | | | | |
|---|---|---|---|---|---|---|---|
| Explosives | LP | Buckshot | BSR001 | 1973 £50 | £100 | US |
| Here Are The Sonics | LP | Etiquette | LP024 | 1965 £37.50 | £75 | US |
| Introducing The Sonics | LP | Jerden | JRL7007 | 1967 £37.50 | £75 | US |
| Merry Christmas | LP | Etiquette | ALB025 | 1965 £50 | £100 | US, with the Wailers & the Galaxies |
| Sonics Boom | LP | Etiquette | LP(S)027 | 1966 £37.50 | £75 | US |

## SONLIGHT

| | | | | | | |
|---|---|---|---|---|---|---|
| Sonlight | LP | Light | | £30 | £60 | |

## SONN, LARRY

| | | | | | | |
|---|---|---|---|---|---|---|
| Larry Sonn Orchestra | LP | Vogue Coral | LVA9040 | 1957 £6 | £15 | |

## SONNY

| | | | | | | |
|---|---|---|---|---|---|---|
| Inner Views | LP | Atco | SD33329 | 1967 £8 | £20 | US |
| Laugh At Me | 7" EP | Atco | 107 | 1965 £4 | £8 | French |

## SONNY & CHER

| | | | | | | |
|---|---|---|---|---|---|---|
| Baby Don't Go | 7" EP | Reprise | RVEP60076 | 1965 £4 | £8 | French, B side by Jerry Keller |
| Baby Don't Go | 7" | Reprise | R20309 | 1964 £1.50 | £4 | |
| Beat Goes On | 7" EP | Atco | 118 | 1967 £4 | £8 | French |
| I Got You Babe | 7" EP | Atco | 101 | 1965 £5 | £10 | French |
| Je m'en balance car je l'aime | 7" EP | Atco | 108 | 1965 £4 | £8 | French |
| Just You | 7" EP | Atco | 102 | 1965 £4 | £8 | French |
| Look At Us | LP | Atlantic | ATL/STL5036 | 1964 £4 | £10 | |
| Petit homme | 7" EP | Atco | 117 | 1966 £4 | £8 | French |
| Plastic Man | 7" EP | Atco | 125 | 1967 £4 | £8 | French |
| Sonny And Cher And Caesar And Cleo | 7" EP | Reprise | R30056 | 1965 £5 | £10 | |
| What Now My Love | 7" EP | Atco | 112 | 1966 £4 | £8 | French |

## SONNY & THE CASCADES

| | | | | | | |
|---|---|---|---|---|---|---|
| Exciting New Liverpool Sound | LP | Columbia | CL2172 | 1964 £8 | £20 | US |

## SONNY & THE DAFFODILS

| | | | | | | |
|---|---|---|---|---|---|---|
| Sonny And The Daffodils | 7" EP | Ember | EMBEP4538 | 1963 £10 | £20 | |

## SONS & LOVERS

| | | | | | | |
|---|---|---|---|---|---|---|
| Matters | 7" | Camp | 602002 | 1967 £1.50 | £4 | |

## SONS OF CHAMPLIN

| | | | | | | |
|---|---|---|---|---|---|---|
| Follow Your Heart | LP | Capitol | ST675 | 1971 £6 | £15 | US |
| Loosen Up Naturally | LP | Capitol | SWBB200 | 1969 £15 | £30 | US double |
| Minus Stems And Seeds | LP | private | | 1971 £50 | £100 | US |
| Sons | LP | Capitol | SKAO322 | 1969 £8 | £20 | US |
| Welcome To The Dance | LP | CBS | 65663 | 1973 £5 | £12 | |

## SONS OF FRED

| | | | | | | |
|---|---|---|---|---|---|---|
| I, I, I | 7" | Parlophone | R5391 | 1965 £20 | £40 | |
| Sweet Love | 7" | Columbia | DB7605 | 1965 £37.50 | £75 | |
| You Told Me | 7" | Parlophone | R5415 | 1966 £25 | £50 | |

## SONS OF MAN

| | | | | | | |
|---|---|---|---|---|---|---|
| Sons Of Man | 7" EP | Oak | RGJ612 | 1967 £100 | £200 | best auctioned |

## SONS OF PILTDOWN MEN

| | | | | | | |
|---|---|---|---|---|---|---|
| Mad Goose | 7" | Pye | 7N25206 | 1963 £5 | £10 | |

## SONS OF SOUL

| | | | | | | |
|---|---|---|---|---|---|---|
| Yea Yea Baby | 7" | Doctor Bird | DB1037 | 1966 £5 | £10 | |

## SONS OF THE PIONEERS

| | | | | | | |
|---|---|---|---|---|---|---|
| Cowboy Classics | 10" LP | RCA | LPM3032 | 1952 £15 | £30 | US |
| Cowboy Hymns And Spirituals | 10" LP | RCA | LPM3095 | 1952 £15 | £30 | US |
| Favorite Cowboy Songs | LP | RCA | LPM1130 | 1955 £6 | £15 | US |
| How Great Thou Art | LP | RCA | LPM1431 | 1957 £5 | £12 | US |
| One Man's Songs | LP | RCA | LPM1483 | 1957 £6 | £15 | US |
| Sons Of The Pioneers | LP | RCA | RD27016 | 1957 £6 | £15 | |
| Sons Of The Pioneers | 7" EP | HMV | 7EG8069 | 1954 £4 | £8 | |
| Western Classics | 10" LP | RCA | LPM3162 | 1953 £15 | £30 | US |

## SOPWITH CAMEL

| | | | | | | |
|---|---|---|---|---|---|---|
| Hello Hello | LP | Kama Sutra | KSBS2063 | 1973 £4 | £10 | US |
| Hello Hello | 7" | Kama Sutra | KAS205 | 1966 £1.50 | £4 | |
| Miraculous Hump Returns From The Moon | LP | Reprise | K44251 | 1973 £4 | £10 | |
| Postcard From Jamaica | 7" EP | Kama Sutra | 617109 | 1967 £15 | £30 | French |
| Sopwith Camel | LP | Kama Sutra | KLP(S)8060 | 1967 £6 | £15 | US |

## SORCERERS

The German single by the Sorcerers is the first recording to feature drummer Cozy Powell. The group subsequently changed its name to Young Blood and released several singles in the UK.

| | | | | | | |
|---|---|---|---|---|---|---|
| Love Is A Beautiful Thing | 7" | Paletten | 667711 | 1967 £100 | £200 | German, best auctioned |

## SORROWS

| | | | | | | | |
|---|---|---|---|---|---|---|---|
| Baby | 7" | Piccadilly | 7N35230 | 1965 | £12.50 | £25 | |
| I Don't Wanna Be Free | 7" | Piccadilly | 7N35219 | 1965 | £15 | £30 | |
| Let Me In | 7" EP | Pye | PNV24168 | 1966 | £37.50 | £75 | French |
| Let Me In | 7" | Piccadilly | 7N35336 | 1966 | £12.50 | £25 | |
| Let The Love Live | 7" | Piccadilly | 7N35309 | 1966 | £12.50 | £25 | |
| Old Songs New Songs | LP | Miura | 10011 | 1968 | £50 | £100 | Italian |
| Pink, Purple, Yellow, Red | 7" | Piccadilly | 7N35385 | 1967 | £30 | £60 | |
| Take A Heart | LP | Pye | NPL38023 | 1965 | £50 | £100 | |
| Take A Heart | 7" EP | Pye | PNV24150 | 1965 | £37.50 | £75 | French |
| Take A Heart | 7" | Piccadilly | 7N35260 | 1965 | £6 | £12 | |
| You've Got What I Want | 7" | Piccadilly | 7N35277 | 1966 | £6 | £12 | |
| You've Got What I Want | 7" | Piccadilly | 7N35277 | 1966 | £12.50 | £25 | ... export picture sleeve |

## SORT SOL

| | | | | | | | |
|---|---|---|---|---|---|---|---|
| Marble Station | 7" | 4AD | AD101 | 1981 | £2.50 | £6 | |

## S.O.S.

| | | | | | | | |
|---|---|---|---|---|---|---|---|
| Skidmore-Osborne-Surman | LP | Ogun | OG400 | 1974 | £8 | £20 | |

## SOUL, HORATIO

| | | | | | | | |
|---|---|---|---|---|---|---|---|
| Ten White Horses | 7" | Island | WI3132 | 1968 | £2 | £5 | |

## SOUL, JIMMY

| | | | | | | | |
|---|---|---|---|---|---|---|---|
| I Hate You Baby | 7" | Stateside | SS274 | 1964 | £2 | £5 | |
| If You Wanna Be Happy | LP | SPQR | E16001 | 1963 | £10 | £25 | US |
| If You Wanna Be Happy | 7" EP | Stateside | SE1010 | 1964 | £7.50 | £15 | |
| If You Wanna Be Happy | 7" | Stateside | SS178 | 1963 | £2.50 | £6 | |
| Jimmy Soul And The Belmonts | LP | Spinorama | 123 | 1963 | £6 | £15 | US |
| Twisting Mathilda | 7" | Stateside | SS103 | 1962 | £2 | £5 | |

## SOUL, JUNIOR

| | | | | | | | |
|---|---|---|---|---|---|---|---|
| Chattie Chattie | 7" | Big Shot | BI503 | 1968 | £2.50 | £6 | |
| Hustler | 7" | Big Shot | BI527 | 1969 | £1.50 | £4 | |
| Miss Cushie | 7" | Doctor Bird | DB1112 | 1967 | £5 | £10 | Lyn Taitt B side |

## SOUL, SHARON

| | | | | | | | |
|---|---|---|---|---|---|---|---|
| How Can I Get To You? | 7" | Stateside | SS411 | 1965 | £20 | £40 | |

## SOUL AGENTS

| | | | | | | | |
|---|---|---|---|---|---|---|---|
| Don't Break It Up | 7" | Pye | 7N15768 | 1965 | £15 | £30 | |
| I Just Want To Make Love To You | 7" | Pye | 7N15660 | 1964 | £15 | £30 | |
| Seventh Son | 7" | Pye | 7N15707 | 1964 | £15 | £30 | |

## SOUL AGENTS (2)

| | | | | | | | |
|---|---|---|---|---|---|---|---|
| For Your Education | 7" | Coxsone | CS7018 | 1967 | £5 | £10 | .. Summertaires B side |
| Lecture | 7" | Coxsone | CS7027 | 1967 | £5 | £10 | ...... Soul Boys B side |

## SOUL BROTHERS

| | | | | | | | |
|---|---|---|---|---|---|---|---|
| Carib Soul | LP | Coxsone | CSL8002 | 1967 | £37.50 | £75 | |
| Green Moon | 7" | Island | WI282 | 1966 | £5 | £10 | |
| Hi Life | 7" | Island | WI3039 | 1967 | £5 | £10 | Delroy Wilson B side |
| Hot Shot Ska | LP | Coxsone | CSL8001 | 1967 | £50 | £100 | |
| James Bond Girl | 7" | Ska Beat | JB258 | 1967 | £5 | £10 | .. Summertaires B side |
| Our Man Flint | 7" | Island | WI3016 | 1967 | £5 | £10 | |
| Ska Shuffle | 7" | Rio | R119 | 1966 | £4 | £8 | .. Hortense & Delroy B side |
| Sound One | 7" | Island | WI296 | 1966 | £5 | £10 | . Emillo Straker B side |

## SOUL BROTHERS (2)

| | | | | | | | |
|---|---|---|---|---|---|---|---|
| Good Lovin' Never Hurt | 7" | Mercury | MF916 | 1965 | £1.50 | £4 | |
| I Can't Believe It | 7" | Parlophone | R5321 | 1965 | £4 | £8 | |
| I Keep Ringing My Baby | 7" | Decca | F12116 | 1965 | £2 | £5 | |

## SOUL BROTHERS SIX

| | | | | | | | |
|---|---|---|---|---|---|---|---|
| Some Kind Of Wonderful | 7" | Atlantic | 584118 | 1967 | £7.50 | £15 | |

## SOUL CARAVAN

| | | | | | | | |
|---|---|---|---|---|---|---|---|
| Gettin' High | LP | CBS | 63268 | 1967 | £8 | £20 | German |

## SOUL CHILDREN

| | | | | | | | |
|---|---|---|---|---|---|---|---|
| Friction | LP | Stax | STX1005 | 1974 | £4 | £10 | |
| Genesis | LP | Stax | 2325076 | 1972 | £4 | £10 | |

## SOUL CITY

| | | | | | | | |
|---|---|---|---|---|---|---|---|
| Everybody Dance Now | 7" | Cameo Parkway | C103 | 1962 | £10 | £20 | |

## SOUL CITY EXECUTIVES

| | | | | | | | |
|---|---|---|---|---|---|---|---|
| Happy Chatter | 7" | Soul City | SC109 | 1969 | £1.50 | £4 | |

## SOUL CLAN

| | | | | | | | |
|---|---|---|---|---|---|---|---|
| Soul Meeting | 7" | Atlantic | 584202 | 1968 | £1.50 | £4 | |
| Soul Meeting | 7" | Atlantic | 584202 | 1968 | £2.50 | £6 | picture sleeve |

## SOUL DEFENDERS

| | | | | | | | |
|---|---|---|---|---|---|---|---|
| Way Back Home | 7" | Banana | BA354 | 1971 | £1.50 | £4 | .... Soul Rebels B side |

## SOUL FLAMES
Mini Really Fit Dem .............................. 7" ...... Nu Beat .......... NB020 .................. 1968 £1.50 ......... £4 ...................................

## SOUL KINGS
Magnificent Seven ................................ 7" ...... Blue Cat .......... BS169 .................. 1969 £2.50 ..... £6  *Rupie Edwards B side*

## SOUL LEADERS
Pour On The Sauce ............................... 7" ...... Rio .............. R134 ................... 1967 £4 ............. £8

## SOUL PURPOSE
Hummin' .............................................. 7" ...... Island .......... WIP6040 ............... 1968 £5 ......... £10 ...................................

## SOUL RUNNERS
Grits 'n' Cornbread ............................... 7" ...... Polydor ......... 56732 ................. 1967 £2 ............ £5

## SOUL SEARCHERS
Salt Of The Earth .................................. LP ...... Sussex ............ LPSX4 ................ 1974 £6 ........ £15

## SOUL SISTERS
Good Time Tonight ................................. 7" ...... London .......... HLC9970 ............. 1965 £7.50 ..... £15 ...................................
I Can't Stand It ...................................... 7" ...... Sue ................ WI312 ............... 1964 £7.50 ..... £15 ...................................
Loop De Loop ........................................ 7" ...... Sue ............. WI336 ............... 1964 £10 ....... £20
Soul Sisters .......................................... LP ..... Sue ............. ILP913 ............... 1964 £15 ....... £30 ...................................

## SOUL SISTERS (2)
Wreck A Buddy ...................................... 7" ...... Amalgamated ... AMG839 ............... 1969 £2 ............ £5

## SOUL SOUNDS
*Soul Survival* is an album of R&B instrumentals played by various ex-Savages and Rebel Rousers. Soul Sounds was not a working group, but the musicians could play this kind of music with one arm tied behind their backs and the record is a convincing addition to the genre, if a little out of date for 1967.

Soul Survival ........................................ LP ...... Columbia ........ SX6158 ............... 1967 £4 ........ £10 ...................................

## SOUL STIRRERS
Soul Stirrers Featuring Sam Cooke ............. LP ...... London ............ HAU8232 .............. 1965 £8 ........ £20 ...................................

## SOUL SURVIVORS
Explosion ............................................ 7" ...... Stateside ......... SS2094 ............. 1968 £1.50 ...... £4 ...................................
Expressway To Your Heart ...................... 7" ...... Stateside ......... SS2057 ............. 1967 £4 ........ £8 ...................................
When The Whistle Blows Anything Goes .. LP ...... Crimson .......... LP502 ............... 1967 £15 ........ £30 ..................... *US*

## SOUL VENDORS
Captain Cojoe ....................................... 7" ...... Studio One ...... SO2070 ............. 1968 £6 ........ £12 ...*Jackie Mittoo B side*
Drum Song ........................................... 7" ...... Coxsone ........ CS7031 ............ 1967 £5 ......... £10 .... *Cool Spoon B side*
Evening Time ........................................ 7" ...... Studio One ...... SO2048 ............. 1968 £6 ........ £12 ...... *Righteous Flames*
Fat Fish ............................................... 7" ...... Coxsone ........ CS7029 ............ 1967 £5 ......... £10 *Marcia Griffiths B side*
Grooving Steady ................................... 7" ...... Coxsone ........ CS7037 ............ 1968 £5 ......... £10 .. *Roy Richards B side*
Hot Rod ............................................... 7" ...... Studio One ...... SO2034 ............. 1967 £6 ........ £12 ......... *Gaylads B side*
On Tour ............................................... LP ...... Coxsone ........ CSL8010 ............ 1967 £50 ....... £100 ...................................
Real Rock ............................................ 7" ...... Coxsone ........ CS7057 ............ 1968 £5 ......... £10 ...*Al Campbell B side*
Rocking Sweet Pea ................................ 7" ...... Studio One ...... SO2018 ............. 1967 £6 ........ £12 ...... *Joe Higgs B side*
Sixth Figure ......................................... 7" ...... Coxsone ........ CS7084 ............ 1969 £5 ......... £10 ..*Denzil Laing B side*
Soul Joint ............................................ 7" ...... Studio One ...... SO2066 ............. 1968 £6 ........ £12 ...................................
To Sir With Love ................................... 7" ...... Blue Cat .......... BS112 .............. 1968 £4 ........ £8 ..... *Righteous Flames B side*
You Troubled Me ................................... 7" ...... Coxsone ........ CS7028 ............ 1967 £5 ......... £10 ..*Bop & The Beltones B side*

## SOULE, GEORGE
Get Involved ......................................... 7" ...... United Artists .. UP35771 ............... 1975 £2.50 ...... £6 ...................................

## SOULETTES
My Desire ............................................ 7" ...... Jackpot ............ JP766 .................. 1971 £1.50 ...... £4

## SOULFUL STRINGS
Burning Spear ....................................... 7" ...... Chess ............. CRS8068 ............. 1967 £5 ......... £10
Groovin' With The Soulful Strings ............. LP ...... Chess ............. CRLS4534 ............ 1969 £4 ......... £10

## SOULMATES
Bring Your Love Back Home ...................... 7" ...... Parlophone ... R5407 ............... 1966 £2 ............ £5
Is That You .......................................... 7" ...... Parlophone ... R5601 ............... 1967 £1.50 ...... £4
Mood Melancholy ................................... 7" ...... Parlophone ... R5506 ............... 1966 £1.50 ...... £4
Too Late To Say You're Sorry ................... 7" ...... Parlophone ... R5334 ............... 1965 £2 ............ £5

## SOULMATES (2)
On The Move ........................................ 7" ...... Amalgamated ... AMG842 ............... 1969 £2.50 ...... £6
Them A Laugh And A Ki Ki ...................... 7" ...... Amalgamated ... AMG836 ............... 1969 £2.50 ...... £6

## SOUND
Physical World ...................................... 7" ...... Tortch ............ TOR003 .............. 1979 £6 ......... £12
Sound ................................................. LP ...... Tortch ............ TOR008 .............. 1979 £6 ......... £15

## SOUND BARRIER
She Always Comes Back To Me ................. 7" ...... Beacon ............ BEA109 ............... 1968 £1.50 ...... £4 ...................................

## SOUND DIMENSION

| | | | | | | | |
|---|---|---|---|---|---|---|---|
| Baby Face | 7" | Bamboo | BAM7 | 1969 | £1.50 | £4 | Gladiators B side |
| Black Onion | 7" | Bamboo | BAM14 | 1969 | £1.50 | £4 | |
| Doctor Sappa Too | 7" | Bamboo | BAM5 | 1969 | £1.50 | £4 | |
| In The Summertime | 7" | Banana | BA313 | 1970 | £1.50 | £4 | |
| Jamaica Rag | 7" | Bamboo | BAM9 | 1969 | £1.50 | £4 | C. Marshall B side |
| More Scorcia | 7" | Coxsone | CS7093 | 1969 | £5 | £10 | Lennie Hibbert B side |
| My Sweet Lord | 7" | Banana | BA338 | 1970 | £1.50 | £4 | Dennis Brown B side |
| Poison Ivy | 7" | Bamboo | BAM18 | 1970 | £1.50 | £4 | |
| Scorcia | 7" | Coxsone | CS7083 | 1969 | £5 | £10 | Cecil & Jackie B side |
| Soulful Strut | 7" | Coxsone | CS7090 | 1969 | £5 | £10 | |
| Time Is Tight | 7" | Coxsone | CS7097 | 1969 | £5 | £10 | Barry Llewellyn B side |
| Whoopee | 7" | Bamboo | BAM13 | 1969 | £1.50 | £4 | Norma Fraser B side |

## SOUND NETWORK

| | | | | | | |
|---|---|---|---|---|---|---|
| Watching | 7" | Mercury | MF944 | 1965 | £6 | £12 |

## SOUND OF REFLECTION

| | | | | | | |
|---|---|---|---|---|---|---|
| Brave New World | 7" | Reflection | RS6001 | 1968 | £2 | £5 |

## SOUND RIDERS

| | | | | | | | |
|---|---|---|---|---|---|---|---|
| Sound Riders | LP | Ariola | 72657IT | 1964 | £50 | £100 | German |

## SOUNDGARDEN

| | | | | | | | |
|---|---|---|---|---|---|---|---|
| Flower | CD-s | SST | SST231CD | 1989 | £2 | £5 | |
| Hands All Over | CD-s | A&M | AMCD560 | 1990 | £2.50 | £6 | |
| Hands All Over | 10" | A&M | AMX560 | 1990 | £2.50 | £6 | |
| Jesus Christ Pose | CD-s | A&M | AMCD691 | 1991 | £2 | £5 | |
| Louder Than Love | 12" | A&M | AMY574 | 1989 | £2.50 | £6 | 1 side etched |
| Rusty Cage | CD-s | A&M | AMCD723 | 1992 | £2 | £5 | |

## SOUNDS AROUND

| | | | | | | |
|---|---|---|---|---|---|---|
| Red White And You | 7" | Piccadilly | 7N35396 | 1967 | £2.50 | £6 |
| What Does She Do? | 7" | Piccadilly | 7N35345 | 1966 | £2.50 | £6 |

## SOUNDS INCORPORATED

| | | | | | | | |
|---|---|---|---|---|---|---|---|
| Emily | 7" | Parlophone | R4815 | 1961 | £2.50 | £6 | |
| Go | 7" | Decca | F11590 | 1963 | £1.50 | £4 | |
| I'm Coming Through | 7" | Columbia | DB7737 | 1965 | £2.50 | £6 | |
| Keep Moving | 7" | Decca | F11723 | 1963 | £5 | £10 | |
| Rinky Dink | LP | Regal | SREG1071 | 1965 | £4 | £10 | |
| Sounds Incorporated | LP | Columbia | SX/SCX3531 | 1964 | £4 | £10 | |
| Sounds Incorporated | LP | Studio Two | TWO1449 | 1966 | £4 | £10 | |
| Top Gear | 7" EP | Columbia | SEG8360 | 1964 | £4 | £8 | |
| Twist At The Star Club Hamburg | LP | Philips | P48036L | 1964 | £8 | £20 | German |

## SOUNDS NICE

| | | | | | | | |
|---|---|---|---|---|---|---|---|
| Love At First Sight | LP | Parlophone | PMC/PCS7089 | 1969 | £8 | £20 | |

## SOUNDS OF MODIFICATION

| | | | | | | | |
|---|---|---|---|---|---|---|---|
| Sounds Of Modification | LP | London | SHAU111 | 1967 | £8 | £20 | German |

## SOUNDS PROGRESSIVE

| | | | | | | |
|---|---|---|---|---|---|---|
| Kid Jensen Introduces Sounds Progressive | LP | Eyemark | EMCL1009 | 1970 | £25 | £50 |

## SOUNDS SENSATIONAL

| | | | | | | |
|---|---|---|---|---|---|---|
| Love In The Open Air | 7" | HMV | POP1584 | 1967 | £2 | £5 |

## SOUNDSVILLE

| | | | | | | | |
|---|---|---|---|---|---|---|---|
| Soundsville | LP | Spectrum | 187 | 1962 | £25 | £50 | US |

## SOUNDTRACK RECORDINGS

| | | | | | | | |
|---|---|---|---|---|---|---|---|
| Addams Family | LP | RCA | LPM/LSP3421 | 1964 | £8 | £20 | US, by Vic Muzzy |
| Africa | LP | MGM | (S)E4462 | 1967 | £8 | £20 | US, by Alex North |
| Agony And The Ecstasy | LP | Capitol | (S)MAS2427 | 1965 | £15 | £30 | US, by Alex North |
| Alakazam The Great | LP | Vee Jay | LP6000 | 1961 | £10 | £25 | US, by Les Baxter |
| Alfred The Great | LP | MGM | CS8112 | 1969 | £75 | £150 | by Raymond Leppard |
| All Night Long | LP | Fontana | STFL591 | 1961 | £8 | £20 | by Ira Newborn & Richard Hazard |
| Amorous Adventures Of Moll Flanders | LP | RCA | LOC/LSO1113 | 196– | £8 | £20 | US, by John Addison |
| Apartment | LP | United Artists | UAL3105/ UAS6105 | 1960 | £15 | £30 | US, by Mitchell Powell |
| Barabbas | LP | Colpix | (S)CP510 | 1962 | £20 | £40 | US, by Mario Nascimbene |
| Barbarella | LP | Stateside | (S)SL10260 | 1968 | £30 | £60 | by Bob Crewe |
| Barefoot In The Park | LP | London | HAD8337 | 1967 | £8 | £20 | by Neal Hefti |
| Behold A Pale Horse | LP | Colpix | (S)CP519 | 1964 | £15 | £30 | US, by Maurice Jarre |
| Blue Max | LP | Mainstream | 5/S6081 | 1966 | £8 | £20 | US, by Jerry Goldsmith |
| Boccaccio '70 | LP | RCA | FOC/FSO5 | 1962 | £15 | £30 | US |
| Bullitt | LP | Warner Bros | WS1777 | 1968 | £15 | £30 | US, by Lalo Schifrin |
| Burke's Law | LP | Liberty | LRP3374/LST7374 | 1964 | £8 | £20 | US, by Herschel Burke Gilbert |
| Captain Horatio Hornblower | LP | Delyse | D3057/DS6057 | 1960 | £30 | £60 | by Robert Farnon |
| Checkmate | LP | Columbia | CL1591/CS8391 | 1960 | £15 | £30 | US, by John Williams |
| Cherry And Harry And Raquel | LP | Beverly Hills | BHS23 | 1968 | £25 | £50 | US, by Bill Loose |
| Chimes At Midnight | LP | Fontana | TL5417 | 1967 | £20 | £40 | by Angelo Lavagnino |

| Title | Format | Label | Catalogue | Year | Price | Price | Notes |
|---|---|---|---|---|---|---|---|
| Circus Of Horrors | LP | Imperial | 9132 | 1960 | £37.50 | £75 | US, by Muir Mathieson |
| Collector | LP | Fontana | (S)TL5259 | 1965 | £20 | | by Maurice Jarre |
| Custer Of The West | LP | Stateside | (S)SL10222 | 1968 | £10 | £25 | by Bernardo Segall |
| Decline And Fall Of A Birdwatcher | LP | Stateside | (S)SL10259 | 1968 | £25 | £50 | by Ron Goodwin |
| Dick Powell Presents | LP | Dot | DLP3421/25421 | 1962 | £10 | £25 | US |
| Dr. Faustus | LP | CBS | 63189 | 1967 | £30 | £60 | by Mario Nascimbene |
| Experiment In Terror | LP | RCA | LPM/LSP2442 | 1962 | £15 | £30 | US, by Henry Mancini, Lee Remick sleeve |
| Fathom | LP | Stateside | (S)SL10213 | 1967 | £10 | £25 | by John Dankworth |
| Flying Clipper | LP | Ace Of Clubs | ACL1166 | 1964 | £8 | £20 | by Riz Ortolani |
| Fox | LP | Warner Bros | WS1738 | 1968 | £10 | £25 | US, by Lalo Schifrin |
| Francis Of Assisi | LP | Twentieth Century Fox | FOX/SFX3053 | 1961 | £30 | £60 | US, by Mario Nascimbene & Franco Ferrara |
| Get Smart | LP | United Artists | UAL3533/ UAS6533 | 1965 | £8 | £20 | US, by Don Adams |
| Girl From UNCLE | LP | MGM | C(S)8034 | 1966 | £10 | £25 | by Jerry Goldsmith & Teddy Randazzo |
| Goliath And The Barbarians | LP | American International | 1001M/S | 1960 | £8 | £20 | US, by Les Baxter |
| Gone With The Wave | LP | Colpix | (S)CP492 | 1965 | £8 | £20 | US, by Lalo Schifrin |
| Gospel According To St. Matthew | LP | Mainstream | (S)54000 | 1966 | £10 | £25 | US |
| Great Race | LP | RCA | RD7759 | 1965 | £10 | £25 | by Henry Mancini |
| Green Hornet | LP | Twentieth Century Fox | TF/S3186 | 1966 | £20 | £40 | US, by Billy May |
| Gypsy | LP | Warner Bros | WM/WS8120 | 1962 | £8 | £20 | by Jule Styne |
| Harper | LP | Mainstream | (S)6078 | 1966 | £8 | £20 | US, by Johnny Mandel |
| Heidi | LP | Capitol | SKA02995 | 1968 | £20 | £40 | US, by John Williams |
| Hell To Eternity | LP | Warwick | W(ST)2030 | 1960 | £10 | £25 | US, by Leith Stevens |
| Hell's Bells | LP | Sidewalk | 5919 | 1969 | £15 | £30 | US, by Les Baxter |
| Hemingway's Adventures Of A Young Man | LP | RCA | MOC1074 | 1962 | £10 | £25 | US, by Franz Waxman |
| Hong Kong | LP | ABC | (S)367 | 1961 | £8 | £20 | US |
| How To Murder Your Wife | LP | United Artists | (S)ULP1098 | 1964 | £8 | £20 | by Neal Hefti |
| How To Steal A Million | LP | Stateside | (S)SL10187 | 1966 | £10 | £25 | by John Williams |
| Hustler | LP | Kapp | KL/KS1264 | 1961 | £15 | £30 | US, by Kenyon Hopkins |
| In Harm's Way | LP | RCA | LOC/LSO1100 | 1965 | £8 | £20 | US, by Jerry Goldsmith |
| In Like Flint | LP | Stateside | (S)SL10207 | 1967 | £15 | £30 | by Jerry Goldsmith |
| Interlude | LP | RCA | RD/SF7990 | 1968 | £8 | £20 | by Georges Delarue |
| It Started In Naples | LP | Dot | DLP3324/25324 | 1960 | £15 | £30 | US, by Alessandro Cicognini |
| Italian Job | LP | Paramount | SPFL256 | 1969 | £20 | £40 | by Quincy Jones |
| Jack And The Beanstalk | LP | HBR | HLP8511 | 1967 | £10 | £25 | US, by James Van Heusen |
| Jack The Ripper | LP | RCA | CAL590 | 1960 | £20 | £40 | US, by Stanley Black |
| Juliet Of The Spirits | LP | Fontana | (S)TL5317 | 1967 | £15 | £30 | by Nino Rota |
| Justine | LP | Monument | SLP18123 | 1969 | £10 | £25 | US, by Jerry Goldsmith |
| Kaleidoscope | LP | Warner Bros | W(S)1663 | 1966 | £15 | £30 | US, by Stanley Myers |
| Khartoum | LP | United Artists | (S)ULP1139 | 1966 | £10 | £25 | by Frank Cordell |
| La Dolce Vita | LP | RCA | RD27202 | 1961 | £30 | £60 | by Nino Rota |
| Lady In Cement | LP | Stateside | (S)SL10267 | 1969 | £10 | £25 | by Hugo Montenegro |
| Lion | LP | London | M76001 | 1962 | £50 | £100 | US, by Malcolm Arnold |
| Long Ships | LP | Colpix | (S)CP517 | 1964 | £25 | £50 | US, by Dusan Radic |
| Loss Of Innocence | LP | Colpix | CP508 | 1962 | £15 | £30 | US, by Richard Addinsell |
| Lost Command | LP | Cinema | LP8017 | 1966 | £10 | £25 | US, by Franz Waxman |
| Man For All Seasons | LP | RCA | RB6712/3 | 1966 | £10 | £25 | by Georges Delarue, double |
| Mayerling | LP | Philips | SBL7876 | 1969 | £25 | £50 | by Francis Lai |
| McLintock | LP | United Artists | UAL4112/ UAS5112 | 1963 | £8 | £20 | US, by Frank DeVol |
| Midas Run | LP | Citadel | CT6016 | 1968 | £30 | £60 | US, by Elmer Bernstein |
| Misfits | LP | United Artists | CLP1481 | 1961 | £8 | £20 | by Alex North |
| Mission: Impossible | LP | Dot | (S)LPD503 | 1968 | £10 | £25 | by Lalo Schifrin |
| Modesty Blaise | LP | Fontana | TL5347 | 1966 | £15 | £30 | by John Dankworth |
| Monte Carlo Or Bust! | LP | Paramount | SPFL255 | 1969 | £10 | £25 | by Ron Goodwin |
| Munsters | LP | Decca | DL(7)4588 | 1964 | £10 | £25 | US |
| Murder Inc. | LP | Canadian American | CALP1003 | 1960 | £15 | £30 | US, by Frank DeVol |
| Murderer's Row | LP | Colgems | COMO/ COSO5003 | 1967 | £15 | £30 | US, by Lalo Schifrin |
| My Geisha | LP | RCA | LOC/LSO1070 | 1962 | £10 | £25 | US, by Franz Waxman |
| Nevada Smith | LP | Dot | DLP3718/25718 | 1966 | £8 | £20 | US, by Alfred Newman |
| Night Of The Generals | LP | Colgems | COMO/ COSO5002 | 1967 | £8 | £20 | US, by Maurice Jarre |
| Nine Hours To Rama | LP | Decca | LK4527 | 1962 | £37.50 | £75 | by Malcolm Arnold |
| Octopussy | CD-s | A&M | 3949672 | 1983 | £6 | £15 | |

| | | | | | | | |
|---|---|---|---|---|---|---|---|
| Our Man Flint | LP | Stateside | (S)SL10174 | 1966 | £10 | £25 | .... by Jerry Goldsmith |
| Our Mother's House | LP | MGM | (S)E4495 | 1967 | £8 | £20 | ........US, by Georges Delarue |
| Panic Button | LP | Musicor | MM2026/MS3026 | 1964 | £10 | £25 | ........US, by Georges Garavarentz |
| Parrish | LP | Warner Bros | W(S)1413 | 1961 | £8 | £20 | ..US, by Max Steiner & George Creeley |
| Play Time/Les Vacances de M. Hulot etc. | LP | Philips | SBL7858 | 1968 | £10 | £25 | ......... by Jacques Tati |
| Pretty Boy Floyd | LP | Audio Fidelity | AFLP1936/SD5936 | 1960 | £8 | £20 | ...... US, by William Sandford |
| Professionals | LP | RCA | RD/SF7876 | 1976 | £10 | £25 | ...... by Maurice Jarre |
| Pulp Fiction | CD | MCA | MCD11103 | 1994 | £10 | £25 | ...... with bonus CD featuring Tarantino interview |
| Red And Blue | LP | United Artists | (S)ULP1184 | 1967 | £10 | £25 | ....... with Vanessa Redgrave |
| Rocket To The Moon | LP | Polydor | 583013 | 1967 | £30 | £60 | .......... by John Scott |
| Sergeants Three | LP | Reprise | R2013 | 1962 | £10 | £25 | ........... by Billy May |
| Shalako | LP | Philips | SBL7867 | 1968 | £8 | £20 | ....by Robert Farnon |
| Silencers | LP | RCA | RD7792 | 1966 | £10 | £25 | ..by Elmer Berstein |
| Ski On The Wild Side | LP | MGM | (S)E4439 | 1967 | £8 | £20 | ....US, by Billy Allen |
| Sodom And Gomorrah | LP | RCA | LOC/LSO1076 | 1963 | £30 | £60 | US, by Miklos Rozsa |
| Sons Of Katie Elder | LP | CBS | BPG62558 | 1965 | £8 | £20 | ..by Elmer Bernstein, with Johnny Cash |
| Stagecoach | LP | Fontana | (S)TL5354 | 1966 | £10 | £25 | ....; by Jerry Goldsmith |
| Summer And Smoke | LP | RCA | LOC/LSO1067 | 1961 | £15 | £30 | ........ US, by Elmer Bernstein |
| Sweet Charity | LP | MCA | MUCS133 | 1969 | £8 | £20 | ..by Cy Coleman and Dorothy Fields |
| Taming Of The Shrew | LP | RCA | VDM117 | 1967 | £15 | £30 | ...US, by Nino Rota |
| Tender Is The Night | LP | Twentieth Century Fox | FOX/SFX3054 | 1962 | £37.50 | £75 | . US, by Sammy Fain & Bernard Herrmann |
| They Came To Rob Las Vegas | LP | Philips | SBL7898 | 1969 | £15 | £30 | by Georges Gavarentz |
| Those Magnificent Men In Their Flying Machines | LP | Stateside | SL10136 | 1965 | £8 | £20 | ...... by Ron Goodwin |
| Three Worlds Of Gulliver | LP | Colpix | CP414 | 1961 | £20 | £40 | ......US, by Bernard Herrmann |
| To Kill A Mockingbird | LP | Ava | A(S)20 | 1964 | £8 | £20 | ......US, by Elmer Bernstein |
| Trap | LP | Polydor | | 1966 | £10 | £25 | ...... by Ron Goodwin |
| Trouble With Angels | LP | Mainstream | 5/S6073 | 1966 | £15 | £30 | ...........US, by Jerry Goldsmith |
| Tunes Of Glory | LP | United Artists | UAL4086/ UAS5086 | 1961 | £8 | £20 | ......US, by Malcolm Arnold |
| Twisted Nerve/Les Bicyclettes de Belsize | LP | Polydor | 583728 | 1968 | £62.50 | £125 | by Bernard Herrmann Reed and Mason |
| Unforgiven | LP | United Artists | UAL4068/ UAS5068 | 1960 | £15 | £30 | ...... US, by Dmitri Tiomkin |
| Valley Of The Dolls | LP | Stateside | (S)SL10228 | 1968 | £10 | £25 | ...... by André & Dory Previn & John Williams |
| Viva Maria! | LP | United Artists | (S)ULP1126 | 1966 | £10 | £25 | ... by Georges Delarue |
| Vixen | LP | Beverly Hills | BHS22 | 1968 | £25 | £50 | ....US, by Bill Loose |
| Walk With Love And Death | LP | Citadel | CT6025 | 1969 | £20 | £40 | ....US, by Georges Delarue |
| War Lord | LP | Brunswick | STA8636 | 1966 | £10 | £25 | ...... by Jerome Moross |
| Who's Afraid Of Virginia Woolf? | LP | Warner Bros | 2B1657 | 1966 | £15 | £30 | .. US double, by Alex North |
| Wild Bunch | LP | Warner Bros | WS1814 | 1969 | £15 | £30 | ...... by Jerry Fielding |
| Yojimbo | LP | MGM | (S)E4096 | 1962 | £25 | £50 | . US, by Masaru Sato |

## SOUP

| | | | | | | | |
|---|---|---|---|---|---|---|---|
| Soup | LP | Arf Arm | 1 | 1970 | £10 | £25 | US, insert but no cover |

## SOUP DRAGONS

| | | | | | | | |
|---|---|---|---|---|---|---|---|
| Deep Trash (Lovegod) | cass | Raw TV Products | | 1989 | £4 | £10 | |
| I'm Free | CD-s | Raw TV Products | RTV9CD | 1990 | £2 | £5 | |
| Mother Universe | CD-s | Raw TV Products | RTV8CD | 1990 | £2 | £5 | |
| Sun Is In The Sky | 7" | Subway | SUBWAY2 | 1986 | £5 | £10 | |

## SOUP GREENS

| | | | | | | | |
|---|---|---|---|---|---|---|---|
| Like A Rolling Stone | 7" | Stateside | SS457 | 1965 | £20 | £40 | |

## SOUTH, JOE

| | | | | | | | |
|---|---|---|---|---|---|---|---|
| Introspect | LP | Capitol | E(S)T108 | 1969 | £4 | £10 | |
| Masquerade | 7" | Oriole | CB1752 | 1962 | £1.50 | £4 | |
| Walk A Mile In My Shoes | 7" | Capitol | CL15625 | 1970 | £1.50 | £4 | |

## SOUTH COAST SKA STARS

| | | | | | | | |
|---|---|---|---|---|---|---|---|
| South Coast Rumble | 7" | Safari | SAFE27 | 1980 | £2 | £5 | |

## SOUTH FORTY

| | | | | | | | |
|---|---|---|---|---|---|---|---|
| Live At The Someplace Else | LP | Metrobeat | MBS1000 | 1964 | £8 | £20 | US |

## SOUTHERN, JERI

| | | | | | | | |
|---|---|---|---|---|---|---|---|
| At The Crescendo | LP | Capitol | (S)T1278 | 1960 | £4 | £10 | |
| Caresses | 7" EP | Brunswick | OE9438 | 1959 | £4 | £8 | |
| Coffee, Cigarettes And Memories | LP | Columbia | 33SX1134 | 1958 | £4 | £10 | |
| Fire Down Below | 7" | Brunswick | 05665 | 1957 | £1.50 | £4 | |
| Jeri Gently Jumps | LP | Brunswick | LAT8209 | 1957 | £6 | £15 | |
| Man That Got Away | 7" | Brunswick | 05367 | 1955 | £2 | £5 | |
| Meets Cole Porter | LP | Capitol | (S)T1173 | 1959 | £4 | £10 | |
| Meets Johnny Smith | LP | Columbia | 33SX1155 | 1959 | £4 | £10 | |
| Occasional Man | 7" | Brunswick | 05490 | 1955 | £2 | £5 | |
| Prelude To A Kiss | LP | Decca | DL8745 | 1958 | £5 | £12 | US |
| Remind Me | 7" | Brunswick | 05343 | 1954 | £2 | £5 | |
| Ridin' High | 7" EP | Columbia | SEG7935 | 1959 | £4 | £8 | |
| Southern Breeze | LP | Columbia | 33SX1110 | 1958 | £4 | £10 | |
| Southern Hospitality | LP | Decca | DL8761 | 1958 | £5 | £12 | US |
| Southern Style | LP | Brunswick | LAT8100 | 1956 | £6 | £15 | |
| Warm | 10" LP | Brunswick | LA8699 | 1955 | £8 | £20 | |
| When Your Heart's On Fire | LP | Decca | DL8394 | 1957 | £6 | £15 | US |
| Where Walks My True Love | 7" | Brunswick | 05529 | 1956 | £1.50 | £4 | |
| You Better Go Now | LP | Decca | DL8214 | 1956 | £6 | £15 | US |

## SOUTHERN, JOHNNY

| | | | | | | | |
|---|---|---|---|---|---|---|---|
| She's Long, She's Tall | 7" | Melodisc | 1434 | 1957 | £1.50 | £4 | |
| We Will Make Love | 7" | Melodisc | 1413 | 1958 | £1.50 | £4 | |

## SOUTHERN DEATH CULT

| | | | | | | | |
|---|---|---|---|---|---|---|---|
| Moya | 7" | Situation 2 | SIT19 | 1982 | £1.50 | £4 | poster sleeve |

## SOUTHERN SOUND

| | | | | | | | |
|---|---|---|---|---|---|---|---|
| Just The Same As You | 7" | Columbia | DB7982 | 1966 | £150 | £250 | best auctioned |

## SOUTHERN TONES

| | | | | | | | |
|---|---|---|---|---|---|---|---|
| Waiting On The Lord | 7" EP | Collector | JEN10 | 1962 | £2 | £5 | |

## SOUTHLANDERS

| | | | | | | | |
|---|---|---|---|---|---|---|---|
| Ain't That A Shame | 7" | Parlophone | MSP6182 | 1955 | £6 | £12 | |
| Alone | 7" | Decca | F10946 | 1957 | £1.50 | £4 | |
| Choo-Choo-Choo Cha-Cha-Cha | 7" | Decca | F11067 | 1958 | £1.50 | £4 | |
| Down Deep | 7" | Decca | F11014 | 1958 | £1.50 | £4 | |
| Hush A Bye Rock | 7" | Parlophone | MSP6236 | 1956 | £4 | £8 | |
| Peanuts | 7" | Decca | F10958 | 1957 | £1.50 | £4 | |
| Put A Light In The Window | 7" | Decca | F10982 | 1958 | £5 | £10 | |
| Southlanders No. 1 | 7" EP | Decca | DFE6508 | 1958 | £10 | £20 | |
| Torero | 7" | Decca | F11032 | 1958 | £4 | £8 | |

## SOUTHSIDE JOHNNY & THE ASBURY DUKES

| | | | | | | | |
|---|---|---|---|---|---|---|---|
| Juke Up Album Network | CD | Impact | | 1992 | £8 | £20 | US promo |
| Little Girl So Fine | 7" | Epic | EPC5230 | 1977 | £5 | £10 | |
| Live At The Bottom Line | LP | Epic | AS275 | 1976 | £6 | £15 | US promo |

## SOUTHWEST F.O.B.

| | | | | | | | |
|---|---|---|---|---|---|---|---|
| Smell Of Incense | LP | Hip | HIS7001 | 1969 | £15 | £30 | US |
| Smell Of Incense | 7" | Stax | STAX107 | 1968 | £1.50 | £4 | |

## SOVEREIGNS

| | | | | | | | |
|---|---|---|---|---|---|---|---|
| Bring Me Home Love | 7" | King | KG1050 | 1966 | £1.50 | £4 | |

## SOVIET FRANCE

| | | | | | | | |
|---|---|---|---|---|---|---|---|
| Garista | CD | Charrm | CHARRMCD001 | 1988 | £5 | £12 | |
| Hessian | CD | Charrm | CHARRMCD002 | 1989 | £5 | £12 | |
| Look Into Me | CD | Charrm | CHARRMCD014 | 1990 | £5 | £12 | |
| Norsche | CD | Charrm | CHARRMCD003 | 1984 | £5 | £12 | |
| Soviet France | 12" | Red Rhino | RED12 | 1982 | £4 | £10 | hessian sleeve |

## SOVINE, RED

| | | | | | | | |
|---|---|---|---|---|---|---|---|
| Country Music | 7" EP | Top Rank | JKP3015 | 1962 | £4 | £8 | |
| Giddy-Up Go | LP | London | HAB8288 | 1966 | £4 | £10 | |
| I Didn't Jump The Fence | LP | London | HAB8343 | 1967 | £4 | £10 | |
| One And Only Red Sovine | LP | Starday | SLP132 | 1961 | £6 | £15 | US |
| Red Sovine | LP | MGM | E3465 | 1957 | £8 | £20 | US |
| Sixteen Tons | 7" | Brunswick | 05513 | 1956 | £15 | £30 | |

## SOXX, BOB B. & THE BLUE JEANS

| | | | | | | | |
|---|---|---|---|---|---|---|---|
| Not Too Young To Get Married | 7" | London | HLU9754 | 1963 | £5 | £10 | |
| Why Do Lovers Break Each Other's Hearts | 7" | London | HLU9694 | 1963 | £4 | £8 | |
| Zip A Dee Doo Dah | LP | London | HAU8121 | 1963 | £30 | £60 | |
| Zip A Dee Doo Dah | LP | Philles | PHLP4002 | 1963 | £37.50 | £75 | US |
| Zip A Dee Doo Dah | 7" | London | HLU9646 | 1963 | £2.50 | £6 | |

## SPACE

| | | | | | | | |
|---|---|---|---|---|---|---|---|
| If It's Real | 12" | Hug | HUGG1T | 1993 | £10 | £20 | |

## SPACE (2)

| | | | | | | | |
|---|---|---|---|---|---|---|---|
| Just Blue | LP | Pye | NSPH28275 | 1979 | £6 | £15 | picture disc |
| Space | LP | KLF | SPACELP1 | 1990 | £8 | £20 | |
| Space | CD | KLF | SPACECD1 | 1990 | £15 | £30 | |

## SPACE (3)
Space.............................................. LP ...... Hand ............. ST5167 ................. 1968 £8............£20 ...................... US

## SPACE ART
Space Art......................................... LP ...... Ariola Hansa.... AHAL8001............. 1977 £4............£10 ..........................

## SPACE OPERA
Space Opera...................................... LP ...... Epic ............. 32117..................... 1973 £6............£15 ...................... US

## SPACEMEN
Clouds.............................................. 7" ...... Top Rank ....... JAR228................. 1959 £5............£10 ..........................
Music For Batman And Robin................... LP ...... Roulette ......... MG/SR25322 ........ 1966 £6............£15 ...................... US
Rockin' In The 25th Century................... LP ...... Roulette ......... MG/SR25275 ........ 1964 £6............£15 ...................... US

## SPACEMEN 3
First Genesis and then Spacemen 3 emerged to prove public schools as an effective, if unlikely, breeding ground for innovative rock music. Spacemen 3 developed rapidly from the first album catalogue of their sixties influences, finding a variety of imaginative ways of texturing electric guitar drones. Though not all of the songs are equally successful, at their best (such as on the album length 12" single 'Transparent Radiation' and on all of the records of the group's main successor, Spiritualized) the result is music that is both moving and magisterial. The demise of the Glass label has ensured that original pressings of the group's records are rising in value, even though album reissues on the Fire label are readily available.

Big City ......................................... CD-s .. Fire................. BLAZE41CD ........ 1991 £2............£5 ............................
Big City (remix)/I Love You.................... 12"..... Fire................. BLAZE41TR ........ 1991 £25...........£50 .......... test pressing
Dreamweapon................................... LP ...... Fierce ............. FRIGHT042 .......... 1990 £4............£10 ............................
Dreamweapon................................... CD.... Fierce ............. FRIGHT042CD.... 1990 £6............£15 ............................
Extract From A Contemporary Sitar ........ 7" ...... Cheree............. CHEREE5............. 1989 £4............£8 ...flexi, B side by Bark
  Evening                                                                                                                                    Psychosis & Fury
                                                                                                                                             Things
Hypnotized...................................... CD-s .. Fire................. BLAZE36CD ........ 1989 £2............£5 ............................
Perfect Precription.............................. LP ...... Glass .............. GLALP026 ............ 1987 £6............£15 ............................
Performance..................................... LP ...... Glass .............. GLALP030 ............ 1988 £6............£15 ............................
Performance..................................... CD.... Glass .............. GLACD030.... 1988 £6............£15 ............................
Revolution....................................... CD-s .. Fire................. BLAZE29CD ........ 1988 £2............£5 ............................
Revolution....................................... 12"..... Fire................. THREEBIE3........ 1989 £10...........£20 ............................
Sound Of Confusion............................ LP ...... Glass .............. GLALP018 ............ 1986 £6............£15 ............................
Take Me To The Other Side................... 12"..... Glass .............. GLASS12054 ........ 1988 £6............£15 ............................
Taking Drugs.................................... LP ...... private.............. FYPL25 ................ 1986 £4............£10 ............................
Transparent Radiation ......................... 12"..... Glass .............. GLAEP108 ............ 1987 £30...........£60 ............................
Walkin' With Jesus.............................. 12"..... Glass .............. GLAEP105 ............ 1986 £20...........£40 ...............lyric insert

## SPADES
Subsequent issues of 'You're Gonna Miss Me' were credited to the group's new name – the Thirteenth Floor Elevators.

You're Gonna Miss Me............................ 7" ...... Zero ............. 10002..................... 1966 £75.......£150 ...................... US

## SPAGHETTI JUNCTION
Work's Nice – If You Can Get It ............. 7" ...... Columbia ....... DB8935 ................. 1972 £2.50............£6 ....................

## SPANDAU BALLET
Be Free With Your Love ........................ CD-s .. CBS............... SPANSP4............. 1989 £2............£5 ...............picture disc

## SPANIELS
Goodnite, It's Time To Go .................... LP ...... Vee Jay ........... LP1002 ................. 1958 £150....£250 ...................... US
Spaniels ............................................ LP ...... Vee Jay ........... LP1024 ................. 1960 £50......£100 ...................... US

## SPANIER, MUGGSY
Broadcasts This Is Is Jazz....................... 10" LP Vogue............. LDE015 ................. 1953 £8............£20 ............................
Gem Of The Ocean ............................. LP ...... MGM ............. C936..................... 1963 £4............£10 ............................
Great Sixteen .................................... LP ...... RCA ............. RD27132 ............. 1959 £8............£20 ............................
Muggsy Spanier And His Band ................ 10" LP Brunswick ...... LA8722 ................. 1955 £8............£20 ............................
Muggsy Spanier And His Dixieland Band .. LP ...... Mercury .......... MPL6516 ............. 1957 £6............£15 ............................
Muggsy Spanier And His Ragtime Band ..... 10" LP HMV............. DLP1031............. 1954 £8............£20 ............................
Muggsy Spanier And The Bucktown Five... 10" LP London .......... AL3528 ................. 1954 £8............£20 ............................

## SPANISH BOYS
I Am Alone ....................................... 7" ...... Blue Beat ....... BB331................. 1965 £6............£12 ............................

## SPANISHTOWN SKABEATS
Solomon........................................... 7" ...... Blue Beat ....... BB320................. 1965 £6............£12 ............................

## SPANKY & OUR GANG
Like To Get To Know You ...................... LP ...... Mercury.......... SMCL20121 ........... 1968 £4............£10 ............................
Spank's Greatest Hits ........................... LP ...... Mercury.......... SR61227 ............. 1970 £4............£10 ...................... US
Spanky & Our Gang ............................ LP ...... Mercury.......... (S)MCL20114........ 1967 £4............£10 ............................
Without Rhyme Or Reason .................... LP ...... Mercury.......... SR61183 ............. 1968 £4............£10 ...................... US

## SPANN, OTIS
Biggest Thing Since Colossus .................. LP ...... Blue Horizon... 763217 ................. 1969 £25...........£50 ...with Fleetwood Mac
Blues Are Where It's At ........................ LP ...... HMV............. CLP/CSD3609 ..... 1963 £6............£15 ............................
Blues Never Die .................................. LP ...... Stateside ......... SL10169 ................. 1966 £6............£15 ............................
Blues Of Otis Spann ............................ LP ...... Decca ............ LK4615 ................. 1964 £25...........£50 ............................
Bottom Of The Blues ........................... LP ...... Stateside ......... (S)SL10255 ........... 1968 £6............£15 ............................
Can't Do Me No Good ......................... 7" ...... Blue Horizon... 573142 ................. 1968 £2............£5 ............................
Cracked Spanner Head.......................... LP ...... Deram ............ DML/SML1036... 1969 £15...........£30 ............................
Good Morning Mr. Blues....................... LP ...... Storyville.......... SLP157 ................. 1964 £6............£15 ............................

| | | | | | | |
|---|---|---|---|---|---|---|
| Nobody Knows My Troubles | LP | Bounty | BY6037 | 1967 £5 | £12 | |
| Nobody Knows My Troubles | LP | Polydor | 545030 | 1967 £5 | £12 | |
| Otis Spann Is The Blues | LP | Candid | CJS9001 | 1960 £20 | £40 | US |
| Piano Blues | LP | Storyville | SLP168 | 1965 £6 | £15 | ...with Memphis Slim |
| Portraits In Blues Vol. 3 | LP | Storyville | 670157 | 1967 £4 | £10 | |
| Raised In Mississippi | LP | Python | KM4 | 1969 £8 | £20 | |
| Stirs Me Up | 7" | Decca | F11972 | 1964 £2.50 | £6 | |
| Walkin' | 7" | Blue Horizon | 573155 | 1969 £5 | £10 | ...with Fleetwood Mac |

## SPARKERS
| | | | | | | |
|---|---|---|---|---|---|---|
| Dip It Up | 7" | Blue Cat | BS155 | 1969 £4 | £8 | |

## SPARKLES
| | | | | | | |
|---|---|---|---|---|---|---|
| Tell Me | 7" EP | DMF | | 196– £6 | £12 | French |

## SPARKS
| | | | | | | |
|---|---|---|---|---|---|---|
| Gratuitous Sax And Senseless Violins | CD | Logic | 74321243022 | 1994 £30 | £60 | promo sampler |
| I Like Girls | 7" | Island | WIP6377 | 1976 £1.50 | £4 | |
| I Want To Hold Your Hand | 7" | Island | WIP6282 | 1976 £4 | £8 | |
| Introducing Sparks | LP | Columbia | PC34901 | 1976 £15 | £30 | ... US red vinyl promo |
| Wonder Girl | 7" | Bearsville | K15505 | 1972 £4 | £8 | |

## SPARKS, RANDY
| | | | | | | |
|---|---|---|---|---|---|---|
| Birmingham Train | 7" | HMV | POP683 | 1959 £1.50 | £4 | |

## SPARROW
| | | | | | | |
|---|---|---|---|---|---|---|
| Carnival Boycott | 7" | Kalypso | XX10 | 1960 £1.50 | £4 | |
| Clara Honey Bunch | 7" | Melodisc | CAL17 | 1964 £1.50 | £4 | |
| Goaty | 7" | Melodisc | CAL18 | 1964 £1.50 | £4 | |
| Leading Calypsonians | 7" | Melodisc | CAL15 | 1964 £1.50 | £4 | |
| Mighty Sparrow | 7" EP | Kalypso | XXEP1 | 1961 £2 | £5 | |
| Mr. Herbert | 7" | Kalypso | XX22 | 196– £1.50 | £4 | |
| Mr. Walker | 7" | Nems | 3558 | 196– £1.50 | £4 | |
| Party With The Sparrow | 7" EP | Kalypso | XXEP3 | 196– £2 | £5 | |
| Sack | 7" | Kalypso | XX17 | 1960 £1.50 | £4 | |
| Slave | LP | Island | ILP902 | 1963 £20 | £40 | |
| Sparrow Come Back | LP | RCA | SF7516 | 1962 £10 | £25 | |
| Village Ram | 7" | Jump Up | JU523 | 1967 £1.50 | £4 | |

## SPARROW (2)
| | | | | | | |
|---|---|---|---|---|---|---|
| Tomorrow's Ship | 7" | CBS | 202342 | 1966 £10 | £20 | |

## SPARROW, JACK
| | | | | | | |
|---|---|---|---|---|---|---|
| Ice Water | 7" | Doctor Bird | DB1005 | 1966 £5 | £10 | |
| More Ice Water | 7" | Doctor Bird | DB1027 | 1966 £5 | £10 | |

## SPARROWS
| | | | | | | |
|---|---|---|---|---|---|---|
| Mersey Sound | LP | Elkay | 3009 | 1964 £6 | £15 | US |

## SPEAR, ROGER RUSKIN
| | | | | | | |
|---|---|---|---|---|---|---|
| Electric Shocks | LP | United Artists | UAS29381 | 1972 £5 | £12 | |
| Rebel Trouser | 7" | United Artists | UP35221 | 1971 £1.50 | £4 | |
| Unusual | LP | United Artists | UAG29508 | 1972 £5 | £12 | |

## SPEAR OF DESTINY
| | | | | | | |
|---|---|---|---|---|---|---|
| Never Take Me Alive | CD-s | Virgin | CDT17 | 1988 £2 | £5 | 3" single |
| Outlands | CD | 10 | DIXCD59 | 1987 £5 | £12 | |
| Price You Pay | CD | Virgin | CDV2549 | 1988 £5 | £12 | |
| Prisoner Of Love | 7" | Epic | DA4068 | 1984 £1.50 | £4 | double |
| Radio Radio | CD-s | Virgin | VSCD1144 | 1988 £2 | £5 | 3" single in metal can |
| So In Love With You | CD-s | Virgin | VSCD1123 | 1988 £2 | £5 | |
| Was That You | CD-s | 10 | TENZ173 | 1987 £2.50 | £6 | |
| Wheel | 7" | Epic | WA3372 | 1983 £2 | £5 | picture disc |

## SPECIALS
| | | | | | | |
|---|---|---|---|---|---|---|
| Specials | CD | Chrysalis | CD25CR02 | 1994 £5 | £12 | Chrysalis 25 pack |

## SPECKLED RED
| | | | | | | |
|---|---|---|---|---|---|---|
| Dirty Dozens | LP | Esquire | 32190 | 1963 £10 | £25 | |
| Dirty Dozens | LP | Storyville | SLP117 | 1964 £5 | £12 | |
| Oh Red | LP | VJM | LC11 | 1971 £4 | £10 | |
| Storyville Blues Anthology Vol. 4 | 7" EP | Storyville | SEP384 | 1962 £4 | £8 | |

## SPECTOR, PHIL

Despite the growing importance in the late eighties of record producers as artists, Phil Spector is still the only producer with the status of a star. His Christmas album, released a number of times over the years, is the perfect seasonal recording. Various artists associated with Spector are given traditional songs to perform (none of them carols, interestingly) and surrounded by dense arrangements that stay just on the right side of mawkishness.

| | | | | | | |
|---|---|---|---|---|---|---|
| Christmas Album | LP | Apple | APCOR24 | 1972 £6 | £15 | |
| Christmas Gift For You | LP | London | HAU8141 | 1963 £15 | £30 | |
| Christmas Gift For You | LP | Philles | PHLP4005 | 1963 £25 | £50 | US blue label |
| Christmas Gift For You | LP | Philles | PHLP4005 | 1964 £8 | £20 | US yellow label |
| Presents Today's Hits | LP | Philles | PHLP4004 | 1963 £30 | £60 | US |

## SPECTOR, RONNIE
| | | | | | | |
|---|---|---|---|---|---|---|
| Try Some Buy Some | 7" | Apple | 33 | 1971 £4 | £8 | picture sleeve |

## SPECTRES
The three singles recorded by the Spectres are the first releases by the group that was eventually to gain international success as Status Quo.

| | | | | | | | |
|---|---|---|---|---|---|---|---|
| Hurdy Gurdy Man | 7" | Piccadilly | 7N35352 | 1966 | £100 | £200 | best auctioned |
| I Who Have Nothing | 7" | Piccadilly | 7N35339 | 1966 | £100 | £200 | best auctioned |
| We Ain't Got Nothin' Yet | 7" | Piccadilly | 7N35368 | 1967 | £100 | £200 | best auctioned |

## SPECTRES (2)
| | | | | | | | |
|---|---|---|---|---|---|---|---|
| Facts Of Life | 7" | Lloyd Sound | UEDQU1 | 1965 | £75 | £150 | |

## SPECTRUM
| | | | | | | | |
|---|---|---|---|---|---|---|---|
| I'll Be Gone | 7" | Parlophone | R5908 | 1971 | £1.50 | £4 | |
| Light Is Dark Enough | LP | RCA | INTS1118 | 1970 | £15 | £30 | |
| Portobello Road | 7" | RCA | RCA1619 | 1967 | £1.50 | £4 | |

## SPEDDING, CHRIS
| | | | | | | | |
|---|---|---|---|---|---|---|---|
| Backwoods Progression | LP | Harvest | SHSP4004 | 1970 | £6 | £15 | |
| Only Lick I Know | LP | Harvest | SHSP4017 | 1972 | £6 | £15 | |
| Rock And Roll Band | 7" | Harvest | HAR5013 | 1970 | £2.50 | £6 | B side by Battered Ornaments |

## SPEED GLUE SHINKI
| | | | | | | | |
|---|---|---|---|---|---|---|---|
| | LP | | | | £330 | £500 | Japanese |

## SPEEDBALL
| | | | | | | | |
|---|---|---|---|---|---|---|---|
| No Survivor | 7" | Dirty Dick | DD1/2 | 1980 | £5 | £10 | |
| No Survivor | 7" | Dirty Dick | DD1/2 | 1980 | £7.50 | £15 | printed sleeve |

## SPEIRS, DAVID
| | | | | | | | |
|---|---|---|---|---|---|---|---|
| David Speirs | LP | Beltona | LBA/LBS61 | 1969 | £5 | £12 | |

## SPELLBINDERS
| | | | | | | | |
|---|---|---|---|---|---|---|---|
| Chain Reaction | 7" | CBS | 202622 | 1967 | £5 | £10 | |
| Chain Reaction | 7" | Direction | 583970 | 1969 | £1.50 | £4 | |
| Help Me | 7" | CBS | 202453 | 1966 | £5 | £10 | |
| Since I Don't Have You | 7" | CBS | 2776 | 1967 | £1.50 | £4 | |
| Sweet Sweet Lovin' | 7" | CBS | 202435 | 1967 | £4 | £8 | |

## SPELLMAN, BENNY
| | | | | | | | |
|---|---|---|---|---|---|---|---|
| Fortune Teller | 7" | London | HLP9570 | 1962 | £15 | £30 | |

## SPELMAN, BRUCE
| | | | | | | | |
|---|---|---|---|---|---|---|---|
| You Don't Know What You're Paddling In | LP | Montagu | | 1972 | £10 | £25 | |

## SPENCE, SKIPP
The solo album made by singer-guitarist Skip Spence after his departure from Moby Grape is rather less weird and a lot less impressive than some critics would have us believe. *Oar* was not released in the UK until it was reissued in the eighties, but US copies do turn up from time to time.

| | | | | | | | |
|---|---|---|---|---|---|---|---|
| Oar | LP | Columbia | CS9831 | 1968 | £10 | £25 | US |

## SPENCER, DON
| | | | | | | | |
|---|---|---|---|---|---|---|---|
| Fireball | 7" | HMV | POP1087 | 1962 | £4 | £8 | |
| Fireball & Other Titles | 7" EP | HMV | 7EG8802 | 1963 | £10 | £20 | |

## SPENCER, JEREMY
| | | | | | | | |
|---|---|---|---|---|---|---|---|
| Jeremy Spencer | LP | Reprise | K44105 | 1971 | £10 | £25 | |
| Jeremy Spencer | LP | Reprise | RSLP9002 | 1970 | £15 | £30 | |
| Linda | 7" | Reprise | RS27002 | 1970 | £1.50 | £4 | |

## SPENCER, SONNY
| | | | | | | | |
|---|---|---|---|---|---|---|---|
| Oh Boy | 7" | Parlophone | R4611 | 1959 | £6 | £12 | |

## SPERRMULL
| | | | | | | | |
|---|---|---|---|---|---|---|---|
| Sperrmüll | LP | Brain | 1026 | 1973 | £37.50 | £75 | German |

## SPHYNKTA
| | | | | | | | |
|---|---|---|---|---|---|---|---|
| Death And Violence | 7" | Sultanic | SUL999 | 1983 | £2.50 | £6 | red vinyl |
| In The Shade Of The Gods | 7" | Sultanic | SUL666 | 1983 | £5 | £10 | red vinyl |

## SPICE
| | | | | | | | |
|---|---|---|---|---|---|---|---|
| Union Jack | 7" | Olga | OLE013 | 1968 | £25 | £50 | |
| What About The Music | 7" | United Artists | UP2246 | 1968 | £25 | £50 | |

## SPICER, GEORGE
| | | | | | | | |
|---|---|---|---|---|---|---|---|
| Blackberry Fold | LP | Topic | 12T235 | 1974 | £4 | £10 | |

## SPIDELLS
| | | | | | | | |
|---|---|---|---|---|---|---|---|
| Find Out What's Happening | 7" | Sue | WI4019 | 1966 | £7.50 | £15 | |

## SPIDER
| | | | | | | | |
|---|---|---|---|---|---|---|---|
| Comedown Song | 7" | Decca | F12430 | 1966 | £5 | £10 | |

## SPIDER (2)
| | | | | | | | |
|---|---|---|---|---|---|---|---|
| Children Of The Street | 7" | Alien | ALIEN14 | 1980 | £1.50 | £4 | |

827

## SPIDERS

| | | | | | | |
|---|---|---|---|---|---|---|
| I Didn't Wanna Do It | LP | Imperial | LP9140 | 1961 £50 £100 | | US |
| I'm Slippin' In | 78 | London | HL8086 | 1954 £15 £30 | | |

## SPIDERS (2)

The Spiders were led by Vincent Furnier – later to adopt the stage name of Alice Cooper.

| | | | | | |
|---|---|---|---|---|---|
| Don't Blow Your Mind | 7" | Santa Cruz | 003 | 1966 £250 £400 | .... US, best auctioned |
| Why Don't You Love Me? | 7" | Nascot | 112 | 1965 £500 £750 | .... US, best auctioned |

## SPIN

| | | | | | |
|---|---|---|---|---|---|
| Let's Pretend | CD-s | Foundation | TFL9CD | 1991 £5 £12 | |
| Scratches In The Sand | CD-s | Foundation | TFL7CD | 1990 £5 £12 | |

## SPINNERS

| | | | | | |
|---|---|---|---|---|---|
| Heebie Jeebies | 7" | Columbia | DB4693 | 1961 £50 £100 | |
| Original Spinners | LP | Motown | 639 | 1967 £6 £15 | US |
| Party My Pad | LP | Time | 52092 | 1963 £25 £50 | US |
| Sweet Thing | 7" | Tamla Motown | TMG514 | 1965 £50 £100 | demo only |

## SPINNERS (2)

| | | | | | |
|---|---|---|---|---|---|
| Spinners | LP | Fontana | TL5201 | 1963 £4 £10 | |

## SPIRAL STAIRCASE

| | | | | | |
|---|---|---|---|---|---|
| Baby What I Mean | 7" | CBS | 3507 | 1968 £2.50 £6 | |
| More Today Than Yesterday | 7" | CBS | 4187 | 1969 £7.50 £15 | |
| No One For Me To Turn To | 7" | CBS | 4524 | 1969 £5 £10 | |

## SPIRALS

| | | | | | |
|---|---|---|---|---|---|
| Rocking Cow | 7" | Capitol | CL14958 | 1958 £5 £10 | |

## SPIRIT

Listening to any of the recordings made by the original line-up of Spirit (the first four albums) makes it impossible to avoid the claim that the group was one of the great bands of the sixties. Like the Byrds (although Spirit's music is not at all similar), the group created a body of work that has hardly dated at all, because it failed to take on the fashionable trappings of its own time in the first place. Fans of intelligent, slightly jazz-inflected rock songs, with distinctive melodies linked to imaginative and incisive playing, can safely purchase any of the recordings made before 1971. Personnel changes at this point rendered the subsequent albums considerably less than essential, although versions of Spirit including guitarist Randy California and drummer Ed Cassidy (proudly wearing his status as one of the oldest working musicians in rock) managed to recapture much of the fire of the original group whenever they played versions of the original material.

| | | | | | |
|---|---|---|---|---|---|
| 12 Dreams Of Dr. Sardonicus | LP | Epic | EPC64191 | 1970 £5 £12 | |
| 1984 | 7" | CBS | 4773 | 1970 £1.50 £4 | |
| Animal Zoo | 7" | CBS | 5149 | 1970 £1.50 £4 | |
| Clear | LP | CBS | 63729 | 1969 £5 £12 | |
| Dark Eyed Woman | 7" | CBS | 4511 | 1969 £1.50 £4 | |
| Dark Eyed Woman | 7" | CBS | 4565 | 1969 £1.50 £4 | |
| Family That Plays Together | LP | CBS | 63523 | 1968 £5 £12 | |
| Highlights Of Spirit Of '76 | LP | Mercury | 001 | 1976 £4 £10 | promo |
| I Got A Line On You | 7" | CBS | 3880 | 1969 £1.50 £4 | |
| Potatoland | LP | Beggars Banquet | BEGA23 | 1981 £4 £10 | with cartoon book |
| Spirit | LP | CBS | 63278 | 1968 £6 £15 | |
| Uncle Jack | 7" | CBS | 3523 | 1968 £1.50 £4 | |

## SPIRIT OF JOHN MORGAN

| | | | | | |
|---|---|---|---|---|---|
| Age Machine | LP | Carnaby | CNLS6007 | 1970 £25 £50 | |
| Age Machine | 7" | Carnaby | CNS4019 | 1970 £2 £5 | |
| Kaleidoscope | LP | Carnaby | 6302010 | 1972 £25 £50 | |
| Live At Durrant House | LP | SWP | 1007 | 197– £50 £100 | |
| Spirit Of John Morgan | LP | Carnaby | 6437503 | 1971 £6 £15 | |
| Spirit Of John Morgan | LP | Carnaby | CNLS6002 | 1969 £25 £50 | |
| Train For All Reasons | 7" | Carnaby | CNS4005 | 1969 £2 £5 | |

## SPIRIT OF MEMPHIS QUARTET

| | | | | | |
|---|---|---|---|---|---|
| Negro Spirituals | LP | Vogue | LAE1033 | 1965 £4 £10 | |
| Negro Spirituals | 10" LP | Parlophone | PMD1070 | 1958 £6 £15 | |

## SPIRITS AND WORM

| | | | | | |
|---|---|---|---|---|---|
| Spirits And Worm | LP | A&M | SP4229 | 1969 £150 £250 | US |

## SPIRITUALIZED

| | | | | | |
|---|---|---|---|---|---|
| Anyway That You Want Me | CD-s | Dedicated | ZD43784 | 1990 £2.50 £6 | |
| Anyway That You Want Me (Remix) | 12" | Dedicated | ZT43784 | 1990 £3 £8 | |
| Electric Mainline | CD | Dedicated | DEDCD0175 | 1995 £5 £12 | glow-in-the-dark case |
| Feel So Sad | 7" | Fierce | FRIGHT053 | 1991 £7.50 £15 | |
| Feel So Sad | CD-s | Dedicated | SPIRT001CD | 1991 £2 £5 | |
| Fucked Up Inside | LP | Decicated | DEDLP008 | 1993 £4 £10 | |
| Fucked Up Inside | CD | Dedicated | DEDCD008 | 1993 £6 £15 | mail order only |
| Lazer Guided Melodies | CD-s | Dedicated | SPIRT004CD | 1992 £2 £5 | mail order sampler |
| Run | CD-s | Dedicated | SPIRIT002CD | 1991 £2 £5 | |
| Smile | CD-s | Dedicated | SPIRIT003CD | 1991 £2 £5 | |

## SPIROGYRA

Having as manager a university professor of chemistry (the father of the band's violinist) was perhaps not the best way of ensuring stardom, and although Spirogyra's brand of folk-rock managed to see the group through three albums, none sold well and all are very scarce today.

Lead singer Barbara Gaskin subsequently worked with ex-Hatfield and the North keyboard player Dave Stewart, gaining a number one hit in 1981 with a high-tech cover of 'It's My Party'.

| | | | | | | |
|---|---|---|---|---|---|---|
| Bells Boots & Shambles | LP | Polydor | 2310246 | 1973 | £100 ... £200 | |
| Dangerous Dave | 7" | Pegasus | PGS3 | 1972 | £2.50 ... £6 | picture sleeve |
| Old Boot Wine | LP | Pegasus | PEG13 | 1972 | £30 ... £60 | |
| St. Radigunds | LP | B&C | CAS1042 | 1971 | £30 ... £60 | |

## SPITFIRE BOYS

| | | | | | | |
|---|---|---|---|---|---|---|
| British Refugee | 7" | RK | RK1001 | 1977 | £2 ... £5 | |

## SPIVEY, VICTORIA

| | | | | | | |
|---|---|---|---|---|---|---|
| Treasures Of North American Negro Music No. 5. | 7" EP | Fontana | TFE17264 | 1960 | £2.50 ... £6 | |
| Victoria Spivey | LP | XTRA | XTRA1022 | 1965 | £8 ... £20 | |
| Victoria Spivey | 7" EP | HMV | 7EG8190 | 1956 | £5 ... £10 | |

## S.P.K.

| | | | | | | |
|---|---|---|---|---|---|---|
| Dekompositiones | 12" | Side Effekts | SER003 | 1983 | £4 ... £10 | |
| Leichenschrei | LP | Side Effekts | SER002 | 198– | £4 ... £10 | |
| Meat Processing Section | 7" | Industrial | IR0011 | 1980 | £5 ... £10 | |

## SPLASH

| | | | | | | |
|---|---|---|---|---|---|---|
| Splash | LP | Polydor | PLA3001 | 1974 | £10 ... £25 | Norwegian |
| Ut Pa Vischan | LP | Polydor | 2379036 | 1972 | £10 ... £25 | Swedish |

## SPLINTER

| | | | | | | |
|---|---|---|---|---|---|---|
| untitled – known as 'The White Album' | LP | Dark Horse | DH2 | 1975 | £25 ... £50 | demo |

## SPLIT KNEE LOONS

| | | | | | | |
|---|---|---|---|---|---|---|
| Special Collectors EP | 7" | Avatar | AAA111 | 1981 | £2 ... £5 | |

## SPOELSTRA, MARK

| | | | | | | |
|---|---|---|---|---|---|---|
| 5 & 20 Questions | LP | Elektra | EKL283 | 1965 | £6 ... £15 | US |
| Mark Spoelstra | LP | Columbia | CS9793 | 1969 | £5 ... £12 | US |
| State Of Mind | LP | Elektra | EKL307 | 1966 | £6 ... £15 | US |

## SPOKESMEN

| | | | | | | |
|---|---|---|---|---|---|---|
| Dawn Of Correction | LP | Decca | DL(7)4712 | 1965 | £6 ... £15 | US |
| Michelle | 7" EP | Decca | 60003 | 1966 | £5 ... £10 | French |

## SPONTANEOUS COMBUSTION

| | | | | | | |
|---|---|---|---|---|---|---|
| Gay Time Night | 7" | Harvest | HAR5060 | 1972 | £1.50 ... £4 | |
| Leaving | 7" | Harvest | HAR5046 | 1971 | £1.50 ... £4 | |
| Sabre Dance | 7" | Harvest | HAR5066 | 1973 | £1.50 ... £4 | |
| Spontaneous Combustion | LP | Harvest | SHVL801 | 1972 | £10 ... £25 | |
| Triad | LP | Harvest | SHVL805 | 1972 | £10 ... £25 | |

## SPONTANEOUS MUSIC ENSEMBLE

The name of the group formed by drummer John Stevens describes exactly what the group was about and although Stevens led and played with many other groups (including that of John Martyn in the mid-seventies), it is the S.M.E. for which he will be best remembered. The group, with a variable personnel, but including at various times many of the best-known names in British jazz, was the first to record free improvisation in the UK and has proved to be enormously influential.

| | | | | | | |
|---|---|---|---|---|---|---|
| Biosystem | LP | Incus | INCUS24 | 1977 | £5 ... £12 | |
| Birds Of A Feather | LP | Byg | 529023 | 1972 | £8 ... £20 | French |
| Bobby Bradford And The SME | LP | Freedom | SLP40111 | 1974 | £8 ... £20 | |
| Bobby Bradford, John Surman & S.M.E. | LP | Nessa | 17 | 1971 | £8 ... £20 | |
| Challenge | LP | Eyemark | EMPL1002 | 1966 | £37.50 ... £75 | |
| Face To Face | LP | Emanen | 303 | 1973 | £6 ... £15 | |
| For CND For Peace And You To Share | LP | A Records | | 1970 | £15 ... £30 | |
| How Ya Doin? | LP | Nondo | 003 | 1973 | £6 ... £15 | |
| Karyobin | LP | Island | ILPS9079 | 1968 | £25 ... £50 | pink label |
| Live Big Band And Quartet | LP | Vinyl | VS0015 | 1971 | £8 ... £20 | |
| S.M.E. = S.M.O. | LP | A Records | | 1975 | £6 ... £15 | |
| S.M.E./S.M.O. In Concert | LP | Sweet Folk And Country | SFA112 | 1981 | £6 ... £15 | |
| So What Do You Think? | LP | Tangent | TGS118 | 1971 | £8 ... £20 | |
| Source From & Towards | LP | Tangent | TNGS107 | 1971 | £8 ... £20 | double |
| Spontaneous In Concert | LP | Emanen | 311/312 | 1974 | £8 ... £20 | |
| Spontaneous Music Ensemble | LP | Marmalade | 608008 | 1969 | £15 ... £30 | credited to John Stevens |
| Spontaneous Music Ensemble | LP | Polydor | 2384009 | 1972 | £4 ... £10 | |

## SPOOKY TOOTH

Spooky Tooth's frequent personnel changes prevented the group from ever achieving stardom. The best material, however (which includes the first two albums and much of *The Last Puff*, although this is as much the work of the Grease Band as of the original Spooky Tooth), provides a distinctive approach to blue-eyed soul that has worn very much better than some of its trendier companions from the time. All the original group members subsequently turned up elsewhere. Singer/keyboard players Gary Wright and Mike Harrison made solo albums; guitarist Luther Grosvenor joined Mott the Hoople and became Ariel Bender; bass player Greg Ridley joined Humble Pie; while drummer Mike Kellie became a member of Three Man Army and then the Only Ones. The album *Ceremony* sees Spooky Tooth cast as session musicians for a project by avant-garde composer Pierre Henry and is not generally liked by fans of the group!

| | | | | | | |
|---|---|---|---|---|---|---|
| Ceremony | LP | Island | ILPS9107 | 1969 | £6 ... £15 | with Pierre Henry, pink label |
| It's All About | LP | Island | ILP980/ILPS9080 | 1968 | £15 ... £30 | pink label |
| Last Puff | LP | Island | ILPS9117 | 1970 | £6 ... £15 | pink label |

| | | | | | | | |
|---|---|---|---|---|---|---|---|
| Love Really Changed Me | 7" | Island | WIP6037 | 1968 | £1.50 | £4 | |
| Mirror | LP | Island | ILPS9292 | 1974 | £4 | £10 | export |
| Nobody There At All | 7" | Island | WIP6048 | 1969 | £10 | £20 | demo only |
| Son Of Your Father | 7" | Island | WIP6060 | 1969 | £1.50 | £4 | |
| Spooky Two | LP | Island | ILPS9098 | 1969 | £8 | £20 | pink label |
| Sunshine Help Me | 7" | Island | WIP6022 | 1967 | £1.50 | £4 | |
| Weight | 7" | Island | WIP6046 | 1968 | £1.50 | £4 | |

## SPOTLIGHTERS

| | | | | | | | |
|---|---|---|---|---|---|---|---|
| Please Be My Girlfriend | 7" | Vogue | V9130 | 1959 | £150 | £250 | best auctioned |

## SPOTLIGHTS

| | | | | | | | |
|---|---|---|---|---|---|---|---|
| Batman And Robin | 7" | Philips | BF1485 | 1966 | £1.50 | £4 | |

## SPOTNICKS

The Spotnicks were Sweden's answer to the Shadows (and are still playing in fact). The lead guitarist was impressive in a Hank Marvinish sort of way, and the two singles 'Orange Blossom Special' and 'Rocket Man' (which also turn up on the EP *On The Air* and the LP *Out-a Space*) are as good as anything produced by the English group. The Spotnicks also had two gimmicks – they performed wearing rather unserviceable-looking space suits, and they used radio-controlled guitars rather than electric leads, although the equipment tended to be somewhat temperamental!

| | | | | | | | |
|---|---|---|---|---|---|---|---|
| Anna | 7" | Oriole | CB1886 | 1963 | £2.50 | £6 | |
| Around The World | LP | Swedisc | SWELP42 | 1966 | £8 | £20 | Swedish |
| At Home In Gothenberg | LP | Swedisc | SWELP33 | 1965 | £8 | £20 | Swedish |
| Back In The Race | LP | Polydor | 2379005 | 1971 | £5 | £12 | Swedish |
| Bo Winberg And The Spotnicks Today | LP | Polydor | 2379060 | 1973 | £4 | £10 | Swedish |
| By Request | LP | Swedisc | SWELP67 | 1968 | £6 | £15 | Swedish |
| Donner Wetter | 7" | Oriole | CB1981 | 1964 | £2.50 | £6 | |
| Hava Nagila | 7" | Oriole | CB1790 | 1963 | £1.50 | £4 | |
| In Acapulco | LP | Swedisc | SWELP60 | 1967 | £8 | £20 | Swedish |
| In Paris | LP | Oriole | PS40040 | 1963 | £6 | £15 | |
| In Spain | LP | Oriole | PS40054 | 1964 | £8 | £20 | |
| In Stockholm | LP | Swedisc | SWELP20 | 1964 | £8 | £20 | Swedish |
| In The Groove | LP | Swedisc | SWELP63 | 1968 | £6 | £15 | Swedish |
| In Tokyo | LP | Swedisc | SWELP38 | 1966 | £8 | £20 | Swedish |
| In Winterland | LP | Swedisc | SWELP48 | 1966 | £8 | £20 | Swedish |
| Just Listen To My Heart | 7" | Oriole | CB1818 | 1963 | £1.50 | £4 | |
| Live In Berlin '74 | LP | Polydor | 2480201 | 1974 | £4 | £10 | German |
| Live In Japan | LP | Swedisc | SWELP53 | 1966 | £8 | £20 | Swedish |
| Lovesick Blues | 7" | Oriole | CB1953 | 1964 | £2.50 | £6 | |
| On The Air | 7" EP | Oriole | EP7075 | 1963 | £5 | £10 | |
| Orange Blossom Special | 7" | Oriole | CB1724 | 1962 | £1.50 | £4 | |
| Out-a Space/In London | LP | Oriole | PS40036 | 1962 | £5 | £12 | |
| Out-A Space: The Spotnicks In London | LP | Oriole | SPS40037 | 1963 | £10 | £25 | stereo |
| Rocket Man | 7" | Oriole | CB1755 | 1962 | £1.50 | £4 | |
| Something Like Country | LP | Polydor | 2379032 | 1972 | £4 | £10 | Swedish |
| Spotnicks At The Olympia Paris | 7" EP | Oriole | EP7079 | 1964 | £6 | £12 | |
| Spotnicks In Berlin | LP | Oriole | PS40064 | 1965 | £10 | £25 | |
| Spotnicks In Paris | 7" EP | Oriole | EP7078 | 1964 | £5 | £10 | |
| Valentina | 7" | Oriole | CB1844 | 1963 | £1.50 | £4 | |
| Volume 1 | LP | Swedisc | SWELP50001 | 1967 | £6 | £15 | Swedish |
| Volume 2 | LP | Swedisc | SWELP50002 | 1967 | £6 | £15 | Swedish |

## SPRATT, JACK

| | | | | | | | |
|---|---|---|---|---|---|---|---|
| Give Me Your Love | 7" | Coxsone | CS7100 | 1969 | £5 | £10 | |

## SPRIGUNS

| | | | | | | | |
|---|---|---|---|---|---|---|---|
| Nothing Else To Do | 7" | Decca | F13676 | 1976 | £2 | £5 | |
| Revel Weird And Wild | LP | Decca | SKL5262 | 1976 | £50 | £100 | |
| Rowdy Dowdy Day | cass | private | | 1974 | £8 | £20 | |
| Time Will Pass | LP | Decca | SKL5286 | 1977 | £50 | £100 | |
| White Witch | 7" | Decca | F13739 | 1977 | £2 | £5 | |

## SPRIGUNS OF TOLGUS

| | | | | | | | |
|---|---|---|---|---|---|---|---|
| Jack With A Feather | LP | Alida Star Cottage | ASC7755A | 1975 | £700 | £1000 | |

## SPRING

| | | | | | | | |
|---|---|---|---|---|---|---|---|
| Spring | LP | Neon | NE6 | 1971 | £50 | £100 | double |

## SPRINGFIELD, DUSTY

| | | | | | | | |
|---|---|---|---|---|---|---|---|
| All I See Is You | 7" | Philips | BF1510 | 1966 | £2 | £5 | picture sleeve |
| Arrested By You | CD-s | Parlophone | CDR6266 | 1990 | £2 | £5 | |
| Cameo | LP | Philips | 6308152 | 1973 | £4 | £10 | |
| Demain tu peux changer | 7" EP | Philips | 433570 | 1963 | £10 | £20 | French |
| Dusty | 7" EP | Philips | BE12564 | 1964 | £5 | £10 | |
| Dusty Definitely | LP | Philips | (S)BL7864 | 1968 | £5 | £12 | |
| Dusty In Memphis | LP | Philips | SBL7889 | 1969 | £5 | £12 | |
| Dusty In New York | 7" EP | Philips | BE12572 | 1965 | £5 | £10 | |
| Dusty Springfield | LP | World Record Club | ST848 | 1968 | £4 | £10 | |
| Everything Is Coming Up Dusty | LP | Philips | (S)BL1002 | 1965 | £5 | £12 | |
| From Dusty With Love | LP | Philips | SBL7927 | 1970 | £4 | £10 | |
| Girl Called Dusty | LP | Philips | (S)BL7594 | 1964 | £5 | £12 | |
| Give Me Time | 7" | Philips | BF1577 | 1967 | £1.50 | £4 | |
| Hits Of Dusty Springfield | cass-s | Philips | MCP100 | 1968 | £3 | £8 | |

| Hits Of The Walker Brothers & Dusty Springfield | cass-s | Philips | MCP1004 | 1968 | £3 | £8 | |
| I Only Want To Be With You | 7" EP | Philips | 433664 | 1963 | £5 | £10 | French |
| I Only Want To Be With You | 7" EP | Philips | BE12560 | 1964 | £4 | £8 | |
| I'll Try Anything | 7" | Philips | BF1553 | 1967 | £1.50 | £4 | |
| If You Go Away | 7" EP | Philips | BE12605 | 1968 | £5 | £10 | |
| In Private | CD-s | Parlophone | CDR6234 | 1989 | £2 | £5 | |
| Mademoiselle Dusty | 7" EP | Philips | BE12579 | 1965 | £6 | £12 | |
| Nothing Has Been Proved | CD-s | Parlophone | CDR6207 | 1989 | £2 | £5 | |
| Oh Holy Child | 7" | Philips | BF1381 | 1964 | £2 | £5 | picture sleeve, Springfields B side |
| Reputation | CD-s | Parlophone | CDR6253 | 1990 | £2 | £5 | |
| See All Her Faces | LP | Philips | 6308117 | 1972 | £4 | £10 | |
| Star Dusty | 7" EP | Philips | 6850751 | 1968 | £2 | £5 | |
| Warten Und Hoffen | 7" | Philips | | 1964 | £6 | £12 | German |
| What's It Gonna Be | 7" | Philips | BF1608 | 1967 | £4 | £8 | |
| Where Am I Going | LP | Philips | (S)BL7820 | 1967 | £5 | £12 | |

## SPRINGFIELD, TOM

| Love's Philosophy | LP | Decca | LK/SKL5003 | 1969 | £6 | £15 | |

## SPRINGFIELDS

| Christmas With The Springfields | 7" EP | Woman's Own | P125 | 1962 | £2.50 | £6 | |
| Folk Songs From The Hills | LP | Philips | 632304BL | 1963 | £4 | £10 | |
| Hit Sounds | 7" EP | Philips | BE12538 | 1963 | £2 | £5 | |
| Kinda Folksy | LP | Philips | BBL7551/SBBL674 | 1962 | £4 | £10 | |
| Kinda Folksy No. 1 | 7" EP | Philips | 433622BE | 1962 | £4 | £8 | |
| Kinda Folksy No. 2 | 7" EP | Philips | 433623BE | 1962 | £5 | £10 | |
| Kinda Folksy No. 3 | 7" EP | Philips | 433624BE | 1962 | £5 | £10 | |
| Springfields | 7" EP | Philips | BBE12476 | 1961 | £4 | £8 | |
| Springfields | 7" EP | Philips | SBBE9068 | 1961 | £6 | £12 | stereo |
| Springfields Story | LP | Philips | BET606 | 1964 | £5 | £12 | double |
| Swahili Papa | 7" | Philips | 326536BF | 1962 | £1.50 | £4 | |

## SPRINGFIELDS (2)

| Sunflower | 7" | Sarah | 010 | 1988 | £4 | £8 | with poster |

## SPRINGSTEEN, BRUCE

Jon Landau's accolade in which he described Bruce Springsteen as the future of rock 'n' roll was proved to be not too far from the mark by Springsteen's subsequent rise to the ranks of megastardom. The corresponding simplification in the man's material, however, is much to be regretted by those who thrilled to the narrative adventures of the songs on his first four great albums. Like Bob Dylan, Bruce Springsteen is an artist for whom a full appreciation depends on the collector obtaining some of his many bootleg recordings – both for the discarded out-takes, which include many songs easily the equal of those chosen for release, and for a sampling of Springsteen's magisterial live performances, whose impact is sadly diluted in the official live recordings.

| 57 Channels (And Nothin' On) | CD-s | Sony | 6581385 | 1992 | £2 | £5 | picture disc |
| As Requested Around The World | LP | Columbia | AS978 | 1981 | £8 | £20 | US promo sampler |
| Atlantic City | 7" | CBS | A2794 | 1982 | £6 | £12 | picture sleeve |
| Badlands | 7" | CBS | A6532 | 1978 | £2 | £5 | |
| Blinded By The Light | 7" EP | Columbia | AS45 | 1973 | £75 | £150 | US, with special sleeve, questionnaire, booklet |
| Born In The USA | LP | CBS | 86304 | 1984 | £8 | £20 | picture disc |
| Born In The USA | 7" | CBS | | | £12.50 | £25 | 5 track promo |
| Born In The USA – The 12" Collection | 12" | CBS | BRUCE1 | 1985 | £6 | £15 | 4 x 12", 1 x 7", poster, boxed |
| Born To Run | LP | Columbia | HC43795 | 1980 | £8 | £20 | US audiophile |
| Born To Run | LP | Columbia | PC33795 | 1975 | £100 | £200 | US, cover titles in script |
| Born To Run | 7" | CBS | A3661 | 1975 | £1.50 | £4 | |
| Born To Run | 7" | CBS | A3661 | 1975 | £7.50 | £15 | picture sleeve |
| Born To Run | 7" | CBS | A7077 | 1985 | £6 | £12 | |
| Born To Run | 7" | CBS | BRUCEB2 | 1987 | £4 | £8 | 2 x 7", boxed |
| Born To Run | 7" | CBS | BRUCEBP2 | 1987 | £1.50 | £4 | with badge |
| Born To Run | 48" | CBS | | 1975 | £37.50 | £75 | US unplayable promo! |
| Born To Run (live) | CD-s | CBS | BRUCEC2 | 1987 | £3 | | |
| Bruce Springsteen | LP | CBS | 66353 | 1979 | £10 | £25 | 3 LPs, boxed |
| Cadillac Ranch | 7" | CBS | A1557 | 1981 | £6 | £12 | |
| Circus Song | 7" EP | Columbia | AS52 | 1973 | £150 | £250 | US, with special sleeve, questionnaire, booklet |
| Cover Me | 7" | CBS | A4662 | 1984 | £2.50 | £6 | poster picture sleeve |
| Cover Me | 7" | CBS | DA4662 | 1984 | £2.50 | £6 | double |
| Cover Me | 7" | CBS | WA4662 | 1984 | £6 | £12 | shaped picture disc, stand |
| Dancing In The Dark | 7" | CBS | WA4436 | 1984 | £7.50 | £15 | shaped picture disc |
| Darkness On The Edge Of Town | LP | Columbia | HC45318 | 1981 | £8 | £20 | US audiophile |
| Darkness On The Edge Of Town | LP | Columbia | PAL35318 | 1978 | £62.50 | £125 | US promo picture disc |
| Ghost Of Tom Joad | CD | Sony | SAMPCD3006 | 1995 | £20 | £40 | promo with lyric booklet |
| Greetings From Asbury Park, N.J. | LP | CBS | 65480 | 1973 | £4 | £10 | gatefold sleeve, orange label |
| Hungry Heart | 7" | CBS | A9309 | 1980 | £6 | £12 | picture sleeve |
| I'm On Fire | 7" | CBS | A6342 | 1985 | £1.50 | £4 | with card |
| I'm On Fire | 7" | CBS | WA6342 | 1985 | £4 | £8 | shaped picture disc |
| I'm On Fire | 12" | CBS | TA6342 | 1985 | £2.50 | £6 | |
| Interviews | 7" | CBS | | 1986 | £5 | £10 | 2 x 7", boxed |

| | | | | | | | |
|---|---|---|---|---|---|---|---|
| Joe Grushecky and Bruce Springsteen In Conversation | CD | Pinnacle | PLR003 | 1995 | £20 | £40 | ...............promo |
| Leap Of Faith | CD-s | Sony | 6583692 | 1992 | £2 | £5 | |
| Live 1975–85 | LP | CBS | SAMP1104 | 1986 | £4 | £10 | ...............promo |
| Nebraska | CD | Columbia | CK38358 | 1983 | £8 | £20 | ...US, early copy with different mix |
| Open All Night | 7" | CBS | A2969 | 1982 | £6 | £12 | |
| Prodigal Son | CD | Dare International | | 1994 | £20 | £40 | |
| Prodigal Son | cass | Dare International | | 1984 | £15 | £30 | ...............demo |
| Promised Land | 7" | CBS | A6720 | 1978 | £2 | £5 | |
| Prove It All Night | 7" | CBS | A6424 | 1978 | £4 | £8 | |
| River | 7" | CBS | A1179 | 1981 | £4 | £8 | |
| River | 12" | CBS | A121179 | 1981 | £3 | £8 | |
| Rosalita | 7" EP | Columbia | AS66 | 1973 | £75 | £150 | ...... US, with special sleeve, questionnaire, booklet |
| Sherry Darling | 7" | CBS | A9568 | 1980 | £4 | £8 | |
| Sherry Darling/Independence Day | 7" | CBS | A9568 | 1980 | £25 | £50 | ...............promo |
| Sherry Darling/Independence Day | 7" | CBS | A9568 | 1980 | £62.50 | £125 | .. promo, picture sleeve |
| Spare Parts | CD-s | CBS | BRUCEB4 | 1988 | £5 | £12 | ...............in tin |
| Spare Parts | CD-s | CBS | BRUCEC4 | 1988 | £2 | £5 | |
| Tenth Avenue Freeze-Out | 7" | CBS | A3940 | 1976 | £2 | £5 | |
| Tougher Than The Rest | CD-s | CBS | BRUCEC3 | 1988 | £4 | £10 | |
| Tunnel Of Love | CD-s | CBS | 6512952 | 1987 | £6 | £15 | |
| Tunnel Of Love | CD | CBS | CDCBS4602709 | 1987 | £5 | £12 | ...............picture disc |
| Tunnel Of Love | 12" | CBS | 6512955 | 1987 | £3 | £8 | ..... shaped picture disc |
| Tunnel Of Love | 12" | CBS | 6512956 | 1987 | £2.50 | £6 | ...............with poster |
| Viva Las Vegas | CD-s | NME | CDPRO1990 | 1990 | £20 | £40 | ......promo, Paul McCartney B side |
| Viva Las Vegas | 10" | NME | PRO101990 | 1990 | £15 | £30 | ...........promo, Paul McCartney B side |
| Wild, The Innocent & E Street Shuffle | LP | CBS | 65780 | 1973 | £4 | £10 | yellow sleeve lettering, Ashbury label |

## SPROUD, BILLY & THE ROCK & ROLL SIX

| | | | | | | | |
|---|---|---|---|---|---|---|---|
| Rock Mister Piper | 7" | Columbia | DB3893 | 1957 | £12.50 | £25 | |

## SPROUTS

| | | | | | | | |
|---|---|---|---|---|---|---|---|
| Teen Billy Baby | 7" | RCA | RCA1031 | 1958 | £20 | £40 | |

## SPUD

| | | | | | | | |
|---|---|---|---|---|---|---|---|
| Happy Handful | LP | Philips | 9108003 | 1975 | £4 | £10 | |
| Silk Purse | LP | Philips | 9108002 | 1975 | £4 | £10 | |
| Smoking In The Bog | LP | Sonet | SNTF742 | 1977 | £4 | £10 | |

## SPUR

| | | | | | | | |
|---|---|---|---|---|---|---|---|
| Spur Of The Moment | LP | Cinema | CSLP1500 | | £30 | £60 | ...............US |

## SPUTNIKS

| | | | | | | | |
|---|---|---|---|---|---|---|---|
| Die Fruhen Jahre | LP | Amiga | 850872 | 1981 | £8 | £20 | ...........East German |

## SPYROGYRA

| | | | | | | | |
|---|---|---|---|---|---|---|---|
| Morning Dance | LP | MCA | INF9004 | 1979 | £6 | £15 | ..... US picture disc, 2 B-side designs |

## SQUEEZE

| | | | | | | | |
|---|---|---|---|---|---|---|---|
| Cool For Cats | 7" | A&M | AMS7426 | 1979 | £1.50 | £4 | .... brilliant pink vinyl |
| Cool For Cats | 7" | A&M | AMS7426 | 1979 | £2.50 | £6 | ............... red vinyl |
| Cool For Cats | 12" | A&M | AMSP7426 | 1979 | £2.50 | £6 | ...............pink vinyl |
| Packet Of Three | 12" | Deptford Fun City | 01 | 1977 | £3 | £8 | ...............pink sleeve |
| Play | CD | Reprise | | 1991 | £10 | £25 | US promo picture disc, plant pot |
| Singles 45s And Under | CD | A&M | 394922 | 1984 | £5 | £12 | .American track listing |
| Six Squeeze Songs Crammed On To One Ten Inch Record | 10" LP | A&M | SP3719 | 1980 | £4 | £10 | ...............US |
| UK Squeeze | LP | A&M | SP4687 | 1978 | £4 | £10 | ...US red vinyl |

## SQUIRE

| | | | | | | | |
|---|---|---|---|---|---|---|---|
| Does Stephanie Know | 7" | Hi Lo | LOX1 | 1985 | £2 | £5 | ...............flexi |
| Get Ready To Go | 7" | Rok | ROKI/II | 1979 | £2.50 | £6 | ..... B side by Coming Shortly |
| Something Old, Something New, Something Borrowed | LP | fan club | L0004 | 1984 | £4 | £10 | |
| Young Idea | 7" | Squire Fan Club | SFC2 | 1984 | £2.50 | £6 | |

## SQUIRES

The scarce single by the Squires marks the recording debut of Neil Young, who was a member of the group.

| | | | | | | | |
|---|---|---|---|---|---|---|---|
| Sultan | 7" | V | 109 | 1961 | £75 | £150 | .... US, best auctioned |

## SQUIRES, DOROTHY

| | | | | | | | |
|---|---|---|---|---|---|---|---|
| Dorothy Squires | 7" EP | Pye | NEP24036 | 1957 | £4 | £8 | |

## SRC

SRC (short for Scott Richard Case, after the lead singer) made three albums, with limited commercial success, before quitting in 1970. Led by the delightfully named Quackenbush brothers, the group is in many ways the quintessential American psychedelic band. Scott Richardson's earnest, slightly fragile vocals are the first word in cool glamour, while the piercing sustain of Gary Quackenbush's lead guitar lines is the sound that the likes of Bevis Frond and Screaming Trees have been trying to emulate for years. The single 'Black Sheep', taken from the first album, is a genuine sixties classic. An extremely rare album made by an earlier version of the group is listed under the name of the Fugitives.

| | | | | | | | |
|---|---|---|---|---|---|---|---|
| Black Sheep | 7" | Capitol | CL15576 | 1969 | £4 | £8 | |
| Milestones | LP | Capitol | (S)T134 | 1969 | £20 | £40 | |
| SRC | LP | Capitol | (S)T2991 | 1968 | £20 | £40 | |
| Traveller's Tale | LP | Capitol | (S)T273 | 1970 | £20 | £40 | |

## ST. CHRISTOPHER

| | | | | | | | |
|---|---|---|---|---|---|---|---|
| Crystal Clear | 7" | Bluegrass | GM001 | 1984 | £2.50 | £6 | |
| Forevermore Starts Here | 7" | Veston | VOD001 | 1987 | £1.50 | £4 | flexi |
| Go Ahead Cry | 7" | Bluegrass | GM003 | 1986 | £2 | £5 | |

## ST. CLAIR, CHERYL

| | | | | | | | |
|---|---|---|---|---|---|---|---|
| My Heart's Not In It | 7" | CBS | 202041 | 1966 | £2 | £5 | |

## ST. JOHN, BARRY

| | | | | | | | |
|---|---|---|---|---|---|---|---|
| Bread And Butter | 7" | Decca | F11975 | 1964 | £1.50 | £4 | |
| Come Away Melinda | 7" | Columbia | DB7783 | 1965 | £1.50 | £4 | |
| Everything I Touch Turns To Tears | 7" | Columbia | DB7868 | 1966 | £15 | £30 | |
| Hey Boy | 7" | Decca | F12145 | 1965 | £1.50 | £4 | |
| Little Bit Of Soap | 7" | Decca | F11933 | 1964 | £1.50 | £4 | |
| Mind How You Go | 7" | Decca | F12111 | 1965 | £2 | £5 | |

## ST. JOHN, BRIDGET

| | | | | | | | |
|---|---|---|---|---|---|---|---|
| Ask Me No Questions | LP | Dandelion | 63750 | 1969 | £10 | £25 | |
| Fly High | 7" | Polydor | 2001280 | 1972 | £1.50 | £4 | picture sleeve |
| If You've Got Money | 7" | Warner Bros | WB8019 | 1970 | £1.50 | £4 | |
| Jumble Queen | LP | Chrysalis | CHR1062 | 1974 | £5 | £12 | |
| Songs For The Gentle Man | LP | Dandelion | DAN8007 | 1971 | £10 | £25 | |
| Thank You For | LP | Dandelion | 2310193 | 1972 | £10 | £25 | |

## ST. JOHN, JEFF COPPERWINE

| | | | | | | | |
|---|---|---|---|---|---|---|---|
| Joint Effort | LP | Spin | SEL933742 | 1970 | £8 | £20 | New Zealand |

## ST. JOHN, RICH

| | | | | | | | |
|---|---|---|---|---|---|---|---|
| Thru' His Eyes | LP | Polydor | 623034 | 1966 | £8 | £20 | German |

## ST. JOHN, ROY

| | | | | | | | |
|---|---|---|---|---|---|---|---|
| Immigration Declaration | LP | Caroline | CA2008 | 1975 | £4 | £10 | |

## ST. JOHN, TAMMY

| | | | | | | | |
|---|---|---|---|---|---|---|---|
| Boys | 7" | Pye | 7N15682 | 1964 | £1.50 | £4 | |
| Dark Shadows And Empty Hallways | 7" | Pye | 7N15948 | 1965 | £1.50 | £4 | |
| Nobody Knows What's Goin' On | 7" | Pye | 7N17042 | 1966 | £7.50 | £15 | |

## ST. PATRICK, OLIVER

| | | | | | | | |
|---|---|---|---|---|---|---|---|
| I Want To Be Loved By You | 7" | Trojan | TR005 | 1967 | £5 | £10 | |

## ST. PETERS, CRISPIAN

| | | | | | | | |
|---|---|---|---|---|---|---|---|
| Almost Persuaded | 7" EP | Decca | DFE8678 | 1967 | £6 | £12 | |
| At This Moment | 7" | Decca | F12080 | 1965 | £1.50 | £4 | |
| Changes | 7" EP | Decca | 457126 | 1966 | £6 | £12 | French |
| Follow Me | LP | Decca | LK4805 | 1966 | £8 | £20 | |
| No No No | 7" | Decca | F12207 | 1965 | £1.50 | £4 | |
| Simply | LP | Square | SQA102 | 1970 | £4 | £10 | |
| So Long | 7" | Decca | F13055 | 1970 | £4 | £8 | |
| You Were On My Mind | 7" EP | Decca | 457110 | 1966 | £6 | £12 | French |

## ST. LOUIS JIMMY

| | | | | | | | |
|---|---|---|---|---|---|---|---|
| Goin' Down Slow | LP | Bluesville | BV1028 | 1961 | £6 | £15 | US |

## ST. LOUIS UNION

| | | | | | | | |
|---|---|---|---|---|---|---|---|
| Behind The Door | 7" | Decca | F12386 | 1966 | £7.50 | £15 | |
| East Side Story | 7" | Decca | F12508 | 1966 | £20 | £40 | |
| Girl | 7" | Decca | F12318 | 1966 | £2 | £5 | |

## ST. VALENTINE'S DAY MASSACRE

| | | | | | | | |
|---|---|---|---|---|---|---|---|
| Brother Can You Spare A Dime | 7" | Fontana | TF883 | 1967 | £37.50 | £75 | |
| Brother Can You Spare A Dime | 7" | Fontana | TF883 | 1967 | £50 | £100 | picture sleeve |

## STACCATOS

| | | | | | | | |
|---|---|---|---|---|---|---|---|
| Butchers And Bakers | 7" | Fontana | TF966 | 1968 | £5 | £10 | |

## STACCATOS (2)

| | | | | | | | |
|---|---|---|---|---|---|---|---|
| Half Past Midnight | 7" | Capitol | CL15505 | 1967 | £2 | £5 | |
| Let's Run Away | 7" | Capitol | CL15478 | 1966 | £2 | £5 | |

## STACCATOS (3)

| | | | | | | | |
|---|---|---|---|---|---|---|---|
| Main Line | 7" | Parlophone | R4828 | 1961 | £2.50 | £6 | |

## STACEY, CLARENCE
Just Your Love ........................................ 7" ...... Pye ................ 7N25025 ............... 1959 £2 ......... £5 ..................................................

## STACKIE, BOB
Grab It Hold It Feel It ............................ 7" ...... Collins ........... CR009 ................. 1968 £1.50 ........ £4 ...............................
Downbeat .......

## STACKRIDGE
Stackridge ............................................... LP ..... MCA ............. MDKS8002 ............ 1971 £4 ...... £10 ................................................

## STACKWADDY
Bugger Off .............................................. LP ..... Dandelion ...... 2310231 ............... 1972 £25 ....... £50 ..............................
Roadrunner ............................................. 7" ...... Dandelion ...... 5119 .................... 1970 £2 ......... £5 ...................................
Stackwaddy ............................................. LP ..... Dandelion ...... 2310154 ............... 1971 £20 ...... £40 ..............................
Stackwaddy ............................................. LP ..... Dandelion ...... DAN8003 ............ 1971 £20 ...... £40 ..............................
You Really Got Me ................................. 7" ...... Dandelion ...... 2001331 ............... 1972 £1.50 ........ £4 ..............................

## STACY, JESS
Jess Stacy ............................................... 10" LP Brunswick ...... LA8737 ............... 1956 £6 ......... £15 .............................
Jess Stacy And The Famous Sidemen ......... LP ..... London ............. LTZK15012 ......... 1957 £6 ......... £15 ................................

## STAEHELY BROTHERS
Sta-Hay-Lee ............................................ LP ..... Epic ............... 32385 ................... 1973 £10 ....... £25 ...................... US

## STAFFORD, JO
American Folk Songs .............................. 10" LP Capitol ........... LC6500 ............... 1950 £6 ......... £15 .............................
As You Desire Me ................................... 10" LP Columbia ........ 33S1024 .............. 1954 £8 ......... £20 .............................
Autumn In New York .............................. 10" LP Capitol ........... H197 .................... 195– £8 ......... £20 ...................... US
Ballad Of The Blues ............................... LP ..... Philips ............. BBL7327 ............. 1959 £4 ......... £10 .............................
Capitol Presents ...................................... 10" LP Capitol ........... LC6575 ............... 1953 £6 ......... £15 .............................
Capitol Presents Vol. 2 ........................... 10" LP Capitol ........... LC6635 ............... 1954 £6 ......... £15 .............................
Chow, Willy ............................................ 7" ...... Columbia ........ SCM5064 ............ 1953 £5 ......... £10 ....with Frankie Laine
Floatin' Down To Cotton Town ................. 10" LP Philips ............. BBR.8075 ............ 1956 £8 ......... £20 ....with Frankie Laine
Greatest Hits .......................................... LP ..... Columbia ........ CL1228 ............... 1959 £8 ......... £20 ...................... US
Happy Holiday ......................................... LP ..... Philips ............. BBL7100 ............. 1956 £5 ......... £12 .............................
I'll Be Seeing You ................................... LP ..... Philips ............. BBL7290 ............. 1959 £4 ......... £10 .............................
It Is No Secret ........................................ 7" ...... Columbia ........ SCM5012 ............ 1953 £4 ......... £8 .............................
Jo Jazz .................................................... LP ..... Philips ............. BBL7428/SBBL595. 1960 £4 ......... £10 .............................
Jo Jazz .................................................... 7" EP . Philips ............. BBE12459 ........... 1961 £2 ......... £5 .............................
Jo Stafford ............................................. 7" EP . Philips ............. BBE12014 ........... 1955 £5 ......... £10 .............................
Jo Stafford ............................................. 7" EP . Philips ............. BBE12141 ........... 1957 £2 ......... £5 .............................
Jo Stafford And Nelson Eddy .................. 7" EP . Columbia ........ SEG7516 ............. 1954 £2 ......... £5 .....with Nelson Eddy
Jo Stafford No. 2 .................................... 7" EP . Philips ............. BBE12138 ........... 1957 £2 ......... £5 .............................
Keep It A Secret ..................................... 7" ...... Columbia ........ SCM5026 ............ 1953 £4 ......... £8 .............................
Kiss Me Kate ........................................... 10" LP Capitol ........... LC6515 ............... 1951 £4 ......... £10 .. with Gordon MacRae
Musical Portrait Of New Orleans .............. LP ..... Columbia ........ CL578 ................. 195– £8 ......... £20 ..... US, with Frankie
Laine
My Heart's In The Highlands .................... 10" LP Philips ............. BBR8011 ............. 1954 £6 ......... £15 .............................
On London Bridge ................................... 7" ...... Philips ............. JK1003 ................ 1957 £2 ......... £5 .............................
Once Over Lightly ................................... LP ..... Philips ............. BBL7169 ............. 1957 £5 ......... £12 .............................
Pine Top's Boogie ................................... 7" ...... Philips ............. PB935 ................. 1959 £2 ......... £5 .............................
Settin' The Woods On Fire ....................... 7" ...... Columbia ........ SCM5014 ............ 1953 £4 ......... £8 .............................
Show Songs ............................................. 7" EP . Columbia ........ SEG7548 ............. 1954 £2 ......... £5 .............................
Showcase ................................................. LP ..... Philips ............. BBL7395 ............. 1960 £4 ......... £10 .............................
Ski Trails ............................................... LP ..... Philips ............. BBL7187 ............. 1957 £5 ......... £12 .............................
Something To Remember You By .............. 7" ...... Columbia ........ SCM5046 ............ 1953 £2.50 ....... £6 .............................
Songs Of Scotland ................................... LP ..... Columbia ........ CL1043 ............... 1957 £8 ......... £20 ...................... US
Star Of Hope .......................................... 7" ...... Columbia ........ SCM5011 ............ 1953 £2.50 ....... £6 .............................
Sunday Evening Songs ............................. 10" LP Capitol ........... LC6611 ............... 1953 £6 ......... £15 .. with Gordon MacRae
Swingin' Down Broadway .......................... LP ..... Philips ............. BBL7243 ............. 1958 £4 ......... £10 .............................
TV Series ................................................ 7" EP . Philips ............. BBE12214 ........... 1958 £2.50 ....... £6 .............................
Voice Of Your Choice .............................. 10" LP Philips ............. BBR8076 ............. 1956 £6 ......... £15 .............................
With A Little Bit Of Luck ....................... 7" ...... Philips ............. PB818 ................. 1958 £1.50 ........ £4 .............................
You Belong To Me ................................... 7" ...... Columbia ........ SCM5013 ............ 1953 £6 ......... £12 .............................

## STAFFORD, TERRY
Follow The Rainbow ................................ 7" ...... London ............. HLU9923 ............. 1964 £2 ......... £5 .............................
Heartache On The Way ............................ 7" ...... Stateside .......... SS225 .................. 1963 £2 ......... £5 .............................
I'll Touch A Star .................................... 7" ...... London ............. HLU9902 ............. 1964 £1.50 ........ £4 .............................
Suspicion ................................................ LP ..... London ............. HAU8200 ............ 1964 £20 ...... £40 .............................
Suspicion ................................................ 7" EP . London ............. REU1436 ............. 1964 £12.50 .. £25 .............................
Suspicion ................................................ 7" ...... London ............. HLU9871 ............. 1964 £1.50 ........ £4 .............................

## STAINED GLASS
Aurora .................................................... LP ..... Capitol ........... ST242 ................. 1971 £10 ....... £25 ...................... US
Crazy Horse Roads ................................. LP ..... Capitol ........... ST154 ................. 1969 £10 ....... £25 ...................... US

## STAINED GLASS (2)
Open Road .............................................. LP ..... Sweet Folk ...... SFA019 ................. 1975 £62.50 .. £125 .............................
And Country ...

## STAIRWAY
Moonstone .............................................. CD ..... New World ..... NWCD168 ............ 1986 £6 ......... £15 .............................

## STAMFORD BRIDGE & FRIENDS
Come Up And See Us Some Time ............. LP ...... Penny Farthing  PELS507 ................. 1970 £25 ....... £50 ...............................

834

## STAMP, TERRY
Fat Sticks .................................................. LP ...... A&M ............. AMLH63329 .......... 1975 £6 .......... £15

## STAMPEDE
Days Of Wine And Roses ........................ 7" ...... Polydor .......... POSP507 ............. 1982 £2 .......... £5
Days Of Wine And Roses ........................ 12" ..... Polydor .......... POSPX507 ............ 1982 £2.50 .......... £6

## STAMPEDERS
From The Fire ...................................... LP ...... Regal .......... SLRZ1039 ............. 1974 £6 .......... £15
                                                                Zonophone .....
Stampeders ......................................... LP ...... Regal .......... SLRZ1032 ............. 1972 £6 .......... £15
                                                                Zonophone .....

## STANBACK, JEAN
I Still Love You ................................... 7" ...... Deep Soul ....... DS9101 ................. 1970 £4 .......... £8

## STANDELLS
The Standells were responsible for a definitive garage punk performance in the single 'Dirty Water'. Much of the group's other material is in the same league, apart from the *Hot Ones* album, which is an ill-advised collection of cover versions. Gary Leeds, who was subsequently one of the Walker Brothers, is the drummer on the first LP, *In Person At P.J.'s*.

Dirty Water ......................................... LP ...... Tower .......... (S)T5027 .......... 1966 £15 .......... £30 .................. US
Dirty Water ......................................... 7" EP . Capitol .......... EAP122009 ............ 1966 £75 .......... £150 .................. French
Dirty Water ......................................... 7" ...... Capitol .......... CL15446 .......... 1966 £6 .......... £12
Help Yourself ....................................... 7" ...... Liberty .......... LIB55722 .......... 1964 £6 .......... £12
Hot Ones ............................................. LP ...... Tower .......... (S)T5049 .......... 1966 £10 .......... £25 .................. US
In Person At P.J.'s ................................ LP ...... Liberty .......... LBY1243 .......... 1965 £15 .......... £30 .................. US
In Person At P.J.s ................................ 7" EP . Liberty .......... LEP2211 .......... 1964 £50 .......... £100 .................. French
Live & Out Of Sight ............................. LP ...... Sunset .......... SUM1186/ .......... 1966 £8 .......... £20 .................. US
                                                                SUS5186 ...............
Try It ................................................. LP ...... Tower .......... (S)T5098 .......... 1967 £10 .......... £25 .................. US
Why Pick On Me .................................. LP ...... Tower .......... (S)T5044 .......... 1966 £10 .......... £25 .................. US

## STANG, ARNOLD
Ivy Will Cling ...................................... 7" ...... Fontana .......... H226 .......... 1959 £1.50 .......... £4

## STANSFIELD, LISA
I Got A Feeling .................................... 7" ...... Polydor .......... POSP651 .......... 1983 £2 .......... £5
Listen To Your Heart ............................ 7" ...... Polydor .......... POSP556 .......... 1983 £2 .......... £5
Only Way ............................................ 7" ...... Polydor .......... POSP521 .......... 1982 £2.50 .......... £6
Your Alibis ......................................... 7" ...... Devil .......... DEV2 .......... 1981 £7.50 .......... £15 .......... picture sleeve

## STANSHALL, VIV
The former lead singer of the Bonzo Dog Band made a number of eccentric records after the demise of that group. One recording not listed here is the alternative ending to Mike Oldfield's *Tubular Bells* (included in the four-album boxed set of Oldfield's first Virgin recordings) in which Stanshall is the commentator for a drunken guided tour of the Manor recording-studio complex. This favourite caricature of a vacuous aristocrat was the inspiration behind Stanshall's classic comedy recording *Sir Henry At Rawlinson End*, versions of which were first broadcast on the radio. 'Labio-Dental Fricative' would be an unlikely title for a single by anyone but Stanshall – it is one for Eric Clapton completists, as the guitarist lends his support to the musical proceedings.

Labio-Dental Fricative .......................... 7" ...... Liberty .......... LBS15309 .......... 1970 £6 .......... £12 ...... with Eric Clapton
Lakanga ............................................. 7" ...... Warner Bros ... K16424 .......... 1974 £1.50 .......... £4
Men Opening Umbrellas Ahead ................ LP ...... Warner Bros .... K56052 .......... 1974 £6 .......... £15
Question ............................................. 7" ...... Harvest .......... HAR5114 .......... 1976 £1.50 .......... £4
Sir Henry At Rawlinson End .................... LP ...... Charisma .......... CAS1139 .......... 1978 £5 .......... £12
Suspicion ........................................... 7" ...... Fly .......... BUG4 .......... 1970 £2.50 .......... £6
Teddy Boys Don't Knit ......................... LP ...... Charisma .......... CAS1153 .......... 1981 £4 .......... £10
Terry Keeps His Clips On ...................... 7" ...... Charisma .......... CB373 .......... 1980 £1.50 .......... £4

## STAPLE SINGERS
Beatitude/Respect Yourself ..................... LP ...... Stax .......... 2325069 .......... 1970 £4 .......... £10
City In The Sky ................................... LP ...... Stax .......... STX1001 .......... 1972 £4 .......... £10
For What It's Worth .............................. 7" ...... Columbia .......... DB8292 .......... 1967 £2.50 .......... £6
For What It's Worth .............................. 7" ...... Soul City .......... SC117 .......... 1969 £2 .......... £5
Freedom Highway .................................. LP ...... Columbia .......... SX6023 .......... 1966 £8 .......... £20
Hammer And Nails .................................. LP ...... Riverside ....... RLP3501 .......... 1963 £10 .......... £25
Hammer And Nails .................................. 7" ...... Riverside ....... 106902 .......... 1963 £2.50 .......... £6
Saviour Is Born .................................... 7" EP . Riverside ....... REP3220 .......... 1962 £2.50 .......... £6
Soul Folk In Action ............................... LP ...... Stax .......... 2363011 .......... 1971 £4 .......... £10
Swing Low ........................................... LP ...... Stateside .......... SL10015 .......... 1963 £8 .......... £20
Uncloudy Day ....................................... LP ...... Fontana .......... 688515ZL .......... 1965 £6 .......... £15
We'll Get Over ..................................... LP ...... Stax .......... SXATS1018 .......... 1969 £4 .......... £10

## STAPLETON, CYRIL
Blue Star ............................................ 7" ...... Decca .......... F10559 .......... 1955 £2 .......... £5
Come Twistin' ...................................... LP ...... Ace Of Clubs .. ACL1114 .......... 1962 £6 .......... £15
Elephant Tango .................................... 7" ...... Decca .......... F10488 .......... 1955 £2 .......... £5
Fanfare Boogie ..................................... 7" ...... Decca .......... F10470 .......... 1955 £1.50 .......... £4
Forgotten Dreams .................................. 7" ...... Decca .......... F10912 .......... 1957 £1.50 .......... £4
Happy Whistler ..................................... 7" ...... Decca .......... F10735 .......... 1956 £2 .......... £5
Italian Theme ...................................... 7" ...... Decca .......... F10703 .......... 1956 £2 .......... £5
Presenting ........................................... 7" EP . Decca .......... DFE6288 .......... 1956 £2 .......... £5
Presenting No. 2 ................................... 7" EP . Decca .......... DFE6340 .......... 1956 £2 .......... £5

## STAPREST
Schooldays ........................................... 7" ...... Avatar .......... AAA103 .......... 1981 £5 .......... £10

## STARCASTLE

| | | | | | | |
|---|---|---|---|---|---|---|
| Citadel | LP | Epic | 34935 | 1978 £4 | £10 | US picture disc |

## STARCHER, BUDDY

| | | | | | | |
|---|---|---|---|---|---|---|
| And His Mountain Guitar Vol. 1 | 7" EP | London | REB1424 | 1964 £2.50 | £6 | |
| And His Mountain Guitar Vol. 2 | 7" EP | London | REB1425 | 1964 £2.50 | £6 | |
| And His Mountain Guitar Vol. 3 | 7" EP | London | REB1426 | 1964 £2.50 | £6 | |

## STARFIRES

| | | | | | | |
|---|---|---|---|---|---|---|
| Starfires Play | LP | Ohio Recording Service | 34 | 1964 £15 | £30 | US |
| Teenbeat A Go-Go | LP | La Brea | LS8018 | 1965 £15 | £30 | US |

## STARGAZERS

| | | | | | | |
|---|---|---|---|---|---|---|
| 365 Kisses | 7" | Decca | F10379 | 1954 £1.50 | £4 | |
| Close The Door | 7" | Decca | F10594 | 1955 £4 | £8 | |
| Crazy Otto Rag | 7" | Decca | F10523 | 1955 £4 | £8 | |
| Happy Wanderer | 7" | Decca | F10259 | 1954 £4 | £8 | |
| Honky Tonk Song | 7" | Decca | F10898 | 1957 £1.50 | £4 | |
| I See The Moon | 7" | Decca | F10213 | 1953 £5 | £10 | |
| Presenting The Stargazers | 10" LP | Decca | LF1186 | 1954 £10 | £25 | |
| Rocking And Rolling | 7" EP | Decca | DFE6362 | 1956 £7.50 | £15 | |
| Rocking And Rolling | 7" | Decca | F10731 | 1956 £4 | £8 | |
| Rose Of The Wildwood | 7" | Decca | F10412 | 1954 £1.50 | £4 | |
| She Loves To Rock | 7" | Decca | F10775 | 1956 £4 | £8 | |
| Skiffling Dogs | 7" | Decca | F10969 | 1957 £1.50 | £4 | |
| Somebody | 7" | Decca | F10437 | 1955 £4 | £8 | |
| South Of The Border | LP | Decca | LK4309 | 1959 £6 | £15 | |
| Stargazers | 7" EP | Decca | DFE6341 | 1956 £7.50 | £15 | |
| Tender Trap | 7" | Decca | F10668 | 1956 £1.50 | £4 | |
| Twenty Tiny Fingers | 7" | Decca | F10626 | 1955 £4 | £8 | |
| Who Is It? | 7" | Decca | F10916 | 1957 £1.50 | £4 | |
| You Won't Be Around | 7" | Decca | F10867 | 1957 £1.50 | £4 | |
| Zambesi | 7" | Decca | F10696 | 1956 £1.50 | £4 | |

## STARK, PETER

| | | | | | | |
|---|---|---|---|---|---|---|
| Mushroom Country | LP | Montage | | 1976 £25 | £50 | US |

## STARK NAKED

| | | | | | | |
|---|---|---|---|---|---|---|
| Stark Naked | LP | RCA | SP4592 | 1971 £10 | £25 | US |

## STARR, CINDY & THE MOPEDS

| | | | | | | |
|---|---|---|---|---|---|---|
| Way I Do | 7" | Columbia | DB110 | 1968 £1.50 | £4 | |
| Pain Of Love | 7" | Columbia | DB107 | 1968 £1.50 | £4 | |

## STARR, EDWIN

| | | | | | | |
|---|---|---|---|---|---|---|
| 25 Miles | LP | Tamla Motown | (S)TML11115 | 1969 £5 | £12 | |
| 25 Miles | 7" | Tamla Motown | TMG672 | 1968 £1.50 | £4 | |
| Agent OO-Soul | 7" | Tamla Motown | TMG790 | 1971 £1.50 | £4 | |
| Headline News | 7" | Polydor | 56717 | 1966 £2 | £5 | |
| I Am The Man For You Baby | 7" | Tamla Motown | TMG646 | 1968 £4 | £8 | |
| I Want My Baby Back | 7" | Tamla Motown | TMG630 | 1967 £5 | £10 | |
| It's My Turn Now | 7" | Polydor | 56726 | 1967 £5 | £10 | |
| Soul Master | LP | Tamla Motown | (S)TML11094 | 1969 £10 | £25 | |
| Stop Her On Sight | 7" | Polydor | 56702 | 1966 £2 | £5 | |
| Stop Her On Sight | 7" | Polydor | 56753 | 1968 £1.50 | £4 | |
| Time | 7" | Tamla Motown | TMG725 | 1970 £1.50 | £4 | |
| War | 7" | Tamla Motown | TMG754 | 1970 £1.50 | £4 | |
| Way Over There | 7" | Tamla Motown | TMG692 | 1969 £1.50 | £4 | |

## STARR, EDWIN & BLINKY

| | | | | | | |
|---|---|---|---|---|---|---|
| Just We Two | LP | Tamla Motown | (S)TML11131 | 1970 £4 | £10 | |
| Oh How Happy | 7" | Tamla Motown | TMG720 | 1969 £50 | £100 | demo only |
| Oh How Happy | 7" | Tamla Motown | TMG748 | 1970 £1.50 | £4 | |

## STARR, FRANK

| | | | | | | |
|---|---|---|---|---|---|---|
| Little Bitty Feeling | 7" | London | HLU9545 | 1962 £4 | £8 | |

## STARR, FREDDIE

Comedian Freddie Starr's inspired impersonations of Elvis Presley are made slightly poignant by the knowledge that Starr is a failed rock singer made good. His group, the Midnighters, was one of the many Merseybeat outfits to emerge in the wake of the Beatles, but none of its singles managed to enter the charts. Starr's drummer was Keef Hartley, who subsequently played with the Artwoods and John Mayall before leading his own band.

| | | | | | | |
|---|---|---|---|---|---|---|
| Baby Blue | 7" | Decca | F11786 | 1963 £10 | £20 | |
| Never Cry On Someone's Shoulder | 7" | Decca | F12009 | 1964 £10 | £20 | |
| This Is Liverpool Beat | LP | Vogue | LDVS17006 | 1964 £25 | £50 | German |
| Who Told You | 7" | Decca | F11663 | 1963 £7.50 | £15 | |

## STARR, JIMMY

| | | | | | | |
|---|---|---|---|---|---|---|
| It's Only Make Believe | 7" | London | HL8731 | 1958 £12.50 | £25 | |

## STARR, KAY

| | | | | | | |
|---|---|---|---|---|---|---|
| Am I A Toy Or A Treasure? | 7" | Capitol | CL14151 | 1955 £5 | £10 | |
| Blue Starr | LP | RCA | RD27056 | 1958 £4 | £10 | |

| | | | | | | | | |
|---|---|---|---|---|---|---|---|---|
| Capitol Presents | 10" LP | Capitol | LC6574 | 1953 | £6 | £15 | |
| Fool Fool Fool | 7" | Capitol | CL14167 | 1954 | £7.50 | £15 | |
| Foolin' Around | 7" | Capitol | CL15194 | 1961 | £1.50 | £4 | |
| Foolishly Yours | 7" | HMV | 7M307 | 1955 | £2.50 | £6 | |
| Heavenly Kay Starr | 7" EP | Top Rank | JKP2042 | 1960 | £2.50 | £6 | |
| Hits Of Kay Starr | 10" LP | Capitol | LC6835 | 1956 | £6 | £15 | |
| If Anyone Finds This, I Love You | 7" | HMV | 7M300 | 1955 | £2.50 | £6 | |
| In A Blue Mood | LP | Capitol | T580 | 1957 | £4 | £10 | |
| Jamie Boy | 7" | HMV | POP357 | 1957 | £1.50 | £4 | |
| Kay Starr | 7" EP | Vogue | EPV1014 | 1955 | £5 | £10 | |
| Kay Starr | 10" LP | Capitol | LC6630 | 1954 | £6 | £15 | |
| Kay Stars Again | 7" EP | HMV | 7EG8184 | 1956 | £2 | £5 | |
| Little Loneliness | 7" | HMV | POP345 | 1957 | £1.50 | £4 | |
| Moving Pt. 1 | 7" EP | Capitol | EAP11254 | 1960 | £2 | £5 | |
| Moving Pt. 2 | 7" EP | Capitol | EAP21254 | 1960 | £2 | £5 | |
| Moving Pt. 3 | 7" EP | Capitol | EAP31254 | 1960 | £5 | £10 | |
| Riders In The Sky | 7" | Capitol | CL15105 | 1959 | £1.50 | £4 | |
| Rock And Roll Waltz | 7" | HMV | 7M371 | 1956 | £7.50 | £15 | |
| Rockin' With Kay | LP | RCA | LPM1720 | 1958 | £8 | £20 | US |
| Second Fiddle | 7" | HMV | 7M420 | 1956 | £4 | £8 | |
| Stroll Me | 7" | RCA | RCA1065 | 1958 | £1.50 | £4 | |
| Swinging With The Starr | LP | London | HAU2039 | 1957 | £8 | £20 | |
| Well I Ask You | 7" EP | Capitol | EAP120210 | 1962 | £2 | £5 | |
| What A Star Is Kay | 7" EP | HMV | 7EG8165 | 1956 | £2 | £5 | |
| Wheel Of Fortune | 7" EP | Capitol | EAP120063 | 1961 | £4 | £8 | |
| Wheel Of Fortune | 7" | Capitol | CL15137 | 1960 | £1.50 | £4 | |
| Where, What Or When? | 7" | HMV | 7M315 | 1955 | £2.50 | £6 | |

## STARR, RANDY

| | | | | | | | |
|---|---|---|---|---|---|---|---|
| After School | 7" | London | HL8443 | 1957 | £10 | £20 | |
| Count On Me | 7" | Felsted | AF106 | 1958 | £2.50 | £6 | |
| Workin' On The Santa Fe | 7" | Top Rank | JAR264 | 1960 | £1.50 | £4 | |

## STARR, RINGO

The rarest Ringo Starr record typifies the variety of work that Starr has undertaken since the break-up of the Beatles. *Scouse The Mouse* is a children's story produced by Donald Pleasence and dramatized with Ringo Starr playing the title role (and singing eight songs). A projected TV version never happened so that the album failed to attract any attention at the time of its release.

| | | | | | | | |
|---|---|---|---|---|---|---|---|
| Back Off Boogaloo | 7" | Apple | R5944 | 1972 | £2 | £5 | picture sleeve |
| Beaucoups Of Blues | LP | Apple | PAS10002 | 1970 | £6 | £15 | |
| Dose Of Rock 'n' Roll | 7" | Polydor | 2001694 | 1976 | £1.50 | £4 | |
| Drowning In A Sea Of Love | 7" | Polydor | 2001734 | 1977 | £15 | £30 | |
| Hey Baby | 7" | Polydor | 2001699 | 1976 | £1.50 | £4 | |
| It Don't Come Easy | 7" | Apple | R5898 | 1971 | £2 | £5 | picture sleeve |
| It Don't Come Easy | 7" | Old Gold | OG4513 | 1984 | £2 | £5 | picture sleeve |
| Lipstick Traces | 7" | Polydor | 2001782 | 1978 | £30 | £60 | demo |
| Oh My My | 7" | Apple | R6011 | 1976 | £4 | £8 | |
| Old Wave | LP | Bellaphon | 26016029 | 1983 | £20 | £40 | German |
| Old Wave/Stop And Smell The Roses | CD | Right Stuff | DPRO66732 | 1994 | £50 | £100 | US promo sampler with bonus track |
| Only You | 7" | Apple | PSR374 | 1974 | £50 | £100 | interview promo |
| Only You | 7" | Apple | R6000 | 1974 | £1.50 | £4 | picture sleeve |
| Ringo | LP | Apple | SWAL3413 | 1973 | £5 | £12 | US, with long version of 'Six O'Clock' |
| Ringo | CD | DCC | GZS1066 | 1994 | £6 | £15 | US audiophile |
| Ringo Starr And His All Starr Band | CD | Ryko | | 1990 | £8 | £20 | US, with bonus CD-s |
| Scouse The Mouse | LP | Polydor | 2480429 | 1978 | £37.50 | £75 | with other artists |
| Scouse The Mouse | cass | Polydor | 3194429 | 1978 | £6 | £15 | with other artists |
| Sentimental Journey | r-reel | Apple | TAPMC7101 | 1970 | £8 | £20 | mono |
| Sentimental Journey | r-reel | Apple | TDPCS7101 | 1970 | £6 | £15 | stereo |
| Sentimental Journey | LP | Apple | PCS7101 | 1970 | £6 | £15 | |
| Tonight | 7" | Polydor | 2001795 | 1978 | £15 | £30 | |

## STARR, STELLA

| | | | | | | | |
|---|---|---|---|---|---|---|---|
| Bring Him Back | 7" | Piccadilly | 7N35366 | 1967 | £12.50 | £25 | |

## STARR, TONY

| | | | | | | | |
|---|---|---|---|---|---|---|---|
| Rocket To The Moon | 7" | Decca | F11847 | 1964 | £7.50 | £15 | |

## STARRY EYED AND LAUGHING

| | | | | | | | |
|---|---|---|---|---|---|---|---|
| Starry Eyed And Laughing | LP | CBS | 80450 | 1974 | £4 | £10 | |
| Thought Talk | LP | CBS | 80907 | 1975 | £4 | £10 | |

## STARS OF HEAVEN

| | | | | | | | |
|---|---|---|---|---|---|---|---|
| Clothes Of Pride | 7" | Hotwire | HWS853 | 1985 | £4 | £8 | |

## STATE OF MICKEY & TOMMY

| | | | | | | | |
|---|---|---|---|---|---|---|---|
| Frisco Bay | 7" | Mercury | MF1009 | 1967 | £20 | £40 | |
| Frisco Bay | 7" EP | Mercury | 152102 | 196– | £30 | £60 | French |
| With Love From | 7" EP | Mercury | 152095 | 196– | £30 | £60 | French |
| With Love From One To Five | 7" | Mercury | MF996 | 1967 | £20 | £40 | |

## STATESMEN

| | | | | | | | |
|---|---|---|---|---|---|---|---|
| I've Just Fallen In Love | 7" | Fontana | TF432 | 1964 | £1.50 | £4 | |
| Look Around | 7" | Decca | F11687 | 1963 | £1.50 | £4 | |

## STATIC

| | | | | | | | |
|---|---|---|---|---|---|---|---|
| When You Went Away | 7" | Page One | POF039 | 1967 | £2 | £5 | |

## STATION SKIFFLE GROUP

| | | | | | | | |
|---|---|---|---|---|---|---|---|
| Station Skiffle Group | 7" EP | Esquire | EP161 | 1958 | £15 | £30 | |

## STATON, DAKOTA

| | | | | | | | |
|---|---|---|---|---|---|---|---|
| Ballads And The Blues | LP | Capitol | (S)T1387 | 1960 | £4 | £10 | |
| Confessin' The Blues | 7" | Capitol | CL14917 | 1959 | £2 | £5 | |
| Crazy He Calls Me | LP | Capitol | T1170 | 1959 | £4 | £10 | |
| Don't Leave Me Now | 7" | Capitol | CL14314 | 1955 | £2.50 | £6 | |
| Dynamic Dakota Staton | LP | Capitol | (S)T1054 | 1959 | £4 | £10 | |
| Dynamic Dakota Staton | 7" EP | Capitol | EAP11054 | 1959 | £2 | £5 | |
| Dynamic Dakota Staton Pt. 2 | 7" EP | Capitol | EAP21054 | 1959 | £2 | £5 | |
| Dynamic Dakota Staton Pt. 3 | 7" EP | Capitol | EAP31054 | 1959 | £2 | £5 | |
| I Never Dreamt | 7" | Capitol | CL14339 | 1955 | £1.50 | £4 | |
| Late, Late Show | LP | Capitol | T876 | 1958 | £4 | £10 | |
| More Than The Mood | LP | Capitol | (S)T1325 | 1960 | £4 | £10 | |
| Party's Over | 7" | Capitol | CL14870 | 1958 | £1.50 | £4 | |
| Time To Swing | LP | Capitol | (S)T1421 | 1961 | £4 | £10 | |

## STATUES

| | | | | | | | |
|---|---|---|---|---|---|---|---|
| Blue Velvet | 7" | London | HLG9192 | 1960 | £10 | £20 | |

## STATUS QUO

Status Quo are one of the more unlikely success stories of rock music, having stuck with the same Chuck Berry and boogie style ever since first deciding on it some time around 1970. The group's earlier recordings – as the Spectres and Traffic Jam before becoming Status Quo – are more varied in style, but perhaps not very expertly performed. The slightly psychedelic 'Pictures Of Matchstick Men' was a considerable hit, of course, but no one bought the accompanying album, which is now extremely scarce. Its awkward title probably did not help its sales when released: *Picturesque Matchstickable Messages*. The succeeding *Spare Parts* is also highly sought-after today, as is the Marble Arch release *Status Quotations*, even though this is only a compilation of singles and tracks from the first LP.

| | | | | | | | |
|---|---|---|---|---|---|---|---|
| 1982 | CD | Vertigo | 8000352 | 1983 | £6 | £15 | |
| Ain't Complainin' | CD-s | Vertigo | QUOCD22 | 1988 | £3 | £8 | |
| Ain't Complaining | CD-s | Vertigo | 0803222 | 1988 | £15 | £30 | CD video |
| Anniversary Waltz | CD-s | Vertigo | QUOCD28 | 1990 | £2 | £5 | |
| Anniversary Waltz Part 2 | CD-s | Vertigo | QUOCD29 | 1990 | £2 | £5 | |
| Anniversary Waltz Parts 1 & 2 | 7" | Vertigo | QUODJ28 | 1990 | £5 | £10 | promo |
| Anniversary Waltz Parts 1 & 2 | 12" | Vertigo | QUO2812 | 1990 | £5 | £12 | B side plays 'Little Lady' & 'Paper Plane' |
| Are You Growing Tired Of My Love | 7" | Pye | 7N17728 | 1969 | £5 | £10 | |
| Back To Back | CD | Vertigo | 814662 | 1983 | £5 | £12 | |
| Black Veils Of Melancholy | 7" | Pye | 7N17497 | 1968 | £5 | £10 | |
| Burning Bridges | CD-s | Vertigo | 0806202 | 1988 | £10 | £20 | CD video |
| Burning Bridges | CD-s | Vertigo | QUOCD25 | 1988 | £2 | £5 | |
| Can't Give You More | CD-s | Vertigo | QUOCD30 | 1991 | £2 | £5 | |
| Can't Give You More | 7" | Vertigo | STATUS30 | 1991 | £5 | £10 | promo |
| Caroline | 7" | Vertigo | QUOP10 | 1982 | £2.50 | £6 | picture disc |
| Caroline (Live) | 12" | Vertigo | QUO1012 | 1982 | £2.50 | £6 | |
| Down Down Down | 7" | Lyntone | LYN3154/5 | 1976 | £2.50 | £6 | flexi, picture sleeve |
| Dreamin' | 7" | Vertigo | QUOP21 | 1986 | £2.50 | £6 | with poster |
| Fakin' The Blues | CD-s | Vertigo | QUOCD31 | 1993 | £5 | £12 | no case |
| Fakin' The Blues | 7" | Vertigo | QUO31 | 1991 | £50 | £100 | |
| Fakin' The Blues | 12" | Vertigo | QUO3112 | 1991 | £62.50 | £125 | |
| File Series | LP | Pye | FILD005 | 1977 | £5 | £12 | double |
| From The Makers Of | LP | Vertigo | PROBX1 | 1982 | £6 | £15 | 3 LPs in metal box |
| Gerdundula | 7" | Pye | 7N45253 | 1973 | £1.50 | £4 | |
| Hello | LP | Vertigo | 6360098 | 1973 | £4 | £10 | with inner sleeve & poster |
| In My Chair | 7" | Pye | 7N17998 | 1970 | £15 | £30 | picture sleeve |
| In The Army Now | 7" | Vertigo | QUODP20 | 1986 | £2.50 | £6 | double |
| In The Army Now | 7" | Vertigo | QUOPD20 | 1986 | £10 | £20 | picture disc |
| In The Army Now | 12" | Vertigo | QUO2012 | 1986 | £4 | £10 | with poster |
| Jealousy | 7" | Vertigo | QUO9 | 1982 | £25 | £50 | Irish promo |
| Just For The Record | LP | Pye | NSPL18607 | 1979 | £4 | £10 | red vinyl |
| Little Dreamer | CD-s | Vertigo | QUOCD27 | 1989 | £2 | £5 | |
| Make Me Stay A Bit Longer | 7" | Pye | 7N17665 | 1969 | £6 | £12 | |
| Marguerita Time | 7" | Vertigo | QUOP14 | 1983 | £5 | £10 | picture disc |
| Marguerita Time | 7" | Vertigo | QUOP1414 | 1983 | £6 | £12 | double Xmas gift pack |
| Mess Of Blues | 12" | Vertigo | QUO1212 | 1983 | £2.50 | £6 | |
| Never Too Late | CD | Vertigo | 8000532 | 1983 | £6 | £15 | |
| Not At All | CD-s | Vertigo | QUOCD26 | 1989 | £2 | £5 | |
| Ol' Rag Blues | 12" | Vertigo | QUO1112 | 1983 | £2.50 | £6 | |
| Pictures Of Matchstick Men | 7" | Pye | 7N17449 | 1968 | £1.50 | £4 | '75cc Minimum' on label |
| Pictures Of Matchstick Men | 7" | Pye | FBS2 | 1979 | £2 | £5 | yellow vinyl |
| Picturesque Matchstickable Messages | LP | Pye | N(S)PL18220 | 1968 | £25 | £100 | |
| Price Of Love | 7" | Pye | 7N17825 | 1969 | £6 | £12 | |
| Red Sky | 7" | Vertigo | QUOD19 | 1986 | £2.50 | £6 | double |
| Red Sky | 12" | Vertigo | QUO1912 | 1986 | £4 | £10 | poster sleeve |
| Rock 'Til You Drop | CD-s | Vertigo | QUOCD32 | 1991 | £2 | £5 | |
| Rock Till You Drop | 12" | Vertigo | QUO3212 | 1992 | £2.50 | £6 | 2 tracks |
| Rock 'n' Roll | 7" | Vertigo | QUOJB6 | 1981 | £2 | £5 | jukebox issue, no picture sleeve |
| Rockin' All Over The World | 7" | Vertigo | 6059184 | 1977 | £2.50 | £6 | picture sleeve, poster |
| Rollin' Home | 7" | Vertigo | QUOP18 | 1986 | £4 | £8 | shaped picture disc |

| | | | | | | | | |
|---|---|---|---|---|---|---|---|---|
| Running All Over The World | CD-s | Vertigo | QUACD1 | 1988 | £2 | £5 | |
| Spare Parts | LP | Pye | N(S)PL18301 | 1968 | £25 | £100 | |
| Status Quotations | LP | Marble Arch | MAL(S)1193 | 1969 | £20 | £40 | |
| Technicolour Dreams | 7" | Pye | 7N17650 | 1968 | £700 | £1000 | best auctioned |
| Technicolour Dreams | 7" | Pye | 7N17650 | 1968 | £330 | £500 | demo, best auctioned |
| Tune To The Music | 7" | Pye | 7N45077 | 1971 | £5 | £10 | |
| Wanderer | 12" | Vertigo | QUOP16 | 1984 | £6 | £15 | clear vinyl, picture disc centre |
| Who Gets The Love? | CD-s | Vertigo | QUOCD23 | 1988 | £2 | £5 | |

## STAVELY MAKEPEACE

| | | | | | | | | |
|---|---|---|---|---|---|---|---|---|
| Tarzan Harvey | 7" | Pyramid | PYR6082 | 1969 | £2.50 | £6 | test pressing only |

## STAVERTON BRIDGE

| | | | | | | | |
|---|---|---|---|---|---|---|---|
| Staverton Bridge | LP | Saydisc | SDL266 | 1975 | £10 | £25 |

## STEAMHAMMER

Steamhammer arrived at the tail end of the British blues boom amidst publicity that spoke of them being a next-generation group who would find ways of going beyond the blues. For once, this was no hype, the second LP in particular being a fine example of jazz-rock, in which Martin Pugh's fluid guitar playing is ably complemented by Steve Joliffe's flute and saxophone. The long 'Another Travelling Tune' shows how improvised rock can be entirely successful when the musicians are as inspired as these.

| | | | | | | | | |
|---|---|---|---|---|---|---|---|---|
| Autumn Song | 7" | CBS | 4496 | 1969 | £1.50 | £4 | |
| Junior's Wailing | 7" | CBS | 4141 | 1969 | £1.50 | £4 | |
| Mountains | LP | B&C | CAS1024 | 1970 | £8 | £20 | |
| Speech | LP | Brain | 1009 | 1972 | £10 | £25 | German |
| Steamhammer | LP | CBS | 63611 | 1968 | £15 | £30 | |
| Steamhammer | LP | Reflection | REFL1 | 1970 | £10 | £25 | |
| Steamhammer Mark 2 | LP | CBS | 63694 | 1969 | £10 | £25 | |

## STEEL

| | | | | | | | |
|---|---|---|---|---|---|---|---|
| Rock Out | 7" | Neat | NEAT14 | 1981 | £2.50 | £6 |

## STEEL MILL

Bruce Springsteen once led a group called Steel Mill, but the hard rock group who recorded the scarce *Green Eyed God* album has no connection with this.

| | | | | | | | |
|---|---|---|---|---|---|---|---|
| Get On The Line | 7" | Penny Farthing | PEN783 | 1971 | £6 | £12 |
| Green Eyed God | LP | Penny Farthing | PELS549 | 1975 | £100 | £200 |
| Green Eyed God | 7" | Penny Farthing | PEN770 | 1971 | £6 | £12 |
| Green Eyed God | 7" | Penny Farthing | PEN894 | 1975 | £1.50 | £4 |

## STEEL RIVER

| | | | | | | | |
|---|---|---|---|---|---|---|---|
| Better Road | LP | Evolution | Z3006 | 1971 | £4 | £10 |
| Weighing Heavy | LP | Evolution | E2018 | 1970 | £4 | £10 |

## STEELE, BETTE ANN

| | | | | | | | |
|---|---|---|---|---|---|---|---|
| Barricade | 7" | Capitol | CL14315 | 1955 | £2 | £5 |

## STEELE, DAVY

| | | | | | | | |
|---|---|---|---|---|---|---|---|
| Long Time Getting | LP | Bracken | BKN1001 | 1983 | £8 | £20 |

## STEELE, JAN & JOHN CAGE

| | | | | | | | |
|---|---|---|---|---|---|---|---|
| Voices & Instruments | LP | Obscure | OBS5 | 1976 | £5 | £12 |

## STEELE, SANDRA & JON

| | | | | | | | |
|---|---|---|---|---|---|---|---|
| I'm Crazy With Love | 7" | Parlophone | MSP6166 | 1955 | £1.50 | £4 |

## STEELE, TOMMY

| | | | | | | | | |
|---|---|---|---|---|---|---|---|---|
| Butterfingers | 7" | Decca | F10877 | 1957 | £2 | £5 | |
| Come On Let's Go | 7" EP | Decca | DFE6551 | 1958 | £2.50 | £6 | |
| Come On Let's Go | 7" | Decca | F11072 | 1958 | £1.50 | £4 | |
| Doomsday Rock | 7" | Decca | F10808 | 1956 | £7.50 | £15 | |
| Dream Maker | 7" | Columbia | DB7070 | 1963 | £1.50 | £4 | |
| Duke Wore Jeans | 7" EP | Decca | DFE6472 | 1958 | £4 | £8 | |
| Duke Wore Jeans | 10" LP | Decca | LF1308 | 1958 | £5 | £12 | |
| Get Happy | LP | Decca | LK4351 | 1960 | £4 | £10 | |
| Happy Guitar | 7" | Decca | F10976 | 1958 | £1.50 | £4 | |
| Hey You | 7" | Decca | F10941 | 1957 | £2 | £5 | |
| Knee Deep In The Blues | 7" | Decca | F10849 | 1957 | £4 | £8 | |
| Little White Bull | 7" | Decca | F11177 | 1959 | £2 | £5 | picture sleeve |
| Nairobi | 7" | Decca | F10991 | 1958 | £1.50 | £4 | |
| Only Man On The Island | 7" | Decca | F11041 | 1958 | £1.50 | £4 | |
| Rock With The Caveman | 7" | Decca | F10795 | 1956 | £12.50 | £25 | |
| Shiralee | 7" | Decca | F10896 | 1957 | £2.50 | £6 | |
| Singing The Blues | 7" EP | Decca | DFE6389 | 1956 | £5 | £10 | |
| Singing The Blues | 7" | Decca | F10819 | 1956 | £5 | £10 | |
| Tallahassie Lassie | 7" | Decca | F11152 | 1959 | £2 | £5 | |
| Tommy Steele | 7" EP | Decca | DFE6592 | 1959 | £2.50 | £6 | |
| Tommy Steele Stage Show | 10" LP | Decca | LF1287 | 1957 | £8 | £20 | |
| Tommy Steele Story | 10" LP | Decca | LF1288 | 1957 | £6 | £15 | |
| Tommy Steele Story Vol. 1 | 7" EP | Decca | DFE6398 | 1957 | £4 | £8 | |
| Tommy Steele Story Vol. 2 | 7" EP | Decca | DFE6424 | 1957 | £4 | £8 | |
| Tommy The Toreador | 7" EP | Decca | DFE6607 | 1959 | £2 | £5 | |
| Trial | 7" | Decca | F11117 | 1959 | £1.50 | £4 | |
| Water Water | 7" | Decca | F10923 | 1957 | £1.50 | £4 | |
| What A Mouth | 7" EP | Decca | DFE6660 | 1960 | £2 | £5 | |

Young Love ........................................... 7" EP . Decca ............. DFE6388 ................ 1956 £5 .......... £10 ......................................

## STEELEYE SPAN
Adam Catched Eve ................................. LP ..... Boulevard ........ BD3004 ................ 1979 £5 .......... £12 .......................................
All Around My Hat ................................ LP ..... Mobile Fidelity MFSL1027 ... 1978 £5 .......... £12 ......... US audiophile
Hark The Village Wait ........................... LP ..... RCA ............. SF8113 ................ 1970 £6 .......... £15 .......................................
Please To See The King ......................... LP ..... B&C ............ CAS1029 ............... 1971 £6 .......... £15 ......... textured sleeve
Rave On ............................................... 7" ..... B&C ............ CB164 .................. 1971 £1.50 ........ £4 ......... picture sleeve
Ten Man Mop ....................................... LP ..... Pegasus ........... PEG9 .................. 1971 £4 .......... £10 ......... with booklet

## STEELY DAN
Aja ....................................................... LP ..... Mobile Fidelity MFSL1033 ... 1979 £6 .......... £15 ......... US audiophile
Aja ....................................................... CD ... Mobile Fidelity UDCD515 .... 1988 £6 .......... £15 ......... US audiophile
Can't Buy A Thrill ................................. LP ..... Command ...... QD40009 ............... 1974 £4 .......... £10 ......... US quad
Countdown To Ecstasy .......................... LP ..... Command ...... QD40010 ............... 1974 £4 .......... £10 ......... US quad
Gaucho ................................................ CD ... Mobile Fidelity UDCD545 ..... 1991 £6 .......... £15 ......... US audiophile
Katy Lied .............................................. LP ..... Mobile Fidelity MFSL1007 ... 1978 £6 .......... £15 ......... US audiophile
Pretzel Logic ........................................ LP ..... Command ....... QD40015 ............... 1974 £4 .......... £10 ......... US quad

## STEEPLECHASE
Lady Bright ........................................... LP ..... Polydor ........... 2489001 ............... 1970 £8 .......... £20 ......................................

## STEGMEYER, BILL
On The Waterfront ................................ 7" ...... London ........... HL8078 ............... 1954 £10 ........ £20 ......................................

## STEIG, JEREMY
Wayfaring Stranger ................................ LP ..... Blue Note ...... BST84354 .......... 1970 £4 .......... £10 ......................................

## STEIN, LOU
Almost Paradise ..................................... 7" ...... London ........... HLZ8419 ........... 1957 £4 .......... £8 ......................................
Who Slammed The Door ......................... 7" ...... Mercury ......... 7MT226 ............ 1958 £1.50 ........ £4 ......................................

## STENSON, BOBO
Underwear ............................................ LP ..... ECM ............. ECM1012ST .......... 1971 £6 .......... £15 ......................................

## STEPHENS, LEIGH
Cast Of Thousands ................................ LP ..... Charisma ........ CAS1040 ............... 1971 £5 .......... £12 ......................................
Red Weather ......................................... LP ..... Philips ............. SBL7897 ............... 1969 £8 .......... £20 ......................................

## STEPPENWOLF
Although their recorded output is quite large, John Kay's Steppenwolf is quite adequately summed up by three great songs – 'Magic Carpet Ride', 'The Pusher' and especially 'Born To Be Wild'. Apart from being a glorious rocker, the last song also contains the first use of the phrase 'heavy metal'. The album *Early Steppenwolf*, recorded live at the Matrix, San Francisco in 1967, is best avoided. Long improvisations clearly did not really suit the group, who tend to use random noise as a substitute for genuine inspiration.

At Your Birthday Party ......................... LP ..... Stateside ......... (S)SL5011 ............ 1969 £4 .......... £10 ......................................
Born To Be Wild ................................... 7" ...... RCA ............. RCA1735 ............ 1968 £1.50 ........ £4 ......................................
Early Steppenwolf ................................. LP ..... Stateside ......... (S)SL5015 ............ 1969 £4 .......... £10 ......................................
Live ...................................................... LP ..... Stateside ......... SSL5029 ............. 1970 £4 .......... £10 ......................................
Magic Carpet Ride ................................. 7" ...... Stateside ......... SS8003 ............... 1968 £1.50 ........ £4 ......................................
Monster ................................................ LP ..... Stateside ......... SSL5021 ............. 1970 £4 .......... £10 ......................................
Second .................................................. LP ..... Stateside ......... (S)SL5003 ............ 1968 £4 .......... £10 ......................................
Sookie Sookie ....................................... 7" ...... RCA ............. RCA1679 ............ 1968 £1.50 ........ £4 ......................................
Steppenwolf .......................................... LP ..... RCA ............. RD/SF7974 .......... 1968 £5 .......... £12 ......................................

## STEREOLAB
Crumb Duck ......................................... 10" ..... Clawfist ........... 20 ..................... 1993 £6 .......... £15 ......... hand made sleeve
Harmonium .......................................... 7" ...... Duophonic ...... DS4504 ............... 1992 £5 .......... £10 ......... amber vinyl
Light (That Will Cease To Fail) ............. 7" ...... Big Money Inc BMI025 .............. 1992 £2.50 ........ £6 ......... pink vinyl
Music For The Amorphous Body Study   CD ... Duophonic ...... ..................... 1995 £8 .......... £20 ..ltd edn soundtrack to
    Center ..........................................................................................................................................................sound and sculpture
                                                                                                                                            exhibition
Stunning Debut Album ........................... 7" ...... Duophonic ...... DS4502 ............... 1991 £7.50 ...... £15 ......... clear vinyl
Stunning Debut Album ........................... 7" ...... Duophonic ...... DS4502 ............... 1991 £10 ........ £20 ... multi-coloured vinyl
Super 45 ................................................ 10" ..... Duophonic ...... DS4501 ............... 1991 £10 ........ £20 ......................................
Super 45 ................................................ 10" ..... Duophonic ...... DS4501 ............... 1991 £15 ........ £30 ..handpainted picture
                                                                                                                                            sleeve

## STEREOS
Big Knock ............................................. 7" ...... MGM ............ MGM1149 ............ 1961 £7.50 ...... £15 ......................................
Big Knock ............................................. 7" ...... MGM ............ MGM1328 ............ 1966 £2.50 ...... £6 ......................................
Please Come Back To Me ....................... 7" ...... MGM ............ MGM1143 ............ 1961 £7.50 ...... £15 ......................................

## STERLING, LESTER
Africkaan Beat ...................................... 7" ...... Coxsone .......... CS7080 ............... 1968 £5 .......... £10 ......... Paragons B side
Air Raid Shelter .................................... 7" ...... R&B ........... JB111 ................. 1963 £5 .......... £10 Roy & Annette B side
Bangarang ............................................. LP ..... Pama ............. SECO15 ............... 1969 £15 ........ £30 ......................................
Bangarang ............................................. 7" ...... Unity ............. UN502 ............... 1968 £1.50 ........ £4 ... with Stranger Cole
Clean The City ...................................... 7" ...... Island ............ WI121 ............... 1963 £5 .......... £10 ......................................
Forest Gate Rock ................................... 7" ...... Big Shot ......... BI507 .................. 1968 £2 .......... £5 ......................................
Gravy Cool ............................................ 7" ...... R&B ........... JB115 ................. 1963 £5 .......... £10 ..... Winston & Bibby
                                                                                                                                            B side
Indian Summer ...................................... 7" ...... R&B ........... JB172 ................. 1964 £5 .......... £10 ...... Stranger & Patsy
                                                                                                                                            B side
Lonesome Feeling .................................. 7" ...... Unity ............. UN531 ............... 1969 £1.50 ........ £4 ......................................
Man About Town ................................... 7" ...... Unity ............. UN518 ............... 1969 £1.50 ........ £4 ......................................
One Thousand Tons Of Megaton ............. 7" ...... Unity ............. UN517 ............... 1969 £1.50 ........ £4 ..King Cannon B side

| | | | | | | | |
|---|---|---|---|---|---|---|---|
| Reggae In The Wind | 7" | Gas | GAS103 | 1969 | £1.50 | £4 | Soul Set B side |
| Regina | 7" | Unity | UN512 | 1969 | £1.50 | £4 | |
| Sir Collins Special | 7" | Collins Downbeat | CR001 | 1967 | £4 | £8 | |
| Soul Voyage | 7" | Doctor Bird | DB1107 | 1967 | £5 | £10 | *Alva Lewis B side* |
| Spoogy | 7" | Unity | UN509 | 1969 | £1.50 | £4 | *... Tommy McCook B side* |
| Zigaloo | 7" | Blue Cat | BS116 | 1968 | £4 | £8 | |

## STEVE & STEVIE

| | | | | | | | |
|---|---|---|---|---|---|---|---|
| Steve And Stevie | LP | Toast | TLP2 | 1968 | £20 | £40 | |

## STEVENS, APRIL

| | | | | | | | |
|---|---|---|---|---|---|---|---|
| Falling In Love Again | 7" | MGM | MGM1366 | 1967 | £25 | £50 | |
| How Could Red Riding Hood | 7" | Parlophone | MSP6088 | 1954 | £2 | £5 | |
| Soft Warm Lips | 7" | Parlophone | MSP6060 | 1953 | £2 | £5 | |
| Teach Me Tiger | LP | Imperial | LP9055/12055 | 1961 | £6 | £15 | *US* |
| Torrid Tunes | LP | Audio Lab | AL1534 | 1959 | £10 | £25 | *US* |

## STEVENS, CAT

| | | | | | | | |
|---|---|---|---|---|---|---|---|
| Bad Night | 7" EP | Deram | 15006 | 1967 | £5 | £10 | *French* |
| Buddha And The Chocolate Box | LP | A&M | QU53623 | 1974 | £4 | £10 | *US quad* |
| Catch Bull At Four | LP | A&M | QU54365 | 1972 | £4 | £10 | *US quad* |
| Cats And Dogs | LP | Deram | | 1967 | £15 | £30 | *test pressing* |
| Foreigner | LP | A&M | QU54391 | 1974 | £4 | £10 | *US quad* |
| Greatest Hits | LP | A&M | QU54519 | 1975 | £4 | £10 | *US quad* |
| I Love My Dog | 7" EP | Deram | 15000 | 1966 | £5 | £10 | *French* |
| I'm Gonna Get Me A Gun | 7" EP | Deram | 15003 | 1967 | £5 | £10 | *French* |
| Matthew And Son | LP | Deram | DML/SML1004 | 1967 | £4 | £10 | |
| Mona Bone Jakon | LP | Island | ILPS9118 | 1970 | £4 | £10 | *pink label* |
| New Masters | LP | Deram | DML/SML1018 | 1967 | £4 | £10 | |
| Saturday Night Live | LP | A&M | | 1975 | £6 | £15 | *US promo* |
| Tea For The Tillerman | LP | A&M | QU54280 | 1972 | £4 | £12 | *US quad* |
| Tea For The Tillerman | LP | Island | ILPS9135 | 1970 | £8 | £20 | *pink label* |
| Tea For The Tillerman | LP | Mobile Fidelity | MFSL1035 | 1979 | £5 | £12 | *US audiophile* |
| Tea For The Tillerman | LP | Mobile Fidelity | MFSL1035 | 1984 | £50 | £100 | *US audiophile (UHQR)* |
| Teaser And The Firecat | LP | A&M | QU54313 | 1972 | £4 | £10 | *US quad* |

## STEVENS, CONNIE

| | | | | | | | |
|---|---|---|---|---|---|---|---|
| As Cricket | 7" EP | Warner Bros | WEP6007 | 1960 | £2 | £5 | |
| As Cricket | 7" EP | Warner Bros | WSE6007 | 1962 | £4 | £8 | *stereo* |
| As Cricket No. 2 | 7" EP | Warner Bros | WEP6105 | 1963 | £2 | £5 | |
| As Cricket No. 2 | 7" EP | Warner Bros | WSE6105 | 1963 | £4 | £8 | *stereo* |
| As Cricket No. 3 | 7" EP | Warner Bros | WEP6112 | 1963 | £2 | £5 | |
| As Cricket No. 3 | 7" EP | Warner Bros | WSE6112 | 1963 | £4 | £8 | *stereo* |
| Conchetta | LP | Warner Bros | W1208 | 1958 | £6 | £15 | *US* |
| Connie | LP | Warner Bros | WM4061/WS8061 | 1962 | £5 | £12 | |
| Connie Stevens From Hawaiian Eye | LP | Warner Bros | W(S)1382 | 1960 | £6 | £15 | *US* |
| Hank Williams Song Book | LP | Warner Bros | WM/WS8111 | 1963 | £4 | £10 | |
| Hawaiian Eye | LP | Warner Bros | W(S)1335 | 1959 | £6 | £15 | *US* |
| They're Jealous Of Me | 7" | Warner Bros | WB128 | 1964 | £1.50 | £4 | |

## STEVENS, DODIE

| | | | | | | | |
|---|---|---|---|---|---|---|---|
| Dodie Stevens | LP | Dot | DLP3212/25212 | 1960 | £6 | £15 | *US* |
| I Wore Out The Record | 7" | Liberty | LIB83 | 1964 | £1.50 | £4 | |
| Over The Rainbow | LP | Dot | DLP3323/25323 | 1960 | £6 | £15 | *US* |
| Pink Shoe Laces | 7" | London | HLD8834 | 1959 | £5 | £10 | |
| Pink Shoelaces | LP | Dot | DLP3371/25371 | 1961 | £6 | £15 | *US* |
| Yes I'm Lonesome Tonight | 7" | London | HLD9280 | 1961 | £1.50 | £4 | |

## STEVENS, JOHN

John Stevens, the erstwhile motivator behind the Spontaneous Music Ensemble, began to move into more commercial areas during the seventies. He is the drummer on John Martyn's *Live At Leeds*, and for the single 'Anni', John Martyn returned the favour – playing guitar and singing on a version of the piece that is quite different from the one found on the LP *John Stevens Away*.

| | | | | | | | |
|---|---|---|---|---|---|---|---|
| Anni | 7" | Vertigo | 6059140 | 1976 | £4 | £8 | *with John Martyn* |

## STEVENS, JOHN & EVAN PARKER

| | | | | | | | |
|---|---|---|---|---|---|---|---|
| Longest Night Vol. 2 | LP | Ogun | OG420 | 1978 | £5 | £12 | |

## STEVENS, KIRK

| | | | | | | | |
|---|---|---|---|---|---|---|---|
| Once | 7" | Decca | F10863 | 1957 | £1.50 | £4 | |

## STEVENS, MEIC

Meic Stevens is a major folk-rock artist, whose career is unknown to most collectors apart from the solitary cult favourite album, *Outlander*. The obscurity that is Stevens's lot has nothing to do with his output, which is large, but everything to do with the fact that he has chosen to stay true to his Celtic roots and performs almost exclusively in the Welsh language. Most of his early records are much harder to find than their values might suggest – 'Did I Dream' will prove near-impossible, although it is an essential item for Led Zeppelin completists, being produced by John Paul Jones. Further Stevens items are listed under Bara Menyn, a folk band of which he was a member. The discographical information included here (together with the other Welsh language items to be found in this guide) was provided by dealer Andrew Hawkey, who operates a thriving mail order company in Lampeter.

| | | | | | | | |
|---|---|---|---|---|---|---|---|
| Ballad Of Old Joe Blind | 7" | Warner Bros | WB8007 | 1970 | £7.50 | £15 | |
| Byw Yn Y Wlad | 7" EP | Wren | WRE1107 | 1971 | £7.50 | £15 | |
| Can Nana | 7" | Theatr Yr Ymylon | YMSP01 | 1978 | £4 | £8 | |

| | | | | | | |
|---|---|---|---|---|---|---|
| Caneuon Cynnar | LP | TicToc | TTL001 | 1979 | £50 | £100 |
| Did I Dream | 7" | Decca | F12174 | 1965 | £25 | £50 |
| Diolch Yn Fawr | 7" EP | Sain | SAIN13 | 1971 | £7.50 | £15 |
| Gog | LP | Sain | 1065M | 1977 | £25 | £50 |
| Gwymon | LP | Wren | WRL536 | 1972 | £37.50 | £75 |
| Lapis Lazuli | LP | Sain | 1312M | 1983 | £6 | £15 |
| Meic Stevens | 7" EP | Newyddion Da | ND1 | 1970 | £15 | £30 |
| Meic Stevens | 7" EP | Wren | WRE1045 | 1968 | £10 | £20 |
| Mwg | 7" EP | Wren | WRE1073 | 1969 | £10 | £20 |
| Nid Oes Un Gwydr Ffenestr | 7" | Wren | WSP2005 | 1970 | £7.50 | £15 |
| Nos Du Nos Da | LP | Sain | 1239M | 1982 | £8 | £20 |
| Outlander | LP | Warner Bros | WS3005 | 1970 | £62.50 | £125 |
| Pe Medrwn | 7" | Theatr Yr Ymylon | YMSP02 | 1978 | £4 | £8 |
| Rhif 2 | 7" EP | Wren | WRE1053 | 1968 | £10 | £20 |
| Y Brawd Houdini | 7" EP | Sain | SAIN4 | 1970 | £7.50 | £15 |

## STEVENS, RAY

| | | | | | | | |
|---|---|---|---|---|---|---|---|
| 1,837 Seconds Of Humor | LP | Mercury | MG2/SR60732 | 1962 | £4 | £10 | US |
| Ahab The Arab | 7" | Mercury | AMT1184 | 1962 | £1.50 | £4 | |
| Crying Goodbye | 7" | Capitol | CL14881 | 1958 | £1.50 | £4 | |
| Harry The Hairy Ape | 7" | Mercury | AMT1207 | 1963 | £1.50 | £4 | |
| Jeremiah Peabody | 7" | Mercury | AMT1158 | 1961 | £1.50 | £4 | |

## STEVENS, RICKY

| | | | | | | |
|---|---|---|---|---|---|---|
| I Cried For You | 7" EP | Columbia | SEG8172 | 1962 | £10 | £20 |

## STEVENS, SHAKIN'

| | | | | | | | |
|---|---|---|---|---|---|---|---|
| Bop Won't Stop | LP | Epic | BX86301 | 1983 | £6 | £15 | LP, cassette, autograph book, boxed |
| Cry Just A Little Bit | 7" | Epic | WA3774 | 1983 | £2 | £5 | picture disc |
| Down On The Farm | 7" | Parlophone | R5860 | 1970 | £12.50 | £25 | |
| Endless Sleep | 7" | Epic | 6845 | 1979 | £4 | £8 | |
| Honey Honey | 7" | Emerald | MD1176 | 1974 | £6 | £12 | |
| I'm No J.D. | LP | CBS | 52901 | 1971 | £20 | £40 | |
| It's Late | 7" | Epic | WA3565 | 1983 | £2.50 | £6 | shaped picture disc |
| It's Raining | 7" | Epic | EPCA1643 | 1981 | £2 | £5 | picture disc |
| Jungle Rock | 7" | Mooncrest | MOON51 | 1976 | £5 | £10 | |
| Justine | 7" | Track | 2094141 | 1978 | £4 | £8 | |
| Legend | LP | Parlophone | PCS7112 | 1970 | £25 | £50 | |
| Never | 7" | Track | 2094134 | 1977 | £4 | £8 | |
| Somebody Touched Me | 7" | Track | 2094136 | 1977 | £2 | £5 | |
| Somebody Touched Me | 7" | Track | 2094136 | 1977 | £5 | £10 | picture sleeve |
| Spooky | 7" | Epic | 7235 | 1979 | £4 | £8 | |
| Sweet Little Rock 'n' Roller | 7" | Polydor | 2058213 | 1972 | £7.50 | £15 | |
| Teardrops | 7" | Epic | DA4882 | 1984 | £2.50 | £6 | double |
| Tiger | 7" | Everest | EV10000 | 1983 | £2 | £5 | picture disc |

## STEWART, AL

As soon as he achieved a small measure of success, Al Stewart decided that his first LP was not as he would have liked it to be, and managed to persuade CBS to issue a new version, with a slightly different track selection and with the whole album re-mixed. The original *Bedsitter Images* is now quite scarce. As for the even scarcer 'Elf' single, Al Stewart would probably prefer to forget about it altogether.

| | | | | | | | |
|---|---|---|---|---|---|---|---|
| Al Stewart Concert | LP | Arista | SP40 | 1977 | £5 | £12 | US promo |
| Bedsitter Images | LP | CBS | (S)BPG63087 | 1967 | £25 | £50 | |
| Bedsitter Images | 7" | CBS | 3034 | 1967 | £2 | £5 | |
| Elf | 7" | Decca | F12467 | 1966 | £37.50 | £75 | |
| First Album (Bedsitter Images) | LP | CBS | 64023 | 1970 | £6 | £15 | |
| Love Chronicles | LP | CBS | 63460 | 1969 | £5 | £12 | |
| Year Of The Cat | LP | Mobile Fidelity | MFSL1009 | 1978 | £5 | £12 | US audiophile |
| Year Of The Cat | CD | Mobile Fidelity | MFCD8039 | 1986 | £6 | £15 | US audiophile |
| Zero She Flies | LP | CBS | 63848 | 1970 | £5 | £12 | |

## STEWART, ANDY

| | | | | | | |
|---|---|---|---|---|---|---|
| Donald, Where's Your Troosers? | 7" | Top Rank | JAR427 | 1960 | £1.50 | £4 |

## STEWART, BILLY

| | | | | | | | |
|---|---|---|---|---|---|---|---|
| Because I Love You | 7" | Chess | CRS8028 | 1966 | £4 | £8 | |
| Billy Stewart Remembered | LP | Chess | LPS1547 | 1968 | £4 | £10 | US |
| I Do Love You | LP | Chess | LP(S)1496 | 1965 | £6 | £15 | US |
| I Do Love You | 7" EP | Chess | CRE6024 | 1966 | £5 | £10 | |
| I Do Love You | 7" | Chess | CRS8009 | 1965 | £2 | £5 | |
| Love Me | 7" | Chess | CRS8038 | 1966 | £1.50 | £4 | |
| Ol' Man River | 7" | Chess | CRS8050 | 1966 | £1.50 | £4 | |
| Reap What You Sow | 7" | Pye | 7N25164 | 1962 | £1.50 | £4 | |
| Secret Love | 7" | Chess | CRS8045 | 1966 | £2 | £5 | |
| Sitting In The Park | 7" | Chess | CRS8017 | 1965 | £2 | £5 | |
| Strange Feeling | 7" | Pye | 7N25222 | 1963 | £1.50 | £4 | |
| Summertime | 7" | Chess | CRS8040 | 1966 | £1.50 | £4 | |
| Teaches Old Standards New Tricks | LP | Chess | LP(S)1513 | 1967 | £5 | £12 | US |
| Unbelievable | LP | Chess | CRL4523 | 1966 | £5 | £12 | |

## STEWART, BOB

| | | | | | | |
|---|---|---|---|---|---|---|
| Unique Sound Of The Psaltery | LP | Argo | ZDA207 | 1975 | £4 | £10 |
| Up Like The Swallow | LP | Broadside | BRO131 | 1978 | £4 | £10 |
| Wraggle Taggle Gypsies O | LP | Crescent | ARS105 | 1976 | £4 | £10 |

## STEWART, DAVE & BRIAN HARRISON
| | | | | | | |
|---|---|---|---|---|---|---|
| Deep December | 7" | Multicord | | 197– £6 | £12 | |
| Girl | 7" EP | Multicord | MULTSH1 | 1971 £6 | £12 | |

## STEWART, DAVIE
| | | | | | | |
|---|---|---|---|---|---|---|
| Davie Stewart | LP | Topic | 12T293 | 1978 £4 | £10 | |

## STEWART, DELANO
| | | | | | | |
|---|---|---|---|---|---|---|
| Got To Come Back | 7" | High Note | HS027 | 1969 £1.50 | £4 | |
| Hallelujah | 7" | High Note | HS034 | 1969 £1.50 | £4 | |
| Let's Have Some Fun | 7" | High Note | HS004 | 1968 £2.50 | £6 | |
| Rocking Sensation | 7" | High Note | HS014 | 1969 £2.50 | £6 | Gaytones B side |
| Stay A Little Bit Longer | LP | Trojan | TBL138 | 1970 £4 | £10 | |
| That's Life | 7" | Doctor Bird | DB1138 | 1968 £5 | £10 | |

## STEWART, IAN
| | | | | | | |
|---|---|---|---|---|---|---|
| Plays The Million Sellers | LP | Fontana | 886105TY | 1968 £6 | £15 | Dutch |

## STEWART, JOHN
| | | | | | | |
|---|---|---|---|---|---|---|
| Signals Through The Glass | LP | Capitol | (S)T2975 | 1968 £4 | £10 | US |

## STEWART, RED
| | | | | | | |
|---|---|---|---|---|---|---|
| Favorite Old Songs | LP | Audio Lab | AL1528 | 1959 £10 | £25 | US |

## STEWART, REX
| | | | | | | |
|---|---|---|---|---|---|---|
| Rendezvous With Rex | LP | Felsted | FAJ7001 | 1959 £5 | £12 | |
| Rex Stewart Orchestra | 10" LP | Felsted | EDL87017 | 1955 £10 | £25 | |

## STEWART, ROD

The fact that Rod Stewart often performs indifferent material should not be allowed to obscure the fact that he is one of the great rock singers. His early Vertigo LPs are fine records that successfully blend acoustic and electric styles into a very satisfying whole. Even better is Stewart's powerful blues singing on Jeff Beck's two sixties albums, *Truth* and *Beckola*. Before this, Rod Stewart learnt his craft as a member of Long John Baldry's Hoochie Coochie Men and of Steampacket – his first singles come from this period and still hold up well, especially a version of 'Shake', backed by Brian Auger's Trinity (who were also a part of Steampacket), which is actually more dynamic than Sam Cooke's original.

| | | | | | | |
|---|---|---|---|---|---|---|
| Blondes Have More Fun | LP | Mobile Fidelity | MFSL1054 | 1981 £4 | £10 | US audiophile |
| Camouflage | LP | Warner Bros | 9250951 | 1984 £6 | £15 | ... with 1 sided picture disc and cassette |
| Day Will Come | 7" | Columbia | DB7766 | 1965 £15 | £30 | |
| Do Ya Think I'm Sexy | 12" | Riva | SAM92 | 1978 £2.50 | £6 | promo |
| Do Ya Think I'm Sexy | 12" | Riva | SAM92 | 1978 £6 | £15 | ...promo, green or blue vinyl |
| Every Picture Tells A Story | CD | Mobile Fidelity | UDCD532 | 1990 £6 | £15 | US audiophile |
| Forever Young | CD-s | WEA | W7796CD | 1988 £2 | £5 | 3" single |
| Gasoline Alley | LP | Vertigo | 6360500 | 1970 £4 | £10 | spiral label |
| Good Morning Little Schoolgirl | 7" | Decca | F11996 | 1964 £15 | £30 | |
| Infatuation | 7" | Warner Bros | SAM194 | 1984 £5 | £10 | ....1 sided picture disc, interview tape |
| It's All Over Now | 7" | Vertigo | 6086002 | 1970 £2 | £5 | |
| Little Miss Understood | 7" | Immediate | IM060 | 1967 £15 | £30 | |
| Lost In You | CD-s | WEA | W7927CD | 1988 £2 | £5 | |
| Old Raincoat Won't Ever Let You Down | LP | Vertigo | VO4 | 1970 £4 | £10 | spiral label |
| Old Raincoat Won't Let You Down | CD | Mercury | 8305722 | 1987 £5 | £12 | |
| Reason To Believe | LP | St. Michael | 21020102 | 1978 £6 | £15 | |
| Sailing | 7" | Riva | RIVA9 | 1977 £25 | £50 | ....blue vinyl, picture sleeve |
| Shake | 7" | Columbia | DB7892 | 1966 £15 | £30 | |
| Sing It Again Rod | CD | Mercury | 8248822 | 1985 £5 | £12 | |
| This Old Heart Of Mine | CD-s | WEA | W2686CD | 1989 £2 | £5 | 3" single |
| Tonight's The Night/First Cut Is The Deepest | 7" | Riva | RIVA3 | 1977 £2.50 | £6 | |
| You're Insane | 12" | Riva | DISCO1A | 1980 £5 | £12 | promo |

## STEWART, SANDY
| | | | | | | |
|---|---|---|---|---|---|---|
| Certain Smile | 7" | London | HLE8683 | 1958 £4 | £8 | |

## STEWART, WINSTON
| | | | | | | |
|---|---|---|---|---|---|---|
| All Of My Life | 7" | Port-O-Jam | PJ4002 | 1964 £5 | £10 | |
| But I Do | 7" | R&B | JB147 | 1964 £5 | £10 | |

## STEWART, WYNN
| | | | | | | |
|---|---|---|---|---|---|---|
| Wishful Thinking | 7" | London | HL7087 | 1960 £10 | £20 | export |

## STEWARTS OF BLAIR
| | | | | | | |
|---|---|---|---|---|---|---|
| Stewarts Of Blair | LP | Topic | 12T138 | 1966 £8 | £20 | |

## STIDHAM, ARBEE
| | | | | | | |
|---|---|---|---|---|---|---|
| Tired Of Wandering | LP | Bluesville | BV1021 | 1961 £8 | £20 | US |

## STIFF LITTLE FINGERS
| | | | | | | |
|---|---|---|---|---|---|---|
| Listen | 7" | Chrysalis | CHSDJ2580 | 1982 £2 | £5 | juke box issue |
| Peel Sessions | CD-s | Strange Fruit | SFPSCD004 | 1988 £2 | £5 | |
| Suspect Device | 7" | Rigid Digits | SRD1 | 1978 £5 | £10 | ..red label, hand-made picture sleeve |
| Suspect Device | 7" | Rigid Digits | SRD1 | 1978 £2.50 | £6 | yellow label |

## STILL LIFE

| | | | | | | |
|---|---|---|---|---|---|---|
| Still Life | LP | Vertigo | 6360026 | 1971 £37.50 £75 | | spiral label |
| What Did We Miss | 7" | Columbia | DB8345 | 1968 £10 £20 | | |

## STILLS, STEPHEN

| | | | | | | |
|---|---|---|---|---|---|---|
| Stephen Stills | LP | Atlantic | 2401004 | 1970 £4 £10 | | |

## STING

| | | | | | | |
|---|---|---|---|---|---|---|
| Acoustic Live In Newcastle | CD | A&M | 3971712 | 1991 £10 £25 | | boxed with book |
| All This Time | CD-s | A&M | AMCD713 | 1991 £2 £5 | | with 12" print |
| Compact Hits | CD-s | A&M | AMCD911 | 1988 £2 £5 | | |
| Dream Of The Blue Turtles | LP | A&M | DREMP1 | 1985 £4 £10 | | picture disc |
| Englishman In New York | CD-s | A&M | AMCD431 | 1987 £2 £5 | | |
| Englishman In New York | CD-s | A&M | AMCDR580 | 1988 £2 £5 | | picture disc |
| Fragile | CD-s | A&M | AMCD439 | 1988 £2 £5 | | |
| It's Probably Me | CD-s | A&M | AMCD883 | 1992 £2 £5 | | with Eric Clapton |
| Mad About You | CD-s | A&M | AMCDR721 | 1991 £2 £5 | | |
| Nado Como El Sol | CD | A&M | | 1988 £8 £20 | | German, songs in Spanish |
| Someone To Watch Over Me | CD-s | A&M | AMC911 | 1988 £2 £5 | | |
| Soul Cages | CD-s | A&M | AMCD759 | 1991 £2 £5 | | |
| Soul Cages | CD | A&M | | 1991 £10 £25 | | US promo box set |
| Soul Cages Interview Disc | CD | A&M | | 1991 £10 £25 | | Canadia promo |
| Ten Summoners' Tales | CD | A&M | | 1993 £10 £25 | | Australian double, with live disc |
| Ten Summoners' Tales – Interview Disc | CD | A&M | 8029 | 1993 £10 £25 | | US promo |
| They Dance Alone | CD-s | A&M | AMCD458 | 1988 £2 £5 | | |
| They Dance Alone | 10" | A&M | AMX458 | 1988 £2.50 £6 | | promo |
| We'll Be Together | CD-s | A&M | AMCD410 | 1987 £2 £5 | | 3" single, boxed |

## STIRLING, PETER LEE

| | | | | | | |
|---|---|---|---|---|---|---|
| You Don't Live Twice | 7" | Decca | F12628 | 1967 £1.50 £4 | | |

## STITES, GARY

| | | | | | | |
|---|---|---|---|---|---|---|
| Lawdy Miss Clawdy | 7" | London | HLL9082 | 1960 £4 £8 | | |
| Lonely For You | LP | Carlton | (ST)LP120 | 1960 £8 £20 | | US |
| Lonely For You | 7" | London | HLL8881 | 1959 £5 £10 | | |
| Starry Eyed | 7" | London | HLL9003 | 1959 £2 £5 | | |

## STITT, SONNY

| | | | | | | |
|---|---|---|---|---|---|---|
| 37 Minutes And 48 Seconds | LP | Vogue | LAE12208 | 1960 £8 £20 | | |
| Blows The Blues | LP | HMV | CLP1420/CSD1341 | 1961 £8 £20 | | |
| Deuces Wild | LP | Atlantic | 3008 | 1968 £6 £15 | | |
| Kaleidoscope | LP | Esquire | 32112 | 1961 £10 £25 | | |
| New York Jazz | LP | Columbia | 33CX10114 | 1958 £20 £40 | | |
| Only The Blues | LP | HMV | CLP1280 | 1959 £8 £20 | | |
| Personal Appearance | LP | HMV | CLP1363 | 1960 £8 £20 | | |
| Quartet/Quintet | LP | Vogue | LAE12196 | 1960 £8 £20 | | |
| S. P. J. Jazz | LP | Esquire | 32049 | 1958 £20 £40 | | with Bud Powell & J. J. Johnson |
| Sonny Side Up | LP | Columbia | 33CX10140 | 1959 £6 £15 | | with Dizzy Gillespie & Sonny Rollins |
| Sonny Stitt-Bud Powell Quartet | 10" LP | Esquire | 20013 | 1953 £37.50 £75 | | |
| Stitt Plays Bird | LP | Atlantic | SD1418 | 1965 £6 £15 | | US |
| Stitt's Bits | LP | Esquire | 32078 | 1959 £20 £40 | | |
| With The New Yorkers | LP | Vogue | LAE12191 | 1959 £8 £20 | | |
| With The Oscar Peterson Trio | LP | HMV | CLP1384 | 1960 £8 £20 | | |

## STIVELL, ALAN

| | | | | | | |
|---|---|---|---|---|---|---|
| A l'Olympia | LP | Fontana | 6399005 | 1972 £4 £10 | | |
| E Langonned | LP | Fontana | 9101500 | 1975 £4 £10 | | |
| From Celtic Roots | LP | Fontana | 6325304 | 1974 £4 £10 | | |
| In Dublin | LP | Fontana | 9299547 | 1975 £4 £10 | | |
| Reflections | LP | Fontana | 6399008 | 1974 £4 £10 | | |
| Renaissance Of The Celtic Harp | LP | Philips | 6414406 | 1971 £4 £10 | | |

## STOCKER, GREENWOOD & FRIENDS

| | | | | | | |
|---|---|---|---|---|---|---|
| Billy Plus Nine | LP | Changes | CR1400 | 1979 £25 £50 | | |

## STOCKHAUSEN, KARLHEINZ

Stockhausen has always tended to be the first port of call for those wishing to investigate the classical avant-garde, and with good reason, for he pioneered most of it. Amongst his vast output are to be found purely electronic works (try *Telemusik* and *Kontakte* for starters); works that mix electronics with voices and acoustic instruments (*Gesang der Jünglinge* and *Mixtur*); works that experiment with spatial effects (*Carré*); essentially mantric exercises (*Stimmung*); orchestral freak-outs (*Trans*); and free improvisation (*Aus den Sieben Tagen*). None of it is rock music and yet his ideas have been a considerable influence on many of the more open rock musicians.

| | | | | | | |
|---|---|---|---|---|---|---|
| Aus Den Sieben Tagen | LP | Deutsche Grammophon | 2720073 | 1971 £37.50 £75 | | 7 LP boxed set |
| Ceylon/Bird Of Passage | LP | Chrysalis | CHR1110 | 1976 £4 £10 | | |
| Elektronische Studie I & II | LP | Deutsche Grammophon | LP16133 | £4 £10 | | |
| Gesang Der Jünglinge/Kontakte | LP | Deutsche Grammophon | 138811 | 1962 £4 £10 | | also a later remixed issue |
| Gruppen/Carre | LP | Deutsche Grammophon | 137002 | 1968 £4 £10 | | |

| | | | | | | | |
|---|---|---|---|---|---|---|---|
| Hymnen | LP | Deutsche Grammophon | 2707039 | 1969 £6 | £15 | double |
| Klavierstücke 8 | LP | Vox | STGBY637 | 1971 £4 | £10 | |
| Klavierstücke 9,11 | LP | Philips | 6500101 | 1971 £4 | £10 | |
| Klavierstücken | LP | CBS | 72591/2 | £6 | £15 | double |
| Kontakte (piano version)/Refrain | LP | Vox | STGBY638 | 1970 £4 | £10 | |
| Kurzwellen | LP | Deutsche Grammophon | 2707045 | 1971 £6 | £15 | double |
| Mantra | LP | Deutsche Grammophon | 2530208 | 1972 £4 | £10 | |
| Mikrophonie I and II | LP | Deutsche Grammophon | 2530583 | 197– £4 | £10 | |
| Momente | LP | Deutsche Grammophon | 2709055 | 1976 £8 | £20 | triple |
| Momente | LP | Nonesuch | H71157 | 196– £4 | £10 | |
| Opus 1970 | LP | Deutsche Grammophon | 139461 | 197– £4 | £10 | |
| Prozession | LP | Deutsche Grammophon | 2530582 | 197– £4 | £10 | |
| Prozession | LP | Vox | STGBY615 | 1969 £4 | £10 | |
| Solo | LP | Deutsche Grammophon | 137005 | 196– £4 | £10 | |
| Stimmung | LP | Deutsche Grammophon | 2543003 | 1970 £4 | £10 | |
| Stop/Ylem | LP | Deutsche Grammophon | 2530442 | 1974 £4 | £10 | |
| Telemusik/Mixtur | LP | Deutsche Grammophon | 137012 | 1970 £4 | £10 | |
| Trans | LP | Deutsche Grammophon | 2530726 | 1976 £4 | £10 | |
| Zyklus | LP | Erato | STU70603 | £4 | £10 | |

## STOCKTON'S WING

| | | | | | | | |
|---|---|---|---|---|---|---|---|
| Stockton's Wing | LP | Tara | 2004 | 1978 £4 | £10 | Irish |
| Take A Chance | LP | Tara | 30041980 | 1980 £4 | £10 | Irish |

## STOEBER, ORVILLE

| | | | | | | | |
|---|---|---|---|---|---|---|---|
| Songs | LP | UNI | 6369611 | 1970 £6 | £15 | German |

## STOKES

| | | | | | | | |
|---|---|---|---|---|---|---|---|
| Whipped Cream | 7" | London | HLU9955 | 1965 £1.50 | £4 | |

## STOLLER, RHET

| | | | | | | | |
|---|---|---|---|---|---|---|---|
| Bandit | 7" | Windsor | PS118 | 1964 £7.50 | £15 | demo |
| Caravan | 7" | Windsor | PS119 | 1964 £4 | £8 | |
| Chariot | 7" | Decca | F11302 | 1960 £2 | £5 | |
| Countdown | 7" | Decca | F11738 | 1963 £2 | £5 | |
| Ricochet | 7" | Windsor | PS130 | 1964 £4 | £8 | |
| Sunshine Anytime | 7" EP | Mosaic | MOSAIC1 | 196– £2 | £5 | |
| Treble Gold One | 7" | Melodisc | 1595 | 1964 £4 | £8 | |
| Uncrowned King | 7" | Columbia | DB8013 | 1966 £7.50 | £15 | demo |
| Walk Don't Run | 7" | Decca | F11271 | 1960 £2.50 | £6 | |

## STOMPERS

| | | | | | | | |
|---|---|---|---|---|---|---|---|
| Foolish Idea | 7" | Fontana | H385 | 1962 £4 | £8 | |

## STONE, CLIFFIE

| | | | | | | | |
|---|---|---|---|---|---|---|---|
| Cool Cowboy | LP | Capitol | (S)T1230 | 1959 £5 | £12 | US |
| Popcorn Song | 7" | Capitol | CL14330 | 1955 £25 | £50 | |

## STONE, GEORGE

| | | | | | | | |
|---|---|---|---|---|---|---|---|
| Hole In The Wall | 7" | Stateside | SS479 | 1965 £1.50 | £4 | |

## STONE, KIRBY FOUR

| | | | | | | | |
|---|---|---|---|---|---|---|---|
| Honey Hush | 7" | Vogue Coral | Q72129 | 1956 £2.50 | £6 | |
| Man, I Flipped | LP | London | HAA2164 | 1959 £4 | £10 | |

## STONE, MARK

| | | | | | | | |
|---|---|---|---|---|---|---|---|
| Stroll | 7" | London | HLR8543 | 1958 £30 | £60 | |

## STONE, ROLAND

| | | | | | | | |
|---|---|---|---|---|---|---|---|
| Just A Moment | LP | Ace | LP1018 | 1961 £6 | £15 | US |

## STONE ANGEL

| | | | | | | | |
|---|---|---|---|---|---|---|---|
| Stone Angel | LP | private | SSLP04 | 1975 £100 | £200 | |

## STONE CIRCUS

| | | | | | | | |
|---|---|---|---|---|---|---|---|
| Stone Circus | LP | Mainstream | S6119 | 1969 £37.50 | £75 | US |

## STONE HARBOUR

| | | | | | | | |
|---|---|---|---|---|---|---|---|
| Emerges | LP | private | | 1974 £330 | £500 | US |

## STONE PONEYS

Lead singer with the Stone Poneys was Linda Ronstadt – these are her first recordings.

| | | | | | | | |
|---|---|---|---|---|---|---|---|
| Different Drum | 7" | Capitol | CL15523 | 1967 £1.50 | £4 | |
| Evergreen | LP | Capitol | ST2763 | 1967 £4 | £10 | US |

| | | | | | | | |
|---|---|---|---|---|---|---|---|
| Stone Poneys | LP | Capitol | ST2666 | 1967 | £4 | £10 | *US* |
| Stone Poneys & Friends | LP | Capitol | ST2863 | 1968 | £4 | £10 | *US* |

## STONE ROSES

| | | | | | | | |
|---|---|---|---|---|---|---|---|
| Complete Stone Roses | CD | Silvertone | ORECD535 | 1995 | £5 | £12 | *with bonus CD single* |
| Elephant Stone | CD-s | Silvertone | ORECD1 | 1990 | £2 | £5 | |
| Fools Gold | CD-s | Silvertone | ORECD13 | 1990 | £2 | £5 | |
| I Want To Be Adored | CD-s | Silvertone | ORECD31 | 1991 | £2 | £5 | |
| Made Of Stone | CD-s | Silvertone | ORECD2 | 1990 | £2 | £5 | |
| One Love | CD-s | Silvertone | ORECD17 | 1990 | £2 | £5 | |
| Sally Cinnamon | 12" | Black | 12REV36 | 1987 | £4 | £10 | *'printed in England' on rear sleeve* |
| She Bangs The Drum | CD-s | Silvertone | ORECD6 | 1989 | £2 | £5 | |
| So Young | 12" | Thin Line | THIN001 | 1985 | £15 | £30 | |

## STONE THE CROWS

| | | | | | | |
|---|---|---|---|---|---|---|
| Continuous Performance | LP | Polydor | 2391043 | 1972 | £4 | £10 |
| Ode To John Law | LP | Polydor | 2425042 | 1970 | £5 | £12 |
| Stone The Crows | LP | Polydor | 2425017 | 1970 | £6 | £15 |
| Teenage Licks | LP | Polydor | 2425071 | 1971 | £5 | £12 |

## STONEFIELD TRAMP

| | | | | | | |
|---|---|---|---|---|---|---|
| Dreaming Again | LP | Acorn | CF247 | 1974 | £75 | £150 |

## STONEHENGE MEN

| | | | | | | |
|---|---|---|---|---|---|---|
| Big Feet | 7" | HMV | POP981 | 1962 | £15 | £30 |

## STONEHOUSE

| | | | | | | |
|---|---|---|---|---|---|---|
| Stonehouse Creek | LP | RCA | SF8197 | 1971 | £50 | £100 |

## STONE'S MASONRY

The recorded evidence is that Martin Stone was one of the great sixties guitarists, even if he seems to have long ago vanished from rock music. The blues instrumental 'Flapjacks', which was released on Mike Vernon's pre-Blue Horizon Purdah label, is a good demonstration of his talents. The group folded, before it could record anything else, when Stone joined Savoy Brown – moving from there to Mighty Baby and on to Chilli Willi and the Red Hot Peppers.

| | | | | | | |
|---|---|---|---|---|---|---|
| Flapjacks | 7" | Purdah | 453504 | 1966 | £37.50 | £75 |

## STONEWALL

| | | | | | | | |
|---|---|---|---|---|---|---|---|
| Stonewall | LP | private | | 1974 | £700 | £1000 | *US* |

## STOREY SISTERS

| | | | | | | |
|---|---|---|---|---|---|---|
| Bad Motorcycle | 7" | London | HLU8571 | 1958 | £25 | £50 |

## STORM

| | | | | | | | |
|---|---|---|---|---|---|---|---|
| Storm | LP | Vamp | 25004 | 1974 | £62.50 | £125 | *Swiss* |

## STORM (2)

| | | | | | | | |
|---|---|---|---|---|---|---|---|
| At The Top | LP | Harvest | 7C06435179 | 1975 | £4 | £10 | *Swedish* |
| Stormvarning | LP | Harvest | 7C06435010 | 1974 | £15 | £30 | *Swedish* |

## STORM, BILLY

| | | | | | | | |
|---|---|---|---|---|---|---|---|
| Billy Storm | LP | Buena Vista | BV3315 | 1963 | £15 | £30 | *US* |
| Sure As You're Born | 7" | London | HLK9236 | 1960 | £2 | £5 | |
| This Is The Night | LP | Famous | F504 | 1969 | £6 | £15 | *US* |

## STORM, DANNY

| | | | | | | | |
|---|---|---|---|---|---|---|---|
| Honest I Do | 7" | Piccadilly | 7N35025 | 1962 | £2.50 | £6 | *picture sleeve* |
| I Just Can't Fool My Heart | 7" | Piccadilly | 7N35091 | 1962 | £2.50 | £6 | |
| Just You | 7" | Piccadilly | 7N35053 | 1962 | £2 | £5 | |
| Say You Do | 7" | Piccadilly | 7N35143 | 1963 | £2.50 | £6 | |

## STORM, GALE

| | | | | | | | |
|---|---|---|---|---|---|---|---|
| Dark Moon | 7" | London | HLD8424 | 1957 | £5 | £10 | |
| Don't Be That Way | 7" | London | HLD8311 | 1956 | £10 | £20 | |
| Farewell To Arms | 7" | London | HLD8570 | 1958 | £5 | £10 | |
| Gale Storm | LP | Dot | DLP3011 | 1956 | £10 | £25 | *US* |
| Heart Without A Sweetheart | 7" | London | HLD8329 | 1956 | £7.50 | £15 | |
| Hits | LP | Dot | DLP3098 | 1958 | £10 | £25 | *US* |
| I Hear You Knocking | 7" | London | HLD8222 | 1956 | £12.50 | £25 | |
| Ivory Tower | 7" | London | HLD8283 | 1956 | £12.50 | £25 | |
| Lucky Lips | 7" | London | HLD8393 | 1957 | £10 | £20 | |
| Memories Are Made Of This | 7" | London | HLD8232 | 1956 | £10 | £20 | |
| Orange Blossoms | 7" | London | HLD8413 | 1957 | £5 | £10 | |
| Presenting Gale Storm | 10" LP | London | HBD1056 | 1956 | £15 | £30 | |
| Sentimental Me | LP | London | HAD2104 | 1958 | £10 | £25 | |
| Why Do Fools Fall In Love | 7" | London | HL7008 | 1956 | £5 | £10 | *export* |
| Why Do Fools Fall In Love | 7" | London | HLD8286 | 1956 | £10 | £20 | |
| You | 7" | London | HLD8632 | 1958 | £4 | £8 | |

## STORM, RORY & THE HURRICANES

| | | | | | | |
|---|---|---|---|---|---|---|
| America | 7" | Parlophone | R5197 | 1964 | £5 | £10 |
| Doctor Feelgood | 7" | Oriole | CB1858 | 1963 | £10 | £20 |

## STORME, ROBB

| | | | | | | |
|---|---|---|---|---|---|---|
| Earth Angel | 7" | Decca | F11388 | 1961 | £2.50 | £6 |
| Here Today | 7" | Columbia | DB7993 | 1966 | £1.50 | £4 |

| | | | | | | | |
|---|---|---|---|---|---|---|---|
| I Don't Need Your Love Anymore | 7" | Decca | F11282 | 1960 | £1.50 | £4 | |
| Wheels | 7" EP | Decca | DFE6700 | 1962 | £25 | £50 | |
| Where Is My Girl | 7" | Columbia | DB7756 | 1965 | £1.50 | £4 | |

## STORMSVILLE SHAKERS

| | | | | | | | |
|---|---|---|---|---|---|---|---|
| Number One | 7" EP | Odeon | MEO148 | 1967 | £10 | £20 | French |

## STORYTELLER

Storyteller's blend of poetry and folk song was greeted with ecstatic reviews and the chance of a performance at the Royal Festival Hall while still very much an up-and-coming group. The first track on the *Storyteller* LP is a delightful piece of folk-rock, with a sparkling guitar solo from Peter Frampton, but its companion tracks are not often in the same league. Singer Caroline Attard married the group's producer, Andy Bown (who was formerly a member of the Herd and subsequently the keyboard player with Status Quo), but her attractive voice has not been heard on record since the early seventies. Poet and singer Terry Durham, the brother of the Seekers' Judith Durham, also has a solo album listed under his name.

| | | | | | | | |
|---|---|---|---|---|---|---|---|
| More Pages | LP | Transatlantic | TRA232 | 1971 | £6 | £15 | |
| Remarkable | 7" | CBS | 7182 | 1971 | £1.50 | £4 | |
| Storyteller | LP | Transatlantic | TRA220 | 1970 | £6 | £15 | |

## STOUGHTON, DAVID

| | | | | | | | |
|---|---|---|---|---|---|---|---|
| Transformer | LP | Elektra | EKS74034 | 1968 | £6 | £15 | US |

## STOWAWAYS

| | | | | | | | |
|---|---|---|---|---|---|---|---|
| In Our Time | LP | Justice | 148 | 196– | £100 | £200 | US |

## STRANGE, BILLY

| | | | | | | | |
|---|---|---|---|---|---|---|---|
| Few Dollars More | 7" | Vocalion | VP9289 | 1967 | £2 | £5 | |
| Get Smart | 7" | Vocalion | VP9259 | 1966 | £4 | £8 | |
| Goldfinger | 7" | Vocalion | VP9231 | 1964 | £6 | £12 | |
| James Bond Theme | 7" | Vocalion | VP9228 | 1964 | £2.50 | £6 | |
| Thunderball | 7" | Vocalion | VP9257 | 1966 | £2.50 | £6 | |
| Where Your Arms Used To Be | 7" | London | HLG9321 | 1961 | £2 | £5 | |

## STRANGE, STEVE

| | | | | | | | |
|---|---|---|---|---|---|---|---|
| In The Year 2525 | 7" | Palace | 1 | | £25 | £50 | test pressing, picture sleeve |
| In The Year 2525 | 7" | Palace | 1 | 1982 | £12.50 | £25 | test pressing only |

## STRANGE DAYS

| | | | | | | | |
|---|---|---|---|---|---|---|---|
| Nine Parts To The Wind | LP | Retreat | RTL6005 | 1975 | £10 | £25 | |

## STRANGE FOX

| | | | | | | | |
|---|---|---|---|---|---|---|---|
| Bring It On Home | 7" | Parlophone | R5876 | 1970 | £1.50 | £4 | |

## STRANGE FRUIT

| | | | | | | | |
|---|---|---|---|---|---|---|---|
| Cut Across Shorty | 7" | Village Thing | VTSX1001 | 1971 | £4 | £8 | |

## STRANGELOVES

| | | | | | | | |
|---|---|---|---|---|---|---|---|
| Cara Lin | 7" | Immediate | IM007 | 1965 | £2 | £5 | |
| Cara-Lin | 7" | Immediate | IM007 | 196– | £1.50 | £4 | pink label |
| Dansez Le Monkiss | 7" EP | Atlantic | 750006 | 1965 | £12.50 | £25 | French |
| Hand Jive | 7" | London | HLZ10063 | 1966 | £2 | £5 | |
| Honey Do | 7" | London | HLK10238 | 1969 | £2 | £5 | |
| I Want Candy | LP | Bang | BLP(S)211 | 1965 | £20 | £40 | US |
| I Want Candy | 7" | London | HLM10481 | 1975 | £1.50 | £4 | |
| I Want Candy | 7" | Stateside | SS446 | 1965 | £5 | £10 | |
| Night Time | 7" | London | HLZ10020 | 1966 | £6 | £12 | |

## STRANGERS

| | | | | | | | |
|---|---|---|---|---|---|---|---|
| One And One Is Two | 7" | Philips | BF1335 | 1964 | £10 | £20 | with Mike Shannon |
| Ram-Bunk-Shush | 7" EP | President | 281 | 1964 | £12.50 | £25 | French |
| Strangers With Mike Shannon | 7" EP | Pathe | EGF795 | 1964 | £15 | £30 | French |

## STRANGERS (2)

| | | | | | | | |
|---|---|---|---|---|---|---|---|
| I'm On An Island | 7" | Pye | 7N17585 | 1968 | £1.50 | £4 | |
| Look Out | 7" | Pye | 7N17240 | 1967 | £5 | £10 | |
| You Didn't Have To Be So Nice | 7" | Pye | 7N17351 | 1967 | £1.50 | £4 | |

## STRANGLERS

| | | | | | | | |
|---|---|---|---|---|---|---|---|
| 96 Tears | CD-s | Epic | TEARSC1 | 1990 | £2 | £5 | 2 versions |
| All Day And All Of The Night | CD-s | Epic | CDVICE1 | 1988 | £4 | £10 | |
| All Day And All Of The Night | 7" | Epic | VICE1 | 1988 | £1.50 | £4 | Monica Couglan sleeve |
| Always The Sun | CD-s | Epic | 6564302 | 1990 | £2 | £5 | 2 versions |
| Bear Cage | 12" | United Artists | 12BP344 | 1980 | £6 | £15 | picture sleeve |
| Black And White | LP | A&M | SP4706 | 1978 | £6 | £15 | US, black & white vinyl |
| Dreamtime | LP | Epic | EPC1126648 | 1986 | £4 | £10 | picture disc |
| European Female | 7" | Epic | EPCA112893 | 1983 | £2 | £5 | picture disc |
| Golden Brown | CD-s | Epic | 6567612 | 1991 | £2 | £5 | |
| Gospel According To The Men In Black | LP | Liberty | LBG30313 | 1981 | £8 | £20 | test pressing |
| Greatest Hits | CD | Epic | 4675419 | 1990 | £5 | £12 | picture disc |
| Grip '89 | CD-s | Liberty | CDEM84 | 1989 | £4 | £10 | |
| N'Emmenes pas Harry | 7" | United Artists | | 1979 | £4 | £8 | sung in French |
| Nice In Nice | 7" | Epic | EPC6500550 | 1986 | £1.50 | £4 | shaped picture disc |
| Night Tracks | CD-s | Strange Fruit | SFNTCD020 | 1989 | £2 | £5 | |
| No Mercy | 7" | Epic | WA4921 | 1984 | £1.50 | £4 | shaped picture disc |
| No More Heroes | 7" | United Artists | FREE8 | 1977 | £10 | £20 | 1 sided promo |

| | | | | | | | | |
|---|---|---|---|---|---|---|---|---|
| Peaches | 7" | United Artists | FREE4 | 1977 | £25 | £50 | promo |
| Peaches | 7" | United Artists | UP36248 | 1977 | £100 | £200 | picture sleeve, newspaper lettering & group picture |
| Peaches | 7" | United Artists | UP36248 | 1978 | £5 | £10 | mispress, B side plays Buzzcocks |
| Rattus Norvegicus | LP | United Artists | UAG30045 | 1977 | £4 | £10 | with 7" (FREE3) |
| Raven | LP | United Artists | UAG30262 | 1979 | £4 | £10 | 3-D cover |
| Something Better Change | 7" | A&M | AM1973 | 1977 | £2 | £5 | US, pink marbled vinyl |
| Stranglers Singles Collection | LP | Liberty | LBG30353 | 1982 | £6 | £15 | with original dark cover |
| Sverge | 7" | United Artists | UP36459 | 1978 | £4 | £8 | sung in Swedish |
| Sweet Smell Of Success | CD-s | Epic | TEARSC2 | 1990 | £2 | £5 | |

## STRATUS

| | | | | | | | |
|---|---|---|---|---|---|---|---|
| Throwing Shapes | LP | Steel Trax | STEEL31001 | 1985 | £4 | £10 | |

## STRAWBERRY ALARM CLOCK

The Strawberry Alarm Clock recorded several American singles as the Sixpence, before adopting a suitably trippy name for their big pop-psychedelic hit, 'Incense And Peppermints'. Though the group made several more records, they remained peripheral to the real centre of rock innovation. Lead guitarist Ed King was later a member of Lynyrd Skynyrd.

| | | | | | | | |
|---|---|---|---|---|---|---|---|
| Best Of The Strawberry Alarm Clock | LP | Uni | 73074 | 1970 | £8 | £20 | US |
| Changes | LP | Vocalion | 73915 | 1971 | £8 | £20 | US |
| Good Morning Starshine | LP | Uni | 73054 | 1969 | £10 | £25 | US |
| Good Morning Starshine | 7" | MCA | MU1080 | 1969 | £2 | £5 | |
| Incense & Peppermints | LP | Pye | N(S)PL28106 | 1968 | £10 | £25 | |
| Incense And Peppermints | 7" | Pye | 7N25436 | 1967 | £5 | £10 | |
| Sit With The Guru | 7" | Pye | 7N25456 | 1968 | £4 | £8 | |
| Tomorrow | 7" | Pye | 7N25446 | 1968 | £4 | £8 | |
| Wake Up It's Tomorrow | LP | Uni | 73025 | 1967 | £15 | £30 | US |
| World In A Sea Shell | LP | Uni | 73035 | 1968 | £10 | £25 | US |

## STRAWBERRY CHILDREN

Songwriter and producer Jimmy Webb made his first bid for stardom as a performer with the one single released by the Strawberry Children – a trio fronted by Webb himself.

| | | | | | | | |
|---|---|---|---|---|---|---|---|
| Love Years Coming | 7" | Liberty | LBF15012 | 1967 | £2.50 | £6 | |

## STRAWBERRY JAM

| | | | | | | | |
|---|---|---|---|---|---|---|---|
| Personally | 7" | Pye | 7N17711 | 1969 | £1.50 | £4 | |

## STRAWBERRY SWITCHBLADE

| | | | | | | | |
|---|---|---|---|---|---|---|---|
| Jolene | 7" | Korova | KOW42 | 1985 | £2 | £5 | shaped picture disc |
| Let Her Go | 7" | Korova | KOW39 | 1985 | £2 | £5 | shaped picture disc |
| Strawberry Switchblade LP Sampler | 7" | Korova | FLX3881 | 1985 | £2.50 | £6 | clear square flexi, booklet |
| Trees And Flowers | 7" | 92 Happy Customers | HAP1 | 1983 | £1.50 | £4 | |
| Trees And Flowers | 12" | 92 Happy Customers | HAPT1 | 1983 | £2.50 | £6 | |

## STRAWBS

The earlier editions of the *Price Guide* list a Strawbs LP called *Heartbreak Hill*, which would be worth a tidy sum if it ever appeared on the market. Alas, the music was recorded in 1979 but never actually committed to vinyl – there are not even any test pressings for collectors to discover. During the eighties, however, Dave Cousins was selling cassettes of the actual music, so that a version of *Heartbreak Hill* does exist, albeit not in a form that is likely to reach any kind of high value.

| | | | | | | | |
|---|---|---|---|---|---|---|---|
| Benedictus | 7" | A&M | AM874 | 1971 | £1.50 | £4 | |
| Burning For You | LP | Oyster | 2391287 | 1977 | £4 | £10 | |
| Bursting At The Seams | LP | A&M | AMLH68144 | 1973 | £4 | £10 | |
| Dead Lines | LP | Arista | SPART1036 | 1978 | £4 | £10 | |
| Deep Cuts | LP | Oyster | 2391234 | 1976 | £4 | £10 | |
| Dragonfly | LP | A&M | AMLS970 | 1970 | £8 | £20 | |
| Forever | 7" | A&M | AM791 | 1970 | £2 | £5 | |
| From The Witchwood | LP | A&M | AMLS64304 | 1971 | £4 | £10 | |
| Ghosts | LP | A&M | AMLH68277 | 1975 | £4 | £10 | |
| Grave New World | LP | A&M | AMLS68078 | 1972 | £4 | £10 | with booklet |
| Hero And Heroine | LP | A&M | AMLH63607 | 1974 | £4 | £10 | |
| Just A Collection Of Antiques And Curios | LP | A&M | AMLS994 | 1970 | £5 | £12 | |
| King | 7" | LO | LO1 | 1980 | £2.50 | £6 | picture sleeve |
| Man Who Called Himself Jesus | 7" | A&M | AM738 | 1968 | £2 | £5 | |
| Nomadness | LP | A&M | AMLH68331 | 1976 | £4 | £10 | |
| Oh How She Changed | 7" | A&M | AM725 | 1968 | £1.50 | £4 | |
| Strawberry Music Sampler No. 1 | LP | private | | 1969 | £330 | £500 | |
| Strawbs | LP | A&M | AMLS936 | 1969 | £8 | £20 | |
| Witchwood | 7" | A&M | AM837 | 1971 | £2.50 | £6 | promo |

## STRAWHEAD

| | | | | | | | |
|---|---|---|---|---|---|---|---|
| Fortunes Of War | LP | Tradition | TSR032 | 1978 | £4 | £10 | |

## STRAY

| | | | | | | | |
|---|---|---|---|---|---|---|---|
| Only What You Make It | 7" | Transatlantic | PROMO1 | 1970 | £2 | £5 | promo |
| Stray | LP | Transatlantic | TRA216 | 1970 | £5 | £12 | |

## STRAY CATS

| | | | | | | | |
|---|---|---|---|---|---|---|---|
| She's Sexy And Seventeen | 7" | Arista | SCAT6 | 1983 | £5 | £10 | shaped picture disc |

## STRAYHORN, BILLY
| | | | | | | | |
|---|---|---|---|---|---|---|---|
| Cue For Saxophone | LP | Felsted | FAJ7008/SJA2008 | 1960 | £10 | £25 | |

## STREAPLERS
| | | | | | | | |
|---|---|---|---|---|---|---|---|
| Times They Are A-Changin' | 7" EP | Columbia | ESRF1786 | 1966 | £5 | £10 | French |

## STREET, HILLARD
| | | | | | | | |
|---|---|---|---|---|---|---|---|
| River Love | 7" | Capitol | CL14960 | 1958 | £1.50 | £4 | |

## STREISAND, BARBRA
| | | | | | | | |
|---|---|---|---|---|---|---|---|
| All I Ask Of You | CD-s | CBS | CDBARB3 | 1989 | £2 | £5 | |
| All I Ask Of You | CD-s | CBS | CPBARB3 | 1989 | £6 | £15 | picture disc |
| Barbra Joan Streisand | LP | Columbia | PCQ30792 | 1971 | £4 | £10 | US quad |
| Barbra Streisand | 7" EP | CBS | AGG20054 | 1964 | £2 | £5 | |
| Butterfly | LP | Columbia | PCQ33005 | 1974 | £4 | £10 | US quad |
| Color Me Barbra | LP | Columbia | CL2478 | 1966 | £20 | £40 | US, red vinyl |
| En Francais | 7" EP | CBS | EP6048 | 1965 | £4 | £8 | |
| Event Of The Decade – A Retrospective | CD | CBS | XPCD417 | 1994 | £75 | £150 | promo double |
| Funny Girl | LP | Columbia | SQ30992 | 1972 | £4 | £10 | US quad |
| Funny Lady | LP | Arista | AQ9004 | 1975 | £4 | £10 | US quad |
| Greatest Hits Volume 2 | LP | Columbia | HC45679 | 1982 | £4 | £10 | US audiophile |
| Guilty | LP | Columbia | HC46750 | 1982 | £4 | £10 | US audiophile |
| Just For The Record – Selection One | CD | Columbia | CSK4196 | 1991 | £10 | £25 | US promo compilation |
| Just For The Record – Selection Two | CD | Columbia | CSK4200 | 1991 | £10 | £25 | US promo compilation |
| Lazy Afternoon | LP | Columbia | PCQ33815 | 1975 | £4 | £10 | US quad |
| Live In Concert At The Forum | LP | Columbia | PCQ31760 | 1972 | £4 | £10 | US quad |
| Lover Come Back To Me | 7" EP | CBS | AGG20042 | 1964 | £2 | £5 | |
| Memories | LP | Columbia | HC47678 | 1982 | £4 | £10 | US audiophile |
| My Man | 7" EP | CBS | EP6068 | 1966 | £2 | £5 | |
| Ordinary Miracles Tour CD | CD | Columbia | CSK6120 | 1994 | £20 | £40 | US promo compilation |
| Places That Belong To You | CD-s | CBS | 6577945 | 1992 | £2 | £5 | |
| Places That Belong To You | CD-s | CBS | 6577949 | 1992 | £6 | £15 | picture disc |
| Second Barbra Streisand Album | LP | Columbia | CS8854 | 1963 | £25 | £50 | US, blue vinyl |
| Second Hand Rose | 7" EP | CBS | EP6150 | 1967 | £2 | £5 | |
| Stoney End | LP | Columbia | PCQ30378 | 1971 | £4 | £10 | US quad |
| Till I Loved You | CD-s | CBS | CDBARB2 | 1988 | £2 | £5 | with Don Johnson |
| Way We Were | LP | Columbia | PCQ32801 | 1974 | £4 | £10 | US quad |
| We're Not Making Love Anymore | CD-s | CBS | CDBARB4 | 1989 | £2 | £5 | |
| We're Not Making Love Anymore | CD-s | CBS | CPBARB4 | 1989 | £5 | £12 | picture disc |

## STRENGTH, TEXAS BILL
| | | | | | | | |
|---|---|---|---|---|---|---|---|
| Yellow Rose Of Texas | 7" | Capitol | CL14357 | 1955 | £6 | £12 | |

## STRETCH
| | | | | | | | |
|---|---|---|---|---|---|---|---|
| Elastique | LP | Anchor | ANCL2014 | 1975 | £5 | £12 | |
| Forget The Past | LP | Hot Wax | HW1 | 1978 | £6 | £15 | |

## STRICKLAND, WILLIAM R.

William Strickland was reputed to have made his songs up as he went along and certainly they sound ramshackle enough for him to have done so. At the time, the Deram label was willing to try anything, but in the end, all that can really be said about Mr Strickland is that he is no Syd Barrett.

| | | | | | | | |
|---|---|---|---|---|---|---|---|
| Is Only The Name | LP | Deram | DML/SML1041 | 1969 | £5 | £12 | |

## STRIDER
| | | | | | | | |
|---|---|---|---|---|---|---|---|
| Exposed | LP | GM | GML1002 | 1973 | £4 | £10 | |
| Misunderstanding | LP | GM | GML1012 | 1974 | £4 | £10 | |

## STRING CHEESE
| | | | | | | | |
|---|---|---|---|---|---|---|---|
| String Cheese | LP | RCA | SF8222 | 1971 | £6 | £15 | |

## STRING DRIVEN THING
| | | | | | | | |
|---|---|---|---|---|---|---|---|
| Another Night | 7" | Concord | CON7 | 1970 | £6 | £12 | |
| Machine That Cried | LP | Charisma | CAS1070 | 1973 | £4 | £10 | |
| String Driven Thing | LP | Charisma | CAS1062 | 1972 | £4 | £10 | |
| String Driven Thing | LP | Concord | CON1001 | 1970 | £50 | £100 | |

## STRINGALONGS
| | | | | | | | |
|---|---|---|---|---|---|---|---|
| Brass Buttons | 7" | London | HLU9354 | 1961 | £1.50 | £4 | |
| Matilda | 7" | London | HLD9652 | 1963 | £2.50 | £6 | |
| Mina Bird | 7" | London | HLU9452 | 1961 | £2 | £5 | |
| Spinnin' My Wheels | 7" | London | HLD9588 | 1962 | £2 | £5 | |
| Stringalong With The Stringalongs | 7" EP | London | REU1398 | 1963 | £7.50 | £15 | |
| Stringalongs | 7" EP | London | REU1322 | 1961 | £7.50 | £15 | |
| Stringalongs | 7" EP | London | REU1350 | 1963 | £7.50 | £15 | |
| String-Alongs | LP | London | HAD/SHD8054 | 1963 | £8 | £20 | |
| Twistwatch | 7" | London | HLD9535 | 1962 | £2 | £5 | |

## STRIPES OF GLORY
| | | | | | | | |
|---|---|---|---|---|---|---|---|
| Denial | 7" | Vogue | V9194 | 1962 | £5 | £10 | |

## STROLLERS
| | | | | | | | |
|---|---|---|---|---|---|---|---|
| Come On Over | 7" | London | HLL9336 | 1961 | £5 | £10 | |
| Jumping With Symphony Sid | 7" | Vogue | V9113 | 1958 | £10 | £20 | |
| Little Bitty Pretty One | 7" | Vogue | V9124 | 1958 | £10 | £20 | |

## STROLLERS (2)
Cuckoo .................................................... 7" ...... Fontana ............ TF598 .................... 1965 £1.50 ....... £4 ........................................

## STRONG, BARRETT
Money ..................................................... 7" ...... London ............ HLU9088 .............. 1960 £50 ....... £100 ........................................

## STRONG, NOLAN & THE DIABLOS
| | | | | | | | |
|---|---|---|---|---|---|---|---|
| Fortune Of Hits | LP | Fortune | LP8010 | 1961 | £15 | £30 | US |
| Fortune Of Hits Vol. 2 | LP | Fortune | LP8012 | 1962 | £15 | £30 | US |
| Mind Over Matter | LP | Fortune | LP8015 | 1963 | £15 | £30 | US |

## STUART, CHAD & JEREMY CLYDE
| | | | | | | | |
|---|---|---|---|---|---|---|---|
| Before And After | 7" EP | CBS | 6101 | 1965 | £5 | £10 | French |
| Before And After | 7" | CBS | 201769 | 1965 | £2.50 | £6 | |
| Best Of Chad And Jeremy | LP | Ember | (ST)NR5036 | 1967 | £4 | £10 | |
| Chad Stuart And Jeremy Clyde | 7" EP | United Artists | UEP1008 | 1965 | £2.50 | £6 | |
| Early In The Morning | 7" | Ember | EMBS186 | 1964 | £1.50 | £4 | |
| I Don't Want To Lose You | 7" | CBS | 201814 | 1965 | £1.50 | £4 | |
| Like I Love You Today | 7" EP | Pathe | EGF716 | 1963 | £5 | £10 | French |
| Sing For You | LP | Ember | NR5021 | 1965 | £4 | £10 | |
| Summer Song | 7" EP | Pathe | EGF775 | 1964 | £5 | £10 | French |
| What Do You Want With Me | 7" EP | Pathe | EGF850 | 1965 | £5 | £10 | French |
| Yesterday's Gone | LP | World Artists | WAM2002/ WAS3002 | 1964 | £4 | £10 | US |
| Yesterday's Gone | 7" EP | Ember | EMBEP4543 | 1964 | £4 | £8 | |
| Yesterday's Gone | 7" | Ember | EMBS180 | 1963 | £1.50 | £4 | |

## STUART, MIKE SPAN
| | | | | | | | |
|---|---|---|---|---|---|---|---|
| Children Of Tomorrow | 7" | Jewel | JL01 | 1968 | £150 | £250 | best auctioned |
| Come On Over To Our Place | 7" | Columbia | DB8066 | 1966 | £7.50 | £15 | |
| Dear | 7" | Columbia | DB8206 | 1967 | £7.50 | £15 | |
| You Can Understand Me | 7" | Fontana | TF959 | 1968 | £4 | £8 | |

## STUD
| | | | | | | | |
|---|---|---|---|---|---|---|---|
| Goodbye Live At Command | LP | BASF | 2029117 | 1973 | £8 | £20 | German |
| September | LP | BASF | 2029054 | 1972 | £10 | £25 | German |
| Stud | LP | Deram | SMLR1084 | 1971 | £10 | £25 | |

## STUDD PUMP
Spare The Children .................................. 7" ...... Penny Farthing  PEN757 ............. 1971 £1.50 ....... £4 ........................................

## STUDIO ONE ALL STARS
Sherry .................................................... 7" ...... Island ............. WI3038 ............... 1967 £5 ........... £10 ........................................

## STUDIO SIX
| | | | | | | | |
|---|---|---|---|---|---|---|---|
| Strawberry Window | 7" | Polydor | BM56219 | 1967 | £5 | £10 | |
| Times Were When | 7" | Polydor | BM56189 | 1967 | £1.50 | £4 | |
| When I See My Baby | 7" | Polydor | BM56131 | 1966 | £1.50 | £4 | |

## STUDIO SWEETHEARTS
I Believe ................................................. 7" ...... DJM ............. DJS10915 ............ 1979 £2.50 ....... £6 ............ picture sleeve

## STUPIDS
Violent Nun ............................................ 7" ...... Children Of The Revolution ...... COR3 .............. 1985 £5 ........... £10 ........................................

## STYLE COUNCIL
| | | | | | | | |
|---|---|---|---|---|---|---|---|
| Agent 88 EP | CD-s | Polydor | TSCCD103 | 1987 | £2 | £5 | |
| Birds And The B's EP | CD-s | Polydor | TSCCD102 | 1987 | £2 | £5 | |
| Café Bleu | CD | Polydor | 8175352 | 1984 | £5 | £12 | |
| Café Bleu EP | CD-s | Polydor | TSCCD101 | 1987 | £2 | £5 | |
| Confessions Of A Pop Group | CD-s | Polygram | 0803849 | 1988 | £4 | £10 | CD video |
| Confessions Of A Pop Group | CD | Polydor | 8357852 | 1988 | £5 | £12 | |
| Confessions Of A Pop Group | CD | Polydor | 8357852 | 1988 | £20 | £40 | promo briefcase set, with video, cassette, towel, biog |
| Cost Of Loving | CD | Polydor | 8314432 | 1987 | £5 | £12 | |
| Have You Ever Had It Blue | CD-s | Polygram | 0803362 | 1988 | £4 | £10 | CD video |
| How She Threw It All Away | CD-s | Polydor | TSCCD16 | 1988 | £2 | £5 | |
| How She Threw It All Away | CD-s | Polygram | 0804002 | 1988 | £4 | £10 | CD video |
| It Just Came To Pieces (live) | 7" | Lyntone | LYN15344/5 | 1984 | £2.50 | £6 | flexi |
| Life At A Top People's Health Club | CD-s | Polygram | 0805602 | 1989 | £4 | £10 | CD video |
| Life At A Top People's Health Farm | CD-s | Polydor | TSCCD1 | 1988 | £2 | £5 | |
| Long Hot Summer | CD-s | Polygram | 0802062 | 1988 | £4 | £10 | CD video |
| Long Hot Summer – '89 remix | CD-s | Polydor | LHSCD1 | 1989 | £2 | £5 | |
| Promised Land | CD-s | Polydor | TSCCD17 | 1989 | £2 | £5 | |
| Showbiz | CD-s | Polygram | 0800381 | 1988 | £4 | £10 | CD video |
| You're The Best Thing | CD-s | Polygram | 0803302 | 1988 | £4 | £10 | CD video |

## STYLOS
Head Over Heels ...................................... 7" ...... Liberty ........... LIB10173 ............ 1964 £37.50 .... £75 ........................................

## STYX
| | | | | | | | |
|---|---|---|---|---|---|---|---|
| Best Of Styx | LP | RCA | 3597 | 1979 | £4 | £10 | Canadian blue vinyl |
| Collection Of Styx | LP | A&M | SAMP3 | 1979 | £8 | £20 | promo, 3 LPs, boxed |
| Compact Hits | CD-s | A&M | AMCD904 | 1988 | £2 | £5 | |

| | | | | | | | |
|---|---|---|---|---|---|---|---|
| Cornerstone | LP | A&M | SP3711 | 1979 | £5 | £12 | US silver vinyl |
| Cornerstone | LP | Nautilus | | 198– | £5 | £12 | US audiophile |
| Grand Illusion | LP | A&M | SP4637 | 1977 | £4 | £10 | Canadian gold vinyl |
| Grand Illusion | LP | Mobile Fidelity | MFSL1026 | 1978 | £5 | £12 | US audiophile |
| Paradise Theatre | LP | Nautilus | | 198– | £5 | £12 | US audiophile |
| Pieces Of Eight | LP | A&M | PR4724 | 1978 | £5 | £12 | US picture disc |
| Pieces Of Eight | LP | Nautilus | | 198– | £5 | £12 | US audiophile |
| Styx Radio Show | LP | A&M | SP8431 | 1976 | £6 | £15 | US promo |
| Styx Radio Special | LP | A&M | SP17053 | 1977 | £8 | £20 | US promo |

## SUB
| | | | | | | | |
|---|---|---|---|---|---|---|---|
| In Concert | LP | Help | | 197– | £180 | £300 | |

## SUBHUMANS
| | | | | | | | |
|---|---|---|---|---|---|---|---|
| Incorrect Thoughts | LP | Friends | FR008 | 1980 | £10 | £25 | |
| No Wishes No Prayers | LP | | | | £6 | £15 | Canadian |

## SUBJECT ESQ.
| | | | | | | | |
|---|---|---|---|---|---|---|---|
| Subject Esq. | LP | Epic | EPC64998 | 1972 | £6 | £15 | German |

## SUBOTNICK, MORTON
| | | | | | | | |
|---|---|---|---|---|---|---|---|
| Silver Apples Of The Moon | LP | Nonesuch | H71174 | 1967 | £8 | £20 | |
| The Wild Bull | LP | Nonesuch | H71208 | 1968 | £8 | £20 | |

## SUBSTITUTE
| | | | | | | | |
|---|---|---|---|---|---|---|---|
| One | 7" | Ignition | IR2 | 1979 | £2.50 | £6 | |
| One | 7" | Ignition | IR2 | 1979 | £5 | £10 | picture sleeve |

## SUDDEN SWAY
| | | | | | | | |
|---|---|---|---|---|---|---|---|
| Jane's Third Party | 7" | Chant | CHANT1 | 1980 | £4 | £8 | |
| Spacemate | 12" | WEA | BYN8B | 1986 | £3 | £8 | double boxed set |
| Traffic Tax Scheme | 12" | Chant | CHANT3 | 1984 | £3 | £8 | |

## SUE & SUNNY
| | | | | | | | |
|---|---|---|---|---|---|---|---|
| I Like Your Style | 7" | Columbia | DB8099 | 1967 | £1.50 | £4 | |
| Show Must Go On | 7" | CBS | 3874 | 1968 | £1.50 | £4 | |
| Sue & Sunny | LP | CBS | 63740 | 1970 | £4 | £10 | |
| Sue And Sunny | LP | Reflection | REFL4 | 1972 | £6 | £15 | |

## SUEDE
| | | | | | | | |
|---|---|---|---|---|---|---|---|
| Be My God | 12" | RML | RML001 | 1990 | £50 | £100 | test pressing |
| Drowners | 7" | Nude | NUD1S | 1992 | £4 | £8 | |
| My Insatiable One | 7" | Nude | SUEDE1 | 1993 | £2.50 | £6 | clear flexi |

## SUGAR
| | | | | | | | |
|---|---|---|---|---|---|---|---|
| Beaster | CD | Ryko | | 1993 | £8 | £20 | US promo, leatherette sleeve |
| Copper Blue | CD | Ryko | RCD10239 | 1992 | £8 | £20 | US promo, copper cover |
| Life Before Sugar | CD | Ryko | VRCD0239 | 1992 | £15 | £30 | US promo double – Copper Blue plus compilation |

## SUGAR & DANDY
| | | | | | | | |
|---|---|---|---|---|---|---|---|
| I Want To Be Your Lover | 7" | Carnival | CV7029 | 1965 | £1.50 | £4 | |
| I'm Into Something Good | 7" | Carnival | CV7024 | 1965 | £1.50 | £4 | |
| I'm Not Crying Now | 7" | Carnival | CV7016 | 1964 | £1.50 | £4 | |
| Let's Ska | 7" | Carnival | CV7023 | 1965 | £1.50 | £4 | |
| Let's Ska | 7" | Page One | POF23044 | 1967 | £1.50 | £4 | |
| Meditation | 7" | Blue Beat | BB367 | 1966 | £6 | £12 | Jetliners B side |
| Oh Dear What Can The Matter Be | 7" | Carnival | CV7009 | 1964 | £1.50 | £4 | |
| One Man Went To Mow | 7" | Carnival | CV7006 | 1963 | £1.50 | £4 | |
| Ska's The Limit | LP | Page One | FOR006 | 1967 | £6 | £15 | |
| Think Of The Good Times | 7" | Carnival | CV7027 | 1965 | £1.50 | £4 | |
| What A Life | 7" | Carnival | CV7015 | 1964 | £1.50 | £4 | |

## SUGAR & PEEWEE
| | | | | | | | |
|---|---|---|---|---|---|---|---|
| One Two Let's Rock | 7" | Vogue | V9112 | 1958 | £250 | £400 | best auctioned |

## SUGAR CREEK
| | | | | | | | |
|---|---|---|---|---|---|---|---|
| Please Tell A Friend | LP | Metromedia | MD1020 | 1969 | £30 | £60 | US |

## SUGAR SHOPPE
| | | | | | | | |
|---|---|---|---|---|---|---|---|
| Skip Along Sam | 7" | Capitol | CL15555 | 1968 | £1.50 | £4 | |

## SUGARBEATS
| | | | | | | | |
|---|---|---|---|---|---|---|---|
| Alice Designs | 7" | Polydor | 56120 | 1966 | £1.50 | £4 | |
| I Just Stand Here | 7" | Polydor | 56069 | 1966 | £1.50 | £4 | |

## SUGARCUBES (SYKURMOLARNIR)
| | | | | | | | |
|---|---|---|---|---|---|---|---|
| Einn Mol'a Mann | 7" | Smekkleysa | SM3/86 | 1986 | £30 | £60 | Icelandic |
| Luftgitar | 12" | Smekkleysa | SM7 | 1987 | £10 | £25 | Icelandic |
| Skytturnar | 12" | Gramm | GRAMM31 | 1986 | £10 | £25 | Icelandic |

## SUGARCUBES
| | | | | | | | |
|---|---|---|---|---|---|---|---|
| 12.11 | 12" | One Little Indian | TPBOX1 | 1990 | £10 | £20 | 11 x 12", boxed |

| | | | | | | | |
|---|---|---|---|---|---|---|---|
| 7.8 | 7" | One Little Indian | TPBOX2 | 1990 | £7.50 | £15 | 8 x 7", boxed |
| Birthday | CD-s | One Little Indian | 7TP7CD | 1987 | £2.50 | £6 | |
| Birthday Christmas Mix | CD-s | One Little Indian | 12TP11CD | 1988 | £2 | £5 | ... with Jesus & Mary Chain |
| CD.6 | CD-s | One Little Indian | TPBOX3 | 1990 | £15 | £30 | 6 x CD-s, boxed |
| Cold Sweat | CD-s | One Little Indian | 7TP9CD | 1988 | £2 | £5 | |
| Deus | CD-s | One Little Indian | 7TP10CD | 1988 | £2 | £5 | |
| Planet | CD-s | One Little Indian | 7TP32CD | 1990 | £2 | £5 | |
| Regina | CD-s | One Little Indian | 7TP26CD | 1989 | £2 | £5 | |

## SUICIDAL TENDENCIES
| | | | | | | | |
|---|---|---|---|---|---|---|---|
| Possessed To Skate | 12" | Virgin | VS96712 | 1987 | £2.50 | £6 | picture disc |

## SUICIDE
| | | | | | | | |
|---|---|---|---|---|---|---|---|
| 23 Minutes In Brussels | LP | Bronze | FRANKIE1 | 1978 | £8 | £20 | |
| Alan Vega – Martin Rev | LP | Ze | ILPS7007 | 1980 | £4 | £10 | |
| Cheree | 7" | Bronze | BRO57 | 1978 | £2 | £5 | |
| Suicide | LP | Bronze | BRON508 | 1977 | £4 | £10 | |

## SUICIDE COMMANDOS
| | | | | | | | |
|---|---|---|---|---|---|---|---|
| Commandos Commit Suicide Dance Concert | LP | Twintone | TTR7906 | 1979 | £6 | £15 | US |

## SULLIVAN, BIG JIM
| | | | | | | | |
|---|---|---|---|---|---|---|---|
| She Walks Through The Fair | 7" | Mercury | MF928 | 1965 | £7.50 | £15 | |
| Sitar A Go-Go | LP | Mercury | SML30001 | 1968 | £8 | £20 | |
| You Don't Know What You've Got | 7" | Decca | F11387 | 1961 | £1.50 | £4 | |

## SULLIVAN, IRA
| | | | | | | | |
|---|---|---|---|---|---|---|---|
| Billy Taylor Introduces Ira Sullivan | LP | HMV | CLP1236 | 1959 | £8 | £20 | |

## SULLIVAN, JOE
| | | | | | | | |
|---|---|---|---|---|---|---|---|
| Joe Sullivan | LP | Columbia | 33CX10047 | 1956 | £6 | £15 | |
| Joe Sullivan | LP | London | HAU2011 | 1956 | £6 | £15 | |
| Joe Sullivan Plays Fats Waller | 10" LP | Philips | BBR8091 | 1956 | £8 | £20 | |

## SULLIVAN, MAXINE
| | | | | | | | |
|---|---|---|---|---|---|---|---|
| Boogie Woogie Maxine | 7" | Parlophone | MSP6086 | 1954 | £1.50 | £4 | |

## SULTANS
| | | | | | | | |
|---|---|---|---|---|---|---|---|
| Les Sultans | LP | Telediscs | 356 | 1966 | £8 | £20 | Canadian |
| Vol. 2 | LP | Idole | 306 | 1967 | £4 | £10 | Canadian |

## SUM PEAR
| | | | | | | | |
|---|---|---|---|---|---|---|---|
| Sum Pear | LP | Euphoria | EST1 | 1971 | £15 | £30 | US |

## SUMAC, YMA
| | | | | | | | |
|---|---|---|---|---|---|---|---|
| Miracles | LP | London | SHU8431 | 1972 | £8 | £20 | |
| Voice Of The Xtaby | 10" LP | Capital | LC6522 | 1953 | £15 | £30 | |

## SUMLIN, HUBERT
| | | | | | | | |
|---|---|---|---|---|---|---|---|
| Across The Board | 7" | Blue Horizon | 451000 | 1965 | £50 | £100 | |

## SUMMER, DONNA
| | | | | | | | |
|---|---|---|---|---|---|---|---|
| Hot Stuff | 12" | Casablanca | CANL151 | 1979 | £4 | £10 | red vinyl |

## SUMMER SET
| | | | | | | | |
|---|---|---|---|---|---|---|---|
| Farmer's Daughter | 7" | Columbia | DB8004 | 1966 | £5 | £10 | 2 different B-sides |
| It's A Dream | 7" | Columbia | DB8215 | 1967 | £15 | £30 | |

## SUMMERFIELD, SAFFRON
| | | | | | | | |
|---|---|---|---|---|---|---|---|
| Fancy Meeting You Here | LP | Mother Earth | MUM1202 | 1976 | £20 | £40 | |
| Salisbury Plain | LP | Mother Earth | MUM1001 | 1974 | £20 | £40 | |

## SUMMERHILL
| | | | | | | | |
|---|---|---|---|---|---|---|---|
| Summerhill | LP | Polydor | 583746 | 1969 | £15 | £30 | |

## SUMMERS, BOB
| | | | | | | | |
|---|---|---|---|---|---|---|---|
| Excitement | 7" | Capitol | CL15063 | 1959 | £1.50 | £4 | |
| Little Brown Jug | 7" | Capitol | CL15130 | 1960 | £2 | £5 | |

## SUMPIN' ELSE
| | | | | | | | |
|---|---|---|---|---|---|---|---|
| I Can't Get Through To You | 7" EP | Liberty | LEP2268 | 1967 | £4 | £8 | French |

## SUN ALSO RISES
| | | | | | | | |
|---|---|---|---|---|---|---|---|
| Sun Also Rises | LP | Village Thing | VTS2 | 1970 | £6 | £15 | |

## SUN DIAL
| | | | | | | | |
|---|---|---|---|---|---|---|---|
| Exploding In Your Mind | 12" | Tangerine | no number | 1991 | £20 | £40 | test pressing |
| Other Way Out | LP | Tangerine | MM07 | 1990 | £10 | £25 | |

## SUN RA

Despite the lengthy list of records by avant-garde jazz eccentric Sun Ra, there are actually many other albums in existence, whose details have thus far remained obscure. Over the years Sun Ra issued a large number of albums on his own El Saturn label, with a minority being subsequently reissued on more widely distributed labels. Only in recent years has the man's enormous contribution to jazz begun to be at all widely appreciated (whether performing on electric piano or synthesizer, whether leading his band through free improvisation or world-music chanting, he seemed to do most things before anyone else) and his albums are becoming increasingly collectable.

| | | | | | | | |
|---|---|---|---|---|---|---|---|
| Angels And Demons At Play | LP | Impulse | AS9245 | 1973 | £8 | £20 | US |
| Art Forms From Dimension Tomorrow | LP | El Saturn | 404/9956 | 1965 | £15 | £30 | US |
| Astro Black | LP | Impulse | AS9255 | 1973 | £8 | £20 | US |
| Atlantis | LP | El Saturn | | | £15 | £30 | US |
| Atlantis | LP | Impulse | AS9239 | 1973 | £8 | £20 | US |
| Continuation | LP | El Saturn | ESR29691/520 | | £15 | £30 | US |
| Cosmo Sun Connection | LP | El Saturn | SRRRD1 | 1985 | £15 | £30 | US |
| Cosmos | LP | Inner City | IC1020 | 1977 | £8 | £20 | US |
| Dance Of Innocent Passion | LP | El Saturn | 1981 | 1981 | £15 | £30 | US |
| Disco 3000 | LP | El Saturn | CMIJ78 | 1978 | £15 | £30 | US |
| Dreams Come True | LP | El Saturn | 485 | 1984 | £15 | £30 | US |
| Fate In A Pleasant Mood | LP | El Saturn | 202 | | £15 | £30 | US |
| Fate In A Pleasant Mood | LP | Impulse | AS9270 | 1974 | £8 | £20 | US |
| Futuristic Sounds Of Sun Ra | LP | BYG | 529111 | 197– | £8 | £20 | French |
| Futuristic Sounds Of Sun Ra | LP | Savoy | MG12169 | 1960 | £20 | £40 | US |
| Heliocentric Worlds Vol. 1 | LP | Fontana | STL5514 | 1965 | £10 | £25 | |
| Heliocentric Worlds Vol. 2 | LP | Fontana | STL5499 | 1966 | £10 | £25 | |
| Hiroshima | LP | El Saturn | 1183 | 1983 | £15 | £30 | US |
| Horizon | LP | El Saturn | 121771 | 1972 | £15 | £30 | US |
| It's After The End Of The World | LP | MPS | MPS15047 | 1970 | £10 | £25 | French |
| Jazz By Sun Ra | LP | Sonet | SLP23 | 196– | £15 | £30 | |
| Jazz By Sun Ra | LP | Transition | TRLP10 | 1956 | £50 | £100 | US |
| Jazz In Silhouette | LP | El Saturn | 205 | 1958 | £25 | £50 | US |
| Jazz In Silhouette | LP | Impulse | ASD9265 | 1975 | £8 | £20 | US |
| Live At Montreux | LP | Inner City | IC1039 | 1977 | £15 | £30 | US double |
| Live At Praxis '84 Vol. 1 | LP | Praxis | CM108 | 1984 | £6 | £15 | Greek |
| Magic City | LP | El Saturn | LPB711/403 | | £15 | £30 | US |
| Magic City | LP | Impulse | AS9243 | 1973 | £8 | £20 | US |
| My Brother The Wind | LP | El Saturn | ESR521 | | £15 | £30 | US |
| My Brother The Wind Vol. 2 | LP | El Saturn | SRA2000/523/ SR1970 | | £15 | £30 | US |
| Nidhamu | LP | El Saturn | 7771 | 1972 | £15 | £30 | US |
| Nubians Of Plutonia | LP | El Saturn | LP406 | | £15 | £30 | US |
| Nubians Of Plutonia | LP | Impulse | AS9242 | 1974 | £8 | £20 | US |
| Nuits de la Fondation Maeght | LP | Recommended | RRELEVEN | 1981 | £8 | £20 | |
| Nuits de la Fondation Maeght Vol. 1 | LP | Shandar | SR10001 | 1972 | £10 | £25 | French |
| Nuits de la Fondation Maeght Vol. 2 | LP | Shandar | SR10003 | 1972 | £10 | £25 | French |
| Oblique Parallax | LP | El Saturn | SR72881 | 1981 | £15 | £30 | US |
| Pathways To Unknown Worlds | LP | El Saturn | 564 | 1973 | £15 | £30 | US |
| Pathways To Unknown Worlds | LP | Impulse | ASD9298 | 1975 | £8 | £20 | US |
| Pictures Of Infinity | LP | Black Lion | BLP30103 | | £6 | £15 | |
| Pictures Of Infinity | LP | Polydor | 2460106 | 1971 | £8 | £20 | |
| Saturn Research | LP | El Saturn | 1978 | 1978 | £15 | £30 | US |
| Secrets Of The Sun | LP | El Saturn | 9954 | 196– | £20 | £40 | |
| Sleeping Beauty | LP | El Saturn | 11179 | 1979 | £15 | £30 | US |
| Solar-Myth Approach Vol. 1 | LP | Affinity | AFF10 | 1978 | £6 | £15 | |
| Solar-Myth Approach Vol. 2 | LP | Affinity | AFF76 | 1983 | £6 | £15 | |
| Solo Piano Vol. 1 | LP | Improvising Arts | IA1373850 | 1978 | £6 | £15 | |
| Solo Piano Vol. 2 | LP | Improvising Arts | IA1373858 | 1978 | £6 | £15 | |
| Soul Vibrations Of Man | LP | El Saturn | 771 | 1976 | £15 | £30 | US |
| Sound Of Joy | LP | Delmark | DS414 | 1968 | £10 | £25 | |
| Springtime Again | LP | El Saturn | 11179 | 1979 | £15 | £30 | US |
| Strange Celestial Road | LP | Y | Y19 | 1980 | £6 | £15 | |
| Sun Ra | LP | Concert Hall | J1348 | 197– | £8 | £20 | French |
| Sun Song | LP | Delmark | DL411 | 1967 | £10 | £25 | |
| Sunrise In Different Dimensions | LP | Hat Art | 2017 | 198– | £8 | £20 | double |
| Sunrise In Different Dimensions | LP | Hat Hut | HH2R17 | 1981 | £10 | £25 | double |
| Super-Sonic Sounds | LP | El Saturn | 204 | | £15 | £30 | US |
| Super-Sonic Sounds | LP | Impulse | AS9271 | 1974 | £8 | £20 | US |
| Supersonic Jazz | LP | El Saturn | LP0216 | 196– | £20 | £40 | |
| Unity | LP | Horo | HDP19/20 | 1978 | £15 | £30 | Italian double |
| Universe In Blue | LP | El Saturn | ESR200/ESR5000 | | £15 | £30 | US |
| Visions | LP | Steeplechase | SCS1126 | 1979 | £8 | £20 | US, with Walt Dickerson |
| Voice Of The Eternal Tomorrow | LP | El Saturn | 91780 | 1980 | £15 | £30 | US |

## SUNDAE TIMES

| | | | | | | | |
|---|---|---|---|---|---|---|---|
| Us Coloured Kids | LP | Joy | JOYS159 | 1969 | £5 | £12 | |

## SUNDANCE

| | | | | | | | |
|---|---|---|---|---|---|---|---|
| Chuffer | LP | Decca | SKL5183 | 1974 | £4 | £10 | |
| Rain Steam Speed | LP | Decca | TXS111 | 1973 | £5 | £12 | |

## SUNDAY AFTERNOON

| | | | | | | | |
|---|---|---|---|---|---|---|---|
| Sunday Afternoon | LP | Longman | | | £37.50 | £75 | |

## SUNDAYS

| | | | | | | | | |
|---|---|---|---|---|---|---|---|---|
| Can't Be Sure | CD-s | Rough Trade | RT218CD | 1989 | £2 | £5 | 3" single |
| Can't Be Sure | 12" | Rough Trade | RTTX218 | 1989 | £2.50 | £6 | export |
| Reading, Writing And Arithmetic | LP | Rough Trade | ROUGH148P | 1990 | £4 | £10 | picture disc |

## SUNDOWN PLAYBOYS

| | | | | | | | |
|---|---|---|---|---|---|---|---|
| Saturday Night Special | 78 | Apple | 44 | 1972 | £100 | £200 | promo, best auctioned |
| Saturday Night Special | 7" | Apple | 44 | 1972 | £1.50 | £4 | |
| Saturday Night Special | 7" | Apple | 44 | 1972 | £7.50 | £15 | picture sleeve |

## SUNDOWNERS

| | | | | | | | |
|---|---|---|---|---|---|---|---|
| Dr. J.Wallace-Browne | 7" | Columbia | DB8339 | 1968 | £1.50 | £4 | |
| House Of The Rising Sun | 7" | Piccadilly | 7N35142 | 1963 | £1.50 | £4 | |
| Shot Of Rhythm And Blues | 7" | Piccadilly | 7N35162 | 1964 | £1.50 | £4 | |
| Where Am I | 7" | Parlophone | R5243 | 1965 | £1.50 | £4 | |

## SUNDRAGON

| | | | | | | | |
|---|---|---|---|---|---|---|---|
| Blueberry Blue | 7" | MGM | MGM1391 | 1968 | £2 | £5 | |
| Five White Horses | 7" | MGM | MGM1458 | 1968 | £1.50 | £4 | |
| Green Tambourine | LP | MGM | C(S)8090 | 1968 | £15 | £30 | |
| Green Tambourine | 7" | MGM | MGM1380 | 1968 | £2 | £5 | |

## SUNFOREST

| | | | | | | |
|---|---|---|---|---|---|---|
| Sound Of Sunforest | LP | Nova | SDN7 | 1969 | £25 | £50 |

## SUNNIES

| | | | | | | | |
|---|---|---|---|---|---|---|---|
| Stimmung In Beat | LP | Philips | 843941PY | 1967 | £6 | £15 | German |

## SUNNY & THE SUNGLOWS

| | | | | | | | |
|---|---|---|---|---|---|---|---|
| All Night Worker | LP | Tear Drop | 2019 | 196– | £6 | £15 | US |
| Peanuts | LP | Sunglow | SLP103 | 1965 | £6 | £15 | US |
| Talk To Me | 7" | London | HL9792 | 1963 | £6 | £12 | |
| Talk To Me/Rags To Riches | LP | Tear Drop | 2000 | 1963 | £8 | £20 | US |

## SUNNYLAND SLIM

| | | | | | | | |
|---|---|---|---|---|---|---|---|
| I Done You Wrong | LP | Storyville | SLP169 | 1965 | £6 | £15 | |
| Midnight Jump | LP | Blue Horizon | 763213 | 1969 | £20 | £40 | |
| Portraits In Blues | LP | Storyville | 670169 | 1968 | £4 | £10 | |
| Slim's Got This Thing Goin' On | LP | Liberty | LBS83237 | 1969 | £8 | £20 | |
| Slim's Shout | LP | Bluesville | BV1016 | 1961 | £8 | £20 | US |
| Sunnyland Slim | LP | Storyville | 616012 | 1970 | £6 | £15 | |

## SUNNYSIDERS

| | | | | | | |
|---|---|---|---|---|---|---|
| Banjo Woogie | 7" | London | HLU8180 | 1955 | £20 | £40 |
| Doesn't He Love Me | 7" | London | HLU8246 | 1956 | £20 | £40 |
| Hey Mister Banjo | 7" | London | HL8135 | 1955 | £30 | £60 |
| I Love You Fair Dinkum | 7" | London | HLU8202 | 1955 | £15 | £30 |
| Oh Me Oh My | 7" | London | HL8160 | 1955 | £20 | £40 |

## SUNRAYS

| | | | | | | | |
|---|---|---|---|---|---|---|---|
| Andrea | LP | Tower | (S)T5017 | 1966 | £8 | £20 | US |
| Andrea | 7" | Capitol | CL15433 | 1966 | £1.50 | £4 | |
| I Live For The Sun | 7" | Capitol | CL15416 | 1965 | £1.50 | £4 | |

## SUNSETS

| | | | | | | | |
|---|---|---|---|---|---|---|---|
| Cry Of The Wild Goose | 7" | Ember | EMBS125 | 1960 | £2 | £5 | |
| Surfing With The Sunsets | LP | Palace | 752 | 1963 | £6 | £15 | US |

## SUNSHINE, MONTY

| | | | | | | |
|---|---|---|---|---|---|---|
| Gonna Build A Mountain | 7" EP | London | RER1368 | 1963 | £2 | £5 |

## SUNSHINE COMPANY

| | | | | | | |
|---|---|---|---|---|---|---|
| Sunshine & Shadows | LP | Liberty | LBL/LBS83159 | 1968 | £4 | £10 |
| Sunshine Company | LP | Liberty | LBL/LBS83120 | 1968 | £4 | £10 |

## SUNTREADER

| | | | | | | |
|---|---|---|---|---|---|---|
| Zin-Zin | LP | Island | HELP13 | 1973 | £4 | £10 |

## SUPERBOYS

| | | | | | | |
|---|---|---|---|---|---|---|
| Ain't That A Shame | 7" | Giant | GN22 | 1968 | £2 | £5 |
| You're Hurtin' Me | 7" | Giant | GN31 | 1968 | £2 | £5 |

## SUPERFINE DANDELION

| | | | | | | | |
|---|---|---|---|---|---|---|---|
| Superfine Dandelion | LP | Mainstream | S6102 | 1968 | £15 | £30 | US |

## SUPERGRASS

| | | | | | | | |
|---|---|---|---|---|---|---|---|
| Caught By The Fuzz | 7" | Backbeat | no number | 1994 | £7.50 | £15 | |
| Mansize Rooster | 7" | Backbeat | no number | 1994 | £12.50 | £25 | green vinyl |

## SUPERSISTER

| | | | | | | | |
|---|---|---|---|---|---|---|---|
| Iskander | LP | Polydor | 2925021 | 1973 | £6 | £15 | Dutch |
| Present From Nancy | LP | Polydor | 2419061 | 1972 | £5 | £12 | |
| Pudding And Gisteren | LP | Polydor | 2419058 | 1972 | £5 | £12 | |
| Super Starshine Vol. 3 | LP | Polydor | 2419030 | 1971 | £8 | £20 | |
| Sweet Okay | LP | Polydor | 2441048 | 1974 | £4 | £10 | Dutch |
| To The Highest Bidder | LP | Dandelion | 2310146 | 1971 | £8 | £20 | |

## SUPERSONICS
| | | | | | | | | |
|---|---|---|---|---|---|---|---|---|
| Second Fiddle | LP | Trojan | TRL6 | 1968 | £8 | £20 | |

## SUPERSTOCKS
| | | | | | | | | |
|---|---|---|---|---|---|---|---|---|
| School Is A Drag | LP | Capitol | (S)T2190 | 1964 | £20 | £40 | US |
| Surf Route 101 | LP | Capitol | (S)T2113 | 1964 | £20 | £40 | US |
| Thunder Road | LP | Capitol | (S)T2060 | 1964 | £20 | £40 | US |

## SUPERTONES
| | | | | | | | | |
|---|---|---|---|---|---|---|---|---|
| Freedom Blues | 7" | Banana | BA312 | 1970 | £1.50 | £4 | |

## SUPERTRAMP
| | | | | | | | | |
|---|---|---|---|---|---|---|---|---|
| Breakfast In America | LP | Mobile Fidelity | MFSL1045 | 1980 | £4 | £10 | US audiophile |
| Compact Hits | CD-s | A&M | AMCD914 | 1988 | £2 | £5 | |
| Crime Of The Century | LP | Mobile Fidelity | MFSL1005 | 1978 | £4 | £10 | US audiophile |
| Crime Of The Century | LP | Mobile Fidelity | MFSL1005 | 1982 | £20 | £40 | US audiophile (UHQR) |
| Crisis? What Crisis | LP | A&M | | | £4 | £10 | audiophile |
| Even In The Quietest Moments | LP | A&M | | | £4 | £10 | audiophile |
| Famous Last Words | LP | A&M | | | £4 | £10 | audiophile |
| Paris | LP | A&M | | | £6 | £15 | audiophile double |

## SUPREMES
| | | | | | | | | |
|---|---|---|---|---|---|---|---|---|
| A Go-Go | LP | Tamla Motown | (S)TML11039 | 1966 | £5 | £12 | |
| At The Copa | LP | Tamla Motown | TML11026 | 1966 | £6 | £15 | |
| Baby Love | 7" | Stateside | SS350 | 1964 | £1.50 | £4 | |
| Back In My Arms Again | 7" | Tamla Motown | TMG516 | 1965 | £4 | £8 | |
| Breathtaking Guy | 7" | Motown | 1044 | 1963 | £7.50 | £15 | US |
| Come See About Me | 7" | Stateside | SS376 | 1965 | £2.50 | £6 | |
| Country, Western & Pop | LP | Tamla Motown | TML11018 | 1965 | £15 | £30 | |
| Happening | 7" | Tamla Motown | TMG607 | 1967 | £1.50 | £4 | |
| I Hear A Symphony | LP | Tamla Motown | TML11028 | 1966 | £4 | £10 | |
| I Hear A Symphony | 7" | Tamla Motown | TMG543 | 1965 | £2 | £5 | |
| I Want A Guy | 7" | Tamla | 1008 | 1961 | £700 | £1000 | US demo, best auctioned |
| I Want A Guy | 7" | Tamla | T54038 | 1961 | £50 | £100 | US |
| L'Amore Verra | 7" | Tamla Motown | TM8004 | 1966 | £37.50 | £75 | sung in Italian |
| Little Bit Of Liverpool | LP | Motown | M/S623 | 1964 | £15 | £30 | US |
| Little Bit Of Liverpool | LP | Stateside | LES501 | 1965 | £50 | £100 | export |
| Love Is Here And Now You're Gone | 7" | Tamla Motown | TMG597 | 1967 | £1.50 | £4 | |
| Love Is Like An Itching In My Heart | 7" | Tamla Motown | TMG560 | 1966 | £7.50 | £15 | |
| Meet The Supremes | LP | Motown | M/S606 | 1964 | £25 | £50 | US |
| Meet The Supremes | LP | Motown | M606 | 1964 | £75 | £150 | US, group seated on stools on cover |
| Meet The Supremes | LP | Stateside | SL10109 | 1964 | £8 | £20 | |
| Merry Christmas | LP | Motown | M/S638 | 1965 | £20 | £40 | US |
| Moonlight And Kisses | 7" | Tamla Motown | GO42625 | 1967 | £10 | £20 | Dutch, B side sung in French |
| More Hits | LP | Tamla Motown | TML11020 | 1965 | £6 | £15 | |
| My Heart Can't Take It No More | 7" | Motown | 1040 | 1963 | £7.50 | £15 | US |
| My World Is Empty Without You | 7" | Tamla Motown | TMG548 | 1966 | £5 | £10 | |
| Nothing But Heartaches | 7" | Tamla Motown | TMG527 | 1965 | £6 | £12 | |
| Shake | 7" EP | Tamla Motown | TME2011 | 1966 | £15 | £30 | |
| Sing Motown | LP | Tamla Motown | (S)TML11047 | 1967 | £5 | £12 | |
| Sing Rodgers & Hart | LP | Tamla Motown | (S)TML11054 | 1967 | £4 | £10 | |
| Stop In The Name Of Love | 7" | Tamla Motown | TMG501 | 1965 | £1.50 | £4 | |
| Supremes Hits | 7" EP | Tamla Motown | TME2008 | 1965 | £5 | £10 | |
| Thank You Darling | 7" | Tamla Motown | GO42609 | 1967 | £10 | £20 | Dutch, B side sung in French |
| We Remember Sam Cooke | LP | Tamla Motown | TML11012 | 1965 | £15 | £30 | |
| When The Lovelight Starts Shining | 7" | Stateside | SS257 | 1964 | £12.50 | £25 | |
| Where Did Our Love Go | LP | Motown | M/S621 | 1964 | £8 | £20 | US |
| Where Did Our Love Go | 7" | Stateside | SS327 | 1964 | £1.50 | £4 | |
| Who's Loving You | 7" | Tamla | T54045 | 1961 | £50 | £100 | US |
| With Love From Us To You | LP | Tamla Motown | TML11002 | 1965 | £15 | £30 | |
| You Can't Hurry Love | 7" | Tamla Motown | TMG575 | 1966 | £1.50 | £4 | |
| You Keep Me Hanging On | 7" | Tamla Motown | TMG585 | 1966 | £1.50 | £4 | |
| Your Heart Belongs To Me | 7" | Motown | 1027 | 1962 | £100 | £200 | US, picture sleeve |

## SURF STOMPERS
| | | | | | | | | |
|---|---|---|---|---|---|---|---|---|
| Original Surfer Stomp | LP | Del Fi | DFS1236 | 1964 | £10 | £25 | US |

## SURF TEENS
| | | | | | | | | |
|---|---|---|---|---|---|---|---|---|
| Surf Mania | LP | Sutton | 339 | 1964 | £15 | £30 | US |

## SURFARIS
| | | | | | | | | |
|---|---|---|---|---|---|---|---|---|
| Fun City | LP | Brunswick | LAT8582 | 1964 | £8 | £20 | |
| Hit City '64 | LP | Brunswick | LAT8567 | 1964 | £8 | £20 | |
| Hit City '65 | LP | Brunswick | LAT8605 | 1965 | £8 | £20 | |
| It Ain't Me Babe | LP | Brunswick | LAT/STA8631 | 1965 | £6 | £15 | |
| Point Panic | 7" | Brunswick | 05894 | 1963 | £1.50 | £4 | |
| Scatter Shield | 7" | Brunswick | 05902 | 1964 | £2 | £5 | |
| Surfaris Play | LP | Brunswick | LAT8561 | 1963 | £8 | £20 | |
| Wipe Out | LP | Dot | DLP3535 | 1966 | £5 | £12 | |
| Wipe Out | LP | London | HAD8110 | 1963 | £15 | £30 | |
| Wipe Out | 7" EP | Dot | VDEP34019 | 1963 | £12.50 | £25 | French |
| Wipe Out | 7" EP | London | RED1405 | 1963 | £12.50 | £25 | |

| | | | | | | |
|---|---|---|---|---|---|---|
| Wipe Out | 7" | London | HLD9751 | 1963 £1.50 | £4 | |

## SURFERS
| | | | | | | |
|---|---|---|---|---|---|---|
| Mambo Jambo | 7" | Vogue | V9147 | 1959 £2.50 | £6 | ... Alan Kalani B side |

## SURFRIDERS
| | | | | | | |
|---|---|---|---|---|---|---|
| Surfbeat | LP | Vault | V(S)105 | 1963 £5 | £12 | US |

## SURFSIDE FIVE
| | | | | | | |
|---|---|---|---|---|---|---|
| Recorded Live | LP | Intermountain | 153 | 196– £37.50 | £75 | US |

## SURMAN, JOHN
| | | | | | | |
|---|---|---|---|---|---|---|
| Alors! | LP | Futura | GER12 | 1970 £25 | £50 | |
| How Many Clouds Can You See? | LP | Deram | DMLR/SMLR1045 | 1969 £20 | £40 | |
| Jazz Double Vol. 1 | LP | Vogue | VJD505/1 | 1974 £15 | £25 | French |
| Jazz Double Vol. 2 | LP | Vogue | VJD505/2 | 1974 £15 | £25 | French |
| John Surman | LP | Deram | DML/SML1030 | 1968 £20 | £40 | |
| Live At Moers Festival | LP | Ring | 1006 | 1975 £6 | £15 | |
| Live At Woodstock Town Hall | LP | Daw | DNLS3072 | 1975 £4 | £10 | with Stu Martin |
| Obeah Wedding | 7" | Deram | DM224 | 1969 £1.50 | £4 | |
| Sonatinas | LP | Stream | SJ106 | 1978 £6 | £15 | |
| Tales Of The Algonquin | LP | Deram | SML1094 | 1971 £20 | £40 | with John Warren |
| Westering Home | LP | Island | HELP10 | 1972 £8 | £20 | |

## SURPRIEZE
| | | | | | | |
|---|---|---|---|---|---|---|
| Zeer Oude Klanken En Heel Nieuwe Geluiden | LP | private | | 1973 £400 | £600 | Dutch |

## SURPRISE PACKAGE
| | | | | | | |
|---|---|---|---|---|---|---|
| Free Up | LP | LHI | S12006 | 1968 £20 | £40 | US |

## SURPRIZE
| | | | | | | |
|---|---|---|---|---|---|---|
| Keep On Truckin' | LP | East Coast | EC1049 | 1974 £37.50 | £75 | US |

## SURVIVOR
| | | | | | | |
|---|---|---|---|---|---|---|
| Eye Of The Tiger | 7" | Scotti Brothers | A2411P | 1982 £1.50 | £4 | picture disc |

## SURVIVORS
| | | | | | | |
|---|---|---|---|---|---|---|
| Rawhide Ska | 7" | Rio | R70 | 1965 £5 | £10 | Owen Gray B side |
| Take Charge | 7" | Rio | R55 | 1965 £5 | £10 | |

## SURVIVORS (2)
Not only was the single by the Survivors written and produced by Brian Wilson, but the Survivors themselves were actually the Beach Boys. The group wanted to see if they could have a hit under another name – with the result that a typically classy performance has become the great lost Beach Boys track.

| | | | | | | |
|---|---|---|---|---|---|---|
| Pamela Jean | 7" | Capitol | 5102 | 1964 £100 | £200 | US |

## SUSTAIN
| | | | | | | |
|---|---|---|---|---|---|---|
| Sustain | LP | Unidentified Artist Productions | UAP2 | 1978 £50 | £100 | Dutch |

## SUTCH, SCREAMING LORD
That a small-time rock 'n' roll singer who has never had a hit record can still be a celebrity is a tribute to David Sutch's skills at self-publicity. Well-known as the leader of the Monster Raving Loony Party, Sutch has also never let it be forgotten that he is also a rock performer. His concerts, however, have always been chaotic affairs. In the wake of his *Lord Sutch And Heavy Friends* LP, expectations were high that he would appear accompanied by some of those same heavy friends – Jeff Beck, Jimmy Page and the rest. People turned up in droves to watch Sutch chase members of an anonymous backing group around the stage with a mop!

| | | | | | | |
|---|---|---|---|---|---|---|
| Cause I Love You | 7" | Atlantic | 2091006 | 1970 £2 | £5 | |
| Cause I Love You | 7" | Atlantic | 584321 | 1970 £2.50 | £6 | |
| Cheat | 7" | CBS | 202080 | 1966 £10 | £20 | |
| Dracula's Daughter | 7" | Oriole | CB1962 | 1964 £10 | £20 | |
| Election Fever | 7" | Atlantic | 2091017 | 1970 £2 | £5 | |
| Good Golly Miss Molly | 7" | HMV | POP953 | 1961 £5 | £10 | |
| Gotta Keep A-Rockin' | 7" | Atlantic | K10221 | 1972 £2 | £5 | |
| Hands Of Jack The Ripper | LP | Atlantic | K40313 | 1972 £6 | £15 | |
| Honey Hush | 7" | CBS | 201767 | 1965 £12.50 | £25 | |
| I'm A Hog For You | 7" | Decca | F11747 | 1963 £4 | £8 | |
| Jack The Ripper | 7" EP | Decca | 457063 | 1965 £15 | £30 | French |
| Jack The Ripper | 7" | Decca | F11598 | 1963 £4 | £8 | |
| Lord Sutch & Heavy Friends | LP | Atlantic | 2400008 | 1970 £6 | £15 | |
| Screaming Lord Sutch Meets The Meteors | 10" LP | Ace | MAD1 | 1981 £37.50 | £75 | |
| She's Fallen In Love With A Monster | 7" | Oriole | CB1944 | 1964 £7.50 | £15 | |
| Train Kept A-Rollin' | 7" EP | CBS | 6104 | 1965 £15 | £30 | French |

## SUTCLIFFE, ROGER
| | | | | | | |
|---|---|---|---|---|---|---|
| Death Letter | LP | Look | LKLP6038RS | 1976 £25 | £50 | |

## SUTHERLAND, ISABEL
| | | | | | | |
|---|---|---|---|---|---|---|
| Bank Of Red Roses | 7" EP | Collector | JES11 | 1961 £2 | £5 | |
| Vagrant Songs Of Scotland | LP | Topic | 12T151 | 1966 £4 | £10 | |

## SUTTON, RALPH
| | | | | | | |
|---|---|---|---|---|---|---|
| I Got Rhythm | 10" LP | Brunswick | LA8719 | 1955 £8 | £20 | |
| Music of Fats Waller | 10" LP | Columbia | 33S1025 | 1954 £8 | £20 | |

| | | | | | | |
|---|---|---|---|---|---|---|
| Piano Moods | 10" LP | Columbia | 33S1018 | 1954 | £8 | £20 |
| Ralph Sutton Quartet | LP | Columbia | 33CX10061 | 1956 | £5 | £12 |
| Stride Piano | 10" LP | Audio Fidelity.. | AF2 | 1953 | £8 | £20 |

## SUZI & BIG DEE IRWIN
| | | | | | | |
|---|---|---|---|---|---|---|
| Ain't That Lovin' You Baby | 7" | Polydor | BM65715 | 1966 | £2 | £5 |

## SUZUKI, PAT
| | | | | | | |
|---|---|---|---|---|---|---|
| I Enjoy Being A Girl | 7" | RCA | RCA1171 | 1960 | £1.50 | £4 |

## SUZY & THE RED STRIPES
| | | | | | | | |
|---|---|---|---|---|---|---|---|
| Seaside Woman | 7" | A&M | AM7461 | 1979 | £4 | £8 | yellow vinyl |
| Seaside Woman | 7" | A&M | AMS7548 | 1980 | £2.50 | £6 | |
| Seaside Woman | 7" | A&M | AMSP7461 | 1979 | £12.50 | £25 | yellow vinyl, boxed |
| Seaside Woman | 7" | EMI | EMI5572 | 1986 | £1.50 | £4 | |
| Seaside Woman | 12" | A&M | AMSP7548 | 1980 | £3 | £8 | |
| Seaside Woman | 12" | EMI | 12EMI5572 | 1986 | £2.50 | £6 | |

## SVANTE
| | | | | | | |
|---|---|---|---|---|---|---|
| Baby I Need Your Loving | 7" | United Artists .. | UP2224 | 1968 | £1.50 | £4 |

## SVENSK
| | | | | | | |
|---|---|---|---|---|---|---|
| Dream Magazine | 7" | Page One | POF036 | 1967 | £5 | £10 |
| You | 7" | Page One | POF050 | 1967 | £5 | £10 |

## SVENSSON, REINHOLD
| | | | | | | | |
|---|---|---|---|---|---|---|---|
| New Sounds From Sweden Vol. 4 | 10" LP | Esquire | 20024 | 1954 | £37.50 | £75 | with Putte Wickman |
| Reinhold Svensson Quintet | 10" LP | Esquire | 20004 | 1953 | £37.50 | £75 | |

## SWALLOWS
| | | | | | | |
|---|---|---|---|---|---|---|
| Roll Roll Pretty Baby | 78 | Vogue | V2136 | 1952 | £7.50 | £15 |

## SWAMP DOGG
| | | | | | | |
|---|---|---|---|---|---|---|
| Total Destruction To Your Mind | LP | Polydor | 2916014 | 1972 | £5 | £12 |

## SWAMP RATS
| | | | | | | | |
|---|---|---|---|---|---|---|---|
| Disco Sucks | LP | Keystone | K11154139 | 1979 | £6 | £15 | US |

## SWAN
| | | | | | | | |
|---|---|---|---|---|---|---|---|
| From Swan With Love | LP | SLP | | 1981 | £25 | £50 | Dutch |

## SWAN ARCADE
| | | | | | | |
|---|---|---|---|---|---|---|
| Matchless | LP | Stoof | MU7428 | 1976 | £4 | £10 |
| Swan Arcade | LP | Trailer | LER2032 | 1973 | £10 | £25 |

## SWANEE RIVER BOYS
| | | | | | | | |
|---|---|---|---|---|---|---|---|
| Do You Believe | 7" | Parlophone | CMSP7 | 1954 | £1.50 | £4 | export |

## SWANN, BETTYE
| | | | | | | |
|---|---|---|---|---|---|---|
| Don't Touch Me | 7" | Capitol | CL15586 | 1969 | £5 | £10 |
| Heading In The Right Direction | 7" | Atlantic | K10851 | 1976 | £2.50 | £6 |
| Make Me Yours | 7" | CBS | 2942 | 1967 | £10 | £20 |
| Today I Started Loving You Again | 7" | Atlantic | K10273 | 1972 | £2 | £5 |
| Victim Of A Foolish Heart | 7" | Atlantic | K10174 | 1972 | £2.50 | £6 |

## SWANS
| | | | | | | | |
|---|---|---|---|---|---|---|---|
| Boy With The Beatle Hair | 7" | Cameo Parkway | C302 | 1964 | £2.50 | £6 | |
| Burning World | CD-s .. | MCA | DMCG6047 | 1989 | £2 | £5 | |
| Can't Find My Way Home | CD-s .. | MCA | CDDMCAT1347 ... | 1989 | £2 | £5 | |
| He's Mine | 7" | Stateside | SS224 | 1963 | £2.50 | £6 | |
| Love Of Life/White Light From The Mouth Of Infinity | CD | Young God .... | YGCD3/5 | 1992 | £8 | £20 | boxed 2 CD set |
| Love Will Tear Us Apart | CD-s .. | Product Inc .... | PROD23CD | 1988 | £2 | £5 | |
| Saved | CD-s .. | MCA | DMCAT1332 | 1989 | £2 | £5 | |

## SWANS (2)
| | | | | | | |
|---|---|---|---|---|---|---|
| Filth | LP | Zensor | NDO3 | 1985 | £10 | £25 |

## SWANSON, BERNICE
| | | | | | | |
|---|---|---|---|---|---|---|
| Baby I'm Yours | 7" | Chess | CRS8008 | 1965 | £10 | £20 |

## SWARBRICK, DAVE
| | | | | | | |
|---|---|---|---|---|---|---|
| Ceilidh Album | LP | Sonet | SNTF764 | 1978 | £4 | £10 |
| Rags, Reels And Airs | LP | Bounty | BY6030 | 1967 | £30 | £60 |
| Rags, Reels And Airs | LP | Polydor | 236514 | 1967 | £30 | £60 |
| Smiddyburn | LP | Logo | 1029 | 1981 | £5 | £12 |
| Swarbrick | LP | Transatlantic ... | TRA337 | 1976 | £4 | £10 |
| Swarbrick 2 | LP | Transatlantic ... | TRA341 | 1977 | £4 | £10 |

## SWARBRICK, DAVE & SIMON NICOL
| | | | | | | |
|---|---|---|---|---|---|---|
| Close To The Wind | LP | Woodworm .... | WR006 | 1984 | £5 | £12 |
| Live At The White Bear | LP | White Bear | WBR001 | 1982 | £10 | £25 |

## SWARBRIGGS
| | | | | | | |
|---|---|---|---|---|---|---|
| That's What Friends Are For | 7" | MCA | MCA179 | 1975 | £1.50 | £4 |

## SWEAT, ROSALYN & THE PARAGONS
Blackbird Singing ....................................... LP ..... Horse ............... HRLP703 ............. 1973 £4 ........ £10 ..........................

## SWE-DANES
| | | | | | | | |
|---|---|---|---|---|---|---|---|
| Skandinavian Shuffles ................................... | LP | Warner Bros | 1388 | 1960 £8 | £20 | | German |
| Swe-Danes ............................................. | 7" EP | Warner Bros | SWEP2017 | 1961 £6 | £12 | | stereo |
| Swe-Danes ............................................. | 7" EP | Warner Bros | WEP6017 | 1961 £5 | £10 | | |

## SWEENEY'S MEN
| | | | | | | |
|---|---|---|---|---|---|---|
| Rattlin' & Roarin' Willy .......................... | LP | Transatlantic | TRA170 | 1968 £25 | £50 | |
| Sullivan's John ........................................ | 7" | Transatlantic | TRASP19 | 1968 £2 | £5 | |
| Sweeney's Men ........................................ | LP | Transatlantic | TRASAM37 | 1976 £5 | £12 | |
| Tracks Of Sweeney ................................. | LP | Transatlantic | TRA200 | 1969 £37.50 | £75 | |
| Tracks Of Sweeney ................................. | LP | Transatlantic | TRASAM40 | 1977 £5 | £12 | |
| Waxies Dargle ........................................ | 7" | Pye | 7N17459 | 1968 £2.50 | £6 | |

## SWEET
Beginning as a teeny-bopper group, the Sweet's music gradually became heavier as it progressed. At the same time, the group aligned itself with the glamour-rock movement, and as the only way for anyone to adopt the kind of extravagant image favoured by the likes of Gary Glitter was with his tongue placed firmly in his cheek, so the Sweet became high princes of camp, mocking themselves and their music even while playing it. In the end, of course, this rebounded on them, and the classy 'Love Is Like Oxygen' apart, the group failed to convince when they tried to become serious artists.

| | | | | | | |
|---|---|---|---|---|---|---|
| All You'll Ever Get From Me ................... | 7" | Parlophone | R5826 | 1970 £10 | £20 | |
| All You'll Ever Get From Me ................... | 7" | Parlophone | R5902 | 1971 £7.50 | £15 | |
| Ballroom Blitz ........................................ | 7" | RCA | RCA2403 | 1973 £5 | £10 | ... plays slow – matrix 2403-A-1E |
| Big Apple ............................................. | 7" | Polydor | POSP73 | 1979 £7.50 | £15 | |
| California Nights ................................... | 7" | Polydor | POSP5 | 1978 £10 | £20 | demo |
| Call Me ............................................... | 7" | Polydor | POSP36 | 1979 £1.50 | £4 | |
| Cut Above The Rest .............................. | LP | Capitol | SO11929 | 1979 £10 | £25 | ... US, different 'Hold Me' & cover |
| Cut Above The Rest .............................. | LP | Polydor | POLD5022 | 1979 £5 | £12 | |
| For AOR Radio Only ............................ | LP | Capitol | SPRO8371/73 | 1975 £15 | £30 | US promo |
| Fox On The Run .................................... | 7" | RCA | PE5226 | 1980 £5 | £10 | |
| Funny How Sweet Coco Can Be ............ | LP | RCA | SF8288 | 1971 £6 | £15 | |
| Get On The Line ................................... | 7" | Parlophone | R5848 | 1970 £20 | £40 | |
| Give The Lady Some Respect ................. | 7" | Polydor | POSP131 | 1980 £1.50 | £4 | |
| Identity Crisis ........................................ | LP | Polydor | 23111179 | 1982 £8 | £20 | |
| It's It's The Sweet Mix .......................... | 12" | Anagram | 12ANA28 | 1984 £2.50 | £6 | |
| Lollipop Man ........................................ | 7" | Parlophone | R5803 | 1969 £50 | £100 | |
| Off The Record ..................................... | LP | RCA | PL25072 | 1977 £4 | £10 | |
| Sixties Man/Tall Girls ........................... | 7" | Polydor | POSP160 | 1980 £7.50 | £15 | mispress |
| Slow Motion .......................................... | 7" | Fontana | TF958 | 1968 £330 | £500 | best auctioned |
| Stairway To The Stars ............................ | 7" | RCA | PB5046 | 1977 £2 | £5 | |
| Sweet Sixteen ....................................... | LP | Anagram | PGRAM16 | 1984 £10 | £25 | picture disc |
| Water's Edge ........................................ | LP | Polydor | POLS1021 | 1980 £8 | £20 | |

## SWEET CHARIOT
Sweet Chariot And Friends ...................... LP ... De Wolfe ....... ................... 1972 £37.50 ... £75 ...........................

## SWEET CHARLES
| | | | | | | |
|---|---|---|---|---|---|---|
| For Sweet People ................................... | LP | People | PE6603 | 1974 £10 | £25 | US |
| For Sweet People ................................... | LP | Urban | URBLP9 | 1988 £4 | £10 | |

## SWEET FEELING
All So Long Ago ...................................... 7" ...... Columbia ....... DB8195 ................. 1967 £15 ... £30 ...........................

## SWEET INSPIRATIONS
| | | | | | | |
|---|---|---|---|---|---|---|
| Let It Be Me .......................................... | 7" | Atlantic | 584132 | 1967 £1.50 | £4 | |
| Sweet Inspiration ................................... | 7" | Atlantic | 584167 | 1968 £1.50 | £4 | |
| Sweets For My Sweet .............................. | 7" | Atlantic | 584279 | 1969 £1.50 | £4 | |
| What The World Needs Now Is Love ....... | 7" | Atlantic | 584233 | 1968 £1.50 | £4 | |
| Why Am I Treated So Bad ...................... | 7" | Atlantic | 584117 | 1967 £1.50 | £4 | |

## SWEET MARIE
Stuck In Paradise ...................................... LP ... Yardbird ...... YDBS771 ......... 1972 £8 ...... £20 ............ US

## SWEET PAIN
| | | | | | | |
|---|---|---|---|---|---|---|
| Sweet Pain ............................................ | LP | Mercury | SMCL20146 | 1969 £15 | £30 | |
| Timber Gibbs ........................................ | 7" | United Artists | UP35268 | 1971 £1.50 | £4 | |

## SWEET PANTS
Fat Peter Presents .................................... LP ...... private ........... LP1141 ................. 1969 £100 ..... £200 ............ US

## SWEET PLUM
| | | | | | | |
|---|---|---|---|---|---|---|
| Lazy Day ............................................... | 7" | Middle Earth | MDS103 | 1969 £2.50 | £6 | |
| Set The Wheels In Motion ...................... | 7" | Middle Earth | MDS105 | 1969 £2.50 | £6 | |

## SWEET SAVAGE
Killing Time ............................................ 7" ...... Sweet Savage ... 1980 .............. 1981 £5 ......... £10 ...........................

## SWEET SLAG
| | | | | | |
|---|---|---|---|---|---|
| Tracking With Close Ups ........................ | LP | XTRA | XTRA1112 | 1971 £10 | £25 |
| Tracking With Close-Ups ........................ | LP | President | PTLS1042 | 1971 £10 | £25 |

## SWEET SMOKE
Just A Poke .................................................... LP ...... Catfish ............ 5C05424311 ........... 1972 £4 ......... £10 .................... Dutch

## SWEET THURSDAY
Sweet Thursday ............................................... LP ...... CBS ............... 65573 ................. 1973 £4 ........ £10 ...........................
Sweet Thursday ............................................... LP ...... Polydor .......... 2310051 .......... 1969 £6 ........ £15 ...........................

## SWEET TOOTHE
Testing ............................................................ LP ...... Dominion ...... NR7360 ................ 1971 £50 ....... £100 ................... US

## SWEETING, HARRY
From Jamaica With Love ......................... 7" ...... Coxsone ........ CS7012 .............. 1967 £5 .......... £10 ...........................

## SWEGAS
Child Of Light ........................................ LP ...... Trend ............. 6480002 ............... 1971 £8 ........ £20 ...........................

## SWELL MAPS
Read About Seymour ............................. 7" ...... Rather ........... GEAR1 ............... 1977 £2.50 ....... £6 ...........................
Trip to Marineville .................................. LP ...... Big Rather ...... TROY1 ............... 1979 £4 ........ £10 ... with 7" (GEAR5)
What A Nice Way To Turn Seventeen        7" ...... Rather ........... GEAR17 ............... 1984 £2.50 ....... £6 ...... with other artists
   No. 2 .........................................................
Whatever Happens Next ......................... LP ...... Rough Trade... ROUGH21 ........... 1981 £5 .......... £12 .................... double

## SWERVEDRIVER
Rave Down EP ...................................... CD-s .. Creation ........ CRESCD088 ........ 1990 £2 .......... £5 ...........................
Sandblasted EP ...................................... CD-s .. Creation ........ CRESCD102 ........ 1991 £2 .......... £5 ...........................
Swervedriver EP .................................... CD-s .. Creation ........ CRESCD79 .......... 1990 £2 .......... £5 ...........................

## SWIFT, T. & THE ELECTRIC BAG
Are You Experienced? ........................... LP ...... Custom .......... 1115 .................. 1967 £15 ........ £30 .................... US

## SWIFT, TUFTY
How To Make A Bakewell Tart ............... LP ...... Free Reed ...... FRR017 .......... 1977 £6 ........ £15 ...........................
You'll Never Die For Love ...................... LP ...... Shark ............. 04 .................. 1985 £4 ........ £10 ...........................

## SWINDLEFOLK
Swindled .............................................. LP ...... Ace Of Clubs .. ACL1273 ............... 1970 £10 ........ £25 ...........................

## SWINGERS
Love Makes The World Go Round ........... 7" ...... Vogue ............ V9158 ............... 1960 £2 .......... £5 ...........................

## SWINGING BLUE JEANS
Blue Jeans A' Swinging ......................... LP ...... HMV ............ CLP1802/CSD1570 1964 £20 ........ £40 ...........................
Brand New And Faded ........................... LP ...... Dart .............. BULL1001 .......... 1974 £4 ........ £10 ...........................
Crazy 'Bout My Baby ............................ 7" ...... HMV ............ POP1477 ........... 1965 £1.50 ........ £4 ...........................
Do You Know ...................................... 7" ...... HMV ............ POP1206 ........... 1963 £2.50 ........ £6 ...........................
Don't Go Out Into The Rain ................. 7" ...... HMV ............ POP1605 ........... 1967 £1.50 ........ £4 ...........................
Don't Make Me Over ........................... 7" ...... HMV ............ POP1501 ........... 1966 £1.50 ........ £4 ...........................
Good Golly Miss Molly ......................... 7" EP . Pathe ............ EGF736 ........... 1964 £15 ........ £30 .................... French
Good Golly Miss Molly ......................... 7" ...... HMV ............ POP1273 ........... 1964 £1.50 ........ £4 ...........................
Hippy Hippy Shake .............................. LP ...... Imperial ......... LP9261/12261 .... 1964 £25 ........ £50 .................... US
Hippy Hippy Shake .............................. CD-s .. EMI .............. CDEM83 ............ 1989 £2 .......... £5 ...........................
Hippy Hippy Shake .............................. 7" EP . Pathe ............ EGF707 ........... 1963 £15 ........ £30 .................... French
Hippy Hippy Shake .............................. 7" ...... HMV ............ POP1242 ........... 1963 £1.50 ........ £4 ...........................
It Isn't There ...................................... 7" ...... HMV ............ POP1375 ........... 1964 £1.50 ........ £4 ...........................
It's So Right ........................................ 7" EP . Pathe ............ EGF782 ........... 1964 £15 ........ £30 .................... French
It's Too Late Now ................................ 7" ...... HMV ............ POP1170 ........... 1963 £1.50 ........ £4 ...........................
Make Me Know You're Mine ................. 7" ...... HMV ............ POP1409 ........... 1965 £1.50 ........ £4 ...........................
Promise You'll Tell Her ........................ 7" ...... HMV ............ POP1327 ........... 1964 £1.50 ........ £4 ...........................
Rumours, Gossip, Words Untrue ........... 7" EP . Pathe ............ EGF950 ........... 1966 £15 ........ £30 .................... French
Rumours, Gossip, Words Untrue ........... 7" ...... HMV ............ POP1564 ........... 1966 £1.50 ........ £4 ...........................
Sandy ................................................. 7" ...... HMV ............ POP1533 ........... 1966 £1.50 ........ £4 ...........................
Shake With The Swinging Blue Jeans ...... 7" EP . HMV ............ 7EG8850 ........... 1964 £7.50 ........ £15 ...........................
Swinging Blue Jeans .............................. LP ...... MFP .............. MFP1163 .......... 1967 £4 ........ £10 ...........................
Tremblin' ............................................ 7" ...... HMV ............ POP1596 ........... 1967 £1.50 ........ £4 ...........................
Tutti Frutti .......................................... LP ...... Regal ............. SREG1073 ......... 1964 £15 ........ £30 .................... export
You're No Good ................................... 7" ...... HMV ............ POP1304 ........... 1964 £1.50 ........ £4 ...........................
You're No Good Miss Molly .................. 7" EP . HMV ............ 7EG8868 ........... 1964 £10 ........ £20 ...........................

## SWINGING MEDALLIONS
Double Shot ........................................ LP ...... Smash ............ MGS2/SRS67083 ... 1966 £8 .......... £20 .................... US
She Drives Me Out Of My Mind ............. 7" ...... Philips............ BF1515 ............. 1966 £2 .......... £5 ...........................

## SWINGING SWEDES
Swinging Swedes .................................. LP ...... Telefunken ...... LGX66050 ............ 1957 £8 ......... £20 ...........................

## SWINGTONES
Geraldine ............................................ 7" ...... HMV ............ POP471 .............. 1958 £50 ....... £100 ...........................

## SYDNEY ALL STARS
Return Of Batman ................................ 7" ...... Bullet ............ BU436 ............... 1970 £1.50 ........ £4 ...........................

## SYKES, ERIC & HATTIE JACQUES
Eric, Hattie And Things ........................ LP ...... Decca ............. LK4507 .............. 1963 £4 .......... £10 ...........................

## SYKES, JOHN
Please Don't Leave Me .......................... 7" ...... MCA .............. MCA792 ........... 1982 £12.50 .... £25 ...........................

## SYKES, ROOSEVELT

| Title | Format | Label | Cat. No. | Year | | | Notes |
|---|---|---|---|---|---|---|---|
| Back To The Blues | 7" EP | Delmark | DJB2 | 1966 | £7.50 | £15 | |
| Big Man Of The Blues | LP | Encore | ENC183 | 1959 | £5 | £12 | |
| Blues From Bar Rooms | LP | 77 | LEU1250 | 1967 | £5 | £12 | |
| Face To Face With The Blues | LP | Columbia | 33SX1343 | 1961 | £8 | £20 | |
| Hard Drivin' Blues | LP | Delmark | DS607 | 1970 | £5 | £12 | |
| Honeydripper | LP | Columbia | 33SX1422 | 1962 | £8 | £20 | |
| Mr. Sykes Blues 1929–1932 | LP | Riverside | RLP8819 | 1967 | £6 | £15 | |
| Return Of Roosevelt Sykes | LP | Bluesville | BV1006 | 1960 | £10 | £25 | US |
| Sings The Blues | LP | Ember | EMB3391 | 196– | £4 | £10 | |
| Too Hot To Hold | 7" | Vogue | V2389 | 1956 | £20 | £40 | |
| Walking This Boogie | 7" | Vogue | V2393 | 1956 | £25 | £50 | |

## SYKO & THE CARIBS

| Title | Format | Label | Cat. No. | Year | | | |
|---|---|---|---|---|---|---|---|
| Do The Dog | 7" | Blue Beat | BB213 | 1964 | £6 | £12 | |
| Sugar Baby | 7" | Blue Beat | BB223 | 1964 | £6 | £12 | |

## SYLTE SISTERS

| Title | Format | Label | Cat. No. | Year | | | |
|---|---|---|---|---|---|---|---|
| Summer Magic | 7" | London | HLU9753 | 1963 | £1.50 | £4 | |

## SYLVESTER, C.

| Title | Format | Label | Cat. No. | Year | | | |
|---|---|---|---|---|---|---|---|
| Going South | 7" | Blue Beat | BB206 | 1964 | £6 | £12 | |

## SYLVIA

| Title | Format | Label | Cat. No. | Year | | | |
|---|---|---|---|---|---|---|---|
| I Can't Help It | 7" | Soul City | SC103 | 1968 | £2 | £5 | |

## SYLVIAN, DAVID

| Title | Format | Label | Cat. No. | Year | | | Notes |
|---|---|---|---|---|---|---|---|
| Damage | CD | Virgin | DAMAGE1 | 1994 | £8 | £20 | gold disc, slip case, booklet, with Robert Fripp |
| Forbidden Colours | CD-s | Virgin | CDT18 | 1988 | £2 | £5 | 3" single, with Ryuichi Sakamoto |
| God's Monkey, A Retrospective | CD | Virgin | DPRO12805 | 1994 | £8 | £20 | US promo, with Robert Fripp |
| Heartbeat | CD-s | Virgin | VUSDG57 | 1992 | £2 | £5 | boxed with cards, with Ryuichi Sakamoto |
| Pop Song | CD-s | Virgin | VSCD1211 | 1989 | £2 | £5 | 2 versions |
| Red Guitar | 7" | Virgin | VSY633 | 1984 | £1.50 | £4 | picture disc |
| Secrets Of The Beehive | CD | Virgin | CDV2471 | 1987 | £5 | £12 | |
| Taking The Veil | 7" | Virgin | VSY815 | 1986 | £1.50 | £4 | square picture disc |
| Weatherbox | CD-s | Virgin | DSCD1 | 1989 | £20 | £40 | 5 CD boxed set |
| Words With The Shaman | CD-s | Virgin | CDT23 | 1988 | £2 | £5 | 3" single |

## SYMARIP

| Title | Format | Label | Cat. No. | Year | | | |
|---|---|---|---|---|---|---|---|
| Skinhead Moon Stomp | LP | Trojan | TBL102 | 1968 | £8 | £20 | |
| Skinhead Moon Stomp | 7" | Treasure Isle | TI7050 | 1969 | £1.50 | £4 | |

## SYMBOLS

| Title | Format | Label | Cat. No. | Year | | | |
|---|---|---|---|---|---|---|---|
| Best Part Of The Symbols | LP | President | PTL1018 | 1968 | £6 | £15 | |
| Canadian Sunset | 7" | President | PT113 | 1968 | £1.50 | £4 | |
| One Fine Girl | 7" | Columbia | DB7459 | 1965 | £1.50 | £4 | |
| You're My Girl | 7" | Columbia | DB7664 | 1965 | £1.50 | £4 | |

## SYMON & PI

| Title | Format | Label | Cat. No. | Year | | | |
|---|---|---|---|---|---|---|---|
| Got To See The Sunrise | 7" | Parlophone | R5719 | 1968 | £2 | £5 | |
| Sha La La La Lee | 7" | Parlophone | R5662 | 1968 | £2 | £5 | |

## SYN

The Syndicats eventually metamorphosed into the Syn, none of whose members had been in the original Syndicats line-up. The Yes connection continued, however, for the bass player and guitarist on the Syn's psychedelic singles were Chris Squire and Peter Banks.

| Title | Format | Label | Cat. No. | Year | | | |
|---|---|---|---|---|---|---|---|
| Created By Clive | 7" | Deram | DM130 | 1967 | £30 | £60 | |
| Flowerman | 7" | Deram | DM145 | 1967 | £30 | £60 | |

## SYNANTHESIA

| Title | Format | Label | Cat. No. | Year | | | |
|---|---|---|---|---|---|---|---|
| Synanthesia | LP | RCA | SF8058 | 1969 | £30 | £60 | |

## SYNDICATE OF SOUND

| Title | Format | Label | Cat. No. | Year | | | Notes |
|---|---|---|---|---|---|---|---|
| Little Girl | LP | Stateside | (S)SL10185 | 1966 | £20 | £40 | |
| Little Girl | 7" EP | Columbia | ESRF1794 | 1966 | £15 | £30 | French |
| Little Girl | 7" | Stateside | SS523 | 1966 | £7.50 | £15 | |
| Rumours | 7" | Stateside | SS538 | 1966 | £4 | £8 | |

## SYNDICATS

The singles made by the Syndicats are collectable on three counts. They are good examples of mid-sixties British R&B; they were produced by legendary producer Joe Meek; and the group's guitarist was Steve Howe, of later Yes fame.

| Title | Format | Label | Cat. No. | Year | | | Notes |
|---|---|---|---|---|---|---|---|
| Crawdaddy Simone | 7" | Columbia | DB7686 | 1965 | £250 | £400 | best auctioned |
| Howlin' For My Baby | 7" | Columbia | DB7441 | 1965 | £37.50 | £75 | |
| Maybelline | 7" | Columbia | DB7238 | 1964 | £37.50 | £75 | |

## SYNERGY

| Title | Format | Label | Cat. No. | Year | | | Notes |
|---|---|---|---|---|---|---|---|
| Audion | LP | Logo | LOGO1033 | 1982 | £5 | £12 | |
| Chords | LP | Passport | PB6000 | 1979 | £5 | £12 | US |
| Electronic Realizations | LP | Sire | 9299752 | 1976 | £6 | £15 | |
| Games | LP | Passport | PB6003 | 1979 | £5 | £12 | US |

| | | | | | | | |
|---|---|---|---|---|---|---|---|
| Jupiter Menace | LP | Shanghai | HAI105 | 1984 | £4 | £10 | |
| Semi-Conductor | LP | Passport | PB11002 | 1984 | £4 | £10 | *US* |
| Sequencer | LP | Sire | 9103326 | 1976 | £6 | £15 | |

## SYRINX

| | | | | | | | |
|---|---|---|---|---|---|---|---|
| Long Lost Relatives | LP | True North | TN5 | 1971 | £8 | £20 | *Canadian* |
| Syrinx | LP | True North | TN2 | 1970 | £8 | £20 | *Canadian* |

## SYSTEM

| | | | | | | | |
|---|---|---|---|---|---|---|---|
| Other Side Of Time | LP | private | | 1977 | £50 | £100 | |

## SYSTEM 7

| | | | | | | | |
|---|---|---|---|---|---|---|---|
| Miracle | 12" | Ten | | 1990 | £4 | £10 | *clear vinyl* |

## SYSTEME CRAPOUTCHIK

| | | | | | | | |
|---|---|---|---|---|---|---|---|
| Aussi loin que je me souvienne | LP | Flamophone | FL3301 | 1969 | £100 | £200 | *French* |
| Flop | LP | Flamophone | FL3302 | 1971 | £100 | £200 | *French double* |

## SZABO, GABOR

| | | | | | | | |
|---|---|---|---|---|---|---|---|
| Sorcerer | LP | Impulse | MIPL/SIPL506 | 1968 | £5 | £12 | |

# T

## T2
It'll All Work Out In Boomland ................. LP ...... Decca ............. SKL5050 ............... 1970 £25 ......... £50 ...................................

## TABLETOPPERS
Rocking Mountain Dew .......................... 7" ...... Starlite ........... ST45069 .............. 1962 £4 ........... £8 ...................................

## TABOR, CHARLIE
Blue Atlantic ....................................... 7" ...... Island ............. WI061 ................ 1963 £2 ............ £5 ...................................

## TABOR, JUNE
Airs And Graces ................................... LP ...... Topic ............ 12TS298 .............. 1976 £4 .......... £10 ..................................
Ashes And Diamonds .......................... LP ...... Topic ............ 12TS360 .............. 1977 £4 .......... £10 ..................................

## TAD & THE SMALL FRY
Checkered Continental Pants ................... 7" ...... London ........... HLU9542 ............. 1962 £1.50 ........ £4 ...............................

## TAGES
Contrast ............................................. LP ...... Parlophone ..... PMCS313 ............. 1967 £15 ......... £30 ............... Swedish
Crazy 'Bout My Baby .......................... 7" ...... Columbia ....... DB8019 .............. 1966 £1.50 ........ £4 ...................................
Extra Extra ........................................ LP ...... Platina .............................. 1966 £15 ......... £30 ............... Swedish
In My Dreams ..................................... 7" EP . Impact ............ 200006 ............... 1967 £10 ......... £20 ................ French
Lilac Years ........................................ LP ...... Fontana .............................. 1969 £10 ......... £25 ............... Swedish
So Many Girls ..................................... 7" ...... HMV .............. POP1515 ............. 1966 £10 ......... £20 ...............................
Studio ............................................... LP ...... Parlophone ........................... 1967 £15 ......... £30 ............... Swedish
Tages ................................................ LP ...... Platina .............................. 1965 £15 ......... £30 ............... Swedish
There's A Blind Man Playing ................. 7" ...... Parlophone ..... R5702 ............... 1968 £1.50 ........ £4 ...................................
Treat Me Like A Lady .......................... 7" ...... Parlophone ..... R5640 ............... 1967 £1.50 ........ £4 ...................................
Two ................................................... LP ...... Platina .............................. 1966 £15 ......... £30 ............... Swedish

## TAGMEMICS
Chimneys ........................................... 7" ...... Index ............. 003 ..................... 1980 £4 ............ £8 ...................................

## TAIEB, JACQUELINE
Tonight I'm Going Home ....................... 7" ...... Fontana ........... TF952 ................ 1968 £15 ......... £30 ...................................

## TAITT, LYN
Dial 609 ............................................ 7" ...... Ska Beat ......... JB264 ................. 1967 £5 .......... £10 ... Tommy McCook B
side
El Casino Royale ................................. 7" ...... Amalgamated ... AMG810 ............. 1968 £4 ............ £8 ...................................
Glad Sounds ....................................... LP ...... Big Shot ......... BBTL4002 ........... 1968 £25 ......... £50 ..................................
I Don't Want To Make You Cry ............. 7" ...... Island ............. WI3075 .............. 1967 £5 .......... £10 ...............................
Napoleon Solo .................................... 7" ...... Island ............. WI3139 .............. 1968 £5 .......... £10 ...............................
Something Stupid ................................ 7" ...... Island ............. WI3066 .............. 1967 £5 .......... £10 ...............................
Soul Food .......................................... 7" ...... Pama .............. PM723 ............... 1968 £2.50 ........ £6 ...............................
Sounds Rock Steady ............................ LP ...... Island ............. ILP969 ............... 1968 £30 ......... £60 ............... pink label
Spanish Eyes ...................................... 7" ...... Doctor Bird ..... DB1047 .............. 1966 £5 .......... £10 ........... with Tommy
McCook, Stranger
Cole B side
Vilmas Jump Up .................................. 7" ...... Doctor Bird ..... DB1006 .............. 1966 £5 .......... £10 .... Glen Miller B side

## TAKE THAT
Confounding the expectations of many observers (including those of the author of this *Price Guide*), Take That managed to maintain a high level of popularity for far longer than the couple of years that is the normal lot of groups of their type (predecessors the Bay City Rollers and New Kids on the Block were enormous in their day, but ceased to sell records as soon as their teenage fans grew old enough to want something different). It seems likely, therefore, that the collectors' items listed here will retain their values for quite a while to come.

Could It Be Magic ............................... CD-s .. RCA ............. 74321123132 ......... 1992 £2 ........... £5 ...................................
Could It Be Magic ............................... 12" ..... RCA ............. 743211123131 ........ 1992 £10 ......... £20 ............ poster sleeve
Do What U Like ................................. cass-s .. Dance UK ...... CADUK2 ............. 1991 £6 .......... £15 ...................................
Do What U Like ................................. 7" ...... Dance UK ...... DUK2 ................. 1991 £15 ......... £30 ...................................
Do What U Like ................................. 12" ..... Dance UK ...... 12DUK2 .............. 1991 £20 ......... £40 ...................................
I Found Heaven ................................... CD-s .. RCA ............. 74321108132 ......... 1992 £2 ........... £5 ...................................
I Found Heaven ................................... 7" ...... RCA ............. 74321108137B ........ 1992 £7.50 ....... £15 ........... picture disc
I Found Heaven ................................... 7" ...... RCA ............. 74321108147 ......... 1992 £2.50 ....... £6 ...................................
It Only Takes A Minute ........................ CD-s .. RCA ............. 74321101002 ......... 1992 £10 ......... £20 ...................................
It Only Takes A Minute ........................ 7" ...... RCA ............. 74321101007 ......... 1992 £2.50 ....... £6 ...................................
It Only Takes A Minute ........................ 7" ...... RCA ............. 74321101007 ......... 1992 £12.50 ...... £25 frame pack with one of
2 sets of prints
Million Love Songs .............................. CD-s .. RCA ............. 74321116002 ......... 1992 £6 .......... £15 ...................................
Once You've Tasted Love ...................... cass-s .. RCA ............. PK45257 ............. 1992 £4 .......... £10 ............ with stencil
Once You've Tasted Love ...................... 7" ...... RCA ............. PB45257 ............. 1992 £4 ............ £8 ...................................
Once You've Tasted Love ...................... 7" ...... RCA ............. PB45265 ............. 1992 £10 ......... £20 ......... with calendar

| Title | Format | Label | Catalogue | Year | | | Notes |
|---|---|---|---|---|---|---|---|
| Once You've Tasted Love | 12" | RCA | PT45258 | 1992 | £10 | £25 | picture disc |
| Pray | CD-s | RCA | 74321154502 | 1993 | £4 | £10 | 2 versions |
| Promises | cass-s | RCA | PK45085 | 1991 | £3 | £8 | |
| Promises | 7" | RCA | PB45085 | 1991 | £2.50 | £6 | |
| Promises | 7" | RCA | PB45085P | 1991 | £6 | £15 | poster picture sleeve |
| Promises | 12" | RCA | PT45085 | 1991 | £6 | £15 | |
| Take That Special | CD | Our Price | no number | 1995 | £50 | £100 | promo |
| Why Can't I Wake Up With You | CD-s | RCA | 74321133102 | 1993 | £2 | £5 | |
| Yellow Tape | cass | private | | 1990 | £180 | £300 | |

## TAKERS
| Title | Format | Label | Catalogue | Year | | | Notes |
|---|---|---|---|---|---|---|---|
| If You Don't Come Back | 7" | Pye | 7N15690 | 1964 | £4 | £8 | |

## TALBOT BROTHERS
| Title | Format | Label | Catalogue | Year | | | Notes |
|---|---|---|---|---|---|---|---|
| Bloodshot Eyes | 7" | Melodisc | 1507 | 1959 | £2 | £5 | |
| Bloodshot Eyes | 7" | Melodisc | CAL20 | 1964 | £1.50 | £4 | |

## TALENT, ZIGGY
| Title | Format | Label | Catalogue | Year | | | Notes |
|---|---|---|---|---|---|---|---|
| Cheek To Cheek | 7" | Brunswick | 05506 | 1955 | £1.50 | £4 | |

## TALES OF JUSTINE
Tim Rice and Andrew Lloyd-Webber made their first venture into pop music with Tales of Justine.

| Title | Format | Label | Catalogue | Year | | | Notes |
|---|---|---|---|---|---|---|---|
| Albert | 7" | HMV | POP1614 | 1967 | £7.50 | £15 | |
| Albert | 7" | HMV | POP1614 | 1967 | £12.50 | £25 | picture sleeve |

## TALISMAN
| Title | Format | Label | Catalogue | Year | | | Notes |
|---|---|---|---|---|---|---|---|
| Primrose Dreams | LP | Argo | ZFB33 | 1972 | £4 | £10 | |
| Stepping Stones | LP | Argo | ZDA161 | 1973 | £4 | £10 | |

## TALISMEN
| Title | Format | Label | Catalogue | Year | | | Notes |
|---|---|---|---|---|---|---|---|
| Masters Of War | 7" | Stateside | SS408 | 1965 | £10 | £20 | |
| Talismen's Style | LP | RCA | S15 | 1965 | £50 | £100 | Italian |

## TALIX
| Title | Format | Label | Catalogue | Year | | | Notes |
|---|---|---|---|---|---|---|---|
| Spuren | LP | Vogue | LDVS17237 | 1971 | £8 | £20 | German |

## TALK TALK
| Title | Format | Label | Catalogue | Year | | | Notes |
|---|---|---|---|---|---|---|---|
| I Believe In You | CD-s | Parlophone | CDR6189 | 1988 | £2 | £5 | |
| It's My Life | CD-s | Parlophone | CDR6254 | 1990 | £2 | £5 | |
| Laughing Stock | CD | Verve | 8477172 | 1991 | £25 | £50 | promo in wooden box with stationery items |
| Life's What You Make It | CD-s | Parlophone | CDR6264 | 1990 | £2 | £5 | |
| Living In Another World | 7" | EMI | EMIP5551 | 1986 | £1.50 | £4 | shaped picture disc |
| Such A Shame | CD-s | Parlophone | CDR6276 | 1990 | £2 | £5 | |
| Talk Talk | 7" | EMI | EMIP5352 | 1982 | £1.50 | £4 | picture disc |
| Talk Talk Demos | 7" | EMI | EMID5433 | 1984 | £4 | £8 | double |

## TALKING HEADS
| Title | Format | Label | Catalogue | Year | | | Notes |
|---|---|---|---|---|---|---|---|
| Blind | CD-s | EMI | CDEM68 | 1988 | £2 | £5 | |
| Fear Of Music | LP | Sire | K56707 | 1979 | £4 | £10 | with 'Psycho Killer' 7 |
| Live At The Roxy | LP | Warner Bros | WBMS104 | 1979 | £10 | £25 | promo |
| Love Goes To Building On Fire | 7" | Sire | 6078604 | 1977 | £1.50 | £4 | picture sleeve |
| Naked | CD | Sire | | 1988 | £10 | £25 | US promo with on-screen graphics |
| Nothing But Flowers | CD-s | EMI | CDEM53 | 1988 | £2 | £5 | |
| Psycho Killer | 12" | Sire | 6078610 | 1977 | £2.50 | £6 | |
| Pulled Up | 7" | Sire | 6078620 | 1978 | £2 | £5 | picture sleeve |
| Radio Head | CD-s | EMI | CDEM1 | 1987 | £2 | £5 | |
| Road To Nowhere | 7" | EMI | EMIP5530 | 1985 | £1.50 | £4 | picture disc |
| Speaking In Tongues | LP | EMI | 9238831 | 1983 | £4 | £10 | clear vinyl |
| Storytelling Giant | CD | Polygram | 0805061 | 1988 | £6 | £15 | CD video |
| Take Me To The River | 7" | Sire | SIR4004 | 1979 | £2.50 | £6 | double |

## TALL, TOM
| Title | Format | Label | Catalogue | Year | | | Notes |
|---|---|---|---|---|---|---|---|
| Are You Mine | 7" | London | HL8150 | 1955 | £7.50 | £15 | with Ginny Wright |
| Country Songs Vol. 2 | 7" EP | London | REU1035 | 1955 | £12.50 | £25 | with Ginny Wright |
| Don't You Know | 7" | London | HLU8429 | 1957 | £7.50 | £15 | with Ruckus Taylor |
| Give Me A Chance | 7" | London | HLU8216 | 1955 | £10 | £20 | |
| Underway | 7" | London | HLU8231 | 1956 | £10 | £20 | |

## TALMY/STONE BAND
| Title | Format | Label | Catalogue | Year | | | Notes |
|---|---|---|---|---|---|---|---|
| Roses Are Red & Other Hits | LP | Ace Of Clubs | ACL1134 | 1962 | £4 | £10 | |

## TALULAH GOSH
| Title | Format | Label | Catalogue | Year | | | Notes |
|---|---|---|---|---|---|---|---|
| Who Needs The Bloody Cartel Anyway | 7" | Sha La La | 002 | 1986 | £1.50 | £4 | flexi |

## TAM, TIM & THE TURN ONS
| Title | Format | Label | Catalogue | Year | | | Notes |
|---|---|---|---|---|---|---|---|
| Wait A Minute | 7" | Island | WIP6007 | 1967 | £5 | £10 | |

## TAMALONE
| Title | Format | Label | Catalogue | Year | | | Notes |
|---|---|---|---|---|---|---|---|
| New Acres | LP | Crossroad | | 1979 | £10 | £25 | Dutch |

## TAMLIN, JAMES
| Title | Format | Label | Catalogue | Year | | | Notes |
|---|---|---|---|---|---|---|---|
| Is There Time | 7" | Columbia | DB7438 | 1965 | £2.50 | £6 | |

## TAMPA RED

| | | | | | | | |
|---|---|---|---|---|---|---|---|
| Don't Jive With Me | LP | Bluesville | BV1043 | 1962 | £6 | £15 | US |
| Don't Tampa With The Blues | LP | Bluesville | BV1030 | 1961 | £6 | £15 | US |
| R&B Vol. 3 | 7" EP | RCA | RCX7160 | 1964 | £7.50 | £15 | |

## TAMPA RED & GEORGIA TOM

| | | | | | | |
|---|---|---|---|---|---|---|
| Male Blues Vol. 2 | 7" EP | Collector | JEL3 | 1959 | £2 | £5 |

## TAMS

| | | | | | | | |
|---|---|---|---|---|---|---|---|
| Be Young, Be Foolish, Be Happy | LP | Stateside | SSL10304 | 1970 | £4 | £10 | |
| Be Young, Be Foolish, Be Happy | 7" | Stateside | SS2123 | 1969 | £2 | £5 | |
| Concrete Jungle | 7" | HMV | POP1464 | 1965 | £2.50 | £6 | |
| Hey Girl Don't Bother Me | LP | ABC | (S)499 | 1964 | £6 | £15 | US |
| Hey Girl Don't Bother Me | 7" | HMV | POP1331 | 1964 | £10 | £20 | |
| It's All Right | 7" | HMV | POP1298 | 1964 | £2 | £5 | |
| Little More Soul | LP | Stateside | (S)SL10258 | 1968 | £4 | £10 | |
| Presenting The Tams | LP | ABC | (S)481 | 1964 | £6 | £15 | US |
| Untie Me | 7" | Stateside | SS146 | 1963 | £1.50 | £4 | |
| What Kind Of Fool | 7" | HMV | POP1254 | 1963 | £4 | £8 | |

## TANDEM

| | | | | | | |
|---|---|---|---|---|---|---|
| Song Of My Life | 7" | Chapter One | CH102 | 1968 | £1.50 | £4 |

## TANDY, SHARON

The reissue specialists, who have turned their attention on to some of the most obscure sixties artists, have nevertheless managed to ignore Sharon Tandy. Her numerous near-miss singles contain many impressive blue-eyed soul performances, which are made even more compelling in some cases by the fiery support of cult favourites, the Fleur De Lys. Tracks like 'Hold On' and 'Our Day Will Come' emerge as rather fine and distinctive pieces of psychedelic soul.

| | | | | | | |
|---|---|---|---|---|---|---|
| Fool On The Hill | 7" | Atlantic | 584166 | 1968 | £4 | £8 |
| Gotta Get Enough Time | 7" | Atlantic | 584242 | 1969 | £2 | £5 |
| Hold On | 7" | Atlantic | 584219 | 1968 | £5 | £10 |
| I've Found Love | 7" | Pye | 7N15939 | 1965 | £1.50 | £4 |
| Love Is Not A Simple Affair | 7" | Atlantic | 584181 | 1968 | £2 | £5 |
| Love Makes The World Go Round | 7" | Mercury | MF898 | 1965 | £2 | £5 |
| Now That You've Gone | 7" | Pye | 7N15806 | 1965 | £1.50 | £4 |
| Our Day Will Come | 7" | Atlantic | 584137 | 1967 | £4 | £8 |
| Stay With Me | 7" | Atlantic | 584124 | 1967 | £6 | £12 |
| Toe-Hold | 7" | Atlantic | 584098 | 1967 | £2.50 | £6 |
| Way She Looks At You | 7" | Atlantic | 584214 | 1968 | £2 | £5 |
| You Gotta Believe It | 7" | Atlantic | 584194 | 1968 | £2 | £5 |

## TANEGA, NORMA

| | | | | | | |
|---|---|---|---|---|---|---|
| Walking My Cat Named Dog | LP | Stateside | (S)SL10182 | 1966 | £4 | £10 |

## TANGERINE DREAM

Perhaps it has something to do with the German character that the rock musicians in that country seized on the newly developed synthesizer, not as a device for creating previously unheard sounds, but as a means for performing mathematically precise patterns of notes. Such is the main approach of Tangerine Dream, as it is of Klaus Schulze and Kraftwerk. 'Ultima Thule' is a particularly rare non-album track, and is atypical in style.

| | | | | | | | |
|---|---|---|---|---|---|---|---|
| Alpha Centauri | LP | Ohr | OMM556012 | 1971 | £4 | £10 | German |
| Alpha Centauri | CD | Jive | CTANG5 | 1988 | £5 | £12 | |
| Atem | LP | Ohr | OMM556031 | 1973 | £6 | £15 | German |
| Atem | CD | Jive | CTANG2 | 1988 | £5 | £12 | |
| Betrayal | 7" | MCA | PSR413 | 1977 | £5 | £10 | promo |
| Das Mädchen Auf Der Treppe | 12" | Virgin | 60065213 | 1982 | £2.50 | £6 | German |
| Electronic Meditation | LP | Ohr | OMM556004 | 1971 | £8 | £20 | German |
| Electronic Meditation | LP | Ohr | OMM56004 | 1970 | £10 | £25 | German |
| Electronic Meditation | CD | Jive | CTANG4 | 1988 | £5 | £12 | |
| Flashpoint | CD | Heavy Metal | HMXD29 | 1985 | £20 | £40 | non-faulty CD! |
| Green Desert | CD | Jive | CTANG1 | 1987 | £5 | £12 | |
| Le Parc | CD | Jive | CHIP26 | 1987 | £5 | £12 | UK pressing |
| Live Miles | CD | Jive | CHIP62 | 1988 | £5 | £12 | |
| Phaedra | 7" | Virgin | PR214 | 1974 | £2.50 | £6 | promo |
| Poland | CD | Jive | CHIP22 | 1988 | £5 | £12 | |
| Poland – The Warsaw Concert | LP | Jive Electro | HIPX22 | 1984 | £6 | £15 | double picture disc |
| Stratosfear | 7" | Virgin | VDJ17 | 1976 | £2.50 | £6 | promo |
| Tangerine Dream '70–'80 | LP | Virgin | VBOX2 | 1980 | £10 | £25 | 4 LP boxed set |
| Thief | LP | Elektra | SE521 | 1981 | £4 | £10 | US promo picture disc |
| Tyger | CD | Jive | CHIP47 | 1987 | £5 | £12 | |
| Ultima Thule | 7" | Ohr | OSS7006 | 1972 | £25 | £50 | German |
| Underwater Sunlight | CD | Jive | CHIP40 | 1986 | £5 | £12 | |
| Warsaw In The Sun | 7" | Jive Electro | JIVEP74 | 1984 | £2.50 | £6 | picture disc |
| Zeit | LP | Ohr | OMM2/56021 | 1972 | £8 | £20 | German double |
| Zeit | CD | Jive | CTANG3 | 1987 | £5 | £12 | |

## TANGERINE PEEL

| | | | | | | | |
|---|---|---|---|---|---|---|---|
| Every Christian Lion-Hearted Man Will Show You | 7" | United Artists | UP1193 | 1967 | £4 | £8 | |
| Soft Delights | LP | RCA | LSA3002 | 1970 | £6 | £15 | US |

## TANGERINE ZOO

| | | | | | | | |
|---|---|---|---|---|---|---|---|
| Outside Looking In | LP | Mainstream | S6116 | 1968 | £30 | £60 | US |
| Tangerine Zoo | LP | Mainstream | S6107 | 1968 | £15 | £30 | US |

## TANNAHILL WEAVERS
Are Ye Sleeping Maggie ............................ LP ...... Plant Life ........ PLR001 ................ 1976 £4 ......... £10 .......................................
Old Woman's Dance .................................. LP ...... Plant Life ........ PLR010 ................ 1978 £4 ......... £10 .......................................

## TANNED LEATHER
Child Of Never Ending Love ................... LP ...... Harvest .......... 1C06229440 .......... 1972 £4 ......... £10 ................. German

## TANNED LEATHER (2)
Saddle Soap ............................................. LP ...... Response ....... RFSP013 .............. 1977 £25 ......... £50 ...........................

## TANNEN, HOLLY & PETE COOPER
Frosty Morning ....................................... LP ...... Plant Life ........ PLR015 ............... 1979 £4 ......... £10 ...........................

## TANSEY, SEAMUS
Masters Of Irish Music ........................... LP ...... Leader ........... LEA2005 .............. 1970 £4 ......... £10 ...with Eddie Corcoran
Traditional Music From Sligo .................. LP ...... Outlet ........... SDLP1022 ............. 1973 £5 ......... £12 ................................ Irish

## TANTONES
So Afraid ............................................... 7" ...... Vogue ............ V9085 .................. 1957 £180 ..... £300 ............ best auctioned

## TAPESTRY
Carnaby Street ....................................... 7" ...... London .......... HLZ10138 ............ 1967 £2 ......... £5 .......................................

## TAPPI TIKARRASS
Tappi Tikarrass was a band playing in Iceland during 1981–3, whose lead singer was the very youthful Björk. In addition to the mini album listed here, the band also made an LP called *Miranda*, which is still available new.

Bitid Fast I Vitid ................................... LP ...... Spor ............... SPOR4 ................. 1981 £20 ......... £40 .......................................

## TARA
Happy .................................................... 7" ...... Polydor ......... 2066009 .............. 1971 £2 ......... £5 .......................................

## TARANTULA
Tarantula .............................................. LP ...... A&M ............. AMLS959 ............ 1970 £4 ......... £10 .......................................

## TARBUCK, JIMMY
Someday ................................................ 7" ...... Immediate ...... IM018 ................. 1965 £2 ......... £5 .......................................

## TARDENSKJOLDS SOLDATER
Peace ..................................................... LP ...... Spectator ....... SL1019 ............... 1970 £15 ......... £30 ................. Danish

## TARGEL, JEM
Lucky Guy ............................................. LP ...... Sheany ........................... 1978 £25 ......... £50 ................................. US

## TARGUS
Somebody's Watching You ....................... LP ...... Crossroad ........ .................. 1981 £8 ......... £20 ................... Dutch

## TARHEEL SLIM & LITTLE ANN
You Make Me Feel So Good ................... 7" ...... Sue ............... WI390 ................. 1965 £4 ......... £8 .......................................

## TARRA
Hard Nipples ........................................ LP ...... Platerie ........... .................. 1981 £8 ......... £20 ................... Dutch

## TARRIERS
Banana Boat Song .................................. 7" ...... Columbia ........ DB3891 ............... 1957 £1.50 ......... £4 .......................................
Dunya .................................................. 7" ...... Columbia ........ DB4025 ............... 1957 £1.50 ......... £4 .......................................
Hard Travellin' ...................................... LP ...... United Artists .. UAL4033/ ............ 1959 £4 ......... £10 ...................... US
                                                                    UAS5033 ...............
Hard Travellin' Vol. 1 ............................. 7" EP . London ........... RET1236 ............... 1960 £2 ......... £5 .......................................
Hard Travellin' Vol. 2 ............................. 7" EP . London ........... RET1237 ............... 1960 £2 ......... £5 .......................................
I Know Where I'm Going .......................... 7" ...... Columbia ........ DB4148 ............... 1958 £1.50 ......... £4 .......................................
Lonesome Traveller ................................. 7" ...... London ........... HLU8600 .............. 1958 £2.50 ......... £6 .......................................
Tarriers ................................................ 10" LP Columbia ........ 33S1115 .............. 1957 £6 ......... £15 .......................................
Tell The World About This ....................... LP ...... Atlantic .......... (SD)8042 .............. 1960 £4 ......... £10 ...................... US
Tom Dooley ........................................... 7" ...... Columbia ........ DB3961 ............... 1957 £1.50 ......... £4 .......................................

## TARTANS
Awake The Town ................................... 7" ...... Caltone .......... TONE115 ............... 1968 £4 ......... £8 .......................................
Coming On Strong .................................. 7" ...... Caltone .......... TONE117 ............... 1968 £4 ......... £8 .......................................
Dance All Night ..................................... 7" ...... Island ............. WI3058 ................. 1967 £5 ......... £10 .......................................

## TASAVALLAN PRESIDENTTI
Hailing from Finland, Tasavallan Presidentti played top quality progressive jazz-rock, sounding like a cross between John McLaughlin's Mahavishnu Orchestra and Jethro Tull. Further albums by the group were issued under the name of guitarist Jukka Tolonen – a virtuoso and distinctive player who deserves to be much better known than he is, although the early, group-credited albums are inevitably the best.

Lambertland .......................................... LP ...... Sonet ............. SNTF636 ............... 1973 £5 ......... £12 .......................................
Milky Way Moses ................................... LP ...... Sonet ............. SNTF658 ............... 1974 £4 ......... £10 .......................................
Tasavallan Presedentti ............................. LP ...... Love .............. LRLP7 .................. 1969 £6 ......... £15 ................. Swedish

## TASSELS
To A Soldier Boy ................................... 7" ...... London ........... HL8885 ................. 1959 £25 ......... £50 .......................................
To A Young Lover .................................. 7" ...... Top Rank ....... JAR229 ................. 1959 £7.50 ......... £15 .......................................

## TASTE

Guitarist Rory Gallagher began his long career with this trio. The titles issued as singles can be found on the *Taste* LP, but these are re-recordings. The Major Minor originals sound significantly different.

| | | | | | | |
|---|---|---|---|---|---|---|
| Blister On The Moon | 7" | Major Minor | MM560 | 1968 £2.50 | £6 | |
| Born On The Wrong Side Of Time | 7" | Major Minor | MM718 | 1970 £1.50 | £4 | |
| Born On The Wrong Side Of Time | 7" | Polydor | 56313 | 1969 £1.50 | £4 | |
| Live At The Isle Of Wight | LP | Polydor | 2383120 | 1972 £4 | £10 | |
| Live Taste | LP | Polydor | 2310082 | 1971 £4 | £10 | |
| On The Boards | LP | Polydor | 583083 | 1970 £5 | £12 | |
| Taste | LP | Polydor | 583042 | 1969 £6 | £15 | |

## TATE, BUDDY

| | | | | | | |
|---|---|---|---|---|---|---|
| Swinging Like Tate | LP | Felsted | FAJ7004/SJA2004 | 1958 £6 | £15 | |

## TATE, ERIC QUINCY

| | | | | | | |
|---|---|---|---|---|---|---|
| Can't Keep A Good Band Down | LP | EQT | | 1977 £20 | £40 | US |

## TATE, HOWARD

| | | | | | | |
|---|---|---|---|---|---|---|
| Ain't Nobody Home | 7" | Verve | VS541 | 1966 £2 | £5 | |
| Baby I Love You | 7" | Verve | VS555 | 1967 £1.50 | £4 | |
| Get It While You Can | LP | Verve | (S)VLP9179 | 1967 £5 | £12 | |
| Get It While You Can | 7" | Verve | VS552 | 1967 £1.50 | £4 | |
| I Learned It All The Hard Way | 7" | Verve | VS556 | 1967 £1.50 | £4 | |
| Look At Granny Run Run | 7" | Verve | VS549 | 1967 £2.50 | £6 | |
| Look At Granny Run Run | 7" | Verve | VS584 | 1968 £1.50 | £4 | |
| Night Owl | 7" | Verve | VS571 | 1968 £2 | £5 | |
| Stop | 7" | Verve | VS565 | 1968 £1.50 | £4 | |

## TATE, PHIL

| | | | | | | |
|---|---|---|---|---|---|---|
| Tunes For Twisters | 7" EP | Oriole | EP7060 | 1962 £2.50 | £6 | |

## TATE, TOMMY

| | | | | | | |
|---|---|---|---|---|---|---|
| Big Blue Diamonds | 7" | Columbia | DB8046 | 1966 £7.50 | £15 | |

## TATUM, ART

| | | | | | | |
|---|---|---|---|---|---|---|
| Art | LP | Fontana | FJL904 | 1967 £4 | £10 | |
| Art Of Tatum | LP | Brunswick | LAT8358 | 1961 £6 | £15 | |
| Art Tatum | LP | Columbia | 33CX10115 | 1958 £8 | £20 | |
| Art Tatum | LP | XTRA | XTRA1007 | 1964 £4 | £10 | |
| Art Tatum | 7" EP | Columbia | SEB10003 | 1955 £2 | £5 | |
| Art Tatum | 7" EP | Columbia | SEG7540 | 1955 £2 | £5 | |
| Art Tatum | 7" EP | Vogue | EPV1008 | 1954 £2 | £5 | |
| Art Tatum | 7" EP | Vogue | EPV1212 | 1957 £2 | £5 | |
| Art Tatum | 10" LP | Capitol | LC6524 | 1951 £15 | £30 | |
| Art Tatum No. 1 | 7" EP | Fontana | TFE17235 | 1960 £2 | £5 | |
| Art Tatum No. 2 | 7" EP | Fontana | TFE17236 | 1960 £2 | £5 | |
| Art Tatum No. 3 | 7" EP | Fontana | TFE17237 | 1960 £2 | £5 | |
| Art Tatum Trio | 7" EP | Melodisc | EPM7108 | 195– £2 | £5 | |
| Art Tatum Trio | 10" LP | Vogue Coral | LRA10011 | 1955 £10 | £25 | |
| Art Tatum–Ben Webster Quartet | LP | Columbia | 33CX10137 | 1959 £8 | £20 | |
| Art Tatum–Buddy De Franco Quartet | 7" EP | Columbia | SEB10101 | 1958 £2 | £5 | |
| Art Tatum–Buddy De Franco Quartet | 7" EP | HMV | 7EG8619 | 1960 £2 | £5 | |
| Art Tatum–Roy Eldridge–Alvin Stoller–John Simmons Quartet | LP | Columbia | 33CX10042 | 1956 £20 | £40 | |
| At Hollywood Bowl | 7" EP | Columbia | SEB10084 | 1958 £2 | £5 | |
| Delicate Touch | 7" EP | Columbia | SEB10116 | 1959 £2 | £5 | |
| Discoveries | LP | Top Rank | 35067 | 1960 £5 | £12 | |
| Encores | 10" LP | Capitol | LC6638 | 1954 £10 | £25 | |
| Genius Of Art Tatum | LP | Columbia | 33CX10005 | 1955 £10 | £25 | |
| Genius Of Art Tatum No. 2 | LP | Columbia | 33CX10053 | 1956 £10 | £25 | |
| Genius Of Art Tatum No. 3 | 10" LP | Columbia | 33C9033 | 1957 £10 | £25 | |
| Greatest Piano Of Them All | 7" EP | HMV | 7EG8604 | 1960 £2 | £5 | |
| Here's Art Tatum | LP | Vogue Coral | LVA9047 | 1957 £10 | £25 | |
| Incomparable Music | 7" EP | HMV | 7EG8684 | 1961 £2 | £5 | |
| Just Jazz | 10" LP | Vogue | LDE081 | 1954 £15 | £30 | |
| Memories | LP | Ember | EMB3314 | 1961 £4 | £10 | |
| Memories | 7" EP | Ember | EMBEP4502 | 1962 £2 | £5 | |
| Memories Vol. 2 | LP | Ember | EMB3326 | 1961 £4 | £10 | |
| Out Of Nowhere | 10" LP | Capitol | LC6625 | 1953 £15 | £30 | |
| Presenting The Art Tatum Trio | 10" LP | Columbia | 33C9039 | 1957 £10 | £25 | |
| Tatum-Carter-Bellson Trio | 7" EP | Columbia | SEB10027 | 1956 £2 | £5 | |
| Tatum-Carter-Bellson Trio | 7" EP | Columbia | SEB10062 | 1957 £2 | £5 | |
| Unforgettable Art | 7" EP | Philips | BBE12136 | 1957 £2 | £5 | |

## TAUPIN, BERNIE

| | | | | | | |
|---|---|---|---|---|---|---|
| An Interview With Bernie Taupin double promo | LP | RCA | | 1987 £5 | £12 | US |

## TAVENER, JOHN

Of all the surprising records to have been issued on the Apple label, the pair of works composed by John Tavener are perhaps the most surprising of all. They have nothing to do with rock music at all in themselves, being prime examples of the classical avant-garde, but they were apparently included in the Beatles' release schedule because Ringo Starr liked them. Tavener's more recent work is inspired by his devout religious beliefs and is considerably less way-out than these early works. His tranquil *The Protecting Veil* gained considerable acclaim in some quarters and not a little commercial success during the nineties.

| | | | | | | | |
|---|---|---|---|---|---|---|---|
| Celtic Requiem | LP | Apple | SAPCOR20 | 1971 | £62.50 | £125 | |
| Whale | LP | Apple | SAPCOR15 | 1970 | £20 | £40 | |
| Whale | LP | Ring O' | 2320104 | 1977 | £8 | £20 | |

## TAVERNERS
| | | | | | | | |
|---|---|---|---|---|---|---|---|
| Blowing Sand | LP | Trailer | LER2080 | 1973 | £4 | £10 | |
| Seldom Sober | LP | Saga | EROS8146 | 1969 | £6 | £15 | |
| Times Of Old England | LP | Folk Heritage | FHR062 | 1974 | £4 | £10 | |

## TAW FOLK
| | | | | | | | |
|---|---|---|---|---|---|---|---|
| Devonshire Cream And Cider | LP | Sentinel | SENS1030 | 1975 | £5 | £12 | |

## TAWNEY, CYRIL
| | | | | | | | |
|---|---|---|---|---|---|---|---|
| Down Among The Barley Straw | LP | Trailer | LER2095 | 1976 | £4 | £10 | |
| I Will Give My Love | LP | Argo | ZFB87 | 1973 | £4 | £10 | |
| In Port | LP | Argo | ZFB28 | 1972 | £5 | £12 | |
| Mayflower Garland | LP | Argo | ZFB9 | 1970 | £10 | £25 | |
| Outlandish Knight | LP | Polydor | 236577 | 1970 | £10 | £25 | |
| Sings Children's Songs From Devon And Cornwall | LP | Argo | ZFB4 | 1970 | £10 | £25 | |

## TAYLES
| | | | | | | | |
|---|---|---|---|---|---|---|---|
| Who Are These Guys? | LP | Cineviste | CV1001 | 1972 | £50 | £100 | US |

## TAYLOR, ALLAN
| | | | | | | | |
|---|---|---|---|---|---|---|---|
| American Album | LP | United Artists | UAG29468 | 1973 | £6 | £15 | |
| Lady | LP | United Artists | UAS29275 | 1972 | £6 | £15 | |
| Roll On The Day | LP | Rubber | RUB040 | 1980 | £4 | £10 | |
| Sometimes | LP | Liberty | LBG83483 | 1971 | £10 | £25 | |
| Traveller | LP | Rubber | RUB026 | 1978 | £4 | £10 | |

## TAYLOR, ART
| | | | | | | | |
|---|---|---|---|---|---|---|---|
| A. T.'s Delight | LP | Blue Note | BLP/BST84047 | 196– | £20 | £40 | |

## TAYLOR, AUSTIN
| | | | | | | | |
|---|---|---|---|---|---|---|---|
| Push Push | 7" | Top Rank | JAR511 | 1960 | £2 | £5 | |

## TAYLOR, BILLY
| | | | | | | | |
|---|---|---|---|---|---|---|---|
| And His Rhythm | 10" LP | Felsted | L87001 | 195– | £20 | £40 | |
| At The London House | LP | HMV | CLP1176 | 1958 | £4 | £10 | |
| Billy Taylor | 7" EP | Esquire | EP115 | 195– | £2 | £5 | |
| Billy Taylor Trio | LP | Esquire | 32010 | 1955 | £10 | £25 | |
| Billy Taylor Trio | 7" EP | Esquire | EP169 | 1958 | £2 | £5 | |
| Billy Taylor Trio | 10" LP | Esquire | 20053 | 1955 | £25 | £50 | |
| Evergreens | 10" LP | HMV | DLP1171 | 1958 | £4 | £10 | |
| Jazz At Storyville | 10" LP | Felsted | EDL87009 | 1954 | £20 | £40 | |
| My Fair Lady Loves Jazz | 10" LP | HMV | DLP1181 | 1958 | £4 | £10 | ...with Quincy Jones |
| New Billy Taylor Trio | LP | HMV | CLP1231 | 1959 | £4 | £10 | |
| Taylor Made | 10" LP | Esquire | 20020 | 1953 | £20 | £40 | |
| Taylor Made Piano | LP | Vogue | LAE12192 | 1960 | £4 | £10 | |

## TAYLOR, BOBBY
| | | | | | | | |
|---|---|---|---|---|---|---|---|
| Taylor Made Soul | LP | Tamla Motown | (S)TML11125 | 1970 | £20 | £40 | |

## TAYLOR, BOBBY & THE VANCOUVERS
| | | | | | | | |
|---|---|---|---|---|---|---|---|
| Bobby Taylor & The Vancouvers | LP | Tamla Motown | (S)TML11093 | 1969 | £8 | £20 | |
| Does Your Mama Know About Me | 7" | Tamla Motown | TMG654 | 1968 | £10 | £20 | |

## TAYLOR, BRYAN

Taylor's 'The Donkey's Tale' is listed elsewhere as a considerable collectors' item. The author of this guide finds this to be rather mysterious, as, in his experience, the market for children's Christmas songs performed by a boy soprano with no subsequent claim to fame is rather limited.

| | | | | | | | |
|---|---|---|---|---|---|---|---|
| Donkey's Tale | 7" | Piccadilly | 7N35018 | 1961 | £1.50 | £4 | |

## TAYLOR, CECIL
| | | | | | | | |
|---|---|---|---|---|---|---|---|
| At The Café Montmartre | LP | Fontana | SFJL928 | 1969 | £8 | £20 | |
| Conquistador | LP | Blue Note | BLP/BST84260 | 1967 | £10 | £25 | |
| Hard Driving Jazz/Stereo Drive | LP | United Artists | UAL4014/ UAS5014 | 1959 | £20 | £40 | US |
| Innovations | LP | Polydor | 2383094 | 1972 | £6 | £15 | |
| Jazz Advance | LP | Transition | TRLP19 | 1956 | £37.50 | £75 | US |
| Looking Ahead | LP | Contemporary | LAC12216 | 1959 | £10 | £25 | |
| Love For Sale | LP | United Artists | UAL4046/ UAS5046 | 1959 | £20 | £40 | US |
| Nefertiti, The Beautiful One Has Come | LP | Fontana | SFJL926 | 1969 | £8 | £20 | |
| Newport Jazz Festival 1957 | LP | Columbia | 33CX10102 | 1958 | £10 | £25 | side 2 by Gigi Gryce & Donald Byrd |
| Nuits de la Fondation Maeght Vol. 1 | LP | Shandar | 83507 | 1969 | £8 | £20 | French |
| Nuits de la Fondation Maeght Vol. 2 | LP | Shandar | SR10011 | 1969 | £8 | £20 | French |
| Unit Structures | LP | Blue Note | BLP/BST84237 | 1966 | £10 | £25 | |
| World Of Cecil Taylor | LP | Candid | 8/9006 | 1960 | £20 | £40 | US |

## TAYLOR, EARL
| | | | | | | | |
|---|---|---|---|---|---|---|---|
| Bluegrass Taylor Made | LP | Capitol | (S)T2090 | 1963 | £5 | £12 | US |

## TAYLOR, EDDIE & FLOYD JONES
Eddie Taylor & Floyd Jones ........................ 7" EP . XX ............... MIN712 ................. 196– £2.50 ........ £6 .........................

## TAYLOR, ELIZABETH
In London ...................................................... LP ..... Colpix ............ PXL459 ................. 1963 £20 ........ £40 ........ with John Barry

## TAYLOR, FELICE
I Can Feel Your Love .................................. 7" ..... President ........ PT193 ............... 1968 £1.50 ........ £4 .........................
I Feel Love Comin' On ............................... 7" ..... President ........ PT155 ............... 1967 £1.50 ........ £4 .........................

## TAYLOR, GLORIA
You Gotta Pay The Price ........................... 7" ..... Polydor ........... 56788 ................. 1970 £1.50 ........ £4 .........................

## TAYLOR, HOUND DOG
Christine ..................................................... 7" ...... Outasite .......... 45504 ................... 1966 £12.50 .... £25 .........................

## TAYLOR, JAMES QUARTET
Blow Up ...................................................... 7" ...... Re-Elect ........ FORD1 ............... 1987 £1.50 ........ £4 .........................
                                                                        President ..........
Breakout ...................................................... CD-s .. Urban ........... URCD38 ............. 1989 £2 ............ £5 .........................
It Doesn't Matter ........................................ CD-s .. Urban ........... URCD43 ............. 1989 £2 ............ £5 .........................
Killing Time ................................................ CD-s .. Urban ........... URBCD61 ............ 1990 £2 ............ £5 .........................
Love The Life .............................................. CD-s .. Urban ........... URBCD57 ............ 1990 £2 ............ £5 .........................

## TAYLOR, JAMES
Carolina In My Mind .................................. 7" ...... Apple .............. 32 ..................... 1970 £2 ............ £5 .........................
Gorilla ......................................................... LP ..... Warner Bros ... BS42866 ............. 1975 £4 ............ £10 ........................ US quad
James Taylor ............................................... LP ..... Apple .............. APCOR3 ............. 1968 £15 ........... £30 ........................ mono
James Taylor ............................................... LP ..... Apple .............. SAPCOR3 ............ 1968 £5 ............ £12 ........ orange lettering
James Taylor ............................................... LP ..... Apple .............. SAPCOR3 ............ 1968 £6 ............ £15 .. stereo, black lettering
Live ............................................................. CD .... Columbia ........ CSK5342 ............. 1994 £8 ............ £20 ........................ US promo
Never Die Young ........................................ CD-s .. CBS ................ 6512042 .............. 1988 £2 ............ £5 .........................
One Man Dog ............................................. LP ..... Warner Bros .... BS42660 ............. 1974 £4 ............ £10 ........................ US quad

## TAYLOR, JEREMY
Always Something New ............................... LP ..... Decca .............. LK4731 ............... 1966 £8 ............ £20 .........................
His Songs ................................................... LP ..... Fontana ........... STL5475 .............. 1968 £5 ............ £12 .........................
Jobsworth ................................................... LP ..... Canon .............. CPT3982 ............. 1973 £4 ............ £10 .........................
More Of His Songs ..................................... LP ..... Fontana ........... STL5523 .............. 1969 £5 ............ £12 .........................
Piece Of Ground ........................................ LP ..... Galliard .......... GAL4018 ............. 1972 £6 ............ £15 .........................
Wait A Minim Songs .................................. 7" EP . Decca .............. DFE8581 ............. 1964 £2.50 ........ £6 .........................

## TAYLOR, JOHN
Pause And Think Again ............................... LP ...... Turtle ............ TUR302 ............... 1971 £25 ........... £50 .........................

## TAYLOR, JOHNNIE
Ain't That Loving You ................................ 7" ...... Stax ............... 601003 ................ 1967 £1.50 ........ £4 .........................
Friday Night ............................................... 7" ...... Stax ............... STX2025 .............. 1968 £1.50 ........ £4 .........................
Looking For Johnnie Taylor ........................ LP ..... Atco ............... 228008 ................ 1969 £4 ............ £10 .........................
Philosophy Continues ................................. LP ..... Stax ............... SXATS1024 .......... 1969 £4 ............ £10 .........................
Raw Blues ................................................... LP ..... Stax ............... STS2008 .............. 1969 £4 ............ £10 ........................ US
Steal Away .................................................. 7" ...... Stax ............... STAX150 ............. 1970 £1.50 ........ £4 .........................
Wanted: One Soul Singer ........................... LP ..... Stax ............... 589008 ................ 1967 £5 ............ £12 .........................
Who's Making Love? ................................... LP ..... Stax ............... (S)XATS1006 ......... 1969 £4 ............ £10 .........................

## TAYLOR, JOSEPH
Unto Brigg Fair ........................................... LP ..... Leader............. LEA4050 ............. 1972 £10 ........... £25 ........ with other artists

## TAYLOR, KARL
Taylor Maid ................................................. LP ..... Polydor ........... 2907023 .............. 1976 £25 ........... £50 ............... Australian

## TAYLOR, KINGSIZE & THE DOMINOES
Keep On Rockin' ......................................... LP ..... Brunswick ....... LP2911109 ........... 1973 £8 ............ £20 .................... German
Kingsize Taylor And The Dominoes ............ LP ..... Ariola ............. 71765IT .............. 1964 £37.50 ...... £75 . German, with Bobby
                                                                                                                                                            Patrick Big Six
Memphis Tennessee ..................................... 7" ...... Polydor ........... NH66990 ............. 1963 £4 ............ £8 .........................
Real Gonk Man ........................................... LP ..... Midnight .......... HLP/HST2101 ...... 1964 £20 ........... £40 ........................ US
Somebody's Always Trying ......................... 7" ...... Decca .............. F11935 ................ 1964 £4 ............ £8 .........................
Star Club Time ........................................... LP ..... Ariola ............. 71431 .................. 1964 £50 ........... £100 ................... German
Stupidity ..................................................... 7" ...... Decca .............. F11874 ................ 1964 £4 ............ £8 .........................
Teenbeat 2 – Teanbeat From The Star ........ 7" EP . Decca .............. DFE8569 ............. 1964 £25 ........... £50 .........................
    Club Hamburg .......................................
Thinkin' ...................................................... 7" ...... Polydor ........... BM56152 ............. 1965 £6 ............ £12 .........................
Twist And Shake ......................................... 7" EP . Polydor ........... EPH21628 ............ 1963 £25 ........... £50 .........................
Twist Time Im Star Club Hamburg ............. LP ..... Ariola ............. 70953 .................. 1964 £50 ........... £100 . German, with Bobby
                                                                                                                                                            Patrick Big Six

## TAYLOR, KOKO
Koko Taylor ................................................ LP ..... Chess .............. LPS1532 .............. 1968 £6 ............ £15 ........................ US
Wang Dang Doodle ..................................... 7" ...... Chess .............. CRS8035 ............. 1966 £2.50 ........ £6 .........................

## TAYLOR, LITTLE JOHNNY
Little Johnny Taylor .................................... LP ..... Galaxy ............ (8)203 ................. 1963 £8 ............ £20 ........................ US
Little Johnny Taylor .................................... LP ..... Vocalion ......... VAP8031 ............. 1965 £8 ............ £20 .........................
One More Chance ....................................... 7" ...... Vocalion ......... VF9264 ............... 1966 £2.50 ........ £6 .........................
Part Time Love ........................................... 7" ...... Vocalion ......... VP9234 ............... 1965 £2.50 ........ £6 .........................

## TAYLOR, MICK

If the single by Mick Taylor has acquired any value by reason of its authorship by the future Bluesbreaker and Rolling Stone, then the justification for this is a little dubious. The Mick Taylor who joined John Mayall in 1967 was only seventeen at the time and a confirmed blues guitarist. It is not at all likely that he would have had a single released two years earlier under the title of 'London Town/Hoboin''.

| | | | | | | |
|---|---|---|---|---|---|---|
| London Town | 7" | CBS | 201770 | 1965 | £5 | £10 |

## TAYLOR, MIKE

Mike Taylor showed every sign of developing into a major talent before his premature death in the late sixties. He co-wrote songs for Cream ('Those Were The Days', 'Passing The Time') and for Colosseum ('Jumping Off The Sun') and was also a fine jazz pianist. The two rare albums he made have Jack Bruce, Tony Reeves and Jon Hiseman among the small supporting cast.

| | | | | | | |
|---|---|---|---|---|---|---|
| Pendulum | LP | Columbia | SX6042 | 1965 | £100 | £200 |
| Trio | LP | Columbia | SX6137 | 1966 | £100 | £200 |

## TAYLOR, NEVILLE

| | | | | | | | |
|---|---|---|---|---|---|---|---|
| Baby Lay Sleeping | 7" | Parlophone | R4493 | 1958 | £2 | £5 | |
| Dance With A Dolly | 7" | Oriole | CB1546 | 1960 | £2 | £5 | |
| First Words Of Love | 7" | Parlophone | R4524 | 1959 | £5 | £10 | |
| Joshua Fit The Battle Of Jericho | 7" | Honey Hit | TB127 | 196– | £1.50 | £4 | picture sleeve |
| Mercy Mercy Percy | 7" | Parlophone | R4447 | 1958 | £5 | £10 | |
| Tears On My Pillow | 7" | Parlophone | R4476 | 1958 | £4 | £8 | |

## TAYLOR, PADDY

| | | | | | | | |
|---|---|---|---|---|---|---|---|
| Boy In The Gap | LP | Claddagh | CC8 | 1969 | £4 | £10 | Irish |

## TAYLOR, R. DEAN

| | | | | | | | |
|---|---|---|---|---|---|---|---|
| Ain't It A Sad Thing | 7" | Rare Earth | RES101 | 1971 | £5 | £10 | TMG786 matrix |
| Ain't It A Sad Thing | 7" | Tamla Motown | TMG786 | 1971 | £20 | £40 | demo only |
| Gotta See Jane | 7" | Tamla Motown | TMG656 | 1968 | £1.50 | £4 | |
| Indiana Wants Me | LP | Tamla Motown | STML11185 | 1971 | £5 | £12 | |

## TAYLOR, ROGER

| | | | | | | |
|---|---|---|---|---|---|---|
| Fun In Space | LP | EMI | EMC3369 | 1981 | £4 | £10 |
| Future Management | 7" | EMI | EMI5157 | 1981 | £5 | £10 |
| I Wanna Testify | 7" | EMI | EMI2679 | 1977 | £20 | £40 |
| Man On Fire | 7" | EMI | EMI5478 | 1984 | £5 | £10 |
| Man On Fire | 12" | EMI | EMI125478 | 1984 | £15 | £30 |
| My Country | 7" | EMI | EMI5200 | 1981 | £10 | £20 |
| Nazis 1994 | CD-s | Parlophone | CDR6379 | 1994 | £2 | £5 |
| Strange Frontier | LP | EMI | EJ2401371 | 1984 | £4 | £10 |
| Strange Frontier | 7" | EMI | EMI5490 | 1984 | £5 | £10 |
| Strange Frontier | 12" | EMI | EMI125490 | 1984 | £15 | £30 |

## TAYLOR, SAM

| | | | | | | |
|---|---|---|---|---|---|---|
| Please Be Kind | 7" | MGM | SP1106 | 1954 | £7.50 | £15 |
| Sam Taylor Orchestra | 7" EP | MGM | MGMEP531 | 1956 | £7.50 | £15 |

## TAYLOR, TED

| | | | | | | |
|---|---|---|---|---|---|---|
| Cat's Eyes | 7" | Oriole | CB1628 | 1961 | £1.50 | £4 |
| Fried Onions | 7" | Oriole | CB1574 | 1961 | £1.50 | £4 |
| Haunted Pad | 7" | Oriole | CB1630 | 1961 | £2 | £5 |
| Jericho | 7" | Oriole | CB1713 | 1962 | £2 | £5 |
| M1 | 7" | Oriole | CB1573 | 1961 | £1.50 | £4 |
| Son Of Honky Tonk | 7" | Oriole | CB1464 | 1958 | £1.50 | £4 |
| Surfrider | 7" | Oriole | CB1767 | 1962 | £5 | £10 |

## TAYLOR, TRUE

True Taylor is one of several names tried by Paul Simon during the early years of his recording career.

| | | | | | | | |
|---|---|---|---|---|---|---|---|
| True Or False | 7" | Big | 614 | 1958 | £20 | £40 | US |

## TAYLOR, VERNON

| | | | | | | |
|---|---|---|---|---|---|---|
| Mystery Train | 7" | London | HLS9025 | 1960 | £25 | £50 |

## TAYLOR, VIC

| | | | | | | |
|---|---|---|---|---|---|---|
| Does It His Way | LP | Trojan | TRLS38 | 1971 | £4 | £10 |
| Heartaches | 7" | Treasure Isle | TI7021 | 1967 | £5 | £10 |

## TAYLOR, VINCE

| | | | | | | | |
|---|---|---|---|---|---|---|---|
| Brand New Cadillac | 7" | Parlophone | R4539 | 1959 | £12.50 | £25 | |
| Jet Black Machine | 7" | Palette | PG9001 | 1960 | £5 | £10 | |
| Luv | 10" LP | Big Beat | BBR0004 | 1962 | £37.50 | £75 | French |
| Right Behind You Baby | 7" | Parlophone | R4505 | 1958 | £12.50 | £25 | |
| Sweet Little Sixteen | 7" EP | Barclay | 70394 | 1961 | £15 | £30 | French |
| Whatcha Gonna Do | 7" | Palette | PG9020 | 1961 | £6 | £12 | |

## TAYLOR MAIDS

| | | | | | | |
|---|---|---|---|---|---|---|
| Theme From I Am A Camera | 7" | Capitol | CL14322 | 1955 | £1.50 | £4 |

## T-BONES

| | | | | | | | |
|---|---|---|---|---|---|---|---|
| I Am Louisiana Red | 7" EP | Riviera | 231075 | 1965 | £50 | £100 | French |
| I'm A Lover | 7" | Columbia | DB7401 | 1964 | £10 | £20 | |
| Won't You Give Me One More Chance | 7" | Columbia | DB7489 | 1965 | £7.50 | £15 | |

## T-BONES (2)

| | | | | | | | |
|---|---|---|---|---|---|---|---|
| No Matter What Shape | 7" EP | Liberty | LEP2248 | 1965 | £4 | £8 | French |

## T.C. ATLANTIC
Live At Bel-Rae Ballroom........................ LP ..... Dove ............. LP4459 ................ 1967 £50........ £100 ....................... US

## TEA & SYMPHONY
Asylum For The Musically Insane ............ LP ..... Harvest .......... SHVL761 ................ 1969 £30....... £60
Boredom ................................................. 7" ..... Harvest .......... HAR5005 .............. 1969 £2.50...... £6
Jo Sago ................................................. LP ..... Harvest .......... SHVL785 .............. 1970 £30........ £60

## TEA COMPANY
Come & Have Some Tea ........................ LP ..... Mercury ......... SMCL20127 .......... 1968 £15........ £30

## TEA SET
Join The Tea Set .................................. 7" ..... King .............. KG1048 ................ 1966 £2............ £5

## TEACHO & THE STUDENTS
Rocket................................................ 7" ...... Felsted ........... AF104 ................ 1958 £12.50.. £25

## TEAGARDEN, JACK
At The Round Table............................. LP ..... Columbia ....... 33SX1235/ ........... 1960 £4............ £10
                                                                              SCX3312 ............
Big T's Jazz........................................ LP ..... Brunswick ....... LAT8229............ 1958 £6........... £15
Jack Teagarden's Dixieland Band ........... LP ..... Capitol........... T1095 ............... 1959 £5........... £12
Jazz Great ......................................... LP ..... London........... LTZN15077 ....... 1957 £8........... £20
This Is Teagarden ............................... LP ..... Capitol........... T721 ............... 1956 £5........... £12

## TEAL, J. BAND
Cooks ............................................... LP ..... Mother Cleo ... ..................... 1977 £10........ £25 ................. US

## TEAM-BEATS
It's Liverpool Time............................... LP ..... Vogue............. LDV17003 ........... 1964 £15........ £30 ................ German

## TEAR GAS
Tear Gas was a Scottish heavy rock group, whose *Piggy Go Getter* LP received a considerable publicity campaign to little avail. The members'
fortunes gained a considerable boost, however, when Tear Gas was taken on entire by singer Alex Harvey, to become the Sensational Alex
Harvey Band.

Piggy Go Getter ................................... LP ..... Famous .......... SFMA5751 ............ 1971 £10........ £25
Tear Gas ............................................ LP ..... Regal            SLRZ1021 ............ 1971 £62.50.. £125
                                                            Zonophone .....

## TEARDROP EXPLODES
Bouncing Babies................................... 7" ..... Zoo ............... CAGE005 ............ 1979 £2.50...... £6 ........ *picture sleeve*
Count To Ten And Run For Cover ......... CD-s .. Mercury.......... DROCD2.............. 1990 £2............ £5
Ha Ha I'm Drowning ............................ 7" ..... Mercury.......... TEAR4................ 1981 £10........ £20 ....... *picture sleeve*
Ha Ha I'm Drowning ............................ 7" ..... Mercury.......... TEAR44.............. 1981 £2............ £5 ............. *double*
Serious Danger ................................... CD-s .. Fontana........... DROCD1.............. 1990 £2............ £5
Sleeping Gas ...................................... 7" ..... Zoo ............... CAGE003 ............ 1979 £2.50...... £6 ..... *blue picture sleeve*
Sleeping Gas ...................................... 7" ..... Zoo ............... CAGE003 ............ 1979 £4............ £8 ...... *red picture sleeve*
Treason ............................................ 7" ..... Zoo ............... CAGE008 ............ 1980 £2............ £5

## TEARS
It's So Easy ........................................ LP ..... Spectator........ SL1031................ 1972 £8............ £20 ............. *Danish*
Tears................................................ LP ..... Spectator........ SL1011................ 1971 £25.......... £50 ............. *Danish*

## TEARS FOR FEARS
Advice For The Young At Heart ............. CD-s .. Fontana.......... IDCD14.............. 1990 £2............ £5
Everybody Wants To Rule The World ...... CD-s .. Polygram......... 0800322............. 1988 £4............ £10 ........... *CD video*
Everybody Wants To Rule The World ...... 7" ..... Mercury.......... IDEA99 .............. 1985 £1.50...... £4 ............... *double*
Famous Last Words............................... CD-s .. Fontana.......... IDCD15............. 1990 £2............ £5
Head Over Heels.................................. CD-s .. Polygram......... 0800622............. 1988 £4............ £10 ........... *CD video*
Head Over Heels.................................. 7" ..... Mercury.......... IDEP10.............. 1985 £2............ £5 ..... *shaped picture disc*
I Believe ........................................... CD-s .. Polygram......... 0800682............. 1988 £4............ £10 ........... *CD video*
Mad World......................................... 7" ..... Mercury.......... IDEA33 .............. 1982 £2............ £5 ............... *double*
Mother's Talk .................................... 7" ..... Mercury.......... IDEP7................ 1984 £2.50...... £6 .......... *picture disc*
Pale Shelter ....................................... 7" ..... Mercury.......... IDEAB5.............. 1983 £1.50...... £4 ............ *blue vinyl*
Pale Shelter ....................................... 7" ..... Mercury.......... IDEAG5.............. 1983 £1.50...... £4 ........... *green vinyl*
Pale Shelter ....................................... 7" ..... Mercury.......... IDEAP5.............. 1983 £2.50...... £6 .......... *picture disc*
Pale Shelter ....................................... 7" ..... Mercury.......... IDEAR5.............. 1983 £1.50...... £4 ............. *red vinyl*
Pale Shelter ....................................... 7" ..... Mercury.......... IDEAW5.............. 1983 £1.50...... £4 ........... *white vinyl*
Scenes From The Big Chair.................... CD-s .. Polygram......... 0801721............. 1988 £4............ £10 ........... *CD video*
Shout ............................................... CD-s .. Polygram......... 0800642............. 1988 £4............ £10 ........... *CD video*
Sowing The Seeds Of Love .................... CD-s .. Mercury.......... IDCD12............. 1989 £2............ £5
Way You Are ...................................... 7" ..... Mercury.......... IDEAS6.............. 1983 £2............ £5 ............... *double*
Woman In Chains ................................ CD-s .. Mercury.......... IDCD13............. 1989 £2............ £5 ............ *2 versions*

## TEATIME
Teatime.............................................. LP ..... Incus.............. INCUS15............. 1975 £6............ £15

## TEAZE
Live In Japan....................................... LP ..... Aquarius.......... AQR520............. 1978 £4............ £10 ............ *Canadian*
One Night Stands ................................. LP ..... Capitol........... 11919................ 1979 £4............ £10 ................ US

## TECHNIQUES
Hey Little Girl .................................... 7" ..... Columbia ....... DB4072 ............. 1958 £10........ £20

## TECHNIQUES (2)

| | | | | | | | |
|---|---|---|---|---|---|---|---|
| Devoted | 7" | Treasure Isle | TI7038 | 1968 | £5 | £10 | *with Tommy McCook* |
| I Wish It Would Rain | 7" | Duke | DU1 | 1968 | £4 | £8 | |
| It's You I Love | 7" | Treasure Isle | TI7040 | 1968 | £5 | £10 | |
| Love Is Not A Gamble | 7" | Treasure Isle | TI7026 | 1967 | £5 | £10 | |
| Man Of My Word | 7" | Duke | DU6 | 1968 | £4 | £8 | |
| My Girl | 7" | Treasure Isle | TI7031 | 1968 | £5 | £10 | *with Tommy McCook* |
| Queen Majesty | 7" | Treasure Isle | TI7019 | 1967 | £5 | £10 | |
| What Am I To Do | 7" | Duke | DU22 | 1969 | £1.50 | £4 | |
| Where Were You | 7" | Duke | DU60 | 1969 | £1.50 | £4 | |
| Who You Gonna Run To | 7" | Camel | CA10 | 1969 | £1.50 | £4 | |
| You Don't Care | 7" | Treasure Isle | TI7001 | 1967 | £5 | £10 | *Tommy McCook B side* |

## TEDDY & THE PANDAS

| | | | | | | | |
|---|---|---|---|---|---|---|---|
| Basic Magnetism | LP | Tower | ST5125 | 1968 | £6 | £15 | *US* |

## TEDDY & THE TIGERS

| | | | | | | |
|---|---|---|---|---|---|---|
| Hold On I'm Coming | 7" | Spin | SP2004 | 1967 | £6 | £12 |

## TEDDY & THE TWILIGHTS

| | | | | | | |
|---|---|---|---|---|---|---|
| I'm Just Your Clown | 7" | Stateside | SS167 | 1963 | £2.50 | £6 |

## TEDDY BEARS

Although Phil Spector is famous as a producer – indeed he was the first such to attain fame independently of the artists he produced – he started his career as a singer. He was one-third of a group, the Teddy Bears, whose best-known song is remembered as a particularly golden oldie – 'To Know Him Is To Love Him'.

| | | | | | | | |
|---|---|---|---|---|---|---|---|
| If Only You Knew | 7" | London | HLP8889 | 1959 | £10 | £20 | |
| Oh Why | 7" | London | HLP8836 | 1959 | £6 | £12 | |
| Teddy Bears Sing | LP | Imperial | LP9067 | 1959 | £100 | £200 | *US, mono* |
| Teddy Bears Sing | LP | Imperial | SLP12067 | 1959 | £180 | £300 | *US, stereo* |
| Teddy Bears Sing | LP | London | HAP2183 | 1959 | £50 | £100 | |
| To Know Him Is To Love Him | 7" | London | HLN8733 | 1958 | £4 | £8 | |

## TEE, WILLIE

| | | | | | | |
|---|---|---|---|---|---|---|
| Thank You John | 7" | Atlantic | 584116 | 1967 | £5 | £10 |
| Walkin' Up A One Way Street | 7" | Mojo | 2092025 | 1971 | £1.50 | £4 |

## TEE SET

| | | | | | | | |
|---|---|---|---|---|---|---|---|
| In The Morning Of My Days | LP | Negram | ELS963 | 1972 | £5 | £12 | *Dutch* |
| Ma belle amie | LP | Columbia | SCX6419 | 1970 | £5 | £12 | |

## TEEMATES

| | | | | | | | |
|---|---|---|---|---|---|---|---|
| Jet Set Dance Discotheque | LP | Audio Fidelity | DFS7042 | 1964 | £30 | £60 | *US* |

## TEEN BEATS

| | | | | | | |
|---|---|---|---|---|---|---|
| Slop Beat | 7" | Top Rank | JAR342 | 1960 | £5 | £10 |

## TEEN KINGS

When reissued as the more common Sun label recording, 'Ooby Dooby' was credited to the Teen Kings' lead singer, Roy Orbison.

| | | | | | | | |
|---|---|---|---|---|---|---|---|
| Ooby Dooby | 7" | Jewel | 101 | 1956 | £330 | £500 | *US, best auctioned* |
| Ooby Dooby | 7" | Jewel | 102 | 1956 | £250 | £400 | *US, best auctioned* |

## TEEN QUEENS

| | | | | | | | |
|---|---|---|---|---|---|---|---|
| Eddie My Love | LP | Crown | CLP5022 | 1957 | £30 | £60 | *US* |
| Eddie My Love | 7" | R&B | MRB5000 | 1965 | £15 | £30 | |
| Teen Queens | LP | Crown | CLP5373 | 1963 | £10 | £25 | *US* |

## TEENAGE FANCLUB

| | | | | | | | |
|---|---|---|---|---|---|---|---|
| Ballad Of John And Yoko | 7" | Paperhouse | PAPER005 | 1990 | £2 | £5 | *1 side etched* |
| Everything Flows | 7" | Paperhouse | PAPER003 | 1990 | £5 | £10 | |
| King | LP | Creation | LP096 | 1991 | £4 | £10 | *sprayed paint cover* |
| King | CD | Creation | CD096 | 1991 | £6 | £15 | *sprayed paint cover* |

## TEENAGE FILMSTARS

| | | | | | | | |
|---|---|---|---|---|---|---|---|
| Cloud Over Liverpool | 7" | Clockwork | COR002 | 1979 | £2.50 | £6 | |
| Cloud Over Liverpool | 7" | Clockwork | COR002 | 1979 | £15 | £30 | *picture sleeve* |
| I Helped Patrick McGoohan Escape | 7" | Fab Listening | FL1 | 1980 | £2.50 | £6 | |
| Odd Man Out | 7" | Blueprint | BLU2013 | 1980 | £2.50 | £6 | *picture sleeve* |
| Odd Man Out | 7" | Wessex | WEX275 | 1980 | £4 | £8 | *no picture sleeve* |

## TEENAGERS

| | | | | | | |
|---|---|---|---|---|---|---|
| Teenagers | 7" EP | RCA | RCX102 | 1957 | £7.50 | £15 |

## TEENMAKERS

| | | | | | | | |
|---|---|---|---|---|---|---|---|
| Teenmakers | LP | Triola | TLD216 | 1966 | £6 | £15 | *Danish* |

## TEESIDE FETTLERS

| | | | | | | |
|---|---|---|---|---|---|---|
| Ring Of Iron | LP | Tradition | TSR016 | 1974 | £4 | £10 |

## TELESCOPES

| | | | | | | | |
|---|---|---|---|---|---|---|---|
| Ever So | CD-s | Creation | CRESCD092 | 1990 | £2 | £5 | |
| Kick The Wall | 7" | Cheree | CHEREE2 | 1989 | £5 | £10 | *2 different picture sleeves* |

| | | | | | | | |
|---|---|---|---|---|---|---|---|
| Precious Little | CD-s | Creation | CRECD81 | 1990 £2 | £5 | |
| Trade Mark of Quality | CD | Fierce | FRIGHTCD039 | 1990 £5 | £12 | |

## TELEVISION

It is curious how the music of Television, which was conceived as a vehicle for the lengthy display of lead guitar expertise, managed to become considered as part of the seventies punk movement, which generally had no time for such excesses. There was, of course, no denying the freshness and sheer excitement of the *Marquee Moon* album, whose status as a classic recording is never likely to be undermined.

| | | | | | | | |
|---|---|---|---|---|---|---|---|
| Little Johnny Jewel | 7" | Ork | 81975 | 1975 £4 | £8 | | US |
| Little Johnny Jewel | 12" | Ork | NYC1 | 1979 £3 | £8 | | US |

## TELEVISION PERSONALITIES

| | | | | | | | |
|---|---|---|---|---|---|---|---|
| 14th Floor | 7" | Teen | CUS77089 | 1978 £15 | £30 | | *3 picture sleeves* |
| And Don't The Kids Just Love It | LP | Rough Trade | RT24 | 1981 £10 | £25 | | *with insert* |
| Biff Bang Pow! | 7" | Creation/ Lyntone | LYN13546 | 1982 £6 | £12 | | *flexi* |
| How I Learned To Love The Bomb | 7" | Dreamworld | DREAM10 | 1986 £5 | £10 | | |
| How I Learned To Love The Bomb | 12" | Dreamworld | DREAM4 | 1986 £3 | £8 | | |
| I Know Where Syd Barrett Lives | 7" | Rough Trade | RT063 | 1981 £6 | £12 | | |
| I Still Believe In Magic | 7" | Caff | CAFF5 | 1989 £7.50 | £15 | | |
| Mummy You're Not Watching Me | LP | Dreamworld | BIGDREAM4 | 1986 £4 | £10 | | |
| Mummy You're Not Watching Me | LP | Whaam! | BIG1 | 1982 £10 | £25 | | *with insert* |
| Painted Word | LP | Illuminated | JAMS37 | 1984 £10 | £25 | | |
| Sense Of Belonging | 7" | Rough Trade | RT109 | 1983 £4 | £8 | | |
| Smashing Time | 7" | Rough Trade | RT051 | 1980 £5 | £10 | | |
| They Could Have Been Bigger Than The Beatles | LP | Dreamworld | BIGDREAM2 | 1986 £4 | £10 | | |
| They Could Have Been Bigger Than The Beatles | LP | Whaam! | BIG5 | 1982 £10 | £25 | | |
| Three Wishes | 7" | Whaam! | WHAAM4 | 1982 £4 | £8 | | *2 sleeves* |
| Where's Bill Grundy Now | 7" | King's Road | LYN5976/7 | 1978 £5 | £10 | | *4 picture sleeves* |
| Where's Bill Grundy Now | 7" | Rough Trade | RT033 | 1979 £2.50 | £6 | | |

## TELHAM TINKERS

| | | | | | | |
|---|---|---|---|---|---|---|
| Hot In Alice Springs | LP | Eron | 031 | 1984 £4 | £10 | |

## TELLERS

| | | | | | | |
|---|---|---|---|---|---|---|
| A-Ya-It-Deh | 7" | Dragon | DRA1031 | 1974 £1.50 | £4 | |
| Innocent People Cry | 7" | Pyramid | PYR7012 | 1974 £1.50 | £4 | |
| No Work No Pay | 7" | Pyramid | PYR7011 | 1974 £1.50 | £4 | |

## TELSTARS

| | | | | | | | |
|---|---|---|---|---|---|---|---|
| Eurovision Team | LP | Nashville | 30107 | 1966 £10 | £25 | | *Swedish* |

## TEMPEST

| | | | | | | |
|---|---|---|---|---|---|---|
| Living In Fear | LP | Bronze | ILPS9267 | 1974 £6 | £15 | |
| Tempest | LP | Bronze | ILPS9220 | 1973 £6 | £15 | |

## TEMPEST, BOBBY

| | | | | | | |
|---|---|---|---|---|---|---|
| Love Or Leave | 7" | Decca | F11125 | 1959 £2 | £5 | |

## TEMPLE, BOB

| | | | | | | |
|---|---|---|---|---|---|---|
| Vim Vam Vamoose | 7" | Parlophone | R4264 | 1957 £1.50 | £4 | |

## TEMPLE, GERRY

| | | | | | | |
|---|---|---|---|---|---|---|
| Angel Face | 7" | HMV | POP1114 | 1963 £5 | £10 | |
| Lovin' Up A Storm | 7" | RCA | RCA1670 | 1968 £2.50 | £6 | |
| No More Tomorrows | 7" | HMV | POP823 | 1961 £5 | £10 | |
| Seventeen Come Sunday | 7" | HMV | POP939 | 1961 £5 | £10 | |

## TEMPLE, SHIRLEY

| | | | | | | |
|---|---|---|---|---|---|---|
| I Remember | 7" EP | Top Rank | JKR8003 | 1959 £5 | £10 | |

## TEMPLE ROW

| | | | | | | |
|---|---|---|---|---|---|---|
| King And Queen | 7" | Polydor | 2058254 | 1972 £2 | £5 | |
| Walk The World Away | 7" | Polydor | 2058329 | 1973 £1.50 | £4 | |

## TEMPLEAIRES

| | | | | | | |
|---|---|---|---|---|---|---|
| He Spoke | 7" | Vogue | V2421 | 1970 £2 | £5 | |

## TEMPO, NINO

| | | | | | | |
|---|---|---|---|---|---|---|
| Rock 'n' Roll Beach Party | 10" LP | London | HBU1075 | 1957 £37.50 | £75 | |
| Tempo's Tempo | 7" | London | HLU8387 | 1957 £87.50 | £175 | |

## TEMPO, NINO & APRIL STEVENS

| | | | | | | | |
|---|---|---|---|---|---|---|---|
| All Strung Out | LP | London | HAU/SHU8314 | 1967 £6 | £15 | | |
| All Strung Out | 7" | Teen | HLU10084 | 1966 £1.50 | £4 | | |
| Deep Purple | LP | London | HAK8168 | 1964 £8 | £20 | | |
| Deep Purple | 7" EP | London | REK1412 | 1964 £5 | £10 | | |
| Deep Purple | 7" | London | HLK9782 | 1963 £1.50 | £4 | | |
| Great Songs | LP | Atlantic | ATL/STL5006 | 1964 £6 | £15 | | |
| Habit Of Lovin' You Baby | 7" | London | HLU10106 | 1967 £1.50 | £4 | | |
| I'm Confessing | 7" | London | HLK9890 | 1964 £1.50 | £4 | | |
| Stardust | 7" | London | HLK9859 | 1964 £1.50 | £4 | | |
| Sweet And Lovely | 7" | London | HLK9580 | 1962 £2 | £5 | | *Top Notes B side* |
| Whispering | 7" | London | HLK9829 | 1964 £1.50 | £4 | | |

## TEMPOS
See You In September ............................... 7" ...... Pye ................. 7N25026 ................ 1959 £5 .......... £10 ..................

## TEMPOS (2)
Speaking Of The Tempos ........................ LP ..... Justice ............ 104 ..................... 1966 £150 ..... £250 ...................... *US*

## TEMPREES
Love Men .................................................. LP ..... Stax ................ 2325083 .............. 1972 £4 .......... £10
Three ....................................................... LP ..... Stax ................ STX1040 ............. 1974 £6 .......... £15

## TEMPTATIONS
Ain't Too Proud To Beg ......................... 7" ...... Tamla Motown TMG565 .......... 1966 £4 .......... £8
Ain't Too Proud To Beg ......................... 7" ...... Tamla Motown TMG699 .......... 1969 £1.50 ...... £4
All I Need .............................................. 7" ...... Tamla Motown TMG610 .......... 1967 £2 ........... £5
Ball Of Confusion .................................. 7" ...... Tamla Motown TMG749 .......... 1970 £1.50 ...... £4
Beauty Is Only Skin Deep ...................... 7" ...... Tamla Motown TMG578 .......... 1966 £2.50 ...... £6
Cloud Nine ............................................ LP ..... Tamla Motown (S)TML11109 .. 1969 £4 .......... £10
Cloud Nine ............................................ 7" ...... Tamla Motown TMG707 .......... 1969 £1.50 ...... £4
Get Ready .............................................. 7" ...... Tamla Motown TMG557 .......... 1966 £5 .......... £10
Get Ready .............................................. 7" ...... Tamla Motown TMG688 .......... 1969 £1.50 ...... £4
Gettin' Ready .......................................... LP ..... Tamla Motown (S)TML11035 .. 1966 £10 ......... £25
Greatest Hits .......................................... LP ..... Tamla Motown (S)TML11042 .. 1967 £4 .......... £10
I Can't Get Next To You ........................ 7" ...... Tamla Motown TMG722 .......... 1970 £1.50 ...... £4
I Could Never Love Another .................. 7" ...... Tamla Motown TMG658 .......... 1968 £1.50 ...... £4
I Wish It Would Rain .............................. 7" ...... Tamla Motown TMG641 .......... 1968 £1.50 ...... £4
I'll Be In Trouble ................................... 7" ...... Stateside .......... SS319 .............. 1964 £12.50 ... £25
I'm Losing You ....................................... 7" ...... Tamla Motown TMG587 .......... 1966 £2 ........... £5
In A Mellow Mood .................................. LP ..... Tamla Motown (S)TML11068 .. 1968 £5 .......... £12
It's Growing ........................................... 7" ...... Tamla Motown TMG504 .......... 1965 £6 .......... £12
It's The Temptations ............................... 7" EP . Tamla Motown TME2010 .......... 1966 £7.50 ...... £15
It's You That I Need ............................... 7" ...... Tamla Motown TMG633 .......... 1967 £6 .......... £12
Just My Imagination ............................... 7" ...... Tamla Motown TMG773 .......... 1971 £1.50 ...... £4
Live ....................................................... LP ..... Tamla Motown (S)TML11053 .. 1967 £4 .......... £10
Live At The Copa ................................... LP ..... Tamla Motown (S)TML11104 .. 1969 £4 .......... £10
Live At The Talk Of The Town ............... LP ..... Tamla Motown (S)TML11141 .. 1970 £4 .......... £10
Meet The Temptations ............................ LP ..... Tamla Motown TML11009 ...... 1965 £37.50 ... £75
Memories ............................................... 7" ...... Tamla Motown TMG948 .......... 1975 £2.50 ...... £6 ...... *demo, picture sleeve*
My Baby .................................................. 7" ...... Tamla Motown TMG541 .......... 1965 £6 .......... £12
My Girl .................................................. 7" ...... Stateside .......... SS378 .............. 1965 £10 ......... £20
Papa Was A Rolling Stone ...................... 7" ...... Tamla Motown TMG839 .......... 1973 £1.50 ...... £4
Psychedelic Shack .................................. LP ..... Tamla Motown (S)TML11147 .. 1970 £6 .......... £15
Psychedelic Shack .................................. 7" ...... Tamla Motown TMG741 .......... 1970 £1.50 ...... £4
Puzzle People ......................................... LP ..... Tamla Motown (S)TML11133 .. 1970 £4 .......... £10
Runaway Child Running Wild .................. 7" ...... Tamla Motown TMG716 .......... 1969 £1.50 ...... £4
Since I Lost My Baby ............................... 7" ...... Tamla Motown TMG526 .......... 1965 £7.50 ...... £15
Sing Smokey .......................................... LP ..... Tamla Motown TML11016 ...... 1965 £15 ......... £30
Temptations ........................................... 7" EP . Tamla Motown TME2004 .......... 1965 £10 ......... £20
Temptations Show .................................. LP ..... Gordy ............... GS933 .............. 1969 £4 .......... £10 ...................... *US*
Temptations Wish It Would Rain ............ LP ..... Tamla Motown (S)TML11079 .. 1968 £6 .......... £15
Temptin' Temptations ............................ LP ..... Tamla Motown TML11023 ...... 1966 £8 .......... £20
Way You Do The Things You Do ............ 7" ...... Stateside .......... SS278 .............. 1964 £12.50 ... £25
Why Did You Leave Me Darling .............. 7" ...... Tamla Motown TMG671 .......... 1968 £1.50 ...... £4
Why You Wanna Make Me Blue .............. 7" ...... Stateside .......... SS348 .............. 1964 £20 ......... £40
With A Lot O'Soul ................................. LP ..... Tamla Motown (S)TML11057 .. 1967 £5 .......... £12
You're My Everything ............................. 7" ...... Tamla Motown TMG620 .......... 1967 £1.50 ...... £4

## TEMPTATIONS (2)
Barbara .................................................. 7" ...... Top Rank ....... JAR384 ............. 1960 £10 ......... £20

## TEMPUS FUGIT
Come Alive ............................................ 7" ...... Philips ............. BF1802 ............. 1969 £7.50 ...... £15

## TEN CC
Greatest Hits .......................................... LP ..... Mercury .......... HS9102504 .......... 1982 £4 .......... £10 .............. *audiophile*
Original Soundtrack ............................... LP ..... Mercury .......... HS9102500 .......... 1982 £4 .......... £10 .............. *audiophile*

## TEN FEET
Got Everything But Love ........................ 7" ...... RCA ................ RCA1544 ............. 1966 £7.50 ...... £15
Shot On Sight ........................................ 7" ...... CBS ................. 3045 .................. 1966 £7.50 ...... £15

## TEN FEET FIVE
Two members of Ten Feet Five left to join the Troggs soon after the release of the group's only single – guitarist Chris Britton and bass player Pete Staples.

Baby's Back In Town .............................. 7" ...... Fontana .......... TF578 ................. 1965 £7.50 ...... £15

## TEN THOUSAND MANIACS
Can't Ignore The Train ........................... 12" ... Elektra ............ EKR11T .............. 1985 £3 ........... £8
Human Conflict #5 ................................. 12" ... Press .............. P2010 ................ 1984 £10 ......... £20
Just As The Tide Was A-Flowin' .............. 7" ...... Elektra ............ EKR19 ............... 1985 £2.50 ...... £6
My Mother The War ............................... 12" ... Reflex ............. 12RE1 ................ 1984 £6 .......... £15
Secrets Of The I Ching ........................... LP ..... Press .............. P3001LP ............. 1984 £20 ......... £40 ...................... *US*
Trouble Me ............................................ CD-s .. Elektra ............ EKR93CD ............ 1989 £2 ........... £5
Trouble Me ............................................ CD-s .. Elektra ............ EKR93CDX .......... 1989 £2.50 ...... £6 ............. *3" single in elephant-shaped pack*

## TEN YEARS AFTER

Before Woodstock showed Alvin Lee the mileage he could get from guitar excess, Ten Years After had a light, jazzy sound that made them stand out from the mass of blues bands emerging at the time. *Undead* shows off this quality well – it even includes a lengthy jam on 'Woodchopper's Ball', which succeeds in dragging the Woody Herman original into the rock age with its dignity intact. *Stonedhenge* is still impressive too as the work of a band thinking hard and imaginatively of ways in which to break free of the constraints of playing the blues, even if that imagination was largely placed on hold for subsequent recordings.

| | | | | | | | |
|---|---|---|---|---|---|---|---|
| Cricklewood Green | LP | Deram | SML1065 | 1970 | £4 | £10 | |
| Hear Me Calling | 7" | Deram | DM221 | 1968 | £1.50 | £4 | |
| Love Like A Man | 7" | Deram | DM299 | 1970 | £1.50 | £4 | |
| Portable People | 7" | Deram | DM176 | 1967 | £1.50 | £4 | |
| Recorded Live | LP | Chrysalis | CHR1049 | 1973 | £4 | £10 | |
| Rock 'n' Roll To The World | LP | Chrysalis | CHR1009 | 1972 | £4 | £10 | |
| Space In Time | LP | Chrysalis | CHR1001 | 1972 | £4 | £10 | |
| Space In Time | LP | Columbia | CQ30801 | 1972 | £4 | £10 | *US quad* |
| Ssssh! | LP | Deram | DML1052 | 1969 | £6 | £15 | *mono* |
| Ssssh! | LP | Deram | SML1052 | 1969 | £4 | £10 | |
| Ssssh! | CD | Chrysalis | CD25CR05 | 1994 | £5 | £12 | *Chrysalis 25 pack* |
| Stonedhenge | LP | Deram | DML1029 | 1968 | £6 | £15 | *mono* |
| Stonedhenge | LP | Deram | SML1029 | 1968 | £4 | £10 | |
| Stonedhenge | CD | Deram | 8205342 | 1989 | £5 | £12 | |
| Ten Years After | LP | Deram | DML1015 | 1967 | £8 | £20 | *mono* |
| Ten Years After | LP | Deram | SML1015 | 1967 | £6 | £15 | |
| Ten Years After | CD | Deram | 8205322 | 1988 | £5 | £12 | |
| Undead | LP | Deram | DML1023 | 1968 | £6 | £15 | *mono* |
| Undead | LP | Deram | SML1023 | 1968 | £4 | £10 | |
| Undead | CD | Deram | 8205332 | 1988 | £5 | £12 | |
| Watt | LP | Deram | SML1078 | 1970 | £4 | £10 | |

## TENDER SLIM & COUSIN LEROY

| | | | | | | | |
|---|---|---|---|---|---|---|---|
| Tender Slim & Cousin Leroy | 7" EP | XX | MIN702 | 196– | £2 | £5 | |

## TENNORS

| | | | | | | | |
|---|---|---|---|---|---|---|---|
| Another Scorcher | 7" | Big Shot | BI517 | 1969 | £1.50 | £4 | |
| Copy Me Donkey | 7" | Island | WI3140 | 1968 | £5 | £10 | *Romeo Stewart B side* |
| Grampa | 7" | Island | WI3156 | 1968 | £5 | £10 | *Romeo Stewart B side* |
| Hopeful Village | 7" | Duke Reid | DR2502 | 1969 | £2.50 | £6 | *Tommy McCook B side* |
| Khaki | 7" | Blue Cat | BS127 | 1968 | £4 | £8 | *Leroy Reid B side* |
| Let Go Yah Donkey | 7" | Fab | FAB50 | 1968 | £4 | £8 | *Romeo Stewart B side* |
| Massie Massa | 7" | Doctor Bird | DB1152 | 1968 | £5 | £10 | *Clive Allstars B side* |
| Pressure And Slide | 7" | Coxsone | CS7024 | 1967 | £5 | £10 | *Soul Brothers B side* |
| Ride Your Donkey | 7" | Fab | FAB41 | 1968 | £4 | £8 | |
| Ride Your Donkey | 7" | Island | WI3133 | 1968 | £5 | £10 | |
| Sufferer | 7" | Doctor Bird | DB1175 | 1968 | £5 | £10 | |
| You're No Good | 7" | Big Shot | BI514 | 1969 | £1.50 | £4 | |

## TERJE, JESPER OG JOACHIM

| | | | | | | | |
|---|---|---|---|---|---|---|---|
| Jesper Og Joachim Terje | LP | Spectator | 1037 | 1970 | £75 | £150 | *Danish* |

## TERMITES

| | | | | | | | |
|---|---|---|---|---|---|---|---|
| Tell Me | 7" | Oriole | CB1989 | 1965 | £6 | £12 | |

## TERMITES (2)

| | | | | | | | |
|---|---|---|---|---|---|---|---|
| Do It Right Now | 7" | Coxsone | CS7025 | 1967 | £5 | £10 | *Summertaires B side* |
| Do The Rock Steady | LP | Studio One | SOL9003 | 1967 | £50 | £100 | |
| It Takes Two To Make Love | 7" | Studio One | SO2029 | 1967 | £6 | £12 | |
| Mama Didn't Know | 7" | Coxsone | CS7039 | 1968 | £5 | £10 | |
| Mercy Mr. Percy | 7" | Studio One | SO2006 | 1967 | £6 | £12 | *Soul Brothers B side* |
| Mr. DJ | 7" | Studio One | SO2040 | 1968 | £6 | £12 | |
| Push It Up | 7" | Pama | PM729 | 1968 | £2.50 | £6 | |
| Push Push | 7" | Nu Beat | NB017 | 1968 | £2.50 | £6 | |
| Show Me The Way | 7" | Pama | PM738 | 1968 | £2.50 | £6 | |
| Sign Up | 7" | Coxsone | CS7008 | 1967 | £5 | £10 | *Delroy Wilson B side* |

## TERRACE, PETE

| | | | | | | | |
|---|---|---|---|---|---|---|---|
| At The Party | 7" | Pye | 7N25427 | 1967 | £2 | £5 | |
| Boogaloo | LP | Pye | NPL28102 | 1967 | £6 | £15 | |
| Shotgun Boogaloo | 7" | Pye | 7N25440 | 1967 | £5 | £10 | |

## TERRAPLANE

| | | | | | | | |
|---|---|---|---|---|---|---|---|
| Moving Target | CD | Epic | 4601572 | 1987 | £5 | £12 | |

## TERRELL, LLOYD

| | | | | | | | |
|---|---|---|---|---|---|---|---|
| Bang Bang Lulu | 7" | Pama | PM710 | 1968 | £1.50 | £4 | *Mrs. Miller B side* |
| Birth Control | 7" | Pama | PM792 | 1969 | £2.50 | £6 | |
| How Come | 7" | Pama | PM740 | 1968 | £1.50 | £4 | *Mrs. Miller B side* |
| Lulu Returns | 7" | Pama | PM752 | 1968 | £1.50 | £4 | *Mrs. Miller B side* |
| Mr. Rhya | 7" | Nu Beat | NB023 | 1969 | £1.50 | £4 | |

## TERRELL, TAMMI

| | | | | | | | |
|---|---|---|---|---|---|---|---|
| Come On And See Me | 7" | Tamla Motown | TMG561 | 1966 | £20 | £40 | |
| Irresistible Tammi Terrell | LP | Tamla Motown | (S)TML11103 | 1969 | £10 | £25 | |

## TERRORVISION

| | | | | | | | |
|---|---|---|---|---|---|---|---|
| American TV | CD-s | Total Vegas | CDPVEGAS3 | 1993 | £2 | £5 | |

| | | | | | | | |
|---|---|---|---|---|---|---|---|
| Formaldehyde | LP | Total Vegas | ATVRLP1 | 1992 £8 | £20 | . 14 tracks, green vinyl |
| Formaldehyde | CD | Total Vegas | ATVRCD1 | 1992 £8 | £20 | 14 tracks |
| Live At Don Valley Stadium | CD | Total Vegas | BOOT1 | 1993 £8 | £20 | promo |
| My House | CD-s | Total Vegas | CDVEGAS2 | 1992 £10 | £20 | |
| My House | 12" | Total Vegas | 12VEGAS2 | 1992 £2.50 | £6 | |
| Prime Time Terrorvision | CD | Total Vegas | CDPRIMEDJ1 | 1994 £8 | £20 | promo |
| Problem Solved | CD-s | Total Vegas | CDATVR1 | 1993 £10 | £20 | |
| Thrive EP | CD-s | Total Vegas | CDVEGAS1 | 1992 £10 | £20 | |
| Thrive EP | 12" | Total Vegas | 12VEGAS1 | 1992 £5 | £12 | |

## TERRY, CLARK

| | | | | | | | |
|---|---|---|---|---|---|---|---|
| Clark Terry | LP | Emarcy | EJL1256 | 1957 £8 | £20 | |
| Duke With A Difference | LP | Riverside | RLP12246 | 1961 £6 | £15 | |
| Gingerbread Men | LP | Fontana | (S)TL5394 | 1967 £4 | £10 | |
| It's What's Happenin' | LP | Impulse | MIPL/SIPL507 | 1968 £4 | £10 | .with Bob Brookmeyer |
| Mumbles | LP | Fontana | TL5373 | 1966 £4 | £10 | |
| Power Of Positive Swinging | LP | Fontana | TL5290 | 1966 £4 | £10 | .with Bob Brookmeyer |
| Tonight | LP | Fontana | TL5265 | 1965 £4 | £10 | .with Bob Brookmeyer |

## TERRY, GORDON

| | | | | | | |
|---|---|---|---|---|---|---|
| Country Clambake | 7" EP | London | REA1098 | 1957 £7.50 | £15 | |

## TERRY, SONNY

| | | | | | | | |
|---|---|---|---|---|---|---|---|
| Blues | 10" LP | Stinson | 55 | | £6 | £15 | US |
| Blues And Folk Songs | 10" LP | Folkways | 2327 | | £6 | £15 | US |
| City Blues | 10" LP | Vogue | LDE165 | 1955 £6 | £15 | |
| Folk Blues | 10" LP | Vogue | LDE137 | 1955 £6 | £15 | |
| Fox Chase | 78 | Vogue | V2326 | 1955 £2.50 | £6 | |
| Harmonica | 10" LP | Folkways | 2035 | | £6 | £15 | US |
| Harmonica | 10" LP | Folkways | 35 | | £6 | £15 | US |
| Harmonica Blues | 10" LP | Topic | 10T30 | 1958 £8 | £20 | |
| Hooting Blues | 7" | Parlophone | MSP6017 | 1953 £10 | £20 | |
| Sonny Is King | LP | Bluesville | BV1059 | 1963 £6 | £15 | US |
| Sonny Terry | LP | Everest | 206 | 196– £6 | £15 | US |
| Sonny Terry | 7" EP | Vogue | EPV1095 | 1956 £5 | £10 | |
| Sonny Terry And His Mouth Harp | LP | Riverside | 12644 | | £6 | £15 | US |
| Sonny's Story | LP | Bluesville | BV1025 | 1961 £6 | £15 | US |
| Sonny's Story | LP | XTRA | XTRA5025 | 1966 £4 | £10 | |
| Talkin' 'Bout The Blues | LP | Washington | W702 | 1961 £8 | £20 | US |
| Washboard Band | 10" LP | Folkways | 2006 | | £6 | £15 | US |
| Whoopin' The Blues | 10" LP | Melodisc | MLP516 | 1958 £6 | £15 | |

## TERRY, SONNY & BROWNIE MCGHEE

| | | | | | | | |
|---|---|---|---|---|---|---|---|
| At The Second Fret | LP | Bluesville | BV1058 | 1962 £6 | £15 | US |
| Back Country Blues | LP | CBS | 52165 | 1963 £5 | £12 | |
| Back Country Blues | LP | Savoy | MG14019 | 195– £15 | £30 | US |
| Blues | LP | Folkways | F63557 | 1959 £8 | £20 | US |
| Blues All Around My Head | LP | Bluesville | BV(S)1020 | 1961 £6 | £15 | US |
| Blues And Folk | LP | Bluesville | BV(S)1005 | 1960 £6 | £15 | US |
| Blues And Shouts | LP | Fantasy | F3317 | 1962 £6 | £15 | US |
| Blues And Shouts | LP | Fantasy | F3317 | 1962 £15 | £30 | US, red vinyl |
| Blues In My Soul | LP | Bluesville | BV(S)1033 | 1961 £6 | £15 | US |
| Blues Is A Story | LP | Vogue | LAE12247 | 1961 £6 | £15 | mono |
| Blues Is A Story | LP | Vogue | SAE5014 | 1961 £10 | £25 | stereo |
| Blues Is My Companion | LP | Columbia | 33SX1223 | 1960 £8 | £20 | |
| Brownie McGhee And Sonny Terry | LP | Vogue | LAE552 | 1964 £6 | £15 | |
| Brownie's Blues | LP | Bluesville | BV(S)1042 | 1962 £6 | £15 | US |
| Down Home Blues | LP | Bluesville | BV(S)1002 | 1960 £6 | £15 | US |
| Down South Smmit Meeting | LP | Vogue | LAE12266 | 1961 £6 | £15 | |
| Folk Songs Of Sonny And Brownie | LP | Roulette | R25074 | 1959 £8 | £20 | US |
| Going Down Slow | 7" | Oriole | CBA1946 | 1964 £4 | £8 | |
| Guitar Highway | LP | Verve | (S)VLP5010 | 1966 £4 | £10 | |
| Hometown Blues | LP | Fontana | TL5289 | 1966 £4 | £10 | |
| In London | LP | Nixa | NJL18 | 1958 £8 | £20 | |
| Just A Closer Walk With Thee | LP | Fantasy | F3296 | 1962 £6 | £15 | US |
| Just A Closer Walk With Thee | LP | Fantasy | F3296 | 1962 £15 | £30 | US, red vinyl |
| Key To The Highway | LP | XTRA | XTRA1004 | 1964 £5 | £12 | |
| Livin' With The Blues | LP | Fontana | 688006ZL | 1965 £4 | £10 | |
| Me And Sonny | 7" EP | Melodisc | EPM783 | 1958 £2.50 | £6 | |
| Pawn Shop Blues | 7" EP | Realm | REP4002 | 1964 £2.50 | £6 | |
| Penetentiary Blues | LP | Fontana | 688007ZL | 1965 £5 | £12 | |
| R And B From S And B | 7" EP | Topic | TOP121 | 1964 £4 | £8 | |
| Rocking And Whooping | 7" | Columbia | DB4433 | 1960 £5 | £10 | |
| Simply Heavenly | LP | Columbia | OL5240 | 1957 £8 | £20 | US |
| Sonny & Brownie At Sugar Hill | LP | Fantasy | F8091 | 1962 £6 | £15 | US |
| Sonny & Brownie At Sugar Hill | LP | Fantasy | F8091 | 1962 £15 | £30 | US, blue vinyl |
| Sonny Terry & Brownie McGhee | LP | Fantasy | F3254 | 1961 £6 | £15 | US |
| Sonny Terry & Brownie McGhee | LP | Fantasy | F3254 | 1961 £15 | £30 | US, red vinyl |
| Sonny Terry & Brownie McGhee | 7" EP | Ember | EMBEP4562 | 1964 £2.50 | £6 | |
| Sonny Terry & Brownie McGhee & Chris Barber | 7" EP | Pye | NJE1073 | 1957 £2 | £5 | |
| Sonny Terry And Brownie McGhee | LP | Topic | 12T29 | 1958 £8 | £20 | |
| Sonny Terry And Brownie McGhee | 7" EP | Vocalion | EPV1274 | 1963 £4 | £8 | |
| Sonny Terry And Brownie McGhee | 7" EP | Vocalion | EPVF1279 | 1964 £4 | £8 | |
| Sonny, Brownie And Chris | 10" LP | Pye | NJT515 | 1958 £8 | £20 | .... with Chris Barber |
| Terry & McGhee In London | 7" EP | Pye | NJE1074 | 1957 £2.50 | £6 | |
| Traditional Blues Vol. 1 | LP | Folkways | F2421 | 1961 £6 | £15 | US |
| Traditional Blues Vol. 2 | LP | Folkways | F2422 | 1961 £6 | £15 | US |

| | | | | | | |
|---|---|---|---|---|---|---|
| Way Down South Summit Meeting | LP | World Pacific | WP(S)1296 | 1960 £6 | £15 | US |
| Where The Blues Began | LP | Fontana | SFJL979 | 1968 £4 | £10 | |
| Whoopin' The Blues | LP | Capitol | T20906 | 1967 £4 | £10 | |
| Work-Play-Faith-Fun Songs | 7" EP | Top Rank | JKP3007 | 1961 £2.50 | £6 | |

## TERRY & JERRY

| | | | | | |
|---|---|---|---|---|---|
| People Are Doing It Every Day | 7" | R&B | MRB5009 | 1965 £2 | £5 |

## TERRY & THE BLUE JEANS

| | | | | | | |
|---|---|---|---|---|---|---|
| Black And Beach | LP | King | SKD390 | 1976 £15 | £30 | Japanese |
| Blue Star | LP | King | SKA106 | 1975 £15 | £30 | Japanese |
| Electric Guitar Folk | LP | King | SKA96 | 1974 £8 | £20 | Japanese |
| Great Tracks | LP | King | SKM1297/98 | 1974 £15 | £30 | Japanese double |
| Pealing Shells | LP | Toshiba | 7071 | 1965 £62.50 | £125 | Japanese |
| Samba Pa Ti | LP | King | SKA87 | 1973 £10 | £25 | Japanese |
| Surfin' | LP | Toshiba | 7031 | 1964 £75 | £150 | Japanese red vinyl |

## TERRY SISTERS

| | | | | | |
|---|---|---|---|---|---|
| It's The Same Old Jazz | 7" | Parlophone | R4364 | 1957 £2.50 | £6 |

## TEST DEPARTMENT

| | | | | | | |
|---|---|---|---|---|---|---|
| Beating The Retreat | 12" | Some Bizarre | TEST2/3 | 1984 £3 | £8 | boxed double with inserts |
| Compulsion | 12" | Test | TEST112 | 1983 £2.50 | £6 | |
| Ecstasy Under Duress | cass | Pleasantly Surprised | PS5 | 198– £5 | £12 | in bag with inserts |
| Godaddin | 12" | Media City | CMC1 | 1988 £4 | £10 | |
| Pax Americana | CD-s | Ministry Of Power | MOP5CD | 1990 £2 | £5 | |

## TETRAGON

| | | | | | | |
|---|---|---|---|---|---|---|
| Nature | LP | Soma | SM1 | 1971 £75 | £150 | German |

## TEX, JOE

| | | | | | | |
|---|---|---|---|---|---|---|
| Best Of Joe Tex | LP | London | HAU8334 | 1967 £8 | £20 | |
| Buying A Book | LP | Atlantic | 588193 | 1969 £4 | £10 | |
| Go Home And Do It | 7" | Atlantic | 584212 | 1968 £1.50 | £4 | |
| Greatest Hits | LP | Atlantic | 587/588089 | 1967 £5 | £12 | |
| Hold On | LP | Checker | 2993 | 1964 £8 | £20 | US |
| Hold On To What You've Got | LP | Atlantic | (SD)8106 | 1965 £6 | £15 | US |
| Hold On To What You've Got | 7" | Atlantic | 584096 | 1967 £1.50 | £4 | |
| Hold On To What You've Got | 7" | Atlantic | AT4015 | 1965 £1.50 | £4 | |
| I Want To Do Everything | 7" | Atlantic | AT4045 | 1965 £1.50 | £4 | |
| I've Got To Do A Little Better | LP | Atlantic | 587053 | 1967 £4 | £10 | |
| Live And Lively | LP | Atlantic | 587/588104 | 1968 £4 | £10 | |
| Love You Save | LP | Atlantic | (SD)8124 | 1966 £6 | £15 | US |
| Love You Save | 7" | Atlantic | AT4081 | 1966 £1.50 | £4 | |
| Men Are Getting Scarce | 7" | Atlantic | 584171 | 1968 £1.50 | £4 | |
| New Boss | LP | Atlantic | 587/588059 | 1967 £4 | £10 | |
| New Boss | LP | Atlantic | ATL5043 | 1965 £8 | £20 | |
| Papa Was Too | 7" | Atlantic | 584068 | 1967 £1.50 | £4 | |
| S.Y.S.L.J.F.M. | 7" | Atlantic | 584016 | 1966 £1.50 | £4 | |
| Show Me | 7" | Atlantic | 584102 | 1967 £1.50 | £4 | |
| Skinny Legs And All | 7" | Atlantic | 584144 | 1967 £1.50 | £4 | |
| Soul Country | LP | Atlantic | 587/588118 | 1968 £4 | £10 | |
| Sweet Woman Like You | 7" | Atlantic | AT4058 | 1965 £1.50 | £4 | |
| We Can't Sit Down Now | 7" | Atlantic | 584296 | 1969 £1.50 | £4 | |
| Woman Can Change A Man | 7" | Atlantic | AT4027 | 1965 £1.50 | £4 | |
| Woman Like That, Yeah | 7" | Atlantic | 584119 | 1967 £1.50 | £4 | |
| You Better Believe It Baby | 7" | Atlantic | 584035 | 1966 £1.50 | £4 | |
| You Better Get It | LP | Atlantic | 587/588130 | 1968 £5 | £12 | |
| You Better Get It | 7" | Atlantic | AT4021 | 1965 £2.50 | £6 | |
| Yum Yum Yum | 7" | Sue | WI370 | 1965 £6 | £12 | |

## TEXAS ALEXANDER

| | | | | | |
|---|---|---|---|---|---|
| Treasures Of North American Negro Music Vol. 7 | 7" EP | Fontana | 467136TE | 1961 £4 | £8 |

## TEXAS RANGERS

| | | | | | |
|---|---|---|---|---|---|
| Way Out West | 7" EP | HMV | 7EG8387 | 1957 £2 | £5 |

## TEXTOR SINGERS

| | | | | | |
|---|---|---|---|---|---|
| Sobbin' Women | 7" | Capitol | CL14211 | 1954 £1.50 | £4 |

## THACKER, RUDY & THE STRINGBEANS

| | | | | | |
|---|---|---|---|---|---|
| Ballad Of Johnny Horton | 7" | Starlite | ST45087 | 1962 £4 | £8 |

## THACKRAY, JAKE

| | | | | | |
|---|---|---|---|---|---|
| Jake's Progress | LP | Columbia | SCX6345 | 1969 £4 | £10 |
| Last Will And Testament | LP | Columbia | SX/SCX6178 | 1967 £4 | £10 |
| Live Performance | LP | Columbia | SCX6453 | 1971 £4 | £10 |

## THARPE, SISTER ROSETTA

| | | | | | |
|---|---|---|---|---|---|
| Gospel Train | LP | Mercury | MPL6529 | 1957 £4 | £10 |
| Gospel Truth | LP | Mercury | MMC14057 | 1961 £4 | £10 |
| If I Can Help Somebody | 7" | MGM | MGM1072 | 1960 £1.50 | £4 |
| Sister Rosetta Tharpe | LP | Brunswick | LAT8290 | 1959 £4 | £10 |

## THAT PETROL EMOTION

| | | | | | | | |
|---|---|---|---|---|---|---|---|
| Cellophane | CD-s | Virgin | VSCD1116 | 1988 | £2 | £5 | |
| Genius Move | CD-s | Virgin | CDEP13 | 1988 | £2 | £5 | |
| Groove Check | CD-s | Virgin | VSCD1159 | 1989 | £2 | £5 | |
| Keen | 7" | Pink | PINKY4 | 1985 | £2 | £5 | |
| V2 | 7" | Noise A Noise | NAN1 | 1985 | £1.50 | £4 | |
| V2 | 12" | Noise A Noise | NAN1T | 1985 | £2.50 | £6 | |

## THE THE

| | | | | | | | |
|---|---|---|---|---|---|---|---|
| Alive | CD | Epic | ESK1867 | 1989 | £10 | £25 | US promo |
| Armageddon Days Are Here Again | CD-s | Epic | CDEMU10 | 1989 | £2 | £5 | |
| Beaten Generation | CD-s | Epic | CDEMU8 | 1989 | £2 | £5 | 2 versions |
| Cold Spell Ahead | 7" | Some Bizarre | BZS4 | 1981 | £10 | £20 | |
| Controversial Subject | 7" | 4AD | AD10 | 1980 | £10 | £20 | |
| Flesh And Bones | 7" | Some Bizarre | | 1985 | £4 | £8 | 1 sided promo |
| Gravitate To Me | CD-s | Epic | CDEMU9 | 1989 | £2 | £5 | |
| Infected | 12" | Epic | TRUTHD3 | 1986 | £2.50 | £6 | double |
| Infected | 12" | Epic | TRUTHQ3 | 1986 | £4 | £10 | uncensored picture sleeve |
| Live In New York | CD | Epic | ESK5300 | 1993 | £10 | £25 | US promo |
| Perfect | 7" | Epic | EPCA3119 | 1983 | £2 | £5 | |
| Perfect | 12" | Epic | EPCA133119 | 1983 | £3 | £8 | |
| Soul Mining | LP | Epic | 25525 | 1983 | £4 | £10 | with 12" |
| Sweet Bird Of Truth | CD-s | Epic | CDTHE2 | 1987 | £2 | £5 | |
| This Is The Day | 7" | Epic | A3710 | 1983 | £6 | £12 | double |
| This Is The Day | 12" | Epic | TA3710 | 1983 | £2.50 | £6 | |
| Uncertain Smile | 7" | Epic | EPCA2787 | 1982 | £2.50 | £6 | with insert |
| Uncertain Smile | 12" | Epic | EPC132787 | 1982 | £3 | £8 | insert |
| Uncertain Smile | 12" | Epic | EPC132787 | 1982 | £10 | £25 | yellow vinyl, insert |

## THEATRE OF HATE

| | | | | | | | |
|---|---|---|---|---|---|---|---|
| Original Sin | 7" | SS | SS3 | 1980 | £2.50 | £6 | |
| Rebel Without A Brain | 7" | Burning Rome | BRR1 | 1981 | £1.50 | £4 | |
| Wake | 7" | Bliss | TOH1EP | 1985 | £4 | £8 | ...with T shirt in 12" pack |

## THEE

| | | | | | | | |
|---|---|---|---|---|---|---|---|
| Each And Every Day | 7" | Decca | F12163 | 1965 | £15 | £30 | |

## THEE MIDNIGHTERS

| | | | | | | | |
|---|---|---|---|---|---|---|---|
| Bring You Love Special Delivery | LP | Whittier | W5000 | 1966 | £8 | £20 | US |
| Giants | LP | Whittier | WS5002 | 1967 | £8 | £20 | US |
| Land Of A Thousand Dances | 7" EP | Vogue | EPL8314 | 1966 | £7.50 | £15 | French |
| Thee Midnighters | LP | Chattahoochee | CS1001 | 1965 | £8 | £20 | US |
| Unlimited | LP | Whittier | W5001 | 1966 | £8 | £20 | US |

## THEE MUFFINS

| | | | | | | | |
|---|---|---|---|---|---|---|---|
| Pop Up | LP | Fan Club | | 1966 | £180 | £300 | US |

## THELWALL, LLANS & THE CELESTIALS

| | | | | | | | |
|---|---|---|---|---|---|---|---|
| Choo Choo Ska | 7" | Island | WI262 | 1966 | £5 | £10 | |

## THEM

Despite being continually plagued by management and record company problems, Them managed to produce some of the toughest and most enduring of British R&B. Much of the credit for this inevitably goes to the group's lead singer – Van Morrison – already a distinctive and commanding vocalist.

| | | | | | | | |
|---|---|---|---|---|---|---|---|
| Angry Young Them | LP | Decca | LK4700 | 1965 | £30 | £60 | |
| Angry Young Them | LP | Decca | LK4700 | 1969 | £6 | £15 | boxed Decca logo |
| Baby Please Don't Go | CD-s | London | LONCD292 | 1991 | £2 | £5 | |
| Baby Please Don't Go | 7" | Decca | F12018 | 1964 | £1.50 | £4 | |
| Being Em On In | 7" EP | Decca | 457108 | 1966 | £30 | £60 | French |
| Call My Name | 7" | Decca | F12355 | 1966 | £2 | £5 | |
| Don't Start Crying Now | 7" EP | Decca | 457069 | 1965 | £30 | £60 | French |
| Don't Start Crying Now | 7" | Decca | F11973 | 1964 | £12.50 | £25 | |
| Gloria | 7" EP | Decca | 457073 | 1965 | £30 | £60 | French |
| Gloria | 7" | Major Minor | MM509 | 1967 | £2 | £5 | |
| Gloria's Dream | 7" EP | Vogue | INT18079 | 1966 | £37.50 | £75 | French |
| Here Comes The Night | 7" | Decca | F12094 | 1965 | £1.50 | £4 | |
| In Reality | LP | Happy Tiger | HT1012 | 1971 | £10 | £25 | US |
| It Won't Hurt Half As Much | 7" | Decca | F12215 | 1965 | £2 | £5 | |
| Mystic Eyes | 7" | Decca | F12281 | 1965 | £2 | £5 | |
| Now & Them | LP | Tower | ST5104 | 1968 | £20 | £40 | US |
| One More Time | 7" | Decca | F12175 | 1965 | £2 | £5 | |
| Portland Town | 7" EP | Vogue | INT18135 | 1967 | £37.50 | £75 | French |
| Richard Cory | 7" | Decca | F12403 | 1966 | £2 | £5 | |
| Story Of Them | 7" | Major Minor | MM513 | 1967 | £2.50 | £6 | |
| Them | LP | Happy Tiger | HT1004 | 1970 | £25 | £30 | US |
| Them | 7" EP | Decca | DFE8612 | 1965 | £30 | £60 | |
| Them | 7" EP | Decca | DFE8612 | 1965 | £37.50 | £75 | export |
| Them Again | LP | Decca | LK4751 | 1966 | £30 | £60 | |
| Them Again | LP | Decca | LK4751 | 1969 | £6 | £15 | boxed, Decca logo |
| Time Out,Time In For Them | LP | Tower | ST5116 | 1968 | £20 | £40 | US |

## THEN JERICHO

| | | | | | | | |
|---|---|---|---|---|---|---|---|
| Big Sweep | 12" | Immaculate | TJ1 | 1985 | £6 | £15 | |

| | | | | | | | |
|---|---|---|---|---|---|---|---|
| Fault | 12" | London | LONX63 | 1985 | £2.50 | £6 | |
| Prairie Rose | CD-s | London | LONCD131 | 1987 | £2 | £5 | |

## THERAPY
| | | | | | | | |
|---|---|---|---|---|---|---|---|
| One Night Stand | LP | Indigo | IRS5124 | 1973 | £6 | £15 | Irish |

## THERAPY?
| | | | | | | | |
|---|---|---|---|---|---|---|---|
| Have A Merry Fucking Christmas | 7" | A&M | THX1 | 1992 | £10 | £20 | |
| Meat Abstract | 7" | Multifucking-national | MFN1 | 1990 | £10 | £20 | |

## THESE FADING COLOURS
| | | | | | | | |
|---|---|---|---|---|---|---|---|
| Just Like Romeo And Juliet | 7" | Ember | EMB5229 | 1966 | £1.50 | £4 | |

## THESE TRAILS
| | | | | | | | |
|---|---|---|---|---|---|---|---|
| These Trails | LP | Sinergia | | 1973 | £50 | £100 | US |

## THIELMANS, JEAN 'TOOTS'
| | | | | | | | |
|---|---|---|---|---|---|---|---|
| Sound | LP | Philips | BBL7058 | 1956 | £6 | £15 | |

## THIN LIZZY
| | | | | | | | |
|---|---|---|---|---|---|---|---|
| Boys Are Back In Town | CD-s | Vertigo | LIZCD15 | 1991 | £2 | £5 | |
| Dedication | CD-s | Vertigo | LIZCD14 | 1991 | £2 | £5 | |
| Farmer | 7" | Parlophone | DIP513 | 1970 | £400 | £600 | Irish, best auctioned |
| Hollywood | 10" | Vertigo | LIZZY10 | 1982 | £2.50 | £6 | 1 sided |
| Little Darling | 7" | Decca | F13507 | 1974 | £2 | £5 | |
| New Day EP | 7" | Decca | F13208 | 1972 | £50 | £100 | |
| Randolph's Tango | 7" | Decca | F13402 | 1973 | £5 | £10 | 2 versions |
| Rocker | CD | Castle Collector | CCSCD117 | 1987 | £8 | £20 | box set with 20 track CD 'The Collection' plus biography, in 6 x9" box |
| Rocker | 7" | Decca | F13467 | 1973 | £2 | £5 | |
| Shades Of A Blue Orphanage | LP | Decca | TXS108 | 1972 | £5 | £12 | |
| Thin Lizzy | LP | Decca | SKL5082 | 1971 | £8 | £20 | |
| Thunder And Lightning | 12" | Vertigo | LIZZY1212 | 1983 | £4 | £10 | with poster |
| Vagabonds Of The Western World | LP | Decca | SKL5170 | 1973 | £4 | £10 | with insert |

## THIRD EAR BAND
| | | | | | | | |
|---|---|---|---|---|---|---|---|
| Alchemy | LP | Harvest | SHVL756 | 1969 | £6 | £15 | |
| Experiences | LP | Harvest | SHSM2007 | 1976 | £4 | £10 | |
| Music From Macbeth | LP | Harvest | SHSP4019 | 1972 | £5 | £12 | |
| Third Ear Band | LP | Harvest | SHVL773 | 1970 | £5 | £12 | |

## THIRD ESTATE
| | | | | | | | |
|---|---|---|---|---|---|---|---|
| Years Before The Wine | LP | private | | 1976 | £330 | £500 | US |

## THIRD POWER
| | | | | | | | |
|---|---|---|---|---|---|---|---|
| Believe | LP | Vanguard | VSD6554 | 1970 | £15 | £30 | US |

## THIRD QUADRANT
| | | | | | | | |
|---|---|---|---|---|---|---|---|
| Seeing Yourself As You Really Are | LP | Rock Cottage | no number | 1982 | £50 | £100 | |

## THIRD RAIL
| | | | | | | | |
|---|---|---|---|---|---|---|---|
| Id Music | LP | Epic | LN24327/BN26327 | 1967 | £15 | £30 | US |
| Run Run Run | 7" | Columbia | DB8274 | 1967 | £10 | £20 | |

## THIRD WORLD WAR
| | | | | | | | |
|---|---|---|---|---|---|---|---|
| Ascension Day | 7" | Fly | BUG7 | 1971 | £1.50 | £4 | picture sleeve |
| Third World War | LP | Fly | FLY4 | 1971 | £4 | £10 | |
| Third World War II | LP | Track | 2406108 | 1972 | £10 | £25 | |

## THIRSTY MOON
| | | | | | | | |
|---|---|---|---|---|---|---|---|
| Blitz | LP | Brain | 1079 | 1975 | £4 | £10 | German |
| Thirsty Moon | LP | Brain | 1021 | 1973 | £4 | £10 | German |
| You'll Never Come Back | LP | Brain | 1041 | 1974 | £4 | £10 | German |

## THIRTEENTH FLOOR ELEVATORS

The group led by Roky Erickson were apparently the first to describe themselves as psychedelic and the first LP has a suitably colourful cover. Musically, however, the group pales next to more celebrated artists like Jefferson Airplane and the Grateful Dead. The Elevators' brand of garage punk is further undermined by the inclusion of an 'electric jug' player, who sounds for the most part like a slightly demented chicken.

| | | | | | | | |
|---|---|---|---|---|---|---|---|
| Bull Of The Woods | LP | International Artists | IA9 | 1969 | £30 | £60 | US |
| Easter Everywhere | LP | International Artists | IA5 | 1968 | £87.50 | £175 | US |
| Easter Everywhere | LP | Radar | RAD15 | 1979 | £4 | £10 | |
| Fire In My Bones | LP | Texas Archive | TAR4 | 1985 | £4 | £10 | US |
| Live | LP | International Artists | IA8 | 1968 | £30 | £60 | US |
| Psychedelic Sounds | LP | International Artists | LP1 | 1966 | £37.50 | £75 | US |
| Psychedelic Sounds | LP | Radar | RAD13 | 1978 | £4 | £10 | |
| Reverberation | 7" EP | Riviera | 231240 | 1966 | £500 | £750 | French, best auctioned |

## THIRTY SECOND TURN OFF
Thirty Second Turn Off............................ LP ...... Jay Boy ........... JSL1 ....................... 1969 £20.........£40 ....................................

## THIRTY-FIRST OF FEBRUARY
Butch Trucks, one of the two drummers in the Allman Brothers Band, played in this band previously, while guitarist Scott Boyer went on to play with the sub-Allmans group, Cowboy.

Thirty-First Of February ...................... LP ...... Vanguard ........ VSD6503 .............. 1969 £15.........£30 ....................... US

## THIS DRIFTIN'S GOTTA STOP
This Driftin's Gotta Stop ........................... LP ...... private............. .................... 197– £15.........£30 ....................................

## THIS HEAT
Deceit.................................................. LP ...... Rough Trade... ROUGH26.............. 1981 £4.........£10 ....................................
Health And Efficiency............................... 12" ...... Piano ........... THIS1201 .............. 1980 £4.........£10 ....................................
This Heat ................................................ LP ...... Piano ........... THIS1 .................... 1979 £5.........£12 ....................................

## THIS MORTAL COIL
Come Here My Love ............................. 10" ...... 4AD ............... BAD608................ 1986 £2.50.........£6 ....................................

## THIS 'N' THAT
Someday................................................ 7" ...... Mercury........... MF938 .................... 1966 £5.........£10 ....................................

## THOLLOT, JACQUES
Quand le son devient trop aigu ................. LP ...... Futura............. 24........................ 1971 £4.........£10 ....................... French

## THOMAS, B. J.
B. J. Thomas And The Triumphs............... LP ...... Pacemaker....... PLP3001 .............. 196– £8.........£20 ....................... US
Very Best Of B. J. Thomas........................ LP ...... Hickory ........... LP(S)133 .............. 1966 £4.........£10 ....................... US

## THOMAS, CARLA
B-a-b-y.................................................. 7" ...... Atlantic .......... 584042............. 1966 £1.50.........£4 ....................................
Best Of Carla Thomas............................. LP ...... Atlantic .......... SD8232 .............. 1969 £4.........£10 ....................... US
Carla ................................................... LP ...... Stax .............. 589004.............. 1967 £6.........£15 ....................................
Comfort Me .......................................... LP ...... Stax .............. ST(S)706 .......... 1966 £6.........£15 ....................... US
Comfort Me .......................................... 7" ...... Atlantic .......... AT4074............. 1966 £1.50.........£4 ....................................
Gee Whiz .............................................. LP ...... Atlantic .......... 8057 .................. 1961 £15.........£30 ....................... US
Gee Whiz .............................................. 7" ...... London ............ HLK9310............. 1961 £4.........£8 ....................................
I Like What You're Doing To Me .............. 7" ...... Stax .............. STAX112............. 1969 £1.50.........£4 ....................................
I'll Bring It On Home To You .................. 7" ...... London ............ HLK9618............. 1962 £2.........£5 ....................................
I've Got No Time To Lose ....................... 7" ...... Atlantic .......... AT4005.............. 1964 £1.50.........£4 ....................................
Let Me Be Good To You .......................... 7" ...... Atlantic .......... 584011.............. 1966 £1.50.........£4 ....................................
Love Of My Own .................................... 7" ...... London ............ HLK9359............. 1961 £2.........£5 ....................................
Memphis Queen ...................................... LP ...... Stax .............. SXATS2019 .......... 1969 £4.........£10 ....................................
Pick Up The Pieces ................................. 7" ...... Stax .............. 601032.............. 1968 £1.50.........£4 ....................................
Queen Alone .......................................... LP ...... Stax .............. 589012.............. 1967 £6.........£15 ....................................
Something Good...................................... 7" ...... Stax .............. 601002.............. 1967 £1.50.........£4 ....................................
When Tomorrow Comes............................ 7" ...... Stax .............. 601008.............. 1967 £1.50.........£4 ....................................
Where Do I Go ...................................... 7" ...... Stax .............. STAX103............. 1968 £1.50.........£4 ....................................

## THOMAS, CLAUDETTE
Roses Are Red My Love........................... 7" ...... Caltone ........... TONE116.............. 1968 £4.........£8 ....................................

## THOMAS, CREEPY JOHN
Creepy John Thomas................................ LP ...... RCA .............. SF8061................ 1969 £20.........£40 ....................................
Ride A Rainbow ..................................... 7" ...... RCA .............. RCA1912.............. 1970 £2.........£5 ....................................

## THOMAS, DAVID
Didn't Have A Very Good Time ................ 7" ...... Recommended REDT7 ................. 1983 £4.............£8 ..........1 side painted

## THOMAS, DOC GROUP
The rare LP recorded in Italy by the British Doc Thomas Group achieves its high value by virtue of its connection with Mott the Hoople, whose guitarist Mick Ralphs and bassist Pete (Overend) Watts played in the earlier band. There was, incidentally, no Mr Thomas.

Doc Thomas Group.................................. LP ...... Interrecord ...... ILP280 .................. 1966 £62.50..£125 .................... Italian

## THOMAS, GENE
Baby's Gone .......................................... 7" ...... United Artists .. UP1047.................. 1964 £4.............£8 ....................................

## THOMAS, IRMA
Don't Mess With My Man ........................ 7" ...... Sue ................ WI372 .................. 1965 £6.........£12 ....................................
I'm Gonna Cry Till My Tears Run Dry ..... 7" ...... Liberty ........... LIB66106 ................ 1965 £6.........£12 ....................................
It's A Man's Woman's World .................... 7" ...... Liberty ........... LIB66178 ................ 1966 £2.........£5 ....................................
Some Things You Never Get Used To....... 7" ...... Liberty ........... LIB66095 ................ 1965 £5.........£10 ....................................
Take A Look .......................................... LP ...... Minit ............. MLL/MLS40004.... 1966 £8.........£20 ....................................
Take A Look .......................................... 7" ...... Liberty ........... LIB66137 ................ 1966 £5.........£10 ....................................
Time Is On My Side ................................ 7" EP .. Liberty ........... LEP4035 ................ 1965 £12.50.........£25 ....................................
Time Is On My Side ................................ 7" ...... Liberty ........... LIB66041 ................ 1964 £7.50.........£15 ....................................
True True Love ....................................... 7" ...... Liberty ........... LIB66080 ................ 1965 £2.50.........£6 ....................................
Wish Someone Would Care ...................... LP ...... Imperial .......... LP9266/12266 ...... 1964 £8.........£20 ....................... US
Wish Someone Would Care ...................... 7" ...... Liberty ........... LIB66013 ................ 1964 £5.........£10 ....................................

## THOMAS, JAMO
I Spy (For The FBI)................................. 7" ...... Polydor........... 56709.................... 1966 £2.........£5 ....................................
I Spy (For The FBI)................................. 7" ...... Polydor........... 56755.................... 1969 £1.50.........£4 ....................................
I'll Be Your Fool..................................... 7" ...... Chess .............. CRS8098 .............. 1969 £2.........£5 ....................................

## THOMAS, JIMMY
Beautiful Night .................................. 7" ...... Parlophone ...... R5773 ................. 1969 £**37.50**...£**75** ..............................
Beautiful Night .................................. 7" ...... Parlophone ...... R5773 ................. 1969 £**30**........£**60** ......................*demo*

## THOMAS, KID
Victory Walk ................................ LP ..... 77 .............. LA1226 ........... 1964 £**4** ......... £**10**

## THOMAS, LEON
Blues And Soulful Truth ...................... LP ...... Philips.............. 6369417 ................. 1973 £**4** ......... £**10**

## THOMAS, NICKY
If I Had A Hammer............................... 7" ..... Trojan............ TR7807 .............. 1970 £**1.50**........£**4**
Love Of The Common People ............... LP ...... Trojan............ TBL143 ............. 1970 £**4**.........£**10**

## THOMAS, RUFUS
Can Your Monkey Do The Dog ............. 7" ...... London ...... HLK9850 ............... 1964 £**2** ........ £**5**
Did You Hear Me?................................ LP ..... Stax ......... 2362028 ........... 1972 £**6**.........£**15**
Do The Dog.................................. 7" EP . Atlantic ....... AET6001 ........... 1964 £**7.50**...£**15**
Doing The Push And Pull.................... LP ..... Stax ......... 2362010 ........... 1971 £**4**........£**10**
Down To My House ...................... 7" ..... Stax ......... 601028 .......... 1968 £**1.50**........£**4**
Funky Chicken ............................... LP ..... Stax ......... SXATS1033 ......... 1970 £**4**........£**10**
Greasy Spoon .............................. 7" ..... Stax ......... 601013 .......... 1967 £**1.50**........£**4**
Jump Back ................................. 7" ..... Atlantic ....... 584089 .......... 1967 £**1.50**........£**4**
Jump Back ................................. 7" ..... Atlantic ....... AT4009 .......... 1964 £**2**.........£**5**
Jump Back With Rufus Thomas ............... 7" EP . Atlantic ....... AET6011 .......... 1965 £**7.50**...£**15**
Memphis Train ............................. 7" ..... Stax ......... 601037 .......... 1968 £**1.50**........£**4**
Somebody Stole My Dog...................... 7" ..... London ...... HLK9884 .......... 1964 £**2**.........£**5**
Walking The Dog .......................... LP ..... London ...... HAK8183 .......... 1964 £**10**........£**25**
Walking The Dog .......................... 7" ..... London ...... HLK9799 .......... 1963 £**5**........£**10**
Willy Nilly .............................. 7" ..... Atlantic ....... 584029 .......... 1966 £**1.50**........£**4**

## THOMAS, TERRY
Sweet Old Fashioned Boy ..................... 7" ...... Decca ............ F10804 .......... 1956 £**2**.........£**5**

## THOMOPOULOUS, ANDREAS
Born Out Of The Tears Of The Sun......... LP ..... Mushroom ...... 150MR4 ........... 1971 £**37.50**...£**75**
So Long Suzanne ........................... 7" ..... Mushroom ...... ........... 1970 £**20**.......£**40**
Songs Of The Street ....................... LP ..... Mushroom ...... 100MR1 ........... 1970 £**37.50**...£**75**

## THOMPSON, BOBBY
That's How Strong My Love Is................. 7" ..... Columbia........ DB113 ......... 1969 £**1.50**........£**4**
That's How Strong My Love Is................. 7" ...... Jolly.............. JY001 ........... 1968 £**2**.........£**5**

## THOMPSON, CHRIS
Chris Thompson .......................... LP ..... Village Thing... VTS21 ............... 1973 £**6** ........ £**15**

## THOMPSON, DON
Don Thompson .......................... LP ..... Sunday........... 1975 £**62.50**...£**125** ....................... *US*

## THOMPSON, EDDIE
His Master's Jazz.......................... LP ..... Tempo............. TAP24 .............. 1960 £**10**.........£**25**

## THOMPSON, HANK
Anybody's Girl.......................... 7" ..... Capitol....... CL15014 ........ 1959 £**1.50**........£**4**
At The Golden Nugget...................... LP ..... Capitol....... (S)T1632 ....... 1962 £**4**........£**10**
Favorite Waltzes......................... LP ..... Capitol....... T1111 ........ 1959 £**5**........£**12** .......... *US*
Favourite Waltzes........................ 7" EP . Capitol....... EAP11111 ........ 1959 £**2**........£**5**
Gathering Flowers ....................... 7" ..... Capitol....... CL14945 ........ 1958 £**2**........£**5**
Hank .................................... LP ..... Capitol....... T826 ........ 1957 £**6**........£**15** .......... *US*
Hank .................................... 7" EP . Capitol....... EAP1826 ........ 1957 £**2.50**...£**6**
Hank Thompson Favorites .................. LP ..... Capitol....... T911 ........ 1957 £**6**........£**15** .......... *US*
Hank Thompson Favorites .................. 10" LP Capitol....... H911 ........ 1956 £**10**........£**25** .......... *US*
Hank Thompson's Dance Ranch ............. LP ..... Capitol....... T975 ........ 1958 £**6**........£**15** .......... *US*
Honey, Honey Bee Ball .................... 7" ..... Capitol....... CL14517 ........ 1956 £**4**........£**8**
I Guess I'm Getting Over You ............. 7" ..... Capitol....... CL15074 ........ 1959 £**1.50**........£**4**
I'm Not Mad, Just Hurt ................... 7" ..... Capitol....... CL14668 ........ 1956 £**2.50**...£**6**
I've Run Out Of Tomorrows ............... 7" ..... Capitol....... CL14961 ........ 1958 £**1.50**........£**4**
Li'l Liza Jane ........................... 7" ..... Capitol....... CL14869 ........ 1958 £**2.50**...£**6**
Most Of All ............................... LP ..... Capitol....... (S)T1360 ........ 1960 £**5**........£**12** .......... *US*
New Recordings Of Hank's All-Time Hits. LP ..... Capitol....... T729 ........ 1956 £**8**........£**20** .......... *US*
New Recordings Of Hank's All-Time Hits. 10" LP Capitol....... H729 ........ 1956 £**10**........£**25** .......... *US*
North Of The Rio Grande.................. LP ..... Capitol....... T618 ........ 1956 £**8**........£**20** .......... *US*
North Of The Rio Grande.................. 10" LP Capitol....... H618 ........ 1955 £**10**........£**25** .......... *US*
Six Pack To Go ........................... 7" ..... Capitol....... CL15114 ........ 1960 £**4**........£**8**
Songs For Rounders ....................... LP ..... Capitol....... (S)T1246 ........ 1959 £**4**........£**10**
Songs Of The Brazos Valley ............... LP ..... Capitol....... T418 ........ 1956 £**8**........£**20** .......... *US*
Songs Of The Brazos Valley ............... 10" LP Capitol....... H418 ........ 1953 £**10**........£**25** .......... *US*
Songs Of The Brazos Valley No. 1 ........ 7" EP . Capitol....... EAP1028 ........ 1956 £**2.50**...£**6**
This Broken Heart Of Mine ................ LP ..... Capitol....... (S)T1469 ........ 1960 £**4**........£**10**

## THOMPSON, HAYDEN
Here's Hayden Thompson...................... LP ...... Kapp.............. KL1507/KS3507 ..... 1966 £**5** ........ £**12** ....................... *US*

## THOMPSON, KAY
Eloise ................................. 7" ...... London ...... HLA8268 ........ 1956 £**7.50**...£**15**
Kay Thompson .......................... LP ..... MGM............ E3146 .......... 195– £**6**........£**15** ....................... *US*

## THOMPSON, LUCKY

| | | | | | | | |
|---|---|---|---|---|---|---|---|
| Lucky Thompson | LP | HMV | CLP1237 | 1958 | £10 | £25 | |
| Recorded In Paris '56 | 10" LP | Ducretet-Thomson | D93098 | 1956 | £8 | £20 | |
| With The Gerard Pochonet Orchestra | LP | Vogue | LAE12022 | 1956 | £8 | £20 | |

## THOMPSON, MAYO

| | | | | | | | |
|---|---|---|---|---|---|---|---|
| Corky's Debt To His Father | LP | Texas Revolution | CFS2270 | 1970 | £20 | £40 | US |

## THOMPSON, MIKE

| | | | | | | | |
|---|---|---|---|---|---|---|---|
| Rocksteady Wedding | 7" | Island | WI3090 | 1967 | £5 | £10 | |

## THOMPSON, RICHARD

Since leaving Fairport Convention, Richard Thompson has matured, not only into a songwriter of particularly fine material, but also into a brilliant and highly individual guitarist. Inevitably, a man who is a major but not especially fashionable talent had trouble in the eighties in finding suitable recording contracts. The relative scarcity of the *Strict Tempo* album is an immediate consequence of this. Happily, Thompson's fortunes have risen in recent years, and following a run of superb albums for Capitol (it is remarkable enough that any rock musician should make the best music of his career over twenty years after starting it) his profile is higher than it has ever been.

| | | | | | | | |
|---|---|---|---|---|---|---|---|
| Guitar, Vocal | LP | Island | ICD8 | 1976 | £6 | £15 | double |
| Henry The Human Fly | LP | Island | ILPS9197 | 1972 | £5 | £12 | |
| I Feel So Good | CD-s | Capitol | CDCL617 | 1991 | £2 | £5 | |
| Live | CD | Capitol | | 1992 | £10 | £25 | US promo |
| Read About Love | CD-s | Capitol | CDCL638 | 1991 | £2 | £5 | |
| Reckless Kind | CD-s | Capitol | CDCL550 | 1989 | £2 | £5 | |
| Strict Tempo | LP | Elixir | LP1 | 1981 | £4 | £10 | |
| Watching The Dark | CD | Ryko | VRCD5303 | 1991 | £8 | £20 | US promo sampler |

## THOMPSON, RICHARD & LINDA

| | | | | | | | |
|---|---|---|---|---|---|---|---|
| First Light | LP | Chrysalis | CHR1177 | 1978 | £4 | £10 | |
| Hokey Pokey | LP | Island | ILPS9305 | 1974 | £4 | £10 | |
| I Want To See The Bright Lights Tonight | LP | Island | ILPS9266 | 1974 | £4 | £10 | |
| Pour Down Like Silver | LP | Island | ILPS9348 | 1975 | £4 | £10 | |
| Sunny Vista | LP | Chrysalis | CHR1247 | 1979 | £4 | £10 | |

## THOMPSON, ROY

| | | | | | | | |
|---|---|---|---|---|---|---|---|
| Sookie Sookie | 7" | Columbia | DB8108 | 1967 | £2 | £5 | |

## THOMPSON, SIR CHARLES

| | | | | | | | |
|---|---|---|---|---|---|---|---|
| Allstars With Charlie Parker | 10" LP | Vogue | LDE032 | 1953 | £30 | £60 | |
| And His Band Featuring Coleman Hawkins | 10" LP | Vanguard | PPT12011 | 1956 | £20 | £40 | |
| Sir Charles Thompson Quartet | 10" LP | Vanguard | PPT12007 | 1956 | £15 | £30 | |
| Sir Charles Thompson Trio | 10" LP | Vanguard | PPT12020 | 1958 | £15 | £30 | |

## THOMPSON, SONNY

| | | | | | | | |
|---|---|---|---|---|---|---|---|
| Houseful Of Blues | 78 | Esquire | 10320 | 1953 | £6 | £12 | |
| Mellow Blues For The Late Hours | LP | King | 655 | 1959 | £20 | £40 | US |
| Moody Blues | LP | King | 568 | 1956 | £25 | £50 | US |
| Real Real Fine | 78 | Vogue | V2143 | 1952 | £6 | £12 | |
| Screamin' Boogie | 78 | Esquire | 10339 | 1953 | £6 | £12 | |
| Screaming Boogie | 7" | Starlite | ST45008 | 1960 | £62.50 | £125 | |

## THOMPSON, SUE

| | | | | | | | |
|---|---|---|---|---|---|---|---|
| Bad Boy | 7" | Hickory | 451255 | 1964 | £2 | £5 | |
| Big Daddy | 7" | Hickory | 451240 | 1964 | £1.50 | £4 | |
| Have A Good Time | 7" | Polydor | NH66979 | 1962 | £1.50 | £4 | |
| I Like Your Kind Of Love | 7" | Polydor | NH66989 | 1963 | £2 | £5 | with Bob Luman |
| I'm Looking For A World | 7" | Hickory | 451359 | 1965 | £1.50 | £4 | |
| It's Break-Up Time | 7" | Hickory | 451328 | 1965 | £2 | £5 | |
| James | 7" | Fontana | 267244TF | 1962 | £2 | £5 | |
| Norman | 7" | Polydor | NH66973 | 1962 | £2 | £5 | |
| Paper Tiger | LP | Hickory | LPM102 | 1964 | £6 | £15 | |
| Paper Tiger | 7" | Hickory | 451284 | 1965 | £1.50 | £4 | |
| Sad Movies | 7" | Polydor | NH66967 | 1961 | £2 | £5 | |
| Two Of A Kind | 7" | Polydor | NH66976 | 1962 | £1.50 | £4 | |
| What's Wrong Billy | 7" | Polydor | NH66987 | 1963 | £1.50 | £4 | |
| Willie Can | 7" | Fontana | 267262TF | 1963 | £1.50 | £4 | |

## THOMPSON TWINS

| | | | | | | | |
|---|---|---|---|---|---|---|---|
| She's In Love With Mystery | 7" | Latent | LATE1 | 1980 | £1.50 | £4 | |
| Squares And Triangles | 7" | Dirty Discs | RANK1 | 1980 | £4 | £8 | |

## THORN, GUNILLA

| | | | | | | | |
|---|---|---|---|---|---|---|---|
| Merry Go Round | 7" | HMV | POP1239 | 1963 | £25 | £50 | |

## THORNE, DAVID

| | | | | | | | |
|---|---|---|---|---|---|---|---|
| Alley Cat Songster | LP | Stateside | SL10036 | 1963 | £6 | £15 | |
| What Will I Tell My Heart | 7" EP | Stateside | SE1020 | 1964 | £2 | £5 | |

## THORNE, WOODY

| | | | | | | | |
|---|---|---|---|---|---|---|---|
| Sadie Lou | 7" | Vogue | V9202 | 1962 | £75 | £150 | |

## THORNHILL, CLAUDE

| | | | | | | | |
|---|---|---|---|---|---|---|---|
| Claude On A Cloud | LP | Brunswick | LAT827-/STA3003 | 1959 | £4 | £10 | |
| Dream Music | 10" LP | London | HAPB1021 | 1954 | £10 | £25 | |

| | | | | | | | | |
|---|---|---|---|---|---|---|---|---|
| Goes Modern | 7" EP . | London | REP1009 | 1954 | £2 | £5 | |
| Goes Modern | 10" LP | London | HAPB1019 | 1954 | £10 | £25 | |
| Pussyfooting | 7" | London | HL8042 | 1954 | £10 | £20 | |

### THORNTON, EDDIE
| | | | | | | | |
|---|---|---|---|---|---|---|---|
| Baby Be My Gal | 7" | Instant | IN003 | 1969 | £2 | £5 | |

### THORNTON, FRADKIN & UNGER
| | | | | | | | | |
|---|---|---|---|---|---|---|---|---|
| Pass On This Side | LP | ESP-Disk | 63019 | 1968 | £10 | £25 | US |

### THORNTON, WILLIE MAE (BIG MAMA)
| | | | | | | | | |
|---|---|---|---|---|---|---|---|---|
| Hound Dog | 78 | Vogue | V2284 | 1954 | £10 | £20 | |
| Tom Cat | 7" | Sue | WI345 | 1964 | £37.50 | £75 | |
| Way It Is | LP | Mercury | SRM161249 | 1970 | £4 | £10 | US |

### THOR'S HAMMER
| | | | | | | | | |
|---|---|---|---|---|---|---|---|---|
| If You Knew | 7" | Parlophone | DP567 | 1966 | £50 | £100 | export |
| Once | 7" | Parlophone | DP565 | 1966 | £50 | £100 | export |
| Thor's Hammer | LP | Metronome | MLP15412 | 1971 | £62.50 | £125 | Danish |
| Thor's Hammer | 7" EP . | Parlophone | CGEP62 | 1966 | £400 | £600 | export, with bonus 7", best auctioned |

### THORSON, LINDA
| | | | | | | | |
|---|---|---|---|---|---|---|---|
| Here I Am | 7" | Ember | EMBS257 | 1968 | £5 | £10 | |

### THORUP, PETER
| | | | | | | | | |
|---|---|---|---|---|---|---|---|---|
| Thin Slices | LP | Metronome | MLP15635 | 1978 | £4 | £10 | German |

### THOUGHTS
| | | | | | | | |
|---|---|---|---|---|---|---|---|
| All Night Stand | 7" | Planet | PLF118 | 1966 | £25 | £50 | |

### THOUGHTS AND WORDS
| | | | | | | | |
|---|---|---|---|---|---|---|---|
| Thoughts And Words | LP | Liberty | LBL83224 | 1969 | £4 | £10 | |

### THOUSAND YARD STARE
| | | | | | | | | |
|---|---|---|---|---|---|---|---|---|
| Strange | 12" | Stifled Aardvark | AARD6T | 1991 | £2.50 | £6 | 1 sided |
| Weatherwatching | 12" | Stifled Aardvark | AARD003 | 1990 | £2.50 | £6 | with insert |

### THRASHING DOVES
| | | | | | | | |
|---|---|---|---|---|---|---|---|
| Angel Visit | CD-s | A&M | CDEE497 | 1989 | £2 | £5 | |
| Another Deadly Sunset | CD-s | A&M | CDEE523 | 1989 | £2 | £5 | |
| Lorelei | CD-s | A&M | CDEE511 | 1989 | £2 | £5 | |
| Reprobate's Hymn | CD-s | A&M | CDEE479 | 1989 | £2 | £5 | |

### THREADS OF LIFE
| | | | | | | | |
|---|---|---|---|---|---|---|---|
| Threads Of Life | LP | Alco | ALC530 | 1972 | £250 | £400 | |

### THREE BELLS
| | | | | | | | |
|---|---|---|---|---|---|---|---|
| Cry No More | 7" | Columbia | DB7980 | 1966 | £1.50 | £4 | |

### THREE CAPS
It comes as a surprise to many people who remember the Capitols' delightful 'Cool Jerk' to find copies credited to the Three Caps. This is the same group, of course, and all the records by the Three Caps are listed in the guide under the Capitols.

### THREE CHUCKLES
| | | | | | | | | |
|---|---|---|---|---|---|---|---|---|
| Runaround | 7" | HMV | 7M292 | 1955 | £7.50 | £15 | |
| Three Chuckles | LP | Vik | LX1067 | 1956 | £30 | £60 | US |
| Times Two, I Love You | 7" | HMV | 7M333 | 1955 | £5 | £10 | |
| We're Gonna Rock Tonight | 7" | HMV | POP292 | 1957 | £37.50 | £75 | |

### THREE CITY FOUR
| | | | | | | | |
|---|---|---|---|---|---|---|---|
| Smoke And Dust | LP | CBS | 63039 | 1967 | £50 | £100 | |
| Three City Four | LP | Decca | LK4705 | 1965 | £62.50 | £125 | |

### THREE CROWS
| | | | | | | | | |
|---|---|---|---|---|---|---|---|---|
| At The Junction | LP | private | JNC1 | 1973 | £10 | £25 | |

### THREE DEGREES
| | | | | | | | |
|---|---|---|---|---|---|---|---|
| Close Your Eyes | 7" | Stateside | SS459 | 1965 | £12.50 | £25 | |
| Gee Baby I'm Sorry | 7" | Stateside | SS413 | 1965 | £5 | £10 | |

### THREE DOG NIGHT
| | | | | | | | | |
|---|---|---|---|---|---|---|---|---|
| It Ain't Easy | LP | Dunhill | DS50078 | 1970 | £6 | £15 | US, nude group on cover |

### THREE DOLLS
| | | | | | | | |
|---|---|---|---|---|---|---|---|
| Living End | 7" | MGM | MGM958 | 1957 | £1.50 | £4 | |

### THREE FLAMES
| | | | | | | | | |
|---|---|---|---|---|---|---|---|---|
| At The Bon Soir | LP | Mercury | MG20239 | 1957 | £6 | £15 | US |

### THREE GOOD REASONS
| | | | | | | | |
|---|---|---|---|---|---|---|---|
| Nowhere Man | 7" | Mercury | MF899 | 1966 | £1.50 | £4 | |

## THREE JOHNS
English White Boy Engineer ........................ 7" ..... CNT ............. CNT003 ............... 1982 £2 ........ £5
Pink Headed Bug .......................................... 7" ...... CNT .............. CNT011 ............... 1983 £1.50 ...... £4

## THREE MAN ARMY
Mahesha ...................................................... : LP ..... Polydor .......... 2310241 .......... 1974 £15 ..... £30 ..................... German
Third Of A Lifetime ................................... LP ..... Pegasus ........ PEG3 ................... 1971 £8 ...... £20
Three Man Army ......................................... LP ..... Reprise ......... K44254 ............... 1973 £6 ...... £15
Three Man Army 2 ...................................... LP ..... Reprise ......... K54015 ............... 1974 £8 ...... £20

## THREE QUARTERS
Pleasure Girls ............................................. 7" ...... Columbia ....... DB7576 ............. 1965 £1.50 ....... £4

## THREE SOUNDS
Black Orchid .............................................. LP ..... Blue Note ...... BLP/BST84155 ..... 1963 £8 ...... £20
Coldwater Flat ............................................ LP ..... Blue Note ...... BST84285 .......... 1968 £4 ...... £10
Elegant Soul ............................................... LP ..... Blue Note ...... BST84301 .......... 1968 £4 ...... £10
Feelin' Good .............................................. LP ..... Blue Note ...... BLP/BST84072 ..... 1961 £15 ..... £30
Gene Harris And The Three Sounds ......... LP ..... Blue Note ...... BST84378 .......... 1970 £4 ...... £10
Here We Come ........................................... LP ..... Blue Note ...... BLP/BST84088 ..... 1961 £10 ..... £25
Hey There! ................................................ LP ..... Blue Note ...... BLP/BST84102 ..... 1962 £10 ..... £25
It Just Got To Be ...................................... LP ..... Blue Note ...... BLP/BST84120 ..... 1963 £10 ..... £25
Live At The Lighthouse ............................. LP ..... Blue Note ...... BLP/BST84265 ..... 1967 £6 ...... £15
Moods ....................................................... LP ..... Blue Note ...... BLP/BST84044 ..... 196– £10 ..... £25
Out Of This World .................................... LP ..... Blue Note ...... BLP/BST84197 ..... 1965 £8 ...... £20
Soul Symphony .......................................... LP ..... Blue Note ...... BST84341 .......... 1969 £4 ...... £10
Vibrations ................................................. LP ..... Blue Note ...... BLP/BST84248 ..... 1966 £8 ...... £20

## THREE SOUNDS (2)
Makin' Bread Again .................................... 7" ...... Liberty ........... LBF15062 ............. 1968 £1.50 ....... £4

## THREE STOOGES
Sing For Kids ............................................. LP ..... Vocalion ........ VL73823 .............. 1968 £6 ...... £15 ..................... US

## THREE SUNS
High Fi And Wide ...................................... LP ..... RCA ............. LPM1249 ............ 1956 £6 ...... £15 ..................... US
Midnight For Two ...................................... LP ..... RCA ............. LPM1333 ............ 1957 £6 ...... £15 ..................... US
Soft And Sweet .......................................... LP ..... RCA ............. LPM1041 ............ 1955 £6 ...... £15 ..................... US

## THREE TOPS
Do It Right ................................................ 7" ..... Treasure Isle .... TI7008 ............... 1967 £5 ...... £10
Great Train In '68 ...................................... 7" ..... Coxsone ........ CS7051 .............. 1968 £5 ...... £10
It's Raining ............................................... 7" ..... Trojan ........... TR003 ................ 1967 £5 ...... £10
Moving To Progress ................................... 7" ..... Studio One ..... SO2023 .............. 1967 £6 ...... £12

## THREE WISE MEN
Thanks For Christmas ................................ 7" ...... Virgin ............ VS642 ................. 1983 £1.50 ....... £4

## THREE'S A CROWD
Look Around The Corner ........................... 7" ...... Fontana .......... TF673 ................. 1966 £4 ...... £8

## THRESHOLD OF PLEASURE
Rain, Rain, Rain ........................................ 7" ...... Decca ............. F12785 ............... 1968 £1.50 ....... £4

## THRICE MICE
Thrice Mice ............................................... LP ..... Philips ............ 6305104 ............. 1970 £8 ........... £20 ................. German

## THRILLINGTON, PERCY 'THRILLS'
Thrillington ............................................... LP ..... Regal           EMC3175 .............. 1975 £75 ....... £150
                                                         Zonophone .....
Uncle Albert, Admiral Halsey .................... 7" ...... EMI ............... EMI2594 .............. 1977 £15 ..... £30

## THRILLS
No One ..................................................... 7" ...... Capitol ........... CL15469 ............. 1966 £15 ......... £30

## THROBBING GRISTLE
Throbbing Gristle emerged at about the same time as punk, yet their music was more profoundly revolutionary than anything produced by the Sex Pistols or their colleagues. Designed to counterpoint the squalor and cruelty that the group saw in late-twentieth-century city life, Throbbing Gristle's music consisted of ugly and angry sound, with none of the melodic or rhythmic landmarks that are normally taken for granted. Due to the group's habit of taping all their live performances, the amount of available Throbbing Gristle material is vast and much of it has become very collectable.

24 Hours ................................................... cass ..... Industrial ........ IRC1-24 ............. 198– £87.50 .. £175 ...26 tapes in case with inserts
Adrenalin .................................................. 7" ...... Industrial ........ IR.0015 .............. 1980 £2.50 ...... £6 .polythene bag, picture sleeve
Assume Power Focus ................................. LP ..... Cause For       POWER                1982 £6 ...... £15
                                                        Concern .....    FOCUS001 ............
Best Of Vol. 2 ........................................... cass .... Industrial ........ IR0001 ................ 1975 £25 ..... £50
Boxed Set ................................................. LP ..... Fetish ............. FX001 ................ 1981 £37.50 ... £75  5 LPs, booklet, badge
D.o.A. The Third And Final Report .......... LP ..... Industrial ........ IR0004 ............... 1978 £6 ...... £15 ...... with calendar and postcard
D.o.A. The Third And Final Report .......... LP ..... Industrial ........ IR0004 ............... 1979 £4 ...... £10  16 equal length tracks
Discipline .................................................. 12" ..... Fetish ............. FET006 ............... 1981 £4 ...... £10
Editions Frankfurt – Berlin ....................... LP ..... Svensk          SJAMS31 ............. 1983 £6 ...... £15
                                                        Illuminated ......

| | | | | | | | |
|---|---|---|---|---|---|---|---|
| Führer Der Menschheit | 10" | American Phonogram | 1JAPSO36 | 1983 | £5 | £12 | |
| Führer Der Menschheit | 10" | Bundestag-rucksache | 29681 | 1982 | £6 | £15 | *some orange vinyl* |
| Funeral In Berlin | LP | Zensor | ZENSOR01 | 1981 | £6 | £15 | *German* |
| Greatest Hits – Entertainment Through Pain | LP | Rough Trade | ROUGHUS23 | 1981 | £4 | £10 | |
| Heathen Earth | LP | Industrial | IR0009 | 1980 | £4 | £10 | |
| Heathen Earth | LP | Industrial | IR0009 | 1980 | £25 | £50 | *blue vinyl* |
| Journey Through A Body | LP | Walter Ulbricht | ST3382 | 1982 | £8 | £20 | |
| Mission Is Terminated | LP+ 12" | Nice | EX39LY2 | 1983 | £6 | £15 | *with booklet* |
| Music From The Death Factory | LP | Death | 01 | 1982 | £50 | £100 | |
| Once Upon A Time | LP | Casual Abandon | CAS1J | 1984 | £4 | £10 | |
| Second Annual Report | LP | Fetish | FET2001 | 1978 | £6 | £15 | *.... with questionnaire, insert* |
| Second Annual Report | LP | Fetish | FET2001 | 1979 | £4 | £10 | *glossy sleeve* |
| Second Annual Report | LP | Fetish | FET2001 | 1981 | £6 | £15 | *backwards version, 2 sleeves* |
| Second Annual Report | LP | Industrial | IR0002 | 1977 | £30 | £60 | *with questionnaire* |
| Subhuman | 7" | Industrial | IR0013 | 1980 | £2.50 | £6 | *.polythene bag, picture sleeve* |
| Thee Psychick Sacrifice | LP | Karnage | KILL1 | 1982 | £6 | £15 | *double* |
| Twenty Jazz Funk Greats | LP | Industrial | IR0008 | 1979 | £4 | £10 | |
| Twenty Jazz Funk Greats | LP | Industrial | IR0008 | 1979 | £6 | £15 | *with poster* |
| United | 7" | Industrial | IR0003 | 1978 | £2 | £5 | |
| United | 7" | Industrial | IR0003 | 1980 | £5 | £10 | *extended B side, white or clear vinyl* |
| We Hate You Little Girls | 7" | Sordide Sentimentale | SS45001 | 1979 | £25 | £50 | *..A4 sleeve, numbered* |

## THROWING MUSES

| | | | | | | | |
|---|---|---|---|---|---|---|---|
| Dizzy | CD-s | 4AD | BAD903CD | 1989 | £2 | £5 | |
| Red Heaven | CD | 4AD | CADD2013 | 1992 | £6 | £15 | *double* |

## THUNDER

| | | | | | | | |
|---|---|---|---|---|---|---|---|
| Backstreet Symphony | CD-s | EMI | CDEM137 | 1990 | £2 | £5 | |
| Dirty Love | CD-s | EMI | CDEM126 | 1990 | £2 | £5 | |
| Gimme Some Lovin' | CD-s | EMI | CDEM148 | 1990 | £2 | £5 | |
| She's So Fine | CD-s | EMI | CDEM111 | 1989 | £2 | £5 | |
| She's So Fine | CD-s | EMI | CDEM158 | 1990 | £2 | £5 | |

## THUNDER, JOHNNY

| | | | | | | | |
|---|---|---|---|---|---|---|---|
| Loop De Loop | LP | Stateside | SL10029 | 1963 | £6 | £15 | |

## THUNDER AND ROSES

| | | | | | | | |
|---|---|---|---|---|---|---|---|
| King Of The Black Sunrise | LP | United Artists | UAS6709 | 1969 | £15 | £30 | *US* |

## THUNDER COMPANY (BRIAN BENNETT)

| | | | | | | | |
|---|---|---|---|---|---|---|---|
| Riding On The Gravy Train | 7" | Columbia | DB8706 | 1970 | £10 | £20 | |

## THUNDERBIRDS

| | | | | | | | |
|---|---|---|---|---|---|---|---|
| Ayuh Ayuh | 7" | London | HL8146 | 1955 | £20 | £40 | |

## THUNDERBIRDS (2)

| | | | | | | | |
|---|---|---|---|---|---|---|---|
| New Orleans Beat | 7" | Oriole | CB1625 | 1961 | £4 | £8 | |
| Wild Weekend | 7" | Oriole | CB1610 | 1961 | £4 | £8 | |

## THUNDERBIRDS (3)

| | | | | | | | |
|---|---|---|---|---|---|---|---|
| Your Ma Said You Cried | 7" | Polydor | 56710 | 1966 | £12.50 | £25 | |

## THUNDERBIRDS (4)

| | | | | | | | |
|---|---|---|---|---|---|---|---|
| Meet The Fabulous Thunderbirds | LP | Red Feather | TH1 | 1964 | £100 | £200 | *US* |

## THUNDERBOLTS

| | | | | | | | |
|---|---|---|---|---|---|---|---|
| Fugitive | 7" | Decca | F11522 | 1962 | £1.50 | £4 | |

## THUNDERBOYS

| | | | | | | | |
|---|---|---|---|---|---|---|---|
| Fashion | 7" | Recent | EJSP9339 | 1980 | £2 | £5 | |

## THUNDERCLAP NEWMAN

For a group not particularly intended to be a novelty outfit, Thunderclap Newman was one of the oddest ever to top the charts. Andy Newman, after whom the group was named, was a middle-aged pianist, whose passion was the traditional jazz of Bix Beiderbecke rather than anything to do with rock. Guitarist Jimmy McCulloch, on the other hand, was just sixteen years old. In between came John 'Speedy' Keene, a moderately talented singer-songwriter, with one dynamite song to his name, 'Something In The Air'. The song was a well-deserved number one hit (and was revived in 1996 for a telephone company advert on television). Sadly, nothing else by the group was in the same league and even the sponsorship of the Who's Pete Townshend, who played bass on the record, could not keep the group together for more than one album.

| | | | | | | | |
|---|---|---|---|---|---|---|---|
| Hollywood Dream | LP | Track | 2406003 | 1970 | £6 | £15 | |
| Peter Townshend Talks To, And About, Thunderclap Newman | LP | Track | PR160 | 1969 | £6 | £15 | *...US interview promo* |
| Something In The Air | 7" | Track | 604301 | 1969 | £1.50 | £4 | |

## THUNDERPUSSY
Documents Of Captivity .......................... LP ..... MRT ............. RL31748 ............... 1973 £**50** ....... £**100** ...................... *US*

## THUNDERS, JOHNNY
Dead Or Alive ......................................... 7" ...... Real ............... ARE1 ................... 1978 £**4** ........... £**8** ........... *picture sleeve*
Vintage '77 ........................................... 12" ..... Jungle ............ JUNG5 ................ 1983 £**2.50** ...... £**6** ..............................
You Can't Put Your Arms Around A ....... 7" ...... Real ............... ARE3 ................... 1978 £**2.50** ... £**6** ........... *picture sleeve*
   Memory..................................................

## THUNDERTHUMBS & TOETSENMAN
Freedom............................................... 7" ...... Polydor .......... POSP480 .......... 1982 £**5** ........... £**10** ..............................
Freedom............................................... 12" ..... Polydor .......... POSPX480 ......... 1982 £**6** .......... £**15** ..............................

## THUNDERTRAIN
Teenage Suicide .................................. LP ...... Jelly ............... JPLP1 .................... 1977 £**6** .......... £**15** ..............................

## THUNDERTREE
Thundertree........................................ LP ...... Roulette ......... SR42038 ............... 1970 £**20** ......... £**40** ...................... *US*

## THYRDS
The Thyrds did well in the *Ready Steady Go* beat group competition won by the Bo Street Runners, but were no more able than the winners to launch any kind of successful career from the exposure. The two issues of 'Hide 'n' Seek' are different recordings, with different songs on the two B sides.

Hide 'n' Seek ....................................... 7" ...... Decca ............. F12010 ............... 1964 £**12.50** .. £**25** ..............................
Hide 'n' Seek ....................................... 7" ...... Oak ................ RGJ133............... 1964 £**62.50** .. £**125** ..............................

## TIBET
Tibet.................................................... LP ...... Bellaphon........ BBS2581 ............... 1978 £**10** ......... £**25** ................. *German*

## TICKAWINDA
With scarce folk albums attracting increasing collectors' interest these days, the private pressing made by Tickawinda earns its high value through a combination of real rarity with easily likeable songwriting and performance. That the group also contained the talents of Clive Gregson – later to be heard with Any Trouble, Richard Thompson and the Clive Gregson-Christine Collister duo – comes as a bonus.

Rosemary Lane ..................................... LP ...... Pennine .......... PSS153................. 1975 £**180** .... £**300** ..............................

## TICKET
Awake.................................................. LP ...... Atlantic .......... SD1008 ................ 1972 £**62.50** .. £**125** ............... *Australian*

## TICKLE
Subway ............................................... 7" ...... Regal       RZ3004 ................ 1967 £**50** ....... £**100** ..............................
                                          Zonophone .....

## TICO & THE TRIUMPHS
The group name hides the identity of the young Paul Simon.

Cards Of Love ....................................... 7" ...... Amy ............... 876 ..................... 1963 £**15** ......... £**30** ...................... *US*
Cry, Little Boy, Cry ............................... 7" ...... Amy ............... 860 ..................... 1962 £**10** ......... £**20** ...................... *US*
Express Train ........................................ 7" ...... Amy ............... 845 ..................... 1962 £**10** ......... £**20** ...................... *US*
Motorcycle ........................................... 7" ...... Amy ............... 835 ..................... 1962 £**10** ......... £**20** ...................... *US*
Motorcycle ........................................... 7" ...... Madison .......... 169 ..................... 1961 £**10** ......... £**20** ...................... *US*

## TIDAL WAVE
Spider Spider ....................................... 7" ...... Storm .............. PD9616............... 1969 £**5** ........... £**10** ..............................
With Tears In My Eyes............................ 7" ...... Decca ............. F22973................. 1969 £**2** ........... £**5** ..............................

## TIDE
Almost Live .......................................... LP ...... Mouth ............ 7237 .................... 1971 £**30** ......... £**60** ...................... *US*

## TIEKIN, FREDDIE & THE ROCKERS
By Popular Demand ............................. LP ...... IT.................... 2301 .................... 1957 £**8** ........... £**20** ...................... *US*
Freddie Tiekin & The Rockers................. LP ...... IT.................... 2304 .................... 1958 £**8** ........... £**20** ...................... *US*

## TIELMAN BROTHERS
East-West ............................................. LP ...... Ariola .............. IHLP1 .................. 1965 £**25** ......... £**50** ...................... *Dutch*
Little Bird ............................................ LP ...... Negram........... ELS895 ................ 1969 £**8** ........... £**20** ...................... *Dutch*
Live ..................................................... LP ...... Ariola .............. 72129.................. 1964 £**25** ......... £**50** ................. *German*
Tielman Brothers................................... LP ...... Imperial .......... 1015 .................... 1964 £**30** ......... £**60** ...................... *Dutch*

## TIERNEY'S FUGITIVES
Did You Want To Run Away................... 7" ...... Decca ............. F12247................. 1965 £**2** ........... £**5** ..............................

## TIETCHENS, ASMUS
Nachtstucke......................................... LP ...... Egg.................. 91040.................. 1977 £**8** ........... £**20** ...................... *French*

## TIFFANIES
It's Got To Be A Great Song ................... 7" ...... Chess .............. CRS8059 ............. 1967 £**12.50** .. £**25** ..............................

## TIFFANY
I Know................................................. 7" ...... Parlophone...... R5311 ................. 1965 £**1.50** ...... £**4** ..............................

## TIFFANY SHADE
Tiffany Shade........................................ LP ...... Fontana............ (S)TL5469 ............. 1968 £**20** ......... £**40** ..............................

## TIFFANY'S THOUGHTS
Find Out What's Happening .................... 7" ..... Parlophone ...... R5439 ................. 1966 £7.50 ...... £15 .............................

## TIGER
Souls Of Africa ................................... 7" ..... New Beat ........ NB052 ................. 1970 £1.50 ........ £4

## TIGER B. SMITH
Tigerrock ......................................... LP ..... Vertigo ......... 6360610 ............... 1972 £10 ....... £25 ................... German
We're The Tiger Bunch ........................... LP ..... Bacillus ...... BLPS19176Q ......... 1974 £6 ......... £15 ................... German

## TIGER LILY
The single by Tiger Lily was the first release by the group that issued all its subsequent records as Ultravox.

Monkey Jive ..................................... 7" ..... Gull ............... GULS12 .............. 1975 £4 ......... £8 .............................
Monkey Jive ..................................... 7" ..... Gull ............... GULS12 .............. 1975 £10 ....... £20 ......... picture sleeve
Monkey Jive ..................................... 7" ..... Gull ............... GULS54 .............. 1977 £2.50 ..... £6 ......... picture sleeve

## TIGG, JIMMY & LOUIS
Who Can I Turn To ............................... 7" ..... Deep Soul ....... DS9105 ................. 1970 £2.50 ........ £6

## TIGHT LIKE THAT
Hokum ......................................... LP ..... Village Thing... VTS12 .............. 1972 £6 ......... £15

## TIKARAM, TANITA
Cathedral Song ................................. CD-s .. WEA ............ YZ331CD ........... 1989 £2 ......... £5
Good Tradition ................................. CD-s .. WEA ............ YZ196CD ........... 1988 £2 ......... £5
Little Sister Leaving Town ..................... CD-s .. WEA ............ YZ459CDP .......... 1990 £2 ......... £5 ............. picture disc
Twist In My Sobriety ........................... CD-s .. WEA ............ YZ321CD ........... 1988 £2 ......... £5
World Outside Your Window .................. CD-s .. WEA ............ YZ363CDX ......... 1989 £2 ......... £5 ................... boxed

## TIL TUESDAY
Believed You Were Lucky ....................... CD-s .. Epic ............... 6530642 ............ 1989 £2 ......... £5

## TILLIS, MEL
Mr. Mel ......................................... LP ..... London .......... HAR8345 ......... 1968 £4 ......... £10

## TILLMAN, BERTHA
Oh My Angel .................................... 7" ..... Oriole ............. CB1746 ............. 1962 £12.50 ... £25

## TILLOTSON, JOHNNY
Alone With You ................................. LP ..... MGM ............ C972 ................. 1964 £8 ......... £20
Angel ........................................... 7" ..... MGM ............ MGM1266 ............ 1964 £1.50 ...... £4
Cabaret ........................................ 7" ..... MGM ............ MGM1393 ........... 1968 £1.50 ...... £4
Dreamy Eyes .................................... 7" ..... London .......... HLA9514 ........... 1962 £1.50 ...... £4
Earth Angel ..................................... 7" ..... London .......... HLA9101 ........... 1960 £7.50 ...... £15
Funny How Time Slips Away .................... 7" ..... London .......... HLA9811 ........... 1963 £1.50 ...... £4
Heartaches By The Number ..................... 7" ..... MGM ............ MGM1281 ........... 1965 £1.50 ...... £4
Hello Enemy .................................... 7" ..... MGM ............ MGM1300 ........... 1966 £1.50 ...... £4
I Can't Help It .................................. 7" ..... London .......... HLA9642 ........... 1962 £1.50 ...... £4
I'm Watching My Watch ......................... 7" ..... MGM ............ MGM1235 ........... 1963 £1.50 ...... £4
It Keeps Right On A-Hurtin' .................... LP ..... London .......... HAA8019 ........... 1962 £15 ....... £30
It Keeps Right On A-Hurtin' .................... 7" ..... London .......... HLA9550 ........... 1962 £1.50 ...... £4
J. T. ............................................ 7" EP . London .......... REA1388 ........... 1963 £10 ....... £20
Jimmy's Girl ................................... 7" ..... London .......... HLA9275 ........... 1961 £1.50 ...... £4
Johnny Tillotson ............................... 7" EP . London .......... REA1345 ........... 1962 £7.50 ...... £15
Johnny Tillotson ............................... 7" EP . MGM ............ MGMEP788 .......... 1963 £7.50 ...... £15
Johnny Tillotson's Best ........................ LP ..... London .......... HAA2431 ........... 1961 £20 ....... £40
Johnny Tillotson's Hit Parade ................ 7" EP . MGM ............ MGMEP790 .......... 1964 £7.50 ...... £15
Me Myself And I ................................ 7" ..... MGM ............ MGM1311 ........... 1966 £1.50 ...... £4
No Love At All .................................. LP ..... MGM ............ C(S)8025 ........... 1966 £5 ......... £12
No Love At All .................................. 7" ..... MGM ............ MGM1319 ........... 1966 £1.50 ...... £4
Our World ...................................... 7" ..... MGM ............ MGM1290 ........... 1965 £1.50 ...... £4
Out Of My Mind ................................ 7" ..... London .......... HLA9695 ........... 1963 £1.50 ...... £4
Poetry In Motion ............................... 7" ..... London .......... HLA9231 ........... 1960 £1.50 ...... £4
Send Me The Pillow You Dream On ........ 7" ..... London .......... HLA9598 ........... 1962 £1.50 ...... £4
She Understands Me ............................ 7" ..... MGM ............ MGM1252 ........... 1964 £1.50 ...... £4
Sings Our World ................................ LP ..... MGM ............ C(S)8005 ........... 1965 £5 ......... £12
Suffering From A Heartache ................... 7" ..... MGM ............ MGM1247 ........... 1964 £1.50 ...... £4
Talk Back Trembling Lips ...................... 7" ..... MGM ............ MGM1214 ........... 1963 £1.50 ...... £4
Then I'll Count Again .......................... 7" ..... MGM ............ MGM1275 ........... 1965 £1.50 ...... £4
True True Happiness ............................ 7" ..... London .......... HLA8930 ........... 1959 £15 ....... £30
Why Do I Love You So .......................... 7" ..... London .......... HLA9048 ........... 1960 £7.50 ...... £15
Without You .................................... 7" ..... London .......... HLA9412 ........... 1961 £1.50 ...... £4
Worried Guy .................................... 7" ..... MGM ............ MGM1225 ........... 1963 £1.50 ...... £4
You Can Never Stop Me Loving You ........ LP ..... Cadence .......... CLP3067/25067 ..... 1963 £10 ....... £25 ................... US

## TILSLEY ORCHESTRA
Thunderbirds Theme ........................... 7" ..... Fontana .......... TF783 ............. 1966 £2 ......... £5
Top TV Themes .................................. LP ..... Fontana .......... (S)TL5411 ............. 1967 £4 ......... £10

## TILSTON, STEVE
Acoustic Confusion ............................. LP ..... Village Thing... VTS5 ................. 1971 £10 ........ £25
Collection ...................................... LP ..... Transatlantic .... TRA252 ............. 1972 £4 ......... £10
Songs From The Dress Rehearsal ............... LP ..... Cornucopia ..... CR1 ................. 1977 £6 ......... £15

886

## TIME

| | | | | | | | |
|---|---|---|---|---|---|---|---|
| First Time I Saw The Sunshine | 7" | Pye | 7N17146 | 1966 | £5 | £10 | |
| Take A Bit Of Notice | 7" | Pye | 7N17019 | 1965 | £12.50 | £25 | |

## TIME (2)

| | | | | | | | |
|---|---|---|---|---|---|---|---|
| Time | LP | Buk | BULP2005 | 1975 | £37.50 | £75 | |

## T.I.M.E.

| | | | | | | | |
|---|---|---|---|---|---|---|---|
| Smooth Ball | LP | Liberty | LBS83232 | 1969 | £6 | £15 | |
| T.I.M.E. | LP | Liberty | LST7558 | 1968 | £6 | £15 | US |
| Take Me Along | 7" | Liberty | LBF15082 | 1969 | £1.50 | £4 | |

## TIMEBOX

Timebox were an interesting soul-inflected group, several of whose songs employ touches of psychedelia to worthwhile effect. In the seventies, the group became Patto.

| | | | | | | | |
|---|---|---|---|---|---|---|---|
| Baked Jam Roll In Your Eye | 7" | Deram | DM246 | 1969 | £2.50 | £6 | |
| Beggin' | 7" | Deram | DM194 | 1968 | £2 | £5 | |
| Don't Make Promises | 7" | Deram | DM153 | 1967 | £2.50 | £6 | |
| Girl Don't You Make Me Wait | 7" | Deram | DM219 | 1968 | £2.50 | £6 | |
| I'll Always Love You | 7" | Piccadilly | 7N35369 | 1967 | £6 | £12 | |
| Original Moose On The Loose | LP | Cosmos | CCLPS9016 | 1977 | £15 | £30 | US |
| Soul Sauce | 7" | Piccadilly | 7N35379 | 1967 | £10 | £20 | |
| Yellow Van | 7" | Deram | DM271 | 1969 | £2.50 | £6 | |

## TIMELORDS

| | | | | | | | |
|---|---|---|---|---|---|---|---|
| Doctorin' The Tardis | CDV | KLF | KLFCD003 | 1988 | £2.50 | £6 | |
| Doctorin' The Tardis | 7" | KLF | KLF003P | 1988 | £2 | £5 | shaped picture disc |
| Gary Glitter Joins The Jams | 12" | KLF | KLF003R | 1988 | £2.50 | £6 | |
| Gary In The Tardis | 7" | KLF | KLF003GG | 1988 | £5 | £10 | promo with Gary Glitter |

## TIMERS

Brian Wilson performs on the A side of this single by the Timers.

| | | | | | | | |
|---|---|---|---|---|---|---|---|
| No-Go Showboat | 7" | Reprise | 231 | 1963 | £25 | £50 | US |

## TIMES

| | | | | | | | |
|---|---|---|---|---|---|---|---|
| Boys About Town | 7" | Artpop | 43DOZ | 1985 | £2.50 | £6 | |
| Boys Brigade | 7" | Artpop | POP46 | 1984 | £1.50 | £4 | |
| Here Comes The Holidays | 7" | Artpop | POP50 | 1982 | £4 | £8 | |
| I Helped Patrick McGoohan Escape | 7" | Artpop | POP49 | 1983 | £4 | £8 | |
| I Helped Patrick McGoohan Escape | 12" | Artpop | No1 | 1983 | £3 | £8 | |
| Pop Goes Art | LP | Artpop | ART20 | 1984 | £4 | £10 | |
| Pop Goes Art | LP | Whaam! | WHAAMLP1 | 1982 | £8 | £20 | |
| Red With Purple Flashes | 7" | Whaam! | WHAAM002 | 1981 | £10 | £20 | |

## TIMES (2)

| | | | | | | | |
|---|---|---|---|---|---|---|---|
| Love We Knew | 7" | Columbia | DB7904 | 1966 | £5 | £10 | |
| Ooh Wee | 7" EP | Columbia | 7ES24 | 1965 | £20 | £40 | demo, no picture sleeve |
| Think About The Times | 7" | Columbia | DB7804 | 1966 | £6 | £12 | |

## TIMMONS, BOBBY

| | | | | | | | |
|---|---|---|---|---|---|---|---|
| Easy Does It | LP | Riverside | RLP363 | 1961 | £6 | £15 | |
| In Person | LP | Riverside | RLP(9)391 | 1961 | £6 | £15 | |
| Moanin' | 7" | Riverside | 3204 | 1967 | £1.50 | £4 | |
| Soul Time | LP | Riverside | RLP334 | 1960 | £6 | £15 | |
| This Here Is Bobby Timmons | LP | Riverside | RLP12317 | 1960 | £6 | £15 | |

## TIMON

| | | | | | | | |
|---|---|---|---|---|---|---|---|
| Bitter Thoughts Of Little Jane | 7" | Pye | 7N17451 | 1968 | £10 | £20 | |

## TIMONEERS

| | | | | | | | |
|---|---|---|---|---|---|---|---|
| Roasted Live | LP | WHM | | | 1976 | £8 | £20 |

## TIN HOUSE

| | | | | | | | |
|---|---|---|---|---|---|---|---|
| Tin House | LP | Epic | BN26291 | 1971 | £6 | £15 | Dutch |

## TIN MACHINE

| | | | | | | | |
|---|---|---|---|---|---|---|---|
| Prisoner Of Love | CD-s | EMI | CDMT76 | 1989 | £2 | £5 | |
| Prisoner Of Love | 7" | EMI | MTPD76 | 1989 | £1.50 | £4 | shaped picture disc |
| Tin Machine | CD-s | EMI | CDMT73 | 1989 | £2 | £5 | |
| Tin Machine | CD | EMI | | | 1989 | £30 | £60 | US promo boxed set with video, cassette, biography |
| Under The God | CD-s | EMI | CDMT68 | 1989 | £2 | £5 | |
| You Belong In Rock 'n' Roll | CD-s | London | LOCDT305 | 1991 | £2 | £5 | round pack |

## TINGLING MOTHER'S CIRCUS

| | | | | | | | |
|---|---|---|---|---|---|---|---|
| Circus Of The Mind | LP | Musicor | MS3167 | 1968 | £15 | £30 | US |

## TINKERBELL'S FAIRYDUST

The records made by this obscure group are typical of the slightly psychedelic late-sixties pop that is still sought after by enthusiasts looking for that elusive lost 'masterpiece' of the period. The album is a recent discovery – at the time of writing only one copy of a demo in a finished sleeve is known to have surfaced, but others must presumably exist.

| | | | | | | | | |
|---|---|---|---|---|---|---|---|---|
| In My Magic Garden | 7" | Decca | F12705 | 1967 | £7.50 | £15 | |
| Sheila's Back In Town | 7" | Decca | F12865 | 1969 | £12.50 | £25 | |
| Tinkerbell's Fairydust | LP | Decca | LK5028 | 1969 | £500 | £750 | demo only |
| Twenty Ten | 7" | Decca | F12778 | 1968 | £7.50 | £15 | |

## TINKERS
| | | | | | | | |
|---|---|---|---|---|---|---|---|
| Spring Rain | LP | Argo | ZFB35 | 1970 | £5 | £12 | |
| Til The Wild Birds | LP | Fontana | 6438020 | 1970 | £5 | £12 | |

## TINO, BABS
| | | | | | | | |
|---|---|---|---|---|---|---|---|
| Forgive Me | 7" EP | London | RER1377 | 1963 | £15 | £30 | |
| Forgive Me | 7" | London | HLR9589 | 1962 | £5 | £10 | |

## TINO & THE REVLONS
| | | | | | | | |
|---|---|---|---|---|---|---|---|
| By Request At The Sway-Zee | LP | Dearborn | | 1966 | £30 | £60 | US |

## TINTERN ABBEY
| | | | | | | | |
|---|---|---|---|---|---|---|---|
| Beeside | 7" | Deram | DM164 | 1967 | £62.50 | £125 | |

## TINY TIM
| | | | | | | | |
|---|---|---|---|---|---|---|---|
| For All My Little Friends | LP | Reprise | 6351 | 1969 | £4 | £10 | US |
| God Bless Tiny Tim | LP | Reprise | RSLP6292 | 1968 | £5 | £12 | |
| Great Balls Of Fire | 7" | Reprise | R20802 | 1968 | £1.50 | £4 | |
| Second Album | LP | Reprise | RSLP6323 | 1968 | £4 | £10 | |
| There'll Always Be An England | 78 | Reprise | RS27004 | 1969 | £5 | £10 | |
| Tip Toe Thru The Tulips | 7" | Reprise | R23258 | 1968 | £1.50 | £4 | |

## TIP TOPS
| | | | | | | | |
|---|---|---|---|---|---|---|---|
| Oo-Kook-A-Boo | 7" | Cameo Parkway | P868 | 1963 | £5 | £10 | |

## TIPPETT, JULIE
| | | | | | | | |
|---|---|---|---|---|---|---|---|
| Sunset Glow | LP | Utopia | UTS601 | 1975 | £5 | £12 | credited to Julie Tippetts |
| Voice | LP | Ogun | OG110 | 1977 | £6 | £15 | with Maggie Nichols, Phil Minton, Brian Eley |

## TIPPETT, KEITH
| | | | | | | | |
|---|---|---|---|---|---|---|---|
| Blueprint | LP | RCA | SF8290 | 1972 | £15 | £30 | |
| Dedicated To You But You Weren't Listening | LP | Vertigo | 6360024 | 1971 | £10 | £25 | spiral label |
| Frames | LP | Ogun | OGD003/4 | 1978 | £8 | £20 | double |
| T 'n' T | LP | Steam | SJ104 | 1976 | £5 | £12 | with Stan Tracey |
| Warm Spirits Cool Spirits | LP | Vinyl | VS101 | 1977 | £5 | £12 | |
| You Are Here I Am There | LP | Polydor | 2384004 | 1969 | £25 | £50 | |

## TIPPI & THE CLOVERS
| | | | | | | | |
|---|---|---|---|---|---|---|---|
| My Heart Said | 7" | Stateside | SS160 | 1963 | £4 | £8 | |

## TIPTON, LESTER
| | | | | | | | |
|---|---|---|---|---|---|---|---|
| This Won't Change | 7" | Grapevine | GRP138 | 1979 | £2 | £5 | Masqueraders B side |

## TIR NA NOG
| | | | | | | | |
|---|---|---|---|---|---|---|---|
| Strong In The Sun | LP | Chrysalis | CHR1047 | 1973 | £4 | £10 | |
| Tear And A Smile | LP | Chrysalis | CHR1006 | 1972 | £4 | £10 | |
| Tir Na Nog | LP | Chrysalis | ILPS9153 | 1971 | £4 | £10 | |

## TITANS
| | | | | | | | |
|---|---|---|---|---|---|---|---|
| Don't You Just Know It | 7" | London | HLU8609 | 1958 | £30 | £60 | |
| Today's Teen Beat | LP | MGM | (S)E3992 | 1961 | £6 | £15 | US |

## TITUS GROAN
| | | | | | | | |
|---|---|---|---|---|---|---|---|
| Open The Door Homer | 7" | Dawn | DNX2053 | 1970 | £10 | £20 | picture sleeve |
| Titus Groan | LP | Dawn | DNLS3012 | 1970 | £25 | £50 | |

## TITUS OATS
| | | | | | | | |
|---|---|---|---|---|---|---|---|
| Jungle Lady | LP | Lips | | 1974 | £75 | £150 | US |

## TJADER, CAL
| | | | | | | | |
|---|---|---|---|---|---|---|---|
| Best Of Cal Tjader | LP | Verve | (S)VLP9192 | 1968 | £4 | £10 | |
| Cal Tjader Group/Don Elliott Group | LP | London | LTZC15050 | 1957 | £6 | £15 | |
| Hip Vibrations | LP | Verve | (S)VLP9215 | 1968 | £4 | £10 | |
| Solar Heat | LP | Fontana | STL5527 | 1969 | £4 | £10 | |
| Soul Sauce | 7" | Verve | VS529 | 1965 | £7.50 | £15 | |

## TOAD
| | | | | | | | |
|---|---|---|---|---|---|---|---|
| Dreams | LP | Frog | | 1975 | £37.50 | £75 | Italian |
| Toad | LP | RCA | SF8241 | 1972 | £62.50 | £125 | |
| Tomorrow Blue | LP | Hallelujah | X626 | 1973 | £50 | £100 | Swiss |

## TOAD THE WET SPROCKET
| | | | | | | | |
|---|---|---|---|---|---|---|---|
| Pete's Punk Song | 7" | Sprocket | | 1979 | £5 | £10 | |
| Reaching For The Sky | 7" | Sprockets | BRS008 | 1980 | £2.50 | £6 | |

## TOADS
| | | | | | | | |
|---|---|---|---|---|---|---|---|
| Toads | LP | Wiggins | 64021 | 1964 | £50 | £100 | US |

## TOBY JUG

| | | | | | | | | |
|---|---|---|---|---|---|---|---|---|
| Greasy Quiff | LP | private | | 1969 | £330 | £500 | | |

## TOBY TWIRL

| | | | | | | | | |
|---|---|---|---|---|---|---|---|
| Harry Faversham | 7" | Decca | F12728 | 1968 | £6 | £12 | |
| Movin' In | 7" | Decca | F12867 | 1969 | £5 | £10 | |
| Toffee Apple Sunday | 7" | Decca | F12804 | 1968 | £10 | £20 | |

## TODD, ART & DOTTIE

| | | | | | | | |
|---|---|---|---|---|---|---|---|
| Chanson D'Amour | 7" | London | HLB8620 | 1958 | £5 | £10 | |
| Straight As An Arrow | 7" | London | HLN8838 | 1959 | £5 | £10 | |

## TODD, GARRY & ROGER TURNER

| | | | | | | | |
|---|---|---|---|---|---|---|---|
| Sunday Best | LP | Incus | INCUS32 | 1979 | £4 | £10 | |

## TODD, NICK

| | | | | | | | |
|---|---|---|---|---|---|---|---|
| At The Hop | 7" | London | HLD8537 | 1958 | £5 | £10 | |
| Plaything | 7" | London | HLD8500 | 1957 | £12.50 | £25 | |
| Tiger | 7" | London | HLD8902 | 1959 | £7.50 | £15 | |

## TODD, PATSY

| | | | | | | | |
|---|---|---|---|---|---|---|---|
| We Were Lovers | 7" | High Note | HS012 | 1968 | £1.50 | £4 | |

## TODD, SHARKEY & THE MONSTERS

| | | | | | | | |
|---|---|---|---|---|---|---|---|
| Cool Ghoul | 7" | Parlophone | R4536 | 1959 | £5 | £10 | |

## TODD, WILF

| | | | | | | | |
|---|---|---|---|---|---|---|---|
| He Took Her Away | 7" | Blue Beat | BB240 | 1964 | £6 | £12 | |

## TODOROW, CAMY

| | | | | | | | |
|---|---|---|---|---|---|---|---|
| Bursting At The Seams | 7" | Virgin | VS816 | 1985 | £2 | £5 | |
| Bursting At The Seams | 12" | Virgin | VS81612 | 1985 | £3 | £8 | |

## TOEFAT

Toefat's LP is most notable for its unsettling cover, showing human figures with enormous toes replacing their heads. The group was one of Cliff Bennett's attempts to revive his career after the demise of the Rebel Rousers – on this occasion he effectively took over a pre-existing band, the Gods.

| | | | | | | | |
|---|---|---|---|---|---|---|---|
| Bad Side Of The Road | 7" | Parlophone | R5829 | 1970 | £1.50 | £4 | |
| Brand New Band | 7" | Chapter One | CH175 | 1972 | £1.50 | £4 | |
| Toefat | LP | Parlophone | PCS7097 | 1970 | £15 | £30 | |
| Toefat II | LP | Regal Zonophone | SLRZ1015 | 1971 | £20 | £40 | |

## TOGETHER

| | | | | | | | |
|---|---|---|---|---|---|---|---|
| Henry's Coming Home | 7" | Columbia | DB8491 | 1968 | £20 | £40 | |

## TOGGERY FIVE

| | | | | | | | |
|---|---|---|---|---|---|---|---|
| I'd Much Rather Be With The Boys | 7" | Parlophone | R5249 | 1965 | £12.50 | £25 | |
| I'm Gonna Jump | 7" | Parlophone | R5175 | 1964 | £10 | £20 | |

## TOKENS

| | | | | | | | |
|---|---|---|---|---|---|---|---|
| B'wa Nina | 7" EP | RCA | 75701 | 1962 | £4 | £8 | French |
| December 5th | LP | B.T.Puppy | BTPS1014 | 1971 | £5 | £12 | US |
| Greatest Moments | LP | B.T.Puppy | BTPS1012 | 1970 | £5 | £12 | US |
| He's In Town | 7" | Fontana | TF500 | 1964 | £1.50 | £4 | |
| I Hear Trumpets Blow | LP | B.T.Puppy | BTLP(S)1000 | 1966 | £5 | £12 | US |
| It's A Happening World | 7" EP | Warner Bros | WEP1457 | 1967 | £4 | £8 | French |
| Lion Sleeps Tonight | LP | RCA | RD27256/SF5128 | 1962 | £15 | £30 | |
| Lion Sleeps Tonight | 7" EP | RCA | 75688 | 1962 | £6 | £12 | French |
| Tokens Again | LP | RCA | LPM/LSP3685 | 1966 | £5 | £12 | US |
| Tokens Of Gold | LP | B.T.Puppy | BTPS1006 | 1969 | £5 | £12 | US |
| Tonight I Fell In Love | 7" | Parlophone | R4790 | 1961 | £2 | £5 | |
| We Sing Folk | LP | RCA | SF7535 | 1962 | £4 | £10 | |
| Wheels | LP | RCA | LPM/LST2886 | 1964 | £5 | £12 | US |

## TOLONEN, JUKKA

| | | | | | | | |
|---|---|---|---|---|---|---|---|
| Crossection | LP | Sonet | SNTF699 | 1975 | £4 | £10 | |
| Hook | LP | Love | LRLP113 | 1974 | £4 | £10 | Finnish |
| Hysterica | LP | Love | LRLP149 | 1975 | £4 | £10 | Finnish |
| Summer Games | LP | Love | LRLP91 | 1973 | £5 | £12 | Finnish |
| Tolonen | LP | Sonet | SNTF652 | 1974 | £4 | £10 | |

## TOM & JERRY

The Tom and Jerry who made the single 'Baby Talk' were Tom Graph and Jerry Landis, otherwise known (in the reverse order) as Simon and Garfunkel.

| | | | | | | | |
|---|---|---|---|---|---|---|---|
| Baby Talk | 7" | Big | 621 | 1958 | £20 | £40 | US |
| Baby Talk | 7" | Gala | GSP806 | 1959 | £10 | £20 | US |
| Hey Schoolgirl | 7" | Big | 613 | 1957 | £15 | £30 | US |
| Hey Schoolgirl | 7" | King | 5167 | 1957 | £15 | £30 | US |
| I'll Drown In My Tears | 7" | Mercury | 71930 | 1961 | £10 | £20 | US |
| I'm Lonesome | 7" | Ember | 1094 | 1959 | £15 | £30 | US |
| I'm Lonesome | 7" | Pye | 7N25202 | 1963 | £15 | £30 | |
| Our Song | 7" | Big | 616 | 1958 | £15 | £30 | US |
| Surrender, Please Surrender | 7" | Paramount | 10363 | 1962 | £10 | £20 | US |

| | | | | | | | | |
|---|---|---|---|---|---|---|---|---|
| That's My Story | 7" | Big | 618 | 1958 | £15 | £30 | | US |
| That's My Story | 7" | Hunt | 319 | 1958 | £15 | £30 | | US |

## TOM & JERRY (2)

| | | | | | | |
|---|---|---|---|---|---|---|
| Johann Mouse | 7" EP | MGM | MGMEP688 | 1958 | £4 | £8 |

## TOM & JERRYO

| | | | | | | |
|---|---|---|---|---|---|---|
| Boogaloo | 7" | HMV | POP1435 | 1965 | £4 | £8 |

## TOM CATS

| | | | | | | | |
|---|---|---|---|---|---|---|---|
| Tom Tom Cat | 7" | Starlite | ST45054 | 1961 | £7.50 | £15 | |
| A Tu Vera | 7" EP | Philips | 436388PE | 1966 | £5 | £10 | Spanish |
| La Neurastenia | 7" EP | Philips | 436826PE | 1966 | £10 | £20 | Spanish |
| Somebody Help Me | 7" EP | Philips | 436849PE | 1966 | £10 | £20 | Spanish |
| Yesterday | 7" EP | Philips | 436387PE | 1966 | £10 | £20 | Spanish |

## TOMLIN, LEE

| | | | | | | |
|---|---|---|---|---|---|---|
| Sweet Sweet Lovin' | 7" | CBS | 202455 | 1966 | £2 | £5 |

## TOMLINSON, ALBERT

| | | | | | | | |
|---|---|---|---|---|---|---|---|
| Don't Wait For Me | 7" | Giant | GN28 | 1968 | £2.50 | £6 | ... Lloyd Evans B side |

## TOMLINSON, ROY

| | | | | | | | |
|---|---|---|---|---|---|---|---|
| I Stand For I | 7" | Coxsone | CS7056 | 1968 | £5 | £10 | Martin B side |

## TOMORROW

Tomorrow are usually held up as the classic psychedelic group, but this reputation derives less from their album, which is very uneven in quality, than from the two wonderful singles, 'My White Bicycle' and 'Revolution'. The chaotic, anarchist streak within the group (Twink) carried through into the Pink Fairies; the musically inventive part (Steve Howe) joined the group Yes.

| | | | | | | |
|---|---|---|---|---|---|---|
| My White Bicycle | 7" | Parlophone | R5597 | 1967 | £7.50 | £15 |
| My White Bicycle | 7" | Parlophone | R5813 | 1969 | £7.50 | £15 |
| Revolution | 7" | Parlophone | R5627 | 1967 | £7.50 | £15 |
| Tomorrow | LP | Harvest | SHSM2010 | 1976 | £6 | £15 |
| Tomorrow | LP | Parlophone | PMC/PCS7042 | 1968 | £50 | £100 |

## TOMORROW COME SOMEDAY (ITHACA)

| | | | | | | |
|---|---|---|---|---|---|---|
| Tomorrow Come Someday | LP | private | SNP97 | 1969 | £400 | £600 |

## TOMORROW'S CHILDREN

| | | | | | | |
|---|---|---|---|---|---|---|
| Bang Bang Rock Steady | 7" | Island | WI3073 | 1967 | £5 | £10 |

## TOMORROW'S GIFT

| | | | | | | | |
|---|---|---|---|---|---|---|---|
| Goodbye Future | LP | Amok | 28515 | 1973 | £10 | £25 | German |
| Tomorrow's Gift | LP | Plus | 12 | 1970 | £37.50 | £75 | German double |

## TON STEINE SCHERBEN

| | | | | | | | |
|---|---|---|---|---|---|---|---|
| Keine Macht Fur Niemand | LP | Volksmund | TSS2 | 1972 | £5 | £12 | German double |
| Warum Geht Es Mir So Dreckig | LP | Volksmund | TSS13 | 1971 | £5 | £12 | German |
| Wenn Die Nacht Am Tiefsten | LP | Volksmund | TSS3 | 1975 | £5 | £12 | German double |

## TONER, ELEANOR

| | | | | | | |
|---|---|---|---|---|---|---|
| All Cried Out | 7" | Decca | F12119 | 1965 | £1.50 | £4 |
| Will You Still Love Me Tomorrow | 7" | Decca | F12192 | 1965 | £1.50 | £4 |

## TONES ON TAIL

| | | | | | | |
|---|---|---|---|---|---|---|
| Bigger Splash | 12" | 4AD | BAD203 | 1982 | £3 | £8 |

## TONETTES

| | | | | | | |
|---|---|---|---|---|---|---|
| Love That Is Real | 7" | Island | WI064 | 1962 | £5 | £10 |

## TONEY JR., OSCAR

| | | | | | | |
|---|---|---|---|---|---|---|
| For Your Precious Love | LP | Stateside | (S)SL10211 | 1967 | £4 | £10 |
| For Your Precious Love | 7" | Stateside | SS2033 | 1967 | £1.50 | £4 |
| No Sad Songs | 7" | Bell | BLL1011 | 1968 | £1.50 | £4 |
| Turn On Your Lovelight | 7" | Stateside | SS2046 | 1967 | £1.50 | £4 |
| You Can Lead Your Woman To The Altar | 7" | Stateside | SS2061 | 1967 | £1.50 | £4 |

## TONGUE & GROOVE

| | | | | | | |
|---|---|---|---|---|---|---|
| Tongue & Groove | LP | Fontana | STL5528 | 1969 | £8 | £20 |

## TONIK, TERRY

| | | | | | | |
|---|---|---|---|---|---|---|
| Just A Little Mod | 7" | Posh | TOFF1 | 1980 | £7.50 | £15 |

## TONTON MACOUTE

| | | | | | | |
|---|---|---|---|---|---|---|
| Tonton Macoute | LP | Neon | NE4 | 1971 | £25 | £50 |

## TONTO'S EXPANDING HEADBAND

Tonto is an instrument (The Original New Timbral Orchestra) – a huge synthesizer – played by Robert Margouleff and Malcolm Cecil. These two are among the more imaginative electronic keyboard performers and *Zero Time* is a good example of what can be achieved. They take advantage of the possibilities afforded to them, by such stratagems as using a ten-note, equally tempered scale (impossible on conventional instruments) and yet the music still manages to be as accessible as it is interesting. Margouleff and Cecil also worked as advisers to Stevie Wonder and their sounds can be heard on many of his records.

| | | | | | | |
|---|---|---|---|---|---|---|
| Zero Time | LP | Atlantic | 2400150 | 1971 | £5 | £12 |

## TONY & DENNIS
Folk Song................................ 7" ...... Trojan............. TR002................. 1967 £4.............£8 ...... *Tommy McCook*
*B side*

## TONY & JOE
Freeze ................................ 7" ...... London.......... HLN8694............... 1958 £15........£30 ..............................

## TONY & LOUISE
Ups And Downs................................ 7" ...... Island............. WI059 ............ 1962 £2............£5 ..............................

## TONY & TANDY
Two Can Make It Together .................... 7" ...... Atlantic......... 2091075 ................. 1971 £1.50......£4 ..............................
Two Can Make It Together .................... 7" ...... Atlantic........... 584262............... 1969 £4.............£8 ..............................

## TONY & THE GRADUATES
Statue .................... 7" ...... Hit ......... HIT13 ............... 196– £20........£40 ..............................

## TONY'S DEFENDERS
Since I Lost My Baby................................ 7" ...... Columbia........ DB7996................. 1966 £6............£12 ..............................
Yes I Do................................ 7" ...... Columbia........ DB7850................. 1966 £7.50....£15 ..............................

## TOOMORROW
Toomorrow was a group put together, Monkees-style, for the purpose of making a rather silly film. This was the flop it deserved to be, but the group's lead singer, Olivia Newton-John, persevered with her musical career.

I Could Never Live Without Your Love .... 7" ...... Decca ............ F13070............... 1970 £15........£30 ..............................
Toomorrow.................................... LP ...... RCA ......... LSA3008 ............... 1970 £37.50....£75 ..............................
You're My Baby Now ........................ 7" ...... RCA ......... RCA1978 ............... 1970 £15........£30 ..............................

## TOOP, DAVID
New And Rediscovered Musical ....... LP ...... Obscure .......... OBS4................... 1976 £4..........£10 ..............................
  Instruments ................................

## TOOTS
Do You Like It ................................ 7" ...... Upsetter .......... US327................... 1970 £1.50........£4 ...... *Upsetters B side*

## TOP DRAWER
Solid Oak ................................ LP ...... Resurrection.... CX1185 ............ 198– £30........£60 ...... *US*
Solid Oak ................................ LP ...... Wishbon ........ 83615................... 1969 £180.....£300 ...... *US*

## TOP TEN ALLSTARS
Beat Party................................ LP ...... Decca ............ 16434............... 1966 £15........£30 ...... *German*
Three O'Clock In The Mornin' ............... LP ...... Decca ............ SLK16387P ............ 1965 £25........£50 ...... *German*

## TOPHAM, TOP
Top Topham was the original lead guitarist with the Yardbirds, but he was replaced by the young Eric Clapton before the group made any recordings. His later solo album consists of a set of blues guitar instrumentals, proving Topham to be a worthy first link in the Yardbirds' lead guitar chain.

Ascension Heights ........................ LP ...... Blue Horizon.. 763857................. 1970 £30........£60 ..............................
Christmas Cracker ........................ 7" ...... Blue Horizon.. 573167................. 1969 £4............£8 ..............................

## TOPICS
The Topics shortly afterwards changed their name to the Four Seasons.

Girl In My Dreams ........................ 7" ...... Perri ............. 1007 .................... 1961 £37.50....£75 ...... *US*

## TOPSY, TINY & THE CHARMS
After Marriage Blues ........................ 7" ...... Pye .............. 7N25104 ............ 1961 £7.50......£15 ..............................
Come On Come On Come On ............... 7" ...... Parlophone..... R4397 ............... 1958 £20........£40 ..............................
You Shocked Me ........................ 7" ...... Parlophone..... R4427 ............... 1958 £20........£40 ..............................

## TORA TORA
Red Sun Setting........................ 7" ...... Mancunian .... TT5000................. 1980 £2.50........£6 ..............................
  Metal .............

## TORME, BERNIE
I'm Not Ready ........................ 7" ...... Jet................. JET126 ................ 1978 £2.............£5 ...... *orange vinyl*

## TORME, MEL
All Of You ................................ 7" ...... Vogue Coral.... Q72202................. 1956 £1.50......£4 ..............................
And The Marty Paich Dektette................ LP ...... London ...... LTZN15009 ......... 1956 £6............£15 ..............................
At The Crescendo ........................ LP ...... Parlophone .... PMC1096 ............ 1959 £4............£10 ..............................
At The Crescendo ........................ LP ...... Vogue Coral.... LVA9004 ............ 1955 £6............£15 ..............................
At The Red Hill........................ LP ...... London ...... HAK/SHK8021 ...... 1963 £4............£10 ..............................
Back In Town........................ LP ...... HMV.......... CLP1382............. 1960 £6............£15 ..............................
Blue Moon ................................ 7" ...... Vogue Coral.... Q72159................. 1956 £2............£5 ..............................
California Suite ........................ LP ...... Bethlehem...... BCP6016 .............. 1958 £8............£20 ...... *US*
Comin' Home Baby ........................ LP ...... London ...... HAK8065............... 1963 £4............£10 ..............................
Comin' Home Baby ........................ 7" ...... London ...... HLK9643............. 1962 £2............£5 ..............................
I Can't Give You Anything But Love...... 7" ...... MGM.......... MGM922............. 1956 £1.50......£4 ..............................
It's A Blue World........................ LP ...... London ...... HAN2016 ............ 1956 £6............£15 ..............................
Love Is Here To Stay ........................ 7" ...... Vogue Coral.... Q72185................. 1956 £1.50......£4 ..............................
Lullaby Of Birdland ........................ 7" ...... London ...... HLN8322............. 1956 £5............£10 ..............................
Lulu's Back In Town ........................ 7" ...... London ...... HLN8305............. 1956 £5............£10 ..............................
Magic Of Mel ........................ 7" EP . London .......... REK1372............... 1963 £2.50........£6 ..............................

| Title | Format | Label | Catalogue | Year | | | |
|---|---|---|---|---|---|---|---|
| Meets The British | LP | Philips | BBL7205 | 1957 | £15 | £30 | |
| Meets The British | 7" EP | Philips | BBE12181 | 1958 | £2.50 | £6 | |
| Mel Tormé | LP | Bethlehem | BCP52 | 1956 | £8 | £20 | US |
| Mel Tormé | LP | HMV | CLP1238 | 1958 | £4 | £10 | |
| Mountain Greenery | 7" | Vogue Coral | Q72150 | 1956 | £2 | £5 | |
| Musical Sounds | LP | Coral | CRL57044 | 1954 | £8 | £20 | US |
| Musical Sounds Are The Best Songs | LP | Vogue Coral | LVA9032 | 1956 | £6 | £15 | |
| My Kind Of Music | LP | HMV | CLP1584/CSD1442 | 1962 | £4 | £10 | |
| My Rosemarie | 7" | Vogue Coral | Q72217 | 1957 | £1.50 | £4 | |
| Olé Tormé | LP | HMV | CLP1315 | 1960 | £4 | £10 | |
| Sings At The Crescendo Pt. 1 | 7" EP | Coral | FEP2026 | 1959 | £2 | £5 | |
| Sings At The Crescendo Pt. 2 | 7" EP | Coral | FEP2027 | 1959 | £2 | £5 | |
| Sings At The Crescendo Pt. 3 | 7" EP | Coral | FEP2028 | 1959 | £2 | £5 | |
| Sings Fred Astaire | LP | London | LTZN15076 | 1957 | £4 | £10 | |
| Sings Fred Astaire Pt. 1 | 7" EP | London | EZN19027 | 1958 | £2 | £5 | |
| Sings Fred Astaire Pt. 2 | 7" EP | London | EZN19028 | 1958 | £2 | £5 | |
| Sings Fred Astaire Pt. 3 | 7" EP | London | EZN19039 | 1958 | £2 | £5 | |
| Songs For Any Taste | 10" LP | MGM | 552 | 1952 | £10 | £25 | US |
| Songs For Any Taste | LP | Parlophone | PMC1114 | 1959 | £6 | £15 | |
| Sunday In New York | LP | Atlantic | (SD)8091 | 1963 | £5 | £12 | US |
| Swingin' On The Moon | LP | HMV | CLP1449/CSD1349 | 1961 | £6 | £15 | |
| Swings Schubert Alley | LP | HMV | CLP1405/CSD1330 | 1960 | £6 | £15 | |
| Torme | LP | Verve | V2105 | 1958 | £5 | £12 | US |
| Voice In Velvet | 7" EP | MGM | MGMEP562 | 1956 | £2.50 | £6 | |
| Voice In Velvet No. 2 | 7" EP | MGM | MGMEP591 | 1957 | £2.50 | £6 | |
| Walkin' Shoes | 7" EP | Decca | DFE6384 | 1956 | £2 | £5 | |
| Walkin' Shoes | 7" | Decca | F10800 | 1956 | £1.50 | £4 | |

## TORMENTORS
| Hanging Round | LP | Royal | RLP111 | 196– | £75 | £150 | US |
|---|---|---|---|---|---|---|---|

## TORNADOES
| Bustin' Surfboards | LP | Josie | 4005 | 1963 | £25 | £50 | US |
|---|---|---|---|---|---|---|---|

## TORNADOS
| | | | | | | | |
|---|---|---|---|---|---|---|---|
| Away From It All | LP | Decca | LK4552 | 1963 | £15 | £30 | |
| Dragonfly | 7" | Decca | F11745 | 1963 | £1.50 | £4 | |
| Earlybird | 7" | Columbia | DB7589 | 1965 | £5 | £10 | |
| Exodus | 7" | Decca | F11946 | 1964 | £4 | £8 | |
| Globetrotter | 7" | Decca | F11562 | 1963 | £1.50 | £4 | |
| Granada | 7" | Columbia | DB7455 | 1965 | £5 | £10 | |
| Hot Pot | 7" | Decca | F11838 | 1964 | £1.50 | £4 | |
| Ice Cream Man | 7" | Decca | F11662 | 1963 | £1.50 | £4 | |
| Is That A Ship I Hear | 7" | Columbia | DB7984 | 1966 | £10 | £20 | |
| Love And Fury | 7" | Decca | F11449 | 1962 | £2.50 | £6 | |
| Monte Carlo | 7" | Decca | F11889 | 1964 | £4 | £8 | |
| More Sounds From The Tornados | 7" EP | Decca | DFE8521 | 1963 | £5 | £10 | |
| Pop Art Goes Mozart | 7" | Columbia | DB7856 | 1966 | £6 | £12 | |
| Robot | 7" | Decca | F11606 | 1963 | £1.50 | £4 | |
| Sounds Of The Tornados | LP | London | LL3293 | 1963 | £8 | £20 | US |
| Sounds Of The Tornados | 7" EP | Decca | DFE8510 | 1962 | £5 | £10 | |
| Stingray | 7" | Columbia | DB7687 | 1965 | £10 | £20 | |
| Telstar | LP | London | LL3279 | 1962 | £10 | £25 | US |
| Telstar | CD | Decca | | 1988 | £25 | £50 | |
| Telstar | 7" EP | Decca | DFE8511 | 1962 | £6 | £12 | |
| Tornado Rock | 7" EP | Decca | DFE8533 | 1963 | £7.50 | £15 | |
| World Of The Tornados | LP | Decca | SPA253 | 1972 | £4 | £10 | |

## TOROK, MITCHELL
| | | | | | | | |
|---|---|---|---|---|---|---|---|
| Caribbean | LP | London | HAW2279 | 1960 | £15 | £30 | |
| Caribbean | 7" | London | HL8004 | 1954 | £10 | £20 | |
| Drink Up And Go Home | 7" | Brunswick | 05642 | 1957 | £4 | £8 | |
| Haunting Waterfall | 7" | London | HL8083 | 1954 | £12.50 | £25 | |
| Havana Huddle | 7" | Brunswick | 05626 | 1956 | £7.50 | £15 | |
| Hootchy Coochy | 7" | London | HL8048 | 1954 | £12.50 | £25 | |
| Louisiana Hayride | 7" EP | London | REP1014 | 1954 | £15 | £30 | |
| Pink Chiffon | 7" | London | HLW9130 | 1960 | £1.50 | £4 | |
| Pledge Of Love | 7" | Brunswick | 05657 | 1957 | £2.50 | £6 | |
| Two Words | 7" | Brunswick | 05718 | 1957 | £2 | £5 | |
| When Mexico Gave Up The Rhumba | 7" | Brunswick | 05586 | 1956 | £5 | £10 | |
| World Keeps Turning Around | 7" | Brunswick | 05423 | 1955 | £5 | £10 | |

## TORQUES
| Live | LP | Lemco | 604 | 196– | £25 | £50 | US |
|---|---|---|---|---|---|---|---|
| Zoom! | LP | Wiggins | 64010 | 1964 | £37.50 | £75 | US |

## TORRENCE, GEORGE & THE NATURALS
| Lickin' Stick | 7" | London | HLZ10181 | 1968 | £2.50 | £6 | |
|---|---|---|---|---|---|---|---|

## TORRIANI, VICO
| All The Big Italian Hits | LP | Decca | LF1589 | 1960 | £20 | £40 | German |
|---|---|---|---|---|---|---|---|

## TORTILLA FLAT
| Fur Eine 3/4 Stunden | LP | | TF0175 | 1974 | £62.50 | £125 | German |
|---|---|---|---|---|---|---|---|
| Little Heroes | LP | Catfish | 5C05624381 | 1971 | £20 | £40 | Dutch |

## TOSH, PETER

| | | | | | | | |
|---|---|---|---|---|---|---|---|
| Bush Doctor | LP | Rolling Stones | CUN39109 | 1978 | £5 | £12 | ....with scratch & sniff sticker |
| Crimson Pirate | 7" | Jackpot | JP706 | 1969 | £5 | £10 | |
| Equal Rights | 7" | Virgin | V2081 | 1977 | £5 | £12 | |
| Hoot Nanny Hoot | 7" | Island | WI211 | 1965 | £12.50 | £25 | |
| I Am The Toughest | 7" | Island | WI3042 | 1967 | £10 | £20 | Marcia Griffiths B side |
| Legalise It | LP | Virgin | V2061 | 1976 | £5 | £12 | |
| Maga Dog | 7" | Bullet | BU486 | 1971 | £5 | £10 | ....... Third & Fourth Generation B side |
| Return Of Al Capone | 7" | Unity | UN525 | 1969 | £2.50 | £6 | Lennox Brown B side |
| Rudies Medley | 7" | Punch | PH91 | 1972 | £1.50 | £4 | |
| Selassie Serenade | 7" | Bullet | BU414 | 1971 | £1.50 | £4 | ... Glen Adams B side |
| Sun Valley | 7" | Unity | UN529 | 1969 | £2.50 | £6 | Hedley Bennett B side |
| Them A Fi Get A Beatin' | 7" | Pressure Beat | PB5509 | 1972 | £5 | £10 | ....... Third & Fourth Generation B side |

## TOTO

| | | | | | | | |
|---|---|---|---|---|---|---|---|
| Africa | CD-s | CBS | 6562982 | 1990 | £2 | £5 | |
| Africa | 7" | CBS | A2510 | 1982 | £1.50 | £4 | ..... shaped picture disc |
| Pamela | CD-s | CBS | 6516072 | 1988 | £2 | £5 | |
| Rosanna | 7" | CBS | A2079 | 1982 | £1.50 | £4 | ..... shaped picture disc |
| Stop Loving You | CD-s | CBS | 6514112 | 1988 | £2 | £5 | |
| Toto | LP | Epic | PJC35317 | 1978 | £5 | £12 | ..... French picture disc |

## TOTTERDELL, DAVE

| | | | | | | | |
|---|---|---|---|---|---|---|---|
| Whitby Bells | LP | Cottage | COT711 | 1977 | £4 | £10 | |

## TOUCH

| | | | | | | | |
|---|---|---|---|---|---|---|---|
| Miss Teach | 7" | Deram | DM243 | 1969 | £2 | £5 | |
| This Is Touch | LP | Deram | DML/SML1033 | 1969 | £15 | £30 | ..............with poster |

## TOUCH (2)

| | | | | | | | |
|---|---|---|---|---|---|---|---|
| Don't You Know What Love Is | 7" | Ariola | ARO243 | 1980 | £2.50 | £6 | |
| Touch | LP | Ariola | ARL5036 | 1980 | £4 | £10 | |
| When The Spirit Moves You | 7" | Ariola | ARO209 | 1980 | £2 | £5 | |

## TOUCH (3)

| | | | | | | | |
|---|---|---|---|---|---|---|---|
| Street Suite | LP | Mainline | LP2001 | 1969 | £875 | £1250 | ....................... US |

## TOUCH OF VELVET

| | | | | | | | |
|---|---|---|---|---|---|---|---|
| Touch Of Velvet | LP | Statik | MADLP002 | | £10 | £25 | |

## TOUCHSTONE

Drummer Chicken Hirsh was previously a member of Country Joe and the Fish, while keyboard player Tom Constanten has managed to sustain a lengthy career following his membership of the Grateful Dead.

| | | | | | | | |
|---|---|---|---|---|---|---|---|
| Tarot | LP | United Artists | UAS5563 | 1972 | £20 | £40 | ....................... US |

## TOUFF, CY

| | | | | | | | |
|---|---|---|---|---|---|---|---|
| Having A Ball | LP | Vogue | LAE12040 | 1957 | £6 | £15 | |

## TOURISTS

| | | | | | | | |
|---|---|---|---|---|---|---|---|
| Blind Among The Flowers | 7" | Logo | GOD350 | 1979 | £1.50 | £4 | ...................... double |
| Loneliest Man In The World | 7" | Logo | GOP360 | 1979 | £2 | £5 | .............picture disc |

## TOUSAN, AL

| | | | | | | | |
|---|---|---|---|---|---|---|---|
| Naomi | 7" | London | HLU9291 | 1961 | £2 | £5 | |

## TOUSSAINT, ALLEN

| | | | | | | | |
|---|---|---|---|---|---|---|---|
| We The People | 7" | Soul City | SC119 | 1969 | £2.50 | £6 | |
| Wild Sound Of New Orleans | LP | RCA | LPM1767 | 1958 | £20 | £40 | ....................... US |

## TOVEY, ROBERTA

| | | | | | | | |
|---|---|---|---|---|---|---|---|
| Who's Who | 7" | Polydor | 56021 | 1965 | £7.50 | £15 | |

## TOWER OF POWER

| | | | | | | | |
|---|---|---|---|---|---|---|---|
| Back To Oakland | LP | Warner Bros | K46282 | 1974 | £4 | £10 | |
| Bump City | LP | Warner Bros | K46167 | 1972 | £4 | £10 | |
| East Bay Grease | LP | San Francisco | SD204 | 1970 | £5 | £12 | ....................... US |
| Tower Of Power | LP | Warner Bros | K46223 | 1974 | £4 | £10 | |
| Urban Renewal | LP | Warner Bros | K56093 | 1975 | £4 | £10 | |

## TOWERS

| | | | | | | | |
|---|---|---|---|---|---|---|---|
| To Know Him Is To Love Him | 7" | Capitol | CL14944 | 1958 | £1.50 | £4 | |

## TOWNER, RALPH

| | | | | | | | |
|---|---|---|---|---|---|---|---|
| Diary | LP | ECM | ECM1032ST | 1973 | £5 | £12 | |
| Solstice | LP | ECM | ECM1060ST | 1975 | £5 | £12 | |
| Sound And Shadows | LP | ECM | ECM1095T | 1976 | £4 | £10 | |
| Trios Solos | LP | ECM | ECM1025ST | 1972 | £5 | £12 | ... with Glen Moore |

## TOWNLEY, JOHN

| | | | | | | | |
|---|---|---|---|---|---|---|---|
| Townley | LP | EMI | EMC3298 | 1979 | £6 | £15 | |

## TOWNSEL SISTERS

| | | | | | | | |
|---|---|---|---|---|---|---|---|
| Will I Ever | 7" | Polydor | NH66954 | 1960 | £2 | £5 | |

## TOWNSEND, ED
Ed Townsend......................................... 7" EP . Capitol............ EAP11091 .............. 1959 £2............£5 ...............................

## TOWNSEND, HENRY
Tired Of Bein' Mistreated ......................... LP ...... Bluesville......... BV1041.................... 1962 £5...........£12 ..........................US

## TOWNSEND, PETE
Friend Is A Friend ................................. CD-s .. Virgin ......... VSCD1198 ............. 1989 £2............£5 .....................3" single
Interview With A Psychoderelict .............. CD..... Atlantic .......... PRCD51612 ........... 1993 £8............£20 ............... US promo
Iron Man.............................................. CD..... Atlantic .......... ........................... 1989 £15............£30 . US promo pack, with
                                                                                                                              CD-s, book, press kit
Pete's Listening Time.............................. LP ...... Atco .............. SAM150.................. 1982 £5............£12 ...... interview promo
Pete's Listening Time.............................. LP ...... Atco .............. SAM150.................. 1982 £10............£25 ...... interview promo,
                                                                                                                                       autographed
Psychoderelict .................................... CD..... Atlantic .......... PRCD51032 ........... 1993 £10............£25 ... US promo double
Townshend Tapes .................................. LP ...... Atco .............. SAM121/2 ............. 1980 £10............£25 double interview promo
Townshend Tapes .................................. LP ...... Atco .............. SAM121/2 ............. 1980 £15............£30 ......... double interview
                                                                                                                              promo, autographed
Uniforms.............................................. 12" .... Atco .............. K11751PT.............. 1982 £2.50............£6 .............picture disc
Who Came First.................................... LP ...... Track ............ 2408201 ................ 1972 £4............£10 ...............................
Won't Get Fooled Again .......................... 7" ...... Island ............ SPB1.................... 1981 £2.50............£6 ... 1 sided promo, with
                                                                                                                                       John Williams

## TOWNSHEND, PETE & MEHER BABA
All Time Star ....................................... LP ...... Universal       MBO1.................. 1975 £30............£60 ....reissue of USL001
                                                        Spiritual
                                                        League ............
Happy Birthday..................................... LP ...... Universal       USL001.................. 1970 £37.50....£75
                                                        Spiritual
                                                        League ............
I Am .................................................. LP ...... Universal       MBO2.................. 1975 £30............£60
                                                        Spiritual
                                                        League ............
I Am .................................................. LP ...... Universal       USL002.................. 1973 £37.50....£75
                                                        Spiritual
                                                        League ............
With Love ............................................ LP ...... Universal       USL003.................. 1974 £37.50....£75
                                                        Spiritual
                                                        League ............

## TOY DOLLS
Everybody Jitterbug................................ 7" ...... Zonophone ..... Z31 ..................... 1982 £2.50............£6
Nellie The Elephant ............................... 7" ...... Volume........... VOL3................... 1983 £2............£5
Tommy Kowie's Car ............................... 7" ...... GBH ............ GRC104................ 1981 £5............£10
Tommy Kowie's Car ............................... 7" ...... GBH ............ SSM005................ 1981 £7.50............£15 ... no picture sleeve

## TOY DOLLS (2)
Little Tin Soldier ................................... 7" ...... London .......... HLN9647.............. 1963 £5............£10

## TOYS
Attack ................................................. 7" ...... Stateside ....... SS483................... 1966 £1.50............£4
Baby Toys ............................................ 7" ...... Stateside ....... SS539................... 1966 £1.50............£4
Ciao Baby ............................................ 7" ...... Philips........... BF1563................. 1967 £1.50............£4
Lover's Concert/Attack........................... LP ...... Stateside ....... (S)SL10175............ 1966 £8............£20
Lover's Concerto ................................... 7" ...... Bell.............. BLL1053............... 1969 £1.50............£4
Lover's Concerto ................................... 7" ...... Stateside ....... SS460................... 1965 £1.50............£4
May My Heart Be Cast To Stone.............. 7" ...... Stateside ....... SS502................... 1966 £2............£5
My Lover's Sonata................................. 7" ...... Philips........... BF1581................. 1967 £2............£5
Silver Spoon ........................................ 7" ...... Stateside ....... SS519................... 1966 £2............£5

## T.P. SMOKE
Smoke................................................. LP ...... Telefunken...... PT12033 .............. 1970 £15............£30 .................German

## T'PAU
Bridge Of Spies .................................... CD..... Siren ............ CDPSRN8............. 1988 £5............£12 ..........picture disc
China In Your Hand ............................... CD-s .. Siren ............ SRNCD64............. 1987 £2............£5 ...............................
I Will Be With You................................ CD-s .. Siren ............ SRNCD87............. 1988 £2............£5 ..........picture disc
Only The Lonely.................................... CD-s .. Siren ............ SRNCD107 ........... 1989 £2............£5 ...............3" single
Road To Our Dream................................ CD-s .. Siren ............ SRNCD100 ........... 1988 £2............£5
Secret Garden ...................................... CD-s .. Siren ............ SRNCD93............. 1988 £2............£5 ..........picture disc
Sex Talk ............................................. CD-s .. Siren ............ SRNCD80............. 1988 £2............£5 ..........picture disc
Valentine ............................................ CD-s .. Siren ............ SRNCD69............. 1988 £2............£5
View From A Bridge ............................... CD-s .. Polygram......... 0804989 ............... 1988 £4............£10 ...............CD video

## TRACEY, GRANT & THE SUNSETS
Everybody Shake.................................... 7" ...... Decca ........... F11741................. 1963 £2............£5
Love Me.............................................. 7" ...... Ember............ EMBS130............. 1961 £4............£8
Please Baby Please ................................ 7" ...... Ember............ EMBS126............. 1961 £5............£10
Taming Tigers ...................................... 7" ...... Ember............ EMBS155............. 1962 £4............£8
Tears Came Rolling Down ........................ 7" ...... Ember............ EMBS148............. 1962 £4............£8
Teenbeat ............................................ LP ...... Ember............ EMB3352............. 1964 £8............£20

## TRACEY, MARK
Caravan Of Lonely Men .......................... 7" ...... Parlophone ..... R4944 ................ 1962 £1.50............£4

## TRACEY, STAN
Alice In Jazzland................................... LP ...... Columbia ........ SX/SCX6051 ......... 1966 £10............£25

| | | | | | | | |
|---|---|---|---|---|---|---|---|
| Alone At Wigmore Hall | LP | Cadillac | SGC1003 | 1974 | £6 | £15 | |
| Captain Adventure | LP | Steam | SJ102 | 1975 | £6 | £15 | |
| Free 'n' One | LP | Columbia | SCX6385 | 1970 | £10 | £25 | |
| In Person | LP | Columbia | SX/SCX6124 | 1967 | £10 | £25 | |
| Jazz Suite | LP | Columbia | 33SX1774/ SCX3589 | 1965 | £10 | £25 | |
| Latin American Caper | LP | Columbia | SCX6358 | 1969 | £10 | £25 | |
| Little Klunk | LP | Ace Of Clubs | ACL1259 | 1969 | £6 | £15 | |
| Little Klunk | LP | Vogue | VA160155 | 1959 | £15 | £30 | |
| New Departures Quartet | LP | Transatlantic | TRA134 | 1964 | £10 | £25 | |
| Perspectives | LP | Columbia | SCX6485 | 1971 | £10 | £25 | |
| Seven Ages Of Man | LP | Columbia | SCX6413 | 1970 | £10 | £25 | |
| Showcase | LP | Vogue | VA160130 | 1958 | £15 | £30 | |
| Under Milk Wood | LP | Steam | SJ101 | 1975 | £6 | £15 | |
| We Love You Madly | LP | Columbia | SX/SCX6320 | 1969 | £10 | £25 | |
| With Love From Jazz | LP | Columbia | SX/SCX6205 | 1968 | £10 | £25 | |

## TRACEY, WENDALL

| | | | | | | | |
|---|---|---|---|---|---|---|---|
| Who's To Know | 7" | London | HLM8664 | 1958 | £7.50 | £15 | |

## TRACK

| | | | | | | | |
|---|---|---|---|---|---|---|---|
| Why Do Fools Fall In Love | 7" | Columbia | DB7987 | 1966 | £2.50 | £6 | |

## TRACTOR

| | | | | | | | |
|---|---|---|---|---|---|---|---|
| No More Rock And Roll | 7" | Cargo | CRS002 | 1977 | £2.50 | £6 | |
| Stone Glory | 7" | Polydor | 2001282 | 1972 | £2.50 | £6 | |
| Tractor | LP | Dandelion | 2310217 | 1972 | £37.50 | £75 | |

## TRAD GRADS

| | | | | | | | |
|---|---|---|---|---|---|---|---|
| Runnin' Shoes | 7" | Decca | F11403 | 1961 | £2.50 | £6 | |

## TRADE WINDS

| | | | | | | | |
|---|---|---|---|---|---|---|---|
| Crossroads | 7" | RCA | RCA1141 | 1959 | £4 | £8 | |

## TRADE WINDS (2)

| | | | | | | | |
|---|---|---|---|---|---|---|---|
| Excursions | LP | Kama Sutra | KLP(S)8057 | 1967 | £5 | £12 | US |
| Mind Excursion | 7" EP | Kama Sutra | 617104 | 1966 | £5 | £10 | French |
| Mind Excursion | 7" | Kama Sutra | KAS202 | 1966 | £1.50 | £4 | |
| New York's A Lonely Town | 7" | Red Bird | RB10020 | 1965 | £4 | £8 | |

## TRADER HORNE

Trader Horne was a folky group formed by Jackie McAuley, who had played keyboards with Them for a while, and Judy Dyble, who was the original lead singer with Fairport Convention. Their one album was followed by a Jackie McAuley solo LP in a similar style, but neither was sufficiently distinctive to make much headway in the market place.

| | | | | | | | |
|---|---|---|---|---|---|---|---|
| Here Comes The Rain | 7" | Dawn | DNS1003 | 1970 | £1.50 | £4 | |
| Morning Way | LP | Dawn | DNLS3004 | 1970 | £30 | £60 | |
| Sheena | 7" | Pye | 7N17846 | 1969 | £2 | £5 | |

## TRAFFIC

The first two albums made by Traffic are near-perfect examples of why so many rock music collectors view the sixties through rose-coloured glasses. Presenting a blend of inspirational songwriting, ever-imaginative arranging and skilful playing, these qualities emerging relatively undiminished by the passing of time, the albums are far more satisfying than any number of more expensive 'progressive' rarities. (Sadly, the reformed 1994 model of Traffic is not the same at all – some of the sound is the same, but the white heat of inspiration has cooled to charcoal.)

| | | | | | | | |
|---|---|---|---|---|---|---|---|
| Best Of Traffic | LP | Island | ILPS9112 | 1969 | £5 | £12 | pink label |
| Far From Home | CD | Virgin | CDVDJ2727 | 1994 | £6 | £15 | promo, card sleeve |
| Feelin' Alright | 7" | Island | WIP6041 | 1968 | £1.50 | £4 | |
| Gimme Some Lovin' | 7" | Island | | 1971 | £2.50 | £6 | promo |
| Heaven Is In Your Mind | LP | United Artists | UAS6651 | 1968 | £5 | £12 | US |
| Here We Go Round The Mulberry Bush | 7" | Island | WIP6025 | 1967 | £1.50 | £4 | |
| Here We Go Round The Mulberry Bush | 7" | Island | WIP6025 | 1967 | £2 | £5 | picture sleeve |
| Hole In My Shoe | 7" | Island | IEP7 | 1978 | £2 | £5 | picture disc |
| Hole In My Shoe | 7" | Island | WIP6017 | 1967 | £1.50 | £4 | |
| Hole In My Shoe | 7" | Island | WIP6017 | 1967 | £2 | £5 | picture sleeve |
| John Barleycorn Must Die | LP | Island | ILPS9116 | 1970 | £5 | £12 | pink label |
| Last Exit | LP | Island | ILPS9097 | 1969 | £6 | £15 | pink label |
| Last Exit | CD | Island | CID9097 | 1988 | £5 | £12 | |
| Live At The Fillmore | LP | Island | ILPS9124 | 1970 | £50 | £100 | demo only |
| Low Spark Of High Heeled Boys | LP | Island | ILPS9180 | 1971 | £4 | £10 | cube cover |
| Low Spark Of High Heeled Boys | CD | Mobile Fidelity | UDCD609 | 1994 | £6 | £15 | US audiophile |
| Medicated Goo | 7" | Island | WIP6050 | 1968 | £1.50 | £4 | |
| Mr. Fantasy | LP | Island | ILP961 | 1967 | £8 | £20 | mono, pink label |
| Mr. Fantasy | LP | Island | ILPS9061 | 1967 | £6 | £15 | stereo, pink label |
| Mr. Fantasy | CD | Mobile Fidelity | UDCD572 | 1992 | £6 | £15 | US audiophile |
| No Face, No Name, No Number | 7" | Island | WIP6030 | 1968 | £1.50 | £4 | |
| On The Road | LP | Island | ILPSD2 | 1973 | £5 | £12 | double |
| Paper Sun | 7" | Island | WIP6002 | 1967 | £1.50 | £4 | |
| Paper Sun | 7" | Island | WIP6002 | 1967 | £4 | £8 | picture sleeve |
| Shoot Out At The Fantasy Factory | LP | Island | ILPS9224 | 1973 | £4 | £10 | cube cover |
| Traffic | LP | Island | ILP981 | 1968 | £6 | £15 | mono, pink label |
| Traffic | LP | Island | ILPS9081 | 1968 | £5 | £12 | stereo, pink label |
| Traffic | CD | Mobile Fidelity | | 1995 | £6 | £15 | US audiophile |
| Traffic Control | CD | Island | PR2300 | 1989 | £8 | £20 | US promo compilation |
| Traffic Report | CD | Island | PR2158 | 1988 | £8 | £20 | US promo compilation |
| Walking In The Wind | 7" | Island | WIP6207 | 1974 | £1.50 | £4 | |

| | | | | | | |
|---|---|---|---|---|---|---|
| Welcome To The Canteen | LP | Island | ILPS9166 | 1971 £4 | £10 | |
| When The Eagle Flies | LP | Island | ILPS9273 | 1974 £4 | £10 | *pink rim label* |
| You Can All Join In | 7" | Island | WIP6041 | 1968 £5 | £10 | *demo only* |

## TRAFFIC JAM

The Spectres changed their name to Traffic Jam for one single, before deciding that the possible confusion with Stevie Winwood's new group, Traffic, was not helping their career. Accordingly, they changed names yet again, this time to Status Quo.

| | | | | | | |
|---|---|---|---|---|---|---|
| Almost But Not Quite There | 7" | Piccadilly | 7N35386 | 1967 £75 | £150 | |

## TRAIN
| | | | | | | |
|---|---|---|---|---|---|---|
| Costumed Cuties | LP | Vanguard | 6542 | 1970 £8 | £20 | *US* |

## TRAINER, PHIL
| | | | | | | |
|---|---|---|---|---|---|---|
| Trainer | LP | BASF | 2029107 | 1973 £8 | £20 | *German* |

## TRAITS
| | | | | | | |
|---|---|---|---|---|---|---|
| Harlem Shuffle | 7" | Pye | 7N25404 | 1967 £2.50 | £6 | |

## TRAMLINE
| | | | | | | |
|---|---|---|---|---|---|---|
| Moves Of Vegetable Centuries | LP | Island | ILPS9095 | 1969 £15 | £30 | *pink label* |
| Somewhere Down The Line | LP | Island | ILPS9088 | 1968 £15 | £30 | *pink label* |

## TRAMMELL, BOBBY LEE
| | | | | | | |
|---|---|---|---|---|---|---|
| Arkansas Twist | LP | Atlantic | LPM1503 | 1962 £15 | £30 | *US* |
| New Dance In France | 7" | Sue | WI326 | 1964 £6 | £12 | |

## TRAMP
| | | | | | | |
|---|---|---|---|---|---|---|
| Each Day | 7" | Youngblood | SBY4 | 1969 £1.50 | £4 | |
| Put A Record On | LP | Spark | SRLP112 | 1974 £15 | £30 | |
| Tramp | LP | Music Man | SMLS603 | 1969 £50 | £100 | |
| Tramp | LP | Spark | SRLM2001 | 1973 £15 | £30 | |
| Vietnam Rose | 7" | Youngblood | 1014 | 1970 £1.50 | £4 | |

## TRANSATLANTICS
| | | | | | | |
|---|---|---|---|---|---|---|
| Don't Fight It | 7" | Mercury | MF948 | 1965 £7.50 | £15 | |
| Louie Go Home | 7" | King | KG1040 | 1966 £2 | £5 | |
| Many Things From Your Window | 7" | Fontana | TF593 | 1965 £2 | £5 | |
| Run For Your Life | 7" | King | KG1033 | 1965 £2 | £5 | |
| Stand Up And Fight Like A Man | 7" | Fontana | TF638 | 1965 £2 | £5 | |

## TRANSVISION VAMP
| | | | | | | |
|---|---|---|---|---|---|---|
| Baby I Don't Care | CD-s | MCA | DTVVT6 | 1989 £2 | £5 | |
| Born To Be Sold | CD-s | MCA | DTVVT9 | 1989 £2 | £5 | |
| I Want Your Love | CD-s | MCA | DTVV3 | 1988 £6 | £15 | *3" single* |
| Landslide Of Love | CD-s | MCA | DTVVT8 | 1989 £2 | £5 | |
| Only One | CD-s | MCA | DTVVT7 | 1989 £2 | £5 | |
| Revolution Baby | CD-s | MCA | DTVVT4 | 1988 £2 | £5 | |
| Sister Moon | CD-s | MCA | DTVV5 | 1988 £3 | £8 | |
| Tell That Girl To Shut Up | CD-s | MCA | DVVT2 | 1988 £6 | £15 | *picture disc* |

## TRAPEZE
| | | | | | | |
|---|---|---|---|---|---|---|
| Final Swing | LP | Threshold | THS11 | 1974 £6 | £15 | |
| Medusa | LP | Threshold | THS4 | 1970 £8 | £20 | |
| Trapeze | LP | Threshold | THS2 | 1970 £8 | £20 | |
| You Are The Music | LP | Threshold | THS8 | 1972 £6 | £15 | |

## TRAPEZE (2)
| | | | | | | |
|---|---|---|---|---|---|---|
| Don't Ask Me How I Know | 7" | Aura | AUS114 | 1979 £2 | £5 | |
| Running Away | 7" | Aura | AUS116 | 1980 £2 | £5 | |

## TRASH
| | | | | | | |
|---|---|---|---|---|---|---|
| Golden Slumbers | 7" | Apple | 17 | 1969 £4 | £8 | |

## TRASHMEN
| | | | | | | |
|---|---|---|---|---|---|---|
| Bad News | 7" EP | Columbia | ESRF1564 | 1964 £20 | £40 | *French* |
| Bird Dance Beat | 7" | Stateside | SS276 | 1964 £6 | £12 | |
| Surfin' Bird | LP | Garrett | GA(S)200 | 1964 £37.50 | £75 | *US* |
| Surfin' Bird | 7" EP | Columbia | ESRF1491 | 1964 £20 | £40 | *French* |
| Surfin' Bird | 7" | Stateside | SS255 | 1964 £10 | £20 | |
| Whoa Dad | 7" EP | Columbia | ESRF1627 | 1964 £30 | £60 | *French* |

## TRAUM, HAPPY & ARTIE
| | | | | | | |
|---|---|---|---|---|---|---|
| Doubleback | LP | Capitol | ST799 | 1971 £4 | £10 | |
| Happy & Artie Traum | LP | Capitol | ST586 | 1969 £4 | £10 | |
| Mud Acres | LP | Matchbox | 239 | 1972 £4 | £10 | |

## TRAVEL AGENCY
| | | | | | | |
|---|---|---|---|---|---|---|
| Travel Agency | LP | Viva | 36017 | 1968 £8 | £20 | *US* |

## TRAVELING WILBURYS
| | | | | | | |
|---|---|---|---|---|---|---|
| End Of The Line | CD-s | WEA | W7637CD | 1989 £2.50 | £6 | |
| End Of The Line | 12" | Warner Bros | W7637T | 1989 £3 | £8 | *with stickers* |
| Handle With Care | CD-s | WEA | W7732CD | 1988 £2 | £5 | |
| Handle With Care | 7" | Warner Bros | W7732 | 1988 £1.50 | £4 | *..gatefold picture sleeve* |
| Handle With Care | 10" | Warner Bros | W7732TE | 1988 £2.50 | £6 | |
| Nododdy's Child | CD-s | WEA | W9973CD | 1990 £2.50 | £6 | |

| Title | Format | Label | Catalogue | Year | Price | Price | Notes |
|---|---|---|---|---|---|---|---|
| She's My Baby | CD-s | WEA | W9523CD | 1990 | £3 | £8 | |
| Volume One | CD | Wilbury Record Co. | | 1988 | £8 | £20 | US promo picture disc |
| Volume Three | CD | Wilbury Record Co. | 9263242DJ | 1990 | £8 | £20 | US promo picture disc |
| Wilbury Twist | CD-s | Warner Bros | W0018CD | 1991 | £2.50 | £6 | |
| Wilbury Twist | 7" | Warner Bros | W0018W | 1991 | £1.50 | £4 | with cards |

## TRAVELLING STEWARTS

| Travelling Stewarts | LP | Topic | 12T179 | 1968 | £10 | £25 | |

## TRAVIS

| Shine On Me | LP | A&M | AMLS68120 | 1973 | £15 | £30 | |

## TRAVIS, DAVE

| Dave Travis | LP | Polydor | 236557 | 1969 | £6 | £15 | ...with Dave Cousins |

## TRAVIS, MERLE

| Back Home | LP | Capitol | T891 | 1957 | £6 | £15 | |
| Back Home | 7" EP | Capitol | EAP1891 | 1957 | £4 | £8 | |
| Merle Travis Guitar | LP | Capitol | T650 | 1956 | £10 | £25 | US |
| Merle Travis Guitar No. 1 | 7" EP | Capitol | EAP1032 | 1956 | £7.50 | £15 | |
| Merle Travis Guitar No. 2 | 7" EP | Capitol | EAP2650 | 1956 | £4 | £8 | |
| Walkin' The Strings | LP | Capitol | T1391 | 1960 | £6 | £15 | US |
| Walkin' The Strings | 7" EP | Capitol | EAP41391 | 1960 | £4 | £8 | |

## TRAVIS, NICK

| Panic Is On | LP | HMV | CLP1036 | 1955 | £10 | £25 | |

## TRAVIS & BOB

| Tell Him No | 7" | Pye | 7N25018 | 1959 | £1.50 | £4 | |

## TREASURE ISLE BOYS

| Love Is A Treasure | 7" | Trojan | TR010 | 1967 | £5 | £10 | Tommy McCook B side |

## TREDJE, ANNA SJALV

| Tussilago Fanfara | LP | Silence | SR4646 | 1979 | £8 | £20 | Swedish |

## TREE

| Tree | LP | Goat Farm | 580 | 1970 | £37.50 | £75 | US |

## TREE, VIRGINIA (SHIRLEY KENT)

| Fresh Out | LP | Minstrel | 0001 | 1975 | £15 | £30 | |

## TREES

Despite the inclusion of tracks by Trees on two of the best-selling CBS rock album samplers, the group's albums sold poorly. They are, however, superior folk-rock and have been sought-after by collectors for a long time (without, however, changing very much in value over the years). Many of the same musicians formed the seventies band Casablanca, but for some reason their album is almost completely ignored by collectors.

| Garden Of Jane Delawney | LP | CBS | 63837 | 1970 | £30 | £60 | |
| Nothing Special | 7" | CBS | 5078 | 1970 | £2.50 | £6 | |
| On The Shore | LP | CBS | 64168 | 1970 | £30 | £60 | |
| On The Shore | LP | Decal | LIK12 | 1987 | £4 | £10 | |

## TREESE, JACK

| Maitoo The Truffle Man | LP | Savanah | | 197– | £6 | £15 | French |

## TREETOPS

| California My Way | 7" | Parlophone | R5669 | 1968 | £1.50 | £4 | |
| Don't Worry Baby | 7" | Parlophone | R5628 | 1967 | £1.50 | £4 | |
| Mississippi Valley | 7" | Columbia | DB8727 | 1970 | £1.50 | £4 | |
| Without The One You Love | 7" | Columbia | DB8799 | 1971 | £1.50 | £4 | |

## TREKKAS

| Please Go | 7" | Planet | PLF105 | 1965 | £15 | £30 | |

## TREKKERS

| Trekkers Go Uptown | 10" LP | Advision | | 1963 | £37.50 | £75 | |

## TREMELOES

| 58/68 World Explosion | LP | CBS | BN26388 | 1968 | £4 | £10 | US |
| Blessed | 7" | Decca | F12423 | 1966 | £2 | £5 | |
| Chip, Rick, Alan And Dave | LP | CBS | (S)BPG63138 | 1967 | £4 | £10 | |
| Here Come The Tremeloes | LP | CBS | (S)BPG63017 | 1967 | £4 | £10 | |
| Live In Cabaret | LP | CBS | 63547 | 1969 | £4 | £10 | |
| Master | LP | CBS | 64242 | 1970 | £4 | £10 | |
| My Little Lady | 7" EP | CBS | EP6402 | 1968 | £2 | £5 | |

## TREMORS

| Beaten An Knuller | LP | Elite | SOLPS246 | 1965 | £5 | £12 | German |

## TREND

| Shot On Sight | 7" | Page One | POF004 | 1966 | £5 | £10 | |

## TRENDS
| | | | | | | | |
|---|---|---|---|---|---|---|---|
| All My Loving | 7" | Piccadilly | 7N35171 | 1964 | £2 | £5 | |
| Way You Do The Things You Do | 7" | Pye | 7N15644 | 1964 | £2 | £5 | |

## TRENDSETTERS
| | | | | | | | |
|---|---|---|---|---|---|---|---|
| At The Hotel De France | 7" EP | Oak | RGJ999 | 196– | £10 | £20 | |
| You Don't Care | 7" | Silver Phoenix | 1001 | 1964 | £15 | £30 | |

## TRENDSETTERS LTD

The roots of King Crimson lie in the four unprepossessing singles made by Trendsetters Ltd, which feature the early work of Michael and Peter Giles.

| | | | | | | | |
|---|---|---|---|---|---|---|---|
| Funny Way Of Showing Your Love | 7" | Parlophone | R5324 | 1965 | £5 | £10 | |
| Go Away | 7" | Parlophone | R5191 | 1964 | £5 | £10 | |
| Hello Josephine | 7" | Parlophone | R5161 | 1964 | £5 | £10 | |
| In A Big Way | 7" | Parlophone | R5118 | 1964 | £5 | £10 | |

## TRENIERS
| | | | | | | | |
|---|---|---|---|---|---|---|---|
| | 10" LP | | | 195– | £75 | £150 | |
| Go Go Go | 7" | Fontana | H137 | 1958 | £37.50 | £75 | |
| Ooh La La | 7" | Coral | Q72319 | 1958 | £7.50 | £15 | |
| Souvenir Album | LP | Dot | DLP3257 | 1960 | £10 | £25 | US |
| Treniers On TV | LP | Epic | LG3125 | 195– | £25 | £50 | US |
| When Your Hair Has Turned Silver | 7" | London | HLD8858 | 1959 | £10 | £20 | |

## TRENT, JACKIE
| | | | | | | | |
|---|---|---|---|---|---|---|---|
| If You Love Me | 7" | Piccadilly | 7N35165 | 1964 | £1.50 | £4 | |
| Magic Of Jackie Trent | LP | Pye | NPL18125 | 1965 | £4 | £10 | |
| Where Are You Now | 7" EP | Pye | NEP24225 | 1965 | £2 | £5 | |
| You Baby | 7" | Pye | 7N17047 | 1966 | £4 | £8 | |

## TREPTE, ULI
| | | | | | | | |
|---|---|---|---|---|---|---|---|
| Spacebox | LP | Spacebox | SP1 | 1981 | £5 | £12 | German, record mailer sleeve |

## TRESPASS
| | | | | | | | |
|---|---|---|---|---|---|---|---|
| Bright Lights | 7" | Trial | CASE3 | 1982 | £4 | £8 | |
| Jealousy | 7" | Trial | CASE2 | 1980 | £4 | £8 | |
| One Of These Days | 7" | Trial | CASE1 | 1979 | £5 | £10 | |

## TRETOW, MICHAEL B.
| | | | | | | | |
|---|---|---|---|---|---|---|---|
| Michael B.Tretow | LP | CBS | 81143 | 1976 | £8 | £20 | German |

## TREVOR
| | | | | | | | |
|---|---|---|---|---|---|---|---|
| Down In Virginia | 7" | Blue Beat | BB228 | 1964 | £6 | £12 | |
| Everyday Like A Holiday | 7" | Blue Cat | BS153 | 1969 | £1.50 | £4 | with The Maytones |

## TRIADE
| | | | | | | | |
|---|---|---|---|---|---|---|---|
| 1998: La Storia Di Sabazio | LP | Derby | DBR65801 | 1973 | £15 | £30 | Italian |

## TRIANA
| | | | | | | | |
|---|---|---|---|---|---|---|---|
| Hyos Del Agobio | LP | Movie Play | 1709079 | 1977 | £6 | £15 | Spanish |
| Sombra Y Luz | LP | Movie Play | 1714394 | 1979 | £5 | £12 | Spanish |
| Triana | LP | Movie Play | 1706787 | 1975 | £6 | £15 | Spanish |
| Un Encuentro | LP | Movie Play | 5506785 | 1980 | £5 | £12 | Spanish |

## TRIANGLE
| | | | | | | | |
|---|---|---|---|---|---|---|---|
| Vol. 1 | LP | Select | 298193 | 1970 | £8 | £20 | Canadian |

## TRIANGLE (2)
| | | | | | | | |
|---|---|---|---|---|---|---|---|
| How Now Blue Cow | LP | Capitol | ST5001 | 1969 | £15 | £30 | US |

## TRIBAN
| | | | | | | | |
|---|---|---|---|---|---|---|---|
| Black Paper Roses | 7" | Decca | F13115 | 1970 | £2 | £5 | |
| Leaving On A Jet Plane | 7" | CSP | 707 | 1969 | £2 | £5 | |
| Rainmaker | LP | Cambrian | | 1972 | £15 | £30 | |
| Triban | LP | Cambrian | MCT592 | 1969 | £15 | £30 | |

## TRIBE
| | | | | | | | |
|---|---|---|---|---|---|---|---|
| Gamma Goochi | 7" | Planet | PLF108 | 1966 | £20 | £40 | |
| Love Is A Beautiful Thing | 7" | RCA | RCA1592 | 1967 | £5 | £10 | |

## TRIBE (2)
| | | | | | | | |
|---|---|---|---|---|---|---|---|
| Dancin' To The Beat Of My Heart | 7" | Polydor | 56510 | 1970 | £5 | £10 | |

## TRIBE, TONY
| | | | | | | | |
|---|---|---|---|---|---|---|---|
| Red Red Wine | 7" | Down Town | DT419 | 1969 | £1.50 | £4 | Rico B side |

## TRIBE OF TOFFS
| | | | | | | | |
|---|---|---|---|---|---|---|---|
| John Kettley Is A Weatherman | 7" | Completely Different | DAFT1 | 1988 | £1.50 | £4 | |

## TRIFFIDS
| | | | | | | | |
|---|---|---|---|---|---|---|---|
| Bury Me Deep In Love | CD-s | Islad | CID424 | 1989 | £2 | £5 | |
| Falling Over You | CD-s | Island | CID413 | 1989 | £2 | £5 | |
| Goodbye Little Boy | CD-s | Island | CID420 | 1989 | £2 | £5 | |

Holy Water.................................................. CD-s .. Island.............. CID367.................... 1988 £2........... £5 ......................

## TRIFFIDS (2)
Are Really Folk........................................ LP ..... Fontana........... TL5231 ................ 1965 £4........... £10

## TRIFFIDS (3)
Lookin' Around ....................................... 7" ...... Columbia........ DB7084 .............. 1963 £1.50..... £4

## TRIFLE
First Meeting .......................................... LP ..... Dawn............ DNLS3017............. 1971 £6........... £15

## TRIKHA, PANDIT KANWAR SAIN
Three Sitar Pieces.................................... LP ..... Mushroom ...... 100MR7 ............... 1970 £20........ £40

## TRILOGY
I'm Beginning To Feel It ......................... LP ..... Mercury......... 6338034 ................. 1970 £4........... £10

## TRIO
Trio ...................................................... LP ..... London .......... LTZC15017 ........... 1956 £15........ £30
Trio With Guests ..................................... LP ..... London .......... LTZC15046 ........... 1957 £10........ £25

## TRIO (2)
In the heady days of the early seventies, the Trio ( John Surman, Barre Phillips, and Stu Martin) achieved the remarkable feat of playing uncompromising avant-garde jazz while gaining a record contract with one of the major record companies. The group even managed a tour of rock venues on the strength of this, yet actually managed to sell very few records, as their scarcity today testifies.

By Contract ............................................. LP ..... Ogun............ OG529.................... 1978 £5........... £12
Conflagration ......................................... LP ..... Dawn............ DNLS3022............. 1971 £15........ £30
Trio ...................................................... LP ..... Dawn............ DNLS3006............. 1970 £20........ £40 .................. double

## TRIOS, CHUCK & AMAZING MAZE
Call On You.............................................. 7" ...... Action............ ACT4517.............. 1968 £1.50....... £4

## TRIP
Atlantide................................................... LP ..... RCA .......................................... 1972 £25.......... £50

## TRIPPERS
Dance With Me ........................................ 7" ...... Pye .............. 7N25388 ............... 1966 £5........... £10

## TRIPSICHORD MUSIC BOX
San Francisco Sound ............................... LP ..... Janus............. JLS3016................ 1971 £75....... £150 ..................... US

## TRISHA
Darkness Of My Night ............................. 7" ...... CBS.............. 201800 ................. 1965 £1.50....... £4

## TRISTANO, LENNIE
Bebop .................................................... LP ..... Mercury......... SMWL21028 ....... 1969 £4........... £10 .... with tracks by Red
                                                                                                                                                                    Rodney
Lennie Tristano ....................................... LP ..... London ......... LTZK15033 .......... 1957 £15........ £30
Lines ..................................................... LP ..... Atlantic .......... 590031................. 1969 £4........... £10
New Tristano........................................... LP ..... Atlantic .......... 590017................. 1968 £5........... £12

## TRISTAR AIRBUS
Travellin' Man ......................................... 7" ...... RCA ............. RCA2170 ............. 1972 £1.50....... £4

## TRISTRAM SHANDY
Tristram Shandy ...................................... LP ..... Silvermore....... SIL0001 ............... 1979 £4........... £10

## TRIUMPH
Rock 'n' Roll Machine............................. LP ..... Attic ............. LATX1036............ 1977 £5.......... £12 ....Canadian, vinyl &
                                                                                                                                                                    metal

## TRIXIE'S BIG RED MOTORBIKE
Norman And Narcissus ............................ 7" ...... Lobby Ludd..... L100001 .............. 1984 £2.50....... £6
Splash Of Red......................................... 7" ...... Chew ............ CH9271............... 1982 £2.50....... £6
Splash Of Red......................................... 7" ...... Lobby Ludd..... L100002 .............. 1984 £2........... £5
Trixie's Big Red Motorbike EP ................ 7" ...... Chew ............ RAM510.............. 1982 £2.50....... £6
Trixie's Big Red Motorbike EP ................ 7" ...... Lobby Ludd..... L100003 .............. 1984 £2........... £5

## TRO, MARCUS
Tell Me................................................... 7" ...... Ember............ EMBS203.............. 1965 £2........... £5

## TROGGS
When the Trogg's 'Wild Thing', with its novelty ocarina solo offsetting the Louie Louie riff, climbed to the top of the charts, Jonathan King offered to treat the group to a slap-up meal if they were still in the charts three years later. He lost his bet – but only just. The Troggs' simple hard(ish) rock bordered on the inept, but they have managed to create a considerable affection in the minds of the record-collecting public. All the Troggs' original recordings are becoming increasingly sought-after, especially the LP Mixed Bag, which includes the group's over-the-top attempts at psychedelia.

Anyway That You Want Me ...................... 7" EP. Fontana........... 460987.................. 1966 £12.50... £25 ........................ French
Anyway That You Want Me ...................... 7" ...... Page One ........ POF010 ................ 1966 £1.50....... £4
Best Of Vol. 1......................................... LP ..... Page One ........ FOR001 ............... 1967 £6........... £15
Best Of Vol. 2......................................... LP ..... Page One ........ FOR002 ............... 1967 £6........... £15
Cellophane ............................................. LP ..... Page One ........ POL003 ............... 1967 £15........ £30
Contrasts ............................................... LP ..... DJM ............. DJML009 ............. 1970 £6........... £15
Easy Livin' ............................................. 7" ...... Page One ........ POF164 ............... 1970 £1.50....... £4
Every Little Thing................................... 7" ...... 10............... TENY21 .............. 1984 £1.50....... £4 .............picture disc

899

| | | | | | | | |
|---|---|---|---|---|---|---|---|
| Evil Woman | 7" | Page One | POF114 | 1969 | £1.50 | £4 | |
| From Nowhere | LP | Fontana | (S)TL5355 | 1966 | £10 | £25 | |
| From Nowhere | CD | Fontana | 8329572 | 1989 | £5 | £12 | |
| Give It To Me | 7" EP | Fontana | 460203 | 1967 | £12.50 | £25 | French |
| Give It To Me | 7" | Page One | POF015 | 1967 | £1.50 | £4 | |
| Hi Hi Hazel | 7" | Page One | POF030 | 1967 | £1.50 | £4 | |
| Hip Hip Hooray | 7" | Page One | POF092 | 1968 | £1.50 | £4 | |
| I Can't Control Myself | 7" EP | Fontana | 460981 | 1966 | £12.50 | £25 | French |
| I Can't Control Myself | 7" | Page One | POF001 | 1966 | £1.50 | £4 | |
| Just A Little Too Much | 7" | Raw | RAW25 | 1978 | £1.50 | £4 | |
| Little Girl | 7" | Page One | POF056 | 1968 | £1.50 | £4 | |
| Lost Girl | 7" | CBS | 202038 | 1966 | £7.50 | £15 | |
| Love Is All Around | 7" | Page One | POF040 | 1967 | £1.50 | £4 | |
| Lover | 7" | Page One | POF171 | 1970 | £1.50 | £4 | |
| Mixed Bag | LP | Page One | POLS012 | 1968 | £37.50 | £75 | |
| My Lady | 7" | Page One | POF022 | 1967 | £12.50 | £25 | |
| Night Of The Long Grass | 7" EP | Fontana | 460212 | 1967 | £12.50 | £25 | French |
| Night Of The Long Grass | 7" | Page One | POF022 | 1967 | £1.50 | £4 | |
| On Tour | LP | Page One | POL1 | 1968 | £75 | £150 | export |
| Raver | 7" | Page One | POF182 | 1970 | £1.50 | £4 | |
| Surprise Surprise | 7" | Page One | POF064 | 1968 | £1.50 | £4 | |
| Trogg Tops Vol. 1 | 7" EP | Page One | POE001 | 1967 | £5 | £10 | |
| Trogg Tops Vol. 2 | 7" EP | Page One | POE002 | 1967 | £7.50 | £15 | |
| Trogglodynamite | LP | Page One | POL001 | 1966 | £10 | £25 | |
| Trogglomania | LP | Page One | POS602 | 1969 | £8 | £20 | |
| Wild Thing | LP | Fontana | SRF27556 | 1966 | £15 | £30 | US |
| Wild Thing | 7" EP | Fontana | 460974 | 1966 | £12.50 | £25 | French |
| Wild Thing | 7" | Fontana | TF689 | 1966 | £1.50 | £4 | |
| With A Girl Like You | 7" EP | Fontana | 465321 | 1966 | £12.50 | £25 | French |
| With a Girl Like You | 7" | Fontana | TF717 | 1966 | £1.50 | £4 | |
| You Can Cry If You Want To | 7" | Page One | POF082 | 1968 | £1.50 | £4 | |

### TROJANS
| | | | | | | | |
|---|---|---|---|---|---|---|---|
| Man I'm Gonna Be | 7" | Decca | F11065 | 1958 | £6 | £12 | |

### TROLL
| | | | | | | | |
|---|---|---|---|---|---|---|---|
| Animated Music | LP | Smash | SRS67114 | 1968 | £25 | £50 | US |

### TROLL BROTHERS
| | | | | | | | |
|---|---|---|---|---|---|---|---|
| You Turn Me On | 7" | SRT | SRT733316 | 197– | £2.50 | £6 | |

### TROMBONES INC.
| | | | | | | | |
|---|---|---|---|---|---|---|---|
| Trombones Inc. | LP | Warner Bros | WM4023/WS8023 | 1961 | £5 | £12 | |

### TRONICS
| | | | | | | | |
|---|---|---|---|---|---|---|---|
| Cantina | 7" | Fontana | H348 | 1961 | £2.50 | £6 | |

### TROOPERS
| | | | | | | | |
|---|---|---|---|---|---|---|---|
| Get Out | 7" | Vogue | V9087 | 1957 | £150 | £250 | best auctioned |

### TROTT, ARCHIBALD
| | | | | | | | |
|---|---|---|---|---|---|---|---|
| Get Together | 7" | Black Swan | WI407 | 1964 | £5 | £10 | |

### TROTTO
| | | | | | | | |
|---|---|---|---|---|---|---|---|
| Trotto | LP | Free Reed | FRR005 | 1976 | £4 | £10 | |

### TROUBADOUR SINGERS
| | | | | | | | |
|---|---|---|---|---|---|---|---|
| Sing Out Big | LP | London | HAF8275 | 1965 | £10 | £25 | |

### TROUBADOURS
| | | | | | | | |
|---|---|---|---|---|---|---|---|
| Fascination | 7" | London | HLR8469 | 1957 | £2.50 | £6 | |
| Lights Of Paris | 7" | London | HLR8541 | 1958 | £2.50 | £6 | |
| Troubadours | 7" EP | London | RER1135 | 1958 | £2 | £5 | |

### TROUBLE
| | | | | | | | |
|---|---|---|---|---|---|---|---|
| After The War | LP | Sonet | SLPS1521 | 1970 | £8 | £20 | Danish |

### TROUP, BOBBY
| | | | | | | | |
|---|---|---|---|---|---|---|---|
| Bobby Troup | 7" EP | Capitol | EAP1484 | 1955 | £2 | £5 | |
| Bobby Troup | 10" LP | Capitol | LC6660 | 1954 | £4 | £10 | |
| Julie Is Her Name | 7" | Capitol | CL14219 | 1954 | £1.50 | £4 | |

### TROW, BOB
| | | | | | | | |
|---|---|---|---|---|---|---|---|
| Soft Squeeze Baby | 7" | London | HL8082 | 1954 | £10 | £20 | |

### TROWER, ROBIN

The former guitarist with Procol Harum was never entirely happy with a group that provided limited opportunity for guitar excess. The albums made by his own power trio were a different matter. Heavily influenced by Jimi Hendrix, Trower was actually one of the few guitarists working in the seventies who was able to impose something of himself on to the Hendrix sound. Bass player Jimmy Dewar, who also proved himself to be a fine lead vocalist, had previously been a member of Stone the Crows – and earlier still was rhythm guitarist with Lulu and the Luvvers – while the drummer on the first two albums, Reg Isadore, played with Peter Bardens amongst other people, and was later to be found supporting Peter Green on a couple of his rare visits to the recording studio.

| | | | | | | | |
|---|---|---|---|---|---|---|---|
| Bridge Of Sighs | LP | Charisma | CHR1057 | 1974 | £4 | £10 | |
| Bridge Of Sighs | CD | Chrysalis | CD25CR15 | 1994 | £5 | £12 | Chrysalis 25 pack |
| For Earth Below | LP | Charisma | CHR1073 | 1975 | £4 | £10 | |
| Twice Removed From Yesterday | LP | Charisma | CHR1039 | 1973 | £4 | £10 | |

## TROY, DORIS

| | | | | | | | |
|---|---|---|---|---|---|---|---|
| Ain't That Cute | 7" | Apple | 24 | 1970 | £1.50 | £4 | |
| Ain't That Cute | 7" | Apple | 24 | 1970 | £4 | £8 | picture sleeve |
| Doris Troy | LP | Apple | SAPCOR13 | 1970 | £8 | £20 | |
| Heartaches | 7" | Atlantic | AT4032 | 1965 | £2 | £5 | |
| I'll Do Anything | 7" | Cameo Parkway | C101 | 1962 | £20 | £40 | |
| I'll Do Anything | 7" | Toast | TT507 | 1968 | £1.50 | £4 | |
| Jacob's Ladder | 7" | Apple | 28 | 1970 | £2 | £5 | |
| Just One Look | LP | Atlantic | (SD)8088 | 1964 | £8 | £20 | US |
| Just One Look | 7" | Atlantic | 584148 | 1968 | £1.50 | £4 | |
| Just One Look | 7" | London | HLK9749 | 1963 | £2.50 | £6 | |
| One More Chance | 7" | Atlantic | AT4020 | 1965 | £2 | £5 | |
| Rainbow Testament | LP | Polydor | 2956001 | 1972 | £4 | £10 | |
| Whatcha Gonna Do About It | 7" EP | Atlantic | AET6007 | 1965 | £15 | £30 | |
| Whatcha Gonna Do About It | 7" | Atlantic | AT4011 | 1964 | £2 | £5 | |

## TROY & THE T-BIRDS

| | | | | | | |
|---|---|---|---|---|---|---|
| Twistle | 7" | London | HL9476 | 1961 | £1.50 | £4 |

## TRUBROT

| | | | | | | | |
|---|---|---|---|---|---|---|---|
| Trubrot | LP | Parlophone | 027 | 1969 | £50 | £100 | Danish |
| Undir Ahrifum | LP | Parlophone | 023 | 1970 | £62.50 | £125 | Danish |

## TRUMPETEERS

| | | | | | | | |
|---|---|---|---|---|---|---|---|
| Milky White Way | LP | Score | 4021 | 1960 | £25 | £50 | US |

## TRUTH

| | | | | | | |
|---|---|---|---|---|---|---|
| Baby Don't You Know | 7" | Pye | 7N15923 | 1965 | £2.50 | £6 |
| Girl | 7" | Pye | 7N17035 | 1966 | £1.50 | £4 |
| I Go To Sleep | 7" | Pye | 7N17095 | 1966 | £7.50 | £15 |
| Jingle Jangle | 7" | Deram | DM105 | 1966 | £10 | £20 |
| Seuno | 7" | Decca | F22764 | 1968 | £2.50 | £6 |
| Walk Away Renee | 7" | Decca | F12582 | 1967 | £1.50 | £4 |
| Who's Wrong | 7" | Pye | 7N15998 | 1965 | £4 | £8 |

## TRUTH (2)

| | | | | | | | |
|---|---|---|---|---|---|---|---|
| Truth | LP | People | PLP5002 | 1970 | £20 | £40 | US |

## TRUTH & JANEY

| | | | | | | | |
|---|---|---|---|---|---|---|---|
| Just A Little Bit Of Magic | LP | Bee Bel | | 1979 | £5 | £12 | US |
| Live | LP | Rock And Bach | | 1988 | £6 | £15 | US double |
| No Rest For The Wicked | LP | Montrose | MR376 | 1976 | £37.50 | £75 | US |

## TRUTH OF TRUTHS

| | | | | | | | |
|---|---|---|---|---|---|---|---|
| Truth Of Truths | LP | Oak | OR1001 | 1971 | £10 | £25 | double |

## TUBB, ERNEST

| | | | | | | | |
|---|---|---|---|---|---|---|---|
| All Time Hits | LP | Decca | DL(7)4046 | 1961 | £5 | £12 | US |
| Daddy Of 'Em All | LP | Brunswick | LAT8260 | 1958 | £6 | £15 | |
| Daddy Of 'Em All | LP | Decca | DL8553 | 1956 | £8 | £20 | US |
| Daddy Of 'Em All Pt. 1 | 7" EP | Brunswick | OE9372 | 1958 | £4 | £8 | |
| Daddy Of 'Em All Pt. 2 | 7" EP | Brunswick | OE9373 | 1958 | £4 | £8 | |
| Daddy Of 'Em All Pt. 3 | 7" EP | Brunswick | OE9374 | 1958 | £4 | £8 | |
| Ernest Tubb Record Shop | LP | Brunswick | LAT8349 | 1960 | £6 | £15 | |
| Ernest Tubb Story Vol. 1 | LP | Brunswick | LAT8313 | 1959 | £4 | £10 | |
| Ernest Tubb Story Vol. 2 | LP | Brunswick | LAT8314 | 1960 | £4 | £10 | |
| Favorites | LP | Decca | DL8291 | 1956 | £8 | £20 | US |
| Favorites | 10" LP | Decca | DL5301 | 1951 | £10 | £25 | US |
| Favourites | LP | Brunswick | LAT8161 | 1957 | £6 | £15 | |
| Golden Favorites | LP | Decca | DL(7)4118 | 1961 | £5 | £12 | US |
| Importance Of Being Ernest | LP | Decca | LAT8292 | 1959 | £6 | £15 | |
| Jimmie Rodgers Songs | 10" LP | Brunswick | LA8736 | 1956 | £8 | £20 | |
| Jimmie Rodgers Songs | 10" LP | Decca | DL5336 | 1951 | £10 | £25 | US |
| Just Call Me Lonesome | LP | Decca | DL(7)4385 | 1964 | £5 | £12 | US |
| Midnight Jamboree | LP | Decca | DL(7)4045 | 1960 | £5 | £12 | US |
| Old Rugged Cross | 10" LP | Decca | DL5334 | 1951 | £10 | £25 | US |
| On Tour | LP | Decca | DL(7)4321 | 1962 | £5 | £12 | US |
| Sing A Song Of Christmas | 10" LP | Decca | DL5497 | 1954 | £10 | £25 | US |
| So Doggone Lonesome | 7" | Brunswick | 05587 | 1956 | £5 | £10 | |
| Thirty Days | 7" | Brunswick | 05527 | 1956 | £15 | £30 | |
| What Am I Living For | 7" | Decca | BM31214 | 195– | £2.50 | £6 | export |

## TUBB, JUSTIN

| | | | | | | |
|---|---|---|---|---|---|---|
| Take A Letter Miss Gray | 7" EP | RCA | RCX7133 | 1964 | £7.50 | £15 |

## TUBES

| | | | | | | | |
|---|---|---|---|---|---|---|---|
| Prime Time | 7" | A&M | AMS7423 | 1979 | £12.50 | £25 | .7 x coloured vinyl 7" plus picture disc, boxed, promo |
| Remote Control | LP | A&M | AMLH9964751 | 1979 | £4 | £10 | Dutch picture disc |
| Tubes First Clean Album | LP | A&M | SP17012 | 1978 | £5 | £12 | US promo |

## TUBEWAY ARMY

| | | | | | | | |
|---|---|---|---|---|---|---|---|
| Are 'Friends' Electric? | 7" | Beggars Banquet | BEG18P | 1979 | £2.50 | £6 | picture disc, insert |

| | | | | | | | |
|---|---|---|---|---|---|---|---|
| Are 'Friends' Electric? | 12" | Intercord | INT126501 | 1979 | £4 | £10 | German |
| Bombers | 7" | Beggars Banquet | BEG8 | 1978 | £2 | £5 | |
| Down In The Park | 12" | Beggars Banquet | BEG17T | 1979 | £5 | £12 | |
| That's Too Bad | 7" | Beggars Banquet | BEG5 | 1978 | £2 | £5 | |
| This Is My Life | 7" | Beggars Banquet | TUB1 | 1985 | £12.50 | £25 | promo |
| Tubeway Army | LP | Beggars Banquet | BEGA4 | 1978 | £15 | £30 | blue vinyl |
| Tubeway Army '78–'79 Vol. 2 | 12" | Beggars Banquet | BEG123E | 1984 | £2.50 | £6 | red vinyl |
| Tubeway Army '78–'79 Vol. 3 | 12" | Beggars Banquet | BEG124E | 1984 | £2.50 | £6 | blue vinyl |

## TUCKER, BESSIE
| Blues By Bessie | 7" EP | HMV | 7EG8085 | 1955 | £7.50 | £15 | |

## TUCKER, BILLY JOE
| Boogie Woogie Bill | 7" | London | HLD9455 | 1961 | £25 | £50 | |

## TUCKER, CY
| My Prayer | 7" | Fontana | TF424 | 1963 | £1.50 | £4 | |

## TUCKER, MAUREEN
| Playin' Possum | LP | Trash | TLP1001 | 1981 | £4 | £10 | US |

## TUCKER, SOPHIE
| Cabaret Days | LP | Mercury | MG20046 | 1954 | £4 | £10 | |
| My Dream | LP | Mercury | MG20035 | 1954 | £4 | £10 | |

## TUCKER, TOMMY
| Hi Heel Sneakers | LP | Checker | 2990 | 1964 | £10 | £25 | US |
| Hi Heel Sneakers | 7" EP | Pye | NEP44027 | 1964 | £6 | £12 | |
| Hi Heel Sneakers | 7" | Chess | CRS8086 | 1969 | £2 | £5 | |
| Hi Heel Sneakers | 7" | Pye | 7N25238 | 1964 | £4 | £8 | |
| Long Tall Shorty | 7" | Pye | 7N25246 | 1964 | £4 | £8 | |
| Oh What A Feeling | 7" | London | HLU9932 | 1964 | £7.50 | £15 | |

## TUCKY BUZZARD
| Alright On The Night | LP | Purple | TPSA7510 | 1973 | £4 | £10 | |
| Buzzard | LP | Purple | TPSA7512 | 1973 | £4 | £10 | |
| Coming On Again | LP | Capitol | 864 | 1971 | £5 | £12 | US |
| Warm Slash | LP | Capitol | EST864 | 1969 | £6 | £15 | |

## TUDOR LODGE
| Lady's Changing Home | 7" | Vertigo | 6059044 | 1971 | £5 | £10 | |
| Tudor Lodge | LP | Vertigo | 6360043 | 1971 | £75 | £150 | |

## TUDOR MINSTRELS
| Family Way | 7" | Decca | F12536 | 1966 | £5 | £10 | |

## TUESDAY'S CHILDREN
| Baby's Gone | 7" | Pye | 7N17406 | 1967 | £2 | £5 | |
| High On A Hill | 7" | Columbia | DB8018 | 1966 | £2 | £5 | |
| In The Valley Of The Shadow Of Love | 7" | Pye | 7N17474 | 1968 | £1.50 | £4 | |
| Strange Light From The East | 7" | King | KG1051 | 1967 | £4 | £8 | |
| When You Walk In The Sun | 7" | Columbia | DB7978 | 1966 | £2 | £5 | |

## TULLY
| Loving Hard | LP | Harvest | SHVL607 | 1971 | £25 | £50 | Australian |
| Sea Of Joy | LP | Harvest | SHVL605 | 1971 | £25 | £50 | Australian |
| Tully | LP | Harvest | SRXO7926 | 1970 | £25 | £50 | Australian |

## TULLY, LEE
| Around The World With Elwood Pretzel | 7" | London | HL8363 | 1957 | £20 | £40 | gold label |

## TUNDRA
| Kentish Garland | LP | Sweet Folk | SFA078 | 1978 | £4 | £10 | |

## TUNEROCKERS
| Green Mosquito | 7" | London | HLT8717 | 1958 | £10 | £20 | |

## TUNETOPPERS
| At The Madison Dance Party | LP | Amy | A1 | 1960 | £8 | £20 | US |

## TUNEWEAVERS
| Happy Happy Birthday Baby | 7" | London | HL8503 | 1957 | £50 | £100 | B side by Paul Gayten |

## TUNNEY, PADDY
| Flowery Vale | LP | Topic | 12TS289 | 1976 | £4 | £10 | |
| Ireland Her Own | LP | Topic | 12T153 | 1966 | £4 | £10 | with Arthur Kearney |
| Irish Edge | LP | Topic | 12T165 | 1966 | £6 | £15 | |
| Wild Bees Nest | LP | Topic | 12T139 | 1965 | £6 | £15 | |

## TURNER, BRUCE
| Bruce Turner | 10" LP | Polygon | JTL2 | 1955 | £15 | £30 | |

## TURNER, GORDON

| | | | | | | |
|---|---|---|---|---|---|---|
| Meditation | LP | Charisma | CAS1009 | 1969 £8 | £20 | |

## TURNER, IKE & TINA

| Title | Format | Label | Cat. No. | Year/Price | Price | Notes |
|---|---|---|---|---|---|---|
| Anything I Wasn't Born With | 7" | HMV | POP1544 | 1966 £5 | £10 | |
| Crazy 'Bout You Baby | 7" | Liberty | LIB15233 | 1969 £2 | £5 | |
| Dance With Ike & Tina Turner | LP | Sue | LP2003 | 1962 £15 | £30 | US |
| Don't Play Me Cheap | LP | Sue | LP2005 | 1963 £15 | £30 | US |
| Dynamite | LP | Sue | LP2004 | 1963 £15 | £30 | US |
| Finger Poppin' | 7" | Warner Bros | WB153 | 1965 £2 | £5 | |
| Fool In Love | 7" | London | HLU9226 | 1960 £2.50 | £6 | |
| Goodbye So Long | 7" | Stateside | SS551 | 1966 £1.50 | £4 | |
| Greatest Hits | LP | London | HAC8248 | 1965 £6 | £15 | |
| Greatest Hits | LP | Sue | LP1038 | 1965 £10 | £25 | US |
| Hunter | LP | Harvest | SHSP4001 | 1970 £10 | £25 | |
| Hunter | 7" | Harvest | HAR5018 | 1970 £2 | £5 | |
| I Can't Believe What You Say | 7" | Sue | WI350 | 1964 £5 | £10 | |
| I'll Never Need More Than This | 7" | London | HLU10155 | 1967 £1.50 | £4 | |
| I'm Gonna Do All I Can | 7" | Minit | MLF11016 | 1969 £2.50 | £6 | |
| I'm Hooked | 7" | HMV | POP1583 | 1967 £7.50 | £15 | |
| Ike & Tina Turner Revue | LP | Ember | EMB3368 | 1966 £4 | £10 | |
| Ike & Tina Turner Show II | LP | Warner Bros | WB5904 | 1967 £4 | £10 | |
| Ike & Tina Turner Show Vol. 1 | 7" EP | Warner Bros | WEP619 | 1965 £8 | £20 | |
| Ike And Tina Turner Show | LP | Warner Bros | W1579 | 1966 £4 | £10 | |
| Ike And Tina Turner Show | LP | Warner Bros | WM8170 | 1965 £6 | £15 | |
| In Person | LP | Minit | MLS40014 | 1969 £4 | £10 | |
| It's Gonna Work Out Fine | LP | Sue | LP2007 | 1963 £15 | £30 | US |
| It's Gonna Work Out Fine | 7" | London | HL9451 | 1961 £5 | £10 | |
| It's Gonna Work Out Fine | 7" | Sue | WI306 | 1964 £5 | £10 | |
| Love Like Yours | 7" | London | HLU10083 | 1966 £1.50 | £4 | |
| Make Em Wait | 7" | A&M | AMS783 | 1970 £2.50 | £6 | |
| Please Please Please | 7" | Sue | WI376 | 1965 £5 | £10 | |
| Poor Fool | 7" | Sue | WI322 | 1964 £5 | £10 | |
| River Deep & Mountain High | LP | London | HAU/SHU8298 | 1966 £6 | £15 | |
| River Deep & Mountain High | LP | Philles | PHLP4011 | 1966 £875 | £1250 | US, no cover |
| River Deep Mountain High | 7" | A&M | AMS829 | 1971 £1.50 | £4 | |
| River Deep Mountain High | 7" | London | HLU10046 | 1966 £1.50 | £4 | |
| River Deep, Mountain HIgh | CD | Mobile Fidelity | MFCD849 | 1987 £6 | £15 | US audiophile |
| So Fine | LP | London | HAU/SHU8370 | 1969 £4 | £10 | |
| So Fine | 7" | London | HLU10189 | 1968 £1.50 | £4 | |
| Somebody | 7" | Warner Bros | WB5766 | 1966 £2 | £5 | |
| Somebody Needs You | 7" EP | Warner Bros | WEP620 | 1966 £10 | £20 | |
| Soul Of Ike & Tina Turner | 7" EP | Sue | IEP706 | 1966 £37.50 | £75 | |
| Sound Of Ike & Tina Turner | LP | Sue | LP2001 | 1961 £20 | £40 | US |
| Tell Her I'm Not At Home | 7" | Warner Bros | WB5753 | 1966 £1.50 | £4 | |
| We Need An Understanding | 7" | London | HLU10217 | 1968 £1.50 | £4 | |

## TURNER, JESSE LEE

| Title | Format | Label | Cat. No. | Year/Price | Price | |
|---|---|---|---|---|---|---|
| Do I Worry | 7" | Top Rank | JAR516 | 1960 £4 | £8 | |
| I'm The Little Space Girl's Father | 7" | London | HLP9108 | 1960 £7.50 | £15 | |
| Shake Baby Shake | 7" | London | HLL8785 | 1959 £20 | £40 | |
| Teenage Misery | 7" | Top Rank | JAR303 | 1960 £5 | £10 | |
| Voice Changing Song | 7" | Vogue | V9201 | 1962 £4 | £8 | |

## TURNER, JOE

| Title | Format | Label | Cat. No. | Year/Price | Price | Notes |
|---|---|---|---|---|---|---|
| Best Of Joe Turner | LP | Atlantic | 8081 | 1963 £10 | £25 | US |
| Big Joe Is Here | LP | London | HAE2231 | 1960 £25 | £50 | |
| Big Joe Rides Again | LP | London | LTZK15205/ SAHK6123 | 1960 £25 | £50 | |
| Boogie Woogie Country Girl | 7" | London | HLE8332 | 1956 £250 | £400 | best auctioned |
| Boss Of The Blues | LP | Atlantic | 590006 | 1967 £4 | £10 | |
| Boss Of The Blues | LP | London | LTZK15053/ SAHK6019 | 1957/ 1959 £25 | £50 | |
| Careless Love | LP | Savoy | MG14106 | 1963 £8 | £20 | US |
| Corrine Corrina | 7" | London | HLE8301 | 1956 £150 | £250 | best auctioned |
| Honey Hush | 7" | London | HLE9055 | 1960 £15 | £30 | |
| Joe Turner | LP | Atlantic | 8005 | 1957 £30 | £60 | US |
| Joe Turner & Pete Johnson | LP | EmArcy | 36014 | 1955 £30 | £60 | US |
| Joe Turner & Pete Johnson Group | 7" EP | Emarcy | ERE1500 | 1956 £12.50 | £25 | |
| Joe Turner & The Blues | LP | Savoy | MG14012 | 1962 £8 | £20 | US |
| Jumpin' The Blues | LP | Fontana | 688802ZL | 1965 £4 | £10 | |
| Kansas City Jazz | LP | Atlantic | 1243 | 1956 £30 | £60 | US |
| Lipstick Powder And Paint | 7" | London | HLE8357 | 1957 £250 | £400 | gold label, best auctioned |
| Mardi Gras Boogie | 78 | MGM | MGM253 | 1949 £6 | £12 | |
| Midnight Cannonball | 7" | Atlantic | AT4026 | 1965 £4 | £8 | |
| My Little Honeydripper | 7" | London | HLK9119 | 1960 £15 | £30 | |
| Presenting Joe Turner | 7" EP | London | REE1111 | 1957 £37.50 | £75 | tri-centre |
| Rockin' The Blues | LP | London | HAE2173 | 1959 £30 | £60 | |
| Singing The Blues | LP | Stateside | (S)SL10226 | 1967 £4 | £10 | |
| Stride By Stride | LP | 77 | LEU1232 | 1964 £5 | £12 | |

## TURNER, JOHN

| | | | | | | |
|---|---|---|---|---|---|---|
| Jewel | LP | private | SKL1016 | 1985 £8 | £20 | |

## TURNER, MEL

| | | | | | | |
|---|---|---|---|---|---|---|
| Doing The Ton | 7" | Columbia | DB7076 | 1963 £1.50 | £4 | |

| | | | | | | | |
|---|---|---|---|---|---|---|---|
| Don't Cry | 7" | Columbia | DB4963 | 1963 | £1.50 | £4 | |
| Let Me Hold Your Hand | 7" | Melodisc | 1580 | 1964 | £1.50 | £4 | |
| Mohican Crawl | 7" | Carnival | CV7003 | 1963 | £1.50 | £4 | |
| Swing Low Sweet Chariot | 7" | Columbia | DB4791 | 1962 | £1.50 | £4 | |
| Welcome Home Little Darlin' | 7" | Island | WI276 | 1966 | £1.50 | £4 | |
| What's The Matter With Me | 7" | Carnival | CV7005 | 1963 | £1.50 | £4 | |

## TURNER, NIK

| | | | | | | | |
|---|---|---|---|---|---|---|---|
| Pass Out | LP | Riddle | RID002 | 1980 | £4 | £10 | |
| Xitintoday | LP | Charisma | CDS4011 | 1978 | £4 | £10 | |
| Xitintoday | LP | Charisma | CDS4011 | 1978 | £8 | £20 | with booklet |

## TURNER, NIK & ROBERT CALVERT

| | | | | | | | |
|---|---|---|---|---|---|---|---|
| Ersatz | LP | Pompadour | POMP001 | 1982 | £8 | £20 | |

## TURNER, SAMMY

| | | | | | | | |
|---|---|---|---|---|---|---|---|
| Always | 7" | London | HLX8963 | 1959 | £2 | £5 | |
| Lavender Blue | 7" | London | HLX8918 | 1959 | £4 | £8 | |
| Lavender Blue Moods | LP | London | HAX2246 | 1960 | £20 | £40 | |
| Paradise | 7" | London | HLX9062 | 1960 | £2 | £5 | |
| Raincoat In The River | 7" | London | HLX9488 | 1962 | £5 | £10 | |

## TURNER, SPYDER

| | | | | | | | |
|---|---|---|---|---|---|---|---|
| Stand By Me | LP | MGM | (S)E4450 | 1967 | £6 | £15 | US |
| Stand By Me | 7" | MGM | MGM1332 | 1967 | £5 | £10 | |

## TURNER, TINA

| | | | | | | | |
|---|---|---|---|---|---|---|---|
| Addicted To Love | CD-s | Capitol | CDCL484 | 1988 | £2 | £5 | |
| Best | CD-s | Capitol | CDCL543 | 1989 | £2 | £5 | |
| Break Every Rule | CD | Capitol | CLP452 | 1987 | £1.50 | £4 | picture disc |
| Collected Recordings – Sixties To Nineties | CD | Capitol | DPRO79449 | 1994 | £8 | £20 | US promo compilation |
| Foreign Affair | CD | Capitol | CDP7931292 | 1989 | £5 | £12 | US passport package |
| Help | 7" | Capitol | CLP325 | 1984 | £1.50 | £4 | picture disc |
| I Don't Wanna Lose You | CD-s | Capitol | CDCL553 | 1989 | £2 | £5 | |
| Play This – In Store | CD | Capitol | DPRO79777 | 1993 | £8 | £20 | US promo compilation |
| Rio '88 | CD | Polygram | 0803481 | 1988 | £6 | £15 | CD video |
| Simply The Best | CD | Capitol | DPRO79963 | 1991 | £8 | £20 | US promo with CD-s |
| Tina Live, Private Dancer Tour | CD | EMI | | 1994 | £15 | £30 | CD and video set |
| We Don't Need Another Hero | 7" | Capitol | CLP364 | 1985 | £1.50 | £4 | picture disc |

## TURNER, TITUS

| | | | | | | | |
|---|---|---|---|---|---|---|---|
| Miss Rubberneck Jones | 7" | Blue Beat | BB32 | 1961 | £6 | £12 | |
| Pony Train | 7" | Oriole | CB1611 | 1961 | £5 | £10 | |
| Sound Off | LP | Jamie | JLP(70)3018 | 1961 | £10 | £25 | US |
| Sound Off | 7" | Parlophone | R4746 | 1961 | £7.50 | £15 | |
| We Told You Not To Marry | 7" | London | HLU9024 | 1960 | £6 | £12 | |

## TURNQUIST REMEDY

| | | | | | | | |
|---|---|---|---|---|---|---|---|
| Turnquist Remedy | LP | Pentagram | 10004 | 1970 | £15 | £30 | US |

## TURNSTYLE

| | | | | | | | |
|---|---|---|---|---|---|---|---|
| Riding A Wave | 7" | Pye | 7N17653 | 1968 | £25 | £50 | |

## TURQUOISE

| | | | | | | | |
|---|---|---|---|---|---|---|---|
| 53 Summer Street | 7" | Decca | F12756 | 1968 | £10 | £20 | |
| Woodstock | 7" | Decca | F12842 | 1968 | £10 | £20 | |

## TURRENTINE, STANLEY

| | | | | | | | |
|---|---|---|---|---|---|---|---|
| Always Something There | LP | Blue Note | BST84298 | 1968 | £5 | £12 | |
| Another Story | LP | Blue Note | BST84336 | 1970 | £5 | £12 | |
| Blue Hour | LP | Blue Note | BLP/BST84057 | 1964 | £15 | £30 | |
| Chip Off The Old Block | LP | Blue Note | BLP/BST84150 | 1965 | £10 | £25 | |
| Common Touch | LP | Blue Note | BST84315 | 1969 | £5 | £12 | |
| Dearly Beloved | LP | Blue Note | BLP/BST84081 | 1964 | £10 | £25 | |
| Easy Walker | LP | Blue Note | BLP/BST84268 | 1967 | £8 | £20 | |
| Hustlin' | LP | Blue Note | BLP/BST84162 | 1965 | £10 | £25 | |
| Joyride | LP | Blue Note | BLP/BST84201 | 1966 | £8 | £20 | |
| Look Of Love | LP | Blue Note | BST84286 | 1968 | £5 | £12 | |
| Look Out! | LP | Blue Note | BLP/BST84039 | 1961 | £15 | £30 | |
| Never Let Me Go | LP | Blue Note | BLP/BST84129 | 1964 | £10 | £25 | |
| Never Let Me Go | 7" | Blue Note | 451894 | 1964 | £2 | £5 | |
| Rough 'n' Tumble | LP | Blue Note | BLP/BST84240 | 1966 | £8 | £20 | |
| Spoiler | LP | Blue Note | BLP/BST84256 | 1967 | £6 | £15 | |
| That's Where It's At | LP | Blue Note | BLP/BST84096 | 1962 | £10 | £25 | |
| Tiger Tail | LP | Fontana | TL5300 | 1966 | £5 | £12 | |
| Up At Minton's | LP | Blue Note | BLP/BST84069 | 1962 | £15 | £30 | |
| Up At Minton's Part 2 | LP | Blue Note | BLP/BST84070 | 1964 | £15 | £30 | |

## TURTLES

| | | | | | | | |
|---|---|---|---|---|---|---|---|
| Battle Of The Bands | LP | London | HAU/SHU8376 | 1968 | £5 | £12 | |
| Can I Get To Know You Better | 7" | London | HLU10095 | 1966 | £1.50 | £4 | |
| Golden Hits | LP | White Whale | (S7)115 | 1967 | £4 | £10 | US |
| Happy Together | LP | London | HAU8330 | 1967 | £6 | £15 | |
| Happy Together | 7" EP | London | REU10185 | 1967 | £7.50 | £15 | French |
| Happy Together | 7" | London | HLU10115 | 1967 | £1.50 | £4 | |
| It Ain't Me Babe | LP | White Whale | (S7)111 | 1965 | £15 | £30 | US |
| It Ain't Me Babe | 7" EP | Polydor | 27770 | 1965 | £7.50 | £15 | French |
| It Ain't Me Babe | 7" EP | Pye | NEP44089 | 1967 | £7.50 | £15 | |

| Title | Format | Label | Cat. No. | Year | | | Notes |
|---|---|---|---|---|---|---|---|
| It Ain't Me Babe | 7" | Pye | 7N25320 | 1965 | £1.50 | £4 | |
| Let Me Be | 7" EP | Polydor | 27780 | 1966 | £7.50 | £15 | French |
| Let Me Be | 7" | Pye | 7N25341 | 1966 | £1.50 | £4 | |
| Let Me Be | 7" | Pye | 7N25421 | 1967 | £1.50 | £4 | |
| She'd Rather Be With Me | 7" EP | London | REU10189 | 1967 | £7.50 | £15 | French |
| She'd Rather Be With Me | 7" | London | HLU10135 | 1967 | £1.50 | £4 | |
| She's My Girl | 7" | London | HLU10168 | 1967 | £1.50 | £4 | |
| Sound Asleep | 7" | London | HLU10184 | 1968 | £1.50 | £4 | |
| Story Of Rock And Roll | 7" | London | HLU10207 | 1968 | £1.50 | £4 | |
| Turtle Soup | LP | White Whale | S7124 | 1969 | £4 | £10 | US |
| Wooden Head | LP | White Whale | WW7133 | 1971 | £4 | £10 | US |
| You Baby | LP | White Whale | (S7)112 | 1966 | £15 | £30 | US |
| You Baby | 7" | Immediate | IM031 | 1966 | £2.50 | £6 | |
| You Know What I Mean | 7" | London | HLU10153 | 1967 | £1.50 | £4 | |

## TUSHINGHAM, RITA & LYNN REDGRAVE
| | | | | | | | |
|---|---|---|---|---|---|---|---|
| Smashing Time | 7" | Stateside | SS2081 | 1968 | £1.50 | £4 | |

## TU-TONES
| | | | | | | | |
|---|---|---|---|---|---|---|---|
| Still In Love With You | 7" | London | HLW8904 | 1959 | £37.50 | £75 | |

## TUTTLE, WESLEY & MARILYN
| | | | | | | | |
|---|---|---|---|---|---|---|---|
| Jim, Johnny And Jonas | 7" | Capitol | CL14291 | 1955 | £1.50 | £4 | |

## TV 21
| | | | | | | | |
|---|---|---|---|---|---|---|---|
| Ambition | 7" | Powbeat | AAARGH!2 | 1980 | £5 | £10 | |
| Playing With Fire | 7" | Powbeat | AAARGH!1 | 1980 | £4 | £8 | |

## T.V. & THE TRIBESMEN
| | | | | | | | |
|---|---|---|---|---|---|---|---|
| Barefootin' | 7" | Pye | 7N25375 | 1966 | £4 | £8 | |

## TV PRODUCT
| | | | | | | | |
|---|---|---|---|---|---|---|---|
| Nowhere's Safe | 7" | Limited Edition | TAKE3 | 1979 | £2 | £5 | B side by the Pratts |

## TWARDZIK, RICHARD
| | | | | | | | |
|---|---|---|---|---|---|---|---|
| Last Set | LP | Vogue | LAE12117 | 1959 | £8 | £20 | ... with tracks by Russ Freeman |

## TWELFTH NIGHT
| | | | | | | | |
|---|---|---|---|---|---|---|---|
| First 7" Album | 7" | Twelfth Night | TN001 | 1980 | £2.50 | £6 | |

## TWENTIETH CENTURY
| | | | | | | | |
|---|---|---|---|---|---|---|---|
| Folk Passion | LP | Reflection | RL305 | 1972 | £50 | £100 | |

## TWENTIETH CENTURY ZOO
| | | | | | | | |
|---|---|---|---|---|---|---|---|
| Thunder On A Clear Day | LP | Vault | 122 | 1965 | £15 | £30 | US |

## TWENTY SEVEN DOLLAR SNAP ON FACE
| | | | | | | | |
|---|---|---|---|---|---|---|---|
| Heterodyne State Hospital | LP | Heterodyne | 00100200001 | 1977 | £30 | £60 | US, blue vinyl |

## TWENTY SIXTY-SIX AND THEN
| | | | | | | | |
|---|---|---|---|---|---|---|---|
| Reflections Of The Future | LP | United Artists | UAS29314 | 1972 | £50 | £100 | German |

## TWENTY-FIVE RIFLES
| | | | | | | | |
|---|---|---|---|---|---|---|---|
| World War Three | 12" | 25 Rifles | TFR1 | 1979 | £2.50 | £6 | |

## TWENTY-THIRD TURNOFF
| | | | | | | | |
|---|---|---|---|---|---|---|---|
| Michael Angelo | 7" | Deram | DM150 | 1967 | £15 | £30 | |

## TWENTY-THREE SKIDOO
| | | | | | | | |
|---|---|---|---|---|---|---|---|
| Ethics | 7" | Pineapple | PULP23 | 1981 | £2 | £5 | |
| Last Words | 7" | Fetish | FE10 | 1981 | £2 | £5 | no picture sleeve |

## TWICE AS MUCH
| | | | | | | | |
|---|---|---|---|---|---|---|---|
| Crystal Ball | 7" | Immediate | IM042 | 1967 | £2 | £5 | |
| Own Up | LP | Immediate | IMLP/IMSP007 | 1966 | £8 | £20 | |
| Sittin' On A Fence | 7" | Immediate | IM033 | 1966 | £1.50 | £4 | |
| Step Out Of Line | 7" | Immediate | IM036 | 1966 | £1.50 | £4 | |
| That's All | LP | Immediate | IMSP013 | 1968 | £8 | £20 | |
| True Story | 7" EP | Columbia | ESRF1818 | 1966 | £7.50 | £15 | French |
| True Story | 7" | Immediate | IM039 | 1966 | £1.50 | £4 | |

## TWIGGY
| | | | | | | | |
|---|---|---|---|---|---|---|---|
| Beautiful Dreams | 7" EP | Pathe | EGF966 | 1966 | £7.50 | £15 | French |
| Beautiful Dreams | 7" | Ember | EMBS239 | 1966 | £2.50 | £6 | |
| Beautiful Dreams | 7" | Ember | EMBS239 | 1966 | £5 | £10 | picture sleeve |

## TWILIGHT ZONERZ
| | | | | | | | |
|---|---|---|---|---|---|---|---|
| Zero Zero One EP | 7" | Zip/Dining Out | ZEROZERO1 | 1979 | £2.50 | £6 | many different sleeves |

## TWILIGHTS
| | | | | | | | |
|---|---|---|---|---|---|---|---|
| Cathy Come Home | 7" | Columbia | DB8396 | 1968 | £5 | £10 | |
| Needle In A Haystack | 7" | Columbia | DB8065 | 1966 | £2.50 | £6 | |
| What's Wrong With The Way | 7" | Columbia | DB8125 | 1967 | £2.50 | £6 | |

## TWILIGHTS (2)
| | | | | | | | |
|---|---|---|---|---|---|---|---|
| Take What I Got | 7" | London | HLU9992 | 1965 | £4 | £8 | |

## TWIN TONES
| | | | | | | | |
|---|---|---|---|---|---|---|---|
| Jo Ann | 7" | RCA | RCA1040 | 1958 | £12.50 | £25 | |

## TWIN TUNES QUINTET
| | | | | | | | |
|---|---|---|---|---|---|---|---|
| Baby Lover | 7" | RCA | RCA1046 | 1958 | £2 | £5 | |

## TWINK
| | | | | | | | |
|---|---|---|---|---|---|---|---|
| Think Pink | LP | Polydor | 2343032 | 1970 | £30 | £60 | |
| Think Pink | LP | Polydor | 2343032 | 1970 | £75 | £150 | pink vinyl |

## TWINKLE
| | | | | | | | |
|---|---|---|---|---|---|---|---|
| End Of The World | 7" | Decca | F12305 | 1965 | £1.50 | £4 | |
| Golden Lights | 7" EP | Decca | 457059 | 1965 | £10 | £20 | French |
| Golden Lights | 7" | Decca | F12076 | 1965 | £1.50 | £4 | |
| Lonely Singing Doll | 7" EP | Decca | 457077 | 1965 | £10 | £20 | French |
| Lonely Singing Doll | 7" EP | Decca | DFE8621 | 1965 | £10 | £20 | |
| Micky | 7" | Instant | IN005 | 1969 | £1.50 | £4 | |
| Poor Old Johnny | 7" | Decca | F12219 | 1965 | £1.50 | £4 | |
| Terry | 7" | Decca | F12013 | 1964 | £1.50 | £4 | |
| Tommy | 7" | Decca | F12139 | 1965 | £2 | £5 | |
| What Am I Doing Here With You | 7" | Decca | F12464 | 1966 | £2.50 | £6 | |

## TWINS
| | | | | | | | |
|---|---|---|---|---|---|---|---|
| Teenagers Love The Twins | LP | RCA | LPM1708 | 1958 | £8 | £20 | US |

## TWINSET
| | | | | | | | |
|---|---|---|---|---|---|---|---|
| Tremblin' | 7" | Decca | F12629 | 1967 | £2 | £5 | |

## TWIST
| | | | | | | | |
|---|---|---|---|---|---|---|---|
| This Is Your Life | LP | Polydor | 2383552 | 1979 | £6 | £15 | |

## TWISTED ACE
| | | | | | | | |
|---|---|---|---|---|---|---|---|
| Firebird | 7" | Heavy Metal | HEAVY9 | 1981 | £4 | £8 | |

## TWISTED SISTER
| | | | | | | | |
|---|---|---|---|---|---|---|---|
| Kids Are Back | 7" | Atlantic | A9827P | 1983 | £2 | £5 | shaped picture disc |
| Ruff Cuts | 12" | Secret | SHH13712 | 1982 | £2.50 | £6 | |

## TWISTERS
| | | | | | | | |
|---|---|---|---|---|---|---|---|
| Doin' The Twist | LP | Treasure | TLP890 | 1962 | £6 | £15 | US |
| Peppermint Twist Time | 7" | Windsor | PSA106 | 1962 | £2.50 | £6 | |
| Turn The Page | 7" | Capitol | CL15167 | 1960 | £1.50 | £4 | |

## TWISTIN' KINGS
| | | | | | | | |
|---|---|---|---|---|---|---|---|
| Twistin' The World Around | LP | Motown | MLP601 | 1960 | £50 | £100 | US |

## TWITTY, CONWAY
| | | | | | | | |
|---|---|---|---|---|---|---|---|
| C'est si bon | 7" | MGM | MGM1118 | 1961 | £1.50 | £4 | |
| Comfy 'n' Cozy | 7" | MGM | MGM1170 | 1962 | £1.50 | £4 | |
| Conway Twitty Sings | LP | MGM | C781 | 1959 | £20 | £40 | |
| Conway Twitty Touch | LP | MGM | (S)E3943 | 1961 | £15 | £30 | US |
| Go On And Cry | 7" | HMV | POP1258 | 1963 | £1.50 | £4 | |
| Greatest Hits | LP | MGM | (S)E3849 | 1960 | £10 | £25 | US |
| Greatest Hits | LP | MGM | (S)E3849 | 1960 | £25 | £50 | US, with poster |
| Handy Man | 7" | MGM | MGM1201 | 1963 | £2 | £5 | |
| Here's Conway Twitty | LP | MCA | MUP(S)342 | 1968 | £4 | £10 | |
| Hey Little Lucy | 7" EP | MGM | MGMEP698 | 1959 | £20 | £40 | |
| Hey Little Lucy | 7" | MGM | MGM1016 | 1959 | £1.50 | £4 | |
| Hit The Road | LP | MGM | (S)E4217 | 1964 | £6 | £15 | US |
| Hurt In My Heart | 7" | MGM | MGM1066 | 1960 | £1.50 | £4 | |
| I Need Your Lovin' | 7" EP | Mercury | ZEP10069 | 1960 | £50 | £100 | |
| Is A Bluebird Blue | 7" EP | MGM | MGMEP738 | 1960 | £15 | £30 | |
| Is A Bluebird Blue | 7" | MGM | MGM1082 | 1960 | £1.50 | £4 | |
| It's Drivin' Me Wild | 7" | MGM | MGM1137 | 1961 | £1.50 | £4 | |
| It's Only Make Believe | 7" EP | MGM | MGMEP684 | 1958 | £20 | £40 | |
| It's Only Make Believe | 7" | MGM | MGM992 | 1958 | £1.50 | £4 | |
| Lonely Blue Boy | LP | MGM | C829 | 1960 | £20 | £40 | |
| Lonely Blue Boy | 7" | MGM | MGM1056 | 1960 | £1.50 | £4 | |
| Mona Lisa | 7" | MGM | MGM1029 | 1959 | £1.50 | £4 | |
| Next In Line | LP | MCA | MUPS363 | 1969 | £4 | £10 | |
| Next Kiss | 7" | MGM | MGM1129 | 1961 | £1.50 | £4 | |
| Pick-Up | 7" | MGM | MGM1187 | 1962 | £2 | £5 | |
| Portrait Of A Fool | LP | MGM | (S)E4019 | 1962 | £8 | £20 | US |
| R&B '63 | LP | MGM | C950 | 1963 | £10 | £25 | |
| Rock And Roll Story | LP | MGM | (S)E3907 | 1961 | £10 | £25 | US |
| Rock And Roll Story | LP | MGM | C(S)8100 | 1968 | £8 | £20 | |
| Rock And Roll Story | 7" EP | MGM | MGMEP752 | 1961 | £20 | £40 | |
| Rosaleena | 7" | MGM | MGM1047 | 1959 | £1.50 | £4 | |
| Saturday Night With Conway | LP | MGM | C801 | 1959 | £20 | £40 | |
| Saturday Night With Conway | 7" EP | MGM | MGMEP719 | 1960 | £15 | £30 | |
| Shake It Up | 78 | Mercury | MT173 | 1957 | £15 | £30 | |
| She Ain't No Angel | 7" | MGM | MGM1209 | 1963 | £2 | £5 | |
| Story Of My Love | 7" | MGM | MGM1003 | 1959 | £1.50 | £4 | |
| Tell Me One More Time | 7" | MGM | MGM1095 | 1960 | £1.50 | £4 | |

| | | | | | | |
|---|---|---|---|---|---|---|
| Tower Of Tears | 7" | MGM | MGM1152 | 1962 £**1.50** | £**4** | |
| Whole Lotta Shakin' Goin' On | 7" | MGM | MGM1108 | 1960 £**2** | £**5** | |

## TWO AND A HALF

| | | | | | | |
|---|---|---|---|---|---|---|
| I Don't Need To Tell You | 7" | Decca | F22715 | 1967 £**2.50** | £**6** | |
| Midnight Swim | 7" | CBS | 202248 | 1966 £**1.50** | £**4** | |
| Questions | 7" | CBS | 202404 | 1966 £**1.50** | £**4** | |
| Suburban Early Morning Station | 7" | Decca | F22672 | 1967 £**4** | £**8** | |
| Walls Are High | 7" | CBS | 202526 | 1967 £**1.50** | £**4** | |

## TWO KINGS

| | | | | | | |
|---|---|---|---|---|---|---|
| Hit You Let You Feel It | 7" | Island | WI249 | 1965 £**5** | £**10** | |
| Rolling Stone | 7" | Island | WI240 | 1965 £**5** | £**10** | |

## TWO NINETEEN SKIFFLE GROUP

| | | | | | | |
|---|---|---|---|---|---|---|
| Two Nineteen Skiffle Group | 7" EP | Esquire | EP126 | 1957 £**6** | £**12** | |
| Two Nineteen Skiffle Group | 7" EP | Esquire | EP146 | 1957 £**10** | £**20** | |
| Two Nineteen Skiffle Group | 7" EP | Esquire | EP176 | 1958 £**10** | £**20** | |
| Two Nineteen Skiffle Group | 7" EP | Esquire | EP196 | 1958 £**15** | £**30** | |

## TYE, ARLYNE

| | | | | | | |
|---|---|---|---|---|---|---|
| Universe | 7" | London | HLL8825 | 1959 £**5** | £**10** | |

## TYLER, BIG T

| | | | | | | |
|---|---|---|---|---|---|---|
| King Kong | 7" | Vogue | V9079 | 1957 £**50** | £**100** | |

## TYLER, FRANKIE

This was a pseudonym used by Frankie Valli, lead singer with the Four Lovers – later the Four Seasons.

| | | | | | | |
|---|---|---|---|---|---|---|
| I Go Ape | 7" | OKeh | 7103 | 1958 £**30** | £**60** | US |

## TYLER, JIMMY

| | | | | | | |
|---|---|---|---|---|---|---|
| Fool 'Em Devil | 7" | Parlophone | MSP6215 | 1956 £**2.50** | £**6** | |

## TYLER, RED

| | | | | | | |
|---|---|---|---|---|---|---|
| Junk Village | 7" | Top Rank | JAR306 | 1960 £**2.50** | £**6** | |
| Rockin' And Rollin' | LP | Ace | LP1006 | 1960 £**10** | £**25** | US |

## TYLER, T. TEXAS

| | | | | | | |
|---|---|---|---|---|---|---|
| Country Round Up | 7" EP | Parlophone | GEP8788 | 1959 £**7.50** | £**15** | |
| Deck Of Cards | LP | Sound | 607 | 1958 £**10** | £**25** | US |
| Great Texan | LP | King | 686 | 1960 £**8** | £**20** | US |
| Man With A Million Friends | LP | London | HAB8322 | 1967 £**4** | £**10** | |
| Songs Along The Way | LP | King | 734 | 1961 £**8** | £**20** | US |
| T. Texas Tyler | LP | King | 664 | 1959 £**8** | £**20** | US |
| T. Texas Tyler | LP | King | 721 | 1961 £**8** | £**20** | US |

## TYMES

| | | | | | | |
|---|---|---|---|---|---|---|
| Come With Me To The Sea | 7" | Cameo Parkway | P884 | 1963 £**1.50** | £**4** | |
| Come With Me To The Sea | 7" | Cameo Parkway | P884 | 1963 £**5** | £**10** | picture sleeve |
| Here She Comes | 7" | Cameo Parkway | P924 | 1964 £**15** | £**30** | |
| Magic Of Our Summer Love | 7" | Cameo Parkway | P919 | 1964 £**1.50** | £**4** | |
| So Much In Love | LP | Cameo Parkway | P7032 | 1963 £**8** | £**20** | |
| So Much In Love | 7" | Cameo Parkway | P871 | 1963 £**1.50** | £**4** | |
| Somewhere | LP | Parkway | P7039 | 1964 £**6** | £**15** | US |
| Somewhere | 7" | Cameo Parkway | P891 | 1964 £**1.50** | £**4** | |
| Sound Of Wonderful Tymes | LP | Parkway | P7038 | 1963 £**6** | £**15** | US |
| To Each His Own | 7" | Cameo Parkway | P908 | 1964 £**1.50** | £**4** | |
| Twelfth Of Never | 7" | Cameo Parkway | P933 | 1964 £**25** | £**50** | |

## TYNER, MCCOY

The pianist who accompanied master saxophonist John Coltrane on his ground-breaking early-sixties records hit his stride as a band-leader in his own right some ten years later. The albums issued by McCoy Tyner through the seventies are masterpieces of modern jazz and include some inspired post-Coltrane playing from some of the same musicians as were employed by Miles Davis during the same period. In many ways, Tyner's music acted as an acoustic counterpoint to Davis's electric experiments, with records like *Sama Layuca*, *Song For My Lady* and the live *Enlightenment* emerging as absolutely essential documents.

| | | | | | | |
|---|---|---|---|---|---|---|
| Asante | LP | Blue Note | BNLA223G | 1974 £**6** | £**15** | US |
| Atlantis | LP | Milestone | 55002 | 1975 £**8** | £**20** | US double |
| Echoes Of A Friend | LP | Milestone | M9055 | 1973 £**6** | £**15** | US |
| Enlightenment | LP | Milestone | 55001 | 1973 £**8** | £**20** | US double |
| Expansions | LP | Blue Note | BST84338 | 1969 £**8** | £**20** | |
| Extensions | LP | Blue Note | BNLA006F | 1973 £**6** | £**15** | US |
| Fly With The Wind | LP | Milestone | M9067 | 1976 £**5** | £**12** | US |
| Focal Point | LP | Milestone | M9072 | 1976 £**4** | £**10** | US |
| Inception | LP | HMV | CLP1638 | 1962 £**8** | £**20** | |
| Live At Newport | LP | Impulse | A48 | 1963 £**8** | £**20** | US |
| Night Of Ballads | LP | Impulse | A39 | 1963 £**8** | £**20** | US |

| | | | | | | | |
|---|---|---|---|---|---|---|---|
| Plays Ellington | LP | Impulse | A79 | 1965 | £8 | £20 | US |
| Reaching Fourth | LP | Impulse | A33 | 1963 | £8 | £20 | US |
| Real McCoy | LP | Blue Note | BLP/BST84264 | 1967 | £8 | £20 | |
| Sahara | LP | Milestone | MSP9039 | 1972 | £6 | £15 | US |
| Sama Layuca | LP | Milestone | M9056 | 1974 | £6 | £15 | US |
| Song For My Lady | LP | Milestone | MSP9044 | 1973 | £6 | £15 | US |
| Song Of The New World | LP | Milestone | M9049 | 1973 | £6 | £15 | US |
| Tender Moments | LP | Blue Note | BST84275 | 1968 | £8 | £20 | |
| Time For Tyner | LP | Blue Note | BST84307 | 1969 | £8 | £20 | |
| Today And Tomorrow | LP | Impulse | A63 | 1964 | £8 | £20 | US |
| Trident | LP | Milestone | M9063 | 1975 | £5 | £12 | US |

## TYPHOONS

| | | | | | | | |
|---|---|---|---|---|---|---|---|
| Needles And Pins | 7" EP | Festival | FX451384 | 196– | £10 | £20 | French |
| Presenting The Fabulous Typhoons | LP | Ray | 50 | 1964 | £25 | £50 | South African |

## TYRANNOSAURUS REX

Tyrannosaurus Rex was originally a duo consisting of Marc Bolan on vocals and acoustic guitar, and Steve Peregrine-Took on bongos — the style of their acoustic music being determined less by a burning desire to create modern folk music than by the fact that they had all their electric equipment stolen just as they were starting out. The duo did have a very distinctive sound, although this became considerably diluted once they began to expand the line-up and switched the electricity back on.

| | | | | | | | |
|---|---|---|---|---|---|---|---|
| Beard Of Stars | LP | Regal Zonophone | SLRZ1013 | 1970 | £10 | £25 | with insert |
| By The Light Of A Magical Moon | 7" | Regal Zonophone | RZ3025 | 1970 | £15 | £30 | |
| Debora | 7" | Magnifly | ECHO102 | 1972 | £2 | £5 | picture sleeve |
| Debora | 7" | Regal Zonophone | RZ3008 | 1968 | £7.50 | £15 | |
| Debora | 7" | Regal Zonophone | RZ3008 | 1968 | £250 | £400 | picture sleeve, best auctioned |
| King Of The Rumbling Spires | 7" | Regal Zonophone | RZ3022 | 1969 | £15 | £30 | |
| King Of The Rumbling Spires | 7" | Regal Zonophone | RZ3022 | 1969 | £250 | £400 | picture sleeve, best auctioned |
| My People Were Fair | LP | Regal Zonophone | LRZ1003 | 1968 | £15 | £30 | with insert, mono |
| My People Were Fair | LP | Regal Zonophone | SLRZ1003 | 1968 | £10 | £25 | with insert |
| One Inch Rock | 7" | Regal Zonophone | RZ3011 | 1968 | £15 | £30 | |
| One Inch Rock | 7" | Regal Zonophone | RZ3011 | 1968 | £250 | £400 | picture sleeve, best auctioned |
| Pewter Suitor | 7" | Regal Zonophone | RZ3016 | 1969 | £15 | £30 | |
| Prophets, Seers And Sages | LP | Regal Zonophone | LRZ1005 | 1968 | £15 | £30 | mono, with insert |
| Prophets, Seers, And Sages | LP | Regal Zonophone | SLRZ1005 | 1968 | £10 | £25 | stereo, with insert |
| Unicorn | LP | Regal Zonophone | LRZ1007 | 1969 | £15 | £30 | mono |
| Unicorn | LP | Regal Zonophone | SLRZ1007 | 1969 | £10 | £25 | stereo |

## TYTAN

| | | | | | | | |
|---|---|---|---|---|---|---|---|
| Blind Men And Fools | 7" | Kamaflage | KAM6 | 1982 | £1.50 | £4 | |
| Blind Men And Fools | 12" | Kamaflage | KAMA6 | 1982 | £2.50 | £6 | |

## TZUKE, JUDIE

| | | | | | | | |
|---|---|---|---|---|---|---|---|
| God Only Knows | CD-s | CBS | TZUKEC1 | 1990 | £2 | £5 | |
| Stay With Me Till Dawn | 7" | Rocket | XPRES17 | 1979 | £2.50 | £6 | picture sleeve |
| We'll Go Dreaming | CD-s | Polydor | PZCD31 | 1989 | £2 | £5 | |

## TZUKE & PAXO

Tzuke and Paxo are Judie Tzuke and her writing partner, Mike Paxman.

| | | | | | | | |
|---|---|---|---|---|---|---|---|
| These Are The Laws | 7" | Good Earth | GD12 | 1976 | £12.50 | £25 | |

# U

## U2

The transformation of U2 from punk camp-followers into international superstars was one of the highlights of rock music in the eighties. In fact, the growth in confidence and originality of the group was extremely rapid in the early days. Bootlegs of U2's very first efforts suggest the group's abilities to be very limited even by the dubious standards of punk. Yet the first album has a freshness and poise that might as well be the work of a different group, while by the time of the live *Under A Blood Red Sky*, U2 had managed to stockpile a considerable armoury of anthemic choruses and had developed a way with an audience that already marked them as great. The various coloured vinyl Irish versions of the early releases have long been collectable; they are joined today by fan-inspired issues appropriate to the group's station, like the limited edition 'Melon' remixes and the promotional sampler CD, *Previously*.

| Title | Format | Label | Cat. No. | Year | | | Notes |
|---|---|---|---|---|---|---|---|
| 11 O'Clock Tick Tock | 7" | CBS | 8687 | 1980 | £15 | £30 | *Irish, yellow vinyl* |
| 11 O'Clock Tick Tock | 7" | Island | WIP6601 | 1980 | £4 | £8 | |
| 4 U2 Play | 7" | CBS | PAC1 | 1982 | £20 | £40 | *Irish, 4-pack* |
| 4 U2 Play | 7" | CBS | PAC1 | 1982 | £75 | £150 | *Irish, 4-pack, coloured vinyl* |
| Achtung Baby | CD | Island | | 1991 | £15 | £30 | *Australian, first day cover* |
| All I Want Is You | CD-s | Island | CDCIDP422 | 1989 | £2.50 | £6 | *picture disc* |
| All I Want Is You | CD-s | Island | CID422 | 1989 | £2 | £5 | |
| All I Want Is You | 7" | Island | IS422 | 1989 | £1.50 | £4 | *in tin box* |
| Angel Of Harlem | CD-s | Island | CIDP402 | 1988 | £2.50 | £6 | *picture disc* |
| Another Day | 7" | CBS | 8306 | 1980 | £12.50 | £25 | *Irish* |
| Another Day | 7" | CBS | 8306 | 1980 | £15 | £30 | *Irish, yellow or orange vinyl* |
| Another Day | 7" | CBS | 8306 | 1980 | £25 | £50 | *white vinyl* |
| Boy | CD | Island | CID9646 | 1986 | £6 | £15 | *ten tracks* |
| Celebration | 7" | Island | WIP6770 | 1982 | £5 | £10 | |
| Day Without Me | 7" | Island | WIP6630 | 1980 | £4 | £8 | |
| Desire | CD-s | Island | CIDP400 | 1988 | £2 | £5 | *picture disc* |
| Even Better Than The Real Thing | CD-s | Island | CID525 | 1992 | £2 | £5 | |
| Even Better Than The Real Thing (Perfecto Remix) | CD-s | Island | CREAL2 | 1992 | £3 | £8 | |
| Fire | 7" | Island | UWIP6679 | 1981 | £2.50 | £6 | *double* |
| Fire | 7" | Island | WIP6679 | 1981 | £1.50 | £4 | |
| Fly | CD-s | Island | CID500 | 1991 | £2 | £5 | |
| Gloria | 7" | Island | WIP6733 | 1981 | £2 | £5 | |
| I Still Haven't Found What I'm Looking For | CD-s | Island | 659152 | 1988 | £2 | £5 | *Dutch import* |
| I Still Haven't Found What I'm Looking For | CD-s | Island | CID328 | 1987 | £12.50 | £25 | |
| I Will Follow | 7" | CBS | 9065 | 1980 | £12.50 | £25 | *Irish, yellow vinyl* |
| I Will Follow | 7" | CBS | 9065 | 1980 | £15 | £30 | *Irish, white vinyl* |
| I Will Follow | 7" | Island | WIP6656 | 1980 | £2 | £5 | |
| Joshua Tree | CD | Island | CIDU26 | 1987 | £75 | £150 | *promo box set, with cassette and LP* |
| Joshua Tree | CD | Island | CIDU26 | 1987 | £15 | £30 | *promo picture disc* |
| Joshua Tree | 7" | Island | | 1987 | £25 | £50 | *box set, 5 x 7"* |
| Lemon | CD-s | Island | LEMCD1 | 1993 | £12.50 | £25 | *promo only* |
| Lemon | 12" | Island | 12LEMDJ1 | 1993 | £30 | £60 | *promo double* |
| Melon | CD | Island | MELONCD1 | 1995 | £15 | £30 | *9 track fan club remix CD* |
| Mysterious Ways | CD-s | Island | CID509 | 1991 | £2 | £5 | |
| New Year's Day | 7" | Island | UWIP6848 | 1983 | £2.50 | £6 | *double* |
| New Year's Day | 7" | Island | WIP6848 | 1983 | £2.50 | £6 | *B side plays Martha Reeves* |
| Night And Day | 12" | Island | RHB1 | 1990 | £20 | £40 | *promo* |
| Numb | CD-s | Island | NUMCD1 | 1993 | £20 | £40 | *promo only* |
| October 1991 | CD-s | Island | U23 | 1991 | £15 | £30 | *promo* |
| One | CD-s | Island | CID515 | 1992 | £2 | £5 | |
| Out Of Control (U2:3) | cass | CBS | 40-7951 | 1985 | £3 | £8 | *Irish* |
| Out Of Control (U2:3) | 7" | CBS | 7951 | 1979 | £7.50 | £15 | *Irish* |
| Out Of Control (U2:3) | 7" | CBS | 7951 | 1979 | £50 | £100 | *Irish, brown vinyl* |
| Out Of Control (U2:3) | 7" | CBS | 7951 | 1979 | £25 | £50 | *Irish, white vinyl* |
| Out Of Control (U2:3) | 7" | CBS | 7951 | 1979 | £15 | £30 | *Irish, yellow or orange vinyl* |
| Out Of Control (U2:3) | 12" | CBS | 127951 | 1979 | £6 | £15 | *Irish* |
| Out Of Control (U2:3) | 12" | CBS | 127951 | 1979 | £50 | £100 | *Irish, numbered* |
| PAC2 | 7" | CBS | PAC2 | | £12.50 | £25 | *Irish, 4-pack* |
| PAC3 | 7" | CBS | PAC3 | | £10 | £20 | *Irish, 4-pack* |
| Previously | CD | Island | PRECD1 | 1996 | £10 | £25 | *promo sampler* |
| Pride | cass-s | Island | CIS202 | 1984 | £2.50 | £6 | |
| Pride | 7" | Island | ISD202 | 1984 | £2 | £5 | *double* |
| Pride | 7" | Island | ISP202 | 1984 | £6 | £12 | *picture disc* |

| | | | | | | | |
|---|---|---|---|---|---|---|---|
| Pride | 12" | Island | ISX202 | 1984 £4 | £10 | 5 tracks |
| Rattle And Hum | LP | Island | U27 | 1988 £50 | £100 | studio versions of 2 live tracks |
| Rattle And Hum | CD | Island | CIDU27 | 1988 £50 | £100 | ..promo briefcase, with cassette and LP |
| Salome | 12" | Island | 12IS550DJ | 1992 £20 | £40 | promo |
| Two Hearts Beat As One | 7" | Island | ISD109 | 1983 £2.50 | £6 | double |
| Two Sides Live | LP | Warner Bros | BUG101 | 1981 £50 | £100 | US promo |
| Under A Blood Red Sky | LP | Island | IMA3 | 1983 £25 | £50 | red vinyl |
| Under A Blood Red Sky | LP | Island | US1PR | 1983 £15 | £30 | .promo with interviews |
| Unforgettable Fire | CD-s | Island | 664974 | 198– £2 | £5 | Austrian import |
| Unforgettable Fire | CD | Mobile Fidelity | UDCD624 | 1995 £6 | £15 | ..........US audiophile |
| Unforgettable Fire | 7" | Island | ISD220 | 1985 £2 | £5 | double |
| Unforgettable Fire | 7" | Island | ISP220 | 1985 £7.50 | £15 | shaped picture disc |
| War | LP | Island | ILPS9733 | 1983 £25 | £50 | picture disc |
| War | CD | Mobile Fidelity | UDCD571 | 1992 £6 | £15 | US audiophile |
| When Love Comes To Town | CD-s | Island | CIDP411 | 1989 £2.50 | £6 | picture disc |
| When Love Comes To Town | CD-s | Island | CIDX411 | 1989 £2 | £5 | |
| Where The Streets Have No Name | CD-s | Island | CID340 | 1987 £2.50 | £6 | |
| Who's Gonna Ride Your Wild Horses | CD-s | Island | CID550 | 1992 £2 | £5 | |
| Who's Gonna Ride Your Wild Horses | CD-s | Island | CIDX550 | 1992 £5 | £12 | digipak with prints |
| With Or Without You | CD-s | Island | CID319 | 1987 £2.50 | £6 | |

## UB40

| | | | | | | | |
|---|---|---|---|---|---|---|---|
| Breakfast In Bed | CD-s | DEP International | DEPX29 | 1988 £2 | £5 | ..with Chrissie Hynde |
| Come Out To Play | CD-s | DEP International | DEPX31 | 1989 £2 | £5 | 3" single |
| Here I Am | CD-s | DEP International | DEPX34 | 1990 £2 | £5 | |
| Homely Girl | CD-s | DEP International | DEPX33 | 1989 £2 | £5 | 3" single |
| I Would Do For You | CD-s | DEP International | DEPX32 | 1989 £2 | £5 | 3" single |
| Impossible Love | CD-s | DEP International | DEPXT37 | 1990 £2 | £5 | |
| Kingston Town | CD-s | DEP International | DEPXT35 | 1990 £2 | £5 | |
| Promises And Lies | CD | Virgin | UBCDJ94 | 1994 £8 | £20 | ...promo with calendar |
| UB40 | CD | DEP International | DEPCDP13 | 1988 £5 | £12 | ...........picture disc |
| Wear You To The Ball | CD-s | DEP International | DEPXT36 | 1990 £2 | £5 | |
| Where Did I Go Wrong? | CD-s | DEP International | DEPX30 | 1988 £2 | £5 | |

## UFO

| | | | | | | | |
|---|---|---|---|---|---|---|---|
| Boogie For George | 7" | Beacon | BEA172 | 1971 £2 | £5 | |
| Come Away Melinda | 7" | Beacon | BEA165 | 1971 £5 | £10 | |
| Flying | LP | Beacon | BES19 | 1972 £5 | £12 | |
| Prince Kajuki | 7" | Beacon | BEA181 | 1971 £2 | £5 | |
| Shake It About | 7" | Beacon | BEA161 | 1970 £5 | £10 | |
| UFO | LP | Beacon | BEAS12 | 1971 £6 | £15 | |

## UGLY CUSTARD

Hardly a real group, the musicians recording this low-budget set of rock instrumentals were taking time out from their regular work as members of Blue Mink. The music is essentially workman-like rather than inspired, with Alan Parker demonstrating the proper overdriven tone for turn-of-the-decade 'progressive' guitar, yet without ever really breaking into a sweat.

| | | | | | | | |
|---|---|---|---|---|---|---|---|
| Ugly Custard | LP | Kaleidoscope | KAL100 | 1971 £25 | £50 | |

## UGLY DUCKLINGS

| | | | | | | | |
|---|---|---|---|---|---|---|---|
| Off The Wall | LP | Razor | 003 | 1968 £6 | £15 | Canadian |
| Somewhere Outside | LP | Yorktown | 50001 | 1966 £37.50 | £75 | Canadian |

## UGLYS

| | | | | | | | |
|---|---|---|---|---|---|---|---|
| End Of The Season | 7" | Pye | 7N17178 | 1966 £7.50 | £15 | |
| Good Idea | 7" | Pye | 7N17027 | 1966 £7.50 | £15 | |
| I See The Light | 7" | MGM | MGM1465 | 1969 £250 | £400 | demo, best auctioned |
| It's Alright | 7" | Pye | 7N15968 | 1965 £5 | £10 | |
| Squire Blew His Horn | 7" | CBS | 2933 | 1967 £20 | £40 | |
| Wake Up My Mind | 7" | Pye | 7N15858 | 1965 £7.50 | £15 | |

## UK

| | | | | | | | |
|---|---|---|---|---|---|---|---|
| UK | CD | Editions EG | EGCD35 | 1988 £5 | £12 | |

## UK DECAY

| | | | | | | | |
|---|---|---|---|---|---|---|---|
| UK Decay | 7" | Plastic | PLAS001 | 1979 £6 | £12 | .B side by Pneumania |

## UK SUBS

| | | | | | | | |
|---|---|---|---|---|---|---|---|
| C.I.D. | 7" | City | NIK5 | 1978 £1.50 | £4 | various coloured vinyls |
| Crash Course | LP | Gem | GEMLP111 | 1980 £4 | £10 | purple vinyl, with 12" (GEMEP1) |
| Party In Paris | 7" | Ramkup | CAC2 | 1981 £10 | £20 | 1 sided, no picture sleeve |

## U.K.'S
| | | | | | | |
|---|---|---|---|---|---|---|
| Ever Faithful Ever True | 7" | HMV | POP1310 | 1964 £4 | £8 | |
| I Will Never Let You Go | 7" | HMV | POP1357 | 1964 £4 | £8 | |

## ULMER, JAMES 'BLOOD'
James 'Blood' Ulmer is a guitarist and occasional singer whose thrilling blend of harmelodic jazz (he was once a member of Ornette Coleman's group) and blues would be enough to make him into a Jimi Hendrix for the nineties if only his kind of cutting-edge music was not so marginalized these days.

| | | | | | | |
|---|---|---|---|---|---|---|
| Are You Glad To Be In America? | LP | Rough Trade | ROUGH16 | 1980 £5 | £12 | |
| Black Rock | LP | CBS | 25064 | 1982 £4 | £10 | |
| Eye Level | 12" | Rough Trade | RTT128 | 1984 £2.50 | £6 | |
| Freelancing | LP | CBS | 85224 | 1981 £4 | £10 | |
| Part Time | LP | Rough Trade | ROUGH65 | 1984 £4 | £10 | |
| Tales Of Captain Black | LP | Artists House | AH7 | 1979 £4 | £10 | . US, credited to James Blood |

## ULTIMATE SPINACH
Given a group name like Ultimate Spinach, any sixties collector will know exactly what to expect, especially with song titles like 'Gilded Lamp Of The Cosmos' and 'Mind Flowers'. If one is prepared to forgive the frequent preciousness of the lyrics, then the first two albums emerge as interesting and worthwhile bodies of music, although the female singer is given too little to do and the much weaker male singer too much (but he wrote the material). The third album is the work of an almost completely different line-up and is much less impressive.

| | | | | | | |
|---|---|---|---|---|---|---|
| Behold And See | LP | MGM | C8094 | 1968 £25 | £50 | |
| Ultimate Spinach | LP | MGM | C8071 | 1968 £25 | £50 | |
| Ultimate Spinach | LP | MGM | SE4600 | 1969 £15 | £30 | US |

## ULTRA VIVID SCENE
| | | | | | | |
|---|---|---|---|---|---|---|
| Mercy Seat | CD-s | 4AD | BADCD906 | 1989 £2 | £5 | |
| Mercy Seat | 12" | 4AD | BAD906 | 1989 £6 | £15 | |
| She Screamed | CD-s | 4AD | BAD806CD | 1988 £2 | £5 | |
| Something To Eat | 7" | 4AD | AD908 | 1989 £2 | £5 | |
| Special One | CD-s | 4AD | BAD0016CD | 1990 £2 | £5 | |
| Staring At The Sun | CD-s | 4AD | BADCD0004 | 1990 £2 | £5 | |

## ULTRAFUNK
| | | | | | | |
|---|---|---|---|---|---|---|
| Ultrafunk | LP | Contempo | CLP509 | 1975 £4 | £10 | |

## ULVAEUS, BJÖRN & BENNY ANDERSSON
*Lycka* is the album made by the two male members of Abba immediately before forming the group.

| | | | | | | |
|---|---|---|---|---|---|---|
| Lycka | LP | Polar | POLL113 | 1970 £6 | £15 | Swedish, mono |
| Lycka | LP | Polar | POLS226 | 1970 £4 | £10 | Swedish, stereo |

## UMPS AND DUMPS
| | | | | | | |
|---|---|---|---|---|---|---|
| Moon's In A Fit | LP | Topic | 12TS416 | 1980 £4 | £10 | |

## UNBEATABLES
| | | | | | | |
|---|---|---|---|---|---|---|
| Live At Palisades Park | LP | Fawn | LP5050 | 1964 £15 | £30 | US |

## UNCLE DOG
| | | | | | | |
|---|---|---|---|---|---|---|
| Old Hat | LP | Signpost | SG4253 | 1972 £4 | £10 | |

## UNCLE JOHN'S BAND
| | | | | | | |
|---|---|---|---|---|---|---|
| Different Game | LP | private | | 1980 £20 | £40 | |

## UNDER THE SUN
| | | | | | | |
|---|---|---|---|---|---|---|
| Under The Sun | LP | Redball | | £30 | £60 | |

## UNDERGROUND
| | | | | | | |
|---|---|---|---|---|---|---|
| Psychedelic Visions | LP | Wing | WC16337 | 1967 £6 | £15 | US |

## UNDERGROUND SET
| | | | | | | |
|---|---|---|---|---|---|---|
| Underground Set | LP | Pan | PAN6302 | 1970 £10 | £25 | |

## UNDERGROUND SUNSHINE
| | | | | | | |
|---|---|---|---|---|---|---|
| Birthday | 7" | Fontana | TF1049 | 1969 £1.50 | £4 | |
| Let There Be Light | LP | Intrepid | IT4003 | 1969 £6 | £15 | US |

## UNDERGROUNDS
| | | | | | | |
|---|---|---|---|---|---|---|
| Psychedelic Visions | LP | Mercury | MG/SR16337 | 1967 £6 | £15 | US |

## UNDERNEATH
| | | | | | | |
|---|---|---|---|---|---|---|
| Imp Of The Perverse | 7" | El | GPO17 | 1986 £2 | £5 | |
| Imp Of The Perverse | 12" | El | GPO17T | 1986 £2.50 | £6 | |
| Lunatic Dawn Of The Dismantler | LP | Acme | ACME9 | 1986 £4 | £10 | |

## UNDERTAKERS
The Undertakers were rated as one of the most exciting of the Merseybeat groups, but like their rivals the Big Three they were not particularly successful in translating this reputation on to record. Of the group's four singles (the last credited to the Takers), only 'Just A Little Bit' managed to dent the charts, although this was a fine example of the genre. The group used to follow the implications of their name to the full, travelling in a hearse and dressing in black morning suits. Singer Jackie Lomax tried very hard to maintain a solo career after the group split up, but managed only limited success, despite the enthusiastic patronage of George Harrison. Sax player Brian Jones's name caused much confusion when a saxophone was credited to 'Brian Jones' on the Beatles' single 'You Know My Name', but, surprisingly, this was actually the Rolling Stone. The Undertakers' Jones did, however, join Gary Glitter's Glitter Band in the seventies.

| | | | | | | | |
|---|---|---|---|---|---|---|---|
| Everybody Loves A Lover | 7" | Pye | 7N15543 | 1963 | £4 | £8 | |
| Just A Little Bit | 7" | Pye | 7N15607 | 1964 | £4 | £8 | |
| What About Us | 7" | Pye | 7N15562 | 1963 | £4 | £8 | |

## UNDERTONES

| | | | | | | | |
|---|---|---|---|---|---|---|---|
| Get Over You | 7" | Sire | SIR4010 | 1979 | £1.50 | £4 | |
| Peel Sessions | CD-s | Strange Fruit | SFPSCD016 | 1988 | £2 | £5 | |
| Sin Of Pride | LP | Ardeck | ARD104 | 1983 | £8 | £20 | ...with tracks 'Bittersweet' and 'Stand So Close' |
| Teenage Kicks | 7" | Good Vibrations | GOT4 | 1978 | £2.50 | £6 | poster sleeve |

## UNDISPUTED TRUTH

| | | | | | | | |
|---|---|---|---|---|---|---|---|
| Best Of The Undisputed Truth | LP | Tamla Motown | STML8029 | 1977 | £4 | £10 | |
| Save My Love For A Rainy Day | 7" | Parlophone | TMG776 | 1971 | £2.50 | £6 | mispressed label |
| Smiling Face Sometimes | 7" | Tamla Motown | TMG789 | 1971 | £1.50 | £4 | |

## UNFOLDING

| | | | | | | | |
|---|---|---|---|---|---|---|---|
| How To Blow Your Mind | LP | Audio Fidelity | 6184 | 1967 | £30 | £60 | US |

## UNFOLDING BOOK OF LIFE

| | | | | | | | |
|---|---|---|---|---|---|---|---|
| Vol. 1 | LP | Island | ILPS9093 | 1969 | £8 | £20 | pink label |
| Vol. 2 | LP | Island | ILPS9094 | 1969 | £8 | £20 | pink label |

## UNICORN

| | | | | | | | |
|---|---|---|---|---|---|---|---|
| Going Home | 7" | Hollick & Taylor | HT1258 | 196– | £10 | £20 | |

## UNIFICS

| | | | | | | | |
|---|---|---|---|---|---|---|---|
| Court Of Love | 7" | London | HLZ10231 | 1968 | £2 | £5 | |

## UNIQUES

| | | | | | | | |
|---|---|---|---|---|---|---|---|
| A-Yuh | 7" | Trojan | TR645 | 1968 | £4 | £8 | |
| Absolutely The Uniques | LP | Trojan | TRL15 | 1969 | £20 | £40 | |
| Beatitude | 7" | Island | WI3123 | 1967 | £5 | £10 | Keith Blake B side |
| Beatitude | 7" | Unity | UN527 | 1969 | £1.50 | £4 | |
| Build My World Around You | 7" | Island | WI3114 | 1967 | £5 | £10 | Lloyd Clarke B side |
| Crimson And Clover | 7" | Nu Beat | NB034 | 1969 | £1.50 | £4 | |
| Dry The Water | 7" | Collins Downbeat | CR002 | 1967 | £4 | £8 | |
| Girl Of My Dreams | 7" | Island | WI3145 | 1968 | £5 | £10 | Lester Stirling B side |
| Gypsy Woman | 7" | Island | WI3084 | 1967 | £5 | £10 | Ken Ross B side |
| I'll Make You Love Me | 7" | Nu Beat | NB037 | 1969 | £1.50 | £4 | |
| Lesson Of Love | 7" | Island | WI3107 | 1967 | £5 | £10 | Delroy Wilson B side |
| Let Me Go Girl | 7" | Island | WI3086 | 1967 | £5 | £10 | Soulettes B side |
| More Love | 7" | Island | WI3117 | 1967 | £5 | £10 | Val Bennett B side |
| More Love | 7" | Trojan | TR610 | 1968 | £4 | £8 | Race Dans B side |
| My Conversation | 7" | Island | WI3122 | 1967 | £5 | £10 | Slim Smith B side |
| Never Let Me Go | 7" | Island | WI3087 | 1967 | £5 | £10 | Don Tony Lee B side |
| People Rock Steady | 7" | Island | WI3070 | 1967 | £5 | £10 | |
| Speak No Evil | 7" | Island | WI3106 | 1967 | £5 | £10 | Glen Adams B side |
| Too Proud To Beg | 7" | Gas | GAS117 | 1969 | £2.50 | £6 | |

## UNIQUES (2)

| | | | | | | | |
|---|---|---|---|---|---|---|---|
| Fast Way Of Living | 7" | Pye | 7N25303 | 1965 | £20 | £40 | |
| Uniquely Yours | LP | Pye | NPL28094 | 1966 | £30 | £60 | |

## UNIT FOUR PLUS TWO

| | | | | | | | |
|---|---|---|---|---|---|---|---|
| Baby Never Say Goodbye | 7" | Decca | F12333 | 1966 | £1.50 | £4 | |
| Butterfly | 7" | Fontana | TF840 | 1967 | £2.50 | £6 | |
| Concrete And Clay | 7" EP | Decca | 457070 | 1965 | £10 | £20 | French |
| Concrete And Clay | 7" | Decca | F12071 | 1965 | £1.50 | £4 | |
| For A Moment | 7" | Decca | F12398 | 1966 | £2 | £5 | |
| Green Fields | 7" | Decca | F11821 | 1964 | £4 | £8 | |
| Hark | 7" | Decca | F12211 | 1965 | £1.50 | £4 | |
| I Was Only Playing Games | 7" | Decca | F12509 | 1966 | £2 | £5 | |
| Loving Takes A Little Understanding | 7" | Fontana | TF891 | 1967 | £1.50 | £4 | |
| Sorrow And Pain | 7" | Fontana | TF1994 | 1964 | £2.50 | £6 | |
| Three Thirty | 7" | Fontana | TF990 | 1969 | £7.50 | £15 | |
| Too Fast, Too Slow | 7" | Fontana | TF834 | 1967 | £4 | £8 | |
| Unit Four Plus Two | LP | Decca | LK4697 | 1965 | £20 | £40 | |
| Unit Four Plus Two | LP | Fontana | SFL13123 | 1969 | £20 | £40 | |
| Unit Four Plus Two | 7" EP | Decca | DFE8619 | 1965 | £7.50 | £15 | |
| You Ain't Goin' Nowhere | 7" | Fontana | TF931 | 1968 | £2.50 | £6 | |
| You've Got To Be Cruel To Be Kind | 7" | Decca | F12299 | 1965 | £1.50 | £4 | |
| You've Never Been In Love Like This Before | 7" EP | Decca | 457087 | 1965 | £10 | £20 | French |
| You've Never Been In Love Like This Before | 7" | Decca | F12144 | 1965 | £1.50 | £4 | |

## UNITED ISLANDS

| | | | | | | | |
|---|---|---|---|---|---|---|---|
| I Love This Day | LP | Audio Art | | 1986 | £8 | £20 | Dutch |

## UNITED STATES DOUBLE QUARTET

| | | | | | | | |
|---|---|---|---|---|---|---|---|
| Life Is Groovy | LP | B.T.Puppy | BTPS1005 | 1969 | £6 | £15 | US |

## UNITED STATES OF AMERICA

| Title | Format | Label | Cat No | Year | Price | Price | Notes |
|---|---|---|---|---|---|---|---|
| Garden Of Earthly Delights | 7" | CBS | 3745 | 1968 | £2 | £5 | |
| United States Of America | LP | CBS | 63340 | 1968 | £10 | £25 | |

## UNIVERIA ZEKT

| Title | Format | Label | Cat No | Year | Price | Price | Notes |
|---|---|---|---|---|---|---|---|
| Unnamables | LP | Theleme | 6332501 | 1972 | £20 | £40 | French |

## UNIVERS ZERO

| Title | Format | Label | Cat No | Year | Price | Price | Notes |
|---|---|---|---|---|---|---|---|
| Ceux du dehors | LP | Recommended | RRTEN | 1981 | £4 | £10 | |
| Hérésie | LP | Recommended | RR4 | 1979 | £5 | £12 | |
| Triomphe des mouches | 7" | Recommended | RR10.5 | 1981 | £4 | £8 | 1 side painted |
| Univers zero | LP | Atem | 7001 | 1978 | £5 | £12 | French |

## UNIVERSALS

| Title | Format | Label | Cat No | Year | Price | Price | Notes |
|---|---|---|---|---|---|---|---|
| Green Veined Orchid | 7" | Page One | POF049 | 1967 | £4 | £8 | |
| I Can't Find You | 7" | Page One | POF032 | 1967 | £7.50 | £15 | |

## UNO

| Title | Format | Label | Cat No | Year | Price | Price | Notes |
|---|---|---|---|---|---|---|---|
| Uno | LP | Pan Ariola | 88397 | 1974 | £8 | £20 | German |

## UNREST WORK AND PLAY

| Title | Format | Label | Cat No | Year | Price | Price | Notes |
|---|---|---|---|---|---|---|---|
| Informs | LP | Recommended | RRC19 | 1984 | £4 | £10 | |

## UNTAMED

| Title | Format | Label | Cat No | Year | Price | Price | Notes |
|---|---|---|---|---|---|---|---|
| Daddy Longlegs | 7" | Planet | PLF113 | 1966 | £20 | £40 | as Lindsay Muir's Untamed |
| I'll Go Crazy | 7" | Stateside | SS431 | 1965 | £20 | £40 | |
| It's Not True | 7" | Planet | PLF103 | 1966 | £20 | £40 | |
| Once Upon A Time | 7" | Parlophone | R5258 | 1965 | £25 | £50 | |
| So Long | 7" | Decca | F12045 | 1964 | £20 | £40 | |

## UNTOUCHABLES

| Title | Format | Label | Cat No | Year | Price | Price | Notes |
|---|---|---|---|---|---|---|---|
| Prisoner In Love | 7" | Blue Cat | BS137 | 1968 | £4 | £8 | |
| Tighten Up | 7" | Trojan | TR613 | 1968 | £2.50 | £6 | |

## UNUSUAL WE

| Title | Format | Label | Cat No | Year | Price | Price | Notes |
|---|---|---|---|---|---|---|---|
| Unusual We | LP | Pulsar | 10608 | 1969 | £5 | £12 | US |

## UNWANTED

| Title | Format | Label | Cat No | Year | Price | Price | Notes |
|---|---|---|---|---|---|---|---|
| Memory Man | 7" | Raw | RAW30 | 1978 | £4 | £8 | |
| Secret Police | 7" | Raw | RAW15 | 1978 | £2 | £5 | |
| Withdrawal | 7" | Raw | RAW6 | 1977 | £5 | £10 | picture sleeve |
| Withdrawal | 12" | Raw | RAWT6 | 1978 | £3 | £8 | |

## UNWIN, STANLEY

| Title | Format | Label | Cat No | Year | Price | Price | Notes |
|---|---|---|---|---|---|---|---|
| Rotatety Diskers | LP | Pye | NPL18062 | 1961 | £4 | £10 | |

## UPBEATS

| Title | Format | Label | Cat No | Year | Price | Price | Notes |
|---|---|---|---|---|---|---|---|
| Keep Cool Crazy Heart | 7" | Pye | 7N25016 | 1959 | £2 | £5 | |
| My Foolish Heart | 7" | London | HLJ8688 | 1958 | £5 | £10 | |
| Teeny Weeny Bikini | 7" | Pye | 7N25028 | 1959 | £2 | £5 | |

## UPCHURCH, PHIL

| Title | Format | Label | Cat No | Year | Price | Price | Notes |
|---|---|---|---|---|---|---|---|
| Feeling Blue | LP | Milestone | 9010 | 1968 | £4 | £10 | US |
| Nothing But Soul | 7" | Sue | WI4017 | 1966 | £4 | £8 | |
| Twist The Big Hit Dances | LP | United Artists | 6175 | 1960 | £5 | £12 | US |
| You Can't Sit Down | LP | Boyd | 398 | 1960 | £6 | £15 | US |
| You Can't Sit Down | 7" | HMV | POP899 | 1961 | £7.50 | £15 | |
| You Can't Sit Down | 7" | Sue | WI4005 | 1966 | £5 | £10 | |
| You Can't Sit Down II | LP | United Artists | 6162 | 1960 | £5 | £12 | US |

## UPSETTERS

The records credited to the Upsetters are all the work of star reggae producer Lee Perry, who has also made numerous records under his own name, as well as producing several other artists' records.

| Title | Format | Label | Cat No | Year | Price | Price | Notes |
|---|---|---|---|---|---|---|---|
| Battle Axe | LP | Trojan | TBL167 | 1971 | £6 | £15 | |
| Clint Eastwood | LP | Pama | PSP1014 | 1969 | £10 | £25 | |
| Clint Eastwood | 7" | Punch | PH21 | 1969 | £1.50 | £4 | |
| Cold Sweat | 7" | Upsetter | US315 | 1969 | £1.50 | £4 | |
| Double Seven | LP | Trojan | TRLS70 | 1974 | £6 | £15 | |
| Dry Acid | 7" | Punch | PH19 | 1970 | £1.50 | £4 | Reggae Boys B side |
| Eastwood Rides Again | LP | Trojan | TBL125 | 1970 | £10 | £25 | |
| Eight For Eight | 7" | Duke | DU11 | 1969 | £2.50 | £6 | |
| Eight For Eight | 7" | Upsetter | US300 | 1969 | £1.50 | £4 | |
| Good, The Bad And The Upsetters | LP | Trojan | TBL119 | 1970 | £10 | £25 | |
| Kiddyo | 7" | Upsetter | US309 | 1969 | £1.50 | £4 | |
| Live Injection | 7" | Upsetter | US313 | 1969 | £1.50 | £4 | Bleechers B side |
| Man From MI5 | 7" | Upsetter | US310 | 1969 | £1.50 | £4 | West Indians B side |
| Many Moods Of The Upsetters | LP | Pama | SECO24 | 1970 | £15 | £30 | |
| Night Doctor | 7" | Upsetter | US307 | 1969 | £1.50 | £4 | Termites B side |
| Prisoner | LP | Trojan | TBL127 | 1970 | £6 | £15 | |
| Return Of Django | LP | Trojan | TRL19 | 1969 | £8 | £20 | |
| Return Of Django | 7" | Upsetter | US301 | 1969 | £1.50 | £4 | |
| Return Of The Ugly | 7" | Punch | PH18 | 1969 | £1.50 | £4 | |
| Stranger On The Shore | 7" | Upsetter | US321 | 1969 | £1.50 | £4 | |
| Taste Of Killing | 7" | Camel | CA13 | 1969 | £1.50 | £4 | |

| | | | | | | | |
|---|---|---|---|---|---|---|---|
| Ten To Twelve | 7" | Upsetter | US303 | 1969 | £1.50 | £4 | |
| Three In One | 7" | Island | WIP6328 | 1976 | £1.50 | £4 | |
| Vampire | 7" | Upsetter | US317 | 1969 | £1.50 | £4 | Bleechers B side |
| Walk Down The Aisle | 7" | Rio | R70 | 1965 | £5 | £10 | |
| Wildcat | 7" | Doctor Bird | DB1034 | 1966 | £5 | £10 | |

## URCHIN

| | | | | | | | |
|---|---|---|---|---|---|---|---|
| Black Leather Fantasy | 7" | DJM | DJS10776 | 1977 | £15 | £30 | |
| She's A Roller | 7" | DJM | DJS10850 | 1978 | £12.50 | £25 | |

## URE, MIDGE

| | | | | | | | |
|---|---|---|---|---|---|---|---|
| Dear God | CD-s | Chrysalis | URECD6 | 1988 | £2 | £5 | in tin box |

## URIAH HEEP

| | | | | | | | |
|---|---|---|---|---|---|---|---|
| Demons And Wizards | LP | Island | ILPS9193 | 1972 | £4 | £10 | |
| Salisbury | LP | Bronze | ILPS9152 | 1971 | £4 | £10 | |
| Salisbury | LP | Island | ILPS9152 | 1971 | £8 | £20 | |
| Salisbury | LP | Vertigo | 6360028 | 1971 | £20 | £40 | spiral label |
| Very 'Eavy, Very 'Umble | LP | Bronze | ILPS9142 | 1971 | £4 | £10 | |
| Very 'Eavy, Very 'Umble | LP | Vertigo | 6360006 | 1970 | £15 | £30 | spiral label |

## URSO, PHIL

| | | | | | | | |
|---|---|---|---|---|---|---|---|
| Phil Urso | 10" LP | London | LZC14016 | 1955 | £15 | £30 | |

## U.S. T-BONES

| | | | | | | | |
|---|---|---|---|---|---|---|---|
| Proper Thing To Do | 7" | Liberty | LIB55951 | 1967 | £1.50 | £4 | |
| Sippin' And Chippin' | 7" | Liberty | LIB55867 | 1966 | £1.50 | £4 | |

## USE OF ASHES

| | | | | | | | |
|---|---|---|---|---|---|---|---|
| Castle Of Fair Welcome | LP | Rosebud | | 1989 | £37.50 | £75 | Dutch |

## USERS

| | | | | | | | |
|---|---|---|---|---|---|---|---|
| Sick Of You | 7" | Raw | RAW1 | 1977 | £2 | £5 | numbered picture sleeve |
| Sick Of You | 12" | Raw | RAWT1 | 1978 | £2.50 | £6 | |

## UTOPIA

| | | | | | | | |
|---|---|---|---|---|---|---|---|
| Utopia | LP | Kent | | 1967 | £30 | £60 | US |

## UTOPIA (2)

| | | | | | | | |
|---|---|---|---|---|---|---|---|
| Utopia | LP | Kent | KST566 | 1967 | £8 | £20 | US |

## UV POP

| | | | | | | | |
|---|---|---|---|---|---|---|---|
| Just A Game | 7" | Pax | PAX9 | 1982 | £2 | £5 | |

# V

### V2
| | | | | | |
|---|---|---|---|---|---|
| Speed Freak | 7" | Bent | SMALLBENT1 | 1978 £2 £5 | red or black vinyl |

### VACELS
| | | | | | |
|---|---|---|---|---|---|
| Can You Please Crawl Out Of Your Window | 7" | Pye | 7N25330 | 1965 £2.50 £6 | |

### VAGABONDS
| | | | | | |
|---|---|---|---|---|---|
| Presenting The Fabulous Vagabonds | LP | Island | ILP916 | 1964 £20 £40 | |
| Ska Time | LP | Decca | LK4617 | 1964 £8 £20 | |

### VAGINA DENTATA ORGAN
| | | | | | |
|---|---|---|---|---|---|
| Cold Meat | 12" | | WSNS004 | 198– £6 £15 | picture disc |
| Music For Hashasins | LP | Temple | TOPY012 | 1987 £8 £20 | |

### VAGRANTS
| | | | | | |
|---|---|---|---|---|---|
| Great Lost Album | LP | Arista | AL8459 | 1987 £10 £25 | US |
| I Can't Make A Friend | 7" | Fontana | TF703 | 1966 £15 £30 | |

### VALADIERS
| | | | | | |
|---|---|---|---|---|---|
| I Found A Girl | 7" | Oriole | CBA1809 | 1963 £400 £600 | best auctioned |

### VALANCE, RICKY
| | | | | |
|---|---|---|---|---|
| Bobby | 7" | Columbia | DB4680 | 1961 £1.50 £4 |
| Don't Play Number Nine | 7" | Columbia | DB4864 | 1962 £1.50 £4 |
| I Never Had A Chance | 7" | Columbia | DB4725 | 1961 £1.50 £4 |
| Jimmy's Girl | 7" | Columbia | DB4586 | 1961 £1.50 £4 |
| Lipstick On Your Lips | 7" | Columbia | DB4543 | 1960 £1.50 £4 |
| Tell Laura I Love Her | 7" | Columbia | DB4493 | 1960 £1.50 £4 |
| Try To Forget Her | 7" | Columbia | DB4787 | 1962 £1.50 £4 |
| Why Can't We | 7" | Columbia | DB4592 | 1961 £1.50 £4 |

### VALE, RICKY & HIS SURFERS
| | | | | | |
|---|---|---|---|---|---|
| Everybody's Surfin' | LP | Strand | SL(S)1104 | 1963 £6 £15 | US |

### VALENS, RITCHIE
| | | | | | |
|---|---|---|---|---|---|
| C'mon Let's Go | 7" | Pye | 7N25000 | 1958 £37.50 £75 | |
| Donna | 7" | London | HL7068 | 1959 £5 £10 | |
| Donna | 7" | London | HL8803 | 1959 £7.50 £15 | |
| Donna | 7" | President | PT126 | 1967 £1.50 £4 | |
| Greatest Hits | LP | London | HA8196 | 1964 £15 £30 | |
| Greatest Hits Vol. 2 | LP | Del-Fi | 1247 | 1965 £15 £30 | US |
| I Remember Ritchie Valens | LP | President | PTL1001 | 1967 £4 £10 | |
| In Concert At Pacoima Jr.High | LP | Del-Fi | 1214 | 1960 £30 £60 | US |
| La Bamba | 7" | London | HL9494 | 1962 £6 £12 | |
| La Bamba | 7" | Sue | WI4011 | 1966 £15 £30 | demo |
| Ritchie | LP | London | HA2390 | 1961 £25 £50 | |
| Ritchie Valens | LP | Del-Fi | 1201 | 1959 £37.50 £75 | US |
| Ritchie Valens | LP | MGM | GAS117 | 1970 £4 £10 | US |
| Ritchie Valens | 7" EP | London | RE1232 | 1959 £50 £100 | tri-centre |
| That's My Little Suzie | 7" | London | HL8886 | 1959 £7.50 £15 | |

### VALENTE, CATERINA
| | | | | | |
|---|---|---|---|---|---|
| A l'Olympia | 10" LP | Decca | 133893 | 1958 £20 £40 | French |
| Arriba Caterina | LP | Polydor | 46073 | 1962 £10 £25 | German |
| Bravo Caterina | 7" EP | Polydor | 20605EPH | 1957 £15 £30 | German |
| Bravo Caterina | 7" EP | Polydor | EPH20282 | 1963 £2 £5 | |
| Breeze And I | 7" | Polydor | NH66953 | 1960 £2 £5 | |
| Caterina Chérie | LP | Polydor | LPHM46310 | 1961 £5 £12 | |
| Caterina Valente | 7" EP | Polydor | EPH20106 | 1963 £2 £5 | |
| Caterina Valente | 7" EP | Polydor | EPH20501 | 1963 £2 £5 | |
| Caterina Valente | 7" EP | Polydor | EPH21613 | 1963 £2 £5 | |
| Caterina Valente No. 2 | 7" EP | Polydor | EPH20528 | 1963 £2 £5 | |
| Caterina Valente No. 3 | 7" EP | Polydor | EPH20545 | 1963 £2 £5 | |
| Caterina Valente Singers | LP | Decca | SLK16317 | 1965 £8 £20 | German |
| Catrin | LP | Decca | T74036 | 1962 £20 £40 | German |
| Classics With A Chaser | LP | RCA | RD27240 | 1960 £15 £30 | |
| Cosmopolitan Lady | LP | Polydor | LPHM46065 | 1960 £5 £12 | |
| Date With Caterina Valente | 10" LP | Polydor | LPH45517 | 1955 £10 £25 | German |
| De Paris à Grenade | 7" EP | Polydor | EPH20547 | 1963 £2 £5 | |
| Ein Gruss Von Caterina Valente | 10" LP | Polydor | LPH45077 | 1953 £30 £60 | German |
| Frenesi | 7" EP | London | GEB7001 | 1962 £2 £5 | |
| Great Continental Hits | LP | Decca | LK/SKL4508 | 1962 £5 £12 | |

| Title | Format | Label | Catalogue | Year | | | |
|---|---|---|---|---|---|---|---|
| Haiti Cherie | 7" EP | Polydor | EPH20516 | 1963 | £2 | £5 | |
| I Happen To Like New York | LP | Decca | LK/SKL4630 | 1964 | £5 | £12 | |
| I Wish You Love | LP | London | PS275 | 1962 | £20 | £40 | US |
| In Italia | LP | Decca | BLK16211P | 1962 | £25 | £50 | German |
| Intimate Valente | LP | Decca | SKL4756 | 1966 | £8 | £20 | |
| Kleine Geschichten Von Grosser Liebe | 7" EP | Polydor | EPH20231 | 1956 | £10 | £20 | German |
| La Malaguena | 7" | Polydor | NH66816 | 1960 | £2.50 | £6 | |
| Many Voices Of Caterina Valente | LP | Decca | BLK16214 | 1963 | £10 | £25 | German |
| My Hawaiian Melody | 7" EP | Decca | DFE8544 | 1963 | £2 | £5 | |
| Olé Caterina | LP | Polydor | 46029 | 1961 | £10 | £25 | German |
| On Tour | LP | Decca | BLK16213P | 1962 | £20 | £40 | German |
| Pariser Chic, Pariser Charme | LP | Decca | BLK16266P | 1963 | £8 | £20 | German |
| Plenty Caterina | 7" EP | Polydor | 20578EPH | 1957 | £12.50 | £25 | French |
| Rendezvous With Caterina | LP | Decca | LK4350 | 1960 | £5 | £12 | |
| Serenata D'Amore | LP | Polydor | 45529LPH | 1958 | £20 | £40 | German |
| Silk 'n' Latin | LP | London | SP44125 | 1969 | £20 | £40 | US double |
| Sombreros Y Guitarras | 7" EP | Polydor | EPH20596 | 1963 | £2 | £5 | |
| Superfonics | LP | RCA | RD27216/SF5099 | 1961 | £5 | £12 | |
| Third Deutsches Jazz Festival | 7" EP | Brunswick | 10021EPB | 1955 | £30 | £60 | German |
| Third Deutsches Jazz Festival 2 | 7" EP | Brunswick | 10025EPB | 1955 | £30 | £60 | German |
| Toast To The Girls | LP | Decca | DL8755 | 1958 | £10 | £25 | US |
| Toast To The Girls | 7" EP | Polydor | 20622EPH | 1958 | £5 | £10 | German |
| Valente And Violins | LP | Decca | LK/SKL4646 | 1965 | £5 | £12 | |
| Valente In Swingtime | LP | Decca | LK/SKL4537 | 1963 | £4 | £10 | |
| Valente On TV | LP | Decca | LK4604 | 1964 | £4 | £10 | |
| Veel Liefs Van Caterina Valente | LP | Capri | CA1G | 1972 | £20 | £40 | Dutch |

## VALENTE, DINO

| Dino | LP | CBS | 65715 | 1968 | £5 | £12 | |
|---|---|---|---|---|---|---|---|
| Dino Valente | LP | CBS | 63443 | 1968 | £10 | £25 | |

## VALENTINE, BILLY

| It's A Sin | 7" | Capitol | CL14320 | 1955 | £4 | £8 | |
|---|---|---|---|---|---|---|---|

## VALENTINE, DICKIE

| Belonging To Someone | 7" EP | Decca | DFE6549 | 1958 | £2 | £5 | |
|---|---|---|---|---|---|---|---|
| Blossom Fell | 7" | Decca | F10430 | 1955 | £5 | £10 | |
| Chapel Of The Roses | 7" | Decca | F10874 | 1957 | £1.50 | £4 | |
| Christmas Alphabet | 7" | Decca | F10628 | 1955 | £10 | £20 | |
| Christmas Island | 7" | Decca | F10798 | 1956 | £4 | £8 | |
| Day Dreams | 7" | Decca | F10766 | 1956 | £2 | £5 | |
| Dickie Goes Dixie | 7" EP | Decca | DFE6427 | 1957 | £2.50 | £6 | |
| Dickie Valentine's Rock 'n' Roll Party | 7" | Decca | F10820 | 1956 | £2 | £5 | |
| Dreams Can Tell A Lie | 7" | Decca | F10667 | 1956 | £2 | £5 | |
| Endless | 7" | Decca | F10346 | 1954 | £5 | £10 | |
| Finger Of Suspicion Points At You | 7" | Decca | F10394 | 1954 | £7.50 | £15 | |
| Hello Mrs. Jones | 7" | Decca | F10517 | 1955 | £2.50 | £6 | |
| Here Is Dickie Valentine | 10" LP | Decca | LF1211 | 1955 | £6 | £15 | |
| Hit Parade | 7" EP | Pye | NEP24120 | 1959 | £2 | £5 | |
| I Wonder | 7" | Decca | F10493 | 1955 | £4 | £8 | |
| Long Before I Knew You | 7" | Decca | F10949 | 1957 | £1.50 | £4 | |
| Love Me Again | 7" | Decca | F11005 | 1958 | £1.50 | £4 | |
| Ma chère amie | 7" | Decca | F10484 | 1955 | £4 | £8 | |
| Mister Sandman | 7" | Decca | F10415 | 1954 | £10 | £20 | |
| My Impossible Castle | 7" | Decca | F10753 | 1956 | £1.50 | £4 | |
| No Such Luck | 7" | Decca | F10549 | 1955 | £2.50 | £6 | |
| Old Pianna Rag | 7" | Decca | F10645 | 1955 | £4 | £8 | |
| Only For You | 7" EP | Decca | DFE6363 | 1956 | £2.50 | £6 | |
| Over My Shoulder | 10" LP | Decca | LF1257 | 1956 | £6 | £15 | |
| Presenting | 7" EP | Decca | DFE6279 | 1956 | £5 | £10 | |
| Presenting Dickie Valentine | 10" LP | Decca | LF1163 | 1954 | £6 | £15 | |
| Puttin' On The Style | 7" | Decca | F10906 | 1957 | £1.50 | £4 | |
| Snowbound For Christmas | 7" | Decca | F10950 | 1957 | £2 | £5 | |
| Swing Along | 7" EP | Decca | DFE6236 | 1955 | £2.50 | £6 | |
| Venus | 7" | Pye | 7N15192 | 1959 | £1.50 | £4 | |
| Voice | 7" | Decca | F10714 | 1956 | £2 | £5 | |
| With Vocal Refrain By | LP | Decca | LK4269 | 1958 | £4 | £10 | |
| With Vocal Refrain By | 7" EP | Decca | DFE6529 | 1958 | £2.50 | £6 | |

## VALENTINE, HILTON

| All In Your Head | LP | Capitol | ST330 | 1969 | £25 | £50 | US |
|---|---|---|---|---|---|---|---|

## VALENTINES

| Hey Baby | 7" | Ember | EMBS123 | 1960 | £20 | £40 | |
|---|---|---|---|---|---|---|---|

## VALENTINO, ANNA

| Calypso Joe | 7" | London | HLD8421 | 1957 | £5 | £10 | |
|---|---|---|---|---|---|---|---|

## VALENTINO, DANNY

| Biology | 7" | MGM | MGM1067 | 1960 | £4 | £8 | |
|---|---|---|---|---|---|---|---|
| Pictures | 7" | MGM | MGM1109 | 1960 | £1.50 | £4 | |
| Stampede | 7" | MGM | MGM1049 | 1959 | £7.50 | £15 | |

## VALENTINO, MARK

| Do It | 7" | Stateside | SS186 | 1963 | £1.50 | £4 | |
|---|---|---|---|---|---|---|---|
| Jiving At The Drive In | 7" | Stateside | SS233 | 1963 | £5 | £10 | |
| Mark Valentino | LP | Swan | LP508 | 1963 | £6 | £15 | US |
| Push And Kick | 7" | Stateside | SS148 | 1963 | £1.50 | £4 | |

## VALENTINOS
| | | | | | | | |
|---|---|---|---|---|---|---|---|
| It's All Over Now | 7" | Soul City | SC106 | 1968 | £2 | £5 | |
| Tired Of Being Nobody | 7" | Stateside | SS2137 | 1969 | £1.50 | £4 | |
| Valentinos/The Sims Twins | LP | Soul City | SCM001 | 1969 | £6 | £15 | with The Sims Twins |

## VALERIE & THE ROCK & ROLL YOUNGSTERS
| | | | | | | | |
|---|---|---|---|---|---|---|---|
| Tonight You Belong To Me | 7" | Columbia | DB3832 | 1956 | £4 | £8 | |

## VALINO, JOE
| | | | | | | | |
|---|---|---|---|---|---|---|---|
| Garden Of Eden | 7" | HMV | POP283 | 1957 | £2 | £5 | |
| God's Little Acre | 7" | London | HLT8705 | 1958 | £4 | £8 | |

## VALKYRIES
| | | | | | | | |
|---|---|---|---|---|---|---|---|
| Rip It Up | 7" | Parlophone | R5123 | 1964 | £4 | £8 | |

## VALLADARES, DIORIS
| | | | | | | | |
|---|---|---|---|---|---|---|---|
| Authentic Merengue | 7" EP | Sue | IEP703 | 1966 | £5 | £10 | |

## VALLEY, JIM
| | | | | | | | |
|---|---|---|---|---|---|---|---|
| Harpo | LP | Panorama | 104 | 1969 | £6 | £15 | US |

## VALLI, FRANKIE
| | | | | | | | |
|---|---|---|---|---|---|---|---|
| My Mother's Eye | 7" | Corona | 1234 | 1953 | £330 | £500 | .... US, best auctioned |
| Please Take A Chance | 7" | Decca | 30994 | 1959 | £37.50 | £75 | US |
| Real | 7" | Cindy | 3012 | 1959 | £37.50 | £75 | US |
| Somebody Else Took Her Home | 7" | Mercury | 70381 | 1954 | £37.50 | £75 | US |
| You're Gonna Hurt Yourself | 7" | Philips | BF1467 | 1966 | £1.50 | £4 | |
| You're Ready Now | 7" | Philips | BF1512 | 1966 | £2.50 | £6 | |

## VALLI, FRANKIE & THE FOUR SEASONS
| | | | | | | | |
|---|---|---|---|---|---|---|---|
| Night | 7" | Mowest | MW3002 | 1972 | £2 | £5 | |

## VALLI, JUNE
| | | | | | | | |
|---|---|---|---|---|---|---|---|
| Anonymous Letter | 7" | Mercury | AMT1048 | 1959 | £1.50 | £4 | |
| Answer To A Maiden's Prayer | 7" | Mercury | AMT1034 | 1959 | £1.50 | £4 | |
| Apple Green | 7" | Mercury | AMT1091 | 1960 | £1.50 | £4 | |
| I Understand | 7" | HMV | 7M245 | 1954 | £2.50 | £6 | |
| Por Favor | 7" | HMV | 7M347 | 1956 | £2 | £5 | |
| Tell Me, Tell Me | 7" | HMV | 7M259 | 1954 | £2.50 | £6 | |
| Wrong, Wrong, Wrong | 7" | HMV | 7M284 | 1955 | £2 | £5 | |

## VALLONS, JOHNNY & THE DEEJAYS
| | | | | | | | |
|---|---|---|---|---|---|---|---|
| Non-Stop Show At Kingside | LP | Swedisc | SWELP8 | 1966 | £50 | £100 | Swedish |

## VALUES
| | | | | | | | |
|---|---|---|---|---|---|---|---|
| Return To Me | 7" | Ember | EMBS211 | 1966 | £10 | £20 | |

## VAMP
Andy Clark and Mick Hutchinson, who recorded three albums together in the early seventies, were previously members of the short-lived Vamp. The group's line-up was completed by the former drummer with the Pretty Things, Viv Prince, and by Pete Sears, who was later a member of Jefferson Starship.

| | | | | | | | |
|---|---|---|---|---|---|---|---|
| Floatin' | 7" | Atlantic | 584213 | 1968 | £25 | £50 | |
| Green Pea | 7" | Atlantic | 584263 | 1969 | £25 | £50 | demo |

## VAMPIRES
| | | | | | | | |
|---|---|---|---|---|---|---|---|
| Do You Wanna Dance | 7" | Pye | 7N17553 | 1968 | £1.50 | £4 | |

## VAMPIRES (2)
| | | | | | | | |
|---|---|---|---|---|---|---|---|
| Swinging Ghosts | 7" | Parlophone | R4599 | 1959 | £4 | £8 | |

## VAMPIRE'S SOUND INCORPORATED
| | | | | | | | |
|---|---|---|---|---|---|---|---|
| Psychedelic Dance Party | LP | Mercury | MCY134615 | 1969 | £20 | £40 | German |

## VAN DAMME, ART
| | | | | | | | |
|---|---|---|---|---|---|---|---|
| Art Van Damme Quintet | 10" LP | Capitol | LC6622 | 1954 | £5 | £12 | |

## VAN DER GRAAF GENERATOR
Peter Hammill's complicated songs, each incorporating several melodic themes and intricate instrumental passages, are well served by Van Der Graaf Generator's musicians. Hugh Banton, in particular, shines as one of the very few organ players in rock to have made a serious attempt to fully explore the potential of the electronic instrument. Peter Hammill's voice too has some of the characteristics of an instrument, as he varies its tonal qualities considerably from moment to moment – sometimes with a little electronic assistance. It is the combination of instrumental bravado and compositional depth that arguably makes these albums, by a short head, the most durable of all the progressive rock canon. With regard to the group's rare singles, it should be noted that 'Refugees' is a different version to that found on *The Least We Can Do Is Wave To Each Other.* 'Firebrand' – the rarest Van Der Graaf release of all – is actually the B side of the single, but this is always the named title to appear on dealers' and collectors' want lists, due to it being the more experimental and dynamic side.

| | | | | | | | |
|---|---|---|---|---|---|---|---|
| Aerosol Grey Machine | LP | Fontana | 6430083 | 1975 | £4 | £10 | |
| Aerosol Grey Machine | LP | Mercury | SR61238 | 1968 | £10 | £25 | US |
| Firebrand | 7" | Polydor | 56758 | 1968 | £150 | £250 | |
| H To He Who Am The Only One | LP | Charisma | CAS1027 | 1970 | £4 | £10 | |
| Least We Can Do Is Wave | LP | Charisma | CAS1007 | 1970 | £15 | £30 | with poster |
| Least We Can Do Is Wave To Each Other | LP | Charisma | CAS1007 | 1969 | £5 | £12 | |
| Long Hello | LP | no label | no number | 1973 | £8 | £20 | |
| Pawn Hearts | LP | Buddah | | 1971 | £6 | £15 | US, with 'Theme One' |

| | | | | | | |
|---|---|---|---|---|---|---|
| Pawn Hearts | LP | Charisma | CAS1051 | 1971 £4 | £10 | |
| Refugees | 7" | Charisma | CB122 | 1970 £15 | £30 | |
| Theme One | 7" | Charisma | CB175 | 1972 £10 | £20 | picture sleeve |
| Wondering | 7" | Charisma | CB297 | 1976 £2 | £5 | |

### VAN DER REE, PAUL (THE HAPPIEST BAND THAT EVER PLAYED)
| | | | | | | |
|---|---|---|---|---|---|---|
| In The Balancing Of Night And Day | LP | Goldfish | LP0001 | 1970 £250 | £500 | Dutch |

### VAN DOREN, MAMIE
| | | | | | | |
|---|---|---|---|---|---|---|
| Something To Dream About | 7" | Capitol | CL14850 | 1958 £1.50 | £4 | |

### VAN DYKE, EARL
| | | | | | | |
|---|---|---|---|---|---|---|
| All For You | 7" | Tamla Motown | TMG506 | 1965 £25 | £50 | |
| Earl Of Funk | LP | Soul | SS715 | 1970 £8 | £20 | US |
| Six By Six | 7" | Tamla Motown | TMG759 | 1970 £1.50 | £4 | |
| Soul Stomp | 7" | Stateside | SS357 | 1964 £30 | £60 | |
| That Motown Sound | LP | Tamla Motown | TML11014 | 1965 £37.50 | £75 | |

### VAN DYKE, LEROY
| | | | | | | |
|---|---|---|---|---|---|---|
| Big Man In A Big House | 7" | Mercury | AMT1173 | 1962 £1.50 | £4 | |
| Broken Promise | 7" | Mercury | AMT1183 | 1962 £1.50 | £4 | |
| It's All Over Now, Baby Blue | 7" | Warner Bros | WB5650 | 1965 £1.50 | £4 | |
| Movin' | LP | Mercury | MMC14118 | 1963 £8 | £20 | |
| Walk On By | LP | Mercury | MMC14101 | 1961 £8 | £20 | |
| Walk On By | 7" | Mercury | AMT1166 | 1961 £1.50 | £4 | |

### VAN DYKE & THE BAMBIS
| | | | | | | |
|---|---|---|---|---|---|---|
| Doin' The Mod | 7" | Piccadilly | 7N35180 | 1964 £1.50 | £4 | |

### VAN DYKES
| | | | | | | |
|---|---|---|---|---|---|---|
| I've Gotta Go On Without You | 7" | Stateside | SS530 | 1966 £5 | £10 | |
| No Man Is An Island | 7" | Stateside | SS504 | 1966 £2.50 | £6 | |
| Tellin' It Like It Is | LP | Bell | 6004 | 1967 £6 | £15 | US |

### VAN EATON, LON & DERREK
| | | | | | | |
|---|---|---|---|---|---|---|
| Brother | LP | Apple | SAPCOR25 | 1973 £6 | £15 | |
| Warm Woman | 7" | Apple | 46 | 1973 £10 | £20 | picture sleeve |

### VAN HALEN
| | | | | | | |
|---|---|---|---|---|---|---|
| Dance The Night Away | 7" | Warner Bros | K17371 | 1979 £1.50 | £4 | |
| Dance The Night Away | 7" | Warner Bros | K17371 | 1979 £2.50 | £6 | picture disc |
| Dreams | 7" | Warner Bros | W8642P | 1986 £2.50 | £6 | shaped picture disc, plinth |
| Feels So Good | CD-s | WEA | W7565CD | 1989 £2 | £5 | |
| Jump | CD-s | Warner Bros | W0155CDX | 1993 £2 | £5 | in metal tin |
| When It's Love | CD-s | WEA | W7816CD | 1988 £2 | £5 | 3" single |
| Why Can't This Be Love | 7" | Warner Bros | W8740P | 1986 £2 | £5 | shaped picture disc, plinth |

### VAN RONK, DAVE
| | | | | | | |
|---|---|---|---|---|---|---|
| Ballads And Blues And Spirituals | LP | Folkways | F3818 | 1959 £6 | £15 | US |

### VAN SPYK, ROB
| | | | | | | |
|---|---|---|---|---|---|---|
| Follow The Sun | LP | private | | 197– £20 | £40 | |

### VAN ZANDT, TOWNES
| | | | | | | |
|---|---|---|---|---|---|---|
| For The Sake Of A Song | LP | Poppy | PYS40001 | 1968 £4 | £10 | US |

### VANCE
| | | | | | | |
|---|---|---|---|---|---|---|
| Epitaph For Mary | LP | VRL | | 1982 £25 | £50 | Dutch |

### VANCE, TOMMY
| | | | | | | |
|---|---|---|---|---|---|---|
| Off The Hook | 7" | Columbia | DB8062 | 1966 £1.50 | £4 | |
| You Must Be The One | 7" | Columbia | DB7999 | 1966 £1.50 | £4 | |

### VANDER, CHRISTIAN
| | | | | | | |
|---|---|---|---|---|---|---|
| Tristan et Iseult | LP | Egg | 90171 | 1978 £4 | £10 | French |

### VANGELIS
| | | | | | | |
|---|---|---|---|---|---|---|
| Chariots Of Fire/China/Opera Sauvage | LP | Polydor | BOX1 | 1982 £6 | £15 | 3 LP boxed set |
| Will Of The Wind | CD-s | Arista | 661767 | 1988 £2 | £5 | |

### VANILLA FUDGE
| | | | | | | |
|---|---|---|---|---|---|---|
| Beat Goes On | LP | Atlantic | 587/588100 | 1968 £4 | £10 | |
| Eleanor Rigby | 7" | Atlantic | 584139 | 1967 £1.50 | £4 | |
| Renaissance | LP | Atlantic | 587/588110 | 1968 £4 | £10 | |
| Shotgun | 7" | Atlantic | 584257 | 1969 £1.50 | £4 | |
| Some Velvet Morning | 7" | Atlantic | 584276 | 1969 £1.50 | £4 | |
| Vanilla Fudge | LP | Atlantic | 587/588086 | 1967 £5 | £12 | |
| Where Is My Mind | 7" | Atlantic | 584179 | 1968 £1.50 | £4 | |
| You Keep Me Hanging On | 7" | Atlantic | 584123 | 1967 £1.50 | £4 | |

### VANITY FARE
| | | | | | | |
|---|---|---|---|---|---|---|
| Sun, The Wind And Other Things | LP | Page One | POLS010 | 1968 £4 | £10 | |

### VANN, TEDDY
| | | | | | | |
|---|---|---|---|---|---|---|
| Cindy | 7" | London | HLU9097 | 1960 £5 | £10 | |

## VARDAS, PETER
He Threw A Stone .................................... 7" ...... Top Rank ....... JAR173 ................. 1959 £1.50 ........ £4 ...............................

## VARDIS
If I Were King ............................................. 7" ...... Castle .............. QUEL2/100 ........ 1980 £2.50 ........ £6 ...............................
Let's Go ...................................................... 7" ...... Logo .............. VAR1 .................. 1980 £1.50 ........ £4 ..................... *double*

## VARIATIONS
Man With All The Toys ........................... 7" ...... Immediate ...... IM019 ................ 1965 £2.50 ........ £6 ...............................

## VARICOSE VEINS
Geographical Problem .............................. 7" ...... Warped ........... WARP1 ................ 1978 £7.50 ...... £15 ...............................

## VARIOUS

Various artists albums can become collectable for a number of reasons. Some contain tracks that are only available on that particular record. One of the most valuable of this sort is the *Glastonbury Fayre* triple album, which within its extravagant packing and multiple inserts contains material by artists like David Bowie, Marc Bolan and the Grateful Dead, none of which has been released anywhere else. Other albums are on labels that are themselves collectable, like the various Tamla Motown anthologies, or the United Dairies compilation. Others simply seem to epitomize an area or era of music particularly well – the classic example here being the *Nuggets* double, which gathers together a number of the American groups whose music represents what was meant by 'punk rock' in the sixties. For jazz collectors, various artist compilations are not popular, and the large number of such albums from the fifties do not, in general, appear in these listings, even when they feature artists who do have substantial collectors' discographies to their names.

| | | | | | | | | |
|---|---|---|---|---|---|---|---|---|
| .................................................. | LP ..... | Treasure Isle .... | TI101 ..................... | 1966 | £30 ........ | £60 | ............................... |
| 18 Original Hits Performed By 18 Unoriginal Artists ................................... | CD ..... | Polygram ......... | PMP011 ................ | 1995 | £25 ........ | £50 | ............... *US promo* |
| 1968 Memphis Country Music Festival ...... | LP ..... | Blue Horizon .. | 763210 ................ | 1968 | £15 ........ | £30 | |
| 49 Greek Street ........................................ | LP ..... | RCA ............. | SF8118 ................ | 1970 | £4 .......... | £10 | |
| 50 Minutes & 24 Seconds Of Recorded Dynamite ...................................... | LP ..... | Sue ................. | ILP920 ................ | 1965 | £15 ........ | £30 | |
| Abbey Tavern Traditional Music And Song | LP ..... | Abbey Tavern .. | ATP101 ................ | 1970 | £8 .......... | £20 | ...................... *Irish* |
| Acid Dreams ............................................. | LP ..... | Acid ............... | 5199 ................... | 1980 | £50 ........ | £100 | ........................... *US* |
| Action Packed Soul .................................. | LP ..... | Action ............ | ACLP6005 ........... | 1969 | £6 .......... | £15 | |
| Afflicted Man's Musica Box ...................... | LP ..... | United Dairies . | UD012 ................ | 1982 | £6 .......... | £15 | |
| Afflicted Man's Musica Box ...................... | LP ..... | United Dairies . | UD012 ................ | 1982 | £20 ........ | £40 | ........ *gatefold sleeve* |
| African Melody ......................................... | LP ..... | Pama .............. | PMP2004 ............. | 1970 | £4 .......... | £10 | |
| Album Full Of Soul .................................. | LP ..... | Stateside ......... | SL10172 .............. | 1966 | £8 .......... | £20 | |
| Alive In The Living Room ........................ | LP ..... | Creation .......... | CRELP001 .......... | 1984 | £4 .......... | £10 | |
| Alive! ....................................................... | LP ..... | Key ................. | KL002 ................ | 1969 | £10 ........ | £25 | |
| All Cops In Delirium ................................ | LP ..... | private ............ | no number ........... | 1980 | £25 ........ | £50 | ........................... *US* |
| All For Art And Art For All ...................... | LP ..... | Whaam! .......... | BIG8 .................. | 1984 | £8 .......... | £20 | |
| All Good Clean Fun ................................. | LP ..... | United Artists .. | UDX201/2 ........... | 1971 | £5 .......... | £12 | ..................... *double* |
| All Star Hit Parade ................................... | 7" EP . | Pye ................. | NEP24168 ........... | 1963 | £2 .......... | £5 | |
| All Star Hit Parade ................................... | 7" ...... | Decca ............. | F10752 ................ | 1956 | £2.50 ..... | £6 | |
| All Star Hit Parade Vol. 2 ........................ | 7" EP . | Pye ................. | NEP24172 ........... | 1964 | £2 .......... | £5 | |
| American Country Jubilee No. 1 .............. | 7" EP . | Decca ............. | DFE8571 ............. | 1964 | £2.50 ..... | £6 | |
| American Folk Blues Festival .................... | LP ..... | Polydor ........... | LPHM46397/ SLPHM237597 ...... | 1963 | £4 .......... | £10 | |
| American Folk Blues Festival 1963 ........... | LP ..... | Fontana ........... | TL5204 ................ | 1964 | £4 .......... | £10 | |
| American Folk Blues Festival 1964 ........... | LP ..... | Fontana ........... | TL5225 ................ | 1965 | £4 .......... | £10 | |
| American Folk Blues Festival 1965 ........... | LP ..... | Fontana ........... | TL5286 ................ | 1966 | £4 .......... | £10 | |
| American Folk Blues Festival 1966 ........... | LP ..... | Fontana ........... | (S)TL5389 ........... | 1966 | £6 .......... | £15 | |
| Angola Prisoners' Blues ............................ | LP ..... | Collector ......... | JGN1003 ............. | 1960 | £5 .......... | £12 | |
| Anniversary Issue ..................................... | 7" ...... | Recommended | RRR&RE .............. | 1985 | £75 ........ | £150 | ....... *15 single set* |
| Anthology Of British Blues Vol. 1 ............ | LP ..... | Immediate ...... | IMAL03/04 ......... | 1969 | £6 .......... | £15 | ..................... *double* |
| Anthology Of British Blues Vol. 2 ............ | LP ..... | Immediate ...... | IMAL05/06 ......... | 1969 | £6 .......... | £15 | ..................... *double* |
| Apollo Saturday Night .............................. | LP ..... | London ............ | HAK/SHK8174 .... | 1964 | £10 ........ | £25 | |
| At The Cavern .......................................... | LP ..... | Decca ............. | LK4597 ............... | 1964 | £10 ........ | £25 | |
| Atlantic Discotheque ................................ | LP ..... | Atlantic ........... | ATL5020 ............. | 1965 | £4 .......... | £10 | |
| Atlantic Is Soul ........................................ | LP ..... | Atlantic ........... | AP2 ..................... | 196– | £4 .......... | £10 | |
| Atlanticlassics ........................................... | LP ..... | Atlantic ........... | AC3 ..................... | 196– | £10 ........ | £25 | |
| Attack Of The Jersey Teens ...................... | LP ..... | Bona Fide ....... | BFRNJ6601 ......... | 1984 | £5 .......... | £12 | ........................... *US* |
| Authentic Rhythm And Blues ................... | LP ..... | Stateside ......... | SL10068 .............. | 1964 | £8 .......... | £20 | |
| Authentic Ska ........................................... | LP ..... | Stateside ......... | SL10107 .............. | 1964 | £8 .......... | £20 | |
| Avant Garde .............................................. | LP ..... | Deutsche Grammophon .. | | 196– | £30 ........ | £60 | ......... *6 LP boxed set* |
| Avant Garde Vol. 2 ................................... | LP ..... | Deutsche Grammophon .. | 643541/46 .......... | 196– | £30 ........ | £60 | ......... *6 LP boxed set* |
| Avant Garde Vol. 3 ................................... | LP ..... | Deutsche Grammophon .. | 2561039/044 ......... | 197– | £30 ........ | £60 | ......... *6 LP boxed set* |
| Backwoods Blues ...................................... | 10" LP | London ........... | AL3535 ................ | 1954 | £10 ........ | £25 | |
| Badger A Go-Go ....................................... | LP ..... | Night Owl ...... | KTV3 ................. | 1968 | £6 .......... | £15 | ........................... *US* |
| Ballin' ...................................................... | LP ..... | Fontana ........... | 688200ZL ........... | 1962 | £4 .......... | £10 | |
| Bang Bang Lulu ........................................ | LP ..... | Pama .............. | PMLP4 ................ | 1968 | £8 .......... | £20 | |
| Barrelhouse Piano .................................... | 10" LP | Vogue Coral ... | LRA10022 ........... | 1955 | £6 .......... | £15 | |
| Barrelhouse Piano Vol. 2 ......................... | 10" LP | Vogue Coral ... | LRA10023 ........... | 1955 | £6 .......... | £15 | |
| Barrelhouse, Boogie Woogie, And Blues .... | 10" LP | Fontana .......... | TFR6018 ............. | 1959 | £5 .......... | £12 | |
| Battle Of The Bands ................................. | LP ..... | Onyx .............. | ES80689 ............. | 1966 | £50 ........ | £100 | ........................... *US* |
| Battle Of The Bands ................................. | LP ..... | Onyx .............. | ES80689 ............. | 198– | £10 ........ | £25 | ........................... *US* |
| Battle Of The Bands ................................. | 10" LP | Capitol ............ | LC6510 ............... | 1951 | £6 .......... | £15 | |
| Battle Of The Bands Vol. 1 ...................... | LP ..... | Panorama ........ | 103 ..................... | 1966 | £25 ........ | £50 | ........................... *US* |
| Battle Of The Bands Vol. 1 ...................... | LP ..... | Ren-Vell ......... | 317 ..................... | 196– | £50 ........ | £100 | ........................... *US* |
| Battle Of The Bands Vol. 2 ...................... | LP ..... | Panorama ........ | 108 ..................... | 1967 | £25 ........ | £50 | ........................... *US* |
| Battle Of The Giants ................................ | LP ..... | Melodisc ......... | 12192 .................. | 196– | £4 .......... | £10 | |
| Bay State Rock Vol. 1 .............................. | LP ..... | Star Rhythm .... | LP101 ................. | 1980 | £5 .......... | £12 | ........................... *US* |
| Beat – Wettbewerb Der Stadt Frankfurt ...... | LP ..... | CBS ................ | 52330 .................. | 1966 | £20 ........ | £40 | ..................... *German* |

| Title | Format | Label | Number | Year | Price1 | Price2 | Notes |
|---|---|---|---|---|---|---|---|
| Beat For You | LP | Polydor | 94042 | 1964 | £20 | £40 | German |
| Beat In Liverpool | 10" LP | Europaische Verlagsanstalt | 101 | 1965 | £25 | £50 | German |
| Beat Party | LP | CBS | 52327 | 1966 | £10 | £25 | German |
| Beater's Hit Parade | LP | Philips | 75283 | 1966 | £25 | £50 | German |
| Bebop Era | LP | RCA | RD7909 | 1967 | £4 | £10 | |
| Bee Jay Demo Record | LP | Tener | 1014 | 1967 | £180 | £300 | US |
| Bells Are Ringing | 7" EP | Philips | BBE12148 | 1957 | £2 | £5 | |
| Best Of Bluegrass | 7" EP | Melodisc | EPM7115 | 195– | £2.50 | £6 | |
| Best Of Camel | LP | Pama | SECO18 | 1969 | £6 | £15 | |
| Best Of The Hideouts | LP | Hideout | HLP1002 | 1965 | £50 | £100 | US |
| Best Wishes For Christmas | 7" EP | Philips | BBE12225 | 1958 | £2 | £5 | |
| Big Beat | LP | Fontana | TFL5080 | 1959 | £25 | £50 | |
| Big D Jamboree | LP | London | HAB8199 | 1964 | £4 | £10 | |
| Big Four | 7" EP | Fontana | TE17469 | 1966 | £2.50 | £6 | |
| Big Four | 7" EP | Philips | BBE12021 | 1956 | £4 | £8 | |
| Big Four | 7" EP | Philips | BE12593 | 1966 | £2 | £5 | |
| Big Four No. 2 | 7" EP | Philips | BBE12040 | 1956 | £4 | £8 | |
| Big Four No. 3 | 7" EP | Philips | BBE12088 | 1956 | £2 | £5 | |
| Big Four No. 4 | 7" EP | Philips | BBE12091 | 1956 | £4 | £8 | |
| Big Four No. 5 | 7" EP | Philips | BBE12114 | 1957 | £2 | £5 | |
| Big Four No. 6 | 7" EP | Philips | BBE12139 | 1957 | £2 | £5 | |
| Big Four No. 7 | 7" EP | Philips | BBE12145 | 1957 | £4 | £8 | |
| Big Four No. 8 | 7" EP | Philips | BBE12158 | 1957 | £2 | £5 | |
| Big Four No. 9 | 7" EP | Philips | BBE12165 | 1957 | £2.50 | £6 | |
| Big Four No. 10 | 7" EP | Philips | BBE12190 | 1958 | £2.50 | £6 | |
| Big Four No. 11 | 7" EP | Philips | BBE12288 | 1959 | £2.50 | £6 | |
| Big Four No. 12 | 7" EP | Philips | BBE12336 | 1959 | £2.50 | £6 | |
| Big Hits Of Mid-America Vol. 1 | LP | Soma | 1245 | 1964 | £25 | £50 | US |
| Big Hits Of Mid-America Vol. 2 | LP | Soma | 1246 | 1965 | £25 | £50 | US |
| Big One | LP | Minit | MML40007E | 1969 | £4 | £10 | |
| Birth Control | LP | Pama | SECO32 | 1970 | £5 | £12 | |
| Bitter End Years | LP | Roxbury | RX3300 | 1976 | £10 | £25 | US triple |
| Black Country Night Out | LP | Broadside | BRO120 | 1976 | £4 | £10 | |
| Black Country Night Out Vol. 2 | LP | Broadside | BRO122 | 1977 | £4 | £10 | |
| Black Diamond Express To Hell | LP | Matchbox | SDX207/8 | 1970 | £5 | £12 | double |
| Black Slacks And Bobby Socks | LP | HMV | CLP1167 | 1958 | £37.50 | £75 | |
| Black, Whites And Blues | LP | CBS | 52796 | 1970 | £4 | £10 | |
| Blackpool Nights | LP | Columbia | 33SX1244 | 1960 | £6 | £15 | |
| Blue Beat Special | LP | Coxsone | CSP1 | 1968 | £25 | £50 | |
| Blue Ridge Mountain Field Trip | LP | Leader | LEA4012 | 1970 | £4 | £10 | |
| Bluebird Blues | LP | RCA | RD7786 | 1966 | £4 | £10 | |
| Bluegrass | 7" EP | Range | JRE7005 | 196– | £2 | £5 | |
| Blues | LP | Chess | CRL4003 | 1964 | £4 | £10 | |
| Blues | LP | Columbia | 33SX1417 | 1962 | £8 | £20 | |
| Blues Anytime Vol. 1 | LP | Immediate | IMLP014 | 1968 | £4 | £10 | |
| Blues Anytime Vol. 2 | LP | Immediate | IMLP015 | 1968 | £4 | £10 | |
| Blues Anytime Vol. 3 | LP | Immediate | IMLP019 | 1968 | £4 | £10 | |
| Blues At Newport | LP | Vanguard | VSD79145 | 1965 | £4 | £10 | US |
| Blues Came Down From Memphis | LP | London | HAS8265 | 1966 | £10 | £25 | |
| Blues Fell This Morning | LP | Philips | BBL7369 | 1960 | £15 | £30 | |
| Blues Festival | 7" EP | Pye | NEP44038 | 1964 | £7.50 | £15 | |
| Blues From Chicago | LP | Python | PLP6 | 1969 | £8 | £20 | |
| Blues From Chicago Vol. 2 | LP | Python | PLP9 | 1970 | £8 | £20 | |
| Blues From Chicago Vol. 3 | LP | Python | PLP15 | 1970 | £8 | £20 | |
| Blues From Maxwell Street | LP | Heritage | 1004 | 196– | £8 | £20 | |
| Blues From The Bayou | LP | Pye | NPL28142 | 1971 | £4 | £10 | |
| Blues From The Windy City | LP | Python | PLP21 | 1971 | £8 | £20 | |
| Blues Is My Companion | LP | Sunflower | no number | 196– | £6 | £15 | |
| Blues Keep Falling | LP | Sunflower | no number | 196– | £6 | £15 | |
| Blues Like Showers Of Rain | LP | Matchbox | SDM142 | 1967 | £25 | £50 | |
| Blues Like Showers Of Rain Vol. 2 | LP | Saydisc | SDM167 | 1968 | £30 | £60 | |
| Blues Now | LP | Decca | LK4681 | 1965 | £10 | £25 | |
| Blues Obscurities Vol. 1 | LP | Blues Obscurities | | 1972 | £8 | £20 | |
| Blues Obscurities Vol. 1 | LP | London | HAU8454 | 1974 | £4 | £10 | |
| Blues Obscurities Vol. 2 | LP | Blues Obscurities | | 1972 | £8 | £20 | |
| Blues Obscurities Vol. 2 | LP | London | HAU8455 | 1974 | £4 | £10 | |
| Blues Obscurities Vol. 3 | LP | Blues Obscurities | | 1972 | £8 | £20 | |
| Blues Obscurities Vol. 3 | LP | London | HAU8456 | 1974 | £4 | £10 | |
| Blues Obscurities Vol. 4 | LP | Blues Obscurities | | 1972 | £8 | £20 | |
| Blues Obscurities Vol. 5 | LP | Blues Obscurities | | 1972 | £8 | £20 | |
| Blues Obscurities Vol. 6 | LP | Blues Obscurities | | 1972 | £8 | £20 | |
| Blues Obscurities Vol. 7 | LP | Blues Obscurities | | 1972 | £8 | £20 | |
| Blues Obscurities Vol. 8 | LP | Blues Obscurities | | 1972 | £8 | £20 | |
| Blues Obscurities Vol. 9 | LP | Blues Obscurities | | 1972 | £8 | £20 | |
| Blues Obscurities Vol. 10 | LP | Blues Obscurities | | 1972 | £8 | £20 | |
| Blues On Parade No. 1 | 7" EP | Columbia | SEG8226 | 1963 | £4 | £8 | |
| Blues Package '69 | LP | Mercury | SMXL77 | 1969 | £4 | £10 | |

| Title | Format | Label | Catalogue | Year | | | Notes |
|---|---|---|---|---|---|---|---|
| Blues People | LP | Highway 51 | H102 | 1969 | £20 | £40 | |
| Blues Piano – Chicago Plus | LP | Atlantic | K40404 | 1972 | £5 | £12 | |
| Blues Potpourri | LP | Kokomo | K1001 | 1968 | £20 | £40 | |
| Blues Rarities Vol. 1 | LP | Rarities | | 1971 | £6 | £15 | double |
| Blues Roots Vol. 1 | LP | Poppy | PYM11001 | 1969 | £5 | £12 | |
| Blues Southside Chicago | LP | Decca | LK4748 | 1966 | £20 | £40 | |
| Blues Today – Southern Style | LP | Python | PLP16 | 1971 | £8 | £20 | |
| Blues Vol. 1 | LP | Pye | NPL28030 | 1964 | £4 | £10 | |
| Blues Vol. 1 | 7" EP | Pye | NEP44029 | 1964 | £5 | £10 | |
| Blues Vol. 1 Pt. 2 | 7" EP | Pye | NEP44035 | 1964 | £5 | £10 | |
| Blues Vol. 2 | LP | Pye | NPL28035 | 1964 | £4 | £10 | |
| Blues Vol. 2 Part 1 | 7" EP | Chess | CRE6011 | 1966 | £5 | £10 | |
| Blues Vol. 3 | LP | Pye | NPL28045 | 1964 | £4 | £10 | |
| Bluescene USA Vol. 1 | LP | Storyville | SLP176 | 1965 | £4 | £10 | |
| Bluescene USA Vol. 2 | LP | Storyville | SLP177 | 1965 | £4 | £10 | |
| Bluescene USA Vol. 3 | LP | Storyville | SLP181 | 1965 | £4 | £10 | |
| Bluescene USA Vol. 4 | LP | Storyville | SLP189 | 1967 | £4 | £10 | |
| Bocastle Breakdown | LP | Topic | 12TS240 | 1974 | £4 | £10 | |
| Bolo Bash | LP | Bolo | BLP8002 | 1964 | £10 | £25 | US |
| Bonnie Lass Come O'er The Burn | LP | Topic | 12T128 | 1965 | £8 | £20 | |
| Bonny North Tyne | LP | Topic | 12TS239 | 1974 | £4 | £10 | |
| Boogie Woogie Rarities | LP | Milestone | MLP2009 | 197– | £4 | £10 | |
| Boogie Woogie With The Blues | 10" LP | London | AL3544 | 1955 | £6 | £15 | |
| Boskoop Project | LP | private | | 1981 | £15 | £30 | Dutch |
| Boss Reggae | LP | Pama | SECO17 | 1969 | £25 | £50 | |
| Both Sides Of The Downs | LP | Eron | 002 | 1974 | £5 | £12 | |
| Bothy Ballads | LP | Tangent | TNGM109 | 1971 | £4 | £10 | |
| Bouquet Of Steel | LP | Aardvark | STEAL2 | 1980 | £4 | £10 | blue vinyl |
| Brave Plough Boy | LP | XTRA | XTRA1150 | 1975 | £8 | £20 | |
| Breeze From Erin | LP | Topic | 12T184 | 1969 | £4 | £10 | |
| Bristol Recorder Vol. 2 | LP | Bristol Recorder | BR002 | 1981 | £5 | £12 | |
| British Blue-Eyed Soul | LP | Island | ILP966/ILPS9066 | 1968 | £15 | £30 | pink label |
| Broadside Ballads Vol. 1 | LP | Broadside | BR301 | 1964 | £6 | £15 | US |
| Brum Beat – Live At The Barrel Organ | LP | Big Bear | BRUM1 | 1979 | £5 | £12 | double |
| Brumbeat | LP | Dial | DLP1 | 1964 | £25 | £50 | |
| Built To Blast | 7" | Fierce Panda | NING04 | 1994 | £2.50 | £6 | double |
| Bumper Bundle – 16 Hits | LP | Decca | LK4734 | 1965 | £6 | £15 | |
| Burghers Vol. 1 | LP | private | 304083 | 1983 | £5 | £12 | US |
| Buskers | LP | Columbia | SX/SCX6356 | 1969 | £10 | £25 | |
| Busted At Oz | LP | Autumn | AU2 | 1981 | £6 | £15 | |
| Buttons And Bows Vol. 1 | LP | Dambusters | DAM003 | 1984 | £6 | £15 | double |
| Buttons And Bows Vol. 2 | LP | Dambusters | DAM006 | 1985 | £6 | £15 | double |
| Bye Bye Birdie | 7" EP | Pye | NEP24142 | 1961 | £2 | £5 | |
| Cabaret Night In Paris | 7" EP | Columbia | 33S1083 | 1956 | £2 | £5 | |
| Cabaret Night In Paris No. 4 | 7" EP | Columbia | 33S1099 | 1957 | £2 | £5 | |
| Cabaret Night In Paris No. 5 | 7" EP | Columbia | 33S1105 | 1957 | £2 | £5 | |
| California Acid Folk | LP | Penguin Egg | 11/12 | 1985 | £10 | £25 | US double |
| California Christmas | LP | Penguin Egg | 6/7 | 1983 | £10 | £25 | US double |
| California Christmas Vol. 2 | LP | Penguin Egg | 9/10 | 1983 | £10 | £25 | US double |
| California Halloween | LP | Penguin Egg | | 198– | £10 | £25 | US double |
| California New Year | LP | Penguin Egg | | 198– | £10 | £25 | US double |
| Calypso Time | 7" EP | Melodisc | EPM767 | 1956 | £2 | £5 | |
| Cameo Big Four | 7" EP | Cameo Parkway | CPE552 | 1963 | £2.50 | £6 | |
| Canny Newcassel | LP | Topic | 12TS219 | 1972 | £8 | £20 | |
| Carolina Country Blues | LP | Flyright | LP505 | 1973 | £4 | £10 | |
| Cerne Box Set | LP | Cerne | CERNE123 | 198– | £15 | £30 | 3 LPs, boxed |
| Changes | LP | Magistral | 2000 | 1980 | £50 | £100 | US |
| Chaplin Revue | LP | Brunswick | LAT8345 | 1960 | £6 | £15 | |
| Charge Of The Light Brigade | LP | United Artists | UAS5177 | 1968 | £4 | £10 | US |
| Chicago – The Blues Today | LP | Fontana | TFL6068 | 1966 | £6 | £15 | |
| Chicago – The Blues Today Vol. 1 | LP | Vanguard | SVRL19020 | 1969 | £6 | £15 | |
| Chicago – The Blues Today Vol. 2 | LP | Fontana | TFL6069 | 1966 | £6 | £15 | |
| Chicago – The Blues Today Vol. 2 | LP | Vanguard | SVRL19021 | 1969 | £6 | £15 | |
| Chicago – The Blues Today Vol. 3 | LP | Fontana | TFL6070 | 1966 | £6 | £15 | |
| Chicago – The Blues Today Vol. 3 | LP | Vanguard | SVRL19022 | 1969 | £6 | £15 | |
| Chicago House Bands | LP | Sunflower | ET1401 | 1968 | £6 | £15 | |
| Chicago Sessions Vol. 1 | LP | Kokomo | K1005 | 1969 | £15 | £30 | |
| Chicken Stuff | LP | Flyright | LP4700 | 1970 | £4 | £10 | |
| Chocolate Soup For Diabetics Vol. 1 | LP | Relics | LSD1 | 1980 | £10 | £25 | |
| Chocolate Soup For Diabetics Vol. 2 | LP | Relics | ACID1 | 1981 | £10 | £25 | |
| Chocolate Soup For Diabetics Vol. 3 | LP | Relics | CSFD3 | 198– | £10 | £25 | |
| Chosen Few Vol. 1 | LP | A-Go-Go | 1966 | 1982 | £25 | £50 | US |
| Chosen Few Vol. 2 | LP | Tom-Tom | 3752 | 1983 | £25 | £50 | US |
| Christmas | 10" LP | Philips | BBR8112 | 1957 | £4 | £10 | |
| Christmas Dedication | LP | Chess | CRLS4541 | 1968 | £4 | £10 | |
| Christmas Reggae | 7" EP | Coxsone | SCE1 | 1967 | £20 | £40 | |
| Classic Scots Ballads | LP | Tangent | TNGM199D | 1975 | £6 | £15 | double |
| Classics Of Irish Traditional Music | LP | Morning Star | 45001 | 1973 | £5 | £12 | US |
| Club Rock Steady | LP | Trojan | TTL54 | 1970 | £8 | £20 | |
| Club Rock Steady '68 | LP | Island | ILP965 | 1968 | £30 | £60 | pink label |
| Club Ska '67 | LP | Island | ILP948 | 1967 | £25 | £50 | |
| Club Ska '67 Vol. 2 | LP | Island | ILP956 | 1967 | £30 | £60 | |
| Club Ska Vol. 1 | LP | Trojan | TTL48 | 1970 | £8 | £20 | |
| Club Ska Vol. 2 | LP | Trojan | TTL51 | 1970 | £8 | £20 | |
| Club Soul | LP | Island | ILP964 | 1968 | £10 | £25 | pink label |
| Club Spangle No. 1 | 7" | Fierce Panda | SPANG01 | 1994 | £2.50 | £6 | |

| Title | Format | Label | Catalogue | Year | | | Notes |
|---|---|---|---|---|---|---|---|
| Coca Cola | LP | Coca Cola | PD2945 | 1980 | £15 | £30 | ... German picture disc |
| Collection Of 16 Big Hits Vol. 6 | LP | Tamla Motown | (S)TML11074 | 1968 | £5 | £12 | |
| Collection Of 16 Original Big Hits Vol. 4 | LP | Tamla Motown | TML11043 | 1967 | £8 | £20 | |
| Collection Of 16 Original Big Hits Vol. 5 | LP | Tamla Motown | TML11050 | 1967 | £5 | £12 | |
| Collection Of 16 Tamla Motown Hits | LP | Tamla Motown | TML11001 | 1965 | £10 | £25 | |
| Collection Of Big Hits Vol. 7 | LP | Tamla Motown | (S)TML11092 | 1969 | £4 | £10 | |
| Collectors Blues Series Vol. 1 | LP | Chicago | 202 | 1975 | £6 | £15 | |
| Collectors Blues Series Vol. 2 | LP | Chicago | 205 | 1975 | £6 | £15 | |
| Collectors Blues Series Vol. 3 | LP | Chicago | 210 | 1975 | £6 | £15 | |
| Collectors Blues Series Vol. 4 | LP | Chicago | 212 | 1975 | £6 | £15 | |
| Collectors Blues Series Vol. 5 | LP | Chicago | 213 | 1975 | £6 | £15 | |
| Collectors Items Vol. 1 | 10" LP | London | AL3514 | 1954 | £4 | £10 | |
| Collectors Items Vol. 2 | 10" LP | London | AL3533 | 1954 | £4 | £10 | |
| Collectors Items Vol. 3 | 10" LP | London | AL3550 | 1956 | £4 | £10 | |
| Come Fly With Me | LP | Blue Beat | BBLP803 | 1964 | £50 | £100 | |
| Connecticut's Greatest Hits | LP | Co-op | CP101 | 1968 | £10 | £25 | US |
| Cool Music For A Hot Night | LP | Tempo | TAP10 | 1957 | £10 | £25 | |
| Country & Western Hits Vol. 1 | 7" EP | CBS | AGG20033 | 1963 | £2 | £5 | |
| Country & Western Hits Vol. 2 | 7" EP | CBS | AGG20041 | 1964 | £2 | £5 | |
| Country And Western | 7" EP | Range | JRE7001 | 196– | £2 | £5 | |
| Country And Western | 7" EP | Range | JRE7004 | 196– | £2 | £5 | |
| Country And Western Express Vol. 1 | 7" EP | Top Rank | JKP2055 | 1960 | £2 | £5 | |
| Country And Western Express Vol. 4 | 7" EP | Top Rank | JKP2063 | 1960 | £2 | £5 | |
| Country And Western Express Vol. 6 | 7" EP | Top Rank | JKP2065 | 1960 | £5 | £10 | |
| Country And Western Golden Hit Parade Vol. 1 | LP | London | HAB8145 | 1964 | £4 | £10 | |
| Country And Western Golden Hit Parade Vol. 2 | LP | London | HAB8146 | 1964 | £4 | £10 | |
| Country And Western Showcase Vol. 2 | 7" EP | Hickory | LPE1505 | 1965 | £2 | £5 | |
| Country And Western Spectacular | 7" EP | Philips | BBE12149 | 1957 | £4 | £8 | |
| Country And Western Trail Blazers No. 1 | 7" EP | Mercury | ZEP10038 | 1959 | £2.50 | £6 | |
| Country Blues | LP | RBF | RF1 | 1961 | £6 | £15 | |
| Country Blues | 7" EP | Heritage | 105 | 196– | £7.50 | £15 | |
| Country Blues Vol. 2 | LP | RBF | RBF9 | 1964 | £6 | £15 | |
| Country Favourites Vol. 1 | 10" LP | Brunswick | LA8729 | 1956 | £4 | £10 | |
| Country Guitar Hall Of Fame | LP | London | HAB8243 | 1965 | £4 | £10 | |
| Country Guitar Vol. 1 | 7" EP | RCA | RCX107 | 1958 | £2 | £5 | |
| Country Guitar Vol. 2 | 7" EP | RCA | RCX110 | 1958 | £2 | £5 | |
| Country Guitar Vol. 5 | 7" EP | RCA | RCX127 | 1959 | £2 | £5 | |
| Country Guitar Vol. 6 | 7" EP | RCA | RCX141 | 1959 | £2 | £5 | |
| Country Guitar Vol. 8 | 7" EP | RCA | RCX147 | 1959 | £2 | £5 | |
| Country Guitar Vol. 9 | 7" EP | RCA | RCX159 | 1959 | £2 | £5 | |
| Country Guitar Vol. 10 | 7" EP | RCA | RCX176 | 1959 | £2 | £5 | |
| Country Guitar Vol. 11 | 7" EP | RCA | RCX177 | 1959 | £2 | £5 | |
| Country Guitar Vol. 12 | 7" EP | RCA | RCX185 | 1960 | £2 | £5 | |
| Country Jubilee Vol. 1 | 7" EP | Decca | DFE8522 | 1963 | £2 | £5 | |
| Country Jubilee Vol. 2 | 7" EP | Decca | DFE8523 | 1963 | £2 | £5 | |
| Crab – Biggest Hits | LP | Pama | ECO2 | 1969 | £8 | £20 | |
| Crazed And Confused | 7" | Fierce Panda | NING02 | 1994 | £10 | £20 | double |
| Damn Yankees | 7" EP | Mercury | MEP9509 | 1956 | £2 | £5 | |
| Dance Craze | 7" EP | Capitol | EAP1518 | 1955 | £2.50 | £6 | |
| Dancebusters Volume One | CD | Wau! Mr. Modo | WAMCD002 | 1990 | £5 | £12 | |
| Dancing Down Orange Street | LP | Big Shot | BSLP5002 | 1968 | £25 | £50 | |
| Dandelion Sampler | 7" | Dandelion | DS7001 | 1971 | £1.50 | £4 | |
| Dark Horse Records '76 | LP | Dark Horse | DH1 | 1976 | £20 | £40 | promo |
| Dark Muddy Bottom | 7" EP | XX | MIN706 | 196– | £2.50 | £6 | |
| Decade Of The Blues – The 1950's | LP | Highway 51 | H100 | 1966 | £20 | £40 | |
| Decade Of The Blues – The 1950's Vol. 2 | LP | Highway 51 | H104 | 1966 | £15 | £30 | |
| Decca Showcase Vol. 5 | 10" LP | Decca | LF1265 | 1955 | £4 | £10 | |
| Deep In My Heart | 7" EP | MGM | MGMEP652 | 1958 | £2 | £5 | |
| Demention Of Sound: British Beat And R&B From 1964-65 | LP | Feedback | LESSON1 | 1983 | £8 | £20 | |
| Depression Blues | 7" EP | Poydras | 102 | 195– | £4 | £8 | |
| Devastate To Liberate | LP | YANGKI | 1 | 1985 | £4 | £10 | |
| Diana's Rooten Tooten Rock And Roll Party | LP | Romulan | UFOX01 | 198– | £10 | £25 | US |
| Ding Dong Dollar Anti-Polaris And Scottish Republican Songs | LP | Folkways | FD5444 | 1962 | £8 | £20 | US |
| Dingles Regatta | LP | Dingles | DIN301 | 1976 | £4 | £10 | |
| Dirt Blues | LP | Minit | MLL/MLS40005 | 1969 | £6 | £15 | |
| Dirty Water – The History Of Eastern Iowa Rock Vol. 2 | LP | Unlimited Productions | RRRLP003 | 1986 | £5 | £12 | US |
| Disc A Dawn | LP | BBC | REC65M | 1970 | £6 | £15 | |
| Discs A Go Go | 7" EP | Decca | DFE8520 | 1962 | £7.50 | £15 | |
| Doctor Soul | LP | Island | ILP943 | 1967 | £15 | £30 | |
| Down Home Blues – Sixties Style | 7" EP | Jan & Dil | JR450 | 196– | £2.50 | £6 | |
| Down In Hogan's Alley | LP | Flyright | LP4703 | 1971 | £4 | £10 | |
| Downhome Blues | LP | Python | | 1970 | £8 | £20 | |
| Downhome Blues Vol. 2 | LP | Python | PLP14 | 1970 | £8 | £20 | |
| Downhome Blues Vol. 3 | LP | Python | PLP22 | 1971 | £8 | £20 | |
| Downhome Harp | 7" EP | XX | MIN709 | 196– | £2 | £5 | |
| Dr. Kitch | LP | Island | ILP954 | 1967 | £20 | £40 | |
| Drumbeat | LP | Parlophone | PMC1101 | 1959 | £10 | £25 | |
| Drumbeat | 7" EP | Fontana | TFE17146 | 1959 | £7.50 | £15 | |
| Duke And The Peacock | LP | Island | ILP976 | 1968 | £25 | £50 | pink label |
| Duke Reid's Golden Hits | LP | Trojan | TTL8 | 1969 | £8 | £20 | |
| Duke Reid's Rock Steady | LP | Island | ILP958 | 1967 | £50 | £100 | pink label |

| Title | Format | Label | Cat. No. | Year | Price 1 | Price 2 | Notes |
|---|---|---|---|---|---|---|---|
| Duke Reid's Rock Steady | LP | Trojan | TTL53 | 1970 | £15 | £30 | |
| Dulcimer Players | LP | Transatlantic | LTRA502 | 1978 | £4 | £10 | |
| Dungeon Folk | LP | BBC | REC355 | 1969 | £5 | £12 | |
| Ear-Piercing Punk | LP | Trash | 0001 | 1983 | £10 | £25 | US |
| Early Blues Vol. 1 | LP | Saydisc | SDR199 | 1970 | £4 | £10 | |
| Early Blues Vol. 2 | LP | Saydisc | SDR206 | 1970 | £4 | £10 | |
| Early Chicago | LP | Happy Tiger | HT1017 | 1972 | £6 | £15 | US |
| Earthed | LP | Middle Earth | MDLS20 | 1970 | £25 | £50 | |
| East | LP | Dead Good | GOOD1 | 1980 | £5 | £12 | |
| East Vernon Blues | LP | Southern Sound | SD200 | 1973 | £8 | £20 | |
| Easy Rider | LP | Stateside | SSL5018 | 1969 | £4 | £10 | |
| Echoes In Time Vol. 1 | LP | Solar | S000 | 1983 | £10 | £25 | US |
| Echoes In Time Vol. 1 | LP | Solar | SR2000 | 1983 | £10 | £25 | US |
| Edinburgh Folk Festival | LP | Decca | LK4546 | 1963 | £25 | £50 | |
| Edinburgh Folk Festival Vol. 2 | LP | Decca | LK4563 | 1964 | £30 | £60 | |
| Edinburgh Students Charity Appeal | 7" EP | E.S.C. | ESC02 | 1965 | £10 | £20 | |
| Edinburgh Students Charity Appeal | 7" EP | E.S.C. | ESC03 | 1966 | £10 | £20 | |
| Electric Blues | LP | Chess | 109597/8/9 | 1969 | £15 | £30 | German, 3 LPs in metal box |
| Electric Muse | LP | Island/ Transatlantic | FOLK1001 | 1975 | £20 | £40 | 4 LP set |
| Electric Newspaper | LP | ESP-Disk | 1034 | 1966 | £25 | £50 | US |
| Electric Sugar Cube Flashbacks | LP | Archive International Productions | AIP10008 | 1983 | £6 | £15 | |
| Electric Sugar Cube Flashbacks Vol. 2 | LP | Archive International Productions | AIP10010 | 1983 | £6 | £15 | |
| Endless Journey Phase 1 | LP | Psycho | 1 | 1982 | £10 | £25 | US |
| Endless Journey Phase 2 | LP | Psycho | 3 | 1983 | £10 | £25 | US |
| Endless Journey Phase 3 | LP | Psycho | 19 | 1983 | £6 | £15 | US |
| England's Greatest Hitmakers | LP | London | LL3430 | 1968 | £20 | £40 | US |
| English Country Music | LP | Topic | 12T296 | 1976 | £4 | £10 | |
| English Country Music From East Anglia | LP | Topic | 12TS229 | 1973 | £4 | £10 | |
| English Melodeon Players | LP | Plant Life | PLR073 | 1986 | £4 | £10 | |
| Epitaph For A Legend | LP | International Artists | 13 | 1980 | £10 | £25 | US double |
| Esquire's Jazz | LP | RCA | RD7904 | 1967 | £4 | £10 | |
| Eternity Project One | CD | Gee Street | GEEACD002 | 1989 | £8 | £20 | |
| European Song Cup 1963 | 7" EP | Decca | DFE8534 | 1963 | £2 | £5 | |
| Every Day I Have The Blues | LP | Speciality | SPE6601 | 1967 | £4 | £10 | |
| Everything's Alright | LP | Decca | SLK16333P | 1964 | £20 | £40 | German |
| Everywhere Chainsaw Sound | LP | CSR | 001 | 1982 | £50 | £100 | US |
| Everywhere Interferences | LP | Chanesaw Sound | CSR002 | 1983 | £25 | £50 | US |
| Excello Story | LP | Blue Horizon | 2683007 | 1972 | £30 | £60 | double |
| Explosive Rocksteady | LP | Amalgamated | AMGLP2002 | 1968 | £25 | £50 | |
| Extracts From Stiff's Greatest Hits | 7" | Stiff | FREEBIE2 | 1978 | £2.50 | £6 | |
| Ey Up Mi Duck! A Celebration Of Derbyshire | LP | RAM | 1 | 1978 | £4 | £10 | |
| Fantastic Folk | LP | Elektra | EUK259 | 1968 | £4 | £10 | |
| Farewell Nancy | LP | Topic | 12T110 | 1964 | £8 | £20 | |
| Fashioned To A Device Behind A Tree | LP | Come Organisation | WDC881021 | 198- | £30 | £60 | |
| FCU (Folk Centrum Utrecht) '69 | LP | private | | 1969 | £100 | £200 | Dutch |
| Feast Of Irish Folk | LP | Polydor | 2475605 | 1977 | £4 | £10 | Irish |
| Festival Of British Jazz | LP | Decca | LK4180 | 1957 | £6 | £15 | |
| Festival Of The Blues Vol. 1 | 7" EP | Pye | NEP44030 | 1964 | £5 | £10 | |
| Fifteen Flaming Groovies | CD | Fire | FIRECD19 | 1989 | £5 | £12 | promo only |
| Fifteen Oldies But Goodies | LP | Melodisc | MS4 | 196- | £4 | £10 | |
| Fifth Pipe Dream | LP | San Francisco Sound | 11680 | 1968 | £37.50 | £75 | US |
| Filling The Gap | LP | Obscure World | 001 | 1989 | £20 | £40 | US 4 LP boxed set |
| Fillmore Last Days | LP | Warner Bros | K66013 | 1972 | £15 | £30 | boxed set, with booklet, ticket, poster |
| Fillmore Last Days | LP | Warner Bros | K66013 | 1972 | £25 | £50 | promo boxed set with interview single |
| Fingers On Fire | LP | London | HAB8205 | 1965 | £4 | £10 | |
| Fings Ain't Wot They Used To Be | LP | HMV | CLP1358/CSD1298 | 1960 | £6 | £15 | |
| Firepoint | LP | Spark | SRLM2003 | 1969 | £8 | £20 | |
| First Lame Bunny Album | LP | Spaceward | 3S1/EDENLP53 | 1973 | £6 | £15 | |
| First National Skiffle Contest | 10" LP | Esquire | 20089 | 1957 | £8 | £20 | |
| First O T'Sort | LP | Transatlantic | LTRA505 | 1978 | £4 | £10 | |
| First Rock 'n' Roll Party | 10" LP | Mercury | MPT7512 | 1956 | £6 | £15 | |
| Flashback Vol. 1 | LP | Flashback | 1001 | 1980 | £10 | £25 | US |
| Flashback Vol. 2 | LP | Flashback | 1002 | 1980 | £10 | £25 | US |
| Flashback Vol. 3 | LP | Flashback | 1003 | 1981 | £25 | £50 | US |
| Flashback Vol. 4 | LP | Flashback | 1004 | 1981 | £25 | £50 | US |
| Flashback Vol. 5 | LP | Flashback | 1005 | 1982 | £25 | £50 | US |
| Flashback Vol. 6 | LP | Flashback | 1006 | 1982 | £25 | £50 | US |
| Fleadh Ceoil 1975 | LP | Dolphin | DOLM5013 | 1975 | £5 | £12 | Irish |
| Folk At The Black Horse | LP | Eron | 012 | 1976 | £4 | £10 | |
| Folk At The Wren | LP | private | | 1969 | £50 | £100 | |
| Folk Box | LP | Elektra | EUK251/2 | 1966 | £5 | £12 | double |
| Folk Centrum Utrecht 1970 | LP | private | | 1970 | £100 | £200 | Dutch |
| Folk Festival | LP | World Record Club | ST890 | 1964 | £8 | £20 | |

| Title | Format | Label | Catalogue | Year | Price | Price | Notes |
|---|---|---|---|---|---|---|---|
| Folk Festival At Newport 1959 Vol. 1 | LP | Top Rank | 35070 | 1960 | £6 | £15 | |
| Folk Festival At Newport 1959 Vol. 2 | LP | Top Rank | 35071 | 1960 | £6 | £15 | |
| Folk Festival At Newport 1959 Vol. 3 | LP | Top Rank | 35072 | 1960 | £6 | £15 | |
| Folk Festival At Newport Vol. 1 | LP | Fontana | TFL6000 | 1962 | £6 | £15 | |
| Folk Festival At Newport Vol. 2 | LP | Fontana | TFL6004 | 1962 | £6 | £15 | |
| Folk Festival At Newport Vol. 3 | LP | Fontana | TFL6009 | 1962 | £6 | £15 | |
| Folk Festival Of The Blues | LP | Pye | NPL28033 | 1964 | £6 | £15 | |
| Folk From McTavish's Kitchen | LP | Counterpoint | CPT3994 | 1973 | £5 | £12 | |
| Folk Now | LP | Decca | LK4683 | 1965 | £10 | £25 | |
| Folk On Friday | LP | BBC | REC955 | 1970 | £10 | £25 | |
| Folk Song Today | 10" LP | HMV | DLP1143 | 1957 | £20 | £40 | |
| Folk Songs Of Britain Vol. 1 | LP | Topic | 12T157 | 1966 | £5 | £12 | |
| Folk Songs Of Britain Vol. 2 | LP | Topic | 12T158 | 1966 | £5 | £12 | |
| Folk Songs Of Britain Vol. 3 | LP | Topic | 12T159 | 1966 | £5 | £12 | |
| Folk Songs Of Britain Vol. 4 | LP | Topic | 12T160 | 1966 | £5 | £12 | |
| Folk Songs Of Britain Vol. 5 | LP | Topic | 12T161 | 1966 | £5 | £12 | |
| Folk Songs Of Britain Vol. 6 | LP | Topic | 12T194 | 1969 | £5 | £12 | |
| Folk Songs Of Britain Vol. 7 | LP | Topic | 12T195 | 1969 | £5 | £12 | |
| Folk Songs Of Britain Vol. 8 | LP | Topic | 12T196 | 1969 | £5 | £12 | |
| Folk Songs Of Britain Vol. 9 | LP | Topic | 12T197 | 1969 | £5 | £12 | |
| Folk Songs Of Britain Vol. 10 | LP | Topic | 12T198 | 1969 | £5 | £12 | |
| Folk Trailer | LP | Trailer | LER2019 | 1970 | £5 | £12 | |
| Folksound Of Britain | LP | HMV | CLP1910 | 1965 | £8 | £20 | |
| Folksound Of Britain | 7" EP | HMV | 7EG8911 | 1965 | £7.50 | £15 | |
| Four Bob Dylan Songs | 7" EP | Riviera | 231160 | 1966 | £10 | £20 | French |
| Four Great Movie Themes | 7" EP | Philips | BBE12140 | 1957 | £4 | £8 | |
| Four Of The Tops | 7" EP | Pye | NEP24300 | 1968 | £2 | £5 | |
| Fourteen | LP | Decca | LK4695 | 1965 | £6 | £15 | |
| Freak Out USA | LP | Sidewalk | 5901 | 1967 | £6 | £15 | US |
| Freedom Sounds | LP | Bamboo | BLP205 | 1970 | £20 | £40 | |
| Fresh From The Can | LP | Polydor | 2675004 | 1970 | £10 | £25 | German, 3 LPs in metal box |
| From Bam Bam To Cherry Oh Baby | LP | Trojan | TRL51 | 1972 | £4 | £10 | |
| From Greer To Eternity | 7" | Fierce Panda | NING05 | 1994 | £2 | £5 | double |
| From Torture To Conscience | LP | New European | BADVC666 | 198– | £5 | £12 | |
| Funky Chicken | LP | Trojan | TBL137 | 1970 | £6 | £15 | |
| Funky Reggae | LP | Bamboo | BLP206 | 1970 | £15 | £30 | |
| Fylde Acoustic | LP | Trailer | LER2105 | 1977 | £8 | £20 | |
| Garage Punk Unknowns Vol. 1 | LP | Stone Age | no number | 1985 | £10 | £25 | US, black and white sleeve |
| Garage Punk Unknowns Vol. 2 | LP | Stone Age | no number | 1985 | £10 | £25 | US, black and white sleeve |
| Garage Punk Unknowns Vol. 3 | LP | Stone Age | no number | 1985 | £10 | £25 | US, black and white sleeve |
| Garage Punk Unknowns Vol. 4 | LP | Stone Age | no number | 1985 | £10 | £25 | US, black and white sleeve |
| Garage Punk Unknowns Vol. 5 | LP | Stone Age | SA665 | 1986 | £10 | £25 | US, black and white sleeve |
| Garage Punk Unknowns Vol. 6 | LP | Stone Age | SA666 | 1986 | £10 | £25 | US, black and white sleeve |
| Garage Punk Unknowns Vol. 7 | LP | Stone Age | SA667 | 1986 | £10 | £25 | US, black and white sleeve |
| Garage Zone Box Set | LP | Moxie | MLP16/17/20/21/1055 | 1990 | £20 | £40 | US, 4 LP plus 1 EP boxed set |
| Gas – Greatest Hits | LP | Pama | ECO4 | 1969 | £8 | £20 | |
| Gathering At The Depot | LP | Beta | S80471414S | 1970 | £20 | £40 | US |
| Gathering Of The Tribe | LP | Bona Fide | 5913330001 | 1982 | £25 | £50 | US |
| Gathering Of The Tribe 4 | LP | Myst | 001 | 1987 | £10 | £25 | US |
| Gayfeet | LP | Doctor Bird | DLM5001 | 1966 | £37.50 | £75 | |
| Gene Norman's Just Jazz | LP | Vogue | LAE12001 | 1955 | £8 | £20 | |
| Genesis – Memphis To Chicago | LP | Chess | 6641125 | 1973 | £20 | £40 | 4 LPs, boxed |
| Genesis – Sweet Home Chicago | LP | Chess | 6641174 | 1975 | £20 | £40 | 4 LPs, boxed |
| Genesis – The Beginnings Of Rock | LP | Chess | 6641047 | 1972 | £20 | £40 | 4 LPs, boxed |
| Georgia Guitars 1927 – 1938 | LP | Kokomo | K1004 | 1969 | £15 | £30 | |
| Get Ready Rock Steady | LP | Coxsone | CSL8007 | 1967 | £50 | £100 | |
| Giants Of Modern Jazz | LP | Concert Hall | BJ1204 | 1955 | £5 | £12 | |
| Gift From Pama | LP | Pama | SECO20 | 1970 | £8 | £20 | |
| Girls And More Girls | 7" EP | MGM | MGMEP703 | 1959 | £2 | £5 | |
| Glastonbury Fayre | LP | Revelation | REV1 | 1974 | £50 | £100 | triple, 4 inserts, printed polythene outer |
| Glimpses Vol. 1 | LP | Wellington | 201085 | 1982 | £25 | £50 | US |
| Glimpses Vol. 2 | LP | Wellington | no number | 1982 | £25 | £50 | US |
| Glimpses Vol. 3 | LP | Wellington | no number | 1983 | £10 | £25 | US |
| Glimpses Vol. 4 | LP | Wellington | W1004 | 1989 | £6 | £15 | US |
| Go | LP | Columbia | SX6062 | 1966 | £15 | £30 | |
| Goin' Away Walkin' | LP | Flyright | LP103 | 1972 | £4 | £10 | |
| Goin' Back To Chicago | LP | Python | LP1 | 1970 | £8 | £20 | |
| Goin' Up The Country | LP | Decca | LK4931 | 1968 | £4 | £10 | |
| Going To California | LP | Heritage | 1003 | 196– | £8 | £20 | |
| Gold | LP | Mother | MO4001 | 1972 | £15 | £30 | |
| Golden Hits | LP | Philips | BBL7331 | 1959 | £5 | £12 | |
| Golden Hits Vol. 2 | LP | Philips | BBL7422 | 1960 | £4 | £10 | |
| Golden Hits Vol. 3 | LP | Philips | BBL7581 | 1961 | £5 | £12 | |
| Golden Pops | LP | Deram | SML1027 | 1968 | £10 | £25 | |
| Gonks Go Beat | LP | Decca | LK4673 | 1965 | £25 | £50 | |
| Good Folk Of Kent | LP | Eron | 004 | 1975 | £25 | £50 | |
| Good Time Music | LP | Elektra | EUK/EUKS7260 | 1967 | £8 | £20 | |

| Title | Format | Label | Cat. No. | Year | | | Notes |
|---|---|---|---|---|---|---|---|
| Gospel Sound | LP | CBS | 67234 | 1972 | £6 | £15 | double |
| Grand Airs Of Connemara | LP | Topic | 12T177 | 1968 | £4 | £10 | |
| Grand Old Fifties | LP | Atlantic | ATL5004 | 1964 | £8 | £20 | |
| Greasy Truckers Live At Dingwalls Dance Hall | LP | Greasy Truckers | GT4997 | 1973 | £6 | £15 | double |
| Greasy Truckers Party | LP | United Artists | UDX203/4 | 1974 | £6 | £15 | double |
| Great Blues Singers | LP | Riverside | RLP12121 | 1961 | £5 | £12 | |
| Great Blues Singers | 10" LP | London | AL3530 | 1954 | £8 | £20 | |
| Great Country And Western Hits | 7" EP | Philips | BBE12318 | 1959 | £2.50 | £6 | |
| Great White Dap | 7" EP | Village Thing | VTSX1000 | 1970 | £7.50 | £15 | |
| Greater Jamaica | LP | Trojan | TBL111 | 1970 | £8 | £20 | |
| Greatest Jamaican Beat | LP | Doctor Bird | DLM5009 | 1967 | £37.50 | £75 | |
| Greatest On Stage | 7" EP | Pye | NEP44054 | 1966 | £2.50 | £6 | |
| Grooving With Bamboo | LP | Bamboo | BDLP215 | 1971 | £15 | £30 | |
| Group Beat '63 | LP | Realm | RM149 | 1963 | £10 | £25 | |
| Group Of Goodies | LP | London | HAU8086 | 1963 | £6 | £15 | |
| Group Of Goodies | 7" EP | London | REU1393 | 1963 | £5 | £10 | |
| Groups Galore | 7" EP | Mercury | ZEP10010 | 1959 | £30 | £60 | |
| Gulf Coast Blues | LP | Sunnyland | KS102 | 1971 | £6 | £15 | |
| Guns Of Navarone | LP | Trojan | TTL16 | 1969 | £8 | £20 | |
| Guy Stevens' Testament Of Rock 'n' Roll | LP | Island | ILP977 | 1968 | £8 | £20 | pink label |
| Guys And Dolls | 7" EP | Philips | BBE12077 | 1956 | £2 | £5 | |
| Hallucinations Off 2 – Psychedelic Underground | LP | Elektra/Metronome | KMLP310 | 1969 | £10 | £25 | German picture disc |
| Handmade Films Music – The Tenth Anniversary | CD | Handmade Films | no number | 1988 | £50 | £100 | promo only |
| Harlem Piano Roll | 10" LP | London | AL3553 | 1956 | £6 | £15 | |
| Harvest Sampler | LP | Harvest | HARSPSLP118 | 1969 | £30 | £60 | promo |
| Havin' A Good Time – Chicago Blues Anthology | LP | Sunnyland | KS101 | 1971 | £6 | £15 | |
| Headline News | LP | Polydor | 582701 | 1966 | £4 | £10 | |
| Heads Together, First Round | LP | Vertigo | 6360045 | 1971 | £5 | £12 | double, spiral label |
| Heather And Glen | LP | Tradition | TLP1047 | 1963 | £6 | £15 | US |
| Heavy Christmas | LP | Pilz | 15211142 | 1971 | £20 | £40 | German |
| Here Come The Girls | LP | Pye | NPL18122 | 1965 | £4 | £10 | |
| Here Comes The Duke | LP | Trojan | TRL6 | 1968 | £15 | £30 | |
| Hey Boy Hey Girl | LP | Pama | PSP1002 | 1969 | £8 | £20 | |
| Hickory Showcase Vol. 1 | 7" EP | Hickory | LPE1500 | 1964 | £2 | £5 | |
| Highway To Heaven | LP | Parlophone | PMC1085 | 1959 | £5 | £12 | |
| Hillside '66 | LP | Hillside | 2520961 | 1966 | £180 | £300 | US |
| Hipsville 29 B.C. | LP | Kramden | KRANMAR101 | 1983 | £10 | £25 | US |
| Hipsville 29 B.C. Vol. 2 | LP | Kramden | KRANMAR102 | 1985 | £6 | £15 | US |
| Hipsville Vol. 3 | LP | Kramden | KRANMAR103 | 1986 | £6 | £15 | US |
| History Of Jazz Part 1 | 10" LP | Capitol | LC6507 | 1951 | £6 | £15 | |
| History Of Jazz Part 2 | 10" LP | Capitol | LC6508 | 1951 | £6 | £15 | |
| History Of Northwest Rock Vol. 1 | LP | Great Northwest | GNW4003 | 1976 | £6 | £15 | US |
| History Of Northwest Rock Vol. 2 | LP | Great Northwest | GNW4008 | 1977 | £6 | £15 | US |
| History Of Northwest Rock Vol. 3 | LP | Great Northwest | GNW4009 | 1981 | £6 | £15 | US |
| History Of Northwest Rock Vol. 4 | LP | Great Northwest | GNW4010 | 1983 | £6 | £15 | US |
| History Of R&B Vol. 1 | LP | Atlantic | 587094 | 1968 | £4 | £10 | |
| History Of R&B Vol. 2 | LP | Atlantic | 587095 | 1968 | £4 | £10 | |
| History Of R&B Vol. 3 | LP | Atlantic | 587096 | 1968 | £4 | £10 | |
| History Of R&B Vol. 4 | LP | Atlantic | 587097 | 1968 | £4 | £10 | |
| History Of R&B Vol. 5 | LP | Atlantic | 587140 | 1968 | £4 | £10 | |
| History Of R&B Vol. 6 | LP | Atlantic | 587141 | 1968 | £4 | £10 | |
| History Of Ska Vol. 1 | LP | Bamboo | BDLP203 | 1969 | £20 | £40 | |
| Hit Parade | 7" EP | Brunswick | OE9340 | 1957 | £2 | £5 | |
| Hit Parade Of 1956 | 10" LP | Pye | NPT19015 | 1957 | £5 | £12 | |
| Hit Parade Vol. 1 | 7" EP | Mercury | MEP9003 | 1956 | £5 | £10 | |
| Hit Parade Vol. 2 | 7" EP | Brunswick | OE9450 | 1959 | £2 | £5 | |
| Hit Parade Vol. 2 | 7" EP | Mercury | MEP9510 | 1956 | £5 | £10 | |
| Hit The Road Stax | LP | Stax | 589005 | 1967 | £5 | £12 | |
| Hitmakers | LP | Jerden | 7005 | 1965 | £6 | £15 | US |
| Hitmakers | 7" EP | Piccadilly | NEP34100 | 1966 | £2 | £5 | |
| Hitmakers International | 7" EP | Pye | NEP44065 | 1966 | £2.50 | £6 | |
| Hitmakers No. 1 | 7" EP | Pye | NEP24213 | 1965 | £2 | £5 | |
| Hitmakers No. 2 | 7" EP | Pye | NEP24214 | 1965 | £4 | £8 | |
| Hitmakers No. 3 | 7" EP | Pye | NEP24215 | 1965 | £2.50 | £6 | |
| Hitmakers Vol. 1 | 7" EP | Pye | NEP24241 | 1966 | £2 | £5 | |
| Hitmakers Vol. 2 | 7" EP | Pye | NEP24242 | 1966 | £2.50 | £6 | |
| Hitmakers Vol. 3 | 7" EP | Pye | NEP24243 | 1966 | £2.50 | £6 | |
| Hits From Can Can | 7" EP | Capitol | EAP1482 | 1955 | £2 | £5 | |
| Hits Vol. 1 | 7" EP | Decca | DFE8648 | 1965 | £2 | £5 | |
| Hits Vol. 2 | 7" EP | Decca | DFE8649 | 1965 | £2 | £5 | |
| Hits Vol. 3 | 7" EP | Decca | DFE8653 | 1965 | £2.50 | £6 | |
| Hits Vol. 4 | 7" EP | Decca | DFE8662 | 1966 | £2 | £5 | |
| Hits Vol. 5 | 7" EP | Decca | DFE8663 | 1966 | £2.50 | £6 | |
| Hits Vol. 6 | 7" EP | Decca | DFE8667 | 1966 | £2.50 | £6 | |
| Hits Vol. 7 | 7" EP | Decca | DFER8675 | 1967 | £2.50 | £6 | |
| Hitsville | 7" EP | Mercury | ZEP10133 | 1962 | £7.50 | £15 | |
| Hitsville USA | LP | Tamla Motown | TML11019 | 1965 | £8 | £20 | |
| Hitsville USA No. 1 | 7" EP | Tamla Motown | TME2001 | 1965 | £20 | £40 | |
| Hitsville Vol. 1 | 7" EP | Coral | FEP2034 | 1959 | £15 | £30 | |
| Hitsville Vol. 2 | 7" EP | Coral | FEP2035 | 1959 | £6 | £12 | |

| Title | Format | Label | Cat. No. | Year | | | Notes |
|---|---|---|---|---|---|---|---|
| Hobos And Drifters | 7" EP | Postwar Blues | 100 | 1966 | £5 | £10 | |
| Hoisting The Black Flag | LP | United Dairies | UD06 | 1981 | £25 | £50 | |
| Honeys | LP | Melodisc | 12216 | 196– | £4 | £10 | |
| Honky Tonk Train | LP | Riverside | RLP8806 | 1967 | £6 | £15 | |
| Hoot'nanny Show Vol. 1 | LP | Waverley | | 1964 | £6 | £15 | |
| Hoot'nanny Show Vol. 2 | LP | Waverley | ZLP2032 | 1964 | £6 | £15 | |
| Hootenanny In London | LP | Decca | LK4544 | 1963 | £10 | £25 | |
| Hootenanny New York City | 7" EP | Topic | TOP37 | 1959 | £4 | £8 | |
| Hot Calypsos | 7" EP | Capitol | EAP1852 | 1957 | £2 | £5 | |
| Hot Numbers | LP | Pama | PMP2006 | 1971 | £6 | £15 | |
| Hot Numbers Vol. 2 | LP | Pama | PMP2009 | 1971 | £6 | £15 | |
| Hot Shots Of Reggae | LP | Trojan | TBL128 | 1970 | £6 | £15 | |
| House That Track Built | LP | Track | 613016 | 1969 | £5 | £12 | |
| Houston Hallucinations | LP | Texas Archive | TAR2 | 1982 | £5 | £12 | US |
| Houston Jump | 7" EP | Solid Sender | SEP100 | 1975 | £2 | £5 | |
| How Blue Can We Get? | LP | Blue Horizon | PR45/46 | 1970 | £8 | £20 | double |
| I Love You Gorgo | LP | Suemi | 1090 | 1969 | £10 | £25 | US |
| I'm Your Country Man | LP | Highway 51 | H104 | 1970 | £10 | £25 | |
| In Crowd | LP | CBS | | 1966 | £6 | £15 | |
| In Crowd | 7" EP | Chess | CRE6010 | 1966 | £4 | £8 | |
| In Fractured Silence | LP | United Dairies | UD015 | 198– | £10 | £25 | |
| In Loving Memory | LP | Tamla Motown | (S)TML11124 | 1969 | £20 | £40 | |
| In Our Own Way/Oldies But Goodies | LP | Blue Horizon | PR37 | 1969 | £6 | £15 | |
| Independent Jamaica | LP | Trojan | TTL15 | 1969 | £8 | £20 | |
| Industrial Records Story | LP | Illuminated | JAMS39 | 1984 | £6 | £15 | |
| International Artists | 7" | Radar | SAM88 | 1978 | £2 | £5 | |
| Irish Folk Night | LP | Decca | LK4633 | 1964 | £6 | £15 | |
| Irish Music In London Pubs | LP | Folkways | FG3575 | 1965 | £8 | £20 | US |
| Irish Music In London Pubs | LP | XTRA | XTRA1090 | 1969 | £5 | £12 | |
| Irish Pipering | LP | Claddagh | CC11 | 1971 | £5 | £12 | Irish |
| Irish Reels, Jigs, Hornpipes And Airs | LP | Kicking Mule | SNKF153 | 1979 | £4 | £10 | |
| Irish Traditional Concertina Styles | LP | Free Reed | FRS506 | 1977 | £4 | £10 | |
| Iron Muse | LP | Topic | 12T86 | 1963 | £10 | £25 | |
| Isle Of Wight/Atlanta Festival | LP | CBS | 66311 | 1971 | £8 | £20 | triple |
| It's All Happening | LP | Columbia | SCX3486 | 1963 | £4 | £10 | |
| It's Beat Time In Liverpool | LP | Ariola | 72756 | 1965 | £25 | £50 | German |
| It's Cha Cha Time | 7" EP | Mercury | ZEP10001 | 1959 | £2 | £5 | |
| It's Great To Be Young | 7" EP | Columbia | SEG7639 | 1956 | £2.50 | £6 | |
| It's Trad Dad | LP | Columbia | 33SX1412 | 1962 | £6 | £15 | |
| Items From Guys And Dolls | 7" EP | Mercury | MEP9503 | 1956 | £4 | £8 | |
| Jack Good's Oh Boy! | LP | Parlophone | PMC1072 | 1958 | £15 | £30 | |
| Jackpot Of Hits | LP | Amalgamated | CSP3 | 1969 | £20 | £40 | |
| Jamaica Ska | LP | Atlantic | 587075 | 1968 | £20 | £40 | |
| Jamaica's Greatest Hits | LP | Melodisc | MLP12158 | 197– | £5 | £12 | |
| Jamaican Blues | LP | Blue Beat | BBLP801 | 1961 | £50 | £100 | |
| Jamaican Memories | LP | Blue Cat | BCL1 | 1968 | £25 | £50 | |
| Jambalaya On The Bayou Vol. 1 | LP | Flyright | LP3502 | 1968 | £6 | £15 | |
| Jambalaya On The Bayou Vol. 2 | LP | Flyright | LP3503 | 1969 | £6 | £15 | |
| James Bond Collection | LP | United Artists | UAS60027/8 | 1972 | £6 | £15 | double |
| Jazz Explosion | LP | Columbia | SLJS1 | 1969 | £4 | £10 | |
| Jazz Juice | LP | Streetsounds | MUSIC1 | 1984 | £8 | £20 | |
| Jazz Juice | LP | Streetsounds | SOUND1 | 1985 | £6 | £15 | |
| Jazz Juice 2 | LP | Streetsounds | SOUND4 | 1986 | £5 | £12 | |
| Jazz Juice 3 | LP | Streetsounds | SOUND5 | 1986 | £5 | £12 | |
| Jazz Juice 4 | LP | Streetsounds | SOUND6 | 1986 | £5 | £12 | |
| Jazz Juice 5 | LP | Streetsounds | SOUND8 | 1987 | £5 | £12 | |
| Jazz Juice 6 | LP | Streetsounds | SOUND9 | 1987 | £5 | £12 | |
| Jazz Juice 6 | CD | Streetsounds | CDSND9 | 1987 | £5 | £12 | |
| Jazz Juice 7 | LP | Streetsounds | SOUND10 | 1988 | £5 | £12 | |
| Jazz Juice 7 | CD | Streetsounds | CDSND10 | 1988 | £5 | £12 | |
| Jazz Juice 8 | LP | Streetsounds | SOUND11 | 1988 | £4 | £10 | |
| Jazz Juice 8 | CD | Streetsounds | CDSND11 | 1988 | £5 | £12 | |
| Jazz Juice 9 | LP | Streetsounds | SOUND12 | 1988 | £4 | £10 | |
| Jazz Juice 9 | CD | Streetsounds | CDSND12 | 1988 | £5 | £12 | |
| Joe Meek Story | LP | Decca | DPA3035/6 | 1977 | £5 | £12 | double |
| John Peel Presents Top Gear | LP | BBC | REC52S | 1969 | £10 | £25 | |
| Journey To Tyme Vol. 1 | LP | Phantom | PRS1001 | 1982 | £6 | £15 | US |
| Journey To Tyme Vol. 2 | LP | Phantom | PRS1002 | 1985 | £6 | £15 | US |
| Journey To Tyme Vol. 3 | LP | Phantom | PRS1003 | 1985 | £6 | £15 | US |
| Journey To Tyme Vol. 4 | LP | Phantom | PRS1006 | 1986 | £6 | £15 | US |
| Journey To Tyme Vol. 5 | LP | Phantom | PRS1007 | 1986 | £6 | £15 | US |
| Jug Bands Vol. 1 | 7" EP | Natchez | NEP701 | 1967 | £5 | £10 | |
| Jug Of Punch | LP | HMV | CLP1327 | 1960 | £20 | £40 | |
| Jug Of Punch | LP | HMV | XLP50003 | 1960 | £20 | £40 | |
| Jugs And Washboards | LP | Ace Of Hearts | AH163 | 1967 | £4 | £10 | |
| Jugs, Washboards And Kazoos | LP | RCA | RD7893 | 1967 | £4 | £10 | |
| Jump Jamaica Jump | LP | R&B | JBL1111 | 1964 | £50 | £100 | |
| Jumping At The Go Go | LP | RCA | RS1066 | 1976 | £5 | £12 | |
| Just For Fun | LP | Decca | LK4524 | 1963 | £10 | £25 | |
| Just For Kicks | LP | CBS | | | £5 | £12 | Irish |
| KDWB Radio: 21 All Time Dream Hits Vol. 1 | LP | Take Six | 2033 | 1967 | £6 | £15 | US |
| Kerbside Entertainers | LP | Jayboy | JSX2009 | 1971 | £10 | £25 | |
| Kicks And Chicks Vol. 1 | LP | Eleventh Hour | EH5806 | 1990 | £5 | £12 | US |
| King Size Reggae | LP | Trojan | TBL140 | 1970 | £8 | £20 | |
| Kings Of Memphis Town 1927–1930 | LP | Saydisc | RL333 | 196– | £4 | £10 | |
| Kings Of The Blues Vol. 1 | 7" EP | RCA | RCX202 | 1961 | £2 | £5 | |
| Kings Of The Blues Vol. 2 | 7" EP | RCA | RCX203 | 1961 | £4 | £8 | |

| Title | Format | Label | Catalogue | Year | Low | High | Notes |
|---|---|---|---|---|---|---|---|
| Kings Of The Blues Vol. 3 | 7" EP | RCA | RCX204 | 1961 | £4 | £8 | |
| Kings Of The Twelve String Guitar | LP | Flyright | LP101 | 1971 | £4 | £10 | |
| Kings Of The Twelve String Guitar | LP | Gryphon | 13159 | 196– | £5 | £12 | |
| Kinney Collection | LP | Kinney | KC1 | 1971 | £4 | £10 | |
| Kosmische Musik | LP | Ohr | OMM256027 | 1973 | £15 | £30 | German double |
| Kralingen | LP | Wild Thing | WC2001 | 1970 | £30 | £60 | Dutch triple |
| Label – Sofa | LP | The Label | TRLP002S | 1979 | £15 | £30 | picture disc |
| Lark In The Morning | LP | Tradition | TLP1004 | 1955 | £10 | £25 | US |
| Last Thing On My Mind | 7" EP | Holyground | HG111 | 1966 | £12.50 | £25 | |
| Let Me Tell You About The Blues | LP | Blue Horizon | LP2 | 1966 | £150 | £250 | |
| Let's Go | 7" EP | Top Rank | JKR8008 | 1959 | £4 | £8 | |
| Let's Go Down South | LP | Neshoba | N11 | 1966 | £10 | £25 | |
| Let's Go Vol. 2 | 7" EP | Top Rank | JKR8012 | 1959 | £5 | £10 | |
| Let's Have A Party | LP | Brunswick | LAT8271 | 1958 | £4 | £10 | |
| Levi Commercials | 10" LP | Levi Strauss | 6720 | 1967 | £50 | £100 | US |
| Liberty/United Artists Sampler | LP | United Artists | REP102 | 1971 | £10 | £25 | promo |
| Live At The Cavern | LP | Decca | SLK16294 | 1965 | £25 | £50 | German |
| Live At The Funny Farm | LP | Scene | 200 | 1966 | £50 | £100 | US |
| Live At The Liverpool Hoop Vol. 1 | LP | Telefunken | SLE14395 | 1965 | £37.50 | £75 | German |
| Live At The Liverpool Hoop Vol. 2 | LP | Telefunken | SLE14411 | 1965 | £37.50 | £75 | German |
| Live At The Vortex | LP | NEMS | NEL6013 | 1977 | £4 | £10 | |
| Live It Up | LP | Big Shot | BBTL4000 | 1968 | £30 | £60 | |
| Live Recording From The Top Ten Beat Club Vol. 1 | LP | Decca | SLK16330P | 1965 | £25 | £50 | German |
| Liverpool And Blue Beat | LP | Eurocord | J022 | 1964 | £25 | £50 | German |
| Liverpool Beat | LP | Embassy | WLP6065 | 1964 | £5 | £12 | |
| Liverpool Beat Time | LP | Discoton | 72351 | 1964 | £37.50 | £75 | German |
| Liverpool Hoop | LP | Columbia | SMC83983 | 1964 | £25 | £50 | German |
| Lleisiau | LP | private | ADF1 | 1975 | £30 | £60 | |
| Loch Ness Monster | LP | Trojan | TBL135 | 1970 | £6 | £15 | |
| London Boys | 7" | Decca | FR13864 | 1979 | £1.50 | £4 | |
| London Hit Parade Vol. 1 | 7" EP | London | RED1075 | 1957 | £4 | £8 | |
| London Hit Parade Vol. 2 | 7" EP | London | REP1096 | 1957 | £15 | £30 | |
| London Hit Parade Vol. 3 | 7" EP | London | RED1097 | 1958 | £4 | £8 | |
| London Hit Parade Vol. 4 | 7" EP | London | RED1130 | 1958 | £4 | £8 | |
| London Hit Parade Vol. 5 | 7" EP | London | RED1145 | 1958 | £4 | £8 | |
| London Really Swings | LP | Columbia | 0301 | 1965 | £37.50 | £75 | US triple |
| Lonely Is An Eyesore | CD/vid/cass | 4AD | CADX703 | 1987 | £75 | £150 | wooden box, etching, screen print |
| Louisville Scene | LP | Rod 'n' Custom | 3001 | 196– | £180 | £300 | US |
| Lovely Dozen | LP | Pama | PSP1001 | 1969 | £10 | £25 | |
| Made In Cornwall | LP | Cornish Legend | CLM 1 | | £30 | £60 | |
| Magic Carpet Ride | LP | TVAA | 001 | 1986 | £10 | £25 | US |
| Magic Cube | 9" LP | Evatone | EVA116811 | 1982 | £5 | £12 | US flexi |
| Male Blues Singers | LP | Collectors' Classics | CC3 | 196– | £4 | £10 | |
| Man From Carolina | LP | Trojan | TBL129 | 1970 | £5 | £12 | |
| Matchbox Days | LP | Village Thing | VTSAM16 | 1972 | £8 | £20 | |
| Maxi Track Record | 7" EP | Track | 2094011 | 1970 | £37.50 | £75 | blue sleeve |
| Maxi Track Record | 7" EP | Track | 2094011 | 1970 | £2 | £5 | maroon & gold sleeve |
| Maxi Track Record | 7" EP | Track | 2094011 | 1970 | £20 | £40 | red & white sleeve, press pack |
| Meet The Beat | 10" LP | Polydor | J73557 | 1965 | £62.50 | £125 | German |
| Memories Are Made Of Hits Vol. 1 | LP | London | HA8129 | 1964 | £4 | £10 | |
| Memories Are Made Of Hits Vol. 2 | LP | London | HA8130 | 1964 | £4 | £10 | |
| Memories Are Made Of Hits Vol. 3 | LP | London | HA8131 | 1964 | £4 | £10 | |
| Memories Are Made Of Hits Vol. 4 | LP | London | HA8138 | 1964 | £4 | £10 | |
| Memories Are Made Of Hits Vol. 5 | LP | London | HA8148 | 1964 | £4 | £10 | |
| Memories Are Made Of Hits Vol. 6 | LP | London | HA8171 | 1964 | £4 | £10 | |
| Memories Are Made Of Hits Vol. 7 | LP | London | HA8189 | 1964 | £4 | £10 | |
| Memories Are Made Of Hits Vol. 8 | LP | London | HA8213 | 1965 | £4 | £10 | |
| Merry Christmas | 7" EP | Decca | DFE6408 | 1957 | £2 | £5 | |
| MGM Evergreens | 7" EP | MGM | MGMEP749 | 1960 | £2 | £5 | |
| Midwest vs Canada Vol. 2 | LP | Unlimited Productions | UPLP1002 | 1984 | £25 | £50 | US |
| Midwest vs The Rest Vol. 1 | LP | Unlimited Productions | UPLP1001 | 1983 | £25 | £50 | US |
| Million-Airs | LP | Coral | LVA9126 | 1960 | £5 | £12 | |
| Milwaukee Sentinel Rock 'n' Roll Revue | LP | Century | 23214 | 196– | £50 | £100 | US |
| Mind Blowers Vol. 1 | LP | White Rabbit | WRLP001 | 1983 | £10 | £25 | US |
| Miniatures | LP | Pipe | PIPE2 | 1980 | £4 | £10 | |
| Miss Labba Labba Reggae | LP | Trojan | TBL174 | 1971 | £6 | £15 | |
| Modern Chicago Blues | LP | Bounty | BY6025 | 1966 | £8 | £20 | |
| Modern Chicago Blues | LP | Polydor | 545031 | 1967 | £4 | £10 | |
| Money Music | LP | August | 100 | 1967 | £180 | £300 | US |
| Monsters Of The Midwest Vol. 2 | LP | Titan | 1002 | 1985 | £5 | £12 | US |
| Month's Best From The Country And West | 7" EP | RCA | RCX7159 | 1964 | £2 | £5 | |
| Month's Best From The Country And West Vol. 2 | 7" EP | RCA | RCX7162 | 1964 | £2 | £5 | |
| Month's Best From The Country And West Vol. 3 | 7" EP | RCA | RCX7171 | 1964 | £2 | £5 | |
| Month's Best From The Country And West Vol. 4 | 7" EP | RCA | RCX7172 | 1965 | £2 | £5 | |

| Title | Format | Label | Catalogue | Year | Price | Price | Notes |
|---|---|---|---|---|---|---|---|
| Month's Best From The Country And West Vol. 5 | 7" EP | RCA | RCX7178 | 1965 | £2 | £5 | |
| Month's Best From The Country And West Vol. 6 | 7" EP | RCA | RCX7181 | 1965 | £2 | £5 | |
| Month's Best From The Country And West Vol. 7 | 7" EP | RCA | RCX7186 | 1967 | £2 | £5 | |
| Moonlight Groover | LP | Trojan | TTL31 | 1970 | £8 | £20 | |
| More American Graffiti | LP | MCA | | 1979 | £6 | £15 | US promo picture disc, 4 different B sides |
| More Down Home Blues | 7" EP | Jan & Dil | JR451 | 196– | £2.50 | £6 | |
| More Singing At The Count House | LP | private | | 1965 | £75 | £150 | |
| Morpeth Rant Northumbrian Country Music | LP | Topic | 12TS267 | 1975 | £4 | £10 | |
| Most Happy Fella | 7" EP | Philips | BBE12348 | 1960 | £2 | £5 | |
| Motortown Revue | LP | Tamla Motown | TML11007 | 1965 | £37.50 | £75 | |
| Motortown Revue Live In Paris | LP | Tamla Motown | TML11027 | 1966 | £20 | £40 | |
| Motown Magic | LP | Tamla Motown | TML11030 | 1966 | £8 | £20 | |
| Motown Memories | LP | Tamla Motown | TML11064 | 1968 | £10 | £25 | |
| Motown Memories Vol. 2 | LP | Tamla Motown | TML11077 | 1968 | £15 | £30 | |
| Motown Memories Vol. 3 | LP | Tamla Motown | STML11143 | 1970 | £10 | £25 | |
| Motown Story | LP | Tamla Motown | TMSP1130 | 1972 | £8 | £20 | boxed set |
| Motown Story – The First 25 Years | LP | Tamla Motown | TMSP6019 | 1983 | £6 | £15 | boxed set |
| Mrs. Ackroyd Superstar! | LP | Free Reed | FRR015 | 1977 | £5 | £12 | |
| Murderer's Home | LP | Pye | NJL11 | 1957 | £5 | £12 | |
| Murderer's Home part 1 | 7" EP | Pye | NJE1062 | 1957 | £2 | £5 | |
| Murderer's Home part 2 | 7" EP | Pye | NJE1063 | 1957 | £2 | £5 | |
| Murderer's Home part 3 | 7" EP | Pye | NJE1064 | 1957 | £2 | £5 | |
| Murderer's Home part 4 | 7" EP | Pye | NJE1065 | 1957 | £2 | £5 | |
| Murderers' Home | LP | Golden Guinea | GGL0317 | 1964 | £4 | £10 | |
| Murray The K Presents | LP | Brooklyn | 302 | 1967 | £15 | £30 | US |
| Murray The K's Greatest Holiday | LP | Brooklyn | 301 | 1967 | £15 | £30 | US |
| Mushroom Folk Sampler | LP | Mushroom | 100MR16 | 1971 | £25 | £50 | |
| Music For The Boy Friend | LP | Brunswick | LAT8201 | 1957 | £8 | £20 | |
| Music House | LP | Trojan | TBL170 | 1971 | £4 | £10 | |
| Music House Vol. 2 | LP | Trojan | TBL177 | 1971 | £4 | £10 | |
| Na Ceirnini 78 | LP | Gael Linn | CEF075 | 1978 | £4 | £10 | Irish |
| Napton Folk Club | 7" EP | Eden | | 1971 | £25 | £50 | |
| Natural Reggae Vol. 1 | LP | Bamboo | BLP201 | 1969 | £20 | £40 | |
| Natural Reggae Vol. 2 | LP | Bamboo | BLP204 | 1970 | £20 | £40 | |
| Natures Mortes – Still Lives | LP | 4AD | CAD117 | 1981 | £25 | £50 | export |
| Nederbiet | LP | Decca | DQL662507 | 1967 | £25 | £50 | Dutch |
| Negro Folklore From Texas State Prison | LP | Bounty | BY6012 | 1966 | £6 | £15 | |
| Negro Folklore From Texas State Prisons | LP | Polydor | 236511 | 1966 | £5 | £12 | |
| Negro Spirituals | LP | Vogue | LAE12033 | 1957 | £6 | £15 | |
| Negro Spirituals | 7" EP | Vogue | EPV1106 | 1956 | £4 | £8 | |
| Negro Spirituals | 7" EP | Vogue | EPV1271 | 1962 | £4 | £8 | |
| Negro Spirituals | 7" EP | Vogue | EPV1276 | 1962 | £4 | £8 | |
| Neue Deutsche Volksmusik | LP | Pilz | 20292262 | 1972 | £10 | £25 | German |
| New England Teen Scene | LP | Moulty | MLP101 | 1983 | £10 | £25 | US |
| New England Teen Scene Vol. 2 | LP | Moulty | MLP103 | 1984 | £6 | £15 | US |
| New Faces From Hitsville | 7" EP | Tamla Motown | TME2014 | 1966 | £37.50 | £75 | |
| New Hi: Dallas 1971 Part 1 | LP | Tempo | 2 | 1971 | £10 | £25 | US |
| New Orleans R&B Vol. 1 | LP | Flyright | LP4708 | 1974 | £4 | £10 | |
| New Orleans R&B Vol. 2 | LP | Flyright | LP4709 | 1974 | £4 | £10 | |
| New Sounds In Folk | 7" EP | Halcyon | HAL1 | 196– | £25 | £50 | |
| New Sounds In Folk | 7" EP | Harlequin | HW349 | 1966 | £62.50 | £125 | |
| New Voices From Scotland | LP | Topic | 12T133 | 1965 | £10 | £25 | |
| New York City Blues | LP | Flyright | LP4706 | 1972 | £4 | £10 | |
| New York Rhythm And Blues | LP | Flyright | LP4707 | 1972 | £4 | £10 | |
| Newport Broadside | LP | Fontana | TFL6038 | 1965 | £8 | £20 | |
| Newport Folk Festival 1964 Evening Concerts Vol. 2 | LP | Fontana | TFL6051 | 1965 | £4 | £10 | |
| Newport Folk Festival 1964 Evening Concerts Vol. 3 | LP | Fontana | TFL6052 | 1965 | £4 | £10 | |
| Newport Folk Festival Evening Concerts Vol. 1 | LP | Fontana | TFL6041 | 1965 | £8 | £20 | |
| Newport Folk Festival Vol. 1 | LP | Fontana | TFL6050 | 1965 | £4 | £10 | |
| Newport Spiritual Stars | LP | London | LTZC15155 | 1959 | £5 | £12 | |
| Night At The Apollo | LP | Vanguard | PPL11004 | 1957 | £4 | £10 | |
| Nixa Hit Parade No. 1 | 7" EP | Pye | NEP24052 | 1957 | £2.50 | £6 | |
| Nixa Hit Parade No. 2 | 7" EP | Pye | NEP24064 | 1958 | £5 | £10 | |
| Nixa Hit Parade No. 3 | 7" EP | Pye | NEP24071 | 1958 | £2 | £5 | |
| Nixa Hit Parade No. 4 | 7" EP | Pye | NEP24078 | 1958 | £2 | £5 | |
| Nixa Hit Parade No. 5 | 7" EP | Pye | NEP24082 | 1958 | £2 | £5 | |
| Nixa Hit Parade No. 6 | 7" EP | Pye | NEP24090 | 1958 | £2 | £5 | |
| Nixa Hit Parade No. 7 | 7" EP | Pye | NEP24100 | 1959 | £2 | £5 | |
| No Introduction | LP | Spark | SRLM107 | 1968 | £6 | £15 | |
| No More Heartaches | LP | Trojan | TTL14 | 1969 | £5 | £12 | |
| No Wave | LP | A&M | PR4738 | 1978 | £6 | £15 | US picture disc |
| Norman Granz Jazz Concert No. 1 | LP | Columbia | 33CX10059 | 1956 | £8 | £20 | |
| Norman Granz Jazz Concert No. 2 | LP | Columbia | 33CX10060 | 1956 | £8 | £20 | |
| Northland Shopping Center 3rd Annual Battle Of The Bands | LP | Magna | | 1967 | £50 | £100 | US |
| Northumbrian Minstrelry | LP | Concert Hall | AM2339 | 1964 | £15 | £30 | |
| Northwest Collection Vol. 1 | LP | Etiquette | 1018 | 196– | £25 | £50 | US |
| Nothin' But The Blues | LP | Fontana | TFL5123 | 1960 | £4 | £10 | |
| Nothing But The Blues | LP | CBS | 66278 | 1971 | £8 | £20 | double |
| Nova Sampler | LP | Nova/Decca | SPA72 | 1970 | £4 | £10 | |

| Title | Format | Label | Number | Year | | | Notes |
|---|---|---|---|---|---|---|---|
| Nubeat – Greatest Hits | LP | Pama | ECO6 | 1969 | £8 | £20 | |
| Nuggets | LP | Elektra | K62012 | 1972 | £15 | £30 | double |
| Nuggets | LP | Sire | SASH37162 | 1976 | £8 | £20 | US double |
| Oakland Blues | LP | Liberty | LBS83234 | 1969 | £4 | £10 | |
| Off The Wall Vol. 1 | LP | Wreckford Wrack | LP1025 | 1982 | £10 | £25 | US |
| Off The Wall Vol. 2 | LP | Wreckford Wrack | LP1301 | 1983 | £10 | £25 | US |
| Oh No It's More From Raw | LP | Raw | RAWLP2 | 1978 | £4 | £10 | |
| Oil Stains | LP | dB | DB101 | 1982 | £25 | £50 | US |
| Oil Stanes Vol. 2 | LP | Bone | 1001 | 1988 | £5 | £12 | US |
| Old British Ballads Of Donegal and Derry | LP | Leader | LEA4055 | 1975 | £4 | £10 | |
| Oldies R&B | LP | Stateside | SL10094 | 1964 | £6 | £15 | |
| On Stage | LP | Stateside | SL10065 | 1963 | £20 | £40 | |
| On The Road Again | LP | XTRA | XTRA1133 | 1973 | £6 | £15 | |
| On The Scene | LP | Columbia | 33SX1662 | 1964 | £20 | £40 | |
| On The Scene | 7" EP | Columbia | SEG8413 | 1965 | £10 | £20 | |
| Once A Week's Enough | LP | private | C2005 | 1977 | £8 | £20 | |
| Once More | LP | Big Shot | BBTL4001 | 1968 | £30 | £60 | |
| One Night Stand | LP | Columbia | 33SX1536 | 1963 | £8 | £20 | |
| Open Up Your Door | LP | Frog Death | GLP101 | 1984 | £6 | £15 | US |
| Open Up Your Door Vol. 2 | LP | Frog Death | GLP102 | 1987 | £6 | £15 | US |
| Original Cool Jamaican Ska | LP | Rio | RLP1 | 1964 | £30 | £60 | |
| Original Golden Oldies Vol. 2 | LP | Prince Buster | PB10 | 1973 | £8 | £20 | |
| Original Great Northwest Hits Vol. 1 | LP | Jerden | JRL7001 | 1964 | £10 | £25 | US |
| Original Great Northwest Hits Vol. 2 | LP | Jerden | JRL7002 | 1964 | £10 | £25 | US |
| Original Hits | LP | London | HAG2308 | 1960 | £10 | £25 | |
| Original Hits | 7" EP | London | REK1390 | 1963 | £5 | £10 | |
| Original Hits | 7" EP | MGM | MGMEP787 | 1963 | £7.50 | £15 | |
| Original Hits Vol. 2 | LP | London | HAG2339 | 1961 | £10 | £25 | |
| Original Hits Vol. 2 | 7" EP | Atlantic | AET6006 | 1965 | £5 | £10 | |
| Original Liverpool Sound | LP | Decca | BD5526 | 1963 | £37.50 | £75 | German |
| Original Rhythm And Blues Hits | 7" EP | Ember | EMBEP4522 | 1962 | £10 | £20 | |
| Original USA Hit Parade | LP | Heliodor | 343001 | 1958 | £20 | £40 | German |
| Ossiach Live | LP | BASF | 49211193 | 1971 | £20 | £40 | German triple |
| Our Choice | 7" EP | Columbia | SEG7669 | 1957 | £2.50 | £6 | |
| Our Significant Hits | LP | London | HAU2404 | 1962 | £10 | £25 | |
| Out Came The Blues | LP | Ace Of Hearts | AH72 | 1964 | £4 | £10 | |
| Out Came The Blues Vol. 2 | LP | Ace Of Hearts | AH158 | 1967 | £4 | £10 | |
| Out Of Sight | LP | Design | DLP269 | 1968 | £8 | £20 | US |
| Owdham Edge Popular Song And Verse From Lancashire | LP | Topic | 12T204 | 1970 | £4 | £10 | |
| Package Tour | LP | Golden Guinea | GGL0268 | 1963 | £6 | £15 | |
| Paddy In The Smoke | LP | Topic | 12T176 | 1968 | £4 | £10 | |
| Pain In My Belly | LP | Blue Beat | BBLP804 | 1965 | £50 | £100 | |
| Pajama Game | 7" EP | London | REA1036 | 1955 | £2 | £5 | |
| Pakistani Soul Session | LP | Island | ILP945 | 1967 | £6 | £15 | |
| Party Time In Jamaica | LP | Studio One | SOL9009 | 1968 | £50 | £100 | |
| Pennsylvanian Unknowns | LP | Time Tunnel | TTR1217425 | 1982 | £10 | £25 | US |
| Perfumed Garden | LP | Psycho | 6 | 1983 | £6 | £15 | |
| Perfumed Garden II | LP | Psycho | 15 | 1983 | £6 | £15 | |
| Piano Blues 1927–1933 | LP | Riverside | RLP8809 | 1967 | £5 | £12 | |
| Picnic | LP | Harvest | SHSS1/2 | 1970 | £5 | £12 | double |
| Piedmont Blues | LP | Flyright | LP104 | 1972 | £4 | £10 | |
| Pinch Of Salt | LP | HMV | CLP1362 | 1960 | £20 | £40 | |
| Pinch Of Salt | LP | HMV | XLP50004 | 1960 | £20 | £40 | |
| Pioneers Of Boogie Woogie | 10" LP | London | AL3506 | 1953 | £10 | £25 | |
| Pioneers Of Boogie Woogie Vol. 2 | 10" LP | London | AL3537 | 1954 | £10 | £25 | |
| Pipeline | LP | Trojan | TBL203 | 1973 | £5 | £12 | |
| Pop Parade Vol. 1 | 10" LP | Mercury | | 1956 | £4 | £10 | |
| Pop Parade Vol. 2 | 10" LP | Mercury | | 1956 | £4 | £10 | |
| Pop Parade Vol. 3 | 10" LP | Mercury | MPT7519 | 1957 | £4 | £10 | |
| Pop Parade Vol. 4 | 10" LP | Mercury | MPT7523 | 1957 | £4 | £10 | |
| Pop Parade Vol. 5 | 10" LP | Mercury | MPT7525 | 1957 | £4 | £10 | |
| Pops Go Stereo | 7" EP | Pye | NSEP85000 | 1958 | £2.50 | £6 | |
| Post War Blues: Chicago | LP | Post War Blues | PWB1 | 1965 | £8 | £20 | |
| Post War Blues: Detroit | LP | Post War Blues | PWB5 | 1968 | £8 | £20 | |
| Post War Blues: Eastern And Gulf Coast States | LP | Post War Blues | PWB3 | 1967 | £8 | £20 | |
| Post War Blues: Memphis On Down | LP | Post War Blues | PWB2 | 1966 | £8 | £20 | |
| Post War Blues: Texas | LP | Post War Blues | PWB4 | 1968 | £8 | £20 | |
| Post War Blues: The Deep South | LP | Post War Blues | PWB7 | 1969 | £8 | £20 | |
| Post War Blues: West Coast | LP | Post War Blues | PWB6 | 1969 | £8 | £20 | |
| Post War Collector Series Vol. 1 | LP | Python | PWBC1 | 1969 | £8 | £20 | |
| Pot Of Flowers | LP | Mainstream | S6100 | 1967 | £6 | £15 | US |
| Pre-War Texas Blues | LP | Kokomo | K1006 | 1970 | £15 | £30 | |
| Preachin' The Blues | LP | Stateside | SL10046 | 1963 | £4 | £10 | |
| Presages | LP | 4AD | BAD11 | 1980 | £4 | £10 | |
| Pride Of Cleveland Past | LP | private | NR15744 | 198– | £5 | £12 | US |
| Primitive Piano | LP | Jazz Collector | ABC1 | 1959 | £8 | £20 | |
| Psilotripitaka | LP | United Dairies | UD134 | 198– | £30 | £60 | 4 LP set |
| Psilotripitaka | LP | United Dairies | UD134 | 198– | £62.50 | £125 | 4 LP set, leather bag |
| Psilotripitaka | CD | United Dairies | UD134CD | 198– | £30 | £60 | 4 CD set |
| Psilotripitaka | CD | United Dairies | UD134CD | 198– | £62.50 | £125 | 4 CD set, leather bag |
| Psychedelic Disaster Whirl | LP | Frantic | 555777 | 1986 | £10 | £25 | US |
| Psychedelic Dream | LP | Columbia | CS38025 | 1982 | £6 | £15 | US double |
| Psychedelic Patchwork Vol. 1 | LP | private | PP101 | 1986 | £10 | £25 | US |
| Psychedelic Salvage Co. Vol. 1 | LP | private | no number | 1990 | £6 | £15 | |

| Title | Format | Label | Number | Year | | | Notes |
|---|---|---|---|---|---|---|---|
| Psychedelic Salvage Co. Vol. 2 | LP | private | no number | 1990 | £6 | £15 | |
| Psychedelic Unknowns Vol. 1 | 7" EP | Calico | EP0001 | 1979 | £10 | £25 | US double |
| Psychedelic Unknowns Vol. 2 | 7" EP | Calico | EP0002 | 1979 | £10 | £25 | US double |
| Psychedelic Unknowns Vol. 3 | LP | Calico | EP0003 | 1981 | £25 | £50 | US |
| Psychedelic Unknowns Vol. 4 | LP | Dayglow-Freon | DFLP001 | 1982 | £10 | £25 | US |
| Psychedelic Unknowns Vol. 5 | LP | Starglow-Neon | SN00001 | 1983 | £10 | £25 | US |
| Psychedelic Unknowns Vol. 6 | LP | Scrap | SCLP1 | 1985 | £5 | £12 | US |
| Psychedelic Unknowns Vol. 7 | LP | Scrap | SCLP2 | 1986 | £5 | £12 | US |
| Psychedelic Unknowns Vol. 8 | LP | Scrap | SCLP3 | 1986 | £5 | £12 | US |
| Psychotic Moose And The Soul Searchers | LP | Psychotic Moose | PMS101 | 1982 | £25 | £50 | US |
| Pure Blues Vol. 1 | LP | Sue | ILP919 | 1965 | £8 | £20 | |
| Put It On, It's Rock Steady | LP | Island | ILP978 | 1968 | £25 | £50 | pink label |
| Pye Sales Sampler | LP | Pye | PSA6 | 1971 | £5 | £12 | promo |
| Queen Of The World | LP | Trojan | TBL136 | 1970 | £5 | £12 | |
| Querschnitt Berlin | LP | private | | 1982 | £8 | £20 | German |
| R&B Chartmakers | 7" EP | Stateside | SE1009 | 1964 | £20 | £40 | |
| R&B Chartmakers No. 2 | 7" EP | Stateside | SE1018 | 1964 | £20 | £40 | |
| R&B Chartmakers No. 3 | 7" EP | Stateside | SE1022 | 1964 | £20 | £40 | |
| R&B Chartmakers No. 4 | 7" EP | Stateside | SE1025 | 1964 | £15 | £30 | |
| R&B Greats Vol. 1 | LP | Realm | RM101 | 1963 | £6 | £15 | |
| R&B Greats Vol. 2 | LP | Realm | RM175 | 1964 | £6 | £15 | |
| R&B Party | LP | Mercury | MCL20019 | 1964 | £5 | £12 | |
| Ragtime Piano Roll | 10" LP | London | AL3515 | 1954 | £6 | £15 | |
| Ragtime Piano Roll Vol. 2 | 10" LP | London | AL3523 | 1954 | £6 | £15 | |
| Ragtime Piano Roll Vol. 3 | 10" LP | London | AL3542 | 1955 | £6 | £15 | |
| Ragtime Piano Roll Vol. 4 | 10" LP | London | AL3563 | 1957 | £6 | £15 | |
| Raptor Presents | 12" | Raptor | RAP1 | 1993 | £25 | £50 | |
| Raw Blues | LP | Ace Of Clubs | ACL/SCL1220 | 1967 | £5 | £12 | |
| Ready Steady Go | LP | Decca | LK4577 | 1964 | £8 | £20 | |
| Ready Steady Go Rocksteady | LP | Pama | PMLP3 | 1968 | £15 | £30 | |
| Ready Steady Win | LP | Decca | LK4634 | 1964 | £25 | £50 | |
| Real R&B | LP | Stateside | SL10112 | 1965 | £6 | £15 | |
| Recommended Records Sampler | 7" | Recommended | RR.8.9 | 1982 | £4 | £8 | clear vinyl, 1 side painted |
| Recording The Blues | LP | CBS | 52797 | 1970 | £4 | £10 | |
| Red Bird Goldies | LP | Red Bird | RB20102 | 1965 | £8 | £20 | |
| Red, Red Wine Vol. 1 | LP | Trojan | TTL11 | 1969 | £5 | £12 | |
| Red, Red Wine Vol. 1 | LP | Trojan | TTL11 | 1969 | £20 | £40 | pink Island label |
| Red, Red Wine Vol. 2 | LP | Trojan | TBL116 | 1970 | £5 | £12 | |
| Reggae Flight 404 | LP | Trojan | TBL115 | 1970 | £5 | £12 | |
| Reggae Girl | LP | Big Shot | BIL3000 | 1968 | £20 | £40 | |
| Reggae Hit The Town | LP | Pama | PTP1001 | 1969 | £8 | £20 | |
| Reggae Hits '69 Vol. 1 | LP | Pama | ECO3 | 1969 | £8 | £20 | |
| Reggae Hits '69 Vol. 2 | LP | Pama | ECO11 | 1969 | £8 | £20 | |
| Reggae In The Grass | LP | Studio One | SOL9007 | 1968 | £50 | £100 | |
| Reggae Jamaica | LP | Trojan | TBL181 | 1971 | £4 | £10 | |
| Reggae Movement | LP | Trojan | TBL144 | 1970 | £5 | £12 | |
| Reggae Power | LP | Trojan | TBL189 | 1972 | £4 | £10 | |
| Reggae Reggae Reggae | LP | Trojan | TBL130 | 1970 | £5 | £12 | |
| Reggae Reggae Reggae Vol. 2 | LP | Trojan | TBL176 | 1971 | £5 | £12 | |
| Reggae Special | LP | Coxsone | CSP2 | 1969 | £20 | £40 | |
| Reggae Steady Go | LP | Trojan | TBL151 | 1970 | £5 | £12 | |
| Reggae Time | LP | Coxsone | CSL8017 | 1968 | £50 | £100 | |
| Reggae To Reggae | LP | Pama | PMP2012 | 1971 | £10 | £25 | |
| Reggae To UK With Love | LP | Pama | PSP1004 | 1969 | £8 | £20 | |
| Reggaematic Sounds | LP | Bamboo | BDLP208 | 1971 | £20 | £40 | |
| Relics – Collectors' Obscurities From The First Psychedelic Era | LP | dB | DB102 | 1982 | £10 | £25 | US |
| Return Of The Young Pennsylvanians | LP | Bona Fide | BFR1672466 | 1983 | £5 | £12 | US |
| Return To Splendour | 7" | Fierce Panda | NING03 | 1994 | £12.50 | £25 | double |
| Revolution | LP | United Artists | UAS29069 | 1969 | £5 | £12 | |
| Rhythm & Blues | LP | Decca | LK4616 | 1964 | £15 | £30 | |
| Rhythm & Blues Showcase Vol. 1 | 7" EP | Pye | NEP44021 | 1964 | £5 | £10 | |
| Rhythm & Blues Showcase Vol. 2 | 7" EP | Pye | NEP44022 | 1964 | £5 | £10 | |
| Rhythm And Blues Classics Vol. 1 | LP | Minit | MLS40008 | 1969 | £5 | £12 | |
| Rhythm And Blues Classics Vol. 2 | LP | Minit | MLS40009 | 1969 | £5 | £12 | |
| Rhythm And Blues Party | LP | Philips | 6436028 | 1976 | £4 | £10 | |
| Rhythm And Blues Vol. 1 | LP | Liberty | LBL83216 | 1969 | £4 | £10 | |
| Rhythm And Blues Vol. 2 | LP | Liberty | LBL83328 | 1969 | £4 | £10 | |
| Rhythm 'n' Blues | LP | Decca | 31031-2 | 1964 | £15 | £30 | German double |
| Ric Tic Relics | LP | Tamla Motown | STML11232 | 1973 | £6 | £15 | |
| Ride Me Donkey | LP | Coxsone | CSL8015 | 1968 | £50 | £100 | |
| Ride Your Donkey | LP | Trojan | TTL18 | 1969 | £8 | £20 | |
| Riot On Sunset Strip | LP | Tower | 5065 | 1967 | £10 | £25 | US |
| Rivertown Blues | LP | London | SHU8245 | 1971 | £4 | £10 | |
| Rock All Night | 10" LP | Mercury | MPT7527 | 1957 | £75 | £150 | |
| Rock And Roll | 7" EP | Vogue | VE170111 | 1958 | £30 | £60 | |
| Rock Und Beat Im Star-Club Hamburg | LP | Ariola | 70983 | 1964 | £37.50 | £75 | German |
| Rock 'n' Roll | 10" LP | London | HBC1067 | 1956 | £15 | £30 | |
| Rock 'n' Roll Forever | LP | London | HAE2180 | 1959 | £20 | £40 | |
| Rock 'n' Roll Music | LP | Vogue | LDVS17198 | 1970 | £10 | £25 | German |
| Rock, Rock, Rock | LP | Chess | LP1425 | 1957 | £25 | £50 | US |
| Rock-A-Hits | LP | London | HAA2338 | 1961 | £15 | £30 | |
| Rocket Along | 10" LP | HMV | DLP1204 | 1960 | £8 | £20 | |
| Rockin' At The 2 I's | 10" LP | Decca | LF1300 | 1958 | £15 | £30 | |
| Rockin' Together | LP | London | HAE2167 | 1959 | £20 | £40 | |

| Title | Format | Label | Catalogue | Year | | | Notes |
|---|---|---|---|---|---|---|---|
| Rocksteady Cool | LP | Pama | PMLP7 | 1969 | £15 | £30 | |
| Rocksteady Coxsone Style | LP | Coxsone | CSL8013 | 1968 | £50 | £100 | |
| Rollercoaster EP | CD-s | Warner Bros | SAM986 | 1982 | £2 | £5 | *Melody Maker disc* |
| Roofgarden Jamboree | LP | Iglus | 103 | 1967 | £100 | £200 | *US* |
| Roots '66 Vol. 1 | LP | Paraquat | TPLP84 | 1984 | £5 | £12 | *US* |
| Round Up | 7" EP | Capitol | EAP120197 | 1962 | £4 | £8 | |
| Rubble 1 – The Psychedelic Snarl | LP | Bam-Caruso | KIRI024 | 1984 | £6 | £15 | |
| Rubble 2 – Pop-Sike Pipe-Dreams | LP | Bam-Caruso | KIRI025 | 1986 | £6 | £15 | |
| Rubble 3 – Nightmares In Wonderland | LP | Bam-Caruso | KIRI026 | 1986 | £6 | £15 | |
| Rubble 4 – 49 Minute Technicolour Dream | LP | Bam-Caruso | KIRI027 | 1984 | £6 | £15 | |
| Rubble 5 – The Electric Crayon Set | LP | Bam-Caruso | KIRI044 | 1986 | £6 | £15 | |
| Rubble 6 – The Clouds Have Groovy Faces | LP | Bam-Caruso | KIRI049 | 1986 | £6 | £15 | |
| Rubble 7 – Pictures In The Sky | LP | Bam-Caruso | KIRI083 | 1988 | £6 | £15 | |
| Rubble 8 – All The Colours Of Darkness | LP | Bam-Caruso | KIRI051 | 1991 | £6 | £15 | |
| Rubble 9 – Plastic Wilderness | LP | Bam-Caruso | KIRI079 | 1991 | £6 | £15 | |
| Rubble 10 – Professor Jordan's Magic Sound Show | LP | Bam-Caruso | KIRI098 | 1988 | £6 | £15 | |
| Rubble 11 – Adventures In The Mist | LP | Bam-Caruso | KIRI069 | 1986 | £6 | £15 | |
| Rubble 12 – Staircase To Nowhere | LP | Bam-Caruso | KIRI070 | 1986 | £6 | £15 | |
| Rubble 13 – Freakbeat Fantoms | LP | Bam-Caruso | KIRI102 | 1989 | £6 | £15 | |
| Rubble 14 – The Magic Rocking Horse | LP | Bam-Caruso | KIRI106 | 1988 | £6 | £15 | |
| Rubble 15 – 5,000 Seconds Over Toyland | LP | Bam-Caruso | KIRI084 | 1991 | £6 | £15 | |
| Rubble 16 – Glass Orchid Aftermath | LP | Bam-Caruso | KIRI096 | 1991 | £6 | £15 | |
| Rubble 17 – A Trip In A Painted World | LP | Bam-Caruso | KIRI099 | 1991 | £6 | £15 | |
| Rural Blues | LP | XTRA | XTRA1035 | 1969 | £6 | £15 | *double* |
| Rural Blues Vol. 1 | LP | Liberty | LBL83213 | 1969 | £5 | £12 | |
| Rural Blues Vol. 2 | LP | Liberty | LBL83214 | 1969 | £5 | £12 | |
| Rural Blues Vol. 3 | LP | Liberty | LBL83329 | 1969 | £5 | £12 | |
| Samantha Promotions | LP | Transworld | SPLP101 | 1970 | £500 | £750 | |
| Samantha Promotions | LP | Transworld | SPLP102 | 1970 | £500 | £750 | |
| San Francisco Interntional Pop Festival | LP | Colstar | 5001 | 196– | £180 | £300 | *US* |
| San Francisco Roots | LP | Vault | SLP119 | 1969 | £6 | £15 | *US* |
| Sandy Bell's Ceilidh | LP | Alba | MAR056 | 1979 | £5 | £12 | |
| Saturday Club | LP | Decca | LK4583 | 1964 | £8 | £20 | |
| Saturday Club | LP | Parlophone | PMC1130 | 1960 | £10 | £25 | |
| Saturday Night At The Apollo | LP | Atlantic | 590007 | 1966 | £4 | £10 | |
| Saturday Night At The Uptown | LP | Atlantic | ATL5018 | 1964 | £6 | £15 | |
| Scene '65 | LP | Columbia | 33SX1730 | 1965 | £20 | £40 | |
| Scorcha From Bamboo | LP | Bamboo | BDLP202 | 1969 | £20 | £40 | |
| Scotia Folk | LP | Fontana | 6438021 | 1970 | £8 | £20 | |
| Screening The Blues | LP | CBS | 66208 | 1968 | £6 | £15 | *double* |
| Scum Of The Earth Part 1 | LP | Killdozer | KILL001 | 1984 | £25 | £50 | *US* |
| Scum Of The Earth Part 2 | LP | Killdozer | KILL002 | 1984 | £50 | £100 | *US* |
| Sea Shanties | LP | Topic | 12TS234 | 1974 | £4 | £10 | |
| Second Coming | LP | Come Organisation | WDC881008 | 1980 | £25 | £50 | |
| Second Folk Review Record | LP | Folksound | FS107 | 1976 | £15 | £30 | |
| Secret Policeman's Other Ball | 10" | Springtime | RARA1001 | 1981 | £4 | £10 | *promo sampler* |
| Select Elektra | LP | Elektra | EUK261/ EUKS7261 | 1968 | £4 | £10 | |
| Seoda Ceoil 2 | LP | Gael Linn | CEF002 | 1969 | £4 | £10 | *Irish* |
| Shades Of Gospel Soul | LP | Motown | M/S701 | 1969 | £6 | £15 | *US* |
| Shagging In The Streets | 7" | Fierce Panda | NING01 | 1994 | £4 | £8 | *double* |
| Shake It Baby | LP | Polydor | 623002 | 1965 | £15 | £30 | *German* |
| Shake, Rattle And Roll | LP | Atlantic | 587109 | 1968 | £4 | £10 | |
| Shepway Folk | LP | Eron | 003 | 1974 | £5 | £12 | |
| Short Circuit – Live At The Electric Circus | 10" LP | Virgin | VCL5003 | 1978 | £4 | £10 | *blue vinyl* |
| Short Circuit – Live At The Electric Circus | 10" LP | Virgin | VCL5003 | 1978 | £37.50 | £75 | *orange vinyl* |
| Short Circuit – Live At The Electric Circus | 10" LP | Virgin | VCL5003 | 1978 | £10 | £25 | *yellow vinyl* |
| Signed D.C. | LP | Satan | SR666 | 1984 | £5 | £12 | *US* |
| Sing A Song Of Soul | LP | Chess | CRL4519 | 1966 | £4 | £10 | |
| Singer Songwriter Project | LP | Elektra | EKL/EKS7299 | 1965 | £15 | £30 | *US* |
| Singing In The Rain | 7" EP | MGM | MGMEP671 | 1958 | £2 | £5 | |
| Singing The Blues | 7" EP | London | REP1403 | 1963 | £7.50 | £15 | |
| Six Five Special | LP | Parlophone | PMC1047 | 1957 | £15 | £30 | |
| Six Five Special | 7" EP | Decca | DFE6485 | 1958 | £5 | £10 | |
| Sixteen Beat Groups From The Hamburg Scene | LP | Polydor | 237639 | 1964 | £37.50 | £75 | *German* |
| Sixteen Dynamic Reggae Hits | LP | Pama | PMP2015 | 1971 | £5 | £12 | |
| Sixteen Dynamic Reggae Hits | LP | Trojan | TBL191 | 1972 | £4 | £10 | |
| Sixteen Original R&B Golden Hits | LP | Starclub | 158011STY | 1965 | £50 | £100 | *German* |
| Ska at The Jamaican Playboy Club | LP | Island | ILP930 | 1966 | £50 | £100 | |
| Ska To Rocksteady | LP | Studio One | SOL9000 | 1967 | £50 | £100 | |
| Skiffle | LP | Ace Of Clubs | ACL1250 | 1967 | £6 | £15 | |
| Soft Beat '66 | LP | Decca | H210 | 1966 | £25 | £50 | *German* |
| Solid Gold | LP | Bamboo | BDLP212 | 1971 | £20 | £40 | |
| Solid Gold Soul | LP | Atlantic | ATL5048 | 1966 | £4 | £10 | |
| Solid On Soul | LP | United Artists | LBR1007 | 197– | £4 | £10 | |
| Some Cleveland And Dales Folk Vol. 1 | LP | Pied Piper | MIK1001 | 1976 | £5 | £12 | |
| Some Cold Rainy Day | LP | Flyright | LP114 | 1975 | £4 | £10 | |
| Some Cold Rainy Day | LP | Southern Preservation | SPR1 | 1972 | £6 | £15 | |
| Some Folk In Leicester | LP | Lestar | LLP101 | 1965 | £25 | £50 | |
| Something Sweet From The Lady | LP | Pama | PMP2003 | 1970 | £6 | £15 | |
| Something To Brighten The Morning – The Story Of Mill Reef | LP | York | | 1974 | £62.50 | £125 | |

| Title | Format | Label | Cat. No. | Year | | | Notes |
|---|---|---|---|---|---|---|---|
| Son Of The Gathering Of The Tribe | LP | BF | 20183 | 1983 | £10 | £25 | US |
| Songs And Ballads Of The Industrial North West | LP | Topic | 12T188 | 1969 | £4 | £10 | |
| Songs From Washington Davy Lamp Folksong Club | LP | DLFC | 110 | 1974 | £20 | £40 | |
| Soul '66 | LP | Sue | ILP934 | 1966 | £15 | £30 | |
| Soul Food | LP | Minit | MLL40011E | 1968 | £6 | £15 | |
| Soul From The City | LP | Soul City | SCB001 | 1969 | £6 | £15 | |
| Soul Of Jamaica | LP | Trojan | TRL3 | 1968 | £15 | £30 | |
| Soul Sauce From Pama | LP | Pama | PMLP8 | 1969 | £6 | £15 | |
| Soul Seller | LP | Polydor | 236554 | 1969 | £4 | £10 | |
| Soul Sixteen | LP | Stateside | SL10186 | 1966 | £5 | £12 | |
| Soul Sounds Of The Sixties | LP | HMV | CLP3617 | 1967 | £6 | £15 | |
| Soul Supply | LP | Stateside | SL10203 | 1967 | £6 | £15 | |
| Sound Of The Grapevine | LP | Grapevine | GRAL1001 | 197– | £5 | £12 | |
| Sound Of The R&B Hits | LP | Stateside | SL10077 | 1964 | £15 | £30 | |
| Sound Of The Sixties | LP | Eva | 12021/2 | 1983 | £8 | £20 | French double |
| Sound Of The Sixties: San Francisco Part 1 | LP | Phantom | PLP1004 | 1985 | £5 | £12 | US |
| Sound Of The Sixties: San Francisco Part 2 | LP | Phantom | PLP1005 | 1985 | £5 | £12 | US |
| Sound Of The Stars | 7" | Lyntone | LYN995 | 1966 | £7.50 | £15 | Disc And Music Echo flexi, envelope |
| Sounds Of Savile | 7" EP | Lyntone | LYN951/2 | 1965 | £20 | £40 | |
| Soundsville | LP | Design | DLP187 | 1965 | £25 | £50 | US |
| Southern Sanctified Singers | LP | Saydisc | RL328 | 196– | £4 | £10 | |
| Southside Chicago | LP | Python | PLP10 | 1971 | £8 | £20 | |
| Speak Low – More Music In The Modern Manner | LP | Tempo | TAP17 | 1958 | £10 | £25 | |
| Spin With The Stars No. 2 | 10" LP | Pye | NPT19019 | 1957 | £5 | £12 | |
| Spin With The Stars No. 3 | 10" LP | Pye | NPT19021 | 1957 | £5 | £12 | |
| Spree '73 | LP | Key | KL021 | 1973 | £4 | £10 | |
| Star Club Center Of Beat | LP | Brunswick | 2910502 | 1965 | £25 | £50 | German |
| Star Club Information Record | LP | Starclub | 111371L | 1964 | £87.50 | £175 | German |
| Star Parade | 7" EP | Decca | DFE6147 | 1955 | £2.50 | £6 | |
| Star Souvenir Greetings | 7" | 208 Radio Luxembourg | | 196– | £5 | £10 | flexi |
| Star-Club Scene '65 | LP | Starclub | 158018 | 1965 | £30 | £60 | German |
| Star-Club Show 6 | LP | Starclub | 148005STL | 1965 | £30 | £60 | German |
| Stars Of Liberty | LP | Liberty | LBY1001 | 1960 | £8 | £20 | |
| Stars Of the 6.5 Special | 10" LP | Decca | LF1299 | 1957 | £15 | £30 | |
| Statik Compilation One | LP | Statik | POL274 | 1985 | £6 | £15 | |
| Stax/Volt Tour In London Vol. 1 | LP | Stax | 589010 | 1967 | £6 | £15 | |
| Stax/Volt Tour In London Vol. 2 | LP | Stax | 589011 | 1967 | £6 | £15 | |
| Steam Ballads | LP | Broadside | BRO121 | 1977 | £5 | £12 | |
| Stiff Box Set No. 1 | 7" | Stiff | BUY1-10 | 1979 | £15 | £30 | 10 x 7", boxed |
| Story Of Oak Records | LP | Tenth Planet | TP010 | 1994 | £8 | £20 | double |
| Story Of The Blues Vol. 2 | LP | CBS | 66232 | 1970 | £6 | £15 | double |
| Straighten Up | LP | Pama | PMP2002 | 1970 | £6 | £15 | |
| Straighten Up Vol. 2 | LP | Pama | PMP2007 | 1971 | £6 | £15 | |
| Straighten Up Vol. 3 | LP | Pama | PMP2014 | 1971 | £6 | £15 | |
| Straighten Up Vol. 4 | LP | Pama | PMP2017 | 1972 | £6 | £15 | |
| Strangers From A Strange Land | LP | private | | 1991 | £6 | £15 | US |
| Street To Street – A Liverpool Compilation | LP | Open Eye | OELP501 | 1979 | £5 | £12 | |
| Strictly Canadian | LP | Birchmont | BM523 | 1971 | £15 | £30 | Canadian |
| Sue Sampler Record For Clubs | LP | Sue | ILP919 | 1965 | £50 | £100 | promo only |
| Sue Story | LP | London | HAC8239 | 1965 | £10 | £25 | different to Sue LP |
| Sue Story | LP | Sue | ILP925 | 1965 | £15 | £30 | |
| Sue Story Vol. 2 | LP | Sue | ILP933 | 1966 | £15 | £30 | |
| Sue Story Vol. 3 | LP | Sue | ILP938 | 1966 | £15 | £30 | |
| Summer '75 | LP | Island | ISS1 | 1975 | £8 | £20 | |
| Super Duper Blues | LP | Blue Horizon | PR31 | 1969 | £4 | £10 | |
| Super Soul | LP | Pye | NPL28107 | 1968 | £4 | £10 | |
| Surf Party | LP | Ava | AVA28 | 1962 | £20 | £40 | US |
| Swamp Blues | LP | Blue Horizon | 766263 | 1970 | £20 | £40 | double |
| Sweet Beat | LP | Starclub | 158022STY | 1966 | £50 | £100 | German |
| Sweet Beat | 7" EP | Top Rank | JKR8007 | 1959 | £7.50 | £15 | |
| Sweet Home Chicago | LP | Delmark | DS618 | 1970 | £5 | £12 | |
| Sweet Soul Sounds | LP | Stateside | (S)SL10243 | 1968 | £6 | £15 | |
| Swing Easy | LP | Coxsone | CSL8018 | 1968 | £50 | £100 | |
| Swingin' Set | LP | MGM | C8012 | 1966 | £6 | £15 | |
| Swingin' The Blues | LP | Tempo | TAP21 | 1958 | £10 | £25 | |
| Syde Tryps Four | LP | Tenth Planet | TP008 | 1994 | £6 | £15 | |
| Syde Tryps One | LP | Tenth Planet | TP002 | 1993 | £6 | £15 | |
| Syde Tryps Three | LP | Tenth Planet | TP006 | 1993 | £6 | £15 | |
| Syde Tryps Two | LP | Tenth Planet | TP004 | 1993 | £6 | £15 | |
| Take Off Your Head And Listen | LP | Rubber | LP001 | 1971 | £4 | £10 | |
| Take Six | 7" EP | Oriole | EP7080 | 1964 | £12.50 | £25 | |
| Talk Of THe Grapevine | LP | Grapevine | GRAL1000 | 1978 | £4 | £10 | |
| Tamla Motown Box | 7" | Tamla Motown | TMG956-975,1000 | 1975 | £50 | £100 | boxed set of demos |
| Tear It Up | 7" EP | Mercury | ZEP10015 | 1959 | £30 | £60 | |
| Teen Scene '64 | 7" EP | Ember | EMBEP4540 | 1964 | £7.50 | £15 | |
| Teenage Rock | LP | Capitol | T1009 | 1958 | £15 | £30 | |
| Teenage Rock | 7" EP | Mercury | MEP9522 | 1957 | £25 | £50 | |
| Teenage Tops | 7" EP | RCA | RCX111 | 1958 | £10 | £20 | |
| Teenager Party '64 | LP | Polydor | 237340 | 1964 | £30 | £60 | German stereo |
| Teenager Party '64 | LP | Polydor | 46840 | 1964 | £25 | £50 | German mono |
| Texas Blues | LP | Fountain | FV205 | 197– | £4 | £10 | |
| Texas Reverberations | LP | Texas Archive | TAR1 | 1982 | £5 | £12 | US |
| Texas-Louisiana Blues | LP | Highway 51 | H103 | 1969 | £20 | £40 | |

| Title | Format | Label | Catalogue | Year | | | Notes |
|---|---|---|---|---|---|---|---|
| Thank Your Lucky Stars | LP | Ace Of Clubs | ACL1108 | 1962 | £6 | £15 | |
| Thank Your Lucky Stars Vol. 2 | LP | Decca | LK4554 | 1963 | £8 | £20 | |
| That's Underground | LP | CBS | SPR23 | 1970 | £6 | £15 | German, multi-coloured vinyl |
| Themes From James Bond Films | 7" EP | CBS | WEP1126 | 1967 | £2 | £5 | |
| There Is Some Fun Going Forward | LP | Dandelion | 2485021 | 1972 | £25 | £50 | with poster |
| These Kind Of Blues Vol. 1 | LP | Action | ACLP6009 | 1969 | £6 | £15 | |
| They Sold A Million No. 4 | 7" EP | Brunswick | OE9420 | 1959 | £2 | £5 | |
| They Sold A Million No. 9 | 7" EP | Brunswick | OE9425 | 1959 | £5 | £10 | |
| They Sold A Million No. 10 | 7" EP | Brunswick | OE9426 | 1959 | £2 | £5 | |
| They Sold A Million No. 11 | 7" EP | Brunswick | OE9427 | 1959 | £4 | £8 | |
| They Sold A Million No. 12 | 7" EP | Brunswick | OE9428 | 1959 | £2 | £5 | |
| They Sold A Million No. 13 | 7" EP | Brunswick | OE9429 | 1959 | £2 | £5 | |
| Third Irish Folk Festival In Concert | LP | Intercord | INT181008 | 1976 | £10 | £25 | German double |
| Thirteen Year Itch | CD | 4AD | SHUFFLE | 1993 | £8 | £20 | |
| This Is Blue Beat | LP | Island | ILP910 | 1964 | £50 | £100 | test pressing |
| This Is Blues | LP | Island | IWP5 | 1970 | £8 | £20 | pink label |
| This Is Merseybeat Vol. 1 | LP | Oriole | PS40047 | 1963 | £20 | £40 | |
| This Is Merseybeat Vol. 2 | LP | Oriole | PS40048 | 1963 | £20 | £40 | |
| This Is Northern Soul | LP | Grapevine | GRAL1002 | 197– | £6 | £15 | |
| This Is Reggae | LP | Pama | PSP1003 | 1969 | £8 | £20 | |
| This Is Reggae Vol. 2 | LP | Pama | PMP2005 | 1971 | £6 | £15 | |
| This Is Reggae Vol. 3 | LP | Pama | PMP2008 | 1971 | £6 | £15 | |
| This Is Reggae Vol. 4 | LP | Pama | PMP2016 | 1972 | £6 | £15 | |
| This Is Sue! | LP | Island | IWP3 | 1969 | £5 | £12 | pink label |
| Those Cakewalkin' Babies From Home | LP | Saydisc | SDR182 | 1970 | £4 | £10 | |
| Three O'Clock Merrian Webster Time | LP | Cicadelic | CICLP999 | 1982 | £5 | £12 | US |
| Tighten Up | LP | Trojan | TBL120 | 1969 | £4 | £10 | |
| Tighten Up | LP | Trojan | TTL1 | 1969 | £5 | £12 | |
| Tighten Up Vol. 2 | LP | Trojan | TBL131 | 1970 | £4 | £10 | |
| Tighten Up Vol. 2 | LP | Trojan | TTL7 | 1969 | £4 | £10 | |
| Tighten Up Vol. 2 | LP | Trojan | TTL7 | 1969 | £20 | £40 | pink Island label |
| Tighten Up Vol. 3 | LP | Trojan | TBL145 | 1970 | £4 | £10 | |
| Tighten Up Vol. 4 | LP | Trojan | TBL163 | 1971 | £4 | £10 | |
| Tighten Up Vol. 5 | LP | Trojan | TBL165 | 1971 | £4 | £10 | |
| Tighten Up Vol. 6 | LP | Trojan | TBL185 | 1972 | £4 | £10 | |
| Tijd For Teenagers 1 | 10" LP | Philips | 600369 | 1965 | £20 | £40 | Dutch |
| Tijd For Teenagers 2 | 10" LP | Philips | 600701 | 1965 | £20 | £40 | Dutch |
| To The Shores Of Lake Placid | LP | Zoo | ZOO4 | 1982 | £4 | £10 | |
| Tobacco A-Go-Go | LP | Blue Mold | BMLP101 | 1984 | £5 | £12 | US |
| Together Sound Of Reading | LP | Airport | MO70870 | 1970 | £10 | £25 | US |
| Top Teen Bands Vol. 1 | LP | Bud-Jet | 311 | 1965 | £25 | £50 | US |
| Top Teen Bands Vol. 2 | LP | Bud-Jet | 312 | 1965 | £25 | £50 | US |
| Top Teen Bands Vol. 3 | LP | Bud-Jet | 313 | 1965 | £25 | £50 | US |
| Top Teen Dances | 7" EP | Stateside | SE1004 | 1963 | £5 | £10 | |
| Top TV Themes | 7" EP | Pye | NEP24276 | 1967 | £2 | £5 | |
| Topic Sampler No. 1 | LP | Topic | TPS114 | 1964 | £6 | £15 | |
| Topic Sampler No. 2 | LP | Topic | TPS145 | 1965 | £5 | £12 | |
| Topic Sampler No. 3 | LP | Topic | TPS166 | 1966 | £4 | £10 | |
| Topic Sampler No. 4 | LP | Topic | TPS168 | 1966 | £4 | £10 | |
| Topic Sampler No. 5 | LP | Topic | TPS169 | 1967 | £4 | £10 | |
| Topic Sampler No. 6 | LP | Topic | TPS201 | 1968 | £4 | £10 | |
| Topic Sampler No. 7 | LP | Topic | TPS205 | 1969 | £4 | £10 | |
| Topic Sampler No. 8 | LP | Topic | TPSS221 | 1972 | £5 | £12 | |
| Tops In Pops No. 1 | 7" EP | Decca | DFE6411 | 1957 | £4 | £8 | |
| Tops In Pops No. 3 | 7" EP | Decca | DFE6467 | 1958 | £2.50 | £6 | |
| Tops In Pops No. 7 | 7" EP | Decca | DFE6583 | 1959 | £2 | £5 | |
| Traditional Music Of Ireland Vol. 1 | LP | Folkways | FW8781 | 1963 | £6 | £15 | US |
| Traditional Music Of Ireland Vol. 2 | LP | Folkways | FW8782 | 1963 | £6 | £15 | US |
| Travelling Folk | LP | Eron | 006 | 1976 | £5 | £12 | |
| Treasures Of North American Negro Music Vol. 6 | 7" EP | Fontana | TFE17265 | 1960 | £2.50 | £6 | |
| Treasury Of Field Recordings | LP | 77 | LA122 | 1960 | £6 | £15 | |
| Treasury Of Field Recordings Vol. 2 | LP | 77 | LA123 | 1960 | £6 | £15 | |
| Tribute To Michael Holliday | LP | Columbia | 33SX1635 | 1964 | £8 | £20 | |
| Triple Treat | LP | Parlophone | PMC1139 | 1961 | £5 | £12 | |
| Trojan Reggae Party | LP | Trojan | TBL172 | 1971 | £4 | £10 | |
| Trojan Story | LP | Trojan | | 1972 | £20 | £40 | triple |
| Trojan Story | LP | Trojan | TALL100 | 1980 | £10 | £25 | 3 LP box set |
| Trojan Story | LP | Trojan | TALL200 | 1982 | £8 | £20 | 3 LP box set |
| Trojan's Greatest Hits | LP | Trojan | TBL180 | 1971 | £4 | £10 | |
| Trojan's Greatest Hits Vol. 2 | LP | Trojan | TBL190 | 1972 | £4 | £10 | |
| Troublemakers | LP | Warner Bros. | PROA857 | 1981 | £8 | £20 | promo double |
| Tub Jug Washboard Bands | LP | Riverside | RLP8802 | 1967 | £6 | £15 | |
| TV Themes | 7" EP | Decca | DFE8585 | 1964 | £15 | £30 | |
| TV Themes 1966 | 7" EP | Pye | NEP24244 | 1966 | £4 | £8 | |
| Twelve Big Hits | LP | Melodisc | 12193 | 196– | £4 | £10 | |
| Twelve Carat Gold | LP | Melodisc | 12217 | 196– | £4 | £10 | |
| Twist At The Star Club | LP | Philips | BL7578 | 1963 | £25 | £50 | |
| Twist Festival Live '64 In Berlin | LP | Metronome | HLP10020 | 1964 | £20 | £40 | German |
| Twist Off | 7" EP | Starlite | STEP31 | 1962 | £20 | £40 | |
| Twist On | 7" EP | Starlite | STEP29 | 1962 | £25 | £50 | |
| Twist Time Im St. C.Hamburg 3 | LP | Ariola | 70954IT | 1964 | £25 | £50 | German |
| Twrw Tanllyd | LP | Sain | 1201M | 1981 | £5 | £12 | |
| Ulster's Flowery Vale | LP | BBC | REC28M | 1968 | £10 | £25 | |
| Unholy Montage | 7" | Fierce | FRIGHT38 | 198– | £10 | £20 | |
| Unity's Great Reggae Hits | LP | Pama | ECO7 | 1969 | £8 | £20 | |
| Urban Blues Vol. 1 | LP | Liberty | LBL83215 | 1969 | £4 | £10 | |

| Title | Format | Label | Cat. No. | Year | | | Notes |
|---|---|---|---|---|---|---|---|
| Urban Blues Vol. 2 | LP | Liberty | LBL83327 | 1969 | £4 | £10 | |
| Valley Of Son Of Gathering Of The Tribe | LP | Gott | 3 | 1984 | £10 | £25 | US |
| Vaudeville Blues | LP | VJM | VLP30 | 1970 | £4 | £10 | |
| Version Galore Vol. 2 | LP | Trojan | TBL175 | 1971 | £5 | £12 | |
| Version Galore Vol. 3 | LP | Trojan | TBL200 | 1973 | £5 | £12 | |
| Version To Version | LP | Trojan | TBL182 | 1972 | £5 | £12 | |
| Version To Version Vol. 3 | LP | Trojan | TBL206 | 1973 | £5 | £12 | |
| Vertigo Annual 1970 | LP | Vertigo | 6499407/8 | 1970 | £5 | £12 | double |
| Vile Vinyl Vol. 1 | LP | High Noon | HINLP001 | 1985 | £5 | £12 | US |
| Vile Vinyl Vol. 2 | LP | High Noon | HINLP002 | 1985 | £5 | £12 | US |
| Vogue Surprise Partie | 7" EP | Vogue | VRE5002 | 1965 | £2 | £5 | |
| Voices Record One | LP | Argo | PLP1112 | 1968 | £15 | £30 | |
| Voices Record Two | LP | Argo | PLP1115 | 1968 | £8 | £20 | |
| Wagon Train | 7" EP | RCA | RCX128 | 1959 | £2 | £5 | |
| Wakey Wakey | LP | Columbia | 33SX1385 | 1962 | £6 | £15 | |
| Walking By Myself | LP | Pye | NPL28041 | 1964 | £8 | £20 | |
| Walking The Blues | LP | Pye | NPL28044 | 1964 | £6 | £15 | |
| Walls Ice Cream Presents | 7" EP | Apple | CT1 | 1969 | £20 | £40 | |
| Washboard Rhythm | LP | Ace Of Hearts | AH55 | 1963 | £4 | £10 | |
| We Like Girls | LP | Coral | LVA9096 | 1959 | £5 | £12 | |
| We Like Guys | LP | Coral | LVA9098 | 1959 | £5 | £12 | |
| We Love You Beatles | 7" EP | CBS | 5649 | 1965 | £10 | £20 | French |
| We Sing The Blues | LP | Liberty | LBY3051 | 1965 | £6 | £15 | |
| We Sing The Blues | LP | London | HAP8061 | 1963 | £10 | £25 | |
| We Sing The Blues | LP | Sue | ILP921 | 1965 | £10 | £25 | |
| We Sing The Blues | 7" EP | Liberty | LEP4036 | 1965 | £5 | £10 | |
| We've Moved | LP | MPL | MPL1 | 197– | £30 | £60 | promo |
| West Coast Love In | LP | Vault | SLP113 | 1967 | £6 | £15 | US |
| West Side Chicago | 7" EP | Solid Sender | SEP101 | 1975 | £2.50 | £6 | |
| What A Way To Die: 15 Forgotten Losers From The Mid-Sixties | LP | Satan | SR1313 | 1983 | £5 | £12 | US |
| What Am I Do | LP | Trojan | TTL34 | 1970 | £6 | £15 | |
| What's Shakin' | LP | Elektra | EKS7304 | 1968 | £5 | £12 | |
| Where It's At – Live At The Cheetah | LP | Audio Fidelity | AFLP2168 | 1966 | £10 | £25 | US |
| Wholly Grail | LP | Grail | | 1972 | £37.50 | £75 | |
| Wide Midlands | LP | Topic | 12TS210 | 1971 | £4 | £10 | |
| Wild Beach Weekend | 7" EP | RCA | 86466 | 1964 | £5 | £10 | French |
| Wir Im Scheinwerfer | LP | Resono | 13003 | 1970 | £8 | £20 | German |
| Women Of The Blues | LP | RCA | RD7840 | 1967 | £6 | £15 | |
| WONE: The Dayton Scene | LP | Prism | | 1966 | £50 | £100 | US |
| Woodstock | LP | Atlantic | 2663001 | 1970 | £6 | £15 | triple |
| Woodstock 2 | LP | Atlantic | 2400130/1 | 1971 | £5 | £12 | double |
| Woorden – Poetry And Experimental Music | LP | Omega | 333023 | 1966 | £15 | £30 | Dutch |
| World Of Blues | LP | London | HAP8099 | 1963 | £10 | £25 | |
| World Of Blues Power Vol. 3 | LP | Decca | SPA263 | 1973 | £4 | £10 | |
| World Of Bullet | LP | Pama | SECO19 | 1969 | £5 | £12 | |
| World Of Folk | LP | Argo | SPA132 | 1971 | £6 | £15 | |
| Yes L.A. | LP | Dangerhouse | EW79 | 1979 | £6 | £15 | 1 sided clear picture disc |
| You Can't Wine | LP | Trojan | TBL142 | 1970 | £5 | £12 | |
| You Left Me Standing | LP | Trojan | TTL9 | 1969 | £8 | £20 | |
| You're Either On The Train | LP | Stiff | DEAL1 | 1978 | £5 | £12 | promo |
| Your Chess Requests | 7" EP | Chess | CRE6026 | 1968 | £5 | £10 | |
| Your Choice | 7" EP | Mercury | MEP9525 | 1957 | £6 | £12 | |
| Your Choice No. 2 | 7" EP | Mercury | MEP9532 | 1958 | £4 | £8 | |
| Your Jamaican Girl | LP | Bamboo | BDLP211 | 1971 | £20 | £40 | |
| Zebra Selection | LP | private | | 1968 | £25 | £50 | US |

## VARTAN, SYLVIE

| Title | Format | Label | Cat. No. | Year | | | Notes |
|---|---|---|---|---|---|---|---|
| Ihre Grossen Erfolge | LP | RCA | CAS10264 | 1974 | £10 | £25 | German |
| L'Avventura E L'Avventura | LP | United Artists | UAS29296 | 1972 | £15 | £30 | Italian |
| Le Locomotion | 7" EP | RCA | 76593 | 1963 | £20 | £40 | French |
| Sylvie | LP | RCA | 440103 | 1963 | £8 | £20 | French |
| Sylvie | LP | RCA | FSP225 | 1968 | £8 | £20 | US |

## VASELINES

| Title | Format | Label | Cat. No. | Year | | | Notes |
|---|---|---|---|---|---|---|---|
| Dum Dum | LP | 53rd And 3rd | AGAS7 | 1990 | £4 | £10 | |
| Dying For It | 12" | 53rd And 3rd | AGARR17T | 1988 | £2.50 | £6 | |
| Son Of A Gun | 7" | 53rd & 3rd | AGARR10 | 1987 | £4 | £8 | |

## VASHTI

| Title | Format | Label | Cat. No. | Year | | | Notes |
|---|---|---|---|---|---|---|---|
| Some Things Just Stick In Your Mind | 7" | Decca | F12157 | 1965 | £15 | £30 | |
| Train Song | 7" | Columbia | DB7917 | 1966 | £7.50 | £15 | |

## VATTEN

| Title | Format | Label | Cat. No. | Year | | | Notes |
|---|---|---|---|---|---|---|---|
| Tungt Vatten | LP | Prophone | PROP7756 | 1975 | £30 | £60 | Swedish |

## VAUGHAN, FRANKIE

| Title | Format | Label | Cat. No. | Year | | | Notes |
|---|---|---|---|---|---|---|---|
| Cuff Of My Shirt | 7" | HMV | 7M182 | 1954 | £2.50 | £6 | |
| Frankie Vaughan | 7" EP | Philips | BBE12022 | 1956 | £2 | £5 | |
| Frankie Vaughan | 7" EP | Philips | BBE12071 | 1956 | £2 | £5 | |
| Frankie Vaughan | 7" EP | Philips | BBE12111 | 1957 | £2 | £5 | |
| Frankie Vaughan | 7" EP | Philips | BBE12220 | 1958 | £2 | £5 | |
| Garden Of Eden | 7" | Philips | JK1002 | 1957 | £4 | £8 | |
| Give Me The Moonlight | 7" | Philips | PB423 | 1955 | £2.50 | £6 | |
| Gotta Have Something In The Bank, Frank | 7" | Philips | JK1030 | 1957 | £2.50 | £6 | |
| Happy Days And Lonely Nights | 7" | HMV | 7M270 | 1954 | £2.50 | £6 | |

| | | | | | | | |
|---|---|---|---|---|---|---|---|
| Happy Go Lucky | LP | Philips | BBL7198 | 1957 | £4 | £10 | |
| Happy Go Lucky | 7" EP | Philips | BBE12171 | 1958 | £2 | £5 | |
| Heart Of A Man | 7" EP | Philips | BBE12299 | 1959 | £2 | £5 | |
| Istanbul | 7" | HMV | 7M167 | 1953 | £5 | £10 | |
| It's Frankie | 7" EP | Philips | BBE12157 | 1957 | £2 | £5 | |
| Kisses Sweeter Than Wine | 7" | Philips | JK1035 | 1957 | £4 | £8 | |
| Lady Is A Square | 7" EP | Philips | BBE12247 | 1959 | £2 | £5 | |
| Let Me Sing & I'm Happy | 7" EP | Philips | BBE12484 | 1961 | £2 | £5 | |
| Let Me Sing & I'm Happy | 7" EP | Philips | SBBE9071 | 1961 | £2.50 | £6 | stereo |
| Let Me Sing & I'm Happy No. 2 | 7" EP | Philips | BBE12485 | 1961 | £2 | £5 | |
| Let Me Sing & I'm Happy No. 2 | 7" EP | Philips | SBBE9072 | 1961 | £2.50 | £6 | stereo |
| Let Me Sing & I'm Happy No. 3 | 7" EP | Philips | BBE12486 | 1961 | £2 | £5 | |
| Let Me Sing & I'm Happy No. 3 | 7" EP | Philips | SBBE9073 | 1961 | £2.50 | £6 | stereo |
| Mister Elegant | 7" EP | HMV | 7EG8245 | 1957 | £2 | £5 | |
| My Son, My Son | 7" | HMV | 7M252 | 1954 | £2.50 | £6 | |
| Showcase | LP | Philips | BBL7233 | 1958 | £4 | £10 | |
| These Dangerous Years | 7" | Philips | JK1022 | 1957 | £2.50 | £6 | |
| Too Many Heartaches | 7" | HMV | 7M298 | 1955 | £2.50 | £6 | |
| What's Behind That Strange Door | 7" | Philips | JK1014 | 1957 | £2.50 | £6 | |

## VAUGHAN, MALCOLM

| | | | | | | | |
|---|---|---|---|---|---|---|---|
| Chapel Of The Roses | 7" | HMV | POP325 | 1957 | £1.50 | £4 | |
| Hello No. 1 | 7" EP | HMV | GES5785 | 1959 | £2 | £5 | stereo |
| Hello No. 2 | 7" EP | HMV | GES5793 | 1959 | £2 | £5 | stereo |
| More Than A Millionaire | 7" | HMV | 7M317 | 1955 | £1.50 | £4 | |
| Only You | 7" | HMV | 7M389 | 1956 | £1.50 | £4 | |
| Requests | 7" EP | HMV | GES5799 | 1959 | £2 | £5 | stereo |
| Sincerity In Song | 7" EP | HMV | 7EG8272 | 1957 | £2.50 | £6 | |
| Sincerity In Song No. 2 | 7" EP | HMV | 7EG8377 | 1957 | £2 | £5 | |
| Sincerity In Song No. 3 | 7" EP | HMV | 7EG8453 | 1957 | £2 | £5 | |
| St. Therese Of The Roses | 7" | HMV | POP250 | 1956 | £1.50 | £4 | |
| With Your Love | 7" | HMV | 7M338 | 1955 | £2 | £5 | |
| World Is Mine | 7" | HMV | POP303 | 1957 | £1.50 | £4 | |

## VAUGHAN, SARAH

| | | | | | | | |
|---|---|---|---|---|---|---|---|
| After Hours At The London House | LP | Mercury | MMC14001 | 1959 | £5 | £12 | |
| At Mister Kelly's | LP | Mercury | MPL6542 | 1958 | £4 | £10 | |
| Best Of Berlin Vol. 1 | 7" EP | Mercury | SEZ19016 | 1961 | £2 | £5 | stereo |
| Close To You | LP | Mercury | CMS18040 | 1961 | £4 | £10 | stereo |
| Count Basie – Sarah Vaughan | LP | Columbia | SCX3403 | 1962 | £4 | £10 | stereo |
| Divine One | LP | Columbia | SCX3390 | 1962 | £4 | £10 | stereo |
| Dreamy | LP | Columbia | SCX3324 | 1960 | £4 | £10 | stereo |
| Explosive Side Of Sarah Vaughan | LP | Columbia | SCX3479 | 1963 | £4 | £10 | |
| Great Songs From Hit Shows Part 1 | LP | Mercury | CMS18019 | 1960 | £4 | £10 | stereo |
| Great Songs From Hit Shows Part 2 | LP | Mercury | CMS18023 | 1960 | £4 | £10 | stereo |
| Hit Parade | 7" EP | Mercury | MEP9511 | 1956 | £2 | £5 | |
| Images | 10" LP | Mercury | MG26005 | 1955 | £5 | £12 | |
| Images | 10" LP | Mercury | MPT7518 | 1957 | £4 | £10 | |
| In Romantic Mood | LP | Mercury | MPL6540 | 1958 | £4 | £10 | |
| In The Land Of Hi Fi | 10" LP | Emarcy | EJL100 | 1956 | £5 | £12 | |
| Linger Awhile | LP | Philips | BBL7165 | 1957 | £4 | £10 | |
| Live For Love | 7" EP | Mercury | SEZ19006 | 1961 | £2.50 | £6 | stereo |
| Make Yourself Comfortable | 10" LP | Mercury | MPT7503 | 1956 | £5 | £12 | |
| Sarah Vaughan | LP | Philips | BBL7082 | 1956 | £4 | £10 | |
| Sarah Vaughan | 7" EP | London | REU1065 | 1956 | £2 | £5 | |
| Sassy | LP | Emarcy | EJL1258 | 1957 | £4 | £10 | |
| Sings | 10" LP | London | HBU1049 | 1956 | £6 | £15 | |
| Sings George Gershwin Vol. 1 | LP | Mercury | CMS18011 | 1959 | £5 | £12 | stereo |
| Sings George Gershwin Vol. 1 | LP | Mercury | MPL6525 | 1959 | £4 | £10 | |
| Sings George Gershwin Vol. 2 | LP | Mercury | CMS18012 | 1959 | £5 | £12 | stereo |
| Sings George Gershwin Vol. 2 | LP | Mercury | MPL6527 | 1957 | £4 | £10 | |
| Sings Great Songs From Hit Shows Part 1 | LP | Mercury | MPL6522 | 1957 | £4 | £10 | |
| Sings Great Songs From Hit Shows Part 2 | LP | Mercury | MPL6523 | 1957 | £4 | £10 | |
| Swingin' Easy | LP | Emarcy | EJL1273 | 1958 | £4 | £10 | |
| Vaughan And Violins | LP | Mercury | CMS18003 | 1959 | £4 | £10 | stereo |
| Wonderful Sarah | LP | Mercury | MPL6532 | 1958 | £4 | £10 | |

## VAUGHAN, STEVIE RAY

| | | | | | | | |
|---|---|---|---|---|---|---|---|
| Tick Tock | CD-s | CBS | 6563525 | 1990 | £2 | £5 | |

## VAUGHN, BILLY

| | | | | | | | |
|---|---|---|---|---|---|---|---|
| Billy Vaughn | 7" EP | London | RED1285 | 1961 | £2 | £5 | |
| Golden Instrumentals | LP | London | HAD2025 | 1957 | £4 | £10 | |
| Golden Instrumentals | LP | London | SAHD6018 | 1959 | £6 | £15 | |
| Golden Instrumentals No. 1 | 7" EP | London | RED1083 | 1957 | £2 | £5 | |
| Golden Instrumentals No. 2 | 7" EP | London | RED1084 | 1957 | £2 | £5 | |
| Johnny Tremain | 7" | London | HLD8511 | 1957 | £1.50 | £4 | |
| Melodies Of Love | 10" LP | London | HBD1048 | 1956 | £4 | £10 | |
| Melody Of Love | 7" | London | HL8112 | 1955 | £10 | £20 | gold label |
| Petticoats Of Portugal | 7" | London | HLD8342 | 1956 | £4 | £8 | gold label |
| Plays The Million Sellers | LP | London | SAHD6003 | 1958 | £4 | £10 | stereo |
| Raunchy | 7" | London | HLD8522 | 1957 | £1.50 | £4 | |
| Sail Along Silvery Moon | LP | London | SAHD6037 | 1958 | £4 | £10 | stereo |
| Sail Along Silvery Moon | 7" EP | London | RED1189 | 1959 | £2 | £5 | |
| Swingin' Safari | 7" EP | London | RED1352 | 1963 | £2 | £5 | |
| Theme From The Threepenny Opera | 7" | London | HLD8238 | 1956 | £5 | £10 | gold label |
| Tumbling Tumbleweeds | 7" | London | HLD8612 | 1958 | £1.50 | £4 | |
| When The Lilac Blooms Again | 7" | London | HLD8319 | 1956 | £5 | £10 | gold label |

## VAUGHT, BOB & THE RENAGADES

| | | | | | | | |
|---|---|---|---|---|---|---|---|
| Surf Crazy | LP | GNP-Crescendo | (S)83 | 1963 | £6 | £15 | US |

## VEDDAR, CHUCK

| | | | | | | |
|---|---|---|---|---|---|---|
| Spanky Boy | 7" | London | HLU8951 | 1959 | £7.50 | £15 |

## VEE, BOBBY

| | | | | | | | |
|---|---|---|---|---|---|---|---|
| Bobby Tomorrow | 7" | Liberty | LIB55530 | 1963 | £1.50 | £4 | |
| Bobby Vee | LP | London | HAG2352 | 1961 | £15 | £30 | |
| Bobby Vee Meets The Crickets | 7" EP | Liberty | LEP2116 | 1963 | £6 | £12 | |
| Bobby Vee Meets The Crickets | 7" EP | Liberty | SLEP2116 | 1963 | £10 | £20 | stereo |
| Bobby Vee Meets The Crickets Vol. 2 | 7" EP | Liberty | LEP2149 | 1963 | £7.50 | £15 | |
| Bobby Vee No. 1 | 7" EP | London | REG1278 | 1961 | £7.50 | £15 | |
| Bobby Vee No. 2 | 7" EP | London | REG1299 | 1961 | £7.50 | £15 | |
| Bobby Vee No. 3 | 7" EP | London | REG1308 | 1961 | £7.50 | £15 | |
| Bobby Vee No. 4 | 7" EP | London | REG1323 | 1961 | £10 | £20 | |
| Bobby Vee's Biggest Hits | 7" EP | Liberty | LEP2102 | 1963 | £6 | £12 | |
| Bobby Vee's Biggest Hits | 7" EP | Liberty | SLEP2102 | 1963 | £7.50 | £15 | stereo |
| Buddy's Song | 7" | Liberty | LIB10141 | 1963 | £2 | £5 | |
| Devil Or Angel | 7" | Liberty | HLG9179 | 1960 | £7.50 | £15 | |
| Do What You Gotta Do | LP | Liberty | LBL/LBS83130 | 1968 | £4 | £10 | |
| Forever Kind Of Love | 7" EP | Liberty | LEP2089 | 1963 | £6 | £12 | |
| Forever Kind Of Love | 7" | Liberty | LIB10046 | 1962 | £1.50 | £4 | |
| Golden Greats | LP | Liberty | (S)LBY1112 | 1962 | £8 | £20 | |
| Hickory, Dick And Dock | 7" | Liberty | LIB55700 | 1964 | £1.50 | £4 | |
| Hits Of The Rockin' Fifties | LP | London | HAG2406/SAHG6206 | 1961 | £15 | £30 | |
| Hits Of The Rockin' Fifties | 7" EP | London | REG1324 | 1961 | £10 | £20 | |
| How Many Tears | 7" | London | HLG9389 | 1961 | £1.50 | £4 | |
| I Remember Buddy Holly | LP | Liberty | (S)LBY1188 | 1963 | £8 | £20 | |
| I'm Gonna Make It Up To You | 7" | Liberty | LBF15234 | 1969 | £1.50 | £4 | |
| Just For Fun | 7" EP | Liberty | LEP2084 | 1963 | £6 | £12 | with The Crickets |
| Just Today | LP | Liberty | LBL/LBS83112 | 1968 | £4 | £10 | |
| Keep On Trying | 7" | Liberty | LIB10197 | 1965 | £1.50 | £4 | |
| Like You've Never Known Before | 7" | Liberty | LIB10272 | 1967 | £1.50 | £4 | |
| Live On Tour | LP | Liberty | (S)LBY1263 | 1965 | £6 | £15 | |
| Look At Me Girl | LP | Liberty | (S)LBY1341 | 1966 | £6 | £15 | |
| Look At Me Girl | 7" | Liberty | LIB55877 | 1966 | £1.50 | £4 | |
| Love's Made A Fool Of You | 7" | London | HLG9459 | 1961 | £4 | £8 | |
| Meets The Crickets | LP | Liberty | (S)LBY1086 | 1962 | £4 | £10 | |
| Meets The Ventures | LP | Liberty | (S)LBY1147 | 1963 | £8 | £20 | |
| Meets The Ventures | 7" EP | Liberty | LEP2212 | 1965 | £7.50 | £15 | |
| Merry Christmas From Bobby Vee | LP | Liberty | LRP3267/LST7267 | 1962 | £8 | £20 | US |
| More Than I Can Say | 7" | London | HLG9316 | 1961 | £1.50 | £4 | |
| New Sound From England | LP | London | LRP3352/LST7352 | 1964 | £8 | £20 | US |
| New Sounds | 7" EP | Liberty | LEP2181 | 1964 | £7.50 | £15 | |
| Night Has A Thousand Eyes | LP | Liberty | (S)LBY1139 | 1963 | £8 | £20 | |
| Night Has A Thousand Eyes | 7" | Liberty | LIB10069 | 1963 | £1.50 | £4 | |
| Please Don't Ask About Barbara | 7" | Liberty | LIB55419 | 1962 | £1.50 | £4 | |
| Recording Session | LP | Liberty | (S)LBY1084 | 1962 | £8 | £20 | |
| Rubber Ball | 7" | London | HLG9255 | 1961 | £2 | £5 | |
| Run Like The Devil | 7" | Liberty | LIB55828 | 1965 | £2 | £5 | |
| Run To Him | 7" | Liberty | LIB55388 | 1962 | £1.50 | £4 | |
| Run To Him | 7" | Liberty | HLG9470 | 1961 | £1.50 | £4 | |
| Sharing You | 7" | Liberty | LIB55451 | 1962 | £1.50 | £4 | |
| Sincerely | 7" EP | Liberty | LEP2053 | 1962 | £6 | £12 | |
| Sings Your Favourites | LP | Liberty | HAG2320 | 1961 | £15 | £30 | |
| Stranger In Your Arms | 7" | Liberty | LIB10124 | 1963 | £1.50 | £4 | |
| Take Good Care Of My Baby | LP | Liberty | (S)LBY1004 | 1961 | £6 | £15 | |
| Take Good Care Of My Baby | LP | London | HAG2428/SAHG6224 | 1961 | £10 | £25 | |
| Take Good Care Of My Baby | 7" | London | HLG7111 | 1961 | £2 | £5 | export |
| Take Good Care Of My Baby | 7" | London | HLG9438 | 1961 | £1.50 | £4 | |
| Thirty Big Hits From The 60s | LP | Liberty | LRP3385/LST7385 | 1964 | £8 | £20 | US |
| True Love Never Runs Smooth | 7" | Liberty | LIB10213 | 1965 | £1.50 | £4 | |
| With Strings And Things | LP | London | HAG2374/SAHG6174 | 1961 | £15 | £30 | |

## VEGA, SUZANNE

| | | | | | | | |
|---|---|---|---|---|---|---|---|
| Compact Hits | CD-s | A&M | AMCD912 | 1988 | £2 | £5 | |
| Left Of Center | CD-s | A&M | CDQ320 | 1986 | £6 | £15 | |
| Small Blue Thing | 7" | A&M | AM294 | 1985 | £1.50 | £4 | double |
| Solitude Standing | CD-s | A&M | VEGCD3 | 1988 | £3 | £8 | |
| Tom's Diner | CD-s | A&M | VEGCD2 | 1987 | £3 | £8 | |

## VEGAS, PAT & LOLLY

| | | | | | | | |
|---|---|---|---|---|---|---|---|
| At The Haunted House | LP | Mercury | MG2/SR61059 | 1966 | £6 | £15 | US |

## VEJTABLES

| | | | | | | | |
|---|---|---|---|---|---|---|---|
| I Still Love You | 7" EP | Vogue | INT18051 | 1965 | £12.50 | £25 | French |
| I Still Love You | 7" | Pye | 7N25339 | 1965 | £4 | £8 | |

## VELEZ, MARTHA

| | | | | | | | |
|---|---|---|---|---|---|---|---|
| Boogie Kitchen | 7" | Blue Horizon | 2096010 | 1972 | £2.50 | £6 | |
| Fiends And Angels | LP | London | HAK/SHK8395 | 1969 | £5 | £12 | |
| Fiends And Angels Again | LP | Blue Horizon | 763867 | 1970 | £10 | £25 | |

| | | | | | | |
|---|---|---|---|---|---|---|
| It Takes A Lot To Laugh | 7" | London | HLK10266 | 1966 | £1.50 | £4 |
| Tell Mama | 7" | London | HLK10280 | 1969 | £1.50 | £4 |

## VELVELETTES

| | | | | | | |
|---|---|---|---|---|---|---|
| He Was Really Sayin' Something | 7" | Stateside | SS387 | 1965 | £15 | £30 |
| Lonely Lonely Girl Am I | 7" | Tamla Motown | TMG521 | 1965 | £30 | £60 |
| Needle In A Haystack | 7" | Stateside | SS361 | 1964 | £10 | £20 |
| Needle In A Haystack | 7" | Tamla Motown | TMG595 | 1967 | £4 | £8 |
| These Things Keep Me Loving You | 7" | Tamla Motown | TMG580 | 1966 | £7.50 | £15 |

## VELVET HUSH

| | | | | | | |
|---|---|---|---|---|---|---|
| Broken Heart | 7" | Oak | RGJ648 | 1968 | £37.50 | £75 |

## VELVET OPERA

| | | | | | | |
|---|---|---|---|---|---|---|
| Anna Dance Square | 7" | CBS | 4189 | 1969 | £1.50 | £4 |
| Black Jack Davy | 7" | CBS | 4802 | 1970 | £1.50 | £4 |
| Ride A Hustler's Dream | LP | CBS | 63692 | 1969 | £20 | £40 |

## VELVET UNDERGROUND

The Velvet Underground's sponsorship by artist Andy Warhol on their first album derives from the group's early involvement with the New York avant-garde. Distinctive and innovative though their albums are, they are to some extent a commercial version of the music the group liked to play live. Bootleg recordings exist of extended performances of 'Sister Ray' and unnamed instrumental pieces, where the meditational drone music of La Monte Young is given a quasi-rock'n'roll setting to create a sound like no other of its time. The song 'Venus In Furs' from the first album found unlikely employment as music for a tyre advert in the nineties, but it remains a stunning performance. The late guitarist Sterling Morrison proudly referred to the song in a television interview as being totally unlike any other sixties track (by anybody) and he is right. Nico appears only on the first album – the inclusion of her songs giving the record an effectively schizophrenic feel. John Cale's departure after *White Light/White Heat* had a more serious effect, while Lou Reed's exit from the group he had created himself means that *Squeeze* is essentially the work of an entirely different group.

| | | | | | | | |
|---|---|---|---|---|---|---|---|
| All Tomorrow's Parties | 7" | Verve | 10427 | 1966 | £75 | £150 | US |
| Andy Warhol's Velvet Underground Featuring Nico | LP | MGM | 2683006 | 1971 | £6 | £15 | double |
| Candy Says | 7" | MGM | 2006283 | 1973 | £2 | £5 | |
| Index Cardboard Picture Disc | 7" | Index | | 1966 | £100 | £200 | US |
| Loaded | LP | Atlantic | 2400111 | 1970 | £6 | £15 | |
| Loop | 7" | Aspen | | 1966 | £100 | £200 | US flexi |
| Radio Spot | 7" | MGM | VU1 | 1969 | £150 | £250 | US promo, best auctioned |
| Squeeze | LP | Polydor | 2383180 | 1972 | £5 | £12 | |
| Sunday Morning | 7" | Verve | 10466 | 1966 | £62.50 | £125 | US |
| Sweet Jane | 7" | Atlantic | K10339 | 1973 | £2 | £5 | |
| Velvet Underground | LP | MGM | CS8108 | 1969 | £15 | £30 | |
| Velvet Underground | LP | Polydor | VUBOX1 | 1986 | £20 | £40 | 5 LP boxed set |
| Velvet Underground And Nico | LP | MGM | 2315056 | 1971 | £5 | £12 | |
| Velvet Underground And Nico | LP | MGM | 2315056 | 1971 | £25 | £50 | with US peelable banana cover |
| Velvet Underground And Nico | LP | Verve | SVLP9184 | 1967 | £20 | £40 | |
| Velvet Underground And Nico | LP | Verve | V5008 | 1967 | £37.50 | £75 | US, peelable banana cover, male torso airbrushed out, mono |
| Velvet Underground And Nico | LP | Verve | V5008 | 1967 | £75 | £150 | US, peelable banana cover, male torso frames group photo, mono |
| Velvet Underground And Nico | LP | Verve | V5008 | 1967 | £50 | £100 | US, peelable banana cover, sticker covers group photo, mono |
| Velvet Underground And Nico | LP | Verve | V65008 | 1967 | £37.50 | £75 | US, peelable banana cover, male torso airbrushed out, stereo |
| Velvet Underground And Nico | LP | Verve | V65008 | 1967 | £62.50 | £125 | US, peelable banana cover, male torso frames group photo, stereo |
| Velvet Underground And Nico | LP | Verve | V65008 | 1967 | £37.50 | £75 | US, peelable banana cover, sticker covers group photo, stereo |
| Velvet Underground And Nico | LP | Verve | VLP9184 | 1967 | £25 | £50 | mono |
| Velvet Underground And Nico | CD | Polydor | C88115 | 1988 | £6 | £15 | box set |
| What Goes On? | 7" | MGM | 14057 | 1969 | £25 | £50 | US promo |
| White Light, White Heat | 7" | Verve | 10560 | 1968 | £25 | £50 | US promo, 2 different B sides |
| White Light/White Heat | LP | Verve | SVLP9201 | 1967 | £20 | £40 | stereo |
| White Light/White Heat | LP | Verve | VLP9201 | 1967 | £25 | £50 | mono |
| Who Loves The Sun | 7" | Atlantic | 2091088 | 1971 | £5 | £10 | |
| Who Loves The Sun | 7" | Cotillion | 44107 | 1971 | £15 | £30 | US promo |

## VELVETS

| | | | | | | |
|---|---|---|---|---|---|---|
| Laugh | 7" | London | HLU9444 | 1961 | £7.50 | £15 |
| That Lucky Old Sun | 7" | London | HLU9328 | 1961 | £7.50 | £15 |
| Tonight | 7" | London | HLU9372 | 1961 | £7.50 | £15 |
| Velvets | 7" EP | London | REU1297 | 1961 | £30 | £60 |

## VELVETT FOGG

| | | | | | | | |
|---|---|---|---|---|---|---|---|
| Telstar '69 | 7" | Pye | 7N17673 | 1969 | £5 | £10 | |
| Velvet Fogg | LP | Pye | NSPL18272 | 1967 | £37.50 | £75 | laminated sleeve |

## VELVETTES

| | | | | | | | |
|---|---|---|---|---|---|---|---|
| He's The One I Want | 7" | Mercury | MF802 | 1964 | £2 | £5 | |
| He's The One I Want | 7" | Mercury | MF802 | 1964 | £4 | £8 | *picture sleeve* |

## VENDORS

| | | | | | | | |
|---|---|---|---|---|---|---|---|
| Peace Pipe | 7" | Domino Studios | no number | 1964 | £250 | £400 | *.. demo, best auctioned* |

## VENOM

| | | | | | | | |
|---|---|---|---|---|---|---|---|
| Blood Lust | 7" | Neat | NEAT13 | 1982 | £1.50 | £4 | |
| Die Hard | 7" | Neat | NEAT027 | 1983 | £2.50 | £6 | *export picture disc* |
| In League With Satan | 7" | Neat | NEAT08 | 1982 | £1.50 | £4 | |
| Manitou | 7" | Neat | NEATSHAPE43 | 1985 | £2.50 | £6 | *..., shaped picture disc* |
| Nightmare | 12" | Neat | NEATSP4712 | 1985 | £2.50 | £6 | *picture disc* |

## VENTURA, CHARLIE

| | | | | | | | |
|---|---|---|---|---|---|---|---|
| Concert | LP | Brunswick | LAT8023 | 1953 | £15 | £30 | |
| Gene Norman Concert Recordings | 10" LP | Vogue | LDE107 | 1954 | £15 | £30 | |

## VENTURA, TOBY

| | | | | | | | |
|---|---|---|---|---|---|---|---|
| If My Heart Were A Story Book | 7" | Decca | F11581 | 1963 | £7.50 | £15 | |

## VENTURAS

| | | | | | | | |
|---|---|---|---|---|---|---|---|
| Here They Are | LP | Drum Boy | DB(S)1003 | 1964 | £10 | £25 | US |

## VENTURES

The Ventures are the American equivalent of the Shadows, maintaining a long and still buoyant career by playing melodic guitar instrumentals with no more than a token regard of the prevailing musical fashions. The size of the Ventures' output is astonishing – they have released far more albums than are listed here, including many that have been issued only in Japan. Despite this, the group still found it necessary to issue an album on their own label in 1964, thereby producing the only real rarity in their catalogue.

| | | | | | | | |
|---|---|---|---|---|---|---|---|
| A Go-Go | LP | Liberty | LBY1274 | 1965 | £4 | £10 | |
| Another Smash | LP | London | HAG2376/SAHG6176 | 1961 | £8 | £20 | |
| Another Smash | 7" EP | London | REG1326 | 1961 | £7.50 | £15 | |
| Batman Theme | LP | Dolton | BLP2042/BST8042 | 1966 | £6 | £15 | US |
| Beach Party | LP | Dolton | BLP2016/BST8016 | 1963 | £6 | £15 | US |
| Blue Moon | 7" | London | HLG9465 | 1961 | £2 | £5 | |
| Christmas Album | LP | Liberty | LBY1285 | 1965 | £6 | £15 | |
| Colourful Ventures | LP | London | HAG2409/SAHG6209 | 1961 | £8 | £20 | |
| Colourful Ventures | 7" EP | London | REG1328 | 1961 | £6 | £12 | |
| Dance Party | LP | Liberty | (S)LBY1110 | 1962 | £6 | £15 | |
| Dance With The Ventures | LP | Dolton | BLP2014/BST8014 | 1963 | £6 | £15 | US |
| Dance! | LP | Dolton | BLP2010/BST8010 | 1963 | £6 | £15 | US |
| Diamond Head | 7" | Liberty | LIB303 | 1965 | £1.50 | £4 | |
| El Cumbanchero | 7" | Liberty | LIB68 | 1964 | £1.50 | £4 | |
| Fabulous Ventures | LP | Dolton | BLP2029/BST8029 | 1964 | £6 | £15 | US |
| Flights Of Fantasy | 7" | Liberty | LBF15075 | 1968 | £1.50 | £4 | |
| Go With The Ventures | LP | Liberty | LBY1323 | 1966 | £4 | £10 | |
| Guitar Freakout | LP | Liberty | LBY1345 | 1967 | £4 | £10 | |
| Hawaii Five-O | 7" | Liberty | LBF15221 | 1969 | £1.50 | £4 | |
| In Space | LP | Liberty | (S)LBY1189 | 1964 | £6 | £15 | |
| Journey To The Stars | 7" | Liberty | LIB91 | 1964 | £1.50 | £4 | |
| Knock Me Out | LP | Liberty | (S)LBY1252 | 1965 | £4 | £10 | |
| Lady Of Spain | 7" | London | HLG7113 | 1961 | £7.50 | £15 | *export* |
| Let's Go | LP | Liberty | LBY1169 | 1963 | £4 | £10 | |
| Lolita Ya Ya | 7" | Liberty | LIB60 | 1964 | £1.50 | £4 | |
| Lullaby Of The Leaves | 7" | London | HLG9344 | 1961 | £1.50 | £4 | |
| Mashed Potatoes And Gravy | LP | Dolton | BLP2016/BST8016 | 1962 | £8 | £20 | US |
| Ninth Wave | 7" | Liberty | LIB78 | 1964 | £1.50 | £4 | |
| On Stage | LP | Liberty | LBY1270 | 1965 | £4 | £10 | |
| Penetration | 7" | Liberty | LIB10142 | 1964 | £1.50 | £4 | |
| Perfidia | 7" EP | London | REG1279 | 1960 | £6 | £12 | |
| Perfidia | 7" | London | HLG9232 | 1960 | £1.50 | £4 | |
| Play Guitar With The Ventures | LP | Dolton | BLP16501 | 1965 | £6 | £15 | US |
| Play Guitar With The Ventures Vol. 2 | LP | Dolton | BLP16502 | 1966 | £6 | £15 | US |
| Play Guitar With The Ventures Vol. 3 | LP | Dolton | BLP16503 | 1966 | £6 | £15 | US |
| Play Guitar With The Ventures Vol. 4 | LP | Dolton | BLP16504 | 1966 | £6 | £15 | US |
| Ram Bunk Shush | 7" EP | London | REG1288 | 1961 | £7.50 | £15 | |
| Ram Bunk Shush | 7" | London | HLG9292 | 1961 | £1.50 | £4 | |
| Secret Agent Man | 7" EP | Liberty | LEP2250 | 1966 | £7.50 | £15 | |
| Secret Agent Man | 7" | Liberty | LIB316 | 1966 | £1.50 | £4 | |
| Slaughter On Tenth Avenue | 7" | Liberty | LIB300 | 1965 | £1.50 | £4 | |
| Sleigh Ride | 7" | Liberty | LIB10219 | 1965 | £1.50 | £4 | |
| Smash Hits | 7" EP | Liberty | LEP2131 | 1963 | £6 | £12 | |
| Stranger | 7" | Liberty | LIB308 | 1965 | £1.50 | £4 | |
| Strawberry Fields Forever | 7" | Liberty | LIB55967 | 1967 | £1.50 | £4 | |
| Super Psychedelics | LP | Liberty | LBL/LBS83033 | 1968 | £4 | £10 | |
| Super Psychedelics | LP | Liberty | LBY1372 | 1967 | £5 | £12 | |
| Surfing | LP | Liberty | LBY1150 | 1963 | £6 | £15 | |
| Swingin' Creeper | 7" | Liberty | LIB306 | 1965 | £1.50 | £4 | |
| Telstar, The Lonely Bull | LP | Dolton | BLP2019/BST8019 | 1963 | £8 | £20 | US |
| Tenth Anniversary Album | LP | Liberty | LST35000 | 1970 | £4 | £10 | US |
| Theme From Silver City | 7" | London | HLG9411 | 1961 | £1.50 | £4 | |
| Theme From The Wild Angels | 7" | Liberty | LIB10266 | 1967 | £1.50 | £4 | |

| | | | | | | | | |
|---|---|---|---|---|---|---|---|---|
| Twist Party | LP | Liberty | LBY1072 | 1962 | £6 | £15 | |
| Twist With The Ventures | LP | London | HAG2429/ SAHG6225 | 1962 | £8 | £20 | |
| Twist With The Ventures | 7" EP | Liberty | LEP2058 | 1962 | £6 | £12 | |
| Two Thousand Pound Bee | 7" | Liberty | LIB67 | 1964 | £1.50 | £4 | |
| Ventures | LP | Dolton | BLP2042/BST8042 | 1966 | £6 | £15 | US |
| Ventures | LP | London | HAG2340 | 1961 | £10 | £25 | |
| Ventures | LP | London | SAHG6143 | 1961 | £15 | £30 | stereo |
| Ventures | LP | Ventures | BG101 | 1964 | £25 | £50 | US |
| Ventures Play Country Greats | 7" EP | Liberty | LEP2174 | 1964 | £6 | £12 | |
| Ventures Play Telstar & Lonely Bull | 7" EP | Liberty | LEP2104 | 1963 | £6 | £12 | |
| Ventures Play The Country Classics | LP | Dolton | BLP2023/BST8023 | 1963 | £8 | £20 | US |
| Versatile Ventures | LP | Liberty | SCR5 | 1966 | £6 | £15 | US |
| Walk Don't Run | LP | Liberty | LBY1002 | 1960 | £6 | £15 | |
| Walk Don't Run | 7" | Top Rank | JAR417 | 1960 | £1.50 | £4 | |
| Walk Don't Run '64 | 7" | Liberty | LIB96 | 1964 | £1.50 | £4 | |
| Walk Don't Run Vol. 2 | LP | Liberty | LBY1228 | 1964 | £6 | £15 | |
| Where The Action Is | LP | Liberty | LBY1297 | 1966 | £4 | £10 | |
| Wild Things | LP | Dolton | BLP2047/BST8047 | 1966 | £6 | £15 | US |

## VENUS IN FURS

| | | | | | | | | |
|---|---|---|---|---|---|---|---|---|
| Momento Mori | 7" | Backs | PNCH105 | 1985 | £2 | £5 | picture disc |
| Momento Mori | 7" | Movement | MOO1 | 1984 | £2 | £5 | |

## VENUTI, JOE

| | | | | | | | |
|---|---|---|---|---|---|---|---|
| Joe Venuti | 10" LP | Brunswick | LA8522 | 1951 | £10 | £25 | |

## VERLANDER, TIM

| | | | | | | | |
|---|---|---|---|---|---|---|---|
| Tim Verlander | LP | Midas | MR007 | 1972 | £8 | £20 | |

## VERNE, LARRY

| | | | | | | | | |
|---|---|---|---|---|---|---|---|---|
| Mr. Custer | 7" | London | HLN9194 | 1960 | £1.50 | £4 | |
| Mr. Larry Verne | LP | Era | EL104 | 1961 | £6 | £15 | US |
| Mr. Livingston | 7" | London | HLN9263 | 1961 | £1.50 | £4 | |

## VERNON, MIKE

Although he has made the occasional record himself, both under his own name and as a member of the Olympic Runners, Mike Vernon is best known as a producer and as the proprietor of Blue Horizon records. As the producer of John Mayall's pivotal *Bluesbreakers* and *Hard Road* albums, Vernon was ideally placed to take a major role within the development of British blues, and he went on to work with most of the significant talents within the genre, including Fleetwood Mac, Chicken Shack, Savoy Brown and the Groundhogs. Every record on his Blue Horizon label is now a collectors' item, as indeed are the handful of singles issued by the label's predecessor, Purdah.

| | | | | | | | | |
|---|---|---|---|---|---|---|---|---|
| Bring It Back Home | LP | Blue Horizon | 2931003 | 1971 | £30 | £60 | |
| Let's Try It Again | 7" | Blue Horizon | 2096007 | 1971 | £2.50 | £6 | |
| Moment Of Madness | LP | Sire | SAS7410 | 1973 | £5 | £12 | US |

## VERNONS GIRLS

| | | | | | | | | |
|---|---|---|---|---|---|---|---|---|
| Do The Bird | 7" | Decca | F11629 | 1963 | £1.50 | £4 | |
| Don't Look Now | 7" | Parlophone | R4596 | 1959 | £1.50 | £4 | |
| Funny All Over | 7" | Decca | F11549 | 1962 | £1.50 | £4 | |
| He'll Never Come Back | 7" | Decca | F11685 | 1963 | £1.50 | £4 | |
| It's A Sin To Tell A Lie | 7" | Decca | F12021 | 1964 | £1.50 | £4 | |
| Jealous Heart | 7" | Parlophone | R4532 | 1959 | £1.50 | £4 | |
| Let's Get Together | 7" | Parlophone | R4832 | 1961 | £1.50 | £4 | |
| Locomotion | 7" | Decca | F11495 | 1962 | £1.50 | £4 | |
| Lover Please | 7" | Decca | F11450 | 1962 | £1.50 | £4 | |
| Madison Time | 7" | Parlophone | R4654 | 1960 | £1.50 | £4 | |
| Only You Can Do It | 7" | Decca | F11887 | 1964 | £1.50 | £4 | |
| Ten Little Lonely Boys | 7" | Parlophone | R4734 | 1961 | £1.50 | £4 | |
| Tomorrow Is Another Day | 7" | Decca | F11781 | 1963 | £1.50 | £4 | |
| Vernons Girls | LP | Parlophone | PMC1052 | 1958 | £25 | £50 | |
| Vernons Girls | 7" EP | Decca | DFE8506 | 1962 | £6 | £12 | |
| We Like Boys | 7" | Parlophone | R4624 | 1960 | £1.50 | £4 | |
| We Love The Beatles | 7" | Decca | F11807 | 1964 | £1.50 | £4 | |
| White Bucks And Saddle Shoes | 7" | Parlophone | R4497 | 1958 | £5 | £10 | |

## VERONICA

Veronica Bennett was the lead singer of the Ronettes and, not long after these solo releases, became Mrs Phil Spector.

| | | | | | | | | |
|---|---|---|---|---|---|---|---|---|
| So Young | 7" | Phil Spector | 1 | 1964 | £20 | £40 | US |
| Why Don't They Let Us Fall In Love? | 7" | Phil Spector | 2 | 1964 | £20 | £40 | US |

## VERSATILE NEWTS

| | | | | | | | |
|---|---|---|---|---|---|---|---|
| Newtrition | 7" | Shanghai | No. 2 | 1980 | £7.50 | £15 | |

## VERSATILES

| | | | | | | | | |
|---|---|---|---|---|---|---|---|---|
| Children Get Ready | 7" | Crab | CRAB1 | 1968 | £2 | £5 | |
| Just Can't Win | 7" | Amalgamated | AMG802 | 1968 | £4 | £8 | Leaders B side |
| Lu Lu Bell | 7" | Amalgamated | AMG854 | 1969 | £2.50 | £6 | |
| Spread Your Bed | 7" | Crab | CRAB5 | 1969 | £1.50 | £4 | |
| Teardrops Falling | 7" | Island | WI3142 | 1968 | £5 | £10 | |
| Worries A Yard | 7" | Big Shot | BI520 | 1969 | £1.50 | £4 | Val Bennett B side |

## VERSATONES

| | | | | | | | |
|---|---|---|---|---|---|---|---|
| Versatones | LP | RCA | LPM1538 | 1957 | £8 | £20 | US |

## VERTO
| | | | | | | | |
|---|---|---|---|---|---|---|---|
| Krig/Volubilis | LP | Tapioca | 10007 | 1976 | £4 | £10 | *French* |
| Reel 19/36 | LP | Fleau | FL7004 | 1978 | £4 | £10 | *French* |

## VERVE
| | | | | | | | |
|---|---|---|---|---|---|---|---|
| Northern Soul | CD | Hut | DGHUT27 | 1995 | £5 | £12 | *fold-out cover* |

## VETERANS
| | | | | | | | |
|---|---|---|---|---|---|---|---|
| Administration | LP | | NO1406 | 1968 | £10 | £25 | *US* |

## VETTES
| | | | | | | | |
|---|---|---|---|---|---|---|---|
| Rev-up | LP | MGM | (S)E4193 | 1963 | £5 | £12 | *US* |

## VIAN, PATRICK
| | | | | | | | |
|---|---|---|---|---|---|---|---|
| Bruits et temps analogues | LP | Egg | 900541 | 1978 | £4 | £10 | *French* |

## VIBRATIONS
| | | | | | | | |
|---|---|---|---|---|---|---|---|
| Canadian Sunset | 7" | Columbia | DB7895 | 1966 | £2.50 | £6 | |
| Greatest Hits | LP | Direction | 863644 | 1969 | £6 | £15 | |
| Love In Them There Hills | 7" | Direction | 583511 | 1968 | £2 | £5 | |
| Misty | LP | OKeh | OKM4112/ OKS14112 | 1966 | £6 | £15 | *US* |
| My Girl Sloopy | 7" | London | HLK9875 | 1964 | £4 | £8 | |
| New Vibrations | LP | Columbia | SX6106 | 1966 | £6 | £15 | |
| One Mint Julep | 7" | Columbia | DB8319 | 1967 | £2 | £5 | |
| Pick Me | 7" | Columbia | DB8175 | 1967 | £5 | £10 | |
| Shout | LP | OKeh | OKM4111/ OKS14111 | 1965 | £8 | £20 | *US* |
| Talkin' 'Bout Love | 7" | Columbia | DB8318 | 1967 | £2 | £5 | |
| Watusi | LP | Checker | 2978 | 1961 | £10 | £25 | *US* |
| Watusi | 7" | Pye | 7N25107 | 1961 | £5 | £10 | |

## VIBRATORS
| | | | | | | | |
|---|---|---|---|---|---|---|---|
| Halfway To Paradise | CD-s | Revolver | REVXD52 | 1990 | £2 | £5 | |

## VIBRATORS (2)
| | | | | | | | |
|---|---|---|---|---|---|---|---|
| Sloop John B | 7" | Doctor Bird | DB1036 | 1966 | £5 | £10 | |

## VICE VERSA
| | | | | | | | |
|---|---|---|---|---|---|---|---|
| Music 4 | 7" | Neutron | NT001 | 1980 | £2 | £5 | |

## VICEROYS
| | | | | | | | |
|---|---|---|---|---|---|---|---|
| Fat Fish | 7" | Blue Cat | BS121 | 1968 | £4 | £8 | *Octaves B side* |
| Jump In A Fire | 7" | Punch | PH3 | 1969 | £1.50 | £4 | |
| Last Night | 7" | Studio One | SO2064 | 1968 | £6 | £12 | |
| Lips And Tongue | 7" | Island | WI3095 | 1967 | £5 | £10 | *Dawn Penn B side* |
| Lose And Gain | 7" | Studio One | SO2016 | 1967 | £6 | £12 | *Soul Brothers B side* |
| Try Hard To Leave | 7" | Coxsone | CS7036 | 1968 | £5 | £10 | |
| Work It | 7" | Crab | CRAB12 | 1969 | £1.50 | £4 | |

## VICEROYS (2)
| | | | | | | | |
|---|---|---|---|---|---|---|---|
| At Granny's Pad | LP | Bolo | BLP8000 | 1963 | £8 | £20 | *US* |

## VICIOUS PINK PHENOMENA
| | | | | | | | |
|---|---|---|---|---|---|---|---|
| My Private Tokyo | 7" | Mobile Suit Corp | CORP1 | 1982 | £2 | £5 | |
| My Private Tokyo | 12" | Mobile Suit Corp | CORP12 | 1982 | £3 | £8 | |

## VICK, HAROLD
| | | | | | | | |
|---|---|---|---|---|---|---|---|
| Steppin' Out | LP | Blue Note | BLP/BST84138 | 1963 | £20 | £40 | |

## VICKERS, MIKE
| | | | | | | | |
|---|---|---|---|---|---|---|---|
| Air On A String | 7" | Columbia | DB8171 | 1967 | £1.50 | £4 | |
| Captain Scarlet And The Mysterons | 7" | Columbia | DB8281 | 1967 | £4 | £8 | |
| Eleventy One | 7" | Columbia | DB7825 | 1966 | £1.50 | £4 | |
| I Wish I Were A Group Again | LP | Columbia | SX/SCX6180 | 1968 | £5 | £12 | |
| Morgan | 7" | Columbia | DB7906 | 1966 | £1.50 | £4 | |
| Puff Adder | 7" | Columbia | DB7657 | 1965 | £7.50 | £15 | |

## VICKY
| | | | | | | | |
|---|---|---|---|---|---|---|---|
| Colours Of Love | 7" | Philips | B1565 | 1967 | £2.50 | £6 | |

## VICKY & JERRY
| | | | | | | | |
|---|---|---|---|---|---|---|---|
| Don't Cry | 7" | HMV | POP715 | 1960 | £2.50 | £6 | |

## VICTIMS OF CHANCE
| | | | | | | | |
|---|---|---|---|---|---|---|---|
| Victims Of Chance | LP | Crestview | CRS3052 | | £37.50 | £75 | *US* |
| Victims Of Chance | LP | Stable | SLE8004 | 1969 | £15 | £30 | |

## VICTIMS OF PLEASURE
| | | | | | | | |
|---|---|---|---|---|---|---|---|
| When You're Young | 7" | PAM | VOP1 | 1980 | £1.50 | £4 | |

## VICTOR, TONY
| | | | | | | | |
|---|---|---|---|---|---|---|---|
| Dear One | 7" | Decca | F11459 | 1962 | £4 | £8 | |

## VICTORS
Things Come Up To Bump ..................... 7" ...... Studio One...... SO2077................. 1969 £6........... £12 ............. *lyrics B side*

## VIDELS
Mister Lonely................ 7" ...... London ........... HLI9153 ............. 1960 £10.......... £20 ...........................

## VIGILANTES
Eclipse................ 7" ...... Pye ................ 7N25082 ............. 1961 £4.......... £8 ...........................

## VIKINGS
| | | | | | | | |
|---|---|---|---|---|---|---|---|
| Come Into The Parlour ........................... | 7" | ...... | Black Swan... | WI430 | 1964 | £5....... | £10 ........................... |
| Daddy ........................... | 7" | ...... | Island ........... | WI167 | 1965 | £5....... | £10 ........................... |
| Down By The Riverside ........................... | 7" | ...... | Black Swan... | WI423 | 1964 | £5....... | £10 ........................... |
| Fever........................... | 7" | ...... | Island ........... | WI117 | 1963 | £5....... | £10 ........................... |
| Get Ready........................... | 7" | ...... | Island ........... | WI122 | 1963 | £5....... | £10 .......*Don Drummond* |
| | | | | | | | *B side* |
| Hallelujah ........................... | 7" | ...... | Island ........... | WI065 | 1962 | £5....... | £10 ........................... |
| Just Got To Be ........................... | 7" | ...... | Island ........... | WI107 | 1963 | £5....... | £10 ........................... |
| Maggie Don't Leave Me ........................... | 7" | ...... | Island ........... | WI035 | 1962 | £5....... | £10 ........................... |
| Never Grow Old........................... | 7" | ...... | Island ........... | WI101 | 1963 | £5....... | £10 ........................... |
| Six And Seven Books Of Moses ........... | 7" | ...... | Island ........... | WI075 | 1963 | £5....... | £10 ........................... |
| Treat Me Bad........................... | 7" | ...... | Black Swan... | WI428 | 1964 | £5....... | £10 ........................... |

## VIKINGS (2)
Bad News Feeling ................................. 7" ...... Alp ............ 595011 ................. 1966 £5....... £10

## VILLAGE
Man In The Moon ................................. 7" ...... Head............. HDS4002 ............. 1969 £12.50....£25

## VILLAGE STOMPERS
Washington Square................................. 7" ...... Columbia ........ DB7123 ................. 1963 £1.50.......£4

## VINCENT, GENE
| | | | | | | | |
|---|---|---|---|---|---|---|---|
| Anna Annabelle ........................... | 7" | ...... | Capitol........... | CL15169 | 1960 | £5....... | £10 ........................... |
| B I Bickey Bi Bo Bo Go ........................... | 7" | ...... | Capitol........... | CL14722 | 1957 | £25....... | £50 ........................... |
| Baby Blue........................... | 7" | ...... | Capitol........... | CL14868 | 1958 | £10....... | £20 ........................... |
| Baby Don't Believe Him........................... | 7" | ...... | Capitol........... | CL15243 | 1962 | £5....... | £10 ........................... |
| Be Bop A Lula ........................... | 7" | ...... | Capitol........... | CL14599 | 1956 | £10....... | £20 ........................... |
| Be Bop A Lula ........................... | 7" | ...... | Dandelion ...... | 4596 | 1969 | £1.50....... | £4 ........................... |
| Be Bop A Lula '62 ........................... | 7" | ...... | Capitol........... | CL15264 | 1962 | £5....... | £10 ........................... |
| Best Of Gene Vincent........................... | LP | ...... | Capitol........... | T20957 | 1967 | £4....... | £10 ........................... |
| Best Of Gene Vincent Vol. 2........................... | LP | ...... | Capitol........... | (S)T21144 | 1969 | £6....... | £15 ........................... |
| Bird Doggin'........................... | 7" | ...... | London ........... | HLH10079 | 1966 | £5....... | £10 ........................... |
| Bluejean Bop ........................... | LP | ...... | Capitol........... | T764 | 1957 | £25....... | £50 ........................... |
| Bluejean Bop ........................... | LP | ...... | Capitol........... | T764 | 1957 | £100....... | £200 ...... US |
| Bluejean Bop ........................... | 7" | ...... | Capitol........... | CL14637 | 1956 | £20....... | £40 ........................... |
| Crazy Beat........................... | 7" | ...... | Capitol........... | CL15307 | 1963 | £6....... | £12 ........................... |
| Crazy Beat Of Gene Vincent ........................... | LP | ...... | Capitol........... | T20453 | 1963 | £20....... | £40 ........................... |
| Crazy Beat Of Gene Vincent Pt. 1 ........... | 7" EP . | Capitol........... | EAP120453 | 1963 | £20....... | £40 ........................... | |
| Crazy Beat Of Gene Vincent Pt. 2 ........... | 7" EP . | Capitol........... | EAP220453 | 1964 | £20....... | £40 ........................... | |
| Crazy Beat Of Gene Vincent Pt. 3 ........... | 7" EP . | Capitol........... | EAP320453 | 1964 | £20....... | £40 ........................... | |
| Crazy Legs ........................... | 7" | ...... | Capitol........... | CL14693 | 1957 | £25....... | £50 ........................... |
| Crazy Times ........................... | LP | ...... | Capitol........... | ST1342 | 1960 | £30....... | £60 ......*stereo* |
| Crazy Times ........................... | LP | ...... | Capitol........... | T1342 | 1960 | £20....... | £40 ........................... |
| Crazy Times ........................... | LP | ...... | Capitol........... | T1342 | 1960 | £75....... | £150 ...... US |
| Crazy Times ........................... | LP | ...... | MFP........... | MFP1053 | 1965 | £4....... | £10 ........................... |
| Dance To The Bop ........................... | 7" | ...... | Capitol........... | CL14808 | 1957 | £15....... | £30 ........................... |
| Day The World Turned Blue ........... | LP | ...... | Kama Sutra ... | KSBS2027 | 1971 | £4....... | £10 ........................... |
| Day The World Turned Blue ........... | 7" | ...... | Kama Sutra ... | 2013018 | 1971 | £1.50....... | £4 ........................... |
| Gene Vincent........................... | LP | ...... | Kama Sutra ... | KSBS2019 | 1970 | £4....... | £10 ........................... |
| Gene Vincent........................... | LP | ...... | London ........... | HAH8333 | 1967 | £15....... | £30 ........................... |
| Gene Vincent & The Blue Caps........... | LP | ...... | Capitol........... | T811 | 1957 | £25....... | £50 ........................... |
| Gene Vincent & The Blue Caps........... | LP | ...... | Capitol........... | T811 | 1957 | £100....... | £200 ...... US |
| Gene Vincent Record Date ........... | LP | ...... | Capitol........... | T1059 | 1958 | £20....... | £40 ........................... |
| Gene Vincent Record Date ........... | LP | ...... | Capitol........... | T1059 | 1958 | £100....... | £200 ...... US |
| Gene Vincent Record Date Pt. 1 ........... | 7" EP . | Capitol........... | EAP11059 | 1959 | £15....... | £30 ........................... | |
| Gene Vincent Record Date Pt. 2 ........... | 7" EP . | Capitol........... | EAP21059 | 1959 | £30....... | £60 ........................... | |
| Gene Vincent Record Date Pt. 3 ........... | 7" EP . | Capitol........... | EAP31059 | 1960 | £12.50....... | £25 ........................... | |
| Gene Vincent Rocks & The Blue Caps Roll........... | LP | ...... | Capitol........... | T970 | 1958 | £25....... | £50 ........................... |
| Gene Vincent Rocks & The Blue Caps Roll........... | LP | ...... | Capitol........... | T970 | 1958 | £100....... | £200 ...... US |
| Git It........................... | 7" | ...... | Capitol........... | CL14935 | 1958 | £10....... | £20 ........................... |
| Held For Questioning........................... | 7" | ...... | Capitol........... | CL15290 | 1963 | £5....... | £10 ........................... |
| Hot Rod Gang........................... | 7" EP . | Capitol........... | EAP1985 | 1958 | £20....... | £40 ........................... | |
| Humpity Dumpity ........................... | 7" | ...... | Columbia ........ | DB7218 | 1964 | £4....... | £8 ........................... |
| I Got A Baby ........................... | 7" | ...... | Capitol........... | CL14830 | 1958 | £10....... | £20 ........................... |
| I'm Back & I'm Proud ........................... | LP | ...... | Dandelion ...... | 63754 | 1969 | £6....... | £15 ........................... |
| I'm Going Home ........................... | 7" | ...... | Capitol........... | CL15215 | 1961 | £4....... | £8 ........................... |
| If You Could Only See Me Today........... | LP | ...... | Buddah ........ | 2361009 | 1972 | £4....... | £10 ........................... |
| If You Want My Loving ........... | 7" EP . | Capitol........... | EAP120173 | 1961 | £20....... | £40 ........................... | |
| If You Want My Loving ........... | 7" | ...... | Capitol........... | CL15185 | 1961 | £5....... | £10 ........................... |
| Jumps Giggles And Shouts........... | 7" | ...... | Capitol........... | CL14681 | 1957 | £30....... | £60 ........................... |
| La Den Da Den Da Da ........... | 7" | ...... | Columbia ........ | DB7293 | 1964 | £4....... | £8 ........................... |
| Live And Rockin' ........... | 7" EP . | Emidisc/fan club | no number | 1968 | £75....... | £150 ........................... | |
| Lonely Street........................... | 7" | ...... | London ........... | HLH10099 | 1966 | £4....... | £8 ........................... |

| | | | | | | | |
|---|---|---|---|---|---|---|---|
| Maybe | 7" | Capitol | CL15179 | 1961 | £5 | £10 | |
| My Heart | 7" | Capitol | CL15115 | 1960 | £4 | £8 | |
| Over The Rainbow, | 7" | Capitol | CL15000 | 1959 | £5 | £10 | |
| Pistol Packing Mama | 7" | Capitol | CL15136 | 1960 | £4 | £8 | |
| Private Detective | 7" | Columbia | DB7343 | 1964 | £4 | £8 | |
| Race With The Devil | 7" EP | Capitol | EAP120354 | 1962 | £20 | £40 | |
| Race With The Devil | 7" | Capitol | CL14628 | 1956 | £25 | £50 | |
| Rainy Day Sunshine | 7" EP | Magnum Force | MFEP003 | 1981 | £2.50 | £6 | |
| Rainy Day Sunshine | 7" | Rollin' Danny | RD1 | 1979 | £2.50 | £6 | |
| Right Now | 7" | Capitol | CL15053 | 1959 | £5 | £10 | |
| Rip It Up | 7" | Capitol | CL15307 | 1963 | £62.50 | £125 | demo |
| Rocky Road Blues | 7" | Capitol | CL14908 | 1958 | £10 | £20 | |
| Roll Over Beethoven | 7" | BBC | BEEB001 | 1974 | £1.50 | £4 | |
| Say Mama | 7" | Capitol | CL14974 | 1959 | £7.50 | £15 | |
| Say Mama | 7" | Capitol | CL15546 | 1968 | £1.50 | £4 | |
| Say Mama | 7" | Capitol | CL15906 | 1977 | £1.50 | £4 | |
| Shakin' Up A Storm | LP | Columbia | 33SX1646 | 1964 | £15 | £30 | |
| She She Little Sheila | 7" | Capitol | CL15202 | 1961 | £5 | £10 | |
| Sounds Like Gene Vincent | LP | Capitol | T1207 | 1959 | £25 | £50 | |
| Sounds Like Gene Vincent | LP | Capitol | T1207 | 1959 | £75 | £150 | US |
| Summertime | 7" | Capitol | CL15035 | 1959 | £5 | £10 | |
| Temptation Baby | 7" | Columbia | DB7174 | 1963 | £2.50 | £6 | |
| True To You | 7" EP | Capitol | EAP120461 | 1963 | £20 | £40 | |
| Unchained Melody | 7" | Capitol | CL15231 | 1961 | £5 | £10 | |
| Wear My Ring | 7" | Capitol | CL14763 | 1957 | £12.50 | £25 | |
| White Lightning | 7" | Dandelion | 4974 | 1970 | £1.50 | £4 | |
| Wild Cat | 7" | Capitol | CL15099 | 1959 | £4 | £8 | |

## VINE, JOEY

| | | | | | | | |
|---|---|---|---|---|---|---|---|
| Down And Out | 7" | Immediate | IM017 | 1965 | £5 | £10 | |

## VINEGAR

| | | | | | | | |
|---|---|---|---|---|---|---|---|
| Vinegar | LP | Phonofoly | WP710101 | 1971 | £75 | £150 | German |

## VINEGAR JOE

| | | | | | | | |
|---|---|---|---|---|---|---|---|
| Rock 'n' Roll Gypsies | LP | Island | ILPS9214 | 1972 | £4 | £10 | |
| Six Star General | LP | Island | ILPS9262 | 1973 | £4 | £10 | |
| Vinegar Joe | LP | Island | ILPS9183 | 1972 | £5 | £12 | |

## VINNEGAR, LEROY

| | | | | | | | |
|---|---|---|---|---|---|---|---|
| Leroy Walks | LP | Contemporary | LAC12136 | 1959 | £8 | £20 | |

## VINSON, EDDIE 'CLEANHEAD'

| | | | | | | | |
|---|---|---|---|---|---|---|---|
| Backdoor Blues | LP | Riverside | 3502 | 196– | £6 | £15 | US |
| Cherry Red | LP | BluesWay | BL(S)6007 | 1967 | £4 | £10 | US |
| Eddie Cleanhead Vinson Sings | LP | Aamco | 312 | 196– | £4 | £10 | US |
| Eddie Cleanhead Vinson Sings | LP | Bethlehem | BCP5005 | 196– | £6 | £15 | US |
| Jump And Grunt | 78 | Vogue | V2023 | 1951 | £5 | £10 | |

## VINSON, EDDIE 'CLEANHEAD' & JIMMY WITHERSPOON

| | | | | | | | |
|---|---|---|---|---|---|---|---|
| Battle Of The Blues Vol. 3 | LP | King | 634 | 1959 | £180 | £300 | US |

## VINSTRICK, V.

| | | | | | | | |
|---|---|---|---|---|---|---|---|
| Love Is Not A Game | 7" | Doctor Bird | DB1167 | 1968 | £5 | £10 | Cinderella B side |

## VINTON, BOBBY

| | | | | | | | |
|---|---|---|---|---|---|---|---|
| Blue On Blue | LP | Columbia | 33SX1566 | 1963 | £6 | £15 | |
| Blue Velvet | CD-s | Epic | 6505242 | 1990 | £2 | £5 | |
| Blue Velvet | 7" | Columbia | DB7110 | 1963 | £1.50 | £4 | |
| Corrine Corrina | 7" | Fontana | H307 | 1961 | £2.50 | £6 | |
| Dancing At The Hop | LP | Epic | LN3727/LN579 | 1960 | £6 | £15 | US |
| Greatest Hits Of The Greatest Groups | LP | Epic | LN24049/BN26049 | 1963 | £6 | £15 | US |
| I Love The Way You Are | 7" | London | HLU9592 | 1962 | £2.50 | £6 | |
| Mr. Lonely | 7" | Columbia | DB7422 | 1964 | £4 | £8 | |
| My Heart Belongs To Only You | LP | Columbia | 33SX1611 | 1963 | £6 | £15 | |
| Roses Are Red | CD-s | Epic | 6564672 | 1990 | £2 | £5 | |
| Sings The Big Ones | LP | Columbia | 33SX1517 | 1963 | £6 | £15 | |
| Songs Of Christmas | 7" EP | Columbia | SEG8363 | 1964 | £7.50 | £15 | |
| Tell Me Why | LP | Columbia | 33SX1649 | 1965 | £6 | £15 | |
| Young In Heart | 7" EP | Columbia | SEG8212 | 1962 | £6 | £12 | |
| Young Man With A Big Band | LP | Epic | LN3780/LN597 | 1961 | £6 | £15 | US |

## VINYL, MATT

| | | | | | | | |
|---|---|---|---|---|---|---|---|
| Useless Tasks | 7" | Housewife's Choice | | 1977 | £2 | £5 | |

## VIOLATORS

| | | | | | | | |
|---|---|---|---|---|---|---|---|
| NY Ripper | 7" | Violators | FRS0022 | 1980 | £2 | £5 | |

## VIOLENTS

| | | | | | | | |
|---|---|---|---|---|---|---|---|
| Alpens Ros | LP | Sonet | 9926 | 1967 | £4 | £10 | Swedish |
| Complete '61-'64 | LP | Sonet | SLPD2643 | 1979 | £8 | £20 | Swedish double |
| Ghia | 7" | HMV | POP1130 | 1963 | £1.50 | £4 | |
| Live At The Star-Club | LP | Sonet | 9913 | 1966 | £4 | £10 | Swedish |
| String Of Hits | LP | Philips | 107400SNL | 1966 | £8 | £20 | Swedish |

## VIPERS SKIFFLE GROUP

| | | | | | | | |
|---|---|---|---|---|---|---|---|
| Coffee Bar Session | 10" LP | Parlophone | PMD1050 | 1957 | £15 | £30 | |

| | | | | | | | |
|---|---|---|---|---|---|---|---|
| Cumberland Gap | 7" | Parlophone | R4289 | 1957 | £2 | £5 | |
| Don't You Rock Me Daddyo | 7" | Parlophone | R4261 | 1957 | £4 | £8 | |
| Homing Bird | 7" | Parlophone | R4351 | 1957 | £2 | £5 | |
| Jim Dandy | 7" | Parlophone | R4286 | 1957 | £4 | £8 | |
| Make Ready For Love | 7" | Parlophone | R4435 | 1958 | £2 | £5 | |
| No Other Baby | 7" | Parlophone | R4393 | 1958 | £2 | £5 | |
| Pick A Bale Of Cotton | 7" | Parlophone | R4238 | 1956 | £4 | £8 | |
| Skiffle Music Vol. 1 | 7" EP | Parlophone | GEP8615 | 1957 | £4 | £8 | |
| Skiffle Music Vol. 2 | 7" EP | Parlophone | GEP8626 | 1957 | £4 | £8 | |
| Skiffle Party | 7" | Parlophone | R4371 | 1957 | £2 | £5 | |
| Skiffling Along With The Vipers | 7" EP | Parlophone | GEP8655 | 1957 | £5 | £10 | |
| Streamline Train | 7" | Parlophone | R4308 | 1957 | £2 | £5 | |
| Summertime Blues | 7" | Parlophone | R4484 | 1958 | £7.50 | £15 | |

## VIPPS
| | | | | | | | |
|---|---|---|---|---|---|---|---|
| Wintertime | 7" | CBS | 202031 | 1966 | £15 | £30 | |

## V.I.P.'S
| | | | | | | | |
|---|---|---|---|---|---|---|---|
| I Wanna Be Free | 7" EP | Fontana | 460982 | 1966 | £37.50 | £75 | French |
| I Wanna Be Free | 7" | Island | WI3003 | 1966 | £15 | £30 | |
| Mercy Mercy | 7" | Philips | 40387 | 1966 | £15 | £30 | US |
| Stagger Lee | 7" EP | Fontana | 460219 | 1967 | £37.50 | £75 | French |
| Straight Down To The Bottom | 7" EP | Fontana | 460996 | 1967 | £37.50 | £75 | French |
| Straight Down To The Bottom | 7" | Island | WIP6005 | 1967 | £15 | £30 | |
| What's That Sound | 7" EP | Fontana | 460238 | 1968 | £37.50 | £75 | French |

## V.I.P.'S (2)
| | | | | | | | |
|---|---|---|---|---|---|---|---|
| Don't Keep Shouting At Me | 7" | RCA | RCA1427 | 1964 | £12.50 | £25 | |

## V.I.P.'S (3)
| | | | | | | | |
|---|---|---|---|---|---|---|---|
| Music For Funsters | 7" | Bust | SOL3 | 1978 | £1.50 | £4 | |

## VIRGIL BROTHERS
| | | | | | | | |
|---|---|---|---|---|---|---|---|
| Temptation 'Bout To Get Me | 7" | Parlophone | R5787 | 1969 | £1.50 | £4 | |

## VIRGIN PRUNES
| | | | | | | | |
|---|---|---|---|---|---|---|---|
| Heresie | 10" | Baby | BABY011 | 1987 | £3 | £8 | double, clear vinyl |
| Heresie | 10" | Suicide | | 1982 | £10 | £20 | boxed set |
| In The Grey Light | 7" | Rough Trade | RT072 | 1981 | £2.50 | £6 | blue picture sleeve |
| In The Grey Light | 7" | Rough Trade | RT072 | 1981 | £1.50 | £4 | green picture sleeve |
| New Form Of Beauty | 7"/ 10" /12" | Rough Trade | RT089-91 | 1981 | £10 | £20 | 3 records, boxed |
| New Form Of Beauty Part One | 7" | Rough Trade | RT089 | 1981 | £2 | £5 | |
| Pagan Love Song | 7" | Rough Trade | RT106 | 1982 | £2.50 | £6 | |
| Twenty Tens | 7" | Baby | BABY001 | 1981 | £5 | £10 | |

## VIRGIN SLEEP
| | | | | | | | |
|---|---|---|---|---|---|---|---|
| Love | 7" | Deram | DM146 | 1967 | £10 | £20 | |
| Secret | 7" | Deram | DM173 | 1968 | £10 | £20 | |

## VIRGINIA WOLVES
| | | | | | | | |
|---|---|---|---|---|---|---|---|
| Stay | 7" | Stateside | SS563 | 1966 | £7.50 | £15 | |

## VIRGINIANS
| | | | | | | | |
|---|---|---|---|---|---|---|---|
| Limbo Baby | 7" | Pye | 7N25175 | 1963 | £1.50 | £4 | |

## VIRTUES
| | | | | | | | |
|---|---|---|---|---|---|---|---|
| Guitar Boogie Shuffle | LP | Strand | SL1061 | 1960 | £8 | £20 | US |
| Guitar Boogie Shuffle | LP | Wynne | WLP111 | 1960 | £8 | £20 | US |
| Guitar Boogie Shuffle | 7" | HMV | POP621 | 1959 | £4 | £8 | |
| Shuffling Along | 7" | HMV | POP637 | 1959 | £4 | £8 | |

## VIRTUES (2)
| | | | | | | | |
|---|---|---|---|---|---|---|---|
| High Tide | 7" | Doctor Bird | DB1164 | 1968 | £5 | £10 | |
| Your Wife And Your Mother | 7" | Island | WI196 | 1965 | £5 | £10 | |

## VIRTUOSA, FRANK
| | | | | | | | |
|---|---|---|---|---|---|---|---|
| Rollin' And Rockin' | 7" | Melodisc | 1386 | 1958 | £7.50 | £15 | |

## VIRUS
| | | | | | | | |
|---|---|---|---|---|---|---|---|
| Revelation | LP | BASF | CRC015 | 1971 | £10 | £25 | German |
| Thoughts | LP | Pilz | 20211029 | 1971 | £10 | £25 | German |

## VISAGE
| | | | | | | | |
|---|---|---|---|---|---|---|---|
| Pleasure Boys | 12" | Polydor | POSPX523 | 1982 | £3 | £8 | |

## VISCOUNTS
| | | | | | | | |
|---|---|---|---|---|---|---|---|
| Chug A Lug | 7" | Top Rank | JAR388 | 1960 | £2.50 | £6 | |
| Harlem Nocturne | LP | Amy | (S)8008 | 1965 | £8 | £20 | US |
| Harlem Nocturne | 7" | Stateside | SS468 | 1965 | £1.50 | £4 | |
| Harlem Nocturne | 7" | Top Rank | JAR254 | 1959 | £2 | £5 | |
| Night Train | 7" | Top Rank | JAR502 | 1960 | £2 | £5 | |
| Viscounts | LP | Madison | 1001 | 1960 | £20 | £40 | US |
| Viscounts' Rock | 7" EP | Top Rank | JKP3005 | 1961 | £20 | £40 | |

## VISCOUNTS (2)

The Viscounts were a vocal trio, whose easy harmonies were typical of the kind of thing the Beatles blew away. One of the group, however, was Gordon Mills, who later made himself a very comfortable living as manager of both Tom Jones and Engelbert Humperdinck.

| | | | | | | | |
|---|---|---|---|---|---|---|---|
| Money Is The Root Of All Evil | 7" | Pye | 7N15323 | 1961 | £1.50 | £4 | |
| Rockin' Little Angel | 7" | Pye | 7N15249 | 1960 | £1.50 | £4 | |
| Shortnin' Bread | 7" | Pye | 7N15287 | 1960 | £1.50 | £4 | |
| Viscounts' Hit Parade | 7" EP | Pye | NEP24132 | 1960 | £7.50 | £15 | |

## VISION

| | | | | | | | |
|---|---|---|---|---|---|---|---|
| Lucifer's Friend | 7" | MVM | 2885 | 1983 | £2 | £5 | |

## VISITORS

| | | | | | | | |
|---|---|---|---|---|---|---|---|
| Empty Rooms | 7" | Departure | RAPTURE1 | 1980 | £1.50 | £4 | |

## VITA NOVA

| | | | | | | | |
|---|---|---|---|---|---|---|---|
| Vita Nova | LP | Life | LS5010 | 1972 | £37.50 | £75 | Austrian |

## VITOUS, MIROSLAV

| | | | | | | | |
|---|---|---|---|---|---|---|---|
| Mountain In The Clouds | LP | Atlantic | SD1622 | 1973 | £5 | £12 | US |

## VOGUES

| | | | | | | | |
|---|---|---|---|---|---|---|---|
| Younger Girl | 7" | Columbia | DB7985 | 1966 | £2.50 | £6 | |

## VOGUES (2)

| | | | | | | | |
|---|---|---|---|---|---|---|---|
| Five O'Clock World | LP | Co&Ce | 1230 | 1966 | £8 | £20 | US |
| Five O'Clock World | 7" EP | London | RE10176 | 1966 | £5 | £10 | French |
| Five O'Clock World | 7" | London | HLG10247 | 1969 | £1.50 | £4 | |
| Five O'Clock World | 7" | London | HLU10014 | 1966 | £2 | £5 | |
| Magic Town | 7" | King | KG1035 | 1966 | £1.50 | £4 | |
| Meet The Vogues | LP | Co&Ce | 1229 | 1965 | £8 | £20 | US |
| Please Mr. Sun | 7" EP | Vogue | INT18104 | 1966 | £5 | £10 | French |
| You're The One | 7" | London | HLU9996 | 1965 | £2 | £5 | |

## VOICE

| | | | | | | | |
|---|---|---|---|---|---|---|---|
| Train To Disaster | 7" | Mercury | MF905 | 1965 | £62.50 | £125 | |

## VOICE OF THE BEEHIVE

| | | | | | | | |
|---|---|---|---|---|---|---|---|
| Don't Call Me Baby | CD-s | London | LONCD175 | 1988 | £2 | £5 | |
| Don't Call Me Baby | CD-s | Polygram | 0804842 | 1988 | £4 | £10 | CD video |
| Evening Show EP | CD-s | Strange Fruit | SFNTCD017 | 1989 | £2 | £5 | |
| I Say Nothing | CD-s | London | LONCD190 | 1988 | £2 | £5 | |
| I Walk The Earth | CD-s | London | LONCD169 | 1988 | £2 | £5 | |
| I Walk The Earth | CD-s | London | LONCD206 | 1988 | £2 | £5 | |
| Man In The Moon | CD-s | London | LONCD209 | 1988 | £2 | £5 | |

## VOICES

| | | | | | | | |
|---|---|---|---|---|---|---|---|
| Rock & Roll Hit Parade | 7" | Beltona | BL2667 | 1956 | £2 | £5 | |

## VOIDS

| | | | | | | | |
|---|---|---|---|---|---|---|---|
| Come On Out | 7" | Polydor | BM56073 | 1966 | £10 | £20 | |

## VOIGHT, WES

| | | | | | | | |
|---|---|---|---|---|---|---|---|
| I'm Moving In | 7" | Parlophone | R4586 | 1959 | £30 | £60 | |

## VOIZ

| | | | | | | | |
|---|---|---|---|---|---|---|---|
| Boanerges | LP | Grapevine | GRA110 | 1977 | £37.50 | £75 | |

## VOKES, HOWARD COUNTRY BOYS

| | | | | | | | |
|---|---|---|---|---|---|---|---|
| Howard Vokes Country Boys | 7" EP | Starlite | GRK508 | 1966 | £2.50 | £6 | |
| Howard Vokes Country Boys | 7" EP | Starlite | STEP27 | 1962 | £5 | £10 | |
| Mountain Guitar | 7" EP | Starlite | STEP37 | 1963 | £4 | £8 | |

## VOLCANOES

| | | | | | | | |
|---|---|---|---|---|---|---|---|
| Polaris | 7" | Philips | BF1246 | 1963 | £2.50 | £6 | |
| Ruby Duby Du | 7" | Philips | PB1098 | 1961 | £4 | £8 | |
| Tightrope | 7" | Philips | PB1113 | 1961 | £4 | £8 | |
| Volcanoes | 7" EP | Philips | BBE12432 | 1960 | £20 | £40 | |

## VOLMAN, MARK & HOWARD KAYLAN

| | | | | | | | |
|---|---|---|---|---|---|---|---|
| Phlorescent Leech And Eddie | LP | Reprise | K44201 | 1972 | £4 | £10 | |

## VOLUMES

| | | | | | | | |
|---|---|---|---|---|---|---|---|
| Dreams | 7" | Fontana | 270109TF | 1962 | £10 | £20 | |
| I Just Can't Help Myself | 7" | Pama | PM755 | 1968 | £150 | £250 | test pressing, best auctioned |
| Sandra | 7" | London | HL9733 | 1963 | £10 | £20 | |

## VON TRAPP FAMILY

| | | | | | | | |
|---|---|---|---|---|---|---|---|
| Brand New Thrill | 7" | Woronzow | WOO1 | 1980 | £10 | £20 | |

## VONTASTICS

| | | | | | | | |
|---|---|---|---|---|---|---|---|
| Day Tripper | 7" | Chess | CRS8043 | 1966 | £2.50 | £6 | |
| Lady Love | 7" | Stateside | SS2002 | 1967 | £7.50 | £15 | |

## VOOMINS
If You Don't Come Back........................... 7"......  Polydor........... 56001..................... 1965 £2............. £5 .............................

## VOXPOPPERS
Last Drag................................................. 7"...... Mercury.......... 7MT202................ 1958 £12.50.... £25 .............................
Voxpoppers ........................................... 7" EP . Mercury.......... MEP9533.............. 1958 £30........ £60 .............................

## VULCANS
Star Trek ............................................... LP...... Trojan............. TRLS53................ 1971 £5.... £12 .............................

## VULCAN'S HAMMER
True Hearts And Sound Bottoms............... LP...... Brown ............ BVH1 ................... 1973 £400..... £600 .............................

# W

## W. GIMMICS
Hot Rods ................................................ 7" EP . Polydor .......... EPH27125 ........... 1965 £5 ......... £10 ................................

## W.A.S.P.
| | | | | | | | |
|---|---|---|---|---|---|---|---|
| 9.5 N.A.S.T.Y. | 7" | Capitol | CLP432 | 1986 | £1.50 | £4 | picture disc |
| Animal | 7" | Music For Nations | PKUT109 | 1984 | £4 | £8 | shaped picture disc, 2 different designs |
| Animal | 12" | Music For Nations | 12KUT109 | 1984 | £4 | £10 | white vinyl |
| Forever Free | CD-s | Capitol | CDCL546 | 1989 | £2 | £5 | |
| I Wanna Be Somebody | 12" | Capitol | 12CLP336 | 1984 | £2.50 | £6 | picture disc |
| Mean Man | CD-s | Capitol | CDCL521 | 1989 | £2 | £5 | |
| Real Me | CD-s | Capitol | CDCL534 | 1989 | £2 | £5 | |

## WACHTOLZ, BARBEL
Ich Hab Musik Im Blut ........................... LP ..... Amiga ............. 850015 ................... 1964 £10 ........ £25 .......... East German

## WACKERS
| | | | | | | | |
|---|---|---|---|---|---|---|---|
| Girl Who Wanted Fame | 7" | Piccadilly | 7N35210 | 1964 | £1.50 | £4 | |
| I Wonder Why | 7" | Oriole | CB1902 | 1964 | £1.50 | £4 | |
| Love Or Money | 7" | Piccadilly | 7N35195 | 1964 | £1.50 | £4 | |

## WADE, ADAM
| | | | | | | | |
|---|---|---|---|---|---|---|---|
| Adam And Evening | LP | HMV | CLP1451 | 1961 | £6 | £15 | |
| And Then Came Adam | LP | Coed | LPC902 | 1960 | £6 | £15 | US |
| And Then Came Adam | 7" EP | HMV | 7EG8620 | 1960 | £5 | £10 | |
| Four Film Songs | 7" EP | Columbia | SEG8316 | 1964 | £5 | £10 | |

## WADE, WAYNE
Dancing Time ........................................ LP ..... Grove Music ... GMCP3 ................. 1979 £4 ......... £10 ................................

## WADE, WELLINGTON
Let's Turkey Trot ................................... 7" ..... Oriole ............ CB1857 .............. 1963 £5 ......... £10 ................................

## WAGNER, ADRIAN
Distance Between Us ............................... LP ..... Atlantic .......... K50082 ............. 1974 £4 ......... £10 ................................

## WAGNER, ROBERT
Almost Eighteen ..................................... 7" ..... London .......... HLU8491 ........... 1957 £5 ......... £10 ................................

## WAGONER, PORTER
| | | | | | | | |
|---|---|---|---|---|---|---|---|
| Blue Grass Story | LP | RCA | RD7693 | 1965 | £4 | £10 | |
| Little Slice Of Life | 7" EP | RCA | RCX7157 | 1964 | £4 | £8 | |
| Satisfied Mind | LP | RCA | LPM1358 | 1956 | £8 | £20 | US |
| Y'All Come | 7" EP | RCA | RCX7158 | 1964 | £4 | £8 | |

## WAILER, BUNNY
| | | | | | | | |
|---|---|---|---|---|---|---|---|
| Blackheart Man | LP | Island | ILPS9415 | 1976 | £5 | £12 | |
| Protest | LP | Island | ILPS9512 | 1978 | £5 | £12 | |
| Sings The Wailers | LP | Island | ILPS9629 | 1981 | £4 | £10 | |

## WAILERS
| | | | | | | | |
|---|---|---|---|---|---|---|---|
| And I Love Her | 7" | Ska Beat | JB230 | 1966 | £20 | £40 | |
| Bend Down Low | 7" | Island | WI3043 | 1967 | £20 | £40 | |
| Concrete Jungle | 7" | Island | WIP6164 | 1973 | £20 | £40 | |
| Dancing Shoes | 7" | Rio | R116 | 1967 | £20 | £40 | |
| Donna | 7" | Island | WI216 | 1965 | £20 | £40 | |
| Down Presser | 7" | Punch | PH77 | 1971 | £20 | £40 | Junior Byles B side |
| Dreamland | 7" | Upsetter | US371 | 1971 | £20 | £40 | Upsetters B side |
| Get Up Stand Up | 7" | Island | WIP6167 | 1973 | £20 | £40 | |
| Good Good Rudie | 7" | Doctor Bird | DB1021 | 1966 | £20 | £40 | City Slickers B side |
| He Who Feels It Knows It | 7" | Island | WI3001 | 1966 | £20 | £40 | |
| I Made A Mistake | 7" | Ska Beat | JB226 | 1965 | £20 | £40 | Soul Brothers B side |
| I Need You | 7" | Island | WI3035 | 1967 | £20 | £40 | Ken Boothe B side |
| I Stand Predominant | 7" | Studio One | SO2024 | 1967 | £20 | £40 | Norma Frazer B side |
| It Hurts To Be Alone | 7" | Island | WI188 | 1965 | £20 | £40 | |
| Jailhouse | 7" | Bamboo | BAM55 | 1970 | £20 | £40 | John Holt B side |
| Jumbie Jamboree | 7" | Island | WI260 | 1966 | £20 | £40 | Skatalites B side |
| Let Him Go | 7" | Island | WI3009 | 1966 | £20 | £40 | 2 different B sides |
| Lonesome Feelings | 7" | Ska Beat | JB211 | 1965 | £20 | £40 | |
| Lonesome Track | 7" | Ska Beat | JB249 | 1966 | £20 | £40 | |
| Love And Affection | 7" | Ska Beat | JB228 | 1965 | £20 | £40 | |
| Maga Dog | 7" | Island | WI212 | 1965 | £20 | £40 | |

| | | | | | | | |
|---|---|---|---|---|---|---|---|
| Mr. Chatterbox | 7" | Jackpot | JP730 | 1970 | £20 | £40 | *Doreen Shaeffer B side* |
| Nice Time | 7" | Doctor Bird | DB1091 | 1967 | £20 | £40 | |
| Playboy | 7" | Island | WI206 | 1965 | £20 | £40 | |
| Put It On | 7" | Island | WI268 | 1966 | £20 | £40 | |
| Rasta Put It On | 7" | Doctor Bird | DB1039 | 1966 | £20 | £40 | *......Roland Alphonso B side* |
| Reggae On Broadway | 7" | CBS | 8144 | 1972 | £20 | £40 | |
| Rude Boy | 7" | Doctor Bird | DB1013 | 1966 | £20 | £40 | *......Roland Alphonso B side* |
| Shame And Scandal | 7" | Island | WI215 | 1965 | £20 | £40 | |
| Simmer Down | 7" | Ska Beat | JB186 | 1965 | £20 | £40 | |
| Stop The Train | 7" | Summit | SUM8526 | 1972 | £20 | £40 | |
| Version Of Cup | 7" | Upsetter | US342 | 1970 | £20 | £40 | *......Upsetters B side* |
| What's New Pussycat | 7" | Island | WI254 | 1965 | £20 | £40 | |

## WAILERS (2)

| | | | | | | | |
|---|---|---|---|---|---|---|---|
| At The Castle | LP | Etiquette | ALB01 | 1962 | £25 | £50 | *US* |
| Mau Mau | 7" | London | HL8994 | 1959 | £37.50 | £75 | *US* |
| Out Of Our Tree | LP | Etiquette | ALB026 | 1966 | £10 | £25 | *US* |
| Outburst | LP | United Artists | UAL3557/ UAS6557 | 1966 | £10 | £25 | *US* |
| Tall Cool One | LP | Golden Crest | CR3075 | 1959 | £30 | £60 | *US* |
| Tall Cool One | LP | Imperial | LP9262/12262 | 1964 | £10 | £25 | *US* |
| Tall Cool One | 7" | London | HL8958 | 1959 | £6 | £12 | |
| Tall Cool One | 7" | London | HL9892 | 1964 | £2.50 | £6 | |
| Wailers And Company | LP | Etiquette | ALB022 | 1963 | £25 | £50 | *US* |
| Wailers Wailers Everywhere | LP | Etiquette | ALB023 | 1965 | £10 | £25 | *US* |
| Walkin' Through People | LP | Bell | 6016 | 1968 | £8 | £20 | *US* |

## WAILING SOULS

| | | | | | | | |
|---|---|---|---|---|---|---|---|
| Back Out | 7" | Banana | BA307 | 1970 | £1.50 | £4 | |
| Row Fisherman Row | 7" | Banana | BA305 | 1970 | £1.50 | £4 | |
| Walk Walk Walk | 7" | Banana | BA335 | 1971 | £1.50 | £4 | *....King Sporty B side* |

## WAINER, CHERRY

| | | | | | | | |
|---|---|---|---|---|---|---|---|
| Cherry Wainer | 7" EP | Pye | NEP24099 | 1959 | £6 | £12 | |
| Itchy Twitchy Feeling | 7" | Pye | 7N15161 | 1958 | £2 | £5 | |
| Money | 7" | Columbia | DB4528 | 1960 | £5 | £10 | |
| Sleepwalk | 7" | Honey Hit | TB128 | 1963 | £1.50 | £4 | |

## WAINMAN, PHIL

| | | | | | | | |
|---|---|---|---|---|---|---|---|
| Hear Me A Drummer Man | 7" | Columbia | DB7615 | 1965 | £2.50 | £6 | |

## WAITING FOR THE SUN

| | | | | | | | |
|---|---|---|---|---|---|---|---|
| Waiting For The Sun | LP | Profile | GMOR167 | 1978 | £50 | £100 | |

## WAITS, TOM

| | | | | | | | |
|---|---|---|---|---|---|---|---|
| Bone Machine Operators' Manual | CD | Island | | 1992 | £8 | £20 | *...US interview promo* |

## WAKE

| | | | | | | | |
|---|---|---|---|---|---|---|---|
| 23.59 | LP | Carnaby | CNLS6005 | 1970 | £50 | £100 | |
| Angelina | 7" | Pye | 7N17813 | 1969 | £4 | £8 | |
| Boys In The Band | 7" | Carnaby | CNS4014 | 1970 | £4 | £8 | |
| Linda | 7" | Carnaby | 6151001 | 1971 | £4 | £8 | |
| Live Today Little Girl | 7" | Carnaby | CNS4010 | 1970 | £4 | £8 | |
| Noah | 7" | Carnaby | CNS4016 | 1971 | £4 | £8 | |

## WAKE (2)

| | | | | | | | |
|---|---|---|---|---|---|---|---|
| On Our Honeymoon | 7" | Scanlist | SCN1 | 1982 | £5 | £10 | |

## WAKELY, JIMMY

| | | | | | | | |
|---|---|---|---|---|---|---|---|
| Are You Mine | 7" | Vogue Coral | Q72125 | 1956 | £4 | £8 | |
| Are You Satisfied | 7" | Brunswick | 05542 | 1956 | £4 | £8 | |
| Christmas On The Range | 10" LP | Capitol | H9004 | 195– | £8 | £20 | *US* |
| Country Million Sellers | LP | Shasta | SHLP501 | 1959 | £5 | £12 | *US* |
| Enter And Rest And Pray | LP | Decca | DL8680 | 1957 | £6 | £15 | *US* |
| Folsom Prison Blues | 7" | Brunswick | 05563 | 1956 | £5 | £10 | |
| Jimmy Wakely Sings | LP | Shasta | SHLP505 | 1960 | £5 | £12 | *US* |
| Merry Christmas | LP | Shasta | SHLP502 | 1959 | £5 | £12 | *US* |
| Santa Fe Trail | LP | Brunswick | LAT8179 | 1957 | £6 | £15 | |
| Songs Of The West | 10" LP | Capitol | H4008 | 195– | £8 | £20 | *US* |

## WAKEMAN, RICK

Those critics who dismiss Rick Wakeman's music as no more than Muzak will be delighted if they hear the scarce *Piano Vibrations*, as this really is a Muzak LP. Nevertheless, the modest value achieved by this rarity reflects not its paucity of musical imagination, but Rick Wakeman's limited status as a collectable artist. Many records as bland as this do attain high values.

| | | | | | | | |
|---|---|---|---|---|---|---|---|
| Journey To The Centre Of The Earth | LP | A&M | QU53621 | 1975 | £4 | £10 | *US quad* |
| Journey To The Centre Of The Earth | CD | Mobile Fidelity | MFCD848 | 1987 | £6 | £15 | *US audiophile* |
| Myths And Legends Of King Arthur | LP | A&M | QU54515 | 1975 | £4 | £10 | *US quad* |
| Piano Vibrations | LP | Polydor | 2460135 | 1971 | £4 | £10 | |
| Six Wives Of Henry VIII | LP | A&M | QU54361 | 1973 | £4 | £10 | *US quad* |

## WALCOTT, COLLIN

| | | | | | | | |
|---|---|---|---|---|---|---|---|
| Cloud Dance | LP | ECM | ECM1062ST | 1975 | £4 | £10 | |

## WALDRON, MAL

| | | | | | | | |
|---|---|---|---|---|---|---|---|
| Free At Last | LP | ECM | ECM1001ST | 1970 | £5 | £12 | |
| Quest | LP | XTRA | XTRA5006 | 1966 | £6 | £15 | |

## WALHAM GREEN EAST WAPPING C.C.R.B.E. ASSOCIATION

| | | | | | | | |
|---|---|---|---|---|---|---|---|
| Sorry Mr. Green | 7" | Columbia | DB8426 | 1968 | £12.50 | £25 | |

## WALKER, BILLY

| | | | | | | | |
|---|---|---|---|---|---|---|---|
| Certain Girl | 7" | Columbia | DB7724 | 1965 | £1.50 | £4 | |
| Forever | 7" | Philips | PB1001 | 1960 | £1.50 | £4 | |

## WALKER, CLINT

| | | | | | | | |
|---|---|---|---|---|---|---|---|
| Inspiration | 7" EP | Warner Bros | WEP6006/ WSEP2006 | 1960 | £2 | £5 | |

## WALKER, DAVID

| | | | | | | | |
|---|---|---|---|---|---|---|---|
| Ring The Changes | 7" | RCA | RCA1664 | 1968 | £7.50 | £15 | |

## WALKER, GARY

| | | | | | | | |
|---|---|---|---|---|---|---|---|
| Album No. 1 | LP | Philips | SFX7133 | 1970 | £50 | £100 | ...Japanese, credited to Gary Walker & The Rain |
| Come In You'll Get Pneumonia | 7" | Philips | BF1740 | 1968 | £10 | £20 | |
| Here's Gary | 7" EP | CBS | EP5742 | 1966 | £5 | £10 | |
| Spooky | 7" | Polydor | 56237 | 1968 | £1.50 | £4 | |
| Twinkie Lee | 7" | CBS | 202081 | 1966 | £1.50 | £4 | |
| You Don't Love Me | 7" | CBS | 202036 | 1966 | £1.50 | £4 | |

## WALKER, JACKIE

| | | | | | | | |
|---|---|---|---|---|---|---|---|
| Oh Lonesome Me | 7" | London | HLP8588 | 1958 | £62.50 | £125 | |

## WALKER, JERRY JEFF

| | | | | | | | |
|---|---|---|---|---|---|---|---|
| Driftin' Way Of Life | LP | Vanguard | SVRL19049 | 1969 | £4 | £10 | |
| Jerry Jeff Walker | LP | Atco | SD33297 | 1969 | £5 | £12 | US |
| Mr. Bojangles | LP | Atco | SD33259 | 1968 | £4 | £10 | US |
| Mr. Bojangles | 7" | Atlantic | 584200 | 1968 | £1.50 | £4 | |

## WALKER, JOHN

| | | | | | | | |
|---|---|---|---|---|---|---|---|
| If You Go Away | LP | Philips | (S)BL7829 | 1967 | £8 | £20 | |
| This Is John Walker | LP | Carnaby | CNLS6001 | 1969 | £8 | £20 | |

## WALKER, JOHN & SCOTT

| | | | | | | | |
|---|---|---|---|---|---|---|---|
| Solo John – Solo Scott | 7" EP | Philips | BE12597 | 1966 | £5 | £10 | |

## WALKER, JUNIOR & THE ALL STARS

| | | | | | | | |
|---|---|---|---|---|---|---|---|
| Cleo's Mood | 7" | Tamla Motown | TMG550 | 1966 | £6 | £12 | |
| Come See About Me | 7" | Tamla Motown | TMG637 | 1968 | £2 | £5 | |
| Do The Boomerang | 7" | Tamla Motown | TMG520 | 1965 | £20 | £40 | |
| Gasssss | LP | Tamla Motown | STML11167 | 1970 | £4 | £10 | |
| Hip City | 7" | Tamla Motown | TMG667 | 1968 | £1.50 | £4 | |
| Home Cookin' | LP | Tamla Motown | (S)TML11097 | 1969 | £4 | £10 | |
| Home Cookin' | 7" | Tamla Motown | TMG682 | 1969 | £1.50 | £4 | |
| How Sweet It Is | 7" | Tamla Motown | TMG571 | 1966 | £2.50 | £6 | |
| Live | LP | Tamla Motown | STML11152 | 1970 | £5 | £12 | |
| Money | 7" | Tamla Motown | TMG586 | 1966 | £4 | £8 | |
| Pucker Up Buttercup | 7" | Tamla Motown | TMG596 | 1967 | £5 | £10 | |
| Road Runner | LP | Tamla Motown | (S)TML11038 | 1966 | £6 | £15 | |
| Road Runner | 7" | Tamla Motown | TMG559 | 1966 | £2.50 | £6 | |
| Shake & Fingerpop | 7" EP | Tamla Motown | TME2013 | 1966 | £7.50 | £15 | |
| Shake And Fingerpop | 7" | Tamla Motown | TMG529 | 1965 | £7.50 | £15 | |
| Shotgun | LP | Tamla Motown | TML11017 | 1965 | £8 | £20 | |
| Shotgun | 7" | Tamla Motown | TMG509 | 1965 | £7.50 | £15 | |
| Soul Session | LP | Tamla Motown | TML11029 | 1966 | £8 | £20 | |

## WALKER, LUCILLE

| | | | | | | | |
|---|---|---|---|---|---|---|---|
| Best Of Lucille Walker | LP | Checker | 1428 | 1957 | £8 | £20 | US |

## WALKER, ROBERT

| | | | | | | | |
|---|---|---|---|---|---|---|---|
| Excuse Me, It's My First LSD Trip | LP | GNP Crescendo | 2027 | 1966 | £15 | £30 | US |

## WALKER, RONNIE

| | | | | | | | |
|---|---|---|---|---|---|---|---|
| It's A Good Feeling | 7" | Stateside | SS2151 | 1969 | £2 | £5 | |

## WALKER, SCOTT

Scott Walker has followed an unusual musical course. He has the voice and the musical inclinations of a cabaret singer, yet he writes much of his own material in a style which is too unsettling and too idiosyncratic to fit comfortably into a cabaret setting. His tendency towards hermit-like behaviour has added to his enigma and created a climate within which his cult following is steadily increasing. As a result, the LPs he made in the years after the demise of the Walker Brothers are becoming more and more collectable.

| | | | | | | | |
|---|---|---|---|---|---|---|---|
| Any Day Now | LP | Philips | 6308148 | 1973 | £10 | £25 | |
| Best Of Scott Vol. 1 | LP | Philips | SBL7910 | 1969 | £4 | £10 | |
| Fire Escape In The Sky | LP | Zoo | ZOO2 | 1981 | £6 | £15 | |
| Great Scott | cass | Philips | MCP1006 | 1967 | £6 | £15 | |
| Jackie | 7" | Philips | BF1628 | 1967 | £1.50 | £4 | |
| Joanna | 7" | Philips | BF1662 | 1968 | £1.50 | £4 | |

| | | | | | | |
|---|---|---|---|---|---|---|
| Looking Back With Scott Walker | LP | Ember | EMB3393 | 1968 £6 | £15 | |
| Mathilde | 7" EP | Philips | 438402 | 1967 £10 | £20 | *French* |
| Moviegoer | LP | Philips | 6308127 | 1972 £10 | £25 | |
| Romantic Scott Walker | LP | Philips | 6850013 | 197– £10 | £25 | |
| Scott | LP | Philips | BL7816 | 1967 £5 | £12 | |
| Scott | LP | Philips | SBL7816 | 1967 £6 | £15 | *stereo* |
| Scott 2 | LP | Philips | BL7840 | 1968 £5 | £12 | |
| Scott 2 | LP | Philips | BL7840 | 1968 £8 | £20 | *....with picture insert* |
| Scott 2 | LP | Philips | SBL7840 | 1968 £8 | £20 | *stereo* |
| Scott 2 | LP | Philips | SBL7840 | 1968 £10 | £25 | *.....with picture insert, stereo* |
| Scott 3 | LP | Philips | SBL7882 | 1969 £15 | £30 | |
| Scott 4 | LP | Philips | SBL7913 | 1969 £25 | £50 | |
| Sings Songs From His TV Series | LP | Philips | SBL7900 | 1969 £4 | £10 | |
| Spotlight On Scott Walker | LP | Philips | 6625017 | 1976 £6 | £15 | *double* |
| Stretch | LP | CBS | 65725 | 1973 £8 | £20 | |
| Sun Ain't Gonna Shine Anymore | CD-s | Fontana | WALKC1 | 1991 £2 | £5 | |
| Terrific | LP | Philips | 6856022 | 197– £10 | £25 | |
| Till The Band Comes In | LP | Philips | 6308035 | 1970 £20 | £40 | |
| Tilt Interview CD | CD | Fontana | SWINT1 | 1995 £30 | £60 | *promo* |
| We Had It All | LP | CBS | 80254 | 1974 £6 | £15 | |

## WALKER, T-BONE

| | | | | | | |
|---|---|---|---|---|---|---|
| Blues Of T-Bone Walker | LP | MFP | MFP1043 | 1965 £6 | £15 | |
| Classics In Jazz | LP | Capitol | T370 | 1956 £25 | £50 | *US* |
| Classics In Jazz | 10" LP | Capitol | H370 | 1953 £37.50 | £75 | *US* |
| Classics In Jazz | 10" LP | Capitol | LC6681 | 1954 £15 | £30 | |
| Funky Town | LP | Stateside | (S)SL10265 | 1969 £4 | £10 | |
| Hustle Is On | 78 | London | HL8087 | 1954 £7.50 | £15 | |
| I Get So Weary | LP | Imperial | 9146 | 1961 £10 | £25 | *US* |
| Party Girl | 7" | Liberty | LIB12018 | 1965 £4 | £8 | |
| Singing The Blues | LP | Imperial | 9116 | 1960 £10 | £25 | *US* |
| Sings The Blues | LP | Imperial | 9098 | 1959 £10 | £25 | *US* |
| Stormy Monday Blues | LP | Stateside | (S)SL10223 | 1968 £4 | £10 | |
| T B Walker | LP | Capitol | T1958 | 1963 £6 | £15 | |
| T-Bone Blues | LP | Atlantic | SD8020 | 1959 £15 | £30 | *US, black label* |
| T-Bone Blues | LP | Atlantic | SD8020 | 196– £6 | £15 | *US, red label* |
| Travellin' Blues | 7" EP | London | REP1404 | 1963 £10 | £20 | |

## WALKER BROTHERS

Scott Engel, John Morse and Gary Leeds were not called Walker and were not brothers. Gary Leeds did not even seem to do very much – he had no voice to match the rich tones of the other two, and so he sat behind a drum kit and pretended (very unconvincingly) that drumming was a vital ingredient in the group's music. The cult interest in Scott Walker's solo music has extended only slightly towards the Walker Brothers, whose music was too popular to ever acquire the attraction of exclusivity and which has none of the disturbing quality of Scott's best work.

| | | | | | | |
|---|---|---|---|---|---|---|
| Another Tear Falls | 7" | Philips | BF1514 | 1966 £1.50 | £4 | |
| But I Do | 7" EP | Philips | 434560 | 1965 £5 | £10 | *French* |
| Deadlier Than The Male | 7" | Philips | BF1537 | 1966 £1.50 | £4 | |
| I Need You | 7" EP | Philips | BE12596 | 1966 £4 | £8 | |
| Love Her | 7" | Philips | BF1409 | 1965 £1.50 | £4 | |
| My Ship Is Coming In | 7" EP | Philips | 434564 | 1965 £5 | £10 | *French* |
| Pretty Girls Everywhere | 7" | Philips | BF1401 | 1965 £1.50 | £4 | |
| Stay With Me Baby | 7" | Philips | BF1548 | 1967 £1.50 | £4 | |
| Story | LP | Philips | DBL002 | 1967 £5 | £12 | *double* |
| Sun Ain't Gonna Shine Anymore | 7" EP | Philips | 434567 | 1966 £5 | £10 | *French* |
| Take It Easy | LP | Philips | BL7691 | 1965 £4 | £10 | |
| Walker Brothers | 7" EP | Philips | BE12603 | 1967 £12.50 | £25 | *demo* |
| Walking In The Rain | 7" | Philips | BF1576 | 1967 £1.50 | £4 | |

## WALKIE TALKIES

| | | | | | | |
|---|---|---|---|---|---|---|
| Rich And Nasty | 7" | Sire | SIR4023 | 1979 £1.50 | £4 | |

## WALKS, DENNIS

| | | | | | | |
|---|---|---|---|---|---|---|
| Billy Lick | 7" | Blue Cat | BS144 | 1968 £4 | £8 | *Drumbago B side* |
| Having A Party | 7" | Amalgamated | AMG816 | 1968 £4 | £8 | *Groovers B side* |

## WALLACE, GIG

| | | | | | | |
|---|---|---|---|---|---|---|
| Rockin' On The Railroad | 7" | Philips | PB981 | 1960 £1.50 | £4 | |

## WALLACE, JERRY

| | | | | | | |
|---|---|---|---|---|---|---|
| Little Coco Palm | 7" | London | HLH9040 | 1960 £1.50 | £4 | |
| Primrose Lane | 7" | London | HLH8943 | 1959 £1.50 | £4 | |
| With This Ring | 7" | London | HL8719 | 1958 £5 | £10 | |
| With This Ring | 7" | London | HL7062 | 1958 £1.50 | £4 | *export* |
| You're Singing Our Love Song | 7" | London | HLH9110 | 1960 £1.50 | £4 | |

## WALLACE, SIPPIE

| | | | | | | |
|---|---|---|---|---|---|---|
| Sings The Blues | LP | Storyville | 671198 | 1967 £4 | £10 | |

## WALLACE BROTHERS

| | | | | | | |
|---|---|---|---|---|---|---|
| I'll Step Aside | 7" | Sue | WI4036 | 1967 £6 | £12 | |
| Lover's Prayer | 7" | Sue | WI355 | 1965 £6 | £12 | |
| Precious Words | 7" | Sue | WI334 | 1964 £4 | £8 | |
| Soul Connection | LP | Sue | ILP950 | 1967 £50 | £100 | |
| Daydream | 7" | Parlophone | R5764 | 1969 £2 | £5 | |
| Fly Me To The Earth | 7" | Parlophone | R5793 | 1969 £2 | £5 | |

Walk On Out .......................................... 7" ...... Parlophone ...... R5844 .................. 1970 £2 ............ £5 ..........................

## WALLENSTEIN
Blitzkrieg .......................................... LP ..... Pilz ................. 20290646 ............... 1971 £15 ........... £30 ................. German
Blue Eyed Boys .................................... LP ..... RCA ............ PL30061 ............ 1979 £5 ............ £12 ................. German
Charline .......................................... LP ..... RCA ............ PL30045 ............ 1978 £5 ............ £12 ................. German
Cosmic Century .................................. LP ..... Komische ....... KM58006 ............ 1973 £8 ............ £20 ................. German
Fräuleins .......................................... LP ..... Harvest ........ 06445932 ............ 1980 £5 ............ £12 ................. German
Lunatics .......................................... LP ..... Clear Light Of CLOJ783 ........ 1981 £5 ............ £12 ................. Australian
                                                                    Jupiter ............
Mother Universe .................................. LP ..... Pilz ................. 20291138 ........... 1972 £10 ........... £25 ................. German
No More Love ................................... LP ..... RCA ............ PL30010 ............ 1977 £6 ............ £15 ................. German
SSSSS Top ....................................... LP ..... RCA ............ 06446307 ............ 1981 £4 ............ £10 ................. German
Stories, Songs And Symphonies ................ LP ..... Komische ....... KM58014 ............ 1975 £8 ............ £20 ................. German

## WALLER, FATS
By The Light Of The Silvery Moon .......... 7" ...... HMV ............ 7M244 .............. 1954 £2.50 ........ £6
Fats 1935 – 1937 ................................ LP ..... RCA ............ RD27047 ............ 1957 £8 ............ £20
Fats 1938 – 1942 ................................ 10" LP RCA ............ RC24004 ............ 1958 £8 ............ £20
Fats At The Organ ............................... 10" LP London ......... AL3521 ............ 1954 £20 ........... £40
Fats Waller ....................................... 7" EP. HMV ............ 7EG8098 ............ 1955 £2 ............ £5
Fats Waller ....................................... 7" EP. HMV ............ 7EG8212 ............ 1957 £2 ............ £5
Fats Waller ....................................... 7" EP. RCA ............ RCX1010 ............ 1959 £2 ............ £5
Fats Waller And His Rhythm ................... 7" EP. HMV ............ 7EG8022 ............ 1954 £2 ............ £5
Fats Waller And His Rhythm ................... 7" EP. HMV ............ 7EG8042 ............ 1954 £2 ............ £5
Fats Waller And His Rhythm ................... 7" EP. HMV ............ 7EG8054 ............ 1954 £2 ............ £5
Fats Waller And His Rhythm ................... 7" EP. HMV ............ 7EG8078 ............ 1955 £2 ............ £5
Fats Waller And His Rhythm ................... 7" EP. HMV ............ 7EG8148 ............ 1956 £2 ............ £5
Fats Waller And His Rhythm ................... 7" EP. HMV ............ 7EG8242 ............ 1957 £2 ............ £5
Fats Waller And His Rhythm ................... 7" EP. HMV ............ 7EG8255 ............ 1957 £2 ............ £5
Favourites ........................................ 10" LP HMV ............ DLP1008 ............ 1953 £20 ........... £40
Favourites No. 2 ................................. 10" LP HMV ............ DLP1118 ............ 1956 £15 ........... £30
Fun With Fats .................................... 10" LP HMV ............ DLP1082 ............ 1955 £20 ........... £40
Good Man Is Hard To Find .................... 7" ...... HMV ............ 7M157 .............. 1953 £1.50 ........ £4
Handful Of Keys ................................. LP ..... RCA ............ RD27185 ............ 1960 £6 ............ £15
Honey Hush ...................................... 7" ...... HMV ............ 7M142 .............. 1953 £2 ............ £5
In London No. 1 ................................. 7" EP. HMV ............ 7EG8304 ............ 1958 £2 ............ £5
In London No. 2 ................................. 7" EP. HMV ............ 7EG8341 ............ 1958 £2 ............ £5
In London No. 3 ................................. 7" EP. HMV ............ 7EG8602 ............ 1960 £2 ............ £5
Jivin' With Fats ................................. 10" LP London ......... AL3522 ............ 1954 £20 ........... £40
My Very Good Friend The Milkman ......... 7" ...... HMV ............ 7M128 .............. 1953 £2 ............ £5
Plays And Sings ................................. 10" LP HMV ............ DLP1017 ............ 1953 £20 ........... £40
Real Fats Waller ................................ LP ..... RCA ............ CDN131 ............ 1959 £5 ............ £12
Rediscovered Solos ............................. 10" LP London ......... AL3507 ............ 1953 £20 ........... £40
Rhythm And Romance .......................... 10" LP HMV ............ DLP1056 ............ 1954 £20 ........... £40
Spreadin' Rhythm Around ..................... 10" LP HMV ............ DLP1138 ............ 1957 £15 ........... £30
Swinging At The Organ ........................ 7" EP. HMV ............ 7EG8191 ............ 1956 £2 ............ £5
Thomas Fats Waller No. 1 ..................... LP ..... HMV ............ CLP1035 ............ 1955 £8 ............ £20
Thomas Fats Waller No. 2 ..................... LP ..... HMV ............ CLP1042 ............ 1955 £8 ............ £20
You've Been Taking Lessons In Love ........ 7" ...... HMV ............ 7M208 .............. 1954 £1.50 ........ £4
Young Fats Waller ............................... 10" LP HMV ............ DLP1111 ............ 1956 £15 ........... £30
Your Feet's Too Big ............................ 7" EP. RCA ............ RCX1053 ............ 1959 £2 ............ £5

## WALLER, GORDON
Gordon ............................................ LP ..... Vertigo ........... 6360069 ............ 1972 £50 ........ £100 ................. spiral label
Rosecrans Boulevard ............................ 7" ...... Columbia ........ DB8337 ............... 1968 £1.50 ........ £4

## WALLER, JIM & THE DELTAS
Surfin' Wild ...................................... LP ..... Arvee ........... A(S)432 ............ 1963 £8 ............ £20 ................. US

## WALLINGTON, GEORGE
George Wallington ............................... 10" LP Esquire ........... 20025 ................ 1954 £25 ........ £50
George Wallington Trio ......................... 10" LP Esquire ........... 20076 ................ 1956 £15 ........ £30
Jazz For The Carriage Trade .................. LP ..... Esquire ......... 32032 ............... 1957 £50 ........ £100
New Sounds From Europe Vol. 5 ............. 10" LP Vogue ............ LDE059 ............ 1954 £25 ........ £50
Workshop .......................................... 10" LP Columbia ........ 33C9035 ............ 1957 £15 ........ £30

## WALLIS, BOB
Everybody Loves Saturday Night ............. LP ..... Top Rank ....... BUY023 ............ 1960 £4 ............ £10
Ole Man River .................................... LP ..... Pye ............ NJL27 ............... 1961 £4 ............ £10
Travellin' Blues .................................. LP ..... Pye ............ NJL30 ............... 1961 £4 ............ £10
Wallis Collection ................................ LP ..... Pye ............ NJL41 ............... 1962 £4 ............ £10

## WALPURGIS
Queen Of Sheba .................................. LP ..... Ohr .............. OMM556023 ......... 1972 £8 ............ £20 ................. German

## WALRUS
Walrus ............................................. LP ..... Deram ............ SML1072 ............... 1971 £8 ............ £20

## WALSH, JOE
Smoker You Drink The Player You Get ..... LP ..... ABC .............. COQ40016 ............ 1974 £4 ............ £10 ................. US quad

## WALSH, SHEILA & CLIFF RICHARD
Drifting ........................................... 7" ...... DJM ............ SHEIL100 ............ 1983 £2 ............ £5 ................. picture disc
Drifting ........................................... 12" ..... DJM ............ SHEILT100 ........... 1983 £2.50 ........ £6 ................. picture disc

## WALTON, DAVE
After You There Can Be Nothing ........... 7" ...... CBS .............. 202508 .......... 1967 £1.50 ........ £4

| Every Window In The City | 7" | CBS | 202098 | 1966 | £1.50 | £4 | |
| Love Ain't What It Used To Be | 7" | CBS | 202057 | 1966 | £4 | £8 | |

## WAMMACK, TRAVIS
| Scratchy | 7" | Atlantic | AT4017 | 1965 | £7.50 | £15 | |

## WANDERERS
| As Time Goes By | 7" | MGM | MGM1169 | 1961 | £5 | £10 | |
| I Could Make You Mine | 7" | MGM | MGM1102 | 1960 | £10 | £20 | |
| Run Run Senorita | 7" | United Artists | UP1020 | 1964 | £5 | £10 | |

## WANDERERS (2)
| Wiggle Waggle | 7" | Trojan | TR7721 | 1969 | £1.50 | £4 | |

## WANSEL, DEXTER
| Voyager | LP | Philadelphia | PIR82786 | 1978 | £8 | £20 | |

## WAPASSOU
| Wapassou | LP | Prodisc | PS37342 | 1974 | £8 | £20 | French |

## WAR
| All Day Music | LP | United Artists | UAS29269 | 1972 | £4 | £10 | |
| War | LP | Liberty | LBG83478 | 1971 | £4 | £10 | |

## WARD, BILLY & THE DOMINOES
| Billy Ward & His Dominoes | LP | Decca | DL8621 | 1958 | £50 | £100 | US |
| Billy Ward & His Dominoes | LP | Federal | 395548 | 1956 | £250 | £400 | US |
| Billy Ward & His Dominoes | LP | King | LP548 | 1956 | £100 | £200 | US |
| Billy Ward & His Dominoes | 10" LP | Federal | 29594 | 1954 | £500 | £750 | US |
| Billy Ward & His Dominoes Feat. Clyde McPhatter & Jackie Wilson | LP | King | LP733 | 1961 | £50 | £100 | US |
| Billy Ward & The Dominoes | 7" EP | London | REU1114 | 1958 | £50 | £100 | |
| Billy Ward & The Dominoes | 10" LP | Parlophone | PMD1061 | 1958 | £250 | £400 | best auctioned |
| Clyde McPhatter With Billy Ward | LP | Federal | 395559 | 1957 | £250 | £400 | US |
| Clyde McPhatter With Billy Ward | LP | King | LP559 | 1956 | £100 | £200 | US |
| Deep Purple | 7" | London | HLU8502 | 1957 | £7.50 | £15 | |
| Don't Thank Me | 78 | Parlophone | R3789 | 1953 | £10 | £20 | |
| Evermore | 7" | Brunswick | 05656 | 1957 | £7.50 | £15 | |
| Have Mercy Baby | 78 | Vogue | V2135 | 1952 | £6 | £12 | |
| Jennie Lee | 7" | London | HLU8634 | 1958 | £7.50 | £15 | |
| Pagan Love Song | LP | Liberty | LRP3113/LST7113 | 1959 | £20 | £40 | US |
| Please Don't Say No | 7" | London | HLU8883 | 1959 | £5 | £10 | |
| Sea Of Glass | LP | Liberty | LRP3056 | 1959 | £20 | £40 | US |
| Sixty Minute Man | 78 | Vogue | V9012 | 1951 | £10 | £20 | |
| St. Theresa Of The Roses | 7" | Brunswick | 05599 | 1956 | £12.50 | £25 | |
| Stardust | 7" | London | HLU8465 | 1957 | £7.50 | £15 | |
| Three Coins In A Fountain | 7" | Parlophone | MSP6112 | 1954 | £50 | £100 | |
| Twenty-Four Songs | LP | King | LP952 | 1966 | £15 | £30 | US |
| Yours Forever | LP | London | HAU2116 | 1958 | £25 | £50 | |

## WARD, BURT
Burt Ward was the Boy Wonder (Robin in *Batman*), of course – this record is a Frank Zappa creation.

| Boy Wonder, I Love You | 7" | MGM | 13632 | 1967 | £75 | £150 | US |

## WARD, CHRISTINE
| Face Of Empty Me | 7" | Decca | F12339 | 1966 | £2.50 | £6 | |

## WARD, DALE
| Letter from Shirley | 7" | London | HLD9835 | 1964 | £4 | £8 | |

## WARD, ROBIN
| Wonderful Summer | LP | Dot | DLP3555/2555 | 1963 | £8 | £20 | US |
| Wonderful Summer | 7" | London | HLD9821 | 1963 | £2 | £5 | |

## WARD SINGERS
| Famous Ward Singers | 10" LP | London | LZC14013 | 1955 | £4 | £10 | |

## WARDS OF COURT
| All Night Girl | 7" | Deram | DM127 | 1967 | £2 | £5 | |

## WARE, LEON
| Musical Massage | LP | Tamla Motown | STML12050 | 1977 | £5 | £12 | |

## WARHORSE
| Red Sea | LP | Vertigo | 6360066 | 1972 | £20 | £40 | spiral label |
| St. Louis | 7" | Vertigo | 6059027 | 1970 | £2 | £5 | |
| Warhorse | LP | Vertigo | 6360015 | 1970 | £15 | £30 | spiral label |

## WARLEIGH, RAY
| First Album | LP | Philips | SBL7881 | 1969 | £10 | £25 | |

## WARLOCK, OZZIE & THE WIZARDS
| Juke Box Fury | 7" | HMV | POP635 | 1959 | £2.50 | £6 | |

## WARM
| Demo Tapes | 7" | Warm | SMS001 | 1978 | £2.50 | £6 | double |

## WARM DUST
| | | | | | | | |
|---|---|---|---|---|---|---|---|
| And It Came To Pass | LP | Trend | TNLS700 | 1970 | £8 | £20 | |
| It's A Beautiful Day | 7" | Trend | 6099002 | 1970 | £1.50 | £4 | |
| Peace For Our Time | LP | Trend | 6480001 | 1971 | £5 | £12 | |

## WARM EXPRESSION
| | | | | | | | |
|---|---|---|---|---|---|---|---|
| Let No Man Put Asunder | 7" | Columbia | DB8672 | 1970 | £1.50 | £4 | |

## WARM SOUNDS
| | | | | | | | |
|---|---|---|---|---|---|---|---|
| Birds And Bees | 7" | Deram | DM120 | 1967 | £1.50 | £4 | |
| Nite Is A-Comin' | 7" | Deram | DM174 | 1968 | £7.50 | £15 | |
| Sticks And Stones | 7" | Immediate | IM058 | 1967 | £1.50 | £4 | |

## WARNER, MIKE & HIS NEW STARS
| | | | | | | | |
|---|---|---|---|---|---|---|---|
| Mike Warner And His New Stars | LP | Ariola | 72359 | 1964 | £62.50 | £125 | German |

## WARNING, GALE
| | | | | | | | |
|---|---|---|---|---|---|---|---|
| Rock Those Crazy Skins | 78 | Oriole | CB1349 | 1956 | £2 | £5 | |

## WARPIG
| | | | | | | | |
|---|---|---|---|---|---|---|---|
| Warpig | LP | Fonthill | NAS13528 | 1971 | £37.50 | £75 | Canadian |

## WARREN, ALMA
| | | | | | | | |
|---|---|---|---|---|---|---|---|
| Stealin' | 7" | Parlophone | MSP6200 | 1956 | £1.50 | £4 | |

## WARREN, PETER
| | | | | | | | |
|---|---|---|---|---|---|---|---|
| Bass Is | LP | Enja | 2018 | 1974 | £10 | £25 | |

## WARREN J.5
| | | | | | | | |
|---|---|---|---|---|---|---|---|
| Rhythm & Blues | LP | Vedette | VRM36049 | 1967 | £50 | £100 | Italian |

## WARREN OF GHANA, GUY
| | | | | | | | |
|---|---|---|---|---|---|---|---|
| Africa Speaks – America Answers | LP | Brunswick | LAT8237 | 1958 | £15 | £30 | |
| African Soundz | LP | Regal Zonophone | SLRZ1031 | 1972 | £15 | £30 | |
| Afro-Jazz | LP | Columbia | SCX6340 | 1969 | £15 | £30 | |
| Monkeys And Butterflies | 7" | Brunswick | 05791 | 1959 | £2 | £5 | |

## WARRIOR
| | | | | | | | |
|---|---|---|---|---|---|---|---|
| Breakout | 7" | Warrior | W002 | 1984 | £2.50 | £6 | |
| For Europe Only | LP | Warrior | W001 | 1983 | £4 | £10 | |

## WARRIOR (2)
| | | | | | | | |
|---|---|---|---|---|---|---|---|
| Invasion | LP | Eden | LP27 | 1972 | £330 | £500 | |

## WARRIORS

The collectability of the Warriors' single derives from the fact that the group's singer was Jon Anderson. The drummer, meanwhile, was Ian Wallace, who has played on numerous records since, most notably LPs made by King Crimson and Bob Dylan.

| | | | | | | | |
|---|---|---|---|---|---|---|---|
| You Came Along | 7" | Decca | F11926 | 1964 | £15 | £30 | |

## WARSAW PAKT
| | | | | | | | |
|---|---|---|---|---|---|---|---|
| Needletime | LP | Island | ILPS9515 | 1977 | £5 | £12 | |
| Safe And Warm | 7" | Island | PAKT1 | 1978 | £2.50 | £6 | |
| Safe And Warm | 7" | Island | PAKT1 | 1978 | £7.50 | £15 | picture sleeve |

## WARWICK, DEE DEE
| | | | | | | | |
|---|---|---|---|---|---|---|---|
| Gotta Get A Hold Of Myself | 7" | Mercury | MF890 | 1965 | £1.50 | £4 | |
| I Want To Be With You | LP | Mercury | MG2/SR61100 | 1967 | £4 | £10 | US |
| I'll Be Better Off | 7" | Mercury | MF1061 | 1968 | £2 | £5 | |
| Lover's Chant | 7" | Mercury | MF909 | 1966 | £6 | £12 | |
| We're Doing Fine | 7" EP | Mercury | 10036MCE | 1966 | £2.50 | £6 | |
| When Love Slips Away | 7" | Mercury | MF974 | 1967 | £1.50 | £4 | |

## WARWICK, DIONNE
| | | | | | | | |
|---|---|---|---|---|---|---|---|
| Dionne | 7" EP | Pye | NEP44044 | 1965 | £2 | £5 | |
| Do You Know The Way To San Jose | 7" EP | Pye | NEP44090 | 1968 | £2 | £5 | |
| Don't Make Me Over | 7" EP | Pye | NEP44026 | 1964 | £2 | £5 | |
| Don't Make Me Over | 7" | Stateside | SS157 | 1963 | £1.50 | £4 | |
| Forever My Love | 7" EP | Pye | NEP44046 | 1965 | £2 | £5 | |
| Here I Am | 7" EP | Pye | NEP44051 | 1966 | £2 | £5 | |
| I Just Don't Know What To Do With Myself | 7" EP | Pye | NEP44077 | 1966 | £2 | £5 | |
| I Love Paris | 7" EP | Pye | NEP44083 | 1967 | £2 | £5 | |
| It's Love That Really Counts | 7" EP | Pye | NEP44024 | 1964 | £2 | £5 | |
| Make The Music Play | 7" | Stateside | SS222 | 1963 | £2.50 | £6 | demo only |
| Message To Michael | 7" EP | Pye | NEP44067 | 1966 | £2 | £5 | |
| Presenting | LP | Pye | NPL28037 | 1964 | £4 | £10 | |
| Who Can I Turn To | 7" EP | Pye | NEP44049 | 1965 | £2 | £5 | |
| Window Wishing | 7" EP | Pye | NEP44073 | 1966 | £2 | £5 | |
| Wishin' And Hopin' | 7" EP | Pye | NEP44039 | 1965 | £2 | £5 | |
| Wishin' And Hopin' | 7" | Stateside | SS191 | 1963 | £1.50 | £4 | |

## WAS (NOT WAS)
| | | | | | | | |
|---|---|---|---|---|---|---|---|
| Anything Can Happen | CD-s | Polygram | 0804542 | 1988 | £3 | £8 | CD video |
| Out Come The Freaks | CD-s | Fontana | WASCD4 | 1988 | £2 | £5 | |

| | | | | | | | |
|---|---|---|---|---|---|---|---|
| Spy In The House Of Love | CD-s .. | Fontana | WASCD2 | 1987 | £2 | £5 | |
| Walk The Dinosaur | CD-s .. | Polygram | 0804522 | 1988 | £3 | £8 | CD video |

## WASA
| | | | | | | | |
|---|---|---|---|---|---|---|---|
| Wasa | LP | Polar | POLS261 | 1975 | £8 | £20 | Swedish |

## WASHBOARD RHYTHM KINGS
| | | | | | | |
|---|---|---|---|---|---|---|
| Washboard Rhythm Kings | 7" EP . | HMV | 7EG8101 | 1955 | £4 | £8 |
| Washboard Rhythm Kings | 7" EP . | HMV | 7EG8126 | 1955 | £4 | £8 |

## WASHINGTON, ALBERT & THE KINGS
| | | | | | | |
|---|---|---|---|---|---|---|
| Turn On THe Bright Lights | 7" | President | PT242 | 1969 | £1.50 | £4 |
| Woman Love | 7" | President | PT227 | 1969 | £1.50 | £4 |

## WASHINGTON, BABY
| | | | | | | | |
|---|---|---|---|---|---|---|---|
| Get A Hold Of Yourself | 7" | United Artists .. | UP2247 | 1968 | £5 | £10 | |
| I Can't Wait Until I See My Baby | 7" | Sue | WI321 | 1964 | £7.50 | £15 | |
| I Don't Know | 7" | Atlantic | 584299 | 1969 | £1.50 | £4 | |
| Only Those In Love | LP | London | HAC8292 | 1966 | £6 | £15 | |
| Only Those In Love | 7" | London | HLC9987 | 1965 | £2.50 | £6 | |
| That's How Heartaches Are Made | LP | London | HAC8260 | 1963 | £8 | £20 | |
| That's How Heartaches Are Made | 7" | Sue | WI302 | 1963 | £7.50 | £15 | |
| With You In Mind | LP | Veep | 16528 | 1968 | £4 | £10 | US |

## WASHINGTON, DELROY
| | | | | | | |
|---|---|---|---|---|---|---|
| I-Sus | LP | Virgin | V2060 | 1976 | £5 | £12 |
| Rasta | LP | Virgin | V2088 | 1977 | £5 | £12 |

## WASHINGTON, DINAH
| | | | | | | | |
|---|---|---|---|---|---|---|---|
| After Hours With Miss D. | 10" LP | Emarcy | EJT501 | 1956 | £6 | £15 | |
| Blues | LP | Top Rank | RX3006 | 1959 | £4 | £10 | ...with tracks by Betty Roche |
| Dinah | LP | Emarcy | EJL1255 | 1957 | £4 | £10 | |
| Dinah '63 | LP | Columbia | 33SX1608 | 1963 | £4 | £10 | |
| For Lonely Lovers | LP | Mercury | MMC14085 | 1962 | £4 | £10 | |
| I Concentrate On You | LP | Mercury | MMC14063/ CMS18043 | 1961 | £4 | £10 | |
| September In The Rain | LP | Mercury | MMC14107 | 1961 | £4 | £10 | |
| Sings The Best In Blues | LP | Mercury | MPL6519 | 1957 | £4 | £10 | |
| Unforgettable | LP | Mercury | MMC14048 | 1960 | £4 | £10 | |
| What A Difference A Day Made | LP | Mercury | MMC14030 | 1960 | £4 | £10 | |
| What A Difference A Day Made | 7" | Mercury | AMT1051 | 1959 | £1.50 | £4 | |

## WASHINGTON, ELLA
| | | | | | | |
|---|---|---|---|---|---|---|
| He Called Me Baby | 7" | Monument | MON1030 | 1969 | £1.50 | £4 |

## WASHINGTON, GENO & THE RAM JAM BAND
| | | | | | | | |
|---|---|---|---|---|---|---|---|
| Different Strokes | 7" EP . | Pye | NEP24293 | 1968 | £5 | £10 | |
| Hand Clappin', Foot Stompin' | LP | Piccadilly | NPL38026 | 1966 | £5 | £12 | |
| Hi | 7" EP . | Piccadilly | NEP34054 | 1966 | £4 | £8 | |
| Hipsters And Flipsters | LP | Piccadilly | N(S)PL38032 | 1967 | £4 | £10 | |
| I Can't Let You Go | 7" | Pye | 7N17649 | 1968 | £1.50 | £4 | |
| Running Wild | LP | Pye | N(S)PL18219 | 1968 | £4 | £10 | |
| Shake A Tail Feather | LP | Piccadilly | N(S)PL38029 | 1968 | £4 | £10 | |
| She Shot A Hole In My Soul | 7" | Piccadilly | 7N35392 | 1967 | £1.50 | £4 | |
| Small Package Of Hipsters | 7" EP . | Pye | NEP24302 | 1968 | £6 | £12 | |
| Tell It Like It Is | 7" EP . | Pye | PNV24198 | 1967 | £6 | £12 | French |
| Tell It Like It Is | 7" | Piccadilly | 7N35403 | 1967 | £1.50 | £4 | |
| Water | 7" EP . | Pye | PNV24178 | 1966 | £6 | £12 | French |
| Water | 7" | Piccadilly | 7N35312 | 1966 | £1.50 | £4 | |

## WASHINGTON, GROVER
| | | | | | | |
|---|---|---|---|---|---|---|
| All The King's Horses | LP | Kudu | KUL5 | 1973 | £4 | £10 |
| Inner City Blues | LP | Kudu | KUL1 | 1973 | £4 | £10 |

## WASHINGTON, JUSTINE
| | | | | | | | |
|---|---|---|---|---|---|---|---|
| Only Those In Love | LP | Sue | (S)1042 | 1965 | £5 | £12 | US |

## WASHINGTON, KENNETH
| | | | | | | | |
|---|---|---|---|---|---|---|---|
| If I Had A Ticket | 7" | CBS | 202494 | 1967 | £2.50 | £6 | with Chris Barber |

## WASHINGTON, SHERI
| | | | | | | |
|---|---|---|---|---|---|---|
| I Got Plenty | 7" | Vogue | V9070 | 1957 | £87.50 | £175 |

## WASHINGTON, SISTER ERNESTINE
| | | | | | | |
|---|---|---|---|---|---|---|
| Sister Ernestine Washington | 7" EP . | Melodisc | EPM752 | 1955 | £2.50 | £6 |

## WASHINGTON, TONY
| | | | | | | |
|---|---|---|---|---|---|---|
| But I Do | 7" | Black Swan | WI459 | 1965 | £2 | £5 |
| Dilly Dilly | 7" | Black Swan | WI460 | 1965 | £2 | £5 |
| Show Me How | 7" | Sue | WI327 | 1964 | £4 | £8 |
| Surely You Love Me | 7" | Fontana | TF478 | 1964 | £1.50 | £4 |

## WASHINGTON, TYRONE
| | | | | | | |
|---|---|---|---|---|---|---|
| Natural Essence | LP | Blue Note | BST84274 | 1968 | £6 | £15 |

## WASHINGTON DC'S
| | | | | | | |
|---|---|---|---|---|---|---|
| I've Done It All Wrong | 7" | Domain | D9 | 1969 | £2 | £5 |

| | | | | | | | |
|---|---|---|---|---|---|---|---|
| Kisses Sweeter Than Wine | 7" EP | Pathe | EGF761 | 1964 | £6 | £12 | French |
| Kisses Sweeter Than Wine | 7" | Ember | EMBS190 | 1964 | £2.50 | £6 | |
| Seek And Find | 7" | CBS | 202464 | 1967 | £10 | £20 | |
| Seek And Find | 7" | CBS | 202464 | 1967 | £20 | £40 | picture sleeve |
| Thirty-Second Floor | 7" | CBS | 202226 | 1966 | £4 | £8 | |

## WASP (BRIAN BENNETT)

| | | | | | | | |
|---|---|---|---|---|---|---|---|
| Melissa | 7" | EMI | EMI2253 | 1975 | £5 | £10 | |

## WASPS

| | | | | | | | |
|---|---|---|---|---|---|---|---|
| Can't Wait Till '78 | 7" | NEMS | NES115 | 1977 | £2 | £5 | Mean Street B side |

## WASTELAND

| | | | | | | | |
|---|---|---|---|---|---|---|---|
| Friends, Romans, Countrymen | 7" | Invicta | INV014 | 1979 | £5 | £10 | |
| Want Not | 7" | Ellie Jay | EJSP9261 | 1979 | £5 | £10 | |

## WATER INTO WINE BAND

| | | | | | | | |
|---|---|---|---|---|---|---|---|
| Harvest Time | LP | private | CJT002 | 1976 | £100 | £200 | |
| Hill Climbing For Beginners | LP | Myrrh | MYR1004 | 1973 | £25 | £50 | brown cover |
| Hill Climbing For Beginners | LP | Myrrh | MYR1004 | 1974 | £37.50 | £75 | white cover, re-recorded tracks |

## WATERBOYS

| | | | | | | | |
|---|---|---|---|---|---|---|---|
| And A Bang On The Ear | CD-s | Ensign | ENYCD624 | 1989 | £2 | £5 | |
| Best Of The Waterboys | CD | Ensign | CCD1845 | 1991 | £10 | £25 | promo double |
| Big Music | 12" | Ensign | 12ENY508 | 1984 | £3 | £8 | |
| December | 12" | Ensign | 12ENY506 | 1984 | £3 | £8 | |
| Dream Harder – Interview Album | CD | Ensign | PROCD4522 | 1993 | £10 | £25 | US promo |
| Girl Called Johnny | 7" | Chicken Jazz | CJ1 | 1983 | £1.50 | £4 | |
| Girl Called Johnny | 12" | Chicken Jazz | CJT1 | 1983 | £3 | £8 | |
| Kit Number One | CD | Ensign | | 1991 | £30 | £60 | promo box set, with Best Of CD, 2 x 12", CD-s, video, 7" |
| Mike Scott Interview | CD | Ensign | DPRO23719 | 1991 | £10 | £25 | US promo |
| Room To Roam | CD | Ensign | | 1991 | £25 | £50 | promo box set, with Best Of CD, 7", CD-s, interview CD |
| This Is The Sea | CD | Chrysalis | CD25CR23 | 1994 | £5 | £12 | Chrysalis 25 pack |
| Waterboys | CD | Chrysalis | CCD1541 | 1986 | £5 | £12 | |
| Whole Of The Moon | 7" | Ensign | ENY520 | 1985 | £2.50 | £6 | |
| Whole Of The Moon | 12" | Ensign | 12ENY520 | 1985 | £3 | £8 | picture sleeve |

## WATERFALL

| | | | | | | | |
|---|---|---|---|---|---|---|---|
| Beneath The Stars | LP | Gun Dog | LP003 | 1981 | £15 | £30 | |
| Flight Of The Day | LP | Bob | FRR001 | 198– | £20 | £40 | |

## WATERPROOF CANDLE

| | | | | | | | |
|---|---|---|---|---|---|---|---|
| Electronically Heated Child | 7" | RCA | RCA1717 | 1968 | £2 | £5 | |

## WATERS, MUDDY

| | | | | | | | |
|---|---|---|---|---|---|---|---|
| After The Rain | LP | Chess | CRL4553 | 1969 | £15 | £30 | |
| At Newport | LP | Chess | CRL4513 | 1965 | £6 | £15 | |
| At Newport | LP | Pye | NJL34 | 1961 | £8 | £20 | |
| Back In The Good Old Days | LP | Syndicate | 001 | 1970 | £8 | £20 | double |
| Best Of Muddy Waters | LP | London | LTZM15152 | 1959 | £15 | £30 | |
| Blues From Big Bill's Copacabana | LP | Chess | LP(S)1533 | 1968 | £6 | £15 | US |
| Blues Man | LP | Polydor | 236574 | 1969 | £4 | £10 | |
| Country Boy | 7" | Python | P04 | 1969 | £10 | £20 | |
| Down On Stovall's Plantation | LP | Bounty | BY6031 | 1968 | £5 | £12 | |
| Electric Mud | LP | Chess | CRL4542 | 1968 | £20 | £40 | |
| Fathers And Sons | LP | Chess | CRL4556 | 1969 | £6 | £15 | with other artists |
| Folk Singer | LP | Pye | NPL28038 | 1964 | £8 | £20 | |
| Good News | LP | Syndicate | 002 | 1970 | £6 | £15 | |
| Honey Bee | 78 | Vogue | V2372 | 1956 | £10 | £20 | |
| I Got A Rich Man's Woman | 7" | Chess | CRS8019 | 1965 | £2.50 | £6 | |
| I'm Ready | 7" EP | Chess | CRE6006 | 1965 | £15 | £30 | |
| Let's Spend The Night Together | 7" | Chess | CRS8083 | 1969 | £1.50 | £4 | |
| Long Distance Call | 78 | Vogue | V2273 | 1954 | £10 | £20 | |
| McKinley Morganfield AKA Muddy Waters | LP | Chess | 6671001 | 1971 | £4 | £10 | |
| Mississippi Blues | 7" EP | London | REU1060 | 1956 | £37.50 | £75 | gold label |
| More Real Folk Blues | LP | Chess | LP(S)1511 | 1966 | £8 | £20 | US |
| Muddy Waters | LP | Pye | NPL28040 | 1964 | £8 | £20 | |
| Muddy Waters | LP | Python | PLP12 | 1969 | £8 | £20 | |
| Muddy Waters | 7" EP | Pye | NEP44010 | 1963 | £5 | £10 | |
| Muddy Waters Vol. 2 | LP | Python | PLP18 | 1969 | £8 | £20 | |
| Muddy Waters Vol. 3 | LP | Python | PLP19 | 1969 | £8 | £20 | |
| Muddy Waters With Little Walter | 7" EP | Vogue | EPV1046 | 1955 | £50 | £100 | |
| Muddy, Brass, & The Blues | LP | Chess | CRL4525 | 1967 | £6 | £15 | |
| My John The Conqueror Root | 7" | Chess | CRS8001 | 1965 | £4 | £8 | |
| Rare Live Recordings Vol. 1 | LP | Black Bear | LP901 | 1972 | £6 | £15 | |
| Rare Live Recordings Vol. 2 | LP | Black Bear | LP902 | 1972 | £6 | £15 | |
| Rare Live Recordings Vol. 3 | LP | Black Bear | LP903 | 1972 | £6 | £15 | |
| Real Folk Blues | LP | Chess | CRL4515 | 1966 | £6 | £15 | |
| Real Folk Blues Vol. 4 | 7" EP | Chess | CRE6022 | 1966 | £7.50 | £15 | |
| Rollin' Stone | 78 | Vogue | V2101 | 1952 | £10 | £20 | |
| Sail On | LP | Chess | LPS1539 | 1969 | £5 | £12 | US |

| Sings Big Bill Broonzy | LP | Pye | NPL28048 | 1964 | £6 | £15 | |
| Vintage Mud | LP | Sunnyland | KS100 | 1969 | £6 | £15 | |

## WATERS, MUDDY, BO DIDDLEY, HOWLIN' WOLF

| Super Super Blues Band | LP | Chess | CRL4537 | 1968 | £6 | £15 | |

## WATERS, MUDDY, BO DIDDLEY, LITTLE WALTER

| Super Blues | LP | Chess | CRL4529 | 1967 | £6 | £15 | |

## WATERS, ROGER

| 5:06 am (Every Stranger's Eyes) | 7" | Harvest | HAR5230 | 1984 | £2.50 | £6 | |
| Another Brick In The Wall Part 2 | CD-s | Mercury | MERCD332 | 1990 | £2 | £5 | ....with Cyndi Lauper |
| Pros And Cons Of Hitch-Hiking | LP | Harvest | SHVL2401051 | 1984 | £4 | £10 | ....banded promo |
| Radio K.A.O.S. | LP | EMI | KAOSDJ1 | 1987 | £5 | £12 | ....banded promo, no dialogue |
| Radio Waves | CD-s | EMI | CDEM6 | 1987 | £2.50 | £6 | |
| Sunset Strip | 7" | EMI | EM20 | 1987 | £2.50 | £6 | |
| Tide Is Turning | CD-s | EMI | CDEM37 | 1987 | £2 | £5 | |
| What God Wants Part 1 | CD-s | CBS | 6581399 | 1992 | £2 | £5 | boxed set with 2 cards |

## WATERSON, MIKE

| Mike Waterson | LP | Topic | 12TS332 | 1977 | £4 | £10 | |

## WATERSONS

| Bright Phoebus | LP | Trailer | LES2076 | 1972 | £5 | £12 | |
| Frost And Fire | LP | Topic | 12T136 | 1965 | £8 | £20 | |
| New Voices | LP | Topic | 12T125 | 1965 | £10 | £25 | with Harry Boardman and Maureen Craik |
| Watersons | LP | Topic | 12T142 | 1966 | £8 | £20 | |
| Yorkshire Garland | LP | Topic | 12T167 | 1966 | £8 | £20 | |

## WATSON, DOC

| Doc Watson Family | LP | XTRA | XTRA1082 | 1969 | £5 | £12 | |
| Home Again! | LP | Fontana | (S)TFL6083 | 1968 | £6 | £15 | |

## WATSON, JOHN L.

| Mother's Love | 7" | Deram | DM285 | 1970 | £1.50 | £4 | |
| White Hot Blue Black | LP | Deram | SMLR1061 | 1970 | £6 | £15 | |

## WATSON, JOHNNY GUITAR

| Bad | LP | OKeh | OKM4118/OKS14118 | 1967 | £6 | £15 | US |
| Blues Soul | LP | Chess | 1490 | 1965 | £10 | £25 | US |
| I Cried For You | LP | Cadet | LP4056 | 1967 | £4 | £10 | US |
| In The Fats Bag | LP | OKeh | OKM4124/OKS14124 | 1967 | £6 | £15 | US |
| Johnny Guitar Watson | LP | King | LP857 | 1963 | £25 | £50 | US |

## WATT, TOMMY

| It Might As Well Be Swing | LP | Parlophone | PMC1068 | 1959 | £6 | £15 | |
| Watt's Cooking | LP | Parlophone | PMC1107 | 1959 | £6 | £15 | |

## WATTERS, LU

| Dixieland Jamboree | 10" LP | Columbia | 33C9036 | 1957 | £6 | £15 | |
| Lu Watters 1947 | 10" LP | London | HBU1061 | 1956 | £6 | £15 | |
| Lu Watters And His Jazz Band | 10" LP | Vogue | LDE009 | 1952 | £8 | £20 | |
| Lu Watters And The Yerba Buena Jazz Band | LP | Good Time Jazz | LAG12030 | 1956 | £5 | £12 | |
| Lu Watters Jazz Band | LP | Good Time Jazz | LAG12025 | 1956 | £5 | £12 | |
| Lu Watters Jazz Band Vol. 1 | 10" LP | Good Time Jazz | LDG038 | 1954 | £8 | £20 | |
| Lu Watters Yerba Buena Band | 10" LP | Columbia | 33C9004 | 1955 | £8 | £20 | |
| Lu Watters Yerba Buena Band Vol. 1 | 10" LP | Good Time Jazz | LP8 | 1953 | £8 | £20 | |
| Lu Watters' Yerba Buena Jazz Band | LP | Good Time Jazz | LAG12123 | 1958 | £5 | £12 | |

## WATTS 103RD STREET RHYTHM BAND

| Cornbread And Grits | LP | Warner Bros | WS1741 | 1967 | £5 | £12 | US |
| Express Yourself | LP | Warner Bros | 1864 | 1970 | £6 | £15 | US |
| Express Yourself | 7" | Warner Bros | WB7417 | 1970 | £1.50 | £4 | |
| In The Jungle Babe | LP | Warner Bros | WS1801 | 1969 | £4 | £10 | US |
| Spreadin' Honey | 7" | Jay Boy | BOY71 | 1973 | £2 | £5 | |
| You're So Beautiful | LP | Warner Bros | 1904 | 1970 | £4 | £10 | US |

## WATTS, NOBLE THIN MAN

| Hard Times | 7" | London | HLU8627 | 1958 | £15 | £30 | |
| Noble Thin Man Watts & Wild Jimmy Spurrill | 7" EP | XX | MIN717 | 196– | £2.50 | £6 | |
| Noble's Theme | 7" | Sue | WI347 | 1964 | £7.50 | £15 | . June Bateman B side |

## WATUSI WARRIORS

| Wa-chi-bam-ba | 7" | London | HL8866 | 1959 | £2.50 | £6 | |

## WAVE CRESTS

| Surftime USA | LP | Viking | VKS6606 | 1963 | £6 | £15 | US |

## WAY, DARRYL & WOLF

| Title | Format | Label | Catalogue | Year | | | Notes |
|---|---|---|---|---|---|---|---|
| Canis Lupus | LP | Deram | SDL14 | 1973 | £5 | £12 | |
| Saturation Point | LP | Deram | SML1104 | 1973 | £5 | £12 | |

## WAY WE LIVE

| Title | Format | Label | Catalogue | Year | | | Notes |
|---|---|---|---|---|---|---|---|
| Candle For Judith | LP | Dandelion | DAN8004 | 1971 | £50 | £100 | |

## WAYBURN, NANCY

| Title | Format | Label | Catalogue | Year | | | Notes |
|---|---|---|---|---|---|---|---|
| World Goes On Without Me | 7" | Warner Bros | WB5646 | 1965 | £2 | £5 | |

## WAYFARERS

| Title | Format | Label | Catalogue | Year | | | Notes |
|---|---|---|---|---|---|---|---|
| Songs And Dance Tunes | LP | MWM | MWM1017 | 1978 | £8 | £20 | |

## WAYNE, ALVIS

| Title | Format | Label | Catalogue | Year | | | Notes |
|---|---|---|---|---|---|---|---|
| Don't Mean Maybe Baby | 7" | Starlite | ST45104 | 1963 | £100 | £200 | best auctioned |

## WAYNE, BOBBY

| Title | Format | Label | Catalogue | Year | | | Notes |
|---|---|---|---|---|---|---|---|
| Ballad Of A Teenage Queen | 7" | Pye | 7N25315 | 1965 | £2 | £5 | |

## WAYNE, CARL

| Title | Format | Label | Catalogue | Year | | | Notes |
|---|---|---|---|---|---|---|---|
| Carl Wayne | LP | RCA | SF8239 | 1971 | £4 | £10 | |

## WAYNE, CARL & THE VIKINGS

| Title | Format | Label | Catalogue | Year | | | Notes |
|---|---|---|---|---|---|---|---|
| This Is Love | 7" | Pye | 7N15824 | 1965 | £10 | £20 | |
| What's A Matter Baby | 7" | Pye | 7N15702 | 1964 | £10 | £20 | |

## WAYNE, CHUCK

| Title | Format | Label | Catalogue | Year | | | Notes |
|---|---|---|---|---|---|---|---|
| Chuck Wayne Quintet | 10" LP | London | LZC14014 | 1955 | £20 | £40 | |

## WAYNE, FRANCES

| Title | Format | Label | Catalogue | Year | | | Notes |
|---|---|---|---|---|---|---|---|
| Frances Wayne | LP | Brunswick | BL54022 | 1957 | £5 | £12 | US |
| Songs For My Man | LP | Epic | LN3222 | 195– | £5 | £12 | US |
| Warm Sound Of Frances Wayne | LP | Atlantic | 1263 | 1956 | £6 | £15 | US |

## WAYNE, JEFF

| Title | Format | Label | Catalogue | Year | | | Notes |
|---|---|---|---|---|---|---|---|
| War Of The Worlds | LP | CBS | WOW100 | 1979 | £8 | £20 | double LP, 12", book, poster, boxed |

## WAYNE, JERRY

| Title | Format | Label | Catalogue | Year | | | Notes |
|---|---|---|---|---|---|---|---|
| Half Hearted Love | 7" | Vogue | V9169 | 1960 | £6 | £12 | |

## WAYNE, PAT & THE BEACHCOMBERS

| Title | Format | Label | Catalogue | Year | | | Notes |
|---|---|---|---|---|---|---|---|
| Brand New Man | 7" | Columbia | DB7417 | 1964 | £1.50 | £4 | |
| Bye Bye Johnny | 7" | Columbia | DB7262 | 1964 | £4 | £8 | |
| Jambalaya | 7" | Columbia | DB7121 | 1963 | £4 | £8 | |
| Roll Over Beethoven | 7" EP | Columbia | ESRF1502 | 1964 | £15 | £30 | French |
| Roll Over Beethoven | 7" | Columbia | DB7182 | 1963 | £4 | £8 | |

## WAYNE, RICKY

| Title | Format | Label | Catalogue | Year | | | Notes |
|---|---|---|---|---|---|---|---|
| Chick A Roo | 7" | Top Rank | JAR432 | 1960 | £7.50 | £15 | demo |
| Chick A Roo | 7" | Triumph | RGM1009 | 1960 | £15 | £30 | |
| Make Way Baby | 7" | Pye | 7N15289 | 1960 | £6 | £12 | |
| Say You're Gonna Be My Own | 7" | Oriole | CB306 | 1965 | £1.50 | £4 | |

## WAYNE, TERRY

| Title | Format | Label | Catalogue | Year | | | Notes |
|---|---|---|---|---|---|---|---|
| All Mama's Children | 7" | Columbia | DB4067 | 1958 | £5 | £10 | |
| Matchbox | 7" | Columbia | DB4002 | 1957 | £6 | £12 | |
| Oh Lonesome Me | 7" | Columbia | DB4112 | 1958 | £2.50 | £6 | |
| She's Mine | 7" | Columbia | DB4312 | 1959 | £2 | £5 | |
| Slim Jim Tie | 7" | Columbia | DB4035 | 1957 | £5 | £10 | |
| Terrific | 7" EP | Columbia | SEG7758 | 1958 | £25 | £50 | |
| Where My Baby Goes | 7" | Columbia | DB4205 | 1958 | £2 | £5 | |

## WAYNE, THOMAS

| Title | Format | Label | Catalogue | Year | | | Notes |
|---|---|---|---|---|---|---|---|
| Tragedy | 7" | London | HL7075 | 1959 | £5 | £10 | |
| Tragedy | 7" | London | HLU8846 | 1959 | £12.50 | £25 | |

## WAYNE, WEE WILLIE

| Title | Format | Label | Catalogue | Year | | | Notes |
|---|---|---|---|---|---|---|---|
| Travellin' Mood | LP | Imperial | LP9144 | 1961 | £20 | £40 | US |

## WAYS AND MEANS

| Title | Format | Label | Catalogue | Year | | | Notes |
|---|---|---|---|---|---|---|---|
| Little Deuce Coupe | 7" | Columbia | DB7907 | 1966 | £2 | £5 | |
| Sea Of Faces | 7" | Pye | 7N17217 | 1966 | £5 | £10 | |

## WAZOO

| Title | Format | Label | Catalogue | Year | | | Notes |
|---|---|---|---|---|---|---|---|
| Weird Freakout | LP | Zigzag | 212 | 1969 | £6 | £15 | US |

## WE FIVE

| Title | Format | Label | Catalogue | Year | | | Notes |
|---|---|---|---|---|---|---|---|
| Let's Get Together | 7" EP | Pye | NEP44056 | 1966 | £6 | £12 | |
| Let's Get Together | 7" | Pye | 7N25346 | 1966 | £1.50 | £4 | |
| You Were On My Mind | 7" | Pye | 7N25314 | 1965 | £1.50 | £4 | |
| You Were On My Mind | LP" | Pye | NPL28067 | 1965 | £8 | £20 | |

## WE THE PEOPLE

| Title | Format | Label | Catalogue | Year | | | Notes |
|---|---|---|---|---|---|---|---|
| He Doesn't Go About It Right | 7" | London | HLH10089 | 1966 | £37.50 | £75 | |
| St. John's Shop | 7" EP | London | RE10184 | 1966 | £100 | £200 | French |
| You Burn Me Up And Down | 7" EP | London | RE10191 | 1966 | £100 | £200 | French |

## WEASELS
Liverpool Beat ......................................... LP ...... Wing .............. MGW/SRW12282 . 1964 £5 .......... £12 ...................... *US*

## WEATHER REPORT
When the time comes to assess the major innovators of late-twentieth-century music, then the name of Weather Report is likely to loom large. Marketed as jazz, Weather Report's music is of equal appeal to progressive rock fans for the way in which it blends improvisation with composed passages, setting up frequently elaborate structures in which the textures and timbres available to electronic instruments are exploited to the full. Under Josef Zawinul's fingers, the synthesizer begins to achieve some of the potential of which it is obviously capable, but which is so seldom realized. The double Japan-only release *Live In Tokyo* contains the complete concert that was presented in excerpt on the UK album *I Sing The Body Electric*.

| Title | Format | Label | Cat# | Year | | | Notes |
|---|---|---|---|---|---|---|---|
| Black Market ............................................... | CD ..... | CBS ...... | CD81325 ............... | 1987 | £5 ........ | £12 | |
| Domino Theory ........................................... | CD ..... | CBS ...... | CD25839 ............... | 1984 | £5 ........ | £12 | |
| I Sing The Body Electric .......................... | LP ..... | CBS ...... | 64943 ................... | 1972 | £4 ........ | £10 | |
| Live In Tokyo .............................................. | LP ..... | CBS Sony ...... | 40AP942-3 ...... | 1972 | £10 ...... | £25 | ........ *Japanese double* |
| Mysterious Traveller .................................. | LP ..... | CBS ...... | 80027 ................... | 1974 | £4 ........ | £10 | |
| Mysterious Traveller .................................. | CD ..... | CBS ...... | CD80027 ............... | 1984 | £5 ........ | £12 | |
| New Album ................................................. | CD ..... | CBS ...... | CD26367 ............... | 1988 | £5 ........ | £12 | |
| Night Passage ............................................. | CD ..... | CBS ...... | CD84597 ............... | 1983 | £5 ........ | £12 | |
| Sweetnighter .............................................. | LP ..... | CBS ...... | 65532 ................... | 1973 | £5 ........ | £12 | |
| Tale Spinnin' ............................................... | LP ..... | CBS ...... | 80734 ................... | 1975 | £4 ........ | £10 | |
| Weather Report .......................................... | LP ..... | CBS ...... | 64521 ................... | 1971 | £4 ........ | £10 | |

## WEAVERS
| Title | Format | Label | Cat# | Year | | | Notes |
|---|---|---|---|---|---|---|---|
| At Home ...................................................... | LP ..... | Top Rank ...... | RX3008 ............... | 1959 | £4 ........ | £10 | |
| At The Carnegie Hall ............................... | LP ..... | Vanguard ........ | PPL11006 ............... | 1957 | £4 ........ | £10 | |
| Best Of The Weavers ................................ | LP ..... | Brunswick ...... | LAT8357 ............... | 1961 | £4 ........ | £10 | |
| Best Of The Weavers ................................ | LP ..... | Decca ............. | DL8893 ............... | 1959 | £4 ........ | £10 | *US* |
| Folk Songs Around The World ................ | LP ..... | Decca ............. | DL8909 ............... | 1959 | £4 ........ | £10 | *US* |
| On Tour ...................................................... | LP ..... | Vanguard .......... | PPL11011 ............... | 1958 | £4 ........ | £10 | |
| Reunion At Carnegie Hall ....................... | LP ..... | Fontana ............. | TFL6032 ............... | 1963 | £4 ........ | £10 | |

## WEB
| Title | Format | Label | Cat# | Year | | | Notes |
|---|---|---|---|---|---|---|---|
| Baby Won't You Leave Me Alone ............. | 7" ...... | Deram ............. | DM217 ............... | 1968 | £1.50 ...... | £4 | |
| Fully Interlocking ...................................... | LP ..... | Deram ............. | SML1025 ............... | 1968 | £8 ........ | £20 | |
| Hatton Mill Morning ................................ | 7" ...... | Deram ............. | DM201 ............... | 1968 | £2 ...... | £5 | |
| I Spider ....................................................... | LP ..... | Polydor ........... | 2383024 ............... | 1970 | £50 ...... | £100 | |
| Monday To Friday ..................................... | 7" ...... | Deram ............. | DM253 ............... | 1969 | £1.50 ...... | £4 | |
| Theraphosa Blondi ..................................... | LP ..... | Deram ............. | SML1058 ............... | 1970 | £8 ........ | £20 | |

## WEBB, DEAN
| Title | Format | Label | Cat# | Year | | | Notes |
|---|---|---|---|---|---|---|---|
| Hey Miss Fanny ......................................... | 7" ...... | Parlophone ...... | R4549 ............... | 1959 | £5 ........ | £10 | |
| Streamline Baby .......................................... | 7" ...... | Parlophone ...... | R4587 ............... | 1959 | £5 ........ | £10 | |

## WEBB, DON
Little Ditty Baby ......................................... 7" ...... Coral .............. Q72385 ............... 1960 £37.50 .... £75

## WEBB, GEORGE
George Webb Dixielanders ........................ 7" EP . Melodisc ......... WPM770 ............... 195– £2 ............. £5

## WEBB, JIMMY
Jimmy Webb is a songwriter of genius – 'By The Time I Get To Phoenix', 'Didn't We', 'MacArthur Park' and 'Wichita Lineman' are early landmarks in his career. His own records reveal him to be a limited but effective singer, with *Land's End* containing some particularly fine material.

| Title | Format | Label | Cat# | Year | | | Notes |
|---|---|---|---|---|---|---|---|
| And So On .................................................. | LP ..... | Reprise ........... | K44134 ............... | 1971 | £4 ........ | £10 | |
| I Keep It Hid ............................................... | 7" ...... | CBS ............. | 3672 ............... | 1968 | £2.50 ...... | £6 | ..*B side Shane Martin* |
| Jim Webb Sings Jim Webb ........................ | LP ..... | CBS ............. | 63335 ............... | 1968 | £6 ........ | £15 | |
| Land's End .................................................. | LP ..... | Asylum ...... | SYL9014 ............... | 1974 | £4 ........ | £10 | |
| Letters ......................................................... | LP ..... | Reprise ........... | K44173 ............... | 1972 | £4 ........ | £10 | |
| Words And Music ....................................... | LP ..... | Reprise ........... | RSLP6421 ............... | 1970 | £4 ........ | £10 | |

## WEBB, JOHNNY
Dig ................................................................ 7" ...... Columbia ........ DB3805 ............... 1956 £1.50 .... £4

## WEBB, PETTA
I Have Wandered In Exile ........................ LP ..... Topic .............. 12TS223 ............... 1973 £10 ........ £25

## WEBB, PETTA & PETE COOPER
Heart Is True .............................................. LP ..... Heart .............. HR001 ............... 1986 £4 .......... £10

## WEBB, SKEETER
Was It A Bad Dream .................................. 7" ...... Parlophone ...... CMSP32 ............... 1955 £2 ............. £5 ...................... *export*

## WEBB, SONNY & THE CASCADES
| Title | Format | Label | Cat# | Year | | | Notes |
|---|---|---|---|---|---|---|---|
| You've Got Everything ............................... | 7" ..... | Oriole ...... | CB1873 ............... | 1963 | £7.50 .... | £15 | |
| You've Got Everything ............................... | 7" ..... | Polydor ........... | NH52158 ............... | 1963 | £2 ........ | £5 | |

## WEBBER SISTERS
My World ..................................................... 7" ...... Island .............. WI3109 ............... 1967 £5 ........ £10 ..... *Alva Lewis B side*

## WEBER, EBERHARD
| Title | Format | Label | Cat# | Year | | | Notes |
|---|---|---|---|---|---|---|---|
| Colours Of Chloë ........................................ | LP ..... | ECM ............. | ECM1042ST ......... | 1974 | £5 ........ | £12 | |
| Following Morning ..................................... | LP ..... | ECM ............. | ECM1084ST ......... | 1976 | £4 ........ | £10 | |
| Yellow Fields .............................................. | LP ..... | ECM ............. | ECM1066ST ......... | 1975 | £5 ........ | £12 | |

## WEBSTER, BEN

| | | | | | | |
|---|---|---|---|---|---|---|
| Ben Webster | 10" LP | Vogue Coral | LRA10021 | 1955 £30 | £60 | |
| Ben Webster And Associates | LP | HMV | CLP1336 | 1960 £6 | £15 | |
| Ben Webster Meets Oscar Peterson | LP | HMV | CLP1412/CSD1336 | 1960 £6 | £15 | |
| Ben Webster With Strings | LP | Columbia | 33CX10014 | 1955 £8 | £20 | |
| Soulville | LP | Columbia | 33CX10122 | 1958 £8 | £20 | |

## WEBSTER, DEENA

| | | | | | | |
|---|---|---|---|---|---|---|
| You're Losing | 7" | Parlophone | R5699 | 1968 £2 | £5 | |

## WEDDING PRESENT

| | | | | | | |
|---|---|---|---|---|---|---|
| Blue Eyes | 7" | RCA | PB45185 | 1992 £2.50 | £6 | No. 1 of 1992 singles |
| Brassneck | CD-s | RCA | PD43404 | 1990 £2 | £5 | |
| Brassneck | 7" | RCA | PB43403 | 1990 £2.50 | £6 | handpainted cover |
| Come Play With Me | 7" | RCA | PB45313 | 1992 £1.50 | £4 | No. 5 of 1992 singles |
| Don't Try And Stop Me Mother | 12" | Reception | REC002/12 | 1986 £4 | £10 | |
| Evening Show EP | CD-s | Strange Fruit | SFNTCD016 | 1988 £2 | £5 | |
| George Best | LP | Reception | LEEDS1 | 1987 £4 | £10 | .. with 7" (REC005) |
| Go Go Dancer | 7" | RCA | PB45183 | 1992 £2 | £5 | No. 2 of 1992 singles |
| Go Out And Get 'Em Boy! | 7" | City Slang | CSL001 | 1985 £12.50 | £25 | |
| Go Out And Get 'Em Boy! | 7" | Reception | REC001 | 1985 £20 | £40 | |
| Katrusyu | 7" | RCA | | 1989 £4 | £8 | promo only |
| Kennedy | CD-s | RCA | PD43118 | 1989 £2 | £5 | |
| Make Me Smile | CD-s | RCA | PD44022 | 1990 £2 | £5 | |
| Million Miles | 7" | Reception | | 1987 £10 | £20 | promo only |
| My Favourite Dress | 7" | Reception | REC005 | 1987 £2.50 | £6 | white vinyl |
| Nobody's Twisting Your Arm | CD-s | Reception | REC009CD | 1988 £2 | £5 | |
| Once More | 7" | Reception | REC002 | 1986 £7.50 | £15 | |
| Peel Sessions | CD-s | Strange Fruit | SFPSCD009 | 1988 £2 | £5 | |
| Porquoi es-tu devenue si raisonnable? | CD-s | Midnight Music | DONG39CD | 1989 £2 | £5 | |
| Silver Shorts | 7" | RCA | PB45311 | 1992 £1.50 | £4 | No. 4 of 1992 singles |
| This Boy Can Wait | 7" | Reception | REC003 | 1986 £2.50 | £6 | |
| This Boy Can Wait | 12" | Reception | REC003/12 | 1986 £3 | £8 | |
| Three | 7" | RCA | PB45181 | 1992 £1.50 | £4 | No. 3 of 1992 singles |
| Tommy | LP | Reception | LEEDS2 | 1988 £6 | £15 | signed, with poster |
| Why Are You Being So Reasonable Now | CD-s | Reception | REC011CD | 1988 £2 | £5 | |

## WEDGE

| | | | | | | |
|---|---|---|---|---|---|---|
| No One Left But Me | LP | private | | 197– £20 | £40 | US |

## WEDGES

| | | | | | | |
|---|---|---|---|---|---|---|
| Hang Ten | LP | Time | (S)T2090 | 1963 £8 | £20 | US |

## WEE WILLIE & THE WINNERS

| | | | | | | |
|---|---|---|---|---|---|---|
| Get Some | 7" | Action | ACT4624 | 1974 £2 | £5 | |

## WEED

| | | | | | | |
|---|---|---|---|---|---|---|
| Weed | LP | Philips | 6305096 | 1971 £50 | £100 | German |

## WEED, BUDDY

| | | | | | | |
|---|---|---|---|---|---|---|
| Kent Song | 7" | Vogue | V9075 | 1957 £7.50 | £15 | |

## WEEDON, BERT

| | | | | | | |
|---|---|---|---|---|---|---|
| $64,000 Question | 7" | Parlophone | R4256 | 1957 £4 | £8 | |
| Big Note Blues | 7" | Parlophone | R4446 | 1958 £2 | £5 | |
| Boy With The Magic Guitar | 7" | Parlophone | MSP6242 | 1956 £5 | £10 | |
| Demonstration Record With David Gell | 7" EP | Selmer | | 1959 £2 | £5 | |
| Fifi | 7" | Saga | SAG2906 | 1959 £4 | £8 | |
| Guitar Boogie Shuffle | 7" | Top Rank | JAR117 | 1959 £1.50 | £4 | |
| Guitar Man | 7" EP | HMV | 7EG8856 | 1964 £4 | £8 | |
| Honky Tonk Guitar | LP | Top Rank | 35101 | 1961 £8 | £20 | |
| King Size Guitar | LP | Top Rank | BUY026 | 1960 £10 | £25 | |
| Night Cry | 7" | HMV | POP1141 | 1963 £2.50 | £6 | |
| Play That Big Guitar | 7" | Parlophone | R4381 | 1957 £2 | £5 | |
| Roulette | 7" EP | Top Rank | TR5004 | 1959 £2 | £5 | with other artists |
| Soho Fair | 7" | Parlophone | R4315 | 1957 £4 | £8 | |
| Teenage Guitar | 7" | Top Rank | JAR136 | 1959 £1.50 | £4 | |
| Tune For Two | 7" | HMV | POP1039 | 1962 £4 | £8 | demo only |
| Waxing The Winners | 7" EP | Esquire | EP56 | 1956 £6 | £12 | |
| Weedon Winners | 7" EP | Top Rank | JKP3008 | 1961 £5 | £10 | |

## WEGMULLER, WALTER

| | | | | | | |
|---|---|---|---|---|---|---|
| Tarot | LP | Kosmische | KK258003 | 1973 £75 | £150 | German boxed double |

## WEIR, FRANK ORCHESTRA

| | | | | | | |
|---|---|---|---|---|---|---|
| Theme From Journey Into Space | 7" | Decca | F10435 | 1955 £1.50 | £4 | |

## WEIRD STRINGS

| | | | | | | |
|---|---|---|---|---|---|---|
| Criminal Cage | 7" | Ace | ACE009 | 1980 £2 | £5 | |
| Oscar Mobile | 7" | Velvet Moon | VM1 | 1980 £2.50 | £6 | |

## WEIRDOS

| | | | | | | |
|---|---|---|---|---|---|---|
| We Got The Neutron Bomb | 7" | Dangerhouse | SP1063 | 1978 £5 | £10 | |

## WELCH, BOB

| | | | | | | |
|---|---|---|---|---|---|---|
| French Kiss | LP | Capitol | EST11663 | 1977 £5 | £12 | US picture disc |

## WELCH, BRUCE

| Title | Format | Label | Cat# | Year | | | Notes |
|---|---|---|---|---|---|---|---|
| Please Mr. Please | 7" | EMI | EMI2141 | 1974 | £30 | £60 | |

## WELCH, ELIZABETH

| Title | Format | Label | Cat# | Year | | | Notes |
|---|---|---|---|---|---|---|---|
| Stormy Weather | 7" | Industrial | IR002 | 1980 | £2.50 | £6 | |

## WELCH, LENNY

| Title | Format | Label | Cat# | Year | | | Notes |
|---|---|---|---|---|---|---|---|
| Darling Take Me Back | 7" | London | HLR9981 | 1965 | £2 | £5 | |
| Run To My Lovin' Arms | 7" | London | HLR10010 | 1965 | £2.50 | £6 | |
| Since I Fell For You | LP | Cadence | CLP5068/25068 | 1963 | £5 | £12 | US |

## WELCH, TIM

| Title | Format | Label | Cat# | Year | | | Notes |
|---|---|---|---|---|---|---|---|
| Weak In The Knees | 7" | Columbia | DB4529 | 1960 | £1.50 | £4 | |

## WELDON, LIAM

| Title | Format | Label | Cat# | Year | | | Notes |
|---|---|---|---|---|---|---|---|
| Dark Horse On The Wind | LP | Mulligan | LUN066 | 1976 | £10 | £25 | |

## WELFARE STATE

| Title | Format | Label | Cat# | Year | | | Notes |
|---|---|---|---|---|---|---|---|
| Welfare State Songs | LP | Look | LKLP6347 | 1978 | £37.50 | £75 | |

## WELLER, PAUL

Paul Weller's new status as one of the major rock figures of the nineties is an astonishing turn around for a man who floundered in a critical wilderness for most of the eighties. Despite the tremendous success of the Jam, Weller's Style Council seldom impressed, seeming for the most part like the work of a man whose creative inspiration was evaporated. Fortunately, his nineties recordings are something else again, the new influence of late-sixties groups like Traffic proving to be highly beneficial.

| Title | Format | Label | Cat# | Year | | | Notes |
|---|---|---|---|---|---|---|---|
| Above The Clouds | CD-s | Go! Discs | GODCD91 | 1992 | £5 | £12 | |
| Conversation With Paul Weller | CD | London | PRCD70072 | 1995 | £15 | £30 | US promo |
| Hung Up | CD-s | Go! Discs | GODCD111 | 1994 | £3 | £8 | |
| Into Tomorrow | CD-s | Freedom High | FHPCD1 | 1991 | £12.50 | £25 | |
| Into Tomorrow | 7" | Freedom High | FHP1 | 1991 | £5 | £10 | |
| Into Tomorrow | 12" | Freedom High | FHPT1 | 1991 | £6 | £15 | |
| Live Wood | CD | Pony Canyon | PCCY00601 | 1994 | £15 | £30 | ...Japanese with bonus CD single |
| More Wood | CD | Pony Canyon | PCCY00509 | 1994 | £8 | £20 | Japanese |
| Out Of The Sinking | CD-s | Go! Discs | GODCD121 | 1994 | £2 | £5 | |
| Paul Weller Special | CD | Our Price | | 1995 | £30 | £60 | promo |
| Peacock Suit | CD-s | Go! Discs | PWRT1 | 1996 | £12.50 | £25 | promo |
| Sexy Sadie | CD-s | Go! Discs | PNPCD1 | 1994 | £15 | £30 | promo |
| Stanley Road | CD | Go! Discs | 8286192 | 1995 | £6 | £15 | in 12" box |
| Sunflower | CD-s | Go! Discs | GODCD102 | 1993 | £3 | £8 | |
| Uh Huh Oh Yeh | CD-s | Go! Discs | GODCD86 | 1992 | £5 | £12 | |
| Weaver | CD-s | Go! Discs | GODCD107 | 1993 | £2 | £5 | |
| Wild Wood | CD-s | Go! Discs | GODCD104 | 1993 | £2 | £5 | |
| Wild Wood | CD | Go! Discs | 8284352 | 1993 | £5 | £12 | fold-out cover |
| Wild Wood | CD | London | 8285132/CDP1216 | 1993 | £10 | £25 | US with bonus 3 track CD |

## WELLES, ORSON

| Title | Format | Label | Cat# | Year | | | Notes |
|---|---|---|---|---|---|---|---|
| War Of The Worlds | LP | Charisma | DCS10 | 1969 | £5 | £12 | double |

## WELLS, BOBBY

| Title | Format | Label | Cat# | Year | | | Notes |
|---|---|---|---|---|---|---|---|
| Let's Coppa Groove | 7" | Beacon | 3102 | 1968 | £1.50 | £4 | yellow label |

## WELLS, DICKY

| Title | Format | Label | Cat# | Year | | | Notes |
|---|---|---|---|---|---|---|---|
| Bones For The King | LP | Felsted | FAJ7006 | 1959 | £5 | £12 | |
| Trombone Four-In-Hand | LP | Felsted | FAJ7009/SJA2009 | 1960 | £5 | £12 | |

## WELLS, HOUSTON

| Title | Format | Label | Cat# | Year | | | Notes |
|---|---|---|---|---|---|---|---|
| Anna Marie | 7" | Parlophone | R5099 | 1964 | £2.50 | £6 | |
| Blowing Wild | 7" | Parlophone | R5069 | 1963 | £2.50 | £6 | |
| Blue Of The Night | 7" | Parlophone | R5226 | 1965 | £1.50 | £4 | |
| Just For You | 7" EP | Parlophone | GEP8878 | 1963 | £15 | £30 | |
| Livin' Alone | 7" | Parlophone | R5141 | 1964 | £2.50 | £6 | |
| Only The Heartaches | 7" | Parlophone | R5031 | 1963 | £2.50 | £6 | |
| Ramona | 7" EP | Parlophone | GEP8914 | 1964 | £25 | £50 | |
| Shutters And Boards | 7" | Parlophone | R4980 | 1962 | £2.50 | £6 | |
| This Song Is Just For You | 7" | Parlophone | R4955 | 1962 | £2.50 | £6 | |
| Western Style | LP | Parlophone | PMC1215 | 1963 | £20 | £40 | |

## WELLS, JEAN

| Title | Format | Label | Cat# | Year | | | Notes |
|---|---|---|---|---|---|---|---|
| World! Here Comes Jean Wells | LP" | Sonet | SNTF606 | 1970 | £6 | £15 | |

## WELLS, JOHNNY

| Title | Format | Label | Cat# | Year | | | Notes |
|---|---|---|---|---|---|---|---|
| Lonely Moon | 7" | Columbia | DB4377 | 1959 | £2 | £5 | |

## WELLS, JUNIOR

| Title | Format | Label | Cat# | Year | | | Notes |
|---|---|---|---|---|---|---|---|
| Blues With A Beat | 7" EP | Delmark | DJB1 | 1966 | £7.50 | £15 | |
| Coming At You | LP | Vanguard | SVRL19011 | 1968 | £5 | £12 | |
| Hoodoo Man Blues | LP | Delmark | DL612 | 1966 | £6 | £15 | US |
| It's My Life Baby | LP | Fontana | (S)TFL6084 | 1966 | £6 | £15 | |
| It's My Life Baby | LP | Vanguard | SVRL19028 | 1968 | £4 | £10 | |
| Junior Wells | 7" EP | XX | MIN715 | 196- | £4 | £8 | |
| You're Tuff Enough | LP | Mercury | SMCL20130 | 1968 | £4 | £10 | |

## WELLS, KITTY

| Title | Format | Label | Catalogue | Year | Price 1 | Price 2 | Notes |
|---|---|---|---|---|---|---|---|
| After Dark | LP | Decca | DL8888 | 1959 | £5 | £12 | US |
| Country Hit Parade | LP | Decca | DL8293 | 1956 | £6 | £15 | US |
| Dust On The Bible | LP | Decca | DL8858 | 1959 | £5 | £12 | US |
| I Gave My Wedding Dress Away | 7" | Brunswick | 05920 | 1964 | £1.50 | £4 | |
| Kitty Sings | 7" EP | Brunswick | OE9149 | 1955 | £5 | £10 | |
| Kitty Wells Story | LP | Decca | DX(S)B(7)174 | 1963 | £4 | £10 | US, with booklet |
| Kitty's Choice | LP | Brunswick | LAT8361 | 1961 | £4 | £10 | |
| Winner Of Your Heart | LP | Decca | DL8552 | 1956 | £6 | £15 | US |

## WELLS, MARY

| Title | Format | Label | Catalogue | Year | Price 1 | Price 2 | Notes |
|---|---|---|---|---|---|---|---|
| Ain't It The Truth | 7" | Stateside | SS372 | 1965 | £4 | £8 | |
| Bye Bye Baby | LP | Oriole | PS40051 | 1963 | £25 | £50 | |
| Dear Lover | 7" | Atlantic | AT4067 | 1966 | £5 | £10 | |
| Doctor | 7" | Stateside | SS2111 | 1968 | £1.50 | £4 | |
| Greatest Hits | LP | Motown | 616 | 1964 | £10 | £25 | US |
| Greatest Hits | LP | Tamla Motown | TML11032 | 1966 | £6 | £15 | |
| He's A Lover | 7" | Stateside | SS439 | 1965 | £2.50 | £6 | |
| Laughing Boy | 7" | Oriole | CBA1829 | 1963 | £20 | £40 | |
| Live On Stage | LP | Motown | 611 | 1963 | £20 | £40 | US |
| Love Songs To The Beatles | LP | Stateside | (S)SL10171 | 1966 | £8 | £20 | |
| Mary Wells | LP | Stateside | SL10133 | 1965 | £6 | £15 | |
| Mary Wells | 7" EP | Tamla Motown | TME2007 | 1965 | £15 | £30 | |
| Me And My Baby | 7" | Atlantic | 584054 | 1966 | £1.50 | £4 | |
| Me Without You | 7" | Stateside | SS463 | 1965 | £2.50 | £6 | |
| My Baby Just Cares For Me | LP | Tamla Motown | TML11006 | 1965 | £10 | £25 | |
| My Guy | LP | Stateside | SL10095 | 1964 | £15 | £30 | |
| My Guy | 7" | Stateside | SS288 | 1964 | £1.50 | £4 | |
| Never Never Leave Me | 7" | Stateside | SS415 | 1965 | £2.50 | £6 | |
| Nothing But A Man | LP | Motown | (MS)630 | 1965 | £10 | £25 | US |
| One Who Really Loves You | LP | Motown | 605 | 1962 | £30 | £60 | US |
| Ooh | LP | Movietone | 71010/72010 | 1966 | £6 | £15 | US |
| Servin' Up Some Soul | LP | Stateside | (S)SL10266 | 1968 | £4 | £10 | |
| Set My Soul On Fire | 7" | Atlantic | 584104 | 1967 | £1.50 | £4 | |
| Two Lovers | LP | Oriole | PS40045 | 1963 | £25 | £50 | |
| Two Lovers | 7" | Oriole | CBA1796 | 1963 | £15 | £30 | |
| Two Sides Of Mary Wells | LP | Atlantic | 587049 | 1966 | £4 | £10 | |
| Use Your Head | 7" | Stateside | SS396 | 1965 | £2.50 | £6 | |
| Vintage Stock | LP | Motown | 653 | 1966 | £10 | £25 | US |
| You Beat Me To The Punch | 7" | Oriole | CBA1762 | 1962 | £15 | £30 | |
| You Lost The Sweetest Boy | 7" | Stateside | SS242 | 1963 | £6 | £12 | |
| Your Old Standby | 7" | Oriole | CBA1847 | 1963 | £20 | £40 | |

## WELLSTOOD, DICK

| Title | Format | Label | Catalogue | Year | Price 1 | Price 2 |
|---|---|---|---|---|---|---|
| Dick Wellstood | 10" LP | London | HBU1059 | 1956 | £6 | £15 |

## WELSH, ALEX

| Title | Format | Label | Catalogue | Year | Price 1 | Price 2 |
|---|---|---|---|---|---|---|
| Alex Welsh And His Band | 10" LP | Nixa | NJT507 | 1957 | £8 | £20 |
| Alex Welsh And His Band '69 | LP | Columbia | S(C)X6333 | 1969 | £5 | £12 |
| At Home With Alex Welsh | LP | Columbia | S(C)X6213 | 1968 | £5 | £12 |
| It's Right Here For You | LP | Columbia | 33SX1322/SCX3377 | 1961 | £6 | £15 |
| Melrose Folio | 10" LP | Nixa | NJT516 | 1958 | £8 | £20 |
| Music Of The Mauve Decade | LP | Columbia | 33SX1219 | 1960 | £6 | £15 |
| Strike One | LP | Strike | JHL102 | 1967 | £6 | £15 |

## WERKHOVEN, HENK

| Title | Format | Label | Catalogue | Year | Price 1 | Price 2 | Notes |
|---|---|---|---|---|---|---|---|
| Orphical Positions | LP | VMU | | 1981 | £30 | £60 | Dutch |

## WERLWINDS

| Title | Format | Label | Catalogue | Year | Price 1 | Price 2 |
|---|---|---|---|---|---|---|
| Winding It Up | 7" | Columbia | DB4650 | 1961 | £5 | £10 |

## WESLEY, FRED

| Title | Format | Label | Catalogue | Year | Price 1 | Price 2 |
|---|---|---|---|---|---|---|
| House Party | 7" | RSO | RSO67 | 1980 | £2 | £5 |
| House Party | 12" | RSO | RSO67 | 1980 | £5 | £12 |

## WESS, FRANK

| Title | Format | Label | Catalogue | Year | Price 1 | Price 2 |
|---|---|---|---|---|---|---|
| Frank Wess Quintet | 10" LP | Atlantic | ATLLP1 | 195– | £20 | £40 |

## WEST

| Title | Format | Label | Catalogue | Year | Price 1 | Price 2 | Notes |
|---|---|---|---|---|---|---|---|
| Bridges | LP | Epic | 26433 | 1969 | £6 | £15 | US |
| West | LP | Epic | 26380 | 1968 | £6 | £15 | US |

## WEST, ADAM & BURT WARD

| Title | Format | Label | Catalogue | Year | Price 1 | Price 2 | Notes |
|---|---|---|---|---|---|---|---|
| Batman | LP | Twentieth Century | TF(S)4180 | 1966 | £20 | £40 | US |

## WEST, DODIE

| Title | Format | Label | Catalogue | Year | Price 1 | Price 2 |
|---|---|---|---|---|---|---|
| Going Out Of My Head | 7" | Decca | F12046 | 1964 | £1.50 | £4 |

## WEST, HEDY

| Title | Format | Label | Catalogue | Year | Price 1 | Price 2 | Notes |
|---|---|---|---|---|---|---|---|
| Ballads | LP | Topic | 12T163 | 1967 | £10 | £25 | |
| Getting Folk Out Of The Country | LP | Folk Variety | FV12008 | 1973 | £6 | £15 | German, with Bill Clifton |
| Hedy West | LP | Vanguard | VRS9124 | 1963 | £8 | £20 | US |
| Hedy West Vol. 2. | LP | Vanguard | VRS/VSD79162 | 1964 | £8 | £20 | US |
| Love, Hell And Biscuits | LP | Bear Family | BF15003 | 1976 | £5 | £12 | German |

| | | | | | | |
|---|---|---|---|---|---|---|
| New Folks | LP | Vanguard | VRS9096 | 1963 £8 £20 | | US |
| Old Times And Hard Times | LP | Topic | 12T117 | 1965 £10 £25 | | |
| Pretty Saro | LP | Topic | 12T146 | 1966 £10 £25 | | |
| Serves 'Em Fine | LP | Fontana | STL5432 | 1967 £10 £25 | | |

## WEST, KEITH

Keith West was the singer with Tomorrow, and his solo singles featured at least some of the members of that group. Certainly guitarist Steve Howe can be heard on West's hit, 'Excerpt From A Teenage Opera'. The opera from which this song was supposedly taken never did appear, although a 1996 CD compilation of songs and out-takes made by Keith West and Mark Wirtz created a shadow of the work – the closest we are ever likely to get to the real thing. In any event, the single works brilliantly in isolation as a tantalizing glimpse of something much larger, but invisible.

| | | | | | |
|---|---|---|---|---|---|
| Excerpt From A Teenage Opera | 7" | Parlophone | R5623 | 1967 £1.50 £4 | |
| On A Saturday | 7" | Parlophone | R5713 | 1968 £10 £20 | |
| Sam | 7" | Parlophone | R5651 | 1967 £1.50 £4 | |
| Smashing Time | LP | Stateside | (S)SL10224 | 1968 £5 £12 | |

## WEST, LESLIE

| | | | | | |
|---|---|---|---|---|---|
| Leslie West Band | LP | Phantom | 701 | 1975 £4 £10 | US |
| Mountain | LP | Bell | SBLL126 | 1969 £8 £20 | |

## WEST, MAE

| | | | | | |
|---|---|---|---|---|---|
| Fabulous Mae West | LP | Brunswick | LAT8082 | 1956 £6 £15 | |
| Twist And Shout | 7" | Stateside | SS2021 | 1967 £4 £8 | |
| Way Out West | LP | Stateside | (S)SL10197 | 1967 £4 £10 | |

## WEST, SPEEDY

| | | | | | |
|---|---|---|---|---|---|
| Guitar Spectacular | LP | Capitol | (S)T1835 | 1962 £6 £15 | US |
| Steel Guitar | LP | Capitol | (S)T1341 | 1960 £8 £20 | US |
| West Of Hawaii | LP | Capitol | T956 | 1958 £10 £25 | US |

## WEST, SPEEDY & JIMMY BRYANT

| | | | | | |
|---|---|---|---|---|---|
| Capitol Presents | 10" LP | Capitol | LC6619 | 1953 £8 £20 | |
| Two Guitars Country Style | LP | Capitol | T520 | 1956 £20 £40 | US |
| Two Guitars Country Style | 10" LP | Capitol | H520 | 1954 £37.50 £75 | US |
| Two Guitars Country Style | 10" LP | Capitol | LC6694 | 1955 £8 £20 | |
| Two Guitars Country Style Part 1 | 7" EP | Capitol | EAP1520 | 1955 £5 £10 | |
| Two Guitars Country Style Part 2 | 7" EP | Capitol | EAP2520 | 1955 £5 £10 | |

## WEST COAST CONSORTIUM

| | | | | | |
|---|---|---|---|---|---|
| Colour Sergeant Lillywhite | 7" | Pye | 7N17482 | 1968 £5 £10 | |
| Some Other Someday | 7" | Pye | 7N17352 | 1967 £1.50 £4 | |

## WEST COAST DELEGATION

| | | | | | |
|---|---|---|---|---|---|
| Reach The Top | 7" | Deram | DM113 | 1967 £2 £5 | |

## WEST COAST KNACK

| | | | | | |
|---|---|---|---|---|---|
| I'm Aware | 7" | Capitol | CL15497 | 1967 £4 £8 | |

## WEST COAST POP ART EXPERIMENTAL BAND

| | | | | | |
|---|---|---|---|---|---|
| Child's Guide To Good & Evil | LP | Reprise | RSLP6298 | 1968 £37.50 £75 | |
| Help I'm A Rock | 7" EP | Reprise | RVEP60104 | 1966 £62.50 £125 | French |
| Part One | LP | Reprise | R(S)6247 | 1967 £25 £50 | US |
| Volume 2 | LP | Reprise | R(S)6270 | 1967 £25 £50 | US |
| West Coast Pop Art Experimental Band | LP | Fifo | M101 | 1966 £1050 £1500 | US |
| Where's My Daddy | LP | Amos | AAS7004 | 1969 £20 £40 | US |

## WEST COAST WORKSHOP

| | | | | | |
|---|---|---|---|---|---|
| Wizard Of Oz And Other Trans Love Trips | LP | Capitol | ST2776 | 1967 £15 £30 | US |

## WEST FIVE

| | | | | | |
|---|---|---|---|---|---|
| But If It Doesn't Work Out | 7" | HMV | POP1513 | 1966 £1.50 £4 | |
| Congratulations | 7" | HMV | POP1396 | 1965 £7.50 £15 | |
| Just Like Romeo And Juliet | 7" | HMV | POP1428 | 1965 £4 £8 | |

## WEST INDIANS

| | | | | | |
|---|---|---|---|---|---|
| Falling In Love | 7" | Doctor Bird | DB1127 | 1968 £5 £10 | |
| Right On Time | 7" | Doctor Bird | DB1121 | 1968 £5 £10 | |
| Strange Whisperings | 7" | Camel | CA16 | 1969 £1.50 £4 | . Carl Dawkins B side |

## WEST POINT SUPERNATURAL

| | | | | | |
|---|---|---|---|---|---|
| Time Will Tell | 7" | Reaction | 591013 | 1967 £2.50 £6 | |

## WEST WON

| | | | | | |
|---|---|---|---|---|---|
| Control | CD-s | Fun After All | CDFAA116D | 1992 £2 £5 | |

## WESTBROOK, MIKE

| | | | | | |
|---|---|---|---|---|---|
| Celebration | LP | Deram | DML/SML1013 | 1967 £25 £50 | |
| Citadel/Room 315 | LP | RCA | SF8433 | 1975 £6 £15 | |
| Cortège | LP | Original | ORA309 | 1982 £10 £25 | 3 LP set |
| For The Record | LP | Transatlantic | TRA312 | 1975 £15 £30 | |
| Goose Sauce | LP | Original | ORA001 | 1978 £6 £15 | |
| Life Of Its Own | 7" | Deram | DM234 | 1969 £2 £5 | |
| Little Westbrook Music | LP | Westbrook | LWN1 | 1983 £6 £15 | |
| Live | LP | Cadillac | SGC1001 | 1974 £8 £20 | |
| London Bridge | LP | Venture | VEB13 | 1988 £10 £25 | 3 LP boxed set |

| Title | Format | Label | Catalogue | Year | | | Notes |
|---|---|---|---|---|---|---|---|
| Love Songs | LP | Deram | SML1069 | 1970 | £37.50 | £75 | |
| Love, Dream And Variations | LP | Transatlantic | TRA323 | 1975 | £8 | £20 | |
| Mama Chicago | LP | RCA | PL25252 | 1979 | £10 | £25 | double |
| Marching Song Vol. 1 | LP | Deram | DML/SML1047 | 1969 | £25 | £50 | |
| Marching Song Vol. 2 | LP | Deram | DML/SML1048 | 1969 | £25 | £50 | |
| Metropolis | LP | Neon | NE10 | 1971 | £20 | £40 | |
| Metropolis | LP | RCA | SF8396 | 1974 | £10 | £25 | |
| Metropolis/Citadel/Room 315 | LP | RCA | | 1979 | £8 | £20 | double |
| On Duke's Birthday | LP | Hat Art | 2021 | 1984 | £6 | £15 | |
| Original Peter | 7" | Deram | DM311 | 1970 | £25 | £50 | with Norma Winstone |
| Piano | LP | Original | ORA002 | 1978 | £6 | £15 | |
| Release | LP | Deram | DML/SML1031 | 1968 | £25 | £50 | |
| Requiem | 7" | Deram | DM286 | 1970 | £2 | £5 | |
| Tyger | LP | RCA | SER5612 | 1971 | £15 | £30 | |
| Westbrook Blake | LP | Original | ORA203 | 1980 | £6 | £15 | |
| Westbrook-Rossini | LP | Hat Art | 2040 | 1987 | £5 | £12 | |

## WESTFAUSTER

| Title | Format | Label | Catalogue | Year | | | Notes |
|---|---|---|---|---|---|---|---|
| In A King's Dream | LP | Nasco | 9008 | 1971 | £37.50 | £75 | US |

## WESTLAKE, KEVIN

| Title | Format | Label | Catalogue | Year | | | Notes |
|---|---|---|---|---|---|---|---|
| Stars Fade | LP | Utopia | 1388 | 1976 | £5 | £12 | US |

## WESTMINSTER FIVE

| Title | Format | Label | Catalogue | Year | | |
|---|---|---|---|---|---|---|
| Railroad Blues | 7" | Carnival | CV7017 | 1964 | £2 | £5 |
| Sticks And Stones | 7" | Carnival | CV7019 | 1965 | £2 | £5 |

## WESTON, KIM

| Title | Format | Label | Catalogue | Year | | |
|---|---|---|---|---|---|---|
| For The First Time | LP | MGM | C(S)8055 | 1967 | £10 | £25 |
| Helpless | 7" | Tamla Motown | TMG554 | 1966 | £30 | £60 |
| I Got What You Need | 7" | MGM | MGM1338 | 1967 | £2.50 | £6 |
| I'm Still Loving You | 7" | Tamla Motown | TMG511 | 1965 | £30 | £60 |
| Kim Weston | 7" EP | Tamla Motown | TME2005 | 1965 | £30 | £60 |
| Little More Love | 7" | Stateside | SS359 | 1964 | £30 | £60 |
| Nobody | 7" | MGM | MGM1382 | 1968 | £2 | £5 |
| Rock Me A Little While | 7" EP | Tamla Motown | TME2015 | 1966 | £75 | £150 |
| Take Me In Your Arms | 7" | Tamla Motown | TMG538 | 1965 | £12.50 | £25 |
| That's Groovy | 7" | MGM | MGM1357 | 1967 | £1.50 | £4 |

## WESTON, RANDY

| Title | Format | Label | Catalogue | Year | | |
|---|---|---|---|---|---|---|
| Cole Porter In Modern Mood | 10" LP | London | HAPB1040 | 1955 | £15 | £30 |
| Randy Weston Trio | LP | London | HAU2018 | 1956 | £8 | £20 |
| Randy Weston Trio | 10" LP | London | HBU1046 | 1956 | £15 | £30 |

## WESTWIND

| Title | Format | Label | Catalogue | Year | | |
|---|---|---|---|---|---|---|
| Love Is | LP | Penny Farthing | PELS505 | 1970 | £75 | £150 |

## WESTWOOD

| Title | Format | Label | Catalogue | Year | | |
|---|---|---|---|---|---|---|
| Winner Takes All | LP | Intercord | INT145610 | 1980 | £10 | £25 |

## WET WET WET

| Title | Format | Label | Catalogue | Year | | | Notes |
|---|---|---|---|---|---|---|---|
| Angel Eyes | CD-s | Polygram | 0802742 | 1988 | £6 | £15 | CD video |
| Angel Eyes | CD-s | Precious Organisation | JWLCD6 | 1987 | £2 | £5 | |
| Broke Away | CD-s | Mercury | JWLCD10 | 1989 | £2 | £5 | |
| Hold Back The River | CD-s | Precious Organisation | JWLCD11 | 1990 | £2 | £5 | |
| I Can Give You Everything | 7" | Lyntone | | 1990 | £2.50 | £6 | flexi |
| I Remember | 7" | Precious | JEWEL5 | 1987 | £2.50 | £6 | |
| I Remember | 12" | Precious | JEWEL512 | 1987 | £4 | £10 | |
| Stay With Me Heartache | CD-s | Precious Organisation | JWLCD13 | 1990 | £2 | £5 | |
| Sweet Little Mystery | 7" | Precious | JWLS4 | 1987 | £2 | £5 | shaped picture disc |
| Sweet Little Mystery | 12" | Precious | JEWEL412 | 1987 | £4 | £10 | 'wet' cover |
| Sweet Surrender | CD-s | Precious Organisation | JWLCD9 | 1989 | £2 | £5 | |
| Temptation | CD-s | Polygram | 0804762 | 1988 | £4 | £10 | CD video |
| Temptation | CD-s | Precious | JWLCD7 | 1988 | £2 | £5 | |
| Video Singles | CD-s | Polygram | 0803389 | 1988 | £6 | £15 | CD video |
| Wishing I Was Lucky | 12" | Precious | JWLD3 | 1987 | £5 | £12 | double |

## WETTLING, GEORGE

| Title | Format | Label | Catalogue | Year | | |
|---|---|---|---|---|---|---|
| George Wettling Jazz Band | 10" LP | Columbia | 33S1019 | 1954 | £5 | £12 |

## WHALEFEATHERS

| Title | Format | Label | Catalogue | Year | | | Notes |
|---|---|---|---|---|---|---|---|
| Declare | LP | Nasco | 9003 | 1969 | £50 | £100 | US |
| Whalefeathers | LP | Blue Horizon | 2431009 | 1971 | £20 | £40 | |
| Whalefeathers | LP | Nasco | 9005 | 1970 | £37.50 | £75 | US |

## WHAM!

| Title | Format | Label | Catalogue | Year | | | Notes |
|---|---|---|---|---|---|---|---|
| Bad Boys | 7" | Innervision | IVL3143 | 1983 | £5 | £10 | picture disc |
| Bad Boys | 7" | Innervision | IVL3143 | 1983 | £2 | £5 | poster picture sleeve |
| Club Tropicana | 7" | Innervision | IVL3613 | 1983 | £5 | £10 | picture disc |
| Final | LP | Epic | WHAM2 | 1986 | £15 | £30 | 2 gold vinyl discs, inserts, boxed |
| Freedom | 7" | Epic | QA4743 | 1984 | £5 | £10 | shaped picture disc |
| Freedom | 7" | Epic | WA4743 | 1984 | £4 | £8 | shaped picture disc |
| Last Christmas | 7" | Epic | GA4949 | 1984 | £1.50 | £4 | gatefold sleeve |

| | | | | | | | |
|---|---|---|---|---|---|---|---|
| Wake Me Up Before You Go-Go | 12" | Epic | TA4440 | 1984 | £4 | £10 | poster sleeve |
| Wham Rap | 12" | Innervision | IVLA122442 | 1982 | £4 | £10 | |

## WHAT KEEPS US RUNNING
| | | | | | | | |
|---|---|---|---|---|---|---|---|
| What Keeps Us Running | LP | Seagull | | 1979 | £10 | £25 | Dutch |

## WHAT'S NEW
| | | | | | | | |
|---|---|---|---|---|---|---|---|
| Early Morning Rain | 7" EP | Number One | LOU2013 | 196– | £4 | £8 | French |
| Get Away | 7" EP | Number One | LOU2014 | 196– | £4 | £8 | French |

## WHEELER, KENNY
| | | | | | | | |
|---|---|---|---|---|---|---|---|
| Gnu High | LP | ECM | ECM1069ST | 1975 | £5 | £12 | |
| Song For Someone | LP | Incus | INCUS10 | 197– | £10 | £25 | |
| Windmill Tilter | LP | Fontana | STL5494 | 1968 | £20 | £40 | with Johnny Dankworth |

## WHEELS

Herbie Armstrong has enjoyed a lengthy and varied career – gaining chart hits as a member of Fox and of Yellow Dog, playing on several Van Morrison LPs and doing much other session work besides. His roots, however, go back to Belfast and an R&B group called Wheels. The group made two singles, then changed its name to Wheels-A-Way for a third.

| | | | | | | | |
|---|---|---|---|---|---|---|---|
| Bad Little Woman/Call My Name | 7" | Columbia | DB7827 | 1966 | £37.50 | £75 | |
| Bad Little Woman/Road Block | 7" | Columbia | DB7827 | 1966 | £100 | £200 | best auctioned |
| Gloria | 7" | Columbia | DB7682 | 1965 | £37.50 | £75 | |
| Kicks | 7" | Columbia | DB7981 | 1966 | £37.50 | £75 | |

## WHEELS OF TIME
| | | | | | | | |
|---|---|---|---|---|---|---|---|
| 1984 | 7" | Spin | 62008 | 1967 | £12.50 | £25 | |

## WHICHWHAT
| | | | | | | | |
|---|---|---|---|---|---|---|---|
| Whichwhat's First | LP | Beacon | BEAS14 | 1970 | £15 | £30 | |

## WHIRLWINDS

The Whirlwinds were led by Graham Gouldman, of later songwriting and Ten cc fame.

| | | | | | | | |
|---|---|---|---|---|---|---|---|
| Look At Me | 7" | HMV | POP1301 | 1964 | £20 | £40 | |

## WHISKERS
| | | | | | | | |
|---|---|---|---|---|---|---|---|
| Beat Parade '65 | LP | Ariola | 73967 | 1965 | £15 | £30 | German |

## WHISKEY, NANCY
| | | | | | | | |
|---|---|---|---|---|---|---|---|
| Nancy Whiskey | 8"EP | Topic | T7 | 195– | £10 | £20 | |

## WHISKEY, NANCY & CHAS MCDEVITT
| | | | | | | | |
|---|---|---|---|---|---|---|---|
| Intoxicating Miss Whiskey | LP | Mercury | MG10018 | 1957 | £10 | £25 | |

## WHISKY, NANCY & THE SKIFFLERS
| | | | | | | | |
|---|---|---|---|---|---|---|---|
| Bowling Green | 7" | Fontana | TF612 | 1965 | £1.50 | £4 | |
| He's Solid Gone | 7" | Oriole | CB1394 | 1957 | £5 | £10 | |
| Hillside In Scotland | 7" | Oriole | CB1452 | 1958 | £2.50 | £6 | |
| Old Grey Goose | 7" | Oriole | CB1485 | 1959 | £2 | £5 | |

## WHISPERS OF TRUTH
| | | | | | | |
|---|---|---|---|---|---|---|
| Whispers Of Truth | LP | Key | | £10 | £25 | |

## WHISTLER
| | | | | | | | |
|---|---|---|---|---|---|---|---|
| Ho-Hum | LP | Deram | SML1083 | 1971 | £8 | £20 | |

## WHITBREAD, SHARON
| | | | | | | |
|---|---|---|---|---|---|---|
| Spice Of LIfe | LP | Ra | | £25 | £50 | |

## WHITCOMB, IAN
| | | | | | | | |
|---|---|---|---|---|---|---|---|
| Good Hard Rock | 7" EP | Capitol | EAP122008 | 1966 | £4 | £8 | French |
| Good Hard Rock | 7" | Capitol | CL15431 | 1966 | £1.50 | £4 | |
| Nervous | 7" EP | Capitol | EAP122004 | 1965 | £5 | £10 | French |
| Sporting Life | 7" EP | Capitol | EAP160002 | 1965 | £4 | £8 | French |
| You Turn Me On | LP | Ember | NR5065 | 1967 | £8 | £20 | |
| You Turn Me On | 7" | Capitol | CL15395 | 1965 | £2 | £5 | |

## WHITE, BUKKA
| | | | | | | | |
|---|---|---|---|---|---|---|---|
| Blues Masters Vol. 4 | LP | Blue Horizon | 4604 | 1972 | £5 | £12 | US |
| Bukka White | LP | CBS | 52629 | 1969 | £15 | £30 | |
| Memphis Hot Shots | LP | Blue Horizon | 763229 | 1969 | £15 | £30 | |
| Sic 'Em Dogs | LP | Herwin | 201 | 1965 | £8 | £20 | US |
| Sky Songs | LP | Fontana | 688804ZL | 1966 | £4 | £10 | |

## WHITE, DANNY
| | | | | | | | |
|---|---|---|---|---|---|---|---|
| Keep My Woman Home | 7" | Sue | WI4031 | 1967 | £7.50 | £15 | |

## WHITE, DUKE
| | | | | | | | |
|---|---|---|---|---|---|---|---|
| It's Over | 7" | Island | WI084 | 1963 | £5 | £10 | |
| Sow Good Seeds | 7" | Black Swan | WI444 | 1965 | £5 | £10 | |

## WHITE, GEORGIA
| | | | | | | | |
|---|---|---|---|---|---|---|---|
| Was I Drunk? | 78 | Vocalion | V1038 | 1954 | £6 | £12 | |

## WHITE, IAN
Ian White ............................................. LP ..... private ............ ............................ 1970 £8 .......... £20 .........................................

## WHITE, JAY
Faraway Places ...................................... 7" EP . London .......... REF1045 .............. 1956 £2 .......... £5 .........................................

## WHITE, JEANETTE
Music ................................................... 7" ...... A&M ............. AMS761 ............... 1969 £7.50 ...... £15 .........................................

## WHITE, JOE
Downtown Girl .................................... 7" ...... Island ............. WI166 ............... 1965 £5 .......... £10 ... *Don Drummond B side*
Hog In A Coco ..................................... 7" ...... Island ............ WI159 ................. 1964 £5 .......... £10 ...*Roland Alphonso B side*
I Need A Woman ................................. 7" ...... Doctor Bird .... DB1090 .............. 1967 £5 .......... £10
If It Don't Work Out ........................... 7" ...... Gayfeet .......... GS202 ............. 1973 £1.50 ....... £4
Irene ................................................... 7" ...... Island ............ WI201 ............. 1965 £5 .......... £10
Lonely Nights ...................................... 7" ...... Doctor Bird .... DB1080 ............. 1967 £5 .......... £10
My Love For You ................................. 7" ...... Doctor Bird .... DB1024 ............. 1966 £5 .......... £10 . *Sammy Ismay B side*
Punch You Down ................................ 7" ...... Ska Beat ........ JB180 ............. 1965 £5 .......... £10 ... *Tommy McCook B side*
Rudies All Around ............................... 7" ...... Doctor Bird .... DB1069 ............. 1966 £5 .......... £10
Since The Other Day ............................ LP ..... Magnet .......... MGT006 .......... 197– £5 .......... £12
Sinners ................................................ 7" ...... R&B ............... JB137 ............. 1964 £5 .......... £10 ...*Roland Alphonso B side*
Try A Little Tenderness ....................... 7" ...... Blue Cat ......... BS119 ............. 1968 £4 .......... £8 ......*Lyn Taitt B side*
Way Of Life .......................................... 7" ...... Blue Cat ......... BS120 ............. 1968 £4 .......... £8
When You Are Young ........................... 7" ...... Island ............ WI145 ............. 1964 £5 .......... £10

## WHITE, JOHN & GAVIN BRYARS
Machine Music ..................................... LP ..... Obscure ......... OBS8 ............. 1978 £4 .......... £10 .........................................

## WHITE, JOSH
Ballads And Blues ................................ 10" LP Brunswick ...... LA8562 ............. 1953 £5 .......... £12
Ballads And Blues Vol. 2 ...................... 10" LP Brunswick ...... LA8653 ............. 1954 £5 .......... £12
Beginning ............................................. LP ..... Mercury ......... 20039MCL ......... 1964 £4 .......... £10
Blues And Josh White ........................... LP ..... Nixa ............... NJL2 .............. 1957 £4 .......... £10
Blues And Pt. 1 ..................................... 7" EP . Pye ................ NJE1057 ........... 1957 £2 .......... £5
Blues And Pt. 2 ..................................... 7" EP . Pye ................ NJE1058 ........... 1957 £2 .......... £5
Blues And Pt. 3 ..................................... 7" EP . Pye ................ NJE1059 ........... 1957 £2 .......... £5
Blues Singer And Balladeer .................. LP ..... Storyville ........ SLP175 ............. 1965 £4 .......... £10
Josh ..................................................... LP ..... Elektra ........... EKL114 ............ 195– £8 .......... £10 ......................... US
Josh At Midnight .................................. LP ..... Elektra ........... EKL102 ............ 195– £4 .......... £10 ......................... US
Josh Comes A-Visitin' .......................... 10" LP London .......... HAPB1038 ......... 1955 £5 .......... £12
Josh White ........................................... LP ..... Decca ............. DL8665 ............ 1957 £5 .......... £12 ......................... US
Josh White ........................................... 7" EP . Mercury ......... 10006MCE ......... 1964 £2 .......... £5
Josh White ........................................... 10" LP London .......... 338 ................ 195– £5 .......... £12 ......................... US
Josh White Program ............................. 10" LP London .......... HAPB1005 ......... 1951 £5 .......... £12
Josh White's Blues ............................... LP ..... Mercury ......... MG20203 ........... 1956 £5 .......... £12 ......................... US
Sings Vol. 2 ......................................... 10" LP London .......... HAPB1032 ......... 1954 £5 .......... £12
Songs By Josh White ............................ 10" LP Mercury ......... MG25014 ........... 1954 £5 .......... £12
Southern Blues ..................................... 7" EP . Mercury ......... YEP9504 ........... 1956 £2 .......... £5
Storyville Blues Anthology Vol. 8 ......... 7" EP . Storyville ........ SEP388 ............ 1964 £2 .......... £5
Twenty-Fifth Anniversary Album .......... LP ..... Elektra ........... EKL123 ............ 195– £4 .......... £10 ......................... US

## WHITE, JOSH & BEVERLY
Beverly And Josh White Jnr .................. 7" EP . Realm ............ REP4003 ........... 1964 £2 .......... £5

## WHITE, JOSH & BIG BILL BROONZY
Josh White & Big Bill Broonzy ............. LP ..... Period ............ 1209 ............... 196– £5 .......... £12 ......................... US

## WHITE, KITTY & DAVID HOWARD
Jesse James ........................................... 7" ...... London .......... HL8102 ............. 1954 £10 .......... £20

## WHITE, LOUISA JANE
When the Battle Is Over ....................... 7" ...... Philips ............ BF1810 ............. 1969 £2 .......... £5

## WHITE, TAM
Lewis Carroll ....................................... 7" ...... Middle Earth ... MDS104 ............ 1970 £1.50 ....... £4
Tam White ........................................... LP ..... Middle Earth ... MDLS304 ........... 1970 £10 .......... £25
That Old Sweet Roll ............................. 7" ...... Deram ............ DM261 ............. 1969 £1.50 ....... £4

## WHITE, TERRY
Rock Around The Mailbag ................... 7" ...... Decca ............. F11133 ............. 1959 £10 .......... £20

## WHITE, TONY JOE
Black And White ................................. LP ..... Monument ...... SMO5027 .......... 1968 £4 .......... £10
Continued ............................................ LP ..... Monument ...... SMO5035 .......... 1969 £4 .......... £10
Tony Joe .............................................. LP ..... Monument ...... SMO5043 .......... 1970 £4 .......... £10

## WHITE LIGHT
White Light .......................................... LP ..... Century .......... 39955 .............. 1969 £180 ..... £300 ......................... US

## WHITE NOISE
Electric Storm ...................................... LP ..... Island ............ ILPS9099 .......... 1969 £5 .......... £12 ............... *pink label*

## WHITE PLAINS
| | | | | | | |
|---|---|---|---|---|---|---|
| When You Are A King | LP | Deram | SML1092 | 1971 £4 | £10 | |
| White Plains | LP | Deram | SML1067 | 1970 £4 | £10 | |

## WHITE SPIRIT
| | | | | | | |
|---|---|---|---|---|---|---|
| Midnight Chaser | 7" | MCA | MCA638 | 1981 £2.50 | £6 | |

## WHITE TRASH
| | | | | | | |
|---|---|---|---|---|---|---|
| Road To Nowhere | 7" | Apple | 6 | 1969 £4 | £8 | |

## WHITEHORN, GEOFF
| | | | | | | |
|---|---|---|---|---|---|---|
| Whitehorn | LP | Stateside | ISS80164 | 1974 £6 | £15 | Japanese |

## WHITEHOUSE

The disturbing, aggressive industrial music made by Whitehouse was issued on a number of privately pressed LPs during the eighties. A distressing Fascist theme runs through much of it, which is apparently intended to be ironic, but within work that is not otherwise notable for any trace of humour it is easy to mistake the irony for the real thing.

| | | | | | | |
|---|---|---|---|---|---|---|
| Birthdeath Experience | LP | Come Organisation | WDC881004 | 1980 £37.50 | £75 | |
| Buchenwald | LP | Come Organisation | WDC881013 | 1981 £25 | £50 | |
| Dedicated To Peter Kurten | LP | Come Organisation | WDC881010 | 1981 £30 | £60 | |
| Erector | LP | Come Organisation | WDC881007 | 1980 £30 | £60 | |
| Great White Death | LP | Come Organisation | WDC881069 | 1981 £25 | £50 | |
| Live Action 1 | cass | Come Organisation | WDC881020 | 1982 £5 | £12 | |
| Live Action 2 | cass | Come Organisation | WDC881022 | 1982 £5 | £12 | |
| New Britain | LP | Come Organisation | WDC881017 | 1982 £37.50 | £75 | |
| One Hundred And Fifty Murderous Passions | LP | Come Organisation | | 198– £20 | £40 | |
| Psychopathia Sexualis | LP | Come Organisation | WDC881027 | 198– £50 | £100 | clear or black vinyl |
| Right To Kill | LP | Come Organisation | WDC881033 | 198– £25 | £50 | |
| Total Sex | LP | Come Organisation | WDC881005 | 1980 £37.50 | £75 | |

## WHITESNAKE
| | | | | | | |
|---|---|---|---|---|---|---|
| Bloody Mary | 7" | EMI | INEP751 | 1978 £2 | £5 | ... picture sleeve, white vinyl |
| Deeper The Love | CD-s | EMI | CDEM128 | 1990 £2 | £5 | |
| Fool For Your Loving | 7" | United Artists | BP352 | 1980 £2 | £5 | luminous sleeve |
| Give Me All Your Love | CD-s | EMI | CDEM23 | 1988 £2 | £5 | |
| Give Me All Your Love | 12" | EMI | 12EM23 | 1988 £2.50 | £6 | white vinyl |
| Give Me All Your Love | 12" | EMI | 12EMP23 | 1988 £2.50 | £6 | picture disc |
| Guilty Of Love | 7" | Liberty | BP420 | 1983 £2 | £5 | picture disc |
| Here I Go Again | 7" | Liberty | BP416 | 1982 £2 | £5 | picture disc |
| Here I Go Again | 10" | EMI | 10EMI35 | 1987 £2.50 | £6 | white vinyl |
| Is This Love | CD-s | EMI | CDEM3 | 1987 £2 | £5 | |
| Is This Love | 7" | EMI | EMP3 | 1987 £1.50 | £4 | shaped picture disc |
| Live At Hammersmith | LP | Polydor | MPF1288 | 1980 £4 | £10 | Japanese |
| Now You're Gone | CD-s | EMI | CDEM150 | 1990 £2 | £5 | |
| Now You're Gone | 7" | EMI | EMPD150 | 1990 £1.50 | £4 | ... shaped picture disc, plinth |
| Slide It In | LP | Liberty | LBGP2400000 | 1984 £4 | £10 | picture disc |
| Standing In The Shadow | 7" | Liberty | BPP423 | 1984 £1.50 | £4 | picture disc |
| Still Of The Night | 7" | EMI | EMIW5606 | 1987 £2.50 | £6 | white vinyl, with poster |
| Still Of The Night | 12" | EMI | 12EMIP5606 | 1987 £2.50 | £6 | picture disc |
| Take Me With You | 12" | Liberty | | 1982 £2.50 | £6 | 1 sided promo |
| Victim Of Love | 7" | Liberty | BP418 | 1982 £7.50 | £15 | |
| Whitesnake 1987 | LP | EMI | EMC3528 | 1987 £4 | £10 | picture disc |

## WHITFIELD, DAVID
| | | | | | | |
|---|---|---|---|---|---|---|
| Adoration Waltz | 7" | Decca | F10833 | 1957 £2 | £5 | |
| Alone | 7" EP | Decca | STO158 | 1962 £2 | £5 | stereo |
| Beyond The Stars | 7" | Decca | F10458 | 1955 £4 | £8 | |
| Book | 7" | Decca | F10242 | 1954 £5 | £10 | |
| Cara Mia | 7" EP | Decca | DFE6225 | 1955 £4 | £8 | |
| Cara Mia | 7" | Decca | F10327 | 1954 £5 | £10 | |
| David Whitfield No. 1 | 7" EP | Decca | DFE6342 | 1956 £2 | £5 | |
| David Whitfield No. 2 | 7" EP | Decca | DFE6400 | 1957 £2 | £5 | |
| David Whitfield No. 3 | 7" EP | Decca | DFE6434 | 1957 £2 | £5 | |
| Everywhere | 7" | Decca | F10515 | 1955 £4 | £8 | |
| From David With Love | LP | Decca | LK4270 | 1958 £4 | £10 | |
| I'll Find You | 7" | Decca | F10864 | 1957 £2 | £5 | |
| I'll Never Stop Loving You | 7" | Decca | F10596 | 1955 £1.50 | £4 | |
| Lady | 7" | Decca | F10562 | 1955 £1.50 | £4 | |
| My September Love | 7" | Decca | F10690 | 1956 £2 | £5 | |
| My Son John | 7" | Decca | F10769 | 1956 £2 | £5 | |

| Title | Format | Label | Cat. No. | Year | | | Notes |
|---|---|---|---|---|---|---|---|
| Santo Natale | 7" | Decca | F10399 | 1954 | £2.50 | £6 | |
| Smile | 7" | Decca | F10355 | 1954 | £2 | £5 | |
| When You Lose The One You Love | 7" | Decca | F10627 | 1955 | £2 | £5 | |
| Whitfield Favourites | LP | Decca | LK4242 | 1958 | £4 | £10 | |
| Yours From The Heart | 10" LP | Decca | LF1165 | 1954 | £5 | £12 | |

## WHITFIELD, WILBUR & THE PLEASERS

| Title | Format | Label | Cat. No. | Year | | | Notes |
|---|---|---|---|---|---|---|---|
| Heart To Heart | 7" | Vogue | V9097 | 1958 | £100 | £200 | best auctioned |
| P. B. Baby | 7" | Vogue | V9078 | 1957 | £75 | £150 | |
| Plaything | 7" | Vogue | V9091 | 1957 | £150 | £250 | best auctioned |

## WHITING, LEONARD

| Title | Format | Label | Cat. No. | Year | | | Notes |
|---|---|---|---|---|---|---|---|
| Piper | 7" | Pye | 7N15943 | 1965 | £6 | £12 | |

## WHITING, MARGARET

| Title | Format | Label | Cat. No. | Year | | | Notes |
|---|---|---|---|---|---|---|---|
| Capitol Presents | 10" LP | Capitol | LC6585 | 1953 | £5 | £12 | |
| Goin' Places | LP | London | HAD2109 | 1958 | £6 | £15 | |
| Heat Wave | 7" | Capitol | CL14242 | 1955 | £2 | £5 | |
| Hot Spell | 7" | London | HLD8662 | 1958 | £1.50 | £4 | |
| I Can't Help It | 7" | London | HLD8562 | 1958 | £1.50 | £4 | |
| I Love A Mystery | 7" | Capitol | CL14527 | 1956 | £1.50 | £4 | |
| Just A Dream | LP | London | HAD2321 | 1961 | £5 | £12 | |
| Just Like A Man | 7" | London | HLD10114 | 1967 | £1.50 | £4 | |
| Kill Me With Kisses | 7" | London | HLD8451 | 1957 | £1.50 | £4 | |
| Lover Lover | 7" | Capitol | CL14375 | 1955 | £2 | £5 | |
| Maggie Isn't Margaret Anymore | LP | London | HAU8332 | 1967 | £4 | £10 | |
| Man | 7" | Capitol | CL14348 | 1955 | £2 | £5 | |
| Margaret Whiting | 10" LP | Capitol | LC6811 | 1956 | £5 | £12 | |
| My Own True Love | 7" | Capitol | CL14213 | 1954 | £2 | £5 | |
| Stowaway | 7" | Capitol | CL14307 | 1955 | £2 | £5 | |
| Wheel Of Hurt | LP | London | HAU/SHU8317 | 1967 | £4 | £10 | |

## WHITLEY, RAY

| Title | Format | Label | Cat. No. | Year | | | Notes |
|---|---|---|---|---|---|---|---|
| I've Been Hurt | 7" | HMV | POP1473 | 1965 | £20 | £40 | |

## WHITMAN, SLIM

| Title | Format | Label | Cat. No. | Year | | | Notes |
|---|---|---|---|---|---|---|---|
| All Time Favorites | LP | Imperial | LP9252 | 1964 | £4 | £10 | US |
| America's Favorite Folk Artist | 10" LP | Imperial | LP3004 | 1954 | £15 | £30 | US |
| And His Singing Guitar | 7" EP | London | REP1006 | 1954 | £5 | £10 | gold label |
| And His Singing Guitar | 10" LP | London | HAPB1015 | 1954 | £15 | £30 | gold label |
| And His Singing Guitar Vol. 2 | LP | London | HAU2015 | 1956 | £10 | £25 | |
| And His Singing Guitar Vol. 2 Pt. 1 | 7" EP | London | REP1064 | 1956 | £5 | £10 | gold label |
| And His Singing Guitar Vol. 2 Pt. 2 | 7" EP | London | REP1070 | 1956 | £5 | £10 | gold label |
| And His Singing Guitar Vol. 2 Pt. 3 | 7" EP | London | REP1100 | 1957 | £5 | £10 | gold label |
| Annie Laurie | LP | Imperial | LP9077 | 1959 | £6 | £15 | US |
| Beautiful Dreamer | 7" | London | HL8080 | 1954 | £10 | £20 | gold label |
| Candy Kisses | 7" | London | HLP8642 | 1958 | £2.50 | £6 | |
| Curtain Of Tears | 7" | London | HLP8416 | 1957 | £4 | £8 | |
| Dear Mary | 7" | London | HLU8327 | 1956 | £10 | £20 | gold label |
| Favorites | LP | Imperial | LP9003 | 1956 | £10 | £25 | US |
| First Visit To Britain | LP | Imperial | LP9135 | 1960 | £5 | £12 | US |
| Gone | 7" | London | HLP8420 | 1957 | £10 | £20 | gold label |
| Haunted Hungry Heart | 7" | London | HL8141 | 1955 | £10 | £20 | gold label |
| Heart Songs And Love Songs | LP | London | HAP8059 | 1963 | £6 | £15 | |
| I Never See Maggie Alone | 7" | London | HLP8835 | 1959 | £2 | £5 | |
| I'll Never Stop Loving You | 7" | London | HLU8167 | 1955 | £10 | £20 | gold label |
| I'll Take You Home Again Kathleen | 7" | London | HLP8403 | 1957 | £5 | £10 | gold label |
| I'll Walk With God | LP | Imperial | LP9088 | 1960 | £5 | £12 | US |
| I'm A Fool | 7" | London | HLU8252 | 1956 | £7.50 | £15 | |
| I'm A Lonely Wanderer | LP | London | HAP8093 | 1963 | £6 | £15 | |
| I'm Casting My Lasso | 7" | London | HLU8350 | 1956 | £7.50 | £15 | gold label |
| Indian Love Call | 7" | London | HL1149 | 1954 | £7.50 | £15 | gold label |
| Indian Love Call | 7" | London | L1149 | 1954 | £12.50 | £25 | gold label |
| Irish Songs The Slim Whitman Way | 7" EP | Liberty | LEP4018 | 1964 | £2.50 | £6 | |
| Irish Songs The Whitman Way | LP | Imperial | LP9245 | 1963 | £5 | £12 | US |
| Just Call Me Lonesome | LP | London | HAP2392 | 1961 | £6 | £15 | |
| Lovesick Blues | 7" | London | HLP8459 | 1957 | £4 | £8 | |
| Many Times | 7" | London | HLP8434 | 1957 | £4 | £8 | |
| Million Record Hits | LP | Imperial | LP9102 | 1960 | £5 | £12 | US |
| North Wind | 7" | London | HL1226 | 1954 | £10 | £20 | gold label |
| North Wind | 7" | London | L1226 | 1954 | £15 | £30 | gold label |
| Once In A Lifetime | LP | Imperial | LP9156 | 1961 | £5 | £12 | US |
| Roll River Roll | 7" | London | HLP9103 | 1960 | £1.50 | £4 | |
| Rose Marie | 7" | London | HL8061 | 1954 | £5 | £10 | gold label |
| Satisfied Man | 7" EP | Liberty | LEP4046 | 1966 | £4 | £8 | |
| Secret Love | 7" | London | HL8039 | 1954 | £12.50 | £25 | gold label |
| Serenade | 7" | London | HLU8287 | 1956 | £7.50 | £15 | gold label |
| Singing Hills | 7" | London | HL8091 | 1954 | £10 | £20 | gold label |
| Sings | LP | Imperial | LP9064 | 1959 | £6 | £15 | US |
| Slim Whitman | LP | Imperial | LP9056 | 1958 | £6 | £15 | US |
| Slim Whitman | LP | London | HAP2343 | 1961 | £6 | £15 | |
| Slim Whitman Sings | LP | Imperial | LP9026 | 1957 | £10 | £25 | US |
| Slim Whitman Sings | LP | London | HAP2139 | 1959 | £6 | £15 | |
| Slim Whitman Sings | 7" EP | London | REP1199 | 1959 | £5 | £10 | tri-centre |
| Slim Whitman Sings And Yodels | 10" LP | RCA | LPM3217 | 1954 | £15 | £30 | US |
| Slim Whitman Sings More Irish Songs | 7" EP | Liberty | LEP4027 | 1965 | £2.50 | £6 | |
| Slim Whitman Sings No. 2 | 7" EP | London | REP1258 | 1960 | £4 | £8 | |
| Slim Whitman Sings Vol. 2 | LP | London | HAP2199 | 1959 | £6 | £15 | |

| | | | | | | | | |
|---|---|---|---|---|---|---|---|---|
| Slim Whitman Sings Vol. 3 | LP | London | HAP2443 | 1962 | £6 | £15 | |
| Slim Whitman Sings Vol. 3 | LP | London | SAHP6232 | 1962 | £8 | £20 | stereo |
| Slim Whitman Sings Vol. 4 | LP | London | HAP8013 | 1962 | £6 | £15 | |
| Song Of The Wild | 7" EP | London | REP1042 | 1955 | £5 | £10 | gold label |
| Song Of The Wild | 7" | London | HLU8196 | 1955 | £10 | £20 | gold label |
| Stairway To Heaven | 7" | London | HL8018 | 1954 | £20 | £40 | gold label |
| There's A Rainbow In Every Teardrop | 7" | London | HL1214 | 1954 | £10 | £20 | gold label |
| There's A Rainbow In Every Teardrop | 7" | London | L1214 | 1954 | £12.50 | £25 | gold label |
| Tumbling Tumbleweeds | 7" | London | HLU8230 | 1956 | £7.50 | £15 | gold label |
| Unchain My Heart | 7" | London | HLP8518 | 1957 | £4 | £8 | |
| Vaya Con Dios | 7" | London | HLP9302 | 1961 | £1.50 | £4 | |
| Very Precious Love | 7" | London | HLP8590 | 1958 | £4 | £8 | |
| Wayward Wind | 7" EP | London | REP1360 | 1963 | £5 | £10 | |
| When I Grow Too Old To Dream | 7" | London | HL8125 | 1955 | £10 | £20 | gold label |
| Wherever You Are | 7" | London | HLP8708 | 1958 | £2.50 | £6 | |

## WHITNEY, MARVA

| | | | | | | | | |
|---|---|---|---|---|---|---|---|---|
| Daddy Don't Know About The Sugar Beat | 7" | Mojo | 2092041 | 1972 | £2 | £5 | |
| I Sing Soul | LP | King | K1053 | 1969 | £25 | £50 | US |
| It's My Thing | LP | Polydor | 583767 | 1969 | £50 | £100 | |
| Live And Lowdown At The Apollo | LP | King | K1079 | 1970 | £25 | £50 | US |
| This Girl's In Love With You | 7" | Polydor | 2001036 | 1970 | £5 | £10 | |

## WHITSETT, TIM

| | | | | | | | | |
|---|---|---|---|---|---|---|---|---|
| Macks By The Tracks | 7" | Sue | WI318 | 1964 | £4 | £8 | |

## WHITSETT, TIM & STICKS HERMAN

| | | | | | | | | |
|---|---|---|---|---|---|---|---|---|
| Rhythm And Blues | 7" EP | Range | JRE7002 | 196– | £5 | £10 | |

## WHITSUNTIDE EASTER

| | | | | | | | | |
|---|---|---|---|---|---|---|---|---|
| Next Time You Play A Wrong Note | LP | Grapevine | GRA109 | 1977 | £100 | £200 | at least 2 different covers |

## WHITTLE, TOMMY

| | | | | | | | | |
|---|---|---|---|---|---|---|---|---|
| New Horizons | LP | Tempo | TAP27 | 1960 | £10 | £25 | |
| Tommy Whittle | 10" LP | Esquire | 20048 | 1955 | £8 | £20 | |
| Tommy Whittle Orchestra | 10" LP | Esquire | 20061 | 1956 | £4 | £10 | |
| Tommy Whittle Quartet | 10" LP | Esquire | 20068 | 1956 | £4 | £10 | |
| Waxing With Whittle | 10" LP | Esquire | 20028 | 1954 | £8 | £20 | |

## WHO

The Who's status as one of the world's most popular rock groups has inevitably led to a considerable interest in their early recordings, which fetch respectable prices even where they were chart hits. The three different B sides for the original issues of 'Substitute' are the result of a dispute between Brunswick and Reaction as to the ownership of the track 'Circles'. 'Instant Party' is the same track, whose change of title did not fool anyone, but 'Waltz For A Pig', credited to the Who Orchestra, is actually a Graham Bond Organisation instrumental. The 1976 reissue of 'Substitute' has the distinction of being the first twelve-inch single ever made, but stubbornly resists becoming a collectors' item. Meanwhile, the most expensive rarities include a withdrawn mail order compilation, *Who Did It*, and scarce picture sleeves for the singles 'Anyway, Anyhow, Anywhere' and 'My Generation'.

| | | | | | | | | |
|---|---|---|---|---|---|---|---|---|
| Acid Queen | 7" | Track | PRO3 | 1969 | £12.50 | £25 | promo |
| Anyway, Anyhow, Anywhere | 7" | Brunswick | 05935 | 1965 | £5 | £10 | |
| Anyway, Anyhow, Anywhere | 7" | Brunswick | 05935 | 1965 | £50 | £100 | picture sleeve |
| Athena/Why Did I Fall For That | 12" | Polydor | WHOPX6 | 1982 | £4 | £10 | picture disc |
| Christmas | 7" | Track | PRO4 | 1969 | £12.50 | £25 | promo |
| Circles | 7" | Brunswick | 05951 | 1966 | £50 | £100 | demo |
| Direct Hits | LP | Track | 612/613006 | 1969 | £6 | £15 | |
| Dogs | 7" | Track | 604023 | 1968 | £2 | £5 | |
| Excerpts From Tommy | 7" EP | Track | 2252001 | 1970 | £2.50 | £6 | |
| Extracts From Thirty Years Of Maximum R&B | CD | Polydor | WHOBOX2 | 1994 | £8 | £20 | promo sampler |
| Face Dances | LP | Mobile Fidelity | MFSL1115 | 1984 | £4 | £10 | US audiophile |
| Filling In The Gaps | LP | Polydor | WHOT1 | 1981 | £15 | £30 | double interview promo |
| Go To The Mirror | 7" | Track | PRO2 | 1969 | £12.50 | £25 | promo |
| Happy Jack | LP | Decca | DL(7)4892 | 1967 | £8 | £20 | US |
| Happy Jack | 7" EP | Polydor | 27799 | 1966 | £25 | £50 | French |
| Happy Jack | 7" | Reaction | 591010 | 1966 | £1.50 | £4 | |
| I Can See For Miles | 7" | Track | 604011 | 1967 | £1.50 | £4 | |
| I Can't Explain | 7" EP | Brunswick | 10668 | 1965 | £50 | £100 | French |
| I Can't Explain | 7" | Brunswick | 05926 | 1965 | £5 | £10 | |
| I'm A Boy | 7" EP | Polydor | 27789 | 1966 | £25 | £50 | French |
| I'm A Boy | 7" | Reaction | 591004 | 1966 | £1.50 | £4 | |
| I'm Free | 7" | Track | PRO1 | 1969 | £12.50 | £25 | promo |
| Instant Party | LP | Brunswick | BDV173269 | 1965 | £25 | £50 | Dutch |
| It's Hard | LP | Warner Bros | 237311 | 1982 | £8 | £20 | US audiophile promo |
| It's Hard | CD | Polydor | 8001062 | 1983 | £5 | £12 | |
| Join Together | CD-s | Virgin | VSCDT1259 | 1990 | £2 | £5 | |
| Join Together | 7" | Polydor | 2094102 | 1972 | £5 | £10 | export, picture sleeve |
| Kids Are Alright | LP | Brunswick | 177026 | 1967 | £25 | £50 | Dutch |
| Kids Are Alright | 7" EP | Decca | 60008 | 1966 | £25 | £50 | French |
| Kids Are Alright | 7" | Brunswick | 05965 | 1966 | £7.50 | £15 | |
| Kids Are Alright | 7" | Brunswick | 05956 | 1966 | £7.50 | £15 | |
| La La La Lies | 7" | Brunswick | 05968 | 1966 | £7.50 | £15 | |
| Legal Matter | 7" | Brunswick | 05956 | 1966 | £6 | £12 | |
| Legal Matter | 7" | Brunswick | 05956 | 1966 | £50 | £100 | export with Scandinavian picture sleeve |
| Legal Matter | 7" | Decca | AD1002 | 1968 | £20 | £40 | export |

| Title | Format | Label | Catalogue | Year | | | Notes |
|---|---|---|---|---|---|---|---|
| Live At Leeds | LP | Track | 2406001 | 1970 | £4 | £10 | 12 inserts |
| Live At Leeds | CD | Polydor | 5271692 | 1995 | £10 | £25 | boxed set |
| Long Live Rock | 7" | MCA | 41053 | 1979 | £7.50 | £15 | US picture disc, 6 different backs |
| Magic Bus | LP | Decca | DL75064 | 1968 | £8 | £20 | US |
| Magic Bus | 7" | Track | 604024 | 1968 | £1.50 | £4 | |
| Making Of Tommy | LP | Polydor | SA010 | 1975 | £10 | £25 | US interview promo |
| My Generation | LP | Brunswick | LAT8616 | 1965 | £37.50 | £75 | |
| My Generation | LP | Decca | DL(7)4664 | 1966 | £20 | £40 | US |
| My Generation | CD-s | Polydor | POCD907 | 1988 | £2 | £5 | |
| My Generation | 7" EP | Brunswick | 10671 | 1965 | £25 | £50 | French |
| My Generation | 7" EP | Decca | 60002 | 1965 | £25 | £50 | French |
| My Generation | 7" | Brunswick | 05944 | 1965 | £2.50 | £6 | |
| My Generation | 7" | Brunswick | 05944 | 1965 | £75 | £150 | picture sleeve |
| My Generation | 7" | Decca | AD1001 | 1968 | £20 | £40 | export |
| My Generation | 7" | Decca | AD1001 | 1968 | £50 | £100 | export, picture sleeve |
| Out In The Street | 7" EP | Decca | 60004 | 1966 | £25 | £50 | French |
| Phases | LP | Polydor | 2675216 | 1981 | £30 | £60 | German 9 LP boxed set |
| Pictures Of Lily | 7" EP | Polydor | 27805 | 1967 | £25 | £50 | French |
| Pictures Of Lily | 7" | Track | 604002 | 1967 | £1.50 | £4 | |
| Pinball Wizard | 7" | Track | 604027 | 1969 | £1.50 | £4 | |
| Quadrophenia | LP | Track | 2657013 | 1973 | £5 | £12 | double |
| Quadrophenia | CD | Mobile Fidelity | UDCD2550 | 1991 | £10 | £25 | US audiophile double |
| Quick One | LP | Reaction | 593002 | 1966 | £20 | £40 | |
| Ready Steady Who | 7" EP | Polydor | 27801 | 1966 | £20 | £40 | French |
| Ready Steady Who | 7" EP | Reaction | 592001 | 1966 | £12.50 | £25 | |
| Ready Steady Who | 7" EP | Reaction | WHO7 | 1983 | £2 | £5 | |
| Roger Daltrey & Pete Townshend Talk About Quadrophenia | LP | Polydor | PRO114 | 1979 | £8 | £20 | US interview promo |
| See Me Feel Me | 7" | Track | 2094004 | 1970 | £4 | £8 | |
| Seeker | 7" | Track | 604036 | 1970 | £1.50 | £4 | |
| Substitute/Circles | 7" | Reaction | 591001 | 1966 | £5 | £10 | |
| Substitute/Instant Party | 7" | Reaction | 591001 | 1966 | £5 | £10 | |
| Substitute/Waltz For A Pig | 7" | Reaction | 591001 | 1966 | £2.50 | £6 | |
| Summertime Blues | 7" | Track | 2094002 | 1970 | £1.50 | £4 | |
| Thirty Years Of Maximum R&B | CD | Polydor | WHOBOX1 | 1994 | £8 | £20 | promo sampler |
| Tommy | LP | Track | 613013/014 | 1969 | £6 | £15 | double, book |
| Tommy Part 1 | LP | Track | 2406007 | 1970 | £4 | £10 | |
| Tommy Part 2 | LP | Track | 2406008 | 1970 | £4 | £10 | |
| Under My Thumb | 7" | Track | 604006 | 1967 | £15 | £30 | |
| Who | LP | Polydor | 623025 | 1966 | £25 | £50 | German |
| Who Are You | LP | MCA | | 1978 | £5 | £12 | US interview promo |
| Who Are You | LP | MCA | P14950 | 1978 | £4 | £10 | US picture disc |
| Who Are You | LP | Superdisk | SD166108 | 1981 | £5 | £12 | US audiophile |
| Who Are You | CD | Mobile Fidelity | UDCD561 | 1992 | £6 | £15 | US audiophile |
| Who Did It | LP | Track | 2856001 | 1971 | £210 | £350 | |
| Who Sell Out | LP | Track | 612002 | 1967 | £20 | £40 | mono |
| Who Sell Out | LP | Track | 612002 | 1967 | £75 | £150 | with poster |
| Who Sell Out | LP | Track | 613002 | 1967 | £15 | £30 | stereo |
| Who's Next | CD | Polydor | C88113 | 1988 | £6 | £15 | box set |
| Won't Get Fooled Again | CD-s | Polydor | POCD917 | 1988 | £2 | £5 | |
| Won't Get Fooled Again | 7" | Track | 2094009 | 1971 | £2.50 | £6 | picture sleeve |
| Won't Get Fooled Again | 7" | Track, | A4112 | 1971 | £4 | £8 | 1 sided promo |

## WHO & STRAWBERRY ALARM CLOCK

| Title | Format | Label | Catalogue | Year | | | Notes |
|---|---|---|---|---|---|---|---|
| Who/Strawberry Alarm Clock | LP | Decca | DL734568 | 1969 | £15 | £30 | US |

## WHYTON, WALLY

| Title | Format | Label | Catalogue | Year | | | Notes |
|---|---|---|---|---|---|---|---|
| All Over This World | 7" | Parlophone | R4630 | 1960 | £1.50 | £4 | |
| Don't Tell Me Your Troubles | 7" | Parlophone | R4585 | 1959 | £2 | £5 | |
| It's A Rat Race | 7" | Pye | 7N15304 | 1960 | £1.50 | £4 | |
| Little Red Pony | 7" | Piccadilly | 7N35089 | 1961 | £1.50 | £4 | |

## WIEBELFETZER

| Title | Format | Label | Catalogue | Year | | | Notes |
|---|---|---|---|---|---|---|---|
| Live | LP | Bazillus | 111–112 | 1971 | £15 | £30 | Swiss double |

## WIEDLIN, JANE

| Title | Format | Label | Catalogue | Year | | | Notes |
|---|---|---|---|---|---|---|---|
| Inside A Dream | CD-s | EMI | CDMT55 | 1988 | £2 | £5 | |
| Rush Hour | CD-s | EMI | CDMT36 | 1988 | £2 | £5 | |

## WIFFEN, DAVID

| Title | Format | Label | Catalogue | Year | | | Notes |
|---|---|---|---|---|---|---|---|
| David Wiffen | LP | Fantasy | 8411 | 1969 | £8 | £20 | US |

## WIG

| Title | Format | Label | Catalogue | Year | | | Notes |
|---|---|---|---|---|---|---|---|
| Live At The Jade Room | LP | Texas Archive | TAR3 | 1982 | £8 | £20 | US |

## WIGGINS, GERALD

| Title | Format | Label | Catalogue | Year | | | Notes |
|---|---|---|---|---|---|---|---|
| Music From Around The World In 80 Days | LP | London | LTZU15109 | 1958 | £6 | £15 | |

## WIGGINS, PERCY

| Title | Format | Label | Catalogue | Year | | | Notes |
|---|---|---|---|---|---|---|---|
| Book Of Memories | 7" | Atlantic | 584113 | 1967 | £2.50 | £6 | |

## WIGGINS, SPENCER

| Title | Format | Label | Catalogue | Year | | | Notes |
|---|---|---|---|---|---|---|---|
| I'm A Poor Man's Son | 7" | Pama | PM794 | 1969 | £2.50 | £6 | |
| Uptight Good Woman | 7" | Stateside | SS2024 | 1967 | £2 | £5 | |

## WIGGONS

| | | | | | | | |
|---|---|---|---|---|---|---|---|
| Rock Baby | 7" | Blue Beat | BB29 | 1961 | £6 | £12 | |

## WIGWAM

| | | | | | | | |
|---|---|---|---|---|---|---|---|
| Being | LP | Love | LRLP92 | 1974 | £6 | £15 | Swedish |
| Dark Album | LP | Love | LRLP227 | 1978 | £6 | £15 | Swedish |
| Fairyport | LP | Love | LRLP44/55 | 1971 | £15 | £30 | Swedish double |
| Hard And Horny | LP | Love | LRLP9 | 1969 | £8 | £20 | Swedish |
| Live From The Twilight Zone | LP | Love | LXPS517/8 | 1975 | £10 | £25 | Swedish double |
| Lucky Golden Stripes And Starpose | LP | Virgin | V2051 | 1976 | £4 | £10 | |
| Rumours On The Rebound | LP | Virgin | VD3503 | 1979 | £5 | £12 | double |
| Tombstone Valentine | LP | Love | LRLP19 | 1970 | £8 | £20 | Swedish double |
| Wicked Ivory | LP | Love | LRLP52 | 1972 | £6 | £15 | Swedish |
| Wigwam | LP | Love | LRLP511 | 1972 | £6 | £15 | Swedish |

## WILBURN BROTHERS

| | | | | | | | |
|---|---|---|---|---|---|---|---|
| Livin' In God's Country | LP | Decca | DL(7)8959 | 1959 | £4 | £10 | US |
| Silver Haired Daddy Of Mine | 7" | Brunswick | 05799 | 1959 | £1.50 | £4 | |
| Wilburn Brothers | LP | Decca | DL8576 | 1957 | £5 | £12 | US |
| Wonderful Wilburn Brothers | LP | King | 746 | 1961 | £8 | £20 | US |

## WILD & WANDERING

| | | | | | | | |
|---|---|---|---|---|---|---|---|
| 2000 Light Ales From Home | 12" | Iguana | VYK14 | 1986 | £15 | £30 | |

## WILD ANGELS

| | | | | | | | |
|---|---|---|---|---|---|---|---|
| Buzz Buzz | 7" | B&C | CB114 | 1970 | £2 | £5 | |
| Nervous Breakdown | 7" | Major Minor | MM569 | 1968 | £4 | £8 | |
| Sally Ann | 7" | B&C | CB123 | 1970 | £1.50 | £4 | |

## WILD COUNTRY

| | | | | | | | |
|---|---|---|---|---|---|---|---|
| Silent Country | 7" | Trafalgar | TRAF01 | 1970 | £2 | £5 | |

## WILD FLOWERS

| | | | | | | | |
|---|---|---|---|---|---|---|---|
| Melt Like Ice | 7" | No Future | FS11 | 1984 | £2 | £5 | |
| Things Have Changed | 7" | Reflex | RE2 | 1984 | £1.50 | £4 | |

## WILD GEESE

| | | | | | | | |
|---|---|---|---|---|---|---|---|
| Flight Two | LP | Joke | JLP207 | 1979 | £6 | £15 | German |

## WILD HAVANA

| | | | | | | | |
|---|---|---|---|---|---|---|---|
| Wild Havana | LP | private | | 1977 | £25 | £50 | Dutch |

## WILD MAGNOLIAS

| | | | | | | | |
|---|---|---|---|---|---|---|---|
| They Call Us Wild | LP | Barclay | XBLY90033 | 1975 | £6 | £15 | French |
| They Call Us Wild | 7" | Barclay | BAR34 | 1975 | £2 | £5 | |
| Wild Magnolias | LP | Barclay | 80529 | 1975 | £6 | £15 | French |

## WILD OATS

| | | | | | | | |
|---|---|---|---|---|---|---|---|
| Wild Oats | 7" EP | Oak | RGJ117 | 1963 | £250 | £400 | best auctioned |

## WILD ONES

| | | | | | | | |
|---|---|---|---|---|---|---|---|
| Bowie Man | 7" | Fontana | TF468 | 1964 | £12.50 | £25 | |

## WILD SILK

| | | | | | | | |
|---|---|---|---|---|---|---|---|
| Help Me | 7" | Columbia | DB8611 | 1969 | £2 | £5 | |
| Plaster Sky | 7" | Columbia | DB8534 | 1969 | £2.50 | £6 | |

## WILD SWANS

| | | | | | | | |
|---|---|---|---|---|---|---|---|
| Revolutionary Spirit | 7" | Zoo | CAGE009 | 1982 | £7.50 | £15 | test pressing |
| Revolutionary Spirit | 12" | Zoo | CAGE009 | 1981 | £6 | £15 | 'Lament For Icarus' picture sleeve |
| Revolutionary Spirit | 12" | Zoo | CAGE009 | 1982 | £2.50 | £6 | |

## WILD THING

| | | | | | | | |
|---|---|---|---|---|---|---|---|
| Partyin' | LP | Polydor | 2410003 | 1971 | £6 | £15 | |

## WILD THYME

| | | | | | | | |
|---|---|---|---|---|---|---|---|
| Plays Fallibroome | LP | Saydisc | SDL339 | 1983 | £4 | £10 | |

## WILD TURKEY

| | | | | | | | |
|---|---|---|---|---|---|---|---|
| Battle Hymn | LP | Chrysalis | CHR1002 | 1971 | £4 | £10 | |
| Turkey | LP | Chrysalis | CHR1010 | 1972 | £4 | £10 | |

## WILD UNCERTAINTY

| | | | | | | | |
|---|---|---|---|---|---|---|---|
| Man With Money | 7" | Planet | PLF120 | 1966 | £12.50 | £25 | |

## WILDCATS

| | | | | | | | |
|---|---|---|---|---|---|---|---|
| Bandstand Record Hop | LP | United Artists | UAL3031 | 1958 | £8 | £20 | US |
| Gazachstahagen | 7" | London | HLT8787 | 1959 | £5 | £10 | |

## WILDE, KIM

| | | | | | | | |
|---|---|---|---|---|---|---|---|
| Another Step | CD | MCA | DMCF3339 | 1987 | £5 | £12 | |
| Close | CD | MCA | DMCG6030 | 1988 | £5 | £12 | |
| Dancing In The Dark | 12" | Rak | 12RAK365 | 1983 | £3 | £8 | with poster |
| Four Letter Word | CD-s | MCA | DKIM10 | 1988 | £2 | £5 | |
| Heart Over Mind | CD-s | MCA | KIMTD16/ KIMXD16 | 1992 | £6 | £15 | 2 single pack |

| Title | Format | Label | Catalogue | Year | | | Notes |
|---|---|---|---|---|---|---|---|
| Hey Mr. Heartache | CD-s | MCA | DKIM7 | 1988 | £5 | £12 | |
| I Can't Say Goodbye | CD-s | MCA | DKIMT14 | 1990 | £2 | £5 | |
| It's Here | CD-s | MCA | DKIMT12 | 1990 | £2 | £5 | |
| Love In The Natural Way | CD-s | MCA | DKIM11 | 1989 | £6 | £15 | picture disc |
| Never Trust A Stranger | CD-s | MCA | DKIM9 | 1988 | £5 | £12 | |
| Rage To Love | 7" | MCA | KIMP3 | 1985 | £2 | £8 | shaped picture disc |
| Second Time | 7" | MCA | KIMP1 | 1984 | £5 | £10 | picture disc |
| Teases And Dares | CD | MCA | DMCF3250 | 1984 | £5 | £12 | |
| Time (7" Version) | CD-s | MCA | DKIMT13 | 1990 | £2 | £5 | |
| Time (Extended) | CD-s | MCA | DKIM13 | 1990 | £2 | £5 | |
| Touch | 7" | MCA | KIMP2 | 1984 | £4 | £8 | shaped picture disc |
| You Came | CD-s | MCA | DKIM8 | 1988 | £2.50 | £6 | 3" single |

## WILDE, MARTY

| Title | Format | Label | Catalogue | Year | | | Notes |
|---|---|---|---|---|---|---|---|
| Bad Boy | LP | Epic | LN3686 | 1960 | £15 | £30 | US |
| Bad Boy | 7" | Philips | PB972 | 1959 | £1.50 | £4 | |
| Bye Bye Birdie | LP | Philips | ABL3383 | 1961 | £5 | £12 | |
| Bye Bye Birdie | 7" EP | Philips | BBE12472 | 1961 | £2.50 | £6 | |
| Bye Bye Birdie No. 2 | 7" EP | Philips | BBE12473 | 1961 | £2.50 | £6 | |
| Bye Bye Birdie No. 3 | 7" EP | Philips | BBE12474 | 1961 | £2.50 | £6 | |
| Bye Bye Birdie No. 4 | 7" EP | Philips | BBE12475 | 1961 | £2.50 | £6 | |
| Come Running | 7" EP | Philips | BBE12517 | 1962 | £7.50 | £15 | |
| Come Running | 7" | Philips | PB1206 | 1961 | £1.50 | £4 | |
| Donna | 7" | Philips | PB902 | 1959 | £2 | £5 | |
| Endless Sleep | 7" | Philips | PB835 | 1958 | £2.50 | £6 | |
| Ever Since You Said Goodbye | 7" | Philips | 326546BF | 1962 | £1.50 | £4 | |
| Fight | 7" | Philips | PB1022 | 1960 | £2 | £5 | |
| Hide And Seek | 7" | Philips | PB1161 | 1961 | £1.50 | £4 | |
| Honeycomb | 7" | Philips | JK1028 | 1958 | £15 | £30 | |
| I Wanna Be Loved By You | 7" | Philips | PB1037 | 1960 | £1.50 | £4 | |
| I've Got So Used To Loving You | 7" | Philips | BF1490 | 1966 | £1.50 | £4 | |
| Jezebel | 7" | Philips | PB1240 | 1962 | £1.50 | £4 | |
| Johnny Rocco | 7" | Philips | PB1002 | 1960 | £1.50 | £4 | |
| Kiss Me | 7" | Columbia | DB7285 | 1964 | £1.50 | £4 | |
| Little Girl | 7" | Philips | PB1078 | 1960 | £1.50 | £4 | |
| Lonely Avenue | 7" | Columbia | DB4980 | 1963 | £1.50 | £4 | |
| Love Bug Crawl | 78 | Philips | PB781 | 1958 | £2 | £5 | |
| Marty | 7" EP | Philips | 433638BE | 1963 | £7.50 | £15 | |
| Marty Wilde Favourites | 7" EP | Philips | BBE12422 | 1960 | £7.50 | £15 | |
| Mexican Boy | 7" | Decca | F11979 | 1964 | £1.50 | £4 | |
| More Of Marty | 7" EP | Philips | BBE12200 | 1958 | £10 | £20 | |
| My Lucky Love | 7" | Philips | PB850 | 1958 | £1.50 | £4 | |
| No One Knows | 7" | Philips | PB875 | 1958 | £2 | £5 | |
| No! Dance With Me | 7" | Philips | 326579BF | 1963 | £1.50 | £4 | |
| Oh Oh I'm Falling In Love Again | 7" | Philips | PB804 | 1958 | £10 | £20 | |
| Presenting Marty Wilde | 7" EP | Philips | BBE12164 | 1957 | £15 | £30 | |
| Rubber Ball | 7" | Philips | PB1101 | 1961 | £1.50 | £4 | |
| Save Your Love For Me | 7" | Columbia | DB7145 | 1963 | £1.50 | £4 | |
| Sea Of Love | 7" EP | Philips | BBE12327 | 1959 | £10 | £20 | |
| Sea Of Love | 7" | Philips | PB959 | 1959 | £1.50 | £4 | |
| Showcase | LP | Philips | BBL7380 | 1960 | £10 | £25 | |
| Teenager In Love | 7" | Philips | PB926 | 1959 | £1.50 | £4 | |
| Tomorrow's Clown | 7" | Philips | PB1191 | 1961 | £1.50 | £4 | |
| Versatile Mr. Wilde | LP | Philips | BBL7385 | 1960 | £10 | £25 | |
| Versatile Mr. Wilde | LP | Philips | SBBL570 | 1960 | £15 | £30 | stereo |
| Versatile Mr. Wilde | 7" EP | Philips | BBE12385 | 1960 | £10 | £20 | |
| When Does It Get To Be Love | 7" | Philips | PB1121 | 1961 | £1.50 | £4 | |
| Wilde About Marty | LP | Philips | BBL7342 | 1960 | £15 | £30 | |

## WILDE THREE

| Title | Format | Label | Catalogue | Year | | | Notes |
|---|---|---|---|---|---|---|---|
| I Cried | 7" | Decca | F12232 | 1965 | £20 | £40 | |
| Since You've Gone | 7" | Decca | F12131 | 1965 | £15 | £30 | |

## WILDER, JOE

| Title | Format | Label | Catalogue | Year | | | Notes |
|---|---|---|---|---|---|---|---|
| Jazz From Peter Gunn | LP | Philips | BBL7321 | 1959 | £6 | £15 | |
| Joe Wilder | LP | London | LTZC15027 | 1957 | £6 | £15 | |

## WILDER BROTHERS

| Title | Format | Label | Catalogue | Year | | | Notes |
|---|---|---|---|---|---|---|---|
| I Want You | 7" | HMV | POP365 | 1957 | £50 | £100 | |

## WILDHEARTS

| Title | Format | Label | Catalogue | Year | | | Notes |
|---|---|---|---|---|---|---|---|
| Caffeine Bomb | CD-s | East West | YZ794CD | 1994 | £6 | £15 | |
| Caffeine Bomb | 7" | East West | YZ794 | 1994 | £2.50 | £6 | green vinyl |
| Caffeine Bomb | 12" | East West | YZ794T | 1994 | £6 | £15 | |
| Don't Be Happy Just Worry | CD | East West | 4509912021 | 1992 | £6 | £15 | double |
| Fishing For Luckies | CD | East West | 4509990392 | 1994 | £5 | £12 | mail order only |
| Fishing For More Luckies | LP | East West | | 1995 | £37.50 | £75 | |
| Greetings From Shitsville | 7" | East West | YZ773 | 1993 | £2.50 | £6 | brown vinyl, insert |
| Mondo Akimbo A-Go-Go EP | CD-s | East West | YZ669CD | 1992 | £20 | £40 | |
| Mondo Akimbo A-Go-Go EP | 12" | East West | YZ669T | 1992 | £20 | £40 | |
| Mondo Akimbo A-Go-Go EP | 12" | East West | YZ669TX | 1992 | £25 | £50 | white vinyl |
| Naivety Play | CD | East West | SAM1555 | 1995 | £20 | £40 | promo |
| Suckerpunch | CD-s | East West | YZ828CD | 1994 | £2 | £5 | |
| Suckerpunch | CD-s | East West | YZ828CDDJ | 1994 | £10 | £20 | promo |
| Suckerpunch | 10" | East West | YZ828TE | 1994 | £4 | £10 | 1 side etched |
| TV Tan | CD-s | East West | YZ784CD | 1993 | £2 | £5 | |
| TV Tan | 7" | East West | YZ784P | 1993 | £2 | £5 | 1 sided picture disc |
| TV Tan | 12" | East West | YZ784T | 1993 | £5 | £12 | |

## WILDWEEDS
It Was Fun While It Lasted..................... 7" ...... Chess .............. CRS8065 ............... 1967 £1.50........£4 ...............................................
Wildweeds.......................................... LP ..... Vanguard ........ VSD6552 .............. 1970 £6...........£15 ...............................US

## WILEY, LEE
Touch Of The Blues............................. LP ..... RCA ................ SF5003.................. 1958 £4..........£10 ......................stereo

## WILFRED & MILLIE
Vow................................................... 7" ...... Island ............ WI190 .................. 1965 £5...........£10 ...............................

## WILHELM, MIKE
Mike Wilhelm ..................................... LP ..... United Artists .. ZZ1 ..................... 1976 £6...........£15 ...............................

## WILKERSON, DON
Elder Don........................................... LP ..... Blue Note ....... BLP/BST84121 ...... 1963 £20.........£40 ...............................
Preach, Brother! ................................. LP ..... Blue Note ....... BLP/BST84107 ...... 1962 £20.........£40 ...............................
Shoutin' ............................................. LP ..... Blue Note ....... BLP/BST84145 ...... 1963 £20.........£40 ...............................

## WILKINS, ERNIE
Top Brass ........................................... LP ..... London ........... LTZC15013 .......... 1956 £6...........£15 ...............................
Trumpets All Out ................................ LP ..... London ........... LTZC15093 .......... 1957 £6...........£15 ...............................

## WILKINS, ROBERT
Rev. Robert Wilkins............................. LP ..... Piedmont ........ PLP13162.............. 196– £8...........£20 ...............................

## WILKINS, ROGER
Before The Reverence.......................... LP ..... Spokane .......... SPL1002.............. 1970 £15.........£30 ...............................

## WILKINSON, ARTHUR
Beatle Cracker Suite ........................... 7" EP . HMV............. 7EG8919............... 1965 £2...............£5 ...............................

## WILKINSON TRI-CYCLE
Wilkinson Tri-Cycle.............................. LP ..... Date .............. TES4016 ............... 1969 £15.........£30 ...............................US

## WILLETT, SLIM
Slim Willett ........................................ LP ..... Audio Lab ....... AL1542 ................. 1961 £10.........£25 ...............................US

## WILLETT FAMILY
Roving Journeyman .............................. LP ..... Topic.............. 12T84 ................... 1962 £8...........£20 ...............................

## WILLETTE, BABY FACE
Face To Face ....................................... LP ..... Blue Note ....... BLP/BST84068 ...... 1961 £30.........£60 ...............................
Stop And Listen ................................... LP ..... Blue Note ....... BLP/BST84084 ...... 1961 £25.........£50 ...............................

## WILLIAMS, AL
I Am Nothing....................................... 7" ...... Grapevine ....... GRP136................ 1979 £1.50........£4 ...............................

## WILLIAMS, ANDY
Are You Sincere................................... 7" ...... London ........... HLA8587 .............. 1958 £2.50........£6 ...............................
Baby Doll............................................ 7" ...... London ........... HLA8360 .............. 1956 £6...........£12 ..................gold label
Best.................................................. 7" EP . London ........... REA1394 ............. 1963 £4.............£8 ...............................
Big Hits ............................................. 7" EP . London ........... REA1088 ............. 1957 £5...........£10 ...............................
Big Hits No. 2 ..................................... 7" EP . London ........... REA1102 ............. 1957 £5...........£10 ...............................
Butterfly ............................................ 7" ...... London ........... HLA8399 .............. 1957 £5...........£10 ...............................
Canadian Sunset.................................. 7" ...... London ........... HL7013 ............... 1956 £1.50........£4 ..................export
Canadian Sunset.................................. 7" ...... London ........... HLA8315 .............. 1956 £6...........£12 ..................gold label
House Of Bamboo ............................... 7" ...... London ........... HLA8784 .............. 1959 £2.............£5 ...............................
I Like Your Kind Of Love ..................... 7" ...... London ........... HLA8437 .............. 1957 £4.............£8 ...............................
Lips Of Wine ...................................... 7" ...... London ........... HLA8487 .............. 1957 £4.............£8 ...............................
Lonely Street....................................... LP ..... London ........... HAA2238 ............. 1960 £4...........£10 ...............................
Lonely Street....................................... 7" ...... London ........... HLA8957 .............. 1959 £1.50........£4 ...............................
Promise Me, Love ............................... 7" ...... London ........... HLA8710 .............. 1958 £2.50........£6 ...............................
Sings Rodgers And Hammerstein .......... LP ..... London ........... HAA2113 ............. 1958 £4...........£10 ...............................
Sings Steve Allen ................................ LP ..... London ........... HAA2054 ............. 1957 £6...........£15 ...............................
Two Time Winners............................... LP ..... London ........... HAA2203 ............. 1959 £4...........£10 ...............................
Village Of St. Bernadette ..................... 7" ...... London ........... HLA9018 .............. 1959 £1.50........£4 ...............................
Wake Me When It's Over ..................... 7" ...... London ........... HLA9099 .............. 1960 £1.50........£4 ...............................
Walk Hand In Hand ............................. 7" ...... London ........... HLA8284 .............. 1956 £6...........£12 ..................gold label

## WILLIAMS, AUDREY
Living It Up ........................................ 7" ...... MGM............. SP1179.................. 1956 £4.............£8 ...............................

## WILLIAMS, BIG JOE
Back To The Country ........................... LP ..... Bounty............ BY6018................ 1966 £6...........£15 ...............................
Big Joe Williams.................................. LP ..... Storyville ......... 616011 ................ 1970 £4...........£10 ...............................
Big Joe Williams.................................. LP ..... XTRA .............. XTRA1033............ 1966 £6...........£15 ...............................
Big Joe Williams.................................. 7" EP . XX ................. MIN700............... 196– £2.............£5 ...............................
Blues For Nine Strings .......................... LP ..... Bluesville ........ BV1056................ 1963 £6...........£15 ...............................US
Blues On Highway 49 ........................... LP ..... Delmark .......... DL604 ................ 1962 £6...........£15 ...............................US
Blues On Highway 51 ........................... LP ..... Esquire ........... 32191................. 1963 £10.........£25 ...............................
Classic Delta Blues............................... LP ..... CBS................ BPG63813............ 1964 £4...........£10 ...............................
Crawlin' King Snake............................. LP ..... RCA ............... INTS1087 ............ 1970 £4...........£10 ...............................
Hand Me Down My Old Walking Stick .... LP ..... Liberty ........... LBL/LBS83207 ...... 1968 £4...........£10 ...............................
Hell Bound And Heaven Sent ................ LP ..... Folkways ......... 31004................. 1967 £4...........£10 ...............................US
Mississippi's Big Joe Williams............... LP ..... Folkways ......... F(S)3820.............. 1962 £6...........£15 ...............................US
On The Highway.................................. 7" EP . Delmark .......... DJB4................... 1966 £2.............£5 ...............................
Piney Woods Blues............................... LP ..... 77 ................. LA1219 ............... 1963 £6...........£15 ...............................

| Title | Format | Label | Catalog | Year | Price | Price | Notes |
|---|---|---|---|---|---|---|---|
| Portraits In Blues Vol. 4 | LP | Storyville | SLP158 | 1964 | £4 | £10 | |
| Portraits In Blues Vol. 7 | LP | Storyville | SLP163 | 1964 | £4 | £10 | |
| Starvin' Chain Blues | LP | Delmark | DL/DSD609 | 1966 | £4 | £10 | US |
| Studio Blues | LP | Bluesville | BV1083 | 1964 | £6 | £15 | US |
| Tough Times | LP | Fontana | 688800ZL | 1965 | £4 | £10 | |

## WILLIAMS, BILLY

| Title | Format | Label | Catalog | Year | Price | Price | Notes |
|---|---|---|---|---|---|---|---|
| Billy Williams Quartet | LP | MGM | E3400 | 1957 | £8 | £20 | US |
| Billy Williams Singing Oh Yeah | LP | Mercury | MG20317 | 1958 | £8 | £20 | US |
| Butterfly | 7" | Vogue Coral | Q72241 | 1957 | £5 | £10 | |
| Crazy Little Palace | 7" | Vogue Coral | Q72149 | 1956 | £7.50 | £15 | |
| Don't Let Go | 7" | Coral | Q72303 | 1958 | £5 | £10 | |
| Follow Me | 7" | Vogue Coral | Q72222 | 1957 | £5 | £10 | |
| Goodnight Irene | 7" | Coral | Q72369 | 1959 | £1.50 | £4 | |
| Got A Date With An Angel | 7" | Vogue Coral | Q72295 | 1957 | £5 | £10 | |
| I Cried For You | 7" | Coral | Q72402 | 1960 | £1.50 | £4 | |
| I'll Get By | 7" | Coral | Q72331 | 1958 | £2.50 | £6 | |
| I'm Gonna Sit Right Down | 7" | Vogue Coral | Q72266 | 1957 | £6 | £12 | |
| Love Me | 7" | Vogue Coral | Q2039 | 1954 | £7.50 | £15 | |
| Nola | 7" | Coral | Q72359 | 1959 | £1.50 | £4 | |
| Pray | 7" | Vogue Coral | Q72180 | 1956 | £4 | £8 | |
| Steppin' Out Tonight | 7" | Coral | Q72316 | 1958 | £12.50 | £25 | |
| Telephone Conversation | 7" | Coral | Q72377 | 1959 | £2 | £5 | |
| Vote For Billy Williams | LP | Wing | MGW12131 | 1959 | £8 | £20 | US |

## WILLIAMS, BOBBY

| Title | Format | Label | Catalog | Year | Price | Price | Notes |
|---|---|---|---|---|---|---|---|
| Baby I Need Your Love | 7" | Action | ACT4509 | 1968 | £4 | £8 | |
| Let's Jam | 7" | Contempo | C17 | 1973 | £2.50 | £6 | |

## WILLIAMS, CHRIS & HIS MONSTERS

| Title | Format | Label | Catalog | Year | Price | Price | Notes |
|---|---|---|---|---|---|---|---|
| Kicking Around | 7" | Triumph | RGM1003 | 1960 | £100 | £200 | best auctioned |
| Monster | 7" | Columbia | DB4383 | 1959 | £5 | £10 | |

## WILLIAMS, CLARENCE

| Title | Format | Label | Catalog | Year | Price | Price | Notes |
|---|---|---|---|---|---|---|---|
| Back Room Special | 10" LP | Columbia | 33S1067 | 1955 | £10 | £25 | |
| Clarence Williams And His Orchestra | 10" LP | London | AL3526 | 1954 | £10 | £25 | |
| Clarence Williams And His Orchestra Vol. 2 | 10" LP | London | AL3561 | 1957 | £10 | £25 | |
| Clarence Williams Vol. 1 | LP | Philips | BBL7521 | 1962 | £6 | £15 | |
| Clarence Williams' Washboard Band | 7" EP | Parlophone | GEP8733 | 1959 | £2 | £5 | |
| High Society | 7" | Columbia | SCM5134 | 1954 | £5 | £10 | |
| Jazz Originators | 7" EP | Collector | JEL18 | 1964 | £2 | £5 | |
| Sidney Bechet Memorial | LP | Fontana | TFL5087 | 1960 | £6 | £15 | |
| Treasures Of North American Music Vol. 3 | 7" EP | Fontana | TFE17053 | 1958 | £2 | £5 | |

## WILLIAMS, DAN

| Title | Format | Label | Catalog | Year | Price | Price | Notes |
|---|---|---|---|---|---|---|---|
| Donkey City | 7" | London | CAY110 | 1955 | £2 | £5 | |

## WILLIAMS, DANNY

| Title | Format | Label | Catalog | Year | Price | Price | Notes |
|---|---|---|---|---|---|---|---|
| Danny Williams | LP | HMV | CLP1458/CSD1369 | 1961 | £5 | £12 | |
| Days Of Wine And Roses | 7" EP | HMV | 7EG8800 | 1963 | £2.50 | £6 | |
| Forget Her, Forget Her | 7" | HMV | POP1372 | 1964 | £1.50 | £4 | |
| Go Away | 7" | HMV | POP1410 | 1965 | £1.50 | £4 | |
| Hits | 7" EP | HMV | 7EG8748 | 1962 | £2.50 | £6 | |
| Moon River | LP | HMV | CLP1521 | 1961 | £5 | £12 | |
| Rain | 7" | HMV | POP1560 | 1966 | £1.50 | £4 | |
| So High – So Low | 7" | HMV | POP655 | 1959 | £1.50 | £4 | |
| Swings With Tony Osborne | 7" EP | HMV | 7EG8763 | 1962 | £2.50 | £6 | |
| Tall Tree | 7" | HMV | POP624 | 1959 | £1.50 | £4 | |
| White On White | 7" | HMV | POP1263 | 1963 | £1.50 | £4 | |
| Youthful Years | 7" | HMV | POP703 | 1959 | £1.50 | £4 | |

## WILLIAMS, EDDIE & LITTLE SONNY WILLIS

| Title | Format | Label | Catalog | Year | Price | Price | Notes |
|---|---|---|---|---|---|---|---|
| Going To California | 7" EP | XX | MIN707 | 196– | £2 | £5 | |

## WILLIAMS, GRANVILLE ORCHESTRA

| Title | Format | Label | Catalog | Year | Price | Price | Notes |
|---|---|---|---|---|---|---|---|
| Hi-Life | LP | Island | ILP971 | 1968 | £20 | £40 | pink label |
| Hi-Life | 7" | Island | WI3062 | 1967 | £2 | £5 | |

## WILLIAMS, HANK

| Title | Format | Label | Catalog | Year | Price | Price | Notes |
|---|---|---|---|---|---|---|---|
| Authentic Sound Of The Country Hits | 7" EP | MGM | MGMEP770 | 1963 | £6 | £12 | |
| Beyond The Sunset | LP | MGM | E4138 | 1961 | £5 | £12 | US |
| Blue Love | 7" | MGM | MGM931 | 1956 | £6 | £12 | |
| Cold Cold Heart | 78 | MGM | MGM459 | 1951 | £3 | £8 | |
| Crazy Heart | 7" | MGM | SP1085 | 1954 | £6 | £12 | |
| Dear John | 78 | MGM | MGM405 | 1951 | £3 | £8 | |
| First, Last And Always | LP | MGM | E3928 | 1961 | £6 | £15 | US |
| Greatest Hits | LP | MGM | E3918 | 1961 | £5 | £12 | US |
| Half As Much | 78 | MGM | MGM527 | 1952 | £3 | £8 | |
| Hank Williams | 7" EP | MGM | MGMEP551 | 1956 | £10 | £20 | |
| Hank Williams & His Drifting Cowboys | 7" EP | MGM | MGMEP512 | 1954 | £7.50 | £15 | |
| Hank Williams Favorites | 7" EP | MGM | MGMEP757 | 1961 | £6 | £12 | |
| Hank Williams Sings | 10" LP | MGM | D105 | 1952 | £15 | £30 | |
| Hank Williams Story | LP | MGM | E4267 | 1966 | £8 | £20 | US |
| Hank's Laments | 7" EP | MGM | MGMEP675 | 1958 | £7.50 | £15 | |
| Hey Good Lookin' | 78 | MGM | MGM454 | 1951 | £3 | £8 | |
| Honky Tonk Blues | 78 | MGM | MGM505 | 1952 | £3 | £8 | |
| Honky Tonk Blues | 7" EP | MGM | MGMEP614 | 1957 | £7.50 | £15 | |
| Honky Tonkin' | LP | MGM | E3412 | 1957 | £15 | £30 | US |

| | | | | | | |
|---|---|---|---|---|---|---|
| Honky Tonkin'...................................... | 7" EP . MGM ............. | MGMEP582 ........... | 1957 £7.50 ... £15 | |
| Honky Tonkin'...................................... | 10" LP MGM ............ | E242 .................... | 1954 £20 ........ £40 | | US |
| I Ain't Got Nothing But Time ................ | 7" ...... MGM ............ | SP1102 .................. | 1954 £6 ......... £12 | |
| I Can't Help It ..................................... | 78 ...... MGM ............ | MGM471 ............... | 1952 £3 ................ £8 | |
| I Saw The Light .................................. | LP ...... MGM ............ | E3331 ................... | 1956 £15 ........ £30 | | US |
| I Saw The Light .................................. | 78 ...... MGM ............ | MGM630 ............... | 1953 £3 ................ £8 | |
| I Saw The Light .................................. | 10" LP MGM ............ | E243 .................... | 1954 £20 ........ £40 | | US |
| I Saw The Light No. 1 .......................... | 7" EP . MGM ............ | MGMEP569 ........... | 1956 £7.50 ... £15 | |
| I Saw The Light No. 2 .......................... | 7" EP . MGM ............ | MGMEP608 ........... | 1957 £7.50 ... £15 | |
| I Wish I Had A Nickel .......................... | 7" ...... MGM ............ | MGM921 ............... | 1956 £6 ......... £12 | |
| I'll Never Get Out Of This World Alive..... | 7" ...... MGM ............ | SP1016 .................. | 1953 £7.50 ... £15 | |
| I'm Blue Inside ................................... | LP ...... MGM ............ | C8021 ................... | 1966 £5 ......... £12 | |
| I'm Blue Inside ................................... | LP ...... MGM ............ | E3926 ................... | 1961 £5 ......... £12 | | US |
| I'm Gonna Sing .................................. | 78 ...... MGM ............ | MGM799 ............... | 1955 £3 ................ £8 | |
| I'm So Lonesome I Could Cry ................ | 7" ...... MGM ............ | MGM1309 ............. | 1966 £2 ................ £5 | |
| Immortal Hank Williams ...................... | LP ...... MGM ............ | E3605 ................... | 1958 £8 ............ £20 | | US |
| Immortal Hank Williams ...................... | 10" LP MGM ............ | D154 .................... | 1958 £10 ........ £25 | |
| In Memory Of Hank Williams ................ | LP ...... MGM ............ | C8020 ................... | 1966 £4 ............ £10 | |
| Jambalaya........................................... | 78 ...... MGM ............ | MGM566 ............... | 1952 £3 ................ £8 | |
| Kaw Liga ............................................ | 7" ...... MGM ............ | SP1034 .................. | 1953 £7.50 ... £15 | |
| Kaw-Liga ............................................ | 7" ...... MGM ............ | MGM1322 ............. | 1966 £2 ................ £5 | |
| Leave Me Alone With The Blues ............. | 7" ...... MGM ............ | MGM966 ............... | 1957 £5 ......... £10 | |
| Let Me Sing A Blue Song ...................... | LP ...... MGM ............ | E3924 ................... | 1961 £5 ......... £12 | | US |
| Lives Again ......................................... | LP ...... MGM ............ | E3923 ................... | 1961 £5 ......... £12 | | US |
| Lonesome Sound Of Hank Williams ......... | LP ...... MGM ............ | C811 .................... | 1960 £8 ............ £20 | |
| Love Songs, Comedy & Hymns .............. | LP ...... MGM ............ | C8040 ................... | 1967 £5 ......... £12 | |
| Lovesick Blues ..................................... | 78 ...... MGM ............ | MGM269 ............... | 1950 £3 ................ £8 | |
| Low Down Blues .................................. | 7" ...... MGM ............ | MGM942 ............... | 1957 £6 ......... £12 | |
| Luke The Drifter .................................. | LP ...... MGM ............ | C8022 ................... | 1966 £4 ............ £10 | |
| Luke The Drifter .................................. | LP ...... MGM ............ | E3267 ................... | 1955 £20 ........ £40 | | US |
| Luke The Drifter .................................. | 10" LP MGM ............ | D119 .................... | 1953 £15 ........ £30 | |
| Many Moods Of Hank Williams .............. | LP ...... MGM ............ | C8023 ................... | 1966 £4 ............ £10 | |
| May You Never Be Alone ...................... | LP ...... MGM ............ | C8019 ................... | 1966 £5 ......... £12 | |
| Memorial Album .................................. | LP ...... MGM ............ | E3272 ................... | 1955 £15 ........ £30 | | US |
| Memorial Album .................................. | 10" LP MGM ............ | D137 .................... | 1955 £10 ........ £25 | |
| Mind Your Own Business ...................... | 78 ...... MGM ............ | MGM553 ............... | 1952 £3 ................ £8 | |
| Moanin' The Blues ............................... | LP ...... MGM ............ | E3330 ................... | 1956 £15 ........ £30 | | US |
| Moanin' The Blues ............................... | 78 ...... MGM ............ | MGM381 ............... | 1951 £3 ................ £8 | |
| Moanin' The Blues ............................... | 10" LP MGM ............ | D144 .................... | 1956 £15 ........ £30 | |
| More Greatest Hits ............................... | LP ...... MGM ............ | E4040 ................... | 1961 £5 ......... £12 | | US |
| More Greatest Hits Vol. 3 ..................... | LP ...... MGM ............ | E4140 ................... | 1962 £5 ......... £12 | | US |
| My Bucket's Got A Hole In It ................ | 7" ...... MGM ............ | SP1048 .................. | 1953 £7.50 ... £15 | |
| On Stage Recorded Live ........................ | LP ...... MGM ............ | C893 .................... | 1962 £6 ......... £15 | |
| Ramblin' Man ..................................... | LP ...... MGM ............ | E3219 ................... | 1955 £15 ........ £30 | | US |
| Ramblin' Man ..................................... | 7" ...... MGM ............ | SP1049 .................. | 1954 £7.50 ... £15 | |
| Ramblin' Man ..................................... | 10" LP MGM ............ | E291 .................... | 1954 £20 ........ £40 | | US |
| Rootie Tootie ....................................... | 7" ...... MGM ............ | MGM957 ............... | 1957 £6 ......... £12 | |
| Sing Me A Blue Song ........................... | LP ...... MGM ............ | E3560 ................... | 1958 £8 ............ £20 | | US |
| Sing Me A Blue Song ........................... | 10" LP MGM ............ | D150 .................... | 1958 £10 ........ £25 | |
| Someday You'll Call My Name ............... | 7" ...... MGM ............ | SP1163 .................. | 1956 £6 ......... £12 | |
| Songs For A Broken Heart ..................... | 7" EP . MGM ............ | MGMEP639 ........... | 1958 £7.50 ... £15 | |
| Songs For A Broken Heart No. 2 ............. | 7" EP . MGM ............ | MGMEP649 ........... | 1958 £7.50 ... £15 | |
| Spirit Of Hank Williams........................ | LP ...... MGM ............ | C956 .................... | 1963 £6 ......... £15 | |
| Thirty-Six Greatest Hits ........................ | LP ...... MGM ............ | 3E2 ...................... | 1957 £25 ........ £50 | | US, triple |
| Thirty-Six More Greatest Hits ................ | LP ...... MGM ............ | 3E4 ...................... | 1958 £25 ........ £50 | | US, triple |
| Unforgettable Hank Williams ................. | LP ...... MGM ............ | C784 .................... | 1959 £8 ............ £20 | |
| Unforgettable Hank Williams ................. | 7" EP . MGM ............ | MGMEP710 ........... | 1960 £6 ......... £12 | |
| Unforgettable Hank Williams No. 2 ........ | 7" EP . MGM ............ | MGMEP726 ........... | 1960 £6 ......... £12 | |
| Unforgettable Hank Williams No. 3 ........ | 7" EP . MGM ............ | MGMEP732 ........... | 1960 £6 ......... £12 | |
| Wait For The Light To Shine ................. | LP ...... MGM ............ | C834 .................... | 1960 £6 ......... £15 | |
| Wanderin' Around ............................... | LP ...... MGM ............ | E3925 ................... | 1961 £5 ......... £12 | | US |
| Weary Blues ........................................ | 7" ...... MGM ............ | SP1067 .................. | 1954 £7.50 ... £15 | |
| Why Don't You Love Me........................ | 78 ...... MGM ............ | MGM483 ............... | 1952 £3 ................ £8 | |
| Window Shopping ................................ | 78 ...... MGM ............ | MGM678 ............... | 1953 £3 ................ £8 | |
| Your Cheatin' Heart............................. | 78 ...... MGM ............ | MGM896 ............... | 1956 £3 ................ £8 | |

## WILLIAMS, HANK & HANK WILLIAMS JR.

| | | | | |
|---|---|---|---|---|
| Singing Together.................................. | LP . MGM ............ | C1008 ............... | 1965 £4 ........... £10 | |

## WILLIAMS, HANK JR.

| | | | | |
|---|---|---|---|---|
| Long Gone Lonesome Blues...................... | 7" ...... MGM ............. | MGM1223 ............. | 1963 £1.50 ..... £4 | |

## WILLIAMS, JEANETTE

| | | | | |
|---|---|---|---|---|
| Hound Dog ......................................... | 7" ...... Action............. | ACT4557 ............... | 1969 £4 ......... £8 | |
| Stuff.................................................. | 7" ...... Action............. | ACT4534 ............... | 1969 £4 ......... £8 | |

## WILLIAMS, JERRY & THE VIOLENTS

| | | | | |
|---|---|---|---|---|
| Jerry Williams And The Violents............... | LP ...... Grand Prix ...... | GP9938 ................. | 1968 £6 ......... £15 | Swedish |
| Rock And Roll Time .............................. | LP ...... Clan ............... | 7012 .................... | 1968 £20 ........ £40 | Italian |
| Star Club Show 5 ................................. | LP ...... Starclub........... | 148004STL ............ | 1965 £37.50 ... £75 | German |

## WILLIAMS, JIMMY

| | | | | |
|---|---|---|---|---|
| Walking On Air ................................... | 7" ...... Atlantic ........... | AT4042 ................. | 1965 £2.50 ..... £6 | |

## WILLIAMS, JOE

| | | | | |
|---|---|---|---|---|
| Ballad And Blues ................................. | 7" EP . Columbia ........ | SEG7984 ............... | 1960 £2 ......... £5 | |
| Everyday I Have The Blues ..................... | 7" EP . Columbia ........ | SEG8001 ............... | 1960 £2.50 ...... £6 | |
| Greatest ............................................. | LP ...... HMV ............... | CLP1109 ............... | 1957 £6 ......... £15 | |

| | | | | | | | |
|---|---|---|---|---|---|---|---|
| Groovy Joe Williams | 7" EP | Columbia | SEB10110 | 1959 | £2 | £5 | |
| Joe Sings The Blues | 7" EP | Columbia | SEG8016 | 1960 | £2.50 | £6 | |
| Joe Williams & Count Basie's Orchestra | 7" EP | Columbia | SEG7810 | 1958 | £2 | £5 | |
| Man Ain't Supposed To Cry | LP | Columbia | 33SX1087 | 1958 | £6 | £15 | |
| Sings | 10" LP | London | HBC1065 | 1956 | £4 | £10 | |
| Sings About You | LP | Columbia | 33SX1229/ SCX3308 | 1960 | £5 | £12 | |

## WILLIAMS, JOHN

| | | | | | | | |
|---|---|---|---|---|---|---|---|
| Can't Find Time For Anything Now | 7" | Columbia | DB8251 | 1967 | £2.50 | £6 | |
| John Williams | LP | Columbia | SX6169 | 1967 | £37.50 | £75 | |
| She's That Kind Of Woman | 7" | Columbia | DB8128 | 1967 | £2.50 | £6 | |

## WILLIAMS, KENNETH

| | | | | | | | |
|---|---|---|---|---|---|---|---|
| Extracts From Pieces Of Eight | 7" EP | Decca | DFE8548 | 1963 | £2 | £5 | |
| In Season | 7" EP | Decca | DFE8671 | 1966 | £2 | £5 | |
| On Pleasure Bent | LP | Decca | LK4856 | 1967 | £4 | £10 | |
| Rambling Syd Rumpo In Concert No. 1 | 7" EP | Parlophone | GEP8965 | 1967 | £2 | £5 | |
| Rambling Syd Rumpo In Concert No. 2 | 7" EP | Parlophone | GEP8966 | 1967 | £2 | £5 | |

## WILLIAMS, LARRY

| | | | | | | | |
|---|---|---|---|---|---|---|---|
| Baby Baby | 7" | London | HLM9053 | 1960 | £7.50 | £15 | |
| Bony Moronie | 7" | London | HLU8532 | 1958 | £12.50 | £25 | |
| Dizzy Miss Lizzy | 7" | London | HLU8604 | 1958 | £15 | £30 | |
| Greatest Hits | LP | OKeh | OKM2123/ OKS12123 | 1967 | £5 | £12 | US |
| Here's Larry Williams | LP | Speciality | SP2109 | 1959 | £30 | £60 | US |
| I Can't Stop Loving You | 7" | London | HLU8911 | 1960 | £7.50 | £15 | |
| Larry Williams | 7" EP | London | REU1213 | 1959 | £30 | £60 | |
| Larry Williams Show | LP | Decca | LK4691 | 1965 | £15 | £30 | with Johnny Guitar Watson |
| On Stage | LP | Sue | ILP922 | 1965 | £15 | £30 | |
| Shake Your Body Girl | 7" | MGM | MGM1447 | 1968 | £2 | £5 | |
| She Said Yeah | 7" | London | HLU8844 | 1959 | £7.50 | £15 | |
| Short Fat Fannie | 7" | London | HLN8472 | 1957 | £12.50 | £25 | |
| Strange | 7" | Sue | WI371 | 1965 | £5 | £10 | |
| Turn On Your Lovelight | 7" | Sue | WI381 | 1965 | £6 | £12 | |

## WILLIAMS, LARRY & JOHNNY GUITAR WATSON

| | | | | | | | |
|---|---|---|---|---|---|---|---|
| Mercy Mercy Mercy | 7" | Columbia | DB8140 | 1967 | £12.50 | £25 | |
| Sweet Little Baby | 7" | Decca | F12151 | 1965 | £5 | £10 | |
| Too Late | 7" | Epic | EPC4421 | 1976 | £1.50 | £4 | |
| Two For The Price Of One | LP | OKeh | OKM4122/ OKS14122 | 1967 | £6 | £15 | US |

## WILLIAMS, LITTLE JERRY

| | | | | | | | |
|---|---|---|---|---|---|---|---|
| Baby You're My Everything | 7" | Cameo Parkway | C100 | 1962 | £7.50 | £15 | |

## WILLIAMS, LLOYD

| | | | | | | | |
|---|---|---|---|---|---|---|---|
| Funky Beat | 7" | Treasure Isle | TI7029 | 1968 | £5 | £10 | |
| Sad World | 7" | Doctor Bird | DB1051 | 1966 | £5 | £10 | Tommy McCook B side |
| Wonderful World | 7" | Doctor Bird | DB1135 | 1968 | £5 | £10 | Tommy McCook B side |

## WILLIAMS, LORETTA

| | | | | | | | |
|---|---|---|---|---|---|---|---|
| Baby Cakes | 7" | Atlantic | 584032 | 1966 | £6 | £12 | |

## WILLIAMS, MARY LOU

| | | | | | | | |
|---|---|---|---|---|---|---|---|
| At The Piano | 7" EP | Parlophone | GEP8567 | 1956 | £2 | £5 | |
| Chug A Lug Jug | 7" | Sue | WI311 | 1964 | £6 | £12 | |
| Don Carlos Meets Mary Lou Williams | 7" EP | Vogue | EPV1042 | 1955 | £2 | £5 | |
| In Paris | 10" LP | Felsted | EDL87012 | 1955 | £15 | £30 | |
| Mary Lou Williams | 7" EP | Columbia | SEG7608 | 1956 | £2 | £5 | |
| Mary Lou Williams Quartet | 7" EP | Esquire | EP66 | 195– | £2 | £5 | |
| Piano Panorama | 10" LP | Esquire | 20026 | 1954 | £20 | £40 | |
| Plays In London | 10" LP | Vogue | LDE022 | 1953 | £20 | £40 | |

## WILLIAMS, MAURICE & THE ZODIACS

| | | | | | | | |
|---|---|---|---|---|---|---|---|
| At The Beach | LP | Snyder | 5586 | 196– | £10 | £25 | US |
| Come Along | 7" | Top Rank | JAR563 | 1961 | £4 | £8 | |
| I Remember | 7" | Top Rank | JAR550 | 1961 | £2 | £5 | |
| Stay | LP | Herald | HLP1014 | 1961 | £30 | £60 | US |
| Stay | LP | Sphere Sound | SSR7007 | 1964 | £10 | £25 | US |
| Stay | 7" EP | Top Rank | JKP3006 | 1961 | £30 | £60 | |
| Stay | 7" | Top Rank | JAR526 | 1960 | £2 | £5 | |

## WILLIAMS, MEL & JOHNNY OTIS

| | | | | | | | |
|---|---|---|---|---|---|---|---|
| All Through The Night | LP | Dig | 103 | 1955 | £25 | £50 | US |

## WILLIAMS, MIKE

| | | | | | | | |
|---|---|---|---|---|---|---|---|
| Lonely Soldier | 7" | Atlantic | 584027 | 1966 | £2 | £5 | |

## WILLIAMS, OTIS & THE CHARMS

| | | | | | | | |
|---|---|---|---|---|---|---|---|
| Hearts Of Stone | 7" | Parlophone | MSP6155 | 1955 | £180 | £300 | best auctioned |
| I'm Waiting Just For You | 7" | Parlophone | R4293 | 1957 | £180 | £300 | best auctioned |
| It's All Over Now | 7" | Parlophone | R4210 | 1956 | £100 | £200 | best auctioned |

| | | | | | | | | |
|---|---|---|---|---|---|---|---|---|
| Ivory Tower | 7" | Parlophone | CMSP36 | 1955 | £87.50 | £175 | export |
| Ivory Tower | 7" | Parlophone | MSP6239 | 1956 | £180 | £300 | best auctioned |
| Secret | 7" | Parlophone | R4495 | 1958 | £25 | £50 | |
| Their All Time Hits | LP | Deluxe | 750 | 1957 | £100 | £200 | US |
| Their All Time Hits | LP | King | 560 | 1957 | £37.50 | £75 | US |
| This Is Otis Williams And The Charms | LP | King | 614 | 1959 | £37.50 | £75 | US |
| Two Hearts | 7" | Parlophone | DP423 | 1955 | £180 | £300 | export, best auctioned |
| Two Hearts | 7" | Parlophone | R4860 | 1961 | £20 | £40 | |

## WILLIAMS, PAUL

| | | | | | | | |
|---|---|---|---|---|---|---|---|
| Gin House | 7" | Columbia | DB7421 | 1964 | £5 | £10 | |
| Many Faces Of Love | 7" | Columbia | DB7768 | 1965 | £5 | £10 | with Zoot Money |
| My Sly Sadie | 7" | Decca | F12844 | 1968 | £1.50 | £4 | |

## WILLIAMS, PAUL (2)

| | | | | | | | |
|---|---|---|---|---|---|---|---|
| Delta Blues Singer | LP | Sonet | SNTF654 | 1973 | £4 | £10 | |
| In Memory Of Robert Johnson | LP | Intercord | 28754 | 1973 | £5 | £12 | German |

## WILLIAMS, POOR JOE

| | | | | | | | |
|---|---|---|---|---|---|---|---|
| Man Sings The Blues | 7" EP | Collector | JEN3 | 1960 | £4 | £8 | |
| Man Sings The Blues Vol. 2 | 7" EP | Collector | JEN4 | 1960 | £4 | £8 | |

## WILLIAMS, REEK & THE FIGHTING CATS

| | | | | | | | |
|---|---|---|---|---|---|---|---|
| Favourites | LP | Delta | 210 | 1967 | £8 | £20 | Dutch |

## WILLIAMS, ROBERT PETE

| | | | | | | | |
|---|---|---|---|---|---|---|---|
| Robert Pete Williams | LP | Saydisc | AMS2002 | 1972 | £4 | £10 | |
| Sugar Farm | LP | Blues Beacon | 1932101ST | 197– | £4 | £10 | |
| Those Prison Blues | LP | 77 | LA1217 | 1963 | £5 | £12 | |

## WILLIAMS, ROGER

| | | | | | | | |
|---|---|---|---|---|---|---|---|
| Almost Paradise | 7" | London | HLR8422 | 1957 | £1.50 | £4 | |
| Anastasia | 7" | London | HLU8379 | 1957 | £2 | £5 | |
| Arrivederci Roma | 7" | London | HLR8572 | 1958 | £1.50 | £4 | |
| Autumn Leaves | 7" | London | HLU8214 | 1955 | £4 | £8 | |
| Till | 7" | London | HLR8516 | 1957 | £1.50 | £4 | |
| Two Different Worlds | 7" | London | HLU8341 | 1956 | £5 | £10 | with Jane Morgan |

## WILLIAMS, SMITTY

| | | | | | | | |
|---|---|---|---|---|---|---|---|
| Cure | 7" | MGM | MGM1167 | 1962 | £1.50 | £4 | |

## WILLIAMS, SONNY

| | | | | | | | |
|---|---|---|---|---|---|---|---|
| Bye Bye Baby Goodbye | 7" | London | HLD8931 | 1959 | £6 | £12 | |

## WILLIAMS, TEX

| | | | | | | | |
|---|---|---|---|---|---|---|---|
| All Time Greats | 7" EP | Brunswick | OE9147 | 1955 | £2 | £5 | |
| Be Sure You're Right | 7" | Brunswick | 05516 | 1956 | £1.50 | £4 | |
| Country Music Time | LP | Decca | DL4295 | 1962 | £4 | £10 | US |
| Dance-O-Rama | LP | Decca | DL5565 | 1955 | £15 | £30 | US |
| Keeper Of Boot Hill | 7" | Top Rank | JAR330 | 1960 | £2 | £5 | |
| Money | 7" | Brunswick | 05393 | 1955 | £2.50 | £6 | |
| River Of No Return | 7" | Brunswick | 05327 | 1954 | £4 | £8 | |
| Smoke! Smoke! Smoke! | LP | Capitol | (S)T1463 | 1960 | £4 | £10 | |
| Talking To The Blues | 7" | Brunswick | 05684 | 1957 | £4 | £8 | |
| Tex Williams' Best | LP | Camden | CAL363 | 1958 | £5 | £12 | US |
| This Ole House | 7" | Brunswick | 05341 | 1954 | £4 | £8 | with Rex Allen |

## WILLIAMS, TONY (1)

| | | | | | | | |
|---|---|---|---|---|---|---|---|
| Life Time | LP | Blue Note | BLP/BST84180 | 1964 | £8 | £20 | |
| Spring | LP | Blue Note | BLP/BST84216 | 1965 | £8 | £20 | |

## WILLIAMS, TONY (2)

| | | | | | | | |
|---|---|---|---|---|---|---|---|
| Girl Is A Girl Is A Girl | LP | Mercury | MMC14027 | 1960 | £4 | £10 | |
| How Come | 7" | Philips | BF1282 | 1962 | £10 | £20 | |

## WILLIAMS, TONY LIFETIME

*Emergency* and *Turn It Over* are densely electric albums like no others. Tony Williams, the group's leader, was the drummer with Miles Davis during the sixties. Lifetime was his idea of a rock group but, filtered through his jazz background, it did not sound very much like anyone else's. Larry Young makes the organ sound like a banshee, pressing adjacent treble keys down all at the same time; John McLaughlin, who has just discovered the delights of high amplification, employs a ferocious fuzz-tone; while Tony Williams plays his customary churning, multi-layered rhythms. Unfortunately, the group was plagued by management problems and when Jack Bruce joined during the recording of *Turn It Over* these only became worse. Later Lifetime recordings are much more routine affairs, although *Believe It*, with Allan Holdsworth in fine form on guitar, has its moments.

| | | | | | | | |
|---|---|---|---|---|---|---|---|
| Believe It | LP | CBS | 69201 | 1976 | £4 | £10 | |
| Emergency | LP | Polydor | 583574 | 1969 | £20 | £40 | double |
| Lifetime | LP | Polydor | 2482179 | 1975 | £4 | £10 | |
| Million Dollar Legs | LP | CBS | 81510 | 1976 | £4 | £10 | |
| One Word | 7" | Polydor | | 1970 | £4 | £8 | |
| Turn It Over | LP | Polydor | 2425019 | 1970 | £8 | £20 | |

## WILLIAMSON, CLAUDE

| | | | | | | | |
|---|---|---|---|---|---|---|---|
| Claude Williamson Trio | 10" LP | Capitol | KPL103 | 1955 | £8 | £20 | |
| Claude Williamson Trio | 10" LP | Capitol | LC6804 | 1956 | £8 | £20 | |

## WILLIAMSON, DUDLEY

| | | | | | | | |
|---|---|---|---|---|---|---|---|
| Coming On The Scene | 7" | Doctor Bird | DB1117 | 1967 | £5 | £10 | |

## WILLIAMSON, ROBIN

| | | | | | | | |
|---|---|---|---|---|---|---|---|
| American Stonehenge | LP | Criminal | STEAL4 | 1978 | £5 | £12 | |
| Glint At The Kindling | LP | Criminal | STEAL6 | 1979 | £5 | £12 | |
| Journey Edge | LP | Flying Fish | FF033 | 1977 | £5 | £12 | US |
| Myrrh | LP | Island | HELP2 | 1972 | £5 | £12 | |
| Songs Of Love And Parting | LP | Flying Fish | FF257 | 1981 | £5 | £12 | US |

## WILLIAMSON, SONNY BOY

It has long been a matter of some confusion that there were two Sonny Boy Williamsons. John Lee 'Sonny Boy' Williamson was a successful blues harmonica player who recorded in the thirties and forties, but who was murdered in 1948 at the age of thirty-four. Sonny Boy Williamson II was christened Alec Ford, but later adopted the surname of his stepfather and the nickname Rice. At the beginning of the forties, Rice Miller began calling himself Sonny Boy Williamson in a deliberate attempt to gain some success on the back of the man who was, at the time, the better-known artist. Ironically, Miller, who was actually the older man by some seventeen years, went on to achieve considerably more success than his namesake – and not because of the name confusion, but because he was himself a fine and innovative harmonica player. During the early sixties, he spent some time in the UK, touring and recording with several of the up-and-coming British R&B groups.

| | | | | | | | |
|---|---|---|---|---|---|---|---|
| Blues Of Sonny Boy Williamson | LP | Storyville | SLP170 | 1965 | £6 | £15 | |
| Bring It On Home | 7" | Chess | CRS8030 | 1966 | £2 | £5 | |
| Bummer Road | LP | Chess | 1536 | 1969 | £4 | £10 | US |
| Down And Out Blues | LP | Pye | NPL28036 | 1964 | £8 | £20 | |
| From The Bottom | 7" | Blue Horizon | 451008 | 1966 | £50 | £100 | |
| Help Me | 7" EP | Chess | CRE6001 | 1965 | £7.50 | £15 | |
| Help Me | 7" | Pye | 7N25191 | 1963 | £2.50 | £6 | |
| In Memoriam | LP | Chess | CRL4510 | 1965 | £6 | £15 | |
| In Memoriam | 7" EP | Chess | CRE6013 | 1966 | £7.50 | £15 | |
| Last Sessions | LP | Rarity | RLP1 | 1974 | £8 | £20 | |
| Lonesome Cabin | 7" | Pye | 7N25268 | 1964 | £2.50 | £6 | |
| More Real Folk Blues | LP | Chess | 1509 | 1966 | £8 | £20 | US |
| No Nights By Myself | 7" | Sue | WI365 | 1965 | £4 | £8 | |
| Portraits In Blues | LP | Fontana | 670158 | 1966 | £5 | £12 | |
| Real Folk Blues | LP | Chess | 1503 | 1966 | £8 | £20 | US |
| Real Folk Blues Vol. 2 | 7" EP | Chess | CRE6018 | 1966 | £5 | £10 | |
| Sonny Boy Williamson | LP | Checker | 1437 | 1959 | £25 | £50 | US |
| Sonny Boy Williamson | 7" EP | Pye | NEP44037 | 1964 | £5 | £10 | |

## WILLIAMSON, SONNY BOY I

| | | | | | | | |
|---|---|---|---|---|---|---|---|
| Sonny Boy And His Pals | LP | Saydisc | SDR169 | 1969 | £6 | £15 | |

## WILLIAMSON, STU

| | | | | | | | |
|---|---|---|---|---|---|---|---|
| Sapphire | 10" LP | London | LZN14030 | 1956 | £20 | £40 | |
| Stu Williamson | LP | London | LTZN15123 | 1958 | £8 | £20 | |

## WILLIE & THE RED RUBBER BAND

| | | | | | | | |
|---|---|---|---|---|---|---|---|
| We're Coming Up | LP | RCA | LSP4193 | 1969 | £6 | £15 | US |
| Willie & The Red Rubber Band | LP | RCA | LSP4074 | 1968 | £6 | £15 | US |

## WILLING, FOY & THE RIDERS OF THE PURPLE SAGE

| | | | | | | | |
|---|---|---|---|---|---|---|---|
| Cowboy | LP | Roulette | R25035 | 1958 | £5 | £12 | US |
| Cowboy No. 1 | 7" EP | Columbia | SEG7834 | 1958 | £2 | £5 | |
| Cowboy No. 2 | 7" EP | Columbia | SEG7855 | 1958 | £2 | £5 | |

## WILLINGHAM, DORIS

| | | | | | | | |
|---|---|---|---|---|---|---|---|
| You Can't Do That | 7" | Jay Boy | BOY1 | 1969 | £2.50 | £6 | |

## WILLIS, CHUCK

| | | | | | | | |
|---|---|---|---|---|---|---|---|
| Betty And Dupree | 7" | London | HLE8595 | 1958 | £15 | £30 | |
| C.C. Rider | 7" | London | HLE8444 | 1957 | £20 | £40 | |
| Chuck Willis Wails The Blues | LP | Epic | LN3425 | 1958 | £50 | £100 | US |
| I Remember Chuck Willis | LP | Atlantic | ATL5003 | 1965 | £15 | £30 | |
| I Remember Chuck Willis | LP | Atlantic | 588145 | 1968 | £4 | £10 | |
| King Of The Stroll | LP | Atlantic | 8018 | 1958 | £50 | £100 | US, black label |
| King Of The Stroll | LP | Atlantic | 8018 | 1959 | £20 | £40 | US, red label |
| My Life | 7" | London | HLE8818 | 1959 | £12.50 | £25 | |
| That Train Has Gone | 7" | London | HLE8489 | 1957 | £15 | £30 | |
| Tribute To Chuck Willis | LP | Epic | LN3728 | 1960 | £30 | £60 | US |
| What Am I Living For | 7" | London | HLE8635 | 1958 | £12.50 | £25 | |
| Willis Wails The Blues | 7" EP | Fontana | TFE17138 | 1959 | £75 | £150 | |

## WILLIS, RALPH

| | | | | | | | |
|---|---|---|---|---|---|---|---|
| Goodbye Blues | 78 | Esquire | 10370 | 1954 | £6 | £12 | |
| Old Home Blues | 78 | Esquire | 10380 | 1954 | £6 | £12 | |
| Ralph Willis | 7" EP | Esquire | EP241 | 1961 | £7.50 | £15 | |
| Ralph Willis | 7" EP | XX | MIN703 | 196– | £2 | £5 | |
| Ralph Willis | 7" EP | XX | MIN711 | 196– | £2 | £5 | |

## WILLIS, SLIM

| | | | | | | | |
|---|---|---|---|---|---|---|---|
| Running Around | 7" | R&B | MRB5004 | 1965 | £5 | £10 | |

## WILLOWS

| | | | | | | | |
|---|---|---|---|---|---|---|---|
| Church Bells May Ring | 7" | London | HLL8290 | 1956 | £330 | £500 | best auctioned |

## WILLS, BOB

| | | | | | | | |
|---|---|---|---|---|---|---|---|
| Best Of Bob Wills | LP | Harmony | HL7304 | 1963 | £6 | £15 | US |
| Bob Wills And His Texas Playboys | LP | Decca | DL8727 | 1957 | £20 | £40 | US |
| Bob Wills And Tommy Duncan | LP | Liberty | LRX/LSX1912 | 1961 | £6 | £15 | US |

| | | | | | | | | |
|---|---|---|---|---|---|---|---|---|
| Bob Wills Sings And Plays | LP | Liberty | LRP3303/LST7303. | 1963 | £6 | £15 | US |
| Bob Wills Special | LP | Harmony | HL7036 | 1957 | £8 | £20 | US |
| Dance-O-Rama | 10" LP | Decca | DL5562 | 1955 | £30 | £60 | US |
| Great Bob Wills | LP | Harmony | HL7345 | 1965 | £6 | £15 | US |
| Heart To Heart Talk | 7" | London | HL7102 | 1960 | £4 | £8 | ..export, with Tommy Duncan |
| Keepsake Album £1 | LP | Longhorn | LP001 | 1965 | £15 | £30 | US |
| Living Legend | LP | Liberty | LRP3182/LST7182. | 1961 | £6 | £15 | US |
| Mr. Words And Music | LP | Liberty | LRP3194/LST7194. | 1961 | £6 | £15 | US |
| Old Time Favorites | 10" LP | Antones | LP6000 | 195– | £30 | £60 | US |
| Old Time Favorites | 10" LP | Antones | LP6010 | 195– | £30 | £60 | US |
| Ranch House Favorites | LP | MGM | E3352 | 1956 | £30 | £60 | US |
| Ranch House Favorites | 10" LP | MGM | E91 | 1951 | £30 | £60 | US |
| Round Up | 10" LP | Columbia | HL9003 | 195– | £30 | £60 | US |
| San Antonio Rose | LP | Starday | SLP375 | 1965 | £6 | £15 | US |
| Together Again | LP | Liberty | LRP3173/LST7173. | 1960 | £5 | £12 | .... US, with Tommy Duncan |
| Western Swing Band | LP | Vocalion | VL(7)3735 | 1965 | £6 | £15 | US |

## WILLS, MICK

| | | | | | | | |
|---|---|---|---|---|---|---|---|
| Fern Hill | LP | Woronzow | WOO9 | 1988 | £10 | £25 | |

## WILLS, TOMMY & HARRY LEWIS

| | | | | | | | |
|---|---|---|---|---|---|---|---|
| Rhythm And Blues | 7" EP | Range | JRE7006 | 196– | £2 | £5 | |

## WILLS, VIOLA

| | | | | | | | |
|---|---|---|---|---|---|---|---|
| Lost Without The Love Of My Guy | 7" | President | PT108 | 1968 | £1.50 | £4 | |

## WILMER & THE DUKES

| | | | | | | | |
|---|---|---|---|---|---|---|---|
| Give Me One More Chance | 7" | Action | ACT4500 | 1968 | £1.50 | £4 | |
| Wilmer & The Dukes | LP | Aphrodisiac | 6001 | 1969 | £5 | £12 | US |

## WILSON, ADA

| | | | | | | | |
|---|---|---|---|---|---|---|---|
| In The Quiet Of My Room | 7" | Ellie Jay | EJSP9288 | 1979 | £2.50 | £6 | |

## WILSON, AL

| | | | | | | | |
|---|---|---|---|---|---|---|---|
| Do What You Gotta Do | 7" | Liberty | LBF15044 | 1968 | £2.50 | £6 | |
| Searching For The Dolphins | LP | Liberty | LBS83173 | 1969 | £6 | £15 | |
| Searching For The Dolphins | LP | Soul City | SCS92006 | 1970 | £6 | £15 | |
| Snake | 7" | Liberty | LIB15121 | 1968 | £5 | £10 | |

## WILSON, ANN & THE DAYBREAKS

This is the same Ann Wilson as the later co-leader of Heart.

| | | | | | | | |
|---|---|---|---|---|---|---|---|
| Standin' Watchin' You | 7" | Topaz | 1311 | 1967 | £25 | £50 | US |
| Through Eyes And Glass | 7" | Topaz | 1312 | 1967 | £25 | £50 | US |

## WILSON, BRIAN

| | | | | | | | |
|---|---|---|---|---|---|---|---|
| Brian Wilson | CD | WEA | 9256692 | 1988 | £5 | £12 | |
| Caroline No | 7" | Capitol | CL15438 | 1966 | £4 | £8 | |
| I Just Wasn't Made For These Times | CD | MCA | MCA5P3575 | 1996 | £8 | £20 | ...US interview promo |
| Love And Mercy | CD-s | Sire | W7814CD | 1988 | £2 | £5 | |
| Words And Music | LP | Warner Bros | WBWM154 | 1988 | £5 | £12 | US promo |

## WILSON, BRIAN & MIKE LOVE

| | | | | | | | |
|---|---|---|---|---|---|---|---|
| Gettin' Hungry | 7" | Capitol | CL15513 | 1967 | £5 | £10 | |

## WILSON, CLIVE

| | | | | | | | |
|---|---|---|---|---|---|---|---|
| Mango Tree | 7" | R&B | JB144 | 1964 | £5 | £10 | |

## WILSON, COLIN

| | | | | | | | |
|---|---|---|---|---|---|---|---|
| Cloudburst | LP | Tabitha | | 1975 | £37.50 | £75 | |

## WILSON, DELROY

| | | | | | | | |
|---|---|---|---|---|---|---|---|
| 1-2-3 | 7" | Island | WI103 | 1963 | £5 | £10 | |
| Better Must Come | LP | Trojan | TRLS44 | 1972 | £5 | £12 | |
| Captivity | LP | Big Shot | BILP102 | 197– | £5 | £12 | |
| Come Down From Your Palms And Pray... | 7" | R&B | JB132 | 1963 | £5 | £10 | |
| Dancing Mood | 7" | Island | WI3013 | 1966 | £5 | £10 | . Soul Brothers B side |
| Easy Snappin' | 7" | Studio One | SO2074 | 1969 | £6 | £12 | .Webber Sisters B side |
| Feel Good All Over | 7" | Studio One | SO2057 | 1968 | £6 | £12 | |
| Get Ready | 7" | Island | WI3050 | 1967 | £5 | £10 | . Roy Richards B side |
| Give Me A Chance | 7" | Doctor Bird | DB1022 | 1966 | £5 | £10 | |
| Good All Over | LP | Coxsone | CSL8016 | 1968 | £50 | £100 | |
| Goodbye | 7" | Black Swan | WI420 | 1964 | £5 | £10 | |
| I Am Not A King | 7" | Studio One | SO2031 | 1967 | £6 | £12 | Heptones B side |
| I Shall Not Remove | LP | R&B | JBL1112 | 1964 | £50 | £100 | |
| I Shall Not Remove | 7" | Island | WI097 | 1963 | £5 | £10 | |
| I'm The One Who Loves You | 7" | High Note | HS015 | 1969 | £1.50 | £4 | Afrotones B side |
| Lion Of Judah | 7" | R&B | JB108 | 1963 | £5 | £10 | |
| Lover Mouth | 7" | R&B | JB148 | 1964 | £5 | £10 | |
| Mr. Cool Operator | LP | Eji | EJI1001 | 1977 | £5 | £12 | |
| Never Conquer | 7" | Studio One | SO2019 | 1967 | £6 | £12 | |
| Once Upon A Time | 7" | Island | WI3127 | 1967 | £5 | £10 | |
| Pick Up The Pieces | 7" | Island | WI205 | 1965 | £5 | £10 | |
| Prince Pharoah | 7" | R&B | JB128 | 1963 | £5 | £10 | |
| Put Yourself In My Place | 7" | High Note | HS011 | 1968 | £1.50 | £4 | |

| Title | Format | Label | Cat. No. | Year | | | Notes |
|---|---|---|---|---|---|---|---|
| Rain From The Skies | 7" | Studio One | SO2046 | 1968 | £6 | £12 | |
| Riding For A Fall | 7" | Island | WI3033 | 1967 | £5 | £10 | |
| Sad Mood | 7" | Camel | CA15 | 1969 | £1.50 | £4 | Stranger Cole B side |
| Sammy Dead | 7" | R&B | JB168 | 1964 | £5 | £10 | Cynthia & Archie B side |
| Spit In The Sky | 7" | Black Swan | WI405 | 1964 | £5 | £10 | |
| Spit In The Sky | 7" | Blue Beat | BB172 | 1963 | £6 | £12 | |
| This Heart Of Mine | 7" | Island | WI3099 | 1967 | £5 | £10 | Glen Adams B side |
| True Believer | 7" | Coxsone | CS7064 | 1968 | £5 | £10 | Marshall Williams B side |
| Won't You Come Home Baby | 7" | Studio One | SO2009 | 1967 | £6 | £12 | Peter & Hortense B side |
| You Bend My Love | 7" | Island | WI116 | 1963 | £5 | £10 | |
| Your Number One | 7" | High Note | HS022 | 1969 | £1.50 | £4 | |

## WILSON, DENNIS

| Title | Format | Label | Cat. No. | Year | | | Notes |
|---|---|---|---|---|---|---|---|
| Sound Of Free | 7" | Stateside | SS2184 | 1970 | £12.50 | £25 | |

## WILSON, DOYLE

| Title | Format | Label | Cat. No. | Year | | | Notes |
|---|---|---|---|---|---|---|---|
| Hey Hey | 7" | Vogue | V9117 | 1958 | £100 | £200 | best auctioned |

## WILSON, EDDIE

| Title | Format | Label | Cat. No. | Year | | | Notes |
|---|---|---|---|---|---|---|---|
| Get Out On The Street | 7" | Action | ACT4555 | 1969 | £1.50 | £4 | |
| Shing A Ling A Stroll | 7" | Action | ACT4536 | 1969 | £2.50 | £6 | |

## WILSON, EDITH

| Title | Format | Label | Cat. No. | Year | | | Notes |
|---|---|---|---|---|---|---|---|
| With Johnny Dunn's Jazzhounds | LP | Fountain | FB302 | 196– | £6 | £15 | |

## WILSON, ERNEST

| Title | Format | Label | Cat. No. | Year | | | Notes |
|---|---|---|---|---|---|---|---|
| If I Were A Carpenter | 7" | Studio One | SO2058 | 1968 | £6 | £12 | Soul Vendors B side |
| Money Worries | 7" | Studio One | SO2032 | 1967 | £6 | £12 | Soul Vendors B side |
| Storybook Children | 7" | Coxsone | CS7044 | 1968 | £5 | £10 | Little Freddie B side |
| Undying Love | 7" | Coxsone | CS7059 | 1968 | £5 | £10 | Soul Vendors B side |

## WILSON, FRANK

| Title | Format | Label | Cat. No. | Year | | | Notes |
|---|---|---|---|---|---|---|---|
| Last Kiss | LP | Josie | JS4006 | 1964 | £8 | £20 | US |
| Last Kiss | 7" | Fontana | TF505 | 1964 | £2 | £5 | |

## WILSON, FRANK (2)

| Title | Format | Label | Cat. No. | Year | | | Notes |
|---|---|---|---|---|---|---|---|
| Do I Love You | 7" | Motown | TMG1170 | 1979 | £10 | £20 | demo, picture sleeve |

## WILSON, JACK

| Title | Format | Label | Cat. No. | Year | | | Notes |
|---|---|---|---|---|---|---|---|
| Easterly Winds | LP | Blue Note | BST84270 | 1968 | £15 | £30 | |
| Jack Wilson Quartet | LP | London | HAK/SHK8170 | 1964 | £6 | £15 | |
| Something Personal | LP | Blue Note | BLP/BST84251 | 1967 | £10 | £25 | |
| Song For My Daughter | LP | Blue Note | BST84328 | 1969 | £5 | £12 | |

## WILSON, JACKIE

The dynamic singer with big hits in four decades (the *tour de force* vocal gymnastics of 'Reet Petite' in the fifties; 'Higher And Higher' in the sixties; 'I Get The Sweetest Feeling' in the seventies; and a reissued 'Reet Petite' in the eighties – when a memorable animated video helped propel the song to number one in the UK) is sadly perhaps best remembered for having died in 1984 after spending nearly nine years in a coma. Apart from some of his joyous performances, he should be remembered as the man who indirectly got the Tamla Motown company going. For Wilson's earliest hits were written by the young Berry Gordy, who was able to use the resulting windfall to start his own label.

| Title | Format | Label | Cat. No. | Year | | | Notes |
|---|---|---|---|---|---|---|---|
| All My Love | 7" | Coral | Q72407 | 1960 | £2 | £5 | |
| Alone At Last | 7" | Coral | Q72412 | 1960 | £2 | £5 | |
| At The Copa | LP | Coral | LVA9209 | 1962 | £10 | £25 | mono |
| At The Copa | LP | Coral | SVL9209 | 1962 | £15 | £30 | stereo |
| Baby Workout | LP | Brunswick | BL(7)54110 | 1963 | £10 | £25 | US |
| Baby Workout | 7" | Coral | Q72460 | 1963 | £2 | £5 | |
| Big Boss Line | 7" | Coral | Q72474 | 1964 | £2 | £5 | |
| Body And Soul | LP | Coral | LVA9202 | 1962 | £10 | £25 | |
| By Special Request | LP | Coral | LVA9151 | 1962 | £20 | £40 | mono |
| By Special Request | LP | Coral | SVL3018 | 1962 | £25 | £50 | stereo |
| Do Your Thing | LP | MCA | MUPS405 | 1970 | £6 | £15 | |
| Dogging Around | 7" | Coral | Q72393 | 1960 | £2.50 | £6 | |
| Dynamic Jackie Wilson | 7" EP | Coral | FEP2043 | 1960 | £20 | £40 | tri-centre |
| For Your Precious Love | 7" | Decca | AD1008 | 1968 | £4 | £8 | export |
| Greatest Hurt | 7" | Coral | Q72450 | 1962 | £2 | £5 | |
| He's So Fine | LP | Coral | LVA9087 | 1958 | £37.50 | £75 | |
| Higher And Higher | LP | MCA | MUP(S)304 | 1967 | £4 | £10 | |
| Higher And Higher | 7" | Coral | Q72493 | 1967 | £2.50 | £6 | |
| I Get The Sweetest Feeling | LP | MCA | MUPS361 | 1969 | £4 | £10 | |
| I Just Can't Help It | 7" | Coral | Q72454 | 1962 | £2 | £5 | |
| I'll Be Satisfied | 7" | Coral | Q72372 | 1959 | £2.50 | £6 | |
| I'm Comin' On Back To You | 7" | Coral | Q72434 | 1961 | £2 | £5 | |
| I'm Wandering | 7" | Coral | Q72332 | 1958 | £4 | £8 | |
| Jackie Sings The Blues | LP | Coral | LVA9130 | 1960 | £30 | £60 | |
| Lonely Teardrops | LP | Coral | LVA9108 | 1959 | £37.50 | £75 | |
| Lonely Teardrops | 7" EP | Coral | FEP2016 | 1959 | £25 | £50 | tri-centre |
| Lonely Teardrops | 7" | Coral | Q72347 | 1958 | £5 | £10 | |
| Lonely Teardrops | 7" | Coral | Q72482 | 1965 | £2.50 | £6 | |
| Merry Christmas | LP | Brunswick | BL(7)54112 | 1963 | £10 | £25 | US |
| My Golden Favorites Vol. 2 | LP | Brunswick | BL(7)54115 | 1964 | £10 | £25 | US |
| My Golden Favourites | LP | Coral | LVA9135 | 1960 | £20 | £40 | |
| My Heart Belongs To Only You | 7" | Coral | Q72444 | 1961 | £2 | £5 | |

| | | | | | | | |
|---|---|---|---|---|---|---|---|
| New Breed | 7" | Coral | Q72467 | 1963 | £2 | £5 | |
| No Pity In The Naked City | 7" | Coral | Q72481 | 1965 | £2.50 | £6 | |
| Please Tell Me Why | 7" | Coral | Q72430 | 1961 | £2 | £5 | |
| Reet Petite | 7" | Coral | Q72290 | 1957 | £2.50 | £6 | |
| Reet Petite | 7" | Vogue Coral | Q72290 | 1957 | £6 | £12 | |
| Shake A Hand | LP | Brunswick | BL(7)54113 | 1963 | £10 | £25 | US |
| Shake A Hand | 7" | Coral | Q72464 | 1963 | £2 | £5 | .. with Linda Hopkins |
| Shake Shake Shake | 7" | Coral | Q72465 | 1963 | £2 | £5 | |
| Since You Showed Me How To Be Happy | 7" | Coral | Q72496 | 1967 | £4 | £8 | |
| Sing | 7" | Coral | Q72453 | 1962 | £2 | £5 | |
| So Much | LP | Coral | LVA9121 | 1960 | £25 | £50 | |
| Somethin' Else | LP | Brunswick | BL(7)54117 | 1964 | £10 | £25 | US |
| Soul Galore | LP | Coral | LVA9232 | 1966 | £10 | £25 | mono |
| Soul Galore | LP | Coral | SVL9232 | 1966 | £15 | £30 | stereo |
| Soul Time | LP | Brunswick | BL(7)54118 | 1965 | £10 | £25 | US |
| Spotlight On Jackie Wilson | LP | Coral | LVA9231 | 1965 | £10 | £25 | |
| Squeeze Her, Tease Her | 7" | Coral | Q72476 | 1964 | £2 | £5 | |
| Talk That Talk | 7" | Coral | Q72384 | 1959 | £2.50 | £6 | |
| Tear Of The Year | 7" | Coral | Q72421 | 1961 | £7.50 | £15 | demo |
| Tear Of The Year | 7" | Coral | Q72424 | 1961 | £2 | £5 | |
| Tenderly | 7" | Ember | JBS705 | 1962 | £75 | £150 | Clyde McPhatter B side |
| That's Why | 7" | Coral | Q72366 | 1959 | £2.50 | £6 | |
| To Be Loved | 7" | Coral | Q72306 | 1958 | £4 | £8 | |
| To Make A Big Man Cry | 7" | Coral | Q72484 | 1966 | £2.50 | £6 | |
| We Have Love | 7" | Coral | Q72338 | 1958 | £4 | £8 | |
| Whispers | LP | Coral | LVA9235 | 1967 | £10 | £25 | |
| Whispers Gettin' Louder | 7" | Coral | Q72487 | 1966 | £2.50 | £6 | |
| Woman, A Lover, A Friend | LP | Coral | LVA9144 | 1961 | £25 | £50 | |
| World's Greatest Melodies | LP | Coral | LVA9214 | 1962 | £10 | £25 | mono |
| World's Greatest Melodies | LP | Coral | SVL9214 | 1962 | £15 | £30 | stereo |
| Years From Now | 7" | Coral | Q72439 | 1961 | £2 | £5 | |
| Yes Indeed | 7" | Coral | Q72480 | 1965 | £2 | £5 | |
| You Ain't Heard Nothing Yet | LP | Coral | LVA9148 | 1961 | £20 | £40 | |
| You Better Know | 7" | Coral | Q72380 | 1959 | £2 | £5 | |

## WILSON, MARTY & THE STRATOLITES

| | | | | | | |
|---|---|---|---|---|---|---|
| Hey Eula | 7" | Brunswick | 05750 | 1958 | £4 | £8 |

## WILSON, MURRY

At least John Lennon's father only got to make a single: they let the father of the Beach Boys make a whole album! The result consists of light instrumental music that would be of marginal interest were it not for Mr Wilson's superstar connections.

| | | | | | | |
|---|---|---|---|---|---|---|
| Many Moods Of Murry Wilson | LP | Capitol | (S)T2819 | 1967 | £4 | £10 |

## WILSON, NANCY

| | | | | | | |
|---|---|---|---|---|---|---|
| Don't Look Over Your Shoulder | 7" | Capitol | CL15508 | 1967 | £2 | £5 |
| Face It Girl It's Over | 7" | Capitol | CL15547 | 1968 | £7.50 | £15 |
| How Glad I Am | 7" | Capitol | CL15352 | 1964 | £1.50 | £4 |
| Uptight | 7" | Capitol | CL15466 | 1966 | £4 | £8 |
| Where Does That Leave Me | 7" | Capitol | CL15412 | 1965 | £2 | £5 |

## WILSON, PEANUTS

| | | | | | | | |
|---|---|---|---|---|---|---|---|
| Cast Iron Arm | 7" | Coral | Q72302 | 1958 | £150 | £250 | best auctioned |

## WILSON, PHIL

| | | | | | | |
|---|---|---|---|---|---|---|
| Better Days | 7" | Caff | CAFF3 | 1989 | £2.50 | £6 |

## WILSON, REUBEN

| | | | | | | |
|---|---|---|---|---|---|---|
| Blue Mode | LP | Blue Note | BST84343 | 1970 | £4 | £10 |
| Cisco Kid | LP | People | PLEO1 | 1973 | £4 | £10 |
| Got To Get Your Own | 7" | Chess | 6078700 | 1976 | £2.50 | £6 |
| Groovy Situation | LP | Blue Note | BST84365 | 1970 | £4 | £10 |
| I'll Take You There | 7" | People | PEO109 | 1974 | £1.50 | £4 |
| Love Bug | LP | Blue Note | BST84317 | 1969 | £4 | £10 |
| On Broadway | LP | Blue Note | BST84295 | 1968 | £4 | £10 |
| Set Us Free | LP | Blue Note | BST84377 | 1970 | £4 | £10 |
| Sweet Life | LP | People | PLEO20 | 1974 | £4 | £10 |

## WILSON, SMILEY

| | | | | | | |
|---|---|---|---|---|---|---|
| Running Bear | 7" | London | HLG9066 | 1960 | £15 | £30 |

## WILSON, TEDDY

| | | | | | | | |
|---|---|---|---|---|---|---|---|
| For Quiet Lovers | 10" LP | HMV | DLP1162 | 1957 | £10 | £25 | |
| I Got Rhythm | LP | HMV | CLP1230 | 1958 | £8 | £20 | |
| Mr. Wilson And Mr. Gershwin | LP | Philips | BBL7344 | 1960 | £4 | £10 | |
| Newport Jazz Festival 1957 | LP | Columbia | 33CX10107 | 1958 | £6 | £15 | ...with Gerry Mulligan |
| Teddy Wilson | 10" LP | Columbia | 33C9019 | 1956 | £15 | £30 | |
| Teddy Wilson | 10" LP | Columbia | 33S1066 | 1955 | £20 | £40 | |
| Teddy Wilson | 10" LP | Philips | BBR8065 | 1955 | £20 | £40 | |
| Teddy Wilson Orchestra With Billie Holiday | 10" LP | Philips | BBR8061 | 1955 | £20 | £40 | |
| Teddy Wilson Trio | 10" LP | Esquire | 20009 | 1953 | £25 | £50 | |

## WILSON, TONY

| | | | | | | |
|---|---|---|---|---|---|---|
| Tony Wilson | LP | Bearsville | K55513 | 1976 | £10 | £25 |

## WILSON, TREVOR
You Couldn't Believe ................................ 7" ...... Ska Beat .......... JB207 ................... 1965 £5 .......... £10 ...................................

## WILTSHIRE, JOHNNY
If The Shoe Fits ................................................ 7" ...... Oriole ............. CB1494 ................ 1959 £7.50 ... £15 ...................................

## WIMPLE WINCH
The expensive singles recorded by Wimple Winch are over-rated, third-division examples of the genre that has come to be called 'freakbeat'. The newly invented fuzzbox – ubiquitous on British beat records from 1966 – 7 – is much in evidence, as are the influences from the Yardbirds, the Who, and the other true innovators of the time. The group evolved out of Just Four Men, whose singles are also very collectable, but which have even less relevance to the creative mainstream.

Rumble On Mersey Square South ............. 7" ...... Fontana .......... TF781 ................... 1967 £50 ....... £100 ...................................
Rumble On Mersey Square South/ ........... 7" ...... Fontana .......... TF781 ................... 1967 £210 ..... £350 ............ best auctioned
   Atmospheres ...............................................
Save My Soul .............................................. 7" ...... Fontana .......... TF718 ................... 1966 £50 ....... £100 ...................................
What's Been Done ...................................... 7" ...... Fontana .......... TF686 ................... 1966 £50 ....... £100 ...................................

## WINCHESTER, JESSE
Jesse Winchester ......................................... LP ...... Ampex ............. A10104 ................. 1970 £4 .......... £10 ................... US

## WIND
Morning ...................................................... LP ...... CBS ................. 65007 ................... 1972 £30 ......... £60 ............... German
Seasons ....................................................... LP ...... Plus ................. 3 .......................... 1971 £30 ......... £60 ............... German

## WIND IN THE WILLOWS
Lead singer with the Wind in the Willows was Debbie Harry. The folky music played by the group is as different from that of Blondie as is Debbie Harry's own hippy appearance from that of the blonde bombshell she decided to become.

Moments Spent ........................................... 7" ...... Capitol ............ CL15561 ................ 1968 £5 .......... £10 ...................................
Wind In The Willows ................................. LP ...... Capitol ............ SKAO2956 ............. 1968 £15 ......... £30 ............ US, gatefold

## WINDING, KAI
Comin' Home Baby ...................................... 7" ...... Verve ............... VS512 ................... 1965 £1.50 ...... £4 ...................................
East Coast Jazz No. 7 ................................... LP ...... London ............. LTZN15003 .......... 1956 £8 .......... £20 ...................................
Swingin' States ........................................... LP ...... Philips ............. BBL7316/SBBL509. 1959 £8 .......... £20 ...................................
Trombone Panorama .................................... LP ...... Philips ............. BBL7275 ............... 1959 £8 .......... £20 ...................................
Trombone Sound .......................................... LP ...... Philips ............. BBL7150 ............... 1957 £8 .......... £20 ...................................

## WINE OF LEBANON
Wine Of Lebanon ........................................ LP ...... Dovetail .......... DOVE46 ................ 1976 £15 ......... £30 ...................................

## WINSOR, MARTIN & REDD SULLIVAN
Hosts Of The Troubadour ............................ LP ...... Deacon ............ DEA1045 ............... 1971 £4 .......... £10 ...................................

## WINSTON, JIMMY & HIS REFLECTIONS
Jimmy Winston was the original organist with the Small Faces and plays on their first single. His own singles, however, recorded as Winston's Fumbs and as Jimmy Winston and His Reflections, were not at all successful.

Sorry She's Mine ......................................... 7" ...... Decca ............... F12410 ................... 1966 £50 ....... £100 ...................................

## WINSTON & ERROL
Fay Is Gone ................................................. 7" ...... Blue Beat ........ BB272 ................... 1964 £6 ........... £12 ...................................

## WINSTON & GEORGE
Keep The Pressure On .................................. 7" ...... Pyramid .......... PYR6002 ............... 1966 £4 ............ £8 ...................................

## WINSTON & PAT
Pony Ride ................................................... 7" ...... Trojan .............. TR605 ................... 1968 £1.50 ...... £4 ...................................

## WINSTON & ROY
Babylon Gone .............................................. 7" ...... Blue Beat ........ BB80 .................... 1962 £6 ........... £12 ...................................

## WINSTONE, ERIC
Dr. Who Theme ........................................... 7" ...... Pye ................... 7N15603 ................ 1964 £2 ............. £5 ...................................

## WINSTONE, NORMA
Edge Of Time .............................................. LP ...... Argo ................ ZDA148 ................. 1971 £25 ......... £50 ...................................
Let's Make Love .......................................... LP ...... BBC ................ TSRP7568 ............. 197– £10 ......... £25 ...................................
   Radioplay ........

## WINSTONS
Colour Him Father ...................................... 7" ...... Pye ................... 7N25493 ................ 1969 £2 ............. £5 ...................................

## WINSTON'S FUMBS
Real Crazy Appartment ................................ 7" ...... RCA ................ RCA1612 ............... 1967 £100 ..... £200 ...................................

## WINTER, JOHNNY
First Winter ................................................ LP ...... Buddah ............ 2359011 ................ 1970 £4 .......... £10 ...................................
John Dawson Winter III .............................. LP ...... Blue Sky .......... PZQ33292 ............ 1974 £4 .......... £10 ............ US quad
Johnny Winter ............................................ LP ...... CBS ................. 63619 ................... 1969 £4 .......... £10 ...................................
Johnny Winter And ..................................... LP ...... CBS ................. 64117 ................... 1971 £4 .......... £10 ...................................
Johnny Winter And Live .............................. LP ...... CBS ................. 64289 ................... 1971 £4 .......... £10 ...................................
Johnny Winter And/Live .............................. LP ...... Columbia ......... CG33651 ............... 1971 £6 .......... £15 ............ US double
Progressive Blues Experiment ....................... LP ...... Liberty ............ LBS83240 .............. 1969 £4 .......... £10 ...................................
Saints And Sinners ....................................... LP ...... Columbia ........ CQ32715 ............... 1974 £4 .......... £10 ............ US quad

| Title | Format | Label | Catalogue | Year | | | Notes |
|---|---|---|---|---|---|---|---|
| Second Winter | LP | CBS | 66231 | 1970 | £5 | £12 | 3 sides |
| Still Alive And Well | LP | Columbia | CQ32188 | 1973 | £4 | £10 | US quad |

## WINTER, PAUL
| | | | | | | | |
|---|---|---|---|---|---|---|---|
| Winter Consort | LP | A&M | AMLS942 | 1969 | £4 | £10 | |

## WINTERHALTER, HUGO ORCHESTRA
| | | | | | | | |
|---|---|---|---|---|---|---|---|
| Canadian Sunset | 7" | HMV | POP241 | 1956 | £1.50 | £4 | |

## WINTERS, DON
| | | | | | | | |
|---|---|---|---|---|---|---|---|
| Someday Baby | 7" | Brunswick | 05827 | 1960 | £4 | £8 | |

## WINTERS, LIZ & BOB CORT
| | | | | | | | |
|---|---|---|---|---|---|---|---|
| Liz Winters & Bob Cort | 7" EP | Decca | DFE6409 | 1957 | £5 | £10 | |
| Love Is Strange | 7" | Decca | F10878 | 1957 | £4 | £8 | |
| Maggie May | 7" | Decca | F10899 | 1957 | £2.50 | £6 | |

## WINTERS, LOIS
| | | | | | | | |
|---|---|---|---|---|---|---|---|
| Japanese Farewell Song | 7" | London | HLD8266 | 1956 | £6 | £12 | |

## WINTERS, MIKE & BERNIE
| | | | | | | | |
|---|---|---|---|---|---|---|---|
| How Do You Do? | 7" | Parlophone | R4384 | 1957 | £2.50 | £6 | |

## WINTERS, RUBY
| | | | | | | | |
|---|---|---|---|---|---|---|---|
| Baby Lay Down | 7" | Creole | CR171 | 1979 | £1.50 | £4 | |
| Back To Love | 7" | Creole | CR174 | 1979 | £1.50 | £4 | |
| I Want Action | 7" | Stateside | SS2090 | 1968 | £2.50 | £6 | |

## WINWOOD, STEVE
| | | | | | | | |
|---|---|---|---|---|---|---|---|
| Arc Of A Diver | CD | Mobile Fidelity | UDCD579 | 1993 | £6 | £15 | US audiophile |
| Back In The High Life | CD | Mobile Fidelity | UDCD611 | 1994 | £6 | £15 | US audiophile |
| Conversation With Steve Winwood | LP | Island | SWCLP1 | 1986 | £5 | £12 | promo |
| Don't You Know What The Night Can Do? | CD-s | Virgin | VSCD1107 | 1988 | £2 | £5 | |
| Holding On | CD-s | Virgin | VSCD1135 | 1988 | £2 | £5 | |
| One And Only Man | CD-s | Virgin | VSCDT1299 | 1990 | £2 | £5 | |
| Refugee Of The Heart | CD | Virgin | | 1990 | £8 | £20 | US gold promo in black velvet bag |
| Roll With It | CD-s | Virgin | VSCD1085 | 1988 | £2 | £5 | |
| Roll With It | CD | Virgin | CDV2532 | 1988 | £6 | £15 | Virgin Megastore 1st day issue, red inner tray |
| Roll With It | CD | Virgin | CDVP2532 | 1988 | £5 | £12 | picture disc |
| Time Is Running Out | 12" | Island | | 1977 | £2.50 | £6 | promo, no picture sleeve |
| Valerie | CD-s | Island | CID336 | 1987 | £2 | £5 | |
| Winwood | LP | United Artists | UAS9950 | 1971 | £4 | £10 | US, with booklet |

## WIRE
| | | | | | | | |
|---|---|---|---|---|---|---|---|
| 154 | LP | Harvest | SHSP4105 | 1979 | £4 | £10 | with 7" (PSR444) |
| Document And Eyewitness | LP | Rough Trade | ROUGH29 | 1984 | £4 | £10 | with 12" (ROUGH2912) |
| Dot Dash | 7" | Harvest | HAR5161 | 1978 | £2 | £5 | picture sleeve |
| Eardrum Buzz | CD-s | Mute | CDMUTE87 | 1989 | £2 | £5 | |
| Eardrum Buzz | 7" | Mute | MUTE87 | 1989 | £4 | £8 | picture sleeve, clear vinyl |
| I Am The Fly | 7" | Harvest | HAR5151 | 1978 | £2 | £5 | picture sleeve |
| In Vivo | CD-s | Mute | CDMUTE98 | 1989 | £2 | £5 | |
| Mannequin | 7" | Harvest | HAR5144 | 1977 | £4 | £8 | picture sleeve |
| Outdoor Miner | 7" | Harvest | HAR5172 | 1979 | £2 | £5 | picture sleeve, white vinyl |
| Question Of Degree | 7" | Harvest | HAR5187 | 1979 | £2 | £5 | picture sleeve |

## WIRELESS
| | | | | | | | |
|---|---|---|---|---|---|---|---|
| No Static | LP | Anthem | ANR11025 | 1980 | £10 | £25 | Canadian |

## WIRTZ, MARK
| | | | | | | | |
|---|---|---|---|---|---|---|---|
| He's Our Dear Old Weatherman | 7" | Parlophone | R5668 | 1968 | £5 | £10 | |
| Mrs. Raven | 7" | Parlophone | R5683 | 1968 | £1.50 | £4 | |

## WISDOM, NORMAN
| | | | | | | | |
|---|---|---|---|---|---|---|---|
| Follow A Star | 7" | Top Rank | JAR246 | 1959 | £1.50 | £4 | |
| Narcissus | 7" | Columbia | SCD2160 | 1961 | £2 | £5 | |
| Norman And Ruby | 7" EP | Columbia | SEG7687 | 1957 | £2 | £5 | with Ruby Murray |
| Norman Wisdom | 7" EP | Columbia | SEG7612 | 1956 | £2.50 | £6 | |
| Two Rivers | 7" | Columbia | SCM5222 | 1956 | £2.50 | £6 | |
| Up In The World | 7" | Columbia | DB3864 | 1957 | £1.50 | £4 | |
| Where's Charly? | LP | Columbia | 33SX1085 | 1958 | £4 | £10 | |
| Wisdom Of A Fool | 7" | Columbia | DB3903 | 1957 | £2 | £5 | |

## WISE BOYS
| | | | | | | | |
|---|---|---|---|---|---|---|---|
| Why Why Why | 7" | Parlophone | R4693 | 1960 | £2 | £5 | |

## WISE GUYS
| | | | | | | | |
|---|---|---|---|---|---|---|---|
| Big Noise | 7" | Top Rank | JAR271 | 1960 | £4 | £8 | |

## WISEMAN, MAC
| | | | | | | | |
|---|---|---|---|---|---|---|---|
| Beside The Still Waters | LP | Dot | DLP3135/ | 1959 | £8 | £20 | US |

| | | | | | | | |
|---|---|---|---|---|---|---|---|
| | | | DLP25135 | | | | |
| Fireball Mail | LP | Dot | DLP3408 | 1961 | £**8** | £**20** | *US* |
| Fireball Mail | 7" | London | HLD8259 | 1956 | £**20** | £**40** | |
| Great Folk Ballads | LP | London | HAD2217 | 1960 | £**15** | £**30** | |
| Jimmy Brown The Newsboy | 7" | London | HL7084 | 1959 | £**10** | £**20** | *export* |
| Keep On The Sunny Side | LP | Dot | DLP3336 | 1960 | £**8** | £**20** | *US* |
| Kentuckian Song | 7" | London | HLD8174 | 1955 | £**20** | £**40** | |
| My Little Home In Tennessee | 7" | London | HLD8226 | 1956 | £**15** | £**30** | |
| Songs From The Hills | 7" EP | London | RED1056 | 1956 | £**7.50** | £**15** | |
| Songs From The Hills | 10" LP | London | HBD1052 | 1956 | £**15** | £**30** | |
| Songs From The Hills Vol. 2 | 7" EP | London | RED1147 | 1958 | £**7.50** | £**15** | |
| Songs From The Hills Vol. 3 | 7" EP | London | RED1242 | 1960 | £**7.50** | £**15** | |
| Step It Up And Go | 7" | London | HLD8412 | 1957 | £**150** | £**250** | *best auctioned* |
| Tis Sweet To Be Remembered | LP | Dot | DLP3084 | 1958 | £**8** | £**20** | *US* |

## WISHART, TREVOR

| | | | | | | | |
|---|---|---|---|---|---|---|---|
| Journey Into Space Parts One And Two | LP | private | YU3-6 | 1973 | £**50** | £**100** | *double* |

## WISHBONE ASH

| | | | | | | | |
|---|---|---|---|---|---|---|---|
| Evening Program With Wishbone Ash | LP | Decca | | 1972 | £**5** | £**12** | *US promo* |
| Live Dates Vol. 2 | LP | MCA | MCG4012 | 1980 | £**5** | £**12** | *with bonus LP* |
| Live From Memphis | LP | MCA | L331922 | 1974 | £**8** | £**20** | *US promo* |
| Pilgrimage | LP | MCA | MDKS8004 | 1971 | £**4** | £**10** | |
| Raw To The Bone | LP | Neat | NEAT1027 | 1985 | £**5** | £**12** | |
| Raw To The Bone | LP | Neat | NEATP1027 | 1985 | £**10** | £**25** | *picture disc* |
| Wishbone Ash | LP | MCA | MKPS2014 | 1970 | £**4** | £**10** | |

## WISHFUL THINKING

| | | | | | | | |
|---|---|---|---|---|---|---|---|
| Alone | 7" | Decca | F22742 | 1968 | £**1.50** | £**4** | |
| Hiroshima | LP | B&C | CAS1038 | 1971 | £**6** | £**15** | |
| Live Vol. 1 | LP | Decca | SKL4900 | 1967 | £**8** | £**20** | |
| Meet The Sun | 7" | Decca | F22673 | 1967 | £**1.50** | £**4** | |
| Turning Round | 7" | Decca | F12438 | 1966 | £**1.50** | £**4** | |

## WITCHFINDER GENERAL

| | | | | | | | |
|---|---|---|---|---|---|---|---|
| Burning A Sinner | 7" | Heavy Metal | HEAVY6 | 1981 | £**2** | £**5** | |
| Music | 7" | Heavy Metal | HEAVY21 | 1983 | £**1.50** | £**4** | |
| Music | 7" | Heavy Metal | HMPD21 | 1983 | £**2** | £**5** | *picture disc* |
| Soviet Invasion | 12" | Heavy Metal | 12HM17 | 1982 | £**4** | £**10** | |

## WITCHFYNDE

| | | | | | | | |
|---|---|---|---|---|---|---|---|
| I'd Rather Go Wild | 7" | Expulsion | OUT3 | 1983 | £**4** | £**8** | |

## WITHERS, BILL

| | | | | | | | |
|---|---|---|---|---|---|---|---|
| Ain't No Sunshine | CD-s | CBS | 6531982 | 1988 | £**2** | £**5** | |
| Live At Carnegie Hall | LP | A&M | AMLD3001 | 1973 | £**5** | £**12** | *double* |
| Lovely Day | CD-s | CBS | 6530012 | 1988 | £**2** | £**5** | |

## WITHERSPOON, JIMMY

| | | | | | | | |
|---|---|---|---|---|---|---|---|
| All That's Good | 7" | Vogue | V2420 | 1964 | £**12.50** | £**25** | |
| At The Monterey Jazz Festival | LP | Hi Fi | 421 | 1959 | £**8** | £**20** | *US* |
| At The Renaissance | LP | Vogue | LAE12253 | 1961 | £**5** | £**12** | |
| Back Door Blues | LP | Polydor | 623256 | 1969 | £**4** | £**10** | |
| Blue Point Of View | LP | Verve | (S)VLP9156 | 1967 | £**4** | £**10** | |
| Blue Spoon | LP | Stateside | SL10139 | 1965 | £**6** | £**15** | |
| Blues Around The Clock | LP | Stateside | SL10105 | 1965 | £**8** | £**20** | |
| Blues For Easy Livers | LP | Transatlantic | PR7475 | 1968 | £**4** | £**10** | |
| Blues Is Now | LP | Verve | (S)VLP9181 | 1968 | £**5** | £**12** | *with Brother Jack McDuff* |
| Blues Singer | LP | Stateside | (S)SL10289 | 1969 | £**4** | £**10** | |
| Come And Walk With Me | 7" | Stateside | SS429 | 1965 | £**2.50** | £**6** | |
| Evenin' Blues | LP | Stateside | SL10088 | 1964 | £**6** | £**15** | |
| Evenin' Blues | LP | Transatlantic | PR7300 | 1967 | £**4** | £**10** | |
| Falling By Degrees | 78 | Vogue | V2261 | 1955 | £**6** | £**12** | |
| Feelin' The Spirit | LP | Hi Fi | 422 | 1959 | £**8** | £**20** | *US* |
| Feeling The Spirit Vol. 1 | 7" EP | Vocalion | VEH170158 | 1964 | £**6** | £**12** | |
| Feeling The Spirit Vol. 2 | 7" EP | Vocalion | VEH170159 | 1964 | £**6** | £**12** | |
| Goin' To Kansas City Blues | LP | RCA | LPM1639 | 1958 | £**8** | £**20** | *US* |
| Hey Mrs. Jones | LP | Reprise | R(9)6012 | 1962 | £**6** | £**15** | *US* |
| Highway To Happiness | 7" | Parlophone | MSP6125 | 1954 | £**15** | £**30** | |
| I Done Told You | 7" | Parlophone | MSP6142 | 1954 | £**15** | £**30** | |
| I Never Will Marry | 7" | Stateside | SS325 | 1964 | £**2.50** | £**6** | |
| If There Wasn't Any You | 7" | Stateside | SS503 | 1966 | £**2.50** | £**6** | |
| In Person | LP | Vogue | VRL3005 | 1965 | £**6** | £**15** | |
| It's All Over But The Crying | 7" | Verve | VS538 | 1966 | £**1.50** | £**4** | |
| Jimmy Witherspoon | LP | Ember | EMB3369 | 1966 | £**4** | £**10** | |
| Jimmy Witherspoon | 7" EP | Vocalion | EPVH1278 | 1964 | £**6** | £**12** | |
| Jimmy Witherspoon At Monterey No. 1 | 7" EP | Vocalion | EPV1269 | 1962 | £**10** | £**20** | |
| Jimmy Witherspoon At Monterey No. 2 | 7" EP | Vocalion | EPV1270 | 1962 | £**10** | £**20** | |
| Jump Children | 78 | Vogue | V2356 | 1956 | £**6** | £**12** | |
| Live | LP | Stateside | (S)SL10232 | 1968 | £**6** | £**15** | |
| Love Me Right | 7" | Stateside | SS461 | 1965 | £**2.50** | £**6** | |
| Money Is Getting Cheaper | 7" | Stateside | SS304 | 1964 | £**2.50** | £**6** | |
| New Orleans Blues | LP | Atlantic | 1266 | 1956 | £**15** | £**30** | *US* |
| New Orleans Blues | LP | London | LTZK15150 | 1959 | £**6** | £**15** | |
| No Rolling Blues | 7" | Vogue | V2060 | 1956 | £**12.50** | £**25** | |
| Outskirts Of Town | 7" EP | Vocalion | EPVH1284 | 1965 | £**6** | £**12** | |
| Rhythm & Blues Concert | 7" EP | Vogue | EPV1198 | 1958 | £**15** | £**30** | *with Helen Humes* |

| | | | | | | | |
|---|---|---|---|---|---|---|---|
| Roots | LP | Reprise | R(9)6059 | 1962 | £6 | £15 | US |
| Singin' The Blues | LP | Vogue | LAE12218 | 1960 | £5 | £12 | |
| Some Of My Best Friends Are The Blues | LP | Stateside | SL10114 | 1965 | £8 | £20 | |
| Some Of My Best Friends Are The Blues | LP | Transatlantic | PR7356 | 1968 | £4 | £10 | |
| Spoon | LP | Reprise | R(9)2008 | 1961 | £6 | £15 | US |
| Spoon In London | LP | Transatlantic | PR7418 | 1968 | £4 | £10 | |
| Spoon Sings And Swings | LP | Fontana | (S)TL5382 | 1967 | £8 | £20 | |
| Spoonful Of Soul | LP | Verve | (S)VLP9216 | 1968 | £4 | £10 | |
| Take This Hammer | LP | Constellation | M1422 | 1964 | £6 | £15 | US |
| There's Good Rockin' Tonight | LP | Fontana | 688005ZL | 1965 | £4 | £10 | |
| Who's Been Jivin' With You | 78 | Vogue | V2295 | 1954 | £5 | £12 | |
| You're Next | 7" | Stateside | SS362 | 1964 | £2.50 | £6 | |

## WITTHUSER & WESTRUPP

| | | | | | | | |
|---|---|---|---|---|---|---|---|
| Bauer Plath | LP | Pilz | 20291154 | 1972 | £6 | £15 | German |
| Der Jesuspilz | LP | Pilz | 20210987 | 1971 | £6 | £15 | German |
| Lieder Von Vampiren, Nonnen Und Toten | LP | Ohr | OMM56002 | 1970 | £8 | £20 | German |
| Live 68–73 | LP | Komische | KM258004 | 1973 | £8 | £20 | German double |
| Trips Und Träume | LP | Ohr | OMM56016 | 1971 | £6 | £15 | German |

## WIZARD

| | | | | | | | |
|---|---|---|---|---|---|---|---|
| Original Wizard | LP | Peon | 1069 | 1971 | £100 | £200 | US |

## WIZARDS FROM KANSAS

| | | | | | | | |
|---|---|---|---|---|---|---|---|
| Wizards From Kansas | LP | Mercury | SR61309 | 1970 | £37.50 | £75 | US |

## WIZZARD

| | | | | | | | |
|---|---|---|---|---|---|---|---|
| I Wish It Could Be Christmas Every Day | 7" | Warner Bros | K16336 | 1973 | £2.50 | £6 | ..gatefold picture sleeve |

## WOLF

| | | | | | | | |
|---|---|---|---|---|---|---|---|
| Head Contact | 12" | Chrysalis | CHS122592 | 1982 | £3 | £8 | |

## WOLFE, CHARLES

| | | | | | | | |
|---|---|---|---|---|---|---|---|
| Dance Dance Dance | 7" | NEMS | 563675 | 1968 | £1.50 | £4 | |

## WOLFETONES

| | | | | | | | |
|---|---|---|---|---|---|---|---|
| Across The Broad Atlantic | LP | Triskel | TRL1002 | 1976 | £4 | £10 | Irish |
| Belt Of The Celts | LP | Triskel | TRL1003 | 1978 | £4 | £10 | Irish |
| Foggy Dew | LP | Fontana | | 196– | £6 | £15 | |
| Irish To The Core | LP | Triskel | TRL1001 | 1976 | £4 | £10 | Irish |
| Let The People Sing | LP | Dolphin | DOL1004 | 1972 | £4 | £10 | Irish |
| Live Alive Oh! | LP | Triskel | TRL1005 | 1980 | £5 | £12 | Irish double |
| Rifles Of The I.R.A. | LP | Dolphin | DOL1002 | 1976 | £4 | £10 | Irish |
| Rights Of Man | LP | Fontana | STL5462 | 1968 | £6 | £15 | |
| Teddy Bear's Head | LP | Dolphin | DOLM5005 | 1976 | £4 | £10 | Irish |
| Till Ireland's A Nation | LP | Dolphin | DOL1006 | 1974 | £4 | £10 | Irish |
| Up The Rebels | LP | Dolphin | DOLM5003 | 1976 | £4 | £10 | Irish |
| Up The Rebels | LP | Fontana | | 196– | £6 | £15 | |

## WOLFF, HENRY & NANCY HENNINGS

| | | | | | | | |
|---|---|---|---|---|---|---|---|
| Tibetan Bells | LP | Island | HELP3 | 1972 | £4 | £10 | |

## WOLFGANG PRESS

| | | | | | | | |
|---|---|---|---|---|---|---|---|
| King Of Soul | CD-s | 4AD | BAD804CD | 1988 | £2 | £5 | |
| Raintime | CD-s | 4AD | BAD907CD | 1989 | £2 | £5 | |
| Scarecrow | 12" | 4AD | BAD409 | 1984 | £3 | £8 | |
| Water | 12" | 4AD | BAD502 | 1985 | £2.50 | £6 | |

## WOLFMAN JACK

| | | | | | | | |
|---|---|---|---|---|---|---|---|
| And The Wolf Pack | LP | Bread | BD0170 | 1963 | £15 | £30 | US |
| Fun And Romance | LP | Columbia | KC33501 | 1975 | £5 | £12 | US |

## WOLFRILLA

| | | | | | | | |
|---|---|---|---|---|---|---|---|
| Song For Jimi | 7" | Concord | CON015 | 1970 | £4 | £8 | |

## WOLVENLEI

| | | | | | | | |
|---|---|---|---|---|---|---|---|
| Wolvenlei | LP | Spoof | | 1978 | £10 | £25 | Dutch |

## WOLVES

| | | | | | | | |
|---|---|---|---|---|---|---|---|
| At The Club | 7" | Pye | 7N17013 | 1965 | £5 | £10 | |
| Journey Into Dreams | 7" | Pye | 7N15676 | 1964 | £2 | £5 | |
| Lust For Life | 7" | Parlophone | R5511 | 1966 | £20 | £40 | |
| Now | 7" | Pye | 7N15733 | 1964 | £7.50 | £15 | |

## WOMACK, BOBBY

| | | | | | | | |
|---|---|---|---|---|---|---|---|
| Across 110th Street | LP | United Artists | UAS29451 | 1973 | £4 | £10 | |
| Broadway Talk | 7" | Minit | MLF11001 | 1968 | £4 | £8 | |
| Communication | LP | United Artists | UAS29306 | 1973 | £4 | £10 | |
| Facts Of Life | LP | United Artists | UAG29456 | 1973 | £4 | £10 | |
| I Can Understand It | LP | United Artists | UAS29715 | 1975 | £4 | £10 | |
| I Don't Know What The World Is Coming To | LP | United Artists | UAG29762 | 1975 | £4 | £10 | |
| Lookin' For A Love Again | LP | United Artists | UAS29574 | 1974 | £4 | £10 | |
| Roads Of Life | LP | Arista | ARTY165 | 1979 | £6 | £15 | |
| Safety Zone | LP | United Artists | UAG29907 | 1976 | £4 | £10 | |
| Understanding | LP | United Artists | UAS29365 | 1972 | £4 | £10 | |
| What Is This | 7" | Jayboy | BOY75 | 1974 | £1.50 | £4 | |
| What Is This | 7" | Minit | MLF11005 | 1968 | £2 | £5 | |

## WOMB

| | | | | | | | |
|---|---|---|---|---|---|---|---|
| Overdub | LP | Dot | DLP25959 | 1969 £6 | £15 | | US |
| Womb | LP | Dot | DLP25433 | 1969 £6 | £15 | | US |

## WOMEGA

| | | | | | | |
|---|---|---|---|---|---|---|
| Quick Step | LP | Skruup | 162210751 | 1975 £5 | £12 | Belgian |

## WONDER, STEVIE

| | | | | | | |
|---|---|---|---|---|---|---|
| Blowin' In The Wind | 7" | Tamla Motown | TMG570 | 1966 £4 | £8 | |
| Castles In The Sand | 7" | Stateside | SS285 | 1964 £12.50 | £25 | |
| Down To Earth | LP | Tamla Motown | (S)TML11045 | 1967 £8 | £20 | |
| Eivets Rednow | LP | Gordy | GS932 | 1968 £5 | £12 | US |
| Fingertips | 7" | Oriole | CBA1853500 | 1963 £10 | £20 | |
| For Once In My Life | LP | Tamla Motown | (S)TML11098 | 1969 £4 | £10 | |
| For Once In My Life | 7" | Tamla Motown | TMG679 | 1968 £1.50 | £4 | |
| Hey Harmonica Man | LP | Stateside | SL10108 | 1965 £30 | £60 | |
| Hey Harmonica Man | 7" | Stateside | SS323 | 1964 £10 | £20 | |
| Hi Heel Sneakers | 7" | Tamla Motown | TMG532 | 1965 £6 | £12 | |
| I Call It Pretty Music | 7" EP | Stateside | SE1014 | 1964 £25 | £50 | |
| I Was Made To Love Her | LP | Tamla Motown | (S)TML11059 | 1968 £6 | £15 | |
| I Was Made To Love Her | 7" | Tamla Motown | TMG613 | 1967 £1.50 | £4 | |
| I'm Wondering | 7" | Tamla Motown | TMG626 | 1967 £1.50 | £4 | |
| Innervisions | CD | Mobile Fidelity | UDCD554 | 1991 £6 | £15 | US audiophile |
| Jazz Soul Of Little Stevie | LP | Stateside | SL10078 | 1964 £30 | £60 | |
| Kiss Me Baby | 7" | Tamla Motown | TMG505 | 1965 £7.50 | £15 | |
| Live | LP | Tamla Motown | (S)TML11150 | 1970 £4 | £10 | |
| Live At The Talk Of The Town | LP | Tamla Motown | STML11164 | 1970 £4 | £10 | |
| My Chérie Amour | 7" | Tamla Motown | TMG690 | 1969 £1.50 | £4 | |
| Nothing's Too Good For My Baby | 7" | Tamla Motown | TMG558 | 1966 £7.50 | £15 | |
| Place In The Sun | 7" | Tamla Motown | TMG588 | 1966 £4 | £8 | |
| Shoo-Be-Doo-Be-Doo-Da-Day | 7" | Tamla Motown | TMG653 | 1968 £1.50 | £4 | |
| Someday At Christmas | LP | Tamla Motown | (S)TML11085 | 1969 £8 | £20 | |
| Stevie Wonder | 7" EP | Tamla Motown | TME2006 | 1965 £20 | £40 | ? |
| Talking Book | LP | EMI | 5CP06293880 | 1979 £6 | £15 | Dutch picture disc |
| Talking Book | CD | Motown | C88114 | 1988 £6 | £15 | box set |
| Travelling Man | 7" | Tamla Motown | TMG602 | 1967 £1.50 | £4 | |
| Tribute To Uncle Ray | LP | Oriole | PS40049 | 1963 £37.50 | £75 | |
| Twelve Year Old Genius | LP | Oriole | PS40050 | 1963 £25 | £50 | |
| Uptight | LP | Tamla Motown | (S)TML11036 | 1966 £6 | £15 | |
| Uptight | 7" | Tamla Motown | TMG545 | 1966 £2.50 | £6 | |
| We Can Work It Out | 7" | Tamla Motown | TMG772 | 1971 £4 | £8 | picture sleeve |
| With A Song In My Heart | LP | Tamla | T250 | 1964 £25 | £50 | US |
| Workout Stevie Workout | 7" | Stateside | SS238 | 1963 £12.50 | £25 | |
| Workout Stevie, Workout | LP | Tamla | TS248 | 1963 £25 | £50 | US |
| You Met Your Match | 7" | Tamla Motown | TMG666 | 1968 £1.50 | £4 | |

## WONDER STUFF

| | | | | | | |
|---|---|---|---|---|---|---|
| Circlesquare | CD-s | Polydor | GONCD10 | 1990 £2 | £5 | |
| Don't Let Me Down Gently | CD-s | Polydor | GONECD7 | 1989 £2 | £5 | |
| Eight-Legged Groove Machine | CD | Polydor | GONECD1 | 1988 £8 | £20 | with 'Wish Away' printed on front cover |
| Give Give Give Me More More More | CD-s | Polydor | GONECD3 | 1988 £4 | £10 | |
| Give Give Give Me More More More | CD-s | Polygram | 0805822 | 1989 £4 | £10 | CD video |
| Give Give Give Me More More More | 7" | Polydor | GONE3 | 1988 £2.50 | £6 | |
| Give Give Give Me More More More | 12" | Polydor | GONEX3 | 1988 £4 | £10 | |
| Golden Green | CD-s | Polydor | GONCD8 | 1989 £2 | £5 | |
| It's Yer Money I'm After Baby | CD-s | Polydor | GONCD5 | 1988 £3 | £8 | |
| It's Yer Money I'm After Baby | 12" | Polydor | GONEX5 | 1988 £2.50 | £6 | with inner |
| Unbearable | 7" | Far Out | GONE002 | 1987 £2 | £5 | no picture sleeve |
| Unbearable | 7" | Farout | GONE002 | 1987 £7.50 | £15 | |
| Waffle And Maple Syrup | LP | Polydor | STUFF1 | 198– £8 | £20 | promo |
| Who Wants To Be The Disco King? | CD-s | Polydor | GONECD6 | 1989 £2 | £5 | |
| Who Wants To Be The Disco King? | 12" | Polydor | GONEX6 | 1989 £2.50 | £6 | with inner |
| Wish Away | CD-s | Polydor | GONECD4 | 1988 £3 | £8 | |
| Wish Away | 12" | Polydor | GONEX4 | 1988 £3 | £8 | |
| Wonderful Day | 7" | Farout | GONE ONE | 1987 £25 | £50 | |

## WONDER WHO

The Wonder Who were the Four Seasons, recording under a pseudonym to see if they could still sell records. With a voice as distinctive as Frankie Valli's, however, they did not succeed in fooling anyone for very long.

| | | | | | | |
|---|---|---|---|---|---|---|
| Don't Think Twice It's Alright | 7" | Philips | BF1440 | 1965 £1.50 | £4 | |
| Lonesome Road | 7" | Philips | BF1600 | 1967 £1.50 | £4 | |
| On The Good Ship Lollipop | 7" | Philips | BF1504 | 1966 £1.50 | £4 | |

## WONDERLAND

| | | | | | |
|---|---|---|---|---|---|
| Poochy | 7" | Polydor | 56539 | 1968 £2.50 | £6 |

## WONDERLAND, ALICE

| | | | | | |
|---|---|---|---|---|---|
| He's Mine | 7" | London | HLU9783 | 1963 £1.50 | £4 |

## WONDERLAND BAND

| | | | | | | |
|---|---|---|---|---|---|---|
| Best Of The Wonderland Band | LP | Karussell | 2415078 | 1973 £10 | £25 | German |
| No. 1 | LP | Polydor | 2371125 | 1971 £15 | £30 | German |

## WONG, ROYCE
Everything's Gonna Be Alright ................. 7" ...... Blue Beat ........ BB301 .................... 1965 £6 .......... £12 ..............................

## WOOD, ANITA
Dream Baby ........................................ 7" ...... Sue .............. WI328 ...................... 1964 £5 ........ £10 ..............................
I'll Wait Forever ................................. 7" ...... London ......... HLS9585 ................ 1962 £7.50 ...... £15 ..........................

## WOOD, BOBBY
I'm A Fool For Loving You .................... 7" ...... Pye .............. 7N25264 ................ 1964 £1.50 ...... £4 ..............................

## WOOD, BRENTON
Baby You Got It ................................. LP ..... Double Shot .... 1003/5003 ............. 1967 £4 .......... £10 ...................... US
Gimme Little Sign .............................. LP ..... Liberty ........... LBL/LBS83088E .... 1967 £4 .......... £10 ..........................
Gimme Little Sign .............................. 7" ...... Liberty ........... LBF15021 .............. 1967 £1.50 ...... £4 ..........................

## WOOD, CHUCK
Seven Days Too Long ......................... 7" ...... Transatlantic .... BIG104 ................ 1967 £2 ............ £5 ....................

## WOOD, DEL
Ragtime Annie ................................... 7" ...... London ......... HL8036 ................ 1954 £10 ......... £20 ........................
Ragtime Piano ................................... 7" EP . London ......... REP1007 .............. 1954 £2.50 ....... £6 ........................

## WOOD, ROBERT
Sonabular ......................................... LP ..... Edici ............ ED6103 ............... 1973 £4 .......... £10 .................. French
Tarot And Tombac .............................. LP ..... Edici ............ ED6102 ............... 1972 £5 .......... £12 .................. French
Vibrarock ......................................... LP ..... Polydor ......... 2393137 ............... 1976 £4 .......... £10 .................. French

## WOOD, ROY
Roy Wood Story ................................. LP ..... Harvest ......... SHDW408 ............ 1976 £5 .......... £12 .................. double

## WOOD, ROY & ANNIE HASLAM
I Never Believed In Love ...................... 7" ...... Warner Bros ... K17028 ............... 1977 £1.50 ...... £4 ..............................

## WOOD, ROYSTON & HEATHER
No Relation ....................................... LP ..... Transatlantic .... TRA342 ............... 1977 £25 ......... £50 ..........................

## WOODBINE LIZZIE
By Numbers ...................................... LP ..... Fellside .......... FE019 ................. 1979 £8 .......... £20 ..........................

## WOODEN HORSE
Pick Up The Pieces ............................. 7" ...... York .............. SYK526 ............... 1972 £2 ............ £5 ..........................
Wooden Horse .................................. LP ..... York .............. FYK403 ............... 1972 £50 ..... £100 ..........................
Wooden Horse II ................................ LP ..... York .............. FYK413 ............... 1973 £180 .... £300 ..........................
Wooden Horses ................................. 7" ...... York .............. SYK543 ............... 1973 £2 ............ £5 ..........................

## WOODEN O
Handful Of Pleasant Delites .................. LP ..... Middle Earth ... MDLS301 ............ 1969 £30 ......... £60 ..........................

## WOODMAN, KEN & HIS PICCADILLY BRASS
That's Nice ....................................... LP ..... Strike ........... JLH101 ................ 1966 £6 .......... £15 ..........................

## WOODPECKERS
Hey Little Girl ................................... 7" ...... Oriole ............ CB311 ................. 1965 £2 ............ £5 ..........................

## WOODS, DONALD
Memories Of An Angel ......................... 7" ...... Vogue ........... V9107 ................. 1958 £150 ..... £250 ........... best auctioned

## WOODS, GAY & TERRY
Backwoods ....................................... LP ..... Polydor ......... 2383322 ............... 1975 £20 ......... £40 ..........................
Renowned ........................................ LP ..... Polydor ......... 2383406 ............... 1976 £20 ......... £40 ..........................
Tenderhooks ..................................... LP ..... Rockburgh ...... ROC104 .............. 1978 £5 .......... £12 ..........................
Time Is Right .................................... LP ..... Polydor ......... 2383375 ............... 1976 £15 ......... £30 ..........................
Woods Band ..................................... LP ..... Greenwich ...... GSLP1004 ............ 1971 £25 ......... £50 ..........................
Woods Band ..................................... LP ..... Mulligan ........ LUN015 .............. 1977 £6 .......... £15 different cover to 1971
                                                                                                                                         issue
Woods Band ..................................... LP ..... Rockburgh ...... CREST29 ............. 1977 £8 .......... £20 ..........................

## WOODS, NICK
Ballad Of Billy Bud ............................ 7" ...... London .......... HLU9621 .............. 1962 £1.50 ...... £4 ..........................

## WOODS, PHIL
New Jazz Quintet ............................... 10" LP Esquire ......... 20055 ................. 1955 £25 ......... £50 ..........................
Phil Woods Quartet ............................ LP ..... Esquire .......... 32020 ................. 1957 £15 ......... £30 ..........................
Phil Woods Septet .............................. LP ..... Esquire .......... 32026 ................. 1957 £15 ......... £30 ..........................

## WOODWARD, MAGGIE
Ali Bama .......................................... 7" ...... Vogue ........... V9148 ................. 1959 £2 ............ £5 ..........................

## WOODY KERN
Awful Disclosures Of Maria Monk ........... LP ..... Pye .............. NSPL18273 .......... 1967 £8 .......... £20 ..........................
Biography ......................................... 7" ...... Pye .............. 7N17672 .............. 1969 £1.50 ...... £4 ..........................

## WOODY'S TRUCK STOP
Woody's Truck Stop ........................... LP ..... Smash ........... SRS67111 ............ 1969 £6 .......... £15 ...................... US

## WOOFERS
Dragsville ......................................... LP ..... Wyncote ......... 9001 ................. 196– £8 .......... £20 ...................... US

## WOOLEY, SHEB

| | | | | | | | |
|---|---|---|---|---|---|---|---|
| Hootenanny Hoot | 7" | MGM | MGM1257 | 1965 | £1.50 | £4 | |
| I Flipped | 7" | MGM | SP1130 | 1955 | £6 | £12 | |
| Jest Plain, Wild And Wooley | 7" EP | MGM | MGMEP540 | 1956 | £10 | £20 | |
| Laughing The Blues | 7" | MGM | MGM1162 | 1962 | £2 | £5 | |
| Luke The Spook | 7" | MGM | MGM1081 | 1960 | £2 | £5 | |
| Meet Mr. Lonely | 7" | MGM | MGM1147 | 1961 | £2 | £5 | |
| More | 7" | MGM | MGM1017 | 1959 | £1.50 | £4 | |
| Purple People Eater | 7" | MGM | MGM981 | 1958 | £2 | £5 | |
| Santa & The Purple People Eater | 7" | MGM | MGM997 | 1958 | £1.50 | £4 | |
| Sheb Wooley | LP | MGM | E3299 | 1956 | £10 | £25 | US |
| Songs From The Day Of Rawhide | LP | MGM | C859 | 1961 | £4 | £10 | |
| Spoofing The Big Ones | LP | MGM | C945 | 1963 | £4 | £10 | |
| Tales Of How The West Was Won | LP | MGM | C955 | 1963 | £4 | £10 | |
| That's My Ma & That's My Pa | LP | MGM | C903 | 1962 | £4 | £10 | |
| Wayward Wind | 7" | MGM | MGM1132 | 1961 | £1.50 | £4 | |

## WOOLIES

| | | | | | | | |
|---|---|---|---|---|---|---|---|
| Basic Rock | LP | Split | 96452001 | 1970 | £20 | £40 | US |
| Live At Lizard's | LP | Spirit | 2005 | 1973 | £20 | £40 | US |
| Who Do You Love? | 7" | RCA | RCA1602 | 1967 | £10 | £20 | |

## WOOTTON, BRENDA

| | | | | | | | |
|---|---|---|---|---|---|---|---|
| Starry Gazey Pie | LP | Sentinel | | | £37.50 | £75 | |

## WOOTTON, BRENDA & JOHN THE FISH

| | | | | | | | |
|---|---|---|---|---|---|---|---|
| Pipers Folk | LP | private | VRC1 | 1968 | £37.50 | £75 | |

## WORK, JIMMY

| | | | | | | | |
|---|---|---|---|---|---|---|---|
| Country Songs | 7" EP | London | RED1039 | 1955 | £12.50 | £25 | |
| When She Said You All | 7" | London | HLD8270 | 1956 | £25 | £50 | |
| You've Got A Heart Like A Merry-Go-Round | 7" | London | HLD8308 | 1956 | £12.50 | £25 | |

## WORLD

| | | | | | | | |
|---|---|---|---|---|---|---|---|
| Angelina | 7" | Liberty | LBF15402 | 1970 | £1.50 | £4 | |
| Lucky Planet | LP | Liberty | LBS83419 | 1970 | £6 | £15 | |

## WORLD DOMINATION ENTERPRISES

| | | | | | | | |
|---|---|---|---|---|---|---|---|
| Asbestos Lead Asbestos | 7" | Karbon | KAR008 | 1985 | £2 | £5 | |

## WORLD OF OZ

| | | | | | | | |
|---|---|---|---|---|---|---|---|
| King Croesus | 7" | Deram | DM205 | 1968 | £1.50 | £4 | |
| Muffin Man | 7" | Deram | DM187 | 1968 | £2.50 | £6 | |
| Willow's Harp | 7" | Deram | DM233 | 1969 | £2.50 | £6 | |
| World Of Oz | LP | Deram | DML/SML1034 | 1969 | £20 | £40 | |

## WORLD PARTY

| | | | | | | | |
|---|---|---|---|---|---|---|---|
| Message In The Box | CD-s | Ensign | ENYCD631 | 1990 | £2 | £5 | |
| Ship Of Fools | CD-s | Ensign | ENYCD606 | 1987 | £2 | £5 | |
| Way Down Now | CD-s | Ensign | ENYCD634 | 1990 | £2 | £5 | |

## WORRYING KYNDE

| | | | | | | | |
|---|---|---|---|---|---|---|---|
| Call Out The Name | 7" | Piccadilly | 7N35370 | 1967 | £15 | £30 | |

## WORTH, JOHNNY

| | | | | | | | |
|---|---|---|---|---|---|---|---|
| Just Because | 7" | Columbia | DB3962 | 1957 | £1.50 | £4 | |
| Nightmare | 7" | Oriole | CB1545 | 1960 | £1.50 | £4 | |

## WORTH, MARION

| | | | | | | | |
|---|---|---|---|---|---|---|---|
| Are You Willing, Willie | 7" | London | HL7089 | 1960 | £2.50 | £6 | export |
| That's My Kind Of Love | 7" | London | HL7097 | 1960 | £2.50 | £6 | export |

## WRANGLERS

| | | | | | | | |
|---|---|---|---|---|---|---|---|
| Liza Jane | 7" | Parlophone | R5163 | 1964 | £20 | £40 | |

## WRAY, LINK

| | | | | | | | |
|---|---|---|---|---|---|---|---|
| Batman Theme | 7" | Chiswick | NS32 | 1978 | £5 | £10 | demo |
| Good Rockin' Tonight | 7" | Stateside | SS397 | 1965 | £4 | £8 | |
| Great Guitar Hits | LP | Vermillion | 1924 | 1966 | £10 | £25 | US |
| Jack The Ripper | LP | Swan | SLP510 | 1963 | £10 | £25 | US |
| Jack The Ripper | 7" | Stateside | SS217 | 1963 | £4 | £8 | |
| Link Wray | LP | Polydor | 2489029 | 1971 | £4 | £10 | |
| Link Wray And The Wraymen | LP | Epic | LN3661 | 1960 | £15 | £30 | US |
| Link Wray Sings And Plays Guitar | LP | Vermillion | 1925 | 1966 | £10 | £25 | US |
| Mr. Guitar | 7" EP | Stateside | SE1015 | 1964 | £20 | £40 | |
| Rumble | 7" | London | HLA8623 | 1958 | £7.50 | £15 | |
| Sweeper | 7" | Stateside | SS256 | 1964 | £2.50 | £6 | |
| There's Good Rockin' Tonight | LP | Union Pacific | UP002 | 1971 | £4 | £10 | |
| Yesterday And Today | LP | Record Factory | 1929 | 196- | £4 | £10 | US |

## WRAY, RAY QUARTET

| | | | | | | | |
|---|---|---|---|---|---|---|---|
| When You Lover Has Gone | 7" | Salvo | SLO1808 | 1962 | £2.50 | £6 | |

## WRAY, VERNON & LINK WRAY

| | | | | | | | |
|---|---|---|---|---|---|---|---|
| Wasted | LP | Vermillion | 1972 | 196- | £5 | £12 | US |

## WREN, JENNY

| | | | | | | | |
|---|---|---|---|---|---|---|---|
| Chasing My Dreams All Over Town | 7" | Fontana | TF672 | 1966 | £12.50 | £25 | |

## WRIGGLERS

| | | | | | | | |
|---|---|---|---|---|---|---|---|
| Cooler | 7" | Giant | GN26 | 1968 | £4 | £8 | |
| Get Right | 7" | Blue Cat | BS106 | 1968 | £4 | £8 | |

## WRIGHT, DALE

| | | | | | | | |
|---|---|---|---|---|---|---|---|
| She's Neat | 7" | London | HLH8573 | 1958 | £50 | £100 | |
| That's Show Biz | 7" | Pye | 7N25022 | 1959 | £12.50 | £25 | |

## WRIGHT, GARY

| | | | | | | | |
|---|---|---|---|---|---|---|---|
| Extraction | LP | A&M | AMLS2004 | 1970 | £4 | £10 | |
| Foot Print | LP | A&M | AMLS64296 | 1971 | £4 | £10 | |

## WRIGHT, GINNY

| | | | | | | | |
|---|---|---|---|---|---|---|---|
| Indian Moon | 7" | London | HL8119 | 1955 | £12.50 | £25 | |

## WRIGHT, GINNY & TOMMY CUTRER

| | | | | | | | |
|---|---|---|---|---|---|---|---|
| Wonderful World | 7" | London | HL8093 | 1954 | £12.50 | £25 | |

## WRIGHT, NAT

| | | | | | | | |
|---|---|---|---|---|---|---|---|
| Anything | 7" | HMV | POP629 | 1959 | £15 | £30 | |

## WRIGHT, O. V.

| | | | | | | | |
|---|---|---|---|---|---|---|---|
| 8 Men 4 Women | 7" | London | HLZ10137 | 1967 | £1.50 | £4 | |
| 8 Men, 4 Women | LP | Island | ILP975 | 1968 | £15 | £30 | pink label |
| Gone For Good | 7" | Vocalion | VP9272 | 1966 | £2 | £5 | |
| I Want Everyone To Know | 7" | Action | ACT4527 | 1969 | £2 | £5 | |
| If It's Only For Tonight | LP | Back Beat | 61 | 1965 | £6 | £15 | US |
| O. V. Wright | 7" EP | Vocalion | VEP170165 | 1965 | £12.50 | £25 | |
| Oh Baby Mine | 7" | Action | ACT4505 | 1968 | £4 | £8 | |
| Poor Boy | 7" | Vocalion | VP9255 | 1966 | £2 | £5 | |
| What About You | 7" | Sue | WI4043 | 1968 | £6 | £12 | |
| You're Gonna Make Me Cry | 7" | Vocalion | VP9249 | 1965 | £2.50 | £6 | |

## WRIGHT, OTIS

| | | | | | | | |
|---|---|---|---|---|---|---|---|
| It Will Soon Be Done | LP | Doctor Bird | DLM5006 | 1967 | £37.50 | £75 | |
| Over In Gloryland | LP | Coxsone | TLP1001 | 196– | £37.50 | £75 | |
| Peace Perfect Peace | LP | Doctor Bird | DLM5005 | 1967 | £37.50 | £75 | |

## WRIGHT, RITA

| | | | | | | | |
|---|---|---|---|---|---|---|---|
| I Can't Give Back The Love | 7" | Tamla Motown | TMG643 | 1968 | £7.50 | £15 | |
| I Can't Give Back The Love I Feel For You | 7" | Tamla Motown | TMG791 | 1971 | £1.50 | £4 | |
| Love Is All You Need | 7" | Jet | UP36382 | 1978 | £4 | £8 | |

## WRIGHT, RUBEN

| | | | | | | | |
|---|---|---|---|---|---|---|---|
| Hey Girl | 7" | Capitol | CL15460 | 1966 | £6 | £12 | |

## WRIGHT, RUBY

| | | | | | | | |
|---|---|---|---|---|---|---|---|
| Bimbo | 7" | Parlophone | MSP6073 | 1954 | £7.50 | £15 | |
| I Fall In Love With You Every Day | 7" | Parlophone | MSP6209 | 1956 | £4 | £8 | |
| Santa's Little Sleigh Bells | 7" | Parlophone | MSP6133 | 1954 | £5 | £10 | |
| Three Stars | 7" | Parlophone | R4556 | 1959 | £4 | £8 | |
| Three Stars Girl | 7" EP | Parlophone | GEP8785 | 1959 | £12.50 | £25 | |
| Till I Waltz Again With You | 7" | Parlophone | MSP6025 | 1953 | £7.50 | £15 | |
| What Have They Told You? | 7" | Parlophone | MSP6150 | 1955 | £4 | £8 | |
| You're Just A Flower From An Old Bouquet | 7" | Parlophone | R4589 | 1959 | £1.50 | £4 | |

## WRIGHT, STEVE

| | | | | | | | |
|---|---|---|---|---|---|---|---|
| Wild Wild Women | 7" | London | HLW8991 | 1959 | £50 | £100 | |

## WRIGHT, WINSTON

| | | | | | | | |
|---|---|---|---|---|---|---|---|
| Five Miles High | 7" | Doctor Bird | DB1308 | 1969 | £5 | £10 | |

## WRIGHT, ZACHARIAH

| | | | | | | | |
|---|---|---|---|---|---|---|---|
| Lumumba Limbo | 7" | Bamboo | BAM403 | 197– | £1.50 | £4 | |

## WRITING ON THE WALL

| | | | | | | | |
|---|---|---|---|---|---|---|---|
| Aries | 7" | Middle Earth | MDE201 | 1969 | £15 | £30 | promo, with tracks by Wooden O & Arcadium |
| Child On A Crossing | 7" | Middle Earth | MDS101 | 1969 | £7.50 | £15 | |
| Man Of Renown | 7" | Pye | 7N45251 | 1973 | £5 | £10 | |
| Power Of The Picts | LP | Middle Earth | MDLS303 | 1969 | £62.50 | £125 | |

## WYATT, JOHNNY

| | | | | | | | |
|---|---|---|---|---|---|---|---|
| This Thing Called Love | 7" | President | PT109 | 1968 | £1.50 | £4 | |

## WYATT, ROBERT

| | | | | | | | |
|---|---|---|---|---|---|---|---|
| End Of An Ear | LP | CBS | 64189 | 1970 | £5 | £12 | |
| Las Vegas Fandango | LP | Pinguin | 4 | 1974 | £20 | £40 | Italian |

## WYLIE, PETE

| | | | | | | | |
|---|---|---|---|---|---|---|---|
| Fourelevenfortyfour | CD-s | Siren | SRNCD59 | 1987 | £2 | £5 | |

## WYLIE, RICHARD
Brand New Man ..................................... 7" ...... Columbia ........ DB7012 ................ 1963 £7.50 ...... £15 ...................................

## WYMAN, BILL
Monkey Grip ............................................. LP ..... Rolling Stones . QD79100 ............... 1974 £4 .......... £10 ................ US quad
Stone Alone ............................................. LP ..... Rolling Stones . QD79103 ............... 1976 £4 .......... £10 ................ US quad

## WYNDHAM-READ, MARTYN
Andy's Gone ............................................ LP ..... Broadside ....... BRO134 ............... 1979 £8 .......... £20 ...................................
Ballad Singer ............................................ LP ..... Autogram ....... ALLP218 .............. 1977 £8 .......... £20 ................ German
Harry The Hawker Is Dead ..................... LP ..... Argo ............. ZFB82 ................. 1973 £15 ........ £30 ...................................
Martyn Wyndham-Read ............................ LP ..... Trailer ............ LER2028 .............. 1971 £10 ........ £25 ...................................
Maypoles To Mistletoe ........................... LP ..... Trailer ............ LER2092 .............. 1975 £8 .......... £20  with Geoff and Pennie
                                                                                                                                                                       Harris
Ned Kelly And That Gang ...................... LP ..... Trailer ............ LER2009 .............. 1970 £8 .......... £20 ...................................
Rose From The Bush ............................. LP ..... Greenwich      GVR222 ............... 1984 £5 .......... £12 ...................................
                                                                           Village ...........
Songs And Music Of The Redcoats .......... LP ..... Argo ............. ZDA147 ............... 1971 £25 ........ £50  with The Druids

## WYNDRUSH
Let It Shine .............................................. LP ..... Wealden ..........  ....................................  1972 £75 ....... £150

## WYNGARDE, PETER
La Ronde de l'amour ............................... 7" ...... RCA ............... RCA1967 .............. 1970 £4 .......... £8
Peter Wyngarde ....................................... LP ..... RCA ............. SF8087 ............... 1970 £100 .... £200

## WYNNS, SANDY
Touch Of Venus ...................................... 7" ...... Fontana .......... TF550 ................. 1965 £75 ....... £150 ...................................

## WYNTER, MARK
Can I Get To Know You Better ............... 7" ...... Pye ............... 7N15771 ............... 1965 £1.50 .... £4
Dream Girl ............................................... 7" ...... Decca ............ F11323 ................ 1961 £1.50 .... £4
Exclusively Yours ..................................... 7" ...... Decca ............ F11354 ................ 1961 £1.50 .... £4
Girl For Everyday ..................................... 7" ...... Decca ............ F11380 ................ 1961 £1.50 .... £4
Heaven's Plan .......................................... 7" ...... Decca ............ F11434 ................ 1962 £1.50 .... £4
I Love Her Still ........................................ 7" ...... Decca ............ F11467 ................ 1962 £1.50 .... £4
Image Of A Girl ....................................... 7" ...... Decca ............ F11263 ................ 1960 £1.50 .... £4
It's Mark Time ......................................... 7" EP . Pye ............... NEP24176 ............. 1962 £6 .......... £12
Kickin' Up The Leaves ............................. 7" ...... Decca ............ F11279 ................ 1960 £1.50 .... £4
Mark Time ............................................... 7" EP . Decca ............ DFE6674 ............. 1960 £10 ........ £20
Mark Wynter ............................................ LP ..... Ace Of Clubs .. ACL1141 .............. 1962 £8 .......... £20
Mark Wynter ............................................ LP ..... Golden Guinea GGL0250 ............. 1963 £4 .......... £10
Warmth Of Wynter ................................... LP ..... Decca ............ LK4409 ............... 1961 £15 ........ £30
Wynter Time ............................................ 7" EP . Pye ............... NEP24185 ............. 1964 £6 .......... £12

# X

| | | | | | | | |
|---|---|---|---|---|---|---|---|
| Wild Thing | CD-s | RCA | ZD49338 | 1989 | £2 | £5 | |

## X MEN
| | | | | | | | |
|---|---|---|---|---|---|---|---|
| Ghosts | 7" | Creation | CRE006 | 1984 | £2.50 | £6 | |
| Spiral Girl | 7" | Creation | CRE014 | 1985 | £2 | £5 | |

## XERO
| | | | | | | | |
|---|---|---|---|---|---|---|---|
| Oh Baby | 7" | Brickyard | XERO1 | 1983 | £1.50 | £4 | |
| Oh Baby | 12" | Brickyard | XERO1T | 1983 | £4 | £10 | |

## XHOL
| | | | | | | | |
|---|---|---|---|---|---|---|---|
| Electrip | LP | Hansa | 80099 | 1969 | £15 | £30 | German |
| Hauruk | LP | Ohr | OMM56014 | 1970 | £10 | £25 | German |
| Motherfuckers GmbH And Co Kg | LP | Ohr | OMM556024 | 1972 | £10 | £25 | German |

## XIT
| | | | | | | | |
|---|---|---|---|---|---|---|---|
| Entrance | LP | Canyon | C7114 | 1974 | £37.50 | £75 | US |
| Relocation | LP | Canyon | C721 | 1978 | £6 | £15 | US |

## XL5
| | | | | | | | |
|---|---|---|---|---|---|---|---|
| XL5 | 7" | HMV | POP1148 | 1963 | £4 | £8 | |

## XMAL DEUTSCHLAND
| | | | | | | | |
|---|---|---|---|---|---|---|---|
| Incubus Succubus II | 7" | 4AD | AD311 | 1983 | £1.50 | £4 | |

## X-RAY SPEX
| | | | | | | | |
|---|---|---|---|---|---|---|---|
| Germ Free Adolescents | LP | EMI | INS3023 | 1978 | £5 | £12 | |
| Oh Bondage, Up Yours | 7" | Virgin | VS189 | 1977 | £5 | £10 | picture sleeve |

## X-RAYS
| | | | | | | | |
|---|---|---|---|---|---|---|---|
| Out Of Control | 7" | London | HLR8805 | 1959 | £10 | £20 | |

## XS ENERGY
| | | | | | | | |
|---|---|---|---|---|---|---|---|
| Eighteen | 7" | World | WRECK1 | 1978 | £2.50 | £6 | |

## XTC
| | | | | | | | |
|---|---|---|---|---|---|---|---|
| 3D EP (Science Friction) | 7" | Virgin | VS188 | 1977 | £100 | £200 | |
| Dear God | CD-s | Virgin | CDEP3 | 1987 | £2 | £5 | |
| Drums And Wires | LP | Virgin | V2129 | 1979 | £4 | £10 | with 7" (VDJ30) |
| Go 2 | LP | Virgin | V2108 | 1978 | £4 | £10 | with Go plus 12" |
| King For A Day | CD-s | Virgin | VSCD1177 | 1988 | £2 | £5 | |
| Love On A Farmboy's Wages | 7" | Virgin | VS613 | 1983 | £1.50 | £4 | double |
| Loving | CD-s | Virgin | VSCD1201 | 1989 | £2 | £5 | |
| Mayor Of Simpleton | CD-s | Virgin | VSCD1158 | 1989 | £2 | £5 | 3" single |
| Oranges And Lemons | CD-s | Virgin | CDVT2581 | 1988 | £5 | £12 | album on 3 CD single boxed set |
| Radios In Motion, A History Of XTC | CD | Geffen | PROCD4397 | 1992 | £8 | £20 | US promo |
| Senses Working Overtime | CD-s | Virgin | CDT9 | 1988 | £2 | £5 | 3" single |
| Sgt. Rock Is Going To Help Me | CD-s | Virgin | VVCS9 | 1990 | £2 | £5 | |
| Skylarking | CD | Mobile Fidelity | UDCD625 | 1994 | £6 | £15 | US audiophile |

## XTRAVERTS
| | | | | | | | |
|---|---|---|---|---|---|---|---|
| Blank Generation | 7" | Spike | SRTSSP001 | 198– | £5 | £10 | no picture sleeve |

## XXX
| | | | | | | | |
|---|---|---|---|---|---|---|---|
| Live | LP | private | | | £37.50 | £75 | US |

# Y

### Y BLEW
Maes B .................................... 7" ...... Qualiton ......... QSP7001 ............... 1967 £4 ............ £8 ............ *picture sleeve*

### Y TRWYNAU COCH
| | | | | | | | |
|---|---|---|---|---|---|---|---|
| Merched Dan 15 .................................. | 7" ...... | Recordian Sqwar ............ | RSROC002 ........... | 1978 £2 ........... | £5 | |
| Rhedeg Rhag Y Torpidos ....................... | LP ..... | Recordian Coch .............. | OCHR2198 ........... | 198– £6 ........... | £15 | |
| Wastod Ar Y Tu Fas ............................... | 7" ...... | Recordian Sqwar ............. | RSROC1 ............... | 197– £2 ........... | £5 | |

### YA HO WA 13
A complete list of the albums made by hippy band Ya Ho Wa 13 finally appears in the fourth edition of this guide. All apart from *Golden Sunrise* (which includes collaborations with the former leader of the Seeds, Sky Saxon) were issued on the group's own Higher Key label. They have long been sought after, but are so seldom seen that information on them continues to be somewhat sketchy.

| | | | | | | | |
|---|---|---|---|---|---|---|---|
| All Or Nothing At All .......................... | LP ..... | Higher Key ..... | 3304 ..................... | 1974 £100 .... £200 | | | US |
| Father Yod And The Spirit Of '76 – Kohoutek ............................................... | LP ..... | Higher Key ..... | 3301 | 1973 £100 .... £200 | | | US |
| Golden Sunrise .................................... | LP ..... | Psycho ............ | PSYCHO2 ............ | 1982 £20 ........ £40 | | | |
| I'm Gonna Take You Home .................. | LP ..... | Higher Key ..... | 3309 ..................... | 1975 £700 .. £1000 | | | US |
| Penetration – An Aquarian Symphony ...... | LP ..... | Higher Key ..... | | 1974 £100 .... £200 | | | US |
| Principles Of The Children .................. | LP ..... | Higher Key ..... | | 1978 £700 .. £1000 | | | US |
| Savage Sons Of Ya Ho Wa .................. | LP ..... | Higher Key ..... | 3306 ..................... | 1974 £100 .... £200 | | | US |
| Spirit Of 76 – Contraction .................. | LP ..... | Higher Key ..... | | 1976 £500 .... £750 | | | US |
| Spirit Of 76 – Expansion ..................... | LP ..... | Higher Key ..... | | 1976 £500 .... £750 | | | US |
| Ya Ho Wa 13 ...................................... | LP ..... | Higher Key ..... | | 1974 £37.50 .... £75 | | | US |
| Ya Ho Wa 13 ...................................... | LP ..... | Higher Key ..... | | 1974 £150 .... £250 | | US, *sheep shag cover, double* |

### YAKS
Yakety Yak .................................... 7" ...... Decca ............. F12115 ................. 1965 £2.50 ........ £6 ..................................

### YAMA & THE KARMA DUSTERS
Up From The Sewers ............................. LP ...... Manhole ......... no number ............ 1970 £150 ..... £250 ....................... US

### YAMASH'TA, STOMU
Japanese percussionist Stomu Yamash'ta came to Britain during the early seventies and amazed the classical music world with his virtuosity. The two LPs listed here contain works by some of the leading contemporary classical composers which allow Yamash'ta to show off his formidable technique – the L'Oiseau Lyre record has percussion as the only instrumentation. Interestingly, Yamash'ta discovered progressive rock and completely changed his musical policy with a number of jazz-rock albums. Perhaps he realized that this was where the most vital musical developments were taking place, although the cynic might argue that he merely realized that there was more money to be made out of rock music.

| | | | | | |
|---|---|---|---|---|---|
| Henze/Takemitsu/Maxwell Davies ............ | LP ...... | L'Oiseau Lyre .. | DSLO1 .................. | 1972 £5 ........... £12 | ..................................... |
| Takemitsu Ishii ...................................... | LP ...... | EMI ................. | EMD5508 .............. | 1973 £5 ........... £12 | ..................................... |

### YANA
| | | | | | |
|---|---|---|---|---|---|
| Climb Up The Wall ............................... | 7" ...... | HMV ............... | POP252 ................. | 1956 £4 ........... £8 | ..................................... |
| I Miss You Mama .................................. | 7" ...... | HMV ............... | POP481 ................. | 1958 £2 ........... £5 | ..................................... |
| Mr. Wonderful ...................................... | 7" ...... | HMV ............... | POP340 ................. | 1957 £2.50 ........ £6 | ..................................... |
| Papa And Mama .................................... | 7" ...... | HMV ............... | POP546 ................. | 1958 £1.50 ........ £4 | ..................................... |

### YANCEY, JIMMY
| | | | | | | |
|---|---|---|---|---|---|---|
| Jimmy And Mama Yancey ........................ | 10" LP | Atlantic ............ | 130 ...................... | 195– £15 ........... £30 | | US |
| Jimmy And Mama Yancey ........................ | 10" LP | Atlantic ............ | 134 ...................... | 195– £15 ........... £30 | | US |
| Jimmy Yancey ........................................ | 7" EP . | HMV ............... | 7EG8062 .............. | 1954 £5 ........... £10 | | |
| Jimmy Yancey ........................................ | 7" EP . | Vogue .............. | EPV1203 .............. | 1958 £5 ........... £10 | | |
| Jimmy Yancey ........................................ | 10" LP | Vogue .............. | LDE166 ............... | 1956 £8 ........... £20 | | |
| Lost Recording Date .............................. | 10" LP | London ............. | AL3525 ............... | 1954 £8 ........... £20 | | |
| Lowdown Dirty Blues ............................. | LP ...... | Atlantic ............ | 590018 ................ | 1968 £4 ........... £10 | | |
| Pure Blues ............................................ | LP ...... | Atlantic ............ | 1231 .................... | 1956 £10 ........... £25 | | US |
| Yancey Special ...................................... | 10" LP | Atlantic ............ | 103 ...................... | 195– £15 ........... £30 | | US |
| Yancey's Piano ...................................... | 7" EP . | HMV ............... | 7EG8083 .............. | 1955 £5 ........... £10 | | |

### YANCEY, MAMA & DON EWELL
Mama Yancey And Don Ewell ................. 10" LP Tempo ............ LAP7 ..................... 1957 £15 ........ £30

### YANKEE DOLLAR
Yankee Dollar ....................................... LP ...... Dot ................. DLP25874 ............ 1968 £5 ........... £12 ....................... US

## YANOVSKY, ZALMAN

| | | | | | | | | |
|---|---|---|---|---|---|---|---|---|
| Alive & Well In Argentina | LP | Buddah | BDS5019 | 1968 | £5 | £12 | | US |
| Alive And Well In Argentina | LP | Kama Sutra | 2316003 | 1971 | £4 | £10 | | |
| As Long As You're Here | 7" | Pye | 7N25438 | 1967 | £1.50 | £4 | | |

## YARDBIRDS

All of the Yardbirds' innovative original records are now collectable – even the chart hits – although the rarest come from right at the start of the group's career, and right at the end. The single 'Goodnight Sweet Josephine' definitely does exist, despite occasional murmurings to the contrary, although possibly only as a demo. Meanwhile, the LP *Live Yardbirds*, ruined, according to the group, by the engineers miking Jimmy Page's monitor speaker rather than the real thing, and also by its extravagant over-dubbed applause, was given two releases and rapidly withdrawn each time. Counterfeits exist, but these have black and white covers, rather than the colour of the originals.

| | | | | | | | |
|---|---|---|---|---|---|---|---|
| Evil Hearted You | 7" | Columbia | DB7706 | 1965 | £1.50 | £4 | |
| Face And Place | LP | Direction | | 1964 | £25 | £50 | New Zealand |
| Five Live Yardbirds | LP | Columbia | 33SX1677 | 1964 | £20 | £40 | |
| Five Live Yardbirds | LP | Columbia | 33SX1677 | 1969 | £4 | £10 | black and white label |
| Five Yardbirds | 7" EP | Columbia | SEG8421 | 1965 | £25 | £50 | |
| For Your Love | LP | Epic | LN24167/BN26167 | 1965 | £15 | £30 | US |
| For Your Love | CD-s | Charly | CDS4 | 1989 | £2 | £5 | |
| For Your Love | 7" EP | Riviera | 231074 | 1965 | £25 | £50 | French |
| For Your Love | 7" | Columbia | DB7499 | 1965 | £1.50 | £4 | |
| Good Morning Little Schoolgirl | 7" | Columbia | DB7391 | 1964 | £4 | £8 | |
| Goodnight Sweet Josephine | 7" | Columbia | DB8368 | 1968 | £75 | £150 | demo, best auctioned |
| Greatest Hits | LP | Epic | LN24246/BN26246 | 1966 | £10 | £25 | US |
| Happening Ten Years Time Ago | 7" EP | Riviera | 231220 | 1966 | £25 | £50 | French |
| Happening Ten Years Time Ago | 7" | Columbia | DB8024 | 1966 | £7.50 | £15 | |
| Having A Rave Up | LP | Columbia | SCXC28 | 1966 | £37.50 | £75 | export |
| Having A Rave Up | LP | Epic | LN24177/BN26177 | 1965 | £10 | £25 | US |
| Heart Full Of Soul | 7" EP | Riviera | 231099 | 1965 | £25 | £50 | French |
| Heart Full Of Soul | 7" | Columbia | DB7594 | 1965 | £1.50 | £4 | |
| I Wish You Would | 7" | Columbia | DB7283 | 1964 | £5 | £10 | |
| Little Games | LP | Epic | LN24313/BN26313 | 1967 | £20 | £40 | US |
| Little Games | 7" EP | Riviera | 231242 | 1967 | £37.50 | £75 | French |
| Little Games | 7" | Columbia | DB8165 | 1967 | £10 | £20 | |
| Live Featuring Jimmy Page | LP | Columbia | P13311 | 1972 | £15 | £30 | US, colour cover |
| Live Featuring Jimmy Page | LP | Epic | KE30615 | 1971 | £20 | £40 | US, colour cover |
| Our Own Sound | LP | Riviera | 4210305 | 1972 | £62.50 | £125 | French |
| Over Under Sideways Down | LP | Epic | LN24210/BN26210 | 1966 | £10 | £25 | US |
| Over Under Sideways Down | 7" EP | Riviera | 231196 | 1966 | £25 | £50 | French |
| Over Under Sideways Down | 7" | Columbia | DB7928 | 1966 | £4 | £8 | |
| Paf Bum | 7" | Ricordi International | SIR20010 | 1966 | £10 | £20 | Italian |
| Shapes Of Things | 7" EP | Riviera | 231170 | 1966 | £25 | £50 | French |
| Shapes Of Things | 7" | Columbia | DB7848 | 1966 | £1.50 | £4 | |
| Still I'm Sad | 7" EP | Riviera | 231131 | 1965 | £25 | £50 | French |
| With Sonny Boy Williamson | LP | Fontana | SFJL960 | 1968 | £8 | £20 | |
| With Sonny Boy Williamson | LP | Fontana | TL5277 | 1964 | £30 | £60 | |
| With Sonny Boy Williamson | LP | Philips | 6435011 | 1971 | £4 | £10 | |
| Yardbirds | LP | Columbia | SSX1018 | 1965 | £50 | £100 | Swedish, different cover |
| Yardbirds | LP | Columbia | SX/SCX6063 | 1966 | £20 | £40 | |
| Yardbirds | LP | Epic | EG30135 | 1970 | £8 | £20 | US |
| Yardbirds | LP | Epic | HE38455 | 1983 | £8 | £20 | US audiophile |
| Yardbirds | 7" EP | Columbia | SEG8521 | 1966 | £87.50 | £175 | |

## YARDBIRDS & HERBIE HANCOCK

| | | | | | | | |
|---|---|---|---|---|---|---|---|
| Blow-Up | LP | MGM | C8039 | 1967 | £10 | £25 | |

## YATES, CHRIS

| | | | | | | | |
|---|---|---|---|---|---|---|---|
| New Born | LP | ILSM | | 1977 | £25 | £50 | US |

## YATES, TOM

| | | | | | | | |
|---|---|---|---|---|---|---|---|
| Love Comes Well Armed | LP | President | PTLS1053 | 1973 | £15 | £30 | |
| Second City Spiritual | LP | CBS | BPG63094 | 1967 | £10 | £25 | |
| Song Of The Shimmering Way | LP | Satril | SATL4007 | 1977 | £4 | £10 | |

## YATHA SIDHRA

| | | | | | | | |
|---|---|---|---|---|---|---|---|
| Meditation Mass | LP | Brain | 1045 | 1974 | £25 | £50 | German |

## YAZOO

| | | | | | | | |
|---|---|---|---|---|---|---|---|
| Situation | CD-s | Mute | YAZ4CD | 1990 | £2 | £5 | |
| Upstairs At Eric's | LP | Mute | STUMM7 | 1983 | £4 | £10 | inner sleeve with happy faces/sad faces |

## YELLO

| | | | | | | | |
|---|---|---|---|---|---|---|---|
| Blazing Saddles | CD-s | Mercury | YELCD4 | 1989 | £2 | £5 | |
| Call It Love | CD-s | Mercury | 8883112 | 1988 | £2 | £5 | |
| Goldrush | 12" | Mercury | MERXD218 | 1986 | £2.50 | £6 | double |
| Of Course I'm Lying | CD-s | Mercury | YELCD3 | 1989 | £2 | £5 | 2 versions |
| Race | CD-s | Mercury | YELCD1 | 1988 | £2 | £5 | |
| Race | CD-s | Polygram | 0805282 | 1989 | £4 | £10 | CD video |
| Rhythm Divine | 12" | Mercury | MERXR253 | 1987 | £10 | £20 | |
| Tied Up | CD-s | Mercury | YELCD2 | 1988 | £2 | £5 | |
| Tied Up | CD-s | Polygram | 0806442 | 1989 | £4 | £10 | CD video |
| Tied Up In Life | 12" | Mercury | YELLR212 | 1988 | £2.50 | £6 | |
| Video Race | CD-s | Polygram | 0807202 | 1988 | £5 | £12 | CD video |

## YELLOW
Roll It Down The Hill .......................... 7" ...... CBS ............... 4869 ..................... 1970 £5 ........ £10 ........................

## YELLOW BALLOON
Yellow Balloon ......................................... LP ..... Canterbury ...... CLPM/CLPS1502 .. 1967 £20 ........ £40 .................. US
Yellow Balloon ....................................... 7" ...... Stateside .......... SS2008 ................... 1967 £4 ........... £8

## YELLOW BELLOW ROOM BOOM
Seeing Things Green ............................. 7" ...... CBS ............... 3205 .................... 1968 £4 ........... £8

## YELLOW MAGIC ORCHESTRA
| | | | | | | | |
|---|---|---|---|---|---|---|---|
| Behind The Mask | 7" | A&M | AMS7559 | 1980 | £4 | £8 | yellow vinyl |
| Behind The Mask | 12" | A&M | AMSP7559 | 1980 | £2.50 | £6 | |
| Computer Game | 7" | A&M | AMS7502 | 1980 | £1.50 | £4 | |
| Computer Game | 7" | A&M | AMS7502 | 1980 | £4 | £8 | yellow vinyl |
| Computer Game | 12" | A&M | AMSP7502 | 1980 | £4 | £10 | |
| Computer Game | 12" | A&M | AMSP7502 | 1980 | £6 | £15 | yellow vinyl |
| Multiplies | LP | A&M | AMLH68516 | 1980 | £6 | £15 | yellow vinyl |
| Nice Age | 7" | A&M | JAPAN2 | 1980 | £1.50 | £4 | yellow vinyl |
| Nice Age | 12" | A&M | JAPAN122 | 1980 | £4 | £10 | |
| Rydeen | 7" | Alfa | ALF2145 | 1979 | £1.50 | £4 | white vinyl |
| Tighten Up | 12" | A&M | AMSP8104 | 1981 | £4 | £10 | |
| Tong Poo | 12" | A&M | AMSP7447 | 1979 | £6 | £15 | yellow vinyl |
| Yellow Magic Orchestra | LP | A&M | AMLH68506 | 1979 | £5 | £12 | yellow vinyl |

## YELLOW PAYGES
Little Woman .......................................... 7" ...... UNI ........... UNS516 ............... 1970 £1.50 ........ £4
Volume One ............................................ LP ..... Uni ........... 73045 ................ 1969 £4 ........... £10 .................. US

## YELLOWSTONE & VOICE
Yellowstone & Voice ............................. LP ..... Regal ....... SRZA8511 ............. 1972 £4 ........... £10
Zonophone .....

## YEMM AND YEMEN
Black Is The Night .............................. 7" ...... Columbia ........ DB8022 ................. 1966 £4 ........... £8

## YES
Sometimes the extended compositions for which Yes are best known have sounded a little forced, as though the group has initially written quite short pop songs and then cast around for ways of stretching them out. Indeed, over the first few albums one can hear this process being developed. *Yes* and *Time And A Word* and the associated singles contain a variety of intelligent harmony pop, in which the songs are carefully arranged, but fairly straightforward in structure. With *The Yes Album*, however, a process begins where the melodies are expanded and chopped about – which works well here because the melodies are strong enough to withstand the treatment, but which is much less successful on *Fragile*. Nevertheless, there are sufficient high points across Yes's catalogue to demonstrate that the symphonic approach to rock is an entirely valid one.

| | | | | | | | |
|---|---|---|---|---|---|---|---|
| Classic Yes | LP | Atlantic | K50842 | 1980 | £10 | £25 | test pressing, different sleeve |
| Close To The Edge | LP | Mobile Fidelity | MFSL1077 | 1980 | £6 | £15 | US audiophile |
| Fragile | LP | Atlantic | 2401019 | 1971 | £4 | £10 | |
| Going For The One | LP | Atlantic | DSK50379 | 1977 | £5 | £12 | 3 x 12", boxed |
| Interview | 7" | Atlantic | SAM7 | 1972 | £2.50 | £6 | promo |
| Interview/Five Songs | 7" | Lyntone | LYN2536 | 197– | £2 | £5 | |
| Looking Around | 7" | Atlantic | 584298 | 1969 | £25 | £50 | |
| Sweet Dreams | 7" | Atlantic | 2091004 | 1970 | £7.50 | £15 | |
| Sweetness | 7" | Atlantic | 584280 | 1969 | £12.50 | £25 | |
| Time And A Word | LP | Atlantic | 2400006 | 1970 | £4 | £10 | lyric sheet |
| Time And A Word | 7" | Atlantic | 584323 | 1970 | £7.50 | £15 | |
| Union | CD | Arista | | 1991 | £8 | £20 | US promo picture disc |
| Yes | LP | Atlantic | 588190 | 1969 | £4 | £10 | lyric sheet |
| Yes Album | LP | Atlantic | 2400101 | 1971 | £4 | £10 | |
| Yes Solos | LP | Atlantic | PR260 | 1976 | £8 | £20 | US promo compilation |
| Yesyears | CD | Atco | PRCD4009 | 1991 | £8 | £20 | US promo sampler |

## YESTERDAY'S CHILDREN
To Be Or Not To Be ......................... 7" EP . DiscAZ ........... 1101 .................. 1967 £15 ........ £30 .................. French

## YETTIES
Dorset Is Beautiful ............................... LP ..... Argo ............ ZFB38 ............... 1972 £4 ........... £10
Fifty Stone Of Loveliness ..................... LP ..... Acorn ............ CF203 ............... 1969 £5 ........... £12

## YETTI-MEN
Yetti-Men ............................................ LP ..... LAK ............ KB4348 ............ 1963 £330 ..... £500 .................. US

## YOGI, MAHARISHI MAHESH
Maharishi Mahesh Yogi ....................... LP ..... Liberty ........... LBS83075E ..... 1967 £4 ........... £10

## YOLANDA
With This Kiss ...................................... 7" ...... Triumph ........ RGM1007 ............ 1960 £7.50 ........ £15

## YORK, PETE
Pete York Percussion Band ................... LP ..... Decca ............ TXS109 ................ 1972 £5 ........... £12

## YORK, RUSTY
Peggy Sue ............................................ 7" ...... Parlophone ...... R4398 ............ 1958 £180 ..... £300 ........ demo only, best auctioned

## YORK BROTHERS
| | | | | | | | |
|---|---|---|---|---|---|---|---|
| Country And Western | 7" EP | Parlophone | GEP8736 | 1958 £5 | £10 | |
| Country And Western No. 2 | 7" EP | Parlophone | GEP8753 | 1958 £6 | £12 | |
| Sixteen Great Country & Western Hits | LP | King | 820 | 1963 £5 | £12 | US |
| Strange Town | 7" | Parlophone | CMSP22 | 1954 £2 | £5 | export |
| Why Don't You Open The Door | 7" | Parlophone | CMSP5 | 1954 £2 | £5 | export |
| York Brothers | LP | King | 586 | 1958 £6 | £15 | US |
| York Brothers Vol. 2 | LP | King | 591 | 1958 £6 | £15 | US |

## YORK POP MUSIC PROJECT
| | | | | | |
|---|---|---|---|---|---|
| All Day | LP | private | | 1973 £50 | £100 |

## YOU, YABBY
| | | | | | |
|---|---|---|---|---|---|
| Deliver Me From My Enemies | LP | Grove Music | GMLP001 | 1978 £5 | £12 |

## YOU KNOW WHO GROUP
| | | | | | | |
|---|---|---|---|---|---|---|
| My Love | 7" EP | Kapp | KEV13016 | 1965 £6 | £12 | French, B side by Angelo & Initials |
| Roses Are Red My Love | 7" | London | HLR9947 | 1965 £4 | £8 | |
| You Know Who Group | LP | International Allied | 420 | 1965 £15 | £30 | US |

## YOULDEN, CHRIS
| | | | | | |
|---|---|---|---|---|---|
| City Child | LP | Deram | SML1112 | 1974 £5 | £12 |
| Nowhere Road | LP | Deram | SML1099 | 1973 £5 | £12 |

## YOUNG, BARBARA
| | | | | | |
|---|---|---|---|---|---|
| No Game At All | LP | Corridor | 020 | £20 | £40 |

## YOUNG, CECIL
| | | | | | |
|---|---|---|---|---|---|
| Cool Jazz | 10" LP | Vogue | LDE003 | 1953 £8 | £20 |

## YOUNG, DARREN
| | | | | | |
|---|---|---|---|---|---|
| My Tears Will Turn To Laughter | 7" | Parlophone | R4919 | 1963 £2.50 | £6 |

## YOUNG, FARON
| | | | | | | |
|---|---|---|---|---|---|---|
| Every Time I'm Kissing You | 7" | Capitol | CL14891 | 1958 £2 | £5 | |
| Five Dollars And It's Saturday Night | 7" | Capitol | CL14655 | 1956 £5 | £10 | |
| Hello Walls | 7" EP | Capitol | EAP11549 | 1961 £4 | £8 | |
| I Can't Dance | 7" | Capitol | CL14860 | 1958 £4 | £8 | |
| I Hate Myself | 7" | Capitol | CL14930 | 1958 £1.50 | £4 | |
| I Hear You Talkin' | 7" | Capitol | CL15050 | 1959 £1.50 | £4 | |
| If You Ain't Lovin' | 7" | Capitol | CL14574 | 1956 £5 | £10 | |
| Live Fast, Love Hard, Die Young | 7" | Capitol | CL14336 | 1955 £7.50 | £15 | |
| Long Time Ago | 7" | Capitol | CL14975 | 1959 £1.50 | £4 | |
| Moonlight Mountain | 7" | Capitol | CL14762 | 1957 £2 | £5 | |
| Object Of My Affection | LP | Capitol | T1004 | 1958 £4 | £10 | |
| Shrine Of St. Cecilia | 7" | Capitol | CL14735 | 1957 £2.50 | £6 | |
| Snowball | 7" | Capitol | CL14822 | 1958 £2 | £5 | |
| Sweethearts Or Strangers | LP | Capitol | T778 | 1957 £6 | £15 | US |
| Sweethearts Or Strangers Pt. 1 | 7" EP | Capitol | EAP1778 | 1957 £4 | £8 | |
| Sweethearts Or Strangers Pt. 2 | 7" EP | Capitol | EAP2778 | 1957 £4 | £8 | |
| Sweethearts Or Strangers Pt. 3 | 7" EP | Capitol | EAP3778 | 1957 £4 | £8 | |
| That's The Way It's Gotta Be | 7" | Capitol | CL15004 | 1959 £1.50 | £4 | |
| This Is Faron Young | LP | Capitol | T1096 | 1963 £4 | £10 | |
| Vacation's Over | 7" | Capitol | CL14793 | 1957 £4 | £8 | |

## YOUNG, GEORGIE
| | | | | | |
|---|---|---|---|---|---|
| Nine More Miles | 7" | London | HLU8748 | 1958 £2 | £5 |

## YOUNG, HARRY
| | | | | | |
|---|---|---|---|---|---|
| Show Me The Way | 7" | Dot | DS16756 | 1965 £2.50 | £6 |

## YOUNG, JESSE COLIN
| | | | | | | |
|---|---|---|---|---|---|---|
| Soul Of A City Boy | LP | Capitol | (S)T2070 | 1964 £6 | £15 | US |
| Youngblood | LP | Mercury | MG2/SR61005 | 1965 £6 | £15 | US |

## YOUNG, JIM SAN FRANCISCO AVANTGARDE
| | | | | | | |
|---|---|---|---|---|---|---|
| Puzzle Box | LP | Polydor | 623226 | 1966 £10 | £25 | German |

## YOUNG, JIMMY
| | | | | | |
|---|---|---|---|---|---|
| Baby Cried | 7" | Decca | F10232 | 1954 £2.50 | £6 |
| Chain Gang | 7" | Decca | F10694 | 1956 £4 | £8 |
| Deep Blue Sea | 7" | Decca | F10948 | 1957 £1.50 | £4 |
| Give Me Your Word | 7" | Decca | F10406 | 1954 £2.50 | £6 |
| If Anyone Finds This | 7" | Decca | F10483 | 1955 £2 | £5 |
| Jimmy Young | 7" EP | Decca | DFE6404 | 1957 £2 | £5 |
| Jimmy Young Sings | 7" EP | Pye | NEP24004 | 1955 £2 | £5 |
| Lovin' Baby | 7" | Decca | F10842 | 1957 £1.50 | £4 |
| Man From Laramie | 7" | Decca | F10597 | 1955 £5 | £10 |
| Man On Fire | 7" | Decca | F10925 | 1957 £1.50 | £4 |
| More | 7" | Decca | F10774 | 1956 £2.50 | £6 |
| Presenting Jimmy Young | 7" EP | Decca | DFE6277 | 1956 £2 | £5 |
| Rich Man Poor Man | 7" | Decca | F10736 | 1956 £2.50 | £6 |
| Round And Round | 7" | Decca | F10875 | 1957 £1.50 | £4 |
| Someone On Your Mind | 7" | Decca | F10640 | 1955 £4 | £8 |
| These Are The Things We'll Share | 7" | Decca | F10444 | 1955 £2 | £5 |

| Unchained Melody | 7" | Decca | F10502 | 1955 £5 | £10 | |

## YOUNG, JOHNNY
| Fat Mandolin | LP | Blue Horizon | 763852 | 1970 £15 | £30 | |

## YOUNG, JOHNNY (2)
| Step Back | 7" | Decca | F22548 | 1967 £2 | £5 | |

## YOUNG, KAREN
| Are You Kidding | 7" | Mercury | MF943 | 1965 £1.50 | £4 | |
| Me And My Mini Skirt | 7" EP | Fontana | 460979 | 1966 £5 | £10 | French |
| Too Much Of A Good Thing | 7" | Major Minor | MM584 | 1968 £2 | £5 | |
| We'll Start The Party Again | 7" | Pye | 7N15956 | 1965 £2 | £5 | |

## YOUNG, KATHY & THE INNOCENTS
| Happy Birthday Blues | 7" | Top Rank | JAR554 | 1961 £5 | £10 | |
| Innocently Yours | LP | Indigo | 503 | 1961 £25 | £50 | US |
| Sound Of Kathy Young | LP | Indigo | 504 | 1961 £25 | £50 | US |
| Thousand Stars | 7" | Top Rank | JAR534 | 1961 £7.50 | £15 | |

## YOUNG, LA MONTE
Avant-garde composer La Monte Young is the founding father of minimalism. Much of his output consists of extracts from an ongoing work entitled *The Tortoise, His Dreams And Journeys*, whose electronic drones are intended to be a permanent feature of a special room, the Dream House.

| La Monte Young Marian Zazeela | LP | Edition X | 1079 | 1969 £30 | £60 | German |
| La Monte Young Marian Zazeela | LP | Edition X | 1079 | 1969 £50 | £100 | German, autographed |
| Theatre Of Eternal Music | LP | Shandar | 83510 | 1973 £8 | £20 | French, with Marian Zazeela |

## YOUNG, LARRY
| Contrasts | LP | Blue Note | BLP/BST84266 | 1967 £15 | £30 | |
| Heaven On Earth | LP | Blue Note | BST84304 | 1968 £10 | £25 | |
| Into Somethin' | LP | Blue Note | BLP/BST84187 | 1964 £25 | £50 | |
| Of Love And Peace | LP | Blue Note | BLP/BST84242 | 1966 £15 | £30 | |
| Unity | LP | Blue Note | BLP/BST84221 | 1965 £20 | £40 | |

## YOUNG, LEON STRINGS
| Glad All Over | 7" | Pye | 7N15646 | 1964 £5 | £10 | |

## YOUNG, LESTER
| Battle Of The Saxes | 10" LP | Felsted | EDL87014 | 1955 £25 | £50 | |
| Blue Lester | LP | London | LTZC15132 | 1958 £15 | £30 | |
| Greatest | LP | Vogue | LAE12194 | 1960 £8 | £20 | |
| Jazz Giants '56 | LP | Columbia | 33CX10054 | 1956 £20 | £40 | |
| Leaps Again | LP | Fontana | FJL128 | 1966 £4 | £10 | |
| Lester Young | LP | Vogue | LAE12016 | 1956 £15 | £30 | |
| Lester Young | 7" EP | Vogue | EPV1127 | 1956 £2 | £5 | |
| Lester Young | 10" LP | Columbia | 33C9015 | 1956 £25 | £50 | |
| Lester Young And His Tenor Sax | LP | Liberty | LBY3048 | 1965 £4 | £10 | |
| Lester Young And The Kansas City Five | LP | Stateside | SL10002 | 1962 £5 | £12 | |
| Memorial Album Vol. 1 | LP | Fontana | TFL5064 | 1959 £8 | £20 | |
| Memorial Album Vol. 2 | LP | Fontana | TFL5065 | 1960 £8 | £20 | |
| Pres | LP | Columbia | 33CX10070 | 1957 £20 | £40 | |
| Pres And Teddy | LP | HMV | CLP1302 | 1959 £10 | £25 | ... with Teddy Wilson |
| President | LP | Columbia | 33CX10031 | 1956 £25 | £50 | |
| Prez | LP | Fontana | TL5260 | 1965 £5 | £12 | |
| With The Oscar Peterson Trio | 10" LP | Columbia | 33C9001 | 1955 £25 | £50 | |

## YOUNG, MIGHTY JOE
| Why Don't You Follow Me | 7" | Parlophone | R5794 | 1969 £4 | £8 | |

## YOUNG, NEIL
Neil Young's blend of electric guitar overkill and acoustic folkiness was established quite early in his long career. It seems extraordinary, therefore, how his reputation among modern critics has become transformed in recent years. The man who was once dismissed as a 'boring old fart' is now extravagantly lauded for music that is hardly distinguishable from that which earned the condemnation. This critic finds Young's electric music to be frequently exhilarating, is bored by much of the acoustic stuff, but is glad that Neil Young is still around to show that a rock attitude and rock creativity do not have to be the exclusive preserve of youth.

| After The Goldrush | LP | Reprise | RSLP6383 | 1970 £4 | £10 | |
| After The Goldrush | CD | Reprise | C8817 | 1988 £6 | £15 | box set |
| Complex Sessions | CD-s | Reprise | PROCD7342 | 1995 £10 | £20 | US promo |
| Conversation With Neil Young | LP | Warner Bros | | 1980 £8 | £20 | US promo |
| Don't Be Denied | 7" | Reprise | SAM15 | 197– £2.50 | £6 | 1 sided promo |
| Down By The River | 7" | Reprise | RS23462 | 1969 £2 | £5 | |
| Everybody Knows This Is Nowhere | LP | Reprise | RSLP6349 | 1969 £5 | £12 | |
| Everybody Knows This Is Nowhere | 7" | Reprise | 0819 | 1969 £25 | £50 | US promo, alternative version |
| Everybody's Rockin' | LP | Geffen | | 1983 £6 | £15 | US audiophile promo |
| For The Turntables | CD | WEA | SAM1310 | 1994 £15 | £30 | promo compilation |
| Freedom | CD | Reprise | 258992 | 1989 £8 | £20 | US promo picture disc |
| Harvest | LP | Nautilus | | 1981 £5 | £12 | US audiophile |
| Loner | 7" | Reprise | RS23405 | 1969 £1.50 | £4 | |
| Neil Young | LP | Reprise | RSLP6317 | 1969 £5 | £12 | |
| Neil Young | LP | Reprise | RSLP6317 | 1969 £8 | £20 | no name on front cover |
| Oh Lonesome Me | 7" | Reprise | RS20861 | 1970 £1.50 | £4 | |
| Only Love Can Break Your Heart | 7" | Reprise | RS20958 | 1970 £1.50 | £4 | |

| | | | | | | |
|---|---|---|---|---|---|---|
| Sleeps With Angels – remastered | CD | Reprise | PROCD7136R | 1994 £8 | £20 | *US promo* |
| Trans | LP | Geffen | GHS2018 | 1982 £6 | £15 | *. US audiophile promo* |
| When You Dance I Can Really Love | 7" | Reprise | RS23488 | 1971 £1.50 | £4 | |

## YOUNG, RALPH

| | | | | | |
|---|---|---|---|---|---|
| Bible Tells Me So | 7" | Brunswick | 05466 | 1955 £2.50 | £6 |
| Bring Me A Bluebird | 7" | Brunswick | 05500 | 1955 £1.50 | £4 |

## YOUNG, ROGER

| | | | | | |
|---|---|---|---|---|---|
| Sweet Sweet Morning | 7" | Columbia | DB7869 | 1966 £2 | £5 |

## YOUNG, ROY

| | | | | | |
|---|---|---|---|---|---|
| Big Fat Mamma | 7" | Fontana | H200 | 1959 £5 | £10 |
| Four And Twenty Thousand Kisses | 7" | Ember | EMBS128 | 1961 £2 | £5 |
| Hey Little Girl | 7" | Fontana | H215 | 1959 £2.50 | £6 |
| I Hardly Know It | 7" | Fontana | H237 | 1960 £4 | £8 |
| I'm In Love | 7" | Fontana | H247 | 1960 £2 | £5 |
| Plenty Of Love | 7" | Fontana | H290 | 1961 £2.50 | £6 |
| Roy Young Band | LP | RCA | SF8161 | 1971 £4 | £10 |

## YOUNG, STEVE

| | | | | | | |
|---|---|---|---|---|---|---|
| Rock Salt And Nails | LP | A&M | 4177 | 1969 £8 | £20 | *US* |

## YOUNG, VICKI

| | | | | | |
|---|---|---|---|---|---|
| Bye Bye Just For A While | 7" | Capitol | CL14528 | 1956 £2 | £5 |
| Hearts Of Stone | 7" | Capitol | CL14228 | 1955 £5 | £10 |
| Live Fast Love Hard Die Young | 7" | Capitol | CL14281 | 1955 £4 | £8 |
| Spanish Main | 7" | Capitol | CL14653 | 1956 £2 | £5 |
| Vicki Young | 7" EP | Capitol | EAP1593 | 1956 £10 | £20 |

## YOUNG, VICTOR

| | | | | | |
|---|---|---|---|---|---|
| Cherry Pink And Apple Blossom White | 7" | Brunswick | 05448 | 1955 £1.50 | £4 |

## YOUNG & MOODY BAND

| | | | | | |
|---|---|---|---|---|---|
| Don't Do That | 7" | Bronze | BRO130 | 1981 £1.50 | £4 |

## YOUNG BLOOD

| | | | | | |
|---|---|---|---|---|---|
| Continuing Story Of Bungalow Bill | 7" | Pye | 7N17696 | 1969 £2 | £5 |
| Green Light | 7" | Pye | 7N17495 | 1968 £5 | £10 |
| I Can't Stop | 7" | Pye | 7N17627 | 1968 £2 | £5 |
| Just How Loud | 7" | Pye | 7N17588 | 1968 £2 | £5 |

## YOUNG BROTHERS

| | | | | | | |
|---|---|---|---|---|---|---|
| High Energy Rock | LP | GDM | | 1978 £10 | £25 | *US, gold vinyl* |

## YOUNG FLOWERS

| | | | | | | |
|---|---|---|---|---|---|---|
| Blomsterpistolen | LP | Sonet | 1258 | 1968 £37.50 | £75 | *Danish* |
| No. 2 | LP | Polydor | 2444007 | 1969 £37.50 | £75 | |

## YOUNG GROWLER

| | | | | | |
|---|---|---|---|---|---|
| V For Victory | 7" EP | Columbia | SEG8502 | 1966 £2 | £5 |

## YOUNG IDEA

| | | | | | |
|---|---|---|---|---|---|
| With A Little Help From My Friends | 7" | Columbia | DB8205 | 1967 £1.50 | £4 |

## YOUNG JESSIE

| | | | | | |
|---|---|---|---|---|---|
| Shuffle In The Gravel | 7" | London | HLE8544 | 1958 £87.50 | £175 |

## YOUNG ONES

| | | | | | |
|---|---|---|---|---|---|
| Baby That's It | 7" | Decca | F11705 | 1963 £2 | £5 |

## YOUNG RASCALS

The group that scored early hits with such songs as 'Groovin'', 'Good Lovin'' and 'Too Many Fish In The Sea', decided in 1967 that they could no longer credibly be described as 'young'. For the sake of continuity, all the group's collectable releases are listed in this guide under their adult name, the Rascals.

## YOUNG SISTERS

| | | | | | |
|---|---|---|---|---|---|
| Cassanova Brown | 7" | London | HLU9610 | 1962 £1.50 | £4 |

## YOUNG SOULS

| | | | | | |
|---|---|---|---|---|---|
| Why Did You Leave | 7" | Amalgamated | AMG844 | 1969 £2.50 | £6 |

## YOUNG TRADITION

| | | | | | |
|---|---|---|---|---|---|
| Boar's Head Carol | 7" | Argo | AFW115 | 1974 £1.50 | £4 |
| Chicken On A Raft | 7" EP | Transatlantic | TRAEP164 | 1968 £7.50 | £15 |
| Galleries | LP | Transatlantic | TRA172 | 1968 £8 | £20 |
| Galleries Revisited | LP | Transatlantic | TRASAM30 | 1973 £4 | £10 |
| So Cheerfully Round | LP | Transatlantic | TRA155 | 1967 £10 | £25 |
| Young Tradition | LP | Transatlantic | TRA142 | 1966 £8 | £20 |
| Young Tradition Sampler | LP | Transatlantic | TRASAM13 | 1969 £4 | £10 |

## YOUNGBLOODS

| | | | | | | |
|---|---|---|---|---|---|---|
| Darkness Darkness | 7" | RCA | RCA1821 | 1969 £1.50 | £4 | |
| Earth Music | LP | RCA | LPM/LSP3865 | 1967 £4 | £10 | *US* |
| Elephant Mountain | LP | RCA | SF8026 | 1969 £4 | £10 | |
| Get Together | 7" | RCA | RCA1877 | 1969 £1.50 | £4 | |
| Jesse Colin Young & The Youngbloods | LP | Mercury | SR61005 | 1965 £5 | £12 | *US* |

| | | | | | |
|---|---|---|---|---|---|
| Rock Festival | LP | Warner Bros | WS1878 | 1970 £4 £10 | |
| Two Trips | LP | Mercury | 6338019 | 1970 £4 £10 | |
| Youngbloods | LP | RCA | LPM/LSP3724 | 1967 £4 £10 | *US* |

## YOUNGFOLK
| | | | | | |
|---|---|---|---|---|---|
| Lonely Girl | 7" | President | PT136 | 1968 £2 £5 | |

## YOUNG-HOLT TRIO
| | | | | | |
|---|---|---|---|---|---|
| Wack Wack | 7" | Coral | Q72489 | 1967 £2 £5 | |

## YOUNG-HOLT UNLIMITED
| | | | | | |
|---|---|---|---|---|---|
| Country Slicker Joe | 7" | MCA | MU1053 | 1969 £2 £5 | |
| Soulful Strut | LP | MCA | MUPS368 | 1969 £6 £15 | |

## YOUTH
| | | | | | |
|---|---|---|---|---|---|
| As Long As There Is Your Love | 7" | Polydor | 56121 | 1966 £2.50 £6 | |

## YOUTH (2)
| | | | | | |
|---|---|---|---|---|---|
| Empty Quarter | LP | Illuminated | JAMS36 | 1984 £5 £12 | |

## YPER, LES SOUND
| | | | | | |
|---|---|---|---|---|---|
| Too Fortiche | 7" | Fontana | TF880 | 1967 £20 £40 | |

## YURO, TIMI
| | | | | | |
|---|---|---|---|---|---|
| Amazing Timi Yuro | LP | Mercury | 20032MCL | 1964 £4 £10 | |
| As Long As There Is You | 7" | Liberty | LIB15182 | 1969 £50 £100 | |
| Best Of Timi Yuro | LP | Liberty | (S)LBY1290 | 1966 £4 £10 | |
| Get Out Of My Life | 7" | Mercury | MF859 | 1965 £10 £20 | |
| Great Performances | LP | Liberty | LBL/LBS83115 | 1968 £4 £10 | |
| Hurt | LP | Liberty | LBY1247 | 1965 £6 £15 | |
| Hurt | 7" | Liberty | LIB10177 | 1964 £1.50 £4 | |
| Hurt | 7" | London | HLG9403 | 1961 £2.50 £6 | |
| I Ain't Gonna Cry No More | 7" | Liberty | LIB55519 | 1963 £5 £10 | |
| I Must Have Been Out Of My Mind | 7" | Liberty | LBF15142 | 1968 £5 £10 | |
| In The Beginning | LP | Liberty | LBL/LBS83128 | 1968 £4 £10 | |
| Let Me Call You Sweetheart | LP | Liberty | (S)LBY1275 | 1966 £4 £10 | |
| Make The World Go Away | LP | Liberty | LBY1192 | 1963 £4 £10 | |
| Make The World Go Away | 7" EP | Liberty | LEP2252 | 1966 £5 £10 | |
| Make The World Go Away | 7" | Liberty | LIB55587 | 1963 £1.50 £4 | |
| Satan Never Sleeps | 7" | Liberty | LIB55410 | 1962 £1.50 £4 | |
| Something Bad On My Mind | LP | Liberty | LBL/LBS83198 | 1968 £6 £15 | |
| Soul | LP | Liberty | LBY1042 | 1962 £5 £12 | |
| Soul | 7" EP | Liberty | LEP2214 | 1965 £5 £10 | |
| Talented | LP | Mercury | SMWL21019 | 1969 £4 £10 | |
| Timi Yuro | LP | London | HAG2415 | 1962 £20 £40 | |
| What's A Matter Baby | LP | Liberty | (S)LBY1154 | 1963 £4 £10 | |
| What's A Matter Baby | 7" | Liberty | LIB55469 | 1962 £5 £10 | |
| You Can Have Him | 7" | Mercury | MF848 | 1965 £1.50 £4 | |

## YWIS
| | | | | | |
|---|---|---|---|---|---|
| Ywis | LP | Minirock | 001 | 1983 £8 £20 | *Dutch* |

# Z

## ZACHERLEY, JOHN
| | | | | | | | |
|---|---|---|---|---|---|---|---|
| Dinner With Drac | 7" | London | HLU8599 | 1958 | £7.50 | £15 | |
| Monster Mash | LP | Parkway | P7018 | 1962 | £8 | £20 | US |
| Scary Tales | LP | Parkway | P7023 | 1963 | £8 | £20 | US |
| Spook Along With Zacherley | LP | Elektra | EKL/EKS7190 | 1960 | £8 | £20 | US |
| Zacherley's Monster Gallery | LP | Crestview | CR(S7)803 | 1963 | £8 | £20 | US |

## ZAKARRIAS
| | | | | | | | |
|---|---|---|---|---|---|---|---|
| Zakarrias | LP | Deram | SML1091 | 1971 | £210 | £350 | |

## ZAKARY THAKS
| | | | | | | | |
|---|---|---|---|---|---|---|---|
| Zakary Thaks | LP | Moxie | MLP2 | 1980 | £8 | £20 | US |

## ZANG, TOMMY
| | | | | | | | |
|---|---|---|---|---|---|---|---|
| Break The Chain | 7" | HMV | POP611 | 1959 | £2 | £5 | |
| Hey, Good Lookin' | 7" | Polydor | NH66957 | 1962 | £4 | £8 | |
| I Can't Hold Your Letters | 7" | Polydor | NH66977 | 1962 | £1.50 | £4 | |
| I'm Gonna Slip You Offa My Mind | 7" | Polydor | NH66955 | 1962 | £1.50 | £4 | |
| Just Call My Name | 7" | Polydor | NH66980 | 1962 | £2.50 | £6 | |
| Take These Chains From My Heart | 7" | Polydor | NH66960 | 1962 | £1.50 | £4 | |

## ZAPPA, FRANK

Critics have never known quite what to make of Frank Zappa. He was such a vastly talented musician and produced such a variety of material that they have tended to focus on just one of the things that he did (usually his satire) and then criticize the rest of his output for failing to measure up in this one area. The fact that Zappa was inclined to hide his art behind a smokescreen of vulgarity does not help, of course, nor does the fact that he was quite self-deprecating about works that are actually little short of being masterpieces. In ages past, many composers were virtuoso instrumentalists who wrote music which would enable them to display their prowess in public performance. Frank Zappa continued this tradition, and because he was working in the rock age and in America, his instrument was the electric guitar and the music he played is easily categorized as rock music. His best work, however (and much of his output qualifies), transcends all the usual categories, emerging as a classical music for our time that is far more relevant, and probably far more durable, than most of what is actually produced under that name. The proof is as close as a copy of *Studio Tan*, or *Uncle Meat*, or *Ship Arriving Too Late To Save A Drowning Witch*, or *The Perfect Stranger*, or *The Grand Wazoo*, or *Make A Jazz Noise Here*, or . . . Frank Zappa will be much missed.

| | | | | | | | |
|---|---|---|---|---|---|---|---|
| 200 Motels | LP | United Artists | UDF50003 | 1971 | £8 | £20 | with booklet |
| Absolutely Free | LP | Verve | (S)VLP9174 | 1967 | £15 | £30 | |
| Absolutely Free | LP | Verve | 2317035 | 1971 | £8 | £20 | |
| Apostrophe | LP | Discreet | K59201 | 1973 | £4 | £10 | |
| Apostrophe | LP | Discreet | MS42175 | 1973 | £8 | £20 | US quad |
| Baby Snakes | LP | Barking Pumpkin | BPR1115 | 1983 | £8 | £20 | picture disc |
| Big Leg Emma | 7" | Verve | VS557 | 1967 | £15 | £30 | US |
| Bongo Fury | LP | Discreet | DS2234 | 1975 | £4 | £10 | |
| Bongo Fury | LP | Discreet | K59209 | 1975 | £37.50 | £75 | test pressing only |
| Burnt Weeny Sandwich | LP | Reprise | K44083 | 1971 | £4 | £10 | |
| Burnt Weeny Sandwich | LP | Reprise | RSLP6370 | 1969 | £6 | £15 | |
| Burnt Weeny Sandwich/Weasels Ripped My Flesh | LP | Reprise | K64024 | 1979 | £5 | £12 | double |
| Chunga's Revenge | LP | Reprise | K44020 | 1971 | £4 | £10 | |
| Chunga's Revenge | LP | Reprise | RSLP2030 | 1970 | £5 | £12 | green cover |
| Chunga's Revenge | LP | Reprise | RSLP2030 | 1970 | £4 | £10 | red cover |
| Clean Cuts From Sheik Yerbouti | LP | Zappa | MK78 | 1980 | £8 | £20 | US promo |
| Clean Cuts From Tinseltown Rebellion | LP | Barking Pumpkin | AS995 | 1981 | £8 | £20 | US promo |
| Clean Cuts From You Are What You Is | LP | Barking Pumpkin | AS1294 | 1981 | £8 | £20 | US promo |
| Cosmic Debris | 7" | Discreet | K19201 | 1973 | £2 | £5 | |
| Ditties And Beer | CD | Ryko | ZAP2 | 1996 | £20 | £40 | US promo compilation |
| Don't Eat The Yellow Snow | 7" | Discreet | K19205 | 1973 | £2 | £5 | |
| Fillmore East 1971 | LP | Reprise | K44150 | 1971 | £4 | £10 | |
| Frank Zappa & The Mothers Of Invention | LP | Verve | 2352057 | 1975 | £5 | £12 | |
| Freak Out | LP | Verve | (S)VLP9154 | 1966 | £20 | £40 | |
| Freak Out | LP | Verve | 2683004 | 1971 | £10 | £25 | double |
| Freak Out | LP | Verve | V(6)5005 | 1966 | £25 | £50 | US, with map insert |
| Grand Wazoo | LP | Reprise | K44209 | 1972 | £4 | £10 | |
| Hot Rats | LP | Reprise | K44078 | 1971 | £4 | £10 | |
| Hot Rats | LP | Reprise | RSLP6356 | 1969 | £6 | £15 | |
| Hot Rats | LP | Reprise | RSLP6356 | 1969 | £30 | £60 | with Zappa Beefheart argument |
| Hot Rats | CD | Ryko | | 1992 | £8 | £20 | US gold picture disc |
| It Can't Happen Here | 7" | Verve | VS545 | 1966 | £30 | £60 | |
| Joe's Garage | 7" | CBS | 7950 | 1980 | £7.50 | £15 | mispress with Bob Dylan B side |

| Title | Format | Label | Catalog | Year | Price | Price | Notes |
|---|---|---|---|---|---|---|---|
| Joe's Garage Act 1 | LP | CBS | 86101 | 1979 | £4 | £10 | ...with lyric sheet |
| Joe's Garage Acts 2/3 | LP | CBS | 88475 | 1979 | £5 | £12 | ..... double, lyric sheets |
| Just Another Band From L.A. | LP | Reprise | K44179 | 1972 | £4 | £10 | |
| Lather | LP | Columbia | 41500 | 1976 | £700 | £1000 | .. 4 LPs, test pressings |
| Lumpy Gravy | LP | Verve | (S)VLP9223 | 1968 | £15 | £30 | |
| Lumpy Gravy | LP | Verve | 2317046 | 1971 | £8 | £20 | |
| Make A Jazz Noise Here | CD | Barking Pumpkin | CDDZAP41 | 1991 | £10 | £25 | original with Bartok & Stravinsky tracks |
| Man From Utopia | 7" | CBS | XPS180 | 1983 | £1.50 | £4 | ............ promo only |
| Mothermania | LP | Verve | (S)VLP9239 | 1969 | £10 | £25 | |
| Mothermania | LP | Verve | 2317047 | 1971 | £8 | £20 | |
| Mothermania | LP | Verve | 2352017 | 1972 | £8 | £20 | |
| Mothers Of Invention | LP | MGM | GAS112 | 1970 | £8 | £20 | ................. US |
| No Commercial Potential | CD | Ryko | FZZAP1 | 1995 | £15 | £30 | ..... promo compilation |
| One Size Fits All | LP | Discreet | K59207 | 1974 | £4 | £10 | |
| Orchestral Favourites | LP | Discreet | K59212 | 1978 | £4 | £10 | |
| Overnight Sensation | LP | Discreet | K41000 | 1973 | £4 | £10 | |
| Overnight Sensation | LP | Discreet | MS42149 | 1973 | £8 | £20 | ............ US quad |
| Roxy And Elsewhere | LP | Discreet | K69201 | 1974 | £5 | £12 | ............... double |
| Ruben And The Jets | LP | Verve | (S)VLP9327 | 1968 | £15 | £30 | |
| Ruben And The Jets | LP | Verve | 2317069 | 1971 | £8 | £20 | |
| Ruben And The Jets | LP | Verve | V65055 | 1968 | £25 | £50 | US, with three inserts |
| Ship Arriving Too Late Sampler | LP | Barking Pumpkin | AS1569 | 1982 | £4 | £10 | ............... US promo |
| Shut Up And Play Your Guitar | LP | CBS | 66368 | 1981 | £10 | £25 | ............... triple |
| Sleep Dirt | LP | Discreet | K59211 | 1978 | £4 | £10 | |
| Specialised Digital Audio Gratification | CD | Barking Pumpkin | CDPROMO1111 | 1988 | £20 | £40 | ............... promo |
| Studio Tan | LP | Discreet | K59210 | 1978 | £4 | £10 | |
| Tears Began To Fall | 7" | Reprise | K14100 | 1971 | £10 | £20 | |
| Tears Began To Fall | 7" | Reprise | K14120 | 1971 | £6 | £12 | |
| Thingfish | LP | EMI | 2402943 | 1985 | £10 | £25 | ......... with libretto |
| Uncle Meat | LP | Bizarre | 2MS2024 | 1969 | £6 | £15 | ............... double |
| Uncle Meat | LP | Transatlantic | TRA197 | 1969 | £10 | £25 | ............... double |
| Uncle Meat | LP | Transatlantic | TRA197 | 1969 | £15 | £30 | ......... double, booklet |
| Waka Jawaka | LP | Reprise | K44203 | 1972 | £4 | £10 | |
| We're Only In It For The Money | LP | Verve | (S)VLP9199 | 1967 | £15 | £30 | |
| We're Only In It For The Money | LP | Verve | (S)VLP9199 | 1967 | £20 | £40 | ......... with insert |
| We're Only In It For The Money | LP | Verve | 2317034 | 1971 | £8 | £20 | |
| Weasels Ripped My Flesh | LP | Reprise | K44019 | 1971 | £4 | £10 | |
| Weasels Ripped My Flesh | LP | Reprise | RSLP2028 | 1970 | £5 | £12 | |
| Welcome To Joe's Garage | LP | Zappa | MK129 | 1981 | £8 | £20 | ......... US promo |
| What Will This Evening | 7" | United Artists | UP35319 | 1971 | £10 | £20 | |
| Worst Of The Mothers | LP | MGM | SE4754 | 1971 | £8 | £20 | .................. US |
| XXXX Of The Mothers Of Invention | LP | Verve | V65074 | 1969 | £8 | £20 | .................. US |
| You Are What You Is | 12" | CBS | A121622 | 1981 | £3 | £8 | ............ picture disc |
| You Can't Do That On The Radio Anymore | CD | Ryko | RCCPRO9003 | 1990 | £10 | £25 | US promo compilation |
| Zappa In New York | LP | Discreet | K69204 | 1977 | £5 | £12 | ............... double |
| Zappa In New York | LP | Discreet | K69204 | 1977 | £20 | £40 | double, with 'Punky's Whips' |
| Zapped | LP | Warner Bros | PRO368 | 1969 | £15 | £30 | ...... US, collage cover |
| Zapped | LP | Warner Bros | PRO368 | 1969 | £10 | £25 | ....... US, photo cover |
| Zoot Allures | LP | Warner Bros | K56298 | 1976 | £4 | £10 | |

## ZARATHUSTRA

| Title | Format | Label | Catalog | Year | Price | Price | Notes |
|---|---|---|---|---|---|---|---|
| Zarathustra | LP | Metronome | MLP15421 | 1971 | £37.50 | £75 | ............... German |

## ZEAR, PETE

| Title | Format | Label | Catalog | Year | Price | Price | Notes |
|---|---|---|---|---|---|---|---|
| Tomorrow's World | 7" | | 22-1 | 1984 | £2.50 | £6 | |

## ZENITH SIX

| Title | Format | Label | Catalog | Year | Price | Price | Notes |
|---|---|---|---|---|---|---|---|
| At The Royal Festival Hall | 7" EP | Decca | DFE6255 | 1956 | £2.50 | £6 | |
| Zenith Six | 7" EP | Tempo | EXA42 | 1957 | £2.50 | £6 | |
| Zenith Six | 7" EP | Tempo | EXA58 | 1957 | £2.50 | £6 | |

## ZEPHYR

| Title | Format | Label | Catalog | Year | Price | Price | Notes |
|---|---|---|---|---|---|---|---|
| Going Back To Colorado | LP | Warner Bros | BS1897 | 1971 | £8 | £20 | .................. US |
| Sunset Ride | LP | Warner Bros | BS2603 | 1972 | £8 | £20 | .................. US |
| Zephyr | LP | Probe | SPB1006 | 1970 | £10 | £25 | |

## ZEPHYRS

| Title | Format | Label | Catalog | Year | Price | Price | Notes |
|---|---|---|---|---|---|---|---|
| I Just Can't Take It | 7" | Columbia | DB7571 | 1965 | £5 | £10 | |
| Little Bit Of Soap | 7" | Columbia | DB7324 | 1964 | £5 | £10 | |
| She's Lost You | 7" | Columbia | DB7481 | 1965 | £5 | £10 | |
| Sweet Little Baby | 7" | Columbia | DB7199 | 1964 | £5 | £10 | |
| What's All That About | 7" | Decca | F11647 | 1963 | £7.50 | £15 | |
| Wonder What I'm Gonna Do | 7" | Columbia | DB7410 | 1964 | £5 | £10 | |

## ZERFAS

| Title | Format | Label | Catalog | Year | Price | Price | Notes |
|---|---|---|---|---|---|---|---|
| Zerfas | LP | 700 West | LH730710 | 1973 | £330 | £500 | .................. US |

## ZETTERLINK, ZIPPO

| Title | Format | Label | Catalog | Year | Price | Price | Notes |
|---|---|---|---|---|---|---|---|
| In The Poor Sun | LP | Orschewski | OR001 | 1971 | £8 | £20 | ............... German |

## ZETTERLUND, MONICA

| Title | Format | Label | Catalog | Year | Price | Price | Notes |
|---|---|---|---|---|---|---|---|
| Make Mine Swedish Style | LP | Philips | BL7647 | 1964 | £4 | £10 | |

998

## ZEVON, WARREN

| | | | | | | | |
|---|---|---|---|---|---|---|---|
| Leave My Monkey Alone | CD-s.. | Virgin | CDEP2 | 1988 | £2 | £5 | |
| Wanted Dead Or Alive | LP | Imperial | LP12456 | 1969 | £5 | £12 | US |
| Werewolves Of London | 12" | Asylum | AS11386 | 1978 | £4 | £10 | US picture disc |

## ZIMMERMAN, TUCKER

| | | | | | | | |
|---|---|---|---|---|---|---|---|
| Ten Songs By Tucker Zimmerman | LP | Regal Zonophone | SLRZ1010 | 1969 | £5 | £12 | |
| Tucker Zimmerman | LP | Village Thing | VTS13 | 1972 | £5 | £12 | |

## ZIOR

| | | | | | | | |
|---|---|---|---|---|---|---|---|
| Cat's Eyes | 7" | Nepentha | 6129003 | 1973 | £2 | £5 | |
| Every Inch A Man | LP | Global Intercord | 26009U | 1973 | £50 | £100 | German |
| Za Za Za Zilda | 7" | Nepentha | 6129002 | 1971 | £2 | £5 | |
| Zior | LP | Nepentha | 6437005 | 1971 | £20 | £40 | |

## ZIP CODES

| | | | | | | | |
|---|---|---|---|---|---|---|---|
| Mustang | LP | Liberty | LRP3367/LST7367 | 1964 | £6 | £15 | US |

## ZIPPER

| | | | | | | | |
|---|---|---|---|---|---|---|---|
| Zipper | LP | Whizeagle | W0001 | 1975 | £25 | £50 | US |

## ZITRO

| | | | | | | | |
|---|---|---|---|---|---|---|---|
| Zitro | LP | ESP-Disk | 1052 | 1967 | £10 | £25 | US |

## ZODIAC MOTEL

| | | | | | | | |
|---|---|---|---|---|---|---|---|
| Story Of Roland Flagg | 7" | Swordfish | SWF1 | 1987 | £2.50 | £6 | 1 sided promo |
| Sunshine Miner | 7" | Swordfish | SWF004 | 1987 | £2.50 | £6 | |

## ZOMBIES

With sixties rock music keenly seeking wider credibility within the arts generally, much used to be made of the Zombies' educational qualifications. In fact, the Zombies' brand of pop-R&B was particularly distinctive, but this had rather more to do with Rod Argent's skilful keyboard playing and Colin Blunstone's attractive, breathy singing than with any qualifications. *Odessey And Oracle* (the mispelling is on the record), recorded as the group was breaking up, is something of a pop masterpiece, inspired by the Beatles no doubt, but nevertheless retaining the Zombies' stamp.

| | | | | | | | |
|---|---|---|---|---|---|---|---|
| Begin Here | LP | Decca | LK4679 | 1965 | £62.50 | £125 | |
| Bunny Lake A Disparu | 7" EP | RCA | 86507 | 1965 | £20 | £40 | French |
| Bunny Lake Is Missing | LP | RCA | RD7791 | 1965 | £20 | £40 | French |
| Care Of Cell 44 | 7" | CBS | 3087 | 1967 | £4 | £8 | |
| Friends Of Mine | 7" | CBS | 2960 | 1967 | £4 | £8 | |
| Goin' Out Of My Head | 7" | Decca | F12584 | 1967 | £1.50 | £4 | |
| Gotta Get A Hold Of Myself | 7" | Decca | F12495 | 1966 | £2 | £5 | |
| I Love You | 7" | Decca | F12798 | 1968 | £1.50 | £4 | |
| Indication | 7" | Decca | F12426 | 1966 | £2 | £5 | |
| Is This The Dream | 7" EP | Decca | 457100 | 1966 | £20 | £40 | French |
| Is This The Dream | 7" | Decca | F12296 | 1965 | £1.50 | £4 | |
| Kind Of Girl | 7" EP | Decca | 457083 | 1965 | £20 | £40 | French |
| Leave Me Be | 7" | Decca | F12004 | 1964 | £1.50 | £4 | |
| Odessey And Oracle | LP | CBS | (S)BPG63280 | 1968 | £20 | £40 | |
| Remember You | 7" | Decca | F12322 | 1966 | £2 | £5 | |
| She's Coming Home | 7" | Decca | F12125 | 1965 | £1.50 | £4 | |
| She's Not There | 7" EP | Decca | 457051 | 1964 | £20 | £40 | French |
| She's Not There | 7" | Decca | F11940 | 1964 | £1.50 | £4 | |
| Tell Her No | 7" | Decca | F12072 | 1965 | £1.50 | £4 | |
| Time Of The Season | 7" | CBS | 3380 | 1968 | £4 | £8 | |
| Time Of The Zombies | LP | Epic | EPC65727 | 1973 | £8 | £20 | double |
| What More Can I Do | 7" EP | Decca | 457075 | 1965 | £20 | £40 | French |
| Whenever You're Ready | 7" | Decca | F12225 | 1965 | £1.50 | £4 | |
| Zombies | 7" EP | Decca | DFE8598 | 1965 | £20 | £40 | |
| Zombies EP | CD-s.. | Special Edition | CD312 | 1988 | £2 | £5 | 3" single |

## ZOO

| | | | | | | | |
|---|---|---|---|---|---|---|---|
| I Shall Be Free | LP | Riviera | 521147 | 1971 | £6 | £15 | French |
| Zoo | LP | Barclay | 521172 | 1971 | £6 | £15 | French |
| Zoo | LP | Major Minor | SMLP74 | 1970 | £6 | £15 | |

## ZOO (2)

| | | | | | | | |
|---|---|---|---|---|---|---|---|
| Presents Chocolate Moose | LP | Sunburst | 7500 | 1968 | £20 | £40 | US |

## ZOROASTER

| | | | | | | | |
|---|---|---|---|---|---|---|---|
| Ahriman | LP | | | | £330 | £500 | |

## ZOSKIA

| | | | | | | | |
|---|---|---|---|---|---|---|---|
| Be Like Me | 12" | Temple | TOPY005 | 1985 | £4 | £10 | clear vinyl |
| J.G. | 7" | Temple | TOPY021 | 1987 | £2 | £5 | test pressing |

## ZOUNDS

| | | | | | | | |
|---|---|---|---|---|---|---|---|
| La Vache qui rit | 7" | Not So Brave | NSB001 | 1982 | £1.50 | £4 | |

## ZUIDERZEE

| | | | | | | | |
|---|---|---|---|---|---|---|---|
| Peace Of Mind | 7" | CBS | 202235 | 1966 | £1.50 | £4 | |

## ZUKIE, TAPPER

| | | | | | | | |
|---|---|---|---|---|---|---|---|
| In Dub | LP | Front Line | FL1029 | 1978 | £5 | £12 | |

| | | | | | | | | |
|---|---|---|---|---|---|---|---|---|
| MPLA | LP | Front Line | FL1006 | 1978 | £5 | £12 | |
| Peace In The Ghetto | LP | Front Line | FL1009 | 1978 | £5 | £12 | |
| Tapper Roots | LP | Front Line | FL1032 | 1978 | £5 | £12 | |

## ZWEISTEIN

| | | | | | | | |
|---|---|---|---|---|---|---|---|
| Trip, Flipout, Meditation | LP | Philips | 6630002 | 1970 | £25 | £50 | German triple |

## ZYGOAT

| | | | | | | | |
|---|---|---|---|---|---|---|---|
| Zygoat | LP | Polydor | 2383270 | 1974 | £4 | £10 | |

## ZZ & THE MASKERS

| | | | | | | | |
|---|---|---|---|---|---|---|---|
| ZZ And The Maskers | LP | Artone | PDR138 | 1965 | £8 | £20 | Dutch |

## ZZ TOP

| | | | | | | | |
|---|---|---|---|---|---|---|---|
| Arrested For Driving While Blind | 7" | London | HLU10547 | 1977 | £2.50 | £6 | |
| Arrested For Driving While Blind | 7" | London | HLU10547 | 1977 | £5 | £10 | mispress with Ray Charles B side |
| Beer Drinkers And Hell Raisers | 7" | London | HLU10458 | 1974 | £2.50 | £6 | |
| Cheap Sunglasses (Live) | 12" | Warner Bros | PRO887 | 1980 | £4 | £10 | promo |
| Double Back | CD-s | WEA | W9812CD | 1990 | £2 | £5 | |
| Eliminator | LP | Warner Bros | W3774P | 1985 | £4 | £10 | picture disc |
| Eliminator | CD | Warner Bros | 237742 | 1987 | £20 | £40 | mispressing – plays Beatles' Revolver |
| Francene | 7" | London | HLU10376 | 1972 | £2.50 | £6 | |
| Gimme All Your Lovin' | 7" | Warner Bros | W9693P | 1983 | £5 | £10 | shaped picture disc |
| Give It Up | CD-s | WEA | W9509CD | 1990 | £2 | £5 | |
| It's Only Love | 7" | London | HLU10538 | 1976 | £2 | £5 | |
| La Grange | 7" | London | HLU10475 | 1975 | £2.50 | £6 | |
| Legs (Dance) | 12" | Warner Bros | PRO2146 | 1983 | £3 | £8 | promo |
| Legs (Extended) | 12" | Warner Bros | PRO2127 | 1983 | £3 | £8 | promo |
| Recycler | CD | Warner Bros | | 1990 | £10 | £25 | US promo with spoken intros |
| Recycler | CD | Warner Bros | 26458 | 1990 | £10 | £25 | US promo picture disc, metal case |
| Rough Boy | 7" | Warner Bros | W2003FP | 1986 | £2 | £5 | interlocking shaped picture disc |
| Sleeping Bag | 7" | Warner Bros | W2001DP | 1985 | £2.50 | £6 | shaped picture disc |
| Sleeping Bag | 7" | Warner Bros | W2001P | 1985 | £2 | £5 | interlocking shaped picture disc |
| Sleeping Bag | 7" | Warner Bros | W2001P | 1985 | £2.50 | £6 | shaped picture disc |
| Stages | 7" | Warner Bros | W2002BP | 1986 | £2 | £5 | interlocking shaped picture disc |
| Taste Of The Sixpack | CD | Warner Bros | PROCD2875 | 1987 | £10 | £25 | US promo sampler |
| Tejas | LP | London | LDU1 | 1976 | £4 | £10 | |
| Tush | 7" | London | HLU10495 | 1975 | £2 | £5 | |